~~For Reference~~

~~Not to be taken from this room~~

ALMANACS OF AMERICAN WARS

CIVIL WAR ALMANAC

John C. Fredriksen

Facts On File
An imprint of Infobase Publishing

Civil War Almanac

Facts On File, Inc.
An imprint of Infobase Publishing
132 West 31st Street
New York NY 10001

ISBN-10: 0-8160-6459-8
ISBN-13: 978-0-8160-6459-5

Library of Congress Cataloging-in-Publication Data

Fredriksen, John C.
Civil War almanac / John C. Fredriksen.
       p. cm.
Includes bibliographical references and index.
Audience: Grades 9–12.
ISBN 0-8160-6459-8 (hardcover : alk. paper) 1. United States—History—Civil War, 1861–1865—Miscellanea. 2. Almanacs, American. I. Title.
E468.F85 2007
973.702′02—dc22   2006029985

Facts On File books are available at special discounts when purchased in bulk quantities for businesses, associations, institutions or sales promotions. Please call our Special Sales Department in New York at (212) 967-8800 or (800) 322-8755.

You can find Facts On File on the World Wide Web at http://www.factsonfile.com

Text design by Erika K. Arroyo
Cover design by Salvatore Luongo
Illustrations by Dale Williams

Printed in the United States of America

VB Hermitage 10 9 8 7 6 5 4 3 2 1

This book is printed on acid-free paper.

Contents

Introduction

By 1860, America's uneasy coexistence with slavery was headed for a violent and dramatic denouement. The election of Abraham Lincoln to the presidency in November proved a catalyst that unleashed long-suppressed urgings for secession among the Southern polity. Commencing with South Carolina in December, the national union quickly unraveled as a majority of slave-holding states voted to end their association with the United States voluntarily, much as the thirteen colonies had departed the British Empire in 1776. Lincoln, who had never campaigned to abolish the "peculiar institution" and, instead, had sought merely to contain it, suddenly confronted a crisis that neither he nor the nation had ever envisioned and for which they were certainly unprepared. The new Confederate States of America underscored its determination to achieve national sovereignty by firing on the Union garrison at Fort Sumter, Charleston, in April 1861. This singular act in and of itself became an immediate catalyst for Northern opinion. Heretofore hesitant as to civil conflict, Northern sentiment suddenly fell in lockstep behind the president in a war to preserve America. The ensuing conflagration proved bigger, more costly, and ultimately more cleansing than any of the contestants could have imagined in the balmy days prior to Bull Run, when myriads of raw recruits merrily tramped off in gaudy uniforms to martial music, beneath flowing banners. By the time the guns fell silent four years later, more than 620,000 of them lay dead, a bigger toll than that exacted in World War II. Large swaths of the South lay in ruins with cities gutted, thousands displaced, and grinding poverty a common lot for years to come. Yet the incubus of slavery had finally been expunged from the political landscape and exchanged for citizenship under a constitution that trumpeted equality for all. But the magnitude of the slaughter and the inspiring heroics and willing sacrifice on both sides forever seared America's consciousness. Appreciably, the Civil War remains a topic of continuing fascination and seemingly endless discourse, as exemplified by the sheer volume of books, essays, and movies produced annually on the subject.

The book you hold is designed to highlight military facets and occurrences as they transpired in the United States throughout the period 1861–65. Due to the sheer scope of events covered and constraints on word length, only passing references can be made to events in other spheres such as politics and diplomacy. In essaying this task, I chose a relatively conventional format made up of two distinct but integral parts. The first is a near-daily almanac of happenings arrayed along a topical/geographical axis. Because the thrust of this almanac is preponderantly military in tenor, great emphasis is paid to recording battles and skirmishes on land, significant troop movements, promotions or demotions of leading personnel, and the capture of individual vessels at sea. Daily subject content varies as to actual events recorded, but in cases in which more than one event transpires the invariable order is diplomacy, politics, North, South, West, Southwest, and naval. Given the expanse of the conflict, some explanation of geographical boundaries is also in order. North refers to Union states from Maryland to Vermont; South covers the Confederacy from Virginia to Florida and then Southern states as far as Louisiana; the West begins at the Shenandoah Valley and extends across the northern tier of the Middle South to regions astride the Mississippi River. Southwest refers to Texas, California, and the Indian Territory. Naval includes both actions at sea and on and along numerous inland waterways. The second part of this book consists of a biographical dictionary containing 107 detailed sketches of military and naval figures associated (Lincoln and Davis are included because of their roles as commander in chief) with this war. All entries are uniform in style and consist of a name, title, dates, text, and bibliography. Special care has also been given to the selection of photos chosen to insure good visuals and subjects in military, not civilian, attire. Textual cross-references, where relevant, then are indicated by small capital letters. In sum, this book is especially designed to afford prospective users immediate access to chronological data, with varying degrees of useful detail contingent upon relative significance, while the biographies proffer a useful cross-section of notable personalities relevant to the military equation, 1861–65.

The Civil War remains a perennially popular topic for reference books, and library shelves abound with almanaclike publications. However, most share an Achilles' heel in that they either contain outdated bibliographic citations or lack them completely. By contrast, I feel it incumbent as an author of reference books to list only the very latest scholarship available, seeing how older items usually are cited in their bibliographies and footnotes anyway. I achieve this by repeatedly combing the Library of Congress and WorldCat Web sites, along with frequent forays into periodical databases found at any college library. Inquiring minds are thereby exposed to rich and varied sources such as master's theses and doctoral dissertations in addition to more traditional materials such as books and articles. Readers can thus enjoy the fullest and most recent intellectual discourse on events and personages covered in this book. Moreover, I also append a detailed bibliography of the very latest Civil War publications, 2000–05, listing materials that would not fit logically in the essays. These two compilations, mutually exclusive, render this almanac very much a reference source for 21st-century scholars, students, or general readers.

I hope that the *Civil War Almanac* will promote a chronological sense for the complex interplay of strategic events and tactical variables on land and sea, 1861–65, that took place in the course of so large and protracted a struggle. It will go far to update or replace existing volumes on the topic and bring to the attention of students and scholars the latest trends in scholarship. I wish to thank my editor, Owen Lancer, for calling this project to my attention. I found it challenging to research and daunting to compile; in sum, it has been a valuable learning experience for myself and one for which I am very grateful.

—John C. Fredriksen, Ph.D.

Chronology

1860

February 1
POLITICS: After 44 ballots, Democrat William F. Pennington emerges as Speaker of the U.S. House of Representatives. He does so only after the withdrawal of fellow Democrat John Sherman, whose own candidacy was hobbled by his endorsement of an antislavery tract. The contest highlights growing factionalism within the Democratic Party over that "peculiar institution."

February 2
POLITICS: Senator Jefferson Davis of Mississippi introduces extreme resolutions defending the legality of slavery in both slaves states and the territories, which also guarantee the return of fugitive slaves to rightful owners.

February 23
POLITICS: The Kansas Territorial Legislature adopts the antislavery Wynadotte Constitution over the veto of Governor Samuel Medary.

February 27
POLITICS: Abraham Lincoln, speaking at New York's Cooper Union in his first memorable eastern address, strongly denounces the extremism of "popular sovereignty" and remains conciliatory and reassuring toward the South. However, he reiterates his adamant opposition toward the extension of slavery in the territories.

April 23–May 3
POLITICS: In the face of a mounting sectional schism, the Democratic Party holds its nominating convention at Charleston, South Carolina. However, when the majority fails to approve a territorial slave code, representatives from Alabama, Arkansas, Florida, Georgia, Louisiana, and South Carolina withdraw in protest on April 30. The remaining participants, unable to muster a two-thirds majority behind any one candidate, vote instead to adjourn and reassemble on June 18.

May 9–10
POLITICS: Baltimore, Maryland, is the site of the Constitutional Union Party nominating convention; this entity is formed from remnants of the American and Whig parties. They choose John Bell of Tennessee as their candidate for president with Edward Everett of Massachusetts as his vice president. They also strongly denounce sectionalism and secessionism.

May 16

POLITICS: The Republican Party convenes its nominating convention in Chicago, Illinois. The leading candidate, William H. Seward, is regarded as too radical on the issue of abolition, so he succumbs on the third ballot to Abraham Lincoln of Illinois. Hannibal Hamlin of Maine is then selected as vice president. Lincoln triumphs by positing himself as a moderate on the subject of slavery; he opposes its expansion into the territories but pledges not to interfere where it already exists.

May 24–25

POLITICS: The U.S. Senate, controlled 36 to 26 by the Democrats, adopts Senator Jefferson Davis's proslavery resolutions. However, the acrimony this engenders only widens the rift between northern and southern delegates, particularly within the Democratic Party.

June 11

POLITICS: Southern Democrats who abandoned the party convention in Charleston, South Carolina, assemble in Richmond, Virginia, to plan a strategy session. They vote to reconvene again in Baltimore on the 28th.

June 18–23

POLITICS: The Democratic Party reconvenes its nominating convention in Baltimore, Maryland, in the absence of many Southern delegates. They nonetheless nominate Stephen A. Douglas for president with Herschel V. Johnson of Georgia as his vice presidential running mate. Their platform also endorses the notion of "popular sovereignty" in the territories.

June 28

POLITICS: Southern delegates, who previously had absented themselves from the Democratic Party convention, likewise convene in Baltimore, Maryland, as National Democrats. They nominate former vice president John C. Breckinridge of Kentucky as their standard-bearer with Joseph Lane of Oregon as vice president; the party's platform unequivocally supports the expansion of slavery into the territories.

August 31

DIPLOMACY: Secretary of State Lewis Cass, alarmed by a major French incursion into Mexico, warns the government of Napoleon III that military occupation of that country is unacceptable to the United States.

November 6

POLITICS: Abraham Lincoln and Hannibal Hamlin win the presidential contest by carrying 18 free states with 1,866,452 popular votes and 180 electoral votes—although none are from Southern states. The Northern Democratic ticket of Stephen A. Douglas and Herschel V. Johnson registers second with 1,376,957 votes and 12 electoral votes while the competing Southern Democratic ticket of John C. Breckinridge and Joseph Lane are third with 11 slave states, 849,781 votes, and 72 electoral votes. Finishing fourth is the Constitutional Unionist ticket of John Bell and Edward Everett with 588,879 popular votes and 39 electoral votes. Lincoln's triumph proves short-lived and precipitates secessionist tremors throughout the South.

November 7
POLITICS: Defiant authorities in Charleston, South Carolina, take umbrage over Abraham Lincoln's recent victory; they raise the traditional Palmetto flag over the city and detain a U.S. officer caught in the act of transferring military supplies from the Charleston arsenal to Fort Moultrie.

November 9
POLITICS: President James Buchanan summons his very divided cabinet to discuss the possible secession crisis. Northerners Lewis Cass, Jeremiah S. Black, and Joseph Holt clearly favor preserving the Union by armed force if necessary, whereas Southerners Howell Cobb, Jacob Thompson, and John B. Floyd oppose military intervention of any kind.
SOUTH: Partisans in Charleston, South Carolina, attempt to seize U.S. arms stored at Fort Moultrie.

A campaign banner for Republican candidates Abraham Lincoln and Hannibal Hamlin, printed in *Harper's Weekly* *(Library of Congress)*

November 10
POLITICS: The South Carolina legislature reacts to Abraham Lincoln's victory by authorizing a convention to contemplate secession from the Union. Senators James Chestnut and James H. Hammond from that state also resign from the government.

November 13
POLITICS: The South Carolina legislature authorizes raising 10,000 volunteers to defend the state from a possible invasion by U.S. forces.

November 14
POLITICS: Georgia congressman Alexander H. Stephens addresses the state legislature at Milledgeville and implores them to oppose secession and uphold constitutional law.

November 15
SOUTH: Major Robert Anderson, U.S. Army, himself a Southerner and sympathetic toward the issue of slavery, is ordered to take command of the garrison at Fort Moultrie in Charleston Harbor.

NAVAL: Lieutenant Thomas A. Craven, commanding naval installations at Key West, Florida, orders landing parties to secure nearby Forts Taylor and Jefferson against possible seizure by "bands of lawless men."

November 18
POLITICS: The Georgia legislature, following South Carolina's lead, procures $1 million to purchase arms and begin to train troops.

November 20
POLITICS: President Buchanan is advised by Attorney General Jeremiah S. Black of his obligation to protect public property from illegal seizure and of the necessity of refraining from military force unless violence is initiated by the secessionists. He is further counseled not to wage offensive warfare against rebellious states but rather to rely on the courts to uphold the law.

November 23
SOUTH: Major Robert Anderson reports on the defensive weaknesses of Fort Moultrie, Charleston Harbor, and suggests transferring the garrison to nearby Fort Sumter, offshore.

November 30
POLITICS: The Mississippi state legislature begins to draw up articles of secession.

December 1
POLITICS: The Florida legislature convenes in order to ponder and debate the growing sectional crisis.

December 3
POLITICS: The 36th Congress convenes its second session in Washington, D.C.

December 4
POLITICS: President James Buchanan makes his final State of the Union message to Congress, noting with trepidation that different sections of the Union were "now arrayed against each other." He attributes the mounting crisis to the machinations of free states, and he questions the constitutionality of using military force to interfere with secession. Buchanan nonetheless opposes secession, despite his strong sympathies for the South.

December 5
POLITICS: President-elect Abraham Lincoln strongly rebukes President James Buchanan's recent State of the Union address.

December 6
POLITICS: The House of Representatives appoints the Committee of Thirty-Three, with one member representing each state, to discuss the present crisis and to suggest possible solutions.

December 8
POLITICS: Secretary of the Treasury Howell Cobb, a Georgian, feels that secession is inevitable at this juncture and tenders his resignation. He is succeeded briefly by Philip F. Thomas of Maryland.

President-elect Abraham Lincoln approaches political rival William H. Seward and asks him to serve as secretary of state under his new administration. Seward readily agrees, although less out of altruism than from a sense that the "incompetent" Lincoln needed an experienced politician to serve as his de facto "prime minister."

December 10
POLITICS: A delegation of South Carolinians meets with President James Buchanan in Washington, D.C., assuring him that U.S. troops and installations will not be disturbed in the event of secession. The president remains unconvinced and begins to mobilize military resources for action. Buchanan continues wrestling with the issue of dispatching reinforcements to the South, however.

The South Carolina legislature endorses a secession convention that is set to convene in Columbia on December 17.

December 11
SOUTH: Major Don C. Buell arrives at Fort Moultrie, Charleston Harbor, with instructions from the War Department for Major Robert Anderson. Apparently, Secretary of War John B. Floyd, a Virginian, refuses to dispatch reinforcements there to avoid provoking a confrontation.

December 12
POLITICS: Secretary of State Lewis Cass, furious over President James Buchanan's unwillingness to send military reinforcements and protect military installations in Charleston, South Carolina, resigns in protest.

The Committee of Thirty-Three, meeting in the U.S. House of Representatives, concocts more than 30 well-intentioned suggestions for avoiding war and secession—none of which prove viable.

December 13
POLITICS: President James Buchanan declines to send reinforcements to Fort Sumter, South Carolina, despite the urging of several cabinet members.

In Washington, D.C., seven senators and 23 representatives from across the South sign a manifesto encouraging secession and independence.

December 14
POLITICS: The Georgia state legislature entreats Alabama, Florida, Mississippi, and South Carolina to appoint delegates for a possible secession convention. All willingly comply.

December 17
POLITICS: The secession convention convenes in Columbia, South Carolina.

Attorney General Jeremiah S. Black, a close confidant of President James Buchanan, is appointed as temporary secretary of state to succeed Lewis Cass. However, Black cannot prevail on Buchanan to reinforce the threatened posts; the president is convinced that the Southern polity will be more pliable if new troops are withheld.

December 18
POLITICS: In an attempt to stave off violence and conciliate Southerners, Senator John J. Crittenden of Kentucky promulgates the Crittenden Compromise, restrict-

ing slavery to the boundaries of the old Missouri Compromise (1819) and extending that line across the continent. Slavery is thus kept out of northern territories, but otherwise the "peculiar institution" is left intact. Significantly, President-elect Abraham Lincoln opposes the measure.

December 19
POLITICS: Delegates to the South Carolina Convention declare that no Federal soldiers can be sent to the forts in Charleston Harbor.

December 20
POLITICS: In light of the mounting sectional crisis, the U.S. Senate appoints the Committee of Thirteen to investigate state affairs and seek possible solutions.

Democrat Edward M. Stanton is appointed attorney general to replace Jeremiah S. Black.

The South Carolina State Convention meeting at Charleston votes 169 to 0—unanimously—to secede from the United States, declaring all prior associations with that entity null and void. This single act sets in motion a chain of events culminating in a mammoth military confrontation between North and South. Charleston's inhabitants nonetheless slip into near-delirious celebrations.

December 22
POLITICS: The South Carolina State Convention demands that the federal government yield control of Fort Moultrie, Fort Sumter, and the U.S. arsenal in Charleston to state authorities. Three commissioners are then dispatched to Washington, D.C., to reiterate those demands.

December 24
POLITICS: Governor Francis W. Pickens of South Carolina declares his state free and independent from the United States, consistent with the "Declaration of Immediate Causes" issued by the convention.

In Washington, D.C., Senator William J. Seward proffers a last-minute constitutional amendment mandating that Congress must not interfere with slavery as it exists in the states. He also seeks jury trials for any fugitive slaves apprehended in free states.

December 26
SOUTH: Major Robert Anderson, commanding the Union garrison at Fort Moultrie, South Carolina, remains cognizant of the dangers to his command. Henceforth, under the cover of darkness, he surreptitiously transfers soldiers from the mainland to the more defensible position at nearby Fort Sumter in Charleston Harbor. This is a large, pentagonal-shaped, casemate (brick) structure that was first constructed on an artificial island in 1829 but never was completed fully. Anderson also undertakes his move without prior authorization from Secretary of War John B. Floyd. Once situated, his soldiers begin to mount cannons and to strengthen their defensive works.

December 27
POLITICS: President James Buchanan expresses his surprise and regrets to Southern congressmen that the garrison of Charleston shifted itself to Fort Sumter, but he declines ordering them back to the mainland.

SOUTH: South Carolina state forces occupy Fort Moultrie and Castle Pinckney in Charleston Harbor. This constitutes the first overt act of military aggression against the U.S. government.

NAVAL: South Carolina forces seize the U.S. revenue cutter *William Aiken* in Charleston Harbor.

December 28

POLITICS: A South Carolina delegation arrives in Washington, D.C., demanding that President James Buchanan transfer all Federal troops from Charleston. He receives them only as private citizens and again declines all demands for removing U.S. troops. Meanwhile, General in Chief Winfield Scott opposes abandoning the fort and urges Secretary of War John B. Floyd to dispatch immediate supplies and reinforcements.

December 29

POLITICS: President James Buchanan requests and receives the resignation of Secretary of War John B. Floyd after Floyd insists on removing Federal forces from Charleston, South Carolina, and the president declines.

December 30

POLITICS: Continuing seizure of Federal property by South Carolina authorities prompts threats of additional resignations among President James Buchanan's cabinet if he fails to take more forceful action.

SOUTH: The U.S. arsenal at Charleston, South Carolina, is seized by state forces. They also occupy all remaining Federal property in the city save one—Fort Sumter in the harbor.

December 31

POLITICS: Postmaster General Joseph Holt is appointed acting secretary of war following the resignation of John B. Floyd. President James Buchanan also refuses another demand by South Carolina commissioners to withdraw Federal troops from Charleston. Upon repeated insistence by Secretary of State Jeremiah S. Black, he finally and reluctantly orders the army and navy departments to mobilize troops and ships for the relief of Fort Sumter. Lines are being drawn inexorably in the sand and will have to be crossed soon.

The Senate Committee of Thirteen fails to reach agreement on any possible political solutions, including the so-called "Crittenden Compromise."

1861

January 2

POLITICS: President James Buchanan refuses to accept a letter from the South Carolina commissioners. The nominally sympathetic executive then instructs that preparations be made to reinforce the garrison at Fort Sumter, Charleston. General Winfield Scott then prevails upon the president to dispatch reinforcements by means of a civilian steamer, which would arrive more quickly than a warship—and attract less attention.

NORTH: The defense of Washington, D.C., is entrusted to Colonel Charles P. Stone, who begins to organize the District of Columbia militia.

SOUTH: South Carolina forces seize the inactive post of Fort Johnson in Charleston Harbor.

NAVAL: The USS *Brooklyn* at Norfolk, Virginia, receives orders to ready itself for a possible relief effort at Fort Sumter, Charleston Harbor.

January 3

POLITICS: The War Department summarily cancels former secretary of war John B. Floyd's instructions to transfer heavy cannon from Pittsburgh, Pennsylvania, to various points throughout the South.

The South Carolina commission departs Washington, D.C., deeming its mission a failure.

The Delaware legislature, although permitting slavery, votes unanimously to remain in the Union.

The Florida State Convention assembles in Tallahassee to weigh secession.

SOUTH: Fort Pulaski, near the mouth of the Savannah River, is peacefully occupied by Georgia state troops on the orders of Governor Joseph E. Brown.

January 4

SOUTH: The U.S. arsenal at Mount Vernon, Mobile, is occupied by Alabama state forces under orders from Governor Andrew B. Moore.

January 5

POLITICS: Senators from seven Southern states—Alabama, Arkansas, Florida, Georgia, Louisiana, Mississippi, and Texas—confer in Washington, D.C., over the possibility of secession. They ultimately urge slaves states to leave the union and establish a confederacy of their own.

SOUTH: The Federal installations of Fort Morgan and Fort Gaines, which guard the entrance to Mobile Bay, Alabama, are taken over by state forces.

NAVAL: A detachment of 40 U.S. Marines is detailed from the Washington Navy Yard and shuttled to Fort Washington on the Maryland side of the Potomac River, as a precaution against seizure.

The supply vessel *Star of the West* departs New York for Fort Sumter, South Carolina, carrying food, supplies, and 250 soldiers as reinforcements. The warship USS *Brooklyn*, originally intended for the mission, is detained by General Winfield Scott, who feels that use of a civilian vessel is less provocative.

January 6

POLITICS: Governor Thomas H. Hicks of Maryland, which is a slave state, wades in heavily against secession.

SOUTH: The U.S. arsenal at Apalachicola, Florida, is seized by state forces.

January 7

POLITICS: The U.S. House of Representatives approves Major Robert Anderson's recent and unauthorized transfer of Federal forces to Fort Sumter, South Carolina.

State conventions in Mississippi and Alabama begin to debate secession.

SOUTH: The U.S. Army post of Fort Marion, St. Augustine, is seized by Florida forces.

January 8

POLITICS: President James Buchanan urges Congress to consider adopting the Crittenden Compromise.

Secretary of the Interior Jacob Thompson, the last remaining Southerner in President James Buchanan's cabinet, tenders his resignation over the *Star of the West*'s departure. Before leaving Washington, D.C., he cables authorities in Charleston, South Carolina, that the transport has been dispatched.

SOUTH: Federal troops garrisoning Fort Barrancas, Pensacola, fire warning shots at a group of individuals approaching them.

January 9

POLITICS: The Mississippi State Convention meeting at Jackson votes to secede on a vote of 84 to 15—becoming the second state to depart.

SOUTH: Fort Johnson, North Carolina, is expropriated by state forces.

Artillery manned by South Carolina state forces at Fort Moultrie and Morris Island fire on the transport *Star of the West* as it approaches Charleston Harbor. No damage is inflicted and it returns to New York unscathed. Technically speaking, these are the first shots of the Civil War, and Major Robert Anderson, commanding the Fort Sumter garrison, protests the action to Governor Francis W. Pickens. However, Anderson orders the garrison to stand down and makes no attempt to interfere.

NAVAL: A detachment of 30 U.S. Marines marches from the Washington Navy Yard to occupy Fort McHenry, Baltimore harbor, until they can be relieved by regular army troops.

January 10

POLITICS: Senator Jefferson Davis addresses the Senate, requesting immediate action on and approval of Southern demands. However, he decries any use of force and seeks to resolve the crisis through constitutional means.

William H. Seward gains appointment as secretary of state.

The Florida State Convention adopts secession on a 62 to 7 vote, becoming the third state to secede.

SOUTH: Fort Caswell, North Carolina, is seized by state forces.

Federal troops under Lieutenant Adam J. Slemmer, garrisoning Fort Barrancas at Pensacola, Florida, spike their cannon and relocate offshore to Fort Pickens on nearby Santa Rosa Island. Local troops soon confiscate the navy yard, but Fort Pickens remains in Union hands for the duration of hostilities.

The U.S. arsenal and barracks at Baton Rouge, Louisiana, are confiscated by state forces under Braxton Bragg on the orders of Governor Thomas O. Moore.

January 11

POLITICS: The Mississippi delegation to the U.S. House of Representatives walks out of Congress.

The New York legislature underscores its determination to uphold the Union by passing several pro-government resolutions.

The Alabama State Convention at Montgomery approves secession on a 61 to 39 vote, becoming the fourth state to secede.

SOUTH: South Carolina governor Francis W. Pickens demands the surrender of Fort Sumter, Charleston Harbor. Major Robert Anderson politely yet curtly declines.

Louisiana state forces occupy the U.S. Marine Hospital in New Orleans, along with Fort Jackson and Fort St. Philip on the Mississippi River.

January 12

POLITICS: The Ohio legislature votes overwhelmingly to support continuation of the Union.

SOUTH: The Federal outposts of Fort Barrancas, Fort McCree, and the Pensacola Navy Yard are occupied by Florida state forces. However, continuing demands for the surrender of Fort Pickens offshore are ignored.

January 13

POLITICS: President James Buchanan entertains an envoy dispatched from South Carolina governor Francis W. Pickens, declaring that Fort Sumter will not be surrendered to state authorities. The president also receives a messenger from Major Robert Anderson, who alerts him of the worsening situation there.

SOUTH: An unofficial truce emerges between South Carolina authorities and the garrison at Fort Sumter, Charleston Harbor.

January 14

POLITICS: The U.S. House Committee of Thirty-Three fails to agree on any compromise solution. Chairman Thomas Corwin next proposes a constitutional amendment to protect slavery where it exists; it passes but is never ratified by any state.

The South Carolina legislature summarily declares that any Union attempt to reinforce Fort Sumter is tantamount to war.

SOUTH: Federal forces under Captain John M. Brannan hurriedly garrison Fort Taylor on Key West, Florida, transforming it into a coaling station of strategic significance.

The Federal installation at Fort Pike, New Orleans, is occupied by Louisiana state forces.

January 15

SOUTH: Major Robert Anderson receives a second summons to surrender Fort Sumter, Charleston Harbor; he declines again.

WEST: Colonel Albert S. Johnston assumes command of the newly formed Department of the Pacific (California and Oregon).

The commander of Fort Pickens, Florida, again refuses a summons to surrender his post.

January 16

POLITICS: The U.S. Senate effectively defeats the Crittenden Compromise; insisting that the U.S. Constitution must be obeyed, not amended.

January 18

POLITICS: Former postmaster general Joseph Holt becomes secretary of war.

The legislature of Massachusetts votes to offer the federal government both men and money to preserve the Union.

SOUTH: South Carolina officials make a third demand for the surrender of Major Robert Anderson and Fort Sumter, Charleston Harbor, which is declined.

Fort Pickens, Florida, turns down a third demand to surrender.

Fort Jefferson, Key West, Florida, is occupied by Federal forces under Major Lewis G. Arnold, and subsequently serves as a detention center for political prisoners.

NAVAL: Alabama state forces seize the lighthouse tender USS *Alert* at Mobile.

January 19

POLITICS: The Georgia State Convention in Milledgeville approves secession on a 208 to 89 vote, becoming the fifth state to secede.

The Virginia General Assembly entreats all states to send delegates to a National Peace Convention in Washington, D.C.

January 20

SOUTH: Mississippi forces occupy Fort Massachusetts on Ship Island, at the mouth of the Mississippi River.

January 21

POLITICS: Jefferson Davis of Mississippi together with Clement C. Clay and Benjamin Fitzpatrick of Alabama and Stephen R. Mallory and David L. Yulee of Florida make a dramatic departure from the U.S. Senate chamber in Washington, D.C., and head for home. Nonetheless, Davis remains deeply troubled by the course of events and allegedly prays for peace that evening.

The New York legislature agrees to uphold the Union by force, if necessary.

NORTH: Rabid abolitionist Wendell Phillips hails the decision of slave states to secede, feeling that their continued presence is detrimental to the United States.

January 22

POLITICS: New York governor Edwin Morgan orders all weapons and gunpowder previously sold to Georgia impounded. This prompts a sharp rebuke from Governor Joseph E. Brown, who seizes several Northern vessels in retaliation.

The Wisconsin legislature votes to agree with New York's stand on the Union.

January 23

POLITICS: The Massachusetts legislature votes in agreement with New York's pledge to support the Union.

NAVAL: Commander John A. B. Dahlgren removes cannon and ammunition from the Washington Navy Yard in the event of a possible attack, storing the latter in the attic of a building.

January 24

SOUTH: The U.S. arsenal at Augusta, Georgia, is seized by state forces.

NAVAL: Federal forces from Fortress Monroe, Virginia, are loaded onboard ships and dispatched to reinforce Fort Pickens, Florida. The squadron consists of the USS *Brooklyn, Sabine, Macedonia,* and *St. Louis.*

January 26

POLITICS: At Baton Rouge, the Louisiana State Convention approves secession on a vote of 113 to 17, becoming the sixth state to secede.

SOUTH: Georgia forces occupy the Oglethorpe barracks and Fort Jackson, Savannah, as per orders from Governor Joseph E. Brown.

January 28

SOUTH: The Federal installation at Fort Macomb, New Orleans, is occupied by Louisiana forces.

January 29

POLITICS: Following a congressional vote, Kansas joins the Union as the 34th state; significantly, its constitution explicitly outlaws slavery.

NAVAL: Louisiana forces seize the U.S. revenue cutter *Robert McClelland* at New Orleans.

To avoid provoking a fight, the Navy Department orders a Marine Corps detachment onboard the USS *Brooklyn,* steaming for Fort Pickens, Florida, not to disembark unless that post is attacked.

January 30

NAVAL: The U.S. revenue cutter *Lewis Cass* surrenders to state forces at Mobile Bay, Alabama.

January 31

SOUTH: Louisiana officials orchestrate the seizure of the U.S. Mint and Customs House at New Orleans, along with the U.S. revenue schooner *Washington.*

February 1

POLITICS: The Texas State Convention, convening in Austin, votes 166 to 7 in favor of secession, becoming the seventh state to secede. A public referendum is also scheduled to solicit public opinion on the measure.

February 3

POLITICS: Senators Judah P. Benjamin and John Slidell of Louisiana withdraw from the U.S. Senate and return home.

February 4

POLITICS: The Peace Convention, summoned by Virginia, assembles in Washington, D.C., under former president John Tyler. It consists of 131 members from 21 states, but none of the seceded states are represented.

Representatives from Alabama, Florida, Georgia, Louisiana, Mississippi, and South Carolina assemble in Montgomery, Alabama, and a Provisional Congress of the Confederate States of America forms with Howell Cobb of Georgia serving as president.

February 5
POLITICS: President James Buchanan reiterates to South Carolina officials his determination that Fort Sumter, Charleston Harbor, will not be surrendered to state authorities.

The Peace Conference convening in Washington, D.C., earnestly votes to resolve the outbreak of sectional violence both diplomatically and constitutionally.

February 7
POLITICS: The Secession Convention at Montgomery, Alabama, begins to draft plans for a provisional form of government, a confederacy of states.

The Choctaw Nation declares its allegiance to the South.

February 8
POLITICS: President James Buchanan authorizes a $25 million loan for current expenses and redemption of treasury notes.

Southern delegates at Montgomery, Alabama, proffer and unanimously approve the Provisional Constitution of the Confederate States—thereby founding the Confederacy. This document, while similar to its Northern equivalent, explicitly declares and protects the right to own slaves. While the importation of slaves remains banned, the existing fugitive slave law is strengthened.

WEST: The U.S. Arsenal at Little Rock, Arkansas, is seized by state troops under orders of Governor Henry M. Rector.

February 9
POLITICS: Jefferson Davis of Mississippi, who is absent from the constitutional convention in Montgomery, Alabama, is unanimously elected provisional president of the Confederate States of America. Alexander H. Stephens of Georgia likewise becomes provisional vice president. Moreover, the Provisional Congress of the Confederacy pledges that all laws extant under the U.S. Constitution, which do not conflict with the Confederate constitution, will be maintained.

Voters in Tennessee roundly defeat a move to convene a secession convention, 68,282 to 59,449.

WEST: General David E. Twiggs appoints a military commission to confer with civilian authorities in Texas.

NAVAL: The steamer USS *Brooklyn* arrives at Pensacola, Florida, to reinforce the garrison at Fort Pickens, but a Marine Corps detachment remains onboard so as not to upset the status quo.

February 10
POLITICS: In Mississippi, a rather surprised Jefferson Davis is alerted by telegram of his election to the Confederate presidency. He has been anticipating a military commission, but nonetheless he agrees to the appointment.

February 11
POLITICS: President-elect Abraham Lincoln departs Springfield, Illinois, and wends his way toward Washington, D.C. He will never return alive.

Jefferson Davis travels from his plantation in Brierfield, Mississippi, to attend inauguration ceremonies at Montgomery, Alabama.

February 12
POLITICS: The Provisional Congress of the Confederacy at Montgomery, Alabama, votes to establish a Peace Commission to the United States.
WEST: State forces seize U.S. Army munitions stored at Napoleon, Arkansas.

February 13
POLITICS: The electoral college completes counting all votes and declares Abraham Lincoln the new chief executive.
WEST: A detachment of U.S. Army troops under Colonel Bernard J. Dowling defeats a band of Chiricahua Apaches at Apache Pass, Arizona; in January 1894 he receives the Congressional Medal of Honor for this action.

February 15
NAVAL: Lieutenant Raphael Semmes resigns his U.S. Navy commission and leaves for the South.

February 16
POLITICS: President-elect Jefferson Davis arrives at Montgomery, Alabama, amid thunderous applause.
WEST: The U.S. arsenal at San Antonio, Texas, is seized by state forces under Ben McCulloch.

Texas civilian commissioners demand the surrender of all Federal posts and property within their state.

February 18
POLITICS: Jefferson Davis of Mississippi is inaugurated as provisional president of the Confederate States of America, declaring, "Obstacles may retard, but they cannot long prevent the progress of a movement sanctified by its justice and sustained by a virtuous people." Alexander H. Stephens of Georgia, who initially opposed secession, then becomes vice president. Military bands then serenade the proceedings with a catchy air popularly known as "Dixie," which gradually gains wide acceptance as an unofficial national anthem of the Confederacy.
WEST: In an act widely condemned as treasonable, General David E. Twiggs surrenders all U.S. Army installations in Texas to state authorities.

February 19
POLITICS: The Confederate Convention in Montgomery, Alabama, elects Judah P. Benjamin of Louisiana attorney general, Christopher G. Memminger of South Carolina secretary of the treasury, John H. Reagan of Texas postmaster general, Robert Toombs of Georgia secretary of state, and Leroy P. Walker of Alabama secretary of war.
SOUTH: Louisiana forces appropriate the U.S. Paymaster's Office in New Orleans.

Colonel Carlos A. Waite replaces General David E. Twiggs as commander of the Department of Texas.

February 20

POLITICS: The Provisional Confederate Congress, acting in the absence of an established body, declares the Mississippi River open to commerce. It also passes legislation creating a Department of the Navy.

February 21

POLITICS: President Jefferson Davis receives a missive from South Carolina governor Francis W. Pickens requesting immediate action on Fort Sumter. Pickens regards the continuing presence of the Federal garrison an affront to "honor and safety."

The former U.S. senator from Florida, Stephen R. Mallory, is chosen as Confederate secretary of the navy.

SOUTHWEST: Federal troops abandon Camp Cooper, Texas.

February 22

POLITICS: While in Baltimore, Maryland, President-elect Abraham Lincoln is warned of a possible attempt on his life and completes his journey to Washington, D.C., on board a secret train.

WEST: A mass gathering at San Francisco, California, declares itself for the Union.

February 23

POLITICS: President-elect Abraham Lincoln arrives in Washington, D.C., amidst a mounting sense of national foreboding.

Texas voters affirm secession by a margin of three to one.

February 25

POLITICS: Judah P. Benjamin is sworn in as Confederate attorney general; this multitalented individual will hold several positions within the new government.

February 26

SOUTHWEST: Federal forces under Captain Edmund Kirby-Smith abandon Camp Colorado, Texas.

February 27

POLITICS: As a continuing gesture to avoid hostilities, President Jefferson Davis appoints three commissioners for possible peace negotiations in Washington, D.C.

The Peace Commission suggests adoption of no less than six constitutional amendments to forestall any possibility of violence.

NAVAL: Congress authorizes the Navy Department's request for seven heavily armed steam sloops to augment the existing fleet strength.

February 28

POLITICS: The House of Representatives adopts an amendment proposed by Thomas Corwin that reaffirms slavery's status where it already exists. President-elect Abraham Lincoln fully concurs with the legislation.

Calls for a state convention to weigh the possibility of secession are narrowly defeated by a popular vote held in North Carolina.

The Confederate Congress agrees to a $15 million domestic loan.

WEST: The Colorado Territory is formed from the western part of the Kansas Territory and William Gilpin gains appointment as governor.

March 1
POLITICS: President-elect Abraham Lincoln appoints Pennsylvania politician Simon Cameron his new secretary of war.

The Provisional Confederate States of America assumes formal control of events at Charleston, South Carolina.

SOUTH: Pierre G. T. Beauregard is commissioned brigadier general, C.S.A.

Major Robert Anderson alerts the government that the garrison at Fort Sumter, Charleston Harbor, must be either supplied, reinforced, or evacuated without further delay. He is running out of provisions rapidly and must capitulate soon by default.

March 2
POLITICS: The U.S. Senate refuses compromise resolutions advanced by the Peace Convention, over the objections of Kentucky senator John J. Crittenden. This act concludes all attempts at political compromise.

WEST: President James Buchanan approves establishment of the new territories of Nevada and Dakota.

NAVAL: The U.S. revenue schooner *Henry Dodge* is captured by state forces at Galveston, Texas.

March 3
POLITICS: President-elect Abraham Lincoln dines with his cabinet for the first time and tours the Senate. Meanwhile, General Winfield Scott, commander in chief of the U.S. Army, dourly informs Secretary of State William H. Seward that mounting a major relief effort to rescue Fort Sumter, Charleston Harbor, appears impractical.

SOUTH: President Jefferson Davis appoints General Pierre G. T. Beauregard commander of Confederate forces in the vicinity of Charleston, South Carolina. He is instructed to prepare for military action against the Federal garrison sequestered inside Fort Sumter in the harbor.

March 4
POLITICS: Abraham Lincoln is formally inaugurated as the 16th president of a less-than-united United States, and he is sworn in by Chief Justice Roger B. Taney. His first address declares that the Union is "perpetual" and cannot be undone by secession. The chief executive also reiterates his stance to preserve all Federal property within the states now seceded. Moreover, he affirms his belief that slavery cannot be allowed in the territories, but he is willing to leave it intact where it already exists. He remains conciliatory, assures the South it will not be attacked, and appeals to "the better angels of our nature." Hannibal Hamlin of Maine becomes vice president, along with William H. Seward as secretary of state, Salmon P. Chase as secretary of the treasury, and Edward Bates as attorney general.

The Confederate Convention assembled at Montgomery, Alabama, officially adopts the "Stars and Bars" flag of seven stars and three stripes as its official symbol.

NAVAL: The Navy Department, which currently operates 42 warships, recalls all but three from foreign stations to assist in the impending crisis.

March 5
POLITICS: President Abraham Lincoln discusses the plight of Major Robert Anderson at Fort Sumter, South Carolina. The major telegraphs him that his supplies are due to run out within four to six weeks, after which he will have little recourse but to surrender. Furthermore, both Anderson and General Winfield Scott concur that the post cannot be held successfully with less than 20,000 troops. Time is running out for a peaceful solution, but Lincoln continues nuancing the delicate situation.

March 6
POLITICS: The Confederate Congress authorizes recruitment of 100,000 volunteers for 12 months. President Jefferson Davis appoints Martin J. Crawford, John Forsyth, and A. B. Roman special commissioners to deal with Republican officeholders in Washington, D.C., once it becomes apparent that President Abraham Lincoln refuses to receive them.

March 7
POLITICS: Gideon Welles, a former Connecticut newspaper editor, is sworn in as the 24th secretary of the navy.

   The Missouri State Convention displays a strong pro-Union streak and votes against secession, yet also considers the Crittenden Compromise a possible avenue for avoiding war.
SOUTH: Braxton Bragg and Samuel Cooper are appointed brigadier generals in the Confederate army.
SOUTHWEST: Federal forces abandon Ringgold Barracks and Camp Verde, Texas.

March 9
POLITICS: At Montgomery, Alabama, the Confederate Convention authorizes the raising of military forces. Delegates also pass a coinage bill and issue treasury notes in denominations from $50 to $1 million.

March 11
POLITICS: The constitution of the Confederacy is unanimously adopted by the Confederate Convention at Montgomery, Alabama, and passed along to constituent states for ratification. It is based primarily on the U.S. Constitution but differs in explicitly condoning the practice of slavery.
SOUTH: General Braxton Bragg assumes command of Confederate forces in Florida and proves himself to be a competent disciplinarian and organizer.

March 12
SOUTHWEST: Federal forces abandon Fort McIntosh, Texas.

March 13
POLITICS: Despite pressure from within his own cabinet, President Abraham Lincoln directly orders Secretary of State William H. Seward not to receive Confederate

emissaries. Through this expedient, he avoids any appearance of recognition of the Confederate government in Montgomery. He also dispatches former navy officer Gustavus V. Fox on a mission to Fort Sumter, South Carolina, to evaluate all possibilities of succoring the garrison.

WEST: Captain Nathaniel Lyon, a pugnacious, aggressive officer by nature, becomes commander of the U.S. arsenal at St. Louis, Missouri.

March 15

POLITICS: President Abraham Lincoln inquires of his cabinet whether or not a relief attempt ought to be mounted to resupply the garrison of Fort Sumter, Charleston Harbor. The majority, especially Secretary of State William H. Seward, view such a move as provocative and advise against it.

The Confederate Congress thanks the state of Louisiana for enriching its coffers with $536,000 appropriated from the U.S. Mint at New Orleans.

SOUTHWEST: Camp Wood, Texas, is abandoned by Federal forces.

March 16

DIPLOMACY: President Jefferson Davis appoints three special ministers, William L. Yancey, Pierre A. Rost, and Dudley Mann, to visit Europe in a quest for diplomatic recognition. They are instructed to use cotton as economic leverage, whenever possible, for securing support.

POLITICS: The Confederate Convention at Montgomery, Alabama, adjourns.

SOUTHWEST: The Arizona Territory Convention at Mesilla votes in favor of secession.

March 17

SOUTHWEST: Federal troops abandon Camp Hudson, Texas.

NAVAL: Agents of the Confederate navy department arrive in New Orleans to arrange for the purchase and construction of gunboats.

March 18

DIPLOMACY: President Abraham Lincoln appoints Charles Francis Adams as minister to Great Britain.

POLITICS: The Arkansas State Convention defeats the move to secede on a 39 to 35 vote and then schedules a public referendum on the issue that summer.

SOUTH: Lieutenant Adam J. Slemmer, commanding Fort Pickens, Florida, returns four fugitive slaves to their owners.

General Braxton Bragg forbids the passing of supplies or communications to either Fort Pickens, Florida, or the navy squadron offshore.

SOUTHWEST: Governor Sam Houston of Texas, having refused to take an oath of allegiance to the Confederacy, is forced to retire from office.

March 19

SOUTHWEST: Federal forces abandon Forts Clark, Inge, and Lancaster, Texas.

March 20

SOUTHWEST: Federal troops yield Fort Brown and Fort Duncan, Texas.

NAVAL: The sloop USS *Isabella,* stocked with supplies for the garrison at Pensacola, is seized by state forces at Mobile, Alabama.

March 21
NAVAL: Former navy officer Gustavus V. Fox, pursuant to orders from President Abraham Lincoln, reconnoiters Fort Sumter and Charleston Harbor, South Carolina, with a view toward relieving the garrison.

March 22
WEST: Governor Claiborne F. Jackson fails to convince his fellow Missourians to join the Confederacy, after which the polity sharply divides into pro- and anti-Federal camps.

Colonel William W. Loring becomes commander of the Department of New Mexico.

March 26
SOUTHWEST: Colonel Earl Van Dorn arrives in Texas to support the Confederate cause.

March 28
POLITICS: To break the impasse, President Abraham Lincoln resolves to mount a sea-borne expedition to succor the Federal garrison at Fort Sumter, Charleston Harbor, and he orders it to sail no later than April 6, 1861. His cabinet also divides on the matter, 3 to 2 in favor with Secretary of War Simon Cameron abstaining. In effect, the wily president is maneuvering his Southern counterpart into firing the first shot.
SOUTHWEST: Federal forces abandon Fort Mason, Texas.

March 31
POLITICS: President Abraham Lincoln orders a relief expedition to assist the Federal garrison at Fort Pickens, Florida, guarding the entrance to Pensacola harbor.
SOUTHWEST: Federal forces abandon Fort Bliss, Texas.
NAVAL: Secretary of the Navy Gideon Welles orders 250 personnel transferred from the New York Navy Yard to Norfolk, Virginia, to bolster the garrison.

April 1
POLITICS: Secretary of State William H. Seward strongly recommends that President Abraham Lincoln abandon Fort Sumter, Charleston Harbor, while more tenable posts along the Gulf of Mexico be fortified. He also suggests that a war with Europe would serve as a "panacea" to unify the country. Lincoln courteously thanks the secretary for such sage advice—then declares that he intends to run his own administration.

April 3
NAVAL: Confederate artillery on Morris Island, Charleston Harbor, fires upon the Union vessel *Rhoda H. Shannon.*

April 4
POLITICS: President Abraham Lincoln approves the strategy suggested by Gustavus V. Fox and informs Major Robert Anderson at Fort Sumter, Charleston, of an

impending relief expedition. However, he still grants that officer complete latitude on any response necessary should the Confederates attack.

The Virginia State Convention in Richmond rejects an ordinance of secession, 89 to 45.

April 5
SOUTHWEST: Federal forces abandon Fort Quitman, Texas.

NAVAL: A squadron consisting of USS *Pawnee, Pocahontas,* and U.S. revenue cutter *Harriet Lane* are assembled under the command of Captain Samuel Mercer. Meanwhile, the *Powhatan* continues steaming toward Fort Pickens, Florida.

April 6
POLITICS: South Carolina governor Francis W. Pickens is advised by President Abraham Lincoln that an expedition is being mounted to supply—not reinforce—the garrison at Fort Sumter, Charleston Harbor. Moreover, if no resistance is encountered, he pledges that no additional troops will be dispatched.

NAVAL: Lieutenant John L. Worden is ordered overland to Fort Pickens; he carries secret orders for the squadron offshore to land reinforcements.

April 7
SOUTH: To increase pressure on Major Robert Anderson, General Pierre G. T. Beauregard forbids any further communications between Fort Sumter, Charleston Harbor, and the shore.

General Braxton Bragg, commanding Confederate forces in Pensacola, requests and receives permission to fire on any reinforcements being landed at Fort Pickens from the squadron offshore.

April 8
SOUTH: In response to the approaching relief expedition to Fort Sumter, Charleston Harbor, Confederate authorities begin to undertake military preparations around the harbor.

NAVAL: Federal troops onboard the U.S. revenue cutter *Harriet Lane* land to bolster the garrison of Fort Pickens, Florida.

April 10
NAVAL: The steamer *Baltic* departs New York in a second attempt to relieve the garrison at Fort Sumter, Charleston Harbor, with naval agent Gustavus V. Fox onboard. En route, it is joined by the USS *Pawnee* off Hampton Roads, Virginia.

Lieutenant John L. Worden arrives at Pensacola, Florida, on official business and receives permission from General Braxton Bragg to visit Fort Pickens.

April 11
POLITICS: Three Confederate peace emissaries depart Washington, D.C., having failed to reach an agreeable solution with Secretary of State William H. Steward. Meanwhile, Federal troops are ordered into the nation's capital, which is completely surrounded by potentially hostile territory.

SOUTH: As a sovereign entity, the Confederate government cannot allow the presence of foreign troops—or their flag—in a major port. The impending arrival of a Union supply ship to further sustain the Fort Sumter garrison constitutes an egregious affront to Southern independence and cannot be permitted. Therefore, General Pierre G. T. Beauregard is ordered by Confederate authorities to demand the immediate capitulation of Fort Sumter, Charleston Harbor. He receives careful instructions not to take offensive action if Major Robert Anderson agrees to evacuate by a strict time table. However, when these new terms are delivered to the Union commander, he flatly refuses. As a sop to Southern sensitivities, Anderson also informs Beauregard that he is nearly out of supplies and must yield by April 15, regardless. The Federals receive a deadline of 24 hours.

SOUTHWEST: Colonel Earl Van Dorn becomes Confederate commander in Texas and is ordered to arrest any U.S. soldiers refusing to join the Southern cause.

April 12

SOUTH: At 3:20 A.M., the tempo of events dramatically escalates once General Pierre G. T. Beauregard dispatches Colonel James Chesnut and Captain Stephen D. Lee to Fort Sumter, Charleston Harbor. They demand a precise time for the evacuation of that post. Major Robert Anderson, acknowledging the inevitable, declares noontime on April 15, provided he does not receive additional supplies or instructions from the government. Anderson then is informed summarily that the Confederates will commence bombarding within one hour. The Civil War, a monumental struggle in military history and a defining moment for the United States, is about to unfold.

At 4:30 A.M., the shoreline around Charleston Harbor erupts into flame as 18 mortars and 30 heavy cannon, backed by 7,000 troops, bombard Fort Sumter. Major Robert Anderson, commanding only 85 men, 43 civilian engineers, and 48 cannon, weathers the storm and waits until daybreak before responding with six cannon of his own. Captain Abner Doubleday receives the honor of firing the first Union shot of the war.

NAVAL: The USS *Pawnee,* the U.S. revenue cutter *Harriet Lane,* and the steamship *Baltic,* commanded by Gustavus V. Fox, arrive in Charleston Harbor, South Carolina, with supplies for Fort Sumter. Having appeared too late to reinforce the garrison they remain helpless spectators as the fort is bombarded.

The naval squadron consisting of USS *Sabine, Brooklyn, St. Louis,* and *Wynandotte* begins to land reinforcements at Fort Pickens, Florida.

April 13

SOUTH: After 34 hours of continuous shelling, a lucky Confederate shot slices through Fort Sumter's flagstaff at 12:48 P.M., while hotshot ignites several fires. This act induces former Texas senator Louis T. Wigfall to commandeer a boat, row out to the fort, and again demand its surrender. At this juncture, Major Robert Anderson concludes this is the wiser course, and he raises a white flag at 2:30 P.M. Firing upon Fort Sumter then ceases and surrender ceremonies are planned for the following day. Curiously, the Federals have sustained no casualties despite 4,000 shells hitting their post. The garrison, for its part, managed to fire off 1,000 rounds, again with little damage to the city or its military facilities. But this perceived Southern aggression galvanizes heretofore tepid sentiments throughout the

North, granting President Abraham Lincoln the political wherewithal necessary for waging war.

SOUTHWEST: Federal forces abandon Fort Davis, Texas.

NAVAL: Relief ships under Gustavus V. Fox continue loitering outside Charleston Harbor, South Carolina, unwilling to approach closer in the face of hostile fire.

His mission completed, Navy lieutenant John L. Worden returns to Washington, D.C., from Fort Pickens, Florida. En route, he is arrested by Confederate authorities near Montgomery, Alabama, and is imprisoned.

The USS *Sabine* assumes blockading stations off Pensacola, Florida.

April 14

SOUTH: Major Robert Anderson formally capitulates Fort Sumter, Charleston Harbor, to Confederate authorities. Ironically, despite the intensity of the bombardment, the only fatalities, two killed and four wounded, occur when a pile of ordnance accidently ignites during a 100-gun salute to the U.S. flag. Anderson's surrender also signals the eruption of euphoric celebrations on the shore and in the city. The captives are subsequently entertained by the cream of Charleston society and depart onboard the provisional squadron commanded by Gustavus V. Fox. "We have met them and we have conquered," Governor Francis Pickens subsequently crows as the first act in a long and bloody drama concludes.

Interior view of Fort Sumter on April 14, 1861, after its evacuation *(National Archives)*

April 15

POLITICS: In a move designed to deny the Confederacy diplomatic recognition, President Abraham Lincoln declares not war but, rather, a state of insurrection and calls for raising 75,000 three-month volunteers to suppress it. However, service by African Americans is declined. He also requests a special meeting of Congress to convene on July 4, Independence Day. Not surprisingly, Lincoln's call to arms is ignored entirely by the governments of North Carolina, Kentucky, and Virginia. However, New York's legislature militantly embraces the Union cause and votes $3 million to support war efforts.

Federal installations at Fort Macon, North Carolina, are seized by state forces.

NAVAL: Naval authorities apprehend 17 Southern vessels at New York harbor.

April 16

POLITICS: Virginia governor John Lechter informs President Abraham Lincoln that his state will not furnish troops for what he considers the "subjugation" of the South.

SOUTH: North Carolina state forces seize Forts Caswell and Johnson.

SOUTHWEST: Federal forces abandon Fort Washita, Chickasaw Nation.

April 17

POLITICS: Secessionists gather in Baltimore in large numbers.

The Virginia State Convention, reacting strongly against President Abraham Lincoln's call for troops, votes 88 to 55 for secession. The proposal is then forwarded to the public for ratification.

President Jefferson Davis begins to solicit applications for Confederate letters of marque and reprisal, in effect, establishing a force of privateers.

WEST: The governments of Missouri and Tennessee refuse to raise the requisite numbers of militia forces.

NAVAL: Southern sympathizers attempt to block Gosport Navy Yard, Norfolk, Virginia, by placing obstacles in the channel, but the attempt proves ineffectual.

The USS *Powhatan* under Lieutenant David D. Porter arrives at Fort Pickens, Florida, and disembarks an additional 600 troops to bolster the sailors and marines already deployed. Thus the best harbor on the Gulf of Mexico is secured for use by Union forces for the remainder of the war.

April 18

NORTH: The 6th Massachusetts rides the rails from New York to Baltimore, Maryland, en route to Washington, D.C.

Colonel Robert E. Lee declines an offer from Abraham Lincoln to command all Union forces. Lee does not support secession, but he feels compelled to follow his native state of Virginia.

Five companies of Pennsylvania Volunteers arrive to protect Washington, D.C.

SOUTH: Virginia forces seize the U.S. Customs Office at Richmond.

Colonel Harvey Brown takes command of Fort Pickens, Pensacola, and establishes the new Department of Florida.

WEST: Lieutenant Roger Jones orders his command of 50 men to burn the U.S. armory at Harper's Ferry, western Virginia, thereby preventing its tooling facilities from falling into enemy hands. Fire destroys the buildings and with it some 15,000 rifled muskets, but the local population extinguishes the flames before valuable factory equipment is destroyed.

Arkansas state forces seize U.S. Army stores at Pine Bluff.

NAVAL: Captain Hiram Paulding is ordered to assemble 1,000 U.S. Marines for the purpose of burning Federal supplies and equipment in the Norfolk Navy Yard, Virginia.

April 19

POLITICS: To interrupt any flow of food or war materiel from abroad, President Abraham Lincoln declares a naval blockade of the Confederate coastline. This effort encompasses all the ports of South Carolina, Georgia, Alabama, Florida, Mississippi, Louisiana, and Texas and so overwhelms the relatively small U.S. Navy that its implementation is gradual, by stages. This is the only part of General Winfield Scott's so-called Anaconda Plan that is enacted from the onset of the war, and Lincoln does so after the urging of Secretary of State William H. Seward. In time the blockade intensifies to reach stranglehold proportions and emerges as a major factor in the downfall of the Confederacy.

NORTH: The 6th Massachusetts, transferring between railroad stations in Baltimore, Maryland, is violently attacked by rioters. Shots are exchanged; four soldiers are killed and 36 are wounded. These are the first Union casualties incurred by hostile action; 11 civilians were also slain. Seething Southerners also begin to cut rail and telegraph lines leading to the capital. For several anxious days, Washington, D.C., remains temporarily cut off from the rest of the country.

Dorothea Dix volunteers to recruit and direct women nurses for the Federal army.

NAVAL: Captain Samuel F. Du Pont embarks from Philadelphia, Pennsylvania, with reinforcements for the beleaguered Union capital. The 8th Massachusetts under General Benjamin F. Butler also sails for Annapolis, Maryland, aboard the ferryboat *Maryland.*

The steam transport *Star of the West* is seized by state forces under General Earl Van Dorn at Indianola, Texas.

Southern-born captain David G. Farragut remains loyal to the Union and relocates his family from Norfolk, Virginia, to New York.

April 20

NORTH: Colonel Robert E. Lee tenders his resignation from the U.S. Army.

To obstruct the passage of Federal troops to Washington, D.C., secessionist mobs burn several railways out of Baltimore, Maryland. This forces Federal troops to arrive by water and then rebuild the tracks as they proceed on foot.

The 8th Massachusetts under General Benjamin F. Butler parades through Annapolis en route to Washington, D.C.

SOUTH: The 4th Massachusetts arrives at Fortress Monroe, on the tip of the Yorktown Peninsula, Virginia.

WEST: Confederate sympathizers seize the U.S. arsenal at Liberty, Missouri.

NAVAL: Captain Charles S. McCauley hurriedly and prematurely orders the Gosport Navy Yard in Norfolk, Virginia, burned and evacuated. He does so despite the arrival of 1,000 U.S. Marines under Commodore Hiram Paulding as reinforcements. The resulting destruction is less than complete, and the dry docks become operative again in a few weeks. The Confederates also retrieve no less than 1,200 heavy naval cannon, which they implant at fortifications as far west as Vicksburg, Mississippi. Among the aged vessels hurriedly destroyed or scuttled are ships of the line USS *Pennsylvania, Columbus, Delaware*; frigates *Raritan, Columbia, Merrimac*; and sloops *Dolphin, Germantown*, and *Plymouth*—mostly obsolete but potentially useful for enforcing the initial Union blockade. McCauley's badly botched withdrawal from Norfolk proves an embarrassing windfall for the Confederate war effort.

The venerable USS *Constitution*, "Old Ironsides" of War of 1812 fame, is towed safely offshore from Annapolis by the steamer USS *Maryland*.

The U.S. Naval Academy at Annapolis is abandoned and transferred north to Newport, Rhode Island. The buildings remain occupied by Federal troops for the remainder of the war.

Texas authorities confiscate the U.S. Coast survey schooner *Twilight* at Aransas Pass.

April 21
NORTH: Rioting and civil disorder continue in Baltimore, Maryland, including sabotage of nearby railroad lines.

WEST: Pro-Union delegates meeting in Monongahela County in western Virginia discuss a secession movement of their own from the Confederacy.

NAVAL: Confederate forces rapidly reoccupy Gosport Navy Yard, Norfolk, Virginia, and commence reconstruction efforts. Due to the hasty Union withdrawal, many tons of valuable weapons and equipment are recovered. Among the vessels salvaged is the old steam frigate USS *Merrimack*, which in a few months is reincarnated as the ironclad ram CSS *Virginia*.

The USS *Saratoga* captures the cargo vessel *Nightingale*, which is found laden with 961 African slaves. The U.S. government officially banned trafficking in human cargo in 1808.

April 22
NORTH: The 7th New York arrives at Annapolis, Maryland, onboard the steamer *Boston*.

SOUTH: The U.S. arsenal at Fayetteville, North Carolina, is captured by state forces.

WEST: Militia begins to arrive at Cairo, Illinois, at the confluence of the Ohio and Mississippi rivers.

Governor Henry M. Rector of Arkansas refuses to provide his quota of militia for government use.

NAVAL: Captain Franklin Buchanan, commanding the Washington Navy Yard, tenders his resignation in anticipation of Maryland's seemingly impending secession—he is not reinstated once his state remains loyal, and he ultimately joins the Confederacy. Buchanan is succeeded by Captain John A. B. Dahlgren.

April 23
POLITICS: President Jefferson Davis offers aid to Confederate sympathizers in Missouri if they attack and seize the U.S. arsenal in St. Louis.

NORTH: An assembly of free African Americans in Boston, Massachusetts, demands that Federal laws preventing their enrollment in state militia be repealed.

General George B. McClellan gains appointment as major general, U.S. Army.

SOUTH: General Robert E. Lee becomes commander of Virginia state forces.

WEST: The Federal installation at Fort Smith, Arkansas, is seized by state forces.

SOUTHWEST: U.S. Army officers taken at San Antonio, Texas, are treated as prisoners of war.

NAVAL: The defenses of Washington, D.C., are enhanced by the arrival of USS *Pawnee* under Captain Hiram Paulding.

April 24
NAVAL: The Navy Department formally begins to evacuate the U.S. Naval Academy at Annapolis, Maryland, whereupon Captain S. Blake loads faculty and midshipmen onto the iconic frigate USS *Constitution*.

The USS *Cumberland* captures the Confederate vessels *Young America* and *George M. Smith* off Hampton Roads, Virginia, both heavily laden with military supplies and ammunition.

April 25
NORTH: The 8th Massachusetts under General Benjamin F. Butler defiantly parades through Washington, D.C., following a lengthy march around Baltimore, Maryland.

WEST: In a daring preemptive raid, Union Captain James H. Stokes arrives at St. Louis, Missouri, by steamer, removes 12,000 muskets from the U.S. arsenal there, and returns the weapons to Alton, Illinois, for militia use. This proves a critical blow to pro-Confederate militias forming in the region.

General Edwin V. Sumner replaces Colonel Albert S. Johnston as commander of the Department of the Pacific.

SOUTHWEST: Fort Stockton, Texas, is abandoned by Federal forces.

Major Caleb C. Sibley capitulates 420 Federal troops to Colonel Earl Van Dorn at Indianola, Texas.

April 26
POLITICS: Georgia governor Joseph E. Brown orders all debts owed to Northerners repudiated.

SOUTH: General Joseph E. Johnston arrives and receives command of Virginia state forces defending the capital of Richmond.

NAVAL: The USS *Commerce* captures Confederate blockade-runner *Lancaster* off Havre de Grace, Maryland.

Confederate secretary of the navy Stephen R. Mallory proposes constructing new classes of steam-powered armored warships to offset the stark Union advantage in numbers.

April 27

Politics: President Abraham Lincoln authorizes suspension of writs of habeas corpus between Philadelphia, Pennsylvania, and Washington, D.C. General Winfield Scott is entrusted with adjudicating all incidents arising from the move.

North: General Robert Patterson, Pennsylvania militia, takes command of the Department of Pennsylvania.

The 8th New York makes a belated appearance in the streets of Washington, D.C.

General Benjamin F. Butler assumes command of the Department of Annapolis, Maryland.

South: The Virginia Convention proffers its capital of Richmond as an alternative to Montgomery, Alabama.

West: Confederate colonel Thomas J. Jackson receives command of Virginia troops in the vicinity of Harper's Ferry.

The steamer *Helmick* is seized with military stores intended for the Confederacy at Cairo, Illinois.

Naval: President Abraham Lincoln extends the Union blockade to encompass the coasts of Virginia and North Carolina. Secretary of the Navy Gideon Welles also authorizes the interdiction of Confederate privateers at sea.

April 29

Politics: The Maryland House of Delegates decisively votes down secession by a margin of 53 to 13.

The provisional Confederate Congress convenes its second session at Montgomery, Alabama, granting President Jefferson Davis war powers and authority to raise volunteers, make loans, issue letters of marque, and command land and naval forces. They do so in direct reaction to President Abraham Lincoln's insurrection declaration and his call for volunteers.

North: Elizabeth Blackwell, the nation's first female doctor, establishes the Women's Central Association for Relief to better coordinate the myriads of smaller war-relief groups. Her organization serves as a precursor for the much larger U.S. Sanitation Commission.

April 30

Southwest: Colonel William H. Emory evacuates Fort Washita in Indian Territory near the Texas border and heads north toward Fort Leavenworth, Texas. His withdrawal renders the neighboring Five Civilized Tribes—Cherokee, Chickasaw, Creek, Choctaw, and Seminole—vulnerable to Confederate influence.

May 1

North: Soldiers killed in the Baltimore riots are interred with full military honors in Boston, Massachusetts.

South: General Robert E. Lee orders that additional Confederate forces be concentrated in the vicinity of Harper's Ferry, Virginia, presently commanded by Colonel Thomas J. Jackson.

Joseph E. Johnston is appointed brigadier general, C.S.A.

WEST: Governor Samuel W. Black of the Nebraska Territory calls out volunteer forces to assist the Union.

NAVAL: The USS *Commerce* captures the Confederate steam tug *Lioness* at the mouth of the Patapsco River, Maryland.

The first U.S. Navy vessels establish a blockade of the James River and Hampton Roads, Virginia.

The USS *Hatteras* seizes the Confederate vessel *Magnolia* in the Gulf of Mexico.

May 3

NORTH: President Abraham Lincoln issues a new call for 42,000 three-year volunteers, with 10 new regiments for the U.S. Army and an additional 18,000 seamen for the navy. This brings available manpower ceilings to 156,000 for the army and 25,000 for the navy.

General Winfield Scott, the senior American commander, unveils his so-called Anaconda Plan for defeating the rising tide of secessionism to President Abraham Lincoln. Basically, this entails a gunboat-supported drive down the Mississippi River by 60,000 troops, commencing at Cairo, Illinois, and ending in the Gulf of Mexico. Concurrently, the U.S. Navy would establish a tight blockade of the Southern coast to strangle Confederate trade with Europe. Derided at first by younger general officers who preferred a swift and decisive military campaign, the Scott plan is not adopted formally until 1864, and then in slightly modified form. Nonetheless, the aged "Old Fuss and Feathers" Scott provided a viable, war-winning strategy that ultimately preserved the Union. Lincoln spends nearly three years finding a general to execute it forcefully.

WEST: The Department of the Ohio is formed (Illinois, Indiana, Ohio).

U.S. ordnance stores are seized at Kansas City, Missouri.

May 4

WEST: Confederate sympathizers appropriate U.S. ordnance stores in Kansas City, Missouri.

SOUTHWEST: Fort Arbuckle, Indian Territory, is abandoned by Federal forces.

NAVAL: The USS *Cumberland* captures the *Mary and Virginia* and the *Theresa C.* attempting to run the blockade off Fortress Monroe, Virginia.

The CSS *Star of the West* is recommissioned in the Confederate navy at New Orleans, Louisiana, as a receiving ship.

May 5

NORTH: To deter attempted sabotage, troops under General Benjamin F. Butler occupy buildings along the Baltimore and Ohio Railroad.

SOUTH: Confederate forces temporarily evacuate the town of Alexandria, Virginia, situated on the Potomac River directly across from Washington, D.C.

NAVAL: The USS *Valley City* captures the Confederate vessel *J. O'Neil* off Pamlico River, North Carolina.

May 6

POLITICS: President Jefferson Davis signs a bill passed by the Confederate Congress, declaring a state of war with the United States.

The state legislature in Arkansas approves secession by 69 to 1, becoming the ninth state to depart, while the government of Tennessee likewise votes 66 to 25 to authorize a public referendum on the issue.

WEST: The Confederate-leaning Missouri State Militia under General Daniel M. Frost establishes a training camp near St. Louis at the behest of Governor Claiborne Jackson. Meanwhile, Captain Nathaniel Lyon, commanding the garrison at St. Louis, refuses all public demands to remove his troops from the city.

NAVAL: The Confederate Congress mandates the issuance of letters of marque and reprisal to privateers.

May 7

POLITICS: The Tennessee state legislature formally votes to join the Confederacy while riots erupt between pro- and antisecessionist sympathizers in Knoxville. The eastern half of the state remains a strong Unionist enclave throughout the war.

NORTH: President Abraham Lincoln appoints newly repatriated Major Robert Anderson to recruiting duties in his native state of Kentucky.

NAVAL: The U.S. Naval Academy staff, students, and supplies finally board the steamer USS *Baltic* and the venerable frigate USS *Constitution* at Annapolis, prior to relocating to Newport, Rhode Island.

The USS *Yankee* receives the fire of Confederate batteries stationed at Gloucester Point, Virginia.

May 9

POLITICS: President Jefferson Davis authorizes enlisting more than 400,000 volunteers for three years or the duration of the war. The quotas are met enthusiastically at first.

NORTH: Maryland's pro-Union stance forces all secessionist military units to evacuate the state.

SOUTHWEST: Colonel William H. Emory abandons Fort Cobb in the Chickasaw Indian Nation.

A detachment of Federal troops under Colonel Isaac V. D. Reeve surrenders to Colonel Earl Van Dorn at San Lucas Spring, Texas.

NAVAL: The frigate USS *Constitution* and the steamer *Baltic* arrive at Newport, Rhode Island, with faculty and midshipmen, to reestablish the U.S. Naval Academy.

Confederate secretary of the navy Stephen R. Mallory orders Commander James D. Bulloch to England as Confederate naval agent. There, Bulloch engages in a battle of wits with U.S. Minister Charles Francis Adams while clandestinely acquiring ships, guns, and munitions.

May 10

POLITICS: President Jefferson Davis urges the Confederate Congress to purchase six warships, arms, and supplies from abroad.

SOUTH: General Robert E. Lee is made commander of Confederate troops in Virginia.

WEST: Violence erupts in St. Louis, Missouri, between secessionist sympathizers and U.S. Army troops, backed by a large German-speaking population. About two dozen civilians and two soldiers die in the fighting as Captain Nathaniel Lyon energetically takes General Daniel M. Frost and 625 Confederates prisoner at Camp Jackson. However, his rashness induces many undecided citizens to join secessionist ranks, and 30 citizens die in subsequent rioting.

NAVAL: Confederate secretary of the navy Stephen R. Mallory alerts the Committee of Naval Affairs, Confederate Congress, that the acquisition of a heavily armed iron ship is "a matter of the first necessity."

The steamer USS *Niagara* under Captain William W. McKean assumes a blockading position off Charleston, South Carolina.

May 11

SOUTH: Ben McCulloch is appointed brigadier general, C.S.A.

WEST: Continuing secessionist unrest in St. Louis, Missouri, results in seven civilian deaths at the hands of the 5th Reserve Regiment. Colonel William S. Harney also arrives back in town to succeed Captain Nathaniel Lyon as garrison commander.

NAVAL: The USS *Pawnee* arrives off Alexandria, Virginia, to protect anchored Union vessels from attack.

May 12

NAVAL: The USS *Niagara* captures the Confederate blockade-runner *General Parkhill* at sea while approaching Charleston, South Carolina.

May 13

DIPLOMACY: In a move that antagonizes the Lincoln administration, the government of Great Britain recognizes both the North and the South as belligerents. This amounts to a discreet nod in terms of recognizing the Confederacy as an equal partner in the upcoming struggle, but Queen Victoria's adherence to strict neutrality dashes Southern hopes for military intervention on their behalf.

POLITICS: Virginia delegates from the western portion of the state, who disagree with secession, convene a convention of their own at Wheeling. There, they discuss joining the Union as a new state.

NORTH: Baltimore is reoccupied and secured by Federal forces under General Benjamin F. Butler, who both occupies Federal Hill and imposes martial law without prior authorization.

WEST: General George B. McClellan is appointed commander of the Department of the Ohio.

SOUTHWEST: General Ben McCulloch becomes Confederate commander of the Indian Territory.

NAVAL: The blockade of Pensacola, Florida, resumes under the USS *Sabine*.

May 14

DIPLOMACY: U.S. minister Charles Francis Adams arrives in London, England, where it is expected his pristine abolitionist credentials will resonate favorably at the Court of St. James.

NORTH: John C. Frémont, a popular explorer and one-time presidential candidate, becomes a major general, U.S. Army. Irvin McDowell and Montgomery C. Meigs also are appointed brigadier generals.

General Benjamin F. Butler consolidates his grip on Baltimore, Maryland, and arrests noted secessionists, including Ross Winans, who had invented a steam cannon. Governor Thomas H. Hicks also issues a call for four regiments to defend Maryland and the national capital.

SOUTH: Robert E. Lee is appointed brigadier general, C.S.A.

WEST: Major Robert Anderson is instructed by President Abraham Lincoln to assist Kentucky Unionists wherever possible, despite the state's avowed neutrality.

The South needs rolling stock, so Colonel Thomas J. Jackson orders the seizure of trains and railroad cars at Harper's Ferry, Virginia.

NAVAL: The USS *Minnesota* captures Confederate schooners *Mary Willis, Delaware Farmer,* and *Emily Ann* off Hampton Roads, Virginia.

May 15

NORTH: Major Robert Anderson, defender of Fort Sumter and regarded as a Northern hero, is promoted several steps to brigadier general, U.S. Army.

SOUTH: General Benjamin Butler relinquishes command of the Department of Annapolis and arrives at Fortress Monroe, Virginia, where he advances to major general of volunteers. He is succeeded by General George Cadwalader.

WEST: General Joseph E. Johnston assumes command of Confederate forces near Harper's Ferry, Virginia.

Colonel William S. Harney, commanding at St. Louis, Missouri, implores citizens to ignore secessionist attempts to raise militia. However, he takes no active steps to interfere, which raises eyebrows among union supporters.

NAVAL: The USS *Bainbridge* is ordered to New Grenada (Panama) to protect American shipping from possible Confederate privateers.

May 16

POLITICS: Tennessee is encouraged to enter the Confederacy at the urging of Governor Isham Harris.

SOUTH: Samuel Cooper gains appointment as a full general and senior leader in the Confederate army.

WEST: William S. Rosecrans is promoted to brigadier general, U.S. Army.

Union troops enter Potosi, Missouri, and begin to round up suspected Confederate sympathizers.

NAVAL: The Navy Department orders Commander John Rodgers to establish naval forces on western rivers and to cooperate with troops under General John C. Frémont.

May 17

POLITICS: President Jefferson Davis agrees to a $50 million loan to the Confederate government along with the distribution of treasury notes. He also signs legislation admitting North Carolina into the Confederacy.

NAVAL: The USS *Minnesota* seizes the Confederate bark *Star* at sea en route to Bremen, Germany.

WEST: The California legislature votes its support for the Union.

SOUTHWEST: Chief John Ross declares neutrality for Cherokee throughout the Indian Territory, although the tribe continues splintering into pro- and antisecessionist factions.

May 18

POLITICS: Arkansas formally joins the Confederate States of America.

WEST: Missouri politician Francis Blair contacts President Abraham Lincoln concerning his suspicions about Colonel William S. Harney, commanding officer at St. Louis.

NAVAL: U.S. Navy ships blockade the mouth of the Rappahannock River, Virginia.

The Confederate schooner *Savannah* is commissioned as a privateer.

May 19

WEST: The Confederate garrison at Harper's Ferry in western Virginia is strengthened by additional troops.

NAVAL: Warships USS *Monticello* and *Thomas Freeborn* trade fire with a Confederate battery at Sewell's Point, Virginia.

The CSS *Lady Davis* seizes the Union ship *A. B. Thompson* near Charleston, South Carolina.

May 20

POLITICS: The Provisional Confederate Congress elects to relocate itself from Montgomery, Alabama, to Richmond, Virginia, where it will remain until 1865. This is calculated to strengthen the Old Dominion's ties to the Confederacy but also shifts the locus of the war northward.

At the behest of Governor Beriah Magoffin, the legislature of the strategic state of Kentucky declares neutrality in the upcoming struggle.

The North Carolina State Convention at Raleigh votes to become the 10th state to secede and also ratifies the Confederate Constitution.

SOUTH: William W. Loring is appointed brigadier general, C.S.A.

NAVAL: The USS *Crusader* captures Confederate blockade-runner *Neptune* off Fort Taylor, Florida.

May 21

DIPLOMACY: A bellicose secretary of state William H. Seward issues Dispatch No. 10 for Minister Charles F. Adams in London, which threatens war with England. In light of prevailing military and political realities, Adams simply ignores it.

POLITICS: The Provisional Confederate Congress adjourns its second Session.

SOUTH: General John B. Magruder arrives to take command of Confederate forces at Yorktown, Virginia. Among his best units there is the 1st North Carolina under Colonel Daniel H. Hill.

WEST: General William S. Harney, commanding Federal forces in Missouri, enters into a convention with Missouri State Guard commander General Sterling Price. He then agrees not to introduce Federal troops into the state if the Southerners can maintain order. Both Congressman Francis P. Blair and Captain Nathaniel Lyon condemn the agreement, regarding it as treasonous.

NAVAL: USS *Pocahontas* captures the Confederate steamer *James Guy* off Machdoc Creek, Virginia.

The venerable frigate USS *Constellation,* the navy's oldest operating warship, captures the slaver *Triton* off the west coast of Africa.

May 23

POLITICS: A popular vote for secession in Virginia is 97,750 in favor and 32,134 against. However, efforts continue in the 50 western counties to remain within the Union.

SOUTH: General Benjamin F. Butler, commanding Fortress Monroe, Virginia, refuses to return three runaways slaves to their owner by declaring them "contraband of war." This sets an important precedent for allowing thousands of slaves to escape to Union lines and freedom.

John B. Floyd, the former secretary of war, becomes a brigadier general, C.S.A.

Virginia general Benjamin Huger assumes command at Norfolk, Virginia.

WEST: Federal troops commence extended operations against Indians on the Eel and Mad rivers of California for the next three weeks.

NAVAL: The USS *Mississippi* suffers sabotage to its steam condensers and is forced back to Boston, Massachusetts, for repairs.

May 24

SOUTH: About 13,000 Union soldiers under General Samuel P. Heintzelman occupy Alexandria and Arlington Heights, Virginia, bolstering the defenses of Washington, D.C. The North now enjoys another solid lodgment on Old Dominion soil. However, when 24-year-old Colonel Elmer E. Ellsworth of the 11th New York Regiment (Fire Zouaves) removes a Confederate flag from a hotel in Alexandria, he is shot by innkeeper James T. Jackson, who is then himself killed. Ellsworth enjoys the melancholy distinction of becoming the North's first officer fatality. Both men are enshrined as martyrs by their respective side.

NAVAL: The USS *Pawnee* under Commander Stephen C. Rowan receives the surrender of Alexandria, Virginia, which is occupied promptly by Federal forces under Commodore John A. B. Dahlgren.

May 25

POLITICS: President Abraham Lincoln attends the funeral of Colonel Elmer E. Ellsworth after his remains lay in state at the White House. "So much of promised usefulness to one's country, and of bright hopes for one's self and friends," a somber Lincoln writes, "have rarely been so suddenly dashed, as in his fall."

NORTH: Secessionist John Merryman is imprisoned by Union authorities in Baltimore, Maryland, for recruiting Confederate troops and sabotaging railroad lines and bridges. Chief Justice Roger B. Taney, acting in the capacity of a Federal circuit court judge, issues a writ of habeas corpus on his behalf to release him, but the commanding officer recognizes no authority other than the commander in chief's. Taney subsequently countered that only Congress possesses the power to suspend habeas corpus.

SOUTH: To forestall Confederate moves against Washington, D.C., Union forces destroy seven miles of bridges and rail line between Alexandria and Leesburg, Virginia.

NAVAL: The USS *Pawnee* captures the Confederate steamer *Thomas Collyer* at Alexandria, Virginia.

The USS *Minnesota* captures the Confederate bark *Winfred* off Hampton Roads, Virginia.

May 26

POLITICAL: U.S. postmaster general Francis P. Blair announces the suspension of all service with Confederate states.

WEST: General George B. McClellan orders three columns of Union forces to advance on Grafton in western Virginia to secure the Baltimore and Ohio Railroad. This forms the most important link between the capital and the western states.

NAVAL: The sloop USS *Powhatan* under Lieutenant David D. Porter takes up blockading positions off Mobile, Alabama.

Commander Charles H. Poor of the USS *Brooklyn* assumes blockading stations off New Orleans, Louisiana.

May 27

POLITICS: Chief Justice Roger B. Taney again declares the suspension of the writ of habeas corpus unconstitutional, which President Abraham Lincoln promptly ignores in light of circumstances.

SOUTH: To enlarge the Northern staging area around Fortress Monroe, Virginia, General Benjamin F. Butler advances eight miles and occupies Newport News.

May 28

SOUTH: General Irvin McDowell is appointed commander of the Department of Northeastern Virginia, including newly acquired Alexandria.

NAVAL: The USS *Union* assumes blockading positions off Savannah, Georgia.

May 29

NORTH: Dorothea L. Dix approaches Secretary of War Simon Cameron and offers to assist organizing hospital services for Federal forces.

SOUTH: Albert S. Johnston is appointed a full general in the Confederate army.

The first Confederate Congress convenes its first session in Richmond, Virginia.

NAVAL: The Potomac Flotilla, consisting of steamers USS *Thomas Freeborn, Anacostia, Resolute,* and *Pawnee,* bombard Southern batteries at Aquia Creek, Virginia, for the next three days.

Commander John R. Goldsborough and the steamer USS *Union* establish a blockade off Savannah, Georgia.

The USS *Powhatan* under Lieutenant David D. Porter captures the Confederate schooner *Mary Clinton* near the Southwest Pass, Mississippi River.

The Confederate privateer *J. C. Calhoun* captures the Union brig *Panama* and takes it to New Orleans.

May 30

POLITICS: Secretary of War Simon Cameron instructs General Benjamin F. Butler at Fortress Monroe, Virginia, that fugitive slaves who cross Union lines are not to be returned but, rather, fed and given work around military installations.

WEST: Federal forces under Colonel Benjamin F. Kelley occupy Grafton, western Virginia, to secure passage of the Baltimore and Ohio Railroad as well as encourage the activities of pro-Union inhabitants. General George B. McClellan next dispatches a brigade under General Thomas A. Morris to seize the town at Philippi, west of strategic Harper's Ferry.

NAVAL: Confederate forces raise the scuttled USS *Merrimac* at Norfolk, Virginia, and commence reconstruction work.

The USS *Quaker City* captures the Confederate schooner *Lynchburg* at sea.

May 31

WEST: General John C. Frémont supersedes General William S. Harney as Union commander in Missouri. His prior agreement with General Sterling Price not to introduce Federal troops in the region also is abrogated.

Federal troops, newly removed from Indian Territory, reestablish themselves at Fort Leavenworth, Kansas.

NAVAL: The USS *Perry* seizes the Confederate blockade runner *Hannah M. Johnson* at sea.

June 1

DIPLOMACY In a major defeat for Confederate privateering, the government of Great Britain forbids armed vessels of either side from bringing prizes into English ports. However, this stance does not prevent British shipyards from clandestinely constructing warships for use by the Confederate navy.

SOUTH: Skirmishing commences between Union and Confederate forces at Arlington Mills and Fairfax County Courthouse, Virginia. Captain John Q. Marr becomes the South's earliest officer fatality.

NAVAL: The USS *Union* captures the Confederate vessel *F. W. Johnson* off the North Carolina coast.

June 2

SOUTH: General Pierre G. T. Beauregard, formerly commanding at Charleston, South Carolina, succeeds General Milledge L. Bonham as head of Confederate forces at Manassas Junction, Virginia.

June 3

POLITICS: Democrat Stephen A. Douglas, the "Little Giant" who defeated Abraham Lincoln in his bid for the Senate, dies in Chicago, Illinois, at the age of 48. The North loses one of its most eloquent and forceful spokespeople.

WEST: A brigade of Indiana troops under General Thomas A. Morris surprises and easily defeats a Confederate detachment under Colonel George A. Porterfield at Philippi, in western Virginia. The Northerners successfully attack his camp and send the defenders scurrying with the loss of 15 men, their baggage, and several flags out of roughly 1,000 men who were engaged. Thomas loses two men wounded. This victory, greatly exaggerated in the press as the "Philippi Races," clears the Kanawha Valley of enemy forces and provides greater impetus for the region to break with the Confederacy. General George B. McClellan, commanding but not directly involved in the action, receives both credit and increasing political attention.

June 4
NAVAL: The brig USS *Perry* captures the Confederate privateer *Savannah* at sea, releasing its prize, the American brig *Joseph*.

June 5
NORTH: Federal authorities and U.S. marshals seize powder works in Connecticut and Delaware to prevent possible shipments to the Confederacy.
SOUTH: Earl Van Dorn is appointed brigadier general, C.S.A.
NAVAL: The USS *Quaker City* captures the Confederate ship *General Greene* off the Chesapeake Capes.

The U.S. revenue cutter *Harriet Lane* engages Confederate forces at Pig Point, Hampton Roads, Virginia.

The USS *Niagara* captures the Confederate vessel *Aid* off Mobile, Alabama.

June 6
SOUTH: Colonel John B. Magruder, commanding Confederate forces outside of Yorktown, Virginia, dispatches Colonel Daniel H. Hill and his 1st North Carolina to nearby Big Bethel to observe Union movements. This places them only eight miles from the main Union force gathered at Hampton.
WEST: Responsibility for Missouri is transferred to the Department of the Ohio under General George B. McClellan.

General Henry A. Wise, former Virginia governor, is appointed Confederate commander of the Kanawha Valley, western Virginia.

June 8
POLITICS: Tennessee voters approve secession by a margin of 104,913 to 47,238, and it joins the Confederacy as the 11th and final state to do so. However, the eastern sections of the state remain active in the Union cause.
SOUTH: General Robert S. Garnett is appointed commander of Confederate forces in northwestern Virginia. Governor John Lechter, to enhance the defenses of his state further, transfers all Virginia troops to Confederate control.
NAVAL: The USS *Resolute* captures the Confederate vessel *Somerset* at Breton's Bay, Georgia.

The USS *Mississippi* establishes a blockade off Key West, Florida.

June 9
NORTH: The U.S. Sanitary Commission is founded and organized to provide nursing, sanitation, and other support activities to Federal forces.
SOUTH: General Benjamin F. Butler decides to dislodge Confederate forces entrenched at Big Bethel, Virginia, only eight miles from his main position in Hampton. To do so, he orders the brigade of General Ebenezer Pierce—composed of five

New York regiments, one from Massachusetts and Vermont, and a section of the 2nd U.S. Artillery out from Newport News—on a night march. The transit goes badly, with many units becoming lost. Worse, the 5th New York (Zouaves), resplendent in their gray uniforms, are mistaken for Confederates and are fired upon, sustaining 21 casualties. Butler's plan, which calls for an attack by four converging columns, also proves overly complicated for his inexperienced recruits to execute properly.

NAVAL: The USS *Massachusetts* captures the British blockade-runner *Perthshire* off Pensacola, Florida.

June 10

NORTH: Dorothea L. Dix becomes superintendent of woman nurses to help supervise medical activities within the U.S. Army.

Colonel Charles Stone leads the 14th U.S. Infantry from Washington, D.C., and embarks at Edward's Ferry across the Potomac River en route to Rockville, Maryland.

SOUTH: Federal forces under General Ebenezer Pierce, numbering 4,400, attack 1,500 Confederates led by Colonel John B. Magruder at Big Bethel, Virginia. The green Union troops are committed piecemeal against enemy entrenchments by their commander and are beaten back, principally by the well-trained 1st North Carolina of Colonel Daniel H. Hill. After badly bungling the effort, Pierce withdraws with eight killed, 53 wounded, and five missing. Among the slain is Major Theodore Winthrop, a noted journalist and member of General Benjamin F. Butler's staff. Southern losses are one killed and seven wounded; news of this successful encounter causes joyous celebrations at Richmond. Consequently, both Magruder and Hill gain promotion to brigadier general. Major George W. Randolph, who handled Magruder's artillery, ultimately rises to Confederate secretary of war.

WEST: Federal captain Nathaniel Lyon, commanding the St. Louis garrison, storms out of negotiations with pro-Southern Missouri governor Claiborne F. Jackson and Home Guard commander General Sterling Price. He then "declares war" on the state of Missouri and prepares to dispense his opponents by force. Meanwhile, Claiborne issues an urgent appeal for 50,000 volunteers to fend off Federal troops.

NAVAL: Confederate lieutenant John M. Brooke, a gifted naval engineer, receives orders to convert the former stream frigate USS *Merrimack* into the ironclad CSS *Virginia*.

The USS *Union* captures the Confederate vessel *Hallie Jackson* off Savannah, Georgia.

June 11

POLITICS: Pro-Union delegates meeting at Wheeling, Virginia, form an alternate government in the westernmost reaches of that state and elect Francis H. Pierpont as governor, along with two U.S. senators.

WEST: Colonel Lew Wallace and his 11th Indiana depart Cumberland, Maryland, and advance against Romney in western Virginia, which he intends to occupy.

SOUTHWEST: Colonel William W. Loring resigns his commission as commander of the New Mexico Territory to join the Confederacy and is succeeded by Colonel Edward R. S. Canby.

June 13

WEST: Colonel Lew Wallace and his 11th Indiana brush aside Confederate pickets and occupy Romney in western Virginia.

Pro-Southern militia under Governor Claiborne F. Jackson evacuate St. Louis, Missouri, and set out for the capital at Jefferson City.

NAVAL: The USS *Mississippi* seizes the schooner *Frost King* at Key West, Florida.

June 14

NORTH: Federal troops under Colonel Charles P. Stone skirmish with Confederates at Seneca Falls, Maryland. At Point of Rocks, Maryland, engineers also remove a 100-ton boulder obstructing the Baltimore and Ohio Railroad, rolled there from overhanging cliffs by retreating Confederates.

SOUTH: Robert E. Lee is promoted to full general, C.S.A.

WEST: General Joseph E. Johnston evacuates Harper's Ferry, Virginia, in the face of converging columns under Generals Robert Patterson and George B. McClellan.

Confederate sympathizers under Governor Claiborne F. Jackson hastily depart Jefferson City, Missouri, as Federal forces draw nearer.

NAVAL: The USS *Sumter* captures the slaver *Falmouth* off the West African coast.

June 15

WEST: Federal troops under Captain Nathaniel Lyon forcibly occupy the capital of Jefferson City, Missouri, while 1,500 poorly armed and trained Confederate sympathizers under Governor Claiborne F. Jackson encamp at nearby Booneville.

June 16

WEST: Confederate forces under General Robert S. Garnett seize Laurel Hill in western Virginia and subsequently occupy a similar strong position at Rich Mountain. Badly outnumbered by troops of the nearby Department of the Ohio under General George B. McClellan, he initiates a series of raids on his line of communications to keep Union forces off balance.

June 17

DIPLOMACY: The government of Spain declares its neutrality but, following Britain's lead, recognizes the Confederacy as a belligerent power.

POLITICS: Unionist delegates meeting in Wheeling, Virginia, unanimously declare their independence from the Confederacy.

NORTH: President Abraham Lincoln is treated to a demonstration of balloon technology by Professor Thaddeus S. C. Lowe. Military observers who are present appreciate the potential use of such technology as battlefield reconnaissance platforms.

Union forces under Colonel Charles P. Stones skirmish with Confederates at Conrad's Ferry, Maryland.

SOUTH: In a clever little action, Colonel Maxcy Gregg of the 1st South Carolina Infantry ambushes and captures a locomotive at Vienna, Virginia. Ohio troops are subsequently dispatched there to repair the tracks.

WEST: Pro-Union inhabitants of Greeneville, Tennessee, rally to keep their region of the state out of the Confederacy.

Union General Nathaniel Lyon and 1,700 men aggressively pursue retreating Missouri State Guard under Governor Claiborne F. Jackson up the Missouri River. He then disembarks and attacks 1,500 poorly armed secessionists at Camp Bacon near Boonville. Jackson forms a line to resist an onslaught by the 1st Missouri Infantry and 2nd Missouri Rifles, but his stand is shattered by artillery fire from Lyon's two cannon. In 20 minutes, the governor and his consorts flee to the southwest corner of the state. Both sides lose three dead and 10 wounded apiece, with an additional 60 guardsmen captured. More important, Union forces now control the lower Missouri River—and Lyon sternly warns all inhabitants against possible acts of treason. He then dispatches a column of pro-Union Missouri Volunteers to prevent General Sterling Price from linking up with Confederate forces under General Ben McCulloch in Arkansas.

NAVAL: The USS *Massachusetts* takes the Confederate schooner *Achilles* off Ship Island, Mississippi.

June 18

NAVAL: The USS *Union* captures the blockade-runner *Amelia* at Charleston, South Carolina.

June 19

POLITICAL: Pro-Union delegates meeting at Wheeling, Virginia, elect Francis H. Pierpont provisional governor of the western portion of that state.

WEST: An attack on Cole Camp, Missouri, by German-speaking pro-Unionists is repulsed by secessionist militia. This small victory stiffens the resolve of the fleeing Southerners.

SOUTHWEST: Cherokee chief John Ross repeats his stance of neutrality and reminds fellow tribesmen of previous obligations to the United States.

NAVAL: The USS *Massachusetts* captures the Confederate brig *Nahum Stetson* off Pass al'Outre, Louisiana.

June 20

WEST: The governor of Kansas calls on citizens to organize and repel any pro-secessionist attacks emanating from Missouri.

June 22

SOUTH: Colonel Harvey Brown, commanding Fort Pickens, Florida, informs the War Department that he will not return fugitive slaves to their owners unless ordered to do so.

WEST: Pro-Union sympathizers gather in Greeneville, Tennessee, and formally declare their allegiance to the Federal government.

June 23

SOUTH: Professor Thaddeus S. C. Lowe rises in his balloon to observe Confederate deployments at Falls Church, Virginia.

NAVAL: Armored conversion of the ex-USS *Merrimac* into the new ironclad CSS *Virginia* continues in earnest at Norfolk, Virginia.

The USS *Massachusetts* seizes Confederate schooners *Trois Frese, Olive Branch, Fanny,* and *Basile* in the Gulf of Mexico. It also catches a Mexican schooner, *Brilliant,* as it attempts to slip through the blockade.

June 24
NORTH: In Washington, D.C., President Abraham Lincoln observes demonstrations of rifled cannon and the "Coffee Mill," an experimental, rapid-firing weapon.
NAVAL: The USS *Pawnee* and *Thomas Freeborn* again engage Confederate batteries at Mathias Point, Virginia.

June 25
SOUTH: Leonidas Polk is appointed major general, C.S.A.

June 26
NORTH: General Nathaniel P. Banks is directed to arrest George P. Jane, marshal of Baltimore, Maryland, police, for secessionist activity. He is ordered to apprehend him as discreetly as possible.
WEST: Colonel Lew Wallace skirmishes with Confederates at Patterson Creek, in western Virginia.
NAVAL: The USS *Minnesota* captures the Confederate bark *Sally Magee* off Hampton Roads, Virginia.

June 27
NORTH: A major strategy session is called in Washington, D.C., with representatives of the army, navy, and coast survey in attendance. The newly created Blockade Strategy Board includes Captain Samuel F. Du Pont, Commander Charles H. Davis, and other military notables and becomes a key planning body. The policies they promulgate remain in effect to the end of the war.
NAVAL: A landing party from the USS *Resolute* burns a Confederate supply depot on the southern shore of the Potomac River.

Confederate forces repel an attempt to land forces at Mathias Point, Virginia, by gunboats USS *Pawnee* and *Thomas Freeborn*. Commander James H. Ward, a former superintendent of the U.S. Naval Academy, is killed in action, becoming the first U.S. Navy officer fatality.

June 28
NAVAL: The Blockade Strategy Board resolves to seize a port in South Carolina and Georgia to serve as coaling stations for the blockading fleet offshore.

Confederates posing as passengers under George N. Hollins, C.S.N., board and capture the passenger steamer *St. Nicholas* at Baltimore and then sail into Chesapeake Bay. Hollins hopes to encounter and surprise the USS *Pawnee*, but it fails to appear.

Confederate privateer *Jefferson Davis* slips past the blockade at Charleston, South Carolina, and commences a successful career raiding Union commerce.

June 29
POLITICAL: Amid mounting war fever, President Abraham Lincoln is briefed on military strategy by Generals Winfield Scott and Irvin McDowell. However, Scott

is against committing untrained levies to combat at this stage and argues—unsuccessfully—against seeking victory in a single, decisive campaign.

NORTH: The Washington, D.C., garrison is bolstered by the arrival of the 11th Massachusetts and 12th New York, which encamp about the White House.

SOUTH: A surprise Confederate raid against Harper's Ferry destroys several boats and bridges before withdrawing.

June 30

NAVAL: The USS *Reliance* destroys the Confederate sloop *Passenger* in the Potomac River.

Captain Raphael Semmes, commanding CSS *Sumter,* evades the USS *Brooklyn* off New Orleans, Louisiana, and commences his celebrated career as a commerce raider.

July 1

POLITICS: The War Department decrees that military volunteers will be recruited from both Kentucky and Tennessee, despite the former's neutrality and the latter's secession.

NORTH: At Baltimore, Maryland, Federal troops arrest four members of the local police force for secessionist activities.

NAVAL: The USS *Minnesota* captures the Confederate schooner *Sally Mears* off Hampton Roads, Virginia.

July 2

POLITICS: The new pro-Union legislature of western Virginia convenes at Wheeling.

NORTH: President Abraham Lincoln confers with General John C. Frémont over strategy in the vital and sensitive region of Missouri, which remains wracked by secessionist unrest.

WEST: General Robert Patterson continues advancing into the Shenandoah Valley and crosses the Potomac River at Williamsport, Maryland, to pin down Confederate forces there. Patterson also wins a minor clash at Hoke's Run, Virginia. General Joseph E. Johnston, meanwhile, prepares to hold off Patterson while shifting the bulk of his troops to Confederate troops near Washington, D.C.

NAVAL: The USS *South Carolina* under Commander James Alden assumes blockading positions off Galveston, Texas.

July 3

WEST: General Robert Patterson continues advancing down the Shenandoah Valley and occupies Martinsburg, Virginia. Outnumbered, General Joseph E. Johnston falls back on Winchester, Virginia.

SOUTHWEST: Union forces abandon Fort McLane in the New Mexico Territory. Meanwhile, the new Western Department arises, consisting of Missouri, Arkansas, Kansas, New Mexico, and the Indian Territory.

NAVAL: CSS *Sumter* under Captain Raphael Semmes captures the American vessel *Golden Rocket* off Cuba.

July 4

POLITICS: President Abraham Lincoln addresses a special session of the 37th Congress and pleads for $4 million—and an additional 400,000 men. Having exhausted all avenues for peaceful settlement, he makes clear his intention of waging war solely against the Confederate government—not the South itself. He also explains and justifies his recent suspension of habeas corpus strictly as a wartime expedient.

SOUTH: Joseph E. Johnston is appointed a full general, C.S.A.

WEST: Union and Confederate forces briefly skirmish at Harper's Ferry, Virginia.

NAVAL: The USS *South Carolina* captures the Confederate blockade-runners *Shark, Venus, Ann Ryan, McCanfield, Louisa,* and *Dart* of Galveston, Texas.

July 5

SOUTH: Contending forces under Generals Benjamin Butler and John B. Magruder skirmish near Curtis's Farm, Newport News, Virginia.

WEST: Colonel Franz Sigel, leading a German-speaking detachment of 1,100 volunteers, advances on a larger force of 4,000 Missouri militia under Governor Claiborne F. Jackson near Carthage. The Confederates decide to attack Sigel's line, which is posted on a hill. The Northerners, who lack cavalry to guard their flanks, pelt Jackson's line with some small artillery, which so unnerves their commander that he orders his 2,000 unharmed state cavalry to take shelter in adjoining woods. Sigel, however, interprets this move as a threat to his flank, so he sounds a retreat. Union losses are 13 dead and 31 wounded to a Confederate tally of 40 killed and 64 injured. Sigel subsequently falls back on the army of General Nathaniel Lyon while Jackson moves to unite with forces under General Sterling Price. Elsewhere, General Ben McCulloch captures a detachment of 80 Union soldiers at Neosho.

NAVAL: The USS *South Carolina* captures the Confederate blockade-runners *Falcon* and *Coralia* off Galveston, Texas.

The USS *Dana* captures the Confederate sloop *Teaser* in Nanjemoy Creek, Maryland.

July 6

WEST: George B. McClellan, commanding the Department of the Ohio, orders an Indiana brigade under General Thomas A. Morris to depart Philippi in western Virginia and march toward Confederate troop concentrations at Laurel Hill. He will take the main force of three brigades simultaneously in a movement against enemy forces at nearby Rich Mountain.

NAVAL: Confederate privateer *Jefferson Davis* seizes Union vessels *Enchantress* and *John Welsh* off Cape Hatteras, North Carolina.

The USS *South Carolina* captures the Confederate schooner *George Baker* off Galveston, Texas.

Confederate raider CSS *Sumter* under Captain Raphael Semmes docks at Havana, Cuba, with six Northern prizes in tow.

July 7

NORTH: Union and Confederate troops skirmish at Great Falls, Maryland.

SOUTH: Contending forces skirmish heavily at Bellington and Laurel Hill in western Virginia.

WEST: Union troops arrive at the foot of Laurel Hill in western Virginia. A force of two regiments under Colonel Robert L. McCook probes defenses erected there by Confederate general Robert S. Gannett, and heavy skirmishing erupts.

General Nathaniel Lyon, commanding Union forces at Springfield, Missouri, is reinforced by troops under Major Samuel D. Sturgis. He now possesses 7,000 men but remains outnumbered two to one by invigorated Confederate forces.

NAVAL: The USS *Pocahontas* engages and damages the CSS *George Page* in Aquia Creek, Virginia.

The Confederate privateer *Jefferson Davis* seizes the Northern ship *S. J. Waring* off New Jersey.

The USS *South Carolina* captures the Confederate schooner *Sam Houston* off Galveston, Texas.

July 8

WEST: Union forces attack and disperse a camp of secessionist militia at Florida, Missouri.

Confederate general Henry H. Sibley receives orders to march from Texas and drive Union forces out of the neighboring New Mexico Territory.

While cruising the Potomac River, the screw tug *Resolute* espies and retrieves two mysterious looking objects, which turn out to be the First Confederate "torpedoes" (mines) encountered during the war.

July 9

POLITICS: The U.S. House of Representatives resolves not to oblige Union soldiers to return fugitive slaves.

WEST: General George B. McClellan, angered by guerrilla attacks on his supply lines in the Allegheny Mountains of western Virginia, resolves to attack Confederate forces under General Robert S. Garnett near Beverly. He gathers up four brigades totaling 15,000 troops and marches to Rich Mountain.

Colonel Robert F. Smith, 16th Illinois, skirmishes with Confederates around Monroe Station, Missouri.

NAVAL: The USS *South Carolina* destroys the Confederate schooner *Tom Hicks* off Galveston, Texas.

Confederate privateer *Jefferson Davis* captures the Union brig *Mary E. Thompson* and the schooner *Mary Goodell*.

July 10

POLITICS: President Abraham Lincoln assures General Simon B. Buckner, head of the Kentucky militia, that Union forces will not violate his state's neutrality.

The Creek Nation concludes a peace treaty with Colonel Albert Pike of the Confederacy.

SOUTH: Daniel H. Hill is appointed brigadier general, C.S.A.

WEST: Having reconnoitered enemy positions, General George B. McClellan commences his offensive in western Virginia by dispatching General William S. Rosecrans to dislodge enemy troops from Rich Mountain while another force under

Colonel Thomas A. Morris advances upon Confederates concentrated at Laurel Hill.

SOUTHWEST: Federal forces abandon Fort Breckinridge, New Mexico Territory.

NAVAL: The USS *Minnesota* captures the Confederate brig *Amy Warwick* in Hampton Roads, Virginia.

July 11

POLITICS: The U.S. Senate formally expels absent members from Arkansas, North Carolina, Texas, and Virginia. One senator from Tennessee is also ejected, but Andrew Johnson, a loyalist from the eastern region of that state, retains his seat.

NORTH: General Nathaniel P. Banks becomes commander of the Department of Annapolis.

WEST: General William S. Rosecrans and 2,000 Union troops attack Colonel John Pegram's 1,300 Confederates at Rich Mountain, western Virginia, after marching all night through a heavy downpour. Assisted by local Unionist guide David Hart, the Northerners snake down a secret path turning the Confederate left flank. A stout fight ensues, and Rosecrans drives back a 300-man advance guard before moving on Pegram's main body. The Confederates hastily abandon their position and flee to nearby Beverly. Victory here places Union forces astride General Robert S. Garnett's lines of communication, and he likewise withdraws from Laurel Hill, closely pursued by the main force under General George B. McClellan. Union losses are 12 killed and 62 wounded; Confederate casualties are given as 72.

NAVAL: The USS *South Carolina* seizes the Confederate ship *T. J. Chambers* off Galveston, Texas.

July 12

POLITICS: Colonel Albert Pike arranges treaties between the Confederacy and the Choctaw and Chickasaw tribes of the Indian Territory.

SOUTH: Continued skirmishing erupts between Union and Confederate forces near Newport News, Virginia.

WEST: Colonel John Pegram surrenders 555 men to General William S. Rosecrans at Beverly, western Virginia, which is then occupied by the main Union army under General George B. McClellan. In the same theater, General Jacob D. Cox's Federal troops advance to engage General Henry A. Wise's Confederates in the Great Kanawha Valley. Southern forces under General Robert S. Garnett, anxious to escape the closing pincer movement, hurriedly move from Kaler's Ford on the Cheat River to nearby Corrick's Ford.

July 13

POLITICS: The House of Representatives expels Missouri member John Clark on a vote of 94 to 45.

WEST: General Robert S. Garnett and his Confederates are defeated again at Corrick's Ford (Carricksford) in western Virginia by General Thomas A. Morris's Indiana brigade. After hard slogging through heavy rainfall and steep terrain, the Federals catch Garnett while fording the Cheat River and maul the 23rd Virginia, which constitutes his rear guard. Garnett himself was in the act of rallying his skirmishers when he is struck down and killed. Confederate resistance collapses as Morris captures one cannon and 40 wagons. Union casualties are reported variously from 10 to 53 while the Confederates admit to 20. Garnett is also the first general officer on either side killed in action. McClellan, elevated by success to the status of national hero, next orders the bulk of his forces to advance on nearby Romney.

NAVAL: The USS *Massachusetts* captures the Confederate schooner *Hiland* off Ship Island, Mississippi.

July 14

WEST: Command of Confederate forces in western Virginia reverts to General Henry R. Jackson. Meanwhile, the Union push under General Robert Patterson stalls south of Harper's Ferry after encountering General Joseph E. Johnston's troops. Patterson's overall timidity and reluctance to give battle earns him the unflattering nickname "Granny" from his troops.

NAVAL: The USS *Daylight* under Commander Samuel Lockwood establishes a formal blockade of Wilmington, North Carolina.

July 15

WEST: Confederate forces effect a full retreat from Harper's Ferry in western Virginia.

July 16

SOUTH: Anxious to maintain the strategic initiative on the heel of victories in western Virginia, General Irvin McDowell orders his 32,000 men onto Manassas Junction. Here, the Manassas Gap and Orange and Alexandria railroads intersect only 30 miles southeast of Washington, D.C. "On to Richmond!" becomes a national mantra—although McDowell manages to traverse only six miles to Fairfax Court House. Another two days are required to reach Centreville, 22 miles from the capital, and the delay grants Confederate forces under General Pierre G. T. Beauregard a badly needed respite. The latter musters only 22,000 men, thinly spread along an eight-mile defensive position behind Bull Run Creek, while awaiting reinforcements from the Shenandoah. Previously, both McDowell and General in Chief Winfield Scott expressed reservations to President Lincoln about committing such raw soldiery to combat, but they were overruled by political considerations.

WEST: Skirmishing continues between General Jacob D. Cox's Federals and Confederates under General Henry A. Wise at Barboursville, western Virginia.

NAVAL: The Blockade Strategy Board informs navy secretary Gideon Welles of the importance of interdicting Confederate shipping. They then suggest using "stone fleets" (scuttled vessels) to obstruct Southern waterways.

The USS *St. Lawrence* captures the British blockade-runner *Herald* while running the blockade out of Beaufort, North Carolina.

In a reversal of fortune, the Confederate prize crew onboard the captured *S. J. Waring* is overcome by its crew—led on by William Tilghman, an African-American sailor. The ship arrives at New York six days later.

July 17

SOUTH: President Jefferson Davis orders General Joseph E. Johnston to reinforce General Pierre G. T. Beauregard in Virginia. In the face of General Robert Patterson's lethargic pursuit, Johnston expertly disengages from the Shenandoah Valley and races 11,000 men east by train to Manassas, Virginia. For the first time in military history, large numbers of troops are shuttled strategically from one front to the other by rail, bringing Confederate numbers up nearly to match Union strength.

WEST: Scarey Town, western Virginia, occasions minor actions between General Jacob D. Cox and General Henry A. Wise, C.S.A.

July 18

DIPLOMACY: Secretary of State William H. Seward instructs American ministers in Britain and France to endorse the previously rejected 1856 Declaration of Paris, which outlawed privateering. However, this move is scuttled subsequently when neither government proves willing to apply it to the Confederacy.

SOUTH: General Irvin McDowell dispatches a reconnaissance in force under General Daniel Tyler toward Confederate forces collected at Centreville, Virginia. He is instructed specifically not to bring on a general engagement. After ascertaining intelligence from the local populace, Tyler accompanies Colonel Israel B. Richardson's command as it probes Confederate positions along Blackburn's Ford on Bull Run Creek. This is on the extreme right of General Pierre G. T. Beauregard's line, then arrayed eight miles along and behind Bull Run Creek. Richardson then deploys two cannon and the 1st Massachusetts, who enthusiastically engage enemy skirmishers until they are staggered by volleys fired from three Virginia brigades under Colonel James Longstreet. After heavy fighting, Richardson orders his force withdrawn, but Tyler, against orders, brings additional cannon and regiments into the fray. These skirmish with Confederates across the creek for an hour before the 12th New York makes an ill-advised charge and is blasted back by Southerners lurking in the dense forestry. Then Longstreet, assisted by the brigade of General Jubal A. Early, counterattacks across the line, but his raw troops give way to confusion. Both sides then draw off to sort themselves out, but the Federal attempts to cross the creek are thwarted. Losses are 19 Union killed and 38 wounded to a Confederate tally of 15 dead and 53 wounded. This minor affair, nonetheless, bolsters Southern morale for the impending fight at Bull Run. McDowell further compounds Northern problems by wasting two more days gathering supplies and conducting additional reconnaissance.

Richard H. Anderson is appointed brigadier general, C.S.A.

NAVAL: The USS *Yankee* captures the Confederate schooner *Favorite* on the Yeocomico River, Virginia.

July 19

WEST: General John Pope, newly arrived in northern Missouri, warns the inhabitants that treasonable activity will be punished promptly, "without awaiting civil process."

NAVAL: The captain-general of Cuba releases all prizes brought into Cuban waters by Captain Raphael Semmes of CSS *Sumter*.

July 20

Politics: The *New York Tribune* adopts the pejorative term *Copperhead* (a poisonous snake) for any Northern politician opposing the war effort.

The third session of the first provisional Confederate Congress convenes in Richmond, Virginia. President Jefferson Davis declares that Arkansas, North Carolina, Tennessee, and Virginia have allied themselves with the Confederacy and that the new capital now is established firmly at Richmond.

South: General Joseph E. Johnston arrives at Manassas Junction with reinforcements and technically succeeds General Pierre P. T. Beauregard as senior commander. Both leaders make preparations to receive an attack delivered by General Irvin McDowell to their front. McDowell, meanwhile, decides that the Confederate right is too strong to assail frontally—as demonstrated by the affair at Blackburn's Ford—and he seeks an unguarded crossing point nearer to Beauregard's left flank. When intelligence is received on the relatively weak defenses around Sudley Ford, McDowell devises a concerted plan to crush the Confederates.

The Union attack is slated to begin with feints launched by General Daniel Tyler's First Division, marching west from Centreville along Warrenton Pike, until it makes demonstrations at the stone bridge where the pike crosses Bull Run. Meanwhile, the Second and Third Divisions under Generals David Hunter and Samuel P. Heintzelman would move west behind Tyler before passing him to suddenly descend on Sudley's Ford at about 7:00 A.M. Once across, these two divisions—totaling 13,000 men—would sweep around the Confederate left and rear, destroying them. An additional feint was intended for Blackburn's Ford by one brigade of Colonel S. D. Miles Fourth Division on the far right, while his remaining brigade remained in reserve. All told, McDowell conceived a viable enough strategy, but he entrusted it to men and officers who simply were too inexperienced to execute it properly.

Curiously, General Beauregard also intended to assail the enemy's left, but his operational orders proved contradictory. Many Southern commanders mistakenly assumed they were to remain in place and the attack never developed. Had they moved, spectators would have witnessed both armies, numbering in the thousands, simultaneously turn each other's flank and ultimately reverse their positions.

West: General William W. Loring assumes control of the Confederate's Northwestern Army in western Virginia.

Naval: The USS *Mount Vernon* seizes the Confederate sloop *Wild Pigeon* on the Rappahannock River.

The USS *Albatross* captures the former prize vessel *Enchantress* off Hatteras Inlet, North Carolina.

July 21

South: A momentous day begins with early morning movements by General Daniel Tyler's division, which is roused from its camps and begins to grope through the darkness at 2:00 A.M. Four hours later, his cannon begins to lob shells at Confederate forces behind the stone bridge crossing Bull Run. However, Colonel Nathan G. Evans deduces that Tyler's movement is merely a demonstration, and he rushes troops to the vicinity of Sudley's Ford. General David Hunter, meanwhile, is equally tardy in

The Fourth Alabama, depicted firing the opening shots of the first major battle of the Civil War (*The National Guard Heritage*)

his movements, and it is not until 9:30 A.M. that Union flanking forces are able to ford Bull Run and work their way south. Evans, however, cobbles together 900 men to oppose their advance on Matthews Hill, and he withstands repeated piecemeal attacks. Gradually, Confederate reinforcements arrive under Colonel Francis S. Bartow and General Barnard Bee while additional Union forces likewise are fed into the fray. After two hours of heavy fighting, the Southerners give way in confusion, and the Federals resume advancing in the direction of Henry House Hill.

General Beauregard nearly compromises his own defensive position with a stream of conflicting orders that keep most of his units stationary instead of moving toward his threatened left flank. One unit that did arrive is a brigade of five Virginia regiments under General Thomas J. Jackson. These quickly deploy on Henry House Hill, assisted by several cannon, and they resist ferociously a Union onslaught by 18,000 men. Jackson's stand enables the survivors of Evans's, Bartow's, and Bee's commands to rally behind him. McDowell also arrives to direct matters personally, but he compromises his numerical superiority by launching piecemeal attacks that are easily repelled. Worse, two Union batteries brought up in support are outgunned and eventually are captured by blue-clad Confederate forces who were mistaken for Federals. Jackson's aggressive defense greatly inspires the Southerners, and General Bee allegedly exclaims: "There is Jackson standing like a stonewall. Rally behind the Virginians!" McDowell continues committing additional forces to battle, but at 4:00 P.M., a Confederate brigade under Colonel Philip St. George Cocke arrives and sweeps the Federals from Henry House Hill. The Union army's offensive, spent by its exertions, begins to sputter out in the intense summer heat.

Meanwhile, a separate struggle unfolds west of Henry House Hill along Chinn Ridge. Union troops under Colonel Oliver O. Howard successfully storm the heights, which places them astride Jackson's flank, poised to drive him off. But as Howard maneuvers to perform exactly that, he is himself outflanked by Confederate brigades under Generals Arnold Elzay and Jubal A. Early and is thrown back. Sensing victory and the exhausted state of his antagonists, Beauregard orders a sudden advance by the entire line of Confederates. Flushed with success, they surge forward, shrieking their trademark battlecry, the "Rebel Yell." McDowell's units, finally bested, give ground in orderly fashion initially and recross Bull Run without undue hazard. However, a lucky Confederate shell suddenly turns over a wagon on the Cub Run Bridge, and utter panic ensues. The exhausted, demoralized soldiers run—headlong into the well-dressed and merry throng of civilians gathered by the roadside to witness what they anticipated would be a clear Union triumph. President Jefferson Davis, arriving on the battlefield during the final stages, urges an all-out pursuit to the gates of Washington, D.C. General Joseph E. Johnston, however, perceiving the disorganized and fatigued nature of his men, declines. Fighting gradually peters out after 10 hours of combat.

The first major engagement of the Civil War ends in a tactical triumph for the Confederacy. Southern losses are 387 killed and 1,582 wounded (1,982) to a Union tally of 460 killed, 1,124 wounded, and 1,132 missing (2,896). The spoils of battle also prove impressive, and they include 28 cannon, 37 caissons, 500,000 rounds of ammunition, and nine regimental colors. In retrospect, Bull Run did little to alter the strategic balance of the war. While minuscule in comparison to later encounters, it demonstrated to both sides that the ensuing struggle would be prolonged and costly.

General Pierre G. T. Beauregard is appointed full general, C.S.A. Jubal A. Early also becomes a brigadier general.

WEST: General Nathaniel P. Banks succeeds General Robert Patterson as commander of the Department of the Shenandoah, western Virginia. The latter's failure to pin down Confederate forces in the region proves a major factor in the Union defeat at Bull Run.

General Jacob D. Dox and Henry A. Wise continue skirmishing at Charlestown, western Virginia.

Skirmishing ensues with Native Americans along the Eel River, California.

NAVAL: The U.S. Marine Corps receives its baptism of fire at Bull Run when a battalion commanded by Major John Reynolds loses with 9 killed, 19 wounded, and 16 missing.

The USS *Albatross* engages the CSS *Beaufort* in Oregon Inlet, North Carolina, forcing it to retreat.

The Confederate privateer *Jefferson Davis* seizes the Union bark *Alvarado* at sea.

July 22

POLITICS: Consistent with the Crittenden Resolution, the U.S. House of Representatives votes for war to preserve governance under the Constitution, save the Union, and maintain the status quo with regard to slavery. The measure is likewise approved by the Senate.

NORTH: The three-month enlistment term of many Union volunteers begins to expire, allowing many of them to be discharged. President Abraham Lincoln counters by signing two bills authorizing 1 million three-year volunteers.

SOUTH: General Barnard Bee, C.S.A., succumbs of wounds received at Bull Run.

WEST: General George B. McClellan is ordered to succeed General Irvin McDowell, who is now disgraced.

The Missouri State Convention, convening at Jefferson City, votes overwhelmingly in favor of the Union and also relocates the capital to St. Louis. Secessionist governor Claiborne F. Jackson, meanwhile, declares himself the only legitimate political authority in Missouri.

Federal troops under General Thomas Sweeney occupy Forsyth, Missouri.

General William J. Hardee, C.S.A., assumes command of Confederate forces in northern Arkansas.

July 23

NORTH: General John A. Dix assumes control of the Department of Maryland.

WEST: General William S. Rosecrans succeeds General George B. McClellan as commander of the Department of the Ohio once the latter transfers to Virginia.

SOUTHWEST: Federal forces abandon Fort Buchanan, New Mexico Territory.

July 24

POLITICS: Congress authorizes the position of assistant secretary of the navy, along with legislation "for the temporary increase in the navy."

WEST: General Jacob D. Cox engages and disperses Confederate forces under General Henry A. Wise at Tyler Mountain in western Virginia. The town of Charleston subsequently is evacuated in the face of mounting Union pressure, and the Kanawha Valley is now free of Southern forces. Wise, meanwhile, retreats in the direction of Gauley Bridge.

July 25

POLITICS: Congress authorizes the recruitment of volunteers, offering those who serve two years a $100 bonus.

Tennessee senator Andrew Johnson moves to adopt the Crittenden Resolution in the U.S. Senate, and it passes 30 to 5. This mandates and reaffirms that the war is being fought for the preservation of the Union and not to abolish slavery.

Confederate secretary of state Robert Toombs, having resigned to join the army, is replaced by Robert M. T. Hunter.

SOUTH: John La Mountain conducts the first balloon reconnaissance flights at Fortress Monroe, Virginia.

WEST: General Nathaniel P. Banks formally succeeds General Robert Patterson as commander of Union forces in the Shenandoah Valley.

General John C. Frémont, a celebrated explorer, becomes commander of the Western Department with headquarters at St. Louis, Missouri.

Skirmishes continue between pro-Union and pro-Confederate forces at Harrisville and Dug Springs, Missouri.

SOUTHWEST: A small Federal detachment of 500 men under Major Isaac Lynde repulses a Confederate attack upon their position at Mesilla, New Mexico Territory.

NAVAL: Congress passes legislation intending to overhaul and improve U.S. Marine Corps organization.

The USS *Resolute* docks at Washington, D.C., with two schooners and one sloop as prizes.

The Confederate privateer *Mariner* captures the Union schooner *Nathaniel Chase* off Ocracoke, North Carolina.

The Confederate privateer *Gordon* seizes the Union brig *William McGilvery* off Cape Hatteras, North Carolina.

The Confederate privateer *Dixie* takes the Union schooner *Mary Alice* off the Florida east coast.

The Confederate raider CSS *Sumter* under Captain Raphael Semmes captures the schooner *Abby Bradford* in the Caribbean.

July 26

WEST: General Felix K. Zollicoffer assumes command of Confederate forces in eastern Tennessee.

SOUTHWEST: Major Isaac Lynde surrenders 500 men to a smaller Confederate force under Captain John Baylor at Fort Fillmore, New Mexico Territory. Lynde is disgraced and subsequently is drummed out of the service, but he eventually makes his way back onto the retirement list.

July 27

POLITICS: President Abraham Lincoln confers with General George B. McClellan, newly arrived in Washington, D.C. The chief executive urges a strategic offensive with advances into Tennessee by way of Virginia and Kentucky. McClellan, who is not as easily stampeded into action as his predecessor, respectfully demurs.

NAVAL: The Confederate raider CSS *Sumter* under Captain Raphael Semmes takes the Union bark *Joseph Maxwell* near Venezuela.

July 28

SOUTH: In light of the deteriorating situation in western Virginia and the death of General Robert Garnett at Carricksford, General Robert E. Lee is ordered to take command of Confederate forces there.

WEST: Confederate forces occupy New Madrid, Missouri, on the Mississippi River.

NAVAL: The USS *Union* destroys the Confederate brig *B. T. Martin* north of Cape Hatteras, North Carolina, once it is run aground by its crew.

The Confederate privateer *Gordon* seizes the Union schooner *Protector* off Cape Hatteras, North Carolina.

The USS *St. Lawrence* sinks the Confederate privateer *Petrel* off Charleston, South Carolina.

July 29

POLITICS: Horace Greeley, the previously hawkish editor of the *New York Tribune,* writes to President Abraham Lincoln and suggests peaceful negotiations to end the fighting.

WEST: General John Pope assumes command of Union forces in North Missouri. He takes active measures to protect railroads from sabotage and suppresses local unrest.

NAVAL: The USS *Yankee* and *Reliance* engage Confederate batteries erected at Marlborough Point, Virginia.

Four U.S. Navy steamers trade shots with a Confederate battery at Aquia Creek, Virginia, for several hours.

July 30

POLITICS: The Missouri State Convention votes 56–25 to declare the gubernatorial seat open, thereby deposing Confederate-leaning Claiborne F. Jackson as chief executive.

SOUTH: General Benjamin F. Butler seeks clarification of orders from the War Department as to policies respecting the great number of escaped African Americans in his camp.

WEST: Union forces under General Jacob D. Cox advance from Charleston and into the Great Kanawha River valley of western Virginia.

July 31

POLITICS: Pro-Union forces in Missouri are bolstered by the election of Hamilton R. Gamble as governor.

WEST: President Abraham Lincoln elevates Ulysses S. Grant, an obscure former army officer, to general of volunteers in Illinois.

General John Pope sternly issues Order No. 3 for the purpose of restoring order to northern Missouri and restricting activities by Confederate sympathizers.

General Sterling Price and his Missouri State Guard unite with Texas troops under General Ben McCulloch and Arkansas forces under General Nicholas B. Pearce at Cassville, Missouri. Their combined forces number in excess of 12,000 men—twice the number of Union general Nathaniel Lyon.

NAVAL: The Confederate privateer *Dixie* captures the Union bark *Glenn* at sea and removes it to Beaufort, North Carolina.

August 1

SOUTH: President Jefferson Davis urges General Joseph E. Johnston to maintain the strategic initiative with further offensive actions against Union forces still in Virginia.

West: General Robert E. Lee succeeds General William W. Loring as head of Confederate forces in western Virginia.

A Confederate force of 12,000 men under Generals Ben McCulloch and Sterling Price march up Telegraph Road from Cassville, Missouri, to Springfield, 50 miles distant.

Southwest: Skirmishing erupts between Confederate and Union sympathizers in Arizona and New Mexico Territories after Captain John Baylor declares the entire region for the South.

Naval: Gustavus V. Fox, a former naval officer, gains appointment as assistant secretary of the navy.

August 2

Politics: Congress approves virtually all of President Abraham Lincoln's acts and appropriations deemed necessary to pursue the war effort, along with issuances of bonds and tariff increases. To better secure funding for the war effort, Congress also passes its first-ever national income tax of 3 percent on incomes of more than $800, along with higher tariffs. Seamen are also enlisted for the duration of the war.

West: Union forces under General Nathaniel Lyon and Confederates under General Ben McCulloch clash at Dug Springs, Missouri. Lyon, badly outnumbered, prepares to retrograde back on Springfield and regroup. Consequently, commanding General John C. Frémont dispatches reinforcements down the Mississippi River to assist him.

Southwest: Union forces evacuate Fort Stanton, New Mexico Territory, in light of recent Confederate successes elsewhere.

August 3

Politics: Governor Isham G. Harris of Tennessee seeks to visit with authorities in Richmond, Virginia, and discuss weakening Confederate control of his state.

West: Federal forces skirmish with Indians in the Upper Pitt River valley, California.

Naval: Congress directs the Department of the Navy to design and construct three ironclad prototypes. They also institute a three-officer "Ironclad Board" to study and recommend construction and deployment of ironclad warships. This body ultimately includes Commodore Joseph Smith, Captain Hiram Paulding, and Commander Charles H. Davis.

In an early application of aerial reconnaissance, John La Mountain lifts off from the deck of USS *Fanny* off Hampton Roads, Virginia, to observe Confederate gun positions along Sewell's Point.

The USS *Wabash* recaptures the Union vessel *Mary Alice* from the Confederate privateer *Dixie* and also seizes the blockade-runner *Sarah Starr* off Charleston, South Carolina.

The USS *South Carolina* engages Confederate shore batteries off Galveston, Texas.

August 4

Naval: A cutter dispatched from the USS *Thomas Freeborn* cuts out and captures the Confederate schooner *Pocahontas* and the sloop *Mary Grey* in Pohick Creek, Virginia.

August 5

POLITICS: The first session of the 37th Congress concludes its monumental, 34-day special session and adjourns.

WEST: General Nathaniel Lyon evacuates Dug Springs, Missouri, in the face of superior Confederate numbers and continues falling back upon Springfield.

NAVAL: The USS *Jamestown* burns the Confederate prize bark *Alvarado* off Fernandina, Florida.

The Confederate privateer *Jefferson Davis* captures the Union brig *Santa Clara* near Puerto Rico.

August 6

POLITICS: President Abraham Lincoln signs the First Confiscation Act, which emancipates all African-American slaves found in the employ of Confederate armed forces, either as laborers or as soldiers.

NORTH: General Ambrose E. Burnside is appointed brigadier general, U.S. Army.

WEST: Union forces ignore Kentucky neutrality by establishing "Dick Robinson," a military camp near Lexington.

Advanced elements of Confederate forces under Generals Ben McCulloch and Sterling Price reach Wilson's Creek, 10 miles from Springfield, Missouri.

August 7

SOUTH: Confederate forces under General John B. Magruder abandon and burn Hampton, Virginia, denying its use to Union forces.

WEST: The steamer *Luella* ferries Federal troops under Major John McDonald, 8th Missouri, on an expedition against Price's Landing, Missouri.

NAVAL: The U.S. government authorizes construction of seven ironclad gunboats under engineer James B. Eads of St. Louis, Missouri, for riverine service: USS *Cairo, Carondelet, Cincinnati, Louisville, Mound City, Pittsburgh,* and *St. Louis.* These are subsequently designed by contractor Samuel M. Pooks, and his ships, incorporating a "humpbacked" design, are popularly referred to as "Pooks's Turtles." The vessels gradually emerge as the nucleus of Union naval power along strategic western water routes.

The USS *Massachusetts* captures the Confederate blockade-runner *Charles Henry* off Ship Island, Mississippi.

August 8

POLITICS: Secretary of War Simon Cameron declares that citizens are not obliged to obey the Fugitive Slave Law as it pertains to secessionists. He further orders General Benjamin F. Butler not to return any escaped slaves to their Confederate owners.

WEST: General Ulysses S. Grant takes command of Union forces at Ironton, Missouri.

NAVAL: The USS *Santee* captures the Confederate schooner *C. P. Knapp* in the Gulf of Mexico.

August 9

WEST: A force of 12,000 Confederates under Generals Ben McCulloch and Sterling Price converge on Springfield, Missouri, in the vicinity of Wilson's Creek, 10 miles to the southwest. Once rested, they intend to attack and overpower Union-held positions in the city on the following day. But rather than abandon Springfield without a fight, General Nathaniel Lyon boldly decides on a preemptive strike of his own. Commanding 4,200 men, he is assisted by a German-speaking detachment of 1,200 soldiers under Colonel Franz Sigel, who marches circuitously to take the Confederates from behind.

Naval: The Confederate privateer *York* captures the Union schooner *George C. Baker* and then promptly relinquishes it to the USS *Union*. *York* is run ashore soon after at Cape Hatteras and burned by its crew.

August 10

West: General Ulysses S. Grant skirmishes with Confederate forces at Potosi, Missouri.

Union general Nathaniel Lyon initiates the Battle of Wilson's Creek by storming Confederate campsites at 5:30 A.M. They drive General Sterling Price back and occupy a prominent ridge crest that is soon to be christened "Bloody Hill." The Southerners, overcoming their initial surprise, redress their lines and rebuff a Union column under Captain Joseph Plummer, who tries to storm artillery posted on their right. Sigel, meanwhile, stealthily advances on the Confederate camp from the south and routs Southern cavalry deployed there. General Ben McCulloch, however, reacts quickly to this new threat and dispatches troops that drive Sigel back, securing the Confederate rear. Their success here is due largely to Colonel Louis Hebert's 3rd Louisiana, clad in gray uniforms like many Union troops, who advance to close range and unleash a volley, staggering the defenders. Attention then swings back to Battle Hill, where the struggle continues raging.

Lyon, unaware of Sigel's debacle, holds his ground as Price launches two frontal attacks in superior strength. The Northerners staunchly repel the Missouri State Guard and drive them back with considerable loss. But as Lyon brings up the 1st Iowa and 2nd Kansas to bolster his own line, a bullet strikes and kills him. Command then devolves upon Major Samuel D. Sturgis. The Union lines, somewhat more constricted, easily fight off a charge by Confederate cavalry and brace themselves for a third charge by Price, now reinforced by McCulloch's Texans. The Confederates come on in great strength and grimly fight their way up the slopes, charging at one point to within 20 paces of Sturgis's position. Federal forces are hard pressed but their line still holds and the Southerners fall back a third time.

At this juncture, Sturgis is apprised of Sigel's failure. He also observes Southerners massing for a fourth assault upon his line, already exhausted and low on ammunition after five hours of continuous combat. Sturgis consequently gives orders to retreat, which the men perform in orderly fashion. The equally battered Confederates under McCulloch occupy the Union position, but they decline to pursue. Despite Southern advantages in numbers, losses at Wilson's Creek proved nearly equal, with the Federals suffering 258 killed, 873 wounded, and 186 missing (1,317) to a Southern tally of 277 killed and 945 injured (1,230), rates of 25.5 percent and 12 percent, respectively. The South has won the Civil War's second pitched engagement, while Lyon is the first Northern general slain in combat. The victory also revives Confederate fortunes in Missouri, and Price continues his march to St. Louis. McCulloch and Nicholas Pearce (Brigadier General of Arkansas forces), meanwhile, hasten back to Arkansas.

August 11

WEST: General John B. Floyd is appointed head of Confederate forces in the Kanawha Valley, western Virginia.

General Jeff Thompson assumes command of the Confederate-leaning Missouri State Guard.

NAVAL: The Confederate blockade-runner *Louisa,* closely pursed by the USS *Penguin,* strikes a shoal off Cape Fear, North Carolina, and sinks.

August 12

WEST: Mescalero Apache raiders under Chief Nicholas attack and kill 15 Confederates at Big Bend, Texas.

NAVAL: The wooden gunboats USS *Tyler, Lexington,* and *Conestoga* drop anchor off Cairo, Illinois, and guard the confluence of the Ohio and Mississippi rivers. These are stopgap designs intending to serve until the new ironclads are in commission, but they prove entirely successful.

August 13

NAVAL: The USS *Powhatan* under Lieutenant David D. Porter recaptures the Union schooner *Abby Bradford* near the mouth of the Mississippi River.

August 14

NORTH: A mutiny by discontented volunteers in the 79th New York Regiment near Washington, D.C., is suppressed.

WEST: General John C. Frémont declares martial law in St. Louis, Missouri, and begins to confiscate Confederate property.

SOUTHWEST: General Paul O. Hebert succeeds General Earl Van Dorn as commander of Confederate forces in Texas.

August 15

POLITICS: President Jefferson Davis orders all remaining Northerners out of Confederate territory within 40 days.

NORTH: Disruptions in the 2nd Maine result in 60 transfers from the Army of the Potomac to the distant Dry Tortugas, Florida.

SOUTH: George B. Crittenden is appointed brigadier general, C.S.A.

WEST: General Robert Anderson, formerly commander at Fort Sumter, takes charge of the Department of the Cumberland (Tennessee and Kentucky). However, he continually suffers from nervous exhaustion brought on by his recent ordeal and retires shortly afterward.

In view of Confederate successes in Missouri, General John C. Frémont pleads with the War Department for immediate reinforcements. President Abraham Lincoln, cognizant of the threat to this important border state, authorizes the transfer of troops.

Major John McDonald and men of the 8th Missouri are ferried by the steamer *Hannibal City* on an expedition against Saint Genevieve, Missouri.

Federal troops skirmish with Indians near Kellogg's Lake, California.

NAVAL: Gunboats USS *Tyler* and *Conestoga* conduct a reconnaissance down the Mississippi River and scout for Confederate fortifications, while the USS *Lexington* performs similar tasks upstream as far as Cape Girardeau, Missouri.

The USS *Resolute* bombards Confederate troops assembled at Mathias Point, Virginia.

August 16

POLITICS: President Abraham Lincoln reiterates that the South remains in a state of insurrection and declares that all commercial intercourse between loyal and rebellious states is prohibited.

WEST: Union and Confederate sympathizers clash at Fredericktown and Kirksville, Missouri.

August 17

NORTH: The new Department of the Potomac is constituted by merging the Departments of Northeastern Virginia, Washington, and the Shenandoah.

Henry W. Halleck is promoted to major general, U.S. Army.

SOUTH: The venerable General John E. Wool replaces General Benjamin F. Butler as head of the Department of Virginia, with headquarters at Fortress Monroe at the tip of Yorktown Peninsula.

August 18

POLITICS: New York newspapers *Journal of Commerce, Daily News, Day Book,* and *Freeman's Journal* are banned summarily from publishing for alleged disloyalty.

SOUTH: Troopers of the 1st New York Cavalry skirmish with Confederates 12 miles south of Alexandria, Virginia.

NAVAL: The successful Confederate privateer *Jefferson Davis* runs aground on a sandbar and is destroyed off St. Augustine, Florida.

August 19

POLITICS: The Southern-leaning editor of the Massachusetts *Essex County Democrat* is accosted by a mob, tarred, and feathered. Newspaper offices in Easton and West Chester, Pennsylvania, are also accosted by pro-Union mobs because of suspected pro-Southern sympathies.

Proslavery expatriates from Missouri petition for their state to join the Confederacy even after they have been driven from office.

NORTH: George H. Thomas is appointed brigadier general, U.S. Army.

General Henry W. Halleck is summoned from California to Washington, D.C.

WEST: Union forces defeat the Missouri Home Guard at Charleston, Missouri, directly across the river from Cairo, Illinois.

NAVY: Secretary of the Navy Gideon Welles orders 200 U.S. Marines to join the Potomac Flotilla for the purpose of scouring the countryside for Confederate depots and supplies.

August 20

NORTH: General George B. McClellan formally takes command of the newly constituted Department and Army of the Potomac. This vaunted force becomes a permanent fixture in the struggle for Virginia during the next four years.

John F. Reynolds is appointed brigadier general, U.S. Army.

South: General Richard C. Gatlin becomes commander of the Confederate forces in North Carolina.

August 21
South: General John B. Grayson assumes control of Confederate forces in the Department of Middle and East Florida.

General Roswell S. Ripley takes charge of Confederate forces in the Department of South Carolina.
West: Union and Confederate sympathizers clash at Jonesboro, Missouri.
Naval: The USS *Vandalia* captures the Confederate blockade-runner *Henry Middleton* off Charleston, South Carolina.

August 22
Naval: Commander John Rodgers drives an estimated 600 Confederates from Commerce, Missouri, preventing them from erecting batteries there.

The Federal gunboat USS *Lexington* impounds the steamer *W. B. Terry* at Paducah, Kentucky, for trading with the enemy. Nearby Confederate forces abscond with the steamer *Samuel Orr* and sail it up the Tennessee River.

August 23
Southwest: Union and Confederate forces skirmish near Fort Craig, New Mexico Territory.
Naval: The steamers USS *Release* and *Yankee* trade salvos with Confederate batteries at the mouth of Potomac Creek, Virginia.

August 24
Diplomacy: President Jefferson Davis appoints James M. Mason of Virginia special commissioner to Great Britain, John Slidell of Louisiana special commissioner to France, and Pierre A. Rost of Louisiana special commissioner to Spain. Each is specifically instructed to seek diplomatic recognition for the Confederacy and, with it, the ability to acquire arms and ammunition.
Politics: President Abraham Lincoln informs Governor Beriah Magoffin that he refuses to order the withdrawal of Union troops, despite Kentucky's professed neutrality.
North: The Department of the Potomac is enlarged through absorption of the Department of Pennsylvania.

August 25
West: The encampment of General Henry A. Wise in western Virginia is beset by an outbreak of measles. His force also skirmishes with Federal troops at Piggot's Mill.
Southwest: Federal troops under Lieutenant John R. Pulliam fight with hostile Indians near Fort Stanton, New Mexico Territory.

Confederate troops under Colonel John R. Baylor skirmish with hostile Apaches near Fort Bliss, Texas.

August 26

WEST: Confederates under General John B. Floyd surprise Colonel Erastus B. Tyler's 27th Ohio Regiment in their camp at Cross Lanes (Summersville), western Virginia, routing them.

Union and Confederate forces skirmish heavily at Wayne Court House and Blue's House in the westernmost reaches of Virginia.

NAVAL: A combined expedition assembles at Hampton Roads, Virginia, under Commodore Silas H. Stringham, consisting of the USS *Cumberland, Fanny, Harriet Lane, Minnesota, Monticello, Pawnee, Susquehanna,* and *Wabash.* This powerful force mounts 143 heavy, rifled cannon. Stringham, a capable veteran of many years with the Mediterranean squadron, is well versed in the newest fort-reduction tactics perfected during the Crimean War; he takes onboard 900 soldiers of the 9th Massachusetts and 20th New York under General Benjamin F. Butler. The expedition weighs anchor and makes for Hatteras Inlet, North Carolina, to eliminate privateering operations there. This is also the first large-scale amphibious operation of the war and is intended as a demonstration of Union naval prowess.

The USS *Daylight* attacks and recaptures the Union schooner *Monticello* in the Rappahannock River, Virginia.

The tug USS *Fanny* captures the Confederate sloop *Emma* off the mouth of the Manokin River, Maryland.

Captain Andrew H. Foote is appointed to replace Captain John Rodgers as commander of the gunboat flotilla of the western rivers.

August 27

NAVAL: The naval expedition under Commodore Silas H. Stringham anchors off Hatteras Inlet and makes preparations to land troops and attack nearby Forts Clark and Hatteras. These are garrisoned by 350 men of the 7th North Carolina under Colonel William F. Mountain. They are situated poorly to contend with such a powerful force. Mountain possesses only 12 small, smoothbore cannon in two open positions, and he is thus outgunned and outnumbered.

August 28

NORTH: The Federal garrison at Fort Ellsworth, Washington, D.C., under General William B. Franklin is augmented by the arrival of 400 sailors deployed from the Washington Navy Yard.

SOUTH: The 2nd and 3rd Michigan skirmish with Confederate forces near Bailey's Cross Roads, Virginia.

WEST: General Nathaniel Lyon, recently slain at Wilson's Creek, is interred with full military honors at St. Louis, Missouri.

NAVAL: The USS *Yankee* captures the Confederate schooner *Remittance* off Piney Point, Virginia.

To seal off Pamlico Sound, an important blockade-running route, a combined expedition of eight warships and two transports under Commodore Silas H. Stringham drops anchor off Hatteras Inlet, North Carolina. A preliminary landing of some 300 men nearly goes awry when high surfs swamps many of the landing boats. Nonetheless, at 10 A.M., Stringham forms his vessels into a fast-moving circle, which continuously bombards the Confederate positions with accurate, plunging fire. The Southern artillery in the forts lack sufficient range to hit back, and the defenders gradually drift away before reinforcements arrive under Commodore Samuel Barron.

The U.S. revenue cutter *R. R. Cuyler* attacks and burns the Confederate ship *Finland* as it attempts to run the blockade off Apalachicola, Florida.

August 29

SOUTH: General Benjamin F. Butler lands 900 soldiers and occupies Forts Hatteras and Clark at Hatteras Inlet, North Carolina. The Confederate garrison under Commodore Samuel Barron offers scant resistance before surrendering their posts, which are secured without any Federal fatalities. Butler is ordered to abandon the position after its defenses are dismantled, but noting how control of the inlet strangles Confederate shipping out of Pamlico Sound, he decides to retain them—a wise decision subsequently upheld by the War Department. The Union has secured its first foothold on Southern territory, and Hatteras Inlet performs useful service as a coaling station and supply depot for the blockading squadron offshore. Coming on the heels of Bull Run, the victory also raises Northern morale.

August 30

WEST: Without prior authorization, General Charles Frémont proclaims a conditional emancipation declaration in Missouri and frees slaves belonging to Confederate sympathizers. He also orders the death penalty for any Southern guerrillas apprehended behind Union lines. President Abraham Lincoln, after hearing of Frémont's actions, declares them "dictatorial" and potentially alienating for Union sympathizers in Kentucky.

NAVAL: In a brisk action, the Confederate steam tug *Harmony* attacks and damages the USS *Savannah* at Newport News, Virginia.

August 31

POLITICS: The third session of the Provisional Confederate Congress adjourns.

NORTH: George G. Meade is promoted to brigadier general, U.S. Army.

SOUTH: The 3rd New Jersey Regiment skirmishes with Confederate forces at Munson's Hill, Virginia.

WEST: General William S. Rosecrans takes three brigades of Ohio troops, 6,000 strong and marches south from Clarksburg, western Virginia, intending to attack the Confederate camp of General John B. Floyd at Carnifex Ferry.

NAVAL: The Union Navy Department abolishes the daily rum ration for sailors.

The CSS *Teaser* approaches and bombards Union forces at Newport News, Virginia.

The USS *George Peabody* captures the Confederate brig *Henry C. Brooks* in Hatteras Inlet, North Carolina.

The USS *Jamestown* apprehends the British blockade-runner *Aigburth* off the Florida coast.

September 1

Politics: President Abraham Lincoln is greatly relieved by word of Federal success at Hatteras Inlet, North Carolina, a welcome victory that raises Northern morale.

West: Skirmishing continues at Blue Creek, Boone Court House, and Burlington, in the western reaches of Virginia.

Arriving at Cape Girardeau, General Ulysses S. Grant takes nominal command of Union forces in southeastern Missouri.

South: Mary Chase, an African-American freedwoman, starts the first school for contrabands (escaped slaves) in Alexandria, Virginia.

Naval: The USS *Dana* captures the Confederate schooner *T. J. Evans* as it runs the blockade off Clay Island, Maryland.

September 2

Politics: President Abraham Lincoln, eager to appease slaveholding border states, instructs General Charles C. Frémont to "modify" his emancipation declaration—in effect, he countermands it.

South: Colonel Harvey Brown, commanding Fort Pickens, Florida, orders a sortie across Pensacola Bay to destroy a Confederate floating dry dock, which he believes is intended to be sunk in the channel as an obstacle.

West: General Leonidas Polk assumes command of all Confederate forces in Department No. 2, encompassing Tennessee, Arkansas, and Missouri.

General Jeff Thompson threatens retaliatory measures for any Confederate sympathizers executed under General Charles C. Frémont's directive.

September 3

North: Oliver O. Howard, Daniel E. Sickles, and Lew Wallace are promoted to brigadier generals, U.S. Army.

West: In a major development, General Leonidas Polk orders Confederate forces to violate Kentucky neutrality and preempt any possible Union advances there. General Gideon Pillow responds by occupying Hickman, Chalk Cliffs, and Columbus, establishing a continuous war front that now stretches from Kansas to the Atlantic.

General Gideon J. Pillow and Colonel William H. L. Wallace arrange prisoner exchanges to take place in Missouri.

September 4

North: Union forces under General George A. McCall skirmish with Confederates at Great Falls, Maryland.

West: General Ulysses S. Grant arrives at Cairo, Illinois, to evaluate the new and potentially advantageous situation in Kentucky.

In the face of Confederate pressure, General Stephen A. Hurlbut evacuates Shelbina, Missouri.

Naval: The USS *Jamestown* seizes and scuttles the Confederate schooner *Colonel Long* off the Georgia coast.

The gunboat CSS *Yankee*, assisted by Confederate batteries at Hickman, Kentucky, trades shots with gunboats USS *Tyler* and *Lexington* near Cairo, Illinois.

September 5

WEST: General Ulysses S. Grant prepares his forces at Cairo, Illinois, for an immediate occupation of Paducah, Kentucky, at the confluence of the Tennessee and Ohio rivers. Significantly, the mouth of the Cumberland River is also nearby.

NAVAL: Captain Andrew H. Foote reports for duty at St. Louis, Missouri, replacing Commander John Rodgers.

September 6

DIPLOMACY: The U.S. consul in London, England, is alerted to the purchase of steamers *Bermuda, Adelaide,* and *Victoria* by Confederate agents.

WEST: Union forces under General Ulysses S. Grant advance south from Cairo, Illinois, to Paducah, Kentucky, at the mouth of the Tennessee River, to forestall a Confederate takeover. He also appoints General Charles F. Smith to command troops in western Kentucky once he returns to Cairo. This minor action wields big strategic consequences as it precludes Southern attempts to establish a main line of defense behind the Ohio River.

NAVAL: The gunboats USS *Tyler* and *Lexington* under Commander John Rodgers provide useful support for General Ulysses S. Grant's occupation of Paducah and Smithland, Kentucky, at the mouths of the Tennessee and Cumberland rivers. The operation proceeds smoothly and demonstrates both Grant's understanding of naval power and his uncanny knack for juggling combined operations.

September 7

WEST: Colonel Alvin P. Hovey leads the 24th Indiana on an expedition to Big Springs, Missouri.

September 8

WEST: General Ulysses S. Grant girds for an engagement at Lucas Bend, Missouri, supported by gunfire from USS *Conestoga* and *Lexington.*

General John Pope initiates military operations against Confederate guerrilla bands in northern Missouri.

September 9

POLITICAL: President Abraham Lincoln is advised by his cabinet to relieve the erratic but popular General Charles C. Frémont of command in Missouri. The president nonetheless relents for the time being and instructs General David Hunter to convey troops there as reinforcements.

WEST: Action looms as Federal troops under General William S. Rosecrans advance to Carnifex Ferry in western Virginia, skirmishing with Confederate outposts en route.

NAVAL: The USS *Cambridge* captures the Confederate schooner *Louisa Agnes* off Nova Scotia, Canada.

September 10

SOUTH: General Albert S. Johnston is appointed commander of Confederate forces in the West.

WEST: General William S. Rosecrans and 6,000 Federal troops strike 2,000 Confederates under General John B. Floyd at Carnifex Ferry on a bend in the Gauley River in western Virginia. Previously, Floyd was warned by General Henry B. Wise not to encamp with his back to the river, but he ignored this sound dictum. The Union troops press forward and clear a heavily wooded area, capturing many Confederate supplies. Rosecrans then views Floyd's fortified camp on the bluffs and pauses to regroup before resuming the fight on the morrow. Floyd, however, quickly evacuates his command across the river under the cover of darkness and destroys the ferry to avoid pursuit. Union forces sustain 17 killed and 141 wounded to Confederate claims of only 20, but Rosecrans's offensive tightens the Federal grip on western Virginia. Curiously, General Wise is blamed for not reinforcing Floyd in a timely manner, and ultimately he is relieved.

General Robert E. Lee prepares his command to pass over to the offensive. He formulates a complicated plan to isolate and storm the Union outpost atop Cheat Mountain, as possession of this strategic point would severe Union communications along several mountain passes and the Staunton-Parkersburg Turnpike. However, his efforts are hampered by General William W. Loring, who outranked Lee in the prewar regular army and strongly resents subordination to him. Despite Lee's best efforts to cultivate cordiality, Loring remains sullen and uncooperative.

General George H. Thomas assumes command of the Union training camp Dick Robinson in eastern Kentucky.

General John McClernand leads Federal troops on a reconnaissance of Norfolk, Missouri.

NAVAL: In a sharp action, gunboats USS *Conestoga* and *Lexington* attack and silence a Confederate battery at Lucas Bend, Missouri, and also damage the Confederate gunboat CSS *Yankee.*

The USS *Pawnee* apprehends the Confederate schooner *Susan Jane* in Hatteras Inlet, North Carolina.

The USS *Cambridge* intercepts the British blockade-runner *Revere* off Beaufort, North Carolina.

September 11

POLITICS: President Abraham Lincoln orders the emancipation declaration of General John C. Frémont modified to conform with acts of Congress.

The Kentucky legislature, angered by Confederate violation of its neutrality, demands the immediate removal of all Southern troops. A similar bill applying to Northern forces is defeated by pro-Unionists.

SOUTH: Confederate cavalry under Colonel J. E. B. Stuart clash with Union troops under General William F. Smith outside Lewinsville, Virginia. In light of their good conduct, General George B. McClellan restores the colors of the 79th New York.

WEST: General Robert E. Lee and 15,000 Confederates launch an overly intricate and unsuccessful attack on 2,000 Union soldiers under General J. J. Reynolds at Cheat Mountain Summit and Elkwater, western Virginia. The Confederates are hampered at the onset by rough terrain and heavy rainfall, but after prodigious efforts, they position themselves without arousing Northern concern. The main strike force under Colonel Albert Rust, 3rd Arkansas, numbering 2,000 men, then prepares to storm the summit of Cheat Mountain, guarded by only 300 men of the 14th Indiana under Colonel Nathan Kimball. Rust, unfortunately, is misled by prisoners into thinking he is actually outnumbered. Then, alarmed by the supposed approach of Union reinforcements, he unceremoniously withdraws without attacking—the signal for which Lee and his army in the Tygart Valley are waiting.

After several hours, Lee, realizing that the element of surprise is compromised, calls off General William W. Loring's attack on Reynolds's main force at Elkwater and retreats. Union casualties are 21 killed and 60 captured to Southern losses of about 100. It is an inauspicious debut for a general soon hailed as the Confederacy's premier soldier.

NAVAL: The USS *South Carolina* captures the *Soledad Cos* off Galveston, Texas.

September 12

POLITICS: President Abraham Lincoln dispatches a personal emissary to St. Louis who is to instruct General John C. Frémont to modify his emancipation declaration, which the president considers a dire threat to Kentucky's allegiance. He also orders Federal troops to arrest 31 members of the Maryland legislature who are suspected of collusion with the enemy.

SOUTH: Braxton Bragg is promoted to major general, C.S.A.

WEST: Simon B. Buckner, the Confederate-leaning head of Kentucky militia forces, calls on inhabitants to resist a Union invasion of the state.

A Confederate force of 7,000 men under General Sterling Price approaches a smaller Union garrison of 3,600 under Colonel James Mulligan at Lexington, Missouri.

Union forces under Colonel Jefferson C. Davis skirmish with Confederates at Booneville, Missouri.

September 13

SOUTH: President Jefferson Davis and General Joseph E. Johnston heatedly argue about the seniority of Confederate generals, the beginning of a permanent estrangement between the two men.

WEST: General Robert E. Lee, learning that Union general Joseph J. Reynolds has reinforced Colonel Nathan Kimball atop Cheat Mountain, launches a reconnaissance in force to ascertain Northern intentions. Colonel John A. Washington, his aide-de-camp, is killed in the process.

General Sterling Price, seeking to maintain the strategic initiative, marches from Wilson's Creek toward Lexington, Missouri—midway between Kansas City and St. Louis— with 7,000 Missouri State Guardsmen. There his advance troops skirmish with the picket's of Colonel James A. Mulligan, 23rd Illinois, and he elects to surround and besiege the town. Mulligan, who commands only 3,600 men and seven cannon within a strongly fortified post, has no choice but to await reinforcements promised by General John C. Frémont.

NAVAL: The CSS *Patrick Henry* under Commander John R. Tucker trades fire with the USS *Savannah* and *Louisiana* off Newport News, Virginia; neither side scores any hits.

The USS *Susquehanna* captures the British blockade-runner *Argonaut* at sea as it makes its way to Key West, Florida.

September 14
SOUTH: Simon B. Buckner is appointed brigadier general, C.S.A.
SOUTHWEST: Colonel George Wright, 9th U.S. Infantry, is appointed commander of Federal forces in Southern California.
NAVAL: The USS *Albatross* captures the Confederate schooner *Alabama* off the mouth of the Potomac River.

Lieutenant John H. Russell fights the first pitched naval engagement of the war at Pensacola, Florida, by sailing the frigate USS *Colorado* past Confederate batteries at night and then leading 100 sailors and marines on a cutting-out expedition. Russell's men storm and capture the privateer *Judah* after hand-to-hand fighting, burn it to the waterline, and withdraw unimpeded. Several enemy artillery pieces are also taken and spiked while ashore. Russell subsequently receives personal thanks from President Abraham Lincoln and is feted by the Navy Department. General Braxton Bragg, however, begins to plan a Confederate retaliatory response.

September 15
POLITICS: President Abraham Lincoln confers with his cabinet about the necessity of removing General John C. Frémont as commander of Missouri.
SOUTH: The 28th Pennsylvania Volunteers under Colonel John W. Geary skirmish with Confederates at Pritchards Mill, Virginia.
WEST: General Robert E. Lee, bested at Cheat Mountain, directs the evacuation of Confederates from the westernmost counties of Virginia. Consequently, he earns the unflattering nickname of "Granny." More important, recent operations reflect badly on Lee as a leader, and soon after he is transferred to South Carolina—a quiet sector.

General Albert S. Johnston arrives to replace General Leonidas Polk as commander of Confederate Department No. 2.

General John C. Frémont has politician Frank P. Blair, his most vocal critic, arrested in St. Louis, Missouri.

September 16
WEST: Confederate General Sterling Price is reinforced and tightens his grip around Lexington, Missouri, while Union defenders under Colonel James A. Mulligan, 23rd Illinois, await promised assistance from St. Louis. Unknown to Mulligan, General John C. Frémont fails to help the beleaguered garrison.
NAVAL: The Ironclad Board recommends to Secretary of the Navy Gideon Welles the construction of three new ironclad warships—*Monitor, Galena,* and *New Ironsides.* The former is a revolutionary new turreted design promulgated by Swedish engineer John Ericsson.

The USS *Pawnee* dispatches a landing party against Confederate fortifications on Beacon Island, North Carolina, and subsequently closes the Oracoke Inlet to enemy shipping.

Armed boats from the USS *Massachusetts* seize and occupy Ship Island, Mississippi, on the Gulf of Mexico. This lodges a Union naval base for the still-forming Gulf Blockade Squadron, midway between New Orleans, Louisiana, and Mobile, Alabama.

The gunboat USS *Conestoga* captures the Confederate steamers *V. R. Stephenson* and *Gazelle* on the Cumberland River, Kentucky.

September 17
WEST: General Benjamin M. Prentiss takes charge of Federal forces north of the Hannibal and St. Joseph Railroad, Missouri.
NAVAL: Confederate forces hastily evacuate Ship Island, Mississippi, after fighting landing parties from the USS *Massachusetts.*

September 18
POLITICS: The Kentucky legislature authorizes the use of force to expel Confederate forces from the state.
WEST: Bowling Green, Kentucky, falls to advancing Confederate forces under General Simon B. Buckner, who is newly appointed, and his Central Division of Kentucky.

General Sterling Price's Confederates fiercely assail the Union perimeter at Lexington, Missouri, and cut the garrison off from their water supply. Progress accelerates once the Confederates seize the brick, two-story Anderson house 100 yards outside the Union perimeter, previously used as a hospital and which now serves as a sniper platform for firing into their camp. At day's end—with few losses to either side—Price calls off the attack and allows the intense heat to do its work. Artillery wagons and pieces of ordnance arrive in his camp during the night in preparation for a final assault.
SOUTHWEST: General Paul O. Hebert assumes command of Confederate forces in the Department of Texas.
NAVAL: Commodore Samuel F. Du Pont wins appointment as commander of the South Atlantic Blockading Squadron.

The USS *Rescue* captures the Confederate schooner *Harford* on the Potomac River.

September 19
SOUTH: Earl Van Dorn is promoted to major general, C.S.A.
WEST: Advancing Confederate forces under General Felix K. Zollicoffer drive Union troops from Barboursville, Kentucky. The Southerners then commence the erection of strong defensive positions across Cumberland Gap, Bowling Green, and Columbus.

General Sterling Price's Confederates continue besieging Lexington, Missouri, which now is being reinforced by artillery units. Union forces under Colonel James A. Mulligan resist stoutly, unaware that a nearby relief column of 3,000 men under General Samuel D. Sturgis has been turned back.

NAVAL: The North Atlantic Blockading Squadron under Commodore Louis M. Goldman is ordered to commence operations from the southernmost boundary of North Carolina up through Virginia.

The USS *Gemsbok* seizes the Confederate schooner *Harmony* off Oracoke, North Carolina.

September 20
WEST: Confederate forces abandon Mayfield, Kentucky, in the face of a Union advance, while General Robert Anderson is ordered to establish his headquarters at Louisville.

Colonel J. Mulligan, 23rd Illinois Regiment, surrenders 3,600 Union troops to General Sterling Price at Lexington, Missouri, after a nine-day siege. Price's men ingeniously employed dampened bales of hemp as moveable breastworks, which they pushed ahead of their advance. Outnumbered, surrounded, and lacking water, Mulligan's officers vote to capitulate. Confederate losses are only 25 killed and 72 wounded while Mulligan suffers 39 killed and 120 wounded. Price also seizes seven cannon and 3,000 rifles, which are distributed among his poorly equipped forces. The inability of Union troops to raise the siege causes many in St. Louis and Washington, D.C., to question the competence of General John C. Frémont.

September 21
WEST: General Robert E. Lee arrives and takes personal command of Confederate forces in the Valley of the Kanawha, western Virginia, to oppose advancing Federals under General William S. Rosecrans.

General Ormsby M. Mitchel assumes command of Federal forces in the Department of the Ohio.

General Albert S. Johnston issues a call for 30,000 volunteers from Tennessee for service in the West.

General Leonidas Polk assumes command of the Western Division in Confederate Department No. 2.

NAVAL: A boat launched from the USS *Seminole* attacks and seizes the Confederate sloop *Maryland* on the Potomac River.

September 22
SOUTH: General Joseph E. Johnston issues a call for 10,000 volunteers from Arkansas and Missouri for service in Department No. 2 (Tennessee).

WEST: General Ulysses S. Grant conducts a reconnaissance in the direction of Columbus, Kentucky, and fights a skirmish at Mayfield Creek.

Federal jayhawkers under James H. Lane attack and burn the town of Osceola, Missouri.

NAVAL: The USS *Gemsbok* captures the Confederate schooner *Mary E. Pindar* off Federal Point, North Carolina.

September 23
NORTH: Winfield S. Hancock becomes a brigadier general, U.S. Army.

WEST: Sharp engagements erupt at Romney, Mechanicsburg Gap, and Hanging Rock in western Virginia as Federal forces advance.

General Felix K. Zollicoffer wages a sharp skirmish with Federal troops at Albany, Kentucky.

General Charles C. Frémont closes a St. Louis paper that blamed him for the surrender of Lexington, Missouri.

NAVAL: Commodore Louis M Goldsborough formally takes charge of the North Atlantic Blockading Squadron.

The USS *Cambridge* intercepts the British schooner *Julia* as it approached Beaufort, North Carolina.

The gunboat USS *Lexington* sails down the Ohio River to Owensboro, Kentucky, in a show of force to thwart Confederate sympathizers.

September 24

NORTH: Colonel John Geary and his 28th Pennsylvania Volunteers skirmish with Confederate forces at Point of Rocks, Maryland.

SOUTH: James Ewell Brown (J. E. B.) Stuart is appointed brigadier general of Confederate cavalry.

NAVAL: The USS *Dart* captures the Confederate schooner *Cecelia* off the Louisiana coast.

September 25

SOUTH: In Richmond, Virginia, President Jefferson Davis and General Joseph E. Johnston engage in another heated contretemps, this time over strategy and the allocation of reinforcements.

General William F. Smith leads Federal troops on a reconnaissance near Lewinsville, Virginia.

General Gustavus W. Smith assumes command of the II Corps, Army of Northern Virginia.

WEST: Federal troops under General William S. Rosecrans continue advancing into the Kanawha Valley, western Virginia, intent on eliminating Confederate forces under General Robert E. Lee. A skirmish is fought near Chapmansville.

Confederate general Henry A. Wise is relieved of command in western Virginia following continuous disagreements with his superior, General John P. Floyd.

Union forces occupy Smithland, Kentucky.

SOUTHWEST: The Department of Southern California is organized.

NAVAL: The Navy Department authorizes the employment of African-American "contrabands" on board naval vessels. They will begin to draw pay at the rank of "boy": 10 dollars per month and one ration per day.

The USS *Jacob Bell* and *Seminole* engage Confederate artillery at Freestone Point, Virginia.

Confederate raider CSS *Sumter* under Captain Raphael Semmes captures the Union ship *Joseph Park* off South America.

September 26

WEST: Confederate troops under General Felix K. Zollicoffer capture Salt Works (Clay County), Kentucky, after skirmishing at Laurel Bridge.

General Simon B. Buckner's Confederates destroy the locks at the mouth of Muddy River, Kentucky.

September 27
NORTH: President Abraham Lincoln and General George B. McClellan engage in heated discussions over resuming the offensive in Virginia. The general feels that the Army of the Potomac is not yet ready for prolonged operations, whereas Lincoln is being criticized for the general's alleged inactivity.

September 28
SOUTH: Thomas C. Hindman is appointed brigadier general, C.S.A.

Colonel Edward D. Baker and his 71st Pennsylvania wage a successful skirmish near Vanderburgh's House, Virginia.

NAVAL: The USS *Susquehanna* captures Confederate schooner *San Juan* as it approaches Elizabeth City, North Carolina.

September 29
SOUTH: Fatalities result when the 69th Pennsylvania accidentally fires into the 71st Pennsylvania at Munson's Hill, Virginia.

General Daniel H. Hill is ordered from Virginia to North Carolina in anticipation of Union activity there.

WEST: The 12th Kentucky under Colonel William A. Hoskins skirmishes with Confederates at Albany, Kentucky, and Travisville, Tennessee.

NAVAL: The USS *Susquehanna* seizes the Confederate schooner *Baltimore* off Hatteras Inlet, North Carolina.

September 30
NAVAL: The USS *Dart* captures the Confederate schooner *Zavalla* off Vermillion Bay, Louisiana.

The USS *Niagara* captures the Confederate pilot boat *Frolic* on the South West Pass of the Mississippi River.

SOUTHWEST: Confederate scout Captain R. Hardeman leads an action against hostile Native Americans near Camp Robledo, New Mexico Territory.

October 1
POLITICS: President Abraham Lincoln appoints General Benjamin F. Butler to command the Department of New England, created largely for the purpose of raising and training new troops for future operations. He also requests action on a large naval expedition to the southeastern coast to establish a coaling station.

At Centreville, Virginia, President Jefferson Davis and Generals Joseph E. Johnston, Pierre G. T. Beauregard, and Gustavus W. Smith continue debating strategy. At length, they finally agree to consolidate their positions and restrain from launching offensive operations into Northern territory until at least the following spring.

NAVAL: Secretary of the Navy Gideon Welles opposes issuing letters of marque and reprisal against the South as it inadvertently would imply recognition of the South's national sovereignty.

A Confederate squadron consisting of CSS *Curlew, Raleigh,* and *Junaluska* captures the supply steamer USS *Fanny* while conveying troops off Pamlico Sound, North Carolina.

October 2

POLITICS: The Confederacy reaches an accord with the Osage in the Indian Territory.

Governor Andrew B. Moore of Alabama warns tradespeople against charging exorbitant prices for their services.

SOUTH: Union forces prevail in a large skirmish at Chapmansville, Virginia, while other fighting rages at Springfield Station.

WEST: Pro-Union forces from Cairo, Illinois, attack a Southern camp at Charleston, Missouri, where statewide intermittent strife continues.

October 3

DIPLOMACY: Louisiana governor Thomas O. Moore summarily bans cotton exports in an attempt to force Britain and France to recognize the Confederacy's independence.

SOUTH: General Henry W. Slocum dispatches the 26th New York to capture Pohick Church, Virginia, from Confederate forces.

The 31st New York, dispatched by General William B. Franklin, skirmishes with Confederate cavalry at Springfield Station, Virginia.

WEST: General Joseph J. Reynolds advances from Cheat Mountain with 5,000 men to dislodge a Confederate force stationed at Camp Bartow, along the southern fork of the Greenbrier River in western Virginia. The 1,800 Southerners under General Henry R. Jackson give ground slowly before making a stand behind the river. Reynolds then deploys his men and makes two determined attacks covered by artillery fire but is easily repulsed. Unable to turn Jackson's flanks, Reynold simply withdraws back to Cheat Mountain, and an impasse settles over the region. Union losses are reported as eight killed and 36 wounded to a Confederate tally of six killed, 33 wounded, and 13 missing.

NAVAL: The USS *Sam Houston* arrives off Galveston, Texas, where it sinks the Confederate schooner *Reindeer.*

October 4

NORTH: Colonel Charles P. Stone skirmishes with Confederate forces at Edwards Ferry, Maryland.

SOUTH: Confederate forces fail to dislodge Union defenders, commanded by General John E. Wool, near Chicamacomico, North Carolina.

WEST: The Confederacy concludes a treaty with the Shawnee, Seneca, and Cherokee in the Indian Territory.

SOUTHWEST: Colonel George Wright, 9th U.S. Infantry, assumes command of the new District of Southern California.

NAVAL: President Abraham Lincoln approves a contract for constructing the U.S. Navy's first ironclad warships; among the intended vessels is John Ericsson's revolutionary USS *Monitor.*

The USS *South Carolina* takes Confederate schooners *Ezilda* and *Joseph H. Toone* at the Southwest Pass of the Mississippi River.

October 5

SOUTH: General Joseph K. F. Mansfield takes charge of Union forces garrisoning Hatteras Inlet, North Carolina.

SOUTHWEST: Pro-Union forces sweep through Oak Grove and Temecula Ranch, California, in an attempt to flush out Confederate sympathizers.

NAVAL: At Chincoteague, Virginia, the USS *Louisiana* dispatches two boats, which attack and destroy a Confederate schooner being outfitted as a privateer.

Heavy fire from the USS *Monticello* proves instrumental in repulsing Confederate troops and steamers as they attacked Hatteras Inlet, North Carolina.

October 6

NAVAL: The USS *Flag* captures the blockade-running schooner *Alert* off Charleston, South Carolina.

October 7

POLITICS: President Abraham Lincoln dispatches Secretary of War Simon Cameron with a letter to General Samuel R. Curtis to inquire if General John C. Frémont should be replaced as commander in Missouri.

SOUTH: William J. Hardee, Thomas J. Jackson, James Longstreet, and John B. Magruder gain promotion to major generals, C.S.A.

General Braxton Bragg extends his military authority over all of Alabama.

WEST: Eager to restore his flagging reputation, General Charles Frémont advances 40,000 men from St. Louis, Missouri, toward Lexington. The move prompts General Sterling Price to withdraw south.

NAVAL: The steam-powered ironclad CSS *Virginia* (nee *Merrimack*), completely armored and redesigned by Confederate engineer John M. Brooke, makes its brief but ominous debut off Hampton Roads, Virginia.

The USS *Louisiana* captures the Confederate schooner *S. T. Carrison* off Wallops Island, Virginia.

The gunboat USS *Tyler* exchanges shots with Confederate artillery posted at Iron Bluffs near Columbus, Kentucky.

General Ulysses S. Grant, accompanied by gunboats USS *Lexington* and *Tyler,* conducts a reconnaissance of Lucas Bend, Missouri.

October 8

WEST: General Robert Anderson, who is ailing and commands the Department of the Cumberland, is superseded by General William T. Sherman at Louisville, Kentucky.

October 9

SOUTH: General Braxton Bragg orders 1,000 Confederates under General Richard H. Anderson across Pensacola Bay to attack Union-held Fort Pickens on Santa Rosa Island, Florida. The Southerners, under cover of darkness, safely land and drive the 6th New York from its camp. Union commander Colonel Harvey Brown then brings out several companies of regulars from the fort, assisted by artillery. These troops skirmish heavily with the Confederates, which dissuades Anderson from attacking further. A quick sweep by Union troops nets several stragglers as the Confederates withdraw, but the bulk of Anderson's troops reach the mainland intact. Brown reports losses of 13 killed, 27 wounded, and 21 missing, whereas Anderson loses 18 dead, 39 wounded, and 30 captured.

NAVAL: American naval vessels guarding the Head of Passes, Mississippi River, are attacked by the Confederate steamer CSS *Ivy*. No damage is incurred by either side, but the impressive range of Southern naval ordnance is noted by the Federals.

October 10

POLITICS: President Jefferson Davis, writing to General Gustavus W. Smith, briefly ponders the use of African-American slaves by Confederate forces as laborers.

WEST: General Ormsby M. Mitchel is ordered on an expedition into the heart of pro-Union East Tennessee.

NAVAL: Accurate shooting by the USS *Daylight* silences a Confederate battery at Lynnhaven Bay, Virginia, after it begins to shell the Union vessel *John Clark*.

Confederate forces attack and capture the American sloop *William Batty* in Tampa Bay, Florida.

October 11

SOUTH: Edmund Kirby-Smith is appointed major general, C.S.A.

WEST: General William S. Rosecrans assumes command of Union forces in the Department of Western Virginia.

NAVAL: The USS *Union* dispatches three boat crews under Lieutenant Abram D. Harrell, which cut out and burn a Confederate privateer in Dumfries Creek, Virginia.

October 12

WEST: General John C. Frémont's advance results in heavy skirmishes at Clintonville and Pomme de Terre (Cameron), Missouri. Confederate partisans under Missouri militiaman Jeff Thompson also raid Ironton from their home base in Stoddard County.

NAVAL: Covered by rain and darkness, the Confederate steamer *Theodora* runs the Union blockade off Charleston, South Carolina, and makes for Cuba. On board are special commissioners James M. Mason and John Slidell.

The USS *Dale* captures the Confederate schooner *Specie* east of Jacksonville, Florida.

Newly launched Confederate rammer CSS *Manassas* under Commodore George N. Hollins departs New Orleans, Louisiana, and ventures down the Mississippi River with the armed steamers *Ivy* and *James L. Day*. While clearing the Head of Passes, they encounter a Union squadron consisting of the USS *Richmond, Vincennes, Water Witch, Nightingale,* and *Preble*. A stiff engagement develops in which *Manassas* successfully rams *Richmond* and *Vincennes,* running them aground. The action concludes soon after, and Hollins steams back upstream. The Union vessels subsequently are refloated, and the blockade resumes.

The confederate privateer *Sallie* captures the Union brig *Granada* at sea.

The first Union ironclad, USS *St. Louis,* is launched at Carondelet, Missouri.

October 13
SOUTH: General Thomas Williams succeeds General James K. F. Mansfield as commander of Union forces at Hatteras Inlet, North Carolina.

NAVAL: The USS *Keystone State* seizes the Confederate steamer *Salvor* near Tortugas Island, Florida.

October 14
POLITICS: To discourage treasonable activity, President Abraham Lincoln orders General Winfield Scott to suspend writs of habeas corpus anywhere in the region from Maine to Washington, D.C.

Secretary of War Simon Cameron orders General Thomas W. Sherman to organize and arm fugitive slaves into military squads at Port Royal, South Carolina.

SOUTH: General Braxton Bragg formally takes charge of the newly constituted Department of Alabama and West Florida.

WEST: Former Virginia attorney turned Confederate raider Jeff Thompson establishes his home base in southeastern Missouri.

SOUTHWEST: Colonel James H. Carleton, 1st California Infantry, replaces Colonel George Wright as commander of the District of Southern California.

NAVAL: Lieutenant A. Murray of the USS *Louisiana* administers loyalty oaths to the inhabitants of Chincoteague Island, Virginia.

October 15
SOUTH: Colonel Isaac M. Tucker and the 2nd New Jersey Regiment skirmish with Confederates at Little River Turnpike, Virginia.

WEST: Confederate raiders under Jeff Thompson attack a Union outpost at Potosi, Missouri, taking 33 prisoners of the 38th Illinois and burning the Big River Bridge.

NAVAL: The USS *Roanoke, Flag, Monticello,* and *Vandalia* capture and sink the Confederate blockade-runner *Thomas Watson* off Stono Reef, Charleston, South Carolina.

October 16
POLITICS: President Jefferson Davis denies requests by Confederate soldiers to return home to serve in their state militia.

WEST: Confederate cavalry under Colonel Ashby Turner clashes with Union forces near Harper's Ferry in western Virginia.

Union forces reoccupy Lexington, Missouri.

NAVAL: The USS *South Carolina* captures the Confederate schooner *Edward Barnard* near South West Pass, Mississippi River.

October 17
NAVAL: After some deliberation, Commodore Samuel F. Du Pont informs U.S. Navy secretary Gideon Welles that Port Royal, South Carolina, is an inviting target and would constitute an important asset to the continuing blockade effort.

The Confederate privateer *Sallie* captures the Federal brig *Betsey Ames* on the Bahama Banks.

October 18

POLITICAL: President Abraham Lincoln meets with his cabinet about continuing dissatisfaction with General in Chief Winfield Scott and his probable retirement. He also experiences problems prying troops from the armies of Generals William T. Sherman and George B. McClellan for the upcoming coastal expedition.

SOUTH: General Israel B. Richardson takes Union forces on a reconnaissance of the Occoquan River, Virginia.

WEST: Confederate raiders under Jeff Thompson skirmish with Colonel Joseph B. Plummer's 11th Missouri Regiment around Wardensburg, Missouri.

SOUTHWEST: General Mansfield Lovell replaces General David E. Twiggs as commander of Confederate Department No. 1 (Louisiana and Texas).

NAVAL: The USS *Gemsbok* captures the Confederate brig *Ariel* off Wilmington, Delaware.

October 19

NAVAL: USS *Massachusetts* and CSS *Florida* wage an inconclusive battle in the Mississippi Sound, but Union forces are alarmed by the apparent longer range of Confederate ordnance.

October 20

SOUTH: General George B. McClellan, eager to test Confederate responses and pressured by Radical Republicans to assume the offensive, orders politician-turned-soldier Colonel Charles P. Stone to dispatch troops from his base at Poolesville, Maryland, and demonstrate before enemy lines near Leesburg, Virginia. Stone elects to send a single brigade of 1,700 men under the inexperienced colonel Edward D. Baker, a political appointee and close friend of President Abraham Lincoln. He is ordered to make a "slight demonstration" to test Confederate reactions. When word of Baker's advance reaches Confederate colonel Nathan G. Evans, he energetically makes preparations to receive the intruders.

Union forces under General George A. McCall occupy Dranesville, Virginia, below the Potomac River. He is supposed to be acting in concert with forces dispatched to Leesburg by Colonel Edward P. Stone, but he withdraws his troops without informing the latter.

WEST: Colonel William P. Carlin advances his 38th Illinois to Pilot Knob, Missouri.

Colonel George Wright replaces General Edwin V. Sumner as commander of the Department of the Pacific.

October 21

SOUTH: Acting upon faulty intelligence, Colonel Isaac D. Baker ferries 1,700 men of his brigade across the Potomac River at Ball's Bluff, Virginia, a 100-foot ledge overlooking the waterway. He does so without first reconnoitering the area for enemy troops and remains unaware that Colonel Nathan G. Evans's Confederates are posted in the woods above him. Federal troops clamber up the slope, but senior officer express concern about having their backs against a river. At this juncture the milling soldiers are fired on by Southerners from higher up, enjoying the advantage of position. An unequal battle ensues for three and a half hours until Baker is killed and his command succumbs to panic. Evans then charges down hill and routs the remaining defenders, many of whom tumble over the bluffs and drown while fording the Potomac. Losses in this affair are 49 Union troops killed, 158 wounded, and 714 captured to a Confederate tally of 33 killed, 115 wounded, and one missing. President Abraham Lincoln is notably shaken upon hearing of the death of Baker, a good friend and close confidant.

Nathan G. Evans is promoted to brigadier general, C.S.A., for his performance at Ball's Bluff.

General John B. Magruder skirmishes with Union forces at Young's Mills (Newport News), Virginia.

General John B. Grayson, C.S.A., dies of illness in Tallahassee, Florida.

WEST: Confederates under General Felix K. Zollicoffer skirmish heavily with the Union troops of General Albin F. Schoepf at Rockcastle Hills, Kentucky.

Colonel J. B. Plummer engages in a three-hour battle with Confederate forces near Fredericktown, Missouri, and occupies the town.

October 22
SOUTH: The Confederate Department of Virginia organizes under General Joseph E. Johnston while General Pierre G. T. Beauregard retains command of the District of the Potomac.

General Theophilus Holmes takes command of the Aquia District of Virginia.

General James H. Trapier assumes control of the Confederate Department of Middle and East Florida.

WEST: General Benjamin F. Kelley takes charge of Union forces in the Department of Harper's Ferry.

General Thomas J. Jackson is ordered to lead Confederate forces in the Shenandoah Valley of western Virginia.

NAVAL: Captain Thomas T. Craven, commanding the Potomac River Flotilla, informs superiors that Confederate batteries control access to the Potomac at all points below Alexandria, Virginia.

October 23
WEST: Skirmishing erupts between Union and Confederate forces at West Liberty and Hodgeville, Kentucky. The strength of enemy defenses alarms General William T. Sherman, who is anxious to forestall further Confederate advances into that state.

NAVAL: Crew members of the captured Confederate privateer *Savannah* are tried in New York on charges of piracy and threatened with execution. Though convicted, the sentences are never carried out.

October 24
POLITICS: President Abraham Lincoln relieves General John C. Frémont of command in Missouri and replaces him with General David Hunter. He also attends the funeral of Colonel Edward D. Baker, his close friend, lately killed at Ball's Bluff.

WEST: The inhabitants of western Virginia overwhelmingly endorse plans for forming their own state.

Colonel R. D. Anderson and his 14th Tennessee attack the Union position of Camp Joe Underwood, Kentucky.

Western Union finalizes its transcontinental telegraph; viable communication with the entire country now becomes possible.

October 25
WEST: Union cavalry under Major Charles Zagonyi defeat opposing Confederate forces and occupy Springfield, Missouri.
NAVAL: Swedish inventor and engineer John Ericsson begins to construct his revolutionary, one-turret warship USS *Monitor* at Greenpoint, New York, by laying its keel.

The USS *Rhode Island* captures the Confederate schooner *Aristides* off Charlotte Harbor, Florida.

October 26
SOUTH: General Alexander R. Lawton takes command of the Confederate Department of Georgia.
WEST: Continued skirmishing under General Benjamin F. Kelley at Romney and South Branch Bridge in western Virginia removes the last remaining Confederate forces from the theater.

General John C. Frémont and General Sterling Price of the Missouri Home Guard agree on a prisoner exchange.
NAVAL: CSS *Nashville* successfully clears the blockade out of Charleston, South Carolina.

The gunboat USS *Conestoga* ferries Federal troops to Eddyville, Kentucky, for an impending advance on Saratoga by General Charles F. Smith.

October 27
WEST: General John C. Frémont shepherds his army toward Springfield, Missouri, in the mistaken belief that the main Confederate force under General Sterling Price encamps there. In fact, Price has retreated long since to safety thanks to Frémont's lethargic movements.
NAVAL: The USS *Santee* captures the Confederate brig *Delta* off Galveston, Texas.

October 28
NORTH: Union troops under General Joseph Hooker engage Confederate batteries near Budd's Ferry, Maryland.
WEST: General Albert S. Johnston relieves General Simon B. Buckner as commander of the Confederate Army Corps of Kentucky at Bowling Green.

Federal forces under General Chester Harding advance toward Fulton, Missouri.
NAVAL: Lieutenant Alfred Hopkins of the USS *Louisiana* leads a three-boat expedition that attacks and burns three Confederate vessels anchored in the Chincoteague Inlet, Virginia.

October 29

NAVAL: A huge combined expedition of 17 warships, 25 supply ships, and 25 transports under Commodore Samuel F. Du Pont, conveying 13,000 Union troops under General Thomas W. Sherman, departs Hampton Roads, Virginia. The largest American armada assembled to date, the flotilla is intended to capture Port Royal, South Carolina, midway between Charleston and Savannah, Georgia. En route, the armada is buffeted by heavy seas off the coast and is scattered widely.

October 30

SOUTH: President Jefferson Davis complains to General Pierre G. T. Beauregard about publishing excerpts from Beauregard's report on the Battle of First Manassas "to exalt yourself at my expense." Thereafter, the two leaders are never reconciled.
WEST: Confederate forces near Fort Donelson, Tennessee, begin to sink stone-filled barges on the Cumberland River as an obstacle to Federal gunboats.
NAVAL: The Confederate privateer *Sallie* seizes the American brig *B. K. Eaton* at sea.

October 31

POLITICS: Secessionist-leaning Missouri legislators meet at Neosho, Missouri, and vote to join the Confederacy. The state continues to be claimed simultaneously by both belligerents.
NORTH: Ailing, 75-year-old General in Chief Winfield Scott, once the military doyen of his age, voluntarily resigns as general in chief of Union forces. He then retires in virtual isolation to the U.S. Military Academy at West Point, New York, for the remainder of the war.
WEST: Union soldiers repulse Confederate attackers at Morgantown, Kentucky, with few casualties to either side.

November 1

NORTH: The 34-year-old general George B. McClellan gains appointment as general in chief to succeed the ailing Winfield Scott. In light of his youth, dash, and reputation, much is expected of him.
WEST: Confederate forces under General John B. Floyd botch an attack on General William S. Rosecrans's troops at Gauley Bridge and Cotton Hill in western Virginia. After being repulsed, the Southerners withdraw completely from the area.

General Ulysses S. Grant arrives at Cairo, Illinois, to take charge of the District of Southeast Missouri. Rumpled and nondescript in appearance, he proves to be aggressively disposed and begins to formulate plans to evict Confederate forces from their strong point along the bluffs at Columbus, Kentucky.

General John C. Frémont finally concludes a prisoner-exchange agreement with General Sterling Price, and he also pledges to release civilians held in military detention. The agreement subsequently is negated by President Abraham Lincoln for exceeding local military authority.
NAVAL: The Union armada under Commodore Samuel F. Du Pont continues being buffeted by high seas off Cape Hatteras, North Carolina, and remains widely scattered.

Portrait of a Confederate soldier *(Library of Congress)*

November 2

SOUTH: Former vice president John C. Breckinridge is appointed brigadier general, C.S.A.

WEST: General John C. Frémont, who has proven incorrigible, is relieved of command of the Department of the West at Springfield, Missouri, and is temporarily replaced by General David Hunter.

Southern partisans under General Jeff Thompson are the object of a Federal offensive at Bird's Point, Cape Girardeau, and Ironton, Missouri.

NAVAL: The USS *Sabine* rescues a battalion of U.S. Marines from the sinking transport *Governor* near Georgetown, South Carolina, before it founders.

British steamer *Bermuda* successfully runs the blockade at Charleston, South Carolina.

November 3

NORTH: Union troops under General Oliver O. Howard advance into southern Maryland to clear out remaining pockets of Confederate troops.

November 4

POLITICS: President Jefferson Davis, frustrated in his inability to reach an agreement with General Pierre G. T. Beauregard concerning strategy, solicits support and advice from General Samuel Cooper and General Robert E. Lee. He also is increasingly aware of rumors concerning his alleged military ineptitude.

SOUTH: General John A. Dix forbids all African Americans from entering beyond closely prescribed military lines.

WEST: General Thomas J. "Stonewall" Jackson arrives as commander of Confederate forces in the Shenandoah Valley, headquartered at Winchester, Virginia.

NAVAL: A large naval expedition under Commodore Samuel F. Du Pont gathers off Port Royal Sound, South Carolina. Meanwhile, Confederate vessels under Commodore Josiah Tattnall fire on the coast survey ship *Vixen* and USS *Ottawa* as they reconnoiter the two-mile-wide entrance into the channel. No damage results as the Union ships complete their mission and withdraw.

November 5

SOUTH: General Robert E. Lee assumes responsibilities as head of the newly constituted Department of South Carolina, Georgia, and East Florida.

WEST: Union troops under General William Nelson occupy Prestonburg, Kentucky.

General John C. Frémont, still commanding the Department of the West, orders General Ulysses S. Grant on a diversionary attack against Columbus, Kentucky, to cover Union thrusts in southeastern Missouri. He anticipates that this maneuver will keep Confederate forces preoccupied and unable to cross the Mississippi River and interfere.

NAVAL: The USS *Ottawa, Pembina, Seneca,* and *Pawnee* attack and disperse a Confederate squadron under Commodore Josiah Tattnall in Port Royal Sound, and begin to shell neighboring Forts Walker and Beauregard on the north and south sides of the sound.

November 6

POLITICS: President Jefferson Davis is elected permanent chief executive of the Confederate States of America and is slated to serve a six-year term. Vice President Alexander Stephens likewise is reelected, as are members of the first permanent Confederate Congress.

Portrait of a Union officer *(Library of Congress)*

WEST: General Ulysses S. Grant embarks from Cairo, Illinois, with two brigades of infantry, some cavalry, and an artillery battery for an amphibious descent on nearby Belmont, Missouri. To cover his actions, he orders General Charles F. Smith, commanding Union forces at Paducah, Kentucky, to demonstrate against the main Confederate force under General Leonidas Polk at Columbus, directly opposite Belmont.

NAVAL: The USS *Rescue* attacks and burns the Confederate schooner *Ada* in Curratoman Creek, Virginia.

The USS *Lawrence* captures the British blockade-runner *Fanny Lee* off Darien, Georgia.

November 7

WEST: General Don C. Buell is chosen to command Union forces in Kentucky, and he receives instructions from General George B. McClellan on the legal status of fugitive African-American slaves.

Approximately 3,000 Union troops under General Ulysses S. Grant disembark at Hunter's Farm, three miles above his objective at Belmont, Missouri. His opponent, General Gideon Pillow, commands 2,500 men, and once the firing commences, General Leonidas Polk rushes an additional 2,500 men across the Mississippi River. Meanwhile, Grant's men launch into the Confederates, who are saddled by Pillow's inept leadership and are routed in a four-hour fight. Enthusiastic Union troops storm into the Confederate camp, and, despite the entreaties of Grant and other officers, they embark on headlong plundering. This allows Pillow to regroup and receive reinforcements under Polk, who arrives in person to take charge. With Confederate forces now interposed between his men and his water transport, Grant has little choice but to cut his way through enemy lines to the riverbank—and safety. Union forces again prevail in stiff fighting and successfully embark while vengeful Confederates fire on them from the shoreline. Grant himself nearly stumbles into advancing Confederates in the woods and almost is captured. His first battle proves somewhat of a botched draw, with Federal troops sustaining 607 casualties to a Confederate tally of 641. But, most important, the affair demonstrates Grant's willingness to undertake the offensive, along with his aptitude for combined operations employing both troops and gunboats.

NAVAL: The South Atlantic Blockading Squadron of 77 vessels under Commodore Samuel F. Du Pont disembarks 16,000 troops under General Thomas W. Sherman off Port Royal Sound, South Carolina, halfway between Charleston and Savannah, Georgia. The Union vessels steam directly into the sound, assume a circling oval formation, and subject the Confederates to a steady stream of accurate gunfire from 154 heavy cannon. Forts Beauregard and Walker, whose crews are largely untrained, respond with a sputtering fire from 41 guns that mainly falls short. Ironically, the Southerners are commanded by General Thomas F. Drayton, whose brother, Percival Drayton, is a Union naval commander. By 3:30 P.M., both fortifications are abandoned and overrun by the combined assault. Confederate defenders under Commodore Josiah Tattnall can only harass their antagonists, but they do manage to rescue the garrison at Hilton Head and ferry them ashore. Despite spectacular pyrotechnics, losses are extremely light, with Du Pont losing eight killed and six wounded while Drayton reports 11 killed and 48 wounded. The Union has acquired a second firm lodging on the Confederate coastline; Port Royal Sound/Hilton Head emerges as a major coaling base for the blockading squadrons.

The wooden gunboats USS *Tyler* and *Lexington* afford useful fire support for Union forces at Belmont, Missouri, allowing them to escape a Confederate pursuit to the water's edge. Their success underscores the growing utility and flexibility of naval craft for riverine operations throughout the West.

The British mail steamer *Trent* departs Havana, Cuba, bound for the Danish island of St. Thomas in the Caribbean. Confederate agents James M. Mason and John Slidell are onboard.

November 8

SOUTH: Federal forces under General Thomas W. Sherman advance inland from Hilton Head, South Carolina, toward the city of Beaufort.

General Robert E. Lee arrives at his new headquarters in Savannah, Georgia. Hearing of the success of Union forces at Port Royal Sound, he orders the coastline evacuated save for the garrison of Fort Pulaski, Georgia.

WEST: Pro-Union agitators rise up and attack Southern forces in the mountainous region of eastern Tennessee, destroying railroad lines and forcing General Felix K. Zollicoffer to request immediate reinforcements.

Union troops under General William Nelson engage Confederate forces at Ivy Mountain, Kentucky. While at Prestonburg, Nelson had become aware of Southern recruiting activities under Colonel John S. Williams at Piketon, 28 miles distant, and resolved to entrap them. He then dispatches Colonel Joshua W. Sill, two regiments, and some cannon on a circuitous route to cut Williams off near the Virginia state line. Nelson himself marches three regiments and two batteries directly toward Piketown. The Confederates, badly outnumbered and armed mostly with muskets and shotguns, rapidly fall back to Ivy Mountain and position themselves along a bend in the road. Nelson's troops are then fought to a standstill. The second column under Sill never arrives. Williams manages to disengage and return to Virginia intact. Nelson reports six killed and 24 wounded; Southern losses are unknown.

NAVAL: The USS *Rescue* shells a Confederate battery at Urbana Creek, Virginia, and subsequently nets a large enemy schooner.

In a potentially disastrous move, the screw sloop USS *San Jacinto* under irascible Captain Charles Wilkes, boards the British mail packet *Trent* in Old Bahama Channel and forcibly removes Southern envoys James M. Mason and John Slidell. This proves an egregious violation of international law involving the rights of neutrals on the high seas and threatens to precipitate a war with Great Britain.

A cutting-out expedition under Lieutenant James E. Jouett, launched from USS *Santee,* surprises and burns the Confederate schooner *Royal Yacht* at Galveston, Texas.

November 9

SOUTH: Union forces under Generals Joseph Hooker and Daniel E. Sickles advance on Mathias Point, York River, Virginia.

Federal troops under General Thomas W. Sherman, assisted by gunboats, advance from Port Royal, South Carolina, and capture the city of Beaufort on the Broad River. This severs a vital communications link between Charleston and Savannah, Georgia. Department commander General Robert E. Lee expresses concern to the government in Richmond about the Union's apparent ability to land troops anywhere at will.

George B. Crittenden is promoted to major general, C.S.A.

WEST: In a major shake-up of command, General Henry W. Halleck becomes commander of Federal troops in the newly created Department of Missouri (Missouri, Arkansas, Illinois, and western Kentucky) while General Don C. Buell replaces General William T. Sherman as head of the Department of the Cumberland, subsequently enlarged and renamed the Department of the Ohio (Indiana, Michigan, Tennessee, and western Kentucky).

The Department of Kansas is organized under General David Hunter.

SOUTHWEST: The Department of New Mexico is reorganized under Colonel Edward R. S. Canby, U.S. Army.

November 11

NORTH: Thaddeus Lowe, Union chief of army aeronautics, rides an observation balloon launched from the *G. W. Parke Custis* anchored in the Potomac River. In nearby Washington, D.C., a torchlight parade is held honoring General George B. McClellan, now publicly heralded as savior of the Union.

WEST: General Jacob D. Cox's Federal troops skirmish with Confederate forces at Gauley Bridge in western Virginia.

General Leonidas Polk is wounded when a large Confederate cannon at Columbus, Kentucky, explodes while being test-fired.

General George B. Crittenden assumes command of Confederate troops in the District of Cumberland Gap, Tennessee. His chief subordinate, Felix K. Zollicoffer, is assigned to southeastern Kentucky but is to remain south of the Cumberland River.

Pitched battles erupt between Union Jayhawkers and Southern Bushwhackers at Little Blue, Missouri.

November 12

SOUTH: Renewed Federal reconnaissance of Occoquan Creek by Federal troops under General Samuel P. Heintzelman.

NAVAL: The British-built steamer *Fingal* arrives with a cargo of military stores at Savannah, Georgia. The vessel subsequently is armed and rechristened CSS *Atlanta*.

November 13

POLITICS: George B. Lincoln contemptuously snubs President Abraham Lincoln when the latter calls on his headquarters by retiring to bed. Henceforth, the general will be summoned to the White House when consultations become necessary.

NAVAL: The USS *Water Witch* captures the British blockade-runner *Cornucopia* off Mobile, Alabama.

November 14

NORTH: General Joseph Hooker fights a minor engagement at Mattawoman Creek, Maryland.

NAVAL: The U.S. revenue cutter *Mary* attacks and captures the Confederate privateer *Neva* at San Francisco, California.

November 15

POLITICS: President Abraham Lincoln and his cabinet begin to focus attention on strategic New Orleans, Louisiana, the Confederacy's second-largest city and a port of great significance. In selecting a naval leader to spearhead an amphibious expedition against it, Secretary Gideon Welles chooses Captain David G. Farragut, a 60-year-old Tennessean and War of 1812 veteran known for his aggressive disposition. Welles has been persuaded to do so by Captain David D. Porter, Farragut's stepbrother.

The U.S. Christian Commission is organized as a wartime extension of the Young Men's Christian Association (YMCA). The commission is designated to provide supplies and extend other assistance to Union troops.

WEST: General Don C. Buell arrives at Louisville, Kentucky, as commander of the Department of the Ohio, replacing General William T. Sherman. The president is counting on him for an early advance into pro-Union eastern Tennessee.

A camp occupied by Union sympathizers near Chattanooga, Tennessee, is overrun by Confederate forces. Their leader, William B. Carter, is captured but subsequently escapes.

SOUTHWEST: A mixed Confederate force of 1,400 Texans under Colonel Douglas H. Cooper with allied Cherokee, Choctaw, and Chickasaw warriors arrives at Canadian Creek, Indian Territory, intending to fight a reputed 1,000 pro-Union Creek Indians stationed there under Opothleyahola. However, once arrived, they discovered that the enemy has withdrawn, so Cooper sets off in pursuit toward nearby Round Mountain.

NAVAL: The USS *San Jacinto* under Captain John Wilkes arrives at Fortress Monroe, Virginia, with captured Confederate emissaries James M. Mason and John Slidell onboard. This is the government's first inkling of what had transpired at sea, and Wilkes is hailed as a hero in the press.

The USS *Dale* captures the British schooner *Mabel* east of Jacksonville, Florida.

November 16

POLITICS: To preclude a potentially ruinous war with Great Britain, Postmaster General Montgomery Blair and Senator Charles Sumner of Massachusetts urge the immediate release of Confederate envoys James M. Mason and John Slidell.

NAVAL: Confederate navy secretary Stephen R. Mallory accepts bids for four, heavily armed seagoing ironclads.

November 17

NAVAL: The USS *Connecticut* captures the British schooner *Adeline* off Cape Canaveral, Florida, uncovering a large cache of military stores and supplies onboard.

November 18

POLITICS: The fifth session of the Provisional Confederate Congress convenes.

Confederate Kentuckians meet at Russellville and adopt a secession ordinance. Like Missouri, Kentucky has separate legislatures in both Union and Confederate camps.

A convention of loyal North Carolinians convenes at Hatteras to denounce secession and reaffirm their loyalty to the Union. Marble Taylor Nash is then elected provisional governor of the state.

SOUTH: The 1st Virginia Cavalry under Colonel Fitzhugh Lee skirmishes with Union forces at Fairfax Courthouse, Virginia.

WEST: General Albert S. Johnston repeats his call for a complete mobilization by all militia and volunteers from Tennessee.

Guerrillas under General Jeff Thompson seize a Federal steamer at Price's Landing, Missouri.

General George Wright formally accepts command of the Department of the Pacific.

SOUTHWEST: A detachment of the 9th Texas under Colonel Douglas H. Cooper, assisted by allied Cherokees, fights a skirmish with Creek warriors under Opothleyahola at Round Mountain, Indian Territory. The pro-Union Native Americans are defeated yet skillfully extricate themselves.

NAVAL: Commodore David D. Porter is tasked with acquiring and supplying gunboats for the long-anticipated campaign against New Orleans, Louisiana.

The USS *Monticello* exchanges fire with Confederate artillery near New Inlet, North Carolina.

Heavy and accurate fire from the gunboat USS *Conestoga* silences a Confederate battery at Canton, Kentucky, and disperses accompanying troops.

November 19

NAVAL: The CSS *Nashville* captures and burns the Union clipper *Harvey Birch* at sea.

November 20

NORTH: General George B. McClellan, a superb organizer and disciplinarian, reviews 70,000 men of the Army of the Potomac near Washington, D.C. In contrast with amateurish forces hastily assembled the previous summer, visitors comment favorably on the martial ardor and discipline of all ranks. However, it remains to be seen if McClellan will aggressively engage enemy forces who are defending the Confederate capital, Richmond, Virginia.

WEST: General John B. Floyd hastily withdraws from the Gauley River region of western Virginia, abandoning or destroying valuable tents and other equipment.

General Thomas C. Hindman leads Confederate forces in a skirmish at Brownsville, Kentucky.

General Henry W. Halleck, newly arrived at the Department of the Missouri in St. Louis, declares General Orders No. 3, excluding African-American slaves from military camps in the Department of the Missouri.

SOUTHWEST: Pursuing Union forces corner and capture Confederate sympathizers under Daniel Showalter at Warner's Ranch, southeast of Los Angeles, California.

November 21

POLITICS: The Confederate cabinet is reorganized with Judah P. Benjamin succeeding LeRoy P. Walker as secretary of war.

NORTH: John M. Schofield is appointed brigadier general, U.S. Army.

WEST: Confederate general Lloyd Tilghman becomes commander of strategic Forts Henry and Donelson on the Tennessee and Cumberland rivers, respectively. These are the lynchpins of Confederate defense in the central region of the war and critical to the Southern war effort.

General Albert S. Johnston again summons 10,000 volunteers from Mississippi to assist in the defense of Columbus, Kentucky.

NAVAL: The USS *New London,* assisted by the *R. R. Cuyler* and *Massachusetts,* seizes the Confederate schooner *Olive* in Mississippi Sound. Hours later, they also seize the steamer *Anna.*

November 22

SOUTHWEST: General Albert Pike is appointed commander of the newly instituted Confederate Department of the Indian Territory.

NAVAL: The Navy Department is authorized to recruit an additional 500 marines and officers.

The USS *Niagara* and *Richmond* engage in a two-day duel with Confederate artillery based in Fort McRee, Pensacola, Florida. The vessels are assisted by fire from neighboring Fort Pickens; Confederate positions sustain heavy damage, as does the *Richmond.*

November 23

WEST: Union troops under General George H. Thomas stage a demonstration from Danville, Kentucky, toward eastern Tennessee.

NAVAL: The Confederate raider CSS *Sumter* under Captain Raphael Semmes evades the USS *Iroquois* at Martinique and heads for Europe.

November 24

WEST: Colonel Nathan B. Forrest mounts a prolonged cavalry raid against union garrisons Caseyville and Eddyville, Kentucky, initiating what becomes a spectacular partisan career.

NAVAL: The USS *San Jacinto* under Captain John Wilkes docks in Boston, Massachusetts, whereupon captured Confederate commissioners James M. Mason and John Slidell are imprisoned at Fort Warren.

A U.S. Navy squadron consisting of the USS *Flag, August, Pocahontas, Seneca,* and *Savannah,* the whole under Commander John Rodgers, disembark forces on Tybee Island and seal off the mouth of the Savannah River, Georgia. This acquisition places nearby Fort Pulaski, Savannah's principal fortification, within Union grasp.

November 25

SOUTH: Confederate secretary of war Judah P. Benjamin orders pro-Union guerrillas captured in Tennessee to be tried by court-martial and hanged if found guilty of burning bridges.

NAVAL: The USS *Penguin* captures the Confederate blockade-runner *Albion* near Edisto, North Carolina.

The Confederate raider CSS *Sumter* under Captain Raphael Semmes takes the Union brig *Montmorenci* off the Leeward Islands.

November 26

POLITICS: A constituent convention gathers at Wheeling, Virginia, and adopts a resolution to secede from Virginia and establish a separate state.

NORTH: A banquet honoring Captain Charles Wilkes is held in Boston as diplomats begin to weigh the diplomatic implications of his actions.

SOUTH: General George A. McCall leads Union forces on an expedition to Dranesville, Virginia, engaging in several skirmishes en route.

NAVAL: Commodore Josiah Tattnall sorties with three armed steamers against Union vessels off Cockspur Roads, Georgia. The Confederates withdraw after failing to lure their opponents to within range of Fort Pulaski's guns.

The Confederate raider CSS *Sumter* under Captain Raphael Semmes seizes and burns the American schooner *Arcade* north of the Leeward Islands.

November 27

DIPLOMACY: Indignation runs high in Great Britain as word of the *Trent* affair circulates. Signs and editorials declaring an "outrage on the British flag" begin to manifest publicly while war seems in the offing.

WEST: General Don C. Buell, commanding the Department of the Ohio, is encouraged by General George B. McClellan to advance into the Tennessee heartland.

NAVAL: A large Union naval expedition, destined for Ship Island, Mississippi, departs Hampton Roads, Virginia. This is the preliminary step for launching an expedition against New Orleans, Louisiana.

The USS *Vincennes* boards and seizes the British blockade-runner *Empress* after it runs aground at the mouth of the Mississippi River.

November 28

POLITICS: The Confederate Congress inducts Missouri into the Confederacy as the 12th state.

WEST: General Benjamin M. Prentiss assumes control of Union forces in the Department of North Missouri.

NAVAL: The USS *New London* captures the blockade-runner *Lewis* and the schooner *A. J. View* off Ship Island, Mississippi.

November 29

SOUTH: In an act of defiance, farmers in the vicinity of Charleston, South Carolina, and Savannah, Georgia, burn cotton crops rather than see them confiscated by Northern forces.

WEST: General John M. Schofield takes command of the Union militia in Missouri.

NAVAL: Lieutenant John L. Worden is exchanged and arrives back in Washington, D.C., after seven months of close confinement in Alabama.

November 30

DIPLOMACY: The British cabinet, headed by Foreign Secretary Lord John Russell, greatly incensed by the *Trent* affair, demands a formal apology and the immediate release of detained Confederate agents James M. Mason and John Slidell. The British minister to the United States, Lord Lyons, is also instructed to depart Washington, D.C., if a proper response is not forthcoming within one week.

WEST: A raid by Confederate bushwhackers captures horses belonging to Federal troops under Benjamin F. Kelley.

NAVAL: The USS *Savannah* attacks and captures the Confederate schooner *E. J. Waterman* after it grounds on Tybee Island, Georgia.

The USS *Wanderer* captures the British blockade-runner *Telegraph* near Indian Keys, Florida.

December 1

DIPLOMACY: The British cabinet prepares for war with the United States by dispatching 6,000 troops to Canada and sending Admiral Sir Alexander Milne to Halifax, Nova Scotia, with 40 vessels mounting 1,273 guns.

POLITICS: U.S. secretary of war Simon Cameron reports to President Abraham Lincoln as to what should be done with the thousands of African-American slaves flocking into Union lines. The president, desperate to maintain the loyalty of border states Delaware, Maryland, Kentucky, and Missouri, orders all mention of emancipation or military service struck from the report, preferring instead to allow Congress to address the issue after the war. The president also inquires of General George B. McClellan exactly when he intends to resume offensive operations in Virginia.

WEST: A brigade of Federal troops under General Albin Schoeph advances to engage General Felix K. Zollicoffer's Confederates at Mill Springs and Somerset, Kentucky.

Confederate authorities in Tennessee hang several pro-Union guerrillas charged with burning bridges.

NAVAL: The gunboat USS *Penguin* captures the blockade-runner *Albion* off Charleston, South Carolina, along with a cargo of commodities worth $100,000.

The USS *Seminole* captures the Confederate sloop *Lida* off St. Simon's Sound, Georgia.

The USS *New London* captures the Confederate sloop *Advocate* in Mississippi Sound.

December 2

POLITICS: The second session of the 37th Congress convenes in Washington, D.C.

Secretary of War Simon Cameron reveals that U.S. military forces comprise 20,334 army soldiers and 640,637 volunteers.

WEST: General Henry Halleck is authorized to suspend writs of habeas corpus within the Department of Missouri.

NAVAL: Secretary of the Navy Gideon Welles informs President Abraham Lincoln that 153 enemy vessels have been captured in the previous year. Moreover, he declares naval manpower at 22,000 men and, once all new vessels on the stocks are afloat, that the navy possesses 264 warships of various description.

The CSS *Patrick Henry* under Commander John R. Tucker attacks four Union steamers off Newport News, Virginia, and withdraws two hours later after sustaining damage.

December 3

POLITICS: President Abraham Lincoln, in his message to Congress, suggests that slaves appropriated from Southern owners be allowed to emigrate. He also reiterates his belief that the Union must be preserved by all means at the government's disposal.

SOUTH: Confederate forces at Vienna, Virginia, capture a detachment of the 3rd Pennsylvania Cavalry.

WEST: The 13th Illinois under Colonel John B. Wyman skirmishes with Confederates at Salem, Missouri, while Major George C. Marshall leads the 2nd Missouri Cavalry on a reconnaissance through Saline County.

General John Pope is installed as commander of all Federal forces between the Missouri and Osage rivers.

NAVAL: Two regiments, the first troops of General Benjamin F. Butler's expedition, arrive by sea at Ship Island, Mississippi. The locale is converted rapidly into a major staging area for future operations against New Orleans, Louisiana.

The USS *Santiago de Cuba* captures the British blockade-runner *Victoria* at sea.

The Confederate raider CSS *Sumter* under Captain Raphael Semmes captures and burns the Union ship *Vigilant* at sea near the West Indies.

December 4

DIPLOMACY: The British government forbids all exports to the United States, especially materials capable of being used for armaments.

POLITICS: The U.S. Senate formerly expels former vice president John C. Breckinridge of Kentucky on a vote of 36 to 0. Since the previous November, Breckinridge has been serving as a Confederate major general.

Southern Presbyterians gather in Augusta, Georgia, to separate themselves from their Northern counterparts. They then found the Assembly of the Presbyterian Church in the Confederate States of America.

WEST: Newly arrived at his headquarters at St. Louis, Missouri, General Henry W. Halleck authorizes continuing punitive measures against Confederate sympathizers in his region. These include the death penalty for any citizen caught assisting rebel guerrillas.

Colonel John H. Morgan leads a successful Confederate mounted raid, which burns the Bacon Creek Bridge near Munfordville, Kentucky.

Armed citizens of Dunksburg, Missouri, unite to repel a Confederate raiding party.

NAVAL: The USS *Montgomery* is attacked by the Confederate steamers *Florida* and *Pamlico* at Horn Island Pass, Mississippi Sound. No damage to either side ensues.

December 5

POLITICS: Congress introduces petitions and bills mandating the abolition of slavery.

WEST: General William J. Hardee assumes command of the Confederate Central Army of Kentucky.

Colonel John B. Wyman of the 13th Illinois commences an expedition to Current Hills, Missouri.

NAVAL: A naval squadron consisting of the USS *Ottawa, Seneca,* and *Pembina* conducts a reconnaissance in force along Wassaw Sound, Georgia.

December 6

POLITICAL: Pro-Union newspaper editor William G. Brownlow is arrested by Confederate authorities on charges of treason in Knoxville, Tennessee.

SOUTH: General George G. Meade conducts a successful Union foraging expedition through Gunnell's Farm in Dranesville, Virginia.

NAVAL: The USS *Augusta* seizes the British blockade-runner *Cheshire* off South Carolina.

December 7

WEST: Confederate forces occupy Glasgow, Missouri, without a fight.

NAVAL: The USS *Santiago de Cuba* under Commander Daniel B. Ridgley stops the British ship *Eugenia Smith* at sea and removes Confederate purchasing agent J. W. Zacharie of New Orleans, Louisiana. Coming on the heels of the *Trent* affair, this act exacerbates tensions between the two nations.

December 8

NORTH: The American Bible Society begins to distribute as many as 7,000 Bibles a day to Union soldiers and sailors.

SOUTHWEST: Pro-Union Chief Opothleyahola and Creek 1,000 warriors arrive at Bird Creek (Chusto-Talasah), Indian Territory, and assume defensive positions while pursued by Confederate and allied Indian forces. The chief then dispatches a messenger to the hostile tribes indicating that he does not wish to spill Indian blood, but word of Creek determination to fight unsettles many of Colonel Douglas H. Cooper's warriors. Native Americans begin to desert him.

NAVAL: The USS *Rhode Island* captures the British blockade-runner *Phantom* off Cape Lookout, North Carolina.

The Confederate raider CSS *Sumter* under Captain Raphael Semmes captures and burns the Union bark *Eben Dodge* at sea.

December 9

POLITICS: In light of recent military disasters at Bull Run and Ball's Bluff, Congress votes 33-3 to establish an oversight committee to monitor the conduct of the war. This becomes known infamously as the Joint Committee on the Conduct of the War and is the bane of many senior Union officers.

SOUTHWEST: Pro-Confederate Cherokee, Chicaksaw, and Choctaw, assisted by the 9th Texas under Colonel Douglas H. Cooper, attack pro-Union Creek under Opotheyahola at Bird Creek (Chusto-Talasah), Indian Territory. With his Texans in the center, Cherokees on the left, and Choctaws and Chickasaws on the right, Cooper advances on the Creeks in unison. Resistance proves fierce initially, but finally both of Opothleyahola's flanks retreat, and he falls back with the center. Cooper's losses amount to 15 killed and 37 wounded, while Creek casualties, never tallied, are probably heavier. However, supply shortages dog the Confederate column, and they fail to pursue the fleeing Creek, who eventually make it to Kansas.

NAVAL: The USS *Harriet Lane,* supported by the Potomac Flotilla, engages Confederate artillery at Freestone Point, Virginia.

The USS *New London* seizes the Confederate schooner *Delight* and sloops *Express* and *Osceola* off Cat Island Passage, Mississippi.

December 10

POLITICS: The Confederate Congress admits the expatriate Kentucky "government" into the Confederacy as its 13th state. It thus joins Missouri as having representatives in both belligerent camps.

NAVAL: A landing party under Lieutenant James W. A. Nicholson of the USS *Isaac Smith* captures an abandoned Confederate fort on Otter Island in the Ashepoo River, South Carolina. It subsequently is turned over to Federal forces.

December 11

SOUTH: The city of Charleston, South Carolina, is ravaged by a destructive fire that consumes half of the city.

NAVAL: The USS *South Carolina* captures the Confederate sloop *Florida* as it attempts to run the blockade off Savannah, Georgia.

The USS *Bienville* captures the Confederate schooner *Sarah and Caroline* off St. John's River, Florida.

December 12

NAVAL: Gunfire from the USS *Isaac Smith* covers a landing by U.S. Marines as they destroy a Confederate base in the Ashepoo River, South Carolina. In this manner, Union forces are slowly expanding their base of operations out from Port Royal Sound.

The USS *Alabama* captures the British ship *Admiral* as it attempts to run the blockade off Savannah, Georgia.

December 13

WEST: Newly appointed Union general Robert H. Milroy decides to attack Confederate positions atop nearby Allegheny Mountain in western Virginia. He marches 830 men from Cheat Mountain directly to his objective, then garrisoned by 1,200 Confederates under General Edward Johnson, while another column under Colonel Gideon C. Moody with 930 men takes a circuitous route 12 miles around the enemy's left flank. However, when Moody is delayed several hours by poor terrain, Milroy attacks alone. Charging up the heavily wooded slopes, he is handily repulsed, at which point Johnson charges downhill and completely disperses his antagonists. By the time Moody's column arrives on the scene, the Southerners are ready for him, and both sides engage in a five-hour firefight across the mountain slope. At length, Moody withdraws back toward Cheat Mountain. Union losses are 20 dead, 107 wounded, and 10 missing while the Confederates record 20 killed, 98 wounded, and 28 missing.

December 14

SOUTHWEST: General Henry H. Sibley assumes control of Confederate forces along the Upper Rio Grande River and the New Mexico and Arizona Territories.

December 15

NAVAL: The USS *Stars and Stripes* captures the Confederate blockade-runner *Charity* off Cape Hatteras, North Carolina, while the USS *Jamestown* seizes the sloop *Havelock* at nearby Cape Fear.

December 16

POLITICS: Congressman Clement Vallandigham of Ohio, soon vilified as a "Copperhead," introduces a resolution commending Captain Charles Wilkes for his role in the *Trent* affair.

December 17

DIPLOMACY: Armed forces of Britain, Spain, and France attack and occupy Veracruz, Mexico, ostensibly seeking reparations for foreign debts. However, once Napoleon III begins to maneuver to seize political control of that nation, the other two belligerents withdraw their troops. The French regime seeks to take advantage of America's preoccupation with domestic strife for its own gain.

SOUTH: Confederate troops skirmish and then evacuate Rockville, South Carolina, in the face of advancing Union forces from nearby Hilton Head.

WEST: General Thomas J. Jackson commences operations against Dam No. 5 on the Potomac River, western Virginia.

Union and Confederate forces under Generals Alexander M. McCook and Thomas C. Hindman, respectively, fight a heavy skirmish at Rowlett's Station, Green River, Kentucky, which results in 17 Northern casualties to 33 killed and 55 wounded Southerners.

NAVAL: The U.S. Navy scuttles a "stone fleet" of seven old vessels at the entrance of Savannah Harbor, Georgia. This is comprised of wooden sailing vessels, heavily laden with stones to impede navigation.

Commodore Henry H. Foote institutes regular Sunday services onboard his fleet of gunboats on the Cumberland River.

December 18

WEST: General John Pope reconnoiters Confederate positions along Blackwater Creek, Missouri, prompting General Sterling Price to withdraw.

December 19

DIPLOMACY: Lord Lyons, British minister to the United States, informally alerts Secretary of State William H. Seward of his instructions, namely, his government's insistence that the Americans must unconditionally release the Southern commissioners James M. Mason and John Slidell, who had been illegally removed from the British vessel *Trent*. Seward asks Lyons to make a formal presentation of his government's demands on December 23.

SOUTH: General George A. McCall orders General Edward O. C. Ord to take his 3rd Brigade of Pennsylvania Reserves, march up the Leesburg Pike from Camp Pierpont, and forage in the vicinity of Dranesville, Virginia. Ord takes with him the 6th, 9th, 10th, and 12th Pennsylvania Reserves, and a squadron of the 1st Pennsylvania Cavalry, and he is further buttressed by the attached 13th Pennsylvania "Bucktails."

NAVAL: Confederates destroy the lighthouse on Morris Island, Charleston Harbor, to deny its use to the enemy.

December 20

POLITICS: The influential Joint Committee on the Conduct of the War is instituted formally in the U.S. Congress following a disastrous defeat at Ball's Bluff during the previous October. It is staffed largely by such Radical Republicans as Benjamin F. Wade of Ohio and Zachariah Chandler of Michigan and is tasked with closely scrutinizing the conduct of president and senior commanders throughout the war.

SOUTH: To obviate mounting shortages of animal fodder and food supplies, Generals Joseph E. Johnston and George B. McClellan dispatch competing foraging expeditions in the vicinity of Dranesville, Virginia. The Union effort, led by General Edward O. C. Ord, consists of five infantry regiments, an artillery battery, and a cavalry squadron. The 1,800 Confederates are led by General J. E. B. Stuart with an almost identical force, though hobbled by a very large wagon train. The Northern troops occupy Dranesville first where Colonel Thomas Kane observes Stuart's approach and warns Ord, who rushes up the balance of his force. Stuart remains oblivious to danger until his 1st Kentucky and 6th South Carolina, who had previously fired on each other by mistake, suddenly encounter the 9th Pennsylvania in an adjoining woods. Stuart nonetheless marches up and deploys his remaining troops with alacrity, pushing the Federals back under the cover of their artillery. But Kane's troops subsequently rally around a two-story brick house, which the Confederates attack and are repulsed. The 11th Virginia then swings forward to outflank the Northerners when it is suddenly assailed in the flank by concealed companies of the 10th Pennsylvania and also is driven back. Stuart then calls off the battle and withdraws back to Centreville, having sustained 43 killed, 143 wounded, and eight missing (194) to a Union tally of seven killed and 61 wounded. All told, it is an inauspicious debut for the South's most celebrated cavalryman.

NAVAL: To further deter Confederate blockade-runners, Captain Charles H. Davis scuttles 16 old whaling vessels, heavily laden with heavy rocks, in the main channel of Charleston Harbor, South Carolina.

December 21

POLITICS: The U.S. Congress institutes the Navy Medal of Honor as the nation's highest military award granted to that service. Curiously, it is intended for enlisted ranks, and commissioned officers are not eligible until 1915.

December 22

WEST: General Henry W. Halleck reiterates, in no uncertain terms, that any individuals found sabotaging Union railroads or telegraph lines are to be shot immediately.

December 23

DIPLOMACY: British minister to the United States Lord Lyons formally submits a note to Secretary of State William H. Seward in which his government demands the release of Confederate agents James M. Mason and John Slidell. The American government has one week to respond satisfactorily, after which time Britain will withdraw its ambassador.

WEST: To break up a concentration of Confederate troops and recruits in southeastern Kentucky, Colonel James A. Garfield is dispatched toward Prestonburg with 1,100 infantry and 450 cavalry with orders to drive the enemy back to Virginia.

Union cavalry under General John Pope reach Lexington, Missouri.

December 24

SOUTH: In light of his poor performance, General Henry A. Wise is dismissed from the Virginia theater and reassigned to a quiet sector in North Carolina.

NAVAL: The USS *Gem of the Sea* captures and sinks the British blockade-runner *Prince of Wales* off Georgetown, South Carolina.

December 25

POLITICS: President Abraham Lincoln celebrates Christmas with his family and later that day confers with legal authorities about the disposition of imprisoned Confederate envoys.

WEST: General Ulysses S. Grant orders the expulsion of all fugitive African Americans from Fort Holt, Kentucky.

General Samuel R. Curtis assumes command of Federal forces in the Southwest District of Missouri.

Colonel George G. Todd and his 10th Missouri Infantry advance upon Danville, Missouri.

NAVAL: The USS *Fernandina* captures the Confederate schooner *William H. Northrup* off Cape Fear, North Carolina.

Confederate navy secretary Stephen R. Mallory implores General Leonidas Polk at Columbus, Kentucky, to furlough troops so that they can assist in the construction of ironclads at Memphis, Tennessee.

December 26

DIPLOMACY: An international crisis is averted when President Abraham Lincoln's cabinet concurs that the seizure of James M. Mason and John Slidell is illegal and that the two captives should be released and allowed to continue to Europe. Secretary of State William H. Seward authorizes their release from confinement at Fort Warren, Boston, blaming the entire matter on a "misunderstanding" by Captain John Wilkes.

SOUTH: Confederate Brigadier General Philip St. George Cocke commits suicide after a lengthy illness in Powhatan, Virginia.

WEST: Martial law is again declared in St. Louis, Missouri, and around its attendant railroads by General Henry W. Halleck.

NAVAL: Commodore Josiah Tattnall sorties from the Savannah River, Georgia, with the CSS *Savannah, Resolute, Sampson, Ida,* and *Barton* and temporarily forces a Union blockading squadron into deeper waters.

The USS *Rhode Island* captures the Confederate schooner *Venus* at Sabine Pass off the Louisiana coast.

December 27

POLITICS: Secretary of State William H. Seward alerts the House and Senate Foreign Relations Committees as to President Abraham Lincoln's decision to release Confederate agents James M. Mason and John Slidell from captivity at Fort Warren in Boston, Massachusetts. He also provides British ambassador Lord Lyons with a lengthy diplomatic note—not an apology—explaining the American response.

WEST: Union and Confederate forces clash at Hallsville, Missouri, and General Benjamin M. Prentiss scatters the Southern garrison lodged there.

December 28

WEST: General Lew Wallace leads Union forces on an expedition against Camp Beauregard and Viola, Kentucky.

Confederate cavalry under Colonel Nathan B. Forrest engage the Union forces of General Thomas L. Crittenden. Forrest leads a detachment of 300 Confederate cavalry toward Sacramento, Kentucky. En route, he encounters a smaller force of 168 Union men under Major Eli Murray. After skirmishing breaks out, Forrest recalls his line to reorganize, which Murray misinterprets as a retreat. The Union troopers charge headlong against twice their number and are hit on both flanks before scattering. Forrest, consistent with his nature, is in the thick of fighting and kills two Union officers. His Confederates sustain two dead, having killed 11 and taken 40 prisoner. Triumphant in this first of many scrapes, the future "Wizard of the Saddle" takes his command back to Greenville, hotly pursued by 500 Union troopers under Colonel James Jackson.

General Benjamin M. Prentiss skirmishes with Confederate forces at Mount Zion Church, Missouri.

NAVAL: The USS *New London* seizes the schooner *Gipsy* in Mississippi Sound.

December 29

WEST: Occupation of Beckley and Suttonville by Union forces in western Virginia further consolidates their grip on the region.

Confederate partisans under General Jeff Thompson unsuccessfully attack the Union steamer *City of Alton* near Commerce, Missouri.

NAVAL: The CSS *Sea Bird* dodges Union gunfire and captures an unnamed Union schooner near Hampton Roads, Virginia.

December 30

NAVAL: The USS *Santee* captures the Confederate schooner *Garonne* off Galveston, Texas.

December 31

POLITICS: Noting the inactivity of Union forces in the East, President Abraham Lincoln anxiously cables General Henry W. Halleck in St. Louis, Missouri, in hopes of hearing of offensive operations in that theater soon. "Are you and General Buell in concert?" he inquires.

NAVAL: A landing party dispatched from USS *Mount Vernon* captures and destroys a light ship off Wilmington, North Carolina, which has been outfitted as a gunboat.

An attack by army troops and sailors from gunboats USS *Ottawa, Pembina,* and *Seneca* disperses Confederate forces at Port Royal Ferry and along the Coosaw River. This preemptive strike removes the threat of Southern artillery emplacements that would isolate Union forces on Port Royal Island.

The USS *Augusta* captures the Confederate schooner *Island Belle* as it ran the blockade near Bull's Bay, South Carolina.

A large landing party from USS *Water Witch, New London,* and *Henry Lewis* attacks and captures Biloxi, Mississippi. The Confederate schooner *Captain Spedden* is also seized, and an artillery battery is demolished.

1862

January 1

DIPLOMACY: Confederate agents James M. Mason and John Slidell board the HMS *Rinaldo* off Provincetown, Massachusetts, and sail for Halifax en route to Great Britain.

NORTH: General in Chief George B. McClellan remains sidelined by illness as President Abraham Lincoln frets over his continuing military inactivity.

SOUTH: Federal troops skirmish heavily as they advance toward Port Royal Ferry on the Coosaw River, South Carolina, attempting to enlarge their bridgehead.

Union and Confederate batteries exchange fire in the vicinity of Fort Pickens and Fort Barancas, Pensacola, Florida.

WEST: General Thomas J. Jackson, eager to secure the lightly defended town of Romney in western Virginia, orders his Stonewall brigade and 8,500 troops under General William W. Loring out of their winter abodes at Winchester. However, no sooner do they leave than the temperature plunges to freezing, and soldiers, marching without heavy overcoats, suffer severely.

General George H. Thomas takes 5,000 Union soldiers on a march from Lebanon, Kentucky, toward the Tennessee state line.

Generals Henry W. Halleck at St. Louis, Missouri, and Don C. Buell at Louisville, Kentucky, are encouraged by the War Department to undertake offensive operations against Confederate forces at Columbus and Nashville.

A detachment of the 1st Kansas Cavalry burns the settlement of Dayton, Missouri.

NAVAL: The USS *Yankee* and *Anacostia* exchange fire with Confederate batteries along Cockpit Point on the Potomac River. The latter receives slight damage.

Commodore Andrew H. Foote dispatches the Federal gunboat USS *Lexington* down the Ohio River to assist the *Conestoga* in protecting Union citizens along the river banks.

January 2

NAVAL: Taking advantage of a heavy fog, the Confederate steamer *Ella Warley* evades the USS *Mohican* and slips into Charleston, South Carolina, with a valuable cargo.

January 3

POLITICS: President Jefferson Davis expresses anxiety over the recent Union seizure of Ship Island, Mississippi, and its probable future use as a base of operations against New Orleans, Louisiana.

SOUTH: Union and Confederate outposts skirmish in the vicinity of Big Bethel, Virginia.

WEST: Confederates under General Thomas J. Jackson continue slogging through freezing, damp weather from Winchester, Virginia, and up the Shenandoah Valley to destroy the Baltimore and Ohio Railroad and dams on the Chesapeake and Ohio Canal.

General George B. Crittenden arrives at Mills Springs, Kentucky, to take command of Confederate forces mistakenly deployed north of the Cumberland River by General Felix K. Zollicoffer.

January 4

WEST: The town of Bath, western Virginia, falls to Confederate forces under General Thomas J. Jackson.

January 5

NORTH: Confederate artillery under General Thomas J. Jackson briefly bombard Union positions in and around Hancock, Maryland. Jackson then retires to Unger's Store to rest his shivering troops.

January 6

POLITICAL: President Abraham Lincoln ignores cries by Radical Republican senators to replace General George B. McClellan, then ill from typhoid fever, over allegations of military inactivity. He also continues urging General Don C. Buell, commanding the Army of the Ohio in Kentucky, to assume an offensive posture.

SOUTH: Henry Heth is appointed brigadier general, C.S.A.

NAVAL: In response to critical shortages of trained manpower, Commodore Andrew H. Foote suggests drafting soldiers to serve on the gunboat fleet. The army proves reluctant to do so, and General Ulysses S. Grant recommends that the guardhouses be emptied to assist the navy.

January 7

NORTH: General Ambrose E. Burnside is appointed commander of the future Department of North Carolina.

WEST: Confederate troops begin to shift from Hancock, Maryland, toward Romney, western Virginia. En route, a Union detachment at Blue's Gap scatters its Confederate opposites and captures two cannon. General Thomas J. Jackson nonetheless determines to capture Romney, possession of which grants him control of the South Branch Valley, Potomac River.

NAVAL: The Federal gunboat USS *Conestoga*, recently returned from a reconnaissance of Confederate positions at Fort Donelson, Tennessee, alerts Commodore Andrew H. Foote as to the intrinsic strength of that position and the danger it poses to a naval assault.

January 8

POLITICS: President Jefferson Davis contacts fugitive Missouri governor Claiborne F. Jackson and assures him that his state is not being neglected by the Confederate government. He also presses the governor to raise additional manpower to offset Union advantages.

January 9

POLITICS: President Abraham Lincoln expresses dismay that Generals Henry W. Halleck and Don C. Buell still fail to initiate offensive measures anywhere in the West.

NAVAL: Commodore David G. Farragut of the USS *Hartford* is appointed commander of the Western Gulf Blockading Squadron. In this capacity, he is responsible for orchestrating the capture of New Orleans, Louisiana, an essential facet of Union strategy. Farragut, cognizant of the need to maintain utmost secrecy, instructs his wife to burn any correspondence he exchanges with her.

January 10

POLITICS: President Abraham Lincoln displays concern to Secretary of War Simon Cameron over the apparent lack of military activity in the West.

Confederate-leaning Missourians Waldo P. Johnson and Trusten Polk are expelled from the U.S. Senate.

WEST: Believing themselves heavily outnumbered, Union forces abandon strategic Romney, western Virginia, to advancing Confederates under General Thomas J. Jackson. That esteemed leader also engages in a bitter contretemps with General William W. Loring about charges that he abused his soldiers by marching them during bitterly cold weather.

General James A. Garfield wages an indecisive pitched battle against Confederates under General Humphrey Marshall at Middle Fork near Prestonburg, Kentucky. Marshall gathers 2,200 men slightly west of the town, largely underequipped and in varied states of training and health. Garfield advances against them with 1,100 infantry and 450 cavalry, although his march from Louisa encounters rough, swampy terrain. The battle begins as Union troops attempt to force the Southerners from two hills while Marshall simultaneously tries to turn the Northern left flank. A confused stalemate ensues until Garfield receives 700 reinforcements in the late afternoon. Humphrey, unable to counter Union numbers, withdraws, conceding the field of battle to Garfield. Losses in this minor affair are 10 Confederates killed, 15 wounded, and 25 captured to a Union tally of one killed and 20 injured. Garfield nonetheless is congratulated by General Don C. Buell and is promoted to brigadier general.

Generals Ulysses S. Grant and John A. McClernand ready their forces at Cairo, Illinois, for a concerted campaign to evict Confederates from their stronghold at Columbus, Kentucky.

The Trans-Mississippi District of Confederate Department No. 2 is organized with General Earl Van Dorn as commander.

NAVAL: In light of the advanced state of the Confederate ironclad CSS *Virginia*, officers at the Navy Department ponder probable defensive measures against it. Commodore Louis M. Goldsborough orders the steam tugs USS *Dragon* and *Zouave* off Hampton Roads, Virginia, to tow the sail frigates *Congress* and *Cumberland* to any position deemed advantageous.

Commodore Andrew H. Foote's gunboats begin to ferry Union troops up and down the Tennessee and Mississippi rivers to mask General Ulysses S. Grant's forthcoming advance on Fort Henry, Tennessee.

January 11

POLITICS: Secretary of War Simon Cameron resigns from office amidst charges of corruption and mismanagement. President Lincoln subsequently nominates former attorney general Edwin M. Stanton, a confidant of General George B. McClellan, as his successor. The appointment proves fortuitous, for Stanton infuses military administration with new energy and efficiency.

SOUTH: The Department of Key West, Florida, is organized with General John M. Brannan as commander.

NAVAL: Commodore Louis M. Goldsborough assembles a squadron consisting of the USS *Henry Brinker, Delaware, Philadelphia, Hunchback, Morse, Southfield, Commodore Barney,* and *Commodore Perry* and the schooner *Howard* off Hampton Roads, Virginia. His immediate objective is the capture of Roanoke Island, North Carolina.

Commander David D. Porter of the gunboat USS *Essex,* along with the *St. Louis,* engage Confederate vessels and positions along the Mississippi River near Lucas Bend, Missouri. The Southerners subsequently withdraw under the cover of their batteries at Columbus, Kentucky.

January 12

WEST: The 37th Ohio conducts antiguerrilla sweeps around Logan County Court House and in the Guyandotte Valley, western Virginia.

NAVAL: A naval expedition of 100 vessels under Commodore Louis M. Goldsborough departs Hampton Roads, Virginia, in preparation for an attack on strategic Roanoke Island, North Carolina. He is accompanied by 15,000 Federal troops under General Ambrose E. Burnside.

The USS *Pensacola* successfully runs past Confederate batteries on the Potomac River at Cockpit and Shipping Points, Virginia.

January 13

POLITICS: President Abraham Lincoln again urges generals Henry W. Halleck and Don C. Buell of the necessity to commence offensive operations in the West. He finds their passivity disconcerting.

NORTH: General George B. McClellan refuses to consult with either the president or other officials as to his impending plan of operations. Moreover, he disagrees with Lincoln's overall strategy of attacking along a broad front.

NAVAL: Lieutenant John L. Worden, still convalescing from months of captivity, is appointed to take command of the revolutionary USS *Monitor,* then under construction on Long Island, New York.

Commodore Louis M. Goldsborough and his 100-ship expedition arrive off Hatteras Inlet, North Carolina. Once on station, he reiterates orders that gunners must be trained completely and familiar with the new Bormann fuzes fitted to 9-inch shrapnel shells.

January 14

WEST: Confederates under General Thomas J. Jackson occupy the strategic hamlet of Romney, western Virginia, amid mounting friction with his unruly subordinate, General William W. Loring.

NAVAL: Three Federal gunboats on the Mississippi River begin to probe the Confederate defenses of Columbus, Kentucky, with a brief bombardment.

January 15

POLITICS: Ohioan Edwin M. Stanton is confirmed by the U.S. Senate as the new secretary of war to replace outgoing Simon Cameron of Pennsylvania.

SOUTH: Confederate general Lovell Mansfield confiscates 14 civilian steamers at New Orleans, Louisiana, and impresses them to bolster that city's defenses.

NAVAL: Commodore Andrew H. Foote advises subordinates against wasting scarce ammunition for his scarcely trained gunboat squadron, urging all hands to make every shot count.

January 16

WEST: General Felix K. Zollicoffer disregards orders from General George B. Crittenden by maintaining Confederate troops north of the Cumberland River, Kentucky, where they must fight with the river to their backs. Shortly after, Crittenden arrives with reinforcements, and he decides that the water is running too high to recross safely. He then makes the most of his subordinate's rashness by planning to engage an oncoming Union column at Logan's Cross Roads, nine miles distant.

NAVAL: Accurate gunfire from the USS *Hatteras,* followed up by boat crews and marines, destroys seven vessels, a railroad depot, and a telegraph office at Cedar Keys, Florida.

The USS *Albatross* captures and sinks the British blockade-runner *York* off Bogue Inlet, North Carolina.

The Union enhances it grip on western waters after the Ead gunboats *Carondelet, St. Louis,* and *Cincinnati* are commissioned. This brings the total of armored river gunboats to seven, and they prove indispensable in asserting Union control of strategic waterways.

January 17

WEST: General George H. Thomas arrives from Somerset, Kentucky, and takes charge of 4,000 Union troops in the vicinity of Logan's Crossroads. The nearest Confederate forces are only 10 miles distant at Mills Springs on the Cumberland River, so he anticipates an attack.

General Charles F. Smith boards a gunboat and begins to probe in the direction of Confederate-held Fort Henry on the Tennessee River.

NAVAL: The USS *Connecticut* seizes the British blockade-runner *Emma* off the Florida coast.

Federal gunboats USS *Conestoga* and *Lexington* conduct a preliminary reconnaissance of the Tennessee River past Confederate-held Fort Henry. The detailed knowledge they acquire helps formulate plans for its swift capture.

January 18

POLITICS: Former president John Tyler dies in Richmond, Virginia, at the age of 62.

WEST: 4,000 Union troops under General George H. Thomas, having enticed Confederate troops north of the Cumberland River to attack, encamp at Mill Springs, Kentucky. Strong reconnaissance parties sent toward the river return with positive information that General George B. Crittenden's Confederates are advancing and that they intend to strike the Union camp at dawn. With trademark thoroughness, Thomas methodically and unhurriedly prepares to receive the enemy while ordering two nearby brigades in support.

NAVAL: The USS *Kearsarge* sails to Cádiz, Spain, in order to halt the depredations of the CSS *Sumter*.

The CSS *Sumter* under Captain Raphael Semmes seizes and burns the Union barks *Neapolitan* and *Investigator* in the Strait of Gibraltar.

Union vessels USS *Midnight* and *Rachel Seaman* bombard Confederate positions at Velasco, Texas.

January 19

WEST: At daybreak, a force of 4,000 Confederates under Generals Felix K. Zollicoffer and William H. Carroll marches 10 miles to attack the Union encampment at Logan's Cross Roads, Kentucky. Despite heavy rain and mud, the Southerners slam into Northern pickets at daybreak, driving them back to the main defense line, commanded by General Mahlon D. Manson. General George H. Thomas then rallies his men and withstands several assaults until the 10th Indiana, tired and out of ammunition, bolts for the rear. Thomas counters by feeding the 4th Kentucky under Colonel Speed S. Fry into line, which drives the Confederates back into a ravine. The two forces then trade shots for several tense minutes as they sort themselves out. The Confederates emerge and charge one more time while Thomas, expecting this move, stations the newly arrived brigade of General Samuel P. Carter obliquely, whose troops rake the Southerners with a deadly enfilade fire. At this confused juncture, Zollicoffer mistakenly gallops into Fry's position in the fog and is shot dead in the saddle. The Confederates waver until Crittenden arrives in person to lead another brigade forward. This charge is also fought to a standstill and, judging the moment right, Thomas orders the 12th Kentucky and 9th Ohio to turn both Confederate flanks. Crittenden's men break under this latest onslaught and flee back to their Beech Grove encampment.

The ensuing Union pursuit proves somewhat slow owing to the poor state of the roads, so Thomas only arrives outside Crittenden's camp at Mills Springs that evening. He determines to attack in force on the morrow, but Crittenden evacuates his Confederates by boat across the swollen Cumberland River and withdraws rapidly back to Nashville. Thomas subsequently captures their supply train, 12 cannon, and 1,000 horses. Confederate losses are 125 killed, 309 wounded, and 99 missing to 40 Union dead, 207 wounded, and 15 missing. Mills Springs is the first in a series of disasters, which negates the Southern defensive line in Kentucky. More significantly, the victory revives Union sentiments throughout the region and delivers to Union forces control of the Cumberland Gap—an important invasion route into eastern Tennessee.

NAVAL: The USS *Itasca* captures the Confederate schooner *Lizzie Weston* off the Florida coast.

January 20

NAVAL: At the behest of Secretary of the Navy Gideon Welles, the Union Gulf Blockading Squadron is reorganized into two distinct formations: The Eastern Gulf

Blockading Squadron and the Western Blockading Squadron, with the latter commanded by Commodore David G. Farragut. His fleet consists of 17 steam warships
and 19 mortar boats under his foster brother, Commander David D. Porter. At this
time Farragut announces word of his impending campaign against New Orleans,
Louisiana, to the crews.

Union boarding parties from the USS *R. R. Cuyler*, in concert with the *Huntsville*
and *Potomac*, capture the Confederate schooner *J. W. Wilder* off Mobile, Alabama.

January 21

WEST: Union forces under General John A. McClernand advance on the Confederate stronghold at Columbus, Kentucky, but they do not engage.

NAVAL: The USS *Ethan Allen* captures the Confederate schooner *Olive Branch* off
Cedar Keys along the Florida coast.

January 22

SOUTH: General Henry A. Wise becomes commander of Confederate forces in the
vicinity of Hatteras Inlet, North Carolina, then under an impending Union assault
from the sea.

NAVAL: The Federal gunboat USS *Lexington* trades fire with Confederate batteries
at Fort Henry on the Tennessee River. General Charles F. Smith is onboard as an
observer.

January 23

WEST: General Thomas J. Jackson leads his Stonewall Brigade out from Romney,
western Virginia, and back down to Winchester. The town, however, remains garrisoned by troops under the uncooperative general William W. Loring. Worse,
Loring feels that Jackson deliberately has left his troops in an exposed position
only 20 miles from Union lines, so he and other officers violate the chain of command by petitioning friends in the Confederate Congress for redress and a change
in orders.

At St. Louis, Missouri, General Henry W. Halleck strengthens existing martial
law provisions, making it illegal for individuals to conduct subversive activities. This
includes the failure of pro-Southern inhabitants to pay assessments to support pro-
Union fugitives; their property is now subject to seizure.

NAVAL: Commodore Louis M. Goldsborough reports slow but steady progress
working his warships and heavily laden transports over the bar at Pamlico Sound,
North Carolina.

The Federal schooner USS *Samuel Rotan* seizes the Confederate steamer *Calhoun* in East Bay, Mississippi River.

Commodore Andrew H. Foote, citing chronic manpower shortages, pleads with
Secretary of the Navy Gideon Welles to broach the subject with the War Department
and arrange a draft of army troops to fill out his gunboat squadron.

January 24

WEST: The small Confederate command of General Humphrey Marshall is ordered
withdrawn from Martindale, Kentucky, and back into Virginia via Pound Gap.

NAVAL: The USS *Mercedita* forces the Confederate schooner *Julia* aground at the mouth of the Mississippi River.

January 25
NAVAL: The USS *Arthur* captures the Confederate schooner *J. J. McNeil* off Pass Cavallo, Texas.

January 26
SOUTH: General Pierre G. T. Beauregard transfers from the Eastern Theater to the West and becomes subordinate to General Albert S. Johnston. Command in Virginia remains with General Joseph E. Johnston, still smarting from his contretemps with President Jefferson Davis.

NAVAL: A second stone fleet is sunk to obstruct Maffitt's Channel, Charleston Harbor.

Captain Charles H. Davis leads USS *Ottawa* and *Seneca* on a reconnaissance of Wassaw Sound, Georgia, in the vicinity of strategic Fort Pulaski. He is accompanied by 2,400 men under General Horatio G. Wright.

January 27
DIPLOMACY: Emperor Napoleon III declares that the American conflict infringes on trade relations with France, but he will observe a policy of strict neutrality.

POLITICS: President Abraham Lincoln, exasperated by a lack of initiative by Union commanders, composes General War Order No. 1. This mandates a general offensive against the Confederacy from various points along the line. February 22—George Washington's birthday—is selected as the deadline to commence combined operations by both army and navy forces.

January 28
WEST: Colonel John H. Morgan leads Confederate cavalry in an action against Union forces near Greensburg and Lebanon, Kentucky.

NAVAL: Off Hatteras Inlet, North Carolina, Commodore Louis M. Goldsborough informs the secretary of the navy that getting army transports over the bar has delayed operations, but he puts the time to good use by aggressively reconnoitering Confederate positions on Roanoke Island.

The USS *De Soto* captures the Confederate blockade-runner *Major Barbour* off Isle Derniere, Louisiana.

Commodore Andrew H. Foote advises senior general Henry W. Halleck to commence operations against Forts Henry and Donelson before the water levels on the Tennessee and Cumberland rivers begin to recede.

January 29
WEST: Union forces began an intensive manhunt around Blue Springs, Missouri, looking for noted guerrilla William C. Quantrill.

NAVAL: The USS storeship *Supply* seizes the Confederate schooner *Stephen Hart* off Sarasota, Florida.

January 30
DIPLOMACY: Recently released Confederate envoys James M. Mason and John Slidell arrive at Southampton, England, and are cordially received.

WEST: General Henry W. Halleck, at St. Louis, Missouri, finally authorizes combined operations against Confederate positions at Forts Henry and Donelson, Tennessee. Because recent rains have reduced existing roads to quagmires, he orders all troop movements conducted by gunboat. General Ulysses S. Grant wastes no time putting his command in motion.

NAVAL: John Ericsson's revolutionary ironclad USS *Monitor,* derided by onlookers as "a cheesebox on a raft," is launched at Greenpoint, Long Island, amid thunderous applause. Trial and acceptance runs begin immediately.

The USS *Kingfisher* captures the Confederate blockade-runner *Teresita* in the Gulf of Mexico.

The Federal gunboat USS *Conestoga* conducts a final reconnaissance of the Tennessee River in preparation for movement against Confederate-held Fort Henry.

January 31

DIPLOMACY: Queen Victoria of Great Britain further dashes Southern hopes by reiterating her government's stance of observing strict neutrality in matters of war. Nonetheless, the British advise Confederate agents of European displeasure over having Southern ports blocked by obstacles.

POLITICS: President Abraham Lincoln issues Special War Order No. 1, which mandates an advance on Manassas Junction, Virginia, by the Army of the Potomac no later than February 22, 1862. General George B. McClellan, however, simply ignores the directive and continues honing his recruits to a fine edge.

Congress passes the Railways and Telegraph Act, empowering the president to commandeer any rail facility deemed essential for the conduct of the war effort.

Radical Republicans demand that General George B. McClellan attack Southern positions immediately, along with actively freeing slaves and enlisting them in the military. The general, however, steadfastly declines to turn a war to save the Union into a social crusade to free African Americans held in bondage.

WEST: Confederate secretary of war Judah P. Benjamin, at the behest of friends in the Confederate Congress, orders General Thomas J. Jackson to relocate Confederate troops from the town of Romney, western Virginia, and back to Winchester. An angry Jackson, aware that General William W. Loring has violated the chain of command behind his back, complies with the order—then resigns from the army. Fortunately for the Confederacy, President Jefferson Davis refuses to accept, and, assisted by Virginia governor John Lechter, he persuades Jackson to remain with the army.

February 1

SOUTHWEST: Confederate forces under General Henry H. Sibley advance from El Paso, Texas, into the New Mexico Territory, intent on conquering the entire region for the South.

NAVAL: The USS *Portsmouth* captures the Confederate steamer *Labuan* near the mouth of the Rio Grande.

The USS *Montgomery* seizes the Confederate schooner *Isabel* in the Gulf of Mexico.

February 2

WEST: General Ulysses S. Grant departs Cairo, Illinois, on his campaign against the Confederate-held Fort Henry on the Tennessee River. He embarks 17,000 troops, transporting them on Commodore Andrew H. Foote's gunboats. Grant intends to land on Panther Creek west of the fort, march inland, and quickly seal off the garrison's avenue of escape.

NAVAL: The USS *Hartford,* flagship of Commodore David G. Farragut, departs Hampton Roads, Virginia, en route to Ship Island, Mississippi, there to take charge of the Western Gulf Blockading Squadron prior to an amphibious descent on New Orleans, Louisiana.

Commodore Andrew H. Foote orders Lieutenant Seth L. Phelps to take the timberclad gunboats USS *Conestoga, Lexington,* and *Tyler* on an independent foray down the Tennessee River and destroy the railroad bridge at Danville, Tennessee. Phelps is then at liberty to venture downstream as far as the water depth allows him.

February 3

POLITICS: President Abraham Lincoln and General George B. McClellan continue at loggerheads over an exact timetable for resuming offensive operations in Virginia. They also differ on strategy, the president leaning toward a direct, overland campaign and the general wishing to sidestep Confederate defenses by landing on the enemy coast.

WEST: General Ulysses S. Grant continues his Fort Henry offensive by dispatching Federal gunboats up the Tennessee River while army transports continue departing from Cairo, Illinois.

NAVAL: The Federal government resolves to treat Confederate privateersmen as prisoners of war rather than to prosecute them as pirates. This eliminates any chance that Union naval personnel might be hanged in retaliation.

The CSS *Nashville* weighs anchor at Southampton, England, and sails off while the USS *Tuscarora* is detained in port for 24 hours, pursuant to international law. As a precaution, the British government assigns HMS *Shannon* to observe the Union gunboat closely until the deadline passes.

Commodore Andrew H. Foote diverts Federal gunboats USS *Essex* and *St. Louis* from Paducah, Kentucky, to assist troop landings 65 miles downstream at Pine Bluff. He then leads a riverine spearhead of four gunboats and several rams on an action that precipitates the Confederacy's ultimate downfall.

February 4

POLITICS: Members of the Confederate Congress at Richmond, Virginia, debate virtues and vices of utilizing free African Americans for service in the Confederate army. Such a commonsense remedy to address endemic manpower shortages is never seriously entertained, however.

WEST: General Lloyd Tilghman, commanding at Fort Henry, Tennessee, learns of the large Union expedition that is bearing down on him and telegraphs General Leonidas Polk for immediate reinforcements.

NAVAL: The gunboat squadron of Commodore Andrew H. Foote, consisting of the USS *Essex, Carondelet, St. Louis, Cincinnati, Conestoga, Tyler,* and *Lexington,* assume bombardment positions on the Tennessee River and begin to sound out the defenses of Confederate-held Fort Henry. One Southerner is killed and three wounded during this preliminary exchange. Several moored mines, or torpedoes, have also been worked free by the fast currents and are examined closely by naval personnel.

February 5

DIPLOMACY: The British government lifts all restrictions against transporting guns, ammunition, and other military stores to Confederate ports.

NORTH: The poem "Battle Hymn of the Republic" by Julia Ward Howe appears in an issue of *Atlantic Monthly.* It is musically arranged to the popular tune "John Brown's Body."

WEST: General Charles F. Smith lands Union troops and seizes the unfinished works of Fort Heiman on the Tennessee River, directly opposite Fort Henry, Tennessee. General Lloyd Tilghman considers his position hopeless and prepares to evacuate the bulk of his garrison to Fort Donelson.

NAVAL: The USS *Keystone State* apprehends the British blockade-runner *Mars* off Fernandina, Florida.

February 6

WEST: General Ulysses S. Grant commences his strategic flanking movement with a concerted drive against Confederate-held Fort Henry on the Tennessee River. This is a wretchedly situated, low-lying earthwork near the riverbank, susceptible to flooding when the Tennessee runs high. Grant disembarks 17,000 troops under Generals John A. McClernand and Charles F. Smith two miles below the fort, but they bog down in swampy terrain and advance slowly. Meanwhile, Confederate general Lloyd Tilghman hurriedly evacuates his 3,400-man garrison to Fort Donelson, 10 miles distant on the Cumberland River before all escape is cut off. Little combat ensues, but a Union cavalry detachment pursues the fleeing Confederates, seizing six cannon and 38 stragglers.

NAVAL: The USS *Sciota* captures the Confederate sloop *Margaret* off Isle au Breton, Louisiana.

The powerful ironclad CSS *Louisiana* is launched at Jefferson City, Louisiana.

Commodore Andrew H. Foote leads a flotilla of four ironclads and three wooden gunboats against Confederate Fort Henry on the Tennessee River, and they open fire at a range of 1,700 yards. General Lloyd Tilghman remains behind with 100 artillerists and 17 cannon to mount an "honorable" defense while his garrison escapes overland. Foote, closing to 600 yards, maintains a tremendous cannonade that disables Tilghman's artillery pieces in a two-hour action. Southerner gunners nonetheless fight well against great odds, striking their antagonists 59 times and scoring a direct hit on the USS *Essex,* which bursts its boilers and scalds several sailors. Several naval officers then row through the sallyport and onto the flooded parade ground to accept Tilgham's surrender at 2:00 P.M. Thus the first Union riverine offensive succeeds almost effortlessly. Union losses are 11 killed, 31 injured, and five missing to

Flag Officer Andrew H. Foote's gunboats attacking Fort Henry, February 6, 1862 *(Library of Congress)*

five Confederates dead, six wounded, five missing, and 70 captured. To underscore his strategic mobility, Foote hurriedly deploys several gunboats downstream, which destroy railroad bridges over the Tennessee River as far south as Muscle Shoals, Alabama. More important, a major invasion route into the center of the South has been pried open. Grant now begins to formulate an attack on Fort Donelson, 10 miles away along the Cumberland River.

NAVAL: The fall of Fort Donelson signals Lieutenant Seth L. Phelps to begin his sojourn down the Tennessee River with the gunboats USS *Conestoga, Lexington,* and *Tyler.* It is a clear demonstration of the Union's ability to project military strength down the western waterways.

February 7

WEST: Federal troops reoccupy Romney, western Virginia, as Confederates under General William W. Loring are withdrawn back to Winchester.

General Ulysses S. Grant, having secured Fort Henry, maps out his strategy for attacking Fort Donelson, Tennessee, on the Cumberland River. Unlike Fort Henry, this is a spacious, well-sited position encompassing 100 acres within its outworks, being both amply garrisoned and well armed with heavy cannon. On a lesser note, General John A. McClernand informs Commodore Andrew H. Foote of his decision to rename Fort Henry Fort Foote in his honor.

At Bowling Green, Kentucky, Confederate general Albert S. Johnston confers with William J. Hardee and Pierre G. T. Beauregard as to his rapidly deteriorating position. Reacting to Fort Henry's fall, he orders troops under General Gideon Pillow at Clarksville, Tennessee, and those of General John B. Floyd at Bowling Green, Kentucky, to march rapidly to the defense of Fort Donelson. Their mission is to stave off Union forces long enough to allow the main portion of the army to withdraw safely to Nashville. Entrusting the inexperienced Floyd and Pillow to undertake such a vital mission bears serious consequences for the Confederacy.

NAVAL: A large naval expedition under Commodore Louis M. Goldsborough leaves its anchorage at Hatteras Inlet, North Carolina, steams into Croatan Sound, and attacks Roanoke Island. The flotilla encounters little resistance and brushes aside Captain William F. Lynch's seven-gunboat flotilla with accurate naval gunfire. The defenders gradually flee upstream, burning the CSS *Curlew* to prevent its capture. Then 10,000 troops under General Ambrose E. Burnside splash ashore at Ashby Point and encamp for the evening. General Henry M. Wise, the regional commander, is absent due to illness, so Confederate leadership devolves upon Colonel Henry M. Shaw. Shaw possesses only 2,500 men and a few ill-served cannon. Inexplicably, strategic Roanoke remains undermanned and poorly situated to receive an attack long anticipated.

The USS *Bohio* captures the Confederate schooner *Eugenie* in the Gulf of Mexico.

The Federal gunboat USS *Conestoga* under Lieutenant S. L. Phelps surprises Confederate shipping on the Tennessee River, forcing the Confederates to burn the steamers *Samuel Orr, Appleton Belle,* and *Lynn Boyd.* While stopping at Perry's Landing the crewmen are surprised but pleased to be lauded and assisted by local pro-Unionists.

February 8

POLITICS: The administration of President Jefferson Davis in Richmond, Virginia, reels from the news of the loss of Fort Henry and Roanoke Island, and a sense of mounting gloom pervades the Confederacy.

SOUTH: The three brigades of Generals Jesse Reno, John G. Parke, and John G. Foster, totaling 10,000 men, advance on Confederate defensive works on the northern end of Roanoke Island, North Carolina. This consists of three small forts and three cannon, manned by 2,500 troops under Colonel Henry M. Shaw. As one Union brigade engages the Southerners frontally, General Ambrose E. Burnside directs the other two into adjoining swamps on a three-hour flanking march. The 9th New York Zouaves then charges the main Confederate work as the rest of the force simultaneously turns both flanks. Southern defenses crumble under the onslaught and surrender. Union casualties total 37 killed, 214 wounded, and 13 missing to a Confederate tally of 23 killed, and 2,500 captured. This constitutes the first major Union land victory, and it greatly boosts Northern morale. Moreover, possession of Roanoke Island grants Burnside a platform on Albemarle Sound from which he can suppress blockade-runners and launch expeditions toward the interior. Its fall also compromises communications with Norfolk, Virginia, and proves a major factor in its abandonment.

In light of the Roanoke disaster, the Confederate Congress tasks an investigative committee to explore General Henry A. Wise's behavior and allegations of incompetence against General Benjamin Huger, overall theater commander, and Secretary of War Judah P. Benjamin.

WEST: The recent fall of Fort Henry, Tennessee, prompts General Albert S. Johnston to order Confederate forces under General William J. Hardee to abandon the south bank of the Cumberland River for Nashville.

NAVAL: Federal gunboats depart Roanoke Island, North Carolina, and begin to sail up the Pasquotank River toward Elizabeth City.

The Federal gunboat USS *Conestoga* attacks and captures the Confederate steamers *Sallie Wood* and CSS *Muscle* on the Mississippi River near Chickasaw, Alabama. Three other vessels are likewise destroyed to prevent capture, bringing recent naval losses for the Confederacy to nine. Dropping anchor at Florence, Alabama, Lieutenant Seth L. Phelps respects the wishes of local citizens not to destroy their railroad bridge, and instead his bluejackets simply tap into the local telegraph office and eavesdrop on Confederate communications.

February 9

WEST: General Gideon J. Pillow supplants Generals Bushrod J. Johnson and Simon B. Buckner as commander of Confederate-held Fort Donelson, Tennessee.

NAVAL: The Federal gunboats USS *Tyler, Conestoga,* and *Lexington* seize the Confederate steamer *Eastport* on the Tennessee River and also attack a deserted Confederate army camp, which they burn.

February 10

WEST: Union general Samuel R. Curtis, commanding the 12,000-man Army of the Southwest, departs Rolla, Missouri, and marches against the 8,000 Missouri Home Guard under General Sterling Price. He intends to drive them deep into Arkansas to preclude any possible interference with the main Union thrust then unfolding down the Mississippi River.

NAVAL: A Federal naval flotilla headed by Commander Stephen C. Rowan of the USS *Delaware* sails up the Pasquotank River and attacks Confederate gunboats and batteries off Elizabeth City, North Carolina. The Southerners are drubbed in a very sharp action and hurriedly scuttle the CSS *Seabird, Black Warrior, Fanny,* and *Forrest.* Artillery positions at Cobb's Point also are destroyed by Union naval gunfire.

Captain Franklin Buchanan complains that he still lacks the necessary trained crew members to man his nearly completed steam ram CSS *Virginia* at Norfolk, Virginia.

Commodore Andrew H. Foote feverishly repairs his gunboats at Cairo, Illinois, after requests by General Henry W. Halleck for their immediate deployment on the Cumberland River against Fort Donelson.

The three-gunboat expedition of Lieutenant Seth L. Phelps concludes its foray down the Tennessee River by arriving back at Fort Donelson, Tennessee. They arrive with three captured Confederate steamers of which one, the *Eastport,* is armed and impressed into Union service. Phelps's raid constitutes one of the most successful endeavors of riverine warfare in the western theater.

February 11
POLITICS: The U.S. Military Rail Roads are established by Secretary of War Edwin M. Stanton. These are adopted to insure the safe and efficient coordination of military transport along thousands of miles of rail line nationwide. Consequently, railborne Union logistics achieve a degree of effectiveness unmatched by its Southern counterpart.
WEST: Union forces under Generals John A. McClernand and Charles F. Smith begin to march 15,000 men from Fort Henry to Fort Donelson on the Cumberland River, Tennessee, although impeded by heavy rains. The latter fort's garrison, meanwhile, has been strengthened by the arrival of Confederates under General Gideon Pillow.

February 12
SOUTH: General Ambrose E. Burnside pushes Federal forces inland and seizes Edenton, North Carolina, as he expands his occupation perimeter beyond Roanoke Island and vicinity.
WEST: General Ulysses S. Grant directs 15,000 Union troops 10 miles overland to invest Fort Donelson on the Cumberland River, Tennessee, now defended by 21,000 Confederates under General John B. Floyd, who is newly arrived. The Federal troops of Generals John A. McClernand and Charles F. Smith conduct the actual siege operations in concert with naval support from the gunboat USS *Carondelet.*

February 13
WEST: Southern forces under General William J. Hardee evacuate Bowling Green, Kentucky, just ahead of advancing Union forces.

Outside Fort Donelson, Tennessee, General John A. McClernand disobeys instructions not to precipitate a general action by deeply probing the Confederate defenses. He then attempts storming a battery at the enemy's center, being heavily repulsed.

The Union Army of the Southwest under General Samuel L. Curtis advances and occupies Springfield, Missouri.
NAVAL: The USS *Pembina,* while sounding the Savannah River, Georgia, observes numerous Confederate torpedoes at low tide. The majority subsequently are sunk or exploded by rifle fire.

February 14
POLITICS: President Abraham Lincoln invokes a general amnesty and pardons all political prisoners who consent to a loyalty oath.
WEST: Bowling Green, Kentucky, is occupied by Union troops under General Ormsby M. Mitchel.

Generals John B. Floyd and Gideon Pillow, despite rebuffing a Union gunboat squadron, conclude that their position at Fort Donelson on the Cumberland River is hopeless. They begin to plan a sortie for the next day, intending to break through Union lines and march to safety.
NAVAL: The experimental ironclad USS *Galena* is launched at Mystic, Connecticut.

Armed boats from the USS *Restless* capture and burn the Confederate sloop *Edisto* and the schooners *Wandoo, Elizabeth,* and *Theodore Stoney* near Bull's Bay, North Carolina.

At 3:00 P.M., Union commodore Andrew H. Foote's gunboat squadron begins a concerted bombardment against Fort Donelson on the Cumberland River, at one point closing to within 400 yards. However, heavy Confederate guns are situated on a 150-foot high bluff, and they subject Foote's vessels to severe plunging fire. The one-sided exchange continues for 90 minutes, and three of four ironclads present are badly damaged and drift helplessly downstream. Foote himself is severely wounded by a splinter and orders his battered armada withdrawn. Losses to naval personnel are 11 killed and 43 wounded. The USS *St. Louis* receives no less than 59 hits and loses its steering, as does the *Louisville*. Little damage has been inflicted upon the Confederates, but the attack unnerves generals John B. Floyd and Gideon Pillow.

February 15
SOUTH: William W. Loring gains appointment as major general, C.S.A.
WEST: Confederate defenders under Generals John B. Floyd and Gideon Pillow suddenly sortie from Fort Donelson, Tennessee, at 6:00 A.M. The attack succeeds completely and penetrates the division of General John A. McClernand. General Ulysses S. Grant, meanwhile, who is on the river flotilla conferring with Commodore Andrew H. Foote, hastily repairs back to the lines to direct a counterattack. He is assisted inadvertently by the Confederates, who, despite having opened an escape route, begin to bicker among themselves about what to do next. As they dither, Grant directs General Charles F. Smith's troops to assail the Confederate right, which he suspects has been weakened, and they gain the outer ramparts of Fort Donelson. Additional forces under General Lew Wallace also charge and contain the Confederate thrust, driving them back inside their post.

That night, Grant obtains additional reinforcements, which bring his total manpower up to 27,000. After heated consultations, the Confederate leaders prepare to surrender; however, neither Floyd nor Pillow wish to be taken prisoner, and that night they ferry themselves across the Cumberland along with 5,000 troops. Some cavalry under Colonel Nathan B. Forrest also determine to escape and wade into the flooded landscape at night to safety.

General Albert S. Johnston arrives in Nashville, Tennessee, to coordinate rapidly crumbling Confederate defenses. As a precaution, Governor Isham Harris removes all state papers and flees south.

General John M. Schofield assumes command of the District of St. Louis, Missouri.

SOUTHWEST: A Confederate column of 3,000 men under General Henry H. Sibley, marching from Mesilla, advances on Union-held Fort Craig, New Mexico Territory. This post is presently garrisoned by 1,000 regulars under Colonel Edward R. S. Canby.

NAVAL: Commodore Josiah Tattnall leads Confederate gunboats on an attack against Union batteries stationed at Venus Point on the Savannah River, but they are gradually beaten back.

February 16

WEST: The Confederate bastion of Fort Donelson, Tennessee, surrenders to General Ulysses S. Grant. Previously, Confederate generals John B. Floyd and Gideon Pillow abandoned their command and ignominiously fled, leaving Generals Simon B. Buckner and Bushrod R. Johnson to their fate. When Buckner, an old acquaintance of Grant's, requests terms, the latter brusquely responds: "No terms except unconditional and immediate surrender can be accepted. I propose to move immediately upon your works." He then takes 15,000 Confederates prisoner, along with 20,000 stands of arms, 48 field pieces, 57 heavy cannon, and considerable supplies. The Southerners also sustain 1,500 combat-related casualties. Union losses are 500 killed, 2,108 wounded, and 221 captive or missing (2,832). For winning the first significant western land action, the victorious Grant is lionized in the Northern press and hailed as "Unconditional Surrender Grant." He also gains promotion to major general.

The loss of Fort Donelson renders the Confederate defensive cordon across Kentucky and Tennessee untenable, prompting General Albert S. Johnston to withdraw his Army of Central Kentucky back toward Murfreesboro. An invasion route to the Deep South is now flung wide open.

SOUTHWEST: The Confederate column of General Henry H. Sibley arrives outside Fort Craig, New Mexico Territory. Sibley, however, deems the post too strong to attack and decides to bypass it, possibly luring the garrison out to do battle on the nearby floodplains.

NAVAL: Accurate shelling by the Union gunboat USS *St. Louis* destroys the Tennessee Ironworks near Dover on the Cumberland River.

February 17

POLITICS: The fifth session of the Confederate Provisional Congress adjourns at Richmond, Virginia.

NORTH: Ulysses S. Grant gains promotion to major general of volunteers, U.S. Army.

WEST: Two Confederate regiments advancing to reinforce Fort Donelson fall captive to Union forces.

NAVAL: The formidable Confederate ironclad CSS *Virginia* is commissioned—with Captain Franklin Buchanan, equally redoubtable, at the helm.

Commodore Andrew H. Foote proceeds with several gunboats and mortar boats down the Cumberland River toward Confederate-held Clarksville, Tennessee.

February 18

POLITICS: The first-ever elected Confederate Congress convenes at Richmond, Virginia.

NAVAL: The USS *Ethan Allen* captures the Confederate schooner *Spitfire* and the sloops *Atlanta* and *Caroline* in Clearwater harbor, Florida.

February 19

POLITICS: The Confederate Congress in Richmond, Virginia, orders the release of 2,000 Federal prisoners.

WEST: Union troops commanded by General Charles F. Smith seize and occupy Clarksville, Tennessee, and Fort Defiance.

SOUTHWEST: General Henry H. Sibley orders his Confederate column of 2,600 men across the Rio Grande toward Valverde Ford, five miles north of Union-held Fort Craig, New Mexico Territory, to threaten its line of communications. As anticipated, Colonel Edward R. S. Canby, rather than remain in his works, sorties the 2,800 man garrison—mostly untrained New Mexico Volunteers—and marches to prevent the Southerners from crossing the river.

NAVAL: The USS *Monitor* begins sea trials in New York harbor, where some propulsion deficiencies are noted.

The USS *Delaware* and *Commodore Perry* conduct an armed reconnaissance down the Chowan River, North Carolina. At length they encounter Confederate forces near the town of Winton, and they withdraw.

The USS *Brooklyn* and *South Carolina* capture the Confederate steamer *Magnolia* in the Gulf of Mexico.

Commodore Andrew H. Foote helps capture Fort Defiance and Clarksville, Tennessee, which Confederate forces hastily evacuate on his approach. The commodore then urges General William F. Smith to advance quickly on Nashville while the Cumberland River still runs high.

February 20

POLITICS: President Abraham Lincoln's 12-year-old son William Wallace ("Willie") Lincoln dies at the White House from typhoid fever.

In light of the twin disasters at Forts Henry and Donelson, the Confederate government authorizes an evacuation of troops from Columbus, Kentucky.

Tennessee governor Isham Harris relocates the Confederate state capital to Memphis as Nashville is threatened by advancing Union forces.

SOUTH: General John E. Wool, commanding Union forces at Fortress Monroe, Virginia, receives disturbing intelligence that the ironclad CSS *Virginia* is deploying against them soon.

WEST: General Albert S. Johnston reassembles his scattered Confederate forces at Murfreesboro, Tennessee.

NAVAL: The new Federal ironclad USS *Monitor* is ordered south to Hampton Roads, Virginia, to reinforce the blockade effort there.

Commodore Louis M. Goldsborough comments on the strength of Confederate river obstacles at New Bern, North Carolina, to Assistant Navy Secretary Gustavus Fox.

Union troops, supported by the USS *Delaware* and *Commodore Perry*, disembark and capture the town of Winton, North Carolina, on the Chowan River.

Commodore David G. Farragut arrives at Ship Island, Mississippi, and prepares to launch what Secretary of the Navy Gideon Welles has deemed "the most important operation of the war"—the expedition against New Orleans, Louisiana.

Landing parties from the USS *New London* seize 12 sloops on Cat Island, Mississippi, suspected of serving as pilot vessels for blockade-runners.

The USS *Portsmouth* captures the Confederate sloop *Pioneer* off Boca Chica, Texas.

February 21

POLITICS: Colonel Charles P. Stone is removed from command and arrested by the Committee on the Conduct of the War. He is blamed with betraying troops defeated at Ball's Bluff the previous October and remains imprisoned for 189 days without trial. Stone is eventually pardoned and released, but his fate is held as an example to others who could be scrutinized by the committee.

NORTH: Nathaniel Gordon, a convicted slave trader, is hanged in New York City, which is the first such punishment rendered for this outlawed practice.

SOUTH: Command of the Department of Florida passes to General Lewis G. Arnold.

SOUTHWEST: Union troops under Colonel Edwin R. S. Canby engage General Henry H. Sibley's marauding Confederates at Valverde, New Mexico Territory, roughly five miles north of strategic Fort Craig. Because Sibley is sidelined with illness, actual combat operations devolve on Colonel Thomas Green. The initial Union assault pushes the Texan vanguard back from the fords and into a ravine, pinning them there. The hard-pressed Green, seeing that the key to Canby's position is a battery of six cannon under Captain Alexander McRae, temporarily abandons his left wing, masses the bulk of his forces on the right, and then charges the guns. These fall after a difficult struggle, and the captured ordnance is then turned on its previous owners. Canby consequently orders his troops to disengage and march back to Fort Craig. Federal losses are given as 68 killed, 160 wounded, and 35 missing, compared to 36 slain Southerners, 150 wounded, and one missing. Sibley's troops prevail in combat, but lacking heavy artillery and possessing but three days' supplies, they elect to bypass Fort Craig altogether and continue marching toward Albuquerque. The fort and its garrison remain a menace to Confederate lines of communication.

February 22

POLITICS: President Jefferson Davis is inaugurated as the first elected chief executive of the Confederate States of America. His ensuing address places the blame for the present hostilities squarely on the North, and he states that he considers the North's stance against states rights to violate principles of the American Revolution. Alexander H. Stevens continues as vice president. From this point on, Southerners view their constitution and administration as permanent, not provisional.

SOUTH: The 5th Pennsylvania Cavalry under Colonel Max Friedman executes an expedition to Vienna and Flint Hill, Virginia.

WEST: The Army of Ohio under General Don C. Buell marches south from Bowling Green, Kentucky, toward Nashville, Tennessee.

NAVAL: Union naval vessels begin to penetrate the Savannah River to isolate Fort Pulaski, Georgia.

Commodore David G. Farragut orders the coast survey to study all Mississippi River passes to establish the safest passage.

February 23

POLITICS: U.S. senator Andrew Johnson of Tennessee is nominated to serve as military governor of the pro-Union, eastern portion of his state by President Abraham Lincoln.

SOUTH: General Benjamin F. Butler is tapped to serve as commander of the newly constituted Department of the Gulf.

WEST: General Albert S. Johnston takes charge of the Confederate Central Army in Tennessee, gathering its strength at Murfreesboro.

Confederate forces under General Nathan B. Forrest evacuate Nashville, Tennessee, now threatened by advancing Union troops under General Don C. Buell.

General John Pope gains appointment as commander of the Army of Mississippi at Commerce, Missouri.

Fayetteville, Arkansas, is occupied by Federal troops under General Samuel R. Curtis.

NAVAL: The USS *Harriet Lane* captures the Confederate schooner *Joanna Ward* off the Florida coast.

Commodore Andrew H. Foote, accompanied by General George W. Cullum, army chief of staff, takes his entire flotilla of four ironclads, three "woodenclads," and three transport vessels down the Mississippi River to observe formidable Confederate positions at Columbus, Kentucky. Concurrently, the USS *Tyler* is dispatched to scout the Tennessee River as far south as Eastport, Mississippi.

February 24

WEST: The much-ravaged town of Harper's Ferry, strategically located at the confluence of the Potomac and Shenandoah rivers, is reoccupied by Union troops of General Nathaniel P. Bank's division.

The Army of the Ohio under General Don C. Buell arrives on the north bank of the Cumberland River, opposite Nashville.

NAVAL: Captain Franklin Buchanan, CSS *Virginia*, is ordered by Confederate secretary of the navy Stephen R. Mallory to sortie his James River squadron against Union naval forces off nearby Hampton Roads as soon as practicable.

February 25

POLITICS: The Legal Tender Act is approved by President Abraham Lincoln. This is the nation's first government-sponsored paper money system. The new currency, known popularly as greenbacks, is intended only as a wartime expedient to allow the Treasury Department to pay bills. Ultimately, $400 million are in circulation by war's end.

The War Department is authorized to commandeer all telegraph lines and services to facilitate military communications.

WEST: Union general William Nelson, assisted by the gunboat USS *Cairo*, bloodlessly occupies Nashville, Tennessee. This is the first Southern state capital and significant industrial center captured by the North. It thereupon serves as a base of operations for the Army of the Ohio. Nashville's fate also signals that Kentucky and western Tennessee are irretrievably lost to the South. Meanwhile, Confederate forces continue their precipitous withdrawal from the line of the Cumberland River.

General Edmund Kirby-Smith is ordered to take command of Southern forces in East Tennessee.

NAVAL: The new Union ironclad USS *Monitor* is commissioned at Long Island, New York, with Lieutenant John L. Worden commanding. It features a revolutionary design that incorporates a single, rotating turret housing two 11-inch Dalhgren smoothbore cannon. Largely submerged underwater, the ship incorporates a forced-draft ventilation system for its crew.

The USS *R. B. Forbes* grounds in a gale off Nag's Head, North Carolina, and is burned to prevent capture.

The USS *Mohican* and *Bienville* capture the British blockade-runner *Arrow* near Fernandina, Florida.

The USS *Kingfisher* seizes the Confederate blockade-runner *Lion* after a three-day chase in the Gulf of Mexico.

The USS *Cairo,* escorting seven steam transports, assists in the capture of Nashville, Tennessee.

February 26
SOUTH: Ambrose P. Hill is appointed brigadier general, C.S.A.
NAVAL: The CSS *Nashville* captures and burns the Union schooner *Robert Gilfillan* at sea.

The USS *Bienville* captures the Confederate schooner *Alert* off St. Johns, Florida.

February 27
POLITICS: Like his northern counterpart, President Jefferson Davis finds it necessary to suspend writs of habeas corpus as a wartime expedient. He then declares martial law in Norfolk and Portsmouth, Virginia, then threatened by Union forces.
NAVAL: The much-anticipated departure of USS *Monitor* is delayed by ammunition shortages and intractable steering failures.

Lack of gunpowder delays the sailing of the Confederate ironclad CSS *Virginia* at Norfolk, Virginia.

February 28
POLITICS: An anxious president Jefferson Davis advises General Joseph E. Johnston, commanding Confederate forces in Virginia, to formulate contingency plans for evacuating men and materiel to safety if necessary.
SOUTH: Union forces are unable to initiate action at Harper's Ferry, western Virginia, because boats provided them for a pontoon bridge prove too large for the canal locks.

General Samuel Jones becomes commander of the Department of Alabama and West Florida following General Braxton Bragg's departure.
WEST: Federal troops occupy Charleston in western Virginia.

General John Pope's Army of the Mississippi advances from Commerce, Missouri, down the western shore of the Mississippi River toward the Confederate enclave of New Madrid. This strongly fortified post houses 7,500 men under General John P. McCown, with 19 heavy guns and a flotilla of gunboats under Captain George N. Hollins.
SOUTHWEST: Advancing Confederate forces capture the town of Tucson in the western New Mexico Territory. The region then elects a delegation to attend Congress in Richmond.
NAVAL: CSS *Nashville* skirts Union blockaders and runs safely into Beaufort, North Carolina.

March 1

NORTH: David Hunter and Irvin McDowell are promoted to major general, U.S. Army.

SOUTH: Martial law is declared in Richmond, Virginia, by Confederate authorities under General John H. Winder.

WEST: General Henry W. Halleck, commanding the Department of the West, orders General Ulysses S. Grant to cross the Tennessee River and move against Eastport, Mississippi.

Confederate general Pierre G. T. Beauregard begins to distribute troops on a line stretching from Columbus, Kentucky, past Island No. 10 on the Mississippi River and Fort Pillow, Tennessee, as far south as Corinth, Mississippi. General Albert S. Johnston also starts to move his command from Murfreesboro, Tennessee, toward an eventual union with Beauregard at Corinth, Mississippi.

SOUTHWEST: Federal forces abandon Albuquerque, New Mexico, to advancing Confederates under General Henry H. Sibley.

NAVAL: The USS *Mount Vernon* captures the British blockade-runner *British Queen* off Wilmington, North Carolina.

Federal gunboats USS *Tyler* and *Lexington* engage a Confederate battery guarding Pittsburgh Landing, Tennessee. However, when sailors and army sharpshooters land to scout the position, several casualties are incurred. Henceforth, Commodore Andrew H. Foote forbids naval personnel from disembarking to fight ashore.

Commodore Andrew H. Foote requests the Navy Department for $20,000 to repair and arm the captured Confederate steamer *Eastport,* which he describes as a fine vessel more than 100 feet long.

March 2

WEST: Confederate forces under General Leonidas Polk finally abandon their strong point at Columbus, Kentucky, and retreat south. Its garrison and armament of 140 cannon are subsequently relocated across the Mississippi River to New Madrid, Missouri, and Island No. 10 under General John P. McCown. The Confederate Kentucky line, previously stretching as far east as Cumberland Gap, has now completely vanished.

General Earl Van Dorn arrives at the Boston Mountains, Arkansas, to take command of the Confederate Trans-Mississippi District. There, he unites his forces with those of General Sterling Price and Ben McCulloch into the new Army of the West and countermands their withdrawal from Missouri. Disregarding poor logistical arrangements and freezing weather, Van Dorn orders his men north to confront pursuing Union forces.

March 3

SOUTH: John Bell Hood is appointed brigadier general, C.S.A.

General Robert E. Lee is recalled from Charleston, South Carolina to Richmond, Virginia, to act as a military adviser for President Jefferson Davis.

WEST: Martinsburg, western Virginia, is occupied by Federal troops.

General Henry W. Halleck accuses General Ulysses S. Grant of sloppy administration, and he orders him detained at Fort Henry, Tennessee, until further notice.

General John Pope directs 18,000 men of the Union Army of the Mississippi into siege operations against New Madrid, Missouri, on the Mississippi River.
SOUTHWEST: Advancing Confederates under General Henry H. Sibley capture Cubero, New Mexico Territory.
NAVAL: A naval expedition under Commodore Samuel F. Du Pont attacks and captures Cumberland Island and Sound, Georgia, along with Fernandina and Amelia Island, Florida. Fort Clinch, seized by a crew from the USS *Ottawa,* is the first Federal fortification retaken in the war. The North thus gains another valuable lodgment on the southern Atlantic seaboard while the entire coast of Georgia falls under Union control.

March 4

POLITICS: The U.S. Senate confirms Tennessee senator Andrew Johnson as military governor of Tennessee with a rank of brigadier general.
SOUTH: Patrick R. Cleburne is appointed brigadier general, C.S.A.

General John C. Pemberton succeeds Robert E. Lee as commander of the Department of South Carolina, Georgia, and East Florida.
WEST: General Charles F. Smith is appointed to lead Union advances down the Tennessee River in light of General Ulysses S. Grant's disciplinary difficulties.

General Earl Van Dorn marches 16,000 men from the Boston Mountains toward Missouri. He remains intent on engaging the Union Army of the Southwest under General Samuel R. Curtis somewhere in the extreme northeastern corner of Arkansas.
SOUTHWEST: Santa Fe, New Mexico Territory, is occupied by Confederates under General Henry H. Sibley.
NAVAL: The USS *Santiago de Cuba* seizes the Confederate sloop *O. K.* off Cedar Keys, Florida.

Federal gunboats USS *Cincinnati* and *Louisville* reconnoiter recently abandoned Confederate works at Columbus, Kentucky, previously hailed as "the Gibraltar of the West." Union troops arrive shortly after by river transport.

March 5

WEST: As Federal troops under General Nathaniel P. Banks advance from Harper's Ferry, western Virginia, and into the Shenandoah Valley, skirmishing erupts at Bunker Hill and Pohick Church.

Union forces under General Charles F. Smith position themselves at Savannah, Tennessee, several miles northeast of Corinth, Mississippi.

General Pierre G. T. Beauregard arrives at Jackson, Tennessee, taking charge of the newly established Confederate Army of the Mississippi. General Albert S. Johnston likewise continues massing troops at Corinth, Mississippi, determined to contest any probable Union thrusts down the Tennessee River.

March 6

POLITICS: President Abraham Lincoln urges Congress to offer monetary compensation to any state that willingly abolishes slavery. The measure is rejected soundly by state legislatures.

The Confederate Congress authorizes military authorities to destroy any cotton, tobacco, or other stores deemed of use to the enemy if they cannot be safely relocated.

SOUTH: Sterling Price is appointed major general, C.S.A.

After interminable delays, General George B. McClellan orders the Army of the Potomac southward against Manassas, Virginia. Concurrently, Confederate forces under General Joseph E. Johnston make preparations to fall back on Fredericksburg.

Union forces reoccupy Leesburg, Virginia.

WEST: A force of 10,500 Union troops under General Samuel R. Curtis entrenches itself along Sugar Creek near Pea Ridge and Elkhorn Tavern, Arkansas, in anticipation of a major Confederate assault. After General Earl Van Dorn tests the Union position and finds it too strong to be attacked frontally, he prepares for a prolonged night march around Curtis to cut him off from Missouri—then attack from behind. The Confederate Army of the West has also been recently reinforced by three Cherokee regiments under General Albert Pike and Colonel Stand Watie.

NAVAL: USS *Water Witch* captures the Confederate schooner *William Mallory* near St. Andrew's Bay, Florida.

The USS *Monitor* under Lieutenant John L. Worden departs New York while under tow by tug *Seth Law* and heads for Hampton Roads, Virginia.

The USS *Pursuit* seizes the Confederate schooner *Anna Belle* off Apalachicola, Florida.

March 7

SOUTH: Pressured by the ponderous Army of the Potomac, General Joseph E. Johnston withdraws Confederate forces from Evansport, Dumfries, Manassas, and Occoquan and heads south toward Fredericksburg, Virginia.

A Union landing party commanded by General Thomas W. Sherman captures Fort Clinch on Fernandina Island, Florida.

WEST: Confederate cavalry under Colonel Ashby Turner skirmish with Union forces near Winchester, western Virginia.

Confederate forces under General Earl Van Dorn conduct a complicated night march around the Army of the Southwest near Pea Ridge, northwestern Arkansas. The main strike force under General Sterling Price positions itself behind and opposite the Union left wing, but fatigued Texans of General Ben McCulloch's division deploying against Curtis's right cannot close the gap. Thus two wings of the Confederate army remain widely separated and unable to act in concert. Van Dorn himself is ill and directs operations from an ambulance in the rear of his line. General Samuel R. Curtis, quickly perceiving the danger posed to his command, simply orders his entire line to "about face." The new threat is immediately countered and negates whatever advantage Van Dorn's wearying march sought to achieve. The action commences across the line when Price's Missourians launch two desperate charges that are beaten back. McCulloch's column, however, stumbles badly when both he and his second in command, General James M. McIntosh, are killed. A third charge by Price manages to drive back Curtis's right, but prompt Union counterattacks regain lost ground. A similar effort is made against Pike's Cherokee on the left with good results. A fourth attack at sunset pushes the Union line back 800 yards but still fails to break it. Fighting then subsides with nightfall.

March 8
POLITICS: President Abraham Lincoln issues General War Order No. 2, which reorganizes the Army of the Potomac into four corps. It also stipulates that at least one corps be left behind for the defense of Washington, D.C. General Irvin McDowell's command draws the assignment.

Unionist William G. Brownlow is released from confinement and allowed to cross over to Union lines in eastern Tennessee.
SOUTH: Union forces advance and occupy Leesburg, Virginia.
WEST: Resurgent Confederate forces under General John B. Floyd reoccupy Chattanooga and Knoxville, Tennessee, forcing Unionists in the region to flee.

Confederate cavalryman Colonel John H. Morgan raids the suburbs of Nashville, Tennessee.

Fighting resumes at Pea Ridge, Arkansas, when Confederate artillery bombard the position of General Samuel R. Curtis, who constricts and consolidates his line. However, when Van Dorn's guns are silenced for want of ammunition, Curtis deduces that Van Dorn's entire force must likewise be low, and he orders General Franz Sigel to attack across the front. A surging blue tide sweeps across the battlefield of Confederates as Van Dorn, his army shattered, orders a complete withdrawal. Union losses amount to 20 killed, 980 wounded, and 201 missing, while the Southerners sustain roughly 2,000 casualties, including 300 captured. Pea Ridge is the first major Union victory in the Far West and thwarts Confederate hopes of invading Missouri for the next two years.
NAVAL: The ironclad ram CSS *Virginia* under Captain Franklin Buchanan sorties from Norfolk, Virginia, and engages wooden ships of the Union blockading squadron off Newport News. Buchanan first maneuvers and slams into the sloop USS *Cumberland*, breaking off its metallic ram and sinking that hapless vessel. The *Virginia* then receives heavy fire from the frigate *Congress,* whose cannon balls simply rebound off heavy iron plate. Buchanan next riddles his opponent at close range, driving it ashore and reducing *Congress* to a burning hulk. A third vessel, *Minnesota,* grounds itself in anticipation of being attacked. Buchanan, who is wounded by gunfire from the shoreline, relinquishes command to Lieutenant Catesby ap Roger Jones, who breaks off the action. Union casualties are two vessels sunk and roughly 300 sailors killed and wounded. Moreover, the death knell of wooden warships has sounded.

The USS *Monitor* under Lieutenant John L. Worden, having survived a perilous transit from New York, arrives off Hampton Roads, Virginia, in the evening.

The USS *Bohio* captures the Confederate schooner *Henry Travers* off Southwest Pass, Mississippi River.

March 9
SOUTH: The Army of the Potomac under General George B. McClellan fails to establish contact with enemy forces and returns to Alexandria, Virginia. Meanwhile, the

Turret of the USS *Monitor*. Photo taken after the battle with the CSS *Virginia*. Note dents in the turret next to the gun ports. *(Naval Historical Foundation)*

Confederate army under General Joseph E. Johnston retreats farther south and positions itself behind the Rappahannock River.

WEST: General Edmund Kirby-Smith arrives at Knoxville to command Confederate forces in East Tennessee.

NAVAL: At about 9:00 A.M., Lieutenant Catesby ap Roger Jones takes the undamaged ironclad CSS *Virginia* out of Norfolk, intending to finish off the grounded USS *Minnesota*. As he approaches his quarry, he is startled to see the low-lying and strange-looking *Monitor* sail directly into his path. During the next four hours, the two iron giants duel to the death before thousands of spectators onshore. Both vessels, heavily armed and armored, fire repeatedly at close range yet fail to inflict serious damage. Jones next tries ramming the *Monitor*, but Lieutenant John L. Worden simply dodges his lumbering adversary while firing away. At length, a lucky Confederate shot strikes Worden's pilothouse, wounding his eye with a splinter. His successor, Lieutenant S. Dana Greene, draws off to assess matters and reload, while

Virginia inadvertently grounds in shallow water. Once Jones frees himself, he makes a final lunge at the *Minnesota* and then, mindful of lowering tides, steams back to Norfolk. This dramatic but inconclusive confrontation heralds the dawn of iron warships in naval warfare.

Landing parties from USS *Anacostia* and *Yankee* occupy and raze abandoned Confederate batteries at Cockpit Point and Evansport, Virginia.

The USS *Mohican* and *Pocahontas* seize St. Simon's and Jekyl islands at New Brunswick, Georgia.

The USS *Pinola* captures the Confederate schooner *Cora* in the Gulf of Mexico and deposits it at Ship Island, Mississippi.

March 10

POLITICS: President Abraham Lincoln pays a bedside visit to Lieutenant John L. Worden, seriously wounded in the fight between the USS *Monitor* and the CSS *Virginia.*

SOUTH: John P. McCown is promoted to major general, C.S.A.

NAVAL: The Union tug USS *Whitehall* is accidentally lost to fire off Fortress Monroe, Virginia.

Commodore David G. Farragut methodically begins to work his deep-draft warships over the bar and into the Mississippi River below New Orleans, Louisiana.

March 11

POLITICS: President Abraham Lincoln, disillusioned by General George B. McClellan's lack of aggressiveness, issues War Order No. 3. This removes the slow-to-act leader as general in chief, although he is retained as command of the Army of the Potomac. Henceforth, all generals are to report directly to Secretary of War Edwin M. Stanton.

President Jefferson Davis refuses to accept the reports of General John B. Floyd and Gideon Pillow on the fall of Fort Donelson, and he unceremoniously relieves both of command.

NORTH: The Department of Western Virginia is absorbed by the Mountain Department and is granted to General John C. Frémont.

General Henry W. Halleck is appointed commander of all Union forces in the West through an amalgamation of the Departments of Kansas, the Missouri, and the Ohio into the new Department of the Mississippi.

WEST: General Thomas J. Jackson departs Winchester, western Virginia, at the head of 4,600 men, and he marches up the valley toward Mount Jackson. He is shadowed cautiously by 18,000 Federals under General Nathaniel P. Banks.

NAVAL: A landing party from the USS *Wabash* captures and occupies St. Augustine, Florida.

Confederate authorities at Pensacola, Florida, fearing a Union naval thrust against them, burn two gunboats to prevent their capture.

March 12

SOUTH: Federal troops under General Ambrose E. Burnside board army transports at Roanoke Island, North Carolina, for an expedition against New Bern on the Neuse River.

West: Union forces advance and reoccupy Winchester in western Virginia as Confederates under General Thomas J. Jackson withdraw farther up the Shenandoah Valley.

General John Pope receives and deploys heavy siege artillery to facilitate his siege of New Madrid, Missouri, on the Mississippi River.

Naval: The USS *Gem of the Sea* captures the British blockade-runner *Fair Play* off Georgetown, South Carolina.

A landing party from the USS *Ottawa* seizes and occupies Jacksonville, Florida.

Federal gunboats USS *Tyler* and *Lexington* cruise down the Tennessee River and trade shots with a Confederate battery at Chickasaw, Alabama.

March 13

Politics: President Abraham Lincoln approves of plans for operations along the Virginia coast by forces under General George B. McClellan. He urges the general "at all events, move such remainder of the army at once in pursuit of the enemy."

New army regulations forbid army officers from returning fugitive African-American slaves back to their owners. Failure to comply is punishable by court-martial.

South: General George B. McClellan convenes a war conference at Fairfax Court House, Virginia, and finalizes his strategy against Richmond. Rather than campaign overland from Urbana on the Rappahannock River, he elects to ship the entire Army of the Potomac up the York and James rivers to outflank strong Confederate defenses. To that end, his force is reorganized into five corps under generals Irvin McDowell (I Corps), Edwin V. Sumner (II Corps), Samuel P. Heintzelman (III Corps), Erasmus D. Keyes (IV Corps), and Nathaniel P. Banks (V Corps).

General Ambrose E. Burnside lands three brigades of 12,000 Union soldiers at Slocum's Creek on the Neuse River, North Carolina, supported by 13 gunboats. His objective is New Bern, that state's second-largest city and an important railhead. After learning of his approach, Confederate general Lawrence O. Branch constricts his 4,000-man garrison within defensive works six miles south of New Bern and awaits their approach.

West: A heavy bombardment from General John Pope's siege guns at Point Pleasant, Missouri, induces Confederate forces under General John P. McCown to evacuate their base at New Madrid for Island No. 10, abandoning mounds of valuable supplies in the process.

General William T. Sherman begins to probe from the Union lodgment at Pittsburg Landing on the Tennessee River and into the surrounding Mississippi countryside.

Naval: A naval expedition lands 12,000 Federal troops under General Ambrose E. Burnside on the Neuse River, North Carolina.

Commander David D. Porter assembles his mortar-ship flotilla at Ship Island, Mississippi, to assist in the upcoming New Orleans campaign.

Captain George N. Hollins reassembles his Confederate gunboat squadron at Island No. 10 in the Mississippi River following the fall of New Madrid, Missouri. His squadron then consists of CSS *Livingston, Polk,* and *Pontchartrain*.

March 14

SOUTH: 12,000 Federal troops under General Ambrose E. Burnside land and advance through rain and mud toward New Bern, North Carolina, the former colonial capital. Confederate defenders under General Lawrence O. Branch resist doughtily for several hours until a militia unit in his center suddenly cracks. The gap is exploited by the brigades of generals Jesse Reno and John G. Foster, and Branch retreats toward Kinston. The 26th and 33rd North Carolina under Colonels Zebulon B. Vance and Robert F. Hoke, respectively, are trapped behind enemy lines, yet both energetically grope for a ford across the Trent River and escape certain capture. New Bern is subsequently occupied by Burnside's victorious forces that afternoon. Union losses are 92 killed, 391 wounded, and one missing for a Confederate total of 64 dead, 101 injured, and 413 captured. The loss in materiel to the Confederates is significant, and the Union gains another base for projecting its strength inland. Burnside gains promotion to major general for the effort, while Confederate general Richard C. Gatlin is sacked for failing to prepare New Bern's defenses in advance.

General George Stoneman conducts a Federal reconnaissance toward Cedar Run, Virginia.

General James H. Trapier assumes command of the Confederate Department of Middle and East Florida.

WEST: General William S. Rosecrans takes charge of the Union Mountain Department.

Commanding General William W. Halleck orders the Army of the Ohio under General Don C. Buell to proceed south from Nashville toward Savannah, Georgia.

Confederates under General Edmund Kirby-Smith skirmish with Union forces at Big Creek Gap and Jacksonboro, Tennessee.

General John Pope overruns the Confederate enclave at New Madrid, Missouri, as defenders under General John P. McCown flee to Island No. 10 in the nearby Mississippi River.

NAVAL: Naval landing parties at New Bern, North Carolina, under Commander Stephen C. Rowan capture two Confederate steamers, sizable cotton supplies, and a howitzer battery.

The division of General Stephen Hurlbut joins General William T. Sherman's force that is already deploying at Pittsburg Landing, Tennessee.

Commodore Andrew H. Foote departs Cairo, Illinois, with seven gunboats for an attack on Island No. 10 in the Mississippi River.

March 15

SOUTH: The Department of the South under General David Hunter absorbs the Department of Florida.

WEST: General Ulysses S. Grant is exonerated of misconduct by General Henry W. Halleck and resumes command of Union forces in Tennessee.

NAVAL: Commodore Andrew H. Foote's flotilla of six gunboats and 121 mortar boats unleashes a preliminary bombardment of Confederate defenses on Island No. 10 in the Mississippi River.

March 16

WEST: General James Garfield and 600 Union volunteers attack and destroy a Confederate encampment under General Humphrey Marshall at Pound Gap, Tennessee.

Colonel John H. Morgan leads Confederate raiders in and around Gallatin, Tennessee.

Federal troops under General John Pope, in concert with Commodore Andrew H. Foote's gunboat flotilla, initiate combined operations against Confederate positions on Island No. 10 in the Mississippi River. This post, well manned and heavily armed, presents a formidable obstacle to all river navigation.

NAVAL: Federal gunboats USS *Yankee* and *Anacostia* duel with Confederate batteries at Aquia Creek, Virginia.

The USS *Owasco* captures Confederate schooners *Eugenia* and *President* in the Gulf of Mexico.

March 17

SOUTH: The Army of the Potomac—105,000 strong—begins to embark at Alexandria, Virginia, for an amphibious transit to Fortress Monroe on the York and James rivers. Through this maneuver, General George B. McClellan aspires to outflank Confederate defenses guarding Richmond.

NAVAL: The CSS *Nashville* slips past blockading vessels USS *Cambridge* and *Gemsbok* off Beaufort, North Carolina. The Navy Department was quite embarrassed by its failure to stop the raider, and Assistant Secretary Gustavus V. Fox described the affair as "a Bull Run for the Navy."

Commodore Andrew H. Foote engages Confederate batteries on Island No. 10 with his gunboat flotilla. Some damage is inflicted ashore, but both USS *Benton* and *Cincinnati* receive damage when a gun burst on *St. Louis* kills and wounds several sailors.

March 18

POLITICS: President Jefferson Davis appoints Confederate secretary of war Judah P. Benjamin his new secretary of state to replace Robert M. T. Hunter, who was elected to the Confederate Senate.

NORTH: Ambrose E. Burnside is promoted to major general, U.S. Army.

WEST: The advance guard of Confederate forces under General Albert S. Johnston trudge into Corinth, Mississippi, from Murfreesboro, Tennessee.

NAVAL: The British blockade-runner *Emily St. Pierre* falls captive to the Union blockading squadron off Charleston, South Carolina. However, once at sea, the prize crew is overpowered, and the vessel sails on to Liverpool, England.

March 19

SOUTH: General Joseph R. Anderson assumes command of the Confederate Department of North Carolina.

WEST: Confederates under General Thomas J. Jackson successfully skirmish with the Union troops of General James Shield at Strasburg, western Virginia.

Colonel Powell Clayton leads the 5th Kansas Cavalry on a mounted expedition to Carthage, Missouri.

SOUTHWEST: Union forces skirmish with Indians at Bishop's Creek, Owen's River valley, California.

NAVAL: The gunboat squadron under Commodore Andrew H. Foote continues flailing away at Confederate defenses on Island No. 10 in the Mississippi River, meeting heavy resistance.

March 20

NORTH: General Nathaniel P. Banks and his V Corps are ordered out of the Shenandoah Valley to the defense of Washington, D.C.

SOUTH: Federal forces under General Oliver O. Howard conduct a reconnaissance of Manassas Junction, Virginia.

General Ambrose E. Burnside leads a strong Union force overland against Washington, North Carolina, from New Bern.

General Benjamin F. Butler accedes to command of the Department of the Gulf at Ship Island, Mississippi, prior to operations against New Orleans, Louisiana.

WEST: Confederates under General Thomas J. Jackson depart Strasburg, Virginia, and advance toward Mount Jackson.

March 21

NORTH: Samuel R. Curtis, William S. Rosecrans, and Lew Wallace gain appointment as major generals, U.S. Army.

SOUTH: Union troops under General Ambrose E. Burnside advance and seize Washington, North Carolina.

WEST: Confederate cavalry under Colonel Turner Ashby alert General Thomas J. Jackson that General Nathaniel P. Banks is withdrawing two divisions from Winchester in the Shenandoah Valley. Jackson, fearing that these reinforcements are destined to assist the Army of the Potomac's drive on Richmond, determines to lure them back. He immediately puts two brigades in motion toward Kernstown.

Confederates under General Edmund Kirby-Smith skirmish with Union forces at Cumberland Gap, Tennessee.

March 22

NORTH: Don C. Buell, John Pope, and Franz Sigel are appointed major generals, U.S. Army.

The Middle Department, headquartered at Baltimore, is constituted under General John A. Dix.

SOUTH: General Mansfield Lovell, commanding the Confederate garrison at New Orleans, reports that he has six steamers for the defense of the city but that the inhabitants are dismayed once the bulk of Confederate naval assets deploy upriver.

WEST: Preliminary skirmishing erupts at Kernstown, western Virginia, between Confederate cavalry under Colonel Turner Ashby and Union forces under General James Shield. Ashby then mistakenly reports to General Thomas J. Jackson that Union strength is about 4,000 men, the same as his own. In fact, Shield possesses twice as many men, with most of them hidden in nearby copses.

The 2nd Kansas Cavalry under Colonel Robert B. Mitchell skirmishes with the Confederate guerrillas of William C. Quantrill outside Independence, Missouri.

Naval: The future CSS *Florida,* presently disguised as the British steamer *Oreto,* departs Liverpool for Nassau. There, the vessel is to be renamed and outfitted with four seven-inch guns. This was the first English vessel built expressly for the Confederate navy and clandestinely secured through the efforts of agent James D. Bulloch.

A naval landing party from USS *Penguin* and *Henry Andrew* engages Confederate forces while reconnoitering ashore at Mosquito Inlet, Florida, suffering three killed.

March 23

Politics: George W. Randolph is appointed Confederate secretary of war.

South: General Ambrose E. Burnside orders Union forces under General John G. Parke against Confederate-held Fort Macon (Beaufort), North Carolina. Defenders in the old stone fort, garrisoned by 400 men under Colonel Moses J. White, are summoned to surrender, but White refuses.

West: General Thomas J. Jackson concludes an impressive two-day march by covering 41 miles in two days. He then initiates his diversionary Shenandoah Valley strategy by attacking 9,000 Union troops under General James Shields at Kernstown, Virginia, south of Winchester. His force of 4,500 in three brigades advances confidently and flanks the Union left, driving them back. However, Union commander General Nathan Kimball continuously feeds more men into the fray and fights the Southerners to a draw. A crisis erupts when the Stonewall brigade of General Richard B. Garnett runs out of ammunition and departs without orders, creating a gap in Jackson's line. As increasing numbers of Federal troops surge forward, Jackson's entire line falls back in semiconfusion, losing 80 killed, 355 wounded, and 263 captured (718) men, along with a number of cannon and wagons. Union losses totaled 118 dead, 450 injured, and 22 captives (590).

Kernstown, while a Confederate tactical defeat, harbors immense strategic implications for both contenders. Union authorities are convinced that Jackson would not have attacked down the Shenandoah until he had been massively reinforced, and now Washington, D.C., is perceived as in danger. Accordingly, President Abraham Lincoln orders the I Corps of General Irvin McDowell to be detained indefinitely at the capital, thereby depriving the Army of the Potomac of its services during the upcoming Peninsula Campaign. The two divisions of General Nathaniel P. Banks are likewise frozen at Harper's Ferry and are rendered unavailable as reinforcements. The defeat at Kernstown also heralds the start of Jackson's dazzling Shenandoah Valley campaign, one of the Civil War's legendary endeavors.

Union soldiers commence digging a 12-mile-long, 50-foot wide canal on the Mississippi River to allow Union gunboats to bypass Confederate defensive works at Island No. 10.

March 24

South: General John B. Magruder, commanding Confederate forces in Virginia's Yorktown Peninsula region, advises superiors in Richmond that Union soldiers are arriving at nearby Fortress Monroe.

General Theophilus H. Holmes becomes commander of the Department of North Carolina.

WEST: The continuing unpopularity of emancipation is underscored when radical abolitionist Wendell Phillips is pelted with eggs and stones in Cincinnati, Ohio.

General Albert S. Johnston completes his concentration of Confederate forces at Corinth, Mississippi, while Union troops under General Ulysses S. Grant consolidate their position at Pittsburg Landing, 20 miles distant.

March 25

WEST: General Henry W. Halleck, commanding at St. Louis, expresses alarm to Commodore Andrew H. Foote on the receipt of intelligence that the Confederates are constructing a huge ironclad (CSS *Arkansas*) downstream capable of destroying his smaller Union gunboats.

SOUTHWEST: Major John M. Chivington of the 1st Colorado Volunteers is ordered to attack a Confederate force lodged near Santa Fe, New Mexico Territory. He arrives at the far end of La Glorietta Pass that evening, captures several sentinels, and prepares to storm the enemy camp at dawn.

NAVAL: Confederate secretary of the navy Stephen R. Mallory orders Commodore Josiah Tattnall to replace the wounded Captain Franklin Buchanan at Norfolk, Virginia.

CSS *Oregon* and *Pamlico* engage the USS *New London* off Pass Christian, Mississippi, but subsequently withdraw when their rifled ordnance jams and no damage is inflicted. Meanwhile, an armada of transport vessels arrives off Ship Island, Mississippi, bearing the army of General Benjamin F. Butler.

The USS *Cayuga* captures the Confederate schooner *Jessie L. Cox* at sea.

Landing parties from the Federal gunboat USS *Cairo* occupy recently abandoned Fort Zollicoffer below Nashville, seizing guns and other equipment.

March 26

SOUTH: Daniel H. Hill is promoted to major general, C.S.A.

General John H. Winder is tapped to serve as commander of the Confederate Department of Henrico, which includes Petersburg, Virginia.

SOUTHWEST: A skirmish between Union and Confederate cavalry near Denver City, Colorado Territory, results in 50 Southern prisoners.

In an early morning raid, Colonel John M. Chivington, 1st Colorado Infantry, advances through Glorieta Pass, New Mexico Territory, and attacks Confederate forces under Major Charles L. Pryon that are encamped at Johnson's Ranch. Federal troops capture the 30-man advance guard and then storm the enemy camp. The surprised Confederates respond with artillery fire that stabilizes their line, but Chivington redeploys to catch the Texans in a crossfire, and the Texans retire in confusion. A last-minute charge by Union cavalry against the Confederate rear guard nets several prisoners; Chivington then orders his men back to Kozlowski's Ranch to regroup. Union losses are 19 dead, 5 wounded, and 3 missing while the Southerners report 16 killed, 30 injured, and 79 missing. The shaken Pyron immediately sends for reinforcements.

NAVAL: Armed boats dispatched by the USS *Delaware* capture Confederate schooners *Albemarle* and *Lion* in Pantego Creek, North Carolina.

March 27

SOUTH: Colonel Jonathan W. Geary and the 28th Pennsylvania conduct a reconnaissance of the region between Middleburg and White Plains, Virginia.

General Joseph E. Johnston is ordered to reinforce the Confederate Army of the Peninsula at Yorktown, Virginia, under General John B. Magruder.

WEST: Secretary of War Edwin M. Stanton tells engineer Charles Ellet to commence construction of numerous steam rams at Pittsburgh, Pennsylvania, and Cincinnati, Ohio, capable of thwarting the new Confederate ironclad being assembled at Memphis, Tennessee.

SOUTHWEST: Colonel William R. Scurry's 4th Texas arrives at Johnson's Ranch, New Mexico Territory, to reinforce a detachment under Major Charles L. Pyron. The Confederates then brace themselves for an anticipated Union attack, and when it fails to materialize, Pyron resumes the offensive by marching through Glorieta Pass.

NAVAL: An armed boat from the USS *Restless* captures the Confederate schooner *Julia Warden* and burns the sloop *Mary Louisa* and the schooner *George Washington* off the South Carolina coast.

Commodore Samuel F. Du Pont informs the Navy Department that Confederate batteries have withdrawn from Skiddaway and Greene Island off the Georgia coast, granting his fleet control of Wassaw and Ossabaw sounds, along with the mouths of the Vernon and Wilmington rivers. The approaches to Savannah, Georgia, are now open.

March 28

SOUTH: General Oliver O. Howard's Union troops occupy Shipping Point, Virginia, to sever the Orange and Alexandria Railroad.

WEST: Union general Washington Morgan and his 7th Division are ordered to secure the Cumberland Gap in Tennessee, a strategic mountain pass connecting Tennessee, Kentucky, and western Virginia.

SOUTHWEST: A Union detachment at Johnson's Ranch near Glorietta Ranch, New Mexico Territory, is reinforced by a detachment under Colonel John P. Slough. Slough decides to attack the Confederates at nearby Apache Canyon and orders Major John Chivington, 1st Colorado Volunteers, and 450 men to march circuitously west around and to their right and rear. As this movement unfolds, a Confederate column under Colonel William R. Scurry simultaneously advances through Glorieta Pass and attacks Slough at Pigeon's Ranch. They drive the defenders hard but are gradually stopped by superior artillery and nightfall.

Meanwhile, Chivington marches around Apache Canyon and happens upon the lightly guarded Confederate baggage train at Johnson's Ranch. He immediately attacks, burning 90 supply wagons and killing 800 draft animals. Chivington then retraces his steps and rejoins Slough's main force at Koslowski's Ranch. The engagements at Glorieta Pass prove disastrous to Confederate fortunes in the Southwest. The loss of their entire commissary marked the end of General Henry H. Sibley's offensive, and he has little recourse but to withdraw back to Texas. Scurry reports his losses as 36 dead, 60 injured, and 25 missing out of 1,100, while Slough sustains 31 killed, 50 wounded, and 30 missing out of 1,345 engaged.

NAVAL: Armed boats under Lieutenant Thomas F. Stevens venture up St. John's River, Florida, and capture and raise the racing yacht *America,* which had been scuttled by Confederate sympathizers. The vessel subsequently is taken into U.S. naval service.

Commander Henry H. Bell takes the USS *Kennebec* on a close reconnaissance of Confederate river defenses below Forts Jackson and St. Philip, below New Orleans, Louisiana. This information allows Commodore David G. Farragut to formulate a precise plan of operations to bypass the forts.

March 29
SOUTH: Advanced elements of General John G. Parke's brigade land on Bogue Banks, Beaufort, North Carolina, and begin to surround nearby Fort Morgan.
WEST: Command of the Mountain Department switches from General William S. Rosecrans to General John C. Frémont.

General Albert S. Johnston assembles his Army of the Mississippi at Corinth, Mississippi, by amalgamating the Armies of Kentucky and Mississippi into a single structure with General Pierre G. T. Beauregard as second in command together with commanders Leonidas Polk (I Corps), Braxton Bragg (II Corps), William J. Hardee (III Corps), and George B. Crittenden (Reserve).
NAVAL: An armed boat from USS *Restless* captures the Confederate schooner *Lydia and Mary* in the Santee River, South Carolina.

The USS *R. R. Cuyler* captures the Confederate schooner *Grace E. Baker* off the Cuban coast.

March 30
WEST: Federal troops occupy Union City, Tennessee.

March 31
NORTH: The division of Union general Louis Blenker is ordered up from General George B. McClellan's Army of the Potomac by President Abraham Lincoln for the defense of Washington, D.C.
SOUTH: General David Hunter assumes command of the newly enlarged Department of the South (South Carolina, Georgia, Florida), with headquarters at Hilton Head, South Carolina.
WEST: Federal forces under General Lew Wallace skirmish with Confederates along the Purdy Road, Adamsville, Tennessee.

Federal troops occupy Union City, Tennessee.

Confederate general William W. Mackall arrives to replace General John P. McCown as commander of New Madrid Bend and Island No. 10 in the Mississippi River. McCown is relieved over his premature abandonment of New Madrid, Missouri, on March 13.

April 1
SOUTH: Headquarters, Army of the Potomac, is transferred from Alexandria to Fortress Monroe, Virginia.
WEST: Confederates under General Thomas J. Jackson withdraw up the Shenandoah Valley, screened by cavalry under Colonel Ashby Turner.

General Nathaniel P. Banks directs an advance of Federal troops from Strasburg, Virginia, to Woodstock and Edenburg.

General Benjamin Cheatham leads a Confederate reconnaissance of Federal positions at Pittsburg Landing, Tennessee, and reports that General Ulysses S. Grant apparently has divided his force.

NAVAL: CSS *Gaines* recaptures the former Confederate schooner *Isabelle* off Mobile, Alabama.

A combined expedition escorted by Federal gunboat USS *St. Louis* captures Fort No. 1 on the Tennessee shore, above Island No. 10 in the Mississippi River. The guns are spiked, and the expedition withdraws unmolested.

April 2

NORTH: Confederate spy Rose Greenhow is expelled from Washington, D.C., by Federal authorities.

SOUTH: General George B. McClellan and his staff arrive at Fortress Monroe, Virginia, preparatory to advancing on Confederate defenses at nearby Yorktown.

WEST: Skirmishing continues between opposing vedettes outside Pittsburg Landing, Tennessee, as General Pierre G. T. Beauregard conceives an overly complex order of battle. He places all three Confederate corps in three successive waves of attack, a tactic exacerbating mass confusion in the swirl of battle. The necessity of attacking gains additional currency once it is learned that the Army of the Ohio under General Don C. Buell departed Nashville and is only a few days away from joining General Ulysses S. Grant. General Albert S. Johnston determines to embark on a violent preemptive strike that, if successful, will prevent Federal forces from combining in overwhelming strength.

NAVAL: The USS *Mount Vernon, Fernandina,* and *Cambridge* capture and burn the Confederate schooner *Kate* off Wilmington, North Carolina.

April 3

POLITICS: The U.S. Senate abolishes slavery in the District of Columbia on a 29 to 14 vote.

Secretary of War Edwin M. Stanton, encouraged by the course of events thus far, mistakenly orders all U.S. recruiting offices closed.

NORTH: President Abraham Lincoln is angered that General George B. McClellan disobeys orders and assigns less than 20,000 men to the defense of Washington, D.C. He therefore insists that one full army corps be retained at the capital. Lincoln also orders offensive operations against Richmond, Virginia, to commence as soon as possible.

SOUTH: General George B. McClellan makes final preparations to direct his massive Army of the Potomac into combat. A talented disciplinarian and organizer, he commands a well-appointed force of 112,000 men.

WEST: Massed Confederate forces under General Albert S. Johnston decamp from Corinth, Mississippi, and grope toward Union positions at Pittsburg Landing, Tennessee. Their advance is dogged by driving rain and poor marching discipline, which many senior commanders fear will alert the defenders to their approach.

NAVAL: The USS *Susquehanna* captures the British blockade-runner *Coquette* off Charleston, South Carolina.

Commodore Samuel F. Du Pont orders the USS *Mohican* to reconnoiter up the Wilmington River and establish the best avenues of approach to Fort Pulaski, Georgia.

Armed boats dispatched from the USS *Isaac Smith* seize the British blockade-runner *British Empire* in Matanzas Inlet, Florida.

Armed boats from the USS *Mercedita* and *Sagamore* capture Apalachicola, Florida, seizing schooners *New Island, Floyd,* and *Rose,* along with the sloop *Octavia.*

April 4

NORTH: The new Departments of the Rappahannock and Shenandoah are constituted under Generals Irvin McDowell (I Corps) and Nathaniel P. Banks (V Corps), respectively.

SOUTH: With his army of 112,000 men assembled on the Yorktown Peninsula, General George B. McClellan begins his long-awaited drive on Richmond, Virginia. His first objective is to capture Yorktown and establish a base between the James and York rivers. In contrast to the slap-dash Union forces of the previous year, the Army of the Potomac is well trained and led, well equipped, and eager to prove its mettle in combat.

WEST: Confederate forces under General Albert S. Johnston continue advancing on Pittsburg Landing, Tennessee, impeded by heavy rains, yet Union forces remain blissfully ignorant of their approach.

NAVAL: The USS *Pursuit* captures the Confederate sloop *Lafayette* in St. Joseph's Bay, Florida.

A Union squadron consisting of USS *J. P. Jackson, New London,* and *Hatteras* lands 1,200 sailors and marines at Pass Christian, Mississippi. Confederate vessels CSS *Carondelet, Pamlico,* and *Oregon* briefly oppose their passage and then withdraw.

The USS *J. P. Jackson* captures the Confederate steamer *P. C. Wallis* off New Orleans, Louisiana.

Under the cover of darkness and rain, the USS *Carondelet* under Commander Henry Walke dashes past Confederate batteries on Island No. 10 in the Mississippi River. As a precaution, the vessel is outfitted with cordwood piled around its boilers, thickened deck planking, and an anchor chain placed as additional armor. The Southerners are now cut off from reinforcements downstream, and Union troops under General John Pope can safely cross the Mississippi River to the Tennessee shore.

April 5

POLITICS: General Andrew Johnson, military governor of his home state of Tennessee, suspends several city officials in Nashville for refusing to take an oath of allegiance.

SOUTH: The Army of the Potomac begins its Peninsula campaign with an advance on Yorktown, Virginia, then energetically defended by 15,000 Confederates under General John B. Magruder. Magruder cannot possibly match his adversary in strength, so he conducts elaborate ruses such as erecting false "Quaker guns" along his line and continually marches troops to give an impression of greater numbers. General George B. McClellan is completely duped by the deception, and rather than aggressively probe Confederate defenses along the Yorktown–Warwick River line, he commences siege operations. His overly cautious demeanor keeps the Army of the Potomac fixed in place for a month.

Union forces take and occupy Edisto Island, South Carolina.

WEST: Massed Confederates under General Albert S. Johnston prepare to strike at Union positions along Pittsburg Landing, Tennessee. Despite entreaties by General Pierre G. T. Beauregard and others to relent, Johnston determines to hit the invaders hard on the morrow. "I would fight them if they were a million," he reputedly declares. Curiously, the army of General Ulysses S. Grant bivouacks quiescently in camp, unaware of the swift fate rapidly descending on it.

NAVAL: Commodore David G. Farragut takes the USS *Iroquois* on a close reconnaissance of Forts Jackson and St. Philip on the Mississippi River. Farragut personally views the fortifications from a mast despite heavy enemy fire.

An armed boat launched from USS *Montgomery* captures and sinks the Confederate schooner *Columbia* near San Luis Pass, Texas.

April 6

SOUTH: Braxton Bragg is promoted to full general, C.S.A.

As General George B. McClellan dithers before Yorktown, Virginia, General Joseph E. Johnston accelerates a transfer of troops there from the Rappahannock River.

WEST: A Federal expedition advances from Greeneville, Tennessee, into the Laurel Valley, North Carolina.

On this momentous day, the Battle of Shiloh erupts at dawn as 44,000 Confederates under General Albert S. Johnston surprise 39,000 Federal troops under General Ulysses S. Grant in camp. Grant is then at his headquarters in Savannah, seven miles distant, and actual leadership devolves on General William T. Sherman. Despite continuing signs of an enemy presence to his front, Sherman takes no precautions. Consequently, the massed Southerners spill out of the adjoining woods at 5:30 A.M., and Union forces suffer complete tactical surprise. The three divisions of Generals Sherman, John A. McClernand, and Benjamin Prentiss attempt to form defensive lines but are repeatedly swept back by a surging gray tide. But Prentiss is luckier; he rallies 3,000 troops along a sunken road surrounded by densely wooded thickets situated directly in the enemy's path. Johnston's men sweep across various parts of the field and ultimately lap around both of Grant's flanks, but his drive in the center falters in the face of stout resistance from Prentiss's small band. They fight so fiercely that the Southerners dub this portion of the battlefield the "Hornets' Nest." General Braxton Bragg, wishing to maintain pressure on Prentiss to keep his forces pinned in position, forsakes maneuvering and launches no less than 12 frontal assaults—all of which are blasted back with heavy losses. General Johnston himself is hit while directing combat from his saddle, and he bleeds to death at about 2:30 P.M. General Pierre G. T. Beauregard then assumes tactical control

The 9th Illinois Infantry at the battle in Shiloh, Tennessee, where their 90-minute stand helped prepare the way for a great Union counterattack the next day *(National Guard Heritage)*

of the battle and orders up 62 cannon to bombard the Federals into submission. A tremendous pounding ensues, and Prentiss finally surrenders 2,000 battered survivors at 5:30 P.M. Beauregard is finally free to lead victorious Confederates against the final Union line.

Meanwhile, Grant returns to camp shortly after the fighting commences and begins to reorganize a coherent defense. The gallant stand of the Hornets' Nest grants him precious little time to sort out his shaken units, bring up new troops, and reestablish a defensive perimeter. He also orders the division of General Lew Wallace, stationed at Crump's Landing seven miles away, to march immediately toward Pittsburg Landing. As it turns out, that general botches his line of march and fails to arrive in a timely manner. Meanwhile, as the exhausted Confederates, low on ammunition and disorganized by intense combat push forward, they begin to lose impetus. Grant then strings his survivors out along a ridge crest fronting Pittsburg Landing, deploys his reserve artillery, and receives timely assistance from two navy gunboats on the Tennessee River. Beauregard briefly tests Grant's new line and judges it too compact and well defended to hit frontally with his exhausted soldiers.

He suspends the attack and determines to renew it in the morning. Unknown to the Confederates, Union positions are strengthened materially by the tardy arrival of Wallace's division that evening, along with elements of General Don C. Buell's Army of the Ohio. Grant, manifestly strengthened by this infusion of fresh troops and now enjoying numerical superiority, determines to strike first the following day.

NAVAL: The USS *Pursuit* captures the Confederate steamer *Florida* at North Bay, Florida.

The USS *Carondelet* drops farther down the Mississippi River on a reconnaissance foray from New Madrid, Missouri, to Tiptonville, where armed parties disembark and spike a Confederate shore battery.

Throughout the engagement at Shiloh, heavy and accurate fire from Federal gunboats USS *Tyler* and *Lexington* assists last-ditch Union defenses.

April 7

POLITICS: The U.S. government concludes a new agreement with Great Britain for more aggressive suppression of the slave trade.

SOUTH: Colonel Thomas J. Lucas leads the 16th Indiana on a reconnaissance over the Rappahannock River into Virginia.

Unions forces embark for an amphibious descent on Elizabeth City, North Carolina.

WEST: General John Pope lands four regiments across the Mississippi River to Tiptonville, Tennessee, severing the supply lines of Confederate-held Island No. 10. The garrison is now completely isolated.

General Ormsby M. Mitchel recruits noted Union spy James J. Andrews for a clandestine raid behind Confederate lines to sabotage railroad links between Atlanta, Georgia, and Chattanooga, Tennessee. Andrews then solicits 22 volunteers from General Joshua W. Sill's Ohio brigade and gradually slips them in by small teams to Marietta, Georgia.

The struggle at Shiloh resumes at 7:30 A.M. as Union forces under General Ulysses S. Grant, newly reinforced, mount a spirited counterattack to regain ground lost in the previous day's fighting. The Confederates under General Pierre G. T. Beauregard resist gamely but slowly yield to superior numbers. The blue tide advances inexorably across the field, and by 2:30, the Southerners are in full retreat back to Corinth, 23 miles away. Both sides then begin the grim business of tallying the results of their work.

Casualties at Shiloh shock both North and South alike due to their sheer enormity. Grant, with 65,000 men engaged, loses 1,754 killed, 8,408 wounded, and 2,885 missing (13,047) while the 44,400 Confederates present sustain 1,728 dead, 8,012 injured, and 959 missing (10,694). The grim reality of the Civil War and the carnage it ultimately entails finally emerge in bold relief. Worse, the Confederates staked everything on an all-out assault that failed. Once defeated, their position in the West erodes even further, and only the solitary bastion at Vicksburg, Mississippi, stands between the South and gradual dismemberment. Nor did the victorious Grant escape recriminations for such slaughter; even though Sherman technically commanded at the onset and is culpable of being surprised in camp, Grant's reputation as "the Butcher" begins to be heard in some quarters.

NAVAL: The Confederate raider CSS *Sumter* is laid up at Gibraltar and abandoned by Captain Raphael Semmes after experiencing boiler difficulties. In the course of its brief career, it seized no less than 18 Northern vessels.

The Federal ironclads USS *Pensacola* and *Mississippi* traverse the bar at the Passes and enter the Mississippi River, prior to moving against New Orleans, Louisiana.

The Federal gunboat USS *Pittsburgh* sails past Island No. 10 on the Mississippi River and joins the *Carondelet* in covering General John Pope's army, then ferrying to the Tennessee side. The gunboat squadron under Commodore Andrew H. Foote also captures heavy ordnance and several Confederate steamers moored there. He consequently receives a vote of thanks from Congress.

April 8

POLITICS: President Jefferson Davis proclaims martial law in East Tennessee to suppress activities of pro-Union inhabitants.

SOUTH: General Joseph Finegan assumes control of the Confederate Department of Middle and Eastern Florida.

WEST: General William W. Mackall surrenders the Confederate garrison of 4,500 men on Island No. 10 to General John Pope. Union forces sustain seven killed, 14 wounded, and seven missing, principally among naval personnel. They also capture 109 heavy cannon, four steamers, and vast quantities of military supplies while extending Union control of the Mississippi River as far south as Fort Pillow, Tennessee. Considering the difficult terrain and currents encountered, Pope performed well. Moreover, his victory constitutes another serious breech of Confederate defenses. President Abraham Lincoln consequently assigns him to command the newly organized Army of Virginia back east.

Federal troops under General Ulysses S. Grant advance from Pittsburg Landing, Tennessee, in pursuit of General Pierre G. T. Beauregard's withdrawing Confederates. General William T. Sherman pursues them briefly but is capably contained by General Nathan B. Forrest's rear guard.

SOUTHWEST: Pursuing Union forces under Colonel Edward R. S. Canby harry General Henry H. Sibley's Confederates as they retreat from Albuquerque, New Mexico Territory.

NAVAL: Commodore David G. Farragut runs the last of his West Gulf Blockading Squadron vessels over the Southwest Pass bar and into the Mississippi River. He then assembles 24 warships, mounting 200 large-caliber guns and 19 mortar schooners under Commander David D. Porter, at Head of Passes. But before steaming toward New Orleans, Louisiana, Farragut must first encounter and bypass Forts Jackson and St. Philip, 80 miles from the city.

April 9

POLITICS: President Abraham Lincoln, flummoxed by General George B. McClellan's lack of aggressiveness, confers with his cabinet over what to do. The chief executive then suggests several lines of attack for the Army of the Potomac to consider and entreats McClellan to attack immediately, insisting, "But you must act."

The Confederate Congress approves a conscription measure over the protest of many politicians who consider the practice a violation of their liberties.

WEST: Command of the Confederate Missouri State Guard passes to General Mosby M. Parsons.

NAVAL: Confederate secretary of the navy Stephen R. Mallory, convinced that the biggest threat to New Orleans, Louisiana, is the Mississippi River squadron of Commodore Andrew H. Foote, refuses to allow the Confederate squadron at Fort Pillow, Tennessee, to shift theaters.

Union forces evacuate Jacksonville, Florida, under the cover of USS *Ottawa, Pembina,* and *Ellen.*

April 10

POLITICS: President Abraham Lincoln signs a joint congressional resolution stipulating gradual emancipation of African-American slaves. It is aimed primarily at the border states and offers "pecuniary aid" in exchange for voluntary compliance.

SOUTH: General Joseph E. Johnston takes command of Confederate forces in the Peninsula District of Virginia, and reinforcements gradually bring Southern manpower up to 34,000. Johnston nonetheless remains pessimistic about resisting the Army of the Potomac, thrice his size, for long.

After weeks of methodical preparation, Union artillery commanded by Captain Quincy A. Gilmore commence shelling Fort Pulaski on Cockspur Island in Savannah harbor. This strategic post, boasting masonry walls seven and a half feet thick, is occupied by Colonel Charles H. Olmstead, 48 cannon, and a garrison of 385 Confederates. Gilmore, meanwhile, directs the placement of 11 batteries on Tybee Island, containing 36 heavy guns and mortars that ring the fort at a distance between 1,650 and 3,400 yards. Union general Thomas W. Sherman implores Olmstead to surrender, but he haughtily replies: "I am here to defend this fort, not to surrender it." Gilmore then gives the order to fire at 8:15 A.M., and his highly accurate, rifled Parrott cannons loose penetrating shells that systematically decimate Fort Pulaski's defenses. By nightfall several large breeches are observed in Olmstead's walls, through which Union shells begin to strike his reinforced gunpowder magazine.

WEST: General John M. Schofield assumes command of Union forces in Missouri while General Samuel R. Curtis heads the new District of Kansas.

NAVAL: The USS *Whitehead* captures the Confederate schooners *Comet* and *J. J. Crittenden* and the sloop *America* in Newbegun Creek, North Carolina.

A detachment from USS *Wabash* manned Battery Sigel during the capture of Fort Pulaski, Georgia. They are cordially invited to come ashore and participate by General David Hunter, overall army commander.

The USS *Keystone State* runs the British blockade-runner *Liverpool* aground at North Inlet, South Carolina, where it was burned by its crew.

Gunboat USS *Kanawha* seizes blockade-runners *Southern Independence, Victoria, Charlotte,* and *Cuba* off Mobile, Alabama.

April 11

POLITICS: Following the Senate's cue, the U.S. House of Representatives votes 93–39 to abolish slavery gradually in the District of Columbia.

SOUTH: Fort Pulaski, Georgia, surrenders to Union captain Quincy A. Gilmore following a heavy bombardment by 5,275 shells from nearby Tybee Island. Union losses are one killed while the Confederates sustain one dead, 13 wounded, and 360 captured. This battle marks the first tactical employment of long-range, rifled cannon with impressive results against masonry defenses. Moreover, the Union victory here jeopardizes the city of Savannah, Georgia, eliminating it as a blockade-running port.

WEST: General Henry W. Halleck supersedes General Ulysses S. Grant at Pittsburg Landing, Tennessee, although he still commands the District of West Tennessee. Leadership of the Army of the Tennessee temporarily reverts to General George H. Thomas.

Union forces under General Ormsby M. Mitchel sever the Memphis and Charleston Railroad by occupying Huntsville, Alabama. They defeat the Confederates of General Edmund Kirby-Smith en route, taking several hundred prisoners in the process.

NAVAL: The Confederate ironclad CSS *Virginia* under Commodore Josiah Tattnall suddenly reappears off Hampton Roads, Virginia. Escorting vessels CSS *Jamestown* and Raleigh under Captain John R. Tucker capture three Union transports but fail to bring on a second duel with the USS *Monitor* offshore.

April 12

SOUTH: General Joseph E. Johnston's command authority is enlarged to include the Departments of Norfolk and the Peninsula, Virginia.

General John B. Magruder's Confederate army at Yorktown, Virginia, is augmented by additional divisions under General James Longstreet, Daniel H. Hill, and Gustavus W. Smith. These are arrayed against the full might of the Army of the Potomac, then consisting of the II Corps of General Edwin V. Sumner, the III Corps of General Samuel Heintzelman, and the IV Corps under General Erasmus Keyes. General William B. Franklin's division, detached from I Corps, also hovers in reserve.

WEST: Cavalry dispatched by General Benjamin F. Kelley snares numerous Confederate operatives in Valley River and Boothville in western Virginia.

Major James J. Andrews and 22 Union volunteers steal the Confederate locomotive *General* and three freight cars at Big Shanty, Georgia, and then head north toward Chattanooga, Tennessee. Their mission is to destroy railroad bridges leading into the city, but the plan is thwarted by rainy weather. Worse, Confederate soldiers hotly pursue in another engine, and the chase continues for 90 miles. When the *General* finally runs out of steam and is abandoned, Andrews and his men flee to the woods where the majority are captured. Andrews and seven volunteers, seized out of uniform, are executed as spies on June 7, 1862, but eight men eventually escape captivity while the rest are exchanged. The raiders become the U.S. Army's first recipients of the Congressional Medal of Honor in March 1863. This affair enters popular folklore as the "Great Locomotive Chase."

NAVAL: Secretary of the Navy Gideon Welles implores President Abraham Lincoln to forbid the export of anthracite coal abroad and thus keep it out of Confederate hands. Since this fuel burns cleanly, it allows blockade-runners to approach ports without detection, whereas steam engines powered by regular coal belch forth black clouds more easily perceived at sea.

April 13
SOUTH: General David Hunter, commanding the vicinity of Fort Pulaski, Georgia, declares his region free of slavery and unilaterally begins to free all African Americans within his jurisdiction.

WEST: Federal troops under General Ormsby M. Mitchel occupy Decatur, Alabama, on the Tennessee River.

SOUTHWEST: Union troops under Colonel Edward R. S. Canby skirmish with retreating Confederates at Peralta, New Mexico Territory.

General James H. Carleton leads a column of troops from California into western Arizona and ultimately drives remaining Confederate forces out of New Mexico Territory.

NAVAL: USS *Beauregard* shells the Confederate garrison at Fort Brooke, Tampa Bay, Florida, after it refuses his surrender summons.

A coastal survey party under Ferdinand H. Gerdes begins to map the Mississippi River approaches below Forts Jackson and St. Philip.

Federal gunboats USS *Tyler* and *Lexington* convey Union troops from Shiloh, Tennessee, to Chickasaw, Alabama, and destroy a bridge operated by the Memphis and Charleston Railroad.

April 14
SOUTH: John C. Breckinridge and Thomas C. Hindman are appointed major generals, C.S.A.

A high-level war meeting convenes in Richmond, Virginia, whereby General Joseph E. Johnston, badly outnumbered by the 112,000 strong Army of the Potomac, pleads with superiors to abandon the Yorktown–Warwick River line before General George B. McClellan attacks in overwhelming strength. However, President Jefferson Davis and his chief military adviser, General Robert E. Lee, demur, observing that withdrawing necessitates the abandonment of Norfolk and its valuable naval facilities.

WEST: In Missouri, Union forces tangle with Confederate irregulars under William C. Quantrill.

NAVAL: The Potomac Flotilla sails down the Rappahannock River, Virginia, shelling Confederate positions and capturing three vessels.

Federal mortar boats under Commodore Andrew H. Foote commence bombarding Fort Pillow, Tennessee, on the Mississippi River. This fortification is located 60 miles south of Island No. 10 and guards the northern approaches to Memphis. Intermittent bombardment continues for the next seven weeks.

April 15
SOUTH: At a special war council held in Richmond, Virginia, President Jefferson Davis breaks the strategic impasse by ordering General Joseph E. Johnston to move his army to Yorktown on the Virginia Peninsula and reinforce General John B. Magruder. A somewhat disgruntled Johnston returns to his command and prepares to march.

A detachment of the 1st Maine Cavalry under Captain Robert F. Dyer is repulsed at Bealeton, Virginia.

WEST: Confederate troops commanded by General Earl Van Dorn are ordered to Memphis, Tennessee.

SOUTHWEST: Pursuing Union forces under Colonel Edward R. S. Canby continue skirmishing with General Henry H. Sibley's Confederates at Peralta, 20 miles south of Albuquerque, New Mexico Territory. The Southerners are bested in a series of running battles as they retire toward Fort Bliss.

NAVAL: The USS *Chenango*, anchored at New York, experiences a boiler explosion that kills 25 sailors.

The USS *Keystone State* captures the Confederate blockade-runner *Success* off Georgetown, South Carolina.

April 16

POLITICS: President Abraham Lincoln signs a bill outlawing slavery in the District of Columbia on a compensated basis—$300 per slave. However, slaves escaping from masters loyal to the Union still remain subject to return under the existing Fugitive Slave Law.

With Union forces only 10 miles from his capital and a stream of bad news from the West, President Jefferson Davis authorizes conscription to maintain Confederate military manpower levels. Consequently, all white males aged 18 to 35 become eligible for three years of service. This is the first conscription legislation in U.S. history.

SOUTH: Union General William F. Smith tests Confederate defenses on the Virginia Peninsula by probing Dam No. 1 along the Warwick River line. He then attacks at Burnt Chimneys with the 3rd, 4th, and 6th Vermont regiments and is repelled with 165 casualties. This small reverse convinces General George B. McClellan of the necessity to erect siege works to flush the defenders from their lines.

An advance to Whitemarsh Island, Georgia, by Union general Quincy A. Gilmore results in heavy skirmishing.

WEST: Union forces attack and occupy Tuscumbia, Alabama.

NAVAL: Commodore David G. Farragut begins to mass 17 warships of his West Gulf Blockading Squadron, including the gunboat squadron of Commodore David D. Porter, below Forts Jackson and St. Philip, Louisiana. These aged structures, one on each side of the Mississippi River, are situated 12 miles above Head of Passes, mount 90 cannon, and are further abetted by a "Mosquito Squadron" of small warships under Captain George N. Hollis. Unfortunately for the defenders, the waterway runs extremely high, which floods Confederate defensive positions and lifts Unions vessel above numerous obstacles placed in their path to block them.

April 17

SOUTH: General Irvin McDowell and his Federal troops skirmish near Falmouth, Virginia, and occupy neighboring Fredericksburg.

New Confederate reinforcements bring the strength of General Joseph E. Johnston's force along the Yorktown-Warwick River line up to 53,000. He nonetheless remains badly outnumbered by the nearby Army of the Potomac, which fields roughly twice as many troops.

WEST: Union forces under General Nathaniel P. Banks occupy Mount Jackson in western Virginia, following a skirmish at Rude's Hill. Confederate forces under General Thomas J. Jackson continue withdrawing before them.

The 36th Ohio under Major Ebenezer B. Andrews tangles with Confederate irregulars between Summerville and Addison, western Virginia.

Quick action by General Edmund Kirby-Smith's Confederates snares 475 Union stragglers at Woodson's Gap, Tennessee.

NAVAL: Commodore David G. Farragut's fleet of 17 warships begins to wend its way up the Mississippi River toward New Orleans, Louisiana. He is also accompanied by a flotilla of 20 mortar boats under Commander David D. Porter.

April 18

NORTH: In an attempt to promote younger, more vigorous leadership, Congress suspends seniority within the ranks of the Army Medical Bureau.

SOUTH: General Joseph Finegan takes charge of the Confederate Department of Middle and East Florida.

General Irvin McDowell marches south and occupies the towns of Falmouth and Yorktown, Virginia.

WEST: General Robert E. Lee orders General Edward Johnson and his Army of the Northwest to coordinate his movements in the Shenandoah Valley.

NAVAL: Landing parties from the USS *Crusader* attack Edisto Island, South Carolina.

Commodore David G. Farragut dispatches Commander David D. Porter with 20 mortar boats to bombard Forts Jackson and St. Philip on the Mississippi River. Porter, convinced he can neutralize these positions with firepower alone, pelts them with 200-pound mortar shells for the next five days. Farragut's movement positions him only 70 miles below the strategic port of New Orleans, Louisiana, and Confederates pin their hopes on the two old forts and an array of sunken hulks and river chains to prevent further Union progress upstream.

April 19

SOUTH: The forces of Generals Ambrose E. Burnside and Benjamin Huger tangle at South Mills, Camden County, South Carolina.

WEST: Sparta in western Virginia is occupied by Federal troops under General Nathaniel P. Banks. Confederates under General Thomas J. Jackson, meanwhile, strike their encampment at Rude Hill and head farther south.

NAVAL: The USS *Huron* captures the Confederate schooner *Glide* off Charleston, South Carolina.

Artillery fire from Fort Jackson, Louisiana, sinks the Federal mortar boat USS *Maria J. Carlton.*

Under the cover of darkness, the USS *Itasca* and *Pinola* advance below Forts Jackson and St. Philip to cut the chain and remove obstructions placed on the Mississippi River. They are assisted greatly by the absence of fire rafts that would have illuminated them as targets—a major Confederate oversight. The river gradually is rendered navigable for Commodore David G. Farragut's fleet.

April 20
SOUTH: General Irvin McDowell confers with President Abraham Lincoln at Aquia Creek, Virginia, and subsequently accompanies him to Washington, D.C.
WEST: General Edward Johnson's Confederate army of the Northwest retreats eastward from Shenandoah Mountain, western Virginia, pressured by a larger Union forces under General John C. Frémont.
NAVAL: The Potomac Flotilla captures nine Confederate vessels at the mouth of the Rappahannock River, Virginia.

April 21
POLITICS: To offset the manpower advantages of the North, the Confederate government authorizes creation of guerrilla formations by passing the Partisan Ranger Act and then adjourns its first session.

Members of the Brownlow family and several other Union sympathizers are evicted from Confederate-held East Tennessee.
WEST: Union forces under General John Pope, having secured Island No. 10, cross back over the Mississippi to assist ongoing efforts in Tennessee.
NAVAL: The Federal gunboat USS *Tyler* seizes the Confederate steamer *Alfred Robb* on the Tennessee River.

April 22
POLITICS: Secretary of War Edwin M. Stanton appoints engineer and inventor Herman Haupt to serve as chief of construction and transportation for U.S. military railroads. The appointment proves fortuitous, and Haupt discharges his duties with efficiency and dispatch.
SOUTH: Advancing Union forces occupy Harrisonburg, Virginia.

General William B. Franklin's division arrives at Fortress Monroe, Virginia, to reinforce the Army of the Potomac.
WEST: General Nathaniel P. Banks occupies Luray in western Virginia.
NAVAL: Armed boats from the USS *Arthur* capture three Confederate vessels at Aransas Pass, Texas, and then just as quickly yield them to attacking enemy troops.

April 23
NAVAL: The USS *Lockwood, Whitehead,* and *Putnam* sink a schooner at the mouth of the Albemarle and Chesapeake Canal near Elizabeth City, North Carolina, closing another useful waterway to the South.

Commodore David G. Farragut, impatient for success and concluding that the bombardment of Forts Jackson and St. Philip is having no effect, decides to run his entire fleet past the fortifications at night.

April 24
NAVAL: The CSS *Nashville,* crammed with 60,000 stands of arms and 40 tons of gunpowder, successfully runs the Union blockade and slips into Wilmington, North Carolina.

At 2:00 A.M. in the predawn darkness, Commodore David G. Farragut runs his fleet of 17 vessels past Forts Jackson and St. Philip on the Mississippi River, in

Flag Officer Farragut's squadron passes the forts on the Mississippi, April 24, 1862, and the U.S. frigate *Mississippi* destroys the rebel ram *Manassas*. Lithograph by Currier & Ives *(Library of Congress)*

three divisions. Confederate defenders under General Johnson K. Duncan unleash a heavy cannonade, but they inflict very little loss. Farragut's flagship, USS *Hartford*, is briefly endangered by a fire raft while the USS *Varuna* is rammed and sinks. But in the ensuing scrape, Commander John K. Mitchell's Southern squadron, including CSS *Warrior, Stonewall Jackson, General Lovell,* and *Breckinridge,* along with steamers *Star, Belle Algerine,* and gunboat *General Quitman,* all succumb to concentrated Union fire. The armored ram CSS *Manassas* is also run ashore and destroyed. With this single, decisive stroke, the fate of New Orleans, Louisiana, is decided. Farragut then sails directly down to the helpless city, intent on bombarding it into submission. Union losses tally 39 killed and 146 wounded while the Confederates sustain nine dead and 33 injured.

April 25

NORTH: George H. Thomas is promoted to major general, U.S. Army.

SOUTH: Federal forces under General John G. Parke commence the bombardment of Fort Macon on Bogue Banks Island off Beaufort, North Carolina. The Confederate garrison only could sputter in reply with a few old cannon while sustaining 25 casualties. At length, Colonel Moses J. White surrenders, and 300 Southerners pass into captivity. The main Union force under General Ambrose E. Burnside is now at liberty to conduct deep forays into the surrounding countryside.

General David Hunter proclaims martial law in his Department of the South (South Carolina, Georgia, Florida).

Confederate general Mansfield Lovell and his 4,000 soldiers quickly slip out of New Orleans, Louisiana, and escape inland before Union occupation forces arrive.

WEST: Charles F. Smith, a talented Union general, dies of a septic leg infection at Savannah, Tennessee.

NAVAL: The USS *Maratanza* bombards Gloucester and Yorktown, Virginia, to assist the Army of the Potomac.

The squadron of Commander Samuel Lockwood, consisting of USS *Daylight, State of Georgia, Chippewa,* and *Gemsbok,* bombards Fort Macon, North Carolina, into submission. Confederate blockade-runners *Alliance* and *Gondar* are also captured.

The USS *Santiago de Cuba* captures the Confederate blockade-runner *Ella Warley* off Port Royal, South Carolina.

The Union flotilla under Commodore David G. Farragut captures the city of New Orleans, Louisiana, following a brief duel with Confederate gunners at English Turn. The Mississippi River is running high and enables the fleet to point its guns over the levee. Union landing parties are met nonetheless by angry, hostile demonstrations at the water's edge while hundreds of valuable cotton bales are burned to prevent capture. But the Confederacy loses its largest and wealthiest seaport while the North acquires a splendid base for operations directly into the Southern heartland.

NAVAL: The uncompleted CSS *Mississippi,* one of the largest and most powerful ironclads afloat, is destroyed by Confederate authorities at New Orleans, Louisiana, to prevent its capture.

The USS *Katahdin* captures the Confederate schooner *John Gilpin* below New Orleans, Louisiana.

April 26

POLITICS: President Abraham Lincoln pays a courtesy call on the French warship *Gassendi,* anchored at the Washington Navy Yard.

NORTH: Alfred H. Terry is appointed a brigadier general, U.S. Army.

SOUTH: Fort Macon, North Carolina, is occupied by Union forces under General John G. Parke.

WEST: Union forces under General Nathaniel P. Banks advance into New Market, western Virginia.

NAVAL: The USS *Onward* destroys the Confederate schooner *Chase* off Raccoon Key, South Carolina.

The USS *Flambeau* captures the Confederate blockade-runner *Active* off Stono Inlet, South Carolina.

The USS *Santiago de Cuba* captures the Confederate schooner *Mersey* off Charleston, South Carolina.

The USS *Uncas* captures the Confederate schooner *Belle* off Charleston, South Carolina.

April 27

SOUTH: General Joseph E. Johnston orders General Benjamin Huger to evacuate Norfolk, Virginia, and salvage as much equipment as possible from the Gosport Navy Yard.

NAVAL: The USS *Mercedita* captures the Confederate steamer *Bermuda* northeast of Abaco.

The USS *Wamsutta* and *Potomska* trade fire with dismounted Confederate cavalry at Wookville Island, Riceboro River, Georgia.

U.S. naval forces accept the surrender of Fort Livingston on Bastian Bay, Louisiana, and crew members from the USS *Kittatinny* hoist the Stars and Stripes flag over its ramparts. Nearby Forts Quitman, Pike, and Wood also capitulate that afternoon.

April 28

NORTH: James H. Carleton is appointed brigadier general, U.S. Army.

SOUTH: General John H. Forney assumes command of the Confederate Department of Alabama and West Florida.

WEST: General John Pope directs a skirmish against Confederates at Monterey, Tennessee.

NAVAL: Confederate Forts Jackson and St. Philip on the Mississippi River mutiny against the commanding general, John K. Duncan and surrender 900 prisoners to Union forces under Commander David D. Porter. The unfinished ironclad CSS *Louisiana*, the *Defiance*, and the *McRae* are also burned to prevent capture.

The British steamer *Oreto* arrives at Nassau, Bahamas, where Confederate sailors wait to man it. It eventually emerges as the CSS *Florida*.

April 29

SOUTH: A skittish general Joseph E. Johnston, cognizant of the vast array of Union siege artillery being mounted against his army along the Yorktown–Warwick River line, informs superiors that he is withdrawing inland as soon as it becomes practical. Johnston reasons that it is better to sacrifice Norfolk than his entire army and suggests a new concentration closer to Richmond.

Timothy Webster, a talented spy working for Allan Pinkerton's Federal Secret Service, is hanged by Confederate authorities at Richmond, Virginia.

The 29th Massachusetts skirmishes at Batchelder's Creek, North Carolina.

City officials formally surrender New Orleans, Louisiana, to Federal authorities. Raising of the U.S. flag over the Customs House arouses much indignation from the inhabitants.

WEST: General Thomas J. Jackson departs Staunton, western Virginia, by dispatching cavalry under Colonel Turner Ashby toward Harrisonburg while he leads the main force toward Port Republic.

Union forces occupy Purdy, Tennessee.

General Henry W. Halleck prepares to move from Pittsburg Landing, Tennessee, against Confederate forces under General Pierre G. T. Beauregard at Corinth, Mississippi. Halleck commands in excess of 100,000 troops.

NAVAL: Landing parties from the gunboat USS *E. B. Hale* destroy a Confederate battery on the Dawho River, South Carolina. On the return route, their vessel is ambushed downstream by troops under General Nathan G. Evans, but Lieutenant Alexander C. Rhind, who previously orders his crew and passengers to lay on the deck, sustains no losses and returns to Edisto Island unharmed.

The USS *Kanawha* captures the British blockade-runner *Annie* in the Gulf of Mexico.

April 30

WEST: Confederate forces under General Thomas J. Jackson march from Elk Run, western Virginia, toward Staunton in a driving rain. There, he intends to confront the 20,000-man army under General John C. Frémont, then advancing from the west. For the next four days, Jackson hounds his command as they cover 92 miles on foot and then ride another 25 miles by rail. This proves one of the most impressive forced marches of the entire war and garners to troops involved the sobriquet of Jackson's "Foot Cavalry."

General Henry W. Halleck finalizes a reorganization of his Armies of the Mississippi to include General Ulysses S. Grant as second in command, George H. Thomas and the Army of the Tennessee (right wing), John Pope and the Army of the Mississippi (left wing), John A. McClernand (reserve wing), and Don C. Buell and the Army of the Ohio. This aggregate of 120,000 troops is the largest military force ever assembled in North America to date. Halleck then orders a concerted, cautious advance on the strategic railroad junction at Corinth, Mississippi, presently defended by 53,000 Confederates under General Pierre G. T. Beauregard.

NAVAL: The USS *Santiago de Cuba* captures the Confederate schooner *Maria* off Port Royal, South Carolina.

May 1

NORTH: William T. Sherman is appointed major general, U.S. Army.

WEST: General Richard S. Ewell takes his 8,500-man division to Swift Run Gap, western Virginia, where he relieves forces under General Thomas J. Jackson.

SOUTH: General George B. McClellan begins to deploy heavy siege ordnance to facilitate the fall of Yorktown, Virginia.

New Orleans, Louisiana, is occupied formally by 15,000 Federal troops under General Benjamin F. Butler, who ushers in a period of controversial and acrimonious administration.

WEST: Union troops under General Jacob D. Cox skirmish with Confederates in the Stone River valley in western Virginia.

NAVAL: The USS *Marblehead* bombards Confederate positions at Yorktown, Virginia.

The USS *Jamestown* captures the British blockade-runner *Intended* off the North Carolina coast.

The USS *Huron* captures the Confederate schooner *Albert* off Charleston, South Carolina.

The USS *Onward* forces the crew of the Confederate schooner *Sarah* to scuttle their own vessel.

The USS *Hatteras* captures the Confederate schooner *Magnolia* near Berwick Bay, Louisiana.

May 2

NORTH: John Gibbon is appointed brigadier general, U.S. Army.

SOUTH: Edward Stanly becomes Federal military governor of North Carolina.

The Army of the Potomac, stalled before illusionary defenses along the York-town–Warwick River line in Virginia's Yorktown Peninsula, readies a huge battery of more than 100 heavy guns and mortars. General George B. McClellan prepares to blast the Confederates out of their entrenchments rather than risk heavy casualties from a frontal assault.

WEST: General James G. Blunt takes charge of the newly reconstituted Department of Kansas.

NAVAL: The USS *Restless* captures the British blockade-runner *Flash* off the South Carolina coast.

May 3

SOUTH: General Joseph E. Johnston begins to withdraw 55,000 Confederate troops from Yorktown, Virginia, before heavy Union siege ordnance starts to shoot. At midnight, Southern artillery erupts along the line to distract Union attention from the operation. General George B. McClellan, observing Confederate works the following day, is surprised but relieved that Johnston's army has vanished. The Army of the Potomac now begins to move up the Yorkstown Peninsula as the retreating Southerners funnel through Williamsburg toward Richmond.

WEST: Skirmishing occurs between General Henry W. Halleck and General Pierre G. T. Beauregard at Farmington, Mississippi, as Union forces begin their belated advance on Corinth.

NAVAL: The USS *R. R. Cuyler* captured the Confederate schooner *Jane* off Tampa Bay, Florida.

May 4

SOUTH: After a month-long siege, Union forces finally occupy the Confederate Yorktown-Warwick River line of Virginia's Yorktown Peninsula. General George B. McClellan methodically begins to pursue the enemy by advancing upon the old colonial capital of Williamsburg in overwhelming strength. The movement of both sides is hampered by continual downpours, which turn the roads to mud.

Skirmishing erupts between cavalry forces of Generals George B. Stoneman and J. E. B. Stuart near Williamsburg, Virginia. Fighting there induces a rear guard to form under General James Longstreet, who occupies a prepositioned line of redoubts centering on a bastion dubbed Fort Magruder. The Confederates enjoy the better of the day's fighting once General Lafayette McLaws charges and overturns Union cavalry and artillery commanded by General Philip St. George Cooke.

WEST: Skirmishing continues between General Henry W. Halleck and Pierre G. T. Beauregard at Farmington Heights, Mississippi.

SOUTHWEST: Confederate forces evacuate Tucson, New Mexico Territory, ahead of the "California column" of General James H. Carleton. Meanwhile, the main

Southern force under General Henry H. Sibley straggles into El Paso, Texas, after an arduous, failed endeavor.

Naval: The USS *Corwin* captures the Confederate schooner *Director* in the York River, Virginia.

Crew members of the USS *Wachusetts* hoist the U.S. flag over Gloucester Point, Virginia, while two Confederate schooners are captured.

The USS *Calhoun* captures the Confederate schooner *Charles Henry* of St. Joseph, Louisiana, and also raises the American flag over nearby Fort Pike.

The USS *Somerset* captures the Confederate steamer *Circassian* at sea.

May 5

Politics: President Abraham Lincoln and Secretary of War Edwin M. Stanton board the steamer *Miami* and sail to Hampton Roads, Virginia, to prod General George B. McClellan into greater action.

Congress authorizes creation of the Department of Agriculture.

South: A Union force of 41,000 men commanded by General Edwin V. Sumner confronts a determined Confederate rear guard numbering 32,000 at Williamsburg, Virginia. Sumner initially brings up two divisions under Generals Joseph Hooker and William F. Smith, who deploy to attack the defenders head on. However, Confederate forces under General James Longstreet are positioned ably at Fort Magruder in the center of the line and repulse Hooker's onslaught with heavy casualties. At this juncture, the commanding general, Joseph E. Johnston, gallops up with reinforcements, although he allows Longstreet to continue fighting. Longstreet, sensing confusion in Union ranks, suddenly launches a sharp counterattack against their left, pushing Hooker's men back in confusion and capturing several cannon. For several desperate minutes, it appears that his division might be destroyed piecemeal, save for the appearance of reinforcements under General Philip Kearny, who promptly drives the disorganized Southerners back inside their works.

On the Confederate left, events shape up more favorably for the North. General Smith detaches General William S. Hancock's brigade on a two-hour, circuitous march around Longstreet's flank, and by dint of adroit maneuvering, he suddenly appears behind the Confederate line at about 3:00 p.m. Hancock then pours in a heavy artillery fire on the defenders until two Confederate brigades under General Jubal A. Early and Daniel H. Hill are ordered up to outflank him. Unfortunately, both commanders are disoriented by the intervening march and deploy directly in front of Hancock's well-positioned troops. The aggressive Early and Hill nonetheless launch disjointed frontal assaults against the Union line, which are blasted back with heavy losses. But despite this tactical success, Sumner fails to follow it up with a decisive attack of his own, and an impasse settles across the battlefield. Fighting stops by nightfall, the Confederates withdraw unmolested, Johnston resumes his retrograde movement back toward Richmond.

Williamsburg, the first encounter of the Peninsula campaign, is both indecisive and characterized by heavy casualties: the Union suffers 456 killed, 1,410 wounded, and 373 missing (2,239) while the Confederacy lose 133 dead and 1,570 injured (1,703). Thanks to Sumner's mishandling of events, Union forces waged a contest that they should have won easily, whereas the Confederates again manage to avoid decisive defeat.

WEST: General Thomas J. Jackson's Confederates occupy Staunton in western Virginia, where he unites with General Edward Johnson's Army of the Northwest. Both men then advance with 10,000 men against nearby Union forces under General Robert H. Milroy.

NAVAL: An armed boat from the USS *Corwin* captures the Confederate sloop *Water Witch* near Gloucester, Virginia.

The USS *Calhoun* captures the Confederate schooner *Rover* on Lake Pontchartrain, Louisiana.

May 6

SOUTH: Williamsburg, Virginia, is occupied by the Army of the Potomac under General George B. McClellan.

WEST: General Thomas J. Jackson bests Union troops under General Nathaniel P. Banks in a heavy skirmish at Harrisonburg, western Virginia, and then marches his Confederates on a 35-mile trek through the mountains toward McDowell. Banks, meanwhile, withdraws in confusion to New Market.

NAVAL: The USS *Ottawa* seizes the Confederate schooner *General C. C. Pinckney* off Charleston, South Carolina.

The USS *Calhoun* captures the Confederate steamer *Whiteman* on Lake Pontchartrain, Louisiana.

May 7

SOUTH: Union and Confederate forces under Generals William B. Franklin and Gustavus W. Smith clash at Eltham's Landing, Virginia, to contest the road from Yorktown to Richmond. Franklin lands part of his division on the south bank of the York River to harass the Confederate left flank as it withdraws from Williamsburg. Smith, tasked with guarding the passage of the entire Confederate baggage train, is cognizant of the danger posed by Franklin's presence and orders General William C. Whiting's division to dislodge him. The Confederates, particularly General John B. Hood's Texas brigade, press the Union pickets hard, pushing them through the woods and under the cover of gunboats in the river. At that point Whiting relents and withdraws, and Franklin's men do not follow. The Confederate wagon train thereby retires intact. Southern losses amount to 48, whereas the Union sustains 186, including 46 captured.

The 6th Pennsylvania Cavalry under Major Robert Morris conducts a reconnaissance toward Mulberry Point on the James River, Virginia.

WEST: General Thomas J. Jackson nudges his footsore host from Staunton to the outskirts of McDowell, western Virginia, tangling with the pickets of General Robert H. Milroy's brigade en route. As the 10,000 Confederates deploy to engage the next morning, Milroy receives timely reinforcements in the form of General Robert C. Schenk's brigade, which brings Union numbers up to 6,000.

General Braxton Bragg gains command of the Confederate Army of Mississippi.

NAVAL: President Abraham Lincoln visits and examines the USS *Monitor* off Fortress Monroe, Virginia.

USS *Wachusetts, Chocura,* and *Sebago* ascend the York River and assist the landing of army troops at West Point, Virginia.

The USS *Currituck* captures the Confederate vessels *American Coaster* and *Planter* in the Pamunkey River, Virginia.

May 8

SOUTH: Union forces begin to occupy Baton Rouge, Louisiana.

WEST: 10,000 Confederates under General Thomas J. Jackson move forward to engage 6,000 Federal troops under Generals Robert H. Milroy and Robert C. Schenk at McDowell, western Virginia. Union troops initially are posted near the town, dominated by nearby Setlinger's Hill. When Milroy perceives Jackson's troop advancing toward that strategic point, he considers retreating until Schenk convinces him to attack and cover their withdrawal. Commencing at 4:30 P.M., Union troops charge up the heavily wooded hill, firing into an open copse into which Southerners deployed and inflicting heavy casualties. But Confederates under General Edward Johnson's Army of the Northwest grimly repulse every attack and hold their ground as Jackson labors to bring up additional troops. After a surprisingly stiff fight of four hours, Milroy finally issues orders to retreat. This is successfully accomplished without Southern interference.

Confederate cavalry under Colonel Turner Ashby mount a pursuit, but the bulk of Union forces escape intact. McDowell is an inauspicious debut for Jackson's celebrated Valley Campaign, for his losses are twice that of his opponents— 116 killed and 300 wounded, and 4 missing to 34 Union dead, 220 injured, and 5 missing. Southerners were further deprived of the services of General Johnson, an excellent commander, who is seriously injured and requires a lengthy convalescence. Consequently, his Army of the Northwest is absorbed into Jackson's Army of the Valley.

General William W. Loring is assigned to command the Army of Southwest Virginia.

Union forces under General Henry W. Halleck pause within a few miles of their objective at Corinth, Mississippi, as his "offensive" assumes more the nature of a siege.

NAVAL: The USS *Monitor, Dacotah, Naugatuck, Seminole,* and *Susquehanna* bombard Confederate batteries at Sewell's Point, Virginia, under the direction of President Abraham Lincoln, who also orders the monitor *Galena* up the James River to support General George B. McClellan.

A landing party from the USS *Iroquois* captures the city of Baton Rouge, Louisiana, and also seizes the local arsenal.

Three rams of the Confederate River Defense Fleet briefly sortie on the Mississippi River from Fort Pillow, Tennessee, but they quickly withdraw after confronting larger Union gunboats.

May 9

SOUTH: President Abraham Lincoln diplomatically admonishes General George B. McClellan for not moving more vigorously on the Confederate capital at Richmond, Virginia.

Confederate forces begin to evacuate the port of Norfolk, Virginia, where great quantities of valuable supplies are abandoned.

General David Hunter declares all African-American slaves in the Department of the South (Florida, Georgia, South Carolina) emancipated. Furthermore, all willing slaves are to be armed and incorporated into the military.

Retreating Confederate forces burn and evacuate the navy yard at Pensacola, Florida, destroying the unfinished ironclad CSS *Fulton* in the process.

WEST: General Thomas J. Jackson pursues Federal forces fleeing toward Franklin, western Virginia.

Skirmishing continues between the forces of General Henry W. Halleck and Pierre G. T. Beauregard near Corinth, Mississippi, as Union forces continue inching toward their objective.

NAVAL: Commodore Andrew H. Foote, wounded at the capture of Fort Donelson, is relieved by Captain Charles H. Davis above Fort Pillow, Tennessee.

May 10

SOUTH: The Gosport Navy Yard at Norfolk, Virginia, is occupied by Union forces under General John E. Wool, whose movements are partially directed from offshore by President Abraham Lincoln. The mighty ram CSS *Virginia* now is deprived of a berth as it draws too much water to be sequestered up the James River.

Confederate forces, informed of the fall of New Orleans, promptly evacuate Pensacola, Florida. Union forces under General Lewis G. Arnold then reclaim the base and the navy yard, which functions as a supply depot for various blockading squadrons.

WEST: Union force prevail in a skirmish with Confederates at Bloomfield, Missouri, and capture their supplies.

The impasse continues outside Corinth, Mississippi, as Union forces slowly advance.

NAVAL: The ironclad USS *New Ironsides* is launched at Philadelphia, Pennsylvania.

The USS *Unadilla* captures the Confederate schooner *Mary Theresa* off Charleston, South Carolina.

The scratch-built Confederate River Defense Fleet of eight converted steam rams under Captain James E. Montgomery bravely sorties at Plum Run Bend on the Mississippi River, just north of Fort Pillow, Tennessee. He is seriously outgunned, and his vessels are lightly armed and protected by cotton bales, but their relatively high speed gives them tactical advantages in cramped waters. He then engages seven U.S. ironclads under Commodore Charles H. Davis in one of few squadron actions of the Civil War. Montgomery appears suddenly off Craigshead Point, and he directly attacks the gunboat USS *Cincinnati* and *Gunboat No. 16*. The *Cincinnati* is rammed several times by CSS *General Bragg, General Sterling Price,* and *General Sumter,* yet fights valiantly and inflicts considerable damage before sinking in shallow water. Montgomery's ships then move up to meet Davis's ironclads as they move downstream to engage. The *Mound City* is rammed by the *General Van Dorn,* losing its bow, and grounds itself to avoid sinking. But once the heavy ironclad *Carondelet* moves into firing range, it punishes the Confederates with rifled cannon fire. *General Sumter, Colonel Levell,* and *General Van Dorn* all sustain serious damage before Montgomery signals them to withdraw back to Fort Pillow. The *Cincinnati* and *Mound City* are raised subsequently and repaired but, in view of this rough experience, Davis appeals to the Navy Department for several of the speedy, new Ellet rams.

May 11

WEST: Colonel John H. Morgan's Confederate cavalry seize a train of the Louisville and Nashville Railroad at Cave City, Kentucky.

NAVAL: Because the CSS *Virginia* draws too much water to operate up the James River, Commodore Josiah Tattnall scuttles it off Craney Island, Virginia, to prevent capture. The Northern Blockading Fleet under Commodore Louis M. Goldsborough now enjoys unfettered passage upriver as far as Drewry's Bluff. He makes immediate preparations to dispatch an expedition in the direction of Richmond, Virginia.

The USS *Bainbridge* captures the Confederate schooner *Newcastle* in the Atlantic.

The USS *Kittatinny* captures the British blockade-runner *Julia* off the Southwest Pass, Mississippi River.

The USS *Hatteras* captures the Confederate steamer *Governor A. Mouton* at Berwick Bay, Louisiana.

May 12

POLITICS: President Abraham Lincoln declares the captured ports of Beaufort, North Carolina, Port Royal, South Carolina, and New Orleans, Louisiana, open to trade. He hopes that the resumption of commercial activities will encourage and strengthen political bonds to the North.

Pro-Union sympathizers hold a convention in Nashville, Tennessee, under the watchful eye of Union forces.

SOUTH: The Army of the Potomac under General George B. McClellan advances to White House, Virginia, coming within 22 miles of the Confederate capital at Richmond.

WEST: General Thomas J. Jackson's pursuit of Union forces fleeing from McDowell, western Virginia, falters due to rain and mud. He thereupon stops at Franklin and turns east to confront advancing columns under General Nathaniel P. Banks.

Troops under General Henry W. Halleck seize Natchez, Mississippi, but their advance on Corinth sputters into a continuing series of skirmishes at Farmington.

NAVAL: The USS *Maratanza* and other gunboats sail up the Pamunkey River in support of the Army of the Potomac.

Crew members of the former CSS *Virginia* are collected under Lieutenant Catesby Ap Roger Jones at Drewry's Bluff on the James River, where they man an artillery battery. This is a formidable position, rising 100 feet above the river and only seven miles downriver from Richmond, Virginia. At length, they are joined by General George W. C. Lee, engineering officer and eldest son of General Robert E. Lee, who supervises the construction of redoubts and also directs the placement of numerous hulks in the river to block any Union passage.

May 13

SOUTH: The seemingly inexorable approach of the Army of the Potomac toward Richmond places the Confederate capital in a panic. President Jefferson Davis sends his wife Varina out of the city for safety.

Martial law is declared in Charleston, South Carolina.

WEST: Union troops under General John C. Frémont occupy Franklin, western Virginia, as Confederates under General Thomas J. Jackson withdraw through the Shenandoah Valley.

Rogersville, Alabama, is captured by Federal troops under General Ormsby M. Mitchel.

NAVAL: Harbor pilot Robert Smalls and eight fellow African-American consorts abscond with the Confederate steamer *Planter* and sail it from Charleston Harbor, South Carolina, before surrendering to the USS *Onward* offshore.

The USS *Bohio* captures the Confederate schooner *Deer Island* in the Mississippi Sound.

The USS *Calhoun* captures the Confederate gunboat *Corypheus* at Bayou Bonfouca, Louisiana.

The USS *Iroquois* and *Oneida* under Commander David G. Farragut capture and occupy Natchez, Mississippi, as Union forces gradually move toward the citadel of Vicksburg.

May 14

SOUTH: After skirmishing at Gaines's Cross Roads, Union forces halt at the White House on the Pamunkey River, only 20 miles from Richmond, Virginia. General George B. McClellan, though enjoying numerical superiority over his adversaries, awaits additional reinforcements from General Irwin McDowell.

NAVAL: The USS *Calhoun* captures the Confederate schooner *Venice* on Lake Pontchartrain, Louisiana.

May 15

SOUTH: As General George B. McClellan closes in on Richmond, Virginia, Confederate forces under General Joseph E. Johnston retire along the Chickahominy River to within three miles of the capital.

The 15th Massachusetts under Colonel Thomas J. C. Armory scouts and skirmishes at Trenton Bridge and Pollocksville, North Carolina.

Rude behavior by New Orleans ladies toward Union occupiers angers General Benjamin F. Butler and prompts him to issue his infamous General Order No. 28, the so-called Woman Order. This stipulates that any woman disposed to act disrespectfully toward Union soldiers will be arrested and treated as a prostitute. The act triggers waves of outrage and indignation across the South—and Butler is ultimately threatened with hanging if apprehended. For this reason, he gains the infamous moniker of "Beast Butler."

WEST: General Thomas J. Jackson's Confederates depart McDowell, western Virginia, and return to the Shenandoah Valley.

General Henry Heth, following the defeat of a Confederate detachment under General Humphrey Marshall, falls back on Jackson's River Depot in western Virginia.

General John C. Frémont conducts small actions at Princeton and Ravenswood, western Virginia.

NAVAL: The armed vessel designated "290"—destined to become the infamous CSS *Alabama*—is launched at Liverpool, England.

Commodore John Rodgers leads the ironclads USS *Monitor, Galena,* and *Naugatuck* up the James River, accompanied by three wooden warships. En route, they encounter formidable Confederate defensives along Drewry's Bluff, seven miles from Richmond, Virginia, and give battle. Southern artillery, manned mostly by naval personnel under Commander Ebenezer Ferrand and enjoying a clear advantage of position, unleash a devastating plunging fire. The Union vessels scarcely can elevate their guns high enough to fire back in return. During a four-hour engagement, *Galena* is struck 40 times and is seriously damaged, losing 13 killed and 11 wounded. The *Naugatuck* also suffers when its 100-pound Parrott gun explodes while firing. Wooden gunboats *Aroostock* and *Port Royal* wisely shy away from the proceedings and hover out of range. Seriously outgunned and unable to circumvent obstacles in his path, Rodgers disengages and limps back to Norfolk—Richmond is saved. For heroism under fire, Corporal John B. Mackie also becomes the first member of the U.S. Marine Corps eligible for the Congressional Medal of Honor.

The USS *Sea Foam* under Matthew Vassar captures the Confederate sloops *Sarah* and *New Eagle* off Ship Island, Mississippi.

May 16
NORTH: The venerable John E. Wool is promoted to major general.
SOUTH: General George B. McClellan establishes his headquarters at the stately mansion at the White House, Virginia, on the Pamunkey River. The property was formerly owned by General Robert E. Lee.

Union and Confederate forces clash briefly near Princeton, Virginia.

General Benjamin F. Butler continues tightening the screws at New Orleans, Louisiana, by closing down the newspapers *Bee* and *Delta*.
WEST: Federal troops capture the Confederate steamer *Daniel E. Miller* at Hornersville, Missouri.
NAVAL: Union naval forces under Commander Samuel P. Lee ascend the Mississippi River, pausing only to bombard Grand Gulf, Mississippi, en route.

May 17
SOUTH: General Irvin McDowell's I Corps, stationed at Fredericksburg, Virginia, finally is ordered south against the Confederate capital at Richmond, in concert with the Army of the Potomac.
WEST: Union troops under General Jacob D. Cox commence to move across the Flat Top Mountains of western Virginia, with a view toward severing the Virginia and Tennessee Railroad. To prevent this, General Humphrey Marshall assembles two brigades under himself and General Henry Heth, with which he prepares to assault Cox's headquarters at Princeton. Marshall plans to attack from the east on the following day while Heth is ordered to strike from the south. But Marshall arrives at Princeton that night and, detecting weak Union defenses, attacks and easily captures the town with support. He then learns from captured papers that additional Union

forces were en route and falls back. Heth never rendezvoused as ordered, but Cox, fearing himself outnumbered, withdraws from Princeton completely. Thus the Virginia and Tennessee Railroad is spared while Humphrey's aggressive move captures 29 Union prisoners.

General Henry W. Halleck continues his snail-like approach to Corinth, Mississippi, stopping today to skirmish with Confederates at Russell's House.

NAVAL: The USS *Sebago* and *Currituck* escort the troop transport *Seth Low* several miles down the Pamunkey River, Virginia, forcing Confederates to burn or scuttle 17 vessels to prevent capture. However, the river at this point becomes so narrow that the gunboats are obliged to run backward for several miles before turning their bows around.

The USS *Hatteras* captures the Confederate sloop *Poody* off Vermillion Bay, Louisiana.

May 18

SOUTH: General William B. Franklin takes charge of the VI Corps, Army of the Potomac, while General Fitz John Porter assumes command of the V Corps.

WEST: Advancing Confederates under General Thomas J. Jackson skirmish with General Nathaniel P. Banks at Woodstock, western Virginia.

NAVAL: The USS *Hunchback* and *Shawsheen* capture the Confederate schooner *Smoot* at Potecasi Creek, North Carolina.

Commander Stephen P. Lee demands the surrender of Vicksburg, Mississippi, but Confederate general Martin L. Smith defiantly refuses. More than a year will lapse before the "Gibraltar of the West" succumbs to Union forces.

May 19

POLITICS: President Abraham Lincoln countermands General David Hunter's unauthorized emancipation order as it affects the Department of the South (South Carolina, Georgia, Florida).

SOUTH: The 4th Georgia attacks a Union landing party along the banks of the James River at City Point, Virginia.

WEST: Confederates under General Thomas J. Jackson begin to march up the Shenandoah Valley toward New Market.

Union forces under General Isaac F. Quinby sail down the Mississippi River to attack Fort Pillow near Memphis, Tennessee.

NAVAL: Federal gunboats USS *Unadilla, Pembina,* and *Ottawa* ascend the Stono River, South Carolina, and commence bombarding Confederate positions on Cole Island.

The USS *Whitehead* captures the Confederate schooner *Eugenia* in Bennet's Creek, North Carolina.

May 20

POLITICS: Congress passes the Homestead Act, which insures settlers 160 acres of land if they remain sedentary for five years and work their plots. Southerners heretofore opposed the measure fearing it would attract overwhelming numbers of antislavery homesteaders to the territories. Three million acres are ultimately distributed among 25,000 citizens by war's end, which in turn facilitates the oncoming tide of western settlement.

SOUTH: Having advanced briefly, General George B. McClellan halts only eight miles from the Confederate capital at Richmond, Virginia. He then divides the Army of the Potomac along both banks of the Chickahominy River while awaiting General Irvin McDowell's I Corps to arrive from Washington, D.C.

General Erasmus D. Keyes leads the IV Corps in operations at Bottom's Bridge on the Chickahominy River, Virginia.

WEST: General Thomas J. Jackson's rapidly moving command swells to 17,000 men with the addition of General Richard S. Ewell's contingent in the Luray Valley, western Virginia. He determines to apply maximum pressure in the Shenandoah Valley to prevent General Nathaniel P. Banks from reinforcing General George B. McClellan's Army of the Potomac.

SOUTHWEST: Union forces reoccupy Tucson in the New Mexico Territory.

NAVAL: Armed boats from USS *Hunchback* and *Whitehead* capture the Confederate schooner *Winter Shrub* in Keel's Creek, North Carolina.

The Federal gunboat USS *Oneida* arrives off Vicksburg, Mississippi, and shells the town.

May 21

SOUTH: Stalled eight miles from the Confederate capital of Richmond, Virginia, and ignoring his clear numerical superiority over the Confederates, General George B. McClellan calls for reinforcements. Meanwhile, the I Corps of General Irvin McDowell continues marching overland toward Richmond, Virginia.

WEST: Confederates under General Thomas J. Jackson move northward in the Luray Valley via passes in the Massanutten Mountains and approach the isolated Union outpost at Fort Royal. His movements are masked effectively by cavalry under Colonel Turner Ashby, which completely confounds Union general Nathaniel P. Banks.

NAVAL: Armed boats from the USS *Hunchback* capture the Confederate schooner *Winter Shrub* at Keel's Creek, North Carolina.

May 22

SOUTH: The 6th Pennsylvania Cavalry (Rush's Lancers) conduct reconnaissance operations around the New Castle and Hanovertown ferries, Virginia.

WEST: Confederate forces under General Thomas J. Jackson depart Luray Gap and advance on Front Royal, western Virginia. He intends to surprise and overwhelm the small Union garrison there.

General Henry W. Halleck continues his leisurely advance toward Corinth, Mississippi, with reconnaissance probes of nearby Iuka and Burnsville.

NAVAL: The USS *Mount Vernon* captures the Confederate steamer *Constitution* at Wilmington, North Carolina.

The USS *Whitehead* captures the Confederate sloop *Ella D* off Keel's Creek, North Carolina.

May 23

SOUTH: Ashby Turner is promoted to brigadier general, C.S.A.

President Abraham Lincoln arrives at Fredericksburg, Virginia, and confers with General Irvin McDowell, whose 20,000 troops suddenly are diverted away from Richmond and into the Shenandoah Valley.

WEST: A force of 17,000 Confederates under General Thomas J. Jackson suddenly appears before a rather surprised Union outpost at Front Royal, Virginia. It is garrisoned by 1,000 men of the 1st Maryland under Colonel John R. Kenly, who remains ignorant of enemy strength and intentions. As the Confederates race down the road to engage the defenders, General Richard Taylor is hailed by notorious spy Belle Boyd, who relays useful intelligence as to Union dispositions about the town. Thus informed, Jackson pushes forward men of his own 1st Maryland, C.S.A., to clear Front Royal and prevent Federal troops from burning two valuable bridges. As Southerners pour into town and vengeful Marylanders from both sides clash, Kenly tries to effect an orderly withdrawal, but his command disintegrates around him. A quick pursuit by the 6th Virginia Cavalry nets Kenly and most of his command outside Cedarville, three miles distant. Union losses in this unequal struggle amount to 904, mostly captured, while Confederate losses are about 50. Both Jackson and the main Union army under General Nathaniel P. Banks continue racing north to Winchester.

Federal troops under General Jacob D. Cox defeat Confederate forces of General Henry Heth at Lewisburg, western Virginia.

May 24

POLITICS: The defeat at Front Royal stings Union authorities into action, and President Abraham Lincoln directs General John C. Frémont to advance into the Shenandoah Valley and confront Confederate forces there. General George B. McClellan is also advised that promised reinforcements are not forthcoming at this time.

SOUTH: Colonel Richard Rush takes his 6th Pennsylvania Cavalry on a scouting mission toward Hanover Court House, Virginia.

WEST: Pursuing Confederates under General Thomas J. Jackson maneuver to intercept Federal forces under General Nathaniel P. Banks at Newtown, western Virginia, but they are slowed by the delaying actions of General John P. Hatch's Union cavalry. Finally brushing aside his opponents, Jackson roughly handles Bank's rearguard and wagon train, taking prisoners and several vehicles. He then trundles up his limping legions and marches them on this latest rapid excursion toward Winchester. Jackson's alarming success prompts President Abraham Lincoln to order General Irwin McDowell to halt at Fredericksburg, Virginia, whereupon he is redirected into the Shenandoah Valley. Lincoln hopes that rapid action will cut off all Confederate escape routes.

NAVAL: The USS *Bienville* seizes the British blockade-runner *Stettin* off Charleston, South Carolina.

The USS *Amanda* and *Bainbridge* capture the Confederate steamer *Swan* off the Tortugas, Florida.

May 25

NORTH: President Abraham Lincoln, chafing over the stalled Union offensive, again urges General George B. McClellan to resume advancing. "I think the time is near when you must either attack Richmond or give up the job and come to the defense of Washington," he blithely declares.

SOUTH: The 3rd Pennsylvania Cavalry under Lieutenant Frank C. Davis advances toward the James River from Bottom's Bridge, Virginia.

The Army of the Potomac, slowly advancing on Richmond, Virginia, is divided by the Chickahominy River, with three Union Corps on its north bank and two below. Confederate commander Joseph E. Johnston, desperate to prevent General George B. McClellan from uniting with the 30,000 men of I Corps under General Irvin McDowell near Fredericksburg, starts to plan to attack Union forces along the river's north bank. By throwing his whole weight against the separated corps of Generals Edwin V. Sumner, William B. Franklin, and Fitz John Porter, he hopes to defeat the Federals in detail before marching north to deal with McDowell.

WEST: Having prevailed over Union forces below Winchester, General Thomas J. Jackson hurriedly marches his weary forces toward another engagement. He even disregards his own religious predilection for observing the Sabbath to hurry the men forward. Jackson then perceives the 7,000 men of General Nathaniel P. Banks deployed along a low range of hills just south of the city, with Colonel Dudley Donnelly's 1st Brigade covering the left flank and Colonel George H. Gordon's 3rd brigade arrayed on the right. Jackson seeks to overpower his adversary quickly and sends three brigades of Generals Charles S. Winder, William B. Taliaferro, and John A. Campbell against Banks's center on Bower's Hill. When these veterans recoil from concentrated infantry and artillery fire, General Richard S. Ewell's division likewise is advanced against the Union right while General Richard Taylor's Louisiana brigade simultaneously hits their left. Taylor leads his men on a wild charge that scatters his opponents, and the entire Union line buckles and breaks. Union troops then stampede through the town and do not rally until they cross the Potomac River into Maryland, 35 miles distant—completely out of the Shenandoah Valley. Jackson, lacking sufficient cavalry to pursue, turns south.

Banks's tactical ineptitude costs him 62 killed, 329 wounded, and 1,714 missing (2,019) while the Confederates barely sustain 400 casualties. During the past three days, Jackson captures 3,030 prisoners, 9,000 firearms, and such a trove of quartermaster stores that Confederates refer to their vanquished adversary as "Commissary Banks." Moreover, Jackson is now poised threateningly only 50 miles from Washington, D.C., a fact mandating General James Shield's recall back to Shenandoah. Ultimately, 40,000 Union troops are withheld from service in the Peninsula campaign because of Jackson's success in the Shenandoah Valley.

General Pierre G. T. Beauregard decides to abandon Corinth, Mississippi, to superior Union numbers and to preserve his army of 50,000 men. He then concocts a number of clever stratagems to convince General Henry W. Halleck that the Confederates actually are being reinforced and that they intend to fight.

NAVAL: Federal and Confederate gunboats exchange fire near the James and Dixon Island, Charleston Harbor.

Colonel Charles Ellet assembles seven steam-powered rams of the Army Mississippi Ram Fleet outside Fort Pillow, Tennessee. There they join the flotilla of Union gunboats under Commodore Charles H. Davis, already deployed.

May 26

SOUTH: Ambrose P. Hill is promoted to major general, C.S.A.

WEST: Defeated Union forces under General Nathaniel P. Banks filter across the Potomac River into Williamsport, Maryland. General Thomas J. Jackson's Confederates, meanwhile, occupy Winchester, Virginia, as additional Federal columns under General John C. Frémont and Irvin McDowell maneuver to cut his retreat.

SOUTHWEST: The Confederate Trans-Mississippi Department is expanded to include Arkansas, the Indian Territory, Missouri, West Louisiana, and Texas.

NAVAL: The USS *Huron* captures the British blockade-runner *Cambria* off Charleston, South Carolina.

The USS *Brooklyn*, assisted by gunboats *Kineo* and *Katahdin,* bombards Grand Gulf, Mississippi.

The USS *Pursuit* captures the Confederate schooner *Andromeda* off the Cuban coast.

Lieutenant Isaac N. Brown is ordered to command the armored ram CSS *Arkansas* at Yazoo City, Mississippi, and oversee its completion.

May 27

SOUTH: With the Army of the Potomac poised only eight miles from Richmond, General George B. McClellan evinces concern for his right flank, situated north of the Chickahominy River. His attention specifically is drawn to Hanover Court House, a village on the Virginia Central Railroad just south of the Pamunkey River, where Confederates allegedly are concentrating in strength. To clear them out, he assigns the V Corps under General Fitz John Porter, who braves a heavy downpour and muddy roads to reach his objective at noon. The 25th New York, his most advanced unit, makes contact with 4,000 men of a North Carolina brigade commanded by Lawrence O. Branch, whose 28th North Carolina resists stoutly. Porter feeds additional men into the line and then mistakenly directs them north in search of the main Confederate body. Sensing an advantage, Branch orders an all-out assault on the Federals to his immediate front, never cognizant of how badly outnumbered he is. The Confederates consequently butt up against General John H. Martindale's brigade of Maine and New York troops, assisted by Massachusetts artillery. Branch's men press the Yankees hard and are on the verge of breaking them when Porter, hearing the fighting in his rear, hurriedly returns to the scene. The North Carolinians yield ground slowly after Branch orders a retreat and fighting sputters out once darkness falls. Union forces then tear up the railroad tracks, burn some bridges, and retrace their steps. Although the fight at Hanover Court House is technically an inconclusive skirmish, it occasions heavy casualties. Porter sustains 62 killed, 223 wounded, and 70 missing to a Confederate tally of 73 dead, 192 injured, and 730 captured.

WEST: As Union forces under General Nathaniel P. Banks continue crossing the Potomac River to safety, General Thomas J. Jackson's Confederates engage their rear guard at Loudoun Heights, western Virginia, threatening Harper's Ferry.

NAVAL: The USS *Bienville* captures the British blockade-runner *Patras* off Bull's Island, South Carolina.

The USS *Santiago de Cuba* seizes the Confederate schooner *Lucy C. Holmes* off Charleston, South Carolina.

May 28

POLITICS: President Jefferson Davis expresses disappointment that General Joseph E. Johnston has not commenced an offensive against the much-larger Army of the Potomac. Nonetheless, he insists: "We are steadily developing for a great battle, and under God's favor I trust for a decisive victory."

WEST: Skirmishing continues between General Henry W. Halleck and Pierre G. T. Beauregard outside Corinth, Mississippi.

The Confederate Department of West Louisiana is designated under General Paul O. Hebert.

NAVAL: Assistant Secretary of the Navy Gustavus V. Fox begins to push legislators to abolish the Navy's rum ration.

The USS *State of Georgia* and *Victoria* capture the Confederate steamer *Nassau* off Fort Caswell, North Carolina.

May 29

SOUTH: Confederate cavalry under General J. E. B. Stuart arrive at Richmond, Virginia, with news that the much-feared approach of General Irvin McDowell's I Corps from the vicinity of Fredericksburg will not materialize. Apparently, the success of General Thomas J. Jackson in the Shenandoah Valley has panicked the Northerners, who then order McDowell to redeploy there. This development prompts General Joseph E. Johnston, commanding Confederate forces in Virginia, to cancel his impending lunge at three Union corps on the north bank of the Chickahominy River in favor of attacking the remaining two Union corps on the south bank of the river.

Union forces skirmish outside South Anna River, Virginia, and also capture the town of Ashland.

WEST: Roughly 50,000 Federal troops under Generals Irvin McDowell, John C. Frémont, and Nathaniel P. Banks begin to concentrate in the vicinity of Harper's Ferry, western Virginia, to cut off and possibly capture the Confederates of General Thomas J. Jackson. All are encouraged by an anxious president Abraham Lincoln, who urges, "Put in all the speed you can." But the wily Jackson begins another one of his rapid disengagements from Front Royal and rapidly transits south to Winchester.

Superior Union numbers prompt General Pierre G. T. Beauregard finally to abandon Corinth, Mississippi, and he withdraws 50,000 men toward Tupelo. To cover the move, Beauregard orders troops and trains to make as much noise as possible to give the impression that reinforcements actually are arriving.

NAVAL: The USS *Keystone* captures the British blockade-runner *Elizabeth* off Charleston, South Carolina.

The USS *Bienville* seizes blockade-runners *Providence*, *Rebecca*, and *La Criolla* off Charleston, South Carolina.

May 30

POLITICS: President Abraham Lincoln, anxious for good news from either Richmond or the Shenandoah Valley, urges all his field commanders to fight.

SOUTH: General Joseph E. Johnston makes a close reconnaissance of Union forces looming within 10 miles of Richmond, Virginia, and he observes that they are physically divided by the rain-swollen Chickahominy River. He decides to concentrate 51,000 men against the combined 34,000 men of III and IV Corps of General Samuel P. Heintzelman and Erasmus D. Keyes, now unsupported on the south bank. Johnston then promulgates a tactically sound if somewhat overcomplicated plan with attacks delivered down three main roads, which is designed to catch the Federals from three different directions. The main strike forces are commanded by Generals James Longstreet, Daniel H. Hill, and Benjamin Huger. However, Johnston's plan is compromised by an overreliance on oral commands, instead of written orders, that further complicates matters for his inexperienced troops.

WEST: Confederates under General Thomas J. Jackson withdraw from Winchester, western Virginia, to avoid being engulfed by three converging Union columns. General Ashby Turner and some Confederate cavalry remain behind as a rear guard. However, when a division under Colonel Nathan Kimball approach the town, Turner panics and abandons his command. A quick charge by the 1st Rhode Island Cavalry recaptures Front Royal, along with 156 Confederate prisoners. The town subsequently is secured by Federal troops under General James Shield.

Union forces under General Henry W. Halleck secure 2,000 Confederate prisoners at Corinth, Mississippi, following the withdrawal of General Pierre G. T. Beauregard. Previously, Beauregard ordered his troops to cook three days of rations to give the impression that he was preparing to fight. He also had troops cheer arriving trains during evacuation measures to give the appearance that he was receiving reinforcements. Halleck thus secured a vital transportation link and severed the vital Memphis and Charleston and Mobile and Ohio railroads, but he nonetheless is criticized for a dilatory pace while campaigning. It has taken him 30 days to cover the 22-mile distance from Pittsburg Landing.

May 31

NORTH: Edward R. S. Canby is promoted to brigadier general, U.S. Army.

SOUTH: As Federal forces under General George B. McClellan continue their glacial advance on Richmond, Virginia, topography requires him to split his forces on both banks of the rain-swollen Chickahominy River. The raging water then washes away all available bridges, and Confederate general Joseph E. Johnston seeks to avail himself of an opportunity to destroy the isolated II and IV Corps, under Generals Samuel P. Heintzelman and Erasmus D. Keyes, respectively, on the south bank. But the impending Confederate assault, through well planned, remains hobbled from the onset by poor staff work and overreliance on verbal orders. Consequently, wholesale confusion ensues as the troops of General James Longstreet inadvertently assume a line of advance previously assigned to Generals Benjamin Huger and D. H. Hill. Hours are lost as the intermingling commands extricate themselves from a tangle of regiments, brigades, and divisions. It is not until 1:00 P.M. that Hill's division finally positions itself to strike Union forces in the vicinity of Seven Pines.

The Confederate attack kicks off amid stiff resistance and heavy casualties. By dint of hard fighting, Hill manages to evict General Silas Casey's Federals from their position and storms several batteries, but Union forces promptly re-form and establish new lines to the rear. Excited Confederate units continue arriving on the battlefield in slovenly order and deliver their assaults piecemeal, so General Keyes stems their advance with reinforcements of his own and counterattacks. These are repulsed after more severe fighting and Longstreet orders an advance across the line to clinch the victory. The hard-charging Southerners drive their opponents from the field, but Union resistance proves insurmountable, and their line re-forms anew and holds. Fighting finally peters out along the line at about 6:00 P.M., and both sides withdraw to lick their wounds and assess damage.

Johnston's secondary attack at Fair Oaks fared little better. Here, Union troops under the redoubtable general Phil Kearny fiercely resist General W. H. C. Whiting's advance and expertly repulse him. Meanwhile, troops from General Edwin V. Sumner's II Corps manage to throw a bridge across the Chickahominy and begin to funnel into the fracas. These forces have been personally ordered here by General George B. McClellan, who is sick and takes no further part in the fighting. As Whiting's attack falters again, General Johnston rides up to supervise matters personally, when a musket ball suddenly thuds into his shoulder. Confederate command devolves to a dithering General Gustavus W. Smith, who withdraws his remaining troops from the field. That evening, Smith reconsiders and issues orders to resume fighting on the following day.

WEST: Adroit maneuvering by General Thomas J. Jackson extricates his army from closing pincers formed by Generals Irwin McDowell and John C. Frémont, and he retires in driving rain from Winchester, western Virginia, to Strasburg.

General Thomas C. Hindman assumes control of the Confederate Trans-Mississippi Department.

NAVAL: The USS *Philadelphia* captures the Confederate schooner *W. F. Harris* in Core Sound, North Carolina.

The USS *Keystone State* captures the British blockade-runner *Cora* off Charleston, South Carolina.

June 1

POLITICS: President Abraham Lincoln telegrams and implores General George B. McClellan to "Hold all your ground, or yield any inch by inch and in good order."

NORTH: Joseph Hooker is appointed major general, U.S. Army.

The Department of Virginia is enlarged with General John E. Wool assigned to the Middle Department and General John A. Dix to head Fortress Monroe, Virginia; all are now under the overall command of General George B. McClellan.

SOUTH: Confederate forces at Seven Pines, Virginia, resume their offensive against the Army of the Potomac. General Gustavus W. Smith orders General D. H. Hill to attack, assisted by additional soldiers under General James Longstreet, but once again Southern plans miscarry. The Confederates deliver their charges fiercely but in piecemeal fashion, which enables Union troops to repulse them. At length, General Robert E. Lee arrives from Richmond to succeed Smith, and he orders the battle stopped at 1 P.M. Both sides sustain severe casualties: The Southerners, who did most of the attacking, lose 980 killed, 4,749 wounded, and 405 missing (6,134) to a

Union tally of 790 dead, 3,594 injured, and 647 missing (5,031). The erstwhile cautious McClellan, who retains the battlefield, could claim a tactical victory, but there follows one portentous, unforeseen consequence: When the skittish General Smith asks to be relieved, President Jefferson Davis assigns Robert E. Lee to succeed him. A corner has been turned in the course of military events of the Civil War—and a dazzling new chapter is about to unfold.

WEST: Confederates under General Thomas J. Jackson and Federals under General Irvin McDowell skirmish at Mount Carmel, western Virginia.

June 2

WEST: Union cavalry under General George Bayard brush aside Confederates under General Turner Ashby near Woodstock, western Virginia, as the Federal pursuit of General Thomas J. Jackson intensifies.

Union forces under General John Pope cautiously begin to follow General Pierre G. T. Beauregard's retreating Confederates at Rienzi, Mississippi.

NAVAL: The USS *Unadilla, Pembina, E. B. Hale, Ellen,* and *Henry Andrew* provide supporting gunfire as troops land on James Island, South Carolina.

Armed boats from the USS *Kingfisher* are attacked in the Aucilla River, Florida, suffering two killed and nine wounded.

An armed boat from the USS *New London* captures the Confederate yachts *Comet* and *Algerine* off Near Basin, Louisiana.

June 3

SOUTH: Colonel George F. Shepley, 12th Maine, becomes military governor of Louisiana.

WEST: Fort Pillow, Tennessee, below Island No. 10 on the Mississippi River, is abandoned by Confederate forces following the fall of Corinth, Mississippi.

NAVAL: USS *Gem of the Sea* captures the blockade-runner *Mary Stewart* off the mouth of the South Santee River, South Carolina.

The USS *Montgomery* captures the British schooner *Will-o'-the-Wisp* off the mouth of the Rio Grande, Texas.

Prolonged bombardment by Federal gunboats on the Mississippi River convinces Confederate defenders to abandon Fort Pillow, Tennessee. The nearby city of Memphis likewise is all but undefended, save for a weak Confederate naval squadron.

June 4

WEST: General Thomas J. Jackson's Confederates pause briefly to skirmish at Big Bend, western Virginia, as he withdraws southward down the Shenandoah Valley.

General Ormsby M. Mitchel skirmishes outside Huntsville, Alabama, where he begins to threaten Chattanooga, Tennessee.

Southern farmers along the Yazoo River begin to burn vast crops of cotton to prevent their capture by advancing Union forces.

NAVAL: Fort Pillow on the Mississippi River is abandoned by Confederate forces and the gunboat flotilla under Commodore Charles H. Davis completely bypasses it.

June 5

POLITICS: In another deft blow against slavery, the United States formally recognizes the largely black nations of Liberia and Haiti, and President Abraham Lincoln appoints diplomatic representatives.

SOUTH: The Union drive on Richmond, Virginia, is stalled by inclement weather while Confederates under the heretofore little-known General Robert E. Lee begin to gird for a decisive counterstrike.

The 24th Massachusetts under Colonel Francis A. Osborn fights a pitched battle at Tranter's Creek, North Carolina.

NAVAL: Confederates destroy the steamer *Havana* at Deadman's Bay, Florida, to prevent its capture by USS *Ezilda.*

Having ignored Fort Pillow, Tennessee, four Union gunboats and five rams under Commodore Charles H. Davis and Colonel Charles Ellet steam down the Mississippi River to capture Memphis, Tennessee.

A tug escorting the USS *Benton* captures the Confederate steamer *Sovereign* off Island No. 37 in the Mississippi River.

June 6

WEST: Confederate cavalry leader General Ashby Turner is mortally wounded in a rearguard action near Harrisonburg, western Virginia. Meanwhile, the main column under General Thomas J. Jackson rapidly retrogrades toward Port Republic, covering over 100 miles in five days.

NAVAL: At 4:20 A.M., Union gunboats under Commodore Charles H. Davis weigh anchor off Island No. 45, two miles north of Memphis, Tennessee, and head for the city. He commands the ironclads USS *Benton, Louisville, Carondelet, Cairo,* and *St. Louis,* along with the small but very potent fleet of army rams under Colonel Charles Ellet. Suddenly, Confederates under Captain James E. Montgomery sortie a small squadron of steam rams, *General Beauregard, General Bragg, General Price, General Van Dorn, General Thompson, Colonel Lovell, Sumter,* and *Little Rebel.* At 5:40 A.M., contact is established between the opposing armadas, and cannonading commences below the city as thousands throng the riverbanks to observe. Davis feigns a retreat while Montgomery pursues until he is surprised amidships by Ellet's rams sailing downstream, four abreast. A confused and violent melee erupts as the majority of Confederate vessels systematically are rammed, disabled by superior Union gunfire, and sunk. Only *Van Dorn* escapes the wreckage and slips downstream to safety. On the Union side, *Queen of the West* is rammed and grounds itself to prevent sinking. Confederate losses in this lopsided encounter are nearly 100 killed and wounded with another 100 captured. The only Union casualty, Colonel Ellet, is wounded superficially by a gunshot through the kneecap and dies two weeks later from infection.

Davis, having dispensed with his adversary, wastes no time claiming Memphis as his prize. Two officers row ashore to the city fathers and demand an immediate surrender, which is received at 10:00 A.M. Handfuls of Confederate troops under General Jeff Thompson slip out of the city beforehand and escape. But all of western Tennessee is now firmly in Union hands and Memphis—the Confederacy's fifth

Lithograph by Middleton, Strobridge & Co. In the foreground are various Confederate ships shown sinking, burning, and being rammed, with Federal warships in the background. The city of Memphis is in the right distance, with a wharf boat by the shore. *(Naval Historical Foundation)*

largest city—functions as a vital staging area for subsequent operations against Vicksburg, Mississippi.

The USS *Pembina* captures the Confederate schooner *Rowena* in the Stono River, South Carolina.

June 7

SOUTH: Federal cavalry patrols reach the outskirts of Richmond, Virginia.

General Benjamin F. Butler orders Louisianan William B. Mumford hanged for removing and destroying the U.S. flag atop the New Orleans Mint.

WEST: Federal troops under General Ormsby M. Mitchel attack Confederate positions at Chattanooga, Tennessee, and are repulsed by General Edmund Kirby Smith.

The important rail center at Jackson, Tennessee, falls to Union forces.

NAVAL: The USS *Anacostia* captures the Confederate sloop *Monitor* in the Piankatank River, Virginia.

The USS *Wissahickon* and *Itasca* begin prolonged exchanges of fire with Confederate artillery stationed at Grand Gulf, Mississippi.

June 8

SOUTH: Unionists are defeated in a heavy skirmish on St. John's Island, South Carolina, and subsequently withdraw back to Legareville.

WEST: The main portion of the Army of the Valley under General Thomas J. Jackson reposes at Port Republic, western Virginia, prior to advancing against the Union forces of General James Shields. Early this morning, a surprise raid by Union cavalry nearly overruns Jackson's headquarters in town, capturing three staff officers. But quick action by nearby Confederates repulses the Federals, costing them four cannon.

Seven miles away, General Richard S. Ewell's force of 5,000 men assumes defensive positions at Cross Keys, western Virginia, anticipating a major thrust by Federal troops under General John C. Frémont. He deploys his three brigades along the crest on the south bank of Mill Creek with artillery concentrated toward his center. At length, Frémont approaches Ewell's position from Port Republic with 12,000 men and begins a desultory series of artillery exchanges and half-hearted reconnaissance probes at about 10:00 A.M. Fighting commences in earnest when Union troops under General Julius Stahel haphazardly deploy against Ewell's right and run headlong into General Issac R. Trimble's eager Confederates. The 15th Alabama, in particular, allows the Federals to approach their position in a cornfield when they suddenly rise up and unleash several crushing volleys at point-blank range. Trimble then chases the chastised Yankees down the Keezletown Road even as Union reinforcements under General Henry Bohlen's brigade arrive to assist.

In the center of Ewell's line, General Robert H. Milroy advances to contact before deciding his position is too strong to carry frontally. However, the Confederate right experiences increasing pressure from General Robert C. Schenck's brigade, and Ewell dispatches General Richard Taylor's troops to buttress that flank. But before more serious fighting develops, Frémont suddenly orders his units disengaged, and he falls back down the Keezletown Road. The Confederates follow cautiously and by nightfall occupy the former Union position. Trimble subsequently begs Ewell to pursue vigorously, but that general, acting under Jackson's strict instructions, maintains his defensive posture. The affair at Cross Keyes is but a skirmish, yet it constitutes another timid performance by Frémont. Confederate losses are recorded as 288 while the Union suffers 684 casualties, nearly half among the serried ranks of the 8th New York. Later that evening, Ewell prepares to march and join Jackson at Port Republic on the following day.

General Irvin McDowell's I Corps again is ordered to depart the Shenandoah Valley and march south to assist the attack on Richmond, Virginia.

NAVAL: The USS Penobscot burns the Confederate schooner Sereta off Shallotte Inlet, North Carolina.

June 9

SOUTH: General John E. Wool assumes command of the Middle Military Department, Virginia.

WEST: Confederates under General Thomas J. Jackson cross a narrow wagon bridge over the North River to attack General Erastus B. Tyler's brigade at Port Republic. Tyler arrays his 3,000 men in a line anchored by a seven-gun battery occupying a charcoal plant, which stands on a hilltop. As the Stonewall brigade under General Charles S. Winder files onto the field at about 7:00 A.M., it receives heavy fire from Tyler's entire force and sustains heavy losses. Nonetheless, he advances to within 200 yards of the Union line and bravely maintains an unequal contest for an hour.

Meanwhile, Jackson orders the Louisiana brigade of General Richard Taylor against the Union left to storm their commanding battery on the hill. Braving heavy fire, Taylor accomplishes just that, although he loses the captured guns twice before prevailing on an excruciating third try. As this drama unfolds, the Stonewall brigade recoils in disorder until bolstered by General Richard S. Ewell's division. By 11:00 A.M., Tyler, now badly outnumbered, orders a withdrawal, which degenerates into a rout. The Union army of General Charles C. Frémont also makes a late appearance across the river but is unable to intervene because Ewell burned all the bridges behind him. Frémont's troops could only shell the field from afar, which does little to assist Tyler's shattered command. Union losses amount to 1,108, including 558 prisoners, while the Southerners incur roughly 800 casualties.

Port Republic, although it reflects somewhat badly on Jackson's combat leadership, is the sixth and final encounter of his remarkable Valley campaign. Since the previous March, Jackson's infamous "Foot Cavalry," whose strength peaked at 17,000 men, have slogged 676 miles, won four pitched battles and several skirmishes, and defied all attempts by 60,000 Federals to snare him. Campaign losses also favor the South, amounting to 3,100 Confederates and more than 5,000 Union troops. But most important, Jackson's endeavors repeatedly siphon off manpower assets that are badly needed before Richmond. With Frémont and Shields safely disposed of, Jackson is now at liberty to depart the Shenandoah Valley and reinforce General Robert E. Lee on the Peninsula. "God has been our shield," he modestly concludes, "and to His name be all the glory."

The division of Union general James Shields is ordered from the Shenandoah Valley to rejoin the I Corps of General Irvin McDowell near Fredericksburg, Virginia.

NAVAL: The USS *Commodore Perry, Shawsheen,* and *Ceres* land and disembark troops at Hamilton, North Carolina, capturing the Confederate steamer *Wilson* in the process.

June 10

WEST: The glacial-acting General Henry W. Halleck authorizes General Ulysses S. Grant, John Pope, and Don C. Buell to resume heading their respective corps. Grant, as the senior leader, rebounds as theater commander and the tempo of events rapidly escalates.

NAVAL: The Federal gunboats USS *Iroquois* and *Katahdin* join *Wissahickon* and *Itasca* in a concerted bombardment of Grand Gulf, Mississippi.

The Federal gunboat USS *Mound City* is damaged by Confederate artillery fire eight miles below Saint Charles on the White River, Arkansas.

June 11

DIPLOMATIC: British prime minister Lord Palmerston protests the behavior of General William F. Butler toward civilians at New Orleans to U.S. minister Charles F. Adams.

SOUTH: General David Hunter, commanding the Department of the South, temporarily leaves and orders his successor, General Henry W. Benham, to refrain from initiating major engagements.

WEST: General John C. Frémont is ordered to withdraw his army from Port Republic and back to Mount Jackson in western Virginia.

SOUTHWEST: Confederate guerrillas under William C. Quantrill unsuccessfully attack a Federal mail escort at Pink Hill, Missouri.

NAVAL: The USS *Susquehanna* captures the Confederate blockade-runner *Princeton* in the Gulf of Mexico.

The USS *Bainbridge* captures the Confederate schooner *Biagorry* in the Gulf of Mexico.

June 12

SOUTH: The Army of the Potomac is strengthened by the arrival of a division commanded by General George A. McCall.

At 2:00 A.M., General J. E. B. Stuart bursts into his headquarters and declares: "Gentlemen, in ten minutes every man must be in the saddle." His 1,200 Virginian troopers then commence a dramatic and celebrated ride from Richmond, Virginia, and around the Army of the Potomac. Stuart is tasked with verifying rumors that parts of General George B. McClellan's right flank are "up in the air" to facilitate a new Confederate offensive envisioned by General Robert E. Lee.

To further confuse Northern military intelligence, General Robert E. Lee dispatches sizable reinforcements to the Shenandoah region to give the impression of a major offensive developing there.

June 13

SOUTH: General J. E. B. Stuart's cavalry reach a threshold after passing through Old Church, Virginia, on the right flank of General George B. McClellan's army. En route, he tangles briefly with a detachment of the 5th U.S. Cavalry, which results in the death of Captain William Latane, 9th Virginia Cavalry—his sole fatality, who is subsequently enshrined as a Southern martyr. No Confederate unit had ever penetrated Union lines this far, but rather than retrace his steps, Stuart boldly plunges ahead and begins his circuitous ride to fame.

June 14

SOUTH: General J. E. B. Stuart's cavalry destroy the bridge over the Chickahominy River at Forge Site to prevent a Union pursuit, and they gallop around the Army of the Potomac's left flank. Ironically, Stuart is chased by Federal cavalry under his father-in-law and fellow Virginian, Colonel Philip St. George Cooke.

NAVAL: The USS *William G. Anderson* captures the Confederate schooner *Montebello* in the Jordan River, Mississippi.

The tug USS *Spitfire* captures the Confederate steamer *Clara Dolsen* in the White River, Arkansas.

June 15

POLITICS: With amazing perspicacity, President Abraham Lincoln informs a worried general John C. Frémont that Confederate reinforcements headed for the Shenandoah Valley are probably a ruse to mask General Thomas J. Jackson's movement toward Richmond, Virginia.

South: General Robert E. Lee formally orders General Thomas J. Jackson, then in the Shenandoah Valley, to join the Army of Northern Virginia on the Peninsula. Lee seeks to annihilate General George B. McClellan's army before it can be reinforced by General Irvin McDowell's I Corps.

General J. E. B. Stuart gallops into Richmond, Virginia, ahead of his troopers with important military intelligence about the Army of the Potomac, which he recently circumnavigated. His 100-mile jaunt captures 165 prisoners, 260 mules and horses, and renders him the darling of the Southern press. More significant, he brings General Robert E. Lee accurate information about the disposition of Union General Fitz John Porter's V Corps, presently unsupported on the north bank of the Chickahominy River. Stuart discerns that Porter's right flank lies unprotected by natural obstacles and is, hence, "in the air." Lee, eager to break the military impasse near Richmond, begins to concoct a plan for Porter's demise.

Federals under General Daniel Sickles advance on Seven Pines, Virginia, skirmishing en route.

West: Union troops under General William T. Sherman skirmish heavily at Tallahatchie Bridge, Mississippi.

Naval: The USS *Corwin* captures the Confederate schooner *Starlight* on the Potopotank River, Virginia.

The USS *Tahoma* and *Somerset* shell a Confederate lighthouse at St. Mary's River, Florida, and subsequently land parties ashore, which capture and burn a battery and a barracks.

June 16

South: The remainder of General J. E. B. Stuart's Confederate cavalry completes its spectacular jaunt around the Union army and canters back to Richmond, Virginia.

At 2:00 A.M., General Henry W. Benham rouses the divisions of General Horatio G. Wright and Isaac I. Stevens from their encampment on James Island, a swampy neck southwest of Charleston, South Carolina. He then orders them to attack Confederate fortifications at nearby Secessionville. This is despite standing orders from his commanding officer, General David Hunter, not to initiate major engagements during his absence. The local Confederate commander, Colonel Thomas G. Lamar of the 1st South Carolina Artillery, is alert to Benham's intentions and prepares a two-mile long position, heavily defended by cannon, to receive the enemy. Possessing but 500 men, Lamar also requests reinforcements from his district commander, General Nathan G. Evans. Federal forces advance stealthily through the darkness, manage to capture an entire Confederate picket, and then confront swampy terrain that funnels their attack directly toward the Confederate works. At 4:00 A.M., Benham orders the first wave of his 6,000 men forward, and they are bloodily repulsed by Lamar's six-inch Columbiad cannon. Two more waves also advance and bravely struggle up the parapet, but the defenders, reinforced now to a strength of 1,500 men, easily shoot down their opponents. At length, Benham ceases the slaughter at 9:30 A.M. and marches back to camp.

The Battle of Secessionville was a minor disaster for the Union and a setback in its campaign to seize Charleston, South Carolina. Benham's recklessness cost his army 107 killed, 487 wounded, and 80 captured to a Confederate tally of 52 dead, 144 injured, and 8 missing. Evans is so pleased with Lamar's performance that his fortifications are officially renamed Fort Lamar in his honor. Benham, however, is subsequently relieved from command and discharged from uniform the following August.

NAVAL: The USS *Somerset* captures the Confederate schooner *Curlew* off Cedar Keys, Florida.

Confederates sink the steamers *Eliza G.* and *Mary Patterson* in the White River, Arkansas, to impede the passage of Union vessels.

June 17

NORTH: General John C. Frémont resigns his commission rather than be subordinated to General John Pope in the new Army of Virginia. He is replaced by General Franz Sigel.

WEST: Confederate forces under General Thomas J. Jackson hurriedly march toward Richmond, Virginia, to join the Army of Northern Virginia under General Robert E. Lee.

General Braxton Bragg, a close friend and confidant of President Jefferson Davis, succeeds the General Pierre G. T. Beauregard, who is ailing, as commander of the Confederate Western Department. The aggressive Bragg is a capable strategist and an accomplished logistician, but his garrulous disposition and indecisive nature alienate all but the most faithful subordinates. Many ranking Confederates openly loath serving under him.

NAVAL: Union forces, assisted by the Federal gunboat USS *New London*, attack Confederate troops at Pass Manchac, Louisiana.

Captain Charles H. Davis is promoted to commodore and commander of U.S. Navy forces along the Mississippi River.

At the behest of General Henry W. Halleck, a naval squadron consisting of the USS *Mound City, St. Louis, Lexington,* and *Conestoga,* engages Confederate batteries at St. Charles, Arkansas. *Mound City* sustains heavy damage when exploding boilers kill or wound 10 sailors, but troops land ashore and successfully carry the position. Victory here closes off the White River to Confederate traffic.

June 18

SOUTH: Union general Samuel D. Sturgis receives command of the Reserve Army Corps in Virginia.

WEST: Federal forces under General George W. Morgan advance and occupy the Cumberland Gap, where mountain trails connecting Tennessee, Kentucky, and Virginia strategically converge. This movement also stirs up long-suppressed Union sentiments throughout the region.

Recent adverse developments prompt the garrison of Vicksburg, Mississippi, to commence building an extensive network of defensive works.

SOUTHWEST: General Paul O. Hebert takes charge of the Confederate District of Texas.

NAVAL: Admiral David G. Farragut begins to assemble his squadron and mortar boat fleet prior to sailing past the guns of Vicksburg on the Mississippi River.

June 19

POLITICS: President Abraham Lincoln signs legislation outlawing slavery in the territories.

SOUTH: The 20th Indiana under Colonel William L. Brown skirmishes along Charles City Road outside Richmond, Virginia, before withdrawing.

At James Island, South Carolina, General Henry W. Benham is arrested for his role in the aborted attack upon Secessionville, and the Judge Advocate General's Office, after weighing the evidence against him, strongly recommends that his brigadier's commission be revoked.

NAVAL: Commander Matthew F. Maury reports to Confederate secretary of the navy Stephen R. Mallory of mining operations on the James River. He also mentions the use of galvanic batteries and the existence of the CSS *Teaser*, the first naval vessel outfitted as a minelayer. It also carries the first Confederate reconnaissance balloon.

The USS *Florida* captures the sloop *Ventura* off Grant's Pass, Mobile Bay, Alabama.

June 20

WEST: General Braxton Bragg arrives at Tupelo, Mississippi, and assumes command of the Confederate Western Department from General Pierre G. T. Beauregard.

A detachment of 3,000 Union troops under General William Thomas boards Admiral David G. Farragut's fleet and heads up the Mississippi River from Baton Rouge. He is ordered to establish a base camp opposite Vicksburg, Mississippi, where a canal can be cut to permit river traffic to bypass the city's formidable armament. Thomas's movement induces General Earl Van Dorn, commanding the Department of Southern Mississippi, to accelerate fortifying the city.

NAVAL: The USS *Keystone State* captures the British blockade-runner *Sarah* off Charleston, South Carolina.

The USS *Madgie* captures the Confederate schooner *Southern Belle* near Darien, South Carolina.

Armed boats from the USS *Albatross* capture the Confederate steam tug *Treaty* and schooner *Louisa* off Georgetown, South Carolina.

The USS *Beauregard* seizes the British blockade-runner *Lucy* at Deadman's Point, Florida.

June 21

SOUTH: Union and Confederate forces skirmish heavily along the Chickahominy River near Richmond, Virginia. Expectations for decisive military action mount, but the nerve-wracking impasse continues.

WEST: General Jeff Thompson's Confederate guerrilla evade a Union attack at Coldwater Station, Mississippi.

NAVAL: Landing parties from the USS *Crusader* and *Planter* drive up the Wadmelaw River, South Carolina, capture Simmons Bluff, and destroy a Confederate encampment there.

The USS *Bohio* captures the Confederate sloop *L. Rebecca* in the Gulf of Mexico.

June 22

SOUTH: The Sisters of Charity dispatch 30 members to serve as nurses in the Army of the Potomac at Fortress Monroe, Virginia.

Union general Erasmus D. Keyes leads a large reconnaissance party in the vicinity of White Oak Swamp, 16 miles south of Richmond, Virginia.

June 23

POLITICS: President Abraham Lincoln, disillusioned by General George B. McClellan's fabled cautiousness, ventures to West Point, New York, and confers with former general in chief Winfield Scott over strategy.

SOUTH: General Robert E. Lee assembles his commanders at the Dabb's House near Richmond, Virginia, and outlines his offensive against the Army of the Potomac's right wing under General Fitz John Porter. He plans to concentrate no less than 55,000 men against Porter's 30,000-strong V Corps by throwing the combined weight of Generals Thomas J. Jackson, James Longstreet, Daniel H. Hill, and Ambrose P. Hill at it in a single, coordinated strike. The lynchpin of Confederate hopes falls on Jackson's Army of the Valley, which is expected to force march to the battlefield and take Porter from behind once he is pinned down frontally by the others. Concurrently, Generals Benjamin Huger and John B. Magruder will fix McClellan's army before Richmond with 25,000 men until Lee's return. Jackson, who had arrived only recently at Richmond alone from the Shenandoah Valley, immediately rejoins his command to accelerate its passage.

WEST: Union general Benjamin Alvord takes charge of the District of Oregon.

June 24

SOUTH: Skirmishing erupts as the Army of the Potomac resumes its belated advance by pressing down on Mechanicsville, Virginia. Confederate forces evacuate White House Landing on their approach.

WEST: General Earl Van Dorn continues fortifying Vicksburg, Mississippi, as 3,000 Federal troops begin encamping nearby across the river.

June 25

SOUTH: The Army of the Potomac edges to within six miles of the Confederate capital at Richmond, Virginia, the closest Union forces will approach in three years. General George B. McClellan, desiring to place heavy cannon on the outskirts of the city and bombard it, orders Oak Grove, a section of swampy, wooded terrain to his front, wrested from the enemy. General Samuel P. Heintzelman's III Corps then advances to dislodge the defenders under General Benjamin Huger and heavy fighting erupts along the front. General Joseph Hooker's division also plunges into the woods at 8:30 A.M., soon supported by the forces led by General Phil Kearny. But the Confederates of General Ambrose R. Wright resist stoutly, slowing Hooker's advance and enabling the brigade of General Robert Ransom to arrive and assist. The exposed Union brigade under General Daniel E. Sickles suddenly breaks and runs for cover, and McClellan next orders all his troops back to their original starting positions. After sorting themselves out and bringing up additional artillery, the Federals advance back upon Oak Grove, methodically raking the Southerners with heavy canister fire. Wright and Ransom both yield ground before darkness envelopes the battlefield and fighting stops. The Union acquires Oak Grove at a cost of 68 killed, 503 wounded, and 55 missing (626), while the Confederates lose 66 dead, 362 injured, and 12 missing (441)—a trifling toll in light of what follows. McClellan congratulates himself on advancing his front another 600 yards toward Richmond, then waxes worried over intelligence that General Thomas J. Jackson's Army of the Valley is approaching. The Army of the Potomac thus concludes its only offensive action of the Peninsula campaign; no one could anticipate that the strategic initiative is passing suddenly into Southern hands.

WEST: The new Army of Virginia is constituted under General John Pope in western Virginia, an amalgam of forces commanded by Generals Irvin McDowell, John C. Frémont, and Nathaniel P. Banks.

To counter the growth of pro-Southern civic organizations, the Union League is organized at Pekin, Illinois, to bolster Northern morale and assist the war effort.

General Thomas Williams division arrives opposite Vicksburg, Mississippi, and establishes a base camp near Swampy Toe.

June 26

SOUTH: Throughout the morning, three Confederate divisions under General James Longstreet, Daniel H. Hill, and Ambrose P. Hill concentrate 47,000 men in the vicinity of Mechanicsville, Virginia. Opposing them are the 30,000-man V Corps of General Fitz John Porter, strongly entrenched behind Beaver Dam Creek. However, Confederate success hinges completely on the arrival of General Thomas J. Jackson's corps in the rear of Union defenses. The Southerners wait patiently for Jackson, whose very arrival constitutes the signal to attack, but he fails to materialize or even establish contact with other commands. His uncharacteristic dilatoriness proves too much for the aggressive A. P. Hill, who orders a frontal assault against Porter at 3:00 P.M. Well-positioned Union forces experience little difficulty blasting back the enthusiastic Confederates, who launch several brave but piecemeal assaults. Three brigades are then committed against the Union right, which likewise are slaughtered by the concentrated artillery and musketry fire of General John F. Reynold's command.

Meanwhile, Jackson's exhausted men finally trudge into Pole Green—three miles from the scene of fighting—where he expects to confer with other commanders. But finding the place deserted with no orders awaiting him, the exhausted general orders his fatigued troops into bivouacs. Back at Mechanicsville, President Jefferson Davis also makes an unexpected appearance at Lee's headquarters, just as brigade-sized attacks by Generals Dorsey Pender and Roswell Ripley are launched. Both men are rebuffed with heavy losses and, with the onset of twilight, the fighting tapers off and stops. Lee's battle plan misfires spectacularly with a loss of 1,484 Confederates to 361 Federals. Union forces waged a set piece defense against steep odds and prevailed in this, the first of the Seven Day's Battles—but victory held unintended consequences. Lee's sudden pugnaciousness completely unnerves General George B. McClellan, who suddenly orders the victorious Porter to abandon his otherwise strong position. The V Corps is now to concentrate four miles east at Gaines' Mill.

In a major move, General George B. McClellan also decides to shift his base of operations from the Pamunkey River to Harrison's Landing on the James River, and he implores Commodore Louis M. Goldsborough to send the bulk of his provision transports there. This is the first move in what many participants on either side begin to ridicule as "the Great Skedaddle."

WEST: The new Federal Army of Virginia under General John Pope assumes responsibility for the former Mountain Department, along with those of the Rappahannock and Shenandoah. General Nathaniel P. Banks commands the II Corps while Irvin McDowell is reassigned the III Corps. General Franz Sigel ultimately is tapped to succeed John C. Frémont as chief of I Corps.

NAVAL: An armed boat from the USS *Mount Vernon* attacks and burns the Confederate blockade-runner Emily off Wilmington, North Carolina, despite heavy fire from nearby Fort Caswell.

The USS *Kensington,* accompanied by mortar boats *Horace Beals* and *Sarah Bruen,* attack and level a Confederate battery at Cole's Creek on the Mississippi River, prior to moving on Vicksburg, Mississippi.

June 27

POLITICS: President Abraham Lincoln formally accepts the resignation of the controversial explorer, soldier, and politician John C. Frémont.

SOUTH: The Union V Corps under General Fitz John Porter retires four miles southeast from Mechanicsville, Virginia, and establishes a new defensive perimeter along a swampy plateau near Gaines' Mill. His 30,000 men deploy in a semicircular line, with General George Sykes's division of U.S. Army regulars holding the right and General George W. Morrell's division on the left and with ample artillery covering his center. The position is buttressed further by the presence of Boatswain Swamp to the front, itself a nearly impassable obstacle.

The Army of Northern Virginia under General Robert E. Lee sharply pursues the Federals and determines to deliver a crushing blow with 56,000 men. To that end, Lee commits the entire division of General Ambrose P. Hill against Porter's center at 2:30 P.M., which is staggered by a maelstrom of artillery and musketry fire. A New York brigade under Colonel Gouverneur K. Warren also distinguishes itself by slamming into the flank of General Maxcy Gregg's South Carolina brigade and driving them off. As this transpires, General James Longstreet's division arrives on the battlefield, but he delays attacking pending the arrival of General Thomas J. Jackson's corps. Jackson, who missed the previous day's fighting at Mechanicsville, performs equally poorly this day and fails to position his men before 3:00 P.M. Meanwhile, Lee resumes attacking Porter's line by forwarding divisions under Generals Daniel H. Hill and Richard S. Ewell up against Porter's left while General George E. Pickett's brigade performs a diversionary thrust on the right. Both attacks, bravely delivered, again are repulsed bloodily by the withering fire of Sykes's regulars and supporting cannon.

Lee's own sloppy staff work means that he cannot assemble the bulk of his army on the field prior to 7:00 P.M. Undeterred by losses, he determines to make a final charge on the tiring Federals, spearheaded by 4,000 fresh troops. Foremost among these is the Texas brigade under General John B. Hood, which takes frightful losses yet crashes through Porter's defenses, netting 14 cannon. This signals the retreat of Union forces, which are covered by a suicidal charge of the U.S. 5th and 2nd Cavalry. As the victorious but weary Confederates surmount the plateau, Porter withdraws in good order toward Chickahominy Creek and closer to General George B. McClellan's main force. Gaines' Mill proves to be the most sanguine of the Seven Days' battles, with Confederate losses of 1,483 dead, 6,401 wounded, and 108 missing (7,993) versus a Union tally of 894 killed, 3,114 wounded, and 2,829 captured (6,837). The combined might of the Army of Virginia had failed again to destroy an isolated Union corps, but Lee's aggressiveness convinces McClellan to abandon Richmond altogether and retreat toward the James River. The much-vaunted Union offensive unravels.

WEST: Federal troops across from Vicksburg, Mississippi, begin digging a canal to alter a bend in the Mississippi River.

General Braxton Bragg directs 3,000 men of General John P. McCown's division to transit by rail from Tupelo, Mississippi, to Chattanooga, Tennessee, and there they join the army of General Edmund Kirby-Smith. The movement takes six days and proceeds smoothly, which convinces Bragg that larger transfers of men and supplies could be shuttled to that theater before Union forces can respond.

NAVAL: The USS *Bienville* captures the Confederate schooner *Morning Star* off Wilmington, North Carolina.

The USS *Cambridge* destroys the blockade-runner *Modern Greece* off Wilmington, North Carolina.

The USS *Bohio* captures the Confederate sloop *Wave* near Mobile, Alabama.

Admiral David G. Farragut formulates plans to run his squadron past the guns of Vicksburg, Mississippi. That accomplished, he will unite with the gunboat flotilla under Admiral Charles H. Davis on the Mississippi River.

June 28

SOUTH: General George B. McClellan withdraws from Richmond and bitterly concludes that he is losing the campaign due to a lack of promised reinforcements. Meanwhile, the Confederates hastily regroup and reorganize to maintain their strategic initiative. General Robert E. Lee, having analyzed McClellan's temperament, now orders his army on an intricate march down four different roads in an attempt to surround and possibly cripple his opponent. He also directs the 11,000-man force under General John B. Magruder to harass the withdrawal of Union forces until the main Confederate body is brought up.

Confederate forces under Colonel George T. Anderson attack a small Union detachment at Garnett's and Golding's farms, Virginia, but they are repulsed in heavy fighting. That night, another force under General (and former Confederate secretary of state) Robert Toombs also probes the Union line only to suffer another defeat. Casualties are recorded as 461 Confederates and 361 Federals.

Federal forces evacuate James Island, South Carolina, temporarily suspending their campaign to capture the city of Charleston.

WEST: Colonel Philip Sheridan takes a brigade of Union cavalry to Boonesboro, 20 miles south of Corinth, Mississippi, and establishes a fortified outpost. He is scouting for possible offensive activity by Confederates under General Braxton Bragg.

General Earl Van Dorn arrives back at Vicksburg, Mississippi, and resumes control of the city's defenses.

NAVAL: Navy vessels sortie from their anchorage at Fortress Monroe, Virginia, and sail to Harrison's Landing to secure communications for the Army of the Potomac as it retires from Richmond.

The USS *Braziliera* captures the Confederate schooner *Chance* off Wassaw Sound, Georgia.

At 2:00 A.M., Admiral David G. Farragut and Commander David D. Porter slip their respective commands past Confederate batteries at Vicksburg, Mississippi, suffering 15 killed and 30 wounded—a trivial toll considering the heavy ordnance poured on them. The mightiest Confederate bastion in the West is about to be challenged.

June 29

SOUTH: The Confederate Department of Alabama and West Florida is disbanded.

General John B. Magruder, advancing east from Williamsburg, Virginia, with 11,000 men, cautiously probes the region for Union forces. He is ordered by General Robert E. Lee to pursue retreating Federal forces aggressively and possibly to destroy their rear guard. Previously, Magruder made arrangements with Generals Thomas J. Jackson and Benjamin Huger to provide cover and support for both of his flanks, but neither force materializes—Jackson is delayed constructing a bridge over Chickahominy Creek while Huger's troops take the wrong road and become lost. Contact with Union troops finally is established at Allen's Farm at about 9:00 A.M., although Magruder suddenly finds himself confronting the entire II Corps of 26,000 men under General Edwin V. Sumner, backed by 40 cannon. He nonetheless attacks and enjoys reasonable success until Federal defenses stiffen. Magruder then suspends the battle at 11:00 A.M. and assumes defensive positions. The equally timorous Sumner then withdraws to new positions at Savage's Station and assumes defensive lines of his own.

Magruder, still unsupported by either Jackson or Huger, cautiously resumes his advance at about 4:00 P.M. and, within the hour, tangles with Sumner's pickets. But Sumner, despite the preponderance of his force, declines to attack and simply lobs shells at Confederate positions for several hours. Confederate General Richard Griffith, reconnoitering Union lines closely, is killed in consequence. Stiff fighting then ensues between the divisions of General Lafayette McLaws and John Sedgwick until an unexpected thunderstorm erupts at about 9:00 P.M., and combat ceases. Thus far, Magruder's "pursuit" availed him little beyond 626 casualties. Sumner's mishandling of affairs cost him 919 men, and he abandons 2,500 sick and injured soldiers before leaving. A major Confederate advance has been stalled. Overnight, the II Corps withdraws to new positions at White Oak Swamp and Glendale.

WEST: General Franz Sigel formally assumes command of the Army of Virginia's I Corps.

NAVAL: The USS *Marblehead* and *Chocura*, anchored in the Pamunkey River, Virginia, provide cover fire for the Army of the Potomac as it withdraws from the vicinity of White House. Transports and armed escorts also sortie up the James and Chickahominy rivers in support of General George B. McClellan.

The USS *Susquehanna* and *Kanawha* capture the British blockade-runner *Ann* off Mobile, Alabama.

The Federal gunboat USS *Lexington* takes fire from Confederate forces on the White River, Arkansas, near St. Charles.

June 30

SOUTH: General Robert E. Lee, intent on destroying at least a portion of General George B. McClellan's Army of the Potomac, issues another set of complicated attack plans to catch the fleeing Federals in a pincer at Glendale, near the junctions of the Charles City Road, Long Bridge Road, and Quaker Road. Orders then are sent out to the divisions of John B. Magruder, Benjamin Huger, Thomas J. Jackson, James Longstreet, and Ambrose P. Hill to converge on Union forces from front, flank, and rear, crushing them. But, once again, Lee is stymied by inept staff work, and his strategy quickly goes awry. Magruder, for his part, becomes lost and spends the entire day marching to and fro behind Confederate lines without seeing action. Huger likewise is unable to surmount obstacles placed in his path along the Charles City Road, and he fails to advance in time. The usually astute Jackson then turns in one of the most lethargic performances of his career by simply remaining north of White Oak Swamp and swapping cannonballs with General William B. Franklin's VI Corps. By 4:00 P.M. that afternoon, an exasperated Lee could count only 19,000 men of Longstreet's and Hill's divisions on the field, and these are seriously depleted by previous fighting.

At length, Longstreet and Hill charge the center of the Union line, posted behind White Oak Swamp Creek, and crash into the division of General George A. McCall, capturing him. But before they can exploit their advantage and seize a vital crossroads, fresh forces under Generals Joseph Hooker, Phil Kearney, and John Sedgewick rush up to engage them. Savage hand-to-hand fighting finally evicts the Confederates and fighting concludes with nightfall. The Union line of retreat is saved. Lee's losses at White Oak are 638 dead, 2,814 wounded, and 221 missing (3,673) while McClellan sustains 297 killed, 1,696 wounded, and 1,804 missing (3,797). Despite a fine performance by his troops, the Union leader continues shifting his base of operations toward Harrison's Landing on the James River and assumes new defensive positions along Malvern Hill, two miles distant.

NAVAL: The USS *South Carolina* is detached from the South Atlantic Blockading Squadron to join the *Wyandotte* off Mosquito Inlet, New Smyrna, Florida, recently used by blockade-runners from Nassau.

The USS *Quaker City* captures the Confederate brig *Model* in the Gulf of Mexico.

The Federal gunboat USS *Lexington* trades fire with Confederate batteries on the White River, Arkansas.

July 1

POLITICS: To meet mounting wartime expenditures, President Lincoln raises the federal income tax to 3 percent on incomes of more than $600 per annum. (The first income tax passed in 1861 was never enacted). The Bureau of Internal Revenue is also founded to collect the levies. Congress then passes the Pacific Railway Act, authorizing construction of the first transcontinental railroad.

SOUTH: Unable to destroy the Army of the Potomac at White Oak Swamp the previous day, General Robert E. Lee is convinced that, nevertheless, General George B. McClellan's force is demoralized by the sledgehammer blows he has dealt them. Now, with Union forces poised to reach Harrison's Landing on the James River safely, he hopes to deliver one last and possibly crushing blow against them at Malvern Hill, a 150-foot high-rise flanked by swamps and other obstacles. That position is defended ably by the V Corps of General Fitz John Porter, who arrays his troops in a defensive semicircle along its crest. Porter's secure flanks also promise to funnel any Confederate assault directly up the center of his waiting line, crowned by 100 pieces of field artillery. The approach is covered further by a thick belt of skirmishers from Colonel Hiram Berdan's elite regiment of green-clad sharpshooters. Finally, even if endangered, Porter could call on any one of four Union additional corps deployed to his rear for assistance.

Confederate general Daniel H. Hill, on surveying the obvious strength of Porter's position, advises Lee to relent, but the general remains determined to attack. Orders then go out for the divisions of General Thomas J. Jackson to deploy against the Union left, that of John B. Magruder to hit their center and of Benjamin Huger's to assail their right. General James Longstreet, meanwhile, strongly suggests that Confederate artillery be massed along either flank and pointed at the center to catch Union gunners in a crossfire. However, as happened repeatedly all week, Lee's sound plan is vexed and undone due to staff errors and misunderstandings. Magruder becomes lost again, countermarching fruitlessly for several hours, and he arrives to find that his position has been taken up by Huger. The Confederate attack, when it developed at 1:00 P.M., is also delivered piecemeal and subject to defeat in detail. The heavy Southern columns present excellent targets to Porter's well-drilled gunners, who rip their formation apart with a deluge of shot, canister, and grape. For several hours, the valiant gray coats fling themselves at the Union position, only to be blasted downhill in tangled heaps. The one-sided slaughter continues until darkness finally closes the contest. Lee's final lunge at McClellan proves catastrophic: His troops sustain losses totaling 869 killed, 4,241 wounded, and 540 missing (5,650) while Union casualties amount to 314 dead, 1,875 wounded, and 818 missing (3,007). A stunned general Daniel H. Hill characterizes Malvern Hill not as war; rather, he says, "it was murder." Porter and other Union generals implore McClellan to counterattack immediately and to resume the drive on Richmond, but he characteristically refuses. The Army of the Potomac then withdraws a final five miles overnight and reestablishes itself at Harrison's Landing, safely under the guns of the Union navy.

The Seven Days' campaign reaches its bloody conclusion with Union forces pushed far from the Southern capital. The Confederacy is preserved for another three and a half years at a cost of 3,286 killed, 15,909 wounded, and 946 missing (20,141). The Army of the Potomac, which handles itself well under excruciating circumstances—not the least of which is McClellan's timorous leadership—loses 1,734 dead, 8,062 injured, and 6,063 missing (15,849). Most important of all, the campaign defines General Robert E. Lee as an assertive, imaginative, and offensive-minded battle captain, much given to bold and calculated risks. Warfare in the eastern theater now largely revolves around his actions.

West: Union forces under General Philip H. Sheridan engage a larger force of 4,700 Confederates under General James R. Chalmers at Booneville, Mississippi, 20 miles south of Corinth. Chalmers presses hard against Sheridan's pickets, carrying the latest Colt revolving rifles, and they make little headway. But Sheridan, while badly outnumbered, orders his 2nd Michigan and 2nd Iowa Cavalry to slip around Chalmer's line and attack his rear. When this move finally transpires at about 3:30 P.M., the Confederates are unnerved completely and withdraw in good order, hotly pursued by Federal troopers. Only 728 Union troops are engaged in this fine defensive action, and they lose one killed, 24 wounded, and 16 missing. Sheridan reportedly counts 65 Confederate dead on the field. Moreover, his aggressive handling of troops catches the attention of General Henry W. Halleck, who arranges for a promotion to brigadier general 10 weeks hence.

Naval: Commodore John Rodgers directs naval cannon fire from the gunboats *Galena, Aroostook,* and *Jacob Bell* against General Robert E. Lee's right flank at Malvern Hill, Virginia, facilitating the final Union withdrawal.

The USS *DeSoto* captures the British schooner *William* off Sabine Pass, Texas.

The Western Flotilla under Commodore Charles H. Davis unites with the naval expedition of Admiral David G. Farragut above Vicksburg, Mississippi. Freshwater and saltwater squadrons thereby are joined for the first time after remarkable efforts by both.

July 2

Politics: President Abraham Lincoln authorizes the "Ironclad test oath" to extract loyalty from all federal employees, and the oath eventually is extended to include federal contractors, attorneys, jurors, and passport applicants. Furthermore, citizens in Federal-occupied regions of the South likewise are required to pledge their allegiance. Lincoln also signs the Land Grant College Act (or Morrill Act), which transfers public lands to educational institutions throughout the North.

South: General George B. McClellan concludes his overall withdrawal to Harrison's Landing, Virginia, derided by many as the "Great Skedaddle."

West: The Confederate districts of the Mississippi and of the Gulf are constituted under Generals Earl Van Dorn and John H. Forney, respectively.

Naval: The USS *Western World* captures the British blockade-runner *Volante* in Winyah Bay, South Carolina.

July 3

Politics: President Abraham Lincoln and General George B. McClellan both endure a firestorm of criticism and recrimination over the recent Peninsula campaign's failure.

West: General Sterling Price becomes commander of the Confederate Army of the West.

Naval: The USS *Quaker City* captures the British blockade-runner *Lilla* off Hole-in-the-Wall, Virginia.

The USS *Hatteras* captures the Confederate schooner *Sarah* off Sabine Pass, Texas.

July 4

POLITICS: General George B. McClellan again advises President Abraham Lincoln that the objective of military operations should be the preservation of the Union, not the elimination of slavery.

NORTH: Philip Kearny, Fitz John Porter, and John Sedgwick are each appointed major general, U.S. Army.

WEST: Confederate cavalry under Colonel John H. Morgan depart Knoxville, Tennessee, with 867 troopers, starting the first of three celebrated raids. Morgan's objective is the town of Gallatin, Tennessee, where he intends to cut the Louisville and Nashville Railroad, then supplying the army of General Don C. Buell.

SOUTHWEST: Pro-union German settlers under Fritz Teneger rally at Bear Creek, Texas, and organize three armed companies for their own protection.

NAVAL: The USS *Maratanza* attacks and captures CSS *Teaser* at Haxall's on the James River, Virginia, as it lays torpedoes. The vessel was also preparing to conduct balloon reconnaissance operations with a device stitched together from old silk frocks.

The USS *Rhode Island* captures the British blockade-runner *R. O. Bryan* off the Texas coast.

July 5

WEST: General William J. Hardee temporarily takes charge of the Army of the Mississippi.

NAVAL: The U.S. Navy Department is reorganized by Act of Congress into eight divisions: Yards and Docks, Equipment and Recruiting, Navigation, Ordnance, Construction and Repair, Steam Engineering, Provisions and Clothing, and Medicine and Surgery.

The USS *Hatteras* captures the Confederate sloop *Elizabeth* off the Louisiana coast.

July 6

SOUTH: General Ambrose E. Burnside sails from the Department of North Carolina with reinforcements slated for the Army of the Potomac, Virginia. His successor is General John G. Foster.

WEST: General Nathan B. Forrest begins to assemble cavalry in Mississippi for an extended raid through Tennessee.

NAVAL: Commodore John Wilkes assumes command of the James River Flotilla, presently a division within the North Atlantic Blockading Squadron under Commodore Louis M. Goldsborough.

July 7

SOUTH: President Abraham Lincoln visits General George B. McClellan at Harrison's Landing, Virginia, to discuss recent events. The general blames his recent setback on a lack of promised reinforcements, and he also urges the president to adopt more conservative approaches to both strategy—and politics.

WEST: Union forces under Generals Samuel R. Curtis and Frederick Steele defeat a body of Confederates at Cache, Arkansas.

NAVAL: The James River Flotilla under Commodore John Rodgers actively escorts and convoys army transports supporting the Army of the Potomac, Virginia.

The USS *Tahoma* captures the Confederate schooner *Uncle Mose* off Yucatán Bank, Mexico.

The USS *Quaker City* and *Huntsville* seize the British schooner *Adela* off the Bahama Islands.

July 8

WEST: Federal troops attack a camp occupied by Confederate guerrilla William C. Quantrill at Pleasant Hill, Missouri.

NAVAL: President Abraham Lincoln arrives onboard the USS *Areil* at Harrison's Landing, Virginia.

Armed boats from the USS *Flag* and *Restless* capture the blockade-runner *Emilie* in Bulls Bay, South Carolina.

July 9

WEST: Tompkinsville, Kentucky, is captured by Confederate cavalry under Colonel John H. Morgan, along with 400 Union prisoners.

NAVAL: An expedition consisting of Federal gunboats USS *Commodore Perry, Shawsheen,* and *Ceres* steams up the Roanoke River, North Carolina, and captures the town of Hamilton, along with the Confederate steamer *Wilson.*

The USS *Arthur* captures the Confederate schooner *Reindeer* off Aransas Pass, Texas.

July 10

WEST: The newly designated Army of Virginia under General John Pope positions itself in the Shenandoah Valley and reminds inhabitants of their obligation to assist Union efforts. He also promises harsh justice for any treasonable or harmful activities against military personnel.

Confederate raider Colonel John H. Morgan captures a Union depot at Glasgow, Kentucky, and issues a dispatch urging inhabitants to "rise and arm, and drive the Hessian invaders from their soil."

Union forces apprehend 90 Confederate guerrillas as they drill between Gallatin and Hartsville, Tennessee.

NAVAL: The USS *Arthur* apprehends the Confederate sloop *Belle Italia* at Aransas Pass, Texas, while the sloop *Monte Christo* is burned to prevent capture.

July 11

POLITICAL: Congress authorizes compensation for the families of Union sailors killed in the action against the CSS *Virginia* at Hampton Roads, Virginia.

NORTH: General Henry W. Halleck gains appointment as general in chief of Union forces.

WEST: Colonel John H. Morgan's occupation of Lebanon, Kentucky, alarms the countryside as far as Cincinnati, Ohio, Evansville, Indiana, and neighboring Lexington and Louisville.

July 12

NORTH: The Congressional Medal of Honor, established in 1861 to honor naval personnel, is expanded to include soldiers.

WEST: Union forces under General Samuel R. Curtis arrive at Helena, Arkansas, from Missouri.

NAVAL: The USS *Mercedita* captures Confederate blockade-runners *Victoria* and *Ida* off Hole-in-the-Wall, Abaco, Bahamas.

Faced with falling water levels on the Yazoo River, the large Confederate ironclad CSS *Arkansas,* under Lieutenant Isaac N. Brown, sorties into the Mississippi River and steams south toward Vicksburg, Mississippi.

July 13

POLITICS: President Abraham Lincoln seeks congressional action to compensate states that are willing to abolish slavery voluntarily. He also informs Secretary of State William H. Seward and Secretary of the Navy Gideon Welles of his intention to read an initial "emancipation proclamation" to the full cabinet on July 22.

SOUTH: Having skirmished with Confederates forces, Union troops burn a bridge along the Rapidan River, Virginia.

WEST: Colonel Nathan B. Forrest and 1,000 Confederate cavalry capture Murfreesboro, Tennessee, by defeating a Union garrison of 1,200 men. He does so by overrunning the camps of the 9th Michigan and 7th Pennsylvania Cavalry before bluffing the still intact 3rd Minnesota to surrender. "I did not come here to make a half job of it," he declares to subordinates after being warned about approaching reinforcements, "I intend to have them all." Union casualties are 29 killed and 120 wounded while Forrest suffers 25 killed and about 50 wounded.

Confederate cavalry under Colonel John H. Morgan raid the vicinity of Harrodsburg, Kentucky.

All remaining Missouri State Guard troops east of the Mississippi River are ordered home to become part of the army under General Thomas C. Hindman.

July 14

POLITICS: President Abraham Lincoln approves legislation for a Federal pension system to assist all widows and children of Union soldiers killed in the war. Meanwhile, 20 representatives from border states announce their opposition to the president's compensated emancipation plan.

SOUTH: Richard H. Anderson is appointed major general, C.S.A.

WEST: General John Pope rallies soldiers of his Army of Virginia in declaring that "The strongest position a soldier should desire to occupy is one from which he can most easily advance against the enemy." He then positions his men between Washington, D.C., and Confederate forces to draw their attention from General George B. McClellan.

Confederate cavalry under Colonel John H. Morgan skirmish with Union forces at Mackville, Kentucky.

July 15

SOUTHWEST: Apaches under Mangas Coloradas and Cochise engage California troops at the Battle of Apache Pass, New Mexico Territory.

NAVAL: Union vessels USS *Carondelet, Tyler,* and *Queen of the West* under Captain Charles H. Davis attack the newly built Confederate ironclad CSS *Arkansas* under Lieutenant Isaac N. Brown once it emerges from the Yazoo River onto the Mississippi. After a heavy exchange of fire, which badly damages *Carondelet* and *Tyler, Arkansas* dashes through 16 Union vessels comprising Commodore David G. Farragut's blockading fleet and steams unscathed on to Vicksburg, Mississippi. Brown then anchors safely under the city's big guns, but Farragut, angered over being surprised, directs his fleet past Vicksburg in broad daylight and attacks the Confederate intruder. Both sides sustain damage, but the *Arkansas* remains afloat and a menace to Union shipping throughout the region. In light of falling water levels on the Mississippi, Farragut continues to New Orleans to recoup his losses. Moreover, Davis's mishandling of the *Arkansas* sortie leads to his eventual replacement by David D. Porter.

July 16

DIPLOMACY: Confederate agent John Slidell requests the French government under Emperor Napoleon III to grant diplomatic recognition.

POLITICS: The western gunboat fleet, constructed and managed by the War Department, is formally transferred by Congress to the Navy Department.

NORTH: Alfred Pleasonton is appointed brigadier general of cavalry.

WEST: General Ulysses S. Grant has his District of West Tennessee enlarged to include the District of the Mississippi and the two armies they contain.

SOUTHWEST: General Theophilus H. Holmes becomes commander of the Confederate Trans-Mississippi Department.

NAVAL: David G. Farragut is formally promoted to rear admiral by Congress, the first officer in United States naval history to hold that rank. President Abraham Lincoln also signs legislation conferring similar promotions on all sitting flag officers.

The USS *Huntsville* captures the British schooner *Agnes* off Abaco, Bahamas.

July 17

POLITICS: President Abraham Lincoln approves the Second Confiscation Act, which mandates freedom for any African-American slaves reaching Union lines. Those wishing to emigrate from the United States will also receive assistance. Various kinds of property useful to the Confederate war effort also are subject to seizure. However, escaped slaves in loyal, border states remain subject to return under the Fugitive Slave Law.

The second session of the 37th Congress adjourns.

SOUTH: General John Pope's Federal troops capture Gordonsville, Virginia, then functioning as a Confederate supply base.

General Daniel H. Hill transfers to the Department of North Carolina.

WEST: Following General Henry S. Halleck's departure for Washington, D.C., General Ulysses S. Grant formally resumes his role as commander of troops in the western theater.

Naval: An armed party of sailors and marines from USS *Potomac, New London,* and *Grey Cloud* ascends the Pascagoula River, Mississippi, on an expedition, but it is turned back by Confederate cavalry.

July 18

West: A small party of Confederate raiders under Captain Adam R. Johnson cross the Ohio River and briefly seize the town of Newburg, Indiana. He then employs two fake cannon constructed from stove pipes across the river to bluff local Indiana Home Guards into compliance lest he "shell" the town. After absconding with guns stored in the Federal arsenal there, the raiders slip quickly back across the river, chased and shelled by a Union gunboat. Hereafter, Johnson is convivially nicknamed "Stovepipe." Two Union soldiers are wounded in the raid, which prompts Governor Oliver P. Morton to wire the War Department for reinforcements.

Confederate cavalry under Colonel John H. Morgan attack and capture the town of Cynthiana, Kentucky, leaving 17 Union and 24 Confederate soldiers dead. He also seizes 400 prisoners.

The Confederate Department No. 2 is enlarged to include Mississippi, East Louisiana, and West Florida.

Naval: Secretary of the Navy Gideon Welles directs naval flag officers to select three enlisted boys annually to become candidates at the U.S. Naval Academy.

July 19

Politics: Horace Greeley, editor of the *New York Tribune,* composes a letter to President Abraham Lincoln and calls on him to free the slaves as a means of weakening the Confederacy.

John S. Phelps of Missouri is named military governor of Arkansas.

Naval: The U.S. Congress approves a pension bill guaranteeing a lifetime subsidy to all naval personnel injured in the line of duty.

A Confederate court of inquiry acquits Commodore Josiah Tattnall for his destruction of the CSS *Virginia* on May 11, 1862.

July 20

West: Colonel John H. Morgan's raiders are surprised by Union cavalry at Owensville, Kentucky, and are dispersed.

July 21

Politics: President Abraham Lincoln discusses with the cabinet the possible employment of African-American soldiers. No action is taken.

South: Nathan B. Forrest is appointed brigadier general, C.S.A.

West: Union forces occupy Luray in western Virginia.

The Confederate Army of Mississippi under General Braxton Bragg advances toward Chattanooga, Tennessee, while command of the District of Tennessee reverts to General Sterling Price.

Naval: The USS *Huntsville* captures the Confederate steamer *Reliance* in the Bahama Channel.

Federal steamers *Clara Dolsen* and *Rob Roy,* along with the tug *Restless,* embark troops at Cairo, Illinois, and transport them to nearby Evansville prior to recapturing Henderson, Kentucky, from Confederate irregulars.

The transport USS *Sallie Woods* is destroyed by Confederate artillery at Argyle Landing on the Mississippi River.

July 22

POLITICS: President Abraham Lincoln unveils a draft of his Emancipation Proclamation to his cabinet, stipulating a grant of freedom to all African Americans held in bondage throughout the Confederacy. However, he heeds Secretary of State William H. Seward's advice to postpone the document's unveiling until after a significant military victory by the North. Secretary of War Edwin M. Stanton also announces that the army can appropriate personal property for military purposes and also employ any freed African Americans as paid laborers.

Federal and Confederate officials reach agreement on a cartel for exchanging prisoners of war. It functions effectively until the fall of 1863 when Union complaints over the treatment of black soldiers force its cancellation.

WEST: Generals John A. Dix and Ambrose E. Burnside assume command of the VII and IX Corps, respectively, in the Department of Virginia.

Confederate raiders under Colonel John H. Morgan return to Livingston, Tennessee, after a spectacular raid through Kentucky. The Federals also learn that a Confederate operative working for Morgan had tapped into their telegraph lines and intercepted army dispatches for the past 12 days.

NAVAL: The USS *Essex* under Captain William B. Porter, accompanied by the ram *Queen of the West,* resumes attacking the Confederate ironclad CSS *Arkansas* off Vicksburg, Mississippi. Both Union vessels are driven off without seriously damaging their opponent, which defiantly steams past Vicksburg's batteries, challenging its opponents to fight. *Queen of the West* nonetheless strikes the ironclad with a heavy broadside and damages its engines before the action concludes.

July 23

NORTH: General Henry W. Halleck, newly arrived as general in chief in Washington, D.C., discusses the possibility of joint operations between Generals George B. McClellan and John Pope.

SOUTH: Union cavalry under Colonel Hugh J. Kirkpatrick, advancing from Fredericksburg, Virginia, raid Confederate supplies gathered at Carmel Church until driven back by General J. E. B. Stuart.

WEST: General John Pope tightens restriction on the inhabitants of the Shenandoah region by insisting that all military-age males take an oath of allegiance or face deportation to the South. Violators, if caught, would be summarily executed and their property would be confiscated.

General Braxton Bragg skillfully transfers by rail 31,000 Confederate troops from Tupelo, Mississippi, to Chattanooga, Tennessee—a distance of 776 miles—in the largest Confederate railroad movement of the war. By invading Kentucky, both Bragg and General Edmund Kirby-Smith intend to take the Union Army of the Ohio from behind. However, in his place Bragg leaves behind two independent commands: Generals Sterling Price at Tupelo and Earl Van Dorn at Vicksburg, each with 16,000 men apiece. A clear line of authority between the two headstrong leaders is never clearly established, again with detrimental effects for the South.

July 24
POLITICS: Martin Van Buren, the eighth president of the United States, dies in Kinderhook, New York, aged 80 years.
SOUTH: Fitzhugh Lee is appointed brigadier general, C.S.A.

Union forces attack and rout a Confederate detachment at Benton's Ferry, Louisiana.

Federal troops under General John Gibbon commence the reconnoitering of Orange Court House, Virginia, from Fredericksburg.

General John G. Foster initiates a Union overland campaign against Trenton, North Carolina, from New Bern.
NAVAL: Falling water levels on the Mississippi River and rising sickness induce Admiral David G. Farragut to remove his squadron from below Vicksburg, Mississippi, to New Orleans, Louisiana, following a two-month hiatus. His experience outside Vicksburg has convinced him that naval forces alone can never take the city. That will require the services of a large, well-equipped army.

The gunboat flotilla of Admiral Charles H. Davis on the Mississippi River steams off toward Helena, Arkansas, from which a steady flow of men and supplies from Texas and Arkansas originates. Both Davis and General Samuel R. Curtis plan sweeping raids along the Arkansas shore and interdict enemy lines of communication.

The USS *Octorara* captures the British blockade-runner *Tubal* Cain off Savannah, Georgia.

The USS *Quaker City* captures the blockade-runner *Orion* off Key West, Florida.

July 25
SOUTH: J. E. B. Stuart is appointed major general, C.S.A.
WEST: Confederate cavalry under General Joseph Wheeler penetrate 70 miles behind Union lines from Holly Springs, Mississippi, and attacks bridges and communications.
NAVAL: The Confederate steamer *Cuba* skirts the Union blockade and enters Mobile, Alabama.

July 26
WEST: General Braxton Bragg's men compel a Federal retreat from Spangler's Mill at Jonesboro, Alabama.
NAVAL: Confederates burn the Union schooner *Louisia Reed* in the James River.

The Southern steamer *Romain* successfully runs the Union blockade off Charleston, South Carolina.

July 27
NORTH: John Buford is appointed brigadier general of cavalry, U.S. Army.

NAVAL: The USS *Yankee* and *Satellite* capture the Confederate schooner *J. W. Sturges* in Chippoak Creek, Virginia.

July 28

POLITICS: Confederate governors of Texas, Missouri, Arkansas, and Louisiana appeal to President Jefferson Davis for men, supplies, money, and a senior commanding general to bolster their military defenses.

SOUTH: Richard Taylor is appointed major general, C.S.A.

Captain Charles D. Sanford conducts the 12th Massachusetts Cavalry on a reconnaissance expedition from Bachelder's Creek, North Carolina, down the Neuse River Road.

WEST: Colonel John H. Morgan's raiders arrive at Livingston, Tennessee.

Confederate forces are ejected from Bollinger's Mills, Missouri, by Federal troops.

NAVAL: The USS *Hatteras* captures the Confederate brig *Josephine* off Ship Shoal, Louisiana.

July 29

SOUTH: General John Pope departs Washington, D.C., to join the Army of Virginia in the field.

WEST: Federal authorities arrest Confederate spy Bell Boyd at Warrenton, Virginia, and she is sent to the Old Capital Prison in Washington, D.C.

Advance elements of the Confederate Army of Mississippi arrive at Chattanooga, Tennessee, constituting a strategic transfer of resources from the Deep South back to its center. General Braxton Bragg skillfully cobbles together a force of 30,000 men there for an offensive into Kentucky.

Confederate cavalry rout General John Logan's troopers at Hatchie Bottom, Tennessee.

Union forces rout Confederate defenders at Moore's Mills, Missouri, inflicting 62 killed and 100 wounded for a Northern loss of 16 dead and 30 injured.

NAVAL: Ship "290," christened *Enrica*, departs Liverpool, England, ostensibly for sea trials. It actually is headed for Nassau for service with the Confederate navy as the infamous commerce raider CSS *Alabama*.

The USS *Mount Vernon* and *Mystic* capture the British blockade-runner *Napier* near Wilmington, North Carolina.

July 30

SOUTH: General George B. McClellan, commanding the Army of the Potomac, Virginia, receives orders to transfer all sick and wounded soldiers from Harrison's Landing. This is a preliminary step for relocating his entire command back to Washington, D.C.

At New Orleans, Louisiana, General Benjamin Butler further roils public sentiments by confiscating a load of church bells cast in Boston; he orders them auctioned.

SOUTHWEST: Major Alfred Hobby arrives at Corpus Christi, Texas, with 300 men of the 8th Texas. His purpose is to guard the town against attacks mounted by the offshore Union squadron under Captain John W. Kittredge.

July 31

DIPLOMACY: U.S. minister Charles F. Adams badgers Foreign Secretary Lord Russell not to allow the newly launched *Enrica* (the future CSS *Alabama*) to leave port. The British government dithers for five days before Lord Russell issues the requested orders, but Confederate agents slip aboard and it sails away under the pretense of conducting sea trials. Ultimately, this vessel accounts for the destruction of 60 Union merchant ships and becomes a major source of friction between the two governments.

POLITICS: President Jefferson Davis directs that any Union officer captured from General John Pope's Army of Virginia is to be treated as a felon. This is in retaliation for the order that hostile Southern citizens should be shot for treason under Pope's draconian administration of the Shenandoah Valley.

WEST: General Braxton Bragg and Genevoe Edmund Kirby-Smith confer at Chattanooga, Tennessee, and hammer out a strategy for the upcoming campaign in Kentucky. The former, while senior, fails to exert his authority over Kirby-Smith, who insists on a virtually independent command. The Confederate offensive thus is compromised from the onset and promises to be poorly coordinated.

NAVAL: The USS *Cimarron* engages a Confederate battery at Coggin's Point, Virginia, after it sinks two army transports.

The USS *Magnolia* captures the Confederate steamer *Memphis* off Cape Romain, South Carolina.

August 1

NORTH: George Crook is appointed brigadier general, U.S. Army.

SOUTH: Federal and Confederate artillery duels at Harrison's Landing, Virginia.

WEST: A heavy skirmish erupts at Newark, Missouri, with Confederates losing 100 killed and wounded while capturing 70 Union troops.

SOUTHWEST: Fritz Teneger convinces 65 pro-Union German settlers at Turtle Creek, Texas, to cross the Rio Grande into Mexico, sail to New Orleans, and join the Union army there. When Confederate authorities learn of the plan they dispatch 94 men to intercept them.

NAVAL: The USS *Thomas Freeborn* captures the Confederate schooner *Mail* in the Coan River, Virginia.

The USS *Penobscot* captures the Confederate sloop *Lizzie* off New Inlet, North Carolina.

August 2

DIPLOMACY: Secretary of State William H. Seward orders American minister to Britain Charles F. Adams to officially ignore any British overtures for mediation.

SOUTH: Malvern Hill, Virginia, is reoccupied by Union troops under General George B. McClellan.

Union forces under General John Pope storm into Orange Court House, Virginia, killing 11 Confederates and taking 52 prisoners for a loss of five wounded.

NAVAL: English authorities prepare to release CSS *Florida* for sea duty after it had been seized at Nassau. August 3

SOUTH: General Henry W. Halleck orders the Army of the Potomac to begin shifting from Harrison's Landing on the Yorktown Peninsula to Aquia Landing near Fredericksburg, Virginia, to protect the national capital better. The transfer occasions much umbrage from General George B. McClellan, who seeks a renewed offensive against Richmond.

WEST: General Jeff Thompson's Confederates are defeated near Memphis, Tennessee.

NAVAL: The USS *Santiago de Cuba* seizes the blockade-runner *Columbia* north of Abaco, Bahamas, along with its cargo of several thousand British-made Enfield rifles, 12 cannon, and tons of munitions.

The Confederate ironclad CSS *Arkansas,* despite persistent engine problems, is ordered out of its berth at Vicksburg, Mississippi, and steams downstream to assist an attack on Baton Rouge, Louisiana. Lieutenant Henry K. Stevens, fearing the worse for his temperamental warship, complies only reluctantly.

August 4

POLITICS: President Abraham Lincoln issues a call for 300,000 drafted militia to serve nine months; this levy was never enacted. But despite persistent manpower shortages, he declines the services of two African-Americans regiments from Indiana, suggesting instead that they be employed as laborers.

SOUTH: Confederate cavalry under General J. E. B. Stuart commence an expedition from Hanover Court House to Fredericksburg, Virginia.

General Ambrose E. Burnside's IX Corps arrives at Aquia Creek, near Fredericksburg, Virginia, to assist the Army of Virginia under General John Pope.

At New Orleans, Louisiana, General Benjamin F. Butler assesses "secessionists" $341,000 to assist the city's poor.

NAVAL: The USS *Huron* captures the Confederate schooner *Aquilla* near Charleston, South Carolina.

The USS *Unadilla* captures the British steamer *Lodona* as it ran the blockade at Hell Gate, Georgia.

August 5

SOUTH: General John Gibbon leads a Federal expedition from Fredericksburg, Virginia, to Frederick's Hall Station, skirmishing en route.

General John C. Breckinridge is ordered by General Earl Van Dorn to attack the Union enclave at Baton Rouge, Louisiana, with a force of 2,600 Confederates, accompanied by the ironclad CSS *Arkansas.* An important part of his mission is to secure Port Hudson on the Mississippi River halfway between Vicksburg and Baton Rouge and to fortify it as a choke point. The Union garrison of 2,500 men under General Thomas Williams deploys to receive him, and a sharp action erupts in very dense fog at about 4:30 A.M. Confusion reigns on both sides but a party of Southerners under General Charles Clark gradually flanks the Union left and pushes the defenders back into the city. Williams is killed while rallying his disorganized troops, but the Confederate advance is thwarted by accurate gunfire from Union gunboats anchored offshore. Fighting finally subsides at about 10:00 A.M. when Breckinridge, realizing that the *Arkansas* is not coming, orders his men back. The Confederates then return to Vicksburg, Mississippi, pausing only to fortify Port Hudson en route. Union losses are 84 dead and 299 wounded to a Southern tally of 84 dead and 372 injured. General Clark, severely wounded, is abandoned on the battlefield and captured.

NAVAL: Union forces commence an expedition up the White River, Arkansas, accompanied by the gunboats *Benton, Iatan, Louisville,* and *Mound City.*

The large Confederate ironclad CSS *Arkansas* under Lieutenant Henry K. Stevens continues down the Mississippi River to assist the expedition against Baton Rouge, Louisiana. Stevens's mission is to neutralize Union gunboats offshore; however, his ship experiences a broken propellor shaft en route to the city, and he is unable to support military efforts ashore. Confederate troops driving against Union positions thus are deprived of badly needed naval support and largely are repulsed by Federal gunboats enfilading their right flank.

August 6

NORTH: William S. Rosecrans is promoted to major general, U.S. Army.

SOUTH: Heavy skirmishing is reported at Malvern Hill and Thornburg, Virginia, and Federal forces withdraw.

WEST: A large skirmish takes place between Federals under General John D. Cox and Confederates under General William W. Loring at Packs Ferry, western Virginia.

Union general Robert L. McCook is murdered by Confederate guerrillas while riding in an ambulance near Decherd, Tennessee.

A starving band of Mdewkanton Santee (Sioux) tribe members arrive at the Lower Agency, where chief Little Crow (Taoyateduta) pleads with Agent Andrew J. Myrick for promised foodstuffs. However, war activities delay the arrival of treaty payments from Washington, D.C., and local authorities refuse to lend Little Crow the credit necessary to feed his people. Despite desperate entreaties for help, Myrick rebuffs the Native Americans, declaring: "So far as I am concerned, if they are hungry, let them eat grass." The chiefs angrily depart the agency, incensed at official indifference.

NAVAL: A Federal naval flotilla under Commander David D. Porter of the USS *Essex* attacks and damages the ironclad CSS *Arkansas,* mechanically unsound and suffering from engine trouble, near Baton Rouge, Louisiana. Once the *Arkansas* is grounded, Stevens orders it set afire and scuttled. The Confederacy never again deploys such a large warship on the Mississippi.

August 7

SOUTH: A force of 24,000 Confederates under General Thomas J. Jackson decamps Gordonsville, Virginia, and marches north to Orange Court House. However, because General Ambrose P. Hill completely misinterprets Jackson's orders and fails to leave camp, the usually hard-marching Southerners cover only eight miles. The incident remains a sore point between the two leaders for the rest of their lives.

SOUTHWEST: Union troops under General Edward R. S. Canby defeat Confederate stragglers near Fort Fillmore, New Mexico Territory.

NAVAL: President Abraham Lincoln, Secretary of War Edwin M. Stanton, and Secretary of State William H. Seward are guests of Admiral John A. B. Dahlgren at the Washington Navy Yard, were they witness the test firing of an experimental repeating cannon christened "Rafael."

The CSS *Florida* sails from Nassau to commence a celebrated raiding career under Lieutenant John N. Maffitt.

August 8

POLITICS: Secretary of War Edwin Stanton suspends writs of habeas corpus throughout the country to facilitate cases against treason and draft evasion.

NORTH: Federal authorities release and parole Confederate spy Belle Boyd from Old Capitol Prison, Washington, D.C., citing lack of evidence to detain her further.

SOUTH: General John Pope orders General Nathaniel P. Banks's division of 9,000 men to proceed south on the Culpeper Road.

General Thomas J. Jackson departs from Orange Court House, Virginia, crosses the Rapidan River with 24,000 men, and advances to evict 9,000 Union troops under General Nathaniel P. Banks from Culpeper County.

WEST: The Army of Mississippi of 30,000 men under General Braxton Bragg departs Chattanooga, Tennessee, and invades Kentucky.

Union and Confederate forces clash heavily at Cumberland Gap, Tennessee, with losses of three Union dead and 15 wounded to 125 Southern casualties.

A spate of attacks on trains by Confederate guerrillas near Huntsville, Alabama, forces Union authorities to arrest secessionist clergy members and place them as passengers on the trains.

August 9

WEST: Aware that Confederates under General Thomas J. Jackson are converging on his position near Cedar Mountain, nine miles south of Culpeper, Virginia, General Nathaniel P. Banks deploys his 9,000 men at its base with cavalry covering open farmland along Cedar Run while his artillery unlimbers atop nearby hills. The overconfident Jackson then approaches from the south with General Richard S. Ewell's division on his right and General Henry S. Winder to his left. His third division under General Ambrose P. Hill is strung out several miles to the rear, en route. After preliminary artillery duels and a hasty, improper reconnaissance, Jackson orders his two divisions forward around 4:30 P.M. The men march sloppily across the field with a considerable gap between them. Jackson, however, is unaware that Banks has stationed two brigades under Generals Samuel W. Crawford and George Gordon in the woods to the left of Winder. These suddenly emerge and hit the Confederates hard, routing Winder's command, including the famous Stonewall Brigade. As General Jubal A. Early advances on the Union center, he also sustains serious losses from Federal artillery and halts to dress ranks. Banks then commits all his reserves to the onslaught, which outflank Jackson and threaten to roll up his line. Confusion increases once the capable Winder is killed by artillery fire, and his command scatters. Jackson grows so perturbed by these unexpected reverses that he draws his sword—allegedly for the only time in the war—grasps a flag, and commences rallying his men. For a few moments it appears that Banks had achieved a startling upset over the previously unstoppable Confederates.

Events began to turn in Jackson's favor at about 5:30 P.M., once the first elements of Hill's division came trudging up the road. These forces plug gaps in the sagging

Confederate line and begin to drive the tiring and outnumbered Federals back. After a failed charge by the 1st Pennsylvania Cavalry, which loses 95 men out of 164, Banks withdraws his men, and the Confederates retain possession of the field. Jackson's losses are 223 killed, 1,060 wounded, and 31 missing (1,334) to a Union tally of 314 killed, 1,445 wounded, and 622 captured (2,353)—a toll that leads participants to dub the encounter "Slaughter Mountain." His victory is tempered by the loss of the capable and talented Winder. Nonetheless, Cedar Mountain forces General Pope to postpone a general advance south, thereby granting General Robert E. Lee additional time to dispatch General James Longstreet north to reinforce Jackson.

August 10
SOUTH: Having elected not to renew the struggle at Cedar Mountain, Virginia, Generals Nathaniel P. Banks and Thomas J. Jackson arrange a truce to collect and bury their dead.

SOUTHWEST: Texas troops under Lieutenant C. D. Macrae attack a sleeping camp of 65 pro-Union German settlers along the Nueces River, Texas, killing 19, wounding nine, and capturing the rest. The nine injured are subsequently removed from camp and executed. Confederate losses are two killed and 18 wounded. The affair permanently dampens outward German disaffection in Texas.

NAVAL: The USS *Resolute* seizes the Confederate schooner *S. S. Jones* off the Virginia coast.

Union forces capture the Confederate steamer *General Lee* outside of Fort Pulaski, Georgia.

Admiral David G. Farragut, in response to guerrilla attacks from the shore on his vessels, partially destroys the town of Donaldsonville, Louisiana, warning inhabitants that the rest will be destroyed if the sniping persists.

August 11
SOUTH: Confederate forces under General Thomas J. Jackson withdraw south of the Rapidan River and back to Gordonsville, Virginia.

WEST: Confederate raiders under William C. Quantrill capture and briefly hold Independence, Missouri.

General Ulysses S. Grant, headquartered at Corinth, Mississippi, declares that all fugitive African American slaves will be employed in his department as laborers.

August 12
WEST: Colonel John H. Morgan stealthily seizes Gallatin, Tennessee, along with 124 Union soldiers under Colonel William P. Boone, without firing a shot. His troopers then destroy tunnels belonging to the Louisville and Nashville Railroad, cutting the supply lines of General Don C. Buell and halting his advance on Chattanooga, Tennessee, for three months.

A Union expedition leaves Fort Leavenworth, Kansas, to secure Independence, Missouri, from Confederate irregulars.

NAVAL: The USS *Arthur* captures the Confederate armed schooner *Breaker* off Aransas Pass, Texas, while the schooners *Elma* and *Hannah* are burned to prevent being captured.

August 13

SOUTH: General Robert E. Lee begins to advance his Army of Northern Virginia from the Peninsula to Gordonsville, Virginia. He begins by dispatching 30,000 troops under General James Longstreet by rail, where they are scheduled to link up with the corps of General Thomas J. Jackson.

SOUTHWEST: Captain John W. Kittredge, commanding U.S. Navy vessels off Corpus Christi, Texas, lands under a flag of truce and urges Confederate authorities to evacuate civilians in light of his impending attack.

WEST: Confederates wage an unsuccessful fight at Yellow Creek, Missouri, losing 60 captives to Union forces.

NAVAL: A collision between Union steamers *George Peabody* and *West Point* on the Potomac River, Virginia, results in 83 deaths, mostly convalescents.

The USS *Kensington* captures the Confederate schooner *Troy* off Sabine Pass, Texas.

August 14

POLITICS: President Abraham Lincoln confers with a delegation of free African Americans at the White House and suggests Central America as a possible venue for colonization. The suggestion is badly received by many black leaders, particularly Frederick Douglass, who accuses the president of "contempt for Negroes."

SOUTH: The III and V Corps are taken by transports from Harrison's Landing, Virginia, and deposited at Aquia Creek near Fredericksburg.

Colonel Charles A. Heckman leads the 9th New Jersey on a reconnaissance from Newport, North Carolina, toward Swansborough.

NAVAL: The USS *Pocahontas* and steam tug *Treaty* exchange fire with Confederate forces on the Black River near Georgetown, South Carolina. This interference allows the steamer *Nina* to escape capture.

August 15

SOUTH: General Robert E. Lee's Army of Northern Virginia reposes at Gordonsville, Virginia, 54,000 strong. From there, he deduces that a lightning strike by Confederate cavalry on bridges over the Rappahannock would isolate Union general John Pope's Army of Virginia on the south bank and was liable to be defeated in detail. He plans to order the march immediately but is dissuaded by General Fitzhugh Lee, who feels that his cavalry horses are worn and require rest.

NAVAL: Commander John Rodgers of the USS *Galena*, in concert with *Port Royal* and *Satellite*, covers the Army of the Potomac as it embarks at Harrison's Landing, Virginia, and is transported over the Chickahominy River.

The USS *Arthur* captures the Confederate steamer *A. B.* after it grounds at the entrance of the Nueces River, Corpus Christi, Texas.

August 16

SOUTH: The Army of the Potomac is relocated completely from Harrison's Landing to Aquia Creek (Alexandria), Virginia, to protect Washington, D.C., better. This withdrawal concludes the so-called Peninsula campaign.

The Army of Northern Virginia under General Robert E. Lee continues advancing toward Gordonsville, Virginia, in anticipation of engaging General John Pope's Army of Virginia.

WEST: General Edmund Kirby-Smith departs Knoxville, Tennessee, with 10,000 men and plunges through the Cumberland Gap and into Kentucky. This act initiates a major Southern offensive to reclaim that state for the Confederacy.

NAVAL: A naval expedition consisting of the USS *Mound City, Benton,* and *General Bragg,* assisted by rams *Monarch, Samson, Lioness,* and *Switzerland,* convey army troops under Colonel Charles R. Woods up the Mississippi River as far as the Yazoo River. They repeatedly land parties along the shore to capture batteries and disperse troop encampments.

August 17

SOUTH: General J. E. B. Stuart assumes command of all Confederate cavalry in the Army of Northern Virginia.

WEST: Half-starved Sioux tribe members stage an uprising in southwest Minnesota by killing five settlers on their farm in Acton Township. Chief Little Crow, when informed of the action, realizes that war with the whites is inevitable and takes to the warpath. The result is a savage, six-week uprising claiming approximately 600 lives.

NAVAL: An armed party from the USS *Ellis* destroys a Confederate battery and a nearby saltworks at Swansboro, North Carolina.

The USS *Sachem, Reindeer, Bella Italia,* and *Corypheus* shell Confederate positions at Corpus Christi, Texas. However, steady fire from Confederate shore emplacements commanded by Major Alfred Hobby keep the Union vessels at a distance. After an ineffectual four-hour exchange, Captain John W. Kittredge calls off his attack and prepares to renew the struggle on the morrow.

Off Nassau, Bahamas, Lieutenant John N. Maffitt assumes formal command of the newly armed and commissioned Confederate raider CSS *Florida.* However, his initial cruise is beset by an outbreak of yellow fever among the crew.

August 18

POLITICS: President Jefferson Davis, addressing the newly convened second session of the Confederate Congress, excoriates the behavior of Union general Benjamin F. Butler at New Orleans.

SOUTH: The Union Army of Virginia under General John Pope withdraws behind the Rappahannock River in the face of advancing Confederate forces. He there awaits reinforcements from General George B. McClellan's 100,000-strong Army of the Potomac.

WEST: General Kirby-Smith and 10,000 Confederates occupy the town of Barboursville, Kentucky. From there, impending supply shortages induce him to commence moving against Lexington.

Confederate forces recapture the town of Clarksville, Tennessee, without a shot being fired. The garrison commander, Col. R. Mason of the 71st Ohio, subsequently is dismissed from the service for cowardice.

Rampaging Sioux warriors attack the Upper and Lower Indian agencies, Minnesota, killing 20 people, including Agent Andrew J. Myrick, whose mouth is symbolically stuffed with the very grass he told the tribes to eat. A detachment of 46 soldiers under Captain John Marsh, 5th Minnesota, advances to rescue the workers and is ambushed at Redwood Ferry and nearly annihilated with the loss of 24 soldiers.

NAVAL: A landing party of 30 sailors and a howitzer disembark from USS *Bella Italia* near Corpus Christi, Texas. A party of 25 men from the 8th Texas engages them on the beach for several tense minutes, at which point Captain John W. Kittredge suspends his attack and returns to the ships offshore. Confederate losses are one dead and a handful wounded.

August 19

NORTH: James B. McPherson is appointed brigadier general, U.S. Army.

SOUTH: General John Pope continues relocating 51,000 Union troops from the Rapidan River to behind the Rappahannock River, Virginia, while awaiting additional forces under General George B. McClellan.

WEST: The Union Department of the Ohio is reconstituted (Illinois, Indiana, Michigan, Ohio, Wisconsin, and eastern Kentucky) under General Horatio G. Wright.

Confederate cavalry under Colonel John H. Morgan begin to probe and raid along the Louisiana and Nashville Railroad.

Federal troops commence a four-month expedition against the Snake Indians of Idaho.

NAVAL: The USS *St. Louis* runs the Confederate steamer *Swallow* aground below Memphis, Tennessee, and then burns it.

August 20

SOUTH: Skirmishes erupt between Federal troops under General John Pope and advancing Confederates under General Thomas J. Jackson at Raccoon Ford, Stevensburg, Brandy Station, and Kelly's Ford, Virginia. Meanwhile, after continuing delays, General Robert E. Lee abandons his plan to strike at bridges over the Rappahannock River to isolate the Army of Virginia under General John Pope.

The Confederate Trans-Mississippi Department absorbs the Districts of Arkansas, Louisiana, and Texas, with General Richard Taylor commanding the District of West Louisiana.

WEST: A mob of Mdewkanton Santee (Sioux) warriors hastily attacks the outskirts of New Ulm, Minnesota, and are repulsed by armed settlers and militia.

SOUTHWEST: General Hamilton P. Bee arrives at Corpus Christi, Texas, to help organize Confederate defenses there.

August 21

POLITICS: The Federal government begins to issue postage stamps to raise money.

Confederate military authorities issue orders to execute any Northern officers found commanding African-American troops. Generals David Hunter and John W. Phelps, in particular, are to be treated as felons if captured for their role in freeing and arming slaves for service in the Union army. Ironically, Phelps resigns his commission this same day because the government has disavowed his efforts.

SOUTH: Confederate forces attempting to cross the Rappahannock River are rebuffed strongly by Union troops, suffering 700 casualties and 2,000 prisoners.

WEST: General Braxton Bragg positions his Confederates above Chattanooga, Tennessee, while the city of Gallatin surrenders.

A large gathering of Mdewkanton band Santee (Sioux) warriors under Chief Little Crow attacks Fort Ridgely, Minnesota, and is repulsed by 180 soldiers and three cannon commanded by Lieutenant Timothy Sheehan. The garrison loses six killed and 20 wounded while Santee losses are considerably heavier. The Indians draw off but continue the siege while awaiting reinforcements.

NAVAL: The USS *Bienville* captures the British blockade-runner Eliza in the Atlantic.

Union forces evacuate Baton Rouge, Louisiana, covered by the USS *Essex* and *Gunboat No. 7.*

August 22

SOUTH: General J. E. B. Stuart crosses the Rappahannock River with 1,500 troopers and two cannon, intending to sever the Orange and Alexandria Railroad, a major Union supply artery. They soon occupy the town of Warrenton, Virginia, without any sign of the enemy and subsequently advance on Catlett's Station under a driving rainstorm.

General Benjamin F. Butler issues orders to recruit African-American slaves into the Union army at New Orleans, Louisiana.

WEST: Confederate cavalry under General Albert G. Jenkins begin an extended raid into western Virginia and Ohio.

Chief Little Crow of the Mdewkanton band of Santee (Sioux) is joined by 400 warriors from the Sisseton and Wahpeton bands, for a total of nearly 800. These forces then make another aborted attack on the 180-man garrison at Fort Ridgley, Minnesota, and are repulsed with 100 casualties. Federal troops sustain three killed and 13 wounded.

NAVAL: Secretary of the Navy Gideon Welles instructs Admiral Louis M. Goldsborough to cooperate closely with the army during its evacuation from Fortress Monroe, Virginia.

The USS *Keystone State* captures the British schooner *Fanny* off St. Simon's Sound, Georgia.

August 23

SOUTH: Northern and Southern artillery duel along the Rappahannock River for five hours.

General J. E. B. Stuart is informed by a captured African American that Catlett's Station, Virginia, is the headquarters of General John Pope. Stuart then attacks with 1,500 troopers under the cover of a rainstorm. They seize 300 prisoners and Pope's personal baggage and uniform, along with his military correspondence. Once in receipt of the latter, General Robert E. Lee is apprised of Union intentions to unite Pope's 51,000-man Army of Virginia with the 100,000-strong Army of the Potomac under General George B. McClellan. Lee, realizing he never could counter such a force successfully, begins to formulate plans to disperse Pope before the two forces can merge.

WEST: General Horatio G. Wright formally accepts command of the Department of the Ohio.

As a Confederate column under General Edmund Kirby-Smith marches on Lexington, Kentucky, the cavalry of his van under Colonel John S. Scott drive off a Union detachment from Big Hill, south of Richmond, where other Federal forces have begun to mass.

The town of New Ulm, Minnesota, is attacked again by 400 rampaging Mdewkanton Santee (Sioux) warriors under Chief Little Crow. The town, stoutly defended by civilians under Judge Charles Flandreu, nearly is consumed by fire, but the Sioux are repulsed and withdraw. The whites lose 36 dead and 23 wounded; Native American losses are unknown but presumed equally heavy.

NAVAL: The USS *Bienville* captures the British blockade-runner *Louisa* near Cape Romain, South Carolina.

The USS *Adirondack* grounds on a reef off Man of War Cay, Little Bahamas, and is abandoned.

The USS *James S. Chambers* captures the Confederate schooner *Corelia* off the Cuban coast.

The USS *Essex* shells Bayou Sara, Louisiana, after guerrillas fire on a landing party.

August 24

SOUTH: In a stunningly bold maneuver, General Robert E. Lee divides the Army of Northern Virginia by detaching 25,000 men of General Thomas J. Jackson's corps on a rapid march to destroy the Orange and Alexandria Railroad, thereby cutting Union general John Pope's supply line. Through this expedient, Lee hopes to draw Union forces up from central Virginia where he can deal with them in the open. Meanwhile, the 30,000 Confederates under General James Longstreet are to remain stationary until Jackson's men are in place.

WEST: General John P. McCown temporarily assumes command of the Department of East Tennessee.

NAVAL: The USS *Henry Andrew* is wrecked in a gale near Cape Henry, Virginia.

The USS *Isaac N. Seymour* sinks in the Neuse River, North Carolina.

The USS *Stars and Stripes* captures British blockade-runner *Mary Elizabeth* off Wilmington, North Carolina.

The USS yacht *Corypheus* captures the Confederate schooner *Water Witch* off Aransas Bay, Texas.

Having received its armament, CSS *Alabama* is commissioned into the Confederate navy off Terceira, Azores, with celebrated raider Raphael Semmes as captain.

August 25

POLITICS: To placate Radical Republicans and alleviate manpower shortages, Secretary of War Edwin M. Stanton authorizes the recruitment of as many as 5,000 African-American soldiers. Orders are then dispatched to General Rufus Saxton, military governor of the South Carolina Sea Islands, to raise five regiments of black troops for military service.

SOUTH: General Thomas J. Jackson's corps detaches from the Army of Northern Virginia and advances to the Rappahannock River. He then commences a wide flanking movement around General John Pope's right flank to cut his line of communications. Jackson's command consists of three crack divisions under Generals Richard S. Ewell, Ambrose P. Hill, and William Taliaferro. By dint of hard slogging, the Southerners cover 56 miles in only two days—one of the most impressive performances of the entire war—and arrive behind the Union Army of Virginia. Through this expedient, Jackson also interposes himself between Pope and the Union capital at Washington, D.C.

WEST: The settlement of New Ulm, Minnesota, is evacuated in the face of possible renewed Sioux attacks. Nearly 1,000 survivors pack up their belongings and flee 30 miles east to Mankato.

August 26

SOUTH: In a surprise move, Confederate forces led by General Isaac Trimble storm into Manassas Junction, Virginia, capturing General John Pope's main supply base. The nominally malnourished Confederates of General Thomas J. Jackson, famously looking more like scarecrows than soldiers, gleefully gorge themselves on the cornucopia within their grasp. At the cost of 12 casualties, the Southerners also net 300 prisoners, eight cannon, and 175 horses.

WEST: General James H. Carleton, takes command of the Department of New Mexico.

NAVAL: Captain Franklin Buchanan is promoted to rear admiral for his conduct in the engagement involving the CSS *Virginia* on March 8, 1862. He remains the only Southerner so honored.

A joint expedition under General Samuel R. Curtis and Commodore Charles H. Davis captures the Confederate steamer *Fair Play* on the Yazoo River in Arkansas. More than 1,200 imported English Enfield rifles are seized.

August 27

SOUTH: Union and Confederate forces begin to grope around the old battlefield of Manassas, Virginia, in anticipation of a major clash. General John Pope, stung by the capture of his supply base at Manassas Junction, rapidly marches from behind the Rappahannock River in search of Confederates under General Thomas J. Jackson. Jackson, meanwhile, ambushes a New Jersey brigade under General George W. Taylor, killing the general, inflicting 135 casualties, and taking 300 prisoners. He then digs in along the Warrenton Turnpike and awaits the balance of the army under General James Longstreet.

The Union division of General Joseph Hooker wins a skirmish at Kettle Run, Virginia, against General Richard S. Ewell, driving him from the field. Hooker's success induces General Thomas J. Jackson to abandon Manassas, and he falls back on Groveton on the Warrenton Turnpike.

WEST: General Nathan B. Forrest is repulsed by the Union garrison at Round Mountain, Tennessee.

Confederate cavalry under General Joseph Wheeler fords the Tennessee River at Chattanooga, ahead of General Braxton Bragg's Army of Mississippi.

A relief column commanded of 1,400 soldiers under Colonel Henry H. Sibley arrives at Fort Sibley, Minnesota, from distant Fort Snelling. Meanwhile, a detachment of troops under Major Joseph R. Brown is ambushed by the Santee (Sioux) at Birch Coulee, losing 16 killed and 44 wounded.

NAVAL: The USS *South Carolina* destroys the Confederate schooner *Patriot* off Mosquito Inlet, Florida.

The USS *Santiago de Cuba* captures the Confederate blockade-runner *Lavinia* off Abaco, Bahamas.

August 28

NORTH: Confederate spy Belle Boyd is released from Old Capital Prison in Washington, D.C., for lack of evidence and sent South with a warning not to return.

SOUTH: Generals Robert E. Lee and James Longstreet force a passage through Thoroughfare Gap, Virginia, to engage the main Union army. In the process, they engage and brush aside a Union division under General James B. Ricketts and cavalry forces under General John Buford.

Two Confederate divisions of General Thomas J. Jackson surprise and engage a force of 2,800 Union troops under General Rufus King at Groveton, Virginia. However, as the heady Southerners advance anticipating an easy victory, they run headlong into the western brigade of General John Gibbon near Brawner's Farm. An intense firefight ensues at 100 yards between Gibbon's black-hatted troops and the famous Stonewall Brigade under General William B. Taliaferro—with both sides oblivious to the carnage marking their respective lines. At length, Jackson tries clinching the victory by outflanking Gibbon, but he is thwarted by a valiant stand by the 19th Indiana under Colonel Solomon Meredith behind a stone wall. After two hours of fierce fighting, both sides withdraw exhausted. Jackson loses not only 1,200 men out of 4,500 present but also the service of Generals Taliaferro and Richard S. Ewell, both seriously injured. General King, who was sidelined for most of the battle by an epileptic seizure, sustains 1,100 casualties out of 2,800 engaged. And for their splendid performance in this, their first engagement, Gibbon's troops gained the famous moniker of "Iron Brigade."

By deliberately precipitating a fight at Groveton, Jackson sought to lure the Army of Virginia under General John Pope to his vicinity, where it could be attacked and destroyed in detail by the combined Confederate force. Pope, as anticipated, took the bait, marched north, and began to concentrate his forces near Jackson's position.

WEST: General Braxton Bragg's Confederate Army of Mississippi, soon to be redesignated the Army of Tennessee, proceeds north from Chattanooga into Kentucky, several days behind a second column under General Edmund Kirby-Smith.

NAVAL: The Federal gunboat USS *Pittsburgh*, accompanied by the steamers *Iatan* and *White Cloud,* leads an expedition from Helena, Arkansas, to Eunice.

August 29

SOUTH: General Thomas J. Jackson begins to assume strong defensive positions behind an unfinished railroad near Groveton, Virginia, as Union forces under General John Pope mass 65,000 men for an attack. The Second Battle of Manassas begins as blue-coated columns under General Franz Sigel and General Joseph Hooker assail Jackson's line, safely ensconced behind an unfinished railroad, from which he easily repels their advance. The problem is that Pope, while enjoying local superiority in numbers, squanders his advantage through piecemeal attacks. Next came the brigades of General Philip Kearny and John F. Reynolds. These forces charge Jackson's left flank and drive General Ambrose P. Hill's defenders hard along Stony Ridge, but they are finally repulsed by timely reinforcements under General Jubal A. Early. On Pope's left flank, the V Corps of General Fitz John Porter deploys and prepares to engage when it detects the approach of General James Longstreet and 30,000 Confederates. This brings available Southern strength up to 55,000 men. Porter immediately notifies Pope of the danger to his army, but he ignores it and remains fixated on Jackson's unbroken line to his front. He also orders Porter to attack Jackson immediately, but Porter demurs and prepares to receive Longstreet. This insubordination ultimately costs Porter his military career, but it probably spared the Army of Virginia from annihilation.

After a hard day of fighting and heavy losses, Pope compounds his difficulties this evening as he perceives Jackson withdrawing slightly to readjust and shorten his line. He mistakenly misinterprets this as a Confederate retreat and, instead of making arrangements to counter Longstreet's corps on his left, begins to deploy

The Second Battle of Bull Run/Manassas August 29, 1862 *(Library of Congress)*

his men for a pursuit. Longstreet, meanwhile, has been ordered by General Robert E. Lee to attack Union forces directly to his front, but he dallies, not knowing the enemy's strength. Thus, the first day of strife at Second Manassas ends with sizable portions of both contesting armies unwilling or unable to engage.

General Pierre G. T. Beauregard relieves General John C. Pemberton as commander of the Department of South Carolina and Georgia.

WEST: The advance guard of General Edmund Kirby-Smith's Confederate column skirmishes with Union forces under General Mahlon D. Manson at Rogersville, outside Richmond, Kentucky. Both sides then summon reinforcements in expectation of a full-scale battle.

WEST: General Frederick Steele assumes command of the Union Army of the Southwest in Arkansas.

NAVAL: The USS *Pittsburgh,* escorting the steamers *White Cloud* and *Iatan,* bombards Confederate emplacements at Carson's Landing on the Mississippi River.

Commodore John Wilkes is transferred from the James River Flotilla to the command of the Potomac Flotilla.

August 30

SOUTH: General Gustavus W. Smith assumes command of Richmond, Virginia, defenses.

The Second Battle of Manassas rages on as Union troops who were ordered by General John Pope to pursue supposedly defeated Confederate forces instead find them deployed in strong defensive positions. Nonetheless, Pope directs General Fitz John Porter to attack the Confederate right, and waves of blue-coated infantry surge forward. Porter makes three concerted charges on General Thomas J. Jackson's men; the first two are repulsed with heavy losses, while the third, delivered directly into Confederate lines, bends yet fails to break them. But Jackson endures several heart-stopping moments as his ammunition begins to give out, and several units have no recourse but to pick up rocks and hurl them at the enemy. Federal troops under Generals Franz Sigel and Joseph Hooker likewise press back Jackson's left wing severely before grinding to a halt. Suddenly, a roll of cannon fire rakes Porter's left flank as General James Longstreet's massed artillery opens fire. This is followed up by a massed charge, spearheaded by General John B. Hood's Texas brigade, which simply rolls up the Union left. Jackson, seeing his blue-clad opponents suddenly waver, orders his own men to charge the enemy in front, and Pope's entire army dissolves. Desperate fighting ensues as a handful of intact Union brigades labor to stem the Confederate tide, first along Chinn Ridge and then Henry House Hill, and their sacrifice enables the Army of Virginia to escape to Centreville. A tough division of U.S. Army regulars under General George Sykes distinguishes itself by trading lives and space for time. A heavy downpour also dampens the ensuing Confederate pursuit. Pope's army, roughly handled, thus escapes to fight another day. General Robert E. Lee, by dint of an exceptionally bold tactical gambit, flawlessly executed, scores another impressive victory for the Southern cause.

Losses at Second Manassas are severe with Pope reporting 1,724 killed, 8,372 wounded, and 5,958 missing (16,054) while Lee counts 1,481 dead, 7,627 injured, and 89 missing (9,197). Moreover, with Pope in headlong retreat and the strategic initiative firmly in his grasp, Lee remains positioned to take the war northward into Maryland. That night, he orders Jackson's perpetually exhausted corps on another forced march to Chantilly in a final attempt to cut Pope's withdrawal toward Washington, D.C.

WEST: General Mahlon D. Manson, bolstered by the arrival of troops under General Charles Cruft, pours 6,500 Union troops—mostly new recruits—into defensive positions six miles below Richmond, Kentucky. His pickets then detect the approach of a Confederate division under General Patrick R. Cleburne, and fighting erupts along the line. When Cleburne sustains a severe mouth injury, he is succeeded by Colonel Preston Smith. The veteran Confederates easily dislodge Manson from his post, and he falls back forming a new line two miles below Richmond at Rogersville. Fighting resumes, and Smith, now reinforced by General James Churchill's division to a strength of 6,850 men, rebuffs a Union counterattack. The discouraged Federals fall back in confusion through the streets of Richmond. There, they are rallied forcefully by newly arrived General William "Bull" Nelson, who stands six-foot, six-inches and weighs 300 pounds. But the Confederates easily disperse this third line, and the Northerners quit the field completely. Kirby-Smith losses are 98 killed, 492 wounded, and 10 missing while Union losses tally 206 killed, 844 wounded, and 4,303 captured. General Nelson is among the wounded, while Manson is captured along with his artillery and wagon train. Worse, as surviving Union troops stampede for Louisville, Kirby-Smith's invasion route is clear as far as the Ohio River.

SOUTHWEST: The Union Department of Arizona is created from the New Mexico Territory.

NAVAL: The large new ironclad monitor USS *Passaic* is launched at Greenpoint, New York.

The USS *R. R. Cuyler* captures the Confederate schooner *Anne Sophie* east of Jacksonville, Florida.

August 31
SOUTH: The Union Army of Virginia under General John Pope consolidates and regroups at Centreville, Virginia, while General Robert E. Lee dispatches Confederates under General Thomas J. Jackson on a forced march around Pope's left flank to possibly cut his retreat to Washington, D.C. This move presages what Lee anticipates will be a decisive blow to destroy the Federal force altogether. After a difficult slog through mud and rain, Jackson arrives at Chantilly and awaits promised reinforcements under General James Longstreet.

Federal troops evacuate Fredericksburg, Virginia, abandoning great quantities of military stores.

A stiff action ensues at Weldon, Virginia, where 100 Confederates are left dead on the ground in exchange for five Union soldiers killed.

WEST: Confederates capture Weston in western Virginia.

NAVAL: The USS *William G. Anderson* captures the Confederate schooner *Lily* off the Louisiana coast.

Confederate forces capture the Union transport *W. B. Terry* after it grounds at Duck River Shoals on the Tennessee River.

September 1

SOUTH: Confederates forces under General Thomas J. Jackson, deployed around Ox Hill and Chantilly, Virginia, are accosted suddenly by Union forces from General Joseph Hooker's division. Jackson initially intended to engage the marauders beforehand but is dissuaded from doing so by General J. E. B. Stuart, who finds their position too strong to assail. Fighting commences at about 4:00 P.M. when Union troops under General Isaac I. Stevens, IX Corps, advance down Warrenton Pike and charge. This clash coincides with a tremendous downpour that does little to temper the ferocity of the combatants. Stevens's attack forces a Louisiana brigade to recoil when he is killed suddenly and his line falters. A determined advance by the Stonewall brigade under General William E. Starke likewise is repelled. Union troops are then bolstered by the appearance of General Philip Kearny's brigade, which plunges into the Confederates and plugs a gap in the Union line. Unfortunately, Kearny, while conducting a personal reconnaissance ahead of his troops, stumbles into Confederate lines and is shot dead. By 6:30 P.M., fighting dies down, and both sides withdraw. Losses in this brief but deadly conflict are estimated at 500 Confederates and 700 Federals; the Union army is weakened further by the loss of two effective leaders. After Chantilly, the curtain lowers on the spectacular Second Manassas campaign.

General Ormsby M. Mitchel assumes control of the Department of South Carolina.

WEST: The approach of Confederate forces under General Edmund Kirby-Smith into Kentucky causes consternation in the capital at Lexington, and the legislature votes to adjourn and relocate to Louisville.

General John P. McCown is appointed commander of the Confederate Department of East Tennessee.

NAVAL: Commodore Louis M. Goldsborough is relieved as commander of the North Atlantic Blockading squadron and replaced by Samuel P. Lee.

The Confederate raider CSS *Florida* under Lieutenant John N. Maffitt puts into Havana, Cuba, beset by an outbreak of yellow fever.

September 2

NORTH: President Abraham Lincoln, ignoring the advice of his cabinet, restores General George B. McClellan as head of the Army of the Potomac, a decision immediately hailed by soldiers in the ranks. The bumbling and recently disgraced general John Pope, meanwhile, continues on without an official command.

WEST: Union forces abandon Winchester, in the Shenandoah Valley, Virginia.

Confederate cavalry under General Albert G. Jenkins captures the Union garrison at Spencer Court House, western Virginia.

Lexington, Kentucky, is occupied by Confederates under General Edmund Kirby-Smith.

Martial law is declared in Cincinnati, Ohio, for fear of a Confederate attack from neighboring Richmond, Kentucky.

A detachment of soldiers is attacked in camp at Birch Coulee, Minnesota, by a band of Santee (Sioux) warriors under Big Eagle (Wambdi Tanka). They manage to keep the attackers at bay for the next 31 hours.

NAVAL: The USS *Restless* captures the Confederate sloop *John Thompson* off the South Carolina coast.

September 3

POLITICS: Kentuckian Joseph Holt is appointed judge advocate general of the United States.

NORTH: General John Pope remonstrates to General in Chief Henry W. Halleck that his recent debacle is due to General Fitz John Porter's refusal to obey orders and George B. McClellan's failure to provide timely support.

SOUTH: General Robert E. Lee, unable to find appreciable openings in Washington, D.C.'s defenses, declines to attack and instead advances toward Leesburg, Virginia, and the Potomac River.

WEST: Generals Alpheus S. Williams and Jesse L. Reno take command of the II Corps and III Corps, respectively, in the Army of Virginia.

Confederate forces reoccupy Winchester, Virginia, while skirmishing erupts at Harper's Ferry, Falls Church, and Bunker Hill.

General Edmund Kirby-Smith's Confederates occupy the provisional Confederate state capital at Frankfort, Kentucky, amid cheering supporters.

NAVAL: The USS *Essex* under Commander William D. Porter bombards the city of Natchez, Mississippi, and it surrenders.

September 4

POLITICS: The Naval Investigating Committee of the Confederate Congress reports favorably on the activities of Secretary of the Navy Stephen R. Mallory, despite the loss of New Orleans and other naval setbacks.

NORTH: The 40,000 men of the Army of Northern Virginia cross the Potomac River at White's Ford, Virginia, and into Maryland.

Union troops begin to evacuate Frederick, Maryland.

SOUTH: Federal forces, ambushed by Texas Rangers at Boutte Station, Louisiana, vigorously pursue their assailants into nearby swamps, capturing several.

WEST: General Albert G. Jenkins takes Confederate cavalry briefly across the Ohio River for a raid in the Point Pleasant region of western Virginia and then returns.

Confederate cavalry under Colonel John H. Morgan unite with the army of General Edmund Kirby-Smith at Lexington, Kentucky.

NAVAL: The USS *Shepherd Knapp* captures the Confederate bark *Fannie Laurie* near the South Edisto River, South Carolina.

The CSS *Florida* under Lieutenant John N. Maffitt plunges past the USS *Oneida, Winona,* and *Rachel Seaman* and enters into Mobile Bay, Alabama. His success results in an official rebuke for local commanders and calls for better management of the blockade effort.

The USS *William G. Anderson* captures the Confederate schooner *Theresa* in the Gulf of Mexico.

September 5

NORTH: General John Pope is formally relieved of command and is recalled back to Washington, D.C., for reassignment. General in Chief Henry W. Halleck orders that his Army of Virginia is to be consolidated within the Army of the Potomac under General George B. McClellan.

SOUTH: General John M. Brannan temporarily takes command of the Department of South Carolina.

WEST: Confederates under General William W. Loring commence campaigning in the Kanawha Valley, western Virginia.

Union troops advance from Fort Donelson, Tennessee, toward Confederate-held Clarksville.

General Don C. Buell withdraws the Army of the Ohio from northern Alabama and back toward Murfreesboro, Tennessee.

General Benjamin H. Grierson leads a mounted reconnaissance to Holly Springs, Mississippi, skirmishing en route.

The Union Department of the Northwest is created out of Wisconsin, Iowa, Minnesota, and the Nebraska and Dakota territories.

NAVAL: The Confederate raider CSS *Alabama* under Captain Raphael Semmes seizes and burns the Union whaler *Ocmulgee* near the Azores.

September 6

NORTH: General John Pope receives the military equivalent of political exile by assuming command of the Department of the Northwest (Wisconsin, Iowa, Minnesota, and the Nebraska and Dakota territories). There he is concerned primarily with curbing a deadly Sioux uprising under Little Crow.

Confederate troops under General Thomas J. Jackson occupy Frederick, Maryland, expecting to be greeted as liberators, yet they are coolly received by the inhabitants.

SOUTH: Federal forces abandon the depot at Aquila Creek, Virginia, leaving tons of valuable supplies.

NAVAL: The USS *Louisiana* assists repelling a Confederate attack on Washington, North Carolina, while an accidental explosion destroys the U.S. Army gunboat *Picket*.

September 7

NORTH: The Union capital at Washington, D.C., panics as Confederate forces under General Robert E. Lee occupy Frederick, Maryland—within striking distance. General George B. McClellan, hastily reappointed commander of the Army of the Potomac, advances north from the capital to engage them.

General Joseph Hooker relieves Irvin McDowell as commander of III Corps, Army of Virginia.

WEST: Clarksville, Tennessee, is occupied by Union forces, as is Bowling Green, Kentucky. Meanwhile, as Confederate general Braxton Bragg marches the Army of Mississippi into Kentucky, he bypasses Union troops under General Don C. Buell at Murfreesboro and Nashville, Tennessee.

NAVAL: The CSS *Alabama* under Captain Raphael Semmes captures and burns the Union schooner *Starlight* off the Azores.

The USS *Essex* under Commodore David D. Porter receives 14 hits as it cruises past Confederate batteries at Port Hudson, Louisiana, on the lower Mississippi River.

September 8

NORTH: The defenses of Washington, D.C., are entrusted to General Nathaniel P. Banks. Meanwhile, General Robert E. Lee issues a proclamation to the inhabitants of Maryland, reassuring them that "We know no enemies among you, and will protect all, of every opinion." Attitudes toward the Confederates remain nonetheless tepid.

WEST: A mounted expedition rides from Fort Leavenworth, Kansas, in pursuit of William C. Quantrill's Confederate guerrillas.

NAVAL: Armed boats from USS *Kingfisher* destroy saltworks along St. Joseph's Bay, Florida.

Commodore John Wilkes assembles the West India Squadron (a mobile or "flying squadron") consisting of USS *Wachusett, Dacotah, Cimarron, Sonoma, Tioga, Octorara,* and *Santiago de Cuba.* He is tasked with halting the depredations by the Confederate raiders CSS *Alabama* and *Florida.*

The CSS *Alabama* under Captain Raphael Semmes captures and burns the Union whaling vessel *Ocean Rover* off the Azores.

September 9

NORTH: As the Army of Northern Virginia filters through Frederick, Maryland, General Robert E. Lee grows concerned that a sizable Union garrison at Harper's Ferry, below him, could threaten his rear. Therefore, he composes Special Order No. 191, which audaciously dispatches the corps of General Thomas J. Jackson back into the Shenandoah Valley to capture that strategic position, while the divisions of Generals Lafayette McLaws and John G. Walker take different routes to the same objective. Lee then instructs General James Longstreet's corps to advance toward Hagerstown, Maryland, daringly—and dangerously—splitting his army in two.

SOUTH: General Samuel P. Heintzelman takes charge of the Washington, D.C., defenses south of the Potomac.

Fighting erupts at Williamsburg, Virginia, where Union forces prevail after a heavy skirmish.

NAVAL: The CSS *Alabama* under Captain Raphael Semmes captures and burns the Union whaling vessels *Alert* and *Weather Gauge* off the Azores.

September 10

NORTH: The Confederate corps of General Thomas J. Jackson and the divisions of General Lafayette McLaws and John G. Walker march from their cantonments near Frederick, Maryland, and commence a converging movement on Harper's Ferry in western Virginia. Meanwhile, General James Longstreet is also sent in the direction of Hagerstown, leaving the Army of Northern Virginia badly scattered and subject to defeat in detail. Timing is thus essential as the larger Army of the Potomac under General George B. McClellan is feared to be bearing down on General Robert E.

Lee. Lee, while advancing with Longstreet, deploys the division of General Daniel H. Hill to guard the passages around South Mountain as a precaution. Meanwhile McClellan, on learning that Lee has abandoned Frederick, moves up cautiously to occupy that position.

WEST: The inhabitants of Cincinnati, Ohio, brace themselves for a possible Confederate raid across the Ohio River from approaching Confederates under General Edmund Kirby-Smith.

September 11

NORTH: Governor Andrew G. Curtin of Pennsylvania, alarmed by the Confederate incursion into neighboring Maryland, calls for 50,000 militia to defend the state.

Hagerstown, Maryland, is occupied by General Robert E. Lee's Confederate forces while the Army of the Potomac under General George B. McClellan inches up to former Southern positions at Frederick.

WEST: Confederates under General Edmund Kirby-Smith capture Maysville, Kentucky, within range of Cincinnati, Ohio. His approach results in thousands of marksmen and squirrel hunters from the Ohio Valley volunteering their services as home guards.

NAVAL: The USS *Patroon* and *Uncas* trade shots with Confederate artillery at St. John's Bluff, Florida, and withdraw after receiving damage.

Armed parties from USS *Sagamore* land at St. Andrew's Bay, Florida, to destroy Confederate saltworks.

September 12

NORTH: As a precaution, the Pennsylvania state archives and treasury relocate from Harrisburg and Philadelphia to New York.

The former Union Army of Virginia is disbanded and absorbed into the Army of the Potomac with its I, II, and III Corps redesignated as I, XI, and XII Corps.

Confederate troops abandon Frederick, Maryland, in the face of pursuing Union forces. This afternoon, General George B. McClellan arrives with 75,000 men from the Army of the Potomac, who begin to scour the countryside for elusive Southerners.

WEST: General Thomas J. Jackson shepherds his corps into the Shenandoah Valley toward Harper's Ferry, western Virginia. A detachment of 2,000 Union troops under General Julius White abandons Martinsdale on their approach and flees to join the main garrison at the ferry.

The town of Glasgow, Kentucky, falls to Confederates under General Edmund Kirby-Smith.

September 13

NORTH: Private Barton W. Mitchell of the 27th Indiana accidentally finds a copy of General Robert E. Lee's Special Order No. 191 wrapped around a cigar. When Mitchell brings his trophy to the attention of Colonel Robert H. Chilton, Chilton immediately dispatches, through channels, the information to commanding General George B. McClellan. McClellan, in turn, suddenly realizes that the Confederates are badly dispersed and subject to defeat by division. Inexplicably, he waits almost 16 hours before putting troops in motion while his golden opportunity ebbs.

General John Sedgwick assumes command of XII Corps, Army of the Potomac.

WEST: Harper's Ferry in western Virginia is enveloped by a three-pronged Confederate movement. General Lafayette McLaws's division occupies neighboring Maryland Heights across the river after a six-hour battle with Union defenders, while General John G. Walker's division positions itself on nearby Loudoun Heights. Subsequently, three more divisions under General Thomas J. Jackson align themselves along School House Ridge to cut off the town. The 12,000-man Union garrison under Colonel Dixon S. Miles thus is trapped speedily by 23,000 Confederates enjoying superiority in both numbers and position. However, Jackson labors under a strict timetable to seize the town within two days—or abandon it and rejoin the badly dispersed main army.

Union forces evacuate Charleston in western Virginia under pressure from Confederates under General William W. Loring.

General Kirby-Smith's Confederates occupy Frankfort, Kentucky, a two-day march from Cincinnati, Ohio.

The Union garrison at Munfordville, Kentucky, is surrounded by a brigade of Mississippi troops under General James R. Chalmers. He summons Union commander Colonel John T. Wilder to surrender. Wilder refuses.

NAVAL: The CSS *Alabama* under Captain Raphael Semmes seizes and burns the Union whaler *Altamaha* off the Azores.

September 14

NORTH: General George B. McClellan sorties the entire Army of the Potomac, intending to catch dispersed Confederates under General Robert E. Lee before they can regroup. He orders the IX Corps under General Jesse L. Reno and the I Corps of General Joseph Hooker to march their respective ways through Fox and Turner's Gap at South Mountain by 9:00 A.M. The pass is held by 3,000 men under General Daniel H. Hill, who, though completely surprised by the attack, resists tenaciously in rough terrain. Hill nonetheless takes a terrific pounding with General Samuel Garland killed and his brigade of North Carolinians largely captured. But at 4:00 P.M., General James Longstreet arrives with reinforcements and feeds brigades under Robert Rodes and John B. Hood back into the fray. The Union attack, now abetted by Hooker's corps and additional troops under General Ambrose E. Burnside, finally clears South Mountain by 10. P.M., with 28,500 Federals pressing on 17,850 Confederates. But because of their slow movements, Northerners lose a golden opportunity to catch the Southerners who besiege Harper's Ferry from behind and destroy them. Nonetheless, Lee is fortunate to draw off the bulk of his army intact. Losses in this severe action amount to 443 Union dead—including General Reno—1,807 wounded, and 75 missing (2,325) to a Confederate tally of 325 killed, 1,560 wounded, and 800 missing (2,685).

Cognizant of General Robert E. Lee's dispersed Army of Northern Virginia, General George B. McClellan dispatches the VI Corps under General William B. Franklin to advance with all haste through Crampton's Gap, Maryland. Once through, he is at liberty to trap the vastly outnumbered division of General Layfayette McLaws near Harper's Ferry and destroy it. Franklin proceeds as ordered and, on approaching Crampton's Gap, encounters advanced elements of a small Confederate holding force under Colonel William A. Parham—an understrength infantry and cavalry brigade totaling 1,000 men. For most of the day, Franklin's two divisions of 12,800 men under General Henry Slocum and William F. Smith methodically batter their way up the slopes of Crampton's Gap, systematically flushing Parham from the densely wooded terrain. The Confederates receive reinforcements in the form of a brigade under General Howell Cobb, but these too are dispersed. By 6:00 P.M., the exhausted, outnumbered Southerners begin to stream down the mountainside in confusion and are rallied in Pleasant Valley only by General McLaws himself. Union casualties tally 533, the Confederates about 800.

Franklin is well positioned to pitch full-force into McLaws division at Harper's Ferry, trapping it against the Potomac River. However, he vastly overestimates the size of Confederate forces opposing him and, as darkness approaches, encamps for the evening instead. Franklin's dilatoriness holds fatal consequences for the Union garrison at Harper's Ferry.

General Jacob D. Cox assumes control of IX Corps, Army of the Potomac.

WEST: Confederate artillery ranges across Union positions at Harper's Ferry, western Virginia, to bombard the garrison of Colonel Dixon S. Miles into submission. The shelling is intense and intimidating, but it injures very few soldiers. Worse, in light of Union advances after the Battle of South Mountain, Jackson must seize the town no later than the morrow, lest General Robert E. Lee be forced to cancel his invasion of Maryland. That night, he slips around General Ambrose P. Hill's division of 3,000 men on the Union left on Bolivar's Heights, prior to launching a general assault. Meanwhile, 1,400 Union cavalry under Colonel Benjamin F. "Grimes" Davis, an enterprising Mississippian in Federal employ, find an unguarded road, and he gallops the 8th New York and 12th Illinois cavalries to safety. Adding insult to injury, Davis also seizes a Confederate supply train of 97 wagons en route to Maryland.

The Army of the Ohio under General Don C. Buell approaches Bowling Green, Kentucky, to stave off a Confederate advance against his rear.

As the main Confederate force under General Braxton Bragg approaches Munfordville, Kentucky, Mississippi troops under General James R. Chalmers launch an attack. The Union commander, Colonel John T. Wilder, reinforced overnight to a strength of 4,000 men, rebuffs the assault on his two blockhouses. Southern losses are 35 killed and 253 wounded to a Federal tally of 15 dead and 57 injured. Chalmers then again demands Wilder's surrender. He again refuses.

General Sterling Price occupies Iuka, Mississippi, with 15,000 soldiers prior to joining General Braxton Bragg in Tennessee. This places him only 20 miles southeast of the main Union staging area at Corinth, and General Ulysses S. Grant sees an opportunity to trap and destroy the exposed Confederates. He therefore orders columns under General Williams S. Rosecrans and Edward O. C. Ord to approach Iuka from two directions to catch the Confederates in a pincer movement.

NAVAL: The CSS *Alabama* under Captain Raphael Semmes captures and burns the Union whaler *Benjamin Tucker* off the Azores.

September 15
NORTH: General Robert E. Lee instructs his Army of Northern Virginia, presently strung out along the hills of Sharpsburg, Maryland, to begin to consolidate and to thwart an attack by superior Union forces. He also orders General Thomas J. Jackson to depart the Shenandoah Valley and rejoin him with all possible haste.

General Joseph Mansfield is appointed commander of the XII Corps, Army of the Potomac.

WEST: After a prolonged bombardment in which Colonel Dixon A. Miles is mortally wounded, General Julius White surrenders the Union garrison at Harper's Ferry, western Virginia, to General Thomas J. Jackson. This proves another stunning setback for the Union. For a loss of 39 dead and 247 injured, the Southerners kill 44, wound 173, and take 12,520 prisoners, a like number of small arms, 73 cannon, tons of valuable equipment, and innumerable livestock. This is the largest Union capitulation of the Civil War, and it represents the largest number of Americans captured in a single action until Bataan in 1942. Jackson quickly rounds up his prisoners and proceeds with celerity to Antietam Creek, Maryland, where a major engagement seems in the offing. Lethargic Union leadership proves General Robert E. Lee's greatest ally in the race to concentrate his army.

General Braxton Bragg envelopes the town of Mundfordville, Kentucky, and besieges the Union garrison there under Colonel John T. Wilder. Intent on settling the matter by a coup de main, Bragg sends one corps under General Leonidas Polk to the north side while another under General William J. Hardee deploys on the south side. Curiously, Bragg is dissuaded from attacking by General Simon B. Buckner, who owns a house in Munfordville and fears for the lives of former neighbors.

Confederates under General Edmund Kirby-Smith advance briefly on Covington, Kentucky—directly opposite Cincinnati, Ohio—and then falls back to Lexington.

General Sterling Price's Southerners occupy the town of Iuka, Mississippi, apparently unaware of Union forces bearing down on them.

NAVAL: The USS *Thomas Freeborn* burns the Confederate schooner *Arctic* in the Great Wicomico River, Maryland.

September 16
POLITICS: The Confederate Congress issues a vote of thanks to Commander Ebenezer Farrand, senior naval officer commanding at Drewry's Bluff on May 15, 1862.
NORTH: General Robert E. Lee, buoyed by the recent seizure of Harper's Ferry, determines not to leave Maryland without a fight and positions his army along a series of low hills at Sharpsburg (Antietam). He initially musters only 18,000 troops, but glacial movements by the Army of the Potomac allows two divisions of General Thomas J. Jackson's corps to arrive and deploy on the Confederate left flank. Jackson's final division under General Ambrose P. Hill is still at Harper's Ferry, 17 miles distant, processing paroles and gathering captured supplies. Hill is ordered to march immediately once he completes his work there. Toward evening, General

George B. McClellan and the main Union army arrive and make a leisurely deployment with 75,000 men—nearly twice the Confederates's strength.

WEST: General John Pope, newly appointed commander of the Department of the Northwest, arrives at St. Paul, Minnesota, to direct military operations against the Santee (Sioux).

NAVAL: The Confederate raider CSS *Alabama* under Captain Raphael Semmes captures and burns the Union whaler *Courser* off the Azores.

September 17

NORTH: The Battle of Antietam commences at 5:30 A.M. when 12,000 soldiers of General Joseph Hooker's I Corps advance against the Confederate left under General Thomas J. Jackson. In stiff fighting Hooker sweeps away the first rows of defenders past the North Wood and onto a nearby Cornfield. Suddenly, General John B. Hood's Texas Brigade bursts on the scene, crashes into Hooker's Federals, and hurls them back. Action recommences when the XII Corps under General Joseph Mansfield approaches to the left of Hooker, seizes the East Woods, and begins to press Jackson back from Dunker Church. Severe fighting ensues and, once Mansfield is killed in action, the Confederates again drive the Northerners back. Fighting then flares anew when General John Sedgwick's division of General Edwin V. Sumner's Corps charges back into the West Woods and is riddled from three sides by Jackson's remaining troops. Sedgwick hastily falls back as two fresh Confederate divisions are shunted over from the right flank by General Robert E. Lee. Jackson is then ordered to counterattack across the line and he does so, being heavily repulsed in turn. The frightful carnage attests to little gain by either army, but Jackson still stands his ground. Momentum consequently shifts to the Confederate center where an equally brutal contest is shaping up.

General Daniel H. Hill, without additional support, commands 5,000 men deployed along the length of a sunken road. At midday, he is hit by two remaining divisions of Sumner's V Corps, and a tremendous firefight erupts along the line. Both sides endure grievous casualties but Hill clings tenaciously to his embattlements. The Southern position then is suddenly compromised when an officer mistakenly takes his regiment out of line and Union reinforcements pour through. Hill then withdraws through a deadly enfilade fire that drops men in clumps and bequeaths to his position the unsavory nickname of "Bloody Lane." The Confederate center is now laid bare after tremendous sacrifice, and all General George B. McClellan needs to do is to order the 25,000 man V Corps under General Fitz John Porter out of reserves and forward. This he fails to do, again squandering an excellent chance to destroy the Army of Northern Virginia.

As fighting dies down across Lee's center, the locus of combat shifts again to the Confederate right. Here the IX Corps under General Ambrose E. Burnside makes several ineffectual attempts to cross a stone bridge over Antietam Creek, which finally succeeds at 3:00 P.M. Burnside then brings up four fresh divisions against the Confederates, whose right flank has been picked clean by earlier fighting, and he is opposed by only 500 Georgia infantry under Colonel Robert Toombs. Another moment of decision has arrived, and swift marching would have destroyed

Battle of Antietam/Sharpsburg September 17, 1862 *(Library of Congress)*

the Confederates, but Burnside advances slowly. Just as he begins to position units to attack, his own left is assailed suddenly by General Ambrose P. Hill's "Light Division," which has been marched rapidly from Harper's Ferry since noon. Furious fighting drives the Federals back to their starting point at about 4:00 P.M., which saves the Confederate army. When McClellan declines to resume the contest, the fighting ends at about 5:00 P.M.

Antietam is technically a drawn battle, but it exacts a horrific toll for both contestants. McClellan, with 75,000 present (although 25,000 were not engaged) suffers 2,108 killed, 9,549 wounded, and 753 missing (12,410). Lee, who can ill-afford such attrition, loses almost as many: 1,512 killed, 7,816 wounded, and 1,844 missing (11,172). The combined total of 3,500 dead and 17,000 wounded renders this the single bloodiest day in American military history, a toll unexceeded by any battle in any conflict, including World War II. The battle also underscores McClellan's inadequacy as a combat commander for he continually frittered away his numerical superiority in uncoordinated, piecemeal attacks. Lee, meanwhile, is fortunate enough to survive intact and has little recourse but to conclude his Maryland campaign on a very bloody note and retreat back into Virginia. His failure also grants President

Abraham Lincoln the military pretext he is seeking to announce his Emancipation Proclamation.

Generals George G. Meade and Alpheus S. Williams become commanders of the I Corps and XII Corps, Army of the Potomac, respectively.

SOUTH: General Ormsby M. Mitchel becomes commander of the Department of the South (South Carolina, Georgia, Florida),

WEST: General Braxton Bragg's 30,000 Confederates capture 4,000 Federal troops under Colonel John T. Wilder at Munfordsville, Kentucky, but only after a unique play of chivalry unfolds. Wilder, an amateur soldier, is perplexed at what to do next and arrives unannounced at General Simon B. Buckner's headquarters under a flag of truce. He is seeking Buckner's personal advice as a gentleman. Buckner willingly obliges his adversary by leading him around Confederate lines to highlight their stark superiority in numbers. Only then does Wilder agree to lay down his arms, and his entire command is paroled and released. Bragg's success subsequently forces Union general George W. Morgan back through the Cumberland Gap, exposing newly emergent Unionists in eastern Tennessee to retaliation.

NAVAL: The CSS *Alabama* under Captain Raphael Semmes captures and burns the Union whaler *Virginia* off the Azores.

The USS *William G. Anderson* seizes the Confederate schooner *Reindeer* in the Gulf of Mexico.

September 18
NORTH: General Robert E. Lee disengages and begins to ferry the Army of Northern Virginia across the Potomac at Blackford's Ford, Maryland, and back into Virginia. He departs, leaving thousands of casualties in his wake. Superior Union forces under General George B. McClellan, however, fail to interfere or even actively to pursue.

SOUTH: General Earl Van Dorn, commanding the Confederate garrison at Vicksburg, Mississippi, orders General Sterling Price and his 15,000 men to rendezvous with him at Pocahontas, Tennessee, and to assist the campaign of General Braxton Bragg. He remains unaware that two Union columns are closing on Price's base at Iuka, to prevent him from doing exactly that.

SOUTHWEST: General James H. Carleton succeeds General Edward R. S. Canby to command the Department of New Mexico.

NAVAL: The Confederate raider CSS *Alabama* under Captain Raphael Semmes captures and burns the Union whaler *Elisha Dunbar* off the Azores.

September 19
NORTH: Pursuing Union forces skirmish with withdrawing Confederates at Boteler's Ford on the Potomac River near Shepherdstown Ford, Maryland. General Robert E. Lee previously had posted chief of artillery General William N. Pendleton at the ford with 45 cannon, a small detachment of infantry, and orders to hold off pursuers until the next day. Around noon, General Fitz John Porter's V Corps appears on the other bank and begins to slip infantry brigades of General Charles Griffin and Colonel James Barnes across the river. As heavy fighting breaks across the line, Pendleton loses his nerve, gallops back to Lee's headquarters, and announces that all his artillery has been captured. Counteracting this loss, General Thomas J. Jackson

is instructed to push General Ambrose P. Hill's division toward the ford and block any possible Union pursuit.

The Confederate Department of North Carolina and Southern Virginia is established with General Gustavus W. Smith as commander.

WEST: The 30,000-man Army of Tennessee of General Braxton Bragg occupies Glasgow, Kentucky, 30 miles east of Bowling Green.

Union columns of 9,000 men each under Generals William S. Rosecrans and Edward O. C. Ord march west and south of Iuka, Mississippi, attempting to crush 15,000 Confederates under General Sterling Price between them. However, Price's cavalry alert him of their approach, and he prepares to attack Rosecrans before both columns unite. General Henry Little's division then spearheads the assault, crumpling the Union left and seizing nine cannon of the 11th Ohio Battery. Fortunately for Rosecrans, he is able to rush up reinforcements and form a new line 600 yards to the rear, which the Confederates assail but, after the death of General Little, fail to break. As night falls, Price abandons his attack and withdraws. Casualties include 86 Southerners killed, 408 wounded, and 200 captured to Union losses of 141 men dead, 613 injured, and 36 missing.

In a curious turn of events, Ord's force, which could have tipped the balance decisively, never budges. He is ordered to move as soon as he hears the sound of gunfire, but owing to a phenomenon called acoustic shadow, he never hears a shot. Moreover, Ord assumes that smoke rising on the skyline is that of Iuka being burned to prevent capture. Rosecrans thus is forced to bear the brunt of battle unsupported, which allows Price to escape. This embarrassment also generates considerable friction among Rosecrans, Ord, and Ulysses S. Grant. Nevertheless, the discouraged Price withdraws southward, now unable to support the army of General Braxton Bragg in Tennessee. He thereupon elects to link up with Confederate forces under General Earl Van Dorn in Mississippi, who is himself planning an eventual attack on Corinth.

The Department of the Missouri is reconstituted while that of Kansas is disbanded.

NAVAL: The Federal ram USS *Queen of the West* trades shots with Confederate batteries and infantry near Bolivar, Mississippi.

September 20

SOUTH: A Confederate division under General Ambrose. P. Hill advances against two Union brigades crossing Boteler's Ford into Virginia. As he deploys to attack, several of his brigades come under severe fire from 70 Union cannon posted across the river. The Confederates nonetheless charge and drive the Federals back across the stream in a stiff fight. The 118th Pennsylvania is particularly hard hit, being forced over a high bluff and into the Potomac River while Confederates man the high bank, shooting at them as they swim. As events turn out, General William N. Pendleton's alarm is completely unfounded: the Southerners lose only four cannon. Thereafter Pendleton is restricted to administrative functions. Casualties in this sharp action total 261 Confederates and 363 Federals. With his rear now secure, General Robert E. Lee next orders the main army back upon Opequon Creek.

WEST: General Braxton Bragg takes his army of 30,000 men out of Munfordville, Kentucky, and proceeds northeast to Bardsville. There, he hopes to engage the looming Army of the Ohio under General Don C. Buell.

NAVAL: Admiral Samuel F. Du Pont warns Assistant Secretary of the Navy Gustavus V. Fox of the perils of attacking so heavily a fortified port as Charleston, South Carolina. "It is a cul de sac," he declares, "and resembles a porcupine's hide turned outside in than anything else, with no outlet—you go into the bag—no running forts as at New Orleans." His admonitions go unheeded by the Navy Department.

The USS *Albatross* captures the Confederate schooner *Two Sisters* near the Rio Grande, Texas.

September 21

SOUTH: Union forces crossing the Potomac River into Virginia skirmish heavily with Confederates at Shepherdstown before disengaging.

WEST: General Braxton Bragg advances Confederate forces toward Bardstown, Kentucky, for the purpose of uniting with General Edmund Kirby-Smith. Meanwhile, Union forces under General Don C. Buell occupy Louisville ahead of the Southerners. Other Federal troops recapture Mumsfordville.

NAVAL: The USS *Albatross* captures the Confederate schooner *Two Sisters* off the Rio Grande River, Texas.

September 22

POLITICS: The Emancipation Proclamation is unveiled by President Abraham Lincoln, which promises freedom for all African Americans currently held in secessionist states. However, he carefully skirts the issue as it pertains to slaveholding border states. Public reaction in the North decidedly is mixed and ranges from wild enthusiasm in New England to angry protests elsewhere. But his stance lessens chances that France or Britain will intervene on the Confederacy's behalf to preserve the institution of slavery, long banned in Europe.

WEST: Union forces reoccupy Harper's Ferry in western Virginia.

NAVAL: The USS *Wyandank* captures the Confederate schooner *Southerner* on the Coan River, Virginia.

September 23

POLITICS: President Abraham Lincoln's Emancipation Proclamation first appears in the Northern press; reaction is mixed and ranges from antipathy to admiration.

WEST: The Department of the Tennessee arises with General George H. Thomas as commander.

After Confederate guerrillas attack the steamer *Eugene* on the Mississippi River near Randolph, Tennessee, Union troops land and raze the town in retaliation.

Little Crow's band of 800 Mdewkanton Santee (Sioux) warriors flee up the Minnesota Valley, pursed by 1,600 volunteer and troops under Colonel Henry H. Sibley. Sibley then encamps for the evening at Lone Tree Lake (reported as Wood Lake), and Little Wolf suddenly turns on his pursuers and prepares to attack at dawn. Fortunately for Sibley, when several of his men attempt to desert, they run headlong into the Indian ambush, and the entire camp is alerted. The ensuing Santee assault is heavily repelled by artillery, and Chief Mankato, along with 30 of his warriors, is killed. The Americans sustain seven dead and 30 wounded. Sibley then presses ahead, and the bulk of the Santee nation surrenders en masse. The Union troops rescue 269 white hostages while taking 2,000 Native Americans prisoners. Several captives will hang for their role in the uprising, but the bulk of the tribe's members are slated for eventual settlement along the Niobrara River, Nebraska Territory.

Naval: The USS *Alabama* captures the British blockade-runner *Nelly* near Ossabaw Sound, Georgia.

September 24

Politics: President Abraham Lincoln authorizes suspension of all writs of habeas corpus as enunciated by Secretary of War Edwin M. Stanton. Furthermore, military trials are now required for all persons suspected of dodging the draft or encouraging disloyal practices.

A three-day conference of Union governors convenes in Altoona, Pennsylvania, at the behest of Governor Andrew G. Curtin. They gather to pledge continuing support for the president and to discuss new ideas on how to best prosecute the war.

The Confederate Congress adopts the seal of the Confederacy.

South: General Pierre G. T. Beauregard replaces General John C. Pemberton as commander of the Confederate Department of South Carolina and Georgia.

West: General Samuel R. Curtis takes charge of the Department of Missouri.

September 25

West: The Army of the Ohio under General Don C. Buell reaches Louisville, Kentucky, and prepares for a possible confrontation with Confederate forces under General Braxton Bragg.

Naval: The USS *Florida* captures the British schooner *Agnes* as it tries running the blockade at St. Andrew's Sound, Georgia.

The USS *Kensington* and *Rachel Seaman,* assisted by mortar schooner *Henry James,* shell Confederate batteries along Sabine Pass, Texas. The city then surrenders to landing parties who go ashore, march inland, and burn a bridge.

September 26

Naval: Admiral Samuel F. Du Pont proposes employing floating, coal-carrying hulks, attended by coaling schooners, that can directly transfer fuel to ships still on station. This visionary suggestion anticipates the 20th-century practice of employing fleet oilers to fuel warships at sea.

The USS *State of Georgia* and *Mystic* sink an unnamed blockade-runner off New Inlet, North Carolina.

September 27

Politics: The Second Confederate Conscription Act is enacted, mandating that all men between 35 and 45 years of age are subject to conscription. It does make allowances for religious conscientious objectors, provided that they pay a $500 exemption tax.

SOUTH: The first regiment of former African-American slaves, the *Chasseurs d'Afrique,* musters into Union service at New Orleans, Louisiana, at the behest of General Benjamin F. Butler.

NAVAL: The USS *Kittatinny* captures the Confederate schooner *Emma* off the Texas coast.

September 28

WEST: The armies of General Sterling Price and Earl Van Dorn unite at Ripley, Tennessee, prior to offensive operations against the vital railroad junction at Corinth, Mississippi. Van Dorn, who enjoys seniority over Price, enjoys grudging overall command.

NAVAL: The USS *State of Georgia* and *Mystic* capture the British blockade-runner *Sunbeam* off New Inlet, North Carolina.

September 29

SOUTH: General John F. Reynolds becomes commander of the I Corps, Army of the Potomac.

WEST: Union general Jefferson C. Davis has a heated contretemps with his superior, General William "Bull" Nelson, and fatally shoots him at a hotel in Louisville, Kentucky.

The combined armies of Generals Earl Van Dorn and Sterling Price, numbering 22,000 men, depart Ripley, Mississippi, and begin to maneuver toward the important railroad junction at Corinth.

September 30

WEST: The Army of Mississippi under General Braxton Bragg begins to concentrate at Bardstown, Kentucky, 30 miles southeast of General Don C. Buell's main Union force at Louisville.

A strong detachment of 4,500 Union and territorial troops under General Colonel Edward Salomon skirmishes with a small Confederate detachment at Newtonia, Missouri; the skirmish rapidly escalates into a battle as reinforcements arrive from both sides. Newly arrived Southerners under Colonel Douglas H. Cooper are handled roughly by Salomon's men, firing from enfilade, and they are rescued only by the timely appearance of Colonel Joseph O. Shelby's 5th Missouri Cavalry and several battalions of mounted Cherokee, Chickasaw, and Choctaw. This new infusion of numbers gives Cooper 6,000 men, and he presses the Federals hard on both flanks. Salomon consequently orders his men to retreat toward Sarcoxie, which is accomplished under close pursuit. Cooper reports his losses at 12 killed, 63 wounded, and three missing; Union casualties number about 400.

October 1

WEST: President Abraham Lincoln confers with General George B. McClellan at Harper's Ferry, western Virginia, over impending strategy.

The 50,000-man Army of the Ohio under General Don C. Buell departs Louisville, Kentucky, in four columns; three of these will concentrate at Perryville while a fourth is assigned to demonstrate toward Confederate-held Frankfort. Their movements are complicated by incessant heat and growing lack of water.

General John C. Pemberton arrives at Vicksburg, Mississippi, supplanting Earl Van Dorn as commander of the Department of Mississippi and East Louisiana.

NAVAL: All army vessels of the Western Gunboat Fleet are formally transferred from the War Department to the Navy Department. Command of the newly designated Mississippi Squadron now devolves on Captain David D. Porter, who replaces the less aggressive, scientifically oriented Charles H. Davis.

October 2

POLITICS: President Abraham Lincoln sets up his tent right next to General George B. McClellan's headquarters in an attempt to spur the reluctant dragon into action.

WEST: The Army of the Ohio under General Don C. Buell slowly begins to press on Bardstown, Kentucky, prior to a further advance toward Frankfort, the provisional Confederate capital. His movement is detected by scouts commanded by General Patrick R. Cleburne, who then alert Confederate headquarters.

A force of 22,000 Confederates under Generals Earl Van Dorn and Sterling Price enter Chewalla, Tennessee, 10 miles northwest of their intended target, Corinth, Mississippi. By this subterfuge, Van Dorn hopes to dupe the Union commander, General William S. Rosecrans, into thinking that his forces actually are marching north into Tennessee to assist General Braxton Bragg.

October 3

SOUTH: A combined expedition under General John M. Brannon captures a Confederate battery at St. John's Bluff and then occupies Jacksonville, Florida.

WEST: Confederate forces numbering 22,000 troops under General Earl van Dorn and Sterling Price attack 23,000 Union troops commanded by General William S. Rosecrans at Corinth, Mississippi. Van Dorn arrays his three divisions under Generals Mansfield Lovell, Dabney Maury, and Louis Hebert in an arc along the northern fringes of the town. Rosecrans, meanwhile, deploys his men in several, mutually supporting lines of defense with all intervals between covered by carefully sited cannon. These fortifications lie 400 yards distant from the main defensive lines constructed in town. The impetuous Van Dorn encounters the first line of Union earthworks at about 9:30 A.M., after which the Confederates, with great gallantry and heavy losses, grind the defenders back toward their second line. This action, however, has the effect of further concentrating and compacting the Union line, and resistance stiffens while heat, fatigue, and a lack of water weaken the Southerners. By nightfall, Van Dorn redeploys his command in a semicircle around Rosecrans's fieldworks and five lunettes (fixed batteries). Ignoring heavy casualties, he intends to attack on the morrow and clinch the victory before Union reinforcements arrive from outlying areas.

NAVAL: The USS *Commodore Perry, Hunchback,* and *Whitehead* trade shots with Confederate forces along the Blackwater River, Virginia, for six hours. However, they are thwarted in their attempt to reach Franklin by obstacles thrown into the river.

The USS *Westfield, Harriet Lane, Owasco,* and *Clifton,* accompanied by the mortar schooner *Henry James,* pound Confederate positions at Galveston, Texas. Landing parties subsequently arrive ashore and capture the city.

The Confederate raider CSS *Alabama* under Captain Raphael Semmes seizes and burns the Union ship *Brilliant* on the high seas.

October 4

POLITICS: In the Confederate-held capital of Frankfort, Kentucky, Governor Richard Hawes is sworn into office with General Braxton Bragg in attendance. However, the attendant festivities are cancelled when word of 20,000 approaching Union troops arrives.

NORTH: President Abraham Lincoln returns from the headquarters of General George B. McClellan after a day of visiting the campsite and hospitals.

WEST: At 4:00 A.M., Confederate forces under General Earl Van Dorn resume attacking General William S. Rosecrans's defensive works at Corinth, Mississippi. General Louis Hebert previously reported himself ill and is replaced by General Martin E. Green, a switch entailing some command confusion. Worse still for the Confederates, General Mansfield Lovell, fearful of wasting his men in headlong attacks against an entrenched foe, remains deliberately unengaged. By dint of hard fighting and heavy sacrifice, part of Green's force storms and seizes the Robinson lunette, Rosecrans's main battery, while his remaining brigades force their way into the town. In both instances, they encounter intractable resistance and soon are evicted in vicious hand-to-hand fighting. Van Dorn finally concedes defeat at about 1:00 P.M. and orders a withdrawal back to Ripley. Rosecrans, astutely planning and conducting an able defense in depth, finally prevails in one of the war's most hard-fought encounters. Federal losses are put at 355 killed, 1,841 wounded, and 324 missing (2,520) while Van Dorn sustains 473 dead, 1,997 injured, and 1,763 captured or missing (4,233)—losses the Confederacy could ill afford in this theater. Generals Lovell and Hebert are also relieved of command, pending a military tribunal. Control of western Tennessee and northern Mississippi begins to pass irrevocably into Union hands, and the locus of war in the West gradually shifts to Vicksburg.

Confederate Indians under Colonel Douglas H. Cooper retreat from Newtonia, Missouri, and back onto the Indian Territory in the face of Union advances directed by General John M. Schofield. Cooper's cavalry, under Colonel Joseph O. Shelby, withdraws separately to the Boston Mountains in southwestern Arkansas and regroups.

NAVAL: Landing parties from the USS *Thomas Freeborn* occupy Dumfries, Virginia, to destroy the telegraph office and its numerous wires.

Armed boats from USS *Somerset* and *Tahoma* destroy Confederate saltworks at Depot Key, Florida.

October 5

DIPLOMACY: British prime minister Lord Palmerston and Foreign Secretary Lord Russell had been leaning in favor of recognizing the Confederacy, a fact made easier by the embarrassing Union defeats of the spring and summer. Their plans are derailed on receiving word of Antietam and the Emancipation Proclamation as much of British public opinion finds the preservation of slavery unpalatable.

WEST: Confederate forces under General Braxton Bragg withdraw from Bardstown, Kentucky, cautiously pursued by the Army of the Ohio under General Don C. Buell.

General Earl Van Dorn's Confederates retreat from Corinth, Mississippi, to Holly Springs. They are intercepted by Union troops under General Edward O. C. Ord along the Hatchie River, Tennessee. An intense but indecisive clash erupts, and the Southerners continue retrograding, covered by cavalry under General Joseph Wheeler. This movement signifies the end of the hard-fought, but badly waged Corinth campaign.

October 6

NORTH: President Abraham Lincoln, frustrated at the dithering of General George C. McClellan, orders General Henry W. Halleck to prod the general to advance into Virginia to engage the enemy. "The President directs that you cross the Potomac and give battle to the enemy or drive him south," Halleck's telegram reads, "Your army must move now while the roads are good." McClellan, as usual, largely ignores the directive.

General Jacob D. Cox is promoted to major general, U.S. Army.

SOUTH: General Joseph Finegan becomes commander of Confederate forces in East Florida; those in West Florida are assigned to General John H. Forney.

WEST: The Army of the Ohio under General Don C. Buell occupies Bardstown, Kentucky, as Confederates under General Braxton Bragg continue withdrawing toward Harrodsburg. Skirmishing intensifies as the two forces close.

NAVAL: The USS *Rachel Seaman* captures the British blockade-runner *Dart* off Sabine Pass, Texas.

October 7

NORTH: General George B. McClellan, who is himself opposed to the Emancipation Proclamation, issues a general order reminding many disgruntled officers of their legal subordination to civilian authority.

General Darius N. Couch replaces General Edwin V. Sumter aa commander of II Corps, Army of the Potomac.

WEST: The III Corps of General Charles C. Gilbert, Army of the Ohio, trudges down the Springfield Road near the vicinity of Perryville, Kentucky, suffering greatly from intense heat. He then dispatches General Philip Sheridan's brigade to seize nearby watering holes from enemy skirmishers commanded by General William J. Hardee lurking to his front. Gilbert's arrival induces General Braxton Bragg to begin to mass the 16,000 men of his Army of Mississippi for an attack. However, due to poor cavalry reconnaissance, Bragg remains unaware that two more Union corps under General Don C. Buell also arrive later in the day, granting him a total of 25,000 men. An additional 32,000 Federal troops are also within marching distance.

General Gordon Granger assumes command of the Union Army of Kentucky.

Union general Eugene A. Carr becomes commander of the Army of the Southwest.

NAVAL: The army transport *Darlington* attacks and captures the Confederate steamer *Governor Milton* in St. John's River, Florida.

Confederate raider CSS *Alabama* under Captain Raphael Semmes captures and burns the Union bark *Wave Crest* and the brig *Dunkirk* off Nova Scotia.

October 8

NORTH: James N. McPherson is promoted to major general, U.S. Army.

General Orlando B. Wilcox succeeds General Jacob D. Cox as head of IX Corps, Army of the Potomac.

WEST: General Franz Sigel leads a reconnaissance from Fairfax Court House to Aldie, Virginia, skirmishing en route.

General Don C. Buell arranges his 25,000 men for battle near Perryville, Kentucky. Today, he deploys the I Corps of General Alexander McCook on his left, the III Corps of General Charles Gilbert in his center, and the II Corps under General Thomas Crittenden on his right. Previously, Confederates under General Leonidas Polk had advanced to attack the Union force, then reported as a single corps, but Polk assumes defensive positions after perceiving their superior numbers. At 10:00 A.M., General Braxton Bragg arrives at the front and orders the Confederates forward against the Union left, regardless. General William J. Hardee is also directed to position his troops along the center to keep Union forces at bay. Bragg's attack kicks off at about 2:00 P.M. when Polk's command, infiltrating through a ravine that remained propitiously undefended, suddenly turns McCook's left flank and violently drives him back. The Federals stumble away in confusion for nearly a mile before new lines can be stabilized. Buell, meanwhile, remains in his tent at some distance to the rear, unaware of the fighting owing to "acoustic shadow." This phenomenon prevents the noise of battle from being heard at headquarters, although the general is eventually alerted by messengers. Buell then spurs his horse onward, arriving on the field at about 4:00 P.M.

In the re-formed center, Gilbert's III Corps handily repulses a Confederate attack by Colonel Samuel Powell's brigade as troops under General Phil Sheridan begin to press through their lines. Sheridan, however, lends no assistance to the hard-pressed McCook on his left, having been ordered by Buell to ignore that sector. Fighting rages on until darkness when Bragg, though he wins a tactical victory of sorts, finally perceives that he is badly outnumbered. That evening he issues orders to fall back on Harrodsburg, capably screened by horsemen under Colonel Joseph Wheeler. The Battle of Perryville proves a costly encounter for both sides: Buell records his losses as 845 killed, 2,851 wounded, and 515 missing (4,211) while Bragg sustains 510 killed, 2,635 wounded, and 251 missing (3,405). Buell's casualties, although slightly heavier, also constitute a smaller percentage of his overall force, whereas the Confederates suffer a staggering loss rate of 20 percent. Moreover, Perryville signals the end of Bragg's promising Kentucky campaign; hereafter, the state is secured and brought more firmly into the Union fold.

NAVAL: Confederates burn the steamer *Blanche* off Havana, Cuba, to prevent its capture by the USS *Montgomery*.

The Confederate raider CSS *Alabama* under Captain Raphael Semmes captures and then releases the Union packet *Tonawanda* on bond off Nova Scotia.

October 9
SOUTH: James Longstreet and Edmund Kirby-Smith are promoted to lieutenant general, C.S.A.

October 10
POLITICS: President Jefferson Davis encourages the Confederate Congress to draft 4,500 African Americans for the purpose of constructing fortifications in and around Richmond, Virginia.

NORTH: 1,800 Confederate cavalry under General J. E. B. Stuart clatter out of Darkesville, Virginia, and ford the Potomac River near Black Creek, Maryland. Their orders are to destroy the Cumberland Valley Railroad bridge near Chambersburg, Pennsylvania, a major supply artery for the Army of the Potomac. This is the genesis of Stuart's second celebrated foray around General George B. McClellan's army.

SOUTH: William J. Hardee, Thomas J. Jackson, John C. Pemberton, and Leonidas Polk gain appointment as lieutenant generals, C.S.A.

John B. Hood and George E. Pickett are appointed major generals, C.S.A.

SOUTHWEST: General John B. Magruder is assigned command of the Department of Texas.

October 11
POLITICS: President Jefferson Davis modifies the draft law to exempt all persons owning 20 or more slaves. This rule serves to heighten a pervasive sense of class conflict, and many politicians accuse Davis of waging "a rich man's war and a poor man's fight."

NORTH: Chambersburg, Pennsylvania, is captured briefly and held by Confederate general J. E. B. Stuart, who destroys several locomotives, paroles 300 Union prisoners, and makes off with 500 horses. However, his main objective, the iron railroad bridge in town, could not be wrecked in time. Stuart then cuts east to Cashtown, south to Emmitsburg, Maryland, and finally fords the Potomac at White's Ferry. His latest venture covers 180 miles in two days without serious Union opposition, and he also seizes 1,200 horses.

WEST: Union forces reoccupy Harrodsburg, Kentucky, in the wake of retreating Confederates under General Braxton Bragg.

NAVAL: The USS *Monticello* captures the British schooner *Revere* off Frying Pan Shoals, North Carolina.

The USS *Maratanza* is damaged by Confederate artillery fire off Cape Fear, North Carolina.

The Confederate raider CSS *Alabama* under Captain Raphael Semmes captures and burns the Union vessel *Manchester*. Reading captured New York newspapers, he also learns of the dispositions of several U.S. Navy warships looking for him.

October 12
SOUTH: Confederate cavalry under General J. E. B. Stuart recross the Potomac near Poolesville, Virginia, completing another famous sojourn from the saddle.

The military results of the raid prove insignificant, but they completely discourage General George B. McClellan, rendering him even more cautious than usual.

West: General Earl Van Dorn is appointed formally commander of all Confederate forces in Mississippi.

Federal troops gather at Ozark, Missouri, to begin a campaign headed for Yellville, Arkansas.

Naval: The USS *Restless* captures the Confederate schooner *Elmira Cornelius* off the South Carolina coast.

Confederate commander and noted oceanographer Matthew F. Maury skillfully pilots the *Herald* past the Union blockade off Charleston, South Carolina, and then sails for Britain to purchase warships for the South.

October 13

Politics: The second session, first Confederate Congress, adjourns in Richmond, Virginia.

North: President Abraham Lincoln again urges General George B. McClellan to resume offensive operations. "Are you not being overcautious when you assume that you cannot do what the enemy is constantly doing?" the president inquires pointedly. McClellan nonetheless refuses to budge and spends several days reorganizing the Army of the Potomac.

West: General Jacob D. Cox accepts command of the Federal District of Western Virginia.

Defeated Confederates under General Braxton Bragg and Edmund Kirby-Smith filter through the Cumberland Gap and back into Tennessee. The much-heralded Kentucky offensive fails, representing the high point of Confederate fortunes in the center region.

Naval: The USS *America* seizes the Confederate schooner *David Crockett* as it runs the blockade off Charleston, South Carolina.

October 14

Politics: Elections held in Pennsylvania, Iowa, Ohio, and Indiana result in Democratic Party gains. The new members largely oppose emancipation and favor peaceful accommodation with the Confederacy.

West: General John C. Pemberton assumes command of the Department of Mississippi and East Louisiana at Vicksburg from General Earl Van Dorn.

Naval: The USS *Memphis* captures the British blockade-runner *Ouachita* off Cape Romain, South Carolina.

October 15

North: Troops from the Army of the Potomac advance from Sharpsburg, Maryland, to Smithfield in western Virginia, while also conducting reconnaissance operations in and around Harper's Ferry.

West: General John H. Morgan proposes to General Edmund Kirby-Smith another protracted raid on Union lines of communication throughout central Kentucky. Permission is granted.

NAVAL: Landing parties from the USS *Fort Henry,* while scouting up the Apalachicola River, Florida, encounter and capture the Confederate sloop *G. L. Brockenborough.*

Armed boats from the USS *Rachel Seaman* and *Kensington* bombard and destroy a railroad bridge at Taylor's Bayou, Texas, to prevent the transit of heavy cannon through Sabine Pass. They then burn schooners *Stonewall* and *Lone Star,* along with a Confederate barracks.

The Confederate raider CSS *Alabama* under Captain Raphael Semmes captures and burns the Union bark *Lamplighter* off Nova Scotia.

October 16

NORTH: Several Pennsylvania counties experience violent resistance to a Federal militia draft.

General George B. McClellan finally is prodded into launching two probing actions from Sharpsburg, Maryland, and Harper's Ferry, Virginia.

WEST: General John Echols supplants General William W. Loring as commander of the Confederate Department of Western Virginia.

Confederate forces under General Braxton Bragg continue their leisurely withdrawal through the Cumberland Gap bottleneck without interference from Union forces under General Don C. Buell.

The Department of the Tennessee is resurrected with General Ulysses S. Grant as commander. He begins to marshal men and resources for an immediate campaign against Vicksburg, Mississippi.

October 17

WEST: Colonel John H. Morgan takes 1,800 cavalry and departs from the Confederate camp, 25 miles southeast of Richmond, Kentucky, on his second major raid of the war. He rides toward the lightly guarded town of Lexington, intending to storm it.

October 18

WEST: Colonel John H. Morgan and 1,800 raiders suddenly attack and evict the Union garrison from Lexington, Kentucky, seizing both the town and 125 prisoners. During the next 12 days, Morgan cuts a circuitous swath across Kentucky, damaging railroad tracks and bridges.

October 19

WEST: General Braxton Bragg continues leading elements of his defeated Army of Tennessee south through the Cumberland Gap, Kentucky. General Don C. Buell is subject to increasing criticism for allowing Confederate forces to withdraw unmolested.

October 20

NORTH: General Henry W. Slocum is appointed commander of XII Corps, Army of the Potomac.

WEST: Union forces collecting on the Gallatin Pike near Nashville, Tennessee, repulse a cavalry attack by General Nathan B. Forrest.

Confederate marauders operating near Bardstown, Kentucky, capture a train of 81 Union wagons.

President Abraham Lincoln instructs former-politician-turned general John A. McClernand to command the newly formed Army of the Mississippi and with it to mount an expedition with troops from Indiana, Illinois, and Iowa against Vicksburg, Mississippi. This action complicates, and infringes on, efforts already underway by General Ulysses S. Grant.

October 21
POLITICS: President Abraham Lincoln urges elections in Tennessee for new state and congressional officials.

President Jefferson Davis advises General Theophilus H. Holmes of Confederate plans for an offensive to clear Tennessee and Arkansas of Federal forces.
NAVAL: The USS *Louisville* and the troop transport *Meteor* capture Bledsoe's Landing and Hamblin's Landing, Arkansas, burning both towns in retaliation for guerrilla attacks on vessels.

October 22
WEST: General Braxton Bragg leisurely evacuates the last of his Confederate forces through the Cumberland Gap, two weeks after his defeat at Perryville and unimpeded by Union troops under General Don C. Buell.

Confederate cavalry under General Joseph Wheeler capture London, Kentucky.

Union forces prevail in a heavy engagement at Maysville, Arkansas, capturing Confederate artillery and horses.
NAVAL: The USS *Penobscot* seizes the British brig *Robert Bruce* off Cape Fear, North Carolina.

The USS *Ellis* destroys the blockade-runner *Adelaide* off New Topsail Inlet, North Carolina.

Battery crews from the USS *Wabash* man three 12-pounder boat howitzers and assist Union troops in a battle at Pocotaglico (Yemassee), South Carolina. The Northerners nonetheless are repulsed and withdraw.

October 23
NAVAL: The CSS *Alabama* under Captain Raphael Semmes captures and burns the Union bark *Lafayette* near Halifax, Nova Scotia.

October 24
WEST: General Don C. Buell is sacked as commander of the Army of the Ohio for failing to aggressively pursue and destroy General Braxton Bragg's defeated army, now safely reposing at Knoxville and Chattanooga, Tennessee.

Command of the Department of the Cumberland passes to General William S. Rosecrans.

A Federal expedition out of Independence, Missouri, skirmishes heavily with Confederate irregulars near Greenton, Chapel Hill, and Hopewell.
NAVAL: The Confederate raider SS *Alabama* under Captain Raphael Semmes captures and burns the Federal whaler *Lafayette* off Halifax, Nova Scotia.

An armed party of mounted sailors from the USS *Baron de Kalb* skirmishes with Confederates scouts at Hopefield, Arkansas, and captures them after a running fight of nine miles.

October 25

POLITICS: President Abraham Lincoln again urges General George B. McClellan to commit the Army of the Potomac to offensive operations in Virginia. When the general informs the president of his fatigued horses, an angry chief executive cables back, "Will you pardon me for asking what the horses of your army have done since the battle of Antietam that fatigue anything?"

SOUTH: Union forces under General Benjamin F. Butler attack and seize Donaldsonville, Louisiana, from Confederates under General Godfrey Weitzel.

WEST: General Ulysses S. Grant receives control of the newly constituted XIII Corps within the Department of the Tennessee.

October 26

NORTH: General Samuel P. Heintzelman succeeds Nathaniel P. Banks as commander of the Washington, D.C., defenses.

SOUTH: After continual prodding, General George B. McClellan finally crosses the Potomac River back into Virginia, but he moves so slowly that General Robert E. Lee's Confederates easily interpose themselves between the invaders and Richmond. Nevertheless, President Abraham Lincoln "rejoiced" at the news.

WEST: The Union Army of the Mississippi under General John A. McClernand is disbanded and reassigned, largely through the machinations of General Ulysses S. Grant.

NAVAL: The Confederate raider CSS *Alabama* under Captain Raphael Semmes captures and burns the Union schooner *Crenshaw* off Halifax, Nova Scotia.

October 27

WEST: General William S. Rosecrans receives command of the XIV Corps in Tennessee.

Union forces prevail in a heavy skirmish at Labadieville, Louisiana, losing 18 killed and 74 wounded to a Southern tally of six killed, 15 wounded, and 208 captured.

NAVAL: Boats from the USS *Flag* capture the British steamer *Anglia* in Bulls Bay, South Carolina.

October 28

SOUTH: General George B. McClellan continues advancing—albeit it at a snail's pace—against Confederate forces at Warrenton, Virginia. General Robert E. Lee counters by falling back to prevent being encircled.

WEST: Confederate general John C. Breckinridge becomes commander of the Army of Middle Tennessee.

Roughly 1,000 Federals under General Samuel R. Curtis of the Army of the Frontier prepare to engage three times their number at Fayetteville, Arkansas, as the latter continues retreating through the Boston Mountains.

NAVAL: A quick raid by Confederates under Lieutenant John T. Wood, C.S.N., captures and burns the Union ship *Alleghanian* off the mouth of the Rappahannock River, Chesapeake Bay.

The USS *Montgomery* captures the Confederate steamer *Caroline* off Pensacola, Florida.

The USS *Sagamore* captures the British blockade-runner *Trier* at Indian River Inlet, Florida.

The Confederate raider CSS *Alabama* under Captain Raphael Semmes captures and burns the Union bark *Lauraetta* off Halifax, Nova Scotia.

October 29

POLITICS: President Abraham Lincoln, ignoring the dilatory pace of General George B. McClelland's movement in Virginia, nonetheless is relieved to see the army in motion. "When you get entirely across the river let me know," he pens, "What do you know of the enemy."

The steady stream of bad news from the West convinces President Jefferson Davis that the Confederacy lacks the resources to defend everything. "Our only alternatives are to abandon important points," he cautions, "or to use our limited resources as effectively as circumstances will permit."

WEST: Pursuing Federal troops recapture 200 head of cattle from Confederate cavalry under General J. E. B. Stuart at Petersburg, western Virginia.

NAVAL: Landing parties from the USS *Ellis* destroy Confederate saltworks at New Topsail Inlet, North Carolina.

The USS *Dan* bombards Sabine Pass, Texas. Landing parties subsequently capture and burn a mill and several buildings.

The CSS *Alabama* under Captain Raphael Semmes seizes the old vessel *Baron de Castine*, which he converts into a cartel vessel, deposits 45 prisoners, and releases on a ransom bond.

October 30

DIPLOMACY: Emperor Napoleon III suggests that France, Russia, and Great Britain conduct a joint mediation effort to end the American war. Failing that, he recommends recognition of the Confederacy.

NORTH: Command of III Corps, Army of the Potomac, passes from General Samuel P. Heintzelman to General George Stoneman.

SOUTH: Joseph Wheeler is appointed brigadier general, C.S.A.

General John M. Brannan resumes command of the Union Department of the South following the death of Ormsby M. Mitchel from illness at Beaufort, South Carolina.

WEST: General William S. Rosecrans formally supplants General Don C. Buell as head of the Department of the Cumberland.

NAVAL: The U.S. Navy Department announces a $500,000 reward for the capture of the Confederate raider "290" (CSS *Alabama*). A dozen warships, better employed elsewhere, are necessarily sent off in pursuit.

The USS *Daylight* captures the Confederate schooner *Racer* near New Topsail Inlet, North Carolina.

The USS *Connecticut* captures the British schooner *Hermosa* at the mouth of the Sabine River, Texas.

October 31

WEST: Union forces under General Ulysses S. Grant begin to mass 30,000 troops at Grand Junction, Tennessee, in preparation for an advance on Vicksburg, Mississippi.

NAVAL: To compensate for its lack of warships, the Confederate Congress authorizes a Torpedo Bureau under General Gabriel J. Rains and an embryonic Naval Submarine Battery Service headed by Lieutenant Hunter Davidson. The numerous devices they test and deploy prove a menace to Union vessels at sea, in harbors, and especially on rivers—ultimately sinking 40 ships.

The USS *Reliance* captures the Confederate sloop *Pointer* off Alexandria, Virginia.

Landing parties from the USS *Mahaska* destroy a Confederate artillery emplacement on Wormley's Creek and West Point, Virginia.

The USS *Commodore Perry, Hetzel, Hunchback, Valley City,* and the gunboat *Vidette* shell a Confederate camp at Plymouth, North Carolina.

The USS *Restless* captures the Confederate sloop *Susan McPherson* off the South Carolina coast.

November 1

SOUTH: General Benjamin F. Butler, commanding the garrison of New Orleans, Louisiana, imposes new restrictions on movements in and out of the city. He also emancipates all the African-American slaves from nonloyal owners.

WEST: General Braxton Bragg assumes control over all Confederate forces in the Department of East Tennessee. To that end, the Army of Mississippi and the Army of Kentucky are merged into a new entity, the Army of Tennessee.

Colonel John H. Morgan concludes his second successful raid through Kentucky by arriving at Springfield, Tennessee.

General Ulysses S. Grant prepares his 30,000 troops at Grand Junction, Tennessee, and orders three columns to advance down the Mississippi Central Railroad toward the important rail junction at Holly Springs.

Federal forces commence sweeps against Confederate guerrillas under William C. Quantrill in Boone and Jackson counties, Missouri.

NAVAL: The USS *Thomas Freeborn* captures three Confederate vessels on the Potomac River near Maryland Point.

The USS *Louisville* captures the Confederate steamer *Evansville* near Island No. 36 on the Mississippi River.

The Confederate raider CSS *Alabama* under Captain Raphael Semmes captures and burns the Union whaler *Levi Starbuck* off Bermuda.

November 3

SOUTH: General James Longstreet's corps deploys along Culpeper Court House, Virginia, and assumes blocking positions in front of the Army of the Potomac under General George B. McClellan.

Union landings on the coasts of Georgia and Florida involve the 1st South Carolina Volunteers under Colonel Thomas W. Higginson, the first African-American unit committed to combat operations.

WEST: Confederate guerrillas under William C. Quantrill attack and capture a Union wagon train at Harrisonville, Missouri.

NAVAL: Commander Henry K. Thatcher contacts Assistant Naval Secretary Gustavus V. Fox and implores that more warships be deployed to the Mediterranean station to prelude any chance of Confederate commerce raiding there.

The USS *Penobscot* runs the British blockade-runner *Pathfinder* aground at Shallotte Inlet, North Carolina.

Federal gunboats USS *Kinsman, Estella, St. Mary, Calhoun,* and *Diana* attack the CSS *Cotton* and Confederate shore batteries at Berwick Bay, Louisiana, and are repulsed.

November 4

POLITICS: Northern Democrats win significant elections in New York, New Jersey, Illinois, and Wisconsin, but Republican victories in California and Michigan offset these losses, and the party maintains control of the U.S. House of Representatives.

NORTH: Richard J. Gatling receives a government patient for his revolutionary, rapid-fire Gatling gun, a precursor to modern machine guns. Functional models are developed by the end of the war but rarely are committed to combat operations.

WEST: Union troops under General Ulysses S. Grant occupy La Grange, Tennessee, prior to a coordinated descent on Vicksburg with forces already collected at Grand Junction.

NAVAL: The USS *Jacob Bell* captures and burns the Confederate schooner *Robert Wilbur* on Nomini Creek, a tributary of the Potomac River.

The USS *Coeur de Lion, Teaser,* and *S. H. Poole* evacuate Union sympathizers off Gwynn's Island, Virginia.

The USS *Daylight* and *Mount Vernon* run the British blockade-runner *Sophia* aground at Masonboro Inlet, North Carolina.

A large naval expedition consisting of the USS *Hetzel, Commodore Perry, Hunchback, Valley City,* and *Seymour,* accompanied by the army gunboat *Vidette,* advance on Hamilton, North Carolina, but they withdraw once troops under General John G. Foster fail to rendezvous as planned.

The USS *Hale* captures the Confederate pilot boat *Wave* off Nassau Sound, Florida.

November 5

NORTH: President Abraham Lincoln, exasperated by General George B. McClellan's dilatoriness, finally orders him replaced by General Ambrose E. Burnside as commander of the Army of the Potomac.

WEST: Confederate cavalry under General Nathan B. Forrest skirmishes with General James S. Negley's Union troops at Nashville, Tennessee.

NAVAL: The USS *Louisiana* captures the Confederate schooner *Alice L. Webb* off Rose Bay, North Carolina.

November 6

SOUTH: Generals James Longstreet and Thomas J. Jackson receive command of the 1st and 2nd Army Corps in the Army of Northern Virginia, respectively.

WEST: General Ulysses S. Grant orders an extended reconnaissance of the region from La Grange, Tennessee, into neighboring Mississippi.

Federal forces out of Fort Scott, Kansas, skirmish with Confederate guerrillas under William C. Quantrill.

NAVAL: The USS *Teaser* captures the Confederate sloop *Grapeshot* in Chesapeake Bay.

November 7

NORTH: General George B. McClellan formally steps down as commander of the Army of the Potomac. While never popular with politicians, "Little Mac" remains adored by his men.

WEST: Generals Leonidas Polk and William J. Hardee receive command of the 1st and 2nd Corps, Army of the Mississippi, respectively.

    The Union Army of the Cumberland under General William S. Rosecrans begins to march from Kentucky to Nashville, Tennessee.

NAVAL: Armed parties from the USS *Potomska* and the army transport *Darlington* disembark on the Sapelo River, Georgia, and destroy Confederate saltworks at Fairhope.

    The USS *Kinsman* and the steamer *Seger* burn the Confederate steamers *Osprey* and *J. P. Smith* at Bayou Cheval, Louisiana.

    On the urging of Admiral David D. Porter, President Abraham Lincoln authorizes the army's Ellet Rams on the Mississippi River to be transferred to the Mississippi Squadron over War Department objections.

November 8

SOUTH: General William C. Whiting assumes command of Confederate defenses on Cape Fear River, North Carolina.

    After a stormy and controversial tenure commanding the Department of the Gulf at New Orleans, General Benjamin F. Butler is replaced by General Nathaniel P. Banks. To preempt any celebrations by the populace, Butler peremptorily closes all breweries and distilleries within his jurisdiction.

WEST: Confederate colonel John D. Imboden's partisan rangers capture St. George in western Virginia.

    General Ulysses S. Grant continues massing several thousand Union troops near La Grange, Tennessee, prior to leading them across the state line into Mississippi and, ultimately, to the Confederate citadel of Vicksburg. He plans his axis of attack down the Mississippi Central Railroad leading directly into the city.

NAVAL: The USS *Resolute* captures the Confederate sloop *Capitola* off Glymount, Maryland.

    The Confederate raider CSS *Alabama* under Captain Raphael Semmes captures and burns the Union vessel *T. B. Wales* near Bermuda.

November 9

SOUTH: General Ambrose E. Burnside assumes command of the Army of the Potomac, a position he never really sought and initially tried to refuse. Acting on his instructions, Union cavalry under Colonel Ulric Dahlgren dash spectacularly through Confederate positions at Fredericksburg, Virginia, taking 54 prisoners for a loss of one killed. This affair proves that the town's defenses are weak, and Burnside begins to draw up plans for an offensive there.

WEST: Partisan rangers under Colonel John D. Imboden skirmish with Federal troops under General Benjamin F. Kelley on the South Fork of the Potomac.

NAVAL: A combined Army-Navy landing party from the USS *Louisiana* captures Greenville, North Carolina.

November 10
NORTH: General Joseph Hooker replaces Fitz John Porter as V Corps commander in the Army of the Potomac. Porter is slated to undergo court-martial proceedings for his role at Second Manassas.

SOUTH: General George B. McClellan, highly respected and beloved by the men he commanded, bids a final farewell to his Army of the Potomac at Warrenton, Virginia.

WEST: The Confederate Department of Western Virginia passes to General John S. Williams.

November 11
NAVAL: The USS *Kensington* captures the Confederate schooner *Course* off the coast of Florida.

November 12
NAVAL: The USS *Kensington* captures the British blockade-runner *Maria* off the coast of Florida.

November 13
WEST: The important rail junction at Holly Springs, Mississippi, is occupied by Union forces as part of a larger campaign directed at Vicksburg by General Ulysses S. Grant.

General Braxton Bragg leads the Confederate Army of Tennessee from Chattanooga, Tennessee, toward Murfreesboro. There, he intends to unite with forces under General John C. Breckinridge.

November 14
NORTH: Newly installed General Ambrose E. Burnside, commanding the Army of the Potomac, effects a major reorganization of his charge by placing Generals Joseph Hooker, Edwin V. Sumner, and William B. Franklin as commanders of the Right, Center, and Left Grand Divisions, respectively. Their respective commands then are organized as "grand divisions" of two corps each. He also prepares for an immediate advance toward Fredericksburg, Virginia, prior to an eventual move on Richmond.

WEST: The Confederate Army of Tennessee under General Braxton Bragg begins to concentrate around Tullahoma, Tennessee.

November 15
POLITICS: George W. Randolph resigns suddenly as Confederate secretary of war.

NORTH: General Ambrose E. Burnside initiates an advance on Falmouth, Virginia, by first launching a feint toward Warrenton. An excellent organizer, Burnside's troops cover 40 miles in two days of hard slogging and arrive opposite the town of Fredericksburg on the Rappahannock River. His alacrity also leaves the Confederates perplexed as to his locale and intentions.

NAVAL: President Abraham Lincoln and several cabinet members narrowly escape injury when an experimental Hyde rocket accidentally explodes during a demonstration at the Washington Navy Yard.

The Confederate raider CSS *Alabama* under Captain Raphael Semmes steams into Martinique harbor, followed closely by the USS *San Jacinto,* which establishes a loose blockade.

November 16

NORTH: Generals Daniel Butterfield and William F. Smith assume command of the V Corps and VI Corps, respectively.

NAVAL: The USS *T. A. Ward* captures the Confederate sloop *G. W. Greene* along St. Jerome's Creek, Maryland.

November 17

POLITICS: General Gustavus W. Smith is appointed acting Confederate secretary of war at the behest of President Jefferson Davis.

SOUTH: The Union Right Grand Division under General Edwin V. Sumner deploys at Falmouth, Virginia, just across from Fredericksburg on the Rappahannock River. This move concludes an impressive 40-mile march by the usually plodding Army of the Potomac, one orchestrated by the new commander, General Ambrose E. Burnside. This maneuver proves so stealthy that Confederate general Robert E. Lee temporarily loses contact with his adversary's whereabouts. Moreover, Fredericksburg at this time is only lightly defended, but despite Sumner's urging, Burnside declines to send troops across the Rappahannock and occupy it. Worse, pontoon bridges and other equipment that Burnside requested have failed to materialize due to bureaucratic snares, and, by waiting for them to arrive, he gradually loses his advantage of surprise.

NAVAL: The USS *Cambridge* runs the British blockade-runner *J. W. Pindar* aground at Masonboro Inlet, North Carolina, burning it.

The USS *Kanawha* and *Kennebec* chase an unnamed Confederate blockade-runner ashore near Mobile, Alabama.

November 18

SOUTH: The Army of the Potomac under General Ambrose E. Burnside continues occupying Falmouth, Virginia, behind the Rappahannock River and directly opposite the heights of Fredericksburg. However, Burnside takes no offensive actions during the next three weeks, allowing Confederates under General James Longstreet to arrive and greatly strengthen their defensive arrangements.

NAVAL: The USS *Monticello* runs the British blockade-runners *Ariel* and *Ann Maria* aground near Shallotte Inlet, North Carolina, burning them.

November 19

SOUTH: General Ambrose E. Burnside arrives to take charge of the Army of the Potomac at Falmouth, Virginia. The Army of Northern Virginia, meanwhile, begins to adjust defensive arrangements near Fredericksburg by posting General James Longstreet's corps at Culpeper while Confederate cavalry under General J. E. B. Stuart occupy Warrenton Junction.

WEST: General Ulysses S. Grant continues probing Confederate lines from Grand Junction, Tennessee, toward Ripley, Mississippi, prior to advancing on Vicksburg.

NAVAL: USS *Wissahickon* and *Dawn*, while blockading the CSS *Nashville* in Ossabaw Sound, Georgia, trade fire with Fort McAllister on the Ogeechee River. *Wissahickon* sustains serious damage and draws off.

The Confederate raider CSS *Alabama* under Captain Raphael Semmes departs Martinique under the cover of a storm, eluding the blockading USS *San Jacinto*.

November 20

SOUTH: General Robert E. Lee arrives at Fredericksburg to direct the Army of Northern Virginia personally as a buildup of troops continues on both sides.

WEST: General Braxton Bragg's Confederate Army of Tennessee is reconstituted with three corps commanded by Generals Edmund Kirby-Smith, Leonidas Polk, and William J. Hardee.

NAVAL: The USS *Seneca* captures the Confederate schooner *Annie Dees* off Charleston, South Carolina.

The USS *Montgomery* captures the Confederate sloop *William E. Chester* in Pensacola Bay, Florida.

November 21

POLITICS: James A. Seddon succeeds George W. Randolph as Confederate secretary of war.

SOUTH: General Ambrose E. Burnside demands that the mayor of Fredericksburg, Virginia, surrender. When he refuses, Burnside strongly advises him to evacuate women and children from the town.

WEST: General Braxton Bragg dispatches Confederate cavalry under General Nathan B. Forrest to disrupt Union lines of communication in western Tennessee.

November 22

POLITICS: Secretary of War Edwin M. Stanton releases the majority of political prisoners in army custody.

SOUTH: General Ambrose E. Burnside reverses himself and assures the mayor of Fredericksburg, Virginia, that he will not fire into the town. In exchange, he expects no hostile action on behalf of its inhabitants.

NAVAL: Joint army-navy landing parties from the USS *Mahaska* capture Matthews Court House, Virginia, destroying numerous saltworks in the area. They also seize three schooners, several small boats, and ample provisions.

November 23

NAVAL: An armed party from the USS *Ellis* under Lieutenant William B. Cushing seizes two schooners off Jacksonville, North Carolina, before they ground and are burned by crews. Cushing later escapes in one of the captured vessels.

November 24

WEST: Confederates under General Thomas J. Jackson march from Winchester, western Virginia, toward the main army at Fredericksburg, Virginia.

President Jefferson Davis elevates General Joseph E. Johnston to commander of Confederate troops in the west, succeeding Generals John C. Pemberton and Braxton Bragg. His military authority embraces the regions of western North

Carolina, Tennessee, northern Georgia, Alabama, Mississippi, and eastern Louisiana. Johnston is tasked specifically with guiding Pemberton in the defense of Vicksburg, Mississippi.

Union troops scour Jasper and Barton counties, Missouri, in search of Confederate bushwhackers under William C. Quantrill.

NAVAL: The USS *Reliance* captures the Confederate longboat *New Moon* on the Potomac River near Alexandria, Virginia.

Landing parties from the USS *Monticello* capture and destroy Confederate saltworks at Little River Inlet, North Carolina.

November 25

WEST: General Samuel Jones succeeds General John S. Williams as commander of the Confederate Western Department of Virginia.

NAVAL: The USS *Kittatinny* captures the British blockade-runner *Matilda* at sea.

November 26

NORTH: President Abraham Lincoln confers with General Ambrose E. Burnside at Aquia Creek, Virginia, over his prospective assault on Fredericksburg. The general wishes for a direct attack while the president argues for a multipronged approach. At length, the president's suggestion is rejected.

WEST: The retiring Confederate Army of Tennessee under General Braxton Bragg occupies the settlement at Murfreesboro, Tennessee. Having abandoned Kentucky to its fate, the general grimly determines to maintain a Confederate presence in central Tennessee.

NAVAL: The USS *Mount Vernon* captures the Confederate blockade-runner *Levi Rowe* off New Inlet, North Carolina.

The USS *Kittatinny* seizes the Confederate schooner *Diana* in the Gulf of Mexico.

November 28

SOUTH: Federal forces rout Southern counterparts in a heavy skirmish at Frankfort, Virginia, seizing 100 prisoners.

WEST: In a preemptive strike, Union general James G. Blunt and 5,000 men attack 2,000 Confederate cavalry under General John S. Marmaduke at Cane Hill, Arkansas. In a nine-hour running battle, the Southerners are driven into the Boston Mountains. Fortunately, they are covered by a skillful rearguard action by General Joseph O. Shelby's troopers and escape intact with 45 casualties to a Union tally of 41. Blunt declines to pursue for fear of being surrounded, but his presence, 100 miles from the nearest Union reinforcements, induces Confederate general Thomas C. Hindman to march overland and attack his isolated column.

November 29

NORTH: Winfield S. Hancock, George G. Meade, John F. Reynolds, John M. Schofield, and Daniel E. Sickles are appointed major generals, U.S. Army.

SOUTHWEST: General John B. Magruder arrives to take charge of the District of Texas, New Mexico, and Arizona. He makes the recapture of the port city of Galveston an immediate priority and begins to marshal the men and ships necessary for a surprise attack.

NAVAL: In an attempt to better facilitate distribution of coal among blockading vessels, Captain H. A. Adams gains appointment as coordinator of coal supply at Philadelphia, Pennsylvania. Fuel consumption in the South Atlantic Blockading Squadron alone is running at 950 tons a week.

General John B. Magruder orders the Confederate steamers *Bayou City* and *Neptune* outfitted with bales of cotton "armor" and transformed into "cottonclads." They will figure prominently in the upcoming attack on Galveston, Texas.

November 30

SOUTH: After incessant delays, pontoons and other bridging equipment requested by General Ambrose E. Burnside finally arrive at Falmouth, Virginia. The Army of the Potomac is now able to cross the Rappahannock River to Fredericksburg, but during this interval, General Robert E. Lee rushes 35,000 men under General James Longstreet to the heights on the city.

NAVAL: The Confederate raider CSS *Alabama* successfully eludes the pursuing warship USS *Vanderbilt* and captures the Union bark *Parker Cook* off the Leeward islands, Atlantic Ocean.

December 1

POLITICS: President Abraham Lincoln proffers a plan for compensated emancipation to the 37th Congress, but it elicits little enthusiasm. "In giving freedom to the slave, we assure freedom to the free," he insists. Lincoln also promises to help colonize those wishing to depart.

The third session, 37th Congress convenes.

SOUTH: General Thomas J. Jackson's corps occupies defensive positions on the right flank of General Robert E. Lee's army at Fredericksburg.

WEST: General Ulysses S. Grant dispatches the XIII Cavalry Corps, a cavalry force of four regiments under Colonel Theophilus L. Dickie, to pursue Confederates fleeing southward from his base at Oxford, Mississippi, across the Tallahatchie River.

NAVAL: Secretary of the Navy Gideon Welles makes his second annual report to President Abraham Lincoln. He announces that 427 ships are in commission, mounting an aggregate of 1,577 guns, while personnel have risen to 28,000 crew, with an additional 12,000 mechanics and laborers.

The USS *Sagamore* captures the British blockade-runner *By George* off Indian River, Florida.

The USS *Tioga* captures the Confederate schooner *Nonsuch* off the Bahama Banks.

December 2

NAVAL: Armed boats from the USS *Sachem* chase the Confederate steamer *Queen of the Bay* until it grounds on Padre Island, Texas. Ensign Alfred H. Reynolds is seriously wounded, however, and is forced to abandon his boats on Mustang Island. The sailors end up retreating 30 miles overland before rejoining their vessel at Aransas Bay.

December 3

WEST: The Union XIII Cavalry Corps under Colonel Theophilus L. Dickie skirmishes heavily with Confederate forces dug in along the Yocknapatalfa River, Mississippi. Dickie then tries skirting the resistance by extending his pursuit in the direction of Coffeeville.

Union troops under General Alvin P. Hovey occupy Grenada, Mississippi, after fleeing Confederates destroy 15 locomotives and 100 railroad cars to prevent their capture.

General Thomas C. Hindman marches his Confederate Army of the Trans-Mississippi, 11,000 strong, out from Van Buren, Arkansas, in bitter winter weather. His goal is to strike and destroy the isolated and outnumbered Union division of General James G. Blunt at Cane Hill. However, once Blunt is alerted to Hindman's approach, he appeals to General Francis J. Herron's division at Springfield, Missouri, 100 miles distant, for help.

NAVAL: The USS *Cambridge* captures the Confederate schooners *J. C. Roker* and *Emma Tuttle* off the North Carolina coast.

The USS *Daylight* apprehends the British blockade-runner *Brilliant* off Wilmington, North Carolina.

December 4

SOUTH: Union and Confederate outposts skirmish along the Rappahannock River.

WEST: Union forces capture Winchester, western Virginia, along with 145 Southern prisoners.

General Joseph E. Johnston arrives to coordinate the military operations of General John C. Pemberton at Vicksburg, Mississippi, and General Braxton Bragg at Nashville, Tennessee. This additional level of control further complicates an already Byzantine command structure.

NAVAL: The USS *Anacostia, Coeur de Lion, Cuttituck,* and *Jacob Bell* trade fire with Confederate batteries at Port Royal, Virginia, before withdrawing.

December 5

POLITICS: President Abraham Lincoln pardons the bulk of 303 Sioux tribesmen slated for execution for their role in a bloody uprising. The final number of condemned and hanged is 39.

WEST: The Union XIII Cavalry Corps, scouting in the vicinity of Coffeeville, Mississippi, engages superior Confederate forces under Generals Mansfield Lovell and Lloyd Tilghman. Harsh fighting ensues as the troopers are forced back by numbers, yet they skillfully withdraw with alternating defensive lines. Colonel Theophilus L. Dickey then breaks off the battle and rides back to Union lines, concluding his five-day pursuit of General Earl Van Dorn. For his effort, Dickey seizes 750 captives, 200 horses, and four wagons at a cost of 10 killed, 63 wounded, and 43 captured. Lovell reports his casualties as seven killed and 43 wounded.

NAVAL: Armed boats from the USS *Mahaska* and *General Putnam* capture the schooners *Seven Brothers* and *Galena* and destroy an additional schooner and two sloops in the Severn River, Maryland.

The USS *Baron de Kalb* captures the Confederate steamer *Lottie* near Memphis, Tennessee.

The Confederate raider CSS *Alabama* under Captain Raphael Semmes captures the Federal schooner *Union* off Haiti, releasing it on a bond.

December 6

WEST: General Joseph Wheeler attacks and captures part of a Federal wagon train at Mill Creek, Tennessee.

In one of the most amazing forced marches of the entire Civil War, two Union divisions from the Army of the Frontier under General Francis J. Herron slog from Springfield, Missouri, and speedily arrive at Fayetteville, Arkansas, to assist General James G. Blunt's force at Cane Hill. Herron, braving rough terrain and bitter cold, covers the distance in only three days—a remarkable accomplishment that literally preserves the Union war effort in Arkansas.

NAVAL: The USS *Diana* seizes the Confederate steamers *Southern Methodist* and *Naniope* on the Mississippi River near Vicksburg.

December 7

POLITICS: President Jefferson Davis, anxious for the fate of Vicksburg, Mississippi, contacts General John C. Pemberton and inquires: "Are you in communication with General J. E. Johnston? Hope you will be reinforced in time."

WEST: A force of 2,400 Confederate raiders under General John H. Morgan surprises and captures Hartsville, Tennessee, along with 1,800 Union captives under Colonel Absalom B. Moore. Morgan's losses in this hotly waged affair total 21 dead and 104 wounded, but he inflicts 58 killed and 204 wounded on the defenders.

Troops in the Confederate Department of Mississippi and East Louisiana are organized into two army groups under Generals Sterling Price and Earl Van Dorn.

General Thomas C. Hindman commences the Battle of Prairie Grove by dispatching a small Confederate cavalry force under Colonel J. C. Monroe to distract and occupy the attention of General James G. Blunt at Cane Hill. Meanwhile, Hindman advances on the footsore and recently arrived host of General Francis J. Herron at Prairie Grove, eight miles from Fayetteville. He possesses 11,000 men and badly outnumbers his opponent, but after achieving strategic surprise, he inexplicably assumes defensive positions. Fighting commences at 9:30 A.M. when the aggressive Herron attacks what he perceives to be a small Confederate force, unaware that Hindman's entire army is present. He is repelled badly in a series of charges while subsequent Confederate advances are likewise defeated by superior Union artillery. Neither side can end the impasse, although Hindman's fortunes dim considerably when Blunt, surmising that Monroe's cavalry is a feint, hurriedly marches to Prairie Grove with his fresh troops. Additional attacks and counterattacks ensue with little gain to either side until nightfall finally ends the contest.

Prairie Grove is a hard-fought and bloody draw, considering the numbers engaged. Union forces totaling 8,000 men sustain 175 dead, 813 wounded, and 263 captured (1,251) while 10,000 Confederates present suffer 164 killed, 817 wounded, and 336 missing (1,317). Moreover, Hindman, his army rapidly disintegrating through desertion, evacuates the field that night and heads back to Van Buren. His defeat signals the continuing Union domination of Missouri and northern Arkansas.

NAVAL: The Confederate raider CSS *Alabama* under Captain Raphael Semmes captures the steamer *Ariel* off Cuba, taking 700 captives, including 150 U.S. Marines under Commander Louis C. Sartori.

December 8

POLITICS: President Abraham Lincoln recommends Captain John L. Worden for a vote of thanks from the U.S. Congress for his role in commanding the USS *Monitor*.

NAVAL: The USS *Daylight* captures the Confederate sloop *Coquette* off New Topsail Inlet, North Carolina.

December 9

WEST: Confederate cavalry under General Joseph Wheeler attack a Union wagon train at La Vergne, Tennessee.

December 10

POLITICS: The U.S. House of Representatives approves a bill creating the new state of West Virginia on a vote of 96–55.

SOUTH: A Confederate attack on Plymouth, North Carolina, partially burns the town and damages Union shipping offshore.

NAVAL: The USS *Currituck* trades fire with a Confederate battery at Brandywine Hill, Virginia.

The ironclad USS *Southfield* takes artillery fire while supporting Federal troops off Plymouth, North Carolina.

The USS *Sagamore* captures the British blockade-runner *Alicia* in the Indian River, Florida.

December 11

SOUTH: John H. Morgan is promoted to brigadier general, C.S.A.

The Army of the Potomac under General Ambrose E. Burnside begins to bridge its way across the Rappahannock River, opposite Fredericksburg, Virginia. However, as the fog lifts, Burnside's engineers receive heavy and effective sniper fire from General William Barksdale's Mississippi brigade. Burnside then orders his artillery to bombard Fredericksburg in retaliation, which inflicts considerable damage but fails to dislodge the snipers. At length, several boatloads of volunteers row themselves across the river under fire and finally flush the Southerners from the town. The Army of the Potomac begins to ferry troops en masse at night, but Barksdale's tenacity brings General Robert E. Lee another 24 hours to strengthen and perfect his defensive works on the heights overlooking the city.

WEST: Confederate general Nathan B. Forrest rides with 2,500 troopers out of Columbia, Tennessee, intending to harass Union lines of communication. His goal is to wreck portions of the Mississippi Central Railroad and the Mobile and Ohio Railroad. Forrest's first objective, however, is the town of Lexington.

December 12

SOUTH: Vengeful troops of the Union Army of the Potomac are preoccupied in a looting binge at Fredericksburg, Virginia. Meanwhile, General Robert E. Lee, realizing that the enemy has crossed in strength for a major effort, hastily summons the corps of General Thomas J. Jackson from positions downstream, and he gradually occupies the right flank of Lee's line. By nightfall, General Ambrose E. Burnside masses 112,000 troops (16 divisions) below the Confederate positions and plans for an assault at dawn.

NAVAL: The USS *Delaware, Shawsheen, Lockwood,* and *Seymour* sail up the Neuse River, North Carolina, to support an army expedition against nearby Goldsboro. Low-water levels ultimately thwart their mission.

The Federal ironclad USS *Cairo* under Commander Thomas O. Selfridge strikes a Confederate "torpedo" (mine) on the Yazoo River, Mississippi, and sinks. This is the first of 40 Union vessels ultimately lost to submerged Southern ordnance.

WEST: General John C. Pemberton appoints the recently disgraced general Earl Van Dorn to assume command of a three-brigade division of Confederate cavalry. His command includes mounted units from Texas, Tennessee, Missouri, and Mississippi, totaling 3,500 troopers.

December 13

SOUTH: Patrick R. Cleburne is prompted to major general, C.S.A.

The Battle of Fredericksburg, Virginia, commences at 10:00 A.M. as a dense fog suddenly lifts and reveals to Southerners the awe-inspiring sight of serried ranks of blue-coated infantry advancing below them. The first thrust is hurled against General Robert E. Lee's lines on the Confederate right when General William B. Franklin commits divisions under Generals George G. Meade and John Gibbon to strike General Thomas J. Jackson. Advancing through heavy fire, Meade and Gibbon find a convenient gap midway through Jackson's erstwhile strong position and pour through. The Federals then surprise a brigade under General Maxcy Gregg, killing him and routing his South Carolinians, but Franklin fails to follow up this surprising breakthrough with reinforcements. Consequently, Jackson's riposte proves sharp and effective: He dispatches the divisions of Jubal A. Early and Daniel H. Hill to slash at both Union flanks, and the Federals flee down the hill with heavy losses. The only real chance for a Northern victory that day is squandered.

As Burnside's main attack develops, it is directed against Lee's left flank, along a steep hill called Marye's Heights. This is defended by General James Longstreet, who prides himself on his defensive expertise, and it ostensibly proves the strongest part of the Confederate line. Longstreet carefully arrays his men behind strong stone walls fronting the open fields that Union forces have to pass. Moreover, any advance also takes them into the teeth of interlocking fields of fire from Colonel Edward P. Alexander's artillery. The drama unfolds as the grand division of General Edwin V. Sumner and part of General Joseph Hooker's command, 60,000 strong, charge bravely uphill—with predictable slaughter. On and on they come in 16

Battle of Fredericksburg, Virginia December 13, 1862 Lithograph by Currier & Ives *(Library of Congress)*

waves, only to be blasted back with heavy losses. Despite Herculean courage and terrible sacrifice, no Federal soldier gets closer than 20 yards to Longstreet's line before succumbing to concentrated rifle and cannon fire. The one-sided slaughter continues well into the evening before Burnside finally calls off the attack. Undeterred by staggering losses, he intends to renew the struggle on the following day, but senior subordinates convince him to relent.

In a long string of Union defeats this year, Fredericksburg is the worst. Burnside's losses amount to 1,284 killed, 9,600 wounded, and 1,769 missing (12,653). The well-protected Confederates predictably sustain half as much carnage, 608 dead, 4,116 injured, and 653 missing (5,377). In reviewing mountains of bodies literally piled before Marye's Heights, Lee aptly remarks, "It is well that war is so terrible. We should grow too fond of it." Meanwhile President Abraham Lincoln, on hearing of Union losses, sullenly declares, "If there is a worse place than Hell I am in it." Northern morale and support for the war plunges to its lowest ebb.

WEST: President Jefferson Davis arrives at Murfreesboro, Tennessee, to review Confederate forces under General Braxton Bragg.

Confederate raiders under General Nathan B. Forrest pause at the Tennessee River near Clifton, Tennessee, to construct flatboats.

Federal troops defeat Confederate forces in a large skirmish at Tuscumbia, Alabama.

December 14

SOUTH: The Army of the Potomac under General Ambrose E. Burnside begins withdrawing back across the Rappahannock River as Confederate forces under General Robert E. Lee continue strengthening their defensive works. Lee summarily ignores General Thomas J. Jackson's urgings to counterattack decisively and possibly destroy the Union force.

General John G. Foster leads Union troops on a successful sortie from New Bern, North Carolina, that captures nearby Kinston.

The Confederate Department of the Gulf is assigned to General Simon B. Buckner.

WEST: General Ulysses S. Grant orders a Union cavalry force from Spring Dale, Mississippi, under Colonel Theophilus L. Dickie to cut the Mobile and Ohio Railroad.

Texas Rangers launch a surprise raid against Union pickets at Helena, Arkansas, capturing 23 soldiers.

December 15

SOUTH: The Army of the Potomac completes its withdrawal across the Rappahannock River, covered by darkness and heavy rainfall. Prior to retreating, General Ambrose E. Burnside sends a flag to General Robert E. Lee requesting a temporary truce to retrieve the Union dead—and those still alive after two days of exposure to the cold. Lee magnanimously grants his request.

WEST: General Nathan B. Forrest and his 2,500 troopers cross the Tennessee River at Clifton, Tennessee, sinking their flatboats in shallow water to retrieve them later.

NAVAL: Assistant Naval Secretary Gustavus V. Fox broaches a possible attack against Wilmington, North Carolina, to Admiral Stephen P. Lee. "Though the popular clamor centers upon Charleston," he notes, "I consider Wilmington a more important point in a military and political point of view."

December 16

SOUTH: The Army of the Potomac reoccupies Falmouth, Virginia, where General Ambrose E. Burnside issues a directive accepting full responsibility for the disaster at Fredericksburg.

General Benjamin F. Butler bids farewell to his command at New Orleans, Louisiana, and is formally succeeded by General Nathaniel P. Banks, who brings additional reinforcements for extended operations upriver.

WEST: A Union force of 700 men and two cannon under Colonel Robert G. Ingersoll, 11th Illinois Cavalry, is dispatched from Jackson, Tennessee. They trot 28 miles east to the town of Lexington with orders to obstruct and delay an impending Confederate raid under General Nathan B. Forrest. Unfortunately, only about 200 of Ingersoll's men are veterans, and the balance are hastily trained recruits.

December 17

POLITICS: Radical Republican senators precipitate a cabinet crisis for President Abraham Lincoln by demanding the resignation of Secretary of State William H. Seward and replacing him with the present treasury secretary, Salmon P. Chase.

Highly insulted, Seward tenders his resignation to the president, who summarily refuses to accept it.

SOUTH: Advancing Union forces reoccupy Baton Rouge, Louisiana.

WEST: General Nathan B. Forrest and 2,500 raiders make preparations to storm Lexington, Tennessee. The garrison commander, Colonel Robert G. Ingersoll, gives orders to destroy all crossings approaching the town, but his men somehow overlook a bridge on the Lower Road.

General Ulysses S. Grant issues General Order No. 11, expelling Jews from his theater of operations. "The Jews, as a class violating every regulation of trade established by the Treasury Department, and also department orders," it reads, "are hereby expelled from the department within twenty-four hours from the receipt of this order." Grant is pressured to rescind the directive in a few weeks.

A division of 3,500 Confederate cavalry under General Earl Van Dorn clatters out of Grenada, Mississippi, intent on raiding the main Federal supply depot at Holly Springs. To confuse Union military intelligence, he takes an indirect route and initially rides north toward Tennessee as far as Ripley before suddenly cutting west, splitting up his columns, and hitting his objective from three different directions.

December 18

WEST: General Nathan B. Forrest and 2,500 Confederates attack a Union cavalry detachment under Colonel Robert G. Ingersoll defending Lexington, Tennessee. The fighting actually begins at dawn when Union troopers raid a Confederate encampment, which is beaten off. Forrest then draws up his men in an elaborate feint, as if they intend to strike the Union left flank. Instead, the Confederates clatter across an unburned bridge on the Lower Road, enabling them to flank a portion of the defenders under Colonel Isaac R. Hawkins. Ingersoll tries desperately to realign his men and repels three headlong charges by Southern veterans, but eventually he is overrun and surrenders. Forrest sustains 35 casualties to a Federal total of 17 killed and injured, with an additional 170 captured.

Federal army units are reorganized in the Army of the Tennessee under General Ulysses S. Grant: General John A. McClernand, XIII Corps; William T. Sherman, XV Corps; Stephen A. Hurlbut, XVI Corps; and James B. McPherson, XVII Corps.

NAVAL: Admiral David G. Farragut strongly suggests reoccupying Baton Rouge, Louisiana, to General Nathaniel P. Banks, who is newly arrived, as a preliminary for the eventual campaign against Port Hudson on the Mississippi River.

December 19

WEST: Confederate cavalry under General Nathan B. Forrest skirmish heavily with Union forces at Spring Creek and Jackson, Tennessee.

General Ulysses S. Grant, alerted to the presence of a large Confederate raiding column in the vicinity of his main supply depot at Holly Springs, Mississippi, warns garrison commander Colonel Robert C. Murphy to prepare his defenses.

December 20

WEST: The XIII Corps, consisting of 32,000 Union troops in four divisions under General William T. Sherman, embarks aboard transports at Memphis, Tennessee, and sails down the Mississippi River. Sherman intends to flank Confederate defenses at Vicksburg, Mississippi, in concert with demonstrations farther inland by General Ulysses S. Grant. These maneuvers are calculated to pin Confederate reinforcements at Grenada and prevent them from reaching the city.

A lightning Confederate raid by General Nathan B. Forrest on Humbolt, Tennessee, results in 50 Union casualties.

In a spectacularly devastating move, Confederate cavalry under General Earl Van Dorn capture a primary Union stockpile at Holly Springs, Mississippi, worth $1.5 million, along with 1,500 prisoners. He does so by utilizing superb marching discipline en route, which keeps Union forces—and his own men—unsure as to his ultimate objective. Van Dorn is further abetted by garrison commander Colonel Robert C. Murphy who, while forewarned, takes no precautions to increase patrolling or prepare adequate defenses. Consequently, the Confederates swoop into town at dawn unopposed, except by a detachment of the 2nd Illinois Cavalry, which is quickly subdued. Van Dorn then orders the bulk of supplies burned, tracks torn up, and telegraph wires cut. This activity takes the raiders 10 hours to accomplish—a good indication of the mountain of stores captured. His mission complete, Van Dorn rides north to elude any Union pursuers. Holly Springs is one of the most devastating cavalry raids in U.S. military history and harbors dire consequences for General Ulysses S. Grant's upcoming Vicksburg campaign.

NAVAL: Commander David D. Porter and the USS *Black Hawk* join forces with the army under General William T. Sherman at Helena, Arkansas, in preparation for joint operations against Vicksburg, Mississippi.

December 21

WEST: General John H. Morgan departs Alexandria, Tennessee, with 3,100 Confederate cavalry, on his third Kentucky raid. His mission is to sever the Louisville and Nashville Railroad, thereby cutting General William S. Rosecrans's principal supply route back to Louisville.

Confederate cavalry under General Nathan B. Forrest capture Union City, Tennessee.

General Ulysses S. Grant, having lost his main supply base at Holly Springs, Mississippi, to rampaging Confederate cavalry under General Earl Van Dorn, evacuates Oxford and marches back to Memphis, Tennessee. This withdrawal terminates his first attempt to attack the Confederate citadel at Vicksburg. Defeated but undeterred, Grant intends to dispense with his dependency on railroads for supplies the next time, but because Confederate raiders have also cut available telegraph lines, Grant loses contact with General William T. Sherman, then poised to attack Vicksburg, Mississippi. He cannot inform him of his withdrawal.

December 22

NORTH: President Abraham Lincoln salutes the courage of the Army of the Potomac, downplays its recent defeat at Fredericksburg, and confers with General Ambrose E. Burnside.

SOUTH: General Robert C. Schenck replaces General John E. Wool as commander of the Middle Military Department, Virginia.

WEST: Confederate cavalry under General John H. Morgan ford the Cumberland River and gallop into Kentucky on another extended raid.

NAVAL: The USS *Huntsville* captures the Confederate schooner *Courier* off Tortugas, Florida.

December 23

POLITICS: President Jefferson Davis excoriates Union general Benjamin F. Butler for his treatment of civilians in New Orleans, Louisiana, and promises to hang him if captured.

SOUTH: General Simon B. Buckner becomes commander of the Confederate Department of the Gulf.

WEST: General Edmund Kirby-Smith resumes command of the Department of East Tennessee.

Texas Rangers stage a successful raid on Union pickets on St. Francis Road, Helena, Arkansas, capturing 18 soldiers.

December 24

SOUTH: The Union XVIII Corps is constituted as the Department of North Carolina under General John G. Foster.

NAVAL: The USS *Charlotte* captures the Confederate steamer *Bloomer* in Choctawhatchee River, Florida.

The army garrison at Columbus, Kentucky, is strengthened against possible Confederate attack by the arrival of the gunboat USS *New Era*.

December 25

NORTH: President and Mrs. Lincoln spend Christmas Day visiting Union wounded in various hospitals.

WEST: Confederate raiders under Colonel John H. Morgan fight Union troops at Bear Wallow, Kentucky, as the town of Glasgow is also captured.

December 26

NORTH: General John Sedgwick succeeds Darius N. Couch as commander of II Corps, Army of the Potomac.

SOUTH: General J. E. B. Stuart takes 1,800 Confederate cavalry on his latest raid behind Union lines by fording the Rappahannock River at Brandy Station, Virginia. This time, he is ordered to capture supply bases along Telegraph Road.

WEST: Union cavalry under General Samuel P. Carter depart Manchester, Kentucky, on an extended raid against Confederate railroad lines in the upper Tennessee Valley.

Confederate cavalry under Colonel John H. Morgan capture Nolin, Kentucky, to disrupt Union communications.

The 43,000-man Army of the Cumberland under General William S. Rosecrans begins to advance from Nashville, Tennessee, toward General Braxton Bragg's Confederates at Murfreesboro. However, his advance is dogged by cold, wet weather along with effective mounted resistance by Confederate cavalry under General Joseph Wheeler.

The XIII Corps under General William T. Sherman disembarks 32,000 men at Johnson's Plantation, at the mouth of the Yazoo River. This places his Union forces on the northern outskirts of Confederate defenses at Vicksburg, Mississippi, roughly six miles from the city itself. However, the defenders, numbering only 6,000 men, are being reinforced by troops from nearby Grenada to a strength of nearly 14,000. Furthermore, Sherman's approach is beset by intractable swampland that funnels any contemplated attack on Chickasaw Bluffs toward its center.

Federal authorities at Mankato, Minnesota, simultaneously hang 38 Santee (Sioux) warriors for their complicity in a bloody insurrection. This killing remains the largest mass execution in American history.

NAVAL: The Federal gunboat flotilla under Commodore David D. Porter, having escorted General William T. Sherman's expedition up the Yazoo River, begins to shell Confederate positions on nearby Haynes's Bluff to cover the landing.

December 27

SOUTH: General J. E. B. Stuart, intent on attacking a Union supply depot at Dumfries, Virginia, is thwarted after learning that the garrison is as large as his 1,800-man mounted column. Another force under Colonel Wade Hampton successfully scatters the 17th Pennsylvania Cavalry at Occoquan Creek, taking 19 captives.

WEST: Confederate cavalry under General John H. Morgan capture 600 Union prisoners in a surprise attack on Elizabethtown, Kentucky. He then begins to uproot tracks and trestles belonging to the Louisville and Nashville Railroad.

General Williams S. Rosecrans skirmishes with Confederate forces as he advances down Murfreesboro Pike, Tennessee.

Advancing Union forces under General William T. Sherman encounter increasing Confederate resistance north of Vicksburg, Mississippi, including the destruction of the Vicksburg and Shreveport Railroad. Worse, as they press southward, they traverse nearly impassable terrain, bayous, and swampland before reaching their objective at Chickasaw Bluffs. Once deployed, they advance under the cover of bombardment provided by gunboats under Commodore David D. Porter. Sherman gradually discovers only four practical approaches to the bluffs, all swept by well-sited Confederate batteries.

NAVAL: The USS *Roebuck* seizes the British schooner *Kate* at the mouth of the St. Mark's River, Florida.

The USS *Magnolia* captures the British schooner *Carmita* off the Marquesas Keys, Florida.

The USS *Cincinnati, Baron de Kalb, Louisville, Lexington, Marmora,* and the ram *Queen of the West* duel with a large Confederate battery on Drumgould's Bluff above the Yazoo River.

December 28

POLITICS: In an attempt to diffuse rising class tensions, the Confederate Congress strikes a clause in its Conscription Act that allows draftees to hire substitutes to take their place.

SOUTH: A column of Confederate cavalry under General J. E. B. Stuart successfully tangles with Federal cavalry near Selectman's Fort on Occoquan Creek, taking 100 prisoners. His subsequent pursuit captures an amply stocked Union camp. He then gallops on to Burke's Station, only 12 miles from Washington, D.C., and telegraphs a humorous message to Quartermaster General Montgomery C. Meigs about the poor quality of Union mules. The Confederates then spur their mounts across the Rappahannock River to safety.

WEST: Confederate raiders under Colonel John H. Morgan destroy the bridge at Muldraugh's Hill, Kentucky.

General Earl Van Dorn, commanding 3,500 Confederate cavalry, slips through Union lines, crosses the Tallahatchie River, and arrives safely back at Grenada, Mississippi. His spectacularly successful raid covers 500 miles in two weeks and completely cripples the developing Union attack against Vicksburg. Union cavalry under Colonel Benjamin Grierson ride hard to intercept the fleeing raiders, but to no avail.

Outside Chickasaw Bluffs, Mississippi, General Frederick Steele's 4th Division makes a preliminary probe of Confederate defenses near Blake's Levee, but he is halted by heavy artillery fire and defensive works erected in his path. Every indication of impenetrable defenses manifests before him, but General William T. Sherman is determined to attack in force. Thanks to telegraph wires that have been cut, he also remains uninformed about General Ulysses S. Grant's disaster at Holly Springs and that the Confederates have reinforced Chickasaw Bluffs to a strength of 14,000 men.

New Madrid, Missouri, is evacuated by Federal troops.

Union forces under General James G. Blunt successfully engage Confederate forces under General Thomas C. Hindman at Dripping Springs (Van Buren), Arkansas, taking 100 captives, 40 wagons, and numerous supplies. Five Confederate steamers are also sunk or burned to prevent capture. Hindman promptly falls back on Little Rock with his remaining 4,000 men.

NAVAL: The USS *Anacostia* captures the Confederate schooner *Exchange* in the Rappahannock River, Virginia.

The USS *Sagamore* captured the British blockade-runner *Elizabeth* off the coast of Florida.

December 29

WEST: General John H. Morgan and his Confederate cavalry seize Boston, Kentucky.

Union cavalry under General Samuel Carter secure numerous Confederate prisoners as he raids along the Blountsville Road, Tennessee.

Skirmishing continues at Lizzard, Tennessee, as General William S. Rosecrans continues advancing on Confederate-held Murfreesboro.

The 32,000 Union troops of XIII Corps under General William T. Sherman attack prepared Confederate positions along Chickasaw Bluffs, six miles north of Vicksburg, Mississippi. Opposing them are 14,000 defenders in carefully prepared defenses under General Stephen D. Lee. Sherman's plan requires a direct assault on the Confederate center in overwhelming force, assisted by supporting fire from Admiral David D. Porter's gunboats. Accordingly, the 3rd Division and 4th Division under Generals Frederick Steel and George W. Morgan skirt the swampland to their front and advance directly on Walnut Hills. Once at the base of the bluffs, they brave a maelstrom of Confederate artillery and rifle fire delivered from the heights and are driven back bloodily. Further attacks throughout the day achieve little beyond depleting Union ranks, and Sherman finally suspends the action at nightfall. Union losses in this lopsided affair amount to 208 killed, 1,005 wounded, and 563 missing (1,776). Confederates casualties are 63 dead, 134 wounded, and 10 missing (207). Defeat here ends the first Union campaign to capture Vicksburg; six months will elapse before efforts can resume.

NAVAL: The USS *Magnolia* captures the British blockade-runner *Flying Fish* off Tortugas, Florida.

Admiral David D. Porter's gunboat squadron renders close artillery support to the army of General William T. Sherman at Chickasaw Bluffs, Mississippi, and then covers their withdrawal.

December 30

WEST: Colonel John H. Morgan skirmishes with Union forces outside of New Haven, Kentucky.

Union troops under General Samuel P. Carter continue raiding Confederate positions in Tennessee, destroying several railroad bridges and capturing the towns of Union and Carter's Depot.

Confederate raiders under General Nathan B. Forrest encamp at Parker's Cross Roads (Red Mound), Tennessee, prior to refloating their sunken flatboats at Clifton and crossing the Tennessee River to safety. However, when his scout detects an approaching Union force, he decides to fight rather than run. As a precaution, he dispatches a scouting force under his brother William to watch the Confederate rear from the direction of Clarksville.

General William S. Rosecrans and 43,000 men of his Army of the Cumberland trudge into Murfreesboro, Tennessee, from Nashville, having taken three days to cover 30 miles in bad weather. He then establishes his line running roughly north to south behind Stone's River, across which sit 37,000 men of the Confederate Army of Tennessee under General Braxton Bragg. In a curious turn of events, both leaders are intending to attack the following day by hitting their opponent's right flank. However, Rosecrans inadvertently assists Bragg by ordering his left flank under General Alexander McCook to extend his line with false campfires to give an impression of greater strength. The ploy backfires when Bragg laboriously deploys and strengthens troops around McCook's real flank so that, when the attack kicks off at dawn, the Confederates enjoy better numbers than they otherwise might have possessed. But a curious play of chivalry also unfolds the evening before battle as military bands in the opposing camps serenade each with competing tunes—then strike up the sentimental "Home Sweet Home."

December 31

POLITICS: President Abraham Lincoln approves an act establishing West Virginia as the 35th state.

SOUTH: A cavalry column under General J. E. B. Stuart concludes its latest foray behind Union lines by riding into Culpeper Court House, Virginia. He has seized 200 captives and 20 wagons at a cost of a single trooper dead, 13 injured, and 13 missing.

WEST: General John H. Morgan's command skirmishes with Union forces at New Market, Kentucky.

At 6:00 A.M., the Confederate army of General Braxton Bragg launches an all-out assault against the Union Army of the Cumberland along Stone's River near Murfreesboro, Tennessee. This move, spearheaded by the corps of General William J. Hardee, catches Union forces off their guard and destroys the division of General Richard W. Johnson. Fleeing Federals withdraw nearly three miles before General Alexander McCook organizes new defensive lines on the right flank. Meanwhile, the corps of General Leonidas Polk assails the Union center, butting up against the well-handled brigades of Generals Philip H. Sheridan and Jefferson C. Davis. Once Confederate cavalry under General Joseph Wheeler spill over from the Union right and onto the Nashville Pike to their rear, however, Sheridan and Davis likewise retreat. General William S. Rosecrans, meanwhile, watching his army disintegrate around him, energetically visits threatened parts of his line, brings up new units, and consolidates his defenses. He has to maintain control of the Nashville Pike, which is his principal line of communication back to Nashville.

Fortunately for Rosecrans, Bragg remains far behind at headquarters, relying solely on reports to stay abreast of battlefield developments. For this reason, a fresh division of four brigades under General John C. Breckinridge remains uncommitted, when they might have proved decisive. Polk's assault then bogs down after he encounters, without reinforcements, a heavily wooded section called the Round Forest. This defensive point, known popularly as "Hell's Half Acre," witnesses some of the battle's most desperate fighting. But despite costly charges bravely delivered, Polk's graycoats fail to pry the defenders out. By this time, Rosecrans's entire line resembles the letter "V," with both flanks drawn sharply back from the center, capably defended by General George H. Thomas's division. Sheridan's troops, running low on ammunition, gradually fall back again just as Confederate attacks along the line peter out at 3:00 P.M. By the slimmest of margins, the Army of the Cumberland survives what comes perilously close to an embarrassing rout. Rosecrans also stubbornly refuses to retreat, despite the pleas of subordinates. Bragg, meanwhile, is convinced that he has won the contest and telegraphs word of his "victory" to the capital at Richmond. Moreover, he fully expects the Federals to abandon their positions before daylight.

General Nathan B. Forrest and 2,100 Confederate cavalry engage the 2nd Union brigade under Colonel Cyrus L. Dunham at Parker's Cross Roads, Tennessee. In preliminary fighting, Forrest manages to surround Dunham and hem him in on three sides. He then demands his surrender, as many Union soldiers are already flying white flags and coming forward in small groups. Dunham, however, refuses and Forrest prepares to decide the issue by a coup de main.

However, Confederate plans are suddenly overturned when Colonel John W. Fuller's 3rd Cavalry Brigade suddenly appears from the direction of Clarksville and attacks the Confederates from behind. Apparently, Forrest's brother William, tasked with patrolling the Confederate rear, took the wrong road and failed to detect their advance. Panic ensues as the Confederate troopers hastily abandon their captured wagons and cannon. Only quick thinking on Forrest's part saves his command: He speedily orders his remaining men to charge against both Dunham and Fuller. In the ensuing confusion, the Confederates ride through Union lines and find a narrow avenue of escape. Forrest's losses amount to 60 killed and wounded, along with 300 captured. Union casualties are given as 27 killed, 140 wounded, and a like number of prisoners. Parker's Cross Roads proves a rare setback for Forrest, and his sheer survival adds further luster to his mounting reputation. Furthermore, Confederate raiding further cripples the Union campaign against Vicksburg, Mississippi, for several months.

Confederate forces under General John S. Marmaduke advance from Lewisburg, Arkansas, into Missouri.

NAVAL: The famous ironclad USS *Monitor*, en route from Hampton Roads, Virginia, to Beaufort, North Carolina, sinks in a gale off Cape Hatteras while under tow. Sixteen crewmen perish, and 47 are rescued by the USS *Rhode Island*.

1863

January 1

POLITICS: "I do order and declare that all persons held as slaves within said designated states, and parts of states, are, and henceforward shall be free," President Abraham Lincoln declares. His Emancipation Proclamation becomes law, although it only affects African Americans in the Confederacy. Slaves in Union-held areas and the strategic border states of Maryland, Kentucky, and Missouri are exempt and remain in bondage for the time being. However, all blacks liberated by force remain eligible to be armed and trained for military service. As anticipated, Lincoln's ploy garners plaudits from France and Britain, further diminishing European sympathy for the South and, with it, the likelihood of intervention on its behalf.

NORTH: General Ambrose E. Burnside tenders his resignation to President Abraham Lincoln, who declines to accept. The general also expresses anxiety that none of his divisional commanders demonstrate faith in his capacity as either a strategist or a leader.

WEST: Combat at Murfreesboro, Tennessee, is suspended as both sides redress ranks and tend to their wounded. At daybreak, General Braxton Bragg is flummoxed to find that the Union Army of the Cumberland is standing its ground defiantly before him. In fact, General William S. Rosecrans, while abandoning the Round Forest salient that had anchored his line the day before, simply withdraws a short distance and establishes new lines farther back along Stone's River. Moreover, tonight he orders Colonel William Beatty's troops to cross the river to occupy the high ground immediately facing General John C. Breckinridge's division on the Confederate right. Both sides then begin to gird themselves for a resumption of combat on the following day.

Union forces skirmish with Confederate cavalry under General Nathan B. Forrest at Clifton, Tennessee.

General William T. Sherman commences to pull Federal troops out of the Yazoo region north of Vicksburg, Mississippi.

An attack by Texas Rangers against Union outposts in Helena, Arkansas, nets 30 prisoners.

SOUTHWEST: A surprise Confederate attack is mounted by General John B. Magruder on Galveston, Texas. In the predawn darkness, he quickly moves 1,500 men and several cannon onto Galveston Island and attacks a Union garrison consisting of 250 men of Colonel Isaac Burrell's 42nd Massachusetts. However, the Southerners are quickly detected and blasted back by accurate naval gunfire from the squadron offshore. By daylight, Magruder judges his attack a failure and withdraws while an intense naval battle unfolds in the harbor. The Confederates finally prevail, and the Union garrison surrenders. Once Galveston is secure, it remains in Southern hands for the rest of the war, serving as a major port.

NAVAL: The USS *Currituck* captures the Confederate sloop *Polter* off the Potomac River.

A sortie by Confederate "cottonclads" CSS *Bayou City* and *Neptune* under Major Leon Smith, C.S.A., pitches into a Union blockade force under Commander William B. Renshaw off Galveston, Texas. To facilitate the attack, the Confederate vessels carry 300 volunteer sharpshooters into battle. Renshaw's squadron, consisting of the USS *Harriet Lane, Owasco, Corypheus, Sachem, Clifton,* and *Westfield,* is caught flatfooted and scatters in the face of what they perceive to be heavily armed Confederate ironclads. Ships on both sides are rammed in the ensuing melee, and the *Westfield,* Renshaw's flagship, runs hard aground. The cutter *Harrier Lane* is also taken in a fierce hand-to-hand battle in which its captain dies, although the Southern steamer *Bayou City* sustains heavy damages and the *Neptune* sinks. Renshaw, seeing the battle lost, orders his squadron into open water, but rather than see the *Westfield* captured, he remains behind to set off charges to destroy it. He and 12 other sailors die when the explosives detonate prematurely. All told, the Confederate victory at Galveston is an impressive, hard-fought affair. Magruder's forces lose 26 killed and 117 wounded while Union losses are 21 dead, 36 injured, and 250 captured.

January 2

NORTH: General James S. Wadsworth assumes temporary command of the I Corps, Army of the Potomac.

WEST: In a manner reminiscent of General J. E. B. Stuart, 1,100 Confederate cavalry under General Joseph Wheeler ride twice around the Army of the Cumberland at Murfreesboro, Tennessee, destroying 1,000 wagons and taking hundreds of prisoners.

General Braxton Bragg, surveying the new line held by General William S. Rosecrans at Stone's River (Murfreesboro), elects to renew the struggle. However, he possesses relatively few intact formations with which to wage it. The largest is General John C. Breckinridge's Kentuckian division, and Bragg commits them against the Union left wing partially anchored on Stone's River. Breckinridge, perceiving the strength of the enemy position, protests the command but orders his men to a frontal assault at 3:00 P.M. The initial Southern charge sweeps two Union brigades from the ridge, forcing them to re-form at the water's edge. The 4,500 Kentuckians then fall on the survivors with a yell, forcing them back across Stone's

River. But Rosecrans, observing his left in danger of crumbling, directs Captain John Mendenhall, chief of artillery, to mass 57 cannon on the river's west bank. This position is significantly higher than the east bank and clearly sweeps the open ground before them.

At about 4:45 P.M. Breckinridge moves forward and charges directly into the teeth of concentrated artillery fire from across the river. His men are repulsed bloodily with 1,700 casualties and withdraw under cover. Suddenly, the Kentuckians are decisively assailed in the flank by fresh Union troops under General James S. Negley and driven back. Breckinridge's defeat signals the end of the battle, and many senior Confederates, including General Leonidas K. Polk, implore Bragg to retreat. He does so only reluctantly and that night puts his army in motion for Shelbyville and Tullahoma, 30 miles distant. Rosecrans, meanwhile, tends to his own shattered army and does not attempt a pursuit.

In proportion to actual numbers engaged, the clash outside Murfreesboro is among the war's bloodiest. There are few laurels to either side. Rosecrans held the field and claims a narrow tactical victory but at the cost of 1,730 dead, 7,802 wounded, and 3,717 missing (13,249) among 41,400 present. Confederate losses are slightly lower with 1,294 killed, 7,945 injured, and 1,027 missing (10,266) out of 34,739. But the already outnumbered Army of Tennessee can scarcely afford such attrition, and Bragg's leadership suffers from a rising tide of criticism. The door to Middle Tennessee is being forced open, but six months lapses before the Army of the Cumberland is rebuilt and resumes offensive operations.

Confederate cavalry under General Nathan B. Forrest recross the Tennessee River at Clifton, Tennessee.

General John H. Morgan's Confederate raiders ford the Cumberland River back into Tennessee. His latest effort culminates in 1,800 prisoners and $2 million in wrecked equipment and railroad tracks. Morgan sustains only 2 killed, 24 wounded, and 64 missing, and he is thanked by the Confederate Congress for his actions.

General John A. McClernand accepts command of the 32,000-strong Army of the Mississippi at Milliken's Bend, Louisiana. His independent command includes General George W. Morgan's I Corps and General William T. Sherman's II Corps.

New Madrid, Missouri, is reoccupied by Federal troops.

Union forces skirmish with Confederates under General John S. Marmaduke at White Spring, Arkansas.

January 3
WEST: General Braxton Bragg's rear guard tangles with Union forces at Burnsville, Tennessee, as the Confederates continue falling back toward Shelbyville and Tullahoma. Two Union brigades push forward in pursuit, although General William S. Rosecrans does not press vigorously.

NAVAL: The USS *Currituck* captures the Confederate sloop *Potter* between the Potomac and Rappahannock rivers.

January 4
NORTH: General John F. Reynolds is reinstated as commander of I Corps, Army of the Potomac.

General in Chief Henry W. Halleck orders General Ulysses S. Grant to rescind his controversial General Order No. 11, which expels all Jews from his department.

WEST: Ignoring prior authorization, General John A. McClernand moves 32,000 Federal troops of his Army of the Mississippi from Milliken's Bend, Louisiana, on an expedition into Arkansas. He embarks the corps of Generals George W. Morgan and William T. Sherman onto transports and sails up the Arkansas River, intending to capture the large Confederate outpost at Arkansas Post 50 miles upstream. This impressive, well-armed fortification, constructed on a high bluff overlooking the waterway, poses a menace to Union river traffic in that region.

NAVAL: The USS *Quaker City* seizes the Confederate sloop *Mercury* near Charleston, South Carolina. Confederate diplomatic dispatches are seized, containing reports on ironclads under construction in Britain for the Confederate navy.

Admiral David D. Porter's squadron, consisting of the gunboats USS *Baron de Kalb, Louisville, Cincinnati, Signal, Marmora, Lexington, New Era, Rattler, Glide,* and *Black Hawk,* escorts army troops up the White River, Arkansas, to seize Fort Hindman in conjunction with General John A. McClernand.

January 5

NORTH: General Ambrose E. Burnside, still tussling with subordinates over his proposed thrust across the Rappahannock, again tenders his resignation to President Abraham Lincoln "to relieve you from all embarrassment in my case." It is again declined.

WEST: Federal forces under General William S. Rosecrans occupy the city of Murfreesboro, Tennessee, as the Army of Tennessee under General Braxton Bragg continues withdrawing southward.

General William T. Sherman accepts command of II Corps, Army of the Mississippi, while en route on the expedition against Fort Hindman, Arkansas.

NAVAL: Armed boats from USS *Sagamore* capture the British blockade-runner *Avenger* in Jupiter Inlet, Florida.

January 6

WEST: Confederate forces under General John S. Marmaduke attack Beaver Station, Missouri, and burn Fort Lawrence.

NAVAL: The USS *Mahaska* and *Commodore Morris* escort a joint expedition up the Pamunkey River, Virginia, as far as White House and West Point, destroying small craft and stores en route.

The USS *Pocahontas* captures the Confederate blockade-runner *Antona* off Cape San Blas, Florida.

January 7

POLITICS: The Democratic-controlled Illinois state legislature roundly condemns President Abraham Lincoln's Emancipation Proclamation and excoriates the chief executive for turning the war into a crusade for liberating African-American slaves.

NORTH: General Henry W. Halleck accepts General Ambrose E. Burnside's proposed attack plan across the Rappahannock River, even though it is to be executed in the deep of winter.

WEST: Ozark, Missouri, is occupied by Confederate forces under Generals Sterling Price and John S. Marmaduke.

NAVAL: General Erasmus D. Keyes and Commander Foxhall A. Parker lead a joint army-navy expedition from Yorktown, Virginia, up the Pamunkey River to West Point and White House.

January 8

POLITICS: John P. Usher is appointed secretary of the interior.

WEST: General Joseph Wheeler leads Confederate cavalry on an extended raid into Tennessee, hitting the settlements of Mill Creek, Harpeth Shoals, and Ashland.

Confederates under General John S. Marmaduke launch an unsuccessful attack on Springfield, Missouri.

A Union ambush at Berryville, Arkansas, kills 10 Confederate bushwhackers.

NAVAL: The USS *Sagamore* captures the British blockade-runner *Julia* off Jupiter Inlet, Florida.

The USS *Tahoma* seizes the Confederate vessel *Silas Henry* after running it aground at Tampa Bay, Florida.

January 9

SOUTH: Confederate troops under General Roger A. Pryor are defeated by General Michael Corcoran outside Suffolk, Virginia.

WEST: General William S. Rosecrans reorganizes his Army of the Cumberland into the XIV Corps under General George H. Thomas, the XX Corps under General Alexander M. McCook, and the XXI Corps under General Thomas L. Crittenden.

General John S. Marmaduke captures the Union garrison at Hartville, Missouri.

NAVAL: Armed boats from USS *Ethan Allen* land and destroy a Confederate salt-works near St. Joseph, Florida.

The transport *Sparking Sea* strikes a reef near Key West, Florida, and sinks; its crew is rescued by the gunboat USS *Sagamore*.

January 10

NORTH: In a celebrated court-martial, General Fitz John Porter is cashiered and dropped from the army rolls for disobeying orders at the Battle of Second Manassas. Not only does this deprive the Union army of a highly capable leader, but also the verdict remains in contention for many years until it is finally overturned in 1879.

General Franz Sigel is appointed commander of the Grand Reserve Division, Army of the Potomac.

General Thomas W. Sherman is appointed commander of the New Orleans, Louisiana, garrison.

A combined expedition of 32,000 men under General John A. McClernand and Admiral David D. Porter continues sailing 50 miles up the Arkansas River to break up a Confederate concentration at Fort Arkansas (Arkansas Post). This formida-ble position is garrisoned by 5,000 men under General Thomas J. Churchill. Once landed, Union troops under Generals George W. Morgan and William T. Sherman are to envelop and isolate the post while heavy naval guns silence its batteries.

NAVAL: The USS *Octorara* seizes the British blockade-runner *Rising Dawn* in the North West Providence Channel, Bahamas.

Admiral David G. Farragut orders Commander Henry H. Bell to reconstitute the blockade of Galveston, Texas, as soon as practicable. Bell's USS *Brooklyn* consequently bombards Confederate defenses of that town.

The gunboat squadron of Admiral David D. Porter, consisting of USS *Baron de Kalb, Louisville, Cincinnati, Lexington, Rattler,* and *Black Hawk,* engages in a heavy exchange of fire with the 11-gun battery at Fort Hindman on the Arkansas River. After covering the landing of troops, the vessels shell Confederate positions but fail to run past the fort.

January 11

WEST: General James B. McPherson takes control of the XVII Corps in Tennessee.

A force of 32,000 Union troops under John A. McClernand and Admiral David D. Porter attacks Hindman (Arkansas Post) under General Thomas J. Churchill. The assault occurs in conjunction with a nearby squadron of Federal gunboats on the White River, whose accurate fire silences the Confederate batteries. However, the ground assault, when it develops at 3:00 P.M., is repelled roundly with losses. Churchill nonetheless realizes the hopelessness of his position and surrenders later that day. McClernand captures 4,791 Southerners, who also lose 28 dead and 81 wounded, along with 17 cannon, thousands of weapons, and tons of ammunition. Union losses are recorded as 134 dead, 898 wounded, and 29 missing. This victory not only restores Union control of the Arkansas River but also bolsters Northern morale.

Confederates under General John S. Marmaduke lose 150 men while skirmishing with Union forces under Colonel Lewis Merrill at Wood's Fork, Missouri. Federal casualties tally 35.

NAVAL: The USS *Matthew Vassar* captures the Confederate schooner *Florida* off Little River Inlet, Florida.

The paddle steamer USS *Hatteras,* cruising 30 miles off Galveston, Texas, is approached at night by a mysterious vessel. This turns out to be the Confederate raider CSS *Alabama* under Captain Raphael Semmes, which sinks the *Hatteras* in a fierce engagement of only 13 minutes. Semmes rescues the entire crew, after which Union ships redouble their efforts to track and corner this elusive foe.

Confederate guerrillas capture the Federal gunboat USS *Grampus No. 2* on the Mississippi River north of Memphis, Tennessee.

Federal gunboats under Admiral David D. Porter effectively shell the Confederate works of Fort Hindman, Arkansas (Arkansas Post), on the Arkansas River. Naval fire proves entirely effective in reducing both guns and fortifications, and Porter notes: "No fort ever received a worse battering, and the highest compliment I can pay to those engaged is to repeat what the rebels said: 'You can't expect men to stand up against the fire of those gunboats.'" His gunboats also managed to corner and sink the ram CSS *Pontchartrain* near Little Rock.

January 12

POLITICS: The third session of the 1st Confederate Congress convenes at Richmond, Virginia, where President Jefferson Davis addresses the legislators, stating that he still hopes eventual European recognition. Davis also vehemently castigates the Union's recent Emancipation Proclamation.

NORTH: The venerable general John E. Wool is appointed commander of the Department of the East.

WEST: Confederate cavalry under General Joseph Wheeler destroys the huge Union supply depot at Ashland, Tennessee, effectively immobilizing the Army of the Cumberland for nearly six months.

NAVAL: The USS *Currituck* destroys a Confederate saltworks at Dividing Creek, Virginia.

January 13

SOUTH: In South Carolina, Union colonel Thomas W. Higginson begins to recruit former African-American slaves for his 1st South Carolina Volunteer Infantry.

WEST: Federal troops under General John A. McClernand capture St. Charles and other settlements along the White River, Arkansas.

NAVAL: The USS *Currituck* captures the Confederate schooner *Hampton* in Dividing Creek, Virginia.

The steamer USS *Hastings* is captured on the Cumberland River by cavalry under General Joseph Wheeler. Wheeler also seizes three steamboats full of wounded troops; these he places on one vessel and allows them to move on. The remaining boats are burned.

A combined army-navy expedition is mounted along the Mississippi River from USS *General Bragg* against Confederate guerrillas known to be operating from Mound City, Arkansas. Several buildings consequently are burned.

January 14

SOUTH: Federal forces under General Godfrey Weitzel wage a successful battle against Confederates at Bayou Teche, Louisiana.

SOUTHWEST: General Edmund Kirby-Smith is appointed commander of the Confederate Army of the Southwest.

NAVAL: The USS *Columbia* grounds on the coast of North Carolina and two days later is burned by its crew to prevent capture.

Federal gunboats USS *Kinsman, Estrella, Calhoun,* and *Diana* attack and sink the Confederate gunboat CSS *Cotton* at Bayou Teche, Louisiana.

A joint expedition under Commander John G. Walker and General Willis A. Gorham steams up the White River, Arkansas, to St. Charles. There, troops from two transports seize the town while the USS *Baron de Kalb* continues upstream in search of CSS *Blue Wing.*

January 15

POLITICS: President Abraham Lincoln takes a break from his usual routine and visits the Washington Navy Yard to confer with Admiral John A. B. Dahlgren and to observe new weapons testing.

WEST: Union troops burn the town of Mound City, Arkansas, in retaliation for supporting guerrilla activities.

NAVAL: The USS *Octorara* captures the British sloop *Brave* in the North West Providence Channel, Bahamas.

January 16

SOUTH: General John Sedgwick assumes command of the IX Corps, Army of the Potomac, in Virginia.

NAVAL: Confederate raider CSS *Florida* under Lieutenant John N. Maffitt skillfully evades Union blockaders under the cover of darkness and slips out of Mobile Bay, Alabama. This celebrated raider eventually seizes 15 Union vessels.

The USS *Baron de Kalb* captures Devall's Bluff, Arkansas, while pursuing CSS *Blue Wing* up the White River.

January 17

POLITICS: President Abraham Lincoln signs legislation allowing for the immediate payment of military personnel. He also asks Congress for currency reforms to halt mounting inflation throughout the North.

SOUTH: Jubal A. Early gains appointment as a major general, C.S.A.

Frederick A. Hoke is promoted to brigadier general, C.S.A.

WEST: General Ulysses S. Grant, resenting General John A. McClernand's disregard for proper channels in mounting his recent expedition against Fort Hindman, Arkansas, summarily orders him to rejoin his main force at Milliken's Bend, Louisiana.

NAVAL: The USS *Baron de Kalb, Forest Rose,* and *Romeo* ply the White River and arrive off Des Arc, Arkansas, where Confederate supplies are seized.

January 18

SOUTH: Acting on the orders of General Henry Heth, the 64th North Carolina under Colonel James A. Keith sweeps through Shelton Laurel, western North Carolina, in search of Northern sympathizers operating there. At length, he nets 15 male captives, most of whom are not associated with bushwhacking operations, and marches them off to a mountain gorge. Ignoring pleas for mercy, they are lined up, shot, and buried in shallow graves. Word of the massacre outrages Confederate secretary of War James A. Seddon and North Carolina Governor Zebulon B. Vance, who demand an immediate inquiry. Confederate army officials drag their feet over the ensuing months, and none of the perpetrators are ever punished.

NAVAL: The USS *Zouave* captures the Confederate sloop *J. C. McCabe* on the James River, Virginia.

The USS *Wachusett,* under Captain Charles Wilkes, and the *Sonoma* capture the Confederate steamer *Virginia* off Mugeres Island, Mexico.

Admiral David D. Porter, concluding operations on the White River, Arkansas, renews his efforts against the Confederate citadel at Vicksburg, Mississippi, by ordering all available gunboats to Milliken's Bend on the Yazoo River.

January 19

SOUTH: In an attempt to redeem his reputation, General Ambrose E. Burnside orders two grand divisions under General Joseph Hooker and General William B. Franklin across the Rappahannock River at Bank's Ford, Virginia. This move places the Army of the Potomac within 10 miles of Fredericksburg and behind Robert E. Lee's Army of Northern Virginia. The winter weather has been excellent of late, but this quickly and dramatically changes.

General Carl Schurz assumes command of the XI Corps, Army of the Potomac.

NAVAL: The Confederate raider CSS *Florida* under Lieutenant John N. Maffitt captures the Union brig *Estelle* at sea.

January 20

SOUTH: Joseph Wheeler is promoted to major general, C.S.A.

The Army of the Potomac under General Ambrose E. Burnside begins its infamous "mud March." The general intends to bolster his flagging reputation by a surprise march around the Army of Northern Virginia's left flank and a rapid crossing of the Rappahannock to force it into battle in the open. But no sooner does his turning maneuver commence than inclement weather sets in, and troops, supplies, and the all-important pontoon bridges bog down on roads, churned to knee-deep mud.

General David Hunter resumes his post as commander of the Department of the South.

WEST: Confederates under General John S. Marmaduke seize Patterson, Missouri.

NAVAL: The Confederate raider CSS *Florida* under Lieutenant John N. Maffitt enters Havana, Cuba.

January 21

POLITICS: President Abraham Lincoln endorses revocation of the infamous "Jew Order" of General Ulysses S. Grant because it "proscribed an entire religious class, some of whom are fighting in our ranks."

President Jefferson Davis dispatches General Joseph E. Johnston to Manchester, Tennessee, to confer with General Braxton Bragg over his unexplained abandonment of Murfreesboro. He does so amid a demonstrated lack of confidence in Bragg's ability to lead from senior subordinates.

NORTH: President Abraham Lincoln approves the court-martial verdict against General Fitz John Porter, and he is formally cashiered and dismissed from the military.

SOUTH: The march of the Army of the Potomac under General Ambrose E. Burnside is stymied by heavy rain and inclement weather conditions during its attempted flank march to the Rappahannock River, Virginia. His columns are bedeviled by roads choked with mud that exhaust soldiers and beasts alike. The Confederates have since become aware of Burnside's move and harass the struggling Federals with jocular offers of assistance.

NAVAL: The USS *Daylight* destroys an unnamed blockade-runner off New Topsail Inlet, North Carolina.

The USS *Ottawa* captures the Confederate schooner *Etiwan* off Charleston, South Carolina.

The USS *Chocura* seizes the British blockade-runner *Pride* off Cape Romain, South Carolina.

A sudden sortie by Confederate cottonclads CSS *Josiah Bell* and *Uncle Ben* under Major Oscar M. Watkins, C.S.A., captures the steamers USS *Morning Light* and *Velocity* off Sabine Pass, Texas. This temporarily interrupts the Union blockade.

January 22

SOUTH: General Ambrose E. Burnside's offensive across the Rappahannock River into Virginia stumbles and ends because of heavy rain and mud-choked roads. The suffering troops, stiffened by rations of liquor, begin to brawl among themselves as morale continues to sink. After heated consultations with subordinates, Burnside concludes that his master stroke has failed and orders the men back into camp at Falmouth, Virginia. They thus endure another round of exhaustive marching in mud so thick that entire wagon trains sink to their axles.

WEST: General Ulysses S. Grant takes charge of Union forces in Arkansas while General John A. McClernand is punitively reduced to commander of the XIII Corps, Army of the Tennessee. Grant then begins construction of an ambitious canal at Swampy Toe Peninsula, opposite Vicksburg, Mississippi, to allow Union shipping to circumvent its defenses on the Mississippi River.

General Joseph Wheeler assumes command of all Confederate cavalry in Middle Tennessee.

NAVAL: The USS *Commodore Morris* captures the Confederate vessels *John C. Calhoun, Harriet,* and *Music* in Chuckatuck Creek, Virginia.

The Confederate raider CSS *Florida* under Lieutenant John N. Maffitt seizes and burns the Union brigs *Windward* and *Corris Ann* off Cuba.

January 23

NORTH: A demoralized—and rather soggy—Army of the Potomac settles into winter quarters at Falmouth, Virginia, directly across from Fredericksburg. General Ambrose E. Burnside, agitated by the performance of several subordinates, issues General Order No. 8, which peremptorily strips Generals Joseph Hooker, Edwin V. Sumner, and William B. Franklin of their commands. The general then rides to Washington, D.C., to confer with President Abraham Lincoln and to defend his decision.

NAVAL: The USS *Cambridge* captures the Confederate schooner *Time* off Cape Fear, North Carolina.

January 24

NAVAL: Admiral David D. Porter arrives back at the Yazoo River and prepares to ascend that body as a way of outflanking the defenses of Vicksburg, Mississippi, from the north.

January 25

POLITICS: Massachusetts governor John A. Andrew authorizes recruitment of the 54th Massachusetts Infantry, which is composed entirely of African Americans and led by white officers.

NORTH: General Ambrose E. Burnside is removed as commander of the Army of the Potomac and replaced by General Joseph "Fighting Joe" Hooker, a boisterous individual and one of Burnside's loudest critics. Generals William B. Franklin and Edwin V. Sumner, however, remain relieved of duties pending a court of inquiry.

SOUTH: The Virginia Partisan Rangers under Lieutenant John S. Mosby skirmish with Federal troops at Fairfax Court House, Virginia.

WEST: Confederates under General John S. Marmaduke end their raid into Missouri by arriving back at Batesville, Arkansas.

NAVAL: The USS *Currituck* captures the Confederate sloop *Queen of the Fleet* in Tapp's Creek, Virginia.

January 26

POLITICS: President Abraham Lincoln orders a major shakeup in the Army of the Potomac leadership with General Darius N. Couch assuming command of the Right Grand Division, General George G. Meade taking charge of the Central Grand Division, and General Oliver O. Howard leading the Left Grand Division. General Charles Griffin is also appointed to take temporary command of the V Corps. The president also congratulates General Joseph Hooker as commander of the Army of the Potomac, despite rumors that he feels a military dictatorship is necessary to win the war. "Only those generals who gain successes can set up dictators," Lincoln notes. "What I ask of you is military success, and I will risk the dictatorship."

NAVAL: The Confederate raider CSS *Alabama* under Captain Raphael Semmes seizes and burns the Union ship *Golden Rule* off Haiti.

January 27

POLITICS: Philadelphia newspaperman A. D. Boileau is arrested for allegedly publishing an anti-Union editorial in his *Journal*.

WEST: In response to Shoshone attacks on settlers and miners in the Great Basin region, Colonel Patrick E. Connor of the 1st California Cavalry leads 300 soldiers on an expedition against the encampment of Chief Bear Hunter on the Bear River, Idaho Territory. The site is well chosen by the Native Americans, who have mustered 300 warriors—it is located along the sides of a deep ravine. For this reason, Connor orchestrates a two-pronged assault that flanks the camp and allows soldiers to fire down from the heights. After a raging conflict of several hours, Bear Hunter and 224 warriors are cut down, and the soldiers take an additional 164 women and children prisoners. Federal losses are 21 dead and 46 wounded. The humbled Shoshone sign a treaty forfeiting their claims to the Great Basin region; Connor gains promotion to brigadier general.

NAVAL: The USS *Hope* seizes the British blockade-runner *Emma Tuttle* off Charleston, South Carolina.

The ironclad USS *Montauk* under Captain John L. Worden spearheads a Federal assault on Fort McAllister on the Ogeechee River, Georgia. This is a test run for the new vessels in preparation for an assault on the more formidable defenses of Charleston, South Carolina. Accompanied by USS *Seneca, Wissahickon, Dawn,* and mortar boat *C. P. Williams,* Worden engages Confederate batteries for four hours. Fighting proves inconclusive, and the squadron is withdrawn. The *Montauk* receives 14 hits, none of them serious. But Admiral Samuel F. Du Pont, who orders the attack, is disappointed by the results, especially the slow firing rate and inaccurate aim of his vessels. "If one ironclad cannot take eight guns," he ponders, "how are five to take 147 guns in Charleston Harbor."

The Confederate raider CSS *Alabama* under Captain Raphael Semmes captures and burns the Union brig *Chastelaine* in the Caribbean.

January 28

POLITICS: President Jefferson Davis warns General Theophilus Holmes of the dangers confronting his Trans-Mississippi Department. "The loss of either of the two positions—Vicksburg or Port Hudson—would destroy communication with the Trans-Mississippi Department," he writes, "and inflict upon the Confederacy an injury which I am sure you have not failed to appreciate."

SOUTH: John D. Imboden is appointed brigadier general, C.S.A.

NAVAL: The USS *Sagamore* sinks the British blockade-runner *Elizabeth* off Jupiter Inlet, Florida.

January 29

POLITICS: The Confederate Congress authorizes a loan of $15 million from French financiers.

A pensive president Jefferson Davis inquires of General John C. Pemberton at Vicksburg, Mississippi, "Has anything or can anything be done to obstruct the navigation from Yazoo Pass down?"

WEST: Colonel James H. Wilson, an engineer, is ordered to depart Helena, Arkansas, with specialists and equipment for an expedition down Yazoo Pass. This turns out to be a major drive to flank the Confederate defenses of Vicksburg from behind, although the region is known to be a tangled, swampy morass.

NAVAL: The USS *Unadilla* seizes the British blockade-runner *Princess Royal* near Charleston, South Carolina.

The USS *Brooklyn*, assisted by Federal gunboats *Scotia*, *Owasco*, and *Katahdin*, bombards Confederate positions at Galveston, Texas. Its captain notes with some trepidation that enemy shot sails easily over his squadron, at a range of two and a half miles.

The Federal gunboat USS *Lexington* is attacked by Confederate artillery while steaming down the Cumberland River between Cairo, Illinois, and Nashville, Tennessee, but accurate counterfire quickly disperses the antagonists.

January 30

WEST: General Ulysses S. Grant, officially placed in charge of western operations at Milliken's Bend, Louisiana, begins to formulate a new strategic campaign against Vicksburg, Mississippi.

NAVAL: A joint expedition sailing with the USS *Commodore Perry* lands armed parties near Hertford, North Carolina. Two bridges are destroyed and several small vessels sunk.

The Federal gunboat USS *Isaac Smith* is caught in a heavy crossfire while steaming up the Stono River, South Carolina, runs aground, and is captured.

Admiral David D. Porter instructs the USS *Linden* to cooperate with army forces under General Ulysses S. Grant while his men dig a canal to circumvent Confederate defenses at Vicksburg, Mississippi. He also orders the squadron to sweep the Yazoo River for supplies of cotton to deprive the Confederacy of this valuable commodity. Captured bales are also to be employed as additional armor for his ships.

January 31

WEST: Union and Confederate forces skirmish heavily in the wake of General Braxton Bragg's withdrawal from Murfreesboro, Tennessee. A heavy engagement at Dover results in 300 Southern captives for a Federal loss of five.

NAVAL: Obscured by a thick haze, Confederate steam rams CSS *Palmetto State* and *Chicora* under Commanders Duncan N. Ingraham and John R. Tucker sortie against the South Atlantic Blockading Squadron of Admiral Samuel F. Du Pont off Charleston, South Carolina. The converted merchantman *Mercedita*, rammed and riddled by cannon fire, surrenders; the USS *Keystone State* sustains heavy damage and is rescued by the *Memphis*. Union losses are 24 killed and 24 wounded, most by scalding. The Confederate vessels then withdraw back to Charleston, having dented the Union blockade but accomplishing little else.

The Confederate raider CSS *Retribution* seizes the Union schooner *Hanover* in the West Indies.

February 1

POLITICS: By this period in the war, inflation erodes the Confederate dollar such that it yields the purchasing power of only 20 cents.

SOUTH: General George Sykes temporarily takes command of the V Corps, Army of the Potomac.

WEST: Advancing Union forces capture the town of Franklin, Tennessee.

NAVAL: The ironclad USS *Montauk* under Captain John L. Worden, assisted by *Seneca, Wissahickon, Dawn,* and the mortar boat *C. P. Williams,* again attack Fort McAllister on the Ogeechee River, Georgia. This time, the vessels initiate action at much closer range and manage to inflict heavy damage. *Montauk* sustains 48 hits in the four-hour exchange, none of them serious.

The USS *Passaic* under Captain Percival Drayton, accompanied by the *Marblehead,* conducts a detailed reconnaissance up the Wilmington River, Georgia.

The USS *Tahoma* and *Hendrick Hudson* capture the British blockade-runner *Margaret* off St. Petersburg, Florida.

The USS *Two Sisters* seizes the Confederate sloop *Richards* off Boca Grande, Mexico.

February 2

NORTH: The Department of Washington, D.C., is constituted while its attendant garrison is designated XXII Corps.

WEST: Colonel James H. Wilson cuts into the Mississippi River levee, spilling water into the Yazoo Pass region and raising its level to support gunboats.

NAVAL: The USS *Mount Vernon* drives the Confederate schooner *Industry* aground at New Topsail Inlet, North Carolina. The vessel is subsequently burned.

The Federal ram USS *Queen of the West* under Colonel Charles R. Ellet runs past the batteries of Vicksburg, Mississippi, and is struck 12 times without sus-

Line engraving depicting the February 2, 1863, attack by U.S. ram *Queen of the West* on the Confederate steamer *City of Vicksburg* off Vicksburg, Mississippi, published in *Harper's Weekly,* 1863 *(Naval Historical Foundation)*

taining serious damage. It then attacks the Confederate vessel *City of Vicksburg* before proceeding farther up the Red River to destroy supply caches deposited there.

February 3
DIPLOMACY: Secretary of State William H. Seward receives an offer made through the French embassy to mediate the war.

POLITICS: The U.S. Congress votes Captain John L. Worden its thanks for service rendered as captain of the USS *Monitor.*

WEST: Confederate cavalry under General Nathan B. Forrest unsuccessfully attacks Union forces under Colonel Abner C. Harding, garrisoning Fort Donelson, Tennessee. Harding reports a loss of 12 dead and 30 injured; the Southerners lose over 100 killed, 400 wounded, and 300 prisoners.

General Joseph Wheeler's Confederate raiding column is repulsed at the Cumberland Iron works, Tennessee.

The levee at Yazoo Pass, Mississippi, is opened to allow access to Vicksburg from behind. A combined expedition consisting of 5,000 troops under General Leonard F. Ross then departs upstream.

Naval: The USS *Midnight* seizes the British blockade-runner *Defy* off the Georgia coast.

The USS *Sonoma* captures the British blockade-runner *Springbo* off the Bahamas.

The Confederate raider CSS *Alabama* under Captain Raphael Semmes seizes and burns the Union schooner *Palmetto* off Puerto Rico.

The USS *Lexington, Fairplay, St. Clair, Brilliant, Robb,* and *Silver Lake* provide supporting fire to army troops at Fort Donelson, Tennessee, repelling a Confederate attack by General Nathan B. Forrest.

A combined expedition under General Leonard F. Ross proceeds down the Yazoo River, accompanied by the gunboats USS *Baron de Kalb* and *Chillicothe*.

February 4

South: General John Sedgwick succeeds William F. Smith as commander of VI Corps, Army of the Potomac.

West: Confederate troops under General John S. Marmaduke are driven from Batesville, Arkansas, by pursuing Union forces.

Naval: The USS *New Era* captures the Confederate steamer *W. A. Knapp* near Island No. 10 in the Mississippi River.

February 5

Politics: Queen Victoria outlines to Parliament her government's reasons for refusing to pursue mediation efforts between the North and the South, namely, because there are few reasonable expectations for success.

North: General Joseph Hooker reorganizes the Army of the Potomac and dispenses with his predecessor's "grand divisions" scheme. A new nine corps structure is implemented under Generals John F. Reynolds (I), Darius N. Couch (II), Daniel E. Sickles (III), George G. Meade (V), John Sedgwick (VI), William F. Smith (IX), Franz Sigel (XI), Henry W. Slocum (XII), and George Stoneman (U.S. Cavalry Corps).

February 6

Diplomacy: Secretary of State William H. Seward unilaterally rejects a French offer to mediate hostilities.

South: The Union IX Corps under General William F. Smith relocates to Newport News, Virginia, to increase pressure on Richmond from the east.

February 7

North: Command of the Department of Washington, D.C., is delegated to General Samuel P. Heintzelman.

Naval: The new Confederate ironclads CSS *Tuscaloosa* and *Huntsville* are launched at Selma, Alabama, and then taken to Mobile to be outfitted.

The gunboat USS *Glide* is destroyed by fire at Cairo, Illinois.

The USS *Forest Rose* is damaged by low hanging trees while traversing Yazoo Pass, Mississippi.

February 8

Politics: Allegedly disloyal statements lead the *Chicago Times* to be suspended temporarily from publication.

NAVAL: At the behest of General John G. Foster, the Federal gunboat *Commodore McDonough* traverses the Stono River, South Carolina, looking for newly erected Confederate batteries. None are noted.

February 9
SOUTHWEST: The Confederate Army of the Southwest under General Edmund Kirby-Smith extends its authority to the entire Trans-Mississippi Department.
NAVAL: The USS *Coeur de Lion* captures the Confederate schooner *Emily Murray* near Machadoc Creek, Virginia.

February 10
NAVAL: The Federal ram USS *Queen of the West* steams farther down the Red River, Louisiana.

The Federal ram USS *Dick Fulton* sustains damage from Confederate forces at Cyrus Bend, Arkansas.

February 11
DIPLOMACY: In London, Confederate agent James M. Mason addresses the lord mayor's banquet and promotes the desirability of recognition for the Confederacy.

February 12
NAVAL: The Confederate raider CSS *Florida* under Lieutenant John N. Maffitt seizes and burns the Union clipper ship *Jacob Bell*, along with cargo estimated at $2 million.

The USS *Conestoga* captures the Confederate steamers *Rose Hambleton* and *Evansville* on the White River, Arkansas.

The USS *Queen of the West* steams up the Red and Atchafalaya rivers, Louisiana, destroying a Confederate wagon train.

February 13
NAVAL: The USS *New Era* captures the Confederate steamers *White Cloud* and *Rowena* near Island No. 10 on the Mississippi River.

The ironclad USS *Indianola* runs past Confederate batteries at Vicksburg, Mississippi, intending to join the *Queen of the West* at the mouth of the Red River as a blockading force.

A combined, light-draft expedition into Yazoo Pass, consisting of USS *Rattler, Romeo, Forest, Rose, Chillicothe, Baron de Kalb,* and *Matamora,* arrives off Helena, Arkansas.

February 14
NAVAL: The USS *Tioga* captures the British blockade-runner *Avon* off the Bahamas.

The USS *Forest Rose* captures the Confederate steamer *Chippewa Valley* at Island No. 63 on the Mississippi River.

The U.S. ram *Queen of the West* under Colonel Charles R. Ellet moves 15 miles up the Black River and captures the steamer CSS *New Era No. 5.* While returning back downstream, his vessel is bracketed by Confederate artillery, run aground, and captured intact. The Union crew, however, escapes by transferring to its prize and sailing off.

February 15

WEST: Confederate raiders under General John H. Morgan are repulsed by Union troops near Cainsville, Tennessee.

NAVAL: The USS *Sonoma* captures the Confederate brig *Atlantic* at sea.

February 16

POLITICS: The U.S. Congress authorizes the Conscription Act, making all men aged between 20 and 45 liable for military service to address the inadequacies of voluntary enlistment. However, substitutes can still be hired for $300.

WEST: General Stephen A. Hurlbut gains control of the XVI Corps, Army of the Mississippi.

February 17

POLITICS: The order suspending publication of the *Chicago Times* is rescinded by General Ulysses S. Grant.

WEST: Federal troops burn the town of Hopefield, Arkansas, in retaliation for Confederate attacks on shipping.

NAVAL: Confederate forces seize the Federal tug USS *Hercules* opposite Memphis, Tennessee.

The Federal ironclad USS *Indianola* arrives at the mouth of the Red River, having successfully run the Confederate gauntlet at Vicksburg, Mississippi. It stations itself there to maintain the Union blockade.

February 18

POLITICS: Union troops break up a convention by Democrats in Frankfort, Kentucky, which they construe as pro-Confederate.

SOUTH: General James Longstreet is ordered to transfer two divisions of his corps from the Army of Northern Virginia near Fredericksburg to bolster the defenses of Richmond, Virginia.

NAVAL: The USS *Victoria* captures the Confederate brig *Minna* off Shallotte Inlet, North Carolina.

Armed boats from the USS *Somerset* capture the blockade-runner *Hortense* at sea.

February 19

POLITICS: Federal troops convalescing in a hospital at Keokuk, Iowa, angered by antiwar sentiments expressed in the local newspaper *Constitution,* hobble over and ransack the news offices.

SOUTH: President Jefferson Davis contacts General Joseph E. Johnston, noting anxiously how little confidence General Braxton Bragg solicits from his senior subordinates. "It is scarcely possible in that state of the case for him to possess the requisite confidence of the troops," Davis notes. However, the president is not disposed toward removing his old friend and confidant from command.

WEST: Skirmishing between Federals and Confederates under General Nathan B. Forrest at Yazoo Pass north of Vicksburg, Mississippi.

NAVAL: The Confederate raider CSS *Retribution* captures the Federal brig *Emily* in the Caribbean.

February 20

WEST: Union troops under Colonel Alfred H. Terry skirmish with Santee (Sioux) outcasts in the Dakota Territory.

NAVAL: The USS *Crusader* captures the Confederate schooner *General Taylor* in Mobjack Bay, Virginia.

February 21

NAVAL: The USS *Thomas Freeborn* and *Dragon* trade fire with Confederate batteries below Fort Lowry, Virginia.

The USS *Dacotah* and *Monticello* exchange salvos with Confederate batteries at Fort Caswell, North Carolina.

The Confederate raider CSS *Alabama* under Captain Raphael Semmes seizes and burns the Federal ship *Golden Eagle* and bark *Olive Jane*.

February 22

WEST: Union cavalry surprise General Earl Van Dorn's supply column at Tuscumbia, Alabama, taking supplies and prisoners.

February 23

POLITICS: Pennsylvanian Simon Cameron, former secretary of war, resigns his post as minister to Russia.

NAVAL: The USS *Dacotah* and *Monticello* engage Confederate batteries at Fort Caswell, North Carolina.

The USS *Potomska* captures the British blockade-runner *Belle* off Sapelo Sound, Georgia. Armed boats from USS *Caswell* and *Arago* capture the Confederate blockade-runner *Glide* off Little Tybee Island, Georgia.

The USS *Kinsman* hits a snag and sinks in Berwick Bay, Louisiana, losing six crew members.

February 24

WEST: After three weeks of intense work, Union troops finally clear the Yazoo Pass of overhanging vegetation. General Leonard F. Ross reassembles an armada of transports and ironclads to venture downstream.

SOUTHWEST: The Arizona Territory is carved out of the New Mexico Territory by an act of Congress.

NAVAL: Armed boats from the USS *Mahaska* capture and sink the Confederate sloop *Mary Jane* and barge *Ben Bolt* in the York River, Virginia.

The USS *State of Georgia* captures the blockade-runner *Annie* off Cape Romain, South Carolina.

The USS *Tahoma* captures the Confederate schooner *Stonewall* off Key West, Florida.

A Confederate naval deserter informs Union blockaders of submarines and other "infernal machines" being assembled and tested at Mobile, Alabama.

The Confederate vessels CSS *William H. Webb* and *Beatty*, assisted by the newly acquired *Queen of the West*, repeatedly ram the ironclad USS *Indianola* of Commander George Brown below Warrenton, Mississippi. Outnumbered and outmaneuvered by speedier craft, *Indianola* sustains serious damage and partially sinks, so Brown surrenders. The Confederates, cognizant of their valuable prize, undertake immediate steps to raise and salvage it. This loss convinces Admiral David D. Porter to abandon efforts to blockade the Red River with single vessels detached from the main fleet.

February 25

POLITICS: The U.S. Congress approves a national banking system drawn up by Secretary of the Treasury Salmon P. Chase, whereby participating institutions reserve up to one-third of their capital in U.S. Securities. These, in turn, serve as a basis for issuing national bank notes (currency) to the public to facilitate long-term financing of the war effort. This system lasts with little modification until establishment of the Federal Reserve in 1913.

SOUTH: Confederate cavalry under General Fitzhugh Lee surprise a Union cavalry outpost at Hartwood Church, Virginia, taking 150 prisoners.

General Daniel H. Hill receives command of Confederate forces in North Carolina.

NAVAL: The USS *Conemaugh* runs the British blockade-runner *Queen of the Waves* aground at the mouth of the North Santee River, South Carolina.

The USS *Vanderbilt* captures the British merchant vessel *Peterhoff* off St. Thomas in the Caribbean, sparking a British diplomatic protest over the disposition of mail found on the vessel. Eventually, President Abraham Lincoln orders the craft and all confiscated mail returned to their owners.

A force of light-draft Federal gunboats enters the Yazoo Pass after army troops clear away trees and other obstructions from the riverbanks.

Confederates scuttle the newly acquired USS *Indianola* to prevent its recapture at the hands of a fast-approaching, formidable Union "warship"; actually, this is an old coal barge disguised as an ironclad with dummy stacks, guns, and superstructure, being floated downstream for that purpose by Admiral David D. Porter.

February 26

SOUTH: General James Longstreet becomes commander of Confederate forces in the Department of Virginia and North Carolina. At this time, his I Corps consists of divisions under Generals John B. Hood and George E. Pickett.

Confederate rangers under Captain John S. Mosby rout a Union detachment near Germantown, Virginia.

WEST: Confederate irregulars burn a Union train near Woodburn, Tennessee.

General Sterling Price is transferred formally back to the Confederate Trans-Mississippi Department.

SOUTHWEST: On further reflection, the National Council of Cherokee Indians abolishes slavery, renounces its prior alliance with the Confederacy, and rejoins the Union.

February 27

Naval: The Confederate raider CSS *Alabama* under Captain Raphael Semmes seizes the Union ship *Washington* in the mid-Atlantic and then releases it on bond.

February 28

Naval: The USS *Wynandank* captures the Confederate schooners *Vista* and *A. W. Thompson* off Piney Point, Virginia.

The ironclad USS *Montauk* under Captain John L. Worden, accompanied by *Seneca*, *Wissahocken*, and *Dawn*, sails up the Ogeechee River and sinks the blockade-runner CSS *Rattlesnake* (nee *Nashville*) near Fort McAllister, Georgia. However, *Montauk* strikes a torpedo and temporarily grounds itself on a mudbank to affect repairs.

The USS *New Era* seizes the Confederate steamer *Curlew* off Island No. 10 in the Mississippi River.

The Yazoo River expedition glides onto the Coldwater River several days ahead of army transports. They are joined by the rams USS *Fulton* and *Lioness* and the gunboat *Petrel*.

March 1

West: Confederate raiders under General Nathan B. Forrest skirmish with Union forces at Bradyville, Tennessee.

Union forces capture and occupy Bloomfield, Missouri.

March 2

North: The U.S. Congress authorizes four major generals and nine brigadier generals for the U.S. Army, with an additional 40 major generals and 200 brigadier generals for the volunteers. Conversely, 33 ranking officers are dismissed from the service on a variety of charges.

Southwest: Federal troops depart New Orleans on an expedition to the mouth of the Rio Grande.

Naval: The Confederate raider CSS *Alabama* under Captain Raphael Semmes seizes and burns the Federal ship *John A. Parks*.

March 3

Diplomacy: The U.S. Congress passes a resolution condemning all offers of mediation as "foreign intervention."

Politics: President Abraham Lincoln signs the Enrollment or Federal Draft Act, whereby all able-bodied males between 20 and 46 years of age are eligible for military service. This is the first such legislation enacted by the Federal government.

The U.S. Congress approves a loan of $300 million for the year 1863. It also formally and finally suspends writs of habeas corpus as a wartime expedient.

Jay Cooke is named Federal agent tasked with promoting the sale of war bonds.

The U.S. Congress establishes the National Academy of Sciences.

The 37th U.S. Congress adjourns.

West: The Idaho Territory is formed by act of Congress, sliced from parts of the adjoining Washington and Dakota territories, and incorporates parts of present-day Montana and Wyoming.

NAVAL: An armed boat from the USS *Matthew Vassar* proceeds up the Little River Inlet, North Carolina, and burns a large vessel there, but on the return trip, the crew is captured by Confederates.

The ironclads USS *Passaic, Nahant,* and *Patapsco,* accompanied by gunboats *Seneca, Dawn,* and *Wissahocken* and three mortar boats, engage the batteries of Fort McAllister, Georgia, for six hours. Little damage is inflicted, but the attack gives Union boat crews practical training for their upcoming moves against Charleston, South Carolina.

March 4

WEST: Confederates under General Earl Van Dorn successfully surround and skirmish with Federal troops at Franklin, Tennessee. Union cavalry manage to ride to safety, but the infantry component of the expedition is forced to surrender.

NAVAL: The USS *James S. Chambers* captures the Spanish blockade-runner *Relampago* at sea and the Confederate schooner *Ida* after it runs ashore at Sanibel Island, Florida.

March 5

POLITICS: In Columbus, Ohio, rampaging Union troops gut the editorial offices of the newspaper *Crisis* for allegedly printing pro-Southern editorials.

WEST: General Earl Van Dorn advances with 6,000 Confederates against a Union position at Thompson's Station, Tennessee. The defenders consist of 2,857 Federal soldiers and cavalry supported by six cannon under Colonel John Coburn. Rather than retreat, Coburn elects to attack the enemy camp and is assailed in turn by cavalry under General Nathan B. Forrest. When these are driven off, the remaining Union infantry stubbornly defend two hills and beat back numerous Confederate charges. At length, a final attempt is mounted by Forrest that finally breaks Union resistance and Coburn surrenders. The Confederates sustain 357 casualties while capturing 1,221 Federals. Bad blood subsequently ensues when Van Dorn accuses Forrest of hoarding captured Union supplies for his own use, a charge Forrest vehemently denies. These two headstrong cavaliers nearly come to dueling before calmer heads prevail.

NAVAL: The USS *Lockwood* safely returns from an armed expedition up the Pungo River to destroy a bridge and break up enemy supply dumps.

The USS *Aroostook* chases the Confederate blockade-runner *Josephine* aground near Fort Morgan, Mobile Bay, Alabama, destroying it by gunfire.

March 6

NAVAL: The Confederate raider CSS *Florida* under Lieutenant John N. Maffitt captures and burns the Union ship *Star of Peace* at sea.

March 7

POLITICS: Federal troops in Baltimore, Maryland, confiscate all song sheets that are deemed "secession music."

SOUTH: A Federal expedition from New Bern, North Carolina, to Mattamuskeet ends in controversy when Colonel Charles C. Dodge, commanding, accuses the

103rd Pennsylvania Volunteers of unauthorized burning, plundering, and disrespectful conduct toward local women.

WEST: Federal forces under General Nathaniel P. Banks advance from New Orleans toward Port Hudson, Louisiana, to campaign in concert with General Ulysses S. Grant at Vicksburg, Mississippi.

General Edmund Kirby-Smith arrives to assume command of all Confederate forces in the Trans-Mississippi Department.

NAVAL: Admiral Samuel P. Lee of the North Atlantic Blockading Squadron, having detached many officers and sailors as prize crews, requests reinforcements to make up manpower deficiencies.

March 8

SOUTH: A sudden raid by Captain John S. Mosby and his Confederate rangers captures General Edwin H. Stoughton in his headquarters at Fairfax County Court House, Virginia, along with 32 prisoners and 58 horses. The general was sleeping in bed at the time and rudely was awakened by a slap on his backside—delivered by Mosby himself. This was one of the most daring—if embarrassing—acts of the entire war.

General Daniel H. Hill's troops skirmish heavily with Union defenders outside Fort Anderson near New Bern, North Carolina.

WEST: Progress on the Yazoo River expedition, slow to begin with, is hindered further by trees felled along the way by retreating Confederates, as well as by the usual overhanging vegetation on the riverbanks. Two additional days are required to clear away all obstacles before additional progress can be made downstream.

NAVAL: The USS *Sagamore* captures the Confederate sloop *Enterprise* near Mosquito Inlet, Florida.

March 9

NAVAL: The USS *Quaker City* captures the British blockade-runner *Douro* near Wilmington, North Carolina.

The USS *Bienville* captures the Confederate schooner *Lightning* off Port Royal, South Carolina.

The 22-boat combined expedition to the Yazoo River under General Leonard F. Ross finally clears the Talluhatchie River and reaches the confluence of the Yalobusha and Tazoo rivers. There, they encounter a small Confederate fortification christened Fort Pemberton near Greenwood, Mississippi, and prepare to bombard it.

March 10

POLITICS: In the Prize Cases, the Supreme Court approves the legality of the Union naval blockade on a 5–4 vote. They do so by declaring the right of a sovereign state to conduct a blockade while simultaneously denying that the Confederate States of America actually exists. The Court also rules that while only Congress has the power to declare war, Lincoln, as commander in chief, has the authority to suppress a rebellion.

President Abraham Lincoln signs a general amnesty for all soldiers, presently absent without leave, to rejoin their units by April 1, 1863.

President Jefferson C. Davis ventures to Vicksburg, Mississippi, where he confers with General John C. Pemberton about affairs in the West.

SOUTH: Federal forces, including a large number of African-American soldiers, seize and occupy Jacksonville, Florida.

NAVAL: The USS *Gem of the Sea* sinks the Confederate sloop *Petee* off Indian River Inlet, Florida.

The USS *Norwich* and *Uncas* ships troops up the St. John's River, Florida, where armed parties land and recapture Jacksonville.

The USS *Chillicothe* destroys a bridge spanning the Tallahatchie River above Fort Pemberton, Mississippi. The Confederate steamer *Thirty-fifth Parallel* is also sunk to prevent capture.

March 11

NAVAL: A Federal gunboat expedition moving up the Tallahatchie River engages Confederate batteries under General William W. Loring at Fort Pemberton, Greenwood, Mississippi. In the course of battle, the ironclad USS *Chillicothe* receives repeated hits and withdraws in damaged condition.

March 12

NAVAL: The USS *Kittatinny* captures the Confederate vessel *D. Sargent* in the Gulf of Mexico.

Admiral David G. Farragut arrives at Baton Rouge, Louisiana, with his flagship USS *Hartford* and prepares to advance past Confederate defenses at Port Hudson on the Mississippi River.

March 13

SOUTH: A horrific explosion rocks the Confederate Ordnance Laboratory on Brown's Island, Richmond, Virginia, killing 70 workers, principally women. This accident highlights how far men have been supplanted as industrial workers due to wartime conditions in the South.

Confederate forces under General Daniel H. Hill launch a night attack against Fort Anderson on the Neuse River, North Carolina, which is repulsed by naval gunfire.

NAVAL: Federal gunboats USS *Hunchback, Hetzel, Ceres,* and *Shawsheen* render invaluable support fire during a surprise Confederate attack on Fort Anderson, North Carolina.

The USS *Huntsville* captures the British blockade-runner *Surprise* near Charlotte Harbor, Florida.

The USS *Octorara* captures the British blockade-runner *Florence Nightingale* in North East Providence Channel, Bahamas.

The Confederate raider CSS *Florida* under Lieutenant John N. Maffitt captures and burns the Union ship *Aldebaran* at sea.

The ironclad USS *Chillicothe*, accompanied by gunboats *Baron de Kalb* and *Matamora,* again engage Confederate batteries at Fort Pemberton at Greenwood, Mississippi. In two hours, the *Chillicothe* receives an additional 38 hits, and the flotilla withdraws back up the Tallahatchie River.

March 14

South: General Nathaniel P. Banks advances his Army of the Gulf on Port Hudson, Louisiana, with 30,000 men. He establishes several artillery batteries to assist the passage of Admiral David G. Farragut's fleet and then returns to Baton Rouge when the attempt fails. It is now painfully apparent to Union authorities that Port Hudson, a position second only in strength to Vicksburg, Mississippi, must be reduced by assault in the near future.

Naval: Admiral David G. Farragut's squadron of seven ships runs past Confederate batteries at Port Hudson, Louisiana, at 11:00 p.m. The admiral's flagship USS *Hartford,* lashed together alongside the *Albatross,* weathers a storm of shot and shells and makes the passage intact. The remaining vessels are supported by mortar fire from army units, but resistance proves fierce and they are driven back downstream. The *Mississippi* grounds, catches afire, and drifts helplessly until exploding with a loss of 64 lives. Moreover, Farragut is cut off from his surviving warships, *Monongahela* and *Richmond,* for several weeks.

Admiral David D. Porter pushes the gunboats USS *Louisville, Cincinnati, Carondelet, Pittsburgh,* and *Mound City,* four mortar boats, and four tugs up the Yazoo River to secure Steele's Bayou near Vicksburg, Mississippi. Over the next weeks, they pass successively upstream hoping to turn the city's defenses from the rear, but progress is slow due to the overgrown riverbanks.

March 15

Naval: The Confederate raider CSS *Alabama* under Captain Raphael Semmes captures the Union ship *Punjab* off the Brazilian coast and releases it on bond.

Armed boats from the USS *Cyane* seize the schooner and suspected Confederate blockade-runner *J. M. Chapman* in San Francisco Bay, California. Various military stores found in its cargo holds demonstrate its belligerent intent.

March 16

North: Philip H. Sheridan is promoted to major general, U.S. Army.

West: Cavalry under Generals Earl Van Dorn and Joseph Wheeler are designated Confederate army corps within the Army of Tennessee.

General William T. Sherman arrives at Hill's Plantation, Mississippi, with the 2nd Division, XV Corps, to support a riverine advance to Steele's Bayou by Admiral David D. Porter.

Naval: The USS *Octorara* captures the Confederate sloop *Rosalie* and schooner *Five Brothers* off the east coast of Florida.

Federal gunboats of the Yazoo River expedition again engage Fort Pemberton, Greenwood, Mississippi, whereupon the ironclad USS *Chillicothe* receives eight more hits, suffers 22 casualties, and drifts helplessly. The attack finally is halted by General Leonard F. Ross, and he makes ready to withdraw downstream in defeat. Failure here terminates General Ulysses S. Grant's attempts to circumvent the Confederate defenses of Vicksburg, Mississippi, through the backdoor.

Admiral David D. Porter confers with General Ulysses S. Grant at Hill's Plantation at the head of Black Bayou, Mississippi, and then leads five of his ironclads up Deer Creek in an attempt to reach Steele's Bayou from the northeast.

March 17

SOUTH: General Ambrose E. Burnside is reassigned to command of the IX Corps, Army of the Potomac, although he subsequently shares this position with General John G. Parke.

A force of 2,100 Union cavalry and six guns under General William W. Averell advances from Morrisville, Virginia, and heads for the Rappahannock River intending to surprise Confederate cavalry stationed at Culpeper Court. While crossing at Kelley's Ford, Union troops are delayed by Confederate sentinels who alert General Fitzhugh Lee to their presence. The Confederates quickly take to their saddles and advance to meet the intruders with 800 men. Averell then lines up his five regiments abreast behind a stone wall, lets the Confederates gallop to within close range, and mows them down with intense artillery and carbine fire. Lee withdraws to a second position farther back and regroups as Union troopers advance in turn. A series of charges and countercharges ensue throughout the afternoon with little advantage to either side before Averell ends the contest at 5:30 P.M. and withdraws across the river in good order. As a parting jest, he leaves Lee, a former West Point roommate, a sack of coffee and a note inquiring if he enjoyed his visit. Union losses total 58 while the Confederates report 133 killed and wounded. Foremost among the fallen is the youthful Southern artillerist Major John Pelham, who is mortally struck by an artillery fragment. Kelley's Ford also puts Southern horsemen on notice of the proficiency their Union opposites have acquired with greater experience.

Captain John S. Mosby surprises and captures a 25-man picket at Herndon Station, Virginia.

NAVAL: The Yazoo River expedition, stymied by Fort Pemberton near Greenwood, Mississippi, steams back down the Tallahatchie River.

March 18

POLITICS: The Democratic-controlled state legislature of New Jersey passes a number of peace resolutions condemning all aspects of the war effort and demanding a negotiated ending. This prompts a sharp response from state regiments in the field, who pass resolutions of their own condemning the legislature's activities as "wicked" and "cowardly."

WEST: General Theophilus H. Holmes is appointed commander of the Confederate District of Arkansas.

NAVAL: The USS *Wissahickon* destroys the Confederate steamer *Georgiana* as it attempts to run the blockade off Charleston, South Carolina.

March 19

SOUTH: General William F. Smith transfers two divisions from his IX Corps at Newport News, Virginia, to the Department of the Ohio.

NAVAL: The USS *Octorara* captures the British blockade-runner *John Williams* off the Bahamas.

Admiral David G. Farragut continues northward by running his steam sloop USS *Hartford* and the ironclad *Albatross* past Confederate guns at Grand Gulf, south of Vicksburg, Mississippi. Despite heavy fire, he sustains only eight casualties and safely anchors the following day off Warrenton.

The Steele's Bayou expedition of Admiral David D. Porter continues up Deer Creek, Mississippi, and begins to encounter Confederate snipers from the shoreline. Porter disembarks 300 sailors to clear the banks of infantry and remove obstacles placed in the river by fleeing Southerners.

March 20
SOUTH: General Daniel H. Hill rings the Union garrison at Washington, North Carolina, with several batteries and deploys several brigades to obstruct possible reinforcements from New Bern. Washington itself is invested by a brigade under General Richard B. Garnett. The garrison commander, General John G. Foster, endures several days of bombardment before Federal gunboats in the nearby Pamlico River arrive to assist.
NAVAL: The USS *Ethan Allen* seizes the British blockade-runner *Gypsy* near St. Joseph's Bay, Florida.

The Steele's Bayou expedition of Admiral David D. Porter no sooner steams past Rolling Fork on Deer Creek, Mississippi, than Confederate forces begin to fell trees and other obstacles behind the fleet to trap it there. Three Southern regiments are then dispatched from Haynes's Bluff to attack and possibly capture the entire squadron.

March 21
NORTH: General Edwin V. Sumner dies of natural causes in Syracuse, New York.
WEST: General William T. Sherman's expedition to Steele's Bayou gropes along the tree-choked river banks, much harassed by snipers and man-made obstacles. Progress is steady but slow, but he increases the tempo to rescue Admiral David D. Porter's squadron, trapped by obstacles at Deer Creek. Protracted skirmishing erupts along the banks as Sherman tries to obstruct a force of 3,000 Confederates from attacking the gunboats in narrow waters.

The Yazoo River expedition of General Leonard F. Ross, now reinforced by troops under General Isaac F. Quinby on Moon Lake, turns around and steams back toward Fort Greenwood, Mississippi.
NAVAL: The USS *Victoria* and *William Bacon* seize the British blockade-runner *Nicolai I* off Cape Fear, North Carolina.

March 22
WEST: Confederate forces under General John Pegram embark on an extended raid into Kentucky.

Mount Sterling, Kentucky, is captured by Confederate troopers belonging to General John H. Morgan's command.
NAVAL: The USS *Tioga* captures British blockade-runners *Granite City* and *Brothers* off Abaco, Bahamas.

Admiral David D. Porter concedes that efforts to seize Steele's Bayou from the Yazoo River have failed, and he commences sailing back to Hill's Plantation, Mississippi, with General William T. Sherman's infantry onboard. Natural obstacles in the river and along the shoreline, complicated by trees felled by fleeing Confederates, thwart another attempt to outflank Vicksburg via inland waterways.

March 23

SOUTH: Virginia Partisan Rangers under Captain John S. Mosby defeat a Federal detachment at Little River Turnpike, Virginia, but then they are surprised and almost captured in turn by Union cavalry.

NAVAL: The USS *Arizona* captures the Confederate sloop *Aurelia* near Mosquito Inlet, Florida.

The Confederate raider CSS *Alabama* under Captain Raphael Semmes captures and burns the Union ship *Morning Star* and the whaler *Kingfisher* off the Brazilian coast.

Admiral David G. Farragut orders the USS *Hartford* and *Albatross* to bombard Confederate works off Warrenton, Mississippi.

March 24

WEST: Confederate forces under General John Pegram skirmish with Union forces at Danville, Kentucky.

Union cavalry under Colonel Benjamin H. Grierson fight a skirmish with pursuing Confederates near La Grange, Tennessee.

NAVAL: The USS *Mount Vernon* captures the British blockade-runner *Mary Jane* off New Inlet, North Carolina.

Admiral David D. Porter's ironclad squadron safely reaches Black Bayou, Mississippi, after almost being trapped on Deer Creek by Confederate infantry. His expedition sustains one engineer killed and four sailors wounded for the effort.

March 25

NORTH: General Ambrose E. Burnside transfers as commanding officer of the Department of the Ohio, succeeding General Horatio G. Wright, who reports back to the Army of the Potomac to command a division.

WEST: General Nathan B. Forrest and his Confederate cavalry column attack Union troops garrisoning in Brentwood, Tennessee. These consist of 520 men of the 22nd Wisconsin under Colonel Edward Bloodgood, with an additional 230 men of the 19th Michigan in a small stockade south of town. Forrest, who had cut all Union telegraph lines beforehand, approaches with two brigades and surrounds both detachments. Some skirmishing ensues, but both Union detachments surrender. But as the Confederate marauders withdraw along the Little Harpeth River, they are set on by a third party of Union cavalry under General Green C. Smith, who recaptures some wagons and supplies. Forrest, nevertheless, concludes another successful raid and escapes with 700 prisoners to Columbia, Tennessee.

NAVAL: The USS *State of Georgia* and *Mount Vernon* capture the Confederate schooner *Rising Dawn* off New Inlet, North Carolina.

The USS *Fort Henry* captures the Confederate schooner *Ranger* at Cedar Keys, Florida.

The USS *Kanawha* captures the Confederate schooner *Clara* off Mobile, Alabama.

The USS *Wachusett* takes the British blockade-runner *Dolphin* off St. Thomas in the Caribbean.

The Confederate raider CSS *Alabama* under Captain Raphael Semmes burns the Union ships *Charles Hill* and *Nora* off the Brazilian coast.

Confederate batteries at Vicksburg, Mississippi, engage rams USS *Lancaster* and *Switzerland* as they attempt to run past their position. The former, struck 30 times, sinks while the latter is so heavily damaged that a planned assault against Warrenton is postponed.

March 26

POLITICS: Voters in the new state of West Virginia approve the gradual emancipation of all slaves.

The Confederate Congress in Richmond, Virginia, approves the Impressment Act, authorizing government agents to seize slaves and foodstuffs to supply the Confederate military. Waste and abuse in its enforcement lead several state governments to condemn the practice.

March 27

POLITICS: President Abraham Lincoln entertains numerous American Indian leaders at the White House and implores them to take up agriculture. "I can see no way in which your race is to become as numerous and prosperous as the white race," he lectured, "except by living as they do, by the cultivation of the earth."

NAVAL: The USS *Pawnee* provides close support fire during an army expedition against Cole's Island, South Carolina.

The USS *Kendrick Hudson* captures the British schooner *Pacifique* off St. Mark's Florida.

The USS *Hartford* under Admiral David G. Farragut bombards Confederate defenses at Warrenton, Mississippi, below Vicksburg.

March 28

WEST: Confederates under General John Pegram skirmish with Union forces at Danville and Hickman's Bridge, Kentucky.

NAVAL: The USS *Stettin* captures the British steamer *Aries* off Bull's Bay, South Carolina.

The Confederate raider CSS *Florida* under Lieutenant John N. Maffitt captures the Union bark *Lapwing* and impresses it as a tender under the new name *Oreto.*

The Federal gunboat USS *Diana* under Captain Thomas L. Peterson sails up the Atchafalaya River, Louisiana, toward Pattersonville, with several companies from the 160th New York and 12th Connecticut onboard. En route, Peterson is ambushed by 500 Confederates on the riverbank, supported by cavalry and artillery. Accurate cannon fire rakes the *Diana*, killing Peterson and driving the infantry from its decks. After a running battle of three hours, *Diana* loses its steering mechanism, grounds, and finally surrenders with a loss of 33 Federals killed and 120 captured. This vessel, which previously had been seized by Union forces at New Orleans in April 1862, reenters Confederate service under General Richard Taylor at Bayou Teche.

March 29

SOUTH: General Carl Schurz is appointed to command the XI Corps, Army of the Potomac.

Southern forces fail to secure Fort Magruder at Williamsburg, Virginia, with a surprise attack.

WEST: General Ulysses S. Grant dispatches General John A. McClernand with troops to Milliken's Bend, Louisiana, on the west bank of the Mississippi River, with orders to march south to New Carthage. Grant now begins the process of divesting himself from supply bases at Memphis, Tennessee.

NAVAL: The USS *South Carolina* seizes the Confederate schooner *Nellie* at Port Royal, South Carolina.

Personnel from the USS *Norwich* evacuate Jacksonville, Florida, after razing most of the town.

The USS *Albatross* joins Admiral David G. Farragut's *Hartford* in a sustained bombardment of Confederate batteries at Warrenton, Mississippi.

March 30

POLITICS: President Abraham Lincoln announces that April 30, 1863, will be designated a national day of fasting and prayer.

SOUTH: Confederate forces under General Daniel H. Hill enact a siege of Union forces at Washington, North Carolina, the course of which is interrupted by Federal gunboats offshore.

NAVAL: The USS *Monticello* captures the British blockade-runner *Sue* near the Little River, North Carolina.

The Confederate raider CSS *Florida* under Lieutenant John N. Maffitt captures and burns the Union bark *M. J. Colcord* at sea.

March 31

NORTH: Oliver O. Howard is appointed major general, U.S. Army.

SOUTH: Captain John S. Mosby and his Virginia Partisan Rangers engage and defeat a Union cavalry detachment at Drainesville, Virginia, inflicting 60 casualties and prisoners.

NAVAL: The USS *Memphis* captures the British schooner *Antelope* off Charleston, South Carolina.

The USS *Two Sisters* captures the Confederate schooner *Agnes* off the Tortugas, Florida.

Admiral David G. Farragut sails USS *Hartford*, *Albatross*, and the recently repaired ram *Switzerland* past Confederate batteries at Grand Gulf, Mississippi. They continue to the Red River and establish a blockade there.

April 1

SOUTH: Captain John S. Mosby's 65 men are surprised in camp by 200 Union cavalry at Broad Run, Virginia, but they repulse their antagonists with 107 casualties.

WEST: General Francis J. Herron succeeds General John M. Schofield as commander of the Army of the Frontier in Missouri.

NAVAL: The USS *Commodore Morris* proceeds up the Ware River, Virginia, where it seizes Patterson Smith's Plantation and burns 22,000 bushels of grain. A body of Confederate cavalry attempting to interfere is driven off.

The USS *Tuscumbia* under Admiral David D. Porter hosts General Ulysses S. Grant and William T. Sherman on a grand reconnaissance of the Yazoo River as far as Haynes's Bluff. The sheer nature of the terrain and other obstacles convince Grant to abandon any advance on Vicksburg, Mississippi, from this direction. The general now turns his attention to operations below the city.

April 2

POLITICS: Richmond, Virginia, is the scene of an infamous "Bread Riot." This morning, a small crowd of women and boys announce that they are going to proceed from Capital Square to obtain bread. Numerous onlookers gradually join the procession, which swells to more than 1,000 and grows increasingly unruly. Full-scale rioting and looting then erupts with many businesses being ransacked. President Jefferson Davis, upon hearing of the outbreak, bravely races over, throws himself in the midst of the angry throng, and demands that they disperse or be fired on by the militia. His warning chills the participants, and they gradually disperse.

SOUTH: General Oliver O. Howard replaces General Carl Schurz as commander of the XI Corps, Army of the Potomac.

WEST: General Ulysses S. Grant meets with Admiral David D. Porter to promulgate a final plan of operations against Vicksburg, Mississippi. They decide that while forces under General William T. Sherman mount a large-scale diversion along Haynes's Bluff to the north, the main force under Grant will march south down the west bank of the Mississippi River. Porter likewise will sail south past the city to reunite with Grant at Hard Times, 30 miles south of Vicksburg. There the entire army will embark and be carried across to the Confederate shore.

NAVAL: Naval gunboats in the Pamlico River, North Carolina, race to the rescue of besieged Union forces at Washington under General John G. Foster. Heavy naval gunfire silences several Confederate guns on the shoreline, painfully demonstrating that Union lines of communication to the garrison remain functional.

Armed boats from the USS *Fort Henry* begin a week-long reconnaissance of Bayport, Florida.

April 3

NAVAL: The USS *New London* and *Cayuga* capture the British blockade-runner *Tampico* off Sabine Pass, Texas.

A Federal expedition consisting of the gunboats USS *Lexington, Brilliant, Robb, Silver Lake,* and *Springfield* bombard and destroy the town of Palmyra, Tennessee, in retaliation for recent Confederate attacks on Union shipping.

April 4

DIPLOMACY: American minister Charles F. Adams loudly protests the impending departure of the vessel *Alexandra*, destined for eventual service in the Confederate navy.

SOUTH: Union forces attack a Confederate battery at Rodman's Point, Washington, North Carolina, but are repulsed.

WEST: The Yazoo River expedition of Generals Leonard F. Ross and Isaac F. Quinby fails again to bombard Fort Pemberton, Greenwood, Mississippi, into submission, and steams back to the Mississippi River in defeat.

NAVAL: The Confederate raider CSS *Alabama* under Captain Raphael Semmes captures and eventually burns the Union ship *Louisa Hatch* off the Brazilian coast.

April 5

POLITICS: President Abraham Lincoln meets with General Joseph Hooker at Fredericksburg, Virginia, to discuss strategy. At this time, both leaders concur that the object of future military operations should center upon the destruction of General Robert E. Lee's army, with Richmond, Virginia, a secondary concern.

NAVAL: Admiral Samuel F. Du Pont marshals his ironclads and steams from North Edisto, South Carolina, intending to attack the harbor defenses of Charleston.

April 6

DIPLOMACY: The British government seizes the newly completed warship *Alexandra* to placate the U.S. government. However, the vessel eventually will be released to the Confederacy by the courts.

NAVAL: With the Stono bar safely buoyed, Admiral Samuel F. Du Pont leads his squadron of nine heavily armed ironclads into the outer fringes of Charleston Harbor, South Carolina, and anchors there for the night.

The USS *Huntsville* captures the Confederate sloop *Minnie* off Charlotte Harbor, Florida.

April 7

WEST: Confederate cavalry under General Joseph Wheeler hit the Louisville and Nashville and Nashville and Chattanooga railroads at Antioch Station, Tennessee.

NAVAL: Adverse tides keep Admiral Samuel F. Du Pont's ironclad squadron from deploying within range of Fort Moultrie and Sumter, Charleston Harbor, South Carolina, until nearly 3:00 P.M. He then finds the channels to the city not only lined with submerged obstacles but also filled with floating range markers to assist gunnery from the forts. Moreover, as the battle intensifies, Du Pont's slow-firing monitors are able to loose only 139 rounds while 77 well-handled Confederate cannon fire off 2,200 shells. The USS *Weehawken* is hardest hit, striking a mine and sustaining 53 hits in only 40 minutes before withdrawing. The remaining eight ironclads in the squadron likewise are battered by heavy and accurate shore fire. *Keokuk* alone suffers 90 hits, many near or below the waterline, which render it nearly uncontrollable.

Du Pont, who had anticipated the worst, finally suspends the action at nightfall and withdraws, thankful that it was "a failure instead of a disaster." The admiral seeks to renew the contest on the morrow but is dissuaded by his captains, who regard the attempt as suicidal. The rebuff off Charleston represents the U.S. Navy's biggest defeat in the Civil War and painfully underscores Du Pont's oft-expressed belief that the city simply is too strong to be taken by sea power alone.

The USS *Barataria* runs aground on Lake Maurepas, Louisiana, and is burned to prevent capture.

April 8

SOUTH: President Abraham Lincoln and General Joseph Hooker review the Army of the Potomac at Falmouth, Virginia, across the Rappahannock River from Fredericksburg.

Naval: The badly damaged ironclad USS *Keokuk* sinks outside of Charleston, South Carolina. However, its signal books eventually are recovered by the Confederates, who can now discern the squadron's communications.

The USS *Gem of the Sea* captures the British blockade-runner *Maggie Fulton* near the Indian River Inlet, Florida.

This night, Edward C. Gabaudan, secretary to Admiral David G. Farragut, joins his superior by sailing downstream past Vicksburg, Mississippi, in a small boat covered with branches. Its somewhat large size attracts Confederate sentinels, who, upon rowing closer, simply pronounce his vessel "a log" and return to shore.

April 9
Naval: Off the French coast, the former merchant vessel *Japan* secretly is commissioned into the Confederate navy as the commerce raider CSS *Georgia* under Commander William L. Maury. This vessel ultimately seizes nine Union ships on a cruise to the Cape of Good Hope, but its questionable sailing abilities result in an early decommissioning.

April 10
Politics: President Jefferson Davis exhorts his countrymen to forego the planting of cotton and tobacco in favor of foodstuffs that are desperately needed by Confederate forces. "Let fields be devoted exclusively to the production of corn, oats, beans, peas, potatoes, and other food for man and beasts," he lectured, "and let all your efforts be directed to the prompt supply of these articles in the districts where our armies are operating."

South: Confederate general Alfred Moulton arrives at Bisland, Louisiana, on the Teche River. There, he constructs Fort Bisland to obstruct the Union advance under General Nathaniel P. Banks. Moulton is joined there eventually by General Richard Taylor, bringing Confederate strength up to 4,000 men and two steamers.

West: General Earl Van Dorn attacks Union troops at Franklin, Tennessee, but he is repulsed by cavalry under General Gordon Granger, losing nearly 300 men.

Naval: A landing party from the USS *Kingfisher* surprises and captures Confederate pickets on Edisto Island, South Carolina.

Armed boats from the USS *New London,* while reconnoitering at Sabine City, Texas, accost a small Confederate sloop and seize Captain Charles Fowler of the CSS *Josiah Bell.*

Landing parties from the USS *Conestoga* scour the banks of Beulah Bend, Mississippi, destroying several guerrilla posts.

April 11
South: General James Longstreet leads 20,000 veteran soldiers on a loose "siege" of Suffolk, Virginia, south of the James River. There, he confronts 25,000 Federals of the IX Corps under General John J. Peck behind a series of elaborate fortifications.

General Henry A. Wise's Confederates again fail to surprise the Union garrison at Fort Magruder, Williamsburg, Virginia.

West: Colonel Abel D. Streight leads 1,700 Union cavalry on a raid into Georgia from Nashville, Tennessee. However, his force consists entirely of infantrymen who have been mounted on mules to negotiate the rough terrain anticipated in northern Alabama.

Naval: The USS *Flag* and *Huron* run the Confederate blockade-runner *Stonewall Jackson* aground near Charleston, South Carolina, destroying it with gunfire.

Admiral Samuel P. Lee of the North Atlantic Blockading Squadron dispatches several gunboats under Lieutenant William B. Cushman to assist in the defense of Suffolk, Virginia.

April 12

Politics: President Abraham Lincoln is informed by General Joseph Hooker that he wishes to swing around General Robert E. Lee's left flank and threaten Richmond, Virginia. The president reminds his general that the destruction of Lee's army remains paramount.

South: The XIX Corps of General Nathaniel P. Banks, numbering 16,000 men in three divisions, moves up the Teche River toward Irish Bend on Bayou Teche, Louisiana, hoping to engage 4,000 Confederates under General Richard Taylor. Banks marches two divisions overland while ordering 4,500 men of General Cuvier Grover's division to land north of the fort to cut their retreat. As Grovier comes ashore, his troops engage Fort Bisland in a three-hour artillery duel that ends with nightfall. Taylor then prepares to have General Henry H. Sibley's Texas Brigade attack Banks's left flank on the morrow to drive him back.

Naval: The Federal gunboats USS *Stepping Stones, Commodore Barney, Commodore Morris,* and *Crusader* take up stations along the Nansemond River, Virginia, to prevent Confederate troops from crossing.

A Confederate boat crew captures the Union steamer *Fox* at Pass l'Outre, Mississippi, and two days later, it runs the blockade outside Mobile, Alabama.

April 13

South: At Irish Bend, Louisiana, Confederate forces gird to deliver an early morning strike against superior forces under General Nathaniel P. Banks. Unfortunately, General Henry H. Sibley, the officer entrusted with that operation, is either inebriated or too ill to comply. The opportunity passes quickly, and the Federals, greatly outnumbering the defenders, push their earthworks to within 400 yards of Fort Bisland. General Richard Taylor, rather than be crushed between Banks and the Union division of General Cuvier Grover once it begins to press down from the north, resolves to abandon his position. His men skillfully skirt Union soldiers along the river and deploy to attack at dawn and to allow the garrison at Fort Bisland to escape.

West: General Ambrose E. Burnside, commanding the Department of the Ohio, suppresses Copperhead (Peace Democrat) activities with a general order instituting military tribunals—and the firing squad—for treasonable activities. Furthermore, any individuals displaying wanton sympathy for the South can expect prompt deportation to Confederate lines.

Naval: President Abraham Lincoln instructs Admiral Samuel F. Du Pont to maintain his position with Charleston Harbor and keep the Confederates apprehensive over another attack.

The USS *Annie* captures the Confederate schooner *Mattie* off the Florida coast.

The USS *Rachel Seaman* captures the Confederate schooner *Maria Alfred* off the Mermentau River, Louisiana.

April 14

SOUTH: Confederates under General Richard Taylor abandon Fort Bisland, Louisiana, in the face of strong Union forces. En route, his men attack and surprise Federal troops under General Cuvier Grover while the main force under General Nathaniel P. Banks, farther south, cautiously occupies the fort. Grover remains in camp and fails to pursue, so Taylor's small command escapes intact. Union casualties amount to about 600 men. Confederate losses are not known but are presumed lighter. However, Taylor is forced to scuttle the recently recaptured CSS *Diana*.

NAVAL: Accurate gunfire from Federal gunboats USS *Mount Washington, Steeping Stones,* and *Commodore Barney* thwarts Confederate efforts to surround the Union garrison at Suffolk, Virginia.

The USS *Huntsville* seizes the British blockade-runner *Ascension* off the Florida Gulf coast.

The USS *Sonoma* captures the Confederate schooner *Clyde* in the Gulf of Mexico.

A task force consisting of USS *Estrella, Arizona,* and *Calhoun* attacks and sinks the Confederate ram CSS *Queen of the West* in Grand Lake, Louisiana.

April 15

SOUTH: Union general John G. Foster sails down the Pamlico River from Washington, North Carolina, past Confederate shore batteries, and into New Bern for reinforcements. General Daniel H. Hill then abandons his siege and withdraws inland.

Advancing Union forces under General Nathaniel P. Banks occupy Franklin, Louisiana.

WEST: General Ulysses S. Grant assembles 45,000 troops at Milliken's Bend, Mississippi, 10 miles north of the Confederate bastion of Vicksburg. He next orders the corps of General James B. McPherson south down the left bank of the Mississippi River to New Carthage, to join the troops of General John A. McClernand already there. Meanwhile, General William T. Sherman's command begins to demonstrate before Chickasaw Bluffs as a feint.

A Federal expedition under General Grenville M. Dodge advances from Corinth, Mississippi, into Courtland, Alabama.

NAVAL: Union gunboats under Lieutenant William B. Cushing silence several Confederate batteries while operating on the Nansemond River near Suffolk, Virginia.

The USS *Monticello* captures the Confederate schooner *Odd Fellow* off Little River, North Carolina.

The USS *William G. Anderson* captures the Confederate schooner *Royal Yacht* on the Gulf of Mexico.

The Confederate raider CSS *Alabama* under Captain Raphael Semmes captures and burns the whalers *Kate Cory* and *Lafayette* off Fernando de Noronha, Brazil.

April 16

POLITICS: President Jefferson Davis signs legislation permitting minors under 18 to hold military commissions.

South: Federal forces advance from Washington, North Carolina, and briefly tangle with the Confederate rear guard under General Daniel H. Hill at nearby Kinston.

West: A gala ball held at Vicksburg, Mississippi, to celebrate the city's perceived impregnability is interrupted suddenly by defiantly heavy gunfire as the Union fleet once again sallies past on the Mississippi River.

Naval: The Federal gunboat USS *Mount Washington* is severely damaged by masked Confederate batteries while steaming along the Nansemond River, Virginia.

The USS *Hendrick Hudson* captures the British blockade-runner *Teresa* off the Florida coast.

The USS *Vanderbilt* seizes the British blockade-runner *Gertrude* off the Bahamas.

Admiral David D. Porter, from his flagship USS *Benton,* successfully passes 12 vessels southward past Confederate batteries on the Vicksburg bluffs, Mississippi. The action lasts two and a half hours, and despite a withering cannonade, Porter succeeds completely. Most of his vessels are struck, but only the transport *Henry Clay* sinks, and the gunboat *Forest Queen* is disabled. The squadron then berths off New Carthage, Mississippi, and prepares to transport the army of General Ulysses S. Grant.

April 17

West: Colonel Benjamin H. Grierson embarks on an ambitious, 16-day diversionary cavalry raid from La Grange, Tennessee, down through Mississippi and on to Baton Rouge, Louisiana. He is ordered to tear up tracks and telegraph wires and take prisoners, thereby deflecting attention away from General Ulysses S. Grant's impending move toward Vicksburg, Mississippi. To complete this 600-mile sojourn, Grierson commands 1,700 troopers of the 6th and 7th Illinois Cavalry, the 2nd Iowa, and a battery of horse artillery.

Confederate cavalry under General John S. Marmaduke departs Arkansas and commences a second raid into Missouri.

Naval: The USS *Wanderer* captures the Confederate schooner *Annie B.* near Egmont, Florida.

The Confederate raider *CSS Florida* under Lieutenant John N. Maffitt captures and burns the Union ship *Commonwealth* off the Brazilian coast.

April 18

Politics: The Confederate Congress authorizes a volunteer navy to encourage the outfitting of warships at private expense.

South: The Federal gunboat USS *Stepping Stones* under Lieutenant William B. Cushing, carrying 270 soldiers of the 8th Connecticut and 89th New York, suddenly appears before Confederate-held Fort Huger on the Nansemond River, Virginia. Before the garrison can react, the Federals push into the fort, seizing 137 prisoners and five cannon. Cushing then escapes unmolested while blame for the defeat is heaped upon the 55th North Carolina, entrusted with defending that post. Duels of honor are subsequently waged between several officers of General Evander M. Law's staff as to where blame lays.

WEST: Colonel Benjamin H. Grierson's Union cavalry column skirmishes on its line of march with Confederates at New Albany, Mississippi.

A force of 3,000 Confederates under General John S. Marmaduke is repulsed at Fayetteville, Arkansas, by a 2,000-man Union garrison.

NAVAL: The USS *Stettin* captures the Confederate steamer *St. John* off Cape Romain, South Carolina.

The USS *Gem of the Sea* sinks the British blockade-runner *Inez* at Indian River Inlet, Florida.

The USS *Susquehanna* captures the Confederate schooner *Alabama* off the Florida Gulf coast.

Armed boats from the USS *New London* and *Cayuga* are attacked and driven back to sea by Confederate forces at Sabine City, Texas.

April 19

SOUTH: President Abraham Lincoln, accompanied by General in Chief Henry W. Halleck and Secretary of War Edwin M. Stanton, visit Aquia Creek, Virginia, to ascertain military matters.

NAVAL: The USS *Housatonic* captures the Confederate sloop *Neptune* near Charleston, South Carolina.

The USS *Powhatan* seizes the Confederate schooner *Major E. Willis* off Charleston, South Carolina.

April 20

POLITICS: President Abraham Lincoln declares that the new state of West Virginia be established from the westernmost counties of Virginia as of June 20, 1863.

SOUTH: Opelousas and Washington, Louisiana, are occupied by Federal forces under General Nathaniel P. Banks.

WEST: General John D. Imboden departs Shenandoah Mountain, Virginia, with 3,365 men on a raid against the Baltimore and Ohio Railroad.

Confederate cavalry under General John S. Marmaduke skirmishes with Union troops at Patterson, Missouri.

NAVAL: A joint expedition captures a Confederate fortification at Hill's Point on the Nansemond River, Virginia, along with five cannon and 160 prisoners.

The USS *Lodona* captures the British blockade-runner *Minnie* off Bulls Bay, South Carolina.

The USS *Octorara* seizes the British blockade-runner *W. Y. Letch* off the Florida coast.

Landing parties from the USS *Port Royal* seize a large cache of cotton at Apalachicola, Florida.

The USS *Estrella, Clifton, Arizona,* and *Calhoun* bombard and capture Fort Burton, Butte á la Rose, Louisiana.

The Confederate raider CSS *Oreto* under Lieutenant Samuel W. Averett captures the Union ship *Kate Dyer* at sea, releasing it on bond.

The USS *Sterling Price* and *Tuscumbia* reconnoiter down the Mississippi River to Grand Gulf, soon to be the object of a Union assault.

April 21

WEST: General William E. Jones leads a large Confederate foray against the Baltimore and Ohio Railroad in West Virginia. He intends to rendezvous with General John D. Imboden near Oakton and Grafton.

Union cavalry under Colonel Benjamin H. Grierson skirmishes with Confederates at Palo Alto, Mississippi. Grierson, hotly pursued by Southern cavalry, cleverly splits his column in two by sending Colonel Edward Hatch of the 2nd Iowa Cavalry off to threaten the Mobile and Ohio Railroad, after which he is to beat a hasty retreat back to La Grange, Tennessee. The Confederates, as anticipated, mistakenly chase Hatch, leaving Grierson free to gallop through the heart of Mississippi virtually unopposed.

NAVAL: The USS *Octorara* captures the British blockade-runner *Handy* off the east coast of Florida.

The USS *Rachel Seaman* captures the Confederate schooner *Nymph* off Pass Cavallo, Texas.

The USS *Lafayette*, under Admiral David D. Porter's direction, bombards a Confederate battery under construction at Grand Gulf, Mississippi.

A convoy of army transports passes the batteries at Vicksburg, Mississippi, at night and under heavy fire. Of six vessels, the steamer *Tigress* sinks while *Empire City* and *Moderator* are badly damaged. The remainder join the main army under General Ulysses S. Grant at New Carthage, Mississippi, granting him the amphibious lift necessary to ferry across the Mississippi River en masse.

April 22

POLITICS: President Jefferson Davis, ever alarmed for the security of Vicksburg, Mississippi, suggests to General John C. Pemberton that he disrupt Federal activities on the Mississippi River by launching fire rafts.

WEST: Union forces under General Grenville M. Dodge battle with Confederate forces at Rock Cut, Alabama.

General John S. Marmaduke skirmishes with Union defenders at Fredericktown, Missouri.

NAVAL: The USS *Mount Vernon* captures the Confederate schooner *St. George* off New Inlet, North Carolina.

April 23

NAVAL: Confederate steamers *Merrimac, Charleston,* and *Margaret and Jessie* dart past the Union blockade and enter Wilmington, North Carolina.

The USS *Pembina* captures the Confederate sloop *Elias Beckwith* off Mobile, Alabama.

The USS *Tioga* captures the British blockade-runner *Justina* at sea.

The Confederate raider CSS *Florida* under Lieutenant John N. Maffitt captures and burns the Union bark *Henrietta* at sea.

April 24

POLITICS: President Abraham Lincoln authorizes General Order No. 100, the so-called Liber Code, an early attempt to codify and standardize laws pertaining to war.

To combat spiraling inflation, the Confederate Congress levies a 10 percent "tax kind" on all produce harvested throughout the South. This move is resented greatly by the agrarian sector, which is already subject to requisition by the Confederate commissary and quartermaster offices.

SOUTH: Union forces under General Grenville M. Dodge capture Tuscumbia, Alabama.

WEST: The Army of the Tennessee under General Ulysses S. Grant reaches Hard Times Plantation, Louisiana, on the left bank of the Mississippi River. There, he immediately prepares to ferry directly across to Bruinsville, Mississippi, and implement his strategy of encircling Vicksburg from below.

Colonel Benjamin H. Grierson's Union cavalry storms into Newton Station, Mississippi, seizing a newly arrived ammunition train and tearing up miles of valuable track belonging to the Southern Mississippi Railroad. This places Union raiders only 100 miles east of the Confederate bastion of Vicksburg, and General John C. Pemberton orders several infantry and artillery regiments from Jackson to intercept them.

Confederate cavalry under General John S. Marmaduke battle with Union forces at Mill Creek Bridge, Missouri.

NAVAL: The USS *Western World* and *Samuel Rotan* seize the Confederate schooners *Martha Ann* and *A. Carson* off Horn Harbor, Virginia.

The USS *De Soto*, obviously having a good day, captures the Confederate schooners *General Prim* and *Rapid,* along with sloops *Jane Adelie* and *Bright* in the Gulf of Mexico.

The USS *Pembina* seizes the Confederate schooner *Joe Flanner* at sea.

The Confederate raider CSS *Alabama* under Captain Raphael Semmes captures the Union whaler *Nye* off the Brazilian coast.

The Confederate raider CSS *Florida* under Lieutenant John N. Maffitt captures and sinks the Union ship *Oneida* at sea.

Admiral David D. Porter stations gunboats on the Mississippi River off the mouth of the Big Black River to isolate Confederate batteries at Grand Gulf, Mississippi.

April 25

WEST: General Dabney H. Maury assumes command of the Confederate Department of East Tennessee.

SOUTHWEST: Pro-Confederate Cherokees under Colonel Stand Watie skirmish with Union troops at Webber's Falls, Indian Territory.

Apache Indians attack Federal troops near Fort Bowie, Arizona Territory, and then withdraw.

NAVAL: The Confederate raider CSS *Georgia* under Lieutenant William L. Maury captures and sinks the Union ship *Dictator* off the Cape Verde Islands.

April 26

SOUTH: A suddenly sortie by Union troops under General Michael Corcoran surprises outposts belonging to General George E. Pickett outside of Suffolk, Virginia, but they are driven back to their lines.

WEST: Confederate cavalry under General John D. Imboden ride from Beverly, West Virginia, toward Buchannon, but newly arrived Union reinforcements in that area force them back to Beverly.

A column of mule-mounted Union infantry under Colonel Abel Streight rides south from Tuscumbia, Alabama, to Rome, Georgia, to wreck the Western and Atlantic Railroad.

Union forces under General John McNeil repel an attack by General John S. Marmaduke's Confederates at Cape Girardeau, Missouri, inflicting 40 dead and 200 wounded for a loss of six killed and six wounded.

NAVAL: The USS *Sagamore* captures the Confederate schooner *New Year* off Tortugas, Florida.

The USS *De Soto* captures the British blockade-runner *Clarita* in the Gulf of Mexico.

The Confederate raider CSS *Alabama* under Captain Raphael Semmes seizes and burns the Union ship *Dorcas Prince* east of Natal, Brazil.

April 27

SOUTH: At Falmouth, Virginia, the 134,000-strong Army of the Potomac is put in motion under General Joseph Hooker. Hooker takes 75,000 men down the banks of the Rappahannock River, intending to deploy them in the region known as the Wilderness, 10 miles behind Confederate lines. Meanwhile, an additional 40,000 troops under General John Sedgwick remain behind at Fredericksburg, Virginia, threatening the main Confederate force under General Robert E. Lee. No previous Union commander has enjoyed such a numerical preponderance over Southern forces.

WEST: General Simon B. Buckner replaces General Dabney H. Maury as commander of the Department of East Tennessee. Maury consequently transfers south to head the District of the Gulf in Louisiana.

Union forces surprise the Texas Legion of General Earl Van Dorn at Carter Creek Pike, Tennessee.

NAVAL: Armed boats from the USS *Monticello* and *Matthew Vassar* attack and sink the British blockade-runner *Golden Liner* in Murrell's Inlet, South Carolina.

The USS *Preble* is accidently destroyed by fire while at anchor off Pensacola, Florida.

April 28

SOUTH: General Joseph Hooker orders his Army of the Potomac across the Rappahannock River and into positions around Chancellorsville, Virginia, while General John Sedgwick remains with 40,000 men at Fredericksburg; hoping to distract and contain the Army of Northern Virginia under General Robert E. Lee.

WEST: Confederate general John S. Bowen, observing the large Union flotilla sailing toward Grand Gulf, Mississippi, hastily wires General John C. Pemberton at Vicksburg to dispatch all available reinforcements to his position. The brigades of Generals Edward D. Tracy and William E. Baldwin are put in motion that evening, racing south.

NAVAL: The tug *Lily* is rammed accidently by USS *Choctaw* on the Yazoo River, Mississippi, and sinks.

April 29

SOUTH: General John Stoneman's Union cavalry division crosses the Rappahannock River into Virginia and commences a major raid. He then dispatches General William W. Averell's brigade toward Gordonsville to tear up the Orange and Alexandria Railroad while he accompanies the main body under General John Buford against the Richmond, Fredericksburg and Potomac Railroad. Unfortunately, not only does this endeavor prove ineffectual, but it also strips the Army of the Potomac of its cavalry and thus its ability to scout and reconnoiter in dense terrain.

WEST: Confederate cavalry under General William E. Jones capture the Union depot at Buchannon, Virginia, taking 500 prisoners and 1,500 horses and burning several bridges.

NAVAL: The USS *Juanita* captures the Confederate schooner *Harvest* at sea north of the Bahamas.

A joint expedition consisting of the USS *Tyler, Choctaw, Baron de Kalb, Signal, Romeo, Linden, Petrel, Black Hawk,* three mortar boats, and 10 transports, wend their way up the Yazoo River in an elaborate feint toward Haynes's Bluff, Mississippi. This evolves to prevent Confederate reinforcements from shifting southward to Grand Gulf.

Admiral David D. Porter's gunboat squadron bombards Confederate batteries on the Mississippi River at Grand Gulf, Mississippi. After five hours of continuous combat, Southern cannon are silenced while the USS *Benton, Tuscumbia,* and *Pittsburgh* receive damage. That same evening, Porter's transports skirt the remaining batteries without incident as Federal forces bypass Grand Gulf altogether. Total Union losses are 18 killed and 57 wounded; the Confederates sustain three dead and 19 injured.

April 30

SOUTH: The Army of the Potomac under General Joseph Hooker marches 30 miles down the banks of the Rappahannock River and crosses 10 miles behind General Robert E. Lee's position at Fredericksburg, Virginia. Considering the size and complexity of his operation, Hooker executes it brilliantly and catches the Confederates off guard. But Lee reacts with typical boldness by once again dividing his army in the face of the enemy: Leaving 10,000 men under General Jubal A. Early to watch the Federals near Fredericksburg, he hastily marches with 50,000 men toward the crossroads at Chancellorsville.

WEST: General Ulysses S. Grant ferries the XIII Corps of General James A. McClernand and the XVII Corps of General James B. McPherson—23,000 men—across the Mississippi River at Bruinsburg, Mississippi. This critical maneuver establishes a Union bridgehead on the east bank of the river only 35 miles below the Confederate bastion of Vicksburg. "All the campaigns, labors, hardships, and exposures, from the month of December previous to this time, that had been made and endured, were for the accomplishment of this one object," Grant later reflects. Moreover, with Confederate attention fixed on General William T. Sherman's feint at Haynes's Bluff to the north and Colonel Benjamin H. Grierson's raid to the south, it is an opportune time to advance inland almost unopposed. By nightfall, Federal troops have pushed several miles inland to confront General John S. Bowen's division at Port Gibson.

NAVAL: The gunboat squadron and transports of Admiral David D. Porter cover and ferry the army of General Ulysses S. Grant across the Mississippi River at Bruinsburg, 10 miles below Grand Gulf, Mississippi. With a single, masterful stroke, Confederate defenses are neutralized, and Union forces are now able to approach the citadel of Vicksburg from the rear.

May 1

POLITICS: The third session, first Confederate Congress, adjourns. Previously, they authorized military tribunals to execute any white Union officers caught commanding African-American soldiers. Black soldiers seized in uniform, if not killed outright, are likewise to be sold into slavery.

Peace Democrat Clement L. Vallandigham gives a speech at Mount Vernon, Ohio, in which he denounces "this wicked, cruel, and unnecessary war." Such sentiments mark him for eventual arrest.

SOUTH: Advanced elements of the Army of Northern Virginia under General Thomas J. Jackson arrive near Chancellorsville, Virginia, and tangle with Union pickets nearby. However, their aggressive demeanor apparently unnerves General Joseph Hooker, who inexplicably orders his Army of the Potomac off clear terrain and into the woody morass known as the Wilderness. By this single expedient, he forfeits the strategic initiative to General Robert E. Lee, as well as neutralizes his advantages in artillery. Meanwhile, Confederate cavalry under General J. E. B. Stuart skillfully discern that the Union right flank is "in the air" and subject to be turned. Lee, sizing up his adversary's intentions, defies all tenets of military wisdom by dividing his forces a second time. He orders Jackson to take 30,000 men—the bulk of his army—on a circuitous, 14-mile end run around Hooker's right, there to deliver a crushing flank attack. Lee himself will hold Hooker's attention by aggressively posturing his remaining 20,000 men as skirmishers. Considering the sheer odds—Hooker fields 75,000 men—this is a dire expedient at best. Lee, however, is gambling on the Union leader's timidity.

General John Stoneman and his Union cavalry column skirmishes with Confederates at Rapidan Station, Virginia.

WEST: Advancing inland from Bruinsburg, Mississippi, General Ulysses S. Grant masses 23,000 men and attacks 8,000 Confederates under General John S. Bowen at Port Gibson. Grant arrays his two brigades to cover the Bruinsburg and Rodney roads, which run parallel atop a high ridge and are flanked by impassable ravines. The XIII Corps of General John A. McClernand, mustering 18,000 men, is assigned most of the fighting. The terrain, unfortunately, strongly favors the defense and Union troops wage a hard fight to evict General Martin E. Green's brigade from Rodney Road. At length, numbers prevail and Southerners gradually relinquish the field. Meanwhile, fighting along Bruinsburg Road proves equally fierce and occasions the death of Brigadier General Edward D. Tracy, but again the Confederates yield. Southern hopes are revived suddenly when Bowen receives last-minute reinforcements from Vicksburg and promptly counterattacks along Rodney Road. The Federals are unable to contain the surge until Grant personally brings up additional troops that finally turn the tide of battle. Having lost his strong defensive position, Bowen retreats rapidly beyond Bayou Pierre, burning the bridge behind him. The Union lodgement is now secure.

Port Gibson was a protracted contest, lasting from 6:00 A.M. to nearly sunset. Union losses are 131 dead, 719 wounded, and 25 missing to a Confederate tally of 68 killed, 380 wounded, and 384 missing. The Southerners perform extremely well, considering the odds, and tied up two entire Union divisions for a day. Nevertheless, Grant consolidates his beachhead as his offensive gathers momentum. The race to Vicksburg now begins in earnest. To facilitate his advance, Grant takes the bold expedient of cutting his own supply lines by carrying all essential impedimenta on his soldiers's backs and foraging off the land. Unconstrained by lines of communication, he now enjoys complete freedom of maneuver.

Confederates under General John S. Marmaduke end their latest raid into Missouri by fighting a final skirmish at Chalk Bluff along the St. Francis River, Arkansas.

NAVAL: Armed boats from the USS *Western World* and *Crusader* burn two Confederate schooners at Milford Haven, Virginia.

The USS *Kanawha* captures the Confederate schooner *Dart* at sea.

Union gunboats exchange fire with Confederate batteries along Haynes's Bluff, Mississippi. The USS *Choctaw* receives 53 hits, but none of the vessels are seriously impaired.

May 2

SOUTH: Proceeding all night with celerity and great marching discipline, 30,000 Confederates under General Thomas J. Jackson steal their way around the Army of the Potomac's right flank at Chancellorsville, Virginia. En route, he is observed by General Daniel E. Sickles, who sends troops off in pursuit. Jackson's move is also perceived by General Oliver O. Howard, commanding the largely German-speaking XI Corps, but he takes no precautions to guard his exposed flank. Jackson, meanwhile, competently arranges his troops into a two-mile long line across Howard's right, and at 6:00 P.M. he slashes into the Federals with a vengeance. The Germans, struck while preparing dinner, crumble under the Confederate onslaught, fleeing two miles. By then Federal resistance stiffens once they bump up against Hooker's center, and fighting bogs down in thick woods and fading light. Jackson, ignoring the mounting confusion around him, then rides forth on a personal reconnaissance mission and he is accidently shot by men of the 18th North Carolina. Nonetheless, Hooker is completely unnerved by this unexpected onslaught, and he retreats back farther into the woods, abandoning the strategic knoll called Hazel Grove without a fight. Confederate general Ambrose P. Hill assumes temporary control of II Corps after Jackson is hit, but he himself is subsequently wounded. Command then reverts to General J. E. B. Stuart.

Confederate forces under General James Longstreet abandon their siege of Suffolk, Virginia, and withdraw back to rejoin the Army of Northern Virginia.

WEST: Federal forces under General Ulysses S. Grant bridge Bayou Pierre outside Port Gibson, Mississippi, and fan out into the countryside. He next seeks to seize the town of Edwards Station, 16 miles east of Vicksburg, to cut the Vicksburg and Jackson Railroad and isolate the garrison.

Union cavalry raiders under Colonel Benjamin H. Grierson fight their final skirmish with Confederate forces at Robert's Ford on the Comite River, Louisiana, before clattering into Baton Rouge, Louisiana. Grierson concludes his spectacular raid with a loss of three dead, seven injured, nine missing, and five ill soldiers left behind for treatment. Confederates losses are estimated at 100 dead, 500 captured, 3,000 weapons taken, and more than 50 miles of railroad and telegraph lines destroyed. In light of his success, essential for masking General Ulysses S. Grant's movement across the Mississippi River, Grierson receives promotion to brigadier general.

NAVAL: The USS *Sacramento* captures the British blockade-runner *Wanderer* at Murrell's Inlet, North Carolina.

Armed boats from the USS *Roebuck* attack and seize the British blockade-runner *Emma Amelia* near St. Joseph's Bay, Florida.

The USS *Perry* captures the Confederate schooner *Alma* at sea.

The Federal gunboats USS *Cricket, Conestoga, Rattler,* and *General Bragg* commence escorting steamers to dissuade guerrilla attacks around Greenville, Mississippi.

May 3

SOUTH: At first light, the struggle renews around Chancellorsville, Virginia. General J. E. B. Stuart mounts 50 cannon atop Hazel Grove and bombards the Union forces of General Joseph Hooker. Hooker, though still outnumbering the Southerners by nearly two to one, will not relinquish his defensive posture, and terrible, confused fighting erupts in the thickly wooded Wilderness. Gradually, both Union flanks are perilously bent back. Then Hooker, suddenly stunned by a falling column, orders his army to retreat gradually toward the Rappahannock River—a move protested by many subordinates.

General Robert E. Lee arrives to take command, and he is greeted by delirious cheering from his troops. However, he has yet to make preparations to attack Hooker when intelligence is received that General John Sedgwick is advancing from Fredericksburg behind him. Convinced that Hooker is spent and lacks offensive spirit to attack, Lee unhesitatingly divides his force the third time in as many days, leaving 20,000 men to contain Hooker while he marches General Richard H. Anderson's division to meet the Union threat.

Combat at Chancellorsville occasions very heavy losses on both sides: Hooker suffers 1,606 dead, 9,762 injured, and 5,919 captured or missing (17,287) while Lee sustains 1,649 killed, 9,106 wounded, and 1,708 missing (12,463). In addition, Lee and the South are deprived of "Stonewall" Jackson, who dies shortly afterward. This loss irreparably shatters the most outstanding tactical duo of the Civil War, and the Army of Northern Virginia, while still formidable, is never quite as devastatingly effective.

General John Sedgwick's VI Corps, numbering 19,000 men, is ordered by General Joseph Hooker to storm the heights of Fredericksburg, Virginia, and then attack the Army of Northern Virginia from the west. Twice Union forces charge General Jubal A. Early's division along Marye's Heights and are as often repelled. On his third try, Sedgwick orders the men forward with unloaded muskets to settle the issue with cold steel alone. The change in tactics works stunningly, and Early is ejected from his field-works. Union losses are roughly 1,100 to 475 Southerners.

As Early's Confederates withdraw to the southwest, the VI Corps proceeds west toward Chancellorsville until it encounters General Cadmus M. Wilcox's brigade on a high ridge, on which sits Salem Church. Fighting develops further once additional Confederates under General Lafayette McLaws arrive to strengthen Wilcox. Sedgwick's men charge several times, but the Southerners, enjoying an advantage in elevation, invariably blast them back. Combat ceases once darkness settles. Sedgwick incurs 1,523 casualties while the Confederates sustain only 674.

Captain John S. Mosby surprises and defeats Union cavalry at Warrenton Junction, Virginia, and is then surprised by the 1st West Virginia Cavalry.

Union forces under General John J. Peck heavily probe Confederate lines outside of Suffolk, Virginia, eagerly ascertaining that their main body under General James

The Battle of Chancellorsville May 1–4, 1863 Lithograph by Currier & Ives *(Library of Congress)*

Longstreet has retired. Longstreet, meanwhile, leads the bulk of his command over the Blackwater River to safety. Casualties from operations around Suffolk amount to roughly 900 Confederates and 260 Federals.

WEST: Colonel Abel D. Streight surrenders 1,500 men of his "Mule Brigade" to General Nathan B. Forrest at Cedar Bluff, Alabama. Forrest, possessing only 600 men, surrounds his opponent and, by constantly parading them and a single battery of guns, bluffs Streight into believing he is actually outnumbered.

Confederate positions along Grand Gulf, Mississippi, are hastily abandoned as General Ulysses S. Grant pushes Union troops inland.

NAVAL: Confederate troops drive off armed boats from the USS *William G. Andrews* at St. Joseph's Island, Texas.

The Confederate CSS *Alabama* under Captain Raphael Semmes captures and burns the Union bark *Sea Lark* off Brazil, carrying a cargo estimated at $500,000.

The gunboat squadron of Admiral David D. Porter moves to engage Confederate batteries at Grand Gulf, Mississippi, and finds that the defenders have evacuated the post beforehand. "The Navy holds the door to Vicksburg," he writes General Ulysses S. Grant. Immediately afterward, Porter rendezvouses with Admiral David G. Farragut off the mouth of the Red River, Louisiana.

May 4

SOUTH: The Battle of Salem Church, Virginia, continues as General John Sedgwick renews his attack on Confederate positions. However, General Robert E. Lee, convinced that the main Union army at Chancellorsville is inert, boldly divides his army by dispatching General Robert Anderson's division to assist the defenders. Additional reinforcements under General Jubal A. Early also arrive and begin to press Sedgwick's men from three sides. Outnumbered and nearly outflanked, the Federals skillfully withdraw toward the Rappahannock River and entrench. After several Southern attacks are repulsed, Lee calls off the action and determines to destroy Sedgwick's force the following day. Union casualties for the day total 4,700; Confederate losses are unknown but probably as severe.

NAVAL: The USS *Chocura* and *Maratanza* capture the Confederate sloop *Express* off Charleston, South Carolina.

The USS *Kennebec* seizes the Confederate schooner *Juniper* at sea.

Admiral David D. Porter leads an expedition up the Red River consisting of USS *Benton, Lafayette, Pittsburgh, Sterling Price,* the ram *Switzerland,* and the tug *Ivy.* Meanwhile, Admiral David G. Farragut departs and sails downstream to New Orleans, Louisiana.

The USS *Albatross* and several gunboats steam up the Red River to engage Fort De Russy at Alexandria, Louisiana.

May 5

POLITICS: Having denounced the war as "wicked and cruel," Ohio senator Clement L. Vallandigham, a Northern Democrat and an outspoken Southern sympathizer, or "Copperhead," is arrested at his home by Union soldiers. As he is removed to the headquarters of General Ambrose E. Burnside at Cincinnati, Ohio, riots ensue and culminate in the burning of several pro-administration newspapers.

South: Over the protest of subordinates, General Joseph Hooker leads his recently humbled Army of the Potomac back over the Rappahannock River.

The Union VI Corps under General John Sedgwick, having been repulsed from Salem Church, Virginia, crosses the Rappahannock River at Bank's Ford to safety. This is the final action of the Chancellorsville campaign, and it occasions Union losses of 900 men to a Confederate tally of 1,200.

Naval: The USS *Tahoma* captures the Confederate schooner *Crazy* off Charlotte Harbor, Florida.

Federal gunboats under Admiral David D. Porter approach Fort De Russy on the Red River, Louisiana, finding it abandoned.

May 6

South: A recovering General Ambrose P. Hill succeeds General Thomas J. Jackson, who is mortally wounded, as commander of II Corps, Army of Northern Virginia.

West: A skirmish at Sherwood, Missouri, results in the death of 30 white and black Union soldiers. Vengeful Federals return the following day and burn the town.

Naval: The USS *Dragon* captures the Confederate schooner *Samuel First* off Potomac Creek, Virginia.

The USS *R. R. Cuyler* captures the Confederate steamer *Eugenie* at sea.

The Confederate raider CSS *Florida* under Lieutenant John N. Maffitt captures the Union brig *Clarence* off the Brazilian coast. The vessel is then impressed into Confederate service under Lieutenant Charles W. Read and commences raiding operations in the mid-Atlantic.

May 7

Politics: A pensive president Jefferson Davis wires General John C. Pemberton at Vicksburg, Mississippi, that he is "anxiously expecting further information of your active operations. . . . You may expect whatever it is in my power to do for your aid."

South: A Union cavalry column under General John Stoneman crosses Racoon Ford, Virginia, ending a less than spectacular "raid."

West: As General William T. Sherman begins to march his XV Corps overland from Milliken's Bend, Mississippi, the Army of the Tennessee under General Ulysses S. Grant begins a concerted drive on the state capital of Jackson.

Confederate general Earl Van Dorn is murdered in his tent at Spring Hill, Tennessee, by the angry husband of an alleged suitor.

Naval: Admiral David D. Porter steps ashore and accepts the surrender of Alexandria, Louisiana.

May 8

Politics: President Abraham Lincoln declares that all foreigners wishing to become citizens remain eligible for the draft.

South: General George Stoneman concludes his lackluster cavalry raid through northern Virginia by rejoining the Army of the Potomac, having lost only 17 killed and 75 wounded. Compared to Confederate efforts elsewhere, this effort fails to exert any impact on events at Chancellorsville and leads to Stoneman's transfer as cavalry corps commander.

West: General William T. Sherman's XV Corps joins General Ulysses S. Grant's main army in Mississippi.

Naval: The USS *Primrose* captures the Confederate schooner *Sarah Lavinia* off Corrotoman Creek, Virginia.

The USS *Canandaigua* captures the Confederate blockade-runner *Cherokee* near Charleston, South Carolina.

The USS *Flag* seizes the Confederate schooner *Amelia* off Charleston, South Carolina.

The USS *Richmond,* accompanied by several mortar boats, bombards Confederate fortifications at Port Hudson, Louisiana.

May 9

Politics: To oversee the new national bank, Congress appoints Hugh McCulloch to serve as comptroller of currency.

South: General Joseph E. Johnston is ordered to Mississippi to assume command of Confederate defenses there.

General Thomas W. Sherman's Federal soldiers proceed along the Amite River, Louisiana, capturing supplies and numerous prisoners.

West: Union oil facilities at Oiltown, West Virginia, are destroyed in a Confederate raid conducted by General William E. "Grumble" Jones.

Union forces under General Ulysses S. Grant continue advancing on Utica, Mississippi, skirmishing en route.

Naval: The USS *Aroostook* captures the Confederate schooner *Sea Lion* at sea.

May 10

South: General Thomas J. Jackson, known famously as "Stonewall" and admired by soldiers on both sides, dies of pneumonia at Guiney's Station, Virginia. His passing proves an irreparable loss to General Robert E. Lee and the Confederate war effort.

Naval: Armed boats from USS *Owasco* and *Katahdin* capture and sink the Confederate blockade-runner *Hanover* off Galveston, Texas.

The USS *Mound City* shells and destroys a Confederate battery at Warrenton, Mississippi.

May 11

Politics: Secretary of the Treasury Salmon P. Chase, after disputing an appointment, angrily offers to resign from President Abraham Lincoln's cabinet, but the president declines to accept.

West: General John C. Pemberton learns that Union forces under General Ulysses S. Grant are approaching Edwards Station rapidly, 16 miles east of Vicksburg, Mississippi, apparently to sever the Jackson and Vicksburg Railroad into the city. He therefore instructs the 4,000 men of General John Gregg's brigade to depart the capital of Jackson and contest the town of Raymond to slow their advance. Gregg arrives and accordingly sets up roadblocks, assumes defensive positions, and awaits Grant's approach.

Union cavalry under Colonel Benjamin H. Grierson cut the New Orleans and Jackson Railroad at Crystal Springs, Mississippi.

Confederate cavalry under General John S. Marmaduke skirmish with Union troops at Mount Vernon and Taylor's Creek, Arkansas.

May 12

WEST: At 9:00 A.M., General John A. Logan's 3rd Division of General James B. McPherson's XVII Corps advances on Raymond, Mississippi, encountering strong resistance from General John Gregg's Confederates. An intense firefight erupts at close range owing to the densely forested terrain, and neither side wields effective control over their units. The ground, together with intense smoke and dust, also keeps Gregg from perceiving how badly outnumbered he is. Nonetheless, he leads a charge that nearly routs the 23rd Indiana and 20th Ohio regiments until Logan personally rallies them and halts the Confederate onslaught. Additional Union forces arrive, and the long blue line surges back across the field, sweeping the rebels before them. McPherson then commits his entire corps, 12,000 strong, and cracks the Southern right wing. Gregg, finally realizing his predicament, orders a general disengagement and retreats in good order toward Jackson. McPherson spends the evening quietly bivouacked on the battlefield.

Raymond is a sharp little action lasting several hours and costs the Union 72 dead, 252 wounded, and 190 missing while the Confederates sustain 66 killed, 339 injured, and 37 missing. More significantly, the stoutness of Confederate defenses convinces General Ulysses S. Grant to alter his approach toward Vicksburg: Rather than be caught between the two fires of General John C. Pemberton in the west and General Joseph E. Johnston to the east, he seeks to overwhelm disparate Confederate forces piecemeal before they can unite.

NAVAL: The USS *Conemaugh* and *Monticello* shell and sink five Confederate schooners in Murrell's Inlet, South Carolina.

Federal gunboats ferry Union cavalry across the Tennessee River for an impending assault on Linden, Tennessee.

May 13

SOUTH: Governor Zebulon B. Vance of North Carolina complains about the high levels of Confederate deserters to President Jefferson Davis.

WEST: General Ulysses S. Grant resumes his advance toward Jackson, Mississippi, with the XV Corps of William T. Sherman and the XIII Corps of James B. McPherson moving rapidly up the Mississippi Springs Road while the XVII Corps of General John A. McClernand moves north in the direction of Clinton.

General Joseph E. Johnston arrives at Jackson, Mississippi, to find a small garrison of 6,000 men under General John Gregg and woefully predicts "I am too late." He realizes that two full Union corps presently are marching up the road toward the city, so Johnston gives the order to evacuate troops and other supplies immediately. He also instructs General John C. Pemberton to take 22,000 men from the Vicksburg garrison, march east, and catch the Federals between them. Meanwhile, Gregg makes preparations to cover Johnston's impending withdrawal.

NAVAL: Armed boats from the USS *Kingfisher* raid Edisto, South Carolina, destroying 800 bushels of cotton collected there.

The USS *Daffodil* seizes the British blockade-runner *Wonder* off Port Royal, South Carolina.

The USS *Huntsville* captures the Confederate schooner *A. J. Hodge* off the east coast of Florida.

The USS *De Soto* captures the Confederate schooner *Sea Bird* near Pensacola Bay, Florida.

The Confederate raider CSS *Florida* under Lieutenant John N. Maffitt captures and burns the Union ship *Crown Point* off the Brazilian coast.

Admiral David D. Porter, having deployed his gunboat fleet along the Red River, Louisiana, returns to Grand Gulf, Mississippi.

May 14

SOUTH: General Robert E. Lee attends a high-level strategy conference in Richmond, Virginia, where he advocates a risky but potentially rewarding scheme to invade Pennsylvania and defeat Northern forces on their own soil. Such a ploy would further discredit the Republican Party and possibly secure European intervention on the Confederacy's behalf.

General Nathaniel P. Banks begins to advance 30,000 Federal troops from Baton Rouge toward the Confederate bastion at Port Hudson, Louisiana. After Vicksburg, this is the only remaining Southern strong point on the Mississippi River; it is defended by 5,000 men under General Franklin Gardner.

WEST: At about 9:00 A.M., the advance guard of General James B. McPherson's XIII Corps makes contact with Confederate outposts before Jackson, Mississippi. However, Union movements from the west are suddenly hampered by heavy downpours, and McPherson is content simply to fire his artillery and skirmish. Meanwhile, the XV Corps of General William T. Sherman plunges ahead from the south, which forces Confederate general John Gregg to spread his 6,000 men in a thin line to contain both forces. Once the rain stops, McPherson, perceiving the fragility of Confederate defenses, suddenly orders a bayonet charge that quickly overruns Gregg's earthworks. Sherman also sends his men forward, and they seize several poorly guarded cannon. Gregg's remaining troops nevertheless fight doggedly until he receives word from General Joseph E. Johnston that army trains have evacuated the city. Gregg then expertly disengages and escapes north from the city.

Union losses at Jackson were 42 killed, 251 wounded, and seven missing whereas Confederates casualties are estimated at 200. General Ulysses S. Grant now obtains a strategic railroad junction east of Vicksburg, Mississippi, completing his stranglehold of the city. He next prepares to deal with Confederate forces under General John C. Pemberton approaching from the west.

NAVAL: Armed boats from the USS *Currituck* seize the Confederate schooner *Ladies' Delight* off Urbana, Virginia.

The USS *Fort Henry* captures the Confederate sloop *Isabella* on Waccasassa Bay, Florida.

May 15

POLITICS: Angry Federal troops storm the offices of the newspaper *Jeffersonian* at Richmond, Indiana, and ransack it on account of purported anti-Union sentiments.

WEST: General John C. Pemberton, ordered by General Joseph E. Johnston to march east from Edward's Station, Mississippi, with 22,000 men and trap General Ulysses S. Grant's Union army between them, disobeys orders. Instead, he marches south from Edwards Station toward Grand Gulf to cut the Union supply line—unaware that Grant has already done so and is living off the land.

Confederate guerrillas under William C. Quantrill skirmish with Union troops at Pleasant Hill, Missouri.

NAVAL: The USS *Canandaigua* captures the Confederate sloop *Secesh* off Charleston, South Carolina.

The USS *Kanawha* seizes the British blockade-runner *Comet* near Fort Morgan, Mobile Bay, Alabama.

Commodore James Palmer receives command of naval forces assisting in the reduction of Port Hudson, Louisiana.

May 16

WEST: General John C. Pemberton deploys his 22,000 men along a commanding elevation known locally as Champion's Hill, Mississippi, roughly halfway between Jackson and Vicksburg. He places General William W. Loring's division on his left with John S. Bowen holding the center and Carter L. Stevenson on the right. The three-mile field is dominated by thick woods and undulating fields favoring the defense, although less so at Steven's end. Pemberton also receives new orders from General Joseph E. Johnston that direct him to combine forces immediately outside Jackson, but it is too late. On comes the 32,000-strong Union army of General Ulysses S. Grant, who deploys the XIII Corps of General James B. McPherson on his right and the XVII Corps under General John A. McClernand on the left. General William T. Sherman's XV Corps is left as a garrison at Jackson to protect the Union rear.

Fighting commences at 10:00 A.M. as McPherson hits Stevenson's division on the left and a tremendous struggle ensues at close quarters. A Confederate counterattack almost pushes Union forces back into Grant's headquarters, but they are enfiladed by concentrated artillery fire and driven off in disorder. Champion's Hill changes hands no less than three times before Pemberton, running short of men, orders Loring to shift unengaged portions of his division to support the center and left. When the temperamental Loring refuses to comply, the unaided Confederates begin to collapse. By 5:30 P.M., Pemberton's army is in full flight across Baker's Creek, burning the bridge behind him. Loring's division is cut off from the main body, so he retreats to the northeast and eventually joins Johnston's forces east of Jackson.

Champion's Hill is the hardest-fought and most decisive engagement of the Vicksburg campaign. Through rapidity of movement, Grant prevents two disparate Confederate forces from uniting against him and defeats each piecemeal. Union losses are 410 dead, 1,844 wounded, and 187 missing (1,838) to a Confederate tally of 381 killed, 1,018 wounded, and 2,441 missing or captured (3,840). The Northerners also capture no less than 27 cannon. Grant finally is poised to move on Vicksburg itself.

NAVAL: The USS *Courier* captures the Confederate vessels *Angelina* and *Emeline* off the South Carolina coast.

The USS *Powhatan* captures the Confederate sloop *C. Routereau* off Charleston, South Carolina.

The USS *Two Sisters* captures the Confederate schooner *Oliver S. Breese* off the Anclote Keys. Florida.

May 17

SOUTH: A sudden Confederate cavalry raid against Union forces on the west bank of the Mississippi River secures numerous prisoners and cattle destined for the army of General Nathaniel P. Banks.

WEST: General John C. Pemberton, routed at Champion Hill the day before, prepares to defend a bridgehead along the west bank of the Big Black River 12 miles east of strategic Vicksburg, Mississippi. He places 5,000 men and 18 cannon under General John S. Bowen behind a hastily erected loop of entrenchments and cotton bales, with both flanks anchored on the Big Black. Better defensive positions are available in hills to the west, but Pemberton chose his position to reestablish contact with General William W. Loring's division, which had become separated from the main body. Unknown to Pemberton, Loring presently is marching off in the opposite direction to join General Joseph E. Johnston at Jackson.

At 5:00 A.M., the first elements of General John A. McClernand's XVII Corps encounter Bowen's pickets, and both sides gird for combat. General Eugene A. Carr sends the fresh brigade of General Michael Lawler forward to probe Confederate defenses, and he uncovers a small gap on their left. Lawler quickly orders the 21st and 23rd Indiana into the breech, with the 11th Wisconsin and 22nd Iowa in support. These units completely surprise and overpower Southerners in their sector and began to roll up their line. Bowen desperately tries shoring up his flagging formation, but additional Union units crash through his center and the entire perimeter collapses. By 10:00 A.M., Confederate forces are streaming back across the Big Black. Pemberton manages to fire the bridges over the river, but the Southerners do not stop running until they reach the outskirts of Vicksburg.

Big Black River is another debacle for the Confederates, who lose 1,751 killed, wounded, and missing, along with 18 artillery pieces. Union casualties amount to 279. In two weeks of dazzling campaigning, the road to Vicksburg is completely open to General Ulysses S. Grant.

NAVAL: The USS *Minnesota* captures the Confederate schooner *Almira Ann* on the Chickahominy River, Virginia.

The USS *Courier* seizes the Confederate schooner *Maria Bishop* off Cape Romain, South Carolina.

The USS *Kanawha* captures the Confederate schooner *Hunter* at sea.

The Confederate blockade-runner *Cuba* burns itself rather than be captured in the Gulf of Mexico by the USS *De Soto*.

May 18

DIPLOMACY: In yet another blow to Confederate aspirations, Foreign Secretary Lord Russell declares to the House of Lords that Great Britain harbors no intention of intervening in the American conflict.

WEST: General William T. Sherman leads a diversionary force up the Yazoo River, intending to storm Snyder's Bluff and Haynes's Bluff north of Vicksburg, Mississippi.

Union forces under General Ulysses S. Grant cross the Big Black River and take up storming positions outside the Confederate bastion of Vicksburg. The Confederate position appears outwardly hopeless, but General John C. Pemberton declares his intention to fight to the last. That same day, General Joseph E. Johnston wires the general and warns him against becoming trapped in the city. But for Pemberton, Vicksburg, and the Confederacy, it is all too late.

NAVAL: Armed boats from the USS *R. R. Cuyler* capture and sink the Confederate schooner *Isabel* near Fort Morgan, Mobile Bay, Alabama.

The USS *Octorara* seizes the British blockade-runner *Eagle* off the Bahamas.

The USS *Kanawha* captures the Confederate schooner *Ripple* at sea.

The USS *Shepherd Knapp* hits a reef near Cap Haitien, Haiti, and is scuttled.

Commander John Grimes leads Federal gunboats USS *Baron de Kalb, Choctaw, Linden, Romeo, Petrel,* and *Forest Rose* up the Yazoo River in concert with General William T. Sherman. The vessels subsequently shell the defenses of Vicksburg itself.

The gunboat USS *Linden,* accompanied by five army transports, attacks and destroys a Confederate battery on Island No. 82 in the Mississippi River.

May 19

POLITICS: To end divisive sentiments arising from the arrest and detainment of Congressman Clement L. Vallandigham (D-Ohio), who advocates peace, Secretary of War Edwin M. Stanton orders him released and deported to Confederate lines.

WEST: General Ulysses S. Grant, eager to attack Confederate defenses at Vicksburg, Mississippi, before they are consolidated, orders General William T. Sherman's XV Corps to attack the north fringes of the city. Despite commendable bravery and desperate fighting, the blue-clad infantry are flung back with heavy losses at the Stockade Redan. Other attacks around the city's perimeter by Generals John B. McPherson and John B. McClernand suffer similar defeat. Grant then suspends the action before trying again. Meanwhile, growing numbers of army and navy siege guns begin to play havoc on the city's inhabitants with a continuous bombardment that plays out for seven weeks.

NAVAL: The USS *Sopronia* captures the Confederate schooner *Mignnonette* off Piney Point, Virginia.

The USS *Huntsville* captures the Spanish blockade-runner *Union* off St. Petersburg, Florida.

The USS *De Soto* captures the Confederate schooner *Mississippian* in the Gulf of Mexico.

May 20

SOUTH: Union forces under General John G. Foster pursue retreating Confederates beyond Kinston, North Carolina, as Southern troops withdraw to support other threatened areas.

NAVAL: Armed boats from the USS *Louisiana* capture the Confederate schooner *R. T. Renshaw* at Tar River, North Carolina.

The USS *Amanda* is driven ashore on the Florida coast during a storm and is wrecked.

May 21

SOUTH: General Joseph E. Johnston orders General Franklin Gardner to abandon Port Hudson, Louisiana, and come to the aid of Vicksburg, Mississippi. Gardner, however, disobeys and remains strongly ensconced behind four and a half miles of earthworks and natural fortifications on a sharp bend along the Mississippi River. The following day, he is surrounded by 30,000 Federal troops under General Nathaniel P. Banks.

WEST: Confederate forces hastily abandon Yazoo City, Mississippi, in the face of an approaching Union flotilla, destroying a number of tooling shops and boat under construction.

NAVAL: The USS *Currituck, Anacostia,* and *Satellite* capture the Confederate schooner *Emily* off the mouth of the Rappahannock River.

The USS *Union* seizes the British blockade-runner *Linnet* off Charlotte Harbor, Florida.

Federal gunboats USS *Baron de Kalb, Choctaw, Forest Rose, Linden,* and *Petrel,* all directed by Commander John Grimes, steam up the Yazoo River from Haynes's Bluff, Mississippi, to Yazoo City. There they shell a Confederate navy yard and destroy three warships under construction—including one described as "a monster, 310 feet long and 70 beam . . . she would have given us much trouble."

May 22

POLITICS: The U.S. War Department establishes the Bureau of Colored Troops to better coordinate the recruitment of African Americans from all regions of the nation.

President Jefferson Davis implores General Braxton Bragg in Tennessee to come to the assistance of Vicksburg, Mississippi, if possible.

SOUTH: General Winfield S. Hancock assumes command of the II Corps, Army of the Potomac.

General Alfred Pleasonton is appointed commander of the Cavalry Corps, Army of the Potomac, replacing General George Stoneman.

WEST: General Ulysses S. Grant again launches a frontal assault on the defenses of Vicksburg, Mississippi, hitting a three-mile stretch of entrenched positions following a continuous and heavy bombardment. This time, both General William T. Sherman's XV Corps and James B. McPherson's XVII Corps are to attack simultaneously in an attempt to overpower the defenders. However, infantry movements are negated by deep, narrow ravines fronting the six strong points selected, which are also backed by a line of high breastworks. Hard fighting and heavy sacrifice avail little to the attackers, and Grant calls the action off. Of the 45,000 Union troops committed, they suffer 502 killed, 2,550 wounded, and 147 missing (3,199). Confederate casualties amount to fewer than 500. Grant then resigns himself to the formal siege operations he sought to avoid. Food shortages, intense summer heat, and unparalleled suffering by civilians are nonetheless taking their toll on the defenders.

NAVAL: The army steamer *Allison* sinks the Confederate schooner *Sea Bird* near New Bern, North Carolina.

Armed boats from USS *Fort Henry* capture the Confederate sloop *Isabella* in Waccasassa Bay, Florida.

The USS *Benton, Mound City, Carondelet,* and *Tuscumbia* resume their bombardment of Vicksburg, Mississippi. All are hit by return fire but are not seriously damaged.

May 23

POLITICS: Secretary of War John A. Seddon strongly suggests to President Jefferson Davis that Confederate forces in the Trans-Mississippi Department mount an offensive operation of some kind to relieve the pressure on Vicksburg, Mississippi. Specifically, he cites the recapture of Helena, Arkansas, as a possible objective, for it partially serves as a supply base for the army of General Ulysses S. Grant.
SOUTH: Richard S. Ewell is promoted to lieutenant general, C.S.A.
WEST: The Army of the Gulf under General Nathaniel P. Banks continues encircling Port Hudson, Louisiana, prior to making a general assault. Banks brings 30,000 men to bear against a Confederate garrison of 7,000 under General Franklin Gardner, a former New Jersey resident married into a prominent Southern family.

May 24

SOUTH: Ambrose P. Hill is appointed lieutenant general, C.S.A.

Henry Heth is appointed major general, C.S.A.
WEST: General John A. Schofield replaces General Samuel R. Curtis as commander of the Department of the Missouri.
NAVAL: Armed boats from the USS *Port Royal* capture the Confederate sloop *Fashion,* burn a repair dock at Devils's Elbow, Florida, and then move on to capture the Confederate sloop *Fashion* near Apalachicola.

Federal gunboats of the Yazoo River expedition begin to move up the adjoining Sunflower River to destroy stocks of grain gathered along its banks.

May 25

POLITICS: Peace Democrat Clement L. Vallandigham is released from prison prior to his deportation across Confederate lines at Murfreesboro, Tennessee.
WEST: An attempt by Federal forces to mine their way through Confederate defenses at Vicksburg, Mississippi, fails when a tunnel, crammed with 2,200 pounds of gunpowder is detonated, only to reveal additional enemy lines beyond.
NAVAL: Union forces skirmishing near Port Hudson, Louisiana, seize the Confederate steamers *Starlight* and *Red Chief* on the Mississippi River.

The Confederate raider CSS *Alabama* under Captain Raphael Semmes captures and burns the Union ship *Gildersleeve* off Bahía, Brazil.

May 26

POLITICS: Peace Democrat Clement L. Vallandigham is finally banished to the Confederacy for the duration of the war and is handed over at Murfreesboro, Tennessee.

SOUTH: General Nathaniel P. Banks assembles a council of war and decides to attack the formidable defenses of Port Hudson, Louisiana, directly. Banks settles on a heavy naval bombardment followed by a mass infantry assault at select points of the Confederate line. He originally intends to hit the Confederates simultaneously at several points, but coordinating the actions of subordinates proves nearly impossible over the rough terrain encountered.

NAVAL: The USS *Ceres, Shawsheen,* and *Brinker* steam up the Neuse River in support of army operations against Wilkinson's Point, North Carolina.

May 27

SOUTH: At 6:00 A.M., General Nathaniel P. Banks launches his long-anticipated attack on Confederate defenses at Port Hudson, Louisiana. The combined assaults on the northern breastworks by General Christopher Auger and Godfrey Wetzel become separated inadvertently in bad terrain and are driven off piecemeal. Once the Confederates repel their blue-clad assailants here, Gardner immediately shifts his garrison to cover other threatened portions of the line. Fighting rages for six straight hours, and Union forces gain a foothold on the embankment but are inevitably driven off. A subsequent advance by General Thomas W. Sherman also is repulsed, and Banks finally suspends the effort. Union losses are 293 dead, 1,545 wounded, and 157 missing (1,995) while the Confederates record 235 casualties.

The first attack on Port Hudson also occasions the first large-scale employment of African-American troops in battle. Mustering on the combat line are the 1st and 3rd Regiments of Louisiana Native Guards, with the former a French-speaking battalion raised among the Creole elite of New Orleans. The unit is distinguished further in its being commanded by black officers, while the newly recruited 3rd Regiment consists of former slaves led by whites. Their ill-fated charge against the 39th Mississippi at the northernmost fringes of the Confederate line is badly repulsed, but the Native Guards perform extremely well throughout their baptism of fire.

WEST: General William T. Sherman attacks Fort Hill on the Mississippi River and is repulsed.

NAVAL: The USS *Coeur de Lion* sinks the Confederate schooners *Gazelle* and *Flight* in the Yeocomico River, Virginia.

The CSS *Chattahoochee* is sunk accidently by a boiler explosion in the Chattahoochee River, Georgia, killing 18 sailors.

The USS *Brooklyn* captures the Confederate schooner *Blazer* at Pass Cavallo, Texas.

Admiral David G. Farragut's squadron, consisting of the USS *Hartford, Richmond, Genesee, Essex,* and *Monongahela,* remains actively engaged in the reduction of Port Hudson, Louisiana.

The Federal gunboat USS *Cincinnati* under Lieutenant George M. Bache is sunk by cannon fire at Fort Hill, near Vicksburg, Mississippi, suffering 25 killed and 15 missing. The vessel nonetheless goes down with it colors flying defiantly from the mast, eliciting praise from General William T. Sherman.

May 28

NORTH: The 54th Massachusetts Infantry, composed entirely of African Americans, parades through Boston under Colonel Robert G. Shaw, a wealthy Brahmin and devoted abolitionist. The unit then ships out to Hilton Head, South Carolina, for service in the siege of Charleston.

WEST: General George L. Hartsuff rises to command XXIII Corps, Army of the Tennessee.

NAVAL: The USS *Brooklyn* captures the Confederate sloop *Kate* off Point Isabel, Texas.

May 29

WEST: General Ambrose E. Burnside protests the release of Copperhead Clement L. Vallandigham from imprisonment and tenders his resignation to President Abraham Lincoln, who refuses it.

NAVAL: The USS *Cimarron* captures the Confederate blockade-runner *Evening Star* near Wassaw Sound, Georgia.

The Confederate raider CSS *Alabama* under Captain Raphael Semmes captures and burns the Union ship *Jabez Snow* in the South Atlantic.

May 30

SOUTH: General Robert E. Lee reorganizes his Army of Northern Virginia into four corps: General James Longstreet (I), General Richard S. Ewell (II), General Ambrose P. Hill (III), and General J. E. B. Stuart (Cavalry Corps).

Virginia Partisan Rangers under Captain John S. Mosby attack and burn a railroad train near Bealton, Virginia.

NAVAL: The USS *Forest Rose* and *Linden* capture and sink the Confederate vessels *Dew Drop* and *Emma Bett* on the Quiver River, Mississippi.

A Union boat expedition captures the Confederate schooner *Star* and the sloop *Victoria* at Brazos Santiago, Texas.

The USS *Rhode Island* runs the Confederate steamer *Margaret and Jessie* ashore at Eleuthera Island, Bahamas.

May 31

POLITICS: In a high-level strategy session at Richmond, Virginia, President Jefferson Davis openly expresses to General Robert E. Lee his dissatisfaction over General Joseph E. Johnston's failure to handle affairs outside Vicksburg, Mississippi, in a timely way. "Genl. Johnson did not, as you thought advisable, attack Grant promptly," he declares, "and I fear the result is that which you anticipated if time was given."

NAVAL: The USS *Pawnee* and *E. B. Hale* cover Federal troops embarkations on James Island, South Carolina.

In his latest display of interservice cooperation, Admiral David D. Porter offers General William T. Sherman two large naval guns for service ashore at Vicksburg, Mississippi, manned by naval personnel.

The USS *Carondelet* and *Forest Queen* assist Union troops to evacuate Perkins Landing on the Mississippi River, Louisiana, while keeping Confederate troops at bay with heavy support fire.

June 1

WEST: General Ambrose E. Burnside closes offices belonging to the *Chicago Times* over seemingly disloyal pronouncements, creating an uproar and another political headache for President Abraham Lincoln.

June 2

POLITICS: President Jefferson Davis orders Peace Democrat Clement L. Vallandigham transported to Wilmington, North Carolina, for detention there as an enemy alien.

NAVAL: The USS *Anacostia* and *Primrose* capture the Confederate sloop *Flying Cloud* at Tapp's Creek, Virginia.

The Confederate raider CSS *Alabama* under Captain Raphael Semmes captures and burns the Union bark *Amazonian* in the South Atlantic after an eight-hour chase.

June 3

NORTH: Benjamin H. Grierson is promoted to brigadier general, U.S. Army.

SOUTH: General Robert E. Lee begins his second invasion of the North by moving 75,000 men of the Army of Virginia from Fredericksburg, Virginia, toward the Shenandoah Valley. General Ambrose P. Hill's corps is detained temporarily near Fredericksburg until needed.

Union general Quincy A. Gilmore assumes temporary command of the Department of the South in South Carolina.

The African-American 54th Massachusetts Infantry under Colonel Robert G. Shaw disembarks at Port Royal, South Carolina. This is the first black unit raised in the North to be committed to combat operations.

WEST: Elements of the Union IX Corps under General John G. Parke begin to reinforce General Ulysses S. Grant outside Vicksburg, Mississippi.

NAVAL: The USS *Stars and Stripes* captures the Confederate sloop *Florida* at St. Mark's Bay, Florida.

The Federal ram USS *Switzerland* reconnoiters up the Atchafalaya River, Louisiana, as far as Simmesport, where it encounters heavy resistance and withdraws.

June 4

POLITICS: President Abraham Lincoln orders Secretary of War Edwin M. Stanton to revoke General Ambrose E. Burnside's suspension of the *Chicago Times*.

WEST: Skirmishing erupts between Confederates under General Braxton Bragg and General William S. Rosecrans's Union troops at Snow Hill, Tennessee.

NAVAL: The USS *Commodore McDonough, Island City,* and *Cossack* support Federal troop landings at Bluffton, South Carolina.

A naval force consisting of USS *Switzerland, Lafayette,* and *Pittsburgh* bombards Confederate positions at Simmesport, Louisiana, driving the defenders off.

June 5

SOUTH: Fighting erupts at Franklin's Crossing on the Rappahannock River as troops of General Ambrose P. Hill's command skirmish with the Union VI Corps under General John Sedgwick. Sedgwick has orders to test Confederate defenses across the river to determine whether they are still there in strength; if not, it is assumed that the Army of Northern Virginia under General Robert E. Lee has headed north to invade Maryland. Accordingly, Sedgwick's 26th New Jersey and 5th Vermont masses at Franklin's Crossing and wade across. They encounter severe sniper fire from Confederate sharpshooters along the riverbank and are driven back. Sedgwick then arrives to oversee personally the deployment of pontoon bridges across the Rappahannock, which are laid under fire. Additional Union troops then dash across, overrunning the Confederate rifle pits and taking 35 captives. Federal losses are six killed and 35 injured. The stiff resistance encountered convinces Sedgwick that the Southerners are still present in force, and he reports his findings to General Joseph Hooker. Hooker, unconvinced, next orders several cavalry forays into the country-side for further reconnaissance. Hill, meanwhile, lingers at Franklin's Crossing for another day before heading off to join Lee in Maryland.

WEST: General John G. Park arrives from North Carolina to assume command of the IX Corps near Vicksburg, Mississippi.

NAVAL: A combined expedition consisting of the USS *Commodore Morris* and *Commodore Jones*, the army gunboat *Smith Briggs*, and the transport *Winnissimet* ascend the Mattapony River, Virginia, to attack Confederate ordnance works at Walkerton. Confederate general Henry A. Wise characterizes the ensuing affair as "a daring and destructive raid."

The USS *Wissahickon* sinks an unidentified Confederate steamer off Charleston, South Carolina.

The Confederate raider CSS *Alabama* under Captain Raphael Semmes captures and burns the Union ship *Talisman* in the mid-Atlantic.

June 6

SOUTH: At Brandy Station, Virginia, General J. E. B. Stuart holds a grand review of 8,000 Confederate cavalry for a large assembly of political dignitaries and spectators gathered on railroad cars.

WEST: General Richard Taylor is ordered by Edmund Kirby-Smith to attack Union positions along Milliken's Bend, Louisiana, and relieve pressure on Vicksburg, Mississippi, across the river. Taylor musters 4,500 men for the effort, with the brigade of General Henry E. McCulloch advancing directly on the town while two others cover the northern and southern flanks. En route, the Confederate advance is detected by elements of the 10th Illinois Cavalry, who alert the commander at Milliken's Bend, Colonel Hermann Lieb. Union forces hastily make preparations to receive their visitors.

NAVAL: The USS *Tahoma* captures the grounded Confederate schooner *Statesman* near Gadsen's Point, Florida.

The Confederate raider CSS *Florida* under Lieutenant John N. Maffitt captures and burns the Union ship *Southern Cross* at sea.

The Confederate raider CSS *Clarence* under Lieutenant Charles Read, formerly a prize of CSS *Florida*, captures the Union bark *Whistling Wind* off Cape Romain, South Carolina.

The Federal gunboat USS *Tyler* seizes the Confederate steamer *Lady Walton* off the mouth of the White River, Arkansas.

June 7

SOUTH: Union forces burn Brierfield, President Jefferson Davis's plantation, as they advance below Vicksburg, Mississippi.

At 5:30 a.m., 1,500 Confederate soldiers under General Henry E. McCulloch attack 1,061 Federals at Milliken's Bend, Louisiana, and push them back onto the river bank. Federal troops under Colonel Hermann Lieb then make a determined stand, aided by the 9th and 13th Louisiana, and 1st Mississippi, three regiments of newly recruited African Americans, who fight courageously. At length, the gunboats USS *Choctaw* and *Lexington* appear on the Mississippi River at about 7:00 a.m. and pound the attackers with heavy and accurate cannon fire. After three hours of intense fighting the Confederates withdraw. The African Americans, who suffer disproportionately high casualties, subsequently murder several Confederate prisoners after learning that they previously had killed black captives in their custody. Union losses in this affair tally 101 dead, 285 injured, and 266 missing while the Confederates sustain 44 killed, 131 wounded, and 10 missing.

SOUTHWEST: French forces occupy Mexico City at the behest of Emperor Napoleon III.

NAVAL: The Confederate raider CSS *Clarence* under Lieutenant Charles Read captures the Union schooner *Alfred H. Partridge* at sea, releasing it on a bond.

Good shooting by the Federal gunboat USS *Lexington* and ironclad *Choctaw* enfilades and helps defeat a strong Confederate thrust at Milliken's Bend, Louisiana.

June 8

SOUTH: The Army of Northern Virginia under General Robert E. Lee arrives at Culpeper Court House, Virginia, where General J. E. B. Stuart stages another elaborate cavalry review. Stuart, a jaunty, supremely confident gamecock, delights in displaying his finely honed troopers, but nonetheless he is slated to receive some rather unexpected—and very unwelcome—visitors.

At Falmouth, Virginia, General Alfred Pleasonton musters his Union cavalry corps, two infantry brigades, and six light batteries (11,000 men in all) for a reconnaissance in force across the Rappahannock River. His mission is to locate the main body of Confederates and ascertain if they are moving north on an offensive into Union territory.

NAVAL: Armed Confederate boats board and capture the Union steam tug *Boston* at Pass à l'Outre on the Mississippi River. The rebels then go on to take and burn the Union barks *Lenox* and *Texana* before boldly sailing the *Boston* past the blockading squadron and into Mobile Bay, Alabama.

The Confederate raider CSS *Georgia* seizes the Union ship *George Griswold*, releasing it on bond.

June 9

SOUTH: At 4:00 a.m., General John Buford's cavalry brigade splashes across the Rappahannock River at Beverly while, four miles downstream, a similar force under General David M. Gregg crosses at Kelly's Ford. General Alfred Pleasonton has thrown two columns against the known headquarters of General J. E. B. Stuart in an attempt to catch the wily trooper in a coordinated pincer attack. Buford, covered by a morning fog, pitches into the pickets of General William E. Jones's Confederate cavalry, rolls them back from the river, and seizes 150 prisoners. He then gallops ahead to Brandy Station, Virginia, in search of Stuart's main body.

Several of Jones's troopers frantically gallop back into Stuart's headquarters, informing him of Buford's approach. The general, with 9,500 veteran troopers scattered over a wide area, immediately dispatches riders out to reassemble the command at Brandy Station while he organizes defenses along Fleetwood Hill. Buford, meanwhile, wastes no time in driving Confederate cavalry back until they are reinforced by General Wade Hampton's brigade. A violent charge by the 12th Virginia Cavalry brings the Union advance to a halt, and combat degenerates into a series of spectacular charges and countercharges. Fleetwood Hill changes hands several times in a flurry of flashing sabers as both sides feed addition squadrons and artillery into the swirling fray, and a stalemate ensues.

At this juncture, Gregg's division surprises Stuart by making a sudden appearance south of the Confederate camp at about noon. Previously, Gregg weakened his force by detaching a column under Colonel Alfred N. Duffie on a circuitous march around the Southern position, but he remains nowhere in sight. The Union advance hesitates after encountering a single Confederate cannon, while Jackson brings up the remnants of Jones's brigade to confront this latest threat. Just then, Hampton's division finally drives Buford's tiring troopers off Fleetwood Hill while Duffie attacks Confederate outposts at Stevensburg, five miles away. Charges and countercharges continue at Brandy Station amid great displays of bravery from both sides until Pleasonton, perceiving dust clouds on the horizon, assumes that columns of Confederate infantry are approaching. He then signals his men to fall back, and the fighting dies down across the line. Union forces then draw off in good order and recross the Rappahannock.

Brandy Station is the largest mounted engagement of the war and a tactical victory for the Confederates, who held the field and inflict 936 Union casualties for the loss of 523. However, the 10-hour struggle underscores the excellent progress Union cavalry have achieved under capable leadership. Henceforth, they remain capable adversaries until the end of the war. Pleasonton also proves to General Joseph Hooker that the Army of Northern Virginia indeed is advancing northward. But most significant of all, Stuart, whose quick actions twice retrieve the day from brushes with disaster, is criticized sharply for allowing himself to be surprised. Thereafter, this dashing but sensitive leader seeks out some kind of spectacular accomplishment, worthy of praise, to retrieve his sullied reputation. The upcoming invasion of Pennsylvania promises him such an opportunity, although with fatal consequences for the South.

A total of 20 Federals are killed and another 14 wounded after a powder magazine accidentally explodes at Alexandria, Virginia.

NAVAL: The Confederate raider CSS *Clarence* under Lieutenant Charles Read captures and burns the Union brig *Mary Alvina* at sea.

A naval battery is landed under Commander Edward Terry to assist in the reduction of Port Hudson, Louisiana.

Union mortar boats resume their protracted bombardment of Vicksburg, Mississippi, attempting to cut off resupply efforts and undermine civilian morale. On average, they hurl 175 heavy explosive shells into the city every day while citizens cower in nearby caves.

June 10

NORTH: General Thomas H. Brooks assumes control of the Department of the Monongahela, Pennsylvania.

General Darius N. Couch becomes head of the Department of the Susquehanna, Pennsylvania.

SOUTH: The fateful Gettysburg campaign begins as the Confederate II Corps under General Richard S. Ewell departs Culpeper, Virginia, and tramps northward toward Maryland.

Partisans under Captain John S. Mosby surprise Union troops in camp at Seneca Mills, Maryland, and retire quickly across the Potomac River to Virginia.

WEST: The Confederate Army of Tennessee experiences something of a religious revival as General Braxton Bragg is confirmed in the Episcopalian Church.

NAVAL: Confederate prisoners overpower the Union steamer *Maple Leaf* and conduct themselves to Cape Henry, Virginia.

Admiral Samuel F. Du Pont, cognizant of the danger posed to his wooden vessels by the new Confederate ram CSS *Atlanta,* orders the ironclads USS *Weehawken* and *Nahant* to proceed immediately from Port Royal, South Carolina, to Wassaw Sound, Georgia.

June 11

POLITICS: In an act of defiance by Peace Democrats in Ohio, they nominate Clement L. Vallandigham as their gubernatorial candidate, despite the fact that the Confederate government shipped him off to Canada.

SOUTH: The African-American 54th Massachusetts Infantry participates in the burning of Darien, Georgia.

WEST: Confederate cavalry under General Nathan B. Forrest skirmish with Union troops at Triune, Tennessee.

NAVAL: The USS *Florida* captures the Confederate steamer *Calypso* trying to run the blockade off Wilmington, North Carolina.

The USS *Memphis, Stettin,* and *Ottawa* run the Confederate steamer *Havelock* aground on Folly Island in Charleston Harbor and then destroy it with gunfire.

June 12

NORTH: In light of approaching Confederate forces, Pennsylvania governor Andrew Curtin calls out the state militia.

SOUTH: The Confederate II Corps under General Richard S. Ewell crosses the Blue Ridge Mountains and descends into the Shenandoah Valley, Virginia.

Federal forces advance out of Suffolk, Virginia, and engage Confederate forces under General Daniel H. Hill at Blackwater.

General Quincy A. Gilmore formally replaces General David Hunter as commander of the Department of the South in South Carolina.

WEST: General Richard S. Ewell, advancing along the Blue Ridge Mountains of western Virginia, detaches General Richard E. Rodes's division and a cavalry brigade of General Albert G. Jenkins toward the town of Berryville. Once there, they are to drive out the 1,800-man Union garrison of Colonel Andrew T. McReynolds before marching on to Martinsburg. While en route, however, McReynolds is alerted to the Confederate approach, and he cleverly marches his unit out of town and off to Summit Point, where it will double back to the main garrison at Winchester. The garrison commander in that town, General Robert H. Milroy, had grown aware of enemy activity below him, but owing to cut telegraph wires, he never receives an order to fall back on Harper's Ferry.

NAVAL: The CSS *Clarence* under Lieutenant Charles Read captures the Union bark *Tacony* off Cape Hatteras, North Carolina, then transfers his crew and continues raiding in the new vessel. Two prizes, the schooner *Schindler* and the brig *Arabella,* are also caught and burned along with *Clarence.*

June 13

SOUTH: To counter recent Confederate moves, the Union Army of the Potomac under General Joseph Hooker repositions itself from behind the Rappahannock River to Centreville, Virginia.

Following a severe bombardment, General Nathaniel P. Banks summons General Franklin Gardner to surrender Port Hudson, Louisiana, but he steadfastly declines.

WEST: A brigade of Confederate cavalry under General Albert G. Jenkins fails to catch the retreating garrison of Colonel Andrew T. McReynolds at Berryville, Virginia, and after much riding can only engage his rear guard at Opequon Creek. The hard-marching McReynolds then joins General Robert H. Milroy's main force at Winchester that evening and prepares for defensive action there. Jenkins, meanwhile, continues to Martinsdale with the division of General Robert E. Rodes close behind in support.

General Richard S. Ewell's II Corps, meanwhile, occupies Berryville, Virginia, while planning an immediate strike against Winchester to drive out or possibly capture the Union garrison. To that end, he dispatches two divisions under General Jubal A. Early and Edward Johnson to encircle the town from three directions. The defenders are unaware of these preparations.

NAVAL: The USS *Sunflower* captures the Confederate schooner *Pushmahata* off the Tortugas, Florida.

The USS *Juniata* captures the Confederate schooner *Fashion* off the Cuban coast.

Federal gunboats resume their prolonged bombardment of Port Hudson, Louisiana, softening up that position for another Union assault on the following day.

The Confederate raider CSS *Georgia* under Lieutenant William L. Maury captures and burns the Union bark *Good Hope* at sea.

June 14

POLITICS: President Abraham Lincoln anxiously goads General Joseph Hooker into some kind of action to oppose this latest Confederate incursion. "If the head of Lee's army is at Martinsburg and the tail of it on the Plank road between Fredericksburg and Chancellorsville, the animal must be very slim somewhere. Could you not break him?"

NORTH: Hugh J. Kilpatrick is promoted to brigadier general of cavalry U.S. Army.

SOUTH: At 4:00 A.M., General Nathaniel P. Banks hurls another assault against Confederate defenses at Port Hudson, Louisiana. This time, an entire infantry division under General Halbert E. Payne charges against the strong point at Priest Cap and, despite brave efforts, recoils with heavy loss. Several hours of savage fighting ensue before Banks suspends the action and draws off with 203 killed, 1,401 wounded, and 188 missing (1,805). The well-protected Confederates lose 22 killed and 25 wounded. The Union siege then resumes, and because the fort's supply line remains cut, time is on Banks's side.

WEST: A Confederate cavalry brigade under General Albert G. Jenkins hastens on the town of Martinsburg, western Virginia, garrisoned by Colonel Benjamin F. Smith 1,500 Federal troops. Despite the odds, Smith aggressively deploys his artillery and skirmishers, halting Jenkins squarely in his tracks. As Confederates dither, Union troops strip the town of everything useful, place all materials on waiting trains, and cart them away. It is not until 5:00 P.M. that infantry under General Robert E. Rodes arrives and finally attacks the town, sweeping away a handful of remaining defenders and seizing 200 captives. But for the second time in two days, an outnumbered Union garrison eludes superior Confederate forces.

The Confederate II Corps of General Richard S. Ewell engages a Federal force under General Robert H. Milroy at Winchester, western Virginia. Milroy initially believes that Confederates to his front are simply a large raiding party, but by the time he realizes that the entire Army of Northern Virginia is bearing down on him, it is too late. He now has few options beyond sequestering his command in numerous forts as the divisions of Generals Jubal A. Early and Edward Johnson surround the town. At 6:00 P.M., 22 Confederate cannon open up on the Union works while the Louisiana brigade overruns the Star Fort, one of Milroy's key positions. The general then hastily convenes a war council that elects to spike its artillery, burn its baggage trains, and evacuate Winchester in the early morning. General Richard S. Ewell, who next appears with the remainder of the II Corps, anticipates such a withdrawal, so after nightfall, he instructs Johnson to reposition men along the Martinburg Turnpike at Stevenson's Depot and cut Milroy's retreat.

General Theophilus H. Holmes, commanding the Confederate District of Arkansas, receives orders from the Confederate War Department to mount an offensive against Helena, Arkansas. This move is perceived as the best possible way of relieving Union pressure on Vicksburg, Mississippi. But nearly three weeks elapse before the lethargic Holmes can scrape together sufficient manpower and supplies to comply.

Federal soldiers torch the town of Eunice, Arkansas, following attacks on the USS *Marmora*.

NAVAL: The USS *Lackawanna* captures the Confederate steamer *Neptune* at sea.

The Confederate raider CSS *Florida* under Lieutenant John N. Maffitt captures and burns the Union ship *Red Gauntlet* in the West Indies.

The Confederate raider CSS *Georgia* under Lieutenant William L. Maury captures the Union bark *J. W. Seaver*, releasing it on a bond.

June 15

POLITICS: President Abraham Lincoln calls for 100,000 militia to muster in Pennsylvania, Maryland, Ohio, and western Virginia to thwart recent Confederate advances northward.

NORTH: The approach of the Army of Northern Virginia on Pennsylvanian soil causes outbreaks of excitement and panic at Baltimore, Maryland.

WEST: Confederates under General Edward Johnson prepare to ambush the retiring forces of General Robert H. Milroy at Stevenson's Depot, four miles north of Winchester, Virginia. Milroy's garrison quietly departs at 1:00 A.M., taking the Martinburg Turnpike running north and then east—the most obvious route out of town. His 6,000 men continue groping along in the dark until 3:30 A.M. when they encounter General Edward Johnson's division in blocking positions. Desperate fighting erupts as Milroy attempts to outflank the Confederates, but only he and roughly 2,700 men cut their way to freedom. Among the huge haul subsequently captured by the Confederates are 2,500 prisoners, 300 wagons, 300 horses, and 23 cannon. Union combat losses add an additional 905 dead and 348 wounded to the tally while Ewell sustains 47 killed, 219 wounded, and three missing. This impressive victory removes Federal forces from the Shenandoah Valley, thereby clearing the way for General Robert E. Lee's invasion of Pennsylvania.

General Stephen A. Hurlbut orders 1,600 Union cavalry from his XVI Corps on a major sweep through northwestern Mississippi to gather supplies and disrupt the enemy.

Confederate general Joseph E. Johnston frantically wires General John C. Pemberton at Vicksburg, Mississippi, that his position is hopeless and that he must abandon the city immediately to save his army. However, Pemberton never receives the message owing to cut telegraph wires, and he remains trapped within his works by Federal forces under General Ulysses S. Grant.

NAVAL: The formidable new Confederate steam ram CSS *Atlanta* under Commander William Webb sails into the Wassaw Sound, Georgia, intending to engage Union blockaders. That evening, he positions his vessel to surprise the monitors at dawn.

The Confederate raider CSS *Tacony* under Lieutenant Charles Read captures and burns the Union brig *Umpire* off the Virginian coast.

The USS *Lackawanna* captures the Confederate steamer *Planter* in the Gulf of Mexico.

The USS *Juliet* captures the Confederate steamer *Fred Nolte* on the White River, Arkansas.

The USS *Marmora* and *Prairie Bird* land parties ashore that burn buildings and railroad equipment at Gaines Landing and Eunice, Arkansas.

The USS *General Sterling Price* and *Mound City* begin a three-day reconnaissance of the Mississippi River below Vicksburg, Mississippi, during the course of which 70 small Confederate boats are destroyed.

June 16

NORTH: General Robert E. Lee begins to ford the Potomac River at Point of Rocks, Maryland, and commences his second invasion of the North. Panic grows throughout Washington, D.C., from fear of a outright Confederate attack.

The new Confederate offensive leads to a furious spate of telegrams between General in Chief Henry W. Halleck and General Joseph Hooker as to General Robert E. Lee's intentions. Hooker wants to rush his troops north and confront Lee above Washington, D.C., while Halleck insists that he follow the Confederates and relieve the garrison at Harper's Ferry, West Virginia, en route.

SOUTH: Responding to the Southern invasion of Maryland, General Joseph Hooker begins to position the Army of the Potomac at Fairfax Court House, Virginia, to pursue.

NAVAL: The USS *Circassian* captures the Confederate sloop *John Wesley* off St. Mark's, Florida.

The Confederate raider CSS *Florida* under Lieutenant John N. Maffitt captures and burns the Union ship *B. F. Hoxie* in the West Indies.

The USS *New Era* sinks nine boats gathered by Confederates on an island north of Island No. 10 in the Mississippi River for an impending attack there.

June 17

SOUTH: As the Army of Northern Virginia under General Robert E. Lee advances north into Maryland, General J. E. B. Stuart is ordered to screen his right flank from prying Federal eyes. His Union opposite, General Alfred Pleasonton, is both determined to uncover Confederate intentions and come to grips with his grey-coated adversaries. Stuart previously had dispatched Colonel Thomas Munford, 5th Virginia Cavalry, to scout the vicinity of Aldie, Virginia, where he brushes against Union troopers under General Hugh J. Kilpatrick. An intense, four-hour fight for possession of the town ensues, with Kilpatrick getting the worst of it, but he is reinforced continually by General David M. Gregg. Simultaneously, another engagement erupts several miles away at Middleburg, when the 1st Rhode Island Cavalry of Colonel Alfred Duffie fights bravely but is overpowered by Stuart's main body. The Union troopers gradually surrender, but Duffie manages to escape with 35 men still in the saddle. Fighting then dies down for the evening; Union losses for the day total about 300 to a Confederate tally of 100.

NAVAL: The ironclads USS *Weehawken* under Captain John Rodgers, assisted by the *Nahant,* engage Commander William A. Webb and the formidable steam ram CSS *Atlanta* as it challenges the Union blockade in Wassaw Sound, Georgia. *Atlanta* grounds in the channel during its approach and subsequently is worked free, but its rudder is damaged and the ship steers erratically. *Weehawken* and *Nahant* then slip quickly into point-blank range and pound their armored adversary to good effect, dismounting two of *Atlanta*'s guns and injuring crew members. When the lumbering giant grounds again, Webb finally surrenders along with 145 prisoners. This constitutes a major loss to the ever-shrinking Confederate navy.

Armed boats from the USS *Itasca* capture the Confederate blockade-runner *Miriam* off Brazos Santiago, Texas.

June 18

SOUTH: General Alfred Pleasonton, angered about losses to his cavalry command at Aldie and Middleburg, Virginia, on the previous day, makes arrangements to storm the latter town. The 16th Pennsylvania Cavalry under Colonel J. Irwin Gregg accomplishes that feat after hard fighting but then receives orders to ride quickly back to Aldie, and Middletown is abandoned and reoccupied by Southerners.

WEST: General Ulysses S. Grant summarily relieves General John A. McClernand from command of the XIII for continued insubordination and replaces him with General Edward O. C. Ord. The final straw comes when McClernand issues unauthorized laudatory statements to his men for their role in the failed assault on Vicksburg, in which he also denigrates the performance of other units.

NAVAL: The USS *Tahoma* captures the British blockade-runner *Harriet* off the Anclote Keys, Florida, and subsequently forces the British vessel *Mary James* ashore at Clearwater.

The USS *James C. Chambers* captures the Confederate schooner *Rebekah* near Tampa Bay, Florida.

The USS *Winona* breaks up a concentration of Confederate cavalry outside Plaquemine, Louisiana, thereby defeating a Confederate attempt to seize nearby Donaldsonville and cut off Union forces that are besieging Port Hudson.

June 19

NORTH: The Confederate II Corps under General Richard S. Ewell continue crossing the Potomac River into Maryland and approaches southern Pennsylvania as Generals Ambrose P. Hill and James Longstreet prepare to follow en masse.

SOUTH: In continuing actions to penetrate the Confederate cavalry screen, Colonel J. Irwin Gregg's 16th Pennsylvania retakes the town of Middleburg, Virginia, after hard fighting and 100 casualties.

NAVAL: The USS *Para* captures the Confederate schooner *Emma* off Mosquito Inlet, Florida.

A naval battery planted ashore engages and repulses Confederates forces near Cerro Gordo, Tennessee.

June 20

POLITICS: Financier Jay Cooke oversees creation of the first national bank in Philadelphia and helps spearhead the drive for Union war bonds.

NORTH: The city of Baltimore, Maryland, erects breastworks to preclude any Confederate raids there.

Skirmishing erupts between contending forces at Upperville and Haymarket, Maryland.

SOUTH: Union cavalry under General Alfred Pleasonton increases pressure on the mounted screen of General J. E. B. Stuart, now left unsupported east of the Blue Ridge Mountains. Accordingly, General David M. Gregg's division is ordered to attack General Wade Hampton's force at Goose Creek, Virginia, while another force under General John Buford threatens to flank the Confederates. Stuart, seeking to preserve his command, withdraws in good order to Upperville for the night.

WEST: West Virginia joins the Union as the 35th state and a stalwart Northern ally. Moreover, its constitution mandates the gradual elimination of slavery.

NAVAL: The USS *Primrose* captures the Confederate sloop *Richard* Vaux at Blakestone Island in the Potomac River.

The Confederate raider CSS *Alabama* under Captain Raphael Semmes captures and burns the Union bark *Conrad* at sea.

The Confederate raider CSS *Tacony* under Lieutenant Charles Read seizes the Union vessel *Isaac Webb* and releases it on a bond.

June 21

SOUTH: Union cavalry under General Hugh J. Kilpatrick skirmish with screening elements of the Army of Northern Virginia at Upperville, Virginia. The Confederate troopers of General J. E. B. Stuart, though pressured, withdraw in good order and form new defensive positions along Ashby's Gap. In light of four days of intense fighting, General Alfred Pleasonton informs General Joseph Hooker that the Confederates are definitely on the move, apparently into the Shenandoah Valley.

NAVAL: The USS *Florida* captures the Confederate schooner *Hattie* off Frying Pan Shoals, North Carolina.

The USS *Owasco* and *Cayuga* capture the Confederate sloop *Active* at Sabine Pass, Texas.

The Confederate raider CSS *Tacony* under Lieutenant Charles Read captures and burns the Union ship *Byzantium* off the New England coast.

The USS *Santiago de Cuba* captures the British blockade-runner *Victory* off Palmetto Point, Eleuthera Island, Bahamas.

June 22

NORTH: Alfred Pleasonton is appointed major general, of cavalry U.S. Army.

SOUTH: General J. E. B. Stuart receives discretionary and somewhat vague instructions from General Robert E. Lee ordering him alternately to raid Union supply lines and to guard the army's right flank as it advances northward into Pennsylvania.

WEST: General William S. Rosecrans prepares to launch his strategic flanking movement from Murfreesboro, Tennessee, toward Tullahoma to force General Braxton Bragg's Army of Tennessee behind the Tennessee River. He undertakes the offensive to preclude the chance of any Southern reinforcements reaching the besieged city of Vicksburg, Mississippi.

NAVAL: The USS *Shawsheen* captures the Confederate schooner *Henry Clay* in Spring Creek, Bay River, North Carolina.

The USS *Itasca* captures the British blockade-runner *Sea Drift* off Matagorda Island, Texas.

The Confederate raider CSS *Tacony* under Lieutenant Charles Read seizes five fishing schooners off the New England coast, burning four and releasing 75 prisoners of the fifth.

June 23

NORTH: The Army of Northern Virginia under General Robert E. Lee nears Chambersburg, Pennsylvania, with several disparate Northern columns groping along in pursuit.

SOUTH: General John A. Dix, commanding the Department of Virginia, spurs Union troops forward in an expedition from Yorktown, Virginia, to South Anna Bridge.

Confederate forces capture 1,000 Union troops at Brashear City, Louisiana.

WEST: The Army of the Cumberland under General William S. Rosecrans ends six months of inactivity at Murfreesboro, Tennessee, by advancing several columns toward Tullhoma. By moving east around General Braxton Bragg's flank, Rosecrans aspires to maneuver the enemy out of strong defensive positions and also prevent them from shipping reinforcements to aid in the defense of Vicksburg, Mississippi.

Union troops burn the town of Sibley, Missouri, after being fired on by Confederate bushwhackers.

NAVAL: Commander Pierce Crosby leads a naval expedition consisting of the Federal gunboats USS *Commodore Barney, Commodore Morris, Western World,* and *Morse* in a combined operation up the Pamunkey River, Virginia. They venture goes unmolested as far upriver as White House.

The USS *Flambeau* seizes the British blockade-runner *Bettie Cratzer* at Murrell's Inlet, South Carolina.

The USS *Pursuit* captures the Confederate sloop *Kate* at Indian River, Florida.

The Confederate raider CSS *Tacony* under Lieutenant Charles Read captures fishing schooners *Ada* and *Wanderer.*

June 24

NORTH: The I and III Corps of Generals James Longstreet and Ambrose P. Hill, respectively, reach the Potomac River and cross into Maryland en route to Pennsylvania. Skirmishing erupts in the vicinity of Antietam.

WEST: The Union Department of West Virginia is set up under the aegis of General Benjamin F. Kelley.

Elements of the Army of the Cumberland and the Army of Tennessee skirmish at Big Spring Branch, Tennessee. The flanking movement initiated by General William S. Rosecrans remains beset by inclement weather and heavy downpours, which hamper marching.

NAVAL: Admiral John A. B. Dahlgren is relieved of duties at the Washington Navy Yard and is ordered to succeed Admiral Samuel F. Du Pont as new commander of the South Atlantic Blockading Squadron.

The Confederate raider CSS *Tacony* under Lieutenant Charles W. Read captures the Union ship *Shatemuc* in New England waters and releases it on bond. At this juncture, Read decides to burn the *Tacony* and transfers his crew to a new capture, the schooner *Archer.*

The USS *Sumpter* collides with the steamer *General Meigs* in a dense fog off Hampton Roads, Virginia, and sinks.

The USS *Santiago de Cuba* captures the Confederate steamer *Britannia* off Palmetto Point, Eleuthera Island, Bahamas.

June 25

NORTH: Having briefly crossed the Potomac River into Maryland, Confederate cavalry under General J. E. B. Stuart capture 125 Union wagons and 400 prisoners at Rockville. Then, while approaching the town of Haymarket, Stuart bumps against troops of the II Corps under General Winfield S. Hancock. Stiff resistance induces him to continue circling farther east around the Union flank—and farther away from the Army of Northern Virginia.

South: General Joseph Hooker dispatches three corps under General John F. Reynolds to intercept the Army of Northern Virginia as it moves north, but the Federals depart too late and can only follow.

General J. E. B. Stuart leads three cavalry brigades north from Salem Depot, Virginia, to join the main Confederate army north of the Potomac River. However, Stuart's interpretation of his otherwise discretionary orders ultimately takes him away from the main theater of operations. Furthermore, they hinder Confederate intelligence-gathering abilities at a time when the whereabouts of pursuing Union forces are unknown.

West: Union forces besieging Vicksburg, Mississippi, explode 2,200 pounds of gunpowder that had been tunneled under the 3rd Louisiana redoubt. Two regiments then try to rush a gap in Confederate defenses but are stopped by additional fortifications farther back.

Naval: The USS *Crusader* lands armed parties, which burn several houses along Pepper Creek, Point Comfort, Virginia, in retaliation for being fired on.

The USS *Sagamore* captures the British blockade-runner *Frolic* near Crystal River, Florida.

The Confederate raider CSS *Georgia* under Lieutenant William L. Maury captures the Union ship *Constitution* at sea.

June 26

North: General Jubal A. Early's division of Confederates presses on through Gettysburg, Pennsylvania, toward York.

South: Confederate cavalry under General J. E. B. Stuart continue detouring 23 miles around Union forces, heading toward Fairfax Court House, Virginia.

West: Large-scale fighting erupts between General William S. Rosecrans and General Braxton Bragg at Shelbyville, Tennessee. The Federals sustain 45 dead, 463 injured, and 13 missing while the Confederate tally amounts to 1,634, including many captured.

Naval: Admiral Andrew H. Foote dies in New York City of wounds received at the siege of Fort Donelson in February 1862.

The Confederate schooner CSS *Archer* under Lieutenant Charles W. Read boldly attacks and sinks the U.S. revenue cutter *Caleb Cushing* at Portland, Maine, but subsequently surrenders to the USS *Forest City* after expending its last ammunition. This concludes the naval career of Read who, in the span of only 19 days, captures 22 vessels, despite the 47 Union ships looking for him.

A gunboat squadron consisting of the USS *Commodore Barney, Commodore Morris, Western World,* and *Morse* covers the landing of army troops at White House on the Pamunkey River, Virginia.

Admiral David G. Farragut's vessels, including USS *Richmond, Genesee,* and *Essex* commence a heavy bombardment of Confederate positions at Port Hudson, Louisiana.

The American ship *Pembroke,* while navigating the Shimonoseki Straits of southern Japan, is fired on by coastal fortifications commanded by the local daimyo. No casualties or damage result, but the incident is reported to U.S. Navy authorities in Yokohama.

June 27

NORTH: President Abraham Lincoln appoints General George G. Meade to replace General Joseph Hooker as commander of the Army of the Potomac.

General Robert E. Lee begins to consolidate the Army of Northern Virginia around Chambersburg, Pennsylvania, with a view toward threatening the state capital of Harrisburg. The towns of Carlisle and York are occupied temporarily by Southern forces.

SOUTH: Confederate cavalry under General J. E. B. Stuart clash with Union forces at Fairfax Court House, Virginia, taking some prisoners. He approaches the town eager to secure supplies abandoned by General Joseph Hooker but is surprised and nearly captured in a sudden charge by 86 troopers of the 11th New York Cavalry. Fortunately, Stuart and his suite are quickly rescued by the 1st North Carolina Cavalry under Colonel Laurence S. Baker, who abruptly pushes the attackers back. The Confederate horsemen then easily occupy Fairfax Court House, dining on captured food, and helping themselves to ample supplies of boots and gloves. Stuart is apparently so pleased with himself that he intends to continue raiding the Union rear— instead of rejoining the Army of Northern Virginia as planned. His force crosses the Potomac River into Maryland that evening.

Confederate forces under General Thomas H. Taylor attack Donaldsonville, Louisiana, but they are repelled.

WEST: As Union forces under General William S. Rosecrans occupy Manchester, Tennessee, General Braxton Bragg decides to withdraw southward to stronger positions at Chattanooga.

NAVAL: The USS *Tioga* captures the British blockade-runner *Julia* near the Bahamas.

The Confederate raider CSS *Florida* under Lieutenant John N. Maffitt captures the Union whaler *V. H. Hill* near Bermuda and releases it on a bond.

June 28

NORTH: Confederate cavalry under General Albert G. Jenkins gallops to within four miles of Harrisburg, Pennsylvania, alarming the population.

General Robert E. Lee is startled to learn that Union forces are gathering at Frederick, Maryland, threatening his rear. Their exact intentions remain hazy as all of Lee's cavalry under General J. E. B. Stuart have departed on a raid deep into Union territory. The Confederates remain virtually blind for several days; therefore, Lee, as a precaution, orders his dispersed command to concentrate in the vicinity of Gettysburg, an important road junction in Pennsylvania.

The division of General Jubal A. Early enters York, Pennsylvania, demanding shoes, clothing, rations, and $100,000. He has to be content with some minor supplies and $28,000.

WEST: A column of Union infantry from the Army of the Cumberland captures Decherd, Tennessee, immediately following its evacuation by General Braxton Bragg's Confederates.

General John C. Pemberton, defending the vital Confederate bastion at Vicksburg, Mississippi, is petitioned by his soldiers to surrender rather than see the entire force starve to death. After a seven-week siege, the final curtain is about to fall.

General Benjamin M. Prentiss, commanding the Union garrison at Helena, Arkansas, is apprised of an impending attack by Confederate forces under General Theophilus H. Holmes. He immediately strengthens his position and solicits gunboat support from the navy.

NAVAL: Admiral Samuel P. Lee detaches vessels from the North Atlantic Blockading Squadron to assist in the defense of Baltimore and Annapolis, Maryland.

Armed boats from the USS *Fort Henry* capture the Confederate schooner *Anna Maria* in the Steinhatchee River, Florida.

The Confederate raider CSS *Georgia* under Lieutenant William L. Maury takes the Union ship *City of Bath* off the Brazilian coast.

June 29

NORTH: George A. Custer is promoted to brevet brigadier general, of cavalry U.S. Army.

The Army of the Potomac under General George G. Meade marches northward through Maryland to engage a marauding Confederate army.

General J. E. B. Stuart's cavalry, scouting for the Army of Northern Virginia, pause long enough at Halt's Woods, Maryland, to wreck tracks belonging to the Baltimore and Ohio Railroad. Then they gallop off to Westminster, brushing aside some Union skirmishers.

NAVAL: The USS *Susquehanna* and *Kanawha* capture the British blockade-runner *Ann* near Mobile Bay, Alabama.

June 30

POLITICS: President Abraham Lincoln ignores continuing pressure to reappoint General George B. McClellan as head of the Army of the Potomac.

NORTH: General John F. Reynolds is ordered by General George M. Meade to occupy the road junction at Gettysburg, Pennsylvania. Several Confederate columns are presently converging on that very point. The town is then occupied by a cavalry division under General John Buford, who, recognizing the value of the intersection, prepares his command to defend it. He briefly tangles with a Confederate brigade that withdraws in the waning daylight. Those soldiers form part of General Henry Heth's division, sent to Gettysburg to collect shoes, but when Heth reports the presence of Union forces to III Corps commander General Ambrose P. Hill, Hill blithely dismisses the notion, insisting that the Federals were still in Maryland.

Marauding Confederate cavalry under General J. E. B. Stuart skirmish with Union troops under General Elon Farnsworth at Hanover, Pennsylvania. A battle then unfolds as Union reinforcements arrive under Generals Hugh J. Kilpatrick and George Custer while the Confederates are assisted by General Fitzhugh Lee. During intense fighting in the streets of the town, Stuart exposes himself recklessly and a countercharge by Kilpatrick nearly captures him. Stuart's gray-clad troopers momentarily fall back to the edge of town to regroup, at which point Custer sends dismounted troopers to attack Confederate artillery on Stuart's right and force them back. These troops then are driven off in turn, but Stuart is convinced that his force is imperiled so he breaks off contact by nightfall. Union losses are 19 dead, 73

injured, and 123 missing to a Confederate tally of nine killed, 50 wounded, and 58
missing. The fight at Hanover, while inconclusive, holds dire implications for the
rapidly unfolding events at Gettysburg, 10 miles west. Rather than join the Army of
Northern Virginia concentrating there, Stuart takes an even wider detour around
pursuing Union forces and rests for the evening at Dover, Pennsylvania.

WEST: General Braxton Bragg's Army of Tennessee, outflanked by approaching
Union forces, abandons Tullahoma, Tennessee, and begins to withdraw across the
Tennessee River toward Chattanooga.

NAVAL: The USS *Ossipee* captures the Confederate schooner *Helena* off Mobile,
Alabama.

July 1

POLITICS: The Missouri State Convention votes to end slavery on July 4, 1870.

NORTH: On this fateful morning, the Confederate division of General Henry
Heth forages in the vicinity of Gettysburg, Pennsylvania, when they unexpectedly
encounter dismounted Union cavalry under General John Buford. A sharp battle
quickly develops as the Southerners impulsively charge and are repulsed by rapidly
firing Spencer carbines. General William D. Pender's division then arrives to assist
Heth just as the Union I Corps under General John F. Reynolds begins to deploy
around Gettysburg. Reynolds is killed early on, and his celebrated Iron Brigade suffers severely as terrific fighting erupts along McPherson's Ridge. Gradually, Federal
troops yield to the mounting Confederate onslaught and are driven back into the
town. Combat intensifies further as Generals Oliver O. Howard and Abner Doubleday arrive with the XI and III Corps, respectively, as does the entire Confederate II
Corps of General Richard S. Ewell. Quick maneuvering allows the rebels to roll up
Howard's line, and soon union troops are also streaming through Gettysburg in
confusion.

Disaster is averted when General Winfield S. Hancock comes galloping up at
the head of his II Corps and occupies high ground immediately below Gettysburg
along Cemetery Hill. He then rallies the shaken survivors of I and XI Corps, further
strengthening the Union line. At this juncture, General Robert E. Lee rides up to
supervise affairs and orders Ewell's corps to attack Union positions "if possible."
Ewell, however, is concerned about the exhausted condition of his men and the
strength of the craggy hills before him, so no attack ever develops. The absence
of Thomas "Stonewall" Jackson at the head of the II Corps is never more keenly
felt. Ewell's well-intentioned delay grants Union forces a badly needed respite and
allows the bulk of the Army of the Potomac to occupy excellent defensive terrain
around Gettysburg that evening. General George G. Meade arrives on the battlefield at midnight and, after reviewing his positions, determines to defend them on
the morrow. Casualties for the day amount to 9,000 Federals and 6,800 Confederates. The Southerners obtain a fine tactical victory but inadvertently fumble their
chances for a strategic one.

A Confederate staff rider finally locates the elusive cavalry of General J. E. B.
Stuart and orders him to join General Robert E. Lee at Gettysburg, Pennsylvania,
with all haste.

SOUTH: Elements of the IV and VII Corps, Army of the Potomac, under Generals George W. Getty and Erasmus D. Keyes, respectively, press ahead from White House, Virginia, in the direction of South Anna River and Bottom's Bridge.

General Daniel H. Hill gains temporary command of the Department of Richmond, Virginia, to help thwart recent Union advances.

WEST: General William S. Rosecrans climaxes his successful Tullahoma Campaign by bloodlessly occupying Chattanooga, Tennessee. This is one of the outstanding contests of maneuvering during the war, and he performs brilliantly.

General Joseph E. Johnston, commanding 32,000 men at Jackson, Mississippi, begins to push forward to assist the Confederate defenders of Vicksburg. En route, he finds his path blocked by the XV Corps of General William T. Sherman, strongly deployed behind the Big Black River.

July 2

POLITICS: Confederate vice president Alexander H. Stephens writes to President Abraham Lincoln about prisoner exchanges and potential discussions to end the war. Lincoln declares that he is not interested.

NORTH: At Gettysburg, Pennsylvania, 75,000 Confederates confront 85,000 Federals whose defensive line resembles a fish hook with its right anchored on Culp's Hill to the north and then running the length of Cemetery Ridge to a large hill called Little Round Top on its extreme left. General George G. Meade, an engineer by training, skillfully crams nearly the entire Army of the Potomac on the rugged, low-lying hills and carefully places his men and batteries to make the rough terrain work against the Confederates. The scenario is crystal clear to General James Longstreet, who remonstrates against attacking further and urges General Robert E. Lee to withdraw. Lee, however, determines to defeat the enemy where he finds them. Over Longstreet's continuing objections, he orders strong advances on both Union flanks. On the right, Ewell makes several futile and costly attempts to storm Culp's Hill, ably defended by General George S. Greene's New Yorkers, and finally earns a minor foothold on Cemetery Hill. This lodgment subsequently is lost to a sudden charge by the Union XII Corps at dawn the following day.

The bulk of fighting occurs at the Union left where Longstreet orchestrates a major drive of several divisions. The massed Confederates then suddenly encounter the Union III Corps of General Dan E. Sickles, who, against orders, pushes his command a mile ahead of the main defensive line while seeking better positions. The result creates an exposed salient that Generals John B. Hood and Lafayette McLaws charge and force themselves through, routing Sickles in the process and carrying the Peach Orchard, the Wheatfield, and Devil's Den after strenuous combat. At one point, the Southern advance actually carries them through the Union center, but a sharp countercharge by General Winfield S. Hancock seals the gap and pushes the Confederates back downhill. The crisis of the day develops on the extreme Union left at Little Round Top, which has been left ungarrisoned and on which the Confederates rapidly march. Southern artillery posted here could perilously command the entire Union left center but, at the last possible moment, General Gouverneur K. Warren rushes men and guns up on top of the hill to prevent a possible disaster.

The First Minnesota Infantry fighting at the Battle of Gettysburg, where it incurred the highest casualty rate of any unit in the Civil War *(The National Guard Heritage)*

A tremendous firefight then unfolds between Colonel Joshua Chamberlain's 20th Maine and an Alabama brigade sent to dislodge them. Chamberlain, his ammunition spent and with men falling fast around him, orders a last-ditch bayonet charge down the slopes of Little Round Top that routs the Confederates and saves Meade's left flank. Both sides subsequently draw off in the waning daylight to assess their losses and gird for another day of sacrifice. Meade, during a late night strategy session, then correctly predicts that Lee, foiled on either flank, will direct the bulk of his efforts at the Union center. This proves the most fortuitous intuition of the war—and, overnight, Meade rushes men and artillery to the threatened sector in advance.

Late in the afternoon, General J. E. B. Stuart stumbles into the headquarters of General Robert E. Lee at Gettysburg, Pennsylvania. An exasperated Lee, who entered the fight without accurate information for lack of proper reconnaissance, curtly declares, "Well, General Stuart, you are here at last."

WEST: Confederate cavalry under Colonel William L. Jackson and Union troopers led by General William W. Averill spar at Beverly, West Virginia.

General John H. Morgan leads 2,500 Confederate cavalry across the Cumberland River at Burkesville, Tennessee, on an extended foray through Kentucky, Indiana, and Ohio.

NAVAL: The USS *Samuel Rotan* seizes the Confederate schooner *Champion* off the Piantatank River, Virginia.

The USS *Cayuga* captures the Confederate sloop *Blue Bell* in the Mermentau River, Louisiana.

The USS *Covington* captures the Confederate steamer *Eureka* near Commerce, Mississippi.

The USS *Juanita* captures the British blockade-runner *Don Jose* at sea.

The Confederate raider CSS *Alabama* under Captain Raphael Semmes captures and burns the Union ship *Anna F. Schmidt* in the South Atlantic.

July 3

NORTH: Throughout the morning, General Robert E. Lee masses additional infantry and artillery along Missionary Ridge, intending to crush the Union center. Again he does so over the protests of General James Longstreet, who favors a wide turning movement around the Union left. But Lee prevails, and at 1:00 P.M., the 140 cannon of General Alexander E. Porter commence to bombard the Union line. The Federals fight back with 100 cannon of their own, initiating the largest artillery duel in American history. Most of the Southern ordnance fired overshoots the Union line, inflicting only minor damage, and after an hour, the Union cannon cease shooting to conserve ammunition. At 3:00 P.M., 15,000 Confederates from the divisions of Generals George E. Pickett, Johnston Pettigrew, and Isaac Trimble advance from the nearby wood lines in paradelike fashion. They traverse what amounts to an absolute killing ground, for the Union batteries are sited carefully to achieve mutual and interlocking fields of fire. Losing heavily at every step, the Southerners nonetheless close the distance and are greeted with concentrated rifle fire. Only a handful of surviving Confederates penetrate Meade's line and are quickly swallowed up or thrown back by Union reserves. Eventually, thousands of wounded and stunned survivors—about half the number committed—stream back across the field toward Seminary Ridge in abject defeat. Lee, surveying the carnage, is heard to murmur, "It's all my fault, my fault."

One act remained to play out. Confederate cavalry under General J. E. B. Stuart, conspicuously absent in the first two days of fighting, are now ordered to seek out and assail the Union rear. En route, Stuart encounters Union cavalry under General David M. Gregg, who fights the Southerners to a standstill in one of the biggest cavalry encounters of the war. The overworked brigade of General George A. Custer particularly distinguishes itself in repeated, headlong charges, after which Stuart draws back, his mission unfulfilled.

The debacle at Gettysburg represents the high tide of Confederate fortunes. Lee's ill-advised switch from a strategic to tactical offensive fails and proves prohibitively costly. Three days of ferocious combat against an enemy enjoying terrain advantages deprives the Army of Northern Virginia of 2,592 killed, 12,709 wounded, and 5,150 missing (20,451)—the actual loss may have been upward of 28,000—a horrific toll of irreplaceable, trained manpower. The Army of the Potomac opposing him, while victorious, is also savaged, sustaining 3,155 dead, 14,529 injured, and 5,365 missing (23,049). Magnifying the Union victory is the fact that the North can far more easily make up such losses. So with Gettysburg, along with events farther west at Vicksburg, a turning point is reached in the course of military events and fortunes. From this date forward, it is no longer a matter of if the Confederacy will lose its bid for independence but rather when.

SOUTH: Union forces abandon Suffolk, Virginia, and withdraw back to Norfolk.

WEST: Confederate cavalry under General John H. Morgan skirmish with Union troops at Columbia, Kentucky, and sustain considerable loss.

The Army of the Cumberland crosses the Elk River, Tennessee, at which point General William S. Rosecrans halts his pursuit of General Braxton Bragg. The Tullahoma campaign to maneuver his adversary out of strong defensive positions succeeds brilliantly, costing Union forces 560 casualties to a Confederate tally of 1,634, 11 cannon, and several tons of supplies captured.

General John C. Pemberton and General Ulysses S. Grant arrange an armistice and confer about surrender terms at Vicksburg, Mississippi. Grant bluntly informs his opposite: "You will be allowed to march out, the officers taking with them their side arms and clothing, and the field, staff, and cavalry officers one horse each. The rank and file will be allowed all their clothing but no other property."

General Theophilus H. Holmes, leading the Confederate District of Arkansas, assembles an army of 7,600 infantry and cavalry to attack Union positions at Helena, Arkansas. His opponent, General Benjamin M. Prentiss, is amply forewarned, diligent, and well prepared for battle.

NAVAL: Armed boats from the USS *Fort Henry* capture the Confederate sloop *Emma* off Sea Horse Key, Florida.

The onset of surrender negotiations at Vicksburg, Mississippi, signals an end to the ongoing bombardment there. Naval personnel fire 16,000 rounds from a variety of ships, gunboats, and mortar boats, in addition to 13 heavy naval guns hauled and handled ashore.

July 4

POLITICS: Confederate vice president Alexander H. Stephens rides the CSS *Torpedo* down the James River under a flag of truce and steams to Hampton Roads, Virginia. There he hopes to meets with Union officials in an attempt to spur dialogue between the two governments, but Federal authorities turn him back.

NORTH: Despite pleas and entreaties from President Abraham Lincoln, General George G. Meade declines to pursue or hound the fleeing Confederates. In light of the horrific casualties recently sustained by his Army of the Potomac, its many officer losses and depleted units, his reluctance is understandable.

The Army of Northern Virginia under General Robert E. Lee withdraws in good order from Gettysburg, Pennsylvania, and marches for Williamsport, Maryland, to recross the Potomac River back to Virginia. Progress is slow owing to incessant rain and a wagon train of wounded stretching 17 miles, but the Federals decline to push the Southerners hard.

West: General John H. Morgan's Confederate cavalry are rebuffed at Green River Bridge, Kentucky.

Vicksburg surrenders to General Ulysses S. Grant after a brutal, seven-week siege. Union losses for the entire campaign amount to roughly 800 killed, 3,900 injured, and 200 missing out of 77,000 committed. The Confederates suffer 900 dead, 2,500 wounded, 200 missing, and 29,491 captured. Surrender at Vicksburg also facilitated the capture of Port Hudson, downstream, four days later. The Confederacy now is cut completely in twain along the Mississippi River, with virtually no ability left to transfer desperately needed food, manpower, or munitions to either side. Thanks to Grant's offensive brilliance, tactical savvy, and ruthlessness to succeed, another tipping point has been reached in military affairs—henceforth, there is no turning back. "Grant is my man," an ebullient president Abraham Lincoln beams, "and I am his the rest of the war."

Union forces defending Helena, Arkansas, under General Benjamin M. Prentiss withstand a determined Confederate attack from Generals Theophilus H. Holmes and Sterling Price. At about 5:00 A.M., Price launches an early morning assault that manages to overrun Union Battery C, but that post then is bombarded thoroughly by surrounding batteries and the gunboat USS *Tyler* on the Mississippi River. Unable to make further headway and unwilling to withstand the a withering cannonade, Price concedes defeat and withdraws at about 11:00 A.M. Southern losses in this badly bungled venture are 380 killed, 1,100 wounded, and another 1,100 taken captive from 7,600 present. The 4,100 Federals lose only 239 killed, wounded, or missing.

Chief Little Crow, who initiated the Santee (Sioux) uprising in Minnesota almost a year earlier, is shot dead by farmers while picking berries.

Naval: Following Vicksburg's capitulation, Admiral David D. Porter's gunboat squadron hoists anchor and sails south to facilitate Port Hudson's reduction.

The Federal gunboat USS *Tyler* intervenes decisively in the defense of Helena, Arkansas, against large Confederate forces, and heavy fire prompts them to retreat.

July 5

North: The retreating Army of Northern Virginia under General Robert E. Lee skirmishes with pursuing Union forces at Cunningham's Cross Roads, Pennsylvania.

South: General Henry W. Wessels leads a Union expedition from Plymouth, North Carolina, toward Confederate troop concentrations at nearby Williamston.

West: Confederate cavalry under General John H. Morgan skirmish with Union troops at Bardstown and Lebanon, Kentucky, taking 400 prisoners. Among the Confederates slain is Morgan's younger brother Thomas.

General William T. Sherman marches from Vicksburg, Mississippi, with 40,000 men in three corps (11 divisions) under Generals Frederick Steele, Edward O. C. Ord, and John G. Parke to recapture Jackson. His first mission is to drive General Joseph E. Johnston's army from behind the Big Black River. The contending forces skirmish along Birdsong Ferry before Union troops construct several bridges and begin to ford. Johnston then retires in good order back to Jackson as Sherman methodically pushes his army forward in pursuit.

July 6

NORTH: The battered Confederate Army of Northern Virginia tramps through Hagerstown, Maryland, unhurried and in excellent marching order. The column then halts at Williamsport to construct pontoon bridges, but the rain-swollen Potomac River remains unfordable for several days. In a desperate and heroic rearguard action, General John D. Imboden thwarts a surprise attack on the Confederate wagon train by General Hugh J. Kilpatrick and John Buford. Imboden skillfully resists until reinforcements under General J. E. B. Stuart arrive and force the Union troopers off.

WEST: The Knights of the Golden Circle, a violent Copperhead group, seize guns and ammunition from a Federal arsenal at Huntington, Indiana.

General William T. Sherman continues pursuing Confederate forces under General Joseph E. Johnston to the vicinity of Jackson, Mississippi.

NAVAL: Admiral John A. Dahlgren relieves Admiral Samuel F. Du Pont of command of the North Atlantic Blockading Squadron off Port Royal, South Carolina. Du Pont's removal is as much about mounting friction with Secretary of the Navy Gideon Welles as it is about his failure before Charleston.

The USS *De Soto* captures the Confederate blockade-runner *Lady Maria* off Clearwater, Florida.

The Confederate raider CSS *Alabama* under Captain Raphael Semmes captures and burns the Union ship *Express* off the Brazilian coast.

July 7

POLITICS: President Abraham Lincoln, buoyed by the news of Vicksburg's surrender, writes, "if General Meade can complete his work, so gloriously prosecuted thus far, by the literal or substantial destruction of Lee's army, the rebellion will be over."

NORTH: The Army of the Potomac under General George G. Meade reoccupies Maryland Heights, Maryland, while President Abraham Lincoln frets over the lack of a more vigorous pursuit.

WEST: Confederate cavalry under General John H. Morgan skirmish with Union troops at Shepherdsville, Kentucky.

General Joseph E. Johnston deploys 26,000 in earthworks in and around Jackson, Mississippi, awaiting an onslaught by superior Union forces under General William T. Sherman. He possesses the divisions of General William W. Loring, John C. Breckinridge, Samuel G. French, and William H. T. Walker, along with a cavalry division under William H. Jackson.

SOUTHWEST: Colonel Kit Carson recruits Ute and Zuni Indians in his continuing campaign against the Navajo.

NAVAL: Confederate raiders under Colonel John H. Morgan seize the steamers *John T. McCombs* and *Alice Dean* at Brandenburg, Kentucky.

The USS *Monongahela* and *New London* trade shots with Confederates batteries near Donaldsonville, Louisiana.

The Confederate raider CSS *Florida* under Lieutenant John N. Maffitt captures the Union ship *Sunrise,* releasing it on a bond.

July 8

NORTH: General Andrew A. Humphreys is designated chief of staff, Army of the Potomac.

SOUTH: Generals Nathaniel P. Banks and Franklin Gardner negotiate for the surrender of Port Hudson, Louisiana. Gardner, while low on food, initially balks at capitulation until hearing of Vicksburg's demise.

WEST: General John H. Morgan crosses the Ohio River at Cumming's Ferry, Kentucky, and begins to raid Indiana and southern Ohio. There is some apprehension that Morgan's presence might rekindle pro-Confederate Copperhead activities in that region.

NAVAL: Armed boats from the USS *Restless* and *Rosalie* seize the Confederate schooner *Ann* in Horse Creek, Florida.

A Federal gunboat squadron sails 500 miles up the Ohio River to help thwart a Confederate cavalry raid mounted by Colonel John H. Morgan. En route, they recapture the steamers *John T. McCombs* and *Alice Dean*.

July 9

SOUTH: An accidental ordnance explosion at Fort Lyon, Virginia, kills 20 Union soldiers and wounds 14 more.

General Quincy A. Gillmore orders the landing of troops on James Island, west of Morris Island, Charleston Harbor, South Carolina, as a diversion prior to launching an all-out assault on Battery Wagner. The operation concludes without serious resistance.

After a heroic, 47-day siege, Confederate general Franklin Gardner surrenders Port Hudson, Louisiana, to the Army of the Gulf under General Nathaniel P. Banks. The Southerners lose roughly 146 killed, 447 wounded and 6,400 captured while Union losses top 708 dead, 3,336 injured, and 319 missing. Another 4,000 to 5,000 men are incapacitated by disease or heat stroke. But victory here removes the last Confederate obstruction on the Mississippi River, which can now be navigated freely as far north as St. Louis, Missouri.

WEST: General John H. Morgan's Confederate raiders skirmish with Union troops at Corydon, Indiana.

General William T. Sherman and three corps continue advancing on Jackson, Mississippi, skirmishing while approaching the town of Clinton. General Joseph E. Johnston, commanding the Confederate Department of the West, hastily makes preparations to resist his onslaught.

NAVAL: Armed boats from the USS *Tahoma* seize a large flatboat loaded with supplies near Manatee River, Florida.

July 10

NORTH: Quincy A. Gillmore is promoted to major general, U.S. Army, replacing General David Hunter as commander of the Department of the South. He inherits a force of 11,000 soldiers, 350 cannon, and 400 engineers, along with orders to capture Charleston, South Carolina. This he prepares to do in earnest.

General Robert E. Lee begins to concentrate his forces around Williamsport, Maryland, while Union forces skirmish with his rear guard.

South: The siege of Charleston, South Carolina, begins as General Quincy A. Gillmore lands 3,700 Federal troops of General George C. Strong's brigade on Morris Island, overpowering Confederate forces stationed there. Gillmore next begins to prepare to carry Battery Wagner, a strategic point garrisoned by General William B. Taliaferro. This officer commands 900 men and several cannon in a stout, low-lying sand-and-palmetto fortification whose strength belies its nondescript appearance. Many Northerners also regard Charleston as the "cradle of the Confederacy," and its capture remains a political imperative. Initial operations here cost Union forces 15 dead and 91 injured; Confederate losses are 294 killed, wounded, and missing.

As a diversion for the impending assault against Battery Wagner, Gilmore dispatches Colonel Thomas W. Higginson on an expedition to burn a bridge on the South Edisto River below Morris Island. This consists of 250 men of his own 1st South Carolina Colored Infantry and the 1st Connecticut Battery, carried by a steamer, a tug, and a transport. Things quickly go awry when progress up the Edisto halts at the confluence of the Pon Pon River, where sharp timber spikes were thrown across the river's neck. While negotiating these obstacles, the tug *Governor Milton* and the transport *Enoch Dean* ground while being shelled by Confederate land batteries along Willstown Bluff. After several failed attempts to attack the bridge, Higgson orders the grounded ships burned, and he steams back to base.

West: Confederate raiders under General John H. Morgan skirmish with Union troops at Salem, Indiana.

A quick raid on Union City, Tennessee, by Confederate troops under Colonel J. B. Biffle nets 100 Federal prisoners.

Union forces under General William T. Sherman begin to invest the state capital of Jackson, Mississippi, intending to drive off Confederates under General Joseph E. Johnston.

Naval: The USS *Shenandoah* and *Ethan Allen* sortie from Boston Navy Yard, Massachusetts, to scour the seas for the Confederate raider CSS *Florida*.

Admiral John A. Dahlgren initiates a second naval siege of Charleston, South Carolina, by bombarding Confederate positions on Morris Island. The ironclads USS *Nahant, Weehawken, Catskill,* and *Montauk* subsequently are damaged by Confederate artillery fire, none seriously. This attack also signals another prolonged period of shelling at Charleston.

The USS *New London,* steaming from Donaldsonville, Louisiana, to New Orleans, is attacked en route by Confederate artillery and damaged.

July 11

Diplomacy: American minister to Britain Charles F. Adams strongly denounces the British practice of building ironclads and outfitting blockade-runners for the Confederacy. He makes clear to Foreign Secretary Earl John Russell that Northern patience is running out over such transgressions.

North: The implementation of the draft law stirs resentment among New York's lower classes, which are mostly Irish and highly resentful toward African Americans.

South: General Daniel H. Hill is appointed lieutenant general, C.S.A., over the objections of President Jefferson Davis, who resents Hill's criticism of his good friend and confidant General Braxton Bragg.

A Union assault on Battery Wagner, Charleston Harbor, South Carolina, is launched by General Quincy A. Gillmore. The force consists of several companies of the 7th Connecticut, backed up by additional men from the 9th Maine and 76th Pennsylvania. However, Gillmore seriously underestimates Southern defenses and is unaware that the garrison had been enlarged to 1,200 men recently. Owing to the island's peculiar geography, all attacks funneling along a narrow strip of beach are amply covered by the fort's heavy cannon. The ensuing assault is easily beaten back with a Union loss of 49 killed, 123 wounded, and 167 missing while the Confederates sustain only six dead and six wounded. The besiegers then bring up an assortment of 40-rifled cannon and mortars and maintain a relentless barrage until another attack can be mounted.

Naval: The USS *Yankee* captures the Confederate schooner *Cassandra* at Jones Point on the Rappahannock River.

July 12

North: The Army of the Potomac under General George G. Meade advances to Williamsport, Maryland, to confront the Army of Northern Virginia under General Robert E. Lee. Once Meade beholds the array of Confederate earthworks stretching for several miles, however, he relents from attacking and builds fortifications of his own.

West: General John H. Morgan's raiding party reaches Vernon, Indiana.

Troops under Generals William T. Sherman and Joseph E. Johnston spar in the vicinity of Clinton, Mississippi. Union forces unleash a lengthy bombardment of Confederate fortifications, and suddenly a brigade under Colonel Isaac Pugh attacks Confederate redoubts defended by General John C. Breckinridge. Pugh does so unsupported and without authorization, losing 500 out of 800 men. Consequently, General Jacob G. Lauman, Pugh's divisional commander, is relieved of command.

Naval: The USS *Penobscot* forces the Confederate blockade-runner *Kate* ashore at Smith's Island, North Carolina, but fails to destroy it.

July 13

Politics: President Abraham Lincoln admonishes General John M. Schofield, commanding in Missouri, over his arrest of William McKee, editor of the *St. Louis Missouri Democrat,* for alleged antiwar activity.

North: Violent antidraft riots erupt in New York shortly after the first names are drawn for induction. At length, a seething mob of 50,000 Irish émigrés attacks the draft office, burning it to the ground. During the next four days, violence escalates until Federal troops are brought in to restore order. More than 1,000 people, principally African Americans targeted by the Irish, are killed or injured.

At Williamsport, Maryland, General Robert E. Lee orders pontoon bridges thrown immediately across the Potomac River, as waters levels begin to subside. That same day, General George G. Meade orders a cavalry reconnaissance of Confederate positions at Williamsport for the following morning.

SOUTH: The Army of Northern Virginia under General Robert E. Lee begins to cross the Potomac River back into Virginia, ending his celebrated and costly second invasion of the North.

Major fighting erupts along Bayou La Fourche, Louisiana, as the Union brigades of Colonel Nathan A. M. Dudley and Joseph S. Morgan advance down both banks to dislodge a Confederate force under General Joseph Green. Green, however, decides to strike first and, with only 700 troops at his disposal, strikes Dudley on both flanks simultaneously. The Federal force quickly folds and falls back in confusion. On the east bank, Morgan's brigade advances to engage with a smaller party of 400 Confederates, but their commander inexplicably panics and withdraws. The emboldened Southerners then charge, routing their opponents. The disgraced Morgan retreats all the way back to Donaldsonville, Louisiana, where he is accused of inebriation and is discharged.

WEST: General John H. Morgan takes his Confederate cavalry into Ohio, and martial law is declared in Cincinnati.

Yazoo City and Natchez, Mississippi, fall to Union forces under General Francis J. Herron.

NAVAL: Commodore Hiram Paulding positions gunboats around New York City to help restore order during the draft riots there.

The USS *Katahdin* captures the British blockade-runner *Excelsior* at San Luis Pass, Texas.

The USS *Forest Rose* and *Petrel* capture the Confederate steamer *Elmira* on the Tensas River, Louisiana.

The USS *Rattler* and *Manitou* capture the Confederate steamer *Louisville* in the Little Red River, Louisiana.

A river squadron consisting of the USS *Baron de Kalb, Kenwood, Signal, New National,* and *Black Hawk* convoys 5,000 Union troops up the Yazoo River to attack Yazoo City, Mississippi. The town falls, and 17 Confederate vessels are scuttled, but the *Baron de Kalb* hits a mine and sinks.

Commander David S. McDougal of the USS *Wyoming,* apprised of the unprovoked attack on the American vessel *Pembroke* in the Shimonoseki Straits, Japan, weighs anchor at Yokohama and prepares to deal directly with the offenders.

July 14

POLITICS: President Abraham Lincoln, disillusioned by General George G. Meade's lax pursuit of retreating Confederates, indelicately informs him, "Your golden opportunity is gone and I am distressed immeasurably because of it."

NORTH: The Army of Northern Virginia steadily evacuates Willamsport, Maryland, after throwing pontoon bridges across the Potomac River and marching back into Virginia. The main force arrives in safety, leaving behind two divisions under General Henry Heth as a rear guard. However, at 7:00 A.M., General George A. Custer's cavalry brigade sweeps into nearby Falling Waters, rounding up several stragglers. General John Buford's division is also en route, but General Hugh J. Kilpatrick arrives first and orders two companies of the 6th Michigan Cavalry to charge two entire Confederate brigades. They sacrifice themselves heroically, and in the ensuing melee manage to mortally wound the capable Confederate general James J. Petti-grew, a popular and effective officer. Custer then throws the balance of his regiment forward as skirmishers, just as Buford's division deploys behind the Southerners. In brief fighting, the Federals capture 719 prisoners, three battle flags, and two can-non, but Confederate losses would have been far greater had Kilpatrick restrained himself until all his cavalry was up in force. This action concludes General Robert E. Lee's second invasion of the north.

SOUTH: Union forces capture Fort Powhatan on the James River, Virginia, which opens that waterway to naval forces as far as Drewry's Bluff.

WEST: General John H. Morgan's Confederate raiders skirmish with Union troops at Camp Dennison, outside Cincinnati, Ohio.

General Joseph E. Johnston, entrenched at Jackson, Mississippi, learns of a large Federal ammunition supply wagon headed from Vicksburg to reinforce the army of General William T. Sherman before him. He thereupon dispatches his entire cavalry force under General William H. Jackson to intercept these supplies and preclude Sherman's anticipated bombardment. After the effort fails, Johnston feels he has little recourse but to abandon the town in the face of overwhelming numbers.

NAVAL: The Federal gunboat squadron under Admiral Samuel P. Lee consisting of USS *Sagamon, Lehigh, Mahaska, Morse, Commodore Barry, Commodore Jones, Sho-kokon,* and *Seymour* capture Fort Powhatan on the James River, Virginia.

The USS *R. R. Cuyler* captures the Confederate steamer *Kate Dale* off the Tor-tugas, Florida.

The USS *Jasmine* seizes the Confederate sloop *Relampago* off the Florida Keys.

July 15

POLITICS: Stricken by news of Gettysburg, Vicksburg, and Port Hudson, a somber president Jefferson Davis intones, "The clouds are truly dark over us."

WEST: Confederate raiders under General John H. Morgan, stymied by stiffening Federal resistance, swing west of Cincinnati, preparing to recross the Ohio River. Union forces on both land and water are in hot pursuit and are closing the gap.

SOUTHWEST: After the Arkansas River becomes fordable, Union general James G. Blunt assembles 3,000 men (mostly Indians and African Americans) and two bat-teries for a preemptive strike against 6,000 Confederates gathering at Elk Creek, Indian Territory. He intends to disperse General Douglas H. Cooper's command before he is reinforced by 3,000 additional Confederates under General William L. Cabell. Should such a preponderance of numbers concentrate, they will force Federal troops to surrender Fort Gibson, Indiana Territory, thereby ceding control of the region to the South.

NAVAL: The USS *Yankee* captures the Confederate schooner *Nanjemoy* in the Coan River, Virginia.

Armed boats from the USS *Stars and Stripes* and *Somerset* destroy Confederate saltworks at Marsh's Island, Florida.

The USS *Santiago de Cuba* captures the Confederate steamer *Lizzie* off the Flor-ida coast.

July 16

SOUTH: Union troops under General Alfred H. Terry repel a determined Confederate attack on James Island, South Carolina, despite heavy shelling from Grimball's Landing on the nearby Stono River.

WEST: General Joseph E. Johnston begins a nighttime evacuation of Jackson, Mississippi, rather than face envelopment by General William T. Sherman. He accordingly falls back across the Pearl River in the darkness and withdraws to Morton, 30 miles farther east. Confederate casualties in the "siege" of Jackson total about 600 while Sherman's losses are 1,122.

NAVAL: The steamer *Imperial* docks at New Orleans, Louisiana, from St. Louis, Missouri. It is the first vessel to travel the Mississippi River in uninterrupted fashion for more than two years.

The USS *Pawnee* and *Marblehead* are hit repeatedly during a Confederate assault on Union positions on James Island, South Carolina. They nonetheless respond with heavy supporting fire, and the attackers are driven off with loss.

Armed boats from the USS *Port Royal* seize a cotton shipment ready for departure through the blockade at Apalachicola, Florida.

The Confederate raider CSS *Georgia* under Lieutenant William L. Maury captures the Union ship *Prince of Wales* and releases it on a bond.

The USS *Wyoming* under Commander David S. McDougal is fired on by several Japanese shore batteries while passing Shimonoseki Straits, Japan. A flotilla of small junks and steamers then sorties to engage him. *Wyoming* counters by firing heavy guns at close range, completely gutting the Japanese vessels and silencing the batteries. American losses are four dead and seven wounded. The attack had been mounted by the daimyo of Chosu, who determines to embarrass the Tokugawa shogunate and possibly hasten its downfall.

Confederate naval agent James D. Bulloch contracts with the French firm of Lucien Arman to construct an ironclad warship that eventually emerges as CSS *Stonewall*.

July 17

SOUTH: Federal siege guns continue flailing away at Battery Wagner, Charleston Harbor, South Carolina, in preparation for a second assault. The 1,300 Confederate defenders remain safely ensconced in their bombproofs and, despite a deluge of ordnance pouring down on them, suffer only eight killed and 20 wounded in two days.

WEST: Jackson, Mississippi, falls a second time to Union forces under General William T. Sherman. He orders the division of General Frank P. Blair to protect the civilian population from looting, but the town is sacked nonetheless by vengeful Northerners.

SOUTHWEST: A force of 3,000 Union troops under General James G. Blunt attack General Douglas H. Cooper's 6,000 Confederate Choctaw, Cherokee, and Texans at Honey Springs, Indian Territory. Cooper enjoys larger numbers, but Blunt possesses more cannon and higher-quality ammunition. Following a protracted artillery duel, Blunt sends his 1st Kansas Colored Infantry and 2nd Indian Home Guard forward against the Confederate center. They are received hotly by the dismounted 20th and 29th Texas Cavalry, whose heavy fire routs the Federal Indians. This induces the Texans to charge home against the 1st Colored, which bravely holds its ground and allows the screaming rebels to approach closely before devastating them with point-blank volleys. The Texans suddenly turn and run, taking a large part of Cooper's center with them.

Aggressive by nature, Blunt advances and outflanks Douglas twice before his Indians mount a whooping counterattack that fails, but that buys them sufficient time to cross the Elk River to safety. Union forces then charge into the Confederate encampment at Elk Creek, burning tons of valuable supplies and safely withdrawing before General William L. Cabell's division arrives. Blunt's prompt action saves the Indian Territory for the Union. Honey Springs is also the largest encounter waged in the Indian territory; Union losses are recorded as 13 dead and 47 captured to a Confederate loss estimated at 134 killed and wounded, with 47 missing. Curiously, this was the first time that Native Americans found themselves pitted against African Americans, who greatly distinguished themselves in combat.

NAVAL: The Federal ram USS *Monarch* assists Union troops in recapturing Hickman, Kentucky, from Confederate cavalry.

July 18

SOUTH: A second Federal assault on Battery Wagner, Charleston Harbor, South Carolina, devolves on two brigades of 6,000 men under Colonel H. S. Putnam and General Thomas G. Stevenson. The attack, which kicks off at 7:45 P.M., is courageously spearheaded by Colonel Robert G. Shaw's African-American 54th Massachusetts, which, ignoring heavy fire and losses, clambers up the Confederate parapet and plants its flag. Consequently, Sergeant William H. Carney becomes the first African-American soldier to win the Medal of Honor in this conflict. Other Union columns also score minor lodgments elsewhere, but the roused Confederates quickly contain or eject all of them. Extremely heavy losses ensue, including five out of six regimental commanders, and General Quincy A. Gillmore calls off the attempt. Union casualties total 246 dead, 880 wounded, and 389 missing (1,515), including the heroic Colonel Shaw. Moreover, the exemplary conduct of his 54th Massachusetts Infantry affords dramatic proof that African Americans will and can fight well if only given the chance. The Confederates, meanwhile, suffer only 36 killed, 133 wounded, and five missing. This latest repulse induces Gilmore to initiate formal siege operations.

General Edward E. Potter leads a Federal expedition from New Bern, North Carolina, against nearby Rocky Mount.

General John G. Foster takes command of the Department of Virginia and North Carolina.

WEST: A skirmish at Pomeroy, Ohio, indicates that Federal troops are closing their noose around Confederate raiders under General John H. Morgan.

NAVAL: Gunfire from the USS *Jacob Bell*, *Resolute*, and *Racer* drive off Confederate infantry attempting to capture the Federal vessel *George Peabody*, which had run aground at Matthias Point, Virginia.

Admiral John A. B. Dahlgren's ironclad squadron, consisting of the USS *Montauk*, *New Ironsides*, *Catskill*, *Nantucket*, *Weehawken*, and *Patapsco*, lends heavy supporting fire during the failed assault on Battery Wagner. Firing begins at 12:00 P.M., and the vessels close to within 300 yards of Confederate works, but the moment

The 54th Massachusetts Volunteer Infantry Regiment fighting on Morris Island, where their heroic actions in battle helped dispel skepticism in those who believed that blacks could not be good soldiers *(The National Guard Heritage)*

his vessels cease fire to allow for the Union infantry assault, the defenders suddenly reemerge and repulse them.

The USS *De Soto, Ossipee,* and *Kennebec* capture the Confederate steamers *James Battle* and *William Bagley* in the Gulf of Mexico.

Armed boats from the USS *Vincennes* and *Clifton* capture the Confederate barge *H. McGuin* on Bay St. Louis, Mississippi.

July 19

NORTH: New York merchants organize relief for African-American victims of the recent draft riots.

WEST: The Army of the Potomac crosses over the Potomac River into Harper's Ferry and down the Shenandoah Valley.

Federal troops under Generals Edward H. Hobson and James M. Shackleford heavily defeat General John H. Morgan's Confederate raiders at Buffington Island on the Ohio River; 800 captives are taken.

Confederate general Daniel H. Hill replaces General William J. Hardee as commander of the II Corps, Army of Tennessee.

NAVAL: The USS *Canandaigua* drives the Confederate steamer *Raccoon* aground in Charleston Harbor, South Carolina.

After traversing 500 miles in the past 10 days, Federal gunboats USS *Moose, Reindeer, Victory, Springfield, Naumkeag, Allegheny, Belle, Fairplay,* and *Silver Lake* outflank Buffington Island in the Ohio River, thereby cutting the retreat of Confederate raiders under Colonel John H. Morgan. Pursuing Union forces take 3,000 prisoners, along with all of Morgan's artillery.

July 20

SOUTH: General George W. Getty assumes command of VII Corps in the Union Department of Virginia and North Carolina.

WEST: The straggling survivors of General John H. Morgan's raid skirmish with Union troops near Hockingport and Coal Hill, Ohio, before riding north from the Ohio River.

NAVAL: The USS *Shawsheen* captures the Confederate schooners *Sally, Helen Jane, Elizabeth, Dolphin,* and *James Brice* off Cedar Island, Neuse River, North Carolina.

July 21

WEST: General John D. Imboden is appointed commander of the Confederate Valley District, Virginia.

NAVAL: Armed boats from the USS *Owasco* and *Cayuga* capture and sink the Confederate schooner *Revenge* off Sabine Pass, Texas.

The transport USS *Sallie Ward* runs aground at Island No. 82 on the Mississippi River and is subsequently destroyed by Confederate artillery fire.

July 22

NAVAL: The New York Chamber of Commerce releases figures stating Union losses to Confederate raiders at 150 vessels worth $12 million. This is stark testimony to the effectiveness of the oceanic raiders CSS *Alabama, Florida,* and *Georgia* and their wily commanders.

The U.S. Navy lands and crews a four-gun battery ashore at Morris Island, Charleston Harbor, South Carolina, to assist bombarding nearby Fort Sumter.

July 23

WEST: Federal forces occupy Manassas Gap, western Virginia, but prove unable to intercept the Army of Northern Virginia and prevent it from moving down the Luray Valley into the Shenandoah region. An advance on Wapping Heights by General William H. French's III Corps, Army of the Potomac, is rebuffed by Confederates under General Richard S. Ewell.

July 24

SOUTH: Federal troops under General Quincy A. Gilmore continue consolidating their hold on Morris Island and Battery Wagner, Charleston Harbor, South Carolina.

In response to perceived French hostility toward the United States, evinced by the occupation of Mexico City, General Nathaniel P. Banks is ordered to prepare troops at New Orleans, Louisiana, for an expedition to the Texas coast.

NAVAL: The USS *Iroquois* captures the Confederate blockade-runner *Merrimac* off the North Carolina coast.

The USS *Arago* seizes the Confederate steamer *Emma* near Wilmington, North Carolina.

Federal warships USS *New Ironsides, Weehawken, Patapsco, Montauk, Catskill, Nantucket, Paul Jones, Ottawa, Seneca,* and *Dai Ching* under Admiral John A. B. Dahlgren bombard Battery Wagner in Charleston Harbor, South Carolina, to support army operations.

July 25

SOUTH: Union forces scouting the region around Goose Creek, Virginia, are twice ambushed and badly mauled by Virginia Partisan Rangers under Major John S. Mosby and withdraw.

A Federal expedition from Portsmouth, Virginia, against Jackson, North Carolina, ends with the death of Confederate general Matt Whitaker.

WEST: Confederate cavalry under Colonel John S. Scott embark on a three-week raid into eastern Kentucky with a pitched battle at Williamsburg.

The Confederate Department of East Tennessee is absorbed into the Department of Tennessee under General Braxton Bragg.

A Federal expedition out of Natchez, Mississippi, burns cotton mills and other buildings at nearby Kingston, Liberty, and Woodville.

After wreaking havoc with Confederate rail lines, General William T. Sherman withdraws from Jackson, Mississippi, and marches back to Vicksburg.

July 26

POLITICS: Kentucky U.S. senator John J. Crittenden, author of the Crittenden Compromise of 1860, dies in Frankfort, Kentucky.

WEST: After a continuous running fight of several days, General John H. Morgan and his remaining 364 troopers surrender at Salineville, Ohio. He is slated for confinement at the Ohio State Penitentiary in Columbus.

Confederate cavalry under Colonel John S. Scott skirmish with Federal troops at Rogersville, Kentucky.

SOUTHWEST: Former Texas governor Sam Houston, who refused to take an oath of allegiance to the Confederacy, dies on his ranch at the age of 70.

July 27

NAVAL: The USS *Clifton,* supported by the *Estrella, Hollyhock,* and *Sachem,* trade shots with Confederate artillery along the Atchafalaya River, Louisiana.

The Confederate raider CSS *Florida* under Lieutenant John N. Maffitt sails from Bermuda with a full complement of coal and ammunition and makes for Brest, France, to effect a major overhaul.

July 28

POLITICS: President Jefferson Davis, taking stock over recent Confederate misfortunes, writes that, "If a victim would secure the success of our cause, I would freely offer myself."

SOUTH: At Aldie, Virginia, Major John S. Mosby and his partisan rangers seize several Union wagons but subsequently lose them to a sharp counterattack.

NAVAL: Armed boats from USS *Beauregard* and *Oleander* raid New Smyrna, Florida, backed by the guns of *Sagamore* and *Para*. Several schooners and a large supply of cotton, ready for export, were all put to the torch.

July 29

DIPLOMACY: Queen Victoria informs Parliament that she sees "No reason to depart from the strict neutrality which Her Majesty has observed from the beginning of the contest." This is the latest blow to Confederate hopes for European military intervention.

SOUTH: General Innis N. Palmer takes charge of the XVIII Corps in the Union Department of Virginia and North Carolina.

NAVAL: The USS *Niphon* captures the British blockade-runner *Banshee* at New Inlet, North Carolina.

The USS *Shawsheen* seizes the Confederate schooner *Telegraph* in Rose Bay, North Carolina.

The USS *Rosalie* captures the British blockade-runner *Georgie* on the Caloosahatchie River, Florida.

Admiral David G. Farragut is relieved of blockading duty along the Texas coast by Admiral Charles H. Bell and sets sail for New York in USS *Hartford*.

July 30

POLITICS: President Abraham Lincoln threatens to execute captured Confederate officers and to subject Southern soldiers to hard labor if captured Union officers are harmed in any manner for leading African-American troops or if former slaves are returned to bondage.

July 31

WEST: General John A. Logan and 1,700 Union cavalrymen skirmish with Confederates at St. Catharine's Creek, Mississippi.

NAVAL: The Confederate raider CSS *Tuscaloosa* under Lieutenant John Low captures the Union ship *Santee* at sea, releasing it on a bond.

August 1

POLITICS: To ameliorate mounting desertion problems, President Jefferson Davis offers an amnesty to all ranks who are present without leave, warning that they have no choice but "victory, or subjugation, slavery, and utter ruin of yourselves, your families, and your country."

The Union IV and VII Corps are broken up and absorbed by other commands.

SOUTH: Vengeful Union troops vigorously corner the partisan rangers of Major John S. Mosby, taking several prisoners at Warrenton Junction, Virginia.

WEST: Noted Confederate spy Belle Boyd is again arrested at Martinsburg, West Virginia, and sent to Washington, D.C., for imprisonment.

A gathering of an estimated 3,000 to 12,000 Democrats at Matton, Illinois, assembles to hear Peace Democrat John R. Eden denounce the administration of

President Abraham Lincoln. Coles County remains a hotbed of antiwar agitation for the rest of the war.

Confederate cavalry under Colonel John S. Scott skirmish with Union troops at Smith's Shoals on the Cumberland River, just prior to crossing back to Tennessee.

A Union cavalry division under General John W. Davidson begins a concerted drive against Confederates at Little Rock, Arkansas.

Naval: The USS *Yankee* captures the sloop *Clara Ann* off the Coan River, Virginia.

Federal gunboats attack the Confederate steamer *Chesterfield* in Charleston Harbor, which thoroughly alarms the defenders.

Admiral David D. Porter formally succeeds Admiral David G. Farragut as commander of all naval forces and operations along the Mississippi River.

August 2

South: General Quincy A. Gillmore, commanding Federals forces outside Charleston, South Carolina, orders the construction of a siege battery built upon the swampy ground of Morris Island in the harbor. This is the future site for on 8-inch rifle Parrot cannon firing 200-pound projectiles, which is quickly dubbed "Swamp Angel" by the troops.

August 3

Politics: To discourage continuing violence, New York governor Horatio Seymour asks President Abraham Lincoln to suspend conscription in his state. The president declines.

South: Wade Hampton and Fitzhugh Lee are appointed major general, C.S.A.

West: The Union IX Corps is transferred from Vicksburg, Mississippi, back to Kentucky.

Naval: A naval reconnaissance consisting of the USS *Sangamon, Cohasset,* and *Commodore Barney* steams up the James River, Virginia, in a naval squadron commanded by Captain Guert Gansevoort.

August 4

South: General John Buford and the 1st Cavalry Division, I Corps, fight with Confederate troops at Brandy Station, Virginia.

Naval: Armed Confederate boat crews from the CSS *Chicora* and *Palmetto State* capture a Union picket at Vincent's Creek, Morris, Island, Charleston.

August 5

West: Union cavalry under General William W. Averell begin a protracted raid from Winchester, Virginia, toward Franklin, West Virginia. He leads a force of 2,000 men, including four mounted regiments and two batteries, with orders to destroy Confederate saltpeter and gunpowder works there.

General Frederick Steele assumes command of Federal forces at Helena, Arkansas.

Naval: The USS *Commodore Barney* is damaged heavily by a Confederate electric mine off Dutch Gap, on the James River, Virginia. The vessel would have been completely destroyed save for the device's premature detonation.

The U.S. Marine detachment under Major Jacob Zeilin, augmented to 500 men, lands on Morris Island, Charleston Harbor, South Carolina.

The Confederate raider CSS *Alabama* under Captain Raphael Semmes captures the Union bark *Sea Bride* off Cape of Good Hope, South Africa; the prize is then sold to an English merchant.

August 6

POLITICS: President Jefferson Davis assures a jittery governor Milledge L. Bonham of South Carolina of his continuing support for the defense of Charleston, "which we pray will never be polluted by the footsteps of a lustful, relentless, inhuman foe."

SOUTH: Major John S. Mosby and his partisan rangers seize Union sutler's wagons near Fairfax Court House, Virginia.

NAVAL: The Federal gunboat expedition up the James River, Virginia, consisting of USS *Sagamon, Cohasset,* and *Commodore Barney* are fired on by Confederate artillery. The latter vessel is struck 30 times, including one shot through the boilers, which disables it.

An armed launch from CSS *Juno* captures a Federal launch from USS *Wabash* in Charleston Harbor, South Carolina.

The USS *Fort Henry* captures the Confederate sloop *Southern Star* off St. Martin's Reef, Florida.

The USS *Antonia* captures the British blockade-runner *Betsey* off Corpus Christi, Texas.

The USS *Paw Paw* hits a snag on the Mississippi River and sinks near Hardin's Point, Arkansas.

The Confederate raider CSS *Florida* under Lieutenant John N. Maffitt captures the Union vessel *Francis B. Cutting* and releases it on bond.

August 7

WEST: The Union XIII Corps under General Cadwallader C. Washburn is transferred from the Department of the Tennessee to the Department of the Gulf.

NAVAL: Naval gunfire from the USS *Mound City* breaks up a Confederate mounted attack near Lake Providence, Louisiana.

August 8

SOUTH: General Robert E. Lee tenders his resignation to President Jefferson Davis because of Lee's recent failure at Gettysburg, but the offer is declined.

NAVAL: The USS *Sagamore* captures the British blockade-runners *Clara Louise, Southern Rights,* and *Shot,* along with the Confederate schooner *Ann* off the Florida coast.

August 10

POLITICS: At a meeting with President Abraham Lincoln, abolitionist Frederick Douglass stridently protests the inequality of pay between white and black soldiers, despite assurances from recruiters that they would be paid the same.

SOUTH: Once the XIII Corps arrives at Carrollton, Louisiana, General Edward O. C. Ord is appointed the new commander.

WEST: General Frederick Steele leads Federal forces toward Little Rock, Arkansas, from Helena.

SOUTHWEST: Confederate regiments at Galveston, Texas, mutiny over a lack of rations and furloughs, but order is gradually restored.

NAVAL: Admiral David G. Farragut receives a tumultuous hero's welcome as the USS *Hartford* arrives at New York City.

The USS *Princess Royal* captures the Confederate vessel *Atlantic* off the Rio Grande, Texas. However, the vessel is recaptured by its crew and sails into Havana, Cuba.

The USS *Cayuga* seizes the Confederate schooner *J. T. Davis* off the Rio Grande, Texas.

August 11

SOUTH: A quick raid by Virginia Partisan Rangers under Major John S. Mosby nets 19 Union wagons at Annandale, Virginia.

Confederate cannon at Battery Wagner, Fort Sumter, and James Island unleash a sudden bombardment of Union positions on Morris Island, Charleston Harbor, South Carolina, forcing fatigue parties to scurry for cover.

August 12

NORTH: President Abraham Lincoln declines to reappoint General John A. McClernand to a new command, effectively ending his military career.

SOUTH: Federal artillerists initiate counterbattery fire with heavy Parrott rifles against Battery Wagner and Fort Sumter, Charleston Harbor, South Carolina. The brick walls of the latter post suffer considerable damage, and within hours, most of its guns are dismounted.

NAVAL: The USS *Princess Royal* captures the British blockade-runner *Flying Scud* off Brazos, Texas.

Admiral Charles H. Bell of the Pacific Squadron orders the USS *Narragansett* to patrol the waters between San Francisco and Acapulco, Mexico, to protect American mail steamers better.

The experimental submarine CSS *Hunley* heads for Charleston, South Carolina, to bolster the defenses of that beleaguered city against a Union flotilla offshore. A novelty, the submarine consists of an iron steam boiler that has been waterproofed and fitted with tapered bow and stern sections. The Hunley is 40 feet long and only 3.5 feet in diameter, being propelled by five men operating a crankshaft-driven propeller.

August 13

NAVAL: A Federal squadron consisting of the USS *Lexington, Cricket,* and *Marmora* steams up the White River, Arkansas, lands at Des Arc, and destroys a telegraph office and some wires. The next day, the Confederate steamers *Kaskakia* and *Thomas Sugg* are also captured en route back to the Red River.

August 14

NORTH: General George G. Meade takes leave of the Army of the Potomac to visit Washington, D.C., to discuss forthcoming strategy with President Abraham Lincoln and his cabinet.

SOUTH: Command of the Union XI Corps reverts to General John J. Peck.

WEST: A building housing the captured sisters of known Confederate guerrillas collapses in Kansas City, Missouri, killing five. This act enrages scattered bands of irregulars, who coalesce and begin to plot grim retaliation.

NAVAL: The USS *Bermuda* captures the British blockade-runners *Carmita* and *Artist* off the Texas coast.

August 15

SOUTH: A Union sweep of the region between Centreville and Aldie, Virginia, fails to snare Confederate raider Major John S. Mosby but acquires several prisoners belonging to his command.

NAVAL: The Confederate submarine CSS *Hunley* arrives at Charleston, South Carolina, from Mobile, Alabama, on two covered railroad cars. General Pierre G. T. Beauregard, commanding the city's defenses, is eager to impress the experimental device into active service.

August 16

SOUTH: General Gouverneur K. Warren assumes command of the II Corps, Army of the Potomac.

WEST: After considerable prodding from the government, General William S. Rosecrans pushes his Army of the Cumberland out of Tullahoma and south toward Chattanooga. He brings with him the XXI Corps of General Thomas L. Crittenden, General George H. Thomas's XIV Corps, and General Alexander M. McCook's XX Corps. Due to mountainous terrain before him, Rosecrans plans to spread the three columns widely to cover all three passes, a risky ploy that endangers his command with defeat in detail. Nonetheless, additional forces under General Ambrose E. Burnside also depart Camp Nelson, Lexington, Kentucky, and advance into East Tennessee. By dint of effective maneuvering, Rosecrans intends to catch General Braxton Bragg's Confederates between himself and Burnside's force.

NAVAL: The USS *Pawnee* narrowly escapes serious damage when an electric torpedo (mine) explodes under its stern at Stono Inlet, South Carolina. In response, Admiral John A. B. Dalhgren orders large nets stretched across the inlet to prevent additional mines from transiting to the fleet.

The USS *De Soto* captures the Confederate steamer *Alice Vivian* in the Gulf of Mexico.

The USS *Gertrude* seizes the Confederate steamer *Warrior* at sea.

The USS *Rhode Island* captures the British blockade-runner *Cronstadt* off Man of War Bay, Abaco, Bahamas.

August 17

SOUTH: General Quincy A. Gilmore orders 11 heavy gun on Morris Island, Charleston Harbor, South Carolina, to commence the first saturation bombardment of Fort Sumter. They fire 938 shots on the first day alone, shattering its remaining brick structures.

NAVAL: The USS *Satellite* captures the Confederate schooner *Three Brothers* in the Great Wicomico River, Maryland.

The USS *Crocus* runs aground at night on Bodlies Island, North Carolina, and subsequently is abandoned.

Admiral John A. B. Dahlgren's squadron takes up bombardment positions in a joint attack on Confederate defenses in Charleston, South Carolina. Present are the ironclads USS *Weehawken, Catskill, Nahant, Montauk, Passaic, Patapsco,* and *New Ironside,* assisted by the gunboats *Canandaigua, Mahaska, Cimarron, Ottawa, Wissahocken, Dai Ching, Seneca,* and *Lodona.* During the next five days, the fleet concentrates its fire on various defensive positions, including Fort Sumter, whose counterfire kills Captain J. W. Rodgers of the *Catskill.*

The USS *De Soto* captures the Confederate steamer *Nita* in Apalachicola Bay, Florida.

August 18

NORTH: Intrigued by new weapons, President Abraham Lincoln test-fires the new, rapid-fire Spencer carbine at Treasury Park, Washington, D.C. This weapon gives Federal units a decided edge in firepower over Confederate units that are still armed with muzzle-loading rifles.

SOUTH: The Union bombardment of Fort Sumter, Charleston Harbor, South Carolina, shows no letup, but the garrison still clings tenaciously behind its masonry ruins.

SOUTHWEST: Federal troops under Colonel Kit Carson skirmish with Pueblo Indians at Pueblo, Colorado.

NAVAL: The USS *Niphon* chases the Confederate steamer *Hebe* aground off Fort Fisher, Wilmington, North Carolina, destroying it by gunfire.

The CSS *Oconee* flounders in heavy seas off St. Catherine's Sound, Georgia.

August 19

NORTH: The military draft resumes in New York without further violence.

WEST: Union cavalry under General William W. Averell destroy Confederate saltpeter works at Franklin, West Virginia.

NAVAL: Landing parties from the USS *Norwich* and *Hale* raid Jacksonville, Florida, and destroy a Confederate signal station.

The USS *Restless* captures the Confederate schooner *Ernti* off the Florida Keys.

August 20

SOUTH: General William B. Franklin takes charge of the Union XXIX Corps in Louisiana.

WEST: Federal forces directed by General Ambrose E. Burnside reach the Tennessee River in East Tennessee.

Three hundred Confederate guerrillas under William C. Quantrill begin their raid into Kansas.

SOUTHWEST: Colonel Kit Carson commences his "scorched earth" policy against the Navajo Indians in the New Mexico Territory, assisted by Ute, Zuni, and Mescalero Apache tribe members. All captives taken then are transferred to a reservation at Bosque Redondo for resettlement.

August 21

SOUTH: The Union bombardment of Fort Sumter, Charleston Harbor, South Carolina, intensifies further as General Quincy A. Gillmore readies "Swamp Angel," a huge Parrott gun lobbing 200-pound incendiary projectiles. Digging an emplacement for this heavy piece and dragging it into position over the swampy ground of Morris Island has taken three weeks. Fully functional, it prepares to fire incendiary rounds at the Charleston waterfront, 7,900 yards distant.

WEST: General Robert B. Potter assumes command of the Union IX Corps in Kentucky.

General John G. Fosters returns to Tennessee to resume command of the Union XVIII Corps.

William C. Quantrill and 450 Confederate and Missouri irregulars storm into Lawrence, Kansas, a noted abolitionist center and hotbed for Union jayhawker activity. During the next four hours, they systematically round up and execute 180 men and boys and then burn 185 buildings before departing. It is the single largest atrocity of the Civil War, condemned by North and South alike.

NAVAL: The CSS *Torch,* a Confederate torpedo boat, attacks and fails to destroy the Federal ironclad USS *New Ironsides* in the channel off Morris Island, Charleston, South Carolina. Having approached to within 40 yards of its target at night, Pilot James Carlin cuts his engines and drifts toward his quarry, but prevailing currents pitch his vehicle alongside the larger navy vessel instead of into it. Carlin's engines then stall for several tense moments as *New Ironsides* labors to depress its cannon low enough to sink the intruder. When the *Torch*'s engine suddenly start, Carlin withdraws his ship back into the harbor, straddled by parting shots from his intended victim.

The Confederate raider CSS *Florida* under Commander John N. Maffitt captures and burns the Union ship *Anglo Saxon* off Brest, France.

August 22

SOUTH: Fort Sumter, Charleston Harbor, South Carolina, endures six days of heavy pounding from Union batteries on nearby Morris Island and sustains heavy damage, yet remains defiant. Meanwhile, the large Union cannon dubbed "Swamp Angel" is disabled while firing its 36th round and abandoned. Beforehand, it lobbed incendiary shells toward the city's waterfront, igniting several fires and panicking the populace.

WEST: Union cavalry under General William W. Averell skirmishes with Colonel William Jackson's Confederates at Huntersville, Virginia, driving them toward Warm Springs.

General William S. Rosecrans dispatches Union forces from Tracy City, Tennessee, to the Tennessee River.

NAVAL: Armed boats from USS *Shohokon* capture and sink the Confederate schooner *Alexander Cooper* at New Topsail Inlet, North Carolina. The men then destroy a nearby saltworks.

The USS *Cayuga* captures the Confederate schooner *Wave* off Corpus Christi, Texas.

Following the latest round of intense bombardment, Admiral John A. B. Dahl-gren moves his ironclad fleet, consisting of USS *Montauk, Weehawken, Nahant, Passaic,* and *Patapsco,* in closer to engage Confederate defenses at Fort Sumter, Charleston Harbor, South Carolina. However, when *Passaic* accidentally grounds near the fort, his attack is delayed in having to get the vessel refloated, and at daylight, the squadron hauls off, having accomplished little.

August 23

SOUTH: Union gunners, having fired 5,009 rounds into Fort Sumter, Charleston Harbor, South Carolina, reduce that post to rubble. But the garrison, with only one cannon still mounted, refuses to yield.

NAVAL: A Confederate expedition under Lieutenant John T. Wood takes four boats filled with 60 sailors and 30 sharpshooters and seizes the Union steamers USS *Reliance* and *Satellite* off Windmill Point on the Rappahannock River, Virginia. The captured vessels subsequently are scuttled a few days later for want of fuel and spare parts.

Admiral John A. B. Dahlgren leads the ironclads USS *New Ironsides, Weehawken, Montauk, Passaic,* and *Patapsco* back into Charleston Harbor, South Carolina, for another round of bombardment. Fort Sumter initially is targeted; then they shift their aim to Fort Moultrie before a thick fog descends and obstructs the gunners of both sides. At daybreak, Dahlgren signals for the squadron to haul off, and fighting ceases.

August 24

SOUTH: Union cavalry under General Hugh J. Kilpatrick skirmish with Confederates near George Court House, Virginia.

Major John S. Mosby begins a protracted raid against Union forces around Warrenton Junction and Alexandria, Virginia.

August 25

SOUTH: Union infantry attacks on Confederate rifle pits outside Battery Wagner, Charleston Harbor, South Carolina, are beaten back.

WEST: Union cavalry under General William W. Averill destroy additional Confederate saltpeter works along Jackson's River, West Virginia. Moving west toward White Sulphur Springs, his command engages a strong force of Confederates before settling in for the evening.

General Thomas Ewing, commanding the Union Border District, issues his controversial General Order No. 11. This edict forces all the inhabitants of Bates, Cass, Jackson, and parts of Vernon counties, Missouri, long suspected of collaborating with Confederate guerrillas, to abandon their homes. The houses then are peremptorily burned in retaliation for the Lawrence massacre. An estimated 20,000 people are displaced, causing enmity and hardship lasting several years beyond the war. Ewing, against his better judgment, drew up the orders on the insistence of General James Lane, a noted Union frontier jayhawker and a popular politician. Lane subsequently threatened to ruin's Ewing's military reputation if he fails to enforce all the measure's harshest provisions.

NAVAL: The newly acquired CSS *Satellite* under Lieutenant John T. Wood attacks and captures the Union schooners *Golden Rod, Coquette,* and *Two Brothers* at the mouth of the Rappahannock River, Virginia.

The USS *William G. Anderson* captures the Confederate schooner *Mack Canfield* off the Rio Grande, Texas.

August 26

POLITICS: In a letter to Unionists in Springfield, Illinois, President Abraham Lincoln writes, "I do not believe any compromise, embracing the maintenance of the Union is now possible. . . . Peace does not appear so distant as it did."

SOUTH: Confederate general John B. Floyd dies of natural causes near Abingdon, Virginia.

Federal troops finally storm the rifle pits fronting Battery Wagner on Morris Island, Charleston Harbor, South Carolina.

WEST: Union cavalry under General William W. Averell skirmish heavily with Confederate forces at White Sulphur Springs, West Virginia. His 2,000 troopers dash headlong into an equal number of Confederates under Colonel George S. Patton, sent there to stop the Union marauders. Averell dismounts, attacks repeatedly across densely wooded terrain, and is defeated. He then remounts and retires in the direction of Callaghan's Station. Union losses are 26 dead, 125 injured, and 67 captured while Patton records 20 killed, 129 wounded, and 13 missing.

SOUTHWEST: Union troops under General James G. Blunt defeat Colonel Stand Watie's Confederate Cherokee in a skirmish at Perryville, Indian Territory.

NAVAL: Armed boats from the USS *Beauregard* seize the Confederate schooner *Phoebe* near Jupiter Inlet, Florida.

August 27

NORTH: Confederate cavalry under General J. E. B. Stuart skirmish with Union forces at Edward's Ferry, Maryland.

WEST: Union cavalry under General William W. Averell trot into Beverly, West Virginia, ending his recent raid.

NAVAL: The USS *Sunflower* captures the Confederate schooner *General Worth* in the Straits of Florida.

The USS *Preble* is accidentally destroyed by fire at Pensacola, Florida.

The USS *William G. Anderson* captures the Confederate schooner *America* off the Texas coast.

The Confederate raiders CSS *Alabama* under Captain Raphael Semmes and CSS *Tuscaloosa* under Lieutenant John Low briefly rendezvous in the Bay of Angra Pequena off the West African coast. Semmes then orders the *Tuscaloosa* to cruise off the Brazilian coast.

August 29

WEST: As Union forces under General William S. Rosecrans flank the city of Chattanooga, Tennessee, Confederates under General Braxton Bragg must soon either fight or fall back.

NAVAL: The experimental submarine CSS *Hunley,* under Lieutenant John A. Payne, tragically sinks on a trial run in Charleston Harbor, South Carolina, killing six crew members. The vessel apparently founders in the wake of the steamer *Etiwan* while its hatches were opened for better ventilation.

The Federal gunboat USS *Estrella* is detached from the West Gulf Blockading Squadron and ordered up the Mississippi River to assist the ironclad *Essex* in anti-guerrilla patrols.

August 30

SOUTH: Union batteries on Morris Island, Charleston Harbor, South Carolina, continue their bombardment of Fort Sumter.

NAVAL: The Confederate steamer CSS *Sumter* is fired on and sunk by shore batteries on Sullivan's Island, Charleston, South Carolina, after mistaking it for a passing Union vessel.

The Confederate raider CSS *Georgia* under Lieutenant William L. Maury captures the Union ship *John Watts* in the mid-Atlantic, releasing it on bond.

A detachment of U.S. Marines assigned to the Mississippi River Squadron captures 35 prisoners, including three Confederate paymasters at Bolivar, Mississippi. They were transporting $2.2 million of Confederate currency at the time.

August 31

SOUTH: General Robert C. Schenck assumes command of the Union VIII Corps along with the Middle Department, Virginia.

General Alpheus S. Williams gains command of the Union XII Corps, Army of the Potomac.

NAVAL: The USS *Gem of the Sea* captures the Confederate sloop *Richard* at Peach Creek, Florida.

September 1

POLITICS: President Jefferson Davis assures Tennessee governor Isham G. Harris that troops and arms are being dispatched to General Braxton Bragg's forces in Tennessee.

SOUTH: Both Fort Sumter and Battery Wagner on Morris Island, Charleston Harbor, South Carolina, remain under continual bombardment from Union cannon, which lob another 627 rounds against their already battered position. Both garrisons, however, continue to resist.

WEST: After preliminary maneuvering, the Union Army of the Cumberland under General William S. Rosecrans finally crosses the Tennessee River and heads for Chattanooga, Tennessee.

Fort Smith, Arkansas, is evacuated by Confederates under General William L. Cabell and subsequently falls to advancing Union forces commanded by General Frederick Steele.

NAVAL: Admiral John A. B. Dahlgren leads his ironclad force in a five-hour night action against Fort Sumter, Charleston Harbor, South Carolina. The vessels steam to within 500 yards of their target before opening fire, and they receive 70 hits from shore batteries before action is suspended at daybreak.

September 2

POLITICS: To curtail mounting manpower shortages, the Alabama state legislature considers the use of slaves in the army.

SOUTH: Union forces establish trench works within 80 yards of Battery Wagner, Morris Island, South Carolina, forcing Confederate authorities to prepare an evacuation effort.

WEST: The Army of the Cumberland under General William S. Rosecrans begins to cross the Tennessee River in pursuit of retreating Confederates.

Union forces under General Ambrose E. Burnside occupy Knoxville, Tennessee, severing the sole remaining direct railhead between eastern and western portions of the Confederacy. Henceforth, the Confederates must employ a tenuous, roundabout route stretching from Virginia to Georgia and thence to Tennessee.

NAVAL: An armed expedition from the USS *Star of the Sea* reconnoiters Peace Creek, Florida, destroying several buildings and small craft.

September 4

SOUTH: Confederate cavalry under General J. E. B. Stuart try unsuccessfully to snare Union general Joseph J. Bartlett at New Baltimore, Virginia.

WEST: General Ulysses S. Grant is badly injured in a fall from his horse at New Orleans, Louisiana.

The Army of the Cumberland under General William S. Rosecrans continues crossing the Tennessee River at Bridgeport, Alabama, below Confederate positions at Chattanooga, Tennessee.

Confederate guerrillas raid the town of Quincy, Missouri, taking four prisoners from the 18th Iowa and subsequently executing them.

Federal forces ambush Confederate bushwhackers at Big Creek, Missouri, killing six guerrillas.

NAVAL: Admiral John H. Bell of the West Gulf Blockading Squadron begins to assemble ships for a joint amphibious expedition from New Orleans to Sabine Pass, Texas. This is undertaken to dissuade French occupation forces in Mexico from crossing the Rio Grande into Texas.

September 5

DIPLOMACY: After being warned by American ambassador Charles F. Adams, British foreign secretary Lord Russell confiscates the two "Laird Rams" before they can be delivered to Confederate agents in Britain. Adams previously advised the British that "it would be superfluous for me to point out to your Lordship that this is war." Government seizure of these dangerous vessels ends a prolonged diplomatic sore point between London and Washington.

POLITICS: A pensive president Jefferson Davis contacts General Braxton Bragg over seemingly flagging Confederate fortunes in Tennessee, asking: "What is your proposed plan of operation? Can you ascertain intention of enemy?"

SOUTH: Union forces tenaciously and methodically push their earthworks to within a few yards of Battery Wagner on Morris Island, South Carolina. Expectations for a final and presumably victorious Federal assault are rife.

WEST: General William S. Rosecrans, convinced that Confederates under General Braxton Bragg are fleeing Chattanooga, Tennessee, into Georgia, daringly divides his army into three parts to cover three, widely spaced mountain passes south of the city.

September 6

SOUTH: Battery Wagner and Battery Gregg, on Morris Island, Charleston Harbor, South Carolina, are evacuated secretly by General Pierre G. T. Beauregard. Barges manned by the crews of CSS *Chicora* and *Palmetto State* row to Cumming Point at night and lift the survivors off, although marauding Federal gunboats snare several prisoners by daylight. This final act concludes 60 days of nearly continuous bombardment by Union land and naval forces—one-third of the 900 defenders have been either killed or wounded. Casualties during the final phase of operations cost the Union 71 dead, 278 wounded, and nine missing while Taliaferro loses 38 dead and 150 wounded.

NAVAL: A landing party from the USS *Argosy* secures Confederate ammunition stores at Bruinsburg, Mississippi.

September 7

SOUTH: Union forces advance on Batteries Wagner and Gregg, Morris Island, South Carolina, finding them desolate and abandoned. Meanwhile Confederate forces under General William B. Taliaferro attack Union pickets on Battery Island, South Carolina, destroying the bridge and landing to nearby Horse Island.

WEST: Union forces reoccupy Cumberland Gap, Tennessee.

SOUTHWEST: A combined army-navy expedition under General William B. Franklin arrives off the bar at Sabine Pass, Texas.

NAVAL: Admiral John A. B. Dahlgren demands the surrender of Fort Sumter in Charleston Harbor, South Carolina, and when the defenders refuse, he conducts a reconnaissance in force with the ironclads USS *Weehawken* and *New Ironsides.* En route, *Weehawken* grounds in the channel, and *New Ironsides* interposes itself between Fort Moultrie and the stricken ship, receiving intense fire and 50 hits. The vessels then retire offshore by daylight to make repairs.

Federal gunboats USS *Clifton, Sachem, Arizona,* and *Granite City* arrive off Sabine Pass, Texas, to support a combined expedition under General William B. Franklin.

September 8

SOUTH: General Quincy A. Gillmore, encouraged by his final conquest of Battery Wagner, Charleston Harbor, South Carolina, prepares for an amphibious expedition against nearby Fort Sumter in conjunction with naval forces under Admiral John A. B. Dahlgren.

WEST: After initial hesitation, General Braxton Bragg abandons Chattanooga, Tennessee, and withdraws 65,000 men toward Lafayette, Georgia.

SOUTHWEST: A small Confederate battery of 42 men under 20-year-old Lieutenant Richard W. Dowling, 1st Texas Heavy Artillery, engages a 4,000-man amphibious expedition under Union general William B. Franklin. Franklin's goal is to seize

Hand-tinted copy of a line engraving by Smyth, depicting USS *New Ironsides* and two monitors in action at Charleston, South Carolina, ca. 1863 *(Naval Historical Foundation)*

the mouth of the Sabine River on the Texas-Louisiana border. Federal gunboats USS *Clifton, Sachem, Arizona,* and *Granite City,* along with several army transports, work themselves across the bar as Confederate gunners hunker down behind their defenses at Fort Griffin. Dowling allowed the vessels to approach to within close range before unleashing a destructive cannonade at 4:00 P.M. Previously, he carefully pre-positioned white poles in the river as range markers, and his six outdated, smoothbore cannon are handled with aplomb. Consequently, the *Sachem* is disabled by a direct shot through its boilers while the *Clifton* grounds directly beneath the Confederate guns and takes a pounding. Both gunboats promptly surrender, after which the expedition withdraws back over the bar and sets sail for New Orleans. Considering the sheer disparity of forces, this is a humiliating defeat for the North, which loses 19 dead, nine wounded, 37 missing, and 315 captured. Dowling suffers no casualties, and President Jefferson Davis hails his stand as "one of the most brilliant and heroic achievements in the history of warfare." Defeat here prompts General Nathaniel P. Banks to shift his attention to the Rio Grande region.

NAVAL: The small Confederate cottonclad CSS *Uncle Ben* assists in the repulse of Union forces at Sabine Pass, Texas.

September 9

DIPLOMACY: The British government formally initiates steps to prevent the two "Laird Rams" from entering into Confederate service.

SOUTH: General James Longstreet's I Corps of 15,000 men begins to embark on trains in Virginia for a nine-day trek to Lafayette, Georgia, to reinforce the Army of Tennessee.

WEST: Union forces under General Ambrose E. Burnside recapture the Cumberland Gap in eastern Tennessee.

The strategic city of Chattanooga, Tennessee, surrenders to the Army of the Cumberland under General William S. Rosecrans without a shot being fired. General Braxton Bragg then falls back 28 miles to Lafayette, Georgia, where he is to receive promised reinforcements.

The Union division of General James S. Negley (XIV Corps) arrives alone and unsupported at McLemore's Cove, Georgia, and General Braxton Bragg orders an assault by Generals Patrick R. Cleburne and Thomas C. Hindman to destroy it. However, Hindman, fretful over being attacked himself, refuses to budge, and Negley escapes intact the next day.

NAVAL: Admiral John A. B. Dahlgren launches a nighttime assault on Fort Sumter, Charleston Harbor, South Carolina, by 413 sailors and U.S. Marines under Commander Thomas H. Stevens. But the Southerners, having earlier recovered the code book from the sunken USS *Keokuk,* are able to decipher Union signals and anticipate the attack. Consequently, the Federals are rebuffed with 100 prisoners. A similar expedition planned by General Quincy A. Gillmore is also summarily cancelled. More significantly, Dahlgren requests additional monitor craft from Secretary of the Navy Gideon Welles; when he refused, the navy stopped its bombardment campaign, and operations against Charleston settle into a blockade.

September 10

SOUTH: Vindictive Georgia troops sack offices of the *North Carolina Standard* in Raleigh, North Carolina, for printing editorials favoring a negotiated settlement with the Union.

WEST: This day finds the Army of the Cumberland under General William S. Rosecrans widely dispersed over a broad area with General Alexander M. Cook (XXI Corps) at Alpine, Georgia, General George H. Thomas (XIV Corps) at McLemore's Cove, and General Thomas L. Crittenden at Chattanooga. He is unaware that General Braxton Bragg actually is regrouping and receiving reinforcements in northern Georgia.

Confederate forces under General Sterling Price evacuate Little Rock, Arkansas, for nearby Rockport, whereupon General Frederick Steele's Federals move in and establish a pro-Union administration. This is another grievous blow to a Confederacy already reeling from the loss of Vicksburg, and it seriously imperils the Trans-Mississippi Department under General Edmund Kirby-Smith. Confederate governor Harris Flanigan is forced to relocate to Washington, Arkansas, where he remains for the next two years.

NAVAL: The USS *Hastings* lends fire support to General Frederick Steele's troops at Devall's Bluff on the White River, Arkansas.

September 11

POLITICS: President Abraham Lincoln authorizes General Andrew Johnson, military governor of Tennessee, to form a civilian government. He also declines to accept General Ambrose E. Burnside's latest attempt to resign.

NAVAL: The USS *Seminole* captures the British blockade-runner *William Peel* off the Rio Grande, Texas.

September 12

WEST: Union and Confederate forces skirmish heavily below Chattanooga, Tennessee.

NAVAL: The USS *Eugenie* captures the Confederate steamer *Alabama* off the Chandeleur Islands, Louisiana.

The Confederate steamer *Fox* is scuttled by its own crew to prevent being captured by the USS *Genesee* at Pascagoula, Mississippi.

September 13

SOUTH: The Army of the Potomac under General George G. Meade occupies Culpeper Court House shortly after it is evacuated by Confederates under General Robert E. Lee. Lee, weakened by the detachment of General James Longstreet's corps to Georgia, falls back across the Rapidan River.

General Henry W. Slocum is restored as commander of the XII Corps, Army of the Potomac.

WEST: The War Department instructs General Ulysses S. Grant to transfer all available forces from Corinth, Mississippi, to Tuscumbia, Alabama, in support of General William S. Rosecrans at Chattanooga, Tennessee.

General Braxton Bragg orders General Leonidas K. Polk to attack and overwhelm the isolated Union XXI Corps of General Thomas L. Crittenden at Lee and Gordon's Mill, northern Georgia. But Polk dithers, demands reinforcements, and fails to move in a timely fashion. Hence, another part of the widely scattered Army of the Cumberland escapes annihilation. General William S. Rosecrans finally recognizes the danger his army faces and orders all three corps to begin to concentrate at Lee and Gordon's Mills along Chickamauga Creek. For the intervening week, both armies race north toward Chattanooga.

NAVAL: The USS *Cimarron* captures the British blockade-runner *Jupiter* near Wassaw Sound, Georgia.

The USS *De Soto* captures the steamer *Montgomery* in the Gulf of Mexico.

A rather unsporting raid by Confederate cavalry nets 20 crew members of the USS *Rattler* as they attend church services at Rodney, Mississippi.

September 14

SOUTH: Union forces under General George M. Meade cross the Rapidan River, Virginia, seeking to engage an elusive Army of Northern Virginia. Skirmishing erupts along the line at Somerville, Racoon, and Robertson's Fords.

September 15

SOUTH: An accidental magazine explosion at Battery Cheves, James Island, South Carolina, kills six Confederate soldiers.

General Edward O. C. Ord arrives to take command of the Union XIII Corps, Louisiana.

WEST: Skirmishing erupts at Catlett's Gap, Georgia, as the armies of Generals William S. Rosecrans and Braxton Bragg begin to concentrate for a final confrontation.

September 16

WEST: The Army of the Cumberland under General William S. Rosecrans continues concentrating along Chickamauga Creek, 12 miles below Chattanooga, Tennessee.

NAVAL: The USS *Coeur de Lion* captures the Confederate schooner *Robert Knowles* in the Potomac River.

The USS *San Jacinto* captures the Confederate steamer *Lizzie Davis* off the Florida west coast.

September 17

WEST: Union and Confederate forces skirmish at Owen's Ford, West Chickamauga Creek, whereby General Braxton Bragg misses yet another opportunity to attack the separated corps of General William S. Rosecrans's Army of the Cumberland. Both sides continue concentrating forces in anticipation of a major clash.

NAVAL: The USS *Adolph Hugel* impounds the sloop *Music* for blockade violations off Alexandria, Virginia.

September 18

WEST: The Army of the Cumberland and the Army of Tennessee confront each other across West Chickamauga Creek, Georgia. For once, the Confederates outnumber Federal forces, having massed 68,000 men to a Union tally of 58,000. General Braxton Bragg seeks to interpose his troops between General William S. Rosecrans and his main supply base at Chattanooga, Tennessee, but increasing skirmishes with Union cavalry along Reed's and Alexander's bridges delay movement a full day. Meanwhile, Rosecrans grows concerned that he is about to be outflanked and hastily summons General George H. Thomas's XIV Corps on a lengthy nighttime march—inadvertently across Bragg's line of march.

September 19

WEST: The Battle of Chickamauga begins once advance elements of General George H. Thomas's XIV Corps encounter Confederate cavalry under General Nathan B. Forrest on the Union left. As fighting escalates, both Generals Braxton Bragg and William S. Rosecrans cancel their respective plans for the day and continually feed additional units into the rapidly expanding fray. Various Union formations remain somewhat disjointed, and a frontal assault by Bragg's entire army might have rolled them up in detail, but that leader remains fixated by the piecemeal struggle to his immediate front. At length, large attacks launched by General Leonidas K. Polk are repulsed with loss. Then General Patrick R. Cleburne also charges Union positions before nightfall and is likewise rebuffed. The day's combat occasioned serious losses to both sides and little else. This evening, following the arrival of General James Longstreet's I Corps, Bragg appoints him to command his left wing while General Leonidas K. Polk directs the right.

NAVAL: A small group of Confederate sailors under Acting Masters John Y. Beall and Edward McGuire attack and capture the Union schooner *Alliance* in Chesapeake Bay, intending to stalk and seize other prizes by stealth.

September 20

SOUTH: John B. Hood is appointed a lieutenant general, C.S.A.

Union cavalry under Generals John Buford and Hugh J. Kilpatrick attack Confederate supply lines near Gordonsville, Virginia, capturing both wagons and cattle.

Major John S. Mosby skirmishes with Union forces at Upperville, Virginia.

WEST: General Braxton Bragg intends to renew combat at Chickamauga at dawn, but confusion and delays down his chain of command preclude any Confederate advance before 9:00 A.M. The pattern of fighting remains similar to the previous day, with General Leonidas K. Polk committing piecemeal attacks on an entrenched, unyielding Union line. The knotty, heavily forested nature of the terrain greatly complicates the movement and deployment of troops en masse, so a "soldier's battle" unfolds between small, determined bands of men. At 9:00 A.M., a forceful Southern charge at the Union center nearly reaches the Lafayette Road, but it is repelled by Federals holding either flank. Another bloody stalemate seems in the offing until fate intervenes.

At about 10:30 A.M., General William S. Rosecrans is mistakenly informed that a gap has developed in the center of his line—in fact there was none—so he orders General Thomas J. Wood's division to plug it. No sooner does Wood remove his troops than General James Longstreet's veterans come pouring through, six brigades deep. The unexpected onslaught completely sweeps away the Union center and right, carrying Rosecrans and several ranking leaders along in a tumultuous retreat.

All that remains to stave off disaster is the XIV Corps of General George H. Thomas, which assumes strong defensive positions along Snodgrass Hill. Longstreet and other Confederate leaders repeatedly assail Thomas's position but are invariably beaten back with losses. Union prospects improve significantly when General Gordon Granger disobeys Rosecrans and rushes his Reserve Corps forward to support Thomas. Granger himself is in the very thick of intense fighting, holding aloft the flag of the 115th Illinois throughout the contest. Clinging to Snodgrass Hill with heroic determination, the beleaguered yet imperturbably calm Thomas gains the moniker "Rock of Chickamauga" by preserving the Army of the Cumberland from otherwise certain destruction. Fighting ceases along the line by nightfall, and Thomas skillfully extricates his command through McFarland's Gap in good order. To accomplish this, Granger orders his 21st and 89th Ohio and 22nd Michigan, whose ammunition is exhausted, to hold the ridge above the pass with bayonets alone. Only after the last of Thomas's column passes through do they finally surrender.

Chickamauga is the bloodiest battle waged in the western theater, with both sides suffering loss rates approaching 28 percent. For the Union, this entails 1,656 dead, 9,749 injured, and 4,774 missing (16,179) while the Confederates lose 2,389 killed, 13,412 wounded, and 2,003 missing (17,804). Among the fatally wounded is Confederate general Ben Hardin Helm, President Abraham Lincoln's brother-in-law, who is mourned by both the president and his wife. General Daniel H. Hill, after scrutinizing the casualty lists, characterizes Chickamauga as "a barren victory." The Army of Tennessee could not sustain such attrition for long, but Bragg compounded his problems by failing to pursue the beaten enemy aggressively. This lackluster leadership causes further rifts in an already fractious chain of command and sullied his already faltering reputation. Rosecrans, his erstwhile sterling persona destroyed, likewise suffers repercussions for his mismanagement of affairs during—and after—the battle.

Confederate forces under General Samuel Jones skirmish with Federal troops at Zollicoffer, Tennessee, and they pursue the defeated troops as far as the villages of Blountsville and Carter's Depot. The former is an important railroad junction through which the Tennessee and Virginia Railroad passes. General Ambrose E. Burnside, wishing to appropriate that rail for his own use, warns Jones to evacuate citizens from the village as he intends to take it back.

September 21

POLITICS: President Abraham Lincoln repeatedly orders General Ambrose E. Burnside at Knoxville, Tennessee, to reinforce General William S. Rosecrans's shattered army at Chattanooga, but the general refuses to budge.

WEST: Five Union divisions under General George H. Thomas abandon their position at Rossville Gap and reach Chattanooga in good order. The Confederate pursuit, when it finally materializes, remains strangely lax in execution.

NAVAL: Confederate raiders on the commandeered vessel *Alliance* seize the Union schooner *J. J. Houseman* in Chesapeake Bay.

September 22

WEST: Union cavalry forces under Colonel John W. Foster charge into Blountsville, Tennessee, to dislodge the 1st Tennessee Cavalry under Colonel James E. Carter. They head directly into prepared Confederate positions, and a four-hour fight erupts after which the bluecoats finally prevail and capture the town. Foster's losses are six dead and 14 injured, and he reports the seizure of 50 Confederates.

General William S. Rosecrans continues rallying the Army of the Cumberland in Chattanooga, Tennessee, while General Ulysses S. Grant dispatches three divisions of the XV Corps from Vicksburg, Mississippi, under General William T. Sherman to assist him. Meanwhile, the Confederate Army of Tennessee leisurely occupies the high ground around the city to commence a siege.

General Joseph O. Shelby takes his "Iron Brigade" of Confederate cavalry out of Arkadelphia, Arkansas, on an extended raid throughout Missouri.

NAVAL: Confederate raiders in the commandeered schooner *Alliance* seize the Union schooners *Samuel Pearsall* and *Alexandria* in Chesapeake Bay.

The USS *Connecticut* captures the British blockade-runner *Juno* off Wilmington, North Carolina.

Landing parties from the USS *Seneca* destroy Confederate saltworks near Darien, Georgia.

The USS *De Soto* recaptures the Federal army tug *Leviathan* in the Gulf of Mexico after its prior seizure by Confederate raiders at South West Pass, Mississippi River.

September 23

NORTH: Secretary of War Edwin M. Stanton begins to orchestrate skillfully the transfer of 20,000 men of the XI and XII Corps from the Army of the Potomac to Chattanooga, Tennessee. They will be shuttled quickly and efficiently along 1,233 miles of railroad track in the biggest transfer of military personnel prior to the Franco-Prussian War.

SOUTH: General George E. Pickett is transferred to the Confederate Department of North Carolina.

NAVAL: The USS *Thomas Freeborn* chases the commandeered schooner *Alliance* until it grounds at Milford Haven, Virginia, and is burned.

September 24

DIPLOMACY: The Confederate government appoints Ambrose D. Mann as its special agent to the Papal States in Rome.

WEST: Rather than defend Missionary Ridge and Lookout Mountain, both natural strong points, General William S. Rosecrans moves all his forces into Chattanooga, Tennessee. This timid display induces General Braxton Bragg to initiate a siege by occupying all high ground surrounding the city without Union interference.

General Joseph Hooker accepts command of the Union XI and XII Corps, then en route to Chattanooga, Tennessee, by rail.

NAVAL: A total of eight Russian warships arrive individually in New York City. They are seeking safety in American ports as Great Britain and France are threatening war over the Polish insurrection, although the move is widely interpreted in the North as a sign of diplomatic support. Another fleet of six vessels eventually anchors in San Francisco, California, and the Russians are warmly received by the political establishments of both cities.

September 25

POLITICS: President Abraham Lincoln castigates General Ambrose E. Burnside at Knoxville, Tennessee, for not reinforcing Union forces besieged at Chattanooga. Having struggled, he wrote, "to get you to assist General Rosecrans, and you have repeatedly declared you would do it, and yet you steadily move the contrary way." On further reflection, the letter is not sent.

WEST: Confederate cavalry under General John D. Imboden launch a successful attack on Cheat River, West Virginia.

General Mahlon D. Manson assumes command of the XXIII Army Corps, Army of the Tennessee.

NAVAL: The USS *Tioga* captures the Confederate steamer *Herald* off the Bahamas.

September 26

SOUTH: General Henry C. Whiting is assigned to command the Confederate District of Cape Fear and the defenses of Wilmington, North Carolina.

SOUTHWEST: General Edmund Kirby-Smith, trying to rally flagging morale in his Confederate Trans-Mississippi Department, declared to fellow citizens: "Your homes are in peril. Vigorous efforts on your part can alone save portions of your state from invasion. You should contest the advance of the enemy, thicket, gully, and stream; harass his rear and cut off his supplies."

September 27

NORTH: President Abraham Lincoln again implores General Ambrose E. Burnside at Knoxville, Tennessee, to forward reinforcements to assist General William S. Rosecrans at Chattanooga. "My order to you meant simply that you should save Rosecrans from being crushed out, believing if he lost his position, you could not hold East Tennessee in any event."

WEST: General Braxton Bragg determines to starve out the Army of the Cumberland from Chattanooga, Tennessee, and orders General Joseph Wheeler's cavalry to raid tenuous Union lines of communication throughout 60-mile-long Sequatchie Valley. Wheeler, who has little experience as a raider, openly doubts his prospects for success, yet declares to subordinates, "I have my orders, gentlemen, and I will attempt the work."

General Joseph O. Shelby's Confederate cavalry skirmishes with Union troops at Moffat's Station, Arkansas.

NAVAL: The USS *Clyde* captures the Confederate schooner *Amaranth* off the Florida Keys.

September 28

WEST: General William S. Rosecrans accuses subordinates, Generals Alexander McCook and Thomas L. Crittenden, of failing to obey his orders at Chickamauga, and both are relieved of command pending a court of inquiry.

September 29

WEST: General John S. Williams and his 1,700 Confederate cavalry drive Union troops from Jonesborough, Tennessee, where they hold their position.

NAVAL: The Federal gunboats USS *Lafayette* and *Kenwood* arrive at Morganza, Louisiana (on Bayou Fordoche), to support General Napoleon J. T. Dana's beleaguered command. His troops had been attacked previously by Confederate forces, losing 400 prisoners, and are now reduced to 1,500 men. The presence of gunboats, however, deters General Thomas Green from renewing his assault.

The USS *St. Louis* under Commander George H. Preble drops anchor at Lisbon, Portugal, after a fruitless 100-day search for Confederate raiders.

September 30

NAVAL: The USS *Rosalie* captures the British blockade-runner *Director* on the Sanibel River, Florida.

October 1

POLITICS: President Abraham Lincoln instructs General John M. Schofield, commanding Union forces in Missouri, to place increasing emphasis on civilian rule and domestic tranquility. "Your immediate duty, in regard to Missouri, now is to advance the efficiency of that establishment and to so use it, as far as practicable, to compel the excited people there to leave one another alone."

SOUTH: General J. E. B. Stuart's Confederate troopers surprise a Union outpost on the north side of Robertson's River, Virginia, taking several prisoners.

WEST: General Robert Ransom arrives at Jonesboro, Tennessee, and orders General John S. Williams to take 1,700 Confederate cavalry on an expedition to seize the Cumberland Gap. Williams, however, exceeds his orders and rides eight miles past Greenville.

Union general Joseph Hooker arrives at Nashville, Tennessee, slightly ahead of his XI and XII Corps.

General Joseph Wheeler leads 4,000 Confederate cavalry in skirmishes with Colonel George Crook's 4th Ohio Cavalry at Smith's Cross Roads, Tennessee, as he clamps down on Northern supply lines. A large Federal wagon train is also captured by the marauding Southerners.

Confederate guerrillas under William C. Quantrill begin to leave Kansas and ride for the relative safety of the Indian Territory to evade Union patrols.

October 2

WEST: Final elements of the Union XI and XII Corps under General Joseph Hooker reach Bridgeport, Alabama, after an impressive journey of 1,159 miles by rail.

Confederate cavalry under General Joseph Wheeler accosts a Union supply train in the Sequatchie Valley, Tennessee, capturing 800 wagons, 1,200 prisoners, and 4,000 mules.

Due to the activities of Confederate cavalry, the Army of the Cumberland, besieged in Chattanooga, is experiencing acute food shortages.

NAVAL: The USS *Bermuda* captures the British blockade-runner *Florrie* off Matagorda, Texas.

October 3

POLITICS: President Abraham Lincoln designates the last Thursday in November Thanksgiving Day.

Secretary of War Edwin M. Stanton authorizes liberated African-American slaves to enlist in Maryland, Tennessee, and Missouri.

SOUTH: Union batteries on Morris Island, Charleston Harbor, South Carolina, cease firing on Fort Sumter after throwing an additional 560 shells at that beleaguered fortification.

WEST: Confederate cavalry under General John S. Williams clash with General Samuel P. Carter's Union troops outside Greenville, Tennessee. After a prolonged skirmish, the Federals withdraw.

The town of McMinnville, Tennessee, is captured by 2,500 Confederate cavalry under General John A. Wharton, who seizes 585 prisoners.

General William B. Franklin leads 19,500 Union troops of his XIX Corps from Fort Bisland, Louisiana, and marches westward from Berwick Bay. His objective is to march up to Bayou Teche as far as Lafayette and then to proceed directly into Texas. Simultaneously, General Cadwallader C. Washburn conducts the XIII Corps from Berwick to Bayou Carrion Crow for the same reason. Both columns are opposed by 8,000 Confederates under General Richard Taylor.

October 4

WEST: General James R. Chalmers leads Confederate cavalry on an extended raid into western Tennessee and northern Mississippi.

Confederate cavalry under General Joseph O. Shelby skirmishes with Union forces at Neosho, Missouri.

October 5

WEST: Union cavalry under General Samuel P. Carter stage a night attack on the Confederate camp at Greenville, Tennessee. However, General John S. Williams mounts a staunch defense, and the Federals eventually withdraw.

The Army of the Cumberland, besieged at Chattanooga, Tennessee, is reinforced by the arrival of the XI and XII Corps under General Joseph Hooker, along with portions of the XV Corps from Vicksburg, Mississippi.

Confederate cavalry under General Joseph Wheeler score a major blow by destroying the Stone's River Railroad bridge at Murfreesboro, Tennessee. However, their rear guard is subsequently scattered by the charge of General Robert B. Mitchell's 2nd Union Cavalry Division.

General Joseph O. Shelby's Confederate raiders skirmish with Union troops at Stockton, Missouri.

NAVAL: The CSS *David,* a torpedo boat with an especially low silhouette and equipped with an exploding spar, steams out of Charleston Harbor, South Carolina, at night intending to jab at the waterline of USS *New Ironsides.* Its approach goes nearly undetected until Federal sentinels open fire with small arms, which is immediately followed by the detonation of the Confederate device. The *New Ironsides* sustains heavy damage while *David,* its own boilers extinguished by the explosion, drifts helplessly alongside its victim for several minutes. Commander W. T. Glassell and a sailor are consequently captured, but the two remaining crew members relight the boilers and steam off to safety. A concerned admiral John A. B. Dahlgren anticipates future attacks. "How far the enemy may seem encouraged I do not know," he wrote the navy secretary, "but I think it will be well to be prepared against a considerable issue of these small craft."

Armed boats from the USS *Granite City* capture the British blockade-runner *Concordia* at Calcasieu Pass, Louisiana.

October 6

WEST: General Joseph Wheeler's Confederate cavalry column is handled roughly by the 2nd Cavalry Division under General Robert B. Mitchell, and nearly driven into the Duck River before escaping.

General James R. Chalmer's Confederate cavalry skirmish along the Coldwater River, Mississippi.

General Joseph O. Shelby's Confederate raiders hit Union positions at Humansville, Missouri.

Confederate guerrillas under William C. Quantrill attack what they think is an isolated Union outpost at Baxter Springs, Kansas. The garrison, consisting of 90 men of the 2nd Kansas Colored Infantry and 3rd Wisconsin Cavalry, are nearly overwhelmed but gradually repel the guerrillas through effective use of a howitzer. Meanwhile, a second column commanded by Quantrill encounters the retinue of General James G. Blunt, then shifting his headquarters from Fort Scott to Fort Smith, Arkansas. The guerrillas, clad in captured blue uniforms, trot right up to the column of 100 men and several wagons before shooting. Only Blunt and a third of his men manage to escape; the rest are captured and murdered in cold blood;

among those slain is the son of General Samuel R. Curtis. This affair leads to Blunt's dismissal for negligence.

NAVAL: The USS *Beauregard* captures the Confederate sloop *Last Trial* off Key West, Florida.

The USS *Virginia* captures the British blockade-runner *Jenny* off the Texas coast.

October 7

SOUTH: Confederate cavalry under General J. E. B. Stuart successfully raid Union pickets at Utz's Ford on the Rapidan River, Virginia.

Union reconnaissance parties report unusual Confederate activity south of the Rapidan River. In fact, General Robert E. Lee, aware that the Army of the Potomac has been weakened by the transfers of two corps to the West, prepares to strike at its right flank.

WEST: Union and Confederate cavalry under Generals Samuel P. Carter and John S. Willliams, respectively, skirmish again outside Greenville, Tennessee.

NAVAL: Landing parties from the USS *Cayuga* destroy the grounded Confederate blockade-runner *Pushmahata* off the Calcasieu River, Louisiana.

A bold overland expedition launched from the USS *Osage* from the Mississippi to the Red River results in the destruction of the Confederate steamers *Robert Fulton* and *Argus*.

October 9

POLITICS: President Jefferson Davis stops in Atlanta, Georgia, en route to Tennessee and harangues the populace to thunderous applause.

SOUTH: General Robert E. Lee advances against the right flank of General George G. Meade's Army of the Potomac by crossing the Rapidan River and marching north toward Washington, D.C. With one corps detached in Tennessee, Lee musters the II Corps of General Richard S. Ewell, the III Corps of newly elevated general Ambrose P. Hill, and the cavalry corps under General J. E. B. Stuart.

WEST: General Joseph Wheeler ends his spectacularly successful strike against Union supply lines by recrossing the Tennessee River at Muscle Shoals, Alabama. In a week, he inflicts 2,000 Union casualties, captures more than 1,000 wagons, burns five bridges, tears up miles of track, and ruins millions of dollars in equipment. This proves one of the most destructive raids of the entire war and nearly throttles the Army of the Cumberland, already on half rations at Chattanooga, Tennessee. However, Wheeler's own losses exceed 2,000 and raise questions as to his abilities as a raider.

NAVAL: The Confederate raider CSS *Georgia* under Lieutenant William L. Maury captures and burns the Union ship *Bold Hunter* off the coast of West Africa.

October 10

NORTH: The War Department requests additional gunboat support for the army of General William T. Sherman at Eastport, Tennessee.

SOUTH: General Robert E. Lee, apprised that the Army of the Potomac has dispatched the VI and VII Corps to assist Union forces at Chattanooga, Tennessee, opts for offensive operations and moves toward the Army of the Potomac. Meanwhile, General George M. Meade informs a disappointed President Abraham Lincoln that he is falling back behind the Rappahannock to thwart Confederate moves to turn his right flank and interpose themselves between him and Washington, D.C.

Confederate authorities are forced to dispatch 1,000 soldiers to suppress mounting Union sentiment in and around Elizabeth City and Edenton, North Carolina. The troops are also there to help enforce local conscription efforts.

WEST: In Tennessee the Union XX and XXI Corps are consolidated into the new IV Corps under General Gordon Granger.

General Ambrose E. Burnside directs a cavalry brigade and an infantry division at Blue Springs, Tennessee, where 1,700 Confederates under General John S. Williams are lurking. The Federals advance in force across broken, heavily wooded terrain and nearly break the Confederate line when they are suddenly bombarded by masked batteries. Burnside, having lost 100 men killed and wounded, orders a withdrawal back to Knoxville. Williams, who also falls back through the Cumberland Gap, records his losses at 261.

President Jefferson Davis arrives at Chattanooga, Tennessee, to confer with General Braxton Bragg over military strategy. He is also there to quell seething unrest between Bragg and his senior subordinates.

October 11

SOUTH: Heavy skirmishing erupts around the Rapidan and Rappahannock rivers as Confederate forces occupy Culpeper, Virginia, and maneuver for advantage in the still-evolving Bristoe Campaign. General Robert E. Lee, wishing to emulate his earlier success at Second Manassas, sends the III Corps under General Ambrose P. Hill on a circuitous march around the Union right while the II Corps of General Richard S. Ewell advances along the Orange and Alexandria Railroad.

WEST: Confederate cavalry under General Joseph O. Shelby capture Boonville, Missouri, on the Missouri River.

NAVAL: The USS *Nansemond* shells the Confederate steamer *Douro* after driving it aground at New Inlet, North Carolina, wrecking it. This vessel previously had been captured on March 9, 1863, and sold, but somehow it ended up back in Confederate hands.

The USS *Madgie* sinks in rough seas while being towed off Frying Pan Shoals, North Carolina.

The USS *Union* captures the Confederate steamer *Spaulding* near St. Andrew Sound, Georgia.

October 12

NAVAL: The USS *Kanawha* and *Eugenie*, while chasing a Confederate steamer into Mobile Bay, Alabama, receive heavy fire from nearby Fort Morgan and draw off.

October 13

POLITICS: The Republican governors prevail during elections held in Indiana, Iowa, and Ohio. Foremost among the victors are Andrew Curtin, Pennsylvania's prowar governor and staunch ally of President Abraham Lincoln. By contrast, Peace Democrat Clement L. Vallandigham, who ran for the Ohio governorship while exiled in Canada, is defeated soundly by a proadministration Republican.

SOUTH: While scouting ahead of the main Confederate army, General J. E. B. Stuart suddenly finds himself surrounded by two Union brigades belonging to the II Corps, which encamp for the evening on either side of Catlett's Station, Virginia. He orders his men sequestered in the nearby woods and silently waits for dawn.

A Federal attempt to snare Confederate guerrilla leader Silas F. Gregory fails at Indiantown, North Carolina.

WEST: President Jefferson Davis, after conferring with General Braxton Bragg in northern Georgia, authorizes that officer to transfer the contentious general Daniel H. Hill from his command.

General Joseph O. Shelby meets with a rare rebuff while attacking the Union garrison at Arrow Rock, Missouri.

NAVAL: An armed boat from the USS *Braziliera* captures the Confederate schooner *Mary* off St. Simon's, Georgia.

October 14

NORTH: General Samuel P. Heintzelman is replaced by General Christopher C. Augur as head of the Department of Washington, D.C., and its attendant XXII Corps.

SOUTH: General Ambrose P. Hill, marching through Warrenton, Virginia, perceives the rear guard of General George G. Meade strung out and fording the Broad Run at Bristoe Station. Hill, anxious to inflict damage, immediately decides to attack. However, he does so impetuously without proper reconnaissance and commits only two brigades of General Henry Heth's division to the assault. Hill's target is the V Corps of General George Sykes but, unknown to him, the entire II Corps of General Gouveneur K. Warren lays in wait behind a railroad embankment at right angles to his advance. No sooner do the North Carolina brigades of General John R. Cooke and William W. Kirkland charge than they are enfiladed immediately by a hail of artillery and musketry. Hit continuously from the front and the side, Heth's attack crumbles after 40 minutes of one-sided slaughter, and he withdraws. By day's end, the Confederates sustain 1,361 casualties, including Cooke and Kirkland wounded, while Union losses are 548. The following day, while traversing the field still strewn with Confederate dead, Hill attempts to explain his embarrassing predicament to General Robert E. Lee, who curtly replies, "Bury these poor men and let us say no more about it."

Confederate cavalry under General J. E. B. Stuart, surrounded by Union forces at Cattlet's Station, Virginia, suddenly charge through the enemy camp in a dense fog. The Southerners are repulsed by troops under General Joshua Owen and Colonel Thomas Smyth, but the bulk of Stuart's cavalry escape in the confusion. The Federals lose 11 killed and 42 wounded while taking 28 prisoners. The only Confederate fatality is Colonel Thomas Ruffin of the 1st North Carolina Cavalry. Once again, Stuart's bold resourcefulness in the face of steep odds voids a potential disaster.

WEST: Union cavalry under General William W. Averell skirmish with Confederates at Salt Lick Bridge, West Virginia.

NAVAL: The USS *Queen City* departs from Helena, Arkansas, and lends close-fire support to army troops engaged at Friar's Point, Mississippi. The expedition nets more than 200 bales of cotton.

October 15

WEST: Union forces capture all 37 men of a Confederate raiding party who were trying to burn the bridge at Hedgesville, West Virginia.

NAVAL: The day before it is to be committed to combat, the experimental Confederate submarine CSS *Hunley* disastrously founders a second time in Charleston Harbor, South Carolina, killing all seven crew members with the craft's inventor, Horace L. Hunley, among them. General Pierre G. T. Beauregard, still impressed with the potential of the craft, orders it raised from a watery grave and pressed back into service.

The USS *Honduras* captures the British blockade-runner *Mail* off St. Petersburg, Florida.

The USS *Commodore* and *Corypheus* destroy a Confederate tannery at Bay St. Louis, Mississippi.

October 16

POLITICS: President Abraham Lincoln, acting through the offices of General in Chief Henry W. Halleck, urges General George G. Meade to attack General Robert E. Lee's forces, but Meade continues resisting such prodding. Lee, meanwhile, falls back and assumes strong defensive positions behind the Rappahannock line.

WEST: General Ulysses S. Grant assumes control of the new Military Division of the Mississippi, which unites the old departments of the Ohio, the Cumberland, and the Tennessee under a single tent. This effectively places him in control of Federal military operations from the Appalachians to the Mississippi River. Grant himself has been summoned to Cairo, Illinois, for a conference with Secretary of War Edwin M. Stanton, although the two will encounter each other accidently at Indianapolis, Indiana.

NAVAL: Landing parties from the USS *Adela* and *Tahoma* march 14 miles overland up the Hillsboro River, Florida, to launch a night attack on known Confederate blockade-runners *Scottish Chief* and *Kate Dale*. Both vessels are burned, but the Federal sailors suffer five killed, 10 wounded, and five captured.

The USS *Tennessee* captures the British blockade-runner *Friendship* near Rio Brazos, Texas, and also drives the Confederate schooner *Jane* ashore.

October 17

POLITICS: President Abraham Lincoln requests the services of 300,000 more volunteers.

SOUTH: General Robert E. Lee disengages the Army of Northern Virginia and marches away from Bull Run, Virginia. To help mask this maneuver, General J. E. B. Stuart divides his cavalry command, sending General Wade Hampton's brigade through Gainesville and Haymarket while General Fitzhugh Lee directs his brigade toward Manassas Junction and Bristoe Station.

WEST: General William S. Rosecrans is relieved formally from the Army of the Cumberland and succeeded by General George H. Thomas. The new commander calmly reviews the perilous situation of his army at Chattanooga, Tennessee, and declares, "We will hold the town till we starve."

NAVAL: Armed boats from the USS *Ward* burn the Confederate schooner *Rover* at Murrell's Inlet, North Carolina.

October 18

SOUTH: Confederate cavalry under General J. E. B. Stuart, approaching Groveton, Virginia, suddenly encounter General Hugh J. Kilpatrick's Union cavalry. Stuart withdraws in the direction of Gainesville and then holds his position until nightfall, awaiting the arrival of his second brigade under General Fitzhugh Lee. Once present, Lee then suggests that on the following morning Stuart should feign retreat and withdraw slowly toward Warrenton. This will enable Lee's troopers to assail Kilpatrick's left flank and rear the moment they cross Broad Run. Stuart agrees to the stratagem and makes dispositions to implement it.

A quick strike by the Virginia Partisan Rangers under Major John S. Mosby leads to the capture of 100 horses, prisoners, and valuable equipment near Annandale, Virginia.

WEST: Confederate forces under General John D. Imboden surround and capture 250 men of the 9th Maryland at Charles Town, West Virginia.

NAVAL: Confederate divers relocate the hull of the submarine CSS *Hunley* in nine fathoms of water and begin recovery operations.

October 19

SOUTH: As anticipated, Confederate cavalry under General J. E. B. Stuart are attacked by General Hugh J. Kirkpatrick's Union troopers at Warrenton, Virginia. Stuart, with the brigade of General Fitzhugh Lee secretly deployed on the Union flank, falls back to Buckland Mills on Broad Run, enticing the impetuous Kilpatrick forward. Kilpatrick willingly obliges, and he sends General George A. Custer's Michigan brigade to commence the affair. Just as the fighting begins, Lee's brigade suddenly strikes Custer's flank and rear with his 2nd Virginia Cavalry. Stuart, observing the trap sprung, instantly orders the 1st North Carolina forward at the charge. Custer's men are predictably routed and flee directly into General Henry E. Davis's brigade as it canters up in support. Chaos reigns as the startled troops try to extricate themselves, and Kilpatrick orders a retreat with vengeful Confederates pursuing hotly. Stuart gradually reins in his men after a five-mile chase from Buckland back to Warrenton, securing 150 prisoners and eight wagons for a loss of 30 casualties. Thereafter, this embarrassing affair becomes jocularly known among Southern horsemen as the "Buckland Races."

Having failed to lure General George G. Meade into battle, the Army of Northern Virginia of General Robert E. Lee settles into defensive positions along the Rappahannock River, with bridgeheads at Rappahannock Station and Kelly's Ford. His aborted Bristoe Campaign cost the Confederacy 205 killed and 1,176 wounded (1,381) to a Federal tally of 136 dead, 733 wounded, and 1,423 missing (2,292).

Nonetheless, Union forces have been pushed back 40 miles in another brilliant offensive maneuver.

October 20
SOUTH: General Cadwallader C. Washburn assumes command of the XIII Corps in Mississippi.

WEST: Confederate cavalry under Colonel George C. Dibrell attack a Union wagon train at Philadelphia, Tennessee, inflicting 479 casualties.

NAVAL: A party from the USS *T. A. Ward* lands at Murrell's Inlet, North Carolina, looking for freshwater, but it is surprised by Confederate cavalry and loses 10 men captured.

The USS *Annie* captures the British blockade-runner *Martha Jane* off Bayport, Florida.

October 21
SOUTH: Union forces under General William B. Franklin occupy Opelousas, Louisiana, the farthest they reach during the so-called Bayou Teche operation.

NAVAL: The USS *Currituck* captures the Confederate steamer *Three Brothers* in the Rappahannock River, Virginia.

The USS *Nansemond* chases the Confederate steamer *Venus* aground near Cape Fear, North Carolina, where it is burned to prevent capture.

The USS *J. P. Jackson* captures the Confederate schooner *Syrena* off Deer Island, Mississippi.

October 22
SOUTH: Pursuing Federal forces attack and overrun a detachment belonging to Major John S. Mosby's partisan rangers near Annandale, Virginia.

NAVAL: The unescorted Union steamer *Mist* is boarded and destroyed by Confederate guerrillas at Ship Island, Mississippi. Hereafter, Admiral David D. Porter advises General William T. Sherman that "steamers should not be allowed to land anywhere but at a military port, or at a place guarded by a gunboat."

October 23
SOUTH: President Jefferson Davis relieves General Leonidas Polk as corps commander in the Army of Tennessee to end tensions with his superior, General Braxton Bragg. He is replaced by General William J. Hardee.

WEST: General Ulysses S. Grant arrives at Chattanooga, Tennessee, and assumes command of the Army of the Cumberland. Accompanied by General George H. Thomas, they advance to within gunshot range of Confederate lines below Lookout Mountain for a peek at enemy positions. Satisfied, Grant next orders a new supply route established from Bridgeport to the beleaguered garrison, the so-called Cracker Line. He also begins to plan an immediate counterstrike against General Braxton Bragg on the heights overlooking the city. Union fortunes are bolstered further by the forthcoming arrival of the XI and XII Corps under General Joseph Hooker, and the XV Corps of General William T. Sherman.

NAVAL: The USS *Norfolk Packet* captures the Confederate schooner *Ocean Bird* near St. Augustine Inlet, Florida.

October 24

WEST: Acting on the advice of Chattanooga's chief engineer, General William F. Smith, General Ulysses S. Grant authorizes a strategy to open up a new supply route on the Tennessee River below Confederate-held Racoon Mountain. This stratagem is necessary to supplant the awkward 60-mile route for supplies from northern Alabama through the Sequatchie Valley, which is also subject to interdiction by Confederate cavalry.

General William T. Sherman is appointed commander of the Army of the Tennessee once it finally arrives at Chattanooga, Tennessee, from Vicksburg, Mississippi.

NAVAL: The USS *Calypso* captures the British blockade-runner *Herald* off Frying Pan Shoals, North Carolina.

The Federal gunboats USS *Hastings* and *Key West* arrive at Eastport, Mississippi, in support of army operations along the Tennessee River under General William T. Sherman.

The USS *Conestoga* captures the Confederate steamer *Lille Martin* and the tug *Sweden* off Napoleon, Mississippi.

October 25

WEST: Confederate forces under General John S. Marmaduke attack and temporarily occupy Pine Bluff, Arkansas.

NAVAL: The USS *Kittatinny* captures the Confederate schooner *Reserve* off Pass Cavallo, Texas.

October 26

SOUTH: Major John S. Mosby's partisans attack a Union wagon train near New Baltimore, Virginia, seizing 145 horses before Union cavalry arrives to chase them off.

Union batteries recommence their second, intensive bombardment of Fort Sumter, Charleston Harbor, South Carolina. They fire 625 heavy shot into the crumbling works on the first day.

General William B. Franklin abandons his proposed offensive into East Texas through the bayou country and halts at Opelousas. He finds the foreboding, swampy terrain, made worse by incessant rainfall, impassible and retraces his steps back to New Iberia. The retreating Federals are followed closely by Confederate forces under ever-aggressive General Richard Taylor, who awaits an opportunity to strike.

WEST: As General Joseph Hooker approaches Chattanooga, Tennessee, with the XI and XII Corps, General William B. Hazen of IV Corps orchestrates laying a pontoon bridge across the Tennessee River at Brown's Ferry, opposite Confederate-held Racoon Mountain, to open up a riverine supply line to the beleaguered city. A brigade under General John B. Turchin then crosses over, defeats a determined charge by the 15th Alabama on the west bank, and secures a bridgehead. Union bases in northern Alabama are now capable of funneling aid directly to the garrison without resorting to the torturous trail running north through the mountains.

NAVAL: The ironclad fleet under Admiral John A. B. Dahlgren commences another intensive, two-week bombardment of Fort Sumter, Charleston Harbor, South Carolina. Despite a terrific pounding, the Confederate garrison holds on.

October 27

WEST: General Joseph Hooker commences operations to reopen the Tennessee River and facilitate the flow of Union supplies to Chattanooga, Tennessee. He advances the XI and XII Corps under his command from Bridgeport, Alabama, toward Brown's Ferry on the Tennessee River, crosses over, and clears Confederates from nearby Racoon Mountain. This move forces General Evander M. Law's division to withdraw to the west side of Lookout Mountain. Hooker also positions a force under General John W. Geary, XII Corps, at Wauhatchie Station to guard his line of communications from possible attack.

General William T. Sherman advances from Vicksburg, Mississippi, toward Chattanooga, Tennessee, having been directed previously by General in Chief Henry W. Halleck to repair Union rail lines en route. General Ulysses S. Grant, however, summarily cancels his instructions and orders him forward to Chattanooga with all speed.

NAVAL: A convoy of Federal troops under General Nathaniel P. Banks departs New Orleans, Louisiana, escorted by the USS *Monongahela, Virginia,* and *Owasco.* They are tasked with capturing Brazos, Santiago, and the mouth of the Rio Grande, Texas. It is anticipated that success here will deter French troops from crossing the river from Mexico.

The USS *Granite City* captures the Confederate schooner *Anita* at Pass Cavallo, Texas.

October 28

WEST: General Braxton Bragg orders General James Longstreet to mount an attack on the Union bridgehead at Brown's Ferry. Instead, Longstreet instructs the division of General Micah Jenkins to hit the Union rear guard at Wauhatchie Station at night. Although the attack is scheduled to kick off at 10:00 P.M., the four Southern brigades became lost in the dark and can only grope their way toward Union positions. Longstreet then cancels the operation and returns to camp, but his messenger never reaches Jenkins in time. At about midnight, the first Union sentries are encountered and eliminated, but General John W. Geary is alert and mounts a strong defense with two brigades.

General John M. Palmer assumes command of the XIV Corps in Tennessee.

NAVAL: The Confederate raider CSS *Georgia* under Lieutenant William L. Maury concludes a seven-month cruise against Union commerce by dropping anchor at Cherbourg, France.

October 29

SOUTH: President Jefferson Davis, continuing on his morale-raising tour of the Deep South, stops at Atlanta, Georgia.

The latest round of Union bombardment at Fort Sumter, Charleston Harbor, South Carolina, amounts to 2,691 shells and 33 slain Confederates, but the defenders still refuse to yield.

WEST: President Jefferson Davis grants a petition by General Nathan B. Forrest to be detached from the Army of Tennessee on the grounds that he has feuded seriously with General Braxton Bragg. The renowned "Wizard of the Saddle" is then granted an independent command based in northern Mississippi.

An early morning Confederate attack unfolds against Union positions at Wauhatchie Station, Tennessee. General Micah Jenkin's division of four brigades hits the Union camp hard in the darkness, but Federal troops under General John W. Geary, firing at muzzle flashes, resist stoutly. The Confederates charge the 'V' shaped Union line repeatedly, but fail to break it, and at 3:00 A.M., Jenkins retreats back to Lookout Mountain. Fighting dies down along the line as General Joseph Hooker dispatches General Carl Schurz's division to Geary's aid, but they became lost and fail to arrive. Confederate losses are 34 killed, 305 wounded, and 69 missing to a Union tally of 78 killed, 327 wounded, and 15 missing. The tenuous union supply line remains secure.

Union cavalry belonging to General George H. Thomas attack and rout a detachment of Confederates at Centerville, Tennessee, taking 90 captives.

General Frank P. Blair assumes command of the XV Corps in Tennessee.

October 30
POLITICS: A gathering of Unionists convenes at Fort Smith, Arkansas, to elect a representative to the U.S. Congress.
NORTH: James H. Wilson is appointed brigadier general, U.S. Army.
WEST: The Federal transport *Chattanooga* arrives up the Tennessee River and docks at Chattanooga, Tennessee, bringing much needed sustenance to the beleaguered Army of the Cumberland.
NAVAL: The USS *Annie* captures the British blockade-runner *Meteor* at Bayport, Florida.

The USS *Vanderbilt* captures the Confederate bark *Saxon* at Angra Pequena, Africa.

Federal gunboats USS *Lexington, Hastings, Key West, Cricket, Tobb, Romeo,* and *Peosta* relocate by steaming from the Mississippi to the Tennessee River in support of General William T. Sherman.

October 31
SOUTH: Union batteries continue with the latest round of shelling at Fort Sumter, Charleston Harbor, South Carolina.
NAVAL: Instruction begins for 52 midshipmen at the Confederate Naval Academy housed aboard the CSS *Patrick Henry* at Drewry's Bluff, James River, Virginia.

November 1
SOUTH: Federal gunners dump another 768 rounds on the shattered remnants of Fort Sumter, South Carolina, but the garrison, holed up in bombproofs, grimly hangs on.

Union forces under General William B. Franklin withdraw from Opelousas, Louisiana, back to New Iberia. This concludes the latest Union attempt to reach Sabine Pass, Texas, via Bayou Teche.
WEST: A force 5,000 Union cavalry and mounted infantry under General William W. Averell clatters out from Beverly, West Virginia, and into the Allegheny Moun-

tains on an extended raid toward Lewisburg. Averell's orders are to destroy the East Tennessee and Virginia Railroad in concert with another column commanded by General Alfred N. Duffie.

Union steamers continue landing supplies at Brown's Ferry on the Tennessee River, signaling the end of General Braxton Bragg's siege of Chattanooga, Tennessee. Because General George H. Thomas's hungry defenders eagerly await the new influx of hardtack, the new route is christened the "Cracker Line."

November 2

POLITICS: A Pennsylvania committee, tasked with organizing festivities surrounding the dedication of a Union cemetery for soldiers fallen at the Battle of Gettysburg, invites President Abraham Lincoln to attend the ceremony, slated for November 19. To their surprise and delight, the chief executive accepts and begins to work on a speech in which to express his justification of the war effort.

SOUTH: President Jefferson Davis is on hand to witness Union artillerists fire another 793 rounds against Fort Sumter, Charleston Harbor, South Carolina. Nonetheless, he "did not believe that Charleston would ever be taken."

November 3

SOUTH: Union gunners pour an additional 661 rounds on the ruins of Fort Sumter, Charleston Harbor, South Carolina, apparently to no effect.

Major John S. Mosby defeats a detachment of Union cavalry at Catlett's Station, Virginia.

Union and Confederate force skirmish heavily along the Bayou Borbeau, Louisiana. Three Federal divisions under General William B. Franklin's XIX Corps encamp carelessly and beyond mutual supporting distance. General Richard Taylor, though outnumbered two to one, masses his Confederates for a sudden attack on General Stephen G. Burbridge's exposed division. Security proves lax, and when Southern cavalry under General Thomas Green suddenly emerge out of a ravine, the Yankees scatter in camp. Burbridge, unable to reform his line, calls the retreat and is hounded all the way back to the camp of General George F. McGinnis, three miles distant. Losses in this sharp and embarrassing affair are 25 Union dead, 129 wounded, and 562 captured, along with one cannon.

WEST: A force 1,700 Union cavalry under General Alfred N. Duffie gallops out from Charleston, West Virginia, on a converted drive against Confederate positions at Lewisburg. Once present, he is to destroy the East Tennessee and Virginia Railroad in concert with a column led by General William W. Averell.

Confederate cavalry under General John R. Chalmers unsuccessfully attack the Union garrison at Collierville, Tennessee, losing 95 men.

General John McNeil assumes command of the Union District of the Frontier.

NAVAL: The USS *Kenwood* captures the Confederate steamer *Black Hawk* off Port Hudson, Louisiana.

Federal gunboats *Monongahela, Owasco,* and *Virginia* support troop landings under General Nathaniel P. Banks as they capture Brazos Island, Texas. The Union finally acquires a toehold in the Lone Star State.

November 4

WEST: General Braxton Bragg directs General James Longstreet to march 15,000 men against Union positions at Knoxville, Tennessee. The actual decision originates with President Jefferson Davis, partially to tie down Union assets in the eastern portion of the state and partially to lessen tensions between two headstrong leaders by separating them. Longstreet takes with him the divisions of General Micah Jenkins, General Lafayette McLaws, two artillery battalions under General Edward P. Alexander, and the cavalry of General Joseph Wheeler. The move itself is a bold expedient, which, if successful, will reopen direct communications with Virginia. Bragg, however, is seriously weakening his own defensive lines just as General Ulysses S. Grant prepares to attack below Chattanooga.

SOUTHWEST: Brownsville, Texas, is formally occupied by Union forces under Generals Napoleon J. T. Dana and Nathaniel P. Banks.

NAVAL: The USS *Virginia* captures the British blockade-runner *Matamoras* off the mouth of the Rio Grande, Texas.

The USS *Monongahela, Virginia,* and *Owasco* assist the army troops of General Napoleon J. T. Dana to seize Brownsville, Texas.

November 5

POLITICS: President Abraham Lincoln rebukes General Nathaniel P. Banks for his tardy efforts at reestablishing a constitutional government in Louisiana, which, he insists, must assure African Americans "on the question of their permanent freedom."

SOUTH: In several operations Major John S. Mosby reports that he has captured 75 prisoners and more than 100 mules and horses in the region Union forces deem "Mosby's Confederacy."

WEST: In light of General James Longstreet's offensive against Knoxville, Tennessee, General Ulysses S. Grant pensively awaits reinforcements under General William T. Sherman so that he finally can break the Confederate stranglehold on Chattanooga. For Grant, it is imperative to strike General Braxton Bragg before Longstreet attacks and possibly defeats General Ambrose E. Burnside's IX Corps at Knoxville.

NAVAL: The USS *Nansemond, Keystone State,* and *Howquah* chase and capture the Confederate vessel *Margaret and Jessie* off Myrtle Beach, South Carolina. This is one of the more enterprising blockade-runners extant, having completed 15 successful trips.

The cannonading of Fort Sumter, South Carolina, continues unabated, and Admiral John A. B. Dahlgren notes: "The only original feature left is the northeast face, the rest is a pile of rubbish."

The USS *Beauregard* seizes the British blockade-runner *Volante* near Cape Canaveral, Florida.

The USS *Virginia* and *Owasco* capture the British blockade-runners *Science* and *Dashing Wave* at the mouth of the Rio Grande, Texas.

November 6

POLITICS: President Jefferson Davis pays a morale-raising visit to Wilmington, North Carolina.

WEST: General William W. Averell encounters a Confederate brigade of 1,700 men and six cannon under General John Echols at Droop Mountain, West Virginia. Averell quickly plans to send his infantry skirting around the enemy left while his own artillery and cavalry demonstrate against Echol's center. At 3:00 P.M., the Confederate line, threatened from two directions, collapses and flees down the mountainside. Averell, having captured a battle flag and a cannon, declines to pursue.

Confederate cavalry under General William E. Jones captures Rogersville, Tennessee, netting 775 prisoners, 32 wagons, and 1,000 horses.

SOUTHWEST: General Nathaniel P. Banks lands and consolidates Union positions at Brownsville and Point Isabelle, Texas.

NAVAL: The Confederate raider CSS *Alabama* under Captain Raphael Semmes captures and burns the Union bark *Amanda* in the Dutch East Indies.

November 7

SOUTH: The Army of the Potomac pushes two brigades over the Rappahannock and into stiff fights at Kelly's Ford and Rappahannock Station. General Robert E. Lee has maintained a bridgehead on the north bank of the Rappahannock River, not really expecting General George G. Meade to attack in force, but when he does, the defenders are caught unawares. General William H. French, commanding the I, II, and II Corps, is ordered to cross the Rappahannock River at Kelly's Ford, then guarded by General Robert Rodes' division. At the onset, the 2nd and 30th North Carolina are overwhelmed in a surprise attack, and many are captured; 349 are casualties. Union forces now are established firmly on the south bank of the Rappahannock.

Five miles upstream, General John Sedgwick moves his V and VI Corps rapidly against Rappahannock Station, defended by the celebrated "Louisiana Tigers" of Colonel Harry T. Hays and a division under General Robert Hoke. Fighting rages throughout the day as Federal troops work their way around the Confederate flanks, but they fail to press their attack home. Combat stops with nightfall, and General Lee somewhat naturally assumes the enemy would not attack further that night, so he declines to reinforce the bridgehead. He intends to counterattack the following day, but Sedgwick preempts him. That evening, through a driving downpour, he leads the 6th Maine in a bayonet charge that startles the "Tigers" and drives them from their rifle pits. The 5th Wisconsin also comes up in support and makes good progress until the coup finally is delivered by a brigade under Colonel Emory Upton. The Confederate bridgehead is crushed, and 1,600 prisoners are taken, including Colonel Archibald C. Godwin. Total Confederate casualties number 2,023, principally captured, while the Federals lose 370. Lee, somewhat embarrassed to find his defensive positions suddenly compromised, rapidly withdraws south toward Culpeper Court House.

WEST: Union cavalry columns under General William W. Averell and Alfred N. A. Duffie unite in Lewisburg, West Virginia, where they destroy numerous Confederate supplies. But finding their path to Dublin blocked by felled trees and other obstacles, both leaders decide to abandon their raid.

NAVAL: Armed boats from the USS *Sagamore* capture the British blockade-runner *Paul* near Bayport, Florida.

Confederate guerrillas capture and burn the steamer *Allen Collier* at Whitworth's Landing, Mississippi, after it left the protection of the Federal gunboat USS *Eastport*.

November 8

WEST: John C. Breckinridge replaces General Daniel H. Hill as commander of the II Corps, Army of Tennessee, because of tensions with commanding General Braxton Bragg.

NAVAL: The USS *James Adger* and *Niphon* capture the Confederate steamer *Cornubia* near New Inlet, North Carolina.

November 9

POLITICS: President Abraham Lincoln attends the theater in Washington, D.C., ironically observing actor John Wilkes Booth perform in *The Marble Heart*.

President Jefferson Davis's train finally chugs into Richmond, Virginia, slowed somewhat by a snowstorm.

NAVAL: Admiral David D. Porter suggests to Secretary of the Navy Gideon Welles that the Coast Survey be employed in making detailed maps of the various creeks and tributaries emanating from the Mississippi River, "where navigation is made up of innumerable lakes and bayous not known to any but the most experienced pilots."

The USS *James Adger* finally seizes the Confederate vessel *Robert E. Lee* off Cape Lookout Shoals, North Carolina. This is another successful blockade-runner with 20 completed trips on its ledgers.

The USS *Niphon* captures the Confederate vessel *Ella and Annie* near Masonboro Inlet, North Carolina.

November 10

SOUTH: The Army of Northern Virginia, falling back, settles into defensive positions behind the Rapidan River to await developments.

For the past three days Union gunners deliver 1,753 artillery rounds against the ruins of Fort Sumter, Charleston Harbor, South Carolina, without prompting a Confederate surrender.

NAVAL: The USS *Howquah* captures the Confederate steamer *Ella* off Wilmington, North Carolina.

After two weeks of concentrated bombardment, the ironclad squadron of Admiral John A. B. Dahlgren reports having fired 9,036 projectiles at Fort Sumter, Charleston Harbor, South Carolina. The post is reduced to rubble yet refuses to yield.

The Confederate raider CSS *Alabama* under Captain Raphael Semmes captures and burns the Union clipper ship *Winged Racer* in the Straits of Sunda off Java.

November 11

POLITICS: President Jefferson Davis, ever concerned about the situation before Chattanooga, Tennessee, warns General Braxton Bragg to "not allow the enemy to get up all his reinforcements before striking him, if it can be avoided."

SOUTH: The politically well-connected general Benjamin F. Butler supersedes General John G. Foster as commander of the Union Department of Virginia and North

Carolina. He immediately orders troops to arrest any civilians using "opprobrious or threatening language" against them.

NAVAL: The Confederate raider CSS *Alabama* under Captain Raphael Semmes burns the Union clipper *Contest* in the Gaspar Straits.

November 12

SOUTH: Union batteries on Morris Island, Charleston Harbor, South Carolina, commence another prolonged bombardment of the still defiant Fort Sumter.

WEST: Generals James Longstreet and Joseph Wheeler mass their respective commands at Loudon, Tennessee, prior to advancing on nearby Knoxville. The weather and marching conditions up to this point have been horrid and greatly impede their progress.

November 14

WEST: General Nathan B. Forrest is assigned to the Confederate command of West Tennessee.

At Chattanooga, General William T. Sherman begins a personal reconnaissance of the northern end of Missionary Ridge, constituting the right wing of General Braxton Bragg's Army of Tennessee.

General James Longstreet's 15,000 Confederates begin to cross the Tennessee River at Loudon, Tennessee, having covered only 60 miles in eight days of hard marching. He then makes a tactical mistake by dispatching the bulk of his cavalry under General Joseph Wheeler on a raid toward the Holston River south of Knoxville. This deprives him of his best fighting troops just as a series of small-scale engagements starts to erupt. Prior to Longstreet's arrival, General Ambrose E. Burnside gallops into Loudon to supervise the evacuation of 5,000 Union troops there personally, and he shepherds them back to Knoxville. This effort turns out to be Burnside's best performance of the entire war, and a curious parallel race then unfolds as the two forces—almost within gunshot of each other—slog through ankle-deep mud vying to reach Knoxville first.

NAVAL: Union forces apprehend Confederate navy master John Y. Beall on the Virginia coast before he and his select band of 14 sailors are able to steal a steamer.

The USS *Dai Ching* captures the Confederate schooner *George Chisholm* at the Santee River, South Carolina.

The USS *Bermuda* recaptures the Union schooner *Mary Campbell* from Confederate forces near Pensacola, Florida.

November 15

SOUTH: Union gunners fire off an additional 2,328 rounds at Fort Sumter, Charleston Harbor, South Carolina, during the past three days without eliciting Confederate capitulation.

WEST: Having reached the Holston River, Confederate cavalry under General Joseph Wheeler arrive on the heights across from Knoxville, Tennessee. Wheeler decides that Union positions are too strong to attack, and so he withdraws.

The army of General James Longstreet and a division of Union troops commanded by General Ambrose E. Burnside slog through a driving rain and mud to reach Knoxville, Tennessee, first. Throughout their ordeal, the contestants are separated only by one mile and a bend in the Tennessee River. Burnside, anxious to avoid being trapped outside the city, redoubles efforts to reach Campbell's Station ahead of the enemy. Longstreet, meanwhile, dispatches General Lafayette McLaw's division to capture the crossroads ahead of him. Both sides encamp in the vicinity of Lenoir for the evening.

Having traversed 675 miles by boat, rail, and road, General William T. Sherman finally arrives at Bridgeport, Alabama, with four divisions, totaling 17,000 men, intended for the relief of Chattanooga, Tennessee. The general rides ahead to confer with General Ulysses S. Grant about his impending offensive.

Union authorities begin to crack down on illicit trade with either the enemy and or by war profiteers throughout western Tennessee and northern Mississippi.

NAVAL: The USS *Lodona* captures the British blockade-runner *Arctic* off Frying Pan Shoals, North Carolina.

The USS *Leigh* grounds under the guns of Fort Moultrie, Charleston Harbor, South Carolina, and has to be rescued and towed by the ironclad *Nahant*. Three of the *Leigh*'s crew members win the Congressional Medal of Honor for carrying a line from their crippled vessel to *Nahant* under heavy enemy fire.

November 16

WEST: Confederate cavalry under General John D. Imboden attack a Union supply train near Burlington, West Virginia, taking 25 captives and 245 horses.

The Confederate corps of General James Longstreet and a retiring Union column under General Ambrose Burnside depart Lenoir, Tennessee, in the early morning darkness. Both sides detach mounted forces ahead of their infantry to capture Campbell's Station, 10 miles distant, first. Burnside, feeling he is losing the race, also burns his baggage and wagons to increase his speed. Continual skirmishing erupts as the Union column fortuitously reach the crossroads just 15 minutes ahead of the Confederates and deploys to give battle. Longstreet then dispatches the brigade of General Evander M. Law around the Union position to strike it from behind while the division of General Lafayette McLaws hits the Union right. Burnside, perceiving this turning movement, falls back a half mile after his main line repulses an attack by McLaws. Law then makes a tardy appearance along the front of the readjusted Union line instead of its rear, and he is likewise beaten back. Fighting ceases at night, and Longstreet concedes both the race and Campbell's Station to the Yankees. Burnside, who conducted his movements with alacrity under trying conditions, suffers 318 casualties to a Confederate tally of 174. Union forces now proceed promptly into Knoxville and prepare for a siege.

SOUTHWEST: Union forces under General Nathaniel P. Banks occupy Corpus Christi, Texas.

November 17

WEST: General William W. Averell concludes his successful Union cavalry raid by returning to New Creek, West Virginia.

General James Longstreet begins to position his corps to besiege Knoxville, Tennessee.

SOUTHWEST: Union forces under General Nathaniel P. Banks storm a Confederate battery on Mustang Island, Aransas Pass, Texas.

NAVAL: The USS *Mystic* captures the Confederate schooner *Emma D.* off Yorktown, Virginia.

The USS *Monongahela* covers the landing of Federal forces under General Nathaniel P. Banks on Mustang Island, Aransas Pass, Texas. Several crew members come ashore to man some howitzers, which bombard the Confederate garrison into surrendering.

November 18

NORTH: President Abraham Lincoln, somewhat depressed over the illness of his son Tad, boards a special train that takes him to Gettysburg, Pennsylvania, for the purpose of dedicating a military cemetery.

SOUTH: Union and Confederate cavalry under Generals George A. Custer and Wade Hampton clash at Germanna Ford, Virginia.

WEST: A Union sweep of the region between Vienna, Virginia, and the Blue Ridge Mountains results in the capture of several of Major John S. Mosby's partisan rangers.

NAVAL: The USS *Granite City* captures the Confederate schooner *Amelia Ann* and the Spanish bark *Teresita* off Aransas Pass, Texas.

Federal gunboats USS *Choctaw, Franklin,* and *Carondelet* bombard Confederate batteries along the Mississippi River at Hog Point, Louisiana.

The Federal schooner *Joseph L. Garrity* is seized by Confederate sympathizers lurking onboard and taken to British Honduras, where it is converted into the blockade-runner *Eureka.*

November 19

NORTH: A gathering of 15,000 citizens at Gettysburg, Pennsylvania, is harangued with stirring oratory for two hours by Edward Everett. Onlookers are next greeted by the spectacle of a gaunt, towering president Abraham Lincoln striding to the podium. In only two minutes, he delivers his "Gettysburg Address," one of the most seminal political speeches in all history. "Four score and seven years ago our fathers brought forth, upon this continent, a new nation, conceived in liberty, and dedicated to the proposition that all men are created equal," it began. The audience listens in raptured silence, applauding lightly and not fully comprehending the import of what they are hearing. But in only 272 words, Lincoln codifies the ideals of the American republic and the absolute, essential necessity for preserving it: "That this nation, under God, shall have a new birth of freedom," he intones, "and that government of the people, by the people, for the people, shall not perish from the earth." This display of timeless eloquence resonates down to the present.

SOUTH: Fort Sumter is hit by an additional 694 shells thrown by a ring of Union siege guns at Charleston Harbor, South Carolina.

WEST: After Union forces under General Ambrose E. Burnside occupy and fortify the city of Knoxville, Tennessee, he orders a cavalry brigade of 700 men under General William P. Sanders to dismount and contest the advance of Confederates under General James Longstreet. Sanders mounts a tenacious defense and contains his antagonists for several hours before being killed, the only Southern-born general in Northern employ to die in combat. Burnside subsequently renames Fort Loudon, on the extreme northwest of the city, Fort Sanders in his honor.

November 20
POLITICS: Considering his recent address at Gettysburg a disappointment, President Abraham Lincoln contacts Edward Everett saying, "I am pleased to know that, in your opinion, the little I did say was not entirely a failure."
SOUTH: Union siege guns fire a further 1,344 rounds at Fort Sumter, Charleston Harbor, South Carolina, killing three defenders and wounding 11.

November 21
SOUTH: A Union sweep of the region between Bealeton and Thoroughfare Gap, Virginia, results in the capture of several partisans belonging to Major John S. Mosby's command.

Virginia Partisan Rangers under Major John S. Mosby attack and capture several Union wagons at Liberty, Virginia.
WEST: Union reinforcements under General William T. Sherman begin to cross the Tennessee River at Brown's Ferry before marching against General Braxton Bragg's right flank along Missionary Ridge. Additional forces under General Joseph Hooker also begin to deploy to storm the Confederate left near the Chattanooga Valley, Tennessee. Union movements are complicated further by a difficult landscape and driving rain, which delays their progress.
NAVAL: The USS *Grand Gulf* and the army transport *Fulton* seize the British steamer *Banshee* off Salter Path, North Carolina.

November 22
WEST: General Braxton Bragg detaches additional troops under General Patrick R. Cleburne from his Army of Tennessee to assist in the siege of Knoxville. Meanwhile, General Ulysses S. Grant orders his men into offensive positions for a major attack against Confederate troops around Chattanooga, Tennessee.
SOUTHWEST: Federal troops under General Nathaniel P. Banks besiege Fort Esperanza, Matagorda Island, Texas.
NAVAL: The USS *Jacob Bell* provides supporting fire for troop landings on St. George's Island, Maryland.

The USS *Aroostook* captures the Confederate schooner *Eureka* near Galveston, Texas.

November 23
WEST: General Ulysses S. Grant, prior to assaulting the main Confederate defenses of Braxton Bragg along Missionary Ridge, orchestrates a clever reconnaissance in force near the enemy's center. He orders General George H. Thomas to parade the IV Corps in full view of enemy positions along Orchard Knob, Tennessee, a long, low mound that would allow Union troops deploying out of Chattanooga to enjoy greater maneuvering room. At a given signal—and without artillery support—the divisions of Generals Thomas J. Woods and Philip H. Sheridan suddenly charge the unsuspecting defenders. What happens next is a minor miracle. At 12:30 P.M.,

Southerners of the 24th and 28th Alabama gathered about Orchard Knob to observe the military movement gradually drift away when they perceive a parade in progress. When a signal gun fires at precisely 1:30 P.M., the Union troops lurch forward, completely dispersing and overrunning their astonished opponents. This easy success enables Union troops to deploy at the very foot of Lookout Mountain and causes Grant to modify further his battle plans for the morrow. Union losses in this minor coup prove light, and 200 Confederates are also taken captive. Orchard Knob also serves as Grant's headquarters for the remainder of the campaign.

Confederate general Carter L. Stevenson, commanding an emaciated division on nearby Lookout Mountain, wires General Braxton Bragg that he lacks sufficient strength to hold his position against a determined Union assault. Stevenson sent his message in the prescribed code, unaware that Federal intelligence could decipher it, and General Ulysses S. Grant now realizes now vulnerable this important facet of the Confederate line is. He quickly instructs General Joseph Hooker to proceed immediately with three divisions to Lookout Mountain, on the Confederate left, and to seize Rossville Gap toward its rear. A redoubtable Union blow is assuming definite form.

General Patrick R. Cleburne's division, previously dispatched to Knoxville to assist General James Longstreet, is recalled hurriedly by General Braxton Bragg back to Chattanooga, Tennessee, and posted on the extreme right along Missionary Ridge.

SOUTHWEST: Federal forces under General Nathaniel P. Banks begin an overland campaign from the Texas coast to Rio Grande City.

November 24

SOUTH: Fort Sumter, Charleston Harbor, South Carolina, is pelted with another 270 Union rounds that leave three killed and two wounded.

WEST: At 8:00 A.M., General Joseph Hooker marches his three divisions—12,000 men—to the foot of Lookout Mountain, Tennessee, and begins to scale the 1,100-foot summit. Their advance is masked conveniently by a dense layer of fog blanketing the slope and blinding the defenders. Confederates under General Carter L. Stevenson, who scarcely can muster 2,693 men to oppose them, resist tenaciously but give ground before the Federal juggernaut. Hooker's attack, spearheaded by General John W. Geary's division, makes good progress, steadily driving the defenders up the slope. Resistance, including artillery fire, stiffens on a plateau halfway up the mountain, and Hooker stops to reorganize and bring up ammunition. Stevenson, having repeatedly requested General Braxton Bragg for reinforcements without response, suddenly is instructed to withdraw and reposition his command on the far right of the line at 2:30 P.M. The fleeing Confederates then burn a bridge behind them and withdraw in the night.

Meanwhile, anxious Union leaders gaze up on the mountain, shrouded with impenetrable, low-laying fog, and wonder how the battle is proceeding. By 8:00 P.M., Hooker has reached all his objectives, and the following morning, when the fog finally disperses, all are immediately relieved to behold the Stars and Stripes flying boldly from the summit. For this reason, the clash at Missionary Ridge becomes popularly known as "the Battle above the Clouds." Casualties are unrecorded by either side but appear to have been light. Furthermore, Hooker is poised to operate against the left and rear of the Confederate defenses by pressing on to Rossville Gap.

At the other end of Bragg's line, troops under General William T. Sherman advance to seize what he thinks is the north end of Missionary Ridge. Instead, the strip of land he captures is separated from the ridge by a wide ravine, thereby tipping off General Braxton Bragg that an assault is imminent.

NAVAL: The USS *Pawnee* and *Marblehead* cover army troops as they sink piles and other obstructions in the Stono River above Legareville, South Carolina.

November 25

SOUTH: Union gunners fire off 517 rounds into the crumbling defenses of Fort Sumter, Charleston Harbor, South Carolina, with little effect.

WEST: At Chattanooga, the final struggle between Generals Ulysses S. Grant, with 64,000 troops, and Braxton Bragg, commanding 46,000, is at hand. At 10:00 A.M., General William T. Sherman, with 16,000 men, begins a concerted drive against the Confederate right anchored on Missionary Ridge. The terrain encountered is rough, favoring the defense, and is manned ably by the 4,000 veterans of General Patrick R. Cleburne's division. Sherman consequently attacks Tunnel Hill all morning and into the afternoon with little to show beyond lengthening casualty lists. This is primarily because Union attacks are delivered piecemeal rather than by means of one crushing blow; hence, Cleburne remains able to shift his troops constantly to each threatened point. Just as the Confederates, whose ammunition is almost exhausted, seem on the verge of being overwhelmed, Cleburne orders a sharp bayonet charge downhill that scatters the tiring bluecoats. Sherman's alarming lack of progress also forces General Ulysses S. Grant to mount diversions elsewhere to prevent General Braxton Bragg from shifting reinforcements over to his right.

General Joseph Hooker's command is then ordered to attack Rossville Gap from Lookout Mountain on Bragg's left, which threatens the Confederate rear. Hooker's progress, however, is delayed because of the necessity to rebuild a bridge over Chickamauga Creek, so Grant next instructs General George H. Thomas, presently holding the Union center, to seize the rifle pits fronting the main Confederate position across Missionary Ridge. Grant simply intends this maneuver as a diversion to tie down Confederate troops until the flank attacks succeed.

At 3:00 P.M., Thomas dutifully masses 20,000 men below Orchard Knob and leads them forward. Cheering Federals under General Thomas J. Wood and Philip H. Sheridan quickly overrun lightly held Confederate positions and then—without orders—continue charging up the slopes of Missionary Ridge. Gathering impetus as they advance and seeking to avenge their humiliation at Chickamauga two months earlier, the surging blue tide drives Confederates from position after position until they stand victorious along the crest of the ridge. General John C. Breckinridge, commanding the Southern center, lacks the manpower necessary to establish a reserve, so the Union advance continues unchecked while

U.S. gunboat *Fort Hindman,* part of the Mississippi River fleet *(Library of Congress)*

the defenders scramble down the opposite slope. This extraordinary "Miracle of Missionary Ridge" suddenly ruptures Bragg's center, and he has no recourse but to order his remaining troops on either flank to withdrawn quickly to Dalton, Georgia.

The Confederate stranglehold on Chattanooga is both decisively—and dramatically—ended through Grant's bold stroke. Union casualties are 684 dead, 4,329 injured, and 322 missing (5,335), only marginally lighter than a Confederate loss of 361 dead, 2,180 injured, and 4,146 missing—mostly captured (6,687). In addition to securing Tennessee for the Union, the victory wields two other benefits of immense import to the conduct of subsequent military events: The road to Georgia is now open and Ulysses S. Grant is slated to receive his well-deserved promotion to lieutenant general.

NAVAL: The USS *Fort Hindman* captures the Confederate steamer *Volunteer* off Natchez Island, Mississippi.

Confederate agents sail the unfinished CSS *Rappahannock* from Britain to preclude its probable seizure by the government. The vessel makes for France.

November 26

SOUTH: Five corps of the Army of the Potomac under General George G. Meade successfully cross the Rapidan River, covered by a fog. Meade is now relying on the speed and stealth of his 85,000 men to crush the dispersed right wing of the Army of Northern Virginia before it can concentrate and oppose him. However, events go quickly awry as the marching order breaks down, units became entangled with each other, and valuable time is lost. The confusion alerts General Robert E. Lee that something is afoot, and he begins to marshal his men to confront the enemy head-on.

WEST: Generals William T. Sherman and George H. Thomas mount a pursuit of fleeing Confederates at Rossville Gap. They continue withdrawing until General Patrick R. Cleburne is ordered to constitute a rear guard at Ringgold Gap and Chickamauga Station, Georgia.

General Washington L. Elliott is ordered to use all available cavalry from the Army of the Cumberland to assist Union forces besieged at Knoxville, Tennessee.

NAVAL: The USS *James Adger* captures the British blockade-runner *Ella* off Masonboro Inlet, North Carolina.

The USS *Antonia* captures the Confederate schooner *Mary Ann* near Corpus Christi, Texas.

November 27

SOUTH: No sooner is the Army of the Potomac successfully across the Rapidan River than the III Corps of General William H. French, leading the advance, takes the wrong road and spends several hours countermarching about. The delays allow the Army of Northern Virginia to deploy General Edward Johnson's division at Payne's Farm, Virginia, directly in his path, and heavy fighting erupts. Johnson first repels the Union division of General Joseph B. Carr and then pitches into them, driving the Federals back onto difficult terrain that slows the Confederate advance. The Southerners subsequently are halted in their tracks and fall back. Meanwhile, elements of General Ambrose P. Hill's III Corps and Jubal A. Early's II Corps arrive in support, at which point Meade suspends the action. Confederate losses are 545 while Union losses, not recorded, are probably as light. The fact that Meade lost the element of surprise fatally compromises his ensuing Mine Run campaign.

Union gunners fire an additional 280 rounds into Fort Sumter, Charleston Harbor, South Carolina.

WEST: General John H. Morgan and several Confederate officers stage a daring escape from the State Penitentiary in Columbus, Ohio.

Confederates under General Patrick R. Cleburne mount an effective rear-guard action at Ringgold Gap, Georgia, as the Army of Tennessee under General Braxton Bragg falls back on Dalton. At 8:00 A.M., Cleburne, mustering only 4,157 muskets, confronts a force twice his size under General Joseph Hooker. That officer, without bothering to reconnoiter, marches one brigade directly into the gap where the Southerners are lying behind ledges and outcrops. The Federals immediately are blasted back with heavy losses while additional Union troops are dispatched to ascend the mountain on Cleburne's flank. These too stumble into a clever ambush and are sent scampering down the slope. Strong Union moves against the Confederate left then are stopped by artillery fire, and renewed attacks develop into a costly stalemate. At 12:00 P.M., Cleburne is ordered by General Joseph Hardee to withdraw from his position, and he disengages. His stiffly fought action bought the Army of Tennessee four precious hours and inflicts 507 Union casualties. The Confederates sustain 20 dead, 190 wounded, and 11 missing.

General William T. Sherman is ordered to provide relief for the Union garrison besieged at Knoxville, Tennessee. He dispatches two divisions from the IV Corps under General Gordon Granger.

NAVAL: The USS *Two Sisters* captures the Confederate schooner *Maria Alberta* off Bayport, Florida.

November 28

SOUTH: General Robert E. Lee continues thwarting a possible attack from the Army of the Potomac under General George M. Meade by assuming strong defensive positions along Mine Run Creek. Astute Confederate moves, such as the construction of extensive trenchworks and field fortifications, doom the Union offensive before it can unfold.

WEST: General Braxton Bragg, hated by his subordinates and humiliated before Chattanooga, formerly submits his resignation to President Jefferson Davis.

Confederate cavalry under General Nathan B. Forrest depart for operations against the Memphis and Charleston Railroad in West Tennessee.

General William T. Sherman marches to the relief of General Ambrose E. Burnside at Knoxville, Tennessee, with parts of the Union XI, XIV, and XV Corps.

General James Longstreet orders an attack on Fort Sanders in an attempt to capture Knoxville, Tennessee. This evening, a heavy fog forces him to cancel the assault, but he nonetheless sends his sharpshooters forward to cover the impending advance. Their presence outside Union lines alerts the defenders, who are strongly ensconced behind a deep, impassable ditch fronting their parapet.

NAVAL: The USS *Chippewa,* while convoying Federal troops up Skull Creek, North Carolina, on reconnaissance duty, engages entrenched Confederate infantry and prevents them from thwarting the mission.

November 29

POLITICS: President Abraham Lincoln recovers from a mild case of smallpox.

WEST: The Confederate attack on Fort Sanders in Knoxville, Tennessee, goes forward at 6:00 A.M., despite frightfully cold winter weather. Prior reconnaissance has been poor, and the attackers have no idea of what was is in store for them. Three brigades of infantry charge forward but, lacking ladders, prove unable to surmount the deep, ice-filled ditch surrounding the works. They also encounter telegraph wire strung out between trees at knee-level as an obstruction—a primitive form of barbed wire. As their momentum fails, Union infantry and artillery on the parapet rake them with murderous fire for 20 minutes. Only a handful of Confederates finally mount the fort's wall before being dispatched, and the rest retreat in disorder. General James Longstreet is willing to launch another attack, but his subordinates dissuade him from doing so. Confederate losses reach 129 killed, 458 wounded, and

226 missing, while the Union sustains five dead and eight wounded. Longstreet's debacle at Fort Sanders signals the end of his "siege" of Knoxville and, on receiving word of Braxton Bragg's rout at Chattanooga, he prepares to withdraw.

SOUTHWEST: Confederate forces evacuate Fort Esperanza on Matagorda Island, Texas.

NAVAL: The USS *Kanawha* captures the schooner *Wenoa* near Mobile, Alabama.

A naval gun crew operates a howitzer battery in support of army operations against Pass Cavallo, Texas.

November 30

SOUTH: General George G. Meade prepares his army for a massive blow on prepared Confederate positions along Mine Run, but he is dissuaded from doing so by General Gouverneur K. Warren.

WEST: President Jefferson Davis grants General Braxton Bragg's request to be relieved of command of the Army of Tennessee at Dalton, Georgia, and he is succeeded temporarily by General William J. Hardee.

SOUTHWEST: Union forces occupy Fort Esperanza on Matagorda Island, Texas.

December 1

POLITICS: Notorious Southern spy Bell Boyd, suffering from typhoid fever, again is released from a Federal prison in Washington, D.C., and warned to steer clear of Union territory.

SOUTH: General George M. Meade begins to wind down his Mine Run campaign by crossing the Army of the Potomac back over the Rapidan River, Virginia, and into winter quarters. General Robert E. Lee starts to position the Army of Northern Virginia for an offensive of its own by dispatching Generals Richard H. Anderson's and Cadmus M. Wilcox's divisions forward to assail Meade's left flank.

WEST: Confederate forces under General Samuel Jones capture $700,000 worth of Union stores at Mount Sterling, Kentucky, along with 250 horses and 100 prisoners without a single loss to his command.

Charging Union cavalry surprise General Joseph Wheeler's command at Jonesville, Virginia, near Cumberland Gap, taking several prisoners.

General James B. McPherson, commanding the Union XVII Corps, attacks and dislodges General Wirt Adams' Confederates from Camp Cotton, Mississippi.

December 2

SOUTH: General George G. Meade concludes his unsuccessful Mine Run Campaign and successfully withdraws Union forces north of the Rapidan River. General Robert E. Lee, rousing his own men for a quick counterstrike, advances on Union positions only to find them deserted. "I am too old to command this army," he opines. "We should have never permitted those people to get away." The Mine Run operation costs the Confederates 601 casualties, the Union sustains 1,653. Furthermore, Lee becomes impressed by the power of entrenchments and intends to employ them in defensive situations whenever possible.

WEST: In an emotional ceremony, General Braxton Bragg surrenders command of the Army of Tennessee to General William J. Hardee at Dalton, Georgia.

NAVAL: Armed boats from the USS *Restless* destroy Confederate saltworks along Lake Ocala, Florida.

December 3

WEST: The I Corps of General James Longstreet abandons Knoxville, Tennessee, and enters into winter quarters at nearby Greenville. From this position, he is at liberty to remain in the theater or march to rejoin General Robert E. Lee in Virginia. General Ambrose E. Burnside, meanwhile, fails to pursue the Confederates vigorously, which forces General Ulysses S. Grant to maintain sizable Union forces in Tennessee until the following spring.

NAVAL: The USS *New London* captures the Confederate schooner *Del Nile* off Padre Pass Island, Texas.

December 4

SOUTH: Nathan B. Forrest is promoted to major general, C.S.A.

The latest round of concentrated bombardment increases at Charleston Harbor, South Carolina, to more than 1,300 rounds in the past seven days.

WEST: General James Longstreet continues to withdraw his 15,000 Confederates northeast of Knoxville, Tennessee, inching toward the Virginia border. General John G. Parke finally initiates a tepid pursuit of Southerners with 4,000 cavalry under General James M. Shackleford.

December 5

SOUTH: General Henry H. Lockwood assumes command of the Union VIII Corps and Middle Department in Virginia.

NAVAL: A boat crew dispatched from the USS *Perry* in search of blockade-runners is captured in Murrell's Inlet, South Carolina. "These blunders are very annoying," Admiral John A. B. Dahlgren concedes, "and yet I do not like to discourage enterprise and dash on the part of our officers and men. Better to suffer from the excess than the deficiencies of these qualities."

December 6

WEST: General William T. Sherman and his staff arrive at the command tent of General Ambrose E. Burnside in Knoxville, Tennessee.

NAVAL: The ironclad USS *Weehawken*, overloaded with ammunition, founders in an ebb tide and sinks outside Charleston Harbor, South Carolina, with a loss of 24 officers and men.

The USS *Violet* and *Aries* capture the British steamer *Ceres* off the mouth of the Cape Fear River, North Carolina.

December 7

POLITICS: The first session of the 38th Congress convenes in Washington, D.C.

The fourth session of the 1st Confederate Congress gathers in Richmond, Virginia. President Jefferson Davis acknowledges the failures of the previous years but declares: "The patriotism of the people has proven equal to every sacrifice demanded by their country's need."

NAVAL: Secretary Gideon Welles makes his third annual report, declaring U.S. Navy strength to be 34,000 seamen and 588 warships, displacing 467,967 tons and carrying

4,443 guns. Moreover, these vessels have accounted for the capture or destruction of more than 1,000 Southern and foreign vessels attempting to run the Union blockade.

A party of 15 Confederate sympathizers under John C. Braine board the Union steamer *Chesapeake* at New York, seize that vessel on its run to Portland, Maine, and conduct it to Nova Scotia, Canada.

December 8

POLITICS: To exacerbate the growing rift in Southern politics, President Abraham Lincoln addresses the opening of the 38th Congress and proffers his Proclamation of Amnesty and Reconstruction to all Southerners who take a loyalty oath. In it, he offers to recognize the sitting government of any seceded state provided that at least 10 percent of voters submit to the oath and abolish slavery. The amnesty does not apply to high-ranking Confederate officials or former military men who resigned to join the Confederacy, but Radical Republicans still find the offer too conciliatory.

WEST: A Union cavalry column under General William W. Averell departs New Creek, West Virginia, on a raid against the Virginia and Tennessee Railroad at Salem, Virginia. Simultaneously, additional cavalry under General Eliakim P. Scammon ride from Charleston toward Lewisburg in support.

NAVAL: The USS *Braziliera* runs the British blockade-runner *Antoinette* aground on Cumberland Island, Georgia, and then burns it.

The USS *Neosho* and *Signal* bombard and destroy a Confederate battery at Morganza, Louisiana, thereby rescuing the merchant steamer *Henry Von Phul*.

December 9

SOUTH: Major John S. Mosby leads an attack on Union camps at Lewinsville, Virginia.

A mutiny by African-American troops at Fort Jackson, Louisiana, is suppressed by white officers. Two transgressors subsequently receive punishment by whipping.

WEST: General John G. Foster succeeds General Ambrose E. Burnside as commander of the Department of the Ohio, principally over his lackadaisical conduct throughout the Chattanooga campaign. Recriminations also follow on the Confederate side as General James Longstreet draws up charges against several of his own staff officers.

NAVAL: The USS *Circassian* captures the British blockade-runner *Minna* off Cape Romain, South Carolina.

The USS *Kennebec* captures the Confederate schooner *Marshall Smith* near Mobile, Alabama.

December 10

NAVAL: The USS *Bloomer* and *Restless* destroy a saltworks and several Confederate schooners at St. Andrews, Florida.

Confederate raiders capture and burn the merchant schooner *Josephine Truxillo* and barge *Stephany* on Bayou Lacomb, Louisiana.

December 11

SOUTH: Union shelling of Fort Sumter, Charleston Harbor, South Carolina, scores a direct hit on an ammunition magazine, killing 11 and wounding 41 Confederates. Despite a veritable hurricane of shot and shell, the defenders pluckily refuse to surrender.

WEST: General John A. Logan replaces General Frank P. Blair as commander of the Union XV Corps in Tennessee.

NAVAL: While attempting to raise the sunken USS *Indianola* from its Mississippi River berth, the Federal ironclad *Carondelet* exchanges fire with Confederate forces along the shoreline, driving them off.

December 12

POLITICS: Henceforth, the Confederate government refuses to accept any supplies sent from the North to Union captives.

SOUTH: A quick raid by Union forces nets 90 Southern prisoners at Charles City Court House, Virginia.

WEST: General Samuel D. Sturgis is assigned to command all Union cavalry in the Department of the Ohio.

December 13

SOUTH: Virginian Partisan Rangers under Major John S. Mosby attack a sleeping Union camp at Germantown, Virginia, killing two soldiers and making off with several horses.

WEST: A force of 4,000 Union cavalry under General James M. Shackleford occupies Bean's Station, Tennessee, while pursuing Confederates under General James Longstreet. Longstreet, observing Shackleford outdistance his infantry support, suddenly turns and enacts a three-pronged attack to catch the Federals in a vise and destroy them. That night, he dispatches four cavalry brigades under General William T. Martin on a circuitous route around the Holston River to assail the Union flank, while an additional two cavalry brigades under General William E. Jones undertake an even longer march to hit Shackleford from behind. Longstreet himself marches with General Bushrod R. Johnson's infantry division to meet the Yankees head on at Bean's Station.

December 14

POLITICS: President Abraham Lincoln grants Mrs Mary Todd's Lincoln's half-sister a general amnesty after she visits the White House and takes a loyalty oath.

WEST: General James Longstreet attacks Bean's Station, Tennessee, at 2:00 A.M., startling but not dislodging Union cavalry under General James M. Shackleford. The Federals post their artillery on a nearby hill overlooking their position and closely engage Longstreet's infantry. This contest is supposed to absorb Shackleford's attention while Confederate cavalry columns strike their flank and rear, but neither General William T. Martin nor William E. Jones appear in time. At length, Shackleford conducts an orderly retreat through Bean's Gap to Blain's Cross Roads and digs in behind a rail breastwork. Pursuing Confederate forces decline attacking him there and withdraw. Fighting in terrible winter weather inflicts roughly 200 casualties on both sides. Bean's Station is the last action of the otherwise dreary Knoxville campaign, which cost the Confederates 182 dead, 768 wounded, and 142 missing (1,142), to a Union tally of 92 killed, 394 wounded, and 207 captured (693).

December 15

SOUTH: Joseph O. Shelby is promoted to major general, C.S.A.

General Jubal A. Early is appointed to command of the Confederate Valley District, Virginia.

WEST: Confederates under General Jubal A. Early sortie from Hanover Junction, Virginia, to cut off Union cavalry under General William W. Averell at nearby Millborough.

General John C. Breckinridge relinquishes command of the II Corps, Army of Tennessee, to General Thomas C. Hindman.

December 16

NORTH: General John Buford dies of tuberculosis in Washington, D.C.

SOUTH: President Jefferson Davis, forgoing past difficulties, appoints General Joseph E. Johnston to supersede General William J. Hardee as commander of the Army of Tennessee. General Leonidas K. Polk also is appointed to head the Army of Mississippi.

WEST: General William W. Averell's cavalry column surprises the inhabitants of Salem, Virginia, as he occupies the town and begins to destroy the depot and railroad bridges found there.

NAVAL: The USS *Huron* captures the Confederate vessel *Chatham* near Doboy Sound, Georgia.

The USS *Ariel* seizes the Confederate sloop *Magnolia* near the west coast of Florida.

December 17

POLITICS: President Abraham Lincoln promulgates plans for a Federal Bureau of Emancipation to assist liberated African Americans. Congress, however, fails to enact it until March 1865.

NAVAL: The USS *Ella and Annie* apprehends the recently commandeered steamer *Chesapeake* in Sambro Harbor, Nova Scotia. A Vice Admiralty Court in Halifax subsequently releases the vessel back to its original owners.

The USS *Roebuck* captures the British blockade-runner *Ringdove* near the Indian River, Florida.

Landing parties from the USS *Moose* report capturing and destroying a distillery operated by Confederate irregulars on Seven Miles Island, Tennessee.

December 18

POLITICS: President Abraham Lincoln, displeased with General John M. Schofield's handling of civilian affairs in Missouri, suggests to Secretary of War Edwin M. Stanton that he simultaneously be sacked and promoted to major general, thereby avoiding any ruffled feathers.

SOUTH: The latest Union sweep between Vienna and Middleburg, Virginia, nets several partisans belonging to Major John S. Mosby's command.

December 19

NAVAL: An expedition consisting of USS *Restless, Bloomer,* and *Caroline* scours St. Andrews Bay, Florida, eliminating 290 saltworks and 268 buildings in a 10-day period.

December 20

NAVAL: The USS *Governor Buckingham* captures the Confederate blockade-runner *Antonica* after it is grounded near Frying Pan Shoals, North Carolina.

The USS *Fox* seizes the Confederate steamer *Powerful* at the mouth of the Suwannee River, Florida.

The USS *Sunflower* takes the Confederates blockade-runner *Hancock* in Tampa Bay, Florida.

The USS *Antona* captures the Confederate schooner *Exchange* off Velasco, Texas.

December 21

WEST: General Jacob D. Cox receives command of the Union XXIII Corps at Knoxville, Tennessee.

December 22

SOUTH: General Leonidas K. Polk is formally transferred as commander of the Confederate Department of Mississippi and Louisiana.

December 23

NAVAL: Admiral David G. Farragut, eager to resume active duty, informs Secretary of the Navy Gideon Welles that his USS *Hartford* is ready to depart save for some crew shortages.

December 24

WEST: General William W. Averell concludes his Union cavalry's third raid for the year by reaching Beverly, West Virginia. The inability of General Samuel Jones to intercept him with superior numbers of Confederates leads to his eventual dismissal as commander of the Western Department.

Cavalry under Generals Benjamin H. Grierson and Nathan B. Forrest clash outside of Estenaula and Jack's Creek, Tennessee.

NAVAL: The USS *Fox* captures the British blockade-runner *Edward* near the mouth of the Suwannee River, Florida.

The USS *Sunflower* captures the Confederate vessel *Hancock* in Tampa Bay, Florida.

The Confederate raider CSS *Alabama* under Captain Raphael Semmes seizes and burns the Union bark *Texan Star* in the Strait of Malacca, Dutch East Indies.

December 25

SOUTH: Federal forces raiding Leesburg, Virginia, capture several men belonging to Major John S. Mosby's partisan rangers.

WEST: Union cavalry under General William W. Averell return to Beverly, West Virginia, concluding a three-week raid against the Virginia and Tennessee Railroad.

NAVAL: Landing parties from the USS *Daylight* and *Howquah* destroy four saltworks at Bear Inlet, North Carolina.

In a surprise bombardment, the USS *Marblehead* receives 20 hits from Confederate batteries off Legareville, Stono River, South Carolina, but landing parties from accompanying vessels *Pawnee* and *C. P. Williams* drive them off.

The Federal gunboat USS *Tahoma* bombards Fort Brooke in Tampa Bay, Florida, for two hours but decides against landing an armed party to seize it.

December 26

WEST: Cavalry under Generals Benjamin H. Grierson and Nathan B. Forrest spar at New Castle and Somerville, Tennessee.

NAVAL: The USS *Reindeer* and army steamer *Silver Lake No. 2* conduct a detailed reconnaissance of the Cumberland River from Nashville, Tennessee, to Creelsboro, Kentucky. During the next five days, they are fired upon but are not seriously damaged.

The Confederate raider CSS *Alabama* under Captain Raphael Semmes captures and burns the Union ships *Sonora* and *Highlander* in the Straits of Malacca.

December 27

NORTH: President Abraham Lincoln and Secretary of War Edwin M. Stanton pay a goodwill visit to Confederate prisoners at Point Lookout, Maryland.

WEST: General Joseph E. Johnston arrives at Dalton, Georgia, to take charge of the Confederate Department of Tennessee with its attendant—and somewhat battered—army.

December 28

POLITICS: The Confederate Congress in Richmond, Virginia, abolishes the practice of hiring draft substitutions and also modifies the detested tax in kind.

Confederate cavalry under General Joseph Wheeler attack a supply train belonging to General George H. Thomas at Charleston, Tennessee.

December 29

SOUTH: General Winfield S. Hancock, seriously wounded at Gettysburg five months earlier, resumes command of the Union II Corps, Army of the Potomac.

NAVAL: A squadron consisting of the USS *Nipsic, Sanford, Geranium, Daffodil,* and *Ethan Allen* steam into Murrel's Inlet, South Carolina, to search for blockade-runners and break up enemy troop concentrations that had attacked Union gunboats.

Armed boats from the USS *Stars and Stripes* burn the Confederate blockade-runner *Caroline Gertrude* at the mouth of the Ocklockonee River, Florida.

December 30

NAVAL: Armed boats from the USS *Pursuit* destroy two Confederate saltworks at St. Joseph's Bay, Florida.

December 31

POLITICS: President Jefferson Davis names North Carolina senator George Davis in an interim appointment to replace outgoing Wade Keyes as Confederate attorney general.

NAVAL: A naval squadron consisting of the USS *Sciota, Granite City, Monongahela, Penobscot,* and *Estrella* attempt to land Federal troops on the Matagorda Peninsula, Texas, but the maneuver is aborted in the face of heavy seas. In the course of sporadic fighting, the Confederate gunboat *John F. Carr* is run ashore and burned.

The USS *Kennebec* seizes the Confederate blockade-runner *Grey Jacket* at sea.

Looking over events of the past year, Navy secretary Gideon Welles is pleased to state: "The war has been waged with success, although there have been in some instances errors and misfortunes. But the heart of the nation is sounder and its hopes higher."

1864

January 1

SOUTH: Major John S. Mosby tangles with Union forces outside Rectortown, Virginia.

WEST: The Department of Kansas is reestablished.

NAVAL: The USS *Huron* intercepts and sinks the British blockade-runner *Sylvanus* in Doboy Sound, Georgia.

January 2

POLITICS: General Patrick L. Cleburne and other officers petition for the possible use of African Americans in the Confederate army to address endemic manpower shortages. Not only does President Jefferson Davis ignore the recommendation, but he ultimately denies Cleburne a well-deserved promotion to lieutenant general because of it.

Senator George Davis of North Carolina formally replaces Wade Keys as Confederate attorney general.

WEST: Federal troops occupy Santa Catalina Island, off the California coast.

January 3

SOUTH: Confederate cavalry under General William E. Jones surprises and defeats General Orlando B. Wilcox at Jonesville, Virginia, taking 383 prisoners, 27 wagons, and three cannon.

WEST: General Fitzhugh Lee's cavalry defeat Union forces in Hardy County, West Virginia, seizing a large supply train belonging to General Benjamin F. Kelley. Among his trophies are 250 head of cattle.

SOUTHWEST: General Francis J. Herron assumes command of Union forces along the Rio Grande, Texas.

NAVAL: Gunfire from the USS *Fort Jackson, Iron Age, Montgomery, Daylight,* and *Fahkee* destroys the beached Confederate steamer *Bendigo* at Lockwood's Folly Inlet, South Carolina.

January 4

POLITICS: President Jefferson Davis instructs General Robert E. Lee to begin to requisition food from civilians as becomes necessary.

WEST: General Edmund Kirby-Smith warns General Richard Taylor of a possible invasion of western Louisiana, insisting, "I still think Red and Washita Rivers, especially the former, are the true lines of operation for an invading column, and that we may expect an attempt to be made by the enemy in force before the rivers fall."

January 5

POLITICS: More than 1,000 African-American citizens of New Orleans, Louisiana, including a handful of War of 1812 veterans, petition for the right to vote and send it to President Abraham, Lincoln.

SOUTHWEST: Federal troops, aided by Apache warriors, rout a large detachment of Navaho along the Pecos River, New Mexico Territory, killing and capturing several in freezing weather.

January 6

SOUTH: General Joseph J. Reynolds is appointed commander of Federal forces at New Orleans, Louisiana.

WEST: The Department of Arkansas is officially constituted.

SOUTHWEST: Colonel Christopher "Kit" Carson begins a protracted winter campaign against hostile Navajo in the Canon de Chelly region of the New Mexico Territory. General James H. Carleton, commanding that department, anxiously wires that his numerous Navajo prisoners are suffering from want of winter clothing and requisitions supplies from the Indian Department.

NAVAL: Confederate guerrillas attack and disable the Federal steamer *Delta* on the Mississippi River.

January 7

POLITICS: President Abraham Lincoln, beset by a rash of army desertions, invariably commutes the death sentence of offenders, insisting, "I am trying to evade the butchering business, lately."

President Jefferson Davis appoints William Preston as envoy to Mexico.

SOUTH: Confederate cavalry under Major John S. Mosby rout a larger Union detachment at Warrenton, Virginia, taking 30 captives and 40 horses.

A detachment of the 21st Georgia Cavalry captures 25 Union prisoners at Waccamaw Neck, South Carolina.

NAVAL: Admiral John A. B. Dahlgren, informed of Confederate submarine technology being tested at Charleston, South Carolina, warns ships of his South Atlantic Blockading Squadron to guard against attacks.

The USS *Montgomery* and *Aries* run the Confederate steamer *Dare* aground at North Inlet, South Carolina; then parties board and burn it.

The USS *San Jacinto* captures the Confederate schooner *Roebuck* at sea.

January 8

SOUTH: General John H. Morgan, recently escaped from the Ohio State Penitentiary, is feted in Richmond, Virginia.

WEST: Seventeen-year-old David O. Dodd is hanged as a Confederate spy in Little Rock, Arkansas.

NAVAL: The USS *Kennebec* captures the Confederate blockade-runner *John Scott* after an eight-hour chase off Mobile, Alabama.

January 9

SOUTH: General Gouverneur K. Warren is appointed commander of the II Corps, Army of the Potomac.

Naval: James O. Putnam, U.S. Consul at Le Havre, France, notifies Captain John Winslow of the USS *Kearsarge* that Confederate vessels CSS *Georgia, Florida,* and *Rappahannock* are planning to attack and overwhelm him once he departs from Brest.

January 10

South: Major John S. Mosby surprises a Union detachment in its camp at Loudoun Heights, Virginia, only to be driven off when the defenders unexpectedly rally.

Naval: The USS *Iron Age* is sunk by Confederate artillery after running aground at Lockwood's Folly Inlet, South Carolina.

The USS *Keystone State, Quaker City,* and *Tuscarora* run the Confederate steamer *Vera* ashore off Little River Inlet, South Carolina, whereupon it is burned by its crew.

Armed boats from the USS *Roebuck* seize the Confederate sloop *Maria Louise* near Jupiter Inlet, Florida.

January 11

Politics: U.S. senator John B. Henderson of Missouri proposes a joint resolution for the abolishment of slavery, which ultimately manifests as the 13th Amendment to the Constitution.

Naval: The USS *Minnesota, Daylight, Aries,* and *Governor Buckingham* intercept the Confederate blockade-runner *Ranger* and force it aground off Lockwood's Folly Inlet, South Carolina, destroying it with gunfire.

The USS *Honeysuckle* captures the British blockade-runner *Fly* off Jupiter Inlet, Florida.

Armed boats from the USS *Roebuck* seize the British blockade-runner *Susan* in Jupiter Inlet, Florida.

January 12

Naval: A naval squadron consisting of the USS *Yankee, Currituck, Anacostia, Tulip,* and *Jacob Bell* supports Union cavalry under General Gilman Marston on an expedition between the Potomac and Rappahannock rivers, Virginia.

January 13

Politics: President Abraham Lincoln instructs Generals Quincy A. Gilmore in Florida and Nathaniel P. Banks in Louisiana to begin to reconstitute civil authority and free governments, "with all possible dispatch."

President Jefferson Davis advises General Joseph E. Johnston against falling back from his present strong position at Dalton, Georgia, declaring, "I trust you will not deem it necessary to adopt such a measure."

Naval: Armed boats from the USS *Two Sisters* capture the Confederate schooner *William* off the Suwannee River, Florida.

January 14

Naval: Armed boats from the USS *Roebuck* force the British blockade-runner *Young Racer* aground at Jupiter Inlet, Florida.

The USS *Union* captures the Confederate steamer *Mayflower* off Tampa Bay, Florida.

The Confederate raider CSS *Alabama* under Captain Raphael Semmes captures and burns the Union vessel *Emma Jane* off the coast of Malabar, India.

January 15

NAVAL: Confederate secretary of the navy Stephen R. Mallory assigns Commander James W. Cooke to command the steam ram CSS *Albemarle,* then under construction at Halifax, North Carolina.

The USS *Beauregard* captures the British blockade-runner *Minnie* off Mosquito Inlet, Florida.

January 16

WEST: General Samuel R. Curtis resumes command of the Union Department of Kansas.

Confederate cavalry attached to General James Longstreet's I Corps defeat their Union opposites under General Samuel D. Sturgis in a heavy skirmish at Dandridge, Tennessee.

NAVAL: Armed boats from the USS *Fernandina* capture the Confederate sloop *Annie Thompson* in St. Catherine's Sound, Georgia.

The USS *Gertrude* captures the Confederate schooner *Ellen* off Mobile Bay, Alabama.

January 17

WEST: General Orlando B. Wilcox succeeds General Robert B. Potter to the command of the Union IX Corps at Knoxville, Tennessee.

January 18

NAVAL: Armed boats from the USS *Roebuck* seize the Confederate sloop *Caroline* off Jupiter Inlet, Florida.

The USS *Stars and Stripes* captures the Confederate steamer *Laura* off the Ocklockonee River, Florida.

Admiral David G. Farragut arrives at Mobile Bay, Alabama, onboard the USS *Hartford* and proceeds to inspect the Confederate defenses. He is especially concerned about the large Confederate steam ram CSS *Tennessee* and begins to enact plans to destroy it.

January 19

WEST: The pro-Union Arkansas constitutional convention embraces antislavery provisions in its new document.

NAVAL: Navy secretary Gideon Welles alerts Admiral David D. Porter as to the possible introduction of Confederate "coal torpedoes"—cast-iron bombs made to resemble pieces of coal and designed to exploded in a ship's boiler. Crews must be alert to prevent enemy agents from placing such devices in Union coal depots. If any are caught, he has "given orders to commanders of vessels not to be very particular about the treatment of any of these desperados if caught—only summary punishment will be effective."

Armed boats from the USS *Roebuck* capture the British blockade-runner *Eliza* and Confederate sloop *Mary* at Jupiter Inlet, Florida.

January 20
POLITICS: President Abraham Lincoln advises General Frederick Steele, commanding the District of Arkansas, to schedule free elections as soon as possible to reestablish a free civilian government.
NAVAL: Federal warships begin to reconnoiter Forts Morgan and Grimes at the mouth of Mobile Bay, Alabama, at the behest of Admiral David G. Farragut.

January 21
POLITICS: A gathering of pro-Union citizens in Nashville, Tennessee, proposes a constitutional convention bent on abolishing slavery.
SOUTHWEST: Federal forces begin a reconnaissance mission on the Matagorda Peninsula, Texas.
NAVAL: The USS *Sciota* and *Granite City* cover disembarking troops at Smith's Landing, Texas, and protect their rear as they advance down the Matagorda Peninsula.

January 22
POLITICS: Isaac Murphy becomes governor of the free-state portions of Arkansas after a vote by the State Convention.
WEST: General William S. Rosecrans is assigned commander of the Federal Department of the Missouri, replacing General John M. Schofield.
 Union forces capture 28 Confederate forage wagons near Wilsonville, Tennessee.
NAVAL: The USS *Restless* captures the Confederate blockade-runner *William A. Kain* in St. Andrew's Bay, Florida.

January 23
POLITICS: President Abraham Lincoln approves a policy whereby plantation owners must recognize freedom for all former slaves and hire them on the basis of contract law.

January 25
SOUTH: Union forces resume their bombardment of Fort Sumter, Charleston Harbor, South Carolina.
WEST: Federal troops abandon Corinth, Mississippi, in a move to consolidate defenses better.

January 26
DIPLOMACY: William L. Drayton, U.S. minister to France, expresses embarrassment about the presence of several Confederate cruisers in French waters and the government's inability to detail a few naval vessels to deal with them.
WEST: General John G. Parke resumes command of the IX Corps at Knoxville, Tennessee, and commences operations to dislodge General James Longstreet's Confederates from Russellville, Tennessee. To facilitate this, he dispatches Union cavalry under General Samuel D. Sturgis south of the French Broad River to harass his communications. That same day, Confederate cavalry under General William

T. Martin engages Sturgis near Fairgrove, Tennessee. Martin, supported by artillery, manages to drive the Federals back toward Sevierville after heavy skirmishing. Sturgis, meanwhile, regroups and prepares to renew the conflict on the morrow.

January 27

POLITICS: President Jefferson Davis summons General Braxton Bragg to Richmond, Virginia, for consultation as long as his "health permits."

WEST: Continuous skirmishing ensues between major forces under General James Longstreet and John G. Parke near Dandridge, Tennessee. General Samuel D. Sturgis's Union cavalry advance on Confederate positions in the vicinity of Fair Gardens, Tennessee, with three regiments and the 18th Indiana Battery. An entire day of charges and countercharges ensues until the 2nd and 4th Indiana Cavalry finally sweep down the Fair Gardens Road, netting 2 cannon and 112 Southern prisoners. Total Confederate losses are around 200 while Sturgis sustains 60 to 70 killed and wounded. Confederate general William T. Martin subsequently falls back to Swann's Island on the French Broad River to await reinforcements.

January 28

WEST: General Jubal A. Early directs Generals Edward L. Thomas and Thomas L. Rossiter on a combined infantry/cavalry raiding force from New Market, Virginia, toward Union positions in the Allegheny Mountains. Their goal is to secure forage for the horses and steal cattle for the men.

General John M. Schofield gains appointment as commander of the Department of the Ohio, while General George Stoneman is designated to lead the XXIII Corps.

After defeating General William T. Martin's Confederates in several skirmishes around Fair Gardens, Tennessee, General Samuel D. Sturgis is beset by strong Confederate infantry forces under General Bushrod R. Johnson. Heavy skirmishing results, and Union troopers fall back to their original positions near Sevierville. General William T. Martin then repositions his Confederate cavalry near Fair Gardens and awaits developments.

General Leonidas K. Polk receives command of the newly designated Confederate Department of Alabama, Mississippi, and East Louisiana.

NAVAL: The USS *Beauregard* captures the British blockade-runner *Racer* off Cape Canaveral, Florida.

The army steamer *Western Metropolis* captures the Confederate steamer *Rosita* off Key West, Florida.

January 29

WEST: Confederate raiders under Generals Edward L. Thomas and Thomas L. Rossiter advance on Moorefield, West Virginia, brushing aside Union detachments blocking the road. While pursuing in the direction of nearby Medley, the 12th Virginia Cavalry stumbles on a Federal wagon train under escort. Rossiter quickly brings up his three remaining regiments, who dismount and pitch into the Federals. A mounted charge by the 35th Battalion of Virginia Cavalry also breaks the Union center as other units turn their flank and the Northerners flee, abandoning 95 wagons. At a cost of 25 casualties, the victorious Rossiter takes 80 captives along with 1,200 cattle and 500 sheep.

January 30
WEST: Confederate raiders under General Thomas L. Rossiter advance from Medley, West Virginia, to nearby Petersburg, where they abscond with Union additional supplies and ammunition. However, alert to the approach of Federal reinforcements, they fall back on General Edward L. Thomas's infantry brigade and gradually ride back into the Shenandoah Valley, concluding a highly successful raid.

Men of the 54th Illinois kill a Democrat who refuses to take a loyalty oath in Mattoon, Illinois.

Recently disgraced general William S. Rosecrans is appointed commander of the Department of the Missouri.

General Frederick Steele becomes commander of the Department of Arkansas.
NAVAL: The Confederate ironclad CSS *Charleston* is launched at Charleston, South Carolina.

Confederate guerrillas fire on the Union steamer *Sir William Wallace* on the Mississippi River.

January 31
POLITICS: President Abraham Lincoln again urges General Nathaniel P. Banks at New Orleans, Louisiana, to begin to institute civilian authority, leaving him, "at liberty to adopt any rule which shall admit to vote any unquestionably loyal free state men and none others. And yet I do wish they would all take the oath."
SOUTH: General George E. Pickett arrives outside New Bern, North Carolina, with orders to capture the city from Union forces, He commands 13,000 troops in three brigades under General Robert F. Hoke, 14 cannon, and a complement of cavalry. Pickett also enjoys the assistance of Commander John T. Wood, an audacious Confederate naval commander. The Southerners conceive a three-pronged attack to catch Union defenders under General Innis N. Palmer in a pincer from both flanks and the center.
WEST: General William T. Sherman instructs General Nathaniel P. Banks to cooperate closely with the gunboats of Admiral David D. Porter in the upcoming Red River campaign, Louisiana.
NAVAL: Commander Charles W. Flusser, accompanied by 40 sailors, 240 soldiers, and a 12-pound howitzer, sails down the Roanoke River and captures the town of Windsor, North Carolina, meeting no resistance.

February 1
POLITICS: President Abraham Lincoln authorizes a draft of 500,000 men to serve three years or until the duration of the war.

The U.S. House of Representative creates the rank of lieutenant general, U.S. Army, with Ulysses S. Grant in mind.
SOUTH: General George E. Pickett attacks Union forces under General Innis N. Palmer at Batchelder's Creek, North Carolina, inflicting 326 casualties and forcing the Northerners back onto New Bern. However, two Confederate columns under

General Seth M. Barton and Colonel James Dearing perceive Federal defenses at Fort Anderson as too formidable, and the attack founders. By nightfall, Pickett cancels his offensive and delays the scheduled advance of General Robert F. Hoke's division.

WEST: General William T. Sherman orders a Union cavalry column under General William Sooy Smith to depart Colliersville, Tennessee, raid southward along the Memphis and Ohio Railroad, and unite with his own main column outside Meridian, Mississippi, no later than February 10.

NAVAL: The USS *Commodore Morris* and *Minnesota* support army landings at Smithfield, Virginia. The attack is repelled in a heavy fog and the force withdraws with the loss of the army transport *Smith Briggs*.

The USS *Sassacus* captures the Confederate blockade-runner *Wild Dayrell* at Stump Inlet, North Carolina, and burns it.

Armed boats from the USS *Braziliera* captures the Confederate sloop *Buffalo* off Brunswick, Georgia.

February 2

SOUTH: General George E. Pickett, frustrated by the doughty defense of New Bern, North Carolina, withdraws General Robert F. Hoke's division back to Kinston. Though a fiasco, his raid gains a measure of notoriety when 22 former Confederate soldiers are caught wearing Union uniforms. They subsequently are all hanged for desertion following a controversial drumhead trial.

WEST: In Chattanooga, Tennessee, 129 Confederate deserters take a loyalty oath to the United States.

NAVAL: In a bold endeavor, the Federal sidewheel steamer USS *Underwriter* suddenly falls to Confederate boats under Commander John T. Wood in the Neuse River near New Bern, North Carolina. However, when the vessel proves unable to get its steam back up, Wood burns his quarry to prevent recapture. This daring act gains him the thanks of the Confederate Congress.

The Federal tug USS *Geranium* captures eight sailors belonging to the Confederate Torpedo Corps near Fort Moultrie, Charleston, South Carolina.

Federal ironclads USS *Leigh*, *Nahant*, and *Pasaic* bombard the grounded Confederate steamer *Presto* in Charleston Harbor, South Carolina.

Admiral John A. B. Dahlgren conducts the USS *Ottawa*, *Norwich*, *Mahaska*, *Dai Ching*, and *Water Witch* up the St. John's River, Florida, in support of army moves against Jacksonville under General Quincy A. Gillmore.

February 3

POLITICS: To suppress espionage, desertion, and disloyalty better, President Jefferson Davis recommends suspending writs of habeas corpus for cases involving spying and desertion.

WEST: General William T. Sherman departs Vicksburg, Mississippi, with 26,800 men of the XVI (General Stephen A. Hurlbut) and XVII Corps (General James B. McPherson), while a separate column of 8,000 cavalry under General William Sooy Smith is supposed to depart from Colliersville, Tennessee. Together, they intend to clear Confederate forces out of northern Mississippi as far as the town of Meridian, 120 miles to the east, and devastate the region to deny Southerners railroads, cotton, wheat, and other foodstuffs. This, in effect, is a dress rehearsal for Sherman's notorious "March to the Sea."

NAVAL: The USS *Midnight* captures the Confederate schooner *Defy* near Doboy Light, Georgia.

Federal gunboats USS *Petrel*, *Marmora*, *Exchange,* and *Romeo* steam up the Yazoo River to knock out a Confederate battery at Liverpool, Mississippi, to assist the Union expedition against Meridian. In response, Southerners burn the steamer *Sharp* to prevent its capture.

February 4

WEST: Union forces under General James B. McPherson link up with General William T. Sherman at Champion's Hill, Mississippi, prior to the final drive on Meridian.

Union forces depart Helena, Arkansas, and begin to push up the White River.

NAVAL: The USS *Sassacus* forces the Confederate steamer *Nutfield* aground off New River Inlet, North Carolina, and then burns it.

Armed boats from the USS *Beauregard* capture the Confederate boat *Lydia* off Jupiter Narrows, Florida.

February 5

SOUTH: Federal troops repel Major John S. Mosby's attack on their rear guard and capture several Confederates. Among them is William E. Ormsby, a Union deserter who joined the Southerners; he is summarily tried by a drumhead court-martial and executed.

Union forces under General Truman Seymour embark at Hilton Head, South Carolina, and sail for Jacksonville, Florida.

WEST: General William T. Sherman's troops approach Jackson, Mississippi, after skirmishing with Confederate forces under General Wirt Adams.

NAVAL: Commander John R. Tucker informs superiors that the boilers aboard the CSS *Chicora* are nonfunctional and that the vessel now can be employed only as a stationary, floating battery.

The USS *De Soto* captures the British blockade-runner *Cumberland* off Santa Rosa Island, Gulf of Mexico.

February 6

POLITICS: The Confederate Congress outlaws the importation of luxuries or the possession of U.S. paper money. It also mandates that half of tobacco and food exports must be surrendered to government agents before ships are allowed to clear ports.

SOUTH: Union forces under General George G. Meade make an aborted crossing of the Rapidan River at Morton's Ford, but they are recalled after heavy fighting.

General Benjamin F. Butler orders a Union expedition from Yorktown, Virginia, against Richmond, but the move is defeated by Confederates under General Eppa Hunton at Baltimore Store.

WEST: General William T. Sherman occupies Jackson, Mississippi, before resuming his drive against the rail junction at Meridian.

NAVAL: The USS *Cambridge* bombards the grounded Confederate steamer *Dee* near Masonboro, North Carolina.

February 7

DIPLOMACY: William Preston becomes the Confederate envoy to French-controlled Mexico. The Confederacy supports Napoleon III's occupation of that country and its puppet the ruler, Emperor Maximilian, in the hope of gaining diplomatic recognition and possibly military intervention.

SOUTH: Federal forces under General Truman Seymour occupy Jacksonville, Florida, and prepare to move west toward the Suwannee River. By invading the center of the state, they hope to deprive the Confederacy of much-needed cattle, grain, and other valuable commodities, as well as accelerate the reintegration of Florida into the Union.

WEST: General Leonidas K. Polk abandons Brandon, Mississippi, as Union forces under General William T. Sherman advance from the state capital at Jackson.

NAVAL: The USS *Norwich* traps the Confederate steamer *St. Mary's* in McGirt's Creek, Florida, where it is scuttled.

February 8

SOUTH: General Truman Seymour advances inland from Jacksonville, Florida, and skirmishes with Confederate forces at Ten-Mile Run.

WEST: The divisions of Generals Stephen D. Lee and William W. Loring unite at Morton, Mississippi, and commence to fall back toward Meridian before the army of General William T. Sherman.

February 9

POLITICS: President Abraham Lincoln sits through a photographic session; one portrait is subsequently utilized on the U.S. five-dollar bill.

SOUTH: 109 Union officers under Colonel Thomas E. Rose tunnel themselves free from Libby Prison in Richmond, Virginia, with 59 ultimately reaching Union lines. Rose and 48 others are recaptured while two die from drowning.

Federal forces seize John's Island in Charleston Harbor, South Carolina.

WEST: General John M. Schofield replaces General John G. Foster as commander of the Federal Department of the Ohio.

Federal forces under General William T. Sherman reoccupy Yazoo City, Mississippi, without resistance.

NAVAL: An armed cutter from the USS *Patapsco* captures the Confederate schooner *Swift* off Cabbage Island, Georgia.

February 10

SOUTH: Union troops continue advancing from Jacksonville, Florida, toward Lake City.

WEST: General William Sooy Smith finally receives the Union cavalry brigade of Colonel George E. Waring and prepares to depart Coliersville, Tennessee, belatedly for Meridian, Mississippi.

NAVAL: The USS *Florida* sinks the Confederate blockade-runners *Fanny and Jenny* and *Emily* once they ground off Masonboro Inlet, North Carolina.

The Confederate raider CSS *Florida* under Lieutenant Charles M. Morris slips out of Brest, France, after seven months of undergoing repairs. Under the cover of a thick fog and rain, he slips past the USS *Kearsarge* and escapes.

February 11

SOUTH: General Joseph Finnegan assembles 600 men at Lake City, Florida, as Confederate defenses coalesce to stop a Union advance commanded by General Truman Seymour.

WEST: A Union train belonging to the Baltimore and Ohio Railroad is thrown off the tracks at Kearneysville, West Virginia, by Confederate guerrillas under Major M. H. Gilmore. The crew and passengers are then robbed of valuables, and the raiders depart.

Ten days late, 8,000 Union cavalry under General William Sooy Smith finally clatter out of Collierville, Tennessee, en route to a rendezvous with General William T. Sherman. Progress is slow owing to rains and swampy terrain. As they advance, more than 1,000 African-American slaves join the column seeking freedom and protection.

NAVAL: The USS *Queen* captures the Confederate schooner *Louisa* at the mouth of the Brazos River, Texas.

February 12

NORTH: President Abraham Lincoln enjoins General Hugh J. Kilpatrick at the White House, whereupon the latter discusses plans for a possible raid against Richmond, Virginia, to free Union prisoners kept there. The president listens intently to the blustery cavalryman and at length grants his approval.

WEST: General William T. Sherman continues his Meridian, Mississippi, campaign by advancing from the west while General William Sooy Smith rides down from the north. Skirmishing ensues but does not hinder either column.

February 13

NAVAL: The USS *Morse,* while conducting a reconnaissance mission up Potopotank Creek, Virginia, captures the Confederate sloop *Margaret Ann.*

The USS *Forrest Rose* helps defeat three Confederate attacks on Waterproof, Louisiana.

February 14

SOUTH: Advancing Federal troops under General Quincy A. Gillmore occupy Gainesville, Florida, without resistance.

WEST: Meridian, Mississippi, falls without resistance to Union forces under General William T. Sherman, who covers 150 miles in 11 days. He then begins systematically to destroy all buildings, supplies, and railroads in his earliest application of what will become known as "Total War." Sherman notes: "For five days, 10,000 men worked hard and with a will in that work of destruction." Ultimately, 115 miles of track, 61 bridges, and 20 locomotives are laid to waste. Confederate general Leonidas K. Polk, too weak to intervene, remains a hapless spectator to the destruction but did remove the bulk of supplies and rolling stock stored there to Demopolis, Alabama. Sherman, meanwhile, awaits the arrival of General William Sooy Smith's cavalry column, now overdue by several days.

February 15

POLITICS: The Confederate Congress appropriates $5 million for a sabotage campaign based in Canada. It is to be orchestrated by Confederate veteran Thomas C. Hines, who intends to meet and coordinate his actions with those of Peace Democrats from the North. Meanwhile, President Jefferson Davis evinces concern that General William T. Sherman might march from Meridian, Mississippi, directly on Montgomery, Alabama.

WEST: Federal troopships land the African-American 12th Louisiana Infantry at Grand Gulf, Mississippi, for the purpose of confiscating cotton stores. No resistance is encountered.

NAVAL: The USS *Forest Rose* lends valuable gunfire support to Union forces under attack at Waterproof, Louisiana.

The USS *Virginia* captures the British blockade-runner *Mary Douglas* off San Luis Pass, Texas.

February 16

SOUTH: Federal troops, attacking Fairfield, North Carolina, in a severe snowstorm, capture an entire company of Confederates in their camp.

WEST: An altercation erupts between soldiers of the 54th Illinois and local Democrats in Paris, Edgar County, Illinois.

Federal troops begin a major campaign against hostile Indians in the vicinity of Fort Walla Walla, Washington Territory.

NAVAL: The USS *Montgomery* captures the British blockade-runner *Pet* near Lockwood's Folly, South Carolina.

The USS *Para* supports an army advance up the St. John's River, Florida, engaging several Confederate batteries en route.

The USS *Octorara* and *J. P. Jackson*, accompanied by six mortar schooners, begin to bombard Fort Powell, Mobile Bay, Alabama.

The USS *St. Clair* and the army steamer *Hope* collide on the Mississippi River during a gale, and the latter sinks.

February 17

POLITICS: The Confederate Congress suspends writs of habeas corpus as it relates to arrests made by authority of the president or the secretary of war. They also expand the draft to include all white males between the ages of 17 and 50. Another act allows the employment of African-American slaves as army laborers. The fourth session, first Confederate Congress then adjourns.

Confederate Vice President Alexander H. Stephen continues protesting the suspension of habeas corpus, insisting it is "Far better that our country be overrun by the enemy, our cities sacked and burned, and our land laid desolate, than that the people should suffer the citadel of their liberties to be entered and taken by professed friends." In light of his opposition, the Georgia legislature counters with a resolution reaffirming the state's support for the war and all measures this may entail.

SOUTH: General William H. French assumes command of the III Corps, Army of the Potomac.

Sepia wash drawing by R. G. Skerrett, 1902, after a painting then held by the Confederate Memorial Literary Society Museum, Richmond, Virginia *(Naval Historical Foundation)*

A surprise attack by Federal troops nets 13 of Major John S. Mosby's partisan rangers at Piedmont, Virginia.

NAVAL: The submarine CSS *Hunley* under Lieutenant George E. Dixon attacks and sinks the 1,934-ton Union screw sloop USS *Housatonic* under Captain Charles W. Pickering in Charleston Harbor, South Carolina. Despite precautions, the attackers are sighted at 8:45 P.M. only 100 yards away, and the Union ship immediately slips its cable and begins to back off. *Hunley* still manages to ram its spar torpedo under the *Housatonic*'s starboard side, which explodes and fatally damages it. Fortunately only five sailors drown, with the rest saved by clinging to the masts as *Housatonic* settles in shallow water. *Hunley* apparently survives the explosion intact and remains topside long enough to signal by lantern that it was returning; then it inexplicably sinks a third time with all hands. Nevertheless, *Housatonic* enjoys the melancholy distinction of being the first warship in history lost to a submarine attack.

The USS *Tahoma* destroys a Confederate saltworks at St. Marks, Florida.

February 18

POLITICS: President Abraham Lincoln declares the port of Brownsville, Texas, open for trade and ends the Federal blockade there.

February 20

SOUTH: Union troops celebrate Confederate raider John S. Mosby's promotion to lieutenant colonel by raiding his headquarters at Front Royal, Virginia; the rebels quickly recover and drive their attackers off.

The Battle of Olustee transpires between General Truman Seymour and Joseph Finnegan, with both sides numbering about 5,000 men apiece. The Northerners encounter Finnegan's force safely dug in behind entrenchments, but Seymour nonetheless orders an advance. First to engage the Confederates is Colonel Joseph Hawley's brigade, consisting of the 7th New Hampshire and the 8th U.S. Colored Infantry, which advances bravely but is decimated by heavy musket fire. As they withdraw in confusion, a battle-hardened Georgia brigade under General Alfred H. Colquett leaps from their entrenchments and charges Colonel William Barton's brigade in the Union center, roughly handling it and taking several cannon. The Confederates then find themselves out of ammunition, their advance falters, and both sides scramble to redress their lines.

Seymour, thoroughly bested, brings his final brigade under Colonel James Montgomery to act as a rear guard. Finnegan then orders an all-out charge against the retreating Federals, but the Confederates are delayed for several minutes by the desperate stand of African-Americans of the 35th U.S. Colored Infantry and the celebrated 54th Massachusetts. Seymour then skillfully extricates his troops and averts a general disaster, principally because Finnegan bungles use of his cavalry and fails to pursue effectively. Casualties at Olustee proportionately equaled or exceeded those of any other Civil War engagement. Seymour sustains a bruising 203 dead, 1,152 wounded, and 506 missing (1,861)—a staggering loss rate of 34 percent, while Finnegan loses 93 killed and 841 injured (946), or 20 percent. More important, the Union's defeat here ensures that Florida remains a vital source of cattle, grain, and other valuable supplies for Confederate armies until the end of hostilities.

WEST: General William Sooy Smith encounters a Confederate cavalry brigade under Colonel Jeffrey E. Forrest at Prairie Station, Mississippi, and begins to skirmish. An extended fire fight erupts as the Northerners lurch toward the town of West Point while Southerners continue gathering in strength.

General William T. Sherman, tired of waiting for General William Sooy Smith's cavalry to reinforce him, abandons Meridian, Mississippi, and retrogrades back to Vicksburg. However, he takes a circuitous northern route attempting to establish contact with his missing cavalry. To date, Union losses are 21 killed, 68 wounded, and 81 missing (170).

NAVAL: Admiral John A. B. Dahlgren, greatly alarmed by the loss of the USS *Housatonic* to a Confederate torpedo attack, suggests to Navy secretary Gideon Welles that the government offer a $20–$30,000 reward for the capture or destruction of any such craft. "They are worth more to us than that," he concludes.

February 21

SOUTH: Partisan rangers under Colonel John S. Mosby disperse a Union raiding party at Dranesville, Virginia, killing 15 and taking 70 captives for a cost of one dead and four wounded.

WEST: Colonel Jeffrey E. Forrest continues skirmishing heavily with Union cavalry at West Point, Mississippi, as his elder brother, General Nathan B. Forrest, arrives with reinforcements. In fact, he is trying to lure Smith into an elaborate ambush staged by the elder Forrest. But General William Sooy Smith, with twice the manpower, is convinced that he is heavily outnumbered and ignominiously withdraws. Smith's retrograde movement ends all attempts to unite with General William T. Sherman at Meridian.

Naval: The USS *Para* captures the Confederate steamer *Hard Times* on the St. John's River, Florida.

February 22

Politics: Senator Samuel Pomeroy of Kansas, viewing President Abraham Lincoln as unelectable, begins a covert attempt to have Secretary of the Treasury Salmon P. Chase nominated as the Republican Party's standard bearer. However, once his "Pomeroy Circular" is printed, it creates an uproar and a backlash against Chase, who ends his candidacy for the presidency. He also offers to resign over the matter, but Lincoln declines to accept.

Michael Hahn is elected governor of the free-state portions of Louisiana.

West: A riot between soldiers and Democrats in Paris, Edgar County, Illinois, results in one civilian death and two wounded soldiers.

General George H. Thomas conducts a large reconnaissance in force of Confederate defenses at Dalton, Georgia, to ascertain if General Joseph E. Johnston has weakened his forces by sending detachments to either General Leonidas Polk in Mississippi or General James Longstreet in Tennessee. To that end, several divisions from General John M. Palmer's XIV Corps proceed through Ringgold Gap and onto the plains near Tunnel Hill.

Confederate cavalry under General Nathan B. Forrest attack and defeat a larger Union rear guard under General William Sooy Smith near Okolona, Mississippi. However, resistance stiffens as the Southerners engage the main Union body, and several Confederate charges are bloodily repelled. The most notable casualty is Colonel Jeffrey E. Forrest, the general's younger brother. Two Union countercharges likewise fail with the loss of six cannon, and Smith then retreats in the direction of Pontotoc. Forrest, whose men are exhausted and low on ammunition, allows them to depart; he records 27 dead and 97 wounded Southerners while claiming 162 prisoners and three stands of colors.

Naval: The USS *Whitehead* shells and destroys a corn mill at Rainbow Bluff, North Carolina.

The USS *Virginia* captures the British blockade-runner Henry Colthirst near San Luis Pass, Texas.

The USS *Linden* hits a snag in the Arkansas River and sinks.

February 23

Politics: Secretary of the Treasury Salmon P. Chase absents himself from cabinet meetings in light of disclosures surrounding the recent Pomeroy Circular.

South: General John A. McClernand receives command of the XIII Corps in Louisiana.

The battered column of General Truman Seymour trudges back into Jacksonville, Florida, concluding that state's only major campaign.

WEST: Confederate cavalry under General Stephen D. Lee unite with General Nathan B. Forrest near West Point, Mississippi, but too late to play a role in defeating Union troopers under General William Sooy Smith.

Skirmishes increase between Union troops under General John M. Palmer's XIV Corps and the Army of Tennessee under General Joseph E. Johnston outside Dalton, Georgia. Despite the strength of the Confederate position, Palmer brings up additional forces and continually presses the Southerners back up higher ground.

NAVAL: The USS *Lancaster,* anchored at Acapulco, Mexico, helps repel an attack by hostile Native Americans.

February 24

POLITICS: President Abraham Lincoln signs legislation to compensate slave owners in Union-controlled regions by paying them $300 when their slaves join the Union army.

The U.S. Senate, following the House's lead, votes to create the rank of lieutenant general.

SOUTH: General Braxton Bragg gains appointment as chief of operations, Confederate army, at Richmond, Virginia. He now serves as President Jefferson Davis's de facto chief of staff.

WEST: Forces under General John M. Palmer's XIV Corps continue skirmishing with Confederate troops at Tunnel Hill, Georgia, testing the strength of their defenses. The division of General Richard W. Johnson begins to ascend the rocky face of the position while under heavy fire from General Alexander P. Stewart's Confederates. The Southerners then fall back in good order and take up strong positions along Tunnel Hill (Buzzard's Roost) to await the Union advance, but nightfall closes the contest.

NAVAL: The USS *Nita* forces the Confederate blockade-runner *Nan Nan* aground in the East Pass of the Suwannee River, Florida.

February 25

WEST: General John C. Breckinridge replaces General Samuel Jones as commander of the Confederate Western Department of Virginia.

General John M. Palmer and his XVI Corps continue probing Confederate positions at Buzzard Roost Gap, Georgia, but they encounter heavy resistance. The division of General Absalom Baird works its way up steep slopes under heavy fire, making steady progress but also taking considerable casualties. After a flanking move by General Jefferson C. Davis stalls along the west side of the imposing ridge, Palmer calls off the effort and withdraws that evening. Union losses are 289 casualties to 140 Confederates, but General George H. Thomas confirms that General Joseph E. Johnston is very strongly entrenched around Dalton. He then divines the strategy, implemented three months later, of sending Union troops through Snake Gap Creek, 15 miles behind Confederate lines, to outflank the defenders. More important, his steady pressure on Johnson necessitates that the corps of General Thomas J. Hardee, recently dispatched to assist General Leonidas Polk in Mississippi, be recalled back to the Army of the Tennessee.

General Oliver O. Howard is reappointed commander of the XI Corps in Tennessee.

Naval: The USS *Roebuck* captures the British blockade-runner *Two Brothers* in the Indian River, Florida.

February 26
Politics: President Abraham Lincoln reaffirms his faith in General Benjamin F. Butler and also commutes all death sentences for desertion to imprisonment for the duration.

South: Edward P. Alexander is appointed brigadier general, C.S.A.

West: Confederate cavalry under Colonel John M. Hughes capture Washington, Tennessee, and they inflict 75 Union casualties.

Union cavalry under General William Sooy Smith straggle back toward Colliersville, Tennessee, following their ill-fated Meridian expedition. Smith claims to have liberated 3,000 slaves, taken 200 captives, and burned 2,000 bales of cotton at a cost of 47 killed, 157 wounded, and 120 missing. Realistically, this is another lackluster effort, and General William T. Sherman laconically dismisses it as "unsatisfactory."

Naval: A boat from the USS *Nipsic* is captured while on picket duty in Charleston Harbor, South Carolina, by the Confederate cutter CSS *Palmetto State*.

February 27
South: Andersonville Prison, near Americus, Georgia, a sixteen-and-one-half-acre log stockade, receives its first Union captives. Crowded and squalid from the onset, it gradually gains infamy as the worst prison site in the South.

West: General George H. Thomas concludes his probing actions outside Dalton, Georgia, and withdraws back into Tennessee.

Naval: Armed boats from the USS *Tahoma* land and destroy Confederate saltworks along Goose Creek, Florida.

The USS *Roebuck* captures the British blockade-runner *Nina* and the Confederate schooner *Rebel* off the Indian River Inlet, Florida.

February 28
South: A force 3,500 Union cavalry under General Hugh J. Kilpatrick prepares for an extended raid toward Richmond, Virginia, in a bid to free Union prisoners held at notorious Libby Prison. The effort has been sanctioned personally by both President Abraham Lincoln and Secretary of War Edwin M. Stanton after they learned of horrendous conditions experienced by Northern prisoners. One of Kilpatrick's principal subordinates is Colonel Ulric Dahlgren, son of Admiral John A. B. Dahlgren, whose participation harbors considerable controversy. The troopers leave camp in high spirits this evening and ford the Rapidan River at Ely's Ford.

To assist the raid on Richmond, General George A. Custer takes his brigade of 1,500 troopers on a raid through Albemarle County, Virginia, while General John Sedgwick's VI Corps creates another diversion in the direction of Madison Court House.

West: General John B. Hood gains appointment as commander of the II Corps, Army of Tennessee.

Naval: The USS *Penobscot* captures the British blockade-runner *Lilly* off Velasco, Texas.

February 29

POLITICS: The U.S. Congress formally revives the rank of lieutenant general at the behest of President Abraham Lincoln.

SOUTH: General Hugh J. Kilpatrick leads 3,500 Federal cavalry across the Rapidan River and gallops toward Richmond, Virginia. On reaching Spotsylvania, he dispatches a column of 500 men under Colonel Ulric Dahlgren toward Goochland Court House to attack Richmond from the south as he hit it from the north. The troopers forge ahead despite inclement weather.

WEST: Union forces begin to reconnoiter the Red River region of Louisiana in preparation for a major offensive there.

NAVAL: Armed boats under Lieutenant William B. Cushing of the USS *Monticello* raid Smithville, North Carolina, in a bold attempt to capture Confederate general Louis Hebert. However, Hebert had departed for Wilmington earlier that day and is not in his tent when Cushing suddenly storms it—being within 50 yards of a Confederate barracks.

Admiral David D. Porter dispatches Commander Frank Ramsey up the Black and Ouachita rivers, Louisiana, with the gunboats USS *Osage, Ouachita, Lexington, Conestoga, Cricket,* and *Fort Hindman.* This move in undertaken in conjunction with and preparation for the much large Red River expedition.

The USS *Penobscot* captures the Confederate schooners *Stingray* and *John Douglas* near Velasco, Texas.

The USS *Virginia* captures the Confederate schooner *Camilla* at Galveston, Texas, and then attacks and burns the sloop *Catherine Holt* off San Luis Pass.

March 1

POLITICS: President Abraham Lincoln nominates General Ulysses S. Grant for the rank of lieutenant general.

SOUTH: General Hugh J. Kilpatrick, meeting resistance as his cavalry column approaches the Confederate capital of Richmond, Virginia (then only lightly defended by invalids and civilians), suddenly cancels his raid, veers away, and recrosses the Chickahominy River. En route, he is pursued sharply by Confederate cavalry under General Wade Hampton, which successfully attack and drive the troopers off in confusion. Colonel Ulric Dalhgren, meanwhile, finding the James River swollen and impassible, decides to shift his attack from the east instead of from the south. He also hangs an African-American guide for mistakenly leading his column astray. But Dalhgren, having approached to within two-and-a-half miles of the city, encounters heavy resistance and becomes separated from his main column with only 100 men. He then calls off the raid and attempts to circle back to rejoin Kilpatrick.

NAVAL: The USS *Connecticut* captures the British blockade-runner *Scotia* off Cape Fear, North Carolina.

The USS *Southfield* and *Whitehead* rescue of the army gunboat *Bombshell,* on the Chowan River, North Carolina, once that vessel is cut off by Confederate batteries.

The USS *Roebuck* captures the British blockade-runner *Lauretta* at Indian River Inlet, Florida.

The Confederate raider CSS *Florida* under Lieutenant Charles M. Morris escapes from Funchal, Madeira, with the USS *St. Louis* in hot pursuit.

March 2
POLITICS: The U.S. Senate confers the rank of lieutenant general on Ulysses S. Grant.

SOUTH: A detachment of 100 Union cavalry under Colonel Ulric Dahlgren is ambushed at Mantapike Hill, King and Queen County, Virginia, and he is killed while 92 of his men are captured. The Confederates then recover papers allegedly suggesting a plot to burn Richmond and to assassinate President Jefferson Davis; both the Union government and General George G. Meade promptly and vehemently deny any complicity. This ill-fated endeavor also costs the North 340 killed, wounded, and captured, in addition to 583 horses lost.

General George A. Custer successfully concludes his own raid through Albemarle County, Virginia, and reaches the safety of Union lines.

NAVAL: Admiral David D. Porter arrives off the mouth of the Red River, Louisiana, with his Mississippi Squadron for the planned expedition against Shreveport and east Texas. He is increasingly concerned by declining water levels on the river but nonetheless resolves to proceed apace.

A naval reconnaissance up the Black River, Louisiana, under Commander Frank Ramsay stops to engage Confederate artillery below Harrisonburg. Ramsay's flagship, USS *Fort Hindman*, is struck 27 times and retires with one engine severely damaged.

March 3
POLITICS: General Ulysses S. Grant is ordered to Washington, D.C., where he is to be promoted to lieutenant general.

NAVAL: The USS *Dan Smith* captures the British blockade-runner *Sophia* off the Altamaha Sound, Georgia. The prize ultimately is abandoned in a gale shortly afterward.

March 4
POLITICS: The U.S. Senate confirms Andrew Johnson to serve as governor of Tennessee.

Pro-Union governor Michael Hahn is sworn into office at New Orleans, Louisiana.

SOUTH: A Confederate advance on Portsmouth, Virginia, is repulsed by Union forces under General David B. Birney and cavalry led by General Hugh J. Kilpatrick.

General James P. Anderson assumes command of the Confederate District of Florida.

WEST: Advanced elements of General William T. Sherman's army reach Vicksburg, Mississippi, escorted by 5,000 slaves and 3,000 captured draft animals. He has covered 360 miles through enemy territory and inflicted great materiel damage on the enemy, while suffering only 113 killed, 385 wounded, and 414 missing (912). Strategically, his Meridian campaign fails to destroy Confederate rail lines or reduce enemy troop levels in northern Mississippi effectively, as both are gradually restored. But the effort convinces Sherman of the intrinsic effectiveness of scorched-earth tactics, and his willful devastation presaged what would be conducted on a far vaster scale through Georgia. The concept of total war against an entire enemy population begins to congeal in his mind. In effect, the Meridian campaign is a dress rehearsal for the destructive policies under which he gains considerable notoriety.

NAVAL: The USS *Pequot* captures the British blockade-runner *Don* off Wilmington, North Carolina.

March 5

POLITICS: Confederate authorities issue new regulations mandating that all Southern vessels donate half their cargo capacity to government shipments. This is undertaken as much to reduce wartime profiteering as to alleviate mounting supply shortages.

WEST: Confederate cavalry under General Joseph Wheeler surprises General Absalom Baird's camp at Leet's Tan-yard, Georgia, capturing his camp, wagons, and numerous prisoners.

NAVAL: A Confederate boarding party under daring commander John T. Wood captures a Union telegraph station at Cherry Point, Virginia. They then attack and capture the Union army transports *Aeolus* and *Titan*, docked nearby. Two days later, Wood scuttles the latter vessel on the Piankatank River.

A naval reconnaissance effort under Commander Frank Ramsay steams down the Black River, Louisiana, reaching the mouth of the Red River.

Federal gunboats USS *Petrel* and *Marmora* lend gunfire ashore to Union troops defending Yazoo City, Mississippi, from a Confederate attack.

March 6

WEST: Federal troops pull out of Yazoo City, Mississippi, under Confederate pressure.

General William T. Sherman appoints General Andrew J. Smith to command lead elements of the Red River expedition, Louisiana, and carefully instructs him to work closely with the gunboat flotilla under Admiral David D. Porter.

NAVAL: The USS *Grand Gulf* captures the British blockade-runner *Mary Ann* off Wilmington, North Carolina.

The USS *Peterhoff* collides with the *Monticello* off New Inlet, North Carolina, and sinks.

A Confederate torpedo boat successfully rams the USS *Memphis* twice in the North Edisto River, South Carolina, but the Union vessel escapes owing to a faulty spar torpedo that fails to detonate. Had it exploded eight feet below the waterline as intended, *Memphis* would undoubtedly have been destroyed.

March 7

WEST: President Jefferson Davis urges General James Longstreet to resume offensive operations in either Kentucky or Tennessee.

March 8

NORTH: General Ulysses S. Grant formally accepts his commission as lieutenant general at a ceremony in the White House and then meets and confers with President Abraham Lincoln for the first time. Grant thus becomes the first American military leader to hold such lofty rank since George Washington.

WEST: General Franz Sigel is appointed commander of the Department of West Virginia, with orders to clear Confederates out of the strategic Shenandoah Valley.

A Union expedition under General Grenville M. Dodge seizes Courtland and Moulton, Alabama, along with valuable supplies, ammunition, and provisions.

NAVAL: The USS *Conestoga* under Commander Thomas O. Selfridge accidentally is rammed by the *General Price* off Grand Gulf, Mississippi, and sinks with the loss of two dead. Ironically, both of Selfridge's previous commands, the *Cumberland* and *Cairo*, were also lost to ramming.

The USS *Virginia* captures the Confederate sloop *Randall* at San Luis Pass, Texas.

March 9

NORTH: General Ulysses S. Grant succeeds General Henry W. Halleck as general in chief, with the latter being demoted to his chief of staff. Grant then ventures to Brandy Station, Virginia, headquarters of the Army of the Potomac. To maintain good relations with officers of that force, General George G. Meade technically remains the commanding officer under Grant.

SOUTH: Union cavalry under General Hugh J. Kilpatrick burn a grain mill and other property in the vicinity of Carlton's Store, King and Queen County, Virginia, to punish the inhabitants for the recent ambush slaying of Colonel Ulric Dahlgren.

NAVAL: The USS *Yankee* conducts a reconnaissance down the Rappahannock River as far as Urbanna, Virginia.

The USS *Shokokon* and General Putnam escort an army expedition under General Isaac J. Wistar up the York and Mattapony rivers, Virginia, as far as Sheppard's Landing.

Admiral David D. Porter assembles his gunboat squadron at the mouth of the Red River, Louisiana, prior to the advance against Shreveport.

March 10

SOUTH: After conferring with General George G. Meade, commander of the Army of the Potomac, General Ulysses S. Grant departs by rail for Nashville, Tennessee, for additional meetings with General William T. Sherman.

Colonel John S. Mosby is bested in a skirmish with superior Federal forces at Charlestown and Kabletown, Virginia.

General Nathaniel P. Banks begins to concentrate troops at New Orleans, Louisiana, in preparation for his Red River expedition to the heartland of the Confederate Trans-Mississippi Department. The bulk of his forces consist of 10,000 men under General Andrew J. Smith, on loan from General William T. Sherman at Vicksburg. Concurrently, a Union column under General Frederick Steele also is slated to leave Little Rick, Arkansas, and advance on Shreveport from the west. This campaign, the brainchild of General Henry W. Halleck, is designed to clear an opening into East Texas. However, it is undertaken over the objections of Generals Ulysses S. Grant and William T. Sherman, who feel that Mobile, Alabama, is a more significant target. Banks, meanwhile, wishes to seize as much Confederate cotton as possible from this highly productive region for that commodity remains highly overpriced in Northern markets and promises to fetch him windfall profits on the open market.

WEST: General Franz Sigel replaces General Benjamin F. Kelley as commander of the Union Department of West Virginia.

NAVAL: The USS *Virginia* captures the Confederate schooner *Sylphide* off San Luis Pass, Texas.

Federal gunboats and ironclads escort army transports carrying General Andrew J. Smith's division down the Mississippi River from Vicksburg, Mississippi, to the mouth of the Red River, Louisiana. Once at the confluence of both rivers, their first objective is Fort De Russy, 30 miles to the west.

March 11

NAVAL: Armed boats from the USS *Beauregard* and *Norfolk Packet* capture the British blockade-runners *Linda* and *Hannah* off Mosquito Inlet, Florida.

The USS *San Jacinto* seizes the Confederate schooner *Lealtad* off Mobile, Alabama.

The USS *Aroostook* captures the British blockade-runner *Mary P. Burton* off Velasco, Texas.

March 12

NORTH: Sweeping leadership changes are finalized in the Union army with General Ulysses S. Grant in overall command of military operations; General Henry W. Halleck serving as his chief of staff; General William T. Sherman leading the Military Division of the Mississippi, including the Departments of the Arkansas, the Cumberland, the Ohio, and the Tennessee; and General James B. McPherson heading both the Department and Army of the Tennessee.

SOUTH: General Nathaniel P. Banks begins to orchestrate his move up the Red River, Louisiana, with a view toward seizing Shreveport. His ultimate goal is to gain a lodgment in the Texas interior and sever the flow of supplies eastward. Advanced forces under General Andrew J. Smith are convoyed up the Red River to Alexandria, Louisiana, their first objective. Banks himself is detained two more weeks at New Orleans to help the struggling civilian administration of Governor Michael Hahn get established.

NAVAL: The USS *Massachusetts* captures the Confederate sloop *Persis* in Wassaw Sound, Georgia.

The USS *Columbine* supports army movements up the St. John's River, Florida, culminating in an attack on Confederate positions at Pilatka.

The USS *Aroostook* captures the Confederate schooner *Marion* off Velasco, Texas.

Admiral David D. Porter leads an armada of 13 ironclads, four tinclads, and four wooden gunboats up the Red River, Louisiana, in concert with the Shreveport expedition of General Nathaniel P. Banks. The USS *Essex, Lafayette, Choctaw, Ozark, Osage, Neosho, Fort Hindman,* and *Cricket* pause to help bombard Fort De Russy, Louisiana, into submission. Meanwhile, army transports convey the 3rd Division, XVI Corps of General Andrew J. Smith up as an advanced force.

March 13

POLITICS: President Abraham Lincoln, after receiving a signed petition from African Americans in Louisiana, encourages Governor Michael Hahn of Louisiana to consider drafting a new state constitution that allows minorities to vote. Curiously, of the 1,000 blacks signing the document, no less than 27 had previously served under General Andrew Jackson in the War of 1812 with a promise of freedom that was subsequently retracted.

NAVAL: Federal gunboats USS *Benton, Chillicothe, Louisville, Pittsburgh, Mound City, Ouachita, Lexington,* and *Gazelle* steam up the Atchafalaya River, Louisiana, and cover troop landings at Simmesport. Meanwhile, the *Eastport* and *Neosho* remain behind to assist in the reduction of Fort De Russy.

March 14

SOUTH: Union forces under General Andrew J. Smith seize Fort De Russy on the Red River, Louisiana, along with 325 prisoners and 12 cannon. This remains the only tactical success of the ensuing campaign.

WEST: General John G. Parke and his IX Corps begin to transfer from eastern Tennessee to Annapolis, Maryland.

March 15

POLITICS: Michael Hahn, newly elected governor of Louisiana, receives powers previously reserved for the military government as civil authority is transferred slowly back to politicians. This proves a forerunner of what ultimately unfolds during Reconstruction.

NAVAL: The USS *Eastport, Lexington,* and *Ouachita* unsuccessfully intercept Confederate vessels fleeing over the Alexandria Rapids, Louisiana. The Southern steamer *Countess* grounds in the process and is destroyed by its crew to prevent capture. The bulk of Admiral David D. Porter's squadron continues working its way toward Alexandria as long as water levels permit.

The USS *Nyanza* captures the Confederate schooner *J. W. Wilder* on the Atchafalaya River, Louisiana.

March 16

SOUTH: Union forces under General Andrew J. Smith occupy Alexandria, Louisiana, supported by nine Federal gunboats.

WEST: General Nathan B. Forrest begins a protracted cavalry raid into West Tennessee and Kentucky.

Confederate cavalry under Colonel John M. Hughs attack the Nashville and Chattanooga Railroad near Tullahoma, Tennessee, destroying a train, taking 60 Union captives, and killing 20 African Americans.

General Sterling Price succeeds General Theophilus H. Holmes as commander of the Confederate District of Arkansas.

NAVAL: Landing parties under Commander Thomas O. Selfridge of the USS *Osage* occupy Alexandria, Louisiana, ahead of General Andrew J. Smith's army troops.

The USS *Neptune* and *Galatea* are ordered into the Caribbean to escort California steamers carrying shipments of gold.

The Confederate raider CSS *Alabama* under Captain Raphael Semmes drops anchor at Capetown, South Africa, to take on supplies.

March 17
SOUTH: General Nathaniel P. Banks, detained at New Orleans, Louisiana, for political reasons, misses his scheduled rendezvous with General Andrew J. Smith at Alexandria.

WEST: Generals Ulysses S. Grant and William T. Sherman meet at Nashville, Tennessee, to coordinate their strategy closely. They then board trains for Cincinnati, Ohio, after Grant declares, "Headquarters will be in the field and, until further orders, will be with the Army of the Potomac."

March 18
POLITICS: Pro-Union Arkansas voters ratify a new constitution mandating the abolishment of slavery.

WEST: General William T. Sherman formally gains appointment as commander of the Military Division of the Mississippi.

NAVAL: General Edmund Kirby-Smith orders the steamer *New Falls City* scuttled at Scopern's Cut-off, below Shreveport on the Red River, Louisiana, as an obstacle. He also instructs that no less than 30 torpedoes be placed below Grand Ecore to further hobble Union advances upstream.

March 19
POLITICS: The Georgia state legislature grants President Jefferson Davis a vote of confidence and, following the next significant Confederate victory, desires that peace talks be conducted with Washington, D.C., but solely on the basis of Southern independence.

SOUTH: Colonel John S. Mosby ambushes and defeats a larger Union detachment at Salem and Orleans, Virginia.

March 20
NAVAL: The USS *Honeysuckle* captures the Confederate sloop *Florida* in the Gulf of Mexico.

The USS *Tioga* captures the Confederate sloop *Swallow* at sea.

March 21
POLITICS: President Abraham Lincoln approves legislation allowing the Nevada and Colorado territories to become states.

SOUTH: Union cavalry under General Joseph A. Mower defeat Confederate troops at Henderson's Hill, Louisiana, taking 250 prisoners, 200 horses, and four cannon. Such losses temporarily cripple General Richard Taylor's ability to conduct adequate scouting and reconnaissance.

NAVAL: The USS *Hendrick Hudson* rams and sinks the Confederate blockade-runner *Wild Pigeon* at sea.

Confederates scuttle the CSS *Clifton* at Sabine Pass, Texas, after it runs aground and cannot be refloated.

March 22
NORTH: General Lew Wallace replaces General Henry H. Lockwood as commander of the Middle Department, headquartered at Baltimore, Maryland.

WEST: General Nathan Kimball succeeds General Frederick Steele as commander of the Union Department of Arkansas once the latter departs Little Rock on an expedition toward the Red River, Louisiana.

March 23
POLITICS: General Ulysses S. Grant hurriedly arrives back in Washington, D.C., eager to put in motion a simultaneous advance from four different armies across the entire South.

SOUTH: The Union I Corps is discontinued, and its troops are reabsorbed by the V Corps, Army of the Potomac under General Gouverneur K. Warren, who has himself replaced General George Sykes.

WEST: General Frederick Steele, ordered into the field by the War Department despite chronic supply shortages, reluctantly leads 10,400 Union troops out of Little Rock, Arkansas. His mission is to proceed east and link up with the Red River expedition of General Nathaniel P. Banks. Steele initially objected to the move as roads, such as they exist, are poor and his flanks remain vulnerable to attack by hard-riding Confederate cavalry. More important, Steele's efforts are dogged by lack of adequate food and fodder for troops and pack animals alike.

NAVAL: A Union naval party seizes an unnamed Confederate steamer on the Santee River, South Carolina, and burns it at the wharf.

March 24
SOUTH: Although never fully recovered from wounds received at Gettysburg, General Winfield S. Hancock resumes command of the II Corps, Army of the Potomac.

The Union III Corps is disbanded, and its troops are distributed among the II and VI Corps, Army of the Potomac.

WEST: A surprise raid by General Nathan B. Forrest captures Union City, Tennessee.

General Nathaniel P. Butler finally arrives at Alexandria, Louisiana, and a week behind schedule before commanding the Union drive up the Red River toward Shreveport. However, he is disconcerted to learn that General Andrew J. Smith's 10,000 troops must revert back to General William T. Sherman no later than April 25 in order to join the advance through Georgia. Banks receives additional bad news in the form of declining levels of water on the Red River itself, which jeopardizes continuing naval support from Admiral David D. Porter's gunboats. Undeterred, Banks orders the campaign to continue.

NAVAL: The USS *Britannia* sails from Beaufort, North Carolina, with 200 soldiers and 50 sailors, in an aborted raid against Swansboro. The expedition is frustrated by unexpectedly heavy seas.

The USS *Stonewall* captures the Confederate sloop *Josephine* off Sarasota Sound, Florida.

March 25
SOUTH: General David M. Gregg replaces General Alfred M. Pleasonton as commander of cavalry forces, Army of the Potomac.

West: General Nathan B. Forrest attacks and captures the town of Paducah, Kentucky, with his force of 2,800 cavalry. However, Colonel Stephen G. Hicks, the garrison commander, refuses to surrender and withdraws his 665 into the safety of nearby Fort Anderson. Forrest, espying the strength of his position, has no intention of attacking, but Colonel Albert P. Thompson nonetheless charges at the head of his 3rd and 7th Kentucky Cavalry. The Confederates are repulsed bloodily with losses of 10 killed (including Thompson) and 40 wounded, while Hicks records 14 killed and 46 wounded. Forrest withdraws with 50 captives and 400 horses, several of which are confiscated from civilians.

Naval: Armed boats from the USS *Winona* capture the Confederate blockade-runner *Little Ada* in the South Santee River, South Carolina, but are driven off by Southern artillery batteries, abandoning their prize.

Cannon fire from the gunboats USS *Peosta* and *Paw Paw* help repel Confederate raiders at Paducah, Kentucky, along the Tennessee River.

March 26

West: The approach of large Union cavalry forces toward Paducah, Kentucky, induces General Nathan B. Forrest to retire in the direction of Fort Pillow, Tennessee, on the Mississippi River.

March 27

South: General Ulysses S. Grant rejoins the Army of the Potomac, now headquartered at Culpeper Court House, Virginia.

Union prisoners begin to arrive en masse at Camp Sumter in Andersonville, Georgia. Once filled to capacity, it becomes the most squalid and infamous prison camp of the South.

March 28

South: General Nathaniel P. Banks continues his advance from Alexandria, Louisiana, toward Shreveport.

West: Charleston, Illinois, is the scene of violent antiwar rioting, aimed at Union soldiers on furlough. Throngs of Democrats gather to hear antiwar congressional candidate John R. Eden speak, as hundreds of soldiers mill around nearby. Once liquor starts to flow, shots are exchanged suddenly between the two parties, and Democrats under Sheriff John O'Hare begin to retrieve hidden weapons from nearby wagons. Six men are killed and 20 injured by Knights of the Golden Circle (Copperheads) before the violence is suppressed by reinforcements. An additional 50 Democrats are arrested, with 29 held indefinitely by military authorities at Springfield, until a clemency order by President Abraham Lincoln releases them.

General Richard Taylor begins to mass 16,000 men to resist a Union advance down the Red River toward Shreveport, Louisiana, an important cotton-producing center.

Union troops under Colonel Powell Clayton, having marched from Pine Bluff, Arkansas, defeat a small Confederate force at Mount Elba.

Naval: The USS *Shokokon* successfully engages a force of Confederate cavalry at Day's Point, Virginia.

The USS *Kingfisher* runs aground off St. Helena Sound, South Carolina, and is scuttled by its crew.

Armed boats from the USS *Sagamore* destroy two unnamed blockade-runners near Cedar Keys, Florida.

Secretary of the Navy Gideon Welles alerts Commander John C. Carter to have the USS *Michigan* ready to sail once the ice breaks on Lake Erie. He has received rumors that Confederates are planning to launch a raid from nearby Canada.

March 29

POLITICS: President Abraham Lincoln prevails on General George G. Meade to forsake a court of inquiry pertaining to his performance at the Battle of Gettysburg. For some time, the general has weathered attacks on his leadership by the Northern press and seeks vindication.

WEST: Union forces under General Nathaniel P. Banks reach Natchitoches, Louisiana, where the general renders a fateful decision: Rather than continue on a road skirting the banks of Red River, protected by the guns of Admiral David D. Porter's gunboats, Banks now veers inland along a more direct route toward his primary objective at Shreveport. Federal troops must now traverse a wilderness region along a single road wide enough for only one wagon. Meanwhile, Confederates under General Richard Taylor burn 10 miles of cotton fields in the Union army's path to deny them that valuable commodity. Taylor then assumes defensive positions at Mansfield, interposing his force between Banks and Shreveport.

A Union column under General Frederick Steele slogs into Arkadelphia, Arkansas, to rest and await reinforcements in the form of two cavalry brigades under General John M. Thayer.

Colonel Powell Clayton, advancing from Mount Elba, Arkansas, rides south and again surprises a Confederate supply train at Long View on the Sabine River. He captures 35 wagons and 260 prisoners.

NAVAL: Armed boats from the USS *Commodore Barney* and *Minnesota* ascend the Chuckatuck Creek and land parties ashore. A quick raid of Confederate headquarters at Cherry Grove, Virginia, nets 20 captives.

Admiral David D. Porter's attempts to get his gunboats over the Alexandria rapids is frustrated by unusually low levels of water on the Red River. The USS *Eastport* is hoisted carefully over the rocks, but the hospital ship *Woodford* strikes a snag and sinks.

The Confederate raider CSS *Florida* under Lieutenant Charles M. Morris captures the Union vessel *Avon* at sea and burns it.

March 30

WEST: Having consolidated his position at Mount Elba, Arkansas, Colonel Powell Clayton opens up a supply route toward Camden to assist the approaching Union column of General Frederick Steele.

March 31

NAVAL: Armed boats from the USS *Sagamore* destroy the Confederate schooner *Etta* and another unnamed vessel near Cedar Keys, Florida.

April 1

WEST: General Frederick Steele, having waited in vain for cavalry reinforcements under General John M. Thayer, departs Arkadelphia, Arkansas, and marches toward the Red River, Louisiana. Dwindling supplies also force him to place the men and pack animals under his command on half rations. Meanwhile, his progress is dogged by Confederate cavalry under Generals Joseph O. Shelby and John S. Marmaduke.

NAVAL: The Federal army transport *Maple Leaf* strikes a Confederate torpedo in the St. John's River, Florida, and sinks off Mandarin Point.

April 2

WEST: Confederate cavalry under General Joseph O. Shelby attack and overturn a Union rear guard at Okolona, Arkansas, taking 160 prisoners.

April 3

SOUTH: General Nathaniel P. Banks and his army reach Grand Ecore, Louisiana, encountering heightened Confederate resistance. He also receives reinforcements in the form of several army transports.

NAVAL: The USS *Eastport, Cricket, Mound City, Chillicothe, Pittsburg, Ozark, Neosho, Osage, Lexington, Fort Hindman,* and *Louisville* escort General Andrew J. Smith's corps up the Red River to Grand Ecore, Louisiana. The troops then slog overland from Natchitoches for an attack on Shreveport with the main force under General Nathaniel P. Banks. However, dwindling water levels remain a concern as Admiral David D. Porter's 13 gunboats and 30 transports barely make it over the Alexandria Rapids.

April 4

DIPLOMACY: In light of French aggression toward Mexico, the U.S. House of Representatives unanimously passes a resolution protesting the policies of Napoleon III. It reaffirms American resolve never to recognize a monarchical regime set up in the Western Hemisphere at the behest of any European power. Meanwhile, the government extends it support of rebel forces under President Benito Juárez.

SOUTH: The Union XI and XII Corps are consolidated into the new XX Corps under General Joseph Hooker; General Jacob D. Dox takes charge of the XXIII Corps and, in a major shift of leadership, the aggressive general Philip H. Sheridan replaces General David M. Gregg as cavalry commander, Army of the Potomac.

WEST: General John M. Schofield becomes commander of the XXIII Corps, Army of the Tennessee.

NAVAL: The USS *Sciota* captures the Confederate schooner *Mary Sorly* (nee U.S. revenue cutter *Dodge*) at Galveston, Texas.

April 6

POLITICS: The Convention of Louisiana, meeting at New Orleans, adopts a new state constitution abolishing slavery.

NORTH: The Union Department of the Monongahela merges with the Department of the Susquehanna in Pennsylvania.

WEST: The army of General Nathaniel P. Banks continues advancing from abandons the banks of the Red River along a narrow road toward Shreveport, Louisiana.

Thus, his force, as it approaches General Richard Taylor's Confederates at Mansfield, becomes literally strung out for miles through the bayou wilderness.

NAVAL: The USS *Estrella* captures the Confederate mail schooner *Julia A. Hodges* in Matagorda Bay, Texas.

April 7

WEST: The Confederate I Corps under General James Longstreet is ordered from Greeneville, Tennessee, and back to the Army of Northern Virginia.

NAVAL: The USS *Beauregard* captures the British blockade-runner *Spunky* off Cape Canaveral, Florida.

Admiral David D. Porter conducts the Federal gunboats USS *Cricket, Fort Hindman, Lexington, Osage, Neosho,* and *Chillicothe* up the Red River to support army troops at Shreveport, Louisiana.

April 8

POLITICS: The U.S. Congress approves the 13th Amendment to the Constitution by a vote of 38 to six. Slavery is now formally abolished in all territories controlled by the United States.

SOUTH: Richard Taylor is appointed lieutenant general, C.S.A.

The Union army of 18,000 men under General Nathaniel Banks moves in single file toward Mansfield, Louisiana, where it confronts General Richard Taylor's 8,000 Confederates at Sabine Crossroads. The Southerners are dug in comfortably behind extensive fieldworks awaiting a Union attack. But once Taylor notices how dispersed the Federals have allowed themselves to become—Banks's wagon train alone is three miles long, which prevents reinforcements from coming up—he orders his men forward. General Alfred Mouton's division attacks the Union left with a cheer but is badly cut up by musketry. Mouton is killed, but his survivors rally under General Camille J. Polignac and press forward, assisted by Texans under General John G. Walker to their right. The Confederates then crash through two Union lines, overrunning Banks's artillery and wagon train, which they immediately stop to plunder. This delay grants Federals under General William H. Emory sufficient time to form a third line; it, too, is attacked heavily but repulses the Southerners. Emory's stand also enables the bulk of Banks's forces to retreat toward Pleasant Hill, 15 miles east, as fighting gradually winds down.

Mansfield proves to be the decisive encounter of the Red River campaign and the largest waged in the Trans-Mississippi theater. Banks is stopped in his tracks and is thrashed soundly due to slovenly deployments. Union losses are also severe considering the numbers engaged and amount to 113 dead, 581 injured, and 1,541 missing (2,235). The victorious Taylor, who captures 20 cannon, 200 wagons, and 1,000 draft animals, suffers more than 1,000 casualties. The Confederates are reinforced tonight by General Thomas J. Churchill's division and immediately pursue the defeated bluecoats downriver.

April 9

NORTH: Union strategy for an all-out push against the Confederacy is finalized into five major components: General Nathaniel P. Banks is to capture Mobile, Alabama;

General William T. Sherman is to drive into Georgia from Tennessee and seize Atlanta; General Franz Sigel is to advance down the Shenandoah Valley, breadbasket of the Confederacy, and General Benjamin F. Butler is to descend on Richmond, Virginia, from the south bank of the James River. But most important, General George G. Meade's Army of the Potomac is to rivet their attention on General Robert E. Lee and the Army of Northern Virginia. "Wherever Lee goes, there you will go also," Grant declares.

SOUTH: General Nathaniel P. Banks consolidates 18,000 men of his shaken army, now reinforced by two veteran divisions from General Andrew J. Smith's XVI Corps, along Pleasant Hill, Louisiana. The Northerners are posted strongly and are ready by the time Confederates under General Richard Taylor appear on the battlefield at 9:00 A.M. However, Taylor's 12,000 men are exhausted by all-night marching, and his attack is delayed by several hours. It is not until 4:30 P.M. that Confederate artillery open up and Churchill's division sweeps forward in a flanking movement around Banks's left. As this transpires, Taylor also commits General Thomas Green's cavalry and a Texas division under General John G. Walker to assail the Union center. These movements are repelled bloodily, although Churchill makes good progress initially and routs two Federal brigades. Suddenly, Churchill is himself assailed in the right flank by a deft counterattack organized by Smith, and he reels backward. Additional charges against the Union line result in nothing but further losses, so Taylor orders combat to cease by nightfall.

Pleasant Hill is a major tactical victory for Banks, who rescues his army from the previous day's humiliation at Mansfield. Union losses are 152 killed, 859 wounded, and 495 captured (1,506) to a Confederate tally of 1,621. However, Union forces continue falling back on Grand Ecore, spelling an end of the Red River campaign. The aggressive Taylor wishes to pursue further, but his superior, General Edmund Kirby-Smith, orders the bulk of his army back into Arkansas to contain a Federal offensive there.

WEST: General George Stoneman transfers from Virginia to the Department of the Ohio as head of all Union cavalry.

General Frederick Steele is reinforced by cavalry under General John M. Thayer at Elkin's Ferry, Arkansas, although this does nothing to alleviate chronic supply shortages. The Union column also is beset persistently by Confederate guerrillas and cavalry.

NAVAL: At 2:00 A.M., the USS *Minnesota* is damaged by a spar torpedo handled by the Confederate torpedo boat CSS *Squib* under Lieutenant Hunter Davidson off Newport News, Virginia. The intruder was detected at 150 yards' distance, but the *Minnesota*'s guns could not be depressed in time. Davidson manages to place his charge in his target's port quarter, but fortunately for the Union vessel, the damage incurred proves slight. *Squib* then steams off to safety under heavy musket fire, thoroughly alarming Union vessels in the area.

April 10

SOUTH: The Red River campaign grounds to an ignominious close as General Nathaniel P. Banks withdraws back to Grand Ecore, Louisiana, General Frederick

Steele stalls in Arkansas. A victorious General Richard Taylor is ordered back to Mansfield by General Edmund Kirby-Smith.

WEST: General Oliver O. Howard replaces General Gordon Granger as commander of the IV Corps, Army of the Tennessee.

Union forces under General Frederick Steele encounter stiff Confederate resistance under General Sterling Price at Prairie D'Ane, Arkansas, and a continuing fight develops during the next four days. With the Red River campaign under General Nathaniel P. Banks concluded, Steele now finds himself marooned deep behind enemy lines with few supplies and no prospect of reinforcements. Nonetheless, he continues advancing toward better positions at Camden to await developments.

NAVAL: Admiral David D. Porter's Mississippi Squadron steams up the Red River and escorts army transports as far as Springfield Landing, Louisiana, 30 miles below Shreveport. Further progress is blocked by the Confederate steamer *New Falls City,* which is sunk in midstream as an obstacle. The vessels are beset further by falling water levels and news of General Nathaniel P. Banks's recent defeat at Sabine Cross Roads.

April 11

POLITICS: The pro-Union administration of Dr. Isaac Murphy is inaugurated at Little Rock, Arkansas.

NAVAL: The USS *Nita* captures the Confederate vessel *Three Brothers* near the mouth of the Homosassa River, Florida.

The USS *Virginia* captures the Confederate blockade-runner *Juanita* at San Luis Pass, Texas.

Admiral David D. Porter's gunboat flotilla slowly begins to work its vessels over the Alexandria rapids while under fire from Confederate artillery and snipers. However, the water level is dipping so low that the majority of his fleet becomes trapped upstream.

April 12

SOUTH: Confederate forces pursuing after the Battle of Pleasant Hill encounter General Thomas K. Smith's division, XVI Corps at Blair's Landing, Louisiana. These troops are covered by several Union gunboats in the adjacent Red River. General Thomas Green nonetheless dismounts his cavalry and artillery to engage them. The aggressive Green, somewhat inebriated, leads a foolish charge against the waiting flotilla and is pummeled by heavy shells fired from the riverfront; he is among the very first killed. The Southerners sustain 300 casualties to a Union tally of only 57.

WEST: General Simon B. Buckner is appointed commander of the Confederate Department of East Tennessee.

A force of 1,500 Confederate cavalry under General James R. Chambers invests Fort Pillow, Tennessee, on the Mississippi River, then defended by 557 Union soldiers, including 262 African Americans, under Major Lionel F. Booth. The fort, a wretchedly designed open earthwork, is partially stormed by Chambers, whose first charge seizes the outer works and renders the Union cannon useless. From

Confederate batteries fire on Union transport ships during the Red River Campaign, March–May 1864. Engraving, *Harper's Weekly*

there, Confederate snipers also fire down into the garrison, killing Major Booth. His successor, Major William F. Bradford, grimly awaits promised reinforcements from downstream and holds on. At 10:00 A.M., General Nathan B. Forrest arrives and, after several more hours of fighting, concludes that the fort cannot be defended. At 3:30 P.M., a flag of truce goes forward demanding Bradford's surrender, but he refuses. Forrest then orders an all-out assault on the last ring of defense, which falls easily. Surviving Federals then either flee over the bluffs and dive into the Mississippi River or try surrendering, but the enraged Confederates apparently go on a rampage. Many Union soldiers, largely African Americans, are apparently murdered in cold blood. The fort is abandoned soon after, and Forrest departs for Jackson, Tennessee. Confederate losses at Fort Pillow are 14 killed and 86 wounded, a pittance compared to Union casualties of 231 dead, 100 wounded, and 226 captured—only 58 African Americans are taken alive. The extent of the slaughter results in charges of massacre being leveled against Forrest, who denies any complicity. But thereafter "Remember Fort Pillow!" becomes a rallying cry for black soldiers.

NAVAL: Armed boats from the USS *South Carolina* and *T. A. Ward* seize the British blockade-runner *Alliance* after it runs aground on Daufuskie Island, South Carolina.

The USS *Estrella*, escorting two army steamers, helps General Fitz H. Warren land troops in Matagorda Bay, Texas, and subsequently captures two small vessels.

The Federal gunboat USS *New Era* assists in the defense of Fort Pillow, Tennessee, but after the fort falls and captured cannon are turned on the vessel, it withdraws upriver.

Admiral David D. Porter's Mississippi Squadron and several army transports begin their trek back down the Red River, Louisiana, engaging enemy troops at Blair's Landing, Louisiana. Heavy and accurate fire from the USS *Neosho, Lexington, Hindman,* and *Osage* drives off Confederate dismounted cavalry and cannon from the riverbanks, killing General Thomas Green in the process. The *Osage* also makes naval history in this engagement by employing for the first time jerry-rigged periscopes to direct naval gunfire.

April 13

NAVAL: A naval expedition consisting of the USS *Stepping Stones, Commodore Morris, Commodore Perry, Commodore Barney, Shokokon,* and *Minnesota* unsuccessfully tries to trap the Confederate torpedo vessel CSS *Squib* on the Nansemond River, Virginia.

The USS *Rachel Seaman* captures the British blockade-runner *Maria Alfred* on the Mermentau River, Louisiana.

The USS *Nyanza* captures the Confederate schooner *Mandoline* at Atchafalaya Bay, Louisiana.

April 14

SOUTH: General John Sedgwick assumes command of the VI Corps, Army of the Potomac.

General Ambrose E. Burnside takes charge of the IX Corps, Army of the Potomac.

WEST: Confederate cavalry under General Abraham Buford, informed by local newspapers that General Nathan B. Forrest's recent raid missed capturing 140 army horses concealed in a foundry at Paducah, Kentucky, suddenly reappear in force. The Union garrison under Colonel Stephen C. Hicks simply withdraws once again into nearby Fort Anderson, and the Southerners make off with valuable new mounts.

NAVAL: The USS *New Era, Platte Valley,* and *Silver Cloud* approach Fort Pillow, Tennessee, and, finding it vacant, fire shells at nearby Confederate forces.

The USS *Peosta, Key West, Fairplay,* and *Victory* approach Paducah, Kentucky, on the Ohio River and drive off Confederate forces gathering along the bank.

The USS *Moose, Hastings,* and *Fairy* engage Confederate cavalry at Columbus, Kentucky, on the Mississippi River.

April 15

POLITICS: Governor Andrew Johnson of Tennessee delivers a speech in Knoxville endorsing the principles of emancipation.

SOUTH: Colonel John S. Mosby ambushes and defeats a large Union contingent at Waterford, Virginia.

WEST: Union cavalry directed by General John M. Schofield surprise Confederates at Greeneville, Tennessee, taking 25 captives.

General Frederick Steele occupies Camden, Arkansas, to gather supplies and rest his hungry men. Meanwhile, Confederates under General Sterling Price continue arriving to threaten his flank and rear.

NAVAL: The USS *Virginia* forces the Confederate sloop *Rosina* aground near San Luis Pass, Texas, destroying it.

The Federal gunboat USS *Eastport* strikes a Confederate torpedo on the Red River below Grand Ecore, Louisiana, and grounds itself in shoal waters to carry out repairs.

April 16
NORTH: An official report by the U.S. government lists 146,634 Confederate prisoners of war.

NAVAL: The army transport *General Hunter* strikes a torpedo and sinks in the St. John's River, Florida.

April 17
NORTH: General Ulysses S. Grant suspends all prisoner exchanges until the Confederates release identical numbers of Union captives—an impossible demand, given their restricted manpower. To this end, Grant also insists: "No distinction whatever will be made in the exchange between white and colored prisoners." Confederate authorities strongly disagree with his dictates, and the practice of prisoner exchanges halts, resulting in longer retention of captives in already overcrowded facilities. Grant's ploy also seriously impairs the South's ability to regain trained manpower.

SOUTH: General Robert F. Hoke gathers up 7,000 men and attacks the Union garrison at Plymouth, North Carolina. His objective is the 2,834 Union infantry, cavalry, and artillery commanded by General Henry W. Wessells, who are supported further by an offshore gunboat squadron.

WEST: To alleviate mounting supply shortages, General Frederick Steele dispatches a foraging expedition from Camden, Arkansas, to confiscate stores of Southern corn. Colonel James M. Williams then marches from camp with 695 men, mostly from the 1st Kansas Colored Volunteers, two cannon, and 198 wagons. En route, he receives additional reinforcements, bringing his numbers up to 1,170 men.

NAVAL: The Federal gunboats USS *Southfield, Ceres,* and *Miami,* accompanied by the army steamer *Bombshell,* assist in the defense of Plymouth, North Carolina. Confederate attackers are driven off, but the *Bombshell* sustains serious damage and sinks.

The USS *Owasco* captures the British blockade-runner *Lilly* off Velasco, Texas.

April 18
SOUTH: General Pierre G. T. Beauregard arrives to replace General Samuel Jones as commander of the Department of North Carolina and Southern Virginia.

General Robert F. Hoke continues his campaign against the Union garrison at Plymouth, North Carolina, by shelling enemy positions and capturing Fort Wessels with several determined charges. However, Federal troops cling stubbornly to nearby Fort Williams, and now Hoke's success hinges on the appearance of the Confederate ram CSS *Albemarle.*

WEST: Confederate cavalry under General John S. Marmaduke detect a party of 1,170 Union soldiers near Poison Springs, Arkansas, and prepare to give battle with 1,700 troopers. He then is joined by General Samuel B. Maxey's command, which brings Confederate numbers up to 3,335. Maxey, although nominally outranking Marmaduke, allows him to take tactical control of the battle. The Confederates then advance, meeting staunch resistance from African Americans of the 1st Kansas Colored Volunteers and are thrown back repeatedly. But Southern numbers gradually assert themselves and the Union troopers suddenly gave way, creating a gap in the Union lines. Colonel James M. Williams strives to close ranks as the Confederates charge again, and he is in the act of covering his wagon train when Marmaduke's masked cannons open fire. The Federal column now is caught in a crossfire and crumbles quickly as survivors flee for the safety of Camden, 10 miles distant. Union losses would have been far higher save for Maxey's decision to overrule Marmaduke and eschew the pursuit in order to secure the wagon train.

Poison Springs is a significant Union defeat for it forces General Frederick Steele's army at Camden on the defensive, where it languishes on half rations. The victorious Marmaduke also captures all 198 wagons and four cannon, and he inflicts 204 killed and missing, along with 97 wounded. Confederate losses are pegged at 13 killed, 81 wounded, and one missing. Sadly, most of the Union dead are African Americans captured in battle and then slaughtered without mercy by Missourians, Arkansans, and Confederate Choctaw.

NAVAL: The USS *Commodore Read* engages and destroys a Confederate supply base at Circus Point on the Rappahannock River, Virginia.

The Confederate ram CSS *Albemarle* departs Hamilton, North Carolina, under Commander James W. Cooke and sails down the Roanoke River. The vessel's appearance is greatly anticipated by Confederate forces currently besieging Plymouth. But while steaming en route, the vessel experiences engine and steering malfunctions and is forced to anchor above the town that evening.

Armed boats from the USS *Beauregard* capture the British blockade-runner *Oramoneta* near Matanzas Inlet, Florida.

The USS *Fox* captures and burns the Confederate schooner *Good Hope* off the Homosassa River, Florida.

April 19

POLITICS: The U.S. Congress passes legislation authorizing the admittance of Nebraska as a state.

SOUTH: Colonel John S. Mosby raids a Union wedding ceremony at Leesburg, Virginia, and then conveys his greetings to Federal troops and Union-leaning inhabitants of the area.

NAVAL: The huge Confederate steam ram CSS *Albemarle* under Commander James W. Cooke attacks the Federal squadron consisting of the USS *Miami, Ceres,* and *Southfield* off Plymouth, North Carolina. Arriving at 3:30 A.M., *Albemarle* strikes and sinks the USS *Southfield,* killing Commander C. W. Flusser. The surviving Union vessels draw off, leaving the Federal garrison ashore unsupported and with Confederate forces commanding all water approaches to Plymouth.

A Confederate torpedo boat makes a failed attempt to strike and sink the USS *Wabash* off Charleston harbor, South Carolina. The attack is detected, and the intended victim manages to raise steam and get underway, but the attackers are finally discouraged by heavy swells.

The USS *Owsaco* captures the British blockade-runner *Laura* in the Gulf of Mexico.

The USS *Virginia* captures the Mexican blockade-runner *Alma* off the Texas coast.

April 20

NORTH: The government reduces rations accorded to Southern prisoners of war in retaliation for mistreatment of Union captives.

SOUTH: General Robert F. Hoke attacks and captures 2,800 Union prisoners and a large quantity of supplies at Plymouth, North Carolina, after a three-day siege. Key to his success is the arrival of the Confederate ram CSS *Albemarle,* which bombards the defenders from offshore. For his success, Hoke receives promotion to major general. Confederate losses are 163 killed and 554 wounded.

WEST: General Edmund Kirby-Smith arrives outside Camden, Arkansas, with three divisions to confront the 13,500 Union troops of General Frederick Steele. The Confederates then begin to maneuver to come between Steele and the capital at Little Rock. Steele, meanwhile, gratefully receives a Union supply train from Pine Bluff, which partially ameliorates his otherwise tenuous supply situation.

April 21

POLITICS: President Abraham Lincoln confers with the governors of Ohio, Indiana, Illinois, and Iowa.

SOUTH: General Nathaniel P. Banks withdraws his army from Grand Ecore, Louisiana, and back to Cloutiersville while closely pursued by Confederate cavalry.

NAVAL: The USS *Eureka* trades fire with a concealed Confederate battery on the Potomac River near Urbanna, Virginia.

Armed boats from the USS *Howquah, Fort Jackson,* and *Niphon* land and destroy Confederate saltworks at Masonboro Sound, North Carolina, taking 160 captives.

Armed boats from the USS *Ethan Allen* attack and destroy a Confederate saltworks at Murrell's Inlet, South Carolina.

Landing parties from the USS *Cimarron* destroy a rice mill and 5,000 bushels of rice at Winyah Bay, South Carolina.

Armed boats from the USS *Sagamore* destroy 400 bales of cotton at Clay Landing, Florida.

The Federal gunboats USS *Petrel* and *Prairie Bird* lend supporting fire to Union forces attacking Yazoo City, Mississippi. However, once *Petrel* steams past Confederate batteries, it proves unable to turn around in the confining waters downstream.

The Federal gunboat USS *Eastport* is refloated after striking a torpedo and limps down the Red River. During the next five days, the damaged vessel grounds itself eight times to effect repairs and covers only 60 miles.

April 22

POLITICS: The first U.S. coins with the inscription "In God We Trust" are minted as per an act of Congress.

President Jefferson Davis writes General Leonidas K. Polk concerning African-American prisoners. "If the negroes are escaped slaves, they should be held safely for recovery by their owners," he states. "If otherwise, inform me."

SOUTH: Fitzhugh Lee is appointed major general, C.S.A.

WEST: To gather additional supplies for his starving forces, General Frederick Steele dispatches 240 wagons on an expedition to Pine Bluff, Arkansas. They are accompanied by Colonel Francis M. Drake, commanding 1,200 infantry and 240 cavalry as an escort.

NAVAL: The Confederate steam ram CSS *Neuse* grounds on its maiden voyage from Kinston, North Carolina, and cannot be refloated. It then is destroyed to prevent capture.

The USS *Petrel* again engages Confederate batteries during a Union assault on Yazoo City, Mississippi. *Petrel* comes off poorly in the exchange, grounds, and is captured by General Wirt Adams with a loss of 10 killed.

The USS *Monticello* boards the British schooner *James Douglas* at sea, only to find it abandoned.

April 23

SOUTH: As the army of General Nathaniel P. Banks retreats from Grand Ecore, Louisiana, a body of Confederate cavalry under General Hamilton P. Bee seizes Monet's Ferry at Cane River Crossing. Because this was the only fordable point in the vicinity, Union troops under General William H. Emory counterattack to regain control of the ferry. Colonel Francis Fessenden dislodges Southerners from behind the high bank they occupy, and Bee withdraws safely to a nearby hillside. Union troops then construct a pontoon bridge on the river, over which Banks's army passes the following day. General Richard Taylor waxes critical over Bee's inept performance and for allowing the Federals to escape. Union losses are estimated at 300; the Confederates sustain about 50 casualties.

WEST: General Frank P. Blair assumes command of the Union XVII Corps in Tennessee.

General James F. Fagan, after learning of the Union wagon train dispatched by General Frederick Steele to Pine Bluff, Arkansas, dispatches 4,000 Confederate cavalry under Generals William L. Cabell and Joseph O. Shelby to intercept the wagon train on the Warren Road.

April 24

WEST: A large Union wagon train wends its way back to Pine Bluff, Arkansas, including 500 Iowa cavalry and 300 former African-American slaves seeking freedom. They proceed down the Warren Road unaware that sizable Confederate forces lurk nearby, preparing to strike.

April 25

SOUTH: Confederate raiders under Colonel John S. Mosby storm a Union outpost at Hunter's Mills, Virginia, capturing men and horses.

General Nathaniel P. Banks's men begin to straggle into Alexandria, Louisiana, concluding their ill-fated campaign up the Red River.

General Robert Ransom is assigned to take charge of the Confederate Department of Richmond.

WEST: A force of 4,000 Confederate cavalry under General William L. Cabell surprises a Union wagon train at Mark's Mills, Arkansas, catching the armed escort of Colonel Francis M. Drake in a pincer. Advanced elements tangle at 8:00 A.M., after which impetuous Southerners drive the Federals back into their wagons. Drake falls seriously wounded before Union defenses can sort themselves out. A final charge from the north delivered by General Joseph O. Shelby clinches the victory, and the Northerners surrender en masse. Cabell seizes 240 wagons and 1,700 prisoners while only 300 Federals escape back to their main force at Camden. Confederate losses are given as 41 killed, 108 wounded, and 144 missing. Moreover, enraged Southerners also murder 150 African-American slaves who had attached themselves to the column. This defeat also impels General Frederick Steele to abandon Camden, Arkansas, in the face of superior numbers and dwindling supplies.

NAVAL: The Confederate raider CSS *Alabama* under Captain Raphael Semmes captures the Federal ship *Rockingham* west of the Cape Verde Islands and sinks it with cannon fire.

April 26

SOUTH: General Ulysses S. Grant orders Union troops to evacuate Washington, North Carolina, following the recent loss of Plymouth. He also orders the town of New Bern held at all costs and has its defenses strengthened.

The battered Union army of General Nathaniel P. Banks continues filtering through Alexandria, Louisiana, and remains two days awaiting the gunboat fleet of Admiral David D. Porter.

WEST: Outnumbered and nearly surrounded by Confederates under Generals Edmund Kirby-Smith and Sterling Price, General Frederick Steele abandons Camden, Arkansas, and marches back to Little Rock. He methodically begins to evacuate that night and skillfully slips past Confederate outposts without detection.

NAVAL: Armed boats from the USS *Ottawa* and *Pawnee* accompany several army transports up the St. John's River in defense of Fort Gates and St. Augustine, Florida.

The Mississippi Squadron under Admiral David D. Porter wages a running fight while passing Confederate batteries near Alexandria on the Red River, Louisiana. In this first round of fighting, the USS *Cricket* sustains heavy damage while the pump steamer *Champion No. 3* is crippled, drifts, and is captured. The wooden gunboat *Juliet* also receives several hits but is fortunately towed out of harm's way by *Champion No. 5.*

The Federal gunboat USS *Eastport,* having grounded six times due to damage from striking a mine, is scuttled on the Red River, Louisiana.

April 27

POLITICS: President Jefferson Davis dispatches a special commissioner to Canada to help to negotiate a possible truce with the United States.

NORTH: In Washington, D.C., General in Chief Ulysses S. Grant begins to issue detailed orders to unleash his multipronged assault on the South.

WEST: General Frederick Steele, having skillfully evacuated Camden, Arkansas, with 13,500 men, begins a laborious slog back to Little Rock. He eludes Confederate vigilance for several hours, but his situation, 70 miles behind enemy lines, low on supplies, and substantially outnumbered, is a perilous one. General Edmund Kirby-Smith then tardily throws a pontoon bridge over the Ouachita River, a feat delaying him several hours, and commences to pursue. The progress of both sides is greatly encumbered by mud and driving rain.

NAVAL: Admiral David D. Porter makes a second attempt to run past Confederate batteries along the Red River near Alexandria, Louisiana. The USS *Fort Hindman* and *Juliet* receive some damage while the pump steamer *Champion No. 5* burns and sinks. The heavy ironclad USS *Neosho* also arrives from downstream to lend assistance. Porter reassembles his surviving craft at Alexandria.

The Confederate raider CSS *Alabama* under Captain Raphael Semmes captures and burns the Federal bark *Tycoon* east of Salvador, Brazil.

April 28

SOUTH: Union batteries in Charleston Harbor, South Carolina, commence to bombard Fort Sumter, throwing an addition 510 rounds throughout the ensuing week.

WEST: General Egbert B. Brown orders Union forces in Johnson County, Missouri, to pursue Confederate guerrilla William C. Quantrill.

NAVAL: Admiral David D. Porter's flotilla remains trapped on the Red River by receding water levels. The admiral himself is resigned to the necessity of scuttling his entire squadron to prevent its capture, and he advises Navy secretary Gideon Welles that, "you may judge my feelings at having to perform so painful a duty."

April 29

POLITICS: The U.S. Congress increases all duties by 50 percent to fund the war effort better.

WEST: General George Crook leads 6,155 men into the Allegheny Mountains, Virginia, for the purpose of cutting the Virginia and Tennessee Railroad. From the onset, his progress is hampered by harsh terrain and drenching rain.

The Union column of General Frederick Steele reaches the rain-swollen banks of the Saline River at Jenkin's Ferry and makes preparations to cross a rickety pontoon bridge. However, the close proximity of pursuing Confederate units necessitates the deployment of a strong rear guard of 4,000 men under General Samuel Rice, VII Corps.

NAVAL: Federal gunboats USS *Yankee, Fuchsia, Thomas Freeborn,* and *Tulip* steam up Carter's Creek, Virginia, to destroy a Confederate base camp.

The USS *Honeysuckle* captures the British blockade-runner *Miriam* off Key West, Florida.

Admiral David D. Porter's gunboat flotilla sits almost completely stranded on the Red River near Alexandria, Louisiana, by declining water levels. Fortunately, succor arrives when army engineer Colonel Joseph Bailey proposes building a series of dams to raise the water. Once the depth reaches seven feet, chutes can be opened to allow the vessels to slip through. "This proposition looked like madness," Porter concedes, "and the best engineers ridiculed it, but Colonel Bailey was so sanguine of success that I requested General Banks to have it done." The result proves to be one of the most remarkable improvisations of the entire war.

April 30
SOUTH: President Jefferson Davis issues orders to return all captured slaves found fighting in Union ranks back to their rightful owners "on proof and payment of charges."

Five-year-old Joe Davis, son of President Jefferson Davis, dies of injuries received in a fall at the Confederate White House in Richmond, Virginia.

WEST: General Franz Sigel leads 6,500 Union troops down the Shenandoah Valley toward Staunton, where he can cut the strategic Virginia Central Railroad.

The Battle of Jenkin's Ferry, Arkansas, develops as Confederate cavalry under John S. Marmaduke approach a Union rear guard under General Samuel Rice. Rice deploys his 4,000 men in a position with strongly secured flanks, which require the Confederates, fielding twice as many men, to attack frontally across a swampy morass. In rapid succession, the brigades of Generals Thomas J. Churchill, Mosby M. Parsons, and John G. Walker all advance and hurl themselves against Rice's position, being invariably driven back with losses. At length, General Frederick Steele passes the bulk of his army over the Sabine River and dutifully extricates his remaining men. General Edmund Kirby-Smith thus loses his final chance to destroy Federal forces in Arkansas completely. Union casualties are 63 dead, 413 wounded, and 45 missing (521), including the skillful general Rice, who is mortally wounded. Confederate losses are 86 killed and 356 wounded (442). As an afternote, men of the U.S. 2nd Colored Infantry murder several Southern prisoners in retaliation for atrocities inflicted on African Americans at Poison Springs the previous April.

NAVAL: The USS *Vicksburg* captures the British blockade-runner *Indian* off Charleston, South Carolina.

The USS *Conemaugh* captures the Confederate schooner *Judson* off Mobile, Alabama.

Confederate blockade-runners *Harriet Lane* and *Alice* slip past the USS *Katahdin* in a heavy rainstorm and evade the Union blockade off Galveston, Texas.

To reserve the Mississippi Squadron of Admiral David D. Porter, Colonel Joseph Bailey begins to construct a dam of logs across the Red River. Through this engineering expedient, the water levels are expected to rise sufficiently to allow Porter's vessels to pass over the Alexandria rapids. "Two or three regiments of Maine men were set to work felling trees," Porter notes, "Everyman seemed to be working with a vigor seldom seen equaled." Their efforts relieve Porter of having to scuttle his squadron to avoid being captured.

May 1
SOUTH: General John P. Hatch is tapped to succeed General Quincy A. Gillmore as commander of the Department of the South.

WEST: Colonel John S. Mosby captures eight wagons belong to General Franz Sigel's army at Bunker Hill, West Virginia.

NAVAL: The USS *Morse, General Putnam,* and *Shawsheen* escort an army expedition up the York River to West Point, Virginia. The vessels subsequently move up the Pamunkey and Mattaponi rivers to patrol for enemy forces.

The USS *Fox* captures the Confederate sloop *Oscar* off St. Marks, Florida.

May 2

POLITICS: The first session, second Confederate Congress convenes in Richmond, Virginia.

President Jefferson Davis addresses the opening session of the second Confederate Congress, accusing Northerners of "barbarism" through their "Plunder and devastation of the property of noncombatants, destruction of private dwellings, and even of edifices devoted to the worship of God."

SOUTH: General William H. Emory replaces General William B. Franklin as commander of the Union XIX Corps, Louisiana.

WEST: General Franz Sigel leads 6,500 Union troops out of Winchester Virginia, and down the Shenandoah Valley Pike toward New Market. His goal is to deny the Confederacy access to any food or cattle grown in this highly productive region.

General William W. Averell leads 2,000 Union cavalry out from Logan's Court House, Virginia, for a diversionary attack against Saltville. He moves in conjunction with another large raid by General George Crook in western Virginia.

May 3

POLITICS: President Abraham Lincoln and his cabinet discuss the recent murder of African-American prisoners at Fort Pillow, Tennessee.

SOUTH: General Ulysses S. Grant orders the the Army of the Potomac, 122,000 strong, to begin to cross the Rapidan River and to move on Richmond, Virginia. General George G. Meade, however, disputes this strategy and argues against traversing the Wilderness to hit the Confederate left flank, but Grant seeks to cut General Robert E. Lee off from Richmond. As the imposing Federal host starts to lurch toward its objective, Lee reacts by moving 66,000 men of the Army of Northern Virginia up from Orange Court House. He anticipates that the harsh terrain will negate Grant's superiority in numbers, ensuring a fairer fight. The ensuing fray promises to be a clash of titans.

WEST: General Frederick Steele's disgruntled Union troops wearily trudge into Little Rock, Arkansas, after their unsuccessful campaign to reach the Red River, Louisiana. His losses amount to 2,750 killed, wounded, and captured, along with nine cannon and 640 wagons lost. Fortunately, deft maneuvering in the face of superior Confederate numbers keeps his army intact and allows the Union to maintain partial control of the Trans-Mississippi Confederacy.

NAVAL: The USS *Chocura* captures the British blockade-runner *Agnes* at the mouth of the Brazos River, Texas, and then snares the Prussian schooner *Frederick the Second* in the same area.

The USS *Virginia* captures and sinks the Confederate schooner *Experiment* in the Gulf of Mexico.

May 4

POLITICS: The U.S. House of Representatives passes the punitively worded Wade-Davis Reconstruction Bill 73 to 59 over President Abraham Lincoln's objections. Curiously, Radical Republican politicians such as Thaddeus Stevens find the measure too conciliatory.

SOUTH: General Ulysses S. Grant and General George G. Meade direct the Army of the Potomac across the Rapidan River, Virginia, toward the heavily forested area known as the Wilderness. They lead a veteran force of 122,000 men, divided into four commands: General Winfield S. Hancock's II Corps, the V Corps under Gouverneur K. Warren, General John Sedgwick's VI Corps, and General Ambrose E. Burnside's IX Corps. Warren and Sedgwick cross the Germanna Ford east of Fredericksburg, Virginia, while Hancock does the same at Ely's Ford, six miles to the east. From there, they march directly into a thick, pine scrub forest of the Wilderness.

General Robert E. Lee, meanwhile, seeking to negate Grant's preponderance in numbers, advances to engage him in the Wilderness, where the rough terrain and thick foliage work to his advantage. He has at his disposal 66,000 veteran troops divided up into General James Longstreet's I Corps, General Richard S. Ewell's II Corps, and General Ambrose P. Hill's III Corps. Longstreet is not in the immediate vicinity and receives orders to march there at once.

General Benjamin F. Butler leads his Army of the James in transports from Fortress Monroe, Virginia, and then down the James River toward Richmond, Virginia.

WEST: General William T. Sherman advances his force of 110,000 men from Chattanooga, Tennessee, against Confederate forces under General Joseph E. Johnston. The Union goal is Atlanta, Georgia, an important communications hub.

NAVAL: The USS *Sunflower, Honduras,* and *J. L. Davis* assist General Daniel Woodbury's soldiers in the seizure of Tampa, Florida. The naval landing party is allowed to hoist the Stars and Stripes over the town.

May 5

SOUTH: The Battle of the Wilderness erupts when General Gouverneur K. Warren's V Corps encounters General Richard S. Ewell's II Corps along the Orange Turnpike Road. Warren is well positioned to sweep the Southerners before him, but his insurmountable delays in attacking grant Ewell time to rush up reinforcements. At 1:00 P.M., a tremendous seesaw struggle erupts in the woods with both sides taking and inflicting heavy casualties but neither side proving able to dislodge the other. General John Sedgwick's VI Corps then deploys and attempts to turn Ewell's left flank but is repulsed. Fighting in this sector dies down at nightfall.

Two miles south, General Winfield S. Hancock's II Corps engages General Ambrose P. Hill's III Corps in fierce fighting. An all-out Confederate advance surges ahead initially, but Hill is halted by General George W. Getty's division, VI Corps, which stands long enough for Hancock to make his greater numbers felt. Hill then is driven back gradually with heavy losses, and Hancock prepares to overwhelm his weakened opponent on the following day.

The Army of the James under General Benjamin F. Butler lands 39,000 men of Generals Quincy A. Gillmore's X Corps and William F. Smith's XVIII Corps at Bermuda Hundred, Virginia. This places Union forces within marching distance of the Confederate capital at Richmond, then lightly defended.

A Confederate assault on New Bern, North Carolina, by General Robert F. Hoke is rebuffed once the CSS *Albemarle* fails to penetrate Union naval defenses. The Southerners then abandon the siege and begin to withdraw.

WEST: Virginian Partisan Rangers under Captain John H. McNeill seize Piedmont, West Virginia, along with several trains, cars, and 104 prisoners.

The 2nd Cavalry Division under General William W. Averell clatters out of Logan Court, Virginia, and advances toward Wyoming Court House. The division skirmishes with the 8th Virginia Cavalry near Saltville.

NAVAL: The ironclad ram CSS *Albemarle* under Commander James W. Cooke, escorted by the smaller *Bombshell*, and *Cotton Plant*, enters Albemarle Sound off Plymouth, North Carolina, to engage Federal warships stationed there. The Union armada under Captain Melancthon Smith mounts 60 cannon to Cooke's two banded Brooke rifles, but the latter's ship is armored heavily and nearly is impervious to cannon fire. Broadsides are exchanged, and the wooden Union vessels sustain damage until Smith orders USS *Sassacus* to charge the *Albemarle* at full steam. The ensuing collision damages both vessels, and once *Albemarle* puts a point-blank cannon shot through *Sassacus*'s boilers, it drifts helplessly out of the fight. Union side-wheelers *Mattabesett* and *Wyalusing* then hurry up to assist and keep the Southerners under a steady bombardment. With *Albemarle* maneuvering badly and *Bombshell* captured, Cooke orders his vessel and *Cotton Plant* back up the Roanoke River. His withdrawal leaves Confederate forces without naval support, and their ongoing attack on New Bern falters.

The Federal gunboats USS *Covington* and *Signal* and the transport *Warner* are sunk near Dunn's Bayou on the Red River, Louisiana, after being attacked by Confederate troops and artillery.

May 6

SOUTH: Stand Watie, a Cherokee chief, is appointed a brigadier general, C.S.A.

The Battle of the Wilderness continues as General Winfield S. Hancock's II Corps, advancing down the Orange Plank Road, smashes into General Ambrose P. Hill's III Corps, nearly breaking it. General Ambrose E. Burnside's IX Corps, which arrives late, is also thrown into the fray, although he blunders into Hill's reserves and is stopped. At that precise moment, General James Longstreet makes his own sudden, if belated, appearance with the veteran I Corps and hits Hancock's left and rear. A hard-fought slugging match at close range ensues until four Confederate brigades discover a secret path around the Union left and attack. Longstreet hammers Hancock back across the line and pushes the Federals onto Brock Road. The hard-charging leader then is wounded seriously by friendly fire while General Micah Jenkins, riding alongside him, is killed. Ironically, Longstreet falls at almost the same spot where "Stonewall" Jackson was wounded fatally a year earlier. Command delays ensue, and the Confederates are unable to resume advancing before

4:00 P.M., which gives Hancock ample time to prepare defenses. When the Confederates finally attack, they encounter entrenched Federals backed by artillery and are repulsed.

Two miles away, General John Sedgwick's VI Corps renews its struggle with General Richard S. Ewell's II Corps along the Orange Turnpike. Ewell strikes first at 4:30 A.M. and is repulsed, as are subsequent Union attacks. The fresh Confederate division under General John B. Gordon then manages to work its way around the Union right and charges, severely disrupting Warren's line. The onset of nightfall dampens further fighting, and both sides settle behind entrenched lines. Worse, the dry vegetation and undergrowth are set ablaze by the fighting, and hundreds of wounded soldiers, unable to crawl to safety, perish horribly in the flames.

The Wilderness is an unequivocal tactical victory for the South as General Lee tackled an opponent twice his size—in an area where he was least expected—and handles him roughly. Grant, who endures the ignominy of having both flanks turned, suffers staggering losses: 2,246 men dead, 12,037 injured, and 3,383 missing (17,666); Confederate casualties, though not recorded, are probably in the vicinity of 8,000. But Grant, unlike Union commanders before him, ignores the setback and, by dint of single-minded determination, completely alters the war's strategic equation. He fully intends to maintain the initiative by sidestepping around Lee's left flank, and inch ever closer to Richmond, Virginia. Lee is thus reduced to following close at hand. "Whatever happens," Grant tells President Abraham Lincoln, "there will be no turning back." This newfound doggedness, missing in the first three years of combat, marks a turning point in the Civil War, whereupon the tide begins to turn inexorably in favor of the North.

The Army of the James under General Benjamin F. Butler slowly advances 39,000 men toward lightly manned Confederate defenses under General George E. Pickett, but he fails to press its advantage. Pickett, commanding only 10,000 men at Petersburg, stands his ground, and Butler timidly starts to entrench. His only offensive action is to order 1,000 troops from the XVIII Corps under General Charles A. Heckman to cut the Richmond and Petersburg railroad, and this is repulsed by Colonel Charles Graham and 600 Confederates.

A Federal expedition from Key West occupies Tampa, Florida.

NAVAL: The side-wheeler USS *Commodore Jones* detonates a 2,000-pound Confederate torpedo and sinks in the James River, Virginia, with a loss of 40 lives. Ironically, the vessel then was dragging the river for mines in concert with the *Mackinaw* and *Commodore Morris*.

Armed boats from the USS *Dawn* support an army attack on Wilson's Wharf, Virginia, and help burn a signal station.

The USS *Eutaw, Osceola, Pequot, Shokokon,* and *Putnam* support landing operations of General Benjamin F. Butler's Army of the James at Bermuda Hundred, Virginia, and subsequently move inland as far as is practicable.

A sortie by the ironclad ram CSS *Raleigh* at New Inlet, North Carolina, forces the USS *Britannia* and *Nansemond* to withdraw, allowing an unnamed blockade-runner to escape.

The USS *Grand Gulf* captures the British blockade-runner *Young Republic* east of Savannah, Georgia.

The Federal steamer USS *Granite City* and the tinclad *Wave* are shelled by Confederate batteries on the Calcasieu River, Louisiana, and are forced to surrender. Union losses total 174; the Confederates report 21 casualties.

May 7

NORTH: Edward R. S. Canby is promoted to major general, U.S. Army.

SOUTH: Richard H. Anderson replaces the critically wounded James Longstreet as commander of the Confederate I Corps, Army of Northern Virginia.

The struggle of the Wilderness concludes as General Ulysses S. Grant maintains the initiative by attempting to slip around the Confederate right and march 12 miles southeast toward Spotsylvania Court House. Possession of this crucial crossroads would grant Union forces an open road to Richmond, Virginia. General Gouverneur K. Warren's VI Corps is then detailed to seize the junction while Federal cavalry under General Philip H. Sheridan move to seize and clear the Brock Road. He has only the division of General Wesley Merritt available, but this is sent trotting down the road toward Spotsylvania.

Sheridan's advanced brigade under General George A. Custer then rides directly into General Fitzhugh Lee's dismounted Confederate troopers at Todd's Tavern, and intense fighting erupts in the underbrush. Additional Union and Confederate cavalry arrive under Generals Wesley Merritt and Wade Hampton, respectively, but the Southerners, though hard pressed, keep their lines intact. To break the impasse, Sheridan directs the cavalry of General David M. Gregg to circle east along the Catharpin Road and catch Lee in a pincer attack. Lee, however, shifts his line accordingly to meet the new threat, and the Union movement bogs down. At nightfall, Sheridan abandons efforts to clear the Brock Road and returns to camp. Union casualties are in the vicinity of 250, with Confederates probably sustaining as many. Consequently, Confederates under General Richard H. Anderson secure Spotsylvania Court House ahead of Union forces.

General Benjamin F. Butler details 8,000 men under General William Brooks to seize the Richmond and Petersburg railroad, and they push back General Bushrod Johnson's 2,700 Confederates from Port Walthall Junction to Swift Creek. Nonetheless, some Union soldiers contemptuously refer to Butler's dilatory campaign as a "stationary advance."

WEST: The Military Division of West Mississippi is created under General Edward R. S. Canby.

The Atlanta campaign begins. General William T. Sherman, commanding the Armies of the Cumberland (General George H. Thomas), the Ohio (General John M. Schofield), and the Tennessee (General James B. McPherson), totaling more than 100,000 men, swiftly advances on Dalton, Georgia. There, he confronts the Army of Tennessee under General Joseph E. Johnston and his 62,000 Confederates. These are organized into two corps under Generals John B. Hood and William J. Hardee, while a third corps under General Leonidas Polk is en route from Mississippi. Southern Confederate cavalry are led by the highly capable general Joseph Wheeler. The contenders are equally matched from a leadership standpoint, and the ensuing campaign comes to resemble a chess match played over impassable terrain.

The Federals begin by marching 25 miles south and applying pressure on Confederates at Rocky Face Ridge, pushing them back as far as Buzzard's Roost Pass. Meanwhile, McPherson's Army of the Tennessee is dispatched below Confederate positions to Snake Gap Creek, 15 miles distant, where he can cut Johnson's rail line decisively and possibly bag his entire force.

NAVAL: The Federal steamer USS *Shawsheen* is attacked by Confederate forces while dragging for torpedoes along the James River, Virginia, and is captured off Chaffin's Bluff. The vessel subsequently is burned and sunk.

The USS *Howquah, Nansemond, Mount Vernon,* and *Kansas* engage the CSS *Raleigh* off New Inlet, North Carolina. The Confederate vessel then grounds at the mouth of the Cape Fear River and is scuttled.

May 8

SOUTH: Thousands of soldiers from both sides file into positions along a three-mile front at Spotsylvania Court House, Virginia. Both General Gouverneur K. Warren's V Corps and General John Sedgwick's VI Corps then charge and attempt to dislodge Confederates from their earthworks, but they are repelled heavily. Moreover, General Robert E. Lee instructs his men to fell trees, dig trenches, and strengthen all defensive lines with earthworks. The most conspicuous feature to arise is a mile-long, half-mile-deep salient dubbed the "Mule Shoe" owing to its protruding shape. General Ulysses S. Grant, undeterred by the growing strength of Lee's position, still probes for Southern weaknesses. Lee's position then gradually assumes a more definite form with General Richard H. Anderson's I Corps on the left, General Richard S. Ewell's II Corps in the center, and General Jubal A. Early's III Corps on the right. All are entrenched heavily with ample reserves to prevent breakthroughs in any given sector.

General Jubal A. Early temporarily replaces the ailing General Ambrose P. Hill as commander of the III Corps, Army of Northern Virginia.

WEST: Union forces under General John Newton, IV Corps, continue pressing against Confederate defenders at Mill Creek Gap, Georgia. The Southerners give ground slowly, falling back and up stronger defensive terrain. At length, General John W. Geary's XX Corps launches three uphill attacks against Dug Gap to flank Buzzard's Roost and is repelled, resulting in 350 casualties.

May 9

SOUTH: The Army of the Potomac deploys on an arc outside Confederate lines erected around Spotsylvania Court House. The far right is occupied by General Winfield S. Hancock's II Corps, followed by General Gouverneur K. Warren's V Corps, General John Sedgwick's VI Corps, and General Ambrose E. Burnside's IX Corps finally anchoring the left. All told, 100,000 Federals confront 60,000 Confederates across the three-mile line that is strongly fortified and skillfully manned.

General John Sedgwick of the VI Corps is killed by a sniper's bullet at Spotsylvania, Virginia, after declaring "They couldn't hit an elephant at this distance." Command then reverts to General Horatio G. Wright.

General Philip H. Sheridan takes seven cavalry brigades, totaling almost 10,000 troopers, on a raid against Richmond, Virginia. He does so in the hopes of luring Confederate cavalry under General J. E. B. Stuart into the open and crushing them with superior numbers. However, this move deprives the Army of the Potomac of its ability to reconnoiter Confederate positions adequately, a deficiency that costs General Ulysses S. Grant dearly.

After a few more half-hearted advances toward Petersburg, General Benjamin F. Butler dispatches General William F. Smith's XVIII Corps toward Petersburg, where they encounter Confederates under General Bushrod Johnson at Swift Creek. Johnson attacks prematurely at Arrowhead Church and is repulsed with losses, but Butler withdraws his Army of the James from Fort Clifton, Virginia, and back to City Point. Several of his generals strongly suggest throwing a pontoon bridge across the Appomattox River for a better approach to the city, but Butler rejects this sagacious advice in favor of throwing up defensive works across Bermuda Neck.

General Stephen D. Lee accepts command of the Confederate Department of Alabama, Mississippi, and East Louisiana.

WEST: General George Crook, riding at the head of 6,155 Union troops, advances into southwestern Virginia, to destroy a portion of the Virginia and Tennessee Railroad. En route, he engages 2,400 Confederates and 10 cannon under General Albert G. Jenkins at Cloyd's Mountain, Virginia. Jenkins, badly outnumbered and commanding a mixed force of tough veterans and local home guards, carefully chooses good defensive positions on a high, wooded bluff and awaits Crook's attack. That general, having surveyed the strength of this deployment, resolves to send Colonel Carr B. White's brigade around the Confederate right. Crook then leads his two remaining brigades against Jenkins's center and traverses an open meadow under heavy fire. As the Federals close in, a brigade of Ohio troops under Colonel Rutherford B. Hayes (a future president) is directed to hit the Confederate right and center.

The ensuing fight proves tenacious and costly to both sides as they form and battle around a rail breastworks. A bloody impasse continues for several hours until White's column suddenly appears on the Confederate left and begins to roll up their line. Resistance collapses and Jenkins, seriously wounded, falls captive along with his cannon. Surviving Confederates subsequently rally under General John McCausland, who forms a successful cavalry rear guard and withdraws. The victorious Crook suffers 688 men to a Confederate tally of 538. He goes on to burn the New River Bridge, thereby cutting the Virginia and Tennessee Railroad, and then rapidly pulls back after receiving word of the Union defeat at the Wilderness.

The Union IV, XIV, and XX Corps renew their attacks on Buzzard's Roost, Georgia, encountering tough resistance from General Alexander P. Stewart's division. Skirmishes and demonstrations also erupt along Rocky Face Ridge where Union cavalry under General Edward M. McCook dispute ground with General Joseph Wheeler's Confederate troopers. Meanwhile, farther south, General James B. McPherson's Army of the Tennessee successfully penetrates Snake Gap Creek, placing him behind General Joseph E. Johnston's main force. But McPherson, perceiving what he thought were impervious Confederate defenses at nearby Resaca, inexplicably retreats. Snake Gap Creek, however, is held by a single brigade of 1,400 infantry under General James Cantey and Union forces squander a golden opportunity to capture General Joseph E. Johnston's entire army.

NAVAL: Admiral David G. Farragut, stationed off Mobile Bay, Alabama, urgently requests the Navy Department to augment his flotilla with Union ironclads and thus neutralize the large Confederate steam ram CSS *Tennessee*. His impending attack on that port depends up on it.

The USS *Connecticut* captures the British blockade-runner *Minnie* at sea.

On the Red River near Alexandria, Louisiana, a log dam constructed by Colonel Joseph Bailey suddenly collapses. This mishap causes a viable chute to form inadvertently over the falls at Alexandria, so Admiral David D. Porter orders ironclads USS *Osage* and *Neosho* and steamers *Fort Hindman* and *Lexington* to run it. Amazingly, all four vessels easily float over the obstacles as 30,000 soldiers and sailors cheer from the riverbanks. Encouraged by success, Bailey commences a new dam to rescue the remaining vessels of Porter's marooned squadron.

May 10

SOUTH: Determined to test Confederate defenses, General Ulysses S. Grant begins to organize large-scale thrust against Spotsylvania Court House, Virginia. He believes that General Robert E. Lee has weakened his center sufficiently by reinforcing his flanks and orders a strong assault against the "Mule Shoe" in consequence. During the afternoon, General Winfield S. Hancock's II Corps manages briefly to work its way around the Confederate left, but the onset of night cancels operations in that sector. But the day's accolades go to Colonel Emory Upton, who arrayed his 12 regiments in a densely packed assault column. At 6:00 P.M., Upton's force charges and penetrates the Mule Shoe's left flank, overturning General Richard Rodes's division and taking 1,000 prisoners. The Union lodgment, unfortunately, is not supported, and General Robert E. Lee directs a strong counterattack that drives Upton's force back to their lines. Grant is nonetheless singularly impressed by Upton's innovation and vows to try the same experiment on a larger scale. He then shifts Hancock's corps to the right of the Union line and prepares to renew the contest.

Three brigades of Confederate troopers under General J. E. B. Stuart arrive at Beaver Dam Station, Virginia, hotly trailing General Philip H. Sheridan's cavalry column. Though outnumbered, Stuart dispatches a brigade under General John B. Gordon to harass the Union rear while deploying Generals William C. Wickham and Lunsford L. Lomax into blocking positions at the junction of Yellow Tavern, six miles north of Richmond. Sheridan's column previously had passed through Beaver Dam Station that morning, burning an estimated 915,000 meat rations and 504,000 bread rations—losses the food-strapped Army of Northern Virginia could scarcely afford. Stuart is determined to stop them from doing more harm.

As General Benjamin F. Butler continues dithering at Bermuda Hundred, General Pierre G. T. Beauregard arrives from Weldon, North Carolina, to take command of the Petersburg, Virginia, defenses. He begins by rushing six Confederate brigades into strong positions along Drewry's Bluff.

WEST: Confederate raiders under Colonel John S. Mosby storms a Union cavalry outpost at Front Royal, Virginia, seizing prisoners and horses.

The Battle of Spotsylvania Court House May 7–20, 1864 Painting by Lewis Prang *(Library of Congress)*

General William W. Averell's cavalry division encounters Confederates under Generals John Morgan and William E. Jones at Wytheville, Virginia. He battles them for four hours, sustaining 114 casualties before withdrawing toward Dublin.

General Benjamin F. Kelley and John D. Imboden clash heavily at Lost River Gap, West Virginia.

General James B. McPherson declines pushing ahead through Snake Creek Gap, Georgia, and commences to fortify his position. Unknown at the time, he is opposed by only a single cavalry brigade under General James Cantey. McPherson, however, is unsupported, wary of his left flank, and fearful that General Joseph E. Johnston might throw the weight of his entire army against him. He digs in and awaits developments. "Such an opportunity does not occur twice in a single life!" an exasperated General William T. Sherman declares. Johnston's line of retreat consequently remains intact and, when apprised of the danger to his army, he immediately prepares to occupy safer ground.

NAVAL: Army transport *Harriet A. Weed* strikes a Confederate torpedo in the St. John's River, Florida, and sinks.

The USS *Connecticut* captures the British blockade-runner *Greyhound* at sea.

Back on the Red River, the dam constructed by Colonel Joseph Bailey to raise water levels is breeched deliberately and the ironclads USS *Mound City, Pittsburgh,* and *Carondelet* successfully shoot over the rapids. Admiral David D. Porter informs Secretary of the Navy Gideon Welles: "The passage of these vessels was a beautiful sight, only to be realized when seen."

May 11

SOUTH: Ignoring heavy losses, General Ulysses S. Grant renews the struggle at Spotsylvania Court House by hitting the Confederate center again. Only this time, he orders the entire II Corps of General Winfield S. Hancock drawn up into dense assault columns to spearhead the assault. Based on events of the previous day, Grant fully expects to overpower Southern forces that are manning the entrenchments at the "Mule Shoe." Meanwhile, General Robert E. Lee carefully monitors reports of Union movement and concludes that Grant is readying to slip around his left flank again. Lee determines to foil him in the act and orders artillery removed from the Mule Shoe, which renders it vulnerable to attack.

At 11:00 A.M., a tremendous cavalry fight ensues as 4,500 Confederates under General J. E. B. Stuart are attacked by twice their number under General Philip H. Sheridan at Yellow Tavern, Virginia. This places a marauding Union cavalry column only six miles north of the Confederate capital at Richmond. Stuart, having deployed his two brigades in a "V" formation, calmly awaits the Union onslaught at the road junction and initially repels moves against his left and center. At 4:00 o'clock, however, the brigade of General George A. Custer masses for a charge on the Confederate left, scatters General Lunsford L. Lomax's brigade, and seizes two cannon. Then Stuart, leading the 1st Virginia Cavalry on a sharp counterattack, successfully drives Custer back to his own lines but is shot mortally in the abdomen and evacuated. The Confederates, badly shaken, repulse additional attacks by Sheridan, and Union forces gradually withdraw eastward down the Chickahominy River. Union losses are estimated at 704 casualties while the Confederates sustain more than 300—including the dashing, irreplaceable Stuart, who dies the following day.

WEST: Confederate cavalry under General John D. Imboden surprise a Union outpost at Port Royal, Virginia, seizing 464 prisoners. This does little to stop General Franz Sigel's leisurely but seemingly inexorable drive down the Shenandoah Valley.

General Edward R. S. Canby is appointed commander of the Federal Military Division of West Mississippi.

May 12

SOUTH: The struggle at Spotsylvania, Virginia, continues as General Ulysses S. Grant launches a crushing assault on the center of General Robert E. Lee's defensive lines. The attack kicks off at 4:35 A.M. as General Winfield S. Hancock's II Corps, arrayed into dense columns, springs forward. The blue wave slams irresistibly into Southern defenses and overwhelms General Edward Johnson's "Stonewall Division," capturing him, 3,000 men, and 20 cannon. Hancock then loses control of his men as they pour through the salient as uncoordinated knots of soldiers. At this crisis, General

Robert E. Lee orders General John B. Gordon's division forward to stop them, which drives Hancock's men back outside the works. The ensuing eight hours witness a vicious, point-blank musketry duel that degenerates into hand-to-hand fighting, bayonet clashing, and rock throwing. In light of the terrible carnage, this sector is christened "Bloody Angle" by the survivors.

As the drama unfolds in Lee's center, Grant launches additional attacks on the Confederate line with General Horatio G. Wright's VI Corps. Wright is beaten back with losses, but the Southerners, losing men heavily, establish new defense lines along the base of the salient and withdraw by 4:00 P.M. Fighting gradually sputters out in a gathering rainstorm, and both sides relent. This latest Union repulse affords stark testimony to the tremendous defensive power of Confederate fieldworks, which have elevated the lowly spade to that of cannon and rifled muskets in tactical significance. Casualties during the two-day period are horrendous: Grant loses 2,725 killed, 13,416 wounded, and 2,258 missing (18,339) men to an estimated Confederate tally of 10,000—including 3,000 captured. General Robert E. Lee triumphs once again over a more numerous adversary, but the vaunted Army of Northern Virginia is being bled white by Grant's determination to fight and his willingness to absorb higher losses.

The Army of the James under General Benjamin F. Butler finally sorties from its defensive works and advances against Confederate lines at Drewry's Bluff, Virginia, with 15,000 men.

WEST: Colonel John S. Mosby captures a large Union wagon train near Strasburg, Virginia.

General John C. Breckinridge arrives at Staunton, Virginia, with 5,500 soldiers, militia, and a contingent of cadets from the Virginia Military Institute.

General Joseph E. Johnston expertly abandons his strong defenses at Dalton, Georgia, and falls back on new positions at Resaca. This pattern of advance and retreat will be repeated continuously over the intervening weeks.

NAVAL: Admiral Samuel P. Lee, alarmed by the recent loss of several warships, establishes an antitorpedo (mine) squadron on the James River, consisting of the USS *Stepping Stones, Delaware,* and *Tritonia.* They are ordered to patrol the waterways constantly for enemy activity and to remain always underway to prevent them from being surprised at night.

The USS *Beauregard* captures the Confederate sloop *Resolute* off the Indian River, Florida.

Armed boats from the USS *Somerset* capture a boatload of Confederate sailors near Apalachicola, Florida, who were themselves intending to capture the USS *Adela.*

May 13

SOUTH: General Philip H. Sheridan withdraws his cavalry column from the Richmond area.

Confederate defenses under General Robert F. Hoke at Drewry's Bluff, Virginia, are seized partially by 15,000 men from the Army of the James under General Benjamin F. Butler. That officer then suspends his attack to form new defense lines of his own. Such vacillation is a good indication of Butler's tactical ineptitude and prompts General Pierre G. T. Beauregard, commanding at Richmond, to counterattack and drive him back into Bermuda Hundred.

Union forces commence a four-day bombardment of Fort Sumter, Charleston Harbor, South Carolina, hurling an additional 1,140 rounds at the derelict but as of yet still defiant fortress.

General Andrew J. Smith's Union troops evacuate Alexandria, Louisiana, completely laying waste to the town and adjoining regions. Reputedly, after the fires recede, only two houses remain standing.

WEST: Union forces finally pour through Snake Creek Gap, Georgia, and occupy Dalton, too late to trap the army of General Joseph E. Johnston, which now lays safely ensconced 13 miles south at Resaca.

Confederate cavalry under General Joseph O. Shelby commences a raid north of the Arkansas River, Arkansas.

NAVAL: The USS *Ceres,* accompanied by the army transport *Rockland,* raids the Alligator River, North Carolina, seizes the Confederate schooner *Ann S. Davenport* and destroys a nearby corn mill.

The USS *Louisville, Chillicote,* and *Ozark,* the last of Admiral David D. Porter's gunboats, dash over a wing dam on the Red River, Louisiana, and float on to safety. The ingenuity of army engineers under Colonel Joseph Bailey, performing their work entirely under fire, saved the squadron from certain destruction after two weeks of intensive exertion. "Words are inadequate to express the admiration I feel for the abilities of Lieutenant Colonel Bailey," Porter wrote, "This is without doubt the best engineering feat ever performed."

May 14

SOUTH: General Pierre G. T. Beauregard begins to marshal forces for a counterattack on the Union Army of the James outside Drewry's Bluff, Virginia. He has available the divisions of Generals Robert F. Hoke and Robert Hanson.

WEST: General John D. Imboden continues skirmishing against the advance of General Franz Sigel as it reaches Mount Jackson, Virginia, seven miles north of New Market.

The armies of Generals William T. Sherman and Joseph E. Johnston confront each other in full battle array at Resaca, Georgia. The Federals muster 100,000 men and the Confederates, recently joined by General Leonidas K. Polk from Mississippi, number 60,000. Sherman begins the battle by launching General John M. Schofield's XXIII Corps in a headlong assault at the intersection of where Generals John B. Hood's and William J. Hardee's corps meet. Schofield charges hard and long all day but is repelled with heavy losses. Fighting then moves down the line to the Confederate right, where General John Logan's XV Corps engages Polk's infantry. The Federals manage to storm a line of earthworks along Camp Creek, situated on some low-lying hills, a significant gain allowing them to mount artillery pieces to shell and possibly destroy the remaining Confederate army. Polk tries repeatedly to dislodge the Federals and fails, but Sherman is slow to recognize the advantage within his grasp, and fighting in this sector dies down.

The day's toughest struggle occurs on the Union left, where the aggressive Hood successfully strikes along the Dalton-Resaca wagon road. However, a division dispatched by General George H. Thomas then halts the Confederate drive and sends them scampering back to their starting point. Resaca concludes with few measurable gains by either side, and more hard fighting is anticipated the following day.

May 15
SOUTH: Outside Richmond, Virginia, General Pierre G. T. Beauregard masses 10 infantry brigades into two divisions commanded by General Robert F. Hoke and Robert Ransom, while holding two brigades in reserve under General Alfred Colquitt. He intends to strike heavily at the right flank of General Benjamin F. Butler's Army of the James on the morrow and hopefully drive it headlong back into the Bermuda Hundred Peninsula.

WEST: General Franz Sigel resumes advancing with 6,500 men toward New Market, Virginia, as 5,500 Confederates under General John C. Breckinridge occupy strong defensive positions. A prolonged artillery duel ensues at long range at which point Breckinridge, tired of waiting for Sigel to charge, orders his own men forward. Two infantry brigades, linked by a force of dismounted cavalry between them, easily clear Sigel's forces from the town amid a cheering populace. However, a large Union battery posted on a hillside directly out of town badly cuts up Breckinridge's men as they clear New Market. A gap opens up in his ranks, and Breckinridge, lacking reserves, reluctantly orders 264 cadets (or "Katydids") from the Virginia Military Institute to fill it. "Put the boys in," he orders, and they advance strongly despite mounting casualties and a heavy downpour. At 3:00 P.M., the Confederates crown the heights and seize two cannon while defeated Federals stream across the Shenandoah River to Strasburg and safety. Union losses are 96 dead, 520 wounded, and 225 missing (841) to a Confederate tally of 43 killed, 474 injured, and three captured (520). The VMI Cadets lose 10 killed and 47 wounded, without wavering, a loss rate of 20 percent.

General William W. Averell concludes another fruitless raid by linking up with Union forces under General George Crook at Union, Virginia.

The Battle of Resaca resumes as Union troops under General Joseph Hooker engage the Confederates of General John B. Hood on the Union left. A confusing, costly battle, fought from ravines and entanglements, ensues with heavy losses to both sides. Meanwhile, General William T. Sherman orders a division of the XVI Corps over the Oostanaula River to seize a strategic railroad bridge in the Confederate rear. General Joseph E. Johnston, his lines of communication now threatened, expertly disengages, throws a pontoon bridge across the river, and withdraws to safety in the predawn darkness. Losses in the two-day struggle amount to 6,000 Federals and 5,000 Confederates, yet Sherman continues pushing ever deeper into Georgia.

The retreating army of General Nathaniel P. Banks skirmishes with Confederate cavalry under General Arthur P. Bagby at Avoyelles, Louisiana, and then continues withdrawing to Marksville.

NAVAL: The USS *Kansas* captures the British blockade-runner *Tristram Shandy* off Fort Fisher, North Carolina.

The Federal gunboat USS *St. Clair,* moving down the Red River, engages and defeats a Confederate battery near Eunice's Bluff, Louisiana.

May 16

SOUTH: A force of 18,000 Confederates under General Pierre G. T. Beauregard launches a sharp attack on the Union Army of the James near Drewry's Bluff, Virginia. Previously, General Benjamin F. Butler drew his 15,000 troops into a defensive line with General Quincy A. Gillmore's X Corps on the left and General William F. Smith's XVIII Corps on the right. But Beauregard, availing himself of a heavy ground fog, directs General Robert Ransom's division to turn Smith's right, which is accomplished skillfully. Ransom then charges and captures General Charles A. Heckman and 400 prisoners before his ammunition fails and brings him to a halt. Meanwhile, Confederate forces under General Robert F. Hoke hit the Union center, but, confused and partially lost in the fog, his attack flounders. Gillmore then counterattacks through a gap in the Southern line, forcing them back. The Confederates of General William H. C. Whiting mass and make one final dash at the Union center and are rebuffed. As fighting dies down, Butler withdraws back behind fortifications along Bermuda Hundred. Confederate losses are 355 dead, 1,941 wounded, and 210 missing (2,506) while the Union sustains 290 killed, 2,380 wounded, and 1,390 missing (4,160). Moreover, Beauregard now completely bottles up his adversary on the peninsula, and Butler remains unable to assist future Union drives on Richmond or Petersburg.

General Nathaniel P. Banks retreats to Mansura, Louisiana, encountering Confederate forces under General Camille A. Polignac. Heavy skirmishing forces the Southerners back, and the Federals continue withdrawing.

WEST: General Joseph E. Johnston begins to abandon positions at Resaca, Georgia, and withdraws toward Calhoun and Adamsville.

NAVAL: The Mississippi Squadron of Admiral David D. Porter finally reenters the Mississippi River after two months of dramatic but unsuccessful campaigning along the Red River, Louisiana.

May 17

SOUTH: Colonel John S. Mosby tangles with Federal cavalry at Waterford, Virginia, inflicting nine casualties.

General Ulysses S. Grant remains eager to resume offensive operations at Spotsylvania Court House, Virginia. Certain that General Robert E. Lee has weakened his left flank by placing the shattered corps of General Richard S. Ewell there, he orders General Winfield S. Hancock's II Corps and General Gouverneur K. Warren's VI Corps to prepare for an assault on the morrow.

General Pierre G. T. Beauregard pushes his Confederates force to just opposite Union defensive lines at Bermuda Hundred, Virginia. This effectively seals the Army of the James on a peninsula, neutralizing it as a threat to either Richmond or Petersburg.

WEST: General Joseph O. Shelby's Confederate cavalry seize Dardanelle, Arkansas.

General William T. Sherman threatens both of General Joseph E. Johnston's flanks near Adamsville, so he retrogrades again toward the Cassville-Kingston region.

May 18

SOUTH: General Ulysses S. Grant attacks Spotsylvania Court House one last time looking for Confederate weaknesses. He feels that recent troop shifts have weakened their left flank, so he directs the V and VI Corps to attempt breaking through. However, General Richard S. Ewell, bolstered by 29 cannon, easily shatters the Federals as they charge across open ground. Grant's forces once again are thrown back, suffering 500 casualties to Ewell's 30. He finally concludes that General Robert E. Lee's position is impregnable and issues orders to sidestep his left flank entirely and march southeast toward Richmond, Virginia.

As General Nathaniel P. Banks's army approaches the Atchafalaya River, it encounters strong Confederate forces at Yellow Bayou, Louisiana. General Andrew J. Smith then dispatches a brigade under General Joseph A. Mower to drive off the rebels, lest they interfere with river-crossing operations. Mower's 4,500 men perform exactly as ordered and pitch into a thick belt of Confederate skirmishers, driving them back onto the main body under General John Wharton. Wharton, in turn, counterattacks as the Union troops become mired in thick underbrush and forces them off in turn. Mower subsequently halts the new Southern assault, and both sides separate once the dense undergrowth catches fire. The ongoing struggle does not interfere with bridging operations across the Atchafalaya River. By the time the battle subsides, Union losses are 350 while the Confederate tally stands at 608. Banks proceeds to move his men across the waterway to safety.

WEST: As General William T. Sherman begins to pursue fleeing Confederates toward Kingston, Georgia, his columns become widely separated and vulnerable to attack. General John B. Hood receives orders to attack the following day, but he uncharacteristically reacts with caution.

Union cavalry under General Kenner Garrard capture Rome, Georgia, after dislodging Confederates there under General Samuel G. French.

NAVAL: Admiral James Buchanan, after much exertion, finally floats the large steam ram CSS *Tennessee* over the Dog River bar and into Mobile Bay, Alabama.

A landing party from the USS *Stockdale* is attacked by Confederate cavalry near the mouth of the Tchefuncta River, Louisiana.

The Confederate raider CSS *Florida* under Lieutenant Charles M. Morris captures and burns the Union schooner *George Latimer* at sea.

May 19

NORTH: Literary circles are saddened by the death of noted New England writer and novelist Nathaniel Hawthorne at Plymouth, New Hampshire.

SOUTH: The Confederate II Corps of General Richard S. Ewell mounts a sudden counterattack at Spotsylvania Court House, hoping to catch Union forces in marching order. However, Federal troops are prepared and hurl back the Southerners with 900 casualties to a Union tally of 1,500. This final burst of activity concludes the bloodshed at Spotsylvania, scene of the Civil War's most vicious fighting.

The army of General Nathaniel P. Banks finally crosses the Atchafalaya River, Louisiana, as the Red River campaign draws to an ignominious conclusion.

West: Union cavalry under Generals William W. Averell and George Crook take Meadow Bluff, West Virginia, thereby ending their raid against the Virginia and Tennessee Railroad.

General Joseph E. Johnston orders General John B. Hood to counterattack the scattered Union XXIII Corps but then countermands his instructions and falls back across the Etowah River toward Allatoona Pass, Georgia. He does so over the protests of Generals William J. Hardee and Leonidas K. Polk, who prefer to stand and fight.

Naval: The USS *General Price* opens fire on a Confederate battery at Tunica Bend, Louisiana, on the Mississippi River and rescues the transport steamer *Superior*. An armed party lands and then pursues the attackers, burning their headquarters.

The USS *De Soto* captures the Confederate schooner *Mississippian* in the Gulf of Mexico.

May 20

South: General Ulysses S. Grant directs the Army of the Potomac south and east in an attempt to outflank the Confederates along the Mattaponi River, Virginia. His objective is Hannover Station, 24 miles north of Richmond, where the Virginia Central Rail Road intersects with the Richmond, Fredericksburg, and Potomac Railroad, a major Southern supply artery.

General Pierre G. T. Beauregard, intending to bottle up General Benjamin F. Butler's Army of the James further at Bermuda Hundred Peninsula, launches a heavy attack on Federal defensive positions held by General Quincy A. Gillmore's X Corps at Ware Bottom Church, Virginia. Initially, the divisions of Generals Alfred H. Terry and Adelbert Ames are hard pressed and driven back. Quincy is forced to spend several hours sorting his command out before finally launching a counterattack that afternoon, which nearly drives the Confederates back to their starting positions. A Southern counterattack also is repulsed bloodily, resulting in the capture of General William S. Walker before Beauregard cancels further assaults. Union losses are roughly 800 to 700 for the Confederates, but Beauregard could now shorten his lines before Bermuda Hundred, and Butler remains effectively hemmed in and unable to assist the ongoing Richmond, Virginia campaign.

The army of General Nathaniel P. Banks completes crossing the 600-yard-wide Atchafalaya River, ending his ill-fated Red River campaign in western Louisiana.

West: Colonel John S. Mosby attacks a Union wagon train near Strasburg, West Virginia, and is repulsed.

Naval: The Mississippi Squadron of Admiral David D. Porter covers the withdrawal of General Nathaniel P. Banks's army across the Atchafalaya River, Louisiana, signaling the end of the Red River campaign.

May 21

Diplomacy: Secretary of State William H. Seward instructs U.S. minister to France John Bigelow that, while he is to remonstrate against French actions in Mexico, he must avoid outright belligerence until after the Civil War has ended.

South: Bested by Southern fortifications around Spotsylvania, General Ulysses S. Grant begins to probe Confederate lines near Milford Station, Virginia. He is surprised by the lack of strong resistance and prepares to sidestep around the Confederate left flank to appear in force across the North Anna River. Grant thus exercises strategic initiative over his opponent, forcing General Robert E. Lee to react and follow.

WEST: General Franz Sigel, having lost the Battle of New Market, is relieved of command in the Shenandoah Valley and replaced by General David Hunter.

NAVAL: The USS *Atlanta* and *Dawn* shell Confederate cavalry attacking Fort Powhatan on the James River, Virginia.

May 22

SOUTH: The Army of Northern Virginia under General Robert E. Lee assumes defensive positions along the North Anna River, slightly ahead of General Ulysses S. Grant. To that end, he deploys General Richard S. Ewell's II Corps on his right, General James Longstreet's I Corps on his center, and General Ambrose P. Hill's III Corps on his left.

WEST: General William T. Sherman again outflanks Confederate defenders under General Joseph E. Johnston and bypasses them at Allatoona, Georgia. Johnson then predictably falls back to new positions at Dallas.

NAVAL: The USS *Crusader* captures the Confederate schooner *Isaac L. Adkins* on the Severn River, Maryland.

May 23

SOUTH: The Union II Corps of General William S. Hancock deploys on the northern bank of the North Anna River at Chesterfield Ford while the IX Corps under General Ambrose E. Burnside lands at Jericho Mills. Meanwhile, the V and VI Corps under Generals Gouverneur K. Warren and Horatio G. Wright, respectively, operate to the west of Jericho Mills. A hasty attack by General Cadmus M. Wilcox's division against Jericho Mills is rebuffed with 642 casualties, and Federal troops commence to dig in.

WEST: General William T. Sherman continues advancing his army from Cassville, Georgia, toward Dallas, where he intends to cross the Etowah River.

General John H. Morgan gallops into Kentucky on another extended raid.

NAVAL: The Federal side-wheeler USS *Columbine* is captured by men of the Confederate 2nd Florida Cavalry at Horse Landing, Palatka, Florida, after grounding on a mud bank. The vessel sustains 20 casualties before capitulating, whereupon the Southerners burn it.

May 24

SOUTH: General Ulysses S. Grant throws pontoon bridges across the North Anna River and continues crossing his Army of the Potomac. Grant also is supported by newly arrived Union cavalry under General Philip H. Sheridan, back from his raid near Richmond, Virginia. General Ambrose E. Burnside's IX Corps next begins to probe Confederate lines at Ox Ford cautiously and finds them too strong to be carried. General Robert E. Lee, again anticipating Union moves, ingeniously deploys the Army of Northern Virginia into an inverted "V" formation, to lure the unsuspecting Federals into a trap. Grant inadvertently nearly obliges him—having scattered his command across the North Anna River and inviting crushing blows in piecemeal—but Lee is suddenly taken ill, and no attack goes forward. Once Grant perceives the danger to his army, he withdraws back across the North Anna River.

Two African-American regiments repel an attack by Confederate cavalry under General Fitzhugh Lee at Wilson's Wharf, Virginia.

WEST: General Joseph E. Johnston orders his Confederates to fall back on new defensive positions at Dallas, Georgia.

Confederate cavalry under General Joseph Wheeler attack Union supply lines at Burnt Hickory, Georgia.

NAVAL: The USS *Dawn* bombards Confederate forces attacking army troops at Wilson's Wharf on the James River, Virginia.

Confederate forces capture and burn the Federal steamer *Lebanon* at Ford's landing, Arkansas.

May 25

SOUTH: The Army of the Potomac under General Ulysses S. Grant, having probed Confederate lines along the North Anna River, Virginia, to no avail, prepares to shift suddenly by marching east toward Cold Harbor. Fortunately, General Robert E. Lee is too ill to order a crushing assault on his widely scattered formations, and the Federals redeploy without interference.

WEST: General David Hunter receives orders to advance down the Shenandoah Valley and capture Lynchburg, Virginia, an important railroad junction. From there, he is to continue south and possibly threaten Charlottesville. It is anticipated that General Robert E. Lee will be forced to dispatch reinforcements to that theater, thereby weakening the defenses of Richmond.

The XX Corps under General Joseph Hooker, advancing on New Hope Church, Georgia, collides head on with General John B. Hood's Confederates. The Federals initially are repulsed until Hooker masses two entire divisions and charges the troops of General Alexander P. Stewart. Stewart, however, clings tenaciously to his ground and, at length, Hooker retires with 1,600 casualties. This encounter places Union forces only 25 miles northeast of Atlanta.

NAVAL: A armed boat from the USS *Mattabesett* unsuccessfully tries to sink the Confederate steam ram CSS *Albemarle* in the Roanoke River, North Carolina. They carefully tow two 100-pound torpedoes up the Middle River, North Carolina, jump overboard, and then swim to within a few yards of their quarry when a sentry detects their approach. The swimmers manage to escape capture, with each ultimately receiving the Congressional Medal of Honor.

The USS *McDonough, E. B. Hale, Dai Ching,* and *Vixen* accompany a combined expedition up the Ashepoo and South Edisto rivers, South Carolina. They advance as far as the town of Williston but, after failing to establish contact with army troops, withdraw back downstream. While moving downstream, the transport *Boston* grounds and is scuttled.

May 26

DIPLOMACY: Robert H. Pruyn, U.S. minister to Japan, requests that the USS *Jamestown* be dispatched to Kanagawa in a preemptive show of force. Japanese authorities are threatening to close that port to all foreign commerce.

POLITICS: The Montana Territory is carved from the eastern portion of the Idaho and Dakota territories.

SOUTH: The Army of the Potomac suddenly pivots east after crossing the North Anna River and heads for the Pamunkey River, turning General Robert E. Lee's right flank. Previous operations in this vicinity result in 2,623 Union casualties and 2,517 Confederate.

General John G. Foster accepts command of the Department of the South.

WEST: A force of 10,000 Union troops under General David Hunter departs Strasburg, Virginia, and commences marching down the Shenandoah Valley toward Staunton. However, 3,000 Confederate cavalry under General John D. Imboden fell trees and other obstacles in Hunter's path, impeding his advance.

Union forces under General James B. McPherson occupy Dallas, Georgia, while General John M. Schofield approaches New Hope Church.

May 27

SOUTH: The Army of Northern Virginia under General Robert E. Lee begin to shift its defensive lines from the North Anna River. Meanwhile, Union cavalry under General George A. Custer cross the Pamunkey River and capture Hanovertown, Virginia. The mounted divisions of Generals Alfred T. A. Torbert and David M. Gregg quickly gallop over and begin to probe westward for Confederates.

WEST: General William T. Sherman conducts several heavy probes of the right flank of Confederate lines along the New Hope–Dallas line, Georgia. An attack mounted by General Oliver O. Howard's IV Corps at Pickett's Mills is repulsed by General Patrick R. Cleburne's Confederates with 1,500 casualties. Encouraged by this tactical success, General Joseph E. Johnston orders General John B. Hood to attack the Union left flank on the following morning.

General Joseph O. Shelby assumes command of all Confederate troops north of the Arkansas River, Arkansas.

NAVAL: The USS *Ariel* captures and burns the Confederate sloop *General Finegan* near Chassahowitzka Bay, Florida.

The USS *Admiral* captures the Confederate steamer *Isabel* off Galveston after a six-hour chase.

May 28

POLITICS: Puppet emperor Maximilian of Austria lands at Vera Cruz, Mexico, in order to assume his throne. A political neophyte, he is backed by the machinations of the French emperor Napoleon III and opposed by Mexican politician-turned-guerrilla Benito Juárez. The United States considers his presence a violation of the long-stated Monroe Doctrine, but Washington is too preoccupied with civil war to do anything beyond diplomatic protests.

SOUTH: General Robert E. Lee shifts his headquarters to Atlee's Station, Virginia, to observe Union army movements toward Richmond better. He then deploys General Ambrose P. Hill's III Corps to guard the Virginia Central Railroad, while the I and II Corps under Generals Richard A. Anderson and Jubal A. Early settle in behind Totopotomo Creek. The Army of the Potomac, meanwhile, continues marching southeast down the north bank of the Pamunkey River, seeking an opening along Lee' right flank.

Union cavalry under General David M. Gregg encounter General Wade Hampton's Confederate troopers at Haw's Shop, Virginia, and a large mounted action ensues. Hampton's South Carolinians, equipped with long-range Enfield rifles, bloodily repulse Gregg's initial charge, and a protracted dismounted fight develops. Confederate numbers prevail as the Union cavalrymen are forced back, but at 2:00 P.M., General George A. Custer's Michigan brigade suddenly dashes onto the field. The "Wolverines" quickly dismount and engage the Southerners with rapid-fire Spencer carbines, forcing Hampton to retreat in turn. After seven hours of fighting, the Confederates withdraw and inform General Robert E. Lee that Union forces are firmly established over the Pamunkey River.

WEST: General John B. Hood, on reconnoitering Union lines, reports that Federal troops are strongly entrenched, so General Joseph E. Johnston cancels his impending assault.

A reconnaissance in force by General William J. Hardee is repulsed at Dallas, Georgia, by General James B. McPherson. The attack was made by General William B. Bates division, which goes forward unsupported and sustains heavy losses from Union defenders.

NAVAL: The USS *Admiral* captures the Confederate steamer *Isabel* off Galveston, Texas, following a six-hour chase. Significantly, this vessel completed 20 successful runs before finally being snared.

May 29

SOUTH: General Ulysses S. Grant, having crossed the Army of the Potomac over the Pamunkey River, Virginia, resumes marching southwest toward the Confederate capital of Richmond, unaware that General Robert E. Lee already is moving troops in the direction of Cold Harbor.

General Jubal A. Early is formally appointed to lead the Confederate II Corps, Army of Northern Virginia—"Stonewall" Jackson's old command.

NAVAL: The USS *Cowslip* captures the Confederate sloop *Last Push* off the Mississippi coast.

May 30

SOUTH: General Ulysses S. Grant's Army of the Potomac, moving along the Totopotomoy Creek, suddenly swings toward Cold Harbor, Virginia, possession of which would place his force within 10 miles of Richmond. Meanwhile, General Robert E. Lee, perceiving that the Union V Corps under General Gouverneur K. Warren is isolated, launches an attack at Bethesda Church to destroy it. The Confederate II Corps under General Jubal A. Early maneuvers around Warren's left flank and charges, routing the Pennsylvania Reserves, but the Federals reform and throw him back. Further attacks under General Stephen D. Ramseur also fail to dislodge the defenders, and the Confederates withdraw to new defenses at Cold Harbor.

WEST: Union cavalry under General George Crook gallop from Meadow Bluff, West Virginia, to join General David Hunter's main Union army in the Shenandoah Valley.

General John H. Morgan begins his final raid against Union lines of communication by entering Kentucky.

NAVAL: The USS *Keystone State* and *Massachusetts* capture the British blockade-runner *Caledonia* off Cape Fear, North Carolina, following a three-hour chase.

May 31

POLITICS: Radical Republicans, dissatisfied with President Abraham Lincoln, nominate former general John C. Frémont in Cleveland, Ohio, as their party candidate for chief executive. They also select General John Cochrane of New York to be vice president. Among Frémont's strongest supporters is African-American abolitionist Frederick Douglass, who feels that Lincoln is far too lenient toward Southerners in his plans for Reconstruction.

SOUTH: General Ulysses S. Grant's Overland Campaign to Richmond, Virginia, while a tactical failure, thus far proves a brilliant strategic success. In one very bloody month, he forces the redoubtable Army of Northern Virginia from positions along the Rapidan River to the gates of the Confederate capital.

General Philip H. Sheridan is ordered to ride and occupy the crossroads at Cold Harbor, Virginia. In the process, he encounters Confederate troopers under General Fitzhugh Lee and drives them off with rapid-fire Spencer carbines.

Richard H. Anderson and Jubal A. Early are promoted to lieutenant general, C.S.A.

NAVAL: The USS *Commodore Perry* trades shot with a Confederate battery on the James River, Virginia, taking six hits over two hours.

June 1

NORTH: Joshua L. Chamberlain is appointed a brigadier general, U.S. Army.

SOUTH: Union cavalry under General Philip H. Sheridan repel a determined attack by General Richard H. Anderson's Confederates at Old Cold Harbor, Virginia, largely through the use of new, rapid-fire Spencer carbines. In the course of the day, Sheridan is relieved by VI and XVIII Corps, who drive the Southerners back until a strong counterattack restores their line. General Ulysses S. Grant, believing that the Confederates are exhausted and their line weakly held, orders General Winfield S. Hancock's II Corps to march all night toward Cold Harbor and prepare for a daylight assault in the morning. Union losses for the day amount to 2,650 while the Confederate casualties are probably as heavy.

WEST: Confederate cavalry under General John H. Morgan attack Union supply lines at Pound Gap, Kentucky.

General Samuel D. Sturgis departs Memphis, Tennessee, at the head of 8,100 men to prevent Confederate raiders under General Nathan B. Forrest from cutting the all-important Nashville and Chattanooga Railroad. He commands a cavalry brigade under General Benjamin H. Grierson and an infantry brigade under Colonel William L. McMillan, along with 22 cannon and 250 supply wagons. From the onset, the column is hampered by heavy rain and progress is slow.

Union cavalry under General George Stoneman seizes Allatoona Pass, Georgia, securing an important railhead. Meanwhile, General William T. Sherman, begins to look for other avenues to outmaneuver the tenacious General Joseph E. Johnston.

Dead being reburied after the Battle of Cold Harbor *(U.S. Army Military History Institute)*

NAVAL: The wooden paddle wheeler USS *Exchange* is damaged by Confederate batteries on the Mississippi River near Columbia, Arkansas.

June 2

SOUTH: At Cold Harbor, Virginia, General Ulysses S. Grant prepares his men for a frontal assault against what he perceives as weak Confederate lines. However, he cancels the action after General Winfield S. Hancock's II Corps, delayed by fatigue and hot weather, arrives in poor condition. Grant reluctantly postpones his attack another day, which grants General Robert E. Lee additional time to dig in and strengthen his lines. In that respect, Cold Harbor is probably the best defensive position that his Army of Northern Virginia ever held. Lee is about to hand Grant another abject lesson in the power of defensive fieldworks.

WEST: Heavy skirmishing develops between 10,000 Union troops under Generals David Hunter and 3,000 Confederates of General John D. Imboden at Coventry, Virginia. The Southerners suffer the worst of it and withdraw.

NAVAL: The USS *Victoria* destroys the Confederate steamer *Georgianna McCaw* after running it aground near Wilmington, North Carolina.

The USS *Wamsutta* chases the British blockade-runner *Rose* aground at Pawley's Island, South Carolina, sinking it.

Armed boats from the USS *Cowslip* conduct a destructive foray up Biloxi Bay, Mississippi, destroying several small craft shops and saltworks.

June 3

SOUTH: The Battle of Cold Harbor unfolds across a continuous, seven-mile front, inundated with earthen fortifications and interlocking fields of fire. The Southern position, manned by 59,000 men, consists of General Jubal A. Early's II Corps on the left, General Richard H. Anderson's I Corps in the center, and General Ambrose P. Hill anchoring the right. Arrayed against them are 108,000 Federal troops of the XI Corps under General Ambrose E. Burnside on the left, followed by the XVIII Corps of General William F. Smith, the VI of General Horatio G. Wright, and General Winfield S. Hancock's II Corps on the right. General Ulysses S. Grant's strategy is simple: Assault the entire Confederate position and, once a weak spot develops, call up reserves to pour through it. But Grant, unaware of the extent of Southern entrenchments before him, is setting the stage for a tragedy.

The Union assault kicks off at 4:30 A.M., as 40,000 Federal troops charge across the open fields in dense columns. The defenders allow them to close, and then they unleash withering torrents of bullets and canister that tear apart formations, cutting men down in droves. Only General Francis Barlow's brigade briefly penetrates Confederate lines on the left before recoiling under heavy fire. Within 30 minutes, the conflict at Cold Harbor ends as suddenly as it began. No less than 7,000 Federals have been killed or wounded, while Southern losses are slightly under 1,500. It is the biggest military blunder of Grant's career, and the Northern press starts assailing him as a "butcher." As he later wrote, "I regret this assault more than any I have ever ordered," and he never again launched frontal attacks against prepared works.

General Robert E. Lee has won his final open field battle, for Cold Harbor marks an end to the mobile phase of Grant's Overland campaign to Richmond. Both sides have endured staggering losses since the beginning of May, with Union casualties exceeding 50,000. The Southern toll amounts to 32,000, which, while lower, is severe. But body counts do not tell the entire story: At the strategic level, Lee's losses actually constitute a higher percentage of his army, 46 to 41 percent. Grant, moreover, receives a constant and steady flow of reinforcements, whereas Confederate manpower resources are dwindling rapidly. But this could scarcely be accomplished, let alone sustained, without equal determination on the political front. President Abraham Lincoln's willingness to both embrace and endure a contest of attrition, with all the heartbreak it entails, ultimately breaks the South's ability to resist and wins the war.

WEST: Union cavalry under General William W. Averell trots out of Bunger's Mills, West Virginia, en route to join the main force under General David Hunter near Lynchburg, Virginia.

Union forces under General William T. Sherman march northwest of the New Hope, Dallas line, and General Joseph E. Johnston begin to abandon his position at New Hope, Georgia.

General Edward R. S. Canby offers to assist Admiral David D. Porter by providing troops for periodic sweeps along the banks of the Mississippi River to prevent further guerrilla-style attacks on shipping.

NAVAL: The USS *Water Witch* is captured by 130 Confederate troops in boats under Lieutenant Thomas P. Pelot in Ossabaw Sound, Georgia. The raiders strike at 2:00 A.M. and were almost on their victim when detected; the ship nonetheless is carried after a wild, hand-to-hand melee. Pelot is one of five Confederates killed while another 17 are injured.

June 4

WEST: General William E. Jones arrives from Bristol, Virginia, to receive command of Confederate forces in the Shenandoah Valley from General John D. Imboden. He brings reinforcements that increase Southern strength up to 5,600 men.

Union cavalry under General Samuel D. Sturgis advance from Memphis, Tennessee, toward Ripley, Mississippi, in search of General Nathan B. Forrest.

The Army of Tennessee under General Joseph E. Johnston departs New Hope Church, Georgia, and begins to occupy ready-made defensive lines around Marietta.

General Andrew J. Smith and 10,000 men of the Union XVI and XVII Corps embark at Vicksburg, Mississippi, and steam north on the Mississippi River to Sunnyside Landing, Arkansas. Once ashore, he is to begin antiguerrilla operations against General John S. Marmaduke.

NAVAL: The USS *Ticonderoga* is assigned patrol duties in the Gulf of St. Lawrence to guard against Confederate raids in New England waters.

The USS *Fort Jackson* captures the Confederate steamer *Thistle* off Charleston, South Carolina.

June 5

SOUTH: General Ulysses S. Grant orders General Philip H. Sheridan, on a mounted raid toward Charlottesville, Virginia, to tear up the Virginia Central Railroad before pressing onward to join General David Hunter in the Shenandoah Valley. Grant anticipates that a raid of this magnitude will distract Confederate attention as he slips his Army of the Potomac over the James River and closer to Richmond.

WEST: A force of 15,000 Union troops under General David Hunter, having advanced down the Shenandoah Valley as far as Harrisonburg before turning east, engages 5,600 Confederates under General William E. Jones at Piedmont, Virginia. The Federals repel Southern skirmishers before encountering their main body under Jones. Hunter then brings up artillery and commences to bombard at 9:00 A.M. before attacking the Confederate left with troops under Colonel Augustus Moor. Moor makes good progress initially but is finally slowed and repelled. Jones then counterattacks until being halted by new troops under Colonel Joseph Thoburn. Moor, meanwhile, rallies his men and, assisted by a cavalry brigade under General Julius Stahel, renews his advance on Jones's right. Charging through a gap in the Southern line, the Federals capture all of Jones's artillery, and his line buckles and shatters. The outnumbered, exhausted Confederates run wildly, and Jones is killed while trying to rally them. Union losses are 780 while the Southerners incur nearly 1,600. Hunter's victory finally clears the way for a Northern invasion of the Shenandoah Valley.

General Andrew J. Smith disembarks on the Mississippi River and lands 10,000 Union troops at Sunnyside Landing, Arkansas. Proceeding inland, they encounter the 3rd Missouri Cavalry under Colonel Colton Greene at Ditch Bayou and run him off after a protracted skirmishing.

NAVAL: The USS *Keystone State* captures the British blockade-runner *Siren* off Beaufort Harbor, North Carolina.

June 6

WEST: The Union Army under General David Hunter occupies Staunton, Virginia, unopposed, and begins to raze both the town and its adjoining countryside.

Union general Joseph A. Mower marches from Sunnyside Landing, Arkansas, with 4,000 troops to evict Colonel Colton Greene's 3rd Missouri Cavalry from Ditch Bayou. Intense skirmishing erupts amid dense undergrowth and swampy land as the Federals push forward and the Southerners yield ground slowly. At length, Greene introduces a handful of cannon whose fire throws Mower's men into confusion as Union artillery become helplessly mired in mud. After seven hours of fighting—in which they held off seven times their number—Greene's troopers fall back beyond Lake Chicot and safety. Union losses in this embarrassing affair total 250; the Confederates admit to only 37.

NAVAL: The USS *Metacomet* captures the Confederate steamer *Donegal* off Mobile, Alabama.

The USS *Louisville* covers the embarkation of 8,000 Federal troops under General Andrew J. Smith near Sunnydale, Arkansas, on the Mississippi River. This activity follows a brief campaign along Bayou Macon to suppress Confederate guerrilla activity.

June 7

POLITICS: The Republican Party convenes at Baltimore, Maryland, to nominate its presidential and vice presidential candidates. With the assistance of several prowar Democrats, they are able to portray themselves as the "National Union Convention."

NORTH: John Gibbon is appointed major general, U.S. Army.

SOUTH: General Philip H. Sheridan rides off from New Castle Ferry, Virginia, with 6,000 troopers under Generals Alfred T. A. Tolbert and David M. Gregg. His mission is to raid the Virginia Central Railroad before proceeding into the Shenandoah Valley to link up with General David Hunter. They assume a line of march northwest toward Trevilian Station to begin their destructive work.

WEST: Union cavalry under Generals William W. Averell and George Crook join the main Union force under General David Hunter near Staunton, Virginia.

A large Union column under General Samuel D. Sturgis trudges into Ripley, Mississippi, having taken a full week to traverse 50 miles. However, General Nathan B. Forrest, fully apprised of Union movements and intentions, begins to lay an elaborate snare for the intruders at Brice's Cross Roads.

Naval: Union batteries on Morris Island, Charleston, South Carolina, bombard the Confederate steam transport *Etiwan,* sinking it off Fort Johnson.

Armed boats from the USS *Clyde* and Sagamore ascend the Suwannee River, Florida, and seize 100 bales of cotton near Clay Landing.

June 8

Politics: A Republican convention held in Baltimore, Maryland, renominates Abraham Lincoln to run for the presidency. However, Vice President Hannibal Hamlin is dropped in favor of Tennessee governor Andrew Johnson, a Southern war Democrat, whose presence should broaden the ticket's appeal. Their platform calls for a military end to the rebellion and ratification of the 13th Amendment to abolish slavery.

South: Alert Confederate scouts inform cavalry leader General Wade Hampton of General Philip H. Sheridan's departure from New Castle Ferry, Virginia. Because the Federals ride northwest, he correctly deduces that Sheridan is headed for Trevilian Station and gallops off with 4,700 cavalry and three batteries to intercept him.

West: Confederate raiders under General John H. Morgan capture the town of Mount Sterling, Kentucky, and rob a bank of $18,000.

General William T. Sherman gathers his men for an advance on Marietta, Georgia, and resumes his flanking tactics. However, General Nathan B. Forrest's activities force him to detach increasing numbers of men to protect rapidly lengthening lines of communication with Tennessee, thereby weakening available field forces.

Naval: Federal gunboats USS *Chillicothe, Neosho,* and *Fort Hindman* steam up the Atchafalaya River, Louisiana, and successfully engage a Confederate battery above Simmesport.

June 9

Politics: President Abraham Lincoln suggests a constitutional amendment to outlaw slavery.

West: Union forces drive General John H. Morgan's raiders out of Mount Sterling, Kentucky, and he withdraws toward Winchester.

Naval: The USS *New Bern* runs the Confederate steamer *Pevensey* aground off Beaufort, North Carolina.

The USS *Rosalie* captures the Confederate steamer *Emma* on Marco Pass, Florida.

The USS *Proteus* captures the British blockade-runner *R. S. Hood* north of the Little Bahama Bank.

June 10

Politics: In light of a growing manpower crisis, the Confederate Congress authorizes military service for all males aged between 17 and 50 years of age.

South: General Richard Taylor is relieved of commanding the District of West Louisiana and replaced by Texas general John G. Walker.

West: Confederate cavalry under General John H. Morgan enter Lexington, Kentucky, seize several hundred horses, and push on to the capital at Frankfort.

In a stunning display of tactical virtuosity, General Nathan B. Forrest and 3,500 Confederate cavalry rout a Union force twice its size at Brice's Cross Roads, Mississippi. Forrest anticipates that General Samuel D. Sturgis will commit his cavalry to battle first, followed by his infantry, and he determines to defeat each in detail as they come up. At 5:30 A.M., a force of 3,300 Union cavalry approaches the crossroads under General Benjamin H. Grierson, and a protracted fight between dismounted troopers commences in earnest. The Confederates, holding high ground and protected by densely wooded terrain, manage to keep Grierson at a standstill while his men are exhausted steadily by the day's intense heat. Around noon, the first elements of Union infantry under Colonel William L. McMillen, also fatigued by a five-mile jog to the battlefield, begin to arrive.

Forrest, eager to maintain the battlefield initiative, begins to launch counterattacks at selected positions along the Union line, all of which are repulsed. However, the effort further tires his opponents. Judging the moment right, at 5:00 P.M., he unleashes a simultaneous attack against the Union left, right, and center while a small force maneuvers around Sturgis's rear. The tiring Federals, hit from all sides, suddenly bolt from the field and career headlong into their extensive wagon and artillery train, overturning both. They are hotly pursued overnight by the Confederates, and the Union retreat degenerates into a rout. Forrest, outnumbered two to one, thus clinches the greatest victory of his already remarkable career: For a loss of 96 dead Confederates and 396 wounded (492), he inflicts 223 killed, 394 wounded, and 1,623 captured (2,240). A further 16 cannon, 1,500 stands of arms, and 192 wagons are also seized. But despite his remarkable success, Forrest remains unable to cut General William T. Sherman's supply line into Georgia.

NAVAL: Colonel Jacob Zeilin becomes the seventh commandant, U.S. Marine Corps.

The USS *Union* captures the Confederate sloop *Caroline* at Jupiter Inlet, Florida.

The USS *Elk* captures the Confederate sloop *Yankee Doodle* at the mouth of the Pearl River, Mississippi Sound.

June 11

SOUTH: General Robert E. Lee dispatches General Jubal A. Early into the Shenandoah Valley to stop Union depredations there under General David Hunter. If successful, he is then at liberty to march up the valley to threaten Washington, D.C., thereby forcing General Ulysses S. Grant to divert reinforcements from the Richmond, Virginia, front. Early's force also receives a new designation, Army of the Valley.

Generals Philip H. Sheridan rides into Trevilian Station, Virginia, where he confronts the division of General Wade Hampton waiting for him in the woods. Sheridan quickly dispatches the Michigan brigade of General George A. Custer to turn Hampton's right flank and slash at his rear, which he does with aplomb. Before the stunned Confederates realize what hits them, Custer dashes in between Hampton and General Fitzhugh Lee's division, capturing 50 wagons, 800 prisoners, and 1,500 horses. Lee is tardy sorting his command out but then begins to pressure the unsupported Custer hard, striking him from front and behind. The Michiganders are hard pressed for several hours, losing their own wagons, and almost overrun before Custer forms a triangular defensive box and beats back Lee's attacks. At the last minute, Sheridan gallops up with reinforcements and scatters the Southerners, taking 500 prisoners as fighting winds down for the evening.

West: Vengeful Union forces under General David Hunter burn the Virginia Military Institute at Lexington, Virginia. Hunter then pauses several days to rest and reorganize his newly constituted Army of West Virginia, a mistake that allows hard-pressed Confederates to rush reinforcements toward the important rail junction at Lynchburg.

Confederate cavalry under General John H. Morgan capture Cynthiana, Kentucky, seizing 300 prisoners and threatening the capital at Frankfort.

General Nathan B. Forrest hotly pursues defeated Union cavalry under General Samuel D. Sturgis, skirmishing with them at Ripley, Mississippi.

The Union XIII Corps is disbanded in the Department of Missouri.

Naval: The Confederate raider CSS *Alabama* under Captain Raphael Semmes docks at Cherbourg, France, to carry out badly needed repairs. His arrival does not escape the attention of the American vice consul in residence, who notifies Captain John A. Winslow of the USS *Kearsarge* at Dover, England, of his presence.

June 12

South: General Ulysses S. Grant begins to shift his Army of the Potomac strategically from Cold Harbor, Virginia, south toward Petersburg—50 miles distant. Union engineers already operating on the James River construct a pontoon bridge 2,100 feet long in only eight hours: One of the greatest engineering triumphs of the war, its existence remains entirely unknown to General Robert E. Lee. Simultaneously, the XVIII Corps of General William F. Smith boards transports down the Pamunkey River and sails for Bermuda Hundred on the south bank of the James River.

General Philip A. Sheridan's cavalry renew their clash with Generals Wade Hampton and Fitzhugh Lee at Trevilian Station, Virginia. General Alfred T. A. Torbert's division is tasked with charging dismounted Confederates at Mallory's Cross Roads while General David M. Gregg's troopers tear up tracks belonging to the Central Virginia Railroad at Louisa Court House. However, Hampton's well-situated soldiers repel seven Union charges, at which point Sheridan concludes his raid and withdraws back to Union lines outside Petersburg. Trevilian Station is one of the largest all-cavalry battles of the Civil War and among the most costly: Sheridan admits to 735 killed, wounded, and missing while Confederate losses are estimated at 1,000. Moreover, Hampton's tactically adroit leadership foils a major Union raid and prevents the Federals from reinforcing the Shenandoah Valley.

West: Union forces under General Stephen G. Burdrige evict General John H. Morgan's 1,300 Confederate raiders from Cynthiana, Kentucky, killing or capturing half. The surviving rebels gallop off in the direction of Abdington, Virginia, and safety.

Naval: Gale winds force the USS *Lavender* onto Lookout Shoal, North Carolina, and it sinks with the loss of nine crewmen. The survivors are rescued two days later by the army steamer *John Farron*.

The USS *Flag* captures the Confederate sloop *Cyclops* off Charleston, South Carolina.

June 13

SOUTH: The campaign for Richmond, Virginia, begins as General Robert E. Lee mistakenly marches troops southward to confront what he believes is the latest Union advance toward the Confederate capital via Malvern Hill and White Oaks Swamp. Meanwhile, General Ulysses S. Grant continues advancing unopposed toward the James River and Petersburg.

To counter recent Union advances in the Shenandoah Valley, General Jubal A. Early's II Corps detaches from the Army of Northern Virginia at Petersburg and moves westward by rail to Lynchburg.

General Richard S. Ewell is appointed commander of the Department of Richmond, Virginia.

WEST: A Union cavalry column under General Samuel D. Sturgis skirmishes with Confederate pursuers at Collierville, Tennessee, ending its mismanaged campaign against General Nathan B. Forrest. Consequently, the inept Sturgis spends the balance of the war at Memphis, "awaiting orders."

NAVAL: The USS *Kearsarge* under Captain John A. Winslow departs Dover, England, en route to Cherbourg, France, and a fateful confrontation with the CSS *Alabama*.

June 14

POLITICS: The first session, second Confederate Congress, adjourns.

SOUTH: Union troops of the XVIII Corps under General William F. Smith disembark at Bermuda Hundred to reinforce General Benjamin F. Butler's Army of the James.

WEST: General Joseph E. Johnston calls a staff conference at his headquarters near the summit of Pine Mountain, Marietta, Georgia. Nearby Union forces fire several rounds from their heavy Parrott cannons, and a shell strikes and kills General Leonidas K. Polk. General Alexander P. Stewart succeeds him as corps commander.

NAVAL: The USS *Courier* runs aground and is wrecked on Abaco Island, Bahamas.

The USS *Kearsarge* under Captain John A. Winslow positions itself in international waters off Cherbourg, France, awaiting the departure of the CSS *Alabama*.

June 15

POLITICS: The 13th Amendment to the U.S. Constitution fails to be ratified in the House of Representatives, falling 13 votes short (95 to 66) of the two-thirds majority needed.

The U.S. Congress passes legislation granting equal pay to African-American soldiers. For many months, black personnel have refused to accept less pay than their white counterparts in protest.

Former congressman and Peace Democrat Clement L. Vallandigham arrives in Ohio following his Canadian exile. He thereupon resumes work for securing a negotiated peace with the Confederacy.

SOUTH: General William F. Smith and 12,500 men of his XVIII Corps make a stumbling approach on the half-manned defenses of Petersburg, Virginia, then poorly held by the 2,200 Confederates of General Henry A. Wise. Smith is reinforced that evening by General Winfield S. Hancock's II Corps, but he elects not to storm the city under a moonlit night. This vacillation permits General Pierre G. T. Beauregard to consolidate Petersburg's defenses rapidly by funneling in additional troops.

General Alfred H. Terry assumes command of the Union X Corps, Army of the Potomac.

WEST: Union forces under General William T. Sherman begin to close with Confederate forces arrayed near Marietta, Georgia.

SOUTHWEST: Confederate Cherokees under General Stand Watie shell and capture the Union steamer *J. R. Williams* at Pleasant Bluffs on the Arkansas River. It is carrying ample rations for the Union garrison at Fort Gibson, Indian Territory, recently burdened by 5,000 Unionist Indian refugees.

NAVAL: Crews from the Federal gunboats USS *Lexington* and *Tyler* detain three northern steamers off Beulah's Landing, Mississippi, that were caught trading with the enemy.

The USS *General Bragg, Winnebago,* and *Naiad* engage a Confederate battery at Como Landing, Louisiana, on the Mississippi River. General Bragg is hit and temporarily disabled by enemy fire.

June 16

POLITICS: President Abraham Lincoln, addressing the Sanitation Fair in Philadelphia, Pennsylvania, declares, "War, at best, is terrible, and this war of ours, in its magnitude and duration, is one of the most terrible." But he continues to assure his audience, stating, "We accepted this war for an object, a worthy object, and the war will end when that object is obtained."

SOUTH: General Pierre G. T. Beauregard masses 14,000 men at Petersburg, Virginia, to stop an unexpected Union advance on the city. Nonetheless, General William F. Smith's XVIII Corps manages to capture several redans and a mile of Confederate trenches on the city's outer perimeter. However, Smith declines to press home his numerical superiority, and his hesitancy is one of the most costly Union mistakes of the war. It prolongs the fighting by nearly a year.

Unknown to the Confederates, General George G. Meade's entire Army of the Potomac silently slips across the James River and steadily advances on Petersburg, Virginia. It is a masterstroke capable of ending the war.

WEST: The Confederate II Corps of General Jubal A. Early reaches Charlottesville, Virginia, although delays in rail service mean that only half of his 8,000 men reach Lynchburg in time to aid its defense.

General Joseph E. Johnston retires to new positions near Mud Creek, Georgia.

NAVAL: The USS *Commodore Perry,* at the behest of General Benjamin F. Butler, bombards Fort Clifton on the James River, Virginia.

A joint Union expedition consisting of the USS *Lockwood, Louisiana,* and army transport *Ella May* begins to operate up the Pamlico and Pungo rivers, North Carolina. They capture and burn the Confederate schooners *Iowa, Mary Emma,* and *Jenny Lind* before returning downstream.

Captain Raphael Semmes, eager to try conclusions with the USS *Kearsarge* offshore, begins to take on supplies of coal and munitions for the CSS *Alabama* at Cherbourg, France.

June 17

NORTH: An explosion rocks part of the Washington Arsenal, killing 18 and injuring 20.

SOUTH: General William F. Smith's XVIII Corps finally launches strong attacks on the newly strengthened defenses of Petersburg, Virginia, and is repulsed by Confederates under General Bushrod R. Johnson.

WEST: Confederate forces under General John C. Breckinridge and John D. Imboden defend Lynchburg, Virginia, against General David Hunter's Union troops. The initial Union drive, delivered by General George Crook, pushes aside Confederate outposts while cavalry under General Alfred N. Duffie advance from the west. Southern resistance then suddenly stiffens following the arrival of General Jubal A. Early, who directs the division of General Stephen Ramseur into the front lines. Hunter elects not to press the conflict further and encamps for the night.

General William T. Sherman begins to probe Confederate positions at Mud Creek, Georgia, seeking a weak spot.

NAVAL: The CSS *Florida* captures and burns the Union brig *W. C. Clarke* at sea.

June 18

SOUTH: The siege of Petersburg, Virginia, begins in earnest once General Robert E. Lee arrives with the Army of Northern Virginia. Lee, commanding 50,000 bedraggled and hungry men, defends a line 26 miles long while simultaneously guarding the four railroads out of the city that constitute his lifeline. Ulysses S. Grant leads 110,000 well-equipped soldiers, backed by a steady stream of replacements that the Confederates cannot match. Yet, to underscore the strength of Southern defenses, a heavy probe by II Corps under General David B. Birney is repulsed. The past four days of fighting in the city's outskirts cost the Union 10,586 casualties while better-protected Southerners sustain about 4,000.

General David B. Birney replaces the ailing General Winfield S. Hancock as commander of the II Corps, Army of the Potomac.

General Thomas W. Sherman takes charge of Union forces in the vicinity of New Orleans, Louisiana.

WEST: General David Hunter's 18,000 Union soldiers renew their attack on Lynchburg, Virginia. However, newly arrived Confederates under General Jubal A. Early boost the defenders to 14,000 men, who resist tenaciously. Hunter is especially foiled by excellent Confederate artillery fire that smothers his own inexperienced gunners. At length, the Union columns under Generals George Crook, William W. Averell, and Jeremiah Sullivan fail to turn Early's position or to score any significant penetrations despite heavy fighting. Hunter concludes that the Confederates have been reinforced heavily overnight and actually outnumber him. He therefore ignominiously halts the engagement and withdraws up the Shenandoah Valley toward Liberty. This timidity emboldens Early, and he regains the strategic initiative by energetically pursuing his larger adversary. Casualties at Lynchburg are not recorded but are believed to be relatively light for both sides.

General Joseph E. Johnston abandons his line at Pine Mountain, Georgia, and falls back to even stronger positions along Kennesaw Mountain, two miles west of Marietta. This elevated ridge line probably constitutes the best defensive terrain his army will hold during the entire Atlanta campaign.

June 19

WEST: Union forces under General David Hunter withdraw from the Shenandoah Valley completely and escape into the Kanawha Valley of West Virginia. Confederates under General Jubal A. Early hotly pursue from behind.

Union forces rout a detachment of Texas Rangers at Hahn's Farm, Arkansas.

NAVAL: The USS *Kearsarge* under Captain John A. Winslow engages the CSS *Alabama* under Captain Raphael Semmes off Cherbourg, France. The Union vessel enjoys a slightly larger crew and marginally heavier armament, but a decided advantage in ordnance since the *Alabama*'s ammunition has deteriorated from lengthy exposure to salt air. Moreover, Winslow takes the precaution of wrapping vulnerable parts of his ship with heavy chains that function as armor. At 11:00 A.M., the antagonists meet seven

Engagement between the CSS *Alabama* and the USS *Kearsarge* June 19, 1864 Painting by Xanthus R. Smith *(Naval Historical Foundation)*

miles offshore and begin to circle at 900 yards distance while 15,000 spectators throng the beach. Semmes commences firing at a mile's distance while Winslow, enjoying superior speed, gradually narrows the range and holds his fire until within a half mile. Both vessels handle their guns well; *Kearsarge* receives 28 hits, including a potentially disastrous strike by a 100-pound shell that fails to explode. But Union gunnery is superb and inflicts tremendous damage on the unprotected *Alabama,* puncturing its hull repeatedly. Within an hour, the celebrated raider begins to list, and Semmes, unable to dash for the French coast, abandons ship. *Alabama* settles beneath the waves stern first as the English yacht *Deerhound* sails in to rescue the wallowing Confederates, including Semmes. Casualties are three Union wounded to 26 Confederate killed, 21 wounded, and 64 captured. This action terminates the Confederacy's most celebrated commerce raider: Since its commissioning in 1862, *Alabama* has sailed 75,000 miles and seized 63 Union ships worth $4.5 million. Winslow subsequently receives a well-deserved promotion to commodore for his lopsided triumph.

June 20

SOUTH: A Union cavalry detachment is routed by Colonel John S. Mosby at Centreville, Virginia, losing 39 captives.

Union forces launch a major expedition from Batchelder's Creek, North Carolina, against nearby Kinston. Some prisoners and horses are taken.

WEST: General William T. Sherman's army moves up against a new Confederate defensive line in the Kennesaw Mountains.

NAVAL: The USS *Morse* and *Cactus* bombard Confederate batteries near White House, Virginia, which have been harassing army supply trains.

The USS *Calypso* and *Nansemond* escort an army expedition up the New River, North Carolina, in an attempt to sever the Wilmington and Weldon Railroad.

June 21

POLITICS: President Abraham Lincoln visits Union troops in the siege lines at Petersburg, Virginia, making a conspicuous target for snipers in his tall, stovepipe hat.

Confederate secretary of the treasury Christopher G. Meminger resigns over criticism of his handling of monetary affairs.

SOUTH: As General Ulysses S. Grant attempts extending Confederate siege lines to the breaking point by moving troops to the south and west of Petersburg, Virginia. However, stiff resistance halts the Federal drive short of the Weldon Railroad. Grant then prepares to hurl two corps and a cavalry division against that vital Confederate supply line.

WEST: General Joseph Hooker's XX Corps reaches Kolb's Farm on the extreme left flank of Confederate positions along Kennesaw Mountain. General Joseph E. Johnston, fearing he will be flanked and ejected from fine defensive terrain, orders the corps of General John B. Hood to march from his right flank over to the endangered point on the left.

NAVAL: Gunfire from the USS *Shokokon* rescues the army transport *Eliza Hancox* from a Confederate attack near Cumberland Point, Virginia.

A Confederate squadron consisting of the CSS *Virginia II, Fredericksburg,* and *Hampton,* backed by land batteries, engages the Union James River squadron at

Trent's and the Varina Reaches. Little damage results to either side and the Confederates withdraw back upstream.

June 22

SOUTH: General Ulysses S. Grant, confronting strong Southern defenses before him at Petersburg, Virginia, tries his time-honored tactic of shifting troops around the Confederate flank in a bid to extend and weaken their lines by cutting the Weldon Railroad. General David B. Birney's II Corps and General Horatio G. Wright's VI Corps, supported by a cavalry division under General James H. Wilson, advance through dense woods to reach their objective. Due to the nature of the terrain, a sizable gap develops between the two forces, a fact which Confederate general Ambrose P. Hill quickly exploits. General Cadmus M. Wilcox's division is ordered to engage Wright's VI Corps as a diversion while Generals William Mahone and Bushrod R. Johnson assail Birney's flank. The assault is delivered savagely and routs the veteran division of General John Gibbon, taking 1,600 prisoners. Further fighting results in a stalemate by nightfall, and the Union leaders fall back to regroup and try again.

Generals James H. Wilson and August V. Kautz take 3,300 Union troopers on a major cavalry raid from Lee's Mill, Virginia, and against the South Side and Danville Railroad.

WEST: General John H. Morgan receives command of the Department of Western Virginia and East Tennessee.

Colonel John S. Mosby captures Duffield's Depot, West Virginia, along with 50 Union prisoners.

General John B. Hood exceeds his orders to extend the Confederate left flank at Kennesaw Mountain by launching an unauthorized assault with 11,000 men against Union positions at Kolb's Farm, Georgia. General Joseph Hooker, commanding 14,000 troops and 40 cannon, is forewarned of Hood's approach and makes careful preparations to receive him in strength. Concentrated musketry and canister fire at close range mows charging Confederates down, and Hood draws off with 1,500 casualties to a Union tally of 250.

NAVAL: The Federal gunboat USS *Lexington* attacks and drives off a body of Confederates from White River Station, Arkansas.

June 23

SOUTH: Union generals David B. Birney and Horatio G. Wright repeat their attack on Confederate defenses along the Weldon Railroad, Petersburg, with their II and VI Corps, respectively. A good initial advance recovers all ground lost on the previous day but a stubborn defense mounted by General William Mahone blocks them from cutting the railroad. At dusk, the Federals again withdraw below the Jerusalem Plank Road with 2,962 casualties. Eight weeks elapse before General Ulysses S. Grant mounts a major effort in this vital sector again.

WEST: General Jubal A. Early energetically conducts 14,000 Confederate troops northward up the Shenandoah Valley in pursuit of General David Hunter. Hunter, retreating rapidly westward, escapes Early's grasp but leaves Washington, D.C., exposed to attack.

NAVAL: The heavy ironclad USS *Tecumseh* is ordered out of the James River, Virginia, and steams off to join the West Gulf Blockading Squadron off Mobile, Alabama.

Lieutenant William B. Cushing rows a small reconnaissance party from the USS *Monticello* up the Cape Fear River and endeavors to obtain the location of the CSS *Raleigh*. They are unaware that this vessel has been scuttled on May 6, but the mission provides Union forces with additional intelligence. Moreover, three seamen, David Warren, William Wright, and John Sullivan, all receive the Congressional Medal of Honor for their participation.

June 24

POLITICS: The Maryland Convention gathers and votes to abolish slavery.
SOUTH: Union cavalry under General Philip H. Sheridan are rebuffed at Samaria Church, Virginia, while returning from their aborted raid toward Lynchburg.
NAVAL: The wooden paddle-wheeler USS *Queen City* is attacked and captured by Confederate forces of General Joseph O. Shelby at Claredon on the White River, Arkansas. The USS *Tyler*, *Fawn*, and *Naumkeag* arrive on the scene shortly after, disperse the attackers, and recapture several Union sailors. However, *Queen City* is sunk by Confederates to prevent its recapture.

June 25

SOUTH: Colonel Henry Pleasant's 48th Pennsylvania, composed mostly of miners from Schuykill County, begin to tunnel beneath Confederate defenses at Petersburg, Virginia. The plan is initially approved by General Ambrose E. Burnside, IX Corps commander, while General Ulysses S. Grant also gives his grudging acceptance. The miners intend to burrow 511 feet long under a South Carolinian battery positioned at Elliott's Salient. Once finished, they will stock 8,000 pounds of gunpowder beneath it and light a fuse. During the next month, Burnside specially trains the African-American division of General Edward Ferrero to spearhead the assault once the changes have been detonated.

General Philip H. Sheridan's cavalry column, thwarted in its drive to Lynchburg, Virginia, ferries across the James River and rejoins the main Union army outside Petersburg.

General James H. Wilson's cavalry raid stumbles at the Staunton River Bridge near Roanoke Station, Virginia, thanks to dogged resistance by 900 Confederate infantry.
SOUTHWEST: Texas Rangers attack and disperse a small Union force at Rancho Las Rinas, Texas, killing 20 men.

June 26

WEST: A force of 14,000 Confederates under General Jubal A. Early occupies Staunton, Virginia, without opposition and then continues marching northward toward Winchester.

The Army of the Ohio under General John M. Schofield, having been ordered to make a "demonstration" against the Confederate position at Kennesaw Mountain, Georgia, sends three brigades across Olley's Creek to secure a foothold on the southern bank. Resistance proves surprisingly light, and he easily accomplishes his mission. However, General William T. Sherman ignores these important gains, calculating that General Joseph E. Johnston's main army is spread dangerously thin along the heights of Kennesaw Mountain. He intends to test his theory by attacking in force on the morrow.

NAVAL: The USS *Norfolk Packet* captures the Confederate sloop *Sarah Mary* off Mosquito Inlet, Florida.

June 27

POLITICS: President Abraham Lincoln formally accepts the Union (Republican) Party's nomination for the presidency.

SOUTH: General William S. Hancock resumes command of the II Corps, Army of the Potomac, following a brief illness.

WEST: General William T. Sherman wages the Battle of Kennesaw Mountain, Georgia, against General Joseph E. Johnston. He impatiently abandons his slow but successful flanking tactics because heavy rains turn the roads into quagmires, which precludes any such maneuvering. He also believes that Johnston, strung along a ridge line seven miles long, is stretched perilously thin. In fact, the Confederates are arrayed skillfully along high ground strewn with large boulders and trees—affording a perfect killing ground to troops advancing from below. Nevertheless, Sherman decides to make several feints on Johnston's flanks before striking him directly in the center—where he is strongest.

The first wave comprises two divisions from General John A. Logan's XV Corps, Army of the Tennessee, which charge uphill and rapidly clear Confederate defenders from their first line of entrenchments. However, as his 5,500 men clamber up the hillside, General William W. Loring's troops respond with intense musketry and artillery fire, dropping Federals in bloody clumps. The attack, suffering heavy losses, is called off after two hours.

The main thrust against Johnston's line occurs farther south along Cheatham's Hill, stoutly held by General William J. Hardee's corps. Up the slopes go 8,000 men from the divisions of Generals Jefferson C. Davis and John Newton, XIV Corps, which quickly overrun the line of defenders in rifle pits. But after pushing beyond the trenches, both commanders are raked by unerring sheets of fire from above that cut down soldiers in droves. Renewed and costly charges ensue, but the second Confederate line under Generals Patrick R. Cleburne and Benjamin F. Cheatham never is imperiled seriously. By the time this advance is suspended, Federals are crumpling within 15 yards of Confederate lines.

Losing heavily by the minute, Sherman finally calls off the assault. His losses range upward of 3,000, including two generals killed, while Johnston incurs about 750 casualties. Kennesaw Mountain proves the most costly mistake of the Atlanta campaign, and Sherman has little recourse but to continue maneuvering once the soggy ground dries out.

NAVAL: The USS *Nipsic* captures the Confederate sloop *Julia* at Sapelo Sound, Georgia.

The USS *Proteus* captures the British blockade-runner *Jupiter* off Man-of-War Cay, Bahamas.

June 28

POLITICS: President Abraham Lincoln signs legislation repealing the fugitive slave acts.

SOUTH: General James H. Wilson's cavalry force pauses at Stoney Creek Station, Virginia, where they are chased by Confederate troopers under General Wade Hampton. The Northerners then are attacked in force and roughly handled, abandoning their artillery, wagons, and wounded.

June 29

WEST: A quick raid by Colonel John S. Mosby on Charlestown and Duffield's Station, West Virginia, nets 25 captives. Numerous storehouses are burned, and telegraph wires are cut.

NAVAL: The USS *Hunchback* and *Saugus* shell Confederate batteries at Deep Bottom, along the James River, Virginia.

June 30

POLITICS: The U.S. Congress approves the Internal Revenue Act to help finance the war. The Morriff Tariff Act of 1861 is also modified to increase the duties levied.

Secretary of the Treasury Salmon P. Chase tenders his resignation to President Abraham Lincoln who, much to his surprise, accepts it. "You and I have reached a point of mutual embarrassment in our official relation which it seems cannot be overcome," Lincoln writes, "or longer sustained, consistently with public service."

WEST: General Jubal A. Early continues his Shenandoah offensive by advancing on New Market, Virginia.

NAVAL: An armed boat from the USS *Roebuck* captures the Confederate sloop *Last Resort* at Indian River Inlet, Florida.

The USS *Glasgow* forces the Confederate steamer *Ivanhoe* to run aground near Fort Morgan, Mobile Bay, Alabama. Four boatloads of sailors from the *Metacomet* and *Kennebec* accost the stricken vessel that night and burn it under the very guns of Fort Morgan.

July 1

POLITICS: President Abraham Lincoln appoints William P. Fessenden as the new secretary of the treasury.

The U.S. Senates passes the Wade-Davis Reconstruction Bill, 26 to 3, with 20 abstaining.

SOUTH: The 3rd Division of U.S. Cavalry under General James H. Wilson staggers back into Peterburg, Virginia, following a disappointing raid against the Petersburg and Weldon Railroad.

WEST: General Irvin McDowell is appointed commander of the Department of the Pacific.

Having abandoned frontal assault tactics, General William T. Sherman initiates a new flanking movement around Kennesaw Mountain and moves in the direction of Marietta, Georgia.

NAVAL: The USS *Merrimac* captures the Confederate sloop *Henrietta* at sea off Tampa, Florida.

The Confederate raider CSS *Florida* under Lieutenant Charles M. Morris captures and burns the Union bark *Harriet Stevens* at sea south of Bermuda.

July 2

SOUTH: Union troops land and gain a lodgment on Johnson Island, Charleston Harbor, South Carolina.

WEST: Confederates under General Jubal A. Early occupy Winchester, Virginia, before commencing their drive on Harper's Ferry, West Virginia.

General Joseph E. Johnston, reacting to the latest Union maneuver, begins to evacuate his position along Kennesaw Mountain, Georgia, and occupies prepared lines below Marietta at Smyrna.

NAVAL: The USS *Keystone State* captures the British blockade-runner *Rouen* near Wilmington, North Carolina.

Federal monitors USS *Leigh* and *Montauk* accompany and support army operations up the Stono River, South Carolina, in an attempt to cut the Charleston-Savannah Railroad.

July 3

SOUTH: Union forces launch attacks on Fort Johnson, Charleston, South Carolina, and are repulsed with 140 prisoners.

WEST: Confederate forces under General Jubal A. Early advance in the region of Buckton, Virginia, driving 5,000 Union troops under General Franz Sigel across the Potomac River at Maryland Heights. Early, declining to assault such a strong position, moves up to cross the river at Shepherdstown.

General George Crook is appointed commander of the Department of West Virginia.

The Army of Tennessee under General Joseph E. Johnston occupies new defensive works near Smyrna, Georgia, astride the Western and Atlantic Railroad. He thereby stands firm north of the Chattahoochee River, a move that General William T. Sherman failed to anticipate.

July 4

POLITICS: President Abraham Lincoln signs legislation modifying certain aspects of the Enrollment Act of 1863, striking the clause allowing substitutes to be purchased for $300.

The president also clashes with Radical Republicans over the tenor of reconstruction by refusing to sign the Wade-Davis Bill, which would have placed conditions for Reconstruction solely in the hands of Congress. He specifically objects to provisions requiring loyalty oaths by 50 percent of each state's 1860 voters.

The first session, 38th Congress adjourns.

WEST: General Jubal A. Early prepares to cross the Potomac River at Patterson's Creek Bridge, West Virginia, and into Maryland.

Union forces under General William T. Sherman stage demonstrations at Nickajack Creek and Turner's Ferry, Georgia, while scouting for a route across the Chattahoochee River. To that end, he sends Generals Oliver O. Howard (IV Corps) and Grenville M. Dodge (XVI Corps) to attack Confederate positions once across the river. Howard moves down on the Western and Atlantic Railroad as ordered, enjoying good progress until he reaches Vining's Station. There, Confederates under General William J. Hardee resist stoutly from a line of entrenchments. Rather than incur heavy casualties, Howard abruptly stops and digs in himself. Dodge, meanwhile, throws a pontoon bridge across Nickajack Creek near Ruff's Mills and pushes inland for nearly a mile before encountering Confederate cavalry and Georgia militia under generals Gustavus W. Smith and William H. Jackson. The Federals are unable to evict the Southerners in hard fighting, so they fall back and consolidate their bridgehead. General Joseph E. Johnston, anticipating that he is about to be flanked again, repositions the Army of Tennessee north of the Chattahoochee and heavily fortifies all bridges and crossings.

A sharp Union counterattack scatters the command of General Joseph O. Shelby in Searcy County, Arkansas.

NAVAL: The USS *Magnolia* captures three small boats laden with supplies several hundred miles east of Florida. That such craft even are dispatched on the open seas is a good indication of the torpid state of the Confederate economy.

The USS *Hastings* trades shots with Confederate sharpshooters along the White River above St. Charles, Arkansas.

July 5

POLITICS: New York journalist Horace Greeley receives peace feelers from the Confederate government and contacts President Abraham Lincoln. Lincoln authorizes Greeley to meet with said individuals at Niagara Falls, New York.

NORTH: General Jubal A. Early sidesteps Harper's Ferry and crosses the Potomac River to Shepherdstown, Maryland, with 12,000 men. His approach triggers an alarm in Washington, D.C., and cries for 24,000 volunteers are raised. The first officer to respond is General Lew Wallace, commander of the Middle Department at Baltimore, who rapidly moves 3,000 troops in the direction of Monocacy Junction, two miles east of Frederick.

SOUTH: General Andrew J. Smith leads a Union force of 14,000 men and 24 cannon from La Grange, Tennessee, toward Tupelo, Mississippi, intending to capture or destroy the army of General Nathan B. Forrest. He is ordered by General William T. Sherman to "bring Forrest to bay and whip him if possible."

WEST: General William T. Sherman brushes against Confederate defenses along the Chattahoochee River, Georgia. Finding General Joseph E. Johnston strongly dug in behind formidable fieldworks, he instructs General George H. Thomas and his Army of the Cumberland to demonstrate before their lines while General James B. McPherson's Army of the Tennessee feints a river crossing at Turner's Ferry, 12 miles downstream. General John M. Schofield also marches the Army of the Ohio across the Chattahoochee to outflank the defenders along Soap Creek.

July 6

NORTH: Confederates under General Jubal A. Early occupy Hagerstown, Maryland, demanding $200,000 for depredations committed earlier by Union forces in the Shenandoah Valley. Meanwhile, Union defenses at Monocacy Junction are bolstered by the arrival of the 8th Illinois Cavalry.

The 3rd Division, VI Corps, begins to move from Virginia to Baltimore, Maryland, to aid in the defense of the city.

July 7

NORTH: General Ulysses S. Grant, realizing the seriousness of Confederate thrusts in Maryland, rushes General James B. Rickett's division (VI Corps) to Baltimore, where it arrives that night, and marches for Monocacy Junction. There, it will join General Lew Wallace, holding the intersection with 3,000 men. Meanwhile, General Jubal A. Early's Confederates commence a leisurely advance on Middletown.

SOUTH: Union troops are forced off James Island, Charleston Harbor, South Carolina, sustaining 330 casualties to a Southern tally of 163. The most recent round of bombardment also drops another 784 rounds on the ruins of Fort Sumter.

NAVAL: The USS *Ariel, Sea Bird, Stonewall,* and *Rosalie* accompany Federal troops on a raid against Brookville and Bayport, Florida. They seize a quantity of cotton and burn a customs house before returning to the Anclote Keys.

July 8

POLITICS: President Abraham Lincoln pocket vetoes the Wade-Davis Reconstruction Act by refusing to sign it. This earns him the ire of Radical Republicans, who redouble their efforts to have Lincoln dropped as the party's standard-bearer in the fall presidential election.

NORTH: A hodgepodge of Union forces under General Lew Wallace assumes defensive positions behind the Monocacy River near Frederick, Maryland, to defend the national capital against General Jubal A. Early's advancing Confederates. On the day before battle, he cobbles together 6,000 men from various sources.

WEST: General Albion P. Howe succeeds Franz Sigel as commander at Harper's Ferry, West Virginia.

Union troops under General John M. Schofield cross the Chattahoochee River, Georgia, at Phillips' Ferry, near the mouth of Soap Creek, Georgia, thereby flanking General Joseph E. Johnston's defensive positions. Here, General Oliver O. Howard throws a pontoon bridge across Powell's Ferry while other troops establish lodgments along Pace's Ferry. Facing three hostile bridgeheads, Johnston orders an immediate withdrawal from the Chattahoochee line and heads for the defenses of Atlanta, only eight miles distant.

NAVAL: The USS *Fort Jackson* captures the British blockade-runner *Boston* off the South Carolina coast.

The USS *Sonoma* captures the Confederate steamer *Ida* near the Stono River, South Carolina.

The USS *Azalea* and *Sweet Briar* seize the Confederate schooner *Pocahontas* near Charleston, South Carolina.

The USS *Kanawha* forces the Confederate blockade-runner *Matagorda* aground near Galveston, where it is destroyed by cannon fire from the Penguin and Aroostook.

The Confederate raider CSS *Florida* under Charles M. Morris seizes and burns the Union whaler *Golconda* southwest of Bermuda.

July 9

POLITICS: The Fabian tactics of General Joseph E. Johnston, which have so infuriated General William T. Sherman, unfortunately draw the ire of President Jefferson Davis. Seeking a possible pretext to relieve Johnston, whom he personally dislikes, Davis dispatches General Braxton Bragg to his headquarters on a "fact-finding" mission. Johnston, meanwhile, withdraws from the Chattahoochee River to Peachtree Creek, only three miles north of Atlanta, Georgia.

NORTH: General Jubal A. Early repeats demands that the city of Hagerstown, Maryland, turn over $200,000 to compensate prior Union abuses in the Shenandoah Valley. He then proceeds to join the Battle of Monocacy, then in its initial stages.

General Lew Wallace and 6,000 Union troops confront 14,000 Confederates under General Jubal A. Early at Monocacy, Maryland. Early intends to turn the Union left flank from the onset and orders his cavalry under General John McCausland to find a ford across the Monocacy River. That accomplished, the corps of John C. Breckinridge crosses over to do battle with General James B. Rickett's division. Rickett's veterans easily repulse two Confederate charges by General John B. Gordon as the Southerners gradually work their way around the Union left. A final charge by General William R. Terry's Virginia brigade dislodges the Federals, and they break in disorder at 4:30 P.M. Wallace then orders his entire line withdrawn up the Baltimore Pike, which is accomplished in reasonably good order; Early declines to pursue. Union losses are 98 killed, 594 wounded, and 1,188 captured (1,880) while the Confederates suffer about 700 lost. The road to Washington, D.C. is now open, but Wallace's stand at Monocacy delays Early's advance an entire day, granting the capital additional time to strengthen its defenses.

WEST: A Union column of 14,000 men under General Andrew J. Smith crosses the Tallahatchie River at New Albany, Mississippi, and continues marching south toward Pontotoc.

The Confederate Army of Tennessee under General Joseph E. Johnston abandons the Chattahoochee River line, the last remaining natural barrier between Union forces and Atlanta, Georgia, and filters into the city's outer chain of defenses. Johnston, cannily outflanked again, had no alternative, but his latest withdrawal distresses the Confederate high command.

NAVAL: The Confederate raider CSS *Florida* under Lieutenant Charles M. Morris captures and burns the Union bark *Greenland* and the schooner *Margaret Y. Davis* off Cape Henry, Virginia.

The USS *Gettysburg* captures the Confederate steamer *Little Ada* off Cape Romain, South Carolina.

July 10

NORTH: Confederates under General Jubal A. Early pass through Rockville, Maryland, to confront Union defenders at Fort Stevens, outside Washington, D.C. The post is held only lightly by 209 inexperienced artillerists, but President Abraham Lincoln blithely exclaims, "Let us be vigilant but keep cool. I hope neither Baltimore nor Washington will be sacked." Fortunately, Union reinforcements are being rushed to the capital from several directions before the Confederates can mount an attack.

WEST: General Lovell H. Rosseau, commanding the District of Tennessee, receives orders from General William T. Sherman to lead a Union raid from Decatur, Alabama, against the Montgomery and West Point Railroad and do "all possible mischief." En route, he is pursued closely by General Stephen D. Lee, commander of the Department of Alabama, Mississippi, and East Louisiana.

NAVAL: The USS *Roebuck* captures the British blockade-runner *Terrapin* at Jupiter Inlet, Florida.

The USS *Monongahela, Lackawanna, Galena,* and *Sebago* attack the Confederate steamer *Virgin* off Fort Morgan, Mobile Bay, Alabama, forcing it aground. Southern cannon fire from the fort keeps the Union vessel at bay while the *Virgin* is subsequently refloated and towed into the bay.

The CSS *Florida* under Lieutenant Charles M. Morris captures and burns the Union bark *General Berry* 35 miles off the Maryland coast. It then proceeds to seize the schooner *Howard,* the bark *Zelinda,* and the steamer *Electric Spark* in the same vicinity. Such depredation alarms government and civilian officials.

The USS *Mount Vernon* and *Monticello* are detached from the South Atlantic Blockading Squadron to search for the CSS *Florida.* The USS *Ino* is disguised further as a merchantman in an attempt to lure the Confederate raider into battle.

July 11

NORTH: General Robert E. Rode's Confederate division marches to within gunshot of Fort Stevens, District of Columbia, then manned by only 209 gunners. Fortunately, General Jubal A. Early's command is exhausted by a combination of intensely hot weather and hard marching and elects not to attack. Had he done so the Confederates might have easily pushed on to Washington, D.C., itself. This fortuitous delay allows Federal defenses to congeal under the direction of General Christopher Augur, who throws skirmishers forward to engage the Southerners. Meanwhile, the 1st and 2nd Divisions of General Horatio G. Wright's VI Corps, joined by elements of General Quincy A. Gilmore's XIX Corps, arrive to bolster the city's defenses. Even President Abraham Lincoln himself shows up as an onlooker and to give encouragement to the outnumbered garrison. That evening, Early decides to attack Fort Stevens on the morrow and then reverses himself after learning of Union reinforcements.

SOUTH: General Edward O. C. Ord assumes command of the VIII Corps and the Union Middle Department, Virginia.

WEST: General Andrew J. Smith's column of 14,000 men reaches Pontotoc, Mississippi, while Confederates under General Nathan B. Forrest begin to mass at nearby Okolona, intending to lure him into a large ambush.

NAVAL: Armed boats from the USS *James L. Davis* land at Tampa, Florida, to destroy a large Confederate saltworks.

July 12

NORTH: Confederates under General Jubal A. Early withdraw from the Washington, D.C., region, cautiously pursued by General Horatio G. Wright's Federal troops. The division of General Richard E. Rodes is somewhat roughly handled in the ensuing chase, but it escapes intact. For a few tense moments, President Abraham Lincoln, visiting the parapets, is under enemy fire, and a young army officer, Oliver Wendell Holmes (a future Supreme Court justice) inadvertently shouts, "Get down, you fool!" While retreating, the Southerners burn down the house of Postmaster General Montgomery Blair.

NAVAL: The USS *Whitehead* and *Ceres,* accompanied by the steamer transport *Ella May,* venture up the Scuppernong River as far as Columbia, North Carolina. There, they destroy a bridge and some grain stores before withdrawing.

The USS *Penobscot* captures the Confederate blockade-runner *James Williams* off Galveston, Texas.

A combined Union expedition against Bayport, Florida, safely returns to the Anclote Keys, having burned several hundred bales of cotton and a customshouse.

July 13

NORTH: General Horatio G. Wright assumes command of Union defenses in and around Washington, D.C., as Confederates under General Jubal A. Early withdraw toward Leesburg to recross the Potomac River.

SOUTH: General Braxton Bragg, sent to General Joseph E. Johnston's headquarters in Georgia to assess matters, files a predictably negative report of that commander to President Jefferson Davis. "It is a sad alternative, but the case seems hopeless in present hands," Bragg writes. "The means are surely adequate if properly employed, especially the cavalry is ample." Davis then prepares to make a dramatic change in commanders.

WEST: General Andrew J. Smith's column, heading south, suddenly veers east to Tupelo, Mississippi, ostensibly to sever the Mobile and Ohio Railroad. Smith actually is concerned that General Nathan B. Forrest is waiting to entrap him in the prairie region around nearby Okolona. Confederate cavalry begin to nip at Smith's rear and flanks, but they are largely deflected. Forrest remains eager to attack but still awaits the arrival of his superior, General Stephen D. Lee, and 2,000 reinforcements.

General William T. Sherman finishes moving the bulk of his forces across the Chattahootchee River, Georgia.

General Napoleon B. Buford leads a column of Union cavalry in pursuit of Confederate raiders under General Joseph O. Shelby in western Tennessee.

NAVAL: Armed boats from the USS *Vicksburg* destroy all bridges over the South River to preclude large-scale Confederate raids near Annapolis, Maryland.

July 14

WEST: General Jubal A. Early crosses the Potomac River at White's Ferry and arrives back in Leesburg, Virginia. Union forces under General Horatio G. Wright decline to pursue.

A force of 7,500 Confederates under Generals Stephen D. Lee and Nathan B. Forrest gathers to attack Union positions outside Tupelo, Mississippi. General Andrew J. Smith has positioned his 14,000 troops expertly along a low ridge with secure flanks and a clear field of fire, awaiting their approach. The Confederate attack launches at 7:00 A.M. and continues for three hours. They make repeated and heroic charges against the waiting Federals, only to be decimated by concentrated musketry and artillery fire. By 1:00 P.M., Lee calls off the action and orders a withdrawal. Smith, enjoying a two-to one advantage in numbers, could have counterattacked and easily smashed the battered Confederates, but he likewise prepares to retreat. The Battle of Tupelo is a surprising tactical victory for the North, but it leaves Forrest's command intact and still functioning. Union losses are 77 killed, 559 wounded, and 39 missing (674) to a Confederate tally of 210 dead and 1,116 injured (1,326).

NAVAL: The USS *Pequot* and *Commodore Morris* bombard Confederate batteries at Malvern Hill, Virginia, in an action lasting four hours.

The USS *Paul Jones* is captured in the Ossabaw Sound, Georgia, while hunting the CSS *Water Witch*.

July 15

NORTH: Union forces under General Horatio K. Wright remain poised north of the Potomac River opposite Leesburg, Virginia, but they do not cross. General Jubal A. Early's Confederates continue loitering in and around that town to rest and recuperate.

WEST: General Andrew J. Smith's Union column files through Tupelo, Mississippi, en route to Tennessee. Confederates under General Nathan B. Forrest, still smarting from their earlier reverse, hound his rear guard incessantly until their leader is painfully wounded.

July 16

POLITICS: A pensive president Jefferson Davis cables General Joseph E. Johnston at Atlanta, Georgia, "I wish to hear from you as to present situation and your plan of operations so specifically as will enable me to anticipate events." Johnston matter of factly replies, "As the enemy is double our number, we must be on the defensive. My plan of operations must therefore depend upon that of the enemy."

SOUTH: While General Joseph E. Johnston continues strengthening the defenses of Atlanta, Georgia, Union forces under General James B. McPherson begin an enveloping movement through Decatur.

WEST: General Jubal A. Early's Confederates reenter the Shenandoah Valley, unencumbered by a Union pursuit, and push on toward Berryville.

NAVAL: Confederate artillery along the James River, Virginia, engage the USS *Mendota*, *Pequot*, and *Commodore Morris* at Four Mile Creek. *Mendota* is struck several times and sustains damage; thereafter, enemy activity temporarily closes navigation on the James River.

July 17

WEST: General Jubal A. Early reaches Strasburg, Virginia, having brushed aside General David Hunter's force at Snicker's Ferry.

General Joseph E. Johnston is preparing to pounce on the isolated Army of the Cumberland under General George H. Thomas at Peachtree Creek, Georgia. Suddenly, a telegraph from President Jefferson Davis arrives at his headquarters, outlining his replacement by General John B. Hood, an impetuous, aggressive fighter. "As you failed to arrest the advance of the enemy to the vicinity of Atlanta," it read, "far in the interior of Georgia, and express no confidence that you can defeat or repel him, your are hereby relieved from the command of the Army and Department of Tennessee." Davis's meddling and personal antipathy for the irritable yet highly capable Johnston marks a dramatic turning point in the course of events. As General William T. Sherman declares, Confederate authorities "rendered us most valuable service."

General William T. Sherman's army crosses the Chattahoochee River, only eight miles from Atlanta, Georgia, and approaches the city and its environs.

July 18

POLITICS: President Abraham Lincoln renews his call for 500,000 volunteers and draftees, an unpopular move that militates against his reelection chances.

President Jefferson Davis appoints George A. Trenholm of South Carolina as the new Confederate secretary of the treasury.

With the Union army nearing the gates of Atlanta, Georgia, Mayor Thomas Calhoun and the city council convene for the last time, thereby concluding the rule of municipal government.

SOUTH: John B. Hood is promoted to lieutenant general, C.S.A., the last such officer appointed, and he succeeds General Joseph E. Johnston.

Union forces under General George H. Thomas push Confederate cavalry across Peachtree Creek, Georgia, prior to crossing three miles north of Atlanta. Capitalizing on plans drawn up by the recently relieved General Joseph E. Johnston, General John B. Hood intends to catch Federal troops in the act of crossing and possibly defeat them piecemeal.

WEST: Confederates under General Jubal A. Early repulse a Union attack on them at Cool Spring, Virginia.

July 19

WEST: Superior Union forces press General Jubal A. Early's Confederates at Berry's Ford and Ashby's Gap, Virginia, as they fall back toward Winchester.

As Union troops under General James B. McPherson push through Decatur, Georgia, the Army of the Cumberland under General George H. Thomas occupies Peachtree Creek to the north. General John B. Hood also begins to marshal Confederate forces for a massive strike against Thomas.

July 20

WEST: Union cavalry under General William W. Averell surprise a brigade from General Stephen D. Ramseur's division at Stephenson's Depot, West Virginia. Confederate losses are 73 dead, 130 wounded, and 267 captured, along with four cannon. Meanwhile, General Jubal A. Early continues withdrawing up the Shenandoah Valley and finally settles in at Strasburg.

No sooner does the 20,000-man Army of the Cumberland under General George H. Thomas cross Peachtree Creek, Georgia, three miles north of Atlanta, than it is heavily attacked by 19,000 Confederates under the newly appointed general John B. Hood. For this purpose, Hood arrays General Alexander P. Stewart's corps on the left, General William J. Hardee's line in the center, and General Benjamin F. Cheatham's corps on the right. However, Cheatham proves slow in getting into position, and the Confederate attack does not materialize until 4:00 P.M., giving the Federals ample time to prepare defenses. Fighting begins on the Union left, where two of Cheatham's divisions charge General John Newton's division, IV Corps. Despite turning Newton's left and taking some headway, the Southerners are repulsed gradually by heavy artillery fire. In the center, Stewart directs General Einfield S. Featherston's division into a gap between the Union divisions of General John W. Geary and William T. Ward. Fighting proves fierce, and the 26th Wisconsin, surrounded on a hillside, scavenges ammunition from Confederate fallen to hold their position. Eventually, a Union countercharge across the line throws Featherston back to his original positions.

The hardest fighting of the day occurs on the right where General Edward C. Walthall's Confederates penetrate the division of Generals Alpheus S. Williams and John W. Geary, XX Corps. Infiltrating along numerous ravines, they manage to surround Geary on three sides and press him hard for three hours. The 61st Ohio, which loses half its strength, shoots down charging Confederates within 10 feet of its line, but holds fast. A Southern breakthrough briefly threatening the flank and rear of General Joseph F. Knipe's division also is repelled by artillery fire. His gambit having failed, Hood suspends the action at 7:00 P.M. and orders a retreat.

Peachtree Creek is the first of Hood's highly audacious but ultimately futile attempts to save Atlanta, and it costs him 2,500 men to a Union tally of 1,779 killed, wounded, and missing. Nonetheless, he prepares to regain lost ground as soon as circumstances favor the offensive.

As the Army of the Tennessee under General James B. McPherson closes in on Atlanta, Georgia, from the east, his troops receive enfilade fire from a position known as Bald Hill. General Walter Q. Gresham is wounded, his 4th Division is galled by Confederate artillery, and McPherson orders troops under General Mortimer D. Leggett to storm the strong point on the morrow.

The Union column under General Andrew J. Smith returns to La Grange, Tennessee, and boards trains for Memphis. His campaign against General Nathan B. Forrest is cancelled, ostensibly for want of supplies, and disappoints the Union high command. However, it did keep the supply lines of General William T. Sherman open for several critical weeks as Confederate raiders are forced to regroup.

July 21

WEST: General George Crook's force of 8,500 men occupies Winchester, Virginia, and he dispatches cavalry under General William W. Averell to divine Confederate intentions farther up the Shenandoah Valley.

General James B. McPherson's Union attack Confederate defenders under General Patrick R. Cleburne at Bald Hill outside Atlanta, Georgia. General Mortimer D. Leggett's men go forward covered by intense Union artillery fire and charge up the slopes. Both sides lose about 350 casualties before the Federals stand victorious on the hillcrest, and Cleburne withdraws. The Union now enjoys a vantage point from which artillery fire can rain down on the city.

Unbeknownst to McPherson, General John B. Hood is preparing a massive strike against his Army of the Tennessee. To that end, he orders the corps of General

William J. Hardee to slip carefully out from behind its fortifications in Atlanta, execute a 15-mile night march to Decatur, and place his troops behind the Union flank and rear. Hood is counting on McPherson's lack of a cavalry screen to render Hardee's approach undetectable.

NAVAL: The USS *Prairie Bird* captures the steamer *Union* on the Mississippi River for trading with the enemy.

July 22

POLITICS: President Jefferson Davis orders General Edmund Kirby-Smith to assist the Army of Tennessee under General John B. Hood. In light of the fact that Federal gunboats patrol the Mississippi River, this proves an impossible order to fulfill.

SOUTH: General Edward O. C. Ord officially is made commander of the XVIII Corps, Army of the Potomac.

WEST: General Horatio K. Wright and his VI Corps are withdrawn from the Shenandoah region, and command devolves on General George Crook at Kernstown, Virginia. General Jubal A. Early, with Confederate forces concentrated behind Cedar Creek near Strasburg, welcomes the news and prepares to advance and attack scattered Union forces.

General Lovell H. Rosseau concludes his successful raid into northern Alabama, having destroyed miles of track belonging to the Montgomery and West Point Railroad. His losses are 12 killed and 30 wounded.

General John B. Hood initiates the Battle of Atlanta by ordering General William J. Hardee's corps to strike at the Army of the Tennessee under General James B. McPherson. The Southerners slightly outnumber their opponents by 36,000 to 30,000. However, Hardee errs by not pushing troops far enough to the east, and instead of turning McPherson's left flank, he strikes it head on. The Confederate divisions of Generals William H. T. Walker and William B. Bate then charge the Federals ferociously but are repelled in bloody fighting by the XVI Corps of General Grenville M. Dodge. Tragedy then strikes Union forces as McPherson, reconnoitering ahead of his troops, encounters a Confederate picket and is shot dead. General James A. Logan succeeds him in command just as the veteran divisions of Generals Patrick R. Cleburne and George E. Manley lace into General Francis M. Blair's XVII Corps on the Union right. Fighting is intense and deadly as Southerners exploit a gap in the Federal line, but the bluecoats hold firm until a reserve brigade arrives and forces their assailants back.

The final act to play out occurs at the Union center, when Hood commits General Benjamin F. Cheatham's corps and General Gustavus W. Smith's Georgia militia against Logan's own XV Corps. Charging Confederates briefly penetrate Union lines as far as the Georgia Railroad and then stall in the face of stiffening resistance. Reinforced Federals then storm across the field in turn, driving the graycoats before them and retaking their position. Repulsed across the line, Hood concedes defeat and withdraws.

Hood's second sortie from Atlanta proves another failure that costs him 8,000 casualties. Union losses are 430 killed, 1,559 wounded, and 1,733 missing (3,722). The foremost fatality is the popular and capable McPherson, a close friend and confident of his fellow Ohioan, General William T. Sherman.

Naval: An armed landing party from the USS *Oneida* captures a Confederate cavalry patrol near Fort Morgan, Mobile Bay, Alabama.

July 23
Politics: The Louisiana State Convention adopts a new constitution that outlaws slavery.
South: General Robert E. Lee, wary of a Union thrust north of the James River, orders General Joseph B. Kershaw to move his division to the vicinity of Darbytown, Virginia, and await developments.

General David B. Birney takes charge of the X Corps, Army of the Potomac.
West: Union cavalry under General Alfred N. Duffie skirmish with Confederate troopers two miles south of Winchester, Virginia, amid telling signs of a Southern resurgence in the Shenandoah Valley. In fact, General Jubal A. Early is close at hand with 14,000 men and intends to strike the 8,500-man garrison of General George Crook's VIII Corps at Kernstown. That commander, alerted as to Confederate intentions, assumes defensive positions below the town.
Naval: The USS *Prairie Bird* rescues 350 survivors from the sinking army transport *B. M. Bunyan* after it hits a snag off Shipworth's Landing, Mississippi.

July 24
West: General Jubal A. Early's 14,000 Confederates engage the smaller Union VIII Corps under General George Crook at Kernstown, Virginia. Early, who deploys his army before the town, orders General John C. Breckinridge to outflank the Federals position on their left as Generals John B. Gordon and Gabriel C. Wharton engage them frontally. Crook's 8,500 men initially withstand several charges until they are finally flanked by Breckinridge while struck frontally by Gordon. They bolt from the field and flee up the Valley Pike toward Bunker Hill, West Virginia, 12 miles distant. Crook's defeat would have been much costlier, but Early mishandles his cavalry, and he escapes intact. Union losses are 1,185, including 479 captured; Confederate casualties are unknown but presumably lighter. This easy triumph further emboldens the aggressive Early, who prepares his command for a new invasion of Pennsylvania. Unfortunately for the South, his success also convinces the political establishment in Washington, D.C., that vigorous new leadership is necessary to secure the Shenandoah region.
Naval: Confederate raiders capture and burn the steamer *Kingston* after it grounds near Windmill Point on the Virginia shore.

July 25
West: Confederates under General Jubal A. Early pursue the defeated Federals of General George Crook to Bunker Hill, West Virginia. Heavy rain impedes marching on both sides.

General William T. Sherman orders the cavalry division of General George Stoneman to prepare for an extended raid into the Georgia countryside for the purpose of cutting the Macon and Western Railroad into Atlanta. He also shifts the axis of his approach toward that city from north and east to west, and orders the Army of the Tennessee, now under General John A. Logan, to march from the right wing to the left. Howard's objective is the town of East Point, Georgia, where the Macon and Western and Atlanta and West Point railroads converge. These tracks represent General John B. Hood's last line of supply to and from Atlanta.

General John Pope, commanding the Department of the Northwest, orders a new expedition against hostile Lakota (Sioux).

NAVAL: Acting master's mate John Woodman leads a daring night reconnaissance effort up the Roanoke River to Plymouth, North Carolina, to ascertain the condition of the Confederate ram CSS *Albemarle*. This imposing warship has remained an object of Union consternation for several months and restricts them from committing offensive operations in and around Plymouth.

The USS *Undine* strikes a snag in the Tennessee River near Clifton, Tennessee, and sinks. Beforehand, acting master John L. Bryant removes several cannon and plants them in the city to defend it from marauding Confederates.

July 26

SOUTH: General Ulysses S. Grant orders Generals Winfield S. Hancock and Philip H. Sheridan to mount a large-scale diversionary attack north of the James River to assist the upcoming assault on Petersburg, slated for July 30. He anticipates that the move will force General Robert E. Lee to shift his men northward, thereby weakening the city's defenses in time for Grant's main attack. Furthermore, should the diversion succeed, Sheridan is to take his troopers on a raid against either Richmond, Virginia, or the Virginia Central Railroad.

General Dabney H. Maury is assigned commander of the Confederate Department of Alabama, Mississippi, and East Louisiana.

WEST: General Oliver O. Howard formally succeeds to command the Army of the Tennessee, replacing the slain James B. McPherson. General David S. Stanley then replaces him as head of the IV Corps.

Union cavalry under General George A. Stoneman depart the Atlanta, Georgia, region on a major raid toward Macon. He is ordered to feint east toward Augusta before turning southwest toward his objective at Lovejoy's Station. There, Stoneman will also link up with another mounted division under General Edward M. McCook.

NAVAL: A landing party from the USS *Shokokon* is attacked at Turkey Bend, Virginia, forcing that vessel to come up and lend supporting fire.

July 27

NORTH: General Henry W. Halleck, chief of staff, assumes new responsibilities as head of the Union Middle Department, and the Departments of Washington, West Virginia, and the Susquehanna.

SOUTH: General Winfield S. Hancock moves his II Corps over the James River, closely followed by General Philip H. Sheridan's cavalry division. Advancing on New Market, Virginia, as far as Deep Bottom Run, their column encounters unexpectedly heavy resistance from Confederates under General Cadmus M. Wilcox. Sheridan, meanwhile, shifts troopers northward around Hancock's right flank and begins to probe down the Darbytown Road before running headlong into General

Henry Heth's division. General Ulysses S. Grant subsequently arrives on the scene to supervise Union operations north of the James River.

WEST: Rather than storm the heavily fortified defenses of Atlanta, Georgia, General William T. Sherman resolves on partial siege while dispatching cavalry raids against railroads and other supply lines into the city.

General Joseph Hooker resigns as commander of the XX Corps in a snit and is replaced by General Alpheus S. Williams.

General George Stoneman disregards orders to ride toward Lovejoy's Station, Georgia, and gallops due south, leaving General Kenner Garrard and 2,000 troopers to hold Flat Rock. Stoneman hopes to score a spectacular coup by liberating thousands of Union prisoners held at Macon and Andersonville.

SOUTHWEST: Confederate Cherokees under General Stand Watie and Texas cavalry under Colonel Richard M. Gano capture a small Union outpost near Fort Smith, Arkansas.

NAVAL: The Federal tugs *Belle, Martin,* and *Hoyt* are fitted with spar torpedoes off New Bern, North Carolina, which are intended for use against any Confederate ironclads in that vicinity.

Union boat crews secretly slip into Mobile Bay, Alabama, at night, and begin to mark Confederate torpedo fields with buoys.

July 28

SOUTH: As Union forces under General Winfield S. Hancock and Philip H. Sheridan continue probing Confederate lines along the Darbytown Road, Virginia, General Joseph B. Kershaw's Confederates surprise and charge the Union troopers. Sheridan's force dismounts and repulses the attack, and they seize 300 prisoners and two battle flags. General Ulysses S. Grant, however, views Southern defenses in the vicinity as impenetrable, and he orders Hancock and Sheridan withdrawn back to the Petersburg lines. Three days of fighting cost the Union 334 casualties.

WEST: General Jubal A. Early dispatches 2,500 cavalry under General John McCausland with orders to seize Chambersburg, Pennsylvania. He is then to demand money and gold from the inhabitants or burn the village to the ground.

General Oliver O. Howard and the Army of the Tennessee advance on East Point, Georgia, determined to sever the last remaining rail lines into Atlanta. But Confederate general John B. Hood divines Howard's intent and tries to stay an elaborate ambush by dispatching the corps of Generals Stephen D. Lee and Alexander P. Stewart to hit the Union left flank near Ezra Church and roll it up. The Southerners advance as ordered, but instead of hitting Howard's flank, they mistakenly veer into the front of General John A. Logan's VX Corps. The tactically astute Logan barricades his men at right angles to Howard's line and is strongly positioned to resist an attack. Lee nonetheless commits his men to charge and is beaten off bloodily three times. Stewart then adds his command to the fray and likewise is defeated. By the time the Confederates depart Ezra Church, they have lost upward of 5,000 men to a Union tally of only 562. The battle did stop Union forces from severing Atlanta's supply line, but it so depletes the Army of Tennessee that General John B. Hood is hereafter forced on the defensive.

Confederate cavalry under General Joseph Wheeler attack and defeat Union troopers under General Kenner Garrard at Flatshoals, Georgia, forcing him to withdraw north.

General Alfred Sully engages a large number of hostile Teton Lakota (Sioux) Indians in their camp at Killdeer Mountain (North Dakota). Sully is looking for remnants of the Santee (Eastern Sioux) warriors who had instigated a bloody uprising in Minnesota two years earlier, especially their notorious chief Inkpaduta. He sought refuge among his Teton brethren, who prepare to give battle rather than surrender him. Sully takes the unusual measure of deploying his 3,000 men in a hollow square and advancing in this formation toward the camp. This walking wall of firepower gradually evicts the Teton from their campsite, and they flee, losing an estimated 150 warriors. Sully sustains five killed and 10 wounded.

SOUTHWEST: Confederate Cherokee under General Stand Watie and Texas cavalry under Colonel Richard M. Gano attack and destroy Union haying operations at Blackburn's Prairie, Indian Territory.

NAVAL: The USS *Agwam* and *Mendota* bombard Confederate artillery at Four Mile Creek on the James River, Virginia.

July 29

NORTH: Confederate cavalry under General John McCausland cross the Potomac River at Cave Spring, west of Williamsport, Maryland, causing a local panic. His progress is somewhat delayed by a small body of Federal troops, whose determined stand enables trains to depart Chambersburg, Pennsylvania, with valuable supplies and equipment.

SOUTH: With an explosive-laden tunnel successfully completed beneath Confederate lines outside Petersburg, Virginia, General Ambrose E. Burnside prepares General Edward Ferrero's division of African Americans to charge into the breech following its detonation. Burnside, however, is stopped by Generals Ulysses S. Grant and George Gordon Meade, who feel they might be accused of sacrificing black troops if the scheme backfires. Burnside thereupon orders one of his three untrained, white divisions into line. Lots are drawn, and it falls on General James H. Ledlie to spearhead the assault.

WEST: Union cavalry under General Edward M. McCook seize Jonesboro, Georgia, and begin to tear up track and demolish rolling stock.

NAVAL: The USS *Whitehead* escorts army steamers *Thomas Coyler* and *Massasoit* up the Chowan River, North Carolina, capturing the Confederate steamer *Arrow* en route.

July 30

NORTH: A force of 2,500 Confederate cavalry under General John McCausland occupies Chambersburg, Pennsylvania, at 5:30 A.M. McCausland then rouses the inhabitants out of bed and demands either $100,000 in gold or $500,00 in cash to compensate for houses previously burned in the Shenandoah Valley. When the residents fail to produce the amount demanded, Southerners, somewhat abetted by liquor, systematically begin to fire the town. By early afternoon, 550 houses smolder in ruins, with 3,000 people homeless. McCausland then gallops off toward McConnellsburg. The damage inflicted amounts to $1.6 million.

SOUTH: At 3:30 A.M., the "Battle of the Crater" unfolds as fuses to an explosive-laden tunnel dug beneath Confederate lines at Petersburg are lit. They fail to explode as planned, so volunteers are sent back down the shaft to relight them. At 4:45 A.M., the ground beneath Elliott's Salient erupts furiously, destroying an artillery emplacement and killing 278 South Carolinian troops. The Union forces, equally stunned, pause for 15 minutes before charging into the smoking crater, measuring 170 feet long, 80 feet wide, and 30 feet deep. But General James H. Ledlie absents himself from the proceedings, and his advance stalls at the bottom of the pit. Confederate forces, recovering from the shock, quickly rush reinforcements to the threatened point and shoot downward into the milling, leaderless Federals. General Edward Ferrero's African-American division is then committed to the fray and is repelled bloodily at the crater's rim by Confederates under General William Mahone. By 1:00 P.M., the attack, a disastrous failure, is called off. Union losses amount to 504 killed, 1,881 wounded, and 1,413 missing (3,798), while the Southerners suffer 361 killed, 727 injured, and 403 missing (1,491). Grant himself calls it "the saddest affair I ever witnessed in the war."

WEST: General Henry W. Slocum becomes commander of the Union XX Corps in Georgia.

Union cavalry under General Edward M. McCook are defeated by General Joseph Wheeler's troopers at Newman, Georgia. Surrounded by five enemy brigades, McCook orders his men to cut their way through enemy lines and regroup north of the Chattahoochee River. This desperate maneuver succeeds, although Union losses include 500 men, their pack train, and two cannon.

General George Stoneman's cavalry engage 2,500 Confederates and Georgia militia outside Macon, Georgia. The Kentucky troopers under his command charge the rebel barricades and are repulsed. But no further attacks are mounted as the enlistment period for these volunteers is about to expire and they are far more interested in surviving than fighting. Disgusted, Stoneman has little recourse but to abandon plans to liberate Union prisoners at Andersonville and spurs his command south toward Pensacola, Florida.

SOUTHWEST: Confederate forces reoccupy Brownstown, Texas.

Confederate Cherokee under General Stand Watie and Texas cavalry under Colonel Richard M. Gano sack and destroy a Fort Smith commissary post, absconding with $130,000 worth of food and clothing.

NAVAL: A landing party from the USS *Potomska* captures and wrecks two Confederate saltworks on the Black River, Georgia. However, the men are hotly pursued by Confederates, and only the presence of their rapid-fire Spencer carbines prevents their capture.

July 31

NORTH: General John McCausland's Confederate cavalry occupy Hancock, Maryland, from which he demands $30,000 and cooked rations. The men then ride onto Bevansville for the evening.

WEST: General George Stoneman's cavalry column departs the outskirts of Macon, Georgia, and attempts circling around the city to cross the Ocmulgee River. He advances as far as Hillsboro before being set upon by General Alfred Iverson and three brigades of Confederate troopers near Sunshine Church. Stoneman tries fighting his way out of encirclement but ultimately surrenders with 700 men. However, brigades under Colonels Horace Capron and Silas Adams cut themselves free and gallop off with Colonel's William C. P. Breckinridge's Confederates giving chase. Stoneman's ambitious raid is the biggest cavalry fiasco of the war and nearly paralyzes General William T. Sherman's mounted arm for several weeks.

NAVAL: With the assistance of the pump steamer *Little Champion,* the USS *Undine* is refloated on the Tennessee River, repaired, and gradually pressed back into service.

August 1

NORTH: General Philip H. Sheridan is chosen to head the Army of the Shenandoah with the specific goal of defeating Confederate forces under General Jubal A. Early.

Confederate cavalry under General John McCausland ride through Cumberland, Maryland, skirmish with Union forces under General Benjamin F. Kelley en route, and then settle in near Old Town for the evening.

WEST: Fighting continues between the mounted forces of Generals Napoleon B. Buford and Joseph O. Shelby at Bardstown and New Haven, Kentucky.

Union artillery commences a protracted bombardment of Atlanta, Georgia.

A Union cavalry column under Colonels Horace Capron and Silas Adams advances toward Athens, Georgia, intending to take the town by storm, but they abandon the attempt after being misled by a guide. The two columns then separate and ride on, hotly pursued by Colonel William C. P. Breckinridge's Confederate troopers.

Union cavalry under General Alfred Pleasonton overrun several guerrilla camps near Independence, Missouri.

August 2

NORTH: General John McCausland's Confederate cavalry column disperses a Union artillery detachment and captures Old Town, Maryland, astride the Potomac River. They then cross the river and set up an encampment at Springfield, West Virginia.

SOUTH: Union forces under General Edward R. S. Canby begin a concerted advance on Mobile, Alabama, while General Gordon Granger commands troops landing in Mobile Bay.

SOUTHWEST: Confederate Cherokee under General Stand Watie and Texas cavalry under Colonel Richard M. Gano briefly shell Fort Smith, Arkansas.

NAVAL: A landing party of 115 Union sailors under Commander George M. Colvocoresses of the USS *Saratoga* raids a Confederate coastal guard meeting at McIntosh Court House, Georgia, and returns with 26 captives and 22 horses.

Confederate agents abandon attempts to sail the CSS *Rappahannock* out of French waters as the government will allow only a 35-man crew.

August 3

NORTH: General Jubal A. Early's Confederates withdraw from Maryland and back into West Virginia.

General David Hunter dispatches 1,500 Union cavalry under General William W. Averell from West Virginia into Maryland to find and defeat Confederate raiders under General John McCausland.

A Union cavalry column under Colonel Horace Capron encamps at Jug Tavern, Georgia, where it is suddenly attacked at dawn by Confederate troopers under Colonel William C. P. Breckinridge. The routed Federals hastily scamper across a nearby bridge until it collapses into Mulberry Creek, drowning scores of men and horses. Union losses are estimated at 250.

SOUTH: General Gordon Granger lands 1,300 Union troops on Dauphin Island, Alabama, but fails to storm Fort Gaines at the entrance of Mobile Bay. He spends the next two days building artillery emplacements for a siege.

WEST: General Andrew J. Smith is dispatched on another expedition to Columbus, Mississippi, against the ever-troublesome General Nathan B. Forrest.

NAVAL: The USS *Miami* bombards Confederate artillery positions at Wilcox's Landing, Virginia.

Armed Union boats make a final nighttime foray into Mobile Bay, Alabama, marking Confederate torpedo fields with buoys and disabling them when practical.

August 4

WEST: Confederate cavalry under General John McCausland attack part of the Baltimore and Ohio Railroad at New Creek, West Virginia, but they are repulsed. They then ride to a new encampment at nearby Moorefield to rest their mounts.

General William T. Sherman, pursuant to a strategy of circling Atlanta, Georgia, from the west, orders General John M. Schofield's Army of the Ohio, reinforced by General John M. Palmers XIV Corps, Army of the Tennessee, to storm Confederate earthworks near Utoy Creek. Success here places him within two miles of the strategic railroad junction at East Point.

General Sterling Price receives permission from Confederate authorities to prepare an invasion of Missouri for the early fall.

NAVAL: The USS *Miami* and *Osceola* attack and disperse Confederate artillery gathered near Harrison's Landing on the James River, Virginia.

August 5

POLITICS: Radical Republicans Benjamin Wade and Henry W. Davis denounce President Abraham Lincoln for vetoing the bill they have sponsored and openly campaign to depose him. "The authority of Congress is paramount and must be respected," they insist.

NORTH: Union cavalry under General William W. Averell is apprised of recent Confederate activity at New Creek, West Virginia, and stealthily begin to approach their encampment at Moorefield.

SOUTH: Confederate forces abandon Fort Powell, Mobile Bay, Alabama, once Federal warships slip past and begin to bombard it from behind.

WEST: General John M. Schofield maneuvers the Army of the Ohio to assault Confederate defenses at Utoy Creek, Georgia, but a command dispute with General John M. Palmer, XIV Corps, delays his projected assault until the following day. During the impasse, General William B. Bate's Confederate division strengthens his position with abatis and earthworks.

NAVAL: At 6:00 A.M., Admiral David G. Farragut launches an all-out attack to capture Mobile Bay, Alabama. He approaches his objective with the ironclad monitors USS *Tecumseh, Manhattan, Winnebago,* and *Chickasaw* in the van while his remaining 14 wooden warships are lashed together in pairs, with smaller vessels tied on the outside and away from Confederate defenses. The armada then approaches the bay, and heavy cannon at Fort Morgan commence to shell them as they pass by. Disaster then suddenly strikes when *Tecumseh* detonates a torpedo and sinks 30 seconds later with the loss of 90 crewmen. *Brooklyn,* the next lead vessel, suddenly reverses its engine and backs up, causing the squadron to jam up dangerously. An anxious Farragut, lashed to the rigging of his screw sloop *Hartford,* inquires what the problem is, and *Brooklyn*'s captain responds "torpedoes!" "Damn the torpedoes, full speed ahead!" is Farragut's immortal (and apocryphal) reply, so *Hartford* plunges directly into the Confederate minefield. The fleet immediately closes up and steams ahead while, miraculously, no other vessels are lost.

Having overcome one major obstacle, Farragut next confronts the large Confederate ram CSS *Tennessee* under Admiral James Buchanan. *Tennessee* sorties against the entire Union fleet, escorted by smaller warships *Selma, Morgan,* and *Gaines,* and tries ramming the *Hartford.* Farragut easily dodges his slower adversary while all 17 ships of the squadron pummel it with intense cannon fire. In short order, the *Gaines* sinks, *Selma* surrenders, and *Morgan* beaches itself. This leaves *Tennessee* alone to face the entire Union fleet, and Buchanan orders it under the protection of Fort Morgan's guns to effect repairs.

Battle of Mobile Bay August 5, 1864 Painting by Xanthus Smith, 1890 *(U.S. Naval Academy Museum)*

By 9:00 A.M., Buchanan judges the battle lost but refuses to surrender. He then leads the *Tennessee* out on a suicide mission against Farragut's squadron in the bay. Faster Union vessels quickly surround the lumbering ram as it fails to strike several targets, while rifled cannon fire blasts away its smokestack and steering chains. His ship now adrift and armor plates buckling under the weight of Union ordnance, the seriously wounded Buchanan finally lowers his flag at 10:00 A.M. By dint of daring and expert seamanship, Farragut wins his second decisive gamble of the Civil War and closes the Confederacy's last remaining port on the Gulf Coast. Union losses are 145 killed and 170 wounded while the defeated Southerners report 12 dead and 20 injured.

August 6

SOUTH: Responding to pleas from General Jubal A. Early in the Shenandoah Valley, General Robert E. Lee dispatches the infantry division of Joseph B. Kershaw and the cavalry division of General Fitzhugh Lee from Richmond, Virginia, as reinforcements. With them, Lee hopes that Early may blunt the new Federal offensive developing against him.

WEST: General Philip H. Sheridan arrives at Harper's Ferry, West Virginia, to assume command of the Army of the Shenandoah. This consists of the VI Corps under General Horatio G. Wright, the VIII Corps under General George Crook, and the XIX Corps under General William H. Emory, and three cavalry divisions under General Alfred T. A. Torbert—a total of 43,000 men.

General William W. Averell passes through Romney, West Virginia, en route to Confederate encampments near Moorefield, taking great precautions to seize all outlying pickets first. Once positioned, he intends to attack the main camp directly while sending a detachment to strike from the east. Averell rests his horses for several hours and then begins to advance on his quarry, covered by early morning darkness.

General John M. Schofield attacks Utoy Creek, Georgia, to seize the nearby railroad junction at East Point. He dispatches two brigades under Generals Jacob B. Cox and Milo Hascall at 10:00 A.M., but the former is pinned down by enemy fire from across Sandtown Road. Cox then rallies and charges three times but is repulsed with heavy losses. On his right, Hascall enjoys better success driving the Southerners back, but fighting ceases after nightfall and a heavy rain.

General Frederick Steele launches a campaign from Little Rock, Arkansas, intending to defeat General Joseph O. Shelby near the Little Red River.

NAVAL: The Confederate raider CSS *Tallahassee* under Lieutenant John T. Wood slips out of Wilmington, North Carolina, commencing a three-week cruise that nets 33 Union vessels.

The much-feared Confederate ram CSS *Albemarle* departs Plymouth, North Carolina, and steams down the Roanoke River, anchoring near its mouth.

The ironclad monitor USS *Chickasaw* commences to bombard Fort Powell, Mobile Bay, Alabama, forcing the garrison under Colonel James M. Williams to evacuate the post. The rest of the Union fleet unleashes a tremendous bombardment against nearby Fort Gaines, which remains defiant. This is despite the fact that Union monitors sail to within point-blank range of its walls, firing 100-pound shells.

August 7
NORTH: General Ulysses S. Grant's choice of 33-year-old General Philip H. Sheridan to lead the newly designated Army of the Shenandoah causes concern for President Abraham Lincoln and Secretary of War Edwin M. Stanton. Both fear that the youthful Sheridan is too inexperienced for so delicate a mission, but Grant reiterates his desire to have this aggressive, headstrong firebrand at the helm.

SOUTH: Having weathered a terrific bombardment from land and sea forces, Colonel Charles D. Anderson receives a flag of truce sent by Admiral David G. Farragut and agrees to surrender Fort Gaines, Mobile Bay, Alabama, on the morrow.

WEST: Union cavalry under General William W. Averell surprise General Bradley T. Johnson's Confederate troopers at Moorefield, West Virginia. The brigade of Major Thomas Gibson gallops through their camp before dawn, routing them and then pursues fleeing survivors of the 8th Virginia Cavalry into the Potomac River. Averell's second brigade under Colonel William H. Powell shortly after strikes General John McCausland's camp in identical fashion, overcomes determined resistance from the 21st Virginia Cavalry, and routs the Southerners. Averell reports taking 420 captives, 400 horses, three flags, and four cannon. Union losses are nine killed and 32 wounded. Johnson subsequently accuses McCausland of neglect of duty, although an inquiry is never held. The defeat also reinforces General Jubal A. Early's perception that his mounted arm is of limited use.

General John M. Schofield moves his Army of the Ohio forward from Utoy Creek to the important rail junction at East Point, Georgia, and beholds extensive Confederate fortifications there. He then declines attacking and orders his men to fortify positions along Sandtown Road. Fighting in the vicinity costs the Union 306 casualties while the Confederates incur less than 100.

August 8
SOUTH: Colonel Charles D. Anderson formally surrenders Fort Gaines, Mobile Bay, Alabama, following a prolonged naval bombardment. The victorious Union fleet then replenishes its ammunition and assumes bombardment positions off Fort Morgan, the final domino to fall.

NAVAL: The USS *Violet* ran aground on a bar off Cape Fear River, North Carolina, and is burned by its crew.

August 9
SOUTH: General Jefferson C. Davis assumes command of the Union XIV Corps in Georgia.

Colonel John S. Mosby routs a larger Union detachment at Fairfax Station, Virginia.

Confederate saboteurs detonate a 12-pound torpedo on a large Union transport at City Point, Virginia. The ensuing explosion ignites chain reactions of stored ordnance throughout the city, showering General Ulysses S. Grant with debris. Casualties total 43 killed and 126 injured.

Federal troops begin formally investing Fort Morgan, Mobile Bay, Alabama, ringing it with cannon and warships, but General Richard L. Page, a former shipmate of Admiral David G. Farragut, refuses to surrender.

WEST: General Philip H. Sheridan marshals his forces for a push from Halltown and Harper's Ferry, West Virginia, down the Shenandoah Valley. His objective is the camp of General Jubal A. Early's Army of the Valley, encamped at Bunker Hill, West Virginia, only 12 miles distant.

General William T. Sherman, having dragged several large Parrott rifles and siege guns up to Bald Hill, Georgia, orders them to begin to bombard Atlanta and its environs. For the next two weeks Union cannon rain down 5,000 shots a day on the beleaguered inhabitants, as much to undermine their morale as to cause damage.

NAVAL: The USS *Catskill* attacks and sinks the Confederate blockade-runner *Prince Albert* off Fort Moultrie, South Carolina.

Admiral David G. Farragut's squadron intensely bombards Fort Morgan, Mobile Bay, Alabama, after General Richard L. Page refuses to surrender. The newly captured CSS *Tennessee* is also towed into position by the USS *Port Royal,* now manned by Union gunners. The fleet is assisted further by 3,000 infantry under General Gordon Granger, who contribute land artillery and sniper fire to the barrage.

August 10

WEST: General Philip H. Sheridan leads Union forces out of Harper's Ferry and into the Shenandoah Valley as General Jubal A. Early falls back on Winchester, Virginia.

Unable to overcome Union superiority in numbers, General John B. Hood dispatches 4,500 crack cavalry under General Joseph Wheeler from Covington, Georgia. There he is to disrupt General William T. Sherman's supply lines north of Atlanta, Georgia, and then wreak havoc throughout eastern Tennessee. Hood anticipates that by sabotaging the critical Macon and Western Railroad, Federal forces will be obliged to either fall back or face starvation.

NAVAL: The Confederate raider CSS *Tallahassee* under Commander John T. Wood takes and burns six Union prizes within 80 miles of Sandy Hook, New Jersey.

The transport steamer *Empress* is attacked by a Confederate battery on the Mississippi River at Gaines Landing, Arkansas. The Federal gunboat USS *Romeo* eventually arrives, silences the Confederates, and tows the hapless vessel to safety. The Southerners are defeated, but both vessels incur serious damage. *Empress* alone sustains 63 hits.

August 11

WEST: Confederates under General Jubal A. Early fall back on Cedar Creek, Virginia, as invigorated Union forces under General Philip H. Sheridan pursue.

NAVAL: Confederate batteries at Gaines's Landing, Arkansas, engage the Federal gunboats USS *Prairie Bird* and *Romeo* in a lengthy exchange before being silenced.

August 12

WEST: Continual skirmishing erupts between the armies of Generals Philip H. Sheridan and Jubal A. Early along Cedar Creek, as neither side feels sufficiently strong to initiative offensive action.

NAVAL: The Confederate raider CSS *Tallahassee* under Commander John T. Wood takes and burns six more prizes off the New York coast.

August 13
SOUTH: On learning that large Southern reinforcements are being transferred to the Shenandoah theater from Deep Bottom Run, Virginia, General Ulysses S. Grant orders General Winfield S. Hancock's II Corps, the X Corps of General David B. Birney, and the 2nd Cavalry Division under General David M. Gregg to strike Confederate defenses there. If successful, Union troops can break through 10 miles southeast of Richmond.

The 43rd Virginia Cavalry under Colonel John S. Mosby captures Berryville, Virginia, along with a Union supply train, 500 horses, 200 head of cattle, and several prisoners.

General John G. Parke is appointed commander of the IX Corps, Army of the Potomac.

WEST: Skirmishing commences between the cavalry forces of General Joseph A. Mower and Nathan B. Forrest at Hurricane Creek, Mississippi.

General Alfred Pleasonton conducts large-scale antiguerrilla actions against William C. Quantrill's raiders in La Fayette, Saline, and Howard counties, Missouri.

NAVAL: The Confederate raider CSS *Tallahassee* under Commander John T. Wood takes and burns the Union schooner *Lammont Du Pont* and the bark *Glenavon* a few miles from New York City, and a greatly alarmed commercial sector appeals to Secretary of the Navy Gideon Welles for navy ships to destroy "the pirate."

The USS *Agwam* trades fire with several Confederate batteries along Forty Mile Creek on the James River.

A Confederate squadron consisting of CSS *Virginia II, Richmond, Fredericksburg, Hampton, Drewry,* and *Nansemond* shells Union army positions at Dutch Gap, Virginia, for 12 hours before withdrawing back up the James River. The damage inflicted is slight.

August 14
SOUTH: General Winfield S. Hancock moves his II Corps, General David B. Birney's X Corps, and the 2nd Cavalry Division over the James River toward Deep Bottom Run, Virginia. However, his initial probes are repulsed with 500 casualties, indicating that Confederate defenses are still fully manned.

WEST: General Richard H. Anderson arrives at Fort Royal, Virginia, with a Confederate infantry and cavalry division, prior to entering the Shenandoah Valley. General Philip H. Sheridan's lines of communication now possibly are threatened, so he orders General Wesley Merritt's cavalry division to reconnoiter Fort Royal and ascertain enemy strength and intentions. Meanwhile, the bulk of Union forces withdraw north of Halltown in the direction of Harper's Ferry, West Virginia.

Confederate cavalry under General Joseph Wheeler attack and destroy tracks belonging to the Western and Atlantic Railroad south of Dalton, Georgia. However, he is unable to overpower the town's Union garrison, so then he gallops north into Tennessee for similar work.

Naval: The Confederate raider CSS *Tallahassee* under Commander John T. Wood captures and sinks the Union ship *James Littlefield* in the Atlantic.

August 15

South: General David B. Birney maneuvers his X Corps down the Charles City Road, intending to attack Fussell's Mills, Virginia, on the following day. General Gouverneur K. Warren also marches his V Corps from the Union right flank to the left for an eventual strike against the strategic Weldon Railroad.

The army of General William T. Sherman continues advancing southwest of Atlanta, Georgia.

Union forces under General John P. Hatch raid the Florida Railroad near Gainesville, Florida.

General Richard Taylor is appointed commander of the Confederate Department of Alabama, Mississippi, and East Louisiana.

West: Union and Confederate forces skirmish at Cedar Creek, Virginia, and once General Philip H. Sheridan withdraws toward Winchester, General Jubal A. Early follows. Sheridan is instructed by General Ulysses S. Grant to act cautiously, as the Confederates opposite him are believed to number 40,000 and, furthermore, given President Abraham Lincoln's precarious political future, an embarrassing defeat must be avoided at all costs. Early, however, misinterprets this behavior as timidity on Sheridan's part, a miscalculation for which he pays dearly.

Naval: The Confederate raider CSS *Tallahassee* under Commander John T. Wood captures and scuttles six more Union schooners off the New England coast.

The USS *Niagara* seizes the British steamer *Georgia* off the coast of Portugal. That vessel, previously serving the Confederacy as CSS *Georgia,* had been sold to British merchants and is now confiscated on account of its prior activity. A prize court in Boston subsequently condemns the vessel.

August 16

South: General David B. Birney's X Corps attacks Confederate positions along the Darbytown Road and achieves a minor breakthrough at Fussell's Mills. However, he lacks manpower to exploit his success, and a swift Southern counterattack by General Charles W. Field seals the breach. Union casualties amount to 2,000, the Confederates half that amount.

West: Union cavalry under General Wesley Merritt engage General Richard H. Anderson's Confederate division at Front Royal, Virginia. A swirling saber melee erupts between the Southern troopers of General William C. Wickham and Union cavalry under General Thomas C. Devlin once Confederates ford the Shenandoah River. A decisive charge by Devlin sends them scampering back across after he seizes two flags and 139 prisoners. At nearby Guard Hill, a Confederate brigade under General William T. Wofford receives a dismounted attack by General George A. Custer's cavalry brigade. The bluecoats, armed with rapid-fire Spencer carbines, gradually outgun and drive the defenders from the hillside, and they break and run across the river in a panic. Merritt thus confirms the presence of strong Confederate forces at Front Royal, a fact inducing General Philip H. Sheridan to continue retreating in the direction of Harper's Ferry, West Virginia.

Colonel John S. Mosby surprises and defeats a Union force at Kernstown and Charlestown, West Virginia.

NAVAL: The Confederate raider CSS *Tallahassee* under Commander John T. Wood captures and burns four more prizes off the New England coast.

The USS *Mount Washington, Delaware, Mackinaw,* and *Canonicus* of the James River Squadron support Federal troops as they advance from Dutch Gap, Virginia.

An armed party from the *USS Saratoga* again raids McIntosh County, Georgia, destroying a bridge and a saltworks and seizing 100 prisoners.

August 17

WEST: General Jubal A. Early attacks the Union rear guard at Winchester, Virginia, as General Philip H. Sheridan continues to retrograde toward Berryville.

NAVAL: The Confederate raider CSS *Tallahassee* under Commander John T. Wood arrives at Halifax, Nova Scotia, to take on a supply of coal. Mortimer M. Jackson, the U.S. consul present, protests its arrival and alerts Commander George A. Steven of the USS *Pontoosuc* at Eastport, Maine.

August 18

NORTH: General Ulysses S. Grant again refuses Confederate requests to resume prisoner exchanges. This deprives the South of critically needed manpower, but it also prolongs the hardships of Union captives languishing in poorly maintained Confederate prisons. In truth, the South can barely feed its own soldiers, let alone thousands of prisoners.

SOUTH: Confederate forces attack General Winfield S. Hancock's II Corps at Deep Bottom Run, Virginia, and are repelled with losses. But General Ulysses S. Grant remains convinced that Confederates defenses north of the James River have not been depleted, and he recalls Hancock's expedition back across the river to Petersburg. Operations in this vicinity cost the Union 2,901 killed, wounded, and captured, to a Southern tally of about 1,500. The seven-day foray does, however, prevent General Robert E. Lee from dispatching additional reinforcements into the Shenandoah Valley.

At 4:00 A.M., General Gouverneur K. Warren's V Corps attacks and captures Globe Tavern and portions of Weldon Railroad outside Petersburg, Virginia. This move threatens to extend Union siege lines around the city and force the Confederates to defend more ground with fewer troops. But General Pierre G. T. Beauregard, commanding at Petersburg, quickly dispatches General Henry Heth's division to slash at Warren's left flank. Heth accordingly attacks out of dense woods around 2:00 P.M., driving the division of General Romeyn B. Ayres before him. Timely Union reinforcements from Generals Samuel W. Crawford and Lysander Cutler's divisions suddenly arrive and drive the Confederates back. Ayres loses about 900 men in heavy fighting. During the night, both sides consolidate their positions and muster additional troops. But General Robert E. Lee cannot allow the Weldon line to be cut, and he prepares to take it back by force.

WEST: General Jubal A. Early harasses General Philip H. Sheridan's withdrawal to Harper's Ferry, West Virginia, by striking at Opequon Creek, Virginia.

A force of 4,000 Union cavalry under General Hugh J. Kilpatrick is dispatched by General William T. Sherman to raid the Atlanta and West Point Railroad at Fairburn, Georgia. That done, he is to spur his command toward Lovejoy's Station for similar work against the Macon and Western Railroad, 20 miles southeast of Atlanta.

August 19

SOUTH: General Gouverneur K. Warren's V Corps at Weldon Station is reinforced by three divisions of the IX Corps, plus General Gershom Mott's division from II Corps. These arrive and deploy in time to meet a large Confederate assault of several brigades orchestrated by General Ambrose P. Hill, maneuvering to recapture the Weldon Railroad at all costs. Due to the thickness of the woods, Confederates under General William Mahone steal to within a few yards of the Union right, then rush fiercely, and nearly collapse it. General Samuel W. Crawford and many of his men fall captive before men of the XI Corps arrive, counterattack, and force Mahone back into the woods. At the center, General Romeyn B. Ayres spars with General Henry Heth inconclusively until the Southerners finally withdraw. By nightfall, Warren's position has been heavily jostled in several places, but he retains control of the Weldon Railroad. Union losses total 198 killed, 1,105 wounded, and 3,152 missing (4,455); Confederate casualties are estimated at 1,600.

WEST: The armies of General Philip H. Sheridan and Jubal A. Early continue skirmishing in the vicinity of Winchester, West Virginia.

Union cavalry under General Hugh J. Kilpatrick arrive at Jonesboro, Georgia, a major supply depot, and burn quantities of stores and equipment before pushing on to their next major objective at Lovejoy's Station.

NAVAL: The Confederate raider CSS *Tallahassee* under Commander John T. Wood departs Halifax, Nova Scotia, and sets sail for Wilmington, North Carolina.

August 20

SOUTH: Fighting dies down along the Weldon Railroad as the V Corps of General Gouverneur K. Warren entrenches and strengthens its position against possible Confederate attacks.

Federal forces operating near Charleston, South Carolina, burn the town of Legareville.

WEST: General Hugh J. Kilpatrick's cavalry column gallops into Lovejoy's Station, Georgia, but has only begun to tear up tracks belonging to the Macon and Western Railroad when it is attacked by Confederate cavalry under General William H. Jackson. Stiff fighting ensues, after which the Union troops break through and escape to rejoin William T. Sherman's main army near Atlanta.

NAVAL: The USS *Pontoosuc* sorties from Eastport, Maine, to Halifax, Nova Scotia, but it arrives seven hours too late to stop the Confederate raider CSS *Tallahassee*. Commander John T. Wood, meanwhile, captures and burns the Union brig *Roan* in the North Atlantic.

August 21

SOUTH: General Robert E. Lee abandons the Weldon Railroad outside Petersburg, Virginia, after renewed attacks by General Ambrose P. Hill fail to dislodge Union defenders from Globe Tavern.

General Richard L. Page, commanding Fort Morgan, Mobile Bay, Alabama, destroys his powder supply to preclude any chance hit by Union shells. By this time, no less than 25 army cannon, 16 mortars, and the guns of Admiral David G. Farragut's entire squadron are playing upon his position.

WEST: Union forces under General Philip H. Sheridan successfully withdraw up and out of the Shenandoah Valley to Harper's Ferry, West Virginia. A planned attack by generals Jubal A. Early and Richard H. Anderson miscarries for want of close cooperation.

A surprise raid by 2,000 Confederate cavalry under General Nathan B. Forrest captures Memphis, Tennessee, and the local Union commander, General Cadwallader C. Washburn, only narrowly escapes in his nightclothes. Forrest then resumes raiding Federal supply lines with almost total impunity during the next two months. His success even elicits backhanded praise from Sherman, who refers to him as "that Devil Forrest."

August 22

SOUTH: The weary II Corps of General Winfield S. Hancock is transferred from the front lines at Petersburg to Reams's Station, a quiet sector, to undertake fatigue duties along the Weldon Railroad. The force consists of infantry divisions under General John Gibbon and Nelson A. Miles, and a cavalry division under General David M. Gregg—tough, veteran troops but completely spent by constant fighting.

WEST: Skirmishing continues at Charlestown, West Virginia, as Confederates under General Jubal A. Early continue pressing General Philip H. Sheridan near Harper's Ferry.

NAVAL: An armed party from the USS *Potomsk* raids the Satilla and White rivers, Georgia, taking numerous prisoners and burning supplies.

August 23

POLITICS: President Abraham Lincoln expresses pessimism over his reelection chances, noting "It will be my duty to co-operate with the President elect, as to save the Union between the election and the inauguration, as he will have secured his election on such ground that he cannot possibly save it afterwards."

SOUTH: General Richard I. Page surrenders Fort Morgan, Mobile Bay, Alabama, after two weeks of intensive bombardment; Federal forces now completely control all adjoining waters. Wilmington, North Carolina, remains the only functioning Confederate port.

WEST: Union cavalry under General Hugh J. Kilpatrick, bested by strong Confederates defenses at Lovejoy's Station, rejoin General William T. Sherman's main force outside Decatur, Georgia. Despite grandiose claims, his recent raid against Southern rail lines is another failure.

NAVAL: Armed boats from the USS *Saratoga, T. A. Ward,* and *Braziliera* conduct an unsuccessful raid up the Turtle River, Georgia. As they approach their objective, the army encampment at Bethel fires at them from the shoreline and forces the vessels back downstream.

August 24

SOUTH: General Ambrose P. Hill sorties the Confederate III Corps out of it trenches, intending to strike Union positions at Reams's Station, Virginia.

WEST: Heavy skirmishing continues between the forces of General Frederick Steele and Joseph O. Shelby at Devall's Bluff, Arkansas.

SOUTHWEST: A party of 420 troopers of the 2nd Kansas Cavalry is attacked in camp by 800 Confederate Cherokee under General Stand Watie and 1,200 Texas cavalry under Colonel Richard M. Gano at Gunter's Prairie, Indian Territory. The defenders lose 20 men. Southerners and Indians then ride northwest of Fort Gibson and strike at a 125-man Union force at Flat Rock Ford, killing 40 more.

NAVAL: The USS *Keystone State* and *Gettysburg* capture the Confederate steamer *Lilian* off Wilmington, North Carolina. The vessel subsequently is acquired by the navy and is assigned to the blockading squadron.

The USS *Narcissus* captures the Confederate schooner *Oregon* in Biloxi Bay, Mississippi Sound.

August 25

SOUTH: At 5:00 P.M., Confederates under General Ambrose P. Hill savagely assault the Union II Corps of General Winfield S. Hancock at Reams' Station, Virginia. Hill's 10,000 men initially rebound off divisions commanded by Generals Nelson A. Miles and David M. Gregg, until parts of the former suddenly buckle. Southerners under Generals Henry Heth and Cadmus M. Wilcox then pour through the breech, capturing several cannon and hundreds of prisoners. Worse, when General John Gibbon's division, exhausted from fatigue work, is ordered up to plug the gap, it stumbles badly and likewise runs. Hancock then withdraws from the area covered by elements of General Orlando Wilcox's IX Corps. Union losses in this embarrassing affair totaled 2,372, the vast majority of whom are prisoners. The Confederates, who suffer only 700 casualties, also seize nine cannon, 3,100 small arms, and several horses.

WEST: General Jubal A. Early, confronting entrenched Union forces at Harper's Ferry, West Virginia, bypasses them with a small holding force in place and moves on to Shepherdstown. From there, he intends another invasion of Maryland.

General William T. Sherman, unwilling to storm the defenses of Atlanta, Georgia, and with the whole of his cavalry having failed to cut Confederate supply lines, resolves to throw the weight of his entire army against the Macon and Western Railroad. This is the sole remaining supply route into the city. He then orders six army corps on a circuitous route to Rough and Ready and Jonesboro where they can best sever this strategic link. As a precaution, Sherman also orders the XX Corps to guard his own railroad bridges spanning the Chattahoochee River.

NAVAL: The Confederate raider CSS *Tallahassee* under Commander John T. Wood successfully runs the Union blockade and reaches Wilmington, North Carolina, having seized 31 prizes.

August 26

POLITICS: A convention of African Americans in Philadelphia, Pennsylvania, advance resolutions calling for the commissioning of black military officers.

NORTH: General Jubal A. Early's Confederate army crosses the Potomac into Maryland for a third time and skirmishes with Union forces at Williamsport.

SOUTH: General Edward O. C. Ord assumes temporary control of the Army of the James outside of Richmond, Virginia.

August 27

SOUTH: Near Atlanta, Georgia, General William T. Sherman dispatches Generals Oliver O. Howard and Hugh J. Kilpatrick on a direct march against General John B. Hood's rail lines at Jonesboro. Hood counters by marching the corps of Generals William J. Hardee and Stephen D. Lee to defeat the Union columns before the Macon and Western Railroad can be interdicted.

NAVAL: The USS *Niphon* and *Monticello* run up Masonboro Inlet, North Carolina, destroy a Confederate battery, and they capture numerous arms and supplies.

Ill-health forces Admiral David G. Farragut to request sick leave from the West Gulf Blockading Squadron inside Mobile Bay, Alabama. "I have now been down in this Gulf and the Caribbean Sea nearly five years out of six," he explains, "with the exception of the short time at home last fall, and the last six months have been a severe drain on me, and I want rest, if it is to be had."

August 28

WEST: General Philip H. Sheridan advances from Harper's Ferry, West Virginia, back toward the Shenandoah Valley without opposition.

General William T. Sherman pushes the Army of the Cumberland under General George H. Thomas onto the Montgomery and Atlanta Railroad while General Oliver O. Howard and his Army of the Tennessee advance on Fairburn, Georgia. Meanwhile, the Army of the Ohio under General John M. Schofield moves up to Mount Gilead Church as General Henry W. Slocum's XX Corps defends Union lines around Atlanta. If successful, these movements threaten General John B. Hood's final rail link out of the city, trapping him inside.

General Sterling Price assumes command of divisions under Generals John S. Marmaduke and James F. Fagan at Camden, Arkansas, prior to marching them across the Arkansas River back into Missouri.

August 29

POLITICS: The Democratic National Convention convenes in Chicago, Illinois, where Copperhead Clement L. Vallandigham delivers the keynote address.

WEST: General Philip H. Sheridan orders his men into action at Smithfield Crossing along the Opequon River, brushing aside a small Confederate detachment.

General Sterling Price continues gathering forces at Princeton, Arkansas, for his final attempt at conquering Missouri for the South.

NAVAL: A Confederate torpedo (mine) explodes in Mobile Bay, Alabama, killing five Union sailors and wounding another nine. Admiral David G. Farragut resolves to eliminate all these potential ship-killing weapons before departing.

August 30

POLITICS: The Democratic National Party Convention in Chicago, Illinois, adopts a peace platform demanding an immediate end to hostilities with the South. The

Democratic Party's political platform is virtually the exact mirror opposite of President Abraham Lincoln and the Republicans.

WEST: General George Crook replaces General David Hunter as commander of the Department of West Virginia.

General Oliver O. Howard, commanding the XV, XVI, XVII Corps and Hugh J. Kilpatrick's cavalry division, crosses the Flint River and marches to within one mile of Jonesboro, Georgia. There, he perceives Confederate forces under General William J. Hardee approaching to engage him. In fact, General John B. Hood has ordered Hardee to strike the Union column in concert with General Stephen D. Lee and drive them back across the Flint.

NAVAL: The USS *Fawn* convoys army transports on an unsuccessful expedition up the White River, Arkansas, in search of Confederate raiders under General Joseph O. Shelby.

August 31

POLITICS: The Democratic National Convention at Chicago, Illinois, nominates former general George B. McClellan as its candidate for the presidency and George H. Pendleton of Ohio for vice president.

SOUTH: A force of 20,000 Confederates under General William J. Hardee attack 20,000 Union soldiers of General Oliver O. Howard at Jonesboro, Georgia. The Federals are strongly posted in a semicircle on high ground and enjoy clear fields of fire. Moreover, Hardee experiences considerable difficulty coordinating the action of subordinates, and his battlefield strategy miscarries. Interminable delays ensue before General Patrick R. Cleburne drives toward Northern positions at 3:00 P.M. under a withering fire. General Stephen D. Lee's columns receive similar treatment and are also thrown back. Hardee's piecemeal attacks disintegrate in the face of determined resistance, and he finally withdraws with 2,000 casualties. Howard loses a mere 178.

The Army of the Ohio under General John M. Schofield severs the Macon and Western Railroad between Jonesboro and Atlanta, Georgia, cutting General John B. Hood's final supply line. The city is now doomed.

NAVAL: The British blockade-runner *Mary Bowers* runs aground near Rattlesnake Shoals, Long Island, South Carolina, and is completely wrecked.

September 1

WEST: The Army of the Shenandoah under General Philip H. Sheridan threatens Winchester, Virginia, as skirmishing flares up along Opequon Creek.

General John B. Hood begins to evacuate Atlanta, Georgia, once Union forces cut the Macon and Western Railroad, and he withdraws down the McDonough Road to Lovejoy's Station. There, he is to unite with General William J. Hardee's battered corps. A large ammunition depot unable to be moved in time is also burned and its detonation resonates at General William T. Sherman's headquarters, 15 miles distant.

Confederates under General William J. Hardee are attacked by superior Union forces as the struggle at Jonesboro, Georgia, continues. General William T. Sherman designs an elaborate movement by several corps to ensnare and possibly capture

General William J. Hardee's corps. General Jefferson C. Davis's XIV Corps advances to engage, only to find the Southerners strongly posted behind impassable terrain. Union attacks are then committed on a piecemeal basis, and the Federals sustain considerable losses, but Davis finally penetrates their thin defenses, taking hundreds of prisoners from General Daniel C. Govan's brigade. Hardee promptly counterattacks with General Benjamin Chetham's division, after which the Union advance grounds to a halt. Davis then passively defends his gains as the Confederates, after nightfall, limp safely to Lovejoy's Station. Union losses are 1,274 out of 20,460 present; the Confederates suffer 911 among the 12,661 engaged. Hardee's determined stand grants General John B. Hood's forces sufficient time to slip out from Sherman's ever-constricting noose.

September 2

POLITICS: To offset critical manpower shortages, General Robert E. Lee advises President Jefferson Davis of the need to replace white laborers with African-American slaves, thereby freeing the former for military service.

SOUTH: General Robert E. Lee, severely pressed in the trenches of Petersburg, Virginia, pressures General Jubal A. Early to return the division of General Richard H. Anderson on loan to him.

"So Atlanta is ours and fairly won," General William T. Sherman telegraphs President Abraham Lincoln, as the city surrenders to the XX Corps of General Henry W. Slocum. This single act immediately rekindles Lincoln's sagging election prospects while exerting a distressing effect throughout the South. During the past four months Union forces have sustained 4,423 dead and 22,822 wounded while the Confederates endure 3,044 killed and 18,952 injured. A further 17,335 from both sides have either been captured or simply lost through desertion.

NAVAL: Secretary of the Navy Gideon Welles receives permission to mount a large amphibious assault against Fort Fisher, Wilmington, North Carolina. Success here will close the Confederacy's sole remaining port.

The USS *Naiad* silences a Confederate battery at Rowe's Landing, Louisiana.

September 3

POLITICS: President Abraham Lincoln, in honor of recent victories at Mobile, Alabama, and Atlanta, Georgia, declares the upcoming September 5 to be a day of national celebration and prayer as such events, "call for devout acknowledgment to the Supreme Being in whose hands are the destinies of nations."

WEST: General Philip A. Sheridan, heavily reinforced, advances again on General Richard H. Anderson's division at Berryville, Virginia, defeating the Confederates as they retreat back to their main force at Winchester.

NAVAL: President Abraham Lincoln orders a 100-gun salute at the Washington Navy Yard in honor of Union successes in Mobile Bay, Alabama.

September 4

SOUTH: The latest 60-day bombardment of Fort Sumter, Charleston Harbor, South Carolina, ends after 14,666 rounds are fired. The Confederate flag still wafts defiantly from the rubble.

WEST: General John H. Morgan is killed by Union forces under General Alvan C. Gillem at Greeneville, Tennessee. An additional 100 Confederates die while 75 are captured.

September 5

POLITICS: Voters in Louisiana ratify a new constitution abolishing slavery.

SOUTH: Confederate sergeant and scout George D. Shadburne informs General Wade Hampton of a weakly held Union corral holding 3,000 cattle at Coggins Point, Virginia. Given critical food shortages in the Army of Northern Virginia, this is an opportunity too good to pass on, so Hampton draws up plans to both raid and rustle the herd.

WEST: Skirmishing continues along Opequon Creek, West Virginia, between Union and Confederate forces.

NAVAL: Admiral David D. Porter replaces Admiral Samuel P. Lee as commander of the North Atlantic Blockading Squadron.

The USS *Keystone State* and *Quaker City* capture the British blockade-runner *Elsie* off Wilmington, North Carolina.

September 6

SOUTH: General Richard Taylor is appointed commander of the Confederate Department of Alabama, Mississippi, and East Louisiana.

WEST: A Confederate force numbering 12,000 men under General Sterling Price finally crosses the Arkansas River at Dardanelle, Arkansas, en route to the Missouri state line. When the Union garrison at Little Rock under General Frederick Steele makes no attempt to intercept or impede his march, moves are undertaken in Washington, D.C., to replace him.

NAVAL: The USS *Proteus* captures the British blockade-runner *Ann Louisa* in the Gulf of Mexico.

September 7

SOUTH: General Benjamin F. Butler resumes command of the Army of the James outside of Richmond, Virginia.

Union gunners at Charleston, South Carolina, fire an additional 573 rounds at Fort Sumter without eliciting its surrender.

General William T. Sherman issues Special Field Order No. 67 to the inhabitants of Atlanta, Georgia, requiring 1,600 families to begin to evacuate the city. "War is cruelty and you cannot refine it," he declares to the city's mayor, "When peace does come you may call on me for anything. Then I will share with you the last cracker."

WEST: General Philip H. Sheridan and Jubal A. Early continue jockeying for position as they skirmish near Winchester, West Virginia.

September 8

POLITICS: George B. McClellan accepts the Democratic Party nomination but rejects a peace platform, declaring, "The Union is the one condition of peace—we ask for no more." He nonetheless continues railing against President Abraham Lincoln's handling of the war as a failure.

NAVAL: The USS *Tritonia, Rodolph,* and *Stockdale* escort an army transport against a large Confederate saltworks on the Bonsecours River near Mobile, Alabama. This factory is so extensive that destroying it consumes nearly an entire day.

September 9

SOUTH: To help break the stalemate before Richmond, Virginia, General Ulysses S. Grant urges the newly victorious general William T. Sherman to resume offensive operations as soon as practicable.

WEST: General Joseph Wheeler, having completed his raid against Union supply lines in Tennessee, concludes his mission by crossing the Tennessee River at Florence, Alabama. In fact, his endeavors achieve very little because Union repair crews quickly restore damaged sections of the railways attacked. The net result of Wheeler's raid is actually to deprive General John B. Hood of cavalry during critical phases of the Atlanta campaign.

NAVAL: The USS *Kanawha* reconstitutes the Federal blockade of Brownsville, Texas, eight months after it had been suspended by President Abraham Lincoln. This is due to the recent evacuation of Union forces from the city.

September 10

NAVAL: A landing party from the USS *Wyalusing* raids Elizabeth City on the Pasquotank River, North Carolina, and takes 29 citizens for interrogation concerning the recent burning of the Federal mail steamer *Fawn* in their vicinity. They then learn that the raid had been conducted by crew members of the CSS *Albemarle.*

The USS *Santiago de Cuba* captures the Confederate steamer *A. D. Vance* off Wilmington, North Carolina.

The USS *Augusta Dinsmore* captures the Confederate schooner *John* near Velasco, Texas.

The USS *Magnolia* seizes the Confederate steamer *Matagorda* off Cape San Antonio, Cuba.

September 11

WEST: General William T. Sherman and John B. Hood conclude a 10-day truce to facilitate evacuating civilians and their belongings from Atlanta, Georgia. When petitioned by the inhabitants to reconsider, Sherman declares, "You might as well appeal against the thunderstorm as against these terrible hardships of war." The age of total war manifests with a vengeance.

NAVAL: A naval expedition consisting of the USS *Rodolph, Stockdale,* and army transport *Planter* ascends the Fish River at Mobile Bay, Alabama, for the purpose of seizing a Confederate sawmill. On the return leg of the voyage, the vessels receive fire by sharpshooters lining the riverbanks, but no injuries result.

September 12

NORTH: President Abraham Lincoln and General Ulysses S. Grant express anxiety to General Philip H. Sheridan about the apparent stalemate in the Shenandoah Valley. Lincoln goes so far as to suggest quietly that Sheridan should be reinforced, thus allowing him to strike with overwhelming force.

WEST: General Sterling Price's Confederates cross the White River, Arkansas, and march to Pocahontas to unite with General Joseph O. Shelby's cavalry division. The

Ruins of a train depot, blown up on Sherman's departure from Atlanta, Georgia *(Library of Congress)*

Army of Missouri is then reorganized into three divisions under Shelby, James F. Fagan, and John S. Marmaduke. Price commands 12,000 men and 14 cannon, but only half his force is armed or trained adequately. The Confederates hope to supply themselves with captured Union weapons as they proceed across Missouri in three distinct columns.

September 13
WEST: More skirmishing takes place between outposts at Bunker Hill and Opequon Creek, West Virginia.

September 14

SOUTH: General Wade Hampton and 4,000 Confederate cavalry, guided by Sergeant George D. Shadburne, embark on a major raid to secure Union cattle corralled at Coggins Point, Virginia. To confuse the Federals, they gallop southwest, then southeast, before veering northeast to the Rowanty Creek.

WEST: General Richard H. Anderson again marches his Confederate division out of the Shenandoah Valley to reinforce the defenses of Richmond, Virginia. This transfer manifestly weakens General Jubal A. Early's army, and his withdrawal is observed by Union spy Rebecca Wright.

September 15

SOUTH: General Wade Hampton and 4,000 Confederate cavalry take a circuitous route for 18 miles until they arrive unseen at Blackwater Creek, Virginia, pausing there until nightfall before advancing on Union pickets at Sycamore Church.

WEST: General Ulysses S. Grant rides north from Petersburg to discuss strategy with General Philip H. Sheridan in the Shenandoah Valley.

September 16

SOUTH: At dawn General Wade Hampton's cavalry charge a Union force at Coggin's Point, Virginia, completely dispersing elements of the 1st D.C. Cavalry and the 13th Pennsylvania Cavalry. They then abscond with 2,486 head of cattle—along with 300 prisoners—in a line stretching seven miles long. Hampton, having sustained only 61 casualties, arrives back behind Confederate lines the following day. This is the largest incidence of cattle rustling in history.

WEST: Rebecca West, a Union spy in Winchester, Virginia, observes the departure of General Joseph Kershaw's Confederate cavalry division and 12 cannon from the army of General Jubal A. Early. She immediately relays the intelligence back to General Philip H. Sheridan, then conferring with General Ulysses S. Grant about strategy at Charlestown, West Virginia. News of this transfer of forces back to Richmond induces Sheridan to attack immediately. Grant fully concurs, laconically stating, "Go in," and then departs.

General Nathan B. Forrest leads 4,500 cavalry out of Verona, Mississippi, on another extended raid against General William T. Sherman's communications in middle Tennessee and northern Alabama.

NAVAL: Armed boats from the USS *Ariel* capture 4,000 pounds of cotton near Tampa Bay, Florida.

September 17

POLITICS: Former general John C. Frémont withdraws his name from the election contest and urges a united Republican effort. The former general and explorer fears that a Democratic victory might lead to either recognition of the Confederacy or the resumption of slavery.

WEST: General Jubal A. Early, though outnumbered three to one by nearby Union forces, advances 12,000 men toward Martinsburg, Virginia, to cut the Baltimore and Ohio Railroad.

September 18

WEST: General Jubal A. Early arrays his 12,000 men defensively at Winchester, Virginia. However, his men are scattered with the divisions of Generals Robert E. Rodes and John B. Gordon sent to Martinsburg, whereas General Stephen D. Ramseur's men straddle the Berryville Pike. Early does so out of a misplaced conviction that General Philip H. Sheridan is cautious and dares not attack. But his disjointed, widely dispersed deployment does not go unnoticed and convinces Sheridan to strike in force the following day.

General John M. Schofield orders a cavalry column under General Stephen O. Burbridge to depart Mount Sterling, Kentucky, and mount a diversion against Saltville on the Virginia border. This is undertaken to mask an even larger raid conducted by General Alvan C. Gillem, who intends to strike into southwestern Virginia from east Tennessee.

September 19

POLITICS: President Jefferson Davis advises the governors of South Carolina, North Carolina, Alabama, Georgia, Virginia, and Florida that recent proclamations requiring aliens to either serve in the army or leave are depriving the Confederacy of many skilled workers. Moreover, he insists that "harmony of action between the States and Confederate authorities is essential to the public welfare."

WEST: At 2:00 P.M., General Philip H. Sheridan's army, numbering 35,000 men, attacks the 12,000 Confederates of General Jubal A. Early at Winchester, Virginia. Sheridan hopes to surprise and annihilate the isolated division of Stephen D. Ramseur, but he errs in pushing General William H. Emory's XIX Corps through the defile at Berryville Canyon. This action not only funnels the Union thrust over a narrow front and alerts Ramseur, but it also enables divisions under Generals Robert E. Rodes and John B. Gordon to arrive in support. Heavy fighting forces Ramseur to give way; then Rodes and Gordon strike back in a vicious counterattack stunning the XIX Corps. Worse, as the newly arriving VI Corps of General Horatio G. Wright begins to deploy, a gap develops between the Union formations, and the Southerners force their way between them. Rodes is killed in the struggle as the Union lines surge back, while Early consolidates his outnumbered force along better lines.

The crisis occurs when Sheridan, judging the moment right, unleashes the VIII Corps under General George Crook. This infusion of new force staggers the weary Confederates, who break and re-form new lines farther back under General John C. Breckinridge. A desperate cavalry charge by General Fitzhugh Lee fails to stop the approach of Union troopers under Generals Wesley Merritt and William W. Averell, and resistance completely crumbles at about 5:00 P.M. Early labors mightily to keep his withdrawal from becoming a rout and gradually assumes new defensive positions at Fisher's Hill, 20 miles south. Significantly, this is the first time that the Confederate II Corps, "Stonewall" Jackson's old command, yields the palm of victory. Early's losses total 276 killed, 1,827 wounded, and 1,818 missing (3,611). The victorious Sheridan incurs 697 dead, 3,983 injured, and 338 missing (5,018).

SOUTHWEST: General John M. Thayer, commanding the District of the Frontier at Fort Smith, Arkansas, dispatches a supply train of 306 wagons and an escort of 610 soldiers to the relief of Fort Gibson. En route, they are attacked by Confederate Indians under General Stand Watie and Texas cavalry under Colonel Richard M. Gano at Cabin Creek, Indian Territory, who eject the defenders from their flimsy stockade, scattering them. The raiders then steal away with 202 wagons and 1,253 mules.

NAVAL: Confederate agents under Master John Y. Beall overpower the crew of the steamer *Philo Parsons* on Lake Erie and conduct it to Johnson's Island to free several prisoners. En route, they also seize and burn the steamer *Island Queen,* but they are thwarted by the timely appearance of the USS *Michigan.* The Confederates then sail *Philo Parsons* to Canada and safety.

Armed boats from the USS *Niphon* land at Masonboro Inlet, North Carolina, to reconnoiter the defenses of nearby Wilmington.

September 20

POLITICS: President Jefferson Davis departs Richmond, Virginia, for Georgia in an attempt to bolster Southern morale there.

SOUTH: Simon B. Buckner is promoted to lieutenant general, C.S.A.

WEST: General Jubal A. Early regroups his scattered forces at Fisher's Hill, Virginia, as Union cavalry pursue them sharply. This is a strong natural position, but Early lacks adequate manpower to man it sufficiently. Meanwhile, rearguard actions erupt at Strasburg, Middletown, and Cedarville as Federal forces under General Philip H. Sheridan approach.

General Stephen O. Burbridge leads 3,500 Union cavalry out of Mount Sterling, Kentucky, and rides toward Saltville, Virginia.

General Sterling Price captures Keytesville, Missouri, as he advances on St. Louis.

September 21

NORTH: General Philip H. Sheridan is appointed permanent commander of the Middle Military District, which encompasses the Shenandoah Valley.

WEST: The Army of the Shenandoah under General Philip H. Sheridan gathers its strength at Strasburg, Virginia, before plunging in full strength at Confederate positions along Fisher's Hill. After surveying General Jubal A. Early's deployment, Sheridan orders the VIII Corps of General George Crook on a wide encircling movement around the Confederate left while detaining divisions of Generals Horatio G. Wright and William H. Emory to his front. As Crook carefully departs this evening, taking every possible precaution not to be observed, the cavalry division of General Alfred T. A. Torbert is also sent clattering into the Luray Valley to swing around Early at New Market Gap and cut his retreat.

Confederate cavalry under General Nathan B. Forrest cross the Tennessee River and move against Athens, Tennessee.

September 22

POLITICS: President Jefferson Davis arrives by train at Macon, Georgia, and assures compatriots that "Our cause is not lost."

WEST: The Battle of Fisher's Hill begins this afternoon when 28,000 Union troops under General Philip H. Sheridan start to make feints and probes along the Confederate line. General Jubal A. Early, who possesses only 9,000 men, suspects that a ruse of some kind is in play and prepares to retreat. Suddenly, the two hidden divisions of the VIII Corps under General George Crook scream down the hillside on the Confederate left, sweeping aside the dismounted cavalry of General Lunsford L. Lomax. One brigade is headed by Colonel Rutherford B. Hayes, a future president of the United States. General Stephen D. Ramseur, whose Confederate division holds the left, tries realigning his men to halt the onslaught, but they are routed by the surging tide. Sheridan then orders Generals Horatio G. Wright and William H. Emory to charge the enemy in front, yelling, "Forward! Forward everything!" The excited Federals then pitch into the enemy, and Early's army crumbles around him. The onset of darkness permits the bulk of his men to retreat, a fact made possible by General Alfred T. A. Torbert's inability to traverse the Luray Valley in time.

Early's Confederates are thrashed thoroughly, although his losses total only 30 killed, 210 injured, and 995 missing (1,235), along with 14 cannon. Considering the natural strength of Fisher's Hill, especially its steep, imposing bluff, Sheridan suffers only 36 killed, 414 wounded, and six missing (456). He then declines to pursue his defeated enemy vigorously, preferring instead to hold back and commence implementing a "scorched earth" policy to devastate the fertile Shenandoah.

September 23
DIPLOMACY: Under European and U.S. pressure the Japanese shogun Tokugawa agrees to keep Yokohama and other ports open to Western vessels.

POLITICS: President Abraham Lincoln requests the resignation of Postmaster General Montgomery Blair as a concession for Radical Republican support in the upcoming election.

SOUTH: General Stephen A. Hurlburt assumes command of the Union Department of the Gulf.

WEST: General Jubal A. Early continues withdrawing back to Woodstock, Virginia, 25 miles from Fisher's Hill as General Philip H. Sheridan's Union forces linger in place while burning crops and farms throughout the Shenandoah Valley.

NAVAL: The side-wheeler USS *Antelope* strikes a snag and sinks in the Mississippi River off New Orleans.

September 24
POLITICS: President Abraham Lincoln appoints William Dennison the new postmaster general to replace the outgoing Montgomery Blair.

WEST: General Philip A. Sheridan moves down the Shenandoah Valley, but instead of pursuing the defeated Confederates, he burns farms and crops to eliminate the Confederacy's breadbasket. He does so with the complete approbation of General Ulysses S. Grant, who advises, "If the war is to last another year we want the Shenandoah Valley to remain a barren waste." Sheridan does not disappoint his superior.

The town of Athens, Tennessee, falls to Confederate cavalry under General Nathan B. Forrest.

NAVAL: The USS *Fuschia*, *Thomas Freeborn*, and *Mercury* raid a boatworks on Stutt's Creek, Virginia. They capture five small boats and destroy a fishery before returning safely.

September 25

SOUTH: President Jefferson Davis arrives at Palmetto, Georgia, to confer with General John B. Hood over strategy. Because of personality clashes, Hood has requested a replacement for ornery General William J. Hardee, which is done. Davis also approves of Hood's strategy for invading Tennessee to strike at Union supply lines, thereby forcing General William T. Sherman's Union army to evacuate Georgia.

WEST: Union forces under General Philip H. Sheridan reach Harrisonburg, Virginia, and continue devastating the surrounding countryside.

General Jubal A. Early's shattered Army of the Valley pulls into Port Republic, Virginia, to rest and regroup. He also is expecting reinforcements from the Army of Northern Virginia to ameliorate earlier losses.

The Confederate army of General Sterling Price enters Fredericktown, Missouri. As the divisions of Generals James F. Fagan and John S. Marmaduke proceed to attack Ironton, cavalry under General Joseph O. Shelby become tasked with cutting rail lines between that town and St. Louis.

NAVAL: The USS *Howquah, Niphon,* and *Governor Buckingham* trade fire with Confederate batteries at Wilmington, North Carolina, and also manage to run the blockade-runner *Lynx* aground, destroying it with cannon fire.

September 26

WEST: Union and Confederate cavalry skirmish at Brown's Gap, Virginia.

Confederate cavalry under General Nathan B. Forrest hit a Union garrison at Pulaski, Tennessee.

A force of 8,000 Confederates under General Sterling Price attacks General Thomas Ewing's 1,450-man Union garrison at Fort Davidson, Pilot Knob, Missouri. This post, though small, is well defended, and Price, declining to employ his artillery train, commits troops to a series of uncoordinated frontal assaults. These are invariably repulsed with upward of 1,000 casualties, but given the stark disparity in numbers, Ewing realizes he cannot hold much longer.

Notorious partisan William "Bloody Bill" Anderson gathers 200 veteran guerrillas four miles south of Centralia, Missouri, 120 miles northwest of St. Louis.

NAVAL: The Confederate raider CSS *Florida* under Lieutenant Charles M. Morris captures and burns the Union bark *Mondamin* off the South American coast.

September 27

WEST: At 2:30 A.M., General Thomas Ewing skillfully evacuates Fort Davidson at Pilot Knob, Missouri, and silently steals through Confederate lines to escape in the darkness. The garrison also detonates all their ammunition and spikes their cannon, so the Confederates gain very little for their sacrifice. By morning, General Sterling Price orders an immediate pursuit, but Ewing covers 66 miles in the next 39 hours and receives reinforcements at Leasburg, south of St. Louis.

Thirty Confederate guerrillas under William "Bloody Bill" Anderson ride into Centralia, Missouri, and systematically rob the town and plunder its inhabitants. What started as brigandage ends up as murder when a train suddenly pulls into town and Anderson apprehends 23 unarmed Union soldiers. These are summarily executed save for Sergeant Thomas Goodman, whom he hopes to exchange for a captive guerrilla. The bushwhackers then ride off back to Singleton's Farm, four miles distant, where Goodman eventually is released unharmed.

Tragedy at Centralia continues when Major A. V. E. Johnson next arrives with 158 men of his newly recruited 39th Missouri Infantry, mounted on mules. Ignoring pleas to refrain from pursuing the guerrillas, he leaves half his command in town and takes the rest directly into a deadly ambush. Johnson and his men all die, and then the guerrillas return to Centralia to kill any remaining soldiers. By the time "Bloody Bill" completes his black deed, 116 soldiers are dead, two are wounded, and six remain missing. This is one of the most reprehensible acts in the violent undercurrents of civil war in Missouri.

NAVAL: Landing parties conduct a second reconnaissance up Masonboro Inlet, North Carolina, for additional intelligence about the defenses of Wilmington.

The USS *Arkansas* captures the Confederate schooner *Watchful* on Barataria Bay, Louisiana.

Admiral David D. Porter bids the men and officers of his Mississippi River Squadron farewell as he departs to assume command of the North Atlantic Blockading Squadron off Wilmington, North Carolina.

September 28

SOUTH: General Ulysses S. Grant begins to probe the defenses of Richmond and Petersburg, Virginia, for weaknesses. He orders General George G. Meade to attack a section of the Confederate line four miles southwest of Petersburg in the vicinity of Poplar Springs Church. Meade accordingly assigns 20,000 men from General Gouverneur K. Warren's V Corps and General John G. Parke's IX Corps to the task. Grant anticipates that this ploy will prevent General Robert E. Lee from shifting men to the defense of Richmond, where another major drive is pending. Lee, however, begins to move General Richard H. Anderson's troops across to the north bank of the James River as a precaution.

General Benjamin F. Butler's Army of the James dispatches General Edward O. C. Ord's XVIII Corps and General David B. Birney's X Corps across the James River for a three-pronged assault on Richmond's outer perimeter. The intended targets are Fort Harrison and New Market Heights, to be struck simultaneously the following day.

WEST: General Jubal A. Early herds his surviving soldiers into Waynesboro, Virginia, to rest and receive reinforcements.

General William J. Hardee is relieved of command in the Army of Tennessee for his inability to coexist with General John B. Hood. He is subsequently dispatched to command the Confederate Department of South Carolina, Georgia, and Florida.

September 29

SOUTH: Two divisions of the V Corps under General Gouverneur K. Warren strike Confederate positions along the Squirrel Level Road near Poplar Springs Church, Virginia. The defenders and their position are quickly overrun, but delays on behalf of General John G. Parke's IX Corps enable General Ambrose P. Hill to rush up reinforcements and counterattack. Struck in the flank by Generals Henry Heth and

Cadmus M. Wilcox, Parke abandons his gains and falls back among Warren's troops at Peeble's Farm. Subsequent Confederate assaults in the vicinity are repulsed by artillery fire.

General Benjamin F. Butler next directs the Union X and XVIII Corps on a two-pronged attack against the defenses of Richmond, Virginia. General David B. Birney's X Corps of 18,000 men attacks up the slopes of New Market Heights, spear-headed by General Charles A. Paine's African-American division. The black troops encounter heavy fire and dogged resistance, losing 800 men in less than an hour, but they tenaciously forge ahead and storm the earthworks in a tremendous display of courage and sacrifice. The Southerners finally are driven off the heights after three costly assaults. Significantly, of 16 Congressional Medals of Honor awarded to African Americans during the war, no less than 14 originate here.

Simultaneously, General Edward O. C. Ord's XVIII Corps surges ahead against Fort Harrison, then garrisoned by 800 inexperienced artillerymen. The Federals have little problem storming their objective and also beat off an attack by Confederates retreating from New Market Heights. Ord then gathers up his men to attack Fort Gilmer atop Chaffin's Bluff, which falters when he falls severely wounded. A body of Union cavalry under General August V. Kautz also probes in strength down the Darbytown Road, only to be rebuffed by heavy artillery fire. The Union troops begin to entrench and strengthen their lines for an inevitable Southern counterattack on the following day.

WEST: Skirmishing resumes between the forces of General Philip H. Sheridan and Jubal A. Early at Waynesborough, Virginia.

General John B. Hood crosses the Army of Tennessee over the Chattahochee River, intending to cut the Western and Atlantic Railroad, a major Union supply artery.

Advanced elements of General Sterling Price's Confederate army clash with Union forces outside Leasburg and Cuba, Missouri. Price since has abandoned the notion of capturing St. Louis, now defended by General Andrew J. Smith's XVI Corps, so he continues westward along the Missouri River.

NAVAL: The USS *Niphon* forces the British blockade-runner *Night Hawk* aground near Fort Fisher, North Carolina, and destroys it.

Confederate sympathizer John C. Braine and his followers seize the Union steamer *Roanoke* off the Cuban coast and bring that vessel to Bermuda. After failing to smuggle coal and other supplies from the island, he burns his vessel and is detained temporarily by British authorities.

September 30

SOUTH: Eager to prevent Union troops from lengthening his trench lines, General Robert E. Lee arrives at Richmond, Virginia, with eight infantry brigades to recapture Fort Harrison. He launches the divisions of Generals Robert F. Hoke and Charles Field in a bid to overwhelm the defenders, but entrenched Federals easily repel four determined charges. Union general George J. Stannard displays conspicuous skill in defending his works, and he falls critically wounded after defeating their final lunge. Lee, finally thwarted, sullenly withdraws to construct new lines of entrenchments closer to the capital. Union losses for the past two days top 3,300 while the Confederates suffer approximately 2,000.

WEST: Union cavalry under General Stephen O. Burbridge skirmish with General Henry L. Giltner's Confederate troopers at Cedar Bluff, Virginia.

NAVAL: Ships of the Confederate James River Squadron under Commodore James K. Mitchell lend naval support fire to the unsuccessful attack on Fort Harrison, Virginia. They also prevent Union troops from occupying strategic Chaffin's Bluff afterward.

October 1

SOUTH: General John G. Parke's IX Corps advances on Confederate siege lines near Poplar Springs Church again but does not attack. Instead, his men dig entrenchments of their own, extending them out to connect with Union lines around Globe Tavern on the Weldon Railroad.

WEST: General John B. Hood moves his surviving forces south around Atlanta to assail General William T. Sherman's railroad lines at Salt Springs, Georgia.

General Nathan B. Forrest's cavalry skirmish with Union garrisons at Athens and Huntsville, Alabama.

General Stephen O. Burbridge's 3,500 cavalry engage and drive back a Confederate rear guard under General Henry L. Giltner at Clinch Mountain, Virginia. The heavily outnumbered Giltner falls back on improvised defenses at nearby Saltville. There Burbridge engages a mixed force of 2,800 soldiers, bushwhackers, and militia under General John S. William, losing heavily with every charge. By the time Federal troopers finally storm Southern defenses, their ammunition is nearly expended and Burbridge orders a retreat back to Kentucky this evening. Union losses are 329 killed, wounded, or missing; the Confederates sustain about 190 casualties.

Advancing Southerners under General Sterling Price engage Federal troops at Franklin and Lake Springs, Missouri.

NAVAL: The USS *Niphon* runs the British blockade-runner *Condor* aground at Port Fisher, North Carolina, and Confederate spy Rose O'Neal Greenhow drowns when the small boat she escapes in capsizes. Greenhow is found with $2,000 in British gold in a bag around her neck. Intense fire from the fort also prevents the Union vessel from destroying the steamer.

October 2

SOUTH: President Jefferson Davis appoints General Pierre G. T. Beauregard commander of the Division of the West to help coordinate the operations of Generals John B. Hood and Richard Taylor. In truth, Davis dislikes Beauregard and resents both his tendency to meddle and his endless penchant for grandiose schemes.

Confederate forces under General Ambrose P. Hill attack Union entrenchments manned by General John G. Parke's IX Corps along Poplar Springs Church but are repulsed. Fighting in this vicinity has depleted Union forces by 2,800 men while the Southerners sustain around 1,300 casualties. Consequently, General Robert E. Lee is obliged to stretch his dwindling manpower resources even thinner to cover the lost ground.

WEST: General John B. Hood begins to cut General William T. Sherman's supply lines between Atlanta and Chattanooga by tearing up tracks belonging to the Western and Atlantic Railroad.

Confederate forces at Saltville, Virginia, most notably guerrillas under Champ Ferguson and a Tennessean brigade under Felix H. Robertson, roam the recent battlefield and execute upward of 100 wounded African-American soldiers of the 5th U.S. Colored Cavalry found alive. Several white Union soldiers are also murdered in cold blood.

General Sterling Price's Confederates occupy Washington, Missouri, on the Missouri River. This action places his force 50 miles from St. Louis.

October 3

POLITICS: President Jefferson Davis, while passing through Columbia, South Carolina, exhorts his fellow citizens to persevere and predicts the defeat of General William T. Sherman.

WEST: General George H. Thomas is dispatched back to Nashville, Tennessee, with orders to curtail any further mischief caused by General John B. Hood to Union lines of communication.

General Alexander P. Stewart's Confederate corps hits Union positions at Big Shanty, Georgia, seizing 175 captives.

Confederates under General Sterling Price engage Union forces at Hermann and Miller's Station, Missouri, outside St. Louis. His success prompts the rerouting of General Andrew J. Smith's corps to that town instead of reinforcing General George H. Thomas's army at Nashville, Tennessee.

NAVAL: Captain Raphael Semmes departs England aboard the English steamer *Tasmanian* and begins to work his way back to the Confederacy.

October 4

POLITICS: Postmaster General William Dennison joins President Abraham Lincoln's cabinet.

Syracuse, New York, is the scene of the "National Convention of Colored Citizens of the United States," with 144 delegates drawn from 18 states. They promulgate the National Equal Rights League, headed by John M. Langston of Ohio.

SOUTH: General William T. Sherman repositions his forces along Kennesaw Mountain for a possible strike at General John B. Hood's army as it marches westward.

WEST: Confederate forces operating against the Western and Atlantic Railroad attack Union positions at Ackworth, Georgia, seizing 250 prisoners.

General Sterling Price, wary of Union reinforcements arriving at St. Louis, Missouri, veers away from the town and heads west.

NAVAL: The Confederate raider CSS *Florida* under Lieutenant Charles M. Morris drops anchor at Bahía, Brazil, closely watched by the USS *Wachusett*.

October 5

POLITICS: President Jefferson Davis appears before cheering crowds at Augusta, Georgia, and lauds them with ringing oratory predicting a complete Confederate victory. "Never before was I so confident that energy, harmony, and determination would rid the country of its enemy," he declares, "and give to the women of the land that peace their good deeds have so well deserved."

SOUTH: A division of Confederates under General Samuel G. French, numbering 3,276 men, becomes tasked with capturing a major Union supply depot at Allatoona Pass, Georgia. That post is defended by 2,025 Union soldiers under the recently arrived General John M. Corse, who counts both rugged terrain and rapid-fire Henry repeating rifles in his favor. For several hours, the Southerners attack from the west and the south, at one point driving the defenders back into their mountaintop fort, but Corse invariably rallies and sweeps his antagonists back down the slopes. French concludes that the position cannot be carried and marches off to join the main army under General John B. Hood. Union losses are 706 while the Confederates sustain 897. This stalwart defense also inspires the noted hymn, "Hold the Fort, For We Are Coming."

General William J. Hardee assumes command of the Department of South Carolina, Georgia, and Florida to separate him from General John B. Hood.

WEST: The Confederate column under General Sterling Price marches west along the Missouri River, occupying the town of Heiman. His rear guard is harassed by Federal cavalry under General Alfred Pleasonton, which induces him to bypass Jefferson City and continue onto Boonville.

NAVAL: A boat expedition from the USS *Restless* enters St. Andrew's Bay, Florida, and destroys a large saltworks along with 150 buildings.

The USS *Mobile* captures the British blockade-runner *Annie Virdon* off Velasco, Texas.

At Bahía, Brazil, the USS *Wachusett* arrives and challenges the smaller CSS *Florida* to a duel in international waters, and the latter respectfully declines. Local authorities extract promises from both captains that Brazilian neutrality will be respected.

October 6

POLITICS: The *Richmond Enquirer* breaks new ground by printing an essay promoting the use of African-American soldiers for the Confederacy. The idea gradually is receiving greater currency, although President Jefferson Davis is never reconciled to it.

WEST: General Philip A. Sheridan, considering the Shenandoah Valley campaign closed, begins to withdraw his army north, destroying everything in its path. General Jubal A. Early, ensconced at Blue Gap, welcomes this turn of events and orders General Thomas L. Rosser's cavalry division to harass withdrawing Federals at every step.

Confederate cavalry under General Nathan B. Forrest harry Union forces at Florence, Alabama.

NAVAL: The USS *Wamsutta* chases the Confederate steamer *Constance* aground on Long Island in Charleston harbor, South Carolina.

October 7

SOUTH: General Robert E. Lee again determines to recapture Fort Harrison, Virginia, in an attempt to restore his siege lines outside Richmond, Virginia. He orders two divisions under General Robert F. Hoke and Charles W. Field, assisted by a cavalry brigade under General Martin W. Gary, to drive Union forces from the Darbytown Road. At dawn these three columns simultaneously fall on 1,700 Union cavalry under General August V. Kautz, driving them back in confusion. Pushing forward, the Confederates encounter stiffer resistance from General Alfred H. Terry's division, X Corps, at Johnson's Farm. Terry uses delays in Field's advance to bring up artillery reinforcements, and at 10:00 A.M., he repulses several piecemeal charges, killing General John Gregg of the famed Texas brigade. Hoke also makes a tardy appearance but fails to advance, at which point Lee calls off the attack and withdraws. Confederate casualties are 1,350 to a Union tally of 399. Defeat here further convinces Lee to begin to dig new lines of trenches closer to Richmond.

WEST: The army of General Philip H. Sheridan continues its policy of burning crops and confiscating livestock at Woodstock, Virginia. To date, his men have destroyed 2,000 barns, 70 flour mills, driven off 4,000 head of cattle, and killed 3,000 sheep. Sheridan vows that when he is finished, the region around Staunton "will have little in it for man or beast." Meanwhile, Confederate cavalry under General Thomas L. Rosser skirmish with the Union rear guard commanded by Generals Wesley Merritt and George A. Custer at Brook's Gap.

NAVAL: The USS *Aster,* while chasing a blockade-runner toward Fort Fisher, North Carolina, runs aground and is destroyed to prevent capture. The crew is rescued by the *Niphon,* which also tows the *Berberry* to safety once it is also disabled while trying to tow the *Aster* off the bar.

The USS *Wachusett* under Commander Napoleon Collins decides to attack and capture the Confederate raider CSS *Florida* at Bahía, Brazil, after learning that Lieutenant Charles M. Morris and most of his crew are ashore. At 3:00 A.M., Collins slips his cable, sneaks past a Brazilian gunboat, and rams his quarry. The *Florida* surrenders after a brief struggle, having previously accounted for 37 Union prizes. However, the nature of its seizure, a blatant violation of Brazilian neutrality, raises acute diplomatic ramifications.

October 8

WEST: General Thomas L. Rosser and his Confederate troopers continue dogging the Union rear guard under Generals Wesley Merritt and George A. Custer. However, their commanding officer, General Alfred T. A. Torbert, denies them permission to engage their opponent. When word of his reluctance reaches General Philip H. Sheridan's ears, he angrily informs Torbert to "start out at daylight and whip the Rebel cavalry or get whipped!" Sheridan further promises to observe the dust up from nearby Round Top Mountain.

Opposing cavalry under General Sterling Price and Alfred Pleasonton skirmish at Jefferson City, Missouri.

NAVAL: The Federal vessel *Steam Picket Boat No. 2* is burned to prevent capture after its crew is captured ashore at Wicomico Bay, Virginia.

The British steamer *Sea King* departs England for Madeira where it will be commissioned as the Confederate raider CSS *Shenandoah.*

October 9

WEST: Union cavalry brigades under Generals George A. Custer and Wesley Merritt engage the Confederate cavalry division of General Thomas L. Rosser at Tom's Brook,

Virginia. As Custer leads 2,500 troopers against Rosser's 3,500 men, he recognizes his adversary as an old West Point roommate and doffs his hat before engaging. Meanwhile, Merrit gallops down the Valley Pike to engage the 1,500 troopers of General Lunsford L. Lomax's division. As Custer and Rosser spar, Merritt crashes headlong into his opponent, routing him. Custer, however, is forced to maneuver around the Confederate left flank to evict the Southerners from their strong position. As Rosser obligingly falls back to Tom's Brook, Custer charges his former acquaintance head-on, routing him, and chases the scampering Southerners 20 miles. Merritt enjoys similar success and pursues Lomax for 26 miles. This is one of the biggest triumphs of the Union mounted arm over its vaunted adversary and is celebrated as "The Woodstock Races." Union losses are nine killed and 48 wounded to a Confederate tally of 350 killed, wounded, or captured, along with 11 cannon and many wagons seized.

General Sterling Price captures Boonsboro, Missouri, while moving steadily northwest away from St. Louis. There, he adds in 2,000 new recruits to his army, which remains chronically short of weapons.

NAVAL: The USS *Sebago* trades fire with Confederate batteries at Freeman's Wharf, Mobile Bay, Alabama, suffering five casualties.

October 10

SOUTH: General John B. Hood skirmishes with Union forces around Rome, Georgia.

WEST: General Philip H. Sheridan moves north and occupies a strong position along Cedar Creek, Virginia, 15 miles south of Winchester, enticing Confederates under General Jubal A. Early to follow.

General Nathan B. Forrest easily disperses a Union boat-borne expedition against him at Eastport, Mississippi.

NAVAL: The USS *Montgomery* captures the British blockade-runner *Bat* off Wilmington, North Carolina.

The Federal gunboats USS *Key West* and *Undine*, escorting the transports *City of Peking, Kenton,* and *Aurora* on an expedition against Eastport, Mississippi, are interdicted on the Tennessee River by Confederate artillery under General Nathan B. Forrest. After a severe exchange, the vessels withdraw down the river.

October 11

POLITICS: The recent round of elections in Pennsylvania, Ohio, and Indiana demonstrates continuing support for President Abraham Lincoln.

WEST: General William T. Sherman concentrates his army at Rome, Georgia, in preparation for attacking Confederates under General John B. Hood as they march west.

General Sterling Price continues lurching northwest through Missouri, skirmishing with Union forces at Boonville and Brunswick.

October 12

POLITICS: U.S. Supreme Court chief justice Roger B. Taney, titular head of that body since 1835, dies in Washington, D.C. He wrote the majority opinion for the infamous *Dred Scott* decision of 1857, which reaffirmed the status of African-American slaves as property, thereby exacerbating sectional tensions.

SOUTH: Continual skirmishing erupts between Union and Confederate forces at Resaca, Georgia, as General John B. Hood marches toward Alabama.

NAVAL: Admiral David D. Porter assumes control of the North Atlantic Blockading Squadron off Wilmington, North Carolina, from Admiral Samuel P. Lee. "It will be almost useless to enjoin on all officers the importance of their being vigilant at all times," he declared. "We have an active enemy to deal with, and every officer and man must be on the alert."

The USS *Chocura* captures the British blockade-runner *Louisa* off Aransas Pass, Texas.

October 13

POLITICS: Maryland narrowly approves a new constitution mandating the abolition of slavery. The tally is 30,174 to 29,799, a margin of only 374 votes.

SOUTH: A drive by General Alfred Terry's X Corps down Darbytown Road, Virginia, is checked by heavy resistance from General Richard H. Anderson's troops.

WEST: General Jubal A. Early advances his greatly reduced Confederate army back to their old position at Fisher's Hill, Virginia.

Confederate raiders under Colonel John S. Mosby capture and burn a train belonging to the Baltimore and Ohio Railroad near Kearneysville, West Virginia, absconding with $173,000 from a Union paymaster.

General John B. Hood's Confederates seize the railroad north of Resaca, Georgia, to cut General William T. Sherman's supply lines back to Tennessee.

NAVAL: Landing parties from the USS *Braziliera* and *Mary Sanford* skirmish with Confederate cavalry at Yellow Bluff, White Oak Creek, Georgia. After freeing several slaves from a nearby plantation, they embark and return downstream.

October 14

WEST: Skirmishing flares anew between Union and Confederate forces in the vicinity of Cedar Creek, Virginia.

General Sterling Price issues an appeal to the people of Missouri to flock to the Confederate banner. His will is largely unheeded.

A force of 2,500 Confederates under General John B. Clark crosses the Missouri River at Arrow Rock and advances on the nearby settlement of Glasgow, Missouri, where a large cache of Union arms reputedly is stored.

October 15

SOUTH: General Braxton Bragg is detached from service at Richmond, Virginia, and sent to Wilmington, North Carolina, to coordinate defenses there.

WEST: Confederate general John B. Clark besieges the town of Glasgow, Missouri, with 2,500 men. The garrison consists of 750 state militia and a handful of Federal troops under Colonel Chester Harding. Harding resists stoutly for several hours until the Southerners capture several buildings on the northeast part of town. Clark then immediately demands his surrender, threatening to unleash guerrilla forces if he resists further. Harding, low on ammunition, complies and is paroled. Union losses are 11 dead and 32 wounded, but they still inflict around 100 casualties on the Confederates.

Worse, the Federals manage to destroy all weapons in their possession, defeating the purpose of the attack.

Paris, Missouri, falls to Confederate forces under General Sterling Price.

October 16

WEST: General Philip H. Sheridan leaves his army at Cedar Creek, Virginia, 15 miles south of Winchester, and makes for a high-level strategy conference with Secretary of War Edwin M. Stanton and General Henry W. Halleck in Washington, D.C. General Horatio G. Wright remains in charge during his absence.

General Sterling Price's army seizes Ridgely, Missouri, as it moves westward along the Missouri River.

General James G. Blunt crosses the Missouri state line from Kansas with 15,000 troops, although his militia refuses to advance any farther than Big Blue River. Blunt nonetheless reaches Lexington with 2,000 soldiers and assumes blocking positions around the town.

October 17

SOUTH: General James Longstreet resumes command of the I Corps, Army of Northern Virginia, following a lengthy convalescence.

WEST: General John B. Gordon and Captain Jedediah Hotchkiss, a topographical engineer, steal on the Union army encamped at Cedar Creek, Virginia, ascend Massanutten Mountain, and examine the Northern encampment closely. They discern that their left is entirely "in the air" and subject to a sudden flanking assault. This intelligence is relayed immediately to General Jubal A. Early.

General Pierre G. T. Beauregard assumes command of the Confederate Military Division of the West to promote better harmony between feuding commanders.

General John B. Hood relents from attacks on Union forces in the vicinity of Gadsden, Alabama, and continues westward in the mistaken belief that General William T. Sherman will follow to protect his line of communications with Tennessee.

Confederates under General Sterling Price occupy Carrollton, Missouri, and commence a drive on Lexington. However, Union forces under General Samuel R. Curtis are approaching from the west, General Andrew J. Smith is marching from the east, and Federal cavalry under General Alfred Pleasonton closely trail the Southerners from behind.

October 18

WEST: Indomitable general Jubal A. Early, learning that General Philip H. Sheridan is absent from his army, plans to attack the Union encampment at Cedar Creek. Acting on General John B. Gordon's advice, he sends three divisions along differing paths that ultimately converge behind the exposed VIII Corp of General George Crook on the left. This march, carried out under extreme secrecy, is one of the most audacious turning movements of the entire war.

October 19

NORTH: Lieutenant Bennet H. Young and his band of 20 Confederate Kentuckians slip across the Canadian border and attack three banks in St. Albans, Vermont, 15 miles from the border. Two citizens are shot, one fatally. After absconding with

$20,000, the Southerners set fire to several buildings and try to recross the border. But as word of the attack spreads, a nearby Union officer forms a posse and chases after the marauders. They catch the raiders on Canadian soil and then turn them over to authorities there for processing and extradition. St. Albans is the northernmost "engagement" of the Civil War.

WEST: At 5:00 A.M., the Battle of Cedar Creek erupts as the Confederate divisions of Generals Clement A. Evans, Stephen Ramseur, and John Pegram plunge out of an early morning fog and into the Union camp at Cedar Creek. The Federal VIII and IX Corps, flanked and completely surprised, simply crumble before the Confederate onslaught. The only real resistance mounted comes from General George W. Getty's division, VI Corps, which resists pluckily and convinces General Jubal A. Early to dislodge the division first before pursuing the beaten troops. Gordon and other leaders advise against the distraction, but at length Getty gradually is pushed back. A break in the fighting develops as the hungry, ragged Confederates pause to loot the Union camp thoroughly. Early, though outnumbered two to one, achieves a striking tactical victory, capturing 1,300 prisoners and 18 cannon. The remnants of three Union corps are reduced to a leaderless throng milling about three miles from camp.

Fortunately, General Philip H. Sheridan is returning from his strategy conference in Washington, D.C., and encounters numerous refugees as he approaches Cedar Creek. Sheridan then spurs his horse for 12 miles and rallies his shaken command. Sheridan's presence is electric, and soon the revitalized Federals regroup and counterattack the exhausted, disorganized Confederates, hitting their left flank at 4:00 P.M. This equally sudden onslaught, spearheaded by General George A. Custer's cavalry, proves too much for Early's men. They bolt from the field, and a vengeful Union pursuit chases them all the way past Fisher's Hill. It a remarkable change in fortunes for Sheridan, who snatches victory from the jaws of defeat. As Early bitterly remonstrates, "The Yankees got whipped and we got scared." Confederate losses are 320 dead, including the talented general Stephen D. Ramseur, 1,540 wounded, and 1,050 missing (2,810) while the Union suffers 644 killed, 3,430 injured, and 1,591 missing (5,671). Sheridan also captures 43 cannon and 300 wagons. More important, Cedar Creek is the straw that finally breaks Southern resistance in the strategic Shenandoah Valley. That this region remains solidly in Union hands for the remainder of the war portends ill for the Confederacy's survival.

General Nathan B. Forrest leads his cavalry out of Corinth, Mississippi, and rides east intending to cooperate with General John B. Hood in Alabama after raiding around Johnsonville, Tennessee.

General Sterling Price's Confederates occupy Lexington, Missouri, ejecting the advance troops of General James G. Blunt. Price, realizing he nearly is surrounded by two converging Federal columns, marches south between his antagonists and determines to defeat each one separately.

NAVAL: The USS *Mobile* captures the Confederate schooner *Emily* at San Luis Pass, Texas.

The English steamer *Sea King* arrives in the Madeira Islands where it is converted into the Confederate raider CSS *Shenandoah* and is commissioned under Lieutenant James I. Waddell.

October 20

POLITICS: President Abraham Lincoln decrees that the last Wednesday of every November will be celebrated as "a day of Thanksgiving and Praise to Almighty God the beneficent Creator and Ruler of the Universe."

WEST: Union cavalry pursue defeated remnants of General Jubal A. Early's army down the Shenandoah Valley. The shattered Confederates continue falling back on New Market.

NAVAL: Armed boats from the USS *Stars and Stripes* ascend the Ocklocknee River, Florida, and destroy a Confederate fishery on Marsh's Island.

October 21

NORTH: General George Crook is appointed a major general, U.S. Army.

WEST: General William T. Sherman halts his pursuit of General John B. Hood at Gaylesville, Alabama, once his Confederate column reaches Gadsden.

A skirmish with Federal cavalry along the Little Blue River alerts General Sterling Price that General James R. Blunt's Army of the Frontier remains within striking distance. Confederate forces experience little difficulty driving off 400 dismounted troopers and two cannon, yet they are rebuffed when they try to pursue across the river. Price's superiority in numbers eventually threatens to run both Union flanks, so Blunt falls back and joins General Samuel R. Curtis's main force at Big Blue River.

NAVAL: The USS *Fort Jackson* captures the Confederate steamer *Wando* off Cape Romain, South Carolina.

The USS *Sea Bird* captures the British blockade-runner *Lucy* off Anclote Keys, Florida.

October 22

WEST: General Sterling Price commits a brigade under Joseph O. Shelby to feint against the main Union line at Big Blue River, Missouri, while launching two brigades under General Sidney D. Jackman against their center. However, General Samuel R. Curtis's command holds firm and forces the Confederates back. Meanwhile, a Southern regiment under Colonel Alonzo Slayback discovers an unprotected ford upstream and crosses to threaten the exposed Union right flank. The fighting gradually dissipates by nightfall, and Curtis falls back in the direction of Westport to regroup.

Simultaneously, General Alfred Pleasonton begins to move up behind the Confederates on the Little Blue River. A Confederate brigade under General William L. Cabell fails to halt the Federal onslaught, losing 400 prisoners and two cannon. The surviving Southerners under General John S. Marmaduke fall back across the river in good order, alerting Price to the danger. The general then girds his command for a fighting withdrawal southward.

NAVAL: Confederate secretary of the navy Stephen R. Mallory writes to President Jefferson Davis, defending his strategy to deploy the CSS *Tallahassee* and *Chickamauga* as commerce raiders rather than detaining them at Wilmington, North Carolina, as part of the city's defenses. "A cruise by the *Chickamauga* and *Tallahassee* against the northern coasts and commerce would at once draw a fleet of fast steamers from the blockading squadron off Wilmington in pursuit of them," he reasons, "and this alone would render such a cruise expedient."

A boat expedition from the USS *Tacony* embarks on a reconnaissance mission up the Roanoke River, North Carolina, where it is fired on by Confederate forces. The Northerners are forced to take cover in a swamp to evade pursuers where they build a makeshift raft to reach the mouth of the river and safety.

The USS *Wamsutta, Geranium,* and *Mingoe* run the British blockade-runner *Flora* aground at Charleston, South Carolina, and it is destroyed by cannon fire from nearby Morris Island the following day.

October 23

WEST: The Battle of Westport, Missouri, erupts between Generals Sterling Price and surrounding Union forces. General James G. Blunt advances against General Joseph O. Shelby across Brush Creek and recoils. However, the Confederates cannot spare the reserves to pursue him because General Alfred Pleasonton's force looms across the Big Blue River, pressing on their rear. At length, General Samuel R. Curtis reinforces Blunt, and he pushes back over Brush Creek just as Pleasonton's column works its way across the river. The Confederates under General John S. Marmaduke resist strongly, but they are ejected from their commanding bluff and a rout ensues. Surrounded and out-numbered, Price's army flees in confusion to the southwest. However, at this juncture the Union leaders begin to squabble among themselves over what to do next, and the Southerners escape with their supply train. Casualties are estimated at 1,500 men for both sides in this action, the last major engagement of the Trans-Mississippi region.

NAVAL: Vessels of the South Atlantic Blockading Squadron sink the grounded block-ade-runner *Flamingo* off Sullivan's Island, South Carolina.

October 24

WEST: General Sterling Price concedes defeat and moves his Confederates south-ward down the border between Kansas and Missouri. His movements are slowed by an enormous baggage train loaded with plunder with which the soldiers are reluctant to part.

NAVAL: The USS *Nita* seizes the abandoned blockade-runner *Unknown* off Clear-water Harbor, Florida, while the *Rosalie* captures an unnamed Confederate sloop off Little Marco down the coast.

October 25

WEST: Confederates under General Sterling Price are attacked by Union cavalry General Alfred Pleasonton at Marais de Cynges River, 60 miles south of Westport on the Kansas border. Though outnumbering their opponents, the demoralized Southerners rapidly give ground, and Price loses one-third of his baggage train. General John S. Marmaduke is also taken prisoner.

NAVAL: An armed party from the USS *Don* lands at Fleet's Point, Great Wicomoco River, Virginia, and burns several barracks.

Admiral George F. Pearson assumes command of the Pacific Squadron from Admiral Charles H. Bell.

October 26

SOUTH: General Ulysses S. Grant wishes to cut the South Side Railroad by launching a small offensive north of the James River. To achieve this, he orders General Benjamin F. Butler to take several divisions of the X and XVIII Corps and advance against Fair Oaks, outside of Richmond, Virginia. Meanwhile, the II, V, and IX Corps are likewise to march toward the Boydton Plank Road, another vital supply route.

WEST: General John B. Hood brushes against a large Union garrison at Decatur, Alabama, sidesteps it, and moves off farther west. He expects to unite with Confederate cavalry under General Nathan B. Forrest soon, but that leader is delayed in Tennessee by independent operations and fails to rendezvous.

Confederate outlaw William "Bloody Bill" Anderson is killed in a Union ambush near Richmond, Missouri.

NAVAL: The USS *Adolph Hugel* captures the Confederate schooner *Coquette* in Wade's Bay on the Potomac River.

Lieutenant William B. Cushing leaves the blockading squadron and arrives in the Roanoke River intending to destroy the CSS *Albemarle* at its moorings. However, his ships ground at the river's mouth, and the attack is postponed until the following evening.

October 27

SOUTH: An advance by 43,000 Union troops commences against the South Side Railroad, south of Petersburg, Virginia, in the early morning rain. Operations entrusted to the Army of the James consist of throwing General Alfred Terry and the X Corps against Charles City while General Godfrey Weitzel leads the XVIII Corps against Fair Oaks. Terry's movement is unimpeded, but General James Longstreet, commanding the defenses of Richmond, Virginia, concludes that Weitzel's maneuver is dangerous and marshals forces to oppose him. As the XVIII Corps moves down the Williamsburg Road, it suddenly confronts the divisions of Generals Robert F. Hoke and Charles W. Field. Weitzel's main thrust is blunted, but an African-American brigade under General John Holman then slips around the Southern flank and charges. Holman's progress is also stopped by dogged resistance from General William Mahone's Confederates, and Weitzel, seeing further gains impractical, orders his men withdrawn. Union losses are 1,103 to a Confederate tally of 451.

Meanwhile even larger operations unfold near Hatcher's Run. The II Corps under General Winfield S. Hancock, the V Corps under General Gouverneur K. Warren, and the IX Corps under General John G. Parke—43,000 men in all—march seven miles southwest of Petersburg through autumn rain. Parke's command meets heavy resistance from General Cadmus M. Wilcox's command and stops. Warren and Hancock nevertheless press forward until they finally reach Boydton Plank Road. There, General Wade Hampton's Confederate cavalry suddenly assails Hancock's left while General Ambrose P. Hill pushes the divisions under Generals Henry Heth against his center and William Mahone strikes his right and rear. The three Confederate forces converge suddenly on the II Corps, causing great confusion, but Hancock calmly sorts out his men and beats back determined Southern assaults. Nightfall closes the engagement at Hatcher's Run, and the Federals fall back to their lines. Hancock suffers 166 dead, 1,028 wounded, and 564 missing, whereas Confederate losses are estimated at about 1,000. General Ulysses S. Grant subsequently concludes offensive operations for the year and settles into winter quarters. The thin gray line prevails again, but its serried ranks grow thinner with every skirmish.

NAVAL: The imposing Confederate ram CSS *Albemarle* is sunk by a spar torpedo operated by 21-year-old Lieutenant William B. Cushing at Plymouth on the Roanoke River, North Carolina. Cushing utilized two 30-foot steam launches, each outfitted with a 14-foot spar torpedo, and a crew of 15. He has the good fortune of passing within 20 feet of the Confederate picket ship *Southfield* without detection and is almost atop the *Albemarle* when sentries observe him in the dark. Cushing then overruns floating log booms placed as protection, strikes his quarry under its port quarter while receiving heavy fire, and detonates the charge. The *Albemarle*, fatally damaged, quickly sinks as does Cushing's own vessel. He then swims to shore alone. At daybreak, the enterprising officer commandeers a small boat and rows eight miles down the Roanoke River to Albemarle Sound, and he is rescued by the USS *Valley City*. Only Cushing and one other member of the expedition make it back; the remaining 13 are captured.

October 28

WEST: In a rare defeat, the 8th Illinois Cavalry routs Confederates under Colonel John S. Mosby, killing eight rangers and capturing nine.

Confederate cavalry under General Nathan B. Forrest arrive at Paris Landing, Tennessee, on the Tennessee River, where they immediately begin to raise obstacles along the waterway to interdict Union water traffic.

General William T. Sherman abandons his own lines of communication at Ladiga, Alabama, and moves westward back toward Atlanta, Georgia. General John B. Hood being beyond his grasp, he next turns his attention to Savannah, Georgia, on the coast.

General James G. Blunt's division surprises and attacks General Sterling Price's retreating army at Newtonia, Missouri. However, quick reactions from General Joseph O. Shelby and his "Iron Brigade" allow the bulk of the Confederates to withdraw intact. After two hours, Blunt nearly runs out of ammunition as Shelby begins to press his left flank, but the timely arrival of General John B. Sanborn and three more Union brigades staves off defeat. Shelby then disengages and slips away. Both sides claim victory, but the Union forfeits its only real chance to destroy Price.

NAVAL: The Confederate raider CSS *Chickamauga* under Lieutenant John Wilkinson slips past the Union blockade off Wilmington, North Carolina.

The USS *Calypso* and *Eolus* capture the British blockade-runner *Lady Sterling* off Wilmington, North Carolina.

The USS *General Thomas* and the army gunboat *Stone River* successfully engage a Confederate battery on the Tennessee River near Decatur, Alabama.

October 29

WEST: In a controversial decision, Department of the Missouri commander General William S. Rosecrans calls all forces under his command back to their respective stations. This leaves General Samuel R. Curtis with only 3,500 cavalry to pursue General Sterling Price's larger Confederate force.

NAVAL: With the fearsome CSS *Albemarle* sunk, a Federal naval squadron consisting of the USS *Valley City, Commodore Hall, Tacony, Shamrock, Otsego, Wyalusing,* and *Whitehead* attack Confederate defenses at Plymouth on the Albemarle River, North Carolina.

October 30

WEST: The Army of Tennessee under General John B. Hood occupies Tuscumbia, Alabama, prior to crossing the Tennessee River. His progress prompts Federal troops to begin to concentrate at Pulsaski, Tennessee.

Confederate cavalry under General Nathan B. Forrest capture the transport *Mazeppa* on the Tennessee River, including its cargo of 9,000 pairs of shoes.

NAVAL: The Confederate raider CSS *Shenandoah* under Lieutenant James I. Waddell captures and sinks the Union bark *Alina* off the Azores.

The Confederate raider CSS *Olustee* (nee *Tallahassee*) under Lieutenant William H. Ward, evades the Union blockade off Wilmington, North Carolina, and begins an Atlantic cruise.

The USS *Undine* and army transports *Venus* and *Cheeseman* are captured by Confederate cavalry under General Nathan B. Forrest on the Tennessee River near Johnsonville, Tennessee. The vessels resist for three hours until *Undine*'s ammunition gives out, and the vessel is beached. Forrest then forms a slapdash Confederate "navy" on the river bend, backed by shore artillery, to interrupt Union river communications.

October 31

POLITICS: Nevada becomes the nation's 36th state. Its two Republican-leaning U.S. senators provide the exact margin necessary to approve the 13th Amendment to the Constitution. The state is also expected to contribute three electoral votes to Lincoln's reelection bid.

WEST: General John B. Hood arrives at Tuscumbia, Alabama, and marches his army northward into Tennessee, still laboring under the mistaken belief that General William T. Sherman will follow.

NAVAL: A Federal navy squadron of seven warships bombards Confederate defenders at Plymouth, North Carolina, until a large magazine is detonated and they evacuate that post. Armed landing parties seize Fort Williams, along with 37 captives and 22 cannon.

The USS *Wilderness* and *Niphon* capture the British blockade-runner *Annie* off New Inlet, North Carolina.

The USS *Katahdin* captures the British blockade-runner *Albert Edward* near Galveston, Texas.

The Confederate raider CSS *Chickamauga* under Lieutenant John Wilkinson captures and sinks the Union ships *Emma L. Hall* and *Shooting Star* off the New England coast.

November 1

Politics: The new Maryland state constitution, abolishing slavery, is enacted.

West: General Nathan B. Forrest advances his cavalry and captured boats down the Tennessee River as far as Johnsonville, Tennessee, where he places artillery on the riverbank and lays in wait for Union river traffic.

General Andrew J. Smith's XVI Corps departs Missouri and heads for Nashville to reinforce the army under General George H. Thomas.

Naval: The Confederate raider CSS *Chickamauga* under Lieutenant John Wilkinson seizes and burns the Union schooners *Goodspeed* and *Otter Rock* in the North Atlantic.

Admiral Samuel P. Lee becomes commander of the Mississippi Squadron at Mound City, Illinois.

November 2

North: Secretary of State William H. Seward informs the major of New York that Confederate agents arriving from Canada are planning to burn the city down by election day.

Naval: The USS *Santiago de Cuba* captures the Confederate steamer *Lucy* off Charleston, South Carolina.

General Nathan B. Forrest proceeds downstream on the Tennessee River with *Venus* and *Undine,* two captured naval vessels. En route, they encounter the Union paddle wheelers USS *Key West* and *Tawah,* whereupon a protracted battle ensues. Eventually *Venus* is driven ashore near Johnsonville, Tennessee, and recaptured while *Undine* remains in Confederate hands and escapes downstream.

The Confederate raider CSS *Chickamauga* under Lieutenant John Wilkinson captures the Union bark *Speedwell* off New Jersey and releases it on a bond.

November 3

West: The Union IV Corps arrives at Pulaski, Tennessee, to help obstruct the advance of General John B. Hood's Confederates.

November 4

West: General John C. Breckinridge leads a small Confederate army from western Virginia into eastern Tennessee. There, he encounters an equally small Federal force at Strawberry Plains, Tennessee, and drives them off.

Naval: Artillery under General Nathan B. Forrest attack and sink the Union paddle wheelers USS *Key West, Tawah,* and *Elfin* on the Tennessee River near Johnsonville, Tennessee. But reinforcements arrive in the form of steamers *Moose, Brilliant, Victory, Curlew, Fairy,* and *Paw Paw,* which force the Confederates to beach and burn CSS *Undine.* Forrest also bombards a large Union depot across the river at Johnsonville, inflicting considerable devastation. His latest raid disrupts the flow of Union supplies and results in considerable damage: Four gunboats, 14 steamers, 17 barges, 33 cannon,

150 captives, and 75,000 tons of supplies ruined. Total loses to the Union exceed $6.7 million.

November 5

WEST: General Nathan B. Forrest, flushed with success, rides south from Johnsonville, Tennessee, toward Corinth, Mississippi, there to join the main Confederate army under General John B. Hood.

NAVAL: The USS *Patapsco* drives an unidentified sloop aground off Fort Moultrie, Charleston harbor, South Carolina, and burns it.

The USS *Fort Morgan* captures the Confederate blockade-runner *John A. Hazard* in the Gulf of Mexico.

The Confederate raider CSS *Shenandoah* under Lieutenant James I. Waddell captures and burns the Union schooner *Charter Oak* off the Cape Verde Islands.

November 6

WEST: More than 100 Copperheads and Confederate sympathizers are arrested by Colonel Benjamin Sweet in Chicago, Illinois. They allegedly were plotting to seize the polls on election day, stuff the ballots, and then burn the city down. None of those arrested are ever prosecuted.

General Sterling Price's men fight a rearguard action at Cane Hill, Arkansas, having evacuated Missouri for the last time.

NAVAL: Armed boats from the USS *Adela* capture the Confederate schooner *Badger* at St. George's Sound, Florida.

The USS *Fort Morgan* captures the Confederate schooner *Lone* off Brazos Pass, Texas.

November 7

POLITICS: The second session of the 2nd Confederate Congress convenes in Richmond, Virginia. President Jefferson Davis declares that the Confederacy still desires a negotiated settlement with the North, but only on the basis of independence. Despite the recent fall of Atlanta, Davis assures Congress, "There are no vital points on the preservation of which the continued existence of the Confederacy depends."

November 8

POLITICS: The Republican ticket of President Abraham Lincoln and Vice President Andrew Johnson decisively wins reelection by 2,330,552 votes to 1,835,985 votes for General George B. McClellan. This translates into 212 Republican electoral votes to 21 for the Democrats; McClellan carries only the states of New Jersey, Delaware, and Kentucky. The margin of 55 percent proves so large that the 81 electoral votes of seceded states would not have altered the outcome. Moreover, Lincoln receives his highest percentage of support from soldiers and sailors fighting in the ranks.

NAVAL: The CSS *Shenandoah* under Lieutenant James I. Waddell captures and burns the Union bark *Godfrey* southwest of the Cape Verde Islands.

November 9

WEST: The army of General William T. Sherman organizes itself into two wings under Generals Oliver O. Howard (XV, XVII Corps) and Henry W. Slocum (XIV, XX Corps) prior to marching on Savannah, Georgia.

Sherman then declares: "The army will forage liberally on the country during the march." All ranks are expected to refrain from destroying private property, if possible, but this is still the first mass application of total war against all segments of society.

NAVAL: The USS *Stepping Stones* seizes the Confederate sloops *Reliance* and *Little Elmer* at Mobjack Bay, Virginia.

November 10

POLITICS: At a party celebrating his election victory, President Abraham Lincoln implores his fellow citizens to remain steadfast in the pursuit of final victory and to reunite the country.

WEST: General Jubal A. Early, while defeated, gives ground slowly and harasses Union advances down the Shenandoah Valley.

General William T. Sherman marches his men from Kingston, Georgia, back to Atlanta, prior to advancing on Savannah.

NAVAL: The Confederate raider CSS *Shenandoah* under Lieutenant James I. Waddell captures and scuttles the Union brig *Susan* southwest of the Cape Verde Islands.

November 11

WEST: Union troops begin to raze the ground in and around Rome, Georgia, leveling bridges, shops, mills, and all useful property as they wend their way back to Atlanta.

General George H. Thomas briefly clashes with Confederates under General John C. Breckinridge at Bull's Gap, eastern Tennessee.

NAVAL: The Federal tug USS *Tulip* sinks in the Potomac River after a boiler explosion that kills 49 members of its crew.

The USS *Lancaster* accosts the steamer *Salvador* and removes Confederate raiders led by Thomas E. Hogg, then en route from Panama to California. The agents were planning to seize the steamer and convert it into a commerce raider.

November 12

WEST: At Rome, Georgia, General William T. Sherman gathers up 60,000 infantry and 5,500 artillery for his proposed "March to the Sea."

NAVAL: Commander Napoleon Collins and the USS *Wachusett* arrive at Norfolk, Virginia, with the captured CSS *Florida* in tow. However, Secretary of State William H. Seward, angered by Collins's overt breach of Brazilian neutrality, orders the vessel returned to Brazil. Collins is also tried by court-martial and is dismissed from the service, but Secretary of the Navy Gideon Welles arranges his reinstatement.

Landing parties from the USS *Hendrick Hudson* and *Nita* attack Confederate saltworks near Tampa, Florida, but they are driven back by enemy cavalry.

The Confederate raider CSS *Shenandoah* under Lieutenant James I. Waddell captures the Union clipper ship *Kate Prince* and the brig *Adelaide,* near the equator, releasing both on a bond.

Sherman's March to the Sea November 1864 Painting by F. O. C. Darley *(Library of Congress)*

November 13

WEST: General Jubal A. Early is ordered back to New Market, Virginia, there to dispatch part of his army from the Shenandoah Valley to the defenses of Richmond and Petersburg, Virginia. This act concludes his celebrated Shenandoah Valley campaign, which involved 1,670 miles of marching and 75 encounters of various sizes.

NAVAL: The Confederate raider CSS *Shenandoah* under Commander James I. Waddell captures and burns the Union schooner *Lizzie M. Stacey* near the equator.

November 14

POLITICS: President Abraham Lincoln accepts General George B. McClellan's resignation from the U.S. Army.

NORTH: Philip H. Sheridan is promoted to major general, U.S. Army.

WEST: Union forces under General William T. Sherman continue pulling up railroads and burning crops and buildings around Atlanta, Georgia. Meanwhile, General Henry W. Slocum leads the XV and XVII Corps out of the city and begins to head off for Savannah.

General John M. Schofield arrives at Pulaski, Tennessee, and assumes command of Union forces concentrating there.

November 15

WEST: General William T. Sherman departs a thoroughly devastated Atlanta, Georgia, and rolls toward Savannah and the sea with 62,000 men. To maximize foraging, his force deploys in two wings of four columns. The right wing is led by General Oliver O. Howard (XIV and XX Corps), his left is under General Henry W. Slocum (XV and XVII Corps), while two cavalry divisions are commanded by General Hugh J. Kilpatrick. Sherman also defies conventional military practice by severing his own lines of communication and living off the land. Most notoriously, he also embarks on a 60-mile-wide swath of destruction across the state, destroying anything of use to the Confederacy. His unequivocal object is to "make Georgia howl," and within 21 days, Sherman's "bummers" inflict damage on the South approaching $100 million, leaving a twisted, blackened landscape in their wake. The age of "total war" has arrived.

November 16

WEST: Union forces under General Hugh J. Kilpatrick brush aside Confederate cavalry under General Joseph Wheeler at Lovejoy Station, Georgia. The principal attack is made by the dismounted 8th Indiana Cavalry, which dislodges the Southerners and drives them in the direction of Beaver Creek. Kilpatrick captures 50 prisoners and two cannon.

General Nathan B. Forrest's cavalry forces finally augment the Confederate Army of Tennessee at Shoal Creek, Tennessee. His arrival signals a general advance by General John B. Hood into Tennessee and the final Confederate offensive of the war.

November 17

POLITICS: President Jefferson Davis dismisses outright any notion proposed by Georgia state senators to conclude a separate peace treaty with the U.S. government.
WEST: General John C. Breckinridge concludes his brief offensive into Tennessee by withdrawing back into western Virginia.
NAVAL: The Federal side-wheelers USS *Otsego* and *Ceres* steam up the Roanoke River, North Carolina, on an extended reconnaissance mission.

November 18

SOUTH: President Jefferson Davis instructs General Howell Cobb to mobilize the state's entire militia force and oppose the advance of General William T. Sherman. He then places the entire force under the command of General William J. Hardee.
WEST: Despite the recent eclipse of Confederate fortunes, guerrilla bands skirmish with Union forces at Fayette, Missouri.

November 19

POLITICS: President Abraham Lincoln lifts the blockades from Norfolk, Virginia, and Pensacola, Florida, declaring them open for business.
SOUTH: Georgia governor Joseph E. Brown orders all men between the ages of 16 and 55 to join the militia to oppose General William T. Sherman, but few actually step forward.
NAVAL: The Confederate raider CSS *Chickamauga* under Lieutenant John Wilkinson runs the Union blockade off Wilmington, North Carolina, covered by a fog, and anchors under the guns of Fort Fisher. The crew then calmly waits for high tide to

lift the vessel over the bar and into the Cape Fear River. The USS *Kansas, Wilderness, Cherokee,* and *Clematis* fire on the vessel once the mist lifts, but *Chickamauga* safely escapes upstream.

November 20

WEST: Union forces under General William T. Sherman skirmish with Confederate defenders at Walnut Creek, East Macon, and Griswoldville, Georgia, as they proceed inexorably toward the coast.

NAVAL: Admiral David D. Porter, acting on the behest of General Benjamin F. Butler, orders the Union steamer USS *Louisiana* sent to Beaufort, North Carolina, crammed with explosives. With it, Butler hopes to damage seriously the Confederate defenses of Fort Fisher, Wilmington, North Carolina.

November 21

WEST: The Army of Tennessee under General John B. Hood advances 31,000 men and 8,000 cavalry out of Florence, Alabama, and toward Nashville, Tennessee, threatening Union lines of communication. He commands three infantry corps under Generals Benjamin F. Cheatham, Stephen D. Lee, Alexander P. Stewart, with a cavalry corps under the redoubtable Nathan B. Forrest. However, his timetable has been delayed three weeks by Forrest's absence, and during that interval, General George H. Thomas strengthens the defenses of Nashville.

General William J. Hardee makes a stand at Macon, Georgia, with a motley assortment of militia and veteran cavalry under General Joseph Wheeler. Union forces do not make an appearance as anticipated. Concluding that Macon is not their objective, Hardee then orders Wheeler to begin to slash attacks on the rear of the enemy columns.

Georgia militiamen under General Gustavus W. Smith ride trains from Macon to Augusta and begin to march toward Griswoldville, Georgia, to impede approaching Union forces.

NAVAL: The USS *Iosco* captures the Confederate schooner *Sybil* off the North Carolina coast.

Armed boats from the USS *Avenger* capture Confederate supplies on the Mississippi River near Bruinsburg, Mississippi.

November 22

SOUTH: General Henry W. Slocum's Union troops approach the state capital of Milledgeville, Georgia, forcing the legislature to flee in panic.

WEST: General John B. Hood rapidly approaches Columbia, Tennessee, intending to cut off Union forces under General John M. Schofield at nearby Pulaski. However, Schofield divines Hood's intentions at the last possible moment and hurriedly maneuvers northward to escape.

General Gustavus W. Smith's division of Georgia militia attacks dismounted Union cavalry under General Hugh J. Kilpatrick at Griswoldville, Georgia. The levies bravely charge several times before being repulsed with 600 casualties; Kilpatrick sustains around 100 casualties.

November 23

SOUTH: Union forces brush aside Confederate defenders at Milledgeville, Georgia, easily occupying the state capital.

WEST: General Edward R. S. Canby departs Vicksburg, Mississippi, and marches toward Jackson to capture supplies destined for General John B. Hood's army in Tennessee.

SOUTHWEST: The surviving Confederates of General Sterling Price's column enter Bonham, Texas.

November 24

WEST: Union cavalry under General John M. Schofield attack and drive off Confederate defenders under General Nathan B. Forrest near Columbia, Tennessee. The Federals then dig in behind the Duck River and await the Army of Tennessee under General John B. Hood.

General William T. Sherman departs Milledgeville, Georgia, and continues his trek toward Savannah. To confuse the Confederates, he orders General Hugh J. Kilpatrick to make a feint 30 miles northwest toward Augusta and then to ride east to sever the Augusta and Savannah Railroad.

SOUTHWEST: An expedition of 300 soldiers and Ute/Apache Indians under Colonel Christopher "Kit" Carson, patrolling the Canadian River in the Texas Panhandle for hostile Commanche and Kiowa bands, detects a large Indian encampment near the ruins of an abandoned trading post called Adobe Walls. Carson secures his own wagon train, conducts a 15-mile night march, and prepares to attack the unsuspecting Indians at dawn.

NAVAL: The USS *Chocura* chases the Confederate schooner *Louisa* onto a bar near the San Bernard River, Texas. A sudden gale subsequently destroys the stricken vessel.

November 25

NORTH: Confederate agents dispatched from Canada set fire to 10 New York hotels in an unsuccessful attempt to burn down the city. One Southern perpetrator is caught and eventually hanged.

SOUTH: General Joseph Wheeler's Confederate cavalry harass General John M. Schofield's Union column near Sandersville, Georgia.

SOUTHWEST: Colonel Christopher "Kit" Carson leads 200 charging cavalry through a hostile Kiowa encampment near Adobe Walls, Texas. Simultaneously, his Ute and Apache steal the warriors's horses. However, the survivors flee into nearby Comanche lodges with pleas for help, and soon hundreds, if not thousands, of angry warriors begin to mass to attack the intruders. Carson, suddenly confronted by the largest aggregation of Native Americans he ever beheld, quickly ducks into the ruins of Adobe Walls. Fortunately for him, the fire of hostile two 12-pound mountain howitzers keeps the Indians at bay. Several hours of shooting at long range ensue, and Carson prepares to withdraw under the cover of darkness. Smoke from a plains fire set by the Kiowa also cloaks his movement. The Americans and their Native-American consorts ride quickly back to the safety of New Mexico. Carson suffers two dead and 10 wounded; Kiowa/Comanche losses are between 50 and 150, due mainly to artillery fire. In point of sheer numbers engaged, Adobe Walls is also the largest Indian battle waged in Texas.

November 26

SOUTH: Advancing Union forces under General William T. Sherman skirmish with Confederates at Sanderson, Georgia.

WEST: General Thomas L. Rosser departs the Shenandoah Valley with two Confederate cavalry brigades, intending to raid the Union depot at New Creek, West Virginia.

The Confederate Army of Tennessee arrives outside Columbia, Tennessee, and finds Federal troops under General John M. Schofield entrenched and ready to receive him.

General Joseph Wheeler encounters the 8th Indiana and 2nd U.S. Cavalry in camp at Sylvian Grove, Georgia, and drives them toward the main Union column at Briar Creek.

November 27

SOUTH: Union troops under General John W. Davidson depart Baton Rouge, Louisiana, intending to cut the Mobile and Ohio Railroad, which is guarded by Confederate forces under General Dabney H. Maury.

WEST: Confederate cavalry under General Thomas L. Rosser engage and defeat a Union detachment sent from New Creek, West Virginia. The Federal commander at New Creek, Colonel George R. Latham, however, takes no special precautions against attack.

General John M. Schofield, confronting a larger Confederate force outside Columbia, Tennessee, begins to pull his men north of the Duck River. He believes that the attack, when mounted, will come from south of the city.

Confederate cavalry lash out at General William T. Sherman's army outside of Waynesboro, Georgia, in a vain effort to slow Union forces down.

A Union cavalry column under General Hugh J. Kilpatrick encamps for the night at Buck Head Creek, Georgia, unaware that Confederate troopers under General Joseph Wheeler are within striking distance.

NAVAL: The Union steamer *Greyhound*, serving as the headquarters ship of General Benjamin F. Butler, explodes and sinks in the James River, Virginia, with a high-ranking conference in attendance. Fortunately, Butler, General Robert Schenck, and Admiral David D. Porter escape unharmed. This was probably the work of a notorious Confederate "coal torpedo" that had been shoveled accidentally or deliberately into the *Greyhound*'s boiler.

Armed boats with Union sailors capture the British blockade-runner *Beatrice* off Charleston, South Carolina.

The USS *Princess Royal* captures the British blockade-runner *Flash* off Brazos Santiago, Texas, and subsequently seizes the schooner *Neptune* later in the day.

The USS *Metacomet* captures the Confederate steamer *Susanna* off Campeche Banks, Mexico.

The Federal ram USS *Vindicator* and stern-wheeler *Prairie Bird* transport and cover the landing of Union cavalry as they destroy railroad tracks and a bridge over the Big Black River near Vicksburg, Mississippi.

November 28

SOUTH: Confederate partisans under Colonel John S. Mosby are bested in a skirmish at Goresville, Virginia, by men of the Independent Battalion of Virginia Cavalry, a Unionist formation.

Union general John G. Foster marches 5,500 men from Hilton Head, South Carolina, to troop transports waiting offshore and sails down the Broad River. He intends to land near Boyd's Neck, stride overland, and cut the Savannah and Charleston Railroad.

WEST: Confederate cavalry under General Thomas L. Rosser stage a surprise attack on Fort Kelley at New Creek, West Virginia. In a swift 30-minute action, they capture the fort and 700 Federals, the majority of whom are cooking lunch. Colonel George R. Lantham fails to prepare the garrison despite ample reports of enemy activity at nearby Moorefield, and he is discharged dishonorably from the service.

General John B. Hood deploys part of his force under General Stephen D. Lee south of Columbia, Tennessee, to give the impression of an attack from south of the city. Hood, however, secretly shifts the bulk of his forces east to cross the Duck River above the town and so cut off any Union retreat. Meanwhile, General Nathan B. Forrest defeats a body of Union cavalry under General James H. Wilson at Spring Hill and drives them in the direction of Franklin. General John M. Schofield then decides to withdraw his army across the Duck River before the trap is sprung. He advances toward Spring Hill.

General Joseph Wheeler orders his Confederate cavalry to attack Union troopers bivouacked along Buck Head Creek, Georgia. Their commander, General Hugh J. Kilpatrick, having unwisely pitched his tent outside the camp, nearly falls captive, while men of the 5th Ohio Cavalry repel the Southerners with rapid-fire carbines. Kilpatrick then forms a new battle line at Reynold's Plantation, repulsing two more Confederate charges. Wheeler finally reins in his men, who regroup, while Kilpatrick escapes intact toward Louisville.

The Union District of Mississippi is constituted with General Napoleon J. T. Dana as commanding officer.

November 29

SOUTH: General John P. Hatch forms a brigade of infantry, a brigade of sailors, and eight cannon to march from Boyd's Neck, South Carolina, toward Grahamville and there to sever an important railroad depot linking Charleston to Savannah, Georgia. However, the Federals, misled by poor maps, march and countermarch aimlessly for several hours, allowing Confederate troops and militia to arrive.

WEST: General John M. Schofield, threatened by Generals John B. Hood and Nathan B. Forrest at Spring Hill, Tennessee, skillfully extricates his forces. He does so after Hood commits three infantry divisions to the attack and fighting breaks down into skirmishing across the line. Tonight, Union forces slip through the very fingers of the Confederates and begin a hard slog toward Franklin, 12 miles distant. That town has been secured earlier by the VI Corps of General David S. Stanley.

Colorado militia and howitzers under Colonel John M. Chivington attack a peaceful Cheyenne camp at Sand Creek, Colorado. The Native Americans under

Chief Black Kettle have been directed there by military authorities with the understanding that they will be safe. Nonetheless, vengeful militiamen attack the sleeping camp at dawn with artillery fire and then charge, killing everyone they encounter. Black Kettle, in an act of desperation, raises an American flag over his tent as a peace gesture but to no avail. "It may perhaps be unnecessary for me to state that I captured no prisoners," Chivington gloats. As many as 149 Native Americans, including women and children, are cut down and scalped, an act that General Nelson A. Miles condemned as "the foulest and most unjustified crime in the annals of America." Militia losses are nine dead and 40 wounded. Chivington is feted subsequently as a hero in Denver, but a congressional inquiry denounces the massacre and ends his military career. The surviving Native Americans go on a rampage lasting several months, but the U.S. government eventually pays the survivors an indemnity.

NAVAL: The monitors USS *Onondaga* and *Mahopac* trade shots inconclusively with a Confederate battery on the James River for three hours.

Commander George H. Preble's 450-man naval brigade, drawn from the South Atlantic Blockading Squadron, disembarks at Boyd's Landing on the Broad River, South Carolina. His mission is to act in concert with nearby army troops and help establish contact with the army of General William T. Sherman.

November 30

SOUTH: General John P. Hatch leads a Union expedition of 4,000 men against Confederate defenses at Honey Hill, South Carolina. There 2,000 Georgia militia under General Gustavus W. Smith are posted strongly along the crest of high ground bordered by streams. Hatch launches three frontal assaults, all of which are repelled by Southern artillery fire. At length, the Federals withdraw with 746 casualties; Smith's losses are about 100. It is an impressive performance by the state levies.

WEST: General John M. Schofield arrives at Franklin, Tennessee, with 15,000 men of his IV and XXII Corps and immediately strengthens existing defensive works. Within hours, he is joined by 23,000 men of the Confederate Army of Tennessee under General John B. Hood, which assumes offensive positions south of town. The corps of General Stephen D. Lee has yet to arrive with the bulk of Confederate artillery, but after surveying Union Lines, the aggressive Hood decides to assault it frontally using the divisions of Generals Patrick R. Cleburne, John Brown, and William Bate. He does so over the objections of General Nathan B. Forrest and Benjamin F. Cheatham. Accordingly, at 4:00 P.M., a tide of graycoats surge forward across two miles of open fields. Hood's initial charge catches two Union brigades under General George D. Wagner out in the open, sweeps them from the ground, and chases them back toward the Federal trenches. The main Union line is therefore obliged to hold its fire until cheering Southerners are nearly on top of them. They then unleash a concentrated fusillade toppling men by the hundreds. Still, the impetus of the Southern attack is so great that Confederates crash through the first line of barricades and enter the town. Colonel Emerson Opdyke's Federal brigade then comes tearing from the reserves, flings itself on the disorganized enemy, and violently ejects them from the trenches. Hood's men, now compressed into a dense mass, resist violently but are cut down from concentrated artillery fire on either flank. Fighting finally ceases about 9:00 P.M. as shattered Southern ranks withdraw from the town. The disputed ground, for all intents and purposes, resembles a slaughter pen.

The Battle of Franklin is a grievous miscalculation by the offensive-minded Hood. No less than six of his generals are killed, including the highly accomplished Cleburne, with another six seriously wounded. Moreover, the Army of Tennessee loses 1,750 dead, 3,800 wounded, and 702 missing (6,252) in another feckless frontal attack. Union losses by comparison are 189 killed, 1,033 injured, and 1,104 missing (2,326), but Schofield resumes withdrawing until reaching Nashville on the following day. Hood then lopes off in pursuit, setting the stage for an even bigger Southern tragedy.

General Andrew J. Smith's XVI Corps arrives at Nashville, Tennessee, to reinforce Union defenders under General George H. Thomas.

NAVAL: Commander George H. Preble leads a naval brigade of 150 marines and 350 sailors from the South Atlantic Blockading Squadron in an army attack on Honey Hill, Grahamville, South Carolina. This action is undertaken to cut the Charleston and Savannah Railroad, as well as to establish contacts with the army of General William T. Sherman. The sailors perform well despite a Northern defeat.

A naval expedition of five boats and 100 Union sailors from the USS *Ethan Allen* and *Dai Ching* sweeps up the South Altamaha River, South Carolina, to find escaped Union prisoners reputedly hiding there.

An armed party from the USS *Midnight* raids and destroys a Confederate saltworks at St. Andrew's Bay, Florida.

The USS *Itasca* captures the British blockade-runner *Carrie Mair* off Pass Cavallo, Texas.

December 1

POLITICS: President Abraham Lincoln appoints Kentuckian James Speed to replace outgoing Edward Bates as attorney general.

WEST: In order to deceive the Confederates as to his real intentions, General William T. Sherman dispatches Union cavalry under General Hugh J. Kilpatrick toward Augusta, Georgia, to give the impression his main force is heading in that direction.

The Union XXIII Corps under General John M. Schofield withdraws to new defensive positions at Nashville, Tennessee, forming part of greater defenses there under General George H. Thomas. The Confederate Army of Tennessee under General John B. Hood also resumes its advance toward the city.

NAVAL: The USS *Rhode Island* captures the British blockade-runner *Vixen* off Cape Fear, North Carolina.

Admiral Samuel P. Lee strengthens his Mississippi River Squadron with the addition of the heavy ironclads USS *Neosho* and *Carondelet*. This is in response to a major Confederate advance across the Tennessee River.

December 2

WEST: Confederate general Thomas L. Rosser, concluding his successful raid against New Creek, West Virginia, returns to camp in the lower Shenandoah Valley.

General John B. Hood arrives before Nashville, Tennessee, with approximately 24,000 men in the corps of Generals Stephen D. Lee, Alexander P. Stewart, and Benjamin F. Cheatham. A sizable force of veteran Confederate cavalry is also present under redoubtable General Nathan B. Forrest, which is soon detached and exerts little influence on events. Hood immediately commences fortifying his position southeast of the city by building several redoubts. Lacking the manpower to attack the Union position outright, he hopes to lure the federals into hitting him instead. He soon will be granted his wish as General George H. Thomas occupies Nashville with 55,000 men, including the VI Corps under General Thomas J. Wood, the XVI Corps under General Andrew J. Smith, and the XXIII Corps under General John M. Schofield. The Union cavalry corps of General James H. Wilson, detached from the city, is also nearby, resting and refitting.

General Thomas J. Wood replaces the wounded general David S. Stanley as commander of the Union IV Corps, Nashville, Tennessee.

General Sterling Price trudges into Laynesport, Arkansas, at the head of his defeated, exhausted column. This concludes Price's final effort to capture Missouri for the Confederacy; he covered 1,488 miles, fought 43 engagements, and lost 4,000 men, chiefly deserters, during his campaign.

General Grenville M. Dodge replaces General William S. Rosecrans as commander of the Department of the Missouri.

Naval: The USS *Chicopee* escorts a combined expedition up the Chowan River to Pitch Landing, North Carolina, where Confederate supply caches are found and burned.

The Federal troop transports *Prairie State, Prima Donna,* and *Magnet* are captured by Confederate forces on the Cumberland River, Tennessee, near Bell's Mill.

December 3

West: Union forces under General William T. Sherman reach Millen, Georgia. Meanwhile, Confederate cavalry under General Joseph Wheeler strike Union positions between Millen and Augusta, whereupon Sherman orders cavalry under General Hugh J. Kilpatrick to hunt down the elusive Southerners.

General George H. Thomas is urged by both President Abraham Lincoln and General Ulysses S. Grant to attack General John B. Hood's army immediately outside Nashville, Tennessee. Instead, Thomas meticulously and unhurriedly begins to strengthen his defenses while awaiting additional reinforcements.

Naval: The USS *Emma* forces the Confederate steamer *Ella* aground at Bald Head Point, North Carolina, and a boarding party subsequently burns it.

The USS *Mackinaw* captures the Confederate schooner *Mary* off Charleston, South Carolina.

Armed parties from the USS *Nita, Stars and Stripes, Hendrick Hudson, Ariel,* and *Two Sisters* attack and destroy a large Confederate saltworks at Rocky Point, Tampa Bay, Florida.

December 4

South: Heavy skirmishing at Waynesboro, Georgia, between cavalry forces of Generals Joseph Wheeler and Hugh J. Kilpatrick. The Union troopers discover the

Southerners behind a series of barricades, which are reduced by horse artillery and flanking attacks by the 9th Michigan and 10th Ohio cavalry. The Confederates then retreat to an even longer line of defenses that cannot be flanked easily, so Kilpatrick orders them stormed by frontal assault. Accordingly, the 9th Pennsylvania, 2nd, 3rd, and 5th Kentucky Cavalry, supported by the dismounted 8th Indiana, charge forward and drive the defenders off. Wheeler then extricates his men across Briar Creek and escapes toward Augusta, having sustained 250 casualties to Kilpatrick's 170.

NAVAL: The USS *R. R. Cuyler, Mackinaw,* and *Gettysburg* capture the Confederate steamer *Armstrong* east of Charleston, South Carolina.

The USS *Pursuit* captures the Confederate vessel *Peep O'Day* off the Indian River, Florida.

The USS *Chocura* captures the Confederate schooner *Lowood* off Velasco, Texas.

The USS *Pembina* captures the Dutch blockade-runner *Geziena Hilligonda* off Brazos Santiago, Texas.

The Confederate raider CSS *Shenandoah* under Lieutenant James I. Waddell captures and burns the Union bark *Edward* off Tristan da Cunha in the South Atlantic.

A naval squadron consisting of the USS *Moose, Carondelet, Fairplay, Reindeer,* and *Silver Lake* attacks Confederate batteries at Bell's Mill on the Cumberland River, Tennessee. Confederate defenders under General John B. Hood and Nathan B. Forrest fail to stop the gunboats, which recapture the three transports *Prairie State, Prima Donna,* and *Magnet,* seized a day earlier along with many Union prisoners.

December 5

POLITICS: The second session, 38th U.S. Congress convenes in Washington, D.C.

WEST: Confederate cavalry under General Nathan B. Forrest trots off to capture Murfreesboro, Tennessee, from Union forces under General L. H. Rosseau.

NAVAL: Secretary of the Navy Gideon Welles submits his fourth annual report to President Abraham Lincoln, stating navy strength at 671 ships, including 62 ironclads, which mount 4,600 cannon and have seized 1,400 Confederate vessels since the war began. "The blockade of a coastline," he declares, "greater in extent than the whole coast of Europe from Cape Trafalgar to Cape North, is an undertaking without precedent in history."

The Federal monitors USS *Saugus, Onondaga, Mahopac,* and *Canonicus* trade shots with Confederate batteries at Howlett's Landing, James River, Virginia.

The Federal tug *Lizzie Freeman* is captured by Confederate forces while anchoring at Smithfield, Virginia.

The naval brigade of Commander George H. Preble lands up the Tulifinny River and supports army operations at Tulifinny Crossroads, Georgia. Confederate resistance proves fierce and Union forces are unable to sever the Savannah-Charleston Railroad.

The USS *Chocura* captured the British blockade-runner *Julia* off Velasco, Texas.

December 6

POLITICS: President Abraham Lincoln, in a conciliatory move, appoints Radical Republican and former secretary of the treasury Salmon P. Chase as the fifth

Chief Justice of the U.S. Supreme Court, succeeding the recently deceased Roger B. Taney.

WEST: General George H. Thomas again is ordered by General Ulysses S. Grant to attack Confederate forces under General John B. Hood at Nashville "and wait no longer for remount of your cavalry." Nonetheless, when Thomas dithers awaiting additional horses, Grant prepares to remove him from command.

Confederate cavalry under General Hylan B. Lyon depart Paris, Tennessee, for an extended raid against Hopkinsville, Kentucky.

NAVAL: Federal monitors USS *Saugus, Onondaga, Mahopac,* and *Canonicus* continue trading fire with Confederate batteries at Howlett's Landing, James River, Virginia.

The USS *Sunflower* captures the Confederate sloop *Pickwick* off St. George's Sound, Florida.

The USS *Chocura* captures the British blockade-runner *Lady Hurley* off Velasco, Texas.

The USS *Princess Royal* forces the Confederate schooner *Alabama* aground at San Luis Pass, Texas, and captures it.

The Federal ironclad USS *Neosho,* along with the steamers *Fairplay, Silver Lake,* and *Moose,* escorts several army transports down the Cumberland River from Nashville. Approaching Bell's Mills, Tennessee, they are beset by heavy fire from Confederate batteries ashore, which is answered by the heavily armored *Neosho.* The Union flag is then shot from its mast and falls onto the deck. Quartermaster John Ditzenback calmly braves a storm of Southern shot, walks on the deck, and reattaches it to the only remaining mast. He obtains the Congressional Medal of Honor. The all-day contest finally concludes at nightfall with *Neosho* having been struck more than 100 times, sustaining minor damage.

December 7

SOUTH: General Benjamin F. Butler begins to mass his forces at Fortress Monroe, Virginia, in anticipation of a large expedition against Wilmington, North Carolina. General Godfrey Wentzel originally had been slated to command the effort, but Butler uses his still considerable political influence to take control.

WEST: Union cavalry under General Robert L. Milroy attack and defeat General Nathan B. Forrest outside Murfreesboro, Tennessee, taking 200 captives and 14 cannon.

NAVAL: Union vessels force the blockade-runner *Stormy Petrel* ashore at Wilmington, North Carolina, and then destroy it with gunfire.

The USS *Narcissus* strikes a torpedo in Mobile Bay, Alabama, and sinks in a heavy storm, although without loss of life.

December 8

NORTH: General Ulysses S. Grant, perplexed over General George H. Thomas's inactivity at Nashville, Tennessee, contacts General Henry W. Halleck and writes, "If Thomas has not struck yet, he ought to be ordered to hand over his command to Schofield."

SOUTH: General Benjamin F. Butler ferries 6,500 men from his Army of the James down the James River to Fortress Monroe, Virginia. There they embark on ships intending to attack Fort Fisher, Wilmington, North Carolina.

Naval: The USS *Cherokee* captures the British blockade-runner *Emma Henry* off the North Carolina coast.

The USS *J. P. Jackson* and *Stockdale* capture the Confederate schooner *Medora* in the Mississippi Sound.

The USS *Itasca* runs the Confederate sloop *Mary Ann* ashore at Pass Cavallo, Texas, and then destroys it with cannon fire.

December 9

North: General Ulysses S. Grant, frustrated by the perceived lack of aggressiveness from General George H. Thomas, orders General John M. Schofield to succeed him. The directive is then suspended when Thomas informs Grant that his intended attack is cancelled because of a winter storm. While the cold weather inconveniences Thomas, it causes the poorly clad and sheltered Confederates under General John B. Hood to shiver in their trenches. The fast-frozen ground also proves impossible to dig through for strengthening field works.

Naval: The USS *Otsego* strikes two Confederate torpedoes and sinks on the Roanoke River near Jamesville, North Carolina. The Federal tug USS *Bazely*, in the act of rescuing survivors, also strikes a device and sinks.

December 10

Politics: President Abraham Lincoln appoints General William F. Smith and Henry Stanberry special commissioners to report on civil and military matters west of the Mississippi River.

West: General William T. Sherman's Union army of 60,000 men reaches the outskirts of Savannah, Georgia. The 18,000 defenders under General William J. Hardee flood the rice fields, forcing prospective Federal attacks to be committed over a very narrow front, so Sherman mounts siege operations instead.

General George Stoneman leads 1,500 Union horsemen on an expedition out of Knoxville, Tennessee, to destroy Confederate salt and lead factories in southwestern Virginia.

Naval: The CSS *Macon, Sampson,* and *Resolute* steam down the Savannah River to engage Union batteries at Tweedside, Georgia. *Resolute* is struck repeatedly, abandoned, and ultimately captured while the remaining vessels flee upstream back to Augusta.

The USS *O. H. Lee* captures the British blockade-runner *Sort* near the Anclote Keys, Florida.

December 11

West: General George H. Thomas, having delayed his planned attack, again is urged by General Ulysses S. Grant to strike John B. Hood's Confederates outside Nashville, Tennessee. Thomas replies that he will attack once the weather, which is dreadful, improves.

December 12

West: General William T. Sherman's army, now stationary, can no longer victual itself, so he orders General Oliver O. Howard to capture Fort McAlister on the Ogeechee River. This move will open a line of supply to the Union fleet offshore.

General George H. Thomas again assures chief of staff General Henry W. Halleck that he will attack Confederates gathered outside Nashville, Tennessee, once weather conditions permit.

December 13

DIPLOMACY: Charles Coursel, a Montreal police magistrate, declares he has no authority to detain Lieutenant Bennet Young and his 20 compatriots for their role in the raid on St. Albans, Vermont, and releases them on bond. A political uproar ensues, and Secretary of State William H. Seward notifies the British government that Washington will nullify the Rush-Bagot Agreement of 1817 in one-year's time. Under this act, the U.S.-Canadian border was demilitarized following the War of 1812.

NORTH: A sorely vexed General Ulysses S. Grant orders General John A. Logan from Virginia to Tennessee to replace General George H. Thomas for failing to take offensive action. Grant also prepares to visit Nashville and supervise matters personally.

WEST: Union cavalry under General George Stoneman defeat General Basil W. Duke's Confederates at Kingsport, Tennessee.

Fort McAllister on the Ogeechee River, Georgia, is attacked by the 2nd Division, XV Corps, under General William B. Hazen. The fort, though formidably armed and constructed, is garrisoned by only 150 Confederates under Major George W. Anderson. Hazen, by comparison, marshals 1,500 picked troops to spearhead the assault, which begins at 4:45 P.M. The Federals quickly clear the ditch and abattis, taking some losses from buried land torpedoes, and the fort falls after hand-to-hand fighting. Union losses are 24 dead and 110 wounded to a Confederate tally of 17 killed and 31 injured. Consequently, General William T. Sherman establishes communication with the South Atlantic Blockading Squadron in Ossabaw Sound, and food supplies are soon steaming their way up the Ogeechee River.

The 13th Colored U.S. Infantry conducts a destructive foray from Barrancas, Florida, to Pollard, Alabama, destroying all public property that cannot be brought off.

NAVAL: An ailing and fatigued admiral David G. Farragut arrives in New York City with the USS *Hartford,* receiving his second hero's welcome.

A large Union expedition under General Benjamin F. Butler departs Fortress Monroe, Virginia, and steams south to attack Fort Fisher, Wilmington, North Carolina. The USS *Sassacus* is detailed to tow the hulk *Louisiana,* laden with explosives, into position off the fort.

December 14

SOUTH: General Edward O. C. Ord is picked to command the Army of the James outside Richmond, Virginia.

WEST: A prompt attack on Bristol, Tennessee, by Union cavalry under General George Stoneman defeats General John C. Vaughn's Confederates and nets 300 Confederate prisoners.

The weather near Nashville, Tennessee, has moderated, and General George H. Thomas wires anxious superiors that he intends to attack General John B. Hood's Confederate army on the following day. True to form, Thomas methodically and unhurriedly arranges his men for the task.

NAVAL: A naval squadron consisting of the USS *Winona, Sonoma,* and several gun-boats is assigned to support the Union advance on Savannah, Georgia, by bombard-ing Forts Beaulieu and Rosedew in Ossabaw Sound.

Seven Union gunboats of the Mississippi River Squadron slip down the Cum-berland River from Nashville, Tennessee, and position themselves opposite the main Confederate battery on the Confederate army's left flank.

December 15

SOUTH: The combined expedition of General Benjamin F. Butler arrives off the North Carolina coast, after missing a rendezvous with the fleet under Admiral David D. Porter.

WEST: A Union cavalry column under General George Stoneman crosses into west-ern Virginia and occupies the town of Abingdon, burning a number of buildings.

General Pierre G. T. Beauregard, commanding the Military Division of the West, instructs General William J. Hardee to save his army rather than be bottled up and captured at Savannah, Georgia.

The Battle of Nashville commences as General George H. Thomas unleashes the XVI and IV Corps against the Confederate left under General Benjamin F. Cheatham. Simultaneously, a large diversionary attack by General James B. Steedman's African-American troops sustains heavy losses but pins down the Confederate right. All the while, General John B. Hood is shifting men furiously to support his overextended line, but it crumbles beforehand. The Southerners, stunned and startled by the weight of Thomas's sledgehammer blows, fall back to a new, more compact position a mile and a half distant. Hood, badly outnum-bered, should have retreated tonight, but he defiantly elects to make another stand.

NAVAL: A quick raid up the Coan River, Virginia, by the USS *Coeur de Lion* and *Mercury* destroys 30 small Confederate craft.

Federal gunboats under Commander Le Roy Fitch, especially the heavy moni-tors *Neosho* and *Carondelet,* actively participate in the Battle of Nashville by bom-barding Confederate formations along the shore line. Their heavy fire helps drive the Southern left flank from the field.

December 16

WEST: The Battle of Nashville continues as General George H. Thomas, startled that General John B. Hood's Confederates have not retreated, renews his drive against their re-formed left wing. The attack rolls forward at 3:30 P.M. with Gen-eral James H. Wilson's cavalry turning the Southern left flank and racing ahead to cut their retreat. This is followed 30 minutes later by a massive attack on the Confederate left-center, which completely overpowers the defenders. Hood's men score better results at the fortified position of Overton Hill on the right, where a major Union thrust is repelled, but the tide of fugitives fleeing down the turnpike becomes irresistible. In the ensuing rout, the Federals capture General Edward Johnson and nearly all of Hood's artillery. Only the onset of darkness and the timely arrival of General Nathan B. Forrest's cavalry prevent his army from being completely annihilated.

Nashville is a decisive Confederate defeat that terminates virtually all organized resistance in the western theater. Hood's losses included 1,500 killed or wounded, along with 4,462 captured (5,962). Thomas, a methodical, if plodding, pugilist, incurs far fewer casualties: 387 dead, 2,558 wounded, and 12 missing (3,057). Nashville is also the only instance in the Civil War when an entire Southern army dissolves in abject panic from the field of battle.

NAVAL: The USS *Mount Vernon* and *New Berne* capture and sink the Confederate schooner *G. O. Bigelow* at Bear Inlet, North Carolina.

December 17

SOUTH: President Jefferson Davis glumly informs General William J. Hardee that he cannot reinforce the Confederate defenders of Savannah, Georgia, with troops drawn from the Army of Northern Virginia.

WEST: Skirmishing erupts between Union cavalry under General George Stoneman and Confederates under General John C. Breckinridge at Wytheville, Virginia. The Southerners are forced back, losing 200 prisoners and eight cannon.

Confederates mount a tenacious rearguard action allowing the army of General John B. Hood to escape. Pursuing Union cavalry under General James H. Wilson prove relentless, however.

General William T. Sherman sends a flag of truce into Confederate lines and formally demands the surrender of Savannah, Georgia.

December 18

POLITICS: President Abraham Lincoln pleads for an additional 300,000 volunteers to bolster the Union army's battered ranks.

WEST: Confederates under General John C. Breckinridge stand at Marion, Virginia, against General George Stoneman's Union cavalry, and they are outflanked. They subsequently retire toward the mountains of North Carolina.

General William J. Hardee refuses General William T. Sherman's demand for surrender at Savannah, Georgia, and prepares to abandon the city.

NAVAL: The USS *Louisiana*, heavily laden with 200 tons of gunpowder for an impending attack on Fort Fisher, Wilmington, North Carolina, is briefly towed out of Charleston Harbor, South Carolina, then returned owning to heavy seas.

December 19

WEST: General George A. Custer's cavalry conduct a destructive romp from Kernstown, Virginia, to Lacey Springs, burning property and disrupting enemy communications. However, his attempt to cut the Virginia Central Railroad proceeds only as far as Harrisonburg before resistance stiffens.

A force of 8,000 Union cavalry under General Alfred T. A. Torbert ranges over portions of the Shenandoah Valley from Winchester to Gordonsville, Virginia, torching crops, farm buildings, and anything of value to the enemy.

Union troops from the XX Corps reach the South Carolina shore outside Savannah, Georgia, thereby threatening the only remaining escape route for General William J. Hardee's Confederates. He orders the city evacuated that evening.

NAVAL: The CSS *Waterwitch,* a former Union vessel, is burned by Confederates on the Vernon River near Savannah, Georgia, to prevent its recapture.

The USS *Princess Royal* captures the Confederate schooner *Cora* off Galveston, Texas.

December 20

SOUTH: Savannah Georgia is evacuated successfully by Confederate forces under General William J. Hardee, which cross the Savannah River on a pontoon bridge constructed from rice boats. However, the defenders are forced to abandon 250 heavy cannon.

WEST: Union cavalry under General George Stoneman storm into Saltville, Virginia, destroying numerous saltworks over the next two days.

NAVAL: Admiral David G. Farragut lowers his flag from the USS *Hartford* in the New York Navy Yard and concludes his naval career.

A boat expedition launched from the USS *Chicopee, Valley City,* and *Wyalusing* against Rainbow Bluff, North Carolina, is rebuffed by Confederate torpedoes and artillery fire along the Roanoke River.

December 21

SOUTH: Savannah, Georgia, falls to Union forces under General William T. Sherman, thereby completing his 285-mile "March to the Sea." He telegrams President Abraham Lincoln, "I beg to present to you as a Christmas gift the city of Savannah with 150 heavy guns and also about 25,000 bales of cotton."

WEST: General Benjamin H. Grierson leads a mounted expedition from Memphis, Tennessee, against the Mobile and Ohio Railroad in northern Alabama and Mississippi.

NAVAL: The Confederate blockade-runner *Owl* slips past Union vessels off Wilmington, North Carolina, and makes for the open sea.

Armed boats from the USS *Ethan Allen* venture up the Altamaha River, South Carolina, on an intelligence-gathering mission.

Confederate sailors scuttle the CSS *Savannah, Isondiga, Firefly,* and the floating battery *Georgia* at Savannah, Georgia, preventing their capture by Union forces.

December 22

WEST: General George Stoneman concludes his raid into western Virginia, departs Saltville, and rides back to Knoxville, Tennessee. In 12 days, he covers 460 miles, taking 900 captives and 19 cannon.

General Joseph J. Reynolds replaces General Frederick Steele as commander of the Department of Arkansas.

December 23

POLITICS: President Abraham Lincoln approves congressional legislation creating the rank of vice admiral; David G. Farragut becomes the first American naval officer so honored, granting him the equivalent rank of lieutenant general.

NAVAL: A belated, combined expedition of 65,000 men under General Benjamin F. Butler and five warships under Admiral David D. Porter arrives off Fort Fisher,

Wilmington, North Carolina. This is possibly the most formidable coastal fortification in the entire Confederacy, being an earthenwork 480 yards long, 60 feet high, and mounting 50 heavy cannon. It currently houses a garrison of 1,500 men under Colonel William Lamb.

The USS *Acacia* captures the British blockade-runner *Julia* near Alligator Creek, South Carolina.

December 24

NAVAL: The USS *Louisiana,* packed with explosives and intended to be detonated under the guns of Fort Fisher, Wilmington, North Carolina, accidently explodes 250 yards away from its objective. When this fails to damage the defenses, 60 Union warships under Admiral David D. Porter begin a concerted bombardment, which strikes the fort at a rate of 115 shells a minute. The pyrotechnics are awe-inspiring but produce relatively little damage.

Federal gunboats under Admiral Samuel D. Lee move down the Tennessee River in a failed attempt to interdict General John B. Hood at Chickasaw, Alabama. The vessels are thwarted by declining water levels below Great Mussel Shoals and withdraw.

December 25

SOUTH: An attack on Fort Fisher, Wilmington, North Carolina, by the Army of the James under General Benjamin F. Butler, transpires. He lands 2,200 men at 2:00 A.M. and advances inland, thinking that the defenses of the fort have been silenced. Suddenly, Confederate gunners unleash a torrent of shot and shell that keeps the attackers 50 yards from their walls. Butler is so nonplussed by stout resistance that he summarily cancels the entire operation and withdraws back to the fleet offshore. Moreover, this retreat is conducted so hastily that 700 Union soldiers remain trapped on the beach for the next two days. Confederate reinforcements under General Robert F. Hoke subsequently arrive to bolster Wilmington's defenses.

December 26

WEST: General John B. Hood begins to ferry the remnants of his army over the Tennessee River at Bainbridge, Tennessee, and heads for Tupelo, Mississippi. This concludes his ill-fated Nashville campaign, the latest nail in the Confederacy's coffin.

The Confederate blockade-runner *Chameleon* (nee *Tallahassee*) successfully evades Union vessels and slips out of Wilmington, North Carolina, after the attack on Fort Fisher.

December 27

SOUTH: General Benjamin F. Butler returns with his expedition to Fortress Monroe, Virginia, where news of his rebuff at Wilmington, North Carolina, enrages the normally detached Ulysses S. Grant.

NAVAL: At midnight an armed boat from the USS *Virginia* cuts out the Confederate schooner *Belle* in Galveston harbor, Texas, only yards away from a Southern guard boat.

December 28

NORTH: General Ulysses S. Grant admits to President Abraham Lincoln that operations against Fort Fisher, North Carolina, are a complete fiasco. Furthermore, he insists that General Benjamin F. Butler be sacked for "gross and culpable failure."

NAVAL: Commander George H. Preble's 500-man naval brigade returns to the South Atlantic Blockading Squadron after four weeks of campaigning ashore.

The USS *Kanawha* destroys an unnamed Confederate sloop at Caney Creek, Texas.

The Confederate raider CSS *Shenandoah* under Lieutenant James I. Waddell captures and burns the Union bark *Delphine* in the Indian Ocean.

December 29

WEST: The Union cavalry column under General George Stoneman finishes its recent raid into western Virginia by galloping into Knoxville, Tennessee.

December 30

POLITICS: Maryland politician Francis P. Blair contacts President Jefferson Davis and suggests meeting with him in Richmond, Virginia, as a peace overture and to "explain the view I entertain in reference to the state of affairs of our Country."

NORTH: President Abraham Lincoln, less vulnerable politically after his landslide election, relieves General Benjamin F. Butler as commander of the Army of the James.

NAVAL: Strong winds drive the USS *Rattler* against a snag, and it sinks near Grand Gulf, Mississippi.

December 31

SOUTH: Union forces settle comfortably into their siege lines outside Petersburg and Richmond, Virginia, constantly reinforced to a strength of 110,000 men and capably led by General Ulysses S. Grant. By contrast, the once-formidable Army of Northern Virginia of General Robert E. Lee, undersupplied and underfed, dwindles steadily through illness, desertion, and combat. His 66,000 gaunt, ragged soldiers remain determined and capable, but they continue perishing in the cold and mud that is the reality of trench warfare. Furthermore, over the succeeding months Lee must contain possible Union breakthroughs at any point along a 35-mile long defensive perimeter. The efficacy of Grant's war-winning strategy—to pin Lee inside his fortifications and bleed him through sheer attrition—is never more apparent. Consequently, the prospects of complete Union victory seldom have appeared brighter.

NAVAL: An exhausted and ailing admiral David G. Farragut is feted by New York City merchants, who present him with a $50,000 government bond.

Armed boats from the USS *Wabash* and *Pawnee* run aground in Charleston Harbor, South Carolina, and 27 Union sailors fall captive.

The USS *Metacomet* captures the Confederate schooner *Sea Witch* off Galveston, Texas.

1865

January 1

SOUTH: Army engineers ignite 12,000 pounds of gunpowder at Dutch Gap, Virginia, to assist a canal excavation. When the dirt tossed by the explosion simply falls back into place, General Benjamin F. Butler abandons efforts to build a detour for Union vessels on the James River, Virginia.

WEST: The 11th U.S. Colored Infantry conducts antiguerrilla sweeps in Arkansas with a heavy skirmish at Bentonville.

Federal troops skirmish fiercely with Snake warriors along the Canyon City Road, Oregon.

NAVAL: The USS *San Jacinto,* progenitor of the notorious *Trent* affair of 1861, is wrecked on No Name Key, Bahamas.

January 2

SOUTH: General Samuel W. Crawford gains temporary command of the V Corps, Army of the Potomac, Virginia.

WEST: Union forces under General Benjamin H. Grierson engage Confederate forces at Franklin and Lexington, Mississippi, as they destroy sections of the Mobile and Ohio Railroad.

NAVAL: Secretary of the Navy Gideon Welles contacts Secretary of War Edwin M. Stanton and expresses the dire necessity for capturing and closing Wilmington, North Carolina, "the only port by which any supplies whatever reach the rebels."

January 3

SOUTH: General Alfred H. Terry receives command of the forthcoming joint expedition against Fort Fisher, Wilmington, North Carolina. At this stage of the war, even General Benjamin F. Butler's political allies cannot salvage his waning fortunes.

General Oliver O. Howard moves the bulk of the Army of the Tennessee from Savannah, Georgia, toward Beaufort on the South Carolina border.

WEST: General Benjamin H. Grierson continues raiding along the Mobile and Ohio Railroad near Mechanicsburg, Mississippi.

NAVAL: The USS *Harvest Moon* transports a detachment of Union troops from Savannah, Georgia, to Beaufort, South Carolina.

The USS *Kanawha* captures the Confederate schooner *Mary Ellen* in the Gulf of Mexico.

January 4

SOUTH: General Alfred H. Terry embarks 8,000 Federal troops at Bermuda Landing, Virginia, as part of the renewed expedition against Fort Fisher, Wilmington, North Carolina.

WEST: General Benjamin H. Grierson concludes his raid against the Mobile and Ohio Railroad with a skirmish at Ponds, Mississippi. To date, he has destroyed 20,000 feet of bridges and other roadways, 20 miles of telegraph wire, 14 locomotives, 95 rail cars, and 300 army wagons.

A Union expedition up the White River culminates in the seizure of 407 head of cattle at Augusta, Arkansas.

NAVAL: Admiral David D. Porter begins to lay down his strategy for the reduction of Fort Fisher, Wilmington, North Carolina. He intends to use a naval infantry brigade of sailors and U.S. Marines to hit the fort frontally while army troops storm the rear.

Armed boats from the USS *Don* seize several Confederate torpedoes on the right bank of the Rappahannock River, Virginia.

January 5
POLITICS: President Abraham Lincoln authorizes James Singleton to pass through Union lines and enter the Confederacy; his mission is to encourage peace negotiations unofficially.

NAVAL: Boats from the USS *Winnebago* land and seize copper kettles, small boats, and other impedimenta at Bon Secours, Alabama.

The Federal ironclad USS *Indianola* is raised from its muddy berth in the Mississippi River after being sunk by enemy action on May 24, 1863.

January 6
POLITICS: Representative J. M. Ashley of Ohio renews the political drive to approve the 13th Amendment to the Constitution. "If slavery is wrong and criminal, as the great body of Christian men admit," he declares, "it is certainly our duty to abolish it."

President Jefferson Davis pens a caustic letter to Vice President Alexander H. Stephens in which he claims that his whispering campaign against him is undermining Confederate morale. "I assure you that it would be to me a source of the sincerest pleasure to see you devoting your great and animated ability exclusively to upholding the confidence and animating the spirit of the people to unconquerable resistance against their foes," he declares.

January 7
SOUTH: General Edward O. C. Ord replaces General Benjamin F. Butler as commander of the Department of Virginia and North Carolina. This is largely done at the behest of General Ulysses S. Grant, who feels that Butler manifestly is incapable of commanding a large force such as the Army of the James. Moreover, by sheer seniority of rank, Butler is next in line to succeed Grant as overall commander in his absence.

WEST: Elements of the Union XIX Corps are transferred from the Shenandoah Valley to Savannah, Georgia.

A large body of around 1,000 Cheyenne and Sioux warriors, still resenting the Sand Creek Massacre, attack frontier settlements at Julesburg and Valley Station, Colorado Territory. The Native Americans send a small detachment forward to lure the garrison out and a party of the 7th Iowa Cavalry under Captain Nicholas J. O'Brien obliges them. However, the intended ambush miscarries when it is sprung too early, and the cavalrymen scamper back into the fort. The frustrated warriors, unable to breach such strong defenses, subsequently loot and burn the town.

NAVAL: Admiral David D. Farragut pays a courtesy call on the White House to discuss current events with President Abraham Lincoln and Secretary of the Navy Gideon Welles.

The French-built ironclad *Sphinx*, sold to Denmark and then relinquished after the Schleswig-Holstein War, is resold secretly to the Confederacy by French emperor Napoleon III. This vessel, soon to be christened CSS *Stonewall*, is potentially the most powerful Confederate warship of the war. Captain Thomas J. Paige then sails it from Copenhagen to Spain on its maiden voyage.

January 8

SOUTH: General Edward O. C. Ord, commanding the Army of the James, also takes control of the Department of Virginia and North Carolina.

WEST: To alleviate near-starvation among his troops, General Thomas L. Rosser leads 300 Confederate cavalry from Staunton, West Virginia, on a raid against well-stocked Union encampments at Beverly. To accomplish this, the Southerners brave high snow drifts and howling winter winds for 75 miles.

General John A. Logan resumes command of the Union XV Corps in Tennessee.

NAVAL: Transports carrying the army of General Alfred H. Terry rendezvous with the naval squadron of Admiral David D. Porter off Beaufort, North Carolina. The two leaders then finalize plans for the impending assault on Fort Fisher, Wilmington, North Carolina.

January 9

POLITICS: President Abraham Lincoln dispatches Secretary of War Edwin M. Stanton to Savannah, Georgia, for discussions with General William T. Sherman. Among the issues raised is Sherman's alleged mistreatment of African-American refugees.

Representative Moses Odell, a New York Democrat, endorses the proposed constitutional amendments to outlaw slavery, insisting: "The South by rebellion has absolved the Democratic party at the North from all obligation to stand up longer for the defense of its 'cornerstone.'"

The Tennessee constitutional convention approves an amendment abolishing slavery and readies the amendment for a popular vote.

SOUTH: General William T. Sherman entertains Secretary of War Edwin M. Stanton at his headquarters in Savannah, Georgia.

WEST: General John B. Hood straggles into Tupelo, Mississippi, with remnants of his once-proud Army of Tennessee. President Jefferson Davis intends to transfer the bulk of the survivors eastward to contest the advance of General William T. Sherman in the Carolinas.

NAVAL: The USS *Wyalusing* captures the Confederate schooner *Triumph* off the mouth of the Perquimans River, North Carolina.

January 10

POLITICS: Heated debate in the U.S. House of Representatives continues as to a constitutional amendment to abolish slavery. Representative Fernando Wood of New York insists its passage negates any chance for peaceful reconciliation with the South.

WEST: A body of 300 Confederate cavalry under General Thomas L. Rosser reaches the Philippi Turnpike north of Beverly, West Virginia, and prepares to storm nearby Union positions at dawn.

NAVAL: The USS *Valley City* seizes the Confederate steamer *Philadelphia* in the Chowan River, Virginia.

January 11
POLITICS: The Missouri constitutional convention approves an ordinance abolishing slavery.
WEST: Despite freezing weather, 300 Confederate cavalrymen under General Thomas L. Rosser attack Union encampments at Beverly, West Virginia. The defenders, comprising detachments from the 8th and 34th Ohio Cavalry, are caught by surprise and overwhelmed before serious resistance is mounted. Rosser secures 583 captives, 100 horses, 600 rifles, and, above all, 10,000 rations to feed his hungry men.

January 12
POLITICS: Secretary of War Edwin M. Stanton confers with African-American leaders in Washington, D.C., about how to best assimilate freed slaves into society. Garrison Frazier, the group's spokesman, suggests that blacks continue farming the land until they are able to purchase it. And, despite allegations of callous indifference by General William T. Sherman toward "contrabands," Frazier states, "We have confidence in General Sherman, and think that what concerns us could not be in better hands."

Senior Maryland politician Francis P. Blair confers with President Jefferson Davis in Richmond, Virginia, sounding out possible overtures for peace. To facilitate a possible rapprochement, Blair suggests mounting a joint military expedition against the French in Mexico. Davis dismisses the scheme as quixotic, but he acquiesces in sending Confederate representatives to a conference with President Abraham Lincoln in February.
SOUTH: General John G. Parke resumes command of the IX Corps, Army of the Potomac, Virginia.
WEST: General Richard Taylor is instructed by President Jefferson Davis to transfer troops from the Army of Tennessee at Tupelo, Mississippi, to bolster Confederate defenses in the Carolinas. "Sherman's campaign has produced bad effect on our people, success against his future operations is needful to reanimate public confidence," he contends, "Hardee requires more aid than Lee can give him, and Hood's army is the only source to which we can now look."
NAVAL: Admiral David D. Porter arrives off Wilmington, North Carolina, with a fleet of 59 warships and 8,000 men commanded by General Alfred H. Terry. This is the largest Union armada and combined expedition of the entire war.

The new and formidable ram CSS *Columbia* grounds in Charleston harbor on its maiden voyage and efforts to refloat it fail.

January 13
SOUTH: General Alfred H. Terry lands four brigades of white troops and one of African Americans, totaling 8,000 men, outside Fort Fisher, Wilmington, North Carolina. As the whites take up assault positions, the black soldiers dig strong fortifications across the peninsula to forestall the arrival of Confederate reinforcements from General Robert F. Hoke's division.

General John B. Hood resigns from the Army of Tennessee at Tupelo, Mississippi, and he is succeeded temporarily by General Pierre G. T. Beauregard.

Naval: Admiral David D. Porter's fleet begins a protracted bombardment of the Confederate defenses at Fort Fisher, Wilmington, North Carolina. During the next two days, his fleet pours an estimated 1.6 million pounds of explosive ordnance on the Southern garrison, commanded by Colonel William Lamb.

Commander Stephen B. Luce takes the USS *Pontiac* 40 miles up the Savannah River to confer with General William T. Sherman. Luce's experience with the general indelibly impresses on him the need to educate navy officers in the principles of warfare and eventually inspires him to found the U.S. Naval War College in Newport, Rhode Island.

January 14

South: Union troops under General Alfred H. Terry resist General Braxton Bragg's efforts to reinforce the Confederate garrison at Fort Fisher, Wilmington, North Carolina. Nonetheless, 350 make it through under General William H. C. Whiting, bringing garrison strength up to roughly 2,000 men.

Naval: The armada of Admiral David D. Porter, mounting 627 heavy cannon, continues its concentrated bombardment of Confederate defenses at Fort Fisher, Wilmington, North Carolina. Porter moves his ships to within 1,000 yards and delivers a meticulously aimed fire that strikes Fort Fisher's defenses at a rate of 100 shells per minute. Within hours, most of the fort's heavy cannon have been rendered useless.

The USS *Seminole* captures the Confederate schooner *Josephine* off the Texas coast.

The Confederate blockade-runner *Leila* founders off the mouth of the Mersey River, England, killing Commander Arthur Sinclair, C.S.N.

January 15

Politics: Edward Everett, a former U.S. congressman from Massachusetts, dies in Boston at the age of 71.

South: General John Gibbon assumes control of the XXIV Corps, Army of the James. This transfer signals that his formally cordial relationship with General Winfield S. Hancock has ended.

General Alfred H. Terry commences an all-out assault on Fort Fisher, Wilmington, North Carolina, with three brigades commanded by Generals Newton M. Curtis, Galusha Pennypacker, and Louis H. Bell. The attack is launched in concert with a large naval brigade that advances against the fort's northeastern salient. Meanwhile, the army troops move inland around the rear of Confederate defenses and storm numerous lines of entrenchments and parapets. Resistance is fierce, and all three Union brigadiers are either killed or wounded in fierce, hand-to hand fighting that lasts eight hours. General William H. C. Whiting and Colonel William Lamb make repeated entreaties for reinforcements, but General Braxton Bragg, with 6,000 men under General Robert F. Hoke nearby, makes no attempt to interfere. At length, Porter sails in closer with concentrated firepower against the defenders while Terry commits his final brigade under General Joseph C. Abbott. The remaining Confederates are overpowered by 10:00 P.M. and surrender.

The Union Assault on Fort Fisher January 15, 1865 Painting by Lewis Prang *(Library of Congress)*

The fall of Fort Fisher is a major victory and demonstrates the Union's skill at massive, combined operations. Terry's and Porter's combined losses are 266 killed, 1,018 wounded, and 57 missing (1,341) with Colonels Pennypacker and Curtis receiving the Congressional Medal of Honor. Confederate losses total around 500 with an additional 1,500 captured. Both General Whiting and Colonel Lamb are wounded, the former mortally. Federal forces finally have slammed the door shut on the South's sole remaining open port, and Confederate vice president Alexander H. Stephens regards its fall as "one of the greatest disasters that had befallen our cause from the beginning of the war."

WEST: General John M. Schofield's XXIII Corps begins to embark on army transports at Clifton, Tennessee to Cincinnati, Ohio, en route to Washington, D.C., and eventual deployment in North Carolina.

NAVAL: Admiral David D. Porter orders the monitors USS *New Ironsides, Saugus, Canonicus, Monadnock,* and *Mahopac* to within 1,000 yards of Fort Fisher, Wilmington, North Carolina, and unleashes a withering, point-blank bombardment. Several hours of cannonading silence virtually all of the fort's heavy cannon, at which point firing ceases and a naval brigade of 1,600 sailors and 400 U.S. Marines lands ashore under Commander K. Randolph Breese. This force is tasked with launching diversionary attacks while army troops work their way around to the rear of Confederate defenses. Three desperate charges are launched and repelled with the loss of 309 casualties, but the defenders are successfully distracted. For their role in the victory, no less than 35 sailors and marines win the Congressional Medal of Honor.

Admiral John A. B. Dahlgren agrees to provide a diversion at Charleston, South Carolina, to draw Confederate attention away from General William T. Sherman's army marching up from Savannah, Georgia. Prior to this decision, several naval vessels are dispatched to find and mark numerous obstacles blocking the harbor. In the course of such activity, the ironclad USS *Patapsco* strikes a torpedo near the entrance of Charleston harbor, South Carolina, sinking 15 seconds later with the loss of 62 officers and men.

January 16
Politics: Maryland politician Francis P. Blair conveys a letter from President Jefferson Davis to President Abraham Lincoln suggesting peace negotiations "between the two nations." Lincoln, like Davis, dismisses any notion of a joint military expedition to expel the French from Mexico, but he agrees to attend a peace conference slated for February.

The Confederate Congress, lacking confidence in President Jefferson Davis's conduct of affairs, passes a resolution 14 to 2 to appoint General Robert E. Lee as general in chief and also restore General Joseph E. Johnston to commander of the Army of Tennessee.

North: Alfred H. Terry is promoted to major general, U.S. Army.

South: Two drunken U.S. sailors accidentally ignite 13,000 pounds of gunpowder at Fort Fisher, Wilmington, North Carolina, killing 25 Federals, injuring 66, and leaving an additional 13 missing.

General Braxton Bragg abandons Smithville and Reeves Point, North Carolina, blowing up Fort Caswell and other defensive works at the mouth of the Cape Fear River.

General William T. Sherman directs his army north from Savannah, Georgia, and toward South Carolina. He also issues Special Field Order No. 15, which confiscates land on the Georgia coast for the express purpose of settling African-American refugees. He later insists this is nothing more than a temporary expedient until the refugees can be settled inland on a more permanent basis.

Naval: Confederate secretary of the navy Stephen R. Mallory urges the James River Squadron under Commander John K. Mitchell to sortie southward and attack a large Union supply depot at City Point, Virginia. This major installation is General Ulysses S. Grant's base of operations. "If we can block the river at or below City Point," he reasons, "Grant might be compelled to evacuate his position."

January 17
South: General George W. Getty takes charge of the VI Corps, Army of the Potomac, Virginia.

Naval: Admiral David D. Porter, surveying the size and strength of Fort Fisher, Wilmington, North Carolina, marvels over its construction yet concludes that "no *Alabamas, Floridas, Chickamaugas,* or *Tallahassees* will ever fit out again from this port, and our merchant vessels very soon, I hope, will be enabled to pursue in safety their avocation." Porter also orders Wilmington's signal lights lit and those of his warships dimmed, to lure any unsuspecting blockade-runners into his grasp.

Boat crews from the USS *Honeysuckle* seize the English blockade-runner *Augusta* in the Suwannee River, Florida.

A combined expedition mounted from the Mississippi Squadron lands at Somerville, Alabama, seizing 90 captives and several horses.

January 18
POLITICS: President Abraham Lincoln hands Francis P. Blair a letter to President Jefferson Davis, demonstrating his willingness to negotiate peace for the inhabitants "of our one common country."
SOUTH: Command of the Savannah, Georgia, region falls to on General John G. Foster and the Department of the South.
WEST: Confederate cavalry under General Thomas L. Rosser surprise Union outposts near Lovettsville, Virginia, and then evade a hasty Federal pursuit.
NAVAL: Lieutenant William B. Cushing of the USS *Monticello* lands at Fort Caswell, North Carolina, and raises the Stars and Stripes.

Confederate blockade-runners *Granite City* and *Wave* successfully evade the Union blockade at Calcasieu Pass, Louisiana.

January 19
POLITICS: President Abraham Lincoln inquires of General Ulysses S. Grant about the possibility of finding Robert Lincoln, his eldest son, a staff position. Grant subsequently appoints him assistance adjutant general with a rank of captain.

President Jefferson Davis, intent on shoring up support for his flagging reputation as a war leader, convinces General Robert E. Lee to serve as general in chief of Confederate forces. Lee reluctantly agrees but cautions, "I must state that with the addition of the immediate command of the army, I do not think I could accomplish any good."
SOUTH: General William T. Sherman orders his army to begin to march north toward the South Carolina border. A two-pronged drive toward Columbia, the state capital, is developing.

January 20
POLITICS: Secretary of War Edwin M. Stanton, recently arrived from Savannah, Georgia, confers with President Abraham Lincoln as to recent conversations held with General William T. Sherman.
SOUTH: General William T. Sherman's army marches north, encountering strong Confederate resistance at Pocotaligo and along the Salkehatchie River, South Carolina.
WEST: Federal troops fight off an attack by hostile Cheyenne and Arapaho at Fort Learned, Kansas.

The Arizona Territory is joined to the Department of the Pacific.
NAVAL: A somewhat surprised admiral David D. Porter, aboard the USS *Malvern*, watches as Confederate blockade-runners *Stag* and *Charlotte* inadvertently anchor

near his vessel in Wilmington harbor and are captured. They are unaware of Fort Fisher's recent capture.

Confederate blockade-runner *City of Richmond* drops anchor at Quiberon Bay, France, and awaits the arrival of the CSS *Stonewall* to transfer men and supplies aboard.

January 21

SOUTH: General William T. Sherman begins to relocate his headquarters from Savannah, Georgia, to Beaufort, South Carolina. Overall, Union movements are delayed two weeks by incessant rains.

WEST: General John M. Schofield's XXIII Corps disembarks from transports at Cincinnati, Ohio, following a five-day journey from Clifton, Tennessee. Here, they entrain for Washington, D.C., and eventual service in North Carolina.

NAVAL: Confederate secretary of the navy Stephen R. Mallory again urges Commander John K. Mitchell of the James River Squadron to strike Union supply depots at City Point, Virginia. "You have an opportunity, I am convinced, rarely presented to a naval operations officer," Mallory insists, "and one which may lead to the most glorious results to your country."

The USS *Penguin* runs the Confederate blockade-runner *Granite City* aground off Velasco, Texas, and destroys it with gunfire.

January 22

NAVAL: An armed boat from the USS *Chocura* captures and burns the Confederate schooner *Delphina* in Calcasieu Pass, Louisiana.

Lieutenant John Low, C.S.N., sails the steamer CSS *Ajax* from Dublin, Ireland, and makes for Nassau to receive its armament. However, adroit diplomacy by American minister Charles F. Adams dissuades the British from allowing any guns to be shipped there.

January 23

POLITICS: President Jefferson Davis, reacting to pressure from the Confederate Congress, signs the General-in-Chief Act, which renders General Robert E. Lee supreme military commander.

WEST: Command of the much-depleted Army of Tennessee formally reverts to General Richard Taylor at Tupelo, Mississippi, where he commands 18,000 men. More than 4,000 soldiers have been transferred to South Carolina to reinforce General William J. Hardee.

NAVAL: Commodore John K. Mitchell sorties down the James River past Richmond, Virginia, to attack a Union supply depot at City Point. Sailing with him are the CSS *Virginia II, Fredericksburg, Drewry, Torpedo, Richmond, Scorpion, Wasp,* and *Hornet.* Mitchell's progress halts once the *Virginia II* and *Richmond* run aground on Union obstacles placed at Trent's Reach. However, Union commander W. A. Parker is criticized severely for declining to engage the Southerners and withdrawing his own ironclad squadron to deeper water.

The USS *Fox* captures the British blockade-runner *Fannie McRae* in the Gulf of Mexico.

January 24

NORTH: Reversing himself, General Ulysses S. Grant now approves of renewed prisoner of war exchanges. The Southerners' arrival home will only exacerbate Confederate food shortages.

SOUTH: General Orlando B. Wilcox takes temporary command of the IX Corps, Army of the Potomac, Virginia.

WEST: General Nathan B. Forrest assumes control of the Confederate District of Mississippi, East Louisiana, and West Tennessee.

NAVAL: The CSS *Drewry* is hit by Union artillery fire on the James River and explodes. Then the USS *Onondaga* and *Massasoit* under Commander W. A. Parker steam up the James River to engage Confederate vessels under Commodore John K. Mitchell, but the Southerners retire upstream.

The Confederate ironclad CSS *Stonewall* anchors at Quiberon Bay, France, to receive a full complement of crew from the blockade-runner *City of Richmond*.

January 25

NAVAL: The USS *Tristram Shandy* captures the Confederate steamer *Blenheim* off New Inlet, North Carolina.

As the army of General William T. Sherman advances from Savannah, Georgia, ships of Admiral John A. B. Dahlgren's South Atlantic Blockading Squadron dip into nearby rivers to provide naval support whenever possible.

The Confederate raider CSS *Shenandoah* under Lieutenant James I. Waddell drops anchor off Melbourne, Australia, to take on supplies and carry out repairs.

January 26

SOUTH: To mask his forthcoming advance on Columbia, South Carolina, General William T. Sherman dispatches a column toward Charleston as a diversion.

NAVAL: The tug USS *Clover* captures the Confederate blockade-runner *Coquette* in the Combahee River, South Carolina. Meanwhile, the *Dai Ching*, which grounds in the same river, is scuttled and abandoned.

January 27

POLITICS: President Jefferson Davis begins to choose a commission to conduct informal peace talks as suggested by Francis P. Blair. This ultimately consists of Vice President Alexander H. Stephens, Senate president Robert Hunter, and Assistant Secretary of War John A. Campbell. They are authorized to discuss possible political moves leading to an armistice.

SOUTH: General Gouverneur K. Warren resumes command of the V Corps, Army of the Potomac, Virginia.

WEST: Command of the Confederate District of Mississippi, East Louisiana, and West Tennessee reverts to General Nathan B. Forrest.

General Robert E. Lee advises President Jefferson Davis of potentially ruinous desertion rates in the Army of Northern Virginia. He ascribes the unrest to a constant lack of food and suggests that the Commissary Department do better.

NAVAL: The USS *Eutaw* steams up the James River, Virginia, and captures the torpedo boat CSS *Scorpion*.

The USS *Ariel* captures an unnamed boat near the Manatee River, Florida.

January 28

SOUTH: Skirmishing occurs as Union forces under General William T. Sherman pass along the Combahee River, South Carolina.

WEST: Union forces repel a Confederate attack on Athens, Tennessee, losing 20 men in the process.

NAVAL: General Ulysses S. Grant arrives onboard the USS *Malvern* to confer with Admiral David D. Porter. Grant then persuades the admiral to provide naval support for an offensive up the Cape Fear River against Fort Anderson, North Carolina.

The USS *Valley City* steams down the Chowan River and helps repel a Confederate night attack against a Union encampment at Colerain, North Carolina.

The Torpedo boat CSS *St. Patrick* successfully strikes the USS *Octorara* at night off Mobile Bay, Alabama, but its spar torpedo fails to detonate. The Confederate vessel then flees undamaged into the darkness.

The Confederate ironclad CSS *Stonewall* departs Quiberon Bay, France, and steams for El Ferrol, Spain, to take on additional coal.

January 30

SOUTH: Advance elements from the Army of Tennessee arrive at Augusta, Georgia, to join Confederate forces under General William J. Hardee.

WEST: The Military Division of the Missouri is set up and includes the Departments of Missouri and the Northwest; General John Pope is appointed commanding officer.

NAVAL: A boat crew from the USS *Henry Brinker,* scouting King's Creek, Virginia, uncovers two 150-pound Confederate torpedoes and the galvanic batteries necessary to detonate them from the shore.

The USS *Cherokee* bombards Confederate troops at Half Moon Battery, North Carolina.

January 31

POLITICS: The U.S. House of Representatives finally musters the two-thirds (119 to 56) majority necessary to approve the 13th Amendment to the Constitution, which abolishes slavery. This legislation had been passed previously by the U.S. Senate on April 8, 1864, and now is handed off to the states for ratification.

SOUTH: General Robert E. Lee is appointed general in chief of Confederate forces in light of continuing dissatisfaction concerning President Jefferson Davis's handling of military affairs.

The Department of North Carolina is created with General John M. Schofield as commanding officer.

General David S. Stanley takes charge of the IV Corps in East Tennessee and North Alabama.

February 1

POLITICS: Illinois becomes the first state to ratify the 13th Amendment to the Constitution, formally abolishing slavery.

John Rock, an African-American attorney from Boston Massachusetts, becomes the first minority lawyer to practice before the U.S. Supreme Court.

Confederate secretary of war James A. Seddon resigns from office due to political pressure.

SOUTH: General William T. Sherman departs Savannah, Georgia, with 62,000 men and heads toward the South Carolina border. His command consists of two wings under Generals Oliver O. Howard's Army of the Tennessee (XV, XVII Corps) and Henry W. Slocum's Army of Georgia (XV and XX Corps), aided by a cavalry division of General Hugh J. Kilpatrick. The Northerners are eager to wreak havoc in the heart of secessionism, and their penchant for destruction—while officially against orders—exceeds anything inflicted on Georgia.

WEST: General John B, Magruder is appointed head of the District of Arkansas.

NAVAL: Boat crews from the USS *Midnight* land and destroy a large saltworks at St. Andrew's Bay, Florida.

February 2

POLITICS: President Abraham Lincoln departs Washington, D.C., to meet with Confederate peace commissioners at Hampton Roads, Virginia.

Rhode Island and Michigan are the second and third states to ratify the 13th Amendment.

SOUTH: General John G. Parke resumes command of the IX Corps, Army of the Potomac, Virginia.

Skirmishing breaks out at Whippy Swamp, South Carolina, between forces under Generals William T. Sherman and William J. Hardee. The approach of Federal troops also induces Confederate authorities to prepare to evacuate Charleston.

WEST: Marauding Cheyenne and Sioux pay a second visit to Julesburg, Colorado, chasing the inhabitants into the nearby fort and burning whatever buildings they find standing.

NAVAL: The USS *Pinola* captures the Confederate schooner *Ben Willis* in the Gulf of Mexico.

February 3

POLITICS: President Jefferson Davis dispatches Confederate vice president Alexander H. Stephens, John A. Campbell, and Robert M. T. Hunter to confer with President Abraham Lincoln and Secretary of State William H. Seward aboard a ship off Hampton Roads, Virginia. The meeting deadlocks since the Southerners insist on independence for the Confederacy as a precondition for peace, whereas Lincoln will accept only their unconditional surrender.

Maryland, New York, and West Virginia ratify the 13th Amendment, for a total of six states.

SOUTH: Federal troops battle with Confederates at Rivers's Bridge, South Carolina, as the army under General William T. Sherman grinds inexorably forward.

WEST: The Confederate District of North Mississippi and West Tennessee is set up under General Marcus J. Wright.

The Confederate District of South Mississippi and East Tennessee is created under General Wirt W. Adams.

NAVAL: The CSS *Macon* and *Sampson,* berthed on the Savannah River, Georgia, are ordered to turn over all powder and ammunition supplies to Confederate army units operating in the vicinity of Augusta.

The USS *Matthew Vassar* seizes the Confederate blockade-runner *John Hale* off the Florida coast following a chase of four hours.

February 4

POLITICS: President Abraham Lincoln returns to Washington, D.C., somewhat distraught that little has been accomplished through peace negotiations. He then assures General Ulysses S. Grant, "Nothing transpired, or transpiring, with the three gentlemen from Richmond is to cause any change, hindrance, or delay of your military plans or operations."

SOUTH: General Ulysses S. Grant, determined to stretch Confederate defenses at Petersburg, Virginia, to the breaking point, orders Union forces to cut off Southern wagon trains near Hatcher's Run along Boydton Plank Road. The II Corps under General Andrew A. Humphreys, the V Corps of General Gouverneur K. Warren, and a cavalry division led by General John M. Gregg draw the assignment.

Fighting erupts at Angley's Post Office and Buford's Bridge, South Carolina, as General William T. Sherman surges farther into the state.

NAVAL: The USS *Wamsutta* and *Potomska* run an unidentified blockade-runner ashore at Breach Inlet, South Carolina.

Armed boats from the USS *Midnight* land and destroy a saltworks at West Bay, Florida.

February 5

POLITICS: President Abraham Lincoln floats the idea of offering $400 million to slave states if they will surrender by April 1. His cabinet uniformly rejects the suggestion, however, so Lincoln abandons it.

SOUTH: General Ulysses S. Grant launches a renewed offensive along the Boydton Plank Road near Hatcher's Run (Dabney's Mill), Virginia. Union cavalry under General David M. Gregg arrive at Dinwiddie Court House, find only a few Confederate wagons and no troops, and subsequently encamp nearby. Meanwhile, General Gouverneur K. Warren's V Corps also moves up to Hatcher's Run while the II Corps of General Andrew A. Humphreys occupies the nearby Vaughan Road. Throughout the course of the day, Confederates launch several strong attacks but are repulsed. Humphreys is then reinforced overnight by Gregg's cavalry, and fighting dies down across the line.

NAVAL: A joint expedition from the USS *Roanoke* up the Pagan and Jones creeks, Virginia, leads to the capture of an unnamed Confederate torpedo boat.

Lieutenant William B. Cushing leads an armed expedition up the Little River, South Carolina, to seize cotton supplies and prisoners.

The Confederate blockade-runner *Chameleon* tries and fails to run the Union blockade off Charleston, South Carolina, then turns and departs for Nassau.

The USS *Niagara* under Commodore Thomas T. Craven, learning of the CSS *Stonewall*'s departure, sails from Dover, England, possibly to intercept it off the coast of Spain.

February 6

POLITICS: In reporting to the Confederate Congress on the recent conference held at Hampton Roads, President Jefferson Davis denounces President Abraham Lincoln for insisting on unconditional surrender as the basis for peace. He declares this unacceptable and vows that the struggle for Southern independence will go on.

General John C. Breckinridge is appointed Confederate secretary of war to replace outgoing James A. Seddon.

SOUTH: Heavy fighting resumes along Hatcher's Run, Virginia, as Confederate forces under General John B. Gordon's division slam into the exposed V Corps of General Gouverneur K. Warren. In the course of fighting, Confederate general John Pegram is killed attacking Union lines. However, a sharp thrust by additional Southerners under General Clement A. Evans contests the Federals along the Boydton Plank Road until nightfall ends the action.

General Robert E. Lee formally is designated general in chief of Confederate armies, although at this stage of the struggle this assignment is merely symbolic.

General Edward O. C. Ord becomes commander of the Department of Virginia.

February 7

POLITICS: Maine and Kansas ratify the 13th Amendment; the Delaware legislature fails to muster a two-thirds majority.

SOUTH: Fighting continues at Hatcher's Run, Virginia, as Union forces successfully extend their siege lines. The Federals sustain 170 dead, 1,100 injured, and 182 missing (1,512). Confederate losses are not known but are presumed to be nearly as heavy. Worse, General Robert E. Lee's defensive perimeter is now stretched to 37 miles in length, increasingly hard for his 46,000 men to hold against superior numbers. This action momentarily concludes General Ulysses S. Grant's efforts to shift forces leftward.

Union troops under General William T. Sherman capture the Edisto River Bridge, South Carolina, and cut the Augusta and Charleston Railroad at Blackville, but progress is slowed by swamps and swollen rivers.

NAVAL: Armed boats from the USS *Bienville* enter Galveston harbor, Texas, and capture the British blockade-runners *Annie Sophie* and *Pet*. However, they fail to apprehend the Confederate blockade-runner *Wren*.

February 8

POLITICS: President Abraham Lincoln signs a U.S. House resolution declaring that 11 states of the soon-to-be-defunct Confederacy should not enjoy representation in the electoral college.

SOUTH: Elements of General John M. Schofield's XXIII Corps trickle into Fort Fisher, Wilmington, North Carolina, following their rapid transfer from the Tennessee interior.

General William T. Sherman responds to a letter from General Joseph Wheeler complaining that Union troops are destroying private homes and property. "Vacant houses being of no use to anybody, I care little about," he writes, "I don't want them destroyed, but do not take much care to preserve them."

WEST: General Grenville M. Dodge assumes command of the Department of Kansas.

February 9

POLITICS: On the recommendation of General Robert E. Lee, now general in chief, President Jefferson Davis enacts a pardon for all Confederate deserters who report back to their units within 30 days.

Unionists in Virginia ratify the 13th Amendment outlawing slavery.

SOUTH: General Quincy A. Gilmore replaces General John G. Foster as commander of the Department of the South.

The Division of Northern Louisiana is formed with General Francis J. Herron as commanding officer.

The Division of Southern Louisiana, centered at New Orleans, is set up under General Thomas W. Sherman.

The XXIII Corps fully deploys at Fort Fisher, Wilmington, North Carolina, under General John M. Schofield, who also commands the Department of North Carolina. His orders are to forge inland, take Wilmington, and affect a new supply route for General William T. Sherman as the latter advances up from South Carolina.

NAVAL: The USS *Pawnee*, *Sonoma*, and *Daffodil* bombard Confederate batteries in Togodo Creek, North Edisto, North Carolina. This action is undertaken in support of General William T. Sherman's army, then moving north near the coast.

February 10

WEST: The Department of Kentucky is created under General John M. Palmer.

The Department of the Cumberland is created with General George H. Thomas as commanding officer.

NAVAL: Captain Raphael Semmes is promoted to rear admiral, C.S.N., for his conduct as commander of the CSS *Alabama,* and he is instructed to take command of the James River Squadron, Virginia.

The USS *Shawmut* and *Huron* bombard Confederate batteries and Fort Anderson on the Cape Fear River, North Carolina.

The ironclad USS *Lehigh,* assisted by several gunboats, cruises the Stono and Folly rivers, South Carolina, in support of army movements and occasionally engages Confederate land batteries.

The USS *Princess Royal* captures and burns the Confederate steamer *Will o' Wisp* off Galveston, Texas.

February 11

SOUTH: The army of General William T. Sherman severs the Augusta and Charleston Railroad, which prevents Charleston, South Carolina, from receiving reinforcements. General William J. Hardee becomes convinced, mistakenly, that the city is Sherman's ultimate objective.

The XXIII Corps under General John M. Schofield makes preparations to steam up the Cape Fear River in transports provided by Admiral David D. Porter, and outflank the defenders of Fort Anderson, North Carolina.

NAVAL: A party of 100 Confederate sailors under Lieutenant Charles W. Read marches from Drewry's Bluff, Virginia, toward City Point on the James River. There, they are to capture several Union vessels, outfit them with spar torpedoes, and then attack and sink any Union ironclads in the area. Success here would leave remaining Federal ships at the mercy of Confederate ironclads waiting upstream. Southern control of the James River could severely compromise the Union army's ability to supply itself at Petersburg.

The USS *Keystone State, Aries, Montgomery, Howquah, Emma,* and *Vicksburg* bombard Half Moon Battery on Cape Fear River, six miles above Fort Fisher, North Carolina.

The USS *Penobscot* captures the British blockade-runner *Matilda* in the Gulf of Mexico.

The USS *Niagara* arrives off La Coruña, Spain, to shadow the CSS *Stonewall* anchored at nearby El Ferrol.

February 12
POLITICS: The Electoral College meets and confirms President Abraham Lincoln's election victory on a vote of 212 to 21.

SOUTH: Union forces under General William T. Sherman advance into Branchville, South Carolina. His soldiers are particularly vengeful during this phase of the march, knowing that the movement for secession commenced here. Sherman's presence forces Confederates under General Pierre G. T. Beauregard across the Edisto River, from whence they begin to concentrate at Cheraw. In effect, Beauregard abandons the central reaches of the state to preserve his army.

WEST: A party of 100 Union soldiers surrounds and attacks the home of noted Confederate guerrilla captain Jeff Williams in Lewisburg, Arkansas, killing him.

General Samuel R. Curtis assumes command of the Department of the Northwest.

NAVAL: A daring Confederate naval expedition conducted by Lieutenant Charles W. Read is cancelled on account of worsening weather and fears of a Union army ambush. He then marches back to Richmond, Virginia, where almost all of his 100 volunteers require medical attention due to exposure.

Confederate blockade-runners *Carolina, Dream, Chicora, Chamelon,* and *Owl* sortie from Nassau and try to run the Union blockade off Charleston, South Carolina, from a variety of directions.

February 13
DIPLOMACY: Lord John Russell informs American diplomats in London of the government's unease over the recent American naval buildup in the Great Lakes region, which negates the 1817 Rush-Bagot Agreement. The British are summarily told that any buildup is in direct response to the Confederate raid on St. Albans, Vermont, on October 19, 1864, which originated from Canada.

POLITICS: Reacting to complaints from west Tennessee politicians, President Abraham Lincoln admonishes military authorities there, insisting that, "the object of the war being to restore and maintain the blessings of peace and good government, I desire you to help, and not hinder, every advance in that direction."

South: The projected movement of General Jacob D. Cox's division, XXII Corps, to outflank Fort Anderson, North Carolina, is hampered by heavy rain and muddy conditions.

Naval: The crews of the Confederate vessels CSS *Chicora, Palmetto State,* and *Charleston,* 300 men and officers in all, are marched from Charleston, South Carolina, under Commander John R. Tucker. They are instructed to assist in the defense of Wilmington, North Carolina.

February 14

South: Wade Hampton is appointed lieutenant general, C.S.A.

General John M. Schofield, citing heavy rain and poor marching conditions, temporarily halts his planned flanking movement by General Jacob D. Cox's division against Fort Anderson, North Carolina.

General William T. Sherman departs Orangeburg, South Carolina, directs Union forces across the Congaree River, and begins to advance on Columbia with both wings of his army. General Pierre G. T. Beauregard makes preparations to flee and also orders the garrison of Charleston under General William J. Hardee to escape possible encirclement.

West: General George Stoneman takes charge of the District of East Tennessee.

Naval: The Confederate blockade-runner *Celt* runs aground while attempting to enter Charleston harbor, South Carolina.

February 15

South: The army of General William T. Sherman halts just south of Columbia, South Carolina, as Confederates continue evacuating the state capital. To mask this move, they bombard the Union encampments from across the Congaree River.

General Alexander Asboth becomes commander of the District of West Florida.

West: General Mosby M. Parsons takes command of the Confederate Department of Arkansas.

Naval: The Union steamer *Knickerbocker* runs hard aground at Smith's Point, Virginia, where it is burned by Confederate forces.

The USS *Merrimac* founders and is allowed to sink off the Florida coast; the crew is rescued by the steamer *Morning Star.*

February 16

Politics: The 13th Amendment is ratified by Indiana, Nevada, and Louisiana.

South: The division of General Jacob D. Cox, XXII Corps, ferries up the Cape Fear River in transports toward Smithville, North Carolina. This movement is part of General John M. Schofield's campaign to evict Confederate defenders from Wilmington.

Federal artillery begin to shell Columbia, South Carolina, while troops under General Oliver O. Howard throw a pontoon bridge across the Broad River north of the city. Meanwhile, the defenders under Generals Pierre G. T. Beauregard and Wade Hampton complete the evacuation of their troops. Farther east, General William J. Hardee is also preparing to flee Charleston rather then become pinned within it.

WEST: Confederate cavalry under General John Crawford capture Union garrisons at Athens and Sweet Water, Tennessee.

NAVAL: Gunboats and transports under Admiral David D. Porter ferry the XXIII Corps of General John M. Schofield from Fort Fisher, North Carolina, to Smithville on the Cape Fear River.

February 17

POLITICS: The U.S. Congress repudiates all debts accrued by various Confederate governments.

SOUTH: General Jacob D. Cox leads 8,000 Federal troops ashore at Smithville on the Cape Fear River, prior to attacking Fort Anderson, North Carolina. Once reinforced by the division of General Adelbert Ames, X Corps, he pushes inland to cut off the Confederate garrison.

Union forces under General William T. Sherman accept the surrender of Columbia, capital of South Carolina, from city officials. Meanwhile, General Wade Hampton's cavalry burn enormous stores of cotton bales prior to retreating, sparks from which ignite several uncontrollable fires. The Federals, flushed with victory and revenge, also enjoy free access to liquor, and discipline begins to dissolve. Fires break out all evening and destroy two-thirds of the city. Southerners are convinced that Columbia has been torched on Sherman's orders, and they mark it as a defining atrocity of the war. Sherman denies any culpability and claims the fire was caused by the sparks that spread from burning cotton bales.

Charleston, South Carolina, is evacuated by Confederate forces under General William J. Hardee, ending an epic siege lasting 567 days. The defenders, who abandon 250 heavy cannon, begin to move north in the direction of Cheraw.

NAVAL: Federal warships under Admiral David D. Porter bombard Fort Anderson, North Carolina. To draw Confederate fire, the Union ships tow "Old Bogey," a fake ironclad assembled from a scow, limber, and canvas, to the head of their line. As expected, it draws the most fire and spares the fleet considerable damage.

Armed boats from the USS *Pawnee, Sonoma, Ottawa, Winona, Potomska, Wando,* and *J. S. Chambers* launch a major diversionary landing at Bull's Bay, South Carolina, to assist the army under General William T. Sherman. Part of this force then unites with the division of General Edward E. Potter and continues driving Confederate forces inland.

The USS *Mahaska* captures the Confederate schooner *Delia* near Bayport, Florida.

February 18

POLITICS: General Robert E. Lee agrees in principle to the notion of arming slaves to fight for Southern independence, but he feels they must be employed as free men to be effective.

SOUTH: General Jacob D. Cox's division begins to maneuver to attack Fort Anderson, Wilmington, North Carolina, closely supported by naval vessels.

General William T. Sherman orders all factories, supply houses, and railroad facilities found in Columbia, South Carolina, burned to deny their use to the Confederacy.

Charleston, South Carolina, is occupied by Union forces under General Alexander Schimmelfenning. For many Federals, capture of this "fire-eater" capital is sweet revenge.

WEST: Men of the 12th U.S. Colored Artillery defeat a Confederate attack on Fort Jones, Colesburg, Kentucky.

The Union XIII under General Gordon Granger and XVI Corps under General Andrew J. Smith are created for service in Mississippi and Missouri, respectively.

NAVAL: The ironclads CSS *Chicora, Palmetto,* and *Charleston* are scuttled by Confederate authorities at Charleston, South Carolina, to prevent their capture by Admiral John A. B. Dahlgren.

The USS *Catskill* seizes the Confederate blockade-runner *Deer* during the Southern evacuation of Charleston, South Carolina.

The USS *Gladiola* captures the Confederate steamer *Syren* near Charleston, South Carolina.

The USS *Pinola* captures and sinks the Confederate schooner *Anna Dale* off Pass Cavallo, Texas.

The USS *Forest Rose* disperses a gathering of Confederates at Cole's Creek, Mississippi.

The Confederate raider CSS *Shenandoah* under Lieutenant James I. Waddell hoists anchor and sails from Port Philip Bay, Melbourne, Australia. During this three-week visit to affect repairs, word of his arrival reaches the Union whaling fleet, which promptly clears out of the South Pacific region.

February 19

SOUTH: Union forces under General William T. Sherman continue wreaking havoc against foundries, railroads, machine shops, and arsenals in Columbia, South Carolina.

As Union troops intensify their drive on Wilimington, North Carolina, General Jacob D. Cox's command begins to load into boats to outflank Fort Anderson along the Cape Fear River. However, General Johnson Hagood evacuates his post this evening, and the garrison escapes to Town Creek, eight miles north.

NAVAL: The Confederate truce vessel *A. H. Schultz,* used for prisoner exchanges, strikes a torpedo on the James River near Chaffin's Bluff and sinks.

The USS *Gertrude* seizes the Mexican brig *Eco* as it attempts to run the blockade off Galveston, Texas.

February 20

POLITICS: The Confederate House of Representatives approves the use of African-American slaves as soldiers.

SOUTH: Union troops under General Jacob D. Cox pursue fleeing Confederates from Fort Anderson, North Carolina, and corner them at Town Creek. The ensuing Federal attack carries their position, and the Southerners withdraw with a loss of 350 casualties. Union losses are recorded as 60.

Having finished their work of destruction at Columbia, South Carolina, the army of General William T. Sherman stakes out a new objective at Goldsborough, North Carolina.

A force of 500 Confederate infantry and cavalry under Major William Footman besieges the Union garrison at Fort Myers, southern Florida. The post is defended by 275 men of the 110th New York, 2nd Florida Cavalry, and the 2nd U.S. Colored Infantry under Captain James Doyle. No assaults are launched, and the contenders engage in an artillery duel at long range for most of the day. At length, Footman moves off with an estimated 40 casualties, while Doyle sustains four wounded and four missing. Thus Union forces prevail in this, the southernmost battle waged in the Civil War.

WEST: General John H. Morgan assumes command of the District of Arizona.

NAVAL: Confederate defenders of Fort Strong, North Carolina, release 200 free-ranging torpedoes down the Cape Fear River at night. Fortunately, most are caught in the nets of rowboats detailed for that purpose and no vessels are lost.

February 21

POLITICS: Citing intense opposition, the Confederate Congress postpones final consideration of a bill authorizing the use of African-American slaves as soldiers.

SOUTH: General Robert E. Lee alerts Confederate secretary of war John C. Breckinridge that, if absolutely necessary, he will abandon Richmond, Virginia, and make all haste for Burkeville to maintain communication with Confederate forces in the Carolinas. He also requests that General Joseph E. Johnston be returned speedily to active duty as the health of General Pierre G. T. Beauregard appears tenuous.

Union forces under General Jacob D. Cox reach the southwestern side of Wilmington, North Carolina. General Braxton Bragg then orders the Confederate division of Robert F. Hoke to evacuate from that city.

WEST: A swift raid by Confederate partisan rangers under Captain Jesse McNeill against Cumberland, Maryland, captures an embarrassed General George Crook and Benjamin F. Kelley in their residence.

Captain Gurnsey W. Davis and 50 men of his 13th Illinois Cavalry float down the Arkansas River from Pine Bluff, Arkansas, and set up a base camp at Douglas Landing. He is aware of a Confederate presence about three miles downriver, but heavy rainfall dissuades him from attacking.

SOUTHWEST: General Douglas H. Cooper takes charge of the Confederate District of the Indian Territory.

NAVAL: The gunboat squadron of Admiral David D. Porter again rings Fort Strong, North Carolina, and pours in concentrated fire as army troops advance up along the banks of Cape Fear River.

February 22

POLITICS: Tennessee voters approve a new state constitution that abolishes slavery while Kentucky rejects the 13th Amendment.

SOUTH: General Robert E. Lee appoints General Joseph E. Johnston commander of the Departments of South Carolina, Georgia, and Florida.

Union forces under General John M. Schofield occupy Wilmington, North Carolina, formerly the last remaining open port of the Confederacy. The Federals are now poised to conduct military operations toward the interior of the state, and to facilitate this, Schofield orders all railroad tracks in the vicinity repaired. When this proves impractical, he shifts his efforts toward converting New Bern into a major staging area.

Confederate forces evacuate Fort Strong, on the Cape Fear River, North Carolina.

General William T. Sherman's Union army approaches Rocky Mount, South Carolina, after intense skirmishing at Camden. He continues giving the impression that his goal is Charlotte, North Carolina, when it is actually Goldsborough, where he can effect a union with General John M. Schofield.

WEST: General John McNeil takes charge of the Union District of Central Missouri.

Confederate guerrillas attack the camp of Captain Gurnsey W. Davis early in the morning, wounding four men. Davis, who prepared for their assault in advance, moves his men back to the Arkansas River to embark and return to Pine Bluff. His experience underscores the dangers that small groups of Federals face while operating in the Arkansas back country.

NAVAL: Admiral David D. Porter personally runs up the Stars and Stripes at Fort Strong, Cape Fear River, North Carolina.

Admiral John A. B. Dahlgren dispatches a squadron of warships to capture Georgetown, South Carolina, thereby establishing lines of communication with General William T. Sherman's advancing army.

February 23

POLITICS: The 13th Amendment is ratified by Minnesota.

SOUTH: General William T. Sherman's XX Corps crosses the Catawba River, South Carolina, while approaching the North Carolina state line.

General John Newton embarks a small force consisting of the 2nd U.S. Florida Cavalry and the 2nd and 99th U.S. Colored Infantry on ships of the East Gulf Coast Blockading Squadron at Key West, Florida. He then sails for St. Marks, intending to close that port to blockade-running.

February 24

SOUTH: General William T. Sherman vigorously protests to General Wade Hampton the alleged murder of several Union soldiers on a foraging expedition. Hampton replies that his government authorizes him to execute any Union soldiers caught burning private property. Moreover, "This order shall remain in force so long as you disgrace the profession of arms by allowing your men to destroy private dwellings."

NAVAL: Secretary of the Navy Gideon Welles instructs Admirals John A. B. Dahlgren and John K. Thatcher, of the South Atlantic Blockading Squadron and West Gulf Squadron, respectively, to detach their least efficient vessels from active duty and send them north in be placed.

February 25

SOUTH: General Joseph E. Johnston arrives at Charlotte, North Carolina, to resume command of the Army of Tennessee and all Confederate forces in South Carolina, Georgia, and Florida. In reality, he leads a skeleton force of roughly 25,000 hungry, ragged men, and "In my opinion, these troops form an army far too weak to cope with Sherman."

General John M. Schofield orders General Innis N. Palmer, commanding Union forces at New Bern, North Carolina, to commence to rebuild all railroad tracks in the direction of Goldsborough.

General Frederick Steele assumes command of Union troops at Pensacola Bay in anticipation of a concerted Union drive against nearby Mobile, Alabama.

NAVAL: Confederates scuttle the CSS *Chickamauga* on the Cape Fear River, North Carolina.

Armed boats from the USS *Catalpa* and *Ningoe* battle with Confederate cavalry at Georgetown, South Carolina, and seize the town.

The USS *Marigold* captures the British blockade-runner *Salvadora* in the Straits of Florida.

The USS *Chenango* captures the Confederate sloop *Elvira* at sea.

February 26

SOUTH: The Union XX Corps of General William T. Sherman approach Hanging Rock, South Carolina, although progress remains somewhat hampered by heavy rains.

WEST: General Winfield S. Hancock assumes command of the Department of West Virginia.

February 27

WEST: Generals Philip H. Sheridan and Wesley Merritt take 10,000 cavalry down the Shenandoah Valley toward Lynchburg, Virginia, intending to sever the Virginia Central Railroad and the James River Canal. His command consists of the 1st Cavalry Division under General Thomas C. Devlin and the 3rd Cavalry Division under General George A. Custer.

NAVAL: Commodore John R. Tucker, heading 350 Confederate sailors and officers, arrives at Fayetteville, North Carolina. From here, he is to march to Richmond, Virginia, and form the nucleus of a naval brigade.

The USS *Proteus* captures the Confederate steamer *Ruby* in the Gulf of Mexico.

The USS *Penobscot* captures and burns the Confederate schooners *Mary Anges* and *Louisa* off Aransas Pass, Texas.

February 28

SOUTH: Nathan B. Forrest is promoted to lieutenant general, C.S.A.

General William T. Sherman's army skirmishes heavily at Rocky Mount and Cheraw, South Carolina, as it nears the North Carolina border.

NAVAL: The USS *Honeysuckle* runs the British blockade-runner *Sort* onto the coast of Florida, capturing it.

The USS *Arizona* is destroyed by a fire and explosion on the Mississippi River below New Orleans.

March 1

POLITICS: The 13th Amendment is ratified by Wisconsin but rejected by New Jersey.

South: General Ulysses S. Grant begins to marshal the Army of the Potomac for a massive strike against Confederate defensive lines around Richmond and Petersburg, Virginia.

West: Union forces under General George A. Custer skirmish with General Thomas L. Rosser's Confederates at Mount Crawford, Virginia. Rosser, possessing only a few hundred men to oppose nearly 5,000 Union troopers, sets fire to the bridge spanning the Middle Fork of the Shenandoah River to delay the blue-coated juggernaut. Before heavy damage results, Custer unexpectedly charges across the bridge in strength, scattering his opponents.

Naval: The side-paddle steamer USS *Harvest Moon* strikes a Confederate torpedo off Georgetown, South Carolina, sinking in five minutes. Admiral John A. B. Dahlgren is aboard at the time but escapes unharmed.

March 2

South: General Robert E. Lee requests a conference with General Ulysses S. Grant although the latter demurs, declaring that he lacks any authority to convene one.

The XX Corps of General William T. Sherman's army occupies Chesterfield, South Carolina.

West: The cavalry division of General George A. Custer clatters up to Waynesboro, Virginia, where it observes the 2,000 Confederates of General Gabriel C. Wharton's division on a ridge line, supported by a few hundred cavalry under General Thomas L. Rosser. This force constitutes the pitiful remnant of General Jubal A. Early's much-feared army, which had ravaged the Shendandoah Valley throughout the previous summer and fall. At a glance, Custer perceives that Rosser lacks the manpower to cover both of his flanks and dispatches three dismounted regiments to encircle the Confederate left without detection. At 3:00 P.M., with his troopers in place, he sounds the charge, and his flankers burst from the wood's on Wharton's left. Custer simultaneously leads his two remaining brigades on a thundering advance through the Confederate center. The Southerners simply dissolve under the onslaught and flee. Quick movements by Union cavalry cut off the majority's escape although Early and his staff gallop off the field.

The Union victory at Waynesboro, while small, finally ends four years of Confederate resistance in the Shenandoah Valley. Custer takes 1,600 prisoners, 17 flags, 11 cannon, and 200 wagons for a loss of nine dead or wounded. The main body under General Philip H. Sheridan arrives shortly after, and Union forces spend the next three weeks laying waste the countryside with scant opposition.

General Benjamin H. Grierson assumes command of all Federal cavalry in the Military Division of West Mississippi.

Naval: The U.S. Congress establishes the Office of Solicitor and Naval Judge Advocate General.

The USS *Pontiac* captures the Confederate steamer *Amazon* off Savannah, Georgia.

The USS *Fox* forces the Confederate schooner *Rob Roy* to be scuttled in Deadman's Bay, Florida.

March 3

POLITICS: President Abraham Lincoln, through Secretary of War Edwin M. Stanton, instructs General Ulysses S. Grant to ignore General Robert E. Lee's intimations toward peace unless he surrenders first.

Congress institutes the Bureau for the Relief of Freedmen and Refugees (Freedmen's Bureau) to assist former African-American slaves to find work, education, and land. This organization, in effect, functions as the nation's first social welfare agency and is tasked with assisting 4 million former slaves adjust to freedom.

To regulate finances better, the U.S. Congress levies a 10-percent tax on state bank notes to drive them out of circulation. These are then replaced by Federal bank notes drawn from institutions belonging to the national banking system. It is a move calculated to improve centralized financing for the war effort.

The second session, 38th Congress adjourns its final session.

SOUTH: General William T. Sherman's army occupies Cheraw, South Carolina, forcing Confederate units across the Pee Dee River.

WEST: Union forces under General Philip H. Sheridan occupy Charlottesville, Virginia, prior to moving onto Petersburg.

A joint expedition is launched against St. Marks Fort near Tallahassee, Florida, under Commander Robert W. Schufeld and General John Newton.

The USS *Honeysuckle* captures the Confederate blockade-runner *Phantom* off the Florida coast.

The USS *Glide* captures the Confederate schooner *Malta-of-Belize* in Vermilion Bayou, Louisiana.

March 4

POLITICS: President Abraham Lincoln is inaugurated for a second term in Washington, D.C. Despite the carnage and acrimony of the past four years, he strikes a conciliatory tone with his adversaries. "With malice toward none; with charity for all, with firmness in the right, as God gives us to see the right, let us strive to finish the work we are in," he declares, "to bind up the nation's wounds, to care for him who shall have borne the battle, and for his widow and his orphan—to do all which may achieve and cherish a just and lasting peace, among ourselves, and with all nations." In contrast to Lincoln's eloquence, newly elected vice president Andrew Johnson delivers a rambling, incoherent speech that offends many in the audience.

Unionist William G. Brownlow is elected governor of Tennessee to replace Andrew Johnson.

SOUTH: The expedition of General John Newton lands at St. Marks, Florida, after delays caused by ship groundings. He then proceeds overland to the nearby town of Newport.

NAVAL: Acting on a request from General Ulysses S. Grant, Secretary of the Navy Gideon Welles dispatches several heavy monitors up the James River, then riding high, to City Point, Virginia. Grant wishes to deter any possible Confederate attacks on his main supply base at this critical juncture of operations against Richmond.

The Union transport *Thorn* strikes a torpedo in the Cape Fear River, North Carolina, and sinks.

General Edward R. S. Canby requests Admiral Samuel P. Lee for additional mortar craft to support his upcoming attack on Mobile, Alabama.

Federal gunboats USS *General Burnside* and *General Thomas* steam down the Tennessee River and bombard the encampment of General Philip D. Roddey at Mussel Shoals, Alabama. Shore parties subsequently land and capture the position.

March 5

POLITICS: Comptroller of Currency Hugh McCulloch is appointed secretary of the treasury, replacing William Fessenden, who resigns after winning reelection as U.S. senator from Maine.

SOUTH: Union troops under General John Newton skirmish with Confederates as they attempt to cross the St. Marks River, Florida, to capture St. Marks. However, finding the enemy strongly dug in along the riverbank and at nearby Newport, he posts a holding force and sends the bulk of his troops north to a position known locally as Natural Bridge.

NAVAL: Armed boats from the USS *Don* skirmish with Colonel John S. Mosby's partisan rangers in Passpatansy Creek, Maryland, capturing a large boat.

March 6

SOUTH: General Joseph E. Johnston formally takes charge of all Confederate forces in North Carolina.

The army of General William T. Sherman crosses the Pee Dee River, South Carolina, and begins to approach Fayetteville, North Carolina. Meanwhile, General Hugh J. Kilpatrick leads 4,000 Union cavalry to cover the left flank of Sherman's advance.

The 600-man expedition of General John Newton encounters strong Confederate defenses under General William Miller at Natural Bridge, Florida. The Federals make repeated attempts to outflank them but find Southern positions too strong to assail. Reinforcements also bring Miller's strength up to about 1,000 men, so Newton falls back and entrenches on an open pine barren. The Confederates subsequently pursue and attack rashly, but they are repulsed. Union forces then withdraw back to the coast unhindered. Newton's losses are 148 men from all causes while the Confederates sustain six dead and between 20 and 30 wounded. This minor Southern victory prevents the state capital at Tallahassee from being attacked.

WEST: General Alexander M. McCook takes command of the District of Eastern Arkansas.

NAVAL: The USS *Commodore Read, Yankee, Delaware,* and *Heliotrope* accompany a joint expedition to Hamilton's Crossing, Virginia, capturing prisoners and supplies and wrecking an important railroad bridge.

The USS *Jonquil* is damaged by a Confederate torpedo while in the act of clearing the Ashley River, South Carolina.

March 7

POLITICS: Admiral David D. Porter testifies before Congress, proffering some salty commentary as to the military abilities of General Benjamin F. Butler and Nathaniel P. Banks.

SOUTH: General Jacob D. Cox and 13,000 Federal troops begin to skirmish outside Fayetteville, North Carolina, while New Bern is converted into a major Federal supply base. Cox's superior, General John M. Schofield, also directs him to repair railroad lines toward Goldsborough prior to uniting with the army of General William T. Sherman. However, progress stalls at Southwest Creek, just short of Kinston, where 6,500 Confederates under Generals Braxton Bragg and Robert F. Hoke have massed. Both sides then engage in a day-long artillery duel at long range as Bragg awaits reinforcements from the Army of Tennessee.

NAVAL: The USS *Chenango* conducts a reconnaissance mission from Georgetown, South Carolina, and 45 miles up the Black River. No serious resistance is encountered.

March 8

POLITICS: The Confederate Senate authorizes African-American slaves to bear arms for military service on a vote of 9-8.

SOUTH: General Braxton Bragg, recently reinforced with 2,000 Confederates from the Army of Tennessee, attacks General Jacob D. Cox's Union forces in the vicinity of Kinston, North Carolina. The main body under General Robert F. Hoke easily crashes through Colonel Charles Upham's advance brigade, but progress stalls as resistance stiffens. Meanwhile, Bragg dispatches General Daniel H. Hill on a wide movement around the Union rear instead of directly supporting Hoke, which accomplishes little. Fighting dies down with nightfall as both side bring up additional forces.

The Union army under General William T. Sherman crosses the state line into North Carolina and begins to ford the Lumber River.

Union cavalry under General Hugh J. Kilpatrick overrun a small Confederate rear guard belonging to General William J. Hardee's army. They then learn that General Wade Hampton's cavalry division is marching right behind, so Kilpatrick devises an elaborate snare to entrap them. He accordingly spreads out his three brigades across the swampy ground near Monroe's Cross Roads, North Carolina, intending to catch his quarry from whatever direction he approaches. In truth, Kilpatrick's overly dispersed deployment nearly causes his own destruction.

WEST: A large cavalry column under General Philip H. Sheridan canters east from the Shenandoah Valley toward Duguidsville, Virginia, en route to joining the main Union force outside Petersburg.

Confederate general Edmund Kirby-Smith, sensitive about letters criticizing him in Southern newspapers, offers to resign from command of the Trans-Mississippi Department. President Jefferson Davis declines to accept.

NAVAL: The USS *Chenango* steams up the Black River and trades fire with Confederate cavalry at Brown's Ferry, South Carolina.

March 9

POLITICS: President Abraham Lincoln accepts the resignation of John P. Usher as secretary of the interior and appoints Assistant Secretary William Otto to succeed him.

Vermont ratifies the 13th Amendment to the Constitution.

South: General Robert E. Lee warns Confederate secretary of war John C. Breck-inridge about endemic supply shortages. "Unless the men and animals can be sub-sisted, the army cannot be kept together, and our present lines must be abandoned," he states.

The Battle of Kinston, North Carolina, resumes, as General Braxton Bragg renews his attack on General Jacob D. Cox's XXII Corps. He dispatches General Robert F. Hoke on another flank attack that dislodges Federals under General Samuel P. Carter while General Daniel H. Hill makes similar gains against Cox's right. But neither commander can dislodge a second line of defenders under General Thomas H. Ruger and the Confederate onslaught stumbles. Bragg, unable to destroy the XXII Corps, then orders his men across the Neuse River and back into Kinston. Union losses are 57 killed, 264 wounded, and 935 captured (1,257) while the Confederates lose 11 dead, 107 wounded, and 16 captured (134).

As General Wade Hampton's Confederate cavalry ride north toward Monroe's Cross Roads, North Carolina, a Union officer from the 5th Kentucky Cavalry unknowingly blunders into his pickets and is captured along with 16 troopers. From him, Hampton learns that General Hugh J. Kilpatrick awaits in ambush—and in a very dispersed deployment. Hampton is also apprised that Colonel George E. Spencer's Union brigade posted no pickets to avoid being detected. He resolves to attack from that direction on the morrow and turn the tables on his antagonist; the two sides are evenly matched with roughly 4,000 veteran troopers apiece.

March 10

South: Having failed to destroy the Union army of General Jacob D. Cox, Confederates under General Braxton Bragg begin to withdraw toward Goldsborough, North Carolina, for an eventual linkup with General Joseph E. Johnston's forces.

Under cover of an early-morning fog, Confederate cavalry under Generals Wade Hampton and Joseph Wheeler successfully attack the Union troopers of General Hugh J. Kilpatrick at Monroe's Cross Roads. Kilpatrick, clad only in his undershirt, narrowly escapes capture as General Matthew Butler's Southerners gallop through his camp, sweeping up all in their path. Suddenly, the rebels stop to plunder Union stores while Wheeler's thrust stumbles while traversing swampy ground. Kilpatrick uses the delay to rally the brigades of Colonels Thomas J. Jordan and Smith D. Atkins and then counterattacks with horse artillery and rapid-fire carbines. The Federals gradually recapture their bivouac as Hampton withdraws in good order toward Fayetteville. Losses are not recorded accurately, but the Southerners claim having inflicted upward of 500 casualties. Kilpatrick insists his losses are no greater than 190 while killing 80 Confederates and taking 30 captives. Thereafter, this affair is jocularly referred to on both sides as the "Battle of Kilpatrick's Pants."

March 11

Politics: President Abraham Lincoln declares an amnesty for all army and navy deserters returning to their units within two months. Failure to do so carries the loss of citizenship.

South: Union cavalry under General Philip H. Sheridan advance to Goochland Court House en route to Petersburg, Virginia.

General William T. Sherman's army occupies Fayetteville, North Carolina, where he grants his army a five-day resting spell. The first Union troops to arrive, a company of 67 cavalrymen under Captain William R. Duncan, trot into town unopposed until they encounter a Confederate rear guard under General Wade Hampton. The Southerners immediately charge and rout their antagonists, killing 11 and capturing 12, including Duncan. Shortly after, the 4th Division, XVII Corps, of General Giles A. Smith marches up and forces Hampton back over the Cape Fear River. Mayor Archibald McLean then surrenders his town to the Federals.

SOUTHWEST: General Lew Wallace meets with Confederate general James Slaughter and Colonel John Ford to arrange an unofficial truce in the Rio Grande region of Texas.

NAVAL: A naval force consisting of the USS *Eolus, Maratanza, Lenapee,* and *Nyjack* sails up the Cape Fear River toward Fayetteville, North Carolina, to assist army troops under General Alfred H. Terry.

The USS *Monroe* is seized and then released by Confederate guerrillas on the Big Black River, Mississippi.

The Confederate steamer CSS *Ajax* under Lieutenant John Low anchors at Nassau, being inspected closely by British authorities for arms or armament.

March 12

SOUTH: A Federal sweep through Loudoun County, Virginia, fails to apprehend Colonel John S Mosby's Confederate Partisan Rangers.

While recuperating at Fayetteville, the army of General William T. Sherman keeps busy by torching all railroad, factory, and storage facilities within their grasp. Among the machinery destroyed are gun-making tools and dies first seized at Harper's Ferry, West Virginia, in 1861.

NAVAL: The USS *Quaker City* captures the British blockade-runner *R. H. Vermilyea* in the Gulf of Mexico.

The tug USS *Althea* strikes a Confederate torpedo in the Blakely River, Alabama, and sinks.

March 13

POLITICS: Desperate to secure additional manpower, President Jefferson Davis signs the "Negro Soldier Law," allowing African Americans to serve in the Confederate army. The legislation implies that slaves who serve may be manumitted at a later date with the permission of their owner and state legislatures. Had such pragmatic measures been approved earlier, they may have mitigated Confederate personnel deficiencies and yielded a positive impact on the Southern war effort.

SOUTH: Union cavalry under General Philip H. Sheridan skirmish with Confederate forces at Beaver Dam Station, Virginia, en route to joining up with the main Federal force outside Petersburg.

NAVAL: A naval force consisting of the USS *Morse, Commodore Read, Delaware,* and *Mosswood* steams up the Rappahannock River to assist army operations near Fort Lowry, Virginia. There they sink eight boats, destroy a bridge, and silence a battery without loss.

March 14

DIPLOMACY: Despite Southern overtures toward emancipation, Lord Palmerston declares to Confederate envoys James M. Mason and Duncan F. Kenner that English diplomatic recognition is now a foregone possibility, seeing how the war will in all likelihood end in a matter of weeks.

SOUTH: Federal troops under General Jacob D. Cox occupy Kinston, North Carolina, prior to advancing on Goldsborough.

NAVAL: The USS *Wyandank* captures the Confederate schooner *Champanero* at St. Inigoes Creek, Maryland.

The USS *Shawmut* and *Commodore Morris* are dispatched up the York and Pamunkey rivers, Virginia, to keep the waterways free of enemy interference.

Armed boats from the USS *Lodona* land at Broro Neck, Georgia, and destroy a large saltwork operating there.

March 15

SOUTH: Union cavalry under General Philip H. Sheridan reach Hanover Court House, Virginia, en route to Petersburg.

General William T. Sherman orders his army out from Fayetteville, North Carolina, and toward Goldsborough, after totally destroying all property of use to the Confederacy, including the city's former U.S. Arsenal. Then Sherman, to keep Confederates confused as to his real intentions, orders the left wing under General Henry W. Slocum to feint in the direction of Raleigh. Meanwhile, Union cavalry under General Hugh J. Kilpatrick advance to Averasboro where they run headlong into General William J. Hardee's division of 6,000 men, strongly posted with a swamp on the right and the Black River to their left. Hardee, ordered to ascertain Union strength for General Joseph E. Johnston, is full of fight and repels Kilpatrick's probes.

March 16

SOUTH: General Pierre G. T. Beauregard becomes second in command of Confederate forces in North Carolina under General Joseph E. Johnston.

General Alexander P. Stewart takes charge of all infantry and artillery forces in the Army of Tennessee.

The Battle of Averasboro, North Carolina, erupts as Union cavalry under General Hugh J. Kilpatrick pushes his 8th Indiana Cavalry forward. These forces drive back the skirmishers of Colonel Alfred Rhett's advance brigade, but they are stopped cold by the main body of Confederates under General Lafayette McLaws. The Southerners gradually work their way around Kilpatrick's flank, forcing him back until additional Federal reinforcements arrive. All four divisions of the Union XX Corps under General Henry W. Slocum then deploy on the field and drive the Confederates back into their strong field fortifications. Fighting continues as Federal troops try and fail to flank McLaw's works, and fighting gradually winds down with nightfall. General William J. Hardee subsequently orders the Confederates to fall back on Smithville, which is accomplished without incident. Union losses total 95 dead, 53 wounded, and 54 missing (202), while the Confederates record 682 from all causes. The result of this insignificant encounter is to delay General

William T. Sherman's left wing significantly, further separating it from the rapidly advancing right wing.

NAVAL: The USS *Pursuit* captures the British blockade-runner *Mary* on the Indian River, Florida.

Admiral Henry K. Thatcher, newly arrived on the scene, offers General Edward R. S. Canby the use of several light draft gunboats to support army operations against Mobile, Alabama.

The USS *Quaker City* captures the Confederate blockade-runner *Telemico* in the Gulf of Mexico.

March 17

SOUTH: General Edward R. S. Canby begins his drive against Mobile, Alabama, with 32,000 men of the XVI and XII Corps; his opponent, General Dabney H. Maury, musters only 2,000. Canby intends to capture the city by means of a pincer's movement, with one column under General Frederick Steele proceeding out of Pensacola to the east as he leads another force from the west along the right shore of Mobile Bay. However, progress by the XIII and XVI Corps proves slow due to muddy conditions and the need to corduroy the roads to allow heavy siege artillery to accompany the march.

NAVAL: The Coastal Survey steamer *Bibb* strikes a Confederate torpedo in Charleston harbor, South Carolina, and is damaged heavily but survives.

The USS *Quaker City* captures the Confederate schooner *George Burkhart* in the Gulf of Mexico.

March 18

POLITICS: The 2nd session, second Confederate Congress adjourns, although in a pique over President Jefferson Davis's insinuations of obstructionism.

SOUTH: Union forces under General John M. Schofield skirmish at the Neuse River Bridge during their advance on Goldsborough, North Carolina.

General Henry W. Slocum's troops skirmish heavily with General Wade Hampton's cavalry as he approaches Bentonville, North Carolina. Meanwhile, General Joseph E. Johnston begins to concentrate troops nearby to attack and possibly destroy the Federal left wing. At the very least, he wants to seriously delay Union forces from concentrating in overwhelming strength near Goldsborough. Johnston then arrays his 21,000 men in an arc across the Goldsboro Road, with General Braxton Bragg on the left, General William J. Hardee in the center, and General Alexander P. Stewart on the right.

NAVAL: A naval force consisting of the USS *Don, Stepping Stones, Heliotrope,* and *Resolute* sails up the Rappahannock River, Virginia, and destroys a Confederate supply base at Montrose that had supported guerrilla operations. A naval party, landed ashore, then scatters a party of Southern cavalry.

March 19

SOUTH: Union cavalry under General Philip H. Sheridan reach White House on the Pamunkey River, Virginia, prior to linking up with the main Federal force at Petersburg.

The Battle of Bentonville, North Carolina, commences as General Henry W. Slocum orders William P. Carlin's division, XX Corps, down the Goldsboro Road toward Cole's Plantation. En route, Carlin encounters large numbers of heavily entrenched Confederates and halts. This is the signal for General Joseph E. Johnston to attack, and he pushes Carlin's division back in confusion until the Federals are reinforced by fresh troops under General William Cogswell. Desperate fighting breaks out along the line as hard-charging Southerners prove unable to break through Union lines. General Braxton Bragg then tardily orders General Robert F. Hoke's division into action, allowing Slocum to strengthen his line. Also, as General William B. Taliaferro's Southerners advance, they are outflanked by Federal troops and forced back with losses. Conflict ceases at nightfall, and both sides rush up reinforcements

General Frederick Steele continues leading 13,000 Federal troops out of Pensacola, Florida, and marches west toward Mobile, Alabama. His first objective is the reduction of Fort Blakely, but progress over the soggy ground remains slow.

General Thomas K. Smith is appointed commander of the District of South Alabama.

NAVAL: The USS *Massachusetts* brushes up against a Confederate torpedo in Charleston harbor, South Carolina, which fortunately fails to explode. The incident occurs only 50 yards from where the ironclad *Patapsco* sank on January 15, 1865.

March 20

SOUTH: The right wing of General William T. Sherman's army under General Oliver O. Howard marches toward Bentonville, North Carolina, to reinforce the left wing under General Henry W. Slocum. His arrival gives him a total of 60,000 veteran troops—three times the size of his Southern opponent. Confederates under General Joseph E. Johnston, meanwhile, take no offensive measures and instead strengthen their fortifications. They are especially eager to protect Mill Creek Bridge, their only escape route, from being seized. Considering the odds, Johnston hopes to wage a defensive battle to his advantage and possibly to inflict crippling losses on the Union army, should they attack.

WEST: A force of 6,000 Union cavalry under General George Stoneman departs Jonesborough, Tennessee, on a wrecking expedition through North Carolina. His primary objective is to destroy tracks and bridges belonging to the Tennessee and Virginia Railroad.

NAVAL: The former Confederate ram *Albemarle* is raised from its muddy berth on the Roanoke River, North Carolina.

March 21

SOUTH: The Battle of Bentonville resumes as General William T. Sherman dispatches General Joseph A. Mower's division to turn the Confederate left and rear while the main Union force demonstrates to their front. Mower makes surprisingly good progress and nearly reaches Mill Creek Bridge before being struck violently on both flanks and driven back. However, Johnston simply lacks the manpower to follow up decisively so he disengages and withdraws across Mill Creek Bridge northwest toward Smithville.

Bentonville is the last conventional clash of the Civil War, and both sides perform exceedingly well under fire. Union casualties are 191 killed, 1,168 wounded, and 287 missing (1,646) to a Confederate tally of 239 killed, 1,694 injured, and 673 missing (2,606). Johnston, unfortunately, is unable to make up his losses and never challenges Sherman again in the field.

General Innis N. Palmer assumes command of the District of Beaufort, South Carolina.

General Edward R. S. Canby lands troops at Dannelly's Mills on the Fish River, Alabama, and proceeds overland toward Spanish Fort as a part of his overall strategy against Mobile. He takes with him the XVI Corps under General Andrew J. Smith, the XIII Corps of General Gordon Granger, and a division of African Americans under General John P. Hawkins.

NAVAL: Commander Arthur R. Yates, commanding the USS *J. P. Jackson,* orders rations issued to the starving inhabitants of Biloxi, Mississippi.

The CSS *Stonewall* under Captain Thomas J. Paige attempts to sail from El Ferrol, Spain, but is detained two days owing to stormy weather.

March 22

SOUTH: After a brief pursuit of General Joseph E. Johnston, the army of General William T. Sherman begins to concentrate in the vicinity of Goldsborough, North Carolina, where he waits for Union reinforcements and supplies advancing from the coast.

General James H. Wilson, at the head of 13,500 Union cavalry, crosses the Tennessee River from Gravelly Springs, Tennessee, into northern Alabama. His objective is to seize the Confederate munitions center at Selma and advances the crack divisions of Generals Edward M. McCook, Eli Long, and Emory Upton; this is the largest cavalry force ever fielded in American history. Moreover, thanks to his rigorous training regime, all ranks are exceptionally well disciplined and armed with the latest repeating rifles. Then Wilson, to confuse the defenders en route, divides his force and moves along three divergent trails. Each column is ordered to remain in mutual supporting distance of the others in the event of Confederate resistance.

March 23

POLITICS: President Abraham Lincoln and his son Tad depart Washington, D.C., for City Point, outside Petersburg, Virginia, to consult with General William T. Sherman and General Ulysses S. Grant.

SOUTH: The combined armies of Generals William T. Sherman and John M. Schofield, numbering in excess of 100,000 men, unite at Goldsborough, North Carolina. Sherman has covered 425 miles from Savannah, Georgia, in only 50 days and without a major mishap. It is an organizational and logistical triumph and far exceeding his better known "March to the Sea" in complexity and difficulty. General Joseph E. Johnston, heavily outnumbered, concedes to General Robert E. Lee that "I can do no more than annoy him."

March 24

POLITICS: President Abraham Lincoln arrives at Fortress Monroe, Virginia, prior to meeting with General Ulysses S. Grant at City Point.

SOUTH: General Robert E. Lee, in light of his slowly eroding defenses in and around Petersburg, conceives his last tactical offensive of the war. He orders General John B. Gordon to take elements of several Confederate corps and seize a portion of nearby Union lines. A breakthrough here will undoubtedly force General Ulysses S. Grant to concentrate his forces near the break, thereby allowing other portions of the Army of Northern Virginia to slip out of Petersburg and join General Joseph E. Johnston in North Carolina. Gordon, an excellent commander, selects Fort Stedman, only 150 yards from Confederate lines and garrisoned by men of the IX Corps under General Orlando B. Wilcox.

NAVAL: The USS *Republic* lands several armed parties ashore up the Cape Fear River, North Carolina, to halt raiding activities by General Joseph Wheeler's cavalry.

The USS *Quaker City* captures the Confederate blockade-runner *Cora* off the Texas coast.

The French-built ironclad ram CSS *Stonewall* departs El Ferrol, Spain, for Havana, Cuba, while the wooden vessels USS *Niagara* and *Sacramento* under Commodore Thomas T. Craven hover at a distance, declining to engage. "At this time the odds in her favor were too great and too certain, in my humble judgement, to admit of the slightest hope of being able to inflict upon her even the most trifling injury," he explains, "whereas, if we had gone out, the *Niagara* would most undoubtedly have been easily and promptly destroyed." Craven, however, subsequently is court-martialed and convicted for failing to engage the enemy, but his verdict is suspended by Secretary of the Navy Gideon Welles.

March 25

POLITICS: President Abraham Lincoln arrives at City Point, Virginia, to confer with General Ulysses S. Grant.

SOUTH: At 4:00 A.M., the Battle of Fort Stedman, Virginia, erupts as Confederate pioneer companies silence outlaying Union pickets and remove their abattis. Then 11,000 Confederates unexpectedly pour into Union trenches near Fort Stedman, surprising the defenders and capturing the fort and Batteries X, XI, and XII. However, as Confederates fan out intending to exploit their breakthrough, resistance intensifies from nearby Fort Haskell and Battery IX, which mires their impetus. Gordon then digs in along a lightly manned perimeter as Federal troops regroup for a major counterattack. At about 7:45 A.M., General John F. Hartranft leads 4,000 men back toward the trenches near Fort Stedman, driving Gordon's veterans back. As the gray masses withdraw across the field, they sustain a particularly withering crossfire from Union batteries posted on either flank. Several thousand Confederates unexpectedly surrender rather then be killed.

Fort Stedman is the last tactical gambit of the Army of Northern Virginia and a heavy defeat for General Robert E. Lee. Lacking the necessary manpower to exploit Gordon's initial surprise, the Southerners lose about 3,500 men, including 1,500 captured. Union casualties amount to 72 killed, 450 wounded, and 522 missing (1,044). Lee now has little recourse but to prepare for the immediate evacuation of Petersburg.

The first Federal supply train from the coast reaches General William T. Sherman's army at Goldsborough, North Carolina.

NAVAL: In light of Confederate military activity, Admiral David D. Porter orders several gunboats up the Appomattox River to guard Union pontoon bridges in and around City Point.

March 26

SOUTH: A force 9,000 Federal cavalry under General Philip H. Sheridan crosses the James River and unites with the main Union force under General Ulysses S. Grant, bringing Union numbers up to 122,000 men—twice the strength of Confederate defenders.

General Robert E. Lee, wary of General William T. Sherman's army catching him from behind while General Ulysses S. Grant pins him frontally, warns President Jefferson Davis to prepare for the inevitable. He tells Davis, "I fear now it will be impossible to prevent a junction between Grant and Sherman, nor do I deem it prudent that this army should maintain its position until the latter shall approach too near."

NAVAL: Armed sailors from the USS *Benton* join an expedition under General Benjamin G. Farrar that captures Trinity, Louisiana, along with numerous prisoners and stores.

March 27

SOUTH: General Alfred H. Terry assumes command of the X Corps in North Carolina.

A force of 32,000 Union troops under General Edward R. S. Canby besieges Spanish Fort, Alabama, by planting 50 siege cannon and 30 field pieces in its vicinity. But the 2,000-man garrison of General Randall L. Gibson proves defiant, and a prolonged artillery duel ensues for the next 13 days.

NAVAL: Secretary of the Navy Gideon Welles orders the USS *Wyoming* to find and destroy the elusive Confederate raider CSS *Shenandoah*.

Admiral Henry K. Thatcher orders several tinclads and gunboats up the Blakely River to support army operations against Spanish Fort. This proves a perilous operation, for the waters have been strewn thickly with Confederate torpedoes.

The CSS *Stonewall* under Captain Thomas J. Paige puts into Lisbon, Portugal, closely followed by the USS *Niagara* and *Sacramento*.

March 28

POLITICS: President Abraham Lincoln, Generals Ulysses S. Grant and William T. Sherman, and Admiral David D. Porter confer on the steamship *River Queen* to discuss postwar policy toward former Confederates. Lincoln, fearful of continuing guerrilla activity, instructs his officers to offer generous terms to their soon-to-be-repatriated countrymen.

WEST: The District of the Plains is formed by combining the Districts of Utah, Colorado, and Nebraska and assigned to General Patrick E. Connor.

NAVAL: The gunboat USS *Milwaukee* strikes a Confederate torpedo and sinks in the Blakely River, Alabama; no lives are lost.

Secretary of the Navy Gideon Welles picks Commodore Sylvanus W. Godon to head up the newly reconstituted Brazil Squadron.

The USS *Niagara,* while sailing up a river to the city of Lisbon, Portugal, is suddenly fired on by guns from a fort and Commodore Thomas T. Craven steams downstream. The Portuguese government subsequently apologizes for the incident.

March 29

SOUTH: The Appomattox campaign begins as 19,000 Confederates under Generals Fitzhugh Lee and George E. Pickett are directed by General Robert E. Lee to outflank Union forces at Lewis Farm, near Gravelly Run, Virginia. General Ulysses S. Grant simultaneously dispatches 13,000 cavalry under General Philip H. Sheridan, supported by 30,000 men of the II Corps and V Corps under Generals General Andrew A. Humphrey and Gouverneur K. Warren, respectively, to turn the extreme far right of Lee's defensive line, southwest of Petersburg, Virginia. Union troops encounter Pickett's skirmish line along the Boydton and Quaker roads and gradually push it back. Warren's V Corps also engages Confederates under General Bushrod Johnson and forces them into new positions along White Oak Road. Fighting dies amid heavy rainfall that evening.

General James H. Wilson's cavalry column passes through Elyton, Alabama, where 1,100 cavalrymen under General John T. Croxton are detached to raid Tuscaloosa and burn all public property.

WEST: General George Stoneman's Union cavalry clash with Confederates at Wilkesborough, North Carolina.

NAVAL: The monitor USS *Osage* strikes a Confederate torpedo in the Blakely River, Alabama, and sinks with a loss of four killed and eight wounded.

March 30

POLITICS: In light of the Confederacy's fading fortunes, President Jefferson Davis confides to a friend: "Faction has done much to cloud our prospects and impair my power to serve the country."

SOUTH: General Philip H. Sheridan concentrates troops at Dinwiddie Court House, southwest of Petersburg, Virginia, and renews his march north in a driving rain. He is repelled gradually in heavy fighting by General Fitzhugh Lee's Confederate cavalry. Meanwhile, the II Corps under General Andrew A. Humphreys and the V Corps under General Gouverneur K. Warren slowly press forward toward Gravelly Run, threatening Confederate positions and the vital Southside Railroad.

General Nathan B. Forrest's cavalry arrive at Scottsville, Alabama, from Tupelo, Mississippi, intending to intercept the roving columns of General James H. Wilson at Elyton.

NAVAL: Lieutenant Charles W. Read takes command of the CSS *William H. Webb* on the Red River, Louisiana. Despite the fact the vessel is unarmed, undermanned, and lacks fuel, he prepares for a dash down the Mississippi River to the open sea—300 miles distant.

March 31

SOUTH: Union forces under General Philip H. Sheridan continue turning the Confederate right flank at Dinwiddie Court House, Virginia. He suddenly is assailed in the left flank by General George E. Pickett's division and shoved back violently. The V Corps under General Gouverneur K. Warren also advances along the White Oak Road, encountering heavy Confederate resistance. In the course of fighting, Warren's 2nd Division is driven off in confusion by General Bushrod Johnson, but a prompt counterstroke by his 3rd Division recaptures all lost ground. Considering that nearly 50,000 Federals prove unable to dislodge 10,000 defenders, the South wins a decided tactical victory. Then Pickett, cognizant of how dangerously thin his force is stretched, withdraws to Five Forks under cover of darkness. There, General Robert E. Lee, fearing the precariousness of his entire perimeter, solemnly instructs Pickett to "Hold Five Forks at all hazards."

The Union cavalry column of General Emory Upton skirmishes with General Nathan B. Forrest's troopers at Montevallo, Alabama. Forrest manages to hit the Union force from behind, temporarily driving them from the field, but they rally and counterattack. A large-scale saber-and-pistol duel erupts as the Confederates gradually retreat toward Ebenezer Church. Federal scouts then capture a Southern courier carrying Forrest's plans, and the information is relayed immediately to Wilson. He dispatches the brigade of General Edward M. McCook to seize and destroy the bridge at Centerville, over which Forrest expects 3,000 men under General William H. Jackson to arrive.

NAVAL: Armed Confederates seizes the Union schooner *St. Mary's* off the Patuxent River, Chesapeake Bay. The vessel then is commandeered to Nassau.

The USS *Iuka* captures the British blockade-runner *Comus* off the Florida coast.

April 1

POLITICS: President Abraham Lincoln returns to Washington, D.C., from the *River Queen.*

Confederate Florida governor John Milton commits suicide at his home.

NORTH: Wesley Merritt is promoted to major general, U.S. Army.

SOUTH: The Battle of Five Forks commences as General Philip H. Sheridan orders cavalry under Generals George A. Custer and Thomas C. Devlin to slash at the Confederate right flank while his remaining forces pin them down frontally. The lynchpin of his attack devolves on General Gouverneur K. Warren's V Corps, which is slated to work its way around the Confederate left and crush it with three divisions. Inexplicably, senior Confederate generals George E. Pickett and Fitzhugh Lee are not present as the struggle develops, being at a fish bake several miles to the rear. Warren, meanwhile, is misled by faulty maps and his turning movement is delayed by several hours. It is not until 4:00 P.M. that General Romeyn B. Ayers's division finally crashes through the wafer-thin Southern defenses. Sheridan then orders his cavalry to charge the entire Confederate line, and it shatters. Thousands of Southerners, finding themselves cut off by Colonel Randall S. Mackenzie's troopers, lay down their arms en masse. The result is a complete and decisive Union victory, though somewhat soured by Sheridan's decision to arbitrarily sack Warren as commander of V Corps. Pickett is also relieved by General Robert E. Lee.

Five Forks cost the Union around 124 killed, 706 injured, and 54 missing (986) while the Confederates lose 450 dead, 750 wounded, and 3,244 captured (4,444) in addition to 11 flags and four cannon. More important, General Robert E. Lee's defensive line is compromised entirely and the South Side Railroad—his final supply line into Petersburg—virtually cut. Lee has no recourse but to abandon Richmond immediately to save his army from imminent capture.

Union cavalry under Generals Eli Long and Emory Upton continue pressing General Nathan B. Forrest at Ebenezer Church, Alabama, where he awaits the arrival of General James R. Chalmer's division. Forrest then deploys three brigades of 1,500 men under Generals Philip D. Roddey and Daniel W. Adams, and Colonel Edward Crossland in a thin line across the Selma Highway. At 4:00 P.M., the first Union wave under Long gallops forward, crashes into the Confederate center, and is repulsed. Forrest is engaged closely in desperate hand-to-hand fighting, receives a severe saber slash before shooting down his antagonist. Upton's command then moves up, dismounts, and charges Adams's troops on the Southern right. The Confederates again prevail in a tough scrap, throwing the Federal troopers back. However, when another part of Upton's men hit Forrest's center-left, held by Alabama militia, they bolt and the entire line collapses. The Confederates then flee pell-mell for Selma, with vengeful Union cavalry pursuing closely. Federal loses amount to 12 dead and 40 wounded to a Confederate tally of 300, mostly captured.

Colonel Andrew B. Spurling's Union cavalry, XIII Corps, engages and defeats the 46th Mississippi Cavalry in a hot action at Sibley's Mills, five miles outside of Fort Blakely, Alabama. The Federals, reinforced by African Americans from General John B. Hawkins's division, trounce the Southerners, capturing a flag and inflicting 74 casualties for a loss of two wounded. Shortly afterward, the 13,000 men of General Frederick Steel's column arrive and besiege the fort.

NAVAL: The tinclad USS *Rodolph* strikes a Confederate torpedo in the Blakely River, Alabama, and sinks with a loss of four killed, 11 wounded, and three missing. Ironically, it was towing an apparatus intended to help raise the *Milwaukee*, sunk by mines four days previously.

The Confederate raider CSS *Shenandoah* under Lieutenant James I. Waddell anchors at Lea Harbor, Ascension Island, in the Eastern Carolines. There it seizes the Union whalers *Pearl, Harvest, Hector,* and *Edward Carey,* which are then stripped of supplies and burned.

April 2

POLITICS: As Confederate defenses around Richmond, Virginia, collapse, a greatly relieved president Abraham Lincoln telegraphs General Ulysses S. Grant, "Allow me to tender to you, and all with you, the nation's grateful thanks for this additional and magnificent success."

SOUTH: General Ulysses S. Grant decisively orders an all-out assault on the crumbling Confederate defenses ringing Petersburg, Virginia. At 4:30 A.M., General Horatio G. Wright's VI Corps storms the Southern right at Fort Fisher as far as Hatcher's Run, fatally rupturing General Robert E. Lee's lines. The XXIV Corps also charges down Boydton Plank Road, routing the defenders while the redoubtable general

Ambrose P. Hill falls while rallying his men. If General Robert E. Lee is to evacuate safely the Army of Northern Virginia to Amelia Court House, he needs additional time to remove them; fortunately, he acquires it once the surging Union tide laps up against Fort Gregg.

Fort Gregg is garrisoned by barely 500 survivors from Generals Nathaniel G. Harris's and Cadmus M. Wilcox's divisions. Around noontime, they are beset by two entire Union divisions under Generals Robert S. Foster and John W. Turner, but the embattled Confederates manage to repel three attacking waves. Federal troops subsequently find an unguarded trench leading into the fort and storm it. Undeterred, the defenders resist fiercely in hand-to-hand fighting before being overwhelmed. Confederate casualties are 57 killed and 129 wounded, and 30 captured to a Union tally of 714.

As the conflict at Fort Gregg rages, the II Corps of General Andrew A. Humphreys inches farther west, seizes the Crow Salient, and pushes up Claiborne Road. General Nelson A. Miles's division, II Corps, is approaching Sutherland's Station when it stumbles on General Henry Heth's Confederates. Miles is ordered personally to exploit Humphrey's initial breakthrough, and he charges the milling Southerners before they can regroup. Heth's men quickly are swept aside and routed, losing 1,000 prisoners and two cannon. Moreover, the South Side Railroad is now firmly in Union hands. But the delays incurred here and at Fort Gregg permit General Robert E. Lee to extricate his remaining troops by nightfall.

General Robert E. Lee begins to evacuate Petersburg, Virginia, and advises President Jefferson Davis to relocate the seat of the Confederate government from Richmond. His 18,500 Confederates no longer can stem a concerted drive by 63,000 Federals, who capture the Petersburg lines at a cost of 625 dead, 3,189 wounded, and 326 missing (4,140); Southern losses are unknown but are considered equally heavy. Lee, however, skillfully shuttles his command over the Appomattox River without Union interference and departs for Amelia Court House, 39 miles southwest of Richmond, and thence begins an overland slog down the Richmond and Danville Railroad to Danville. He intends, or at least hopes, to link up with General Joseph E. Johnston somewhere in North Carolina. Thus, the siege of Petersburg, which commenced on June 15, 1864, successfully terminates with Union losses of 5,100 killed, 24,800 wounded, and 17,500 captured or missing; Confederate casualties are variously estimated at between 28,000 and 38,000.

Meanwhile, General Richard S. Ewell, commanding Southern forces in Richmond, issues orders to burn all military supplies and equipment that cannot be moved. As flames shoot out into the sky, looters take to the streets, adding to the general sense of mayhem. This evening, Ewell removes the last remaining Confederate soldiers from the capital, and he marches them across the Mayo Bridge on the James River. The bridge is burned behind him to prevent a pursuit.

General Joseph A. Mower takes charge of the XX Corps, North Carolina.

General James H. Wilson arrives before Selma, Alabama, a heavily fortified city guarded by 5,000 men under General Nathan B. Forrest. Fortunately for the Federals, they seize the British civil engineer responsible for constructing an elaborate series of fieldworks, redans, palisades, and ditches; he freely informs his captors of the layout. Wilson then dispatches General Eli Long to attack the Confederate right while dismounted; the troopers cross 600 yards of open space, taking heavy losses. Long is wounded, but his men spill over the redoubts as General Emory Upton's dismounted division also threads its way through a swamp on the Confederate left. Wilson then decides the issue with a thundering charge down the Selma Road, which unnerves and finally routs the defenders. By nightfall, the city is secured, and Union forces begin to burn factories, storage facilities, railyards, and anything of use to the Confederacy. Forrest's losses are 2,700 captured and 102 cannon seized; Wilson sustains 46 dead, 300 wounded, and 13 missing.

WEST: General George Stoneman's Union cavalry column crosses into Virginia and divides into three parts to burn bridges at Wytheville, the New River Valley, and the Roanoke River valley.

NAVAL: Confederate secretary of the navy Stephen R. Mallory orders the James River Squadron, consisting of CSS *Virginia II, Richmond, Fredericksburg, Nansemond, Hampton, Roanoke, Torpedo, Shrapnel,* and *Patrick Henry,* scuttled to prevent capture. "The spectacle," Admiral Raphael Semmes writes, "was grand beyond description." All naval remaining personnel are ordered to pick up rifles and serve as an infantry brigade.

A naval expedition consisting of the USS *Shamrock, Wyoming, Hunchback, Valley City,* and *Whitehead* departs Plymouth, North Carolina, and steams up the Roanoke River as far as Stumpy Reach in support of General William T. Sherman's army.

April 3

POLITICS: President Jefferson Davis and his cabinet arrive by special train in Danville, Virginia.

SOUTH: Union forces under General Godfrey Weitzel, commander of the African-American XXV Corps, prepare to occupy Richmond, Virginia. At 5:30 A.M., Weitzel sends a small party under Major Atherton H. Stevens, which is received by the civil authorities at city hall. Richmond then surrenders to Union forces, who promptly raise the Stars and Stripes over the state capitol. Weitzel himself arrives three hours later and orders all fires extinguished, looters arrested, and order restored. An eerie calm settles over the former Confederate capital as President Jefferson Davis's residence is occupied and transformed into a military headquarters.

President Abraham Lincoln, visiting General Ulysses S. Grant in Petersburg, declares, "Thank God I have lived to see this. It seems to me that I have been dreaming a horrid dream for four years, and now the nightmare is gone."

The Army of Northern Virginia disengages and slips out of the Richmond-Petersburg trenches and moves westward to make for Amelia Court House. General James Longstreet takes the point, while General John B. Gordon forms the rear guard. Additional forces join the lengthening column, with General William Mahone marching behind from Bermuda Hundred. Moreover, General Richard S. Ewell is expected to join them from Richmond on the morrow. General Robert E. Lee now commands 30,000 ragged, hungry, and worn out men—aptly pursued by a well-supplied, well-fed force three times their size.

After decisively breaking through at Five Forks, Virginia, General Philip H. Sheridan orders his cavalry on a "Hell for leather" pursuit of fleeing Confederates. General Wesley Merritt's division then canters off in the direction of Amelia Court House, intending to cut off the enemy's retreat. Spearheading this movement is General George A. Custer, a recklessly daring cavalier. Custer, galloping ahead of his column, suddenly perceives a Confederate rear guard at Namozine Creek under General William P. Roberts. He quickly deploys horse artillery to distract the defenders while the 1st Vermont Cavalry crosses farther upstream to turn their flank. The Southerners, quickly perceiving this threat, abandon their position and fall back.

Custer subsequently presses ahead for another five miles toward Namozine Church, where a Confederate cavalry division under General Rufus Barringer is collected. A quick reconnaissance by the 8th New York Cavalry reveals the extent of Southern defenses and Custer orders them around the Southern left flank. En route, they suddenly crash into the 1st North Carolina Cavalry, and an intense melee erupts. Meanwhile, Custer leads the 1st Vermont and 15th New York on a thundering charge toward the Confederate center, routing them. The general's younger brother, Lieutenant Thomas W. Custer, helps capture the colors of the 2nd South Carolina Cavalry and 15 prisoners, winning a Congressional Medal of Honor. Union losses in this sharp encounter are unknown, but they secure 350 captives, 100 horses, and a cannon.

General David S. Stanley leads his IV Corps on an expedition to Asheville, North Carolina.

Fort Blakely, Alabama, is invested by 13,000 Federal troops under General Frederick Steele. It is defended by 4,000 Confederates led by General St. John R. Liddell. The progress of Union siege lines is hampered by enfilading fire from the CSS *Nashville* at the mouth of the Raft River.

NAVAL: A force of 50 midshipmen from the Confederate Naval Academy are chosen to escort the archives and treasury of the government from Richmond, Virginia, to Danville.

The naval brigade of Commodore John R. Tucker departs Drewry's Bluff, Virginia, now attached to the Confederate division of General George W. "Custis" Lee.

As Confederate forces withdraw from Richmond, Virginia, Admiral David D. Porter instructs his fleet to begin extensive antitorpedo sweeps up numerous rivers, creeks, and estuaries.

April 4

POLITICS: President Abraham Lincoln ventures up the James River to Richmond, Virginia, aboard the USS *Malvern.* Once ashore, he is escorted by Admiral David D. Porter and 10 sailors to the Confederate White House, being greeted by throngs of former African-American slaves. Many of these reach out and touch Lincoln's person to convince themselves that he is not an apparition.

President Jefferson Davis, pausing momentarily at Danville, Virginia, calls on fellow Southerners not to lose hope, for ultimate victory is certain to come from "our own unquenchable resolve."

SOUTH: The Army of Northern Virginia, having achieved a day's head start out of Richmond, Virginia, arrives at Amelia Court House to discover that promised rations for the starving troops have failed to arrive. Instead, ordnance supplies have been dispatched by mistake, and General Robert E. Lee orders his men to forage for themselves. Meanwhile, pursuing Union forces quickly close the gap.

Union cavalry under General Philip H. Sheridan advance to Jetersville, Virginia, cutting off the Army of Northern Virginia's retreat. General George G. Meade and the II and V Corps, Army of the Potomac, also arrive. The two commanders then dig in and wait for the Confederates to attack them.

General John T. Croxton's Union cavalry column occupies Tuscaloosa, Alabama, capturing three cannon and burning various public stores.

SOUTHWEST: General John B. Magruder is appointed head of the Confederate District of Texas, New Mexico, and Arizona.

NAVAL: Admiral David G. Farragut and his entourage arrive in Richmond, Virginia, to inspect the city.

Admiral Henry K. Thatcher agrees to supply General Edward R. S. Canby with rowboats and sailors capable of assisting in the assault on Forts Tracey and Huger.

A naval battery consisting of three 30-pound Parrott rifles is landed on the banks of the Blakely River to participate in the reduction of Spanish Fort, Alabama.

April 5

POLITICS: As President Abraham Lincoln delights in sitting in Jefferson Davis's chair, he is approached by Confederate assistant secretary of war John A. Campbell, himself a former U.S. Supreme Court justice, who requests that the president help maintain the rule of law in Virginia.

Secretary of State William H. Seward is severely injured in a carriage accident in Washington, D.C.

SOUTH: Union troopers under General George Crook encounter a Confederate wagon train outside Jetersville, Virginia, and Crook orders the 1st Pennsylvania Cavalry forward. They capture 200 wagons, 11 flags and 320 prisoners. The Confederates react sharply by dispatching General Fitzhugh Lee's cavalry in pursuit, which harry the Federals as far as Amelia Springs before encountering reinforcements under General J. Irvin Gregg. Northern losses are reported as 20 killed and 96 wounded.

General Robert E. Lee, preparing to depart Amelia Court House, is now joined by the troops of General Richard S. Ewell, bringing his strength up to 58,000. Lee now determines to attack Union forces under Generals Philip H. Sheridan and George G. Meade presently entrenching at Jetersville. Three divisions under General James Longstreet are readied to march, but Lee cancels the move after learning that more Federal troops are approaching. To avoid encirclement, he orders a night march around the Union left flank followed by a quick dash to Farmville in the hopes of finding supplies there. Meade, the senior Union commander, declines attacking as the VI Corps has yet to appear. Federal troops continue milling around their fortifications until 10:30 P.M., when General Ulysses S. Grant arrives and personally directs the pursuit.

NAVAL: The Union steamer *Harriet DeFord* is seized by Confederate partisans as it sails up the St. Mary's River, Maryland. The vessel subsequently is taken to Dimer's Creek, Virginia, and burned.

April 6

SOUTH: The Battle of Sayler's Creek unfolds as the Army of Northern Virginia, retreating from Amelia Court House to Farmville, Virginia, inadvertently separates into three parts. Closely pursuing Union forces are thus able to exploit gaps between the commands of Generals Richard S. Ewell, Richard H. Anderson, and John B. Gordon with disastrous effect. Trouble begins when Anderson halts his long wagon train to fend off some Union cavalry, but he fails to inform the lead division under General James Longstreet, which continues marching off. General Horatio G. Wright's Federal troops then assail Ewell's isolated detachment near Harper's Farm near Little Sayler's Creek, supported by 20 cannon. The Confederates initially repulse the Union advance as they pour over the flooded creek, but the division of General George W. Getty effectively flanks the defenders. Ewell's entire line then is double-enveloped promptly, and 3,400 troops surrender.

Another drama develops to Ewell's right and rear, where a Union cavalry division under General Wesley Merritt attacks General Anderson's corps. Here, the weak formations of General George E. Pickett and Bushrod Johnson collapse before a determined onslaught by Generals George A. Custer and Thomas C. Devlin. As Southern defenses crumble, Anderson's survivors flee into the woods while victorious Federals round up another 2,600 captives, 300 wagons, and 15 cannon.

The final act to play out occurs on the Confederate left, where 17,000 men of General Andrew A. Humphrey's II Corps engage General Gordon's rear guard, numbering 7,000. Gordon is protecting a Confederate wagon train bogged down in the mud. The Federals attack, and after heavy fighting proves inconsequential, Humphreys sends a column around the Southern left. Gordon, now nearly outflanked, hastily withdraws from the creek with the loss of 1,700 men.

Sayler's Creek proves disastrous to the Army of Northern Virginia, which loses 7,700 men and eight generals—one fifth of its overall strength. Union losses amount to only 166 killed and 982 wounded. This is one of the largest number of American soldiers captured in a single action prior to Bataan in 1942. General Robert E. Lee, who accompanied Longstreet in the van, rode back to observe the fighting and aptly exclaims, "My God! Has the army been dissolved?" Sayler's Creek thus proves both a black day for the vaunted Army of Northern Virginia and its final encounter with the tenacious Army of the Potomac.

Meanwhile, Confederates under General James Longstreet continue withdrawing toward High Bridge, an important trestle over the Appomattox River. En route, Longstreet perceives that a Union force of three infantry regiments has been detached toward High Bridge by General Edward O. C. Ord to burn it. Longstreet reacts quickly by dispatching two cavalry divisions under Generals Thomas L. Munford and Thomas L. Rosser to stop them. Intense hand-to-hand fighting erupts at the southeast end of the bridge where Union forces are overwhelmed and General

Theodore Read killed. The victorious Southerners capture 800 prisoners while saving the strategic bridge.

Union cavalry under General James H. Wilson spar with General Nathan B. Forrest's troopers at Lanier's Mills, Sipsey Creek, and King's Store, Alabama.

General John T. Croxton's cavalry column skirmishes with pursuing Confederates under General William W. Adams at Eutaw, Alabama, losing 34 men and two ambulances.

WEST: Confederate Partisan Rangers under Colonel John S. Mosby surprise and attack the Unionist Loudoun Country Rangers near Charles Town, West Virginia. This is Mosby's final military action of the war and, typically, a success.

April 7

DIPLOMACY: The U.S. government, having lost millions of dollars in shipping to the English-built CSS *Alabama*, begins litigation to recoup damages.

POLITICS: An anxious president Abraham Lincoln, on hearing that General Robert E. Lee might capitulate if cornered, orders General Ulysses S. Grant to "Let the thing be pressed."

Tennessee ratifies the 13th Amendment while William G. Brownlow, an unabashed Unionist, is inaugurated as governor.

SOUTH: After the Confederate division of General John B. Gordon crosses High Bridge, Virginia, General Andrew A. Humphrey's II Corps shows up in pursuit. The Southerners set fire to the bridge behind them, but Federal troops rush forward to extinguish its flames. Humphrey then hurriedly crosses over to the north bank of the Appomattox River, tangling with a Confederate rear guard under General William Mahone. The Northerners succeed in pushing the Southerners back, and by noon, the entire II Corps forces its way across.

This development proves particularly distressing for General Robert E. Lee, who now abandons his plan for marching to Farmville in favor of moving 38 miles farther west to Appomattox Court House. Union cavalry under General Philip H. Sheridan then suddenly appear and force the Confederates to give battle at Cumberland Church. Humphrey's II Corps also arrives and adds to the general confusion. The Southerners manage to beat off numerous attacks, capturing General J. Irvin Gregg in the process, but Lee leads his weary, hungry troops on their final night march. He is also forced to order two trains, laden with rations for his hungry troops, to depart immediately for Lynchburg and safety.

General Ulysses S. Grant, arriving at Farmville at the head of 80,000 men, suggests to General Robert E. Lee that he surrender and avoid the useless effusion of blood. "The result of the last week must convince you of the hopelessness of further resistance on the part of the Army of Northern Virginia in this struggle," he states, "I feel that it is so, and regard it as my duty to shift from myself the responsibility of any further effusion of blood." Lee initially dismisses the notion and determines to fight on.

April 8

POLITICS: President Abraham Lincoln returns to the White House after an eventful stay at Richmond, Virginia.

SOUTH: Rather than surrender, General Robert E. Lee seeks to break through Union forces blocking his path at Appomattox Court House. But that night, hearts sink as the campfires of 80,000 Union soldiers light up the evening sky in the distance. Federal cavalry under Philip H. Sheridan also arrive at Appomattox, west of Lee's camp, again blocking his withdrawal. At a council of war held late that night, Lee and his generals agree to attack Sheridan in the morning, dislodge his forces, and then press on to Lynchburg. Previously, Sheridan's cavalry capture several trainloads of food intended for the starving Army of Northern Virginia at Pamplin's Station.

At Spanish Fort, Alabama, a charge by the 8th Iowa gains a lodgment in the Confederate defenses. That evening, General Randall L. Gibson evacuates his garrison on a hidden walkway and through the nearby marshes. The Southerners sustain 93 killed and 350 wounded in a two-week period. General Edward R. S. Canby also captures 500 prisoners and 50 cannon.

NAVAL: The party of Confederate midshipmen escorting the archives and treasury of state to Charlotte, North Carolina, is threatened by Union cavalry and veers southward. They also convince Confederate first lady Varina Davis to accompany them for safety's sake.

April 9

SOUTH: Palm Sunday. General Robert E. Lee directs Generals John B. Gordon and Fitzhugh Lee to attack General Philip H. Sheridan's cavalry at Appomattox Court House, Virginia. The Federal troopers are dislodged gradually from their position and Lee discerns that General Edward O. C. Ord's Army of the James is waiting in strength directly behind them. Lee finally acknowledges the hopelessness of his position and parlays with Union authorities to discuss surrender terms. "There is nothing left for me to do but to go and see General Grant," he states, "and I would rather die a thousand deaths."

At 1:30 P.M., General Robert E. Lee, accompanied only by his secretary, meets with General Ulysses S. Grant and formally surrenders the Army of Northern Virginia at Appomattox, Virginia. They convene at the house of Wilbur McLean—an act of significant irony. Previously, McLean lived at Bull Run where, in July 1861, his house served as a hospital for victorious Confederate forces. He thereupon relocated to Appomattox to escape the tumult of war. The terms Grant proffers are quite generous, whereby all of Lee's 30,000 men are paroled and allowed to return home, officers are permitted to retain side arms, and all horses and mules are to remain with their rightful owners. Lee then addresses his men, declaring, "Go to your homes and resume your occupations. Obey the laws and become good citizens as you were soldiers." As a final gesture, Union forces issue 25,000 rations to the half-starved Confederates. The bloody, bitter Civil War reaches a dignified and humane denouement.

General Thomas A. Smyth dies of wounds received two days earlier at Farmville, Virginia, becoming the last Union general fatality.

Fort Blakely, Mobile, Alabama, is besieged by 45,000 Federal troops once General Frederick Steele receives 32,000 reinforcements under General Edward R. S. Canby. An assault force of 16,000 men then attacks the Confederate defenses at

This painting depicts the surrender of Robert E. Lee and his army at Appomattox Court House, Virginia, to General Ulysses S. Grant. *(Library of Congress)*

noon, covered by the fire of 37 field pieces and 75 siege guns. The Federals charge headlong into torpedo-laced fields, taking special care to avoid the visible trip wires, and vault directly into the Confederate works. Their success prompts General St. John R. Liddell to surrender after 20 minutes of fighting. Union losses are 113 killed and 516 wounded (629) while 3,423 Confederates are captured along with 40 cannon. Fort Blakely is also the last, significant pitched engagement of the Civil War.

WEST: The cavalry column of General George Stoneman reunites in western Virginia before raiding Winston-Salem, North Carolina. After destroying all public property, the column gallops off to nearby Salisbury, where a sizable number of Union prisoners are confined.

NAVAL: The Confederate blockade-runner *Chameleon* docks at Liverpool, England, unaware the Civil War is drawing rapidly to a conclusion.

CSS *Nashville* under Lieutenant John W. Bennett sails close to shore and tries to rescue as many Confederates from Fort Blakely as possible before being driven off by Union sharpshooters.

April 10

POLITICS: President Abraham Lincoln is accosted by happy crowds in Washington, D.C., and then asks a military band to strike up "Dixie," "one of the best tunes I have ever heard."

President Jefferson Davis, on learning of General Robert E. Lee's capitulation, departs Danville with his cabinet and makes for Greensborough, North Carolina.

NORTH: News of General Robert E. Lee's capitulation triggers wild celebrations in Northern cities.

SOUTH: General Robert E. Lee issues Order No. 9, bidding a formal farewell to the men and officers of the Army of Northern Virginia. "With an increasing admiration of your constancy and devotion to your country," Lee writes, "and a grateful remembrance of your kind and generous consideration of myself, I bid you an affectionate farewell."

General William T. Sherman departs Goldsborough, North Carolina, and advances on Raleigh to engage remaining Confederate forces under General Joseph E. Johnston. Word of Lee's capitulation reaches Johnston, meanwhile, and he begins to angle for a formal surrender.

As Union siege artillery continue playing on Forts Huger and Tracy in Mobile, Alabama, General Dabney H. Maury makes preparations to abandon the city and retreat.

April 11

POLITICS: President Abraham Lincoln delivers his final public address to enthusiastic crowds gathered about the White House. He again preaches magnanimity and peaceful reconciliation with the inhabitants of former secessionist states.

SOUTH: General William T. Sherman's army advances on Raleigh, North Carolina.

The Confederate government train pulls into Greensborough, North Carolina, carrying President Jefferson Davis and his cabinet.

Union cavalry under General James H. Wilson cross the Alabama River and ride off to attack Montgomery.

General Dabney H. Maury formally abandons Forts Hugar and Tracy at Mobile, Alabama, escaping with 4,500 men and 27 cannon.

NAVAL: The USS *Sea Bird* captures the Confederate sloops *Florida* and *Annie* near the Crystal River, Florida, sinking both.

April 12

SOUTH: The Army of Northern Virginia formally capitulates at Appomattox Court House to General Joshua L. Chamberlain. Confederates under General John B. Gordon then lead a weathered column of Southern troops along the Richmond Stage Road, completely lined by Union forces. As the solemn procession passes, Chamberlain orders his men to present arms in salute, which is promptly returned by the Southerners. Roughly 28,000 Confederates sullenly file down the road, stack arms, roll up their flags, and prepare to return home.

President Jefferson Davis, readying to flee from Greensborough, North Carolina, confers with General Joseph E. Johnston about the potential surrender of Confederate forces. He then authorizes Johnson to meet with General William T. Sherman and ask for terms.

General William T. Sherman's army skirmishes with Confederate forces outside Raleigh, capital of North Carolina.

Mayor R. H. Slough of Mobile, Alabama, formally surrenders to General Gordon Granger.

WEST: A Union cavalry column under General George Stoneman encounters a motley defense force of 800 men under General William M. Gardner at Salisbury,

North Carolina. Fighting in the ranks is former lieutenant general and defender of Vicksburg John C. Pemberton, now functioning as an ordnance inspector. When Stoneman finds his approach to Salisbury blocked by an unplanked bridge and strong Confederate fieldworks across Grants Creek, he dispatches the 12th Kentucky Cavalry to demonstrate in front while the 11th Kentucky and 13th Tennessee Cavalry ford farther upstream to catch the enemy from behind. This action causes the enemy flanks to crumble, at which point Stoneman directs the 6th Tennessee Cavalry to capture Gardner's artillery in a stirring charge. The bridge over Grant's Creek is also repaired under fire, over which General John K. Miller's cavalry surge, routing the Confederates. Stoneman, however, proves unable to rescue any Union captives held in town as they had previously been moved to Charlotte. After his men then burn all public property, Stoneman spurs his command back toward Tennessee.

Montgomery, Alabama, is captured by cavalry under General James H. Wilson, burning all public stores.

Union forces under General Edward R. S. Canby finally occupy Mobile, Alabama, after sustaining losses of 232 dead, 1,303 injured, and 43 missing (1,578).

NAVAL: Fleeing Confederate forces scuttle the CSS *Huntsville* and *Tuscaloosa* at Mobile, Alabama, to prevent capture while the *Nashville, Baltic,* and *Morgan* steam up the Tombigbee River to escape.

April 13

POLITICS: Secretary of War Edwin M. Stanton orders the military draft suspended and also reduces supply requisitions.

SOUTH: Union forces under General William T. Sherman enter Raleigh, North Carolina, and continue to Greensborough.

NAVAL: The tug USS *Ida* strikes a Confederate torpedo near Choctaw Pass, Mobile Bay, Alabama, and sinks. This is the fifth U.S. Navy vessel lost in five weeks.

April 14

POLITICS: In his final cabinet meeting, President Abraham Lincoln reiterates his call for reconciliation with the South.

NORTH: At 10:15 P.M., President Abraham Lincoln, while attending a performance of *Our American Cousin* at Ford's Theater in Washington, D.C., is suddenly shot from behind by actor John Wilkes Booth. Secretary of State William H. Seward, recovering at home from injuries received in a carriage crash, also survives an assassination attempt by Lewis Powell. Secretary of War Edwin M. Stanton declares martial law in the District of Columbia and initiates a massive dragnet to snare the assassins.

SOUTH: General William T. Sherman agrees to enter into surrender negotiations with General Joseph E. Johnston at Durham Station, North Carolina.

General Robert Anderson hoists the American flag over the remnants of Fort Sumter, Charleston Harbor, South Carolina. It is the identical standard lowered by him on April 14, 1861.

NAVAL: The gunboat USS *Sciota* strikes a Confederate torpedo and sinks in Mobile Bay, Alabama. A nearby launch from the USS *Cincinnati* also blows up after brushing against a torpedo, losing three killed.

The Confederate raider CSS *Shenandoah* under Lieutenant James I. Waddell hoists anchor for the East Carolines and sails north toward the Kuriles.

April 15
POLITICS: President Abraham Lincoln dies at 7:22 A.M., leaving Secretary of War Edwin M. Stanton to declare, "Now he belongs to the ages." Vice President Andrew Johnson is then sworn in as the nation's 17th chief executive by Chief Justice Salmon P. Chase; Johnson's first request is to ask members of Lincoln's cabinet to remain in their offices.

President Jefferson Davis departs Greensborough, North Carolina, on horseback and rides all night toward Lexington.
NORTH: George A. Custer is promoted to major general, U.S. Army.

April 16
SOUTH: General James H. Wilson's army occupies Columbus, Georgia, after brushing aside a hodgepodge collection of Confederates and militia and taking 1,200 captives and 52 cannon. The victorious troopers then commence to burn several factories, 100,000 cotton bales, 15 locomotives, and 200 railcars. Meanwhile, another column under General Edward M. McCook seizes West Point, destroying an additional 19 locomotives and 200 railcars.
NAVAL: Confederate forces capture and burn the USS *St. Paul* in the Hatchee River, Tennessee.

April 17
POLITICS: John Wilkes Booth, who injured his leg after assassinating President Abraham Lincoln, hides himself near Port Tobacco, Maryland. He then waits for transportation over the Potomac River to continue his escape.

The body of President Abraham Lincoln lies in state in the East Room of the White House, Washington, D.C.

President Jefferson Davis and his entourage arrive at Salisbury, North Carolina.
SOUTH: General William T. Sherman and Joseph E. Johnston confer at the Bennet House, Durham Station, North Carolina, to draw up surrender terms.
NAVAL: The ironclad CSS *Jackson* (nee *Muscogee*) is destroyed on the Chattahoochee River near Columbus, Georgia, by Union cavalry surging through the town.

The naval escort guarding Confederate archives and treasury arrives safely at Washington, Georgia. First Lady Varina Davis is left behind as the party continues to Augusta.

The USS *Maria A. Wood* clears Confederate obstructions on the Blakely River channel, Mobile Bay, Alabama. The vessel then enters the city of Mobile.

April 18
SOUTH: General Joseph E. Johnston agrees to surrender his 37,000 men to General William T. Sherman at Durham Station, North Carolina. However, terms of their "Memorandum or Basis of Agreement" are viewed as overly generous, and they are disavowed by the government. Sherman is accused of overstepping his authority and is ordered to renegotiate the pact, offering the same terms used at Appomattox.

April 19

POLITICS: Funeral services are held for President Abraham Lincoln in Washington, D.C., and huge crowds throng the proceedings.

President Jefferson Davis and his remaining cabinet flee to Charlotte, North Carolina.

SOUTH: General Henry W. Halleck assumes command of the newly instituted Military of the James, Virginia.

WEST: General Simon B. Buckner receives command of the newly created District of Arkansas and West Louisiana.

General John Pope recommends the surrender of all Confederate forces west of the Mississippi River to General Edmund Kirby-Smith, on the same terms offered to General Robert E. Lee.

NAVAL: The Federal gunboat USS *Lexington* steams up the Red River, Louisiana, bearing terms of surrender for General Edmund Kirby-Smith.

April 20

POLITICS: Arkansas ratifies the 13th Amendment.

SOUTH: General Robert E. Lee writes to President Jefferson Davis, voicing opposition to the latter's plan to wage extended guerrilla warfare throughout the South.

Federal troops under General James H. Wilson occupy Macon, Georgia, without resistance, although skirmishes are still reported in the countryside. Here, Wilson learns of the war's end. His raid is one of the most successful of the war, covering 525 miles in only 28 days, capturing 6,820 prisoners, 23 flags, 288 cannon, and cutting a swath of destruction across Alabama and Georgia. Despite this litany of achievements, Wilson's losses are light and amount to 99 killed, 598 wounded, and 28 missing.

April 21

POLITICS: A train bearing the casket that holds the body of President Abraham Lincoln departs Washington, D.C., for Springfield, Illinois, as immense crowds of mourners gather along the tracks en route.

SOUTH: Colonel John S. Mosby, "the vaunted Gray Ghost," refuses to surrender his 43rd Virginia Cavalry battalion and instead simply disbands them at Millwood, Virginia.

NAVAL: The Union steamer *Sultana* departs New Orleans with 100 passengers and sails up the Mississippi River to Vicksburg, Mississippi. Boiler problems are brought to the attention of Captain J. Cass Mason en route, and he resolves to remedy them at Vicksburg.

The USS *Cornubia* captures an unnamed British schooner off Galveston, Texas.

April 22

POLITICS: John Wilkes Booth and his accomplice David E. Herold escape in a small rowboat from Maryland to Virginia.

SOUTH: Union cavalry under General John T. Croxton occupy Talladega, Alabama, dispersing 500 militia and burning several factories and ironworks.

General Benjamin F. Butler briefly resumes his command of the Department of the Gulf, Louisiana.

NAVAL: The side-wheel steamer USS *Black Hawk* catches fire and explodes on the Ohio River near Mound City, Illinois.

April 23

SOUTH: A Union expedition under General Horatio G. Wright, VI Corps, and General Wesley Merritt's cavalry, takes 500 Southern prisoners at Danville and South Boston, Virginia. General James Dearing dies of wounds at Lynchburg, Virginia, the last ranking Southerner to perish.

NAVAL: Lieutenant Charles W. Read enacts his daring plan to dash down the Mississippi River in CSS *Webb* and make for the open sea past New Orleans. The ironclads USS *Manhattan* and *Fort Hindman* briefly engage Read as he emerges from the Red River, but his vessel proves faster than its plodding pursuers and escapes downstream.

April 24

POLITICS: President Andrew Johnson formally rejects the surrender agreement reached between General William T. Sherman and General Joseph E. Johnston. Sherman is informed by General Ulysses S. Grant himself, who arrives at Raleigh, North Carolina, to do so.

Political assassins John Wilkes Booth and Davis Herold make their way to Port Conway, Virginia.

NAVAL: Admiral Samuel P. Lee urges special vigilance along the Mississippi River "to prevent the carrying across of plunder and property in the hands of Jefferson Davis and his Cabinet, and also to seize their persons."

The Union steamer *Sultana* departs Vicksburg, Mississippi, loaded with 2,100 newly released Union prisoners and 200 civilians—six times its legal carrying capacity. The reason for the overload is that the Federal government is paying steamers to transport prisoners north at a rate of five dollars per soldier and 10 dollars per officer. However, Captain J. Cass Mason decides against having his faulty boilers overhauled and, instead, simply patches them up until he reaches St. Louis, Missouri.

The CSS *Webb* under Lieutenant Charles W. Read passes through New Orleans, Louisiana, at flank speed, easily thwarting slower pursuers. As he passes the city, Federal gunboats score several direct hits, but his vessel proceeds unimpeded toward the sea. However, having reached 25 miles below the city, the USS *Richmond* intercepts the Confederates by moving upstream. Read, trapped between two fires, finally beaches the *Webb* and surrenders.

April 25

POLITICS: Union troops chase political assassins John Wilkes Booth and David E. Herold to Bowling Green, Virginia, just south of the Rappahannock River. The two fugitives then take refuge in the barn of farmer Richard H. Garrett.

April 26

POLITICS: John Wilkes Booth is cornered in a barn near Bowling Green, Virginia, while attempting to escape from Virginia and dies from gunshot wounds. David E. Herold is captured.

President Jefferson Davis departs Charlotte, North Carolina, and ventures to the Trans-Mississippi region, vowing there to carry on a guerrilla struggle for Southern rights and independence.

SOUTH: General Joseph E. Johnston and General William T. Sherman meet again at Durham Station, North Carolina, and renegotiate a surrender agreement with terms similar to those at Appomattox.

April 27

NAVAL: The body of John Wilkes Booth arrives aboard the monitor USS *Montauk* in the Anacostia River outside Washington, D.C., where an autopsy is performed. David E. Herold is also kept in chains in the ship's hold.

Commodore William Radford of the James River Flotilla and the USS *Tristram Shandy* are alerted to watch for the approaching ironclad CSS *Stonewall*.

At 2:00 A.M., boilers on the Union steamer *Sultana* explode with a deafening roar, hurling crew and passengers alike into the frigid waters of the Mississippi River. By the time help finally arrives from Memphis, Tennessee, two hours later, more than 1,700 people perish through burns and hypothermia; only 600 survivors are fished from the waters. *Sultana* remains the single biggest disaster in U.S. maritime history and eclipses the more famous *Titanic*, 47 years later.

April 28

POLITICS: The train bearing President Abraham Lincoln's casket passes through Cleveland, Ohio, where it is viewed by 50,000 citizens.

President Jefferson Davis accepts the resignation of Confederate treasury secretary George A. Trenholm from his cabinet.

April 29

POLITICS: President Andrew Johnson issues an Executive Order lifting commercial restrictions against all Southern states except Texas.

President Jefferson Davis and his entourage reach Yorksville, South Carolina.

NAVAL: The USS *Donegal* is ordered from Bull's Bay, South Carolina, to the Savannah River, Georgia, to search for the CSS *Stonewall*.

An armed party from the USS *Moose* attacks and scatters a Confederate raiding party of the Cumberland River, Tennessee, inflicting 20 casualties, and taking six captives.

April 30

SOUTH: General Edward R. S. Canby holds preliminary talks with General Richard Taylor at Mobile, Alabama, as to the latter's forthcoming surrender. Afterward, Taylor ventures back to his headquarters at Meridian, Mississippi, and makes preparations.

May 1

POLITICS: President Andrew Johnson calls for a board of nine army officers to try eight individuals implicated in President Abraham Lincoln's death. The accused are now subject to military justice rather than civil proceedings.

President Jefferson Davis reaches Cokesbury, South Carolina, en route to the Florida coast. There, he and his party hope to catch a ship and sail to Texas.

SOUTH: The cavalry column of General John T. Croxton arrives at Macon, Georgia, covering 650 miles in 30 days and eluding superior numbers of Confederate pursuers.

WEST: Recently disgraced general Gouverneur K. Warren replaces General Napoleon J. T. Dana as head of the Department of Mississippi.

May 2

POLITICS: President Andrew Johnson accuses a fugitive Jefferson Davis of complicity in the assassination of President Abraham Lincoln and offers $100,000 for his capture.

President Jefferson Davis arrives at Abbeville, South Carolina, and heads for Washington, Georgia, escorted by four brigades of cavalry under General Basil W. Duke. Members of his cabinet begin to object to his intention to renew the struggle through guerrilla warfare.

Confederate secretary of the navy Stephen R. Mallory tenders his resignation to President Jefferson Davis at Washington, Georgia.

NAVAL: Commander Matthew F. Maury departs Britain with $40,000 worth of electrical equipment to manufacture torpedoes at Galveston, Texas. During his sojourn abroad, the talented Maury perfects a controlled mine system whereby torpedoes, planted on a grid pattern and corresponding to a chart, can be selectively detonated when enemy vessels reach their proximity.

May 3

POLITICS: The funeral train bearing the body of President Abraham Lincoln pulls into Springfield, Illinois.

Confederate secretary of state Judah B. Benjamin resigns from office and eventually flees to Britain.

NORTH: The funeral train of President Abraham Lincoln pulls into Springfield, Illinois.

SOUTH: The Army of Tennessee under General Joseph E. Johnston formally lays down its arms near Durham Station, North Carolina. This concludes the Civil War in the East.

Confederate president Jefferson Davis and his cabinet arrive at Washington, Georgia.

May 4

POLITICS: The remains of President Abraham Lincoln are interred at Springfield, Illinois.

SOUTH: General Richard Taylor surrenders all Confederate forces east of the Mississippi River to General Edward R. S. Canby at Citronelle, Alabama. He receives the identical terms proffered to General Robert E. Lee and is further allowed to utilize trains and steamers to send his men home.

NAVAL: Commodore Ebenezer Farrand surrenders Confederate naval forces on the Tombigbee River to Admiral Henry K. Thatcher, including CSS *Morgan, Balti, Black Diamond*, and *Nashville*.

The CSS *Ajax* drops anchor at St. George's, Bermuda, hoping to pick up its armament from Havana, Cuba. However, British governor W. G. Hamley obstructs any such moves.

May 5

POLITICS: President Jefferson Davis and his dwindling party of followers arrive at Sandersville, Georgia.

Connecticut ratifies the 13th Amendment abolishing slavery.

May 6

POLITICS: President Andrew Johnson appoints General David Hunter to head the military commission tasked with trying those accused of assassinating President Abraham Lincoln. The accused are prosecuted by Joseph Holt, judge advocate general of the U.S. Army.

NORTH: James H. Wilson is promoted to major general, U.S. Army.

WEST: General Thomas L. Rosser surrenders his Confederate cavalry at Lexington, Virginia.

May 8

WEST: General Edward R. S. Canby formally accepts the paroles of General Richard Taylor's forces in Mississippi, Alabama, and East Louisiana.

NAVAL: The USS *Insonomia* captures the British blockade-runner *George Douthwaite* near the Warrior River, Florida.

May 9

POLITICS: President Andrew Johnson declares the naval blockade to remain in place for two more weeks to impede any escape by fugitive Confederate leaders.

Francis H. Pierpont receives official recognition as governor of Virginia; previously he headed Unionist Virginians in Federal-held territory.

The trial of eight suspected conspirators begins in Washington, D.C.

President Jefferson Davis is reunited with his wife Varina at Dublin, Georgia.

WEST: General Nathan B. Forrest disbands his men rather than surrender.

May 10

POLITICS: President Andrew Johnson declares armed resistance "virtually at an end," although skirmishing persists in rural parts of the South.

President Jefferson Davis and his wife are captured near Abbeville, Georgia, by men of the 1st Wisconsin and 4th Michigan Cavalry under Lieutenant Colonel Benjamin Pritchard—part of General James H. Wilson's command. His detention signals the end of the Confederate government.

General Samuel Jones surrenders Confederate forces at Tallahassee, Florida.

WEST: Dreaded Confederate guerrilla William C. Quantrill is mortally wounded and captured near Taylorsville, Kentucky.

May 11

WEST: General Jeff Thompson surrenders at Chalk Bluff, Arkansas.

SOUTHWEST: Colonel Theodore H. Barrett, 62nd U.S. Colored Infantry, disregards the unofficial truce along the Rio Grande region of Texas by mustering 250 men of his regiment and 50 troopers of the 2nd Texas Cavalry to attack a Confederate outpost at White's Ranch on the road to Brownstown. The column is commanded by Colonel David Branson, who leads them over the rain-swollen Boca Chica River toward their objective. Finding this position abandoned, Branson rests his men in a thicket for the night.

NAVAL: Captain Thomas J. Paige and the CSS *Stonewall* docks at Havana, Cuba.

May 12

POLITICS: President Andrew Johnson appoints General Oliver O. Howard to head the Freedmen's Bureau.

SOUTH: General Adelbert Ames becomes commander of the X Corps, Florida.

SOUTHWEST: Colonel David Branson's Union column defeats a force of 300 Confederate cavalry at Palmito Ranch, Texas, on the road to Brownsville. After regrouping, the Southerners counterattack and drive the Federal forces back to White's Ranch. Overnight, both sides continue receiving reinforcements.

May 13

WEST: General Edmund Kirby-Smith confers with the Confederate governors of Arkansas, Louisiana, and Missouri in Marshall, Texas. Smith intends to surrender his forces, but General Joseph O. Shelby threatens to arrest him if he tries.

SOUTHWEST: Colonel Theodore H. Barrett arrives to take command of Union troops under Colonel David Branson and leads them back into combat at Palmito Ranch, Texas. They engage a force of Confederate cavalry under Colonel John S. Ford, who deftly outflanks the overconfident Federals. Barrett promptly falls back, hotly pursued by the Southerners, who chase him for 17 miles. The fighting then stops once Barrett reaches his original starting point at White's Ranch. Union losses are estimated at around 130 killed, wounded, or captured; the Confederates suffer far less. While small, Palmito Ranch is also the last pitched encounter of the Civil War. Once Ford interrogates his prisoners and learns that the war is over, he begins to disband Confederate forces along the Rio Grande.

May 16

POLITICS: President Jefferson Davis, his family, and several ranking Confederate officials are placed on steamers and sent down the Savannah River, Georgia, to Port Royal, South Carolina.

May 17

SOUTH: General Philip H. Sheridan becomes commander of all Federal troops west of the Mississippi and south of the Arkansas rivers, where scattered Confederate resistance continues.

General Edward R. S. Canby relieves General Benjamin F. Butler as head of the newly enlarged Department of the Gulf, whose jurisdiction now encompasses Louisiana, Mississippi, Alabama, and Florida.

May 19

NAVAL: Captain Thomas J. Page hands over the CSS *Stonewall* to the captain general of Cuba for $16,000, with which he pays off his crew. The vessel ultimately is sold to Japan.

The USS *Grosbeak* receives the surrender of the 2nd Arkansas at Laconia, Arkansas.

May 20

WEST: Federal soldiers repel an attack by hostile Sioux on Deer Creek, Dakota Territory, killing and wounding around 50.

NAVAL: Secretary of the Navy Gideon Welles appoints a naval board headed by Admiral David G. Farragut to investigate the present affairs of the displaced U.S. Naval Institute and to make recommendations for the future.

Federal authorities arrest former Confederate secretary of the navy Stephen R. Mallory at LaGrange, Georgia.

May 21

NAVAL: The far-ranging CSS *Shenandoah* under Lieutenant James I. Waddell enters the Sea of Okhotsk in search of Union whaling vessels.

May 22

POLITICS: President Andrew Johnson opens all Southern seaports as of July 1 with the exception of four facilities in Texas: Galveston, La Salle, Brazos Santiago, and Brownsville.

President Jefferson Davis arrives in chains at Fortress Monroe, Virginia, and will remain confined there until May 13, 1867.

NAVAL: *Picket Boat No. 5* seizes the Confederate steamers *Skirwan*, *Cotton Plant*, *Fisher*, and *Egypt Mills* in the Roanoke River, North Carolina.

Commander Matthew F. Maury arrives at Havana, Cuba, with thousands of dollars of electrical equipment for building and detonating torpedoes. However, on hearing of the Confederacy's demise, he abandons his attempt to reach Galveston, Texas.

May 23

POLITICS: The Piedmont government, a collection of Unionist politicians from Virginia, occupies the state capital at Richmond.

NORTH: The Grand Armies of the Republic parade in a mass review at Washington, D.C., and flags are permitted to fly at full mast for the first time in four years. Curiously, not one of the 166 African-American regiments raised during the war is present at the festivities.

NAVAL: The USS *Azalea* captures the British blockade-runner *Sarah M. Newhall* off Savannah, Georgia.

May 24

NORTH: The army of General William T. Sherman, sporting a much looser appearance than the spit-and-polish Army of the Potomac, victoriously tramps through Washington, D.C. Sherman also refuses to shake hands with Secretary of War Edwin M. Stanton over their recent imbroglio concerning the surrender of General Joseph E. Johnston.

NAVAL: The USS *Cornubia* and *Princess Royal* sink the Confederate blockade-runner *Denbigh* and the schooner *Le Compt* off Galveston, Texas.

May 25

SOUTH: An accidental explosion of 20 tons of Confederate gunpowder occurs in Mobile, Alabama, wrecking facilities and inflicting 300 casualties. Quartermaster John Cooper, having dashed into the fires and rescued a wounded man on his back, receives his second Congressional Medal of Honor.

NAVAL: The USS *Vanderbilt* tows the captured Confederate ram CSS *Columbia* to Hampton Roads, Virginia.

Admiral Henry K. Thatcher notes that Confederate defenses at Sabine Pass, Texas, have been disbanded and the Stars and Stripes is hoisted over them by men of the USS *Owasco*.

Commander Matthew F. Maury, fearing that his prior work on torpedoes makes him ineligible for a parole, sails from Havana, Cuba, to Mexico.

May 26

SOUTH: General Simon B. Buckner, representing general Edmund Kirby-Smith, surrenders to General Edward R. S. Canby's deputy general Peter J. Osterhaus at New Orleans, Louisiana. This act formally dissolves all remaining Confederate forces west of the Mississippi River. General Joseph O. Shelby, however, defiantly leads 1,000 followers south into Mexico to found a military colony.

May 27

POLITICS: President Andrew Johnson empties the prisons of almost all Southerners held under military jurisdiction.

NORTH: Benjamin H. Grierson is appointed major general, U.S. Army.

NAVAL: Acting on instructions from Admiral John A. B. Dahlgren, the USS *Pontiac* deposits several Confederate torpedoes for examination at the U.S. Naval Academy.

The CSS *Spray* surrenders to Union forces in the St. Mark's River, Florida.

The Confederate raider CSS *Shenandoah* under Lieutenant James I. Waddell captures and burns the Union whaler *Abigail* in the Sea of Okhotsk.

May 29

DIPLOMACY: In a detailed letter, American minister to Britain Charles F. Adams outlines to Foreign Minister Lord John Russell that British-built Confederate warships are responsible for the destruction of 110,000 tons of American shipping—and compensation is in order. This damage is so extensive that the United States forfeits its prior position as the world's largest maritime carrier.

POLITICS: President Andrew Johnson proclaims an amnesty and pardon to any former Confederates submitting to a loyalty oath. He also extends recognition to four new state governments established by his predecessor along with plans for readmitting Southern states into the Union. Johnson's continuation of moderate reconstruction or, as he deems it, "restoration," spells certain trouble at the hands of Radical Republicans.

William H. Holden gains appointment as provisional governor of North Carolina.

June 1

NAVAL: Army troops conveyed by USS *Itasca* occupy Apalachicola, Florida.

The USS *Ouachita* and seven gunboats convoy 4,000 troops under General Francis J. Herron, up the Red River, Louisiana, to secure Confederate forts and posts. In this manner, the large ironclad CSS *Missouri* is secured at Alexandria.

June 2

DIPLOMACY: The government of Great Britain officially rescinds belligerent status for the Confederacy.

POLITICS: President Andrew Johnson pardons Lambdin P. Milligan, a notorious "Copperhead" agitator sentenced to hang.

SOUTHWEST: General Edmund Kirby-Smith formally surrenders Confederate forces at Galveston, Texas, to General Edmund J. Davis. The articles of capitulation are signed aboard the USS *Fort Jackson*.

NAVAL: Secretary of the Navy Gideon Welles begins a downsizing and economizing policy by ordering the Mississippi Squadron of Admiral Samuel P. Lee reduced to 15 ships.

June 3

NAVAL: The CSS *Missouri* surrenders to U.S. naval forces on the Red River, Louisiana.

Admiral Louis M. Goldsborough receives command of the reconstituted European Squadron.

June 5

NAVAL: Captain Benjamin F. Sands directs landing parties from the USS *Cornubia* and *Preston* to occupy Galveston, Texas, and raise the Stars and Stripes.

June 6

POLITICS: President Andrew Johnson orders all remaining Confederate prisoners of war released.

Voters in Missouri ratify a new constitution abolishing slavery.

WEST: Confederate guerrilla William C. Quantrill dies of wounds at Louisville, Kentucky.

NAVAL: Commander Matthew F. Maury, C.S.N., arrives at Veracruz, Mexico, and proceeds to Mexico City to present his credentials to Emperor Maximilian. The receipt of several letters from family members strongly advising him not to return home convinces him that this is the right course to pursue.

June 7

NAVAL: The USS *Ouachita* seizes the CSS *Cotton* and removes it to the mouth of the Red River.

June 8
NORTH: A tardy Union VI Corps parades through Washington, D.C.

June 9
NAVAL: Per order of Secretary of the Navy Gideon Welles, the East and West Gulf squadrons are united under the leadership of Admiral Henry K. Thatcher. The North and South Atlantic squadrons likewise are consolidated under Admiral John A. B. Dahlgren.

The CSS *Ajax* under Lieutenant John Low arrives back at Liverpool, England, where it is interned by authorities. Low himself decides to remain abroad rather than return home.

June 13
POLITICS: President Andrew Johnson appoints William L. Sharkey provisional governor of Mississippi, continuing his policy of restoring civilian authority as quickly as possible.

June 17
POLITICS: President Andrew Johnson appoints James Johnson and Andrew J. Hamilton provisional governors of Georgia and Texas, respectively.

June 21
POLITICS: President Andrew Johnson appoints Lewis E. Parsons provisional governor of Alabama.

June 22
NAVAL: The Confederate raider CSS *Shenandoah* under Lieutenant James I. Waddell fires the last naval shots of the war by capturing the Union whalers *William Thompson, Euphrates, Milo, Sophia Thornton,* and *Jerah Swift* in the Bering Sea. Waddell hears rumors that the war has ended from his captives but disbelieves them for lack of evidence.

June 23
POLITICS: President Andrew Johnson declares the Union naval blockade of all Southern states officially over.

SOUTHWEST: General Stand Watie surrenders his Confederate Cherokee at Doaksville, Indian Territory. He is the last Confederate general to capitulate.

NAVAL: Admiral Samuel F. Du Pont dies unexpectedly at Philadelphia, Pennsylvania, aged 61 years.

The Confederate raider CSS *Shenandoah* under Lieutenant James I. Waddell captures and burns the Union whaler *General Williams* in the Bering Sea.

June 24
POLITICS: President Andrew Johnson lifts all commercial restrictions from states and territories west of the Mississippi River.

June 26
NAVAL: The Confederate raider CSS *Shenandoah* under Lieutenant James I. Waddell seizes and burns the Union whalers *Nimrod, William C. Nye, Catherine, General Pike, Isabella,* and *Gipsey* in the Bering Sea.

June 27
NAVAL: Commander Matthew F. Maury, C.S.N., finally has his audience with Emperor Maximilian in Mexico City, Mexico.

June 28
NAVAL: The Confederate raider CSS *Shenandoah* seizes Union whalers *Brunswick, Favorite, James Murray, Nile, Hillman, Nassau, Isaac Howland, Waverly, Martha, Favorite, Covington,* and *Congress,* bonding a handful and burning the rest. In a voyage traversing 58,000 miles, this is Waddell's most enterprising day.

June 30
POLITICS: A military commission finds all eight conspirators implicated in the assassination of President Abraham Lincoln guilty. David E. Herold, Lewis Payne, George A. Atzerodt, and Mary E. Surratt are sentenced to hang while Dr. Samuel Mudd, Samuel Arnold, and Michael O'Laughlin receive life imprisonment; Edward Spangler receives six-years' imprisonment.

July 1
POLITICS: President Andrew Johnson declares all Southern ports open to foreign commerce and shipping.
  New Hampshire ratifies the 13th Amendment.
NAVAL: The Confederate raider CSS *Shenandoah* under Lieutenant James I. Waddell, threatened by ice floes in the Bering Sea, sails south looking for additional victims.

July 3
WEST: General Patrick E. Conner arrives at Fort Laramie, Wyoming, to orchestrate military activity against ongoing Arapaho raids.

July 7
POLITICS: Four individuals implicated in the assassination of President Abraham Lincoln go to the gallows in Washington, D.C. Four others are relocated to serve their sentences in the Dry Tortugas islands, Florida.

July 13
POLITICS: President Andrew Johnson appoints William Marvin provisional governor of Florida.

July 14
NAVAL: The Confederate blockade-runner *Owl* under Commander John N. Maffitt steams into the Mersey River and drops anchor at Liverpool. He then disbands his crew and turns the vessel over to an English shipping firm.

July 15
NAVAL: The Confederate raider CSS *Shenandoah* under Lieutenant James I. Waddell finally clears the Bering Sea and steers south intending to attack San Francisco, California.

July 16
NAVAL: With the encouragement of Emperor Maximilian, Commander Matthew F. Maury draws up a detailed plan for Confederate immigration to Mexico.

July 18
NAVAL: The USS *Colorado* arrives at Vlissingen, Netherlands, where Admiral Louis M. Goldsborough takes command of the newly reconstituted European Squadron.

July 19
POLITICS: Governor J. Madison Wells implores the inhabitants of Louisiana to take the oath of allegiance or lose their right to vote.

July 20
NAVAL: The army transport *Quinnebaug* strikes a reef outside Beaufort, North Carolina, and sinks with the loss of 25 lives. The survivors are rescued eventually by boats from the USS *Anemone* and *Corwin*.

July 31
NAVAL: The Potomac Flotilla is disbanded.
    The East Indian squadron is established under Commodore Henry H. Bell, commanding the USS *Wachusett, Hartford,* and *Wyoming*. His mission is to patrol waters from the Strait of Sunda to the Sea of Japan.

August 2
NAVAL: Lieutenant James I. Waddell of the CSS *Shenandoah* learns from the British vessel *Barracouta* that the Civil War has in fact ended. Fearing that he and his crew will be charged with piracy and ignoring protests from his crew, he orders the vessel to make for Britain via Cape Horn.

August 12
NAVAL: The Brazil Squadron arrives at Bahía, Brazil, with the USS *Susquehanna, Monadnock, Chippewa, Monticello, Canonicus, Shawmut, Fahkee,* and *Wasp* to protect American interests in the South Atlantic.

August 14
NAVAL: The once-imposing Mississippi Squadron of 80 warships is disbanded by Admiral Samuel P. Lee; henceforth, U.S. Navy presence on the western waterways is reduced to five vessels.

August 21
POLITICS: The Mississippi state legislature negates its secessionist ordinance and also abolishes slavery.

August 23
NAVAL: The USS *Commodore McDonough* sinks while under tow from Port Royal, South Carolina, to New York.

August 24
SOUTH: Clara Barton and Captain James M. Moore conclude their activities to identify and register Union dead at Andersonville Prison, Georgia.

August 28
NAVAL: Admiral David D. Porter is appointed the sixth superintendent of the U.S. Naval Academy and orchestrates its transfer from Newport, Rhode Island, back to Annapolis, Maryland. Porter serves four years, rising there to vice admiral.

September 1

SOUTH: Former general Robert E. Lee becomes president of Washington College, Virginia.

September 3

WEST: A detachment of Federal troops from General Patrick E. Connor's command engages a combined party of Arapaho, Comanche, and Sioux warriors at the Battle of Powder River, Idaho Territory.

September 4

WEST: Roughly 2,000 hostile Indians continue to attack a Federal detachment at Powder River, Montana Territory, killing two soldiers and losing 13 warriors.

September 5

POLITICS: The South Carolina legislature repeals its ordinance of secession, declaring it null and void.

September 11

NAVAL: Emperor Maximilian approves of Commander Matthew F. Maury's plans to encourage Confederate immigration to Mexico.

September 14

WEST: Representatives of nine Native American tribes (Cherokee, Creek, Choctaw, Chickasaw, Osage, Seminole, Seneca, Shawnee, and Quapaw) gather at Fort Smith, Arkansas, and sign a treaty of loyalty to the United States.

September 16

NAVAL: The Confederate raider CSS *Shenandoah* under Lieutenant James I. Waddell rounds Cape Horn and enters the Atlantic Ocean en route to Liverpool, England.

September 18

NAVAL: Emperor Maximilian of Mexico appoints Commander Matthew F. Maury an "Honorary Counselor of the State" and "Director of the National Observatory."

September 23

WEST: Native Americans attack an army encampment in the Harney Lake valley, Oregon Territory; this is the last recorded engagement of the Civil War period.

October 2

SOUTH: Former general Robert E. Lee takes his oath of allegiance to the United States and receives a full pardon.

NAVAL: Commodore John Rodgers leads the USS *Vanderbilt*, *Tuscarora*, *Powhatan*, and *Monadnock* round Cape Horn and into the Pacific Ocean to reinforce the Pacific Squadron.

October 11

POLITICS: Former Confederate vice president Alexander H. Stephens and several high-ranking cabinet officers are paroled by President Andrew Johnson.

October 12

POLITICS: President Andrew Johnson declares an end to martial law in Kentucky.

October 20

NAVAL: The steam tug USS *Nettle* sinks after colliding with an ironclad.

November 3

NAVAL: Secretary of the Navy Gideon Welles instructs all U.S. Navy vessels to render proper honors on entering English ports. This diplomatic nicety is resumed once the British government retracts belligerent status from the now-defunct Confederacy.

November 5

NAVAL: Lieutenant James I. Waddell docks the CSS *Shenandoah* at Liverpool, England, after covering 58,000 miles and seizing 38 prizes without loss of life.

November 6

NAVAL: Lieutenant James I. Waddell surrenders the CSS *Shenandoah* to British authorities. His is the final Confederate flag struck. After a few days in confinement, the crew is released by British authorities. *Shenandoah* subsequently is turned over to U.S. minister Charles F. Adams, who sells the vessel to the Sultan of Zanzibar. Waddell, meanwhile, is reviled by the American government as the "Anglo-American Pirate Captain," which induces him to remain in England until 1875.

The USS *Jacob Bell* sinks while being towed to New York.

The USS *Anna* is wrecked on the Florida coast.

The USS *Itasca* strikes a Confederate mine in Mobile Bay, Alabama, and sinks.

The tug USS *Rose* strikes a Confederate mine in Mobile Bay, Alabama, and sinks.

November 9

POLITICS: The North Carolina legislature overturns its 1861 secession ordinance, outlaws slavery, and elects new members to Congress.

November 10

SOUTH: Captain Henry Wirz is hanged by Union authorities for his role as commandant of notorious Andersonville Prison, Georgia. He is the only former Confederate so punished.

November 13

POLITICS: The South Carolina state legislature ratifies the 13th Amendment.

November 23

NAVAL: The former Confederate ironclad CSS *Stonewall* is escorted by the USS *Rhode Island* and *Hornet* to the Washington Navy Yard, following its purchase from the governor-general of Cuba. The vessel ultimately is sold to Japan.

November 24

POLITICS: The state legislature of Mississippi passes laws concerning vagrancy, labor service, and other "black codes" intending to regulate African Americans and define their roles in the greater society. Henceforth, blacks are not allowed to serve on juries, cannot testify against white persons in a court of law, cannot bear arms, and cannot gather in large numbers. Collectively, this is the first manifestation of what becomes known as "Jim Crow" laws during the 20th century.

December 1
POLITICS: The government revokes wartime suspension of the writ of habeas corpus, except in states of the former Confederacy, the District of Columbia, and the New Mexico and Arizona territories.

December 2
POLITICS: The Alabama state legislature ratifies the 13th Amendment, fulfilling the requisite three-fourths approval by the states.

December 4
POLITICS: The 39th U.S. Congress convenes and institutes the Joint Committee on Reconstruction to oppose President Andrew Johnson. Known as the "Committee of Fifteen," it consists of nine Republicans and six Democrats, and votes repeatedly along party lines. Among its first actions is to dispute the credentials of newly elected senators and representatives from states of the former Confederacy, hence denying them seats in Congress.

The 13th Amendment is ratified by North Carolina but it fails in Mississippi.
NAVAL: Secretary of the Navy Gideon Welles reconstitutes the West India Squadron under Commodore James S. Palmer of the USS *Rhode Island*. His command includes the *De Soto, Swatara, Monongahela, Florida, Augusta, Shamrock, Ashuelot,* and *Monocacy.*

December 5
DIPLOMACY: Secretary of State William H. Seward instructs U.S. minister to France John Bigelow to enunciate to Emperor Napoleon III, in no uncertain terms, American displeasure with the French occupation of Mexico.
POLITICS: The 13th Amendment is ratified by Georgia.

December 6
POLITICS: In his first annual message to Congress, President Andrew Johnson declares, with "gratitude to God in the name of the people for the preservation of the United States," that the Union has been restored.

December 11
POLITICS: The 13th Amendment is ratified by Oregon.

December 14
POLITICS: Representative Thaddeus Stevens of Pennsylvania, an outspoken Radical Republican, assumes the mantle of leadership within the Committee of Fifteen.

December 18
POLITICS: Secretary of State William H. Seward declares the 13th Amendment to the Constitution, approved by 27 states, as adopted. After nearly two and a half

contentious centuries, the incubus of slavery is expunged from the American polity and psyche alike.

December 24

POLITICS: The Ku Klux Klan is founded in Tennessee as a secret society intent on terrorizing African Americans. Former Confederate general Nathan B. Forrest is installed as the first Grand Wizard.

December 27

NAVAL: Secretary of the Navy Gideon Welles makes his annual report to the president, declaring navy strength at nearly 700 warships, a far cry from the 42 vessels in commission at the onset of hostilities. Personnel during this period also mushroomed from 7,600 to 51,000 rank and file. "After the capture of Fort Hatteras and Clark in August 1861," he beams, "port after port was wrested from the insurgents, until the flag of the Union was again restored in every harbor and along our entire coast, and the rebellion wholly suppressed." While less dramatic than events on land, the persistent naval blockade played a major role in the economic and strategic collapse of the Confederacy.

Former Confederate admiral Raphael Semmes is arrested and brought to Washington, D.C., for allegedly violating parole conditions. He remains in custody until April 1866 and is never brought to trial.

Alexander, Edward P. (1835–1910)
Confederate general

Edward Porter Alexander was born in Washington, Georgia, on May 26, 1835, the son of affluent parents. He gained admittance to the U.S. Military Academy, West Point, in 1835 and graduated third in his class by 1839; at the time of his attendance, Robert E. LEE was military superintendent. Alexander also displayed considerable promise as an instructor and taught at West Point until October 1858, when he rose to first lieutenant and accompanied Colonel Albert S. JOHNSTON west as a member of his Mormon expedition. Alexander returned to the academy in 1859 where, in concert with Major Albert J. Myer, he helped perfect the "wigwam" (semaphore) system of signaling with flags or lanterns. This permitted armies in the field to communicate vital information over greater distances. He subsequently transferred back to the frontier as part of the garrison at Fort Steilacom, Washington Territory. Though Southern-born, Alexander did not readily embrace secession, but once the process began in the spring of 1861, he resigned his commission and offered his service to the Confederacy.

On March 16, 1861, Alexander joined the staff of General Pierre G. T. BEAUREGARD as a captain in the signal service. He performed valuable service at the Battle of Bull Run on July 21, 1861, by transmitting information of a Union flanking movement back to headquarters, which enabled Beauregard to parry the blow. During the Peninsula campaign of 1861, Alexander became one of the first Confederate officers employed in balloon

Confederate general Edward P. Alexander *(Massachusetts Commandery Military Order of the Loyal Legion and the U.S. Army Military History Institute)*

reconnaissance at the Battle of Gaines's Mill on June 27, 1862. But as a young officer, he was particularly drawn to the artillery service, and it was here that he made his greatest contributions. General Robert E. Lee, now head of the Army of Northern Virginia, sought out Porter to replace the incompetent general William N. Pendleton as his chief of artillery. Alexander accordingly gained promotion to lieutenant colonel as of July 1862 and became indelibly associated with the "long arm of Lee" thereafter. He displayed great talent in sighting his field pieces at the Battle of Fredericksburg on December 13, 1862, transforming parts of that field into a killing ground. Lee was so pleased by his performance that he arranged Alexander's promotion to colonel in charge of an artillery battalion with General James LONGSTREET's I Corps. In this capacity, he accompanied General Thomas J. JACKSON on his famous flank march at Chancellorsville, Virginia, in May 1863. He proved instrumental in massing 30 cannon at Hazel Grove on May 4, 1863, which drove off the Union army of General Joseph HOOKER.

On July 3, 1863, Alexander performed his most noted deed of the war. At this, the climactic third day of Gettysburg, he massed more than 140 cannons, hub-to-hub, for a sustained bombardment of Union positions. These dueled with 100 Union cannon on the opposite heights, which ceased fire to conserve their ammunition. Confederate gunners kept up a tremendous cannonade, which, owning to the excellent defensive dispositions of General George G. MEADE, mostly passed harmlessly overhead. Following the bloody repulse of General George E. PICKETT, Alexander provided covering fire for the retreating Confederates. In the fall of 1863, he next accompanied General Longstreet west to reinforce the Army of Tennessee under General Braxton BRAGG. Alexander missed the bloody fight at Chickamauga on September 20, 1863, but he did render useful service during the ill-fated siege of Knoxville that December. Bragg's successor, General Joseph E. JOHNSTON, was so impressed with Alexander's abilities that he requested his transfer to the Army

of Tennessee—but General Lee flatly refused to release him.

On March 1, 1864, Alexander rose to brigadier general and resumed his activities as Longstreet's chief of ordnance with the I Corps. He and his cannon were conspicuous in the bloody encounters of the Wilderness and Spotsylvania in May 1864, where a new adversary, General Ulysses S. GRANT, kept maneuvering the Confederates back to their capital of Richmond, Virginia. Alexander next distinguished himself in the bloody fighting at Cold Harbor and Petersburg that summer, in which massed Union attacks invariably were repelled with slaughter. Prior to the July 30, 1864, Battle of the Crater, outside Petersburg, Alexander accurately predicted that the Federals might attempt mining beneath Confederate defensive works and urged his superiors to begin countermining operations. Alexander then was wounded by a sniper and sent to the rear to recuperate before the attack transpired. He rejoined the army just as General Lee was about to abandon the Richmond-Petersburg area, and he subsequently urged his superior against surrendering at Appomattox. Alexander finally laid down his arms on April 9, 1865, with the rest of the Army of Northern Virginia.

In the postwar period, Alexander again distinguished himself as a mathematics and engineering professor at the University of South Carolina, Columbia, where he also penned numerous and well-received treatises about railroad management. In 1885, President Grover Cleveland appointed the former artillerist director of the Union Pacific Railroad, and he subsequently used his surveying skills to settle a boundary dispute between Nicaragua and Costa Rica. Alexander use published numerous memoirs and essays on the Civil War and was one of a handful of officers willing to criticize the military leadership of Robert E. Lee. Alexander died in Savannah, Georgia, on April 28, 1910, the Confederacy's leading artillerist.

Further Reading

Boggs, Marion A., ed. *The Alexander Letters, 1787–1900.* Athens: University of Georgia Press, 1980.

Cole, Philip M. *Civil War Artillery at Gettysburg: Organization, Equipment, Ammunition, and Tactics.* Cambridge, Mass.: Da Capo Press, 2002.

Gallagher, Gary W., ed. *Fighting for the Confederacy: The Personal Recollections of General Edward Porter Alexander.* Chapel Hill: University of North Carolina Press, 1989.

Golay, Michael. *To Gettysburg and Beyond: The Parallel Lives of Joshua Lawrence and Edward Porter Alexander.* New York: Crown, 1994.

Hazlet, James C., Edwin Olmstead, and M. Hume Parks. *Field Artillery Weapons of the Civil War.* Urbana: University of Illinois Press, 2004.

Murray, R. L. E. P. *Alexander and the Artillery Action in the Peach Orchard.* Wolcott, N.Y.: Benedum Books, 2000.

Naisawald, Louis V. *Cannon Blasts: Civil War Artillery in the Eastern Armies.* Shippensburg, Pa.: White Mane Books, 2004.

Anderson, Richard H. (1821–1879)
Confederate general

Richard Heron Anderson was born in Statesburg, South Carolina, on October 7, 1821, the grandson of a Revolutionary War officer. In 1838, he was admitted to the U.S. Military Academy and graduated four years later, 40th in his class. As a second lieutenant, Anderson passed through the Cavalry School at Carlisle, Pennsylvania, and served in the 1st U.S. Dragoons at Little Rock, Arkansas Territory. In 1847, he accompanied General Winfield SCOTT's invasion of Mexico at Veracruz, fought with distinction at St. Augustin on August 17, 1847, and received a brevet promotion to first lieutenant. After the war, Anderson transferred back to Pennsylvania and stayed as a cavalry instructor until 1852. That year, he rose to captain and shipped west to serve in a number of outposts in Texas, New Mexico, and Kansas. In 1858, Anderson was selected to accompany Colonel Albert S. JOHNSTON on his noted Mormon expedition, and the following year, he was posted to Fort Kearney, Nebraska Territory. It was while on this duty that the first rumblings of secession were heard. Anderson, who did not support slavery, felt tremendous pressure from his family to join the

Confederate general Richard H. Anderson *(Massachusetts Commandery Military Order of the Loyal Legion and the U.S. Army Military History Institute)*

Confederacy after South Carolina left the Union in December 1860. Therefore, he reluctantly resigned his commission in February 1861 and offered his services as colonel of the 1st South Carolina Regiment.

Anderson initially served under General Pierre G. T. BEAUREGARD during the fateful bombardment of Fort Sumter, Charleston, on April 12–14, 1861, and subsequently succeeded him as city commander. On July 19, 1861, Anderson advanced to brigadier general and was attached to the army of General Braxton BRAGG at Pensacola, Florida. On October 9, 1861, he first saw combat by organizing and leading a successful overnight raid against Union forces on Santa Rosa Island, and in February 1862, he was transferred to Virginia to command a brigade in General James LONGSTREET's division. Anderson fought exceedingly well throughout the Peninsula campaign of that spring, winning laurels from superiors for aggressive fighting at Williamsburg, Seven Pines, and the Seven Days' battles. He then rose to major general on July 14, 1862, under General Benjamin HUGER. Anderson was in the thick of fighting at Second Bull Run on August 30, 1862, and later accompanied General Thomas J. JACKSON in maneuvers culminating in the capture of Harper's Ferry on September 15, 1862. Two days later, he helped decisively reinforce General Robert E. LEE at Antietam, receiving severe injuries in combat. Anderson recovered in time to participate at Fredericksburg, February 13, 1862, but was only lightly engaged, but by dint of his fearlessness under fire and eagerness to engage the enemy, he acquired a popular reputation as "Fighting Dick."

During the Chancellorsville campaign of May 1863, Anderson commanded one of three brigades entrusted with holding back the far larger army of General Joseph HOOKER while Jackson launched his famous flank attack. On May 4, 1863, he proved instrumental in helping defeat the VI Corps of General John Sedgwick at Salem Church, Virginia. After the death of Jackson, Anderson's division transferred to General Ambrose P. HILL's III Corps, and he accompanied him throughout the Gettysburg campaign. Anderson was closely engaged on the second day of combat, and he helped sweep General Daniel SICKLES III Corps from their positions at the Peach Orchard. The following day, his division marched in support of General George E. PICKETT's memorable charge against the Union center and withdrew with the main army back to Virginia. Anderson temporarily succeeded Longstreet as commander of I Corps once the latter was wounded at the Wilderness on May 6, 1864. That evening, he performed his most famous deed by force-marching to the strategic road junction at Spotsylvania Court House, arriving there only minutes ahead of Union forces, and repelling numerous attacks by General Gouverneur K. Warren. His prompt actions allowed the Army of Northern Virginia under General Lee to erect defensive positions around Spotsylvania, which blunted another determined Union drive on Richmond. Consequently, he received promotion to lieutenant general on May 31, 1864. When Longstreet returned to the field that October, Anderson resumed his duties as a divisional commander. He served capably throughout the siege of Richmond and Petersburg, Virginia, and he helped conduct the army out of that area when Lee abandoned the capital on April 2, 1865. Four days later, Anderson suffered his only defeat at Sayler's Creek, whereby his command nearly was annihilated by Union forces under General Philip H. SHERIDAN. He was then relieved of command and sent home.

After the war, Anderson eked out a marginal existence as a laborer with the South Carolina Railroad for many years, rising to agent. He lived in poverty until 1875 when the position of state phosphate inspector was proffered. Anderson, one of the Confederacy's finest divisional-level leaders, died in relative obscurity at Beaufort, South Carolina, on June 26, 1879.

Further Reading

Elliott, Joseph C. *Lieutenant General Richard Heron Anderson: Lee's Noble Soldier.* Dayton, Ohio: Morningside House, 1985.

Gallagher, Gary W., ed. *The Second Day at Gettysburg: Essays on Confederate and Union Military Leadership.* Kent, Ohio: Kent State University Press, 2001.

Grimsley, Mark. *And Keep Moving On: The Virginia Campaign, May–June, 1864.* Lincoln: University of Nebraska Press, 2002.

Marvel, William. *Lee's Last Retreat: The Flight to Appomattox.* Chapel Hill: University of North Carolina Press, 2002.

Pfanz, Harry W. *Gettysburg—Culp's Hill and Cemetery Ridge.* Chapel Hill: University of North Carolina Press, 1993.

Smith, Derek. *Lee's Last Stand: Sailor's Creek, Virginia, 1865.* Shippensburg, Pa.: White Mane Books, 2002.

Anderson, Robert (1805–1871)

Union general

Robert Anderson was born near Louisville, Kentucky, on June 14, 1805, into a family with deep Southern roots. He graduated from the U.S. Military Academy in 1825 and joined the 3rd U.S. Artillery as a second lieutenant. As such, Anderson fought in the Black Hawk War of 1832, gaining brevet promotion to captain for gallantry, and also served in Florida's Second Seminole War (1836–38). Anderson next participated in General Winfield SCOTT's invasion of Mexico in 1847, winning a second brevet to major for gallantry at Molino del Rey, in which he was also wounded. Thereafter, he spent the next several years serving with various artillery boards and also translated French military texts for army use. Anderson, a proslavery, Southern-born officer, seemed a natural choice to Secretary of War John B. FLOYD to head the Federal garrison at Charleston, South Carolina, in November 1860. That state was being buffeted violently by the winds of secession, and it was hoped that Anderson, by dint of his Southern sensibilities, might diffuse tensions there.

After arriving in Charleston, Anderson remained polite, even deferential, to city authorities but also adamant toward fulfilling his duties. His position worsened considerably after December 20, 1861, when South Carolina passed a secession ordinance and tensions with the federal government—and its troops—increased. At that time, Anderson commanded 137 men at Fort Moultrie, a wretched fortification in Charleston proper that was indefensible from the land side. Fearing for the safety of his men—and without prior authorization from the War Department—Anderson acted decisively. On the evening of December 26, 1860, he quietly and efficiently transferred the garrison from Fort Moultrie to Fort Sumter on an island in the harbor. Once there, he cabled superiors as to his predicament and awaited further instructions. Predictably, the secessionist-leaning secretary Floyd was livid over the unauthorized transfer and demanded it be countermanded, but President James Buchanan refused and settled for the status quo. He was counting on Anderson's well-grounded reputation for tact and intelligence, along with his unswerving loyalty to the Union, to forestall any outbreak of violence.

Charleston authorities naturally were incensed that the U.S. garrison had slipped from their grasp and demanded Anderson's surrender. That officer politely but firmly refused. To underscore his pledge of neutrality, he took no action on January 9, 1861, when Southern batteries fired the first unofficial shots of the Civil War by driving off the supply ship *Star of the West*. However, Confederate leaders, seeking diplomatic recognition for their national sovereignty, simply could not tolerate the presence of Federal troops in one of their largest seaports. General Pierre G. T. BEAUREGARD, the local military commander, was then ordered to bombard the insolent Yankees into submission if they failed to depart. As previously, Anderson politely declined and Southerners began to line the shoreline with heavy cannon. Anderson also informed both Beauregard and President Abraham LINCOLN that his garrison was nearly out of victuals and would have to capitulate within days if not

Union general Robert Anderson *(Massachusetts Commandery Military Order of the Loyal Legion and the U.S. Army Military History Institute)*

resupplied. The crisis mounted when Lincoln announced his decision to send a ship with food—not reinforcements—to the beleaguered garrison. This proved one contingency that Confederate authorities could not allow, and so again, on April 11, 1861, they informed Anderson that either he must surrender immediately or they would open fire. When the stalwart officer again refused to abandon his duty, the slide toward civil war became inevitable.

Confederate batteries opened fire at 4:30 A.M. on the morning of April 12, 1861, and bombarded Fort Sumter continuously for the next 34 hours. Anderson gave Captain Abner Doubleday the honor of firing the first Union shot of the war, but in the end, he was simply overpowered and capitulated at noontime on April 14. His men then were trundled off by the Confederates and allowed to depart by boat. Anderson's heroic stand rendered him the first Northern hero of the Civil War, but privately, he remained grief-stricken over his inability to prevent the outbreak of war. Anderson gained promotion to brigadier general on May 15, 1861, and appointment as commander of the Department of Kentucky (later the Department of the Cumberland) from May to October 1861. His calm presence helped shore up Unionist sympathies in this, his native state. However, Anderson remained dogged by ill health and retired from active service in October 1863 after being replaced by General William T. Sherman. Anderson briefly donned his general's uniform on April 14, 1865, when he personally raised the same American flag over Fort Sumter that had been lowered four years earlier. Anderson, a quiet, efficient professional soldier, died while vacationing in Nice, France, on October 26, 1871.

Further Reading

Detzer, David. *Allegiance: Fort Sumter, Charleston, and the Beginning of the Civil War.* New York: Harcourt, 2002.
Garrison, Webb S. *Lincoln's Little War.* Nashville, Tenn.: Rutledge Hill Press, 1997.
Hendrickson, Robert. *Sumter, the First Day of the Civil War.* Chelsea, Mich.: Scarborough, 1997.
Klein, Maury. *Days of Defiance: Sumter, Secession, and the Coming of the Civil War.* New York: Vintage Books, 1999.
McGinty, Brian. "Robert Anderson: Reluctant Hero." *Civil War Times Illustrated* 31, no. 2 (1992): 44–47, 58, 68.
Ramsey, David M. "Robert Anderson in the Civil War." Unpublished master's thesis, Florida State University, 1974.
Wait, Eugene M. *Opening of the Civil War.* Commack, N.Y.: Nova Science Pub., 1999.

Anderson, William (ca. 1837–1864)
Confederate guerrilla

William Anderson probably was born in Kentucky around 1837 and relocated with his family to Council Grove, Kansas Territory, in 1854. The frontier then was reeling from the effects of the Kansas-Nebraska Act of that year, which allowed new states in the union on the basis of "popular sovereignty." This well-intentioned legislation triggered an onslaught of lawlessness as pro- and antislavery groups violently competed for political supremacy. For good measure, criminal elements frequently sided with either group if it suited their own agenda. The ensuing mayhem and murder bequeathed to the territory an uncomely reputation as "Bleeding Kansas." Tensions between the two groups were exacerbated further following the onset of secessionism in 1861. Anderson's own father, a somewhat shady figure, was gunned down in a confrontation with pro-Union settlers in March 1862. With the Civil War now in full swing, the warring factions coalesced into violent groupings favoring either the South ("Bushwhackers") or the North ("Jayhawkers"). Both sides were utterly ruthless in dealing with the other and frequently committed atrocities against civilians, law enforcement figures, and anyone else who got in their way.

By 1862, Anderson had matured into a tall, willowy youth with a penchant for horse theft. He initially favored the pro-Northern faction and generally helped himself to the plunder they accrued. Following the death of his father, however, he relocated to western Missouri and promptly switched sides. The catalyst for his reversion to barbarism occurred on August 13, 1863, when his two sisters, under arrest for alleged Confederate activities, died when the jail confining them collapsed. Anderson consequently joined a gang of frontier desperados under Captain William C. QUANTRILL and began to wreak his own personal brand of vengeance against Unionists. On August 21, 1863, he waged a full measure of activities at Lawrence, Kansas, which was seized by Quantrill's guerrillas. These ruffians, who included Frank and Jesse James, Cole Younger, and a host of future outlaws, systematically rounded up and murdered 200 men and boys before burning the town to the ground. On October 6, Anderson, wearing Union garb, also helped ambush the military escort of General James G. Blunt at Baxter Springs, Kansas, capturing and killing 110 prisoners. Shortly afterward, Anderson was promoted to lieutenant and wintered with the guerrillas in Texas. He subsequently broke with the violent Quantrill after one of his own men was executed and went on to form his own gang of outlaw marauders. By this time, Anderson has also earned, and apparently reveled in, his grim sobriquet of "Bloody Bill."

Commencing in the spring of 1864, Anderson's gang of 50 guerrillas swept the plains of western and central Missouri, robbing and gunning down soldiers and civilians alike. His career climaxed on September 27, 1864, when he captured the town of Centralia, Missouri, robbing the residents and torching the town. At this point, a train pulled into the station bearing 24 unarmed Union soldiers, of whom 23 were bound and executed in cold blood. Union reinforcements arrived shortly after and pursued the guerrillas, but Anderson led them directly into an ambush, killing an additional 100 prisoners. Despite his notoriety, General Sterling PRICE openly employed Anderson and his men as scouts during his final invasion of Missouri, which came to grief at Westport on October 23, 1864. Four days later, Anderson was patrolling outside the town of Orrick when he

stumbled directly into a Jayhawk ambush. He was killed in the ensuing fight, and his body was propped up for public display by vengeful settlers. Anderson's remains then were interred in an unmarked grave after being dragged through the street by horses. He left a bloody legacy whose tradition of violence was perpetuated in the postwar period by the James brothers and other former and notorious subordinates.

Further Reading
Bird, Roy. *Civil War in Kansas.* Gretna, La.: Pelican Publishing, 2004.
Gilmore, Donald L. *Civil War on the Missouri-Kansas Border.* Gretna, La.: Pelican Publishing, 2006.
Mackey, Robert R. *The Uncivil War: Irregular Warfare in the Upper South, 1861–1865.* Norman: University of Oklahoma Press, 2004.
Nichols, Bruce. *Guerrilla Warfare in Civil War Missouri, 1863.* Jefferson, N.C.: McFarland, 2006.
Stiles, T. J. *Jesse James: Last Rebel Guerrilla of the Civil War.* New York: Alfred A. Knopf, 2002.
Wood, Larry. *The Civil War Story of Bloody Bill Anderson.* Austin, Tex.: Eakin Press, 2003.

Ashby, Turner (1828–1862)
Confederate general
Turner Ashby was born in Fauquier County, Virginia, on October 23, 1828, grandson of a Revolutionary War hero. He entered business as an adult and gained local renown for his striking appearance and abilities as a horseman. In 1859, Ashby had his first brush with military matters when he raised a company of volunteer cavalry to help combat the abolitionist John Brown at Harper's Ferry. His services were not then needed, but he maintained his company and continually patrolled the reaches of western Virginia, searching for abolitionist activity. After the Civil War erupted in April 1861, he and John D. IMBODEN originated a plan to seize the Federal arsenal and valuable gunmaking machinery at Harper's Ferry, although they were thwarted when the garrison burned their outpost to the ground. Ashby also reached a personal turning point in June 1861 when his younger brother was killed in a skirmish with sol-

diers of the 11th Indiana Infantry under Colonel Lew WALLACE. He immediately swore to avenge his loss and nursed a growing hatred for the Unionists. His energetic services came to the attention of Colonel Thomas J. JACKSON, who then prevailed on General Joseph E. JOHNSTON to commission Ashby into the Confederate service. Accordingly, on July 23, 1861, Ashby was inducted as a lieutenant colonel of the 7th Virginia Cavalry.

Ashby quickly emerged as one of the first Southern cavalry leaders of note and an exceptionally enterprising leader. On one occasion, he disguised himself as a doctor and rode for miles behind Union lines to ascertain their strength and intentions. His men also constantly patrolled the lower Shenandoah Valley against Federal incursions and raids. Ashby acquitted himself well, rising to colonel of the 7th Virginia Cavalry that November. However, his regiment had ballooned in size to 27 companies—far too large from an administrative standpoint. He was also somewhat lax in matters of discipline, and his men acquired a reputation for plundering on the battlefield. Such behavior repelled the spit-and-polish Jackson, who threatened to disband Ashby's command and distribute it among other units if he failed to instill a proper military regimen. The enraged cavalier promptly stormed into his superior's tent and threatened in turn to resign from the army. Jackson relented—on condition that he properly instruct his men. Ashby agreed, and on May 23, 1862, he gained promotion to brigadier general in time to participate in the famous Shenandoah Valley campaign of that year.

During the ensuing two months, Ashby performed scouting, screening, and combat activities for Jackson, frequently against superior numbers but usually victorious. His only real error occurred on May 23, 1862, while reconnoitering in the vicinity of Kernstown, when he inadvertently reported that the town was occupied by a handful of Union troops. On the basis of this report, Jackson then advanced to Kernstown—and headlong into General James Shield's division, which largely had been concealed in the nearby woods. The

ensuing repulse was the only blot on Jackson's otherwise illustrious campaign. Ashby subsequently performed well in the Confederate victory at Winchester two days later, but he failed to intercept the retreat of General Nathaniel P. BANKS successfully when his men again reverted to plundering captured enemy wagons.

At length, Jackson began an orderly withdrawal from the Shenandoah Valley in the face of superior numbers, and Ashby provided the rear guard. As the Confederates withdrew toward Port Republic, Union forces under General John C. Frémont pushed troops forward to engage them. Ashby repulsed one determined charge at Chestnut Ridge on June 6, 1862, when the enemy brought up fresh infantry in support. Ashby did likewise and dismounted to encourage his troops. He then led a charge on foot, shouting, "Forward my brave men!" and was shot down and killed. Jackson, who appreciated his talent as a scout, deeply regretted his passing. "As a partisan officer I never knew his superior," Stonewall confided, "His daring was proverbial; his powers of endurance almost incredible; his tone of character heroic; and his sagacity almost intuitive in divining the purposes and movements of the enemy." Ashby, revered by his men as the "White Knight of the Valley," was interred at Winchester, Virginia, having died before achieving his full potential as a combat officer.

Further Reading

Anderson, Paul C. *Blood Image: Turner Ashby in the Civil War and the Southern Mind.* Baton Rouge: Louisiana State University Press, 2002.

Bushong, Millard K. *General Turner Ashby and Stonewall's Valley Campaign.* Verona, Va.: McClure, 1980.

Cochran, Darrell. "First of the Cavaliers: General Turner Ashby's Brief Glory." *Civil War Times Illustrated* 25, no. 10 (1987): 22–28.

Ecelbarger, Gary L. *We Are in for It! The First Battle of Kernstown.* Shippenburg, Pa.: White Mane Books, 1997.

O'Toole, John T. "The Revenge of Turner Ashby." *Civil War* 58 (August 1996): 40–44.

Paterson, Richard. "Schemes and Treachery." *Civil War Times Illustrated* 28, no. 2 (1989): 38–45.

B

Banks, Nathaniel P. (1816–1894)

Union general

Nathaniel Prentiss Banks was born in Waltham, Massachusetts, on January 16, 1816, the son of a textile foreman. He initially worked in the mills, but, disliking physical labor, he studied law in his spare time and was admitted to the state bar in 1839. He then became active within the Democratic Party, rising steadily through the ranks and winning a seat in the state House of Representatives in 1849. Political success whetted Banks's appetite, and in 1853, he successfully stood for a seat in the U.S. House of Representatives, maneuvering himself into the speakership a year later. But Banks grew disillusioned with the Democratic Party's stance on slavery, so in 1856, he joined the newly formed Republican Party. He then quit Congress and successfully ran for the Massachusetts governorship in 1857, being reelected consecutively two more times. In 1860, Banks resigned from politics altogether to replace George B. McCLELLAN as president of the Illinois Central Railroad. He still enjoyed deep political roots in the Republican Party and, as a New Englander, a high national profile. Therefore, when President Abraham LINCOLN put in a call for volunteers in April 1861, Banks gained appointment as major general of volunteers to shore up political support from New England. This was done strictly for geopolitical reasons, for Banks, though a skilled administrator, lacked any prior experience in the art of war.

Following the Union debacle at Bull Run on July 21, 1861, Banks was tapped to succeed the disgraced general Robert Patterson as commander of Federal troops in the strategic Shenandoah Valley. The following spring, he received orders to clear the valley of Confederate forces, and he was trounced soundly by General Thomas J. JACKSON at Winchester on May 25, 1862. Union forces abandoned so many valuable supplies in their flight across the Potomac River that victorious Confederates denegraded him as "Commissary Banks." The following June, Banks's force was reorganized in the II Corps in the Army of Virginia under General John POPE. On August 9, 1862, he again tangled with General Ambrose P. HILL at Cedar Mountain, Virginia, being badly defeated and driven from the field. By this time, complaints about Banks's lackluster leadership reached the ears of the Joint Committee on the Conduct of the War, but Lincoln, who needed the general for political reasons, refused to dismiss him outright. Therefore, in November 1862, he was sent to New Orleans, Louisiana, to replace another controversial "political general," Benjamin F. BUTLER.

Once in charge, Banks moderated Butler's harsh policies toward Southerners, released political prisoners, and opened churches to worship. He also organized new elections under the old state constitution and attempted to enfranchise African Americans. But whatever goodwill these moves

Union general Nathaniel P. Banks *(Massachusetts Commandery Military Order of the Loyal Legion and the U.S. Army Military History Institute)*

generated was irretrievably lost once Banks authorized recruitment of former slaves as the Corps d'Afrique. In the spring of 1863, Banks returned to the field by acting in concert with Union forces under General Ulysses S. GRANT at Vicksburg, Mississippi. His objective was to reduce the fortified enclave at Port Hudson, Louisiana, possession of which would clear navigation along the Mississippi River. But Banks again stumbled badly; despite clear numerical superiority, he proved unable to defeat the garrison of General Franklin Gardner, and he was repulsed bloodily in three major attacks on May 27, June 11, and June 14, 1862. It was not until word of Vicksburg's fall

arrived that Gardner finally capitulated on July 9 after Banks sustained 3,000 casualties. For the rest of the year, he remained occupied with several fruitless expeditions along the Texas coast, which achieved nothing.

Despite open grumbling about ineptitude, Banks received his most important military assignment in the spring of 1864 when General Henry W. HALLECK ordered him to mount a joint expedition up the Red River and into east Texas. As usual, Banks was lackadaisical in his leadership and commenced operations several weeks behind schedule. After bloodlessly seizing Alexandria, Louisiana, he proceeded overland by a narrow road toward his next objective at Shreveport. His tardy deployment induced Confederates under General Richard TAYLOR to attack him at Sabine Cross Roads on April 9, 1864, where Union troops were defeated heavily. The following day, Banks fought Taylor to a draw at Pleasant Hill; nonetheless, he continued his retreat back to New Orleans. En route, the accompanying gunboat squadron of Admiral David D. PORTER nearly was lost on the Red River due to falling water levels, and only the intercession of Colonel Joseph Baily, an engineer, saved the gunboats. Shortly after arriving at New Orleans in June, Banks finally was supplanted by General Edward R. S. CANBY. He never again held a field command and resigned his commission in August 1865.

After the war, Banks resumed his political activities with considerable success, returning to Congress repeatedly. Always eager to gain an advantage, he constantly switched allegiances from Republican to Democratic and back again as suited his needs. Banks died at Waltham, Massachusetts, on September 1, 1894, having been one of the more dismal political appointees of the Civil War.

Further Reading

Ayers, Thomas. *Dark and Bloody Ground: The Battle of Mansfield and the Forgotten Civil War in Louisiana.* Dallas: Taylor Trade, 2001.
Bounds, Steve, and Curtis Milbourn. "The Battle of Mansfield." *North & South* 6, no. 2 (2003): 26–41.

Dawson, Joseph G. "Lincoln's Political Generals." Unpublished Ph.D. diss., Texas A & M University, 2004.

Forsyth, Michael J. *The Red River Campaign of 1864 and the Loss by the Confederacy of the Civil War.* Jefferson, N.C.: McFarland, 2002.

Gallagher, Gary W. *The Shenandoah Valley Campaign of 1862.* Chapel Hill: University of North Carolina Press, 2003.

Goss, Thomas J. *The War within the Union High Command: Politics and Generalship during the Civil War.* Lawrence: University Press of Kansas, 2003.

Joiner, Gary D. *Through the Howling Wilderness: the 1864 Red River Campaign of Union Failure in the West.* Knoxville: University of Tennessee Press, 2006.

Persons, Benjamin S. *From This Valley They Say You Are Leaving: The Union Red River Campaign, March 1864 to May 1865.* Bloomington, Ind.: 1st Books Library, 2003.

Beauregard, Pierre G. T. (1818–1893)

Confederate general

Pierre Gustave Toutant Beauregard was born in St. Bernard Parish, Louisiana, on May 28, 1818, the son of French parents. Throughout life, his somewhat short stature seemed offset by a towering ego. In 1834, he gained admittance to the U.S. Military Academy and, studious disciple of Napoleon that he was, graduated second in his class four years later. Among his friends and classmates was Irvin McDowell, a future Union general. Beauregard, now a second lieutenant in the elite Corps of Engineers, subsequently held a number of important construction positions along the East Coast. He served for a decade, acquitting himself well in numerous assignments, and in 1847, General Winfield Scott appointed him a staff engineer. Beauregard fought with distinction during the Mexican War, being wounded twice and winning two brevet promotions for bravery at Veracruz, Cerro Gordo, and Contreras. Privately—and consistent with his tempestuous disposition—Beauregard fumed over not receiving greater recognition for his talents. After the war, he resumed his construction and engineering activities, which culminated in the prestigious appointment as superintendent of cadets at West Point on January 23, 1861.

Unfortunately, secession was in the wind, and when Beauregard made some impolitic remarks about Southern rights, he was dismissed from office four days later. He lingered on in the military until Louisiana left the Union in February 1861 and then resigned his commission and offered his service to the Confederate States of America.

On March 1, 1861, President Jefferson Davis appointed Beauregard a brigadier general in the Confederate army and appointed him commander of Southern forces at Charleston, South Carolina. This placed him at the very center of secessionist activities, for Confederate authorities remained flummoxed over what to do with the Federal garrison ensconced at Fort Sumter. On April 12, 1861, Beauregard received orders to bombard Major Robert Anderson into submission, an act precipitating the bloodiest conflict in U.S. history. For his role, Beauregard became lionized throughout the South as a Confederate hero. He was next appointed

Confederate general Pierre G. T. Beauregard *(National Archives)*

to command Confederate forces assembled for the defense of Virginia. He was technically second in command to General Joseph E. JOHNSTON, but the latter was diplomatic enough to allow him to conduct the battle and secure the Southern victory over General McDowell at Bull Run on July 21, 1861. However, success exacerbated tensions with President Davis, for Beauregard strongly felt that the defeated Federals should have been pursued to the very gates of Washington, D.C., and his tactless and public remarks about the president led to their permanent estrangement. Nevertheless, on August 13, 1861, the banty leader received promotion to lieutenant general and was sent west to serve with the Army of Mississippi under General Albert S. JOHNSTON. On a lighter note, Beauregard also found the time to design the famous "Stars and Bars" Confederate battle flag, which has symbolized the South ever since.

Beauregard helped formulate the overly complicated plan for the April 6, 1861, Battle of Shiloh, which nearly destroyed the army of General Ulysses S. GRANT. After Johnston was killed in action, Beauregard continued leading the army until an influx of Union reinforcements drove him from the field on April 7. He then skillfully extricated his command but further sullied his reputation with Davis by trying to portray the encounter as a victory. A month later, Beauregard was forced to yield the strategic railroad junction of Corinth, Mississippi, to General Henry W. HALLECK, which did little to endear him to Confederate authorities. Then, reeling from chronic throat pain, Beauregard took an unauthorized medical leave, which handed the president a pretext for relieving him of command—permanently. His fateful replacement was General Braxton BRAGG, a Davis sycophant and a decidedly uneven military leader. After recuperating, Beauregard ventured back east to accept command of the Department of South Carolina, Georgia, and Florida, headquartered at Charleston. His most successful accomplishment was repelling the April 1863 naval assault by Admiral Samuel F. DU PONT, along with lesser attacks mounted by his successor, Admiral John A. B. DAHLGREN. His per-

formance was impressive enough for General Robert E. LEE to invite him to serve with the Army of Northern Virginia, but Beauregard remained coy and held out for an independent command. Accordingly, on April 23, 1864, he was appointed head of the newly renamed Department of North Carolina and Southern Virginia.

Beauregard performed his finest work in the defense of Petersburg, Virginia, which brought the Confederate war effort several additional months of life. On May 16, 1864, he drove back larger Union forces under General Benjamin F. BUTLER from Drewry's Heights, Virginia, effectively sealing his Army of the James in the peninsula of Bermuda Hundred. But Beauregard also took it upon himself to bombard Confederate headquarters with myriads of hopelessly Napoleonic schemes for winning the war, which drove President Davis to distraction. Eager to rid himself of this irksome leader, Davis once again transferred Beauregard to command of the Department of the West, an administrative position created to coordinate all Confederate forces in Mississippi, Alabama, Georgia, and the Carolinas. When his best efforts failed to contain the army of General William T. SHERMAN from taking Atlanta and Savannah, Georgia, Beauregard returned east again to command Southern forces in South Carolina. He and General Joe Johnston both surrendered to Sherman on April 18, 1865, closing a controversial military career.

Back in civilian life, Beauregard served as president of the Jackson and Mississippi Railroad and also managed to direct the Louisiana State Lottery Commission. He also engaged in a heated, no-holds-barred publishing war with Johnston and Davis over who, precisely, lost the Confederacy. The contentious, capable Beauregard, popularly known as "Napoleon in Gray," died at New Orleans on February 21, 1893.

Further Reading

Arnold, James R. *Shiloh, 1862: The Death of Innocence.* Westport, Conn.: Praeger, 2004.

Beauregard, Pierre G. T. *A Commentary on the Campaign and Battle of Manassas.* New York: G. P. Putnam's Sons, 1891.

Detzer, David. *Donnybrook: The Battle of Bull Run.* San Diego: Harcourt, 2004.

Echelberry, Earl. "War Cloud Lowering." *Military Heritage* 3, no. 1 (2001): 48–46, 58–59, 98.

Engel, Stephen D. *Struggle for the Heartland: The Campaign from Fort Henry to Corinth.* Lincoln: University of Nebraska Press, 2001.

Gallagher, Gary W., and Joseph T. Glatthaar, eds. *Leaders of the Lost Cause: New Perspectives on the Confederate High Command.* Mechanicsburg, Pa.: Stackpole Books, 2004.

Jones, Wilmer L. *Generals in Blue and Gray.* 2 vols. Westport, Conn.: Praeger, 2004.

Martin, David G. *The Shiloh Campaign, March–April 1862.* Cambridge, Mass.: Da Capo Press, 2003.

Rafuse, Ethan S. *A Single Grand Victory: The First Campaign and Battle of Manassas.* Wilmington, Del.: Scholarly Resources, 2002.

Bragg, Braxton (1817–1876)

Confederate general

Braxton Bragg was born in Warrenton, North Carolina, on March 22, 1817, the son of a wealthy planter. Well educated at a local military academy, he entered the U.S. Military Academy in 1833 and graduated four years later, fifth in his class. Bragg then received a lieutenant's commission in the 3rd U.S. Artillery and fought competently in the Second Seminole War despite repeated bouts with fever. By this time, he had acquired a reputation as a stern, competent officer, but one combative and garrulously disposed. Bragg also began to exhibit what today might be considered a persecution complex, for he continually complained about being ignored and neglected. None of this interfered with his performance in the Mexican War (1846–48), which proved exemplary. Bragg received three brevet promotions while serving under General Zachary Taylor, and his handling of cannon at the Battle of Buena Vista undoubtedly saved the American army from defeat. After the war, Bragg returned to his usual routine of frontier garrison duty, with its concomitant slow promotions, and he angrily brooded over his lack of official recognition. Fed up with an indifferent military bureaucracy, he resigned his commission

Confederate general Braxton Bragg *(Library of Congress)*

in March 1855 and retired to Louisiana to run a sugar plantation.

As the Civil War approached in the spring of 1861, Bragg, on paper at least, appeared to be one of the more promising Confederate officers. Commissioned a brigadier general on February 23, 1861, he gained appointment as commander of coastal defenses between Pensacola, Florida, and Mobile, Alabama, winning plaudits for military administration and his ability to train raw recruits. Consequently, he rose to major general in January 1862 and received the II Corps in the then-forming Army of Mississippi under General Albert S. JOHNSTON. In this capacity, he distinguished himself at the Battle of Shiloh (April 6–7, 1862) until Union reinforcements prompted a Confederate withdrawal. The following June, General Pierre G. T. BEAUREGARD departed the theater on sick leave, and President Jefferson DAVIS, Bragg's longtime confidant, appointed him head of the Army of Mississippi. Bragg immediately took to the offensive and, in a fine display of administrative mettle, expertly shuttled his troops by rail from Mississippi to the gates of Kentucky. His ensuing invasion kept Union forces off balance for several weeks despite only sullen cooperation from General Edmund KIRBY-SMITH. Bragg was well positioned to capture the strategic Union base at Louisville, but he allowed himself to become caught up in the politics of creating a Confederate government at Frankfort. This distraction allowed Federals under General Don C. BUELL to occupy Louisville, receive reinforcements, and finally confront the Confederates at Perryville, Kentucky, on October 8, 1862. The result was a bloody standoff that ended Bragg's invasion, and he fell back through the Cumberland Gap into Tennessee. The following month, his force was renamed the Army of Tennessee, which faced a new adversary in General William S. ROSECRANS. After retreating before superior Union forces, Bragg suddenly turned and pounced on Rosecrans at the Battle of Murfreesboro (Stone's River) (December 30, 1862–January 3, 1863), another bloody encounter. Both sides suffered heavy losses, and the Confederates came close to driving Rosecrans from the field, but in the end, Bragg was forced to retreat again. Heavy casualties among Kentuckian troops also led to accusations of abuse by their commander, General John C. BRECKINRIDGE. Bragg's inability to win, coupled with a recalcitrant disposition that alienated superiors and subordinates alike, prompted calls for his dismissal. President Davis, unfortunately, remained loyal to his old friend, and no action was taken.

Confederate fortunes in the West continued declining throughout 1863. During the summer months, Rosecrans's Army of the Cumberland brilliantly outmaneuvered Bragg near Tullahoma, Tennessee, forcing the Southerners to abandon the city without a shot. Bragg simply fell back to the mountains of northern Georgia where he was reinforced by General James LONGSTREET's I Corps before suddenly and violently attacking Rosecrans at Chickamauga on September 19–20, 1863. The Confederates finally prevailed in this bloody slugfest, although their casualties were

heavier due to Bragg's repeated use of frontal assaults. Worse, he failed to promptly pursue and destroy Rosecrans's shattered army, now holed up at Chattanooga, Tennessee, which Bragg was content to simply besiege. Discontent with his leadership was rife, and General Nathan B. FORREST became so angered by Bragg's lethargy that they nearly dueled, and he requested a transfer elsewhere. Continuing disagreement with General Longstreet also resulted in the latter's assignment to besiege Knoxville just as Union forces under General Ulysses S. GRANT were building up strength for a counterattack. The hammer fell on Bragg on November 23, 1863, when the Army of Tennessee was routed from heights ringing Chattanooga and he withdrew back to Dalton, Georgia. Bragg, his own confidence severely depleted, requested to be relieved of command, and he was replaced by General Joseph E. JOHNSTON on December 1, 1863.

By the spring of 1864, Bragg was back in Richmond, Virginia, acting as a senior military adviser to his old friend President Davis. In this capacity, one of the most fateful tasks he performed was recommending that General Johnston be replaced by General John B. HOOD. That October, Bragg shifted to North Carolina to assist in the defense of Fort Fisher at Wilmington. When that fort fell to Union forces on January 15, 1865, he was criticized severely for failing to rush badly needed reinforcements to its defense. For the next four months, he functioned as a divisional commander under General Johnston and finally surrendered with him on April 18, 1865. After the war, Bragg found work in Alabama as superintendent of public works and then relocated to Galveston, Texas, where he worked as chief engineer of the Gulf, Colorado, and Santa Fe Railroad. He died in Galveston on September 27, 1876, a good fighter and a talented soldier but temperamentally unsuited for the demanding nuances of high command.

Further Reading

Bradley, Michael R. *Tullahoma: The 1863 Campaign for the Control of Middle Tennessee.* Shippensburg, Pa.: Burd Street Press, 2000.

Broadwater, Robert P. *The Battle of Perryville, 1862: Culmination of the Failed Kentucky Campaign.* Jefferson, N.C.: McFarland, 2006.

Daniel, Larry J. *Cannoneers in Gray: The Field Artillery of the Army of Tennessee, 1861–1865.* Tuscaloosa: University of Alabama Press, 2005.

Gallagher, Gary W., and Joseph T. Glatthaar, eds. *Leaders of the Lost Cause: New Perspectives on the Confederate High Command.* Mechanicsburg, Pa.: Stackpole Books, 2004.

Haughton, Andrew. *Training, Tactics and Leadership in the Confederate Army of Tennessee: Seeds of Failure.* Portland, Ore.: Frank Cass, 2000.

Hess, Earl J. *Banners to the Breeze: The Kentucky Campaign, Corinth, and Stones River.* Lincoln: University of Nebraska Press, 2000.

Lepa, Jack H. *The Civil War in Tennessee, 1862–1863.* Jefferson, N.C.: McFarland, 2007.

McCaslin, Richard B. *The Last Stronghold: The Campaign for Fort Fisher.* Abilene, Tex.: McWhiney Foundation Press, 2003.

Spruill, Mat. *Storming the Heights: A Guide to the Battle of Chattanooga.* Knoxville: University of Tennessee Press, 2003.

Breckinridge, John C. (1821–1875)

Confederate general

John Cabell Breckinridge was born near Lexington, Kentucky, on January 16, 1821, into one of that state's most prominent political families. He was educated at Centre College, the College of New Jersey, and Transylvania College with degrees in law, being carefully groomed to continue the family's tradition of public service. Shortly after opening his law practice in Kentucky, Breckinridge obtained a major's commission in the 3rd Kentucky Regiment and briefly served in the Mexican War (1846–48). He failed to see combat but did act as a legal adviser to General Gideon J. PILLOW in his dispute with General Winfield SCOTT. Once back home, Breckinridge's drive, intellect, and family name catapulted him into the political arena with a seat in the state house of representatives. In 1856, and much to his surprise, the promising young politician was nominated as James Buchanan's vice presidential candidate and won.

At age 35, he thus became the youngest individual ever to occupy that office. Breckinridge was largely ignored by the Buchanan administration as the president's attention was increasingly preoccupied by mounting sectional tensions over the issue of slavery and secession. Though a slave owner himself, Breckinridge felt that the institution was doomed, and he also worked tirelessly against secession among firebrand Southerners. When the Democratic Party split along regional lines in 1860, these same extremists nominated him as their presidential candidate, despite his open disdain for their position. He nonetheless proffered himself as a moderate alternative to Abraham LINCOLN, who went on to win the election. Breckinridge was then appointed to serve in the U.S. Senate by the Kentucky state legislature, commencing in January 1861.

Confederate general John C. Breckinridge *(Massachusetts Commandery Military Order of the Loyal Legion and the U.S. Army Military History Institute)*

In the Senate, Breckinridge defended the right of Southern states to secede, although he invariably cautioned against it. The Civil War commenced in April 1861, and five months later a Federal court in Kentucky ordered Breckinridge arrested for treason. He then fled to the Confederacy, received a brigadier general's commission the following November, and set about organizing the famous "Orphan Brigade" for Kentucky expatriates like himself. Despite his lack of formal military training, Breckinridge performed ably under General Albert S. JOHNSTON at the April 6–7, 1862, Battle of Shiloh, where he commanded the reserves. He rose to major general in June 1862 and, on August 5, 1862, led an ill-fated attack against Union troops at Baton Rouge, Louisiana, that nearly succeeded. He then marched north to serve under General William J. HARDEE's corps in the Army of Tennessee. Breckinridge again distinguished himself in combat at Murfreesboro (December 31, 1862–January 3, 1863), although his brigade sustained heavy losses from Union artillery fire. He consequently quarreled with commanding General Braxton BRAGG over the mistreatment of his men and was urged by many subordinates to duel with him. Breckinridge, fortunately, transferred south again before personal resentments culminated in tragedy.

Breckinridge subsequently joined the army of General Joseph E. JOHNSTON and fought in the defense of Jackson, Mississippi. He then transferred back to the Army of Tennessee as part of General Daniel H. HILL's division, performing well at the bloody Battle of Chickamauga, September 19–20, 1863. His good performance resulted in command of an understrength corps during the Battle of Chattanooga, November 25, 1863, another heavy Confederate defeat. To prevent another collision with Bragg, who accused Breckinridge of being drunk, President Jefferson DAVIS interceded by transferring the disgruntled Kentuckian east to replace General John H. MORGAN as head of the Department of Southwest Virginia. Breckinridge was now responsible for the defense of the Shenandoah Valley, the "breadbasket of the Confederacy," and on May 15, 1864, he defeated a larger Union force under General Franz SIGEL at New Market. This engagement witnessed the deployment of 247 youthful cadets (or "Katydids") from the nearby Virginia Military Institute, whose outstanding behavior that bloody day entered Southern folklore. Breckinridge then transferred again to the Army of Northern Virginia under General Robert E. LEE, where he rendered useful service in fighting at Cold Harbor on June 3, 1864. That summer, he accompanied General Jubal A. EARLY back to the Shenandoah Valley, where he again fought valorously and futilely against superior numbers under General Philip H. SHERIDAN. Breckinridge then returned west once more to the Army of Tennessee, this time under General John B. HOOD and saw active service at the defeat at Nashville, Tennessee, on December 15–16, 1864. In February 1865 President Davis appointed Breckinridge to be his final secretary of war. His most significant contribution was in convincing the president to end the war honorably and not besmirch the Confederacy's name by resorting to guerrilla warfare. "This has been a magnificent epic," he maintained, "In God's name let it not terminate in a farce."

After the fall of Richmond in April 1865, Breckinridge rejoined Johnston in North Carolina, where he served as a negotiator in surrender negotiations with General William T. SHERMAN. Fearing arrest, he then fled to Cuba and Britain, remaining abroad for three years. Breckinridge, under a general amnesty in 1868, finally returned to Kentucky, where he resumed his legal activities. Thereafter, he also served as a spokesman for national reconciliation and formally denounced the infamous Ku Klux Klan for violence against African Americans. Breckinridge died of physical exhaustion in Lexington, Kentucky, on May 17, 1875, aged but 54 years. On balance, he was probably the most gifted "political general" of either side.

Further Reading

Davis, William C. *Honorable Defeat: The Last Days of the Confederate Government.* New York: Harcourt, 2001.

Haines, J. D. *Put the Boys In: The Story of the Virginia Military Institute Cadets at the Battle of New Market.* Austin, Tex.: Eakin Press, 2003.

Heenhan, Jim. "Final Attack at Stones River." *Military Heritage* 5, no. 2 (2003): 52–59.

Hess, Earl J. *Banners to the Breeze: The Kentucky Campaign, Corinth, and Stones River.* Lincoln: University of Nebraska Press, 2000.

Jones, Wilmer L. *Generals in Blue and Gray.* 2 vols. Westport, Conn.: Praeger, 2004.

Lepa, Jack H. *The Shenandoah Valley Campaign of 1864.* Jefferson, N.C.: McFarland, 2003.

Naisawald, L. Van Loan, and James I. Robertson. *The Battle of Lynchburg: Seize Lynchburg–If Only for a Single Day.* Lynchburg, Va.: Warwick House Pub., 2004.

Buchanan, Franklin (1800–1874)

Confederate admiral

Franklin Buchanan was born in Baltimore, Maryland, on September 17, 1800, and he commenced his long association with naval affairs by becoming a midshipman on January 28, 1815. He first sailed with Commodore Oliver H. Perry onboard the frigate USS *Java* and spent the next two decades performing routine work with a variety of squadrons. Buchanan invariably acquitted himself well, rising to lieutenant in January 1825 and commander in September 1841. After he commanded the steam frigate *Mississippi* and the sloop *Vincennes,* Secretary of the Navy George Bancroft tasked him with drafting plans for a new naval academy to be constructed at Annapolis, Maryland. Buchanan's scheme proved so thorough that Bancroft appointed him to serve as the first superintendent in 1845. In this capacity, he grafted his own sense for high academics and no-nonsense discipline onto the curriculum and gave that institution its successful start. Buchanan then petitioned for active duty once the war with Mexico erupted in 1846, and in March 1847 he received command of the sloop *Germantown.* He then accompanied the squadrons of commodores David C. Conner and Matthew C. Perry in various actions around the Gulf of Mexico, winning high praise for competence and bravery. In 1853

Confederate admiral Franklin Buchanan *(U.S. Navy)*

Buchanan was selected to command Perry's flagship *Susquehanna* on its fateful voyage to establish diplomatic relations with Japan. He remained in Asia for two years before returning home to administer the Washington Navy Yard as a captain in 1855.

As a Southerner, Buchanan mistakenly believed that his native state of Maryland was about to secede, and he tendered his resignation on April 22, 1861. Maryland, however, stayed loyal to the Union, but when Buchanan petitioned to withdraw his resignation, Secretary of the Navy Gideon Welles summarily refused it. For many weeks thereafter, Buchanan hovered between the two feuding camps, but in September 1861 he joined the Confederate navy as a captain posted with the Bureau of Orders and Details. He functioned well, but Buchanan, a strident man of action, chafed as a bureaucrat and agitated for a more active role. In February 1862 he then received command of the

James River Squadron and spent several weeks supervising conversion of the captured steam frigate *Merrimac* into the armored ram CSS *Virginia*. On March 8, 1862, Buchanan forever altered the nature of naval warfare by steaming off to engage the Union blockading squadron at Hampton Roads, Virginia. In a fierce, one-sided action, he quickly sank the wooden frigate *Cumberland* and drove another wooden vessel, the *Congress*, aground. Ironically, his younger brother was an officer on board this vessel. This action also marked the immediate ascendancy of iron warships. Buchanan, who exposed himself fearlessly in the battle, was struck by a bullet fired from the shoreline and severely injured. Consequently, he missed the legendary duel with the Union ironclad *Monitor* on the following day. In light of his performance at the helm of *Virginia,* he became the Confederacy's first admiral on August 21, 1862.

For the next two years, Buchanan applied his considerable skills at improving the defenses of Mobile, Alabama, a significant Confederate port. He also oversaw construction of four new ironclads, of which only one, the *Tennessee,* was in service when Union forces attacked on August 5, 1864. That memorable day, Admiral David G. FARRAGUT braved Confederate guns and minefields and ran his squadron directly into the bay, sweeping aside feeble Southern opposition. Buchanan, badly outnumbered, might have enjoyed better success employing his armored ships as floating batteries, but he unhesitatingly threw *Tennessee* against the entire Union squadron and tried repeatedly to ram the *Hartford,* Farragut's flagship. Wounded again and his vessel badly damaged, Buchanan struck his flag and surrendered. He remained a prisoner until March 1865, when he was paroled and returned to Mobile. He surrendered there a second time the following May and left the Confederate service. After the war, Buchanan served as president of the University of Maryland before dying in Talbot County, Maryland, on May 11, 1874. He was among the Confederacy's bravest and most accomplished naval leaders.

Further Reading

Campbell, R. Thomas. *Confederate Phoenix: The CSS Virginia.* Shippensburg, Pa.: Burd Street Press, 2001.

———. *Iron Courage: Confederate Ironclads in the War Between the States.* Shippensburg, Pa.: Burd Street Press, 2002.

Friend, Jack. *West Wind, Flood Tide: The Battle of Mobile Bay.* Annapolis, Md.: Naval Institute Press, 2003.

Garcia, Pedro. "Through a Gate of Fire." *Military Heritage* 4, no. 3 (2002): 62–75.

Park, Carl D. *Ironclad Down: The USS Merrimack-CSS Virginia from Construction to Destruction.* Annapolis, Md.: Naval Institute Press, 2007.

Silverstone, Paul H. *Civil War Navies, 1855–1883.* Annapolis, Md.: Naval Institute Press, 2001.

Symonds, Craig L. "Rank and Rancor in the Confederate Navy." *MHQ* 14, no. 2 (2002): 14–19.

Buell, Don C. (1818–1898)

Union general

Don Carlos Buell was born near Marietta, Ohio, on March 23, 1818, the son of a businessman. He attended the U.S. Military Academy in 1837 and graduated four years later in the lower half of his class. Buell then received his lieutenant's commission in the 3rd U.S. Infantry, with whom he initially fought in the closing stages of Florida's Second Seminole War. He subsequently transferred to General Zachary Taylor's Army of Texas to fight in the Mexican War (1846–48). Buell distinguished himself in combat at Monterrey, Contreras, and Churubusco, winning two brevet promotions and becoming badly wounded. Now a captain, he next fulfilled a variety of outpost duties along the frontier before transferring to the adjutant general's office in the Department of the Pacific. In 1859 he was briefly attached to the secretary of war's office and then returned east just as the Civil War seemed imminent. Recalled to Washington, Buell became a brigadier general on May 17, 1861, and helped organize Washington, D.C.'s defenses before receiving a division in General George B. MCCLELLAN's Army of the Potomac. Holding a well-deserved reputation for efficiency, administration, and strategy, he was considered one of the Union army's most promising officers, and much was expected of him.

In November 1861 Buell transferred west once more, replacing General William T. SHERMAN as head of the Department of the Ohio. He then received orders to secure Nashville, Tennessee, but vacillated until General Ulysses S. GRANT first secured Forts Henry and Donelson in February 1862. Buell was nonetheless promoted to major general of volunteers and ordered to continue advancing down the Tennessee River in support of Grant. On the evening of April 6, 1862, his army reached Pittsburg Landing after the first day of costly fighting at the Battle of Shiloh, and on the following morning, Buell attacked and drove off Confederates under General Pierre G. T. BEAUREGARD. That May, under the jurisdiction of General Henry W. HALLECK, he participated in the glacial campaign against Corinth, Mississippi. On June 10, 1862, Buell commanded four divisions in an attempt to repair the Memphis and Charleston Railroad leading to Chattanooga, Tennessee. This proved tedious work, and his efforts were greatly vexed by Confederate raiding activities under General John H. MORGAN. Consequently, Chattanooga was occupied by the Confederate Army of Tennessee under General Braxton BRAGG, who then prepared to invade Union-held territory farther north.

The turning point in Buell's fortunes occurred in August 1862 when Confederate armies under Generals Bragg and Edmund KIRBY-SMITH invaded Kentucky. With his base at Louisville now threatened, Buell hastily marched north to Louisville and managed to secure it while Bragg was at Frankfort installing a Confederate government. Once reinforced and resupplied, Buell prepared for a military showdown with Bragg. The War Department, however, had tired of what they considered Buell's lethargic leadership and ordered him to turn command of the Army of the Ohio over to General George H. THOMAS. But Thomas, a loyal subordinate, declined the appointment seeing that Buell was nearly ready to attack, and the latter retained his command. On October 8, 1862,

he encountered Bragg at Perryville, Kentucky, and a bloody battle raged. Buell enjoyed numerical superiority of 55,000 to 15,000—roughly three to one—but Bragg nearly managed to drive the Federals from the field before finally retreating. Buell, however, manifestly failed to pursue the defeated Southerners, and they leisurely withdrew through the Cumberland Gap and back into Tennessee. For this reason, he was relieved of command by the War Department on October 24, 1862, and was replaced by General William S. ROSECRANS.

Buell angrily contested his dismissal, claiming he was short on supplies, and demanded a court of inquiry. His claims were then investigated for several months, but the military commission issued a report without recommendation. Buell thus remained "awaiting orders" for the next two years until his term as general of volunteers expired. On June 1, 1864, Buell also resigned his

Don Carlos Buell *(Massachusetts Commandery Military Order of the Loyal Legion and the U.S. Army Military History Institute)*

regular army commission and left the service altogether. He then retired to Louisville as president of the Green River Iron Works until his death there on November 19, 1898. Buell retains the reputation as a talented disciplinarian and administrator but an essentially uninspired and plodding performer.

Further Reading

Broadwater, Robert P. *The Battle of Perryville, 1862: Culmination of the Failed Kentucky Campaign.* Jefferson, N.C.: McFarland, 2006.

Engle, Stephen D. *Don Carlos Buell: Most Promising of All.* Chapel Hill: University of North Carolina Press, 1999.

Hess, Earl J. *Banners to the Breeze: The Kentucky Campaign, Corinth, and Stones River.* Lincoln: University of Nebraska Press, 2000.

Noe, Kenneth. *Perryville: This Grand Havoc of Battle.* Lexington: University Press of Kentucky, 2001.

Prokopowicz, Gerald J. *All for the Regiment: The Army of the Ohio, 1861–1862.* Chapel Hill: University of North Carolina Press, 2001.

Ross, Charles D. *Civil War Acoustic Shadows.* Shippensburg, Pa.: White Mane Books, 2001.

Union general John Buford *(Library of Congress)*

Buford, John (1826–1863)

Union general

John Buford was born in Woodford, Kentucky, on March 4, 1826, and he relocated with his family to Rock Island, Illinois. From there he gained admittance to the U.S. Military Academy in 1844 and graduated four years later as a second lieutenant in the 2nd U.S. Dragoons. Buford then proceeded to the frontier, where he performed routine service in Texas, New Mexico, and Kansas for several years. In 1855 he rose to regimental quartermaster and that year accompanied General William S. Harney in a war against the Sioux. Buford fought well at the Battle of Ash Hollow, September 3, 1855, in which Little Thunder's band was defeated, and he won commendations from Colonel Philip St. George Cooke. Two years later, Buford accompanied Colonel Albert S. JOHNSTON in his Mormon Expedition of 1857–58, expertly handling quartermaster functions across a grueling, 1,000

mile, midwinter march. Buford rose to captain on March 9, 1859, and was serving with the regiment in Utah when the Civil War erupted in April 1861. To underscore his expertise in handling cavalry, he marched the 2nd Dragoons 1,500 miles to Washington, D.C., in only 60 days. Despite his consistently excellent performance, Buford remained unable to secure an independent command and spent the first year of the war as a major on the Inspector General's staff.

In July 1862 General John POPE arrived in the East to command of the newly constituted Army of Virginia and was appalled to find Buford, one of the military's most experienced cavalry officers, behind a desk. He thereupon appointed him a brigade commander with a rank of brigadier general. In this capacity, Buford defeated Confederate cavalry at Verdiersville, Virginia, on August 17, 1862, capturing the plumed hat of General J. E. B. STUART and signed orders from General Robert E. Lee. He fought equally well against superior Confederate numbers at Thoroughfare Gap on August 28–29 before being brushed aside by General James Longstreet's I Corps. In the process, Buford alerted Pope of Longstreet's arrival on his left flank, but the general failed to act on this valuable intelligence, and his army was nearly destroyed. On August 30 Buford received a severe wound while covering the Army of Virginia's retreat, but his good performance resulted in an appointment as chief of cavalry in the Army of the Potomac under General Joseph Hooker. He next bore a conspicuous role in General George Stoneman's raid during the Chancellorsville campaign of May 1863 and again covered the Union retreat. On June 9 Buford gained additional laurels by turning in a fine performance at Brandy Station, June 9, 1863, under General Alfred Pleasonton, affording additional proof that Union troopers had closed the qualitative gap with their Southern counterparts.

The war in the East took a new direction when General Lee struck north into Union territory and invaded Pennsylvania. Buford, having skirmished intermittently with Stuart's troopers at Aldie, Gap, Upperville, Middleburg, and Ashby's Gap, Virginia, covered the left flank of the I Corps under General John Reynolds. On arriving at the strategic road junction at Gettysburg, Buford encountered and drove off Confederate infantry in the area. He then promptly alerted superiors, dismounted his troopers, and prepared for combat along McPherson's Ridge. On July 1, elements of General Henry Heth's Confederate division stumbled headlong into Buford's position while foraging for shoes and were heavily repelled by his rapid-fire Spencer carbines. As more and more combatants were thrown in from both sides, Buford dutifully clung to the crossroads until he was relieved by Reynolds. He then shifted his forces to oppose the approaching corps of General Richard S. Ewell, delaying them several hours. His tenacious conduct allowed the main Union force under General George Meade to occupy the high ground overlooking Gettysburg, a major factor in the ensuing Confederate defeat.

After Gettysburg, Buford skirmished intermittently with the Confederate rear guard and fought in a heavy action near Williamsport, Maryland on July 6, 1863. The following November, his fortunes crested with an appointment as cavalry commander in the Army of the Cumberland. Buford, unfortunately, was stricken with typhoid and obtained a badly needed medical leave. He died in the house of General Stoneman on December 16, 1863, just hours after President Abraham Lincoln promoted him to major general. His death was a serious loss to the Army of the Potomac, particularly its mounted arm.

Further Reading

Longacre, Edward G. *General John Buford: A Military Biography.* Cambridge, Mass.: Da Capo Press, 2003.

McKinney, Joseph W. *Brandy Station, Virginia, June 9, 1863: The Largest Cavalry Battle of the Civil War.* Jefferson, N.C.: McFarland, 2006.

Newton, Steven H. *McPherson's Ridge: The First Battle for the High Ground, July 1, 1863.* Cambridge, Mass.: Da Capo Press, 2002.

Phipps, Michael. *"The Devil's to Pay": General John Buford, United States Army.* Gettysburg, Pa.: Farnsworth House Military Impressions, 1995.

Wittenberg, Eric J. *The Union Cavalry Comes of Age: Hartwood's Church to Brandy Station, 1863.* Dulles, Va.: Brassey's, 2005.

Burnside, Ambrose E. (1824–1881)

Union general

Ambrose Everett Burnside was born in Liberty, Indiana, on May 23, 1824, the son of a former South Carolinian who had emancipated his slaves. After working as a tailor several years, he was admitted to the U.S. Military Academy in 1843 and graduated four years later as a second lieutenant in the 3rd U.S. Artillery. Burnside arrived in Mexico during final phases of the 1846–48 war there, seeing no combat. He subsequently fulfilled routine garrison duties along the western frontier and was slightly wounded in a skirmish with Apaches. His experience in the field convinced him that cavalrymen needed better weapons than the standard-issue Hall carbine, so in 1853 he resigned his commission and established a gun factory in Bristol, Rhode Island. Burnside then designed and manufactured a functional, rapid-fire carbine for military use, but he went bankrupt when anticipated government contracts failed to materialize. Fortunately, his good friend George B. McCLELLAN offered help in 1858 by appointing him treasurer of the Illinois Central Railroad. Burnside worked there until the Civil War broke out in April 1861. That month, he returned east to become colonel of the 1st Rhode Island Volunteers and subsequently led a brigade at Bull Run the following July. He also befriended President Abraham LINCOLN, who arranged his promotion to brigadier general of volunteers on August 6, 1861.

Union general Ambrose E. Burnside *(Library of Congress)*

In October 1861 Burnside received an important assignment: He was to accompany the fleet of Commodore Louis M. Goldsborough to the North Carolina coast, establish a base, and recruit from what were believed to be thousands of Southern Unionists. He performed well at the seizure of Roanoke Island and New Bern in the spring of 1862, capturing 2,500 prisoners and 32 cannon while also closing the Albemarle and Pamlico inlets to blockade-runners. This success made him a national hero, and Lincoln rewarded him with a promotion to major general and command of the IX Corps in the Army of the Potomac under General McClellan. He had previously, perhaps conscious of his own limitations as a leader, declined Lincoln's offer to serve as the army's leader. Lincoln again proffered command of the Army of the Potomac in the wake of General John POPE's debacle at Second Manassas that August, and again Burnside demurred. He next fought at the Battle of Antietam on September 17, 1862, where he commanded both his IX Corps and General Joseph L. HOOKER's I Corps. However, Burnside's performed sluggishly and, by failing to cross the Rohrbach Bridge in time, lost an opportunity to crush the Confederate left flank.

After McClellan was dismissed on November 7, 1861, Lincoln offered Burnside command of the Army of the Potomac a third time, and he reluctantly accepted. He immediately concocted an elaborate scheme to slip behind the Confederates by bridging the Rappahannock River at Fredericksburg, Virginia, and making a sudden dash on Richmond. Burnside anticipated that this maneuver would force General Robert E. LEE's army out into the open where it could be engaged to his advantage. However, pontoons and other bridging equipment were slow in arriving, and Lee had ample time to occupy and fortify Fredericksburg ahead of Union forces. On December 13 Burnside nonetheless put his plan in motion and hurled 122,000 men against Confederate fieldworks with disastrous effects: Union forces were bloodily repulsed with more than 12,000 casualties. In January 1863 Burnside further sullied his reputation by proposing a midwinter march around the Confederates, which, following the onset of heavy rain, quickly degenerated into the infamous "mud march." Lincoln, with few regrets, finally dismissed Burnside from the Army of the Potomac on January 26, 1863, and replaced him with Hooker.

In March 1863 Burnside transferred to the Department of the Ohio, where he again displayed some of his previous energy. He moved quickly to subdue "Copperhead" activities of former congressman Clement L. Vallandigham, arresting him for treason. He then promulgated General Order No. 38, which shut down two newspapers and promised swift imprisonment for any individual suspected of pro-Confederate sympathies. Ultimately, Lincoln repudiated Burnside's measures, but they proved popular with local Unionists. He then orchestrated military movements culminating in the defeat and capture of General John H. MORGAN's raiding party in Ohio. In September 1863 Burnside marshaled his forces, advanced through the Cumberland Gap, and captured Knoxville, Tennessee. Two months later, he artfully withstood a determined siege by General James LONGSTREET's veteran I Corps, thereby prevented him from rushing reinforcements to beleaguered Confederate forces at Chattanooga. For these effective actions, he received the thanks of Congress. Burnside had partially rehabilitated his reputation, so Lincoln also directed him to return to the Army of the Potomac where he resumed command of his old IX Corps under General Ulysses S. GRANT.

In the spring and summer of 1864, Burnside accompanied Grant's overland campaign against Richmond, Virginia. He fought competently at the bloody encounters of Wilderness, Spotsylvania Court House, and in the trenches of Petersburg. His downfall occurred on July 4, 1864, when he failed to support Union troops from his corps adequately as they waged the infamous Battle of the Crater, a stinging Union defeat. A court of inquiry conducted by General George G. MEADE found him at fault, although there was plenty of blame to go around, and Burnside was relieved from active duty. The fact that Meade had removed

a large contingent of specially trained African-American troops from Burnside's command prior to the battle—contributing materially to the debacle—went unmentioned. Burnside finally resigned his commission on April 15, 1865, and reentered the civilian sector.

Burnside subsequently returned to Rhode Island where he enjoyed a highly successful political career. He won three consecutive terms as governor (1866–68) before being elected to the U.S. Senate in 1874. That year, he also served as national commander of the Grand Army of the Republic, a noted veteran's organization. Burnside died in Bristol, Rhode Island, on September 13, 1881, a capable commander promoted beyond his abilities. Ironically, he is best remembered for his bushy facial whiskers, which have since entered popular lexicon as "sideburns."

Further Reading

Brooks, Victor. *The Fredericksburg Campaign: October 1862–January 1863.* Conshohocken, Pa.: Combined Publishing, 2000.

Cannan, John. *Burnside's Bridge, Antietam.* Conshohocken, Pa.: Combined Publishing, 2001.

———. *The Crater: Burnside's Assault on the Confederate Trenches, July 30, 1864.* London: Leo Cooper, 2003.

O'Reilly, Francis A. *The Fredericksburg Campaign: Winter War on the Rappahannock.* Baton Rouge: Louisiana State University Press, 2003.

Pfanz, Donald C. *War So Terrible: A Popular History of the Battle of Fredericksburg.* Richmond, Va.: Page One History Publications, 2003.

Rable, George. *Fredericksburg! Fredericksburg!* Chapel Hill: University of North Carolina Press, 2002.

Taaffe, Stephen R. *Commanding the Army of Potomac.* Lawrence: University Press of Kansas, 2006.

Wert, Jeffrey D. *The Sword of Lincoln: The Army of the Potomac.* New York: Simon and Schuster, 2005.

Butler, Benjamin F. (1818–1893)

Union general

Benjamin Franklin Butler was born in Deerfield, New Hampshire, on November 5, 1818, and, in 1838, he graduated from Waterville (Colby) College, Maine, with a law degree. He eventually

Union general Benjamin F. Butler *(Library of Congress)*

established a practice in Massachusetts but gradually forsook it in favor of a career in politics. Here, Butler demonstrated a knack for canvassing people's sympathies and was repeatedly elected to the state legislature as a Democrat. Butler also served as a major general of state militia. In 1859 he made an unsuccessful run for the governorship, and the following year, he arrived in Charleston, South Carolina, to vote for Jefferson DAVIS as the party's presidential candidate. Staunchly pro-Southern, he threw his support behind John C. BRECKINRIDGE at the breakaway convention held at Baltimore. However, once Southern states began to secede after Abraham LINCOLN's electoral victory that November, Butler quickly professed his loyalty to the Union and received a brigadier general's commission in the state militia. In this capacity, he performed critically important work in the early days of the war by taking the 8th Massachusetts Regiment into Baltimore, Maryland, suppressing pro-Confederate rioters, and then restoring rail lines and other communications to Washington, D.C. A grateful President Lincoln then appointed him the first major general of volunteers and placed him in charge of Union forces at Fortress Monroe, Virginia.

Controversy was never far from Butler's door. While at Fortress Monroe, he electrified the North and antagonized the South by refusing to return three African-American slaves who reached his camp. Declaring them "contraband of war," he allowed them to work for the army. Such a stance made him the darling of Radical Republicans, whose ranks Butler joined to enhance his standing with the government. However, Butler's indelible ineptitude manifested itself on June 10, 1861, when troops under his command badly bungled a skirmish with General John B. MAGRUDER's Confederates at Big Bethel, Virginia. Lincoln, unwilling or unable to remove such a politically valuable asset, then appointed Butler to accompany Commodore Silas H. Strigham on a six-ship expedition to Cape Hatteras, North Carolina. On August 27, 1861, Butler's 800 men helped capture Pamlico Sound, two forts, and 615 prisoners—the first Union victory after the debacle at Bull Run in July. Lincoln then granted him a leave of absence to recruit soldiers in New England while even more ambitious plans for him were developing.

In April 1862, Butler accompanied Commodore David G. FARRAGUT on an ambitious, combined expedition against New Orleans, Louisiana. On May 1, 1862, Farragut successfully ran his fleet past Southern forts and compelled the city to surrender, whereupon Butler acted as military governor. His seven-month tenure proved both controversial and acrimonious. Butler treated Southern defiance harshly. In one instance, he hanged Louisianan William Mumford for lowering an American flag. He also thwarted invective heaped on his troops by Creole ladies through his infamous Order No. 28, the much reviled "Woman Order," which required all disrespectful females to be treated as prostitutes. The Southern press was enraged by Butler's cavalier attitude and dubbed him "Beast Butler." Confederate president Jefferson DAVIS went so far as to brand him an outlaw and to be "immediately executed if captured." On the brighter side, Butler worked conscientiously to improve city sanitation, assist the poor, and actively recruit African-American slaves into the Union army. However, when he and several subordinates became embroiled in financial improprieties, he became more of a liability than an asset. In December 1862, President Lincoln felt emboldened enough to remove Butler from command and replace him with the equally inept general Nathaniel P. BANKS.

Butler remained inactive through 1863 while political allies pressured the president for his reinstatement. In December, he gained appointment as commanding officer of the Department of Virginia and North Carolina, and with it the Union XVIII Corps. In the spring, his command was expanded to include the X Corps and redesignated the Army of the James. With these 40,000 men Butler was supposed to work closely with General Ulysses S. GRANT in coordinating attacks against the Richmond–Petersburg line. However, in May 1864, Butler moved sluggishly against Petersburg, then lightly defended, and he was stopped in his tracks by General Pierre G. T. BEAUREGARD at the Battle of Drewry's Bluff, May 12–16. Thereafter, the Army of the James was effectively "bottled up" on the peninsula of Bermuda Hundred and was unable to participate in the struggle for Richmond. Grant wanted him removed for squandering these military assets, but Lincoln waited until his successful reelection bid in November 1864 before relieving Butler and sending him back to Massachusetts. Butler, however, still possessed powerful allies in the Republican Party, so in December 1864, he was teamed with Admiral David D. PORTER for a joint expedition against Fort Fisher outside of Wilmington, North Carolina. On December 23, Butler launched an ill-fated attempt to destroy the fort with an old vessel crammed with explosives, which this resulted in nothing but spectacular pyrotechnics. He landed his troops on December 25—and then promptly reembarked them after pronounc-

ing Fort Fisher unassailable. Such display of wanton incompetence finally prompted Grant to petition Lincoln for Butler's immediate removal, which finally materialized on January 7, 1865. Eight days later, Fort Fisher was forcefully carried by Admiral Porter and the same force under General Alfred H. TERRY. Butler remained unemployed for the remainder of the war and finally resigned his commission on November 30, 1865.

Back in civilian life, Butler resumed his successful career in politics. He was elected five times to the U.S. House of Representatives as a Radical Republican and also served one term as governor of Massachusetts in 1882. While in Congress, he helped spearhead the impeachment drive against President Andrew Johnson for his alleged lenient treatment of former Confederates. In 1884, Butler, ambitious as ever, also made an unsuccessful bid for the presidency at the head of the Greenback Party. He died in Washington, D.C., on January 1, 1893, one of the most incompetent "political generals" of the Civil War.

Further Reading

Butler, Benjamin F. *Butler's Book: Autobiography and Personal Reminiscences of Major General Benjamin F. Butler.* Boston: A. M. Thayer, 1892.

Dawson, Joseph G. "Lincoln's Political Generals." Unpublished Ph.D. diss., Texas A & M University, 2004.

Goss, Thomas J. *The War within the Union High Command: Politics and Generalship during the Civil War.* Lawrence: University Press of Kansas, 2003.

McCaslin, Richard B. *The Last Stronghold: The Campaign for Fort Fisher.* Abilene, Tex.: McWhiney Foundation Press, 2003.

Morgan, Michael. "The Beast at His Best." *Civil War Times* 42, no. 6 (2004): 24–31.

Pena, Christopher. *General Butler: Beast or Patriot: New Orleans Occupation, May–December, 1862.* Bloomington, Ind.: 1st Books, 2003.

Smith, Michael T. "The Beast Unleashed: Benjamin F. Butler and Conceptions of Masculinity in the Civil War North." *New England Quarterly* 79, no. 2 (2006): 248–276.

C

Canby, Edward R. S. (1817–1873)

Union general

Edward Richard Sprigg Canby was born at Piatt's Landing, Kentucky, on November 9, 1817, and raised in Crawfordsville, Indiana. He graduated from the U.S. Military Academy near the bottom of his class in 1839 and received a second lieutenant's commission in the 2nd U.S. Infantry. Canby then fought in Florida's Second Seminole War between 1839 and 1842 before rotating west for a stint of routine garrison duty. Promoted to captain in 1846, he accompanied General Winfield SCOTT's army the following year in the Mexican War (1846–48), winning two brevet promotions for bravery at Cerro Gordo and Churubusco. After the war, he joined the adjutant general's department of the 10th Military District in California until March 1855, when the rank of major, 10th U.S. Infantry was proffered. In this capacity, Canby marched with Colonel Albert S. JOHNSTON during the famous Mormon expedition of 1857–58 before resuming mundane garrison duties and minor campaigning against the Navajo in 1860–61.

The onset of the Civil War in April 1861 found Canby serving as commander of Fort Defiance, New Mexico Territory, and within months, he rose to colonel of the newly raised 19th U.S. Infantry. In light of his talent for military administration, he gained appointment as commander of the Department of New Mexico, headquartered at Fort Craig. His intense efforts at recruiting, training, and equipping soldiers throughout this desolate region paid dividends in the spring of 1862 when a Confederate column under General Henry H. SIBLEY invaded New Mexico from Texas. Canby unsuccessfully resisted Sibley at a hard-fought encounter near Valverde on February 21, 1862, at which point he resorted to Fabian tactics and lured his opponent farther from supply lines. Once reinforced by Colorado Volunteers under Colonel John M. Chivington, Canby resumed the offensive, attacking Sibley's scattered detachments at Glorieta Pass on March 28, 1862. When the Confederates lost their entire baggage train to a surprise Union assault, Sibley had no recourse but to fall back to Texas. Canby then shadowed the Confederates closely, skirmishing intensely at Peralta on April 15, and then allowing them to withdraw back to El Paso unmolested. His solid, if unspectacular, leadership preserved the New Mexico Territory for the Union and stopped the Confederate drive on California.

Shortly afterward, Canby was reinforced by the California column under Colonel James CARLETON and received a well-deserved promoted to brigadier general on March 31, 1862. The following September, he departed and transferred to the War Department in Washington, D.C., to serve as Secretary of War Edwin M. Stanton's assistant. Canby performed well, and in March 1863, he temporarily assumed control of troops tasked with restoring order in New York City after violent antidraft riots. On May 11, 1864, he advanced to major general and gained appointment as commander of the Military Division of West Mississippi, eventually replacing the inept general Nathaniel P. BANKS. On November 6, 1864, Canby was severely wounded in a Confederate guerrilla attack while steaming up the White River, Arkansas, but he recovered in time to orchestrate a campaign against Mobile, Alabama. In concert with troops under General Frederick Steele and a Union fleet commanded by Admiral Henry K. Thatcher, Canby conducted a methodical campaign that gradually reduced Confederate fortifications and drove the city to capitulate on April 12, 1865. After Southern resistance collapsed, Canby was called on to receive the surrender of General Richard TAYLOR's forces on May 4, 1865, followed by that of General Simon B. Buckner (representing Edmund KIRBY-SMITH) on May 26. These were the final Confederate field armies east of the Mississippi River to lay down their arms.

Canby enjoyed a highly active postwar career commencing in 1866 when he received promotion to brigadier general in the regular army. He also headed on Reconstruction efforts in Virginia and the Carolinas, becoming the only military figure to lead more than one department. In August 1870, Canby became commander of the Department of Columbia, which included the Washington, Idaho, and Alaska territories. Three years later, he accepted responsibility for the Military Division of the Pacific. In March 1873, tensions with the Modoc tribe of northern California exploded into open warfare, and Canby was called to restore the peace. He earnestly tried to achieve a settlement by negotiating directly with aggrieved Modoc leaders in face-to-face talks at Siskiyou. On April 11, 1873, while conversing with Modoc chief Captain Jack, he was suddenly shot and killed. He is the only high-ranking military officer killed at the hands of Native Americans.

Further Reading

Alberts, Don E. *The Battle of Glorieta: Union Victory in the West.* College Station: Texas A & M University Press, 1998.

Edrington, Thomas S. *The Battle of Glorieta Pass: A Gettysburg in the West, March 26–28, 1862.* Albuquerque: University of New Mexico Press, 1998.

Heyman, Max L. *Prudent Soldier: A Biography of Major General E. R. S. Canby.* Glendale, Calif.: Arthur H. Clark, 1959.

O'Brien, Sean M. *Mobile, 1865: Last Stand of the Confederacy.* Westport, Conn.: Praeger, 2001.

Waugh, John C. *Last Stand at Mobile.* Abilene, Tex.: McWhiney Foundation, 2001.

Whitlock, Flint. *Distant Bugles, Distant Drums: The Union Response to the Confederate Invasion of New Mexico.* Boulder, Colo.: University Press of Colorado, 2006.

Carleton, James H. (1814–1873)

Union general

James Henry Carleton was born in Lubec, Maine, on December 27, 1814, and as a young man he aspired to be a writer. To that end, he corresponded with noted novelist Charles Dickens, but Carleton reached a turning point in his life during the so-called Aroostook War between Maine and New Brunswick. He served as a militia lieutenant and took an immediate liking to military service, so Carleton sought out a regular army commission. In 1839 he was commissioned a second lieutenant in the 1st U.S. Dragoons and two years later reported for duty at Fort Gibson, Indian Territory (Oklahoma). During the next few years, Carleton performed routine garrison service at various frontier posts and also accompanied numerous dragoon expedition into the hinterlands. In 1844 Carleton rode with Colonel Stephen W. Kearney, the noted explorer, along the Oregon Trail to South Pass and, consistent with his literary bent, published a colorful account for the frontier newspaper *Spirit of the Times.* When the Mexican War commenced in 1846, Carleton served as aide-de-camp to General John E. Wool and the following year received a brevet promotion to captain at the Battle of Buena Vista. Protracted illness precluded further wartime service, and Carleton resumed garrison duty at posts throughout the Old Southwest. In 1852 he served as commander of Fort Union, New Mexico Territory, and conducted numerous forays against hostile Jicarilla Apache with the noted scout Christopher "Kit" Carson. By the advent of the Civil War in April 1861, Carleton enjoyed a well-deserved reputation as an efficient, if humorless, frontier administrator.

In August 1861, Carleton, then stationed in California, was promoted to colonel of the 1st California Infantry. The following spring, General George Wright, commanding the Department of the Pacific, chose this veteran frontier fighter to lead 2,000 men eastward across the deserts and assist the Union war effort in New Mexico. Carleton did so with commendable efficiency and shepherded the so-called California column into Tucson, Arizona Territory, in May 1862. His approach induced Confederate forces under General Henry H. SIBLEY to abandon the New Mexico Territory altogether and slip back into Texas. Carleton, a brigadier general as of April 28, 1862, next succeeded General Edward R. S. CANBY as head of the Department of New Mexico and immediately subjected the unruly outlands to martial law. Confederate sympathizers such as Sylvester Mowry were promptly arrested and detained while Carleton sparred constantly with Judge Joseph Knapp over the legality of various detentions.

However, the biggest challenge facing Carleton's quest for frontier order came from the Navajo and Mescalero Apache. He summarily ordered both tribes into close confinement on reservations and, when they refused to obliged, conducted a scorched-earth war against them. Carleton then ordered Kit Carson and other scouts to execute any male Native Americans found in arms, but they wisely ignored such punitive measures and simply burned their crops to force them into submission. After the Navajo submitted, Carleton rounded up 9,000 tribe members and marched them 300 miles to reservations at Bosque Redondo in what has become reviled as the "Long Walk." His harshness toward both whites and Native Americans proved unpopular and draconian, but he maintained order throughout a precarious time in frontier history. For his efforts, he gained brevet promotion to major general in 1865

and transferred to a new command in Texas the following year. Two years later, the government reversed Carleton's policies and allowed the Navaho to return home.

In October 1866, Carleton became lieutenant colonel of the 4th U.S. Infantry, then stationed at San Antonio. He remained there seven years before dying of pneumonia on January 7, 1873, a harsh but effective frontier administrator.

Further Reading
Dunlay, Thomas W. *Kit Carson and the Indians*. Lincoln: University of Nebraska Press, 2000.
Hunt, Aurora. *Major General James Henry Carleton, Western Frontier Dragoon*. Glendale, Calif.: Arthur Clark, 1958.
Hutton, Paul A., ed. *Soldiers West: Biographies from the Military Frontier*. Lincoln: University of Nebraska Press, 1987.
Masich, Andrew E. *The Civil War in Arizona: The Story of the California Volunteers*. Norman: University of Oklahoma Press, 2006.
Miller, Darlis. *The California Column in New Mexico*. Albuquerque: University of New Mexico Press, 1982.
Pelzer, Louis, ed. *The Prairie Logbooks: Dragoon Campaigns to the Pawnee Villages in 1844 and to the Rocky Mountains in 1845*. Lincoln: University of Nebraska Press, 1983.

Cleburne, Patrick R. (1828–1864)
Confederate general

Patrick Ronayne Cleburne was born in County Cork, Ireland, on March 16, 1828, the son of a noted physician. He aspired to follow his father by pursuing pharmacology at the University of Dublin, but he failed the entrance exam. Deeply ashamed, Cleburne next joined the British army by enlisting in the 49th Foot in 1846, serving three years. He eventually purchased his release in 1849 and emigrated to the United States. After settling in Helena, Arkansas, in 1850 he worked as a druggist, studied law, and opened a successful law practice in 1855, the same year he became a naturalized citizen. By 1860, with the storm clouds of secession gathering, Cleburne joined the Yell Rifles as a private and eventually was elected captain. This unit subsequently joined nine other companies to form the 1st Arkansas Infantry, in which Cleburne became colonel as of May 14, 1861. As the Civil War unfolded, Cleburne's unit was amalgamated into a division commanded by General William J. HARDEE, and the two leaders became fast friends. During the next three years, their military activities invariably were intermingled.

In the fall of 1861, Cleburne accepted command of a brigade under General Albert S. JOHNSTON's command at Bowling Green, Kentucky, and they accompanied that leader as he fell back to Tennessee. Cleburne, now a brigadier general, first saw action at the Battle of Shiloh on April 6, 1862, where he formed the extreme left wing of the Confederate advance and drove Union forces up against the Tennessee River. The next day, a determined Union counterattack forced Confederates from the field, but Cleburne's brigade formed a successful rear guard preventing the retreat from becoming a rout. Cleburne subsequently accompanied the invasion of Kentucky under General Braxton BRAGG that summer, being severely wounded at the Battle of Richmond on August 30, 1862. Fortunately, he recovered in time to distinguish himself at the Battle of Perryville on October 8, 1862, suffering two additional wounds. Cleburne then fought capably again at the Battle of Stone's River (Murfreesboro) (December 31, 1862–January 3, 1863), where his ruthless attack ran the Union right wing back four miles. Afterward, he accompanied Bragg's army back to Shelbyville and, like many subordinates, came to despise his commanding officer. Nonetheless, he was promoted to major general as of November 1862, becoming the Confederacy's ranking officer of foreign birth.

Cleburne next accompanied the Army of Tennessee throughout the Tullahoma campaign, which afforded no real fighting and resulted in another Confederate retreat. However, Bragg then suddenly turned and struck at the Army of the Cumberland under General William S. ROSE-

CRANS at Chickamauga on September 19–20, and Cleburne was in his element. He so ferociously assailed the Union position that Rosecrans shifted his men away from the center—just as General James LONGSTREET came crashing through the center. Cleburne performed equally well during his dogged defense at the Battle of Missionary Ridge, November 25, 1863, and repulsed several determined attacks by General William T. SHERMAN. Bragg then retreated again, and Cleburne's division, assisted by General Joseph WHEELER's cavalry, remained behind at Ringgold Gap as a rear guard. On November 27, 1863, he expertly repelled several attempts by General Joseph L. HOOKER to force the pass, ensuring a safe Confederate withdrawal. For all his skill in combat, Cleburne twice received the thanks of the Confederate Congress, and he was popularly heralded as the "Stonewall of the West."

Confederate general Patrick R. Cleburne *(Library of Congress)*

Cleburne seemed slated for higher command, but in the winter of 1863–64, his prospects for promotion suddenly waned. Irish by birth and never having owned slaves, he circulated a petition calling on the Confederate government to enlist African Americans into the army in exchange for freedom. Such a move might tap into a half-million willing recruits and, furthermore, also induce the hesitant governments of Britain and France to bestow diplomatic recognition. But Confederate authorities were stunned by his proposal, and President Jefferson DAVIS, who took steps to have Cleburne's suggestion quashed, also withheld his well-deserved promotion to lieutenant general. He nevertheless continued functioning as a divisional leader with fine performances under General Joseph E. JOHNSTON at Kennesaw Mountain and Bald Hill on June 27 and July 22, 1864. Cleburne performed his final duties to the Confederacy while accompanying General John B. HOOD's ill-fated offensive into Tennessee that fall. On November 30, 1864, he led his men in a desperate charge on the entrenched Union forces of General John M. SCHOFIELD at Franklin. Cleburne lost two horses under him, yet he rallied his men and charged on foot—only to be shot dead within 50 yards of Federal lines. He was one of six Southern generals slain that day, and his remains eventually were interred at Helena, Arkansas. Cleburne's natural aggressiveness and tactical finesse renders him the most accomplished Confederate officer of his grade, and he was possibly the finest divisional commander of the entire war.

Further Reading

Brennan, Patrick. "The Battle of Franklin." *North & South* 8, no. 1 (2005): 26–46.

Evans, E. Raymond. *Cleburne's Defense of Ringgold Gap.* Signal Mountain, Tenn.: Mountain Press, 1998.

Farley, M. Foster. "The Battle of Franklin." *Military Heritage* 1, no. 5 (2000): 60–67.

Joslyn, Mauriel L. "The Youth and Irish Military Service of Patrick Cleburne (1828–1864)." *Irish Sword* 23, no. 19 (2002): 87–98.

Joslyn, Mauriel L., ed. *A Meteor Shining Brightly: Essays on the Life an Career of Major General Patrick R. Cleburne.* Macon, Ga.: Mercer University Press, 2000.

Logsdon, David R. *Eyewitnesses at the Battle of Franklin.* Nashville, Tenn.: Kettle Mills Press, 2000.

Crittenden, George B. (1812–1880)
Confederate general

George Bib Crittenden was born in Russellville, Kentucky, on March 20, 1812, the son of a prominent state politician and future governor. He attended the U.S. Military Academy in 1827 and graduated four years later, midway in a class of 45. Crittenden subsequently served as an infantry lieutenant during the Black Hawk War of 1832 and then performed several years of routine garrison work in Alabama and Georgia. However, he resigned his commission in April 1833 to study law at Transylvania University. He was admitted to the bar but then abandoned his profession for military adventurism in the Republic of Texas. In December 1842 Crittenden volunteered to accompany a 250-man expedition against Ciudad Merir, Mexico, under Colonel William S. Fisher. When the entire company was captured, he and his messmates endured harsh captivity in a filthy Mexico City prison. The inmates staged a failed escape attempt, at which point their captors decided to execute every 10th man on the draw of a black bean. Crittenden pulled a white bean, handed it to a friend who had a family, and then drew another white bean and luckily escaped the firing squad. He spent nearly a year in prison before Secretary of State Daniel Webster managed to arrange his release. In 1846 Crittenden resumed his military activities as a captain of mounted Kentucky riflemen, and he received a brevet promotion for bravery at the battles of Contreras and Churubusco. After the war, he reentered the U.S. Army with a rank of major, but his career was jeopardized by frequent dissipation. Nonetheless, Crittenden rose to lieutenant colonel and was a ranking officer in the New Mexico Territory when the Civil War erupted in April 1861.

Back in Kentucky, Crittenden's father, John J. Crittenden, father of the "Crittenden Compromise" to avert war, begged his son not to join the Confederacy. His own younger brother, Thomas

L. Crittenden, joined the Union army as a high-ranking officer. But Crittenden, for reasons of his own, sided with the South and resigned his commission. By June 1861, he was a Confederate brigadier general commanding forces at Knoxville, Tennessee. A popular figure, Crittenden rose to major general the following November, and he was ordered to assume command of Southern forces from Generals Felix K. Zollicoffer and William H. Carroll. That November—and without authorization—Zollicoffer took 4,000 men and entrenched them on the north bank of the Cumberland River near Beech Grove, Kentucky. He did this despite the fact that the state legislature had declared its neutrality and wished combatants from either side to remove their forces.

By January 1862, Zollicoffer's isolated detachment had attracted the attention of Union forces under General George H. THOMAS, and Crittenden marched to reinforce him. Thomas, meanwhile, decided to dislodge the Confederates, then foolishly deployed with a flooded river to their back, and he advanced with 7,000 men. Crittenden, however, resolved to strike first, and he hastily gathered up his small force before Thomas could combine with other Federals. On January 19, 1862, he fiercely assailed the Union camp near Mills Springs (Logan's Crossroads), Kentucky. The Confederates enjoyed success initially until General Zollicoffer became separated from his troops in a fog, blundered into Union lines, and was shot dead. Thomas then adroitly dispersed Crittenden's renewed assaults with a deadly enfilade fire. The battered Southerners withdrew with heavy losses while Thomas pursued them leisurely. Crittenden managed to evacuate Beech Grove and get the bulk of his forces across the rain-swollen Cumberland River, although forced to abandon his baggage and artillery. Mills Springs, though small in scope, harbored huge consequences for it peeled back the first line of Confederate defenses in Kentucky, exposing Forts Henry and Donelson to attack by General Ulysses S. GRANT the following month.

No sooner did Crittenden's command wearily trudge into Murfreesboro, Tennessee, than he faced accusations of being drunk in battle. He strenuously rebuked the charges, whereupon General Albert S. JOHNSTON appointed him to command his reserve at Iuka in northern Mississippi. Crittenden thus received a second chance to rehabilitate his reputation, but on April 1, 1862, General William J. HARDEE arrived at his camp on inspection and found it in disarray. Crittenden was arrested and court-martialed for drunkenness, and he resigned his commission in October 1862. He spent the balance of the war acting as a volunteer aide on the staff of General John S. Williams. Crittenden returned to Frankfort, Kentucky, after the war, where, thanks to family connections, he was installed as the state librarian in 1867. He died in obscurity at Danville on November 27, 1880, one of the least efficient Confederate commanders of the western theater.

Further Reading

Dalton, David C. "Zollicoffer, Crittenden, and the Mill Springs Campaign." *Filson Club Historical Quarterly* 60 (1986): 463–471.

Hafendorfer, Kenneth A. *Mill Springs: Campaign and Battle of Mill Springs, Kentucky.* Louisville, Ky.: KH Press, 2001.

Hess, Earl J. *Banners to the Breeze: The Kentucky Campaigns, Corinth, and Stone's River.* Lincoln: University of Nebraska Press, 2000.

Mason, Kevin G. "Black Sabbath: The Battle of Mill Springs." Unpublished master's thesis, University of Tennessee, 1997.

Myers, Raymond E. *General Felix Zollicoffer and the Battle of Mill Springs.* Louisville, Ky.: Filson Club Historical Society, 1998.

Stevens, Peter F. "The Black Bean Draw." *American History* 32, no. 4 (1997): 36–40, 63–64.

Crook, George (1829–1890)

Union general

George Crook was born near Dayton, Ohio, on September 23, 1829, the son of farmers. After passing through the U.S. Military Academy in 1852, he served as a second lieutenant with the 4th U.S. Infantry at various posts in California and Oregon. Crook partook of innumerable skirmishes

Union general George Crook *(Library of Congress)*

with hostile Native Americans and in 1857 was struck by an arrow, a wound that he carried for life. But Crook, unlike most contemporaries, studied the native tribes closely to learn more about them and thus avail himself more innovative tactics against them. In time, he came to empathize with them and frequently railed against the civilian bureaucrats in Washington, D.C., who exploited them. By 1861, Crook was a lowly infantry captain, and that May he transferred east with expectations for fighting in the then-unfolding Civil War. That September, he was made colonel of the 36th Ohio Infantry and spent a year rendering useful service in westernmost Virginia. Crook then rose to brigadier general of volunteers in August 1862 and acquitted himself well in heavy fighting at South Mountain and Antietam that fall. He subsequently transferred west, commanding a cavalry division in General William S. ROSE-CRANS's Army of the Cumberland. Crook bore a full measure of campaigning at Tullahoma and distinguished himself at the bloody encounter at

Chickamauga on September 19–20, 1863. After Rosecrans fell back to Chattanooga, Tennessee, Crook was entrusted with keeping Union supply lines open, and, on October 6, 1863, he defeated Confederate raiders under General Joseph WHEELER at Farmington and drove them across the Tennessee River. He then rose by brevet to regular colonel shortly afterward.

In the spring of 1864 Crook was back east again as commander of the Department of West Virginia. As such, he conducted several successful raids against Confederate communications throughout the Kanawha District. On July 23–24, he was surprised and heavily defeated at Kernstown, Virginia, by resurgent Confederates under General Jubal A. EARLY. In August 1864 Crook nonetheless succeeded the inept general David Hunter as commander of the Department of West Virginia. He also joined General Philip H. SHERIDAN's Army of the Shenandoah, commanding the VIII Corps, and he was conspicuously engaged in several pitched battles against Early's hard-charging Confederates. These included the Union victories at Winchester, Fisher's Hill, and, last, Cedar Creek on October 19, 1864, where he was initially surprised by Early but then rallied his men and helped win the day. Crook then suddenly fell captive to Confederate partisans led by Captain John H. McNeil and spent several weeks in confinement at Richmond's notorious Libby Prison. He was exchanged and returned to service in time to serve in the final phases of the Richmond–Petersburg campaign. On April 1, 1865, Crook's cavalry was heavily employed at the decisive victory at Five Forks, Virginia, and contributed greatly to the boxing in of General Robert E. LEE at Appomattox. Crook closed the war with the final ranks of brevet major general of volunteers and brevet major general, U.S. Army.

After the war, Crook reverted back to his regular rank of lieutenant colonel, 32nd U.S. Infantry, and returned to the western frontier. He soon emerged as one of America's greatest Indian fighters, commencing with a successful campaign to subdue the Paiutes of Oregon in 1868. Three years later, President Ulysses S. GRANT dispatched him to Arizona, where he helped suppress an Apache uprising led by Cochise. Disregarding army dogma, he pioneered the use of pack-mules for supplies and friendly Apache scouts to track down hostile natives. Moreover, his respect and affection for Native Americans earned him the moniker "Gray Fox" from the people he subdued. In 1876 Crook participated in the great uprising in the Black Hills of the Dakotas, and he was defeated by Chief Crazy Horse at the Rose Bud on March 17, 1876, which indirectly led to the death of Colonel George A. CUSTER one week later. Crook rebounded by attacking and destroying the village of Chief American Horse at Slim Buttes on September 9, 1876. With the Sioux and Cheyenne finally brought under control, Crook made it his personal policy to protect Native Americans from grasping Indian agents and meandering frontiersmen to forestall future outbreaks of violence.

In 1882 frontier violence flared up when the Apache rose under the leadership of Geronimo. Crook pursued the wily chief with a single company of cavalry and 200 friendly Apaches deep into Mexican territory, and he convinced him to surrender. Geronimo again escaped from the reservation in 1885, but Crook's lenient policies had run their course with the government, and he was eventually replaced by General Nelson A. Miles. Ultimately, Miles was forced to employ Apache scouts in similar fashion to bring Geronimo to bay. Crook subsequently took charge of the Division of the Missouri in May 1888, headquartered at Chicago, Illinois, where he directed final phases of the Indian wars. Though far removed from the frontier, he nonetheless remained a strident spokesman on behalf on Native American rights until his death there on March 21, 1890. He was also one of the Union's most capable divisional commanders.

Further Reading

Aleshire, Peter. *The Fox and the Whirlwind: General George Crook and Geronimo: A Paired Biography.* New York: Wiley, 2000.

Alexander, Robert. *Five Forks: Waterloo of the Confederacy.* East Lansing: Michigan State University Press, 2003.

Coffey, David. *Sheridan's Lieutenants: Philip Sheridan, His Generals, and the Final Years of the Civil War.* Wilmington, Del.: Rowman and Littlefield, 2005.

Lepa, Jack H. *The Shenandoah Valley Campaign of 1864.* Jefferson, N.C.: McFarland, 2003.

Longacre, Edward G. *The Cavalry at Appomattox: A Tactical Study of Mounted Operations during the Civil War's Climactic Campaign, March 27–April 9, 1865.* Mechanicsburg, Pa.: Stackpole Books, 2003.

O'Beirne, Kevin. "Crook's Devils." *Military Heritage* 1, no. 4 (2000): 62–75.

Robinson, Charles M. *General Crook and the Western Frontier.* Norman: University of Oklahoma Press, 2001.

Schmitt, Martin F., ed. *General George Crook: His Autobiography.* Norman: University of Oklahoma Press, 1986.

Curtis, Samuel R. (1805–1866)
Union general

Samuel Ryan Curtis was born in Champlain, New York, on February 3, 1805, and raised in Licking County, Ohio. He passed through the U.S. Military Academy in 1831 and was posted as a second lieutenant with the 7th U.S. Infantry. Curtis performed garrison duty at Fort Gibson, Indian Territory, for only a year before resigning his commission. He then successively served as an engineer on the National Road and chief engineer on the Muskingum River before studying law in 1841. During the War with Mexico (1846–48), he became colonel of the 3rd Ohio Infantry, but mostly he performed as adjutant general under General John E. Wool. Curtis also briefly functioned as military governor of Matamoros, Camargo, Monterrey, and Saltillo. Afterward, he relocated to Keokuk, Iowa, as a chief engineer on several river projects and then in St. Louis, Missouri, for the same reason. Curtis then entered politics as a Republican in 1856, serving first as major of Keokuk and then in the U.S. House of Representatives where he ceaselessly advocated creation of a transcontinental railroad. Curtis, a droll, uncharismatic figure, was nonetheless respected for his personal integrity, and he gained reelection to Congress in 1858 and 1860. In 1861 he attended the Peace Conference in Washington, D. C., to possibly avert secession and the violence that would accompany it. After the Civil War commenced in April 1861, he returned to Iowa and helped raise that state's first volunteer regiments; Curtis himself was elected unanimously colonel of the 2nd Iowa Infantry. Moreover, on the recommendation of General in Chief Winfield Scott, he was elevated to brigadier general the following May.

After resigning from Congress, Curtis accepted his first command at St. Louis, Missouri, which he rapidly helped bring under order. His principal activity was in helping to arrange the relief and replacement of the inept general John C. Frémont from command of the Department of the Missouri in November 1861. His successor, General Henry W. Halleck, placed Curtis in charge of the District of Southwest Missouri with orders to eliminate a threat posed by Confederates under General Sterling Price. He performed admirably with the scanty resources allotted him and pushed the Southerners deep into Arkansas. There, Price was unexpectedly reinforced by General Earl Van Dorn, who then turned to attack Curtis's Army of the Southwest at Pea Ridge (Elkhorn Tavern) on March 7–8, 1862. Van Dorn staged an elaborate flanking movement that placed his army behind the Federals, but Curtis simply ordered his entire force to about-face, and assisted by artillery under General Franz Sigel, he decimated several determined, if piecemeal, attacks. The Confederates eventually were driven off in confusion, Missouri was saved for the Union, and Curtis won a promotion to major general.

In September 1862 Curtis succeeded Halleck as head of the Department of the Missouri and quickly ran afoul of internecine politics and personalities. He failed to get along with either General John M. Schofield, his principal subordinate, or Governor H. R. Gamble. Curtis also proved unable to stem systemic outbreaks of guerrilla warfare, and his often draconian responses, such

as imposing levies upon suspected Confederate sympathizers, drove people into the enemy ranks. In May 1863 President Abraham Lincoln removed Curtis from St. Louis and reassigned him to lead the Department of Kansas, a command requiring less political finesse and more administrative skill. Curtis functioned competently until the fall of 1864, when General Price launched a final bid to conquer Missouri for the Confederacy. Curtis quickly raised a force of 4,000 soldiers and confronted twice his numbers at Big Blue River on October 21, 1864. He was driven back but made a tenacious stand at Westport, Missouri, two days later. Here the cavalry of General Alfred Pleasonton hit the Southerners from behind, and Price hastily fell back toward Arkansas. Curtis pursued him doggedly, mauling several Confederate rear guards, but he quarreled with Pleasonton, and the Confederates escaped. In January 1865 he was reassigned to the Department of the Northwest to conduct several peace treaty talks with the Sioux, the Crow, and other neighboring tribes. Curtis finally was discharged from the military in April 1866.

Back in civilian life, Curtis continued advocating his lifelong passion, the transcontinental railroad. In 1866 President Andrew Johnson appointed him to a three-man commission to explore its possible development. Curtis died suddenly at Council Bluffs, Iowa, on December 26, 1866, a brusque but otherwise useful officer of the western theater.

Further Reading

Beckenbaugh, Terry L. "The War of Politics: Samuel Ryan Curtis, Race, and the Political/Military Establishment." Unpublished Ph.D. diss., University of Arkansas, Fayetteville, 2001.

Bird, Roy. *Civil War in Kansas.* Gretna, La.: Pelican Publishing, 2004.

DeBlack, Thomas R. *With Fire and Sword: Arkansas, 1861–1874.* Fayetteville: University of Arkansas Press, 2003.

Gerteis, Louis S. *Civil War St. Louis.* Lawrence: University Press of Kansas, 2001.

Ham, Sharon. "End of Innocence." *Iowa Heritage Illustrated* 85, nos. 2–3 (2004): 64–79.

Johnson, Mark W. *That Body of Brave Men: The U.S. Regular Infantry and the Civil War in the West, 1861–1865.* Cambridge, Mass.: Da Capo Press, 2003.

Shea, William L., and Grady McWhiney. *War in the West: Pea Ridge and Prairie Grove.* Abilene, Tex.: McWhiney Foundation, 2001.

Custer, George A. (1839–1876)

Union general

George Armstrong Custer was born in New Rumley, Ohio, on December 5, 1839, and he taught briefly at an academy in Monroe, Michigan. In 1857 he gained admittance to the U.S. Military Academy and graduated four years later at the bottom of his class. As a cadet, Custer proved sullen, inattentive, and ill-disposed toward discipline. However, after graduating in 1861, he received his lieutenant's commission, 2nd U.S. Cavalry, just as the Civil War erupted, and he compiled one of the most meteoric rises in American military history. During the Battle of Bull Run, he caught the eye of General George B. McClellan, who appointed him an aide-de-camp. Custer performed heroically throughout the Peninsula campaign of 1862 and subsequently requested a combat command. He next served under General Alfred Pleasonton at the Battle of Aldie, June 17, 1863, with such distinction that he received, on Pleasonton's strongest recommendation, promotion to brevet brigadier general. Aged but 23 years, Custer was now the youngest general in the Union army, and his Michigan cavalry brigade, which he dubbed "The Wolverines," became renowned for their dash and discipline—and for donning the flashy red necktie of their commander. The following month, he fought with exceptional valor at Gettysburg, where, on July 3, 1863, his brigade prevented Confederate cavalry under General J. E. B. Stuart from attacking the Union rear.

In 1864 Custer transferred to the division of General Hugh J. Kilpatrick, and he was closely engaged in several severe engagements in General Ulysses S. Grant's overland drive to Richmond. His most noted encounter was at Yellow Tavern on May 11, 1864, in which he conducted the action that fatally wounded General Stuart. That summer, he joined General Philip H. Sheridan's Army of the Shenandoah to command an entire division. Always at the forefront of the action, Custer struck savagely at Confederate armies in Union victories at Winchester, Fisher's Hill, and Cedar Creek, invariably with decisive effect. He then received brevet promotion to major general at the age of 24 and assumed command of the 3rd Cavalry Division from General James H. Wilson. With it, he literally destroyed General Jubal A. Early's army at Waynesboro, Virginia, on March 2, 1865, and the following month added further luster to his name by charging equally hard at Dinwiddie Court House and the decisive Union victory at Five Forks on April 1, 1865. Custer's hard-riding troopers then proved instrumental in pursuing the Confederate army of Northern Virginia to Appomattox, Virginia, and bringing it to

Union general George A. Custer *(Library of Congress)*

bay. On April 9, 1865, when General Robert E. Lee sent forward a white flag to the Union lines, it was received by Custer. In the course of four years of combat, Custer had 11 horses killed underneath him, yet he was only wounded once. War's end found him the darling of the mounted arm and the national press, both totally captivated by his long, blonde hair, indifference to danger, and ravenous appetite for glory.

Custer was retained in the postwar service but reduced in rank to his regular grade of captain as of March 1866. Four months, later the 7th U.S. Cavalry was organized, and he became its lieutenant colonel. Custer next reported for duty in Kansas where he first experienced Indian fighting under General Winfield S. Hancock. Dissatisfied and perplexed by Native American tactics, he took an unauthorized leave of absence, was court-martialed, and was suspended for a year. In 1868 General Sheridan managed to have him reinstated and, on November 27, Custer committed a memorable atrocity by attacking the peaceful village of Chief Black Kettle on the Washita River. Despite official disapproval of this ill-advised action, no disciplinary action resulted, and Custer remained on active duty in Kansas. In 1873 he experienced his first brush with Sioux while protecting miners in the Black Hills region of South Dakota. Three years later, tensions exploded into open warfare, and Custer was assigned to an army column under General Alfred H. Terry. Another force under General George Crook was supposed to be advancing from the east but met defeat at the Rose Bud River and was forced to withdraw. Meanwhile, Custer recklessly forged ahead, and on June 25, 1876, the 7th Cavalry happened upon a large Native-American encampment at Little Big Horn. Despite the fact that the camp was inhabited by thousands of warriors, Custer divided his command and attacked. He was quickly overwhelmed by Chiefs Crazy Hose and Gall and killed along with 261 men of the 7th Cavalry. Six companies of the regiment under Major Marcus A. Reno and Captain Frederick W. Benteen managed to entrench themselves on a hillside and beat off attacks for two days until Terry arrived with the main column. "Custer's Last Stand," as Little Big Horn came to be known, was not the largest defeat suffered at the hands of Native Americans, but it certainly was the most sensationalized. It virtually assured that Custer's larger-than-life persona would remain an essential part of American frontier mythology.

Further Reading

Barnett, Louisek. *Touched by Fire: The Life, Death, & Mythic After Life of George Armstrong Custer.* Lincoln: University of Nebraska Press, 2006.

Coffey, David. *Sheridan's Lieutenants: Phil Sheridan, His Generals, and the Final Year of the Civil War.* Wilmington, Del.: Rowman and Littlefield, 2005.

Hatch, Tom. *The Cavalry of Appomattox: A Tactical Study of Mounted Operations during the Civil War's Climactic Campaign, March 27–April 9, 1865.* Mechanicsburg, Pa.: Stackpole Books, 2003.

Ovies, Adolfo. *Crossed Sabers: General George Armstrong Custer and the Shenandoah Campaign.* Bloomington, Ind.: Author House, 2004.

Robbins, James. *Last in Their Class: Custer, Pickett, and the Goats of West Point.* New York: Encounter Books, 2006.

Walker, Paul D. *The Battle that Saved the Union: Custer vs Stuart at Gettysburg.* Gretna, La.: Pelican Publishing, 2002.

D

Dahlgren, John A. B. (1809–1870)

Union admiral

John Adolphus Bernard Dahlgren was born in Philadelphia, Pennsylvania, on November 13, 1809, the son of a Swedish consul. He attempted to join the U.S. Navy in 1825 but was rejected as too young. However, after accompanying a merchant vessel for a year, he gained an appointment as acting midshipman in March 1826. For the next decade, Dahlgren served on a variety of ships and in several squadrons, and his abilities at mathematics resulted in a posting with the U.S. Coastal Survey. He acquitted himself well in most capacities, but in 1837 he was sidelined with vision problems and received a four-year furlough. While seeking treatment in Europe, he also studied the primitive rocket technology of the day. Dahlgren resumed his naval career as a lieutenant in 1842, and four years later, he requested sea duty during the Mexican War but, in light of his technical expertise, was assigned to the Washington Navy Yard instead. There, he helped found the U.S. Navy Ordnance Department and functioned as assistant inspector. During the next 15 years, Dahlgren became closely identified with the latest developments in naval weaponry. He is best remembered for designing and constructing the famous Dahlgren cannon in 1851, based on his understanding that explosive forces in a cannon are greater at the rear end than at the muzzle. Consequently, his cannons were thicker in back

than in front, and their distinct teardrop shape earned them the moniker "soda bottles." In practice, the 11- and 15-inch diameter Dahlgrens possessed superior muzzle velocity, range, and accuracy than contemporary European designs. He also designed a light-weight howitzer suitable for small boats and landing parties. Dahlgren furthered his reputation as an ordnance authority by writing and publishing several texts on the subject, which were professionally well received.

As the Civil War approached in the spring of 1861, Dahlgren's superior, Captain Franklin BUCHANAN, resigned as head of the Washington Navy Yard to join the South. Dahlgren then took energetic measures to fortify and defend the navy yard against possible Confederate attack. President Abraham LINCOLN so appreciated his performance that he arranged Dahlgren's appointment as director of the Bureau of Ordnance in July 1862 and promotion to captain through a special act of Congress the following August. In the ensuing months, he was actively employed in designing, testing, and mounting stronger weapons for new classes of ironclad warships. Dahlgren performed his tasks capably, and in February 1863, he advanced to rear admiral. The following July, he was ordered to succeed the unfortunate Admiral Samuel F. Du PONT as head of the South Atlantic Blockading Squadron.

On station, Dahlgren's immediate object was the reduction and capture of Charleston, South

Union admiral John A. B. Dahlgren *(Library of Congress)*

Carolina. He sailed his heavy ironclads into the harbor and bombarded the city's defenses on several occasions, but aside from demolishing some old forts, he failed to subdue the port. In the course of several months, he also lost several monitor vessels to the Confederate "torpedoes" (mines). Thereafter, he maintained an iron blockade of Charleston and authorized occasional raids upriver to keep the defenders off balance. In December 1864, Dahlgren played an important role in the capture of Savannah, Georgia, by supplying the army of General William T. SHERMAN with food and supplies. His heavy cannon, meanwhile, enjoyed success equally at sea and on land. Several naval batteries were landed ashore to assist General Ulysses S. GRANT during the July 1863 siege of Vicksburg, Mississippi, where their heavy firepower smothered Confederate defenses. In August 1864, the large-bore Dahlgrens employed on Admiral David G. FARRAGUT's monitors USS *Manhattan* and *Chickasaw* helped damage and

subdue the Confederate ram CSS *Tennessee* under now Admiral Buchanan at Mobile Bay. Dahlgren himself occupied the evacuated city of Charleston in February 1865 and relinquished control of the squadron by war's end. Sadly, his son, Colonel Ulric Dahlgren, had been killed in General Hugh J. KILPATRICK's cavalry raid against Richmond, Virginia, on March 2, 1864.

Dahlgren resumed his technical research in Washington, D.C., as bureau chief, but in 1866, he assumed command of the South Pacific Squadron. In July 1868 he returned to the navy yard, rose to commandant the following year, and died there in that capacity on July 12, 1870. His famous cannon, though rendered obsolete by advances in rifled artillery, saw continued service with the U.S. Navy until the early 1890s.

Further Reading

Browning, Robert M. *Success Is All That Was Expected: The South Atlantic Blockading Squadron during the Civil War.* Washington, D.C.: Brassey's, 2002.

Canfield, Eugene B. "Guns for the Monitors." *Naval History* 14, no. 4 (2000): 48–55.

Fuller, Howard. *Navies and Naval Operations of the Civil War, 1861–65.* London: Conway Marine, 2005.

Phelps, W. Chris. *The Bombardment of Charleston, 1863–1865.* Gretna, La.: Pelican Publishing, 2002.

Roberts, William H. *Now the Contest: Coastal and Oceanic Naval Operations in the Civil War.* Lincoln: University of Nebraska Press, 2004.

Schneller, Robert J. *A Quest for Glory: A Biography of Rear Admiral John A. Dahlgren.* Annapolis, Md.: Naval Institute Press, 1995.

Davis, Charles H. (1807–1887)
Union admiral

Charles Henry Davis was born in Boston, Massachusetts, on January 16, 1807, was well educated, and attended Harvard University in 1824. However, he quit school two years later to join the U.S. Navy as a midshipman and spent a decade cruising the Pacific Ocean and Mediterranean Sea. Davis received his lieutenant's commission in March 1834, and in 1842 he returned to Harvard to complete his degree. In light of his mathematical prowess, he found steady employment with the U.S. Coast Survey, and he published numerous scientific papers on the effects of tides. Davis advanced to commander in June 1854 and three years later assumed control of the Pacific Squadron. In this capacity, he arranged the rescue of American renegade adventurer William Walker from Nicaragua in May 1857. Two years later, he reported to the offices of the Nautical Almanac Office at Harvard, and he continued publishing scientific tracts as they related to naval and maritime service.

When the Civil War erupted in April 1861, Davis initially was assigned to the Bureau of Detail in Washington, D.C. It was his responsibility to provide accurate charts, proper organization, and efficient logistics for a sustained blockade of the lengthy Confederate coastline. He also assisted in planning intricate combined army-navy expeditions against the Confederate coast, most notably Cape Hatteras in August 1861. Three months later, he accompanied Admiral Samuel F. DU PONT on a campaign against Port Royal, South Carolina, and bore a conspicuous role in the victory of November 7, 1861. Success here planted the first Union lodgment on South Carolinian soil since the fall of Fort Sumter the previous April, and he received promotion to captain. Davis also pioneered the use of "stone fleets," namely, old wooden vessels filled with rock and sunk off Confederate harbors to obstruct them.

In the spring of 1862, Davis was tapped to succeed the ailing captain Andrew H. FOOTE as commander of the Mississippi Squadron. On June 5, 1862, once reinforced by several army rams under Colonel Charles Ellet, Davis fought and won the Battle of Plum Run Bend against a small but determined Confederate squadron. That same afternoon, he landed at Memphis, Tennessee, and received the city's surrender. Promoted to commodore, he next sailed south to Vicksburg, Mississippi, and joined forces with the fleet of Admiral David G. FARRAGUT. There, in concert with army units, he energetically conducted a series of raids along the Mississippi River that kept Confederate forces from crossing the river and reinforcing the garrison. His string of luck ended on July 15, 1862, when the large Confederate ram CSS *Arkansas* sortied from the Yazoo River and passed directly through Davis's squadron. The Union vessels, badly outgunned, came off poorly in the engagement, which prompted Secretary of the Navy Gideon Welles to replace the scholarly Davis with a more aggressive officer. On October 1, 1862, Commander David D. PORTER was chosen as his successor, and Davis reported back to Washington, D.C., to resume his scientific inquiries. As a sop to any hurt feelings on the matter, Davis also received a promotion to rear admiral as of February 1863.

Davis effectively managed the Bureau of Navigation, under whose aegis fell the navy's scientific

Union admiral Charles H. Davis *(U.S. Navy)*

office and its academy, until the war concluded in 1865. He was also responsible for creating the new Hydrographic Office to facilitate chart making and navigational aids. Davis also strongly suggested creation of a National Academy of Science, which was founded in 1863. At the conclusion of hostilities, he transferred from the Navy Department to the Naval Observatory as superintendent. He then took to sea in 1867 to command the Brazilian Squadron, remaining at sea for three years. In 1870 Davis came ashore for the last time as commandant of the Norfolk Navy Yard, Virginia, where simmering resentment against Northerners made his tenure decidedly unpleasant. He then resumed his work at the National Observatory, dying there on February 18, 1887. Although not exactly a combat officer of the first rank, Davis made indelible contributions to naval science as one of the most accomplished researchers of his day.

Further Reading

Campbell, R. Thomas. *Confederate Naval Forces on Western Waters: The Defense of the Mississippi River and Its Tributaries.* Jefferson, N.C.: McFarland, 2005.

Davis, Charles H. *Life of Charles Henry Davis, Rear Admiral, 1807–1877.* Boston: Houghton Mifflin, 1899.

Hearn, Chester G. *Ellet's Brigade: The Strangest Outfit of All.* Baton Rouge: Louisiana State University Press, 2000.

Joiner, Gary D. *Mr. Lincoln's Brown Water Navy: The Mississippi Squadron.* Lanham, Md.: Rowman & Littlefield, 2007.

Konstam, Angus. *Mississippi River Gunboats of the American Civil War, 1861–1865.* Oxford, U.K.: Osprey, 2002.

Silverstone, Paul H. *Civil War Navies, 1855–1883.* Annapolis, Md.: Naval Institute Press, 2001.

Davis, Jefferson (1808–1889)

President, Confederate States of America

Jefferson Davis was born in Christian County, Kentucky, on June 3, 1808, and raised in Mississippi. After briefly attending Transylvania University, he opted to apply to the U.S. Military Academy in 1825 and graduated four years later in the middle of his class. As a second lieutenant in the 1st U.S. Infantry, he fought briefly in the Black Hawk War of 1832 under General Zachary Taylor, and he conducted Sauk chief Black Hawk into confinement at Jefferson Barracks, Missouri. In May 1834 he transferred to the 1st U.S. Dragoons while also courting Sarah Knox Taylor, the general's daughter. They were married over his objections, and he resigned his commission to run a plantation in Mississippi. Tragically, Davis lost his young bride to malaria six months later, and he suffered intermittent bouts of illness for the rest of his life. Davis withdrew into seclusion for nearly a decade and finally emerged in 1844 to run for Congress. That year, he successfully stood for a seat in the U.S. House of Representatives and resigned two years later to participate in the war with Mexico that he had so strenuously advocated.

In 1846 Davis was commissioned colonel of the 1st Mississippi Rifle Regiment, and he joined his ex-father-in-law General Taylor at the mouth of the Rio Grande. He fought well at the Battle of Monterrey, where his men distinguished themselves in house-to-house fighting. Afterward, most of Taylor's regular troops were transferred to the army of General Winfield SCOTT, and Taylor, now mustering mostly militia, was attacked by General Antonio López de Santa Anna at Buena Vista on February 22, 1847. Once again, Davis was in the thick of the fray and bravely repulsed a Mexican cavalry charge that threatened artillery commanded by captains Braxton BRAGG and George H. THOMAS. He sustained a foot wound for the effort and returned to Mississippi a hero. He subsequently won appointment to complete an unfinished term in the U.S. Senate. In the wake of the Mexican War, sectional tensions between the North and South magnified exponentially over the issue of expanding slavery into newly acquired territories. Davis, while an articulate defender of Southern rights and slavery, left the Senate in 1851 to run unsuccessfully for the governor's office in his home state. He avoided the public arena for two years until 1853 when President Franklin Pierce appointed him secretary of war. In this

Jefferson Davis, president of the Confederate States of America *(National Archives)*

capacity, Davis displayed considerable foresight and innovation. He introduced badly needed administrative reforms, sought out the newest rifled weapons for the infantry, replaced wooden cannon carriages with metal ones, and at one point even introduced camels into the arid southwest on an experimental basis. By the time he left office in 1857, he was considered one of the War Department's most efficient bureaucrats.

In the spring of 1857, Davis was easily reelected to the Senate, where he forcefully and eloquently championed states rights and slavery. However, unlike many Southern "firebrands," he sought accommodation with the North to preserve the Union. When the Democratic Party split during the election year of 1860, he threw his support behind John C. BRECKINRIDGE and was aghast that Abraham LINCOLN, who opposed the expansion of slavery, won the election. Southern states then began to secede from the Union in December 1860,

and Davis reluctantly but determinedly sided with Mississippi. On January 21, 1861, he delivered an anguish-ridden farewell speech to the Senate before departing to tender his services to the emerging Confederate States of America. Once home, Davis fully expected to become a major general of state forces, but on February 9, 1861, he was genuinely surprised to learn that the secessionist congress, meeting in Montgomery, Alabama, nominated him to serve as president of this new Southern entity. He was inaugurated nine days later in Montgomery and then transferred the seat of Confederate governance to Richmond, Virginia, to shore up support from that state. In July 1861 the initial victory of General Pierre G. T. BEAUREGARD over General Irwin McDOWELL at Bull Run caused elation throughout the South and a premature sense of relief, but victory here belied severe and long-term deficiencies that dogged the Confederacy throughout its brief existence. The North's superior manpower and larger industrial base, coupled with Davis's own inability to secure cooperation between individual states within the Confederacy, doomed the fledgling state as both a political and a military entity. The celebrated prowess of Southern armies notwithstanding, multiplicity of the problems Davis encountered as chief executive simply proved insurmountable.

Davis firmly believed in his cause, stridently defended it, and remained fixated upon an ultimate Confederate victory to the bitter end. However, as chief executive, he had a tendency to meddle with his generals and interfere with military matters. He also was blinded to the incompetence of his friends Braxton BRAGG and Leonidas POLK, and he refused to remove them from power despite repeated displays of ineptitude. Moreover, Davis clashed repeatedly with talented yet headstrong leaders such as Beauregard and Joseph E. JOHNSTON, and periodically relieved them at inopportune times. Fortunately for the South, he commiserated well with his most successful field commander, General Robert E. LEE, and he worked closely with him. The eastern theater thus received the greater part of the administration's attention while events in the West, where the war would be lost, remained a consistent lower priority.

As Confederate fortunes waned, Davis lacked the authority to shift manpower decisively from one theater to the next owing to resistance from state governments. He thus was forced to invoke measures such as conscription, taxation, and confiscation to strengthen the overall Confederate position. These policies struck at the very heart of states's rights—the philosophical underpinning of his regime—and led to a chorus of condemnation from Southern politicians. He further compounded his problems by refusing to entertain the notion of employing African-American slaves in the military in exchange for freedom. This recalcitrance negated a pool of manpower numbering 2 million—at a period when the North ultimately added 180,000 black soldiers to their own roster. By the time such pragmatic measures were forced on him by the Confederate Congress in the spring of 1865, they arrived far too late to alter the outcome of events. After the fall of Richmond in April 1865, Davis and his cabinet hastily fled south, intending to reach the trans-Mississippi region and carry on the struggle for Southern independence through guerrilla warfare. When he and his entourage were seized by General James H. WILSON's cavalry at Irwinville, Georgia, on May 10, 1865, the Confederate States of America had reached its climactic denouement.

Davis was incarcerated in chains at Fortress Monroe, Virginia, although public outcry mitigated his harsh conditions. He remained confined for two years before being released and, though indicted for treason, was never brought to trial. Davis subsequently returned to a life of poverty in Mississippi with his faithful wife Varina, where he penned an extensive apologia for the war. In it, he vehemently blamed men such as Beauregard and Johnston for defeat while minimizing his own role in the debacle. Davis, who never applied for a pardon and never renewed his citizenship, died at Beauvior, Mississippi, on December 6, 1889. For many decades thereafter, in the minds of many fel-

low Southerners, he remained the embodiment and symbol of the Confederacy's proud and defiant "Lost Cause."

Further Reading

Cashin, Joan E. *Never at Peace: Varina Howell Davis and the Civil War.* Boston: Houghton Mifflin, 2005.

Collins, Donald E. *The Death and Resurrection of Jefferson Davis.* Lanham, Md.: Rowman and Littlefield, 2005.

Davis, Jefferson. *The Rise and Fall of the Confederate Government.* 2 vols. New York: D. Appleton, 1881.

Detzer, David. *Dissonance: Between Fort Sumter and Bull Run in the Turbulent First Days of the Civil War.* Orlando, Fla.: Harcourt, 2006.

Eicher, David J. *Dixie Betrayed: How the South Really Lost the Civil War.* New York: Little Brown, 2006.

Escott, Paul D. *Military Necessity: Civil-Military Relations in the Confederacy* Westport, Conn.: Praeger Security International, 2006.

Hattaway, Herman, and Richard E. Berlinger. *Jefferson Davis, Confederate President.* Lawrence: University Press of Kansas, 2002.

Jones, Wilmer L. *Generals in Blue and Gray.* 2 vols. Westport, Conn.: Praeger, 2004.

Monroe, Haskell W., and James T. McIntosh, eds. *The Papers of Jefferson Davis.* 10 vols. Baton Rouge: Louisiana State University Press, 1971–1999.

Doubleday, Abner (1819–1893)

Union general

Abner Doubleday was born in Ballston Spa, New York, on June 26, 1819, and attended school in nearby Cooperstown. He enjoyed a close association with athletics as a youth and undoubtedly played baseball there, but the polite fiction surrounding his originating the game has been discredited by historians. Doubleday was admitted to the U.S. Military Academy in 1838 and graduated four years later midway in his class. He was then commissioned a second lieutenant in the 3rd U.S. Artillery and performed several tours of routine garrison work along the Atlantic coast before transferring to the Army of Texas under General Zachary Taylor in 1846. He subsequently fought at the Battle of Monterrey that year, acquitting himself well and gaining promotion to first lieutenant in March 1847. After the war Doubleday reported for duty along the frontier, where he rose to captain in 1855 and fought in Florida's Third Seminole War. In December 1860 he accompanied Major Robert ANDERSON when his company was sent to garrison Fort Moultrie in Charleston, South Carolina. Anderson feared for the safety of his men following that state's secession on December 20, 1861, and he ordered them transferred to the incomplete works of Fort Sumter in Charleston harbor. Doubleday commanded the first company to reach the fort and began to strengthen the works and mount cannon. On April 12, 1861, Confederate forces under General Pierre G. T. BEAUREGARD commenced bombarding Fort Sumter, and Anderson allowed Doubleday the honor of firing the first Union shots of the Civil War in response. The garrison surrendered two days later, and Doubleday departed by boat for the North.

As the Civil War unfolded, Doubleday gained promotion to major and command of the 17th U.S. Infantry. With them, he campaigned in the Shenandoah Valley before advancing to brigadier general in February 1862. He then transferred to the Army of the Potomac under General John POPE and performed well in severe fighting at Groveton and Second Bull Run in August 1862. Doubleday then rose to command a division, was actively engaged at Stone Mountain, Antietam, and Fredericksburg that fall, and received promotion to major general as of November 1862. He next saw action at Chancellorsville in May 1863. Doubleday by now had acquired the reputation of a tenacious fighter but one who moved with such deliberation that his troops nicknamed him "Old Forty-Eight Hours."

During initial stages of the Gettysburg campaign, Doubleday commanded a division in General John F. REYNOLDS's I Corps. In this capacity, he arrived with Reynolds in the late morning of July 1, 1863, to reinforce Union cavalry under General John BUFORD, and he succeeded Reynolds to the command after he was killed. Gettysburg was Doubleday's finest hour. Outnumbered

and outmaneuvered by General Richard S. EWELL's Confederates, he relinquished control of the town slowly until the bulk of his forces were safely ensconced on nearby heights. He acquitted himself well, considering the confused events of the first day, but General George G. MEADE, commanding the Army of the Potomac, disapproved of Doubleday's tendency toward lethargic movements. He therefore appointed General John Newton, an officer with less seniority, to command the I Corps for the remainder of the engagement. Doubleday was appreciably incensed by the slight but returned to his division and performed well during the next two days. His men bore a prominent role in repulsing the climactic charge by General George E. PICKETT on July 3, 1863, but Doubleday, smarting from Meade's treatment, withdrew from active duties two days later.

Doubleday spent the remainder of the war performing administrative duties in Washington,

Union general Abner Doubleday *(Library of Congress)*

D.C. He also testified vindictively against General Meade during an official congressional inquiry in 1864, the strident tenor of which only besmirched his own reputation. His only other active service during the war was commanding a small part of Washington's defenses during General Jubal A. Early's raid of July 1864. After the war, Doubleday reverted back to his lineal rank of lieutenant colonel, 23th U.S. Infantry, and accompanied his men to San Francisco, California. He then rose to colonel in 1867, transferred to the African-American 24th U.S. Infantry in Texas, and served competently until his retirement in December 1873. Never one to let go of a grudge, he also published several tracts on Gettysburg that excoriated General Meade and exaggerated his own role. Doubleday died at Mendham, New Jersey, on January 26, 1893, better remembered for allegedly inventing baseball than for his conscientious service during the Civil War.

Further Reading

Doubleday, Abner. *Chancellorsville and Gettysburg.* New York: Da Capo Press, 1994.

———. *Reminiscences of Fort Sumter and Moultrie, 1860–1861.* Baltimore: Nautical and Aviation Publishing, 1998.

Newton, Steven H. *McPherson's Ridge: The First Battle for the High Ground, July 1, 1863.* Cambridge, Mass.: Da Capo Press, 2002.

Pfanz, Harry W. *Gettysburg—The First Day.* Chapel Hill: University of North Carolina Press, 2001.

Ramsey, David M. "The 'Old Sumter Hero': A Biography of Major General Abner Doubleday." Unpublished Ph.D. diss., Florida State University, 1980.

Du Pont, Samuel F. (1803–1865)

Union admiral

Samuel Francis Du Pont was born in Bergen Point, New Jersey, on September 25, 1803, the scion of a prominent Delaware family. His father, politically connected to former president Thomas Jefferson, prevailed on his old friend to have Du Pont receive a midshipman's commission in 1815. Two years later, he commenced a series of cruises

Union admiral Samuel F. Du Pont *(U.S. Navy)*

in the Mediterranean and South American squadrons, rising to lieutenant in 1826 and commander by 1843. When the Mexican War erupted in 1846, Du Pont commanded the sloop USS *Cyane* in the Pacific, and with it, he transported the troops of Major John C. Frémont from San Francisco to San Diego, California. He then proceeded to clear enemy forces from the towns of Guaymas, Mazatlán, and La Paz, and later he assisted Commander William B. Shubrick in the capture of San Jose. In this last engagement, Du Pont accompanied a landing party ashore and rescued a party of U.S. Marines besieged in a church. He returned to Washington, D.C., in 1848 and served on a number of important boards, including one recommending creation of a naval academy. He rose to captain in 1855 and stirred considerable acrimony that year as a member of the Efficiency Board, which discharged 201 incompetent officers from active service. He also recommended modernization by advocating wholesale adoption of steam propulsion and better weapons for naval vessels. In 1856 Du Pont commanded the *Minnesota* to China, where he witnessed and carefully analyzed the latest Anglo-French amphibious tactics in operations against Chinese forts. He returned home in 1860 and received command of the Washington Navy Yard, his final peacetime assignment.

Once the Civil War broke out in April 1861, Du Pont sat as senior member on the vitally important Blockade Board, a body tasked with drawing up operational strategy and tactics for use against the Confederate coastline and military installations found there. On September 18, 1861, he received command of the strategic South Atlantic Blockading Squadron. Two months later, on November 7, 1861, Du Pont attacked and captured Port Royal, South Carolina, in concert with General Benjamin F. BUTLER. This constituted the first Federal lodgment on South Carolinian soil since the fall of Fort Sumter in April. Du Pont then continued with a string of minor successes by seizing Tybee Island and Fort Pulaski off Savannah, Georgia, along with numerous points on the coast of Florida the following spring. In recognition of his success, Du Pont received both the thanks of Congress and promotion to rear admiral in July 1862.

By the spring of 1863, Northern politicians were agitating for some kind of punitive action against Charleston, South Carolina, long viewed as the seat of secessionism. In light of Du Pont's seemingly effortless victories against other points along the coast, pressure mounted on him to launch an all-out attack on the city. Du Pont, however, demurred. His new and highly touted monitor craft, while heavily armored, possessed few cannon for offensive purposes and would be outgunned badly in any engagement against Charleston's intricate defenses. To prove his point, he staged a test run of tactics on Fort McAllister, Georgia, on March 3, 1863. Here, the monitors *Passaic, Patapsco,* and *Nahant* under Commander John L. WORDEN attacked and bombarded the enemy post, taking heavy fire in return and accomplishing little. Moreover, the cramped waters of Charleston harbor singularly militated against the successful circling and bombarding tactics employed elsewhere, and Du Pont further warned civilian authorities that the city could be taken only in concert with army troops. Secretary of the Navy Gideon Welles nonetheless caved in to political pressure and ordered Du Pont to attack the city. The admiral sullenly complied, fully expecting to be defeated. On April 7, 1863, Du Pont led seven monitors and one armored steamer into Charleston harbor in a lopsided, two-hour duel with numerous shore batteries directed by General Pierre G. T. BEAUREGARD. His ships were all struck repeatedly, and one monitor, the *Keokuk,* sank the next day. A storm of public and private criticism then arose against the admiral, who tendered his resignation. Du Pont still managed to remain on station for three more months, during which time one of his ships under Commander John RODGERS captured the Confederate vessel CSS *Atlanta.* Du Pont was then replaced by Admiral John A. B. DAHLGREN on July 6, 1863, who, like his predecessor, failed to capture Charleston by a coup de main.

Du Pont returned to his home at Wilmington, Delaware, a bitter, disillusioned man and for several months engaged Secretary Welles in a heated public diatribe over responsibility for the Charleston debacle. He died suddenly in Philadelphia, Pennsylvania, on June 23, 1865, a distinguished officer whose career was ended by the very action he strongly opposed.

Further Reading

Browning, Robert M. *Success Is All that Was Expected: The South Atlantic Blockading Squadron during the Civil War.* Washington, D.C.: Brassey's, 2002.

Coombe, Jack D. *Gunsmoke over the Atlantic: First Naval Actions of the Civil War.* New York: Bantam Books, 2002.

Fuller, Howard. *Navies and Naval Operations of the Civil War, 1861–65.* London: Conway Marine, 2005.

Phelps, W. Chris. *The Bombardment of Charleston, 1863–1865.* Gretna, La.: Pelican Publishing, 2002.

Roberts, William H. *Now for the Contest: Coastal and Oceanic Naval Operations in the Civil War.* Lincoln: University of Nebraska Press, 2004.

Weddle, Kevin J. *Lincoln's Tragic Admiral: The Life of Samuel Francis Du Pont.* Charlottesville: University of Virginia Press, 2005.

E

Early, Jubal A. (1816–1894)

Confederate general

Jubal Anderson Early was born in Franklin County, Virginia, on November 3, 1816, and well educated at local academies. He entered the U.S. Military Academy in 1833 and graduated four years later midway in his class. Early initially saw service as a second lieutenant in the 3rd U.S. Artillery and fought briefly in Florida's Second Seminole War. He then lost interest in military matters and resigned his commission in 1839 to study law. Two years later, Early gained election to the Virginia House of Delegates and also served intermittently as state attorney. Once the Mexican War broke out in 1846, he donned a uniform to serve with the 1st Virginia Volunteers under General Zachary Taylor, but he performed little beyond garrison duty. Unfortunately, Early contracted severe rheumatism in Mexico, which rendered him stooped and gangly beyond his years. He then returned home to resume his successful political career and, in April 1861, was elected to attend the state secessionist convention. Here, Early argued strenuously against secession, but once Virginia left the Union on April 17, 1861, he offered his services to his home state as colonel of the 24th Virginia Infantry. In this capacity, he commanded a brigade at Bull Run on July 21, 1861, acquitting himself well and winning promotion to brigadier general the following month.

During the next three years, Early, a coarse, hard-drinking, and rather profane individual, found himself catapulted into the front ranks of Confederate generalship. He performed capably under General Joseph E. JOHNSTON through the Peninsula campaign and was badly wounded at Williamsburg on May 5, 1862. He recovered in time to fight again at Malvern Hill the following July and subsequently served in General Richard S. EWELL's division of General Thomas J. JACKSON's II Corps. Fighting valorously at Second Bull Run, Antietam, and Fredericksburg, he earned praise from both Jackson and General Robert E. LEE, who affectionately referred to his crusty subordinate as "My Bad Old Man." Early advanced to major general in April 1863 and was selected by Lee to contain General John Sedgwick's Union force at Fredericksburg, while he went on to win a stunning offensive victory at Chancellorsville on May 2–3, 1863. He consequently rose to major general and further distinguished himself in hard fighting at Gettysburg, July 1–3, 1863. In May 1864 Early was tapped to succeed General Ambrose P. HILL temporarily as commander of the III Corps at the Wilderness and Spotsylvania, performing well at that level of command. Then, promoted to lieutenant general as of May 31, he succeeded Ewell as commander of the III Corps in June 1864, whereupon General Lee detached him from the Army of Northern Virginia on a special mission.

In June 1864 Early loped into the Shenandoah Valley with orders to clear that strategic region of Union forces. On June 18, 1864, he defeated General David Hunter at Lynchburg, Virginia, and pursued him vigorously out of the area. He then undertook the bold gambit of raiding the Union capital of Washington, D.C., brushing aside a small Union force under General Lew WALLACE at Monocacy on July 9, 1864. His sudden appearance on the outskirts of the District of Columbia forced General Ulysses S. GRANT to siphon off badly needed manpower from his Richmond campaign to defend the seat of government. Ultimately, the VI and XIX Corps were dispatched. Early had toyed with the idea of attacking Fort Stevens on July 11, but he ultimately withdrew back into the

Confederate general Jubal A. Early *(Massachusetts Commandery Military Order of the Loyal Legion and the U.S. Army Military History Institute)*

Shenandoah. Union forces under General Horatio G. Wright pursued him warily and then pulled back with the bulk of his forces. A force under General George CROOK remained behind at Kernstown, where, on July 24, Early suddenly turned on his pursuers, scattering them. He then deployed several cavalry columns northward, one of which burned the town of Chambersburg, Pennsylvania, on July 13, 1864. Confederate success here greatly embarrassed the government and prompted Grant to take drastic measures to end diversions in this theater once and for all.

In September 1864, General Philip H. SHERIDAN entered the Shenandoah with 40,000 men and orders to pursue and crush Early's army of 18,000 veterans. In quick succession, Sheridan defeated the Confederates at Winchester, September 19,1864, and Fisher's Hill two days later. Early was forced to retreat farther down the valley until Sheridan stopped advancing and left to attend a strategy conference in Washington. Then Early, assisted by Generals John C. BRECKINRIDGE and John B. GORDON, unexpectedly struck at Cedar Creek on October 19, 1864, nearly routing the Federals before Sheridan arrived to rally his men and launch a devastating counterattack. This defeat marked the end of Early's celebrated Shenandoah Valley campaign, and he fell back to Waynesboro, Virginia, to recoup the survivors. On March 2, 1865, General George A. CUSTER suddenly attacked the Confederates, finally smashing the remnants of Early's army. General Lee never held Early personally accountable for the debacle, but the Southern press blamed him for losing this strategic region, and he lost his command shortly before hostilities ceased.

After the war ended, Early fled to Mexico and Canada, where he composed his memoirs. He subsequently returned to Virginia in 1867 and played a significant role in the postwar period by championing the "Lost Cause" theory of the Civil War. He enjoyed a wide-ranging, popular audience, since many hard-core Confederates simply refused to accept defeat gracefully. Early also resumed his successful legal practice and served as the first president of the Southern Historical Association, which extolled the virtues of General Lee and blamed the loss of the war on subordinates such as General James LONGSTREET. Early, who never petitioned to have his citizenship restored, died at Lynchburg, Virginia, on March 2, 1894—an "unreconstructed" Confederate to the bitter end.

Further Reading

Cooling, Frank B. "The Campaign That Could Have Changed the War—and Did: Jubal Early's 1864 Raid on Washington, D.C." *Blue & Gray* 7, no. 5 (2004): 12–23.

Early, Jubal A. *A Memoir of the Last Year of the War for Independence in the Confederate States of America.* Columbia: University of South Carolina Press, 2001.

Gallagher, Gary W., ed. *The Shenandoah Campaign of 1864.* Chapel Hill: University of North Carolina Press, 2006.

Jones, Wilmer L. *Generals in Blue and Gray.* 2 vols. Westport, Conn.: Praeger, 2004.

Lepka, Jack H. *The Shenandoah Valley Campaign of 1864.* Jefferson, N.C.: McFarland, 2003.

Naisawald, L. VanLoan, and James I. Robertson. *The Battle of Lynchburg: Seize Lynchburg—If Only for a Single Day!* Lynchburg, Va.: Warwick House Pub., 2004.

Patchan, Scott C. *Shenandoah Summer: The 1864 Valley Campaign.* Lincoln: University of Nebraska Press, 2007.

Evans, Nathan G. (1824–1868)

Confederate general

Nathan George Evans was born in Marion County, South Carolina, on February 3, 1824, and he studied at Randolph-Macon College. In 1844, on the recommendation of John C. Calhoun, Evans gained admittance to the U.S. Military Academy. Uninspired as a cadet, he acquired the lifelong moniker "Shanks" owning to his spindly legs. After graduating in 1848, Evans joined the 1st U.S. Dragoons as a second lieutenant and commenced a wide-ranging tour of frontier posts. In 1855 he transferred to the newly raised 2nd U.S. Cavalry, in which many future Confederate generals rode.

Now a captain, Evans gained a reputation for fearlessness in battle, and on one occasion, he slew two Comanche chiefs at the Battle of Wachita Village, October 1, 1858. The South Carolina state legislature voted him an elaborate sword in consequence. Evans remained on the frontier until his native state seceded from the Union in December 1860, whereupon he resigned his commission in February 1861 and joined the South Carolina cavalry as a major.

Throughout the bombardment of Fort Sumter, April 12–14, 1861, Evans served as an adjutant general for state forces. Two months later, he gained promotion to lieutenant colonel of the 4th South Carolina Infantry and subsequently commanded a brigade under General Pierre G. T. BEAUREGARD in Virginia. While deployed at Manassas Junction on July 21, 1861, it was Evans who first detected the massive Union turning movement of General Irwin MCDOWELL, consisting of 17,000 men. Evans, commanding only 5,000 soldiers, ably defended the Stone Bridge and obstructed their passage until superior numbers forced him back. He was then reinforced by General Barnard E. Bee and Colonel Wade HAMPTON, who were also driven off, but Evans's delaying tactics allowed General Beauregard to react decisively and win the day. For his efforts he gained promotion to colonel, becoming one of South Carolina's earliest wartime heroes. On October 21, 1861, Evans subsequently intercepted a column of Union troops under Colonel Edward D. Baker at Ball's Bluff, Virginia, routing them with a loss of 214 casualties and 714 captives. This little disaster portended very large consequences for it induced Senator Benjamin F. Wade, a Radical Republican, to found the Joint Congressional Committee on the Conduct of the War. The committee operated as a political oversight board and was legally empowered to scrutinize, subpoena, or arrest any Union leader for alleged misbehavior. Evans, meanwhile, received both the thanks of the Confederate Congress and promotion to brigadier general.

Evans acquired such notoriety that his command, popularly known as the "Tramp Brigade," functioned virtually as an autonomous unit. He then marched it back to South Carolina in December 1861 to take command of the 3rd Military District. There, Evans gained additional laurels for defeating several small Union incursions along the coastline. In the summer of 1862, he marched back to Virginia as part of General James LONGSTREET's corps and performed well at Second Bull Run that August. Evans then took temporary command of an entire division during the invasion of Maryland, fighting tenaciously at the battles of South Mountain and Antietam. He then led the "Tramp Brigade" back to North Carolina where, on December 13, 1862, he fiercely resisted General John G. Foster's drive on Kinston. By this time, Evans, a known heavy drinker, was under investigation for dissipation on the battlefield and General Beauregard relieved him of command pending the outcome. Cleared of all charges, he resumed command of the brigade by summer.

In June 1863 Evans was posted to Vicksburg, Mississippi, as part of General William W. LORING's division. In this capacity, he fought under General Joseph E. JOHNSTON at the unsuccessful defense of Jackson, Mississippi, on July 9–16, 1863, and then transferred back east to Savannah, Georgia, for garrison duty. Beauregard, still commanding the district, refused to grant him serious responsibilities, but once he transferred north, Evans became commander of South Carolina's 1st Military District. Shortly after assuming control, he fell off his horse and sustained serious injuries that incapacitated him for the rest of the war. He was in Richmond, Virginia, when it fell to Union forces on April 3, 1865, and fled west with Confederate president Jefferson DAVIS. After the war, Evans relocated to Midway, Alabama, to serve as a school principal. He died there in that capacity on November 30, 1868, a brave officer compromised by his addiction to alcohol.

Further Reading

Conrad, James L. "From Glory to Contention: The Sad History of 'Shanks' Evans." *Civil War Times Illustrated* 22, no. 9 (1983): 32–38.

Detzer, David. *Donnybrook: The Battle of Bull Run*. San Diego: Harcourt, 2004.

Howard, William F. *The Battle of Ball's Bluff: The Leesburg Affair, October 21, 1861*. Lynchburg, Va.: A. E. Howard, 1994.

Priest, John M. *Before Antietam: The Battle of South Mountain*. Shippensburg, Pa.: White Mane Books, 1992.

Silverman, Jason H., Samuel N. Thomas, and Beverly D. Evans. *Shanks: The Life and Wars of Nathan George Evans*. Cambridge, Mass.: Da Capo Press, 2002.

Stone, DeWitt B., ed. *Wandering to Glory: Confederate Veterans Remember Evans Brigade*. Columbia: University of South Carolina Press, 2001.

Ewell, Richard S. (1817–1872)

Confederate general

Richard Stoddert Ewell was born in Washington, D.C., on February 8, 1817, the son of a physician, and was raised in Prince William County, Virginia. In 1836 he matriculated at the U.S. Military Academy and graduated four years later as a second lieutenant in the 1st U.S. Dragoons. Significantly, Ewell rode with his regiment for 20 years. In 1845 he accompanied the dragoon expeditions of Colonel Philip St. George Cooke and Stephen W. Kearny along the Santa Fe and Oregon trails. In the Mexican War (1846–48), he joined General Winfield SCOTT's army and won a brevet promotion to captain for bravery at the battles of Contreras and Churubusco in August 1847. In the latter engagement, he escorted his wounded commander, Captain Philip KEARNY, to the rear and then led his company with distinction. Afterward, he resumed garrison duty along the western frontier and skirmished several times with the Apache under Cochise (1855–57). Two years later, he accompanied noted explorer Colonel Benjamin Bonneville and helped survey the newly acquired lands of the Gadsden Purchase. Ewell next commanded Fort Buchanan, Arizona Territory, in 1860 before illness necessitated a sick leave back to Virginia. Though personally opposed to secession, he resigned his commission and joined the Confederacy once Virginia left the Union in April 1861. Ewell then received a lieutenant colonel's commission in the infantry.

On June 1, 1861, Ewell was slightly injured in a skirmish outside Fairfax, Virginia, becoming in all likelihood the first Southern field officer wounded in action. He was then promoted to brigadier general on June 17, 1861, and commanded troops at Bull Run on July 21, 1861. There, General Pierre G. T. BEAUREGARD directed him to attack Union forces at Centreville, Virginia, but the orders were lost in transit, and he failed to distinguish himself. Nevertheless, on January 24, 1862, Ewell advanced in rank to major general and assumed command of the division formerly led by General Edmund KIRBY-SMITH. He then joined General Thomas J. JACKSON's II Corps and bore conspicuous roles in the spectacular Shenandoah Valley campaign of that spring. Jackson and Ewell worked well in tandem, and they scored victories over General Nathaniel P. BANKS at Winchester, Virginia, on May 25, 1861, and General John C. Frémont at Cross Keys on June 8. Jackson's corps then shifted to Virginia's peninsula to join the Army of Northern Virginia under General Robert E. LEE. During the Second Bull Run campaign against General John POPE, Ewell was heavily engaged at Groveton on August 28, 1862, and lost his left leg. He convalesced for nine months and returned to the field a lieutenant general as of May 23, 1863.

After the smashing Confederate victory at Chancellorsville (May 5–6, 1862), Ewell was chosen to replace the mortally wounded Jackson as commander of II Corps. He then helped spearhead Lee's invasion of Pennsylvania with a brilliant victory over Union forces at Winchester, Virginia (June 13–15, 1863), taking nearly 4,000 prisoners. Ewell was preparing to march against Harrisburg, Pennsylvania, when Lee suddenly ordered him to assist General Ambrose P. HILL's III Corps at the strategic road junction called Gettysburg. On July 1, 1863, after a hard slog, Ewell nursed his footsore command into the town and drove out the Union XI Corps of General Oliver O. HOWARD. Then, in one of the war's most controversial decisions, he elected not to storm the

Confederate general Richard S. Ewell *(Massachusetts Commandery Military Order of the Loyal Legion and the U.S. Army Military History Institute)*

lightly defended heights of Cemetery Hill nearby. At the time, Ewell was acting under discretionary orders from Lee to attack, "If possible." However, this hesitation enabled Union forces under General George G. MEADE to consolidate their defenses on highly favorable terrain, which cost the Confederates heavily during the next two days. Ewell justified his actions as pursuant to Lee's instructions, but thereafter he was highly criticized for potentially losing the battle. On July 2 and 3, his corps mounted numerous attacks against Culp's Hill in the rear of Union positions but was invariably driven back downhill. Ewell subsequently fell back with the main army to Virginia. From May 5–12, 1864, his command again was engaged actively in the bloody battles of the Wilderness and Spotsylvania, suffering heavy losses. Ewell was then severely injured by a fall from his horse and Lee replaced him with General Jubal A. EARLY. While recovering, Lee ordered him to take charge of Richmond's defenses. His most notable service occurred on September 29, 1864, when he rushed reinforcements to Fort Harrison and repelled a serious Union probe of the city's defenses. Ewell capably defended the city until April 3, 1865, when Richmond was evacuated by Confederate forces. While marching west, Ewell's corps was cornered at Sayler's Creek, Virginia, by General Philip H. SHERIDAN and nearly was annihilated on April 7, 1865. He was taken prisoner and endured a brief spell of captivity at Fort Sewall, Massachusetts, before being released. After the war, Ewell retired to a farm in Maury County, Tennessee, where he died of pneumonia on January 25, 1872. "Old Bald Head," as he was affectionately known, was a talented commander with many favorable attributes, but in terms of decisiveness and alacrity of movement, he proved no replacement for "Stonewall."

Further Reading

Casdorph, Paul D. *Confederate General R. S. Ewell: Robert E. Lee's Hesitant Commander.* Lexington: University Press of Kentucky, 2004.

Cox, John D. *Culp's Hill: The Attack and Defense of the Union Flank, July 2, 1863.* Cambridge, Mass.: Da Capo Press, 2003.

Jones, Wilmer L. *Generals in Blue and Gray.* Westport, Conn.: Praeger, 2004.

Newton, Steven H. *McPherson's Ridge: The First Battle for the High Ground, July 1, 1863.* Cambridge, Mass.: Da Capo Press, 2002.

Pfanz, Donald. *Richard S. Ewell: A Soldier's Life.* Chapel Hill: University of North Carolina Press, 1998.

Pfanz, Harry W. *Gettysburg—the First Day.* Chapel Hill: University of North Carolina Press, 2001.

Smith, Derek. *Lee's Last Stand: Sailor's Creek, Virginia, 1865.* Shippensburg, Pa.: White Mane Books, 2002.

Tumilty, Victor. "Filling Jackson's Shoes." *Civil War Times* 42, no. 2 (2003): 24–31.

F

Farragut, David G. (1801–1870)

Union admiral

James Glasgow Farragut was born in Campbell's Station, Tennessee, on July 5, 1801, the son of a U.S. Navy sailing master. He relocated to New Orleans, Louisiana, with his family, and after losing both parents to disease, he was adopted by Captain David Porter in 1808. Porter subsequently arranged for Farragut to receive a midshipman's commission, and during the War of 1812, he accompanied his adopted father on the famous Pacific cruise of the USS *Essex.* Many British whaling vessels were captured, and at one point Farragut, aged but 12 years, served as prize master onboard the *Alexander Barclay.* He became a prisoner when the *Essex* was in turn taken by HMS *Phoebe* and *Cherub* on February 18, 1814, and sailed home. Captain Porter publicly lauded his adopted son for bravery in battle, and Farragut honored his adopted father by changing his name to David. During the next 45 years, Farragut fulfilled a wide-ranging variety of missions both at home and abroad. He then rejoined in father as part of the Caribbean "Mosquito Squadron" to suppress piracy in 1822. Farragut rose to lieutenant three years later and, in 1828, while commanding the sloop *Erie,* witnessed the French and British fleets bombard and capture the Mexican castle of San Juan de Ulloa. This incident underscored to Farragut the vulnerability of fortifications to plunging artillery fire. He next fulfilled an uneventful stint of blockade duty during the Mexican War (1846–48); returned to Washington, D.C., to publish a number of technical treatises; and in 1854 directed construction of naval facilities at Mare Island, San Francisco. By the time Farragut became a captain in 1855, he was regarded as a competent but relatively undistinguished career officer. He was also a longtime resident of Norfolk, Virginia, but after the Civil War commenced in April 1861, his pro-Union sympathies required him to move to New York. He quickly tendered his services to the U.S. government, but the Navy Department, suspicious of his Southern roots, restricted his activities to supervising a retirement board.

After many months of officially imposed inactivity, fate intervened on Farragut's behalf when President Abraham LINCOLN sanctioned an amphibious attack on his home port of New Orleans. It was only after the intercession of his adopted brother, Commander David D. PORTER, that Secretary of the Navy Gideon Welles delegated the mission to Farragut. He now headed the West Gulf Blockading Squadron and for two months meticulously gathered a fleet of 24 wooden warships and 19 mortar gunboats off Ship Island, Mississippi. On April 18, 1862, after carefully plotting his approach to the city, Farragut directed Porter's gunboats to bombard Forts Jackson and St. Philip, on the Mississippi River, into submission. A week elapsed without the desired results, however, and the famously impatient Farragut ordered his fleet to pass the forts at night and take the city by storm. On the night of April 24, 1862, he audaciously accomplished exactly that, sweeping aside a small Confederate flotilla at the cost of one vessel sunk. The river was then running high, and with his guns pointed over the levees toward the city, New Orleans surrendered on April 25 and was occupied by troops under General Benjamin F. BUTLER. This was a major Union victory with significant military consequences: The South lost its biggest port while the Union acquired a strategic base controlling both the Mississippi River and the Gulf of Mexico. A grateful Congress voted Farragut their thanks and promoted him to rear admiral on July 16, 1862; he is the first American naval officer accorded such high rank.

Farragut followed up his success by running the fleet up the Mississippi River and operating for a time off the Confederate bastion at Vicksburg, Mississippi. He tried to capture that vital city with

Union admiral David G. Farragut *(Library of Congress)*

naval power alone but was thwarted by an inability to bombard the high bluffs on which it sat. He was eventually joined by the Mississippi River Squadron of Captain Charles H. DAVIS, whose lack of aggressiveness led to his eventual replacement by Porter. Farragut then sailed back downstream to assist General Nathaniel P. BANKS in the reduction of Port Hudson, Louisiana, on July 8, 1863, which constituted part of General Ulysses S. GRANT's efforts at Vicksburg. Control of the entire Mississippi River from St. Louis to New Orleans then reverted back to Union hands for the remainder of the war. Farragut next began to plan an ambitious assault on the significant port of Mobile, Alabama, but ill health necessitated his return to New York for convalescence. It was not until the spring of 1864 that he felt strong enough to resume duties with the West Gulf Blockading Squadron. He then spent several months assembling his ships, charting the waters in and around Mobile Bay, and marking torpedo (mine) fields as necessary. At dawn on August 5, 1864, Farragut led his squadron of four armored monitors and 14 wooden vessels past the guns of Fort Morgan. En route, the ironclad *Tecumseh* struck a mine and sank quickly, causing the entire squadron to back up. Farragut, lashed to the mainmast of the *Hartford* to better observe events, inquired as to the problem and barked back, "Damn the torpedoes! Full speed ahead!" The Union fleet then crashed into Mobile Bay sinking a small Confederate squadron before tangling with and subduing the ram CSS *Tennessee* under redoubtable Admiral Franklin BUCHANAN. Fort Morgan managed to hold out until August 23, 1864, after which the second-largest Confederate port was firmly in Union hands. In recognition of his second splendid achievement, Congress elevated him to the rank of vice admiral on December 23, 1864.

Farragut returned to New York shortly after to recuperate his health, and he missed the major naval effort at Fort Fisher, Wilmington, North Carolina. He then partook of minor operations along the James River, Virginia, in the spring of 1865 when the war ended. On July 26, 1866, Congress again promoted him to full admiral, and he assumed command of the European Squadron on an extended goodwill tour through 1867. Farragut died in Portsmouth, New Hampshire, on August 14, 1870, one of the boldest exponents of naval power in American history. His contributions to the Union victory were essential.

Further Reading

Duffy, James P. *Lincoln's Admiral: The Civil War Campaigns of David Farragut.* New York: Wiley, 1997.
Friend, Jack. *West Wind, Flood Tide: The Battle of Mobile Bay.* Annapolis, Md.: Naval Institute Press, 2003.
Fuller, Howard. *Navies and Naval Operations of the Civil War, 1861–65.* London: Conway Maritime, 2005.
Garcia, Pedro. "Losing the Big Easy." *Civil War Times Illustrated* 41, no. 2 (2002): 46–53, 64–65.
Harris, William C. "Damn *These* Torpedoes, too!" *Civil War Times Illustrated* 39, no. 1 (2000): 36–42.
Hearn, Chester G. *Admiral David Glasgow Farragut: The Civil War Years.* Annapolis, Md.: Naval Institute Press, 1998.
Schneller, Robert J. *Farragut: America's First Admiral.* Washington, D.C.: Brassey's, 2002.
Sweetman, Jack, ed. *The Great Admirals: Command at Sea, 1587–1945.* Annapolis, Md.: Naval Institute Press, 1997.
———. *Great American Naval Battles.* Annapolis, Md.: Naval Institute Press, 1998.
Suhr, Robert. "A Run for New Orleans." *Military Heritage* 2, no. 1 (2000): 52–59, 86–87.

Floyd, John B. (1806–1863)
Confederate general

John Buchanan Floyd was born in Smithfield, Virginia, on June 1, 1806, the son of a planter. He passed through South Carolina College in 1829 with a law degree and commenced a successful practice at home. In 1847 he parleyed his skills into politics by successfully standing for a seat in the House of Delegates and a year later served as governor of Virginia. As a politician, Floyd fully embraced slavery and states's rights, but he proved ambivalent toward secession. In 1856 he strongly supported the presidential candidacy of James Buchanan and received the appointment of secretary of war in return. Floyd, lacking any practical

military experience, enjoyed a stormy tenure in office amid rising claims of corruption and cronyism. The bulk of accusations arose from his apparent mishandling of Indian trust funds and the alleged channeling of profits into the hands of friends and relatives. Floyd deepened his reputation for controversy in 1860 by appointing Joseph E. JOHNSTON, his brother in law, to be quartermaster general, over the heads of more experienced individuals such as Colonel Robert E. LEE. Once the nation was buffeted by the rising tide of secessionism, Floyd's actions were viewed in a more treasonable light. At one point, he arranged for the transfer of 125,00 small arms to arsenals throughout the South, a move greeted with suspicion by many Northerners. Floyd simply countered that he was making room for new stocks of rifled weapons that were expected soon. A congressional committee investigated Floyd and cleared him of any improprieties in February 1861, but by then the issue was moot. Floyd, angered by what he considered the illegal transfer of Federal troops from Fort Moultrie, Charleston, South Carolina, to Fort Sumter in the harbor, demanded that President Buchanan countermand the move. When Buchanan refused to order Major Robert ANDERSON into compliance, Floyd resigned from office on December 29, 1860, and returned to Virginia.

On May 23, 1861, Floyd became a brigadier general in the Confederate army. The following August, he assumed control of the Army of the Kanawha in western Virginia and was tasked with protecting the Allegheny Mountains from Union attacks. He waged a number of ineffective skirmishes at Cross Lanes and Carnifex Ferry that September, losing valuable ground. However, the following December, he transferred his brigade to the army of General Albert S. JOHNSTON in Kentucky, where he was assigned to command Forts Henry and Donelson. These strategic posts, on the Cumberland and Tennessee rivers, respectively, constituted the first line of Southern defenses in the middle sector, and they were vital to the Confederate cause. For this reason, in the spring of

1862, they became the objects of a concerted Union offensive under General Ulysses S. Grant and Captain Andrew H. Foote. On February 6, 1862, Foote managed to capture Fort Henry with gunboats alone while Grant prepared to march overland to besiege the remaining post.

For several days Floyd, in concert with Generals Gideon J. Pillow and Simon B. Buckner, deliberated about what to do. On February 6, 1862, Fort Donelson's gunners drove off Foote's gunboats, but Floyd believed that his position was hopeless. The Confederates then sortied in strength against Grant's besieging army the following day, and they nearly broke through, but indecisiveness at the last minute allowed a Union counterattack to shut the defenders back into their fort. That evening, Floyd and Pillow made a fateful decision to escape with part of the garrison while Buckner remained behind to surrender. On February 16, 1862, Floyd and Pillow departed before Grant accepted the surrender of Fort Donelson—a major blow to the Confederacy. The entire affairs so disgusted Major Nathan B. Forrest that he disregarded orders and likewise cut his way to safety. Floyd then made his way to Nashville, where Johnston placed him in charge of evacuation efforts. However, once Confederate president Jefferson Davis learned of the circumstances by which Floyd abandoned his command, he relieved him on March 11, 1862. This act should have ended his military career, but Floyd's political connections ran deep, and in April 1862, the Virginia legislature promoted him to major general of militia. He then spent the balance of the year garrisoning saltmines and railroads in the southwestern portion of the state before dying at Abingdon on August 26, 1863. All told, Floyd's flirtation with military command bore disastrous consequences for the Confederacy that he sought so earnestly to serve.

Further Reading

Engle, Stephen D. *Struggle for the Heartland: The Campaign from Fort Henry to Corinth.* Lincoln: University of Nebraska Press, 2001.

Gott, Kendall D. *Where the South Lost the War: An Analysis of the Fort Henry–Fort Donelson Campaign, February 1862.* Mechanicsburg, Pa.: Stackpole Books, 2003.

McKnight, Brian D. *Contested Borderland: The Civil War in Appalachian Kentucky and Virginia.* Lexington: University Press of Kentucky, 2006.

Pinnegar, Charles. *Brand of Infamy: A Biography of John Buchanan Floyd.* Westport, Conn.: Greenwood Press, 2002.

Symonds, Craig, et al. "Who Were the Worst Ten Generals?" *North & South* 7, no. 3 (2004): 12–25.

Tucker, Spencer C. *"Unconditional Surrender": The Captures of Forts Henry and Donelson.* Abilene, Tex.: McWhiney Foundation Press, 2001.

Foote, Andrew H. (1806–1863)
Union admiral

Andrew Hull Foote was born in New Haven, Connecticut, on September 12, 1806, and raised in a strict, religious household. In 1822 he gained admittance to the U.S. Military Academy, but he matriculated only six months before receiving his midshipman's commission in the U.S. Navy. During the next two decades, he held a wide variety of billets both on land and on sea, rising to lieutenant in 1831. Ten years later, he assumed command of the frigate USS *Cumberland* and, consistent with his deeply held religious beliefs, made history by organizing the first shipwide temperance society. Foote subsequently launched a drive to ban alcoholic rations on navy vessels, which finally became official policy in 1862. He also agitated against flogging and zealously pursued antislavery activities off the coast of Africa. Ashore, Foote was active in abolitionist activities, and in 1854, he published an account of his activities entitled *Africa and the American Flag*. In 1856 he advanced to command and took the sloop *Portsmouth* on a tour of Asia, where he witnessed British naval operations during the so-called Arrow War against China. On November 21, 1856, Chinese gunners at Canton mistakenly fired on his vessel, so Foote promptly landed 300 sailors and marines ashore, stormed four barrier forts, and killed an estimated 250 defenders at a cost of 29 killed and wounded. He

Union admiral Andrew H. Foote *(National Archives)*

sailed home in 1858 and received command of the Brooklyn Navy Yard, a post he held when the Civil War commenced.

In June 1861 Foote was ordered to replace Commander John RODGERS as head of the embryonic Mississippi River Squadron, headquartered at St. Louis, Missouri. He assisted engineer James B. Eads in constructing several armored gunboats for use on the western waters. These 12 small vessels, mounting 143 heavy cannon, quickly proved invaluable assets for exploiting riverine warfare against the Confederacy. Foote also struck up cordial relations with the local military commander, General Ulysses S. GRANT, who shared his strate-

gic vision for offensive operations. Their first objective was Fort Henry on the Cumberland River, which Foote bombarded into submission on February 6, 1862, without army assistance. He next sailed on to engage the much stronger position of Fort Donelson on the Tennessee River while Grant marched overland to besiege it. On February 14 Foote engaged the Confederate batteries, situated on a high bluff, which subjected his armada to a plunging fire. He was rebuffed with severe losses and sustained a foot injury but refused to relinquish command. Hobbling on crutches, Foote next deployed his craft in concert with General John POPE's forces at Island No. 10 in the Mississippi River. After several days of ineffectual bombardment, he slipped the ironclad *Carondelet* past Confederate defenses on the night of April 4, 1862, cutting the garrison off and prompting its surrender three days later. The upper Mississippi River was now entirely clear of a Confederate presence, but Foote's declining health necessitated his replacement by Commander Charles H. DAVIS in June 1862.

In light of his exceptional service, Foote received both the thanks of Congress and promotion to rear admiral as of June 16, 1862. He remained actively employed in New York as chief of the Bureau of Equipment and Recruiting, although he chafed in the role of a bureaucrat. Foote then lobbied for an active command, and in June 1863, he succeeded Admiral Samuel F. DU PONT as head of the South Atlantic Blockading Squadron. He never lived to accept command, dying suddenly in New York on June 26, 1863. Foote made invaluable contributions to the Union war effort through his expertise with gunboats and his demonstrated willingness to work closely with army commanders.

Further Reading

Coombe, Jack D. *Thunder along the Mississippi: The River Battles That Split the Confederacy.* New York: Sarpedon, 1996.

Forlenza, Gerald A. "A Navy Life: The Pre-Civil War Career of Rear Admiral Andrew Hull Foote." Unpublished Ph.D. diss., Claremont Graduate School, 1991.

Gott, Kendall D. "Gateway to the Heartland." *North & South* 7, no. 2 (2004): 46–59.

Jackson, Rex T. *James B. Eads: The Civil War Ironclads on His Mississippi.* Bowie, Md.: Heritage Books, 2004.

Konstam, Angus. *Mississippi River Gunboats of the American Civil War.* Oxford: Osprey, 2002.

Tucker, Spencer C. *Andrew Foote: Civil War Admiral on Western Waters.* Annapolis, Md.: Naval Institute Press, 2000.

Forrest, Nathan B. (1821–1877)

Confederate general

Nathan Bedford Forrest was born in Chapel Hill, Tennessee, on July 13, 1821, the son of an impoverished blacksmith. He accompanied his family to Mississippi where his father died in 1837 and left him, at the age of 16, responsible for feeding a large family. Forrest never attended school and remained semiliterate throughout his entire life, but he proved himself a singularly driven man. After working as a day laborer, he learned to trade in cattle and slaves and eventually established a prosperous plantation. Forrest proved so adept at selling cotton that he became a self-made millionaire by the time the Civil War began in April 1861. He initially joined the 7th Tennessee Cavalry as a private and then received permission to raise and equip a regiment at his own expense as its lieutenant colonel. In February 1862 he fought well at the defense of Forts Henry and Donelson, and on the night of the 16th, he escaped rather than surrender. Such initiative brought him promotion to colonel, and he gained additional laurels at the Battle of Shiloh (April 6–7, 1862), capturing a Union battery and advancing to brigadier general. In July 1862 Forrest was assigned to the army of General Braxton BRAGG, a man for whom he expressed strong antipathy. He nonetheless performed well as an independent raider, and on July 13, 1862, he bluffed the Union garrison at Murfreesboro, Tennessee, into surrendering. Bragg, who viewed Forrest as more of a nuisance than an asset, subsequently stripped him of command and ordered him south to raise a new force. Forrest readily complied, and from December 1862 to January 1863, he accompanied General Earl VAN DORN on several effective raids against General Ulysses S. GRANT's supply lines. When Van Dorn later accused Forrest of hoarding captured Union supplies for his own use—a charge Forrest vehemently denied—the two headstrong cavaliers nearly came to blows.

The secret of Forrest's success was his ability to move suddenly, strike unexpectedly, and withdraw quickly along prearranged escape routes. His oft-quoted mantra of "Get there first with the most men" was germane to his success but also a luxury he seldom enjoyed. In fact, Forrest exhibited an uncanny knack for engaging and defeating forces much larger than his own. For example, in April 1863, he surrounded and bluffed the 2,000-man column of Colonel Abel D. Streight into surrendering to his 500 men at Rome, Georgia.

Confederate general Nathan B. Forrest *(Massachusetts Commandery Military Order of the Loyal Legion and the U.S. Army Military History Institute)*

Forrest subsequently rejoined the Army of Tennessee under General Bragg that summer and fought well at the bloody battle of Chickamauga on September 18–20, 1863. However, Forrest became so outraged by Bragg's unwillingness to pursue General William S. ROSECRANS's defeated army that a duel seemed in the offing. He then requested an immediate transfer, and President Jefferson DAVIS allowed him to set up an independent command in nearby Mississippi with a rank of major general as of December 4, 1863. From here, Forrest was at liberty to slash at Union supply routes in Tennessee and northern Alabama while also parrying the occasional Federal thrust against him. The only serious blot on his military reputation was the capture of Fort Pillow, Tennessee, on April 12, 1864, whereby he apparently allowed his men to lose control and massacre part of the African-American garrison. On June 10, 1864, Forrest scored his biggest tactical success by attacking and routing General Samuel G. Sturgis's 10,000 Union soldiers at Brice's Cross Roads, Mississippi. However, he suffered a heavy defeat while operating under General Samuel D. Lee at Tupelo on July 13–15, 1864, and returned to raiding. He scored a spectacular success at Johnston, Tennessee, nearly crippling General William T. SHERMAN's supply lines on his march to Georgia. Sherman grew so exasperated that he declared that Forrest must be destroyed "if it costs ten thousand lives and breaks the treasury." He subsequently served under General John B. HOOD during his ill-fated advance on Nashville, Tennessee, and he skillfully covered the Confederate withdrawal throughout December 1864.

Forrest rose to lieutenant general in February 1865 but his shrinking command confronted insurmountably steep odds. On April 2, 1865, General James H. WILSON's cavalry corps drove Forrest and his troopers out of Selma, Alabama, his last and largest defeat. He finally surrendered to Union authorities at Gainesville, Alabama, on May 9, 1865, and returned home to his ruined plantation. After the war, Forrest tried to recoup his fortune but enjoyed little success. He spent the balance of his remaining years in Memphis, Tennessee, as president of a railroad company. Forrest also acquired considerable notoriety by founding the infamous Ku Klux Klan in 1867, serving as its first and only Grand Wizard. He subsequently disbanded the group in 1869 after failing to curb its violent excesses against African Americans. Forrest died in Memphis on October 29, 1877, at the age of 56. His greatest leadership trait, a single-minded determination to succeed, probably makes him the Confederacy's most accomplished cavalry leader and a partisan raider of the first order. Like Wade HAMPTON and Richard TAYLOR, he is one of only three Confederates who were elevated to lieutenant general without prior military training.

Further Reading

Ashdown, Paul. *The Myth of Nathaniel Bedford Forrest.* Lanham, Md.: Rowman and Littlefield, 2005.

Black, Robert W. *Cavalry Raids of the Civil War.* Mechanicsburg, Pa.: Stackpole Books, 2004.

Bradley, Michael R. *Nathan Bedford Forrest's Escort and Staff.* Gretna, La.: Pelican Pub. Co., 2006.

Browning, Robert M. *Forrest: The Confederacy's Relentless Warrior.* Washington, D.C.: Brassey's, 2004.

Cimprich, John. *Fort Pillow, a Civil War Massacre, and Public Memory.* Baton Rouge: Louisiana State University Press, 2005.

Davidson, Eddy. *Nathan Bedford Forrest: In Search of the Empire.* Gretna, La.: Pelican Pub. Co., 2006.

Keithly, David. "Pay the Devil Asymmetrically: Nathan Bedford Forrest in the American Civil War." *Civil Wars* 5, no. 4 (2002): 77–102.

Russell, Michael B. "Fort Pillow: Press, Propaganda, and Public Perception During the American Civil War." Unpublished master's thesis, University of Arkansas, Fayetteville, 2002.

G

Gibbon, John (1827–1896)

Union general

John Gibbon was born in Holmesburg, Pennsylvania, on April 20, 1827, the son of a physician. He relocated with his family to Charlotte, North Carolina, as a child and was admitted from there to the U.S. Military Academy in 1842. Gibbon graduated five years later, having been held back a year owing to difficulties with an English course. Now a second lieutenant of the 4th U.S. Artillery, he accompanied his gun crew to Mexico in 1847 but saw no action. He next served in Florida by assisting Seminole Indians in their move to the Indian Territory (Oklahoma), from which he acquired lasting sympathy for Native Americans. By 1855, Gibbon was promoted captain and back at West Point as an artillery instructor where, in 1859, he published his seminal *The Artillerist's Manual.* This text is significant in being the first American book on the subject, for prior to its appearance the army simply utilized the latest French manuals. Gibbon was stationed in Utah Territory when the secession crisis erupted in 1861 and his Southern origins caused a degree of suspicion among fellow officers. Nonetheless, and despite the fact that his three brothers served the Confederacy, he remained loyal to the Union.

Gibbon first saw service by commanding a battery in the newly raised Army of the Potomac, and, on November 8, 1861, he joined General Irwin McDowell's division as chief of artillery. A hard-edged professional and an excellent disciplinarian, he rose to brigadier general on May 2, 1862, and led a brigade in General Rufus King's division. In this respect, Gibbon differed from many of his West Point contemporaries by not despising volunteer soldiers. Instead, he paid them due respect, carefully trained them, and cultivated their loyalty. His command consisted of four regiments from Wisconsin and one from Illinois, which he outfitted with white pants and tall black hats to improve esprit de corps. The "Black Hat Brigade," as they were initially known, experienced its baptism of fire at Groveton, Virginia, on August 28, 1862, where it was ambushed by Confederates under General Thomas J. Jackson. Gibbon calmly led his men into a battle in which they suffered 40 percent casualties but held their ground dutifully. He next distinguished himself in bloody fighting at South Mountain and Antietam, where General Joseph Hooker pronounced his troops the "Iron Brigade"—and the moniker stuck. Gibbon subsequently led a division in General John F. Reynolds I Corps at Fredericksburg on December 13, 1862, where he was severely wounded. After recovering, he was assigned to divisional command in the II Corps of General Winfield S. Hancock, and he fought actively in the ill-fated Chancellorsville campaign.

During the first day of Gettysburg, July 1, 1863, the Iron Brigade was one of the first infantry units to reinforce Union cavalry under General

Union general John Gibbon *(Library of Congress)*

capacity, he helped pursue the Army of Northern Virginia from Richmond in April 1865 and was one of three commissioners selected to arrange the surrender of General Robert E. LEE at Appomattox on April 9.

Gibbon was retained in the peacetime establishment with a rank of colonel of the 36th and then the 7th U.S. Infantry, and he was posted back on the frontier. In this capacity, his unit formed part of General George CROOK's column and was the first to reach the survivors of General George A. CUSTER's 7th Cavalry at Little Big Horn. The following year, he played a prominent role in the Nez Perce War against Chief Joseph and was repulsed by the tribe's warriors at the Battle of Big Hole, Montana, on August 9, 1877. Gibbon, who sustained his third and final wound in this fight, afterward befriended the chief. In 1885 he accepted command of the Department of Columbia and the following year took charge of the Department of the Pacific at San Francisco. Gibbon retired from the army in 1891 and eventually settled in Baltimore, Maryland, where he served as commander of the Military Order of the Loyal Legion. He died there on February 6, 1896, a loyal Southerner and an outstanding combat commander.

John BUFORD. Gibbon led it into the thick of combat under General John F. REYNOLDS, where it suffered horrific casualties but again acquitted itself well. On July 3, 1863, Gibbon's command absorbed the main Confederate charge by General George E. PICKETT on Cemetery Hill, driving the Southerners off with heavy losses. At the height of the engagement, Gibbon received a second serious wound and was borne from the battlefield. After months of convalescence, he rejoined Hancock's II Corps in time for General Ulysses S. GRANT's Overland campaign against Richmond, Virginia, in May 1864. Gibbon then fought capably at the bloody battles of the Wilderness, Spotsylvania, and Cold Harbor before settling into the long siege at Petersburg. He rose to major general in June 1864, but his formally cordial relations with Hancock soured, and Gibbon was transferred to command the XXIV Corps, Army of the James. In this

Further Reading

Berkoff, Todd S. "'Our Boys Mowed Their Ranks Like Grass': The Iron Brigade at Brawner's Farm." *Military Heritage* 2, no. 4 (2001): 64–71, 98.

Herdegen, Lance J. *The Men Stood Like Iron: How the Iron Brigade Won Its Name.* Bloomington: Indiana University Press, 1997.

Lavery, Donald S. *Iron Brigade General: John Gibbon, A Rebel in Blue.* Westport, Conn.: Greenwood Press, 1993.

Newton, Steven H. *McPherson's Ridge: The First Fight for the High Ground, July 1, 1863.* Cambridge, Mass.: Da Capo Press, 2002.

Nolan, Alan T., and Sharon E. Vipond. *Giants in Their Tall Hats: Essays on the Iron Brigade.* Bloomington: Indiana University Press, 1998.

Wert, Jeffrey D. *A Brotherhood of Valor: The Common Soldiers of the Stonewall Brigade, C.S.A., and the Iron Brigade, U.S.A.* New York: Simon and Schuster, 1999.

Gordon, John B. (1832–1904)

Confederate general

John Brown Gordon was born in Upson County, Georgia, on February 6, 1832, and he studied at the University of Georgia. However, he quit school briefly to study law and subsequently managed a mine in northwestern Georgia. Gordon was also passionately pro-secessionist, so when the Civil War erupted in April 1861, he joined a company of mountain men called the "Racoon Roughs" and functioned as their captain. When Georgia authorities declined to accept their services, he marched them across the state line to become part of the 6th Alabama Infantry. Gordon, despite his lack of professional military training, adjusted well to mili-

Confederate general John B. Gordon *(National Archives)*

tary life, and in April 1862, he advanced to colonel. He then fought in the Peninsula campaign of 1862 under General Richard Rodes, seeing combat at Seven Pines and Malvern Hill. In the latter engagement, Gordon assumed command of the brigade when Rodes fell wounded. That fall, Gordon helped spearhead the Confederate advance into Maryland, and he saw active duty at the battles of South Mountain and Antietam as part of General Daniel H. HILL's division. On September 17, 1862, Gordon's brigade held the Sunken Road in the center of General Robert E. LEE's position, where it beat off repeated attacks by superior numbers of Union troops. In the course of combat, Gordon was hit no less than five times, with the last bullet smashing into his left cheek, knocking him unconscious. In light of his sterling behavior, he received promotion to brigadier general, although he required several months for recuperation.

In the spring of 1863, Gordon commanded a brigade of Georgia troops in General Jubal A. EARLY's division. He fought well at Chancellorsville and Gettysburg that year and performed exceptionally well during the 1864 Overland campaign against General Ulysses S. GRANT. At the Battle of Spotsylvania on May 12, 1864, Federals under General Winfield S. HANCOCK overran the Confederate salient at the "Mule Shoe" and threatened to break their line when Gordon promptly counterattacked and drove them back. Consequently, he gained promotion to major general and accompanied Early's II Corps throughout the famous Shenandoah campaign of the summer and fall of 1864. As such, he bore conspicuous roles in fighting at Lynchburg, Monocacy, and Kernstown during the initial Confederate resurgence and then at the losing battles of Winchester, Fisher's Hill, and Cedar Creek against General Philip H. SHERIDAN. Afterward, Early's army was broken up, and the survivors returned to the Army of Northern Virginia outside Petersburg, Virginia. Gordon had yet to be promoted to lieutenant general, but he was nevertheless tasked with conducting the final Confederate offensive of the war against Fort Stedman on

March 25, 1865. Defeat here signaled the eventual collapse of Southern defenses, and Gordon conducted a tenacious rearguard action that allowed the Army of Northern Virginia to escape intact. He next fought at Sayler's Creek on April 6, 1865, where most of the II Corps was captured or destroyed, and he briefly succeeded General Richard S. Ewell as commander. Lee then appointed Gordon to draw up documents outlining his surrender to General Grant on April 12, 1865. He also received the special distinction of being allowed to lead the bedraggled Confederates out of camp, past Union troops lining the roads at Appomattox. When General Joshua L. Chamberlain unexpectedly ordered his men to present arms as a token of respect, Gordon had his men do the same, thereby returning "honor for honor."

After the war, Gordon enjoyed a lengthy and successful political career. He gained election to the U.S. Senate in 1873 as a Democrat, becoming the first former Confederate to preside over that body. He also served as a leading voice for national reconciliation and urged Southerners to work wholeheartedly for reunification. He also prevailed on Northern politicians to end the period of Reconstruction and allow self-rule in former states of the Confederacy. As a spokesperson for the "New South," Gordon was also a proponent of modernization and industrialization to assist his region in breaking from its long agrarian tradition. In 1886 Gordon was elected governor of Georgia, and two years later, he served again in the U.S. Senate. In a throwback to his earlier life, when the United Confederate Veterans was established in 1890, Gordon was elected its first commander in chief. He held the post at the time of his death in Miami, Florida, on January 9, 1904. He was among the Confederacy's most successful divisional commanders and the only corps-level leader without professional military instruction.

Further Reading

Bates, Thomas. "One of the Best: John Brown Gordon's Rise in the Army of Northern Virginia." Unpublished master's thesis, James Madison University, 2001.
Eckert, Ralph L. *John Brown Gordon: Soldier, Southerner, American.* Baton Rouge: Louisiana State University Press, 1989.
Lepa, Jack H. *The Shenandoah Campaign of 1864.* Jefferson, N.C.: McFarland, 2003.
Lowry, Joseph E. "Lee's Last Throw of the Dice." *Military Heritage* 6, no. 3 (2004): 62–69.
Gordon, John B. *Reminiscences of the Civil War.* New York: C. Scribner's Sons, 1903.
Smith, Derek. *Lee's Last Stand: Sailor's Creek, Virginia, 1865.* Shippensburg, Pa.: White Mane Books, 2002.

Gorgas, Josiah (1818–1883)
Confederate general

Josiah Gorgas was born in Running Pumps, Pennsylvania, on July 1, 1818, the son of poor farmers, and he was forced to quit school in order to help support his large family. After enduring a hardscrabble existence, he gained admittance to the U.S. Military Academy in 1837 and graduated four years later, sixth in a class of 52. Gorgas was then posted as a second lieutenant in the Ordnance Corps, for which he showed considerable promise. He remained at the Watervliet Arsenal, New York, for many years and in 1845 spent a year in Europe to study foreign ordnance. He returned home in time to fight in the Mexican War (1846–48), with the army under General Winfield Scott. Gorgas acquitted himself well while sighting cannon at the siege of Veracruz, and Scott appointed him head of the ordnance depot there. After the war, Gorgas resumed his routine activities at a number of Federal arsenals around the country. However, while stationed at Mount Vernon, Alabama, in 1853, he married the daughter of a former governor. After this time, he increasingly identified his personal interests with those of the South. Gorgas, who had lost a brevet promotion to internal army politics, finally rose to captain in 1855 and was commanding the Franklin Arsenal in Philadelphia, Pennsylvania, when the Civil War commenced in April 1861. After some initial wavering, his wife and her family prevailed on him to throw his lot in with the South, and he resigned his commission to join the Confederate army.

Gorgas was initially posted as a major within the Confederate Ordnance Corps, but President Jefferson DAVIS, acting on the advice of General Pierre G. T. BEAUREGARD, appointed him chief of Confederate ordnance on April 8, 1861. Thus situated, he was now responsible for procuring, constructing, and repairing all available weapons for Southern armies. On paper, Gorgas faced nearly insurmountable obstacles, for the Confederacy generally lacked an industrial base and possessed but a single cannon foundry in Richmond, Virginia. However, this heretofore unknown ordnance officer demonstrated outright genius at organization and improvisation, and he soon established himself as one of the Confederacy's greatest assets. To augment existing stocks, Gorgas instituted a systematized policy of thoroughly scavenging Union weapons and supplies captured on the battlefield. He next undertook a drastic expansion of existing factories and the addition of new ones, along with the concomitant gunpowder mills, foundries, and arsenals to manufacture rifles, pistols, swords, and cannon. Gorgas also founded the Confederate Nitre and Mineral Bureau to manage the utilization of all natural resources effectively. Realizing that the South could never match Northern industrial output, he dispatched numerous agents abroad to Europe to buy or barter for the requisite weapons, tools, and machinery. These items would then be transported home on a fleet of blockade-runners employed by the Ordnance Department. The system he originated proved highly efficient, and during the next four years, the Confederacy acquired 600,000 weapons, 2 million pounds of saltpeter, and 1.5 million pounds of lead.

Gorgas carried the process a step further through an ingenious system of decentralized distribution to offset the Confederacy's decided lack of railroads. It was administered by capable subordinates handpicked by Gorgas himself, and it worked surprisingly well considering the difficulties under which the South labored. Consequently, he almost singlehandedly kept Confederate field armies relatively well armed and equipped for the duration of the war. The Southern war effort could not have lasted as long as it did without his supervision, and on November 10, 1864, he gained promotion to brigadier general. His supply system remained in play until the very last days of the war, and Gorgas himself surrendered to Union authorities at Washington, North Carolina, on May 14, 1865.

In the postwar period, Gorgas tried his hand at administering an ironworks in Alabama, and after it failed, he turned to education in 1872 in becoming vice president of the University of the South at Sewanee, Tennessee. After a stormy tenure there, he transferred to the University of Alabama as its president in 1878. Poor health soon necessitated his retirement, and Gorgas spent the rest of his life as the university librarian. He died in Tuscaloosa, Alabama, on May 15, 1883, the most accomplished ordnance officer in American history—Union or Confederate.

Further Reading

Bragg, C. L. *Never for Want of Powder: The Confederate Powder Works in Augusta, Georgia.* Columbia: University of South Carolina Press, 2007.

Collins, Steven G. "From Pikes to Gunpowder: Josiah Gorgas and the Arming of an Agrarian Nation." Unpublished master's thesis, Southwest Texas State University, 1992.

Moore, Michael J. "Josiah Gorgas and the Richmond Ordnance Industry: The Arsenal of the Confederacy." Unpublished master's thesis, Old Dominion University, 1996.

Wiggins, Sarah W. *Love and Duty: Amelia and Josiah Gorgas and Their Family.* Tuscaloosa: University of Alabama Press, 2005.

Wiggins, Sarah W., ed. *The Journal of Josiah Gorgas, 1857–1878.* Tuscaloosa: University of Alabama Press, 1995.

Woodward, Steven E., et al. "Who Were the Top Ten Generals?" *North & South* 6, no. 4 (2003): 12–22.

Grant, Ulysses S. (1822–1885)

Union general

Hiram Ulysses Grant was born in Point Pleasant, Ohio, on April 27, 1822, the son of farmers. Listless and idle as a youth, his father managed to secure him an appointment to the U.S. Military Academy in 1839. While in attendance, his name was mistakenly recorded as Ulysses Simpson Grant, which he formally adopted. Grant proved a lackluster student, displaying aptitude for horsemanship and little else, but he graduated midway in his class by 1843 and was commissioned a second lieutenant in the 4th U.S. Infantry. He served briefly at the Jefferson Barracks, Missouri, before joining General Zachary Taylor's Army of Texas in 1846. When the Mexican War broke out, Grant was in the thick of fighting at Palo Alto, Resaca de la Palma, and Monterrey, and he subsequently transferred to the army of General Winfield SCOTT in 1847. During the advance on Mexico City he won two brevet promotions for bravery at the battles of Molino del Rey and Chapultepec. On a personal level, Grant opposed the conflict as an act of aggression against a neighboring country. After the war, he transferred to the western frontier for a long stint of routine garrison duty, rising to captain in 1853. However, the isolation and boredom took a heavy toll on Grant who, like many contemporaries, sought relief through excessive drinking. After officially being reprimanded, he resigned his commission in 1854 and rejoined his family at Galena, Illinois. For six years, Grant tried various business ventures, all of which conspicuously failed, and he ended up clerking in his father's tannery. Only the onset of civil war in 1861 fostered a dramatic turn in his personal fortunes.

Grant initially offered his service to the government and was ignored. After he worked several months for the state adjutant general, Congressman Elihu Washburne secured him an appointment as colonel of the 21st Illinois Volunteers in June 1861. Two months later, he received promotion to brigadier general and command of the District of Southeast Missouri. Early on, Grant revealed his predilection for offensive operations by seizing Paducah, Kentucky, on September 6, 1861, to keep it out of Confederate hands. On November 7, 1861, he attacked Southern forces at

Union general Ulysses S. Grant *(Library of Congress)*

Belmont, Missouri, drove General Gideon PILLOW's Confederates out of camp, and then lost control of his men, who engaged in plunder. A sharp counterattack by General Leonidas K. POLK sent the Federals fleeing back to their riverboats, and Grant luckily evaded capture. Consequently, Grant spent the next few months drilling and disciplining his men while badgering the theater commander, General Henry W. HALLECK, permission to attack Forts Henry and Donelson on the Cumberland and Tennessee rivers, respectively. When Halleck finally acquiesced, Grant energetically attacked and took both fortifications with timely assistance from Captain Andrew H. FOOTE and his gunboats. On February 15, 1862, Union forces experienced a close call when a Confederate sortie out of Fort Donelson surprised the bluecoats in their trenches, and the Southerners nearly escaped, but a prompt counterattack by Grant shut the defenders up in their works. Generals John B. FLOYD and Gideon J. Pillow then ignominiously chose to flee rather than surrender and accorded General Simon B. Buckner that melancholy task. Significantly, when Buckner formally asked Grant, an old acquaintance, for terms, he brusquely demanded and received unconditional surrender on February 16, 1862. Thereafter, the Union press lauded him as "Unconditional Surrender Grant."

Grant, seeking to maintain the strategic initiative, struck south along the Tennessee River and made a lodgment at Pittsburg Landing, Tennessee, better known as Shiloh. On the morning of April 6, 1862, his men were rudely surprised in camp by an entire Confederate army under General Albert S. JOHNSTON, driven to the river, and nearly defeated. That evening, Grant luckily obtained reinforcements from Generals Don C. BUELL and Lew WALLACE, which enabled him to counterattack General Pierre G. T. BEAUREGARD on the following day and regain lost ground. The resulting heavy casualties raised a storm of criticism against Grant in the press, and he consequently was superseded by the tottering Halleck for several weeks. After a glacial campaign against Corinth, Mississippi, Halleck transferred to Washington, D.C., as general in chief, and Grant was restored to command. He then orchestrated an offensive strategy against the Confederate bastion at Vicksburg, Mississippi, so as to cut the South in two. Through the winter and into the spring of 1863, he made no less than four direct and indirect approaches to the city from the north, frequently in concert with General William T. SHERMAN and naval vessels under Commander David D. PORTER, but to no avail. But on the evening of March 20, 1863, he brilliantly broke the impasse by marching down the left bank of the Mississippi

River and, with Porter's help, ferried his troops across below Confederate defenses. Striking inland with 25,000 men, he also launched General Benjamin H. GRIERSON on an extended raid to Baton Rouge, Louisiana, to mask his movements. Grant then cut his own supply lines and foraged off the land as Confederates under General Joseph E. JOHNSTON and John C. PEMBERTON tried frantically to stop him. Federal forces aggressively beat the divided Southerners in four pitched battles, driving off Johnston and trapping Pemberton within Vicksburg. Grant then launched two frontal assaults on the city that were bloodily repelled before settling into a protracted siege of 46 days. When Vicksburg finally surrendered to Grant on July 4, 1863, the Confederacy had been fatally split, and he received promotion to major general and command of the Division of the Mississippi.

Grant next turned his attention to Tennessee, where the Army of the Cumberland under General William S. ROSECRANS was besieged at Chattanooga by General Braxton BRAGG's Confederates. Moving quickly, Grant sacked Rosecrans in favor of General George H. THOMAS, reestablished a reliable supply route (the so-called Cracker Line), and ordered up four divisions under General Sherman. Bragg had unwillingly played into Union hands by dispatching General James LONGSTREET's veteran I Corps to besiege Knoxville, at which point, Grant fell on his diminished forces like a thunderbolt on November 25, 1863, in the twin battles of Lookout Mountain and Missionary Ridge. The Confederates were shattered and reeled back in defeat to Georgia. This unbroken string of victories now propelled Grant to the forefront of Union military leadership, and President Abraham LINCOLN arranged for his promotion to lieutenant general in March 1864. He also summoned his general to Washington to replace Halleck as general-in-chief and formulate an all-encompassing strategy to crush the tottering but as yet defiant Confederacy and end the Civil War. This marks Grant's greatest contribution to the war effort: promulgating a comprehensive, multipronged offensive that brought the full weight of superior Union manpower and resources on the South. In the western theater, General Sherman was to depart Tennessee and march for Atlanta, Georgia, and thence to Savannah and the sea. In the Deep South, General Nathaniel BANKS would lead an offensive up the Red River into western Louisiana as far as Texas to cut off any flow of supplies. In Virginia, the Army of the James under General Benjamin F. BUTLER was to attack along the south banks of the James River to threaten Petersburg. However, the main blow would be delivered by Grant himself to be aimed solely at the redoubtable Army of Northern Virginia under General Robert E. LEE. The contest, when it unfolded, would be a clash of giants.

In the late spring of 1864, Grant directed the Army of the Potomac under General George M. MEADE to begin the advance on Richmond. Lee countered by attacking at the Wilderness, May 5–6, where he repulsed Grant with heavy loses to both sides. But herein marked a paradigm shift in Union strategy: Though defeated, Grant did not withdraw; rather, he simply sidestepped to the left and continued inching toward Richmond. Lee followed and met him at Spotsylvania Court House, May 7–20, in another inconclusive bloody standoff. Absorbing casualties stoically, Grant sidestepped Lee again, forcing him on a march to the North Anna River. The Confederates moved adroitly and blocked him, so, for the only time in the campaign, Grant elected on a frontal attack at Cold Harbor on June 3, 1864, to smash through Lee's defenses. The resulting disaster cost Union forces 6,000 men in an hour and led to renewed accusations of Grant as a "butcher." Since the opening of the campaign, the Army of the Potomac had in fact suffered 50,000 casualties, nearly one-half its strength. Lee, in contrast, sustained an estimated 30,000 to 32,000 casualties, roughly half that amount. But whereas Grant received a steady influx of replacements to keep his manpower levels more or less constant, the Army of Northern Virginia was slowly hemorrhaging to death. Grant's strategy of movement and attrition was slowly paying decisive dividends. Later in June, he

stole a march on Lee, slipped across the James River on June 12–17, 1864, and advanced on a lightly guarded Petersburg. However, Union bungling and a furious reaction from Lee stalled his offensive, and a protracted nine-month siege ensued. Grant's most memorable attack, the so-called Battle of the Crater (July 30, 1864), was another costly fiasco owing to General Ambrose E. BURNSIDE's indecision. But, again, Lee's finely tuned offensive army was immobilized in trenches as Union forces maintained both the strategic and the tactical initiative over their adversaries.

By the fall of 1864, the new Union strategy hastened the Confederacy's downfall. While Grant pinned down Lee in Virginia, Sherman seized Atlanta and approached Savannah with a view toward moving up the Carolinas. Also, a new force under General Philip H. SHERIDAN had cleared Confederates out of the strategic Shenandoah Valley, robbing them of their most important breadbasket. Sheridan then delivered the fatal blow on April 1, 1865, when he finally broke Lee's defenses at Five Forks. Grant, judging the moment right, struck the Petersburg defenses with his entire army, and Confederate resistance crumbled. Lee managed to extricate his army and march westward, where it was surrounded at Appomattox Court House on April 9, 1865. Then, in a solemn ceremony, Lee met Grant and formally surrendered under the latter's very generous terms. Thus, a third Confederate force passed into the hands of "Unconditional Surrender" Grant, closing the bloodiest chapter in American history.

After the war, Grant was retained in the peacetime establishment, and Congress honored him with a rank of four-star general in 1866. Hailed as the savior of his country, he then successfully ran for the presidency in 1868 and 1872, winning easily. However, his tenure in office was marred by scandals that surrounded many of his appointees. No blame was ever attached to Grant who, through it all, remained personally untarnished. He then returned to private life and tried his hand at business, failed miserably, and went bankrupt. The old warrior, stricken by throat cancer, accepted his friend Mark Twain's advice and published his military memoirs, which proved surprisingly successful and rescued his family from insolvency. Grant died at Mount McGregor, New York, on July 23, 1885. With the possible exception of President Lincoln, no individual was more responsible for preserving the United States at a critical moment in its history. Grant's strategic vision and tactical tenacity were the driving forces behind Union victory.

Further Reading

Ballard, Michael B. *U.S. Grant: The Making of a General, 1861–1863.* Lanham, Md.: Rowman and Littlefield, 2005.

Bonekemper, Edward H. *A Victor, Not a Butcher: Ulysses S. Grant's Overlooked Military Genius.* Washington, D.C.: Regnery Pub., 2004.

Flood, Charles B. *Grant and Sherman: The Friendship That Won the Civil War.* New York: Farrar, Straus and Giroux, 2005.

Gott, Kendall D. *Where the South Lost the War: An Analysis of the Fort Henry–Fort Donelson Campaign, February 1862.* Mechanicsburg, Pa.: Stackpole Books, 2003.

Grant, Ulysses S. *The Civil War Memoirs of Ulysses S. Grant.* New York: Forge, 2002.

Hess, Earl J. *Trench Warfare under Grant and Lee: Field Fortifications in the Overland Campaign.* Chapel Hill: University of North Carolina Press, 2007.

Kionka, T. K. *Key Command: Ulysses S. Grant: District of Cairo.* Columbia: University Press of Missouri, 2006.

Longacre, Edward G. *General Ulysses S. Grant: the Soldier and the Man.* Cambridge, Mass.: Da Capo Press, 2006.

Mosier, John. *Grant.* New York: Palgrave Macmillan, 2006.

Taaffe, Stephen R. *Commanding the Army of the Potomac.* Lawrence: University Press of Kansas, 2006.

Walsh, George. *"Whip the Rebellion": Ulysses S. Grant's Rise to Command.* New York: Tom Doherty Associates, 2005.

Grierson, Benjamin H. (1826–1911)

Union general

Benjamin Henry Grierson was born in Pittsburgh, Pennsylvania, on July 8, 1826, and eventually settled in Jacksonville, Illinois. He taught music for many years before entering the mercantile business and watching it fail in the Panic of 1857. When the Civil War commenced in April 1861, Grierson joined an Illinois militia regiment as a private and fought Confederate guerrillas in neighboring Missouri. He impressed his superiors with his bravery and skill, and on October 24, 1861, Grierson became a major in the 6th Illinois Cavalry. The appointment is curious since Grierson, who had been kicked in the face and permanently disfigured by a horse, thoroughly detested the beasts. He then rose by merit to colonel on April 12, 1862, and subsequently distinguished himself by vigorously pursuing Confederate raiders under General Earl VAN DORN in December of that year. His skill and aggressiveness brought him to the attention of General Ulysses S. GRANT, then planning ambitious moves against Vicksburg, Mississippi. Grierson was to play an integral role in his strategy.

On April 17, 1862, Grierson departed La Grange, Tennessee, with the 6th and 7th Illinois Cavalry, the 2nd Iowa Cavalry, and Battery K of the Illinois Light Artillery, totaling 1,700 men. His mission was to drive south through Mississippi and on to Union-held Baton Rouge, Louisiana, and tear up railroad tracks and telegraph wires en route. In this manner, he would create a strategic diversion, masking Grant's impending moves across the Mississippi River. During the next 16 days Grierson galloped hard, eluded numerous pursuers, and completely confounded the Confederate high command at Vicksburg. General John C. PEMBERTON consequently ordered all available units to try to intercept the elusive troopers, thereby committing his strategic reserve just as Grant prepared to strike. By the time Grierson successfully accomplished his mission, he had traversed 600 miles through enemy territory, captured 500 prisoners, and tore up 50 miles of track and telegraph wire. In light of his exceptional behavior, he gained promotion to brigadier general in June 1862 and was retained in the army of General Nathaniel P. BANKS during the successful siege of Port Hudson. Grierson ended the year transferring back to Tennessee, where he commanded a cavalry division in the XVI Corps of General Andrew J. Smith. In this capacity, he accompanied the ill-fated foray against General Nathan B. FORREST at Brice's Cross Roads on June 10, 1864, and was nearly routed. The following month, he was engaged closely under General Smith at the Battle of Tupelo (July 14, 1864), at which Forrest sustained a heavy defeat.

In November 1864 Grierson accepted command of the 4th Cavalry Division in the Military Division of Mississippi, but the following month, he was replaced by General James H. WILSON. He

Union general Benjamin H. Grierson *(Massachusetts Commandery Military Order of the Loyal Legion and the U.S. Army Military History Institute)*

then operated against General John B. HOOD's lines of communication during the Nashville campaign in December and, in February 1865, received promotion to major general. Grierson then joined General Edward R. S. CANBY's Military Division of West Mississippi, where he conducted numerous raids and forays deep into Alabama and Georgia. By war's end, he commanded 4,000 troopers and was widely respected as one of the Union's most adept cavalry leaders.

Grierson was retained in the peacetime establishment as colonel of the newly created 10th U.S. Cavalry, one of four units comprised solely of African Americans and white officers. During the next 25 years, he led his so-called Buffalo Soldiers across the Old Southwest, fighting innumerable skirmishes with Native Americans while also erecting miles of roads and telegraph wire. He also founded and directed construction of Fort Sill, Indian Territory (Oklahoma), which served as a major frontier outpost. Throughout the final phases of the Indian wars on the Southern Plains (1878–81), Grierson's 10th distinguished itself in combat against the Apache under Chief Victorio by eliminating them as a raiding force in West Texas. He was also unique in championing the cause of African-American soldiers at a time when many West Point–trained officers held them in disdain. Moreover, Grierson strove to deal honestly with Native Americans, a policy that brought him into conflict with his superior, General Philip H. SHERIDAN. In November 1866 Grierson assumed control of the District of New Mexico, and two years later, he left his beloved 10th Cavalry to succeed General Nelson A. Miles as commander of the Department of Arizona. Grierson finally resigned from the military in July 1890 and spent the rest of his life at his home in Jacksonville, Illinois. He died while vacationing at Omena, Michigan, on August 31, 1911, being only one of a handful of non-West Point graduates to attain the grade of brigadier general in the regular army. His unstinting defense of Native Americans and African-American soldiers sadly deprived him of well-deserved military promotions for almost 24 years.

Further Reading

Black, Robert W. *Cavalry Raids of the Civil War.* Mechanicsburg, Pa.: Stackpole Books, 2004.

Hutton, Paul A., ed. *Soldiers West: Biographies from the Military Frontier.* Lincoln: University of Nebraska Press, 1987.

Leckie, William H. *Unlikely Warriors: General Benjamin H. Grierson and His Family.* Norman: University of Oklahoma Press, 1984.

———. *The Buffalo Soldiers: A Narrative of the Black Cavalry in the West.* Norman: University of Oklahoma Press, 2003.

York, Neil L. *Fiction as Fact: The Horse Soldiers and Popular Memory.* Kent, Ohio: Kent State University Press, 2001.

H

Halleck, Henry W. (1815–1872)

Union general

Henry Wager Halleck was born in Westernville, New York, on January 16, 1815, the son of farmers. He ran away from home to escape the drudgery of agrarian life, and in 1837, he gained admittance to the U.S. Military Academy. Halleck, a gifted student, graduated third in his class in 1839 and was commissioned a second lieutenant in the elite Corps of Engineers. After strengthening the defenses of New York harbor, he ventured to Europe in 1844 on a grand tour of foreign fortifications. He returned home a year later to deliver in Boston, Massachusetts, a series of lectures on warfare that were subsequently published as *Elements of Military Art & Science* (1846). This was one of the first expressions of American military professionalism and was widely read by soldiers and militia officers alike. When the Mexican War erupted in 1846, Halleck sailed to the West Coast with Commander William B. Shubrick, where he built fortifications and participated in minor military actions. Halleck became a captain in 1847 and spent the next eight years in California as secretary of state in the military administration of General Bennett Riley, where he helped draw up the state constitution. He then resigned from the military in 1854 to pursue law and amassed a small fortune as an attorney and president of the Atlantic and Pacific Railroad. In 1861 Halleck furthered his reputation for scholarship by composing *International Law*, another widely read and highly praised work.

When the Civil War commenced in April 1861, Halleck sought out a regular commission, and General in Chief Winfield Scott prevailed on President Abraham Lincoln to appoint him a major general. Halleck was then assigned to the Department of the Missouri, headquartered at St. Louis, to replace General John C. Frémont and to rectify his organizational chaos. A superb administrator, Halleck quickly reduced corruption and inefficiency, improved military discipline and morale, and suppressed Confederate guerrillas by posting garrisons around the state. By the winter of 1861, the Missouri Valley was firmly in Union hands, and he turned to cracking the first line of Southern defenses in Kentucky and Tennessee. In February 1862 Halleck authorized General Ulysses S. Grant's Army of the Tennessee to attack Forts Henry and Donelson, which was done effectively. The following March, he helped orchestrate the fall of Island No. 10 with General John Pope's Army of the Mississippi while General Samuel R. Curtis's Army of the Southwest won the Battle of Pea Ridge in Arkansas. He then allowed a concerted drive down the Tennessee River by Generals Grant, Don C. Buell, and Lew Wallace, which culminated in the bloody victory at Shiloh (April 6–7, 1862). Halleck, alarmed by rumors that Grant had been drinking heavily, subsequently arrived at his headquarters to take command in the field. His

Union general Henry W. Halleck *(Library of Congress)*

next objective, the strategic railroad junction at Corinth, Mississippi, fell on May 29, 1862, but only after a glacial campaign of three weeks against smaller Confederate forces under General Pierre G. T. BEAUREGARD. Halleck's plodding, uninspiring performance induced Lincoln to restore Grant to command in the western theater. Halleck subsequently was recalled to Washington, D.C., to serve as general in chief. It was hoped his demonstrated talent for military administration would lend greater coordination to the Union war effort.

As Lincoln predicted, Halleck excelled in the role as head military administrator, earning the unflattering but basically accurate moniker of "Old Brains." From his office, he efficiently orchestrated a concerted mass effort to recruit, train, and equip thousands of soldiers over a vast area, thereby placing the Union army on a sounder wartime footing. This proved a very tall order in an army of volunteers, but Halleck managed to graft a veneer of military professionalism on an otherwise unruly lot. His principal failing was as a grand strategist, being overly cautious by nature and too concerned with the possession of strategic points. In an age of modern war, destruction of the enemy's forces had become paramount, a concept that Lincoln the novice fully embraced. Halleck was also something of an aloof individual, who allowed grand strategy to drift over the next two years by failing to challenge commanders in the field. He also quarreled with General Joseph HOOKER over how to handle General Robert E. LEE's invasion of Pennsylvania and ultimately replaced him with General George G. MEADE. In March 1864, Union strategy received a major boost when Grant replaced him as general in chief and Halleck was graciously "kicked upstairs" to serve as chief of staff. Thereafter, his impact on military affairs was minimal, and he contented himself in working as a highly efficient military bureaucrat. In July 1864 he left his office briefly to command Washington's defenses during the celebrated raid of General Jubal A. EARLY. Toward the end of the conflict, Halleck was transferred from the capital to placate Radical Republicans and was placed in charge of the Division of the James at Richmond, Virginia. There, he quarreled with General William T. SHERMAN about surrender terms accorded General Joseph E. JOHNSTON. The two men, previously close friends, were never reconciled from this dispute.

After the war, the government unceremoniously transferred Halleck to the Division of the Pacific, where he remained until 1869. That year, he assumed command of the Division of the South, which he held until his death at Louisville, Kentucky, on January 9, 1872. In terms of overall ability and potential, Halleck was the North's most gifted, yet least successful, soldier.

Further Reading

Engle, Stephen D. *Struggle for the Heartland: The Campaign from Fort Henry to Corinth*. Lincoln: University of Nebraska Press, 2001.

Marszalek, John F. *Commander of All Lincoln's Armies: A Life of General Henry W. Halleck*. Cambridge, Mass.: Belknap Press of Harvard University Press, 2004.

———. "Henry W. Halleck: The Early Seeds of Failure." *North and South* 8, no. 1 (2005): 78–86.

Rafuse, Ethan S. "McClellan and Halleck at War: The Struggle for Control of the Union War Effort in the West, November 1861–March 1862." *Civil War History* 49, no. 1 (2003): 32–51.

Ritter, Charles F., and Jon L. Wakelyn, eds. *Leaders of the American Civil War*. Westport, Conn.: Greenwood Press, 1998.

Smith, Timothy B. "A Siege from the Start: The Spring 1862 Campaign against Corinth, Mississippi." *Journal of Mississippi History* 66, no. 4 (2004): 403–424.

Hampton, Wade (1818–1902)

Confederate general

Wade Hampton was born in Charleston, South Carolina, on March 28, 1818, a scion of one of that state's most distinguished families. Well-educated at academies, he passed through South Carolina College in 1836 with a law degree but declined to practice. Instead, he managed his family's large plantation and estates, and he did this so deftly that he achieved great wealth. In 1852 Hampton parleyed his success into politics by winning a seat in the state legislature, where he functioned as a voice of moderation against a rising tide of secessionism. Curiously, Hampton, though a slave owner, openly questioned the continuing viability of the "peculiar institution" and opposed reopening the slave trade, and while he felt the secession by Southern states was legally and morally justified, Hampton insisted that it should not be attempted until all political and constitutional remedies had been exhausted. However, once South Carolina seceded from the Union in December 1860, he offered his services to the new Confederate States of America. The following April, Governor Francis Pickens authorized him to raise his own legion, a mixed force of cavalry, infantry, and artillery, at his own expense. Hampton obliged and served as its colonel, despite his lack of prior military training. The Hampton Legion first distinguished themselves at Bull Run on July 27, 1861, where Hampton was slightly wounded. On May 23, 1862, he advanced to brigadier general and served under General Thomas J. JACKSON throughout the noted Peninsula campaign of that year. Hampton was wounded again at Seven Pines on May 31, 1862, and the following July, he was transferred to the cavalry corps of General J. E. B. STUART, attached to the Army of Northern Virginia.

Hampton proved himself to be an outstanding leader of mounted troops. He accompanied Jackson throughout the Antietam campaign of September 1862, conducted several successful raids over the winter, and subsequently fought at Brandy Station (June 9, 1863) where his younger brother was killed, and Gettysburg (July 1–3, 1863), receiving three wounds. Hampton, however, came to

Confederate general Wade Hampton *(Massachusetts Commandery Military Order of the Loyal Legion and the U.S. Army Military History Institute)*

resent Stuart's tendency toward grandstanding as well as his reluctance to accord honors to anybody but his own Virginia cavalry. Nonetheless, he rose to major general as of September 3, 1863, and, following Stuart's death in May 1864, succeeded him as chief of the cavalry corps. Hampton's greatest accomplishment in this capacity was the June 11–12, 1864, Battle of Trevilian Station, where he stopped a larger Union force under General Philip H. SHERIDAN from reaching Lynchburg, Virginia. Hampton then assisted in the defeat of General Winfield S. HANCOCK's II Corps at Ream's Station on August 25, 1864. The following month, he led what amounted to the largest rustling operation in history by raiding behind Union lines and absconding with 2,500 head of cattle from Coggin's Point, Virginia. His troopers were then employed as makeshift cowboys as they herded their spoils back to Confederate lines.

By the spring of 1865, horses were becoming a scarce commodity in the Army of Northern Virginia, so Hampton began to drill his men to fight as foot soldiers. General Robert E. LEE then detached his command from the Petersburg area and transferred it to South Carolina to forage for mounts. On February 15, 1865, he was also promoted to lieutenant general. Hampton then transferred to the Army of Tennessee of General Joseph E. JOHNSTON in an attempt to halt Federal troops under General William T. SHERMAN from marching up the Carolinas. When the state capital of Columbia was nearly destroyed by fire, Hampton entered into an angry correspondence with Sherman about responsibility for the act, which the latter firmly denied. He also incurred a measure of notoriety by deliberately executing any Union stragglers found plundering private homes. With the collapse of the Confederacy in April 1865, Hampton made a futile attempt to escort President Jefferson DAVIS across the Mississippi River becoming one of the last high-ranking Confederates to surrender.

Hampton resumed his political career after the war and generally supported President Andrew Johnson's attempt at reconstruction. He also took the unprecedented step of endorsing limited civil rights for newly freed African-American slaves. Hampton, however, came to deplore the excesses of the Radical Republicans and eventually aligned himself with traditional Democratic interests and embraced a racially tinged agenda. He was elected governor in 1876 and also served a term in the U.S. Senate (1879–81) before becoming the commissioner of Pacific Railways (1893–97). Hampton died in Columbia, South Carolina, on April 11, 1902. A gifted, physically impressive individual, he, like Nathan B. FORREST and Richard TAYLOR, was one of three Confederates to become lieutenant general without a professional military background.

Further Reading

Ackerman, Robert K. *Wade Hampton III.* Columbia: University of South Carolina Press, 2007.

Cisco, Walter B. *Wade Hampton: Confederate Warrior, Conservative Statesman.* Washington, D.C.: Brassey's, 2004.

Longacre, Edward G. *Gentleman and Soldier: A Biography of Wade Hampton III.* Nashville: Rutledge Hill Press, 2003.

Simms, William G. *A City Laid Waste: The Capture, Sack, and Destruction of the City of Columbia.* Columbia: University of South Carolina Press, 2005.

Wittenberg, Eric J. *Glory Enough for All: Sheridan's Second Raid and the Battle of Trevilian Station.* London: Brassey's, 2002.

———. *The Battle of Monroe's Crossroads: And the Civil War's Final Campaign.* New York: Savas Beatie, 2006.

Hancock, Winfield S. (1824–1886)

Union general

Winfield Scott Hancock was born in Montgomery Square, Pennsylvania, on February 14, 1824, the son of a schoolteacher with deep roots in the Democratic Party. Hancock used his father's connections to secure an appointment to the U.S. Military Academy in 1840, from which he graduated midway in his class four years later. Now a second lieutenant in the 6th U.S. Infantry, he served three years on the western frontier as a recruiting officer before joining General Winfield SCOTT's army in Mexico. In short order, Hancock distinguished himself in fighting at Contreras and Churubusco, winning a brevet promotion for bravery. He rose to captain in 1855 and saw additional service against the Seminoles in Florida and in Kansas during the period of abolitionist troubles there. Hancock then transferred to southern California in May 1859, where he functioned as quartermaster. Despite his strong pro-Southern sympathies, he deplored secession and after April 1861 took measures to protect Federal property. He also agitated for a combat command and transferred east to become a brigadier general in General George B. McCLELLAN's Army of the Potomac.

Hancock fought steadily through the Peninsula campaign of 1861. Tall, commanding, and impressive in the saddle, he emerged as one of the Union's best commanders at the divisional and corps levels. At Williamsburg on May 4–5, 1862, his brigade outflanked Confederate forces, routing them. McClellan, who had witnessed the event, pronounced his performance "superb"—and the nickname stuck. Good combat leadership at South Mountain and Antietam in September 1862 culminated in command of a division in the II Corps with the rank of major general of volunteers. Hancock next fought at the bloody debacle at Fredericksburg on December 13, 1862, where his formation sustained 50 percent losses yet never wavered. He further distinguished himself at the heavy Union defeat at Chancellorsville, May 2–3, 1863, and mounted a steady rearguard action that allowed the battered forces of General Joseph HOOKER to escape destruction. In consequence of his excellent performance, President Abraham LINCOLN appointed Hancock head of the II Corps in June 1863.

Hancock made his most essential contribution at the three-day ordeal of Gettysburg, Pennsylvania, under General George G. MEADE. On July 1, 1863, he rushed his II Corps to the assistance of General John F. REYNOLDS I Corps, assumed command of Union forces from General Abner DOUBLEDAY, and completely stabilized Union positions

Union general Winfield S. Hancock *(Library of Congress)*

along Cemetery Hill Ridge and Culp's Hill. On July 2, while commanding the Union center, he repaired the damage incurred by General Daniel SICKLES insubordinate deployment of the III Corps and artfully shifted troops to the left to negate General James LONGSTREET's turning movement. On July 3 the locus of combat reverted back to the Union center, and Hancock's II Corps absorbed and bloodily repelled the determined charge by 15,000 Confederates under General George E. PICKETT. In the last few moments of battle, Hancock received a severe leg wound, yet refused assistance until victory was assured. Sadly and ironically, General Lewis A. Armistead, one of Hancock's best friends of the antebellum period, was mortally wounded urging on Southern troops against his position.

Several months of recuperation passed before Hancock rejoined the II Corps, now operating under the aegis of General Ulysses S. GRANT. Though still confined to an ambulance, he fought well in the bloody May 5, 1863, encounter at the Wilderness, driving General Ambrose P. HILL back several miles. At Spotsylvania (May 12, 1863), his II Corps successfully stormed Confederate defenses at the "Mule Shoe" until driven back by a determined charge by General John C. BRECKIN-RIDGE. However, his men suffered inordinate losses at Cold Harbor (June 3, 1864) and entered the siege of Petersburg with decimated ranks. Hancock was also feeling the effects of exhaustion and his old wound, and on June 15, 1864, he passed up an opportunity to storm lightly guarded Petersburg, Virginia. He was then roughly handled by Generals Hill and Wade HAMPTON at Ream's Station on August 25, 1864, and Grant, cognizant of his declining health, removed him from the line. Hancock next assumed new duties commanding the defenses of Washington, D.C., where he also recruited the Veteran Volunteer Corps for garrison purposes.

In 1866 Hancock gained promotion to major general, and the following year, he took charge of the Department of the Missouri. Here, he conducted operations against hostile bands of Cheyenne and Kiowa and also arranged for the court-martial of General George A. CUSTER for being absent without leave. In 1867 President Andrew Johnson transferred him from the frontier and assigned him duties as head of the Fifth Military District (Texas and Louisiana) during Reconstruction. He replaced the testy general Philip H. SHERIDAN as military governor, and his casual friendliness toward Southerners earned him the ire of many Radical Republicans. In keeping with his beliefs, Hancock issued orders to keep recently freed African-American slaves off juries and voter registration lists. General in Chief Grant angrily removed him for refusing to assert military prerogatives over civilian wishes, a stance endearing him to former Confederates, and he was exiled to the distant Department of Dakota. His row with the Republicans caught the eye of fellow Democrats, who needed a national standard-bearer, and

in 1880, he ran an unsuccessful campaign for president against Chester A. Arthur. He then resumed his duties as head of the Department of the East with headquarters on Governor's Island, New York. "Hancock, the Superb" died at that post on February 9, 1886, one of the greatest corps-level commanders on either side.

Further Reading

Cannon, John. *Bloody Angle: Hancock's Assault on the Mule Shoe Salient, May 12, 1864.* Cambridge, Mass.: Da Capo Press, 2002.

Constant, George W. "The Men Who Made Hancock 'Superb.'" *Civil War Times Illustrated* 40, no. 1 (2001): 38–44, 53–55.

Deppen, John. "Hancock the Superb." *Military Heritage* 5, no. 5 (2004): 40–49.

Gambore, A. M. *Hancock at Gettysburg and Beyond.* Baltimore: Butternut and Blue, 2002.

Grimsely, Mark. *And Keep on Moving: The Virginia Campaign, May–June, 1864.* Lincoln: University of Nebraska Press, 2002.

Jamieson, Perry D. *Winfield Scott Hancock: Gettysburg Hero.* Abilene, Tex.: McWhiney Foundation Press, 2003.

Kreisler, Lawrence A. "From Volunteers to Veterans: A Social and Military History of the II Corps, Army of the Potomac, 1861–1865." Unpublished Ph.D. diss., University of Alabama, 2001.

Newton, Steven H. *McPherson's Ridge: The First Battle for the High Ground, July 1, 1863.* Cambridge, Mass.: Da Capo Press, 2002.

Pfanz, Harry W. *Gettysburg—the First Day.* Chapel Hill: University of North Carolina Press, 2001.

Wert, Jeffrey D. *Gettysburg: Day Three.* New York: Simon and Schuster, 2001.

Hardee, William J. (1815–1873)

Confederate general

William Joseph Hardee was born in Little Saltilla, Georgia, on October 12, 1815, the son of a wealthy planter. He matriculated through the U.S. Military Academy and graduated in 1838 as a second lieutenant of the 2nd U.S. Dragoons. Hardee saw fighting in Florida's Second Seminole War but subsequently went to France in 1840 to study for two years at the Royal Cavalry School at Saumur.

In 1844 he joined General Zachary Taylor's Army of Occupation as a captain and patrolled the Texas frontier along the Rio Grande. Ownership of this stretch of land was disputed with Mexico, and during a patrol on April 25, 1846, Hardee was ambushed and captured. Exchanged the following month, he fought under Taylor at Monterrey that September and then joined the army of General Winfield SCOTT during its march on Mexico City. Hardee won two brevet promotions for bravery before the war ended in 1848, and afterward, he resumed routine military activities along the frontier. In 1853 Secretary of War Jefferson DAVIS ordered him to compile a new drill manual, and he wrote *Rifle and Light Infantry Tactics* (1855), which served as a standard text for both Union and Confederate armies during the Civil War. It differed from General Scott's *Infantry Tactics,* first published in 1815, by recognizing the increased range and lethality of rifled weapons and calling for faster marching rates, dispersed formations, and increased reliance on skirmishers. In 1855 Hardee was posted with the newly organized 2nd U.S. Cavalry, in whose ranks rode future luminaries Albert S. JOHNSTON, Robert E. LEE, George H. THOMAS, Earl VAN DORN, Edmund KIRBY-SMITH, and John B. HOOD. This regiment proved so outstanding in containing Comanche attacks in Texas—and was so overstaffed by Southerners—that it was popularly called "Jeff Davis's Own." In 1856 Hardee transferred from the frontier as a lieutenant colonel and served as commandant of cadets at West Point. After four years of useful service, he returned to Georgia on vacation, resigned his commission once his native state seceded on January 19, 1861, and joined the Confederate army as a colonel.

In June 1861 Hardee advanced to brigadier and proceeded to Arkansas to recruit a brigade. He joined General Johnston's Army of Mississippi commanding the III Corps and fought with distinction at Shiloh on April 6–7, 1862. Promoted to major general, he then accompanied General Braxton BRAGG during the ill-fated invasion of Kentucky. Hardee acquitted himself well at the

bloody Battle of Perryville on October 8, 1862, inflicting heavy losses on General Don C. BUELL's Army of the Cumberland and winning promotion to lieutenant general. He then performed impressively at the Battle of Murfreesboro (Stone's River) on December 31, 1862–January 3, 1863, where his clever flanking tactics drove the right flank of General William S. ROSECRANS back three miles. However, Hardee greatly resented Bragg's vacillating leadership, quarreled with him, and transferred out of the Army of Tennessee to train troops in Mississippi. He then rejoined Bragg in time to command his right wing at Missionary Ridge on November 24, 1863, where his valiant stand prevented the Confederate army from being destroyed. When Bragg retired from command, President Davis offered Hardee command of the Army of Tennessee, but he declined and served instead under General Joseph E. JOHNSTON.

Throughout the ensuing Atlanta campaign, Hardee fought well but futilely against superior Union forces under General William T. SHERMAN.

Confederate general William J. Hardee *(Library of Congress)*

When Davis sacked Johnston and replaced him with General John B. Hood on July 17, 1864, he greatly resented being passed over. Moreover, he did not work well with the overly aggressive Hood, who decimated Hardee's command in a series of ill-advised offensives against Sherman. On July 22, 1864, Hardee surprised the army of General James B. McPherson at Peachtree Creek, killing him, but once Atlanta fell on September 2, 1864, he felt he could no longer function under Hood and requested a transfer. Hardee then received reassignment to the Department of South Carolina, Georgia, and Florida, where he continued opposing Sherman's march to the sea. He was forced to abandon Savannah to superior numbers on December 21, 1864, along with Charleston, South Carolina, in February 1865. Reunited with Johnston in North Carolina, he fought bravely at the battles of Averasboro and Bentonville on March 15–20, 1865, with his only son dying in the latter engagement. Hardee finally surrendered with Johnston at Durham's Station on April 21, 1865. After the war, he became a planter in Alabama, and he also served as president of the Selma and Meridian Railroad. Hardee, who acquired the nickname of "Old Reliable" on account of his steady leadership, died at Wytheville, Virginia, on November 6, 1873, a superior corps commander.

Further Reading

Arnold, James R. *Jeff Davis's Own: Cavalry. Comanches, and the Battle for the Texas Frontier.* New York: Wiley, 2000.

Bradley, Mark L., and David E. Roth. *Old Reliable's Finest Hour: The Battle of Averasboro, North Carolina, March 15–16, 1865.* Columbus, Ohio: Blue and Gray Enterprises, 2002.

Broadwater, Robert P. *Battle of Despair: Bentonville and the North Carolina Campaign.* Macon, Ga.: Mercer University Press, 2004.

Davis, Stephen. *Atlanta Will Fall: Sherman, Joe Johnston, and the Yankee Heavy Battalions.* Wilmington, Del.: Scholarly Resources, 2001.

Furqueron, James R. "The Finest Opportunity Lost: The Battle of Jonesborough, August 31–September 1, 1864." *North & South* 6, no. 6 (2003): 48–63.

Lepa, Jack H. *Breaking the Confederacy: The Georgia and Tennessee Campaigns of 1864.* Jefferson, N.C.: McFarland, 2005.

Noe, Kenneth. *Perryville: This Grand Havoc of Battle.* Lexington: University Press of Kentucky, 2001.

Heth, Henry (1825–1899)

Confederate general

Henry Heth was born in Blackheath, Virginia, on December 16, 1825, the son of a navy midshipman. In 1843 he entered the U.S. Military Academy and graduated four years later at the very bottom of his class. Now a lieutenant in the 1st U.S. Infantry, Heth ventured to Mexico in the final phases of the Mexican War and saw no combat. He then spent the next 12 years performing routine garrison duty at various posts along the western frontier. Heth rose to captain of the 10th U.S. Infantry in 1855 and finally fought against the Brule Sioux at Blue Water, Nebraska, performing competently. Two years later, he penned a manual entitled *A System of Target Practice*, which became a standard military treatise. In 1858 Heth accompanied Colonel Albert S. Johnston on his Mormon expedition, again eliciting praise from superiors. He was not particularly interested in politics and did not favor secession, but when Virginia left the Union in April 1861, he resigned his commission and offered his service to the Confederacy.

By August 1861 Heth was a lieutenant colonel in the quartermaster service under General John B. Floyd in western Virginia and commanded the 45th Virginia at Carnifex Ferry on September 10, 1861. President Jefferson Davis sought to have Heth become commander of Confederate forces in Missouri, but Southern commanders there resented his West Point background and politically negated the transfer. Heth nonetheless rose to brigadier general in February 1861 and won appointment as commander of the Lewisburg Military District. In this capacity, he fought and won several skirmishes against Union forces, but on May 9, 1862, he was himself defeated by Colonel George Crook and his 36th Ohio at

Lewisburg. Afterward, he relocated to Kentucky to serve under General Edmund KIRBY-SMITH, but he smarted over being in what he considered a military backwater. Heth began to agitate for another transfer back east, and in the spring of 1863, he was appointed a brigade commander in General Ambrose P. HILL's noted "Light Division." His subsequently tenure with General Robert E. LEE's Army of Northern Virginia was accomplished but fraught with peril for the South. In May 1862 Heth fought under General Thomas J. JACKSON's II Corps during the Chancellorsville campaign. He accompanied Jackson on his masterful turning movement of General Joseph HOOKER's right flank, being slightly wounded. Later that month, his good behavior resulted in promotion to major general and command of his own division. Personally brave but displaying a tendency toward rashness and a disdain for proper reconnaissance, Heth was now positioned to adversely influence upcoming military events.

During General Lee's invasion of Pennsylvania, Heth's Light Division formed part of Hill's III Corps. On July 1, 1863, he was foraging for shoes near the vital road junction of Gettysburg when his skirmishers encountered dismounted cavalry under General John BUFORD. At that time, he was under Lee's strict orders not to precipitate an action until the rest of the army arrived, but nonetheless, he committed a brigade under General James J. Pettigrew to attack. When his men were pushed back by Buford's rapid-firing carbines, Heth brought up additional forces and renewed the struggle. The sound of battle attracted men from both sides, and an unscheduled engagement unfolded. By nightfall, the Southerners had gained the upper hand, winning a solid tactical victory. But the hillsides of Gettysburg were not where Lee had planned to fight, and for the next two days, he waged a bloody battle with Union forces on ground of their own choosing. Heth, by dint of his rashness, was responsible for this, and his behavior engendered dire consequences for the Confederacy. His division had incurred heavy losses while he himself sustained a serious head wound—surviving only because he had stuffed his new hat with paper to make it fit better. He recovered in time to cover the army's retreat, although, at Falling Waters, Maryland, on July 14, 1863, his division was roughly handled by Union cavalry under General Hugh J. KILPATRICK.

Despite his mishandling of affairs at Gettysburg, Heth remained a popular commander with his troops. His division again was savaged by Union troops at Bristoe Station on October 14, 1863, and he subsequently rendered useful service at the Wilderness, Cold Harbor, and in the trenches of Petersburg in 1864. On August 24, 1864, Heth scored a surprising victory over General Winfield S. HANCOCK's II Corps at Ream's Station, Virginia, taking 2,000 prisoners. He then remained with the army until the bitter end and finally surrendered with Lee at Appomattox on April 9, 1865. After the war, Heth settled in Richmond as a businessman, although he eventually found employment with the federal government. He was also active in veteran's affairs, giving speeches, and he also penned an extensive memoir about the war years. Heth died in Washington, D.C., on September 27, 1899, a capable division commander when not given to rashness.

Further Reading

Gragg, Rod. *Covered with Glory: The 26th Carolina Infantry at Gettysburg.* New York: HarperCollins, 2000.

Horn, John. *The Destruction of the Weldon Railroad, Deep Bottom, Globe Tavern, and Ream's Station, August 14–25, 1864.* Lynchburg, Va.: H. E. Howard, 1991.

Morrison, James L., ed. *The Memoirs of Henry Heth.* Westport, Conn.: Greenwood Press, 1974.

Newton, Steven H. *McPherson's Ridge: The First Battle for the High Ground, July 1, 1863.* Cambridge, Mass.: Da Capo Press, 2002.

Pfanz, Harry W. *Gettysburg—The First Day.* Chapel Hill: University of North Carolina Press, 2001.

Robbins, James S. *Last in Their Class: Custer, Pickett, and the Goats of West Point.* New York: Encounter Books, 2006.

Hill, Ambrose P. (1825–1865)

Confederate general

Ambrose Powell Hill was born in Culpeper County, Virginia, on November 9, 1825, and well educated at home. He entered the U.S. Military Academy in 1842 and, after missing a year due to illness, graduated in 1847 as a second lieutenant in the 1st U.S. Artillery. Hill, known as "Little Powell" on account of his short stature, accompanied his regiment south during closing phases of the Mexican War, saw no combat, and spent the postwar period pulling garrison duty in Texas. Between 1850 and 1855, he served in Florida during difficulties with the Seminoles there and subsequently transferred as a captain with the U.S. Coastal Survey. Though a Southerner, Hill opposed slavery on moral grounds, but he also supported the notion of states' rights. Accordingly, he resigned his commission in March 1861 and offered his services to the Confederacy as colonel of the 13th Virginia Infantry. He commanded a brigade at Bull Run in July 1861, but he saw no serious fighting. However, in light of his skill at training and disciplining soldiers, Hill rose to brigadier general in February 1862. It was during the Peninsula campaign of that year that he emerged as one of the finest divisional commanders in the Confederate service.

Hill initially served under General James LONGSTREET, an officer whom he came to dislike intensely. On May 5, 1862, he delivered a crushing blow to Union forces at Williamsburg, Virginia, winning promotion to major general and command of a six-brigade division—the largest in the Confederate army. Under Hill's expert eye and intense training regimen, it promptly became known as the "Light Division" on account of its rapidity of movement. He continued distinguishing himself throughout the internecine fighting of the Seven Days' battles, invariably taking heavy losses but always driving the enemy back. But, as his relations with Longstreet were at the breaking point, General Robert E. LEE arranged his transfer to the II Corps of General Thomas J. JACKSON to forestall a possible duel. The banty Hill, a flam-

Confederate general Ambrose P. Hill *(National Archives)*

boyant figure who disdained regular uniforms and who always went into combat bedecked in a bright red shirt, also failed to befriend the pious, spit-and-polish Jackson. The two men nonetheless worked well together on the battlefield at Cedar Mountain and Second Manassas in August 1862, and Hill received the honor of spearheading the Confederate drive into Maryland. Jackson, however, became incensed by Hill's lack of protocol and his slovenly marching order, and he had him arrested. Hill made the requisite adjustments in discipline and went on to to capture the Union garrison at Harper's Ferry, personally receiving its surrender. He then performed his greatest military feat at Antietam against General George B. MCCLELLAN on September 17, 1862, by hurriedly forwarding the Light Division and rescuing Lee's left flank from certain destruction. This proved to be one of the greatest forced marches of the war.

Hill subsequently performed well at Fredericksburg against General Ambrose E. Burnside on December 13, 1862, and he accompanied Jackson's flank attack at Chancellorsville on May 2–3, which rolled up the army of General Joseph Hooker. Following the death of Jackson, he was promoted to lieutenant general on May 24, 1863, and appointed head of the newly formed III Corps. But Hill, suffering from intermittent kidney problems, was increasingly ill, and his performance became uneven. His behavior at the crucial first day of Gettysburg on July 1, 1863, proved uninspired, and he allowed General Henry Heth's division to precipitate the battle before the rest of the army came up in support. His troops did manage to drive General John F. Reynold's I Corps and General Oliver O. Howard's IX Corps out of the town, but then they failed to seize the heights above. On October 14, 1863, Hill subsequently stumbled into a well-defended Union position, commanded by General Gouverneur K. Warren, without proper reconnaissance, and he lost two brigades in heavy fighting. On May 5–6, 1864, Hill's corps nearly was overwhelmed by General Winfield S. Hancock's command, and he dropped out of active duty from fatigue and illness. He resumed active duty by June and fought in the defense of Petersburg, Virginia, expertly driving off repeated Union attempts to severe Confederate communications. Illness again necessitated a medical furlough of several months, but just as he was returning on April 2, 1865, General Ulysses S. Grant ordered a massive onslaught that penetrated Southern defenses. Hill was shot down trying to rally his command. Irascible and basically promoted beyond his abilities, he still enjoyed a sterling reputation among fellow Confederates; reputedly both Lee and Jackson called for him on their deathbeds.

Further Reading

Cross, David F. *A Melancholy Affair at the Weldon Railroad: The Vermont Brigade, June 23, 1864.* Shippensburg, Pa.: White Mane Books, 2003.

Jones, Wilmer L. *Generals in Blue and Gray.* 2 vols. Westport, Conn.: Praeger, 2004.

Newton, Steven W. *McPherson's Ridge: The First Battle for the High Ground, July 1, 1863.* Cambridge, Mass.: Da Capo Press, 2002.

Pfanz, Harry W. *Gettysburg—The First Day.* Chapel Hill: University of North Carolina Press, 2001.

Sears, Stephen. *Landscape Turned Red: The Battle of Antietam.* Boston: Houghton Mifflin, 2003.

Smith, Derek. *The Gallant Dead: Union and Confederate Generals Killed in the Civil War.* Mechanicsburg, Pa.: Stackpole Books, 2005.

Welsh, William E. "Little Powell's Big Fight." *Military Heritage* 6, no. 6 (2005): 50–57, 182.

Hill, Daniel H. (1821–1889)
Confederate general

Daniel Harvey Hill was born in the York District, South Carolina, on July 12, 1821, the son of farmers. His father died when he was a child, and Hill was raised by his stern Presbyterian mother, who indelibly influenced his social bearings. He also suffered from intermittent pain arising from a congenital spinal defect. Hill nonetheless managed to enter the U.S. Military Academy in 1838 and graduated four years later in the middle of his class. As a second lieutenant in the 1st U.S. Artillery, he fulfilled a long stint of garrison duty in the Southwest before heading south to fight in the Mexican War (1846–48). A lion in combat, Hill marched with the army under General Winfield Scott and garnered brevet promotions for gallantry at the battles of Contreras, Churbusco, and Chapultepec. The South Carolina legislature also voted him an ornate sword as a token of their esteem. But Hill terminated his promising career in February 1849 by resigning his commission to work as a mathematics instructor at Washington College, Virginia. He performed much useful work and also arranged for Thomas J. Jackson to teach at the nearby Virginia Military Institute; Hill subsequently married Jackson's sister. In 1854 he transferred to Davidson College, North Carolina, where his fine grasp of administration rescued that institution from insolvency. Hill departed Davidson in 1859 to perform similar work at the newly created North Carolina Military Institute. When North Carolina seceded from the Union on May 20, 1861, Hill gained an appointment as colonel of the 1st North Carolina Volunteers.

On June 10, 1861, Hill, assisted by Colonel John B. MAGRUDER, fought and won the Civil War's first sizable encounter at Big Bethel, Virginia, by defeating Federal troops under General Benjamin F. BUTLER. This garnered him immediate promotion to brigadier general the following August along with command of the Pamlico District of North Carolina. In the spring of 1862, Hill advanced to major general and commanded a division under General Joseph E. JOHNSTON during initial phases of the Peninsula campaign. He next distinguished himself in the Seven Days' battles under General Robert E. LEE, especially at the very bloody engagement at Malvern Hill on July 1, 1862. However, Hill's outspoken, irascible disposition militated against him when he openly criticized Lee's leadership for the costly repulse there,

Confederate general Daniel H. Hill *(Library of Congress)*

declaring, "It wasn't war, it was murder." He then engendered another controversy in September during the invasion of Maryland when a copy of Lee's secret instructions (Special Order 191) was dispatched to Hill wrapped around some cigars—and ended up in the hands of General George B. MCCLELLAN. As Union forces then converged on the scattered Confederates, Hill greatly distinguished himself at Crampton's Gap (South Mountain) on September 13, 1862, delaying McClellan's advance by four hours and allowing Lee to assemble behind Antietam Creek. He subsequently fought well defending the sunken lane against great odds four days later. However, Lee, still smarting from Hill's inopportune remarks, declined recommending him for promotion to lieutenant general. Hill was so angered by the snub that he threatened to resign, but he was dissuaded from doing so by his brother-in-law, "Stonewall Jackson."

Hill was transferred back to North Carolina in February 1863 and then performed useful work defending Richmond, Virginia, during the Gettysburg campaign. President Jefferson DAVIS was so impressed by his performance that he recommended him for a lieutenant generalship, and he transferred him to the western theater as a corps commander. Hill fought well at the bloody battle of Chickamauga on September 19, 1863, but he was impolitic in criticizing the leadership of General Braxton BRAGG. When Bragg, one of President Davis's closest friends, complained about Hill's behavior, Davis scuttled his forthcoming promotion. In the end, both men were removed from command, and Hill spent several months employed as a volunteer aide to General Pierre G. T. BEAUREGARD at Petersburg, Virginia. It was not until the spring of 1865 that he resumed field operations by commanding a division in General Stephen D. Lee's corps, and he fought at Bentonville, North Carolina, on March 19–21, 1865. Hill finally surrendered with General Johnston at Durham's Station the following April.

After the war, Hill resumed his activities as a highly skilled academic administrator at Arkansas Industrial University (now the University of

Arkansas). He also actively edited and published several Confederate-oriented magazines for Southern consumption, wherein he criticized General Lee's generalship. In 1885 he transferred as president of the Middle Georgia Military and Agricultural College before dying at Charlotte, North Carolina, on September 24, 1889. Hill was among the South's best and most hard-hitting divisional commanders, whose career was perpetually thwarted by his otherwise tactless demeanor.

Further Reading

Bridges, Hal. *Lee's Maverick General, Daniel Harvey Hill.* Lincoln: University of Nebraska Press, 1991.

Burton, Brian K. *Extraordinary Circumstances: The Seven Days Battles.* Bloomington: Indiana University Press, 2001.

Hughes, Nathaniel C., and Timothy D. Johnson, eds. *A Fighter from Way Back: The Mexican War Diary of Lieutenant Daniel Harvey Hill, 4th Artillery, U.S.A.* Kent, Ohio: Kent State University Press, 2002.

Isenbarger, Dennis L. "Perpetual Stubbornness: The Relationship of President Jefferson Davis and Major General Daniel Harvey Hill." Unpublished master's thesis, Western Carolina University, 1997.

Jones, Wilmer L. *Generals in Blue and Gray.* 2 vols. Westport, Conn.: Praeger, 2004.

Sears, Stephen W. "The Twisted Tale of the Lost Order." *North & South* 5, no. 7 (2002): 54–65.

Hindman, Thomas C. (1828–1868)

Confederate general

Thomas Carmichael Hindman was born in Nashville, Tennessee, on January 28, 1828, and relocated with his family to Ripley, Mississippi, where his father served as an Indian agent. He was educated by tutors and at several private schools near Princeton, New Jersey, before joining the 2nd Mississippi Infantry in 1846. He then served in the Mexican War as a captain without seeing combat and returned home in 1848 to study law. After joining the bar in 1851, Hindman expressed an interest in politics, and he ran for office as a states' rights Democrat. That year, he also supported Jefferson Davis's gubernatorial candidacy and displayed real ability as a fiery rabble-rousing orator.

In 1853 Hindman himself won a seat in the Mississippi state legislature, where he remained for three years before relocating to Helena, Arkansas. A short, aggressive man who never minced his words, he made few friends among the political establishment, but his message of defiance toward the national government resonated with the voters, who sent him to Congress as a representative in 1858. There, Hindman functioned as a radical secessionist, and in 1860, he backed the presidential candidacy of John C. Breckinridge. Hindman then resigned his seat in order to serve as colonel of the newly formed 2nd Arkansas Infantry.

Given his ambition and political connections, Hindman's climb up the Confederate chain of command proved rapid. He advanced to brigadier general as of September 28, 1861, and had risen to major general by the spring of 1862. Hindman now commanded a division in General William J. Hardee's corps and acquitted himself well at the bloody Battle of Shiloh (April 6–7, 1862) by repeatedly attacking the so-called Hornet's Nest. He then repaired back to Arkansas as the newly installed commander of the Trans-Mississippi Department. Determined to transform this military backwater into a garrison state, Hindman strongly enforced conscription laws with prescribed punishments for failing to comply, and he raised 18,000 additional soldiers from scratch. However, his tactless and seemingly arbitrary methods incurred considerable resentment, and at length he was replaced by the more accommodating general Theophilus H. Holmes. The elderly Holmes diplomatically kept most of Hindman's methods in place and allowed him to carry out military functions. Consequently, Arkansas was well prepared to receive a Union invasion in the fall of 1862. Eager to engage the enemy, Hindman secretly marched 10,000 men against the divides forces of Generals James G. Blunt and Francis J. Herron at Prairie Grove on December 7, 1862. Having skillfully driven a wedge between the two forces, he inexplicably went on the defensive and gradually squandered his strategic surprise in piecemeal attacks. Thereafter, he requested a transfer out of Arkansas and into the Army of Tennessee.

Hindman remained without a command for several months, and his principal activity involved overseeing the court of inquiry investigating General Mansfield LOVELL for the loss of New Orleans, Louisiana. In July 1862 he was assigned a division under General Leonidas K. POLK at Chattanooga, Tennessee. Hindman subsequently fought well at the bloody encounter at Chickamauga on September 19–20, 1863, being seriously wounded. However, General Braxton BRAGG was displeased by Hindman's performance and relieved him of command. In January 1864 he further complicated his position with the Confederate government by endorsing General Patrick R. CLEBURNE's suggestion to offer African-American slaves freedom in exchange for military service. Hindman finally took charge of a division under General Joseph E. JOHNSTON and fought well during the opening phases of the Atlanta campaign before an eye injury necessitated his removal. He spent the final months of the war at his home in Helena.

After the war, Hindman initially fled to Mexico to escape prosecution, but he returned to Arkansas in 1867 to resume his political career. He remained an outspoken opponent of Radical Reconstruction and railed against what he considered "carpetbagger" rule by outsiders. On September 27, 1868, Hindman was suddenly murdered in his home, probably for political reasons; his death was never solved.

Further Reading

Bailey, Anne J., and Daniel E. Sutherland, eds. *Civil War Arkansas: Beyond Battles and Leaders.* Fayetteville: University of Arkansas Press, 2000.

Collins, Robert. *General James G. Blunt: Tarnished Glory.* Gretna, La.: Pelican Publishing, 2005.

Cozzens, Peter. "Hindman's Grand Delusion." *Civil War Times Illustrated* 39, no. 5 (2000): 28–35, 66–69.

DeBlack, Thomas R. *With Fire and Sword: Arkansas, 1861–1874.* Fayetteville: University of Arkansas Press, 2003.

Frazier, Rodney R. *Broken Swords: The Lives, Times, and Deaths of Eight Former Confederate Generals Mur-*

dered After the Smoke of Battle Had Cleared. New York: Vantage Press, 2003.

Shea, William J., and Grady McWhiney. *War in the West: Pea Ridge and Prairie Grove.* Abilene, Tex.: McWhiney Foundation Press, 2001.

Hoke, Robert F. (1837–1912)
Confederate general

Robert Frederick Hoke was born in Lincolnton, North Carolina, on May 27, 1837, the son of a politician. He was 17 years old and attending the Kentucky Military Institute when his father died, prompting him to quit school and manage the family cotton mill and iron foundry. After North Carolina seceded on May 20, 1861, Hoke joined the 1st North Carolina Infantry under Colonel Daniel H. HILL as a second lieutenant. He then fought with distinction at the Battle of Big Bethel on June 10, 1861, one of the Civil War's first sizable clashes and a Confederate victory. Hoke, by dint of superior performance, continued rising in rank, and by the time he returned home in the spring of 1862, he was lieutenant colonel of the 33rd North Carolina. He again fought well at the defeat of New Bern on March 14, 1862, becoming the only Southern officer there to garner official praise. Hoke's regiment then shuttled back to the Army of Northern Virginia under General Robert E. LEE, where he acquitted himself well and captured an enemy battery at Glendale on June 30, 1862. After conspicuous bravery at Second Manassas in August and Antietam that September, he became colonel of the 21st North Carolina and part of General Jubal A. EARLY's division. In this capacity, he commanded an entire brigade at the December 13, 1862, Battle of Fredericksburg, badly repulsing a determined attack by General George G. MEADE. Against all expectations, Hoke ordered his Tar Heel troops to charge, and they did so ferociously, netting 300 Federal prisoners. Consequently, he rose to brigadier general as of January 19, 1863, at the age of 26.

In the spring of 1863, Hoke arrived in the Piedmont district of his home state to conduct both anti-Unionist operations and round up deserters who had been terrorizing the countryside. He then returned to Virginia and was severely wounded during opening phases of the Battle of Chancellorsville on May 3, 1863, while defending Marye's Heights against General John Sedgwick. Hoke consequently missed Gettysburg and was sent back home to recruit troops and collect deserters. In January 1864 he joined General George E. Pickett's division in the failed siege of New Bern. Fortunately, he received an independent command and instructions to besiege and capture the Union lodgment at Plymouth, North Carolina, garrisoned by 3,000 Union troops under General Henry W. Wessels. Hoke methodically surrounded the Federal position and, assisted by the powerful Confederate ram CSS *Albemarle* offshore, drove the defenders from a series of fortifications. On April 20, 1864, Wessels surrendered in one of the few Confederate victories on North Carolina soil. Consequently, Hoke received the thanks of the Confederate Congress while President Jefferson Davis personally promoted him to major general, the Confederacy's youngest. When Hoke rejoined the Army of Northern Virginia again that summer, much was expected of this accomplished young warrior.

Unfortunately, Hoke had been advanced beyond his abilities. He fought well enough under General Pierre G. T. Beauregard at Drewry's Bluff on May 10, 1864, which sealed General Benjamin F. Butler on the peninsula of Bermuda Hundred. But in a series of battles commencing with Cold Harbor on June 3, 1864, Hoke apparently lost his earlier dash and seemed incapable of coordinating his movement with other leaders. On June 24, 1864, his attack near Petersburg recoiled with heavy losses, and the following September, he failed, after three charges, to capture Union-held Fort Harrison. His division was then pulled from the line and sent to bolster the defenses of Fort Fisher, Wilmington, North Carolina, under General Braxton Bragg. On January 15, Bragg forbade him from launching an attack on Federal troops that may have prevented the fort from fall-

ing to General Alfred H. Terry. Hoke then transferred to the Army of Tennessee under General Joseph E. Johnston, seeing active duty at the Battle of Bentonville (March 19–21, 1865). He finally surrendered his sword to Union forces at Durham Station the following April.

After the war, Hoke resumed his commercial activities and also served as director of the North Carolina Railroad. Despite his wartime celebrity, he avoided publicity and died in near obscurity in Raleigh on July 3, 1912. Hoke County, North Carolina, subsequently was created in honor of his memory.

Further Reading

Barefoot, Daniel W. General Robert F. *Hoke: Lee's Modest Warrior.* Salem, N.C.: John F. Blair, 1996.

Broadwater, Robert P. *Battle of Despair: Bentonville and the North Carolina Campaign.* Macon, Ga.: Mercer University Press, 2004.

Brooks, Victor. *The Fredericksburg Campaign.* Conshohocken, Pa.: Combined Publishing, 2000.

Joyner, Clinton. "Major General Robert Frederick Hoke and the Civil War in North Carolina." Unpublished master's thesis, East Carolina University, 1974.

McCaslin, Richard B. *The Last Stronghold: The Campaign for Fort Fisher.* Abilene, Tex.: McWhiney Foundation Press, 2003.

Moss, Juanita P. *Battle of Plymouth, North Carolina (April 17–20, 1864): The Last Confederate Victory.* Bowie, Md.: Willow Bend Books, 2004.

Hood, John B. (1831–1879)
Confederate general

John Bell Hood was born in Owingsville, Kentucky, on June 1, 1831, the son of a physician. He was admitted to the U.S. Military Academy in 1849, proved something of a sullen, undistinguished student, and graduated four years later as a second lieutenant in the 4th U.S. Infantry. Hood reported for duty in California, but in 1855, he transferred to the newly created 2nd U.S. Cavalry under Colonel Albert S. Johnston. Hood rode with him for several years in Texas, waged numerous skirmishes with the Comanche, and was

Confederate general John B. Hood *(Library of Congress)*

wounded on one occasion. When the Civil War broke out in April 1861, Hood had no reservations about resigning his commission to fight for the South. However, because his native state of Kentucky remained neutral, he entered Confederate service from his adopted state of Texas. Hood spent several months in Virginia where he functioned as a cavalry instructor under General John B. MAGRUDER at Yorktown, Virginia, winning plaudits from superiors, but in October 1861, he switched back to the infantry as a colonel of the 4th Texas, and in February 1862, Hood advanced to brigadier general commanding the famous "Texas Brigade." Leading by example from the front and imposing an iron hand on his unruly recruits, he transformed them into the shock troops of the Confederacy.

Hood fought with great gallantry through the 1862 Peninsula campaign, acquiring the well-deserved reputation as a "fighting general." At the Battle of Gaines's Mill, June 27, 1863, his Texans crashed through Union lines, took several cannon, and forced General Fitz John PORTER to retreat. The following August, Hood distinguished himself in combat at Second Manassas as part of General James LONGSTREET's I Corps, where he delivered a flank attack that sent the Union army of General John POPE reeling. In September, his Texans successfully fended off the attacks of two Union Corps at Antietam, sparing General Robert E. LEE's center—while nearly being annihilated in the process. He consequently rose to the rank of the major general the following October. His next big engagement was at Gettysburg, July 2, 1863, where he drove the advance troops of General Daniel SICKLES from Devil's Den before sustaining a crippling arm wound. He next spent several week recuperating before accompanying Longstreet to reinforce the Army of Tennessee under General Braxton BRAGG. On September 20, 1863, in the bloody battle of Chickamauga, he delivered a crushing assault that nearly destroyed the Army of the Cumberland under General William S. ROSECRANS, losing his left leg in the process. Thereafter, the aggressive Kentuckian had to be strapped into his saddle while campaigning. He then rose to lieutenant general as of February 1864 and to command of a corps under General Joseph E. JOHNSTON in the Atlanta campaign.

Hood, a devotee of massed assaults, did not work well with Johnston, a master of set-piece defensive tactics, and the Army of Tennessee was forced to yield before the superior numbers of General William T. SHERMAN. On July 17, President Jefferson DAVIS, discouraged by Johnston's inability to halt the Union advance, suddenly replaced him with Hood. Predictably, Confederate strategy switched to the offensive, and Hood was heavily repulsed at Peachtree Creek, Atlanta, and Ezra Church on July 20, 22, and 28, 1864. At length, the Confederates were forced to abandon Atlanta to Sherman on September 1, 1864, and General William J. HARDEE, expressing no confidence in Hood's ability to lead, requested a transfer. When Sherman subsequently marched from Atlanta to Savannah and the sea, Hood saw a strategic opportunity to lure him back. He collected the Army of Tennessee and rapidly marched westward in Alabama to attack Union lines of communication. When that ploy failed to distract Sherman, Hood redirected his line of march north into Tennessee and a possible drive to the Ohio River. On November 29, 1864, he failed to trap a portion of the Union army under John M. SCHOFIELD at Spring Hill and then pursued them to Franklin. There, on November 30, 1864—and despite the protests of his subordinates—Hood launched a series of frontal assaults on prepared Union positions that were bloodily and predictably shattered. Six Confederate generals, including the irreplaceable Patrick R. CLEBURNE, fell that day. Hood then followed Schofield until he fell back on General George H. THOMAS's Union army at Nashville. Though severely depleted in numbers and lacking sufficient artillery, the stubborn Kentuckian entrenched his men around the city, daring Thomas to attack him. On December 15–16, 1864, the unhurried Thomas obliged him, completely shattering the Confederates. The once mighty Army of Tennessee dissolved into a mass of refugees, and Hood was relieved of command at his own request on January 23, 1865. He was succeeded by General Richard TAYLOR and, in Mississippi, he finally surrendered to Union authorities at Natchez on May 31, 1865.

Hood retired to New Orleans, Louisiana, to work in the insurance industry, and he also penned an excellent, if vitriolic, set of memoirs which matter of factly blamed Bragg and Johnston for losing the war. Not surprisingly, he studiously downplayed his own role in the western disasters. After surviving poverty for many years, Hood died of yellow fever on August 30, 1879, at the age of 48. Unquestionably one of the Civil War's bravest, most aggressive, and most tenacious division-level fighters, he was simply out of his depth at higher command—with disastrous results for the South.

Further Reading

Bagby, Milton. "Advance and Retreat." *American History* 37, no. 4 (2002): 38–46.

Bailey, Anne J. *The Chessboard of War: Sherman and Hood in the Autumn Campaigns of 1864.* Lincoln: University of Nebraska Press, 2000.

Daniel, Larry J. *Cannoneers in Gray: The Field Artillery of the Army of Tennessee, 1861–1865.* Tuscaloosa: University of Alabama Press, 2005.

Gallagher, Gary W., and Joseph T. Glatthaar, eds. *Leaders of the Lost Cause: New Perspectives on the Confederate High Command.* Mechanicsburg, Pa.: Stackpole Books, 2004.

Haughton, Andrew. *Training, Tactics, and Leadership in the Confederate Army of Tennessee: Seeds of Failure.* Portland, Ore.: Frank Cass, 2000.

Hood, John B. *Advance and Retreat: Personal Experiences in the United States and Confederate Armies.* Lincoln: University of Nebraska Press, 1996.

Jacobsen, Eric A., and Richard A. Rupp. *For Cause & Country: A Study of the Affair at Spring Hill & the Battle of Franklin.* Franklin, Tenn.: O'More Publishing, 2006.

Lepa, Jack H. *Breaking the Confederacy: The Georgia and Tennessee Campaigns of 1864.* Jefferson, N.C.: McFarland, 2005.

McDonough, James L. *Nashville: The Western Confederacy's Final Gamble.* Knoxville: University of Tennessee Press, 2004.

Hooker, Joseph (1814–1879)

Union general

Joseph Hooker was born in Hadley, Massachusetts, on November 13, 1814, the son of a businessman. Declining to follow his father's profession, he gained admission to the U.S. Military Academy in 1837 and graduated four years later as a second lieutenant of artillery. Hooker initially saw active duty in Florida's Second Seminole War, where he rose to first lieutenant, and he subsequently returned to West Point to serve as adjutant. During the Mexican War (1846–48), he served as a staff officer under General Zachary Taylor and Winfield SCOTT, but he managed to see extensive combat and won three consecutive brevet promotions in fighting at Monterrey, National Bridge, and Chapultepec. During the trial of General Gideon PILLOW, he testified favorably on his behalf and gained the lasting enmity of Scott. After the war, Hooker was reassigned to the Division of the Pacific in California where, dissatisfied with slow promotions, he resigned his commission in 1853. Hooker then pursued farming and also served as a colonel in the militia until the Civil War erupted in April 1861. He immediately tendered his services to the army, but he was not offered a commission—possibly because of the obstruction of Scott, now general in chief. Hooker then traveled to Washington, D.C., where he finally landed a brigadier general's commission on May 17, 1861, and assignment to the capital's defenses. He performed well and was chosen by General George B. MCCLELLAN to command a division in the newly formed Army of the Potomac.

Hooker first saw fighting in the Peninsula campaign of 1862, with General Samuel P. Heint-

Union general Joseph Hooker *(Library of Congress)*

zelman's III Corps, and he was closely engaged with General James LONGSTREET in the hard-fought encounter at Williamsburg on May 5, 1862. His bravery proved so conspicuous that he won both promotion to major general and the nickname "Fighting Joe." After more distinguished service under General John POPE at Second Manassas the following August, Hooker was closely engaged at South Mountain and Antietam, Maryland, in September 1862. During the latter contest, he orchestrated a heavy attack against General Robert E. LEE's left wing and might have prevailed had he been properly supported. General Ambrose BURNSIDE subsequently appointed him to command a grand division of two corps at Fredericksburg on December 13, 1862, where he was one of few Union officers to garner any distinction. Hooker, loud and indiscrete, openly complained about Burnside's leadership. President Abraham LINCOLN appointed him the new commander of the Army of the Potomac in January 1863. Hooker also gained a measure of notoriety in political circles by stating that both the army and the nation needed a dictator to win the war. "Only those generals who gain success can set up dictators," Lincoln advised him. "What I ask of you is military success and I will risk the dictatorship."

Hooker displayed considerable skill reorganizing and reinvigorating the much abused Army of the Potomac, and by May 1862, he possessed a splendidly trained and equipped force of 132,000 men—twice the size of General Robert E. Lee's Army of Northern Virginia. He then embarked on a bold strategy to slide around Lee's left flank through a rapid crossing of the Rapidan and Rappahannock rivers. Hooker's ploy worked brilliantly, and on May 1, 1863, his army was massed in a densely wooded area known as the Wilderness, only 10 miles from the unsuspecting Confederates. However, Lee took the even bolder expedient of dividing his army in the face of the enemy and dispatching the II Corps of General Thomas J. JACKSON to swing around and hit Hooker's own exposed right. Hooker, inexplicably, then lost his nerve and went on the defense, forfeiting all tactical initiative to the Confederates. He had also dispatched the bulk of his cavalry under General George Stoneman on a lengthy raid, thereby depriving himself of reconnaissance abilities that may have detected the enemy's approach. On May 2, Jackson launched his masterful flank attack, which routed the XI Corps of General Oliver O. HOWARD. Hooker then ordered his army, largely intact, strongly posted, and full of fight, to retreat over the protests of his generals. This closed the ill-fated Chancellorsville campaign, which ruined Hooker's reputation and cost the Union 17,000 men. Lincoln and General in Chief Henry W. HALLECK apparently also lost confidence in him and so interfered with his initial moves during the Gettysburg campaign that Hooker resigned three days before that fateful encounter transpired. He was hurriedly replaced by General George G. MEADE.

In the fall of 1863, Hooker transferred to the western theater to serve under General Ulysses S. GRANT, where he commanded the XI and XII Corps. In this capacity, he won a striking victory at Lookout Mountain on November 24, 1863, winning a major general's brevet in the regular army. Three days later, he sparred heavily with General Patrick R. CLEBURNE at Ringgold Gap, Georgia, and was unable to push back the Southern rearguard. Nevertheless, the following spring, he led the new XX Corps under General William T. SHERMAN in the Atlanta campaign, again distinguishing himself in several hard-fought battles. However, when General James B. McPHERSON was killed outside Atlanta on July 22, 1864, Sherman appointed General Howard—an officer of far less seniority—to succeeded him as commander of the Army of Tennessee. Hooker, enraged by the snub, promptly submitted his resignation in protest. He spent the balance of the war heading the Northern Department, a quiet sector.

After the war, Hooker led the Department of the East and the Department of the Lakes before resigning in 1868. He then lived in quiet seclusion until his death at Garden City, New York, on October 31, 1879, one of the Union's best corps commanders, an aggressive tactician who invariably inflicted more damage than he received. Unfortunately, his headstrong nature, sharp tongue, and indiscrete behavior alienated many around him and militated against his advancement.

Further Reading

Cubbison, Douglas R. "Tactical Genius above the Clouds: 'Fighting Joe' Hooker and John White Geary at the Battle of Lookout Mountain, November 24, 1863." *Tennessee Historical Quarterly* 61, no. 4 (2002): 266–289.

Dubbs, Carol K. *Defend This Old Town: Williamsburg during the Civil War.* Baton Rouge: Louisiana State University Press, 2002.

Longacre, Edward G. *The Commanders of Chancellorsville: The Gentleman vs the Rogue.* Nashville, Tenn.: Rutledge Hill Press, 2005.

Smith, Carl. *Chancellorsville, 1863: Jackson's Lightning Strike.* Westport, Conn.: Praeger, 2004.

Spruill, Mat. *Storming the Heights: A Guide to the Battle of Chattanooga.* Knoxville: University of Tennessee Press, 2003.

Taaffe, Stephen R. *Commanding the Army of the Potomac.* Lawrence: University Press of Kansas, 2006.

Wert, Jeffrey D. *The Sword of Lincoln: The Army of the Potomac.* New York: Simon and Schuster, 2005.

Howard, Oliver O. (1830–1909)

Union general

Oliver Otis Howard was born in Leeds, Maine, on November 8, 1830, the son of farmers. He graduated from Bowdoin College in 1850 and then entered the U.S. Military Academy. Howard graduated four years later, fourth in his class, and was commissioned a second lieutenant in the Ordnance Corps. After serving briefly in Florida's Third Seminole War, he transferred back to West Point to serve as a mathematics instructor. Howard by this time had undergone a profound religious conversion and seriously considered ordination to the ministry, but the onset of the Civil War induced him to become colonel of the 3rd Maine Infantry in June 1861. He then commanded a brigade at Bull Run the following July, which stampeded like the rest of General Irwin

Union general Oliver O. Howard *(Library of Congress)*

McDowell's army, but Howard performed well enough under fire to merit promotion to brigadier general in September. As part of General George B. McClellan's Army of the Potomac, he fought well in the Peninsula campaign and lost his right arm at the Battle of Fair Oaks on May 31, 1862. After recovering, Howard rejoined the army in time to fight well at Antietam, succeed a wounded general John Sedgwick to command a division, and then advance to major general that November. In the spring of 1863, he replaced the bumbling general Franz Sigel as commander of the XI Corps, which was a largely German-speaking unit. Howard's inadequacies for high command became quickly manifest at Chancellorsville on May 2, 1864, when General Thomas J. Jackson outflanked the XI Corps, routing it. On July 1, 1863, Howard arrived at Gettysburg shortly after the death of General John F. Reynolds and assumed command from General Abner Doubleday. Again, his XI Corps was pummeled heavily by an influx of Confederates under General Richard S. Ewell and driven off McPherson Ridge. Howard, luckily, had stationed his reserves along the high ground of Cemetery Ridge, and the Union line, now bolstered by additional troops under General Winfield S. Hancock, held firm. He subsequently received the thanks of Congress for this act. However, the commanding general, George M. Meade, remained unimpressed with his performance and did not resist when the XI Corps was transferred west to fight under General George H. Thomas in the Army of the Cumberland. On November 24–25, 1863, Howard fought capably at the Union victory of Chattanooga, and he subsequently received command of the new IV Corps under General William T. Sherman.

In the spring of 1864, Howard accompanied Sherman on his famous campaign against Atlanta, performing adequately. Moreover, when General James B. McPherson was killed outside Atlanta on July 22, 1864, Sherman elected Howard to lead the Army of the Tennessee over General Joseph Hooker—a move prompting the latter's resignation. Howard then accompanied Sherman on the march to Savannah and the subsequent campaign north into the Carolinas, again acquitting himself well. By war's end, he held a rank of brevet major general of volunteers.

In the immediate postwar period, Howard was chosen by President Andrew Johnson to head the newly created Freedmen's Bureau to assist liberated African-American slaves. He readily accepted the task, given his religious and abolitionist impulses, but he proved a lax administrator who refused to investigate the activities of subordinates. In 1867 the all-black Howard University was established at his behest, and he served as its first president (1869–72). In 1873 President Ulysses S. Grant dispatched Howard to the western frontier to quell an Apache uprising, and Howard, by dint of sincerity and personal honesty, convinced Chief Cochise to return to the reservation without bloodshed. By 1877 he commanded the Department of Columbia and successfully campaigned against Chief Joseph of the Nez Percé in concert with Generals John GIBBON and Nelson Miles. On October 5, 1877, he received the chief's surrender at Eagle Rock, Montana, ending his famous flight. In January 1881 Howard returned to West Point as superintendent for a year, and then he successively took charge of the Division of the Platte and the East. In 1893 Congress awarded him a Congressional Medal of Honor for his services at Fair Oaks in 1862. Howard retired from the army in 1894 and penned several lucid memoirs about his military experiences. He died in Burlington, Vermont, on October 26, 1909, an earnest, if mediocre, leader.

Further Reading

Howard, Oliver O. *Autobiography of Oliver Otis Howard, Major General, U.S. Army*. New York: Baker and Taylor, 1907.

Newton, Steven H. *McPherson's Ridge: The First Battle for the High Ground, July 1, 1863*. Cambridge, Mass.: Da Capo Press, 2002.

Pfanz, Harry W. *Gettysburg—The First Day*. Chapel Hill: University of North Carolina Press, 2001.

Valuska, David L., and Christian B. Keller. *Damn Dutch: Pennsylvania Germans at Gettysburg*. Mechanicsburg, Pa.: Stackpole Books, 2004.

Weland, Gerald. *O. O. Howard, Union General*. Jefferson, N.C.: McFarland, 1995.

Woodworth, Steven E. *Nothing but Victory: The Army of the Tennessee, 1861–1865*. New York: Alfred A. Knopf, 2005.

Huger, Benjamin (1805–1877)

Confederate general

Benjamin Huger was born in Charleston, South Carolina, on November 22, 1805, into a distinguished family of Huguenot descent. His father had served as aide-de-camp to General James Wilkinson during the War of 1812, while his mother was the daughter of General Thomas Pinckney of the American Revolution. Given this martial background, Huger attended the U.S. Military Academy in 1821 and graduated four years later at the top of his class. He was then commissioned second lieutenant in the 3rd U.S. Artillery and performed topographical duties until 1828,

when he left on a sabbatical to study artillery in Europe. Huger then joined the Ordnance Department, rising to captain in 1832. He commanded Fortress Monroe, Virginia, for 12 years while also sitting on various ordnance boards. During the Mexican War, he served in the army of General Winfield SCOTT as commander of the artillery train. His placement of field pieces at the siege of Veracruz proved masterful and resulted in brevet promotion to major. Huger subsequently was breveted two more times for bravery at Molino del Rey and Chapultepec, ending the war a lieutenant colonel. Afterward, he resumed his duties with the Ordnance Department, helped develop a new artillery system, and commanded a successive series of Federal arsenals from Harper's Ferry, Virginia, to Pikesville, Maryland. Huger's service was so esteemed by his home state that the South Carolina legislature voted him a ceremonial sword. The old soldier did not immediately tender his resignation when his native state seceded in December 1860; he waited until after the bombardment of Fort Sumter in April 1861. Prior to the outbreak of fighting, Huger had been dispatched to the fort to confer with fellow Southerner Major Robert ANDERSON, but the latter had already resolved to remain loyal to the Union, and their discussions came to naught.

The elderly soldier rose rapidly through the Confederate ranks, being commissioned a brigadier general in June 1861 and major general the following October. As such, he was entrusted with command of the Department of Southern Virginia and North Carolina, headquartered at Norfolk. Huger administered his grossly undermanned charge well until February 8, 1862, when a Union fleet under Admiral Louis M. Goldsborough anchored offshore and landed a Union army under General Ambrose E. BURNSIDE. When Huger failed to dispatch reinforcements, Burnside experienced little difficulty capturing the island from General Henry Wise. This proved an embarrassing loss to the South, and the Confederate Congress conducted an investigation into Huger's behavior. Meanwhile, the imposing Army of the

Potomac under General George B. McClellan began to push up Virginia's Peninsula district toward Richmond. Huger, greatly outnumbered, hastily abandoned Norfolk to the Federals, scuttling the famous CSS *Virginia* in the process. He then joined Generals James Longstreet and Daniel H. Hill to command a division in the army under General Joseph E. Johnston. Huger retreated with the main body until May 31, 1862, when Johnston turned and attacked the isolated corps of General Erasmus D. Keyes at Seven Pines (Fair Oaks). Unfortunately, Huger's deployment proved hopelessly inept, and his division became ensnared with Longstreet's men while marching down the same road. His subsequent lethargic movements allowed the Union troops to escape unscathed. Johnston was then replaced by the aggressive general Robert E. Lee, who counterattacked across the line in the Seven Day's battles. Again, Huger performed sluggishly, and furthermore, a congressional committee found him culpable for the loss of Roanoke. He thereupon was relieved of duty on July 12, 1862, and sent west in the less demanding role as inspector of ordnance and artillery. He functioned capably in this office until 1863, when he rose to chief of ordnance in the Trans-Mississippi Department until the end of the war. Afterward, Huger migrated to Fauquier County, Virginia, to farm. He died in Charleston, South Carolina, on December 7, 1877, a soldier of demonstrated technical competence, but too past his prime for the rigors of war.

Further Reading

Burton, Brian K. *Extraordinary Circumstances: The Seven Days Battles.* Bloomington: Indiana University Press, 2001.

Gallagher, Gary W., ed. *The Richmond Campaign of 1862: The Peninsula and the Seven Days.* Chapel Hill: University of North Carolina Press, 2000.

Newton, Steven H. *The Battle of Seven Pines, May 31–June 1, 1862.* Lynchburg, Va.: H. E. Howard, 1993.

Rhoades, Jeffrey L. *Scapegoat General: The Story of Major General Benjamin Huger.* Hamden, Conn.: Archon Books, 1985.

Sauers, Richard. "The Confederate Congress and the Loss of Roanoke Island." *Civil War History* 40, no. 2 (1994): 134–150.

Van Velzer, William R. "Benjamin Huger and the Arming of America, 1825–1861." Unpublished master's thesis, Virginia Polytechnic University, 1994.

Imboden, John D. (1823–1895)

Confederate general

John Daniel Imboden was born in Augusta County, Virginia, on February 16, 1823, and he matriculated at nearby Washington College (1841–42). He then studied law and opened up a successful practice at Staunton while also developing a taste for politics. Imboden was twice elected to the House of Delegates where he served as a staunch secessionist, but he proved unable to win a seat in the state secessionist convention. Concurrent with this, he joined the local militia and helped organize the Staunton artillery. Once Virginia seceded from the Union, Imboden accompanied Turner ASHBY and helped to seize the Federal arsenal at Harper's Ferry on April 19, 1861. He then advanced to colonel and served under General Pierre G. T. BEAUREGARD at the Battle of Bull Run (July 21, 1861). Imboden was conspicuously engaged at the defense of Henry House Hill, where he supported the command of General Bernard E. Bee. He next switched from artillery to cavalry by organizing the 1st Partisan Rangers in the spring of 1862. He led his scouts throughout General Thomas J. JACKSON's brilliant Shenandaoh campaign, and he fought conspicuously at the battles of Cross Keys and Port Republic that June. He subsequently joined the Army of Northern Virginia under General Robert E. LEE in time for the invasion of Maryland that fall, and he assisted in the capture of Harper's Ferry on September 15, 1862.

Imboden's good performance resulted in his promotion to brigadier general on January 28, 1863, and command of the Northwestern Brigade of the Department of Northern Virginia. Two months later, he performed his most impressive military deed by organizing a large mounted raid against the Baltimore and Ohio Railroad. On April 20, 1863, Imboden led 3,200 troopers into the hills of West Virginia while acting in concert with a force of similar size under General William E. "Grumble" Jones. For the next 37 days, the two cavaliers tore up 170 miles of track and absconded with scores of badly needed horses and livestock. Both forces then united to eliminate the petroleum fields at Oiltown, destroying 150,000 barrels of oil. By the time Imboden and Jones concluded their successful foray, they had seized more than 5,000 cattle and 1,200 horses, burned 24 bridges, acquired 1,000 small arms, and inflicted 800 Federal casualties. This was one of the greatest cavalry raids of the Civil War, and it was accomplished at little cost to the Confederacy.

By summer, Imboden's command had been reassigned to the Army of Northern Virginia as it advanced into Pennsylvania. He successfully screened Lee's left flank but arrived at Gettysburg on July 3, 1863, just as the Confederates were withdrawing. He then assisted the exhausted, battered survivors by acting as their rear guard. On July 6, 1863, the Army of Northern Virginia was pressed up against the flooded Potomac River

Confederate general John D. Imboden *(Massachusetts Commandery Military Order of the Loyal Legion and the U.S. Army Military History Institute)*

while Union cavalry nipped at its heels. Imboden, tasked with escorting the army's supply train and thousands of wounded soldiers, suddenly found himself set upon by Federal troopers under Generals Hugh J. Kilpatrick and John Buford near Williamsport, Maryland. However, having scrapped together all available manpower, including the walking wounded, he managed to hold the marauders back until generals Fitzhugh Lee and Wade Hampton arrived to reinforce him. By the

fall, Imboden was active again in the Shenandoah Valley, and he captured the entire 9th Maryland at Charles Town in October. Highly commended by Lee, he next served under General John C. Breckinridge at New Market, Virginia, on May 15, 1864, where he helped defeat Federal forces under General Franz Sigel. He accompanied General Jubal A. Early's famous sortie into the Shenandoah Valley in the summer and fall before being driven out by General Philip H. Sheridan. As the year ended, Imboden contracted typhoid fever, and he was transferred to prison duties at Aiken, South Carolina, until hostilities ceased. Imboden revived his legal career after the war in Washington County, Virginia, and he was also active in Confederate veterans' affairs. He also vocally advocated developing the coal and iron resources of his native state. Imboden, one of the Civil War's most intrepid partisan fighters, died in Damascus, Virginia, on August 15, 1895.

Further Reading

Brown, Kent M. *Retreat from Gettysburg: Lee, Logistics, and the Pennsylvania Campaign.* Chapel Hill: University of North Carolina Press, 2005.

French, Stephen. *The Jones-Imboden Raid against the B & O Railroad at Roalesburg, Virginia, April 1863.* Saline, Mich.: McNaughton and Gunn for the Blue and Gray Education Society, 2001.

Gallagher, Gary W., ed. *The Third Day at Gettysburg and Beyond.* Chapel Hill: University of North Carolina Press, 1994.

Lepa, Jack H. *The Shenandoah Valley Campaign of 1864.* Jefferson, N.C.: McFarland, 2003.

Patchan, Scott C. "Piedmont: The Forgotten Battle." *North & South* 6, no. 3 (2003): 62–75.

Tucker, Spencer C. *Brigadier General John D. Imboden: Confederate Commander in the Shenandoah.* Lexington: University Press of Kentucky, 2003.

J

Jackson, Thomas J. (1824–1863)

Confederate general

Thomas Jonathan Jackson was born in Clarksburg, Virginia (West Virginia) and orphaned at an early age. Raised by an uncle, he possessed only rudimentary educational and social skills on being accepted to the U.S. Military Academy in 1842. Jackson, however, proved himself a willful individual, and by dint of hard work and perseverance, he graduated 17th out of a class of 59 four years later. He then joined the army of General Winfield Scott in Mexico, winning consecutive brevet promotions for bravery at Veracruz, Cerro Gordo, and Chapultepec. After the war, Jackson did routine garrison work in Florida and New York, but he resigned his commission in 1851 after his brother-in-law, Daniel H. Hill, managed to secure him a teaching appointment at the Virginia Military Institute (VMI) in Lexington. A boring instructor, he struggled with tactics and natural philosophy for a decade and was decidedly unpopular with students. Furthermore, Jackson's predilection for observing the strict nuances of Calvinism reinforced his reputation as a religious fanatic. He nonetheless lived quietly and shunned the public eye until 1859, when he commanded the VMI cadets during the capture of abolitionist John Brown at Harper's Ferry. Jackson was also staunchly Unionist in outlook, and it was not until Virginia seceded in April 1861 that he offered his sword to the Confederacy. Little known outside of Lexington, he could secure only the rank of colonel.

Jackson spent several weeks drilling his cadets for military service, and in June 1861, he was assigned to the army of General Joseph E. Johnston in his native Shenandoah Valley. Shortly after, his troops were shunted by rail to assist General Pierre G. T. Beauregard at Manassas Junction, Virginia, and they fought well in the Battle of Bull Run (July 21, 1861). Tasked with defending Henry House Hill, he did so with aplomb, whereupon General Bernard Bee declared, "There is Jackson standing like a stonewall." The sobriquet stuck and a legend was born. On October 7, 1861, Jackson advanced to major general, and he returned to the Shenandoah Valley to conduct one of the most brilliant campaigns in military history. He started off on the wrong foot in February 1862 by marching his command through freezing snow and was highly criticized by General William W. Loring. When Loring went over Jackson's head and complained to authorities, he nearly resigned from the service but was persuaded to remain. The following March, he was ordered to keep Union forces out of the Shenandoah Valley and prevent them from reinforcing General George B. McClellan in his drive on Richmond. Jackson, with 17,000 men facing three Union armies totaling 64,000, immediately seized and kept the initiative by adroit offensive maneuvering. He was initially rebuffed by General James Shields at Kernstown on March 23, 1862, but his aggressiveness caused Union leaders to detain forces in the valley. He then marched rapidly and defeated General Nathaniel P. BANKS at Front Royal and Winchester, May 23 and 25, 1862, while dispatching the division of General Richard S. EWELL to dislodge General John C. Frémont at Cross Keys on June 8, 1862. Jackson himself lunged at Shields again at Port Republic on June 9, driving his superior numbers from the field. In only 48 days, his fast-marching forces, celebrated as "Jackson's foot cavalry," traversed 350 miles, inflicted 7,000 Federal casualties, and captured tons of badly needed supplies and equipment. In terms of rapidity of movement and economy of force, his 1862 Shenandoah campaign remains a singular military accomplishment, and it rendered him a hero throughout the South.

Confederate general Thomas J. Jackson *(Library of Congress)*

Having dispensed with opponents in the valley, Jackson hurried to join General Robert E. LEE's Army of Northern Virginia in time for the fast unfolding Peninsula campaign. His performance here was somewhat erratic owing to mental fatigue and unfamiliarity with local terrain, so his contributions were minimal. Jackson operated more successfully the following August, when he defeated General Banks again at Cedar Mountain on August 9, undertook a secret two day march that covered 51 miles, and captured General John POPE's supply base on the 27th. He next fought off a large Union counterattack at Groveton on the 28th and successfully defended Lee's left flank at Second Manassas on August 29–30. Jackson then spearheaded a Confederate advance back into the Shenandoah Valley by capturing Harper's Ferry on September 15, 1862, along with 12,000 Federals, before rapidly reinforcing Lee's depleted army at Antietam on September 17. There, he successfully fended off numerous Union attacks and won both promotion to lieutenant general and command of the newly organized II Corps. Jackson again commanded the left wing of the army at Fredericksburg (December 13, 1862), tenaciously defending his part of the line against determined Northern attacks by General Ambrose BURNSIDE. On many a far-flung field, the tactical rapport between Lee and Jackson proved an unbeatable combination.

Jackson reached his operational zenith during the Chancellorsville campaign of May 1862. No sooner had General Joseph HOOKER crossed the Rapidan River with 132,000 men than Lee decided to divide his force in the face of the enemy and send Jackson on a circuitous 12-mile march around the Union right flank. On May 2, 1863, "Stonewall" launched a crushing blow against General Oliver O. HOWARD's XI Corps, and he almost rolled up the Union line before darkness and caused the fighting to stop. Advancing ahead to reconnoiter at dusk, Jackson suddenly was shot and wounded by his own men. He lost his left arm in consequence and lingered for eight days before dying of pneumonia at Guinea Station, Virginia, on May 8, 1863. His death represented a catastrophic loss to the Confederacy and Lee, in his own estimation, declared, "I have lost my right arm." Never again would the Army of Northern Virginia possess a commander with such an intuitive grasp of Lee's orders. Moreover, his untimely demise undoubtedly hastened the Confederacy's downfall.

Further Reading

Alexander, Bevin. *Lost Victories: The Military Genius of Stonewall Jackson.* New York: Hippocrene Books, 2004.

Davis, Don. *Stonewall Jackson.* New York: Palgrave Macmillan, 2007.

Gallagher, Gary W. *The Shenandoah Valley Campaign of 1862.* Chapel Hill: University of North Carolina Press, 2003.

Green, Jennifer. "From West Point to the Virginia Military Institute: The Educational Life of Stonewall Jackson." *Virginia Cavalcade* 49, no. 3 (2000): 134–143.

Hall, Kenneth. *Stonewall Jackson and Religious Faith in Military Command.* Jefferson, N.C.: McFarland, 2005.

Krick, Robert K. *Conquering the Valley: Stonewall Jackson at Port Republic.* Baton Rouge: Louisiana State University Press, 2002.

Martin, David G. *Jackson's Valley Campaign: November 1861–June 1862.* Cambridge, Mass.: Da Capo Press, 2003.

Robertson, James I. "The Christian Soldier: General Thomas J. 'Stonewall' Jackson." *History Today* 53, no. 2 (2003): 29–35.

Smith, Derek. *The Gallant Dead: Union and Confederate Generals Killed in the Civil War.* Mechanicsburg, Pa.: Stackpole Books, 2005.

Wilkins, J. Steven. *All Things for Good: The Steadfast Fidelity of Stonewall Jackson.* Nashville, Tenn.: Cumberland House, 2004.

Johnston, Albert S. (1803–1862)

Confederate general

Albert Sidney Johnston was born in Washington, Kentucky, on February 2, 1803, and educated at Transylvania University. There, he met and befriended Jefferson DAVIS, the future Confederate president, before attending the U.S. Military Academy in 1826. Four years later, he graduated as a second lieutenant in the 2nd U.S. Infantry, and he performed garrison duty in the Black Hawk War. However, he resigned two years later to attend to his dying wife and subsequently migrated to Texas to fight in its war for independence. Johnston, a large, strapping individual exuding a commanding persona, enlisted as a private in the Texas army and within a year had risen to brigadier general. His headstrong antics angered many contemporaries, and in 1837, he was injured seriously in a duel. He then relinquished his commission to serve as secretary of war for the new Texas Republic until 1840, when a disagreement with President Sam Houston resulted in his resignation. Johnston then farmed for many before serving as a colonel of the 1st Texas Rifles in the Mexican War (1846–48), fought well under Generals Zachary Taylor and William O. Butler, and won plaudits for his behavior in the September 1846 Battle of Monterrey. He returned to his plantation after the war, but the following year, his fellow Kentuckian Taylor, now president, commissioned him major and paymaster of U.S. troops stationed in Texas. In 1855 Davis, now secretary of war, chose Johnston to head the newly formed and elite 2nd U.S. Cavalry with Robert E. LEE as his lieutenant colonel and George H. THOMAS and William J. HARDEE his majors. In 1857 Johnston replaced Colonel William S. Harney as head of the Department of Texas, and in 1858 he conducted his famous Mormon expedition to restore Federal authority to the Utah Territory. By 1860 he functioned as brigadier general commanding the Department of the Pacific until the cusp of the Civil War. Though offered a position as second in command of Union forces in the Civil War by General Winfield SCOTT, Johnston resigned his commission once his adopted state of Texas seceded in February 1861.

Johnston traveled three months from California to reach Richmond, Virginia, to confer with his old friend Davis. Consequently, he was installed as a full general in the Confederate service and second only to General Samuel Cooper in seniority. He then accepted command of Department No. 2, which encompassed the western frontier from the Appalachian Mountains to the Indian Territory (Oklahoma). Given the vast expanse he was expected to defend, Johnston labored under many disadvantages as the Federals enjoyed superiority in numbers, equipment and, above all, ironclad river boats. Johnston nonetheless pushed his line far north into Kentucky, anchoring it on Forts Henry and Donelson on the Cumberland and Tennessee rivers, respectively. But on January 19, 1862, General George B. CRITTENDEN fumbled an attack at Mill Springs, Kentucky, losing heavily. In February 1862, further mismanagement by Generals Gideon J. PILLOW and John B. FLOYD resulted in the capture of both posts by General Ulysses S. GRANT. Johnston consequently ordered his Kentucky positions abandoned, and after Nashville fell to General Don C. BUELL in late February, he withdrew down to northern Alabama. The easy conquest of valuable land proved disheartening to Southern leaders, but Johnston simply lacked the wherewithal to confront larger Union armies. He then began to mass his forces at Corinth, Mississippi, assisted by reinforcements under General Pierre G. T. BEAUREGARD, and at length cobbled together a force numbering 40,000 men. This force he labeled the Army of Mississippi, which consisted of corps led by Generals Braxton BRAGG, Leonidas K. POLK, John C. BRECKINRIDGE, and his former major Hardee. Furthermore, Johnston decided against retreating another inch.

Once Grant resumed his advance down the Tennessee River by establishing a lodgment at Pittsburg Landing (Shiloh), Tennessee, Johnston sought to strike at him before reinforcements from General Buell's Army of the Ohio arrived. He then led his army from Corinth for several days in driving rain and arrived outside Grant's camp on April 5, 1862. On the following day, his massed corps completely surprised the Union pickets and charged directly into the Federal camp. The Northerners were nearly

swept back to the river before Grant reestablished his defensive perimeter, and Johnston turned to mopping up scattered pockets of resistance. One of these, the so-called Peach Orchard, had repelled several Confederate attacks, and Johnston led the next one in person. There, he was struck in the leg by a bullet and bled to death before medical aid could be rendered. Command then reverted to Beauregard, who halted the battle and withdrew the next day. Johnston was thus the highest-ranking Confederate fatality of the Civil War and was mourned greatly. President Davis especially felt the loss and subsequently recorded that his death was "the turning point in our fate." Johnston's remains initially were interred at New Orleans, Louisiana, and then were transferred to their final resting place in his adopted state of Texas.

Further Reading

Arnold, James R. *Jeff Davis's Own: Cavalry, Comanches, and the Battle for the Texas Frontier.* New York: Wiley, 2000.

———. *Shiloh, 1862: The Death of Innocence.* Westport, Conn.: Praeger, 2004.

Eicher, John H., and David J. Eicher. *Civil War High Commands.* Stanford, Calif.: Stanford University Press, 2001.

Engle, Stephen D. *Struggle for the Heartland: The Campaign from Fort Henry to Corinth.* Lincoln: University of Nebraska Press, 2001.

Gallagher, Gary W., and Joseph T. Glatthaar, eds. *Leaders of the Lost Cause: New Perspectives on the Confederate High Command.* Mechanicsburg, Pa.: Stackpole Books, 2004.

Gott, Kendall D. *Where the South Lost the War: An Analysis of the Fort Henry–Fort Donelson Campaign, February, 1862.* Mechanicsburg, Pa.: Stackpole Books, 2003.

Hanson, Victor D. *Ripples of Battle: How Wars of the Past Still Determine How We Fight, How We Live, and How We Think.* New York: Doubleday, 2003.

Smith, Derek. *The Gallant Dead: Union and Confederate Generals Killed in the Civil War.* Mechanicsburg, Pa.: Stackpole Books, 2005.

Smith, Timothy B. *The Untold Story of Shiloh: The Battle and the Battlefield.* Knoxville: University of Tennessee Press, 2006.

Johnston, Joseph E. (1803–1891)
Confederate general

Joseph Eggleston Johnston was born in Prince Edward County, Virginia, on February 3, 1803, the son of a Revolutionary War veteran. In 1824 he matriculated at the U.S. Military Academy and graduated four years later in the upper third of his class. Johnston then served as a second lieutenant in the 4th U.S. Artillery in the Black Hawk War of 1832 and on the staff of General Winfield SCOTT during initial phases of Florida's Second Seminole War (1836). Johnston quit the military to work as a civilian engineer and then returned in 1837 to serve with the Topographical Engineer Corps. He rose to captain in 1846 and rejoined General Scott for the march on Mexico City in 1847. That year, he distinguished himself in combat at Cerro Gordo and Chapultepec, being wounded five times and receiving three brevet promotions. Johnston resumed his engineering work in Texas, where, in 1855, he became lieutenant colonel of the 1st U.S. Cavalry. Two years later, he accompanied Colonel Albert S. JOHNSTON during his Mormon expedition to Utah, and in 1860 his brother-in-law, Secretary of War John B. FLOYD, appointed him brigadier general and quartermaster of the army. Many questioned this appointment as an example of Floyd's penchant for nepotism. Johnston, however, remained at this post for less than a year, resigning his commission after the Civil War commenced in April 1861.

Johnston initially was employed as a brigadier general, commanding the Army of the Shenandoah, then considered something of a backwater. But in July 1861, he ordered the cavalry of Colonel J. E. B. STUART to confound nearby Union forces while he rushed his army by rail to Manassas Junction, Virginia, to assist General Pierre G. T. BEAUREGARD at the Battle of Bull Run. Johnston's appearance proved decisive and contributed greatly to the Southern victory there. The following August, he won promotion to full general, but controversy arose when Johnston angrily disputed his position as fourth in seniority behind Generals Samuel Cooper, Albert S. Johnston, and Robert E.

Confederate general Joseph Johnston *(National Archives)*

LEE. His quarrelsome disposition also alienated President Jefferson DAVIS and fueled the growing rift between them. Davis's antipathy for Johnston mounted during the 1862 Peninsula campaign when the latter, heavily outnumbered by General George B. MCCLELLAN's Army of the Potomac, continually gave ground and retreated toward Richmond. Johnston finally turned and pounced on a portion of the Federal army at Seven Pines (Fair Oaks) on May 31–June 1, 1862, in which he was severely wounded. He was then replaced permanently by Lee for the rest of the war.

Johnston remained unemployed for several months until May 1863, when Davis reluctantly appointed him to head up the Department of the West to coordinate efforts between Generals John C. PEMBERTON, Braxton BRAGG, and Edmund KIRBY-SMITH. Johnston, however, continually complained—with some validity—that the existing command structure was untenable and that this vast department was undermanned and underequipped. These deficiencies became readily apparent during General Ulysses S. GRANT's Vicksburg campaign: Johnston ordered Pemberton to withdraw from the city to save his army, but Davis countermanded his instructions. On May 14, 1863, Federal forces under General William T. SHERMAN drove Johnston away from his main base at Jackson, Mississippi, and when Vicksburg surrendered on July 4, Davis held him responsible for the debacle. He was again relieved of command and assigned minor duties in Alabama for six months until the next crisis arrived.

In December 1863 Johnston was tapped to replace General Braxton Bragg as head of the much-battered Army of Tennessee. The general, rather than heed Davis's preferences for an immediate offensive, spent the next few months at Dalton, Georgia, drilling, training, and reequipping his charge to counter more effectively Sherman's forthcoming campaign against Atlanta. That May, Sherman advanced with 100,000 troops against Johnston's 60,000, and an elaborate military dance unfolded. Johnston, a master of defensive tactics, continually thwarted Sherman's attempts to destroy him and repeatedly fell back to prepared positions. The Union commander grew so exasperated by these Fabian tactics that Union troops were committed to a frontal assault at Kennesaw Mountain on June 27, 1864, suffering heavy losses. Johnston again withdrew and kept his army intact until he was nearly at the gates of Atlanta. But his willingness to trade space for time angered Davis, who replaced Johnston with the more aggressive John B. HOOD on July 17, 1864. Johnston thus remained marooned without a command for six more months until February 1865 when, on the insistence of General Lee and the Confederate Congress, Davis restored him to lead remnants of the Army of Tennessee in North Carolina. Outnumbered three to one, he waged another futile attempt to halt Sherman's advance despite a bloody battle at Bentonville on March 19–21, 1865. Johnston finally surrendered his sword at Durham's Station

on April 18, 1865, although, when the U.S. government rejected Sherman's overly generous terms, he surrendered again on April 25.

After the war, Johnston sold insurance in Virginia and was elected to Congress as a representative in 1879. Six years later, President Grover Cleveland appointed him railroad commissioner, and while living in Washington, D.C., he befriended his former antagonist, Sherman. Johnston also penned a detailed and highly vitriolic set of memoirs in which he blamed Davis and Hood for losing the war. The pugnacious, combative Johnston, popularly regarded by his troops as "Fighting Joe," died in Washington of pneumonia on March 21, 1891; ironically, he contracted the malady while attending Sherman's funeral as a pallbearer.

Further Reading

Bradley, Mark L. *This Astonishing Close: The Road to Bennett Place.* Chapel Hill: University of North Carolina Press, 2000.

Broadwater, Robert P. *Battle of Despair: Bentonville and the North Carolina Campaign.* Macon, Ga.: Mercer University Press, 2004.

Daniel, Larry J. *Cannoneers in Gray: The Field Artillery of the Army of Tennessee, 1861–1865.* Tuscaloosa: University of Alabama Press, 2005.

Gallagher, Gary W., and Joseph T. Glatthaar, eds. *Leaders of the Lost Cause: New Perspectives on the Confederate High Command.* Mechanicsburg, Pa.: Stackpole Books, 2004.

Haughton, Andrew. *Training, Tactics, and Leadership in the Confederate Army of Tennessee: Seeds of Failure.* Portland, Ore.: Frank Cass, 2000.

Johnston, Joseph E. *Narrative of Military Operations during the Civil War.* New York: Da Capo Press, 1990.

Lepa, Jack H. *Breaking the Confederacy: The Georgia and Tennessee Campaigns of 1864.* Jefferson, N.C.: McFarland, 2005.

Longacre, Edward G. *Worthy Opponents: William T. Sherman, USA, Joseph E. Johnston, CSA.* Nashville, Tenn.: Rutledge Hill Press, 2006.

Symonds, Craig L. "Johnston's Toughest Fight." *MHQ* 16 (winter 2004): 56–61.

Towles, Louis P. "Dalton and the Rebirth of the Army of Tennessee." *Proceedings of the South Carolina Historical Association* (2002): 87–1000.

K

Kearny, Philip (1814–1862)

Union general

Philip Kearny was born in New York City on June 1, 1814, and orphaned at an early age. He was raised by a wealthy grandfather and pressured to attend Columbia College for a law degree in 1833. When his stepfather died three years later, he inherited a small fortune and fulfilled his lifelong ambition by joining the military. Kearny was then commissioned a second lieutenant in the 1st U.S. Dragoons and served along the western frontier alongside his famous uncle, Colonel Stephen W. Kearny, the explorer. After two years of service, he was sent to study cavalry tactics at the Royal Cavalry School in Saumur, France, and he subsequently served with the noted Chasseurs d'Afrique in Algiers. Kearny fought well in the successful campaign against noted rebel Abdel Kader and published an account of his experiences. In 1840 he returned to the United States and was tasked with writing a new cavalry manual for the army. Kearney retired briefly from the army in 1846, but he speedily rejoined following the onset of the Mexican War that year. Attached to General Winfield SCOTT's army, he conducted a gallant charge at Churubusco on August 20, 1847, losing his left arm and gaining brevet promotion to major. Kearney then remained on the frontier and retired again in 1851 to marry and enjoy his riches in New Jersey. Listless as ever, he rejoined the French army in 1859 as part of Emperor Napoleon III's Imperial Guard, and he acquitted himself with distinction against the Austrians in the battles of Magenta and Solferino that year. His excellent service resulted in receipt of the cross of the Légion d'honneur, becoming the first American officer so honored. Kearny remained in Paris until the outbreak of the Civil War in 1861, whenupon he hurriedly returned to New Jersey and joined the army.

Given his reputation, Kearny had no trouble securing a brigadier generalship of New Jersey troops in the division of William B. Franklin's division. Mounted on a beautiful charger, he always led from the front and became known throughout both armies as the "One-armed Devil." In the course of General George B. McCLELLAN's 1862 Peninsula campaign, Kearny fought with distinction at Williamsburg on May 4–5, 1862, delivering a successful charge that rescued the division of General Joseph HOOKER. He also recklessly exposed himself in major fighting at Fair Oaks on June 1, 1862, where his favorite horse was killed and he grieved openly. Kearny then fought doggedly at the Battle of Glendale during McClellan's retreat, thereby preserving a Union withdrawal to Harrison's Landing. The following month, he advanced to major general and received command of a division in General Samuel P. Heintzelman's III Corps. Intent on improving the esprit de corps of his men, he also instituted the so-called Kearny Patch, a forerunner of the corps badge system adopted by the Union army. He then conducted himself exceedingly well under General John POPE at the Battle of Second Manassas on August 29–30, 1862, delivering the most successful Union charge of the day. On September 1, 1862, Kearny found himself arrayed against the redoubtable General Thomas J. JACKSON at Chantilly, and after severe fighting, he stopped a determined Confederate pursuit. In the midst of battle, Kearny recklessly—and typically—spurred his horse forward to reconnoiter and stumbled into a Confederate picket line. He was shot down trying to escape, but General Robert E. LEE sent his body, his horse, and his sword back across Union lines as a token of respect. Kearny's fall was a serious loss to the Army of the Potomac; in his memory, the men of his division instituted their own decoration, the Kearny Cross. The town of Kearny, New Jersey, was also renamed in his honor.

Further Reading

Gottfried, Bradley M. *Kearny's Own: The History of the First New Jersey Brigade in the Civil War.* New Brunswick, N.J.: Rutgers University Press, 2005.

Pindell, Richard. "Phil Kearny—the One-Armed Devil." *Civil War Times Illustrated* 27, no. 3 (1988): 16–21, 44–46.

Styple, William B., ed. *Letters from the Peninsula: The Civil War Letters of General Philip Kearny.* Kearny, N.J.: Belle Grove Publishing, 1988.

Smith, Derek. *The Gallant Dead: Union and Confederate Generals Killed in the Civil War.* Mechanicsburg, Pa.: Stackpole Books, 2005.

Taylor, Paul. *He Hath Loosed the Fateful Lightning: The Battle of Ox Hill (Chantilly), September 1, 1862.* Shippensburg, Pa.: White Mane Books, 2003.

Welker, David A. *Tempest at Ox Hill: The Battle of Chantilly.* Conshohocken, Pa.: Combined Publishing, 2001.

Kilpatrick, Hugh J. (1836–1881)

Union general

Hugh Judson Kilpatrick was born in Deckertown, New Jersey, on January 14, 1836, the son of a militia officer. He entered the U.S. Military Academy in 1857 and, showing some ability, graduated 19th in his class of 45 four years later. He was then commissioned a second lieutenant in the 1st U.S. Artillery but switched to captain in the 5th New York Infantry after the Civil War commenced in April 1861. In this capacity, he fought at Big Bethel, Virginia, on June 10, 1861, and was severely injured. While recovering, he used his political connections—and an uncanny knack for self-promotion—to transfer again to the 2nd New York Cavalry. Kilpatrick remained with the mounted arm for the rest of the war, and in 1862, he performed capably throughout General George B. McCLELLAN's Peninsula campaign. The following August, he fought with distinction at Thoroughfare Gap and Second Manassas, rising to colonel as of December 1862 and brigadier general in June 1863. Kilpatrick fought well at the huge cavalry

Union general Hugh J. Kilpatrick *(Massachusetts Commandery Military Order of the Loyal Legion and the U.S. Army Military History Institute)*

clash at Brandy Station on June 9, 1863, under General Alfred PLEASONTON, and he actively skirmished with the Confederate cavalry of General J. E. B. STUART throughout the approach to Gettysburg that July. In concert with General George A. CUSTER, he managed to delay Stuart at Hanover, Pennsylvania, and prevented him from reaching the battlefield in time. On July 3, 1863, however, Kilpatrick enhanced his reputation for recklessness by ordering the brigade of General Elon J. Farnsworth to charge Confederate infantry head on. This indiscretion cost Farnsworth his life and garnered Kilpatrick the unflattering sobriquet of "Kill-cavalry."

In February 1864 Kilpatrick sought to rehabilitate his reputation by planning an ambitious raid against the Confederate capital at Richmond, Virginia, and liberate thousands of Union captives detained at the infamous Libby Prison. President Abraham LINCOLN reviewed the plan and enthusiastically endorsed it. On February 28, 1864, Kilpatrick galloped off with 4,000 troopers and crossed the Rapidan River. En route, he dispatched a small column of 500 men under Colonel Ulric Dahlgren, son of Admiral John A. D. DAHLGREN, to attack the city from the south. After hard riding in heavy rain and sleet, Kilpatrick arrived before Richmond—guarded by only 500 old men and boys—then suddenly lost his nerve. Some preliminary skirmishing convinced him to suspend the enterprise, and he withdrew. When Confederate cavalry attacked him in his camp that night, he abandoned the expedition altogether. Dahlgren, meanwhile, attacked the southern outskirts of the city and was rebuffed. As he fell back to Union lines, his column was ambushed, and Dahlgren was killed. Papers subsequently found on his body suggested that he was authorized to burn the city down and assassinate President Jefferson DAVIS, if possible, which led to a public uproar throughout the South. General George G. MEADE was forced to disavow publicly any knowledge of the matter, which did little to enhance Kilpatrick's reputation.

In the spring of 1864, Kilpatrick's cavalry division transferred west to the Army of the Cumberland under General George H. THOMAS. He then accompanied General William T. SHERMAN's campaign against Atlanta, Georgia, being heavily engaged in several skirmishes. On May 16, 1864, he fell severely wounded at Resaca and spent several weeks convalescing. Kilpatrick nonetheless accompanied his men in an ambulance as they burned their way across Georgia, sparring constantly with his old West Point rival General Joseph WHEELER. On August 22, 1865, he conducted a devastating raid against Jonesboro, Georgia, partaking fully of Sherman's order to burn or destroy anything of possible use to the Confederacy. Kilpatrick formally returned to the saddle as a brevet major general in 1865 and fought at the capture of Fayetteville, North Carolina. By war's end, he had risen to major general of volunteers and was generally acknowledged as one of the Union army's bravest—and most reckless—cavalry leaders.

After the war, Kilpatrick resigned his commission to serve as U.S. minister to Chile (1865–68). After President Ulysses S. GRANT recalled him, he entered politics by endorsing Horace Greeley for the presidency in 1872, and he also unsuccessfully stood for a congressional seat in 1880. The following year President James Garfield reappointed him minister to Chile, where he died in Santiago on December 4, 1881.

Further Reading

Black, Robert W. *Cavalry Raids of the Civil War.* Mechanicsburg, Pa.: Stackpole Books, 2004.

Mckinney, Joseph W. *Brandy Station, Virginia, June 9, 1863: The Longest Cavalry Battle of the Civil War.* Jefferson, N.C.: McFarland, 2006.

Pritchard, Russ A. *Raiders of the Civil War: Untold Stories of Actions Behind the Lines.* Guilford, Conn.: Lyons Press, 2005.

Rummel, George A. *Cavalry on the Road to Gettysburg: Kilpatrick at Hanover and Hunterstown.* Shippensburg, Pa.: White Mane Books, 2000.

Wittenberg, Eric J. *The Union Cavalry Comes of Age: Hartwood's Church to Brandy Station, 1863.* Dulles, Va.: Brassey's, 2005.

———. *The Battle of Monroe's Crossroads: And the Civil War's Final Campaign.* New York, Savas Beatic, 2006.

Kirby-Smith, Edmund (1824–1893)

Confederate general

Edmund Kirby-Smith was born in St. Augustine, Florida, on May 16, 1824, the son of a distinguished War of 1812 officer, Colonel Joseph Lee Smith. Later in life, he appended his mother's maiden name to his own and referred to himself as Kirby-Smith. He attended a private military academy in Virginia before attending the U.S. Military Academy in 1841, where he proved to be a mediocre student. Kirby-Smith nearly washed out due to nearsightedness, but in 1845 he received his second lieutenant's commission in the 5th U.S. Infantry. He then deployed with General Zachary Taylor as part of the Army of Occupation in Texas, and in 1847 he accompanied General Winfield SCOTT's advance on Mexico City. Kirby-Smith demonstrated prowess in battle by winning consecutive brevet promotions at Cerro Gordo and Contreras. He then performed routine garrison duty in the Southwest until serving as a mathematics instructor at West Point in 1849. Three years later, he shuttled back to the frontier, and in 1855, Kirby-Smith joined the newly raised 2nd U.S. Cavalry under Colonel Albert S. JOHNSTON. He spent the next five years skirmishing with hostile Comanche throughout Texas, acquitting himself well. He then rose to major in 1860 but resigned his commission to become a cavalry colonel in the Confederate service once Florida seceded in March 1861.

Kirby-Smith was initially posted in the Shenandoah Valley as chief of staff under General Joseph E. JOHNSTON and gradually rose to brigadier general. On July 21, 1861, he accompanied Johnston by train to the battlefield of Bull Run where he launched a crushing attack and was severely wounded. In October 1862 Kirby-Smith was promoted to major general and assigned to General Pierre G. T. BEAUREGARD's army in Mississippi. The following spring, he assumed command of the Department of Eastern Tennessee and prepared a small army to drive out Union forces from the Cumberland Gap. In August 1862 Kirby-Smith spearheaded the Confederate invasion of Ken-

Confederate general Edmund Kirby-Smith *(Library of Congress)*

tucky in concert with General Braxton BRAGG. On August 30 he crushed a smaller Union army under General William Nelson at Richmond, taking 4,000 captives, and subsequently occupied the capital of Lexington. However, neither Kirby-Smith nor Bragg coordinated their movements well, and both fell back before General Don C. BUELL's Army of the Ohio. Kirby-Smith fought well in the bloody engagements of Perryville in October and Murfreesboro in December–January, but he grew disenchanted with Bragg's lethargic leadership and requested a transfer.

Kirby-Smith, a lieutenant general as of October 1862, next received command of the Trans-Mississippi Department, encompassing Arkansas, Texas, West Louisiana, and the Indian Territory. The fall of Vicksburg, Mississippi, on July 4, 1863, cut the Confederacy in half, and Kirby-Smith was authorized by President Jefferson DAVIS to conduct his affairs with near autonomy. He now displayed a near genius for administration and, by running the Union blockade off Galveston, Texas, and bartering for weapons with cotton, he rendered his command nearly self-sufficient. In fact, he handled affairs so adroitly that his charge became celebrated as "Kirby-Smithdom." He consequently gained promotion to full general as of February 1864 and took active measures to thwart two Union drives against his department. That spring, he orchestrated the defeat of General Frederick Steele's offensive in Arkansas with generals Sterling PRICE and Joseph O. SHELBY, while his talented subordinate, General Richard TAYLOR, defeated General Nathaniel BANKS along the Red River. He then withdrew the bulk of Taylor's force to finish off Steele, which allowed the fleet of Admiral David D. PORTER to escape and caused a rancorous response from his subordinate. But the Trans-Mississippi Department remained undisturbed for the reminder of the war, and on May 26, 1865, Kirby-Smith surrendered to General Edward R. S. CANBY at Galveston. He was the last senior Confederate commander to do so.

After the war, Kirby-Smith fled to Cuba, but he returned two years later to serve as president of an insurance and telegraph company. In 1870 he joined the faculty of the University of Nashville and then the University of the South as a mathematics instructor, where he taught for the rest of his life. Kirby-Smith died in Suwanee, Tennessee, on March 28, 1893, the longest-surviving full general of the Confederacy.

Further Reading

Broadwater, Robert P. *The Battle of Perryville, 1862: Culmination of the Failed Kentucky Campaign.* Jefferson, N.C.: McFarland, 2006.

Forsyth, Michael J. *The Camden Expedition of 1864 and the Opportunity Lost by the Confederacy to Change the Civil War.* Jefferson, N.C.: McFarland, 2003.

Gallagher, Gary W., and Joseph T. Glatthaar, eds. *Leaders of the Lost Cause: New Perspectives on the Confederate High Command.* Mechanicsburg, Pa.: Stackpole Books, 2004.

Hafendorfer, Kenneth A. *Battle of Richmond, Kentucky, August 30, 1862.* Louisville, Ky.: KH Press, 2006.

Lagvanec, Cyril M. "Chevalier Bayard of the Confederacy: The Life and Career of Edmund Kirby Smith." Unpublished Ph.D. diss., Texas A & M University, 1999.

Prushankin, Jeffrey S. *A Crisis in Confederate Command: Edmund Kirby Smith, Robert Taylor, and the Army of the Trans-Mississippi.* Baton Rouge: Louisiana State University Press, 2005.

L

Lee, Fitzhugh (1835–1905)
Confederate general

Fitzhugh Lee was born in Clermont, Virginia, on November 19, 1835, a grandson of American Revolutionary War hero "Light Horse" Harry Lee. He attended the U.S. Military Academy in 1852, earning mediocre grades and so many disciplinary infractions that Superintendent Robert E. LEE, his uncle, nearly expelled him. Lee nevertheless graduated in 1856 near the bottom of his class and received his second lieutenant's commission. After a brief stint as instructor at the Cavalry School at Carlisle, Pennsylvania, he transferred to the 2nd U.S. Cavalry under Colonel Albert S. JOHNSTON and was posted on the Texas frontier. Lee distinguished himself in combat against the Comanche, and on May 19, 1859, he was severely injured. He recuperated at West Point as an assistant instructor before resigning his commission in April 1861 to offer his sword to the Confederacy.

Lee was initially posted with General Joseph E. JOHNSTON in the Shenandoah Valley, where he served as a staff officer. He then fought well at Bull Run on July 21, 1861, and rose to lieutenant colonel of the noted 1st Virginia Cavalry. Lee's career became indelibly bound up with that of his commander, General J. E. B. STUART, and in the spring of 1862, he participated in the ride around General George B. McCLELLAN's army, rising to brigadier general the following July. He next fought at Second Manassas the following August, where his tardy movements allowed the army of General John POPE to escape destruction, and he subsequently performed well at Antietam in September. On March 17, 1863, General William W. Averell nearly surprised Lee in camp at Kelly's Ford, Virginia, but he fought back tenaciously and gradually drove off superior Union forces. In May he performed his most significant task, that of uncovering the exposed flank of General Oliver O. HOWARD's XI Corps at Chancellorsville, which enabled a swift and crushing Confederate riposte. Lee then fought alongside Stuart at Brandy Station in June and Gettysburg in July, acquitting himself well and rising to major general commanding a division.

The waning fortunes of the Confederacy served to intensify Lee's battlefield performances. On May 7, 1864, his troopers reached strategic Spotsylvania Crossroads ahead of Union forces, and he skillfully withstood repeated attacks until reinforced by General Richard H. ANDERSON. After Stuart's death at Yellow Tavern, he served under another valiant trooper, General Wade HAMPTON. Lee then made a late appearance at Trevilian Station on June 11, 1864, but he managed to stop a concerted advance by General George A. CUSTER. A month later, Lee's division supported General Jubal A. EARLY's drive up the Shenandoah Valley. He participated in all the major battles against General Philip H. SHERIDAN and was critically injured at Third Winchester on September 19,

1864. Lee spent the next three months recuperating, and in March 1865, he succeeded Hampton as cavalry commander in the Army of Northern Virginia. The most notorious incident in his distinguished career occurred at Five Forks, Virginia, on April 1, 1865. Lee was absent from his command along with General George E. PICKETT, and both men were enjoying a shad bake far to the rear when Sheridan struck suddenly and overran Southern positions. On April 9, 1865, Lee conducted the very last Confederate cavalry charge of the war at Farmville, the same day his famous uncle surrendered at Appomattox.

Back in Virginia, Lee developed a taste for politics, and in 1885, he was elected governor as a Democrat. He subsequently lost a bid for the U.S. Senate, but in 1896, President Grover Cleveland appointed him the U.S. consul in Havana, Cuba. Here he displayed overt sympathies toward freedom-seeking Cuban rebels and advised the government to dispatch the battleship USS *Maine* to protect American interests. When the Spanish-American War broke out in 1898, President William McKinley commissioned him one of three former Confederates to hold the rank of brigadier general of volunteers. Lee then took control of the VII Corps but saw no fighting and later served as military governor of Havana. He then collaborated with fellow ex-Confederate general Joseph WHEELER in penning a book, *Cuba's Struggle against Spain* (1898). After a brief stint commanding the Department of the Missouri, Lee retired from the army in March 1901. He died in Washington, D.C., on April 28, 1905, a skilled leader of mounted troops.

Further Reading

Alexander, Robert. *Five Forks: Waterloo of the Confederacy: A Civil War Narrative.* East Lansing: Michigan State University Press, 2003.

Arnold, James R. *Jeff Davis's Own: Cavalry. Comanches, and the Battle for the Texas Frontier.* New York: Wiley, 2000.

Crawford, Mark. *Confederate Courage on Other Fields: Four Lesser Known Accounts of the War between the States.* Jefferson, N.C.: McFarland, 2000.

Longacre, Edward G. *Fitz Lee: A Military Biography of Major General Fitz Hugh Lee, C.S.A.* Cambridge, Mass.: Da Capo Press, 2005.

Morris, Roy, Jr. "Sweltering Summer Collision." *Military History* 9, no. 6 (1993): 42–49.

Nichols, James A. *General Fitzhugh Lee, a Biography.* Lynchburg, Va.: H. E. Howard, 1989.

Confederate general Fitzhugh Lee *(Massachusetts Commandery Military Order of the Loyal Legion and the U.S. Army Military History Institute)*

Lee, Robert E. (1807–1870)

Confederate general

Robert Edward Lee was born at Stratford, Westmoreland County, Virginia, on January 19, 1807, a son of famed Revolutionary War hero "Light Horse Harry" Lee. After being well educated locally, he entered the U.S. Military Academy in

Confederate general Robert E. Lee *(Library of Congress)*

1825 and graduated four years later second in his class—without a single demerit. Lee then received his second lieutenant's commission in the elite Corps of Engineers and acquired distinction in a variety of difficult tasks along the Mississippi River. He rose to captain in 1838 and joined the staff of General Winfield SCOTT during the Mexican War (1846–48). Lee fought with distinction at Cerro Gordo, made a daring reconnaissance of enemy positions, and subsequently performed well at the battles of Churubusco and Chapultepec. He ended the war as a brevet lieutenant colonel and between 1852 and 1855 also served as superintendent of cadets at West Point. In this post, he revitalized the curriculum and nearly expelled his nephew, Fitzhugh LEE, on account of poor grades and disciplinary infractions. In 1855 Lee was tapped to serve as lieutenant colonel of the newly raised 2nd U.S. Cavalry under Colonel Albert S. JOHNSTON, a unit renowned for training

a number of future Confederate generals. He served in Texas until 1859 and then, during a furlough at home, commanded a detachment of U.S. Marines that captured abolitionist John Brown at Harper's Ferry, Virginia. In 1860 Lee received his first line command as colonel of the 1st U.S. Cavalry, and he also headed up the Department of Texas. By then the gathering war clouds induced General in Chief Scott to tender Lee a ranking position within the Federal army to crush the rebellion, but he respectfully declined. Lee, in fact, supported neither secession nor slavery, but he felt obliged to support his native state when it seceded on April 17, 1861. He subsequently accepted the post of major general of state forces.

In May 1861 Lee became a full general of Confederate forces at the behest of President Jefferson DAVIS, and third in seniority behind Generals Samuel Cooper and Albert S. Johnston. He then proceeded to bungle his first assignment in western Virginia, thanks largely to uncooperative subordinates such as General John B. FLOYD, and he acquired the uncomely moniker of "Granny." Davis maintained his faith in Lee, fortunately, and reassigned him to strengthen defenses along the South Atlantic coast. By March 1862 Lee was back at Richmond acting in the capacity of senior military adviser to Davis. His most important work here was encouraging a Confederate offensive up the Shenandoah Valley by General Thomas J. JACKSON to relieve pressure on the Confederate capital. In the spring of 1862, the huge Army of the Potomac under General George B. MCCLELLAN was advancing up the Virginia Peninsula as the main Confederate force under General Joseph E. JOHNSTON continued giving ground. Fate intervened at the Battle of Seven Pines on June 1, 1862, when Johnston was severely wounded and was replaced by Lee. Lee then launched an audacious series of hard-pounding attacks on the surprised Unionists—the Seven Days' battles—which drove McClellan back from the gates of Richmond. Confederate losses were heavy, and he failed to destroy the corps of General Fitz John PORTER, but Lee's offensive completely unnerved his adversary and brought the South a badly needed respite. He then completely overhauled his command, renaming it the Army of Northern Virginia, with two corps under Generals Jackson and James LONGSTREET. The new force successfully met its first test that summer when the Union Army of Virginia under General John POPE was nearly routed with 16,000 casualties at Second Manassas on August 29–30, 1862. Lee's losses, though considerable, were only 9,000.

Having seized the strategic initiative, Lee audaciously gambled on an invasion of Union territory and carried the war directly into Maryland. The result was another hard-fought clash with McClellan at Antietam on September 17, 1862, which nearly proved disastrous until Lee was rescued by the sudden appearance of General Ambrose P. HILL's division. This was the single bloodiest day of the Civil War with 12,400 Union and 13,700 Confederate casualties and a strategic defeat for Lee, who withdrew back to Virginia. Shortly afterward, the Army of the Potomac again was knocking at Virginia's door under a new leader, General Ambrose E. BURNSIDE, who attacked Lee as he sat entrenched behind strong field fortifications at Fredericksburg on December 13, 1862. The result was a lopsided slaughter with 13,000 Federal losses to a Confederate tally of 5,300. The second year of the war thus ended on a high note for Lee—in only six months he had risen from obscurity to an object of veneration, both among his men and among fellow Southerners.

In the spring of 1863, General Joseph HOOKER led a reconstituted Army of the Potomac across the Rapidan River in an attempt to outflank the wily Confederates. On May 2–3, 1863, Lee countered with the dangerous expedient of dividing his force in the face of the enemy and sending Jackson on a lengthy flank march around the Union right at Chancellorsville. The ensuing attack crushed Hooker's flank and induced him to retreat. Lee then boldly divided his force a third time and drove off an approaching force under General John Sedgwick. Chancellorsville is perhaps the best example of Lee's daring tactical virtuosity; he

had suffered 12,000 casualties, inflicted 17,000, and drove an army twice his size back into Union territory. However, the Confederate war effort received a mortal blow when the ever-perceptive Jackson was fatally wounded by friendly fire. Lee, for the remainder of the conflict, depended on subordinates who were equally brave but ultimately less capable.

In the summer of 1863, Lee sought to maintain the strategic initiative by reinvading Northern territory. His plan quickly went awry when General J. E. B. STUART led his cavalry on a spectacular ride into Pennsylvania, which deprived the Army of Northern Virginia of its reconnaissance capabilities. Consequently, when Lee collided with Union forces under General George G. MEADE at Gettysburg, Pennsylvania, on July 1, 1863, he was completely misled as to enemy strength and intentions. For the next two days the Confederates hurled their strength against strong Union positions and were repulsed with losses, culminating in the disastrous attack by General George E. PICKETT on July 3, 1863. Lee's defeat marked the high tide of Confederate military fortunes and, coupled with the surrender of Vicksburg, Mississippi, on July 4, a tipping point had been reached in the course of military events. Union losses of 23,000 nearly matched those of the 25,000 Southern casualties incurred, but the North, enjoying a larger population pool, readily made up such deficiencies.

Lee's next contest of strength occurred in the late spring of 1864, only this time against a new and completely different adversary. General Ulysses S. GRANT, the conqueror of Vicksburg, mustered 120,000 well-trained soldiers against 60,000 Confederates. Significantly, Grant determined to make the destruction of the Army of Northern Virginia his primary goal. He intended to accomplish this by maneuvering incessantly toward Richmond, Virginia, predicting that Lee had no recourse but to follow. A series of bloody encounters ensued at the Wilderness, Spotsylvania Court House, and Cold Harbor, in which Union casualties totaled 50,000 men—but Grant did not retreat. When confronted by insurmountable

Confederate resistance, he simply sidestepped to the left and inched closer toward Richmond. Lee, as anticipated, followed closely and by summer had become pinned within the earthworks of Petersburg, Virginia. With the once formidable Army of Northern Virginia bled white and neutralized from field operations, General William T. SHERMAN was able to break through to Atlanta and Savannah, Georgia, and gradually approach Richmond from behind. Meanwhile, to relieve Union pressure on his dwindling army, Lee dispatched General Jubal A. EARLY on his famous sweep through the Shenandoah Valley, which caused considerable alarm in Washington, D.C., and forced Grant to transfer numerous reinforcements to that theater. But Early's defeat at the hands of General Philip H. SHERIDAN in the fall of 1864 and the loss of the valley's resources that this represented signaled the coming collapse of the Confederacy.

Lee maintained his hungry, understrength forces in the trench works of Richmond and Petersburg for nearly a year as Grant continually received fresh reinforcements. As a sop toward the Confederate Congress, he also accepted the titular assignment as general in chief of all Southern armies in February 1865, but by then the Confederacy was in its death throes. The end came on April 1, 1865, when General Sheridan broke through General Fitzhugh Lee's defenses at Five Forks, Virginia, and Grant ordered a simultaneous assault across the line. Southern defenses crumbled under the repeated blows, and Lee, his position untenable, ordered the capital abandoned. He then extricated his surviving forces and made a run for North Carolina to join General Johnston, only to be halted at Appomattox Court House by Sheridan's cavalry. With superior Union forces closing in from all sides, Lee finally concluded that the game was up and surrendered to Grant with great dignity on April 9, 1865. Defeat had no dampening effect on the soldiers' overt affection for Lee, whom they affectionately called "Marse Robert."

After the war, Lee spurned lucrative offers of employment to work as president of Washington College in Lexington, Virginia. He accepted defeat with grace and urged former compatriots to work for unity and national reconciliation. Lee died at Lexington on October 12, 1870, an iconic figure of the Civil War and one of the most beloved, effective military leaders in American military history.

Further Reading

Cahart, Tom. *Lost Triumph: Lee's Real Plan at Gettysburg—and Why It Failed.* New York: G. P. Putnam's Sons, 2005.

Carmichael, Peter S. *Audacity Personified: The Generalship of Robert E. Lee.* Baton Rouge: Louisiana State University Press, 2004.

Fellman, Michael. *The Making of Robert E. Lee.* Baltimore: Johns Hopkins University Press, 2003.

Gallagher, Gary W., and Joseph T. Glatthaar, eds. *Leaders of the Lost Cause: New Perspectives on the Confederate High Command.* Mechanicsburg, Pa.: Stackpole Books, 2004.

Hess, Earl J. *Trench Warfare under Grant and Lee: Field Fortifications in the Overland Campaign.* Chapel Hill: University of North Carolina Press, 2007.

Jermann, Donald R. *Antietam: The Lost Order.* Gretna, La: Pelican Pub., 2006.

Katcher, Philip R. N. *Robert E. Lee.* London: Brassey's, 2004.

Longacre, Edward G. *The Commanders of Chancellorsville: The Gentleman vs the Rogue.* Nashville: Rutledge Hill Press, 2005.

Reid, Brian H. *Robert E. Lee: Icon for a Nation.* London: Weidenfeld and Nicolson, 2005.

Walsh, George. *Damage Them All You Can: Robert E. Lee's Army of Northern Virginia.* New York: Forge, 2002.

Lincoln, Abraham (1809–1865)
President, United States

Abraham Lincoln was born near Hodgenville, Kentucky, on February 12, 1809, the son of a backwoods family. He endured childhood poverty for many years while living on the frontiers of Indiana, becoming essentially self-taught. Lincoln eventually settled on a career in law in Springfield, Illinois, and briefly served as a militia captain during the brief Black Hawk War of 1832. The future commander in chief saw no combat save for, in his own words, "many bloody battles with mosqui-toes." Lincoln subsequently acquired a taste for politics, joined the Whig Party, and in 1847 won a seat in the U.S. House of Representatives. In this capacity, he stridently opposed both the Mexican War and any expansion of slavery into newly acquired territories. In 1858 Lincoln ran unsuc-cessfully as a Republican for the U.S. Senate against Democrat Stephen A. Douglas, and he cap-tured national attention through a series of lively debates. Consequently, the gaunt and gangly attor-ney saw his political capital soar, and in 1860 he handily won the party's nomination for the presi-dency. He ran—and won—on a platform dedi-cated to halting the expansion of slavery, not its abolition. However, Lincoln's ascension was con-strued as a direct threat to the South's "peculiar institution," and in December 1860 South Caro-lina voted to secede from the Union. This act induced other states to follow, and a new entity, the Confederate States of America, was already extant by the time Lincoln took his inaugural oath of office.

No neophyte chief executive ever confronted a more daunting, dangerous situation that did Lin-coln in the spring of 1861, with a small standing army and the Southern third of the nation up in arms against the federal government. He never-theless remained adamant that the Union would be preserved at any cost. Surprisingly, Lincoln proved himself a forceful and capable commander in chief who was unafraid of taking risks. To solidify his Northern political base, he overruled General In Chief Winfield SCOTT and authorized a relief expedition to resupply the Union garrison trapped at Fort Sumter, South Carolina. For polit-ical consumption, he underscored the fact that this was a humanitarian mission to deliver food, not reinforcements. It was a ploy calculated to force the hand of his Confederate counterpart, Jef-ferson DAVIS, who, as the head of a self-proclaimed sovereign nation, could not tolerate an American garrison residing in a major Southern harbor. On April 12, 1861, Confederate forces under General Pierre G. T. BEAUREGARD commenced bombard-ing the fort, forcing Major Robert ANDERSON to surrender two days later. The Northern populace, waxing indifferent up until now, viewed this act as overt aggression against the United States and began to mobilize for war. Lincoln then moved with characteristic decisiveness by summoning 75,000 three-month volunteers, suspending writs of habeas corpus in threatened regions, and—most important—declaring the Southern coastline under a naval blockade.

Despite his prior lack of military training, Lin-coln displayed an astonishing grasp of strategy based on the North's overwhelming preponderance in terms of manpower and industry. He therefore sought to implement a broad-based offensive to apply maximum pressure against the insurrection-ists from as many directions as possible. Moreover,

President of the United States Abraham Lincoln
(National Archives)

the commander in chief inculcated the very modern view that the destruction of enemy armies, and not the mere acquisition of territory, was tantamount to victory itself. He also agreed in principle to the overarching strategy enunciated by General Scott, whose so-called Anaconda Plan entailed dividing the Confederacy down the Mississippi River and slowly strangling the whole to death. In time this proved a war-winning strategy. Unfortunately for Lincoln, conduct of military operations was entrusted to a series of leaders who eschewed his strategic vision and proved incapable of defeating Southern armies in the field. Worst of all, the steady drum beat of politicians forced the president and his generals into combat long before their raw recruits were ready for it.

Commencing in July 1861, when the barely trained levies of General Irvin McDOWELL were routed at Bull Run, the Federal war effort remained beset by a succession of hesitant, if not outright blundering leaders: Generals George B. McCLELLAN, John POPE, Ambrose E. BURNSIDE, and Joseph HOOKER all tried and failed to defeat the Army of Northern Virginia under the dazzling General Robert E. LEE; other appointees such as General Benjamin F. BUTLER, Nathaniel C. BANKS, and Franz SIGEL proved likewise incompetent but had to be retained out of pressing political concerns. Nor did Lincoln receive much cogent advice from General in Chief Henry W. HALLECK, a splendid administrator but a lackluster strategist. For the first two years of the war, the only real Union success came from the steadily expanding blockade and capture of Southern ports at the hands of such professionals as Admirals Samuel F. Du PONT and David G. FARRAGUT. Their endeavors restricted the flow of Confederate cotton to European markets and throttled the flow of weapons and raw materials returning through an extensive net of Southern blockade-runners. The impasse continued until July 1863 when General George G. MEADE defeated Lee at Gettysburg while another figure, General Ulysses S. GRANT, captured Vicksburg on the Mississippi River, severing the Confederacy in two. Lincoln finally saw in Grant that commodity the lack of which had so hobbled the war effort to date—an aggressive, relentless fighter who fully embraced the president's broad offensive scheme. Once Lincoln appointed Grant general in chief in the spring of 1864, the fate of the Confederacy was sealed.

Throughout the spring and early summer of 1864, the redoubtable Grant singularly failed to humble Lee's stubborn graycoats in the field. A series of bloody encounters at the Wilderness, Spotsylvania Court House, and Cold Harbor led to increasingly long casualty lists and open questioning as to Lincoln's very survival in the fall elections. Defeat and heavy losses took a heavy toll on the president, as did the death of his son Todd, but he willingly bore the burdens to provide Grant with whatever support he needed. The shift occurred by late summer and early fall. Once Grant had finally pinned Lee to the defense of Richmond, Virginia, the army of General William T. SHERMAN had captured Atlanta, Georgia, while forces under General Philip H. SHERIDAN swept the strategic Shenandoah Valley free of Confederates. This string of important victories dramatically resuscitated Lincoln's political fortunes, and in November he handily crushed his Democratic opponent, General McClellan. Six months later, the Confederacy lay in ruins: outnumbered, out of supplies, and flagging in spirit. Lee then surrendered to Grant at Appomattox on April 9, 1865, effectively ending military operations in the East. All the while, Lincoln took to the podium and pleaded for leniency toward the former Confederates and national unification without vindictiveness. The president never lived to see the country reunited: On April 14, 1865, he was cut down by John Wilkes Booth at Ford's Theater in Washington, D.C. Lincoln, the awkward, sad-looking leader who had labored so long and successfully to keep the nation whole, became the first chief executive assassinated in office. But because of his triumph at preserving the Union throughout the worse crisis in its history, Lincoln is frequently cited as America's greatest chief executive.

In addition to saving the United States, Lincoln ushered in a social revolution by finally vanquishing the centuries-old incubus of human bondage. This was a highly emotional issue to both North and South, and the chief executive nuanced the matter with great delicacy. Lincoln himself, while personally against slavery, was quite willing to accommodate it where it already existed. Once the South rejected this stance, he weathered the dire necessity of keeping strategic and slaveholding border states such as Maryland, Kentucky, and Missouri in the Union camp. He thereby completely ignored the demands of abolitionists and Radical Republicans to outlaw slavery altogether. A more incremental approach, one cued closely to the military course of the war, was ultimately preferable. In the fall of 1862, after the Union victory at Antietam, Lincoln issued his famous "Emancipation Proclamation," which only freed slaves in areas still under Confederate control. Furthermore, he consistently negated all attempts by Union commanders to free slaves so as not to lose continuing support from slaveholding Unionists. Despite his caution, these moves reveal much about Lincoln's grasp of foreign affairs: By firmly placing the American government on the side of emancipation, he minimized the risk of European intervention on behalf of the Confederacy. The British government, in particular, would certainly not enter an armed conflict to preserve Southern slavery. Lincoln also initially looked askance at the use of African-American troops until 1863, when shortages of white volunteers had to be remedied. Public opinion may have been mixed, and developments certainly infuriated Confederate sensibilities, but upward of 180,000 black troops flocked to the colors, fought magnificently, and further tipped the manpower scales in favor of the North. Toward the close of the war, Lincoln also embraced creation of the Freedmen's Bureau to help manumitted slaves readjust to living, working, and voting as free citizens. The president died before his dream of peacefully reintegrating former slaves and Confederates into society was realized. The chore consequently fell to individuals of lesser ability and

conviction, with decidedly mixed and frequently unfortunate results. Had Lincoln lived as the guiding spirit behind postwar Reconstruction, the tumult of 20th-century civil rights movements may have been obviated altogether.

Further Reading

Cox, Hank H. *Lincoln and the Sioux Uprising of 1862.* Nashville, Tenn.: Cumberland House, 2005.

Detzer, David. *Dissonance: Between Fort Sumter and Bull Run in the Turbulent First Days of the Civil War.* Orlando, Fla.: Harcourt, 2006.

Griffin, John C. *Abraham Lincoln's Execution.* Gretna, La: Pelican Pub. Co. 2006.

Goodwin, Doris K. *Team of Rivals: The Political Genius of Abraham Lincoln.* New York: Simon and Schuster, 2005.

Harris, William C. *Lincoln's Last Months.* Cambridge, Mass.: Belknap Press of Harvard University Press, 2004.

Mansch, Larry D. *Abraham Lincoln, President-elect: The Four Critical Months from Election to Inauguration.* Jefferson, N.C.: McFarland, 2005.

Marcott, Frank B. *Six Days in April: Lincoln and the Union in Peril.* New York: Algora Publishing, 2005.

Marvel, William. *Mr. Lincoln Goes to War.* Boston: Houghton Mifflin, 2006.

Perret, Geoffrey. *Lincoln's War: The Untold Story of America's Greatest President as Commander in Chief.* New York: Random House, 2004.

Wheeler, Tom. *Mr. Lincoln's T-mails: The Untold Story of How Abraham Lincoln used the Telegraph to win the Civil War.* New York: Collins, 2006.

Longstreet, James (1821–1904)

Confederate general

James Longstreet was born in Edgehill, South Carolina, on January 8, 1821, the son of planters. He gained admittance to the U.S. Military Academy in 1838, compiling a mediocre academic record before graduating near the bottom of his class in 1842. He then served as a second lieutenant in the 4th and 8th U.S. Infantries while performing garrison duty at various posts along the Louisiana and Texas frontiers. When the Mexican War commenced in 1846, Longstreet joined the army of General Zachary Taylor, and he distin-

Confederate general James Longstreet *(Massachusetts Commandery Military Order of the Loyal Legion and the U.S. Army Military History Institute)*

guished himself at the battle of Monterrey. The following year, he accompanied General Winfield SCOTT on his march to Mexico City, winning a brevet promotion to major for gallantry and suffering severe wounds at Chapultepec. After the war, Longstreet returned to the frontier to serve as payroll master for many years. Once the Civil War broke out in April 1861, he resigned his commission and became a brigadier general in the Confederate army of General Pierre G. T. BEAUREGARD. Longstreet proved himself a tremendous fighter, commencing at Blackburn's Ford on July 18, 1861, where he repulsed the advance guard of General Irvin McDOWELL. Three days later, he fought with distinction at Bull Run and pursued

fleeing Federal forces nearly to the gates of Washington, D.C.

Longstreet's fine performance resulted in his promotion to major general and command of a division in General Joseph E. JOHNSTON's army. In this capacity, he conducted a fine rear-guard action against General Samuel P. Heintzelman's III Corps at Williamsburg on May 5, 1862, and he nearly routed a division under General Joseph HOOKER. However, he bungled his next assignment at Seven Pines the following May 31, leading to a Confederate repulse. Longstreet then rebounded under General Robert E. LEE during his Seven Days' battles and subsequently received command of nearly half of Lee's infantry. He then decisively contributed to the overwhelming Confederate victory over General John POPE at Second Manassas on August 29–30, 1862, in concert with General Thomas J. JACKSON. Longstreet's tendency toward caution then manifested itself when he strongly opposed Lee's invasion of Maryland that fall, but he fought exceedingly well at South Mountain and Antietam in September. The following month, Lee, who affectionately referred to Longstreet as his "Old War Horse," promoted him to lieutenant general with command of the newly organized I Corps. With the stodgy general, he capably defended Marye's Heights at the Battle of Fredericksburg on December 13, 1862, against General Ambrose BURNSIDE.

In February 1863 Longstreet was detached on an independent command around Suffolk, Virginia, where he failed to distinguish himself. His lethargic movements also deprived him of participating in the decisive Confederate victory at Chancellorsville (May 2–3, 1863), but following the death of Jackson, he emerged as Lee's senior corps commander and his closest confidant. As a strategist, Longstreet embraced Lee's renewed northern offensive, but only in concert with a tactical defense once a battle situation developed. He therefore was somewhat aghast on July 2, 1863, when Lee decided to attack the strongly posted army of General George G. MEADE at Gettysburg for the next two days. Longstreet sullenly complied with orders to hit the Union center along Cemetery Ridge, where a division under General John B. HOOD dislodged the III Corps of General Daniel SICKLES from the Peach Orchard but failed to turn the Union left at Little Round Top. In fact, Longstreet moved so tardily that it was not until 4:30 P.M. that his attack—scheduled for the morning—got underway. On July 3 he also vehemently remonstrated against Lee's plan to assault the Union center. He contributed only the division of General George E. PICKETT to the ensuing debacle, and as he predicted, the Confederates were turned back with staggering losses. In the fall of 1863, the I Corps temporarily transferred west to bolster the Army of Tennessee under General Braxton BRAGG. Longstreet bore a critical role in the Southern victory at Chickamauga (September 20, 1863), where his men smashed though an inadvertent gap caused by General William S. ROSECRANS. However, deteriorating relations with Bragg resulted in Longstreet's assignment to besiege Knoxville, Tennessee, where he and General Joseph WHEELER failed to overcome Federal troops under General Burnside. The ensuing defeat of Bragg at Chattanooga on November 25, 1863, and the subsequent approach of General William T. SHERMAN with reinforcements induced Longstreet to abandon Knoxville for the winter.

Longstreet rejoined Lee in the spring of 1864 in time to oppose the Overland campaign of General Ulysses S. GRANT. His timely appearance at the Wilderness on May 6, 1864, reinforced General Ambrose P. HILL's corps and drove off Federals under General Winfield S. HANCOCK. Unfortunately, Longstreet was accidently wounded by his own men at the height of the struggle, and he could not resume active duty until the following October. Command of the I Corps reverted to General Richard H. ANDERSON in his absence. Longstreet next commanded the defenses of Richmond, Virginia, until the Union breakthrough of April 2–3, 1865, and he retreated with Lee to Appomattox Court House. He remained in the field beside Lee until the latter's surrender to superior Union forces on April 9, 1865.

After the war, Longstreet entered business and gained the undying enmity of former friends by joining the Republican Party. President Grant, a West Point classmate, then appointed him surveyor of New Orleans in 1869 and postmaster in 1873. Commencing in 1880, he also served as minister to Turkey, U.S. marshal for Georgia, and U.S. railroad commissioner. Throughout this period, Longstreet embraced the vitriolic literary campaign ascribing blame for the loss of the war. He was one of few senior commanders willing to criticize Lee's leadership openly and was, in turn, bitterly assailed by former generals Jubal A. EARLY and Fitzhugh LEE for slowness and insubordination at Gettysburg—in effect, losing the battle. Longstreet, revered and reviled by many as "Old Pete," died at his home in Gainesville, Georgia, on January 2, 1904, an outstanding corps commander but undistinguished in an independent role.

Further Reading

Bloomberg, Arnold. "On They Came Like an Angry Flood." *Military Heritage* 4, no. 6 (2003): 72–80.

Dinardo, Richard L. "Southern by the Grace of God but Prussian by Common Sense: James Longstreet and the Exercise of Command in the U.S. Civil War." *Journal of Military History* 66, no. 4 (2002): 1011–1032.

Dinardo, Richard L., and Albert A. Nofi. *James Longstreet: The Man, the Soldier, the Controversy.* Conshohocken, Pa.: Combined Publishing, 1998.

Franks, Edward C. "In Defense of Braxton Bragg: The Detachment of Longstreet Considered." *North & South* 5, no. 5 (2002): 28–38.

Hastings, Earl C. *A Pitiless Rain: The Battle of Williamsburg.* Shippensburg, Pa.: White Mane Books, 1997.

Longstreet, James. *From Manassas to Appomattox: Memoirs of the Civil War in America.* Philadelphia: J. B. Lippincott, 1896.

Mendoza, Alexander. "Struggle in Command: General James Longstreet and the First Corps in the West, 1863–1864." Unpublished Ph.D. diss., Texas Tech University, 2002.

Rhea, Gordon C. *The Battle of the Wilderness, May 5–6, 1864.* Baton Rouge: Louisiana State University Press, 2004.

Loring, William W. (1818–1886)

Confederate general

William Wing Loring was born in Wilmington, North Carolina, raised in Florida, and served in the militia during the Second Seminole War (1835–42), rising to lieutenant. He then studied law at Georgetown College, gained admittance to the state bar, and won a seat in the state legislature, but when the Mexican War commenced in 1846, he joined the U.S. Army as a captain in the elite 2nd Mounted Riflemen. In this capacity, Loring accompanied the army of General Winfield SCOTT on its march to Mexico City, winning two brevet promotions for bravery at Contreras and Chapultepec. In the latter engagement, Loring lost his left arm. He ended the war a brevet lieutenant colonel

Confederate general William W. Loring *(Florida State Archives)*

and marched his regiment to Fort Leavenworth, Kansas, in anticipation of the famous gold rush to California. He then escorted settlers 2,500 miles to Oregon and back with a train of 600 wagons. Loring discharged his duties well under difficult conditions and consequently received command of the Department of Oregon in 1851. His regiment subsequently transferred to Texas and New Mexico, seeing constant action against hostile Comanche and Kiowa. In December 1856 Loring became the army's youngest colonel and also assumed control of Fort Union, New Mexico. Two years later, he accompanied Colonel Albert S. JOHNSTON on the noted Mormon expedition to Utah and the following year took a leave of absence to study in Europe. He returned in 1860 as commander of the Department of New Mexico. Loring, while a Southerner, did not embrace secession strongly, but after Florida left the Union in January 1861, he tendered his resignation and turned Fort Union over to Colonel Edward R. S. CANBY, another frontier stalwart.

In May 1861 Loring gained appointment as a brigadier general, and the following July he succeeded the slain general Robert B. Garnett as commander of the Northwestern Army in the Shenandoah Valley. This brought him under the aegis of General Robert E. LEE, Loring's junior in prewar days, and the two men failed to get along amicably. Following the Cheat Mountain expedition in September 1861, Lee was transferred to another sector and replaced by General Thomas J. JACKSON. On January 1, 1862, Jackson launched a midwinter offensive to capture the town of Romney, Virginia, and Loring's men suffered terribly from exposure to the elements. Jackson ordered him to remain behind in place, exposed to attack, so Loring violated the chain of command by complaining to friends in the Confederate War Department. When Secretary of War Judah P. Benjamin consequently ordered Jackson to remove Loring's command from Romney, the latter angrily threatened to resign his commission. Loring was then tactfully transferred from the valley on February 9, 1862, and reassigned to Norfolk as a major general.

In December 1862 Loring was again transferred, this time to the Army of the Mississippi under John C. PEMBERTON, whom he also outranked in the prewar army. The two men held each other in thinly veiled contempt and barely cooperated. Nonetheless, on March 11, 1863, Loring's gallant stand at Fort Pemberton, Greenwood, Mississippi, turned back a combined Union expedition along the Tallahatchie River. Mounting the parapet, he paraded back and forth under fire and encouraged his command to "Give them blizzards, boys!" Thereafter, he became jocularly known as "Old Blizzards." Loring's victory spared Vicksburg's defenses from being turned and forced General Ulysses S. GRANT to campaign overland from below the city. On May 16, 1863, Grant caught up to Pemberton at Champion's Hill, Mississippi, driving the Southerners from the field and forcing Loring to break away from the main force. With Pemberton now shut up in Vicksburg, Loring marched to join General Joseph E. JOHNSTON's army at Jackson. Months later, Pemberton vindictively accused Loring of insubordination and blamed him for the city's fall.

By the spring of 1864, Loring had transferred to the corps of General Leonidas K. POLK, and he fought with him against General William T. SHERMAN's advance into Georgia. Once Polk was killed on June 14, 1864, he assumed command of his corps until replaced by General Alexander P. Stewart—a good indication of Johnston's distrust of his abilities. Loring went on to fight well at the battles of Peachtree Creek and Ezra Church under General John B. HOOD in July 1864, and then he accompanied Hood during the ill-fated advance into Tennessee. He again fought conspicuously at the defeats of Franklin and Nashville that fall and afterward took his surviving men back into North Carolina to rejoin Johnston. Loring performed well at Bentonville (March 19–21, 1865) before finally surrendering to Sherman at Greensboro on May 2, 1865.

For a former Confederate, Loring enjoyed an active and varied career throughout the postwar period. After serving as a banker in New York City, he departed for Egypt in 1869 and joined the army of Khedive Ismail I as a *lewan pasha* (brigadier general). He commanded the garrison of Alexandria for five years, led an expedition into the Sudan, and won the Battle of Kaya-Khor in 1874. Loring consequently enjoying the title of *pasha* and command of a division. He returned to the United States in 1879 to write about his experiences. Loring died in New York City on December 30, 1886, a talented, colorful, and stubborn military leader.

Further Reading

Loring, William W. *A Confederate Soldier in Egypt.* New York: Dodd, Mead, 1884.

Oliva, Leo E. *Fort Union and the Frontier Army in the South West.* Santa Fe, N.Mex.: Division of History, National Park Service, 1993.

Raab, James. *W. W. Loring—Florida's Forgotten General.* Manhattan, Kans.: Sunflower Press, 1996.

Rankin, Thomas M. *Stonewall Jackson's Romney Campaign, January 1–February 20, 1862.* Lynchburg, Va.: H. E. Holland, 1994.

Smith, Timothy B. *Champion Hill: Decisive Battle for Vicksburg.* New York: Savas Beatie, 2004.

Wessels, William L. *Born to Be a Soldier: The Military Career of William Wing Loring of St. Augustine, Florida.* Fort Worth, Tex.: Texas Christian University Press, 1971.

Lovell, Mansfield (1822–1884)

Confederate general

Mansfield Lovell was born in Washington, D.C., on October 20, 1822, a son of army surgeon-general Joseph Lovell. Orphaned by the death of his parents, he entered the U.S. Military Academy in 1838 and graduated four years later near the top of his class. Lovell then served as a second lieutenant in the 4th U.S. Artillery, performing garrison duty in Texas under General Zachary Taylor. When the Mexican War broke out, he accompanied Taylor's army and fought with distinction at Monterrey (September 18–21, 1846), being wounded and winning a brevet promotion. After serving as aide-de-camp to General John A. Quitman, he transferred to the army of General Winfield SCOTT in

1847 as it advanced on Mexico City. Lovell fought well at the storming of Chapultepec on September 14, 1847, receiving a second brevet to captain. Afterward, he performed several more tours of garrison duty along the frontier before resigning his commission in 1854. He then worked at an ironworks in New Jersey for four years until 1858, when he relocated to New York City as the city's first superintendent of street improvement. There, he met and befriended Gustavus W. Smith, a future Confederate general. Once the Civil War commenced in April 1861, Smith departed immediately for the South, but Lovell lingered in the city for several months before finally offering his service to the Confederacy that September. His tardiness at joining always produced an undercurrent of suspicion as to his actual loyalties.

On October 7, 1861, Lovell—thanks largely to the intercession of his friend Smith—became a major general in the Confederate army and head of Department No. 1, the city of New Orleans. Though the South's largest city and main port, he inherited a small garrison, few cannon, and inadequate naval resources. He spent the next several months strengthening Forts Jackson and St. Philip, 70 miles below the city on the Mississippi River, which any invading squadron would have to pass. Lovell performed well, considering his material deficiencies, but he proved much given to drink and bragging. Moreover, he stated repeatedly to the Southern press that New Orleans could be easily defended under present conditions. On April 18, 1862, a combined Union fleet of ships and mortar boats under Captains David G. FARRAGUT and David D. PORTER threaded its way up the Mississippi. As anticipated, Forts St. Philip and Jackson held the fleet at bay for a week until Farragut executed a brilliant night passage on April 24, 1862. Once the fleet pulled up alongside the helpless city and landed the army of General Benjamin F. BUTLER, Lovell had little recourse but to evacuate his army to safety. For this, he was immediately condemned in newspapers throughout the South,

even though leaders such as General Robert E. LEE sanctioned the appropriateness of his withdrawal. A court of inquiry also vindicated Lovell, but his subsequent career remained hobbled by a whispering campaign about alleged disloyalty. His own troops added to the hubbub by singing "The New Ballad of Lord Lovell," which satirized the loss of New Orleans and the most obvious consequence of heavy drinking—his conspicuous red nose.

In the fall of 1862, Lovell had succeeded to the command of the I Corps in the army of General Earl VAN DORN, in which he also served as second in command. On October 3–4, 1862, Van Dorn ordered a desperate attempt to retake the strategic railroad junction at Corinth, Mississippi, from Union forces under General William S. ROSECRANS. Lovell performed well on the first day of fighting, which occasioned heavy Confederate losses, but on the second day, Van Dorn ordered his division to assault strongly entrenched Federal troops. Lovell, unwilling to sacrifice his command in a futile attack, only sent skirmishers forward while two other Southern divisions went forward, unsupported, and were mauled. Van Dorn then charged Lovell with insubordination, but he partially redeemed his reputation by conducting a splendid rear-guard action at Coffeeville, Mississippi, on October 5, 1862. Shortly after, Lovell was relieved, and he spent the balance of the war as a volunteer staff officer under General Joseph E. JOHNSTON. Despite repeated entreaties for a new command, Lovell passed the remainder of the war in relative obscurity. In March 1865 General Lee requested that he receive the command of a corps, and the government finally relented, but the war ended before Lovell could reach his headquarters.

After the war, Lovell relocated to Georgia to work as a rice farmer, but in 1869 he lost his estate in a flood. He then returned to New York to hold down various positions as a surveyor and an engineer. Lovell died there on June 1, 1884, a talented officer but seldom employed by a government that never really trusted him.

Further Reading

Cozzens, Peter. *The Darkest Days of the War: Iuka and Corinth.* Chapel Hill: University of North Carolina Press, 1997.

Garcia, Pedro. "Losing the Big Easy." *Civil War Times Illustrated* 41, no. 2 (2002): 46–53, 64–65.

Hearn, Chester G. *The Capture of New Orleans.* Baton Rouge: Louisiana State University Press, 1995.

Heleniak, Roman J., and Lawrence L. Hewitt, eds. *The 1989 Deep Delta Civil War Symposium: Leadership during the Civil War.* Shippensburg, Pa.: White Mane Books, 1992.

Smith, Brier R. *Major General Mansfield Lovell and the Fall of New Orleans: The Downfall of a Career.* Memphis, Tenn.: Memphis Pink Palace Museum, 1973.

Sutherland, Daniel L. "Mansfield Lovell's Quest for Justice: Another Look at the Fall of New Orleans." *Louisiana History* 24, no. 3 (1987): 233–259.

Lyon, Nathaniel (1818–1861)

Union general

Nathaniel Lyon was born in Ashford, Connecticut, on July 14, 1818, the son of farmers. He entered the U.S. Military Academy in 1837 and graduated four years later a second lieutenant in the 2nd U.S. Infantry. Lyon next fought in Florida's Second Seminole War and performed garrison duty at Sacket's Harbor, New York, before accompanying General Winfield SCOTT's army in the Mexican War. Lyon, endowed with flaming red hair and a disposition to match, fought bravely at Contreras and Churubusco in 1847, winning a brevet promotion to captain. He next performed a stint of frontier duties and Indian fighting before being assigned to Fort Riley, Kansas, during the period known as "Bleeding Kansas." Lyon's encounter with slavery affected him profoundly, and he joined the Republican Party as an avid abolitionist. In February 1861, on the cusp of open hostilities, he was installed as commander of the U.S. Arsenal at St. Louis, Missouri. It proved to be a singularly fortuitous appointment for the North.

Throughout the spring of 1861, Missouri was split along Northern and Southern lines with Governor Claiborne F. Jackson firmly in the Confederate camp. Lyon, determined to hold St. Louis for

the Union, began to recruit a Unionist militia known as the Home Guard from thousands of German-speaking immigrants. This move prompted Jackson to call out his own Confederate militia, the State Guard, that Lyon feared would be used to capture the St. Louis arsenal. With typical audacity and dispatch, he surrounded and captured many Confederate sympathizers at Camp Jackson on May 10, 1861, and then paraded them through the streets of the city. Riots broke out in consequence, and when the Home Guard fired into the crowd, killing 28 men, thousands fled the city and joined the Confederate side. Lyon's rash action may have bolstered Jackson's hand for the time being, but it also kept the arsenal out of Confederate hands and possibly saved Missouri for the Union. Lyon also conspired with Congressman Francis P. Blair, a Radical Republican, to remove the Southern-leaning general William S. Harney as commander of the Department of the West. Lyon then advanced to brigadier general of volunteers to succeed him and moved quickly to secure the Potosi lead mines for the Union. Then, to avoid further bloodshed, he conferred with Governor Jackson and State Guard commander Sterling PRICE at a hotel in St. Louis on June 11, 1861. Negotiations came to nothing and Lyon angrily stalked out declaring, "This means war!" He began to mobilize his troops to neutralize the Confederate threat once and for all.

Lyon, true to form, moved swiftly. On June 15, 1861, his troops captured the state capital of Jefferson City, forcing Governor Jackson to flee. Two days later, his Home Guard attacked state troops at Boonville, Missouri, defeating them. He then moved against the major city of Springfield, which fell on July 13, 1861. On August 2, 1861, Lyon engaged and defeated another Southern force at Dug Springs. There, he learned that a large Confederate force consisting of State Guard troops under Price and Texas forces under General Ben McCULLOCH were advancing on him with 11,000 men. Lyon, who possessed only 5,500, should have withdrawn, but, instead, he chose to attack over the objections of his second in command, Major

John M. SCHOFIELD. On August 10, 1861, he surprised the Confederates at Wilson's Creek by driving them from their camp and occupying a nearby ridge line. While Price's men counterattacked, a second Union column under Colonel Franz SIGEL marched to the rear of the Confederate camp and nearly routed the defenders before being defeated in turn. The Confederates, flushed with victory, were gathering for a final assault when Lyon launched his fourth charge of the day and fell mortally wounded. His army then safely extricated itself and withdrew, leaving the field to victorious but disorganized Southerners.

Lyon was the first Union officer of general rank to fall in combat and was enshrined among the North's first martyrs. His headstrong behavior undoubtedly contributed to his demise, but by acting promptly and aggressively in the early days of the crisis, he probably preserved Missouri for the Union. In December 1861 the slain officer posthumously received the thanks of Congress.

Further Reading

Brookshear, William R. *Bloody Hill: The Civil War Battle of Wilson's Creek.* Washington, D.C.: Brassey's, 2000.

Gerteis, Louis S. *Civil War St. Louis.* Lawrence: University Press of Kansas, 2001.

Johnson, Mark W. *That Brave Body of Men: The U.S. Regular Infantry and the Civil War in the West, 1861–1865.* Cambridge, Mass.: Da Capo Press, 2003.

Phillips, Christopher. *Damned Yankee: The Life of General Nathaniel Lyon.* Baton Rouge: Louisiana State University Press, 1990.

Piston, William G., and Richard W. Hatcher. *Wilson's Creek: The Second Battle of the Civil War and the Men Who Fought It.* Chapel Hill: University of North Carolina Press, 2000.

Smith, Derek. *The Gallant Dead: Union and Confederate Generals Killed in the Civil War.* Mechanicsburg, Pa.: Stackpole Books, 2005.

M

McClellan, George B. (1826–1885)
Union general

George Brinton McClellan was born in Philadelphia, Pennsylvania, on December 13, 1826, a member of an established and influential family. After briefly studying at the University of Pennsylvania, he was admitted to the U.S. Military Academy in 1842—aged only 16 years—and graduated four years later, second in his class. He then served as a second lieutenant in the elite Corps of Engineers, joining General Winfield SCOTT's army in time to serve in the Mexican War. McClellan distinguished himself in combat, winning two brevet promotions for bravery at Contreras, Churubusco, and Chapultepec. Afterward, he served as an instructor at West Point until 1851, and he was called on to design and construct Fort Delaware, undertake harbor clearing, and conduct railroad surveys. In 1855 McClellan rose to captain and journeyed to Europe to observe the ongoing Crimean War. He also studied cavalry tactics in Prussia and Austria and designed the so-called McClellan saddle, which remained in use for several decades. However, McClellan ended his promising military career by resigning his commission in 1857 to work as chief engineer of the Illinois Central Railroad. A superb administrator, he had risen to president of the Ohio and Mississippi Railroad by 1860.

When the Civil War began in April 1861, McClellan served as a major general of volunteers, commanding the Department of the Ohio. In this capacity, he helped plan and orchestrate several minor victories over Confederate forces in present-day West Virginia, especially the Battle of Rich Mountain (July 11, 1861). Success here brought him to the attention of President Abraham LINCOLN, then desperately seeking to replace General Irvin McDowELL as commander of Union forces. In July 1861 McClellan, who, while short in stature, cut an impressive military figure on horseback, gained appointment as head of the newly organized Army of the Potomac. That November, he also maneuvered to have himself appointed general in chief at the expense of his old mentor, General Scott. McClellan proved himself to be a superb disciplinarian and a first-class military organizer. Within months, he transformed his charge from an unruly mob into a finely honed military machine, eager for combat. The men came to revere their commander, in turn, christening him "Little Mac." Lincoln, however, grew frustrated by McClellan's lack of aggressiveness or, as he put it, his case of "the slows." McClellan ignored continual prodding by the government to attack, and on January 27, 1862, the president issued General War Order No. 1 mandating a general offensive. When McClellan still refused to budge, he was removed as general in chief and replaced by General Henry W. HALLECK.

It was not until March 1862 that McClellan began his offensive with 118,000 men. He did so

Union general George B. McClellan *(National Archives)*

by transporting his huge army down the Potomac River to the Yorktown Peninsula, thus bypassing the strong fortifications of Richmond, Virginia. But McClellan, while possessing twice as many troops as General Joseph E. JOHNSTON, behaved cautiously and only inched his way inland. He was easily deceived by a smaller force under General John B. MAGRUDER at Yorktown, which he stopped to besiege and thereby squandered a month in preparations. McClellan next easily parried Johnston's careless thrust at Seven Oaks on May 31–June 1, 1862, but he then confronted the infinitely more aggressive general Robert E. LEE. Lee, taking advantage of his opponent's ingrained caution, launched the Seven Days' battles for the next week to intimidate him. McClellan, although besting the Confederates and inflicting heavier

losses, believed himself badly outnumbered and fell back to the James River. Lincoln became so angered by this display of timidity that he removed "Little Mac" in August and had the Army of the Potomac broken up and distributed among the new Army of Virginia under General John POPE. McClellan bitterly complained that his failure resulted from the lack of promised reinforcements, especially the 30,000 men General McDowell's I Corps that had been detained for the defense of Washington, D.C.

Pope's tenure as senior Union commander proved disastrous and came to grief at Second Manassas on August 29–30, 1862. Lee then crossed into Union territory by invading Maryland, and a desperate Lincoln restored McClellan to command. As before, he energetically reinvigorated the Army of the Potomac and was further bolstered by receipt of a copy of General Lee's secret orders. The orders revealed that Confederate forces were badly divided, but McClellan, true to form, reacted slowly. After winning a small victory at South Mountain on September 14, 1862, he confronted Lee's entire army at Antietam three days later. The Confederates were outnumbered badly 90,000 to 55,000 men, but McClellan attacked cautiously, failed to commit his entire army to the fray, and allowed Lee to escape a close brush with destruction. When the Southerners withdrew back to Virginia, McClellan failed to pursue them vigorously and instead called for reinforcements. Confederate cavalry under General J. E. B. STUART then conducted their second celebrated ride around the Army of the Potomac, and Lincoln again relieved McClellan in favor of General Ambrose E. BURNSIDE. Following a tearful farewell from his soldiers, he left the field, never to command again.

After waiting two years for orders that never came, McClellan accepted the Democratic Party's nomination for the presidency in 1864. He disavowed his party's peace platform and calls for a negotiated settlement with the South, but he nonetheless waxed critical of Lincoln's performance as commander in chief. The war weariness of the North coupled with high casualty rates from General Ulysses S. GRANT's Overland campaign to Richmond seemed to dampen Lincoln's political future. The soldiers, however, overwhelmingly rejected their former commander, and the president easily gained reelection with 212 electoral votes to 21. McClellan then resigned from the army altogether and toured Europe for three years. Back home, he became chief engineer for the New York City Department of Docks, and from 1878 to 1881, he served as governor of New Jersey. McClellan died in Orange, New Jersey, on October 29, 1885. He was among the most talented of Civil War leaders yet was simply unwilling to risk the splendid army he had so painstakingly created.

Further Reading

Beatie, Russell H. *Army of the Potomac, Vol. 1: Birth of Command, November 1860–September 1861.* New York: Da Capo Press, 2002.

Bonekemper, Edward H. *McClellan and Failure: A Study of Civil War Fear, Incompetence, and Worse.* Jefferson, N.C.: McFarland, 2007.

Dougherty, Kevin, and J. Michael Moore. *The Peninsula Campaign of 1862: A Military Analysis.* Jackson: University Press of Mississippi, 2005.

Jermann, Donald R. *Antietam: The Lost Order.* Gretna, La.: Pelican Publishing, 2006.

McClellan, George B. *McClellan's Own Story: The War for the Union.* New York: C. L. Webster, 1887.

McPherson, James M. *Crossroads of Freedom: Antietam.* New York: Oxford University Press, 2002.

Rafuse, Ethan S. *McClellan's War: The Failure of Moderation in the Struggle for the Union.* Bloomington: Indiana University Press, 2005.

Taaffe, Stephen R. *Commanding the Army of the Potomac.* Lawrence: University Press of Kansas, 2006.

Wert, Jeffrey D. *The Sword of Lincoln: The Army of the Potomac.* New York: Simon and Schuster, 2005.

McCulloch, Ben (1811–1862)

Confederate general

Ben McCulloch was born in Rutherford, Tennessee, on November 11, 1811, the son of a War of 1812 soldier from that state. He was raised on the frontier, befriended legendary scout Davy Crockett, and accompanied him to Texas in 1836. McCulloch missed dying at the Alamo on account of measles but subsequently distinguished himself at the decisive victory at San Jacinto. He then settled in Texas as a surveyor and also became one of the founding members of the noted Texas Rangers, organized for frontier defense. This ad hoc group of rough-hewn scouts fought well at the August 1840 Battle of Plum Creek in which he defeated the Great Comanche Raid of that year, and despite a reputation for brutality toward Indians and Mexicans, McCulloch became a popular figure in the southwestern press and won a seat in the Texas Congress. When the Mexican War erupted in 1846, he volunteered his services as a scout under General Zachary Taylor and further distinguished himself in the Battle of Monterrey. In February 1847 McCulloch performed particularly valuable service by detecting the approach of General Antonio de Santa Anna's army prior to the Battle of Buena Vista. Consequently, McCulloch received brevet promotion to major of U.S. Volunteers. After the war, he migrated to California at the height of the gold rush and then returned to Texas in 1852 to serve as a federal marshal. In 1858 he accompanied the Mormon expedition of Colonel Albert S. JOHNSTON and remained behind as a peace commissioner.

Once Texas seceded from the Union on February 1, 1861, McCulloch became a colonel of state troops. In that capacity, he received the surrender of U.S. forces under General David E. Twiggs at San Antonio. On May 11, 1861, he was appointed brigadier general at the behest of Confederate president Jefferson DAVIS and was assigned to command the Southwest Division, with troops in Texas, Louisiana, and Arkansas. He also was responsible for military matters in the nearby Indian Territory and arranged the commissioning of Cherokee Stand WATIE to brigadier general. As a military figure, McCulloch cultivated his larger-than-life image by remaining contemptuous of military protocol and regulations. As such, he invariably discarded his Confederate uniform in favor of a trademark black velvet outfit. His first military endeavor of consequence was to march troops into southwestern Missouri and reinforce the Confederate State Guard under General Sterling PRICE. On August 10, 1861, both men were surprised in camp by Union troops under General Nathaniel LYON and nearly routed. However, McCulloch managed to defeat a flanking force under Colonel Franz SIGEL and personally led a charge by Louisiana infantry that captured five cannon. Lyon was killed in the ensuing fracas, and the Confederates were left holding the field.

Victory did little to promote good relations between the headstrong McCulloch and the equally obstinate Price. In January 1862 Confederate authorities responded by creating the new Trans-Mississippi Department under General Earl VAN DORN to keep both in line. Heavy losses and internal disorganization stalled a Southern resurgence in the region for several months, and it was not until the spring that Van Dorn, Price, and McCulloch finally confronted a new threat posed by General Samuel R. CURTIS. Gathering 16,000 men, Van Dorn advanced on the Federals at Pea Ridge, Arkansas, on March 7, 1862. That morning, McCulloch rode ahead of the main body to reconnoiter the Union position, conspicuously decked out in his black uniform. He was then singled out by a sharpshooter and killed. Deprived of his sound judgment, Van Dorn waged a reckless and piecemeal action that forfeited control of northern Arkansas to the North. McCulloch had enjoyed renown as one of the first and greatest of the Texas Rangers, and his passing was greatly lamented. At the time of his death, he was also the second-most senior brigadier in Confederate service.

Further Reading

Brice, Donaly E. *The Great Comanche Raid: Boldest Indian Attack of the Texas Republic.* Austin, Tex.: Eakin Press, 1987.
Cutrer, Thomas W. *Ben McCulloch and the Frontier Military Tradition.* Chapel Hill: University of North Carolina Press, 1993.
DeBlack, Thomas R. *With Fire and Sword: Arkansas, 1861–1874.* Fayetteville: University of Arkansas Press, 2003.
Maberry, Robert T. "Texans and the Defense of the Confederate Northwest, April 1861–April 1862." Unpublished Ph.D. diss., Texas Christian University, 1992.
Piston, William G., and Richard W. Hatcher. *Wilson's Creek: The Second Battle of the Civil War and the Men Who Fought It.* Chapel Hill: University of North Carolina Press, 2000.
Shea, William L., and Grady McWhiney. *War in the West: Pea Ridge and Prairie Grove.* Abilene, Tex.: McWhiney Foundation Press, 2001.

McDowell, Irvin (1818–1885)
Union general

Irvin McDowell was born in Columbus, Ohio, on October 15, 1818, and he attended the Collège de Troyes in France before being admitted to the U.S. Military Academy in 1834. He graduated four years later midway in his class and served as a second lieutenant in the 1st U.S. Artillery during garrison stints along the Canadian border. In 1841 he transferred back to West Point as an instructor, rising there to first lieutenant, and in 1845 he joined the staff of General John E. Wool in Texas as a staff officer. In this capacity, McDowell fought in the Mexican War (1846–48), winning a brevet promotion to captain for gallantry at the Battle of Buena Vista in February 1847. He subsequently arrived at Washington, D.C., and was posted within the adjutant general's department. For the next 12 years, he performed well in staff assignments, rising to major and frequently serving as aide-de-camp to General Winfield SCOTT. After the Civil War commenced, McDowell used political connections through Scott and Secretary of the Treasury Salmon P. Chase to advance three grades to brigadier general as of May 11, 1861. He then accepted command of the Department of Northeastern Virginia and began to cobble together a force composed mainly of 90-day volunteers and poorly trained militia. Despite his lack of experience in handling large numbers of troops, McDowell discharged his duties with energy and dispatch, and, by July, he possessed a scratch force of 50,000 enthusiastic citizen soldiers. Given sufficient time, he would have undoubtedly welded this polyglot assemblage into a finely honed army—but this proved to be a luxury he could not afford. Moreover, his blunt, reserved personality won few admirers or friends among the soldiers and politicians with whom he had to contend.

Ever since the bombardment of Fort Sumter on April 12, 1861, the administration of President Abraham LINCOLN fell under increasing pressure to mount a major offensive against the Confederate capital of Richmond, Virginia, and crush the rebellion in one fell swoop. McDowell, as the commanding general in the theater, also felt the heat and was goaded into committing his troops to combat before they were ready. He nonetheless proffered an excellent plan for outflanking Confederate forces deployed at Manassas Junction under General Pierre G. T. BEAUREGARD. It was anticipated that a crushing victory here would severe Richmond's supply lines and end the rebellion without further bloodshed. On July 16, 1861, McDowell led his overconfident amateurs southward down the Warrenton Turnpike to thunderous cheers of "On to Richmond!" Two days later, he paused at Centreville to reorganize and to leisurely reconnoiter Confederate positions. On July 18 a Union force was bested at Blackburn's Ford by Confederates under General James LONGSTREET, which further reinforced McDowell's caution. His three-day delay also enabled Beauregard to summon 10,000 reinforcements under the highly capable general Joseph E. JOHNSTON, who boarded trains in the Shenandoah Valley. Union forces in the region under elderly general Robert Patterson were supposed to have assisted McDowell by pinning Johnston in place to prevent such a move, but they failed to do so.

The fateful encounter at Bull Run, on July 21, 1861, was ostensibly lost to the Union before the first gun was fired. When McDowell finally attacked, he did so slowly and by piecemeal, allowing the Southerners to feed additional units to the threatened sector and hold the Northerners off. Exhausted by a day of fighting in intense heat, McDowell's levies finally wilted in the face of Johnston's reinforcements and departed the battlefield in an embarrassing stampede. The Southerners, equally disorganized by success, proved unable to mount an effective pursuit. In sum, McDowell originated a fine battle plan but one that proved beyond the ability of raw troops and officers to execute properly. Held as a scapegoat for defeat, he was replaced the following August by General George B. McCLELLAN.

When the Army of the Potomac was organized in August 1861, McDowell received com-

Union general Irvin McDowell *(National Archives)*

mand of the I Corps along with promotion to major general as of March 1862. But he played no role in McClellan's ambitious Peninsula campaign because the activities of General Thomas J. Jackson in the Shenandoah Valley convinced President Lincoln that Washington was threatened. Hence, McDowell's I Corps remained in reserve, guarding the capital, and it saw little fighting: McClellan vocally cited his inaction as a major cause of his defeat at the hands of General Robert E. Lee. McDowell subsequently commanded the III Corps in the Army of Virginia under General John Pope. Like Pope, he received blame for the defeat at Second Manassas on August 29–30, 1862, and he was relieved from field command for the duration of the war. McDowell angrily demanded and received a court of inquiry that exonerated his behavior, but his wartime service concluded. It was not until July 1864 that he received command of the distant Department of the Pacific, followed by the Department of California in 1865.

After the war, McDowell gradually resuscitated his reputation as a fine military administrator. He commanded the Department of the East in 1868, rising to major general in 1872. He next fulfilled four years as head of the Department of the South before returning to the Department of the Pacific in 1876. McDowell finally retired in 1882 and died at San Francisco on May 4, 1885. While a capable staff officer and administrator, he could never live down the stigma of losing the Civil War's first large engagement.

Further Reading

Beatie, Russell H. *Army of the Potomac, Vol. 1: Birth of Command, November 1860–September 1861.* New York: Da Capo Press, 2002.

Davis, William C. *Battle at Bull Run: A History of the First Major Campaign of the Civil War.* Baton Rouge: Louisiana State University Press, 1995.

Detzer, David. *Donnybrook: The Battle of Bull Run, 1861.* San Diego: Harcourt, 2004.

Hennessy, John J. *Return to Bull Run: The Campaign and Battle of Second Manassas.* Norman: University of Oklahoma Press, 1993.

Jones, Wilmer L. *Generals in Blue and Gray.* 2 vols. Westport, Conn.: Praeger, 2004.

Rafuse, Ethan S. *A Single Grand Victory: The First Campaign and Battle of Manassas.* Wilmington, Del.: Scholarly Resources, 2002.

McPherson, James B. (1828–1864)

Union general

James Birdseye McPherson was born near Clyde, Ohio, on November 14, 1828, the son of farmers. He overcame a life of poverty to enter the U.S. Military Academy in 1849 and graduated four years later, first in his class. Posted as a second lieutenant within the elite Corps of Engineers, McPherson remained at the academy as an instructor until 1854, when he performed engineering work at New York and San Francisco. He rose to first lieutenant as of December 1858 and, as a strong Unionist, helped raise a volunteer company once the Civil War commenced in April 1861. Though promoted to captain and desiring a field command, McPherson was ordered to Boston to supervise harbor defenses. He then appealed to his former commander, now General Henry W. Halleck, for help, and Halleck ordered him to St. Louis, Missouri, as his aide-de-camp with a rank of lieutenant colonel. In the winter of 1861, McPherson transferred to General Ulysses S. Grant's staff as his engineering officer and capably discharged his duties at Forts Henry and Donelson in February 1862. He performed equally well in the Shiloh campaign that spring and was entrusted with supervising military railroads in Mississippi as a brigadier general of volunteers. In October 1862 he further distinguished himself by rushing reinforcements to General William S. Rosecrans, then besieged at Corinth, Mississippi, and so effectively pursued Confederates under General Earl Van Dorn that he received both promotion to major general of volunteers and command of a division in the XIII Corps. McPherson next fought throughout the ensuing Vicksburg campaign, commanding the XVII Corps, and he bore prominent roles in the victories at Port Gibson, Jackson, and Champion's Hill in May 1863.

Union general James B. McPherson *(Massachusetts Commandery Military Order of the Loyal Legion and the U.S. Army Military History Institute)*

He then actively partook of the siege operations at Vicksburg and, following its capitulation on July 4, 1863, won appointment as its governor.

On recommendations from both Halleck and Grant, McPherson advanced to brigadier general in the regular army as of August 1863. He participated in General William T. SHERMAN's Meridian offensive in January 1864 and subsequently succeeded Sherman as commander of the Army of the Tennessee during the march to Atlanta. As expected, McPherson performed well in a difficult campaign of maneuver and only faltered once. In May 1864 Sherman dispatched him on a 40-mile march below Dalton, Georgia, where the army of General Joseph E. JOHNSTON was strongly entrenched. He advanced into Snake Gap Creek as ordered and was well positioned to cut off Johnston's entire army, but he suddenly and uncharacteristically grew cautious and retreated. This

proved the most unfortunate mistake of his entire military career, for the pass was then guarded by three weak Confederate brigades, and his hesitation allowed Johnston to escape encirclement speedily. Nonetheless, McPherson's XVII Corps continued marching and fighting competently at Resaca, Dallas, and Kennesaw Mountain on the approach to Atlanta, and he helped to maneuver Johnston out of strong defensive positions.

Johnston's inability to stem Sherman's approach resulted in his replacement with the ever-aggressive general John B. HOOD, a former West Point roommate of McPherson. That officer, cognizant of Hood's well-deserved reputation for offensive tactics, immediately deployed his troops to meet what he anticipated would be an all-out assault. On July 22, 1864, Hood struck violently at Union forces outside Atlanta, and Confederates under General William J. HARDEE hit the Army of the Tennessee hard. After a raging battle of several hours, they were repulsed, thanks to McPherson's excellent dispositions. However, as McPherson was reconnoitering a gap between several of his units, he stumbled into a Confederate picket line and was shot dead at the age of 35. "The country has lost one of its best soldiers," General Grant lamented, "and I have lost one of my best friends." McPherson's death was a serious loss to the Union army, and had he lived, he may have been one of the towering figures of the postwar period.

Further Reading

Block, William. "The Pride of Clyde: James B. McPherson." *Northwest Ohio Quarterly* 74, no. 2 (2002): 50–62.

Cubbison, Douglas. *The Entering Wedge: The Battle of Port Gibson, 1 May 1863: A Scholarly Monograph.* Saline, Mich.: McNaughton and Gunn, 2002.

Melia, Tamara M. "James B. McPherson and the Ideals of the Old Army." Unpublished Ph.D., diss., Southern Illinois University, 1987.

Smith, Derek. *The Gallant Dead: Union and Confederate Generals Killed in the Civil War.* Mechanicsburg, Pa.: Stackpole Books, 2005.

Smith, Timothy B. *Champion's Hill: Decisive Battle for Vicksburg.* New York: Savas Beattie, 2005.

Woodworth, Steven E. *Nothing But Victory: The Army of the Tennessee, 1861–1865.* New York: Alfred A. Knopf, 2005.

Woodworth, Steven E., ed. *Grant's Lieutenants.* 2 vols. Lawrence: University Press of Kansas, 2001.

Magruder, John B. (1807–1871)

Confederate general

John Bankhead Magruder was born in Port Royal, Virginia, on May 1, 1807, the son of an attorney. He entered the U.S. Military Academy in 1826 and graduated in the middle of his class four years later as a second lieutenant in the 7th U.S. Infantry. As a student, Magruder was much given to heavy drinking and nearly was expelled for demerits. In 1831 he transferred to the 1st U.S. Infantry and performed useful service in Florida's Second Seminole War (1836–42). Magruder was next billeted in Texas as part of the Army of Occupation under General Zachary Taylor. He fought conspicuously in the Mexican War, commanding an artillery battery under General Gideon Pillow at Cerro Gordo in 1847 and winning brevet promotions to major and lieutenant colonel. After the war, Magruder resumed a long stint of garrison duty along the frontier and the East Coast, gaining notoriety for his lavish partying, elaborate attire, and a projected sense of superiority that manifested in the sobriquet "Prince John." In 1859 Magruder returned west again to serve as commander of Fort Leavenworth, Kansas, and he also toured as an artillery inspector. He was never overtly sympathetic toward secession, but after Virginia left the Union in April 1861, he resigned his commission and tended his service to the Confederacy as a colonel of infantry.

Magruder's flair for theatrics never deserted him in combat. On June 10, 1861, he led a small detachment of Confederates at Big Bethel, Virginia, defeating an equally small detachment of Federals under General Benjamin F. Butler. The Southern press immediately magnified his victory and lionized him to the point where he gained promotion to brigadier general in June and major general the following October. In the spring of 1862, he performed his best work by completely hoodwinking the vast army of General George B. McClellan at Yorktown into believing that his force of 15,000 men was much larger. Consequently, Union forces squandered an entire month, April 4–May 4, 1862, preparing for an unnecessary siege. However, General Joseph E. Johnston remained less impressed with his deportment, and after quarreling with him, Magruder sought a transfer to the Trans-Mississippi Department. While this transpired, Magruder fought capably at the Battle of Seven Pines (June 1, 1862), and he resumed his bluffing activities against McClellan during General Robert E. Lee's Seven Days' offensive. But after this point, his battlefield performance lessened through either lack of sleep or excessive drinking, and he fumbled assignments at Savage's Station on June 29, 1862, and at Malvern Hill on July 1, 1862. Lee was angered by his dilatoriness and was preparing charges against him when Magruder was transferred to the District of Texas, New Mexico, and Arizona.

Magruder's subsequent activities were competent, if anticlimactic. On January 1, 1863, he orchestrated a surprise attack on Union forces garrisoning the port of Galveston, Texas, capturing them and the revenue cutter *Harriet Lane* and driving off the blockading squadron. This proved a significant victory as Galveston remained a port of considerable blockade-running activity for the rest of the war. In 1864 he also coordinated his efforts with General Richard Taylor in West Louisiana, and his assistance helped defeat the Red River expedition of General Nathaniel C. Banks. Magruder then briefly commanded the District of Arkansas in the fall of 1864 before returning to Texas. He surrendered there to Union authorities on June 2, 1865. Like many disaffected Confederates, Magruder chose to emigrate to Mexico rather than return home. He served Emperor Maximilian as head of the Land Office of Colonization to encourage Southern immigration there. However, in November 1866 he sailed to Havana, Cuba, and then to New York City to practice law before finally settling down in San Antonio, Texas.

"Prince John" died there on February 18, 1871, a colorful, if marginal, military leader.

Further Reading

Casdorph, Paul D. *Prince John Magruder: His Life and Campaigns.* New York: Wiley and Sons, 1991.

Cotham, Edward T. *Battle on the Bay: The Civil War Struggle for Galveston.* Austin: University of Texas Press, 1998.

Moore, J. Michael. "The Damn Failure: The Battles of Lee's Mill and Damn No. 1." *North & South* 5, no. 5 (2002): 62–71.

Schroeder, Glenn B. *A Rebel and a Yankee: Cousins at War.* Greeley, Colo.: Immigrant Press, 2000.

Stever, Rex H. "Magruder's Scorched Earth Policy." *Journal of South Texas* 16, no. 1 (2003): 34–44.

Townsend, Stephen A. *The Yankee Invasion of Texas.* College Station: Texas A & M University Press, 2005.

Meade, George G. (1815–1872)

Union general

George Gordon Meade was born in Cadiz, Spain, on December 31, 1815, the son of a naval agent. The premature death of his father forced him to quit school to support his family, but, in 1831, he gained admittance to the U.S. Military Academy. Meade graduated four years later as a second lieutenant in the 3rd U.S. Artillery, where he fought in Florida's Second Seminole War before contracting a fever. He briefly served at the U.S. Arsenal in Watertown, Massachusetts, and then resigned his commission to work as a surveyor. In 1842 Meade rejoined the service as a lieutenant in the Topographical Engineers, and he performed boundary work in Maine and construction work in Philadelphia. He next accompanied General Zachary Taylor's army during the Mexican War, winning a brevet promotion for valor at the Battle of Monterrey (September 20–24, 1846). After a tour under General Winfield SCOTT in the advance against Mexico City the following year, Meade resumed his surveying work in Philadelphia, Florida, and along the Canadian border, rising to captain as of May 1856. The onset of the Civil War in April 1861 led to a commission as a brigadier general in the Pennsylvania Reserves, and he

spent several months manning the defenses of Washington, D.C.

Meade commenced to campaign actively by leading a brigade in the 1862 Peninsula campaign under General George B. McCLELLAN. He fought conspicuously at Mechanicsville, Gaines's Mill, White Oak Swamp, and especially at Frayser's Farm (Glendale) on June 20, 1862, where he was wounded yet refused to quit the field. He had only partially recovered in time to see additional service under General John POPE at Second Manassas (August 29–30, 1862), and he commanded a division at Antietam on September 17, 1862. When the commander of I Corps, General Joseph HOOKER, fell wounded, Meade replaced him in

Union general George Meade *(Library of Congress)*

battle, performing capably. He consequently rose to major general the following November under General Ambrose E. BURNSIDE, and on December 17, 1862, during the disastrous Battle of Fredericksburg, he scored one of the few Union successes of the day with a minor breakthrough at General Thomas J. JACKSON's position. When command of the Army of the Potomac reverted to Hooker in the spring of 1863, Meade was entrusted with the command of V Corps, which was only slightly engaged at the disastrous defeat of Chancellorsville on May 2, 1863. Shortly after, the Army of Northern Virginia under General Robert E. LEE began its second incursion into Union territory by invading Pennsylvania. Hooker was then relieved of command, and when General John F. REYNOLDS declined to take up the mantle, Meade accepted it on June 28, 1863. He was somewhat taken aback by the appointment and not entirely pleased, but it proved most fortuitous for the country.

On July 1, 1863, Union and Confederate forces collided in an engagement at Gettysburg, Pennsylvania. Generals John BUFORD, Abner DOUBLEDAY, Oliver O. HOWARD, and Winfield S. HANCOCK waged a valiant fight, but they were driven out of town and up the slopes of nearby hills. Meade arrived on the battlefield at midnight, sorted through his jumbled units, and assumed a masterfully defensive position. With his surveyor's eye, he judiciously placed brigades and divisions along Cemetery Ridge, Little Round Top, and Culp's Hill in such a manner as to make the broken, heavily wooded terrain work for him and against the Confederates. Consequently, throughout July 2, 1863, Union forces ably repelled determined attacks by General James LONGSTREET along the critical left flank. The slovenly deployment of General Daniel E. SICKLES and his III Corps caused many anxious moments and heavy casualties, but otherwise Meade's line held firm. At a council of war that evening, Meade decided on a dawn attack to eliminate small Southern gains at the foot of Culp's Hill and cleverly anticipated that Lee, hav-

ing failed against both flanks, would most likely strike the Union center next. Throughout the evening, men and artillery shifted into position to meet the new threat. On July 3, 1863, Confederate artillery under Colonel Edward P. ALEXANDER heavily bombarded Cemetery Ridge for several hours, followed up by an assault by 15,000 infantry under General George E. PICKETT. This was repulsed bloodily by concentrated Union firepower, and Lee retreated back to Virginia after suffering losses of as many as 28,000 men. Meade's own casualties were considerable—at 23,000—so he declined to pursue actively.

Lincoln was gravely disappointed that the victor of Gettysburg failed to destroy Lee's army, but the general nonetheless received the thanks of Congress and promotion to regular brigadier general. General Ulysses S. GRANT arrived at Meade's headquarters the following spring as general in chief, but Meade was allowed to remain titular commander of the Army of the Potomac. Despite an awkward command arrangement, the two men worked well together, and Meade acquitted himself ably in bloody battles at the Wilderness and Spotsylvania Court House. On June 3, 1864, he proved instrumental in dissuading Grant from additional attacks at Cold Harbor, Virginia, which occasioned horrific losses. With Grant's approval, he rose to major general, U.S. Army, in August 1864. Meade continued fighting well throughout the Petersburg campaign and helped direct the final movements at Appomattox Court House with General Philip H. SHERIDAN which finally trapped Lee's army on April 9, 1865.

After the war, Meade remained in the service commanding the Department of the East, and, in 1868, he also performed reconstruction duties in Georgia, Alabama, and Florida. In 1869 he took charge of the Division of the Atlantic, where his final years proved uneventful save for a vitriolic and long-running dispute with Sickles concerning their respective roles at Gettysburg. Meade died in Philadelphia on November 6, 1872, of complications arising from his old wound. A more competent than brilliant leader, his skill at handling troops and effectively utilizing terrain won the Civil War's most decisive battle for the North.

Further Reading

Callihan, David L. "Passing the Test: George G. Meade's Initiation as Army Commander." *Gettysburg Magazine* 30 (July 2004): 30–48.

Hall, Jeffrey C. *The Stand of the United States Army at Gettysburg*. Bloomington: Indiana University Press, 2003.

Hyde, Bill. *The Union Generals Speak: The Meade Hearings on the Battle of Gettysburg*. Baton Rouge: Louisiana State University Press, 2003.

Meade, George W. *Life and Letters of General George G. Meade, Major General, United States Army*. 2 vols. New York: Charles Scribner's Sons, 1913.

Rafuse, Ethan S. *George Gordon Meade and the War in the East*. Abilene, Tex.: McWhiney Foundation Press, 2003.

Sauers, Richard A. *Meade: Victor of Gettysburg*. Washington, D.C.: Brassey's, 2003.

Sears, Stephen W. *Gettysburg*. Boston: Houghton Mifflin, 2003.

Taaffe, Stephen R. *Commanding the Army of the Potomac*. Lawrence: University Press of Kansas, 2006.

Trudeau, Andre N. *Gettysburg: A Testing of Courage*. New York: HarperCollins, 2002.

Wert, Jeffrey D. *The Sword of Lincoln: The Army of the Potomac*. New York: Simon and Schuster, 2005.

Meigs, Montgomery C. (1816–1892)

Union general

Montgomery Cunningham Meigs was born in Augusta, Georgia, on May 3, 1816, the son of a physician. He relocated to Philadelphia, Pennsylvania, with his family and briefly attended college there before transferring to the U.S. Military Academy in 1832. Meigs graduated near the top of his class four years later and was assigned to the elite Corps of Engineers. For the next 16 years, he distinguished himself in a variety of capacities, including a stint in service along the Mississippi River under Captain Robert E. LEE. He faced his biggest challenge in 1853 after being promoted to captain and assigned as chief engineer of the Washington Aqueduct Project, destined to bring supplies of freshwater to the capital, year round.

Union general Montgomery C. Meigs *(Library of Congress)*

Meigs successfully completed this daunting task eight years later by constructing the world's largest masonry arch over the Cabin John Branch, a tributary of the Potomac River. Throughout this same period, he was also responsible for designing and constructing new wings and domes for the Capitol Building. However, in 1860 he ran afoul of Secretary of War John B. FLOYD over the issue of contracts and was punitively reassigned to construction work in the Dry Tortugas off Florida. Meigs was recalled to Washington shortly after Floyd quit the government, and he attended the inauguration of President Abraham LINCOLN in February 1861. He the resumed routine engineering duties until the Civil War commenced the following April.

No sooner had hostilities erupted at Fort Sumter, South Carolina, than Meigs conferred with Commander David D. PORTER and Secretary of State William H. Seward about the necessity of reinforcing Fort Pickens off the coast of Pensacola, Florida. He then helped organize a successful relief expedition to that distant post, winning promotion to colonel, 11th U.S. Infantry in May 1861. But Meigs, disdaining a field command, requested succeeding Colonel Joseph E. JOHNSTON as quartermaster general of the army. Though never trained as a logistician, he was destined to make significant contributions to that field. Meigs inherited a small, chaotic department, totally unsuited to the task of arming and equipping a rapidly expanding army. Fortunately, he rapidly transformed it into a smoothly functioning instrument of war that met the ongoing needs of nearly 1 million soldiers. As quartermaster, Meigs bore responsibilities for acquiring and distributing food, clothing, and equipment for the various Union commands, along with the necessary transportation. He was also instrumental in promoting and paying for ironclad gunboats so essential to riverine warfare in the West. Unfortunately, an overreliance on civilian contractors engendered notoriously corrupt practices, including kickbacks and influence-peddling at every level. Meigs countered such abuse with his own brand of scrupulous honesty and accountability, and, by war's end, his department had distributed over $1.5 billion in materiel. In light of his superb performance, no Union army was ever defeated for want of supplies.

Meigs also demonstrated his bureaucratic prowess in the field by directing and supervising logistical operations in support of General Ulysses S. GRANT's overland campaign to Richmond, Virginia, in 1864. In July, when Confederates under General Jubal A. EARLY threatened Washington, D.C., he briefly commanded a division of War Department employees in the capital's defense. He also organized a complicated convoy of supply ships to assist General William T. SHERMAN's march from Savannah, Georgia, up to coast to Raleigh, North Carolina. Meigs endured a personal tragedy in October 1864 when his son was allegedly murdered by Confederate partisans. His son's commanding officer, General Philip H. SHERIDAN, was so outraged by the act that he literally burned every farm and building within five miles of the incident. Meigs's loss only spurred him on to greater efforts,

and for handling the complex business of army logistics seamlessly, he ended the war a brevet brigadier general. His antipathy for former colleague General Robert E. LEE proved to be so great that he designed and built Arlington National Cemetery on land previously owned by Lee's family.

Meigs resumed his engineering activities in the postwar period by supervising plans for a new War Department building and part of the new Smithsonian Institution. In 1876 he was tapped to visit Europe to observe military affairs and also served on a commission tasked with considering military reforms. He retired from active service in 1882, but he still found time to design the Pension Office Building, to serve as a Smithsonian regent, to join the American Philosophical Society, and to help found the American Academy of Science. The multitalented Meigs died in Washington, D.C., on January 2, 1892. He remains one of the most peerless bureaucrats of American military history and a major contributor to the ultimate Union victory.

Further Reading

Dickinson, William C., Dean A. Herrin, and Donald R. Kennon, eds. *Montgomery C. Meigs and the Building of the Nation's Capitol.* Athens: University of Ohio Press, 2001.

Hagerman, Edward. *The American Civil War and the Origins of Modern Warfare: Ideas, Organizations, and Field Command.* Bloomington: Indiana University Press, 1988.

Miller, David. *Second Only to Grant: Quartermaster General Montgomery C. Meigs: A Biography.* Shippensburg, Pa.: White Mane Books, 2000.

Risch, Erna. *Quartermaster Support for the Army: A History of the Corps, 1775–1939.* Washington, D.C.: Office of the Quartermaster General, 1962.

Stevens, Joseph E. "The North's Secret Weapon." *American History* 37, no. 1 (2002): 42–48.

Woodworth, Steve E., et al. "Who Were the Top Ten Generals?" *North & South* 6, no. 4 (2003): 12–22.

Morgan, John H. (1825–1864)

Confederate general

John Hunt Morgan was born in Huntsville, Alabama, on June 1, 1825, the son of a merchant and planter. He relocated to Lexington, Kentucky, with his family and briefly attended Transylvania University before being expelled for dueling. During the Mexican War, he joined the 1st Kentucky Cavalry as a lieutenant and performed useful service under General Zachary Taylor, especially at the Battle of Buena Vista (1847). Afterward, he returned to Kentucky to become a successful hemp manufacturer. He also maintained his militia contacts and in 1857 founded and led his own company, the Lexington Rifles. Morgan was openly sympathetic to the Confederacy and defiantly flew their flag over his factory throughout the period of Kentucky neutrality. But once the legislature finally declared for the Union in the fall of 1861, he moved to Tennessee and joined the Confederate army as a cavalry captain.

Morgan, handsome, dashing, and more than six feet tall, came to personify the romantic ideals of a cavalry raider. He rose to colonel after good behavior at the Battle of Shiloh in April 1862, and he was subsequently attached to General Joseph WHEELER's cavalry as part of General Braxton BRAGG's Army of Tennessee. In this capacity, he began to launch numerous and devastatingly effective raids against Union installations and lines of communication throughout Kentucky and Tennessee. On July 4, 1862, he commenced a 900-mile raid that netted 1,000 captives, cut railroad and telegraph lines, and delayed the advance of General Don C. BUELL's army by several weeks. On August 21, 1862, he confronted General Richard W. Johnson and 700 pursuing Union troopers; in the ensuing scrape, Johnson was captured and his command scattered. The following October, he advanced with 1,800 men and briefly seized his home town of Lexington for several hours. On December 7, 1862, Morgan launched another lightning foray that stormed into Hartsville, Tennessee, taking 1,700 Union prisoners. He then gained promotion to brigadier general, and President Abraham LINCOLN, frustrated as to the apparent ease of Morgan's movements, angrily wired General Henry W. HALLECK, declaring "They are having a stampede in Kentucky. Please look at it."

Consequently, more than 20,000 Federal troops were detached from field service to guard communication and supply lines. Morgan's daring success induced President Jefferson DAVIS to push through the Partisan Ranger Act on April 21, 1863, which raised mounted units specifically for raiding purposes.

In June 1863 Morgan initiated his most audacious raid by riding northward into Indiana and Ohio on a 24-day ride. He did so against the wishes of General Bragg, who sought a more conventional use for his 2,400 troopers. Morgan nonetheless ferried across the Ohio River and galloped 1,100 miles through the two states with Federal troops and a squadron of gunboats in hot pursuit. Morgan drove his men 50 miles in the saddle per day and at one point wildly galloped

Confederate general John H. Morgan *(Massachusetts Commandery Military Order of the Loyal Legion and the U.S. Army Military History Institute)*

through the suburbs of downtown Cincinnati. However, the bulk of his force was cornered at Buffington Island in the Ohio River and was captured, while Morgan himself managed to elude his pursuers until July 26. Thereafter, he was incarcerated in the Ohio State Penitentiary, Columbus, and was treated like a common brigand. But it was never safe to underestimate Morgan in times of adversity, and, on November 26, 1863, he affected a daring escape.

Morgan returned to the Confederacy with a hero's welcome and won assignment as commander of the Department of Southwestern Virginia. He then resumed his raiding activities, although with less success owing to the loss of skilled leaders and rising indiscipline among his troopers. When his forays began to resemble large-scale plundering expeditions, he was investigated by Confederate authorities and nearly was removed from command. But Morgan, determined to silence his critics, counted on one final raid against Nashville to exonerate his reputation. En route, he encamped at Greeneville, Tennessee, a region known for Unionist sympathies, and the inhabitants tipped off a nearby Federal garrison. On September 4, 1864, they surprised Morgan in camp, killing him. At the time of his death, his activities were of declining military value to the Confederacy and more likely a source of embarrassment, but for many months, Morgan was a formidable Confederate partisan and a hero throughout the South.

Further Reading

Black, Robert W. *Cavalry Raids of the Civil War.* Mechanicsburg, Pa.: Stackpole Books, 2004.

Ervin, Robert E. *The John Hunt Morgan Raid of 1863.* Jackson, Ohio: Jackson County Historical Society, 2003.

Foster, John M. "A Futile Resistance: The Response to Morgan's Raid in Indiana, July 8–13, 1863." Unpublished master's thesis, University of Indianapolis, 2003.

Gorin, Betty J. *"Morgan is Coming!": Confederate Raiders in the Heart of Kentucky.* Louisville, Ky.: Harmony House Publishers, 2006.

Sanders, Stuart W. "A Little Fight between Friends and Family." *Civil War Times Illustrated* 40, no. 5 (2001): 40–44, 66.

Smith, Derek. *The Gallant Dead: Union and Confederate Generals Killed in the Civil War.* Mechanicsburg, Pa.: Stackpole Books, 2005.

Mosby, John S. (1833–1916)
Confederate partisan

John Singleton Mosby was born in Edgemont, Virginia, on December 6, 1833, the son of farmers. He enrolled at the University of Virginia at 15, had an altercation with a bully, and shot him. After serving six months in jail, he studied law and was eventually admitted to the bar in Bristol County, Virginia. When the Civil War broke out in April 1861, Mosby joined the 1st Virginia Cavalry as a private. He fought at Bull Run that July before joining General J. E. B. STUART as a scout and originated the strategy of "riding around" the army of General George B. McCLELLAN during the 1862 Peninsula campaign. Mosby advanced to lieutenant that December and pushed hard for an independent command of rangers to harry Union detachments throughout Loudoun County. Permission was granted in February 1863, and Mosby commenced his soon to be legendary operations with only nine men.

A talented raider, Mosby quickly established himself as the bane of Union rear areas with his sudden attacks and equally quick escapes. He accomplished this by hand-picking his officers, strictly disciplining all ranks, and refraining from the cruel practices usually associated with other Southern partisans. Great emphasis was placed on rapidity of movement, followed by quick dispersion to prearranged regrouping sites. The men were also self-sufficient, bringing their own clothing and weapons, and always divided up captured spoils between them. Mosby's command was thus highly cohesive and tightly knit, and his men deemed no target too daunting for their small-scale, hit-and-run tactics. He underscored this fact on March 9, 1863, when, with only 29 men, he stole past Union sentries at Fair-

Confederate partisan John S. Mosby *(Library of Congress)*

fax Court House, awakened General Edwin H. Stoughton with a slap to his backside, and seized him along with 33 men and 58 horses. Mosby then rose to captain and major following another successful action near Chantilly. Throughout the Gettysburg campaign of July 1863, his men fed General Robert E. LEE a steady stream of accurate military intelligence, while his band of irregulars were incorporated into the Confederate army as Company A, 43rd Battalion, Partisan Rangers. Mosby then continued raiding Union outposts with near impunity, rising to lieutenant colonel in February 1864. His endeavors proved so galling to Union authorities that General George A. CUSTER hanged several partisans as brigands. Mosby countered by hanging several of Custer's men in retaliation, at which point the practice ceased on both sides.

By the fall of 1864, Mosby's rangers constituted the only organized resistance to Union forces in northern Virginia. With such speed and ease did he continue his slashing operations throughout Londoun and Fauquier counties that the region became known informally as "Mosby's Confederacy." In November 1864 an exasperated general Philip H. SHERIDAN dispatched Captain Richard Blazer and 100 Union scouts, armed with the latest Spencer repeating rifles, to eliminate the threat. However, Mosby easily ambushed and captured Blazer's detachment at Kabletown, Virginia, on November 18, 1864. It is estimated that no less than 30,000 Union soldiers became tied down hunting for the elusive raiders. General Ulysses S. GRANT vowed to hang Mosby without trial if he were caught. However, Mosby evaded capture, rose to colonel in December 1864, and continued harassing Union troops successfully until the end of the war. Rather than surrender his command, now numbering 1,900 men, the "Gray Ghost" simply disbanded them and they went home.

Mosby returned to his home a war hero, and he resumed his legal practice in Salem, Virginia. However, he became an anathema to former Confederates by joining the Republican Party and campaigning for President Grant. The admiration between Grant and Mosby proved mutual, and Grant elevated his former adversary to several posts within the government. In 1878 President Rutherford B. Hayes, another Civil War veteran, appointed Mosby U.S. consul to Hong Kong, where he remained until 1885. From 1904 to 1910, he served as assistant general in the State Department before dying at Warrenton, Virginia, on May 30, 1916. In terms of results, Mosby is probably the most successful partisan fighter in American history.

Further Reading

Ashdown, Paul. *The Mosby Myth: A Confederate Hero in Life and Legend.* Wilmington, Del.: Scholarly Resources, 2002.

Black, Robert W. *Cavalry Raids of the Civil War.* Mechanicsburg, Pa.: Stackpole Books, 2004.

Brown, Peter A. *Mosby's Fighting Parson: The Life and Times of Sam Chapman.* Westminster, Md.: Willow Bend Books, 2001.

Mackey, Robert R. *The Uncivil War: Irregular Warfare in the Upper South, 1861–1865.* Norman: University of Oklahoma Press, 2004.

Mosby, John S. *Take Sides with the Truth: The Postwar Letters of John Singleton Mosby to Samuel F. Chapman.* Lexington University Press of Kentucky, 2007.

Ramage, James A. *Gray Ghost: The Life of Colonel John Singleton Mosby.* Lexington: University Press of Kentucky, 1999.

P

Pemberton, John C. (1814–1881)

Confederate general

John Clifford Pemberton was born in Philadelphia, Pennsylvania, on August 10, 1814, the son of a successful businessman. He was well educated by tutors and briefly attended the University of Pennsylvania before transferring to the U.S. Military Academy in 1833. Pemberton graduated four years later as a second lieutenant in the 4th U.S. Infantry, and he saw service in Florida's Second Seminole War up through 1839. That year, he commenced a wide-ranging tour of garrison duty along the coast and frontiers. In 1846 he joined General Zachary Taylor's Army of Occupation and served as an aide to General William J. Worth during initial phases of the Mexican War. The following year, Pemberton transferred to General Winfield SCOTT's army, winning brevet promotions to captain and major for gallantry at Churubusco, Molino del Rey, and Chapultepec. After the war, he was stationed at Fortress Monroe, Virginia, and he married into a prominent family. Thereafter, his personal and political orientation became wedded to the South. He resumed garrison duties on the western frontier, rose to captain, and in 1858 accompanied Colonel Albert S. JOHNSTON's Mormon expedition. Pemberton was serving at Fort Ridgely, Minnesota, in the spring of 1861 when the rising tide of secession—and family ties—convinced him to resign his commission and proffer his services to the Confederacy. This decision was roundly condemned by his family in Philadelphia, and two younger brothers joined the Union army.

Pemberton held various regimental grades until June 1861, when he advanced to brigadier general and was assigned to the defenses of Norfolk, Virginia. The following February 1862, he transferred to the Department of South Carolina, Georgia, and Florida as a major general to replace General Robert E. LEE. Pemberton proved himself to be a hard worker and a skilled engineer, and he constructed Battery Wagner, which proved so essential to the defense of Charleston, South Carolina. However, he was impolitic for suggesting that Fort Sumter, where secessionism began, be considered next to useless. He also went on record as stating that he would abandon his department rather than allow his small army to be captured. A firestorm of criticism erupted in the press, and at length President Jefferson DAVIS, mindful of Pemberton's status as a Northerner, removed him from command. But later that year, the tactless leader gained promotion to lieutenant general and he was entrusted with the Department of Mississippi and East Louisiana. Here, Pemberton's overriding concern was keeping the bastions of Vicksburg, Mississippi, and Port Hudson, Louisiana, in Southern hands.

Pemberton arrived in Vicksburg in November 1862, displacing General Earl VAN DORN, and he immediately set about strengthening its defenses.

An energetic leader, he also dispatched General William W. Loring along the Tallahatchie River to construct Fort Pemberton and help cover backwater approaches to the city. In December 1862 Pemberton ordered Confederate cavalry under General Earl Van Dorn to raid Union supplies at Holly Springs, Mississippi; the resulting destruction forced General Ulysses S. Grant to postpone his impending Vicksburg campaign by several months. Pemberton also took measures to defend the city's northern approaches along Chickasaw Bluffs, and he bloodily repelled determined attacks by General William T. Sherman. His impressive success seemed to underscore Vicksburg's reputation for being unassailable.

Confederate fortunes declined precipitously in the spring of 1863 when Grant finally launched an attack by passing gunboats under Admiral David D. Porter below the city, while he marched his army down the west bank of the Mississippi River and crossed it. He had also ordered Union cavalry under Colonel Benjamin H. Grierson to conduct a large-scale diversionary raid from Tennessee to Baton Rouge, Louisiana, to confuse the defenders. As anticipated, Pemberton was distracted by Grierson and failed to sortie against Grant in the field. Once General Joseph E. Johnston had been driven from the capital of Jackson, Grant swerved west and attacked Pemberton at Champion's Hill and Big Black River on May 16–17, 1863, routing him. All the while Pemberton was also saddled with conflicting orders: Johnston ordered him to quit the city and save his army while President Davis insisted that he stay and fight. When Pemberton chose the latter course, he was shut up quickly by Grant's besieging forces. His Confederates turned back two strong Union assaults but then endured six weeks of close confinement and heavy bombardment. Faced with starvation, he finally surrendered Vicksburg and 30,000 soldiers unconditionally to Grant on July 4, 1863. He thus became an object of intense loathing in the Southern press despite the fact that, on balance, Pemberton had performed well against steep odds.

Once exchanged, Pemberton never again received a field command, ostensibly because Southern troops, more suspicious than ever of his Northern roots, threatened to mutiny rather than serve under him. He therefore resigned his general's commission and spent the remainder of the war as a lieutenant colonel and ordnance inspector in Richmond. He performed well in this capacity before surrendering with Johnston's army in April 1865. Afterward, Pemberton tried his luck at farming in Virginia and failed, so in 1876 he relocated his family back to Philadelphia. He died in Penllyn, Pennsylvania, on July 13, 1881, a talented and well-meaning military leader, transformed by bad luck into one of the most reviled figures of Confederate history.

Further Reading
Ballard, Michael B. *Vicksburg: The Campaign That Opened the Mississippi.* Chapel Hill: University of North Carolina Press, 2004.
Cotton, Gordon A., and Jeff T. Giambrone. *Vicksburg and the War.* Gretna, La.: Pelican Publishing, 2004.
Heathcote, T. A. *Vicksburg.* London: Brassey's, 2004.
Isbell, Timothy T. *Vicksburg: Sentinels of Stone.* Jackson: University Press of Mississippi, 2006.
Shea, William L., and Terrence J. Winschel. *Vicksburg Is the Key: The Struggle for the Mississippi.* Lincoln: University of Nebraska Press, 2003.
Smith, Timothy B. *Champion Hill: Decisive Battle for Vicksburg.* New York: Savas Beatie, 2005.
Winschel, Terrence J. *Triumph and Defeat: The Vicksburg Campaign.* New York: Savas Beatie, 2004.

Pickett, George E. (1825–1875)
Confederate general

George Edward Pickett was born in Richmond, Virginia, on January 25, 1825, the son of prosperous planters. He briefly read law before gaining admittance to the U.S. Military Academy in 1842. Pickett demonstrated slovenly academics and graduated at the very bottom of his famous class in 1846, alongside future luminaries such as George B. McClellan and Thomas J. Jackson. Thereafter, he served as a second lieutenant in the 8th U.S. Infantry in the army of General Winfield Scott during the advance on Mexico City. Pickett conducted himself bravely at the siege of Veracruz and the battles of Contreras and Churubusco, winning brevet promotions to lieutenant and captain. After performing garrison duty in Texas (1849–56), he shipped off for similar work in Washington Territory. In 1859 Pickett singlehandedly confronted three British warships contesting American possession of San Juan Island with only his company of infantry. War was averted through diplomacy, but he emerged as a national hero and was placed in charge of American forces on the island through 1861. When the Civil War erupted that April, he resigned his commission and returned to Virginia as a colonel in the Confederate service.

For many months into the war, Pickett was employed securing the defenses of the Rappahannock region, and, in January 1862, he rose to brigadier general. He then joined General James LONGSTREET's division in time for the Peninsula campaign. Pickett bravely conducted his "Gamecock brigade" at Williamsburg, Fair Oaks, and Gaines's Mill, where he fell severely wounded. Several months of recuperation ensued, but at the instigation of Longstreet, he rose to major general in October 1862. In this capacity, he commanded a division in Longstreet's I Corps at Fredericksburg, acquitting himself well during the bloody business of December 13, 1862. In the spring of 1863, he accompanied Longstreet on his failed campaign in Suffolk, Virginia, and he thus missed the decisive events at Chancellorsville that May. He then advanced with General Robert E. LEE into Pennsylvania in time to fight at Gettysburg. Pickett arrived on the battlefield on the evening of July 2, 1863, and his fresh troops were chosen to spearhead a massive Confederate charge against General George G. MEADE's center along Cemetery Ridge. Southern artillery under General Edward P. ALEXANDER bombarded the Union lines for several hours, unfortunately with little effect, and then Pickett's division advanced alongside that of General James J. Pettigrew and two brigades under General William D. Pender, a total of 15,000 veteran troops. As the men in parade-like fashion crossed a mile-long clearing, they fell under concentrated artillery and rifle fire from General Winfield S. HANCOCK's men, who simply cut them down in droves. A few determined survivors managed to penetrate Union lines briefly before being swept back, and Pickett withdrew with 10,000 casualties. His defeat, commonly regarded as "Pickett's Charge," is generally acknowledged as the high tide of Confederate military fortunes.

Defeat did not diminish Pickett's reputation as a fighting commander, and in the spring of 1864, he assumed command of the Department of Virginia and North Carolina. Thus disposed, he made a failed attempt to capture New Bern, North Carolina, from Union forces. He also gained considerable notoriety by summarily hanging 22 Southern deserters captured in Union uniforms. Thereafter

Confederate general George E. Pickett *(Library of Congress)*

Pickett returned to Virginia, and he helped bottle up the Union Army of the James under General Benjamin F. Butler at Bermuda Hundred in May 1864. He then apparently suffered from a spell of what would be diagnosed today as combat fatigue and was replaced by General Pierre G. T. Beauregard. After recovering, Pickett was posted on the extreme right of the Confederate siege lines at Petersburg, where, on March 31, 1865, he masterfully repulsed a determined attack by Federal cavalry under General Philip H. Sheridan at Dinwiddie Court House. The next day, April 1, 1865, however, he singularly erred by attending a shad bake several miles to the rear with General Fitzhugh Lee, just as Sheridan renewed his assault at Five Forks. Deprived of leadership, Confederate defenses buckled, and Lee was forced to abandon Richmond hastily to escape encirclement. Pickett saw additional fighting at Sayler's Creek on April 6, 1865; then Lee finally relieved him of command. He surrendered at Appomattox Court House with the main army three days later.

Pickett fled to Canada after the war to avoid prosecution for executing the Confederate deserters. Declining an invitation to serve in the armies of the khedive of Egypt, he returned to Virginia under a general amnesty and entered the insurance industry. Pickett also engaged in a lengthy written battle to clear his reputation and openly blamed General Lee for the destruction of his division at Gettysburg. He died in Norfolk, Virginia, on October 25, 1875, an unquestionably brave officer, yet indelibly associated with two of the worst defeats in Confederate military history.

Further Reading

Alexander, Robert. *Five Forks: Waterloo of the Confederacy: A Civil War Narrative.* East Lansing: Michigan State University Press, 2003.
Gordon, Lesley J. *General George Pickett in Life and Legend.* Chapel Hill: University of North Carolina Press, 1998.
Hess, Earl J. *Pickett's Charge—The Last Attack at Gettysburg.* Chapel Hill: University of North Carolina Press, 2001.
Robbins, James S. *Last in Their Class: Custer, Pickett, and the Goats of West Point.* New York: Encounter Books, 2006.
Rollins, Richard, ed. *Pickett's Charge: Eyewitness Accounts at Gettysburg.* Mechanicsburg, Pa.: Stackpole Books, 2005.
Wert, Jeffrey D. *Gettysburg: Day Three.* New York: Simon and Schuster, 2001.

Pillow, Gideon J. (1806–1878)
Confederate general

Gideon Johnson Pillow was born in Williamson, Tennessee, on June 8, 1806, into a family of planters. After graduating from the University of Tennessee in 1827, he studied law and was admitted to the state bar three years later. Pillow, adept as an attorney and a Democratic Party operative, also developed an interest in politics and struck up a successful partnership with fellow lawyer James K. Polk. He played a direct role in securing the party nomination for Polk in 1844, and, two years later, President Polk appointed Pillow a brigadier general of volunteers for the ongoing Mexican War. He initially served as part of General Zachary Taylor's army in Texas, but the general declined to employ his troops. Pillow then transferred to General Winfield Scott's army during the campaign to Mexico City, where he composed several letters criticizing his Whig commander for the president's consideration. In fact, Pillow regarded himself as Polk's personal representative. Scott disliked Pillow in kind, especially after he botched his first combat assignment at Cerro Gordo on April 17, 1847. He nonetheless used political connections to secure promotion to major general and turned in respectable performances at Contreras, Churubusco, and Chapultepec, where he was wounded. However, Pillow used poor judgment by anonymously publishing critical essays about Scott in the *New Orleans Daily Delta*, whereupon he was arrested and court-martialed for insubordination. Pillow, ably defended by John C. Breckinridge, was eventually cleared of all charges, but the affair sullied his reputation. After the war, he returned to Tennessee to resume delving into politics.

A staunch Democratic, Pillow did not favor secession and worked to moderate calls for separation. He remained loyal to the Union until Tennessee seceded in the spring of 1861, whereupon Governor Isham G. Harris appointed him a major general of state forces. President Jefferson DAVIS, never previously impressed by Pillow's ability as a soldier, allowed him to become a brigadier general in the Confederate service the following July. In this capacity, he reported for service under General Leonidas POLK in the western part of the state. There, Pillow eagerly sought to invade nearby Kentucky and seize it for the Confederacy, which he accomplished on September 4, 1861, by occupying and fortifying Columbus. The move was roundly condemned by the Kentucky state legislature, heretofore neutral, which then threw its support behind the Union. On November 7, 1861, Pillow next fought under Polk at the Battle of Belmont, Missouri, in which Federal troops under General Ulysses S. GRANT were defeated and forced back to Illinois. His performance here seemed to enhance his military reputation, and in February 1862, Pillow received command of strategic Fort Donelson on the Cumberland River.

In the spring of 1862, the aggressive Grant set his sights on Forts Henry and Donelson to open up a waterborne invasion of the Confederate heartland. On February 6, 1862, a Union gunboat flotilla under Captain Andrew H. FOOTE cowed Fort Henry into submission as Grant prepared to march overland to Pillow's position at Fort Donelson. Grant knew Pillow from their Mexican War days and thoroughly despised him. Worse, on February 13, 1862, Pillow also was superseded by General John B. FLOYD just as the fort was being surrounded by Grant's forces. The two Confederate leaders bickered about what to do next, and Pillow prevailed on both Floyd and General Simon B. Buckner to cut their way through Union siege lines and escape. On February 15, 1862, the Confederates accomplished exactly that and were on the verge of escaping when Pillow inexplicably lost his nerve and ordered the men back to the fort! Grant then promptly sealed the defenders off within their works. At a council of war held that evening, both Pillow and Floyd elected to abandon their command and leave Buckner to surrender the fort. Colonel Nathan B. FORREST was so disgusted by such wanton cowardice that he galloped his cavalry regiment through Union lines and escaped. On December 16, 1862, Buckner surrendered 15,000 badly needed troops to Grant, opening up an invasion route that ultimately spelled doom for the Confederacy.

President Davis was appreciably livid when he was apprised of what Pillow and Floyd had done, and both were summarily relieved. A court of inquiry found the former guilty of "grave errors of judgment," but he was eventually restored to command a brigade in the division of his old friend General Breckinridge. He then fought at the bloody Battle of Murfreesboro on January 2, 1863, performing adequately. The government next reassigned him as superintendent of the Conscript Bureau for Alabama, Mississippi, and Tennessee. Pillow ran his department with an iron fist and ruthlessly rounded up thousands of new soldiers. In March 1864 he requested command of a cavalry force to protect the iron and coal regions of central Alabama from marauding Union raiders, but he mishandled several encounters that summer and was relieved a second time. Pillow ended the war as commissary general of prisoners, and he surrendered to Union authorities at Montgomery on May 5, 1865.

The postwar period found Pillow a ruined man, and despite resumption of his successful law career in Memphis, he was overwhelmed by debts in 1876 and relocated to Lee County, Arkansas, to escape them. He lived there for several years as a subsistence farmer until his death in Helena on October 8, 1878. Pillow's command of Confederate forces had been rather brief, overall, but his tenure manifested disastrous consequences for the South.

Further Reading
Cooling, Benjamin F. "Lew Wallace and Gideon Pillow: Enigmas and Variations on an American Theme." *Lincoln Herald* 84 (1981): 651–658.

Gott, Kendall D. *Where the South Lost the War: An Analysis of the Fort Henry–Fort Donelson Campaign, February 1862*. Mechanicsburg, Pa.: Stackpole Books, 2003.

Hughes, Nathaniel C., and Roy P. Stonesifer. *The Life and Wars of Gideon J. Pillow*. Chapel Hill: University of North Carolina Press, 1993.

Roberts, Donald J. "Belmont: Grant's First Battle." *Military Heritage* 2, no. 6 (2001): 40–49.

Symonds, Craig, et al. "Who Were the Worst Ten Generals?" *North & South* 7, no. 3 (2004): 12–25.

Tucker, Spencer C. *"Unconditional Surrender": The Captures of Forts Henry and Donelson*. Abilene, Tex.: McWhiney Foundation, 2001.

Pleasonton, Alfred (1824–1897)

Union general

Alfred Pleasonton was born in Washington, D.C., on June 7, 1824, the son of President James Monroe's personal secretary. He matriculated at the U.S. Military Academy in 1840 and graduated near the top of his class four years later. Pleasonton then served as a second lieutenant in the 2nd U.S. Dragoons and served a number of frontier and garrison assignments. During the Mexican War, he accompanied the army of General Zachary Taylor and won a brevet promotion for gallantry at the battles of Palo Alto and Resaca de la Palma in 1846. Afterward, he remained with his regiment in the New Mexico Territory, rising there to adjutant. He advanced to captain in 1855 and served under General William S. Harney through a number of Indian conflicts in Florida, Kansas, Oregon, and Washington Territory. Following the onset of the Civil War in April 1861, he helped conduct his regiment, renamed the 2nd U.S. Cavalry, from Utah to Washington, D.C. Pleasonton became a major in the spring of 1862, fought capably in General George B. McLellan's Peninsula campaign, and won promotion to brigadier general of volunteers as of July. In this capacity, he rendered additional useful services at Second Manassas, South Mountain, and Antietam; while an aggressive leader, he proved less successful at gathering military intelligence.

On May 2, 1863, Pleasonton garnered additional distinction at the Union debacle of Chan-

Union general Alfred Pleasanton *(Library of Congress)*

cellorsville, where he successfully contested the advance of General Thomas J. Jackson's Confederates and rescued the remnants of General Oliver O. Howard's IX Corps. Shortly afterward, General Joseph Hooker appointed him chief of cavalry in the Army of the Potomac to replace the indifferent general George Stoneman. When General Robert E. Lee commenced his second invasion of the North that June, Pleasonton was dispatched to locate his whereabouts and report. On June 9, 1863, his troopers under Generals John Buford and Hugh J. Kilpatrick surprised the vaunted Confederate cavalry of General J. E. B. Stuart in camp at Brandy Station and nearly defeated them. Union forces ultimately relinquished the field, but the action served notice that Pleasonton's vigorous leadership had rendered his cavalry a force to reckon with. On June 22, 1863, he advanced to major general of volunteers and next performed valuable services throughout the three-day engagement at Gettysburg (July 1–3, 1863). Pleasonton again aggressively engaged his Southern counterparts but generally failed to distinguish himself in an intelligence-gathering capacity.

As an officer, Pleasonton was personally fearless, outspoken, and possessed a unique flair for self-promotion in the news media. His career entered a new phase after March 1864 when he publicly criticized the conduct of General George G. MEADE before the Joint Congressional Committee on the Conduct of the War—and he immediately found himself transferred to the nether regions. Pleasonton landed in the remote Department of Missouri as cavalry commander under General William S. ROSECRANS. He arrived in time to contest a large Confederate offensive under General Sterling PRICE, and he kept Price from capturing the capital of Jefferson City (October 8–22). Pleasonton then worked closely with Union forces under General Samuel R. CURTIS to corner Price at Westport, Missouri, where, in a series of battles along the Little Blue, Big Blue, and Marais des Cygnes rivers, the Southerners were defeated soundly and driven back to Arkansas. More damage might have been inflicted on Price had Pleasonton and Curtis not quarreled over the victory and mounted an effective pursuit. He nevertheless received additional brevets to brigadier and major general in the regular army for his fine service.

In the postwar period, Pleasonton reverted back to his lineal rank of lieutenant colonel in the 20th U.S. Infantry, where he resented serving under officers whom he had previously commanded. He resigned his commission in January 1868 and accepted several low-level positions within the federal government. In 1870 he briefly served as commissioner of Internal Revenue, and from 1872 to 1874, he served as president of the Cincinnati and Terre Haute Railroad. Pleasonton died in Washington, D.C., on February 17, 1897, a capable combat leader and the individual most responsible for improving the performance and morale of the cavalry in the Army of the Potomac.

Under his tenure, Federal troopers were able to meet Confederate cavalry on equal terms for the first time in the war.

Further Reading

Crouch, Richard E. *Brandy Station: A Battle Like No Other.* Westminster, Md.: Willow Bend Books, 2002.

Longacre, Edward G. "The Knight of Romance." *Civil War Times Illustrated* 13, no. 8 (1974): 10–23.

———. *Lincoln's Cavalrymen: A History of the Mounted Forces of the Army of the Potomac, 1861–1865.* Mechanicsburg, Pa.: Stackpole Books, 2000.

McKinney, Joseph W. *Brandy Station, Virginia, June 9, 1863: The Largest Cavalry Battle of the Civil War.* Jefferson, N.C.: McFarland, 2006.

Monnett, Howard N. *Action before Westport, 1864.* Niwot: University Press of Colorado, 1994.

Wittenberg, Eric J. *The Union Cavalry Comes of Age: Hartwood Church to Brandy Station, 1863.* Dulles, Va.: Brassey's, 2005.

Polk, Leonidas (1806–1864)

Confederate general

Leonidas Polk was born in Raleigh, North Carolina, on April 10, 1806, the son of affluent planters. After briefly attending the University of North Carolina, he transferred to the U.S. Military Academy in 1823, where he met and befriended future Confederate leaders Jefferson DAVIS, Joseph E. JOHNSTON, and Albert S. JOHNSTON. While in attendance, Polk came under the sway of the academy chaplain and acquired a profound sense of religiosity. He graduated near the top of his class in 1827 as a second lieutenant of artillery but resigned within a year to pursue religious studies. He next attended the Virginia Theological Seminary and was ordained an Episcopal minister in April 1830. After several years of preaching in Richmond, Polk gained an appointment as bishop of the Southwest, with a circuit that included Louisiana, Alabama, Mississippi, and Arkansas. Charismatic and convivial, he enjoyed considerable success spreading the Episcopal message in this thinly populated region, and, in 1841, he became the first bishop of Louisiana. By this time,

Polk, who had married into a wealthy, slave-owning family, had matured into a fiery Southern nationalist. Polk felt strongly that the South needed its own university to expunge itself of various "Yankee" beliefs and influences. During the years, he therefore collected $500,000 and received a 9,500-acre land grant in Sewanee, Tennessee. On October 9, 1860, he personally laid the cornerstone for what emerged as the University of the South, which finally opened its doors in 1868.

As the secession crisis mounted in the spring of 1861, Polk tendered his services to President Davis, who commissioned him a major general in the Confederate service. He was entrusted with Department No. 2, encompassing western Tennessee, eastern Arkansas, and the Mississippi River throughout that region. But Polk, though ambitious, was neither strategic-minded nor politically astute. On September 4, 1861, he erred grievously by dispatching General Gideon J. PILLOW to seize the heights of Columbus, Kentucky, and deny it to Union forces. This move not only angered the Kentucky government, which up until then had been studiously neutral but also forced them to declare their allegiance to the Federal government. This, in turn, facilitated Union moves to secure the headwaters of the Cumberland and Tennessee rivers, which constituted major invasion routes into the Southern heartland. Such subtleties were totally lost on Polk, who went on to attack and defeat a small Union thrust under General Ulysses S. GRANT at Belmont, Missouri, on November 7, 1861.

After the fall of Forts Henry and Donelson in the spring of 1862, Polk withdrew from Kentucky and joined his former West Point roommate, General Albert S. Johnston, at Corinth, Mississippi. There, he assumed command of the I Corps, Army of Mississippi and bravely conducted affairs on the Southern right wing throughout the bloody encounter of Shiloh in April 1862. He then served under Johnston's successor, General Braxton BRAGG, in the same capacity. However, Polk disliked Bragg intensely, and he soon headed the anti-Bragg faction within the western high com-

mand. Nonetheless, on October 8, 1862, Polk behaved competently in the Battle of Perryville, winning promotion to lieutenant general. He next fought at the Confederate defeat of Murfreesboro (December 3, 1862–January 3, 1863), earning scorn from Bragg for allegedly delaying his orders to attack. He fought bravely, however, and at one point mistakenly rode up to the 22nd Indiana Infantry. Polk rather dramatically convinced them that he was actually a Union general; then he spurred his horse and escaped. But command relations with Bragg finally ruptured following the costly Southern victory at Chickamauga on September 19–20, 1863, when Polk was court-martialed for failing to attack as ordered. Polk, meanwhile, used his influence with Davis to undercut Bragg and agitated to have him removed as head of the Army of Tennessee. To maintain peace among his feuding commanders, Davis appointed Polk to succeed General Joseph E. Johnston as head of the Department of Alabama, Mississippi, and East Louisiana.

In January 1864, Polk's Army of Mississippi proved unable to contain a Union offensive by General William T. SHERMAN, which captured Meridian, Mississippi. He then marched east to unite with Johnston's Army of Tennessee in time to oppose the Union march on Atlanta. Polk fought bravely in the various battles that failed to stem the Union advance, and he remained a popular figure with his troops. On June 14, 1864, while reconnoitering Federals positions near Pine Mountain, Georgia, he was struck by a Union cannon shell and killed. Polk, though hailed by his soldiers as the "Fighting Bishop," was at best a marginally competent commander who owed his high rank more to political connections than to ability.

Further Reading

Jones, Wilmer L. *Generals in Blue and Gray*. 2 vols. Westport, Conn.: Praeger, 2004.

Noe, Kenneth. *Perryville: This Grand Havoc of Battle*. Lexington: University Press of Kentucky, 2001.

Roberts, Donald J. "Belmont: Grant's First Battle." *Military Heritage* 2, no. 6 (2001): 40–49.

Robins, Glenn. *The Bishop of the Old South: The Ministry and Civil War Legacy of Leonidas Polk.* Macon, Ga: Mercer University Press, 2006.

Smith, Derek. *The Gallant Dead: Union and Confederate Generals Killed in the Civil War.* Mechanicsburg, Pa.: Stackpole Books, 2005.

Woodworth, Steven E. *No Band of Brothers: Problems in the Rebel High Command.* Columbia: University of Missouri Press, 1999.

Pope, John (1822–1892)

Union general

John Pope was born in Louisville, Kentucky, on March 16, 1822, the son of a judge. He entered the U.S. Military Academy in 1838 and graduated four years later as a second lieutenant in the Topographical Engineers. Pope then conducted survey work along the Canadian border and in Florida before joining the army of General Zachary Taylor in Texas. He subsequently fought well in the Mexican War, winning brevet promotions for bravery at the battles of Monterrey and Buena Vista. He then resumed his survey work on the western frontier, rising to captain in 1856 and serving as chief engineer of the Department of New Mexico. When the Civil War broke out in April 1861, he was performing light-house duty and became one of four army officers chosen to escort President Abraham LINCOLN from Springfield, Illinois, to Washington, D.C. In May 1861 Pope was elevated to the rank of brigadier general of volunteers and assigned to the Department of Missouri. An aggressive officer, he trounced Confederates under General Sterling PRICE at Blackwater on December 18, 1861, seizing 1,200 prisoners. Pope also worked behind the scenes to have the inept general John C. Frémont removed as commander of Missouri. In the spring of 1862, newly arrived general Henry W. HALLECK appointed Pope commander of the Army of the Mississippi with orders to clear Confederate forces out of the region. He then methodically besieged New Madrid, Missouri, taking it on March 14, 1862, before moving on to heavily defended Island No. 10 in the Mississippi River. Here, he worked closely with a gunboat flo-

tilla under Captain Andrew H. FOOTE and cut a canal to allow armed vessels to pass below the island and sever it from the mainland. Consequently. Island No. 10 surrendered along with 3,500 prisoners on April 7, 1862. This victory cleared the upper reaches of the Mississippi to Union navigation as far south as Memphis, Tennessee, and Pope received a well-deserved promotion to major general. His Army of the Mississippi then joined General Ulysses S. GRANT's Army of the Tennessee and General Don C. BUELL's Army of the Ohio in Halleck's campaign against Corinth, Mississippi. Pope's good conduct also caught the attention of President Lincoln, who was anxious to replace the lethargic general George B. McCLELLAN as commander of Union forces in the East. In June 1862 he arrived in the Shenandoah Valley to assume command of the newly created Army of Virginia, succeeding his old nemesis Frémont. But rather then cement cordial relations with officers

Union general John Pope *(National Archives)*

in the Army of the Potomac, he alienated them by bombastically bragging about his victories in the West.

In August 1861, Pope commanded 70,000 men and began a cautious campaign against Richmond, Virginia. His advance was supposed to be supported by McClellan, still smarting over his recent removal from command and whose cooperation proved sullen. General Robert E. LEE used their unsynchronized movements to his advantage by dispatching half of his force under General Thomas J. JACKSON on a raid around Pope's right flank. On August 27, 1862, Jackson stormed into Pope's supply base at Manchester, Virginia, and then dug in and awaited the Union riposte. Pope, thinking that he had Jackson trapped, moved most of his army up to the old Manassas battlefield and began to attack his outnumbered adversary. He was unaware that Lee had dispatched the other half of his army under General James LONGSTREET through Thoroughfare Gap, which completely flanked the Union position. On August 29–30, 1862, while Pope contented himself with piecemeal attacks against Jackson's line, Longstreet suddenly lunged and began to roll up the Union line. Pope's forces recovered from their initial surprise and fell back in good order, heavily repelling an attack by Jackson at Chantilly on September 1, 1862. But another Union army had been humbled by Lee, and President Lincoln was forced to relieve Pope from command. Before leaving, he fixed the blame for his defeat squarely on General Fitz John PORTER, a McClellan ally, and likewise had him removed from command and cashiered. The Army of Virginia was then dissolved and command reverted back to General McClellan.

Thoroughly disgraced, Pope was reassigned to the Department of the Northwest, where he helped suppress an uprising by the Santee Sioux under Little Crow. In January 1865 he assumed command of the Department of the Mississippi while the rank of major general was conferred two months later. Pope subsequently served a stint in reconstruction duty in Alabama, Georgia, and Florida, where he championed civil rights for for-

mer African-American slaves. He then returned to the western frontier where, during the next two decades, he gradually rehabilitated his military reputation as an outstanding administrator. In this capacity, Pope, like Generals George CROOK, Benjamin H. GRIERSON, and Oliver O. HOWARD argued for better treatment of Native Americans to keep the peace and excoriated the graft and corruption of the Indian Bureau. He retired as commander of the Department of California in March 1886 and died at Sandusky, Ohio, on September 23, 1892. Pope was an effective military figure whose skill at bureaucracy always outdistanced his combat abilities.

Further Reading

Cozzens, Peter. *General John Pope: A Life for the Nation.* Urbana: University of Illinois Press, 2000.

———. "Roadblock on the Mississippi." *Civil War Times Illustrated* 41, no. 1 (2002): 40–49.

Cozzens, Peter, and Robert I. Girardi, eds. *The Military Memoirs of General John Pope.* Chapel Hill: University of North Carolina Press, 1998.

Langellier, John P. *Second Manassas, 1862: Robert E. Lee's Greatest Victory.* Westport, Conn.: Praeger, 2004.

Martin, David G. *The Second Bull Run Campaign, July–August 1862.* Cambridge, Mass.: Da Capo Press, 2001.

Shur, Robert C. "Cracking the Nut of Island No. 10." *Military Heritage* 7, no. 1 (2005): 64–71, 77.

Porter, David D. (1813–1891)
Union admiral

David Dixon Porter was born in Chester, Pennsylvania, on June 8, 1813, a son of Commodore David Porter, a naval hero of the War of 1812. His eminent family included foster brother David G. FARRAGUT, the future admiral, while his cousin Fitz John PORTER was a noted general. Porter went to sea at an early age with his father and was educated indifferently. He followed his father into the Mexican navy in 1826, being wounded and captured by Spanish forces. In 1829 he finally joined the U.S. Navy as a midshipman and completed several Mediterranean cruises. Promotion was slow, however, and Porter was only a lieutenant when the Mexican War broke out in 1846. He nonetheless distinguished himself onboard the steamer *Spitfire* and led a naval detachment that captured the town of Tabasco in June 1847. He remained barely employed during the postwar period and nearly quit the service to engage in merchant ship enterprises. Porter was reinstated to active status in 1855 and commanded the USS *Supply* to bring camels to Texas at the behest of Secretary of War Jefferson DAVIS. After 1857, he served as commandant of the Portsmouth, New Hampshire, Navy Yard, remaining there until 1861. After serving almost two decades as a lieutenant, Porter was ready to leave the navy altogether until the onset of the Civil War in April convinced him to remain in the service.

No sooner had the firing commenced than Porter, a highly aggressive, enterprising personality with considerable skill at self-promotion, advanced a bold scheme for the relief of Fort Pickens, Florida. When President Abraham LINCOLN personally approved of the plan, Porter, accompanied by Captain Montgomery C. MEIGS, sailed with the USS *Powhatan* and successfully reinforced the garrison there. En route, he ignored recall signals from Secretary of the Navy Gideon Welles, who had not been privy to the planning, and thereafter he distrusted Porter intensely. Nonetheless Porter rose to commander as of August 1861, and now part of the West Gulf Coast Blockading Squadron, he threw himself energetically into planning the capture of New Orleans, Louisiana. Moreover, he played a crucial role in convincing the government to assign his Southern-born foster brother, Farragut, to orchestrate the campaign. In April 1862 Porter led 20 mortar boats that helped bombard Forts St. Philip and Jackson into submission two days after New Orleans fell to Farragut. After receiving the thanks of Congress, Porter accompanied his brother up the Mississippi River to Vicksburg, Mississippi, which would occupy his attention for more than a year. In October 1862 he also succeeded Admiral Charles H. DAVIS as head of the Mississippi River Squadron, and he was pro-

Union admiral David D. Porter *(Library of Congress)*

moted acting rear admiral over the heads of 80 more senior officers. The headstrong Porter also worked closely with two other forceful personalities, Generals William T. SHERMAN and Ulysses S. GRANT, in the campaigns that followed, establishing a splendid precedent for combined operations in the war.

In January 1863 Porter gave naval support to General John A. McClernand's campaign against Fort Hindman, Arkansas, in another display of joint operations. But his greatest contribution came on April 16, 1863, when he ran his squadron past the batteries of Vicksburg and subsequently transported Grant's army across the Mississippi River to Bruinsburg, effectively sealing that city's fate. The following May, he pushed his gunboats up the narrow confines of the Yazoo River onto Steele's Bayou, forcing the Confederates to abandon several forts and scuttle three unfinished ironclads. Returning to the Mississippi, he next took up bombardment positions around Vicksburg, then besieged by Grant, and contributed to its discomfiture. General John C. PEMBERTON finally surrendered the city on July 4, 1863, and Porter received the thanks of Congress and official promotion to rear admiral.

In the spring of 1864, Porter accompanied General Nathaniel C. BANKS on his ill-fated Red River expedition into western Louisiana. His fleet was continually compromised by Bank's blundering and by declining water levels that nearly grounded all shipping. Only the timely intercession of Colonel Joseph Bailey, who constructed wing dams across the river, enabled Porter's command to run the Alexandria Rapids and escape intact. That fall, he assumed command of the North Atlantic Blockading Squadron and was tasked with capturing Fort Fisher, Wilmington, North Carolina. He had marshalled the largest naval squadron ever assembled in American history—120 vessels—but was thwarted when General Benjamin F. BUTLER ineptly handled the landing and withdrew in December 1864. Porter angrily persuaded superiors to grant him a second attempt, this time in concert with the infinitely more capable General Alfred H. TERRY. On January 15, 1865, Porter pushed his vessels in close support and covered Terry's troops as they successfully overran Fort Fisher, shutting the Confederacy's sole remaining port. Porter spent the final weeks of the war directing the Potomac River flotilla in concert with General Grant, and he forced Admiral Raphael SEMMES to scuttle his vessels. He was also on hand to greet President Lincoln while he toured Richmond shortly before the war ended in April 1865.

Porter was retained in the postwar establishment, and in August 1865 he became superintendent of the U.S. Naval Academy at Annapolis, Maryland. His tenure there was highly constructive, and he modernized the curricula and increased the emphasis on professionalism. He rose to vice admiral in July 1866, and as special adviser to the secretary of war under President Grant, he virtually ran the entire navy. Porter was promoted to full admiral following the death of

Farragut in 1870, becoming senior officer and only the second individual to hold that rank. He spent the next two decades actively employed on various boards until his death in Washington, D.C., on February 13, 1891. Brash, abrasive, and somewhat prone to political plotting, Porter was the most significant naval officer of the Civil War after Farragut.

Further Reading

Fonvielle, Chris E. *The Wilmington Campaign: Last Departing Rays of Hope.* Mechanicsburg, Pa.: Stackpole Books, 2001.

Fuller, Howard. *Navies and Naval Operations of the Civil War, 1861–65.* London: Conway Marine, 2005.

Hearn, Chester. *David Dixon Porter: The Civil War Years.* Annapolis, Md.: Naval Institute Press, 1998.

Joiner, Gary D. *Mr. Lincoln's Brown Water Navy: The Mississippi Squadron.* Lanham, Md.: Rowman & Littlefield, 2007.

McCaslin, Richard B. *The Last Stronghold: The Campaign for Fort Fisher.* Abilene, Tex.: McWhiney Foundation, 2003.

Porter, David D. *Incidents and Anecdotes of the Civil War.* New York: D. Appleton, 1885.

Roberts, William H. *Now for the Contest: Coastal and Oceanic Naval Operations in the Civil War.* Lincoln: University of Nebraska Press, 2004.

Stokes, David M. "Wherever the Sand Is Damp: Union Naval Operations in the Red River Campaign, 12 March–22 May 1864." *North Louisiana History* 34, no. 1 (2003): 45–65.

Porter, Fitz John (1822–1901)

Union general

Fitz John Porter was born in Portsmouth, New Hampshire, on August 31, 1822, the son of a U.S. Navy officer and cousin of the future admiral David D. PORTER. He passed through the prestigious Exeter Academy before gaining admission to the U.S. Military Academy in 1841, and he graduated near the top of his class four years later. Porter then served as a second lieutenant in the 4th U.S. Artillery at various posts along the western frontier before joining the army of General Winfield SCOTT during the Mexican War. He fought exceedingly well at Molino del Rey and Chapultepec in 1847, winning two brevet promotions to captain. Afterward, he returned to West Point as an instructor while also serving as adjutant to Superintendent Robert E. LEE. Porter subsequently transferred to Fort Leavenworth, Kansas, to serve as adjutant general in the Department of the West, and in 1859 he accompanied the Mormon expedition of Colonel Albert S. JOHNSTON. In early 1861, when secession and civil war seemed inevitable, Porter accepted a secret mission to remove Federal troops and stores from Texas, and he relocated five artillery batteries in the process. He then gained promotion to colonel of the 15th U.S. Infantry in May 1861, rising to brigadier general of volunteers a few days later. Porter also rendered impressive service in the Department of Pennsylvania, where he quickly raised, trained, and equipped 30 regiments for active service in short order. His excellent performance brought him to the attention of General George B. MCCLELLAN, who granted him command of a division in General Samuel P. Heintzelman's III Corps. Porter reciprocated by becoming an intensely partisan supporter of McClellan in the charged political atmosphere surrounding the Union high command.

McClellan commenced his long awaited Peninsula campaign in the spring of 1862, and Porter efficiently directed the siege of Yorktown. He then assumed command of the V Corps during the ill-fated drive on Richmond, Virginia. After some awkward maneuvering by McClellan, the V Corps was left stranded on the north bank of the rain-swollen Chickahominy River and thus became the object of General Robert E. LEE's new offensive. On June 26–27, 1862, Porter was attacked by larger numbers of Confederates at Mechanicsville and Gaines's Mill, but he nevertheless pummeled his opponents with heavy losses and withdrew in good order. After joining McClellan's main force, he conducted the tactical defense at Malvern Hill on July 1, 1862, whereby Lee was repulsed with horrific casualties and the Union army safely fell back to Harrison's Landing. For his stirring battlefield performance, Porter received promotion to

major general of volunteers and brigadier general in the regular army.

McClellan's lack of aggressive leadership resulted in his replacement by General John POPE in July 1862. Porter, as a firm supporter of his former commander, came to despise Pope as a braggart and impolitically criticized him in public. Pope returned such disdain in kind toward all McClellan supporters, which undermined unity of command in the newly organized Army of Virginia. On August 28, 1862, Porter found himself arrayed against General Thomas J. JACKSON's Confederates on the old battlefield of Bull Run. From his position on the far left of the Union line, he was ordered by Pope to turn Jackson's flank and attack his rear, but Porter became alarmed at the approach of Southern reinforcements under General James LONGSTREET. He thereby disobeyed orders and held his ground, keeping Longstreet in check for the time being. On August 30, 1862, Porter again received direct orders from Pope to

Union general Fitz John Porter (Library of Congress)

attack Jackson—which he promptly obeyed—and then the entire Union army collapsed when Longstreet finally advanced. Pope had no recourse but to withdraw, and he blamed his defeat on officers still loyal to McClellan. He specifically charged Porter with insubordination in the face of the enemy, and a court-martial was summoned. Porter countered by stating that, by holding Longstreet at bay as long as he did, he saved the entire army from destruction.

Porter remained with V Corps for the next three months after McClellan was restored to command, although he was lightly engaged. In November 1862 he was formally relieved of command and arrested. Porter's trial commenced on January 21, 1863, during which he was convicted by a board of Radical Republican officers closely aligned with Pope. Porter was then summarily cashiered from the service, and the Army of the Potomac lost, through political infighting, one of its finest combat officers. Porter spent the next 16 years of his life seeking official vindication, and in 1878, a board headed by General John M. Scho-field finally recommended exoneration. It was not until 1882 that President Chester A. Arthur remitted the dishonorable part of Porter's sentence, and four years later, an act of Congress reinstated him as a colonel on the retired list. Porter, meanwhile, had flourished in a variety of civilian positions in New York and New Jersey. At one point, the khedive of Egypt offered him command of his entire army, but he declined. Porter died in Morristown, New Jersey, on May 21, 1901. He was a capable soldier whose indiscrete behavior cost him what might have been an outstanding Civil War career.

Further Reading

Anders, Curt. *Injustice of Trial: Second Bull Run. General Fitz John Porter's Courtmartial and the Schofield Board Investigation That Restored His Good Name.* Zionsville, Ind.: Guild Press/Emmis, 2002.

Haydock, Michael D. "The Court-Martial of Fitz John Porter." *American History* 33, no. 6 (1999): 48–57.

Langellier, John P. *Second Manassas, 1862: Robert E. Lee's Greatest Victory.* Westport, Conn.: Praeger, 2004.

Martin, David G. *The Second Bull Run Campaign, July–August, 1862.* Cambridge, Mass.: Da Capo Press, 2001.

Porter, Fitz John. *General Fitz John Porter's Statement of Services of the Fifth Army Corps, in 1862, in Northern Virginia.* New York: Evening Post Steam Presses, 1878.

Sears, Stephen W. "The Case of Fitz John Porter." *MHQ* 5, no. 3 (1993): 70–79.

Price, Sterling (1809–1867)

Confederate general

Sterling Price was born in Prince Edward County, Virginia, on September 20, 1809, the son of wealthy, slave-owning planters. He attended Hampton Sidney College before accompanying his family to Missouri, where he established himself as a wealthy tobacco planter and merchant. Success whetted Price's appetite for politics, and he served several terms in the state legislature before successfully standing for a congressional seat in 1844. He resigned in 1846 to fight in the Mexican War as colonel of the 2nd Missouri Infantry, which formed part of General Stephen W. Kearny's column. Price performed well in various duties and effectively subdued a revolt by Pueblo Indians in New Mexico in 1847. The following year, he led an expedition into northern Mexico, capturing the town of Chihuahua and winning promotion to brigadier general. His men, to whom Price paid particular attention, christened him "Old Pap." Back home, Price parleyed his wartime popularity into political success by being elected governor (1853–57). As the storm clouds of secession grew in 1860, he served as president of a state convention tasked with addressing this divisive issue. Price opposed secession, and he helped defeat the measure by a 69 to 1 vote. The dynamic events changed dramatically when pro-Union officer captain Nathaniel Lyon seized pro-Southern militia at Camp Jackson on May 10, 1861, whereupon Price and thousands of Missourians declared for the Confederacy. Governor Claiborne F. Jackson subsequently appointed Price a major general commanding the militia, or

Confederate general Sterling Price *(Library of Congress)*

State Guard, and both men negotiated a peace pact with General William S. Harney on May 21, 1861, to keep Union forces out of Missouri. When Lyon and Congressman Francis P. Blair subsequently arranged for Haney's dismissal, Price and Claiborne met with them in St. Louis to forestall further violence on June 11, 1861, but Lyon angrily stormed out of the meeting, vowing to crush the rebellion.

Lyon quickly chased Price's ill-armed militia out of Jefferson City, and he was pursued by General Franz SIGEL, whom he repulsed at Carthage, Missouri, on July 5, 1861. Price continued falling back into northern Arkansas until reinforced by Confederates forces under General Ben McCULLOCH and marched back. Lyon, though outnumbered, attacked the secessionist forces at Wilson's Creek on August 10, 1861, and he was killed. Price followed up this victory by

seizing a Union garrison at nearby Lexington, Missouri, on September 20, 1861, taking 3,000 prisoners and a large store of supplies. But a popular uprising failed to materialize, and Price gradually gave ground before a larger army under General John C. Frémont and returned to Arkansas. It was not until the spring of 1862 that he joined forces with McCulloch and General Earl VAN DORN and attacked the smaller army of General Samuel R. CURTIS at Pea Ridge/Elkhorn Tavern, on March 6–7. Federal troops prevailed, McCulloch was killed, and Price was wounded, leaving southern Missouri and northern Arkansas under Union control. In April 1862 Price rose to major general in the Confederate service and led a division of Missourians to assist General Pierre G. T. BEAUREGARD in Mississippi. Price then waged an inclusive battle against General William S. ROSECRANS at Iuka on September 19, 1862, and he was bested again at Corinth on October 3–4, 1862. Price, disgusted with Van Dorn, then ventured to Richmond, Virginia, to confer with President Jefferson DAVIS. There, he prevailed on Davis, who always suspected his loyalty, to allow him to return to the Trans-Mississippi Department and retake Missouri for the Confederacy.

In the summer of 1863, Price served in the Department of Arkansas under aged general Theophilus Holmes. Together, they waged an ill-considered attack on General Benjamin M. Prentiss at Helena on July 4, 1863, and they were badly repulsed. Price's attempt to hold Pine Bluff was also defeated on October 25, 1863. The following year, he found himself yielding ground before a large Union force under General Frederick Steele, then marching to join the Red River expedition of General Nathaniel C. BANKS. Once reinforced by the Confederates of General Edmund KIRBY-SMITH, Price halted Steele at Camden, Arkansas, pursued him as far as Jenkin's Ferry, and attacked his rear guard unsuccessfully on April 30, 1864. However, the western theater was being depleted of Union troops to support war efforts farther east, and Kirby-Smith dispatched Price on his long-sought invasion of Missouri.

Price, assisted by General Joseph O. SHELBY, assembled a force of 12,000 volunteers in September 1864 and crossed the state line into Missouri. However, nearly one-third of his men were unarmed, and most of them were poorly trained. Worse, the thousands of Missourians he expected to flock to his colors failed to materialize. Price then marched his ragtag ensemble and waged a costly encounter at Pilot's Knob on September 27, 1864, failing to capture either the Union garrison or its arms. Losses here compelled him to bypass St. Louis altogether, and on October 8, 1864, he halted outside Jefferson City before a large garrison under General Alfred PLEASONTON. Price's column was finally brought to bay on October 23, 1864, at Westport, Missouri, which the combined forces of Curtis and Pleasonton nearly destroyed. He then executed a hasty withdrawal through Kansas and back into Arkansas, covered by Shelby's cavalry. Price's dreams for conquering his home state for the Confederacy vanished, and after the war ended, he fled to Mexico.

In April 1865 Price offered his services to Emperor Maximilian and sought to encourage a Confederate colony. Illness and the collapse of the Mexican regime forced him back to St. Louis two years later, where he eked out a marginal existence. Price died there on September 29, 1867, a major and largely ineffective player in the Civil War's western theater.

Further Reading

Adams, George R. *General William S. Harney: Prince of Dragoons.* Lincoln: University of Nebraska Press, 2001.

DeBlack, Thomas R. *With Fire and Sword: Arkansas, 1861–1874.* Fayetteville: University of Arkansas Press, 2003.

Eakin, Joanne C. *The Battle of Independence, 11 August, 1862.* Independence, Mo.: Two Trails Pub., 2000.

Forsyth, Michael J. *The Camden Expedition of 1864 and the Opportunity Lost by the Confederacy to Change the War.* Jefferson, N.C.: McFarland, 2003.

Gerteis, Louis S. *Civil War St. Louis.* Lawrence: University Press of Kansas, 2001.

Hatcher, Richard W. *Wilson's Creek: The Second Battle of the Civil War and the Men Who Fought It.* Chapel Hill: University of North Carolina Press, 2000.

Monnett, Howard N. *Action before Westport, 1864.* Niwot: University Press of Colorado, 1995.

Q

Quantrill, William C. (1837–1865)
Confederate guerrilla

William Clarke Quantrill was born in Dover, Ohio, on July 31, 1837, the son of a schoolteacher. Intelligent and well educated, he taught school for many years before relocating to the frontiers of Kansas around 1857. There, he degenerated into a life of debauchery under the assumed name of "Charlie Hart" and became adept at horse theft, gambling, and drinking. These activities blended into the turmoil of "Bloody Kansas," where pro- and antislavery factions staged numerous and invariably bloody confrontations. Quantrill initially joined a group of antislavery "Jayhawkers," and he plundered several proslavery camps and households until he was accused of stealing from his own men. He thereupon changed sides and became a Southern "bushwhacker" as an outlet for his sociopathic behavior. When the Civil War broke out in April 1861, it ushered in a period of intense lawlessness throughout Kansas and neighboring Missouri. Quantrill wasted no time aligning with the Confederacy, and his bandit gang assisted General Sterling PRICE in the capture of Lexington, Missouri, on September 20, 1861. Then he and many frontier ruffians resumed their killing and robbing spree, which induced General Henry W. HALLECK to issue General Order No. 32, stipulating that all parties caught engaging in such activity could expect summary execution. Such decrees provided little more than amusement to men of Quantrill's ilk; as exponents of hit-and-run tactics, most were never caught.

In August 1862 Quantrill was commissioned a captain in the Confederate service through the Partisan Ranger Act, despite unease over his unsavory reputation. In time, his command grew to 450 men, which included William "Bloody Bill" ANDERSON, Cole Younger, and Frank and Jesse James. As the ruthlessness of these men grew, Federal authorities responded in kind by arresting entire communities of suspected sympathizers and burning their homes. At one point, a derelict prison housing several prisoners—including Anderson's sister—collapsed, killing several inmates. Quantrill used the incident as a convenient pretext to extract gruesome revenge. On August 21, 1863, he led his men on a raid against Lawrence, Kansas, a known abolitionist center. Rounding up of men and boys, he executed 200 prisoners in cold blood, robbed the bank, and burned the entire town. This single act helped define Quantrill as the Civil War's most infamous guerrilla. "No fiend in human shape could have acted with more barbarity," an exasperated governor Thomas Carney exclaimed. General Thomas E. Ewing, under intense political pressure from Jayhawkers and Radical Republicans, then issued General Order No. 11, which led to the evacuation of four entire counties suspected of aiding the rebels.

On October 6, 1863, Quantrill again struck terror into his opponents by ambushing General James G. Blunt's mounted escort at Baxter Springs, Kansas, killing more than 100 Union soldiers and noncombatants in cold blood. But fate then intervened when his group, apparently dissatisfied by Quantrill's leadership, splintered into several small groups. Quantrill himself maintained a low profile for nearly a year until the fall of 1864, when he recruited a new band and began to raid in Kentucky. Union general John M. Palmer then recruited the noted Jayhawker, Captain Edward Terrill, to track down and eliminate the elusive raider. On May 10, 1865, Terrill accomplished exactly that, wounding and capturing Quantrill in a surprise raid at Taylorsville, Kentucky. The former guerrilla lingered for nearly a month in prison at Louisville before dying on June 6, 1865. Thus perished an individual universally reviled as the "bloodiest man in American history." Ironically, his legacy of brutality lived on in the postwar period in the actions of several outlaws who learned their bloody trade on the frontiers of Civil War Missouri.

Further Reading

Bird, Roy. *Civil War in Kansas*. Gretna, La.: Pelican Publishing, 2004.

Gilmore, Donald L. *Civil War on the Missouri-Kansas Border*. Gretna, La.: Pelican Publishing, 2005.

Mackey, Robert R. *The Uncivil War: Irregular Warfare in the Upper South, 1861–1865*. Norman: University of Oklahoma Press, 2004.

Nichols, Bruce. *Guerrilla Warfare in Civil War Missouri, 1863*. Jefferson, N.C.: McFarland, 2006.

Petersen, Paul R. *Quantrill of Missouri: The Making of a Guerrilla Warrior*. Nashville, Tenn.: Cumberland House, 2003.

Woodiel, Loftin C. "William C. Quantrill, Deviant or Hero?" Unpublished Ph.D. diss., St. Louis University, 2000.

Reynolds, John F. (1820–1863)
Union general

John Fulton Reynolds was born in Lancaster, Pennsylvania, on September 20, 1820, the son of a newspaper editor. After attending local academies, he gained admittance to the U.S. Military Academy in 1837 and graduated near the middle of his class four years later. He then served many years as a second lieutenant in the 3rd U.S. Artillery during a long stint of garrison duty in Texas. Reynolds accompanied the army of General Zachary Taylor during the Mexican War and won two brevets for bravery at Monterrey in 1846 and Buena Vista in 1847. After the war, he began a series of staff and command assignments that occasioned his rise to major. In 1856 Reynolds distinguished himself in combat against Native Americans of the Rogue River tribe of Oregon, and the following year, he marched with Colonel Albert S. JOHNSTON in the Mormon expedition. After fulfilling another tour of duty at Fort Vancouver, Washington Territory, Reynolds reported back to West Point in 1860, where he served as commandant of cadets and tactics instructor.

When the Civil War began, Reynolds was commissioned lieutenant colonel of the 14th U.S. Infantry on May 14, 1861, and two days later, he gained appointment as brigadier general of volunteers in Pennsylvania. He then garrisoned the defenses of Washington, D.C., for several months before serving as military governor of Fredericks-burg, Virginia, in May 1862, where he impressed the occupants with his fair and judicious behavior. The following June, he fought in General George B. MCCLELLAN's Peninsula campaign at the head of a brigade of Pennsylvania volunteers. In this capacity, he fought exceedingly well at the battles of Mechanicsburg and Gaines's Mill (June 26 and 27, 1862), being captured in the latter struggle. News of his captivity at Richmond's Libby Prison induced citizens of Fredericksburg to petition Confederate authorities for his release, and he was exchanged the following August. Reynolds next led the Pennsylvania Reserve Division at the disastrous Battle of Second Manassas, one of few commanders to win praise from General John POPE. Once General Robert E. LEE invaded Maryland that September, Pennsylvania governor Andrew G. Curtin left the army to serve as commander of Pennsylvania state militia throughout the crisis. Reynolds then advanced to major general as of November 29, 1863, and he succeeded General Joseph HOOKER to command of the I Corps, Army of the Potomac. On December 13, 1862, a division of his men under General George G. MEADE made the only headway against Confederate defenses. In May 1862 Reynolds was present at the disastrous Battle of Chancellorsville, although lightly engaged. Nonetheless, he repeatedly urged General Hooker to attack the Confederate left in strength, which might have turned the tide of battle for the Union.

After Chancellorsville, President Abraham LINCOLN sought a new leader to replace the now disgraced Hooker as commander of the Army of the Potomac. Accordingly, he summoned Reynolds to the White House on May 31, 1863, to sound out his views. Reynolds, however, declined all offers after the president could not promise to restrain political influences on the high command and allow him to maneuver freely. The position therefore went to his old subordinate Meade, only three days prior to the fateful encounter at Gettysburg. At that time, Reynolds commanded the left wing of the army, consisting of the I Corps under General Abner DOUBLEDAY, the III Corps of General Daniel SICKLES, and the IX Corps of General Oliver O. HOWARD. On July 1, 1863, Meade ordered him to hold the vital crossroads at Gettysburg, and he arrived ahead of his troops to find Union cavalry under General John BUFORD heavily pressed by Confederate numbers. He then hastened back to urge his own command forward and was boldly deploying the 2nd Wisconsin Infantry to the front lines when a sniper's bullet killed him. Reynold's sacrifice was not in vain as his remaining troops bought additional precious time for Meade to bring up the rest of the army. Considering his latent ability as a fighting commander, his death was a serious loss to the Union army.

Further Reading

Hoffsommer, Robert D., ed. "Sergeant Charles Veil's Memoir: On the Death of Reynolds." *Civil War Times Illustrated* 21, no. 4 (1982): 16–25.

Jones, Wilmer L. *Generals in Blue and Gray.* 2 vols. Westport, Conn.: Praeger, 2004.

Longacre, Edward G. "John F. Reynolds." *Civil War Times Illustrated* 11, no. 5 (1972): 26, 35–43.

Newton, Steven H. *McPherson's Ridge: The First Battle for the High Ground, July 1, 1863.* Cambridge, Mass.: Da Capo Press, 2002.

Pfanz, Harry W. *Gettysburg—the First Day.* Chapel Hill: University of North Carolina Press, 2001.

Riley, Michael M. *"For God's Sake, Forward": General John F. Reynolds, United States Army.* Gettysburg, Pa.: Farnsworth House Military Impressions, 1995.

Rodgers, John (1812–1882)

Union naval officer

John Rodgers was born near Havre de Grace, Maryland, on August 8, 1812, a son of Commodore John Rodgers, a naval hero from the War of 1812. He went to sea as a midshipman in April 1828 and completed routine service aboard a succession of various squadrons before advancing to passed midshipman in June 1834. He then studied briefly at the University of Virginia and sailed with the Brazilian Squadron (1836–39) before serving in Florida's Second Seminole War. Rodgers rose to lieutenant in January 1840, completed more tours of duty abroad, and then reported for duty with the U.S. Coastal Survey. Having successfully fulfilled his tasks, Rodgers received his first command, the sloop USS *John Hancock,* in October 1852, as part of the North Pacific exploring and surveying expedition. He succeeded the seriously ill commodore Cadwalader Ringgold as expedition leader in 1854 and pushed his vessels farther north into the Bering Sea than any other individual to that time. After returning to Washington, D.C., in 1855 Rodgers advanced to commander and commenced to write a lengthy report of his endeavors. He was awaiting orders in this capacity when the Civil War broke out in April 1861.

Rodgers formed part of the botched Union attempt to destroy the Navy Yard at Norfolk, Virginia, where he was captured and then released by Virginian authorities. In May 1861 his services were requested by Major George B. MCCLELLAN at Cincinnati, Ohio, for the purpose of constructing and outfitting a squadron of armored gunboats for use on western waters. Rodgers then worked closely with engineer Samuel Pook to design and build the so-called Pook Turtles. However, his acerbic temperament led to friction with army personnel, so he was replaced by the more amicable Andrew H. FOOTE, and he was transferred to the converted steamer *Flag* as part of Commodore Samuel F. DU PONT's South Atlantic Blockading Squadron. Eager for action, Rodgers fought well in the November 7, 1861, seizure of Port Royal,

South Carolina, and he personally captured and occupied Fort Walker. Du Pont was so pleased with his performance that Rodgers subsequently hoisted the first American flag over enemy soil since the bombardment of Fort Sumter in April. The following November, he led expeditions that captured Tybee Island off the coast of Georgia and Fernandina Island, Florida, in March 1862. On May 15, 1862, Rodgers conducted the new and experimental ironclad monitor *Galena* up the James River to Drewry's Bluff, Virginia. There, he engaged in a lopsided duel with Confederate batteries on the cliffs and came off a poor second, sustaining 40 hits and 33 casualties. Despite this reverse, he advanced to captain in July 1862 and rejoined Du Pont the following November.

Rodgers next commanded the new, improved monitor *Weehawken,* which was better armored and more seaworthy than its predecessors. To put

Union naval officer John Rodgers *(Library of Congress)*

any doubts to rest, he led his vessel through several storms to confirm its survivability. Thus prepared, the *Weehawken* spearheaded Du Pont's ill-fated attack on Charleston Harbor on April 7, 1863, receiving 53 hits by the time the action was called off. Throughout the engagement, his vessel also pushed an antitorpedo (mine) device, known as a "boot-jack," to deflect and detonate the weapons. Rodgers then made suitable repairs and unhesitatingly engaged the formidable Confederate ram CSS *Atlanta* in Wassaw Sound, Georgia, on June 17, 1862, driving it ashore and capturing it in only 15 minutes. For this display of outstanding seamanship, he received the thanks of Congress and advanced to commodore. He then succeeded to the command of the newly designed monitors *Canonicus* and *Dictator,* which, unfortunately, proved so plagued with technical difficulties that he spent the rest of the war rendering them operational.

Rodgers was retained in the postwar service, and he commanded a small Pacific Squadron and the Boston Navy Yard. He rose to rear admiral in 1869 and the following year took control of the Asiatic Squadron to promote American interests in Korea, the self-styled "Hermit Kingdom." On June 9, 1871, Rodgers, carrying U.S. minister Frederick F. Low onboard, was suddenly fired on by a Korean fort. When no explanation or apology was forthcoming, he landed a detachment of sailors and marines, stormed the offending battery, and killed 243 Korean soldiers. This marked America's first armed intervention in northeast Asia, and after the Korean king refused all diplomatic overtures, Rodgers sailed home. He then finished his career by completing several tours of duty ashore before dying at the Naval Observatory in Washington on May 5, 1882. At the time of his passing, Rodgers was the navy's most senior officer of his grade.

Further Reading

Bradford, James C., ed. *Captains of the Old Steam Navy: Makers of the American Naval Tradition, 1840–1880.* Annapolis, Md.: Naval Institute Press, 1986.

Browning, Robert M. *Success Is All That Was Expected: The South Atlantic Blockading Squadron during the Civil War.* Washington, D.C.: Brassey's, 2002.

Chang, Gordon H. "Whose Barbarism"? Whose "Treachery?" Race and Civilization in the Unknown United States–Korea War of 1871. *Journal of American History* 89, no. 4 (2003): 1331–1365.

Hackemer, Kurt. "The Other Ironclad: The USS *Galena* and the Critical Summer of 1862." *Civil War History* 40, no. 3 (1994): 226–247.

Quarstein, John V. *A History of Ironclads: The Power of Iron Over Wood.* Charleston, S.C.: The History Press, 2006.

Silverstone, Paul H. *Civil War Navies, 1855–1883.* Annapolis, Md.: Naval Institute Press, 2001.

Rosecrans, William S. (1819–1898)

Union general

William Starke Rosecrans was born in Kingston, Ohio, on September 6, 1819, the son of farmers. After his father died, he was forced to quit school and help support his family, and through dint of hard work, he received an appointment to the U.S. Military Academy in 1838. An excellent student, Rosecrans graduated fifth in his class four years later and was commissioned into the elite Corps of Engineers as a second lieutenant. In 1842 he commenced routine construction activities at Hampton Roads, Virginia, and Newport, Rhode Island, and he also served as an instructor at West Point (1843–47). However, Rosecrans grew disillusioned with low pay and slow promotion, so he resigned from the army in 1854 to pursue a career in business. For the next seven years, he worked as a civil engineer in Ohio and also operated his own kerosene distillery. Following the onset of hostilities in April 1861, Rosecrans quickly responded by serving as a volunteer aide-de-camp to Major George B. MCCLELLAN. He shortly after rose to lieutenant colonel of the 23rd Ohio Volunteers in June, and then President Abraham LINCOLN appointed him a brigadier general in the regular army. In this capacity, he served under McClellan in western Virginia, gaining small but significant victories over Confederate forces at Richmond Mountain on July 11, 1861. McClellan, who received overall

Union general William S. Rosecrans *(Massachusetts Commandery Military Order of the Loyal Legion and the U.S. Army Military History Institute)*

credit for success here, was summoned east, and Rosecrans succeeded him as head of the Department of Western Virginia. His most important accomplishment was defeating General John B. FLOYD at Carnifex Ferry on September 10, 1861, which helped clear West Virginia of Confederates.

In the spring of 1862, Rosecrans was succeeded by General John C. Frémont while he transferred west to join the Army of the Mississippi under General John POPE. In this capacity, he commanded the left wing of Pope's force during General Henry W. HALLECK's Corinth campaign, and he succeeded him in command of the Army of the Mississippi in June 1862. This placed Rosecrans under the aegis of General Ulysses S. GRANT, who regarded him as a marginally talented, plodding performer. As if to underscore this perception, Rosecrans defeated General Sterling PRICE at Iuka on September 19, 1862, then repelled General Earl VAN DORN at Corinth (October 3–4, 1862), but he fumbled the pursuit and allowed his foes to escape. He nevertheless received promotion to major general that fall and succeeded General Don C. BUELL as head of the Army of the Ohio, which he renamed the Army of the Cumberland. Rosecrans spent several weeks shadowing the Army of Tennessee under General Braxton BRAGG until he suddenly turned at Murfreesboro (Stones River) and fought from December 31, 1862 to January 3, 1863. A bloody standoff ensued as both sides pummeled each other's right flank, and Rosecrans nearly abandoned the contest before the Southerners were compelled by losses to withdraw. For his efforts here, he also received the thanks of Congress.

Typically, Rosecrans spent the next several months methodically training and preparing his army, a pace that vexed impatient superiors. It took considerable prodding, but he finally moved against Bragg in June 1863 during the so-called Tullahoma campaign, in which the Confederates were completely outmaneuvered and abandoned Chattanooga, Tennessee, without a shot being fired. It was, in truth, a brilliant achievement for which praise was deserved. However, Rosecrans grew careless by pursuing the Confederates into northern Georgia with his army widely dispersed. Bragg, now reinforced by General James LONGSTREET's corps from Virginia, predictably turned and struck back at Chickamauga on September 19–20. Rosecrans handled his troops well initially, until he inadvertently shifted a division and created a gap in his line just as Longstreet attacked. His army was completely shattered save for the magnificent stand of General George H. THOMAS, and he fell back in haste to Chattanooga. When Rosecrans inexplicably allowed Bragg to occupy the high ground surrounding the city and besieged him, Grant arrived on October 19, 1863, and relieved him from command.

Rosecrans subsequently received command of the Department of the Missouri, where he quarreled with Generals Samuel R. CURTIS and Alfred PLEASONTON throughout General Sterling PRICE's invasion of that state. In December 1864 he reported to Cincinnati for orders, which never came, and finally he resigned in disgust in March 1867. Rosecrans served as minister to Mexico until being sacked a second time by President Grant in 1869. He then relocated to California, purchased a ranch, and dabbled in mining. In 1881 he won election to the U.S. House of Representatives, and he vindictively voted against back pay for Grant, then dying of throat cancer. Rosecrans served as register of the U.S. Treasury from 1885 to 1893 before dying at Redondo Beach, California, on March 11, 1898. He was a talented but essentially luckless commander who displayed flashes of brilliance alongside consistent sluggishness in the field.

Further Reading

Bowers, John. *Chickamauga and Chattanooga: The Battles That Doomed the Confederacy.* New York: Post Road Press, 2000.

Castel, Albert. "Victorious Loser: William S. Rosecrans." *Timeline* 19, no. 4–5 (2002): 32–41, 22–37.

———. "West Virginia, 1861: A Tale of a Goose, a Dog, and a Fox." *North & South* 7, no. 7 (2004): 44–55.

Daniel, Larry J. *Days of Glory: The Army of the Cumberland, 1861–1865.* Baton Rouge: Louisiana State University Press, 2004.

Lepa, Jack H. *The Civil War in Tennessee, 1862–1863.* Jefferson, N.C.: McFarland, 2007.

Ross, Charles D. *Civil War Acoustic Shadows.* Shippensburg, Pa.: White Mane Books, 2001.

S

Schofield, John M. (1831–1906)

Union general

John McAllister Schofield was born in Gerry, New York, on September 29, 1831, the son of a Baptist minister. He relocated to Illinois with his family as a child and in 1849 gained an appointment to the U.S. Military Academy. He graduated near the top of his class in 1853 and served as a second lieutenant with the 1st U.S. Artillery in Florida before returning to West Point as an instructor. In 1860 he obtained a leave of absence to teach physics at Washington University, St. Louis, Missouri, but he responded to President Abraham LINCOLN's call for volunteers the following spring. Schofield then became a major in the 1st Missouri Artillery and chief of staff under General Nathaniel LYON. In this capacity, he fought bravely at the defeat of Wilson's Creek on August 10, 1861, eventually winning the Congressional Medal of Honor for exemplary behavior. Prior to the battle, Schofield urged the badly outnumbered Lyon not to attack and also balked at Colonel Franz SIGEL's secret flanking march to the Confederate rear. That November, he became a brigadier general of Missouri militia, and head of the District of St. Louis and enjoyed some success rooting out Confederate guerrillas under William C. QUANTRILL. In November 1862 Schofield gained command of the Army of the Frontier, which was primarily concerned with antiguerrilla activities, but his nomination to major general was held up in Congress by political enemies. His promotion finally was approved in May 1863, at which point he assumed control of the Department of the Missouri. Schofield, however, was ambitious and used his good relationship with President Lincoln to agitate for a combat command. Accordingly, in February 1864, he assumed command of the Department of the Ohio and its constituent army, the XXIII Corps.

Throughout the spring and summer of 1864, Schofield formed part of General William T. SHERMAN's army as it marched to Atlanta, Georgia. He performed capably in the complex maneuvering that turned General Joseph E. JOHNSTON's Confederates out of several fortified positions. However, when Johnston's successor, General John B. HOOD, marched into Tennessee to cut Sherman's supply lines, Schofield was detached from the main army to slow him while General George H. THOMAS assembled a new army for the defense of Nashville. On November 28, 1864, Schofield skillfully extricated his command from a trap laid by Hood at Spring Hill, and then he occupied defensive positions around the city of Franklin. Hood attacked vigorously on November 30, 1864, and was vigorously repulsed with six generals killed and thousands of casualties. Schofield slipped away again, skillfully covered by General James H. WILSON's cavalry, and he rejoined Thomas at Nashville. On December 15–16, his XXIII Corps figured prominently in the rout of Hood and the near annihilation of his Army of Tennessee.

Schofield rose to major general of volunteers and performed an impressive movement of forces from Tennessee by riverboat, train, and ship to North Carolina. There, he helped orchestrate the capture of Wilmington before advancing inland to Goldsborough to link up with Sherman that March. In April 1865 Schofield participated in negotiations to end hostilities and was on hand to accept Johnston's surrender at Durham Station. He ended the war commanding the Department of North Carolina. Shortly afterward, President Andrew Johnson appointed him special envoy to France, where he compellingly convinced the government of Emperor Napoleon III to withdraw its forces from Mexico. He served as acting secretary of war under Johnston and also performed Reconstruction work. President Ulysses S. GRANT appointed him head of the Department of the Missouri in 1869. He later transferred to the Division of the Pacific, and in 1872, he ventured to Hawaii with the recommendation that the United States obtain Pearl Harbor as a naval base. In 1876 Schofield returned to West Point as commandant

and two years later headed a board of inquiry that overturned the court-martial verdict of General Fitz John PORTER.

Schofield's most daunting task occurred in 1888 when, following the death of General Philip H. SHERIDAN, he was elevated to commanding general of the army. Throughout his seven-year tenure, he oversaw improvements in the lot of the common soldiers while also fostering greater professionalism among the officer corps. He also broke precedent by urging that Native Americans be allowed to join the military as regular soldiers while the government helped assume for the care and feeding of their families. Perhaps Schofield's greatest contribution to the U.S. Army was his call for a German-style general staff system, which was adopted at the turn of the 20th century. He resigned from the army in 1895 as a lieutenant general before dying at St. Augustine, Florida, on March 4, 1906. In addition to being an outstanding combat officer, Schofield is widely regarded as among the army's finest peacetime administrators and reformers.

Further Reading

Connelly, Donald B. *John M. Schofield of the Politics of Governorship.* Chapel Hill: University of North Carolina Press, 2006.

Fonvielle, Chris E. *The Wilmington Campaign: Last Departing Rays of Hope.* Mechanicsburg, Pa.: Stackpole Books, 2001.

Lepa, Jack H. *Breaking the Confederacy: The Georgia and Tennessee Campaigns of 1864.* Jefferson, N.C.: McFarland, 2005.

McDonough, James L. *Nashville: The Western Confederacy's Final Gamble.* Knoxville: University of Tennessee Press, 2004.

Nichols, Bruce. *Guerrilla Warfare in Civil War Missouri, 1863.* Jefferson, N.C.: McFarland, 2006.

Schofield, John M. *Forty-Six Years in the Army.* Norman: University of Oklahoma Press, 1998.

Scott, Winfield (1786–1866)

Union general

Winfield Scott was born near Petersburg, Virginia, on June 13, 1786, and he briefly attended William and Mary College. After studying law for several

Union general John M. Schofield *(Library of Congress)*

Union general Winfield Scott *(National Archives)*

months, Scott joined the U.S. Army as a captain of artillery in 1808, commencing a distinguished military career that lasted more than a half-century. He gained national attention during the War of 1812, particularly at the bloody encounters of Chippewa and Lundy's Lane in July 1814, which demonstrated the ability of American troops to withstand professional British adversaries in the field. He ended the war a brevet major general, the nation's youngest. Throughout the postwar period, Scott functioned as the embodiment of military professionalism and composed the first infantry manuals employed since the American Revolution. By dint of superior skills, he became the army's commanding general in 1841, and he held that position for the next 20 years. Scott was also renowned for his towering stature, standing more than six-and-a-half-feet tall, and his equally commanding ego. In fact, his strict insistence on following the various nuances of military etiquette garnered him the nick-

name "Old Fuss and Feathers." Scott demonstrated his abilities as a commander during the Mexican War in 1847, when he conducted a near-flawless advance on Mexico City that constituted a textbook example of military planning and maneuver. Moreover, his example of success and the methods he employed influenced nearly 100 junior officers serving under him, who, over a decade later, rose to be generals in the Civil War. In 1852 he made a clumsy run for the presidency as a Whig and lost decisively to Democrat Franklin Pierce.

The 75-year-old Scott, though himself a Southerner, opposed secession as it unfolded in the fall of 1860. He tried to convince President James Buchanan to reinforce and strengthen army garrisons throughout the South, but his advice was ignored by Secretary of War John B. FLOYD. Once the new chief executive, Abraham LINCOLN, was in power, he advised him to abandon Fort Sumter, South Carolina, on the basis of it being militarily indefensible. Lincoln chose to ignore his advice and instead requested him to proffer a military strategy for subduing the rebellious South. The elderly Scott then articulated a comprehensive plan calling for a tight blockade of the Confederate coastline from Norfolk, Virginia, to Galveston, Texas, followed by a military offensive down the Mississippi Valley that utilized the various waterways as avenues of invasion. Furthermore, he predicted a three-year conflict requiring the service of 300,000 three-year soldiers—a far cry from the 75,000 three-month volunteers initially requested by Lincoln. It was his strategic vision that the South, cut off from trade with Europe and slowly dismembered through control of the Mississippi, would gradually but irrevocably succumb to superior Union numbers and resources. His solution failed to meet quicksilver political expectations for an immediate and decisive victory over the secessionists, so his strategy, ridiculed as the "Anaconda Plan," was initially discarded.

The wizened warrior also urged the administration against precipitously committing raw, barely trained troops to combat operations. Again, politicians scoffed at his caution, and he was strong-armed into approving a hasty offensive under General Irvin McDowell. This operation came to grief at Bull Run on July 21, 1861, as he predicted. Political and military leaders, now taking stock of Scott's advanced age and declining health, openly began to question his relevance to the military matters at hand. Scott undoubtedly hastened his own removal by appointing the young, brash general George B. McClellan who routinely disregarded the old soldier's advice and elbowed himself into the role of Lincoln's de facto military adviser, as head of the Army of the Potomac. Scott, old, ill, and feeling ignored, finally resigned his commission on October 31, 1861. He retired to the U.S. Military Academy, West Point, to write his memoirs. He also lived long enough to see his "Anaconda Plan" vindicated, for the basic outline was eventually adopted with successful results to the Union. Scott died at West Point on May 29, 1866, being both literally and figuratively a towering figure of American military history.

Further Reading
Eisenhower, John S. D. *Agent of Destiny: The Life and Times of General Winfield Scott.* New York: Free Press, 1997.
Johnson, Timothy D. *Winfield Scott: The Quest for Military Glory.* Lawrence: University Press of Kansas, 1998.
MacDonnell, Francis. "The Confederate Spin on Winfield Scott and George Thomas." *Civil War History* 44, no. 4 (1998): 255–266.
Perret, Geoffrey. "Anaconda: The Plan That Never Was." *North & South* 6, no. 4 (2003): 36–43.
Peskin, Allan. *Winfield Scott and the Profession of Arms.* Kent, Ohio: Kent State University Press, 2003.
Rafuse, Ethan S. "Former Whigs in Conflict: Winfield Scott, Abraham Lincoln, and the Secession Crisis Revisited." *Lincoln Herald* 103, no. 1 (2001): 8–22.

Semmes, Raphael (1809–1877)
Confederate admiral
Raphael Semmes was born in Charles County, Maryland, on September 27, 1809, and was orphaned at an early age. Raised by uncles, he joined the navy as a midshipman in 1826 and per-

formed routine duties aboard a succession of vessels. In his spare time, Semmes also studied law and gained admittance to the bar in 1834. He rose to lieutenant in February 1837 and served in that capacity during the Mexican War. In October 1846 he commanded the brig USS *Somers* in the Gulf of Mexico until losing his ship and 40 crew members to a sudden squall. Exonerated by a court of inquiry, Semmes subsequently helped supervise the landing of General Winfield Scott at Veracruz in 1847 and campaigned alongside army troops during the advance on Mexico City. After the war, Semmes settled in Montgomery, Alabama, awaiting orders and practicing law. He rose to commander in 1855 and assumed responsibilities as lighthouse inspector for the Gulf region. Once Alabama seceded from the Union in February 1861, Semmes resigned his commission and joined the newly formed Confederate navy as a commander. His first assignment was to visit New York to purchase naval supplies before the onset of actual hostilities. On his return visit, Semmes stopped in Washington, D.C., to observe the inauguration of President Abraham Lincoln.

Before taking to sea, Semmes held lengthy discussions with Confederate secretary of the navy Stephen R. Mallory as to the probable course of naval events. Given the South's limited assets, both men agreed to pursue a *guerre de course,* namely, the outfitting of commerce destroyers to attack Northern shipping and sap Union economic vitality. On June 30, 1861, he took the converted steamer *Havana,* now armed and outfitted as the commerce raider CSS *Sumter,* out from Pass a L'Outre, Mississippi, and into open ocean. His was the first vessel to display the Confederate flag abroad, and over the course of the next few months Semmes steamed as far north as Maine, taking 18 prizes. His success forced Navy secretary Gideon Welles to dispatch several warships in pursuit, which finally cornered him at Gibraltar in April 1862. Semmes, noting the dilapidated condition of his vessel, decommissioned it and escaped to Nassau. He there awaited delivery of a new and more powerful vessel, the 200-foot steam sloop

CSS *Alabama,* which had been constructed clandestinely in England. In August 1862 Semmes, now a captain, outfitted his new vessel at Terceira in the Azores and sailed off into history. During the next two years, he attacked Union shipping at locales as far away as Singapore, ultimately seizing and burning 66 prizes. One victim, the Union warship USS *Hatteras,* was surprised at night off Galveston, Texas, and sunk in only 15 minutes. Semmes's haul made him the most successful privateer captain in naval history and forced the American government, which branded him a pirate, to redouble efforts to catch him.

After an exhausting cruise of 22 months, Semmes finally put in to Cherbourg, France, for some badly needed repairs. While there, he was blockaded in port by the *Kearsarge,* commanded by Captain John A. Winslow, a former acquaintance. In a rashly based decision, Semmes decided that his ship was more than a match for his opponent, and on June 19, 1864, he left Cherbourg to engage it. The *Kearsarge,* well armed, armored, and trained, proceeded to disable the *Alabama* systematically with accurate gunnery while the Confederate gunners aimed high. Semmes abandoned ship after a 45-minute contest and was rescued from capture by an English yacht—a violation of international law. He returned to the South as a hero, and in February 1865, he was made an admiral. For the final months of the war, Semmes commanded the James River Squadron of three ironclads and three gunboats, but he saw no serious action. He scuttled his ships before Richmond fell to the armies of General Ulysses S. GRANT on April 2, 1865, and he massed his sailors into a naval brigade. Semmes then served as a brigadier general in the army of General Joseph E. JOHNSTON and surrendered at Durham Station with that officer on April 26, 1865.

In December 1865 Semmes was arrested by government authorities and charged with piracy, but he was ultimately released. He then returned to Mobile, Alabama, to teach, edit a newspaper, and practice maritime law. Semmes died at Point Clear, Alabama, on August 30, 1877, but his success in war led to a major diplomatic fracas with England over the so-called Alabama Claims. Because the *Alabama* was built in England for hostile purposes against the United States, the courts viewed it as a breach of international neutrality. In 1872 the British government finally admitted culpability and paid $15.5 million in compensation to Semmes's numerous victims.

Further Reading

Bowcock, Andrew. *CSS Alabama: Anatomy of a Confederate Raider.* London: Chatham, 2002.

Gindlesperger, James. *Fire on the Water: The USS Kearsarge and CSS Alabama.* Shippensburg, Pa.: Burd Street Press, 2004.

Hollet, D. *The Alabama Affair: The British Shipyards Conspiracy in the American Civil War.* Wirral, U.K.: Avid Publications, 2003.

Merli, Frank J. *The Alabama, British Neutrality, and the American Civil War.* Bloomington: Indiana University Press, 2004.

Taylor, John M. *Semmes: Rebel Raider.* Washington, D.C.: Brassey's, 2004.

Tucker, Spencer. *Blue and Gray Navies: The Civil War Afloat.* Annapolis, Md.: Naval Institute Press, 2006.

Shelby, Joseph O. (1830–1897)

Confederate general

Joseph Orville Shelby was born in Lexington, Kentucky, on December 12, 1830, and he attended the University of Transylvania (1845–48). After a year in Pennsylvania to study rope manufacturing, he relocated with his family to Waverly, Missouri, to grow hemp and enter business. As a slaveholder, Shelby opposed abolitionists during the Kansas-Missouri border disputes, and he raised cavalry companies to raid his opponents. When the Civil War erupted in April 1861, Shelby declined a commission in the Union army and offered his services to the Confederacy. As a member of the State Guard, he fought with General Sterling PRICE at Wilson's Creek on August 10, 1861, and then participated in the siege of Lexington. His exemplary conduct as a cavalry leader marked him for additional service with the mounted arm. On March 7–8, 1862, he fought under General Ben McCULLOCH at the defeat of Pea Ridge, skillfully covering the Southern withdrawal. That June, he was commissioned a colonel in Confederate service and given a three-regiment force, which, by dint of hard fighting, gained renown as the "Iron Brigade." Under Shelby's untutored but excellent leadership, it quickly emerged as the finest Southern cavalry unit of the Trans-Mississippi theater.

As the tide of Confederate fortunes in Missouri and Arkansas ebbed and flowed, Shelby was usually on hand as a scout, a combat officer, or a commander of the rear guard. Audacious by nature, in December 1862 he briefly seized the outer defenses of Springfield, Missouri, and subsequently conducted numerous forays behind Union lines in support of General Thomas C. HINDMAN. He next fought under Price during the ill-fated attack on Helena, Arkansas, where he was wounded. That September, Shelby performed his greatest military deed by raiding across the length and breadth of Missouri with the Iron Brigade, capturing Federal garrisons at Boonville, Neosho, Warsaw, and Tipton. His hard-riding troopers covered 1,500 miles in only 36 days, inflicted nearly 600 casualties and destroying nearly $2 million of Union property. It is estimated that his activities tied down the services of 50,000 Union troops who had been sent to oppose him and precluded any reinforcements to Federal armies besieged at Chattanooga, Tennessee. Moreover, this proved not only the longest cavalry raid of the war but also one that gave Shelby a reputation to vie with that of General J. E. B. STUART in the East. In recognition of his accomplishments, he gained promotion to brigadier general on December 15, 1863.

In the spring of 1864, Shelby performed more useful service by successfully opposing 15,000 Union troops under General Frederick Steele at Princeton, Arkansas. That September, he accompanied Price's final invasion of Missouri and waged several successful actions against isolated Union detachments. On October 21–23, 1864, Shelby acquitted himself well during Price's defeat at Westport, Missouri, and his ferocious rearguard

actions undoubtedly saved his army from destruction. At that time, General Alfred PLEASONTON declared Shelby the best Confederate cavalry opponent he ever encountered. After falling back to Texas, he learned of General Robert E. LEE's surrender at Appomattox in April 1865 and vowed never to capitulate. He even threatened General Edmund KIRBY-SMITH with arrest if he attempted to surrender. Once reality prevailed, Shelby took 1,000 of his followers south into Mexico to found a colony for Emperor Maximilian. However, once the French began to withdraw in 1866, Shelby abandoned the effort and returned to Missouri. He farmed for many years in Bates County before serving as a U.S. federal marshal in 1893. He also gained a degree of notoriety by testifying as a defense witness in the trial of noted outlaw Frank James, which led to his acquittal. Shelby continued as sheriff and a popular frontier figure until his death in Adrian County, Missouri, on February 13, 1897. As a cavalry leader, many historians rate him as equal or better than such contemporaries as Nathan B. FORREST and Joseph WHEELER.

Further Reading

Beasley, Conger, Jr., ed. *Shelby's Expedition to Mexico: An Unwritten Leaf of the War.* Fayetteville: University of Arkansas Press, 2002.

Nichols, Bruce. *Guerrilla Warfare in Civil War Missouri, 1863.* Jefferson, N.C.: McFarland, 2006.

Scott, Mark E. *The Fifth Season: General "Jo" Shelby, the Great Raid of 1863.* Independence, Mo.: Two Trails Pubs., 2001.

Sellmeyer, Deryl P. J. *Shelby's Iron Brigade.* Gretna, La.: Pelican Publishing, 2007.

Shea, William L. "Prelude to Prairie Grove: Cane Hill, November 28, 1862." *Arkansas Historical Quarterly* 63, no. 4 (2004): 352–379.

Sheridan, Philip H. (1831–1888)
Union general

Philip Henry Sheridan was born near Albany, New York, on March 6, 1831, the son of Irish immigrants. He matured in Somerset, Ohio, and clerked several years in a dry goods store before winning an appointment to the U.S. Military Academy in

1849 after lying about his age. A mediocre student, Sheridan possessed a ferocious temper and at one point attacked a larger cadet captain with a fixed bayonet because of an alleged insult. He was suspended for a year in consequence and finally graduated in 1854 as a second lieutenant in the 1st U.S. Infantry. After fighting Native Americans along the Rio Grande in Texas, he transferred to the 4th U.S. Infantry and performed similar service against the Yakima tribes of the Oregon Territory. When the Civil War commenced in April 1861, Sheridan was an obscure captain, but he managed to wrangle a staff position under Generals Nathaniel LYON and Henry W. HALLECK. He performed well as a quartermaster but chafed as a bureaucrat and sought a combat command. After badgering Halleck for weeks (for Sheridan was anything if not dogged), he received command of the 2nd Michigan Cavalry in May 1862. With this force, he engaged and defeated 5,000 of General

Union general Philip H. Sheridan *(National Archives)*

William J. HARDEE's Confederate cavalry at Booneville, Mississippi, on July 1, 1862, becoming a brigadier general of volunteers in consequence. He subsequently commanded an infantry division under General Don C. BUELL at the bloody Battle of Perryville, Kentucky, on October 8, 1862, where his relentless attacks convinced General Braxton BRAGG to retreat. At the equally sanguine Battle of Murfreesboro (December 31, 1862–January 3, 1863), his valiant stand against General Leonidas POLK's superior numbers saved the army of General William S. ROSECRANS from certain destruction. His superior performance resulted in a promotion to major general of volunteers in March 1863 at the age of 32.

Sheridan commanded a division in the XX Corps throughout Rosecrans's brilliantly executed Tullahoma campaign in central Tennessee. But both leaders came to grief on September 20, 1863, when Bragg suddenly assailed Union forces at Chickamauga and Sheridan's men were routed by two divisions under General James LONGSTREET. Nevertheless, he rounded up the stragglers and assisted General George H. THOMAS in conducting a successful rear-guard action. Sheridan next fought well at the Battle of Missionary Ridge on November 25, 1863, herding his division up the slopes in an unauthorized advance that routed the Confederates and captured the crest. Sheridan's stomach for fighting brought him to the attention of General Ulysses S. GRANT, who ordered him east as head of his cavalry corps in the much abused Army of the Potomac.

Once in charge, Sheridan completely revamped, retrained, and reequipped the Union cavalry, converting it from a scouting force to a true combat arm. He also brusquely argued with General George G. MEADE about exactly what role troopers should play in the upcoming Overland campaign against Richmond, Virginia. Sheridan, at one point, openly declared that he would destroy Confederate troopers under legendary general J. E. B. STUART, if only allowed to. Grant, impressed by such aplomb, gave him this permission, and Sheridan set out. He defeated Stuart at Yellow Tavern on May 11, 1864, fatally wounding him. The following month, he waged a hard-fought but inconclusive battle with General Wade HAMPTON's troopers at Trevilian Station, Virginia, although he inflicted heavy damage on Confederate lines of communications and railroads in the process. In August Grant tasked him with driving Confederates under General Jubal A. EARLY out of the strategic Shenandoah Valley and laying waste to that fertile region. Sheridan's Army of the Shenandoah accordingly pounced on Early at Winchester on September 19, 1864, and at Fisher's Hill three days later, routing him. Pursuant to orders, he burned large swaths of valuable farmland to deny its use to the South, becoming a thoroughly hated figure in the process. Early subsequently turned and struck at the unsuspecting Federals at Cedar Creek on October 19, 1864, nearly routing them, but Sheridan galloped 15 miles from the rear, rallied his men, and shattered the Confederates in a sweeping counterattack. "Sheridan's Ride," as it came to be known, was celebrated in a famous poem by Thomas Buchanan Read, and victory also brought him the thanks of Congress and promotion to major general.

Sheridan finally dispensed with Early's survivors at Waynesboro, Virginia, on March 2, 1865. He then rejoined Grant outside of Petersburg. Massing his forces on the Confederate right flank, he was rebuffed by General George E. PICKETT at Dinwiddie Court House on March 31, 1865, but on the following day, April 1, he smashed through Confederate lines at the Battle of Five Forks. This masterstroke forced General Robert E. LEE's Army of Northern Virginia to abandon Richmond hastily and to flee westward with Sheridan in hot pursuit. On April 6, 1865, his cavalry caught and captured a third of the Confederate army at Sayler's Creek, and three days later, he cut off Lee's retreat at Appomattox Court House. Lee surrendered and Sheridan, thunderbolt of the Union army, helped close the Civil War in his typically decisive fashion.

After the war, Sheridan was dispatched to Texas where his threatening displays of military strength induced the government of Napoleon III to remove its armies from Mexico. He then oversaw Reconstruction activities in Texas and Louisiana although, as a Radical Republican, his conduct proved so heavy-handed that President Andrew Johnson removed him. In September 1867 Sheridan transferred to the Department of the Missouri as a lieutenant general, and for the next 16 years, he conducted a ruthless war of subjugation against hostile Native-American tribesmen with Generals Alfred H. TERRY, George CROOK, and George A. CUSTER. In 1870 he took a brief furlough to observe the Franco-Prussian War, and in 1878 he assumed command of the Military Division of the Southwest. Sheridan succeeded General William T. SHERMAN as commanding general of the army in November 1883, and in June 1888, he became only the third person, after Grant and Sherman, to pin four stars on his shoulders as a full general. Sheridan died in Noquitt, Massachusetts, on August 5, 1888, at the age of 57, an outstanding combat commander of the Civil War whose triumphs invariably centered around careful preparation, unswerving adherence to the offense, and unflinching concern for the soldiers serving under him.

Further Reading

Alexander, Robert. *Five Forks: Waterloo of the Confederacy: A Civil War Narrative.* East Lansing: Michigan State University Press, 2003.

Coffey, David. *Sheridan's Lieutenants: Philip Sheridan, His Generals, and the Final Year of the Civil War.* Wilmington, Del.: Rowman and Littlefield, 2005.

Hampson, Jeffery J. "Grant and His Disciples in Terror: A Study of the Civil War Campaigns of Grant, Sheridan, and Sherman." Unpublished master's thesis, James Madison University, 2003.

King, Curtis S. "Reconsider, Hell!" *MHQ* 13, no. 4 (2001): 88–95.

Longacre, Edward G. *The Cavalry at Appomattox: A Tactical Study of Mounted Operations during the Civil War's Climactic Campaign, March 2–April 9, 1865.* Mechanicsburg, Pa.: Stackpole Books, 2003.

Wittenberg, Eric J. *Little Phil: A Reassessment of the Civil War Leadership of General Philip H. Sheridan.* Washington, D.C.: Brassey's, 2002.

———. *Glory Enough for All: Sheridan's Second Raid and the Battle of Trevilian Station.* London: Brassey's, 2002.

Sherman, William T. (1820–1891)

Union general

Tecumseh Sherman was born in Lancaster, Ohio, on February 8, 1820, the son of a state judge. Orphaned at an early age, he became a ward of Senator Thomas Ewing, who subsequently christened him William. Sherman, with his stepfather's patronage, gained appointment to the U.S. Military Academy in 1836, and graduated near the top of his class four years later. He joined the 3rd U.S. Artillery as a second lieutenant and fought in Florida's Second Seminole War until 1841. Sherman then fulfilled a long string of garrison duties throughout the Deep South, where he thoroughly familiarized himself with the people and the geography. When the Mexican War broke out in 1846, Sherman sailed to California to join the staff of General Stephen W. Kearny, but he saw no combat. He next performed as a captain in the commissary department, but discouraged by low pay and slow promotions, Sherman resigned his commission in 1853. He then failed in banking and law, but in 1859 he accepted a position as superintendent of the Alexandria Military Academy, Louisiana. Sherman greatly admired the South and evinced genuine affection for the Southern people, but after the Civil War commenced in 1861, he departed Louisiana for St. Louis, Missouri, and he sought to regain his army commission. Before leaving, his many Southern friends implored him to accept a commission in the Confederate army, but he politely declined.

Through the influence of his younger brother John, a U.S. senator, Sherman was reinstated as a colonel of the 13th U.S. Infantry on May 14, 1861. He commanded a brigade under General Irvin McDowell at Bull Run on July 21, 1861, being one of few officers to distinguish himself in combat. Sherman rose to brigadier general the following August and transferred to the Department of the Ohio to assist General Robert Anderson. By

October, he succeeded Anderson in command and entered into a bitter war of words with the local press, which openly regarded him as insane. When the volatile Sherman experienced a nervous breakdown, he was replaced by General Don C. Buell and sent to Missouri as a staff officer under General Henry W. Halleck. Sherman there received command of the District of Cairo, Illinois, where he gained acquaintance with General Ulysses S. Grant during the campaign against Forts Henry and Donelson in February 1862. The high-strung Sherman and the low-key Grant struck up a cordial relationship that lasted the remainder of their lives. He commanded a division in Grant's Army of the Tennessee and fought conspicuously at the bloody Battle of Shiloh (April 5–6, 1862). Sherman, who had commanded the pickets that day, had been surprised by Confederates under General Albert S. Johnston, but he effectively rallied his command and contributed to the final Union victory.

Sherman was promoted to major general the following May and performed useful service during the Union advance on Corinth, Mississippi. Grant then ordered him to secure Memphis, Tennessee, as a major base of operations against the Confederate citadel of Vicksburg. In this capacity, he ruthlessly suppressed guerrilla activity and punished civilian collaborators harshly—noting carefully the effect such moves had on discouraging the population from further resistance. That fall, Sherman performed initial moves against Vicksburg by attacking its northern tier of defenses along Chickasaw Bluffs, Mississippi, but he was badly repulsed on December 29, 1862. When the press widely accused him of incompetence, he publicly swore he would hang the next reporter who annoyed him. President Abraham Lincoln then supplanted Sherman with the politically oriented General John A. McClernand, who appointed him commander of the XV Corps in the newly constituted Army of the Mississippi. Sherman then accompanied combined operations resulting in the capture of Fort Hindman, Arkansas, on January 11, 1863, before Grant reassigned him to his own Army of the Tennessee. Sherman again distinguished himself by driving Confederates under General Joseph E. JOHNSTON from Jackson, Mississippi, on May 14, 1863, which left Grant free to concentrate on Vicksburg. After that city surrendered on July 4, 1863, Sherman advanced to brigadier general in the regular army and succeeded Grant as commander of the Army of the Tennessee. On November 24, 1863, Sherman figured conspicuously in the defeat of General Braxton BRAGG at Chattanooga, Tennessee, and his subsequent advance on Knoxville broke the siege of General James LONGSTREET. In March 1864, once Grant was called east to serve as commanding general, Sherman succeeded him in leading the Military Division of the Mississippi and as head of all Union forces in the western theater.

In the spring of 1864, Sherman conducted a large offensive toward Meridian, Mississippi, against General Leonidas POLK. His campaign occasioned little fighting; rather, it featured the marked destruction of railways, factories, and storage facilities of possible use to the Confederacy—in sum, a dry run for what happened on a much vaster scale that fall. Thus, Sherman's most vital contribution to the war effort unfolded in the spring and summer of 1864 while commanding the Armies of the Ohio, Cumberland, and Tennessee, under Generals John M. SCHOFIELD, George H. THOMAS, and James B. McPHERSON. With these 100,000 veteran troops, he was to capture the strategic railroad junction at Atlanta, Georgia, before pressing on to Savannah and the sea. For the next few months, Union forces were engaged in an intricate campaign of maneuver against General Johnston's 60,000 men in the Army of Tennessee, who skillfully fell back on a succession of defensive positions. Only once, at Kennesaw Mountain, Georgia, on June 27, 1864, did Sherman grow impatient and attack—suffering heavy losses. However, Johnston's Fabian tactics did not sit well with the Confederate high command, and they replaced him with the aggressive General John B. HOOD in July. Hood then proceeded to squander his army in a series of headlong attack's

Union general William T. Sherman *(Library of Congress)*

against Sherman's men, and on September 2, 1864, Atlanta finally fell. Not only was this a significant Union victory, but it also virtually insured President Abraham Lincoln's reelection that fall. Sherman, having dispatched Schofield and Thomas to pursue Hood back to Nashville, marched next with General Oliver O. HOWARD's Army of the Tennessee and General Henry W. Slocum's Army of Georgia toward Savannah. Imitating Grant at Vicksburg, he also severed his own lines of supply and advanced while foraging off the land. But, most significant, Sherman initiated his policy of "total war," whereby property and food stuffs of potential use to the Confederacy were either confiscated or burned outright. "War is cruelty and you cannot refine it," he insisted. In truth, Sherman was determined to break, not simply Confederate armies, but the very will of Southerners to resist. Union forces then carved a 60-mile wide swath of destruction through Georgia, and on December 21, 1864, he forced General William J. HARDEE to abandon Savannah without a fight. Sherman proudly telegraphed his accomplishment to the president and offered to him the city as a Christmas present. For his efforts, so essential to the ultimate Union victory, Sherman again received the thanks of Congress.

In the spring of 1865, Sherman resumed advancing, this time northward into South Carolina. He drove General Wade HAMPTON's troops out of the state capital at Columbia on February 17, 1865, which was then burned to the ground. The Union columns then pressed into North Carolina where, on March 19–20, General Johnston launched his final, last-ditch blow at Bentonville, which was easily parried. On April 26, 1865, Johnston finally capitulated to Sherman at Durham Station, although under terms so generous that the new administration of President Andrew Johnston refused to acknowledge them. Continuing press criticism so angered the general that he also threatened to boycott the grand victory march through Washington, D.C., if retractions were not made. Sherman, never one to forgo a grudge, next snubbed Secretary of War Edwin M. Stanton on the reviewing stand and refused to shake his hand for criticizing the terms under which Johnston surrendered.

Sherman rose to lieutenant general in July 1866 while heading the Division of the Missouri. Three years later, newly elected President Grant appointed him commanding general of the army with four stars, becoming only the second individual in American history to be so honored. For the next decade, Sherman worked earnestly to improve conditions in the army and foster greater professionalism, including the wholesale adoption of German staff methods. In concert with General Philip H. SHERIDAN, he also waged a ruthless pacification program against hostile Native Americans and finally bought the western frontier under American domination. He proved as merciless toward Native Americans as he had toward Con-

federates, with identical results. Sherman retired from the military in November 1883 and resisted repeated calls to enter politics as a Republican. He died in New York City on February 14, 1891, a highly capable, successful—and ruthless—Civil War commander, second only to Grant in the Union's equation of victory. His systematic application of "total war" also anticipated the trend that warfare would follow throughout the 20th century, whereby civilian populations—and the industrial capability they represented—would become legitimate military targets.

Further Reading

Bailey, Anne J. *War and Ruin: William T. Sherman and the Savannah Campaign.* Wilmington, Del.: Scholarly Resources, 2003.

Flood, Charles B. *Grant and Sherman: The Friendship That Won the Civil War.* New York: Farrar, Straus, and Giroux, 2005.

Foster, Buckley T. *Sherman's Mississippi Campaign.* Tuscaloosa: University of Alabama Press, 2006.

Kennett, Lee B. *Sherman: A Soldier's Life.* New York: HarperCollins, 2001.

Marszalek, John F. *Sherman's March to the Sea.* Abilene, Tex.: McWhiney Foundation Press, 2005.

Scales, John R. *Sherman Invades Georgia: Planning the North Georgia Campaign, A Modern Perspective.* Annapolis, Md.: Naval Institute Press, 2006.

Sherman, William T. *Memoirs of General William T. Sherman, Written by Himself.* 2 vols. Bloomington: Indiana University Press, 1957.

Simms, William G. *A City Laid Waste: The Capture, Sack, and Destruction of the City of Columbia.* Columbia: University of South Carolina Press, 2005.

Woodworth, Steven E. *Nothing but Victory: The Army of the Tennessee, 1861–1865.* New York: Alfred A. Knopf, 2005.

Sibley, Henry H. (1816–1886)

Confederate general

Henry Hopkins Sibley was born in Natchitoches, Louisiana, on May 25, 1816, and educated at private schools in Ohio. He gained admission to the U.S. Military Academy in 1833, was held back a year for poor academics, and finally graduated in 1838 as a second lieutenant in the 2nd U.S. Dragoons. Sibley then fought in Florida's Second Seminole War before performing garrison duty throughout the Old Southwest. During the Mexican War, he marched with General Winfield SCOTT's army, winning brevet promotion to major for bravery at the Battle of Medellín on March 25, 1847. Afterward, Sibley resumed routine garrison duties in Texas where, at Fort Belknap, he perfected the so-called Sibley Tent. This was an Indian teepee modified for military use—as a device, it was widely employed by both sides in the Civil War. Sibley suffered from kidney stones, drank heavily to relieve the pain, and became alcoholic. In 1858 he accompanied General Albert S. JOHNSTON's Mormon expedition, where he engaged in a standing feud with his immediate superior, Major Philip St. George Cooke, and was court-martialed. Acquitted, he spent several months at

Confederate general Henry H. Sibley *(Library of Congress)*

Fort Craig, New Mexico, under Colonel Edward R. S. CANBY. Sibley resigned his commission shortly after the Civil War commenced in May 1861, apparently on the same day that his promotion to major arrived.

Now a Confederate colonel, Sibley ventured to Richmond, Virginia, to confer with President Jefferson DAVIS. He impressed on Davis the necessity of a Confederate campaign to sweep Union influence from the Arizona and New Mexico territories and possibly deliver California to the Confederacy. Davis, impressed by the scheme, promoted Sibley to brigadier general on June 17, 1861, and the following July, he was installed as head of the Department of New Mexico. He then hurriedly returned to San Antonio, Texas, to recruit soldiers. By January 1863 he had gathered 2,000 men, enough to outfit three regiments for his so-called Sibley Brigade. He then embarked on his quixotic quest by departing from El Paso and marching westward into New Mexico. Sibley had earlier promised Davis that his men could easily forage off the countryside, an unrealistic assertion considering the barrenness of the region—and the major cause for his ultimate defeat. His first objective was Fort Craig, where Canby awaited his approach with 3,800 soldiers and militia. The opposing forces clashed heavily at Valverde on February 21, 1862, after which Canby retreated within the confines of Fort Craig. Sibley, meanwhile, bypassed that strong point altogether and continued advancing up the Rio Grande. This move left a strong enemy force positioned astride Confederate lines of communications, a major strategic mistake.

Sibley continued advancing deeper into New Mexico, taking Albuquerque on March 10, 1862, despite the fact that Federal troops conducted a scorched earth policy in his path, destroying anything of potential use to the invaders. Facing logistical shortages, he next turned his attention to Fort Union, a major Union supply depot whose seizure would relieve his present difficulties. En route, the Confederates encountered the Colorado militia of Major John M. Chivington at

Glorieta Pass in the Sangre de Cristo Mountains on March 28, 1862. Sibley defeated part of this force, but a column led by Chivington marched through Apache Pass, behind the Confederates, and captured their supply train. Now lacking food and ammunition, Sibley had no recourse but to withdraw back to Texas before the 3,000 man "California Column" of Colonel James H. CARLETON made its appearance. The Texans then were harried by Canby's soldiers at every turn, losing additional men at Peralta on April 15, 1862. Sibley's exhausted column finally trudged into San Antonio that July, having lost 500 men—a quarter of its strength. The Confederacy never renewed its attempt to seize the Southwest, which remained firmly in Union hands until the end of the war.

Sibley was recalled back to Richmond to answer charges of intoxication, but he was cleared by a court of inquiry. He subsequently headed a brigade under General Richard TAYLOR in western Louisiana. Unfortunately, his mishandling of troops at the Battle of Bisland on April 12–14, 1864—attributed to drinking—led to his arrest and court-martial. Sibley was again acquitted, but his reputation was ruined, and he spent the remainder of the war in the Trans-Mississippi Department without a command.

In 1869 Sibley found employment with Ismail I, the khedive of Egypt, and he served as his chief of artillery. He was dismissed from the service in 1874 on account of drinking and settled down in poverty at Fredericksburg, Virginia. He spent the last few months of his life trying to recoup royalties owed him from government purchases of his Sibley tent, which a court ruled null and void after he entered Confederate service. He died at Fredericksburg on August 23, 1886, one of the Confederacy's most ineffectual figures.

Further Reading

Alberts, Don E. *The Battle of Glorieta: Union Victory in the West.* College Station: Texas A & M University Press, 2000.

Hall, Martin H. *Sibley's New Mexico Campaign.* Albuquerque: University of New Mexico Press, 2000.

Healey, Donald W. *The Road to Glorieta: A Confederate Army Marches through New Mexico.* Bowie, Md.: Heritage Books, 2003.

Hubbard, Joe A. "Intelligence and the Confederate Invasion of New Mexico." Unpublished master's thesis, New Mexico State University, 2001.

Thompson, Jerry D., ed. *Civil War in the South War: Recollections of the Sibley Brigade.* College Station: Texas A & M University Press, 2001.

Wilson, John P., and Jerry Thompson, eds. *The Civil War in West Texas and New Mexico: The Lost Letterbook of Brigadier General Henry Hopkins Sibley.* El Paso, Tex.: Texas Western Press, 2001.

Sickles, Daniel E. (1825–1914)

Union general

Daniel E. Sickles was born in New York City on October 20, 1825, the son of a successful lawyer and politician. After briefly studying at New York University, he passed the bar exam in 1846 and became intrigued by politics. As a state legislator, Sickles helped arrange the purchase of what became Central Park in 1853 and subsequently relocated to London, England, as private secretary to U.S. minister James Buchanan. Mercurially disposed, he lost that post by refusing to toast Queen Victoria during an official Fourth of July celebration. Sickles nonetheless advanced his political fortunes in 1856 by winning a seat in the U.S. House of Representatives as a Democrat, serving two terms. He also gained national notoriety for gunning down the son of Francis Scott Key over an alleged affair with his wife. During his trial, he was defended by Edwin M. Stanton, the future secretary of war, and was acquitted on the basis of temporary insanity, the first time such a defense had been employed. He then forgave his wife for infidelity, which ended his political career, and he returned to New York. When the Civil War broke out in 1861, Sickles sensed a return to the public forum and helped raised five regiments for the city's "Excelsior Brigade" with himself as colonel of the 17th New York Infantry. President Abraham LINCOLN, eager to solicit high-profile Democrats to the war effort, subsequently elevated him to brigadier general on September 3, 1861.

Union general Daniel E. Sickles *(Library of Congress)*

Sickles first saw action in the Peninsula campaign of 1862 as part of General Joseph HOOKER's division, III Corps. He performed well at the clashes of Fair Oaks and Malvern Hill (May–June) and also fought admirably at Antietam that September. Sickles then advanced to major general as of November 29, 1862, assuming command of Hooker's old division. In this capacity, he remained in reserve at Fredericksburg on December 13, 1862, and then succeeded Hooker to the command of III Corps once Hooker became army commander in January 1863. Sickles was present at the debacle of Chancellorsville (May 2–3, 1863), where the III Corps was detached from the Union line and was ordered to pursue Confederates under General Thomas J. JACKSON. This movement actually weakened Hooker's position just as Jackson delivered his famous flank attack, which rolled up the Union XI Corps. No blame was attached to Sickles for the debacle, and he continued heading the III Corps during General Robert E. LEE's invasion of Pennsylvania.

On July 1, 1863, Sickles commanded one of three corps constituting the left wing of the Army of the Potomac under General George G. MEADE. He saw little fighting that day, and on July 2 Meade ordered him to defend the hills of Round Top and Little Round Top on the extreme Union left flank. Then, in the most controversial action of his career, Sickles pushed his men beyond his assigned sector and occupied an exposed salient at the Peach Orchard. He felt that this was a better position, but no sooner had the III Corps taken its positions than Confederates under General James LONGSTREET drove them back in confusion. This precipitated a crisis as the center of the Union line nearly collapsed until General Winfield S. HANCOCK arrived in person with reinforcements and finally halted the hard-charging Southerners. Sickles consequently lost nearly half of his command and, after being struck by a cannonball, a leg as well. Historians have disagreed ever since about the impact of Sickles's indiscretion, with many feeling that he should have been court-martialed for disobeying orders. Nevertheless, in 1897 he received a Congressional Medal of Honor for his behavior and, in a macabre twist, also donated his severed limb to the National Museum of Medicine.

Sickles, his active military service ended, subsequently engaged in an acrimonious dispute with Meade about the events of July 2. He appeared before the Joint Committee on the Conduct of the War and roundly accused Meade of incompetence. His testimony, and the vitriol with which he delivered it, damaged the reputations of both men. In 1865 President Lincoln dispatched him to South America on a diplomatic mission—increasing his distance from Meade—and after the war, he also served as governor of the Carolinas during Reconstruction. Sickles, now a Radical Republican, worked so enthusiastically for the civil rights of African Americans that President Andrew Johnson removed him. Still, in July 1866 he advanced to colonel of the 42nd U.S. Infantry, and the following year, he received brevet promotion to brigadier general for services at Gettysburg. Sickles retired from the service in April 1869 with a rank of major general. That year, President Ulysses S. GRANT appointed him minister to Spain where he bungled his handling of American support for Cuban rebels and resigned. He then traveled through Europe for several years before being reelected to Congress as a Democrat in 1892. The combative and controversial Sickles died in New York on May 3, 1914, a talented political general but far from the best.

Further Reading

Gallagher, Gary H., ed. *The Second Day at Gettysburg: Essays on Confederate and Union Leadership.* Kent, Ohio: Kent State University Press, 1993.

Hyde, Bill. *The Union Generals Speak: The Meade Hearings on the Battle of Gettysburg.* Baton Rouge: Louisiana State University Press, 2003.

Jones, Wilmer L. *Generals in Blue and Gray.* 2 vols. Westport, Conn.: Praeger, 2004.

Keneally, Thomas. *American Scoundrel: The Life of the Notorious Civil War General Daniel Sickles.* New York: Doubleday, 2002.

Sauers, Richard A. *Gettysburg: The Meade-Sickles Controversy.* Washington, D.C.: Brassey's, 2003.

Sears, Stephen W. *Gettysburg.* Boston: Houghton Mifflin, 2004.

Sigel, Franz (1824–1902)

Union general

Franz Sigel was born in Sinsheim, Grand Duchy of Baden, Germany, on November 18, 1824, the son of a magistrate. He passed through the military college at Karlsruhe in 1843 and served in the ducal army as a lieutenant but was caught up in swell of radical liberalism. He dueled with a fellow officer over politics in 1847 and was forced to resign his commission. During the Revolution of 1848, Sigel served as a revolutionary commander and was defeated twice by Prussian troops before escaping to Switzerland. The following year, he returned to Baden after a liberal regime had been installed, and he served as the minister of war before the Prussians returned

and drove him out in 1849. Sigel fled again to Switzerland, was deported to England, and in May 1852, he arrived in New York City. He worked there as a schoolteacher while also serving in the local militia, rising to major. In 1857 he relocated to St. Louis, Missouri, home to a large German-speaking population, and he soon served as a prominent spokesperson for the community. When the Civil War erupted in April 1861, Sigel, like most German Americans, strongly favored the Union, and he offered his services to President Abraham LINCOLN. He then helped to raise the 3rd Regiment of Missouri Volunteers, in which he acted as colonel. In this capacity, Sigel assisted Captain Nathaniel LYON in the capture of Camp Jackson on May 10, 1861, and he pursued the rebels to the capital of Jefferson City. There, he received his first independent command, the 2nd Missouri Brigade, and attacked superior numbers under General Sterling PRICE at Carthage, Missouri, on July 5, 1861. Sigel was

Union general Franz Sigel *(Library of Congress)*

badly repulsed and then reunited with Lyon at Springfield in time for an even bigger confrontation with General Ben McCulloch at Wilson's Creek on August 10, 1861. He prevailed on his superior to perform an intricate flanking movement that ultimately failed and led to a Union defeat. Despite his checkered beginning, Sigel was hailed in the press as a hero and a rallying figure for German Americans to gather around.

In the spring of 1862, Sigel was entrusted with command of two infantry divisions in the army of General Samuel R. Curtis. On March 7–8, 1862, he fought competently at the Battle of Pea Ridge/ Elkhorn Tavern, Arkansas, helping defeat Confederate forces under General Earl Van Dorn. President Lincoln, always eager to bolster his political support among German Americans, readily agreed to promoting him to major general on March 22, 1862. In June 1862 Sigel shipped east to the Shenandoah Valley, Virginia, to succeeded General John C. Frémont as commander of I Corps in General John Pope's Army of Virginia. He fought marginally well on the Union right wing during the disastrous Battle of Second Manassas, August 29–30, 1862, and the following fall, he transferred to the Army of the Potomac under General George B. McClellan. By December, he commanded a grand division under General Ambrose E. Burnside, although, during the defeat at Fredericksburg (December 13, 1862), he remained in reserve. When his grand division was broken up in the spring of 1863, Sigel assumed command of the largely German-speaking XI Corps. Poor health necessitated his removal shortly afterward, and he was succeeded by General Oliver O. Howard. By June, Sigel had recovered sufficiently to head the Pennsylvania Reserves during General Robert E. Lee's invasion of that state, but he still used his significant political connections to secure a combat command.

In February 1864 Sigel gained appointment as head of the Department and Army of West Virginia in the Shenandoah Valley. He then received orders to wrest that productive region from the Confederates and launched a invasion

with 5,100 men. Sigel's advance was greatly delayed by the skillfull tactics of General John D. Imboden's cavalry, which allowed additional Southern troops under General John C. Breckinridge to gather at New Market, Virginia. On May 15, 1864, as Sigel dithered before New Market, Breckinridge attacked under the cover of a driving rainstorm, assisted by 247 Virginia Military Institute cadets, and he heavily defeated the Federals. Sigel consequently was stripped of his field command and was placed in charge of the garrison at Harper's Ferry, West Virginia. This post he yielded to General Jubal A. Early in July 1864 and hastily withdrew across the Potomac without a fight. Sigel consequently lacked a command for the remainder of the war and finally resigned his commission on May 4, 1865.

After the war, Sigel worked as an editor of German-language publications in Baltimore, Maryland, and New York. Political connections within the Democratic Party resulted in his appointment as collector of internal revenue in May 1871, and he also won election as city register. Sigel died in New York on August 21, 1902, little remembered as the highest-ranking Union immigrant soldier of the Civil War. Marginally competent at best, he performed more useful service as a symbol for German Americans to rally around.

Further Reading
Duncan, Richard R. "The Raid on Piedmont and the Crippling of Franz Sigel in the Shenandoah Valley." *West Virginia History* 55 (1996): 25–40.

Engle, Stephen D. *Yankee Dutchman: The Life of Franz Sigel.* Baton Rouge: Louisiana State University Press, 1997.

Hinze, David C., and Karen Farnham. *The Battle of Carthage.* Gretna, La.: Pelican Publishing, 2004.

Lepa, Jack H. *The Shenandoah Valley Campaign of 1864.* Jefferson, N.C.: McFarland, 2003.

Piston, William G. *Wilson's Creek: The Second Battle of the Civil War and the Men Who Fought It.* Chapel Hill: University of North Carolina Press, 2004.

Shea, William L., and Grady McWhiney. *Civil War in the West: Pea Ridge and Prairie Grove.* Abilene, Tex.: McWhiney Foundation Press, 2001.

Stuart, J. E. B. (1833–1864)

Confederate general

James Ewell Brown Stuart was born in Patrick County, Virginia, on February 6, 1833, the son of an attorney. After briefly attending Emory and Henry College, he was admitted to the U.S. Military Academy in 1850. Stuart proved himself an adept student and graduated near the top of his class four years later. In 1854 he served as a second lieutenant in the Mounted Rifle Regiment before transferring to the 1st U.S. Cavalry. In this capacity, he saw extensive service in Kansas and Texas against the Cheyenne, and he was badly wounded in a skirmish at Solomon's Fork. He was also actively employed in suppressing frontier violence during the period of frontier difficulties known as "Bleeding Kansas." In 1855 Stuart married the daughter of his commander and fellow Virginian, Colonel Philip St. George Cooke. Four years later, while on leave in Virginia, Stuart served as an aide to Colonel Robert E. LEE during the capture of abolitionist John Brown at Harper's Ferry. He returned to the frontier and rose to captain in April 1861 just as the Civil War was commencing. Stuart remained in the army until Virginia seceded; then he resigned his commission and joined the Confederacy.

Stuart rose quickly to become colonel of the 1st Virginia Cavalry assigned to the army of General Joseph E. JOHNSTON in the Shenandoah Valley. That summer, he expertly screened Johnston's moves to reinforce General Pierre G. T. BEAUREGARD at Bull Run and staged a spectacular cavalry charge that aided in the Confederate victory of July 21, 1861. Stuart then advanced to brigadier general on September 24, 1861, and began to mold his enthusiastic command into highly trained soldiers. Many of his troops fully inculcated his dash and tendency toward flamboyant displays on the battlefield. Stuart gained instant notoriety during the Peninsula campaign of 1862, when he skillfully executed a daring ride around the army of General George B. McCLELLAN (June 12–15). This act gave Lee accurate intelligence necessary to commence his Seven Days' offensive when he drove Union forces from the gates of Richmond. Ironically, Stuart was pursued throughout by Colonel Cooke, his father-in-law, who remained loyal to the Union. Consequently, he became a major general on July 25, 1862, and received command of all 15,000 cavalry in the Army of Northern Virginia. Stuart next gained additional plaudits for his role in the Second Manassas Campaign against the army of General John POPE. Riding hard, he captured Pope's headquarters at Catlett Station on August 22 and his supply base at Manassas Junction on August 27. He effectively supported General Thomas J. JACKSON throughout the battle itself (August 29–30, 1862). His troopers rendered additional valuable service throughout Lee's invasion of Maryland that September, performing another circuitous ride around McClellan's army following severe combat at South Mountain and Antietam. In October he led a dashing raid as far north as Chambersburg, Pennsylvania, and seized more than 1,000 valuable horses. On December 13, 1862, Stuart's command formed the extreme right flank of Lee's army at Fredericksburg, again performing credibly.

The new year ushered in additional opportunities for Stuart to distinguish himself. In May 1863 he detected the advance of General Joseph HOOKER's army across the Rapidan River, granting Lee sufficient time to formulate a counterstrike at Chancellorsville. Soon after, a mounted brigade under General Fitzhugh LEE discovered that the flank General Oliver O. HOWARD's XI Corps was "in the air," setting the stage for a massive Confederate flank attack. During the battle of May 2, Stuart succeeded both Jackson and General Ambrose P. HILL to command the II Corps after they were wounded, and he conducted affairs competently. Lee then orchestrated his second invasion of the North and entrusted Stuart to screen his advance. On June 9, 1863, however, his command was surprised at Brandy Station by Union cavalry under General Alfred PLEASONTON

Confederate general J. E. B. Stuart *(National Archives)*

and nearly defeated in one of the largest cavalry actions of the war. Stuart's fine generalship allowed the Southerners finally to prevail, although he sustained heavy losses and was roundly criticized in the press—and military circles—for being caught unaware. Stung by these remarks, the haughty, sensitive Stuart, who relished official sanction, determined to redeem his reputation with some kind of grand gesture.

In late June 1863, Stuart received discretionary orders from Lee to screen the army's advance and provide intelligence as to the disposition of Union forces, but he remained at liberty to raid inland as circumstances allowed. Stuart, eager for action, chose the latter course and galloped off into Pennsylvania, losing contact with Lee's headquarters for several days. Consequently, the Confederates operated blindly when they encountered Union forces under General George G. Meade at Gettysburg on

July 1, 1863. Stuart did not make his appearance on the battlefield until the following evening, and on July 3, 1863, he unsuccessfully jousted with General George A. Custer's troopers in the Union rear. He concluded the campaign by successfully covering the Southern withdrawal back to Virginia. Many historians have since concluded that Lee's ultimate defeat at Gettysburg revolved around his lack of reliable military intelligence. Only Stuart could have provided him with such information and, on this occasion, he clearly failed in his mission.

Stuart's experience at Gettysburg and the harsh criticism it engendered induced him to maintain closer contact with headquarters at all times. During the initial phases of General Ulysses S. Grant's overland campaign to Richmond, he served brilliantly in that capacity, keeping Lee abreast of all Union movements. An exasperated Grant then unleashed General Philip H. Sheridan and 12,000 troopers on a raid against the Confederate capital to lure his elusive opponent out into the open and destroy him. On May 9, 1864, both sides clashed indecisively at Todd's Tavern, but two days later, a pitched battle erupted at Yellow Tavern, only six miles from Richmond. Stuart's embattled cavalrymen held their ground against double their numbers until he was mortally wounded and evacuated. "I would rather die than be whipped," he declared at the time. Stuart lingered a day in Richmond before dying on May 12, 1864, and he was replaced by General Wade Hampton. His passing was a significant blow to the Army of Northern Virginia. Brave, vainglorious Stuart personified the taste and temperament of "Southern Cavaliers."

Further Reading

Crouch, Richard E. *Brandy Station: A Battle Like None Other.* Westminster, Md.: Willow Bend Books, 2002.

McKinney, Joseph W. *Brandy Station Virginia, June 9, 1863: The Largest Cavalry Battle of the Civil War.* Jefferson, N.C.: McFarland, 2006.

Mitchell, Adele. *The Letters of Major General James E. B. Stuart.* Fairfax, Va.: Stuart-Mosby Historical Society, 1990.

Robinson, Warren C. *Jeb Stuart and the Confederate Defeat at Gettysburg.* Lincoln: University of Nebraska Press, 2007.

Smith, Derek. *The Gallant Dead: Union and Confederate Generals Killed in the Civil War.* Mechanicsburg, Pa.: Stackpole Books, 2005.

Walker, Paul D. *The Cavalry Battle That Saved the Union: Custer vs Stuart at Gettysburg.* Gretna, La.: Pelican Publishing, 2002.

Wittenberg, Eric J., and J. David Petruzzi. *Plenty of Blame to Go Around: Jeb Stuart's Controversial Ride to Gettysburg.* New York: Savas Beatie, 2006.

T

Taylor, Richard (1826–1879)

Confederate general

Richard Taylor was born near Louisville, Kentucky, on January 27, 1826, the son of general and future president Zachary Taylor. He was well educated at private schools and graduated from Yale University in 1843. Taylor, who exhibited a mania for military history, joined his father's staff during the onset of the Mexican War in 1846, and witnessed the battles of Palo Alto and Resaca de la Palma. However, he declined joining the military and returned to Jefferson County, Mississippi, to manage the family's plantation. During this period, another future president, Jefferson DAVIS, married his sister, while he became one of the state's wealthiest planters. Politically, Taylor opposed radical secessionists in the Democratic Party, and during the 1860 presidential convention in Baltimore, Maryland, he tried to arrange compromise between warring factions. Thereafter, he concluded that secession was inevitable, and during the Louisiana secession convention of January 1861, he voted to leave the Union and join the Confederacy. Shortly after, Taylor gained appointment as colonel of the 9th Louisiana Infantry and departed for the East.

Taylor arrived in Virginia too late to fight at Bull Run in July 1861, but the following October, President Davis made him a brigadier general. The appointment raised eyebrows in military circles as Taylor lacked professional military experience, and the move was denounced as favoritism. But drawing on years of studying military history, strategy, and tactics, Taylor settled quickly into his new role. He first saw combat under General Thomas J. JACKSON during the famous Shenandoah campaign of 1862, in which his Louisiana brigade served as an elite strike force. In the fighting at Front Royal, Winchester, and Port Republic (May–June 1862), Taylor's men invariably stormed strong Federal positions and tipped the contest in Jackson's favor. He next joined the Army of Northern Virginia under General Robert E. LEE, again performing credibly during the Seven Days' battles. Taylor then became the Confederacy's youngest major general on July 28, 1862, but prolonged exposure to cold weather triggered bouts of acute arthritis. Therefore, at Taylor's request, Davis appointed him head of the District of West Louisiana and sent him home. His native state had by then reached its lowest ebb, with New Orleans under firm Union control and Federal forces pushing ever farther up the Mississippi River. But Taylor's aggressive handling of troops defeated General Benjamin F. BUTLER in a number of small engagements that kept him confined him to the city, although he ended up dismissing General Henry H. SIBLEY for drunkenness. The impasse continued until the spring of 1864 when a large combined expedition under General Nathaniel C. BANKS and Admiral David D. PORTER began to ascend the Red River in a bid to invade East Texas.

Taylor, who only commanded 9,000 men, entered into a hostile exchange with General Edmund KIRBY-SMITH, commanding the Trans-Mississippi Department, over his scanty allocation of troops and resources. Taylor was then ordered to give ground and avoid combat, a strategy he performed only reluctantly. But on April 8, 1864, as Banks carelessly deployed his men near Mansfield, Louisiana, Taylor could not pass on an opportunity to attack, and he scattered his larger adversary after severe fighting. The next day, Banks fell back to stronger positions on Pleasant Hill, which Taylor promptly attacked on April 9, 1864, and was himself repulsed. Nonetheless, Union forces continued withdrawing to New Orleans as the gunboat armada of Admiral Porter nearly became stranded due to falling water levels. Taylor wanted to attack and capture the fleet intact, but at that exact moment, Kirby-Smith ordered the bulk of his forces to Arkansas to contain a Union offensive under General Frederick Steele. Taylor reluctantly complied and then unleashed a hostile and disrespectful diatribe at his commanding officer. He was asked to be relieved of command. The request was refused, and while events at Red River soured relations between the two men, Taylor's aggressive leadership preserved this productive part of the Confederacy for another year.

In July 1864 President Davis elevated Taylor to lieutenant general, becoming only one of three individuals who did not attend West Point to achieve such status. As such, he assumed command of the Department of Alabama, Mississippi, and East Louisiana. The ensuing year found Taylor coping with increasingly larger Union raids in his jurisdiction and steadily shrinking manpower resources. In January 1865 he assumed control of General John B. HOOD's Army of Tennessee, now decimated by recent fighting at Nashville. Within weeks, most of these troops were marched east to reinforce General Joseph E. JOHNSTON in the Carolinas. Taylor used the remnants to stave off Union raids, assisted by cavalry under General Nathan B. FORREST. Neither men could halt the depredations of Generals James H. WILSON's raiders, and in April, Confederate hopes for independence were finally dashed. On May 4, 1865, Taylor formally surrendered to General Edward R. S. CANBY at Citronelle, Alabama, being the last Confederate commander east of the Mississippi to do so.

After the war, Taylor resumed his activities in the Democratic Party and vocally opposed Reconstruction and the rights of African Americans. He moved to New York City in 1875 to campaign actively for presidential aspirant Samuel J. Tilden. Taylor died there on April 12, 1879, a capable Confederate leader.

Further Reading

Ayres, Thomas. *Dark and Bloody Ground: The Battle of Mansfield and the Forgotten Civil War in Louisiana.* Dallas: Taylor Trade, 2001.

Joiner, Gary D. *One Damn Blunder from Beginning to End: The Red River Campaign of 1864.* Wilmington, Del.: Scholarly Resources, 2003.

———. *Through the Howling Wilderness: The 1864 Red River Campaign and Union Failure in the West.* Knoxville: University of Tennessee Press, 2006.

Jones, Wilmer L. *Generals in Blue and Gray.* 2 vols. Westport, Conn.: Praeger, 2004.

Milbourn, Curtis W. "The Lafourche Offensive: Richard Taylor's Attempt to Relieve Port Hudson." *North & South* 7, no. 5 (2004): 70–83.

Persons, Benjamin S. *From This Valley They Say You Are Leaving: The Union Red River Campaign, March 1863–May 1865.* Bloomington, Ind.: 1st Books Library, 2003.

Prushankin, Jeffrey S. *A Crisis in Confederate Command: Edmund Kirby Smith, Richard Taylor, and the Army of the Trans-Mississippi.* Baton Rouge: Louisiana State University Press, 2005.

Terry, Alfred H. (1827–1890)

Union general

Alfred Howe Terry was born in Hartford, Connecticut, on November 10, 1827, the son of a bookseller. After passing through the local school system, he studied law at Yale University but did not graduate. Instead, he was admitted to the bar and clerked in the New Haven County Court (1853–60) while also serving in the local militia.

Terry was attracted by military service, and he served as colonel of the 2nd Connecticut Militia by the time the Civil War erupted in April 1861. His unit mustered into service as 90-day volunteers, and he fought at Bull Run on the following July 21, 1861. Once his unit disbanded, Terry gained appointment as colonel of the 7th Connecticut Infantry, a three-year outfit. In this capacity, he accompanied General Thomas W. Sherman on the expedition against Port Royal, South Carolina, on November 7, 1861, and he subsequently distinguished himself in the capture of Fort Pulaski, Georgia, on April 11, 1862. He consequently received promotion to brigadier general of volunteers and served as garrison commander. Terry's next assignment was at the siege of Charleston, South Carolina, where he was involved in actions against Morris Island, Fort Sumter, and Fort Wagner. In December 1863 Terry transferred to the Army of the James under General Benjamin F. BUTLER, commanding a division. He fought well in many actions around Petersburg and in the vicinity of the peninsula of Bermuda Hundred. On May 16, 1864, his men successfully covered the retreat of Union forces from Drewry's Bluff, which signaled the end of Butler's offensive operations.

Terry's exceptional performance led to his promotion to major general in August 1864, along with command of the X Corps, Army of the James. In this capacity, he accompanied Butler's ill-fated expedition against Fort Fisher, Wilmington, North Carolina, on December 25, 1864. General Ulysses S. GRANT then allowed him to sail with Admiral David D. PORTER on a renewed attempt against the fort in January 1865. Once ashore, he constructed defenses against possible Confederate reinforcements under General Robert F. HOKE and stood by him while Porter's entire fleet intensely bombarded Fort Fisher for three days. On January 15, 1865, assisted by a naval brigade, Terry successfully stormed and captured Fort Fisher after a hard-fought battle that resulted in 2,000 prisoners and 165 cannon captured. Success also resulted in the thanks of Congress and promotion to brigadier general in the regular army. The latter was quite

distinctive because Terry had never previously served in the military establishment.

After Fort Fisher fell, Terry's command was placed under the auspices of General John M. SCHOFIELD, and he continued with mop-up operations before finally linking up with General William T. SHERMAN's army at Goldsborough. Once the war ended, Terry rose to major general before mustering out of the volunteers and into the regular service. Throughout most of 1865, he performed Reconstruction work in the Department of Virginia, winning praise for his even-handed approach to delicate matters. However, he experienced a major career shift in 1866 when he was transferred to the Department of Dakota. Thereafter, he became indelibly associated with events along the western frontier for the next 22 years, save for 1869–72, when he served as head of the Department of the South in Georgia.

In the West, Terry became inextricably caught up in the tide of white encroachment on Native-

Union general Alfred H. Terry *(Massachusetts Commandery Military Order of the Loyal Legion and the U.S. Army Military History Institute)*

American lands and the inevitable strife that followed. When Chiefs Crazy Horse and Sitting Bull refused to return to their reservations, General Philip H. SHERIDAN ordered him to conduct a three-pronged offensive against the tribes of the Black Hills region. Assisted by Generals John GIBBON and George CROOK, Terry's column, which constituted the main strike force, reached the Big Horn, River and dispatched Colonel George A. CUSTER on a reconnaissance mission. On June 25, 1876, Custer's detachment was wiped out at Little Big Horn, and Terry's force arrived the next day to bury the dead. Through the ensuing political firestorm, he declined to become embroiled and remained silent as to Custer's culpability for the disaster. Subsequent campaigning throughout the winter gradually drove the exhausted tribes back onto reservations, and in 1877 Terry visited Canada and parleyed with Sitting Bull for his return. The following year, he remained east long enough to sit on the board that reversed General Fitz John PORTER's dismissal of 1863.

Terry remained with the Department of Dakota until March 1886, when he rose to major general and succeeded General Winfield S. HANCOCK as head of the Division of the Missouri, headquartered in Chicago. Declining health necessitated his resignation in April 1888 after a long and successful tenure on the frontier, distinguished by his fair treatment of Native Americans. Terry died in New Haven on December 16, 1890, one of few volunteer officers to achieve both distinction and high grade in the regular service.

Further Reading

Fonvielle, Chris E. *The Wilmington Campaign: Last Departing Rays of Hope.* Mechanicsburg, Pa.: Stackpole Books, 2001.

Majeske, Penelope A. "'Your Obedient Servant': The United States Army in Virginia during Reconstruction, 1865–1867." Unpublished Ph.D. diss., Wayne State University, 1980.

Marino, Carl W. "General Alfred Terry Howe: Soldier from Connecticut." Unpublished Ph.D. diss., New York University, 1968.

McCaslin, Richard B. *The Last Stronghold: The Campaign for Fort Fisher.* Abilene, Tex.: McWhiney Foundation Press, 2003.

Robertson, William G. *Back Door to Richmond: The Bermuda Hundred Campaign, April–June, 1864.* Newark: University of Delaware Press, 1987.

Schiller, Herbert M. *Sumter Is Avenged! The Siege and Reduction of Fort Pulaski.* Shippensburg, Pa.: White Mane Books, 1995.

Thomas, George H. (1816–1870)
Union general

George Henry Thomas was born in Southampton County, Virginia, on July 31, 1816, the son of farmers. He originally wished to study botany, but the death of his parents prevented him from attending college, and in 1836 he attended the U.S. Military Academy. Four years later, he became a second lieutenant with the 3rd U.S. Artillery and fought for two years in Florida's Second Seminole War before fulfilling routine garrison duty throughout the South. When the Mexican War broke out in 1846, he formed part of the Army of Occupation in Texas under General Zachary Taylor and served in the artillery company commanded by Captain Braxton BRAGG. Thomas fought well at Monterrey that year and at Buena Vista in 1847, winning two brevets to major. He then returned to West Point as a tactics instructor, rising there to captain by 1853. Two years later, he transferred as major to the newly raised 2nd U.S. Cavalry under Colonel Albert S. JOHNSTON. This distinguished unit possessed so many Southern officers that it was touted as "Jeff DAVIS's Own" and included such future Civil War luminaries as Robert E. LEE, William J. HARDEE, Edmund KIRBY-SMITH, Fitzhugh LEE, and John B. HOOD. Thomas performed quietly but capably, and in 1860 he was furloughed after receiving back injuries that left him with a trademark, lumbering stride. When the Civil War began in April 1861, he was disowned by his family for remaining with the Union. His courageous decision won little applause in Washington, D.C., however, where leaders viewed his Southern roots with suspicion. In contrast, soldiers who knew Thomas gave him the affectionate nickname "Old Pap" for his mild manners and the kindly treatment he afforded them.

Thomas assumed command of the 2nd U.S. Cavalry's remnants at Carlisle Barracks, Pennsylvania, and he advanced to brigadier general in August 1861 after useful service in the Shenandoah Valley. He then transferred to the Army of the Ohio under General Don C. BUELL, and he commanded a division. On January 19, 1862, Thomas won the first significant Union victory in the West by defeating General George B. CRITTENDEN at Mill Springs, Kentucky, although he failed to received a promotion. Thomas then accompanied Buell down the Tennessee River, arriving too late to fight at the bloody Battle of Shiloh (April 6–7, 1862). General Henry W. HALLECK next appointed him to command the left wing of his army during the advance on Corinth, Mississippi, as a major general of volunteers. Thomas returned to the Army of the Ohio that June and, six months later, fought conspicuously in Buell's victory over General Bragg at Perryville on October 8, 1862. Previously, he had refused an offer to command the Army of the Ohio in deference to Buell, whom he considered more experienced. However, once Buell was dismissed for failing to pursue Bragg energetically, Thomas was also passed over in favor of General William S. ROSECRANS. Thomas angrily protested the unwarranted snub and then continued serving as commander of the XIV Corps in the newly renamed Army of the Cumberland.

Thomas next fought well at the sanguine encounter at Murfreesboro (December 31, 1862–January 3, 1863), convincing Rosecrans not to retreat and greatly assisting in the victory. He continued on through the Tullahoma campaign during the summer of 1863, whereby Chattanooga was acquired by the North. But Thomas's greatest contribution occurred at the bloody Battle of Chickamauga (September 19–20, 1863), where Rosecrans inadvertently created a gap in his own line, and the veteran corps of General

Union general George H. Thomas *(Library of Congress)*

James LONGSTREET poured through, shattering his army. Thomas, commanding the right wing, methodically shored up his XIV Corps on Horseshoe Ridge and beat back every Confederate attempt to dislodge him. His magnificent, set-piece defense discouraged Bragg from pursuing, saved the Union army, and gained for him the popular sobriquet "Rock of Chickamauga." For his efforts, he received promotion to brigadier general in the regular army—but no command. It was not until the following October that General Ulysses S. GRANT appointed Thomas head of the Army of the Cumberland, then besieged in Chattanooga. On November 25, 1863, he helped rout Bragg's Confederates through a splendid—and unauthorized—charge up Missionary Ridge. But despite this latest bravura performance, Thomas still was denied a command position and ended up a subordinate under General William T. SHERMAN, an officer with less seniority. Thomas, as usual, took the snub in stride and carried on.

Through the spring and summer of 1864, Thomas accompanied Sherman on his march to Atlanta, Georgia, as his second in command and sparred constantly with Confederate defenders under General Joseph E. JOHNSTON. When Johnston was replaced by the more aggressive general Hood, Thomas effectively parried a serious Confederate counterattack at Peach Tree Creek on July 20, 1864. Sherman then dispatched him in pursuit of Hood once the latter marched into Tennessee. Thomas, tasked with cobbling together a new army as troops arrived in driblets, ordered General John M. SCHOFIELD to slow Hood's advance until his force was assembled and ready. The Confederates arrived outside Nashville in November and dared Thomas to attack them while officials in Washington also pressured him to advance. Thomas, however, remained methodical and imperturbably calm as ever despite repeated warnings from Grant that he would be replaced for failing to attack. Grant, in fact, issued orders to have General John A Logan succeed him when Thomas finally struck on December 15–16, 1864. The ensuing Battle of Nashville proved disastrous for the Confederacy, and Hood's army was nearly annihilated. He consequently received both the thanks of Congress and promotion to major general, along with command of the Departments of the Tennessee and the Cumberland. Lingering doubts as to Thomas's loyalty had finally been laid to rest.

Thomas remained in the peacetime establishment, and in 1868 he requested and received command of the Department of the Pacific, head-quartered at San Francisco, California. He then quietly and unobtrusively administered his charge until his death there on March 28, 1870. Low-key by nature, Thomas was less known nationally than many of his more flamboyant contemporaries, but he accrued a combat record second to none. Sherman, with great justification, eulogized him as "slow but true as steel."

Further Reading

Arnold, James R. *Jeff Davis's Own: Cavalry, Comanches, and the Battle for the Texas Frontier.* New York: Wiley, 2000.

Brennan, Patrick. "Hell on Horseshoe Ridge." *North & South* 7, no. 2 (2004): 22–44.

Daniel, Larry J. *Days of Glory: The Army of the Cumberland, 1861–1865.* Baton Rouge: Louisiana State University Press, 2004.

Einolf, Christopher J. *George Thomas, Virginian for the Union.* Norman: University of Oklahoma Press, 2007.

Hafendorfer, Kenneth A. *Mill Springs: Campaign and Battle of Mill Springs, Kentucky.* Louisville, Ky.: KH Press, 2001.

Lepa, Jack H. *Breaking the Confederacy: The Georgia and Tennessee Campaign of 1864.* Jefferson, N.C.: McFarland, 2005.

McDonough, James L. *Nashville: The Western Confederacy's Final Gamble.* Knoxville: University of Tennessee Press, 2004.

Mills, Brett. "'Time and History Will Do Me Justice': George H. Thomas and His Place in History." *Journal of America's Military Past* 29, no. 4 (2003): 6–24.

Prokopowicz, Gerald J. *All for the Regiment: The Army of the Ohio, 1861–1862.* Chapel Hill: University of North Carolina Press, 2001.

V

Van Dorn, Earl (1820–1863)

Confederate general

Earl Van Dorn was born in Port Gibson, Mississippi, on September 17, 1820, the son of a local magistrate. He gained appointment to the U.S. Military Academy in 1838 and graduated near the bottom of his class four years later. In 1842 Van Dorn became a second lieutenant in the 7th U.S. Infantry and fought briefly against the Seminoles in Florida before joining General Zachary Taylor's army in Texas. In 1847 he transferred to General Winfield Scott's army and won two brevet promotions for gallantry at the battles of Cerro Gordo and Churubusco. In 1855 Van Dorn advanced to captain in the 2nd U.S. Cavalry for service along the Texas frontier. He distinguished himself in many pitched battles with hostile Comanche, being seriously wounded. Van Dorn was promoted to major in 1860, but on January 3, 1861, he resigned his commission and returned to Mississippi. There, he succeeded his friend Jefferson Davis as major general of state forces, and the following March, he was installed as colonel in the Confederate service. In this capacity, he performed useful service in Texas by accepting the surrender of Union forces under General David E. Twiggs. President Davis next arranged Van Dorn's promotion to brigadier general on June 5, 1861, and major general the following September 19. He also received command of the Confederate Trans-Mississippi Department as of January 1862, a sprawl-ing jurisdiction encompassing Texas, Arkansas, and Missouri. For many months, Van Dorn's principal task was to sort out confusion in Confederate ranks, most notably bickering between Generals Sterling Price and Ben McCulloch.

Van Dorn was a brave and capable soldier, but he proved somewhat lacking in administrative ability. Once ordered to clear Union forces out of northern Arkansas, he assembled a scratch force of 16,000 men and attacked a smaller force of Federals under General Samuel R. Curtis at Pea Ridge (March 6–7, 1862). His Confederate Army of the West, assisted by Confederate Cherokee under Colonel Stand Watie, was poorly handled after an exhausting march and was badly defeated. Van Dorn then surrendered command of the Trans-Mississippi Department to General Theophilus H. Holmes while he was sent across the Mississippi to join General Braxton Bragg in Tennessee. At length, Bragg felt it best to leave the mercurial Van Dorn behind in Mississippi to guard his communications. Van Dorn, however, took to the offensive by attacking General William S. Rosecrans at Corinth on October 3–4, 1862. The Federals, strongly entrenched, handily beat off several determined Confederate attacks, inflicting heavy losses. Van Dorn then retreated in confusion, and his men were roughly handled in another encounter along the Hatchie River two days later. The losses incurred resulted in a court of inquiry that exonerated Van Dorn from charges of drunkenness, but he never again held a significant field command.

Despite his tactical ineptitude with large bodies of men, Van Dorn still enjoyed the confidence of President Davis, who then assigned him command of the strategic citadel at Vicksburg, Mississippi. He enjoyed some success when he repulsed an attempt by Admiral David G. FARRAGUT to bombard the city with gunboats, but in November he was succeeded by General John C. PEMBERTON and reassigned to a cavalry command. For the first time in the war, Van Dorn was back in his element, and he demonstrated flashes of brilliance. On December 20, 1863, he artfully orchestrated a surprise attack on the huge Union supply dump at Holly Springs, burning it to the ground. The loss proved so catastrophic to General Ulysses S. GRANT that he rescheduled his impending campaign against Vicksburg by several months. In March 1863, Van Dorn staged another successful action at Thompson's Station in concert with General Nathan B. FORREST, culminating in the capture of 1,000 Federals. This victory seemed to catapult Van Dorn to the front rank of Confederate cavalry commanders. However, his career reached its tragic end at Spring Hill, Tennessee, on May 7, 1863, when he was shot and killed by Dr. George B. Peters, allegedly for having an affair with his wife. This latest indiscretion deprived the Confederacy of a useful leader at a critical juncture of the Vicksburg campaign; at the time of his death, Van Dorn was also the ranking Confederate major general.

Further Reading

Arnold, James R. *Jeff Davis's Own: Cavalry, Comanches, and the Battle for the Texas Frontier.* New York: Wiley, 2000.

Carter, Arthur B. *The Tarnished Cavalier: Major General Earl Van Dorn, C.S.A.* Knoxville: University of Tennessee Press, 1999.

Cozzens, Peter. *The Darkest Days of the War: Iuka and Corinth.* Chapel Hill: University of North Carolina Press, 1997.

DeBlack, Thomas R. *With Fire and Sword: Arkansas, 1861–1874.* Fayetteville: University of Arkansas Press, 2003.

Lowe, Richard. "Van Dorn's Raid on Holly Springs, December, 1862." *Journal of Mississippi History* 61 (1999): 59–71.

Shea, William L., and Grady McWhiney. *War in the West: Pea Ridge and Prairie Grove.* Abilene, Tex.: McWhiney Foundation Press, 2001.

Winschel, Terrence J. "Earl Van Dorn: From West Point to Mexico." *Mississippi History* 62, no. 3 (2000): 179–197.

Wallace, Lew (1827–1905)

Union general

Lewis Wallace was born in Brookville, Indiana, on April 10, 1827, the son of an attorney. As a youth, he obtained rudimentary education, but he was essentially self-taught. Wallace prepared himself for a legal career but interrupted his studies in 1846 to raise a company of infantry for service in the Mexican War as its lieutenant. He saw no combat and was so angered by General Zachary Taylor's disparaging remarks about Indiana troops that he quit the Whig Party and became a Democrat. Wallace subsequently was admitted to the bar in 1849 while also maintaining close ties to the militia. He also set down political roots in 1856 by successfully standing for a seat in the state senate, and in April 1861 the governor appointed him adjutant general of state forces. Wallace then used his skill at raising troops and his political connections to become colonel of the 11th Indiana Infantry, a colorful Zouave unit. Unlike many political appointees, he proved himself a capable soldier who fought well and distinguished himself in minor actions at Romney and Harper's Ferry, Virginia. He rose to brigadier general in consequence on September 3, 1861, and he reported back to the Department of the Ohio to lead a division. In this capacity, Wallace handled his men capably during General Ulysses S. GRANT's campaign against Forts Henry and Donelson in February 1862. That month, he became the first Indiana native pro-moted to the rank of major general of volunteers, and he accompanied Grant down the Tennessee River to Pittsburg Landing, Tennessee. There, on April 6–7, Confederates under General Albert S. JOHNSTON surprised Grant's men in camp during the Battle of Shiloh while Wallace's division was encamped six miles downstream. Grant immediately ordered him to reinforce General William T. SHERMAN's division, but Wallace, saddled by inaccurate maps, took the wrong road and was forced to backtrack. He did not reach the Union camp until midnight, having failed to contribute to the day's fighting. On the following morning, his fresh troops spearheaded a counterattack that drove Confederates from the field, although Grant characterized his overall performance as lethargic.

Wallace had previously criticized General Henry W. HALLECK, who now replaced Grant as theater commander, and consequently Halleck removed him from command. He next reported for duty at Cincinnati, Ohio, and on September 2, 1862, he organized the city's defenses against a possible raid from Kentucky under General Edmund KIRBY-SMITH. Among the troops Wallace recruited was a brigade of African Americans, among the first such formations in the West. The following month, he chaired a military commission investigating the activities of General Don C. BUELL, which led to his ultimate dismissal. Wallace then assumed command of the Middle Department at Baltimore, Maryland, as head of the small VIII Corps. He discharged his duties capably and with little fanfare until midsummer 1864 when 11,000 Confederates under General Jubal A. EARLY marched up the Shenandoah Valley toward Washington, D.C. Though outnumbered two to one, Wallace assembled a scratch force of 6,000 men and confronted the invaders at Monocacy on July 9, 1864. The Federals were swept aside after a stiff fight, and Wallace withdrew back to Baltimore, but the delays incurred allowed General Horatio G. Wright to strengthen the capital's defenses, and a Confederate assault was thwarted. In May 1865, Wallace served on the court that tried conspirators charged with the assassination of President Abraham LINCOLN. The following August, he also sat on a tribunal that condemned Captain Henry Wirz, commander of notorious Andersonville Prison, to hang.

After mustering out, Wallace enjoyed a highly varied, wide-ranging career. He first ventured to Mexico to support Republican forces trying to oust the French-backed emperor Maximilian. Unsuccessful, Wallace then returned to Indiana to resume political activities, and in 1878 his influence helped deliver the state to President Rutherford B. Hayes. He was then appointed governor of the New Mexico Territory as a sinecure, and he expended considerable energy ending a hostile range war with the likes of Billy the Kid. In 1880 Wallace gained lasting renown by writing the novel *Ben Hur*, one of the most popular books ever published in American literature. President James A. Garfield then appointed him minister to Turkey, where he served from 1881 to 1885. Wallace then returned to Crawford, Indiana, to continue writing, and he died there on February 15, 1905. Despite his mixed military record, he was among the most colorful of political generals.

Further Reading

Arnold, James R. *Shiloh, 1862: The End of Innocence.* Westport, Conn.: Praeger, 2004.
Boomhower, Ray E. *The Sword and the Pen: A Life of Lew Wallace.* Indianapolis: Indiana Historical Society Press, 2005.
Leeke, Jim, ed. *Smoke, Sound & Fury: The Civil War Memoirs of Major-General Lew Wallace, U.S. Volunteers.* Philadelphia: Polyglot Press, 2004.
Stephens, Gail M. "Lew Wallace's Fall from Grace." *North & South* 7, no. 3 (2004): 32–46.
Stephens, Gail M., and Gloria B. Swift. "Honor Redeemed: Lew Wallace's Military Career and the Battle of Monocacy." *North & South* 4, no. 2 (2001): 34–46.
Woodworth, Steven L., ed. *Grant's Lieutenants: From Cairo to Vicksburg.* Lawrence: University Press of Kansas, 2001.

Watie, Stand (1806–1871)

Confederate general

Degataga (Stand Firm) was born to the Deer Clan of the Cherokee at Oothcaloga, Georgia, on December 12, 1806, a son of farmers. Educated at mission schools and converted to the Moravian Church, he gradually Anglicized his name to Stand Watie. He also claimed one-quarter Scottish ancestry through his mother, and he became closely associated with the light-skinned tribal elite. In time, both he and his brother Elias Boudinot, editor of the tribal newspaper *Cherokee Phoenix,* aligned themselves with factions who were willing to sell their land to the U.S. government and peacefully relocate to the Indian Territory (Oklahoma) reserved for them. This placed him at odds with Chief John Ross and the bulk of the Cherokee, who resisted deportation from Georgia. Watie was nonetheless one of a handful of chiefs who willingly signed the Treaty of New Echota in December 1835, mandating their removal. He arrived at his new home without incident, but many Cherokee, forced to endure the so-called Trail of Tears under General Winfield SCOTT, resented his cooperation with whites. Thereafter, the tribe was strongly split into two feuding factions under Ross and Watie, with the latter losing a brother, a cousin, and an uncle to assassination. Peace was not restored to the tribe until 1846.

After resettling, Watie established himself as a wealthy, slave-owning planter and was therefore naturally sympathetic to the newly established Confederate State of America. In August 1861 he prevailed on Chief Ross to embrace the Southern cause, and he received command of the 1st Cherokee Mounted Rifle Regiment as its colonel. When Ross subsequently reneged on his commitments and fled to Union-controlled territory, a civil war broke out among the Cherokee in which Watie ultimately prevailed. Thereafter, he mustered all available warriors and joined Confederates armies in the field. Watie fought with General Earl VAN DORN at Pea Ridge (March 7–8, 1862), and, there, he captured a Union battery and covered the Confederate withdrawal. He was also conspicuously engaged in the Southern defeat at Honey Springs on July 17, 1863, in which Confederate Native Americans were pitted against Union African Americans. That year, shifting tides of fortune finally convinced the majority of Cherokee to renounce their alliance with the Confederacy, but Watie remained loyal and advanced to brigadier general as of May 1864. He was also elected the principal tribal war chief and commanded an entire brigade of two mounted regiments and three battalions of Cherokee, Osage, and Seminole infantry. With them, he attacked and captured the Federal steamer *J. R. Williams* in June 1864, along with $41.2 million in supplies. The following September 19, 1864, Watie also seized 200 supply wagons and 1,200 mules at Cabin Crossing. Once hostilities concluded, Watie surrendered to Union officials on June 23, 1865, the last Confederate commander to do so.

After the war, Watie resumed his highly visible profile in tribal politics and worked at reconciling the various factions. He made his greatest contribution in helping to negotiate the Cherokee Reconstruction Treaty of 1866, whereby all slaves in tribal possession were manumitted. He thereafter became a fairly prosperous tobacco grower, minus his slaves. Watie died at Honey Creek, Indian Territory, on September 9, 1871, the only Native American to obtain general's rank during the Civil War. His activities tied down the services of thousands of Federal troops, marking him as one of the conflict's most skilled leaders of irregulars.

Further Reading

Confer, Clarissa W. *The Cherokee Nation in the Civil War*. Norman: University of Oklahoma Press, 2007.

Epple, Jess C. *Honey Springs Depot:, Elk Creek, Creek Nation, Indiana Territory*. Muskogee, Okla.: Thomason Print Co., 2002.

Hatch, Tom. *The Blue, the Gray, and the Red*. Mechanicsburg, Pa.: Stackpole Books, 2003.

Jackson, Rex T. *A Trail of Tears: The American Indian in the Civil War*. Bowie, Md.: Heritage Books, 2004.

Spencer, John D. *American Civil War in Indian Territory*. New York: Osprey, 2006.

Taylor, Ethel. *Dust in the Wind: The Civil War in Indian Territory*. Westminster, Md.: Heritage Books, 2005.

Wheeler, Joseph (1836–1906)
Confederate general

Joseph Wheeler was born in Augusta, Georgia, on September 10, 1836, the son of a banker. After attending private academies in Connecticut, he matriculated through the U.S. Military Academy in 1854 and graduated four years later near the bottom of his class. Wheeler then served as a second lieutenant in the Regiment of Mounted Riflemen in New Mexico, where his willingness to skirmish with hostile Apaches led to the nickname "Fighting Joe." However, once Georgia seceded from the Union in February 1861, he likewise resigned his commission and joined the Confederate army. Wheeler first served as an artillery lieutenant at Pensacola, Florida, under General Braxton BRAGG. He favorably impressed his superiors and consequently became colonel of the 19th Alabama Infantry in September 1861. In this capacity, Wheeler fought well at the Battle of Shiloh (April 6–7, 1862), garnering praise for his conduct of the Confederate rear guard. Bragg, now head of the Army of Mississippi, then appointed Wheeler to command all his cavalry. This proved a fortuitous appointment, for he became one of the hardest riding, most astute mounted leaders on either side. In August 1862 Wheeler's men spearheaded Bragg's drive into Kentucky, where, on October 8, 1862, he distinguished himself at the Battle of Perryville and then expertly covered the Confederate retreat. His

Confederate general Joseph Wheeler *(Library of Congress)*

of eastern Tennessee virtually unopposed. During the course of several days, his men inflicted nearly 2,000 casualties, burned 1,000 supply wagons, and destroyed $3 million of property at a cost of only 212 men. This master stroke nearly destroyed Rosecrans's ability to feed his army at Chattanooga and greatly increased its hardships. Wheeler then accompanied General James LONGSTREET on his aborted siege of Knoxville and, after the crushing Confederate defeat at Missionary Ridge on November 25, 1863, again covered Bragg's retreat into Georgia. Wheeler then acted in concert with General Patrick R. CLEBURNE at Ringgold Gap, Georgia, successfully defending it for several hours against superior numbers under General Joseph HOOKER.

In the spring of 1864, Wheeler found himself attached to the Army of Tennessee under General Joseph E. JOHNSTON. For several weeks, he campaigned hard against the advancing columns of General William T. SHERMAN as they marched toward Atlanta, Georgia. On July 30, 1864, he captured General George Stoneman's cavalry column, along with 700 prisoners, which incapacitated Sherman's mounted arm for several weeks. A new commander, General John B. HOOD, then dispatched Wheeler on another long and fruitless raid against Union communications in Tennessee. He then reunited with Johnston in the Carolinas, offering the only organized Confederate resistance to Union troopers under General Hugh J. KILPATRICK. Wheeler gained promotion to lieutenant general in February 1865, but concern over indiscipline in his command resulted in subordination under General Wade HAMPTON. Wheeler was again closely engaged at the Battle of Bentonville, North Carolina, on March 19–21, 1865, before fleeing back to Georgia. He finally was captured there on May 1865 while assisting the flight of President Jefferson DAVIS. In the course of his Civil War career, Wheeler fought in 200 engagements, lost 16 horses shot from beneath him, was wounded three times, and witnessed 36 staff officers shot down at his side.

good performance led to a promotion to brigadier general on October 30, 1862, and throughout the following December, he competently delayed the advance of Union forces under General William S. ROSECRANS. Wheeler then fought well at the bloody encounter of Murfreesboro (December 31, 1862–January 3, 1863), again covered Bragg's retreat, and served as cavalry commander in his newly organized Army of Tennessee. He also became the South's youngest major general as of January 20, 1863, at the age of 26.

Wheeler next accompanied Bragg throughout the Tullahoma campaign against Rosecrans before fighting again at Chickamauga on September 19–20, 1863. Once Union forces were besieged at Chattanooga, Tennessee, he conducted one of the war's most destructive cavalry raids by crossing the Tennessee River, brushing aside General George CROOK's command on the other bank, and then galloping through the Sequatchie Valley

Wheeler was imprisoned briefly in Delaware during the postwar period, but he relocated to New Orleans, Louisiana, where he flourished as a merchant and lawyer. In 1881 he gained election to the U.S. House of Representatives, returning there eight consecutive times and serving as chairman of the influential Ways and Means Committee. In this capacity, Wheeler became an important symbol of national reconciliation between North and South. For this reason, President William McKinley appointed him a major general of volunteers during the Spanish-American War of 1898. Wheeler again acquitted himself well as a cavalry commander, whose units included Colonel Theodore Roosevelt's "Rough Riders." After the war, he briefly led a convalescent camp at Montauk Point, New York, before leading a brigade in the Philippines. In 1900 Wheeler rose to brigadier general in the regular army as head of the Department of the Lakes. He retired the following year to live in Brooklyn, dying there on January 25, 1906. Wheeler, along with J. E. B. STUART, Joseph O. SHELBY, and Nathan B. FORREST, was among the most talented cavalry leaders of the Civil War. He is one of only a handful of Southern leaders to hold general's rank in both armies or to be interred at Arlington National Cemetery in Washington, D.C.

Further Reading

Black, Robert W. *Cavalry Raids of the Civil War.* Mechanicsburg, Pa.: Stackpole Books, 2004.

Blumberg, Arnold. "Wheeler's 1863 Sequatchie Valley Raid." *Military Heritage* 4, no. 4 (2003): 60–67, 90.

Brookshear, William R., and David K. Schneider. *Glory at a Gallop: Tales of the Confederate Cavalry.* Washington, D.C.: Brassey's, 1993.

Longacre, Edward G. *A Soldier to the Last. Maj. Gen. Joseph Wheeler.* Washington, D.C.: Potomac Books, 2006.

Poole, John R. *Cracker Cavaliers: The 2nd Georgia Cavalry under Wheeler and Forrest.* Macon, Ga.: Mercer University Press, 2000.

Wittenberg, Eric J. *The Battle of Monroe's Crossroads: And the Civil War's Final Campaign.* New York: Savas Bentie, 2006.

Wilkes, Charles (1798–1877)

Union naval officer

Charles Wilkes was born in New York City on April 3, 1798, the son of a banker. Early on, he developed a love of the sea, and after failing to receive a midshipman's commission in 1815, Wilkes joined the merchant marine to acquire nautical experience. Three years later, he was allowed to join the service as a midshipman and during the next 20 years fulfilled a series of routine assignments both afloat and ashore. Wilkes rose

Union naval officer Charles Wilkes *(Massachusetts Commandery Military Order of the Loyal Legion and the U.S. Army Military History Institute)*

to lieutenant by 1826, and in 1838 the government appointed him to command an ambitious exploring expedition that several senior naval leaders declined to accept. The fact that Wilkes had acquired the reputation as a querulous, disagreeable officer rankled contemporaries far less than the fact that he enjoyed less seniority than many officers now serving under him. Nevertheless, Wilkes departed Hampton Roads, Virginia, with a flotilla of six vessels and a bevy of scientists. During the next four years, he ably conducted the U.S. exploring expedition to the farthest reaches of the Pacific, which included the discovery of a new landmass, Antarctica (originally christened Wilkes Land), in December 1839. All told, it was a remarkable episode of discovery covering 80,000 miles, visiting 180 islands, and resulting in the creation of 180 nautical charts that were so accurate that many were still employed during World War II. Moreover, the plants and animals he brought back formed the core collection of what became the Smithsonian Institution. But no sooner had Wilkes docked at New York in June 1842 than he was brought up on charges of abuse leveled by many officers and crew members. A court-martial found him guilty of meting out unauthorized punishment, which only enhanced his reputation as a stiff-necked martinet. Worse, enemies in Congress obstructed the funding to publish his 20-volume record of the expedition. Wilkes simply accepted an assignment ashore and spent 17 years editing and publishing it on his own. During this period, he rose to commander in 1843 and captain in 1855.

When the Civil War commenced in April 1861, Wilkes was assigned to the USS *Merrimac* at Norfolk, but he arrived to find that it had already been scuttled by retreating Union forces. He then received command of the steamer *San Jacinto* with orders to patrol the west coast of Florida for Confederate commerce and possibly to intercept the raider CSS *Sumter* under Commander Raphael SEMMES. While in Havana, he learned that Confederate diplomats John M. Mason and John Slidell were aboard the British

mail ship *Trent* off the Bahamas. Rough-hewn and hardly beholden to the nuances of diplomacy, Wilkes aggressively charted an intercept course, and on November 8, 1861, he fired a shot across the British vessel's bow. Mason and Slidell then were forcibly removed in an egregious violation of international neutrality, but Wilkes arrived at Boston to a hero's welcome. The British government, however, vehemently protested and threatened war if Mason and Slidell were not immediately released. President Abraham LINCOLN, wishing at all hazards to avoid British military intervention on the Confederacy's behalf, ordered both men released on January 1, 1862. The incident subsided much to the relief of both sides.

The contentious Wilkes received promotion to commodore in July 1862 and successively commanded the James River and Potomac River squadrons to assist the Peninsula campaign of General George B. McCLELLAN. That September, he was accorded a rank of acting rear admiral along with command of the West Indies Squadron. Wilkes then was tasked with intercepting Confederate privateers and blockade-runners, which he pursued with vigor. However, he also roughly accosted several British vessels in the process, and he was recalled in June 1863 amid a storm of diplomatic protests. Wilkes then vented his anger against Secretary of the Navy Gideon Welles, whom he publicly denounced as a buffoon, and he was court-martialed a second time in March 1864. He then was demoted to captain and placed on three years' suspension, although President Lincoln reduced the sentence to a single year. His active navy career ended, Wilkes retired in 1864 and resumed editing and publishing his expedition accounts. He advanced to rear admiral on the retired list in July 1866 and composed his lengthy memoirs in 1871 at the age of 73. Wilkes died in Washington, D.C., on February 8, 1877, a highly efficient naval officer, a thoroughly unlikable individual, and the man who almost embroiled the United States in a war with Britain.

Further Reading

Bradford, James C., ed. *Captains of the Old Steam Navy: Makers of the American Naval Tradition, 1840–1880.* Annapolis, Md.: Naval Institute Press, 1986.

Fuller, Howard. *Navies and Naval Operations of the Civil War, 1861–1865.* London: Conway Marine, 2005.

Joyce, Barry A. *The Shaping of American Ethnology: The Wilkes Exploring Expedition, 1838–1842.* Lincoln: University of Nebraska Press, 2001.

Morgan, William J., et al., eds. *Autobiography of Rear Admiral Charles Wilkes, U.S. Navy, 1798–1877.* Washington, D.C.: Naval History Division, 1978.

Philbrick, Nathaniel. *Sea of Glory: America's Voyage of Discovery: The U.S. Exploring Expedition, 1838–1842.* New York: Viking Press, 2003.

Warren, Gordon H. *Fountain of Discontent: The Trent Affair and Freedom of the Seas.* Boston: Northeastern University Press, 1981.

Wilson, James H. (1837–1925)

Union general

James Harrison Wilson was born in Shawneetown, Illinois, on September 2, 1837, the son of farmers. He briefly attended McKendree College before enrolling at the U.S. Military Academy in 1855. An excellent student, Wilson graduated sixth in his class in 1860 and was posted with the elite Corps of Engineers. He then spent a year at Fort Vancouver, Washington Territory, before the Civil War broke out in April 1861, when Wilson hastened back east to fight. He saw his first action as a topographical engineer on the staff of General Thomas W. Sherman at the capture of Port Royal, South Carolina, in November 1861 and subsequently distinguished himself under General David Hunter during the siege of Fort Pulaski, Georgia, in April 1862. Eager for advancement, Wilson next served as a volunteer aide-de-camp to General George B. McClellan throughout the Antietam campaign of September. Good conduct resulted in promotion to lieutenant colonel of volunteers and transfer to the staff of General Ulysses S. Grant the following November 1862. Wilson performed well throughout the ensuing Vicksburg campaign and served as inspector general of the Army of the Tennessee as of July 1863. He rose to brigadier

Union general James Wilson *(Library of Congress)*

general of volunteers that October and fought with distinction at the decisive Union victory of Chattanooga on November 25, 1863. Grant then recommended him as chief of the Cavalry Bureau within the War Department, which office he assumed in January 1864.

Wilson, possessing no prior experience with the mounted arm, nonetheless instituted reforms that completely overhauled the cavalry's equipment and mission. He believed that the days of sword-wielding charges had passed and that troopers were infinitely more valuable serving as mobile infantry, combining movement with firepower. To that end, he issued rapid-fire Spencer rifles to all ranks and trained them vigorously in the art of skirmishing. In April 1864 Grant reassigned Wilson to command the 3rd Cavalry Division as part of General Philip H. Sheridan's cavalry corps, Army of the Potomac. In his first mounted foray, Wilson conducted some minor raids near Richmond, losing his wagon train in one instance and then tangling heavily with General Wade HAMPTON's Confederate cavalry at Ream's Station on August 25, 1864. He subsequently accompanied Sheridan to the Shenandoah Valley and bore a prominent role in the crushing of Confederate forces under General Jubal A. EARLY. Wilson, as he acquired greater experience in handling mounted troops, exhibited signs of operational brilliance, and, in the fall of 1864, he was posted as cavalry chief in the Military Division of the Mississippi under General William T. SHERMAN.

Wilson provided useful services during the Union advance to Atlanta, Georgia, until General John B. HOOD's Confederates marched into Tennessee to attack Union supply lines. After detaching the division of General Hugh J. KILPATRICK to remain with Sherman, he then accompanied Generals George H. THOMAS and John M. SCHOFIELD westward. Wilson's cavalry expertly delayed the Confederate approach to Spring Hill and Franklin, where they suffered terrible losses on November 29, 1864, and he subsequently covered Schofield's retreat to Nashville. On December 16 his men were actively engaged in the decisive Battle of Nashville, which saw Hood's Army of Tennessee virtually destroyed by a vigorous pursuit. Wilson then gained promotion to brevet brigadier general of regulars in March 1865 along with command of his own cavalry corps, 15,000 strong. With it, he launched a series of devastating raids across northern Alabama and Georgia, heavily defeating General Nathan B. FORREST at Selma on April 2, 1865. This success was followed up by the captures of Montgomery on April 12 and Columbus, Georgia, on April 16, along with 7,000 prisoners and 300 cannon. Thus, to Wilson goes the distinction of fighting and winning the Civil War's last land engagement east of the Mississippi River. His men also gained a final measure of distinction on May 10, 1865, by capturing Confederate president Jefferson DAVIS at Irwinville, Georgia. He ended the war as a major general of volunteers at the age of 27.

Wilson was retained in the postwar service as a lieutenant colonel of the 35th U.S. Infantry, and he resigned from the service in December 1870 to pursue railroad engineering. He returned to the colors when the Spanish-American War commenced in 1898 as a major general of volunteers, seeing service in Cuba and Puerto Rico. In 1900 he ventured to China to fight in the Boxer Rebellion under General Adna R. Chaffee and commanded a punitive expedition against the city of Patachow. He then retired with a rank of brigadier general by a special act of Congress. Wilson died in Wilmington, Delaware, on February 23, 1925, a noted "boy general" of the Civil War and one of the longest surviving Union generals.

Further Reading

Black, Robert W. *Cavalry Raids of the Civil War*. Mechanicsburg, Pa.: Stackpole Books, 2004.

Bellware, Daniel A. "The Last Battle of the War. Period. Really." *Civil War Times Illustrated* 42, no. 1 (2003): 48–43, 56.

Coffey, David. *Sheridan's Lieutenants: Phil Sheridan, His Generals, and the Final Year of the Civil War*. Wilmington, Del.: Rowman and Littlefield, 2005.

Jones, James P. *Yankee Blitzkrieg: Wilson's Raid through Alabama and Georgia*. Lexington: University Press of Kentucky, 2000.

Kennan, Jerry. *Wilson's Cavalry Corps: Union Campaigns in the Western Theater, October 1864 through Spring 1865*. Jefferson, N.C.: McFarland, 1998.

Longacre, Edward G. *Lincoln's Cavalrymen: A History of the Mounted Forces of the Army of the Potomac, 1861–1865*. Mechanicsburg, Pa.: Stackpole Books, 2000.

Worden, John L. (1818–1897)

Union naval officer

John Lorimer Worden was born in Westchester County, New York, on March 12, 1818, and he joined the U.S. Navy as a midshipman in 1834. For the next 27 years, he fulfilled a series of routine assignments afloat and ashore, rising to lieutenant in 1846. He still held that rank when the Civil War commenced in April 1861 and immediately requested duty at sea. Worden was dispatched overland to Fort Pickens, Florida, with a secret communiqué for the Federal squadron offshore.

Confederate authorities apprehended him at Montgomery, Alabama, on his return trip, and he experienced close confinement for seven months. Once exchanged, Worden received command of inventor John Ericsson's new and experimental ironclad warship, USS *Monitor*. This unique vessel, frequently derided as a "cheese box on a raft," sat extremely low in the water with a single, revolving turret amidships. Its bizarre appearance greatly belied the dramatic military revolution it embodied.

On February 25, 1862, Worden sailed his charge from Long Island, New York, to Hampton Roads, Virginia, delayed by choppy seas and last-minute mechanical failures. He arrived on the evening of March 7, 1862, to behold the devastation wrought by the Confederate captain Franklin

Union naval officer John L. Worden *(U.S. Navy)*

BUCHANAN and the ironclad CSS *Virginia* (née *Merrimac*), which had sank or had severely damaged the Federal frigates *Cumberland* and *Congress* that afternoon. The following morning, the *Virginia,* now captained by Lieutenant Catesby ap Roger Jones, reappeared to finish off the Union vessels, and Worden placed his *Monitor* squarely in its path. For the next three hours, the armored giants flailed away at each other, inflicting little damage. The *Virginia* also tried to ram its smaller opponent, but it was thwarted by the latter's higher speed and shallower draft. Finally, a lucky Southern shot shattered Worden's pilothouse, wounding him in the eye. He relinquished command to Lieutenant Samuel D. Greene, and after a few more hours of combat, the *Virginia* withdrew back to Norfolk before low tides stranded it. This engagement, though technically a draw, proved a strategic victory for the North as it maintained the blockade of Norfolk and ensured its eventual capture. It also sounded the death knell of wooden warships. Worden's wound required several months of rehabilitation, but he received the thanks of Congress and promotion to commander in July 1862 for his fine performance. President Abraham LINCOLN was so impressed by the doughty sailor that he paid him a bedside visit.

After recovery, Worden assumed command of the new *Passaic*-class monitor *Montauk* in January 1863, and he sailed as part of Admiral Samuel F. Du PONT's South Atlantic Blockading Squadron. A massive naval attack on heavily defended Charleston, South Carolina, was then in the planning stages, and Worden was ordered to attack Fort McAllister, Savannah, Georgia, as an experiment, on January 27, 1863. He traded shots with the fort for several hours, inflicting little damage and sustaining 46 hits. Another attack on February 1, 1863, yielded similar results, but on February 28, he managed to destroy the Confederate raider CSS *Nashville* beneath the fort's guns. That month, he also rose to captain. But despite Du Pont's predictions of disaster, the Navy Department authorized the assault on Charleston, which transpired on the afternoon of April 7, 1863. Worden was actively engaged, receiving a further 14 direct hits, and the rest of the fleet was also heavily damaged. Shortly after, he was relieved of command and recalled to New York to supervise the construction of new monitor vessels. This vital service kept him out of combat for the remainder of the war.

In the postwar period, Worden commanded the *Pensacola* as part of the Pacific Squadron until May 1868, when he advanced to commodore and was appointed superintendent of the U.S. Naval Academy, Annapolis. His five year of tenure was characterized by his implementation of elevated academic standards and rules against hazing, and the founding of the U.S. Naval Institute, in which he served as first president. Worden rose to rear admiral in November 1872 and spent the next 14 years commanding various squadrons. He retired in December 1886 after a special act of Congress allowed him to retain full-pay status for life. Worden died in Washington, D.C., on October 18, 1897, an important leadership figure in the navy's transition from wood to iron.

Further Reading

Clancy, Paul R. *Ironclad: The Epic Battle Calamities, Loss, and Historic Recovery of the USS Monitor.* Camden, Maine: International Marine/McGraw-Hill, 2006.

Holzer, Harold, ed. *The Battle of Hampton Roads: New Perspectives on the USS Monitor and CSS Virginia.* New York: Fordham University Press, 2006.

Nelson, James L. *Reign of Iron: The Story of the First Battling Ironclads, The Monitor and the Merrimack.* New York: William Morrow, 2004.

Roberts, William H. *Civil War Ironclads: The U.S. Navy and Industrial Mobilization.* Baltimore: Johns Hopkins University Press, 2002.

Symonds, Craig L. *Decision at Sea: Five Naval Battles That Shaped American History.* New York: Oxford University Press, 2005.

West, W. Wilson. "Monitor Madness: Union Ironclad Construction at New York City, 1862–1864." Unpublished Ph.D. diss., University of Alabama, 2003.

 # APPENDIX

Casualties and Major Land Battles of the Civil War

TROOPS AVAILABLE FOR DUTY (JANUARY 1)

	Union	Confederacy
1862	527,204	209,852
1863	698,808	253,208
1864	611,250	233,586
1865	620,924	154,910
Total Forces	1,556,678	1,082,119

DEATHS DURING THE CIVIL WAR

	Union	Confederacy
Total forces	1,556,678	1,082,119
Deaths from Wounds	110,070	94,000
Deaths from Disease	249,458	164,000
Death Rate	23 percent	24 percent
Wounded	275,175	100,000

DEATHS IN AMERICAN WARS (U.S. MILITARY CASUALTIES)

Civil War	618,000
World War II	405,000
World War I	112,000
Vietnam War	58,000
Korean War	36,517
American Revolution	25,000
War of 1812	20,000
Mexican War	13,000
Spanish-American War	2,446
Gulf War	299

Major Land Battles

The Ten Costliest Land Battles, Measured by Casualties (Killed, Wounded, Captured, and Missing)

BATTLE (STATE)	DATES	CONFEDERATE COMMANDER	UNION COMMANDER	CONFEDERATE FORCES	UNION FORCES	VICTOR	CASUALTIES
Battle of Gettysburg (Pennsylvania)	July 1–3, 1863	Robert E. Lee	George G. Meade	75,000	82,289	Union	51,112 U: 23,049 C: 28,063
Battle of Chickamauga (Georgia)	September 19–20, 1863	Braxton Bragg	William Rosecrans	66,326	58,222	Conf.	34,624 U: 16,170 C: 18,454
Battle of Chancellorsville (Virginia)	May 1–4, 1863	Robert E. Lee	Joseph Hooker	60,892	133,868	Conf.	30,099 U: 17,278 C: 12,821
Battle of Spotsylvania Court House (Virginia)	May 8–19, 1864	Robert E. Lee	Ulysses S. Grant	50,000	83,000	Draw	27,399 U: 18,399 C: 9,000
Battle of Antietam (Maryland)	September 17, 1862	Robert E. Lee	George B. McClellan	51,844	75,316	Draw	23,134 U: 12,410 C: 10,724
Battle of the Wilderness (Virginia)	May 5–7, 1864	Robert E. Lee	Ulysses S. Grant	61,025	101,895	Draw	25,416 U: 17,666 C: 7,750
Second Battle of Manassas (Virginia)	August 29–30, 1862	Robert E. Lee	John Pope	48,527	75,696	Conf.	25,251 U: 16,054 C: 9,197
Battle of Stones River (Tennessee)	December 31, 1862	Braxton Bragg	William S. Rosecrans	37,739	41,400	Union	24,645 U: 12,906 C: 11,739
Battle of Shiloh (Tennessee)	April 6–7, 1862	Albert Sidney Johnston, P. G. T. Beauregard	Ulysses S. Grant	40,335	62,682	Union	23,741 U: 13,047 C: 10,694
Battle of Fort Donelson (Tennessee)	February 13–16, 1862	John B. Floyd, Simon B. Buckner	Ulysses S. Grant	21,000	27,000	Union	19,455 U: 2,832 C: 16,623

MAPS

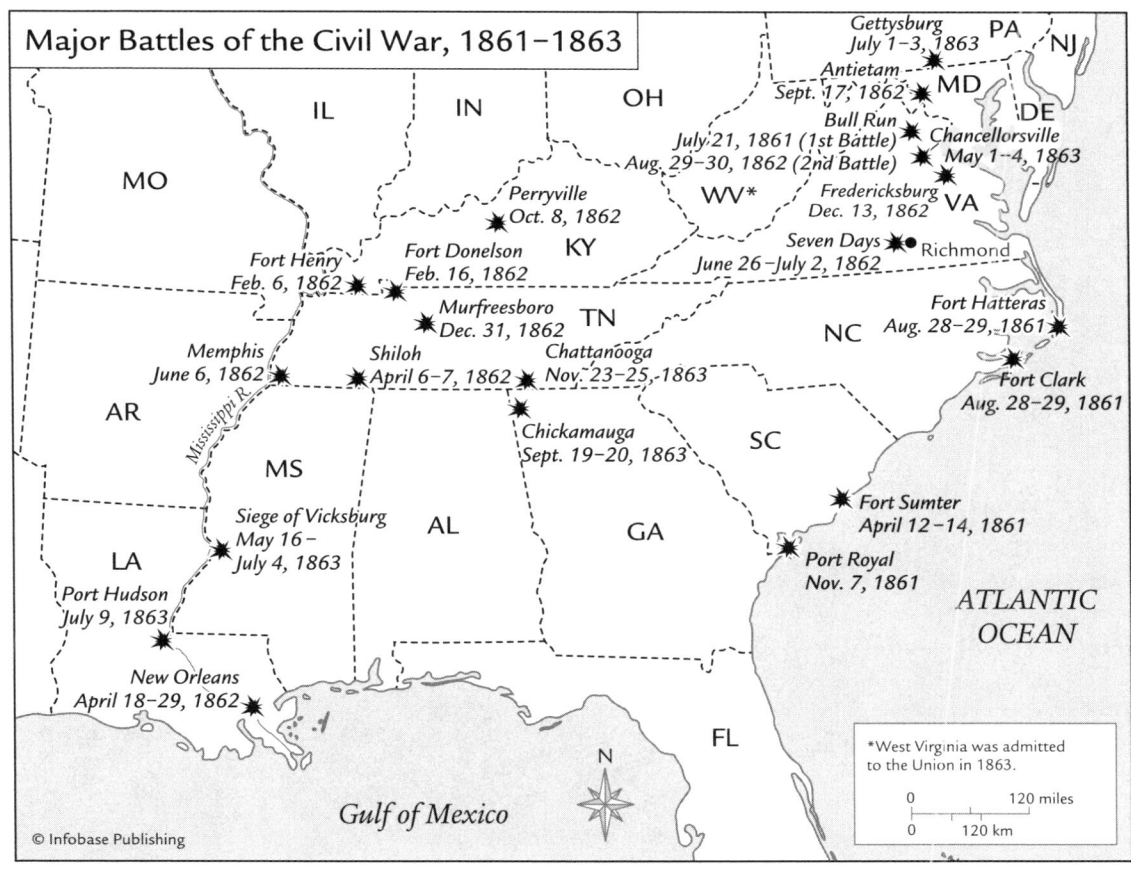

Major Battles of the Civil War, 1861–1863

Gettysburg
July 1–3, 1863 PA NJ

Antietam
Sept. 17, 1862 MD DE

Bull Run
July 21, 1861 (1st Battle) Chancellorsville
Aug. 29–30, 1862 (2nd Battle) May 1–4, 1863

Fredericksburg
Dec. 13, 1862 VA

Perryville
Oct. 8, 1862 WV*

Seven Days
June 26–July 2, 1862 Richmond

Fort Henry
Feb. 6, 1862 Fort Donelson
Feb. 16, 1862 KY

Fort Hatteras
Aug. 28–29, 1861

Murfreesboro
Dec. 31, 1862 TN

NC

Memphis
June 6, 1862 Shiloh
April 6–7, 1862 Chattanooga
Nov. 23–25, 1863

Fort Clark
Aug. 28–29, 1861

AR

Chickamauga
Sept. 19–20, 1863 SC

MS

Fort Sumter
April 12–14, 1861

Siege of Vicksburg
May 16–
July 4, 1863 AL GA

Port Royal
Nov. 7, 1861

LA

ATLANTIC
OCEAN

Port Hudson
July 9, 1863

New Orleans
April 18–29, 1862

FL

*West Virginia was admitted
to the Union in 1863.

0   120 miles
0   120 km

N

Gulf of Mexico

IL IN OH

MO

© Infobase Publishing

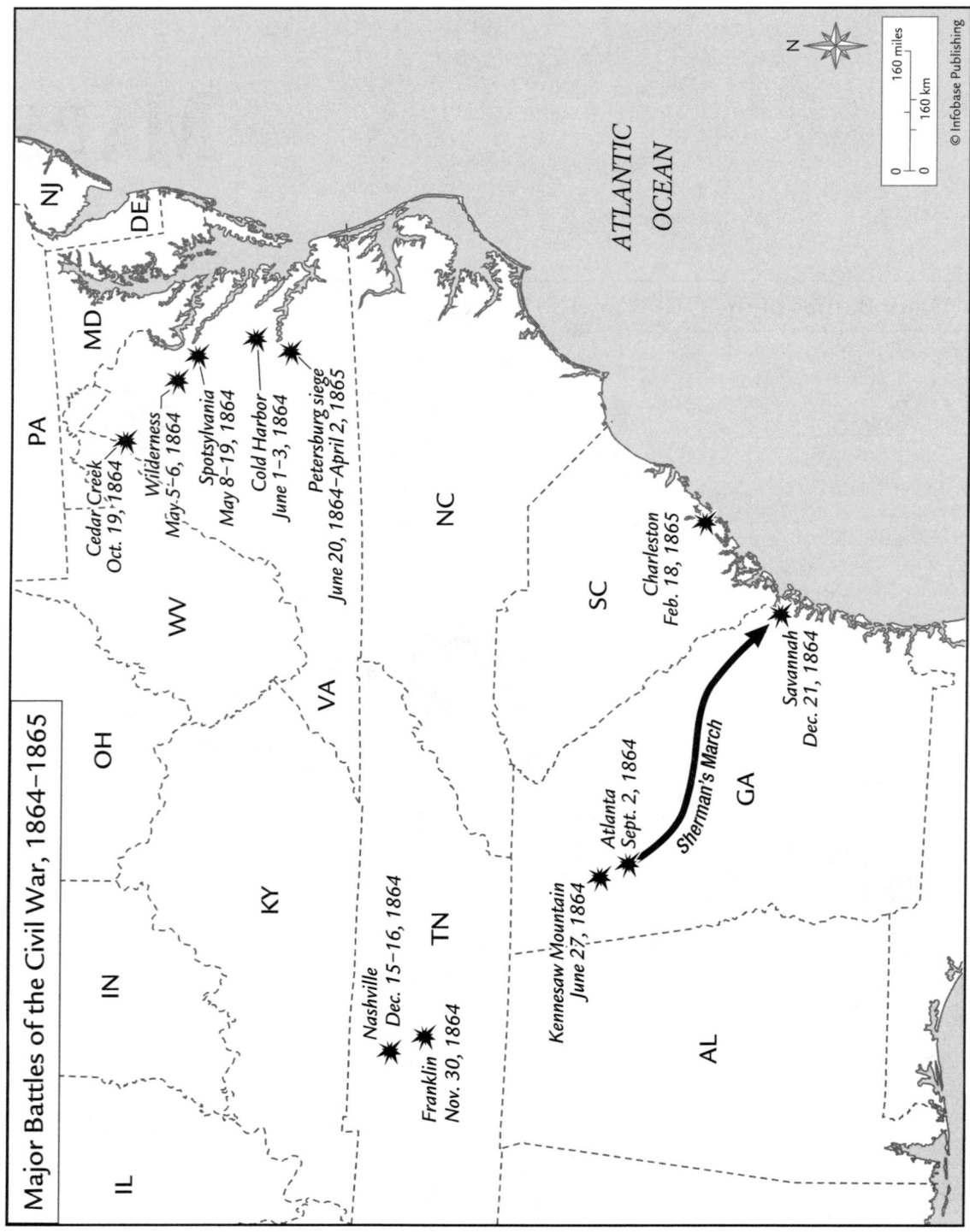

Major Battles of the Civil War, 1864–1865

Cedar Creek
Oct. 19, 1864

Wilderness
May 5–6, 1864

Spotsylvania
May 8–19, 1864

Cold Harbor
June 1–3, 1864

Petersburg siege
June 20, 1864–April 2, 1865

Charleston
Feb. 18, 1865

Savannah
Dec. 21, 1864

Sherman's March

Atlanta
Sept. 2, 1864

Kennesaw Mountain
June 27, 1864

Nashville
Dec. 15–16, 1864

Franklin
Nov. 30, 1864

NJ

DE

MD

PA

WV

VA

NC

SC

GA

AL

OH

KY

TN

IN

IL

ATLANTIC
OCEAN

N

160 miles

160 km

© Infobase Publishing

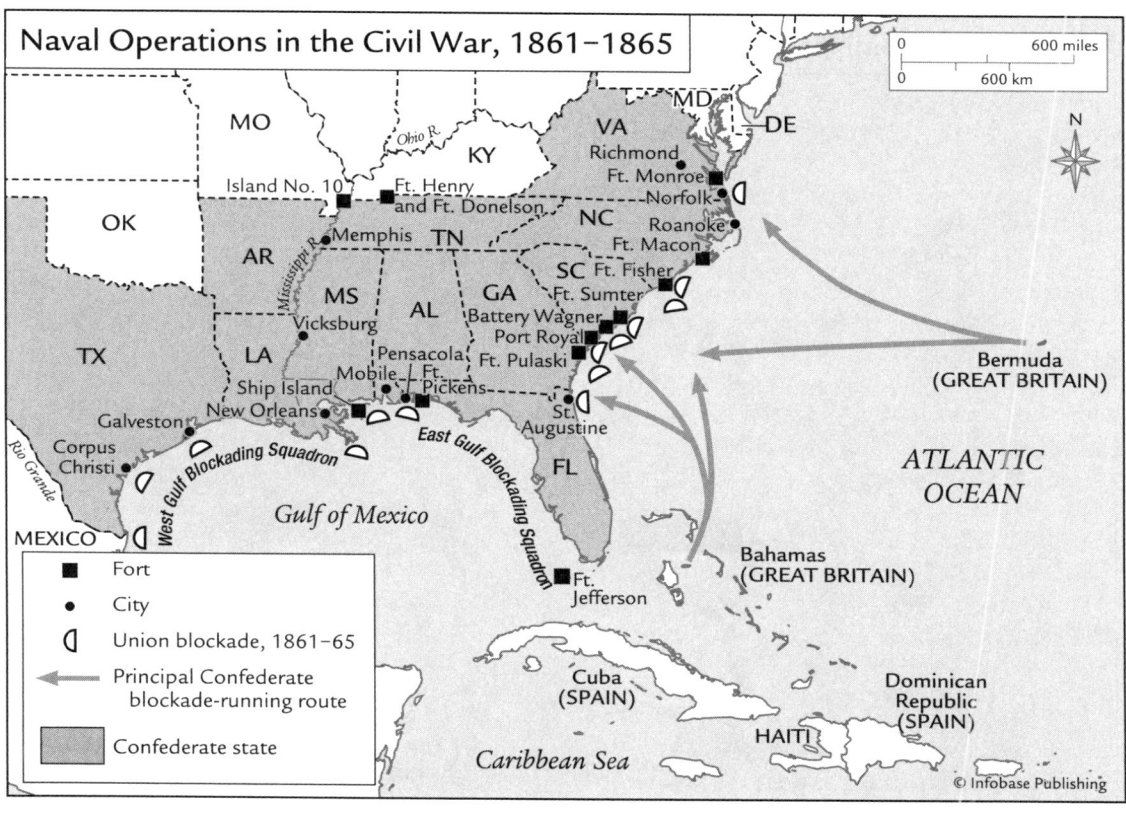

Naval Operations in the Civil War, 1861–1865

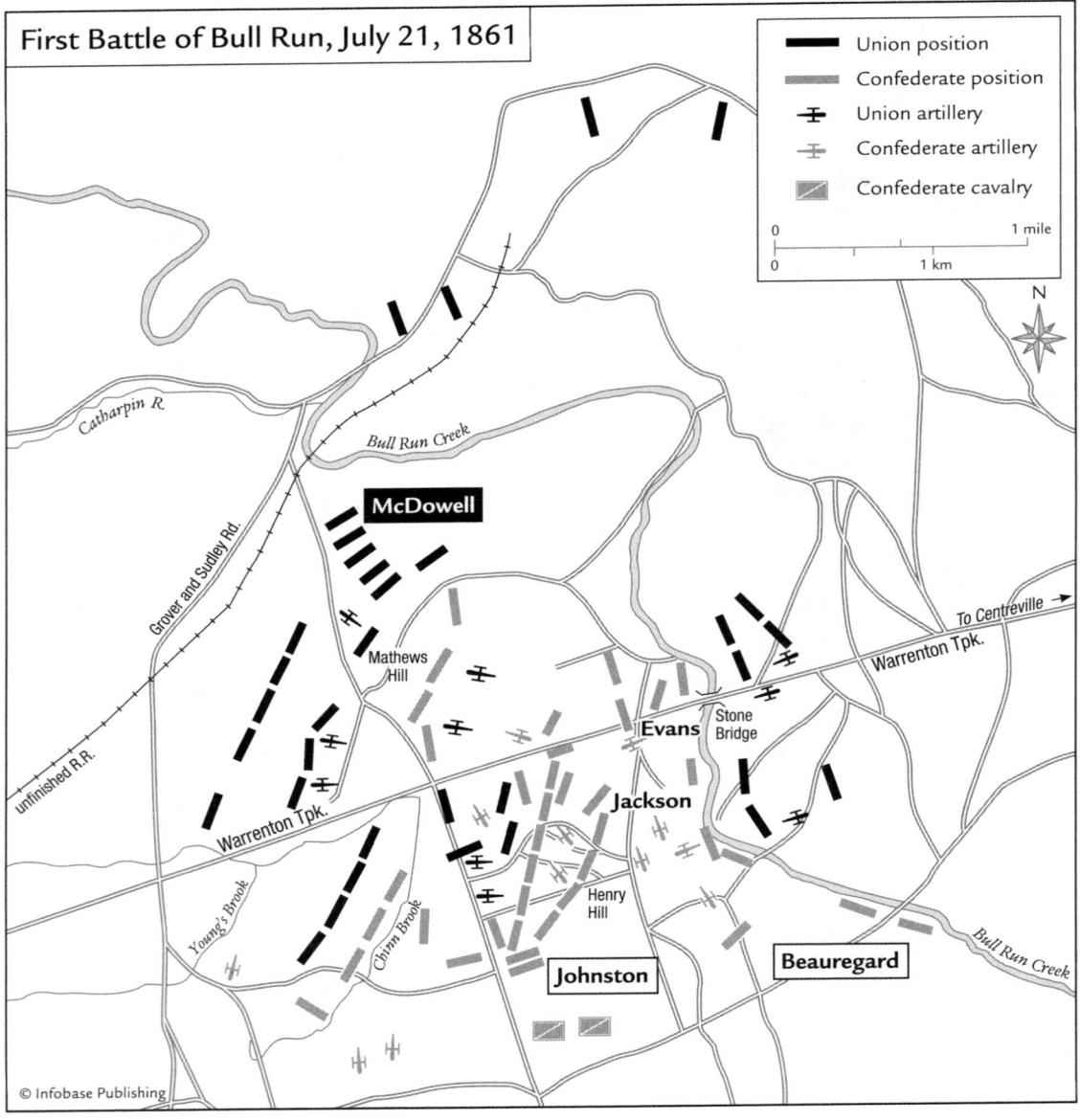

First Battle of Bull Run, July 21, 1861

	Union position
	Confederate position
	Union artillery
	Confederate artillery
	Confederate cavalry

0   1 mile
0   1 km

N

Catharpin R.

Bull Run Creek

Grover and Sudley Rd.

unfinished R.R.

McDowell

Mathews Hill

Warrenton Tpk.

To Centreville →

Warrenton Tpk.

Evans

Stone Bridge

Jackson

Young's Brook

Chinn Brook

Henry Hill

Johnston

Beauregard

Bull Run Creek

© Infobase Publishing

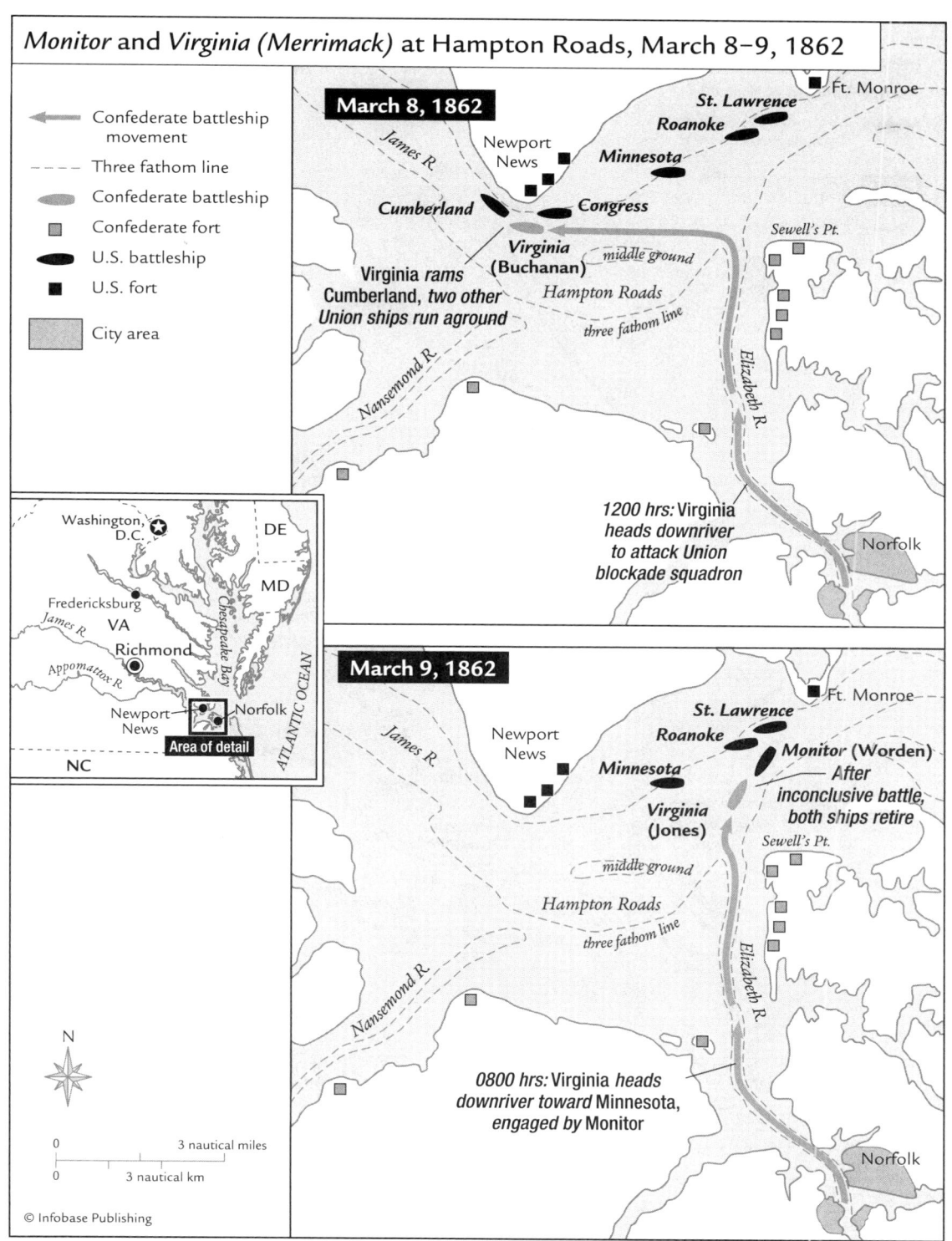

Monitor and *Virginia (Merrimack)* at Hampton Roads, March 8–9, 1862

Confederate battleship movement

Three fathom line

Confederate battleship

Confederate fort

U.S. battleship

U.S. fort

City area

March 8, 1862

St. Lawrence
Roanoke
Ft. Monroe
Newport News
Minnesota
Cumberland   Congress
Virginia (Buchanan)
Virginia *rams* Cumberland, *two other Union ships run aground*
James R.
middle ground
Hampton Roads
three fathom line
Nansemond R.
Sewell's Pt.
Elizabeth R.

1200 hrs: Virginia *heads downriver to attack Union blockade squadron*

Norfolk

Washington, D.C.
DE
MD
Fredericksburg
VA
James R.
Richmond
Appomattox R.
Newport News   Norfolk
Chesapeake Bay
ATLANTIC OCEAN
Area of detail
NC

March 9, 1862

St. Lawrence
Roanoke
Ft. Monroe
Newport News
Minnesota
Monitor (Worden)
Virginia (Jones)
After inconclusive battle, both ships retire
James R.
Sewell's Pt.
middle ground
Hampton Roads
three fathom line
Nansemond R.
Elizabeth R.

0800 hrs: Virginia *heads downriver toward* Minnesota, *engaged by* Monitor

Norfolk

N

0   3 nautical miles
0   3 nautical km

© Infobase Publishing

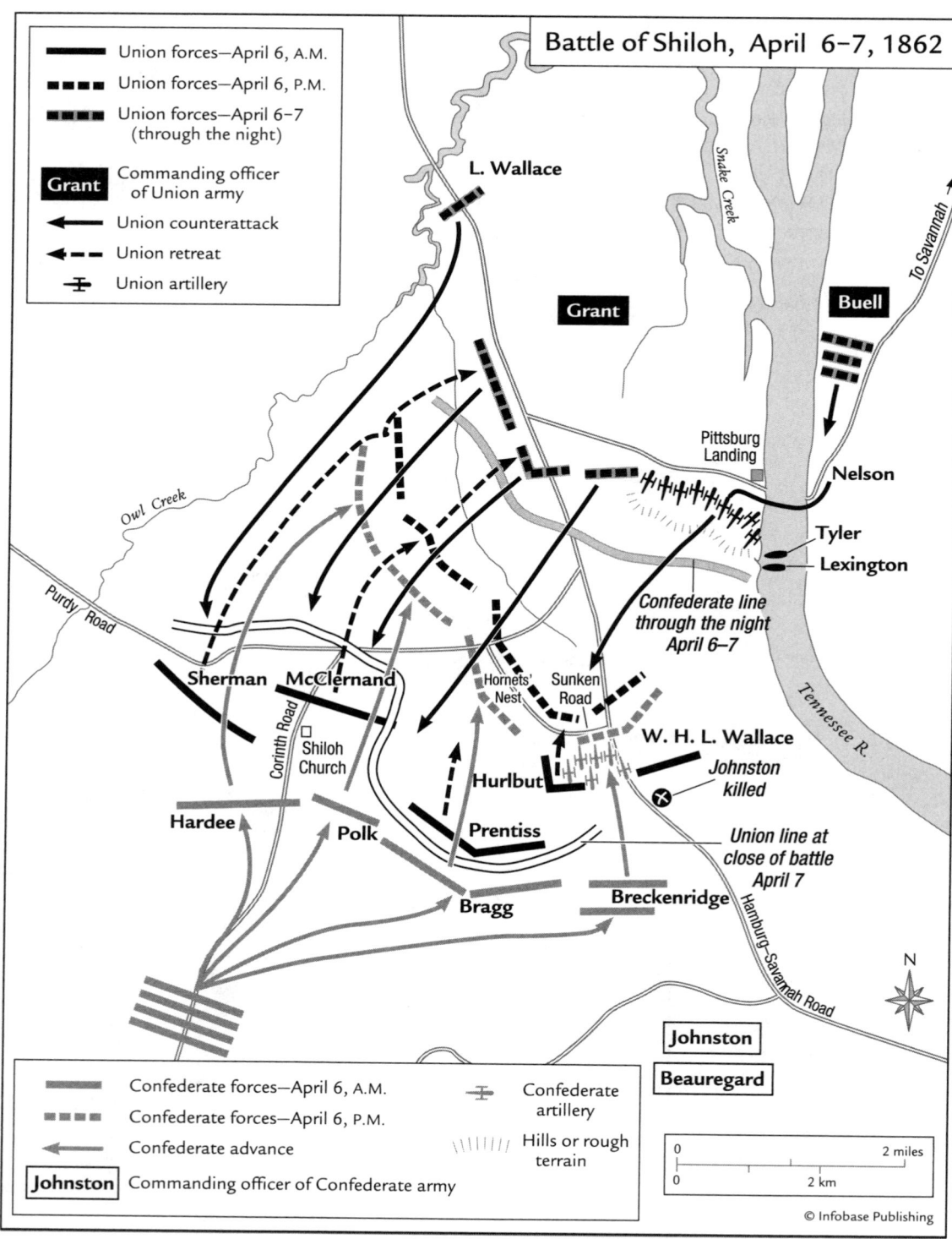

Battle of Shiloh, April 6–7, 1862

Legend:

Union forces—April 6, A.M.
Union forces—April 6, P.M.
Union forces—April 6–7 (through the night)

Grant — Commanding officer of Union army

Union counterattack
Union retreat
Union artillery

Confederate forces—April 6, A.M.
Confederate forces—April 6, P.M.
Confederate advance
Johnston Commanding officer of Confederate army

Confederate artillery
Hills or rough terrain

L. Wallace
Snake Creek
To Savannah
Grant
Buell
Pittsburg Landing
Nelson
Owl Creek
Tyler
Lexington
Confederate line through the night April 6–7
Purdy Road
Sherman
McClernand
Hornets' Nest
Sunken Road
Corinth Road
Shiloh Church
W. H. L. Wallace
Johnston killed
Hurlbut
Union line at close of battle April 7
Hardee
Polk
Prentiss
Tennessee R.
Bragg
Breckenridge
Hamburg-Savannah Road
Johnston
Beauregard
N

0   2 miles
0   2 km

© Infobase Publishing

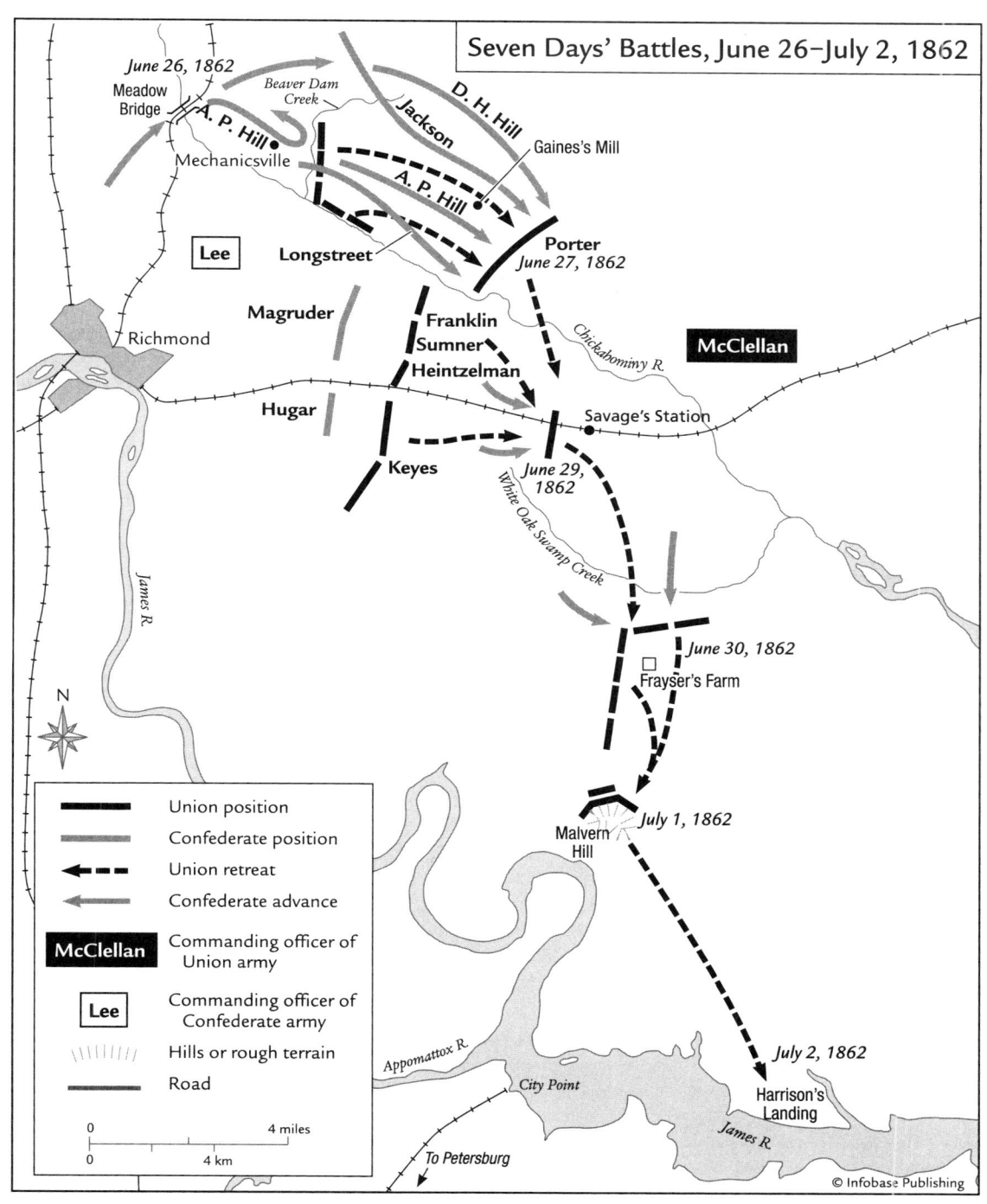

Seven Days' Battles, June 26–July 2, 1862

June 26, 1862
Meadow Bridge
A. P. Hill
Mechanicsville
Beaver Dam Creek
Jackson
D. H. Hill
Gaines's Mill
A. P. Hill
Lee
Longstreet
Porter
June 27, 1862
Magruder
Franklin
Sumner
Heintzelman
Chickahominy R.
McClellan
Richmond
Hugar
Savage's Station
Keyes
June 29, 1862
White Oak Swamp Creek
June 30, 1862
Frayser's Farm
N
July 1, 1862
Malvern Hill
James R.

Union position
Confederate position
Union retreat
Confederate advance
McClellan   Commanding officer of Union army
Lee   Commanding officer of Confederate army
Hills or rough terrain
Road

0   4 miles
0   4 km

Appomattox R.
City Point
To Petersburg
July 2, 1862
Harrison's Landing
James R.
© Infobase Publishing

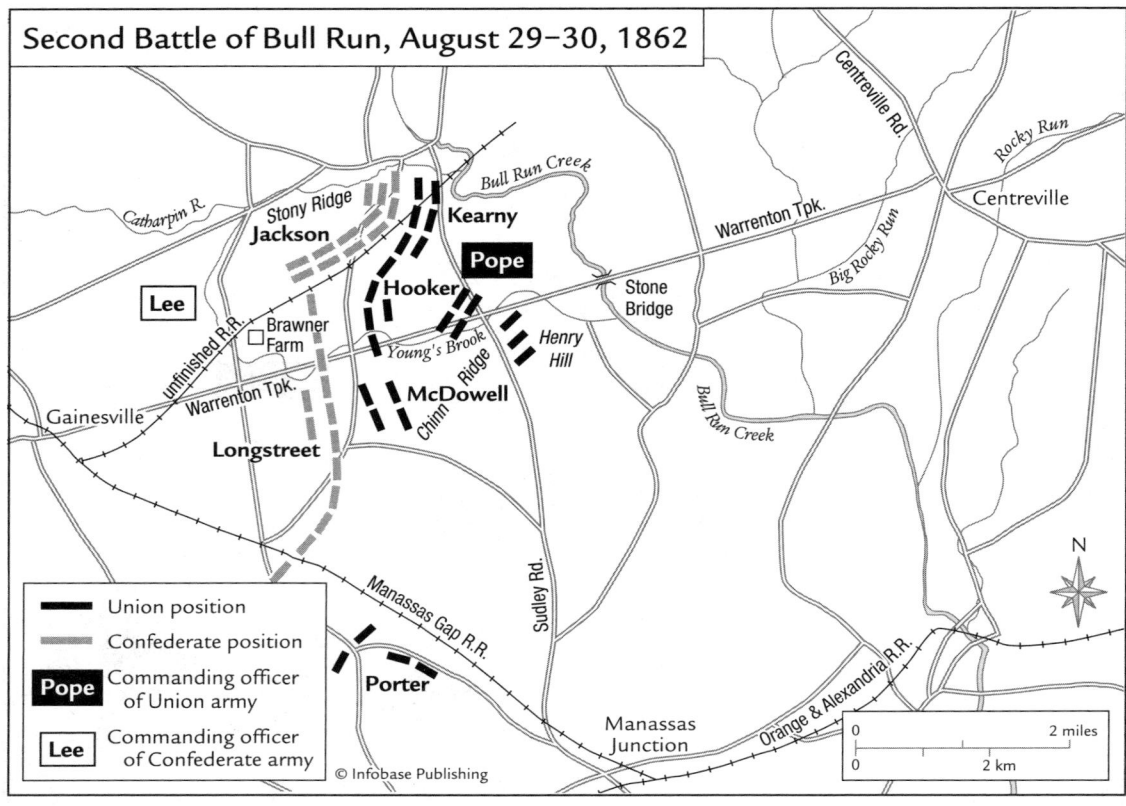

Second Battle of Bull Run, August 29–30, 1862

Union position

Confederate position

Pope Commanding officer of Union army

Lee Commanding officer of Confederate army

© Infobase Publishing

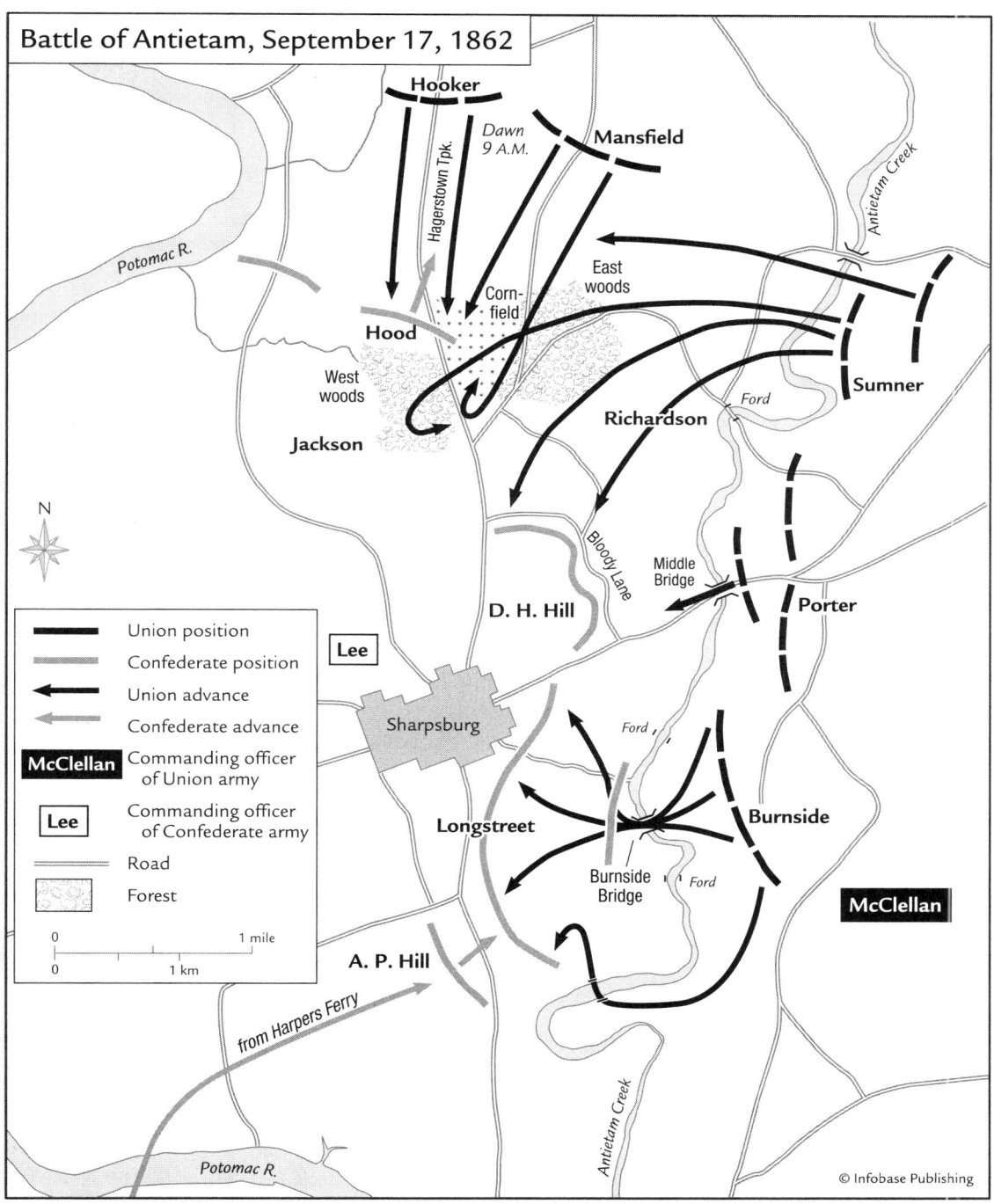

Battle of Antietam, September 17, 1862

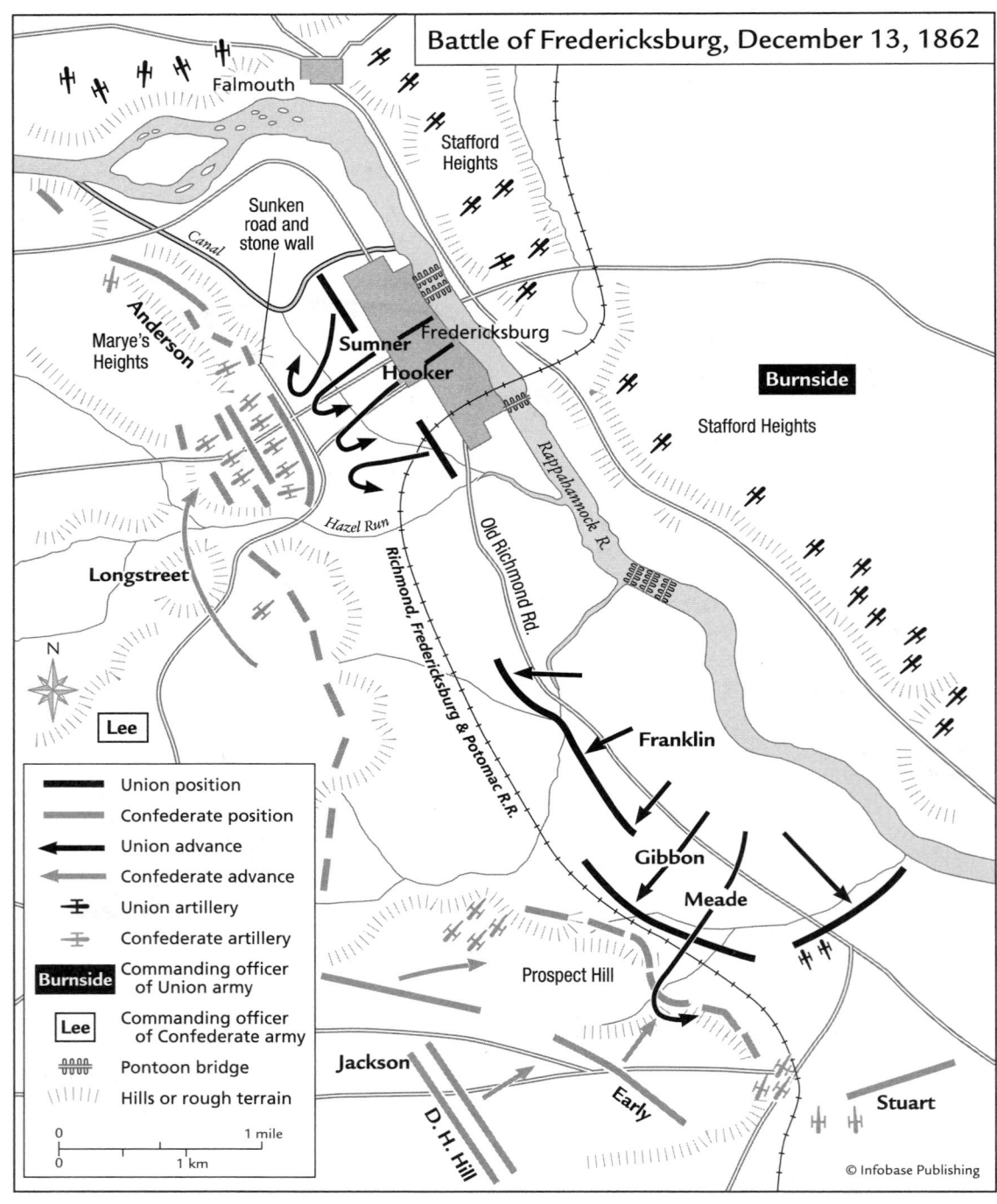

Battle of Fredericksburg, December 13, 1862

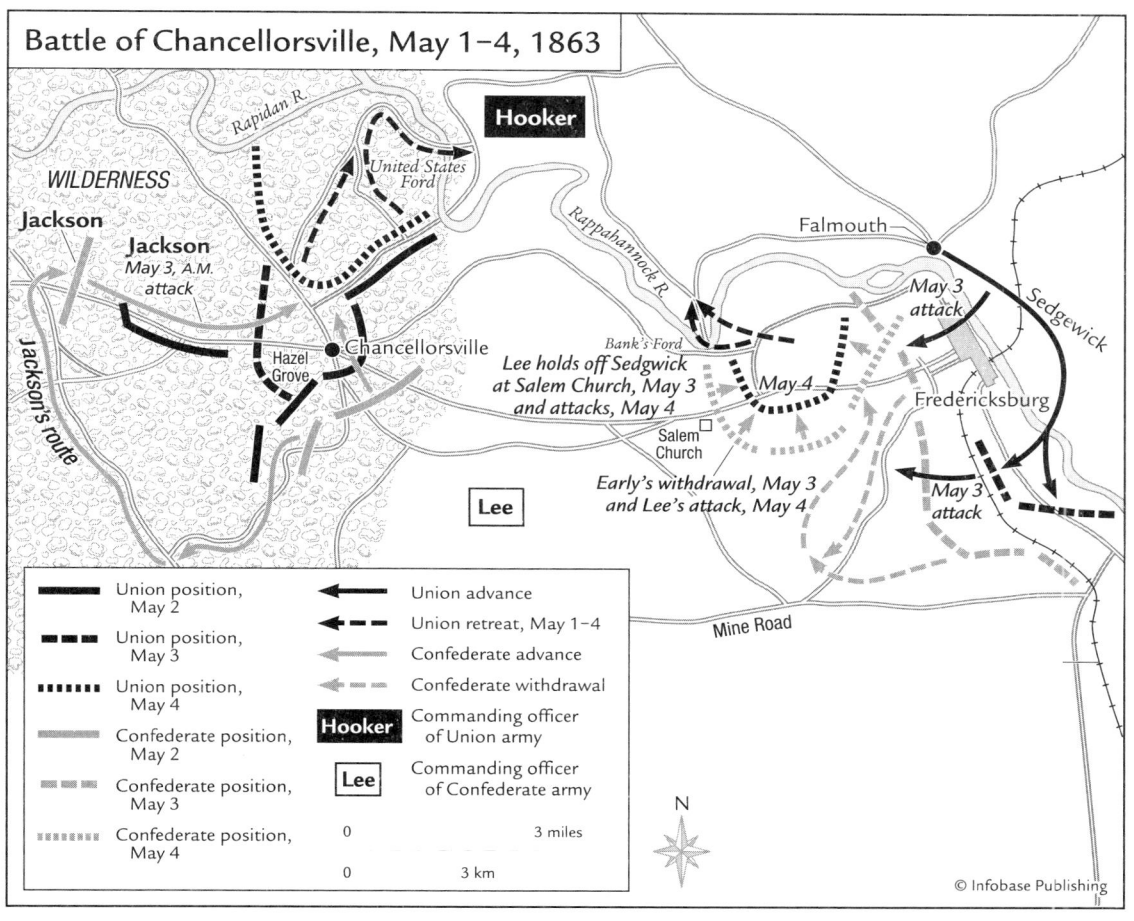

Battle of Chancellorsville, May 1–4, 1863

WILDERNESS

Rapidan R.

United States Ford

Hooker

Jackson

Jackson
May 3, A.M.
attack

Jackson's route

Hazel Grove

Chancellorsville

Rappahannock R.

Falmouth

Bank's Ford

Lee holds off Sedgwick
at Salem Church, May 3
and attacks, May 4

May 4

Salem Church

May 3
attack

Sedgewick

Fredericksburg

May 3
attack

Lee

Early's withdrawal, May 3
and Lee's attack, May 4

Mine Road

N

Legend

▬▬▬	Union position, May 2
▬ ▬ ▬	Union position, May 3
▪▪▪▪▪	Union position, May 4
▬▬▬	Confederate position, May 2
▬ ▬ ▬	Confederate position, May 3
▪▪▪▪▪	Confederate position, May 4
◀▬▬	Union advance
◀ ▬ ▬	Union retreat, May 1–4
◀▬▬	Confederate advance
◀ ▬ ▬	Confederate withdrawal
Hooker	Commanding officer of Union army
Lee	Commanding officer of Confederate army

0   3 miles

0   3 km

© Infobase Publishing

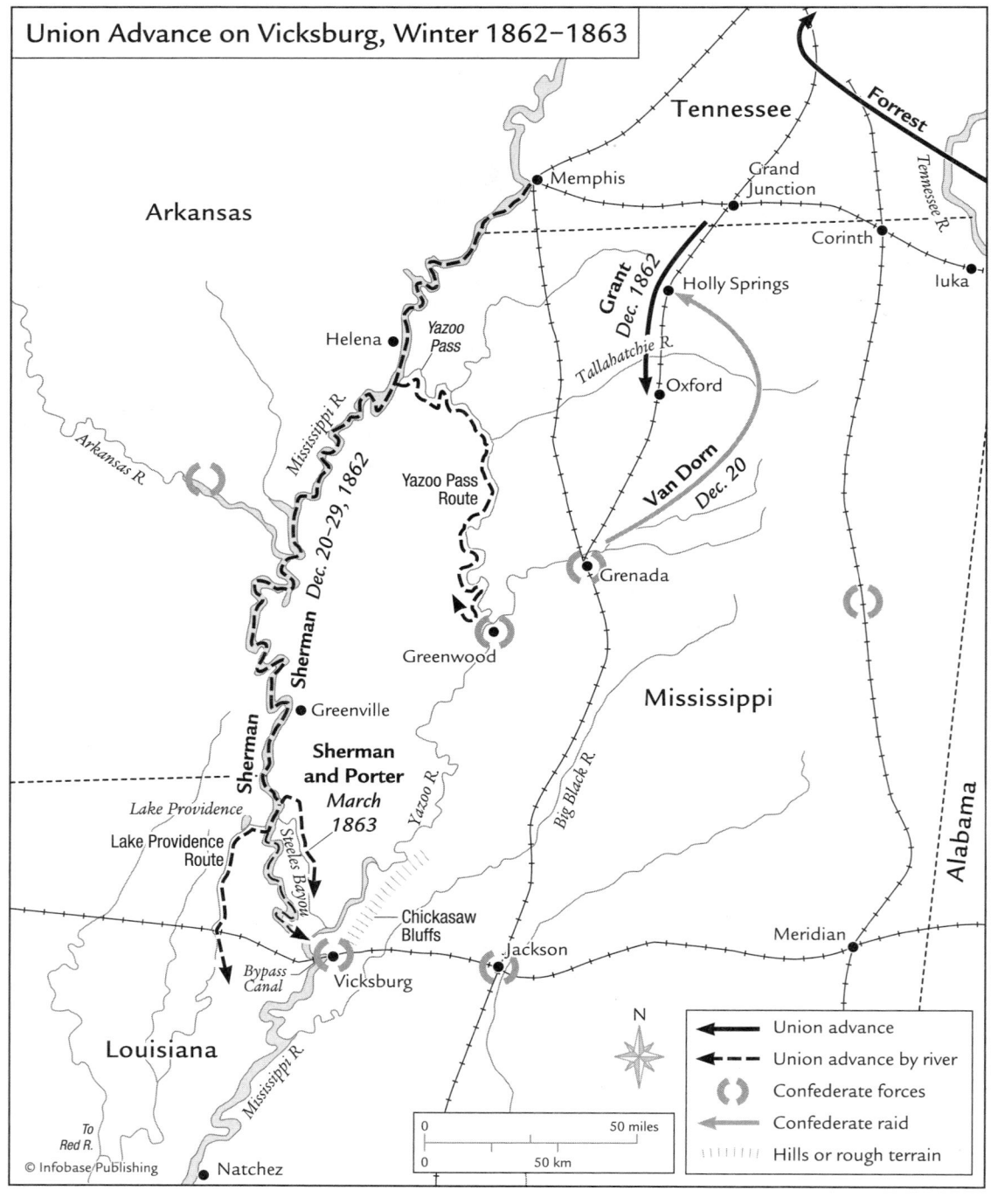

Union Advance on Vicksburg, Winter 1862–1863

Tennessee

Forrest

Arkansas

Memphis

Grand Junction

Corinth

Tennessee R.

Grant Dec. 1862

Holly Springs

Iuka

Helena

Yazoo Pass

Tallahatchie R.

Oxford

Mississippi R.

Yazoo Pass Route

Van Dorn Dec. 20

Arkansas R.

Sherman Dec. 20–29, 1862

Grenada

Greenwood

Greenville

Mississippi

Sherman

Sherman and Porter *March 1863*

Lake Providence

Yazoo R.

Big Black R.

Alabama

Lake Providence Route

Steeles Bayou

Chickasaw Bluffs

Jackson

Meridian

Bypass Canal

Vicksburg

Louisiana

Mississippi R.

N

To Red R.

© Infobase Publishing

Natchez

0 ——— 50 miles	
0 ——— 50 km	

⟵	Union advance
⟵ (dashed)	Union advance by river
↺↻	Confederate forces
⟵ (gray)	Confederate raid
∣∣∣∣∣∣	Hills or rough terrain

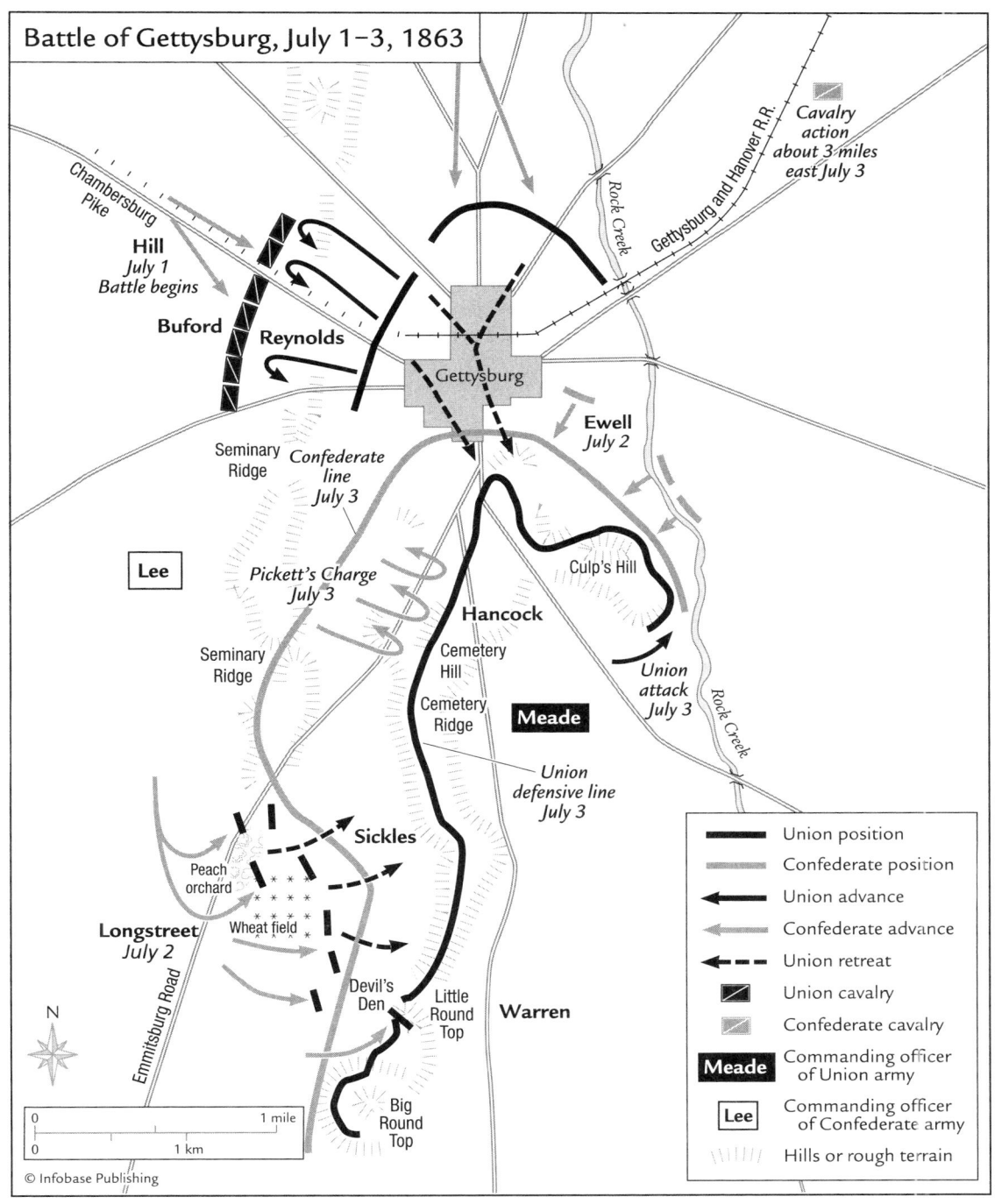

Battle of Gettysburg, July 1–3, 1863

Cavalry action about 3 miles east July 3

Gettysburg and Hanover R.R.

Chambersburg Pike

Rock Creek

Hill
*July 1
Battle begins*

Buford

Reynolds

Gettysburg

Ewell
July 2

Seminary Ridge

Confederate line July 3

Culp's Hill

Lee

Pickett's Charge July 3

Hancock

Seminary Ridge

Cemetery Hill

Union attack July 3

Rock Creek

Cemetery Ridge

Meade

Union defensive line July 3

Sickles

Peach orchard

Wheat field

Longstreet
July 2

Emmitsburg Road

Devil's Den

Little Round Top

Warren

N

Big Round Top

▬▬▬	Union position
▬▬▬	Confederate position
◀━━	Union advance
◀━━	Confederate advance
◀- - -	Union retreat
◣	Union cavalry
◪	Confederate cavalry
Meade	Commanding officer of Union army
Lee	Commanding officer of Confederate army
//////	Hills or rough terrain

0   1 mile
0   1 km

© Infobase Publishing

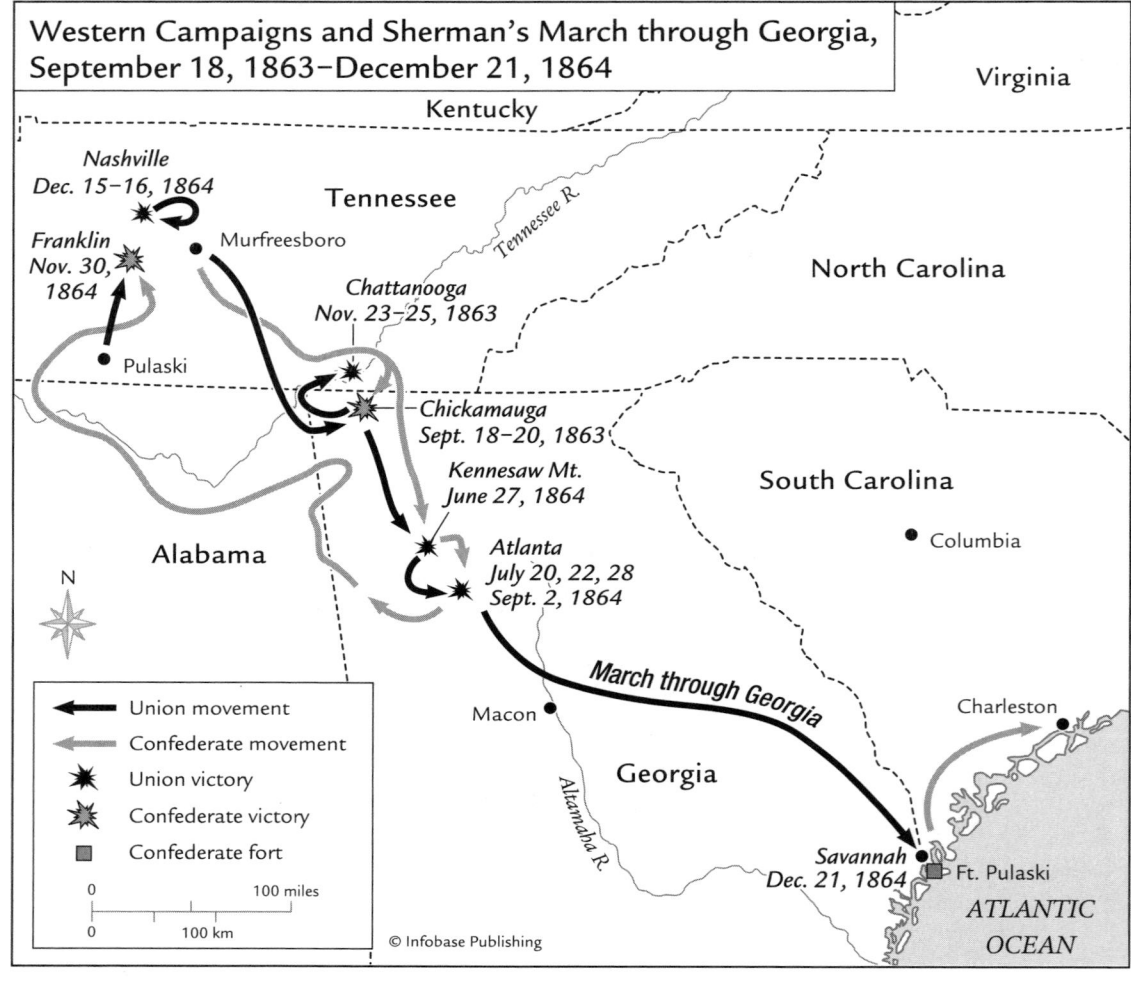

Western Campaigns and Sherman's March through Georgia, September 18, 1863–December 21, 1864

Virginia

Kentucky

Nashville
Dec. 15–16, 1864

Tennessee

Murfreesboro

Tennessee R.

Franklin
Nov. 30,
1864

North Carolina

Chattanooga
Nov. 23–25, 1863

Pulaski

Chickamauga
Sept. 18–20, 1863

South Carolina

Kennesaw Mt.
June 27, 1864

Columbia

Alabama

Atlanta
July 20, 22, 28
Sept. 2, 1864

N

March through Georgia

Charleston

Macon

Georgia

Altamaha R.

Union movement
Confederate movement
Union victory
Confederate victory
Confederate fort

Savannah
Dec. 21, 1864

Ft. Pulaski

ATLANTIC
OCEAN

0   100 miles
0   100 km

© Infobase Publishing

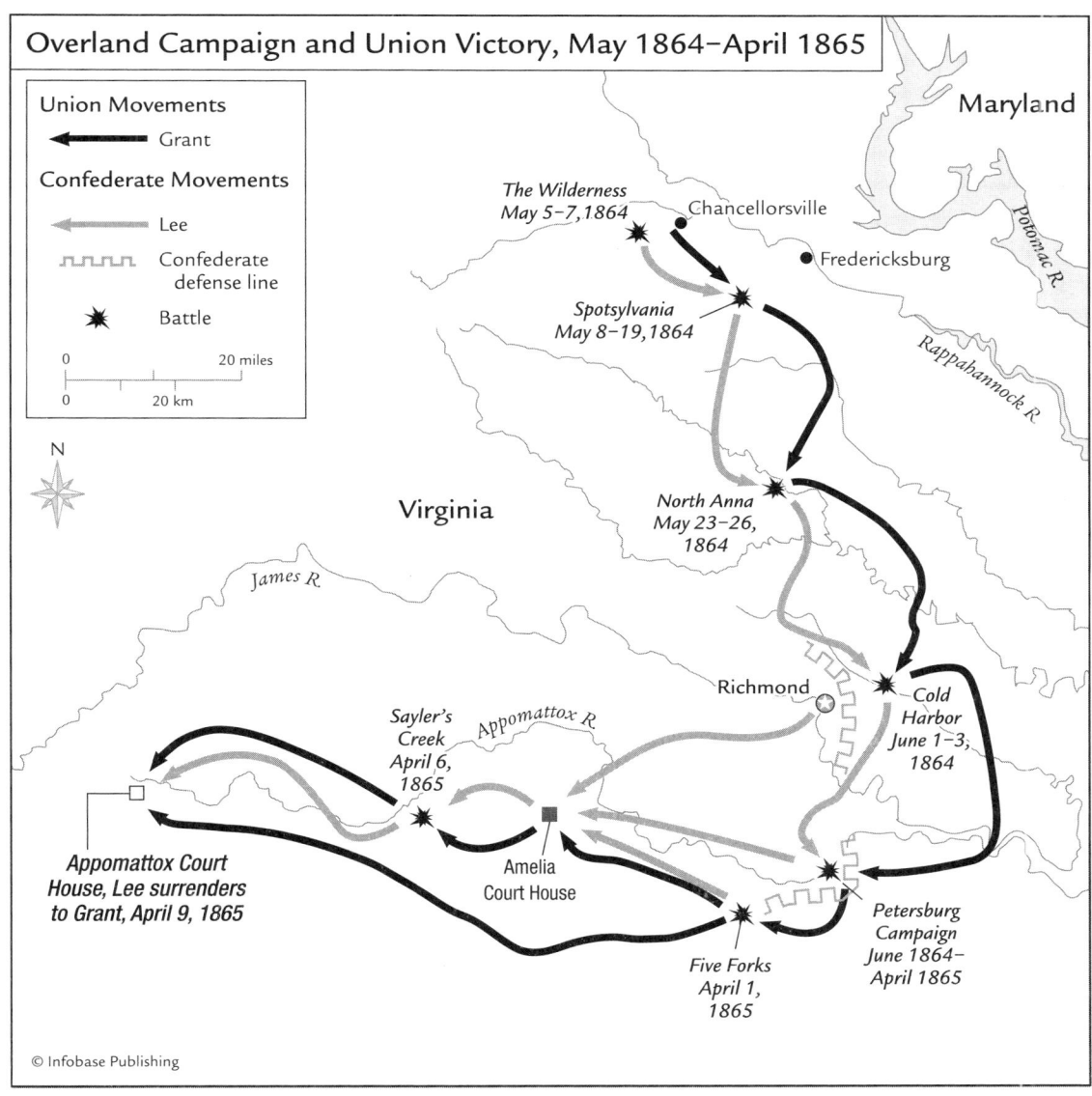

Overland Campaign and Union Victory, May 1864–April 1865

Maryland

Union Movements

— Grant

Confederate Movements

— Lee

⊓⊔⊓⊔ Confederate defense line

✱ Battle

0   20 miles

0   20 km

N

Virginia

The Wilderness May 5–7, 1864

Chancellorsville

● Fredericksburg

Spotsylvania May 8–19, 1864

Rappahannock R.

North Anna May 23–26, 1864

James R.

Richmond

Cold Harbor June 1–3, 1864

Sayler's Creek April 6, 1865

Appomattox R.

Amelia Court House

Appomattox Court House, Lee surrenders to Grant, April 9, 1865

Five Forks April 1, 1865

Petersburg Campaign June 1864– April 1865

© Infobase Publishing

BIBLIOGRAPHY

Adelman, Garry E. *The Myth of Little Round Top: Gettysburg.* Gettysburg, Pa.: Thomas Publications, 2003.

Alberts, Don E. *General Wesley Merritt: Brandy Station to Manila Bay.* Columbus, Ohio: General's Books, 2000.

Alduino, Frank W., and David J. Coles. "'Ye Come from Many a Far Off Clime; and Speak in Many Tongue': The Garabaldi Guard and Italian-American Service in the Civil War." *Italian Americana* 22, no. 1 (2004): 47–63.

Alexander, Ted. "Antietam: The Bloodiest Day." *North & South* 5, no. 7 (2002): 76–89.

Allmon, William B. "Hold Allatoona!" *Military Heritage* 4, no. 1 (2002): 52–59.

Archer, John M. *Culp's Hill at Gettysburg: "The Mountain Trembled.*" Gettysburg, Pa.: Thomas Publications, 2002.

Ayers, Edward L., Gary W. Gallagher, and Andrew J. Torget, eds. *Crucible of the Civil War: Virginia from Secession to Commemoration.* Charlottesville: University of Virginia Press, 2006.

Baehr, Theodore. *Faith in God and Generals: An Anthology of Faith, Hope, and Love in the American Civil War.* Nashville, Tenn.: Broadman, Holman, 2003.

Bak, Richard. *The CSS Hunley: The Greatest Undersea Adventure of the Civil War.* New York: Cooper Square Press, 2003.

Baldwin, John. *Last Flag Down: The Epic Journey of the Last Confederate Warship.* New York: Crown Publishers, 2007.

Banasik, Michael E., ed. *Cavaliers of the Brush: Quantrill and His Men.* Iowa City, Iowa: Camp Pope Bookshop, 2003.

Barefoot, Daniel W. *Let Us Die Like Brave Men: Behind the Dying Words of Confederate Warriors.* Winston-Salem, N.C.: John F. Blair, 2005.

Barnes, Wyatt E. "Harboring the Czar's Fleet." *MHQ* 13, no. 4 (2001): 64–70.

Barnhart, Donald. "Junkyard Ironclad." *Civil War Times Illustrated* 40, no. 2 (2001): 30–37, 67–68.

Barry, Peter J. "The Charleston Riot and Its Aftermath: Civil, Military, and Presidential Responses." *Journal of Illinois History* 7, no. 2 (2004): 82–106.

Baumgartner, Richard A. *Buckeye Blood: Ohio at Gettysburg.* Huntington, W.Va.: Blue Acorn Press, 2003.

Bell, John. *Confederate Seadog: John Taylor Wood in War and Exile.* Jefferson, N.C.: McFarland, 2002.

Bennett, Brian A. *The Beau Ideal of a Soldier and a Gentleman: The Life of Coil. Patrick Henry O'Rourke from Ireland to Gettysburg.* Wheatland, N.Y.: Triphammer Pub., 2002.

Bennett, Michael J. *Union Jacks: Yankee Sailors in the Civil War.* Chapel Hill: University of North Carolina Press, 2004.

———. "Dissenters from the American Mood: Why Men Became Yankee Sailors during the Civil War." *North & South* 8, no. 2 (2005): 12–21.

Bishop, Ronald R. "August Sebelin's Civil War: A German Sailor in the Union Navy, 1861–1865." Unpublished master's thesis, Baylor University, 2002.

Blair, Dan. "'One Good Port': Beaufort Harbor, North Carolina." *North Carolina Historical Review* 79, no. 3 (2002): 301–326.

Blair, Jayne E. *Tragedy at Montpelier: The Untold Story of Ten Confederate Deserters from North Carolina.* Bowie, Md.: Heritage Books, 2003.

Bleser, Carol K. *Intimate Strategies of the Civil War: Military Commanders and Their Wives.* New York: Oxford University Press, 2001.

Bonds, Russell S. *Stealing the General: The Great Locomotive Clause of the First Medal of Honor.* Yardley, Pa.: Westholme, 2007.

Boswell, Evault. *Quantrill's Raiders in Texas.* Austin, Tex.: Eakin Press, 2003.

Bowden, Scott, and Bill Ward. *Last Chance for Victory: Robert E. Lee and the Gettysburg Campaign.* Campbell, Calif.: Savas, 2001.

Bragg, C. L. *Distinction in Every Service: Brigadier General Marcellus A. Stovall, C.S.A.* Shippensburg, Pa.: White Mane Books, 2002.

Brennan, Patrick. "The Army Commander Who Never Was." *North & South* 5, no. 5 (2002): 12–25.

———. "It Wasn't Stuart's Fault." *North & South* 6, no. 5 (2003): 22–37.

———. "'I Had Rather Die than Be Whipped': The Battle of Yellow Tavern." *North & South* 7, no. 4 (2004): 56–73.

Brewer, James D. *Tom Worthington's War: Shiloh, Sherman, and the Search for Vindication.* Jefferson, N.C.: McFarland, 2001.

Brooke, George M., ed. *Ironclads and Big Guns of the Confederacy: The Journals and Letters of John M. Brooke.* Columbia: University of South Carolina Press, 2002.

Brooks, Charles E. "The Social and Cultural Dynamics of Soldiering in Hood's Texas Brigade." *Journal of Southern History* 67, no. 3 (2001): 535–572.

Browning, Robert M. "Defunct Strategy and Divergent Goals: The Role of the United States Navy along the Eastern Seaboard during the Civil War." *Prologue* 33, no. 3 (2001): 168–179.

Brownstein, Elizabeth S. *Lincoln's Other White House.* Hoboken, N.J.: John Wiley and Sons, 2005.

Brubaker, Jack. "Defending the Susquehanna." *Civil War Times* 43, no. 3 (2003): 74–80.

Bruce, Susannah U. "The Harp and the Eagle: The Impact of Civil War Military Service in the Union Army on the Irish in America." Unpublished Ph.D. diss., Kansas State University, 2002.

Budiansky, Stephen. "America's Unknown Intelligence Czar." *American Heritage* 55, no. 5 (2004): 55–63.

Buker, George E. "The Inner Blockade of Florida and the Wildcat Blockade-Runners." *North & South* 4, no. 2 (2001): 70–85.

———. *Blockaders, Refugees, and Contrabands: Civil War on Florida's Gulf Coast.* Tuscaloosa: University of Alabama Press, 2004.

Bundy, Carol. *The Nature of Sacrifice: A Biography of Charles Russell Lowe, Jr., 1835–1864.* New York: Farrar, Straus, and Giroux, 2005.

Burkhardt, George S. *Confederate Rage, Yankee Wrath: No Quarter in the Civil War.* Carbondale: Southern Illinois University Press, 2007.

Butko, Brian, and Nicholas P. Ciotola, eds. *Industry and Infantry.* Pittsburgh: Historical Society of Western Pennsylvania, 2003.

Butts, Michele T. *Galvanized Yankees on the Upper Missouri: The Face of Loyalty.* Boulder: University of Colorado Press, 2003.

Calcutt, Rebecca B. *Richmond's Wartime Hospitals: In Depth Study of Medical Care during the War of 1812.* Gretna, La.: Pelican Publishing, 2005.

Callaghan, Daniel M. *Thomas Francis Meagher and the Irish Brigade in the Civil War.* Jefferson, N.C.: McFarland, 2006.

Callan, J. Sean. *Courage and Country: James Shields: More than Irish Luck.* Lake Forest, Ill.: 1st Books Library, 2004.

Calore, Paul. *Naval Campaigns of the Civil War.* Jefferson, N.C.: McFarland, 2002.

Campbell, Jacqueline G. "'The Most Diabolical Act of All the Barbarous War': Soldiers, Civilians, and the Burning of Columbia, February, 1865." *American Nineteenth Century History* 3, no. 3 (2002): 53–72.

Campbell, R. Thomas. *Sea Hawk of the Confederacy: Lt. Charles Read and the Confederate Navy.* Shippensburg, Pa.: Burd Street Press, 2000.

———. *Hunters of the Night: Confederate Torpedo Boats in the War between the States.* Shippensburg, Pa.: White Mane Books, 2000.

———. *Confederate Navy Quizzes and Facts.* Shippensburg, Pa.: Burd Street Press, 2001.

———. *The Hunley Story: Journey of a Confederate Submarine.* Shippensburg, Pa.: Burd Street Press, 2002.

Campbell, R. Thomas, ed. *Engineer in Gray: Memoirs of Chief Engineer James H. Tomb, CSN.* Jefferson, N.C.: McFarland, 2005.

Campbell, Thomas A. *Storm over Carolina: The Confederate Navy's Struggle for Eastern North Carolina.* Nashville, Tenn.: Cumberland House, 2006.

Canfield, Eugene B. "*Alabama*'s Defeat Was No Surprise." *Naval History* 18, no. 4 (2004): 43–46.

Carlisle, Rodney P. *The Civil War and Reconstruction.* New York: Facts On File, 2007.

Carmichael, Peter S. *The Last Generation: Young Virginians in Peace, War, and Reunion.* Chapel Hill: University of North Carolina Press, 2005.

Carson, Ray M. *The Civl War Soldier: A Photographic Journey.* New York: Gramercy Books, 2007.

Carter, Alice E. *The Civil War on the Web: A Guide to the Very Best Sites.* Wilmington, Del.: SR Books, 2003.

Casstevens, Frances H. *"Out of the Mouth of Hell": Civil War Prisons and Escapes.* Jefferson, N.C.: McFarland, 2005.

———. *Edward A. Wild and the African Brigade in the Civil War.* Jefferson, N.C.: McFarland, 2003.

———. *Clingman's Brigade in the Confederacy, 1862–1865.* Jefferson, N.C.: McFarland, 2002.

Castel, Albert. "Why the North Won and the South Lost." *Civil War Times Illustrated* 39, no. 2 (2000): 56–60.

———. *Articles of War: Winners, Losers, and Some Who Were Both in the Civil War.* Mechanicsburg, Pa.: Stackpole Books, 2001.

———. "So Glorious an Adventure: Major Tom Taylor's March to the Sea." *Timeline* 18, no. 5 (2001): 18–31.

———. "Vicksburg: Myths and Realities." *North & South* 6, no. 7 (2003): 62–69.

Chaffin, Tom. *Sea of Gray: The Around-the-World Odyssey of the Confederate Raider Shenandoah.* New York: Hill and Wang, 2006.

Christ, Mark K., ed. *"All Cut to Pieces and Gone to Hell": The Civil War, Race Relations, and the Battle of Poison Springs.* Little Rock, Ark.: August House, 2003.

Clancy, Paul R. *The Epic Battle, Calamitous Loss, and Historic Recovery of the USS Monitor.* Camden, Maine: International Marine, 2005.

Clark, John E. "Management in the War: The Legacy of the Civil War Railroads." *North & South* 5, no. 5 (2002): 50–59.

Clarke, Francis M. "Sentimental Bonds: Suffering, Sacrifice, and Benevolence in the Civil War North." Unpublished Ph.D. diss., John's Hopkins University, 2002.

Clarke, Hewitt. *He Saw the Elephant: Confederate Naval Saga of Lt. Charles "Savvy" Read, CSN.* Spring, Tex.: Lone Star Press, 2000.

Claxton, Melvin, and Mark Puls. *Uncommon Valor: The Exploit of the New Market Heights Medal of Honor Winners.* Hoboken, N.J.: John Wiley and Sons, 2006.

Clemmer, Gregg S. *Old Alleghany: The Life and Wars of General Ed Johnson.* Staunton, Va.: Hearthside Pub., 2004.

Coddington, Ronald S. *Faces of the Civil War: An Album of Union Soldiers and Their Stories.* Baltimore: Johns Hopkins University Press, 2004.

Coffin, Howard. *The Battered Stars: One State's Civil War Ordeal during Grant's Overland Campaign from the Home Front in Vermont to the Battlefields of Virginia.* Woodstock, Vt.: Countryman, 2002.

Cole, Philip M. *Command and Communication Frictions in the Gettysburg Campaign.* Orrtanna, Pa.: Colecraft Industries, 2006.

Coleman, Wim, and Pat Perrin. *The American Civil War.* Detroit: Greenhaven Press, 2005.

Collins, Robert. *General James G. Blunt: Corrupt Conqueror.* Gretna, La.: Pelican Pub., 2005.

Conrad, James L. *The Young Lions: Confederate Cadets at War.* Columbia: University of South Carolina Press, 2004.

———. *Rebel Reefers: The Organization and Midshipmen of the Confederate States Naval Academy.* Boulder, Colo.: Da Capo Press, 2003.

Cooper, Edward S. *William Babcock Hazen: The Best Hated Man.* Madison, N.J.: Fairleigh Dickinson University Press, 2005.

Coski, John M. *The Confederate Battle Flag: America's Most Embattled Emblem.* Cambridge, Mass.: Belknap Press of Harvard University Press, 2005.

Couper, William. *The Corps Forward: The Biographical Sketches of the VMI Cadets Who Fought in the Battle of New Market.* Buena Vista, Va.: Mariner Publishing, 2005.

Cozzens, Peter. "Jackson Alone." *Civil War Times Illustrated* 40, no. 6 (2001): 30–39, 74–76.

Creighton, Margaret S. *The Colors of Courage: Gettysburg's Forgotten History: Immigrants, Women, and African Americans in the Civil War's Defining Battle.* New York: Basic Books, 2005.

Cross, Coy F. *Lincoln's Man in Liverpool: Consul Dudley and the Legal Battle to Stop Confederate Warships.* Dekalb: Northern Illinois University Press, 2007.

Cunningham, Alvin R. *Conrad Elroy, Powder Monkey: The Role of the Navy in the Civil War.* Logan, Iowa: Perfection Learning, 2003.

Curry, Angus. *The Officers of the CSS Shenandoah.* Gainesville: University Press of Florida, 2006.

Cutler, Thomas J. "A Duel of Iron." *Naval History* 18, no. 4 (2004): 26–31.

Dahlstrom, Neil. "Rock Island Prison, 1863–1865: Andersonville of the North Dispelled." *Journal of Illinois History* 4, no. 4 (2001): 291–306.

Davis, Robert S. *Ghosts and Shadows of Andersonville: Essays on the Secret Social Histories of America's Deadliest Prison.* Macon, Ga.: Mercer University Press, 2006.

Davis, William C. *The Illustrated Encyclopedia of the Civil War: The Soldiers, Generals, Weapons, and Battles.* Guildford, Conn.: Lyons Press, 2001.

———. *The Commanders of the Civil War.* London: Salamander, 2001.

———. *Look Away! A History of the Confederate States of America.* New York: Free Press, 2002.

Davis, William C., Brian C. Pohanka, and Don Troiani, eds. *Civil War Journal: The Leaders.* New York: Gramercy Books, 2003.

Day, Carl F. *Tom Custer: Ride to Glory.* Spokane, Wash.: Arthur H. Clark, 2003.

Dedmondt, Glenn. *The Flags of Civil War North Carolina.* Gretna, La.: Pelican Publishing, 2003.

De Kay, James T. *The Rebel Raiders: The Astonishing History of the Confederacy's Secret Navy.* New York: Ballantine Books, 2002.

Desjardin, Thomas A. *These Honored Dead: How the Story of Gettysburg Shaped American Memory.* Cambridge, Mass.: Da Capo Press, 2003.

Dew, Charles B. "How Samuel E. Pittman Validated Lee's 'Lost Orders' Prior to Antietam: A Historical Note." *Journal of Southern History* 70, no. 4 (2004): 865–870.

Discofarno, Ken. *They Saved the Union at Little Round Top, Gettysburg, July 2, 1863.* Gettysburg, Pa.: Thomas Publications, 2002.

Dollar, Susan E. "The Red River Campaign, Natchitoches Parish, Louisiana: A Case of Equal Opportunity Destruction." *Louisiana History* 43, no. 4 (2002): 411–432.

Dougherty, James J. *Stone's Brigade and the Fight for the McPherson's Farm: Battle of Gettysburg, July 1, 1863.* Conshohocken, Pa.: Combined Publishing, 2001.

Doughtery, Kevin. *The Coastal War in North and South Carolina: An Analysis of the Evolution of Joint Navy-Army Operations, 1861–1865.* Danville, Va.: BGES, 2002.

Dreese, Michael A. *Civil War Leadership and Mexican War Experience.* Jackson: University Press of Mississippi, 2007.

———. *Never Desert the Old Flag: 50 Stories of Union Battle Flags and Color-Bearers at Gettysburg.* Gettysburg, Pa.: Thomas Publications, 2002.

Dreese, Michael E. *Torn Families: Death and Kinship at the Battle of Gettysburg.* Jefferson, N.C.: McFarland, 2007.

Duncan, Richard R. *Beleaguered Winchester: A Virginia Community at War, 1861–1865.* Baton Rouge: Louisiana State University Press, 2007.

Dunkelman, Mark H. "Death to All Foragers." *American History* 37, no. 3 (2002): 28–35.

Durkin, Joseph T. *Confederate Navy Chief: Stephen R. Mallory.* Tuscaloosa: University of Alabama Press, 2005.

Duvall, Sam. "Incident at Hatcher's Run." *Alabama Heritage,* no. 63 (2002): 18–28.

Ecelbarger, Gary L. *Black Jack Logan: An Extraordinary Life in Peace and War.* Guilford, Conn.: Lyon's Press, 2005.

———. "Stonewall Jackson's Fog of War: The Operational Triangle of May 24, 1862." *North & South* 5, no. 3 (2002): 46–55.

Echelberry, Earl. "Death in the Woods." *Military Heritage* 6, no. 5 (2005): 52–59, 82.

Edwards, Whit. *The Prairie Was on Fire: Eyewitness Accounts of the Civil War in the Indian Territory.* Oklahoma City: Oklahoma Historical Society, 2001.

Ehlers, Mark. "The Colors of Courage: White Soldiers' Response to Black Troops in the Civil War." Unpublished master's thesis, James Madison University, 2005.

Eicher, David J. *The Longest Night: A Military History of the Civil War.* New York: Simon and Schuster, 2001.

Ellem, Warren. "The Fall of Fort Fisher: Contested Memories of the Civil War." *North Carolina Historical Review* 79, no. 2 (2002): 198–233.

Elmore, Charles J. *General David Hunter's Proclamation: The Quest for African American Freedom before and during the Civil War.* Fort Washington, Pa.: Eastern National, 2002.

Elmore, Tom. "Head to Head." *Civil War Times Illustrated* 40, no. 7 (2002): 44–52, 54–55.

Escobedo, Santiago. "Iron Men and Wooden Carts: Tejano Freighters during the Civil War." *Journal of South Texas* 17, no. 2 (2004): 51–60.

Escott, Paul D. *The Plea of Military Necessity: Civil-Military Relations in the Confederacy.* Westport, Conn.: Praeger Security International, 2006.

Faust, Drew G. "'We Should Grow Too Fond of It': Why We Love the Civil War." *Civil War History* 50, no. 4 (2004): 368–383.

Feege, Edward H. "The Rehabilitation of James Waddell." *Naval History* 17, no. 3 (2003): 31–35.

Feis, William B. "Lee's Army Is Really Whipped': Grant and Intelligence Assessment from the Wilderness to Cold Harbor." *North & South* 7, no. 4 (2004): 28–37.

———. "Charles S. Bell: Union Scout." *North & South* 4, no. 5 (2001): 26–37.

———. "'There Is a Bad Enemy in This City': Colonel William Truesdail's Army Police and the Occupation of Nashville, 1862–1863." *North & South* 8, no. 2 (2005): 34–45.

Field, Ron. *Uniforms of the Civil War: An Illustrated Guide for Historians, Collectors, and Reenactors.* Guilford, Conn.: Lyon's Press, 2005.

———. *The Confederate Army, 1861–65.* Oxford, UK: Osprey, 2005.

Fitzpatrick, David J. "Emory Upton and the Citizen Soldier." *Journal of Military History* 65, no. 2 (2001): 355–389.

Fordyce, Samuel W., ed. *An American General: The Memoirs of David Sloan Stanley.* Santa Barbara, Calif.: Narrative Press, 2003.

Frazier, Donald S. "'The Battles of Texas Will Be Fought in Louisiana': The Assault of Fort Butler, June 28, 1863." *Southwestern Historical Quarterly* 104, no. 3 (2001): 332–362.

———. "'The Carnival of Death': The Cavalry Battle at Cheneyville, Louisiana, May 20, 1863." *Louisiana History* 42, no. 2 (2001): 193–207.

Freehling, William W. "Why Civil War Military History Must Be Less than 85 Percent Military." *North & South* 5, no. 2 (2001): 14–24.

Freemon, Frank R. *Gangrene and Glory: Medical Care during the American Civil War.* Urbana: University of Illinois Press, 2001.

Fuller, Howard J. "'The Whole Character of Maritime Life': British Reactions to the USS *Monitor* and the American Ironclad Experience." *Mariner's Mirror* 88, no. 3 (2002): 285–300.

———. "'This Country Now Occupies the Vantage Ground': Understanding John Ericsson's Monitors and the American Union's War against British Naval Supremacy." *American Neptune* 62, no. 1 (2002): 91–110.

Furgueron, James R. "The 'Best Hated Man' in the Union Army: The Remarkable Career of General William Babcock Hazen." *North & South* 4, nos. 3–4 (2001): 22–34; 66–79.

Furgurson, Ernest B. *Not War but Murder: Cold Harbor, 1864.* New York: Alfred A. Knopf, 2000.

Garavaglia, Louis A. "Sherman's March and the Georgia Arsenals." *North & South* 6, no. 1 (2002): 12–22.

Garcia, Pedro. "Highway to Victory." *Military Heritage* 4, no. 2 (2002): 74–79.

———. "Confederacy in the Balance." *Military Heritage* 6, no. 2 (2004): 60–67, 87.

Garrison, Nancy S. *With Courage and Delicacy: Civil War on the Peninsula: Women and the S. S. Sanitary Commission.* Cambridge, Mass.: Da Capo Press, 2003.

Giambrone, Jeff T. "Defense of the Mississippi Valley." *North & South* 7, no. 6 (2004): 50–65.

Gibson, Charles D. "Soldiers Take the Tidewater." *Naval History* 16, no. 6 (2002): 27–30.

Gottfried, Bradley M. *Brigades of Gettysburg: The Union and Confederate Brigades at the Battle of Gettysburg.* Cambridge, Mass.: Da Capo Press, 2002.

Goulka, Jeremiah H., ed. *The Grand Old Man of Maine: Selected Letters of Joshua Lawrence Chamberlain, 1865–1914.* Chapel Hill: University of North Carolina Press, 2004.

Grabeau, Warren. *Confusion Compounded: The Pivotal Battle of Raymond, 12 May, 1863: A Scholarly Monograph.* Saline, Mich.: McNaughton and Gunn, 2001.

Gragg, Rod. *A Commitment to Valor: A Character Portrait of Robert E. Lee.* Nashville, Tenn.: Rutledge Hill Press, 2001.

Garrison, Webb. *Mutiny in the Civil War.* Shippensburg, Pa.: White Mane, 2001.

Green, A. Wilson. *Breaking the Backbone of the Rebellion: The Final Battles of the Petersburg Campaign.* Mason City, Iowa: Savas Pub., 2000.

———. *Civil War Petersburg: Confederate City on the Crucible of War.* Charlottesville: University of Virginia Press, 2006.

Griffin, John C. *A Pictorial History of the Confederacy.* Jefferson, N.C.: McFarland, 2004.

Grimsley, Mark. "Second-Guessing Bobby Lee: A Counterfactual Assessment of Lee's Generalship during the Overland Campaign." *North & South* 7, no. 4 (2004): 38–45.

Grimsley, Mark, and Brooks D. Simpson. *The Collapse of the Confederacy.* Lincoln: University of Nebraska Press, 2001.

Grocki, Stan. *1863, Year of Lost Opportunities.* Baltimore: America House Book Publishers, 2002.

Hartwig, D. Scott. "'It Looked like a Task to Storm': The Pennsylvania Reserves Assault South Mountain, September 14, 1862." *North & South* 5, no. 7 (2002): 36–49.

Hattaway, Herman. "The Changing Face of Battle." *North & South* 4, no. 6 (2001): 34–43.

———. *Reflections of a Civil War Historian: Essays on Leadership, Society, and the Art of War.* Columbia: University of Missouri Press, 2003.

Hawkins, Rusty. "A Slight History of Coastal Battles in Texas during the Civil War." Unpublished master's thesis, West Texas A & M University, 2003.

Heiss, Walter R. *Veterinary Service during the American Civil War*. Baltimore: PublishAmerica, 2005.

Hennessy, John J. "Lincoln Wins Back His Army." *Civil War Times Illustrated* 39, no. 7 (2001): 34–42, 65.

Henris, John. "A Legacy of Rebellion: The Short, Tragic Career of William Edmondson (Grumble) Jones." Unpublished master's thesis, Slippery Rock, University of Pennsylvania, 2002.

Hess, Earl J. *Field Armies & Fortifications of the Civil War: The Eastern Campaigns, 1861–1864*. Chapel Hill: University of North Carolina Press, 2005.

Hicks, Brian. *Raising the Hunley: The Remarkable History and Recovery of the Lost Confederate Submarine*. New York: Ballantine Books, 2002.

Hogan, Neil. "Colonel Patrick O'Rorke: Fallen Hero of Gettysburg." *Irish Sword* 23, no. 91 (2002): 33–52.

Holberton, William B. *Homeward Bound: The Demobilization of the Union and Confederate Armies, 1865–66*. Mechanicsburg, Pa.: Stackpole Books, 2001.

Holzer, Harold. "Windows on the Civil War at Sea." *Naval History* 18, no. 4 (2004): 16–21.

Horres, C. Russell. "An Affair at Ft. Sumter." *South Carolina Historical Magazine* 102, no. 1 (2001): 6–26.

Howard, Nathan. "A Two Front Dilemma: The Texas Rangers in the Civil War." *Southern Historian* 23 (2002): 43–55.

Hoyt, Edwin P. *The Voyage of the Hunley*. Short Hills, N.J.: Buford Books, 2002.

Hubbs, Mark. "A Rebel Shot Causes 'Torture and Despair.'" *Naval History* 16, no. 2 (2002): 46–50.

Hughes, Nathaniel C., and Gordon D. Whitney. *Jefferson Davis in Blue: The Life of Sherman's Relentless Warrior*. Baton Rouge: Louisiana State University Press, 2002.

Jackson, Rex T. *The Sultana Saga: The Titanic of the Mississippi*. Bowie, Md.: Heritage Books, 2003.

Jamieson, Perry D. "Background to Bloodshed: The Tactics of the U.S.–Mexican War and the 1850s." *North & South* 4, no. 6 (2001): 24–31.

Johnson, Clint. *In the Footsteps of Robert E. Lee*. Winston-Salem, N.C.: John F. Blair, 2001.

Johnson, John M. *Lead, Salt, and the Railroad: Toland's Raid on Wytheville, July 18, 1863*. Wytheville, Va.: Wythe County Historical Society, 2003.

Jones, Robert A. *Confederate Corsair: The Life of Lt. Charles W. "Savez" Read*. Mechanicsburg, Pa.: Stackpole Books, 2000.

Jones, Terry L., ed. *Campbell Brown's Civil War: With Ewell in the Army of Northern Virginia*. Baton Rouge: Louisiana State University Press, 2001.

Jordan, David M. *"Happiness Is Not My Companion": The Life of G. K. Warren*. Bloomington: Indiana University Press, 2001.

Joyner, Elizabeth H. *The USS Cairo: History of Artifacts of a Civil War Gunboat*. Jefferson, N.C.: McFarland, 2006.

Kelly, Dorothy E. "General William P. Sanders: Son of the South, Defender of the Union." *North & South* 7, no. 2 (2004): 84–92.

Kinard, Jeff. *Lafayette of the South: Prince Camille de Polignac and the American Civil War*. College Station: Texas A & M University Press, 2001.

Konstam, Angus. *Confederate Ironclad, 1861–65*. Oxford, U.K.: Osprey, 2001.

———. *Union Monitor, 1861–65*. Oxford, U.K.: Osprey, 2002.

Konstam, Angus, and Tony Bryan. *USS Monitor & CSS Virginia at Hampton Roads, 1862*. Oxford, U.K.: Osprey, 2003.

———. *Confederate Submarines and Torpedo Vessels, 1861–65*. Oxford, U.K.: Osprey, 2004.

———. *Confederate Raider, 1861–65*. Oxford, U.K.: Osprey, 2003.

———. *Confederate Blockade Runner, 1861–65*. Oxford, U.K.: Osprey, 2004.

Krick, Robert K. *The Smoothbore Volley That Doomed the Confederacy: The Death of Stonewall Jackson and Other Chapters on the Army of Northern Virginia*. Baton Rouge: Louisiana State University Press, 2002.

Kroll, C. Douglas. *Friends in Peace and War: The Russian Navy's Landmark Visit to Civil War San Francisco*. Washington, D.C.: Potomac Books, 2007.

Krumwiede, John F. *Old Waddy's Coming! The Military Career of Brigadier General James S. Wadsworth*. Baltimore: Butternut and Blue, 2002.

Kunstler, Mort, and James I. Robertson. *Gods and Generals: The Paintings of Mort Kunstler*. Shelton, Conn.: Greenwich Workshop Press, 2002.

LaFantasie, Glenn W. "William C. Oates and the Death of General Elon Farnsworth." *North & South* 8, no. 1 (2005): 48–55.

———. "Night and Death on Little Round Top." *American History* 39, no. 6 (2004): 48–55, 71.

———. *Gettysburg Requiem: The Life and Lost Causes of Confederate Colonel William C. Oates*. New York: Oxford University Press, 2006.

Lamm, Alan K. "Wesley Merritt: The Union Army's Other 'Boy General.'" *Journal of America's Military Past* 28, no. 2 (2001): 19–44.

Lane, Mills. *Savannah and the Civil War Sea.* Savannah, Ga.: Ships of the Sea Maritime Museum, 2001.

Lang, J. Stephen. *The Complete's Idiot's Guide to the Confederacy.* Indianapolis, Ind.: Alpha Books, 2003.

Lanning, Michael L. *The Civil War 100: The Stories Behind the Most Influential Battles, People, and Events in the War Between the States.* Naperville, Ill.: Sourcebooks, 2007.

Larabee, Ann. *The Gentleman Bomber: The Chilling Tale of a Confederate Spy, Con Artist, and Mass Murderer.* New York: Palgrave Macmillan, 2005.

Lash, Jeffrey N. *A Politician Turned General: The Civil War Career of Stephen Augustus Hurlbut.* Kent, Ohio: Kent State University Press, 2003.

Lentz, Perry. *Private Fleming at Chancellorville: The Red Badge of Courage and the Civil War.* Columbia: University of Missouri Press, 2006.

Levine, Bruce C. *Confederate Emancipation: Southern Plans to Free and Arm Slaves during the Civil War.* New York: Oxford University Press, 2005.

Longacre, Edward G. *General William Dorsey Pender: A Military Biography.* Conshohocken, Pa.: Combined Publishing, 2001.

Longacre, Glenn, and John C. Haas. *To Battle for God and the Right: The Civil War Letterbooks of Emerson Opdycke.* Urbana: University of Illinois Press, 2003.

Lord, Francis A. *Civil War Collector's Encyclopedia: Arms, Uniforms, and Equipment of the Union and Confederacy.* Mineola, N.Y.: Dover Publications, 2004.

Lowe, Richard G. *Walker's Texas Division, C.S.A.: Greyhounds of the Trans-Mississippi.* Baton Rouge: Louisiana State University Press, 2006.

Lowry, Thomas P. "'I Hope to Get Wounded in the Arse': Military Justice during the Overland Campaign." *North & South* 7, no. 4 (2004): 50–54.

Lundahl, Jeffrey D. "Engineers in Blue: The Engineer Corps Contributions to the Union Victory." Unpublished master's thesis, California State University, Hayward, 2005.

Lundberg, John R. *The Finishing Stroke: Texans in the 1864 Tennessee Campaign.* Abilene, Tex.: McWhiney Foundation Press, 2002.

Lynn, John W. *Confederate Commando and Fleet Surgeon: Dr. Daniel Burr Conrad.* Shippensburg, Pa.: Burd Street Press, 2001.

Macomber, Robert. "Action on the Florida Coast." *Naval History* 17, no. 1 (2003): 38–41.

Maharay, George S. *Vermont Hero: Major General George J. Stannard.* Shippensburg, Pa.: White Mane Books, 2001.

Mahood, Wayne. *General Wadsworth: The Life and Times of Brevet Major General James S. Wadsworth.* Cambridge, Mass.: Da Capo Press, 2003.

———. *Alexander "Fighting Elleck" Hays: The Life of a Civil War General, from West Point to the Wilderness.* Jefferson, N.C.: McFarland, 2005.

Manning, Chandra. *What This Cruel War Was Over: Soldiers, Slavery, and the Civil War.* New York: Alfred A. Knopf, 2007.

Markle, Donald E. *Spies and Spymasters of the Civil War.* New York: Hippocrene Books, 2004.

Marten, James A. *Children for the Union: The War Spirit on the Northern Home Front.* Chicago: Ivan R. Dee, 2004.

Martin, Samuel J. *Matthew Calbraith Butler, Confederate General, Hampton Red Shirt, and U.S. Senator.* Mechanicsburg, Pa.: Stackpole Books, 2001.

Matthews, Gary R. *Basil Wilson Duke, C.S.A.: The Right Man in the Right Place.* Lexington: University Press of Kentucky, 2005.

Mayeux, Steven M. *Earthen Walls, Iron Men: Fort De Russey, Louisiana, and the Defense of the Red River.* Knoxville: University of Tennessee Press, 2007.

McCaslin, Richard B. "In the Shadow of Washington: Robert E. Lee and the Confederacy." *North & South* 4, no. 4 (2001): 14–23.

McKenzie, Kenneth F. "Among the Last to Run." *Naval History* 17, no. 5 (2003): 24–29.

McMurray, Philip. "'Where My Natural Roots Lead Me': Joshua L. Chamberlain—the Origins of a Civil War Officer." Unpublished master's thesis, Kent State University Press, 2001.

McNeil, Jim. *Masters of the Shoals: Tales of the Cape Fear Pilots Who Ran the Union Blockade.* Cambridge, Mass.: Da Capo Press, 2003.

McPherson, James M. *The Mighty Scourge: Perspectives on the Civil War.* New York, Oxford University Press, 2007.

———. *The Atlas of the Civil War.* Philadelphia: Courage Books, 2005.

McPherson, James M., ed. *The Most Fearful Ordeal: Original Coverage of the Civil War by the New York Times.* New York: St. Martin's Press, 2005.

Melton, Brian C. *Sherman's Forgotten General: Henry W. Slocum.* Columbia: University of Missouri Press, 2007.

Melton, Maurice. "Casualties of War: Two Georgia Coast Pilots and the Capture of the USS *Water Witch.*" *Journal of South Georgia History* 16 (2004): 1–14.

Milbourne, Curtis W. "'I Have Been Worse Treated than Any Officer': Confederate Colonel Thomas Green's Assessment of the New Mexico Campaign." *Southwestern Historical Quarterly* 105, no. 2 (2001): 322–337.

Miller, Edward S. "The *Monitor's* Lucky Sister." *Naval History* 18, no. 4 (2004): 32–36.

Miller, Joel M. "Gustavus Vasa Fox and the Expedition to Relieve Fort Sumter." Unpublished master's thesis, Tulane University, 2004.

Miller, William J. *Great Maps of the Civil War: Pivotal Battles and Campaigns Featuring 32 Removable Maps.* Nashville, Tenn.: Rutledge Hill Press, 2004.

Milton, David H. *Lincoln's Spymaster: Thomas Haines Dudley and the Liverpool Network.* Mechanicsburg, Pa.: Stackpole Books, 2003.

Milton, Keith. "Duel at Hampton Roads." *Military Heritage* 3, no. 3 (2001): 38–44, 97.

Monroe, Dan. *Shapers of the Great Debate on the Civil War: A Biographical Dictionary.* Westport, Conn.: Greenwood Press, 2005.

Mulesky, Ray. *Thunder from a Clear Sky: Stovepipe Johnson's Confederate Raid on Newburgh, Indiana.* New York: iUniverse, 2005.

Murray, R. L. *"A Perfect Storm of Lead": George Sears Greene and His New York Brigade in Defense of Culp's Hill.* Wolcott, N.Y.: Benedum Books, 2000.

———. *"The Greatest Battle of the Age": New Yorkers at First Bull Run.* Wolcott, N.Y.: Benedum Books, 2002.

———. *Holding the Line: New Yorkers in Defense of Pickett's Charge.* Wolcott, N.Y.: Benedum Books, 2001.

———. *Antietam: A Strategic and Tactical Analysis of the Maryland Campaign of 1862.* Wolcott, N.Y.: Benedum Books, 2000.

———. *Letters from the Front: New Yorkers at First Bull Run.* Wolcott, N.Y.: Benedum Books, 2002.

———. *Letters from Berdan's Sharpshooters.* Wolcott, N.Y.: Benedum Books, 2005.

Mushkat, Jerome, ed. *A Citizen-Soldier's Civil War: The Letters of Brevet Major General Alvin C. Voris.* Dekalb: Northern Illinois University Press, 2002.

Neely, Mark E. "Was the Civil War a Total War?" *Civil War History* 50, no. 4 (2004): 434–458.

Nelson, Scott R., and Carol Sheriff. *A People at War: Civilians and Soldiers in America's Civil War.* New York: Oxford University Press, 2007.

Newton, Steven H. "Joseph Johnston and Snake Creek Gap." *North & South* 4, no. 3 (2001): 56–67.

———. "The Confederate Home Guard: Forgotten Soldiers of the Lost Cause?" *North & South* 6, no. 1 (2002): 40–50.

Newton, Steven H., et al. "The Ten Greatest Blunders of the Civil War." *North & South* 8, no. 1 (2005): 12–23.

Nosworthy, Brent. *The Bloody Crucible of Courage: Fighting Methods and Combat Experience of the Civil War.* New York: Carroll and Graf, 2003.

Noyalas, Jonathan A. *"My Will is Absolute Law:' A Biography of Union General Robert H. Milroy."* Jefferson, N.C.: McFarland, 2006.

O'Donnell, Patrick D. "Dick Dowling and the Battle of Sabine Pass: The Thermopylae of Lieutenant Dick Dowling." *Irish Sword* 23, no. 91 (2002): 69–86.

Oeffinger, John C. *A Soldier's General: The Civil War Letters of Major General Lafayette McLaws.* Chapel Hill: University of North Carolina Press, 2002.

Owens, Richard H. "An Astonishing Career." *Military Heritage* 3, no. 2 (2001): 64–73.

Palmer, David W. *The Forgotten Hero of Gettysburg: A Biography of General George Sears Greene.* Trenton, N.J.: Xlibris Corp., 2004.

Palmer, Juliette M. "Beyond Black and White in Blue and Gray: The Absence of Ethnic Regiments in Civil War Films." Unpublished master's thesis, Regent University, 2001.

Paradis, James M. *African Americans and the Gettysburg Campaign.* Lanham, Md.: Scarecrow Press, 2005.

Parsons, Philip W. *The Union Sixth Army Corps in the Chancellorsville Campaign.* Jefferson, N.C.: McFarland, 2006.

Patterson, Gerard A. *From Blue to Gray: The Life of Confederate General Cadmus M. Wilcox.* Mechanicsburg, Pa.: Stackpole Books, 2001.

Peladeau, Marius B., and Edwin C. Bearss. *Burnished Rows of Steel: Vermont's Role in the Battle of Gettysburg, July 1–3, 1863.* Newport: Vermont Civil War Enterprises, 2002.

Petrie, Stewart J. *Bloody Path to the Shenandoah: Fighting with the Union VI Corps in the American Civil War.* Shippensburg, Pa.: Burd Street Press, 2004.

Platt, Carolyn V. "'Three Cheers for the Cracker Line': William Gates Le Duc and the Relief of Chattanooga." *Timeline* 22, no. 2 (2005): 36–39.

Polsky, Andrew J. "'Mr. Lincoln's Army': Revisited: Partisanship, Institutional Position, and Union Army Command, 1861–1865." *Studies in American Political Development* 16, no. 2 (2002): 176–207.

Prince, Cathryn J. *Burn the Town and Jack the Banks!: Confederates Attack Vermont!* New York: Carroll and Grant, 2006.

Pritchard, Russ A. *Raiders of the Civil War: Untold Stories of Actions behind the Lines.* Guilford, Conn.: Lyons Press, 2005.

Raab, James W. *J. Patton Anderson, Confederate General: A Biography.* Jefferson, N.C.: McFarland, 2004.

———. *Confederate General Lloyd Tilgham: A Biography.* Jefferson, N.C.: McFarland, 2006.

Rafuse, Ethan S. *The American Civil War.* Aldershot, U.K.: Ashgate, 2005.

Rafuse, Ethan S., ed. *The American Civil War.* Burlington, Vt.: Ashgate, 2005.

Ragan, Mark K. *Submarine Warfare in the Civil War.* Cambridge, Mass.: Da Capo Press, 2002.

Ramold, Steven J. *Slaves, Citizens: African Americans in the Union Navy.* Dekalb: Northern Illinois University Press, 2002.

Raus, Edmund J. *Banners South: A Northern Community at War.* Kent, Ohio: Kent State University Press, 2005.

Reidy, Joseph P. "Black Men in Navy Blue during the Civil War." *Prologue* 33, no. 3 (2001): 154–167.

Rhea, Gordon C. *Carrying the Flag: The Story of Private Charles Whilden, the Confederacy's Unlikely Hero.* New York: Basic Books, 2004.

———. "'Butcher' Grant and the Overland Campaign." *North & South* 4, no. 1 (2000): 44–55.

———. "'The Hottest Place I Ever Was In': The Battle of Haw's Shop, May 28, 1864." *North & South* 4, no. 4 (2001): 42–57.

———. "A Hot Time in Ashland: The Battles of Hanover Court House and Ashland, May 31–June 1, 1864." *North & South* 4, no. 7 (2001): 24–37.

———. *Cold Harbor: Lee and Grant, May 26–June 3, 1864.* Baton Rouge: Louisiana State University Press, 2002.

———. "The Truce at Cold Harbor." *North & South* 7, no. 1 (2004): 76–85.

———. "The Overland Campaign of 1864." *North & South* 7, no. 4 (2004): 12–26.

Richter, William L. *Historical Dictionary of the Civil War and Reconstruction.* Lanham, Md.: Scarecrow Press, 2004.

Ridgway, James M. *Little Mac: Demise of an American.* Princeton, N.J.: Xlibris Corp., 2000.

Ripple, Charles C. "Lion of War and Lamb of God: Thomas Jonathan Jackson, Christian Warrior." Unpublished master's thesis, Wake Forrest University, 2003.

Robinson, Armstead L. *Bitter Fruits of Bondage: The Demise of Slavery and the Collapse of the Confederacy, 1861–1865.* Charlottesville: University of Virginia Press, 2005.

Rodgers, Thomas E. "Billy Yank and G. I. Joe: Am Exploratory Essay on the Sociopolitical Dimensions of Soldier Motivation." *Journal of Military History* 69, no. 1 (2005): 93–121.

Rogers, J. H. "War Comes to Norfolk Harbor, 1861." *Virginia Cavalcade* 50, no. 2 (2001): 64–75.

Roland, Charles P. "Becoming a Soldier." *Register of the Kentucky Historical Society* 101, nos. 1–2 (2003): 75–92.

———. *An American Iliad: The Story of the Civil War.* Lexington: University Press of Kentucky, 2004.

Rosecrans, William S. "King of the Hill." *Civil War Times Illustrated* 49, no. 3 (2001): 24–26, 68–70.

Ross, D. Reid. "Kansas Abolitionists Fight Confederates in Missouri." *Journal of the West* 40, no. 3 (2001): 58–67.

Rubin, Anne S. *A Shattered Nation: The Rise and Fall of the Confederacy, 1861–1868.* Chapel Hill: University of North Carolina Press, 2005.

Rutkow, Ira M. *Bleeding Blue and Gray: The Untold Story of Civil War Medicine.* New York: Random House, 2005.

Samito, Christian G., ed. *Fear Was Not in Him: The Civil War Letters of Major General Francis C. Barlow, U.S.A.* New York: Fordham University Press, 2004.

Sanders, Charles W. *While in the Hands of the Enemy: Military Prisons of the Civil War.* Baton Rouge: Louisiana State University Press, 2005.

Schiller, Laurence D. "Two Tales of Tennessee: The Ups and Downs of Cavalry Command." *North & South* 4, no. 4 (2001): 78–86.

Schmidt, Leone. *For the Honor of the Flag: The Life of General Mason Brayman, 1813–1895.* Warrenville, Ill.: Warrenville Historical Society, 2004.

Schneller, Robert J. *Cushing: Civil War SEAL.* Washington, D.C.: Brassey's, 2004.

Schooler, Lynn. *The Last Shot: The Incredible Story of the C.S.S. Shenandoah and the True Conclusion of the American Civil War.* New York: Ecco, 2005.

Schultz, Duane P. *The Most Glorious Fourth: Vicksburg and Gettysburg, July 4, 1863.* New York: Norton, 2002.

Sears, Stephen W. "Glendale: Opportunity Squandered." *North & South* 5, no. 1 (2001): 12–24.

———. "'We Should Assume the Aggressive': Origins of the Gettysburg Campaign." *North & South* 5, no. 4 (2002): 58–66.

———. "The Lee of Gettysburg." *North & South* 6, no. 5 (2003): 12–19.

Shaw, David. *Sea Wolf of the Confederacy: The Daring Civil War Raids of Naval Lt. Charles W. Read.* New York: Free Press, 2004.

Sheldon, George. *Fire on the River: The Defense of the World's Longest Covered Bridge and How it Changed the Battle of Gettysburg.* Lancaster, Pa.: Quaker Hill Press, 2006.

Shover, Michele. "John Bidwell: Civil War Politics, and the Indian Crisis of 1862." *Dogtown Territorial Quarterly,* no. 46 (2001): 4–24, 34–37.

Sifakis, Stewart. *Compendium of the Confederate Armies.* Bowie, Md.: Willow Bend Books, 2003.

Silber, Nina. *Daughters of the Union: Northern Women Fight the Civil War.* Cambridge, Mass.: Harvard University Press, 2005.

Silverman, Jason H., and Susan R. Silverman. "Blacks in Gray, Myth or Reality." *North & South* 5, no. 3 (2002): 35–43.

Simson, Jay W. *Naval Strategies of the Civil War: Confederate Innovations and Federal Opportunism.* Nashville, Tenn.: Cumberland House, 2001.

Siry, David R. "Confederates in Pennsylvania: Lee's 1863 Invasion of the North, a Thesis in History." Unpublished master's thesis, Pennsylvania State University, 2003.

Sizer, Lyde C., and Jim Cullen. *The Civil War Era: An Anthology of Sources.* Malden, Mass.: Blackwell, 2004.

Sleevi, Nola M. "The Commanders of the Second Corps of the Army of Northern Virginia: Their Religious Beliefs, as Reflected in Their Leadership." Unpublished master's thesis, University of Missouri–Kansas City, 2002.

Small, Stephen C. "The *Wampanoag* Goes on Trial." *Naval History* 16, no. 4 (2002): 32–36.

Smith, Derek. "'This Brilliant Exploit': Attack on the USS *Underwriter.*" *North & South* 8, no. 2 (2005): 76–82.

Smith, John D., ed. *Black Soldiers in Blue: African American Troops in the Civil War Era.* Chapel Hill: University of North Carolina Press, 2002.

Sneden, Robert K. "Pen and Sword at Savage's Station." *Civil War Times Illustrated* 39, no. 5 (2000): 42–51.

Snell, Mark A. *From First to Last: The Life of Major General William B. Franklin.* New York: Fordham University Press, 2002.

Speer, Lonnie R. *Portals to Hell: Military Prisons of the Civil War.* Lincoln: University of Nebraska Press, 2005.

Staats, Richard J. *The Life and Times of Ephraim Cooper: One of Lincoln's First Volunteers.* Bowie, Md.: Heritage Books, 2003.

Stephens, Larry, and Mike Skinner. *Hold the Fort—I Am Coming: The Battle of Altoona Pass, October 5, 1864.* Carrollton, Ga.: Battle Flag Press, 2001.

Suderow, Bryce A. "War Along the James." *North & South* 6, no. 3 (2003): 12–23.

Summers, Mark W. "The Spoils of War." *North & South* 6, no. 2 (2003): 82–89.

Sunderland, Jonathan. *Union Troops of the American Civil War.* Ramsbury, U.K.: Crowood, 2005.

Surdam, David G. "The Confederate Naval Buildup: Could More Have Been Accomplished?" *Naval War College Review* 54, no. 1 (2001): 107–127.

Sutherland, Daniel E. "Guerrilla Warfare, Democracy, and the Fate of the Confederacy." *Journal of Southern History* 68, no. 2 (2002): 259–292.

Swisher, James K. *Warrior in Gray: General Robert Rodes of Lee's Army.* Shippensburg, Pa.: White Mane Books, 2000.

Symonds, Craig L. *American Heritage History of the Battle of Gettysburg.* New York: HarperCollins, 2001.

———. "Generalship at Gettysburg." *North & South* 6, no. 5 (2003): 80–92.

Tagg, Larry. *The Generals of Gettysburg: The Leaders of America's Greatest Battle.* Cambridge, Mass.: Da Capo Press, 2003.

Tanner, Robert G. *Retreat to Victory? Confederate Strategy Reconsidered.* Wilmington, Del.: Scholarly Resources, 2001.

Tap, Bruce. "Amateurs at War: Abraham Lincoln and the Committee on the Conduct of the War." *Journal of the Abraham Lincoln Association* 23, no. 2 (2002): 1–18.

Taylor, John M. "British Observers in Wartime Dixie." *MHQ* 14, no. 2 (2002): 66–71.

Taylor, Lenette S. "Uncle Sam's Landlord: Quartering the Union Army in Nashville in the Summer of 1863."

Tennessee Historical Quarterly 61, no. 4 (2002): 242–265.

Teague, Chuck. "Leadership Impaired? The Health of Robert E. Lee during the Gettysburg Campaign." *North & South* 6, no. 5 (2003): 68–78.

Thompson, Jerry D. *Civil War to the Bloody End: The Life and Times of Major General Samuel P. Heintzelman.* College Station: Texas A&M University Press, 2006.

Thomsen, Brian M., ed. *Blue and Gray at Sea: Naval Memoirs of the Civil War.* New York: Forge, 2003.

Toomey, Daniel C. *The Johnson-Gilmore Raid, July 9–13, 1864.* Baltimore, Md.: Toomey Press, 2005.

Trask, Benjamin H., and Dina B. Hill. *USS Monitor Bibliography.* Newport News, Va.: The Mariners Museum, 2002.

Tucker, Leslie R. *Major General Isaac Ridgeway Trimble: Biography of a Baltimore Confederate.* Jefferson, N.C.: McFarland, 2005.

Tucker, Phillip T. *God Help the Irish!: The History of the Irish Brigade.* Abilene, Tex.: McWhiney Foundation, 2006.

Tucker, Phillip T. *Irish Confederates: The Civil War's Forgotten Soldiers.* Abilene, Tex.: McWhiney Foundation Press, 2006.

Tucker, Spencer C. *A Short History of the Civil War at Sea.* Wilmington, Del.: Scholarly Resources, 2002.

Tulloch, Hugh. *The Routledge Companion to the Civil War.* New York: Routledge, 2006.

Underwood, Rodman L. *Waters of Discord: The Union Blockade of Texas during the Civil War.* Jefferson, N.C.: McFarland, 2003.

———. *Stephen Russell Mallory: A Biography of the Confederate Navy Secretary and United States Senator.* Jefferson, N.C.: McFarland, 2005.

Van Tassel, David D., and John Vacha. *Behind Bayonets: The Civil War in Northern Ohio.* Kent, Ohio: Kent State University Press, 2005.

Varon, Elizabeth R. *Southern Lady, Yankee Spy: The True Story of Elizabeth Van Lew, A Union Agent in the Heart of the Confederacy.* New York: Oxford University Press, 2005.

Wagner, Richard. *For Honor, Flag, and Family: Civil War General Samuel W. Crawford.* Shippensburg, Pa.: White Mane Books, 2005.

Wakefield, John L. *Confederates against the Confederacy: Essays on Leadership and Loyalty.* Westport, Conn.: Praeger, 2002.

Waldrep, Christopher. *Vicksburg's Long Shadow: The Civil War Legacy of Race and Remembrance.* Lanham, Md.: Rowman and Littlefield, 2005.

Walsh, George. *Those Damn Horse Soldiers: True Tales of the Civil War Cavalry.* New York: Forge, 2006.

Walt, Eugene M. *Bull Run and Beyond.* Huntington, N.Y.: Nova History Publications, 2001.

Ward, Mary G. *Civil War Legends of Rich Mountain and Beverly, West Virginia.* Parson, W. Va.: McClain Printing Co., 2004.

Webber, Jennifer L. "'If Ever War Was Holy': Quaker Soldiers and the Union Army." *North & South* 5, no. 3 (2002): 62–72.

Weitz, Mark A. *More Damning than Slaughter: Desertion in the Confederate Army.* Lincoln: University of Nebraska Press, 2005.

———. "'A Justifiable Crime': Desertion in the Confederate Army." *North & South* 8, no. 1 (2005): 66–74.

Welch, Richard F. *The Boy General: The Life and Careers of Francis Channing Barlow.* Kent, Ohio: Kent State University Press, 2005.

Westrick, Robert F. "The U.S.S. *Peterhoff:* An Historical and Archaeological Investigation of a Civil War Shipwreck." Unpublished master's thesis, East Carolina University, 2001.

Whisker, James B. *U.S. and Confederate Arms and Armories during the American Civil War.* 4 vols. Lewiston, N.Y.: E. Mellen Press, 2002–2003.

Whittington, Terry. "In the Shadow of Defeat: Tracking the Vicksburg Parolees." *Journal of Mississippi History* 64, no. 4 (2002): 307–330.

Wideman, John C. *The Sinking of the USS Cairo.* Jackson: University Press of Mississippi, 2004.

Williams, Don. "Devil's Den." *Military Heritage* 3, no. 5 (2002): 68–75.

Williams, Frank J. "Abraham Lincoln: The President Who Changed the Role of Commander in Chief." *White House Studies* 2, no. 1 (2002): 3–15.

Wills, Brian S. *Gone with the Glory: The Civil War in Cinema.* Lanham, Md.: Rowman & Littlefield, 2007.

Wilson, Mark R. *The Business of the Civil War: Military Mobilization and the State, 1861–1865.* Baltimore: Johns Hopkins University Press, 2006.

Winik, Jay. *April, 1865: The Month That Saved America.* New York: HarperCollins, 2001.

Woodworth, Steven E. "The Scapegoat of Arkansas Post." *MHQ* 13, no. 3 (2001): 58–67.

———. *The Loyal, True, and Brave: American's Civil War Soldiers.* Wilmington, Del.: SR Books, 2002.

———. "The Army of the Tennessee and the Elements of Military Success." *North & South* 6, no. 4 (2003): 44–55.

Woodworth, Steven E., and Warren Wilkinson. "Calm Before the Storm." *MHQ* 14, no. 3 (2002): 34–41.

Wylie, Paul R. *The Irish General: Thomas Francis Meagher.* Norman: University of Oklahoma Press, 2007.

Yates, Bernice-Marie., ed. *The Perfect Gentleman: The Life and Letters of George Washington Custis Lee.* Fairfax, Va.: Xulon Press, 2003.

Youngblood, Norman E. "The Development of Landmine Warfare." Unpublished Ph.D. diss., Texas Tech University, 2002.

INDEX

Italic page numbers indicate illustrations. **Boldface** page numbers denote biographies.

Business Law

The Ethical, Global, and Digital Environment

EIGHTEENTH EDITION

18e

Jamie Darin Prenkert

A. James Barnes

Joshua E. Perry

Todd Haugh

Abbey R. Stemler

all of Indiana University

BUSINESS LAW: THE ETHICAL, GLOBAL, AND DIGITAL ENVIRONMENT,
EIGHTEENTH EDITION

Published by McGraw-Hill LLC, 1325 Avenue of the Americas, New York, NY 10121. Copyright © 2022 by
McGraw-Hill LLC. All rights reserved. Printed in the United States of America. Previous editions © 2019, 2016,
and 2013. No part of this publication may be reproduced or distributed in any form or by any means, or stored in
a database or retrieval system, without the prior written consent of McGraw-Hill LLC, including, but not limited
to, in any network or other electronic storage or transmission, or broadcast for distance learning.

Some ancillaries, including electronic and print components, may not be available to customers outside the
United States.

This book is printed on acid-free paper.

1 2 3 4 5 6 7 8 9 LWI 24 23 22 21

ISBN 978-1-260-73689-2 (bound edition)
MHID 1-260-73689-X (bound edition)
ISBN 978-1-264-29658-3 (loose-leaf edition)
MHID 1-264-29658-4 (loose-leaf edition)

Portfolio Manager: *Kathleen Klehr*
Product Developer: *Alexandra Kukla*
Marketing Manager: *Claire McLemore*
Content Project Managers: *Amy Gehl/Jodi Banowetz*
Buyer: *Laura Fuller*
Designer: *Matt Diamond*
Content Licensing Specialists: *Jacob Sullivan*
Cover Image: *bonetta/Getty Images*
Compositor: *SPi Global*

Library of Congress Cataloging-in-Publication Data

Names: Prenkert, Jamie Darin, author. | Barnes, A. James, author. | Perry,
    Joshua E., author. | Haugh, Todd, author. | Stemler, Abbey R., author.
Title: Business law : the ethical, global, and digital environment / Jamie
    Darin Prenkert, A. James Barnes, Joshua E. Perry, Todd Haugh, Abbey R.
Stemler, all of Indiana University.
Description: Eighteenth edition. | New York, NY : McGraw Hill Education,
    [2022] | Includes index. | Audience: Ages 18+
Identifiers: LCCN 2020052156 (print) | LCCN 2020052157 (ebook) | ISBN
    9781260736892 (paperback) | ISBN 126073689X (bound edition) | ISBN
    9781264296583 (loose-leaf edition) | ISBN 1264296584 (loose-leaf
edition) | ISBN 9781264296606 (epub)
Subjects: LCSH: Commercial law–United States.
Classification: LCC KF889 .B89 2022 (print) | LCC KF889 (ebook) | DDC
    346.7307–dc23
LC record available at https://lccn.loc.gov/2020052156
LC ebook record available at https://lccn.loc.gov/2020052157

mheducation.com/highered

Jamie Darin Prenkert, Professor of Business Law and the Charles M. Hewitt Professor, joined the faculty of Indiana University's Kelley School of Business in 2002. He is the Associate Dean of Academics for the Kelley School. He served as chair of the Department of Business Law and Ethics from 2014 to 2016 and from 2019 to 2020, having served as an Associate Vice Provost for Faculty and Academic Affairs for the Indiana University–Bloomington campus from 2016 to 2019. Professor Prenkert is a former editor in chief of the *American Business Law Journal* and is a member of the executive committee of the Academy of Legal Studies in Business. His research focuses on issues of employment discrimination and the human rights obligations of transnational corporations. He has published articles in the *American Business Law Journal*, the *North Carolina Law Review*, the *Berkeley Journal of Employment and Labor Law*, and the *University of Pennsylvania Journal of International Law*, among others. He also coedited a volume titled *Law, Business and Human Rights: Bridging the Gap.* Professor Prenkert has taught undergraduate and graduate courses, both in-residence and online, focusing on the legal environment of business, employment law, law for entrepreneurs, business and human rights, and critical thinking. He is a recipient of the Harry C. Sauvain Undergraduate Teaching Award and the Kelley Innovative Teaching Award.

Professor Prenkert earned a B.A. (*summa cum laude*) from Anderson University and a J.D. (*magna cum laude*) from Harvard Law School. Prior to joining the faculty of the Kelley School, he was a senior trial attorney for the U.S. Equal Employment Opportunity Commission.

A. James Barnes, Professor of Public and Environmental Affairs and Professor of Law at Indiana University-Bloomington (IU), previously served as Dean of IU's School of Public and Environmental Affairs and has taught business law at IU and Georgetown University. His teaching interests include commercial law, environmental law, alternative dispute resolution, law and public policy, and ethics and the public official. He is the co-author of several leading books on business law.

From 1985 to 1988, Professor Barnes served as the deputy administrator of the U.S. Environmental Protection Agency (EPA). From 1983 to 1985, he was the EPA general counsel and in the early 1970s served as chief of staff to the first administrator of EPA. Professor Barnes also served as a trial attorney in the U.S. Department of Justice and as general counsel of the U.S. Department of Agriculture. From 1975 to 1981, he had a commercial and environmental law practice with the firm of Beveridge and Diamond in Washington, D.C.

Professor Barnes is a Fellow of the National Academy of Public Administration, and a Fellow in the American College of Environmental Lawyers. He served as chair of the Environmental Protection Agency's Environmental Finance Advisory Board and as a member of the U.S. Department of Energy's Environmental Management Advisory Board. From 1992 to 1998,

he was a member of the Board of Directors of the Long Island Lighting Company (LILCO). Professor Barnes received his B.A. from Michigan State University and a J.D. (*cum laude*) from Harvard Law School.

Joshua E. Perry, Graf Family Professor and Associate Professor of Business Law and Ethics, joined the faculty of Indiana University's Kelley School of Business in 2009. He currently serves as chair of the Department of Business Law and Ethics, an appointment he has held since 2020. He was formerly the Faculty Chair for the Kelley School's Undergraduate Program. A three-time winner of the IU Trustees' Teaching Award and two-time winner of the Kelley Innovative Teaching Award, he teaches graduate and undergraduate courses on business ethics, critical thinking, and the legal environment of business. Professor Perry earned a B.A. (*summa cum laude*) from Lipscomb University, a Masters of Theological Studies from the Vanderbilt University Divinity School, and a J.D. from the Vanderbilt University Law School, where he was Senior Articles Editor on the *Law Review*. Prior to joining Kelley, he was on faculty at the Center for Biomedical Ethics and Society at Vanderbilt University Medical Center. In that role, he taught medical ethics in the School of Medicine and professional responsibility in the Law School, and served as a clinical ethicist in both the adult and children's hospitals at Vanderbilt. Before entering academe, he practiced law in Nashville, Tennessee, at a boutique litigation firm, where he specialized in dispute resolution and risk mitigation for clients in the health care, intellectual property, and entertainment industries.

Professor Perry's award-winning scholarship explores legal, ethical, and public policy issues in the life science, medical device, and health care industries, as well as in the business of medicine. He is the author of over 30 articles and essays that have appeared in a variety of journals, including the *American Business Law Journal*; the *Georgia Law Review*; the *Notre Dame Journal of Law, Ethics, and Public Policy*; the *Journal of Law, Medicine and Ethics*; and the *University of Pennsylvania Journal of Law and Social Change*, among others. His expertise has been featured in *The New York Times, USA Today, Wired, Fast Company, Huffington Post,* and *Salon*. Since 2015, he also has served on the editorial board for the *Journal of Business Ethics* as section editor for law, public policy, and ethics.

Todd Haugh, Associate Professor of Business Law and Ethics and Weimer Faculty Fellow at Indiana University's Kelley School of Business. His scholarship focuses on white-collar and corporate crime, business and behavioral ethics, and federal sentencing policy. His work has appeared in top law and business journals, including the *Northwestern University Law Review, Notre Dame Law Review, Vanderbilt Law Review,* and the *MIT-Sloan Management Review*. Prof. Haugh's expertise relating to the burgeoning field of behavioral compliance has led to frequent speaking and consulting engagements with major U.S.

companies and ethics organizations. He is also regularly quoted in national news publications such as *The New York Times*, *The Wall Street Journal*, *Forbes*, *Bloomberg News*, and *USA Today*.

A graduate of the University of Illinois College of Law and Brown University, Professor Haugh has extensive professional experience as a white-collar criminal defense attorney, a federal law clerk, and a member of the general counsel's office of the U.S. Sentencing Commission. In 2011, he was chosen as one of four Supreme Court Fellows of the Supreme Court of the United States to study the administrative machinery of the federal judiciary.

Prior to joining the Kelley School, where he teaches courses on business ethics, white-collar crime, and critical thinking, Professor Haugh taught at DePaul University College of Law and Chicago-Kent College of Law. He is a recipient of numerous teaching and scholarly awards, including a Trustees Teaching Award and multiple Innovative Teaching Awards, and a Jesse Fine Fellowship from the Poynter Center for the Study of Ethics and American Institutions, to which he now serves as a board member. In 2019 he was awarded the Distinguished Early Career Achievement Award by the Academy of Legal Studies in Business.

Abbey R. Stemler, Assistant Professor of Business Law and Ethics at Indiana University's Kelley School of Business.

She is a leading scholar on the sharing economy, and her scholarship and teaching have garnered many university and national awards. She is frequently sought out for her expertise on platform-based technology companies, such as Facebook, Uber, and Google.

Professor Stemler has published multiple articles in leading law journals such as the *Iowa Law Review*, *Emory Law Journal*, *Maryland Law Review*, *Georgia Law Review*, and *Harvard Journal on Legislation*. Her research explores the interesting spaces where law has yet to catch up with technology. In particular, her aim is to expose the evolving realities of Internet-based innovations and platforms and to find ways to effectively regulate them without hindering their beneficial uses. As she sees it, many modern firms inhabit a world that operates under alien physics—where free is often costly and "smart" is not always wise. She employs tools and insights from economics, behavioral science, regulatory theory, and rhetoric to understand how we, as a society, can better protect consumers, privacy, and democracy.

Professor Stemler is also a faculty associate at the Berkman Klein Center for Internet & Society at Harvard University, practicing attorney, entrepreneur, and consultant for governments and multinational organizations such as the World Bank Group.

This is the 18th Edition (and the 24th overall edition) of a business law text that first appeared in 1935. Throughout its more than 80 years of existence, this book has been a leader and an innovator in the fields of business law and the legal environment of business. One reason for the book's success is its clear and comprehensive treatment of the standard topics that form the traditional business law curriculum. Another reason is its responsiveness to changes in these traditional subjects and to new views about that curriculum. In 1976, this textbook was the first to inject regulatory materials into a business law textbook, defining the "legal environment" approach to business law. Over the years, this textbook has also pioneered by introducing materials on business ethics, corporate social responsibility, global legal issues, and the law of an increasingly digital world. The 18th Edition continues to emphasize change by integrating these four areas into its pedagogy.

Appendix B: The Uniform Commercial Code

The Uniform Commercial Code, or UCC, was developed by the American Law Institute (ALI) and the National Conference of Commissioners on Uniform State Laws (NCCUSL) as a body of rules intended to make the application of law to commercial transactions consistent across fifty states. The UCC has been adopted in whole by all but one state legislature, Louisiana, which adopted only certain sections. Such widespread use of the UCC, even with the minor deviations some jurisdictions make from the official code, makes possible more efficient and more confident transactions across state lines. The UCC can be accessed here: www.law.cornell.edu/ucc.

Continuing Strengths

The 18th Edition continues the basic features that have made its predecessors successful. They include:

- *Comprehensive coverage.* We believe that the text continues to excel in both the number of topics it addresses and the depth of coverage within each topic. This is true not only of the basic business law subjects that form the core of the book, but also of the regulatory and other subjects that are said to constitute the "legal environment" curriculum.
- *Style and presentation.* This text is written in a style that is direct, lucid, and organized, yet also relatively relaxed and conversational. For this reason, the text lends itself to the flipped classroom, allowing coverage of certain topics by assigning them as reading without lecturing on them. As always, key points and terms are emphasized; examples, charts, figures, and concept summaries are used liberally; and elements of a claim and lists of defenses are stated in numbered paragraphs.
- *Case selection.* We try very hard to find cases that clearly illustrate important points made in the text, that should interest students, and that are fun to teach. Except when older decisions are landmarks or continue to provide the best illustrations of particular concepts, we also try to select recent cases. Our collective in-class teaching experience with recent editions has helped us determine which of those cases best meet these criteria.

Important Changes in This Edition

For this edition, we welcome Todd Haugh and Abbey Stemler, our Indiana University colleagues, to the author team. They bring new teaching, research, and legal practice experiences to our team that have helped shape our approach to the 18th Edition and will allow us to continue to deliver excellent coverage of the ever-changing legal environment of business.

Our longtime co-author Arlen Langvardt decided to retire from authoring the textbook along with retiring from his faculty position at Indiana University. The author team wishes to express our gratitude for his leadership on the textbook for the past couple of editions and to thank him for the profound impact he has made on this text. In his place, Jamie Prenkert has moved into the lead author role. Co-author Jim Barnes remains our connection to the long and vital history of this textbook. With this edition, Jim will have been a co-author of this text for more than 50 years!

In this edition, the combination of new and longstanding authors has led to a number of innovations, while maintaining the thorough yet accessible approach for which the book is well known. Along with a more explicit focus on compliance in addition to ethics (see Ethics and Compliance in Action features), the 18th Edition includes new cases, tracks recent developments in various substantive areas of law, and offers revisions to various textual material in our ongoing commitment to clarity and completeness. The book continues to include both hypothetical examples and real-life cases so that instructors can elucidate important concepts for students while also maintaining student interest and engagement. Key additions and revisions for the 18th Edition include the following:

Chapter 1
- New problem case dealing with a spectator injured by a foul ball at a professional baseball game. The problem case can be used to enrich class discussion around case law reasoning, as illustrated in the *Coomer* case in the main text.
- Introduction of the new Ethics and Compliance in Action feature, which is present throughout the book.

Chapter 2
- New discussion of the Forced Arbitration Injustice Repeal Act (Fair Act).

Chapter 3
- Incorporation in the text of several recent Supreme Court cases, including *Trump v. Vance* (separation of powers and

Supremacy Clause), *Burwell v. Hobby Lobby Stores* and *Master-piece Cakeshop, Ltd. v. Colorado Civil Rights Commission* (First Amendment religion clause, as well as the federal Religious Freedom Restoration Act).

- Reorganization of the Commerce Clause discussion and the addition of 2018 Supreme Court decision *South Dakota v. Wayfair, Inc.*, which illustrates the standard for excessive burden on interstate commerce.
- New figure describing the Food and Drug Administration's tobacco regulations pursuant to the Family Smoking Prevention and Tobacco Control Act and related court challenges, with specific focus on First Amendment speech issues.
- New discussion of the claims against Harvard College and the University of North Carolina related to their admissions practices.

Chapter 4
- New discussion of the Business Roundtable's 2019 statement regarding stakeholder theory.

Chapter 5
- New discussion of Fourth Amendment searches and the third-party doctrine.
- New case note that highlights the importance of *New York Central & Hudson River Railroad v. United States*, which established the concept of corporate criminal liability.
- Revision of discussion of criminal racketeering offenses.
- New problem regarding whether a health care company and its senior executives had standing to challenge a warrant in a tax fraud case based on Fourth Amendment grounds.
- New problem case on the Sixth Amendment's reach in the context of corporate criminal fines based on the *Apprendi* line of Supreme Court cases.

Chapter 7
- New case that provides a clear illustration of negligence elements in the context of an easily understood fact pattern.

Chapter 8
- New case, *ZUP, LLC v. Nash Manufacturing, Inc.*, which provides a relatable example of the patent requirement of nonobviousness.

Chapter 9
- New case, *Grimes v. Young Life, Inc.*, which deals with a hybrid contract and the application of the predominant factor test.
- New case, *PWS Environmental, Inc. v. All Clear Restoration and Remediation, LLC*, which provides a straightforward application of quasi-contract.

Chapter 10
- New Cyberlaw in Action feature dealing with Twitter and offer terms.
- Replacement of the term "insanity" with the more modern concept of "mental incapacity."

Chapter 11
- General update of examples to ensure that concepts and technology references remain relevant.

Chapter 12
- New case, *Mid-American Salt, LLC v. Morris County Cooperative Pricing Council*, which illustrates that requirements contracts, though recognized under the UCC, must create some obligation in order to avoid being illusory.
- Revision of the discussion of forbearance as a form of consideration for added clarity.

Chapter 16
- Discussion of the 21st Century Integrated Digital Experience Act (IDEA).

Chapter 17
- New Ethics and Compliance in Action feature, which explores the ethics of obligating a donee beneficiary to an arbitration clause.

Chapter 18
- New case, *Macomb Mechanical, Inc. v. Lasalle Group Inc.*, which illustrates the operation of a "pay if paid" clause as a condition precedent.

Chapter 19
- New case, *National Music Museum: America's Shrine to Music v. Johnson*, which deals with a contract for the sale of a guitar once owned by Elvis Presley and illustrates the rules concerning the passage of title.

Chapter 20
- New introduction problem, which explores products liability and ethical issues involving JUUL e-cigarettes.
- New Cyberlaw in Action feature that explores the question of whether Amazon, when it sells a defective product via a third-party seller, can be held liable. The box references and discusses recent litigation including *Allstate New Jersey Insurance Co. v. Amazon.com*; *Eberhart v. Amazon.com*; *Oberdorf v. Amazon.com, Inc.*; and *Papataros v. Amazon.com*.
- Revision of discussion of punitive damages to include recent verdicts against Johnson & Johnson and Monsanto.

Chapter 21
- New case, *Hillerich & Bradsby v. Charles Products*, which addresses whether a buyer timely notified the seller that products delivered to the buyer for sale to children in buyer's Louisville Slugger Museum Store were defective (i.e., contained lead content in excess of limits prescribed under the Consumer Products Safety Improvement Act of 2008).

Chapter 22
- New case, *Beau Townsend Ford Lincoln v. Don Hinds Ford*, which illustrates the principle that a buyer is liable for the purchase price of goods that have been received and accepted and that the buyer is not relieved of that obligation when deceived into making payment to someone other than the seller to whom the buyer is contractually obligated to pay.

Chapter 23
- New problem case.

Chapter 24

- Revision to *Francini v. Goodspeed Airport, LLC* to note that the Connecticut Supreme Court upheld the Connecticut Appellate Court's decision (included in the text) in 2018.

Chapter 25

- Revisions to text to clarify state and local variations in the law that have developed in recent years.
- Revision and update to the discussion of a landlord's duty to mitigate damages.

Chapter 26

- Revision to the explanation of the formalities of a will for greater clarity.

Chapter 27

- New Cyberlaw in Action feature discussing the burgeoning cyber insurance market.
- Updates to the status of health care insurance under the Affordable Care Act.

Chapter 28

- New case, *Trump Endeavor 12 LLC v. Fernich, Inc. d/b/a The Paint Spot*, involving a contractor who sued to enforce a lien on property on which it had provided materials but had not been paid by the owner of the property.

Chapter 29

- New case, *Hyman v. Capital One Auto Finance*, where the court held that a debtor had stated a case for conversion and breach of the peace in the course of an attempted repossession of her automobile where the "repo man" involved the state police without judicial authorization.

Chapter 30

- Revision of discussion of preferential liens.
- New case, *Rosenberg v. N.Y State Higher Education Services Corp.*, in which a bankruptcy court granted a discharge of student loans on the grounds their repayment would constitute an undue hardship. The court criticized previous bankruptcy court decisions that produced harsh results for students on the grounds that the courts did not properly apply prior case authority.
- New text concerning the Small Business Organization Act of 2019 that provides a modified procedure to facilitate reorganization under Chapter 11 of small businesses in financial difficulty.

Chapter 32

- New case, *Triffin v. Sinha*, which illustrates the operation of the shelter rule: The assignee of a check was held to be entitled to holder-in-due-course status because the entity that assigned the check to him was a holder in due course.

Chapter 33

- Revision of the text for clarity and to reflect recent changes in the law.

Chapter 34

- New case, *Grodner & Associates v. Regions Bank*, which involves a bookkeeper who defrauded the law firm for which she worked over a period of 15 months by writing checks utilizing facsimile signatures and initiating ACH transactions, which she was not authorized to perform. The bank refused to recredit the account on the grounds the law firm had not notified the bank of the fraud within a year after receiving a statement containing an unauthorized payment and the law firm was unable to show any deviation from the bank's own procedures or local banking standards or from the terms of the parties' deposit agreement.
- Revision of discussion of Check 21, the electronic processing of checks, and Federal Reserve Board Regulations concerning wire transfers.

Chapter 35

- New case, *Krakauer v. Dish Network LLC*, which illustrates the objective standard of manifested assent for agency formation.
- New Cyberlaw in Action feature, which discusses California's judicial and legislative responses to misclassification of gig workers as nonemployee agents in a variety of industries, specifically focusing on sharing-economy platform businesses like Uber and Lyft.

Chapter 36

- New case, *Synergies3 Tec Services, LLC v. Corvo*, in which the court analyzes whether employees' intentional tort was committed in the scope of their employment.

Chapter 37

- Introduction of one of the newest business forms: the benefit corporation.

Chapter 38

- New problem case, which deals with the possible creation of a partnership amid a pandemic.

Chapter 39

- New case, *Gelman v. Buehler*, which demonstrates to students the importance of partnership agreements.

Chapter 40

- New introduction problem, which examines the appropriateness for and tax implications of forming a limited liability company.
- New in-depth discussion of the tax advantages of limited liability companies.
- Removal of discussion of the now-outdated business form: the limited liability limited partnership.

Chapter 41

- New text, which discusses benefit corporations and their growing importance, including a new chart comparing benefit corporations and certified "B corps."
- New case about scholarly critique of benefit corporations suggesting they may actually hurt socially conscious companies that are more traditionally organized.

Chapter 42

- Revision of Ethics and Compliance in Action feature concerning offshore tax havens used by major U.S. companies.

- New problem cases about the policy arguments for holding promoters liable for preincorporation contracts and the equity stakes taken in entrepreneurial ventures on the popular show *Shark Tank*.

Chapter 43
- New text related to CEO compensation, including that of Tesla's Elon Musk and Disney's Bob Iger.
- New text that highlights the duty-of-care obligations related to the oversight of legal compliance.
- New case, *In re Caremark Int'l Inc. Derivative Litig.*, which established the fiduciary obligation of board oversight of compliance and effectively created modern corporate compliance regimes.
- Revised discussion of the foundations of corporate criminal liability and the costs of white-collar crime.
- New problem case about a shareholder suit against Allergan, the company that makes Botox, and the theory of legal liability underlying fiduciary duty claims.

Chapter 44
- New Ethics and Compliance in Action feature about the ethicality of share dissolution at Facebook.
- New problem case regarding dividend distribution under the Model Business Corporation Act.

Chapter 45
- New discussion of the Security and Exchange Commission's powers, including implications of recent Supreme Court opinions *Lucia v. SEC and Kokesh v. SEC*.
- New and revised text about Section 5 of the Securities Act of 1933, including Rules 163A, 135, 169, and the Jumpstart Our Business Startups (JOBS) Act.
- Revision of the Concept Review concerning the communications issuers may provide to the public.
- New text on "gun jumping" violations levied against Google and Salesforce.
- Revisions to text on offering exemptions, including new text concerning Regulation A, Regulation Crowdfunding, and Rule 506, and deletion of text referring to the withdrawn Rule 595.
- Revision of Ethics and Compliance in Action feature related to the trade-offs and criticisms of the JOBS Act.
- Revision of the Concept Review regarding issuers' exemptions from registration requirements.
- New discussion of scienter and the Private Litigation Securities Reform Act.
- Revision of text concerning insider trading, including a new discussion of classical and misappropriation theories, as well as tippee liability under *Dirks v. SEC*.
- New case, *SEC v. Dorozhko*, which considered computer hacking as insider trading under the misappropriation theory.
- New case note comparing *United States v. Newman* and *United States v. Salman*, which address the personal benefit test of tippee liability.
- New problem case on whether Elon Musk violated securities laws based on his tweets.

- New problem case about insider trading prosecution of Mathew Martoma and SAC Capital Advisors.

Chapter 46
- New discussion of Regulation Best Interest, including a summary chart of obligations of broker-dealers.
- New case, *United States v. Goyal*, which concerned the evidence used to convict a former CFO for securities fraud violations under Section 10(b) of the 1934 Act.
- New problem case about whether the suit against a seller of high-performance liquid chromatography systems met the pleading standards for scienter and materiality under the securities laws.

Chapter 47
- Revision to discussion of Federal Communications Commission action about network neutrality regulation.

Chapter 48
- Revision to discussion of the recent actions taken by the FTC to regulate deceptive practices.
- Revision to discussion of the Truth in Lending Act.
- New discussion of the Economic Growth, Regulatory Relief, and Consumer Protection Act (Economic Growth Act) and its impact on the Fair Credit Reporting Act.

Chapter 49
- New case box about *United States v. Apple, Inc.*, in which Apple was held responsible for violating the Sherman Act when it conspired among major book publishers to raise the retail prices of ebooks.
- New Ethics and Compliance in Action feature that discusses how antitrust laws may hinder socially responsible business practices.

Chapter 50
- New Ethics and Compliance in Action feature about consolidation among big tech firms such as Facebook and Instagram.

Chapter 51
- New case concerning workers' compensation, *American Greetings Corp. v. Bunch*, in which an employee is injured during a work-related event but not while performing day-to-day work responsibilities.
- Added discussion of emergency medical and family leave provisions of the Families First Coronavirus Response Act.
- Revised discussion of collective bargaining and unionization to reflect recent Supreme Court cases, including *Janus v. AFSCME* and *Epic Systems Corp. v. Lewis*.
- New discussion of the Equal Pay Act that includes consideration of the U.S. Women's National Soccer Team's pay discrimination claim against U.S. Soccer.
- New case, *Bostock v. Clayton County*, in which the U.S. Supreme Court held that Title VII of the 1964 Civil Rights Act prohibition against discrimination in employment because of sex includes discrimination on the basis of sexual orientation and gender identity.

Chapter 52

- Revision of text to incorporate retrenchment by Trump administration of Environmental Protection Agency regulations to control greenhouse gasses associated with global climate change, including the Clean Power Plan and the automobile fuel economy standards adopted during the Obama administration.

Acknowledgments

We would like to thank the many reviewers who have contributed their ideas and time to the development of this text. We express our sincere appreciation to the following:

Wade Chumney, *California State University-Northridge*

Amanda Foss, *Modesto Junior College*

Richard Guertin, *Orange County Community College*

Gwenda Bennett Hawk, *Johnson County Community College*

Joseph Pugh, *Immaculata University*

Kurt Saunders, *California State University-Northridge*

Henry Lowenstein, *Coastal Carolina University*

Dennis Wallace, *University of New Mexico*

Melanie Stallings Williams, *California State University-Northridge*

We also acknowledge the assistance and substantive contributions of Professor Sarah Jane Hughes of Indiana University's Maurer School of Law and Professors Angela Aneiros (Chapter 25), Victor Bongard (Chapter 24), Shawna Eikenberry (Chapter 18), Goldburn Maynard (Chapter 26), and April Sellers (Chapters 3 and 51) of Indiana University's Kelley School of Business. We further acknowledge the technical contributions of Elise Borouvka and the research assistance of Lin Ye, a student at the Maurer School.

Jamie Darin Prenkert
A. James Barnes
Joshua E. Perry
Todd Haugh
Abbey R. Stemler

A New Kind of Business Law

The 18th Edition of *Business Law* continues to focus on global, ethical, and digital issues affecting legal aspects of business. The new edition contains a number of new features as well as a revised supplements package. Please take a few moments to page through some of the highlights of this new edition.

OPENING VIGNETTES

Each chapter begins with an opening vignette that presents students with a mix of real-life and hypothetical situations and discussion questions. These stories provide a preview of issues addressed in the chapter and help to stimulate students' interest in the chapter content.

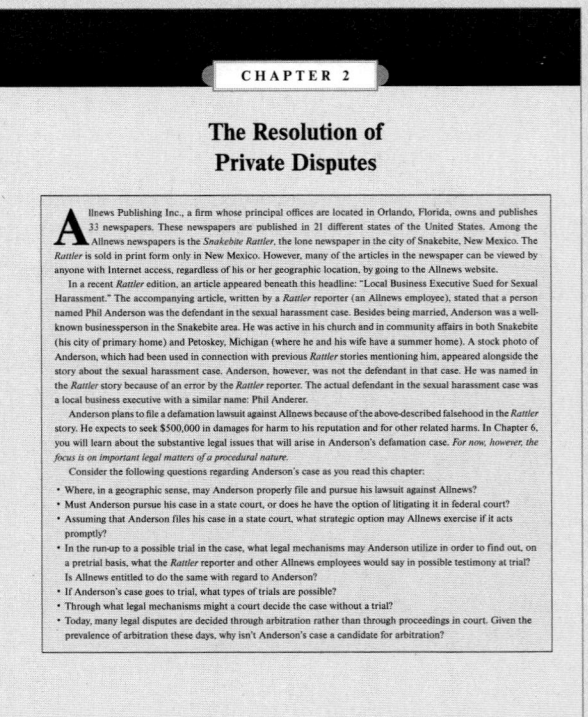

CHAPTER 2

The Resolution of Private Disputes

Allnews Publishing Inc., a firm whose principal offices are located in Orlando, Florida, owns and publishes 33 newspapers. These newspapers are published in 21 different states of the United States. Among the Allnews newspapers is the *Snakebite Rattler*, the lone newspaper in the city of Snakebite, New Mexico. The *Rattler* is sold in print form only in New Mexico. However, many of the articles in the newspaper can be viewed by anyone with Internet access, regardless of his or her geographic location, by going to the Allnews website.

In a recent *Rattler* edition, an article appeared beneath this headline: "Local Business Executive Sued for Sexual Harassment." The accompanying article, written by a *Rattler* reporter (an Allnews employee), stated that a person named Phil Anderson was the defendant in the sexual harassment case. Besides being married, Anderson was a well-known businessperson in the Snakebite area. He was active in his church and in community affairs in both Snakebite (his city of primary home) and Petoskey, Michigan (where he and his wife have a summer home). A stock photo of Anderson, which had been used in connection with previous *Rattler* stories mentioning him, appeared alongside the story about the sexual harassment case. Anderson, however, was not the defendant in that case. He was named in the *Rattler* story because of an error by the *Rattler* reporter. The actual defendant in the sexual harassment case was a local business executive with a similar name: Phil Anderer.

Anderson plans to file a defamation lawsuit against Allnews because of the above-described falsehood in the *Rattler* story. He expects to seek $500,000 in damages for harm to his reputation and for other related harms. In Chapter 6, you will learn about the substantive legal issues that will arise in Anderson's defamation case. *For now, however, the focus is on important legal matters of a procedural nature.*

Consider the following questions regarding Anderson's case as you read this chapter:

- Where, in a geographic sense, may Anderson properly file and pursue his lawsuit against Allnews?
- Must Anderson pursue his case in a state court, or does he have the option of litigating it in federal court?
- Assuming that Anderson files his case in a state court, what strategic option may Allnews exercise if it acts promptly?
- In the run-up to a possible trial in the case, what legal mechanisms may Anderson utilize in order to find out, on a pretrial basis, what the *Rattler* reporter and other Allnews employees would say in possible testimony at trial? Is Allnews entitled to do the same with regard to Anderson?
- If Anderson's case goes to trial, what types of trials are possible?
- Through what legal mechanisms might a court decide the case without a trial?
- Today, many legal disputes are decided through arbitration rather than through proceedings in court. Given the prevalence of arbitration these days, why isn't Anderson's case a candidate for arbitration?

LEARNING OBJECTIVES

Active **Learning Objectives** open each chapter. LOs inform you of specific outcomes you should have after finishing the chapter. Icons reference each LO's reference within the chapter.

LO LEARNING OBJECTIVES

After studying this chapter, you should be able to:

2-1 Describe the basic structures of state court systems and the federal court system.

2-2 Explain the difference between subject-matter jurisdiction and in personam jurisdiction.

2-3 Identify the major legal issues courts must resolve when deciding whether in personam jurisdiction exists with regard to a defendant in a civil case.

2-4 Explain what is necessary in order for a federal court to have subject-matter jurisdiction over a civil case.

2-5 Identify the major steps in a civil lawsuit's progression from beginning to end.

2-6 Describe the different forms of discovery available to parties in civil cases.

2-7 Explain the differences among the major forms of alternative dispute resolution.

CYBERLAW IN ACTION

In recent years, the widespread uses of e-mail and information presented and stored in electronic form have raised questions about whether, in civil litigation, an opposing party's e-mails and electronic information are discoverable to the same extent as conventional written or printed documents. With the Federal Rules of Civil Procedure and comparable discovery rules applicable in state courts having been devised prior to the explosion in e-mail use and online activities, the rules' references to "documents" contemplated traditional on-paper items. Courts, however, frequently interpreted "documents" broadly, so as to include e-mails and certain electronic communications within the scope of discoverable items.

Even so, greater clarity regarding discoverability seemed warranted—especially as to electronic material that might be less readily classifiable than e-mails as "documents." Various states responded by updating their discovery rules to include electronic communications within the list of discoverable items. So did the Federal Judicial Conference. In Federal Rules of Civil Procedure amendments proposed by the Judicial Conference and ratified by Congress in 2006, "electronically stored information" became a separate category of discoverable material. The *electronically stored information (ESI)* category is broad enough to include e-mails and similar communications as well as electronic business records, web pages, dynamic databases, and a host of other material existing in electronic form. So-called e-discovery has become a

objection is valid in light of the particular facts and circumstances. For instance, if requested e-mails appear only on backup tapes and searching those tapes would require the expenditures of significant time, money, and effort, are the requested e-mails "not reasonably accessible because of undue burden or costs"? Perhaps, but perhaps not. The court will rule, based on the relevant situation. The court may deny the discovery request, uphold it, or condition the upholding of it on the requesting party's covering part or all of the costs incurred by the other party in retrieving the ESI and making it available. When a party fails or refuses to comply with a legitimate discovery request and the party seeking discovery of ESI has to secure a court order compelling the release of it, the court may order the noncompliant party to pay the attorney fees incurred by the requesting party in seeking the court order. If a recalcitrant party disregards a court order compelling discovery, the court may assess attorney fees against that party and/or impose evidentiary or procedural sanctions such as barring that party from using certain evidence or from raising certain claims or defenses at trial.

The discussion suggests that discovery requests regarding ESI may be extensive and broad-ranging, with logistical issues often attending those requests. In recognition of these realities, the Federal Rules seek to head off disputes by requiring the parties to civil litigation to meet, at least through their attorneys, soon after the case is filed. The meeting's goal is development of a discovery plan that outlines the parties' intentions regarding ESI discovery and sets forth an agreement on such matters as the form in which the

CYBERLAW IN ACTION BOXES

In keeping with today's technological world, these boxes describe and discuss actual instances of how the Internet is affecting business law today.

ETHICS AND COMPLIANCE IN ACTION BOXES

These boxes appear throughout the chapters and offer critical thinking questions and situations that relate to ethical/public policy concerns.

Ethics and Compliance in Action

The broad scope of discovery rights in a civil case will often entitle a party to seek and obtain copies of e-mails, records, memos, and other documents and electronically stored information from the opposing party's files. In many cases, some of the most favorable evidence for the plaintiff will have come from the defendant's files, and vice versa. If your firm is, or is likely to be, a party to civil litigation and you know that the firm's files contain materials that may be damaging to the firm in the litigation, you may be faced with the temptation to alter or destroy the potentially damaging items. This temptation poses serious ethical dilemmas. Is it morally defensible to change the content of records or documents on an after-the-fact basis, in order to lessen the adverse effect on your firm in pending or probable litigation? Is document destruction or e-mail deletion ethically justifiable when you seek to protect your firm's interests in a lawsuit?

If the ethical concerns are not sufficient by themselves to make you leery of involvement in document alteration or destruction, consider the potential legal consequences for yourself and your firm. The much-publicized collapse of the Enron Corporation in 2001 led to considerable scrutiny of the actions of the Arthur Andersen firm, which had provided auditing and consulting services to Enron. An Andersen partner, David Duncan, pleaded guilty to a criminal obstruction of justice charge that accused him of having destroyed, or having instructed Andersen employees to destroy, certain Enron-related records in order to thwart a Securities and Exchange Commission (SEC) investigation of Andersen. The U.S. Justice Department also launched an obstruction of justice prosecution against Andersen on the theory that the firm altered or destroyed records pertaining to Enron in order to impede the SEC investigation. A jury found Andersen guilty of obstruction of justice. Although the Andersen conviction was later overturned by the

to impose appropriate sanctions on the document-destroying party. These sanctions may include such remedies as court orders prohibiting the document-destroyer from raising certain claims or defenses in the lawsuit, instructions to the jury regarding the wrongful destruction of the documents, and court orders that the document-destroyer pay certain attorney fees to the opposing party.

What about the temptation to refuse to cooperate regarding an opposing party's lawful request for discovery regarding material in one's possession? Although a refusal to cooperate seems less blameworthy than destruction or alteration of documents, extreme instances of recalcitrance during the discovery process may cause a party to experience adverse consequences similar to those imposed on parties who destroy or alter documents. Litigation involving Ronald Perelman and the Morgan Stanley firm provides an illustration. Perelman had sued Morgan Stanley on the theory that the investment bank participated with Sunbeam Corp. in a fraudulent scheme that supposedly induced him to sell Sunbeam his stake in another firm in return for Sunbeam shares whose value plummeted when Sunbeam collapsed. During the discovery phase of the case, Perelman had sought certain potentially relevant e-mails from Morgan Stanley's files. Morgan Stanley repeatedly failed and refused to provide this discoverable material and, in the process, ignored court orders to provide the e-mails.

Eventually, a fed-up trial judge decided to impose sanctions for Morgan Stanley's wrongful conduct during the discovery process. The judge ordered that Perelman's contentions would be presumed to be correct and that the burden of proof would be shifted to Morgan Stanley so that Morgan Stanley would have to disprove Perelman's allegations. In addition, the trial judge prohibited Morgan Stanley from

THE GLOBAL BUSINESS ENVIRONMENT BOXES

Because global issues affect people in many different aspects of business, this material appears throughout the text instead of in a separate chapter on international issues. This feature brings to life global issues that are affecting business law.

The Global Business Environment

Just as statutes may require judicial interpretation when a dispute arises, so may treaties. The techniques that courts use in interpreting treaties correspond closely to the statutory interpretation techniques discussed in this chapter. *Olympic Airways v. Husain*, 540 U.S. 644 (2004), furnishes a useful example.

In *Olympic Airways*, the U.S. Supreme Court was faced with an interpretation question regarding a treaty, the Warsaw Convention, which deals with airlines' liability for passenger deaths or injuries on international flights. Numerous nations (including the United States) subscribe to the Warsaw Convention, a key provision of which provides that in regard to international flights, the airline "shall be liable for damages sustained in the event of the death or wounding of a passenger or any other bodily injury suffered by a passenger, if the accident which caused the damage so sustained took place on board the aircraft or in the course of any of the operations of embarking or disembarking." A separate provision imposes limits on the amount of money damages to which a liable airline may be subjected.

The *Olympic Airways* case centered around the death of Dr. Abid Hanson, a severe asthmatic, on an international flight operated by Olympic. Smoking was permitted on the flight. Hanson was given a seat in the nonsmoking section,

distress, whereupon his wife and a doctor who was on board gave him shots of epinephrine from an emergency kit that Hanson carried. Although the doctor administered CPR and oxygen when Hanson collapsed, Hanson died. Husain, acting as personal representative of her late husband's estate, sued Olympic in federal court on the theory that the Warsaw Convention made Olympic liable for Hanson's death. The federal district court and the court of appeals ruled in favor of Husain.

In considering Olympic's appeal, the U.S. Supreme Court noted that the key issue was one of treaty interpretation: whether the flight attendant's refusals to reseat Hanson constituted an "accident which caused" the death of Hanson. Noting that the Warsaw Convention itself did not define "accident" and that different dictionary definitions of "accident" exist, the Court looked to a precedent case, *Air France v. Saks*, 470 U.S. 392 (1985), for guidance. In the *Air France* case, the Court held that the term "accident" in the Warsaw Convention means "an unexpected or unusual event or happening that is external to the passenger." Applying that definition to the facts at hand, the Court concluded in *Olympic Airways* that the repeated refusals to reseat Hanson despite his health concerns amounted to unexpected and unusual behavior for a flight attendant. Although the refusals were not the sole rea-

LOG ON BOXES

These appear throughout the chapters and direct students, where appropriate, to relevant websites that will give them more information about each featured topic. Many of these are key legal sites that may be used repeatedly by business law students and business professionals alike.

LOG ON

For a great deal of information about the U.S. Supreme Court and access to the Court's opinions in recent cases, see the Court's website at **http://www.supremecourtus.gov**.

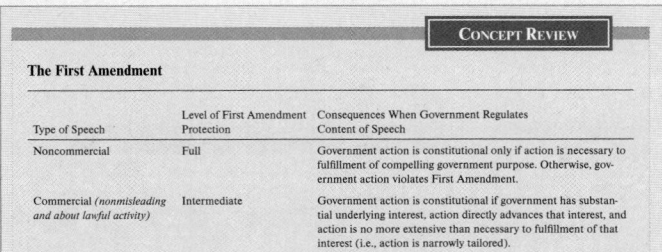

CONCEPT REVIEW

The First Amendment

Type of Speech	Level of First Amendment Protection	Consequences When Government Regulates Content of Speech
Noncommercial	Full	Government action is constitutional only if action is necessary to fulfillment of compelling government purpose. Otherwise, government action violates First Amendment.
Commercial (*nonmisleading and about lawful activity*)	Intermediate	Government action is constitutional if government has substantial underlying interest, action directly advances that interest, and action is no more extensive than necessary to fulfillment of that interest (i.e., action is narrowly tailored).

CONCEPT REVIEWS

These boxes visually represent important concepts presented in the text to help summarize key ideas at a glance and simplify students' conceptualization of complicated issues.

FIGURES

The figures appear occasionally in certain chapters. These features typically furnish further detail on special issues introduced more generally elsewhere in the text.

Figure 2.1 The Thirteen Federal Judicial Circuits

First Circuit (*Boston, Mass.*) Maine, Massachusetts, New Hampshire, Puerto Rico, Rhode Island	**Second Circuit** (*New York, N.Y.*) Connecticut, New York, Vermont	**Third Circuit** (*Philadelphia, Pa.*) Delaware, New Jersey, Pennsylvania, Virgin Islands	**Fourth Circuit** (*Richmond, Va.*) Maryland, North Carolina, South Carolina, Virginia, West Virginia
Fifth Circuit (*New Orleans, La.*) Louisiana, Mississippi, Texas	**Sixth Circuit** (*Cincinnati, Ohio*) Kentucky, Michigan, Ohio, Tennessee	**Seventh Circuit** (*Chicago, Ill.*) Illinois, Indiana, Wisconsin	**Eighth Circuit** (*St. Louis, Mo.*) Arkansas, Iowa, Minnesota, Missouri, Nebraska, North Dakota, South Dakota

---

Abdouch v. Lopez   829 N.W.2d 662 (Neb. 2013)

Helen Abdouch, an Omaha, Nebraska, resident, served as executive secretary of the Nebraska presidential campaign of John F. Kennedy in 1960. Ken Lopez, a Massachusetts resident, and his Massachusetts-based company, Ken Lopez Bookseller (KLB), are engaged in the rare book business. In 1963, Abdouch received a copy of a book titled Revolutionary Road. *Its author, Richard Yates, inscribed the copy with a note to Abdouch. The inscribed copy was later stolen from Abdouch. In 2009, Lopez and KLB bought the inscribed copy from a seller in Georgia. They sold it that same year to a customer from a state other than Nebraska. In 2011, Abdouch learned that Lopez had used the inscription and references to her in an advertisement on KLB's website. The advertisement, which appeared on the website for more than three years after Lopez and KLB sold the inscribed copy, contained a picture of the inscription, the word "SOLD," and this statement:*

This copy is inscribed by Yates: 'For Helen Abdouch—with admiration and best wishes. Dick Yates. 8/19/63.' Yates had worked as a speech writer for Robert Kennedy when Kennedy served as Attorney General; Abdouch was the executive secretary of the Nebraska (John F.) Kennedy organization when Robert Kennedy was campaign manager. . . . A scarce book, and it is extremely uncommon to find this advance issue of it signed. Given the date of the inscription—that is, during JFK's Presidency—and the connection between writer and recipient, it's reasonable to suppose this was an author's copy, presented to Abdouch by Yates.

Because Lopez and KLB did not obtain her permission before mentioning her and using the inscription in the advertisement, Abdouch filed an invasion-of-privacy lawsuit against Lopez and KLB in a Nebraska state district court. Contending that the Nebraska court lacked in personam jurisdiction, Lopez and KLB filed a motion to dismiss the case. The state district court granted the motion. Abdouch then appealed to the Supreme Court of Nebraska. (Further facts bearing upon the in personam jurisdiction issue appear in the following edited version of the Supreme Court's opinion.)

CASES

The cases in each chapter help to provide concrete examples of the rules stated in the text. A list of cases appears at the front of the text.

PROBLEMS AND PROBLEM CASES

Problem cases appear at the end of each chapter for student review and discussion.

Problems and Problem Cases

1. Victoria Wilson, a resident of Illinois, wishes to bring an invasion of privacy lawsuit against XYZ Co. because XYZ used a photograph of her, without her consent, in an advertisement for one of the company's products. Wilson will seek money damages of $150,000 from XYZ, whose principal offices are located in New Jersey. A New Jersey newspaper was the only print media outlet in which the advertisement was published. However, XYZ also placed the advertisement on the firm's website. This website may be viewed by anyone with Internet access, regardless of the viewer's geographic location. Where, in a geographic sense, may Wilson properly file and pursue her lawsuit against XYZ? Must Wilson pursue her case in a state court, or does she have the option of litigating in federal court? Assuming that Wilson files her case in state court, what strategic option may XYZ exercise if it acts promptly?

2. Alex Ferrer, a former judge who appeared as "Judge Alex" on a television program, entered into a contract with Arnold Preston, a California attorney who rendered services to persons in the entertainment industry. Seeking fees allegedly due under the contract, Preston invoked the clause setting forth the parties' agreement to arbitrate "any dispute . . . relating to the terms of [the contract] or the breach, validity, or legality thereof . . . in accordance with the rules [of the American Arbitration Association]." Ferrer countered Preston's demand for arbitration by filing, with the California Labor Commissioner, a petition in which he contended that the contract was unenforceable under residents Anne and Jim Cornelsen. When Anne Cornelson telephoned the Bomblisses and said she was ready to sell two litters of Tibetan mastiff puppies, Ron Bombliss expressed interest in purchasing two females of breeding quality. The Cornelsens had a website that allowed communications regarding dogs available for purchase but did not permit actual sales via the website. The Bomblisses traveled to Oklahoma to see the Cornelsens' puppies and ended up purchasing two of them. The Cornelsens provided a guarantee that the puppies were suitable for breeding purposes. Following the sale, the Cornelsens mailed, to the Bomblisses' home in Illinois, American Kennel Club registration papers for the puppies. Around this same time, Anne Cornelsen posted comments in an Internet chat room frequented by persons interested in Tibetan mastiffs. These comments suggested that the mother of certain Tibetan mastiff puppies (including one the Bomblisses had purchased) may have had a genetic disorder. The comments were made in the context of an apparent dispute between the Cornelsens and Richard Eichhorn, who owned the mother mastiff and had made it available to the Cornelsens for breeding purposes. The Bomblisses believed that the comments would have been seen by other persons in Illinois and elsewhere and would have impaired the Bomblisses' ability to sell their puppies even though, when tested, their puppies were healthy. The Bomblisses therefore sued the Cornelsens in an Illinois court on various legal theories. The Cornelsens asked the Illinois court to dismiss the case on the ground that the court lacked in personam jurisdiction over them. Did the Illinois court lack in personam jurisdiction?

KEY TERMS

Key terms are in color and bolded throughout the text and defined in the Glossary at the end of the text for better comprehension of important terminology.

WRITING ASSIGNMENT

McGraw Hill's new Writing Assignment tool delivers a learning experience that improves students' written communication skills and conceptual understanding with every assignment. Assign, monitor, and provide feedback on writing more efficiently and grade assignments within McGraw Hill Connect®. Writing Assignment gives students an all-in-one-place interface, so you can provide feedback more efficiently.

Features include:

- Saved and reusable comments (text and audio).
- Ability to link to resources in comments.
- Rubric building and scoring.
- Ability to assign draft and final deadline milestones.
- Tablet ready and tools for all learners.

BUSINESS LAW APPLICATION-BASED ACTIVITIES (ABAS)

Application-based activities for business law provide students valuable practice using problem-solving skills to apply their knowledge to realistic scenarios. Students progress from understanding basic concepts to using their knowledge to analyze complex scenarios and solve problems. Application-based activities have been developed for the topics most often taught (as ranked by instructors) in the business law course. These unique activities are assignable and auto-gradable in Connect.

REMOTE PROCTORING & BROWSER-LOCKING CAPABILITIES

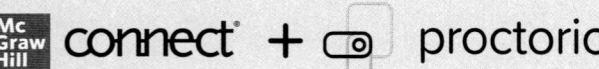

New remote proctoring and browser-locking capabilities, hosted by Proctorio within Connect, provide control of the assessment environment by enabling security options and verifying the identity of the student.

Seamlessly integrated within Connect, these services allow instructors to control students' assessment experience by restricting browser activity, recording students' activity, and verifying students are doing their own work.

Instant and detailed reporting gives instructors an at-a-glance view of potential academic integrity concerns, thereby avoiding personal bias and supporting evidence-based claims.

TEST BUILDER

Available within Connect, Test Builder is a cloud-based tool that enables instructors to format tests that can be printed or administered within an LMS. Test Builder offers a modern, streamlined interface for easy content configuration that matches course needs, without requiring a download. Test Builder allows you to:

- Access all test bank content from a particular title.
- Easily pinpoint the most relevant content through robust filtering options.
- Manipulate the order of questions or scramble questions and/or answers.
- Pin questions to a specific location within a test.
- Determine your preferred treatment of algorithmic questions.
- Choose the layout and spacing.
- Add instructions and configure default settings.

Test Builder provides a secure interface for better protection of content and allows for just-in-time updates to flow directly into assessments.

ROGER CPA

McGraw Hill Education has partnered with Roger CPA Review, a global leader in CPA Exam preparation, to provide students a smooth transition from the accounting classroom to successful completion of the CPA Exam. While many aspiring accountants wait until they have completed their academic studies to begin preparing for the CPA Exam, research shows that those who become familiar with exam content earlier in the process have a stronger chance of successfully passing the CPA Exam. Accordingly, students using these McGraw Hill materials will have access to sample CPA Exam Multiple-Choice questions from Roger CPA Review, with expert-written explanations and solutions. All questions are either directly from the AICPA or are modeled on AICPA questions that appear in the exam. Instructors may assign the auto-gradable Roger CPA Review Multiple-Choice Questions in *Connect*, which are delivered via the Roger CPA Review platform and mirror the look, feel, and functionality of the actual exam. McGraw Hill Education and Roger CPA Review are dedicated to supporting every accounting student along their journey, ultimately helping them achieve career success in the accounting profession. For more information about the full Roger CPA Review program, exam requirements, and exam content, visit www.rogercpareview.com.

TEST BANK AND QUIZZES

The test bank consists of true-false, multiple-choice, and short essay questions in each chapter. Questions adapted from previous CPA exams are also included and highlighted to help Accounting students review for the exam. Instructors can test students using the quiz questions divided by chapter.

BUSINESS LAW CASE REPOSITORY

Available in *Connect*, the Case Repository is a collection of cases from current and previous editions.

INTERACTIVE APPLICATIONS

Assignable in *Connect*, interactive applications offer a variety of automatically graded exercises that require students to apply key concepts. These applications provide instant feedback and progress tracking for students and detailed results for the instructor.

BUSINESS LAW NEWSLETTER

McGraw Hill Education's monthly business law newsletter, *Proceedings*, is designed specifically with the business law educator in mind. *Proceedings* incorporates "hot topics" in business law, video suggestions, an ethical dilemma, teaching tips, and a "chapter key" cross-referencing newsletter topics with the various McGraw Hill Education business law programs. *Proceedings* is delivered via e-mail to business law instructors each month.

POWERPOINT PRESENTATIONS

The PowerPoint presentations provide lecture outline material, important concepts and figures in the text, and summaries of the cases in the book. Notes are also provided within the PowerPoint presentations to augment information and class discussion.

INSTRUCTOR'S MANUAL

A package of supplementary materials is included in the instructor's manual.

Assurance of Learning

Many educational institutions today are focused on the notion of *assurance of learning*, an important element of some accreditation standards. *Business Law* is designed specifically to support your assurance of learning initiatives with a simple, yet powerful solution.

Each test bank question for *Business Law* maps to a specific chapter learning outcome/objective listed in the text. You can easily query for learning outcomes/objectives that directly relate to the learning objectives for your course.

AACSB Statement

McGraw Hill Education is a proud corporate member of AACSB International. The authors of *Business Law* understand the importance and value of AACSB accreditation and recognize the curricular guidelines detailed in the AACSB standards for business accreditation.

The statements contained in *Business Law* are provided only as a guide for the users of this textbook. The AACSB leaves content coverage and assessment within the purview of individual schools, the mission of the school, and the faculty. Although *Business Law* and the teaching package make no claim of any specific AACSB qualification or evaluation, we have within *Business Law* labeled selected questions according to the AACSB general knowledge and skill areas.

Instructors: Student Success Starts with You

Tools to enhance your unique voice

Want to build your own course? No problem. Prefer to use our turnkey, prebuilt course? Easy. Want to make changes throughout the semester? Sure. And you'll save time with Connect's auto-grading too.

65%
Less Time Grading

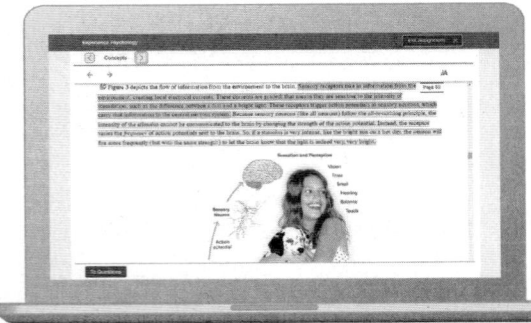

Laptop: McGraw Hill; Woman/dog: George Doyle/Getty Images

Study made personal

Incorporate adaptive study resources like SmartBook® 2.0 into your course and help your students be better prepared in less time. Learn more about the powerful personalized learning experience available in SmartBook 2.0 at **www.mheducation.com/highered/connect/smartbook**

Affordable solutions, added value

Make technology work for you with LMS integration for single sign-on access, mobile access to the digital textbook, and reports to quickly show you how each of your students is doing. And with our Inclusive Access program you can provide all these tools at a discount to your students. Ask your McGraw Hill representative for more information.

Padlock: Jobalou/Getty Images

Solutions for your challenges

A product isn't a solution. Real solutions are affordable, reliable, and come with training and ongoing support when you need it and how you want it. Visit **www. supportateverystep.com** for videos and resources both you and your students can use throughout the semester.

Checkmark: Jobalou/Getty Images

Students: Get Learning that Fits You

Effective tools for efficient studying

Connect is designed to make you more productive with simple, flexible, intuitive tools that maximize your study time and meet your individual learning needs. Get learning that works for you with Connect.

Study anytime, anywhere

Download the free ReadAnywhere app and access your online eBook or SmartBook 2.0 assignments when it's convenient, even if you're offline. And since the app automatically syncs with your eBook and SmartBook 2.0 assignments in Connect, all of your work is available every time you open it. Find out more at **www.mheducation.com/readanywhere**

> *"I really liked this app—it made it easy to study when you don't have your text-book in front of you."*
>
> - Jordan Cunningham, Eastern Washington University

Everything you need in one place

Your Connect course has everything you need—whether reading on your digital eBook or completing assignments for class, Connect makes it easy to get your work done.

Learning for everyone

McGraw Hill works directly with Accessibility Services Departments and faculty to meet the learning needs of all students. Please contact your Accessibility Services Office and ask them to email accessibility@mheducation.com, or visit **www.mheducation.com/about/accessibility** for more information.

Brief Contents

Contents

Part 7   Commercial Paper

Contents   xxxiii

Contents

Foundations of American Law

Pixtal/AGE Fotostock

CHAPTER 1

The Nature of Law

Assume that you have taken on a management position at MKT Corp. If MKT is to make sound business decisions, you and your management colleagues must be aware of a broad array of legal considerations. These may range, to use a nonexhaustive list, from issues in contract, agency, and employment law to considerations suggested by tort, intellectual property, securities, and constitutional law. Sometimes, legal principles may constrain MKT's business decisions; at other times, the law may prove a valuable ally of MKT in the successful operation of the firm's business.

Of course, you and other members of the MKT management group will rely on the advice of in-house counsel (an attorney who is an MKT employee) or of outside attorneys who are in private practice. The approach of simply "leaving the law to the lawyers," however, is likely to be counterproductive. It will often be up to nonlawyers such as you to identify a potential legal issue or pitfall about which MKT needs professional guidance. If you fail to spot the issue in a timely manner and legal problems are allowed to develop and fester, even the most skilled attorneys may have difficulty rescuing you and the firm from the resulting predicament. If, on the other hand, your failure to identify a legal consideration means that you do not seek advice in time to obtain an advantage that applicable law would have provided MKT, the corporation may lose out on a beneficial opportunity. Either way—that is, whether the relevant legal issue operates as a constraint or offers a potential advantage—you and the firm cannot afford to be unfamiliar with the legal environment in which MKT operates.

This may sound intimidating, but it need not be. The process of acquiring a working understanding of the legal environment of business begins simply enough with these basic questions:

- What major types of law apply to the business activities and help shape the business decisions of firms such as MKT?
- What ways of examining and evaluating law may serve as useful perspectives from which to view the legal environment in which MKT and other businesses operate?
- What role do courts play in making or interpreting law that applies to businesses such as MKT and to employees of those firms, and what methods of legal reasoning do courts utilize?
- What is the relationship between legal standards of behavior and notions of *ethical* conduct?

LO LEARNING OBJECTIVES

After studying this chapter, you should be able to:

1-1 Identify the respective makers of the different types of law (constitutions, statutes, common law, and administrative regulations and decisions).

1-2 Identify the type of law that takes precedence when two types of law conflict.

1-3 Explain the basic differences between the *criminal law* and *civil law* classifications.

1-4 Describe key ways in which the major schools of jurisprudence differ from each other.

1-5   Describe the respective roles of adhering to precedent (*stare decisis*) and distinguishing precedent in case law reasoning.

1-6   Identify what courts focus on when applying the major statutory interpretation techniques (plain meaning, legislative purpose, legislative history, and general public purpose).

Types and Classifications of Law

The Types of Law

 LO1-1 Identify the respective makers of the different types of law (constitutions, statutes, common law, and administrative regulations and decisions).

Constitutions Constitutions, which exist at the state and federal levels, have two general functions.[1] First, they set up the structure of government for the political unit they control (a state or the federal government). This involves creating the branches and subdivisions of the government and stating the powers given and denied to each. Through its **separation of powers**, the U.S. Constitution establishes the Congress and gives it power to *make* law in certain areas, provides for a chief executive (the president) whose function is to execute or *enforce* the laws, and helps create a federal judiciary to *interpret* the laws. The U.S. Constitution also structures the relationship between the federal government and the states. In the process, it respects the principle of **federalism** by recognizing the states' power to make law in certain areas.

The second function of constitutions is to prevent the government from taking certain actions or passing certain laws, sometimes even if those actions or laws would otherwise appear to fall within the authority granted to the government under the first function. Constitutions do so mainly by prohibiting government action that restricts certain individual rights. The Bill of Rights to the U.S. Constitution is an example. You could see the interaction of those two functions, for instance, where Congress is empowered to regulate interstate commerce but cannot do so in a way that would abridge the First Amendment's free speech guarantee.

Statutes Statutes are laws created by elected representatives in Congress or a state legislature. They are stated in an authoritative form in statute books or codes. As you will see, however, their interpretation and application are often difficult.

Throughout this text, you will encounter state statutes that were originally drafted as **uniform acts**. Uniform acts are model statutes drafted by private bodies of lawyers and scholars. They do not become law until a legislature enacts them. Their aim is to produce state-by-state uniformity on the subjects they address. Examples include the Uniform Commercial Code (which deals with a wide range of commercial law subjects), the Revised Uniform Partnership Act, and the Revised Model Business Corporation Act.

Common Law The **common law** (also called judge-made law or case law) is law made and applied by judges as they decide cases not governed by statutes or other types of law. Although, as a general matter, common law exists only at the state level, both state courts and federal courts become involved in applying it. The common law originated in medieval England and developed from the decisions of judges in settling disputes. Over time, judges began to follow the decisions of other judges in similar cases, called **precedents**. This practice became formalized in the doctrine of *stare decisis* (let the decision stand). As you will see later in the chapter, *stare decisis* is not completely rigid in its requirement of adherence to precedent. It is flexible enough to allow the common law to evolve to meet changing social conditions. The common law rules in force today, therefore, often differ considerably from the common law rules of earlier times.

The common law came to America with the first English settlers, was applied by courts during the colonial period, and continued to be applied after the Revolution and the adoption of the Constitution. It still governs many cases today. For example, the rules of tort, contract, and agency discussed in this text are mainly common law rules. In some instances, states have codified (enacted into statute) some parts of the common law. States and the federal government have also passed statutes superseding the common law in certain situations. As discussed in Chapter 9, for example, the states have established special rules for contract cases involving the sale of goods by enacting Article 2 of the Uniform Commercial Code.

---

[1]Chapter 3 discusses constitutional law as it applies to government regulation of business.

This text's torts, contracts, and agency chapters often refer to the *Restatement*—or *Restatement (Second)* or (*Third*)—rule on a particular subject. The *Restatements* are collections of common law (and occasionally statutory) rules covering various areas of the law. Because they are written by the American Law Institute rather than by courts, the *Restatements* are not law and do not bind courts. However, state courts often find *Restatement* rules persuasive and adopt them as common law rules within their states. The *Restatement* rules usually are the rules followed by a majority of the states. Occasionally, however, the *Restatements* stimulate changes in the common law by suggesting new rules that the courts later decide to follow.

Because the judge-made rules of common law apply only when there is no applicable statute or other type of law, common law fills in gaps left by other legal rules if sound social and public policy reasons call for those gaps to be filled. As a result, with regard to the common law, judges sometimes serve in the unexpected role of crafting legal rules in addition to interpreting the law.

In *Price v. High Pointe Oil Company, Inc.*, which follows shortly, the court surveys the relevant legal landscape and concludes that a longstanding common law rule should remain in effect. A later section in the chapter will focus on the process of **case law reasoning**, in which courts engage when they make and apply common law rules. That process is exemplified by the first half of the *Price* opinion.

Price v. High Pointe Oil Company, Inc.   828 N.W.2d 660 (Mich. 2013)

In 2006, Beckie Price replaced the oil furnace in her house with a propane furnace. The oil furnace was removed, but the pipe that had been used to fill the furnace with oil remained in place.

At the time the furnace was replaced, Price canceled her contract for oil refills with the predecessor of High Pointe Oil Company, the defendant. Somehow, though, in November 2007, High Pointe mistakenly placed Price's address back on its "keep full list." Subsequently, a High Pointe truck driver pumped around 400 gallons of fuel oil into Price's basement through the oil-fill pipe before realizing the mistake. Price's house and her belongings were destroyed. The house was eventually torn down, the site was remediated, and a new house was built on a different part of Price's property. Price's personal property was all cleaned or replaced. All of her costs related to her temporary homelessness were reimbursed to her, as well. Thus, she was fully compensated for all of her economic losses resulting from High Pointe's error.

Nevertheless, Price sued High Pointe alleging a number of claims. The only of her claims to survive to trial was one focused on her noneconomic losses—for example, pain and suffering, humiliation, embarrassment, and emotional distress. A jury found in Price's favor and awarded her $100,000 in damages.

High Pointe filed an appeal to the intermediate appellate court but lost. High Pointe then appealed to the Michigan Supreme Court, excerpts of whose opinion is below.

Markman, J.

III. Analysis

The question in this case is whether noneconomic damages are recoverable for the negligent destruction of real property. Absent any relevant statute, the answer to that question is a matter of common law.

A. Common Law

As this Court explained in [a prior case], the common law "is but the accumulated expressions of the various judicial tribunals in their efforts to ascertain what is right and just between individuals in respect to private disputes[.]" The common law, however, is not static. By its nature, it adapts to changing circumstances. . . . The common law is always a work in progress and typically develops incrementally, i.e., gradually evolving as individual disputes are decided and existing common-law rules are considered and sometimes adapted to current needs in light of changing times and circumstances.

The common-law rule with respect to the damages recoverable in an action alleging the negligent destruction of property was set forth in [a 1933 case]:

If injury to property caused by negligence is permanent or irreparable, the measure of damages is the difference in its market value before and after said injury, but if the injury is reparable, and the expense of making repairs is less than the value of the property, the measure of damages is the cost of making repairs.

Michigan common law has continually followed [that] rule. . . . Accordingly, the long-held common-law rule in Michigan is that the measure of damages for the negligent destruction of property is the cost of replacement or repair. Because replacement and repair costs reflect *economic* damages, the logical implication of this rule is that the measure of damages excludes *noneconomic* damages.

Lending additional support to this conclusion is the simple fact that, before the Court of Appeals' opinion below, *no* case ever in the history of the Michigan common law has approvingly discussed the recovery of noneconomic damages for the negligent destruction of property. Indeed, no case has even broached this issue except through the negative implication arising from limiting damages for the negligent destruction or damage of property to replacement and repair costs. . . .

Moreover, the Court of Appeals has decided two relatively recent cases concerning injury to *personal* property in which noneconomic damages were disallowed. In *Koester v. VCA Animal Hospital*, the plaintiff dog owner sought noneconomic damages . . . against his veterinarian following the death of his dog . . . . The trial court [ruled in favor of the veterinarian], holding that "emotional damages for the loss of a dog do not exist." On appeal, the Court of Appeals affirmed, noting that pets are personal property under Michigan law and explaining that there "is no Michigan precedent that permits the recovery of damages for emotional injuries allegedly suffered as a consequence of property damage."

Later, in *Bernhardt v. Ingham Regional Medical Center*, the plaintiff [accidentally left] her grandmother's 1897 wedding ring (which was also her wedding ring) and a watch purchased in 1980 around the time of her brother's murder . . . in the [hospital's] washbasin and left the hospital. Upon realizing her mistake, the plaintiff contacted the defendant and was advised that she could retrieve the jewelry from hospital security. However, when she tried to retrieve the jewelry, it could not be located. The plaintiff sued, and the defendant . . . argu[ed] that the plaintiff's damages did not exceed the $25,000 [minimum amount for a valid case in the] trial court. The plaintiff countered that her damages exceeded that limit because the jewelry possessed great sentimental value. The trial court granted the defendant's motion. On appeal, the Court of Appeals affirmed, citing *Koester* for the proposition that there "is no Michigan precedent that permits the recovery of damages for emotional injuries allegedly suffered as a consequence of property damage". . . . In support of its conclusion, *Bernhardt* quoted the following language from the Restatement Second of Torts:

> If the subject matter cannot be replaced, however, as in the case of a destroyed or lost family portrait, the owner will be compensated for its special value to him, as evidenced by the original cost, and the quality and condition at the time of the loss. . . . In these cases, however, damages cannot be based on sentimental value. Compensatory damages are not given for emotional distress caused merely by the loss of the things, except that in unusual circumstances damages may be awarded for humiliation caused by deprivation, as when one is deprived of essential elements of clothing.

While *Koester* and *Bernhardt* both involved negligent injury to *personal* property, they speak of property generally. Although the Court of Appeals in the instant case seeks to draw distinctions between personal and real property, neither that Court nor plaintiff has explained how any of those distinctions, even if they had some pertinent foundation in the law, are relevant with regard to the propriety of awarding noneconomic damages. In short, while it is doubtlessly true that many people are highly emotionally attached to their houses, many people are also highly emotionally attached to their pets, their heirlooms, their collections, and any number of other things. But there is no legally relevant basis that would logically justify prohibiting the recovery of noneconomic damages for the negligent killing of a pet or the negligent loss of a family heirloom but allow such a recovery for the negligent destruction of a house. Accordingly, *Koester* and *Bernhardt* underscore [the long-standing] exclusion of noneconomic damages for negligent injury to real and personal property.

Finally, we would be remiss if we did not address *Sutter v. Biggs*, which the Court of Appeals cited as providing the "general rule" for the recovery of damages in tort actions. *Sutter* stated:

> The general rule, expressed in terms of damages, and long followed in this State, is that in a tort action, the [party that committed the tort] is liable for all injuries resulting directly from his wrongful act, whether foreseeable or not, provided the damages are the legal and natural consequences of the wrongful act, and are such as, according to common experience and the usual course of events, might reasonably have been anticipated. Remote contingent, or speculative damages are not considered in conformity to the general rule.

Although *Sutter* articulates a "general rule," it is a "general rule" that has never been applied to allow the recovery of noneconomic damages in a case involving only property damage, and it is a "general rule" that must be read in light of the more narrow and specific "general rule" [that Michigan has always followed with regard to the noneconomic damages exclusion in cases involving property damage].

The development of the common law frequently yields "general rules" from which branch more specific "general rules" that apply in limited circumstances. Where tension exists between those rules, the more specific rule controls. . . . With respect to this case, although *Sutter* articulated a general rule, [the rule excluding noneconomic damages for property damages is] a more specific "general rule". . . . Accordingly, because this case involves only property damage, the [latter] rule . . . controls.

B. Altering the Common Law

Because the Court of Appeals determined that the "general rule" is that "in a tort action, the [party who committed the tort] is liable for *all* injuries," the Court of Appeals contended that it was not altering the common law but, rather, "declin[ing] to extend" to real property the personal property "exception" set forth in *Koester* and *Bernhardt*. However, as previously mentioned, the Court of Appeals' opinion constitutes the first and only Michigan case to support the recovery of noneconomic damages for the negligent destruction of property. Accordingly, contrary to the Court of Appeals' own characterization and for the reasons discussed [above], the Court of Appeals' holding represents an alteration of the common law. With that understanding, we address whether the common law *should* be altered.

"This Court is the principal steward of Michigan's common law," . . . and it is "axiomatic that our courts have the constitutional authority to change the common law in the proper case. . . ." However, this Court has also explained that alteration of the common law should be approached cautiously with the fullest consideration of public policy and should not occur through sudden departure from longstanding legal rules. . . . Among them has been our attempt to "avoid capricious departures from bedrock legal rules as such tectonic shifts might produce unforeseen and undesirable consequences." . . . As this emphasis on incrementalism suggests, when it comes to alteration of the common law, the traditional rule must prevail absent compelling reasons for change. This approach ensures continuity and stability in the law.

With the foregoing principles in mind, we respectfully decline to alter the common-law rule that the appropriate measure of damages for negligently damaged property is the cost of replacement or repair. We are not oblivious to the reality that destruction of property or property damage will often engender considerable mental distress, and we are quite prepared to believe that the particular circumstances of the instant case were sufficient to have caused exactly such distress. However, we are persuaded that the present rule is a rational one and justifiable as a matter of reasonable public policy. We recognize that might also be true of alternative rules that could be constructed by this Court. In the final analysis, however, the venerability of the present rule and the lack of any compelling argument that would suggest its objectionableness in light of changing social and economic circumstances weigh, in our judgment, in favor of its retention. Because we believe the rule to be sound, if change is going to come, it must come by legislative alteration. A number of factors persuade us that the longstanding character of the present rule is not simply a function of serendipity or of judicial inertia, but is reflective of the fact that the rule serves legitimate purposes and values within our legal system.

First, one of the most fundamental principles of our economic system is that the market sets the price of property. This is so even though every individual values property differently as a function of his or her own particular preferences. . . . Second, economic damages, unlike noneconomic damages, are easily verifiable, quantifiable, and measurable. Thus, when measured only in terms of economic damages, the value of property is easily ascertainable. . . . Third, limiting damages to the economic value of the damaged or destroyed property limits disparities in damage awards from case to case. Disparities in recovery are inherent in legal matters in which the value of what is in dispute is neither tangible nor objectively determined, but rather intangible and subjectively determined. . . . Fourth, the present rule affords some reasonable level of certainty to businesses regarding the potential scope of their liability for accidents caused to property resulting from their negligent conduct. [U]nder the Court of Appeals' rule, those businesses that come into regular contact with real property—contractors, repairmen, and fuel suppliers, for example—would be exposed to the uncertainty of not knowing whether their exposure to tort liability will be defined by a plaintiff who has an unusual emotional attachment to the property or by a jury that has an unusually sympathetic opinion toward those emotional attachments.

Once again, it is not our view that the common-law rule in Michigan cannot be improved, or that it represents the best of all possible rules, only that the rule is a reasonable one and has survived for as long as it has because there is some reasonable basis for the rule and that no compelling reasons for replacing it have been set forth by either the Court of Appeals or plaintiff. We therefore leave it to the Legislature, if it chooses to do so at some future time, to more carefully balance the benefits of the current rule with what that body might come to view as its shortcomings.

IV. Conclusion

The issue in this case is whether noneconomic damages are recoverable for the negligent destruction of real property. No Michigan case has ever allowed a plaintiff to recover noneconomic damages resulting solely from the negligent destruction of property, either real or personal. Rather, the common law of this state has long provided that the appropriate measure of damages in cases involving the negligent destruction of property is simply the cost of replacement or repair of the negligently destroyed property. We continue today to adhere to this rule and decline to alter it. Accordingly, we reverse the judgment of the Court of Appeals and remand this case to the trial court for entry of summary disposition in defendant's favor.

Equity The body of law called **equity** historically concerned itself with accomplishing "rough justice" when common law rules would produce unfair results. In medieval England, common law rules were technical and rigid and the remedies available in common law courts were too few. This meant that some deserving parties could not obtain adequate relief. As a result, separate equity courts began hearing cases that the common law courts could not resolve fairly. In these equity courts, procedures were flexible, and rigid rules of law were deemphasized in favor of general moral maxims.

Equity courts also provided several remedies not available in the common law courts (which generally awarded only money damages or the recovery of property). The most important of these *equitable remedies* was—and continues to be—the **injunction**, a court order forbidding a party to do some act or commanding him to perform some act. Others include the contract remedies of **specific performance** (whereby a party is ordered to perform according to the terms of her contract), **reformation** (in which the court rewrites the contract's terms to reflect the parties' real intentions), and **rescission** (a cancellation of a contract and a return of the parties to their precontractual position).

As was the common law, equity principles were brought to the American colonies and continued to be used after the Revolution and the adoption of the Constitution. Over time, however, the once-sharp line between law and equity has become blurred. Nearly all states have abolished separate equity courts and have enabled courts to grant whatever relief is appropriate, whether it be the legal remedy of money damages or one of the equitable remedies discussed earlier. Equitable principles have been blended together with common law rules, and some traditional equity doctrines have been restated as common law or statutory rules. An example is the doctrine of unconscionability discussed in Chapter 15.

Administrative Regulations and Decisions As Chapter 47 reveals, the administrative agencies established by Congress and the state legislatures have acquired considerable power, importance, and influence over business. A major reason for the rise of administrative agencies was the collection of social and economic problems created by the industrialization of the United States that began late in the 19th century. Because legislatures generally lacked the time and expertise to deal with these problems on a continuing basis, the creation of specialized, expert agencies was almost inevitable.

Administrative agencies obtain the ability to make law through a *delegation* (or grant) of power from the legislature. Agencies normally are created by a statute that specifies the areas in which the agency can make law and the scope of its power in each area. Often, these statutory delegations are worded so broadly that the legislature has, in effect, merely pointed to a problem and given the agency wide-ranging powers to deal with it.

The two types of law made by administrative agencies are *administrative regulations* and *agency decisions*. As do statutes, administrative regulations appear in a precise form in one authoritative source. They differ from statutes, however, because the body enacting regulations is not an elected body. Many agencies have an internal courtlike structure that enables them to hear cases arising under the statutes and regulations they enforce. The resulting agency decisions are legally binding, though appeals to the judicial system are sometimes allowed.

Treaties According to the U.S. Constitution, **treaties** made by the president with foreign governments and approved by two-thirds of the U.S. Senate become "the supreme Law of the Land." As will be seen, treaties invalidate inconsistent state (and sometimes federal) laws.

Ordinances State governments have subordinate units that exercise certain functions. Some of these units, such as school districts, have limited powers. Others, such as counties, municipalities, and townships, exercise various governmental functions. The enactments of counties and municipalities are called **ordinances**; zoning ordinances are an example. Ordinances resemble statutes, and the techniques of statutory interpretation described later in this chapter typically are used to interpret ambiguous language in ordinances.

Executive Orders In theory, the president or a state's governor is a chief executive who enforces the laws but has no law-making powers. However, these officials sometimes have limited power to issue laws called **executive orders**. This power normally results from a legislative delegation.

Priority Rules

 LO1-2 Identify the type of law that takes precedence when two types of law conflict.

Because the different types of law may, from time to time, conflict, rules for determining which type takes priority are necessary. Here, we briefly describe the most important such rules.

1. According to the principle of **federal supremacy**, the U.S. Constitution, federal laws enacted pursuant to it, and treaties are the supreme law of the land. This means that federal law defeats conflicting state law.

2. Constitutions defeat other types of law within their domain. Thus, a state constitution defeats all other state laws inconsistent with it. The U.S. Constitution, however, defeats inconsistent laws of whatever type.

3. When a treaty conflicts with a federal statute over a purely domestic matter, the measure that is later in time usually prevails.

4. Within either the state or the federal domain, statutes defeat conflicting laws that depend on a legislative

delegation for their validity. For example, a state statute defeats an inconsistent state administrative regulation.

5. Statutes and any laws derived from them by delegation defeat inconsistent common law rules. Accordingly, either a statute or an administrative regulation defeats a conflicting common law rule.

Courts are careful to avoid finding a conflict between the different types of law unless the conflict is clear. In fact, one maxim of statutory interpretation (described later in this chapter) instructs courts to choose an interpretation that avoids unnecessary conflicts with other types of law, particularly constitutions that would preempt the statute. Statutes will sometimes explicitly state the enacting legislature's intent to displace a common law rule. In the absence of that, though, courts will look for significant overlap and inconsistency between a statute and a common law rule to determine that there is a conflict for which the statute must take priority. The following *Advance Dental Care, Inc. v. SunTrust Bank* case illustrates this. Notice how the court first looks to the statutory language for explicit instruction regarding displacement of the common law rule. Then it considers whether the statute and common law rule overlap, particularly whether the statute offers a sufficient remedy to replace the common law rule. Finally, the court notes an important inconsistency between the statute and the common law rule.

Advance Dental Care, Inc. v. SunTrust Bank
816 F. Supp. 2d 268 (D. Md. 2011)

Michelle Rampersad was an employee of Advance Dental at its dental office in Prince George's County, Maryland. During a period of more than three years ending in fall 2007, Rampersad took approximately 185 insurance reimbursement checks that were written to Advance Dental and endorsed them to herself. She then took the checks to SunTrust Bank and deposited them into her personal accounts. The checks totaled $400,954.04.

Advance Dental filed a lawsuit against SunTrust after it discovered Rampersad's unauthorized endorsement and deposit of the checks. The lawsuit claimed SunTrust violated two provisions of the Maryland version of the Uniform Commercial Code (UCC) dealing with negligence and conversion. It also stated a claim of negligence pursuant to the common law of Maryland. The court had previously dismissed the UCC negligence claim for reasons not relevant here. In the opinion that follows, the court considers whether Advance Dental's common-law negligence claim has been displaced by the statutory UCC conversion claim.

Alexander Williams, Jr., U.S. District Court Judge

III. Legal Analysis

In this case of first impression, the Court must determine whether section 3-420 of the Maryland U.C.C. [(the U.C.C. conversion provision)] displaces common-law negligence when a payee seeks to recover from a depositary bank that accepted unauthorized and fraudulently endorsed checks.

A. Availability of an Adequate U.C.C. Remedy

[C]ourts have held that common-law negligence claims can proceed only in the absence of an adequate U.C.C. remedy.

In the present case, it is indisputable that Advance Dental has an adequate U.C.C. remedy—conversion—for which Advance Dental has already filed a claim. Therefore, in light of the overwhelming case law, . . . [the U.C.C. conversion provision] displaces common-law negligence because Advance Dental has an adequate U.C.C. remedy.

B. Indistinct Causes of Action with Conflicting Defenses

Statutory authority also emphasizes the necessity of displacing common-law negligence in this case. Section 1-103(b) of the Maryland U.C.C. establishes the U.C.C.'s position regarding the survival of common-law actions alongside the U.C.C.: "[u]nless displaced by the particular provisions of Titles 1-10 of this article, the principles of law and equity . . . shall supplement its provisions. . . ." Since the U.C.C. has no express "displacement" provision, the Court must determine whether [the U.C.C. conversion provision] is a "particular provision" that displaces the common law.

The Court finds significant overlap between [the U.C.C. conversion provision] and common-law negligence. [The U.C.C. conversion provision] defines conversion as "payment with respect to [an] instrument for a person not entitled to enforce the instrument or receive payment." Here, Advance Dental alleges that SunTrust is liable in negligence for allowing Rampersad to fraudulently endorse and deposit checks made payable to Advance Dental into her personal account. Therefore, . . . both negligence and conversion require a consideration of whether there was payment over a wrongful endorsement.

The duplicative nature of these two theories suggests the U.C.C.'s intention to create a comprehensive regulation of payment over unauthorized or fraudulent endorsements. . . . In the presence of such intent, courts have preempted common-law claims. To do otherwise would destroy the U.C.C.'s attempt to establish reliability, uniformity, and certainty in commercial transactions.

Here, Advance Dental's common-law negligence action has no independent significance apart from [the U.C.C. conversion provision]. In fact, when discussing common-law negligence, Advance Dental simply refers to the same conduct alleged in Count I (conversion) to argue that SunTrust has breached its duty of reasonable and ordinary care. . . . In other words, [the U.C.C. conversion provision] has effectively subsumed common-law negligence claims.

Not only is common-law negligence insufficiently distinct from [the U.C.C. conversion provision], but the conflicting defenses available for each cause of action are also problematic. The U.C.C. is based on the principle of comparative negligence. In contrast, contributory negligence remains a defense for common-law negligence.[2] Displacement is thus required since Maryland courts "hesitate to adopt or perpetuate a common law rule that would be plainly inconsistent with the legislature's intent. . . ."

IV. Conclusion

For the foregoing reasons [and reasons not included in this edited version of the opinion], the Court **GRANTS** Defendant's Renewed Motion to Dismiss Count III of Plaintiff's Complaint.

Classifications of Law
Three common classifications of law cut across the different types of law. These classifications involve distinctions between (1) criminal law and civil law; (2) substantive law and procedural law; and (3) public law and private law. One type of law might be classified in each of these ways. For example, a burglary statute would be criminal, substantive, and public; a rule of contract law would be civil, substantive, and private.

 LO1-3 Explain the basic differences between the *criminal law* and *civil law* classifications.

Criminal and Civil Law **Criminal law** is the law under which the government prosecutes someone for committing a crime. It creates duties that are owed to the public as a whole. **Civil law** mainly concerns obligations that private parties owe to each other. It is the law applied when one private party sues another. The government, however, may also be a party to a civil case. For example, a city may sue, or be sued by, a construction contractor. Criminal penalties (e.g., imprisonment or fines) differ from civil remedies (e.g., money damages or equitable relief). Although most of the legal rules in this text are civil law rules, Chapter 5 deals specifically with the criminal law.

Even though the civil law and the criminal law are distinct bodies of law, the same behavior will sometimes violate both. For instance, if A commits an intentional act of physical violence on B, A may face both a criminal prosecution by the state and B's civil suit for damages.

Substantive Law and Procedural Law **Substantive law** sets the rights and duties of people as they act in society. **Procedural law** controls the behavior of government bodies (mainly courts) as they establish and enforce rules of substantive law. A statute making murder a crime, for example, is a rule of substantive law. The rules describing the proper conduct of a trial, however, are procedural. This text focuses on substantive law, although Chapters 2 and 5 examine some of the procedural rules governing civil and criminal cases.

Public and Private Law **Public law** concerns the powers of government and the relations between government and private parties. Examples include constitutional law, administrative law, and criminal law. **Private law** establishes a framework of legal rules that enables parties to set the rights and duties they owe each other. Examples include the rules of contract, property, and agency.

Jurisprudence

LO1-4 Describe key ways in which the major schools of jurisprudence differ from each other.

The various types of law sometimes are called *positive law*. Positive law comprises the rules that have been laid down by a recognized political authority. Knowing the types of positive law is essential to an understanding of the American legal system and the topics discussed in this text.

---

[2]The comparative and contributory negligence defenses are discussed in detail in Chapter 7. They address in different manners whether and to what extent a plaintiff's own negligence in the actions upon which a claim is based ought to excuse the defendant from liability. Here the defenses would be relevant in that SunTrust might argue that Advance Dental was at fault for failing to discover and to prevent Rampersad's fraudulent activities on its own.

Yet defining *law* by listing these different kinds of positive law is no more complete or accurate than defining "automobile" by describing all the vehicles going by that name. To define law properly, some say, we need a general description that captures its essence.

The field known as **jurisprudence** seeks to provide such a description. Over time, different schools of jurisprudence have emerged, each with its own distinctive view of the essence of the law.

Legal Positivism
One feature common to all types of law is their enactment by a governmental authority such as a legislature or an administrative agency. This feature underlies the definition of law that characterizes the school of jurisprudence known as **legal positivism**. Legal positivists define law as the *command of a recognized political authority*. As the British political philosopher Thomas Hobbes observed, "Law properly, is the word of him, that by right hath command over others."

The commands of recognized political authorities may be good, bad, or indifferent in moral terms. To legal positivists, such commands are valid law regardless of their "good" or "bad" content. In other words, positivists see legal validity and moral validity as entirely separate questions. Some (but not all) positivists say that every properly enacted positive law should be enforced and obeyed, whether just or unjust. Similarly, a judge who views the law through a positivist lens would typically try to enforce the law as written, excluding her own moral views from the process. Note, however, that this does not mean that a positivist is bound to accept the law as static or unchangeable. Rather, a positivist who was unhappy with the law as written would point to established political processes as the appropriate mechanism for the law to evolve (e.g., by lobbying a legislature to amend or repeal a statute).

Natural Law
At first glance, legal positivism's "law is law, just or not" approach may seem to be perfect common sense. It presents a problem, however, for it could mean that *any* positive law—no matter how unjust—is valid law and should be enforced and obeyed so long as some recognized political authority enacted it. The school of jurisprudence known as **natural law** rejects the positivist separation of law and morality.

Natural law adherents usually contend that some higher law or set of universal moral rules binds all human beings in all times and places. The Roman statesman Marcus Cicero described natural law as "the highest reason, implanted in nature, which commands what ought to be done and forbids the opposite." Because this higher law determines what is ultimately good and ultimately bad, it serves as a criterion for evaluating positive law. To Saint Thomas Aquinas, for example, "every human law has just so much of the nature of law, as it is derived from the law of nature." To be genuine law, in other words, positive law must resemble the law of nature by being "good"—or at least by not being "bad."

Unjust positive laws, then, are not valid law under the natural law view. As Cicero put it: "What of the many deadly, the many pestilential statutes which are imposed on peoples? These no more deserve to be called laws than the rules a band of robbers might pass in their assembly."

An "unjust" law's supposed invalidity does not translate into a natural law defense that is recognized in court, however. Nonetheless, judges may sometimes take natural law-oriented views into account when interpreting the law. As compared with positivist judges, judges influenced by natural law ideas may be more likely to read constitutional provisions broadly in order to strike down positive laws they regard as unjust. They also may be more likely to let morality influence their interpretation of the law. Of course, neither judges nor natural law thinkers always agree about what is moral and immoral—a major difficulty for the natural law position. This difficulty allows legal positivists to claim that only by keeping legal and moral questions separate can we obtain stability and predictability in the law.

American Legal Realism
To some, the debate between natural law and legal positivism may seem disconnected from reality. Not only is natural law unworkable, such people might say, but sometimes positive law does not mean much either. For example, juries sometimes pay little attention to the legal rules that are supposed to guide their decisions, and prosecutors have discretion concerning whether to enforce criminal statutes. In some legal proceedings, moreover, the background, biases, and values of the judge—and not the positive law—drive the result. An old joke reminds us that justice sometimes is what the judge ate for breakfast.

Remarks such as these typify the school of jurisprudence known as **American legal realism**. Legal realists regard the law in the books as less important than the *law in action*—the conduct of those who enforce and interpret the positive law. American legal realism defines law as the *behavior of public officials (mainly judges) as they deal with matters before the legal system*. Because the actions of such decision makers—and not the rules in the books—really affect people's lives, the realists say, this behavior is what deserves to be called law.

It is doubtful whether the legal realists have ever developed a common position on the relation between law and morality or on the duty to obey positive law. They have been quick, however, to tell judges how to behave. Many realists feel that the modern judge should be a social engineer who weighs all relevant values and considers social science findings when deciding a case. Such a judge would make the positive law only one factor in her decision. Because judges inevitably base their decisions on personal considerations, the realists assert, they should at least do this honestly and intelligently. To promote this kind of decision making, the realists have sometimes favored fuzzy, discretionary standards that allow judges to decide each case according to its unique facts.

Sociological Jurisprudence Sociological jurisprudence is a general label uniting several different approaches that examine law within its social context. The following quotation from Justice Oliver Wendell Holmes is consistent with such approaches:

> The life of the law has not been logic: it has been experience. The felt necessities of the time, the prevalent moral and political theories, intuitions of public policy, avowed or unconscious, even the prejudices which judges share with their fellow-men, have had a good deal more to do than the syllogism in determining the rules by which men should be governed. The law embodies the story of a nation's development through many centuries, and it cannot be dealt with as if it contained only the axioms and corollaries of a book of mathematics.[3]

Despite these approaches' common outlook, there is no distinctive sociological definition of law. If one were attempted, it might go as follows: *Law is a process of social ordering reflecting society's dominant interests and values.*

Different Sociological Approaches By examining examples of sociological legal thinking, we can add substance to the definition just offered. The "dominant interests" portion of the definition is exemplified by the writings of Roscoe Pound, an influential 20th-century American legal philosopher. Pound developed a detailed and changing catalog of the social interests that press on government and the legal system and thus shape positive law. An example of the definition's "dominant values" component is the *historical school* of jurisprudence identified with the 19th-century German legal philosopher Friedrich Karl von Savigny. Savigny saw law as an unplanned, almost unconscious, reflection of the collective spirit of a particular society. In his view,

legal change could only be explained historically, as a slow response to social change.

By emphasizing the influence of dominant social interests and values, Pound and Savigny undermine the legal positivist view that law is nothing more than the command of some political authority. The early 20th-century Austrian legal philosopher Eugen Ehrlich went even further in rejecting positivism. He did so by identifying two different "processes of social ordering" contained within our definition of sociological jurisprudence. The first of these is positive law. The second is the "living law," informal social controls such as customs, family ties, and business practices. By regarding both as law, Ehrlich sought to demonstrate that positive law is only one element within a spectrum of social controls.

The Implications of Sociological Jurisprudence Because its definition of law includes social values, sociological jurisprudence seems to resemble natural law. Most sociological thinkers, however, are concerned only with the *fact* that moral values influence the law, and not with the goodness or badness of those values. Thus, it might seem that sociological jurisprudence gives no practical advice to those who must enforce and obey positive law.

Sociological jurisprudence has at least one practical implication, however: a tendency to urge that the law must change to meet changing social conditions and values. In other words, the law should keep up with the times. Some might stick to this view even when society's values are changing for the worse. To Holmes, for example, "[t]he first requirement of a sound body of law is, that it should correspond with the actual feelings and demands of the community, whether right or wrong."

Other Schools of Jurisprudence During the past half century, legal scholars have fashioned additional ways of viewing law, explaining why legal rules are as they are and exploring supposed needs for changes in legal doctrines. For example, the *law and economics* movement examines legal rules through the lens provided by economic theory and analysis. This movement's influence has extended beyond academic literature, with law and economics-oriented considerations, factors, and tests sometimes appearing in judicial opinions dealing with such matters as contract, tort, or antitrust law.

The *critical legal studies (CLS)* movement regards law as inevitably the product of political calculation (mostly of the right-wing variety) and longstanding class biases on the part of lawmakers, including judges. Articles published by CLS adherents provide controversial assessments and critiques of legal rules. Given the thrust of CLS and the view it takes of

---

[3]Oliver Wendell Holmes, *The Common Law* (1881).

lawmakers, however, one would be hard-pressed to find CLS adherents in the legislature or the judiciary.

Other schools of jurisprudence that have acquired notoriety in recent years examine law and the legal system from the vantage points of particular groups of persons or sets of ideas. Examples include feminist and queer legal theory and critical disability theory.

As you read the excerpts of judicial opinions throughout this text, consider whether one or more of these jurisprudential approaches appear to have influenced the judges' thinking when interpreting or applying the law. Certainly judges seldom, if ever, explicitly reference those influences, but you may find them lurking significantly between the lines of some of the opinions.

The Functions of Law

In societies of the past, people often viewed law as unchanging rules that deserved obedience because they were part of the natural order of things. Most lawmakers today, however, treat law as a flexible tool or instrument for the accomplishment of chosen purposes. For example, the law of negotiable instruments discussed later in this text is designed to stimulate commercial activity by promoting the free movement of money substitutes such as promissory notes, checks, and drafts. Throughout the text, moreover, you see courts manipulating existing legal rules to achieve desired results. One strength of this *instrumentalist* attitude is its willingness to adapt the law to further the social good. A weakness, however, is the legal instability and uncertainty those adaptations often produce.

Just as individual legal rules advance specific purposes, law as a whole serves many general social functions. Among the most important of those functions are:

1. *Peacekeeping.* The criminal law rules discussed in Chapter 5 further this basic function of any legal system. Also, as Chapter 2 suggests, the resolution of private disputes serves as a major function of the civil law.

2. *Checking government power and promoting personal freedom.* Obvious examples are the constitutional restrictions examined in Chapter 3.

3. *Facilitating planning and the realization of reasonable expectations.* The rules of contract law discussed in Chapters 9, 10, 11, 12, 13, 14, 15, 16, 17, and 18 help fulfill this function of law.

4. *Promoting economic growth through free competition.* The antitrust laws discussed in Chapters 48, 49, and 50 are among the many legal rules that help perform this function.

5. *Promoting social justice.* Throughout this century, government has intervened in private social and economic affairs to correct perceived injustices and give all citizens equal access to life's basic goods. Examples include some of the employment laws addressed in Chapter 51.

6. *Protecting the environment.* The most important federal environmental statutes are discussed in Chapter 52.

Obviously, the law's various functions can conflict. The familiar clash between economic growth and environmental protection is an example. Chapter 5's cases dealing with the constitutional aspects of criminal cases illustrate the equally familiar conflict between effective law enforcement and the preservation of personal rights. Only rarely does the law achieve one end without sacrificing others. In law, as in life, there generally is no such thing as a free lunch. Where the law's objectives conflict, lawmakers may try to strike the best possible balance among those goals. This suggests limits on the law's usefulness as a device for promoting particular social goals.

Legal Reasoning

This text seeks to describe important legal rules affecting business. As texts generally do, it states those rules in what lawyers call "black letter" form, using sentences saying that certain legal consequences will occur if certain events happen. Although it provides a clear statement of the law's commands, this black letter approach can be misleading. It suggests definiteness, certainty, permanence, and predictability—attributes the law frequently lacks. To illustrate, and to give you some idea how lawyers and judges think, we now discuss the two most important kinds of legal reasoning: *case law reasoning* and *statutory interpretation.*[4] However, we first must examine legal reasoning in general.

Legal reasoning is basically deductive, or syllogistic. The legal rule is the major premise, the facts are the minor premise, and the result is the product of combining the two. Suppose a state statute says that a driver operating an automobile between 55 and 70 miles per hour must pay a $50 fine (the rule or major premise) and that Jim Smith drives his car at 65 miles per hour (the facts or minor premise). If Jim is arrested, and if the necessary facts can be proved, he will be required to pay the $50 fine. As you will

---

[4]The reasoning courts employ in constitutional cases resembles that used in common law cases, but often is somewhat looser. See Chapter 3.

Ethics and Compliance in Action

Some schools of jurisprudence discussed in this chapter concern themselves with the relationship between law and notions of morality. These schools of jurisprudence involve considerations related to key aspects of ethical theories, which address ethical issues arising in business contexts, corporate governance, and compliance. Chapter 4 defines major ethical theories. Chapter 44 discusses corporate governance issues in more detail. And compliance, which refers to the processes by which an organization polices its own behavior to ensure that it conforms to applicable laws, is addressed throughout this text. In this Ethics and Compliance in Action feature, we will focus on those parallel considerations between two schools of jurisprudence and several ethical theories.

Natural law's focus on rights thought to be independent of positive law has parallels in ethical theories that are classified under the *rights theory* heading. In its concern over unjust laws, natural law finds common ground with the ethical theory known as *justice theory*. When subscribers to sociological jurisprudence focus on the many influences that shape law and the trade-offs involved in a dynamic legal system, they may explore considerations that relate not only to rights theory or justice theory but also to the theory of *utilitarianism* and considerations central to *shareholder theory*. As you study Chapter 4 and later chapters, keep the schools of jurisprudence in mind. Think of them as you consider the extent to which a behavior's probable legal treatment and the possible ethical assessments of it may correspond or, instead, diverge.

now see, however, legal reasoning often is more difficult than this example would suggest.

Case Law Reasoning

LO1-5 Describe the respective roles of adhering to precedent (*stare decisis*) and distinguishing precedent in case law reasoning.

In cases governed by the common law, courts find the appropriate legal rules in prior cases called *precedents*. The standard for choosing and applying prior cases to decide present cases is the doctrine of *stare decisis*, which states that like cases should be decided alike. That is, the present case should be decided in the same way as past cases presenting the same facts and the same legal issues. If no applicable precedent exists, the court is free to develop a new common law rule to govern the case, assuming the court believes that sound public policy reasons call for the development of a new rule. When an earlier case may seem similar enough to the present case to constitute a precedent, but the court deciding the present case nevertheless identifies a meaningful difference between the cases, the court *distinguishes* the earlier decision.

Because every present case differs from the precedents in some respect, it is always possible to spot a factual distinction. For example, one could attempt to distinguish a prior case dealing with a defense to a claim of breach of contract because both parties in that case had black hair, whereas one party in the present case dealing with that same defense has brown hair. Of course, such a distinction would be ridiculous because the difference it identifies is insignificant in moral, social policy, or legal terms. A valid distinction involves a

widely accepted ethical or policy reason for treating the present case differently from its predecessor. Because people disagree about moral ideas, public policies, and the degree to which they are accepted, and because all these factors change over time, judges may differ on the wisdom of distinguishing a prior case. This is a source of uncertainty in the common law, but it gives the common law the flexibility to adapt to changing social conditions.[5]

When a precedent has been properly distinguished, the common law rule it stated does not control the present case. The court deciding the present case may then fashion a new common law rule to govern the case. Consider, for instance, an example involving the employment-at-will rule, the prevailing common law rule regarding employees in the United States. Under this rule, an employee may be fired at any time—and without any reason, let alone a good one—unless a contract between the employer and the employee guaranteed a certain duration of employment or established that the employee could be fired only for certain recognized legal causes. Most employees are not parties to a contract containing such provisions. Therefore, they are employees-at-will. Assume that in a precedent case, an employee who had been doing good work challenged his firing and that the court hearing the case ruled against him on the basis of the employment-at-will rule. Also assume that in a later case, a fired employee has challenged her dismissal. Although the fired employee would appear to be subject to the employment-at-will rule applied in the seemingly similar precedent case, the court deciding the later case nevertheless identifies an important difference: that in the later case,

---

[5]Also, though they exercise the power infrequently, courts sometimes completely *overrule* their own prior decisions.

the employee was fired in retaliation for having reported to law enforcement authorities that her employer was engaging in seriously unlawful business-related conduct. A firing under such circumstances appears to offend public policy notwithstanding the general acceptance of the employment-at-will rule. Having properly distinguished the precedent, the court deciding the later case would not be bound by the employment-at-will rule set forth in the precedent and would be free to develop a public policy–based exception under which the retaliatory firing would be deemed wrongful. (Chapter 51 will reveal that courts in a number of states have adopted such an exception to the employment-at-will rule.)

The *Coomer* case, which follows, provides a further illustration of the process of case law reasoning. In *Coomer*, the Missouri Supreme Court scrutinizes various precedents as it attempts to determine whether Missouri's courts should extend the so-called baseball rule, under which injuries

suffered as a result of certain risks that are inherent to an activity—like being struck by a foul ball at a baseball game — are not legally considered to be the fault of the baseball team or stadium, even though it was theoretically possible for the team or stadium to have done more to protect the injured person from the risk. (Negligence law, upon which Coomer's claim is based, is discussed in depth in Chapter 7.) Ultimately, the court decides not to expand the baseball rule to the facts of Coomer's case, finding his injury did not result from a risk inherent to attending the baseball game.[6]

———
[6]Though mastery of the nuances of the rules of baseball is not necessary to understand the court's reasoning in the *Coomer* case, readers who are unfamiliar with baseball may find an explanation of the basics of the game helpful. One such explanation can be found at www .howbaseballworks.com/FieldofPlay.htm.

Coomer v. Kansas City Royals Baseball Corp.   437 S.W.3d 184 (Mo. 2014)

On September 8, 2009, John Coomer and his father attended a Major League Baseball game between the Kansas City Royals and the Detroit Tigers. The game, which took place in Kansas City at Kauffman Stadium, was less well attended than normal because it rained most of the day leading up to the first pitch. Early in the game, Coomer and his father moved from their assigned seats to better, empty seats six rows behind the visitor's dugout.

Shortly after Coomer moved to the better seats, Sluggerrr, the mascot for the Royals, mounted the dugout to begin the "Hotdog Launch," which had been a feature of every Royals home game since 2000. The Launch happened between innings, when Sluggerrr used an air gun to shoot hotdogs from the roof of the visitor's dugout to fans seated beyond hand-tossing range. When his assistants were reloading the air gun, Sluggerrr tossed hotdogs by hand to the fans seated nearby. Sluggerrr usually tossed the hotdogs underhand while facing the fans, but sometimes he threw them overhand, behind his back, or side-armed.

At the game in question, Sluggerrr began to toss hotdogs by hand to fans seated near Coomer, while Sluggerrr's assistants were reloading the hotdog-shaped air gun. Coomer testified that he saw Sluggerrr turn away from the crowd as if to prepare for a behind-the-back throw, but because Coomer chose that moment to turn and look at the scoreboard, he admits he never saw Sluggerrr throw the hotdog that he claims injured him. Coomer testified only that a "split second later . . . something hit me in the face," and he described the blow as "pretty forceful."

A couple of days later, Coomer reported that he was "seeing differently" and something "wasn't right" with his left eye. The problem progressed until, approximately eight days after the incident, Coomer saw a doctor and was diagnosed with a detached retina. Coomer underwent surgeries to repair the retina and to remove a "traumatic cataract" in the same eye.

Coomer sued the Kansas City Royals Corp. for, among other things, negligence (i.e., that Sluggerrr's careless acts, which were the responsibility of the Royals to oversee and control, caused his injury). The Royals did not deny responsibility for Sluggerrr's acts but instead argued that Sluggerrr did not act negligently and, in any event, that Coomer had accepted the risk posed by Sluggerrr's hotdog toss by buying a ticket and attending the game. The latter is a theory known as implied primary assumption of risk.[7]

Among the instructions the trial judge gave to the jury was one asking the jury to decide whether the risk of being injured by Sluggerrr's hotdog toss is one of the inherent risks of watching a Royals home game, which Coomer assumed merely by attending the game. The jury found in favor of the Royals, and Coomer appealed.

Paul C. Wilson, Judge

In the past, this Court has held that spectators cannot sue a baseball team for injuries caused when a ball or bat enters the

———
[7]Chapter 7 includes a detailed discussion of the negligence defense of assumption of risk.

stands. Such risks are an unavoidable—even desirable—part of the joy that comes with being close enough to the Great American Pastime to smell the new-mown grass, to hear the crack of 42 inches of solid ash meeting a 95-mph fastball, or to watch a diving third baseman turn a heart-rending triple into a soul-soaring double-play. The risk of being injured by Sluggerrr's hotdog toss, on the other hand, is not an unavoidable part of watching the Royals play baseball. That risk is no more inherent in watching a game of baseball than it is inherent in watching a rock concert, a monster truck rally, or any other assemblage where free food or T-shirts are tossed into the crowd to increase excitement and boost attendance.

***

II. Implied Primary Assumption of the Risk and the "Baseball Rule"

Long before the Kansas City Athletics moved to Oakland and the fledging [sic] Royals joined the Junior Circuit, an overwhelming majority of courts recognized that spectators at sporting events are exposed to certain risks that are inherent merely in watching the contest. Accordingly, under [the] implied primary assumption of the risk, these courts held that the home team was not liable to a spectator injured as a result of such risks.

The archetypal example of this application of implied primary assumption of the risk is when a baseball park owner fails to protect each and every spectator from the risk of being injured by a ball or bat flying into the stands. Just as Missouri teams have led (and continue to lead) professional baseball on the field, Missouri courts helped lead the nation in defining this area of the law off the field. More than 50 years ago, this Court was one of the first to articulate the so-called "Baseball Rule":

> [W]here a baseball game is being conducted under the customary and usual conditions prevailing in baseball parks, *it is not negligence to fail to protect all seats in the park by wire netting,* and that the special circumstances and specific negligence pleaded did not aid plaintiff or impose upon the defendant a duty to warn him against hazards which are necessarily incident to baseball and are perfectly obvious to a person in possession of his faculties.

Anderson v. Kansas City Baseball Club, 231 S.W.2d 170, 172 (Mo. 1950) (emphasis added).

Anderson was based on this Court's earlier decision in *Hudson v. Kansas City Baseball Club*, 164 S.W.2d 318, 320 (Mo. 1942), which used the "no duty" language of implied primary assumption of the risk to explain its holding:

> The basis of the proprietor's liability is his superior knowledge and if his invitee knows of the condition or hazard *there is no duty* on the part of the proprietor to warn him and there is no liability for resulting injury because the invitee has as much knowledge as the proprietor does and then by voluntarily acting, in view of his knowledge, assumes the risks and dangers incident to the known condition.

Hudson, 164 S.W.2d at 323 (emphasis added) (applying Restatement (Second) of Torts, § 343). *Hudson* involved a spectator with personal knowledge of the inherent risk of being injured by a foul ball while watching a baseball game. But, when the Court returned to this same issue eight years later in *Anderson*, it continued to rely on section 343 of the Restatement (Second) of Torts (i.e., the "open and obvious dangers" doctrine under the rules of premises liability) to extend Missouri's no-duty rule to cases involving baseball spectators with no prior knowledge of baseball or the risks inherent in watching it.

> All of the cases cited here and many others which are cited in *Hudson v. Kansas City Baseball Club* . . . emphasize that when due care has been exercised to provide a reasonable number of screened seats, there remains a hazard that spectators in unscreened seats may be struck and injured by balls which are fouled or otherwise driven into the stands. *This risk is a necessary and inherent part of the game* and remains after ordinary care has been exercised to provide the spectators with seats which are reasonably safe. It is a risk which is assumed by the spectators because it remains after due care has been exercised and is not the result of negligence on the part of the baseball club. It is clearly *not an unreasonable risk to spectators which imposes a duty* to warn [or protect].

Anderson, 231 S.W.2d at 173 (emphasis added).

Anderson and *Hudson* are just two of the many dozens of cases around the country holding that, as long as some seats directly behind home plate are protected, the team owes "no duty" to spectators outside that area who are injured by a ball or bat while watching a baseball game. Despite being decided by such different courts across so many decades, all of these cases reflect certain shared principles. First, it is not possible for baseball players to play the game without occasionally sending balls or bats (or parts of bats) into the stands, sometimes at unsafe speeds. Second, it is not possible for the home team to protect each and every spectator from such risks without fundamentally altering the game or the spectators' experience of watching it through such means as: (a) substituting foam rubber balls and bats that will not injure anyone (or be very fun to watch); (b) erecting a screen or other barrier around the entire field protecting all spectators while obstructing their view and making them feel more removed from the action; or (c) moving all spectators at least 600 feet away from home plate in all directions. Third, ordinary negligence principles do not produce reliably acceptable results in these circumstances because the risk of injury (and the extent of the harm) to spectators is substantial, yet the justification for not protecting spectators from that risk can be expressed only in terms of the amusement or entertainment value of watching the sport that brought the spectators to the stadium in the first place.

Against this background, *Anderson* and *Hudson* (and dozens of Baseball Rule cases around the country) represent a conscious decision to favor the collective interests of all spectators by rejecting as a matter of law the individual claims of injured spectators. [T]he rationale [is] now identified as implied primary assumption of the risk, [and] these decisions protect the home team from liability for risks that are inherent in watching a baseball game based on the team's failure to take steps that could defeat the reason spectators are there at all, i.e., to get as close as they can to the action without interfering with the game they came to watch.

But the rationale for this rule—and, therefore, the rule itself—extends only to those risks that the home team is powerless to alleviate without fundamentally altering the game or spectator's enjoyment of it. As a result, the solid wall of authority in support of the Baseball Rule is badly cracked in cases where a spectator is injured by a ball *when* the game is not underway or *where* fans ordinarily do expect to have to keep a careful lookout for balls or bats leaving the field. This Court has not had to address such a question and does not do so now.

Moreover, even though the "no duty" rationale of the Baseball Rule applies to risks inherent in watching a baseball game, the home team still owes a duty of reasonable care not to *alter or increase* such inherent risks. One example, useful both for its facts and its analysis, is *Lowe v. California League of Prof. Baseball*, 56 Cal. App. 4th 112 (1997).

In *Lowe*, even though the plaintiff was struck by a foul ball, he claimed that his injuries were not caused by that inherent risk. Instead, the plaintiff claimed he was prevented from watching for foul balls because he was repeatedly jostled and distracted by the team's dinosaur mascot. The court agreed that the Baseball Rule did not bar such a claim:

> [T]he key inquiry here is whether the risk which led to plaintiff's injury involved some feature or aspect of the game which is inevitable or unavoidable in the actual playing of the game.... Can [this] be said about the antics of the mascot? We think not. Actually, the ... person who dressed up as Tremor, recounted that there were occasional games played when he was not there. In view of this testimony, as a matter of law, we hold that the antics of the mascot are not an essential or integral part of the playing of a baseball game. In short, the game can be played in the absence of such antics.

Id. (emphasis added).

Accordingly, even though implied primary assumption of the risk precludes recovery for injuries caused by the inherent risk of being hit by a foul ball while watching a baseball game, *Lowe* holds that the jury can hold the team liable for such injuries if the negligence of its mascot altered or increased that otherwise inherent risk and this negligence causes the plaintiff's injuries.

Accordingly, the proper application of implied primary assumption of the risk in this case ... is this: if Coomer was

injured by a risk that is an inherent part of watching the Royals play baseball, the team had no duty to protect him and cannot be liable for his injuries. But, if Coomer's injury resulted from a risk that is not an inherent part of watching baseball in person—or if the negligence of the Royals altered or increased one of these inherent risks and caused Coomer's injury—the jury is entitled to hold the Royals liable for such negligence....

***

IV. Being Injured by Sluggerrr's Hotdog Toss Is Not a Risk Inherent in Watching Royals Baseball

According to the Royals, the risk to a spectator of being injured by Sluggerrr's hotdog toss shares the same essential characteristics as the other risks that this Court (and many others) determined long ago were inherent in watching a baseball game in person, i.e., risks that a spectator will be injured by a flying ball or bat. The Court disagrees.

The rationale for barring recovery for injuries from risks that are inherent in watching a particular sport under implied primary assumption of the risk is that the defendant team owner cannot remove such risks without materially altering either the sport that the spectators come to see or the spectator's enjoyment of it. No such argument applies to Sluggerrr's hotdog toss. Millions of fans have watched the Royals (and its forebears in professional baseball) play the National Pastime for the better part of a century before Sluggerrr began tossing hotdogs, and millions more people watch professional baseball every year in stadiums all across this country without the benefit of such antics.

Some fans may find Sluggerrr's hotdog toss fun to watch between innings, and some fans may even have come to expect it, but this does not make the risk of injury from Sluggerrr's hotdog toss an "inherent risk" of watching a Royals game. "[I]nherent" means "*structural* or involved in the *constitution or essential character of* something: belonging *by nature or settled habit*," *Webster's Third New International Dictionary* (1966), at 1163 (emphasis added). There is nothing about the risk of injury from Sluggerrr's hotdog toss that is "structural" or involves the "constitution or essential character" of watching a Royals game at Kauffman Stadium.

The Royals concede that Sluggerrr's hotdog toss has nothing to do with watching the game of baseball but contend that the Hotdog Launch is a well-established (even customary) part of the overall stadium "experience." In support, the Royals cite cases that have applied the Baseball Rule to risks that were not created directly from the game. These cases do not support the Royals' argument.

In *Loughran v. The Phillies*, 888 A.2d 872, 876–77 (Pa. Super. 2005), because a plaintiff was injured when a fielder tossed the ball into the stands after catching the last out of the inning, the court held that implied primary assumption of the risk barred the plaintiff's claims. In rejecting the plaintiff's claim that the Baseball Rule should not apply because the throw was not part of the game itself, *Loughran* holds that—even though the "'no duty' rule applies only to 'common, expected, and frequent' risks of the game"—the link between the game and the risk of being hit with a ball tossed into the stands by a player is undeniable. *Id.* at 876. Baseball is the reason centerfielder Marlon Byrd was there, just as it was the reason the fans were in the stands (including the many who were yelling for Byrd to toss the ball to them). Here, on the other hand, there is no link between the game and the risk of being hit by Sluggerrr's hotdog toss. The Hotdog Launch is not an inherent part of the game; it is what the Royals do to entertain baseball fans when there is no game for them to watch. Sluggerrr may make breaks in the game more fun, but Coomer and his 12,000 rain-soaked fellow spectators were not there to watch Sluggerrr toss hotdogs; they were there to watch the Royals play baseball.

Somewhat closer to the mark—but still inapposite—is the Royals' reliance on *Cohen v. Sterling Mets, L.P.*, 840 N.Y.S.2d 527 (N.Y. Sup. Ct. 2007), *aff'd* 58 A.D.3d (N.Y. App. Div. 2009). A vendor sued the team for injuries caused by a fan who hit the vendor while diving for a souvenir T-shirt that had been tossed into the crowd. The court dismissed these claims, stating: "When a ball is tossed into the stands by a player many spectators rush toward the ball in hopes of getting a souvenir, just as what allegedly occurred here during the t-shirt launch." *Id.*

The Royals' reliance on *Cohen* highlights one of the basic flaws in its effort to use implied primary assumption to bar Coomer's claims, and it shows the importance of correctly identifying the risks and activity in each case. [W]hat makes a risk "inherent" for purposes of this doctrine . . . is that the risks are so intertwined (i.e., so "structural" or involved in the "constitution or essential character") with the underlying activity that the team cannot control or limit the risk without abandoning the activity. In *Cohen*, because the Mets could not control how fans reacted to the T-shirt launch, that reaction was an inherent risk—not of watching a baseball game but—of taking part in the T-shirt launch (which the plaintiff's work required him to do). Here, on the other hand, not only is being injured by Sluggerrr's hotdog toss not an inherent risk of watching a Royals game, it is not an inherent risk of the Hotdog Launch. . . .

Accordingly, the Court holds as a matter of law that the risk of injury from Sluggerrr's hotdog toss is not one of the risks inherent in watching the Royals play baseball that Coomer assumed merely by attending a game at Kauffman Stadium. This risk can be increased, decreased or eliminated altogether with no impact on the game or the spectators' enjoyment of it. As a result, Sluggerrr (and, therefore, the Royals) owe the fans a duty to use reasonable care in conducting the Hotdog Launch and can be held liable for damages caused by a breach of that duty.

Conclusion

For the reasons set forth above, this Court vacates the judgment and remands the case.

Statutory Interpretation Because statutes are written in one authoritative form, their interpretation might seem easier than case law reasoning. However, this is not so. The natural ambiguity of language serves as one reason courts face difficulties when interpreting statutes. The problems become especially difficult when statutory words are applied to situations the legislature did not foresee. In some instances, legislators may deliberately use ambiguous language when they are unwilling or unable to deal specifically with each situation the statute was enacted to regulate. When this happens, the legislature expects courts and/or administrative agencies to fill in the details on a case-by-case basis. Other reasons for deliberate ambiguity include the need for legislative compromise and legislators' desire to avoid taking controversial positions.

Ambiguity in statutory language can also arise from the vagaries of grammar, either as a result of sloppiness or because rules of grammar are contested. The following *O'Connor* case, for instance, illustrates just how much can ride on a "missing" comma, namely millions of dollars in unpaid overtime wages. As you read the case, consider what strategies the judges use to resolve the ambiguity. Those strategies correspond to the techniques of statutory interpretation that are described in the text following the case.

O'Connor v. Oakhurst Dairy   851 F.3d 69 (1st Cir. 2017)

A group of delivery drivers for Oakhurst Dairy sued the dairy and its parent company for unpaid overtime wages. Oakhurst Dairy processes, bottles, stores, markets, and distributes milk and other dairy products from facilities in Portland, Waterville, Bangor, and Presque Isle, Maine.

Oakhurst designated the plaintiff drivers as "route salesmen" on their official job descriptions. The drivers, however, claimed they solely engaged in deliveries of Oakhurst's products.

State and federal wage and hour laws generally require employers to pay their employees a premium wage for any hours the employees work in excess of 40 hours in a given week, unless the employees are exempted from overtime rules by the relevant statutory language.

The drivers argued that they were not exempted from the overtime wage requirement in the Maine wage and hour statute, while Oakhurst argued that they were exempt under a provision focused on workers who deal with perishable food products.

The district court considered the question and agreed with Oakhurst.

The drivers appealed.

BARRON, Circuit Judge

For want of a comma, we have this case. It arises from a dispute between a Maine dairy company and its delivery drivers, and it concerns the scope of an exemption from Maine's overtime law. Specifically, if that exemption used a serial comma to mark off the last of the activities that it lists, then the exemption would clearly encompass an activity that the drivers perform. And, in that event, the drivers would plainly fall within the exemption and thus outside the overtime law's protection. But, as it happens, there is no serial comma to be found in the exemption's list of activities, thus leading to this dispute over whether the drivers fall within the exemption from the overtime law or not.

The District Court concluded that, despite the absent comma, the Maine legislature unambiguously intended for the last term in the exemption's list of activities to identify an exempt activity in its own right. But, we conclude that the exemption's scope is actually not so clear in this regard. And because, under Maine law, ambiguities in the state's wage and hour laws must be construed liberally in order to accomplish their remedial purpose, we adopt the drivers' narrower reading of the exemption.

I.

The Maine overtime law is part of the state's wage and hour law.

The overtime law provides that "[a]n employer may not require an employee to work more than 40 hours in any one week unless 1 1/2 times the regular hourly rate is paid for all hours actually worked in excess of 40 hours in that week."

[S]ome workers who fall within the statutory definition of "employee" nonetheless fall outside the protection of the overtime law due to a series of express exemptions from that law. The exemption to the overtime law that is in dispute here is Exemption F.

Exemption F covers employees whose work involves the handling—in one way or another—of certain, expressly enumerated food products. Specifically, Exemption F states that the protection of the overtime law does not apply to: "The canning, processing, preserving, freezing, drying, marketing, storing, packing for shipment or distribution of: (1) Agricultural produce; (2) Meat and fish products; and (3) Perishable foods." The parties' dispute concerns the meaning of the words "packing for shipment or distribution."

The delivery drivers contend that, in combination, these words refer to the single activity of "packing," whether the "packing" is for "shipment" or for "distribution." The drivers further contend that, although they do handle perishable foods, they do not engage in "packing" them. As a result, the drivers argue that, as employees who fall outside Exemption F, the Maine overtime law protects them.

Oakhurst responds that the disputed words actually refer to two distinct exempt activities, with the first being "packing for shipment" and the second being "distribution." And because the delivery drivers do—quite obviously—engage in the "distribution" of dairy products, which are "perishable foods," Oakhurst contends that the drivers fall within Exemption F and thus outside the overtime law's protection.

* * *

III.

Each party recognizes that, by its bare terms, Exemption F raises questions as to its scope, largely due to the fact that no comma precedes the words "or distribution." But each side also contends that the exemption's text has a latent clarity, at least after one applies various interpretive aids. Each side then goes on to argue

Part One   Foundations of American Law

that the overtime law's evident purpose and legislative history confirms its preferred reading.

We conclude, however, that Exemption F is ambiguous, even after we take account of the relevant interpretive aids and the law's purpose and legislative history. For that reason, we conclude that, under Maine law, we must construe the exemption in the narrow manner that the drivers favor, as doing so furthers the overtime law's remedial purposes. Before explaining our reasons for reaching this conclusion, though, we first need to work our way through the parties' arguments as to why, despite the absent comma, Exemption F is clearer than it looks.

A.

First, the text. In considering it, we do not simply look at the particular word "distribution" in isolation from the exemption as a whole. We instead must take account of certain linguistic conventions—canons, as they are often called—that can help us make sense of a word in the context in which it appears. Oakhurst argues that, when we account for these canons here, it is clear that the exemption identifies "distribution" as a stand-alone, exempt activity rather than as an activity that merely modifies the stand-alone, exempt activity of "packing."

Oakhurst relies for its reading in significant part on the rule against surplusage, which instructs that we must give independent meaning to each word in a statute and treat none as unnecessary. To make this case, Oakhurst explains that "shipment" and "distribution" are synonyms. For that reason, Oakhurst contends, "distribution" cannot describe a type of "packing," as the word "distribution" would then redundantly perform the role that "shipment"—as its synonym—already performs, which is to describe the type of "packing" that is exempt. By contrast, Oakhurst explains, under its reading, the words "shipment" and "distribution" are not redundant. The first word, "shipment," describes the exempt activity of "packing," while the second, "distribution," describes an exempt activity in its own right.

Oakhurst also relies on another established linguistic convention in pressing its case—the convention of using a conjunction to mark off the last item on a list. Oakhurst notes, rightly, that there is no conjunction before "packing," but that there is one after "shipment" and thus before "distribution." Oakhurst also observes that Maine overtime law contains two other lists in addition to the one at issue here and that each places a conjunction before the last item.

Oakhurst acknowledges that its reading would be beyond dispute if a comma preceded the word "distribution" and that no comma is there. But, Oakhurst contends, that comma is missing for good reason. Oakhurst points out that the Maine Legislative Drafting Manual expressly instructs that: "when drafting Maine law or rules, don't use a comma between the penultimate and the last item of a

series." In fact, Oakhurst notes, Maine statutes invariably omit the serial comma from lists.

B.

If no more could be gleaned from the text, we might be inclined to read Exemption F as Oakhurst does. But, the delivery drivers point out, there is more to consider. And while these other features of the text do not compel the drivers' reading, they do make the exemption's scope unclear, at least as a matter of text alone.

The drivers contend, first, that the inclusion of both "shipment" and "distribution" to describe "packing" results in no redundancy. Those activities, the drivers argue, are each distinct. They contend that "shipment" refers to the outsourcing of the delivery of goods to a third-party carrier for transportation, while "distribution" refers to a seller's in-house transportation of products directly to recipients. And the drivers note that this distinction is, in one form or another, adhered to in [the *New Oxford English American Dictionary* and *Webster's Third New International Dictionary*] definitions.

Consistent with the drivers' contention, Exemption F does use two different words ("shipment" and "distribution") when it is hard to see why, on Oakhurst's reading, the legislature did not simply use just one of them twice. After all, if "distribution" and "shipment" really do mean the same thing, as Oakhurst contends, then it is odd that the legislature chose to use one of them ("shipment") to describe the activity for which "packing" is done but the other ("distribution") to describe the activity itself.

The drivers' argument that the legislature did not view the words to be interchangeable draws additional support from another Maine statute. That statute clearly lists both "distribution" and "shipment" as if each represents a separate activity in its own right. And because Maine law elsewhere treats "shipment" and "distribution" as if they are separate activities in a list, we do not see why we must assume that the Maine legislature did not treat them that way here as well. After all, the use of these two words to describe "packing" need not be understood to be wasteful. Such usage could simply reflect the legislature's intention to make clear that "packing" is exempt whether done for "shipment" or for "distribution" and not simply when done for just one of those activities.[a]

Next, the drivers point to the exemption's grammar. The drivers note that each of the terms in Exemption F that indisputably names an exempt activity—"canning, processing, preserving," and so forth on through "packing"—is a gerund. By, contrast,

---

[a]We also note that there is some reason to think that the distinction between "shipment" and "distribution" is not merely one that only a lawyer could love. Oakhurst's own internal organization chart seems to treat the two as if they are separate activities.

"distribution" is not. And neither is "shipment." In fact, those are the only non-gerund nouns in the exemption, other than the ones that name various foods.

Thus, the drivers argue, in accord with what is known as the parallel usage convention, that "distribution" and "shipment" must be playing the same grammatical role—and one distinct from the role that the gerunds play. In accord with that convention, the drivers read "shipment" and "distribution" each to be objects of the preposition "for" that describes the exempt activity of "packing." And the drivers read the gerunds each to be referring to stand-alone, exempt activities—"canning, preserving. . . ."

By contrast, in violation of the convention, Oakhurst's reading treats one of the two non-gerunds ("distribution") as if it is performing a distinct grammatical function from the other ("shipment"), as the latter functions as an object of a preposition while the former does not. And Oakhurst's reading also contravenes the parallel usage convention in another way: it treats a non-gerund (again, "distribution") as if it is performing a role in the list—naming an exempt activity in its own right—that gerunds otherwise exclusively perform.

Finally, the delivery drivers circle back to that missing comma. They acknowledge that the drafting manual advises drafters not to use serial commas to set off the final item in a list—despite the clarity that the inclusion of serial commas would often seem to bring. But the drivers point out that the drafting manual is not dogmatic on that point. The manual also contains a proviso—"Be careful if an item in the series is modified"—and then sets out several examples of how lists with modified or otherwise complex terms should be written to avoid the ambiguity that a missing serial comma would otherwise create.

Thus, the drafting manual's seeming—and, from a judge's point of view, entirely welcome—distaste for ambiguous lists does suggest a reason to doubt Oakhurst's insistence that the missing comma casts no doubt on its preferred reading. For, as the drivers explain, the drafting manual cannot be read to instruct that the comma should have been omitted here if "distribution" was intended to be the last item in the list. In that event, the serial comma's omission would give rise to just the sort of ambiguity that the manual warns drafters not to create.

Still, the drivers' textual points do not account for what seems to us to be Oakhurst's strongest textual rejoinder: no conjunction precedes "packing." Rather, the only conjunction in the exemption—"or"—appears before "distribution." And so, on the drivers' reading, the list is strangely stingy when it comes to conjunctions, as it fails to use one to mark off the last listed activity.

To address this anomaly, the drivers cite to Antonin Scalia & Bryan Garner, *Reading Law: The Interpretation of Legal Texts*

(2012), in which the authors observe that "[s]ometimes drafters will omit conjunctions altogether between the enumerated items [in a list]," in a technique called "asyndeton," *id.* at 119. But those same authors point out that most legislative drafters avoid asyndeton. And, the delivery drivers do not provide any examples of Maine statutes that use this unusual grammatical device. Thus, the drivers' reading of the text is hardly fully satisfying.[b]

IV.

The text has, to be candid, not gotten us very far. We are reluctant to conclude from the text alone that the legislature clearly chose to deploy the nonstandard grammatical device of asyndeton. But we are also reluctant to overlook the seemingly anomalous violation of the parallel usage canon that Oakhurst's reading of the text produces. And so—there being no comma in place to break the tie—the text turns out to be no clearer on close inspection than it first appeared. As a result, we turn to the parties' arguments about the exemption's purpose and the legislative history.

A.

Oakhurst contends that the evident purpose of the exemption strongly favors its reading. The whole point of the exemption, Oakhurst asserts (albeit without reference to any directly supportive text or legislative history), is to protect against the distorting effects that the overtime law otherwise might have on employer decisions about how best to ensure perishable foods will not spoil. And, Oakhurst argues, the risk of spoilage posed by the distribution of perishable food is no less serious than is the risk of spoilage posed by the other activities regarding the handling of such foods to which the exemption clearly does apply.

B.

We are not so sure. Any analysis of Exemption F that depends upon an assertion about its clear purpose is necessarily somewhat

---

[b]The drivers do also contend that their reading draws support from the *noscitur a sociis* canon, which "dictates that words grouped in a list should be given related meaning." In particular, the drivers contend that distribution is a different sort of activity than the others, nearly all of which entail transforming perishable products to less perishable forms—"canning," "processing," "preserving," "freezing," "drying," and "storing." However, the list of activities also includes "marketing," which Oakhurst argues undercuts the drivers' noscitur a sociis argument. And even if "marketing" does not mean promoting goods or services, as in the case of advertising, and means only "to deal in a market," . . . it is a word that would have at least some potential commonalities with the disputed word, "distribution." For that reason, this canon adds little insight beyond that offered by the parallel usage convention.

speculative. Nothing in the overtime law's text or legislative history purports to define a clear purpose for the exemption.

Moreover, even if we were to share in Oakhurst's speculation that the legislature included the exemption solely to protect against the possible spoilage of perishable foods rather than for some distinct reason related, perhaps, to the particular dynamics of certain labor markets, we still could not say that it would be arbitrary for the legislature to exempt "packing" but not "distributing" perishable goods. The reason to include "packing" in the exemption is easy enough to conjure. If perishable goods are not packed in a timely fashion, it stands to reason that they may well spoil. Thus, one can imagine the reason to ensure that the overtime law creates no incentives for employers to delay the packing of such goods. The same logic, however, does not so easily apply to explain the need to exempt the activity of distributing those same goods. Drivers delivering perishable food must often inevitably spend long periods of time on the road to get the goods to their destination. It is thus not at all clear that a legal requirement for employers to pay overtime would affect whether drivers would get the goods to their destination before they spoiled. No matter what delivery drivers are paid for the journey, the trip cannot be made to be shorter than it is.

Of course, this speculation about the effect that a legal requirement to pay overtime may or may not have on increasing the risk of food spoilage is just that. But such speculation does make us cautious about relying on what is only a presumed legislative purpose to generate a firm conclusion about what the legislature must have intended in drafting the exemption.

* * *

C.

To be clear, none of this evidence is decisive either way. It does highlight, however, the hazards of simply assuming—on the basis of no more than supposition about what would make sense—that the legislature could not have intended to craft Exemption F as the drivers contend that the legislature crafted it. Thus, we do not find either the purpose or the legislative history fully clarifying. And so we are back to where we began.

V.

We are not, however, without a means of moving forward. The default rule of construction under Maine law for ambiguous provisions in the state's wage and hour laws is that they "should be liberally construed to further the beneficent purposes for which they are enacted." *Dir. of Bureau of Labor Standards v. Cormier*, 527 A.2d 1297, 1300 (Me. 1987). The opening of the subchapter of Maine law containing the overtime statute and exemption at issue here declares a clear legislative purpose: "It is the declared public policy of the State of Maine that workers employed in any occupation should receive wages sufficient to provide adequate maintenance and to protect their health, and to be fairly commensurate with the value of the services rendered." Thus, in accord with *Cormier*, we must interpret the ambiguity in Exemption F in light of the remedial purpose of Maine's overtime statute. And, when we do, the ambiguity clearly favors the drivers' narrower reading of the exemption.

* * *

VI.

Accordingly, the District Court's grant of partial summary judgment to Oakhurst is **reversed**.

LO1-6 Identify what courts focus on when applying the major statutory interpretation techniques (plain meaning, legislative purpose, legislative history, and general public purpose).

To deal with the problems of ambiguity that arise from drafting errors, unclear language, or the application of clear language to unanticipated circumstances, courts use various techniques of statutory interpretation. As you saw in the *O'Connor* case, different techniques may dictate different results in a particular case. Sometimes judges employ the techniques in an instrumentalist or result-oriented fashion, emphasizing the technique that will produce the result they want and downplaying the others. It is, therefore, unclear which technique should control when different techniques yield different results. Judges have considerable latitude in this regard.

A conceptually helpful metaphor here might be to think of a judge approaching a question of statutory interpretation as a repairperson. The various techniques of statutory interpretation described here are the tools he or she might use for a repair job. Sometimes a particular tool is more suited to a particular job, but a repairperson uses his or her judgment in determining which tools to use to accomplish the goal of making the repair. Likewise, a judge retains the freedom to reach in the "statutory interpretation toolbox" for any of the tools described here, but professional norms and experience often guide a judge's choice, just as it would a repairperson's.

Plain Meaning Courts routinely begin their interpretation of a statute with its actual language. If the statute's words have a clear, common, accepted meaning, courts often employ the *plain meaning rule*. This approach calls for the court to apply the statute according to the usual meaning of its words, without concerning itself with anything else. At times, this approach is clear and settles the matter. Often, though, judges find the application of plain meaning unhelpful. It may lead to absurd or patently unjust results, or it might simply fail to resolve the ambiguity at issue. In *James v. City of Costa Mesa*, which follows the description of these statutory interpretation techniques, both the majority and the dissenting judges agree that the plain meaning of the statutory text at issue is ambiguous, even as they disagree as to what that meaning is.

Legislative History and Legislative Purpose Courts sometimes refuse to follow a statute's plain meaning when its legislative history suggests a different result. Almost all courts resort to legislative history when the statute's language is ambiguous. A statute's legislative history includes the following sources: reports of investigative committees or law revision commissions that led to the legislation, transcripts or summaries of hearings of legislative committees that originally considered the legislation, reports issued by such committees, records of legislative debates, reports of conference committees reconciling the chambers' conflicting versions of the law in a **bicameral legislature**, amendments or defeated amendments to the legislation, other bills not passed by the legislature but proposing similar legislation, and discrepancies between a bill passed by one chamber of a bicameral legislature and the final version of the statute.

Sometimes a statute's legislative history provides no information or conflicting information about its meaning, scope, or purposes. Some sources prove to be more authoritative than others. The worth of debates, for instance, may depend on which legislator (e.g., the sponsor of the bill or an uninformed blowhard) is quoted. Some sources are useful only in particular situations; prior unpassed bills and amendments or defeated amendments are examples. Consider, for instance, whether mopeds are covered by an air pollution statute applying to "automobiles, trucks, buses, and other motorized passenger or cargo vehicles." If the statute's original version included mopeds, but this reference was removed by amendment, it is unlikely that the legislature wanted mopeds to be covered. The same might be true if six similar unpassed bills had included mopeds, but the bill that was eventually passed did not, or if one house had passed a bill including mopeds, but mopeds did not appear in the final version of the legislation.

Courts use legislative history in two overlapping but distinguishable ways. They may use it to determine what the legislature thought about the specific meaning of statutory language. They may also use it to determine the overall aim, end, or goal of the legislation. In this second case, they then ask whether a particular interpretation of the statute is consistent with this

legislative purpose. To illustrate the difference between these two uses of legislative history, suppose that a court is considering whether our pollution statute's "other motorized passenger or cargo vehicles" language includes battery-powered vehicles. The court might scan the legislative history for specific references to battery-powered vehicles or other indications of what the legislature thought about their inclusion. The court might also use the same history to determine the overall aims of the statute and then ask whether including battery-powered vehicles is consistent with those aims. Because the history probably would reveal that the statute's purpose was to reduce air pollution from internal combustion engines, the court might well conclude that covering battery-powered vehicles would be inconsistent with the legislative purpose and, therefore, decline to include them within the coverage of the statute.

General Public Purpose Occasionally, courts construe statutory language in the light of various *general public purposes*. These purposes are not the purposes underlying the statute in question; rather, they are widely accepted general notions of public policy. For example, the Supreme Court once used the general public policy against racial discrimination in education as an argument for denying tax-exempt status to a private university that discriminated on the basis of race.

Prior Interpretations Courts sometimes follow prior cases and administrative decisions interpreting a statute, regardless of the statute's plain meaning or legislative history. The main argument for following these prior interpretations is to promote stability and certainty by preventing each successive court that considers a statute from adopting its own interpretation. The courts' willingness to follow a prior interpretation depends on such factors as the number of past courts adopting the interpretation, the authoritativeness of those courts, and the number of years that the interpretation has been followed.[8]

Maxims Maxims are general rules of thumb employed in statutory interpretation. There are many maxims, which courts tend to use or ignore at their discretion. The *O'Connor* court used several maxims to interpret the Maine overtime law exemption in the case at the beginning of this section.

---

[8]Note here that this technique is related to, but distinct from, a court's obligation to follow binding precedent. If a prior interpretation of a statute was handed down by a higher court whose rulings are binding on a lower court, then the lower court must follow that interpretation. As such, the application of binding precedent is not truly considered statutory interpretation. The technique of statutory interpretation that follows prior interpretations of a statute arises when courts look to non-precedential decisions of other courts for guidance.

The court there referred to the maxims as "canons" of statutory interpretation. For our purposes, *maxim* and *canon* are synonyms. The judge in *O'Connor* explained the maxim of *noscitur a sociis* in the second footnote of the opinion. Another example of a maxim is the *ejusdem generis* rule, which says that when general words follow words of a specific, limited meaning, the general language should be limited to things of the same class as those specifically stated. Suppose that the pollution statute quoted earlier listed 12 types of gas-powered vehicles and ended with the words "and other motorized passenger or cargo vehicles." In that instance, *ejusdem generis* probably would dictate that battery-powered vehicles not be included.

The following *James v. City of Costa Mesa* case reports the decision of a three-judge panel of the U.S. Court of Appeals for the Ninth Circuit. Two of the three judges agreed with one interpretation of the statutory language at issue; the third disagreed with that interpretation. The decision of the two judges who agreed is presented as the *majority opinion* of the court, while the disagreeing judge's argument is in the *dissenting opinion*. Notice how each opinion uses plain meaning and legislative history and purpose (with a maxim or two peppered in for good measure) to interpret the language to different conclusions. This illustrates how, regardless of these consistent techniques described here, there is still substantial room for contested judgment in statutory interpretation. Likewise, you should compare and contrast the *James* court's application of those techniques with the earlier *O'Connor* opinion.

James v. City of Costa Mesa   700 F.3d 394 (9th Cir. 2012)

Marla James, Wayne Washington, James Armantrout, and Charles Daniel Dejong (collectively referred to here either as "the plaintiffs" or "James," the name of the lead plaintiff) suffer from serious medical conditions. To alleviate pain associated with their impairments, they each use marijuana, as recommended and monitored by their doctors. In California, where the plaintiffs live, the medical use of marijuana is permissible according to state law. Marijuana, however, remains a controlled substance under the federal Controlled Substances Act (CSA). As a result, it is generally a federal crime to possess and distribute marijuana, even for medical purposes.

The plaintiffs filed a lawsuit against the cities of Costa Mesa and Lake Forest, California, for taking steps to close down or otherwise prohibit the operation of marijuana-dispensing facilities within their boundaries. The plaintiffs claimed that the cities' actions violated Title II of the Americans with Disabilities Act (ADA), which prohibits discrimination on the basis of disability in the provision of public services. The lawsuit asked the court to enjoin the cities' actions (i.e., issue a decision ordering the cities to stop their efforts to close the marijuana-dispensing facilities).

A judge in the U.S. District Court for the Central District of California declined to issue an injunction on the ground that the ADA does not protect against discrimination on the basis of plaintiffs' marijuana use, even medical marijuana use supervised by a doctor in accordance with state law. The judge based his decision on a determination that the plaintiffs are not entitled to the protection of the ADA in this instance because only a "qualified individual with a disability" is protected from being denied the benefit of public services. The ADA states that "the term 'individual with a disability' does not include an individual who is currently engaging in the illegal use of drugs, when the covered entity acts on the basis of such use."

The plaintiffs appealed the District Court's ruling to the U.S. Court of Appeals for the Ninth Circuit.

Raymond C. Fisher, Circuit Judge

This case turns on whether the plaintiffs' medical marijuana use constitutes "illegal use of drugs[.]"

[The ADA] defines "illegal use of drugs" as

the use of drugs, the possession or distribution of which is unlawful under the Controlled Substances Act. Such term does not include the use of a drug taken under supervision by a licensed health care professional, or other uses authorized by the Controlled Substances Act or other provisions of Federal law.

The parties agree that the possession and distribution of marijuana, even for medical purposes, is generally unlawful under the CSA, and thus that medical marijuana use falls within the exclusion set forth in [the above definition's] first sentence. They dispute, however, whether medical marijuana use is covered by one of the exceptions in the second sentence. The plaintiffs contend their medical marijuana use falls within the exception for drug use supervised by a licensed health care professional.

There are two reasonable interpretations of the [ADA]'s language excepting from the illegal drug exclusion "use of a drug taken under supervision by a licensed health care professional, or other uses authorized by the Controlled Substances Act or other provisions of Federal law." The first interpretation—urged by the plaintiffs—is that this language creates *two* exceptions to the illegal drug exclusion: (1) an exception for professionally supervised drug use carried out under *any* legal authority, and (2) an independent exception for drug use authorized by the CSA or other provisions of federal law. The second interpretation—offered by the cities and adopted by the district court—is that the provision contains a *single* exception covering all uses authorized by the CSA or other provisions of federal law, including both CSA-authorized uses that involve professional supervision (such as use of controlled substances by prescription . . . and uses of controlled substances in connection with research and experimentation), and other CSA-authorized uses. Under the plaintiffs' interpretation, their state-sanctioned, doctor-recommended marijuana use is covered under the supervised use exception. Under the cities' interpretation, the plaintiffs' state-authorized medical marijuana use is not covered by any exception because it is not authorized by the CSA or another provision of federal law. Although [the definition of "illegal use of drugs"] lacks a plain meaning and its legislative history is not conclusive, we hold, in light of the text and legislative history of the ADA, as well as the relationship between the ADA and the CSA, that the cities' interpretation is correct.

The meaning of ["illegal use of drugs"] cannot be discerned from the text alone. Both interpretations of the provision are somewhat problematic. The cities' reading of the statute renders the first clause in [the definition]'s second sentence superfluous; if Congress had intended that the exception cover only uses authorized by the CSA and other provisions of federal law, it could have omitted the "taken under supervision" language altogether. But the plaintiffs' interpretation also fails to give effect to each word of [the statute], for if Congress had really intended that the language excepting "other uses authorized by the Controlled Substances Act or other provisions of Federal law" be entirely independent of the preceding supervised use language, it could have omitted the word "other," thus excepting "use of a drug taken under supervision by a licensed health care professional, or uses authorized by the Controlled Substances Act." Moreover, unless the word "other" is omitted, the plaintiffs' interpretation renders the statutory language outright awkward. One would not *naturally* describe "the use of a drug taken under supervision by a licensed health care professional, or *other* uses authorized by the Controlled Substances Act or other provisions of Federal law" unless the supervised uses were a *subset* of the uses authorized by the CSA and other provisions of federal law. The plaintiffs' reading thus results not only in surplusage, but also in semantic dissonance.

The cities' interpretation also makes the most sense of the contested language when it is viewed in context. . . . Here, the context reveals Congress' intent to define "illegal use of drugs" by reference to federal, rather than state, law. [The definition] mentions the CSA by name twice, and [a subsequent provision of the ADA] provides that "[t]he term 'drug' means a controlled substance, as defined in . . . the Controlled Substances Act."

We therefore conclude that the cities' interpretation of the statutory text is the more persuasive, though we agree with the dissent that the text is ultimately inconclusive. We therefore look to legislative history, including related congressional activity.

The legislative history of this provision, like its text, is indeterminate. It is true, as the plaintiffs point out, that Congress rejected an early draft of the "taken under supervision" exception in favor of a broader version. [The early version excepted drugs taken *pursuant to a valid prescription*, rather than the use of a drug taken under *supervision by a licensed health care professional*.] We are not persuaded, however, that this history compels the plaintiffs' interpretation. Although the expansion of the supervised use exception suggests Congress wanted to cover more than just CSA-authorized *prescription-based* use, it does not demonstrate that the exception was meant to extend beyond the set of uses authorized by the CSA and other provisions of federal law. The CSA does authorize some professionally supervised drug use that is not prescription-based, and Congress could have intended simply to expand the supervised use exception to encompass all such uses.

One House Committee Report does include a brief passage that arguably supports the notion that [the] supervised use language and [the] authorized use language are independent, stating "The term 'illegal use of drugs' does not include the use of controlled substances, including experimental drugs, taken under the supervision of a licensed health care professional. It also does not include uses authorized by the Controlled Substances Act or other provisions of federal law." This discussion is of limited persuasive value, however, because it may rest on the unstated assumption—quite plausible at the time—that professionally supervised use of illegal drugs would always be consistent with the CSA. There is no reason to think that the 1990 Congress that passed the ADA would have anticipated later changes in state law facilitating professional supervision of drug use that federal law does not permit. The first such change came six years later, when California voters passed Proposition 215, now codified as the Compassionate Use Act of 1996.

[D]uring and after adoption of the ADA there has been a strong and longstanding federal policy against medical marijuana use outside the limits established by federal law itself. . . . Under the plaintiffs' view, the ADA worked a substantial departure from this accepted federal policy by extending federal protections to federally prohibited, but state-authorized, medical use of marijuana. That would have been an extraordinary departure from policy, and one that we would have expected Congress to take explicitly. It is unlikely that Congress would have wished to legitimize state-authorized, federally proscribed medical marijuana use without debate, in an ambiguously worded ADA provision.

* * *

Affirmed.

DISSENT BY: Marsha S. Berzon, Circuit Judge

The statutory interpretation issue at the core of this case is an unusually tough one, as the majority opinion recognizes. Looking at the language of [the definition of "illegal use of drugs"] alone, I would come out where the majority does—concluding that the statute is ambiguous. But unlike the majority, I would not declare a near-draw. Instead, looking at the words alone, I would conclude that the plaintiffs have much the better reading, but not by enough to be comfortable that their interpretation is surely correct. Turning then to the legislative history, I would again declare the plaintiffs the winner, this time sufficiently, when combined with the language considerations, to adopt their interpretation, absent some very good reason otherwise.

1. Statutory Text

Although [the definition] is not *entirely* clear, James has very much the better reading of the statutory language. In James's view, the phrases "use of a drug taken under supervision by a licensed health care professional" and "other uses authorized by the [CSA]" create *two different* exceptions, so that the ADA protects use of drugs under supervision of a doctor even when that use is not authorized by the CSA. If Congress intended to carve out only drug use authorized by the CSA, after all, the entire first clause—"the use of a drug under supervision by a licensed health care professional"—would have been unnecessary.

a. The use of "other"

[T]he word "other" is not necessarily redundant at all. It *could* be read to indicate that use under supervision of a doctor is meant to be a category of uses entirely subsumed by the larger category of uses authorized by the CSA, but this is not the only possible interpretation. Put another way, omitting the word "other" entirely would certainly have compelled the reading James advances, but its presence does not invalidate her interpretation. There is, after all, a middle ground between these two readings. . . . [T]he two clauses could . . . be seen as *partially* overlapping, with the group of uses supervised by a doctor partially included within the set of uses authorized by the CSA but also partially independent, encompassing in addition a set of uses not authorized by the CSA. This reading strikes me as the most sensible.

Under this interpretation, "other" is not redundant. Instead, it accurately reflects the overlap. Were the "other" not there, the exception would have divided the relevant universe into two non-overlapping sets. Yet, in fact the CSA authorizes some (but not all) uses of "drugs taken under supervision of a licensed health care professional." The "other" serves to signal that there is no strict dichotomy between the two phrases, as the bulk of the CSA-authorized uses are within the broader set covered by the first phrase.

* * *

2. Legislative History

James' reading of the statute also accords *much* better with the overall thrust of the legislative history. That history, while not *entirely* without ambiguity, strongly supports James's interpretation.

a. Evolution of the exception

As the majority observes, Congress replaced a draft of the exception that required that use of drugs be "pursuant to a valid prescription," . . . with the broader language eventually enacted. Critically, the House Committee Report restates the exception, once amended, in precisely the cumulative manner I have suggested most accords with the statutory language: "The term 'illegal use of drugs' does not include the use of controlled substances, including experimental drugs, taken under the supervision of a licensed health care professional. It also does not include uses authorized by the [CSA] or other provisions of Federal law." This summary is in no way ambiguous, and indicates at least that members of the House familiar with the statutory language understood it in the manner that, for reasons I have explained, most accords with ordinary principles of grammar and syntax.

b. Congressional awareness of medical marijuana

The majority discounts any significance in the way the current language is described in the relevant Committee report, observing that California voters did not pass Prop. 215 until 1996 and that there were no state laws in 1990 allowing for professionally supervised use of drugs in a manner inconsistent with the CSA. Congress would not have carefully drafted the exception to include non-CSA authorized medically supervised uses, the majority posits, as no such uses were legal under state law at the time.

That explanation for dismissing the best reading of the statute and the only coherent reading of the Committee's explanation of the statute won't wash, for several reasons. First, while California in 1996 became the first of the sixteen states that currently legalize medical marijuana, the history of medical marijuana goes back much further, so that use for medical purposes was not unthinkable in 1990. At one time, "almost all States . . . had exceptions making lawful, under specified conditions, possession of marihuana by . . . persons for whom the drug had been prescribed or to whom it had been given by an authorized medical person." What's more, the Federal government itself conducted an experimental medical marijuana program from 1978 to 1992, and it continues to provide marijuana to the surviving participants. The existence of these programs indicates that medical marijuana was not a concept utterly foreign to Congress before 1996.

* * *

The upshot is that the statutory language and history, taken together, fit much better with James's version of what Congress meant than the Cities'.

CYBERLAW IN ACTION

Section 230 of the Communications Decency Act (CDA), a federal statute, provides that "[n]o provider or user of an interactive computer service shall be treated as the publisher or speaker of any information provided by another information content provider." Although § 230 appears in a statute otherwise designed to protect minors against online exposure to indecent material, the broad language of § 230 has caused courts to apply it in contexts having nothing to do with indecent expression.

For instance, various courts have held that § 230 protects providers of an interactive computer service (ICS) against liability for defamation when a user of the service creates and posts false, reputation-harming statements about someone else. (ICS is defined in the statute as "any information service, system, or access software provider that provides or enables computer access by multiple users to a computer server.") With courts so holding, § 230 has the effect of superseding a common law rule of defamation that anyone treated as a publisher or speaker of defamatory material is liable to the same extent as the original speaker or writer of that material. Absent § 230, ICS providers could sometimes face defamation liability under the theory that they are publishers of statements made by someone else. (You will learn more about defamation in Chapter 6.) This application of § 230 illustrates two concepts noted earlier in the chapter: first, that federal law overrides state law when the two conflict, and second, that an applicable statute supersedes a common law rule.

Cases in other contexts have required courts to utilize statutory interpretation techniques discussed in this chapter as they determine whether § 230's shield against liability applies. For example, two cases presented the question whether § 230 protects website operators against liability for alleged Fair Housing Act (FHA) violations based on material that appears on their sites. The FHA states that it is unlawful to "make, print or publish" or to "cause" the making, printing, or publishing of, notices, statements, or advertisements that "with respect to the sale or rental of a dwelling[,] . . . indicate[s] any preference, limitation, or discrimination based on race, color,

religion, sex, handicap, familial status, or national origin, or an intention to make any such preference, limitation, or discrimination." A civil rights organization sued Craigslist Inc., which operated a well-known electronic forum for those who sought to buy, sell, or rent housing and miscellaneous goods and services. The plaintiff alleged that Craigslist users posted housing-related statements such as "No minorities" and "No children" and that those statements constituted FHA violations on the part of Craigslist.

In *Chicago Lawyers Committee for Civil Rights Under Law, Inc. v. Craigslist, Inc.*, 519 F.3d 666 (7th Cir. 2008), the U.S. Court of Appeals for the Seventh Circuit affirmed the district court's dismissal of the plaintiff's complaint. The Seventh Circuit held that a "natural reading" of § 230 of the CDA protected Craigslist against liability. The statements that allegedly violated the FHA were those of users of the electronic forum—meaning that Craigslist would be liable only if it were treated as a publisher or speaker of the users' statements. The plain language of § 230, however, prohibited classifying Craigslist as a publisher or speaker of the content posted by the users. Neither did Craigslist "cause" users to make statements of the sort prohibited by the FHA. Using a commonsense interpretation of the word "cause," the court concluded that merely furnishing the electronic forum was not enough to implicate Craigslist in having "cause[d]" the users' statements. There were no facts indicating that Craigslist suggested or encouraged statements potentially running afoul of the FHA.

Very shortly after the *Craigslist* decision, a different federal court of appeals decided *Fair Housing Council v. Roommates. com, LLC.* That case presented the question whether § 230 of the CDA protected Roommates.com against FHA liability for allegedly discriminatory housing-related statements posted by users of Roommates.com's electronic forum. The case's basic facts appear in problem case 10 at the end of this chapter. Review those facts and compare them to the facts of the *Craigslist* case. Then determine whether § 230 protected Roommates.com against liability (as it protected Craigslist) or whether the facts of the *Roommates.com* case warranted a different outcome.

Limits on the Power of Courts

By now, you may think that anything goes when courts decide common law cases or interpret statutes. Many factors, however, discourage courts from adopting a freewheeling approach. Their legal training and mental makeup cause judges to be likely to respect established precedents and the will of the legislature. Many courts issue written opinions, which expose judges to academic and professional criticism if the opinions are poorly reasoned. Lower court judges may be

discouraged from innovation by the fear of being overruled by a higher court. Finally, political factors inhibit judges. For example, some judges are elected, and even judges with lifetime tenure can sometimes be removed.

An even more fundamental limit on the power of courts is that they cannot make or interpret law until parties present them with a case to decide. In addition, any such case must be a real dispute. That is, courts generally limit themselves to genuine, existing "cases or controversies" between real parties with tangible opposing interests in the lawsuit. Courts generally do not issue *advisory opinions* on abstract legal questions unrelated to a genuine dispute, and do not decide *feigned controversies* that parties concoct to seek answers to such questions. Courts may also refuse to decide cases that are insufficiently *ripe* to have matured into a genuine controversy, or that are *moot* because there no longer is a real dispute between the parties. Reflecting similar policies is the doctrine of **standing to sue**, which normally requires that the plaintiff have some direct, tangible, and substantial stake in the outcome of the litigation.

State and federal **declaratory judgment** statutes, however, allow parties to determine their rights and duties even though their controversy has not advanced to the point where harm has occurred and legal relief may be necessary. This enables them to determine their legal position without taking action that could expose them to liability. For example, if Darlene believes that something she plans to do would not violate Earl's copyright on a work of authorship but she recognizes that he may take a contrary view, she may seek a declaratory judgment on the question rather than risk Earl's lawsuit by proceeding to do what she had planned. Usually, a declaratory judgment is awarded only when the parties' dispute is sufficiently advanced to constitute a real case or controversy.

The Global Business Environment

Just as statutes may require judicial interpretation when a dispute arises, so may treaties. The techniques that courts use in interpreting treaties correspond closely to the statutory interpretation techniques discussed in this chapter. *Olympic Airways v. Husain*, 540 U.S. 644 (2004), furnishes a useful example.

In *Olympic Airways*, the U.S. Supreme Court was faced with an interpretation question regarding a treaty, the Warsaw Convention, which deals with airlines' liability for passenger deaths or injuries on international flights. Numerous nations (including the United States) subscribe to the Warsaw Convention, a key provision of which provides that in regard to international flights, the airline "shall be liable for damages sustained in the event of the death or wounding of a passenger or any other bodily injury suffered by a passenger, if the accident which caused the damage so sustained took place on board the aircraft or in the course of any of the operations of embarking or disembarking." A separate provision imposes limits on the amount of money damages to which a liable airline may be subjected.

The *Olympic Airways* case centered around the death of Dr. Abid Hanson, a severe asthmatic, on an international flight operated by Olympic. Smoking was permitted on the flight. Hanson was given a seat in the nonsmoking section, but his seat was only three rows in front of the smoking section. Because Hanson was extremely sensitive to secondhand smoke, he and his wife, Rubina Husain, requested various times that he be allowed, for health reasons, to move to a seat farther away from the smoking section. Each time, the request was denied by an Olympic flight attendant. When smoke from the smoking section began to give Hanson difficulty, he used a new inhaler and walked toward the front of the plane to get some fresher air. Hanson went into respiratory distress, whereupon his wife and a doctor who was on board gave him shots of epinephrine from an emergency kit that Hanson carried. Although the doctor administered CPR and oxygen when Hanson collapsed, Hanson died. Husain, acting as personal representative of her late husband's estate, sued Olympic in federal court on the theory that the Warsaw Convention made Olympic liable for Hanson's death. The federal district court and the court of appeals ruled in favor of Husain.

In considering Olympic's appeal, the U.S. Supreme Court noted that the key issue was one of treaty interpretation: whether the flight attendant's refusals to reseat Hanson constituted an "accident which caused" the death of Hanson. Noting that the Warsaw Convention itself did not define "accident" and that different dictionary definitions of "accident" exist, the Court looked to a precedent case, *Air France v. Saks*, 470 U.S. 392 (1985), for guidance. In the *Air France* case, the Court held that the term "accident" in the Warsaw Convention means "an unexpected or unusual event or happening that is external to the passenger." Applying that definition to the facts at hand, the Court concluded in *Olympic Airways* that the repeated refusals to reseat Hanson despite his health concerns amounted to unexpected and unusual behavior for a flight attendant. Although the refusals were not the sole reason why Hanson died (the smoke itself being a key factor), the refusals were nonetheless a significant link in the causation chain that led to Hanson's death. Given the definition of "accident" in the Court's earlier precedent, the phrasing, the Warsaw Convention, and the underlying public policies supporting it, the Court concluded that the refusals to reseat Hanson constituted an "accident" covered by the Warsaw Convention. Therefore, the Court affirmed the decision of the lower courts.

APPENDIX

Reading and Briefing Cases

Throughout this text, you will encounter cases—the judicial opinions accompanying court decisions. These cases are highly edited versions of their much longer originals. What follows are explanations and pointers to assist you in studying cases.

1. Each case has a *case name* that includes at least some of the parties to the case. Because the order of the parties may change when a case is appealed, do not assume that the first party listed is the plaintiff (the party suing) and the second the defendant (the party being sued). Also, because some cases have many plaintiffs and/or many defendants, the parties discussed in the court's opinion sometimes differ from those found in the case name.

2. Each case also has a *citation*, which includes the volume and page number of the legal reporter in which the full case appears, plus the year the case was decided. *James v. City of Costa Mesa*, for instance, begins on page 394 of volume 700 of the third edition of the *Federal Reporter* (the official reporter that compiles the published opinions of the U.S. Circuit Courts of Appeal) and was decided in 2012. (Each of the many different legal reporters has its own abbreviation. The list is too long to include here.) In parentheses accompanying the date, we also give you some information about the court that decided the case. For example, "1st Cir." is the U.S. Court of Appeals for the First Circuit, "D. Md." is the U.S. District Court for the District of Maryland, "Mich." is the Supreme Court of Michigan, and "Minn. Ct. App." is the Minnesota Court of Appeals (a Minnesota intermediate appellate court). Chapter 2 describes the various kinds of courts.

3. At the beginning of each case, there is a *statement of facts* containing the most important facts that gave rise to the case. These appear in italics and are largely written by the authors of this text, though some of the language may be that of the court.

4. As part of the statement of facts, we give you the case's *procedural history*. This history tells you what courts previously handled the case you are reading, and how they dealt with it.

5. Next comes your major concern: the *body of the court's opinion*. Here, the court determines the applicable law and applies it to the facts to reach a conclusion. The court's discussion of the relevant law may be elaborate; it may include prior cases, legislative history,

applicable public policies, and more. The court's application of the law to the facts usually occurs after it has arrived at the applicable legal rule(s), but also may be intertwined with its legal discussion.

6. At the very end of the case, we complete the procedural history by stating the court's *decision*. For example, "Judgment reversed in favor of Smith" says that a lower court judgment against Smith was reversed on appeal. This means that Smith's appeal was successful and Smith wins.

7. The cases' main function is to provide concrete examples of rules stated in the text. (Frequently, the text tells you what point the case illustrates.) In studying law, it is easy to conclude that your task is finished once you have memorized a black letter rule. Real-life legal problems, however, seldom present themselves as abstract questions of law; instead, they are hidden in particular situations one encounters or particular actions one takes. Without some sense of a legal rule's real-life application, your knowledge of that rule is incomplete. The cases help provide this sense.

8. You may find it helpful to *brief* the cases. There is no one correct way to brief a case, but most good briefs contain the following elements: (1) a short statement of the relevant facts, (2) the case's prior history, (3) the question(s) or issue(s) the court had to decide, (4) the answer(s) to those question(s), (5) the reasoning the court used to justify its decision, and (6) the final result. A brief of *Price v. High Pointe Oil Company, Inc.* (a case included earlier) might look this way:

Price v. High Pointe Oil Company, Inc.

Facts Beckie Price's house and all of her personal belongings were destroyed when High Pointe erroneously filled her basement with 400 gallons of oil through an oil fill pipe that formerly led to an oil furnace in the basement. Price had replaced the oil furnace with a propane furnace a year earlier and canceled her fill order with High Pointe. Somehow, though, her address was mistakenly included on a "keep full list." Despite the fact that Price's house was eventually rebuilt, her land was remediated, her personal belongings cleaned or replaced, and her expenses while she was displaced from her home covered, she sued High Pointe for negligence, including claims for noneconomic damages.

History A Michigan jury found for Price on the claim they heard and awarded her $100,000. The Michigan appellate court affirmed. High Pointe appealed to the Michigan Supreme Court.

Issues Should the Michigan common law include the recognition of noneconomic damages for the negligent destruction of real property?

Holdings Michigan common law has never allowed the recovery of noneconomic damages for the negligent destruction of real or personal property and the court will not adopt a new common law rule doing so in this case.

Reasoning The longstanding rule in Michigan is that the remedy for the negligent destruction of property is the market value of the property if it is destroyed or the repair cost of the property if it is only damaged. No cases have ever held differently. Two recent cases applied the exclusion of noneconomic damages to claims regarding personal property, and the Court found that the current case was not distinguishable from those cases.

Consistent with the proper caution courts should exercise when considering changing the common law, the Court further declined to modify that longstanding rule for a number of reasons. The rule is rational and can be justified by important considerations of public policy, including:

1. A reliance on the market for valuation of property;

2. Easy verifiability, quantifiability, and measurability of economic damages (and concomitant difficulty of those in noneconomic damages);

3. Avoidance of disparity among the valuation of the same property in different cases; and

4. Certainty for businesses that have frequent contact with property and might damage it through negligence.

The Legislature is the appropriate entity to change the rule if it sees fit.

Result The Supreme Court of Michigan reversed the judgment of the Court of Appeals and remanded the case to the trial court to enter judgment in favor of High Pointe.

Problems and Problem Cases

1. In August 2002, Dayle Trentadue, as the daughter and representative of the estate of Margarette Eby, sued various parties for their part in Eby's 1986 murder at the home she rented in Flint, Michigan. The murder had been unsolved from 1986 until 2002, when DNA evidence established that Jeffrey Gorton had committed the crime. Gorton worked for his parents' corporation, which serviced the sprinkler system on the grounds surrounding the rental home where Eby lived.

   In addition to Gorton, Trentadue sued Gorton's parents, their corporation, the estate of the rental-home owner, the property management company that managed the rental home, and two employees of the rental-home owner. The claims against the parties other than Gorton were negligence-based wrongful death theories. Those parties asked the court to dismiss Trentadue's lawsuit against them, claiming the action was barred by Michigan's three-year statute of limitations for wrongful death actions.

   Statutes of limitations require that a plaintiff who wishes to make a legal claim must file her lawsuit within a designated length of time after her claim accrues. Normally a claim accrues at the time the legal wrong was committed. If the plaintiff does not file her lawsuit within the time specified by the applicable statute of limitations, her claim cannot lawfully be pursued.

   The defendants other than Gorton argued that Trentadue's case should be dismissed because her claim accrued when Eby was killed in 1986—meaning that the 2002 filing of the lawsuit occurred long after the three-year period had expired. Trentadue responded that a common law rule known as the "discovery rule" should be applied so as to suspend the running of the limitations period until 2002, when she learned the identity of Eby's killer. Under the discovery rule, the 2002 filing of the lawsuit would have been timely because the limitations period would have been tolled, or suspended, until the 2002 discovery that Gorton was the murderer. The Michigan Compiled Laws (MCL)—the statute that includes the relevant three-year statute of limitations for wrongful death claims—does not include a tolling provision similar to the common law discovery rule for wrongful death claims, even though it does in other areas. Nonetheless, the statute likewise does not explicitly reject the discovery rule.

   How should the court determine whether the common law discovery rule applies to Trentadue's claims or whether it has been displaced by the MCL's statute of limitations?

2. Which of the following types of law will have priority in the event that they present an unresolvable and unavoidable conflict?

   • A federal administrative regulation and a state statute.
   • A federal statute and the U.S. Constitution.
   • A federal statute and a federal administrative regulation.

- A state constitution and a treaty that has been ratified by Congress.

3. The Freedom of Access to Clinic Entrances Act (FACE), a federal statute, provides for penalties against anyone who "by force or threat of force or by physical obstruction . . . intentionally injures, intimidates, or interferes . . . with any person . . . in order to intimidate such person . . . from obtaining or providing reproductive health services." Two persons, Lynch and Moscinski, blocked access to a clinic that offered such services. The federal government sought an injunction barring Lynch and Moscinski from impeding access to, or coming within 15 feet of, the clinic. In defense, the defendants argued that FACE protects the taking of innocent human life, that FACE is therefore contrary to natural law, and that, accordingly, FACE should be declared null and void. A federal district court issued the injunction after finding that Lynch and Moscinski had violated FACE by making entrance to the clinic unreasonably difficult. On appeal, the defendants maintained that the district court erred in not recognizing their natural law argument as a defense. Were the defendants correct?

4. Many states and localities used to have so-called Sunday Closing laws—statutes or ordinances forbidding certain business from being conducted on Sunday. A few may still have such laws. Often, these laws have not been obeyed or enforced. What would an extreme legal positivist tend to think about the duty to enforce and obey such laws? What would a natural law exponent who strongly believes in economic freedom tend to think about this question? What about a natural law adherent who is a Christian religious traditionalist? What observation would almost any legal realist make about Sunday Closing laws? With these laws looked at from a sociological perspective, finally, what social factors help explain their original passage, their relative lack of enforcement today, and their continued presence on the books despite their lack of enforcement?

5. Keith Rawlins and his daughter, Jenna, attended the July 20, 2012, baseball game between the Cleveland Indians and the Baltimore Orioles. That night, following the game, the Indians were hosting a post-game fireworks display. As a result, the Cleveland Fire Department ordered that certain sections of spectator seating had to be vacated prior to the display. The Rawlinses' seats were in one of those sections. Rawlins and his daughter claimed that ushers indicated that they had to vacate their seats prior to the end of the game. Though they did not want to leave, they complied, and as they proceeded up the steps to leave the stadium, Rawlins was struck in the head with a foul ball. Rawlins was seriously injured as a result, and Jenna suffered emotional trauma from seeing her father injured in this way. They sued the Indians. Based on the discussion of the common law "baseball rule" in the *Coomer* case in this chapter and the precedents that applied and declined to apply it, if you were the judge in this case, would you apply the baseball rule to shield the Cleveland Indians from liability or would you distinguish this case from those where the baseball rule applies? Why?

6. Linda Hagan and her sister Barbara Parker drank from a bottle of Coke that they both agreed tasted flat. Hagan then held the bottle up to a light and observed what she and Parker thought was a used condom with "oozy stringy stuff coming out of the top." Both women were distressed that they had consumed some foreign material, and Hagan immediately became nauseated. The bottle was later delivered to Coca-Cola for testing. Concerned about what they had drunk, the women went to a health care facility the next day and were given shots. The medical personnel at the clinic told them that they should be tested for HIV. Hagan and Parker were then tested and informed that the results were negative. Six months later, both women were again tested for HIV, and the results were again negative.

   Hagan and Parker brought a negligence action against Coca-Cola. Coca-Cola's beverage analyst testified at trial that he had initially thought, as Hagan and Parker had, that the object in the bottle was a condom; however, upon closer examination, he concluded that the object was a mold and that, to a "scientific certainty," the item floating in the Coke bottle was not a condom.

   There is case law that lays out the so-called impact rule in negligence claims. The rule requires that before a plaintiff may recover damages for emotional distress, she must demonstrate that the emotional stress suffered flowed from injuries sustained in an impact. Nonetheless, there are a number of exceptions to the impact rule, in which a lack of physical impact would not preclude an otherwise viable claim for emotional distress. Those exceptions include bystander cases, wrongful birth cases, negligent stillbirth cases, and bad-faith claims against insurance carriers. Other courts had found that ingestion of a contaminated product could serve in the place of the traditionally required impact.

   Given that Hagan and Parker's claim is in common law, how should the court go about determining whether the impact rule applies to their case?

7. The federal Age Discrimination in Employment Act (ADEA) makes it unlawful for employers "to fail or refuse to hire or to discharge any individual or otherwise discriminate against any individual with respect to his compensation, terms, conditions, or privileges of employment, because of such individual's age." The ADEA also provides that the statute's protection against discrimination applies only when the affected individual is at least 40 years of age. A pre-1997 collective bargaining agreement between the United Auto Workers (UAW) and General Dynamics Land Systems, Inc. (GDLS) called for GDLS to furnish health benefits to retired employees who had worked for the company for a qualifying number of years. In 1997, however, the UAW and GDLS entered into a new collective bargaining agreement that eliminated the obligation of GDLS to provide health benefits to employees who retired after the effective date of the new agreement, except for then-current workers who were at least 50 years old at the time of the agreement. Employees in that 50-and-over category would still receive health benefits when they retired.

Dennis Cline and certain other GDLS employees objected to the new collective bargaining agreement because they were under 50 years of age when the agreement was adopted, and thus would not receive health benefits when they retired. Cline and the other objecting employees were all at least 40 years of age. In a proceeding before the Equal Employment Opportunity Commission (EEOC), Cline and the similarly situated employees asserted that the 1997 agreement violated the ADEA because they were within the ADEA's protected class of persons (those at least 40 years of age) and because the agreement discriminated against them "with respect to . . . compensation, terms, conditions, or privileges of employment, because of [their] age" (quoting the ADEA). They contended that age discrimination occurred when their under-50 age served as the basis for denying them the more favorable treatment to be received by persons 50 years of age or older. After no settlement occurred despite the EEOC's encouragement, Cline and the similarly situated employees sued GDLS for a supposed violation of the ADEA. In asserting that they had been discriminated against in favor of older workers, did Cline and the other plaintiffs state a valid claim under the ADEA?

8. A federal statute known as the Freedom of Information Act (FOIA) establishes a general rule that federal agencies must make records and documents publicly available upon submission of a proper request. However, if those records or documents fall within certain exemptions set forth in FOIA, they can be withheld from public disclosure.

After the Federal Communications Commission (FCC) conducted an investigation of AT&T regarding AT&T's possible overbilling of the government under an FCC-administered program, the FCC and AT&T entered into an agreement to settle any allegations of wrongdoing. The agreement included a payment from AT&T to the government of $500,000, though AT&T admitted no wrongdoing.

Subsequently, a trade association and some of AT&T's competitors submitted a FOIA request to the FCC for records related to the investigation. The FCC withheld certain documents that contained AT&T trade secrets, pursuant to a specific FOIA exemption. But the FCC determined that other documents not containing trade secrets had to be disclosed despite AT&T's contention that they should not be disclosed under Exemption 7(C), which exempts "records or information compiled for law enforcement purposes" if the records "could reasonably be expected to constitute unwarranted invasion of personal privacy." The FCC determined that Exemption 7(C) did not apply because corporations like AT&T, unlike humans, do not possess "personal privacy" interests.

This dispute ultimately ended up in court, requiring judges to determine the meaning of "personal privacy" in Exemption 7(C). How might a judge go about determining whether Exemption 7(C) applies to AT&T's interests?

9. Law enforcement officers arrived at a Minnesota residence in order to execute arrest warrants for Andrew Hyatt. During the officers' attempt to make the arrest, Hyatt yelled something such as, "Go ahead, just shoot me, shoot me," and struck one of the officers. Another officer then called for assistance from City of Anoka, Minnesota, police officer Mark Yates, who was elsewhere in the residence with his leashed police dog, Chips. Yates entered the room where Hyatt was, saw the injured officer's bloodied face, and observed Hyatt standing behind his wife (Lena Hyatt). One of the officers acquired the impression that Lena may have been serving as a shield for her husband. When Andrew again yelled, "Shoot me, shoot me" and ran toward the back of the room, Yates released Chips from the leash. Instead of pursuing Andrew, Chips apprehended Lena, taking her to the ground and performing a "bite and hold" on her leg and arm. Yates then pursued Andrew, who had fled through a window. When Yates

later reentered the room, he released Chips from Lena and instructed another officer to arrest her on suspicion of obstruction of legal process. Lena was taken by ambulance to a hospital and treated for lacerations on her elbow and knee. She later sued the City of Anoka, seeking compensation for medical expenses and pain and suffering. Her complaint alleged liability on the basis of Minnesota's dog bite statute, which read as follows:

> If a dog, without provocation, attacks or injures any person who is acting peaceably in any place where the person may lawfully be, the owner of the dog is liable in damages to the person so attacked or injured to the full amount of the injury sustained. The term "owner" includes any person harboring or keeping a dog but the owner shall be primarily liable. The term "dog" includes both male and female of the canine species.

In defense, the city argued that the dog bite statute does not apply to police dogs and municipalities that own them. Was the city correct?

10. Roommates.com, LLC ("Roommates") operated a widely used website designed to match people renting out spare rooms with people looking for a place to live. Before subscribers to Roommates could search listings or post housing opportunities on the website, they had to create profiles by answering a series of questions. Besides requesting basic information such as name, location, and e-mail address, Roommates required each subscriber to disclose his or her sex and sexual orientation and whether he or she would bring children to a household. Each subscriber was further required to describe his or her roommate preferences with respect to the same three criteria (sex, sexual orientation, and whether children would be brought to the household). Roommates also encouraged subscribers to provide "Additional Comments" describing themselves and their desired roommate in an open-ended essay. After a new subscriber completed the application, Roommates would assemble his or her answers into a profile page. Subscribers to Roommates were entitled to view their own profile pages and those of others, send personal e-mail messages through the site, and receive notices from Roommates regarding available housing opportunities matching their preferences.

The Fair Housing Councils of the San Fernando Valley and San Diego ("Councils") sued Roommates, alleging that its activities violated the federal Fair Housing Act ("FHA"). The FHA prohibits discrimination in the sale or rental of housing on the basis of "race, color, religion, sex, familial status, or national origin." The FHA also bars

> mak[ing], print[ing], or publish[ing], or caus[ing] to be made, printed, or published, any notice, statement, or advertisement, with respect to the sale or rental of a dwelling that indicates any preference, limitation, or discrimination based on race, color, religion, sex, handicap, familial status, or national origin, or an intention to make any such preference, limitation, or discrimination.

Roommates argued, however, that it was immune from liability under § 230 of the federal Communications Decency Act, which provides that "[n]o provider . . . of an interactive computer service shall be treated as the publisher or speaker of any information provided by another information content provider." Did § 230 protect Roommates against liability?

The Resolution of
Private Disputes

Allnews Publishing Inc., a firm whose principal offices are located in Orlando, Florida, owns and publishes 33 newspapers. These newspapers are published in 21 different states of the United States. Among the Allnews newspapers is the *Snakebite Rattler*, the lone newspaper in the city of Snakebite, New Mexico. The *Rattler* is sold in print form only in New Mexico. However, many of the articles in the newspaper can be viewed by anyone with Internet access, regardless of his or her geographic location, by going to the Allnews website.

In a recent *Rattler* edition, an article appeared beneath this headline: "Local Business Executive Sued for Sexual Harassment." The accompanying article, written by a *Rattler* reporter (an Allnews employee), stated that a person named Phil Anderson was the defendant in the sexual harassment case. Besides being married, Anderson was a well-known businessperson in the Snakebite area. He was active in his church and in community affairs in both Snakebite (his city of primary home) and Petoskey, Michigan (where he and his wife have a summer home). A stock photo of Anderson, which had been used in connection with previous *Rattler* stories mentioning him, appeared alongside the story about the sexual harassment case. Anderson, however, was not the defendant in that case. He was named in the *Rattler* story because of an error by the *Rattler* reporter. The actual defendant in the sexual harassment case was a local business executive with a similar name: Phil Anderer.

Anderson plans to file a defamation lawsuit against Allnews because of the above-described falsehood in the *Rattler* story. He expects to seek $500,000 in damages for harm to his reputation and for other related harms. In Chapter 6, you will learn about the substantive legal issues that will arise in Anderson's defamation case. *For now, however, the focus is on important legal matters of a procedural nature.*

Consider the following questions regarding Anderson's case as you read this chapter:

- Where, in a geographic sense, may Anderson properly file and pursue his lawsuit against Allnews?
- Must Anderson pursue his case in a state court, or does he have the option of litigating it in federal court?
- Assuming that Anderson files his case in a state court, what strategic option may Allnews exercise if it acts promptly?
- In the run-up to a possible trial in the case, what legal mechanisms may Anderson utilize in order to find out, on a pretrial basis, what the *Rattler* reporter and other Allnews employees would say in possible testimony at trial? Is Allnews entitled to do the same with regard to Anderson?
- If Anderson's case goes to trial, what types of trials are possible?
- Through what legal mechanisms might a court decide the case without a trial?
- Today, many legal disputes are decided through arbitration rather than through proceedings in court. Given the prevalence of arbitration these days, why isn't Anderson's case a candidate for arbitration?

BUSINESS LAW COURSES examine many substantive legal rules that tell us how to behave in business and in society. Examples include the principles of contract, tort, and agency law, as well as those of many other legal areas addressed later in this text. Most of these principles are applied by courts as they decide civil cases involving private parties. This chapter lays a foundation for the text's discussion of substantive legal rules by examining the court systems of the United States and by outlining how civil cases proceed from beginning to end. The chapter also explores related subjects, including *alternative dispute resolution*, a collection of processes for resolving private disputes outside the court systems.

State Courts and Their Jurisdiction

 LO2-1   Describe the basic structures of state court systems and the federal court system.

The United States has 52 court systems—a federal system plus a system for each state and the District of Columbia. This section describes the various types of state courts. It also considers the important subject of *jurisdiction*, something a court must have if its decision in a case is to be binding on the parties.

Courts of Limited Jurisdiction
Minor criminal cases and civil disputes involving small amounts of money or specialized matters frequently are decided in *courts of limited jurisdiction*. Examples include traffic courts, probate courts, and small claims courts. Such courts often handle a large number of cases. In some of

these courts, procedures may be informal, and parties often argue their own cases without representation by attorneys. Courts of limited jurisdiction often are not courts of record—meaning that they may not keep a transcript of the proceedings conducted. Appeals from their decisions therefore require a new trial (a trial *de novo*) in a trial court.

Trial Courts
Courts of limited jurisdiction find the relevant facts, identify the appropriate rule(s) of law, and combine the facts and the law to reach a decision. State trial courts do the same but differ from inferior courts in two key ways. First, they are not governed by the subject-matter restrictions or the limits on civil damages or criminal penalties that govern courts of limited jurisdiction. Cases involving significant dollar amounts or major criminal penalties usually begin, therefore, at the trial court level. Second, trial courts are courts of record that keep detailed records of hearings, trials, and other proceedings. These records become important if a trial court decision is appealed. The trial court's fact-finding function may be handled by the judge or by a jury. Determination of the applicable law, however, is always the judge's responsibility. In cases pending in trial courts, the parties nearly always are represented by attorneys.

States usually have at least one trial court for each county. It may be called a circuit, superior, district, county, chancery, or common pleas court. Most state trial courts can hear a wide range of civil and criminal cases, with little or no subject-matter restriction. They may, however, have civil and criminal divisions. If no court of limited jurisdiction deals with these matters, state trial courts may also contain other divisions such as domestic relations courts or probate courts.

Appellate Courts State appeals (or appellate) courts generally decide only legal questions. Instead of receiving new evidence or otherwise retrying the case, appellate courts review the record of the trial court proceedings. Although appellate courts correct legal errors made by the trial judge, they usually accept the trial court's findings of fact. Appellate courts may also hear appeals from state administrative agency decisions. Some states have only one appeals court (usually called the Supreme Court), but most also have an intermediate appellate court. The U.S. Supreme Court sometimes hears appeals from decisions of the state's highest court.

Jurisdiction and Venue

 Explain the difference between subject-matter jurisdiction and in personam jurisdiction.

The party who sues in a civil case (the plaintiff) cannot sue the defendant (the party being sued) in whatever court the plaintiff happens to prefer. Instead, the chosen court—whether a state court or a federal court—must have **jurisdiction** over the case. Jurisdiction is a court's power to hear a case and to issue a decision binding on the parties. In order to render a binding decision in a civil case, a court must have not only subject-matter jurisdiction but also in personam jurisdiction or in rem jurisdiction. Even if a court has jurisdiction, applicable **venue** requirements must also be satisfied in order for the case to proceed in that court.

Subject-Matter Jurisdiction Subject-matter jurisdiction is a court's power to decide the *type* of dispute involved in the case. Criminal courts, for example, cannot hear civil matters. Similarly, a $500,000 claim for breach of contract cannot be pursued in a small claims court.

In Personam Jurisdiction

 Identify the major legal issues courts must resolve when deciding whether in personam jurisdiction exists with regard to a defendant in a civil case.

Even a court with subject-matter jurisdiction cannot decide a civil case unless it also has either **in personam jurisdiction** or **in rem jurisdiction**. In personam jurisdiction is based on the residence, location, or activities of the defendant. A state court has in personam jurisdiction over defendants who are citizens or residents of the state (even if situated out-of-state), who are within the state's borders when

process is served on them (even if nonresidents),[1] or who consent to the court's authority (for instance, by entering the state to defend against the plaintiff's claim).[2] The same principle governs federal courts' in personam jurisdiction over defendants.

In addition, most states have enacted "long-arm" statutes that are designed to give their courts in personam jurisdiction over out-of-state defendants in certain instances. Under these statutes, nonresident individuals and businesses may become subject to the jurisdiction of the state's courts by, for example, doing business within the state, contracting to supply goods or services within the state, committing a tort (a civil wrong) within the state, or committing a tort outside the state if it produces harm within the state. (Some long-arm statutes are phrased with even broader application in mind, so that in personam jurisdiction may extend as far as the U.S. Constitution's Due Process clauses permit.) Federal law, moreover, permits federal courts to rely on state long-arm statutes as a basis for obtaining in personam jurisdiction over nonresident defendants.

Even if a long-arm statute applies, however, a state or federal court's assertion of in personam jurisdiction over a nonresident defendant must also meet due process standards. In *International Shoe Co. v. Washington* (1945), the U.S. Supreme Court held that in order for due process requirements to be satisfied when a state or federal court asserts in personam jurisdiction over a nonresident defendant, the defendant must be shown to have had the requisite "minimum contacts" with the forum state or federal district. These contacts must be significant enough that it would not offend "traditional notions of fair play and substantial justice" to require the nonresident defendant to defend the case in the forum state or federal district.

After *International Shoe*, in personam jurisdiction cases involving nonresident defendants became divided into two categories: general jurisdiction and specific jurisdiction. In *Abdouch v. Lopez*, which follows, the Supreme Court of Nebraska explains each of these types of in personam jurisdiction and goes on to address the specific jurisdiction arguments made in the case. In *Daimler AG v. Bauman*, which serves as a basis of the Global Business Environment box that appears later in the chapter, the U.S. Supreme Court decides whether general jurisdiction exists regarding a German firm sued in the United States over actions that occurred outside the United States.

---

[1]Service of process is discussed later in the chapter.

[2]In many states, however, out-of-state defendants may make a *special appearance* to challenge the court's jurisdiction without consenting to the court's authority.

Abdouch v. Lopez   829 N.W.2d 662 (Neb. 2013)

Helen Abdouch, an Omaha, Nebraska, resident, served as executive secretary of the Nebraska presidential campaign of John F. Kennedy in 1960. Ken Lopez, a Massachusetts resident, and his Massachusetts-based company, Ken Lopez Bookseller (KLB), are engaged in the rare book business. In 1963, Abdouch received a copy of a book titled Revolutionary Road. *Its author, Richard Yates, inscribed the copy with a note to Abdouch. The inscribed copy was later stolen from Abdouch. In 2009, Lopez and KLB bought the inscribed copy from a seller in Georgia. They sold it that same year to a customer from a state other than Nebraska. In 2011, Abdouch learned that Lopez had used the inscription and references to her in an advertisement on KLB's website. The advertisement, which appeared on the website for more than three years after Lopez and KLB sold the inscribed copy, contained a picture of the inscription, the word "SOLD," and this statement:*

> *This copy is inscribed by Yates: 'For Helen Abdouch—with admiration and best wishes. Dick Yates. 8/19/63.' Yates had worked as a speech writer for Robert Kennedy when Kennedy served as Attorney General; Abdouch was the executive secretary of the Nebraska (John F.) Kennedy organization when Robert Kennedy was campaign manager. . . . A scarce book, and it is extremely uncommon to find this advance issue of it signed. Given the date of the inscription—that is, during JFK's Presidency—and the connection between writer and recipient, it's reasonable to suppose this was an author's copy, presented to Abdouch by Yates.*

Because Lopez and KLB did not obtain her permission before mentioning her and using the inscription in the advertisement, Abdouch filed an invasion-of-privacy lawsuit against Lopez and KLB in a Nebraska state district court. Contending that the Nebraska court lacked in personam jurisdiction, Lopez and KLB filed a motion to dismiss the case. The state district court granted the motion. Abdouch then appealed to the Supreme Court of Nebraska. (Further facts bearing upon the in personam jurisdiction issue appear in the following edited version of the Supreme Court's opinion.)

McCormack, Judge

Abdouch argues that the district court erred in finding that the State lacked in personam jurisdiction [, often referred to here as *personal jurisdiction*,] over Lopez and KLB. Abdouch argues that [the defendants'] active website deliberately targeted her with tortious conduct. She alleges these contacts are sufficient to create the necessary minimum contacts for specific jurisdiction.

Personal jurisdiction is the power of a tribunal to subject and bind a particular entity to its decisions. Before a court can exercise personal jurisdiction over a nonresident defendant, the court must determine whether the long-arm statute is satisfied and, if the long-arm statute is satisfied, whether minimum contacts exist between the defendant and the forum state [for due process purposes]. Nebraska's long-arm statute provides: "A court may exercise personal jurisdiction over a person . . . [w]ho has any other contact with or maintains any other relation to this state to afford a basis for the exercise of personal jurisdiction consistent with the Constitution of the United States." Nebraska's long-arm statute, therefore, extends Nebraska's jurisdiction over nonresidents having any contact with or maintaining any relation to this state as far as the U.S. Constitution permits. [T]he issue is whether Lopez and KLB had sufficient contacts with Nebraska so that the exercise of personal jurisdiction would not offend federal principles of due process.

To subject an out-of-state defendant to personal jurisdiction in a forum court, due process requires that the defendant have minimum contacts with the forum state so as not to offend traditional notions of fair play and substantial justice. [*See International Shoe Co. v. Washington*, 326 U.S. 310, 316 (1945).] The benchmark . . . is whether the defendant's minimum contacts with the forum state are such that the defendant should reasonably anticipate being haled into court there. Whether a forum state court has personal jurisdiction over a nonresident defendant depends on whether the defendant's actions created substantial connections with the forum state, resulting in the defendant's purposeful availment of the forum state's benefits and protections.

In analyzing personal jurisdiction, we consider the quality and type of the defendant's activities in deciding whether the defendant has the necessary minimum contacts with the forum state. A court exercises two types of personal jurisdiction depending upon the facts and circumstances of the case: general personal jurisdiction or specific personal jurisdiction. In the exercise of general personal jurisdiction, the plaintiff's claim does not have to arise directly out of the defendant's contacts with the forum state if the defendant has engaged in continuous and systematic general business contacts with the forum state. But if the defendant's contacts are neither substantial nor continuous and systematic, as Abdouch concedes is the case here, and instead the cause of action arises out of or is related to the defendant's contacts with the forum, a court may assert specific jurisdiction over the defendant, depending upon the nature and quality of such contact.

The Internet and its interaction with personal jurisdiction over a nonresident is an issue of first impression for this court. [However,] we take note that technological advances do not render impotent our longstanding principles. With this in mind, [most federal courts of appeal have] adopted the analytical framework set forth in *Zippo Manufacturing Co. v. Zippo Dot Com, Inc.*, 952 F. Supp. 1119 (W.D. Pa. 1997), for Internet jurisdiction cases. In that case, Zippo Manufacturing filed a complaint in Pennsylvania against nonresident Zippo Dot Com, Inc., alleging causes of action under the federal Trademark Act of 1946. Zippo Dot Com's contact with Pennsylvania consisted of over 3,000 Pennsylvania residents subscribing to its website. The court in *Zippo Manufacturing* famously created a "sliding scale" test that considers a website's interactivity and the nature of the commercial activities conducted over the Internet to determine whether the courts have personal jurisdiction over nonresident defendants. The court explained the sliding scale as follows:

> At one end of the spectrum are situations where a defendant clearly does business over the Internet. If the defendant enters into contracts with residents of a foreign jurisdiction that involve the knowing and repeated transmission of computer files over the Internet, personal jurisdiction is proper. . . . At the opposite end are situations where a defendant has simply posted information on an Internet website which is accessible to users in foreign jurisdictions. A passive website that does little more than make information available to those who are interested in it is not grounds for the exercise [of] personal jurisdiction. . . . The middle ground is occupied by interactive websites where a user can exchange information with the host computer. In these cases, the exercise of jurisdiction is determined by examining the level of interactivity and commercial nature of the exchange of information that occurs on the website.

The court in *Zippo Manufacturing* held that Pennsylvania had personal jurisdiction over Zippo Dot Com. In doing so, the court . . . found that the Zippo Dot Com website was a highly interactive commercial site [and] that the trademark infringement causes of action were related to the business contacts with customers in Pennsylvania.

[Although *Zippo Manufacturing*'s test] is widely recognized and accepted, most circuits use it only as a starting point. As the Second Circuit noted, "it does not amount to a separate framework for analyzing Internet-based jurisdiction"; instead, "traditional statutory and constitutional principles remain the touchstone of the inquiry." [Case citation omitted.]

The Seventh Circuit has noted that "[c]ourts should be careful in resolving questions about personal jurisdiction involving online contacts to ensure that a defendant is not haled into court simply because the defendant owns or operates a website that is accessible in the forum state, even if that site is interactive."

[Citation omitted.] Many courts have held that even if the defendant operates a highly interactive website which is accessible from, but does not target, the forum state, then the defendant may not be haled into court in that state without offending the Constitution.

Our precedent states that for there to be specific personal jurisdiction, the cause of action must arise out of or be related to the defendant's contacts with the forum state. This is consistent with the U.S. Supreme Court's precedent which has stated "mere purchases, even if occurring at regular intervals, are not enough to warrant a State's assertion of in personam jurisdiction over a nonresident corporation in a cause of action not related to those purchase transactions." *Helicopteros Nacionales de Colombia v. Hall*, 466 U.S. 408 (1984).

In the case at hand, it is evident that the KLB website is interactive under the *Zippo Manufacturing* test. In his affidavit, Lopez admits that customers can browse and purchase books from the online inventory. Lopez admits that he has two customers in Nebraska who are on the mailing list for KLB's catalogs. He admits that from 2009 through 2011, . . . $614.87 in sales from the website was made to Nebraska residents out of an estimated $3.9 million in total sales. But, beyond the minimal website sales to Nebraska residents and mailing catalogs to two Nebraska residents [who requested them], Lopez's and KLB's contacts with Nebraska are nonexistent. Lopez and KLB do not own, lease, or rent land in Nebraska. They have never advertised directly in Nebraska, participated in bookfairs in Nebraska [despite having participated in many bookfairs in other states], or attended meetings in Nebraska, and neither has paid sales tax in Nebraska.

Furthermore, the Seventh Circuit has recently stated that when "the plaintiff's claims are for intentional torts, the inquiry focuses on whether the conduct underlying the claims was purposely directed at the forum state." [Citation omitted.] The reason for requiring purposeful direction is to "ensure that an out-of-state defendant is not bound to appear to account for merely 'random, fortuitous, or attenuated contacts' with the forum state." *Burger King Corp. v. Rudzewicz*, 471 U.S. 462 (1985). Here, Abdouch's cause of action is an intentional tort based on Nebraska's privacy statute. There is no evidence that Lopez and KLB purposefully directed the advertisement at Nebraska. Further, there is no evidence that Lopez and KLB intended to invade Abdouch's privacy in Nebraska. Rather, the limited Internet sales appear to be random, fortuitous, and attenuated contacts with Nebraska. Therefore, although KLB's website is highly interactive, all of the contacts created by the site with Nebraska are unrelated to Abdouch's cause of action.

Abdouch argues that the effects test formulated by the U.S. Supreme Court in *Calder v. Jones*, 465 U.S. 783 (1984), creates personal jurisdiction over Lopez and KLB. In *Calder*, two Florida residents participated in the publication of [a *National Enquirer*] article about a California resident who brought a libel action in California against the Florida residents. Both defendants asserted that as Florida residents, they were not subject to the jurisdiction of the California court. The Supreme Court rejected the defendants' argument and noted that the defendants [committed]

intentional, and allegedly tortious, actions [that] were expressly aimed at California. [They] wrote and . . . edited an article that they knew would have a potentially devastating impact upon [the plaintiff]. And they knew that the brunt of that injury would be felt by [her] in the State in which she lives and works and in which the National Enquirer has its largest circulation. Under the circumstances, [the defendants] must reasonably anticipate being haled into court there to answer for the truth of the statements made in their article.

[*Calder,* 465 *U.S.* at 789–90.]

In coming to its holding, the U.S. Supreme Court created a test, now known as the *Calder* effects test, which has been explained by the Eighth Circuit: "[A] defendant's tortious acts can serve as a source of personal jurisdiction only where the plaintiff makes a prima facie showing that the defendant's acts (1) were intentional, (2) were uniquely or expressly aimed at the forum state, and (3) caused harm, the brunt of which was suffered—and which the defendant knew was likely to be suffered—[in the forum state]." *Johnson v. Arden,* 614 F.3d 785 (8th Cir. 2010). In the context of Internet intentional tort cases, the federal circuit courts have rejected the argument that [merely] posting defamatory or invasive material to the World Wide Web [is enough to satisfy the *Calder* effects test and give rise to in personam jurisdiction].

[Here,] Lopez's and KLB's placement of the advertisement online was directed at the entire world, without expressly aiming the posting at Nebraska. Abdouch pleaded in her complaint that the advertisement was "broadcast or sent out over the World Wide Web," but Abdouch failed to plead facts that demonstrate that Nebraska residents were targeted with the advertisement. Although the advertisement does mention that "Abdouch was the executive secretary of the Nebraska (John F.) Kennedy organization," the advertisement does not expressly direct its offer of sale to Nebraska. The mention of Nebraska here is incidental and was not included for the purposes of having the consequences felt in Nebraska. Lopez did not know that Abdouch was a resident of Nebraska [until he learned that fact in 2011]. He [initially] assumed that she had passed away and thus had no way of knowing that the brunt of harm would be suffered in Nebraska.

We conclude that Abdouch's complaint fails to plead facts to demonstrate that Lopez and KLB have sufficient minimum contacts with Nebraska. Although the website used to post the advertisement is interactive, the contacts created by the website are unrelated to Abdouch's cause of action. Furthermore, . . . the pleadings fail to establish that Lopez and KLB expressly aimed their tortious conduct at Nebraska. For these reasons, Lopez and KLB could not have anticipated being haled into a Nebraska court for their online advertisement.

Dismissal for lack of in personam jurisdiction affirmed.

The Global Business Environment

Daimler AG v. Bauman   134 S. Ct. 746 (2014)

In 2004, 22 residents of Argentina filed suit in the U.S. District Court for the Northern District of California against Daimler, a German company that manufactures Mercedes-Benz vehicles in Germany. The plaintiffs contended that during Argentina's 1976–1983 "Dirty War," Daimler's subsidiary, Mercedes-Benz Argentina (MB Argentina), collaborated with state security forces to kidnap, detain, torture, and kill certain MB Argentina workers. These workers included the plaintiffs and deceased persons closely related to the plaintiffs. No part of MB Argentina's alleged collaboration with Argentinian authorities took place in California or anywhere else in the United States.

The plaintiffs maintained that Daimler should be held vicariously liable for MB Argentina's actions. They brought claims under U.S. law as well as claims for wrongful death

and intentional infliction of emotional distress under the laws of California and Argentina. Relying on a California long-arm statute that applies to the full extent of what constitutional notions of due process will permit, the plaintiffs contended that in personam jurisdiction over Daimler should be predicated on the California contacts of Mercedes-Benz USA, LLC (MBUSA), another Daimler subsidiary. MBUSA, which is incorporated in Delaware and has its principal place of business in New Jersey, distributes Daimler-manufactured vehicles to dealerships in California and throughout the United States. MBUSA has multiple California-based facilities and is the largest supplier of luxury vehicles to the California market.

Daimler sought dismissal of the case on the ground that the court lacked in personam jurisdiction over it. A federal district court granted Daimler's request. The U.S. Court of Appeals for the Ninth Circuit reversed, concluding that in personam jurisdiction (personal jurisdiction) existed. The U.S. Supreme Court granted Daimler's petition for a writ of certiorari.

Writing for the Supreme Court in *Daimler AG v. Bauman*, Justice Ginsburg noted the landmark decision in *International Shoe Co. v. Washington*, 326 U.S. 310 (1945). That decision's "minimum contacts" doctrine and "fair play and substantial justice" test continue to guide the due process inquiry when in personam jurisdiction over a nonresident defendant is at issue. (See the discussion of *International Shoe* earlier in the chapter.) Justice Ginsburg's *Daimler* majority opinion also outlined the differences between general jurisdiction and specific jurisdiction. (For an explanation of these two types of in personam jurisdiction, see *Abdouch v. Lopez*, a case included earlier in the chapter.) The following excerpts from *Daimler* focus on the question of whether general jurisdiction existed.

Ginsburg, Justice This case concerns the authority of a court in the United States to entertain a claim brought by foreign plaintiffs against a foreign defendant based on events occurring entirely outside the United States. The question presented is whether the Due Process Clause of the Fourteenth Amendment precludes the district court from exercising jurisdiction over Daimler, given the absence of any California connection to the atrocities, perpetrators, or victims described in the complaint.

Plaintiffs invoked the court's general or all-purpose jurisdiction. California, they urge, is a place where Daimler may be sued on any and all claims against it, wherever in the world the claims may arise. For example, as plaintiffs' counsel affirmed, under the proffered jurisdictional theory, if a Daimler-manufactured vehicle overturned in Poland, injuring a Polish driver and passenger, the injured parties could maintain a design defect suit in California. [We must decide whether such] exercises of personal jurisdiction . . . are [permitted or, instead,] barred by due process constraints on the assertion of adjudicatory authority.

In *Goodyear Dunlop Tires Operations, S. A. v. Brown*, 131 S. Ct. 2846 (2011), we addressed the distinction between general or all-purpose jurisdiction, and specific or conduct-linked jurisdiction. As to the former, we held that a court may assert jurisdiction over a foreign corporation "to hear any and all claims against [it]" only when the corporation's affiliations with the State in which suit is brought are so constant and pervasive "as to render [it] essentially at home in the forum State." *Id.* at 2851.

Since [the 1945 decision in] *International Shoe*, "specific jurisdiction has become the centerpiece of modern jurisdiction theory, while general jurisdiction [has played] a reduced role." *Goodyear*, 131 S. Ct. at 2854. Our post-*International Shoe* opinions on general jurisdiction . . . are few. [In] *Perkins v. Benguet Consolidated Mining Co.*, 342 U.S. 437 (1952), an Ohio resident sued Benguet [in an Ohio court] on a claim that neither arose in Ohio nor related to the corporation's activities in that State. [Benguet] was a company incorporated under the laws of the Philippines, where it operated gold and silver mines. [However,] Benguet ceased its mining operations during the Japanese occupation of the Philippines in World War II; its president moved to Ohio, where he kept an office, maintained the company's files, and oversaw the company's activities. We held that [because Ohio was the corporation's principal, if temporary, place of business,] the Ohio courts could exercise general jurisdiction over Benguet without offending due process. *Id.* at 448.

The next case on point, *Helicopteros Nacionales de Colombia, S.A. v. Hall*, 466 U.S. 408 (1984), arose from a helicopter crash in Peru. Four U.S. citizens perished in that accident; their survivors and representatives brought suit in Texas state court against the helicopter's owner and operator, a Colombian corporation. That company's contacts with Texas were confined to "sending its chief executive officer to Houston for a contract-negotiation session; accepting into its New York bank account checks drawn on a Houston bank; purchasing helicopters, equipment, and training services from a Texas-based helicopter company for substantial sums; and sending personnel to Texas for training." *Id.* at 416. Notably, those contacts bore no apparent relationship to the accident that gave rise to the suit. We held that the company's Texas connections did not resemble the "continuous and systematic general business contacts . . . found to exist in *Perkins*." *Id.* "[M]ere purchases, even if occurring at regular intervals," we clarified, "are not enough to warrant a State's assertion of in personam jurisdiction over a nonresident corporation in a cause of action not related to those purchase transactions." *Id.* at 418.

Most recently, in *Goodyear*, we answered this question: "Are foreign subsidiaries of a United States parent corporation amenable to suit in state court on claims unrelated to any activity of the subsidiaries in the forum State?" 131 S. Ct. at 2850. That case arose from a bus accident outside Paris that killed two boys from North Carolina. The boys' parents brought a wrongful-death suit in North Carolina state court alleging that the bus's tire was defectively manufactured. The complaint named as defendants not only Goodyear, an Ohio corporation, but also Goodyear's Turkish, French, and Luxembourgian subsidiaries. Those foreign subsidiaries, which manufactured tires for sale in Europe and Asia, lacked any affiliation with North Carolina. A small percentage of tires manufactured by the foreign subsidiaries were distributed in North Carolina, however, and on that ground, the North Carolina Court of Appeals held the subsidiaries amenable to the general jurisdiction of North Carolina courts.

We reversed, observing that the North Carolina court's analysis "elided the essential difference between case-specific and all-purpose (general) jurisdiction." *Id.* at 2846. Although the placement of a product into the stream of commerce "may bolster an affiliation germane to specific jurisdiction," we explained, such contacts "do not warrant a determination that, based on those ties, the forum has general jurisdiction over a defendant." *Id.* As *International Shoe* itself teaches, a corporation's "continuous activity of some sorts within a state is not enough to support the demand that the corporation be amenable to suits unrelated to that activity." 326 U.S. at 318. Because Goodyear's foreign subsidiaries were "in no sense at home in North Carolina," we held, those subsidiaries could not be required to submit to the general jurisdiction of that State's courts. 131 S. Ct. at 2854.

With this background, we turn directly to the question whether Daimler's affiliations with California are sufficient to subject it to the general (all-purpose) personal jurisdiction of that State's courts. In sustaining the exercise of general jurisdiction over Daimler, the Ninth Circuit relied on an agency theory, determining that MBUSA acted as Daimler's agent for jurisdictional purposes and then attributing MBUSA's California contacts to Daimler. This Court has not yet addressed whether a foreign corporation may be subjected to a court's general jurisdiction based on the contacts of its in-state subsidiary. But we need not pass judgment on invocation of an agency theory in the context of general jurisdiction, for in no event can the appeals court's analysis be sustained.

The Ninth Circuit's agency finding rested primarily on its observation that MBUSA's services were important to Daimler, as gauged by Daimler's hypothetical readiness to perform those services itself if MBUSA did not exist. Formulated this way, the inquiry into importance stacks the deck, for it will always yield a pro-jurisdiction answer: "Anything a corporation does through an independent contractor, subsidiary, or distributor is presumably something that the corporation would do by other means if the independent contractor, subsidiary, or distributor did not exist." [Citation omitted.] The Ninth Circuit's agency theory thus appears to subject foreign corporations to general jurisdiction whenever they have an in-state subsidiary or affiliate, an outcome that would sweep beyond even the sprawling view of general jurisdiction we rejected in *Goodyear.*

Goodyear made clear that only a limited set of affiliations with a forum will render a defendant amenable to all-purpose jurisdiction there. With respect to a corporation, the place of incorporation and principal place of business are paradigm bases for general jurisdiction. Those affiliations have the virtue of being unique—that is, each ordinarily indicates only one place—as well as easily ascertainable. *Cf. Hertz Corp. v. Friend*, 559 U.S. 77 (2010). These bases afford plaintiffs recourse to at least one clear and certain forum in which a corporate defendant may be sued on any and all claims.

Goodyear did not hold that a corporation may be subject to general jurisdiction only in a forum where it is incorporated or has its principal place of business; it simply typed those places paradigm all-purpose forums. Plaintiffs would have us look beyond the exemplar bases *Goodyear* identified, and approve the exercise of general jurisdiction in every State in which a corporation "engages in a substantial, continuous, and systematic course of business" [quoting the plaintiffs' brief]. That formulation, we hold, is unacceptably grasping.

[The relevant] inquiry under [*International Shoe* and] *Goodyear* is not whether a foreign corporation's in-forum contacts can be said to be in some sense "continuous and systematic," it is whether that corporation's "affiliations with the State are so continuous and systematic as to render [it] essentially at home in the forum State." *Goodyear*, 131 S. Ct. at 2851. Here, neither Daimler nor MBUSA is incorporated in California, nor does either entity have its principal place of business there. If Daimler's California activities sufficed to allow adjudication of this Argentina-rooted case in California, the same global reach would presumably be available in every other State in which MBUSA's sales are sizable. Such exorbitant exercises of all-purpose jurisdiction would scarcely permit out-of-state defendants "to structure their primary conduct with some minimum assurance as to where that conduct will and will not render them liable to suit." [Citation omitted.]

It was therefore error for the Ninth Circuit to conclude that Daimler, even with MBUSA's contacts attributed to it, was at home in California, and hence subject to suit there on claims by foreign plaintiffs having nothing to do with anything that occurred or had its principal impact in California.

Ninth Circuit decision reversed; Daimler held not subject to court's in personam jurisdiction.

In Rem Jurisdiction   In rem jurisdiction is based on the presence of *property* within the state. It empowers state courts to determine rights in that property even if the persons whose rights are affected are outside the state's in personam jurisdiction. For example, a state court's decision regarding title to land within the state is said to bind the world.[3]

Venue   Even if a court has jurisdiction, it may be unable to decide the case because **venue** requirements have not been met. Venue questions arise only after jurisdiction is established or assumed. In general, a court has venue if it is a territorially fair and convenient forum in which to hear the case. Venue requirements applicable to state

---

[3]Another form of jurisdiction, *quasi in rem jurisdiction* or *attachment jurisdiction*, also is based on the presence of property within the state. Unlike cases based on in rem jurisdiction, cases based on quasi in rem jurisdiction do not necessarily determine rights in the property itself. Instead, the property is regarded as an extension of the out-of-state defendant—an extension that sometimes enables the court to decide claims unrelated to the property. For example, a plaintiff might attach the defendant's bank account in the state where the bank is located, sue the defendant on a tort or contract claim unrelated to the bank account, and recover the amount of the judgment from the account if the suit is successful.

courts typically are set by state statutes, which normally determine the county in which a case must be brought. For instance, the statute might say that a case concerning land must be filed in the county where the land is located, and that other suits must be brought in the county where the defendant resides or is doing business. If justice so requires, the defendant may be able to obtain a *change of venue*. This can occur when, for example, a fair trial would be impossible within a particular county.

Role of Forum Selection Clauses Contracts sometimes contain a clause reciting that disputes between the parties regarding matters connected with the contract must be litigated in the courts of a particular state. Such a provision is known as a ***forum selection clause***. Depending on its wording, a forum selection clause may have the effect of addressing both jurisdiction and venue issues. Although forum selection clauses may appear in agreements whose terms have been hammered out by the parties after extensive negotiation, they fairly often are found in form agreements whose terms were not the product of actual discussion or give-and-take. For example, an Internet access provider (IAP) may include a forum selection clause in a so-called clickwrap document that sets forth the terms of its Internet-related services—terms to which the IAP's subscribers are deemed to have agreed by virtue of utilizing the IAP's services. Forum selection clauses, whether expressly bargained for or included in a clickwrap agreement, are generally enforced by courts unless they are shown to be unreasonable in a given set of circumstances. Assume, for instance, that the IAP's terms of service document calls for the courts of Virginia to have "exclusive jurisdiction" over its subscribers' disputes with the company, but that a subscriber sues the IAP in a Pennsylvania court. Unless the subscriber performs the difficult task of demonstrating that application of the clickwrap agreement's forum selection clause would be unreasonable, the Pennsylvania court will be likely to dismiss the case and to hold that if the subscriber wishes to litigate the claim, he or she must sue in an appropriate Virginia court.

Federal Courts and Their Jurisdiction

Federal District Courts

 LO2-1 Describe the basic structures of state court systems and the federal court system.

In the federal system, lawsuits usually begin in the federal district courts. As do state trial courts, the federal district courts determine both the facts and the law. The fact-finding function may be entrusted to either the judge or a jury, but determining the applicable law is the judge's responsibility. Each state is designated as a separate district for purposes of the federal court system. Each district has at least one district court, and each district court has at least one judge.

District Court Jurisdiction

LO2-4 Explain what is necessary in order for a federal court to have subject-matter jurisdiction over a civil case.

There are various bases of federal district court civil jurisdiction. The two most important are **diversity jurisdiction** and **federal question jurisdiction**. One traditional justification for diversity jurisdiction is that it may help protect out-of-state defendants from potentially biased state courts. *Diversity jurisdiction* exists when (1) the case is between citizens of different states and (2) the amount in controversy exceeds $75,000. Diversity jurisdiction also exists in certain cases between citizens of a state and citizens or governments of foreign nations, if the amount in controversy exceeds $75,000. Under diversity jurisdiction, a corporation is a citizen of both the state where it has been incorporated and the state where it has its principal place of business. For an example of diversity jurisdiction and an explanation of how a corporation's principal place of business is to be determined for diversity jurisdiction purposes, see the U.S. Supreme Court's *Hertz* decision, which follows shortly.

Federal question jurisdiction exists when the case arises under the Constitution, laws, or treaties of the United States. The "arises under" requirement normally is met when a right created by federal law is a basic part of the plaintiff's case. There is no amount-in-controversy requirement for federal question jurisdiction.

Diversity jurisdiction and federal question jurisdiction are forms of subject-matter jurisdiction. Even if one of the two forms exists, a federal district court must also have in personam jurisdiction in order to render a decision that is binding on the parties. As indicated earlier in the chapter, the analysis of in personam jurisdiction issues in the federal court system is essentially the same as in the state court systems. Further limiting the plaintiff's choice of federal district courts are the federal system's complex venue requirements, which are beyond the scope of this text.

Concurrent Jurisdiction and Removal The federal district courts have *exclusive jurisdiction* over some matters. Patent cases, for example, must be litigated in the federal system. Often, however, federal district courts have *concurrent jurisdiction* with state courts—meaning that both state and federal courts have jurisdiction over the case. For example, a plaintiff might assert state court in personam jurisdiction over an out-of-state defendant or might sue in a federal district court under that court's diversity jurisdiction. A state court, moreover, may sometimes decide cases involving federal questions. Where concurrent jurisdiction exists and the plaintiff opts for a state court, the defendant has the option to *remove* the case to an appropriate federal district court, assuming the defendant acts promptly. The *Hertz* decision, which follows, provides an example of a defendant's ability to have a case removed from state court to federal court in an instance of concurrent jurisdiction.

Hertz Corp. v. Friend   559 U.S. 77 (2010)

Alleging violations of California's wage and hour laws, California citizens Melinda Friend and John Nhieu sued Hertz Corporation in a California state court. Hertz filed a notice seeking removal of the case to a federal court on the basis of diversity-of-citizenship jurisdiction. The relevant federal statute provides that a federal court possesses diversity jurisdiction if the plaintiff and defendant are citizens of different states and the amount in controversy exceeds $75,000. The statute further provides that "a corporation shall be deemed to be a citizen of any State by which it has been incorporated and of the State where it has its principal place of business."

In seeking removal, Hertz argued that diversity jurisdiction was appropriate because the plaintiffs and the defendant were citizens of different states and more than $75,000 was in controversy. The plaintiffs contended, however, that Hertz was a California citizen (just as they were) and that the case should therefore remain in state court. Hertz submitted a declaration meant to demonstrate that its "principal place of business" was in New Jersey rather than in California. Besides stressing that Hertz was a national operation with car rental locations in 44 states, the declaration recited a series of statistics indicating that California accounted for approximately 20 percent of Hertz's rental locations, full-time employees, annual revenue, and annual car rental transactions. The declaration also listed Park Ridge, New Jersey, as the location of Hertz's corporate headquarters and stated that Hertz's core executive and administrative functions are conducted there.

In deciding whether Hertz was a California citizen for purposes of the diversity jurisdiction statute, the U.S. District Court for the Northern District of California applied Ninth Circuit Court of Appeals precedent instructing courts to identify a corporation's principal place of business by first determining the amount of a corporation's business activity state by state. Then, if the amount of activity was significantly larger or substantially predominated in one state, that state would be considered the corporation's principal place of business. Applying the Ninth Circuit's test to the relevant facts, the federal district court reasoned that the extent of Hertz's business activities in California, as compared with its activities in other states, made California Hertz's principal place of business. Because it concluded that Hertz was a California citizen and that diversity jurisdiction did not exist, the district court ordered that the case be remanded to state court. Hertz appealed this order to the Ninth Circuit Court of Appeals, which affirmed. The U.S. Supreme Court agreed to decide the case at Hertz's request.

Breyer, Justice

The federal diversity jurisdiction statute provides that "a corporation shall be deemed to be a citizen of any State by which it has been incorporated and of the State where it has its principal place of business." We seek here to resolve different interpretations that the [federal courts of appeal] have given this phrase. In doing so, we place primary weight upon the need for judicial administration of a jurisdictional statute to remain as simple as possible.

The phrase "principal place of business" has proved . . . difficult to apply. [C]ourts were . . . uncertain as to where to look to determine a corporation's "principal place of business" for diversity purposes. If a corporation's headquarters and executive offices were in the same state in which it did most of its business, the test seemed straightforward. The "principal place of business" was located in that state. But suppose those corporate headquarters, including executive offices, are in one state, while the corporation's plants or other centers of business activity are located in other states? In 1959 a distinguished federal district judge, Edward Weinfeld, answer[ed] this question in part:

Where a corporation is engaged in far-flung and varied activities which are carried on in different states, its principal place of business is the nerve center from which it radiates out to its constituent parts and from which its officers direct, control and coordinate all activities without regard to locale, in the furtherance of the corporate objective. The test . . . is that place where the corporation has an office from which its business was directed and controlled—the place where all of its business was under the supreme direction and control of its officers.

Scot Typewriter Co. v. Underwood Corp., 170 F. Supp. 862, 865 (S.D.N.Y. 1959).

Numerous [circuit courts of appeal] have since followed this rule, applying the "nerve center" test for corporations with "far-flung" business activities. *Scot*'s analysis, however, did not go far enough. For it did not answer what courts should do when the operations of the corporation are not "far-flung" but rather limited to only a few states. When faced with this question, various courts have focused more heavily on where a corporation's actual business activities are located.

Perhaps because corporations come in many different forms, involve many different kinds of business activities, and locate offices and plants for different reasons in different ways in different regions, a general "business activities" approach has proved unusually difficult to apply. Courts must decide which factors are more important than others: for example, plant location, sales or servicing centers, transactions, payrolls, or revenue generation.

The number of factors grew as courts explicitly combined aspects of the "nerve center" and "business activity" tests to look to a corporation's "total activities," sometimes to try to determine what treatises have described as the corporation's "center of gravity." Not surprisingly, different circuit courts of appeal (and sometimes different courts within a single circuit) have applied these highly general multifactor tests in different ways. This complexity . . . is at war with administrative simplicity. And it has failed to achieve a nationally uniform interpretation of federal law, an unfortunate consequence in a federal legal system.

In an effort to find a single, more uniform interpretation of the statutory phrase, we have reviewed the courts of appeals' divergent and increasingly complex interpretations. [W]e now return to, and expand, Judge Weinfeld's approach [in *Scot*]. We conclude that "principal place of business" is best read as referring to the place where a corporation's officers direct, control, and coordinate the corporation's activities. It is the place that courts of appeals have called the corporation's "nerve center." And in practice it should normally be the place where the corporation maintains its headquarters—provided that the headquarters is the actual center of direction, control, and coordination, *i.e.*, the "nerve center," and not simply an office where the corporation holds its board meetings (for example, attended by directors and officers who have traveled there for the occasion).

[Important considerations] convince us that this approach, while imperfect, is superior to other possibilities. First, the statute's language supports the approach. The statute's text deems a corporation a citizen of the "State where it has its principal place of business." The word "place" is in the singular, not the plural.

The word "principal" requires us to pick out the "main, prominent" or "leading" place. And the fact that the word "place" follows the words "State where" means that the "place" is a place *within* a state. It is not the state itself.

A corporation's "nerve center," usually its main headquarters, is a single place. The public often (though not always) considers it the corporation's main place of business. By contrast, the application of a more general business activities test has led some courts, as in the present case, to look, not at a particular place within a state, but incorrectly at the state itself, measuring the total amount of business activities that the corporation conducts there and determining whether they are significantly larger than in the next-ranking state. This approach invites greater litigation and can lead to strange results, as the Ninth Circuit has since recognized. Namely, if a "corporation may be deemed a citizen of California on th[e] basis" of "activities [that] roughly reflect California's larger population . . . nearly every national retailer— no matter how far flung its operations—will be deemed a citizen of California for diversity purposes." [Case citation omitted.] But why award or decline diversity jurisdiction on the basis of a state's population, whether measured directly, indirectly (say proportionately), or with modifications?

Second, administrative simplicity is a major virtue in a jurisdictional statute. Complex jurisdictional tests complicate a case, eating up time and money as the parties litigate, not the merits of their claims, but which court is the right court to decide those claims. [Moreover,] courts benefit from straightforward rules under which they can readily assure themselves of their power to hear a case. Simple jurisdictional rules also promote greater predictability. Predictability is valuable to corporations making business and investment decisions. Predictability also benefits plaintiffs deciding whether to file suit in a state or federal court.

A "nerve center" approach, which ordinarily equates that "center" with a corporation's headquarters, is simple to apply *comparatively speaking*. The metaphor of a corporate "brain," while not precise, suggests a single location. By contrast, a corporation's general business activities more often lack a single principal place where they take place. That is to say, the corporation may have several plants, many sales locations, and employees located in many different places. If so, it will not be as easy to determine which of these different business locales is the "principal" or most important "place."

We recognize that there may be no perfect test that satisfies all administrative and purposive criteria. We recognize as well that, under the "nerve center" test we adopt today, there will be hard cases. For example, in this era of telecommuting, some corporations may divide their command and coordinating functions among officers who work at several different locations, perhaps communicating over the Internet. That said, our test nonetheless points courts in a single direction, towards the center of overall direction, control, and coordination. Courts do not have to try to weigh corporate functions, assets, or revenues different in kind, one from the other.

We also recognize that the use of a "nerve center" test may in some cases produce results that seem to cut against the basic rationale for [diversity jurisdiction]. For example, if the bulk of a company's business activities visible to the public take place in New Jersey, while its top officers direct those activities just across the river in New York, the "principal place of business" is New York. One could argue that members of the public in New Jersey would be *less* likely to be prejudiced against the corporation than persons in New York—yet the corporation will still be entitled to remove a New Jersey state case to federal court. And note too that the same corporation would be unable to remove a

New York state case to federal court, despite the New York public's presumed prejudice against the corporation.

We understand that such seeming anomalies will arise. However, in view of the necessity of having a clearer rule, we must accept them. Accepting occasionally counterintuitive results is the price the legal system must pay to avoid overly complex jurisdictional administration while producing the benefits that accompany a more uniform legal system.

[In this case, Hertz's] unchallenged declaration suggests that Hertz's center of direction, control, and coordination, its "nerve center," and its corporate headquarters are one and the same, and they are located in New Jersey, not in California.

Ninth Circuit's decision vacated, and case remanded for further proceedings in federal district court.

Specialized Federal Courts

The federal court system also includes certain specialized federal courts, including the Court of Federal Claims (which hears claims against the United States), the Court of International Trade (which is concerned with tariff, customs, import, and other trade matters), the bankruptcy courts (which operate as adjuncts of the district courts), and the Tax Court (which reviews certain IRS determinations). Usually, the decisions of these courts can be appealed to a federal court of appeals.

Federal Courts of Appeals

The U.S. courts of appeals do not engage in fact-finding. Instead, they review only the legal conclusions reached by lower federal courts. As Figure 2.1 shows, there are 13 circuit courts of appeals: 11 numbered circuits covering several states each; a District of Columbia circuit; and a separate federal circuit.

Except for the Court of Appeals for the Federal Circuit, the most important function of the U.S. courts of appeals is to hear appeals from decisions of the federal district courts. Appeals from a district court ordinarily proceed to the court of appeals for that district court's region. Appeals from the District Court for the Southern District of New York, for example, go to the Second Circuit Court of Appeals. The courts of appeals also hear appeals from the Tax Court, from many administrative agency decisions, and from some bankruptcy court decisions. The Court of Appeals for the Federal Circuit hears a wide variety of specialized appeals, including some patent and trademark matters, Court of Federal Claims decisions, and decisions by the Court of International Trade.

The U.S. Supreme Court

The United States Supreme Court, the highest court in the land, is mainly an appellate court. It therefore considers only questions of law when it decides appeals from the federal courts of appeals and the highest state courts.[4] Today, most appealable decisions from these courts fall within the Supreme Court's *certiorari* jurisdiction, under which the Court has discretion whether to hear the appeal. The Court hears only a small percentage of the many appeals it is asked to decide under its certiorari jurisdiction.

Nearly all appeals from the federal courts of appeals are within the Court's certiorari jurisdiction. Appeals from the highest state courts are within the certiorari jurisdiction when (1) the validity of any treaty or federal statute has been questioned; (2) any state statute is challenged as repugnant to federal law; or (3) any title, right, privilege, or immunity is claimed under federal law. The Supreme Court usually defers to the states' highest courts on questions of state law and does not hear appeals from those courts if the case involves only such questions.

In certain rare situations, the U.S. Supreme Court has **original jurisdiction**, which means that it acts as a trial court. The Supreme Court has *original and exclusive* jurisdiction over all controversies between two or more states. It has *original*, but not exclusive, jurisdiction over cases involving foreign ambassadors, ministers, and like parties;

---

[4]In special situations that do not often arise, the Supreme Court will hear appeals directly from the federal district courts.

Figure 2.1   The Thirteen Federal Judicial Circuits

First Circuit (*Boston, Mass.*) Maine, Massachusetts, New Hampshire, Puerto Rico, Rhode Island

Second Circuit (*New York, N.Y.*) Connecticut, New York, Vermont

Third Circuit (*Philadelphia, Pa.*) Delaware, New Jersey, Pennsylvania, Virgin Islands

Fourth Circuit (*Richmond, Va.*) Maryland, North Carolina, South Carolina, Virginia, West Virginia

Fifth Circuit (*New Orleans, La.*) Louisiana, Mississippi, Texas

Sixth Circuit (*Cincinnati, Ohio*) Kentucky, Michigan, Ohio, Tennessee

Seventh Circuit (*Chicago, Ill.*) Illinois, Indiana, Wisconsin

Eighth Circuit (*St. Louis, Mo.*) Arkansas, Iowa, Minnesota, Missouri, Nebraska, North Dakota, South Dakota

Ninth Circuit (*San Francisco, Calif.*) Alaska, Arizona, California, Guam, Hawaii, Idaho, Montana, Nevada, Northern Mariana Islands, Oregon, Washington

Tenth Circuit (*Denver, Colo.*) Colorado, Kansas, New Mexico, Oklahoma, Utah, Wyoming

Eleventh Circuit (*Atlanta, Ga.*) Alabama, Florida, Georgia

District of Columbia Circuit (*Washington, D.C.*)

Federal Circuit (*Washington, D.C.*)

controversies between the United States and a state; and cases in which a state proceeds against citizens of another state or against aliens.

Civil Procedure

 Identify the major steps in a civil lawsuit's progression from beginning to end.

Civil procedure is the set of legal rules establishing how a civil lawsuit proceeds from beginning to end.[5] Because civil procedure sometimes varies with the jurisdiction in question,[6] the following presentation summarizes the most widely accepted rules governing civil cases in state and federal courts. Knowledge of these basic procedural matters will be useful if you become involved in a civil lawsuit and will help you understand the cases in this text.

In any civil case, the *adversary system* is at work. Through their attorneys, the litigants take contrary positions before a judge and possibly a jury. To win a civil case, the plaintiff must prove each element of his, her, or its claim by a *preponderance of the evidence.*[7] This standard of proof requires the plaintiff to show that the greater weight of the evidence—by credibility, not quantity—supports the existence of each element. In other words, the plaintiff must convince the fact-finder that the existence of each element is more probable than its nonexistence. The attorney for each party presents his or her client's version of the facts, tries to convince the judge or jury that this version is true, and attempts to rebut conflicting factual allegations by the other party. Each attorney also seeks to persuade the court that his or her reading of the law is correct.

Service of the Summons   A **summons** notifies the defendant that he, she, or it is being sued. The summons typically names the plaintiff and states the time within which the defendant must enter an *appearance* in court (usually through an attorney). In most jurisdictions,

---

[5]Criminal procedure is discussed in Chapter 5.
[6]In the following discussion, the term *jurisdiction* refers to one of the 50 states, the District of Columbia, or the federal government.

[7]In a criminal case, however, the government must prove the elements of the alleged crime beyond a reasonable doubt. This standard of proof is discussed in Chapter 5.

it is accompanied by a copy of the plaintiff's complaint (which is described later).

The summons is usually served on the defendant by an appropriate public official after the plaintiff has filed her case. To ensure that the defendant is properly notified, statutes, court rules, and constitutional due process guarantees set standards for proper service of the summons. For example, personal delivery to the defendant almost always meets these standards. Many jurisdictions also permit the summons to be left at the defendant's home or place of business. Service to corporations often may be accomplished by delivery of the summons to the firm's managing agent. Many state long-arm statutes permit out-of-state defendants to be served by registered mail. Although inadequate service of process may sometimes defeat the plaintiff's claim, the defendant who participates in the case without making a prompt objection to the manner of service will be deemed to have waived the objection.

The Pleadings

The **pleadings** are the documents the parties file with the court when they first state their respective claims and defenses. They include the **complaint**, the **answer**, and, in some jurisdictions, the **reply**. Traditionally, the pleadings' main function was to define and limit the issues to be decided by the court. Only those issues raised in the pleadings were considered part of the case, amendments to the pleadings were seldom permitted, and litigants were firmly bound by allegations or admissions contained in the pleadings. Although many jurisdictions retain some of these rules, most have relaxed them significantly. The main reason is the modern view of the purpose of pleading rules: that their aim is less to define the issues for trial than to give the parties general notice of each other's claims and defenses.

The Complaint The complaint states the plaintiff's claim in separate, numbered paragraphs. It must allege sufficient facts to show that the plaintiff would be entitled to legal relief and to give the defendant reasonable notice of the nature of the plaintiff's claim. The complaint also must state the remedy requested.

The Answer Unless the defendant makes a successful motion to dismiss (described later), he must file an answer to the plaintiff's complaint within a designated time after service of the complaint. The amount of time is set by applicable law, with 30 to 45 days being typical. The answer responds to the complaint paragraph by paragraph, with an admission or denial of each of the plaintiff's allegations.

An answer may also include an **affirmative defense** to the claim asserted in the complaint. A successful affirmative defense enables the defendant to win the case even if all the allegations in the complaint are true and, by themselves, would have entitled the plaintiff to recover. For example, suppose that the plaintiff bases her lawsuit on a contract that she alleges the defendant has breached. The defendant's answer may admit or deny the existence of the contract or the assertion that the defendant breached it. In addition, the answer may make assertions that, if proven, would provide the defendant an affirmative defense on the basis of fraud committed by the plaintiff during the contract negotiation phase.

Furthermore, the answer may contain a **counterclaim**.[8] A counterclaim is a *new* claim by the defendant arising from the matters stated in the complaint. Unlike an affirmative defense, it is not merely an attack on the plaintiff's claim, but is the defendant's attempt to obtain legal relief. In addition to using fraud as an affirmative defense to a plaintiff's contract claim, for example, a defendant might counterclaim for damages caused by that fraud.

The Reply In some jurisdictions, the plaintiff is allowed or required to respond to an affirmative defense or a counterclaim by making a reply. The reply is the plaintiff's point-by-point response to the allegations in the answer or counterclaim. In jurisdictions that do not allow a reply to an answer, the defendant's new allegations are automatically denied. Usually, however, a plaintiff who wishes to contest a counterclaim must file a reply to it.

Motion to Dismiss

Sometimes it is evident from the complaint or the pleadings that the plaintiff does not have a valid claim. In such a situation, it would be wasteful for the litigation to proceed further. The procedural device for ending the case at this early stage is commonly called the **motion to dismiss**. This motion often is made after the plaintiff has filed her complaint. A similar motion allowed by some jurisdictions, the **motion for judgment on the pleadings**, normally occurs after the pleadings have been completed. A successful motion to dismiss means that the defendant wins the case. If the motion fails, the case proceeds.

The motion to dismiss may be made on various grounds—for example, inadequate service of process or lack of jurisdiction. The most important type of motion to dismiss, however, is the motion to dismiss for failure to state a claim upon which relief can be granted, sometimes

---

[8]In appropriate instances, a defendant also may file a *cross claim* against another defendant in the plaintiff's suit, or a *third-party complaint* against a party who was not named as a defendant in the plaintiff's complaint.

called the **demurrer**. This motion basically says "So what?" to the factual allegations in the complaint. It asserts that the plaintiff cannot recover even if all of his allegations are true because no rule of law entitles him to win on those facts. Suppose that Potter sues Davis on the theory that Davis's bad breath is a form of "olfactory pollution" entitling Potter to recover damages. Potter's complaint describes Davis's breath and the distress it causes Potter in great detail. Even if all of Potter's factual allegations are true, Davis's motion to dismiss almost certainly will succeed. There is no rule of law allowing the "victim" of another person's bad breath to recover damages from that person.

Discovery

 Describe the different forms of discovery available to parties in civil cases.

When a civil case begins, litigants do not always possess all of the facts they need to prove their claims or establish their defenses. To help litigants obtain the facts and to narrow and clarify the issues for trial, the state and federal court systems permit each party to a civil case to exercise **discovery** rights. The discovery phase of a lawsuit normally begins when the pleadings have been completed. Each party is entitled to request information from the other party by utilizing the forms of discovery described in this section. Moreover, for civil cases pending in federal court, the Federal Rules of Civil Procedure require each party to provide the other party certain relevant information at an early point in the case without a formal discovery request by the other party.

Discovery is available for information that is not subject to a recognized legal privilege and is relevant to the case or likely to lead to other information that may be relevant. Information may be subject to discovery even if it would not ultimately be admissible at trial under the legal rules of evidence. The scope of permissible discovery is thus extremely broad. The broad scope of discovery stems from a policy decision to minimize the surprise element in litigation and to give each party the opportunity to become fully informed regarding facts known by the opposing party. Each party may then formulate trial strategies on the basis of that knowledge.

The *deposition* is one of the most frequently employed forms of discovery. In a deposition, one party's attorney conducts an oral examination of the other party or of a likely witness (usually one identified with the other party). The questions asked by the examining attorney and the answers given by the deponent—the person being examined—are taken down by a court reporter. The deponent is under oath, just as he or she would be if testifying at trial, even though the deposition occurs on a pretrial basis and is likely to take place at an attorney's office or at some location other than a courtroom. Some depositions are recorded in audiovisual form.

Interrogatories and *requests for admissions* are among the other commonly utilized forms of discovery. Interrogatories are written questions directed by the plaintiff to the defendant, or vice versa. The litigant on whom interrogatories are served must provide written answers, under oath, within a time period prescribed by applicable law (30 days being typical). Requests for admissions are one party's written demand that the other party admit or deny, in writing, certain statements of supposed fact or of the application of law to fact, within a time period prescribed by law (30 days again being typical). The other party's failure to respond with an admission or denial during the legal time period is deemed an admission of the statements' truth or accuracy.

Requests for production of documents or other physical items (e.g., videos, photographs, and the like) are a discovery form employed by the parties in many civil cases. What about e-mail and other electronically stored information? For a discussion of the discoverability of such items, see the Cyberlaw in Action box that appears later in the chapter.

When the issues in a case make the opposing litigant's physical or mental condition relevant, a party may seek discovery in yet another way by filing a *motion for a court order requiring* that the opponent undergo *a physical or mental examination*. With the exception of the discovery form mentioned in the previous sentence, discovery generally takes place without a need for court orders or other judicial supervision. Courts become involved, however, if a party objects to a discovery request on the basis of privilege or other recognized legal ground, desires an order compelling a noncomplying litigant to respond to a discovery request, or seeks sanctions on a party who refused to comply with a legitimate discovery request or abusively invoked the discovery process.

Documents and similar items obtained through the discovery process may be used at trial if they fall within the legal rules governing admissible evidence. The same is true of discovery material such as answers to interrogatories and responses to requests for admissions. If a party or other witness who testifies at trial offers testimony that differs from her statements during a deposition, the deposition may be used to impeach her—that is, to cast doubt on her trial testimony. A litigant may offer as evidence the deposition of a witness who died prior to trial or meets the legal standard of unavailability to testify in person.

CYBERLAW IN ACTION

In recent years, the widespread uses of e-mail and information presented and stored in electronic form have raised questions about whether, in civil litigation, an opposing party's e-mails and electronic information are discoverable to the same extent as conventional written or printed documents. With the Federal Rules of Civil Procedure and comparable discovery rules applicable in state courts having been devised prior to the explosion in e-mail use and online activities, the rules' references to "documents" contemplated traditional on-paper items. Courts, however, frequently interpreted "documents" broadly, so as to include e-mails and certain electronic communications within the scope of discoverable items.

Even so, greater clarity regarding discoverability seemed warranted—especially as to electronic material that might be less readily classifiable than e-mails as "documents." Various states responded by updating their discovery rules to include electronic communications within the list of discoverable items. So did the Federal Judicial Conference. In Federal Rules of Civil Procedure amendments proposed by the Judicial Conference and ratified by Congress in 2006, "electronically stored information" became a separate category of discoverable material. The *electronically stored information (ESI)* category is broad enough to include e-mails and similar communications as well as electronic business records, web pages, dynamic databases, and a host of other material existing in electronic form. So-called e-discovery has become a standard feature of civil litigation because of the obvious value of having access to the opposing party's e-mails and other electronic communications.

Discovery regarding ESI occurs in largely the same manner as discovery regarding conventional documents. The party seeking discovery of ESI serves a specific request for production on the other. The served party must provide the requested ESI if it is relevant, is not protected by a legal privilege (e.g., the attorney–client privilege), and is reasonably accessible. Court involvement becomes necessary only if the party from whom discovery is sought fails to comply or objects on lack of relevance, privilege, or burdensomeness grounds. The Federal Rules allow the party seeking discovery of ESI to specify the form in which the requested copies should appear (e.g., hard copies, electronic files, searchable CD, direct access to database, etc.). The party from whom discovery is sought may object to the specified form, in which event the court may have to resolve the dispute. If the requesting party does not specify a form, the other party must provide the requested electronic material in a form that is reasonably usable.

The Federal Rules provide that if the requested electronic material is "not reasonably accessible because of undue burden or cost," the party from whom discovery is sought need not provide it. When an objection along those lines is filed, the court decides whether the objection is valid in light of the particular facts and circumstances. For instance, if requested e-mails appear only on backup tapes and searching those tapes would require the expenditures of significant time, money, and effort, are the requested e-mails "not reasonably accessible because of undue burden or costs"? Perhaps, but perhaps not. The court will rule, based on the relevant situation. The court may deny the discovery request, uphold it, or condition the upholding of it on the requesting party's covering part or all of the costs incurred by the other party in retrieving the ESI and making it available. When a party fails or refuses to comply with a legitimate discovery request and the party seeking discovery of ESI has to secure a court order compelling the release of it, the court may order the noncompliant party to pay the attorney fees incurred by the requesting party in seeking the court order. If a recalcitrant party disregards a court order compelling discovery, the court may assess attorney fees against that party and/or impose evidentiary or procedural sanctions such as barring that party from using certain evidence or from raising certain claims or defenses at trial.

The discussion suggests that discovery requests regarding ESI may be extensive and broad-ranging, with logistical issues often attending those requests. In recognition of these realities, the Federal Rules seek to head off disputes by requiring the parties to civil litigation to meet, at least through their attorneys, soon after the case is filed. The meeting's goal is development of a discovery plan that outlines the parties' intentions regarding ESI discovery and sets forth an agreement on such matters as the form in which the requested ESI will be provided. If the parties cannot agree on certain ESI discovery issues, the court will become involved to resolve the disputes.

The discoverability of ESI makes it incumbent upon businesses to retain and preserve such material not only when litigation to which the material may be related has already been instituted, but also when potential litigation might reasonably be anticipated. Failure to preserve the electronic communications could give rise to allegations of evidence destruction and, potentially, sanctions imposed by a court. (For further discussion of related legal and ethical issues, see this chapter's Ethics and Compliance in Action box.)

Finally, given the now-standard requests of plaintiffs and defendants that the opposing party provide access to relevant e-mails, one should not forget this important piece of advice: Do not say anything in an e-mail that you would not say in a formal written memo or in a conversation with someone. There is a too-frequent tendency to think that because e-mails often tend to be informal in nature, one is somehow free to say things in an e-mail that he or she would not say in another setting. Many individuals and companies have learned the hard way that comments made in their e-mails or those of their employees proved to be damning evidence against them in litigation and thus helped the opposing parties win the cases.

In addition, selected parts or all of the deposition of the opposing party or of certain persons affiliated with the opposing party may be used as evidence at trial, regardless of whether such a deponent is available to testify "live."

Participation in the discovery process may require significant expenditures of time and effort, not only by the attorneys but also by the parties and their employees. Parties who see themselves as too busy to comply with discovery requests may need to think seriously about whether they should remain a party to pending litigation. The discovery process may also trigger significant ethical issues, such as those associated with uses of discovery requests simply to harass or cause expense to the other party, or the issues faced by one who does not wish to hand over legitimately sought material that may prove to be damaging to him or to his employer.

Summary Judgment   **Summary judgment** is a device for disposing of relatively clear cases without a trial. It differs from a demurrer because it involves factual determinations. To prevail, the party moving for a summary judgment must show that (1) there is no genuine issue of material (legally significant) fact and (2) she is entitled to judgment as a matter of law. A moving party satisfies the first element of the test by using the pleadings, relevant discovery information, and affidavits (signed and sworn statements regarding matters of fact) to show that there is no real question about any significant fact. She satisfies the second element by showing that, given the established facts, the applicable law clearly mandates that she win.

Either or both parties may move for a summary judgment. If the court rules in favor of either party, that party wins the case. (The losing party may appeal, however.) If the parties' summary judgment motions are denied, the case proceeds to trial. The judge may also grant a partial summary judgment, which settles some issues in the case but leaves others to be decided at trial.

The Pretrial Conference   Depending on the jurisdiction, a **pretrial conference** is either mandatory or held at the discretion of the trial judge. At this conference, the judge meets informally with the attorneys for both litigants. He or she may try to get the attorneys to stipulate, or agree to, the resolution of certain issues in order to simplify the trial. The judge may also urge them to convince their clients to settle the case by coming to an agreement that eliminates the need for a trial. If the case is not settled, the judge enters a pretrial order that includes the attorneys' stipulations and any other agreements. Ordinarily, this order binds the parties for the remainder of the case.

The Trial   Once the case has been through discovery and has survived any pretrial motions, it is set for trial. The trial may be before a judge alone (i.e., a bench trial), in which case the judge makes findings of fact and reaches conclusions of law before issuing the court's judgment. If the right to a jury trial exists and either party demands one, the jury finds the facts. The judge, however, continues to determine legal questions.[9] During a pretrial jury screening process known as *voir dire*, biased potential jurors may be removed for cause. In addition, the attorney for each party is allowed a limited number of *peremptory challenges*, which allow him to remove potential jurors without having to show bias or other cause.

Trial Procedure   At either a bench trial or a jury trial, the attorneys for each party make opening statements that outline what they expect to prove. The plaintiff's attorney then presents her client's case-in-chief by calling witnesses and introducing documentary evidence (relevant documents and written records, e-mails, videos, and other evidence having a physical form). The plaintiff's attorney asks questions of her client's witnesses in a process known as direct examination. If the plaintiff is an individual person rather than a corporation, he is very likely to testify. The plaintiff's attorney may choose to call the defendant to testify. In this respect, civil cases differ from criminal cases, in which the Fifth Amendment's privilege against self-incrimination bars the government from compelling the defendant to testify. After the plaintiff's attorney completes direct examination of a witness, the defendant's lawyer cross-examines the witness. This may be followed by redirect examination by the plaintiff's attorney and recross examination by the defendant's lawyer.

Once the plaintiff's attorney has completed the presentation of her client's case, defense counsel presents his client's case-in-chief by offering documentary evidence and the testimony of witnesses. The same process of direct, cross-, redirect, and recross-examination is followed, except that the examination roles of the respective lawyers are reversed. After the plaintiff and defendant have presented their cases-in-chief, each party is allowed to present evidence rebutting the showing made by the other party. Throughout each side's presentations of evidence, the opposing attorney may object, on specified legal grounds, to certain questions asked of

---

[9]The rules governing availability of a jury trial are largely beyond the scope of this text. The U.S. Constitution guarantees a jury trial in federal court cases "at common law" whose amount exceeds $20. Most states have similar constitutional provisions, often with a higher dollar amount. Also, Congress and the state legislatures have chosen to allow jury trials in various other cases.

Ethics and Compliance in Action

The broad scope of discovery rights in a civil case will often entitle a party to seek and obtain copies of e-mails, records, memos, and other documents and electronically stored information from the opposing party's files. In many cases, some of the most favorable evidence for the plaintiff will have come from the defendant's files, and vice versa. If your firm is, or is likely to be, a party to civil litigation and you know that the firm's files contain materials that may be damaging to the firm in the litigation, you may be faced with the temptation to alter or destroy the potentially damaging items. This temptation poses serious ethical dilemmas. Is it morally defensible to change the content of records or documents on an after-the-fact basis, in order to lessen the adverse effect on your firm in pending or probable litigation? Is document destruction or e-mail deletion ethically justifiable when you seek to protect your firm's interests in a lawsuit?

If the ethical concerns are not sufficient by themselves to make you leery of involvement in document alteration or destruction, consider the potential legal consequences for yourself and your firm. The much-publicized collapse of the Enron Corporation in 2001 led to considerable scrutiny of the actions of the Arthur Andersen firm, which had provided auditing and consulting services to Enron. An Andersen partner, David Duncan, pleaded guilty to a criminal obstruction of justice charge that accused him of having destroyed, or having instructed Andersen employees to destroy, certain Enron-related records in order to thwart a Securities and Exchange Commission (SEC) investigation of Andersen. The U.S. Justice Department also launched an obstruction of justice prosecution against Andersen on the theory that the firm altered or destroyed records pertaining to Enron in order to impede the SEC investigation. A jury found Andersen guilty of obstruction of justice. Although the Andersen conviction was later overturned by the U.S. Supreme Court because the trial judge's instructions to the jury on relevant principles of law had been impermissibly vague regarding the critical issue of criminal intent, a devastating effect on the firm had already taken place.

Of course, not all instances of document alteration or destruction will lead to criminal prosecution for obstruction of justice. Other consequences of a noncriminal but clearly severe nature may result, however, from document destruction that interferes with legitimate discovery requests in a civil case. In such instances, courts have broad discretionary authority to impose appropriate sanctions on the document-destroying party. These sanctions may include such remedies as court orders prohibiting the document-destroyer from raising certain claims or defenses in the lawsuit, instructions to the jury regarding the wrongful destruction of the documents, and court orders that the document-destroyer pay certain attorney fees to the opposing party.

What about the temptation to refuse to cooperate regarding an opposing party's lawful request for discovery regarding material in one's possession? Although a refusal to cooperate seems less blameworthy than destruction or alteration of documents, extreme instances of recalcitrance during the discovery process may cause a party to experience adverse consequences similar to those imposed on parties who destroy or alter documents. Litigation involving Ronald Perelman and the Morgan Stanley firm provides an illustration. Perelman had sued Morgan Stanley on the theory that the investment bank participated with Sunbeam Corp. in a fraudulent scheme that supposedly induced him to sell Sunbeam his stake in another firm in return for Sunbeam shares whose value plummeted when Sunbeam collapsed. During the discovery phase of the case, Perelman had sought certain potentially relevant e-mails from Morgan Stanley's files. Morgan Stanley repeatedly failed and refused to provide this discoverable material and, in the process, ignored court orders to provide the e-mails.

Eventually, a fed-up trial judge decided to impose sanctions for Morgan Stanley's wrongful conduct during the discovery process. The judge ordered that Perelman's contentions would be presumed to be correct and that the burden of proof would be shifted to Morgan Stanley so that Morgan Stanley would have to disprove Perelman's allegations. In addition, the trial judge prohibited Morgan Stanley from contesting certain allegations made by Perelman. The jury later returned a verdict in favor of Perelman and against Morgan Stanley for $604 million in compensatory damages and $850 million in punitive damages. The court orders sanctioning Morgan Stanley for its discovery misconduct undoubtedly played a key role in Perelman's victory, effectively turning a case that was not a sure-fire winner for Perelman into just that. The case illustrates that a party to litigation may be playing with fire if he, she, or it insists on refusing to comply with legitimate discovery requests.

---

witnesses or to certain evidence that has been offered for admission. The trial judge utilizes the legal rules of evidence to determine whether to sustain the objection (meaning that the objected-to question cannot be answered by the witness or that the offered evidence will be disallowed) or, instead, overrule it (meaning that the question may be answered or that the offered evidence will be allowed).

The witnesses that plaintiffs and defendants call to testify at trial may include those who can testify as to relevant facts of which they have personal knowledge (often called *lay witnesses*) and, sometimes, so-called expert witnesses. If the court agrees that someone a plaintiff or defendant wishes to use as an expert witness possesses relevant scientific, technical, or other specialized knowledge, skill, experience, or educational background and could provide testimony potentially useful to the judge or jury, the court may permit the expert witness to provide opinion testimony or other insights regarding matters of importance in the case. (Lay witnesses, on the other hand, normally are not permitted to offer opinions in their testimony.)

Before allowing such opinion testimony, however, the court must be satisfied not only that the witness qualifies as an expert by virtue of knowledge, skill, experience, or background, but also that his or her opinion testimony would be based on sufficient facts and would result from reasoned application of principles and methods considered reliable in the relevant field. In a significant number of cases, there may be "dueling experts" on a given matter—one expert witness called by the plaintiff and another by the defendant.

After all of the evidence has been presented by the parties, each party's attorney makes a closing argument summarizing his or her client's position. In bench trials, the judge then usually takes the case under advisement rather than issuing a decision immediately. The judge later makes findings of fact and reaches conclusions of law, renders judgment, and, if the plaintiff is the winning party, states the relief to which the plaintiff is entitled.

Jury Trials   At the close of a jury trial, the judge ordinarily submits the case to the jury after issuing **instructions** that set forth the legal rules applicable to the case. The jury then deliberates, makes the necessary determinations of the facts, applies the applicable legal rules to the facts, and arrives at a **verdict** on which the court's judgment will be based.

The verdict form used the majority of the time is the *general verdict*, which requires only that the jury declare which party wins and, if the plaintiff wins, the money damages awarded. The jury neither states its findings of fact nor explains its application of the law to the facts. Although the nature of the general verdict may permit a jury, if it is so inclined, to render a decision that is based on bias, sympathy, or some basis other than the probable facts and the law, one's belief regarding the extent to which juries engage in so-called jury nullification of the facts and law is likely to be heavily influenced by one's attitude toward the jury system. Most proponents of the jury system may be inclined to believe that "renegade" juries, though regrettable, are an aberration, and that the vast majority of juries make a good-faith effort to decide cases on the basis of the facts and controlling legal principles. Some jury system proponents, however, take a different view, asserting that juries *should* engage in jury nullification when they believe it is necessary to accomplish "rough justice." Those who take a dim view of the jury system perceive it as fundamentally flawed and as offering juries too much opportunity to make decisions that stray from a reasonable view of the evidence and the law. Critics of the jury system have little hope of abolishing it, however. Doing so would require amendments to the U.S. Constitution and many state constitutions, as well as the repeal of numerous federal and state statutes.

Another verdict form known as the *special verdict* may serve to minimize concerns that some observers have about jury decisions. When a special verdict is employed, the jury makes specific, written findings of fact in response to questions posed by the trial judge. The judge then applies the law to those findings. Whether a special verdict is utilized is a matter largely within the discretion of the trial judge. The special verdict is not as frequently employed, however, as the general verdict.

Directed Verdict   Although the general verdict gives the jury considerable power, the American legal system also has devices for limiting that power. One device, the **directed verdict**, takes the case away from the jury and provides a judgment to one party before the jury gets a chance to decide the case. The motion for a directed verdict may be made by either party; it usually occurs after the other (nonmoving) party has presented her evidence. The moving party asserts that the evidence, even when viewed favorably to the other party, leads to only one result and need not be considered by the jury. Courts differ on the test governing a motion for a directed verdict. Some deny the motion if there is *any* evidence favoring the nonmoving party, whereas others deny the motion only if there is *substantial* evidence favoring the nonmoving party. More often than not, trial judges deny motions for a directed verdict.

Judgment Notwithstanding the Verdict   On occasion, one party wins a judgment even after the jury has reached a verdict against that party. The device for doing so is the **judgment notwithstanding the verdict** (also known as the *judgment non obstante veredicto* or judgment n.o.v.). Some jurisdictions provide that a motion for judgment n.o.v. cannot be made unless the moving party previously moved for a directed verdict. In any event, the standard used to decide the motion for judgment n.o.v. usually is the same standard used to decide the motion for a directed verdict.

Motion for a New Trial In a wide range of situations that vary among jurisdictions, the losing party can successfully move for a new trial. Acceptable reasons for granting a new trial include legal errors by the judge during the trial, jury or attorney misconduct, the discovery of new evidence, or an award of excessive damages to the plaintiff. Most motions for a new trial are unsuccessful, however.

Appeal
A final judgment generally prevents the parties from relitigating the same claim. One or more parties still may appeal the trial court's decision, however. Normally, appellate courts consider only alleged errors of law made by the trial court. The matters ordinarily considered "legal" and thus appealable include the trial judge's decisions on motions to dismiss, for summary judgment, for directed verdict or judgment notwithstanding the verdict, and for a new trial. Other matters typically considered appealable include trial court rulings on service of process and admission of evidence at trial, as well as the court's legal conclusions in a nonjury trial, instructions to the jury in a jury case, and decision regarding damages or other relief. Appellate courts may *affirm* the trial court's decision, *reverse* it, or affirm parts of the decision and reverse other parts. One of three things ordinarily results from an appellate court's disposition of an appeal: (1) the plaintiff wins the case, (2) the defendant wins the case, or (3) the case is *remanded* (returned) to the trial court for further proceedings if the trial court's decision is reversed in whole or in part. For example, if the plaintiff appeals a trial court decision granting the defendant's motion to dismiss and the appellate courts affirm that decision, the plaintiff loses. On the other hand, if an appellate court reverses a trial court judgment in the plaintiff's favor, the defendant could win outright, or the case might be returned to the trial court for further proceedings consistent with the appellate decision.

Enforcing a Judgment
In this text, you may occasionally see cases in which someone was not sued even though he probably would have been liable to the plaintiff, who sued another party instead. One explanation is that the first party was "judgment-proof"—so lacking in assets as to make a civil lawsuit for damages a waste of time and money. The defendant's financial condition also affects a winning plaintiff's ability to collect whatever damages she has been awarded.

When the defendant fails to pay as required after losing a civil case, the winning plaintiff must enforce the judgment. Ordinarily, the plaintiff will obtain a *writ of execution* enabling the sheriff or federal marshal to seize designated property of the defendant and sell it at a judicial sale to help satisfy the judgment. A judgment winner may also use a procedure known as *garnishment* to seize property, money, and wages that belong to the defendant but are in the hands of a third party such as a bank or employer. Legal limits exist, however, concerning the portion of wages that may be garnished. If the property needed to satisfy the judgment is located in another state, the plaintiff must use that state's execution or garnishment procedures. Under the U.S. Constitution, the second state must give "full faith and credit" to the judgment of the state in which the plaintiff originally sued. Finally, when the court has awarded an equitable remedy such as an injunction, the defendant may be found in contempt of court and subjected to a fine or a jail term if he fails to obey the court's order.

Class Actions
So far, our civil procedure discussion has proceeded as if the plaintiff and the defendant were single parties. Various plaintiffs and defendants, however, may be parties to one lawsuit. In addition, each jurisdiction has procedural rules stating when other parties can be *joined* to a suit that begins without them.

One special type of multiparty case, the **class action**, allows one or more persons to sue on behalf of themselves and all others who have suffered similar harm from substantially the same wrong. Class action suits by consumers, environmentalists, and other groups now are reasonably common events. The usual justifications for the class action are that (1) it allows legal wrongs causing losses to a large number of widely dispersed parties to be fully compensated and (2) it promotes economy of judicial effort by combining many similar claims into one suit.

The requirements for a class action vary among jurisdictions. The issues addressed by state and federal class action rules include the following: whether there are questions of law and fact common to all members of the alleged class; whether those common questions predominate over other questions; whether the class is small enough to allow all of its members to join the case as parties, rather than use a class action; and whether the plaintiff(s) and their attorney(s) can adequately represent the class without conflicts of interest or other forms of unfairness. To protect the individual class members' right to be heard, some jurisdictions have required that unnamed or absent class members be given notice of the case if this is reasonably possible. The damages awarded in a successful class action usually are apportioned among the entire class. Establishing the total recovery and distributing it to the class, however, pose problems when the class is large, the class members' injuries are indefinite, or some members cannot be identified.

In 2005, Congress moved to restrict the filing of class actions in state courts by enacting a statute giving the federal district courts original jurisdiction over class actions in which the amount in controversy exceeds $5 million and any member of the plaintiff class resides in a state different from the state of any defendant. Proponents of the measure describe it as being designed to curtail "forum shopping" by multistate plaintiffs for "friendly" state courts that might be especially likely to favor the claims of the plaintiffs. Critics assert that the 2005 enactment is too protective of corporate defendants and likely to curtail the bringing of legitimate civil rights, consumer-protection, and environmental-harm claims. Those criticisms have been countered by assertions from other quarters that the 2005 law did not go far enough in restricting class actions. These critics contend that some proposed classes are simply "too big"—meaning that a corporate defendant could face ruinous financial consequences if the court allowed the case to proceed as a class action and liability was established. In such instances, the argument goes, the court should refuse to certify the case as a class action and thereby force individual plaintiffs to sue on a case-by-case basis.

Over the last decade, the Supreme Court has issued important decisions dealing with class action certification issues. In *Wal-Mart Stores, Inc. v. Dukes*, 564 U.S. 338 (2011), the Court rejected class status for a group of 1.5 million females employed, or formerly employed, by Walmart. All 1.5 million claimed to have been the victims of sex discrimination during their Walmart employment as a result of a company practice that allowed local store managers very broad discretion in making salary and promotion decisions regarding store employees. The plaintiffs who sought class recognition alleged that in exercising this discretion, store managers made salary and promotion decisions that discriminated against them on the basis of their sex. In ruling that the case could not go forward as a class action, the Court concluded that even though the plaintiffs all claimed to have experienced sex discrimination as a result of a supposed corporate practice, this surface similarity in the discrimination allegations was not enough to satisfy a key class action certification requirement: the need for the plaintiffs' claims to reflect common questions of law and fact. According to the Court, this "commonality" requirement called for the plaintiffs to show that they "suffered the same injury" in a specific sense. The Court reasoned that they could not do so, given the large number of store managers who exercised discretion in making decisions regarding individual employees and given the variability in the particular harms—and extent of harms—experienced by the employees. Although the Court did not invoke the "too big" argument referred to in an earlier paragraph, it seems possible that such a concern may have lurked in the background.

Of course, the decision in *Wal-Mart* did not mean that the plaintiffs were automatically deprived of legal recourse for the alleged wrongs they claimed. They could still pursue their cases individually. As might be expected, however, only a small percentage of the employees and former employees opted to pursue their own individual cases once the Court denied them the opportunity to band together as a class.

Wal-Mart appeared to suggest that courts should closely scrutinize class action requests and that class action certification would likely become more difficult for plaintiffs to obtain. A 2016 Supreme Court decision, however, reveals that class actions are not necessarily a dying breed after *Wal-Mart*. In *Tyson Foods, Inc. v. Bouaphakeo*, which follows, the Court affirms the lower court's grant of class action certification. Besides concluding that the commonality element held lacking in *Wal-Mart* was present in *Bouaphakeo*, the Court focuses on the related yet separate question of whether the common questions in the dispute predominate over the individual ones. In addition, the Court addresses an important evidentiary question.

Tyson Foods, Inc. v. Bouaphakeo   136 S. Ct. 1036 (2016)

A federal law, the Fair Labor Standards Act (FLSA), requires that if employees covered by the statute work more than 40 hours during a week, their employers must pay them overtime compensation. For those excess hours, employees are to be paid one and one-half times their regular hourly rate. The FLSA also requires employers to pay employees for activities that are integral and indispensable to their regular work, even if those activities do not occur at the employees' workstations. In addition, the FLSA requires employers to keep records of employees' wages, hours worked, and employment conditions.

Peg Bouaphakeo and numerous other employees of Tyson Foods Inc. were covered by the FLSA. They worked in the kill, cut, and re-trim departments of a Tyson pork processing plant. Safety considerations associated with the nature of their work necessitated that these employees wear protective gear. The exact composition of the gear depended on the tasks they were assigned to perform on a given day. Tyson compensated some of the employees for the time spent in donning and doffing the protective gear. These employees were paid for an extra four minutes each day because Tyson estimated that four minutes was the time necessary to put on and take off the protective gear. For certain other employees, Tyson estimated that eight minutes was the relevant amount of time. Tyson, therefore, paid those employees for an extra eight minutes per day. Still other Tyson employees, though required to wear protective gear, were not paid for the donning-and-doffing time. Although Tyson recorded the amount of time each employee spent at his or her actual workstation, it did not record the time each employee spent in putting on and taking off the required protective gear. The employees took the position that this time significantly exceeded the four- and eight-minute estimates Tyson used.

Bouaphakeo and the other employees sued Tyson in a federal district court, alleging that in either not including or not accurately including the donning-and-doffing time in hours the employees worked, Tyson had denied the employees overtime compensation required by the FLSA. The employees contended that wearing the protective gear was integral and indispensable to their work and that if their time spent putting on and taking off the required protective gear had been included in hours worked, they would have exceeded the 40-hours-per-week threshold for overtime pay.

The employees sought to have their claims against Tyson certified as a class action under a collective action provision in the FLSA. Tyson argued that because of the variance in protective gear the respective employees wore, the employees' claims were not sufficiently similar to be resolved in a class action. The district court concluded, however, that class action certification was warranted because common questions, such as whether putting on and taking off required protective gear was compensable under the FLSA, were present even if not all of the workers wore the same gear.

Because Tyson did not keep records of the donning-and-doffing time, the employees relied on evidence stemming from a study by an industrial relations expert. The expert conducted more than 700 videotaped observations of how long various donning-and-doffing activities took and then averaged the time taken. This process yielded an estimate of 18 minutes per day for the cut and re-trim departments and 21.25 minutes per day for the kill department. These estimates were then added to the timesheets of each employee to ascertain which class members worked more than 40 hours in a week and to shed light on a possible class-wide recovery. The jury awarded the class approximately $2.9 million in unpaid wages. Before that amount was paid by Tyson and distributed to class members, Tyson appealed to the U.S. Court of Appeals for the Eighth Circuit. Tyson argued that the district court erred in certifying the case as a class action. After the Eighth Circuit affirmed the lower court's decision, the U.S. Supreme Court agreed to decide the case.

Kennedy, Justice

Tyson challenges the certification of the FLSA collective action. The parties do not dispute that the standard for certifying a collective action under the FLSA is no more stringent than the standard for certifying a class under the Federal Rules of Civil Procedure. This opinion assumes, without deciding, that this is correct. For purposes of this case, then, if certification of respondents' class action under the Federal Rules was proper, certification of the collective action was proper as well.

Federal Rule of Civil Procedure 23(b)(3) requires that, before a class is certified under that subsection, a district court must find that "questions of law or fact common to class members predominate over any questions affecting only individual members." The "predominance inquiry tests whether proposed classes are sufficiently cohesive to warrant adjudication by representation." *Amchem Products, Inc. v. Windsor*, 521 U.S. 591, 623 (1997). This calls upon courts to give careful scrutiny to the relation between common and individual questions in a case. An individual question is one where "members of a proposed class will need to present evidence that varies from member to member," while a common question is one where "the same evidence will suffice for each member to make a prima facie showing [or] the issue is

susceptible to generalized, class-wide proof." [Citation omitted.] The predominance inquiry "asks whether the common, aggregation-enabling, issues in the case are more prevalent or important than the non-common, aggregation-defeating, individual issues." [Citation omitted.] When "one or more of the central issues in the action are common to the class and can be said to predominate, the action may be considered proper under Rule 23(b)(3) even though other important matters will have to be tried separately, such as damages or some affirmative defenses peculiar to some individual class members." [Citation omitted.]

Here, the parties do not dispute that there are important questions common to all class members, the most significant of which is whether time spent donning and doffing the required protective gear is compensable work under the FLSA. To be entitled to recovery, however, each employee must prove that the amount of time spent donning and doffing, when added to his or her regular hours, amounted to more than 40 hours in a given week. Tyson argues that these necessarily person-specific inquiries into individual work time predominate over the common questions raised by the employees' claims, making class certification improper.

The employees counter that these individual inquiries are unnecessary because it can be assumed each employee donned and doffed for the same average time observed [by the industrial rela-tions expert in his review of videotapes of employees putting on protective gear]. Whether this inference is permissible becomes the central dispute in this case. Tyson contends that [the expert's] study manufactures predominance by assuming away the very dif-ferences that make the case inappropriate for classwide resolu-tion. Reliance on a representative sample, Tyson argues, absolves each employee of the responsibility to prove personal injury, and thus deprives petitioner of any ability to litigate its defenses to individual claims.

Calling this unfair, Tyson maintains that the Court should announce a broad rule against the use in class actions of what the parties call representative evidence. A categorical exclusion of that sort, however, would make little sense. A representative or statistical sample, like all evidence, is a means to establish or defend against liability. Its permissibility turns not on the form a proceeding takes—be it a class or individual action—but on the degree to which the evidence is reliable in proving or disproving the elements of the relevant cause of action.

It follows that the Court would reach too far were it to es-tablish general rules governing the use of statistical evidence, or so-called representative evidence, in all class-action cases. Evi-dence of this type is used in various substantive realms of the law. Whether and when statistical evidence can be used to establish classwide liability will depend on the purpose for which the evi-dence is being introduced and on the elements of the underlying cause of action.

In many cases, a representative sample is the only practi-cable means to collect and present relevant data establishing a defendant's liability. In a case where representative evidence is relevant in proving a plaintiff's individual claim, that evi-dence cannot be deemed improper merely because the claim is brought on behalf of a class. One way for the employees to show, then, that the sample relied upon here is a permissible method of proving classwide liability is by showing that each class member could have relied on that sample to establish li-ability if he or she had brought an individual action. If the sam-ple could have sustained a reasonable jury finding as to hours worked in each employee's individual action, that sample is a permissible means of establishing the employees' hours worked in a class action.

In this suit, the employees sought to introduce a representa-tive sample to fill an evidentiary gap created by the employer's failure to keep adequate records. If the employees had proceeded with 3,344 individual lawsuits, each employee likely would have had to introduce [the expert's] study to prove the hours he or she worked. Rather than absolving the employees from proving indi-vidual injury, the representative evidence here was a permissible means of making that very showing. Reliance on [the expert's] study did not deprive Tyson of its ability to litigate individual

defenses. Since there were no alternative means for the employ-ees to establish their hours worked, Tyson's primary defense was to show that [the expert's] study was unrepresentative or inac-curate. That defense is itself common to the claims made by all class members.

Tyson's reliance on *Wal-Mart Stores, Inc. v. Dukes*, 564 U.S. 338 (2011), is misplaced. *Wal-Mart* does not stand for the broad proposition that a representative sample is an impermissible means of establishing classwide liability.

Wal-Mart involved a nationwide Title VII class of over 1½ million employees. In reversing class certification, this Court did not reach Rule 23(b)(3)'s predominance prong, holding instead that the class failed to meet even Rule 23(a)'s more basic require-ment that class members share a common question of fact or law. The plaintiffs in *Wal-Mart* did not provide significant proof of a common policy of discrimination to which each employee was subject. "The only corporate policy that the plaintiffs' evidence convincingly establishe[d was] Wal-Mart's 'policy' of allowing discretion by local supervisors over employment matters"; and even then, the plaintiffs could not identify "a common mode of exercising discretion that pervade[d] the entire company." *Id.* at 355–56.

The plaintiffs in *Wal-Mart* proposed to use representative evi-dence as a means of overcoming this absence of a common pol-icy. Under their proposed methodology, a "sample set of the class members would be selected, as to whom liability for sex discrimi-nation and the backpay owing as a result would be determined in depositions supervised by a master." *Id.* at 367. The aggregate damages award was to be derived by taking the percentage of claims determined to be valid from this sample and applying it to the rest of the class, and then multiplying the number of presump-tively valid claims by the average backpay award in the sample set. The Court held that this "Trial By Formula" was [improper] because it enlarged the class members' substantive right[s] and deprived defendants of their right to litigate statutory defenses to individual claims.

The Court's holding in the instant case is in accord with *Wal-Mart*. The underlying question in *Wal-Mart*, as here, was whether the sample at issue could have been used to establish liability in an individual action. Since the Court held that the employees were not similarly situated, none of them could have prevailed in an individual suit by relying on depositions detailing the ways in which other employees were discriminated against by their particular store managers. By extension, if the employees had brought 1½ million individual suits, there would be little or no role for representative evidence. Permitting the use of that sam-ple in a class action, therefore, would have [been inappropriate because it would have given] plaintiffs and defendants different rights in a class proceeding than they could have asserted in an individual action.

In contrast, the study here could have been sufficient to sustain a jury finding as to hours worked if it were introduced in each employee's individual action. While the experiences of the employees in *Wal-Mart* bore little relationship to one another, in this case each employee worked in the same facility, did similar work, and was paid under the same policy. [U]nder these circumstances the experiences of a subset of employees can be probative as to the experiences of all of them.

This is not to say that all inferences drawn from representative evidence in an FLSA case are just and reasonable. Representative evidence that is statistically inadequate or based on implausible assumptions could not lead to a fair or accurate estimate of the uncompensated hours an employee has worked. Tyson, however, did not raise a challenge to the methodology [used by the employees' expert]. As a result, there is

no basis in the record to conclude it was legal error to admit that evidence.

Once a district court finds evidence to be admissible, its persuasiveness is, in general, a matter for the jury. Reasonable minds may differ as to whether the average time [the expert] calculated is probative as to the time actually worked by each employee. Resolving that question, however, is the near-exclusive province of the jury. The district court could have denied class certification on this ground only if it concluded that no reasonable juror could have believed that the employees spent roughly equal time donning and doffing. The district court made no such finding, and the record here provides no basis for this Court to second-guess that conclusion.

Judgment of Eighth Circuit Court of Appeals affirmed.

Alternative Dispute Resolution

 LO2-7 Explain the differences among the major forms of alternative dispute resolution.

Lawsuits are not the only devices for resolving civil disputes. Nor are they always the best means of doing so. Settling private disputes through the courts can be a cumbersome, lengthy, and expensive process for litigants. With the advent of a litigious society and the increasing caseloads it has produced, handling disputes in this fashion also imposes ever-greater social costs. For these reasons and others, various forms of **alternative dispute resolution (ADR)** have assumed increasing importance in recent years. Proponents of ADR cite many considerations in its favor. These include ADR's (1) quicker resolution of disputes; (2) lower costs in time, money, and aggravation for the parties; (3) lessening of the strain on an overloaded court system; (4) use of decision makers with specialized expertise; and (5) potential for compromise decisions that promote and reflect consensus between the parties. As will be seen in later discussion, however, there are ADR skeptics.

Common Forms of ADR

Settlement The settlement of a civil lawsuit is not everyone's idea of an alternative dispute resolution mechanism. It is an important means, however, of avoiding protracted litigation—one that often is a sensible compromise for the

parties. Most cases settle at some stage in the proceedings described previously. The usual settlement agreement is a contract whereby the defendant, without admitting liability, agrees to pay the plaintiff a sum of money in exchange for the plaintiff's promise to drop the claim against the defendant. Such agreements must satisfy the requirements of contract law discussed later in this text. In some cases, moreover, the court must approve the settlement in order for it to be enforceable. Examples include class actions and litigation involving minors.

Arbitration Arbitration is the submission of a dispute to a neutral, nonjudicial third party (the *arbitrator*) who issues a binding decision resolving the dispute. Arbitration usually results from the parties' agreement. That agreement normally is made before the dispute arises (most often through an *arbitration clause* in a contract). As noted in the *Concepcion* case, which follows shortly, the Federal Arbitration Act requires judicial enforcement of a wide range of agreements to arbitrate claims. This means that if a contract contains a clause requiring arbitration of certain claims but one of the parties attempts to litigate such a claim in court, the court is very likely to dismiss the case and compel arbitration of the dispute.

Arbitration may also be compelled by other statutes. One example is the *compulsory arbitration* many states require as part of the collective bargaining process for certain public employees. Finally, parties who have not agreed in advance to submit future disputes to arbitration may agree upon arbitration after the dispute arises.

Arbitration usually is less formal than regular court proceedings. The arbitrator may or may not be an attorney. Often, she is a professional with expertise in the subject matter of the dispute. Although arbitration hearings often resemble civil trials, the applicable procedures, the rules for admission of evidence, and the record-keeping requirements typically are not as rigorous as those governing courts. Arbitrators sometimes have freedom to ignore rules of substantive law that would bind a court.

The arbitrator's decision, called an *award*, is filed with a court, which will enforce it if necessary. The losing party may object to the arbitrator's award, but judicial review of arbitration proceedings is limited. According to the Federal Arbitration Act (FAA), grounds for overturning an arbitration award include (1) a party's use of fraud, (2) the arbitrator's partiality or corruption, and (3) other misconduct by the arbitrator.

The previously noted advantages of arbitration and the enforceability of arbitration clauses in contracts have combined in recent years to make such clauses common features in various types of contracts. Skeptics of arbitration, however, worry about this development, particularly when the relevant contract is one drafted entirely or almost entirely by the party with greater economic power and business sophistication. These critics point to arbitration's potential for unfairness to ordinary consumers or employees of, say, a large corporation when they find that their dispute with the corporation cannot be resolved in court but must instead be submitted to arbitration because of an arbitration clause in the parties' contract. In such situations, the contract's terms probably would have been dictated by the corporation rather than having been arrived at through a genuine bargaining process.

Although most arbitrators almost certainly strive to be fair, critics cite the supposed danger that some arbitrators may tend to favor parties with greater economic clout because, as the old saying goes, "they know which side their bread is buttered on." These arguments about the potential for second-class justice, whether accurate or overblown, have led to calls in some quarters for legislative action in which Congress would tinker with the FAA by denying or restricting the ability of business organizations to include binding arbitration clauses in their contracts with ordinary consumers or employees (as opposed to contracts with other business entities). In 2019 the U.S. House of Representatives passed the Forced Arbitration Injustice Repeal Act (FAIR Act), which prohibits a forced arbitration agreement from being enforced if it requires forced arbitration of an employment, consumer, or civil rights claim against a corporation. As this book went to press, passage in the Senate and enactment of this legislation was uncertain.

During recent years, this further question about arbitration has arisen: If state law permits the creation of a classwide arbitration that combines individual arbitrations presenting the same issues, is an arbitration clause enforceable under the FAA if it not only requires individual arbitration but also bans classwide arbitration? The two Supreme Court decisions discussed below address that question.

AT&T Mobility LLC v. Concepcion, which follows shortly, addresses the FAA's purposes and emphasizes that the FAA's provision requiring enforcement of agreements to arbitrate controls over nearly all state laws that would stand in the way of enforcement of such an agreement. The Supreme Court goes on to hold that contract provisions requiring arbitration of claims on an individual basis—and prohibiting joinder of those claims with others in a class action–type arbitration—are both permissible and enforceable under the FAA, notwithstanding any state law to the contrary.

In *American Express Co. v. Italian Colors Restaurant*, 133 S. Ct. 2304 (2013), the Supreme Court followed the lead of *Concepcion* and held that a court must respect a contractual waiver of class arbitration even if plaintiffs seeking to bring a class action in court contend that the plaintiffs' costs of individually arbitrating claims for an alleged violation of federal law would exceed the potential recovery. Taken together, the two decisions probably will make class arbitration an increasingly rare species, as corporations seem likely to draft arbitration clauses so that they not only

---

AT&T Mobility LLC v. Concepcion   563 U.S. 333 (2011)

Vincent and Liza Concepcion entered into a contract for the sale and servicing of cellular phones with AT&T Mobility LLC (AT&T). AT&T used the same contract in its dealings with other customers. The agreement called for arbitration of all disputes between the parties but required that claims be brought in the parties' "individual capacity, and not as a plaintiff or class member in any purported class or representative proceeding."

AT&T advertised the service that the Concepcions purchased as including the provision of free phones. Although the Concepcions were not charged for the phones, they were charged $30.22 in sales tax based on the phones' retail value. The Concepcions later sued AT&T in the U.S. District Court for the Southern District of California. Their complaint was consolidated with a class action case alleging, among other things, that AT&T had engaged in false advertising and fraud by charging sales tax on phones it advertised as free.

AT&T filed a motion asking the court to compel arbitration under the terms of its contract with the Concepcions. The Concepcions opposed the motion, contending that the arbitration agreement was unconscionable and otherwise objectionable under California law because it disallowed classwide procedures. Finding the arbitration provision unconscionable because AT&T had not shown that arbitration of individual disputes adequately substituted for the deterrent effects of class actions, the district court denied AT&T's motion. In so ruling, the court relied on the California Supreme Court's decision in Discover Bank v. Superior Court, *113 P.3d 1100 (Cal. 2005). The U.S. Court of Appeals for the Ninth Circuit affirmed on the same ground. The Ninth Circuit also held that the Federal Arbitration Act (FAA) did not preempt the California rule stemming from* Discover Bank. *The U.S. Supreme Court granted AT&T's request that it decide the case.*

Scalia, Justice

Section 2 of the FAA makes agreements to arbitrate "valid, irrevocable, and enforceable, save upon such grounds as exist at law or in equity for the revocation of any contract." We consider whether the FAA prohibits states from conditioning the enforceability of certain arbitration agreements on the availability of classwide arbitration procedures.

The FAA was enacted in 1925 in response to widespread judicial hostility to arbitration agreements. We have described [§ 2 of the FAA] as reflecting both a "liberal federal policy favoring arbitration" and the "fundamental principle that arbitration is a matter of contract." [Case citations omitted.] In line with these principles, courts must place arbitration agreements on an equal footing with other contracts, and enforce them according to their terms.

The final phrase of § 2, however, permits arbitration agreements to be declared unenforceable "upon such grounds as exist at law or in equity for the revocation of any contract." This saving clause permits agreements to arbitrate to be invalidated by "generally applicable contract defenses, such as fraud, duress, or unconscionability," but not by defenses that apply only to arbitration or that derive their meaning from the fact that an agreement to arbitrate is at issue. [Case citations omitted.] The question in this case is whether § 2 preempts California's rule classifying most collective-arbitration waivers in consumer contracts as unconscionable. We refer to this rule as the *Discover Bank* rule.

Under California law, courts may refuse to enforce any contract found "to have been unconscionable at the time it was made," or may "limit the application of any unconscionable clause." [Statutory citation omitted.] A finding of unconscionability requires "a 'procedural' and a 'substantive' element, the former focusing on 'oppression' or 'surprise' due to unequal bargaining power, the latter on 'overly harsh' or 'one-sided' results." [Case citation omitted.] In *Discover Bank*, the California Supreme Court applied this framework to class-action waivers in arbitration agreements and held as follows:

[W]hen the waiver is found in a consumer contract of adhesion in a setting in which disputes between the contracting parties predictably involve small amounts of damages, and when it is alleged that the party with the superior bargaining power has carried out a scheme to deliberately cheat large numbers of consumers out of individually small sums of money, then . . . the waiver becomes in practice the exemption of the party from responsibility for [its] own fraud, or willful injury to the person or property of another. Under these circumstances, such waivers are unconscionable under California law and should not be enforced.

California courts have frequently applied this rule to find arbitration agreements unconscionable.

The Concepcions argue that the *Discover Bank* rule, given its origins in California's unconscionability doctrine and California's policy against exculpat[ory] [agreements] is a ground that "exist[s] at law or in equity for the revocation of any contract" under FAA § 2. Moreover, they argue that even if we construe the *Discover Bank* rule as a prohibition on collective-action waivers rather than simply an application of unconscionability, the rule would still be applicable to all dispute-resolution contracts, since California prohibits waivers of class litigation as well.

When state law prohibits outright the arbitration of a particular type of claim, the analysis is straightforward: The conflicting rule is displaced by the FAA. *Preston v. Ferrer*, 552 U.S. 346, 353 (2008). But the inquiry becomes more complex when a doctrine normally thought to be generally applicable, such as duress or, as relevant here, unconscionability, is alleged to have been applied in a fashion that disfavors arbitration. In *Perry v. Thomas*, 482 U.S. 483 (1987), for example, we noted that the FAA's preemptive effect might extend even to grounds traditionally thought to exist "'at law or in equity for the revocation of any contract.'" We said that a court may not "rely on the uniqueness of an agreement to arbitrate as a basis for a state-law holding that enforcement would be unconscionable, for this would enable the court to effect what . . . the state legislature cannot."

An obvious illustration of this point would be a case finding unconscionable or unenforceable as against public policy consumer arbitration agreements that fail to provide for judicially monitored discovery. The rationalizations for such a holding are neither difficult to imagine nor different in kind from those articulated in *Discover Bank*. A court might reason that no consumer would knowingly waive his right to full discovery, as this would enable companies to hide their wrongdoing [and possibly evade legal responsibility]. And, the reasoning would continue, because such a rule applies the general principle of unconscionability or public-policy disapproval of exculpatory agreements, it is applicable to "any" contract and thus preserved by § 2 of the FAA. In practice, of course, the rule would have a disproportionate impact on arbitration agreements, but it would presumably apply to contracts purporting to restrict discovery in litigation as well.

Although § 2's saving clause preserves generally applicable contract defenses, nothing in it suggests an intent to preserve state-law rules that stand as an obstacle to the accomplishment of the FAA's objectives. The "principal purpose" of the FAA is to "ensur[e] that private arbitration agreements are enforced according to their terms." [Case citation omitted.] [Accordingly,] we have held that parties may agree to limit the issues subject to arbitration, to arbitrate according to specific rules, and to limit with whom a party will arbitrate its disputes. [Case citations omitted.]

The point of affording parties discretion in designing arbitration processes is to allow for efficient, streamlined procedures tailored to the type of dispute. It can be specified, for example, that the decision-maker be a specialist in the relevant field, or that proceedings be kept confidential to protect trade secrets. And the informality of arbitral proceedings is itself desirable, reducing the cost and increasing the speed of dispute resolution.

[O]ur cases . . . have repeatedly described the FAA as "embod[ying] [a] national policy favoring arbitration," and "a liberal federal policy favoring arbitration agreements, notwithstanding any state substantive or procedural policies to the contrary." [Case citations omitted.] Thus, in *Preston v. Ferrer*, holding preempted a state-law rule requiring exhaustion of administrative remedies before arbitration, we said: "A prime objective of an agreement to arbitrate is to achieve 'streamlined proceedings and expeditious results,'" which objective would be "frustrated" by requiring a dispute to be heard by an agency first. That rule, we said, would "at the least, hinder speedy resolution of the controversy."

California's *Discover Bank* rule similarly interferes with arbitration. Although the rule does not *require* classwide arbitration, it allows any party to a consumer contract to demand it *ex post*. The rule also requires that damages be predictably small, and that the consumer allege a scheme to cheat consumers. The former requirement, however, is toothless and malleable, and the latter has no limiting effect, as all that is required is an allegation. Consumers remain free to bring and resolve their disputes on a bilateral basis under *Discover Bank*, and some may well do so; but there is little incentive for lawyers to arbitrate on behalf of individuals when they may do so for a class and reap far higher fees in the process. And faced with inevitable class arbitration, companies would have less incentive to continue resolving potentially duplicative claims on an individual basis.

Although we have had little occasion to examine classwide arbitration, our decision in *Stolt-Nielsen S.A. v. Animal Feeds Int'l*

Corp., 130 S. Ct. 1758 (2010), is instructive. In that case we held that an arbitration panel exceeded its power under . . . the FAA by imposing class procedures based on policy judgments rather than the arbitration agreement itself or some background principle of contract law that would affect its interpretation. We then held that the agreement at issue, which was silent on the question of class procedures, could not be interpreted to allow them because the "changes brought about by the shift from bilateral arbitration to class-action arbitration" are "fundamental." Classwide arbitration includes absent parties, necessitating additional and different procedures and involving higher stakes. Confidentiality becomes more difficult. And while it is theoretically possible to select an arbitrator with some expertise relevant to the class-certification question, arbitrators are not generally knowledgeable in the often-dominant procedural aspects of certification, such as the protection of absent parties. The conclusion follows that class arbitration, to the extent it is manufactured by *Discover Bank* rather than consensual, [interferes with fundamental attributions of arbitration and] is inconsistent with the FAA.

First, the switch from bilateral to class arbitration sacrifices the principal advantage of arbitration—its informality—and makes the process slower, more costly, and more likely to generate procedural morass than final judgment. [B]efore an arbitrator may decide the merits of a claim in classwide procedures, he must first decide, for example, whether the class itself may be certified, whether the named parties are sufficiently representative and typical, and how discovery for the class should be conducted. A cursory comparison of bilateral and class arbitration illustrates the difference. According to the American Arbitration Association (AAA), the average consumer arbitration between January and August 2007 resulted in a disposition on the merits in six months. As of September 2009, the AAA had opened 283 class arbitrations. Of those, 121 remained active, and 162 had been settled, withdrawn, or dismissed. Not a single one, however, had resulted in a final award on the merits. For those cases that were no longer active, the [mean] time from filing to settlement, withdrawal, or dismissal—not judgment on the merits—was . . . 630 days.

Second, class arbitration *requires* procedural formality. The AAA's rules governing class arbitrations mimic the Federal Rules of Civil Procedure for class litigation. And while parties can alter those procedures by contract, an alternative is not obvious. If procedures are too informal, absent class members would not be bound by the arbitration. For a class-action money judgment to bind absentees in litigation, class representatives must at all times adequately represent absent class members, and absent members must be afforded notice, an opportunity to be heard, and a right to opt out of the class. At least this amount of process would presumably be required for absent parties to be bound by the results of arbitration. We find it unlikely that in passing the FAA, Congress meant to leave the disposition of these procedural requirements to an arbitrator. Indeed, class arbitration was not even envisioned by Congress when it passed the FAA in 1925.

Third, class arbitration greatly increases risks to defendants. Informal procedures do of course have a cost: The absence of multilayered review makes it more likely that errors will go uncorrected. Defendants are willing to accept the costs of these errors in arbitration, since their impact is limited to the size of individual disputes, and presumably outweighed by savings from avoiding the courts. But when damages allegedly owed to tens of thousands of potential claimants are aggregated and decided at once, the risk of an error will often become unacceptable.

Faced with even a small chance of a devastating loss, defendants will be pressured into settling questionable claims.

The dissent claims that class proceedings are necessary to prosecute small-dollar claims that might otherwise slip through the legal system. But states cannot require a procedure that is inconsistent with the FAA, even if it is desirable for unrelated reasons. Because it "stands as an obstacle to the accomplishment and execution of the full purposes and objectives of Congress," [case citation omitted,] California's *Discover Bank* rule is preempted by the FAA.

Decision of Ninth Circuit Court of Appeals reversed, and case remanded for further proceedings.

mandate arbitration but require it to be of the individual claim variety.

Court-Annexed Arbitration In this form of ADR, certain civil lawsuits are diverted into arbitration. One example might be cases in which less than a specified dollar amount is at issue. Most often, court-annexed arbitration is mandatory and is ordered by the judge, but some jurisdictions merely offer litigants the option of arbitration. The losing party in a court-annexed arbitration still has the right to a regular trial.

Mediation In mediation, a neutral third party called a *mediator* helps the parties reach a cooperative resolution of their dispute by facilitating communication between them, clarifying their areas of agreement and disagreement, helping them see each other's viewpoints, and suggesting settlement options. Mediators, unlike arbitrators, cannot make decisions that bind the parties. Instead, a successful mediation process results in a *mediation agreement*. Such agreements normally are enforced under regular contract law principles.

Mediation is used in a wide range of situations, including labor, commercial, family, and environmental disputes. It may occur by agreement of the parties after a dispute has arisen. It may also result from a previous contractual agreement by the parties. Increasingly, court-annexed mediation is either compelled or made available by courts in certain cases.

Summary Jury Trial Sometimes settlement of civil litigation is impeded because the litigants have vastly different perceptions about the merits of their cases. In such cases, the summary jury trial may give the parties a needed dose of reality. The summary jury trial is an abbreviated, nonpublic mock jury trial that does not bind the parties. If the parties do not settle after completion of the summary jury trial, they still are entitled to a regular court trial. There is some disagreement over whether courts can compel the parties to take part in a summary jury trial.

Minitrial A minitrial is an informal, abbreviated private "trial" whose aim is to promote settlement of disputes. Normally, it arises out of a private agreement that also describes the procedures to be followed. In the typical minitrial, counsel for the parties present their cases to a panel composed of senior management from each side. Sometimes a neutral advisor such as an attorney or a retired judge presides. This advisor may also offer an opinion about the case's likely outcome in court. After the presentations, the managers attempt to negotiate a settlement.

Other ADR Devices
Other ADR devices include (1) *med/arb* (a hybrid of mediation and arbitration in which a third party first acts as a mediator, and then as an arbitrator), (2) the use of *magistrates* and *special masters* to perform various tasks during complex litigation in the federal courts, (3) *early neutral evaluation (ENE)* (a court-annexed procedure involving early, objective evaluation of the case by a neutral private attorney with experience in its subject matter), (4) *private judging* (in which litigants hire a private referee to issue a decision that may be binding but that usually does not preclude recourse to the courts), and (5) *private panels* instituted by an industry or an organization to handle claims of certain kinds (e.g., the Better Business Bureau). In addition, some formal legal processes are sometimes called ADR devices. Examples include small claims courts and the administrative procedures used to handle claims for veterans' benefits or Social Security benefits.

Problems and Problem Cases

1. Victoria Wilson, a resident of Illinois, wishes to bring an invasion of privacy lawsuit against XYZ Co. because XYZ used a photograph of her, without her consent, in an advertisement for one of the company's products. Wilson will seek money damages of $150,000 from XYZ, whose principal offices are located in New Jersey. A New Jersey newspaper was the only print media outlet in which the advertisement was published. However, XYZ also placed the advertisement on the firm's website. This website may be viewed by anyone with Internet access, regardless of the viewer's geographic location. Where, in a geographic sense, may Wilson properly file and pursue her lawsuit against XYZ? Must Wilson pursue her case in a state court, or does she have the option of litigating in federal court? Assuming that Wilson files her case in state court, what strategic option may XYZ exercise if it acts promptly?

2. Alex Ferrer, a former judge who appeared as "Judge Alex" on a television program, entered into a contract with Arnold Preston, a California attorney who rendered services to persons in the entertainment industry. Seeking fees allegedly due under the contract, Preston invoked the clause setting forth the parties' agreement to arbitrate "any dispute . . . relating to the terms of [the contract] or the breach, validity, or legality thereof . . . in accordance with the rules [of the American Arbitration Association]." Ferrer countered Preston's demand for arbitration by filing, with the California Labor Commissioner, a petition in which he contended that the contract was unenforceable under the California Talent Agencies Act (CTAA) because Preston supposedly acted as a talent agent without the license required by the CTAA. In addition, Ferrer sued Preston in a California court, seeking a declaration that the dispute between the parties regarding the contract and its validity was not subject to arbitration. Ferrer also sought an injunction restraining Preston from proceeding before the arbitrator unless and until the Labor Commissioner concluded that she did not have authority to rule on the parties' dispute. Preston responded by moving to compel arbitration, in reliance on the Federal Arbitration Act. The California court denied Preston's motion to compel arbitration and issued the injunction sought by Ferrer. Was the court correct in doing so?

3. Dog-breeders Ron and Catherine Bombliss lived in Illinois. They bred Tibetan mastiffs, as did Oklahoma residents Anne and Jim Cornelsen. When Anne Cornelson telephoned the Bomblisses and said she was ready to sell two litters of Tibetan mastiff puppies, Ron Bombliss expressed interest in purchasing two females of breeding quality. The Cornelsens had a website that allowed communications regarding dogs available for purchase but did not permit actual sales via the website. The Bomblisses traveled to Oklahoma to see the Cornelsens' puppies and ended up purchasing two of them. The Cornelsens provided a guarantee that the puppies were suitable for breeding purposes. Following the sale, the Cornelsens mailed, to the Bomblisses' home in Illinois, American Kennel Club registration papers for the puppies. Around this same time, Anne Cornelsen posted comments in an Internet chat room frequented by persons interested in Tibetan mastiffs. These comments suggested that the mother of certain Tibetan mastiff puppies (including one the Bomblisses had purchased) may have had a genetic disorder. The comments were made in the context of an apparent dispute between the Cornelsens and Richard Eichhorn, who owned the mother mastiff and had made it available to the Cornelsens for breeding purposes. The Bomblisses believed that the comments would have been seen by other persons in Illinois and elsewhere and would have impaired the Bomblisses' ability to sell their puppies even though, when tested, their puppies were healthy. The Bomblisses therefore sued the Cornelsens in an Illinois court on various legal theories. The Cornelsens asked the Illinois court to dismiss the case on the ground that the court lacked in personam jurisdiction over them. Did the Illinois court lack in personam jurisdiction?

4. Hall Street Associates was the landlord and Mattel Inc. was the tenant under various leases for property that Mattel used as a manufacturing site for many years. The leases provided that the tenant would indemnify the landlord for any costs resulting from the tenant's failure to follow environmental laws while using the premises. Tests of the property's well water in 1998 showed high levels of trichloroethylene (TCE), the apparent residue of manufacturing discharges connected with Mattel's operations on the site between 1951 and 1980. After the Oregon Department of Environmental Quality (DEQ) discovered even more pollutants, Mattel signed a consent order with the DEQ providing for cleanup of the site. After Mattel gave notice of intent to terminate the lease in 2001, Hall Street sued, contesting Mattel's right to vacate on the date it gave and claiming that the leases obliged Mattel to

indemnify Hall Street for the costs of cleaning up the TCE. A federal district court ruled in Mattel's favor on the termination issue. The parties then proposed that they be permitted to submit the indemnification issue to arbitration rather than having the court rule on it. The court was amenable. The parties drew up an arbitration agreement, which the court approved and entered as an order. One paragraph of the agreement provided that

> [t]he United States District Court for the District of Oregon may enter judgment upon any [arbitration] award, either by confirming the award or by vacating, modifying or correcting the award. The court shall vacate, modify or correct any award: (i) where the arbitrator's findings of facts are not supported by substantial evidence, or (ii) where the arbitrator's conclusions of law are erroneous.

The arbitrator initially decided in Mattel's favor on the indemnification question, but the federal district court vacated the arbitrator's decision on the ground of legal error (the basis set forth in the parties' arbitration agreement). On remand, the arbitrator ruled in favor of Hall Street. The district court upheld this ruling. Mattel then appealed to the U.S. Court of Appeals for the Ninth Circuit, arguing that the arbitrator's initial decision in Mattel's favor should be reinstated. In particular, Mattel argued that the agreement calling for the district court to vacate the arbitrator's decision in the event of legal error amounted to an unenforceable attempt to expand the legally permitted grounds for setting aside an arbitrator's decision (as set forth in the Federal Arbitration Act). How did the Ninth Circuit rule?

5. WWP Inc. (WWP) is a charitable organization that furnishes assistance to injured military veterans and their families. WWP conducts its operations under the name "Wounded Warrior Project." After WWP had been in existence for approximately a year, a separate, unaffiliated charitable organization, Wounded Warriors Family Support Inc. (WWFS), began providing assistance to injured veterans and their families. WWFS operated outside the United States as of 2002 but later became active within the United States. WWFS also launched a website whose domain name, "wounded warriors.org," was similar to a domain name used by WWP. In addition, WWFS's website included content referring to a "Wounded Warriors Hospital Fund." Through use of this website, WWFS received large amounts of donated funds. WWP sued WWFS in the U.S. District Court for the District of

Nebraska. Relying on various legal theories, WWP alleged that WWFS created confusion through its website as to whether WWP and WWFS were affiliated and that WWFS had been unjustly enriched through receipt and retention of donations actually meant for WWP. After a jury trial, the district court awarded WWP approximately $1.7 million in damages and issued an injunction meant to curb further instances of confusion. WWFS appealed to the U.S. Court of Appeals for the Eighth Circuit. In its appeal, WWFS argued (among other things) that the district court had erred in denying WWFS's motion to compel WWP to produce "[a]ll documents relating to or evidencing any donations received by [WWP] from January 1, 2002 to the present" after WWP refused to provide the documents. WWFS also argued on appeal that the district court erred in allowing a forensic accountant to testify as an expert witness who offered an opinion regarding the amount of damages allegedly sustained by WWP. WWFS argued that the forensic accountant should not have been permitted to testify as an expert because he utilized what WWFS regarded as simple mathematical calculations and because his opinion on damages was insufficiently connected with the facts of the case. Did the district court err in denying the motion to compel production of the requested documents? Did the district court err in permitting the forensic accountant to offer an expert opinion?

6. Jerrie Gray worked at a Tyson Foods plant where she was exposed to comments, gestures, and physical contact that, she alleged, constituted sexual harassment. Tyson disputed the allegation, arguing that the behavior was not unwelcome; that the complained-about conduct was not based on sex; that the conduct did not affect a term, condition, or privilege of employment; and that proper remedial action was taken in response to any complaint by Gray of sexual harassment. During the trial in federal court, a witness for Gray repeatedly volunteered inadmissible testimony that the judge had to tell the jury to disregard. At one point, upon an objection from the defendant's counsel, the witness asked, "May I say something here?" The judge told her she could not. Finally, after the jury left the courtroom, the witness had an angry outburst that continued into the hallway, in view of some of the jurors.

The jury awarded Gray $185,000 in compensatory and $800,000 in punitive damages. Tyson believed that it should not have been liable, that the awards of damages were excessive and unsupported by evidence, and that the inadmissible evidence and improper conduct had tainted the proceedings. What courses of action may Tyson pursue?

7. Oklahoma resident Samantha Guffey purchased a used 2009 Volvo XC90 (Volvo) from Odil Ostonakulov and Motorcars of Nashville Inc. (MNI). Ostonakulov resides in Tennessee. MNI is a Tennessee corporation with its principal place of business in Nashville, Tennessee. Ostonakulov and MNI operate a used car lot in Nashville. The sale occurred after Guffey was the winning bidder for the car in an auction by MNI on eBay. After receiving the Volvo, Guffey determined that it was not in the condition advertised. She later sued Ostonakulov and MNI in an Oklahoma state trial court for alleged fraud and alleged violations of an Oklahoma consumer protection law. The defendants moved to dismiss for lack of in personam jurisdiction.

In an affidavit Guffey provided for the court as it considered the defendants' jurisdiction objection, Guffey stated that she bid on the Volvo listed on eBay based, in part, on the representation of a 30-day limited warranty on the car. The affidavit also stated that after she submitted her bid, but several days before the closing date of the auction, she received an e-mail solicitation from Ostonakulov suggesting that she contact him by phone and negotiate a "buy-it-now" price for the vehicle. She chose not to do so, but only after calling and speaking with him personally about the matter. After Gulley learned that she had won the auction with the highest bid, she had her father call and speak to Ostonakulov about final details and payment instructions. Ostonakulov mailed a purchase agreement to Gulley's father's office in Oklahoma City. Gulley signed the agreement and returned it to Tennessee. Ostonakulov also helped arrange shipping of the vehicle to Oklahoma, where Guffey took delivery. According to Guffey's affidavit, the eBay sale to her was not an isolated transaction for the defendants and that they have between 12 and 35 cars listed for sale every day on eBay. The affidavit also asserted that the defendants had sold at least three cars in Oklahoma and that they have sold more than 30 cars to Oklahoma residents.

Oklahoma has a long-arm statute that applies to the full extent permitted by due process principles. The Oklahoma trial court dismissed the case after concluding that it did not have in personam jurisdiction over the defendants. Guffey appealed to the Supreme Court of Oklahoma. How did that court rule on the jurisdiction question?

8. Abbott Laboratories manufactured and sold the Life Care PCA, a pump that delivers medication into a person intravenously at specific time intervals. Beverly Lewis sued Abbott in a Mississippi state court, alleging that a defective Life Care PCA had injured her by delivering an excessive quantity of morphine. Abbott served Lewis with a request for admission calling for her to admit that her damages did not exceed $75,000. Lewis did not answer the request for admission. Abbott removed the case to the U.S. District Court for the Southern District of Mississippi, predicating the court's subject-matter jurisdiction on diversity of citizenship and an amount in controversy exceeding $75,000. Contending that her silence had amounted to an admission that her damages were less than $75,000, Lewis filed a motion asking that the federal court remand the case to the state court. Did the federal court have subject-matter jurisdiction? How did the federal court rule on Lewis's motion to send the case back to the state court?

9. The state of New Jersey says it is sovereign over certain landfilled portions of Ellis Island. The state of New York disagrees, asserting that it is sovereign over the whole of the island. New Jersey brings an action in the U.S. District Court for the Southern District of New York. Should the court hear the case?

10. Florian Hinrichs, a citizen of Germany and a member of the German military, had been assigned to Fort Rucker for flight training. Fort Rucker is located in Alabama. Hinrichs and Daniel Vinson were in the same training program. On June 24, 2007 (during the time of his assignment to Fort Rucker), Hinrichs was riding in the front passenger seat of Vinson's 2004 GMC Sierra 1500 pickup truck (the Sierra). Vinson was driving the Sierra. As the vehicle proceeded down an Alabama roadway, it was struck by a vehicle whose intoxicated driver (Kenneth Earl Smith) caused it to run a stop sign. The Sierra rolled over twice, and Hinrichs suffered a spinal-cord injury that left him paralyzed. In the litigation referred to below, Hinrichs alleged that his injuries were caused by the defective design of the Sierra's roof. This design, Hinrichs contended, allowed the roof over the passenger compartment to collapse during the rollover. Hinrichs also alleged that Sierra's seatbelt, which he was wearing at the time of the accident, was defectively designed because it failed to restrain him. General Motors Corp. designed the Sierra. General Motors of Canada Ltd. (GM Canada), whose principal place of business is in Ontario, Canada, is a separate legal entity from

GM. GM Canada was incorporated under Canadian law and has its principal place of business in Ontario, Canada. It does not do business directly in the United States. GM Canada manufactured certain parts of the Sierra eventually purchased by Vinson, assembled the vehicle in Canada, and sold it to GM. The transfer of title to the vehicle (i.e., from GM Canada to GM) occurred in Canada. GM then distributed the Sierra for sale in the United States through a dealer located in Pennsylvania. Vinson purchased the Sierra from the Pennsylvania dealer in 2003. He drove it to Alabama in 2006 when he was assigned to Fort Rucker.

Besides suing Smith (the intoxicated driver) for negligence, Hinrichs brought product liability claims against both GM and GM Canada in an Alabama trial court. Arguing that the Alabama court lacked in personam jurisdiction over it, GM Canada moved for dismissal. In opposition to the motion, Hinrichs stressed that even if GM Canada does not do business directly in the United States, it anticipates that almost all of the vehicles it assembles in Canada will end up in the stream of commerce in the United States and that Alabama is among the states in which the vehicles will be sold or driven. The Alabama trial court dismissed the claim against GM Canada on the ground that in personam jurisdiction was lacking. Hinrichs appealed the dismissal. Was the trial court's ruling correct?

Business and the Constitution

A federal statute and related regulations prohibited producers of beer from listing, on a product label, the alcohol content of the beer in the container on which the label appeared. The regulation existed because the U.S. government believed that if alcohol content could be disclosed on labels, certain producers of beer might begin marketing their brand as having a higher alcohol content than competing beers. The government was concerned that "strength wars" among producers could then develop, that consumers would seek out beers with higher alcohol content, and that adverse public health consequences would follow. Because it wished to include alcohol content information on container labels for its beers, Coors Brewing Co. filed suit against the U.S. government and asked the court to rule that the statute and regulations violated Coors's constitutional right to freedom of speech.

Consider the following questions as you read Chapter 3:

- On which provision in the U.S. Constitution was Coors relying in its challenge of the statute and regulations?
- Does a corporation such as Coors possess the same constitutional right to freedom of speech possessed by an individual human being, or does the government have greater latitude to restrict the content of a corporation's speech?
- The alcohol content disclosures that Coors wished to make with regard to its product would be classified as *commercial speech*. Does commercial speech receive the same degree of constitutional protection that political or other noncommercial speech receives?
- Which party—Coors or the federal government—won the case, and why?
- Do producers and other sellers of alcoholic beverages have, in connection with the sale of their products, special ethical obligations that sellers of other products might not have? If so, what are those obligations and why do they exist?

LO LEARNING OBJECTIVES

After studying this chapter, you should be able to:

3-1 Describe the role of courts in interpreting constitutions and in determining whether statutes or other government actions are constitutional.

3-2 Explain the key role of the U.S. Constitution's Commerce Clause in authorizing action by Congress.

3-3 Explain the burden-on-commerce doctrine's role in making certain state government actions unconstitutional.

3-4 Describe the incorporation doctrine's role in making most guarantees of the Bill of Rights operate to protect persons not only against certain federal government actions, but also against certain state and local government actions.

3-5 Explain the differences among the means-ends tests used by courts when the constitutionality of government action is being determined (strict scrutiny, intermediate scrutiny, and rational basis).

3-6 Describe the differences between noncommercial speech and commercial speech and the respective levels of First Amendment protection they receive.

3-7 Explain the difference between procedural due process and substantive due process.

3-8 Identify the instances when an Equal Protection Clause–based challenge to government action triggers more rigorous scrutiny than the rational basis test.

3-9 Identify the major circumstances in which federal law will preempt state law.

3-10 Explain the power granted to the government by the Takings Clause, as well as the limits on that power.

CONSTITUTIONS SERVE TWO general functions. First, they set up the structure of government, allocating power among its various branches and subdivisions. Second, they prevent government from taking certain actions—especially actions that restrict individual or, as suggested by the Coors scenario that opened this chapter, corporate rights. This chapter examines the U.S. Constitution's performance of these functions and considers how that performance affects government regulation of business.

An Overview of the U.S. Constitution

The U.S. Constitution exhibits the principle of **separation of powers** by giving distinct powers to Congress, the president, and the federal courts. Article I of the Constitution establishes a Congress composed of a Senate and a House of Representatives, gives it sole power to legislate at the federal level, and sets out rules for the enactment of legislation. Article I, § 8 also defines when Congress can make law by stating its *legislative powers*. Three of those powers—the commerce, tax, and spending powers—are discussed later in the chapter.

Article II gives the president the *executive power*—the power to execute or enforce the laws passed by Congress. Section 2 of that article lists other presidential powers, including the powers to command the nation's armed forces and to make treaties. Article III gives the *judicial power* of the United States to the Supreme Court and the other federal courts later established by Congress. Article III also determines the types of cases the federal courts may decide.

Besides creating a separation of powers, Articles I, II, and III set up a system of **checks and balances** among Congress, the president, and the courts. For example, Article I gives the president the power to veto legislation passed by Congress, but allows Congress to override such a veto by a two-thirds vote of each House. Articles I and II provide that the president, the vice president, and other federal officials may be removed from office if, following an impeachment trial in the Senate, two-thirds of the Senate concludes that the impeached office-holder committed "Treason, Bribery, or other high Crimes and Misdemeanors." Article II states that treaties agreed to by the president must be approved by a two-thirds vote of the Senate. Article III gives Congress some control over the Supreme Court's appellate jurisdiction.

The Constitution recognizes the principle of **federalism** in the way it structures power relations between the federal government and the states. After listing the powers Congress holds, Article I lists certain powers that Congress cannot exercise. The Tenth Amendment provides that those powers the Constitution neither gives to the federal government nor denies to the states are reserved to the states or the people.

Article VI, however, makes the Constitution, laws, and treaties of the United States supreme over state law. As will be seen, this principle of federal supremacy may cause federal statutes to *preempt* inconsistent state laws. The Constitution also puts limits on the states' lawmaking powers. One example is Article I's command that states shall not pass laws impairing the obligation of contracts.

Of course, there is sometimes disagreement (between state and federal officials, for example) about whether a particular branch of government has overreached. For example, in 2020, President Trump challenged a subpoena (issued as part of a state criminal investigation) for financial records related to his personal and business financial records. The president argued that a sitting president is absolutely immune from such a process; among other things, he argued that the criminal subpoenas would divert him from his duties and impose an intolerable burden on a president's ability to perform his Article II functions. The Supreme Court found that distraction was not sufficient to confer absolute immunity and held that Article II and the Supremacy Clause do not preclude or require a heightened standard for the issuance of a state criminal subpoena to a sitting president. *Trump v. Vance,* 140 S. Ct. 2412 (2020).

Article V sets forth the procedures for amending the Constitution. The Constitution has been amended 27 times. The first 10 of these amendments comprise the Bill of Rights. Although the rights guaranteed in the first

10 amendments once restricted only federal government action, most of them now limit state government action as well. As you will learn, this results from their *incorporation* within the Due Process Clause of the Fourteenth Amendment.

The Evolution of the Constitution and the Role of the Supreme Court

 LO3-1 Describe the role of courts in interpreting constitutions and in determining whether statutes or other government actions are constitutional.

According to the legal realists discussed in Chapter 1, written "book law" is less important than what public decision makers *actually do*. Using this approach, we discover a Constitution that differs from the written Constitution just described. The actual powers of today's presidency, for instance, exceed anything one would expect from reading Article II. As you will see, moreover, some constitutional provisions have acquired a meaning different from their meaning when first enacted. American constitutional law has evolved rather than being static.

Many of these changes result from the way one public decision maker—the nine-member U.S. Supreme Court—has interpreted the Constitution over time. Formal constitutional change can be accomplished only through the amendment process. Because this process is difficult to employ, however, amendments to the Constitution have been relatively infrequent. As a practical matter, the Supreme Court has become the Constitution's main "amender" through its many interpretations of constitutional provisions. Various factors help explain the Supreme Court's ability and willingness to play this role. Because of their vagueness, some key constitutional provisions invite diverse interpretations. "Due process of law" and "equal protection of the laws" are examples. In addition, the history surrounding the enactment of constitutional provisions sometimes is sketchy, confused, or contradictory.

Under the power of **judicial review**, courts can declare the actions of other government bodies unconstitutional. How courts exercise this power depends on how they choose to read the Constitution. Courts thus have political power—a conclusion especially applicable to the Supreme Court. Indeed, the Supreme Court's justices are, to a considerable extent, public policy makers. Their beliefs are important in the determination of how the United States is governed. This is why the justices'

nomination and confirmation often involve so much political controversy.

Yet even though the Constitution frequently is what the courts say it is, judicial power to shape the Constitution has limits. Certain limits spring from the Constitution's language, which sometimes is quite clear. Others result from the judges' adherence to the *stare decisis* doctrine discussed in Chapter 1. Perhaps the most significant limits on judges' power, however, stem from the tension between modern judicial review and democracy. Legislators are chosen by the people, whereas judges—especially appellate level judges—often are appointed, not elected. Today, judges exercise political power by declaring the actions of legislatures unconstitutional under standards largely of the judiciary's own devising. This sometimes leads to charges that courts are undemocratic, elitist institutions. Such charges put political constraints on judges because courts depend on the other branches of government—and ultimately on public belief in judges' fidelity to the rule of law—to make their decisions effective. Therefore, judges sometimes may be reluctant to declare statutes unconstitutional because they are wary of power struggles with a more representative body such as Congress.

 **LOG ON**

For a great deal of information about the U.S. Supreme Court and access to the Court's opinions in recent cases, see the Court's website at **http://www.supremecourtus.gov**.

The Coverage and Structure of This Chapter

This chapter examines certain constitutional provisions that are important to business; it does not discuss constitutional law in its entirety. These provisions help define federal and state power to regulate the economy. The U.S. Constitution limits government regulatory power in two general ways. First, it restricts *federal* legislative authority by listing the powers Congress can exercise. These are known as the **enumerated powers**. Federal legislation cannot be constitutional if it is not based on a power specifically stated in the Constitution. Second, the U.S. Constitution limits both *state and federal* power by placing certain **independent checks** in the path of each. In effect, the independent checks establish that even if Congress has an enumerated power to legislate on a particular matter or a state constitution authorizes a state to take certain actions, there still are certain protected spheres into which neither the federal government nor the state government may reach.

Accordingly, a federal law must meet two general tests in order to be constitutional: (1) it must be based on an enumerated power of Congress and (2) it must not collide with any of the independent checks. For example, Congress has the power to regulate commerce among the states. This power might seem to allow Congress to pass legislation forbidding women from crossing state lines to buy or sell goods. Yet such a law, though arguably based on an enumerated power, surely would be unconstitutional because it conflicts with an independent check—the equal protection guarantee discussed later in the chapter. Today, the independent checks are the main limitations on congressional power. The most important reason for the decline of the enumerated powers limitation is the perceived need for active federal regulation of economic and social life. Recently, however, the enumerated powers limitation has begun to assume somewhat more importance, as will be seen.

After discussion of the most important state and federal powers to regulate economic matters, the chapter explores certain independent checks that apply to the federal government and the states. The chapter then examines some independent checks that affect the states alone. It concludes by discussing a provision—the Takings Clause of the Fifth Amendment—that both recognizes a governmental power and limits its exercise.

State and Federal Power to Regulate

State Regulatory Power Although state constitutions may do so, the U.S. Constitution does not list the powers state legislatures can exercise. The U.S. Constitution does place certain independent checks in the path of state lawmaking, however. It also declares that certain powers (e.g., creating currency and taxing imports) can be exercised only by Congress. In many other areas, though, Congress and the state legislatures have *concurrent powers*. Both can make law within those areas unless Congress preempts state regulation under the Supremacy Clause. A very important state legislative power that operates concurrently with many congressional powers is the **police power**, a broad state power to regulate for the public health, safety, morals, and welfare.

Federal Regulatory Power Article I, § 8 of the U.S. Constitution specifies a number of ways in which Congress may legislate concerning business and commercial matters. For example, it empowers Congress to coin and borrow money, regulate interstate commerce, establish uniform laws regarding bankruptcies, create post offices,

and enact copyright and patent laws. The most important congressional powers contained in Article I, § 8, however, are the powers to regulate commerce among the states, to lay and collect taxes, and to spend for the general welfare. Because they now are read broadly, these three powers are the main constitutional bases for the extensive federal social and economic regulation that exists today.

The Commerce Power

 LO3-2 Explain the key role of the U.S. Constitution's Commerce Clause in authorizing action by Congress.

Article I, § 8 states that "The Congress shall have Power . . . . To regulate Commerce . . . among the several States." The original reason for giving Congress this power to regulate *interstate commerce* (that is, commerce between or among multiple states) was to nationalize economic matters by blocking the protectionist state restrictions on interstate trade that were common after the Revolution. As discussed later in the chapter, the Commerce Clause serves as an independent check on state regulation that unduly restricts interstate commerce. Our present concern, however, is the Commerce Clause's role as a source of congressional regulatory power.

The literal language of the Commerce Clause simply empowers Congress to regulate commerce that occurs among the states. Supreme Court decisions interpreting the Commerce Clause have held, however, that it sets up three categories of actions in which Congress may engage: first, regulating the channels of interstate commerce; second, regulating and protecting the instrumentalities of interstate commerce, as well as persons or things in interstate commerce; and third, regulating activities that substantially affect interstate commerce. Largely because of judicial decisions regarding congressional action falling within the third category, the Commerce Clause has become a federal power with an extensive regulatory reach. How has this transformation occurred?

The most important step in the transformation was the Supreme Court's conclusion that the power to regulate *interstate* commerce includes the power to regulate *intrastate* (that is, commerce within a state) activities that affect interstate commerce. For example, in a 1914 decision, the Supreme Court upheld the Interstate Commerce Commission's regulation of railroad rates within Texas (an intrastate matter outside the language of the Commerce Clause) because those rates affected rail traffic between Texas and Louisiana (an interstate matter within the clause's language). This "affecting commerce" doctrine eventually was used to justify federal police power measures with significant intrastate reach. For instance, the Supreme Court upheld the application of the 1964 Civil Rights Act's "public accommodations" section to a family-owned restaurant in Birmingham, Alabama. It did so because the restaurant's racial discrimination affected interstate commerce by reducing the restaurant's business and limiting its purchases of out-of-state meat and by restricting the ability of Blacks to travel among the states.

By the early 1990s, broad judicial interpretations of the Commerce Clause led many observers to conclude that the clause established a federal power with almost unlimited reach. Then two Supreme Court decisions, *United States v. Lopez*, 514 U.S. 549 (1995), and *United States v. Morrison*, 529 U.S. 598 (2000), offered clear reminders that the power to regulate interstate commerce is not without limits. Those cases struck down laws that made possessing a gun in a school zone a federal crime (*Lopez*) and addressed gender-motivated violent crimes (*Morrison*). In both cases, the Court held that Congress had exceeded its power.

One area that has tested Congress's Commerce Clause power is the federal ban on marijuana. Though many states and cities have made it legal as a matter of state law, it remains (at least at the time of this writing) illegal under federal law. The Supreme Court has found that Congress has the power to prohibit its use under federal law, finding that there exists an interstate market for the drug and that such a law regulates economic activity. *Gonzales v. Raich*, 545 U.S. 1 (2005).

In the case below, the Court considered whether a state law was an unconstitutional burden on interstate commerce.

South Dakota v. Wayfair, Inc.	**138 S. Ct. 2080 (2018)**

The State of South Dakota (like most states) requires companies to collect a sales tax on goods and services sold in the state and remit the money to the state. That practice is fairly straightforward for businesses that sell their products through physical locations in the state (brick-and-mortar stores, for example), when a customer pays at the point of sale. But online retailers with no physical location in the state had argued that states could not force them to collect the tax. The U.S. Supreme Court had ruled in the past, most recently in a case called Quill Corp. v. North Dakota *(504 U.S. 298 (1992)), that states could not require a business to collect the state's sales tax if that business had no physical presence in the state. That ruling was based on the Commerce Clause: Without a strong connection between the business and the state (such as a physical presence), the tax collection requirement imposed an undue burden on the free flow of interstate commerce.*

South Dakota sued Wayfair and other online retailers, seeking to require them to collect its sales tax from online sales to customers in South Dakota. It argued that the "physical presence" rule was depriving them of needed tax dollars and should be overturned. Because of binding precedent from the U.S. Supreme Court (i.e., the Quill *case and a case before it called* Bellas Hess*), the retailers won on their motions for summary judgment in the trial court and the South Dakota Supreme Court. The U.S. Supreme Court granted certiorari to hear South Dakota's appeal.*

Kennedy, Justice

All concede that taxing the sales in question here is lawful. The question is whether the out-of-state seller can be held responsible for its payment, and this turns on a proper interpretation of the Commerce Clause, U.S. Const., Art. I, § 8, cl. 3.

Under this Court's decisions in *Bellas Hess* and *Quill*, South Dakota may not require a business to collect its sales tax if the business lacks a physical presence in the State. Without that physical presence, South Dakota instead must rely on its residents to pay the use tax owed on their purchases from out-of-state sellers. "[T]he impracticability of [this] collection from the multitude of individual purchasers is obvious." *National Geographic Soc. v. California Bd. of Equalization*, 430 U.S. 551, 555 (1977). And consumer compliance rates are notoriously low. . . . It is estimated that *Bellas Hess* and *Quill* cause the States to lose between $8 and $33 billion every year. . . . In South Dakota alone, the Department of Revenue estimates revenue loss at $48 to $58 million annually. Particularly because South Dakota has no state income tax, it must put substantial reliance on its sales and use taxes for the revenue necessary to fund essential services. Those taxes account for over 60 percent of its general fund.

In 2016, South Dakota confronted the serious inequity *Quill* imposes by enacting S. 106–"An Act to provide for the collection of sales taxes from certain remote sellers, to establish certain Legislative findings, and to declare an emergency." The legislature found that the inability to collect sales tax from remote sellers was "seriously eroding the sales tax base" and "causing revenue losses and imminent harm . . . through the loss of critical funding for state and local services." § 8(1). . . . The Act applies only to sellers that, on an annual basis, deliver more than $100,000 of goods or services into the State or engage in 200 or more separate transactions for the delivery of goods or services into the State.

Respondents Wayfair, Inc., Overstock.com, Inc., and Newegg, Inc., are merchants with no employees or real estate in South

Dakota. . . . Each easily meets the minimum sales or transactions requirement of the Act, but none collects South Dakota sales tax.

II.

The Constitution grants Congress the power "[t]o regulate Commerce . . . among the several States." Art. I, § 8, cl. 3. . . . Although the Commerce Clause is written as an affirmative grant of authority to Congress, this Court has long held that in some instances it imposes limitations on the States absent congressional action.

Modern precedents rest upon two primary principles that mark the boundaries of a State's authority to regulate interstate commerce. First, state regulations may not discriminate against interstate commerce; and second, States may not impose undue burdens on interstate commerce.

[A] State "may tax exclusively interstate commerce so long as the tax does not create any effect forbidden by the Commerce Clause." [*Complete Auto Transit, Inc. v. Brady*, 430 U.S. 274, 285 (1977)]. After all, "interstate commerce may be required to pay its fair share of state taxes." *D. H. Holmes Co. v. McNamara*, 486 U.S. 24, 31 (1988).

In *National Bellas Hess, Inc. v. Department of Revenue of Ill.*, 386 U.S. 753, 754–55 (1967),] . . . [t]he Court held that . . . [unless a] retailer maintained a physical presence such as "retail outlets, solicitors, or property within a State," the State lacked the power to require that retailer to collect a local use tax. *Ibid.*

In 1992, the Court reexamined the physical presence rule in *Quill.*

III

The physical presence rule has "been the target of criticism over many years from many quarters." *Direct Marketing Assn. v. Brohl*, 814 F.3d 1129, 1148, 1150–1151 (10th Cir. 2016) (Gorsuch, J., concurring). . . . *Quill* created an inefficient "online sales tax loophole" that gives out-of-state businesses an advantage. And "while nexus rules are clearly necessary," the Court "should focus on rules that are appropriate to the twenty-first century, not the nineteenth." Hellerstein, *Deconstructing the Debate Over State Taxation of Electronic Commerce*, 13 Harv. J. L. & Tech. 549, 553 (2000). Each year, the physical presence rule becomes further removed from economic reality and results in significant revenue losses to the States. These critiques underscore that the physical presence rule, both as first formulated and as applied today, is an incorrect interpretation of the Commerce Clause.

All agree that South Dakota has the authority to tax these transactions. . . . The central dispute is whether South Dakota may require remote sellers to collect and remit the tax without some additional connection to the State. . . . There just must be "a substantial nexus with the taxing State."

Physical presence is not necessary to create a substantial nexus. The *Quill* majority expressed concern that without the physical presence rule "a state tax might unduly burden interstate commerce" by subjecting retailers to tax collection obligations in thousands of different taxing jurisdictions. But the administrative costs of compliance, especially in the modern economy with its Internet technology, are largely unrelated to whether a company happens to have a physical presence in a State. For example, a business with one salesperson in each State must collect sales taxes in every jurisdiction in which goods are delivered; but a business with 500 salespersons in one central location and a website accessible in every State need not collect sales taxes on otherwise identical nationwide sales.

Quill puts both local businesses and many interstate businesses with physical presence at a competitive disadvantage relative to remote sellers. Remote sellers can avoid the regulatory burdens of tax collection and can offer *de facto* lower prices caused by the widespread failure of consumers to pay the tax on their own. . . . In effect, *Quill* has come to serve as a judicially created tax shelter for businesses that decide to limit their physical presence and still sell their goods and services to a State's consumers—something that has become easier and more prevalent as technology has advanced.

Worse still, the rule produces an incentive to avoid physical presence in multiple States. . . . Rejecting the physical presence rule is necessary to ensure that artificial competitive advantages are not created by this Court's precedents.

Modern e-commerce does not align analytically with a test that relies on the sort of physical presence defined in *Quill.*

Between targeted advertising and instant access to most consumers via any internet-enabled device, "a business may be present in a State in a meaningful way without" that presence "being physical in the traditional sense of the term." *Quill*'s physical presence rule intrudes on States' reasonable choices in enacting their tax systems. And that it allows remote sellers to escape an obligation to remit a lawful state tax is unfair and unjust. It is unfair and unjust to those competitors, both local and out of State, who must remit the tax; to the consumers who pay the tax; and to the States that seek fair enforcement of the sales tax, a tax many States for many years have considered an indispensable source for raising revenue.

In essence, respondents ask this Court to retain a rule that allows their customers to escape payment of sales taxes—taxes that are essential to create and secure the active market they supply with goods and services. An example may suffice. Wayfair offers to sell a vast selection of furnishings. Its advertising seeks to create an image of beautiful, peaceful homes, but it also says that "[o]ne of the best things about buying through Wayfair is that we do not have to charge sales tax." Brief for Petitioner 55. What Wayfair ignores in its subtle offer to assist in tax evasion is that creating a dream home assumes solvent state and local governments. State taxes fund the police and fire departments that protect the homes containing their customers' furniture and ensure goods are safely delivered; maintain the public roads and municipal services that allow communication with and access to customers; support the "sound local banking institutions to support credit transactions [and] courts to ensure collection of the purchase price," *Quill,* 504 U.S., at 328 (opinion of White, J.); and help create the "climate of consumer confidence" that facilitates sales.

IV

* * *

Though *Quill* was wrong on its own terms when it was decided in 1992, since then the Internet revolution has made its earlier error all the more egregious and harmful. . . . In 1992, less than 2 percent of Americans had Internet access. Today that number is about 89 percent. When it decided *Quill,* the Court could not have envisioned a world in which the world's largest retailer would be a remote seller.

The Internet's prevalence and power have changed the dynamics of the national economy. In 1992, mail-order sales in the United States totaled $180 billion. Last year, e-commerce retail sales alone were estimated at $453.5 billion.

This expansion has also increased the revenue shortfall faced by States seeking to collect their sales and use taxes. In 1992, it was estimated that the States were losing between $694 million and $3 billion per year in sales tax revenues as a result of the physical presence rule. Now estimates range from $8 to $33 billion.

Here, the tax distortion created by *Quill* exists in large part because consumers regularly fail to comply with lawful use taxes. Some remote retailers go so far as to advertise sales as tax free.

For these reasons, the Court concludes that the physical presence rule of *Quill* is unsound and incorrect. The Court's decisions in *Quill Corp. v. North Dakota,* 504 U.S. 298 (1992), and *National Bellas Hess, Inc. v. Department of Revenue of Ill.,* 386 U.S. 753 (1967), should be, and now are, overruled.

V

In the absence of *Quill* and *Bellas Hess,* the first prong of the *Complete Auto* test simply asks whether the tax applies to an activity with a substantial nexus with the taxing State. "[S]uch a nexus is established when the taxpayer [or collector] 'avails itself of the substantial privilege of carrying on business' in that jurisdiction." *Polar Tankers, Inc. v. City of Valdez,* 557 U.S. 1, 11 (2009).

Here, the nexus is clearly sufficient based on both the economic and virtual contacts respondents have with the State. The Act applies only to sellers that deliver more than $100,000 of goods or services into South Dakota or engage in 200 or more separate transactions for the delivery of goods and services into the State on an annual basis. This quantity of business could not have occurred unless the seller availed itself of the substantial privilege of carrying on business in South Dakota. And respondents are large, national companies that undoubtedly maintain an extensive virtual presence. Thus, the substantial nexus requirement of *Complete Auto* is satisfied in this case.

The judgment of the Supreme Court of South Dakota is vacated, and the case is remanded for further proceedings not inconsistent with this opinion.

The Taxing Power Article I, § 8 of the Constitution states that "The Congress shall have Power To lay and collect Taxes, Duties, Imposts and Excises." The main purpose of this *taxing power* is to provide a means of raising revenue for the federal government. The taxing power, however, may also serve as a regulatory device. Congress may choose to regulate a disfavored activity by taxing it heavily or may opt to encourage a favored activity by lowering or eliminating a tax on it. Today, the reach of the taxing power is seen as very broad, as evidenced by *National Federation of Independent Business v. Sebelius,* which follows shortly.

The Spending Power If taxing-power regulation uses a federal club, congressional *spending-power* regulation employs a federal carrot. Article I, § 8 also gives Congress a broad ability to spend for the general welfare. By basing the receipt of federal money on the performance of certain conditions, Congress can use the spending power to encourage states to take certain actions and thereby advance specific regulatory ends. Conditional federal grants to the states, for instance, are common today.

Over the past several decades, congressional spending-power regulation routinely has been upheld. There are limits, however, on its use. First, an exercise of the spending power must serve *general* public purposes rather than particular interests. Second, when Congress conditions the receipt of federal money on certain conditions, it must do so clearly. Third, the condition must be reasonably related to the purpose underlying the federal expenditure. This means, for instance, that Congress probably could not condition a state's receipt of federal highway money on the state's adoption of a one-house legislature. Fourth, though Congress may use conditional grants of funding to states to encourage them to take certain regulatory actions, Congress can neither compel states to enact a desired regulatory program nor otherwise coerce them into doing so. For an example of issues arising under this last limit on Congress's spending power, see the *National Federation* case, which follows shortly.

The Necessary and Proper Clause After listing the commerce power, the taxing and spending powers, and various other powers extended to Congress, Article I, § 8 concludes with a provision granting Congress the further power to "make all Laws which shall be necessary and proper for carrying into Execution the foregoing Powers. . . ." The Necessary and Proper Clause is dependent upon Article I, § 8's previously listed powers but augments them by permitting Congress to enact laws that are useful or conducive to the exercise of those enumerated powers.

Figure 3.1   A Note on the Affordable Care Act Decision

Congress enacted the Patient Protection and Affordable Care Act (hereinafter, Affordable Care Act or ACA) in 2010. Several cases filed shortly thereafter in federal courts presented constitutional challenges to two provisions in the statute: (1) the requirement, applicable to most Americans, that they have health insurance in force by a certain date specified in the law or, instead, pay what the statute termed a "[s]hared responsibility payment" (a provision that has come to be known as the *individual mandate* and will be referred to by that designation here) and (2) the requirement that states participate in an expansion of Medicaid, the long-standing federally created program under which the federal government and the states act together to fund health care for low-income persons and others with special needs.

After the lower courts issued conflicting decisions, the Supreme Court agreed to decide the constitutionality of the challenged provisions. *National Federation of Independent Business v. Sebelius* (hereinafter, *NFIB*) proved to be not only an important Commerce Clause case, but also a major decision regarding two other enumerated powers, the taxing power and the spending power. This note focuses on *NFIB*'s treatment of the Commerce Clause issue triggered by the individual mandate referred to above. An edited version of *NFIB* appears in the chapter. It focuses on the 2012 decision's taxing-power and spending-power analyses, which dealt, respectively, with the individual mandate and the Medicaid expansion provision.

When Congress enacted the Affordable Care Act, it relied chiefly on the Commerce Clause as the source of power to enact the law. The federal government, accordingly, placed primary emphasis on the Commerce Clause when it sought to defend the individual mandate in the courts. The government invoked its taxing power as an alternative justification.

Although there was no true majority opinion for the Supreme Court on the commerce-power question in *NFIB*, five justices concluded that the individual mandate exceeded the regulatory authority Congress possesses under the Commerce Clause. Chief Justice Roberts, who wrote for a majority of the Court on the taxing-power question, garnered no official votes for the portion of his opinion dealing with the commerce power. However, the four dissenting justices—Scalia, Kennedy, Thomas, and Alito—joined in an opinion adopting a commerce-power analysis that closely resembled the Chief Justice's analysis. (The dissenters' extreme dissatisfaction with the Chief Justice's treatment of the taxing-power issue probably kept them from joining any part of the Roberts opinion despite their apparent agreement with his Commerce Clause analysis.)

Chief Justice Roberts and the four dissenters separately acknowledged that the Court's precedents contemplated expansive authority for Congress under the Commerce Clause. They concluded, however, that the individual mandate went beyond what those precedents would authorize. The Chief Justice stressed that in giving Congress the power to "regulate" commerce, the Commerce Clause presupposes the existence of relevant activity to be regulated. The individual mandate, he observed, sought to compel persons not otherwise inclined to engage in commercial activity to do so by purchasing insurance. Noting the seemingly unprecedented nature of a congressional requirement that persons make a purchase from a private party, the Chief Justice asserted that the Court's precedents dealing with activities substantially affecting interstate commerce could not be stretched far enough to let Congress reach the absence of commercial activity and regulate it by requiring such activity.

The four dissenters took a similar tack, emphasizing that the individual mandate amounted to an impermissible attempt to regulate inactivity rather than the activity necessary, in their view, to make the Commerce Clause a potential source of regulatory authority. (The other four justices—Ginsburg, Breyer, Sotomayor, and Kagan—regarded the Court's "affecting commerce" precedents as leading logically to the conclusion that the individual mandate should be seen as authorized under the Commerce Clause, given the inevitability that everyone will need health care at some point and the notion that the insurance requirement was largely a payment mechanism designed to help control health care costs. Their Commerce Clause arguments failed, however.)

With five justices concluding that the Commerce Clause did not authorize the individual mandate, it became necessary for the Court to determine whether a separate enumerated power—the taxing power—would provide the necessary constitutional foundation for the provision (which, as noted earlier, required that an individual make a "[s]hared responsibility payment" if he or she did not obtain health insurance). Although the taxing-power argument was its backup argument, the government succeeded with it. Chief Justice Roberts, joined by Justices Ginsburg, Breyer, Sotomayor, and Kagan, determined that the congressional power to tax justified the provision. (See the later edited version of *NFIB*, which focuses on the taxing-power issue as well as the spending-power issue raised by the Affordable Care Act's Medicaid expansion provision.)

Critics of the Affordable Care Act and of the notion that the Commerce Clause permits expansive federal power likely were heartened by the government's failure to succeed with its commerce-power argument in *NFIB*. But if critics won the Commerce Clause battle, they lost the constitutional war. The government's success with the taxing-power argument meant that the individual mandate—often described as the centerpiece of the Affordable Care Act—was every bit as constitutional as it would have been if the government had succeeded with the Commerce Clause argument.

At the time of this writing, the Supreme Court was preparing to consider another challenge to the ACA. In cases brought by a group of states, some plaintiffs claim the entire law should be struck down because of changes that Congress had made to the law. Specifically, Congress changed the penalty for not buying health insurance, making the penalty zero. A legal question the cases present is whether the change to the law means that the entire ACA is now unconstitutional.

National Federation of Independent Business v. Sebelius
567 U.S. 519 (2012)

Congress enacted the Patient Protection and Affordable Care Act in 2010 (hereinafter, ACA) in an effort to increase the number of Americans covered by health insurance and decrease the cost of health care. As noted in Figure 3.1, one key ACA provision has come to be known as the individual mandate. That provision requires most Americans to maintain "minimum essential" health insurance coverage. For persons who are not exempt, and who do not receive health insurance through an employer or government program, the means of satisfying the requirement is to purchase insurance from a private company.

The ACA further requires that those who do not comply with the mandate to have insurance in force must make a "[s]hared responsibility payment" to the federal government. That payment, which the ACA describes as a "penalty," is calculated as a percentage of household income, subject to a floor based on a specified dollar amount and a ceiling based on the average annual premium the individual would have to pay for qualifying private health insurance. The ACA states that this "penalty" will be paid to the Internal Revenue Service (IRS) with an individual's taxes, and "shall be assessed and collected in the same manner" as tax penalties. Some individuals who are subject to the insurance mandate are nonetheless exempt from the shared responsibility payment if their income is below a certain threshold.

As noted in Figure 3.1, the ACA also features a provision calling for an expansion of the Medicaid program, which offers federal funding to states to assist low-income families, children, pregnant women, the blind, the elderly, and the disabled in obtaining medical care. The ACA provision at issue expands Medicaid's scope and increases the number of individuals the states must cover. For example, the ACA calls for state programs to provide Medicaid coverage to adults with incomes up to 133 percent of the federal poverty level, whereas many states historically have covered adults with children only if their income is considerably lower and have not covered childless adults at all. The ACA's Medicaid provision increases federal funding to cover all of the states' costs in expanding Medicaid coverage in early years of the expansion and most of those costs in succeeding years. However, the ACA also provides that if a state does not comply with the new Medicaid coverage requirements, the state could lose not merely the federal funding for those requirements, but potentially all of its federal Medicaid funds.

In various federal court cases, plaintiffs challenged the above-referred-to ACA provisions on constitutional grounds. The cases yielded conflicting results. Included among the cases was one filed by 26 states, several individuals, and the National Federation of Independent Business. In that case, the U.S. Court of Appeals for the Eleventh Circuit concluded that Congress lacked constitutional authority to enact the individual mandate. However, the Eleventh Circuit upheld the Medicaid expansion as a valid exercise of Congress's spending power. The U.S. Supreme Court agreed to decide the case.

As explained in Figure 3.1, five justices concluded in National Federation of Independent Business v. Sebelius *that the Commerce Clause could not be interpreted as authorizing the individual mandate. The following edited version of the opinion authored by Chief Justice Roberts focuses on whether Congress's taxing power authorizes the individual mandate and on whether Congress's spending power justifies the Medicaid expansion. Justices Ginsburg, Breyer, Sotomayor, and Kagan joined the Chief Justice to form a majority on the taxing-power question. On the spending-power question, Justices Breyer and Kagan subscribed to the Chief Justice's analysis. Justices Ginsburg and Sotomayor provided the fourth and fifth votes for the outcome reached by the Chief Justice's opinion on the Medicaid expansion, though they otherwise disagreed with his analysis.*

Roberts, Chief Justice

Today we resolve constitutional challenges to two provisions of the ACA: the individual mandate, which requires individuals to purchase a health insurance policy providing a minimum level of coverage [or, instead, make a "[s]hared responsibility payment"]; and the Medicaid expansion, which gives funds to the states on the condition that they provide specified health care to all citizens whose income falls below a certain threshold.

[R]ather than granting general authority to perform all the conceivable functions of government, the Constitution lists, or enumerates, the federal government's powers. The same does not apply to the states, because the Constitution is not the source of their power. The Constitution may restrict state governments—as it does, for example, by forbidding them to deny any person the equal protection of the laws. But where such prohibitions do not apply, state governments do not need constitutional authorization to act. The states thus can and do perform many of the vital functions of modern government—punishing street crime, running public schools, and zoning property for development, to name but a few. Our cases refer to this general power, possessed by the states but not by the federal government, as the police power.

This case concerns . . . powers that the Constitution does grant the federal government, but which must be read carefully to avoid creating a general federal authority akin to the police power. The Constitution authorizes Congress to "regulate Commerce with foreign Nations, and among the several States, and with the Indian Tribes." Art. I, § 8, cl. 3. Congress may also "lay and collect Taxes, Duties, Imposts and Excises, to pay the Debts and provide for the common Defence and general Welfare of the United States." Art. I, § 8, cl. 1. Put simply, Congress may tax and spend. This grant gives the federal government considerable influence even in areas where it cannot directly regulate. The federal government may enact a tax on an activity that it cannot authorize, forbid, or otherwise control. And in exercising its spending power, Congress may offer funds to the states, and may condition those offers on compliance with specified conditions. These offers may well induce the states to adopt policies that the federal government itself could not impose.

The reach of the federal government's enumerated powers is broader still because the Constitution authorizes Congress to "make all Laws which shall be necessary and proper for carrying into Execution the foregoing Powers." Art. I, § 8, cl. 18. We have long read this provision to give Congress great latitude

in exercising its powers. Our respect for Congress's policy judgments [, however,] can never extend so far as to disavow restraints on federal power that the Constitution carefully constructed.

The Individual Mandate and the Taxing Power

The government advances two theories for the proposition that Congress had constitutional authority to enact the ACA's individual mandate. First, the government argues that Congress had the power to enact the mandate under the Commerce Clause. [Alternatively], the government argues that if the commerce power does not support the mandate, we should nonetheless uphold it as an exercise of Congress's power to tax.

[*Authors' note:* As explained earlier, the government failed to succeed with its Commerce Clause argument. For discussion of the Court's Commerce Clause analysis, see Figure 3.1.]

Because the Commerce Clause does not support the individual mandate, it is necessary to turn to the government's second argument: that the mandate may be upheld as within Congress's enumerated power to "lay and collect Taxes." Under the mandate, if an individual does not maintain health insurance, the only consequence is that he must make an additional payment to the IRS when he pays his taxes. That, according to the government, means the mandate can be regarded as establishing a condition—not owning health insurance—that triggers a tax—the required payment to the IRS. Under that theory, the mandate is not a legal command to buy insurance. Rather, it makes going without insurance just another thing the government taxes, like buying gasoline or earning income. And if the mandate is in effect just a tax hike on . . . taxpayers who do not have health insurance, it may be within Congress's constitutional power to tax. Granting the ACA the full measure of deference owed to federal statutes, it can be so read.

The exaction the Affordable Care Act imposes on those without health insurance looks like a tax in many respects. The "[s]hared responsibility payment," as the statute entitles it, is paid into the Treasury by "taxpayer[s]" when they file their tax returns. It does not apply to individuals who do not pay federal income taxes because their household income is less than the filing threshold in the Internal Revenue Code. For taxpayers who do owe the payment, its amount is determined by such familiar factors as taxable income, number of dependents, and joint filing status. The requirement to pay is found in the Internal Revenue Code and enforced by the IRS, which . . . must assess and collect it "in the same manner as taxes." This process yields the essential feature of any tax: it produces at least some revenue for the government. Indeed, the payment is expected to raise about $4 billion per year by 2017.

It is of course true that the Act describes the payment as a "penalty," not a "tax." But . . . that label . . . does not determine whether the payment may be viewed as an exercise of Congress's taxing power. [We have decided cases in which something labeled as a "penalty" was nevertheless a tax, and other cases in which something labeled a "tax" was nevertheless a penalty.]

The [use of a functional analysis that is not tied to labels] suggests that the shared responsibility payment may for constitutional purposes be considered a tax, not a penalty. First, for most Americans the amount due will be far less than the price of insurance, and, by statute, it can never be more. In 2016, for example, individuals making $35,000 a year are expected to owe the IRS about $60 for any month in which they do not have health insurance. Someone with an annual income of $100,000 a year would likely owe about $200. The price of a qualifying insurance policy is projected to be around $400 per month. It may often be a reasonable financial decision to make the payment rather than purchase insurance, unlike [a situation in which there would be a large] financial punishment. Second, the individual mandate contains no . . . requirement [of knowing wrongdoing or other corrupt intent]. Third, the payment is collected solely by the IRS through the normal means of taxation—except that the IRS is *not* allowed to use those means most suggestive of a punitive sanction, such as criminal prosecution. The [types of] reasons the Court [has used in previous cases for concluding that] what was called a "tax" . . . was a penalty support the conclusion that what is called a "penalty" here may be viewed as a tax.

None of this is to say that the payment is not intended to affect individual conduct. Although the payment will raise considerable revenue, it is plainly designed to expand health insurance coverage. But taxes that seek to influence conduct are nothing new. Some of our earliest federal taxes sought to deter the purchase of imported manufactured goods in order to foster the growth of domestic industry. Today, federal and state taxes can compose more than half the retail price of cigarettes, not just to raise more money, but to encourage people to quit smoking. And we have upheld such obviously regulatory measures as taxes on selling marijuana and sawed-off shotguns.

Indeed, "[e]very tax is in some measure regulatory. To some extent it interposes an economic impediment to the activity taxed as compared with others not taxed." [Citation omitted.] That [the challenged ACA provision] seeks to shape decisions about whether to buy health insurance does not mean that it cannot be a valid exercise of the taxing power. Because the Constitution permits such a tax, it is not our role to forbid it, or to pass upon its wisdom or fairness.

The Medicaid Expansion and the Spending Power

The states also contend that the Medicaid expansion exceeds Congress's authority under [its spending power]. They claim that Congress is coercing the states to adopt the changes it wants by threatening to withhold all of a state's Medicaid grants, unless the state accepts the new expanded funding and complies with the conditions that come with it. This, they argue, violates the basic principle that the "federal government may not compel the states to enact or administer a federal regulatory program." *New York v. United States*, 505 U.S. 144, 188 (1992).

There is no doubt that the ACA [calls for] dramatic[ ] increases [in] state obligations under Medicaid. The current Medicaid program requires states to cover only certain discrete categories of needy individuals—pregnant women, children, needy families, the blind, the elderly, and the disabled. There is no mandatory coverage for most childless adults, and the states typically do not offer any such coverage. The states also enjoy considerable flexibility with respect to the coverage levels for parents of needy families. On average states cover only those unemployed parents who make less than 37 percent of the federal poverty level, and only those employed parents who make less than 63 percent of the poverty line.

The Medicaid provisions of the ACA, in contrast, require states to expand their Medicaid programs by 2014 to cover all individuals under the age of 65 with incomes below 133 percent of the federal poverty line. The ACA provides that the federal government will pay 100 percent of the costs of covering these newly eligible individuals through 2016. In the following years, the federal payment level gradually decreases, to a minimum of 90 percent. In light of the expansion in coverage mandated by the ACA, the federal government estimates that its Medicaid spending will increase by approximately $100 billion per year.

The [Constitution's] Spending Clause grants Congress the power "to pay the Debts and provide for the . . . general Welfare of the United States." Art. I, § 8, cl. 1. We have long recognized that Congress may use this power to grant federal funds to the states, and may condition such a grant upon the states' "taking certain actions that Congress could not require them to take." [Citation omitted.] Such measures "encourage a state to regulate in a particular way, [and] influenc[e] a state's policy choices." [Citation omitted.]

At the same time, our cases have recognized limits on Congress's power under the Spending Clause to secure state compliance with federal objectives. We have repeatedly characterized . . . Spending Clause legislation as "much in the nature of a *contract*." [Citations omitted.] The legitimacy of Congress's exercise of the spending power "thus rests on whether the State voluntarily and knowingly accepts the terms of the contract."

[Citation omitted.] Respecting this limitation is critical to ensuring that Spending Clause legislation does not undermine the status of the states as independent sovereigns in our federal system.

That insight has led this Court to strike down federal legislation that commandeers a state's legislative or administrative apparatus for federal purposes. It has also led us to scrutinize Spending Clause legislation to ensure that Congress is not using financial inducements to exert a "power akin to undue influence." [Citation omitted.] Congress may use its spending power to create incentives for states to act in accordance with federal policies. But when pressure turns into compulsion, the legislation runs contrary to our system of federalism. Spending Clause programs do not pose this danger when a state has a legitimate choice whether to accept the federal conditions in exchange for federal funds. In such a situation, state officials can fairly be held politically accountable for choosing to accept or refuse the federal offer. But when the state has no choice, the federal government can achieve its objectives without accountability.

Congress may attach appropriate conditions to federal taxing and spending programs to preserve its control over the use of federal funds. In the typical case we look to the states to defend their prerogatives by adopting "the simple expedient of not yielding" to federal blandishments when they do not want to embrace the federal policies as their own. [Citation omitted.] The states, however, argue that the Medicaid expansion is far from the typical case. They object that [instead] of simply refusing to grant the new funds to states that will not accept the new conditions, Congress has also threatened to withhold those states' existing Medicaid funds. The states claim that this threat serves no purpose other than to force unwilling states to sign up for the dramatic expansion in health care coverage effected by the ACA. Given the nature of the threat and the programs at issue here, we must agree.

In *South Dakota v. Dole*, 483 U.S. 203 (1987), we considered a challenge to a federal law that threatened to withhold five percent of a State's federal highway funds if the State did not raise its drinking age to 21. The Court found that the condition was "directly related to one of the main purposes for which highway funds are expended—safe interstate travel." [*Id.*] at 208. At the same time, the condition was not a restriction on how the highway funds—set aside for specific highway improvement and maintenance efforts—were to be used. We accordingly asked whether "the financial inducement offered by Congress" was "so coercive as to pass the point at which pressure turns into compulsion." *Id.* at 211. By "financial inducement" the Court meant the threat of losing 5 percent of highway funds; no new money was offered to the states to raise their drinking ages. We found that the inducement was not impermissibly coercive, because Congress was offering only "relatively mild encouragement to the States." *Id.* We observed that "all South Dakota would lose if she adheres to her chosen course as to a suitable minimum drinking age is 5 percent" of her highway funds. *Id.* In fact, the federal funds at stake constituted less than half of one percent of South Dakota's budget at the time. In consequence, "we conclude[d] that [the] encouragement to state action [was] a valid use of the spending power." *Id.* at 212. Whether to accept the drinking age change "remain[ed] the prerogative of the states not merely in theory but in fact." *Id.* at 211–212.

In this case, the financial "inducement" Congress has chosen is much more than "relatively mild encouragement"—it is a gun to the head. A state that opts out of the ACA's expansion in health care coverage . . . stands to lose not merely "a relatively small percentage" of its existing Medicaid funding, but *all* of it. Medicaid spending accounts for over 20 percent of the average state's total budget, with federal funds covering 50 to 83 percent of those costs. It is easy to see how the *Dole* Court could conclude that the threatened loss of less than half of one percent of South Dakota's budget left that state a "prerogative" to reject Congress's desired policy, "not merely in theory but in fact." The threatened loss of over 10 percent of a state's overall budget, in contrast, is economic dragooning that leaves the states with no real option but to acquiesce in the Medicaid expansion.

Nothing in our opinion precludes Congress from offering funds under the ACA to expand the availability of health care, and requiring that states [agreeing to accept] such funds comply with the conditions on their use. What Congress is not free to do is to penalize states that choose not to participate in that new program by taking away their existing Medicaid funding. In light of the Court's holding, the [federal government] cannot . . . withdraw existing Medicaid funds [from states] for failure to comply with the requirements set out in the [ACA's Medicaid] expansion.

The Court today limits the financial pressure the [federal government] may apply to induce states to accept the terms of the Medicaid expansion. As a practical matter, that means states may now choose to reject the expansion. Some states may indeed decline to participate. Other states, however, may voluntarily sign up, finding the idea of expanding Medicaid coverage attractive, particularly given the level of federal funding the ACA offers at the outset.

Judgment of Eleventh Circuit affirmed insofar as it held that individual mandate exceeded commerce power, reversed insofar as it held that individual mandate was not authorized by taxing power, and reversed insofar as it held that Medicaid expansion was justified under spending power.

Burden on, or Discrimination against, Interstate Commerce

 Explain the burden-on-commerce doctrine's role in making certain state government actions unconstitutional.

In addition to empowering Congress to regulate interstate commerce, the Commerce Clause limits the states' ability to *burden* or discriminate against such commerce. This limitation is not expressly stated in the Constitution. Instead, it arises by implication from the Commerce Clause and reflects that clause's original purpose of blocking state protectionism and ensuring free interstate trade. (Because this limitation arises by implication, it is often referred to as the "dormant" Commerce Clause.) The burden-on-commerce limitation and the nondiscrimination principle operate independently of congressional legislation under the commerce power or other federal powers. If appropriate federal regulation is present, the preemption questions discussed in the next section may also arise.

Many different state laws can raise burden-on-commerce problems. For example, state regulation of transportation (e.g., limits on train or truck lengths) has been a prolific source of litigation. The same is true of state restrictions on the importation of goods or resources, such as laws forbidding the sale of out-of-state food products unless they meet certain standards. Such restrictions sometimes benefit local economic interests and reflect their political influence. Burden-on-commerce issues also arise if states try to aid their own residents by blocking the export of scarce or valuable products, thus denying out-of-state buyers access to those products.

In part because of the variety of state regulations it has had to consider, the Supreme Court has not adhered to one consistent test for determining when such regulations impermissibly burden interstate commerce. In a 1994 case, the Court said that if a state law *discriminates* against interstate commerce, the strictest scrutiny will be applied in the determination of the law's constitutionality. Discrimination is *express* when state laws treat local and interstate commerce unequally on their face.

State laws might also discriminate even though on their face, they seem neutral regarding interstate commerce. This occurs when their *effect* is to burden or hinder such commerce. In one case, for example, the Supreme Court considered a North Carolina statute that required all closed containers of apples sold within the state to bear only the applicable U.S. grade or standard. The State of Washington, the nation's largest apple producer, had its own inspection and grading system for Washington apples. This system generally was regarded as superior to the federal system. The Court struck down the North Carolina statute because it benefited local apple producers by forcing Washington sellers to regrade apples sold in North Carolina (thus raising their costs of doing business) and by undermining the competitive advantage provided by Washington's superior grading system.

On the other hand, state laws that regulate evenhandedly and have only incidental effects on interstate commerce are constitutional if they serve legitimate state interests and their local benefits exceed the burden they place on interstate commerce. There is no sharp line between such regulations and those that are almost always unconstitutional under the tests discussed above. In a 1981 Supreme Court case, a state truck-length limitation that differed from the limitations imposed by neighboring states failed to satisfy the tests for constitutionality. The Court concluded that the measure did not further the state's legitimate interest in highway safety because the trucks banned by the state generally were as safe as those it allowed. In addition, whatever marginal safety advantage the law provided was outweighed by the numerous problems it posed for interstate trucking companies.

Laws may also unconstitutionally burden interstate commerce when they *directly regulate* that commerce. This can occur, for example, when state price regulations require firms to post the prices at which they will sell within the state and to promise that they will not sell below those prices in other states. Because they affect prices in other states, such regulations directly regulate interstate commerce and usually are unconstitutional.

Independent Checks on the Federal Government and the States

Even if a regulation is within Congress's enumerated powers or a state's police power, it still is unconstitutional if it collides with one of the Constitution's *independent checks*. This section discusses three checks that limit federal and state regulation of the economy: freedom of speech, due process, and equal protection. Before discussing these guarantees, however, we must consider three foundational matters.

Incorporation

 Describe the incorporation doctrine's role in making most guarantees of the Bill of Rights operate to protect persons not only against certain federal government actions, but also against certain state and local government actions.

The Fifth Amendment prevents the federal government from depriving "any person . . . of life, liberty, or property, without due process of law." The Fourteenth Amendment creates the same prohibition with regard to the states. The literal language of the First Amendment, however, restricts only federal government action. Moreover, the Fourteenth Amendment says that no *state* shall "deny to any person . . . the equal protection of the laws."

Thus, although the due process guarantees clearly apply to both the federal government and the states, the First Amendment seems to apply only to the federal government and the Equal Protection Clause only to the states. The First Amendment's free speech guarantee, however, has been included within the "liberty" protected by Fourteenth Amendment due process as a result of Supreme Court decisions. The free speech guarantee, therefore, restricts state governments as well as the federal government. This is an example of the process of *incorporation*, by which almost all Bill of Rights provisions now apply to the states. The criminal procedure–related provisions in the Fourth, Fifth, and Sixth Amendments (examined in Chapter 5 of this text) are further examples of Bill of Rights protections that the federal government must honor but that state and local governments must respect as well because of the incorporation doctrine. The Fourteenth Amendment's equal protection guarantee, on the other hand, has been made applicable to federal government action through incorporation of it within the Fifth Amendment's Due Process Clause.

Government Action

People often talk as if the Constitution protects them against anyone who might threaten their rights. However, most of the Constitution's individual rights provisions block only the actions of *government* bodies, federal, state, and local.[1] Private behavior that denies individual rights, while perhaps forbidden by statute, is very seldom a constitutional matter. This **government action** or **state action** requirement forces courts to distinguish between governmental behavior and private behavior. Judicial approaches to this problem have varied over time.

Before World War II, only formal arms of government such as legislatures, administrative agencies, municipalities, courts, prosecutors, and state universities were deemed state actors. After the war, however, the scope of government action increased considerably, with various sorts of traditionally private behavior being subjected to individual rights limitations. The Supreme Court, in *Marsh*

v. Alabama, 326 U.S. 501 (1946), treated a privately owned company town's restriction of free expression as government action under the *public function* theory because the town was nearly identical to a regular municipality in most respects. In *Shelley v. Kraemer*, 334 U.S. 1 (1948), the Court held that when state courts enforced certain white homeowners' private agreements not to sell their homes to Blacks, there was state action that violated the Equal Protection Clause. Later, in *Burton v. Wilmington Parking Authority*, 365 U.S. 715 (1961), the Court concluded that racial discrimination by a privately owned restaurant located in a state-owned and state-operated parking garage was unconstitutional state action, in part because the garage and the restaurant were intertwined in a mutually beneficial "symbiotic" relationship. Among the other factors leading courts to find state action during the 1960s and 1970s were extensive government regulation of private activity and government financial aid to a private actor.

The Court, however, severely restricted the reach of state action during the 1970s and 1980s. Since then, private behavior generally has not been held to constitute state action unless a regular unit of government is directly *responsible* for the challenged private behavior because it has coerced or encouraged such behavior. The public function doctrine, moreover, has been limited to situations in which a private entity exercises powers that have *traditionally* been *exclusively* reserved to the state; private police protection is a possible example. In addition, government regulation and government funding have become somewhat less important factors in state action determinations.

Means-Ends Tests

 LO3-5 Explain the differences among the means-ends tests used by courts when the constitutionality of government action is being determined (strict scrutiny, intermediate scrutiny, and rational basis).

Throughout this chapter, you will see tests of constitutionality that may seem strange at first glance. One example is the test for determining whether laws that discriminate on the basis of sex violate equal protection. This test says that to be constitutional, such laws must be substantially related to the achievement of an important government purpose. The Equal Protection Clause does not contain such language. It simply says that "No State shall . . . deny to any person . . . the equal protection of the laws." What is going on here?

The sex discrimination test just stated is a **means-ends test** developed by the Supreme Court. Such tests are judicially created because no constitutional right is absolute and because judges, therefore, must weigh individual rights against the

---

[1]However, the Thirteenth Amendment, which bans slavery and involuntary servitude throughout the United States, does not have a government action requirement. Some state constitutions, moreover, have individual rights provisions that lack a state action requirement.

social purposes served by laws that restrict those rights. In other words, means-ends tests determine how courts strike the balance between individual rights and the social needs that may justify their suppression. The "ends" component of a means-ends test specifies how *significant* a social purpose must be in order to justify the restriction of a right. The "means" component states how *effectively* the challenged law must promote that purpose in order to be constitutional. In the sex discrimination test, for example, the challenged law must serve an "important" government purpose (the significance of the end) and must be "substantially" related to the achievement of that purpose (the effectiveness of the means).

Some constitutional rights are deemed more important than others. Accordingly, courts use tougher tests of constitutionality in certain cases and more lenient tests in other situations. Sometimes these tests are lengthy and complicated. Throughout the chapter, therefore, we will simplify by referring to three general kinds of means-ends tests:

1. *The rational basis test.* This is a very relaxed test of constitutionality that challenged laws usually pass with ease. A typical formulation of the rational basis test might say that government action need only have a *reasonable* relation to the achievement of a *legitimate* government purpose to be constitutional.

2. *Intermediate scrutiny.* This comes in many forms; the sex discrimination test discussed above is an example.

3. *Full strict scrutiny.* Here, the court might say that the challenged law must be *necessary* to the fulfillment of a *compelling* government purpose. (Sometimes a court might choose different phrasing, such as by saying that the challenged law must be *narrowly tailored* to fulfillment of the government's compelling purpose. Despite the different phrasing, the test is substantively the same.) Government action that is subjected to this rigorous test of constitutionality is usually struck down.

Business and the First Amendment

LO3-6 Describe the differences between noncommercial speech and commercial speech and the respective levels of the First Amendment protection they receive.

The First Amendment provides that "Congress shall make no law . . . abridging the freedom of speech." Despite its absolute language ("*no* law"), the First Amendment does not prohibit every law that restricts speech. Although the First Amendment's free speech guarantee is not absolute, government action restricting the content of speech usually receives close scrutiny from the courts. One justification

for this high level of protection is the "marketplace" rationale, under which the free competition of ideas is seen as the surest means of attaining truth. The marketplace of ideas operates most effectively, according to this rationale, when restrictions on speech are kept to a minimum and all viewpoints can be considered.

During recent decades, the First Amendment has been applied to a wide variety of government restrictions on the expression of individuals and organizations, including corporations. This chapter does not attempt a comprehensive discussion of the many applications of the freedom of speech guarantee. Instead, it explores basic First Amendment concepts before turning to an examination of the free speech rights of corporations.

The religion portions of the First Amendment are mostly beyond the scope of this text. Two issues related to business, though, bear mention here. First, in 2017, a company called Hobby Lobby argued that its religious beliefs should exempt it from having to comply with certain Affordable Care Act regulations that it found objectionable—specifically, a rule requiring it to cover the cost of contraceptives for its employees. The Court did not consider the First Amendment implications but instead ruled in Hobby Lobby's favor on the ground that the company had religious beliefs under a statute called the Religious Freedom Restoration Act. *Burwell v. Hobby Lobby Stores,* 573 U.S. 682 (2014).

Second, in one well-publicized case, a baker in Colorado declined to bake a cake for a same-sex wedding, claiming that it violated his religious beliefs. He argued that the cakes he baked, though for a business, were expressive activity protected by the First Amendment. The U.S. Supreme Court ruled in his favor but not on First Amendment grounds (instead, it found that the state administrative agency had acted improperly when considering his claim). It seems inevitable that the Court will address the First Amendment arguments in some similar case in the future, eventually deciding whether a business has such a right. *See Masterpiece Cakeshop, Ltd. v. Colorado Civil Rights Commission,* 138 S. Ct. 1719 (2018).

Restrictions on Content of Speech For constitutional purposes, there is a fundamental distinction between *conduct* and *speech* (or, to use a frequently employed alternative term, *expression*). Because conduct usually does not receive constitutional protection, the government typically has considerable latitude to regulate it. Speech, on the other hand, enjoys First Amendment protection. The line between unprotected conduct and potentially protected speech may seem distinct, but that is not always the case in actual practice. Consider the cases involving so-called expressive conduct—conduct so inherently expressive that it is treated for First Amendment purposes the same as speech uttered verbally or communicated in writing. As the Supreme Court has held, flag-burning is an example of expressive conduct. Most conduct is not considered to be inherently expressive, however, and thus does not receive First Amendment protection.

In a recent Supreme Court decision, *Expressions Hair Design v. Schneiderman*, 137 S. Ct. 1144 (2017), the conduct-versus-speech issue came to the forefront. A New York statute barred merchants from imposing, on customers who paid by credit card, a surcharge in addition to the price charged to cash-paying customers. Expressions Hair Design (EHD) wished to post notices that announced a price for cash-paying customers and that an added fee would be tacked on for credit-card-paying customers. Because it feared that posting such notices could leave it vulnerable to legal proceedings for alleged violations of the statute, EHD challenged the statute on First Amendment grounds. The State of New York argued that the statute merely regulated price and was therefore a conduct regulation undeserving of the First Amendment. The Supreme Court disagreed, classifying the statute as a speech restriction—and hence potentially a violation of the First Amendment—because it had the effect of prohibiting the communication of the price information that EHD wished to convey.

If speech stands to be affected by a law or other government action speech, the next key question is whether the government action restricts the *content* of speech, as opposed to operating in a content-neutral way by regulating such matters as time, place, or manner of speech. Whereas content-neutral restrictions are evaluated under a looser test for First Amendment purposes, content restrictions strike at the heart of the freedom of speech guarantee and are reviewed with strict scrutiny.

An example comes from *Reed v. Town of Gilbert*, 576 U.S. 155 (2015), which pertained to an Arizona town's sign code that prohibited the display of outdoor signs without a permit but set forth various exemptions from the prohibition. One exemption was for "Ideological Signs," another was for "Political Signs," and another was for "Temporary Directional Signs." Signs in the first two categories could be much larger than those in the Temporary Directional Signs category, and either had no placement or time-of-display restrictions (Ideological Signs) or could be displayed during a time period of significant length (Political Signs, which could be displayed during an election season). Temporary Directional Signs, however, had to be much smaller. Moreover, they could only be displayed not more than 12 hours before a qualifying event and not more than one hour afterward. A church that was cited for violating the Temporary Directional Signs time restrictions challenged the town code provisions as a violation of the First Amendment. Rejecting the town's argument that the code's sign provisions were content-neutral because they

did not single out particular viewpoints for adverse treatment, the Supreme Court emphasized that the provisions still were content restrictions because their application depended completely on the communicative content of the signs. The Court concluded that the code provisions could not withstand strict scrutiny because even if it were assumed that the town possessed compelling interests in aesthetics and public safety, there were content-neutral ways of furthering those objectives (such as by consistently regulating such matters as sign size, materials, lighting, and portability). Therefore, the sign provisions violated the First Amendment.

The Court also noted in *Reed* that viewpoint-discrimination, though not present in the case and not necessary for a content restriction to be identified, is a particularly egregious type of content restriction. *Matal v. Tam*, which appears later in the chapter, provides an example of viewpoint discrimination and the role it plays in First Amendment analysis.

Political and Other Noncommercial Speech Political speech—expression that deals in some fashion with government, government issues or policies, public officials, or political candidates—is often described as being at the "core" of the First Amendment. Various Supreme Court decisions have held, however, that the freedom of speech guarantee applies not only to political speech, but also to noncommercial expression that does not have a political content or flavor. According to these decisions, the First Amendment protects speech of a literary or artistic nature; speech dealing with scientific, economic, educational, and ethical issues; and expression on many other matters of public interest or concern. Government attempts to restrict the content of political or other noncommercial speech normally receive full strict scrutiny when challenged in court. Unless the government is able to meet the exceedingly difficult burden of proving that the speech restriction is *necessary* to the fulfillment of a *compelling government purpose*, a First Amendment violation will be found. Because government restrictions on political or other noncommercial speech trigger the full strict scrutiny test, such speech is referred to as carrying "full" First Amendment protection.

Do *corporations*, however, have the same First Amendment rights that individual human beings possess? The Supreme Court has consistently provided a "yes" answer to this question. Therefore, if a corporation engages in political or other noncommercial expression, it is entitled to full First Amendment protection, just as an individual would be if he or she engaged in such speech. In the much-publicized *Citizens United* case, which follows shortly, the Supreme Court ruled on a First Amendment–based challenge to a federal statute that restricted uses of corporate funds for "electioneering communications" close to the time of an election and for advertisements amounting to express advocacy for or against a candidate who was seeking office. Treating the funding restrictions as speech restrictions, a five-justice majority of the Court held that they violated the First Amendment because they could not withstand strict scrutiny. Figure 3.2, which follows the case, describes some observed impacts of the *Citizens United* decision on subsequent election cycles.

Although corporate speakers have First Amendment rights, not all speech of a corporation is fully protected. Some corporate speech is classified as **commercial speech**, a category of expression examined later in the chapter. As

will be seen, commercial speech receives First Amendment protection but not the full variety extended to political or noncommercial speech. The mere fact, however, that a profit motive underlies speech does not make the speech commercial in nature. Books, movies, television programs, musical works, works of visual art, and newspaper, magazine, and journal articles are normally classified as noncommercial speech—and are thus fully protected—despite the typical existence of an underlying profit motive. Their informational, educational, artistic, or entertainment components are thought to outweigh, for First Amendment purposes, the profit motive.

Citizens United v. Federal Election Commission
558 U.S. 310 (2010)

Citizens United, a nonprofit corporation with a $12 million annual budget, receives most of its funds in the form of donations by individuals. A small portion comes from for-profit corporations. In January 2008, Citizens United released a film titled Hillary: The Movie *(hereinafter* Hillary*). It is a 90-minute documentary about then-senator Hillary Clinton, a candidate in the Democratic Party's 2008 presidential primary elections.* Hillary *depicts interviews with political commentators and other persons, most of them quite critical of Senator Clinton.*

Hillary *was released in theaters and on DVD, but Citizens United wanted to increase distribution by making it available through video-on-demand. Although video-on-demand services often require viewers to pay a small fee to view a selected program, Citizens United planned to pay for the service and to make* Hillary *available to viewers free of charge. To promote the film, Citizens United produced two 10-second advertisements and one 30-second ad for airing on broadcast and cable television. Each ad included a pejorative statement about Senator Clinton, followed by the name of the movie and the address of a website for the movie.*

Before the Bipartisan Campaign Reform Act of 2002 (BCRA), federal law prohibited corporations and unions from using general treasury funds for direct contributions to candidates or as independent expenditures expressly advocating, through any form of media, the election or defeat of a candidate in certain qualified federal elections. 2 U.S.C. § 441b. The BCRA amended § 441b to include any "electioneering communication" as well. The statute defined "electioneering communication" as "any broadcast, cable, or satellite communication" that "refers to a clearly identified candidate for Federal office" and is made within 30 days of a primary election or 60 days of a general election.

When combined, the federal law that preexisted the BCRA and the amendments added by the BCRA barred corporations and unions from using their general treasury funds for express advocacy or electioneering communications. However, they were permitted to establish a "separate segregated fund" (known as a political action committee, or PAC) for these purposes. The funds to be received by the PAC were limited to donations from the corporation's stockholders and employees or from the union's members.

Citizens United wanted to make Hillary *available through video-on-demand within 30 days of the 2008 primary elections. It feared, however, that both the film and the ads promoting it would be covered by § 441b's ban on corporate-funded independent expenditures and could thus subject the corporation to civil and criminal penalties. Citizens United therefore sought declaratory and injunctive relief against the FEC, arguing that § 441b was unconstitutional on its face and as applied to* Hillary *and that the BCRA's disclaimer and disclosure requirements were unconstitutional as applied to* Hillary *and to the three ads for the movie. A federal district court granted the FEC's motion for summary judgment. The court held that § 441b was constitutional under previous Supreme Court precedents, as were the statute's disclaimer and disclosure requirements. Citizens United sought review by the Supreme Court (rather than a circuit court of appeals) under a review provision in the challenged law.*

Kennedy, Justice

Federal law prohibits corporations and unions from using their general treasury funds to make independent expenditures for speech defined as an "electioneering communication" or for speech expressly

advocating the election or defeat of a candidate. 2 U.S.C. § 441b. Limits on electioneering communications were upheld in *McConnell v. Federal Election Comm'n*, 540 U.S. 93 (2003). The holding of *McConnell* rested to a large extent on an earlier case, *Austin v. Michigan Chamber of Commerce*, 494 U.S. 652 (1990). In this case we are asked to reconsider *Austin* and, in effect, *McConnell*.

The law before us is an outright ban [on speech], backed by criminal sanctions. Section 441b makes it a felony for all corporations—including nonprofit advocacy corporations—either to expressly advocate the election or defeat of candidates or to broadcast electioneering communications within 30 days of a primary election and 60 days of a general election. These prohibitions are classic examples of censorship.

Section 441b is a ban on corporate speech notwithstanding the fact that a PAC created by a corporation can still speak. A PAC is a separate association from the corporation. So the PAC exemption from § 441b's expenditure ban does not allow corporations to speak. Even if a PAC could somehow allow a corporation to speak—and it does not—the option to form PACs does not alleviate the First Amendment problems with § 441b. PACs are burdensome alternatives; they are expensive to administer and subject to extensive regulations. [Also,] PACs must file detailed monthly reports with the FEC. PACs have to comply with these regulations just to speak. This might explain why fewer than 2,000 of the millions of corporations in this country have PACs.

[P]olitical speech must prevail against laws that would suppress it, whether by design or inadvertence. Laws that burden political speech are subject to strict scrutiny, which requires the Government to prove that the restriction furthers a compelling interest and is narrowly tailored to achieve that interest. Premised on mistrust of governmental power, the First Amendment stands against attempts to disfavor certain subjects or viewpoints. Prohibited, too, are restrictions distinguishing among different speakers, allowing speech by some but not others. The Court has recognized [in various cases] that First Amendment protection extends to corporations. [*E.g.,*] *First National Bank of Boston v. Bellotti*, 435 U.S. 765 (1978). This protection has been extended by explicit holdings to the context of political speech.

At least since the latter part of the 19th century, the laws of some states and of the United States imposed a ban on corporate *direct contributions* to candidates. Yet not until 1947 did Congress first prohibit *independent expenditures* by corporations and labor unions. For almost three decades thereafter, the Court did not reach the question whether restrictions on corporate and union expenditures are constitutional.

In *Buckley v. Valeo*, 424 U.S. 1 (1976), the Court addressed various challenges to the Federal Election Campaign Act of 1971 (FECA), as amended in 1974. [FECA limited direct contributions to candidates, established] an independent expenditure ban . . . that applied to individuals as well as corporations and labor unions, [and included a separate ban on corporate and union independent expenditures.] [*Buckley* considered only the direct contributions provision and the broader independent expenditure ban that applied to individuals as well as corporations and unions.]

Before addressing the constitutionality of [the broader] independent expenditure ban, *Buckley* first upheld . . . FECA's limits on direct contributions to candidates. The *Buckley* Court recognized a "sufficiently important" governmental interest in "the prevention of corruption and the appearance of corruption." This followed from the Court's concern that large contributions could be given "to secure a political *quid pro quo*." The *Buckley* Court explained that the potential for *quid pro quo* corruption distinguished direct contributions to candidates from independent expenditures. The Court emphasized that "the independent expenditure ceiling . . . fails to serve any substantial governmental interest in stemming the reality or appearance of corruption in the electoral process," because "[t]he absence of prearrangement and coordination . . . alleviates the danger that expenditures will be given as a *quid pro quo* for improper commitments from the candidate." *Buckley* invalidated [FECA's broader] restriction on independent expenditures.

Buckley did not consider [FECA's] separate ban [that specifically applied to] corporate and union independent expenditures. Had [that specific ban] been challenged in the wake of *Buckley*, however, it could not have been squared with the reasoning and analysis of that precedent. [Nevertheless], Congress recodified [the] corporate and union expenditure ban at 2 U.S.C. § 441b four months after *Buckley* was decided. Section 441b is the independent expenditure restriction challenged here.

Less than two years after *Buckley*, *Bellotti* reaffirmed the First Amendment principle that the government cannot restrict political speech based on the speaker's corporate identity. *Bellotti* could not have been clearer when it struck down a state-law prohibition on corporate independent expenditures related to *referenda* issues. *Bellotti* did not address the constitutionality of the state's ban on corporate independent expenditures to support *candidates*. In our view, however, that restriction would have been unconstitutional under *Bellotti*'s central principle: that the First Amendment does not allow political speech restrictions based on a speaker's corporate identity.

Thus the law stood until *Austin*, [which] "uph[eld] a direct restriction on the independent expenditure of funds for political speech for the first time in [this Court's] history." (Kennedy, J., dissenting in *Austin*.) [In *Austin*], the Michigan Chamber of Commerce sought to use general treasury funds to run a newspaper ad supporting a specific candidate. Michigan law, however, prohibited corporate independent expenditures that supported or opposed any candidate for state office. The *Austin* Court sustained the speech prohibition. To bypass *Buckley* and *Bellotti*, the Court identified a new governmental interest in limiting political speech: an anti-distortion interest. *Austin* found a compelling governmental interest in preventing "the corrosive and distorting effects of immense aggregations of wealth that are accumulated with the help of the corporate form and that have little or no correlation to the public's support for the corporation's political ideas."

The Court is thus confronted with conflicting lines of precedent: a pre-*Austin* line that forbids restrictions on political speech based on the speaker's corporate identity and a post-*Austin* line that permits them. No case before *Austin* had held that Congress could prohibit independent expenditures for political speech based on the speaker's corporate identity. In its defense of the corporate-speech restrictions in § 441b, the government notes the anti-distortion rationale on which *Austin* and its progeny rest in part, yet . . . the government does little to defend it. And with good reason, for the rationale cannot support § 441b.

If the First Amendment has any force, it prohibits Congress from fining or jailing citizens, or associations of citizens, for simply engaging in political speech. If the anti-distortion rationale were to be accepted, however, it would permit government to ban political speech simply because the speaker is an association that has taken on the corporate form. If *Austin* were correct, the government could prohibit a corporation from expressing political views in media beyond those presented here, such as by printing books. The government responds "that the FEC has never applied this statute to a book," and if it did, "there would be quite [a] good as-applied [constitutional] challenge." This troubling assertion of brooding governmental power cannot be reconciled with the confidence and stability in civic discourse that the First Amendment must secure.

[As noted in *Bellotti*,] [p]olitical speech is "indispensable to decisionmaking in a democracy, and this is no less true because the speech comes from a corporation rather than an individual." This protection for speech is inconsistent with *Austin*'s anti-distortion rationale. *Austin* sought to defend the anti-distortion rationale as a means to prevent corporations from obtaining "an unfair advantage in the political marketplace" by using "resources amassed in the economic marketplace." But *Buckley* rejected the premise that the government has an interest "in equalizing the relative ability of individuals and groups to influence the outcome of elections." *Buckley* was specific in stating that "the skyrocketing cost of political campaigns" could not sustain the governmental prohibition.

The censorship we now confront is vast in its reach. The government has "muffle[d] the voices that best represent the most significant segments of the economy" (opinion of Scalia, J., in *McConnell*). The purpose and effect of this law is to prevent corporations, including small and nonprofit corporations, from presenting both facts and opinions to the public. This makes *Austin*'s anti-distortion rationale all the more an aberration. When government seeks to use its full power, including the criminal law, to command where a person may get his or her information or what distrusted source he or she may not hear, it uses censorship to control thought. This is unlawful. The First Amendment confirms the freedom to think for ourselves.

What we have said also shows the invalidity of [another argument] made by the government. For the most part relinquishing the anti-distortion rationale, the government falls back on the argument that corporate political speech can be banned in order to prevent corruption or its appearance. The *Buckley* Court . . . sustained limits on *direct contributions* in order to ensure against the reality or appearance of corruption. That case did not extend this rationale to *independent expenditures*, and the Court does not do so here.

[The Court stated in *Buckley* that] "[t]he absence of prearrangement and coordination of an expenditure with the candidate or his agent not only undermines the value of the expenditure to the candidate, but also alleviates the danger that expenditures will be given as a *quid pro quo* for improper commitments from the candidate." Limits on independent expenditures, such as § 441b, have a chilling effect extending well beyond the government's interest in preventing *quid pro quo* corruption. The anti-corruption interest is not sufficient to displace the speech here in question.

For the reasons above, it must be concluded that *Austin* was not well reasoned. *Austin* is [also] undermined by experience since its announcement. Political speech is so ingrained in our culture that speakers find ways to circumvent campaign finance laws. Our nation's speech dynamic is changing, and informative voices should not have to circumvent onerous restrictions to exercise their First Amendment rights.

Rapid changes in technology—and the creative dynamic inherent in the concept of free expression—counsel against upholding a law that restricts political speech in certain media or by certain speakers. Today, 30-second television ads may be the most effective way to convey a political message. Soon, however, it may be that Internet sources, such as blogs and social networking websites, will provide citizens with significant information about political candidates and issues. Yet, § 441b would seem to ban a blog post expressly advocating the election or defeat of a candidate if that blog were created with corporate funds. The First Amendment does not permit Congress to make these categorical distinctions based on the corporate identity of the speaker and the content of the political speech.

Due consideration leads to this conclusion: *Austin* should be and now is overruled. We return to the principle established in *Buckley* and *Bellotti* that the government may not suppress political speech on the basis of the speaker's corporate identity. No sufficient governmental interest justifies limits on the political speech of nonprofit or for-profit corporations.

Austin is overruled, so it provides no basis for allowing the government to limit corporate independent expenditures. As the government appears to concede [in its brief], overruling *Austin* "effectively invalidate[s] not only [the BCRA's amendments to § 441(b)] but also § 441b's prohibition on the use of corporate treasury funds for express advocacy." Section 441b's restrictions on corporate independent expenditures are therefore invalid and cannot be applied to *Hillary*. Given our conclusion, we are further required to overrule the part of *McConnell* that upheld [the BCRA's] extension of § 441b's restrictions on corporate independent expenditures.

District court's judgment reversed as to constitutionality of restrictions on corporate independent expenditures.

Stevens, Justice (joined by Ginsburg, Breyer, and Sotomayor, Justices), concurring in part and dissenting in part

Although I concur in the Court's decision to sustain the BCRA's disclaimer and disclosure provisions, I emphatically dissent from its principal holding.

Citizens United is a wealthy nonprofit corporation that runs a PAC with millions of dollars in assets. Under the BCRA, it could have used those assets to televise and promote *Hillary* wherever and whenever it wanted to. It also could have spent unrestricted sums to broadcast *Hillary* at any time other than the 30 days before the last primary election. Neither Citizens United's nor any other corporation's speech has been "banned." All that the parties dispute is whether Citizens United had a right to use the funds in its general treasury to pay for broadcasts during the 30-day period. The notion that the First Amendment dictates an affirmative answer to that question is, in my judgment, profoundly misguided.

The Court today rejects a century of history when it treats the distinction between corporate and individual campaign spending as an invidious novelty born of *Austin*. Relying largely on individual dissenting opinions, the majority blazes through our precedents, overruling or disavowing a [large] body of case law. The only thing preventing the majority from affirming the district court, or adopting a narrower ground that would retain *Austin*, is its disdain for

Austin. The laws upheld in *Austin* and *McConnell* leave open many additional avenues for corporations' political speech.

Roaming far afield from the case at hand, the majority worries that the government will use [the statute at issue] to ban books, pamphlets, and blogs. Yet by its plain terms, [the statute] does not apply to printed material. And . . . we highly doubt that [§ 441b] could be interpreted to apply to a website or book that happens to be transmitted at some stage over airwaves or cable lines, or that the FEC would ever try to do so.

So let us be clear: Neither *Austin* nor *McConnell* held or implied that corporations may be silenced; the FEC is not a "censor"; and in the years since these cases were decided, corporations have continued to play a major role in the national dialogue. Laws such as [§ 441b] target a class of communications that is especially likely to corrupt the political process. Such laws burden political speech, and that is always a serious matter, demanding careful scrutiny. But the majority's incessant talk of a "ban" aims at a straw man.

In [our] democratic society, the longstanding consensus on the need to limit corporate campaign spending [reflects] the common sense of the American people, who have . . . fought against the distinctive corrupting potential of corporate electioneering since the days of Theodore Roosevelt. It is a strange time to repudiate that common sense. While American democracy is imperfect, few outside the majority of this Court would have thought its flaws included a dearth of corporate money in politics.

Figure 3.2   A Note on Post-*Citizens United* Developments

After *Citizens United*, not-for-profit and for-profit corporations were free to spend unlimited sums from their general treasury funds for express advocacy purposes or for other electioneering communications regarding candidates for federal election, as long as the spending took place independently from the campaigns of favored candidates. Corporations could fund such advertisements directly, without being bound by the invalidated requirement of using a PAC to which only employees and shareholders could contribute. Further, they could engage in such independent expenditures by providing unlimited funds to so-called Super PACs—organizations that were not formally affiliated with candidates for office but accepted money from any individual or organization for the purpose of producing advertisements favoring or disfavoring candidates.

In the run-up to the 2012 elections, some corporations donated significant amounts to Super PACs and other not-for-profit organizations in order to help fund such advertisements. So did many individual persons. This tendency became especially pronounced after a federal court of appeals reasoned that given the conclusions drawn in *Citizens United* and the Supreme Court's long-standing position that the First Amendment rights of individuals and corporations are coextensive, individuals should be free to engage in unlimited spending for express advocacy purposes. In the 2012 elections, certain very wealthy individuals proved to be even bigger spenders in this regard than corporate entities were. The total dollars spent in connection with the 2012 elections easily surpassed the spending levels in previous elections. Similar patterns could be observed in the 2014 and 2016 elections.

Commercial Speech The exact boundaries of the commercial speech category are not certain, though the Supreme Court has usually defined commercial speech as speech that proposes a commercial transaction. As a result, most cases on the subject involve advertisements for the sale of products or services or for the promotion of a business. In 1942, the Supreme Court held that commercial speech fell outside the First Amendment's protective umbrella. The Court reversed its position, however, during the 1970s. It reasoned that informed consumer choice would be furthered by the removal of barriers to the flow of commercial information in which consumers would find an interest. Since the mid-1970s, commercial speech has received an intermediate level of First Amendment protection if it deals with a lawful activity and is nonmisleading. Commercial speech receives no protection, however, if it misleads or seeks to promote an illegal activity. As a result, there is no First Amendment obstacle to federal or state regulation of deceptive commercial advertising. (Political or other noncommercial speech, on the other hand, generally receives—with very few exceptions—full First Amendment protection even if it misleads or deals with unlawful matters.)

Because nonmisleading commercial speech about a lawful activity receives intermediate protection, the government has greater ability to regulate such speech without violating the First Amendment than when the government seeks to regulate fully protected political or other noncommercial speech. Nearly four decades ago, the Supreme Court developed a still-controlling test that amounts to intermediate scrutiny. Under this test, a government restriction on protected commercial speech does not violate the First Amendment if the government proves each of these elements: that a *substantial government interest* underlies the restriction, that the restriction *directly advances* the underlying interest, and that the restriction is *no more extensive than necessary* to further the interest (i.e., that the restriction is narrowly tailored). It usually is not difficult for the government to prove that a substantial interest supports the commercial speech restriction. Almost any asserted interest connected with the promotion of public health, safety, or welfare will suffice. The government is likely to encounter more difficulty, however, in proving that the restriction at issue directly advances the underlying interest without being more extensive than necessary—the elements that address the "fit" between the restriction and the underlying interest. If the government fails to prove any element of the test, the restriction violates the First Amendment.

Although the same test has been used in evaluating commercial speech restrictions for nearly four decades, the Supreme Court has varied the intensity with which it has applied the test. From the mid-1980s until 1995, the Court sometimes applied the test loosely and in a manner favorable to the government. The Court has applied the test—especially the "fit" elements—more strictly since 1995, however. For instance, in *Coors v. Rubin*, 514 U.S. 476 (1995), the Court struck down federal restrictions that kept beer producers from listing the alcohol content of their beer on product labels. (The *Coors* case was the subject of the introductory problem that began this chapter.) In *44 Liquormart v. Rhode Island*, 517 U.S. 484 (1996), the Court held that Rhode Island's prohibition on price disclosures in alcoholic beverage advertisements violated the First Amendment. A 1999 decision, *Greater New Orleans Broadcasting Association v. United States*, 527 U.S. 173 (1999), established that a federal law barring broadcast advertisements for a variety of gambling activities could not constitutionally be applied to radio and television stations located in the same state as the gambling casino whose lawful activities were being advertised. *Sorrell v. IMS Health, Inc.*, 564 U.S. 552 (2011), involved a challenge to a Vermont law that barred pharmacies from releasing data about physicians' prescribing practices and tendencies if the release would be to parties wishing to use the information for marketing purposes. The law, however, allowed pharmacies to disclose such information if it would be used for various other purposes. Continuing to display its inclination to afford significant protection to commercial speech, the Court held that in singling out marketing-related uses for adverse treatment while otherwise allowing the disclosure of the information, the statute violated the First Amendment.

In its commercial speech decisions during the past two-plus decades, the Court has tended to emphasize that the government restrictions at issue suffered from a "fit" problem. Sometimes the defective fit consisted of too tenuous a relationship between the restriction and the government interest underlying it. More frequently the restriction prohibited more speech than was necessary because the government failed to adopt alternative measures that would have furthered the underlying public health, safety, or welfare interest just as well, if not better.

Two key conclusions may be drawn from the Court's commercial speech decisions since 1995: (1) the government has found it more difficult to justify restrictions on commercial speech and (2) the gap between the intermediate protection for commercial speech and the full protection for political and other noncommercial speech has effectively become smaller than it was roughly 25 years ago. Although the Court has hinted that it might consider formal changes in the commercial speech doctrine (so as

The First Amendment

Type of Speech	Level of First Amendment Protection	Consequences When Government Regulates Content of Speech
Noncommercial	Full	Government action is constitutional only if action is necessary to fulfillment of compelling government purpose. Otherwise, government action violates First Amendment.
Commercial (*nonmisleading and about lawful activity*)	Intermediate	Government action is constitutional if government has substantial underlying interest, action directly advances that interest, and action is no more extensive than necessary to fulfillment of that interest (i.e., action is narrowly tailored).
Commercial (*misleading or about unlawful activity*)	None	Government action is constitutional.

to enhance First Amendment protection for commercial speech), it had not made formal doctrinal changes as of the time this book went to press.

Matal v. Tam, which appears later in the chapter, addresses the four-part test utilized in determining the constitutionality of commercial speech restrictions, and illustrates the rigor with which the Supreme Court has applied the third and fourth parts of the test in recent years.

The Government Speech Doctrine Previous discussion has revealed that when the government restricts the content of private parties' speech, a First Amendment violation is likely to have occurred. But when the government itself speaks, it is free to convey its preferred viewpoints and to reject contrary views that private parties wish to express. Such is the premise of the recently developed, and still not precisely defined, *government speech doctrine*.

Whether government speech is present depends largely upon the extent to which the government crafted the conveyed messages or supervised, through heavy involvement, the communication of the messages. In *Johanns v. Livestock Marketing Association*, 544 U.S. 550 (2005), for instance, the Supreme Court upheld a federal statute that set up a program of paid advertisements designed to promote the image and sale of beef products. The Court emphasized that the U.S. Department of Agriculture designed the program, established its contours, and exercised close supervisory authority over the messages that were communicated in the advertisements. Therefore, the

Court, reasoned, the government speech doctrine applied and shielded the program against a First Amendment-based challenge by an association that did not want to participate in the government-created program. More recently, in *Walker v. Texas Division, Sons of Confederate Veterans, Inc.*, 576 U.S. 200 (2015), the Supreme Court held that the First Amendment was not violated—and that the government speech doctrine applied—when the State of Texas rejected a group's request for a specialty license plate consisting of an image of the Confederate battle flag. In deciding that the government speech doctrine applied, the Court stressed the government's historic use of license plates to convey messages and the supervisory control maintained by the government in running the specialty license plate program. Figure 3.3, which appears later in the chapter, explores recent requirements to include graphic warnings on tobacco products.

In *Matal v. Tam*, which follows, the Supreme Court struck down, on First Amendment grounds, a provision in federal law that allowed the government to refuse to register a trademark that is disparaging to individuals or groups. (Trademark registration is addressed in Chapter 8. Discussion of *Tam* also appears there.) In so ruling, the Court rejected the government's attempt to invoke the government speech doctrine and reminded readers that the First Amendment protects a great deal of speech that is offensive in nature. *Tam* also explores an issue noted earlier in the chapter: the problematic nature, for First Amendment purposes, of laws that discriminate among speakers on the basis of the viewpoints they express.

Matal v. Tam   137 S. Ct. 1744 (2017)

Simon Tam is the lead singer of a musical group known as "The Slants." Members of the band are Asian Americans. Although "Slants" has been used as a derogatory term for persons of Asian descent, Tam and the other band members believe that by taking the term as the name of their group, they will help to "reclaim" the term and drain its denigrating force.

Tam sought to have THE SLANTS registered as a trademark on the federal principal register. An examining attorney at the U.S. Patent and Trademark Office (PTO) denied Tam's application, invoking a Lanham Act provision (referred to here as the disparagement clause). That provision bars the registration of trademarks that may "disparage . . . or bring . . . into contemp[t] or disrepute" any "persons, living or dead." In the examining attorney's judgment, THE SLANTS was disparaging with regard to persons of Asian descent.

Tam unsuccessfully appealed the examining attorney's denial of registration to the PTO's Trademark Trial and Appeal Board. He then appealed to the U.S. Court of Appeals for the Federal Circuit, which held the disparagement clause unconstitutional under the First Amendment. The PTO filed a petition for certiorari, which the U.S. Supreme Court granted in order to decide whether the disparagement clause violates the First Amendment.

Alito, Justice

"The principle underlying trademark protection is that distinctive marks—words, names, symbols, and the like—can help distinguish a particular artisan's goods from those of others." *B&B Hardware, Inc. v. Hargis Industries, Inc.*, 135 S. Ct. 1293 (2015). A trademark . . . helps consumers identify goods and services that they wish to purchase, as well as those they want to avoid. Trademarks . . . were protected at common law and in equity at the time of the founding of our country. Eventually, Congress stepped in to provide a degree of national uniformity [through] the Lanham Act, enacted in 1946. By that time, trademark had expanded far beyond phrases that do no more than identify a good or service. Then, as now, trademarks often consisted of catchy phrases that convey a message.

Under the Lanham Act, trademarks that are used in commerce may be placed on the [federal] principal register. This system of federal registration helps to ensure that trademarks are fully protected and supports the free flow of commerce. Without federal registration, a valid trademark may still be used in commerce [and] can be enforced against would-be infringers. Federal registration, however, confers important legal rights and benefits on trademark owners who register their marks. [*Authors' note*: Those rights and benefits are summarized in Chapter 8 of the text and will not be discussed here.]

The Lanham Act contains provisions that bar certain trademarks from the principal register. At issue in this case is one such provision, which we will call "the disparagement clause." This provision prohibits the registration of a trademark "which may disparage . . . persons, living or dead, institutions, beliefs, or national symbols, or bring them into contempt, or disrepute."

When deciding whether a trademark is disparaging, an examiner at the PTO generally applies a two-part test [set forth in the Trademark Manual of Examining Procedure]. The examiner first considers "the likely meaning of the matter in question, taking into account not only dictionary definitions, but also . . . the manner in which the mark is used in the marketplace in connection with the goods or services." If that meaning refers to "identifiable persons, institutions, beliefs or national symbols," the examiner moves to the second step, asking "whether that meaning may be disparaging to a substantial [component] of the referenced group." If the examiner finds that a "substantial [component], although not necessarily a majority, of the referenced group would find the proposed mark . . . to be disparaging in the context of contemporary attitudes," a prima facie case of disparagement is made out, and the burden shifts to the applicant to prove that the trademark is not disparaging. What is more, the PTO has specified that "[t]he fact that an applicant may be a member of that group or has good intentions underlying its use of a term does not obviate the fact that a substantial composite of the referenced group would find the term objectionable." [The examiner in this case applied the two-part test in concluding that THE SLANTS was a disparaging term.]

[W]e must decide whether the disparagement clause violates the Free Speech Clause of the First Amendment. And at the outset, we must consider [an argument] that would eliminate any First Amendment protection. Specifically, the Government contends that trademarks are government speech, not private speech.

The First Amendment prohibits Congress and other government entities and actors from "abridging the freedom of speech"; the First Amendment does not say that Congress and other government entities must abridge their own ability to speak freely. And our cases recognize that "[t]he Free Speech Clause . . . does not regulate government speech." *Pleasant Grove City v. Summum*, 555 U.S. 460, 467 (2009). *See Johanns v. Livestock Marketing Association*, 544 U.S. 550, 553 (2005) ("[T]he Government's own speech . . . is exempt from First Amendment scrutiny").

As we have said, "it is not easy to imagine how government could function" if it were subject to the restrictions that the First

Amendment imposes on private speech. *Summum*, 555 U.S. at 468. *See Walker v. Texas Division, Sons of Confederate Veterans, Inc.*, 135 S. Ct. 2239 (2015). [Although] "the First Amendment forbids the government to regulate speech in ways that favor some viewpoints or ideas at the expense of others," [citation omitted,] . . . imposing a requirement of viewpoint-neutrality on government speech would be paralyzing. When a government entity embarks on a course of action, it necessarily takes a particular viewpoint and rejects others. The Free Speech Clause does not require government to maintain viewpoint neutrality when its officers and employees speak about that venture.

Here is a simple example. During the Second World War, the Federal Government produced and distributed millions of posters to promote the war effort. There were posters urging enlistment, the purchase of war bonds, and the conservation of scarce resources. These posters expressed a viewpoint, but the First Amendment did not demand that the Government balance the message of these posters by producing and distributing posters encouraging Americans to refrain from engaging in these activities.

But while the government-speech doctrine is important—indeed, essential—it is a doctrine that is susceptible to dangerous misuse. If private speech could be passed off as government speech by simply affixing a government seal of approval, government could silence or muffle the expression of disfavored viewpoints. For this reason, we must exercise great caution before extending our government-speech precedents.

At issue here is the content of trademarks that are registered by the PTO, an arm of the Federal Government. The Federal Government does not dream up these marks, and it does not edit marks submitted for registration. Except as required by the statute involved here, an examiner may not reject a mark based on the viewpoint that it appears to express. Thus, unless that section is thought to apply, an examiner does not inquire whether any viewpoint conveyed by a mark is consistent with Government policy or whether any such viewpoint is consistent with that expressed by other marks already on the principal register. Instead, if the mark meets the Lanham Act's viewpoint-neutral requirements, registration is mandatory. In light of all this, it is far-fetched to suggest that the content of a registered mark is government speech. If the federal registration of a trademark makes the mark government speech, the Federal Government is babbling prodigiously and incoherently. It is saying many unseemly things. It is expressing contradictory views. (Compare, [for instance, these two registered marks:] "Abolish Abortion" [and] "I Stand With Planned Parenthood.") It is unashamedly endorsing a vast array of commercial products and services. And it is providing Delphic advice to the consuming public.

For example, if trademarks represent government speech, what does the Government have in mind when it advises Americans to "make.believe" (Sony), "Think different" (Apple), "Just do it" (Nike), or "Have it your way" (Burger King)? Was the Government warning about a coming disaster when it registered the mark "EndTime Ministries"?

None of our government speech cases even remotely supports the idea that registered trademarks are government speech. In *Johanns*, we considered advertisements promoting the sale of beef products. A federal statute called for the creation of a program of paid advertising "to advance the image and desirability of beef and beef products." 544 U.S. at 561. Congress and the Secretary of Agriculture provided guidelines for the content of the ads, Department of Agriculture officials attended the meetings at which the content of specific ads was discussed, and the Secretary could edit or reject any proposed ad. Noting that "[t]he message set out in the beef promotions [was] from beginning to end the message established by the Federal Government," we held that the ads were government speech. *Id.* at 560. The Government's involvement in the creation of these beef ads bears no resemblance to anything that occurs when a trademark is registered.

[Moreover, trademarks] have not traditionally been used to convey a Government message. With the exception of the enforcement of [the statute at issue here], the viewpoint expressed by a mark has not played a role in the decision whether to place it on the principal register. And there is no evidence that the public associates the contents of trademarks with the Federal Government.

This brings us to the case on which the Government relies most heavily, *Walker*, which likely marks the outer bounds of the government-speech doctrine. Holding that the messages on Texas specialty license plates are government speech [and that the State of Texas therefore did not violate the First Amendment when it rejected a request for a specialty license consisting of a representation of the Confederate battle flag], the *Walker* Court cited three factors. First, license plates have long been used by the States to convey state messages. Second, license plates "are often closely identified in the public mind" with the State, since they are manufactured and owned by the State, generally designed by the State, and serve as a form of "government ID." Third, Texas "maintain[ed] direct control over the messages conveyed on its specialty plates." As explained above, none of these factors is present in this case.

In sum, the federal registration of trademarks is vastly different from the beef ads in *Johanns* [and] the specialty license plates in *Walker*. Holding that the registration of a trademark converts the mark into government speech would constitute a huge and dangerous extension of the government-speech doctrine. For if the registration of trademarks constituted government speech, other systems of government registration could easily be characterized in the same way.

Perhaps the most worrisome implication of the Government's argument concerns the system of copyright registration. If federal registration makes a trademark government speech and thus eliminates all First Amendment protection, would the registration of the copyright for a book produce a similar transformation? The Government attempts to distinguish copyright on the ground that it is "the engine of free expression," Brief for Petitioner (quoting *Eldred v. Ashcroft*, 537 U.S. 186, 219 (2003)), but as this case illustrates, trademarks often have an expressive content. Companies spend huge amounts to create and publicize trademarks that convey a message. It is true that the necessary brevity of trademarks limits what they can say. But powerful messages can sometimes be conveyed in just a few words.

Trademarks are private, not government, speech.

Having concluded that the disparagement clause cannot be sustained under our government-speech [cases, we note the existence of] a dispute between the parties on the question whether trademarks are commercial speech and are thus subject to the relaxed scrutiny outlined in *Central Hudson Gas & Electric Corp. v. Public Service Commission*, 447 U.S. 557 (1980). The Government and *amici* supporting its position argue that all trademarks are commercial speech. They note that the central purposes of trademarks are commercial and that federal law regulates trademarks to promote fair and orderly interstate commerce. Tam and his *amici*, on the other hand, contend that many, if not all, trademarks have an expressive component. In other words, these trademarks do not simply identify the source of a product or service but go on to say something more, either about the product or service or some broader issue. The trademark in this case illustrates this point. The name "The Slants" not only identifies the band but expresses a view about social issues.

We need not resolve this debate between the parties because the disparagement clause cannot withstand even *Central Hudson* review. Under *Central Hudson*, a restriction of speech must serve "a substantial interest," and it must be "narrowly drawn." *Id.* at 564–565. This means, among other things, that "[t]he regulatory technique may extend only as far as the interest it serves." *Id.* at 565. The disparagement clause fails this requirement.

It is claimed that the disparagement clause serves two interests. The first is phrased in a variety of ways in the briefs. The Government asserts [in its brief] an interest in preventing "underrepresented groups" from being "bombarded with demeaning messages in commercial advertising." An *amicus* supporting the Government refers [in its brief] to "encouraging racial tolerance and protecting the privacy and welfare of individuals." But no matter how the point is phrased, its unmistakable thrust is this: The Government has an interest in preventing speech expressing ideas that offend. And that idea strikes at the heart of the First Amendment. Speech that demeans on the basis of race, ethnicity, gender, religion, age, disability, or any other similar ground is hateful; but the proudest boast of our free speech jurisprudence is that we protect the freedom to express "the thought that we hate." *United States v. Schwimmer*, 279 U.S. 644, 655 (1929) (Holmes, J., dissenting).

The second interest asserted is protecting the orderly flow of commerce. Commerce, we are told, is disrupted by trademarks that "involv[e] disparagement of race, gender, ethnicity, national origin, religion, sexual orientation, and similar demographic classification" [quoting the Federal Circuit's decision in this case]. Such trademarks are analogized to discriminatory conduct, which has been recognized to have an adverse effect on commerce. A simple answer to this argument is that the disparagement clause is not narrowly drawn to drive out trademarks that support invidious discrimination. The clause reaches any trademark that disparages *any person, group, or institution*. It applies to trademarks [such as] the following: "Down with racists," "Down with sexists," "Down with homophobes." It is not an anti-discrimination clause; it is a happy-talk clause. In this way, it goes much further than is necessary to serve the interest asserted.

There is also a deeper problem with the argument that commercial speech may be cleansed of any expression likely to cause offense. The commercial market is well stocked with merchandise that disparages prominent figures and groups, and the line between commercial and non-commercial speech is not always clear, as this case illustrates. If affixing the commercial label permits the suppression of any speech that may lead to political or social "volatility," free speech would be endangered.

For these reasons, we hold that [regardless of whether trademarks are or are not commercial speech,] the disparagement clause violates the Free Speech Clause of the First Amendment. [The disparagement clause] offends a bedrock First Amendment principle: Speech may not be banned on the ground that it expresses ideas that offend.

Justice Kennedy, with whom Justices Ginsburg, Sotomayor, and Kagan join, concurring in part and concurring in the judgment

As the Court is correct to hold, [the disparagement clause] constitutes viewpoint discrimination—a form of speech suppression so potent that it must be subject to rigorous constitutional scrutiny. The Government's action and the statute on which it is based cannot survive this scrutiny. The Court is correct in its judgment, and I join [most] of its opinion. This separate writing explains in greater detail why the First Amendment's protections against viewpoint discrimination apply to the trademark here. It submits further that the viewpoint discrimination rationale renders unnecessary any extended treatment of other questions raised by the parties.

Those few categories of speech that the government can regulate or punish—for instance, fraud, defamation, or incitement—are well established within our constitutional tradition. Aside from these and a few other narrow exceptions, it is a fundamental principle of the First Amendment that the government may not punish or suppress speech based on disapproval of the ideas or perspectives the speech conveys.

A law found to discriminate based on viewpoint is an "egregious form of content discrimination," which is "presumptively unconstitutional." [Citation omitted.] At its most basic, the test for viewpoint discrimination is whether . . . the government has singled out a subset of messages for disfavor based on the views expressed. In the instant case, the disparagement clause the Government now seeks to implement and enforce identifies the relevant subject as "persons, living or dead, institutions, beliefs, or national symbols." Within that category, an applicant may register a positive or benign mark but not a derogatory one. The law thus reflects the Government's disapproval of a subset of messages it finds offensive. This is the essence of viewpoint discrimination.

The parties dispute whether trademarks are commercial speech. [This] issue may turn on whether certain commercial concerns for the protection of trademarks might, as a general matter, be the basis for regulation. However that issue is resolved, the viewpoint based discrimination at issue here [causes the disparagement clause to violate the First Amendment].

Justice Thomas, concurring in part and concurring in the judgment

I join [much of] the opinion of Justice Alito. I also write separately because "I continue to believe that when the government seeks to restrict truthful speech in order to suppress the ideas it conveys, strict scrutiny is appropriate, whether or not the speech in question may be characterized as 'commercial.'" *Lorillard Tobacco Co. v. Reilly*, 533 U.S. 525, 572 (2001) (Thomas, J., concurring in part and concurring in judgment). I nonetheless join . . . Justice Alito's opinion [insofar as it] concludes that the disparagement clause is unconstitutional even under the less stringent test announced in *Central Hudson Gas & Electric Corp. v. Public Service Commission*.

Judgment of Federal Circuit affirmed.

Figure 3.3   A Note on Tobacco Regulations

What about rules that require tobacco companies to print warnings about their products; do those infringe on the companies' First Amendment rights? Congress has passed and amended several laws regulating the labeling and advertising of tobacco products. In 2009, it passed a law known as the Family Smoking Prevention and Tobacco Control Act (TCA). The TCA requires a federal agency, the Food and Drug Administration (FDA), to issue regulations that require color graphics depicting the health risks of smoking.

Here are some examples of the required graphic images the FDA has proposed (see www.fda.gov/tobacco-products/labeling-and-warning-statements-tobacco-products/cigarette-health-warnings#sample):

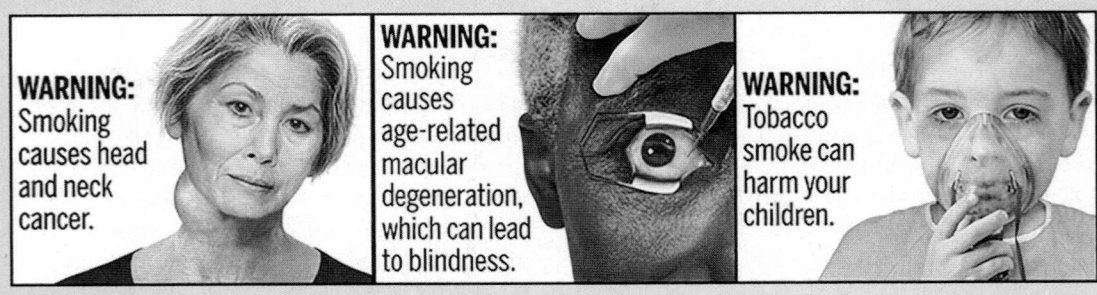

Companies that produce these products have challenged both the FDA's rules and the TCA. The U.S. Court of Appeals for the D.C. Circuit struck down one set of regulations in 2012, holding that the required images proposed by the FDA violated the First Amendment and that the FDA did not provide substantial evidence that graphic warnings on cigarette advertising would directly advance its interest in reducing smoking rates to a material degree. *R.J. Reynolds Tobacco Co. v. Food & Drug Admin.,* 696 F.3d 1205 (D.C. Cir. 2012). In a separate ruling also in 2012, the U.S. Court of Appeals for the Sixth Circuit upheld the TCA's graphic warning requirement, finding the provision did not violate the First Amendment and the graphic warning requirement was reasonably related to the government's interest in preventing consumer deception. *Discount Tobacco City & Lottery, Inc. v. United States,* 674 F.3d 509 (6th Cir. 2012).

Several public health and medical organizations sued in 2016 to force the FDA to issue final regulations on graphic labels, as required by the TCA. The U.S. District Court for the District of Massachusetts ruled in favor of the plaintiffs and ordered the FDA to issue a final rule requiring graphic health warnings by March 15, 2020. *American Academy of Pediatrics v. FDA,* 2019 WL 1047149 (D. Mass. March 5, 2019).

The FDA then issued a new final rule, which at the time of this writing is the subject of litigation. Several tobacco companies filed a lawsuit in the Federal District Court for the Eastern District of Texas against the FDA, seeking to invalidate the graphic health warnings and the requirement under the Tobacco Control Act. The companies argued that the new rule requiring graphic warnings violates the First Amendment, the TCA's requirement that FDA issue a rule requiring the health warning violates the First Amendment, and the FDA acted arbitrarily and capriciously in drafting and issuing the rule.

Philip Morris USA Inc. filed a similar challenge in the U.S. District Court for the District of Columbia. The company alleges that the rule violates the First Amendment rights of tobacco companies by requiring them to "disparage their own products with shocking and inflammatory graphic images." The complaint seeks declaratory and injunctive relief to prevent implementation of the rule.

Due Process

The Fifth and Fourteenth Amendments require that the federal government and the states observe **due process** when they deprive a person of life, liberty, or property. Due process has both *procedural* and *substantive* meanings.

 LO3-7 Explain the difference between procedural due process and substantive due process.

Procedural Due Process The traditional conception of due process, called **procedural due process**, establishes the *procedures* that government must follow when it takes life, liberty, or property. Although the requirements of procedural due process vary from situation to situation, their core idea is that one is entitled to adequate *notice* of the government action to be taken against him and to some sort of *fair trial or hearing* before that action can occur.

For purposes of procedural due process claims, *liberty* includes a very broad and poorly defined range of freedoms. It even includes certain interests in personal reputation. For example, the firing of a government employee may require some kind of due process hearing if it is publicized, the fired employee's reputation is sufficiently damaged, and her future employment opportunities are restricted. The Supreme Court has said that procedural due process *property* is not created by the Constitution but by existing rules and understandings that stem from an independent source such as state law. These rules and understandings must give a person a *legitimate claim of entitlement* to a benefit, not merely some need, desire, or expectation for it. This definition includes almost all of the usual forms of property, as well as utility service, disability benefits, welfare benefits, and a driver's license. It also includes the job rights of tenured public employees who can be discharged only for cause, but not the rights of untenured or probationary employees.

Substantive Due Process Procedural due process does not challenge rules of *substantive law*—the rules that set standards of behavior for organized social life. For example, imagine that State X makes adultery a crime and allows people to be convicted of adultery without a trial. Arguments that adultery should not be a crime go to the substance of the statute, whereas objections to the lack of a trial are procedural in nature.

Sometimes, the due process clauses have been used to attack the substance of government action. For our purposes, the most important example of this **substantive due process** occurred early in the 20th century, when courts struck down various kinds of social legislation as denying due process. They did so mainly by reading freedom of contract and other economic rights into the liberty and property protected by the Fifth and Fourteenth Amendments, and then interpreting "due process of law" to require that laws denying such rights be subjected to means-ends scrutiny. The best-known example is the Supreme Court's 1905 decision in *Lochner v. New York*, 198 U.S. 45 (1905), which struck down a state law setting maximum hours of work for bakery employees because the statute limited freedom of contract and did not directly advance the legitimate state goal of promoting worker health.

Since 1937, however, this "economic" form of substantive due process has been largely abandoned by the Supreme Court and has not amounted to a significant check on government regulation of economic matters. Substantive due process attacks on such regulations now trigger only a lenient type of rational basis review and thus have had little chance of success. During the 1970s and 1980s, however, substantive due process became increasingly important as a device for protecting *noneconomic* rights. The most important examples are the liberty and privacy interests, which consist of several rights that the Supreme Court regards as fundamental and as entitled to significant constitutional protection. The Court has declared that these include the rights to marry, have children and direct their education and upbringing, enjoy marital privacy, use contraception, and, within certain limits, elect to have an abortion. Laws restricting these rights must be narrowly tailored to meet a compelling government purpose in order to avoid being declared unconstitutional. *Obergefell v. Hodges*, which appears later in the chapter, illustrates the influence of substantive due process interests.

Equal Protection

 LO3-8 Identify the instances when an Equal Protection Clause–based challenge to government action triggers more rigorous scrutiny than the rational basis test.

The Fourteenth Amendment's Equal Protection Clause says that "[n]o State shall . . . deny to any person . . . the equal protection of the laws." Because the equal protection guarantee has been incorporated within Fifth Amendment due process, it also restricts the federal government. The equal protection guarantee potentially applies to all situations in which government *classifies* or *distinguishes* people. The law inevitably makes distinctions among people, benefiting or burdening some groups but not others. Equal protection doctrine, as developed by the Supreme Court, sets the standards such distinctions must meet in order to be constitutional.

Economic Regulations The basic equal protection standard is the *rational basis* test described earlier. This is the standard usually applied to social and economic regulations that are challenged as denying equal protection. As the following case illustrates, this lenient test usually does not impede state and federal regulation of social and economic matters.

Fitzgerald v. Racing Association of Central Iowa
539 U.S. 103 (2003)

Before 1989, Iowa permitted only one form of gambling: parimutuel betting at racetracks. A 1989 Iowa statute authorized other forms of gambling, including slot machines on riverboats. The 1989 law established that adjusted revenues from riverboat slot machine gambling would be taxed at graduated rates, with a top rate of 20 percent. In 1994, Iowa enacted a law that authorized racetracks to operate slot machines. That law also imposed a graduated tax upon racetrack slot machine adjusted revenues, with a top rate that started at 20 percent and would automatically rise over time to 36 percent. The 1994 enactment left in place the 20 percent tax rate on riverboat slot machine adjusted revenues.

Contending that the 1994 legislation's 20 percent versus 36 percent tax rate difference violated the federal Constitution's Equal Protection Clause, a group of racetracks and an association of dog owners brought suit against the State of Iowa (through its state treasurer, Michael Fitzgerald). A state district court upheld the statute, but the Iowa Supreme Court reversed. The U.S. Supreme Court granted Iowa's petition for a writ of certiorari.

Breyer, Justice

We here consider whether a difference in state tax rates violates the Fourteenth Amendment's mandate that "no State shall . . . deny to any person . . . the equal protection of the laws." The law in question does not distinguish on the basis of, for example, race or gender. It does not distinguish between in-state and out-of-state businesses. Neither does it favor a State's long-time residents at the expense of residents who have more recently arrived from other States. Rather, the law distinguishes for tax purposes among revenues obtained within the State of Iowa by two enterprises, each of which does business in the State. Where that is so, the law is subject to rational-basis review:

> The Equal Protection Clause is satisfied so long as there is a plausible policy reason for the classification, the legislative facts on which the classification is apparently based rationally may have been considered to be true by the governmental decisionmaker, and the relationship of the classification to its goal is not so attenuated as to render the distinction arbitrary or irrational.

[Case citation omitted.] [We have also held that] rational-basis review "is especially deferential in the context of classifications made by complex tax laws." [Case citation omitted.]

The Iowa Supreme Court found that the 20 percent/36 percent tax rate differential failed to meet this standard because, in its view, that difference frustrated what it saw as the law's basic objective, namely, rescuing the racetracks from economic distress. And no rational person, it believed, could claim the contrary. The Iowa Supreme Court could not deny, however, that the Iowa law, like most laws, might predominately serve one general objective, say, helping the racetracks, while containing subsidiary provisions that seek to achieve other desirable (perhaps even contrary) ends as well, thereby producing a law that balances objectives but still serves the general objective when seen as a whole. After all, if *every* subsidiary provision in a law designed to help racetracks had to help those racetracks and nothing more, then (since any tax rate hurts the racetracks when compared with a lower rate) there could be no taxation of the racetracks at all.

Neither could the Iowa Supreme Court deny that the 1994 legislation, *seen as a whole*, can rationally be understood to do what that court says it seeks to do, namely, advance the racetracks' economic interests. Its grant to the racetracks of authority to operate slot machines should help the racetracks economically to some degree—even if its simultaneous imposition of a tax on slot machine adjusted revenue means that the law provides less help than respondents might like. At least a rational legislator might so believe. And the Constitution grants legislators, not courts, broad authority (within the bounds of rationality) to decide whom they wish to help with their tax laws and how much help those laws ought to provide. "The 'task of classifying persons for . . . benefits . . . inevitably requires that some persons who have an almost equally strong claim to favored treatment be placed on different sides of the line,' and the fact the line might have been drawn differently at some points is a matter for legislative, rather than judicial, consideration." [Case citation omitted.]

Once one realizes that not every provision in a law must share a single objective, one has no difficulty finding the necessary rational support for the 20 percent/36 percent differential here at issue. That difference, harmful to the racetracks, is helpful to the riverboats, which, as [those challenging the 1994 statute] concede, were also facing financial peril. These two characterizations are but opposite sides of the same coin. Each reflects a rational way for a legislator to view the matter. And aside from simply aiding the financial position of the riverboats, the legislators may have wanted to encourage the economic development of river communities or to promote riverboat history, say, by providing incentives for riverboats to remain in the State, rather than relocate to other States. Alternatively, they may have wanted to protect the reliance interests of riverboat operators, whose adjusted slot machine revenue had previously been taxed at the 20 percent rate. All these objectives are rational ones, which lower riverboat tax rates could further and which suffice to uphold the different tax rates.

We conclude that there is "a plausible policy reason for the classification," that the legislature "rationally may have . . . considered . . . true" the related justifying "legislative facts," and that the "relationship of the classification to its goal is not so attenuated as to render the distinction arbitrary or irrational." [Case citation omitted.] Consequently the State's differential tax rate does not violate the Federal Equal Protection Clause.

Iowa Supreme Court decision reversed, and case remanded for further proceedings.

Fundamental Rights The rational basis test is the basic equal protection standard. Some classifications, however, receive tougher means-ends scrutiny. According to Supreme Court precedent, laws that discriminate regarding **fundamental rights** or *suspect classes* must undergo more rigorous review.

Although the list of rights regarded as fundamental for equal protection purposes is not completely clear, it clearly includes the right to marry. As made plain in *Obergefell v. Hodges*, which follows shortly, this right exists regardless of whether the couple to be married is of opposite genders or of the same gender. The list also includes certain criminal procedure protections as well as the rights to vote and engage in interstate travel. Laws creating unequal enjoyment of these rights receive full strict scrutiny. In 1969, for instance, the Supreme Court struck down the District of Columbia's one-year residency requirement for receiving welfare benefits because that requirement unequally and impermissibly restricted the right of interstate travel.

An equal protection claim involving the fundamental right to vote was addressed in high-profile fashion by the Supreme Court in *Bush v. Gore,* 531 U.S. 98 (2000). A five-justice majority in the historic and controversial decision terminated an ongoing vote recount in Florida because, in the majority's view, Florida law's "intent of the voter" test was not a sufficiently clear standard for determining whether a ballot not counted in the initial machine count should be counted as valid during the manual recount. The majority was concerned that in the absence of a more specific standard, vote counters taking part in the recount might apply inconsistent standards in determining what the voter supposedly intended, and might thereby value some votes over others. The termination of the Florida recount meant that then-governor Bush won the state of Florida, giving him enough Electoral College votes to win the presidency despite the fact that candidate Gore tallied more popular votes nationally. The four dissenters in *Bush v. Gore* faulted the majority for focusing on the supposed equal protection violation it identified, when, in the dissenters'

view, the Court ignored a potentially bigger equal protection problem created by termination of the recount: the prospect that large numbers of ballots not counted during the machine count would never be counted, even though they may have been valid votes under Florida's "intent of the voter" test.

In *Crawford v. Marion County Election Board*, 553 U.S. 181 (2008), the Supreme Court again addressed the fundamental right to vote. This time, the Court was faced with determining whether an Indiana law violated the Equal Protection Clause by requiring that voters produce a government-issued photo ID as a precondition to being allowed to vote. Those who raised the equal protection challenge to the requirement asserted that its burdens would fall disproportionately on low-income and elderly voters, who would be less likely than other persons to have a driver's license or other photo ID. The Court upheld the Indiana law, ruling that it did not violate the Equal Protection Clause. Six justices agreed that even though voter fraud at the polls had not been a demonstrated problem in Indiana, the photo ID requirement was a generally applicable and not excessively burdensome way of furthering the state's purposes of preventing voter fraud and preserving voter confidence in the integrity of elections.

Since *Crawford*, lower courts have decided various cases that presented constitutional challenges to voter ID laws enacted in other states. Some such laws have been upheld. In other cases, however, voter ID laws have been struck down if they imposed more onerous ID requirements than the law at issue in *Crawford* and if the showing of a disproportionate adverse effect on certain groups of voters was especially strong.

Obergefell v. Hodges   576 U.S. 644 (2015)

Cases from Michigan, Kentucky, Ohio, and Tennessee—states whose statutes defined marriage as a union between one man and one woman—were consolidated for purposes of the U.S. Supreme Court decision that appears below in edited form. The petitioners before the Supreme Court were 14 same-sex couples and two men whose same-sex partners were deceased. The respondents were state officials responsible for enforcing the laws in question. The petitioners claimed that the respondents violated the Fourteenth Amendment to the U.S. Constitution by denying them the right to marry or by refusing to give full recognition to marriages that were lawfully performed in another state.

The petitioners filed their cases in U.S. district courts in their home states. Each district court ruled in their favor. The respondents appealed these decisions to the U.S. Court of Appeals for the Sixth Circuit, which consolidated the cases and reversed the judgments of the district courts. The Sixth Circuit held that a state has no constitutional obligation to license same-sex marriages or to recognize same-sex marriages performed out of state. This ruling conflicted with rulings by other federal courts of appeals on the same set of issues.

The petitioners sought certiorari from the U.S. Supreme Court, which granted review regarding two questions. The first was whether the Fourteenth Amendment requires a state to issue a marriage license to two persons of the same sex. The second was whether the Fourteenth Amendment requires a state to recognize a same-sex marriage licensed and performed in a state that does grant that right. (Further facts appear in the following edited version of the Supreme Court's decision.)

Kennedy, Justice

The Constitution promises liberty to all within its reach, a liberty that includes certain specific rights that allow persons . . . to define and express their identity. The petitioners seek to find that liberty by marrying someone of the same sex and having their marriages deemed lawful on the same terms and conditions as marriages between persons of the opposite sex.

[T]he annals of human history reveal the transcendent importance of marriage. Marriage is sacred to those who live by their religions and offers unique fulfillment to those who find meaning in the secular realm. There are untold references to the beauty of marriage in religious and philosophical texts spanning time, cultures, and faiths, as well as in art and literature in all their forms. It is fair and necessary to say these references were based on the understanding that marriage is a union between two persons of the opposite sex. That history is the beginning of these cases. The respondents say it should be the end as well. To them, it would demean a timeless institution if the concept and lawful status of marriage were extended to two persons of the same sex. This view long has been held—and continues to be held—in good faith by reasonable and sincere people here and throughout the world.

The petitioners acknowledge this history but contend that these cases cannot end there. [They do not seek] to demean the revered idea and reality of marriage. To the contrary, it is the enduring importance of marriage that underlies the petitioners' contentions. [T]he petitioners seek [the right to marry] because of their respect—and need—for its privileges and responsibilities. And their immutable nature dictates that same-sex marriage is their only real path to this profound commitment.

Recounting the circumstances of three of these cases illustrates the urgency of the petitioners' cause from their perspective. Petitioner James Obergefell, a plaintiff in the Ohio case, met John Arthur over two decades ago. They fell in love and started a life together. In 2011, however, Arthur was diagnosed with amyotrophic lateral sclerosis, or ALS. This debilitating disease is progressive, with no known cure. Two years ago, Obergefell and Arthur decided to commit to one another, resolving to marry before Arthur died. To fulfill their mutual promise, they traveled from Ohio to Maryland, where same-sex marriage was legal, [and were wed there]. Three months later, Arthur died. Ohio law does not permit Obergefell to be listed as the surviving spouse on Arthur's death certificate. By statute, they must remain strangers even in death, a state-imposed separation Obergefell deems "hurtful for the rest of time." He brought suit to be shown as the surviving spouse on Arthur's death certificate.

April DeBoer and Jayne Rowse are co-plaintiffs in the case from Michigan. They celebrated a commitment ceremony to honor their permanent relation in 2007. In 2009, DeBoer and Rowse fostered and then adopted a baby boy. Later that same year, they welcomed another son into their family. The new baby, born prematurely and abandoned by his biological mother, required around-the-clock care. The next year, a baby girl with special needs joined their family. Michigan, however, permits only opposite-sex married couples or single individuals to adopt, so each child can have only one woman as his or her legal parent. If an emergency were to arise, schools and hospitals may treat the three children as if they had only one parent. And, were tragedy to befall either DeBoer or Rowse, the other would have no legal rights over the children she had not been permitted to adopt. This couple seeks relief from the continuing uncertainty their unmarried status creates in their lives.

Army Sergeant Ijpe DeKoe and his partner Thomas Kostura, co-plaintiffs in the Tennessee case, fell in love. In 2011, DeKoe received orders to deploy to Afghanistan. Before leaving, he and Kostura married in New York. When DeKoe returned [from his deployment], the two settled in Tennessee, where DeKoe works for the Army Reserve. Their lawful marriage is stripped from them whenever they reside in Tennessee, returning and disappearing as they travel across state lines. DeKoe . . . endure[s] a substantial burden [as a result].

The ancient origins of marriage confirm its centrality, but [its history] is one of both continuity and change. For example, marriage was once viewed as an arrangement by the couple's parents based on political, religious, and financial concerns; but by the time of the Nation's founding, it was understood to be a voluntary contract between a man and a woman. [Another example involves] the centuries-old doctrine of coverture, [under which] a married man and woman were treated by the State as a single, male-dominated legal entity. As women gained legal, political, and property rights, and as society began to understand that women have their own equal dignity, the law of coverture was abandoned. These and other developments in the institution of marriage . . . worked deep transformations in its structure [and] have strengthened, not weakened, the institution of marriage. Indeed, changed understandings of marriage are characteristic of a Nation where new dimensions of freedom become apparent to new generations, often through perspectives that begin in pleas or protests and then are considered in the political sphere and the judicial process.

This dynamic can be seen in the Nation's experiences with the rights of gays and lesbians. Until the mid-20th century, same-sex intimacy long had been condemned as immoral by the State itself in most Western nations, a belief often embodied in the criminal law. For this reason, among others, many persons did not deem homosexuals to have dignity in their own distinct identity. A truthful declaration by same-sex couples of what was in their hearts had to remain unspoken. Even when a greater awareness of the humanity and integrity of homosexual persons came in the period after World War II, the argument that gays and lesbians had a just claim to dignity was in conflict with both law and widespread social conventions. Same-sex intimacy remained a crime in many States. Gays and lesbians were prohibited from most government employment, barred from military service, excluded under immigration laws, targeted by police, and burdened in their rights to associate. For much of the 20th century, moreover, homosexuality was treated as . . . a mental disorder. Only in more recent years have psychiatrists and others recognized that sexual orientation is both a normal expression of human sexuality and immutable.

In the late 20th century, following substantial cultural and political developments, same-sex couples began to lead more open and public lives and to establish families. This development was followed by a quite extensive discussion of the issue in both governmental and private sectors and by a shift in public attitudes toward greater tolerance. As a result, questions about the rights of gays and lesbians reached the courts.

This Court first gave detailed consideration to the legal status of homosexuals in *Bowers v. Hardwick*, 478 U.S. 186 (1986). There it upheld the constitutionality of a Georgia law deemed to criminalize certain homosexual acts. Ten years later, in *Romer v. Evans*, 517 U.S. 620 (1996), the Court invalidated an amendment to Colorado's Constitution that sought to foreclose any branch or political subdivision of the State from protecting persons against discrimination based on sexual orientation. Then, in 2003, the Court overruled *Bowers*, holding that laws making same-sex intimacy a crime "demea[n] the lives of homosexual persons." *Lawrence v. Texas*, 539 U.S. 558, 575 (2003).

Against this background, the legal question of same-sex marriage arose. In 1993, the Hawaii Supreme Court held Hawaii's law restricting marriage to opposite-sex couples constituted a classification on the basis of sex and was therefore subject to strict scrutiny under the Hawaii Constitution. Although this decision did not mandate that same-sex marriage be allowed, some States [chose to reaffirm] in their laws that marriage is defined as a union between opposite-sex partners. So too in 1996, Congress passed the Defense of Marriage Act (DOMA), defining marriage for all federal-law purposes as "only a legal union between one man and one woman as husband and wife."

The new and widespread discussion of the subject led other States to a different conclusion. In 2003, the Supreme Judicial Court of Massachusetts held that the State's constitution guaranteed same-sex couples the right to marry. After that ruling, some additional States granted marriage rights to same-sex couples, either through judicial or legislative processes. Two terms ago, in *United States v. Windsor*, 133 S. Ct. 2675 (2013), this Court invalidated DOMA to the extent it barred the federal government from treating same-sex marriages as valid even when they were lawful in the State where they were licensed. DOMA, the Court held, impermissibly disparaged those same-sex couples "who wanted to affirm their commitment to one another before their children, their family, their friends, and their community."

Numerous cases about same-sex marriage have reached the United States Courts of Appeals in recent years. With the exception of the opinion here under review and one other, the Courts of Appeals have held that excluding same-sex couples from marriage violates the Constitution. There also have been many thoughtful district court decisions addressing same-sex marriage—and most of them, too, have concluded same-sex couples must be allowed to marry.

Under the Due Process Clause of the Fourteenth Amendment, no State shall "deprive any person of life, liberty, or property, without due process of law." The fundamental liberties protected by this Clause include most of the rights enumerated in the Bill of Rights. In addition, these liberties extend to certain personal choices central to individual dignity and autonomy, including intimate choices that define personal identity and beliefs. *See, e.g., Eisenstadt v. Baird*, 405 U.S. 438, 453 (1972); *Griswold v. Connecticut*, 381 U.S. 479, 484–486 (1965).

The identification and protection of fundamental rights is an enduring part of the judicial duty to interpret the Constitution. [I]t requires courts to exercise reasoned judgment in identifying interests of the person so fundamental that the State must accord them its respect. History and tradition guide and discipline this inquiry but do not set its outer boundaries. That method respects our history and learns from it without allowing the past alone to rule the present. The nature of injustice is that we may not always see it in our own times. The generations that wrote and ratified the Bill of Rights and the Fourteenth Amendment did not presume to know the extent of freedom in all of its dimensions, and so they entrusted to future generations a charter protecting the right of all persons to enjoy liberty as we learn its meaning. When new insight reveals discord between the Constitution's central protections and a received legal stricture, a claim to liberty must be addressed.

Applying these established tenets, the Court has long held that the right to marry is protected by the Constitution. In *Loving v. Virginia*, 388 U.S. 1, 12 (1967), which invalidated bans on interracial unions, a unanimous Court held that marriage is "one of the vital personal rights essential to the orderly pursuit of happiness by free men." The Court reaffirmed that holding in *Zablocki v. Redhail*, 434 U.S. 374, 384 (1978), which held the right to marry was burdened by a law prohibiting fathers who were behind on child support from marrying. Over time and in other contexts, the Court has reiterated that the right to marry is fundamental under the Due Process Clause. [Citations omitted.]

It cannot be denied that this Court's cases describing the right to marry presumed a relationship involving opposite-sex partners. The Court, like many institutions, has made assumptions defined by the world and time of which it is a part. This was evident in *Baker v. Nelson*, 409 U.S. 810, a one-line summary decision issued in 1972, holding the exclusion of same-sex couples from marriage did not present a substantial federal question.

Still, there are other, more instructive precedents. In defining the right to marry, [this Court's] cases have identified essential attributes of that right based in history, tradition, and other constitutional liberties inherent in this intimate bond. *See, e.g., Zablocki; Loving; Griswold.* And in assessing whether the force and rationale of its cases apply to same-sex couples, the Court must respect the basic reasons why the right to marry has been long protected.

This analysis compels the conclusion that same-sex couples may exercise the right to marry. The four principles and traditions to be discussed demonstrate that the reasons marriage is fundamental under the Constitution apply with equal force to same-sex couples.

A first premise of the Court's relevant precedents is that the right to personal choice regarding marriage is inherent in the concept of individual autonomy. This abiding connection between marriage and liberty is why *Loving* invalidated interracial marriage bans under the Due Process Clause. *See* 388 U.S. at 12. Like choices concerning contraception, family relationships, procreation, and childrearing, all of which are protected by the Constitution, decisions concerning marriage are among the most intimate that an individual can make. The nature of marriage is that, through its enduring bond, two persons together can find other freedoms, such as expression, intimacy, and spirituality. This is true for all persons, whatever their sexual orientation. *See Windsor*, 133 S. Ct. 2675. There is dignity in the bond between two men or two women who seek to marry and in their autonomy to make such profound choices.

A second principle in this Court's jurisprudence is that the right to marry is fundamental because it supports a two-person union unlike any other in its importance to the committed individuals. This point was central to *Griswold v. Connecticut*, which held the Constitution protects the right of married couples to use contraception. 381 U.S. at 485.

As this Court held in *Lawrence*, same-sex couples have the same right as opposite-sex couples to enjoy intimate association. But while *Lawrence* confirmed a dimension of freedom that allows individuals to engage in intimate association without criminal liability, it does not follow that freedom stops there. Outlaw to outcast may be a step forward, but it does not achieve the full promise of liberty.

A third basis for protecting the right to marry is that it safeguards children and families and thus draws meaning from related rights of childrearing, procreation, and education. The Court has recognized these connections by describing the varied rights as a unified whole: "[T]he right to marry, establish a home and bring up children is a central part of the liberty protected by the Due Process Clause." *Zablocki*, 434 U.S. at 384. Under the laws of the several States, some of marriage's protections for children and families are material. But marriage also confers more profound benefits. By giving recognition and legal structure to their parents' relationship, marriage allows children "to understand the integrity and closeness of their own family and its concord with other families in their community and in their daily lives." *Windsor*, 133 S. Ct. 2675. Marriage also affords the permanency and stability important to children's best interests.

As all parties agree, many same-sex couples provide loving and nurturing homes to their children, whether biological or adopted. And hundreds of thousands of children are presently being raised by such couples. Most States have allowed gays and lesbians to adopt, either as individuals or as couples, and many adopted and foster children have same-sex parents. This provides powerful confirmation from the law itself that gays and lesbians can create loving, supportive families.

Excluding same-sex couples from marriage thus conflicts with a central premise of the right to marry. Without the recognition, stability, and predictability marriage offers, their children suffer the stigma of knowing their families are somehow lesser. They also suffer the significant material costs of being raised by unmarried parents, relegated through no fault of their own to a more difficult and uncertain family life. The marriage laws at issue here thus harm and humiliate the children of same-sex couples.

That is not to say the right to marry is less meaningful for those who do not or cannot have children. An ability, desire, or promise to procreate is not and has not been a prerequisite for a valid marriage in any State.

Fourth and finally, this Court's cases and the Nation's traditions make clear that marriage is a keystone of our social order. [J]ust as a couple vows to support each other, so does society pledge to support the couple, offering symbolic recognition and material benefits to protect and nourish the union. [States] have throughout our history made marriage the basis for an expanding list of governmental rights, benefits, and responsibilities. These aspects of marital status include: taxation; inheritance and property rights; rules of intestate succession; spousal privilege in the law of evidence; hospital access; medical decisionmaking authority; adoption rights; the rights and benefits of survivors; birth and death certificates; professional ethics rules; campaign finance restrictions; workers' compensation benefits; health insurance; and child custody, support, and visitation rules. Valid marriage under state law is also a significant status for over a thousand provisions of federal law. The States have contributed to the fundamental character of the marriage right by placing that institution at the center of so many facets of the legal and social order.

There is no difference between same- and opposite-sex couples with respect to this principle. Yet by virtue of their exclusion from that institution, same-sex couples are denied the constellation of benefits that the States have linked to marriage. This harm results in more than just material burdens. Same-sex couples are consigned to an instability many opposite-sex couples would deem intolerable in their own lives. As the State itself makes marriage all the more precious by the significance it attaches to it, exclusion from that status has the effect of teaching that gays and lesbians are unequal in important respects. It demeans gays and lesbians for the State to lock them out of a central institution of the Nation's society.

The limitation of marriage to opposite-sex couples may long have seemed natural and just, but its inconsistency with the central meaning of the fundamental right to marry is now manifest. With that knowledge must come the recognition that laws excluding same-sex couples from the marriage right impose stigma and injury of the kind prohibited by our basic charter. Under the Constitution, same-sex couples seek in marriage the same legal treatment as opposite-sex couples, and it would disparage their choices and diminish their personhood to deny them this right.

The right of same-sex couples to marry that is part of the liberty promised by the Fourteenth Amendment is derived, too, from that Amendment's guarantee of the equal protection of the laws. The Due Process Clause and the Equal Protection Clause are connected in a profound way, though they set forth independent principles. Rights implicit in liberty and rights secured by equal protection may rest on different precepts and are not always coextensive, yet in some instances each may be instructive as to the meaning and reach of the other. In any particular case one Clause may be thought to capture the essence of the right in a more accurate and comprehensive way, even as the two Clauses may converge in the identification and definition of the right. This interrelation of the two principles furthers our understanding of what freedom is and must become.

The Court's cases touching upon the right to marry reflect this dynamic. In *Loving*, the Court invalidated a prohibition on interracial marriage under both the Equal Protection Clause and the Due Process Clause. The Court . . . stated: "There can be no doubt that restricting the freedom to marry solely because of racial classifications violates the central meaning of the Equal Protection Clause." 388 U.S. at 12. With this link to equal protection, the Court proceeded to hold that the prohibition offended central precepts of liberty: "To deny this fundamental freedom on so unsupportable a basis as the racial classifications embodied in these statutes, classifications so directly subversive of the principle of equality at the heart of the Fourteenth Amendment, is surely to deprive all the State's citizens of liberty without due process of law." *Id.*

The synergy between the two protections is illustrated further in *Zablocki*. There the Court invoked the Equal Protection Clause as its basis for invalidating the challenged law, which barred fathers who were behind on child-support payments from marrying without judicial approval. The equal protection analysis depended in central part on the Court's holding that the law burdened a right "of fundamental importance." 434 U.S. at 383. It was the essential nature of the marriage right that made apparent the law's incompatibility with requirements of equality. Each concept—liberty and equal protection—leads to a stronger understanding of the other.

Other cases confirm this relation between liberty and equality. In *M. L. B. v. S. L. J.*, 519 U.S. 102, 119–24 (1996), the Court invalidated under due process and equal protection principles a statute requiring indigent mothers to pay a fee in order to appeal the termination of their parental rights. In *Eisenstadt v. Baird*, the Court invoked both principles to invalidate a prohibition on the distribution of contraceptives to unmarried persons but not married persons. *See* 405 U.S. at 446–54.

In *Lawrence*, the Court acknowledged the interlocking nature of these constitutional safeguards in the context of the legal treatment of gays and lesbians. Although *Lawrence* elaborated its holding under the Due Process Clause, it acknowledged, and sought to remedy, the continuing inequality that resulted from laws making intimacy in the lives of gays and lesbians a crime against the State. *See* 539 U.S. at 575. *Lawrence* therefore drew upon principles of liberty and equality to define and protect the rights of gays and lesbians, holding the State "cannot demean their existence or control their destiny by making their private sexual conduct a crime." *Id.* at 578.

This dynamic also applies to same-sex marriage. It is now clear that the challenged laws burden the liberty of same-sex couples, and it must be further acknowledged that they abridge central precepts of equality. Here the marriage laws enforced by the respondents are in essence unequal: same-sex couples are denied all the benefits afforded to opposite-sex couples and are barred from exercising a fundamental right. Especially against a long history of disapproval of their relationships, this denial to same-sex couples of the right to marry works a grave and continuing harm.

These considerations lead to the conclusion that the right to marry is a fundamental right inherent in the liberty of the person, and under the Due Process and Equal Protection Clauses of the Fourteenth Amendment couples of the same-sex may not be deprived of that right and that liberty. The Court now holds that same-sex couples may exercise the fundamental right to marry. No longer may this liberty be denied to them. *Baker v. Nelson* must be and now is overruled, and the State laws challenged by Petitioners in these cases are now held invalid to the extent they exclude same-sex couples from civil marriage on the same terms and conditions as opposite-sex couples.

There may be an initial inclination in these cases to proceed with caution—to await further legislation, litigation, and debate. The respondents warn there has been insufficient democratic discourse before deciding an issue so basic as the definition of marriage. Yet there has been far more deliberation than this argument acknowledges. There have been referenda, legislative debates, and grassroots campaigns, as well as countless studies, papers, books, and other popular and scholarly writings. There has been extensive litigation in state and federal courts. Judicial opinions addressing the issue have been informed by the contentions of parties and counsel, which, in turn, reflect the more general, societal discussion of same-sex marriage and its meaning that has occurred over the past decades. As more than 100 *amici* make clear in their filings, many of the central institutions in American life—state and local governments, the military, large and small businesses, labor unions, religious organizations, law enforcement, civic groups, professional organizations, and universities—have devoted substantial attention to the question. This has led to an enhanced understanding of the issue—an understanding reflected in the arguments now presented for resolution as a matter of constitutional law.

Of course, the Constitution contemplates that democracy is the appropriate process for change, so long as that process does not abridge fundamental rights. But . . . when the rights of persons are violated, the Constitution requires redress by the courts, notwithstanding the more general value of democratic decisionmaking. An individual can invoke a right to constitutional protection when he or she is harmed, even if the broader public disagrees and even if the legislature refuses to act. The idea of the Constitution "was to withdraw certain subjects from the vicissitudes of political controversy, to place them beyond the reach of majorities and officials and to establish them as legal principles to be applied by the courts." *West Virginia Bd. of Ed. v. Barnette*, 319 U.S. 624, 638 (1943). This is why "fundamental rights may not be submitted to a vote; they depend on the outcome of no elections." *Id.*

This is not the first time the Court has been asked to adopt a cautious approach to recognizing and protecting fundamental rights. In *Bowers*, a bare majority upheld a law criminalizing same-sex intimacy. *See* 478 U.S. at 186. That approach might have been viewed as a cautious endorsement of the democratic process, which had only just begun to consider the rights of gays and lesbians. Yet, in effect, *Bowers* upheld state action that denied gays and lesbians a fundamental right and caused them pain and humiliation. Although *Bowers* was eventually repudiated in *Lawrence*, men and women were harmed in the interim, and the substantial effects of these injuries no doubt lingered long after *Bowers* was overruled. Dignitary wounds cannot always be healed with the stroke of a pen.

A ruling against same-sex couples would have the same effect—and, like *Bowers*, would be unjustified under the Fourteenth Amendment. The petitioners' stories[, as detailed earlier in this opinion,] make clear the urgency of the issue they present to the Court.

These cases also present the question whether the Constitution requires States to recognize same-sex marriages validly performed out of State. As made clear by the case of Obergefell and Arthur, and by that of DeKoe and Kostura, the recognition bans inflict substantial and continuing harm on same-sex couples. Being married in one State but having that valid marriage denied in another is one of "the most perplexing and distressing complication[s]" in the law of domestic relations. [Citation omitted.] Leaving the current state of affairs in place would maintain and promote instability and uncertainty. For some couples, even an ordinary drive into a neighboring State to visit family or friends risks causing severe hardship in the event of a spouse's hospitalization while across state lines. In light of the fact that many States already allow same-sex marriage—and hundreds of thousands of these marriages already have occurred—the disruption caused by the recognition bans is significant and ever-growing.

The Court, in this decision, holds that same-sex couples may exercise the fundamental right to marry in all States. It follows that the Court also must hold—and it now does hold—that there is no lawful basis for a State to refuse to recognize a lawful same-sex marriage performed in another State on the ground of its same-sex character.

No union is more profound than marriage, for it embodies the highest ideals of love, fidelity, devotion, sacrifice, and family. [The petitioners'] hope is not to be . . . excluded from one of civilization's oldest institutions. They ask for equal dignity in the eyes of the law. The Constitution grants them that right.

Sixth Circuit's judgment reversed.

Suspect Classes Certain "suspect" bases of classification also trigger more rigorous equal protection review. Although what is considered a "suspect class" is subject to review and change, race, alienage, and national origin generally are considered **suspect classes.**

1. *Race and national origin.* Classifications disadvantaging racial or national minorities receive the most rigorous kind of strict scrutiny and are almost never constitutional. For instance, in a recent decision that dealt not only with the suspect class of race but also the fundamental right to vote, the Supreme Court struck down North Carolina's formulation of certain legislative voting districts because the formulation depended upon impermissible drawing of race-based lines. (The case was *Cooper v. Harris*, 137 S. Ct. 1455 (2017).)

The Supreme Court has sometimes upheld government-required affirmative action plans and what critics have called reverse racial discrimination—government action that benefits racial minorities and allegedly disadvantages whites. In 1989, however, a majority of the Court concluded that state action of this kind should receive the same full strict scrutiny as discrimination *against* racial or national minorities. A 1995 Supreme Court decision held that this is true of federal government action as well as state action. These developments have curtailed certain government-created affirmative action programs but have not eliminated them.

In the companion cases of *Gratz v. Bollinger*, 539 U.S. 244 (2003), and *Grutter v. Bollinger,* 539 U.S. 306 (2003), the Supreme Court considered whether the University of Michigan violated the Equal Protection Clause by taking minority students' race into account in its undergraduate and law school admissions policies. The Court recognized in the two cases that seeking student diversity in a higher education context is a compelling government interest. However, in *Gratz*, a five-justice majority of the Court held that the university's undergraduate admissions policy violated the Equal Protection Clause because the policy's consideration of minority applicants' race became effectively the automatic determining factor in admission decisions regarding minority applicants. In *Grutter*, on the other hand, a different five-justice majority held that the university's law school admissions policy did not violate the Equal Protection Clause. The *Grutter* majority reasoned that the law school's policy, in considering minority applicants' race, did so as part of individualized consideration of applicants and of various types of diversity, not simply race. Thus, the law school's policy did not make race *the* determining factor in the impermissible way that the undergraduate policy did.

In the years following the decisions in *Gratz* and *Grutter*, the composition of the Supreme Court changed. When the Court agreed to decide a challenge to a race-conscious student admissions policy at the University of Texas (a policy patterned in large part after what the Court had approved in *Grutter*), speculation mounted that the Court might use the case as a vehicle for overruling *Grutter* or substantially cutting back on its effect. The Court did not do so, however. In *Fisher v. University of Texas*, 136 S. Ct. 2198 (2016), the Court reiterated a key *Grutter* principle: that seeking diversity in the student body at colleges and universities counts as a compelling government purpose in

the strict scrutiny analysis. The Court also left unaltered *Grutter*'s approach of permitting race to be considered in admissions decisions, as long as it was among a number of other factors taken into account in an individualized consideration of applicants and of various types of diversity. According to the Court, the challenged University of Texas plan passed the constitutional test by being narrowly tailored to achievement of the compelling government interest in achieving student body diversity.

In 2014, the Supreme Court decided an affirmative action–related case that presented a different wrinkle in the form of this question: If consideration of race in state university admission decisions is sometimes permissible (as *Grutter* and *Fisher* indicate), can the voters of a state constitutionally *bar* the use of race as a consideration in such decisions? In a Michigan referendum that took place three years after the decision in *Grutter*, voters approved an amendment to the state constitution that prohibited the use of race-conscious affirmative action in public education, government contracting, and public employment. Ruling on a challenge to this action, the Court emphasized in *Schuette v. Coalition to Defend Affirmative Action*, 572 U.S. 291 (2014), that the case was "not about how the debate about racial preferences should be resolved." Rather, it was "about who may resolve it." The Court went on to hold that there was "no authority in the [U.S.] Constitution . . . or in this Court's precedents for the judiciary to set aside Michigan laws that commit this policy determination to the voters."

A lawsuit against Harvard College claims that Harvard's admissions process violates Asian American applicants. The claim is not based on the Constitution; rather, it alleges violation of a federal law that prohibits discrimination among organizations or programs that receive federal funds (42 U.S.C. §2000d et seq.). But it is relevant for this discussion because the equal protection analysis applies to cases brought under that law. The federal district court in the Harvard case therefore analyzed the issue under the principles set forth in *Fisher* and found in favor of Harvard. At the time of this drafting, the case remained on appeal. *See Students for Fair Admissions, Inc. v. President and Fellows of Harvard College,* 397 F. Supp. 3d 126 (D. Mass. 2019). A similar case (though a direct constitutional challenge) against the University of North Carolina was pending as this book went to press (*see Students for Fair Admission, Inc. v. University of North Carolina,* 2019 WL 4773908 (M.D.N.C. Sept. 30, 2019)).

2. *Sex.* Although the Supreme Court has been hesitant to make a formal declaration that sex is a suspect class, for roughly four decades laws discriminating on the basis

Ethics and Compliance in Action

As discussion in this chapter reveals, Supreme Court precedent establishes that when government action discriminates on the basis of race or sex, the action will receive heightened scrutiny from the court if an equal protection challenge is brought. Despite cases such as *Obergefell v. Hodges* (in which the Supreme Court held that same-sex couples cannot be denied the fundamental right to marry), the Court has not recognized sexual orientation or transgender status as a suspect class for equal protection purposes. Unless and until the Court does so, the government may

have more legal latitude to regulate in ways that draw lines on the basis of persons' sexual orientation or transgender status than in ways that classify on the basis of persons' race or sex. Now view this set of issues from an ethical perspective. Should the government be any freer to take actions that discriminate against gays, lesbians, or transgender persons than it is to take actions that discriminate on the basis of race or sex? As you consider this question, you may wish to examine Chapter 4's discussion of ethical theories and ethical decision making.

of gender have been subjected to a fairly rigorous form of *intermediate scrutiny*. As the Court has said, such laws require an "exceedingly persuasive" justification. The usual test is that government action discriminating on the basis of sex must be *substantially* related to the furtherance of an *important* government purpose. Under this test, measures discriminating against women have almost always been struck down. The Supreme Court has said that laws disadvantaging men receive the same scrutiny as those disadvantaging women, but this has not prevented the Court from upholding men-only draft registration and a law making statutory rape a crime for men alone.

With gender as a longstanding suspect class and with legal developments such as the *Obergefell* decision's extension of the right to marry to same-sex couples, will the Supreme Court formally recognize sexual orientation and transgender status as suspect classes for equal protection purposes? Signs of such a development are at least discernible, but how immediately such a development may occur is an open question.

Independent Checks Applying Only to the States

The Contract Clause   Article I, § 10 of the Constitution states: "No State shall . . . pass any . . . Law impairing the Obligation of Contracts." Known as the *Contract Clause*, this provision deals with state laws that change the parties' performance obligations under an *existing* contract *after* that contract has been made.[2] The original purpose of the Contract Clause was to strike down the many debtor relief statutes passed by the states after the Revolution.

These statutes impaired the obligations of existing private contracts by relieving debtors of what they owed to creditors. In two early 19th-century cases, however, the Contract Clause was also held to protect the obligations of *governmental* contracts, charters, and grants.

The Contract Clause probably was the most important constitutional check on state regulation of the economy for much of the 19th century. Beginning in the latter part of that century, the clause gradually became subordinate to legislation based on the states' police powers. By the mid-20th century, most observers treated the clause as being of historical interest only. In 1977, however, the Supreme Court gave the Contract Clause new life by announcing a fairly strict constitutional test governing situations in which a state impairs *its own* contracts, charters, and grants. Such impairments, the Court said, must be "reasonable and necessary to serve an important public purpose."

During recent decades, the Court has continued its deference toward state regulations that impair the obligations of *private* contracts. Consider, for instance, *Exxon Corp. v. Eagerton*, 462 U.S. 176 (1983). For years, Exxon had paid a severance tax under Alabama law on oil and gas it drilled within the state. As the tax increased, appropriate provisions in Exxon's contracts with the purchasers of its oil and gas allowed Exxon to pass on the amounts of the increases to the purchasers. Alabama, however, enacted a law that not only increased the severance tax but also forbade producers of oil and gas from passing on the increase to purchasers. Exxon filed suit, seeking a declaration that the law's pass-on prohibition violated the Contract Clause. Affirming Alabama's highest court, the U.S. Supreme Court observed that the Contract Clause allows the states to adopt broad regulatory measures without having to be concerned that private contracts will be affected. The pass-on prohibition was designed to advance a broad public interest in protecting consumers against excessive prices and

---

[2]Under the Fifth Amendment's Due Process Cause, standards similar to those described in this section apply to the federal government.

Equal Protection and Levels of Scrutiny

Type of Government Action	Controlling Test	Operation and Effect of Test
Government action that discriminates but neither affects exercise of fundamental right nor discriminates against suspect class (e.g., most social and economic regulation)	Rational basis	Lenient test—government action is constitutional if rationally related to legitimate government purpose.
Government action that discriminates concerning ability to exercise fundamental right	Full strict scrutiny	Very rigorous test—government action is unconstitutional unless necessary to fulfillment of compelling government purpose.
Government action that discriminates on basis of race or national origin	Full strict scrutiny	Very rigorous test—government action is unconstitutional unless necessary to fulfillment of compelling government purpose.
Government action that discriminates on basis of sex (gender)	Intermediate scrutiny	Moderately rigorous test—government action is unconstitutional unless substantially related to fulfillment of important government purpose.

was applicable to all oil and gas producers regardless of whether they were then parties to contracts containing pass-on provisions. Therefore, the Court reasoned, the Alabama statute did not violate the Contract Clause.

Federal Preemption

 LO3-9 Identify the major circumstances in which federal law will preempt state law.

The constitutional principle of **federal supremacy** dictates that when state law conflicts with valid federal law, the federal law is supreme. In such a situation, the state law is said to be *preempted* by the federal regulation. The central question in most federal preemption cases is the intent of Congress. Thus, such cases often present complex questions of statutory interpretation.

Federal preemption of state law generally occurs for one or more of these reasons:

1. *There is a literal conflict between the state and federal measures, so that it is impossible to follow both simultaneously.*

2. *The federal law specifically states that it will preempt state regulation in certain areas.* Similar statements may also appear in the federal statute's legislative history. Courts sometimes find such statements persuasive even when they appear only in the legislative history and not in the statute itself.

3. *The federal regulation is pervasive.* If Congress has "occupied the field" by regulating a subject in great breadth and/or in considerable detail, such action by Congress may suggest an intent to displace state regulation of the subject. This may be especially likely where Congress has given an administrative agency broad regulatory power in a particular area.

4. *The state regulation is an obstacle to fulfilling the purposes of the federal law.* Here, the party challenging the state law's constitutionality typically claims that the state law interferes with the purposes she attributes to the federal measure (purposes usually found in its legislative history).

Arizona v. United States, 567 U.S. 387 (2012), illustrates the principles set forth in the above discussion of grounds for preemption. In that case, the Supreme Court was faced with deciding whether certain provisions in an Arizona law were preempted by federal immigration law, which has been enacted pursuant to the power granted to Congress over immigration matters in Article I, § 8 of the Constitution. The Court held that the so-called show me your papers provision in the Arizona law was not preempted. That provision called for state law enforcement officers to determine the immigration status of anyone they stopped or arrested if there was reason to suspect that the person might be in the country illegally.

However, the Court held that federal immigration law preempted three other provisions in the Arizona law: a provision making it a crime under Arizona law for an immigrant to fail to register under a federal law, a provision making it a crime under Arizona law for illegal immigrants to work or seek work, and a provision allowing Arizona law enforcement officers to make warrantless arrests if the officers have probable cause to believe the arrested persons committed acts that would make them subject to deportation under federal law. The preempted provisions either conflicted with federal law or posed too great an impediment to fulfillment of the federal law's objectives.

The Takings Clause

 LO3-10 Explain the power granted to the government by the Takings Clause, as well as the limits on that power.

The Fifth Amendment states that "private property [shall not] be taken for public use, without just compensation." Because this **Takings Clause** has been incorporated within Fourteenth Amendment due process, it applies to the states. Traditionally, it has come into play when the government formally condemns land through its power of **eminent domain**,[3] but it has many other applications as well.

The Takings Clause both recognizes government's power to take private property and limits the exercise of that power. It does so by requiring that when *property* is subjected to a governmental *taking*, the taking must be for a *public use* and the property owner must receive *just compensation*. We now consider these four aspects of the Takings Clause in turn.

1. *Property.* The Takings Clause protects other property interests besides land and interests in land. Although its full scope is unclear, the clause has been held to cover takings of personal property, liens, trade secrets, and contract rights.

---

[3]Eminent domain and the Takings Clause's application to land use problems are discussed in Chapter 24.

2. *Taking.* Because of the range of property interests it may cover, the Takings Clause potentially has a broad scope. Another reason for the clause's wide possible application is the range of government activities that may be considered takings. Of course, the government's use of formal condemnation procedures to acquire private property is a taking. There may also be a taking when the government physically invades private property or allows someone else to do so.

It has long been recognized, moreover, that overly extensive land use regulation may so diminish the value of property or the owner's enjoyment of it as to constitute a taking. Among the factors courts consider in such "regulatory taking" cases are the degree to which government deprives the owner of free possession, use, and disposition of his property; the overall economic impact of the regulation on the owner; and how much the regulation interferes with the owner's reasonable investment-backed expectations regarding the future use of the property. In *Lucas v. South Carolina Coastal Council*, 505 U.S. 1003 (1992), the Supreme Court held that there is an automatic taking when the government denies the owner *all* economically beneficial uses of the land. When this is not the case, courts tend to apply some form of means-ends scrutiny in determining whether land use regulation has gone too far and thus amounts to a regulatory taking.

3. *Public use.* Once a taking of property has occurred, it is unconstitutional unless it is for a public use. The public use element took center stage in a widely publicized 2005 Supreme Court decision, *Kelo v. City of New London.* For discussion of *Kelo*, see Figure 3.4.

4. *Just compensation.* Even if a taking of property is for a public use, it still is unconstitutional if the property owner does not receive just compensation. Although the standards for determining just compensation vary with the circumstances, the basic test is the fair market value of the property (or of the lost property right) at the time of the taking.

Figure 3.4   Economic Development as Public Use?

Does the government's taking of private property for the purpose of economic development satisfy the *public use* requirement set forth in the Fifth Amendment's Takings Clause? In *Kelo v. City of New London*, 545 U.S. 469 (2005), the U.S. Supreme Court answered "yes."

New London, Connecticut, experienced economic decline for a considerable number of years. The city therefore made economic revitalization efforts, which included a plan to acquire 115 parcels of real estate in a 90-acre area and create, in collaboration with private developers, a multifaceted zone that would combine commercial, residential, and recreational elements. The planned development was designed to increase tax revenue, create jobs, and otherwise capitalize on the economic opportunities that city officials expected would flow from a major pharmaceutical company's already-announced plan to construct a large facility near the area the city wished to develop.

The city was able to negotiate the purchase of most parcels of property in the 90-acre area, but some property owners refused to sell. The latter group included Susette

Kelo and Wilhelmina Dery. Kelo had lived in her home for several years, had made substantial improvements to it, and especially enjoyed the water view it afforded. Dery had lived her entire life in the home the city sought to acquire. Both homes were well maintained. After the city decided to use its eminent domain power to acquire the properties of those owners who refused to sell, Kelo, Dery, and the other nonselling owners filed suit. They contended that the city's plan to take their property for the purpose of economic development did not involve a public use and thus would violate the Fifth Amendment's Takings Clause. The dispute made its way through the Connecticut courts and then to the U.S. Supreme Court, where a five-justice majority ruled in favor of the city.

Writing for the majority in *Kelo v. City of New London*, Justice Stevens noted that earlier decisions had identified three types of eminent domain settings in which the government's acquisition of private property satisfied the constitutional *public use* element: first, when the government planned to develop a government-owned facility (e.g., a military base); second, when the government planned to construct, or allow others to construct, improvements to which the public would have broad access (e.g., highways or railroads); and third, when the government sought to further some meaningful public purpose. Justice Stevens observed that precedents had recognized the *public purpose* type of public use even if the government would not ultimately retain legal title to the acquired property (unlike the military base example) and the acquired property would not be fully opened up for public access (unlike the highway and railroad examples). The Court acknowledged that the public use requirement clearly would not be satisfied if the government took private party A's property simply to give it to private party B. However, the Court stressed, the prospect that private parties might ultimately own or control property the government had acquired through eminent domain would not make the taking unconstitutional if an overriding public purpose prompted the government's use of eminent domain. Similarly, even if certain private parties (e.g., the pharmaceutical company and private developers in the *Kelo* facts) would stand to benefit from the government's exercise of eminent domain, such a fact would not make the taking unconstitutional if a public purpose supported the taking.

The *Kelo* majority stressed the particular relevance of two earlier Supreme Court decisions, *Berman v. Parker*, 348 U.S. 26 (1954), and *Hawaii Housing Authority v. Midkiff*, 467 U.S. 299 (1984). In *Berman*, the Court sustained Washington, D.C.'s use of eminent domain to take property that included businesses and "blighted" dwellings

in order to construct a low-income housing project and new streets, schools, and public facilities. In *Midkiff*, the Court upheld Hawaii's use of eminent domain to effectuate a legislative determination that Hawaii's longstanding land oligopoly, under which property ownership was highly concentrated among a small number of property owners, had to be broken up for social and economic reasons. The *Kelo* majority concluded that significant public purposes were present in both *Berman* and *Midkiff* and that those decisions led logically to the conclusion that economic development was a public purpose weighty enough to constitute public use for purposes of the Takings Clause. Therefore, the Court upheld the city's exercise of eminent domain in *Kelo*.

In his majority opinion, Justice Stevens was careful to point out that because the constitutional question was whether a public use existed, it was not the Court's job to determine the wisdom of the government's attempt to exercise eminent domain. Neither should the Court allow its decision to be guided by the undoubted hardship that eminent domain places on unwilling property owners who must yield their homes to the state (albeit in return for "just compensation"). Justice Stevens emphasized that if state legislatures believed an economic development purpose such as the one the City of New London had in mind should not be used to support an exercise of eminent domain, the legislatures were free to specify, in their state statutes, that eminent domain could not be employed for an economic development purpose. The Court's determination of what is a public use for purposes of the Takings Clause sets a protective floor for property owners, with states being free to give greater protection against takings by the government.

The four dissenting justices in *Kelo* issued sharply worded opinions expressing their disagreement with the majority's characterization of *Berman* and *Midkiff* as having led logically to the conclusion that economic development was a public use. In emotional terms, the dissenters accused the majority of having effectively erased the public use requirement from the Takings Clause. The *Kelo* decision drew considerable media attention, perhaps more because of what appeared to be considerable hardship to property owners such as Kelo and Dery than because of new legal ground—if any—broken in the decision. For many observers, the case's compelling facts led to a perception that the city had engaged in overreaching. The Court's decision in *Kelo* meant that in a legal sense, there was no overreaching on the part of the city. Was there, however, overreaching in an *ethical* sense? How would *utilitarians* answer that question? What about *rights theorists*? (As you consider the questions, you may wish to consult Chapter 4.)

Problems and Problem Cases

1. In 1967, Gary Jones purchased a house on North Bryan Street in Little Rock, Arkansas. He and his wife lived in the house until they separated in 1993. Jones then moved into an apartment in Little Rock, and his wife continued to live in the house. Jones paid his mortgage each month for 30 years. The mortgage company paid the property taxes on the house. After Jones paid off his mortgage in 1997, the property taxes went unpaid. In April 2000, the Arkansas Commissioner of State Lands (Commissioner) attempted to notify Jones of his tax delinquency and his right to redeem the property by paying the past-due taxes. The Commissioner sought to provide this notice by mailing a certified letter to Jones at the North Bryan Street address. Arkansas law approved the use of such a method of providing notice. The packet of information sent by the Commissioner stated that unless Jones redeemed the property, it would be subject to public sale two years later. No one was at home to sign for the letter. No one appeared at the post office to retrieve the letter within the next 15 days. The post office then returned the unopened packet to the Commissioner with an "unclaimed" designation on it. In the spring of 2002, a few weeks before the public sale scheduled for Jones's house, the Commissioner published a notice of public sale in a local newspaper. No bids were submitted, meaning that under Arkansas law, the state could negotiate a private sale of the property.

    Several months later, Linda Flowers submitted a purchase offer. The Commissioner then mailed another certified letter to Jones at the North Bryan Street address, attempting to notify him that his house would be sold to Flowers if he did not pay his delinquent taxes. As with the first letter, the second letter was returned to the Commissioner with an "unclaimed" designation. Flowers purchased the house. Immediately after the expiration of the 30-day period in which Arkansas law would have allowed Jones to make a post-sale redemption of the property by paying the past-due taxes, Flowers had an eviction notice delivered to the North Bryan Street property. The notice was served on Jones's daughter, who contacted Jones and notified him of the tax sale. Jones then filed a lawsuit in Arkansas state court against the Commissioner and Flowers. In his lawsuit, Jones contended that the Commissioner's failure to provide notice of the tax sale and of Jones's right to redeem resulted in the taking of his property without due process. The trial court ruled in favor of the Commissioner and Flowers, and the Arkansas Supreme Court affirmed. The U.S. Supreme Court agreed to decide the case and its central question of whether Jones was afforded due process. How did the U.S. Supreme Court rule?

2. Two Rhode Island statutes prohibited advertising the retail price of alcoholic beverages. The first applied to vendors licensed in Rhode Island as well as to out-of-state manufacturers, wholesalers, and shippers. It prohibited them from "advertising in any manner whatsoever" the price of any alcoholic beverage offered for sale in the state. The only exception to the restriction was for price tags or signs displayed with the merchandise within licensed premises, if the tags or signs were not visible from the street. The second statute barred the Rhode Island news media from publishing or broadcasting advertisements that made reference to the price of any alcoholic beverages. 44 Liquormart Inc., a licensed retailer of alcoholic beverages, operated a store in Rhode Island. Because it wished to advertise prices it would charge for alcoholic beverages, 44 Liquormart filed a declaratory judgment action against the state. 44 Liquormart asked the court to rule that the statutes referred to above violated the First Amendment. The district court concluded that the statutes failed the applicable test for restrictions on commercial speech and therefore struck them down. The U.S. Court of Appeals for the First Circuit reversed, determining that the statutes were constitutionally permissible restrictions on commercial speech. The U.S. Supreme Court granted 44 Liquormart's petition for a writ of certiorari. How did the Supreme Court rule?

3. A federal statute, 8 U.S.C. § 1409, sets requirements for acquisition of U.S. citizenship by a child born outside the United States to unwed parents, only one of whom is a U.S. citizen. If the mother is the U.S. citizen, the child acquires citizenship at birth. Section 1409(a) states that when the father is the citizen parent, the child acquires citizenship only if, before the child reaches the age of 18, the child is legitimized under the law of the child's residence or domicile, the father acknowledges paternity in writing under oath, or paternity is established by a competent court. Tuan Anh Nguyen was born in Vietnam to a Vietnamese mother and a U.S. citizen father, Joseph Boulais. At six years of age, Nguyen came to the United States, where he became a lawful permanent resident and was raised by his father. When Nguyen was 22, he pleaded guilty in a Texas court to two counts of sexual assault.

The U.S. Immigration and Naturalization Service initiated deportation proceedings against Nguyen, and an immigration judge found him deportable. While Nguyen's appeal to the U.S. Board of Immigration Appeals was pending, Boulais obtained from a state court an order of parentage that was based on DNA testing. The board dismissed Nguyen's appeal, denying his citizenship claim on the ground that he had not established compliance with § 1409(a). Nguyen and Boulais appealed to the U.S. Court of Appeals for the Fifth Circuit, which rejected their contention that § 1409 discriminated on the basis of gender and thus violated the Constitution's equal protection guarantee. Was the Fifth Circuit's decision correct?

4. As most other states do, the Commonwealth of Kentucky taxes its residents' income. Kentucky law establishes that interest on bonds issued by Kentucky and its political subdivisions is exempt from Kentucky's income tax, whereas interest on bonds issued by other states and their political subdivisions is taxable. The tax exemption for Kentucky bonds helps make those bonds attractive to in-state purchasers even if they carry somewhat lower rates of interest than other states' bonds or those issued by private companies. Most other states have differential tax schemes that resemble Kentucky's. Kentucky residents George and Catherine Davis paid state income tax on interest from out-of-state municipal bonds, and then sued the Department of Revenue of Kentucky in an effort to obtain a refund. The Davises contended that Kentucky's differential taxation of municipal bond interest impermissibly discriminates against interstate commerce in violation of the U.S. Constitution's Commerce Clause. Were the Davises correct?

5. Nike Inc. mounted a public relations campaign in order to refute news media allegations that its labor practices overseas were unfair and unlawful. The campaign involved the use of press releases, letters to newspapers, a letter to university presidents and athletic directors, and full-page advertisements in leading newspapers. Relying on California statutes designed to curb false and misleading advertising and other forms of unfair competition, California resident Mark Kasky filed suit in a California court on behalf of the general public of the state. Kasky contended that Nike had made false statements in its campaign and that the court should therefore grant the legal relief contemplated by the California statutes. In terms of Nike's potential liability, why would it make a difference whether the speech in which Nike engaged was commercial or, instead, noncommercial? What are the arguments in favor of a conclusion that Nike was engaged in commercial speech? What are the arguments in favor of a conclusion that Nike was engaged in noncommercial speech? How did the court rule on the speech classification issue—that is, whether Nike's speech was commercial or, instead, that it is noncommercial?

6. Public school districts in Seattle, Washington, and Louisville, Kentucky, faced litigation in which it was alleged that they violated the Equal Protection Clause by considering race when assigning students to schools. The Seattle district, which had neither created segregated schools nor been subject to court-ordered desegregation, generally allowed students to choose which high school they wished to attend. However, the district classified students as white or nonwhite. It then used the racial classifications as a "tiebreaker" to allocate available slots in particular high schools and thereby seek to achieve racially diverse schools despite the existence of certain housing patterns that would have produced little racial diversity at certain schools. The Louisville district had been subject to a federal court's desegregation decree during a two-decades-long period, but a court had lifted the desegregation order after concluding that the district had eliminated the vestiges of prior segregation to the greatest extent feasible. The Louisville district then adopted a plan under which students were classified as Black or "other." Using these classifications in making elementary school assignments and in ruling on transfer requests, the district sought to achieve racial diversity in schools that would have reflected less racial diversity in light of traditional housing patterns. The cases challenging the two districts' policies of considering race made their way through the federal courts and were later consolidated for decision by the U.S. Supreme Court.

What test would the Seattle and Louisville school districts need to pass in order to avoid a Supreme Court determination that their policies violate the Equal Protection Clause? Could the school districts pass that test? Why or why not?

7. Marijuana is classified under federal law as an illegal drug. On what enumerated power would Congress have relied when it enacted the federal statute that outlaws marijuana and other specified drugs?

A number of states have legalized marijuana possession and use up to certain levels designated in their laws. Several other states have legalized marijuana possession and use for medicinal purposes, but for those purposes only. As a constitutional matter, could the federal government—if it were so inclined—adopt an aggressive enforcement posture in which it would override the state laws to the contrary? If so, on what constitutional basis? If not, why not?

8. The Minnesota legislature passed a statute banning the sale of milk in plastic nonrefillable, nonreusable containers. However, it allowed sales of milk in other nonrefillable, nonreusable containers such as paperboard cartons. One of the justifications for this ban on plastic jugs was that it would ease the state's solid waste disposal problems because plastic jugs occupy more space in landfills than other nonreturnable milk containers. A group of dairy businesses challenged the statute, arguing that its distinction between plastic containers and other containers was unconstitutional under the Equal Protection Clause. What means-ends test or level of scrutiny applies in this case? Under that test, is easing the state's solid waste disposal problems a sufficiently important *end*? Under that test, is there a sufficiently close "fit" between the classification and that end to make the statutory *means* constitutional? In answering the last question, assume for the sake of argument that there probably were more effective ways of alleviating the solid waste disposal problem than banning plastic jugs while allowing paperboard cartons.

9. The plaintiffs in the case described below were two married same-sex couples who conceived children through anonymous sperm donation. Leigh and Jana Jacobs were married in Iowa in 2010, and Terrah and Marisa Pavan were married in New Hampshire in 2011. Leigh and Terrah each gave birth to a child in Arkansas in 2015. When it came time to secure birth certificates for the newborns, each couple filled out paperwork listing both spouses as parents—Leigh and Jana in one case, Terrah and Marisa in the other. Both times, however, the Arkansas Department of Health issued certificates bearing only the birth mother's name. The department's decision rested on a provision of Arkansas law that specified which individuals will appear as parents on a child's state-issued birth certificate. The statute stated that "[f]or the purposes of birth registration, the mother is deemed to be the woman who gives birth to the child." The statute also instructed that "[i]f the mother was married at the time of either conception or birth, the name of [her] husband shall be entered on the certificate as the father of the child." The requirement that a married woman's husband appear on her child's birth certificate applied, according to the state's

interpretation of the statute, if the couple conceived by means of artificial insemination with the help of an anonymous sperm donor.

The Jacobses and Pavans brought this suit in Arkansas state court against the director of the Arkansas Department of Health in an effort to obtain a declaration that the state's birth-certificate law violated the U.S. Constitution. The trial court so ruled, but the Arkansas Supreme Court reversed the trial court's decision. The U.S. Supreme Court agreed to decide the case. What constitutional provision or provisions do you see as relevant here? How did the Supreme Court rule?

10. While it was preparing a comprehensive land use plan in the area, the Tahoe Regional Planning Agency (TRPA) imposed two moratoria on development of property in the Lake Tahoe Basin. The moratoria together lasted 32 months. A group of property developers affected by the moratoria filed suit in federal court alleging that the moratoria constituted an unconstitutional taking without just compensation. Were the developers correct?

11. A federal statute criminalized the creation, sale, or possession of certain depictions of animal cruelty. For purposes of the statute, a depiction of "animal cruelty" was defined as one "in which a living animal is intentionally maimed, mutilated, tortured, wounded, or killed," if the depicted conduct violated federal or state law at the place where the creation, sale, or possession took place. The legislative history of the statute indicated that it was prompted by a congressional objective of eliminating dissemination of so-called crush videos (videos showing live animals being crushed to death by persons stomping on them).

Robert Stevens operated a website on which he sold videos of pitbulls engaging in dogfighting and otherwise attacking animals. After he was convicted of violating the above-described statute by selling the videos, he appealed on the ground that the statute violated the First Amendment. The case made its way to the U.S. Supreme Court. How did the Court rule? Was Stevens entitled to the protection of the First Amendment?

12. Florida's Code of Judicial Conduct bars judges and candidates running for election to a judgeship from personally soliciting campaign contributions of a financial nature. Attorney Lanell Williams-Yulee, a candidate running for election to a Florida judgeship, drafted and mailed a letter to voters. In the letter, she asked for donations to her campaign. The State Bar

of Florida brought a disciplinary proceeding against Williams-Yulee because of the letter. The proceedings concluded with a finding that a public reprimand was in order because she had violated the Code of Judicial Conduct. The Bar rejected Williams-Yulee's argument that the ban on personal solicitation violated her First Amendment rights. The Supreme Court of Florida also rejected that argument. The U.S. Supreme Court agreed to decide the case. What kind of speech was Williams-Yulee engaging in through her letter soliciting contributions to her campaign? Did the Code of Judicial Conduct's restriction on personal solicitation violate her First Amendment rights?

13. A federal law, the Immigration Reform and Control Act (IRCA), makes it "unlawful for a person or other entity . . . to hire, or to recruit or refer for a fee, for employment in the United States an alien knowing the alien is an unauthorized alien." Employers that violate this prohibition may be subjected to civil and criminal sanctions. IRCA also restricts the ability of states to combat employment of unauthorized workers. It does so by expressly preempting "any state or local law imposing civil or criminal sanctions (other than through licensing and similar laws) upon those who employ, or recruit or refer for a fee for employment,

unauthorized aliens." In addition, IRCA requires employers to take steps to verify an employee's eligibility for employment. Seeking to improve that verification process, Congress created E-Verify, an Internet-based system employers can use to check the work authorization status of employees. Federal law does not require the use of E-Verify, however.

Arizona was among several states that enacted statutes designed to impose sanctions for the employment of unauthorized aliens. According to an Arizona law (the Legal Arizona Workers Act), the licenses of state employers that knowingly or intentionally employ unauthorized aliens may be, and in certain circumstances must be, suspended or revoked. The Arizona law also requires that all Arizona employers use E-Verify. The Chamber of Commerce of the United States and various business and civil rights organizations filed suit against those charged with administering the Arizona law. The plaintiffs argued that the state law's license suspension and revocation provisions were both expressly and impliedly preempted by federal immigration law, and that the mandatory use of E-Verify was impliedly preempted. Were the plaintiffs right? Did federal immigration law preempt the challenged provisions of the Arizona statute?

Business Ethics, Corporate Social Responsibility, Corporate Governance, and Critical Thinking

What defines ethical behavior? Think of a time when you thought that someone or some business did something ethical. Was it someone going out of her way to help another person? Was it, for example, a young man—a customer at a store—helping an elderly woman carry heavy packages to her car? Was it someone entering a building during a pouring rain and giving her umbrella to a father and his small children who were waiting to leave until the rain stopped?

Was it a corporate executive speaking for an hour to a friend's daughter—a young college student—helping her understand how to seek an internship and prepare for a career in the executive's industry? Was it a business giving a second chance to a young man who fell in with the wrong crowd, made a mistake, and served time in prison?

Was it a company recalling and repairing an allegedly defective product, even when not required by the government, at great cost to its profits and shareholders? Was it a business that bought a failing company in the solar industry? Was it a corporation buying a competitor, achieving synergies, improving options and pricing for consumers, and increasing the company's profits?

Was it a business that chose to upgrade its factories in a midwestern town instead of moving manufacturing operations overseas? Was it a business that opened a new plant in Indonesia, creating jobs for 1,000 workers? Was it a corporation with excess cash opting to increase its dividend by 25 percent and buy back 10 percent of its stock, thereby increasing returns to shareholders and the price of the shareholders' stock in the company?

In these and other situations in which you observed what you believed was ethical conduct, what made you think the behavior was ethical? Was it that the ethical actor obeyed some fundamental notion of rightness? Was it that the person treated someone the way you would want to be treated? Was it that the actor gave an opportunity to someone who was in greater need than most people? Was it that the company helped someone who deserved aid?

Was it that most people thought that it was the right thing to do or that the majority wanted it done, whether right or not? Was it that the business took full advantage of the resources entrusted to it by society? Was it that the business helped society use its scarce resources in a productive or fair way?

What ethical responsibilities do businesses and business leaders have and to whom?

What defines ethical behavior?

Why Study Business Ethics?

General Motors hiding that it sold cars with faulty ignitions. Target failing to protect customers' credit card information. Enron maintaining its stock price by moving liabilities off balance sheet. WorldCom using fraudulent accounting to increase its stock price. ImClone executives and their family members trading on inside information. These business names and acts from the past two decades conjure images of unethical and socially irresponsible behavior by business executives. The U.S. Congress, employees, investors, and other critics of the power held and abused by some corporations and their management have demanded that corporate wrongdoers be punished and that future wrongdoers be deterred. Consequently, shareholders, creditors, and state and federal attorneys general have brought several civil and criminal actions against wrongdoing corporations and their executives. Congress has also entered the fray, passing the Sarbanes–Oxley Act of 2002, which increased penalties for corporate wrongdoers and established rules designed to deter and prevent future wrongdoing. The purpose of the statute is to encourage and enable corporate executives to be ethical and socially responsible.

But statutes and civil and criminal actions can go only so far in directing business managers down an ethical path. And while avoiding liability by complying with the law is one reason to be ethical and socially responsible, there are noble and economic reasons that encourage current and future business executives to study business ethics.

Although it is tempting to paint all businesses and all managers with the same brush that colors unethical and irresponsible corporations and executives, in reality corporate executives are little different from you, your friends, and your acquaintances. All of us from time to time fail to do the right thing, and we know that people have varying levels of commitment to acting ethically. The difference between most of us and corporate executives is that they are in positions of power that allow them to do greater damage to others when they act unethically or socially irresponsibly. They also act under the microscope of public scrutiny.

It is also tempting to say that current business managers are less ethical than managers historically. But as former Federal Reserve chair Alan Greenspan said, "It is not that humans have become any more greedy than in generations past. It is that the avenues to express greed have grown enormously."

This brings us to the first and most important reason we need to study business ethics: to make better decisions for ourselves, the businesses we work for, and the society we live in. As you read this chapter, you will not only study the different theories that attempt to define ethical conduct but, more importantly, learn to use a strategic framework for making decisions. This framework provides a process for systematic ethical analysis, which will increase the likelihood you have considered all the facts affecting your decision. By learning a methodology for ethical decision making and studying common thinking errors, you will improve your ability to make decisions that build trust and solidify relationships with your business's stakeholders.

Another reason we study ethics is to understand ourselves and others better. While studying the various ethical theories, you will see concepts that reflect your own thinking and the thinking of others. This chapter, by exploring ethical theories systematically and pointing out the strengths and weaknesses of each ethical theory, should help you understand better why you think the way you do and why others think the way they do. By studying ethical theories, learning a process for ethical decision making, and understanding common reasoning fallacies, you should also be better equipped to decide how you should think and whether you should be persuaded by the arguments of others. Along the way, by better understanding where others are coming from and avoiding fallacious reasoning, you should become a more rigorous, critical thinker, as well as persuasive speaker and writer.

There are also pragmatic reasons for executives to study business ethics. By learning how to act ethically and by, in fact, doing so, businesses forestall public criticism, reduce lawsuits against them, prevent Congress from passing onerous legislation, and make higher profits. For many corporate actors, however, these are not reasons to act ethically, but instead the natural consequences of so acting.

While we are studying business ethics, we will also examine the role of the law and regulations in defining ethical conduct. Some argue that it is sufficient for corporations and executives to comply with the requirements of the law; commonly, critics of the corporation point out that because laws cannot and do not encompass all expressions of ethical behavior, compliance with the law is necessary but not sufficient to ensure ethical conduct. This introduces us to one of the major issues in the corporate social responsibility debate.

The Corporate Social Responsibility Debate

Although interest in business ethics education has increased greatly in the last few decades, that interest is only the latest stage in a long struggle to control corporate misbehavior. Ever since large corporations emerged in the late 19th century, such firms have been heroes to some and villains to others. Large corporations perform essential national and global economic functions, including raw material extraction, energy production, transportation, and communication, as well as providing consumer goods, professional services, and entertainment to millions of people.

Critics, however, claim that in their pursuit of profits, corporations ruin the environment, mistreat employees, sell shoddy and dangerous products, produce immoral television shows and motion pictures, and corrupt the political process. Critics claim that even when corporations provide vital and important services, business is not nearly as accountable to the public as are organs of government. For example, the public has little to say about the election of corporate directors or the appointment of corporate officers. This lack of accountability is aggravated by the large amount of power that big corporations wield in America and throughout much of the world.

These criticisms and perceptions have led to calls for changes in how corporations and their executives make decisions. The main device for checking corporate misdeeds has been the law. The perceived need to check abuses of business power was a force behind the New Deal laws of the 1930s and extensive federal regulations enacted in the 1960s and 1970s. Some critics, however, believe that legal regulation, while an important element of any corporate control scheme, is insufficient by itself. They argue that businesses should adhere to a standard of ethical or socially responsible behavior that is higher than the law.

One such standard is the stakeholder theory of corporate social responsibility. It holds that rather than merely striving to maximize profits for its shareholders, a corporation should balance the interests of investors against the interests of other corporate stakeholders, such as employees, suppliers, customers, and the community. In August 2019, the Business Roundtable endorsed the stakeholder theory approach, noting the importance of delivering value to customers, investing in employees, dealing fairly and ethically with suppliers, supporting local communities, and generating long-term value for shareholders. To promote such behavior, some corporate critics have proposed changes that increase the influence of the various stakeholders in the internal governance of a corporation. We will study many of these proposals later in the chapter in the subsection on shareholder theory and its emphasis on profit maximization. You will also learn later that an ethical decision-making process requires a business executive to anticipate the effects of a corporate decision on the various corporate stakeholders.

Despite concerns about abuses of power, big business has contributed greatly to the unprecedented abundance in America and elsewhere. Partly for this reason and partly because many businesses attempt to be ethical actors, critics have not totally dominated the debate about control of the modern corporation. Some defenders of business argue that in a society founded on capitalism, profit maximization should be the main goal of businesses: The only ethical norms firms must follow are those embodied in the law or those impacting profits. In short, they argue that businesses that maximize profits within the limits of the law are acting ethically. Otherwise, the marketplace would discipline them for acting unethically by reducing their profits.

Former Fed chair Alan Greenspan wrote in 1963 that moral values are the power behind capitalism. He wrote, "Capitalism is based on self-interest and self-esteem; it holds integrity and trustworthiness as cardinal virtues and makes them pay off in the marketplace, thus demanding that [business persons] survive by means of virtue, not of vices." Note that companies that are successful decade after decade, like Procter & Gamble and Johnson & Johnson, adhere to society's core values.

We will explore other arguments supporting and criticizing shareholder theory and its emphasis on profit maximization later in the chapter, where we will consider proposals to improve corporate governance and accountability. For now, however, having set the stage for the debate about business ethics and corporate social responsibility, we want to study the definitions of ethical behavior.

Ethical Theories

For centuries, religious and secular scholars have explored the meaning of human existence and attempted to define a "good life." In this section, we will define and examine some of the most important theories of ethical conduct.

Ethics and Compliance in Action

American physicist, mathematician, and futurist Freeman Dyson provided insights into why we humans may have difficulty determining which ethical viewpoint to embrace. His research also helps explain why different people have different ethical leanings.

The destiny of our species is shaped by the imperatives of survival on six distinct time scales. To survive means to compete successfully on all six time scales. But the unit of survival is different for each of the six time scales. On a time scale of years, the unit is the individual. On a time scale of decades, the unit is the family. On a time scale of centuries, the unit is the tribe or nation. On a time scale of millennia, the unit is the culture. On a time scale of tens of millennia, the unit is the species. On a time scale of eons, the unit is the whole web of life on our planet. That is why conflicting loyalties are deep in our nature. In order to survive, we need to be loyal to ourselves, to our families, to our tribes, to our culture, to our species, to our planet. If our psychological impulses are complicated, it is because they were shaped by complicated and conflicting demands.[1]

Dyson goes on to write, "Nature gave us greed, a robust desire to maximize our personal winnings. Without greed we would not have survived at the individual level." Yet he points out that Nature also gave us the connections and tools to survive at the family level (Dyson calls this tool love of family), the tribal level (love of friends), the cultural level (love of conversation), the species level (love of people in general), and the planetary level (love of nature).

If Dyson is correct, why are humans sometimes vastly different from each other in some of their ethical values? Why do some of us argue, for example, that universal health care is a right for each citizen, while others believe health care is a privilege? The answer lies in the degree to which each of us embraces, innately or rationally, Dyson's six units of survival and the extent to which each of us possesses the connections and tools to survive on each of those levels.

_____

[1] Freeman Dyson, *From Eros to Gaia* (London: Penguin Books, 1993), pp. 341–42.

LO4-1 Appreciate the strengths and weaknesses of the various ethical theories.

As we cover these theories, much of what you read will be familiar to you. The names may be new, but almost certainly you have previously heard speeches and read writings of politicians, religious leaders, and commentators that incorporate the values in these theories. You will discover that your own thinking is consistent with one or more of the theories. You can also recognize the thinking of friends and antagonists in these theories.

None of these theories is necessarily invalid, and many people believe strongly in any one of them. Whether you believe your theory to be right and the others to be wrong, it is unlikely that others will accept what you see as the error of their ways and agree with all your values. Instead, it is important for you to recognize that people's ethical values can be as diverse as human culture. Therefore, no amount of argumentation appealing to theories you accept is likely to influence someone who subscribes to a different ethical viewpoint. The key, therefore, is to understand the complexity of ethical perspectives so that you can better understand both your viewpoint and the viewpoints of others. Only then is it possible to pursue common ground and provide a rational explanation for the decision that must ultimately be made.

This means that if you want to be understood by and to influence someone who has a different ethical underpinning than you do, you must first determine her ethical viewpoint and then speak in an ethical language that will be understood and accepted by her. Otherwise, you and your opponent are like the talking heads on nighttime cable TV news shows, whose debates often are reduced to shouting matches void of any attempt to understand the other side.

LOG ON

Go to
www.iep.utm.edu
The Internet Encyclopedia of Philosophy gives you background on all the world's great philosophers from Abelard to Zizek. You can also study the development of philosophy from ancient times to the present. Many of the world's great philosophers addressed the question of ethical or moral conduct.

The five ethical theories we will highlight are rights theory, justice theory, utilitarianism, shareholder theory, and virtue theory. Some of these theories focus on results of our decisions or actions: Do our decisions or actions produce the right results? Theories that focus on the consequences of a decision are teleological ethical theories. For example, a teleological theory may justify a manufacturing company laying off 5,000 employees because the effect is to keep the price of manufactured goods low for consumers and to increase profits for the company's shareholders.

Other theories focus on the inherent rightness or wrongness of a decision or action itself, irrespective of what results it produces. This rightness or wrongness can be determined by a rule or principle or flow from a duty or responsibility. Theories that focus on decisions or actions alone are deontological ethical theories. For example, a deontological theory may find unacceptable that any competent employee loses his job, even if the layoff's effect is to reduce prices to consumers and increase profits. Or a deontological theory emphasizing the principle that it is wrong to be dishonest might require that one never tell a lie, regardless of the consequences. Deontological theories place great emphasis on the duties and responsibilities that flow from rules, laws, policies, or social norms governing our actions.

First, we will cover rights theory, which is a deontological theory. Next will be justice theory, which has concepts common to rights theory but with a focus primarily on outcomes. Our study of ethical theories will then turn to two additional teleological theories, utilitarianism and shareholder theory. Finally, we'll consider virtue theory, which places the issue of one's character and core virtues at the fore, instead of focusing first on rules and responsibilities or the consequences that inevitably flow from all of our actions.

Rights Theory
Rights theory encompasses a variety of ethical philosophies holding that certain human rights are fundamental and must be respected by other humans. The focus is on each individual member of society and her rights. As an ethically responsible individual, each of us faces a moral compulsion not to harm the fundamental rights of others, especially stakeholders impacted by our business activity.

Kantianism Few rights theorists are strict deontologists, and one of the few is 18th-century philosopher Immanuel Kant. Kant viewed humans as moral actors who are free to make choices. He believed humans are able to judge the morality of any action by applying his famous categorical imperative. One formulation of the categorical imperative is, "Act only on that maxim whereby at the same time you can will that it shall become a universal law." This means that we judge an action by applying it universally.

Suppose you want to borrow money even though you know that you will never repay it. To justify this action using the categorical imperative, you state the following maxim or rule: "When I want money, I will borrow money and promise to repay it, even though I know I won't repay." According to Kant, you would not want this

maxim to become a universal law because no one would believe in promises to repay debts and you would not be able to borrow money when you want. The ability to trust others in society would be completely impossible, and relationships would deteriorate. Thus, your maxim or rule fails to satisfy the categorical imperative. You are compelled, therefore, not to promise falsely that you will repay a loan.

Kant had a second formulation of the categorical imperative: "Always act to treat humanity, whether in yourself or in others, as an end in itself, never merely as a means." Thus arises a rule or principle creating a duty not to use or manipulate others in order to achieve our own happiness. In Kant's eyes, if you falsely promise a lender to repay a loan, you are manipulating that person's trust in you for your own ends because she would not agree to the loan if she knew all the facts.

Modern Rights Theories Strict deontological ethical theories like Kant's face an obvious problem: The duties are often viewed as absolute and universally applicable. A deontologist might argue that one must never lie or kill, even though most of us find lying and killing acceptable in some contexts, such as in self-defense. Responding to these difficulties, some modern philosophers have proposed mixed deontological theories. There are many theories here, but one popular theory requires us to abide by a moral rule unless a more important rule conflicts with it. In other words, our moral compulsion is not to compromise a person's right unless a greater right takes priority over it.

For example, members of society have the right not to be lied to. Therefore, in most contexts you are morally compelled not to tell a falsehood. That is an important right because it is critical in a community or marketplace that one be able to rely on another's word. If, however, you could save someone's life by telling a falsehood, such as telling a lie to a criminal about where a witness who will testify against him can be found, you probably will be required to save that person's life by lying about his whereabouts. In this context, the witness's right to live is a more important right than the criminal's right to hear the truth. In effect, one right "trumps" the other right.

What are these fundamental rights? How do we rank them in importance? Seventeenth-century philosopher John Locke argued for fundamental rights that we see embodied in the constitutions of modern democratic states: the protection of life, liberty, and property. Libertarians and others include the important rights of freedom of contract and freedom of expression. Modern liberals, like Bertolt Brecht, argued that all humans have basic rights to employment, food, housing, and education. In much of the ongoing debate around health care policy in the United States, a key question is whether or not every citizen has a right to health care.

Strengths of Rights Theory The major strength of rights theory is that it recognizes the moral worth of each individual and the importance of protecting fundamental rights. This means that members of modern democratic societies have extensive liberties and rights around which a consensus has formed and citizens need not fear the removal of these rights by their government or other members of society. In the U.S. context, one need look no further than the Declaration of Independence and its emphasis on "life, liberty, and the pursuit of happiness" as those "unalienable rights" that lie beyond the reach of government interference. In the global context, the Universal Declaration of Human Rights was adopted by the United Nations in 1948 as an expression of fundamental rights to which many people believe all are entitled.

Criticisms of Rights Theory Most of the criticisms of rights theory deal with the near absolute yet relative value of the rights protected, sometimes making it difficult to articulate and administer a comprehensive rights theory.

First, it is difficult to achieve agreement about which rights are protected. Rights fundamental to modern countries like the United States (such as many women's or GLBT rights) are more limited in other countries around the world. Even within one country, citizens disagree on the existence and ranking of rights. For example, as noted earlier, some Americans argue that the right to health care is an important need that should be met by government or a person's employer. Other Americans believe funding universal health care would interfere with the libertarian right to limited government intervention in our lives. Balancing rights in conflict can be difficult.

In addition, rights theory does not concern itself with the costs or benefits of requiring respect for another's right. For example, rights theory probably justifies the protection of a neo-Nazi's right to spout hateful speech, even though the costs of such speech, including damage to relations between ethnic groups, may far outweigh any benefits the speaker, listeners, and society receive from the speech.

Moreover, in the context of discussions around public policy and political economy, some argue that rights theory can be perverted to create a sense of entitlement reducing innovation, entrepreneurship, and production.

The Global Business Environment

The Golden Rule in the World's Religions and Cultures

Immanuel Kant's categorical imperative, which is one formulation of rights theory, has its foundations in the Golden Rule. Note that the Golden Rule exists in all cultures and in all countries of the world. Here is a sampling.

BUDDHISM: Hurt not others in ways that you would find hurtful.

CHRISTIANITY: Do to others as you would have others do to you.

CONFUCIANISM: Do not to others what you would not like yourself.

GRECIAN: Do not that to a neighbor which you shall take ill from him.

HINDUISM: This is the sum of duty: do nothing to others which if done to you would cause you pain.

HUMANISM: Individual and social problems can only be resolved by means of human reason, intelligent effort, and critical thinking joined with compassion and a spirit of empathy for all living beings.

ISLAM: No one of you is a believer until he desires for his brother that which he desires for himself.

JAINISM: In happiness and suffering, in joy and grief, we should regard all creatures as we regard our own self.

JUDAISM: Whatever is hateful to you, do not to another.

NATIVE AMERICAN SPIRITUALITY: Respect for all life is the foundation.

PERSIAN: Do as you would be done by.

ROMAN: Treat your inferiors as you would be treated by your superiors.

SHINTOISM: The heart of the person before you is a mirror. See there your own form.

SIKHISM: As you deem yourself, so deem others.

TAOISM: Regard your neighbor's gain as your own gain, and your neighbor's loss as your own loss.

YORUBAN: One going to take a pointed stick to pinch a baby bird should first try it on himself to feel how it hurts.

ZOROASTRIANISM: That nature alone is good which refrains from doing to another whatsoever is not good for itself.

For example, if one is able to claim an entitlement to a job, a place to live, food, and health care—regardless of how hard he is expected to work—motivations to pull one's own weight and contribute to society and the greater good may be compromised, resulting in a financially unsustainable culture of dependency. The overlap between theories of ethics and their political policy implications is explored further as we turn our attention to justice theory.

Justice Theory

In 1971, John Rawls published his book *A Theory of Justice*, the philosophical underpinning for the bureaucratic welfare state. Based upon the principle of justice, Rawls reasoned that it was right for governments to redistribute wealth in order to help the poor and disadvantaged. He argued for a just distribution of society's resources by which a society's benefits and burdens are allocated fairly among its members.

Rawls expressed this philosophy in his Greatest Equal Liberty Principle: Each person has an equal right to basic rights and liberties. He qualified or limited this principle with the Difference Principle: Social inequalities are acceptable only if they cannot be eliminated without making the worst-off class even worse off. The basic structure is perfectly just, he wrote, when the prospects of the least fortunate are as great as they can be.

Rawls's justice theory has application in the business context. Justice theory requires decision makers to be guided by fairness and impartiality and to take seriously what outcomes these principles produce. In the business context, justice theory prompts leadership to ask: Are our employees getting what they deserve? It would mean, for example, that a business deciding in which of two communities to build a new manufacturing plant should consider which community has the greater need for economic development.

Chief among Rawls's critics was his Harvard colleague Robert Nozick. Nozick argued that the rights of the individual are primary and that nothing more was justified than a minimal government that protected against violence and theft and ensured the enforcement of contracts. Nozick espoused a libertarian view that unequal distribution of wealth is moral if there is equal opportunity. Applied to the business context, Nozick's formulation of justice would permit a business to choose between two manufacturing plant sites after giving each community the opportunity to make its best bid for the plant. Instead of picking the community most in need, the business may pick the one offering the best deal.

Strengths of Justice Theory The strength of Rawls's justice theory lies in its basic premise that society owes a duty to protect those who are least advantaged—that

is, positioned unfairly vis-à-vis the distribution of social goods. Its motives are consistent with the religious and secular philosophies that urge humans to help those in need. Many religions and cultures hold basic to their faith the assistance of those who are less fortunate.

Criticisms of Justice Theory Rawls's justice theory shares some of the criticisms of rights theory. It treats equality as an absolute, without examining the potential costs of producing equality, including reduced incentives for innovation, entrepreneurship, and production. Moreover, any attempt to rearrange social benefits requires an accurate measurement of current wealth. For example, if a business is unable to measure accurately which employees are in greater need of benefits due to their wealth level, application of justice theory may make the business a Robin Hood in reverse: taking from the poor to give to the rich.

Utilitarianism

Utilitarianism requires a decision maker to maximize utility for society as a whole. Maximizing utility means achieving the highest level of satisfactions over dissatisfactions. This means that a person must consider the benefits and costs of his actions to everyone in society.

A utilitarian will act only if the benefits of the action to society outweigh the societal costs of the action. Note that the focus is on society as a whole. This means a decision maker may be required to do something that harms her if society as a whole is benefited by her action. A teleological theory, utilitarianism judges our actions as good or bad depending on their consequences. This is sometimes expressed as "the ends justify the means."

Utilitarianism is most identified with 19th-century philosophers Jeremy Bentham and John Stuart Mill. Bentham argued that maximizing utility meant achieving the greatest overall balance of pleasure over pain. A critic of utilitarianism, Thomas Carlyle, called utilitarianism "pig philosophy" because it appeared to base the goal of ethics on the swinish pleasures of the multitude.

Mill thought Bentham's approach too narrow and broadened the definition of utility to include satisfactions such as health, knowledge, friendship, and aesthetic delights. Responding to Carlyle's criticisms, Mill also wrote that some satisfactions count more than others. For example, the pleasure of seeing wild animals free in the world may be a greater satisfaction morally than shooting them and seeing them stuffed in one's den.

How does utilitarianism work in practice? It requires that you consider not just the impact of decisions on yourself, your family, and your friends, but also the impact on everyone in society. Before deciding whether to ride a bicycle to school or work rather than to drive a car, a utilitarian would consider the wear and tear on her clothes, the time saved or lost by riding a bike, the displeasure of riding in bad weather, her improved physical condition, her feeling of satisfaction for not using fossil fuels, the cost of buying more food to fuel her body for the bike trips, the dangers of riding near automobile traffic, and a host of other factors that affect her satisfaction and dissatisfaction.

But her utilitarian analysis doesn't stop there. She has to consider her decision's effect on the rest of society. Will she interfere with automobile traffic flow and decrease the driving pleasure of automobile drivers? Will commuters be encouraged to ride as she does and benefit from doing so? Will her lower use of gasoline for her car reduce demand and consumption of fossil fuels, saving money for car drivers and reducing pollution? Will her and other bike riders' increased food consumption drive up food prices and make it less affordable for poor families? This only scratches the surface of her utilitarian analysis.

The process we used earlier, act utilitarianism, judges each act separately, assessing a single act's benefits and costs to society's members. Obviously, a person cannot make an act utilitarian analysis for every decision. It would take too much time and many variables are difficult to calculate.

Utilitarianism recognizes that human limitation. Rule utilitarianism judges actions by a rule that over the long run maximizes benefits over costs. For example, you may find that taking a shower every morning before school or work maximizes society's satisfactions, as a rule. Most days, people around you will be benefited by not having to smell noisome odors, and your personal and professional prospects will improve by practicing good hygiene. Therefore, you are likely to be a rule utilitarian and shower each morning, even though some days you may not contact other people.

Many of the habits we have are the result of rule utilitarian analysis. Likewise, many business practices, such as a retailer's regular starting and closing times, also are based in rule utilitarianism.

Strengths of Utilitarianism What are the strengths of utilitarianism as a guide for ethical conduct? It is easy to articulate the standard of conduct: You merely need to do what is best for society as a whole. Moreover, many find it intuitive to employ an ethical reasoning that seeks to maximize human flourishing and eliminate harm or suffering.

Criticisms of Utilitarianism Those strengths also expose some of the criticisms of utilitarianism as an ethical construct. It is difficult to measure one's own pleasures and pains and satisfactions and dissatisfactions, let alone those of all of society's members. In short, how does one adequately and accurately measure human flourishing? In addition, those benefits and costs are inevitably distributed unequally across society's members. It can foster a tyranny of the majority that may result in morally monstrous behavior, such as a decision by a 100,000-person community to use a lake as a dump for human waste because only one person otherwise uses or draws drinking water from the lake.

That example exhibits how utilitarianism differs from rights theory. While rights theory may protect a person's right to clean drinking water regardless of its cost, utilitarianism considers the benefits and costs of that right as only one factor in the total mix of society's benefits and costs. In some cases, the cost of interfering with someone's right may outweigh the benefits to society, resulting in the same decision that rights theory produces. But where rights theory is essentially a one-factor analysis, utilitarianism requires a consideration of that factor and a host of others as well, in an attempt to balance pleasure over pain.

A final criticism of utilitarianism is that it is not constrained by law. Certainly, the law is a factor in utilitarian analysis. Utilitarian analysis must consider, for example, the dissatisfactions fostered by not complying with the law and by creating an environment of lawlessness in a society. Yet the law is only one factor in utilitarian analysis. The pains caused by violating the law may be offset by benefits the violation produces. Rational actors may ultimately determine that the cost–benefit analysis justifies deviation from a law or rule. Most people, however, are rule utilitarian when it comes to law, deciding that obeying the law in the long run maximizes social utility.

Shareholder Theory Premised on the concept that corporate leaders are agents who owe contractual obligations to investors, shareholder theory argues that ethical dilemmas should be resolved with a focus on maximizing the firm's long-term profits within the limits of the law. It is based in the *laissez faire* theory of capitalism first expressed by Adam Smith in the 18th century and more recently promoted by the Nobel Prize–winning economist Milton Friedman. Laissez faire economists argue total social welfare is optimized if humans are permitted to work toward their own selfish goals. The role of government, law, and regulation is solely to ensure the workings of a free market by not interfering with economic liberty, by eliminating collusion among competitors, and by promoting accurate information in the marketplace.

By focusing on results—maximizing total social welfare through a corporate focus on profit maximization—a shareholder theory approach to ethical decisions is a teleological- or consequences-oriented ethical theory. It is closely related to utilitarianism, but it differs fundamentally in how ethical decisions are made. While utilitarianism considers all stakeholders as it seeks to maximize social utility by focusing the actor on a broad-based creation of social value and reduction in social harm, a shareholder approach to profit maximization optimizes total social utility by narrowing the actor's focus, requiring the decision maker to make a wealth-maximizing decision that is focused on enhancing profits for those investors or shareholders who can claim a direct financial interest in the organization's bottom line.

Strengths of Focusing on Profit Maximization By working in our own interests, we compete for society's scarce resources (iron ore, labor, and land, to name a few), which are allocated to those people and businesses that can use them most productively. By allocating society's resources to their most efficient uses, as determined by a free market, shareholder theory claims to maximize total social utility or benefits. Thus, in theory, society as a whole is bettered if all of us compete freely for its resources by trying to increase our personal or organizational profits. If we fail to maximize profits, some of society's resources will be allocated to less productive uses that reduce society's total welfare.

In addition, shareholder theory emphasizes that a commitment first and foremost to profit maximization must always be constrained by what is permitted under the law. A profit maximizer theoretically acts ethically by complying with society's mores as expressed in its laws.

Moreover, the emphasis on profit maximization requires the decision maker and business to be disciplined according to the dictates of the marketplace. Consequently, an analysis of the ethical issue pursuant to shareholder theory probably requires a decision maker to consider the rights protected by rights theory, especially the shareholder's or investor's contractual rights to a return on investment, as well as fairness dictates embedded in justice theory. Ignoring important rights of employees, customers, suppliers, communities, and other stakeholders may negatively impact a corporation's long-term profits. A business that engages in behavior that is judged unethical by consumers and other members of society is subject to boycotts, adverse publicity, demands for more restrictive laws, and other reactions that damage its image, decrease its revenue, and increase its costs.

Consider, for example, the reduced sales of Martha Stewart–branded goods at Kmart after Ms. Stewart was accused of trading ImClone stock while possessing inside information. Consider also the fewer number of college

graduates willing to work for Waste Management Inc. in the wake of adverse publicity and indictments against its executives for misstating its financial results. Note also the higher cost of capital for firms like Dell as investors bid down the stock price of companies accused of accounting irregularities and other wrongdoing.

All these reactions to perceived unethical conduct impact the business's profitability in the short and long run, motivating that business to make decisions that comply with ethical views that transcend legal requirements.

Criticisms of Focusing on Profit Maximization The strengths of shareholder theory's emphasis on profit maximization as a model for ethical behavior also suggest criticisms and weaknesses of the theory. Striking at the heart of the theory is the criticism that corporate managers are subject to human failings that make it impossible for them to maximize corporate profits. The failure to discover and process all relevant information and varying levels of aversion to risk can result in one manager making a different decision than another manager. Group decision making in the business context introduces other dynamics that interfere with rational decision making. Social psychologists have found that groups often accept a higher level of risk than they would as individuals. There is also the tendency of a group to internalize the group's values and suppress critical thought.

Furthermore, even if an emphasis on profit maximization results in an efficient allocation of society's resources and maximization of total social welfare, it does not concern itself with how wealth is allocated within society. In the United States, the top wealthiest 1 percent own more than 40 percent of the nation's wealth, and globally, it is estimated that 26 individuals control more wealth than the combined wealth of 50 percent of the global population. To some people, those levels of wealth disparity are unacceptable. To laissez faire economists, wealth disparity is an inevitable component of a free market that rewards hard work, acquired skills, innovation, and risk taking. Yet critics of shareholder theory's emphasis on profit maximization respond that market imperfections, structural barriers, and a person's position in life at birth interfere with his ability to compete.

Critics charge that the ability of laws and market forces to control corporate behavior is limited because it requires lawmakers, consumers, employees, and other constituents to detect unethical corporate acts and take appropriate steps. Even if consumers notice irresponsible behavior and inform a corporation, a bureaucratic corporate structure may interfere with the information being received by the proper person inside the corporation. If, instead, consumers are silent and refuse to buy corporate products because of perceived unethical acts, corporate management may notice a decrease in sales, yet attribute it to something other than the corporation's unethical behavior.

Critics also argue that equating ethical behavior with legal compliance is a tautology in countries like the United States where businesses distort the lawmaking process by lobbying legislators and making political contributions. It cannot be ethical, they argue, for businesses to merely comply with laws reflecting the interests of businesses and over which corporations have enormous influence post–*Citizens United.*

Proponents of the emphasis on profit maximization respond that many laws restraining businesses are passed despite businesses lobbying against those laws. The Sarbanes–Oxley Act, which increases penalties for wrongdoing executives, requires CEOs to certify financial statements, and imposes internal governance rules on public companies, is such an example. So are laws restricting drug companies from selling a drug unless it is approved by the Food and Drug Administration and requiring environmental impact studies before a business may construct a new manufacturing plant. Moreover, businesses are nothing other than a collection of individual stakeholders, which includes employees, shareholders, and their communities. When they act to influence political policies or lobby for legal or regulatory change, their advocacy is arguably in the best interests of all these stakeholders.

Critics respond that ethics transcends law, requiring, in some situations, that businesses adhere to a higher standard than required by law. We understand this in our personal lives. For example, despite the absence of law dictating, for the most part, how we treat friends, we know that ethical behavior requires us to be loyal to friends and to spend time with them when they need our help. In the business context, a firm may be permitted to release employees for nearly any reason, except the few legally banned bases of discrimination (such as race, age, and gender), yet some critics will argue businesses should not terminate an employee for other reasons currently not banned by most laws (such as sexual orientation or appearance). Moreover, these critics further argue that businesses—due to their influential role in a modern society—should be leaders in setting a standard for ethical conduct.

Those who emphasize profit maximization respond that such an ethical standard is difficult to define and hampers efficient decision making. Moreover, they argue that experience shows the law has been a particularly relevant definition of ethical conduct. Consider that many corporate scandals would have been prevented had the executives merely complied with the law and had existing regulations been enforced. For example, Enron executives illegally kept some liabilities off the firm's financial statements, while regulatory oversight also failed. Tyco and Adelphia executives illegally looted corporate assets. Had these executives

Ethics and Compliance in Action

Minimum Wage Laws

In recent years, debate has raged over whether governments in the United States should increase dramatically the federal or state minimum wage that most employers must pay employees, from about $7 per hour to as much as $15 per hour. In 2015, the City of Seattle increased its minimum wage of city workers to $15 per hour, and New York City followed suit in 2019. Between 2020 and 2025, Washington, D.C.; New Jersey; Massachusetts; Maryland; Illinois; and California are scheduled to see similar increases.

The efforts to increase the minimum wage are directed mostly against McDonald's, Walmart, and other employers who employ large numbers of low-skilled or inexperienced workers. For example, one 26-year-old woman who worked at a Chicago McDonald's as a cashier for 10 years claimed she could not support her two children on the wage paid by McDonald's.

Should a government protect employees by increasing the minimum wage? If a minimum wage is imposed by government, what is the right wage? A $15-per-hour wage translates into annual compensation of $30,000, hardly enough to support a family. Should the minimum wage be $25 per hour? Why not make it $50 per hour, which would be $100,000 annual income, enough to permit most families to survive quite well?

Why should government impose a minimum wage on private employers? Are employees without power to demand higher wages? Will a minimum wage distort the employment market? Do employees deserve higher wages than the amount they and their employers agree on? Does a high minimum wage encourage workers to remain in low-skill jobs rather than improving their skills and qualifying for higher-wage jobs? Should a 42-year-old woman be required to improve her lot in life by increasing her education rather than continuing to do a job that any 16-year-old can do? What social barriers or structural inequities might exist to hinder some in society from gaining necessary skills and improving access to better employment options?

Do the answers to those questions depend on the ethical theory to which one subscribes?

simply complied with the law and maximized their firms' long-run profits, none of those ethical debacles would have occurred.

Critics of profit maximization respond that the corporate crises at companies like Enron and WorldCom prove that flaws in corporate governance encourage executives to act unethically. These examples, critics say, show that many executives do not maximize profits for their firms. Instead, driven by short-term, quarterly financial expectations, they maximize their own profits at the expense of the firm and its shareholders. They claim that stock options and other incentives intended to align the interests of executives with those of shareholders promote decisions that raise short-term profits to the long-run detriment of the firms. They point out that many CEOs and other top executives negotiate compensation plans that do not require them to stay with the firm long term and that allow them to benefit enormously from short-term profit taking. Executive greed, encouraged by these perverse executive compensation plans, also encourage CEOs and other executives to violate the law.

Defenders of business, profit maximization, and capitalist economics point out that it is nearly impossible to stop someone who is bent on fraud. A dishonest executive will lie to shareholders, creditors, board members, and the public and also treat the law as optional. Yet enlightened proponents of the modern corporation accept that there are problems with corporate management culture that require changes. They know that an unconstrained CEO; ethically uneducated executives; perverse compensation incentives; and inadequate supervision of executives by the firm's CEOs, board of directors, and shareholders present golden opportunities to the unscrupulous person and make unwitting accomplices of the ignorant and the powerless. Such an awareness highlights the role of corporate culture—for example, an ethical climate—in fostering an environment in which individuals are supported in their desire to act and live according to their moral compass.

Finally, divining the shareholders' ethical viewpoint may be difficult. While nearly all shareholders are mostly profit driven, a small minority of shareholders have other agendas, such as protecting the environment or workers' rights, regardless of the cost to the corporation. It is often not possible to please all shareholders.

Nonetheless, increasing shareholder democracy by enhancing the shareholders' role in the nomination and election of board members is essential to uniting the interests of shareholders and management. So is facilitating the ability of shareholders to bring proposals for ethical policy to a vote of shareholders. In the past several years, for public companies at least, the Securities and Exchange Commission has taken several steps to increase shareholder democracy. These steps, which are covered fully in Chapter 45, are having their intended effect. For example, during the 2014 shareholder meeting season, shareholder proposals included requiring annual election of directors and limiting corporate political lobbying and contributions. Moreover, the New York Stock Exchange and NASDAQ require companies listed on those exchanges to submit for shareholder approval certain actions, such as approval of stock option plans.

Virtue Theory

Differing from both the deontological emphasis on rights and justice flowing from duties and responsibilities, as well as the teleological focus on consequences and outcomes (measured according to either a utilitarian or profit maximization calculus), is a third approach to ethical analysis that highlights the importance of character—for both individuals and an organization. Virtue theory demands that an individual know his values and how they correlate to his identity, habits, and ways of engaging with others. Focusing on an intentional pursuit of virtues, the theory emphasizes questions such as: Who are you? What values are most important to you? Are my stated values and the actions I take aligned? For an organization, the theory inquires: What is your corporate purpose? What are your corporate values? Are our corporate actions and our values integrated?

Virtue theory, therefore, approaches ethical dilemmas from a commitment to integrity and an emphasis on character development. Deontological and teleological considerations are still important components of the ethical analysis, but the starting point is different. Instead of focusing on what action is right, virtue theory focuses on whether the individual (or the corporation) is acting consistently with those virtues or values that will result in a life well lived.

As developed in the West, a virtue-oriented approach owes much to Aristotle and other Greek philosophers, who explored practical notions of the good life and how best to achieve it. In the East, virtue theory was largely cultivated by Confucius, who focused on the centrality of benevolence and righteousness as hallmarks in the development of character. In short, a virtue theory approach emphasizes the person and the daily struggle to become a better person through identification and cultivation—or habituation—of virtues, such as wisdom or courage or benevolence.

As an example, consider a person in need of help. A deontologist might offer assistance out of a sense of duty or responsibility or allegiance to the Golden Rule. A utilitarian might offer aid because the consequences would result in a maximization of overall well-being. One acting according to virtue theory, however, would be helping out of desire to become a more charitable or benevolent person. The giving of aid would flow from a commitment to becoming a person who gives aid. In this instance, one might imagine that a virtue theorist would have predetermined that she values the virtues of charity and benevolence. Upon confronting an opportunity to help someone in need, she would simply have acted in a way that promoted these virtues and made them more habitual in the person's daily activity.

Strengths of Virtue Theory As noted in the previous discussion, acting with regard to one's self-interest is a hallmark of the human condition. Virtue theory offers an opportunity to convert impulses at the heart of selfishness and greed into opportunities to act with a self-interested focus to become more personally virtuous and integrated with regard to one's values, actions, and the habits we wish to cultivate. In organizations, virtue theory can create an aspirational climate and an additional way of emphasizing the importance of manifesting those corporate values that may otherwise be seen as mere words on a website or posters in the break room. Moreover, virtue theory's focus on the development of practical wisdom—that is, moral imagination and sound judgment honed by experience—creates space and structure to encourage personal growth and continuous teaching and training of employees.

Additional value brought by a virtue approach to ethics is its appreciation for the ambiguity of dilemmas where simple maxims or principles are not adequate to the maintenance of human relationships nor accommodating to the complexity of human emotions.

Criticisms of Virtue Theory Some critics argue that virtue theory is ultimately too subjective, too limited in scope, and too difficult to codify to be useful, especially in the corporate context. Certainly, those deontologists or teleologists seeking a universally applicable code of ethics may be unsatisfied, but then any such code is probably unrealistic given the complexities of the 21st-century global business environment. Other concerns have been raised about the inability of virtue theory to apply in a diverse global business environment because virtues that might be recognized and celebrated in one part of the world might be different from those virtues recognized elsewhere. Indeed, cultural relativity is an important issue to be considered when conducting ethical analysis using any theory or framework, as notions of what constitutes "right" and "wrong" are frequently contested.

Improving Corporate Governance and Corporate Social Responsibility Even if
we cannot stop all fraudulent executives, we can modify the corporate governance model to educate, motivate, and supervise executives and thereby improve corporate social responsibility. Corporate critics have proposed a wide variety of cures, all of which have been implemented to some degree and with varying degrees of success.

Ethics Codes Many large corporations and several industries have adopted codes of ethics or codes of conduct to guide executives and other employees. The Sarbanes–Oxley Act requires a public company to disclose whether it has adopted a code of ethics for senior financial officers and to disclose any change in the code or waiver of the code's application.

There are two popular views of such codes. One sees the codes as genuine efforts to foster ethical behavior within a firm or an industry. The other view regards them as thinly disguised attempts to make the firm function better, to mislead the public into believing the firm behaves ethically, to prevent the passage of legislation that would impose stricter constraints on business, or to limit competition under the veil of ethical standards. Even where the first view is correct, ethical codes fail to address concretely all possible forms of corporate misbehavior. Instead, they often emphasize either the behavior required for the firm's effective internal function, such as not accepting gifts from customers, or the relations between competitors within a particular industry, such as prohibitions on some types of advertising.

Better corporate ethics codes make clear that the corporation expects employees not to violate the law in a mistaken belief that loyalty to the corporation or corporate profitability requires it. Such codes work best, however, when a corporation also gives its employees an outlet for dealing with a superior's request to do an unethical act. That outlet may be the corporate legal department, a corporate compliance/ethics officer, or even an anonymous reporting procedure.

Ethical Instruction Some corporations require their employees to enroll in classes that teach ethical decision making. The idea is that a manager trained in ethical conduct will recognize unethical actions before they are taken and deter herself and the corporation from the unethical acts.

While promising in theory, in practice, many managers are resistant to ethical training that requires them to examine their principles. They are reluctant to question a set of long-held principles with which they are comfortable. Therefore, there are some doubts whether managers are receptive to ethical instruction. Even if the training is accepted, will managers retain the ethical lessons of their training and use it, or will time and other job-related pressures force a manager to think only of completing the job at hand?

Moreover, what ethical values should be emphasized? Is it enough to teach only one, a few, or all the theories of ethical conduct? Corporations may favor the simplicity of a shareholder orientation that focuses on maximization of profits. But should a corporation also teach rights theory and expect its employees to follow it? How should concerns over justice and fair distribution of benefits and burdens be addressed?

Most major corporations today express their dedication to ethical decision making by having an ethics officer who is not only responsible for ethical instruction, but also in charge of ethical supervision. The ethics officer may attempt to instill ethical decision making as a component of daily corporate life by sensitizing employees to the perils of ignoring ethical issues. The ethics officer may also be a mentor or sounding board for all employees who face ethical issues.

Whether an ethics officer is effective, however, is determined by the level of commitment top executives make to ethical behavior and the position and power granted to the ethics officer. For example, will top executives and the board of directors allow an ethics officer to nix an important deal on ethical grounds, or will they replace the ethics officer with another executive whose ethical views permit the deal? Therefore, probably more important than an ethics officer is a CEO with the character to do the right thing.

Consider All Stakeholders' Interests Utilitarianism analysis clearly requires an executive to consider a decision's impact on all stakeholders. How else can one determine all the benefits and costs of the decision? Likewise, modern rights theory also dictates considering all stakeholders' rights, including not compromising an important right unless trumped by another. Kant's categorical imperative also mandates a concern for others by requiring one to act as one would require others to act.

For those seeking to maximize profits, the wisdom of considering all stakeholders is apparent because ignoring the interests of any stakeholder may negatively affect profits. For example, a decision may affect a firm's ability to attract high-quality employees, antagonize consumers, alienate suppliers, and motivate the public to lobby lawmakers to pass laws that increase a firm's cost of doing business. This wisdom is reflected in the Guidelines for Ethical Decision Making, which you will learn in the next section.

Nonetheless, there are challenges when a corporate manager considers the interests of all stakeholders. Beyond the enormity of identifying all stakeholders, stakeholders' interests may conflict, requiring a compromise that harms some stakeholders and benefits others. In addition, the impact on each stakeholder group may be difficult to assess accurately.

For example, if a manager is considering whether to terminate the 500 least productive employees during an economic downturn, the manager will note that shareholders will benefit from lower labor costs and consumers may find lower prices for goods, but the manager also knows that the terminated employees, their families, and their communities will likely suffer from the loss of income. Yet if the employees terminated are near retirement and have sizable retirement savings or if the termination motivates employees to return to college and seek better jobs, the impact on them, their families, and their communities may be minimal or even positive. On the other hand, if the manager makes the decision to retain the employees, shareholder wealth may decrease and economic inefficiency may result, which harms all society.

Independent Boards of Directors

In some of the instances in which corporate executives have acted unethically and violated the law, the board of directors was little more than a rubber stamp or a sounding board for the CEO and other top executives. The CEO handpicked a board that largely allowed the CEO to run the corporation with little board supervision.

CEO domination of the board is a reality in most large corporations because the market for CEO talent has skewed the system in favor of CEOs. Few CEOs are willing to accept positions in which the board exercises real control. Often, therefore, a CEO determines which board members serve on the independent board nominating committee and selects who is nominated by the committee. Owing their positions to the CEO and earning handsome fees sometimes exceeding $100,000, many directors are reluctant to oppose the CEO's plans.

For more than four decades, corporate critics have demanded that corporate boards be made more independent of the CEO. The corporate ethical crises of recent years have increased those calls for independence. The New York Stock Exchange and NASDAQ require companies with securities listed on the exchanges to have a majority of directors independent of the company and top management. Their rules also require independent management compensation, board nomination, and audit committees. The Sarbanes–Oxley Act requires public companies to have board audit committees comprising only independent directors.

One criticism of director independence rules is the belief that no director can remain independent after joining the board because every director receives compensation from the corporation. There is a concern that an independent director, whose compensation is high, will side with management to ensure his continuing nomination, election, and receipt of high fees.

More extreme proposals of corporate critics include recommendations that all corporate stakeholders—such as labor, government, environmentalists, and communities—have representation on the board or that special directors or committees be given responsibility over special areas, such as consumer protection and workers' rights. Other critics argue for contested elections for each board vacancy. Few corporations have adopted these recommendations.

While honestly motivated, these laws and recommendations often fail to produce greater corporate social responsibility because they ignore the main reason for management's domination of the board: the limited time, information, and resources that directors have. One solution is to give outside directors a full-time staff with power to acquire information within the corporation. This solution, while providing a check on management, also may produce inefficiency by creating another layer of management in the firm.

In addition, some of the recommendations complicate management by making the board less cohesive. Conflicts between stakeholder representatives or between inside and outside directors may be difficult to resolve. For example, the board could be divided by disputes among shareholders who want more dividends, consumers who want lower prices, and employees who want higher wages.

Changing the Internal Management Structure Some corporate critics argue that the historic shift of corporate powers away from a public corporation's board and shareholders to its managers is irreversible. They recommend, therefore, that the best way to produce responsible corporate behavior is to change the corporation's management structure.

The main proponent of this view, Christopher Stone, recommended the creation of offices dedicated to areas such as environmental affairs and workers' rights, higher educational requirements for officers in positions like occupational safety, and procedures to ensure that important information inside and outside the corporation is directed to the proper person within the corporation. He also recommended that corporations study certain important issues and create reports of the study before making decisions.

These requirements aim to change the process by which corporations make decisions. The objective is to improve decision making by raising the competency of decision makers, increasing the amount of relevant information they hold, and enhancing the methodology by which decisions are made.

More information held by more competent managers using better tools should produce better decisions. Two of the later sections in this chapter in part reflect these recommendations. The Guidelines for Ethical Decision Making require a decision maker to study a decision carefully before making a decision. This includes acquiring all relevant facts, assessing a decision's impact on each stakeholder, and considering the ethics of one's decision from each ethical perspective. In addition, the Thinking Critically section will help you understand when fallacious thinking interferes with a manager's ability to make good decisions.

Eliminating Perverse Incentives and Supervising Management Even if a corporation modifies its internal management structure by improving the decision-making process, there are no guarantees more responsible decisions will result. To the extent unethical corporate behavior results from faulty perception and inadequate facts, a better decision-making process helps. But if a decision maker is motivated solely to increase short-term profits, irresponsible decisions may follow. When one examines closely recent corporate debacles, three things are clear: The corporate wrongdoers acted in their selfish interests; the corporate reward system encouraged them to act selfishly, illegally, and unethically; and the wrongdoers acted without effective supervision. These facts suggest other changes that should be made in the internal management structure.

During the high-flying stock market of the 1990s, stock options were the compensation package preferred by high-level corporate executives. Shareholders and boards of directors were more than willing to accommodate them. On one level, stock options seem to align the interests of executives with those of the corporation and its shareholders. Issued at an exercise price usually far above the current market price of the stock, stock options have no value until the corporation's stock price exceeds the exercise price of the stock options. Thus, executives are motivated to increase the corporation's profits, which should result in an increase in the stock's market price. In the 1990s stock market, in which some stock prices were doubling yearly, the exercise price of executives' stock options was quickly dwarfed by the market price. Executives exercised the stock options, buying and then selling stock and, in the process, generating profits for a single executive in the tens and hundreds of millions of dollars. Shareholders also benefited from the dramatic increase in the value of their stock.

So what is the problem with stock options? As executives accepted more of their compensation in the form of stock options and became addicted to the lifestyle financed by them, some executives felt pressure to keep profits soaring to ever-higher levels. In companies like Enron and WorldCom, which had flawed business models and suspect accounting practices, some executives were encouraged to create business deals that had little, if any, economic justification and could be accounted for in ways that kept profits growing.

In what were essentially pyramid schemes, once the faulty economics of the deals were understood by prospective partners, no new deals were possible, and the schemes crashed like houses of cards. But until the schemes were discovered, many executives, including some who were part of the fraudulent schemes, pocketed tens and hundreds of millions of dollars in stock option profits.

The Sarbanes–Oxley Act, as amended by the Dodd-Frank Wall Street Reform and Consumer Protection Act of 2010, addressed this issue by requiring executive officers to disgorge any bonus and incentive-based or equity-based compensation received during the three-year period prior to which the corporation was required to restate its financial statements.

It is easy to see how fraudulent actions subvert the objective of stock options to motivate executives to act in the best interests of shareholders. Adolph Berle, however, has argued for more than 50 years that stock options are flawed compensation devices that allow executives to profit when stock market prices rise in general, even when executives have no positive effect on profitability. He proposed that the best way to compensate executives is to allow them to trade on inside information they possess about a corporation's prospects, information they possess because they helped produce those prospects. His proposal, however, is not likely ever to be legal compensation because insider trading creates the appearance that the securities markets are rigged.

Even with incentives in place to encourage executives to inflate profits artificially, it is unlikely that the recent fraudulent schemes at Enron, WorldCom, and other companies would have occurred had there been better scrutiny of upper management and its actions by the CEO and the board of directors. At Enron, executives were given great freedom to create partnerships that allowed Enron to keep liabilities off the balance sheet yet generate income that arguably could be recognized in the current period. It is not surprising that this freedom from scrutiny, when combined with financial incentives to create the partnerships, resulted in executives creating partnerships that had little economic value to Enron.

Better supervision of management is mostly the responsibility of the CEO, but the board of directors bears this duty also. We addressed earlier proposals to create boards of directors that are more nearly independent of the CEO and, therefore, better able to supervise the CEO and other top managers. Primarily, however, better supervision is a matter of attitude, or a willingness to devote time and effort to discover the actions of those under your charge and to challenge them to justify their actions. It is not unlike the responsibility a parent owes to a teenage child to scrutinize her actions and her friends to make sure that she is acting consistent with the values of the family. So, too,

boards must make the effort to scrutinize their CEOs and hire CEOs who are able and willing to scrutinize the work of the managers below them.

Yet directors must also be educated and experienced. Poor supervision of management has also been shown to be partly due to some directors' ignorance of business disciplines like finance and accounting. Unless board members are able to understand accounting numbers and other information that suggests management wrongdoing, board scrutiny of management is a process with no substance.

The Law The law has been the primary means of controlling corporate misdeeds. Lawmakers usually assume that corporations and executives are rational actors that can be deterred from unethical and socially irresponsible behavior by the threats law presents. Those threats are fines and civil damages, such as those imposed and increased by the Sarbanes–Oxley Act. For deterrence to work, however, corporate decision makers must know when the law's penalties will be imposed, fear those penalties, and act rationally to avoid them.

To some extent, the law's ability to control executive misbehavior is limited. As we discussed earlier in this chapter, corporate lobbying may result in laws reflecting the views of corporations, not society as a whole. Some corporate executives may not know the law exists. Others may view the penalties merely as a cost of doing business. Some may think the risk of detection is so low that the corporation can avoid detection. Other executives believe they are above the law, that it does not apply to them out of arrogance or a belief that they know better than lawmakers. Some rationalize their violation of the law on the grounds that "everybody does it."

Nonetheless, for all its flaws, the law is an important means by which society controls business misconduct. Of all the devices for corporate control we have considered, only market forces and the law impose direct penalties for corporate misbehavior. Although legal rules have no special claim to moral correctness, at least they are knowable. Laws also are the result of an open political process in which competing arguments are made and evaluated. This cannot be said about the intuitions of a corporate ethics officer, edicts from public interest groups, or the theories of economists or philosophers, except to the extent they are reflected in law. Moreover, in mature political systems like the United States, respect for and adherence to law is a well-entrenched value.

Where markets fail to promote socially responsible conduct, the law can do the job. For example, the antitrust laws discussed in Chapter 49, while still controversial, have eliminated the worst anticompetitive business practices. The federal securities laws examined in Chapters 45 and 46 arguably restored investor confidence in the securities markets after the stock market crash of 1929. Although environmentalists often demand more regulation, the environmental laws treated in Chapter 52 have improved the quality of water and reduced our exposure to toxic substances. Employment regulations discussed in Chapter 51—especially those banning employment discrimination—have forced significant changes in the American workplace. Thus, the law has an accomplished record as a corporate control device.

Indeed, sometimes the law does the job too well, often imposing a maze of regulations that deter socially valuable profit seeking without producing comparable benefits. Former Fed chair Greenspan once wrote, "Government regulation is not an alternative means of protecting the consumer. It does not build quality into goods, or accuracy into information. Its sole 'contribution' is to substitute force and fear for incentive as the 'protector' of the consumer."

The hope was that the Sarbanes–Oxley Act would restore investor confidence in audited financial statements and corporate governance. A 2007 survey by Financial Executives International found that 69 percent of financial executives agreed that compliance with SOX section 404 resulted in more investor confidence in their companies' financial reports. Fifty percent agreed that financial reports were more accurate. As for the cost of SOX compliance, a 2014 Protiviti report found that more than one-third of large companies (at least $10 billion in annual revenue) spent less than $500,000, while 30 percent spent more than $2 million.

Guidelines for Ethical Decision Making

Now that you understand the basics of ethical theories and the issues in the corporate governance debate, how do you use this information to make decisions for your business that are ethical and socially responsible? That is, what

process will ensure that you have considered all the ethical ramifications and arrived at a decision that is good for your business, good for your community, good for society as a whole, and good for you.

 LO4-2 Apply the Guidelines for Ethical Decision Making to business and personal decisions.

Figure 4.1 lists nine factors in the Guidelines for Ethical Decision Making. Let's consider each Guideline and explain how each helps you make better decisions.

What Facts Impact My Decision? This is such an obvious component of any good decision that it hardly seems necessary to mention. Yet it is common that people make only a feeble attempt to acquire *all* the facts necessary to a good decision.

Many people enter a decision-making process biased in favor of a particular option. As a result, they look only for facts that support that option. You have seen this done many times by your friends and opponents, and because you are an honest person, you have seen yourself do this as well from time to time. In addition, demands on our time, fatigue, laziness, ignorance of where to look for facts, and aversion to inconveniencing someone who has information contribute to a reluctance or inability to dig deep for relevant facts.

Because good decisions cannot be made in a partial vacuum of information, it is important to recognize when you need to acquire more facts. That is primarily the function of your other classes, which may teach you how to make stock market investment decisions, how to audit a company's financial records, and how to do marketing research.

For our purposes, let's consider this example. Suppose we work for a television manufacturing company that has a factory in Sacramento, California. Our company has placed

Figure 4.1   Guidelines for Ethical Decision Making
1. What **FACTS** impact my decision?
2. What are the **ALTERNATIVES?**
3. Who are the **STAKEHOLDERS?**
4. How do the alternatives impact **SOCIETY AS A WHOLE?**
5. How do the alternatives impact **MY BUSINESS FIRM?**
6. How do the alternatives impact **ME, THE DECISION MAKER?**
7. What are the **ETHICS** of each alternative?
8. What are the **PRACTICAL CONSTRAINTS** of each alternative?
9. What **COURSE OF ACTION** should be taken and how do we **IMPLEMENT** it?

you in charge of investigating the firm's decision whether to move the factory to Juarez, Mexico. What facts are needed to make this decision, and where do you find those facts?

Among the facts you need are: What are the firm's labor costs in Sacramento, and what will those costs be in Juarez? How much will labor costs increase in subsequent years? What is the likelihood of good labor relations in each location? What is and will be the productivity level of employees in each city? What are and will be the transportation costs of moving the firm's inventory to market? What impact will the move have on employees, their families, the communities, the schools, and other stakeholders in each community? Will Sacramento employees find other jobs in Sacramento or elsewhere? How much will we have to pay in severance pay?

How will our customers and suppliers be affected by our decision? If we move to Juarez, will our customers boycott our products even if our televisions are better and cheaper than before? If we move, will our suppliers' costs increase or decrease? How will our profitability be affected? How will shareholders view the decision? Who are our shareholders? Do we have a lot of Mexican shareholders, or do Americans dominate our shareholder list? What tax concessions and other benefits will the City of Sacramento give our firm if we promise to stay in Sacramento? What will Ciudad Juarez and the government of Mexico give us if we move to Juarez? How will our decision impact U.S.-Mexican economic and political relations?

This looks like a lot of facts, but we have only scratched the surface. You can probably come up with another 100 facts that should be researched. To give you another example of how thorough managers must be to make prudent decisions, consider that the organizers for the Olympics and Boston Marathon must attempt to predict and prevent terrorist attacks. For the 2000 Summer Olympics in Sydney, Australia, organizers created 800 different terrorist scenarios before developing an antiterrorism plan.

You can see that, to some extent, we are discussing other factors in the Guidelines as we garner facts. The factors do overlap to some degree. Note also that some of the facts you want to find are not facts at all, but estimates, such as cost and sales projections. We'll discuss in the Eighth Guideline the practical problems with the facts we find.

What Are the Alternatives?
A decision maker must be thorough in listing the alternative courses of actions. For many of us, the temptation is to conclude that there are only two options: to do something or not to do something. Let's take our decision whether to move our factory to Juarez, Mexico. You might think that the only choices are to stay in Sacramento or to move to Juarez. Yet there are several combinations that fall in between those extremes.

For example, we could consider maintaining the factory in Sacramento temporarily, opening a smaller factory in Juarez, and gradually moving production to Mexico as employees in Sacramento retire. Another alternative is to offer jobs in the Juarez factory to all Sacramento employees who want to move. If per-unit labor costs in Sacramento are our concern, we could ask employees in Sacramento to accept lower wages and fringe benefits or to increase their productivity.

There are many other alternatives that you can imagine. It is important to consider all reasonable alternatives. If you do not, you increase the risk that the best course of action was not chosen only because it was not considered.

Who Are the Stakeholders?
In modern societies, where diversity is valued as an independent virtue, considering the impacts of your decision on the full range of society's stakeholders has taken on great significance in prudent and ethical decision making. While a public corporation with thousands of shareholders obviously owes a duty to its shareholders to maximize shareholder wealth, corporate managers must also consider the interests of other important stakeholders, including employees, suppliers, customers, and the communities in which they live. Stakeholders also include society as a whole, which can be defined as narrowly as your country or more expansively as an economic union of countries, such as the European Union of 27 countries, or even the world as a whole.

Not to be omitted from stakeholders is you, the decision maker who is also impacted by your decisions for your firm. The legitimacy of considering your own selfish interests will be considered fully in the Sixth Guideline.

Listing all the stakeholders is not a goal by itself but helps the decision maker apply more completely other factors in the ethical Guidelines. Knowing whom your decision affects will help you find the facts you need. It also helps you evaluate the alternatives using the next three Guidelines: how the alternatives we have proposed impact society as a whole, your firm, and the decision maker.

How Do the Alternatives Impact Society as a Whole?
We covered some aspects of this Guideline earlier when we made an effort to discover all the facts that impact our decision. We can do a better job discovering the facts if we try to determine how our decision impacts society as a whole.

For example, if the alternative we evaluate is keeping the factory in Sacramento after getting property tax and road building concessions from the City of Sacramento, how is society as a whole impacted? What effect will tax concessions have on the quality of Sacramento schools (most schools are funded with property taxes)? Will lower taxes cause the Sacramento infrastructure (roads and governmental services) to decline to the detriment of the ordinary citizen? Will the economic benefits to workers in Sacramento offset the harm to the economy and workers in Juarez?

Will our firm's receiving preferential concessions from the Sacramento government undermine the ordinary citizen's faith in our political and economic institutions? Will we contribute to the feelings of some citizens that government grants privileges only to the powerful? Will our staying in Sacramento foster further economic growth in Sacramento? Will staying in Sacramento allow our suppliers to stay in business and continue to hire employees who will buy goods from groceries and malls in Sacramento?

What impact will our decision have on efforts to create a global economy in which labor and goods can freely travel between countries? Will our decision increase international tension between the United States and Mexico?

Note that the impact of our decision on society as a whole fits neatly with one of the ethical theories we discussed earlier: utilitarianism. Yet profit maximization, rights theory, and justice theory also require a consideration of societal impacts.

How Do the Alternatives Impact My Business Firm?
The most obvious impact any alternative has on your firm is its effect on the firm's bottom-line profitability. Yet that answer requires explaining because what you really want to know is what smaller things leading to profitability are impacted by an alternative.

For example, if our decision is to keep the factory in Sacramento open temporarily and gradually move the plant to Juarez as retirements occur, what will happen to employee moral and productivity in Sacramento? Will our suppliers in Sacramento abandon us to serve more permanent clients instead? Will consumers in Sacramento and the rest of California boycott our televisions? Will they be able to convince other American laborers to boycott our TVs? Will a boycott generate adverse publicity and media coverage that will damage our brand name? Will investors view our firm as a riskier business, raising our cost of capital?

Again, you can see some redundancy here as we work through the Guidelines, but that redundancy is all right because it ensures that we are examining all factors important to our decision.

How Do the Alternatives Impact Me, the Decision Maker?
At first look, considering how a decision you make for your firm impacts *you* hardly seems to be a component of ethical and responsible decision making. The term *selfish* probably comes to mind.

Many of the corporate ethical debacles of the last few years comprised unethical and imprudent decisions that probably were motivated by the decision makers' selfish interests. Mortgage brokers' desires to earn large fees encouraged them to falsify borrowers' financial status and to make imprudent loans to high-risk clients. Several of Enron's off-balance-sheet partnerships, while apparently helping Enron's financial position, lined the pockets of conflicted Enron executives holding stock options and receiving management fees from the partnerships.

Despite these examples, merely because a decision benefits you, the decision maker, does not always mean it is imprudent or unethical. Even decisions by some Enron executives in the late 1990s, while motivated in part by the desire to increase the value of the executives' stock options, could have been prudent and ethical if the off-balance-sheet partnerships had real economic value to Enron (as they did when Enron first created off-balance-sheet partnerships in the 1980s) and accounting for them complied with the law.

At least two reasons explain why you can and should consider your own interest yet act ethically for your firm. First, as the decision maker, you are impacted by the decision. Whether deservedly or not, the decision maker is often credited or blamed for the success or failure of the course of action chosen. You may also be a stakeholder in other ways. For example, if you are an executive in the factory in Sacramento, you and your family may be required to move to Juarez (or El Paso, Texas, which borders Juarez) if the factory relocates. It is valid to consider a decision's impact on you and your family, although it should not be given undue weight.

A second, and more important, reason to consider your own interest is that your decision may be better for your firm and other stakeholders if you also consider your selfish interest. For example, suppose when you were charged to lead the inquiry into the firm's decision whether to move to Juarez, it was made clear that the CEO preferred to close the Sacramento factory and move operations to Juarez.

Suppose also that you would be required to move to Juarez. Your spouse has a well-paying job in Sacramento, and your teenage children are in a good school system and have very supportive friends. You have a strong relationship with your parents and siblings, who also live within 50 miles of your family in Sacramento. You believe that you and your family could find new friends and good schools in El Paso or Juarez, and the move would enhance your position in the firm and increase your chances of a promotion. Nonetheless, overall you and your spouse have determined that staying in the Sacramento area is best for your family. So you are considering quitting your job with the firm and finding another job in the Sacramento area rather than make an attempt to oppose the CEO's preference.

If you quit your job, even in protest, you will have no role in the decision and your resignation will likely have no impact on the firm's Sacramento–Juarez decision. Had you stayed with the firm, you could have led a diligent inquiry into all the facts that may have concluded that the prudent and ethical decision for the firm was to stay in Sacramento. Without your input and guidance, the firm may make a less prudent and ethical decision.

You can think of other examples where acting selfishly also results in better decisions. Suppose a top-level accounting executive, to whom you are directly responsible, has violated accounting standards and the law by pressuring the firm's auditors to book as income in the current year a contract that will not be performed for two years. You could quit your job and blow the whistle, but you may be viewed as a disgruntled employee and your story given no credibility. You could confront the executive, but you may lose your job or at least jeopardize your chances for a promotion while tipping off the executive, who will cover her tracks. As an alternative, the more effective solution may be to consider how you can keep your job and prospects for promotion while achieving your objective to blow the whistle on the executive. One alternative may be to go through appropriate channels in the firm, such as discussing the matter with the firm's audit committee or legal counsel.

Finding a way to keep your job will allow you to make an ethical decision that benefits your firm, whereas your quitting may leave the decision to someone else who would not act as prudently. The bottom line is this: While, sometimes, ethical conduct requires acting unselfishly, in other contexts, consideration of your self-interest is not only consistent with ethical conduct, but also necessary to produce a moral result.

What Are the Ethics of Each Alternative?

Because our goal is to make a decision that is not only prudent for the firm, but also ethical and defensible in the event we are required to give an accounting for our actions, we must consider the ethics of each alternative, not from one but a variety of ethical viewpoints. Our stakeholders' values comprise many ethical theories; ignoring any one theory will likely cause an incomplete consideration of the issues and may result in unforeseen, regrettable outcomes.

What Would a Utilitarian Do? A utilitarian would choose the alternative that promises the highest net welfare to society as a whole. If we define our society as the United States, moving to Juarez may nonetheless produce the highest net benefit because the benefits to American citizens from a lower cost of televisions and to American shareholders from higher profits may more than offset the harm to our

employees and other citizens of Sacramento. Another benefit of the move may be the reduced cost of the U.S. government dealing with illegal immigration as Mexican workers decide to work at our plant in Juarez. Another cost may be the increased labor cost for a Texas business that would have hired Mexican workers had we not hired them.

If we define society as all countries in the North American Free Trade Agreement (NAFTA was signed by the United States, Mexico, and Canada), the benefit to workers in Juarez may completely offset the harm to workers in Sacramento. For example, the benefit to Juarez workers may be greater than the harm to Sacramento employees if many Juarez employees would otherwise be underemployed and Sacramento employees can find other work or are protected by a severance package or retirement plan.

As we discussed earlier in the discussion of ethical theories, finding and weighing all the benefits and costs of an alternative are difficult tasks. Even if we reject this theory as the final determinant, it is a good exercise for ensuring that we maximize the number of facts we consider when making a decision.

What Would Someone Focused on Maximizing Profits Do? One following traditional shareholder theory and its emphasis on profit maximization would choose the alternative that produces the most long-run profits for the company, within the limits of the law. This may mean, for example, that the firm should keep the factory in Sacramento if that will produce the most profits for the next 10 to 15 years.

This does not mean that the firm may ignore the impact of the decision on Juarez's community and workers. It may be that moving to Juarez will create a more affluent population in Juarez and consequently increase the firm's television sales in Juarez. But that impact is judged not by whether society as a whole is bettered (as with utilitarian analysis) or whether Juarez workers are more deserving of jobs (as with justice theory analysis), but is solely judged by how it impacts the firm's bottom line.

Nonetheless, profit maximization may compel a decision maker to consider stakeholders other than the corporation and its shareholders. A decision to move to Juarez may mobilize American consumers to boycott our TVs, for example, or cause a public relations backlash if our Juarez employees receive wages far below our Sacramento workers. These and other impacts on corporate stakeholders may negatively impact the firm's profits.

Although projecting profits is not a precise science, tools you learned in finance classes should enhance your ability to select an alternative that maximizes your firm's profits within the limits of the law.

What Would a Rights Theorist Do? A follower of modern rights theory will determine whether anyone's rights are negatively affected by an alternative. If several rights are affected, the rights theorist will determine which right is more important or trumps the other rights, and choose the alternative that respects the most important right.

For example, if the alternative is to move to Juarez, the Sacramento employees, among others, are negatively affected. Yet if we do not move, potential employees in Juarez are harmed. Are these equal rights a mere wash, or is it more important to retain a job one already has than to be deprived of a job one has never had?

Are other rights at work here, and how are they ranked? Is it more important to maintain manufacturing production in the firm's home country for national security and trade balance reasons than to provide cheaper televisions for the firm's customers? Does the right of all citizens to live in a global economy that spreads wealth worldwide and promotes international harmony trump all other rights?

While apparently difficult to identify and rank valid rights, this theory has value even to a utilitarian and a profit maximizer. By examining rights that are espoused by various stakeholders, we are more likely to consider all the costs and benefits of our decision and know which rights can adversely affect the firm's profitability if we fail to take them into account.

What Would a Justice Theorist Do? A justice theorist would choose the alternative that allocates society's benefits and burden most fairly. This requires the decision maker to consider whether everyone is getting what he deserves. If we follow the preaching of John Rawls, the firm should move to Juarez if the workers there are less advantaged than those in Sacramento, who may be protected by savings, severance packages, and retirement plans.

If we follow Nozick's libertarian approach, it is sufficient that the firm gives Sacramento workers an opportunity to compete for the plant by matching the offer the firm has received from Juarez workers. Under this analysis, if Sacramento workers fail to match the Juarez workers' offer of lower wages, for example, it would be fair to move the factory to Juarez, even if Sacramento workers are denied their right to jobs.

Even if the firm has difficulty determining who most deserves jobs with our firm, justice theory, like rights theory, helps the firm identify constituents who suffer from our decision and who can create problems impacting the firm's profitability if the firm ignores their claims.

What Does Virtue Theory Require? Virtue theory requires the decision maker to review those personal or corporate virtues and values that are essential to the individual's or organization's flourishing. This approach acknowledges the fact that all business is communal and requires individuals working together in an effort to realize the good life. Virtue theory, therefore, would prompt decision makers to ask what decision is consistent with the corporate identity or character they wish to cultivate.

Practically speaking, this would involve revisiting the corporate statement of values and considering seriously what impact closing the Sacramento facility would have on the corporate culture internally and externally—that is, in terms of reputation in the market—and whether this impact is consistent with the pursuit of excellence in terms of those predetermined corporate values. Again, as noted earlier, this analysis is potentially more ambiguous than a mere determination of what maximizes profits or what produces an overall most efficient allocation of utility, but it does ensure reflection on the implications for a corporation or individual who wants to take seriously a commitment to integrity.

What Are the Practical Constraints of Each Alternative?

As we evaluate alternatives, it is important to consider each alternative's practical problems before we implement it. For example, is it feasible for us to implement an alternative? Do we have the necessary money, labor, and other resources?

Suppose one alternative is to maintain our manufacturing plant in Sacramento as we open a new plant in Juarez, gradually shutting down the Sacramento plant as employees retire and quit. That alternative sounds like an ethical way to protect the jobs of all existing and prospective employees, but what are the costs of having two plants? Will the expense make that alternative infeasible? Will the additional expense make it difficult for the firm to compete with other TV manufacturers? Is it practicable to have a plant in Sacramento operating with only five employees who are 40 years old and will not retire for 15 years?

It is also necessary to consider potential problems with the facts that have led us to each alternative. Did we find all the facts relevant to our decision? How certain are we of some facts? For example, are we confident about our projections of labor and transportation costs if we move to Juarez? Are we sure that sales of our products will drop insubstantially due to consumer boycotts?

What Course of Action Should Be Taken and How Do We Implement It?

Ultimately, we have to stop our analysis and make a decision by choosing one alternative. Yet even then our planning is not over.

We must determine how to put the alternative into action. How do we implement it? Who announces the decision? Who is told of the decision and when? Do some people, like our employee's labor union, receive advance notice of our plans and have an opportunity to negotiate a better deal for our Sacramento employees? When do we tell shareholders, government officials, lenders, suppliers, investments analysts, and the media, and in what order? Do we antagonize a friend or an enemy and risk killing a deal if we inform someone too soon or too late?

Finally, we have to prepare for the worst-case scenario. What do we do if, despite careful investigation, analysis, and planning, our course of action fails? Do we have backup plans? Have we anticipated all the possible ways our plan may fail and readied responses to those failures?

In 1985, the Coca-Cola Company decided to change the flavor of Coke in response to Coke's shrinking share of the cola market. Despite careful market research, Coca-Cola failed to anticipate Coke drinkers' negative response to the new Coke formula and was caught without a response to the outcry. Within three months, Coca-Cola realized it had to revive the old Coke formula under the brand name Coca-Cola Classic. In the meantime, Coke lost significant market share to rival Pepsi. Today, one would expect Coke executives introducing a reformulated drink to predict more consumers' reactions to the drink and to prepare a response to each reaction.

Knowing When to Use the Guidelines

You can probably see that following these factors will result in better decisions in a variety of contexts, including some that appear to have no ethical concerns. For example, in the next few years, most of you will consider what major course of study to select at college or what job to take with which firm in which industry. This framework can help you make a better analysis that should result in a better decision.

The Guidelines can be used also to decide mundane matters in your personal life, such as whether to eat a high-fat hamburger or a healthful salad for lunch, whether to spend the next hour exercising at the gym or visiting a friend in the hospital, and whether or not to brush your teeth every day after lunch. But for most of us, using the Guidelines every day for every decision would occupy so much of our time that little could be accomplished, what is sometimes called "paralysis by analysis."

Practicality, therefore, requires us to use the Guidelines only for important decisions and those that create a potential for ethical problems. We can identify decisions requiring application of the Guidelines if we carefully reflect from time to time about what we have done and are doing. This requires us to examine our past, current, and future actions.

It may not surprise you how seldom people, including business executives, carefully preview and review their

actions. The pressures and pace of daily living give us little time to examine our lives critically. Most people are reluctant to look at themselves in the mirror and ask themselves whether they are doing the right thing for themselves, their families, their businesses, and their communities. Few know or follow the words of Socrates, "The unexamined life is not worth living."

Ask yourself whether you believe that mortgage brokers used anything like the Guidelines for Ethical Decision Making before signing low-income borrowers to loans exceeding $500,000. Did executives at bankrupt energy trader Enron consider any ethical issues before creating off-balance-sheet partnerships with no economic value to Enron? Do you think the employees at accounting firm Arthur Andersen carefully examined their decision to accept Enron's accounting for off-balance-sheet partnerships?

Merely by examining our past and prospective actions, we can better know when to apply the Guidelines. In the next to last section of this chapter, Resisting Requests to Act Unethically, you will learn additional tools to help you identify when to apply the Guidelines.

LOG ON

Go to
www.scu.edu/ethics
This website maintained by the Markkula Center for Applied Ethics at the University of Santa Clara has links to business ethics resources and guides for ethical/moral decision making.

Thinking Critically

Legal reasoning and ethical decision making both require one to think critically—that is, to evaluate arguments logically, honestly, and without bias in favor of your own arguments and against those of others. Thinking critically is a skill, and as with any skill, one can improve through greater awareness of common mistakes and intentional practice of those methods that will lead to improvement.

LO4-3 Recognize critical thinking errors in your own and others' arguments.

Even if someone uses the Guidelines for Ethical Decision Making, there is a risk that they have been misapplied if a person makes errors of logic or uses fallacious arguments. In this section, we want to help you identify when your arguments and thinking may be flawed and how to correct them. Equally important, we want to help you identify flaws in others' thinking. The purpose is to help you think critically and not to accept at face value everything you read or hear and to be careful before you commit your arguments to paper or voice them.

This chapter's short coverage of critical thinking covers only a few of the errors of logic and argument that are covered in a college course or book devoted to the subject. Here are 15 common fallacies and errors in reasoning that, if learned, can help you become a more rigorous and careful thinker.

Non Sequiturs
A *non sequitur* is a conclusion that does not follow from the facts or premises one sets out. The speaker is missing the point or coming to an irrelevant conclusion. For example, suppose a consumer uses a corporation's product and becomes ill. The consumer argues that because the corporation has lots of money, the corporation should pay for his medical expenses. Clearly, the consumer is missing the point. The issue is whether the corporation's product *caused* his injuries, not whether money should be transferred from a wealthy corporation to a poor consumer.

You see this also used when employees attempt to justify stealing pens, staplers, and paper from their employers. The typical *non sequitur* goes like this: "I don't get paid enough, so I'll take a few supplies. My employer won't even miss them."

Business executives fall prey to this fallacy also. Our firm may consider which employees to let go during a downturn. Company policy may call for retaining the best employees in each department, yet instead we release those employees making the highest salary in each position in order to save more money. Our decision does not match the standards the company set for downsizing decisions and is a *non sequitur*, unless we admit that we have changed company policy.

Appeals to Pity
A common fallacy seen in the American press is the appeal to pity or compassion. This argument generates support for a proposition by focusing on a victim's predicament. It usually is also a *non sequitur*. Examples are news stories about elderly, retired people who find it hard to afford expensive, life-prolonging drugs. None of these stories point out that many of these people squandered their incomes when working rather than saving for retirement.

Appeals to pity are effective because humans are compassionate. We have to be careful, however, not to be distracted from the real issues at hand. For example, in the trial against accused 9/11 co-conspirator Zacarias Moussaoui, federal prosecutors wanted to introduce testimony by the families of the victims. While what the families of

9/11 suffered is terrible, the victims' families hold no evidence of Moussaoui's role in 9/11. Instead, their testimonies are appeals to pity likely to distract the jury from its main task of determining whether Moussaoui was a part of the 9/11 conspiracy.

American presidents and other politicians often use appeals to pity, such as having a press conference with children behind the president while he opines about income inequality. Moreover, you see many appeals to pity used against corporations. Here is a typical argument: A corporation has a chemical plant near a neighborhood; children are getting sick and dying in the neighborhood; someone should pay for this suffering; the corporation should pay. You can also see that this reasoning is a *non sequitur*. Better reasoning requires one to determine not whether two events are coincidental or correlated, but whether one (the chemical plant) caused the other (the children's illnesses).

False Analogies
An analogy essentially argues that because something is like something else in one or more ways, it is also like it in another respect. Arguers often use analogies to make a point vividly, and therefore analogies have strong appeal. Nonetheless, while some analogies are apt, we should make sure that the two situations are sufficiently similar to make the analogy valid.

Suppose an executive argues that our bank should not make loans to lower-income borrowers because the bank will suffer huge losses like Countrywide Financial. This analogy may be invalid because we may do a better job verifying a borrower's income and ability to repay a loan than did Countrywide.

Analogies can also be used to generate support for a proposal, such as arguing that because Six Sigma worked for General Electric, it will work for our firm also. It is probable that factors other than Six Sigma contributed to GE's success, factors our firm may or may not share with GE.

Nonetheless, analogies can identify potential opportunities, which we should evaluate prudently to determine whether the analogy is valid. Analogies can also suggest potential problems that require us to examine a decision more carefully before committing to it.

Begging the Question
An arguer begs the question when she takes for granted or assumes the thing that she is setting out to prove. For example, you might say that we should tell the truth because lying is wrong. That is circular reasoning and makes no sense because telling the truth and not lying are the same things. Another example is arguing that democracy is the best form of government because the majority is always right.

Examples of begging the question are difficult to identify sometimes because they are hidden in the language of the speaker. It is best identified by looking for arguments that merely restate what the speaker or questioner has already stated, but in different words. For an example in the business context, consider this interchange between you and someone working under you.

You: Can I trust these numbers you gave to me?

Coworker: Yes, you can trust them.

You: Why can I trust them?

Coworker: Because I'm an honest person.

The coworker used circular reasoning because whether the numbers can be trusted is determined by whether he is honest, yet he provided no proof of his honesty, such as his numbers being backed by facts.

Argumentum ad Populum
Argumentum ad populum means argument to the people. It is an emotional appeal to popular beliefs, values, or wants. The fallacy is that merely because many or all people believe something does not mean it is true. It is common for newspapers to poll its readers about current issues, such as support for a presidential decision. For example, a newspaper poll may show that 60 percent of Americans support the president. The people may be right, but it is also possible that the president's supporters are wrong: They may be uninformed or base their support of the president on invalid reasoning.

Arguments to the people are commonly used by corporations in advertisements, such as beer company ads showing friends having a good time while drinking beer. The point of such ads is that if you want to have a good time with friends, you should drink beer. While some beer drinkers do have fun with friends, you probably can also point to other people who drink beer alone.

Bandwagon Fallacy
The bandwagon fallacy is similar to *argumentum ad populum*. A bandwagon argument states that we should or should not do something merely because one or more other people or firms do or do not do it. *Sports Illustrated* quoted basketball player Diana Taurasi's objection to being arrested for driving drunk: "Why me? Everyone drives drunk!" Some people justify cheating on their taxes for the same reason.

This reasoning can be fallacious because probably not everyone is doing it, and even if many or all people do something, it is not necessarily right. For example, while some baseball players do use steroids, there are serious negative side effects including impotency and acute psychosis, which make its use risky. Cheating on taxes may be common, but it is still illegal and can result in the cheater's imprisonment.

Bandwagon thinking played a large part in the current credit crunch as many loan buyers like Bear Stearns bought high-risk loans only because their competitors were buying the loans, thereby encouraging lenders to continue to make high-risk loans.

Argumentum ad Baculum
Argumentum ad baculum means argument to club. The arguer uses threats or fear to bolster his position. This is a common argument in business and family settings. For example, when a parent asks a child to take out the garbage, the child may ask, "Why?" Some parents respond, "Because if you don't, you'll spend the rest of the afternoon in your room." Such an argument is a *non sequitur* as well.

In the business context, bosses explicitly and implicitly use the club, often generating support for their ideas from subordinates who fear they will not be promoted unless they support the boss's plans. An executive who values input from subordinates will ensure that they do not perceive that the executive is wielding a club over them.

Enron's CFO Andrew Fastow used this argument against investment firm Goldman Sachs when it balked at lending money to Enron. He told Goldman that he would not do anything with a presentation Goldman had prepared unless it made the loan.

By threatening to boycott a company's products, consumers and other interest groups use this argument against corporations perceived to act unethically. It is one reason that profit maximization requires decision makers to consider a decision's impact on all stakeholders.

Argumentum ad Hominem
Argumentum ad hominem means "argument against the man." This tactic attacks the speaker, not his reasoning. For example, a Republican senator criticizes a Democratic senator who supports the withdrawal of American troops from a war zone by saying, "You can't trust him. He never served in the armed forces." Such an argument attacks the Democratic senator's character, not the validity of his reasons for withdrawing troops.

When a CEO proposes a new compensation plan for corporate executives, an opponent may argue, "Of course he wants the new plan. He'll make a lot of money from it." Again, this argument doesn't address whether the plan is a good one or not; it only attacks the CEO's motives. While the obvious conflict of interest the CEO has may cause us to doubt the sincerity of the reasons he presents for the plan (such as to attract and retain better management talent), merely pointing out this conflict does not rebut his reasons.

One form of *ad hominem* argument is attacking a speaker's consistency, such as, "Last year you argued for something different." Another common form is appealing to personal circumstances. One woman may say to another, "As a woman, how can you be against corporate policies that set aside executive positions for women?" By personalizing the argument, the speaker is trying to distract the listener from the real issue. A proper response to the personal attack may be, "As a woman and a human, I believe in equal opportunity for all people. I see no need for any woman or me to have special privileges to compete with men. I can compete on my own. By having quotas, the corporation cheapens my accomplishments by suggesting that I need the quota. Why do you, as a woman, think you need a quota?"

Guilt by association is the last *ad hominem* argument we will consider. This argument attacks the speaker by linking her to someone unpopular. For example, if you make the libertarian argument that government should not restrict or tax the consumption of marijuana, someone may attack you by saying, "Mass murderer Charles Manson also believed that." Your attacker suggests that by believing as you do, you are as evil as Charles Manson. Some corporate critics use guilt by association to paint all executives as unethical people motivated to cheat their corporations. For example, if a CEO asks for stock options as part of her compensation package, someone may say, "Enron's executives wanted stock options also." The implication is that the CEO should not be trusted because some Enron executives who were corrupt also wanted stock options.

No *ad hominem* argument is necessarily fallacious because a person's character, motives, consistency, personal characteristics, and associations may suggest further scrutiny of a speaker's arguments is necessary. However, merely attacking the speaker does not expose flaws in her arguments.

Argument from Authority
Arguments from authority rely on the quality of an expert or person in a position of authority, not the quality of the expert's or authority's argument. For example, if someone says, "The president says we need to stop drug trafficking in the United States, and that is good enough for me," he has argued from authority. He and the president may have good reasons to stop drug trafficking, but we cannot know that from his statement.

Another example is "Studies show that humans need to drink 10 glasses of water a day." What studies? What were their methodologies? Did the sample sizes permit valid conclusions? A form of argument to authority is argument to reverence or respect, such as "Who are you to disagree with the CEO's decision to terminate 5,000 employees?" The arguer is trying to get you to abandon your arguments, not because they are invalid, but because they conflict with the views of an authority. Your response to this question should not attack the CEO (to call the CEO an idiot would be *ad hominem* and also damage your prospects in the firm), but state the reasons you believe the company would be better off not terminating 5,000 employees.

It is natural to rely on authorities who have expertise in the area on which they speak. But should we give credibility to authorities speaking on matters outside the scope of their competency? For example, does the fact that Julia Roberts is an Academy Award–winning actress have any relevance when she is testifying before Congress about Rett Syndrome, a neurological disorder that leaves infants unable to communicate and control body functions? Is she any more credible as a Rett Syndrome authority because she narrated a film on the Discovery Health Channel about children afflicted with the disease?

This chapter includes several examples of arguments from authority when we cite Kant, Bentham, Aristotle, and others who have formulated ethical theories. What makes their theories valid, however, is not whether they are recognized as experts, but whether their reasoning is sound.

False Cause
This fallacy results from observing two events and concluding that there is a causal link between them when there is no such link. Often we commit this fallacy because we do not attempt to find all the evidence proving or disproving the causal connection. For example, if as a store manager you change the opening hour for your store to 6 A.M. from 8 A.M., records for the first month of operation under the new hours may show an increase in revenue. While you may be tempted to infer that the revenue increase is due to the earlier opening hour, you should not make that conclusion until at the very least you examine store receipts showing the amount of revenue generated between 6 A.M. and 8 A.M. The increase in revenue could have resulted from improved general economic conditions unconnected to the new hours: People just had more money to spend.

The fallacy of false cause is important to businesses, which need to make valid connections between events in order to judge the effectiveness of decisions. Whether, for example, new products and an improved customer relations program increase revenues and profits should be subjected to rigorous testing, not some superficial causal analysis. Measurement tools you learn in other business classes help you eliminate false causes.

The Gambler's Fallacy
This fallacy results from the mistaken belief that independent prior outcomes affect future outcomes. Consider this example. Suppose you flip a coin five times and each time it comes up heads. What is the probability that the next coin flip will be heads? If you did not answer 50 percent, you committed the gambler's fallacy. Each coin flip is an independent event, so no number of consecutive flips producing heads will reduce the likelihood that the next flip will also be heads. That individual probability is true even though the probability of flipping six consecutive heads is 0.5 to the sixth power, or only 1.5625 percent.

What is the relevance of the gambler's fallacy to business? We believe and are taught that business managers and professionals with higher skills and better decision-making methods are more likely to be successful than those with lesser skills and worse methods. Yet we have not discussed the importance of luck or circumstance to success. When a corporation has five years of profits rising by 30 percent, is it due to good management or because of expanding consumer demand or any number of other reasons? If a mutual fund has seven years of annual returns of at least 15 percent, is the fund's manager an investment genius or is she lucky? If it is just luck, one should not expect the luck to continue. The point is that you should not be seduced by a firm's, manager's, or even your own string of successes and immediately jump to the conclusion that the successes were the result of managerial excellence. Instead, you should use measurement tools taught in your finance, marketing, and other courses to determine the real reasons for success.

Reductio ad Absurdum

Reductio ad absurdum carries an argument to its logical end, without considering whether it is an inevitable or probable result. This is often called the slippery slope fallacy.

For example, if I want to convince someone not to eat fast food, I might argue, "Eating fast food will cause you to put on weight. Putting on weight will make you overweight. Soon you will weigh 400 pounds and die of heart disease. Therefore, eating fast food leads to death. Don't eat fast food." In other words, if you started eating fast food, you are on a slippery slope and will not be able to stop until you die. Although you can see that this argument makes some sense, it is absurd for most people who eat fast food.

Scientist Carl Sagan noted that the slippery slope argument is used by both sides of the abortion debate. One side says, "If we allow abortion in the first weeks of pregnancy, it will be impossible to prevent the killing of a full-term infant." The other replies, "If the state prohibits abortion even in the ninth month, it will soon be telling us what to do with our bodies around the time of conception."

Business executives face this argument frequently. Human resource managers use it to justify not making exceptions to rules, such as saying, "If we allow you time off to go to your aunt's funeral, we have to let anyone off any time they want." Well, no, that was not what you were asking for. Executives who reason this way often are looking for administratively simple rules that do not require them to make distinctions. That is, they do not want to think hard or critically.

Pushing an argument to its limits is a useful exercise in critical thinking, often helping us discover whether a claim has validity. The fallacy is carrying the argument to its extreme without recognizing and admitting that there are many steps along the way that are more likely consequences.

Appeals to Tradition

Appeals to tradition infer that because something has been done a certain way in the past, it should be done the same way in the future. You probably have heard people say, "I don't know why we do it, but we've always done it that way, and it's always worked, so we'll continue to do it that way." Although there is some validity to continuing to do what has stood the test of time, the reasons a business strategy has succeeded in the past may be independent of the strategy itself. The gambler's fallacy would suggest that perhaps we have just been lucky in the past. Also, changed circumstances may justify departing from previous ways of doing business.

In November 2013, many retailers like Kmart, Walmart, Sears, and The Gap were criticized for opening their retail stores on Thanksgiving Day. Arguments against the openings were mostly appeals to tradition and to pity, that is, that workers in the past have been and should in the future be able to enjoy Thanksgiving Day with family instead of working. The arguments were also *non sequiturs* because critics of the openings continued to consume sports programming, TV shows, electricity, heat, gasoline, and other services provided by employees working on Thanksgiving Day.

The Lure of the New

The opposite of an appeal to tradition is the lure of the new, the idea that we should do or buy something merely because it is "just released" or "improved." You see this common theme in advertising that promotes "new and improved" Tide or iPhone 11. Experience tells us that sometimes new products are better. But we can also recount examples of new car models with defects and new software with bugs that were fixed in a later version.

The lure of the new is also a common theme in management theories as some managers have raced to embrace one new craze after another, depending on which is the hottest fad, be it Strategic Planning, Total Quality Management, Reengineering the Corporation, or Customer Relationship Management. The point here is the same. Avoid being dazzled by claims of newness. Evaluations of ideas should be based on substance.

Sunk Cost Fallacy

The sunk cost fallacy is an attempt to recover invested time, money, and other resources by spending still more time, money, or other resources. It is sometimes expressed as "throwing good money after bad." Stock market investors do this often. They invest $30,000 in the latest tech stock. When the investment declines to $2,000, rather than evaluate whether it is better to withdraw that $2,000 and invest it elsewhere, an investor who falls for the sunk cost fallacy might say, "I can't stop investing now, otherwise what I've invested so far will be lost." While the latter part of the statement is true, the fallacy is in the first part. Of the money already invested, $28,000 is lost whether or not the investor continues to invest. If the tech stock is not a good investment *at this time*, the rational decision is to withdraw the remaining $2,000 and not invest more money.

There are other statements that indicate business executives may fall victim to the sunk cost fallacy: "It's too late for us to change plans now." Or "If we could go back to square one, then we could make a different decision." The best way to spend the firm's remaining labor and money may be to continue a project. But that decision should be unaffected by a consideration of the labor and money already expended. The proper question is this: What project will give the firm the best return on its investment of money and other resources *from this point forward*? To continue to invest in a hopeless project is irrational and may be a pathetic attempt to delay having to face the consequences of a poor decision.

A decision maker acts irrationally when he attempts to save face by throwing good money after bad. If you want a real-world example of ego falling prey to the sunk cost fallacy, consider that President Lyndon Johnson committed American soldiers to the Vietnam Conflict after he had determined that America and South Vietnam could never defeat the Viet Cong. By falling for the sunk cost fallacy, the United States lost billions of dollars and tens of thousands of soldiers in the pursuit of a hopeless cause.

LOG ON

Go to
www.fallacyfiles.org
Maintained by Gary Curtis, *The Fallacy Files* cover more than 150 fallacies with links to explanations and valuable resources.
Go to
www.ethicsunwrapped.utexas.edu
Ethics Unwrapped uses a fun and accessible video format to present the latest research from psychology, neuroscience, and behavioral economics explaining how biases and pressures can cloud our thinking and compromise our ethical decision making.

Common Characteristics of Poor Decision Making

Most business managers during the course of their formal education in school or informal education on the job have learned most of the techniques we have discussed in this chapter for making ethical and well-reasoned decisions. Yet business managers continue to make unethical and poor decisions, most often in disregard of the very principles that they otherwise view as essential to good decision making. Each of us can also point to examples when we have failed to analyze a situation properly before making a decision, even though, at the time, we possessed the ability to make better decisions.

Why do we and other well-intentioned people make bad decisions? What is it that interferes with our ability to use all the decision-making tools at our disposal, resulting sometimes in unethical and even catastrophic decisions? What causes a basically honest accountant to agree to cook the books for his corporation? What causes a drug company to continue to market a drug when internal tests and user experience show a high incidence of harmful side effects? What causes a corporation to continue to operate a chemical plant when its safety systems have been shut down? While business scholars and other writers have suggested several attributes that commonly interfere with good decision making, we believe they can be distilled into three essential traits that are useful to you, a decision maker who has already learned the Guidelines for Ethical Decision Making and the most common critical thinking errors.

Failing to Remember Goals Friedrich Nietzsche wrote, "Man's most enduring stupidity is forgetting what he is trying to do." If, for example, our company's goal as a retailer is to garner a 30 percent market share in the retail market in five years, you may think that would translate into being dominant in each segment of our business, from housewares to video games. But should our retailer strive to dominate a market segment that is declining, such as portable cassette players, when the consumer market has clearly moved to smartphones and other digital recorders? If we focus on the wrong goal—dominating the cassette player market, which may not exist in five years—we have failed to remember our goal of acquiring a 30 percent overall market share.

In another example, suppose we are a luxury homebuilder with two goals that go hand-in-hand: producing high-quality housing and maintaining an annual 15 percent return on equity. The first goal supports the second goal: By having a reputation for producing high-quality housing, we can charge more for our houses. Suppose, however, one of our project managers is under pressure to bring her development in line with cost projections. She decides, therefore, to use lower-quality, lower-cost materials. The consequence is we meet our profit target in the short run, but in the long run, when the shoddy materials are detected and our reputation is sullied, both of our goals of building high-quality housing and achieving a 15 percent return on equity will be compromised. Again, we have failed to remember the most important goal, maintaining high quality, which allowed us to achieve our ROE goal.

Overconfidence The phenomenon known as *overconfidence bias* leads us to be more confident than we should be about the extent of our knowledge and our problem-solving skills. To the extent that this "been there, done that" mindset takes hold in a leader, her ability to learn helpful lessons from the experiences of others may be compromised. In the realm of ethical decision making, the leader who thinks she has mastered everything important and has nothing more to learn may end up teaching those in the organization unfortunate lessons and may unknowingly influence the organization's culture in an undesirable way.

While confidence is a personal trait essential to success, overoptimism is one of the most common reasons for bad decisions. We all have heard ourselves and others say, "Don't worry. Everything will work out OK." That statement is likely a consequence of overconfidence, not careful analysis that is necessary to make sure everything will work out as we hope.

There are several corollaries or other ways to express this overoptimism. Sometimes, business executives will do something that they know to be wrong with the belief that it is only a small or temporary wrong that will be fixed next year. They may rationalize that no one will notice the wrongdoing and that only big companies and big executives get caught, not small companies and little managers like them.

Many major accounting scandals started small, rationalized as temporary attempts to cook the books that would be corrected in the following years when business turned around. As we now know, finance managers and accountants who thought things would turn around were being overconfident about the economy and their companies.

Another aspect of overconfidence is *confirmation bias*; that is, we must be doing things the right way because all has gone well in the past. Or at least we have not been caught doing something wrong in the past, so we will not be caught in the future. In part, this reveals a thinking error we have studied: appeal to tradition. In the earlier homebuilder example, the project manager's cutting quality in years past may not have been detected by homeowners who knew nothing about construction quality. And none of the project manager's workers may have told top management about the project manager's actions. That past, however, does not guarantee the future. New homeowners may be more knowledgeable, and future workers may inform management of the project manager's quality-cutting actions.

If we are not careful, confirmation bias can also cause us to see what we want to see in a given situation and to engage in subconscious favorable spinning of potentially relevant facts even if those facts might fairly be treated as pointing in the other direction. Confirmation bias can cause us to miss the real lessons from an example that we think we are viewing objectively. To guard against the negative effects of confirmation bias and to learn as much as we can from an example or situation, we need to seek out and pay attention to possible disconfirming evidence: evidence indicating that our preferred position or view may not be correct.

Another consequence of overoptimism is believing that complex problems have simple solutions. That leads to the next common trait of bad decision making.

Complexity of the Issues Closely aligned to and aggravated by overconfidence is the failure of decision makers to understand the complexity of an issue. A manager may perceive that the facts are simpler than reality and, therefore, not see that there is little margin for error. Consequently, the executive has not considered the full range of possible solutions and has failed to find the one solution that best matches the facts.

Restated, the decision maker has not done all the investigation and thinking required by the Guidelines for Ethical Decision Making and, therefore, has not discovered all the facts and considered all the reasonable courses of action necessary to making a prudent decision.

The impediments to knowing all the facts, understanding the complexity of a problem, and doing the hard work to create and evaluate all possible solutions to a problem are known to all of us. Fatigue, laziness, overconfidence, and forgetting goals play roles in promoting ignorance of critical facts. We may also want to be team players, by following the lead of a colleague or the order of a boss. These human tendencies deter us from making the effort to find the facts and to consider all options.

Resisting Requests to Act Unethically

Even if we follow the Guidelines for Ethical Decision Making and avoid the pitfalls of fallacious reasoning, not everyone is a CEO or his own boss and able to make decisions that others are expected to follow. Sure, if you control a firm, you will do the right thing. But the reality is that for most people in the business world, other people make many decisions that you are asked to carry out. What do you do when asked to do something unethical? How can you resist a boss's request to act unethically? What could employees at WorldCom have done when its CFO instructed them to falsify the firm's books or mortgage brokers when their bosses asked them to falsify borrowers' incomes?

 LO4-4 Utilize a process to make ethical decisions in the face of pressure from others.

Recognizing Unethical Requests and Bosses
A person must recognize whether he has been asked to do something unethical. While this sounds simple considering we have spent most of this chapter helping you

make just that kind of decision, there are structural problems that interfere with your ability to perform an ethical analysis when a boss or colleague asks you to do something. Many of us are inclined to be team players and "do as we are told" by a superior. Therefore, it is important to recognize any tendency to accept appeals to authority and to resist the temptation to follow orders blindly. We do not want to be like the Enron accounting employee who returned to his alma mater and was asked by a student, "What do you do at Enron?" When considering that question, a question he never posed to himself, he realized that his only job was to remove liabilities from Enron's balance sheet.

For most bosses' orders, such an analysis will be unnecessary. Most of the time, a boss is herself ethical and will not ask us to do something wrong. But there are exceptions that require us to be on the lookout. Moreover, some bosses have questionable integrity, and they are more likely to give us unethical orders. Therefore, it will be helpful if we can identify bosses who have shaky ethics, for whom we should put up our ethical antennae when they come to us with a task.

Business ethicists have attempted to identify executives with questionable integrity by their actions. Ethical bosses have the ability to "tell it like it is," while those with less integrity say one thing and do another. Ethical bosses have the ability to acknowledge that they have failed, whereas those with low integrity often insist on being right all the time. Ethical bosses try to build a consensus before making an important decision; unethical bosses may generate support for their decisions with intimidation through anger and threats. Ethical bosses can think about the needs of others besides themselves. Bosses with low integrity who misuse their workers by asking them to act unethically often mistreat other people also, like secretaries and servers.

If we pay attention to these details, we will be better able to consider the "source" when we are asked to do something by a boss and, therefore, more sensitive to the need to scrutinize the ethics of a boss's request.

Buying Time
If we think a requested action is or might be unethical, what is done next? How can we refuse to do something a boss has ordered us to do? One key is to buy some time before you have to execute the boss's order. Buying time allows you to find more facts, understand an act's impact on the firm's stakeholders, and evaluate the ethics of the action. It also lets you find other alternatives that achieve the boss's objectives without compromising your values. Delay also gives you time to speak with the firm's ethics officer and other confidants.

How do you buy time? If the request is in an e-mail, you might delay responding to it. Or you could answer that you have received the e-mail and will give your attention to it when you finish with the task you are working on. Similar tactics can be used with phone calls and other direct orders. Even a few hours can help your decision. Depending on the order and your ability to stack delay on top of delay, you may be able to give yourself days or weeks to find a solution to your dilemma.

The most important reason for buying time is it allows you to seek advice and assistance from other people, especially those in the firm. That brings us to the next tactic for dealing with unethical requests.

Find a Mentor and a Peer Support Group
Having a support system is one of the most important keys to survival in any organization, and it is best to put a system in place when you start working at the firm. Your support system can improve and help defend your decisions. It can also give you access to executives who hold the power to overrule your boss. Your support system should include a mentor and a network of other employees with circumstances similar to your own.

A mentor who is well established, well respected, and highly placed in the firm will help you negotiate the pitfalls that destroy employees who are ignorant of a firm's culture. A mentor can be a sounding board for your decisions; she can provide information on those who can be expected to help you and those who could hurt you; she can advise you of the procedures you should follow to avoid antagonizing potential allies. A mentor can also defend you and provide protection when you oppose a boss's decision. Many firms have a mentorship program, but if not or if your assigned mentor is deficient, you should find an appropriate mentor soon after you join the firm. Be sure to keep her updated regularly on what you are doing. By letting a mentor know that you care to keep her informed, she becomes invested in you and your career.

You should also build a community of your peers by creating a network of other workers who share your values and interests. You may want to find others who joined the firm at about the same time you did, who are about the same age, who share your passion for the firm's products and services, and who have strong ethical values. To cement the relationship, your peer support group should meet regularly, such as twice a week at work during 15-minute coffee breaks. This group can give you advice, help with difficult decisions, and unite to back up your ethical decisions.

Find Win–Win Solutions
As we learned from the Guidelines for Ethical Decision Making, many times there are more than the two options of doing and not doing something. There are a number of choices in between those

extremes, and the best solution may be one unconnected to them. For example, suppose your boss has ordered you to fire someone who works under you. The worker's productivity may be lagging, and perhaps he has made a few costly mistakes. Yet you think it would be wrong to fire the worker at this time. What do you do?

Find a win-win solution—that is, a compromise that works for you and your boss. First, discover your boss's wants. Probably you will find that your boss wants an employee who makes no or few mistakes and has a certain level of productivity. Next determine what is needed for the affected employee to reach that level. If you find the employee is having emotional problems that interfere with his work, are they temporary or can we help him handle them? Can we make him more productive by giving him more training? Is the employee unmotivated or is he unaware that he lags behind other workers? Should we give him a warning and place him on probationary status for a month, releasing him if there is no satisfactory improvement? These alternatives may address your boss's concerns about the employee without compromising your ethical values.

In other contexts, you may need to approach your boss directly and show that her order is not right for the firm. Using the Guidelines for Ethical Decision Making and valid arguments, you may be able to persuade your boss to accept your perspective and avoid an otherwise unethical decision. Finding a win-win solution is possible only when there is room for compromise. The Ethical Guidelines and logical arguments are effective when your boss respects reason and wants to act ethically. However, when you face an intractable executive demanding you do something illegal, a different response is needed.

Work within the Firm to Stop the Unethical Act
Suppose you receive an order from an executive you know or suspect to be corrupt. For example, a CFO is motivated to increase the price of the firm's stock in order to make her stock options more valuable. She orders you to book in the current year revenue that, in fact, will not be received for at least two years, if ever. Booking that revenue would be fraudulent, unethical, and illegal. You are convinced the CFO knows of the illegality and will find someone else to book the revenue if you refuse. You probably will lose your job if you do not cooperate. What do you do?

This is when your mentor, peer support group, and corporate ethics officer can help you. Your mentor may have access to the CEO or audit committee, who, if honest, should back you and fire the CFO. Your peer support group might

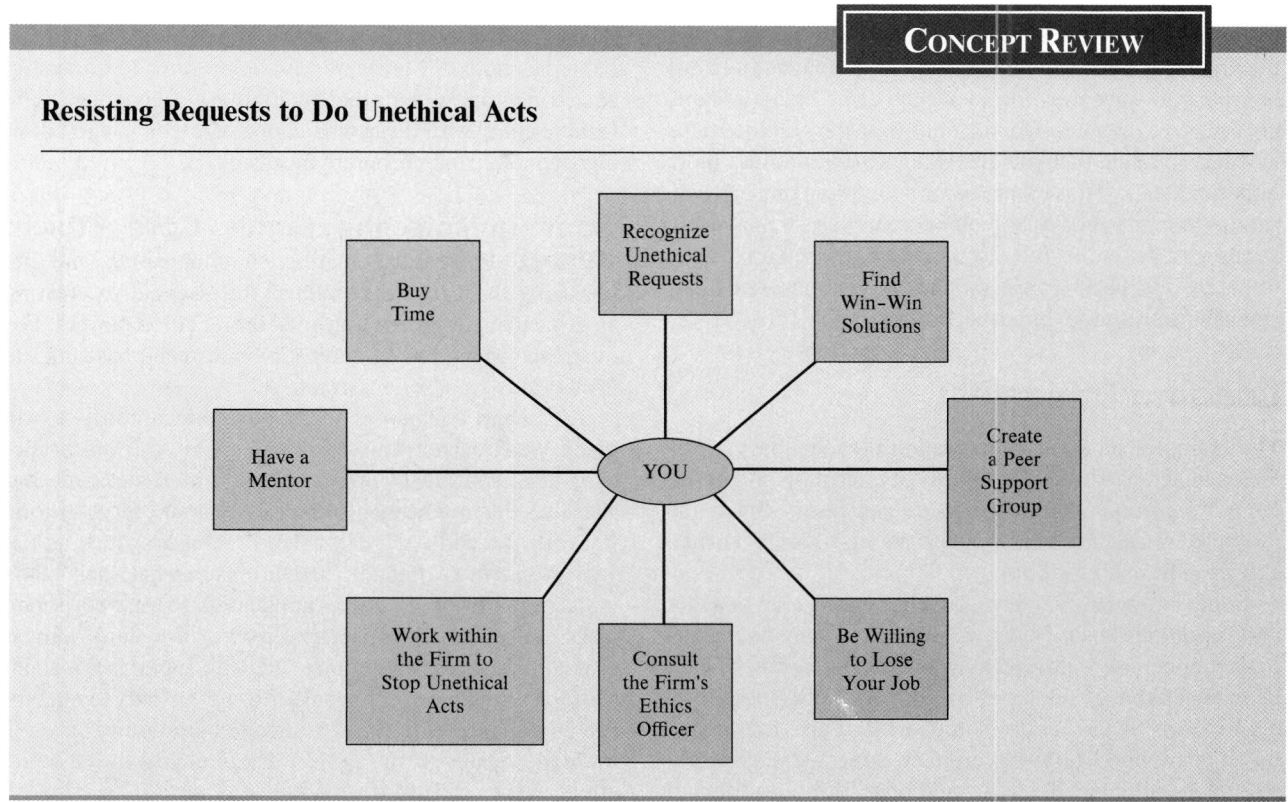

CONCEPT REVIEW

Resisting Requests to Do Unethical Acts

Recognize Unethical Requests

Buy Time

Find Win-Win Solutions

Have a Mentor

Create a Peer Support Group

YOU

Work within the Firm to Stop Unethical Acts

Consult the Firm's Ethics Officer

Be Willing to Lose Your Job

have similar access. The corporate ethics officer, especially if she is a lawyer in the firm's legal department, can also provide her backing and that of the legal department.

There is one large caveat, however. While the situation just described should and probably will result in your support system rallying to your support, in other situations that are ethically ambiguous, you, your mentor, and your support group may find that fighting a battle against a top corporate executive ineffectively expends your and your colleagues' political capital. In other words, you need to pick your battles carefully lest you and your colleagues at the firm be labeled whiners and troublemakers who unnecessarily seek intervention from higher-level corporate executives. This is why we have listed this alternative near the end of our discussion. In most situations, it is better to rely on your colleagues as advisors and to execute win–win solutions in cooperation with your boss.

But if neither compromise nor other intrafirm tactics protect you from unethical requests, you are left with a final tactic.

Prepare to Lose Your Job This is the last tactic because by quitting or losing your job, you are deprived of your ability to help the firm make ethical decisions. Only as an employee can you craft win–win solutions or work within the firm to do the right thing.

But if a firm's executives and its internal governance are so corrupted that neither compromise nor reason can steer the firm away from an unethical and illegal course, you must be willing to walk away from your job or be fired for standing up for your values. Do not want your job and the status it brings so much that you are willing to compromise more important values. It is tough losing a job when one has obligations to family, banks, and other creditors as well as aspirations for a better life. But if you prepare yourself financially from day one, putting away money for an ethical rainy day, you will protect more important values.

Leading Ethically

The examples set by an organization's leaders have a profound effect on the culture of an organization. If the examples are good, a healthy culture can result. But if the examples reflect little seriousness about ethics, a corner-cutting culture may follow.

Someday, perhaps today, you will be in charge of other people in your business organization. You may be managing a four-person team, you may be a vice president of marketing in charge of a department, or you may eventually be a CEO directing an entire company. You give the people under your charge tasks to complete, supervise their work, help them complete the tasks, and provide motivation and

feedback to ensure that the current job will be done well and that future work will be done better. So how do you also ensure that all those people under your charge act ethically? This is the daily challenge of ethical business leaders, who must not only act ethically themselves, but also promote ethical behavior of their workers.

Be Ethical

 LO4-5 Be an ethical leader.

No one can lead ethically who does not attempt—and mostly succeed—in behaving ethically in her business and personal life. Few underlings respect an unethical leader, and many will be tempted to rationalize their own unethical conduct when they see their leaders acting unethically. They fall prey to the bandwagon fallacy, arguing, for example, that because the CFO is doing something wrong, so may they. For the same reason, ethical behavior by good managers encourages ethical behavior by underlings, who often view their bosses as role models and guides for advancing in the corporation. If they see an ethical boss moving up in the business, they will believe that the system is fair and that they, too, by acting ethically, can advance at the firm. As Harvard business ethics professor Lynn Sharp Paine has noted, "Managers who fail to provide leadership and to institute systems that facilitate ethical conduct share responsibility with those who conceive, execute, and knowingly benefit from corporate misdeeds."

Communicate the Firm's Core Ethical Values
For CEOs, creating, communicating, and emphasizing the firm's core values are essential to creating an ethical environment that rubs off on all employees. For other managers, recommunicating and reemphasizing the firm's value are also important.

All public companies today have ethics codes, as do many smaller companies. Yet the CEO who leads ethically must continually emphasize in written messages and speeches the importance and necessity that everyone comply with the code. Other top-level managers, such as the vice president of finance, should ensure that their staffs understand the ethics code's application to their corporate tasks and make ethical reviews part of the staffs' annual evaluations. A lower-level manager who supervises a small staff for a single project should also do his part to encourage compliance with the ethics code by pointing out how the code relates to the project assignment and including ethics in the project team's progress reports.

Connect Ethical Behavior with the Firm's and Workers' Best Interests

It is one thing to educate your staff about ethical behavior and another to obtain compliance. One good way to increase compliance with the firm's core ethical values is to convince the staff that their best interests—and the firm's—are met by acting ethically. Management should help employees understand that the firm's profitability and the employee's advancement in the firm are optimized by each employee taking responsibility for acting ethically. Staff must understand that adverse publicity caused by unethical conduct harms a firm's ability to promote itself and its products and services. The ethical manager also clearly establishes ethical behavior as a prerequisite for salary increases and promotions, or at least that unethical behavior is a disqualifier.

Reinforce Ethical Behavior

When a manager knows a staff member has acted ethically in a situation in which employees in less ethical firms would be tempted to act unethically, the manager should congratulate and find other ways to reinforce the staff member's behavior. For example, if a staff member reports that a supplier has attempted to bribe him in order to do business with the firm, the ethical manager will praise the staff member and may include a letter commending him in his employment file.

In addition, management should set up a mechanism for its employees to report instances of unethical behavior by the staff. While some employees will view whistle-blowing as an act of disloyalty, management should recharacterize whistle-blowing as necessary to the protection of the firm's decision-making processes and reputation. Undetected ethical decisions often lead to poor decisions and harm corporate profits. While management does not want witch hunts, good managers must garner evidence of alleged unethical behavior so they may investigate and stop conduct that is harmful to the firm.

A necessary corollary is not reinforcing unethical behavior, including behavior that may lead to an unethical act or foster an environment that appears tolerant of ethical missteps. It is usually not acceptable to ignore bad behavior. The ethical leader must reprimand staff for unethical actions and must not tolerate statements that suggest the firm should engage in unethical conduct. For example, if, during discussions about how to increase revenue for a product line, one staff member suggests obtaining competitors' agreements to fix prices, a manager running the meeting should make clear that the firm will not engage in that or any other conduct that is illegal. To let the price-fixing comment pass without comment may send the message that the manager and the firm condone illegal or unethical acts.

Additionally, managers should work to create a culture in which employees feel a sense of "ownership" in the organization. Employees who invest themselves in the organization are more likely to be employees with both a greater sense of satisfaction and higher commitment to the overall mission of the firm. Consider the difference between how most people treat an owned car versus a rental car. No one changes the oil, rotates the tires, or washes and waxes a rental car. A rental car serves a short-term, instrumental purpose and carries with it no long-term commitment or investment. Ownership of a vehicle, on the other hand, is accompanied by routine maintenance and proactive attention to any unusual sounds or dashboard indicators. Leaders who can inspire an ownership mentality among their employees are less likely to confront employees content to perform at the bare minimum level or tempted to cut corners.

Collectively, these reinforcing mechanisms should create a culture in which ethical practices define the firm and its employees rather than being imposed on them.

Problems and Problem Cases

1. You are a middle manager with responsibility over a staff of 16 workers. One of your workers is six months pregnant. Over the last month, she has missed work an average of two days a week and seems to be frequently distracted at work. You are concerned about her welfare and about her work performance, but are unsure what to do. What do the Guidelines for Ethical Decision Making suggest you do first?

2. You are an outside director of Crowler Inc., a manufacturer of kitchen and bathroom fixtures such as faucets, shower heads, and shower doors. Crowler has 29,000 employees worldwide, including 18,000 manufacturing employees in the United States, Canada, and Mexico. Its headquarters is in Eden Prairie, Minnesota. The CEO has proposed that Crowler increase its manufacturing capacity by adding a large facility to manufacture kitchen faucets, thereby increasing manufacturing employment by 3,000 workers. The board of directors is considering whether Crowler should expand its manufacturing facility in Brownsville, Texas; open a new factory in Indonesia; or close the Brownsville facility and move its current operations and the new operations to Indonesia. Using the Guidelines for Ethical Decision Making, what do you want to know before you make a decision?

3. You are a debt collections officer for a credit card issuer, NationalOne Corporation. NationalOne generates

73 percent of its profits from credit card fees and interest charged to consumers with annual incomes between $15,000 and $125,000. NationalOne's business model is to charge its credit card customers a low initial interest rate of 10 percent and a nominal annual fee of $10. If a customer defaults on one payment, however, the interest rate jumps to 22 percent, and the annual fee to $100. In the course of collecting debts for NationalOne, you have noticed that once the typical customer defaults, she is able to pay about 50 percent of the original debt had the interest rate and annual fee not changed. NationalOne's policy is not to accept anything less than 100 percent of the amount of the debt until the debtor has been in default for at least two years, by which time you find the customers typically can pay only about 10 percent of the now much larger debt. Many customers threaten to file and do file for bankruptcy protection. Would a rights theorist suggest any changes in NationalOne's policies? Would a profit maximizer suggest changes?

4. When is it appropriate to give a job applicant, employee, associate, colleague, or partner a second chance? Consider the following situations:

a. A manager is very effective in getting maximum efforts and results from her staff. However, the staff complains about suffering continual verbal abuse from the manager, including receiving belittling comments both privately and in public. Should her employer fire the manager or seek to rehabilitate her?

b. An employee is a recovering cocaine addict. Since successfully completing rehabilitation, he has received a college degree and been drug-free for three years. Would you hire him?

c. Donald Sterling, co-owner of the Los Angeles Clippers, a team in the National Basketball Association, made racist remarks in a private conversation that was recorded secretly by his girlfriend. Should the other NBA owners have attempted to oust him from team ownership?

d. Jerry Sandusky, a coach for the Penn State football program, was observed engaging in same-sex relations with a youth attending his program for underprivileged youths. In 2012, he was convicted of 52 counts of sexual abuse of young boys over a 15-year period. Should Penn State have fired him as a coach when it had first notice of one instance of abuse, or should it have attempted to rehabilitate him? After the full extent of his crimes have become known, would it be appropriate for Penn State or any other employer to hire him for a position in which he has contact with young boys? Are there jobs for which you would hire him? Why or why not?

5. Marigold Dairy Corporation sells milk products, including powdered milk formula for infants. Marigold hopes to increase sales of its powdered milk formula in Liberia and other African nations where mothers are often malnourished due to drought and civil war. Marigold's marketing department has created a marketing plan to convince mothers and expectant mothers not to breastfeed their babies and to, instead, use Marigold formula. Doctors generally favor breastfeeding as beneficial to mothers (it helps the uterus return to normal size), to babies (it is nutritious and strengthens the bonds between the infant and the mother), and to families (it is inexpensive). Marigold's marketing plan stresses the good nutrition of its formula and the convenience to parents of using it, including not having to breastfeed.

You are the senior vice president of marketing for Marigold. Do you approve this marketing plan? What would a rights theorist do? What would a utilitarian do? What would a profit maximizer do?

6. During World War II, the insecticide DDT was used successfully to halt a typhus epidemic spread by lice and to control mosquitoes and flies. After World War II, it was used extensively to control agricultural and household pests. Today, DDT may not be used legally in the United States and most other countries. Although DDT has a rather low immediate toxicity to humans and other vertebrates, it becomes concentrated in fatty tissues of the body. In addition, it degrades slowly, remaining toxic in the soil for years after its application. But there has never been any credible evidence that this residue has caused any harm. Even so, DDT has been blamed for the near extinction of bald eagles, whose population has increased greatly since DDT was banned, although evidence tends to point to oil, lead, mercury, stress from noise, and other factors as the likely causes.

In 2013, more than 2,469 people in the United States were infected by and 119 people killed after contracting West Nile virus, which is carried to humans by mosquitoes. CDC director Julie Gerberding called West Nile virus an "emerging, infectious disease epidemic" that could be spread all the way to the Pacific Coast by birds and mosquitoes. Pesticides such as malathion, resmethrin, and sumithrin can be effective in killing mosquitoes but are significantly limited because they do not stay in the environment after spraying. In Mozambique, indoor spraying of DDT has caused malaria rates to drop 88 percent among children.

As an executive for Eartho Chemical Company, you have been asked by Eartho's CEO to study whether Eartho should resume the manufacture of DDT. What would a utilitarian decide? What would a profit maximizer do?

7. *This American Life* is an American Public Media radio program conceived, produced, written, and performed by Ira Glass. In 2012, Episode 454, "Mr. Daisey and the Apple Factory," chronicled the investigation of Apple's Foxconn factory in China by author and monologist Mike Daisey. The episode ran portions of Daisey's monologue that detailed Apple's exploitation of Chinese workers. The episode was the most downloaded episode in the show's history. Less than two months later, Ira Glass and his staff discovered that Daisey had fabricated the claim that the plant guards had guns and exaggerated the number of underage workers with whom he met. Daisey also falsely represented that a man with a mangled hand was injured at Foxconn making iPads and that Daisey's iPad was the first one the man ever saw in operation. What did Ira Glass do with the new information? What would you have done?

8. Jordan Belfort founded Stratton Oakmont, a brokerage firm that focused on selling very risky penny stocks—stocks selling at very low prices—to investors. Belfort encouraged his brokers to use high-pressure tactics to sell the stocks. Belfort paid his brokers handsomely, with commissions reaching 25 percent of the purchase price. As a result, many Stratton Oakmont brokers were able to improve their lives and support their families. Many of the stocks peddled by the brokers were investments in small companies with little chance of becoming profitable. Some of the investors were pressured into buying more stock than they should have purchased, considering their levels of wealth and other security holdings. The investors could have insisted on receiving more information about the stocks before purchasing them. However, the investors' desires to make a large, quick profit deterred them from taking steps to protect themselves. Assess the ethical behavior of both the brokers and the investors.

9. In 2007, NFL commissioner Roger Goodell determined that the New England Patriots and its head coach, Bill Belichick, had violated NFL rules by videotaping opposing teams' sideline signals during games. Goodell docked the Patriots a 2008 first-round draft pick, and he fined Belichick $500,000 and the team $250,000. In 2008, Goodell interviewed the Patriots' employee who had done the videotaping and concluded that the employee's information was consistent with the behavior for which the Patriots and Belichick had been disciplined in 2007. Therefore, Goodell termed the matter over and said it was not necessary to discipline further the Patriots or Belichick. Immediately thereafter, Arlen Specter, a U.S. senator from Pennsylvania, called the NFL investigation "neither objective nor adequate." Specter stated, "If the commissioner doesn't move for an independent investigation, . . . depending on the public reaction, I may ask the Senate Judiciary Committee to hold hearings on the NFL antitrust exemption." Specter further stated that Goodell has made "ridiculous" assertions that wouldn't fly "in kindergarten." The senator said Goodell was caught in an "apparent conflict of interest" because the NFL doesn't want the public to lose confidence in the league's integrity. Terming the videotaping of opposing teams' signals a form of cheating equivalent to steroid use, Specter called for an independent investigation similar to the 2007 Mitchell Report on performance-enhancing drugs in baseball.

   Can you identify the fallacies in Senator Specter's arguments?

10. You are hired as a corporate accountant for Ryco Industries, a public company with shares traded on the New York Stock Exchange. The company has enjoyed consistently higher earnings each quarter, meeting or exceeding the expectations of Wall Street analysts every quarter for the past seven years. Soon after being hired, you discover a "reserve" account in the accounting records. Your inquiry shows that the account is designed to accumulate earnings deficiencies or excesses, that is, to permit Ryco to adjust its earnings each quarter such that earnings not increase too little or too much. You bring your findings to the attention of Ryco's chief accounting officer, who tells you that the account merely allows Ryco to smooth or manage its earnings, something that Wall Street analysts want to see. If earnings fluctuated, she explains, analysts would make less optimistic estimates about the prospects of Ryco, and its stock price would take a hit. The CAO tells you, "Look, we're just doing this to avoid getting hammered in the stock market. Every company does this. And we're not making up earnings. When actual earnings are too high, we just withhold recognizing some of those earnings until we need them in the future. When actual earnings are too low, we know we'll have better quarters in the future from which we can borrow earnings now. It all evens out."

    Can you identify the critical thinking errors and the characteristics of poor decision making that the CAO is exhibiting? Create a plan that will help you resist the CAO's request for you to continue to manage earnings as Ryco has done in the past.

11. You have been a director of sales at Privation Insurance Company for the last five years. Next week, you will be promoted to the position of vice president of sales, leading a staff of 35 sales professionals. Your immediate superior is the senior vice president of marketing and sales. What plan do you adopt for ethically leading your 35-person staff in your new position? List five things you'll do to lead your staff ethically.

Crimes and Torts

Criminal Law and Procedure

Nicolai Caymen worked as a desk clerk at a hotel in Ketchikan, Alaska. After a woman called a Ketchikan business supply store and complained that the store had charged her credit card for a laptop computer she did not purchase, the store discovered that Caymen had used a credit card in placing a telephone order for the laptop and that when he picked up the computer, the store clerk had not asked for identification. Store personnel then contacted the Ketchikan police department to report the incident and to pass along information, acquired from other stores, indicating that Caymen may have attempted similar credit card fraud elsewhere.

In order to look for the laptop and other evidence of credit card fraud, the police obtained a search warrant for the house where Caymen rented a room. Caymen, who was present while his room was searched, denied the allegation that he had used someone else's credit card to acquire the laptop. Instead, he stated that he had bought it with his own credit card. During the search, the police found the laptop and a tower computer. It was later determined that Caymen had rented the tower computer from a store but had never made any of the required payments. In Caymen's wallet, which the police examined in connection with the search of his room, the officers found receipts containing the names and credit card information of guests who had stayed at the hotel where Caymen was employed.

The police seized the laptop and contacted the store where Caymen had acquired it to ask whether officers could examine the laptop's hard drive before they returned the computer to the store. The store's owner consented. In examining the laptop's hard drive for evidence of credit card fraud, the police found evidence indicating Caymen's probable commission of federal crimes unrelated to credit card fraud. The police then temporarily suspended their search of the hard drive and obtained another search warrant because they had probable cause to believe that Caymen had committed federal offenses. Under that search warrant, officers checked the hard drives and storage media from the laptop and tower computers and found further evidence pertaining to the federal crimes.

Caymen was prosecuted in state court for credit card fraud and was indicted in federal court for the separate federal offenses. In the federal proceeding, he asked the court to suppress (i.e., rule inadmissible) the evidence obtained by the police in their examinations of the hard drives of the laptop and tower computers. Caymen based his suppression request on this multipart theory: that the police had no valid warrant for their initial look at the laptop's hard drive; that in the absence of a valid warrant, his consent (rather than the store owner's) was needed to justify a search of the laptop's hard drive; that the evidence obtained during the initial examination of the laptop's hard drive was the result of an unconstitutional search and was therefore inadmissible; and that the evidence obtained in the later examinations of the hard drives of the laptop and tower computers amounted to inadmissible "fruit of the poisonous tree."

As you read Chapter 5, consider these questions:

- On what constitutional provision was Caymen basing his challenge to the validity of the searches conducted by the police?

- Must law enforcement officers always have a warrant before they conduct a search, or are warrantless searches sometimes permissible? If warrantless searches are sometimes permissible, when?

- What is the usual remedy when law enforcement officers conduct an unconstitutional search?
- Did Caymen succeed with his challenge to the validity of the searches conducted by the police? Why or why not?
- What if a guilty person goes free as a result of a court's ruling that he was subjected to an unconstitutional search by law enforcement officers? From an ethical perspective, how would *utilitarians* view that outcome? What about *rights theorists*?

LO LEARNING OBJECTIVES

After studying this chapter, you should be able to:

5-1 Describe the difference between a felony and a misdemeanor.

5-2 Explain why the First Amendment may sometimes serve as a defense to criminal liability.

5-3 Identify the constitutional provisions at issue when a criminal law is challenged as being excessively vague.

5-4 Identify the standard of proof that the government must meet in a criminal prosecution, as well as the constitutional sources of that requirement.

5-5 Identify the major steps in a criminal prosecution.

5-6 Describe the basic protections afforded by the Fourth, Fifth, and Sixth Amendments.

5-7 Describe major exceptions to the Fourth Amendment's usual preference that the government have a warrant before conducting a search.

5-8 Explain what the exclusionary rule is.

5-9 List the components of the *Miranda* warnings and state when law enforcement officers must give those warnings.

5-10 Describe the major elements that must be proven in order to establish a violation of the Computer Fraud and Abuse Act.

THE LIST FEATURES FAMILIAR corporate names: Enron, Arthur Andersen, WorldCom, Adelphia, ImClone, Volkswagen, Wells Fargo, and Tyco. Individuals such as Bernard Ebbers, John and Timothy Rigas, and Dennis Kozlowski also make the list. Don't forget about Bernie Madoff. These names sometimes dominated the business headlines during recent years, but not for reasons any corporation or executive would find desirable. Instead, they acquired the notoriety associated with widely publicized financial scandals, related civil litigation, and criminal prosecutions that were pursued by the government, seriously contemplated by prosecutors, or argued for by the public and political figures of varying stripes.

For instance, former WorldCom CEO Bernie Ebbers was sentenced to 25 years in prison for his role in an $11 billion accounting and securities fraud. The Rigases were sentenced to substantial prison terms because of their involvement in bank and securities fraud while serving as high-level executives at Adelphia. Kozlowski, convicted of financial wrongdoing in connection with his former

position as Tyco's CEO, also faced incarceration. Madoff received a 150-year prison sentence and extensive public scorn after being convicted of crimes associated with the Ponzi scheme through which he defrauded investors.

Criminal convictions because of financial wrongdoing led to the above-mentioned notoriety of certain individuals and the corporations with which they were affiliated, but other sorts of business-related activity may also result in criminal charges. In 2012, for instance, the oil company BP pleaded guilty to offenses connected with the Deepwater Horizon oil-drilling disaster that occurred off the Gulf Coast and caused the deaths of 11 persons as well as extensive environmental damage. A criminal fine of approximately $1.3 billion was imposed on BP, along with even more in civil penalties.

During recent years, the U.S. Department of Justice considered whether to file criminal charges against General Motors for allegedly misleading federal regulators regarding an ignition switch problem that led to crashes in which persons were injured or killed. Volkswagen pleaded guilty in

2017 to criminal charges in connection with its employees' scheme to install devices in vehicles so that the cars would receive false and deceptively positive results on government-required emissions tests. In 2019, Wells Fargo agreed to pay $3 billion to resolve the company's potential criminal and civil liability stemming from a decade-long practice of pressuring employees to meet unrealistic sales goals. That practice led over 5,000 employees to provide millions of accounts and products to customers under false pretenses, often by creating false records or misusing customers' identities. The BP, GM, Volkswagen, and Wells Fargo sagas also featured civil consequences because of regulatory penalties and lawsuits, but there seems little doubt that criminal charges or the possibility of them weighed especially heavily on the minds of those companies' executives and employees.

In an earlier edition of this text, the first paragraph of Chapter 5 noted the importance of studying criminal law as part of a business manager's education but conceded that "[w]hen one lists legal topics relevant to business, criminal law comes to mind less readily than contracts, torts, agency, corporations, and various other subjects dealt with in this text." That statement was written some 25 years ago. Given the media, public, and governmental attention devoted to recent corporate scandals, it might be argued that criminal law now comes to mind *more* readily than certain other subjects on the list of legal topics relevant to business. At the very least, events involving high-profile firms and executives have demonstrated that business managers create considerable risk for themselves and their firms if they ignore the criminal law or lack a working understanding of it.

Role of the Criminal Law

This century has witnessed society's increasing tendency to use the criminal law as a major device for controlling corporate behavior. Many regulatory statutes establish criminal and civil penalties for statutory violations. The criminal penalties often apply to individual employees as well as to their organizational employers.

Advocates of using the criminal law in this way typically argue that doing so achieves a deterrence level superior to that produced by damage awards and other civil remedies. Corporations may be inclined to treat damage awards as simply a business cost and to violate regulatory provisions when doing so makes economic sense. Criminal prosecutions, however, threaten corporations with the reputation-harming effect of a criminal conviction. In some cases, the criminal law allows society to penalize wrongdoing employees who would not be directly affected by a civil judgment against their employer. Moreover, by alerting private parties to a

violation that could also give rise to a civil lawsuit for damages, criminal prosecutions may increase the likelihood that a corporation will bear the full costs of its actions. Proponents of using criminal law against corporations may also point to its expressive function. In other words, in addition to offering higher penalties, the criminal law signals society's moral outrage in a way that a money judgment—even a multibillion-dollar one—cannot.

Our examination of the criminal law's role in today's business environment begins with consideration of the nature and essential components of the criminal law. Next, the chapter discusses procedural issues in criminal prosecutions and explains constitutional issues that may arise in such cases. The chapter then explores various problems encountered in applying the criminal law to the corporate setting.

Nature of Crimes

 LO5-1 Describe the difference between a felony and a misdemeanor.

Crimes are *public wrongs*—acts prohibited by the state or federal government. Criminal prosecutions are initiated by a prosecutor (an elected or appointed government employee) in the name of the state or the United States, whichever is appropriate. Persons convicted of crimes bear the stigma of a criminal conviction and face the punitive force of the criminal sanction, which may include incarceration.

Our legal system also contemplates noncriminal consequences for violations of legal duties. The next two chapters deal with *torts*, private wrongs for which the wrongdoer must pay money damages to compensate the harmed victim. In some tort cases, the court may also assess punitive damages in order to punish the wrongdoer. Only the criminal sanction, however, combines the threat to life or liberty with the stigma of conviction.

Crimes are typically classified as felonies or misdemeanors. A **felony** is a serious crime such as murder, sexual assault, arson, drug-dealing, or a theft or fraud offense of sufficient magnitude. Most felonies involve significant moral culpability on the offender's part. Felonies are punishable by lengthy confinement of the convicted offender to a penitentiary, as well as by a fine. A person convicted of a felony may experience other adverse consequences, such as disenfranchisement (loss of voting rights) and disqualification from the practice of certain professions (e.g., law or medicine). A **misdemeanor** is a lesser offense such as disorderly conduct or battery resulting in minor physical harm to the victim. Misdemeanor offenses usually involve less—sometimes much less—moral culpability than felony offenses. As such, misdemeanors are punishable by lesser fines or limited confinement in jail. Depending on their seriousness and potential for harm to the public, traffic violations are classified either as misdemeanors or as less serious infractions. Really only quasi-criminal, infractions usually are punishable by fines but not by confinement in jail.

Purpose of the Criminal Sanction

Disagreements about when the criminal sanction should be employed sometimes stem from a dispute over its purpose. Persons accepting the *utilitarian* view believe that prevention of socially undesirable behavior is the only proper purpose of criminal penalties. This prevention goal includes three major components: deterrence, rehabilitation, and incapacitation.

Deterrence theorists maintain that the threat or imposition of punishment deters the commission of crimes in two ways. The first, *specific deterrence*, occurs when punishment of an offender deters him from committing further crimes. The second, *general deterrence*, results when punishment of a wrongdoer deters other persons from committing similar offenses. Factors influencing the probable effectiveness of deterrence include the respective likelihoods that the crime will be detected, that detection will be followed by prosecution, and that prosecution will result in a conviction. The severity of the probable punishment also serves as a key factor.

A fundamental problem attending deterrence theories is that we cannot be certain whether deterrence works because we cannot determine reliably what the crime rate would be in the absence of punishment. Similarly, high levels of crime and recidivism (repeat offenses by previously punished offenders) may indicate only that sufficiently severe and certain criminal sanctions have not been employed, not that criminal sanctions in general cannot effectively deter. Deterrence theory's other major problem is its assumption that potential offenders are rational beings who consciously weigh the threat of punishment against the benefits derived from an offense. The threat of punishment, however, may not deter the commission of criminal offenses produced by irrational or unconscious drives. Additionally, deterrence theories presuppose that would-be offenders even know the law and its sanctions, a suspect notion at best.

Rehabilitation of convicted offenders—changing their attitudes or values so that they are not inclined to commit future offenses—serves as another way to prevent undesirable behavior. Rehabilitation was the dominant model of criminal law for much of this nation's history but was called into question in the 1970s and fell out of favor. Critics of rehabilitation commonly point to high rates of recidivism as evidence of the general failure of rehabilitation efforts to date.

Incapacitation of convicted offenders may also contribute to the goal of prevention. While incarcerated, offenders may also have much less ability to commit other crimes. This excludes crimes committed against other inmates and guards. It also ignores the downstream impacts of incarceration on families and communities.

Prevention is not the only asserted goal of the criminal sanction. Some persons see *retribution*—the infliction of deserved suffering on violators of society's most fundamental rules—as the central focus of criminal punishment. Under this theory, punishment satisfies community and individual desires for revenge and reinforces important social values.

As a general rule, state laws on criminal punishments seek to further equally the deterrence, rehabilitation, and incapacitation purposes just discussed. State statutes usually set forth ranges of sentences (e.g., minimum and maximum amounts of fines and imprisonment) for each crime established by law. The court sets the convicted offender's sentence within the appropriate range unless the court places the defendant on probation or otherwise non-carceral sentence.

Probation is effectively a conditional sentence that suspends the usual imprisonment and/or fine if the offender "toes the line" and meets other judicially imposed conditions for the period specified by the court. It is sometimes granted to first-time offenders and other convicted defendants deemed suitable candidates by the court. In deciding whether to order probation or an appropriate sentence within the statutory range, the court normally places considerable reliance on information contained in a presentence investigation conducted by the probation office.

Figure 5.1 explains how federal law approaches the proper determination of a convicted offender's punishment.

Figure 5.1 The Federal Sentencing Guidelines and the *Booker* Decision

The federal approach to sentencing closely resembled the typical state approach discussed in the text until the Federal Sentencing Guidelines took effect in 1987. The significantly different sentencing model contemplated by the Sentencing Guidelines was largely upended, however, by the U.S. Supreme Court's decision in *United States v. Booker*, 543 U.S. 220 (2005), and decisions that followed it. To understand *Booker*, one must first know how the Sentencing Guidelines operated for the approximately 20 years preceding the Supreme Court's decision.

In the Sentencing Reform Act of 1984, Congress created the U.S. Sentencing Commission and authorized it to develop the Sentencing Guidelines. Congress took this action to reduce judicial discretion in sentencing and to minimize disparities among sentences imposed on defendants who committed the same offenses. Although pre–Sentencing Guidelines statutes setting forth sentencing ranges for particular crimes generally remained on the books, the Sentencing Guidelines developed by the Sentencing Commission assumed a legally controlling status under provisions of the Sentencing Reform Act. The Guidelines contain a table with more than 40 levels of seriousness of offense. Where an offender's crime and corresponding sentence range are listed on the table depends on the offender's prior criminal history and on various factors associated with the offense. The Sentencing Reform Act established that federal courts were bound by the table and usually were required to sentence convicted defendants in accordance with the range set in the table for the crime at issue. However, if the court found the existence of certain additional circumstances to be present (such as a leadership role in a crime committed by more than one person or similar facts seeming to enhance the defendant's level of culpability), the Guidelines required the court to sentence the defendant to a harsher penalty than would otherwise have been the maximum under the Guidelines.

Many federal judges voiced displeasure with the Guidelines because their mandatory nature deprived judges of the sentencing discretion they believed they needed in order to do justice in individual cases. In another key effect, the Guidelines led to the imposition of more severe sentences than had previously been imposed. Although the prospect of probation for certain offenses was not eliminated, the Guidelines led to an increased use of incarceration of individuals convicted of serious crimes. (A special subset of rules known as the Organizational Sentencing Guidelines, discussed later in the chapter, pertains to the sentencing of organizations convicted of federal crimes.)

Approximately 20 years ago, questions began arising about the constitutionality of the Sentencing Guidelines. The questions focused on the cases in which the Guidelines effectively required—if the requisite additional circumstances were present—a sentence higher than what would otherwise have been the maximum called for by the Guidelines. These cases were troublesome because nearly always the additional circumstances triggering the enhanced sentence were identified by the trial judge on the basis of evidence submitted to him or her at a post-trial sentencing hearing. The jury, on the other hand, would have heard and seen only the evidence produced at the trial—evidence that went toward guilt and presumably the standard range of punishment, but not toward an enhanced punishment harsher than the usual maximum. All of this was problematic, critics contended, in view of criminal defendants' Sixth Amendment right to a jury trial.

In 2005, *United States v. Booker* provided the Supreme Court an opportunity to address the concerns raised by critics of the Guidelines. A jury had convicted Booker of the offense of possessing, with intent to distribute, at least 50 grams of crack cocaine. The evidence the jury heard at trial was to the effect that Booker possessed approximately 90 grams of crack. The Sentencing Guidelines called for a sentence of 20 to 22 years in prison for possessing at least 50 grams. However, evidence presented to the judge at the sentencing hearing indicated that Booker possessed some 650 grams. Possession of a much larger amount of crack than the amount for which he was convicted was a special circumstance that, under the Guidelines, necessitated a harsher sentence. Upon finding by a preponderance of the evidence that Booker possessed 650 grams (rather than the smaller quantity about which the jury heard evidence), the judge was required by the Guidelines to sentence Booker to at least 30 years in prison—even though the evidence presented to the jury would have justified a lesser sentence of 20 to 22 years. The judge imposed a 30-year sentence on Booker, who contended on appeal that the enhanced sentence required by the Guidelines violated his Sixth Amendment jury trial right.

In the *Booker* decision, the Supreme Court held that in view of the Sixth Amendment, any facts calling for the imposition of a sentence harsher than the usual maximum must be facts found by a jury rather than merely a judge (unless a jury has been validly waived by the defendant or the defendant agreed to the facts in a plea agreement). The Federal Sentencing Guidelines and the statute contemplating their creation were thus unconstitutional insofar as they mandated a sentence going beyond the usual maximum if a judge's factual findings supporting such a sentence were made on the basis of evidence that the jury had not heard. To remedy the constitutional defect, the Court determined it was necessary to excise certain Sentencing Reform Act sections that made the Sentencing Guidelines mandatory. The elimination of those statutory sections caused the Sentencing Guidelines to become *advisory* to judges as they make sentencing decisions. Judges must still consider what the Guidelines call for in regard to sentencing, but they are not required to impose the particular sentences specified in the Guidelines. The Court also stated in *Booker* that when a judge's sentencing decision is challenged on appeal, the governing standard will be one of reasonableness.

After *Booker*, lower courts were faced with determining what the "reasonableness" standard of review meant, as well as how far trial courts' discretion regarding the Guidelines really extended. In *Rita v. United States*, 551 U.S. 338 (2007), the Supreme Court held that it was permissible for courts of appeal to adopt and apply a presumption of reasonableness if the sentence imposed by the trial court fell within the range set by the Guidelines. *Gall v. United States*, 552 U.S. 38 (2007), made clear, however, that the converse was not true. The Court held there that courts of appeals cannot apply a presumption of unreasonableness to a sentence that departed from the range set by the Guidelines. Instead, according to *Gall*, consideration of the Guidelines is only "the starting point and the initial benchmark" for the trial judge as he or she makes an "individualized assessment" based on the facts and circumstances. Appellate courts are to give "due deference" to the trial judge's sentencing determinations, regardless of whether the sentence fell within or outside the Guidelines's range. In *Kimbrough v. United States*, 552 U.S. 85 (2007), a companion case to *Gall*, the Court underscored this standard of review and expressed disapproval of appellate court micro-management of trial judges' sentencing decisions. The Court also suggested in *Kimbrough*—and made explicit in *Spears v. United States*, 555 U.S. 261 (2009)—that considerable deference to the trial judge's sentencing determinations remains

appropriate even if it appears that the sentence departed from the Guidelines because of the judge's policy disagreement with the Guidelines.

Booker and its progeny have restored to trial judges most of the sentencing latitude they had prior to the Guidelines. This latitude is subject to two constraints: First, the sentence must be consistent with relevant *statutes* (as opposed to the now-advisory Guidelines), and second, the sentence must be based upon facts found by the jury. Whether judges actually use this discretion, or are instead "anchored" to the Guidelines' ranges, is an empirical question. As might be expected, it appears that as more time since *Booker* passes, judges seem willing to use more of their inherent discretion.

Essentials of Crime

To convict a defendant of a crime, the government ordinarily must (1) demonstrate that his alleged acts violated a criminal statute; (2) prove beyond a reasonable doubt that he committed those acts; and (3) prove that he had the capacity to form a criminal intent. Crimes are *statutory* offenses. A given behavior is not a crime unless Congress or a state legislature has criminalized it.[1]

Courts also carefully scrutinize, and narrowly construe, criminal statutes in an effort to make certain that they sweep in only those behaviors specifically prohibited by the relevant legislature. In *Sekhar v. United States*, which follows, the U.S. Supreme Court conducts such an examination of the Hobbs Act in order to determine whether the defendant's actions constituted extortion in violation of that federal statute.

---

[1]Infractions of a minor criminal or quasi-criminal nature (such as traffic offenses) are often established by city or county ordinances but will not be considered here. For discussion of ordinances as a type of law, see Chapter 1.

Sekhar v. United States   570 U.S. 729 (2013)

New York's Common Retirement Fund is an employee pension fund for the State of New York and its local governments. The State Comptroller chooses Common Retirement Fund investments. When the Comptroller decides to approve an investment, he issues a "Commitment."

Giridhar Sekhar was a managing partner of FA Technology Ventures (FATV). In 2009, the Comptroller's office was considering whether to invest in a fund managed by that firm. The office's general counsel recommended that the Comptroller decide not to invest in the FATV-managed fund. The Comptroller followed the recommendation, decided not to issue a Commitment, and notified an FATV partner about the decision. This partner had previously heard rumors that the general counsel was having an extramarital affair.

The general counsel then received a series of anonymous e-mails demanding that he recommend moving forward with the investment in the FATV-managed fund. The e-mails also threatened that if the general counsel did not so recommend, the sender would disclose information about his alleged affair to his wife, government officials, and the media. The general counsel contacted law enforcement, which traced some of the e-mails to Sekhar's home computer and other e-mails to FATV offices.

Sekhar was later indicted for attempted extortion in violation of the Hobbs Act, which subjects a person to criminal liability if he "in any way or degree obstructs, delays, or affects commerce or the movement of any article or commodity in commerce, by robbery or extortion or attempts or conspires so to do." 18 U.S.C. § 1951(a). The act defines extortion *to mean "the obtaining of property from another, with his consent, induced by wrongful use of actual or threatened force, violence, or fear, or under color of official right." 18 U.S.C. § 1951(b)(2). On the verdict form used at Sekhar's trial, the jury was asked to specify the property that Sekhar attempted to extort: (1) "the Commitment," (2) "the Comptroller's approval of the Commitment," or (3) "the General Counsel's recommendation to approve the Commitment." The jury chose only the third option in convicting Sekhar of attempted extortion.*

The U.S. Court of Appeals for the Second Circuit affirmed Sekhar's conviction. The Second Circuit held that the general counsel "had a property right in rendering sound legal advice to the Comptroller and, specifically, to recommend—free from threats—whether the Comptroller should issue a Commitment." In addition, the Second Circuit concluded that Sekhar not only attempted to deprive the general counsel of his "property right" but also "attempted to exercise that right by forcing the general counsel to make a recommendation determined by [Sekhar]." The U.S. Supreme Court agreed to review the case.

Scalia, Justice

We consider whether attempting to compel a person to recommend that his employer approve an investment constitutes "the obtaining of property from another" under 18 U.S.C. § 1951(b)(2). Whether viewed from the standpoint of the common law, the text and genesis of the statute at issue here, or the jurisprudence of this Court's prior cases, what was charged in this case was not extortion.

It is a settled principle of interpretation that, absent other indication, "Congress intends to incorporate the well-settled meaning of the common-law terms it uses." [Citation omitted.] Or as Justice Frankfurter colorfully put it [in a 1947 law journal article], "if a word is obviously transplanted from another legal source, whether the common law or other legislation, it brings the old soil with it."

The Hobbs Act punishes "extortion," one of the oldest crimes in our legal tradition. As far as is known, no case predating the Hobbs Act—English, federal, or state—ever identified conduct such as that charged here as extortionate. Extortion required the obtaining of items of value, typically cash, from the victim. It did not cover mere coercion to act, or to refrain from acting.

The text of the statute confirms that the alleged property here cannot be extorted. Enacted in 1946, the Hobbs Act defines its crime of "extortion" as "the *obtaining of property from another*, with his consent, induced by wrongful use of actual or threatened force, violence, or fear, or under color of official right." Obtaining property requires "not only the deprivation but also the acquisition of property." *Scheidler v. National Organization for Women, Inc.*, 537 U.S. 393, 404 (2003). That is, it requires that the victim part with his property, and that the extortionist "gain possession" of it. *Id.* at 403 n.8. The property extorted must therefore be *transferable*—that is, capable of passing from one person to another. The alleged property here lacks that defining feature.

The genesis of the Hobbs Act reinforces that conclusion. The Act was modeled after § 850 of the New York Penal Law (1909). Congress borrowed, nearly verbatim, the New York statute's definition of extortion. The New York statute contained, in addition to the felony crime of extortion, a . . . misdemeanor crime of coercion. Whereas the former required the criminal acquisition of property, the latter required merely the use of threats "to compel another person to do or to abstain from doing an act which such other person has a legal right to do or to abstain from doing" [quoting the New York statute]. Congress did not copy the coercion provision. The omission must have been deliberate, since it was perfectly clear that extortion did not include coercion. At the time of the borrowing (1946), New York courts had consistently held that the sort of *interference* with rights that occurred here was coercion.

And finally, this Court's own precedent similarly demands reversal of Sekhar's conviction. In *Scheidler*, we held that protesters did not commit extortion under the Hobbs Act, even though they "interfered with, disrupted, and in some instances completely deprived" abortion clinics of their ability to run their business. 537 U.S. at 404–05. We reasoned that the protesters may have deprived the clinics of an "alleged property right," but they did not pursue or receive "something of value from" the clinics that they could then "exercise, transfer, or sell" themselves. *Id.* at 405. This case is easier than *Scheidler*, where one might at least have said that physical occupation of property amounted to obtaining that property. The deprivation alleged here is far more abstract. *Scheidler* rested its decision, as we do, on the term "obtaining." The principle announced there—that a defendant must pursue something of value from the victim that can be exercised, transferred, or sold—applies with equal force here. Whether one considers the personal right at issue to be "property" in a broad sense or not, it certainly was not *obtainable property* under the Hobbs Act.

The government's shifting and imprecise characterization of the alleged property at issue betrays the weakness of its case. According to the jury's verdict form, the "property" that Sekhar attempted to extort was "the General Counsel's recommendation to approve the Commitment." But the government expends minuscule effort in defending that theory of conviction. And for good reason—to wit, our decision in *Cleveland v. United States*, 531 U.S. 12 (2000), which reversed a business owner's mail-fraud conviction for "obtaining money or property" through misrepresentations made in an application for a video-poker license issued by the State. We held that a "license" is not "property" while in a state's hands and so cannot be "obtained" from the state. Even less so can an employee's yet-to-be-issued recommendation be called obtainable property, and less so still a yet-to-be-issued recommendation that would merely approve (but not effect) a particular investment.

Hence the government's reliance on an alternative . . . description of the property. Instead of defending the jury's description, the government hinges its case on the general counsel's "intangible property right to give his disinterested legal opinion to his client free of improper outside interference" [quoting the government's brief]. But *what*, exactly, would Sekhar have obtained for himself? A right to give *his own* disinterested legal opinion to *his own* client free of improper interference? Or perhaps, a right to give *the general counsel's* disinterested legal opinion to *the general counsel's* client?

Either formulation sounds absurd, because it is. Clearly, Sekhar's goal was not to acquire the general counsel's "intangible property right to give disinterested legal advice." It was to force the general counsel to offer advice that accorded with Sekhar's wishes. But again, that is coercion, not extortion. No fluent speaker of English would say that Sekhar "*obtained and exercised* the general counsel's right to make a recommendation," any more than he would say that a person "*obtained and exercised* another's right to free speech." He would say that Sekhar "*forced* the general counsel to make a particular recommendation," just as he would say that a person "*forced* another to make a statement." Adopting the government's theory here would not only make nonsense of words, it would collapse the longstanding distinction between extortion and coercion and ignore Congress's choice to penalize one but not the other. That we cannot do.

Second Circuit decision reversed in favor of Sekhar.

Constitutional Limitations on Power to Criminalize Behavior

The U.S. Constitution prohibits *ex post facto* criminal laws. This means that a defendant's act must have been prohibited by statute at the time she committed it and that the penalty imposed must be the one provided for at the time of her offense. In *Peugh v. United States*, 569 U.S. 530 (2013), for example, the U.S. Supreme Court held that a defendant convicted of bank fraud should have been sentenced under the version of the Federal Sentencing Guidelines in effect when he committed the crime rather than under a later version that the lower courts used as the basis for imposing a more severe punishment than the earlier version would have permitted.

The Constitution places other limits on legislative power to criminalize behavior. If behavior is constitutionally protected, it cannot be deemed criminal. For example, the right of privacy held implicit in the Constitution caused the Supreme Court, in *Griswold v. Connecticut* (1965), to strike down state statutes that prohibited the use of contraceptive devices and the counseling or assisting of others in the use of such devices. This decision provided the constitutional basis for the Court's historic *Roe v. Wade* (1973) decision, which limited the states' power to criminalize abortions.

First Amendment

 LO5-2 Explain why the First Amendment may sometimes serve as a defense to criminal liability.

By prohibiting laws that unreasonably restrict freedom of speech, the First Amendment plays a major role in limiting governmental power to enact and enforce criminal laws. As explained in Chapter 3, the First Amendment protects a broad range of noncommercial speech, including expression of a political, literary, or artistic nature as well as speech that deals with economic, scientific, or ethical issues or with other matters of public interest or concern. The First Amendment protection for noncommercial speech is so substantial that it is called "full" protection.

The First Amendment may operate as a defense to a criminal prosecution concerning speech many persons would find offensive. For instance, in *United States v. Alvarez*, 567 U.S. 709 (2012), the Supreme Court struck down a portion of the Stolen Valor Act, a federal law that criminalized false statements made about earning a military medal. Although the defendant had lied repeatedly about having served in the military and earning a Purple Heart, the Court found the statute broadly applied to false statements made at any time, in any place, and to any person,

which conflicted with the First Amendment. In addition, the Court held in *United States v. Stevens,* 559 U.S. 460 (2010), that the First Amendment protected the defendant against criminal responsibility for having violated a statute that barred distribution of videos in which a cruel killing or maiming of an actual animal was depicted. (The First Amendment safeguarded the *speech* present in such videos notwithstanding its offensive character, but would not protect any defendant against criminal responsibility for violating a statute prohibiting the *conduct* of engaging in cruelty to animals.) But First Amendment protection, despite being very substantial, is not absolute. Consider *Holder v. Humanitarian Law Project*, 561 U.S. 1 (2010), in which the Supreme Court rejected a multipronged attack on the constitutionality of a federal statute that criminalized the furnishing of support to foreign groups the government has labeled as terrorist organizations. In upholding the statute, the Court held that it did not violate the First Amendment even as applied to persons who wished to donate money to support and encourage the humanitarian, lawful, and nonviolent activities of those organizations (as opposed to their activities amounting to terrorism). Although donating money in support of social causes may be viewed as speech, the Court concluded that the statute did not violate the First Amendment rights of supporters of the organizations' nonterrorist activities because the prohibition of even those supporters' donations was suitably tailored to the furtherance of the vital government interest in combating terrorism.

Commercial speech, on the other hand, receives a less substantial First Amendment shield known as "intermediate" protection. Does a speaker or writer with a profit motive (e.g., the author who hopes to make money on her book) therefore receive only intermediate First Amendment protection? No, as a general rule, because the mere presence of a profit motive does not keep expression from being fully protected noncommercial speech. Moreover, the commercial speech designation is usually reserved for what the Supreme Court has termed "speech that does no more than propose a commercial transaction." The best example of commercial speech is an advertisement for a product, service, or business.

Despite receiving less-than-full protection, commercial speech is far from a First Amendment outcast. Recent Supreme Court decisions, as noted in Chapter 3, have effectively raised commercial speech's intermediate protection to a level near that of full protection. Therefore, regardless of whether it is full or intermediate in strength, the First Amendment protection extended to expression means that governmental attempts to hold persons criminally liable for the content of their written or spoken statements are often unconstitutional.

Some speech falls outside the First Amendment umbrella, however. In a long line of cases, the Supreme Court has established that *obscene* expression receives no First Amendment protection. Purveyors of obscene books, movies, and other similar works may therefore be criminally convicted of violating an obscenity statute even though it is the works' content (i.e., the speech) that furnishes the basis for the conviction. Expression is obscene only if the government proves each element of the controlling obscenity test, which the Supreme Court established in *Miller v. California* (1973):

> (a) [That] the average person, applying contemporary community standards, would find that the work, taken as a whole, appeals to the prurient interest; (b) [that] the work depicts or describes, in a patently offensive way, [explicit] sexual conduct specifically defined by the applicable state law; and (c) [that] the work, taken as a whole, lacks serious literary, artistic, political, or scientific value.

If any of the three elements is not proven, the work is not obscene; instead, it receives First Amendment protection.

The *Miller* test's final element is the one most likely to derail the government's obscenity case against a defendant. Books, movies, and other materials that contain explicit sexual content are not obscene if they have serious literary, artistic, political, or scientific value—and they generally do. In view of the *Miller* test's final element, moreover, certain publications that might fairly be regarded as "pornographic" are likely to escape being classified as obscene.

Although nonobscene expression carries First Amendment protection, Supreme Court decisions have allowed the government limited latitude to regulate *indecent* speech in order to protect minors from being exposed to such material. Indecent expression contains considerable sexual content but stops short of being obscene, often because of the presence of serious literary, artistic, political, or scientific value (for adults, at least). Assume that a state statute requires magazines available for sale at a store to be located behind a store counter, rather than on an unattended display rack, if the magazines feature nudity and sexual content and the store is open to minors. This statute primarily restricts indecent expression because most magazines contemplated by the law are unlikely to be obscene. If the statute is challenged on First Amendment grounds and the court concludes that it is narrowly tailored to further the protection-of-minors purpose, it will survive First Amendment scrutiny. A law that restricts too much expression suitable for adults, however, will violate the First Amendment even if the government's aim was to safeguard minors.

Recent years have witnessed decisions in which the Supreme Court determined the First Amendment fate of statutes designed to protect minors against online exposure to material that is indecent though not obscene.

In *Reno v. American Civil Liberties Union*, 521 U.S. 844 (1997), the Court struck down most of the Communications Decency Act of 1996 (CDA), which sought to ban Internet distribution of indecent material in a manner that would make the material accessible by minors. The Court reasoned that notwithstanding the statute's protection-of-minors purpose, the sweeping nature of the ban on indecent material extended too far into the realm of expression that adults were entitled to receive. In *Ashcroft v. American Civil Liberties Union*, 542 U.S. 665 (2004), the Court considered the constitutionality of the Child Online Protection Act (COPA), the next congressional attempt to restrict minors' exposure to indecent material in online contexts. According to the Court, the same problem that plagued the CDA—restricting too much expression that adults were entitled to communicate and receive—doomed the COPA to a determination of unconstitutionality.

As noted above, much of the material often referred to as pornography would not be considered obscene under the *Miller* test and thus would normally carry First Amendment protection. Safeguarding-of-minors concerns have proven critical, however, to the very different legal treatment extended to child pornography—sexually explicit visual depictions of actual minors (as opposed to similar depictions of adults). Because of the obvious dangers and harms that child pornography poses for minors, child pornography has long been held to fall outside the First Amendment's protective umbrella. Therefore, the Supreme Court has held that there is no First Amendment bar to criminal prosecutions for purveying or possessing child pornography.

LO5-3 Identify the constitutional provisions at issue when a criminal law is challenged as being excessively vague.

Due Process Clauses In addition to limiting the sorts of behavior that may be made criminal, the Constitution limits the manner in which behavior may be criminalized. The Due Process Clauses of the Fifth and Fourteenth Amendments (discussed in Chapter 3) require that criminal statutes define the prohibited behavior precisely enough to enable law enforcement officers and ordinary members of the public to understand which behavior violates the law. Statutes that fail to provide such fair notice may be challenged as unconstitutionally vague.

For example, in *Skilling v. United States*, 561 U.S. 358 (2010), a defendant brought a vagueness challenge to a federal statute he was convicted of violating. The statute made it a crime to deprive another person of the intangible right to the defendant's "honest services." To avoid the potential vagueness problem suggested by the statute's "honest services" language, the Supreme Court adopted a limited construction of the statute. The Court ruled that for a violation of the honest services law to have occurred, the defendant's actions must have involved the offering, payment, or receipt of bribes or kickbacks. Whatever other misdeeds Skilling—an Enron executive—committed or may have committed, none of them involved bribes or kickbacks. For further discussion of the importance of clarity in criminal statutes, see *Shaw v. United States*, which appears later in the chapter.

Equal Protection Clause The Fourteenth Amendment's Equal Protection Clause (also discussed in Chapter 3) prohibits criminal statutes that discriminatorily treat certain persons of the same class or arbitrarily discriminate among different classes of persons. Legislatures usually are extended considerable latitude in making statutory classifications if the classifications have a rational basis. "Suspect" classifications, such as those based on race, are subjected to much closer judicial scrutiny, however.

Eighth Amendment Finally, the Constitution limits the type of punishment imposed on convicted offenders. The Eighth Amendment forbids cruel and unusual punishments. This prohibition furnishes, for example, the constitutional basis for judicial decisions establishing limits on imposition of the death penalty. Although various Supreme Court cases indicate that the Eighth Amendment may bar a sentence whose harshness is disproportionate to the seriousness of the defendant's offense, the Court has signaled that any Eighth Amendment concerns along these lines are unlikely to be triggered unless the sentence–crime disproportionality is exceedingly gross.

Proof beyond a Reasonable Doubt

 LO5-4 Identify the standard of proof that the government must meet in a criminal prosecution, as well as the constitutional sources of that requirement.

The serious matters at stake in a criminal case—the life and liberty of the accused—justify our legal system's placement of significant limits on the government's power to convict a person of a crime. A fundamental safeguard is the *presumption of innocence*; defendants in criminal cases are presumed innocent until proven guilty. The Due Process Clauses require the government to overcome this presumption by proving beyond a reasonable doubt every element of the offense charged against the defendant.[2] Requiring the government to meet this high burden of proof minimizes the risk of erroneous criminal convictions.

Defendant's Criminal Intent and Capacity Most serious crimes require *mens rea*, or criminal intent, as an element. The level of fault required for a criminal violation depends on the wording of the relevant statute. Many criminal statutes require proof of intentional wrongdoing. Others impose liability for reckless conduct or, in rare instances, mere negligence. In the criminal context, recklessness generally means that the accused consciously disregarded a substantial risk that the harm prohibited by the statute would result from her actions. Negligence means that the accused failed to perceive a substantial risk of harm that a reasonable person would have perceived. As a general rule, negligent behavior is left to the civil justice system rather than being criminalized. *Shaw v. United States*, which follows shortly, addresses criminal intent and related issues.

In *Arthur Andersen LLP v. United States*, 544 U.S. 696 (2005), the Supreme Court issued a reminder regarding the importance of the element of criminal intent. The Andersen firm, which provided auditing and consulting services to Enron prior to its collapse in 2001, had been convicted on obstruction-of-justice charges dealing with destruction of Enron-related documents. The Supreme Court overturned the conviction because the trial judge's instructions to the jury had not sufficiently required the jury to determine whether criminal intent was present when Andersen employees, acting at least in part under the firm's preexisting document-retention policy, destroyed documents that would have been relevant to legal proceedings connected with the Enron debacle.

Criminal intent may be inferred from an accused's behavior because a person is normally held to have intended the natural and probable consequences of her acts. The intent requirement furthers the criminal law's general goal of punishing conscious wrongdoers. Accordingly, proof that the defendant had the capacity to form the required intent is a traditional prerequisite of criminal responsibility. The criminal law recognizes three general types of incapacity: *intoxication*, *infancy*, and *insanity*.

Although it is not a complete defense to criminal liability, voluntary intoxication may sometimes diminish the degree of a defendant's responsibility. For example, many

---

[2]The beyond-a-reasonable-doubt standard required of the government in criminal cases contemplates a stronger and more convincing showing than that required of plaintiffs in civil cases. As explained in Chapter 2, plaintiffs in civil cases need only prove the elements of their claims by a preponderance of the evidence.

first-degree murder statutes require proof of *premeditation*, a conscious decision to kill. One who kills while highly intoxicated may be incapable of premeditation—meaning that he would not be guilty of first-degree murder. He may be convicted, however, of another homicide offense that does not require proof of premeditation.

The criminal law historically presumed that children younger than 14 years of age ("infants," for legal purposes) could not form a criminal intent. Today, most states treat juvenile offenders below a certain statutory age—usually 16 or 17—differently from adult offenders, with special juvenile court systems and separate detention facilities. Current juvenile law emphasizes rehabilitation rather than capacity issues. Repeat offenders or offenders charged with

very serious offenses, however, may sometimes be treated as adults.

An accused's insanity at the time the charged act was committed may constitute a complete defense. This possible effect of insanity has generated public dissatisfaction. The controlling legal test for whether a defendant was insane varies among court systems. The details of the possible tests are beyond the scope of this text. Suffice it to say that as applied by courts, the tests make it a rare case in which the defendant succeeds with an insanity defense.

Shaw v. United States, which follows, deals with criminal intent issues and illustrates the careful attention courts pay to the particular elements required by a criminal statute.

Shaw v. United States   137 S. Ct. 462 (2016)

Lawrence Shaw obtained the identifying numbers of a Bank of America account belonging to a bank customer, Stanley Hsu. Shaw used those numbers, as well as other related information, to transfer funds from Hsu's account to other accounts at different financial institutions. Shaw then obtained, from those other accounts, the funds he had transferred from Hsu's Bank of America account.

A federal statute makes it a crime "knowingly [to] execut[e] a scheme . . . to defraud a financial institution." 18 U.S.C. § 1344(1). A federally insured bank such as Bank of America would be an example of a financial institution contemplated by this statute. A federal district court convicted Shaw of violating 18 U.S.C. § 1344(1). The U.S. Court of Appeals for the Ninth Circuit affirmed his conviction. In his petition for certiorari, Shaw argued that the words "scheme . . . to defraud a financial institution" require the government to prove that the defendant had "a specific intent not only to deceive, but also to cheat, a bank," rather than "a non-bank third party." The U.S. Supreme Court granted review.

Breyer, Justice

Shaw argues that § 1344 does not apply to him because he intended to cheat only a bank depositor, not a bank. We do not accept his arguments.

Section 1344 makes it a crime:

knowingly [to] execut[e] a scheme . . .

(1) to defraud a financial institution; or

(2) to obtain any of the moneys, funds, credits, assets, securities, or other property owned by, or under the custody or control of, a financial institution, by means of false or fraudulent pretenses, representations, or promises.

Shaw makes several related arguments in favor of his basic claim, namely, that the statute does not cover schemes to deprive a bank of customer deposits.

First, he [argues in his brief] that subsection (1) requires "an intent to wrong a victim bank [a 'financial institution'] in its property rights." He adds that the property he took, money in Hsu's bank account, belonged to Hsu, the bank's customer, and that Hsu is not a "financial institution." Hence, [according to this argument,] Shaw's scheme was one "designed" to

obtain only "a bank customer's property," not "a bank's own property."

The basic flaw in this argument lies in the fact that the bank, too, had property rights in Hsu's bank account. When a customer deposits funds, the bank ordinarily becomes the owner of the funds and consequently has the right to use the funds as a source of loans that help the bank earn profits (though the customer retains the right to withdraw funds). Sometimes, the contract between the customer and the bank provides that the customer retains ownership of the funds and the bank merely assumes possession. But even then the bank is entitled to possess the deposited funds against all the world [except for the customer with which the bank contracted]. This right, too, is a property right.

Thus, Shaw's scheme to cheat Hsu was also a scheme to deprive the bank of certain bank property rights. Hence, for purposes of the bank fraud statute, a scheme fraudulently to obtain funds from a bank depositor's account normally is also a scheme fraudulently to obtain property from a "financial institution," at least where, as here, the defendant knew that the bank held the deposits, the funds obtained came from the deposit account, and the defendant misled the bank in order to obtain those funds.

Second, Shaw says he did not intend to cause the bank financial harm. Indeed, the parties appear to agree that, due to standard banking practices in place at the time of the fraud, no bank involved in the scheme ultimately suffered any monetary loss. But the statute, while insisting upon "a scheme to defraud," demands neither a showing of ultimate financial loss nor a showing of intent to cause financial loss. Many years ago Judge Learned Hand pointed out that "[a] man is none the less cheated out of his property, when he is induced to part with it by fraud," even if "he gets a quid pro quo of equal value." *United States v. Rowe*, 56 F.2d 747, 749 (2d Cir. 1932). That is because "[i]t may be impossible to measure his loss by the gross scales available to a court, but he has suffered a wrong; he has lost," for example, "his chance to bargain with the facts before him." *Id. See* O. Holmes, *The Common Law* 132 (1881) ("[A] man is liable to an action for deceit if he makes a false representation to another, knowing it to be false, but intending that the other should believe and act upon it"); *Neder v. United States*, 527 U.S. 1 (1999) (bank fraud statute's definition of fraud reflects the common law).

It is consequently not surprising that, when interpreting the analogous mail fraud statute, we have held it "sufficient" that the victim (here, the bank) be "deprived of its right" to use of the property, even if it ultimately did not suffer unreimbursed loss. [Citation omitted.] Lower courts have explained that, where cash is taken from a bank "but the bank [is] fully insured[,] [t]he theft [is] complete when the cash [i]s taken; the fact that the bank ha[s] a contract with an insurance company enabling it to shift the loss to that company [is] immaterial." [Citation omitted.] We have found no case from this Court interpreting the bank fraud statute as requiring that the victim bank ultimately suffer financial harm, or that the defendant intend that the victim bank suffer such harm.

Third, Shaw appears to argue that, whatever the true state of property law, he did not know that the bank had a property interest in Hsu's account; hence he could not have intended to cheat the bank of its property. Shaw did know, however, that the bank possessed Hsu's account. He did make false statements to the bank. He did correctly believe that those false statements would lead the bank to release from that account funds that ultimately and wrongfully ended up in Shaw's pocket. And the bank did in fact possess a property interest in the account. These facts are sufficient to show that Shaw knew he was entering into a scheme to defraud the bank even if he was not aware of the niceties of bank-related property law. To require more, i.e., to require actual knowledge of those bank-related property-law niceties, would free (or convict) equally culpable defendants depending upon their property-law expertise—an arbitrary result.

We have found no case from this Court requiring legal knowledge of the kind Shaw suggests he lacked. But we have found cases in roughly similar fraud-related contexts where this Court has asked only whether the targeted property was in fact property in the hands of the victim, not whether the defendant knew that the law would characterize the items at issue as "property." *See Pasquantino v. United States*, 544 U.S. 544 (2005) (Canada's right to uncollected excise taxes on imported liquor counted as "property" for purposes of the wire fraud statute); *Carpenter v. United States*, 484 U.S. 19 (1987) (a newspaper's interest in the confidentiality of the contents and timing of a news column counted as property for the purposes of the mail and wire fraud statutes). We conclude that the legal ignorance that Shaw claims here is no defense to criminal prosecution for bank fraud.

Fourth, Shaw argues that the bank fraud statute requires the Government to prove more than his simple knowledge that he would likely harm the bank's property interest; in his view, the government must prove that such was his purpose. Shaw adds that his purpose was to take money from Hsu; taking property from the bank was not his purpose.

But the statute itself makes criminal the "knowin[g] execut[ion of] a scheme . . . to defraud." To hold that something other than knowledge is required would assume that Congress intended to distinguish, in respect to states of mind, between (1) the fraudulent scheme, and (2) its fraudulent elements. Why would Congress wish to do so? Shaw refers us to a number of cases involving fraud against the government and points to language in those cases suggesting that the relevant statutes required that the defendant's purpose be to harm the statutorily protected target and not a third party. [However,] crimes of fraud targeting the government [fall within] an area of the law with its own special rules and protections. We have found no relevant authority in the area of mail fraud, wire fraud, financial frauds, or the like supporting Shaw's view.

[Fifth], Shaw asks us to apply the rule of lenity. We have said that the rule applies if "at the end of the process of construing what Congress has expressed," there is "a grievous ambiguity or uncertainty in the statute." [Citations omitted.] The statute is clear enough that we need not rely on the rule of lenity. As we have said, a deposit account at a bank counts as bank property for purposes of subsection (1). The defendant, in circumstances such as those present here, need not know that the deposit account is, as a legal matter, characterized as bank property. Moreover, in those circumstances, the government need not prove that the defendant intended that the bank ultimately suffer monetary loss. Finally, the statute as applied here requires a state of mind equivalent to knowledge, not purpose.

Judgment of Ninth Circuit vacated; case remanded for further proceedings.

Criminal Procedure

Criminal Prosecutions: An Overview

LO5-5 Identify the major steps in a criminal prosecution.

Persons arrested for allegedly committing a crime are taken to the police station and booked. *Booking* is an administrative procedure for recording the suspect's arrest. In some states, temporary release on bail may be available at this stage. After booking, the police file an arrest report with the prosecutor, who decides whether to charge the suspect with an offense. If she decides to prosecute, the prosecutor prepares a complaint identifying the accused and detailing the charges. Most states require that arrested suspects be taken promptly before a magistrate or other judicial officer (such as a justice of the peace or judge whose court is of limited jurisdiction) for an *initial appearance*. During this appearance, the magistrate informs the accused of the charges and outlines the accused's constitutional rights. In misdemeanor cases in which the accused pleads guilty, the sentence may be (but need not be) imposed without a later hearing. If the accused pleads not guilty to a misdemeanor charge, the case is set for trial. In felony cases, as well as misdemeanor cases in which the accused pleads not guilty, the magistrate sets the amount of bail.

In many states, defendants in felony cases are protected against unjustified prosecutions by an additional procedural step, the *preliminary hearing*. The prosecutor must introduce enough evidence at this hearing to persuade a magistrate that there is *probable cause* to believe the accused committed a felony.[3] If persuaded that probable cause exists, the magistrate binds over the defendant for trial in the appropriate court.

After a bindover, the formal charge against the defendant is filed with the trial court. The formal charge consists of either an *information* filed by the prosecutor or an *indictment* returned by a grand jury. Roughly half of the states require that a grand jury approve the decision to prosecute a person for a felony. Grand juries are bodies of citizens selected in the same manner as the members of a trial (petit) jury; often, they are chosen through random drawings from a list of registered voters. Indictment of an accused prior to a preliminary hearing normally eliminates the need for a preliminary hearing because the indictment serves essentially the same function as a magistrate's probable cause determination.

The remainder of the states allow felony defendants to be charged by either indictment or information, at the prosecutor's discretion. An *information* is a formal charge signed by the prosecutor outlining the facts supporting the charges against the defendant. In states allowing felony prosecution by information, prosecutors elect the information method in the vast majority of felony cases. Misdemeanor cases are prosecuted by information in nearly all states.[4]

Once an information or indictment has been filed with a trial court, an *arraignment* occurs. The defendant is brought before the court, informed of the charges, and asked to enter a plea. The defendant may plead guilty, not guilty, or nolo contendere. Although technically not an admission of guilt, nolo contendere pleas indicate that the defendant does not contest the charges. This decision by the defendant will lead to a finding of guilt. Unlike evidence of a guilty plea, however, evidence of a defendant's nolo plea is inadmissible in later civil cases against that defendant based on the same conduct amounting to the criminal violation. Individuals and corporate defendants therefore may find nolo pleas attractive when their chances of mounting a successful defense to the criminal prosecution are poor and the prospect of later civil suits is likely.

At or shortly after the arraignment, the defendant who pleads not guilty chooses the type of trial that will take place. Persons accused of serious crimes for which incarceration for more than six months is possible have a constitutional right to be tried by a jury of their peers. The accused, however, may waive this right and opt for a bench trial (i.e., before a judge only). Pursuant to the Supreme Court's decision in *Ramos v. Louisiana*, 139 S. Ct. 1318 (2019), the Sixth Amendment requires that jury verdicts for serious crimes must be unanimous in all state and federal cases.

Role of Constitutional Safeguards The preceding text referred to various procedural devices designed to protect persons accused of crime. The Bill of Rights, the first 10 amendments to the U.S. Constitution, sets forth other rights of criminal defendants. These rights guard against unjustified or erroneous criminal convictions and serve as reminders of government's proper role in the administration

---

[3]The state need not satisfy the beyond-a-reasonable-doubt standard of proof at the preliminary hearing stage. The prosecutor sufficiently establishes probable cause by persuading the magistrate to believe it is more likely than not that the defendant committed the felony alleged.

[4]For federal crimes, a prosecutor in the relevant U.S. Attorney's office files an information to institute the case if the offense involved carries a penalty of not more than one year of imprisonment. Federal prosecutions for more serious crimes with potentially more severe penalties are commenced by means of a grand jury indictment.

of justice in a democratic society. Justice Oliver Wendell Holmes aptly addressed this latter point when he said, "I think it less evil that some criminals should escape than that the government should play an ignoble part."

Although the literal language of the Bill of Rights refers only to federal government actions, the U.S. Supreme Court has applied the most important Bill of Rights guarantees to state government actions by "selectively incorporating" those guarantees into the Fourteenth Amendment's due process protection. Once a particular safeguard has been found to be "implicit in the concept of ordered liberty" or "fundamental to the American scheme of justice," it has been applied equally in state and federal criminal trials. This has occurred with the constitutional protections examined earlier in this chapter as well as with the Fourth, Fifth, and Sixth Amendment guarantees discussed in the following sections.

LO5-6 Describe the basic protections afforded by the Fourth, Fifth, and Sixth Amendments.

The Fourth Amendment

The Fourth Amendment protects persons against arbitrary and unreasonable governmental violations of their privacy rights. It states:

> The right of the people to be secure in their persons, houses, papers, and effects, against unreasonable searches and seizures, shall not be violated, and no Warrants shall issue, but upon probable cause, supported by Oath or affirmation, and particularly describing the place to be searched, and the persons or things to be seized.

Key Fourth Amendment Questions

The Fourth Amendment's language and judicial interpretations of it reflect the difficulties inherent in balancing citizens' legitimate expectations of privacy against government's important interest in securing evidence of wrongdoing. The immediately following paragraphs introduce key Fourth Amendment questions and offer answers of a general nature. More complete discussion and explanation of Fourth Amendment issues and principles will then appear in the text material and cases included later in this section of the chapter. In addition, Figure 5.2, which appears later in the chapter, provides further detail.

Two basic questions arise when a government action is challenged under the Fourth Amendment. *First, was there a search or seizure?* If the government action did not constitute a search or seizure, there cannot have been a Fourth Amendment violation. *If there was a search or seizure, this second basic question must be addressed: Was it unreasonable?* The Fourth Amendment furnishes protection only against "unreasonable" searches and seizures.

Questions about the Fourth Amendment language regarding warrants often accompany the fundamental questions noted above. *Must the government have a warrant in order to comply with the Fourth Amendment when it conducts a search or seizure?* The Fourth Amendment's language stops short of making warrants mandatory in all instances. However, cases interpreting and applying the Fourth Amendment indicate that a search conducted in accordance with a properly supported warrant issued by a judge or magistrate will be considered reasonable. *What is necessary for a valid warrant?* "[P]robable cause" for the issuance of the warrant must exist, and the warrant's language must "particularly descri[be]" the relevant place, persons, or things. *May a warrant's validity be challenged for lack of probable cause or on other grounds?* Yes, if the challenging party has standing to do so. *How are warrantless searches treated under the Fourth Amendment?* They tend to be considered unreasonable. As later discussion reveals, however, the Supreme Court has identified various types of warrantless searches that do not violate the Fourth Amendment.

Finally, this important question frequently presents itself: *What is the usual remedy if an unreasonable search or seizure took place?* The exclusionary rule is applied—meaning that evidence obtained in or as the result of the unreasonable search or seizure cannot be used in a criminal case against the party whose Fourth Amendment rights were violated.

We now look in greater depth at the questions introduced above. Whether a search took place for Fourth Amendment purposes depends to a great extent on whether the affected person (whether human or corporate) had a reasonable expectation of privacy that was invaded. The Supreme Court has stated that the Fourth Amendment protects persons rather than places. However, consideration of places and items often becomes necessary because of the amendment's reference to "the right of the people to be secure in their persons, houses, papers, and effects" and because reasonable expectations of privacy often are connected with places and things. Accordingly, the Supreme Court has held that the Fourth Amendment's protection extends to such places or items as private dwellings and immediately surrounding areas (often called the *curtilage*), offices, sealed containers, mail, and telephone booths (nearly a relic of the past). The Court has denied Fourth Amendment protection to places, items, or matters as to which it found no reasonable expectations of privacy, such as open fields, bank records, and voluntary conversations between government informants and criminal suspects or defendants.

Even when the circumstances involve an item or area that might otherwise seem to suggest Fourth Amendment concerns, some government actions may be deemed insufficiently intrusive to constitute a search or seizure. For example, the Supreme Court held in *United States v. Place*, 462 U.S. 696 (1983), that it was not a search when police exposed an airline traveler's luggage to a narcotics detection dog in a public place, given the minimally intrusive nature of the action and the narrow scope of information it revealed. Relying on *Place*, the Supreme Court concluded in *Illinois v. Caballes*, 543 U.S. 405 (2005), that no search occurred when law enforcement officers used a drug-sniffing dog on the exterior of a car whose driver had been stopped for speeding. However, in *Rodriguez v. United States*, 575 U.S. 348 (2015), the Supreme Court limited *Caballes* in both legal and practical effect by holding that if the use of the drug-sniffing dog around the car's exterior lengthened an otherwise lawful traffic stop beyond the time reasonably necessary to complete the purpose of the stop, a Fourth Amendment violation would be present.

On the other hand, the Supreme Court concluded in *Kyllo v. United States*, 533 U.S. 27 (2001), that a search occurred when law enforcement officers, operating from a public street, aimed a thermal-imaging device at the exterior of a private home in an effort to identify heat-emanation patterns that might suggest the presence of a marijuana-growing operation inside the home. The cases just noted set the stage for a later case in which the Supreme Court was faced with deciding whether a search took place when police officers, acting without a warrant, brought drug-sniffing dogs to a suspect's home and put the dogs into service on the suspect's porch. Would the Court rule as it did in the earlier drug-sniffing dog cases (*Place* and *Caballes*), or would it follow the lead of *Kyllo*? Holding that an unreasonable search occurred, the Court emphasized in *Florida v. Jardines*, 569 U.S. 1 (2013), as it had in *Kyllo*, the particular importance of the home and its curtilage when balancing the resident's Fourth Amendment interests against the evidence-gathering interests of the government.

The case that follows provides further illustration of Fourth Amendment principles noted earlier. In *United States v. Jones*, the Supreme Court decides whether a search took place when law enforcement officers, acting without a warrant, attached a GPS device to the underside of a suspect's car in an effort to gather evidence pertaining to possible crimes.

United States v. Jones   565 U.S. 400 (2012)

Antoine Jones, the owner and operator of a District of Columbia nightclub, came under suspicion of trafficking in narcotics. He became the target of an investigation by a joint FBI and Metropolitan Police Department task force. Officers employed various investigative techniques, including visual surveillance of the nightclub, installation of a camera focused on the front door of the club, and a pen register and wiretap covering Jones's cell phone. In addition, the law enforcement agents installed a GPS tracking device on the undercarriage of the Jeep Grand Cherokee that Jones's wife owned but that Jones drove exclusively. The agents installed the GPS device while it was parked in a public parking lot. They did so without a warrant to authorize such action and without informing Jones or his wife.

Over the next 28 days, the government used the GPS device to track the vehicle's movements. By means of signals from multiple satellites, the device established the vehicle's location and communicated that location by cell phone to a government computer. It relayed more than 2,000 pages of data over the four-week period.

The government ultimately obtained a multiple-count indictment charging Jones and several alleged co-conspirators with various drug-trafficking offenses. Before trial, Jones filed a motion asking a federal district court to suppress (i.e., rule inadmissible) the evidence obtained through use of the GPS device. The court denied the motion because "'[a] person traveling in an automobile on public thoroughfares has no reasonable expectation of privacy in his movements from one place to another'" [quoting the district court's decision, which quoted United States v. Knotts, 460 U.S. 276 (1983)]. At the trial, the government introduced as evidence GPS-derived locational data that connected Jones to the alleged conspirators' stash house, where $850,000 in cash and large quantities of illegal drugs were found. The jury found Jones guilty.

The U.S. Court of Appeals for the District of Columbia Circuit reversed the conviction. The D.C. Circuit held that the warrantless use of the GPS device violated the Fourth Amendment and that the lower court therefore should have suppressed the evidence obtained through the device's use. The Supreme Court granted the government's petition for a writ of certiorari.

Scalia, Justice

The Fourth Amendment provides in relevant part that "[t]he right of the people to be secure in their persons, houses, papers, and effects, against unreasonable searches and seizures, shall not be violated." It is beyond dispute that a vehicle is an "effect" as that term is used in the Amendment. We hold that the government's installation of a GPS device on a target's vehicle, and its use of that device to monitor the vehicle's movements, constitutes a "search."

It is important to be clear about what occurred in this case: The government physically occupied private property for the purpose of obtaining information. We have no doubt that such a physical intrusion would have been considered a "search" within the meaning of the Fourth Amendment when it was adopted. The text of the Fourth Amendment reflects its close connection to property, since otherwise it would have referred simply to "the right of the people to be secure against unreasonable searches and seizures"; the phrase "in their persons, houses, papers, and effects" would have been superfluous.

Consistent with this understanding, our Fourth Amendment jurisprudence was tied to common-law trespass, at least until the latter half of the 20th century. Our later cases, of course, have deviated from that exclusively property-based approach. In *Katz v. United States*, 389 U.S. 347, 351 (1967), we said that "the Fourth Amendment protects people, not places," and found a violation in attachment of an eavesdropping device to a public telephone booth. Our later cases have applied the analysis of Justice Harlan's concurrence in that case, which said that a violation occurs when government officers violate a person's "reasonable expectation of privacy." *Id.* at 360.

The government contends that the Harlan standard shows that no search occurred here, since Jones had no "reasonable expectation of privacy" in the area of the Jeep accessed by government agents (its underbody) and in the locations of the Jeep on the public roads, which were visible to all. But we need not address the government's contentions, because Jones's Fourth Amendment rights do not rise or fall with the *Katz* formulation. As explained, for most of our history the Fourth Amendment was understood to embody a particular concern for government trespass upon the areas ("persons, houses, papers, and effects") it enumerates. *Katz* did not repudiate that understanding. Less than two years [after *Katz* was decided,] the Court upheld defendants' contention that the government could not introduce against them conversations between *other* people obtained by warrantless placement of electronic surveillance devices in their homes. The opinion rejected the dissent's contention that there was no Fourth Amendment violation "unless the conversational privacy of the homeowner himself is invaded." *Alderman v. United States*, 394 U.S. 165, 176 (1969). "[W]e [do not] believe that *Katz*, by holding that the Fourth Amendment protects

persons and their private conversations, was intended to withdraw any of the protection which the Amendment extends to the home. . . ." *Id.* at 180.

More recently, in *Soldal v. Cook County*, 506 U.S. 56 (1992), the Court unanimously rejected the argument that although a "seizure" had occurred "in a 'technical' sense" when a trailer home was forcibly removed, no Fourth Amendment violation occurred because law enforcement had not "invade[d] the [individuals'] privacy." *Id.* at 60. *Katz*, the Court explained, established that "property rights are not the sole measure of Fourth Amendment violations," but did not "snuf[f] out the previously recognized protection for property." *Id.* at 64. We have embodied that preservation of past rights in our very definition of "reasonable expectation of privacy," which we have said to be an expectation "that has a source outside of the Fourth Amendment, either by reference to concepts of real or personal property law or to understandings that are recognized and permitted by society." *Minnesota v. Carter*, 525 U.S. 83, 88 (1998). *Katz* did not narrow the Fourth Amendment's scope.

The government contends that several of our post-*Katz* cases foreclose the conclusion that what occurred here constituted a search. It relies principally on two cases in which we rejected Fourth Amendment challenges to "beepers," electronic tracking devices that represent another form of electronic monitoring. The first case, *United States v. Knotts*, 460 U.S. 276 (1983), upheld against Fourth Amendment challenge the use of a beeper that had been placed in a container of chloroform, allowing law enforcement to monitor the location of the container. We said that there had been no infringement of Knotts' reasonable expectation of privacy since the information obtained—the location of the automobile carrying the container on public roads, and the location of the off-loaded container in open fields near Knotts' cabin—had been voluntarily conveyed to the public. But as we have discussed, the *Katz* reasonable-expectation-of-privacy test has been *added to*, not *substituted for*, the common-law trespassory test. The holding in *Knotts* addressed only the former, since the latter was not at issue. The beeper had been placed in the container before it came into Knotts's possession, with the consent of the then-owner. Knotts did not challenge that installation, and we specifically declined to consider its effect on the Fourth Amendment analysis.

The second beeper case, *United States v. Karo*, 468 U.S. 705 (1984), does not suggest a different conclusion. There we addressed the question left open by *Knotts*, whether the installation of a beeper in a container amounted to a search or seizure. As in *Knotts*, at the time the beeper was installed the container belonged to a third party, and it did not come into possession of the defendant until later. Thus, the specific question we considered was whether the installation *"with the consent of the original owner* constitute[d] a search or seizure . . . when the container is delivered to a buyer having no knowledge of the presence of the beeper." *Id.* at 707 (emphasis added). We held not. The government, we said, came into physical contact with the container only before it belonged to the defendant Karo, and the transfer of the container with the unmonitored beeper inside did not convey any information and thus did not invade Karo's privacy. That conclusion is perfectly consistent with the one we reach here. Karo accepted the container as it came to him, beeper and all, and was therefore not entitled to object to the beeper's presence, even though it was used to monitor the container's location. Jones, who possessed the Jeep at the time the government trespassorily inserted the information-gathering device, is on much different footing.

The government also points to our exposition in *New York v. Class*, 475 U.S. 106 (1986), that "[t]he exterior of a car . . . is thrust into the public eye, and thus to examine it does not constitute a 'search.'" *Id.* at 114. That statement is of marginal relevance here since, as the government acknowledges, "the officers in this case did *more* than conduct a visual inspection of respondent's vehicle" [quoting the government's brief, with emphasis added]. By attaching the device to the Jeep, officers encroached on a protected area. In *Class* itself we suggested that this would make a difference, for we concluded that an officer's momentary reaching into the interior of a vehicle did constitute a search. *Id.* at 114–15.

Finally, the government's position gains little support from our conclusion in *Oliver v. United States*, 466 U.S. 170 (1984), that officers' information-gathering intrusion on an "open field" did not constitute a Fourth Amendment search even though it was a trespass at common law. *Id.* at 183. Quite simply, an open field, unlike the curtilage of a home, see *United States v. Dunn*, 480 U.S. 294, 300 (1987), is not one of those protected areas enumerated in the Fourth Amendment. The government's physical intrusion on such an area—unlike its intrusion on the "effect" at issue here—is of no Fourth Amendment significance. Thus, our theory is not that the Fourth Amendment is concerned with [every] trespass that led to the gathering of evidence. The Fourth Amendment protects against trespassory searches only with regard to those items ("persons, houses, papers, and effects") that it enumerates. The trespass that occurred in *Oliver*[, therefore, did not amount to a Fourth Amendment violation].

The government argues in the alternative that even if the attachment and use of the GPS device was a search, it was reasonable—and thus lawful—under the Fourth Amendment because "officers had reasonable suspicion, and indeed probable cause, to believe that [Jones] was a leader in a large-scale cocaine distribution conspiracy" [quoting the government's brief]. We have no occasion to consider this argument. The government did not raise it below, and the D.C. Circuit therefore did not address it. We consider the argument forfeited.

D.C. Circuit decision in favor of Jones affirmed.

[Note: Five justices subscribed to Justice Scalia's majority opinion. The other four justices agreed with the outcome (that the placement and use of the GPS device was a search for Fourth Amendment purposes). However, they would have reached that outcome purely on the basis of the reasonable expectation of privacy test rather than through taking trespass considerations into account.]

Justice Sotomayor's concurrence in *Jones* became especially important in the Court's 2018 opinion in *Carpenter v. United States*, 138 S. Ct. 2206, which addressed whether the government could obtain cell phone location records without a warrant pursuant to the Stored Communications Act. The Court held that data used in tracking a person by cell towers was similar to that of using a GPS tracking device as in *Jones*. In addition, the "third-party doctrine," which provides that people who voluntarily provide information to third parties like phone companies have no reasonable expectation of privacy, did not change the result because consumers do not choose to share their geographic location and movements through cell phones. In reaching this conclusion, the Court stressed "the inescapable and automatic" nature of the collection of cell phone data, and that cell phones hold the "privacies of life" for many Americans.

 LO5-7 Describe major exceptions to the Fourth Amendment's usual preference that the government have a warrant before conducting a search.

Warrantless Searches and the Fourth Amendment

Although the Fourth Amendment is sometimes described as setting up a warrant "requirement," the amendment's literal language does not do so. It is more accurate to say that as interpreted by courts, the Fourth Amendment contemplates a preference for a warrant but does not require one in all instances. Because a judge or magistrate must determine whether probable cause supports the request for the warrant and must ensure that the government's intrusive action is appropriately limited, warrants serve to protect privacy interests and guard against pure "fishing expeditions" by the government. The preference for warrants, therefore, gives rise not only to the rule that a search or seizure conducted in accordance with a proper warrant is reasonable for Fourth Amendment purposes but also to the assumption that a warrantless search or seizure may be unreasonable.

Clearly, however, not all warrantless searches and seizures violate the Fourth Amendment. The Supreme Court has identified various instances in which a warrantless search or seizure will pass muster under the Fourth Amendment. The list of exceptions to the usual preference for a warrant includes the following:

Search incident to lawful arrest. Under this long-recognized exception, officers may conduct a warrantless search of the arrestee himself, the items in his possession, and the items within his control—or to which he has access—at the time of arrest. (This is permitted regardless of whether the arrest itself occurred pursuant to a warrant or whether the arrest was otherwise lawful because there was probable cause to believe that the arrestee committed the relevant offense.) The rationale is twofold: to protect the arresting officers in the possible event that the arrestee has a weapon and to obtain evidence that otherwise might be destroyed or go undiscovered. Weapons and evidence obtained during the search may be seized by the officers.

Does the search-incident-to-arrest exception permit officers to search the content stored on a cell phone or smartphone in the arrestee's possession at the time of the arrest? For consideration of that question, see Figure 5.2.

Certain searches of motor vehicles. Law enforcement officers may conduct a warrantless search of a motor vehicle when the driver or other recent occupant of the vehicle is arrested and either (1) the arrestee is still within reaching distance of the vehicle during the search or (2) the officers have reason to believe the vehicle contains evidence of the crime for which the driver or other occupant was arrested. The rationale here is essentially the same as in the search-incident-to-arrest scenario described above. Weapons and evidence obtained during the search of the vehicle may be seized by the officers.

Investigative stops upon reasonable suspicion. Officers need not have a warrant to stop a vehicle if they have a

---

Figure 5.2   A Note on *Riley v. California*

Nearby discussion in the text outlines the search-incident-to-arrest exception to the usual preference for a warrant. If, as is often the case, an arrestee has a cell phone or smartphone in his or her possession, may law enforcement officers search the content stored on that phone under the search-incident-to arrest doctrine, or is a warrant to search it necessary? In recent years, police fairly routinely conducted such a search, relied on search-incident-to-arrest principles in doing so, and not infrequently found the phone to be a treasure trove of evidence. Critics of such police action asserted that cell phones—and particularly smartphones—are different from other items an arrestee may have in his or her possession because the phones may contain huge quantities of information and because, in their view, arrestees should be seen as having reasonable expectations of privacy in regard to what those devices contain. Lower courts reached differing results when addressing the question whether a warrant is necessary in this setting.

In 2014, the Supreme Court decided *Riley v. California*, 573 U.S. 373. In that case, the Court held unanimously that the search-incident-to-arrest doctrine does not justify a search of an arrestee's cell phone or smartphone and that a warrant is necessary in order for such a search to be reasonable for Fourth Amendment purposes. Writing for the Court, Chief Justice Roberts made it clear that cell phones and smartphones are vastly different from other items that persons may carry with them, given those devices' broad-ranging functions and their capacities to store enormous amounts—as well as various types—of information. The chief justice noted that these devices, on which so many persons rely, may furnish "a digital record of nearly every aspect of the [owners'] lives—from the mundane to the intimate." The privacy interests of cell phone and smartphone owners thus carried more weight in the Court's analysis than did countervailing law enforcement interests.

The Court also emphasized the importance of having a clear rule for law enforcement officers to follow. Rejecting the government's proposal that officers be able to conduct a warrantless search of an arrestee's cell phone or smartphone in an effort to find evidence pertaining to the crime for which he or she was arrested (as opposed to evidence of other possible crimes), the Court regarded that proposal as unworkable. Such a rule would require too many fact-specific judgments by officers in the field and afterward by judges in court proceedings. Moreover, such a rule might be exploited by officers to an unreasonable extent. Hence, the Court stressed that the need for a warrant before searching the cell phone or smartphone exists even when officers believe that the device in the arrestee's possession is likely to contain evidence relevant to the crime for which the arrest occurred. In addition, the Court made no distinction between older cell phones and new smartphones, even though the smartphones can do far more than the cell phones that seemed so remarkable not many years ago. Either way—cell phone or high-powered smartphone—officers are expected to know after the *Riley* decision that a warrant will be necessary before they can search the content of the device.

reasonable suspicion that the driver committed a traffic violation (for which a ticket might be issued but no arrest would be made) or if they have a reasonable suspicion of other wrongdoing on the part of the driver or other vehicle occupant. In such an investigative stop, the detention of the driver and vehicle occupants does not violate the Fourth Amendment if the stop is brief and otherwise reasonably conducted. If no arrest occurs but the officers proceed to conduct a warrantless search of the vehicle, there normally will be a Fourth Amendment violation. However, the officers may search the vehicle if the driver consents or if probable cause to search arises on the basis of the officers' visual observations, other sensory perceptions, or further key facts that come to the officers' attention. If evidence discovered in the search of the vehicle helps to form the basis of criminal charges against the driver or other vehicle occupants, the persons charged have legal standing to challenge the validity of the stop (by arguing that the necessary reasonable suspicion was lacking) and the ensuing search (by arguing that the search stemmed from an improper stop or was unsupported by probable cause).

Stop-and-frisk searches for weapons. If law enforcement officers' observations give them a reasonable suspicion that a person may be engaged in criminal activity, the officers may detain the person briefly for investigative purposes without violating the Fourth Amendment. During that detention—usually called a "*Terry* stop" because of the case in which the Supreme Court held that the Fourth Amendment permits such police action—officers may conduct a pat-down search of the detained person in order to determine whether he is carrying a weapon that could endanger the officers.

Plain view. If an officer sees contraband or other evidence in plain view (meaning that the item is readily visible to the officer without any special efforts), the officer may seize the item and will not violate the Fourth Amendment in doing so.

Consensual searches. Searches that occur with the consent of a person who owns or possesses the relevant place or thing are considered reasonable. Therefore, one who consents to a search of her home, office, or car will normally be regarded as having forfeited any Fourth Amendment objection she might otherwise have been able to make. If there are co-occupants of a residence and any co-occupant gives law enforcement officers consent to search the property, the permission granted by that co-occupant will normally insulate the search against a Fourth Amendment challenge brought later by a nonpresent and nonconsenting co-occupant. As the Supreme Court recognized in *Georgia v. Randolph*, 547 U.S. 103 (2006), however, a consent to search provided by one co-occupant of a residence does not protect the search against a Fourth Amendment challenge by another co-occupant who was present at the time of the search and objected to its occurrence. If the police cannot (as the *Randolph* decision indicates) lawfully conduct a search of a residence when an on-the-premises co-occupant refuses to consent, does the Fourth Amendment permit the police to return to the home when the nonconsenting co-occupant is no longer present, obtain consent from another co-occupant, and conduct the search? The Supreme Court said "yes" in the 2014 case *Fernandez v. California*, 571 U.S. 292.

Searches under exigent circumstances. Courts have upheld warrantless searches of premises that law enforcement officers enter in order to protect persons present there if the officers reasonably believe those persons are at risk of imminent serious harm. The emergency nature of such a situation obviously would not allow time to obtain a warrant. The Supreme Court has ruled that the exigent circumstances exception can also apply to warrantless searches of premises entered by officers when they are in hot pursuit of a fleeing suspect. In *Kentucky v. King*, 563 U.S. 452 (2011), the Court held that this exception justified officers' warrantless entry and search of an apartment. In that case, officers who had been pursuing a fleeing suspect entered the apartment when, after knocking on the door and announcing their presence, they heard sounds that made them think evidence was being destroyed. The Court concluded that the additional exigency of preventing evidence destruction helped to make the warrantless entry and search acceptable under the Fourth Amendment, even though the officers guessed wrong about which apartment the suspect they had been chasing had actually entered.

In *Missouri v. McNeely*, 569 U.S. 141 (2013), however, the Court rejected the state's argument that concern about possible dissipation of evidence of blood alcohol content should justify applying the exigent circumstances doctrine to authorize a warrantless drawing of blood from a motorist suspected of driving under the influence of alcohol. Weighing that law enforcement concern against the invasive nature of a forced drawing of blood (as opposed to a noninvasive breath test) caused the Court to conclude that a warrant was necessary. Yet, in *Mitchell v. Wisconsin*, 139 S. Ct. 2525 (2019), the Court appears to have reopened the door of warrantless blood draws when the motorist is unconscious. The test for exigency is, according to the Court, when there is a compelling need for official action and no time to secure a warrant. In holding that the state met that test merely because the defendant was unconscious, the opinion may have created a presumption of exigent circumstances in such situations.

DNA swabs in the booking process. In *Maryland v. King*, 569 U.S. 435 (2013), the Supreme Court weighed in on a practice engaged in fairly frequently by law enforcement officers in recent years: taking a DNA sample from arrestees—usually those charged with crimes involving violence—without a warrant and as part of the booking process. The sample tends to be taken quickly through insertion of a swab inside the arrestee's cheek. Upholding a Maryland law that permitted such warrantless use of the DNA swab on those arrested for violent crimes, a five-justice majority of the Supreme Court regarded the bodily intrusion as minimal and stressed the usefulness of the resulting evidence in accurately identifying the arrestee. The dissenters were troubled by what they regarded as the real (though unspoken) reason why the Court permitted the gathering of DNA evidence in this way: the usefulness of the resulting evidence in solving crimes *other than the ones for which the arrestee was arrested*—crimes for which law enforcement authorities otherwise had no reason to suspect the arrestee.

Customs searches. Given the importance of controlling the nation's borders and regulating the passage of persons and items into the country, government agents have fairly broad authority to conduct warrantless searches in the customs and border contexts.

Administrative inspections of closely regulated businesses. Various statutes and regulations subject certain types of businesses to inspections by government agents in order to safeguard public health and welfare. To the extent that these inspections come within the scope of the relevant statutes and regulations, they are considered to be reasonable for Fourth Amendment purposes even though they occur without a warrant.

Exclusionary Rule

 LO5-8 Explain what the exclusionary rule is.

The exclusionary rule serves as the basic remedial device in cases of Fourth Amendment violations. Under this judicially crafted rule, evidence seized in illegal searches cannot be used in a subsequent trial against an accused whose constitutional rights were violated.[5] In addition, if information obtained in an illegal search leads to the later discovery of further evidence, that further evidence is considered "fruit of the poisonous tree" and is therefore excluded from use at trial under the rule established in *Wong Sun v. United*

States, 371 U.S. 471 (1963). Because the exclusionary rule may result in suppression of convincing evidence of crime, it has generated controversy. The rule's supporters regard it as necessary to deter police from violating citizens' constitutional rights. The rule's opponents assert that it has no deterrent effect on police who believed they were acting lawfully. A loudly voiced complaint in some quarters has been that "because of a policeman's error, a criminal goes free."

During roughly the past three decades, the Supreme Court has responded to such criticism by rendering decisions that restrict the operation of the exclusionary rule. For example, the Court has held that illegally obtained evidence may be introduced at trial if the prosecution convinces the trial judge that the evidence would inevitably have been obtained anyway by lawful means. The Court has also created a "good-faith" exception to the exclusionary rule. This exception allows the use of evidence seized by police officers who acted pursuant to a search warrant later held invalid if the officers reasonably believed that the warrant was valid. In *Herring v. United States*, 555 U.S. 135 (2009), the Court declined to apply the exclusionary rule to evidence obtained as a result of an arrest made pursuant to a rescinded arrest warrant where a police employee had negligently failed to remove the rescinded warrant from a law enforcement database, but the arresting officer relied in good faith on the warrant's supposed validity.

Although the Court has not extended this good-faith exception to warrantless searches in general, it has declined to apply the exclusionary rule where the search was conducted in reliance on a statute that was later declared invalid or in reliance on earlier Court decisions that gave greater Fourth Amendment leeway to law enforcement officers than an otherwise controlling later decision did.

Finally, *Utah v. Strieff*, 136 S. Ct. 2056 (2016), further illustrates the Supreme Court's tendency in recent years to narrow the application of the exclusionary rule. In that case, a law enforcement officer detained a person without sufficient legal cause but quickly learned that there was an outstanding arrest warrant for the person. The officer then made the arrest, conducted a search incident to the arrest, and discovered that the arrestee was in possession of illegal drugs. In the drug possession prosecution that followed, the defendant argued that because the initial detention of him was without cause, the seized drugs should be excluded from evidence under the previously discussed fruit-of-the-poisonous-tree doctrine. The Supreme Court rejected that argument, holding instead that the detaining officer's prompt discovery of the valid arrest warrant made the connection between the initial stop of the defendant and the officer's discovery of the drugs too attenuated to warrant exclusion of the evidence.

---

[5]The Supreme Court initially authorized application of the exclusionary rule in federal criminal cases only. In *Mapp v. Ohio*, 367 U.S. 643 (1961), the Court made the exclusionary rule applicable to state criminal cases as well.

The USA PATRIOT Act Approximately six weeks after the September 11, 2001, terrorist attacks on the United States, Congress enacted the Uniting and Strengthening America by Providing Appropriate Tools Required to Intercept and Obstruct Terrorism Act. This statute, commonly known as the USA PATRIOT Act or as simply the Patriot Act, contains numerous and broad-ranging provisions designed to protect the public against international and domestic terrorism.

Included in the Patriot Act are measures allowing the federal government significantly expanded ability, in terrorism-related investigations, to conduct searches of property, monitor Internet activities, track electronic communications, and obtain records regarding customers of businesses. Most, though not all, actions of that nature require a warrant from a special court known as the Foreign Intelligence Surveillance Court. The statute contemplates, however, that such warrants may be issued upon less of a showing by the government than would ordinarily be required, and may be more sweeping than usual in terms of geographic application. Moreover, warrants issued by the special court for the search of property can be of the so-called sneak and peek variety, under which the FBI need not produce the warrant for the property owner or possessor to see and need not notify an absent property owner or possessor that the search took place (unlike the rules typically applicable to execution of "regular" warrants).

In addition, the Patriot Act permits warrants for "roving" wiretaps—ones that apply to various communications devices or methods that a person suspected of ties to terrorism may employ, as opposed to being restricted to a single communications device or method.

The Patriot Act also calls for banks to report seemingly suspicious monetary deposits, as well as any deposits exceeding $10,000, not only to the Treasury Department (as required by prior law) but also to the Central Intelligence Agency and other federal intelligence agencies. In addition, the statute enables federal law enforcement authorities to seek a Surveillance Court warrant for the obtaining of individuals' credit, medical, and student records, regardless of state or federal privacy laws that would otherwise have applied.

Commentators critical of the Patriot Act have argued that despite the importance of safeguarding the public against acts of terrorism, the statute tips the balance too heavily in favor of law enforcement. They have characterized the statute's definition of "domestic terrorism" as so broad that various suspected activities not normally regarded as terrorism (or as harboring or aiding terrorists) could be considered as such for purposes of the federal government's expanded investigatory tools. If that happens,

the critics contend, Fourth Amendment and other constitutional rights may easily be subverted. Others with reservations about the statute maintain that its allowance of expanded monitoring of Internet activities and electronic communications and its provisions for retrieval of library records and other records normally protected by privacy laws could give the government ready access to communications and private information of many wholly innocent persons.

In apparent recognition of the extraordinary action it was taking in a time of national crisis, Congress included provisions stating that unless they were renewed, portions of the Patriot Act would expire at the end of 2005. Congress has since renewed the bulk of the Patriot Act on more than one occasion and has made most of its provisions permanent in the sense of not requiring a renewal (though certain provisions, such as the one dealing with roving wiretaps, continue to require periodic renewals). With most of the Patriot Act having been made permanent, those who have raised civil liberties concerns may continue to seek repeal of part or all of the statute. Repeal seems unlikely, however, in a political environment that continues to be shaped in significant ways by the events of 2001.

The expanded investigatory tools provided by the Patriot Act have existed alongside those provided by an older statute, the Foreign Intelligence Surveillance Act (FISA), which was enacted long before the September 11, 2001, attacks and has been amended various times both before and since. Under FISA, monitoring of a suspected terrorist's electronic communications generally required that an individualized warrant be obtained from the previously mentioned Foreign Intelligence Surveillance Court (FISA Court), which operates in secret and whose decisions, unlike those of other courts, are not published. Applications for warrants from the FISA Court have historically been approved a very high percentage of the time.

In December 2005, it was revealed that the White House had implemented a program of monitoring telephone calls of suspected terrorists when one party to the conversation was located outside the United States. This monitoring had occurred without an attempt by the government to obtain warrants from the FISA Court. Critics of this action by the government complained that it violated not only FISA but also the Fourth Amendment. The White House took the position, however, that the monitoring program was within the inherent powers of the executive branch. Disputes over the validity of the monitoring program led to discussions over possible amendments to strengthen or loosen FISA's requirements. These discussions resulted in an amendment under which the FISA Court could issue blanket warrants for electronic monitoring of groups of terrorism suspects for set periods of time (as opposed to the previous sole option of individualized warrants). With such loosening of what it saw as FISA's constraints, the government shut down its warrantless monitoring program and resumed going to the FISA Court for warrants. In 2008, Congress enacted a further amendment to FISA. This amendment expanded the government's ability to monitor the phone calls of suspected terrorists, established FISA's requirement of warrants from the FISA Court as the exclusive way of exercising this surveillance power, and provided immunity from legal liability for telephone companies that had assisted the government in the phone call monitoring activities for which FISA Court warrants had not been obtained.

Revelations in 2013 and 2014 by ex–Central Intelligence Agency contractor Edward Snowden about formerly secret intelligence-gathering by the federal government furnished a further chapter in the ongoing saga of anti-terrorism-related surveillance. Snowden's disclosures regarding the government's collection and analysis of huge amounts of data from phone records led to debates about how much authority the government should or should not have in that sense. Later policy statements and legislative efforts have explored ways to limit and manage the government's access to phone records and similar material in ways that would suitably account for the government's terrorism-prevention interests and the public's privacy interests.

The Fifth Amendment

 LO5-6 Describe the basic protections afforded by the Fourth, Fifth, and Sixth Amendments.

The Fifth and Fourteenth Amendments' Due Process Clauses guarantee basic procedural and substantive fairness to criminal defendants. The Due Process Clauses are discussed earlier in this chapter and in Chapter 3.

Privilege against Self-Incrimination

 LO5-9 List the components of the *Miranda* warnings and state when law enforcement officers must give those warnings.

In another significant provision, the Fifth Amendment protects against *compelled testimonial self-incrimination* by establishing that "[n]o person . . . shall be compelled in any criminal case to be a witness against himself." This provision prevents the government from coercing a defendant

into making incriminating statements and thereby assisting in his own prosecution.

In *Miranda v. Arizona*, 384 U.S. 436 (1966), the Supreme Court established procedural requirements—the now-familiar *Miranda* warnings—to safeguard this Fifth Amendment right and other constitutional guarantees. The Court did so by requiring police to inform criminal suspects, before commencing custodial interrogation of them, that they have the right to remain silent, that any statements they make may be used as evidence against them, and that during questioning they have the right to the presence and assistance of a retained or court-appointed attorney (with court appointment occurring when suspects lack the financial ability to retain counsel).[6] Incriminating statements that an in-custody suspect makes without first having been given the *Miranda* warnings are inadmissible at trial. (The exclusionary rule is thus the remedy for a *Miranda* violation.) If the suspect invokes her right to silence, custodial interrogation must cease. If the suspect knowingly and voluntarily waives her right to silence after having been given the *Miranda* warnings, her statements will be admissible.

The right to silence is limited, however, in various ways. For example, the traditional view that the Fifth Amendment applies only to *testimonial* admissions serves as the basis for allowing the police to compel an accused to furnish nontestimonial evidence such as fingerprints, samples of body fluids, and hair.

Supreme Court decisions have recognized further limitations on the right to silence. For instance, the right has been held to include a corresponding implicit prohibition of prosecutorial comments at trial about the accused's failure to testify. Although Supreme Court decisions still support this prohibition, the Court has sometimes allowed prosecutors to use the defendant's pretrial silence to impeach his trial testimony. For example, the Court has held that the Fifth Amendment is not violated by prosecutorial use of a defendant's silence (either prearrest or postarrest, but in advance of any *Miranda* warnings) to discredit his trial testimony that he killed the victim in self-defense.

More recently, in *Salinas v. Texas*, 570 U.S. 178 (2013), the Court held that there was no Fifth Amendment violation when the prosecutor at a murder trial commented on the defendant's failure, during a pre-custody and prearrest interview, to answer a police officer's question about a shotgun and shell casings found at the scene of the crime, even though he did respond to other questions posed by

---

[6]The portions of the *Miranda* warnings dealing with the right to an attorney further Sixth Amendment interests. The Sixth Amendment is discussed later in this chapter.

the officer. Notwithstanding popular misconceptions, the Fifth Amendment does not establish a complete right to remain silent but only guarantees that criminal defendants may not be compelled to testify against themselves. Therefore, as long as police do not deprive defendants the opportunity to claim a Fifth Amendment privilege, there is no constitutional violation.

In *Berghuis v. Thompkins*, which follows, a five-justice majority of the Supreme Court holds that a suspect who wishes to invoke his *Miranda* right to remain silent must unambiguously invoke that right—a rule characterized by the four dissenting justices as "counterintuitively" requiring a suspect to speak up in order to indicate that he wants to remain silent.

Berghuis v. Thompkins   560 U.S. 370 (2010)

Approximately a year after a Southfield, Michigan shooting in which one person was killed and another was wounded, suspect Van Chester Thompkins was arrested. While Thompkins was in custody, police officers interrogated him. At the beginning of the interrogation, one of the officers, Detective Helgert, informed Thompkins of his Miranda *rights.*

Officers began questioning Thompkins. At no point did Thompkins state that he wished to remain silent, that he did not want to talk with the police, or that he wanted an attorney. Thompkins was largely silent during the interrogation, which lasted approximately three hours. However, he did give a few limited verbal responses such as "yeah," "no," or "I don't know." On occasion, he communicated by nodding his head.

Roughly two hours and 45 minutes into the interrogation, Helgert asked Thompkins, "Do you believe in God?" Thompkins made eye contact with Helgert and said, "Yes," as his eyes (according to the record) "well[ed] up with tears." Helgert also asked, "Do you pray to God?" Thompkins said, "Yes." Helgert then asked, "Do you pray to God to forgive you for shooting that boy down?" Thompkins answered, "Yes," and looked away. Thompkins refused to make a written confession, and the interrogation ended approximately 15 minutes later.

In a Michigan trial court, Thompkins was charged with first-degree murder, assault with intent to commit murder, and certain firearms-related offenses. He moved to suppress the statements made during the interrogation. He argued that he had invoked his Fifth Amendment right to remain silent, that the police officers were therefore required to end the interrogation at once, that he had not waived his right to remain silent, and that his inculpatory statements were involuntary. The trial court denied the motion, and a jury found him guilty on all counts. On appeal, Thompkins contended that the trial court erred in refusing to suppress his pretrial statements under Miranda. *The Michigan Court of Appeals rejected the* Miranda *claim and affirmed the conviction. The Michigan Supreme Court denied discretionary review.*

Thompkins later filed a petition for a writ of habeas corpus in the U.S. District Court for the Eastern District of Michigan on the same grounds. The district court ruled against Thompkins. The Sixth Circuit reversed, ruling for Thompkins because his "persistent silence for nearly three hours in response to questioning and repeated invitations to tell his side of the story offered a clear and unequivocal message to the officers: Thompkins did not wish to waive his [Miranda] rights." The U.S. Supreme Court granted certiorari.

Kennedy, Justice

[In *Miranda*, the Court] formulated a warning that must be given to suspects before they can be subjected to custodial interrogation. The substance of the warning still must be given to suspects today. All concede that the warning given in this case was in full compliance with these requirements. The dispute centers on the response—or nonresponse—from the suspect.

Thompkins makes various arguments that his answers to questions from the detectives were inadmissible. He first contends that he invoked his privilege to remain silent by not saying anything for a sufficient period of time, so the interrogation should have ceased before he made his inculpatory statements.

This argument is unpersuasive. In the context of invoking the *Miranda* right to counsel, the Court in *Davis v. United States*, 512 U.S. 452, 459 (1994), held that a suspect must do so

"unambiguously." [*Davis* established that if] an accused makes a statement concerning the right to counsel "that is ambiguous or equivocal" or makes no statement, the police are not required to end the interrogation, or ask questions to clarify whether the accused wants to invoke his or her *Miranda* rights.

The Court has not yet stated whether an invocation of the right to remain silent can be ambiguous or equivocal, but there is no principled reason to adopt different standards for determining when an accused has invoked the *Miranda* right to remain silent and the *Miranda* right to counsel at issue in *Davis*. Both protect the privilege against compulsory self-incrimination by requiring an interrogation to cease when either right is invoked.

There is good reason to require an accused who wants to invoke his or her right to remain silent to do so unambiguously. A requirement of an unambiguous invocation of *Miranda* rights results in an objective inquiry that "avoid[s] difficulties of proof and . . . provide[s] guidance to officers" on how to proceed in the face of ambiguity. *Davis*, 512 U.S., at 458–459. If an ambiguous act, omission, or statement could require police to end the interrogation, police would be required to make difficult decisions about an accused's unclear intent and face the consequence of suppression if they guess wrong. Suppression of a voluntary confession in these circumstances would place a significant burden on society's interest in prosecuting criminal activity. Treating an ambiguous or equivocal act, omission, or statement as an invocation of *Miranda* rights "might add marginally to *Miranda*'s goal of dispelling the compulsion inherent in custodial interrogation." *Moran v. Burbine*, 475 U.S. 412, 425 (1986). But "as *Miranda* holds, full comprehension of the rights to remain silent and request an attorney are sufficient to dispel whatever coercion is inherent in the interrogation process" [quoting *Burbine*].

Thompkins did not say that he wanted to remain silent or that he did not want to talk with the police. Had he made either of these simple, unambiguous statements, he would have invoked his right to cut off questioning. Here he did neither, so he did not invoke his right to remain silent.

We next consider whether Thompkins waived his right to remain silent. Even absent the accused's invocation of the right to remain silent, the accused's statement during a custodial interrogation is inadmissible at trial unless the prosecution can establish that the accused "in fact knowingly and voluntarily waived *[Miranda]* rights" when making the statement. *North Carolina v. Butler*, 441 U.S. 369, 373 (1979). The waiver inquiry has two distinct dimensions: waiver must be "voluntary in the sense that it was the product of a free and deliberate choice rather than intimidation, coercion, or deception," and [must be] "made with a full awareness of both the nature of the right being abandoned and the consequences of the decision to abandon it" [quoting *Burbine*].

Some language in *Miranda* could be read to indicate that waivers are difficult to establish absent an explicit written waiver or a formal, express oral statement. In addition, *Miranda* stated that "a heavy burden rests on the government to demonstrate that the defendant knowingly and intelligently waived his privilege against self-incrimination and his right to retained or appointed counsel."

The course of decisions since *Miranda*, informed by the application of *Miranda* warnings in the whole course of law enforcement, demonstrates that waivers can be established even absent formal or express statements of waiver. The main purpose of *Miranda* is to ensure that an accused is advised of and understands the right to remain silent and the right to counsel.

One of the first cases to decide the meaning and import of *Miranda* with respect to the question of waiver was *North Carolina v. Butler*. *Butler* interpreted the *Miranda* language concerning the "heavy burden" to show waiver in accord with usual principles of determining waiver, which can include waiver implied from all the circumstances. The prosecution therefore does not need to show that a waiver of *Miranda* rights was express. *Butler* made clear that a waiver of *Miranda* rights may be implied through "the defendant's silence, coupled with an understanding of his rights and a course of conduct indicating waiver." The Court in *Butler* therefore "retreated" from the "language and tenor of the *Miranda* opinion," which "suggested that the Court would require that a waiver . . . be 'specifically made.'" [Citation omitted.]

If the state establishes that a *Miranda* warning was given and the accused made an uncoerced statement, this showing, standing alone, is insufficient to demonstrate a valid waiver of *Miranda* rights. The prosecution must make the additional showing that the accused understood these rights. Where the prosecution shows that a *Miranda* warning was given and that it was understood by the accused, an accused's uncoerced statement establishes an implied waiver of the right to remain silent.

The record in this case shows that Thompkins waived his right to remain silent. There is no basis in this case to conclude that he did not understand his rights; and on these facts it follows that he chose not to invoke or rely on those rights when he did speak. First, there is no contention that Thompkins did not understand his rights; and from this it follows that he knew what he gave up when he spoke. There was more than enough evidence in the record to conclude that Thompkins understood his *Miranda* rights. Thompkins received a written copy of the *Miranda* warnings; Detective Helgert determined that Thompkins could read and understand English; and Thompkins was given time to read the warnings. Thompkins, furthermore, read aloud the fifth warning, which stated that "you have the right to decide at any time before or during questioning to use your right to remain silent and your right to talk with a lawyer while you are being questioned." He was thus aware that his right to remain silent would not dissipate after a certain amount of time and that police would have to honor his right to be silent and his right to counsel during the whole course of interrogation. Those rights, the warning made clear, could be asserted at any time. Helgert, moreover, read the warnings aloud.

Second, Thompkins' answer to Detective Helgert's question about whether Thompkins prayed to God for forgiveness for shooting the victim is a "course of conduct indicating waiver" of the right to remain silent (quoting *Butler*). If Thompkins wanted to remain silent, he could have said nothing in response to Helgert's questions, or he could have unambiguously invoked his *Miranda* rights and ended the interrogation. The fact that Thompkins made a statement about three hours after receiving a *Miranda* warning does not overcome the fact that he engaged in a course of conduct indicating waiver. Police are not required to rewarn suspects from time to time.

Third, there is no evidence that Thompkins's statement was coerced. Thompkins does not claim that police threatened or injured him during the interrogation or that he was in any way fearful. Thompkins knowingly and voluntarily made a statement to police, so he waived his right to remain silent.

In sum, a suspect who has received and understood the *Miranda* warnings, and has not invoked his *Miranda* rights, waives the right to remain silent by making an uncoerced statement to the police. Thompkins did not invoke his right to remain silent and stop the questioning. Understanding his rights in full, he waived his right to remain silent by making a voluntary statement to the police.

Sixth Circuit's judgment reversed; case remanded with instructions to deny petition for writ of habeas corpus.

Sotomayor, Justice, with whom Justices Stevens, Ginsburg, and Breyer join, dissenting

Today's decision turns *Miranda* upside down. Criminal suspects must now unambiguously invoke their right to remain silent—which, counterintuitively, requires them to speak. At the same time, suspects will be legally presumed to have waived their rights even if they have given no clear expression of their intent to do so. Those results . . . find no basis in *Miranda* or our subsequent cases and are inconsistent with the fair-trial principles on which those precedents are grounded.

Production of Records The preceding discussion of the privilege against self-incrimination applies to criminal defendants in general. The Fifth Amendment's scope, however, has long been of particular concern to businesspersons charged with crimes. Documentary evidence often is quite important to the government's case in white-collar crime prosecutions. To what extent does the Fifth Amendment protect business records? More than a century ago, the Supreme Court held, in *Boyd v. United States*, 116 U.S. 616 (1886), that the Fifth Amendment protects individuals against compelled production of their private papers.

In more recent years, however, the Court has drastically limited the scope of the protection contemplated by *Boyd*. The Court has held various times that the private papers privilege is personal and thus cannot be asserted by a corporation, partnership, or other "collective entity." Because such entities have no Fifth Amendment privilege against self-incrimination, the Court has held that when an organization's individual officer or agent has custody of organization records, the officer or agent cannot assert any personal privilege to prevent their disclosure. This rule holds even if the contents of the records incriminate her personally. Finally, various decisions allow the government to require business proprietors to keep certain records relevant to transactions that are appropriate subjects for government regulation. These "required records" are not entitled to private papers protection. They may be subpoenaed and used against the record keeper in prosecutions for regulatory violations.

The Court's business records decisions during the past four decades cast further doubt on the future of the private papers doctrine. Instead of focusing on whether subpoenaed records are private in nature, the Court now considers whether the *act of producing* the records would be sufficiently testimonial to trigger the privilege against self-incrimination. In *Fisher v. United States*, 425 U.S. 391 (1976), the Court held that an individual subpoenaed to produce personal documents may assert his Fifth Amendment privilege only if the act of producing the documents would involve incriminating testimonial admissions. This is likely when the individual producing the records is in effect certifying the records' authenticity or admitting the existence of records previously unknown to the government (demonstrating that he had access to the records and, therefore, possible knowledge of any incriminating contents).

In *United States v. Doe*, 465 U.S. 605 (1984), the Court extended the act-of-production privilege to a sole proprietor whose proprietorship records were subpoenaed. The Court, however, held that normal business records were not themselves protected by the Fifth Amendment because they were voluntarily prepared and thus not the product of compulsion. In view of *Doe*'s emphasis on the testimonial and potentially incriminating nature of the act of producing business records, some observers thought that officers of collective entities under government investigation might be able to assert their personal privileges against self-incrimination as a way to avoid producing incriminating business records.

Braswell v. United States, 487 U.S. 99 (1988), dashed such hopes, however, as the Court refused to extend its *Doe* holding to cover a corporation's sole shareholder who acted in his capacity as custodian of corporate records. The Court held that Braswell (the sole shareholder), having chosen to operate his business under the corporate form, was bound by the rule that corporations and similar entities have no Fifth Amendment privilege. Because Braswell acted in a representative capacity in producing the requested records, the government could not make evidentiary use of his act of production. The government, however, was free to use the contents of the records against Braswell and the corporation.

Double Jeopardy Another important Fifth Amendment provision is the Double Jeopardy Clause, which prevents a second criminal prosecution for the same offense after the defendant has been acquitted or convicted of that offense. Moreover, it bars the imposition of multiple punishments for the same offense.

The Double Jeopardy Clause does not, however, preclude the possibility that a single criminal act may lead to more than one criminal prosecution. One criminal act may produce several statutory violations, all of which may give rise to prosecution. For example, a defendant who commits sexual assault may also be prosecuted for battery, assault with a deadly weapon, and kidnapping if the facts of the case indicate that the relevant statutes were violated. In addition, the Supreme Court has long used a "same elements" test (also known as the *Blockburger* test for the opinion articulating it) to determine what constitutes the same offense. This means that a single criminal act with multiple victims (e.g., a restaurant robbery in which several patrons are robbed) could result in several prosecutions because the identity of

The Global Business Environment

If an arrestee who is a foreign national makes incriminating statements to law enforcement authorities without having been informed of his right under an international agreement to have his detention reported to his country's consulate, does the exclusionary rule apply? The U.S. Supreme Court confronted that question in *Sanchez-Llamas v. Oregon*, 548 U.S. 331 (2006).

The relevant international agreement in *Sanchez-Llamas* was the Vienna Convention on Consular Relations, which was drafted in 1963 with the purpose, as set forth in its preamble, of "contribut[ing] to the development of friendly relations among nations, irrespective of their differing constitutional and social systems." Approximately 170 countries have subscribed to the Vienna Convention. The United States became a party to it in 1969. Article 36 of the Vienna Convention provides that "if he so requests, the competent authorities of the receiving State shall, without delay, inform the consular post of the sending State if, within its consular district, a national of that State is arrested or committed to prison or to custody pending trial or is detained in any other manner." Thus, when a national of one country is detained by authorities in another, the authorities must notify the consular officers of the detainee's home country if the detainee so requests. Article 36 further provides that "[t]he said authorities shall inform the [detainee] without delay of his rights under this sub-paragraph." The Convention also states that the rights provided by Article 36 "shall be exercised in conformity with the laws and regulations of the receiving State, subject to the proviso, however, that the said laws and regulations must enable full effect to be given to the purposes for which the rights accorded under this Article are intended."

Moises Sanchez-Llamas, a Mexican national, was arrested in Oregon in 1999 for alleged involvement in an exchange of gunfire in which a police officer was wounded. Following the arrest, police officers gave Sanchez-Llamas the *Miranda* warnings in both English and Spanish. However, the officers did not inform Sanchez-Llamas that he could ask to have the Mexican Consulate notified of his detention. Article 36 of the Vienna Convention was thus violated. During the interrogation that followed the issuance of the *Miranda* warnings, Sanchez-Llamas made incriminating statements that led to attempted murder charges, as well as various other charges, against him. After he made the incriminating statements and the formal charges were filed, Sanchez-Llamas learned of his Article 36 rights. He then moved for suppression of his incriminating statements (i.e., for an order that those statements be excluded from evidence at the trial) because of the Article 36 violation. The Oregon trial court denied the suppression motion. Sanchez-Llamas was convicted and sentenced to prison. After the appellate courts in Oregon affirmed, the U.S. Supreme Court agreed to decide the case.

Assuming that—but without deciding whether—individuals have a right to invoke Article 36 in a judicial proceeding (as opposed to nations enforcing the Convention through political or other appropriate channels), the Supreme Court held in *Sanchez-Llamas* that the exclusionary rule was not a proper remedy for an Article 36 violation. The Court noted that the Vienna Convention itself said nothing about the exclusionary rule as a remedy. Instead, through the statement that Article 36 rights are to be "exercised in conformity with the laws and regulations of the receiving State," the Convention left the implementation of Article 36 to domestic law. The Court stated that it "would be startling" if the Convention were interpreted as requiring suppression of evidence as a remedy for an Article 36 violation because "[t]he exclusionary rule as we know it is an entirely American legal creation." The Court stressed that there was "no reason to suppose that Sanchez-Llamas would be afforded the relief he seeks here in any of the other 169 countries party to the Vienna Convention." (Presumably, then, a U.S. national should not assume that the exclusionary rule will apply to his case if he is arrested in another Vienna Convention nation and makes incriminating statements to law enforcement officers without having been informed of his Article 36 rights.)

The Court emphasized that "[b]ecause the [exclusionary] rule's social costs are considerable, suppression is warranted only where the rule's 'remedial objectives are thought most efficaciously served.'" [Case citations omitted.] The Court emphasized that "[w]e have applied the exclusionary rule primarily to deter constitutional violations"—normally those involving unreasonable searches in violation of the Fourth Amendment or incriminating statements of accused persons whose Fifth Amendment rights had been violated because their confessions were not voluntary or because they had not been given the *Miranda* warnings. No such problems attended the incriminating statements made by Sanchez-Llamas. From the Court's perspective, "[t]he violation of the right to consular notification . . . is at best remotely connected to the gathering of evidence" and "there is likely to be little connection between an Article 36 violation and evidence or statements obtained by police." The Court reasoned that even if law enforcement officers fail to provide detained foreign nationals notice of their Article 36 rights, the same general interests served by Article 36 would be safeguarded by other protections available to persons in the situation in which Sanchez-Llamas found himself. The Court stressed that "[a] foreign national detained on suspicion of crime, like anyone else in our country, enjoys under our system the protections of the Due Process Clause[,] . . . is entitled to an attorney, and is protected against compelled self-incrimination."

Finally, the Court stated that Vienna Convention rights could be vindicated in ways other than suppression of evidence. The Court observed that a defendant could make an Article 36 argument "as part of a broader challenge to the voluntariness of his statements to police" and that if a defendant alludes to a supposed Article 36 violation at trial, "a court can make appropriate accommodations to ensure that the defendant secures, to the extent possible, the benefits of consular assistance." Having concluded that the exclusionary rule was not an appropriate remedy for the Article 36 violation at issue, the Court upheld the conviction of Sanchez-Llamas.

---

each victim would be an additional fact or element of proof in each case.

In addition, the Double Jeopardy Clause does not protect against multiple prosecutions by different sovereigns. A conviction or acquittal in a state prosecution does not prevent a subsequent federal prosecution for a federal offense arising out of the same event, or vice versa. Finally, the Double Jeopardy Clause does not bar a private plaintiff from pursuing a *civil* case (normally for one or more of the intentional torts discussed in Chapter 6) against a defendant who was criminally prosecuted by the government for the same alleged conduct.

The Sixth Amendment

 LO5-6 Describe the basic protections afforded by the Fourth, Fifth, and Sixth Amendments.

The Sixth Amendment applies to criminal cases in various ways. It entitles criminal defendants to a speedy trial by an impartial jury and guarantees them the right to confront and cross-examine the witnesses against them. The Sixth Amendment also gives the accused in a criminal case the right "to have the assistance of counsel" in her defense. This provision has been interpreted to mean not only that the accused may employ her own attorney but also that an indigent criminal defendant is entitled to court-appointed counsel. Included in the previously discussed *Miranda* warnings is a requirement that the police inform the accused of his right to counsel before custodial interrogation begins. *Edwards v. Arizona*, 452 U.S. 973 (1981), established that once the accused has requested the assistance of counsel, he may not as a general rule be interrogated further until counsel is made available to him.

The Supreme Court later held that the *Edwards* rule against further questioning is triggered only by an *unambiguous* request for counsel.[7] In *McNeil v. Wisconsin*, 501 U.S. 171 (1991), the Court provided further latitude for law enforcement officers by holding that if a defendant has made an in-court request for an attorney's assistance regarding a crime with which he has been formally charged, that request does not preclude police interrogation of him—in the absence of counsel—regarding another unrelated crime.

Finally, an accused is entitled to *effective* assistance of counsel. This means that the accused is entitled to representation at a point in the proceedings when an attorney may effectively assist him, and to reasonably competent representation by that attorney. Inadequate assistance of counsel is a proper basis for setting aside a conviction and ordering a new trial, but the standard applied to these cases makes ineffective assistance of counsel claims difficult ones for convicted defendants to invoke successfully.

White-Collar Crimes and the Dilemmas of Corporate Control

Introduction *White-collar crime* is the term used to describe a wide variety of nonviolent criminal offenses committed by businesspersons and business organizations. This term includes offenses committed by employees against their employers, as well as corporate officers' offenses that harm the corporation and its shareholders. It also includes criminal offenses committed by corporate employers and employees

---

[7]In *Davis v. United States*, 512 U.S. 452 (1994), the court concluded that "Maybe I should talk to a lawyer" was too ambiguous to trigger the *Edwards* rule.

Ethics and Compliance in Action

The highly publicized financial scandals involving Enron, WorldCom, Volkswagen, and other firms mentioned near the beginning of this chapter involved conduct that in some instances was alleged to be criminal. Regardless of whether criminal violations occurred, the alleged conduct was widely perceived to be questionable on ethical grounds and motivated by a desire for short-term gains notwithstanding the costs to others. Consider the broad-ranging and sometimes devastating effects of the perceived ethical lapses and the related legal proceedings (civil and criminal) faced by the firms and certain executives. These effects included:

• The crippling or near-crippling blow to the viability of the firms involved.

• The collapse in value of the firms' stock and the resulting loss to disillusioned and angry shareholders who felt they had been hoodwinked.
• The harm to the professional and personal reputations of the individuals involved in the business decisions that triggered legal scrutiny and raised serious ethical concerns.
• The job losses experienced by large numbers of employees who had nothing whatsoever to do with the questionable actions that effectively brought down the firm or made massive layoffs necessary.
• The effects on the families of those who lost their jobs.
• The lack of confidence on the part of would-be investors in the profit figures and projections put forth every day by corporations—including those that have done nothing irregular.
• The ripple effects of the above on the economy generally.

against society. Each year, corporate crime costs consumers billions of dollars. It takes various forms, from consumer fraud, securities fraud, mail or wire fraud, and tax evasion to price-fixing, environmental pollution, and other regulatory violations. Corporate crime presents our legal system with various problems that are unique.

Corporations form the backbone of the most successful economic system in history. They dominate the international economic scene and provide us with substantial benefits in the forms of efficiently produced goods and services. Yet these same corporations, through their agents, may pollute the environment, swindle their customers, mislead investors, produce dangerously defective products, and conspire with others to injure or destroy competition. How are we to achieve effective control over these large organizations so important to our existence? Increasingly, we have come to rely on the criminal law as a major corporate control instrument. The criminal law, however, was developed with individual wrongdoers in mind. Thus, criminal prosecutions aimed at individual white collar offenders generally follow the same legal and procedural avenues as other prosecutions. But even run-of-the-mill white-collar crime usually occurs within an organizational context. And corporate crime is inherently *organizational* in nature. Any given corporate action may be the product of the combined actions of many individuals acting within the corporate hierarchy. It may be that no individual had sufficient knowledge to possess the *mens rea* necessary for criminal responsibility under usual criminal law principles. Moreover, criminally penalizing corporations raises special problems in view of the obvious inability to apply standard sanctions such as imprisonment to legal entities.

Evolution of Corporate Criminal Liability

The law initially rejected the notion that corporations could be criminally responsible for their employees' actions. Early corporations, small in size and number, had little impact on public life. Their small size made it relatively easy to pinpoint individual wrongdoers within the corporation.

As corporations grew in size and power, however, the social need to control their activities grew accordingly. Corporate criminal liability evolved and expanded in two ways. First, legislatures enacted statutes creating regulatory offenses that did not require proof of *mens rea*. Second, courts began holding corporations responsible for violating criminal laws that previously had been applied only to individuals. Although those laws required proof of *mens rea*, courts tended to conclude that the *mens rea* requirement regarding a corporate defendant could be satisfied by imputing the criminal intent of employees to the corporation in a fashion similar to the imposition of tort liability on corporations under the *respondeat superior* doctrine.[8] The Supreme Court adopted this reasoning in its *New York Central* opinion, which established corporate criminal liability. See Figure 5.3.

Corporations now may face criminal liability for almost any offense if the statute in question indicates a legislative intent to hold corporations responsible. This legislative intent requirement is sometimes problematic. Many state criminal statutes may contain language suggesting an intent to hold only individuals liable. For example, manslaughter statutes often define the offense as "the killing

---

[8]Chapter 36 discusses *respondeat superior* in detail.

Figure 5.3   A Note on *New York Central*

The most important case in white collar and corporate crime has to be the Supreme Court's 1909 opinion in *New York Central & Hudson River Railroad v. United States,* 212 U.S. 481, because it approved the use of criminal sanctions against corporations. In *New York Central,* a railroad and its employee were charged and convicted of violating the Elkins Act, a statute passed in 1903 that authorized the Interstate Commerce Commission to impose heavy fines on railroads that offered rebates and on the shippers that accepted these rebates. Unlike most other statutes at the time, the Elkins Act explicitly imposed criminal liability on the corporation for acts committed by the corporate agent. The statute stated that

> anything done or omitted . . . by a corporation common carrier . . . which, if done or omitted . . . by any director or officer [or other agent] thereof . . . would constitute a misdemeanor under . . . this act, shall also be held to be a misdemeanor committed by such corporation. . . .
>
> In construing and enforcing the provisions of this section, the act, omission, or failure of any officer [or] agent . . . employed by any common carrier, acting within the scope of his employment, shall in every case be also deemed to be the act, omission, or failure of such carrier, as well as that of that person.

The facts were "practically undisputed," in the Court's words, as the corporation stipulated that its agent had given shipping rebates to the American Sugar Refining Company. The agent and the railroad were fined a total of $108,000 (approximately $3 million today).

On appeal, the railroad argued its conviction violated the Amendments discussed earlier in this chapter, namely the Due Process Clause of the Fifth Amendment. The argument was twofold: First, the company's conviction wrongly punished innocent shareholders; and, second, the conviction violated the presumption of innocence because no evidence had been presented that the company's board of directors authorized the agent's illegal acts.

The Supreme Court unanimously rejected these arguments and upheld the convictions. The Court found "no good reason why corporations may not be held responsible for and charged with the knowledge and purposes of their agents, acting within the authority conferred upon them." In reaching its decision, the Court focused on the dominant role that companies played in the U.S. economy. The Court reasoned that without extending the tort doctrine of *respondeat superior* to criminal cases, many offenses would go unpunished. According to the Court, to "give [corporations] immunity from all punishment because of the old and exploded doctrine that a corporation cannot commit a crime would virtually take away the only means of effectually controlling the subject-matter and correcting the abuses aimed at." Thus, the concept of vicarious corporate criminal liability was cemented in U.S. law.

of one human being by the act of another." When statutes are framed, however, in more general terms—such as by referring to "persons"—courts are generally willing to apply them to corporate defendants.

Corporate Criminal Liability Today Under the modern rule, a corporation may be held liable for criminal offenses committed by employees who *acted within the scope of their employment and for the benefit of the corporation.* A major corporate criminal liability issue centers around the classes of corporate employees whose intent can be imputed to the corporation. Some commentators argue that a corporation should be criminally responsible only for offenses committed by high corporate officials or those linked to them by authorization or acquiescence. (Nearly all, if not all, courts impose criminal liability on a corporation under such circumstances.) This argument reflects fairness notions, for if any group of corporate employees can fairly be said to constitute a corporation's mind, that group is its top officers and directors.

The problem with imposing corporate liability only on the basis of top corporate officers' actions or knowledge is that such a policy often insulates the corporation from liability. Many corporate offenses may be directly traceable only to middle managers or more subordinate employees. It may be impossible to demonstrate that any higher-level corporate official had sufficient knowledge to constitute *mens rea.* Recognizing this problem, the federal courts have adopted a general rule that a corporation may be criminally liable for the actions of *any* of its agents, regardless of whether any link between the agents and higher-level corporate officials can be demonstrated.

Problems with Punishing Corporations Despite the legal theories that justify corporate criminal liability, the punishment of corporations remains problematic. Does a criminal conviction stigmatize a corporation in the same way it stigmatizes an individual? Perhaps the only stigma resulting from a corporate criminal conviction is felt by the firm's employees, many of whom are entirely innocent of wrongdoing. Is it just to punish the innocent in an attempt to punish the guilty?

Consider, for instance, the effects that innocent employees of the Arthur Andersen firm experienced as a result of Andersen's obstruction-of-justice conviction in 2002. Although the conviction was overturned by the Supreme Court in 2005 because of faulty jury instructions (see the chapter's earlier discussion of criminal intent), the Andersen firm had already been knocked out of existence. Many partners of the firm acquired positions elsewhere, but nonpartner employees of the firm no doubt experienced hardship despite having had nothing to do with any alleged wrongdoing. Concern about preservation of the firm and minimizing hardship for employees appeared to motivate another leading accounting firm, KPMG, to take the unusual step of acknowledging possibly criminal behavior before being formally charged in connection with certain questionable tax shelters designed by the firm. By acknowledging wrongdoing, it was thought, the firm might be able to head off further criminal difficulty and remain viable as a firm. Similar motivations probably help explain BP's decision to plead guilty to criminal charges in connection with the Deepwater Horizon oil-drilling disaster and Volkswagen's previously noted decision to enter such a plea. (See the discussion of these cases near the outset of the chapter.)

What about the cash fine, the primary punishment imposed on convicted corporations? Most critics of corporate control strategies maintain that fines imposed on convicted firms tend to be too small to provide effective deterrence. These critics urge the use of fines keyed in some fashion to the corporate defendant's wealth. Larger fines may lead to undesirable results, however, if the corporate defendant ultimately passes along the fines to its customers (through higher prices), shareholders (through lower dividends or no dividends), or employees (through lower wages). Moreover, fines large enough to threaten corporate solvency may harm employees and those economically dependent on the corporation's financial well-being. Most of those persons, however, neither had the power to prevent the violation nor derived any benefit from it. Moreover, the managers responsible for a violation may avoid the imposition of direct burdens on them when the fine is assessed against the corporation. In fact, many may already have left the firm at the time of the sanction, sometimes with large bonuses and previously granted stock options.

Still other deficiencies make fines less-than-adequate corporate control devices. Fine strategies assume that all corporations are rationally acting profit-maximizers. Fines of sufficient size, it is argued, will erode the profit drive underlying most corporate violations. Numerous studies of actual corporate behavior suggest, however, that

corporations are not always rational actors. Moreover, many for-profit corporations may not be profit-maximizers all the time. Mature firms with well-established market shares may embrace goals other than profit maximization, such as technological prominence, increased market share, or higher employee salaries. In addition, the interests of managers who make corporate decisions and establish corporate policies may not coincide with the long-range economic interests of their corporate employers. The prospect that their employer could have to pay a substantial fine at some future point may not trouble top managers, who tend to have relatively short terms in office and are often compensated in part by large bonuses keyed to year-end profitability.

Individual Liability for Corporate Crime

Individuals who commit crimes while acting in corporate capacities have always been subjected to personal criminal liability. Many European nations reject corporate criminal liability and rely exclusively on individual criminal responsibility. In view of the problems associated with imposing criminal liability on corporations, individual liability may seem a more attractive control device. Besides being more consistent with traditional criminal law notions about the personal nature of guilt, individual liability may provide better deterrence than corporate liability if it enables society to use the criminal punishment threat against those who make important corporate decisions. The prospect of personal liability may cause individuals to resist corporate pressures to violate the law. If guilty individuals are identified and punished, the criminal law's purposes may be achieved without harm to innocent employees, shareholders, and consumers.

Problems with Individual Liability Attractive as it may sound, individual liability also poses significant problems when applied to corporate acts. Identifying responsible individuals within the corporate hierarchy becomes difficult—and frequently impossible—if we follow traditional notions and require proof of criminal intent. Business decisions leading to corporate wrongs often result from the collective actions of numerous corporate employees, none of whom had complete knowledge or specific criminal intent. Other corporate crimes are structural in the sense that they result from internal bureaucratic failures rather than the conscious actions of any individual or group.

Proving culpability on the part of high-level executives may be particularly difficult. Bad news sometimes does not reach them; other times, they consciously avoid knowledge that would lead to criminal responsibility. It therefore may be possible to demonstrate culpability only on the part of mid-level managers. Juries may be unwilling to convict such individuals, however, if they seem to be scapegoats for their unindicted superiors.

The difficulties in imposing criminal penalties on individual employees have led to the creation of some regulatory offenses that impose strict or vicarious liability on corporate officers. Strict liability offenses dispense with the requirement of proof of criminal intent but ordinarily require proof that the defendant committed some wrongful act. Vicarious liability offenses impose criminal liability on a defendant for the acts of third parties (normally, employees under the defendant's personal supervision), but may require proof of some form of *mens rea*, such as the defendant's negligent or reckless failure to supervise. Statutes often combine these two approaches by making corporate executives liable for the acts or omissions of corporate employees without requiring proof of criminal intent on the part of the employees.

Critics of strict liability offenses often argue that *mens rea* is a basic principle in our legal system and that it is unjust to stigmatize with a criminal conviction persons who are not morally culpable. In addition, critics doubt that strict liability statutes produce the deterrence sought by their proponents. Such statutes may reduce the moral impact of the criminal sanction if they apply it to relatively trivial offenses. Moreover, they may not result in enough convictions or sufficiently severe penalties to produce deterrence because juries and judges are unwilling to convict or punish defendants who may not be morally culpable. Although statutes creating strict liability offenses are generally held constitutional, they are disfavored by courts. Most courts require a clear indication of a legislative intent

to dispense with the *mens rea* element. So far, strict liability criminal offenses applicable to white-collar corporate employees have been limited to the areas of environmental, pharmaceutical, and food safety regulations, where protecting the health and welfare of the public is paramount.

Strict liability offenses are also criticized on the ground that even if responsible individuals within the corporation are convicted and punished appropriately, individual liability unaccompanied by corporate liability is unlikely to achieve effective corporate control. If immune from criminal liability, corporations could benefit financially from employees' violations of the law. Individual liability, unlike a corporate fine, does not force a corporation to give up the profits flowing from a violation. Thus, the corporation would have no incentive to avoid future violations. Incarcerated offenders would merely be replaced by others who might eventually yield to the pressures that produced the violations in the first place. Corporate liability, however, may sometimes encourage corporate efforts to prevent future violations. When an offense has occurred but no identifiable individual is sufficiently culpable to justify an individual prosecution of him or her, corporate liability is uniquely appropriate.

New Directions   The preceding discussion suggests that future efforts at corporate control will continue to include both corporate and individual criminal liability. It also suggests, however, that new approaches are necessary if society is to gain more effective control over corporate activities.

Various novel criminal penalties have been utilized in the individual liability setting. For example, white-collar

Ethics and Compliance in Action

Enron employee Sherron Watkins received considerable praise from the public, governmental officials, and media commentators when she went public with her concerns about certain accounting and other business practices of her employer. These alleged practices caused Enron and high-level executives of the firm to undergo considerable legal scrutiny in the civil and criminal arenas.

In deciding to become a whistleblower, Sherron Watkins no doubt was motivated by what she regarded as a moral obligation. The decision she made was more highly publicized than most decisions of that nature but was otherwise of a type that many employees have faced and will continue to face. You may be among those persons at some point in your career. Various questions, including the ones set forth below, may therefore be worth pondering. As you do so, you may find it useful

to consider the perspectives afforded by the ethical theories discussed in Chapter 4.

- When an employee learns of apparently unlawful behavior on the part of his or her employer, does the employee have an ethical duty to blow the whistle on the employer?
- Do any ethical duties or obligations of the employee come into conflict in such a situation? If so, what are they, and how does the employee balance them?
- What practical consequences may one face if he or she becomes a whistleblower? What role, if any, should those potential consequences play in the ethical analysis?
- What other consequences are likely to occur if the whistle is blown? What is likely to happen if the whistle isn't blown? Should these likely consequences affect the ethical analysis? If so, how?

offenders have sometimes been sentenced to render public service in addition to, or in lieu of, being incarcerated or fined. Some have even suggested the licensing of managers, with license suspensions as a penalty for offenders. The common thread in these and other similar approaches is an attempt to create penalties that are meaningful yet not so severe that judges and juries are unwilling to impose them.

A promising suggestion regarding corporate liability involves imaginative judicial use of corporate probation for convicted corporate offenders. For example, courts could require convicted corporations to do self-studies identifying the source of a violation and proposing appropriate steps to prevent future violations. If bureaucratic failures caused the violation, the court could order a limited restructuring of the corporation's internal decision-making processes as a condition of obtaining probation or avoiding a penalty. Possible orders might include requiring the collection and monitoring of the data necessary to discover or prevent future violations and mandating the creation of new executive positions to monitor such data. Restructuring would minimize the previously discussed harm to innocent persons that often accompanies corporate financial penalties. In addition, restructuring could be a more effective way to achieve corporate rehabilitation than relying exclusively on a corporation's desire to avoid future fines as an incentive to police itself.

The Federal Sentencing Guidelines, discussed earlier in this chapter in Figure 5.1, contain good reasons for corporations to institute measures to prevent regulatory violations. This is true even though, as Figure 5.1 indicates, the Supreme Court's 2005 decision in *Booker* made the Guidelines advisory rather than mandatory. Under the subset of rules known as the Organizational Sentencing Guidelines, organizations convicted of violating federal law may face greatly increased penalties for certain offenses, with some crimes carrying fines as high as roughly $300 million. The penalty that may be imposed on an organization depends on its "culpability score," which increases (thus calling for a more severe penalty) if, for example, high-level corporate officers were involved in the offense or the organization had a history of such offenses. Even apart from the potentially severe penalties, however, the Organizational Sentencing Guidelines provide an incentive for corporations to adopt compliance programs designed "to prevent and detect violations of the law." The presence of an effective compliance program may reduce the corporation's culpability score for sentencing purposes. Prior to the time the Organizational Sentencing Guidelines were developed, courts generally concluded that the existence of a compliance program should not operate as a mitigating factor in the sentencing of a convicted organization.

In recent years, the Justice Department has made increased use of deferred and nonprosecution agreements (DPAs and NPAs), under which corporations avoid formal criminal charges and trials in return for their agreement to pay monetary penalties, make compliance reforms, and submit to outside monitoring of their activities. Proponents of DPAs see them as a way to encourage more responsible behavior from corporations without the "hammer" of the criminal sanction. Critics, however, see the increased use of DPAs as sending a signal to corporations that they may engage in wrongful activities but still have available, in a figurative sense, a "get-out-of-jail-almost-free" card. As noted in earlier discussion, Toyota entered into a DPA regarding its responses to the sudden acceleration problem in some of its vehicles avoiding a criminal conviction despite there being almost 90 driver deaths.

Important White-Collar Crimes

Regulatory Offenses Numerous state and federal regulatory statutes on a wide range of subjects prescribe criminal as well as civil liability for violations. For instance, the federal Food, Drug, and Cosmetic Act obligates pharmaceutical companies to report safety data regarding their medications to the Food and Drug Administration (FDA) and bars such companies from promoting their medications for uses other than those approved by the FDA. In 2012, GlaxoSmithKline pleaded guilty to criminal charges in which the government alleged that the firm had violated these obligations. The charges that the government considered filing against GM in recent years included an alleged failure to disclose material safety information to the National Highway Traffic Safety Administration under provisions in federal law that impose such a disclosure obligation.

Other major federal regulatory offenses are discussed in later chapters. These include violations of the Sherman Antitrust Act, the Securities Act of 1933, the Securities Exchange Act of 1934, and certain environmental laws.

Fraudulent Acts Many business crimes involve some fraudulent conduct. In most states, it is a crime to obtain money or property by fraudulent pretenses, issue fraudulent checks, make false credit statements, or give short weights or measures. Certain forms of fraud in bankruptcy proceedings, such as false claims by creditors or fraudulent concealment or transfer of a debtor's assets, are federal criminal offenses. The same is true of securities fraud and extortion. *Sekhar v. United States*, which appears earlier in the chapter, deals with what does and does not constitute extortion under the federal Hobbs Act.

In addition, the federal mail fraud and wire fraud statutes make criminal the use of the mail, telephones, e-mail, or other similar means of communication to accomplish a fraudulent scheme. In *United States v. Anderson*, which follows, the court outlines the elements the government must prove in mail fraud and wire fraud prosecutions and analyzes the factual record of the case in light of those elements. The court also addresses sentencing issues under the Federal Sentencing Guidelines.

United States v. Anderson	558 F. App'x 454 (5th Cir. 2014)

A federal grand jury returned a 12-count indictment against spouses Andrea and Norman Anderson. Count 1 alleged that the Andersons conspired to commit wire fraud, in violation of 18 U.S.C. § 1349. Counts 2 through 12 alleged that they committed wire fraud, in violation of 18 U.S.C. § 1343.

At the Andersons' jury trial, the government introduced evidence that the Andersons ran a Ponzi scheme under which various persons were defrauded. According to the government's evidence, the Andersons represented to potential victims that they were successful investors and that they wanted to help others find similar success. They would usually tell their victims that Andrea Anderson had a sister, supposedly named "Lenore Lawrence," who purportedly worked at Goldman Sachs. They also claimed that they had a sizable investment account at the firms. The Andersons further represented that "Lenore" would be the one purchasing the stocks for which the victims were paying. Victims provided their money to the Andersons' personal bank accounts in a variety of ways, including wire transfers, cashier's checks, personal checks, and cash.

The evidence further indicated that the Andersons sent the victims e-mails confirming the making of payments and that they sometimes asked for more money in order to complete transactions. The Andersons did own a few investment accounts at TD Ameritrade. Some victims received money from their investments, but usually this was money taken from one victim and given to another. As a U.S. Secret Service special agent testified, "[t]he same day . . . that funds came in from one investor, the money went right back out to another investor." At other times, instead of sending the principal and interest back to the victim as promised, the Andersons would claim that they had reinvested the money because "[n]ow is not the time not to invest."

Victims also received e-mails supposedly sent by Lenore Lawrence, claiming that the victims' instructions (to sell off stocks and return their money) were being followed. No one ever met Lawrence or spoke to her on the phone, however. Some victims demanded their money back repeatedly but to no avail. Andrea Anderson sometimes responded by forwarding e-mails that were supposedly from Goldman Sachs employees. These e-mails were not genuine. According to the evidence, Andrea Anderson would meet with Goldman Sachs employees and act as though she wanted to open an account. When the Goldman Sachs employees would e-mail her to follow up on their initial meeting, Anderson would modify those e-mails and forward them to the victims.

The evidence also revealed that Goldman Sachs did not employ a "Lenore Lawrence" and that the Andersons did not own an investment account at Goldman Sachs. Although the evidence showed that the Andersons did invest some of the money, they never made noteworthy returns on their investments and mostly experienced losses. The Andersons had no other source of income. It appeared that they used the victims' money for personal expenses. Ultimately, according to the evidence, 11 victims lost a total of approximately $915,000.

The jury convicted the Andersons on all 12 counts. The district court sentenced each of them to 57 months of imprisonment and ordered that they pay $915,000 in restitution. The Andersons appealed their convictions and their sentences to the U.S. Court of Appeals for the Fifth Circuit, which issued the following opinion.

Per Curiam

The Andersons first argue that the evidence is insufficient to sustain the jury's verdict of guilty on the 12 counts of conviction. We must affirm [the jury's verdict] if a rational trier of fact could have found that the evidence established the essential elements of the offense beyond a reasonable doubt.

The Andersons were convicted of one count of conspiracy to commit wire fraud under 18 U.S.C. § 1349. To prove a conspiracy to commit wire fraud, the government had to prove beyond a reasonable doubt that (1) two or more persons made an agreement to commit wire fraud; (2) that the defendant knew the unlawful purpose of the agreement; and (3) that the defendant joined in the agreement willfully, in other words, with the intent to further the unlawful purpose. The agreement may be silent and does not need to be formal or spoken. "An agreement may be inferred from concert of action, voluntary participation may be inferred from a collection of circumstances, and knowledge may be inferred from surrounding circumstances." [Case citation omitted.]

The Andersons were also convicted of 11 counts of wire fraud under 18 U.S.C. § 1343. To prove wire fraud, the government had to prove beyond a reasonable doubt "(1) a scheme to defraud and (2) the use of, or causing the use of, wire communications in furtherance of the scheme." Additionally, even though not within the language of § 1343, "materiality of falsehood is an element" of the crime. "A material statement has a natural tendency to influence, or is capable of influencing, the decision of the decision-making body to which it was addressed." "Violation of the wire-fraud statute requires the specific intent to defraud, i.e., a 'conscious knowing intent to defraud.'" [Case citations omitted throughout paragraph.]

[Regarding] the conspiracy conviction, the Andersons assert that there is insufficient evidence as to all the essential elements. However, the government points to evidence from which a rational trier of fact could have drawn the necessary inferences. Several victims testified that the Andersons worked in tandem. For example, victim Phillip Douglas was introduced to the Andersons by another victim, his ex-girlfriend Deborah Ford. "She just said [that she was investing with] Andrea and Norman, because they were like one. One person, basically. They were a couple." Victim Rafael Green testified that he was in frequent e-mail contact with Andrea Anderson, that she forwarded him a "Goldman Sachs" e-mail, and that he later received repayment from Norman Anderson, as promised by the e-mail. [Various other victims testified that both Andersons communicated with them about their investments and in response to complaints by them.]

Not only that, but both spouses were making material misrepresentations. Both spouses met with victims Tom Parrish and his wife: "They told us that they . . . had a private family hedge fund with Andrea's sister and her cousin, her sister Lenore, and her cousin Joy. That one of them worked for Goldman Sachs, and the other worked for BlackRock in New York City." Both statements were false. The record is replete with similar evidence. Given all this evidence, a rational trier of fact could have found all three elements of conspiracy to commit wire fraud beyond a reasonable doubt.

As to the substantive crime of wire fraud, the Andersons argue there is insufficient evidence to show the specific intent to defraud. However, a rational trier of fact could have found this specific intent beyond a reasonable doubt simply from the fact that the Andersons were lying about their connection to Goldman Sachs, among other things. These lies were intended to get people to invest with them. The evidence at trial was sufficient to support the Andersons' convictions on all counts.

The Andersons claim, however, that Count 1 of the indictment should have been dismissed because it fails to state an offense. They argue that 18 U.S.C. § 1349 is a penalty provision only, and that it is unconstitutional to apply it as a criminal offense because it gives no notice to the public of what constitutes a conspiracy to commit wire fraud.

Enacted as part of the Sarbanes–Oxley Act of 2002, 18 U.S.C. § 1349 provides: "Any person who attempts or conspires to commit any offense under this chapter shall be subject to the same penalties as those prescribed for the offense, the commission of which was the object of the attempt or conspiracy." According to the Andersons, the fatal flaw in this language is that it does not contain the requirements of a conspiracy [as set forth in certain other federal laws specifically requiring proof that two or more persons must have worked together in an effort to defraud or otherwise violate the law and that at least one of the conspirators must have engaged in some overt act in furtherance of the alleged conspiracy]. [T]he Andersons complain that § 1349 does not contain the essential elements of an overt act or even conspiratorial agreement between two or more people.

Section 1349 . . . lacks an overt act requirement. But the Supreme Court has held that there is no constitutional problem with the lack of an overt act requirement in [similar statutes], and has upheld convictions under that provision. The Supreme Court has similarly found other conspiracy statutes lacking an overt act requirement constitutional. Similarly, we have clarified [in earlier decisions] that § 1349 indeed does not contain an overt act requirement, and have refused to dismiss an indictment where the defendant was arguing that being charged under both § 1349 and [another federal statute dealing with conspiracies] violated the prohibition on multiplicity. [Citations omitted throughout paragraph.]

The Andersons' contention that § 1349 is [merely a] penalty provision because of the circumstances of its legislative birth is also unpersuasive. Section 1349 was originally in Title IX of the Sarbanes–Oxley Act of 2002, which was entitled "White-Collar Crime Penalty Enhancements." However, as the Supreme Court has previously clarified, the heading of a statute is only helpful if there is some doubt about the meaning of the statute. [Case citation omitted.] Here, this is no ambiguity. Section 1349 is clearly a freestanding criminal charge. The Andersons' contention that the district court erred by not dismissing the indictment fails.

[In challenging the sentences imposed on them,] the Andersons contend that the district court erred in calculating the number of victims. Under [the U.S. Sentencing Guidelines], if the offense involved 10 or more victims, the offense level is increased by two levels [and the potential punishment is therefore more severe]. The commentary to [the Sentencing Guidelines] defines "victim" as, among other things, "any person who sustained any part of the actual loss." "Actual loss" is defined as "the reasonably foreseeable pecuniary harm that resulted from the offense." [Citations omitted.]

We review a district court's application of the Sentencing Guidelines de novo and its factual findings for clear error. No clear error has occurred if the district court's finding is plausible in light of the record as a whole. The Andersons contend that there were just 9, not 11, victims because [one investor] combined his investments with those of two other investors. At the sentencing hearing, the district court rejected this argument [and concluded that there were 11 victims]. This factual finding is clearly plausible in light of the record as a whole. The district court did not clearly err in finding that there were at least 10 victims, justifying the [potential penalty] enhancement [under the Sentencing Guidelines].

The Andersons also argue that the district court imposed a substantively unreasonable sentence. It is well-settled that the Sentencing Guidelines are advisory, and sentencing decisions are examined for reasonableness. "Properly calculated within-Guidelines sentences enjoy a presumption of reasonableness that is rebutted only upon a showing that the sentence does not account for a factor that should receive significant weight, it gives significant weight to an irrelevant or improper factor, or it represents a clear error of judgment in balancing sentencing factors." [Case citation omitted.] When a district court imposes a within-Guidelines sentence, we "infer that the judge has considered all the factors for a fair sentence . . . , and it will be rare for a reviewing court to say such a sentence is unreasonable." [Case citation omitted.]

Here, the district court sentenced the Andersons to 57 months in prison, a within-Guidelines sentence. The district court [stated that] it found the sentences reasonable "in view of the nature and circumstances of the offense." As to both sentences, the court found that they would "serve as just punishment, promote respect for the law, and deter future violations of the law." Given the within-Guidelines sentences and the district court's consideration of [relevant factors], the Andersons have not overcome the presumption of reasonableness.

Convictions of defendants affirmed; sentences imposed on them affirmed.

The Sarbanes–Oxley Act In response to a series of highly publicized financial scandals and accounting controversies involving Enron, Arthur Andersen, Global Crossing, WorldCom, and other firms, Congress enacted the Sarbanes–Oxley Act of 2002 (SOX). SOX created the Public Company Accounting Oversight Board and charged it with regulatory responsibilities concerning public accounting firms' audits of corporations. The statute also established various requirements designed to ensure auditor independence; bring about higher levels of accuracy in corporate reporting of financial information; and promote responsible conduct on the part of corporate officers and directors, auditors, and securities analysts.

Additional portions of the broad-ranging SOX were given separate and more informative titles such as the Corporate and Criminal Fraud Accountability Act and the White-Collar Crime Penalty Enhancement Act. In those other portions of the statute, Congress:

- Established substantial fines and/or a maximum of 20 years of imprisonment as punishment for the knowing alteration or destruction of documents or records with the intent to impede a government investigation or proceeding.
- Made it a crime for an accountant to destroy corporate audit records prior to the appropriate time set forth in the statute and in regulations to be promulgated by the Securities and Exchange Commission.
- Classified debts resulting from civil judgments for securities fraud as nondischargeable in bankruptcy.
- Lengthened the statute of limitations period within which certain securities fraud cases may be filed.
- Provided legal protections for employees who act as whistleblowers regarding instances of fraud engaged in by their employers or, as the Supreme Court held in *Lawson v. FMR LLC*, 571 U.S. 429 (2014), by other firms that use them on an outside-contracting basis for advice or services such as auditing.
- Established substantial fines and/or imprisonment of up to 25 years as the punishment for certain securities fraud offenses.
- Increased the maximum term of imprisonment for mail fraud and wire fraud to 20 years.
- Made attempts and conspiracies to commit such offenses subject to the same penalties established for the offenses themselves.
- Enhanced the penalties for certain criminal violations of the Securities Exchange Act of 1934.
- Instructed the U.S. Sentencing Commission to review the Federal Sentencing Guidelines' treatment of obstruction of justice offenses, white-collar crimes, and securities fraud offenses in order to ensure that deterrence and punishment purposes were being adequately served.

Bribery and Giving of Illegal Gratuities

State and federal law has long made it a crime to offer public officials gifts, favors, or anything of value to influence official decisions for private benefit. In 1977, Congress enacted the Foreign Corrupt Practices Act (FCPA),

The Global Business Environment

At varying times since the 1977 enactment of the Foreign Corrupt Practices Act, the United States has advocated the development of international agreements designed to combat bribery and similar forms of corruption on at least a regional, if not a global, scale. These efforts and those of other nations sharing similar views bore fruit during the past decades.

In 1996, the Organization of American States (OAS) adopted the Inter-American Convention Against Corruption (IACAC). When it ratified the IACAC in September 2000, the United States joined 20 other subscribing OAS nations. The IACAC prohibits the offering or giving of a bribe to a government official in order to influence the official's actions, the solicitation or receipt of such a bribe, and certain other forms of corruption on the part of government officials. It requires subscribing nations to make changes in their domestic laws in order to make those laws consistent with the IACAC. The United States has taken the position that given the content of the Foreign Corrupt Practices Act and other U.S. statutes prohibiting the offering and solicitation of bribes as well as various other forms of corruption, its statutes already are consistent with the IACAC.

The Organization for Economic Cooperation and Development (OECD) is made up of 29 nations that are leading exporters. In 1997, the OECD adopted the Convention on Combating Bribery of Officials in International Business Transactions. The OECD Convention, subscribed to by the United States, 28 other OECD member nations, and five nonmember nations, prohibits the offering or giving of a bribe to a government official in order to obtain a business advantage from the official's action or inaction. It calls for subscribing nations to have domestic laws that contain such a prohibition. Unlike the IACAC, however, the OECD neither prohibits the government official's solicitation or receipt of a bribe nor contains provisions dealing with the other forms of official corruption contemplated by the IACAC.

In 1999, the Council of Europe adopted the Criminal Law Convention on Corruption, which calls upon European Union (EU) member nations to develop domestic laws prohibiting the same sorts of behaviors prohibited by the IACAC. Many European Union members have signed on to this convention, as have three nonmembers of the EU. One of those is the United States.

Because the IACAC, the OECD Convention, and the Criminal Law Convention are relatively recent developments, it is too early to draw firm conclusions about whether they have been effective international instruments for combating bribery and similar forms of corruption. Much depends upon whether the domestic laws contemplated by these conventions are enforced with consistency and regularity.

which criminalized the offering or giving of anything of value to officials of foreign governments in an attempt to influence their official actions. Individuals who violate the FCPA's bribery prohibition may be fined up to $250,000 and/or imprisoned for a maximum of five years. Corporate violators of the FCPA may be fined as much as $2 million. As explained in the nearby Global Business Environment box, the 1990s marked the emergence of international agreements as additional devices for addressing the problem of bribery of government officials.

In recent years, various high-profile companies and their executives or other employees have been the subject of federal investigations for potential violations of the FCPA. Regardless of whether such investigations lead to actual criminal charges, these firms and the individuals associated with them incur substantial legal costs and may take significant hits to their reputations. The experience sometimes convinces investigated companies that enhancement of their legal-compliance programs is a prudent step to lessen the danger of future problems of a similar nature.

Most states in the United States also have commercial bribery statutes. These laws prohibit offering or providing kickbacks and similar payoffs to private parties in order to secure some commercial advantage.

Computer Crime

 LO5-10 Describe the major elements that must be proven in order to establish a violation of the Computer Fraud and Abuse Act.

As computers have come to play an increasingly important role in our society, new opportunities for crime have arisen. In some instances, computers may be used to accomplish crimes such as theft, embezzlement, espionage, and fraud. In others, computers or the information stored there may be targets of crimes such as unauthorized access, vandalism, tampering, or theft of services. The law's response to computer crimes has evolved with this new technology. For example, computer hacking—once viewed by some as a mischievous but clever activity—can now lead to significant prison sentences and fines.

The technical nature of computer crime complicates its detection and prosecution. Traditional criminal statutes have often proven inadequate because they tend not to address explicitly the types of crime associated with the use of computers.

Almost all states have now enacted criminal statutes specifically outlawing certain abuses of computers. Common provisions prohibit such acts as obtaining access to a computer system without authorization, tampering with files or causing damage to a system (e.g., by spreading a virus or deleting files), invading the privacy of others, using a computer to commit fraud or theft, and trafficking in passwords or access codes.

On the federal level, computer crime has been prosecuted with some success under existing federal statutes, primarily those forbidding mail fraud, wire fraud, transportation of stolen property, and thefts of property. As has been true at the state level, successful prosecution of these cases often depends on broad interpretation of the statutory prerequisites. Another federal law deals more directly with improper uses of computers. Among the crimes covered by this federal statute are intentionally gaining unauthorized access to a computer used by or for the U.S. government, trafficking in passwords and other access devices, and using a computer to obtain government information that is protected from disclosure. It is also a crime to gain unauthorized access to the computer system of a private financial institution that has a connection with the federal government (such as federal insurance for the deposits in the financial institution). In addition, the statute criminalizes the transmission of codes, commands, or information if the transmission was intended to damage such an institution's computers, computer system, data, or programs.

The federal Computer Fraud and Abuse Act (CFAA) allows the imposition of criminal and civil liability on one who "knowingly, and with intent to defraud, accesses a protected computer without authorization, or exceeds authorized access, and by means of such conduct furthers the intended fraud and obtains anything of value." In addition, the CFAA provides that criminal and civil liability may attach to one who transmits a program, information, code, or command knowingly, intentionally, and without authorization, if the act results in damage to a computer system used by the government or a financial institution or otherwise in interstate commerce. For a case applying the CFAA, see the nearby Cyberlaw in Action box.

CYBERLAW IN ACTION

May an employee who violates his employer's restrictions on computer access and use be held criminally responsible under the federal Computer Fraud and Abuse Act (CFAA)? The federal courts of appeals that have considered this question have disagreed on the correct answer to it. Here, we consider *United States v. Nosal*, in which the Ninth Circuit Court of Appeals ultimately rejected the government's attempt to hold the defendant criminally responsible under the CFAA. According to other federal courts of appeal, however, the same CFAA provision addressed in *Nosal* contemplates criminal responsibility in cases with facts very similar to those in *Nosal*.

For several years, David Nosal was an executive at Korn/Ferry International, an executive search firm. When Nosal left his job at Korn/Ferry, he signed a separation agreement and an independent contractor agreement. Under these contracts, he agreed to serve as an independent contractor for Korn/Ferry and promised not to compete with the firm for one year. In return, Korn/Ferry agreed to make certain payments to Nosal.

Shortly after leaving the firm, Nosal recruited three Korn/Ferry employees to help him start a competing business. According to the allegations in the indictment referred to below, these employees utilized their user accounts to access the Korn/Ferry computer system and obtain trade secrets and other proprietary information belonging to Korn/Ferry. The particular information obtained by the employees—and allegedly transferred to Nosal—included source lists, names, and contact information from a confidential Korn/Ferry database that the firm regarded as among the world's most comprehensive databases of information regarding executive candidates. The indictment alleged that Korn/Ferry engaged in considerable efforts to keep the database confidential, required its employees to enter into agreements that confined use and disclosure of information in the database to purposes connected with Korn/Ferry's business, and otherwise alerted employees that accessing Korn/Ferry information in the database without authority to do so was prohibited.

A federal grand jury indictment charged Nosal and one of the Korn/Ferry employees with violations of the CFAA (18 U.S.C. § 1030). The CFAA prohibits a variety of computer crimes, most of which involve accessing computers without authorization or in excess of authorization and then taking some prohibited action. The particular subsection under which Nosal was charged, § 1030(a)(4), calls for criminal liability to be imposed on one who "knowingly and with intent to defraud, accesses a protected computer without authorization, or exceeds authorized access, and by means of such conduct furthers the intended fraud and obtains anything of value." According to the indictment, Nosal's co-conspirators exceeded their authorized access to Korn/Ferry's computer system by obtaining information from it in order to defraud their employer and help Nosal establish a competing business.

Nosal moved to dismiss the indictment, arguing that "the CFAA was aimed primarily at computer hackers and . . . does not cover employees who misappropriate information or who violate contractual confidentiality agreements by using employer-owned information in a manner inconsistent with those agreements." Nosal argued that the Korn/Ferry employees could not have acted "without authorization" and could not have "exceed[ed] authorized access" because they had permission under certain circumstances to access the computer system and the information present there. A federal district court agreed with this argument, while acknowledging that courts had split on how to interpret § 1030(a)(4). Opting for the interpretation that an employee does not exceed authorized access to a computer system by accessing information unless the employee is without authority to access the information under *any* circumstances, the district court dismissed various counts in the indictment because the Korn/Ferry employees did have authority to access the database in question under certain circumstances. The federal government appealed to the U.S. Court of Appeals for the Ninth Circuit.

A Ninth Circuit panel initially interpreted § 1030(a)(4) in a manner favorable to the government's case (*United States v. Nosal*, 642 F.3d 781 (9th Cir. 2011)) but the court granted a request that it rehear the case *en banc* (i.e., by the full Ninth Circuit). On rehearing, the court changed course and went Nosal's way. In *United States v. Nosal*, 676 F.3d 854 (9th Cir. 2012), the court stressed that the CFAA was fundamentally an anti-hacking statute and that the relevant statutory language should be interpreted in light of that statutory nature and purpose. According to the Ninth Circuit, the "exceeds authorized access" language in the relevant statutory section applied only to hacking instances in which the alleged violator did not have permission to access the computer system and its contents under any circumstances.

The Ninth Circuit's interpretation of the statute meant that Nosal and his supposed co-conspirators did not violate the statute because they did have authorization from their employer to access the relevant database, even though they then violated the employer's restrictions on use of the database. Nosal and the Korn/Ferry employees may have misappropriated information, the court reasoned, but they did not violate the CFAA provision because it was meant to reach only hacking, not misappropriation. In rejecting the government's argument that the "exceeds authorized access" language should be interpreted as applying to instances in which someone legitimately has access to a computer system and its contents but then exceeds the system owner's restrictions on how the contents can be used, the Ninth Circuit expressed concern that the government's proposed interpretation could make criminals of many employees who have access to their employer's computer system but then sometimes

use it for personal purposes such as checking Facebook, looking up scores of sporting events, or playing games. Purposes of that nature, the court noted, may be likely to violate many employers' use policies even though such uses probably occur with considerable frequency each day. The Ninth Circuit stressed that interpreting "exceeds authorized access" as prohibiting only hacking-type behavior would avoid such anomalous results.

The court conceded that other circuits (the Fifth, Seventh, and Eleventh) had adopted the government's preferred view of the "exceeds authorized access" language and that a case such as the one before it would come out differently under those other circuits' approach. Their approach, however, was too broad an interpretation of the statutory language for the Ninth Circuit to countenance. Hence, the court concluded, there was no CFAA violation in *Nosal*. (The court noted that it was not addressing whether Nosal might face responsibility on another charge brought by the government: for an alleged violation of a trade secrets statute.)

The dissenting judges in *Nosal* vehemently disagreed. They asserted that the majority was preoccupied with unrealistic hypotheticals in which employees who were Facebook users and sports score seekers might be criminally prosecuted by the government if they made such uses of their employer's computer system and the employer's policy prohibited such uses. Apart from the extreme unlikelihood that the government would ever target such users for prosecution, the dissenters noted that the majority was overlooking the critical element of an intent to defraud—an element arguably present in *Nosal* but not in the Facebook-type hypotheticals the majority emphasized. In addition, the dissenters reasoned that instances in which employees seek to help someone else set up a business that competes with their employer (the situation in *Nosal*) are readily distinguishable from the hypotheticals about which the majority was worried.

The split among the circuits on how to interpret the "exceeds authorized access" language in the CFAA could be resolved by the Supreme Court, of course, if the Court would agree to decide an appropriate case at some point.

Note: The Court did just that. In April 2020, certiorari was granted in *Van Buren v. United States*, 2020 U.S.LEXIS 2336 (Apr. 20, 2020), which will address whether a police sergeant who was permitted to use a license plate database for work, but did so for the "improper purpose" of checking on an exotic dancer, violates the CFAA.

Problems and Problem Cases

1. Ahmad Ressam attempted to enter the United States by car ferry at Port Angeles, Washington. Hidden in his rental car's trunk were explosives that he intended to detonate at the Los Angeles International Airport. After the ferry docked, a customs official questioned Ressam. On the customs declaration form the official instructed Ressam to complete, Ressam identified himself by a false name and falsely referred to himself as a Canadian citizen even though he was Algerian. Ressam was then directed to a secondary inspection station, where another official performed a search of his car. This search uncovered explosives and related

items in the car's spare tire well. Ressam was later convicted of a number of crimes, including the felony of making a false statement to a U.S. customs official and the offense of carrying an explosive "during the commission of" the just-noted felony, in violation of 18 U.S.C. § 844(h)(2). The latter offense was Count 9 in the indictment against Ressam. The U.S. Court of Appeals for the Ninth Circuit set aside Ressam's conviction on Count 9 because it interpreted the word *during*, as used in § 844(h)(2), as including an implicit requirement that the explosive be carried *in relation to* the underlying felony. The Ninth Circuit concluded that because Ressam's carrying of explosives did not relate to the underlying felony of making a false statement to a customs official, the conviction on Count 9 could not stand. Did the Ninth Circuit correctly interpret the "during the commission of" language in the statute on which Count 9 was based?

2. A California Highway Patrol officer stopped the pickup truck occupied by Lorenzo and Jose Navarette because it matched the description of a vehicle that an anonymous 911 caller had recently reported as having run her off the road. As he and a second officer approached the truck, they smelled marijuana. They searched the truck's bed, found 30 pounds of marijuana, and arrested both Navarettes. The Navarettes moved to suppress the evidence, arguing that the anonymous call to 911 did not give rise to a reasonable suspicion on the part of the officer and that the traffic stop therefore violated the Fourth Amendment. They further argued that if the traffic stop violated the Fourth Amendment, the evidence obtained in the search should be excluded under the fruit-of-the-poisonous-tree doctrine. The Navarettes' motion was denied. They were later convicted of drug-possession offenses. On appeal, the Navarettes reiterated their objection to the traffic stop and their objection to the use of the evidence obtained in the search. Did the traffic stop violate the Fourth Amendment? Should the evidence obtained in the ensuing search have been suppressed?

3. A federal grand jury was investigating "John Doe," president and sole shareholder of "XYZ" corporation, concerning possible violations of federal securities and money-laundering statutes. During the investigation, the government learned that XYZ had paid the bills for various telephone lines, including those used in Doe's homes and car. Grand jury subpoenas calling for the production of documents were then served on the custodian of XYZ's corporate records, on Doe, and on the law firm Paul, Weiss, Rifkind, Wharton

& Garrison (Paul–Weiss), which represented Doe. These subpoenas sought production of telephone bills, records, and statements of account regarding certain telephone numbers, including those used by Doe. The district court determined after an evidentiary hearing that the documents sought were XYZ's, and not Doe's.

Paul–Weiss, which had received copies of these documents from its client, refused to produce them, arguing that it was exempted from doing so by Doe's privilege against self-incrimination. Was Paul–Weiss correct in its assertion?

4. William Parks, a special agent of the U.S. Customs Service, was investigating allegations that Bet-Air Inc. (a seller of spare aviation parts and supplies) had supplied restricted military parts to Iran. Parks entered Bet-Air's property and removed a bag of shredded documents from a garbage dumpster. The dumpster was located near the Bet-Air offices in a parking area reserved for the firm's employees. To reach the dumpster, Parks had to travel 40 yards on a private paved road. No signs indicated that the road was private. In later judicial proceedings, Parks testified that at the time he traveled on the road, he did not know he was on Bet-Air's property. When reconstructed, some of the previously shredded documents contained information seemingly relevant to the investigation. Parks used the shredded documents and the information they revealed as the basis for obtaining a warrant to search the Bet-Air premises. In executing the search warrant, Parks and other law enforcement officers seized numerous documents and Bet-Air records.

A federal grand jury indicted Bet-Air's chairman, Terence Hall, and other defendants on various counts related to the alleged supplying of restricted military parts to Iran. Contending that the Fourth Amendment had been violated, Hall filed a motion asking the court to suppress (i.e., exclude) all evidence derived from the warrantless search of the dumpster and all evidence seized during the search of the Bet-Air premises (the search pursuant to the warrant). The federal district court denied Hall's motion. Following a jury trial, Hall was convicted on all counts and sentenced to prison. He appealed, again arguing that the Fourth Amendment was violated. How did the appellate court rule? Was there a Fourth Amendment violation?

5. For approximately 20 years, Efrain Santos operated an illegal lottery in Indiana. He employed a number of helpers to run the lottery. At bars and restaurants, Santos's runners gathered bets from gamblers, kept a

portion of the bets as their commissions, and delivered the rest to Santos's collectors. Collectors, one of whom was Benedicto Diaz, then delivered the money to Santos, who used some of it to pay the salaries of collectors (including Diaz) and to pay the lottery winners. These payments to runners, collectors, and winners formed the basis of a 10-count indictment against Santos and Diaz filed in the U.S. District Court for the Northern District of Indiana. A jury found Santos guilty of running and conspiring to run an illegal gambling business, as well as one count of conspiracy to launder money and two counts of money laundering. Diaz pleaded guilty to conspiracy to launder money. The relevant provision of the federal money-laundering statute reads as follows:

> Whoever, knowing that the property involved in a financial transaction represents the proceeds of some form of unlawful activity, conducts or attempts to conduct such a financial transaction which in fact involves the proceeds of specified unlawful activity . . . with the intent to promote the carrying on of specified unlawful activity . . . shall be sentenced to a fine of not more than $500,000 or twice the value of the property involved in the transaction, whichever is greater, or imprisonment for not more than twenty years, or both.

After the district court sentenced Santos and Diaz to prison, the U.S. Court of Appeals for the Seventh Circuit affirmed the convictions and sentences. Santos and Diaz later attacked the validity of the convictions and sentences by seeking a writ of habeas corpus. In the habeas corpus proceeding, the district court rejected all of their claims except for one, a challenge to their money-laundering convictions. The district court concluded that the money-laundering statute's prohibition of transactions involving criminal "proceeds" applies only to transactions involving criminal profits, not criminal receipts. Applying that holding to the cases of Santos and Diaz, the district court found no evidence that the transactions on which the money-laundering convictions were based (Santos's payments to runners, winners, and collectors and Diaz's receipt of payment for his collection services) involved profits, as opposed to receipts, of the illegal lottery. Accordingly, the district court vacated the money-laundering convictions. The Seventh Circuit affirmed. The U.S. Supreme Court granted the government's petition for a writ of certiorari in order to address this question: whether the term *proceeds* in the federal money-laundering statute means "receipts" or, instead, "profits." How did the Supreme Court rule?

6. Police officers arrested Rodney Gant for driving with a suspended license. After they handcuffed him and locked him in the back of a patrol car, the officers searched his car and discovered cocaine in the pocket of a jacket on the backseat. Gant was charged with possession of a narcotic drug for sale and possession of drug paraphernalia (the plastic bag in which the cocaine was found). Gant moved to suppress the evidence seized from his car on the ground that the warrantless search violated the Fourth Amendment. The state resisted Gant's motion by arguing that the search of the car was constitutionally valid pursuant to U.S. Supreme Court decisions allowing a warrantless search incident to arrest and a warrantless search of an arrestee's vehicle if the search was contemporaneous with the arrest. Gant argued that the search of his vehicle should be held a violation of the Fourth Amendment because he posed no threat to the officers after he was handcuffed in the patrol car and because he was arrested for a traffic offense for which no evidence could be found in his vehicle. An Arizona trial court held that the search of the car did not violate the Fourth Amendment. Therefore, the court denied Gant's suppression motion. The case proceeded to trial, and a jury convicted Gant. He was sentenced to prison. After protracted state-court proceedings, Arizona's highest court concluded that Gant's conviction could not stand because the search of his car was unreasonable for Fourth Amendment purposes. The U.S. Supreme Court agreed to decide the case. How did the Supreme Court rule regarding the search of Gant's car? Did the search violate the Fourth Amendment?

7. Muniz was arrested on a charge of driving under the influence of alcohol. He was taken to a booking center, where he was asked several questions by a police officer without first being given the *Miranda* warnings. Videotape (which included an audio portion) was used to record the questions and Muniz's answers. The officer asked Muniz his name, address, height, weight, eye color, date of birth, and current age. Muniz stumbled over answers to two of these questions. The officer then asked Muniz the date of his sixth birthday, but Muniz did not give the correct date. At a later point, Muniz was read the *Miranda* warnings for the first time. He was later convicted of the charged offense, with the trial court denying his motion to exclude the videotape (both video and audio portions) from evidence. Assume that the video portion of the tape violated neither the Fifth Amendment nor *Miranda*.

Should all or any part of the audio portion of the tape (which contained Muniz's stumbling responses to two questions plus his incorrect answer to the sixth birthday date question) have been excluded as a violation of either the Fifth Amendment or *Miranda*?

8. A federal statute, 18 U.S.C. § 1037, prohibits a variety of misleading electronic mail–related actions in commercial settings. These include instances in which a person who, with knowledge of doing so, "materially falsifies header information in multiple commercial electronic mail messages and intentionally initiates the transmission of such messages" (prohibited by § 1037(a)(3)) or "registers, using information that materially falsifies the identity of the actual registrant, for five or more electronic mail accounts or online user accounts or two or more domain names, and intentionally initiates the transmission of multiple commercial electronic mail messages from any combination of such accounts or domain names" (prohibited by § 1037(a)(4)). Violators of these prohibitions may be punished by fines or imprisonment, or both.

   A federal indictment charged that Michael Twombly and Joshua Eveloff violated § 1037(a)(3) and (4). The government claimed that Twombly leased dedicated servers using an alias, including one server from Biznesshosting Inc., and that shortly after it provided logon credentials to Twombly, Biznesshosting began receiving complaints regarding spam electronic mail messages originating from its network. These spam messages allegedly numbered approximately 1 million, followed several days later by another 1.5 million. The spam messages contained computer software advertising and directed recipients to the website of a company with a Canadian address. The government maintained that this site was falsely registered under the name of a nonexistent business and that the messages' routing information and "From" lines had been falsified. As a result, the government contended, recipients, Internet service providers, and law enforcement agencies were prevented from identifying, locating, or responding to the senders. When Biznesshosting investigated the complaints, it traced the spam to the server leased by Twombly. A search conducted by the FBI allegedly uncovered roughly 20 dedicated servers leased by Twombly using false credentials. According to the government, Twombly leased the servers for an unnamed person—later determined to be Eveloff—and received payment from that person for each set of logon credentials provided. Under the government's theory of the case, both Twombly and Eveloff caused the spam messages to be sent. Twombly and Eveloff moved for dismissal of the indictment on the ground that § 1037(a)(3) and (4) were unconstitutionally vague. Did their argument have merit?

9. Suspicious that marijuana was being grown in eventual defendant DK's home, federal agents used a thermal imaging device to scan his home from a public street. The agents sought to determine whether the amount of heat emanating from the home (which was part of a triplex) was consistent with the amount emanated from high-intensity lamps typically used for indoor marijuana growth. The scan showed that the roof and a side wall were relatively hot compared with the rest of the home and substantially warmer than the neighboring units. Based in part on the thermal imaging results, a federal magistrate judge issued a warrant to search the home, where the agents found marijuana growing. After being indicted on a federal drug charge, DK unsuccessfully moved to suppress the evidence seized from his home. He then entered a conditional guilty plea under which, on appeal, he could challenge the use of the thermal imaging device and the validity of the resulting warrant. The government took the position that the use of the device, when operated from a public street, was not a search for purposes of the Fourth Amendment and that DK therefore did not have a basis for his Fourth Amendment–based challenge. Was the government correct in this argument?

10. John Park was CEO of Acme Markets Inc., a national retail food chain with approximately 36,000 employees, 874 retail outlets, and 16 warehouses. Acme and Park were charged with five counts of violating the federal Food, Drug, and Cosmetic Act by storing food shipped in interstate commerce in warehouses where it was exposed to rodent contamination. The violations were detected during FDA inspections of Acme's Baltimore warehouse. Inspectors saw evidence of rodent infestation and unsanitary conditions, such as mouse droppings on the floor of the hanging meat room and alongside bales of Jell-O, as well as a hole chewed by a rodent in a bale of Jell-O. The FDA notified Park of these findings by a letter. Upon checking with Acme's vice president for legal affairs, Park learned that the Baltimore division vice president was investigating the situation immediately and would be taking corrective action. An FDA inspection three months after the first one disclosed continued rodent contamination at the Baltimore warehouse despite improved sanitation there. The criminal charges referred to above were then filed against Acme and Park. Acme pleaded

guilty; Park refused to do so and proceeded to trial. After being convicted on each count, Park appealed. A federal court of appeals overturned his conviction. Was the appellate court correct in doing so?

11. Patrice Seibert's 12-year-old son, Jonathan, had cerebral palsy. When Jonathan died in his sleep, Seibert feared charges of neglect because there were bedsores on his body. In Seibert's presence, two of her teenage sons and two of their friends devised a plan to conceal the facts surrounding Jonathan's death by incinerating his body in the course of burning the family's mobile home. Under the plan, the fire would be set while Donald Rector, a mentally ill teenager who lived with the family, was asleep in the mobile home. The fire and the presence of Rector's body would eliminate any indication that Jonathan had been the victim of neglect. Seibert's son Darian and a friend set the fire as planned, and Rector died.

Five days later, police officers awakened Seibert at 3:00 A.M. at a hospital where Darian was being treated for burns. An officer arrested Seibert but, in accordance with instructions from Officer Hanrahan, refrained from giving *Miranda* warnings at the time of the arrest. After Seibert had been taken to the police station and left alone in an interview room for 15 minutes, Hanrahan questioned her for 30 to 40 minutes without giving *Miranda* warnings. During this questioning, Hanrahan squeezed Seibert's arm and repeated this statement: "Donald [Rector] was also to die in his sleep." When Seibert finally admitted that she knew Rector was meant to die in the fire, she was given a 20-minute coffee and cigarette break. Hanrahan then turned on a tape recorder, gave Seibert the *Miranda* warnings, and obtained a signed waiver of rights from her. He resumed the questioning with "OK, Patrice, we've been talking for a little while about what happened on Wednesday, the twelfth, haven't we?" Hanrahan then confronted Seibert with her pre-*Miranda*-warnings statements about the plan to set the fire and the understanding that Rector would be left sleeping in the mobile home. Specifically, Hanrahan referred to Seibert's pre-*Miranda*-warnings statements by asking, in regard to Rector, "[D]idn't you tell me he was supposed to die in his sleep?" and "So he was supposed to die in his sleep?" Seibert answered "Yes" to the second of these post-warnings questions.

After being charged with murder for her role in Rector's death, Seibert sought to have her pre-*Miranda*-warnings statements and her post-*Miranda*-warnings statements suppressed (i.e., excluded from evidence) as the remedy for supposed Fifth Amendment and *Miranda* violations. At the hearing on Seibert's suppression motion, Hanrahan testified that he decided to withhold *Miranda* warnings and to resort to an interrogation technique he had been taught: question first, then give the *Miranda* warnings, and then repeat the question "until I get the answer that she's already provided once." Hanrahan acknowledged that Seibert's ultimate statement was "largely a repeat" of information obtained prior to the giving of the *Miranda* warnings. The Missouri trial court suppressed Seibert's pre-*Miranda*-warnings statements but permitted use of her post-warnings statements. A jury convicted Seibert, and the Missouri Court of Appeals affirmed. However, the Missouri Supreme Court reversed, holding that Seibert's post-warnings statements should have been suppressed as well. The U.S. Supreme Court agreed to decide the case at the request of the state of Missouri. How did the Supreme Court rule on the suppression issue?

12. Police officers set up a controlled buy of crack cocaine outside an apartment complex. An undercover officer watched the deal take place from an unmarked car in a nearby parking lot. After the buy occurred, the undercover officer radioed uniformed officers to move in on the suspect. He told them that the suspect was moving toward the breezeway of an apartment building, and he urged them to get there quickly before the suspect entered an apartment. In response, the uniformed officers drove into the parking lot, left their vehicles, and ran to the breezeway. As they entered it, they heard a door shut and detected a very strong odor of burnt marijuana. At the end of the breezeway, the officers saw two apartments, one on the left and one on the right; they did not know which apartment the suspect had entered. Because they smelled marijuana smoke emanating from the apartment on the left, they approached that apartment's door.

One of the officers who approached the door later testified that they loudly banged on the door and announced, "This is the police." This officer said that the officers then could hear people and things moving inside the apartment. These sounds led the officers to believe that drug-related evidence was about to be destroyed. After announcing that they would enter the apartment, the officers kicked in the door and entered. They found three people in the front room, including eventual defendant HK. (The suspect they had been chasing was not among the three, however.)

During a protective sweep of the apartment, the officers saw marijuana and powder cocaine in plain view. In a subsequent search, they also discovered crack cocaine, cash, and drug paraphernalia. HK was later charged with drug-possession and drug-trafficking offenses. He unsuccessfully sought to have the evidence suppressed as the result of a search that, in his view, violated the Fourth Amendment. After being convicted, he appealed and renewed his arguments about the search and the evidence obtained. Did the warrantless entry of the apartment violate HK's Fourth Amendment rights? Should the evidence obtained in the search have been suppressed?

13. After a lengthy investigation spearheaded by the Internal Revenue Service (IRS), agents concluded that SDI Future Health, Inc. (SDI) and two of its senior executives—Todd Kaplan (SDI's president) and Jack Brunk (an SDI officer)—had engaged in Medicare fraud and tax fraud. Based on the information obtained during the investigation, the federal government applied for a warrant to search SDI's business premises. The warrant depended heavily on an IRS special agent's affidavit, which contained information the agent had learned from former employees and business associates of SDI. The warrant stated that the premises to be searched were SDI's corporate headquarters, principal business offices, and computers, and it listed categories of documents, records, and other items to be seized. A federal magistrate judge who reviewed the affidavit and the warrant concluded that probable cause existed for the search and therefore issued the warrant. Based on the evidence recovered, SDI, Kaplan, and Brunk were charged with 124 counts of health care fraud; various counts of conspiracy regarding health care fraud, money laundering, and unlawful kickback payments; and other counts of attempting to evade income taxes. Did SDI have standing to challenge the warrant on Fourth Amendment grounds? What about Kaplan and Brunk?

14. Southern Union Company is a natural gas distributor. Its subsidiary stored liquid mercury, an extremely hazardous substance, at a facility in Rhode Island. A group of kids from a nearby apartment complex broke into the facility, played with the mercury, and spread it around the facility and apartment complex, leading to the complex's residents being temporarily displaced during the cleanup. After an investigation, Southern Union was tried and convicted of storing hazardous materials without a permit in violation of the Resource Conservation and Recovery Act, which provides for "a fine of not more than $50,000 for each day of violation." At sentencing, the government argued that the company had violated the statute for 762 days, allowing a maximum fine of $38.1 million. Southern Union objected that this calculation violated its Sixth Amendment rights because the jury was not asked to determine the precise duration of the violation. Southern Union invoked the Supreme Court's line of cases holding that the Sixth Amendment bars judge-found facts to be used to increase a defendant's maximum authorized sentence. The government acknowledged the Court's line of cases but said they did not apply to criminal fines. Who has the better argument?

Intentional Torts

The opening problem in Chapter 2 presented the basic facts underlying a defamation case that business executive Phil Anderson intends to pursue against Allnews Publishing Inc. The questions asked in Chapter 2 pertained to *procedural* matters. We now return to Anderson's case in order to focus on *substantive* legal aspects of defamation, one of the torts about which you will learn in this chapter. Here, again, are the basic facts:

Allnews Publishing Inc., a firm whose principal offices are located in Orlando, Florida, owns and publishes 33 newspapers. These newspapers are published in 21 different states of the United States. Among the Allnews newspapers is the *Snakebite Rattler*, the lone newspaper in the city of Snakebite, New Mexico. The *Rattler* is sold in print form only in New Mexico. However, many of the articles in the newspaper can be viewed by anyone with Internet access, regardless of his or her geographic location, by going to the Allnews website.

In a recent *Rattler* edition, an article appeared beneath this headline: "Local Business Executive Sued for Sexual Harassment." The accompanying article, written by a *Rattler* reporter (an Allnews employee), stated that a person named Phil Anderson was the defendant in the sexual harassment case. Besides being married, Anderson was a well-known businessperson in the Snakebite area. He was active in his church and in community affairs in both Snakebite (his city of primary residence) and Petoskey, Michigan (where he and his wife have a summer home). A stock photo of Anderson, which had been used in connection with previous *Rattler* stories mentioning him, appeared alongside the story about the sexual harassment case. Anderson, however, was not the defendant in that case. He was named in the *Rattler* story because of an error by the *Rattler* reporter. The actual defendant in the sexual harassment case was a local business executive with a similar name: Phil Anderer.

Anderson plans to file a defamation lawsuit against Allnews because of the above-described falsehood in the *Rattler* story. He expects to seek $500,000 in damages for harm to his reputation and for other related harms.

Consider the following questions as you study this chapter:

- How does defamation differ from other torts addressed in this chapter?
- What types of harms, and what corresponding types of money damages, are recognized in defamation cases? How do those types of harms and damages compare to the harms and damages in other tort cases?
- What basic elements of a defamation claim must Anderson prove in order to have a chance of winning his case? Would he be able to prove those elements?
- Because Anderson's defamation claim would be based on speech (the erroneous statement in the *Rattler* article), what role will the First Amendment play in the case?
- Is Anderson a *public figure* or, instead, a *private figure*? Why is the answer to that question important in determining whether Anderson is likely to win the case?

LO   LEARNING OBJECTIVES

After studying this chapter, you should be able to:

6-1 Explain the basic differences among the four types of wrongfulness in tort law (intent, recklessness, negligence, and strict liability).

6-2 Explain the difference between compensatory damages and punitive damages.

6-3 List and explain the elements of battery.

6-4 List and explain the elements of assault.

6-5 Explain what is necessary in order for liability to be imposed on the basis of intentional infliction of emotional distress.

6-6 List and explain the elements of false imprisonment.

6-7 List and explain the common law elements of defamation.

6-8 Explain what a public official plaintiff or a public figure plaintiff must prove, for constitutional reasons, in order to win a defamation case.

6-9 Explain what a private figure plaintiff must prove, for constitutional reasons, in order to win a defamation case.

6-10 Distinguish among the four types of invasion of privacy.

6-11 Identify circumstances in which a celebrity's right of publicity is implicated.

6-12 Explain the difference between trespass to land and private nuisance.

 LO6-1 Explain the basic differences among the four types of wrongfulness in tort law (intent, recklessness, negligence, and strict liability).

A **TORT** IS A *civil wrong* that is not a breach of a contract. Tort cases identify different types of wrongfulness, culpability, or fault and define them in varying ways. In this chapter and in Chapter 7, we will refer to the four types of wrongfulness defined here.

1. *Intent.* We define *intent* as the desire to cause certain consequences or the substantial certainty that those consequences will result from one's behavior. For example, if D pulls the trigger of a loaded handgun while aiming it at P for the purpose of killing him or with a substantial certainty that P would be killed, D intended to kill P. This chapter discusses several *intentional torts*, most of which require, as the name of this category of torts suggests, intent on the part of the defendant.

2. *Recklessness.* The form of intent involving substantial certainty blends by degrees into a different kind of fault: recklessness (sometimes called "willful and wanton conduct"). We define *recklessness* as a conscious indifference to a known and substantial risk of harm created by one's behavior. Suppose that simply because he likes the muzzle flash and the sound, D fires his handgun at random in a crowded subway station. One of D's shots injures P. D acted recklessly if he had no desire to hit P or anyone else

and was not substantially certain that anyone would be hit but, nonetheless, knew that this could easily result from his behavior. When legal responsibility is assigned in the civil context, recklessness is often treated as a near equivalent of intentional wrongdoing. Recklessness is considered a more severe degree of fault than the next type to be discussed: negligence.

3. *Negligence.* We define *negligence* as a failure to use reasonable care, with harm to another party occurring as a result. Negligent conduct falls below the level necessary to protect others against unreasonable risks of harm. Assume that without checking, D pulls the trigger on what he incorrectly and unreasonably thinks is an unloaded handgun. If the gun goes off and wounds P, D has negligently harmed P. Chapter 7 discusses negligence law in detail.

4. *Strict liability.* Strict liability is liability without fault or, more precisely, liability irrespective of fault. In a strict liability case, the plaintiff need not prove intent, recklessness, negligence, or any other kind of wrongfulness on the defendant's part. However, strict liability is not automatic liability. A plaintiff must prove certain things in any strict liability case, but fault is not one of them. Chapter 7 discusses various types of strict liability, some of which are examined more fully in other chapters.

Tort law contemplates civil liability for those who commit torts. This distinguishes it from the criminal law, which also involves wrongful behavior. As you saw in Chapter 1, a civil case is normally a suit between private parties. In criminal cases, a prosecutor represents the government in confronting the defendant. The standard of proof that the plaintiff must satisfy in a tort case is the *preponderance of the evidence* standard, not the more stringent beyond-a-reasonable-doubt standard applied in criminal cases. This means that the greater weight of the evidence introduced at the trial must support the plaintiff's position on every element of the tort case. Finally, the remedy allowed in civil cases (most often, damages) differs from the punishment imposed in criminal cases (e.g., imprisonment or a fine). Of course, the same behavior may sometimes give rise to both civil and criminal liability. For example, one who commits a sexual assault is criminally liable and will also be liable for some or all of the torts of assault, battery, false imprisonment, and intentional infliction of emotional distress.

 LO6-2 Explain the difference between compensatory damages and punitive damages.

A plaintiff who wins a tort case usually recovers **compensatory damages** for the harm she suffered as a result of the defendant's wrongful act. Depending on the facts of the case, these damages may be for direct and immediate harms, such as physical injuries, medical expenses, and lost wages and benefits, or for seemingly less tangible harms, such as loss of privacy, injury to reputation, and emotional distress. If the defendant's behavior was particularly bad, injured victims may also be able to recover **punitive damages**. Punitive damages are not intended to compensate tort victims for their losses. Instead, they are designed to punish flagrant wrongdoers and to deter them, as well as others, from engaging in similar conduct in the future. Punitive damages are reserved for the worst kinds of wrongdoing and thus are not routinely assessed against the losing defendant in a tort case. Certainly, however, some behaviors amounting to recklessness or giving rise to intentional tort liability are regarded as reprehensible enough to justify an assessment of punitive damages.

The *Mathias* case, which follows, reviews the types of fault discussed above and explains the role that punitive damages may play in certain cases.

Mathias v. Accor Economy Lodging, Inc.   347 F.3d 672 (7th Cir. 2003)

Burl and Desiree Mathias were bitten by bedbugs when they stayed at a Motel 6 in downtown Chicago. They sued the corporation that owns and operates the Motel 6 chain. Alleging that the defendant's personnel refused to act in response to the complaints of various guests and otherwise knowingly disregarded clear evidence of a bedbug infestation problem, the plaintiffs sought compensatory and punitive damages on the theory that the defendant had engaged in "willful and wanton conduct." A federal court jury returned a verdict in favor of the Mathiases, awarding them compensatory damages for their injuries and assessing punitive damages against the defendant. On appeal to the U.S. Court of Appeals for the Seventh Circuit, the defendant argued that any fault on its part did not amount to willful and wanton conduct and that the award of punitive damages was therefore unwarranted. Further facts pertinent to the case are discussed in the edited version of the Seventh Circuit's opinion, which appears below.

Posner, Circuit Judge

[B]edbugs . . . are making a comeback in the U.S. as a consequence of more conservative use of pesticides. The plaintiffs claim that in allowing guests to be attacked by bedbugs in a motel that charges upwards of $100 a day for a room and would not like to be mistaken for a flophouse, the defendant was guilty of "willful and wanton conduct" and thus [should be] liable for punitive as well as compensatory damages. The jury agreed and awarded each plaintiff $186,000 in punitive damages, though only $5,000 in compensatory damages.

The defendant argues that at worst it is guilty of simple negligence, and if this is right the plaintiffs were not entitled . . . to any award of punitive damages. [The defendant] also complains that

the [punitive damages] award was excessive. . . . The first complaint has no possible merit, as the evidence of . . . recklessness, in the strong sense of an unjustifiable failure to avoid a *known* risk, was amply shown. In 1998, EcoLab, the extermination service that the motel used, discovered bedbugs in several rooms in the motel and recommended that it be hired to spray every room, for which it would charge the motel only $500; the motel refused. The next year, bedbugs were again discovered in a room but EcoLab was asked to spray just that room. The motel tried to negotiate "a building sweep [by EcoLab] free of charge," but, not surprisingly, the negotiation failed. By the spring of 2000, the motel's manager "started noticing that there were refunds being given by my desk clerks and reports coming back from the guests that there were ticks in the rooms and bugs in the rooms that were biting." She looked in some of the rooms and discovered bedbugs.

Further incidents of guests being bitten by insects and demanding and receiving refunds led the manager to recommend to her superior in the company that the motel be closed while every room was sprayed, but this was refused. This superior, a district manager, was a management-level employee of the defendant, and his knowledge of the risk and failure to take effective steps either to eliminate it or to warn the motel's guests are imputed to his employer for purposes of determining whether the employer should be liable for punitive damages. The employer's liability for compensatory damages is of course automatic on the basis of the principle of *respondeat superior*, since the district manager was acting within the scope of his employment. [Under the *respondeat superior* principle, employers are liable for torts committed by employees if those torts occurred within the scope of employment.]

The infestation continued and began to reach farcical proportions, as when a guest, after complaining of having been bitten repeatedly by insects while asleep in his room in the hotel, was moved to another room only to discover insects there; and within 18 minutes of being moved to a third room he discovered insects in that room as well and had to be moved still again. (Odd that at that point he didn't flee the motel.) By July, the motel's management was acknowledging to EcoLab that there was a "major problem with bedbugs" and that all that was being done about it was "chasing them from room to room." Desk clerks were instructed to call the "bedbugs" "ticks," apparently on the theory that customers would be less alarmed, though in fact ticks are more dangerous than bedbugs because they spread Lyme Disease and Rocky Mountain Spotted Fever. Rooms that the motel had placed on "Do not rent, bugs in room" status nevertheless were rented.

It was in November that the plaintiffs checked into the motel. They were given Room 504, even though the motel had classified the room as "DO NOT RENT UNTIL TREATED," and it had not been treated. Indeed, that night 190 of the hotel's 191 rooms were occupied, even though a number of them had been placed on the same don't-rent status as Room 504.

Although bedbug bites are not as serious as the bites of some other insects, they are painful and unsightly. Motel 6 could not have rented any rooms at the prices it charged had it informed guests that the risk of being bitten by bedbugs was appreciable. Its failure either to warn guests or to take effective measures to eliminate the bedbugs amounted to fraud and probably to [the intentional tort of] battery as well. There was, in short, sufficient evidence of "willful and wanton conduct" [that is, of recklessness as opposed to mere negligence] to permit an award of punitive damages in this case.

But in what amount? In arguing that $20,000 was the maximum amount of punitive damages that a jury could constitutionally have awarded each plaintiff, the defendant points to the U.S.

Supreme Court's recent statement that "few awards [of punitive damages] exceeding a single-digit ratio between punitive and compensatory damages, to a significant degree, will satisfy due process." *State Farm Mutual Automobile Insurance Co. v. Campbell*, 538 U.S. 408 (2003). The Court went on to suggest that "four times the amount of compensatory damages might be close to the line of constitutional impropriety." Hence the defendant's proposed ceiling in this case of $20,000, four times the compensatory damages awarded to each plaintiff. The ratio of punitive to compensatory damages determined by the jury was, in contrast, 37.2 to 1.

The Supreme Court did not, however, lay down a 4-to-1 or single-digit-ratio rule—it said merely that "there is a presumption against an award that has a 145-to-1 ratio"—and it would be unreasonable to do so. We must consider why punitive damages are awarded and why the Court has decided that due process requires that such awards be limited. The second question is easier to answer than the first. The term *punitive damages* implies punishment, and a standard principle of penal theory is that "the punishment should fit the crime" in the sense of being proportional to the wrongfulness of the defendant's action, though the principle is modified when the probability of detection is very low (a familiar example is the heavy fines for littering) or the crime is potentially lucrative (as in the case of trafficking in illegal drugs).

Another penal precept is that a defendant should have reasonable notice of the sanction for unlawful acts, so that he can make a rational determination of how to act; and so there have to be reasonably clear standards for determining the amount of punitive damages for particular wrongs. [A] third precept . . . is that sanctions should be based on the wrong done rather than on the status of the defendant; a person is punished for what he does, not for who he is, even if the who is a huge corporation.

What follows from these principles, however, is that punitive damages should be admeasured by standards or rules rather than in a completely ad hoc manner, and this does not tell us what the maximum ratio of punitive to compensatory damages should be in a particular case. To determine that, we have to consider why punitive damages are awarded in the first place.

[O]ne function of punitive-damages awards is to relieve the pressures on an overloaded system of criminal justice by providing a civil alternative to criminal prosecution of minor crimes. An example is deliberately spitting in a person's face, a criminal assault but because minor readily deterrable by the levying of what amounts to a civil fine through a suit for damages for the tort of battery. Compensatory damages [unaccompanied by punitive damages] would not do the trick in such a case, . . . for three reasons: because [compensatory damages] are difficult to determine in the case of acts that inflict largely [dignity-related] harms; because in the spitting case [compensatory damages] would be too slight to give the victim an incentive to sue, and he might decide instead to respond with violence—and an age-old purpose of the law of torts is to provide a substitute for violent retaliation against wrongful injury; and because to limit the plaintiff to compensatory damages would enable the defendant to commit the offensive act with impunity provided that he was willing to pay.

When punitive damages are sought for billion-dollar oil spills and other huge economic injuries, the considerations that we have just canvassed fade. As the Supreme Court emphasized in *Campbell*, the fact that the plaintiffs in that case had been awarded very substantial compensatory damages—$1 million for a dispute over insurance coverage—greatly reduced the need for giving them a huge award of punitive damages ($145 million) as well in order to provide an effective remedy. Our case is closer to the spitting case. The defendant's behavior was outrageous but the compensable harm done was slight and at the same time difficult to quantify because a large element of it was emotional. And the defendant may well have profited from its misconduct because by concealing the infestation it was able to keep renting rooms. Refunds were frequent but may have cost less than the cost of closing the hotel for a thorough fumigation. The hotel's attempt to pass off the bedbugs as ticks, which some guests might ignorantly have thought less unhealthful, may have postponed the instituting of litigation to rectify the hotel's misconduct. The award of punitive damages in this case thus serves the additional purpose of limiting the defendant's ability to profit from its fraud by escaping detection and (private) prosecution. If a tortfeasor is "caught" only half the time he commits torts, then when he is caught he should be punished twice as heavily in order to make up for the times he gets away.

Finally, if the total stakes in the case were capped at $50,000 (2 × [$5,000 + $20,000]), the plaintiffs might well have had difficulty financing this lawsuit. It is here that the defendant's aggregate net worth of $1.6 billion becomes relevant. A defendant's wealth is not a sufficient basis for awarding punitive damages. *BMW of North America, Inc. v. Gore*, 517 U.S. 559 (1996). That would be discriminatory and would violate the rule of law, as we explained earlier, by making punishment depend on status rather than conduct. Where wealth in the sense of resources enters is in

enabling the defendant to mount an extremely aggressive defense against suits such as this and by doing so to make litigating against it very costly, which in turn may make it difficult for the plaintiffs to find a lawyer willing to handle their case, involving as it does only modest stakes, for the usual 33–40 percent contingent fee. In other words, the defendant is investing in developing a reputation intended to deter plaintiffs. It is difficult otherwise to explain the great stubbornness with which it has defended this case, making a host of frivolous evidentiary arguments despite the very modest stakes even when the punitive damages awarded by the jury are included.

All things considered, we cannot say that the award of punitive damages was excessive, albeit the precise number chosen by the jury was arbitrary. It is probably not a coincidence that $5,000 + $186,000 = $191,000/191 = $1,000: that is, $1,000 per room in the hotel. But as there are no [rigid] punitive-damages guidelines, . . . it is inevitable that the specific amount of punitive damages awarded . . . will be arbitrary. (Which is perhaps why the plaintiffs' lawyer did not suggest a number to the jury.) The judicial function is to police a range, not a point.

But it would have been helpful had the parties presented evidence concerning the regulatory or criminal penalties to which the defendant exposed itself by deliberately exposing its customers to a substantial risk of being bitten by bedbugs. That is an inquiry recommended by the Supreme Court [in *Campbell*]. [However,] we do not think its omission invalidates the award. We can take judicial notice that deliberate exposure of hotel guests to the health risks created by insect infestations [potentially] exposes the hotel's owner to [criminal fines] under Illinois and Chicago law that in the aggregate are comparable in severity to that of the punitive damage award in this case. [W]hat is much more important, a Chicago hotel that permits unsanitary conditions to exist is subject to revocation of its license, without which it cannot operate. We are sure that the defendant would prefer to pay the punitive damages assessed in this case than to lose its license.

District court's judgment in favor of plaintiffs affirmed.

Interference with Personal Rights

This chapter examines two categories of intentional torts: (1) those involving interference with personal rights and (2) those involving interference with property rights. A third category, business or competitive torts, will be discussed in Chapter 8.

Battery

 List and explain the elements of battery.

Battery is the intentional and harmful or offensive touching of another without his consent. Contact is *harmful* if it produces bodily injury. However, battery also includes nonharmful contact that is *offensive*—calculated to offend a reasonable sense of personal dignity. The *intent* required for battery is either (1) the intent to cause harmful or offensive contact or (2) the intent to cause apprehension that such contact is imminent. Assume, for instance, that in order to scare Pine, Delano threatens to "shoot" Pine with a gun that Delano mistakenly believes is unloaded. If Delano ends up shooting Pine even though that had not been his specific intent, Delano is liable for battery. For battery to occur, moreover, the person who suffers the harmful or offensive contact need not be the person the wrongdoer intended to injure. Under a concept known as *transferred intent*, a defendant who intends to injure one person but actually injures another is liable to the person injured, despite the absence of any specific desire to injure him. So, if Dudley throws a rock at Thomas and hits Pike instead, Dudley is liable to Pike for battery.

As the previous examples suggest, the *touching* necessary for battery does not require direct contact between the defendant's body and the plaintiff's body. Dudley is therefore liable if he successfully lays a trap for Pike or poisons him. There is also a touching if the defendant causes contact with anything attached to the plaintiff's body. If the other elements of a battery are present, Dudley is thus liable to Pike if he shoots off Pike's hat. Finally, the plaintiff need not be aware of the battery at the time it occurs. This means that Dudley is liable if he sneaks up behind Pike and knocks Pike unconscious, without Pike's ever knowing what hit him.

There is no liability for battery, however, if the plaintiff *consented* to the touching. As a general rule, consent must be freely and intelligently given to be a defense to battery. Consent may also be inferred from a person's voluntary participation in an activity, but it is ordinarily limited to contacts that are a normal consequence of the activity. A professional boxer injured by his opponent's punches to the head, therefore, would not win a battery lawsuit against the opponent. However, a professional boxer whose ear is partially bitten off by his opponent should have a valid battery claim against the ear-biter. In addition, the law infers consent to many touchings that are customary or reasonably necessary in normal social life. Thus, Preston could not recover for battery if Dean tapped him on the shoulder to ask directions or brushed against him on a crowded street. Of course, many such contacts are neither harmful nor offensive anyway.

In *Banks v. Lockhart*, which follows, the court applies the elements of battery to the facts and explains why battery cases may give rise to awards of punitive damages in addition to compensatory damages.

Banks v. Lockhart   119 So. 3d 370 (Miss. Ct. App. 2013)

Brandon Lockhart and his friend, Lindsay Gibson, visited several Oxford, Mississippi, bars one July evening. While at the Library Bar & Grill, Lockhart and Gibson encountered Harrison Banks. For reasons unknown, Gibson slapped Banks several times. A brief altercation between Banks and Gibson ensued, but the two were quickly separated. After this altercation, Lockhart and Gibson left the Library.

While Lockhart and Gibson were walking in an alleyway near Taylor's Pub, another altercation took place between Gibson and a third party. During this altercation, the third party knocked Gibson to the ground. Lockhart knelt down to assist Gibson and was struck in the face. This blow knocked Lockhart to the ground. At the trial in the case referred to below, Lockhart testified that when he looked up, he saw Banks fleeing the scene. However, Banks testified at trial that he was not present in the alleyway and did not see Lockhart or Gibson after they left the Library.

At the urging of police officers who arrived on the scene shortly after this second altercation, Lockhart went to the local hospital to have his injuries assessed and treated. According to Lockhart's trial testimony, several hospital exams showed that the above-described blow to his face shattered a sinus bone. Lockhart also testified that he underwent several steroid injections and one invasive surgery to remove scar tissue from the side of his face, and that further treatments could be needed.

Based on the above facts, Lockhart sued Banks for the alleged battery that occurred near Taylor's Pub. A Mississippi jury returned a verdict in favor of Lockhart for $300,000 in compensatory damages and $50,000 in punitive damages. Banks filed alternative post-trial motions for a judgment notwithstanding the verdict, a new trial, or a remittitur. (In this context, a remittitur would be a ruling by the court that the amount of damages awarded to the plaintiff by the jury was excessive and that unless the plaintiff agreed to accept a lesser amount as set by the court, the judgment in favor of the plaintiff would be vacated and a new trial on damages issues would be ordered.) After the trial court denied each of these motions, Banks appealed to the Court of Appeals of Mississippi.

Griffis, Judge

On appeal, Banks argues that: (1) the jury's verdict is against the overwhelming weight of the evidence; (2) the trial court erred when it allowed the jury to consider punitive damages; and (3) the trial court erred when it did not grant a remittitur on compensatory and punitive damages.

A battery occurs when a person intends to cause a harmful or offensive contact to another person and such contact actually occurs. To determine whether the verdict was against the overwhelming weight of the evidence, we look at the facts in the light most favorable to the verdict. It is undisputed in the record that Lockhart suffered a harmful or offensive contact [on the relevant July night]. Thus, the central elements of battery that Lockhart had to prove to the jury were that: (1) Banks intended to cause a harmful or offensive contact, and (2) Banks was responsible for the harmful or offensive contact.

Both parties agree that at least one altercation took place that evening in the Library between Gibson and Banks. While Banks claims he was not a party, it is undisputed that a second altercation took place in the alleyway near Taylor's Pub, where Lockhart was struck in the face. Lockhart claims that after he was struck, he observed Banks fleeing from the scene. Additionally, the testimonies of [two police officers who arrived on the scene] were consistent that an altercation took place in the alleyway between Gibson and another party, and that while assisting Gibson after he was knocked to the ground, Lockhart was struck in the face. Banks's only response to these assertions is that he simply was not present and, therefore, did not strike Lockhart. A reasonable, hypothetical juror could make inferences and conclude that, based on the testimony of the witnesses and the fact that a previous altercation had occurred, Banks was a party to the second altercation in the alleyway. As for Banks's intent, a reasonable, hypothetical juror could have concluded that, based on Banks's own statements, involvement in the previous altercation, and involvement in the alleyway altercation, he intended to cause a harmful or offensive contact when he struck Lockhart. Given this scenario, we cannot conclude that the verdict was contrary to the overwhelming weight of the evidence.

Banks argues that Lockhart's testimony lacked credibility. Determining the credibility of a witness or the weight of their testimony is not the province of this court. The weight and credibility of the witnesses was for the jury, [which] determined that Lockhart was a more credible witness than Banks. Furthermore, when applying the standard of review to jury verdicts in civil cases, . . . the jury verdict in favor of [Lockhart means that] this court resolves all conflicts in the evidence in his favor.

[Banks also challenges the damages award as unsupported by the record.] Lockhart stipulated that his medical expenses were $11,654.64. Banks claims that the difference between an award of $350,000 in compensatory and punitive damages and medical expenses of $11,654.64 clearly evidences bias on the part of the jury. However, medical expenses are not the only damages claimed by Lockhart. He also claims past, present, and future physical pain and suffering, and resulting mental anguish.

It is clear from the record that Lockhart sustained an actual injury and incurred damages as a result. However, this court [cannot speculate about] the reason for the difference between the damages claimed by Lockhart and the jury's specific allotment of the award. As such, this court cannot say that a reasonable juror would have concluded otherwise. Thus, taking the evidence in this matter as a whole, we find that a reasonable, hypothetical juror could have found as the jury here found.

Banks's second assignment of error is that the trial court erred in allowing the jury to consider punitive damages. [For punitive damages to have been appropriate, Mississippi law requires a showing that the defendant] acted with . . . willful, wanton, or reckless disregard for the safety of others. [E]ven in situations where an assault or battery occurred from sudden passion, [the requisite willful, wanton, or reckless disregard] on the part of the assailant may still be present in the case [and presumed from the proven facts and circumstances]. *Anderson v. Jenkins*, 70 So. 2d 535, 540 (Miss. 1954). In *Anderson*, the Supreme Court of Mississippi considered whether an assailant possessed [willful, wanton, or reckless disregard] when using a weapon to defend property. The assailant in *Anderson* fired a shotgun, twice, at a vehicle filled with teenage trespassers and one of the teens was struck in the eye with a shotgun. The assailant had the requisite intent to cause an offensive or harmful contact and that contact actually occurred. This court cannot say that simply because fists instead of firearms were used to cause the battery here, that the Supreme Court's presumption no longer applies. Given the facts of this case, such a presumption can be made with respect to Banks's intent when the jury considered punitive damages.

The trial court did not abuse its discretion in allowing the jury to consider the issue of punitive damages. The jury found Banks responsible for the battery to Lockhart and awarded compensatory damages. Taking the totality of the circumstances, a reasonable, hypothetical trier of fact could have found that Banks acted willfully, wantonly, or with reckless disregard by striking Lockhart.

[As explained in the discussion above], a reasonable, hypothetical juror could have found as the jury here found; thus, this court finds the overwhelming weight of the evidence is not against the verdict. The trial court did not abuse its discretion in denying Banks's motion for remittitur.

Furthermore, "[a] jury award should not be disturbed unless its size, in comparison to the actual amount of damage, shocks the conscience." [Citation omitted.] The award of $300,000 in compensatory damages and $50,000 in punitive damages does appear rather substantial, given the totality of the case before the trial court and the record before us. However, this court cannot say that such an award shocks the conscience. Given that the trial court did not abuse its discretion in denying Banks's motion for a remittitur and that, while significant, the award does not shock the conscience, this court finds no merit in Banks's argument.

Judgment in favor of Lockhart affirmed.

Assault

 LO6-4 List and explain the elements of assault.

Assault occurs when there is an intentional attempt or offer to cause a harmful or offensive contact with another person, if that attempt or offer causes a reasonable apprehension of imminent battery in the other person's mind. The necessary *intent* is the same as the intent required for battery. In an assault case, however, it is irrelevant whether the threatened contact actually occurs. Instead, the key thing is the plaintiff's *apprehension* of a harmful or offensive contact. Apprehension need not involve fear; it might be described as a mental state consistent with this thought: "I'm just about to be hit."

The plaintiff's apprehension must pertain to an anticipated battery that would be *imminent or immediate*. Threats of some future battery, therefore, do not create liability for assault. In addition, the plaintiff must experience apprehension *at the time the threatened battery occurs*. For instance, if Dinwiddie fires a rifle at Porter from a great distance and misses him, and only later does Porter learn of the attempt on his life, Dinwiddie is not liable to Porter for assault. The plaintiff's apprehension must also be *reasonable*. As a result, threatening words normally are not an assault unless they are accompanied by acts or circumstances indicating the defendant's intent to carry out the threat.

Intentional Infliction of Emotional Distress

 LO6-5 Explain what is necessary in order for liability to be imposed on the basis of intentional infliction of emotional distress.

For many years, courts refused to allow recovery for purely emotional injuries unless the defendant had committed some recognized tort. Victims of such torts as assault, battery, and false imprisonment could recover for the emotional injuries resulting from these torts, but courts would not recognize an independent tort of infliction of emotional distress. The reasons for this judicial reluctance included a fear of spurious or trivial claims, concerns about proving purely emotional harms, and uncertainty about the proper boundaries of an independent tort. However, increased confidence in our knowledge about emotional injuries and a greater willingness to compensate such harms have helped to overcome these judicial impediments. Most courts today allow recovery for severe emotional distress, under appropriate circumstances, regardless of whether the elements of any other tort are proven.

The courts are not, however, in complete agreement on the elements of this relatively new tort. All courts do require that a wrongdoer's conduct be *outrageous* before liability for emotional distress arises. The *Restatement (Second) of Torts* speaks of conduct "so outrageous in character, and so extreme in degree, as to go beyond all possible bounds of decency, and to be regarded as atrocious, and utterly intolerable in a civilized community." This means that many instances of boorish, insensitive behavior are not "bad enough" to give rise to liability for this tort. Courts also agree in requiring *severe* emotional distress. The *Restatement (Second)* sets forth another clear majority rule: that the defendant must *intentionally* or *recklessly* inflict the distress in order to be liable. A few courts, however, still fear fictitious claims and require proof of some bodily harm resulting from the victim's emotional distress.

In addition, some courts say that the plaintiff's distress must be distress that a reasonable person of ordinary sensibilities would suffer. The focus on whether the severely distressed person had ordinary sensibilities is sometimes minimized, however, when the defendant behaves outrageously by abusing a position or relation that gives him authority over another. Examples include employers, police officers, landlords, and school authorities.

The courts also differ in the extent to which they allow recovery for emotional distress suffered as a result of witnessing outrageous conduct directed at persons other than the plaintiff. The *Restatement (Second)* suggests that, at minimum, plaintiffs should be allowed to recover for severe emotional distress resulting from witnessing outrageous behavior toward a member of their immediate family.

In the *Durham* case, which follows, the court applies the elements of intentional infliction of emotional distress to a set of facts involving a manager's alleged treatment of an employee.

Durham v. McDonald's Restaurants of Oklahoma, Inc.
256 P.3d 64 (Okla. 2011)

Camran Durham filed an intentional infliction of emotional distress lawsuit in an Oklahoma court against his former employer, McDonald's Restaurants of Oklahoma, Inc. Durham based his claim on the behavior of a McDonald's manager (Durham's former supervisor) who, during Durham's employment, denied three requests by Durham that he be allowed to take his prescription anti-seizure medication. In the course of denying the last request, the manager called Durham a "f . . . ing retard." Durham, who was 16 years old at the time, alleged that the manager's refusals caused him to fear he would suffer a seizure. Durham alleged that he left work crying after the incident and did not return.

McDonald's moved for summary judgment but did not controvert Durham's account of the incident. Instead, McDonald's argued that the manager's conduct did not amount to "extreme and outrageous" conduct—a required element of a claim for intentional infliction of emotional distress. In so arguing, McDonald's relied on an earlier federal court disposition of claims made by Durham under the federal Americans with Disabilities Act (ADA). In denying Durham recovery on his ADA claims, the federal court determined that the manager's conduct was "not severe."

The trial court in Durham's state court case concluded that the federal court disposition of the ADA claims constituted a binding determination of the "extreme and outrageous" element of Durham's claim for intentional infliction of emotional distress. Therefore, the trial court granted summary judgment in favor of McDonald's. Durham appealed to the Oklahoma Court of Civil Appeals, which affirmed. Durham appealed to the Supreme Court of Oklahoma.

Reif, Judge

In order to prove the tort of intentional infliction of emotional distress (or outrage), a plaintiff must prove each of the following elements: (1) the alleged tortfeasor acted intentionally or recklessly; (2) the alleged tortfeasor's conduct was extreme and outrageous; (3) the conduct caused the plaintiff emotional distress; and (4) the emotional distress was severe. In the case at hand, McDonald's has argued that the federal court [decision regarding Durham's ADA claims effectively] adjudicated the second and fourth elements of the tort, and, therefore, Durham's claim is barred by [the] issue preclusion [doctrine].

The Court of Civil Appeals found that the federal court had necessarily determined that the manager's conduct was "not severe" in disposing of the federal ADA claims. Noting that *Black's Law Dictionary* treats "extreme" as a synonym for "severe," the Court of Civil Appeals [concluded] that conduct which is not severe cannot be "extreme and outrageous" under the applicable law. [According to Oklahoma case law,] "extreme and outrageous" conduct requires the existence of conduct so extreme in degree as to go beyond all possible bounds of decency, and which is viewed as atrocious and utterly intolerable in a civilized community. In general, a defendant's conduct must be such that an average member of the community would exclaim, "Outrageous!" [Citations omitted.]

The chief problem we have with [the analysis of the Court of Civil Appeals] is that it was not necessary for the federal court to make any determination about the character of the manager's conduct in disposing of the federal litigation. All of Durham's claims under the ADA, including [a] hostile working environment and constructive discharge claim, were dependent upon [Durham's being] a "disabled person." The federal court determined [that Durham] *was not a disabled person.* [Durham's] status as a disabled person was the linchpin of federal question jurisdiction and the determination of this issue adversely to [Durham] ended the court's jurisdiction to decide any other issue concerning the ADA claims. [Under the circumstances, the federal court did not have] power to rule on any other matter affecting the parties. The Court of Civil Appeals [therefore] erred in ruling that the federal court disposition of the ADA claims was preclusive of the extreme and outrageous element of plaintiff's claim for intentional infliction of emotional distress.

When this Court reviews a claim for intentional infliction of emotional distress that has been rejected by the Court of Civil Appeals, we will make the "gatekeeper" or threshold determination of whether the defendant's conduct may reasonably be regarded as extreme and outrageous. The test is whether the conduct is so extreme in degree as to go beyond all possible bounds of decency, and is atrocious and utterly intolerable in a civilized community. In the case at hand, we find that the manager's use of "f . . . ing retard" in addressing a minor employee who is filled with apprehension after being denied permission to take anti-seizure medication may reasonably be regarded as meeting this test. We further find that reasonable people might differ on this issue, but could nonetheless similarly conclude that such conduct meets the test of [being] extreme and outrageous. Where this threshold is satisfied, the issue of whether a defendant's conduct is extreme and outrageous is for a jury to decide.

In its motion for summary judgment, McDonald's also asserted that Durham cannot prove the severe emotional distress element of intentional infliction of emotional distress. The motion pointed out that the trial court could make the "gatekeeper" or threshold determination concerning this element [and resolve it against Durham] based on the federal court disposition of the ADA claims. [It is important to note, however, that] the *federal court did not determine* whether Durham suffered severe emotional distress. Our review of [Durham's] evidentiary materials leads us to the . . . conclusion [that there is a substantial controversy between the parties regarding the severe emotional distress element].

Intentional infliction of emotional distress does not provide redress for every invasion of emotional serenity or every anti-social act that may produce hurt feelings. While emotional distress can include all highly unpleasant mental reactions, such as fright, horror, grief, shame, humiliation, embarrassment, anger, chagrin, disappointment, worry, and nausea, it must be so severe that no reasonable person could be expected to endure it. The intensity and duration of the distress are factors to be considered in determining severity, but the type of distress must be reasonable and justified under the circumstances. It is for the court to determine, in the first instance, whether based upon the evidence presented, severe emotional distress can be found. [Citations omitted.]

At the time the manager refused permission to take the anti-seizure medicine, Durham related that he "was getting scared he might die [or] he could bite off his tongue or fall and hurt himself." After the manager called him a "f . . . ing retard," he ran out the door crying. As a consequence of this treatment, Durham stated he became "withdrawn" and "a recluse." He recounted that "[h]e felt he couldn't do anything [and] was afraid he would suffer the same experience at another job." His mother related that he "wouldn't go outside, slept all day, and had to be home schooled." She stated that he "became depressed and introverted." She reported that "he was no longer active [and] lost interest in everything." Durham believed that a school friend who worked at McDonald's told other school friends about the incident. They began calling plaintiff a "f . . . ing retard" and teased him by saying, "I hear you can't even keep a job at McDonald's because you're a f . . . ing retard."

Viewing the evidentiary materials in a light most favorable to plaintiff Durham [(as we are required to do in reviewing the grant of summary judgment against him)], we hold that the highly unpleasant mental reactions that plaintiff Durham and his mother described are reasonable and justified under the circumstances. We also hold that they go beyond mere hurt feelings, insult, indignity, and annoyance and could be reasonably regarded to constitute emotional distress so severe that no reasonable person could be expected to endure it. In such cases, "[i]t is for the jury to determine whether, on the evidence, severe emotional distress in fact existed." [Citation omitted.]

Grant of summary judgment in favor of McDonald's reversed; case remanded for further proceedings.

Most intentional infliction of emotional distress cases are based on allegedly outrageous *conduct*. What about allegedly outrageous *speech*? May it be the basis of a valid emotional distress claim? The potential First Amendment implications of allowing emotional distress liability to be based on speech—particularly when the plaintiff is a famous person who was the target or subject of the defendant's statements—occupied the attention of the U.S. Supreme Court in *Hustler Magazine, Inc. v. Falwell*, 485 U.S. 46 (1988). On First Amendment grounds, the Court unanimously struck down a damages award received in the lower courts by the Rev. Jerry Falwell as a result of offensive statements about him in an adult magazine. In doing so, the Court severely restricted the ability of *public figures* to win speech-related intentional infliction of emotional distress cases by requiring that such plaintiffs prove the same stern First Amendment–based requirements imposed on public figure plaintiffs in defamation cases. (A later section in this chapter includes extensive discussion of defamation law, including the First Amendment–based requirements that public figures must satisfy when they sue for defamation.)

The Court had no occasion to rule in *Falwell* on whether the First Amendment would restrict the ability of a private figure (i.e., a person who is not well known and thus is not a public figure) to base an emotional distress claim on a defendant's allegedly outrageous speech about him or her. The parallel drawn in *Falwell* to the constitutional requirements in defamation cases could signify somewhat less of a role for the First Amendment in intentional infliction of emotional distress cases brought by private figure plaintiffs regarding speech about them. The matter remains uncertain, however.

What about instances in which the allegedly outrageous speech was not about the plaintiff but caused the plaintiff to experience significant emotional harm? The Supreme Court addressed such an instance in a controversial and much-publicized decision, *Snyder v. Phelps*, 562 U.S. 443 (2011). The plaintiff, Albert Snyder, was the father of a deceased soldier who had been killed in the line of duty. At the time of the soldier's funeral and in relatively close proximity to where it was held, the defendants (the Rev. Fred Phelps and other individuals associated with the Westboro Baptist Church) displayed picket signs communicating strongly worded anti-gay messages. The plaintiff saw the signs on the way to the funeral and learned of their specific content a few hours later. He regarded the defendants' messages and their decision to target the funeral for their protest as a distress-causing, unwelcome intrusion into an intensely personal event for the Snyder family. In his lawsuit, therefore, Snyder alleged claims for intentional infliction of emotional distress and invasion of privacy. This was not the first time the defendants had picketed at a deceased soldier's funeral. They had done so frequently in order to express their view that God hates homosexuals and that American soldiers die because of God's displeasure with attitudes of tolerance toward gays.

The Supreme Court held in *Snyder v. Phelps* that Snyder could not prevail and that the defendants' speech was fully protected under the First Amendment because it dealt with a matter of public concern. The Court acknowledged the offensive nature of the defendants' speech, particularly under the circumstances in which the defendants communicated it, but stressed that the First Amendment protects a great deal of speech that listeners or viewers may find objectionable or unwelcome. After the decisions in *Falwell* and *Snyder*, it is fair to say that the First Amendment makes a *speech-based* intentional infliction of emotional distress case very hard to win. Of course, when a defendant's *conduct*—as opposed to speech—serves as the basis for an emotional distress case, the First Amendment does not even potentially furnish the defendant any protection against liability.

False Imprisonment

 LO6-6 List and explain the elements of false imprisonment.

False imprisonment is the intentional *confinement* of another person for an *appreciable time* (a few minutes is enough) *without his consent.* The confinement element essentially involves the defendant's keeping the plaintiff within a circle that the defendant has created. It may result from physical barriers to the plaintiff's freedom of movement, such as locking a person in a room with no other doors or windows, or from the use or threat of physical force against the plaintiff. Confinement also may result from the unfounded assertion of legal authority to detain the plaintiff, or from the detention of the plaintiff's property (e.g., a purse containing a large sum of money). Likewise, a threat to harm another, such as the plaintiff's spouse or child, can also cause confinement if it prevents the plaintiff from moving.

The confinement must be *complete.* Partial confinement of another by blocking her path or by depriving her of one means of escape where several exist, such as locking one door of a building having several unlocked doors, is not false imprisonment. The fact that a means of escape exists, however, does not relieve the defendant of liability if the plaintiff cannot reasonably be expected to know of its existence. The same is true if using the escape route would present some unreasonable risk of harm to the plaintiff or would involve some affront to the plaintiff's sense of personal dignity.

Although there is some disagreement on the subject, courts usually hold that the plaintiff must have *knowledge* of his confinement in order for liability for false imprisonment to arise. In addition, there is no liability if the plaintiff has *consented* to his confinement. Such consent, however, must be freely given; consent in the face of an implied or actual threat of force or an assertion of legal authority is not freely given.

Today, many false imprisonment cases involve a store's detention of persons suspected of shoplifting. In an attempt to accommodate the legitimate interests of store owners, most states have passed statutes giving them a *conditional privilege* to stop suspected shoplifters. To obtain this defense, the owner usually must act with reasonable cause and in a reasonable manner, and must detain the suspect for no longer than a reasonable length of time. These privilege statutes typically extend to other intentional torts besides false imprisonment.

The *Farrell* case, which follows, examines the elements of false imprisonment and considers the role a privilege statute may play.

Farrell v. Macy's Retail Holdings, Inc.   2016 U.S. App. LEXIS 6791 (4th Cir. 2016)

Stephanie and William Farrell were shopping at a Macy's department store that was located in a Maryland mall. The asset protection manager for Macy's observed William, and then the couple, and saw what is set forth in this statement of facts. Initially, William walked around the store wearing a jacket that he had not yet purchased. Then after removing the jacket, William selected several items from sales racks, removed the items from their hangers, and placed the items into a bag. He also appeared to move away from where he selected the jacket before placing it into the bag and leaving the jacket's hanger on a different rack. After the Farrells began shopping together, the couple selected a robe for William, and he again removed it from the hanger and placed it in the bag. The Farrells then approached the exit to the mall, where two mall security officers, one of whom was wearing his security uniform, were sitting. After getting within 5 to 10 feet of the exit, the Farrells turned back into the store. Suspecting that the Farrells were attempting to shoplift store items, Macy's employees then stopped them, detained them, and questioned them. The store employees released the Farrells after determining that they were not shoplifting.

Relying on diversity of citizenship principles, the Farrells sued Macy's in a federal district court on the theory that the above-described detention constituted false imprisonment. Maryland has a so-called shopkeeper's statute. Such a statute protects store owners and their employees against false imprisonment liability for detaining customers on suspicion of shoplifting even though the customers were innocent in that regard, if there was probable cause for the theft suspicion and the detention was conducted reasonably. Largely on the basis of the shopkeeper's statute, the district court granted summary judgment in favor of Macy's. The Farrells appealed to the U.S. Court of Appeals for the Fourth Circuit.

Per Curiam

The district court granted summary judgment [in favor of Macy's] based on its determination that [the Macy's employees] had probable cause to detain William Farrell. We review de novo a district court's order granting summary judgment. [The Federal Rules of Civil Procedure provide that summary judgment is to be granted] "if the movant shows that there is no genuine dispute as to any material fact and the movant is entitled to judgment as a matter of law." In determining whether a genuine issue of material fact exists, "we view the facts and all justifiable inferences arising therefrom in the light most favorable to . . . the nonmoving party." [Case citation omitted.]

The Farrells argue that the Defendants' employees lacked probable cause to detain them. Under Maryland law, "[f]or a plaintiff to succeed on a false arrest or false imprisonment claim, the plaintiff must establish that the defendant deprived the plaintiff of his or her liberty without consent and without legal justification." *State v. Roshchin*, 130 A.3d 453, 459 (Md. 2016). However, [a Maryland statute provides that] a merchant cannot be held liable for false imprisonment if it "had, at the time of the detention . . . , probable cause to believe that the person committed the crime of 'theft,' as prohibited by [Maryland law]. [Probable cause] is defined in terms of facts and circumstances sufficient to warrant a prudent person in believing that the suspect had committed or was committing an offense." *DiPino v. Davis*, 729 A.2d 354, 361 (Md. 1999).

Maryland defines theft as "willfully and knowingly obtaining unauthorized control over the property or services of another; by deception or otherwise; with intent to deprive the owner of his property. . . . " *Lee v. State*, 474 A.2d 537, 540–41 (Md. Ct. Spec. App. 1984). In *Lee*, the court noted that "several factors should be assessed to determine whether the accused [in a shoplifting case] intended to deprive the owner of property," including "concealment of [the] goods[,]. . . . [o]ther furtive or unusual behavior[,]. . . . [t]he customer's proximity to the store's exits[,] . . . and

possession by the customer of a shoplifting device with which to conceal merchandise." *Id.* at 542–43. Although *Lee* addressed these factors in determining whether sufficient evidence supported a conviction for theft, its discussion also is relevant to whether probable cause existed to believe that a person is committing theft.

We conclude that [on the basis of the observations of the Macy's asset-protection manager, as described in the above statement of facts,] the Macy's employees had probable cause to detain the Farrells at the time of the detention. The Farrells argue that the district court did not view the evidence in the proper light because it failed to consider their deposition testimony that they intended to purchase the items at the sales counter near where they had entered the store and, therefore, that they had not passed all points of sale prior to their apprehension. However, "[w]hether probable cause exists depends upon the reasonable conclusion to be drawn from the facts known to the [detaining] officer at the time of the arrest." *Devenpeck v. Alford*, 543 U.S. 146, 152 (2004). The Farrells have not argued or offered any evidence demonstrating that, at the time he detained them, the asset-protection manager knew they intended to pay for the items William Farrell had placed into the bag he was carrying. Moreover, the court's finding that the Farrells had passed all points of sale is supported by the store's video surveillance; the couple is seen walking toward the exit to the mall and, as Stephanie Farrell testified at her deposition, coming within approximately five to ten feet of the exit while looking at a table displaying merchandise for sale.

[Because the Macy's employees had probable cause to detain the Farrells, the statute referred to above protects Macy's against liability for false imprisonment. The district court, therefore, correctly granted summary judgment in favor of Macy's.]

District court's grant of summary judgment in favor of defendant affirmed.

Defamation

 LO6-7 List and explain the common law elements of defamation.

Claims for defamation are recognized in order to protect the reputational interest of the plaintiff (whether an individual person or a corporation). Defamation is ordinarily defined as the (1) unprivileged (2) publication of (3) false and defamatory (4) statements concerning another. Before examining each of these elements, we must consider the distinction between two forms of defamation: **libel** and **slander**.

The Libel–Slander Distinction Libel refers to written or printed defamation or to other defamation having a physical form, such as a defamatory picture, sign, or statue. Slander refers to all other defamatory statements—mainly oral defamation. Today, however, the great majority of courts treat defamatory statements in radio and television broadcasts as libel. The same is true of defamatory statements made on the Internet.

Why does the libel–slander distinction matter? Because of libel's more permanent nature and the seriousness we usually attach to the written word, the common law has traditionally allowed plaintiffs to recover for libel without proof of **actual damages** (reputional injury and other harm such as emotional distress). Presumed damages have long been allowed by the common law in libel cases. Described by the U.S. Supreme Court as an "oddity of tort law," presumed damages "compensate" for reputational harm that is presumed to have occurred but does not have to be proven by the plaintiff.

Slander, on the other hand, is generally not actionable without proof of special damages, unless the nature of the slanderous statement is so serious that it can be classified as *slander per se*. In cases of slander per se, presumed damages are allowed by the common law. Slander per se ordinarily includes false statements that the plaintiff (1) has committed a crime involving moral turpitude or potential imprisonment, (2) has a loathsome disease, (3) is professionally incompetent or guilty of professional misconduct, or (4) is guilty of serious sexual misconduct.

False and Defamatory Statement Included among the elements of defamation are the separate requirements that the defendant's statement be both *false* and *defamatory*. Truth is a complete defense in a defamation case. A defamatory statement is one that is likely to harm the reputation of another by injuring his community's estimation of him or by deterring others from associating or dealing with him.

"Of and Concerning" the Plaintiff Because the defamation cause of action serves to protect reputation, an essential element of the tort is that the alleged defamatory statement must be "of and concerning" the plaintiff. That is, the statement must be about—and thus bear upon the reputation of—the party who brought the case. This requirement presents problems whose complexities are beyond the scope of this text. The rules sketched below, therefore, are sometimes subject to exceptions not explained here.

What about allegedly *fictional accounts* whose characters resemble real people? Most courts say that fictional accounts may be defamatory if a reasonable reader would identify the plaintiff as the subject of the story. Similarly, *humorous or satirical accounts* ordinarily are not defamation unless a reasonable reader would believe that they purport to describe real events or actual facts.

Statements of pure *opinion* do not amount to defamation because they are not statements of "fact" concerning the plaintiff. However, statements that mix elements of opinion with elements of supposed "fact" may be actionable. *Neumann v. Liles*, which follows shortly, explains and applies the factors courts take into account in deciding whether a statement is actionable as a false statement of supposed fact or is, instead, a nonactionable statement of opinion. The *Obsidian Finance Group* case, which appears later in the chapter, also touches on the fact-versus-opinion issue.

Do defamatory statements concerning particular *groups* of people also defame the individuals who belong to those groups? Generally, an individual member of a defamed group cannot recover for damage to her own reputation unless the group is so small that the statement can reasonably be understood as referring to individual group members.

Finally, courts have placed some limits on the persons or entities that can suffer injury to reputation. No liability attaches, for example, to defamatory statements concerning the dead. Corporations and other business entities have reputational interests and can recover for defamatory statements that harm them in their business or deter others from dealing with them. Statements about a corporation's officers, employees, or shareholders normally are not defamatory regarding the corporation, however, unless the statements also reflect on the manner in which the corporation conducts its business.[1]

---

[1]As Chapter 8 reveals, statements concerning the quality of a corporation's products or the quality of its title to land or other property may be the basis of an injurious falsehood claim.

Neumann v. Liles   369 P.3d 1117 (Ore. 2016)

Carol Neumann is an owner of Dancing Deer Mountain LLC, an Oregon business that arranges and performs wedding events at a property Neumann owns. Christopher Liles attended a wedding and reception held on Neumann's property. Two days after those events, Liles posted a negative review about Neumann and her business on Google Reviews, a publicly accessible website on which individuals may post comments about services or products they have received. The review was titled "Disaster!!!!! Find a different wedding venue." The text of the review was as follows:

> There are many other great places to get married, this is not that place! The worst wedding experience of my life! The location is beautiful the problem is the owners. Carol (female owner) is two faced, crooked, and was rude to multiple guest[s]. I was only happy with one thing. It was a beautiful wedding, when it wasn't raining and Carol and Tim stayed away. The owners did not make the rules clear to the people helping with set up even when they saw something they didn't like they waited until the day of the wedding to bring it up. They also changed the rules as they saw fit. We were told we had to leave at 9pm, but at 8:15 they started telling the guests that they had to leave immediately. The "bridal suite" was a tool shed that was painted pretty, but a shed all the same. In my opinion [s]he will find a why [sic] to keep your $500 deposit, and will try to make you pay even more.

Neumann sued Liles in an Oregon court, alleging that the statements in his review constituted defamation. The court dismissed the case after concluding that Liles's statements amounted to nonactionable opinion and were otherwise protected by the First Amendment.

Neumann appealed to the Oregon Court of Appeals, which reversed the lower court's decision. The Court of Appeals concluded that some of the statements Liles made were capable of a defamatory meaning and seemingly factual—meaning that if the statements were false, they could give rise to a valid defamation claim in favor of Neumann. Among the potentially actionable statements, according to the Court of Appeals, were the statements that Neumann was "rude to multiple guest[s]," that she is "crooked," and that she "will find a [way] to keep your $500 deposit." Liles then appealed to the Supreme Court of Oregon, which agreed to decide the case in order to "determine how an actionable statement of fact is distinguished from a constitutionally protected expression of opinion in a defamation claim and whether the context in which a statement is made affects that analysis."

Baldwin, Judge

This case requires us to decide whether a defamatory statement made in an online business review is entitled to protection under the First Amendment. [More specifically, we must] determine whether a reasonable factfinder could conclude that an allegedly defamatory statement touching on a matter of public concern implies an assertion of objective fact and is therefore not constitutionally protected.

Liles argues that his online review of Neumann's venue is entitled to protection under the First Amendment. He contends that his review, when read in the context of informal online communication, is properly understood as expressing merely his subjective opinion about the venue that he was reviewing. He also contends that the statements in his review are not provable as true or false. Regarding the words that the Court of Appeals concluded to be capable of defamatory meaning, such as "rude" and "crooked," he argues that those words are too vague to imply an assertion of fact.

Although our determination of the legal sufficiency of Neumann's defamation claim hinges on whether Liles's statements are protected under the First Amendment, we begin our analysis by [noting that under the common law elements of defamation, the plaintiff must show that] a defendant made a defamatory statement about the plaintiff and published the statement to a third party. A defamatory statement is one that would subject the plaintiff "to hatred, contempt or ridicule, [or] tend to diminish the esteem, respect, goodwill or confidence in which [the plaintiff] is held, or [tend] to excite adverse, derogatory or unpleasant feelings or opinions against [the plaintiff]." [Citation omitted.] In the professional context, a statement is defamatory if it falsely "ascribes to another conduct, characteristics, or a condition incompatible with the proper conduct of his lawful business, trade, [or] profession." [Citation omitted.]

At early common law, defamatory statements were generally deemed actionable regardless of whether they were statements of fact or expressions of opinion. [Over time, however, the common law began to accord some measure of protection for statements of opinion. Later,] the United States Supreme Court determined that the First Amendment places limits on the application of the state law of defamation. The protection afforded under the First Amendment to statements of opinion on matters of public concern reached what one court called its "high-water mark" in *Gertz v. Robert Welch, Inc.*, 418 U.S. 323 (1974). *Keohane v. Stewart*, 882 P.2d 1293, 1298 (Colo. 1994) (so characterizing the Supreme Court's opinion in *Gertz*). In *Gertz*, the Court stated in *dictum*: "Under the

First Amendment there is no such thing as a false idea. However pernicious an opinion may seem, we depend for its correction not on the conscience of judges and juries but on the competition of other ideas. But there is no constitutional value in false statements of fact." 418 U.S. at 339–40. A majority of state and federal courts interpreted *Gertz* to have announced that expressions of opinion were absolutely privileged under the First Amendment.

In *Milkovich v. Lorain Journal Co.*, 497 U.S. 1 (1990), however, the Supreme Court dispelled the notion that it had announced a "wholesale defamation exemption for anything that might be labeled 'opinion.'" *Id.* at 18. In that case, a newspaper published a column that implied that Milkovich, a high school wrestling coach, had lied under oath in a judicial proceeding after his team was involved in an altercation at a wrestling match and the coach's team was placed on probation. Milkovich filed a libel action against the newspaper and a reporter, alleging that the defendants had accused him of committing the crime of perjury, thereby damaging him in his occupation of coach and teacher. The Supreme Court rejected the defendants' argument that all defamatory statements that are categorized as "opinion" as opposed to "fact" enjoy blanket First Amendment protection. *Id.* at 17–18. The Court clarified that the oft-cited passage in *Gertz* had been "merely a reiteration of Justice Holmes' classic 'marketplace of ideas' concept." *Id.* at 18 (citing *Abrams v. United States*, 250 U.S. 616, 630 (1919) (Holmes, J., dissenting) ("[T]he ultimate good desired is better reached by free trade in ideas. . . . [T]he best test of truth is the power of the thought to get itself accepted in the competition of the market."). Thus, *Gertz* had not created an additional separate constitutional privilege for anything that might be labeled an "opinion." In the Court's view, such an interpretation of *Gertz* would "ignore the fact that expressions of 'opinion' may often imply an assertion of objective fact." *Milkovich*, 497 U.S. at 18.

Ultimately, the Court refused to create a separate constitutional privilege for "opinion," concluding instead that existing constitutional doctrine adequately protected the "uninhibited, robust, and wide-open" debate on public issues. *Id.* at 20–21. Under that existing doctrine, full constitutional protection is afforded to statements regarding matters of public concern that are not sufficiently factual to be capable of being proved false and statements that cannot reasonably be interpreted as stating actual facts. The dispositive question in determining whether a defamatory statement is constitutionally protected, according to the Court, is whether a reasonable factfinder could conclude that the statement implies an assertion of objective fact about the plaintiff. *Id.* at 19–21.

Applying that rule to the facts of *Milkovich*, the Court determined that a reasonable factfinder could conclude that the statements in the newspaper column implied a factual assertion

that Milkovich had perjured himself in a judicial proceeding. The Court considered various factors. First, the Court noted that the column had not used "the sort of loose, figurative, or hyperbolic language" that would negate the impression that the writer was seriously maintaining that Milkovich had committed the crime of perjury. Second, the Court concluded the "general tenor of the article" did not negate that impression. Third, in the Court's view, the accusation that Milkovich had committed perjury was "sufficiently factual to be susceptible of being proved true or false." Accordingly, the Court held that the column did not enjoy constitutional protection. *Id.*

The analytical response of both lower federal courts and state courts to *Milkovich* has been varied. This case presents the first occasion for this court to announce a framework for analyzing whether a defamatory statement is entitled to First Amendment protection. In the absence of existing law from this court, we look to the approaches of other jurisdictions for guidance.

In *Unelko Corp. v. Rooney*, 912 F.2d 1049 (9th Cir. 1990), decided shortly after *Milkovich*, the U.S. Court of Appeals for the Ninth Circuit addressed whether certain statements that Andy Rooney had made during two broadcasts of "60 Minutes" were protected as opinion under the First Amendment. The court concluded that, after *Milkovich*, "the threshold question in defamation suits is not whether a statement might be labeled 'opinion,' but rather whether a reasonable factfinder could conclude that the statement impl[ies] an assertion of objective fact." *Id.* at 1053. To resolve that threshold question, the Ninth Circuit drew from the factors that the Supreme Court had considered in *Milkovich* and announced a three-part test: (1) whether the general tenor of the entire work negates the impression that the defendant was asserting an objective fact; (2) whether the defendant used figurative or hyperbolic language that negates that impression; and (3) whether the statement in question is susceptible of being proved true or false. *Id.* Since *Unelko*, the Ninth Circuit has consistently used that three-part inquiry to determine whether a reasonable factfinder could conclude that a statement implies an assertion of objective fact. Several other courts also have expressly adopted the Ninth Circuit's test.

We agree with those courts that have found the Ninth Circuit's three-part inquiry to be a sound approach for determining whether a statement is entitled to First Amendment protection. The Ninth Circuit's test appropriately considers the totality of the relevant circumstances, including the context in which particular statements were made and the verifiability of those statements. The Ninth Circuit's test is also a reasonable interpretation of *Milkovich*. It explicitly incorporates the factors that the Supreme Court itself considered in deciding *Milkovich*. Accordingly, we follow the Ninth Circuit's three-part framework for whether a reasonable factfinder could conclude that a given statement implies a factual assertion.

[We now] apply that test to the facts of this case. Initially, we conclude that, if false, several of Liles's statements are capable of a defamatory meaning. Throughout his review, Liles ascribed to Neumann conduct that is incompatible with the proper conduct of a wedding venue operator and, as the Court of Appeals noted, "inconsistent with a positive wedding experience." As a result, a reasonable factfinder could conclude that Liles's statements were defamatory if he or she found that the statements were false. The question remains, however, whether they are nevertheless protected under the First Amendment.

To resolve that question, we must first determine, by examining the content, form, and context of Liles's statements, whether those statements involve matters of public concern. Neumann has not disputed that Liles's statements involve matters of public concern, and we readily conclude that they do. Liles's review was posted on a publicly accessible website, and the content of his review related to matters of general interest to the public, particularly those members of the public who are in the market for a wedding venue. Next, we must determine whether a reasonable factfinder could interpret Liles's statements as implying assertions of objective fact. Applying the three-part inquiry that we articulated above, we first consider whether the general tenor of the entire work negates the impression that Liles was asserting objective facts about Neumann. From the outset, it is apparent that the review is describing Liles's personal view of Neumann's wedding venue, calling it a "Disaster!!!!!" The general tenor of the piece, beginning with the word *Disaster*, is that, in Liles's subjective opinion, the services were grossly inadequate and that the business was poorly operated.

However, read independently, two sentences in the review could create the impression that Liles was asserting an objective fact: "Carol (female owner) is two faced, crooked, and was rude to multiple guest[s]. . . . In my opinion [s]he will find a [way] to keep your $500 deposit, and will try to make you pay even more." Standing alone, those statements could create the impression that Liles was asserting the fact that Neumann had wrongfully kept a deposit that she was not entitled to keep. In the context of the entire review, however, those sentences do not leave such an impression. Rather, the review as a whole reveals that Liles was an attendee at the wedding in question and suggests that he did not himself purchase wedding services from Neumann. The general tenor of the review thus reflects Liles's negative personal and subjective impressions and reactions as a guest at the venue and negates the impression that Liles was asserting objective facts.

We next consider whether Liles used figurative or hyperbolic language that negates the impression that he was asserting objective facts. Although the general tenor of the review reveals its hyperbolic nature more clearly than do the individual statements contained therein, several statements can be characterized as hyperbolic. In particular, the title of the review—which starts with the word *Disaster* and is followed by a histrionic series of exclamation marks—is hyperbolic and sets the tone for the review. The review also includes the exaggerative statements that this was "The worst wedding experience of [Liles's] life!" and that Liles was "only happy with one thing" about the wedding. Such hyperbolic expressions further negate any impression that Liles was asserting objective facts.

Finally, we consider whether Liles's review is susceptible of being proved true or false. As discussed, Liles's statements generally reflect a strong personal viewpoint as a guest at the wedding venue, which renders them not susceptible of being proved true or false. Again, the sentences quoted above referring to Neumann as "crooked" and stating that, "[i]n my opinion [s]he will find a [way] to keep your $500 deposit, and will try to make you pay even more" could, standing alone, create the impression that Liles was asserting facts about Neumann. However, viewed in the context of the remainder of the review, those statements are not provably false. The general reference to Neumann as "crooked" is not a verifiable accusation that Neumann committed a specific crime. Moreover, in light of the hyperbolic tenor of the review, the use of the word *crooked* does not suggest that Liles was seriously maintaining that Neumann had, in fact, committed a crime.

Similarly, Liles's statement that "[i]n my opinion [Neumann] will find a [way] to keep your $500 deposit, and will try to make you pay even more" is not susceptible of being proved true or false. That statement is explicitly prefaced with the words, "In my opinion"—thereby alerting the reader to the fact that what follows is a subjective viewpoint. Of course, those words alone will not insulate an otherwise factual assertion from liability. *See Milkovich*, 497 U.S. at 19 (simply couching statements in terms of opinion does not dispel their defamatory implications). However, given that Liles—as a mere guest at the wedding—presumably did not pay the deposit for the wedding involved in this case, his speculation that Neumann would try to keep a couple's deposit is not susceptible of being proved true or false.

Based on the foregoing factors, we conclude that a reasonable factfinder could not conclude that Liles's review implies an assertion of objective fact. Rather, his review is an expression of opinion on matters of public concern that is protected under the First Amendment. We therefore further conclude that the trial court did not err in dismissing Neumann's claim, and we reverse the Court of Appeals determination to the contrary.

Court of Appeals decision reversed; Neumann's defamation claim dismissed.

Publication Liability for defamation requires publication of the defamatory statement. As a general rule, no widespread communication of a defamatory statement is necessary for publication. The defendant's communication of the defamatory statement to one person other than the person defamed ordinarily suffices.

So long as no one else receives or overhears it, however, an insulting message communicated directly from the defendant to the plaintiff is not actionable. The long-standing rule is that publication does not take place when *the plaintiff herself* communicates the offensive statement to another. Courts sometimes make an exception to this rule in cases where a discharged employee is forced to tell a potential future employer about false and defamatory statements made to her by her prior employer.

Some courts still follow the older rule that intracorporate statements (statements by one corporate officer or employee to another officer of the same corporation) do not involve publication. Most courts, however, follow the modern trend and hold that there is publication in such situations.

The general rule is that one who repeats a false and defamatory statement may be liable for defamation. This is true even if he identifies the source of the statement.

A party other than the person who initially made a defamatory statement may be liable along with the original speaker or writer if that other party served as a *publisher* of the defamatory falsehood but not if the other party was a mere *distributor*. According to defamation law's traditional publisher versus distributor distinction, a company that publishes a book or a newspaper may be held liable for defamation on the basis of statements that appear in the book or in the newspaper's articles. The rationale is that the publishing company possessed considerable editorial control over the content of the book or the articles and would have had the ability to remove the defamatory falsehoods. (The writer of the statements, of course, would be liable as well.) Libraries and bookstores, however, are mere distributors because they lack the editorial control that publishers have. Therefore, libraries and bookstores are not liable for defamation even if defamatory falsehoods appear in books they lend to users or sell to customers.

What about Internet service providers and website operators? Can they be held liable as publishers of statements posted online by other parties? The answer might initially seem to be "yes" in instances where the service provider or website operator reserved some measure of editorial control, but the actual answer is "no." Section 230 of the federal Communications Decency Act establishes a national rule that "no provider or user of an interactive computer service shall be treated as the publisher or speaker of any information provided by another information content provider." This section has been applied by courts in a significant number of defamation cases and in various other types of cases in which liability for someone else's online statements is at issue.

Defenses and Privileges Even though defamation is called an intentional tort, the common law contemplated a form of strict liability for defamation. Defenses are available, however, in certain defamation cases. Of course, the truth of the defamatory statement is a complete defense to liability. Defamatory statements may be *privileged* as well. Privileges to defamation liability recognize that in some circumstances, other social interests are more important than an individual's right to reputation. Privileges can be *absolute* or *conditional*.

An absolute privilege shields the author of a defamatory statement regardless of her knowledge, motive, or intent. When such a privilege applies, it operates as a complete defense to defamation liability. Absolutely privileged statements include those made by participants in judicial proceedings, by legislators or witnesses in the course of legislative proceedings, by certain executive officials in the course of their duties, and by one spouse to the other in private. In each case, the theory underlying the privilege is that complete freedom of expression is essential to the proper functioning of the relevant activity, and that potential liability for defamation would inhibit free expression.

Conditional (or qualified) privileges give the defendant a defense unless the privilege is *abused*. What constitutes abuse varies with the privilege in question. In general, conditional privileges are abused when the statement is made with knowledge of its falsity or with reckless disregard for the truth, when the statement does not advance the purposes supporting the privilege, or when it is unnecessarily made to inappropriate people.

There are various conditional privileges. One important conditional privilege involves *statements made to protect or further the legitimate interests of another*. One of the most common business-related examples is the employment reference. Suppose that Parker's former employer, Dorfman, has good reason to believe—and does in fact believe—that Parker embezzled money from Dorfman's business while Parker was a Dorfman employee. Trumbull, who is deciding whether to hire Parker, contacts Dorfman to ask about Parker's work record and performance as an employee. During the conversation, Dorfman tells Trumbull that he believes Parker committed embezzlement while working for him. On these facts, Dorfman will be protected by a conditional privilege against defamation liability to Parker because Dorfman's statement was designed to further Trumbull's legitimate interest in making an intelligent hiring decision. Dorfman's reasonably based belief in the truth of his statement about Parker is critical to his ability to rely on the conditional privilege. If Dorfman had known his statement was false or had made it with reckless disregard for the truth, Dorfman would have abused the conditional privilege and would have lost its protection against liability.

A second important type of conditional privilege concerns *statements made to promote a common interest.* Intracorporate communications serve as an example, as do communications to law enforcement agencies and professional disciplinary bodies.

A further example can be found in the U.S. Supreme Court decision *Air Wisconsin Airlines Corp. v. Hoeper*, 134 S. Ct. 852 (2014). In that case, the Court interpreted a federal statute that establishes a conditional privilege protecting airlines and their employees from civil liability for the content of their reports on suspicious behavior to the Transportation Security Administration (TSA). Hoeper claimed he was defamed when airline officials relayed their concerns about his behavior and "mental stability" to the TSA. When they made this report, the airline officials knew that Hoeper had been visibly angry after failing (for the fourth time) a certification test he had to pass in order to keep his job as a pilot. They also knew he had made a statement to the effect that the testing program was rigged against him. In addition, the airline officials were aware that Hoeper was scheduled to board a flight to go home from the testing center. They were concerned that he could be carrying a firearm because he had been among the pilots permitted to do so. After receiving the report, the TSA had Hoeper removed from the plane he had boarded for his flight home.

In rejecting Hoeper's defamation claim, the Court ruled that the gist of the report to the TSA was not materially false despite the "mental stability" speculation and the report's reference to Hoeper as a terminated employee (when in reality the termination would not occur until the next day). Importantly, Hoeper still would have lost the case even if the report had been materially false. In that event, the defendants would have been protected under the statute's conditional privilege absent a showing—which Hoeper would not have been able to make—that they abused the privilege by making a report with knowledge of its falsity or with reckless disregard for the truth.

Finally, many courts recognize a privilege called *fair comment.* That privilege protects fair and accurate media reports of defamatory statements that appear in proceedings of official government action or originate from public meetings.

Defamation and the Constitution Until approximately 55 years ago, the First Amendment's guarantees of freedom of speech and press were not considered relevant to defamation cases. The common law's strict liability approach meant that unless one of the privileges discussed earlier applied, a speaker or writer who made a false statement believing it to be true had no more protection against defamation liability than the deliberate liar had. In a series of cases dating back to 1964, however, the U.S. Supreme Court has concluded that the common law's approach is too heavily weighted in favor of plaintiffs' reputational interests and not sufficiently protective of defendants' free speech and free press interests. The Court has recognized that when coupled with the potential availability of presumed damages, a strict liability regime could deter would-be speakers from contributing true statements to public debate out of fear of the costly liability that might result if the jury somehow concluded that the statements were false. Recognizing the need to guard against this "chilling effect" and the resulting restriction on the flow of information that is important to a free society, the Court determined in *New York Times Co. v. Sullivan*, 376 U.S. 254 (1964) that the First Amendment has a role to play in certain defamation cases. The Court reasoned that judicial enforcement of the legal rules of defamation served as the government action necessary to trigger application of the First Amendment.

 LO6-8 Explain what a public official plaintiff or a public figure plaintiff must prove, for constitutional reasons, in order to win a defamation case.

Public Official Plaintiff Cases In *New York Times*, the Court held that when a *public official* brings a defamation case, he or she must prove not only the usual elements of defamation but also a First Amendment–based fault requirement known as actual malice. The Court gave actual malice a special meaning: knowledge of falsity or reckless disregard for the truth. Thus, after *New York Times*, a defendant who makes a false and defamatory statement about a public official plaintiff will not be held liable unless the public official proves that the defendant made the statement either (1) knowing it was false or (2) recklessly. Moreover, the Court held in *New York Times* that as a further First Amendment–based safeguard, the public official plaintiff must prove actual malice by *clear and convincing evidence*—a higher standard of proof than the preponderance of the evidence standard applicable to every other element of a defamation claim and to civil cases generally. The public official category includes many high-level government officials, whether elected or appointed.

Public Figure Plaintiff Cases Three years after *New York Times*, the Supreme Court extended the proof-of-actual-malice requirement to defamation cases in which the plaintiff is a *public figure.* The Court also mandated that such a plaintiff prove actual malice by clear and convincing evidence. Individual persons or corporations are public figures if they either (1) are well known to large segments of society through their own voluntary efforts or (2) have voluntarily placed themselves, in the words of the Supreme Court, at "the forefront of a particular public controversy." The first type of public figure, sometimes given the "general-purpose" designation, includes well-known corporations, political candidates who are not already holders of public office, and ex-government officials. It also includes a diverse collection of celebrities, near celebrities, and well-known persons ranging from familiar actors, entertainers, and media figures to famous athletes or coaches and others with high public visibility in their chosen professions. The second type of public figure, sometimes assigned the "limited-purpose" label, is not well known by large segments of society but has chosen to take a prominent leadership role regarding a matter of public debate (e.g., the abortion rights controversy, the debate over whether certain drugs should be legalized, or disputes over the extent to which environmental regulations should restrict business activity). A general-purpose public figure must prove actual malice in any defamation case in which he, she, or it is the plaintiff. A limited-purpose public figure, on the other hand, must prove actual malice when the statement giving rise to the case relates in some sense to the public controversy as to which the plaintiff is a public figure.

The proof-of-actual-malice requirement poses a very substantial hurdle for public officials and public figures to clear. That is by design, according to the Supreme Court. Defendants have especially strong First Amendment interests in regard to statements about public officials and public figures, given the high level of public interest and concern that attaches almost automatically to matters involving such persons.

Knowledge of falsity—one of the two forms of actual malice—is difficult to prove. When the defendant who made a false statement can point to an arguably credible source on which he, she, or it relied as a supposed indicator of the statement's truth, the defendant presumably did not have knowledge of the statement's falsity. Neither did the defendant speak or write with the other form of actual malice—*reckless disregard for the truth*—in such an instance. According to the Supreme Court, reckless disregard has been demonstrated when the plaintiff proves either (1) that the defendant "in fact entertained serious doubts" about the statement's truth but made the statement anyway or (2) that the defendant consciously rejected overwhelming evidence of falsity and chose instead to rely on a much less significant bit of evidence that would have indicated truth only if the contrary evidence had not also been part of the picture. When the defendant relied on an arguably credible source that tended to indicate the statement was true, the defendant presumably did not entertain serious doubts and did not consciously reject overwhelming evidence of falsity. Such a defendant, therefore, did not display reckless disregard for the truth. If a reasonable person in the defendant's position would not have relied on a lone source despite its credibility and would have ascertained the statement's falsity through further investigation, the defendant who failed to investigate further has been negligent. Negligence, however, is not as severe a degree of fault as reckless disregard and does not constitute actual malice.

Most defamation cases brought by public official or public figure plaintiffs are won by the defendant—if not at trial, then on appeal. That is often the result because the plaintiff was unable to prove actual malice even though the statement was false and tended to harm reputation. Sometimes, however, the public official or public figure plaintiff accomplishes the daunting task of proving actual malice. When that occurs, the First Amendment does not bar such a plaintiff from winning the case and recovering compensatory damages (including those of the presumed variety) as well as punitive damages.

In *Bertrand v. Mullin*, which follows, the Supreme Court of Iowa focuses on the actual malice element that public official plaintiffs and public figure plaintiffs must prove if they are to win a defamation case. The decision explores the First Amendment foundations of the actual malice element and illustrates the difficulty of proving either of the forms it may take.

Bertrand v. Mullin   846 N.W.2d 884 (Iowa 2014)

Republican Rick Bertrand and Democrat Rick Mullin were candidates for the Iowa Senate in the 2010 election. Bertrand owned businesses in Sioux City, Iowa. From 1999 until 2009, however, he served as a salesperson and district manager for Takeda Pharmaceuticals. Bertrand worked in a Takeda division that marketed the diabetes drug Actos. Another Takeda division sold Rozerem, a prescription sleep aid. Bertrand never personally sold Rozerem.

In October 2010, Bertrand ran a televised campaign advertisement that contrasted Mullin's current policy positions with positions he had taken in the past. The ad angered Mullin and, according to his campaign's internal polling, adversely affected his support. His campaign manager told him that "Bertrand hit you hard. Hit him back harder."

Research conducted for Mullin revealed a newspaper article about a consumer group's disclosure of a Food and Drug Administration (FDA) report finding that 388 patients had been hospitalized for heart problems after taking Actos. Research also revealed that the FDA had criticized Takeda's marketing of Rozerem—especially an ad in which Rozerem seemingly was being marketed to children. Finally, research uncovered a newspaper article noting that a consumer advocacy group had labeled Takeda "the most unethical drug company in the world."

This research furnished the basis for a televised ad run by Mullin in response to Bertrand's ad. When Mullin and Iowa Democratic Party staff members discussed the proposed script for the ad in mid-October, Mullin disliked its tone. In a later e-mail, Mullin called a rewrite of the script "less vile." He eventually approved the script.

The Mullin ad—titled "Secrets"—first aired on TV on October 17. The audio portion contained these statements:

> Rick Bertrand said he would run a positive campaign but now he is falsely attacking Rick Mullin. Why? Because Bertrand doesn't want you to know he put his profits ahead of children's health. Bertrand was a sales agent for a big drug company that was rated the most unethical company in the world. The FDA singled out Bertrand's company for marketing a dangerous sleep drug to children.
>
> Rick Bertrand. Broken promises. A record of deceit.

At the bottom of the screen during one shot, this statement appeared: "BERTRAND'S COMPANY MARKETED SLEEP DRUG TO CHILDREN." The statements in the ad cited the above-mentioned newspaper articles, which also flashed across the screen. Mullin later admitted that he did not know whether Bertrand had ever sold Rozerem or marketed dangerous drugs to children. In addition, Mullin admitted that when he approved the ad's script, he liked the reference to profiting at the expense of children.

At an October 21 public debate, Bertrand called the Mullin ad false and demanded that Mullin stop airing it. The next day, Bertrand filed a defamation lawsuit against Mullin and the Iowa Democratic Party in a state district court. Mullin kept running the ad through October 31, two days before the election. Bertrand won the election by 222 votes.

The trial court ruled that of the 10 supposedly defamatory statements in the Mullin ad and in related campaign mailings, eight were not actionable as a matter of law. However, the court permitted the jury to consider two statements from the ad: "The FDA singled out Bertrand's company for the marketing of dangerous drugs to children." and "BERTRAND'S COMPANY MARKETED SLEEP DRUG TO CHILDREN." According to the court, "a reasonable jury [could] find that these statements imply a false fact, namely that Rick Bertrand personally sold a dangerous sleep drug to children, or that he owns a company that sold a dangerous sleep drug to children." Besides denying that the statements and implications were false, Mullin argued that Bertrand could not prove they were made with actual malice.

At the close of the evidence, the court denied the defendants' motion for a directed verdict. The jury returned a verdict in favor of Bertrand for $31,000 in damages against Mullin and $200,000 against the Iowa Democratic Party. In response to the defendants' motion for judgment notwithstanding the verdict (JNOV), the court concluded that it should have granted a directed verdict for the defendants regarding the alleged implication that Bertrand owned a company that sold Rozerem. No reasonable juror could conclude that Takeda was Bertrand's company, the court determined, because reasonable viewers of the ad could not ignore the statement that Bertrand had been a Takeda sales agent (a statement that preceded the "Bertrand's company" line in the ad).

The above ruling did not change the case's outcome, however, because the court concluded that in view of "the language and juxtaposition of the phrases," reasonable jurors could have regarded—and apparently did regard—the ad's statement as implying that Bertrand personally sold Rozerem. The court reasoned that even if Mullin literally expressed a legitimate point about the company for which Bertrand had worked, reasonable persons hearing the statement could infer that Bertrand personally sold the product. In addition, the court concluded that sufficient evidence of actual malice had been presented. The court therefore allowed the jury verdict for Bertrand to stand. The defendants appealed to the Supreme Court of Iowa.

Cady, Chief Justice

In an ordinary case, a plaintiff establishes a prima facie claim for defamation by showing the defendant (1) published a statement that (2) was false and defamatory (3) of and concerning the plaintiff, and (4) resulted in injury to the plaintiff. We have previously held the defamatory publication need not be explicit, but may be implied "by a careful choice of words in juxtaposition of statements." [Citation omitted.] A plaintiff who is a candidate for public office [is treated, for defamation purposes, as if he were] a public official. *Monitor Patriot Co. v. Roy*, 401 U.S. 265, 271–72 (1971). When a plaintiff is [a public figure or a] public official, the First Amendment adds [the requirement of proving] actual malice. *New York Times v. Sullivan*, 376 U.S. 254, 279–80 (1964).

[The public official] plaintiff bears the burden of showing actual malice by clear and convincing evidence. The burden to establish actual malice was deliberately set high . . . in *New York Times* [because the First Amendment contemplates] a "profound national commitment to the principle that debate on public issues should be uninhibited, robust, and wide-open, and that it may well include vehement, caustic, and sometimes unpleasantly sharp attacks on government and public officials." *Id.* at 270. At its core, the First Amendment guarantee "has its fullest and most urgent application precisely to the conduct of campaigns for political office." *Monitor Patriot*, 401 U.S. at 272. [C]onstitutional protection for political speech in the context of a campaign extends to "anything which might touch on an official's fitness for office." *Garrison v. Louisiana*, 379 U.S. 64, 77 (1964).

A statement is made with actual malice when accompanied by "knowledge that it was false or with reckless disregard for its truth or falsity." *New York Times*, 376 U.S. at 279–80. A knowing falsehood may be easy to identify in theory, but any effort to peer into the recesses of human attitudes towards the truthfulness of a statement is certain to be difficult.

"Reckless disregard . . . cannot be fully encompassed in one infallible definition." *St. Amant v. Thompson*, 390 U.S. 727, 730 (1968). Yet, in the half century the *New York Times* rule has preserved the First Amendment's guarantee of uninhibited commentary regarding public officials and figures, the Supreme Court has crafted some useful guideposts. Most prominently, an early case nearly contemporaneous with *New York Times* opined that statements made with a "high degree of awareness of their probable falsity" may subject the speaker to civil damages. *Garrison*, 379 U.S. at 74. The negative implication, of course, is that a court may not award damages against one who negligently communicates a falsehood about a public official [or public figure]. *Masson v. New Yorker Magazine, Inc.*, 501 U.S. 496, 510 (1991) ("Mere negligence does not suffice."). The Supreme Court has explained its reasoning:

[R]eckless conduct is not measured by whether a reasonably prudent man would have published, or would have investigated

before publishing. There must be sufficient evidence to permit the conclusion that the defendant *in fact entertained serious doubts as to the truth of his publication*. Publishing with such doubts shows reckless disregard for truth or falsity and demonstrates actual malice.

St. Amant, 390 U.S. at 731 (emphasis added).

Candidly, the *New York Times* standard tilts the balance strongly in favor of negligent defendants. "[F]ailure to investigate before publishing, even when a reasonably prudent person would have done so, is not sufficient to establish reckless disregard." *Harte-Hanks Communications, Inc. v. Connaughton*, 491 U.S. 657, 688 (1989). Similarly, "[r]eliance on a single source, in the absence of a high degree of awareness of probable falsity, does not constitute actual malice." [Citation omitted.] Nor does a "shoddy" investigation constitute actual malice. [Citation omitted.] "[F]ailure to follow journalistic standards and lack of investigation may establish irresponsibility or even possibly gross irresponsibility, but not reckless disregard of truth." [Citation omitted.]

Mullin and the Iowa Democratic Party challenge the judgment entered on the claim of defamation on several grounds, including the sufficiency of evidence to support the actual malice element of the tort. In considering the actual malice element, we must decide if the evidence supports a finding that the defendants "in fact entertained serious doubts as to the truth" of the implied communication in the commercial—that Bertrand personally sold a dangerous drug—or if they had "a high degree of awareness of [its] probable falsity." *St. Amant*, 390 U.S. at 731 (first quotation); *Garrison*, 379 U.S. at 74 (second quotation).

Bertrand argues actual malice was supported by the evidence in a number of ways. First, he claims the evidence showed that the defendants knew the implication in the commercial at issue was false because they knew that none of his Sioux City companies sold drugs and [because they neither knew] which pharmaceutical company [division] Bertrand worked in [nor] which division of the company sold the drug in dispute. Second, Bertrand claims Mullin and the Iowa Democratic Party should have known the implication in the commercial was false because Mullin expressed doubts about the commercial before it aired. Third, Bertrand claims actual malice was supported by evidence that the defendants acquired ill will towards him after he aired his own hard-hitting commercial. Fourth, Bertrand asserts the jury could have found actual malice because the purpose of the commercial was to curtail electoral support for Bertrand.

We first consider the evidence to support a finding that Mullin and the Iowa Democratic Party had actual knowledge of the falsity of the implied statement in the commercial. In doing so, we clarify that the district court ultimately found the only actionable defamation claim was based on the implication that Bertrand sold drugs to children, reported to be dangerous, when he worked for a pharmaceutical company. Thus, any knowledge by the defendants that Bertrand's Sioux City businesses never marketed drugs to children has no impact on the pertinent question whether they knew that Bertrand never sold a dangerous drug to children when he worked for the pharmaceutical company. [T]he evidence of actual malice necessary to support the implied defamation in this case [would need to center] on knowledge of the falsity of the implied statement that Bertrand personally marketed Rozerem, not on knowledge that he did not own the company that marketed the drug or that the businesses he actually owned did not market the drug.

The evidence at trial established that Mullin and the Iowa Democratic Party did *not* know [whether] Bertrand was personally responsible in any way for marketing or selling the drug. They conducted some research . . . and concluded from [it] that Bertrand worked for the drug company and the company marketed the drug. The research revealed that the FDA and others criticized Takeda for selling Rozerem. These statements were true and formed the basis for their claim that Bertrand was associated with an unethical business. Yet, Mullin and the Iowa Democratic Party did not look into the matter further to uncover the complete story. The truth, of course, was that Bertrand never worked in the particular division of the company that marketed the drug and never sold the drug. Nevertheless, there was no evidence that Mullin or the Iowa Democratic Party knew the implied statement that Bertrand sold the drug was false.

Without evidence of actual knowledge, we consider [whether] the implied statement was made with reckless disregard for its truth or falsity. We begin by considering the degree of awareness of the probable falsity and any doubts that may have existed about the truth or falsity of the implied statement.

Mullin and the Iowa Democratic Party asserted the implication that Bertrand sold a dangerous drug was made in good faith because they only wanted to inform voters that Bertrand was associated with an unethical company. While this assertion is alone insufficient to conclusively establish the absence of actual malice, it is important to recognize that the nondefamatory implication the defendants sought to communicate—Bertrand was associated with an unethical company that sold a dangerous drug—can be [inferred] from the advertisement. [Even if the false implication that Bertrand personally sold the drug is also present in the ad], the general background story from which both implications were derived was not false. Thus, the defamatory statement in this case was not built on a totally fabricated story.

It is also important to observe that the sources [used in gathering] the background information for the advertisement were not so unreliable as to be unworthy of credence and indicative of reckless disregard for the truth. Some of the reports may not have been neutral, but mere reliance on sources with predisposed viewpoints does not establish actual malice.

We next consider the evidence that Mullin initially [disliked] the tone of the commercial as proof of actual malice. There was no evidence[, however,] that the concerns expressed by Mullin pertained to the falsity of any statements. The expressions of doubt were not evidence of actual malice, but were pragmatic and expedient considerations of tenor and political image-crafting with which the First Amendment is fundamentally unconcerned.

We next consider the evidence that Mullin was angry at Bertrand for running his negative campaign advertisement and sought to "hit back" hard at him. This is the type of evidence, however, that demonstrates common law malice, [not] actual malice. As used in the First Amendment context, actual malice . . . "has nothing to do with bad motive or ill will." *Harte-Hanks Communications*, 491 U.S. at 666 n.7. "[U]nlike the common law definition of malice, *New York Times* actual malice focuses upon the attitudes of defendants vis-à-vis the truth of their statements, as opposed to their attitudes towards plaintiffs." [Citation omitted.]

We next consider the claim by Bertrand that actual malice was established because the very purpose of the commercial was to attack, and thereby negatively affect, a candidate's reputation. An intent to inflict harm is insufficient to demonstrate a reckless disregard for the truth. The very point of the trenchant public discourse protected under the legal standards of *New York Times* is oftentimes to weaken the support for political rivals in future elections. The standards of *New York Times* do not constrain First Amendment protection to political discourse of a sterile, academic character or an undiluted high-minded nature.

[Although] the ordinary purpose of a defamation action is to vindicate and protect a person's common law reputational interest[, the] First Amendment protects public discourse—even in the form of withering criticism of a political opponent's past dealings or associations—unless the lodged attack is clearly shown to be false and made with actual malice. After all, *New York Times* and its progeny even reach so far as to protect pillorying barbs some may regard as offensive and outrageous. *See Hustler Magazine, Inc. v. Falwell*, 485 U.S. 46, 55 (1988) (rejecting an "outrageous[ness]" exception to traditional public official [and public figure] tort suit rules).

Overall, we conclude the evidence failed to establish actual malice. The failure to write the advertisement in a way to avoid the false implication may have been negligence, but it did not rise to the level of reckless disregard for the truth. The evidence failed to support [the] high degree of subjective awareness of falsity needed for a public official to recover for defamation.

The result of this case is not to imply that actual malice cannot exist within the rough and tumble Wild West approach to negative commercials that have seemingly become standard discourse in many political campaigns. Protection from defamatory statements does exist and should exist, but the high standards established under the First Amendment to permit a free exchange of ideas within the same discourse must also be protected. Among public figures and officials, an added layer of toughness is expected, and a greater showing of culpability is required under our governing legal standards to make sure the freedom of political speech . . . is not suppressed or chilled. [T]he protective constitutional line

of free speech in the arena of public officials is drawn at actual malice. Within this arena, speech cannot become actionable defamation until the line has been crossed. It was not in this case.

Jury verdict in favor of Bertrand reversed; case dismissed.

Private Figure Plaintiff Cases

 LO6-9 Explain what a private figure plaintiff must prove, for constitutional reasons, in order to win a defamation case.

What about defamation cases brought by *private figures*, those corporations that are not public figures and those individual persons who are neither public figures nor public officials? In *Gertz v. Robert Welch, Inc.*, 418 U.S. 323 (1974), the Supreme Court concluded that private figure plaintiffs should not be expected to prove actual malice in order to win defamation cases, despite defendants' meaningful free speech and press interests. The Court noted that such plaintiffs have neither sought, nor do they command, the higher level of attention desired and achieved by public officials and public figures. Requiring private figure plaintiffs to prove actual malice would tip the balance too heavily in favor of defendants' First Amendment interests and would do so at the expense of plaintiffs' reputational interests. The Court sought to balance the respective interests more suitably by developing, in *Gertz*, a two-rule approach under which the first rule focused on liability and the second focused on damages.

The first *Gertz* rule provided that in order to win a defamation case, the private figure plaintiff must prove some level of fault as set by state law, so long as that level of fault was at least negligence (in the sense discussed earlier). After *Gertz*, almost every state chose negligence as the applicable fault requirement. The second *Gertz* rule addressed recoverable damages. It provided that if a private figure plaintiff proved only negligence on the defendant's part—the level of fault necessary to enable the plaintiff to win the case—the recoverable damages would be restricted to compensatory damages for proven reputational harm and other actual injury. Presumed damages and punitive damages would not be recoverable in such an instance. The second *Gertz* rule also spoke to the availability of presumed and punitive damages by providing that if the private figure plaintiff wanted to recover such damages (either instead of or in addition to damages for demonstrated harm), he, she, or it would need to prove actual malice by clear and convincing evidence.

In a 1985 decision, *Dun & Bradstreet, Inc. v. Greenmoss Builders, Inc.*, 472 U.S. 749, the Court injected a *public concern versus private concern* distinction into at least the second, if not both, of the two *Gertz* rules. The Court held in *Dun & Bradstreet* that the second *Gertz* rule (the one requiring proof of actual malice as a condition of recovering presumed and punitive damages) applies only when the private figure plaintiff's case is based on a statement that addressed a matter of public concern. If the private figure plaintiff's case pertains to a statement that addressed a matter of only private concern, the second *Gertz* rule does not apply—meaning that presumed and punitive damages are recoverable instead of or in addition to damages for proven actual injury, even though the plaintiff established nothing more than the negligence presumably necessary to win the case. "Presumably necessary" is an apt characterization because it is a matter of interpretation and debate whether, after *Dun & Bradstreet*, the basic fault requirement of negligence still applies to a private figure plaintiff case involving a statement on a matter of private concern.

Only the second *Gertz* rule was at issue in *Dun & Bradstreet*, which, according to the Court, was a private figure–private concern case. Negligence on the defendant's part was present in the facts and was not a contested issue when the case reached the Supreme Court. Even so, it is not unreasonable to assert that if the Court was injecting a public concern qualifier into the second *Gertz* rule, it logically would also have been contemplating a public concern qualifier for the first *Gertz* rule (the rule requiring proof of at least negligence to establish liability). Under this reading of *Dun & Bradstreet*, the common law's liability-without-fault approach would again govern defamation cases of the private figure–private concern variety. Those who read *Dun & Bradstreet* more narrowly, however, are inclined to restrict it to what the Supreme Court actually held (i.e., that a public concern element is part of the second *Gertz* rule) and to assume that the basic fault requirement of negligence continues to apply to *all* private figure plaintiff cases until the Supreme Court specifically holds to the contrary. The narrower reading of *Dun & Bradstreet* may have slightly more adherents among lower courts and legal commentators, but it is a close call.

The *Obsidian Finance Group* case, which follows shortly, illustrates the application of the two *Gertz* rules to a private figure plaintiff case.

As the above discussion indicates, public concern determinations have become important in private figure plaintiff cases. (Note that the Supreme Court has not made the public concern–private concern distinction a requirement for public officials' and public figures' defamation cases—probably because the public concern character of statements about such prominent persons is essentially a "given.") What sorts of statements, then, deal with matters of public concern? The Supreme Court provided little guidance on this issue in *Dun & Bradstreet*. Lower court decisions, however, have consistently established that statements dealing with crime address matters of public concern. The same is true of a broad range of statements dealing with public health, safety, or welfare, or with comparably important matters that capture society's attention. For further discussion of what may constitute a public concern, see the *Obsidian Finance Group* case.

The Media–Nonmedia Issue (or Nonissue?) A final set of issues concerning defamation's First Amendment–based fault requirements is whether they apply only when the defendant is a member of the media (i.e., the press), or in all defamation cases. In phrasing its holdings in certain defamation decisions, the Supreme Court has sometimes employed media-oriented language. That may have been done, however, because the cases involved media defendants. The

Court contributed to confusion on this point in one decision with an inaccurate footnote asserting that the Court had never decided whether the First Amendment–based fault requirements apply in nonmedia defendant cases. Yet the Court clearly had done so. The landmark *New York Times* case included media and nonmedia defendants. There, the Court held that the public official plaintiff needed to prove actual malice on the part of all of the defendants.

Although the Court has not officially addressed the media–nonmedia issue in recent decisions, some justices over the years have unofficially rejected such a distinction by making comments along those lines in concurring and dissenting opinions. In view of those comments, the decision in *New York Times*, the equal billing the First Amendment gives to freedom of "speech" and freedom of the "press," and the disapproval of a media–nonmedia distinction by most lower courts and an overwhelming majority of legal commentators, it seems extremely likely that if the Supreme Court now faced the issue squarely, it would hold that the First Amendment–based fault requirements apply to all defamation cases without regard for whether the defendant is a member of the media.

Besides addressing the rules for private figure plaintiff cases and the role of the public concern element, the court in *Obsidian Finance Group* rejects the argument that the First Amendment aspects of defamation should apply only in cases against media defendants. That decision appears next. Figure 6.1's summary of the relevant First Amendment rules follows.

Obsidian Finance Group, LLC v. Cox   740 F.3d 1284 (9th Cir. 2014)

Kevin Padrick was a principal in Obsidian Finance Group, which provides advice to financially distressed businesses. Summit Accommodators Inc. retained Obsidian in connection with a contemplated bankruptcy. After Summit filed for reorganization, the bankruptcy court appointed Padrick as the Chapter 11 trustee. Because Summit had misappropriated funds from clients, Padrick's main task was to marshal the firm's assets for the benefit of those clients.

After Padrick's appointment, Crystal Cox published blog posts on several websites that she created. These blog posts accused Padrick and Obsidian of fraud, corruption, money laundering, and other illegal activities in connection with the Summit bankruptcy. Despite a cease-and-desist letter from Padrick and Obsidian, Cox continued posting allegations. Padrick and Obsidian then sued her for defamation.

The federal district court held that all but one of Cox's blog posts were constitutionally protected opinions because they employed figurative and hyperbolic language and could not be proven true or false. The court held, however, that a December 25 blog post on bankruptcycorruption.com made "fairly specific allegations [that] a reasonable reader could understand . . . to imply a provable fact assertion"—that is, that Padrick, in his capacity as bankruptcy trustee, failed to pay $174,000 in taxes owed by Summit. The district judge therefore allowed that single defamation claim to proceed to a jury trial.

In a pretrial memorandum, dealing with proposed jury instructions, Cox argued that because the December 25 blog post involved a matter of public concern, Padrick and Obsidian had the burden of proving her negligence in order to recover for defamation and that they could not recover presumed damages absent proof that she acted with actual malice. Cox alternatively argued that Padrick and Obsidian were public figures and thus were required to prove that Cox made the statements against them with actual malice. Rejecting both of Cox's arguments, the district court explained that Padrick and Obsidian were not required to prove either negligence or actual damages because Cox had failed to submit "evidence suggestive of her status as a journalist." The court also ruled that neither Padrick nor Obsidian was a public figure.

After the parties presented their evidence and made their closing arguments, the district judge instructed the jury that the plaintiffs "are entitled to receive reasonable compensation for harm to reputation, humiliation, or mental suffering even if [they did] not present evidence that proves actual damages . . . because the law presumes that the plaintiffs suffered these damages." The jury returned a verdict in favor of Padrick and Obsidian, awarding Padrick $1.5 million and Obsidian $1 million in compensatory damages. After the district court denied her motion for a new trial, Cox appealed to the U.S. Court of Appeals for the Ninth Circuit. Obsidian and Padrick cross-appealed, contending that their defamation claims about the other blog posts should have gone to the jury.

Hurwitz, Circuit Judge

Cox does not contest the district court's finding that the December 25 blog post contained an assertion of fact; nor does she contest the jury's conclusions that the post was false and defamatory. She challenges only the district court's rulings that (a) liability could be imposed without a showing of fault or actual damages, and (b) Padrick and Obsidian were not public officials.

The Supreme Court's landmark opinion in *New York Times Co. v. Sullivan*, 376 U.S. 254 (1964), began the construction of a First Amendment framework concerning the level of fault required for defamation liability. *New York Times* held that when a public official seeks damages for defamation, the official must show "actual malice"—that the defendant published the defamatory statement "with knowledge that it was false or with reckless disregard of whether it was false or not." *Id.* at 280. A decade later, *Gertz v. Robert Welch, Inc.*, held that the First Amendment required only a "negligence standard for private defamation actions." 418 U.S. 323, 350 (1974). This case involves the intersection between *New York Times* and *Gertz*, an area not yet fully explored by this Circuit, in the context of a medium of publication—the Internet—entirely unknown at the time of those decisions.

Padrick and Obsidian first argue that the *Gertz* negligence requirement applies only to suits against the institutional press. [They] are correct in noting that *Gertz* involved an institutional media defendant and that the Court's opinion specifically cited the need to shield "the press and broadcast media from the rigors of strict liability for defamation." 418 U.S. at 348. We conclude, however, that the holding in *Gertz* sweeps more broadly.

The *Gertz* court did not expressly limit its holding to the defamation of institutional media defendants. And, although the Supreme Court has never directly held that the *Gertz* rule applies beyond the institutional press, it has [applied the *New York Times* rules in defamation cases against non-media defendants].

[In addition, the Supreme Court has] repeatedly refused in non-defamation contexts to accord greater First Amendment protection to the institutional media than to other speakers. The Supreme Court recently emphasized the point in *Citizens United v. Federal Election Commission*: "We have consistently rejected the proposition that the institutional press has any constitutional privilege beyond that of other speakers." 558 U.S. 310, 352 (2010). In construing the constitutionality of campaign finance statutes, the Court cited with approval the position of five Justices in *Dun &*

Bradstreet, Inc. v. Greenmoss Builders, Inc., that "in the context of defamation law, the rights of the institutional media are no greater and no less than those enjoyed by other individuals engaged in the same activities." 472 U.S. 749, 784 (1985) (Brennan, J., dissenting); *id.* at 773 (White, J., concurring in the judgment). *Dun & Bradstreet* held that presumed and punitive damages are constitutionally permitted in defamation cases without a showing of actual malice when the defamatory statements at issue do not involve matters of public concern. *See* 472 U.S. at 763.

Like the Supreme Court, the Ninth Circuit has not directly addressed whether First Amendment defamation rules apply equally to both the institutional press and individual speakers. But every other circuit to consider the issue has held that the First Amendment defamation rules in *New York Times* and its progeny apply equally to the institutional press and individual speakers. We agree with our sister circuits. The protections of the First Amendment do not turn on whether the defendant was a trained journalist, formally affiliated with traditional news entities, engaged in conflict-of-interest disclosure, went beyond just assembling others' writings, or tried to get both sides of a story. As the Supreme Court has accurately warned, a First Amendment distinction between the institutional press and other speakers is unworkable: "With the advent of the Internet and the decline of print and broadcast media . . . the line between the media and others who wish to comment on political and social issues becomes far more blurred." *Citizens United*, 558 U.S. at 352. In defamation cases, the public-figure status of a plaintiff and the public importance of the statement at issue—not the identity of the speaker—provide the First Amendment touchstones.

We therefore hold that the *Gertz* negligence requirement for private defamation actions is not limited to cases with institutional media defendants. But this does not completely resolve the *Gertz* dispute. Padrick and Obsidian also argue that they were not required to prove Cox's negligence because *Gertz* involved a matter of public concern and this case does not.

The Supreme Court has "never considered whether the *Gertz* balance obtains when the defamatory statements involve no issue of public concern." *Dun & Bradstreet*, 472 U.S. at 757 (plurality opinion). *Dun & Bradstreet* dealt only with the *Gertz* rule on presumed damages, not the *Gertz* negligence standard. *See* 472 U.S. at 754–55. But even assuming that *Gertz* is limited to statements involving matters of public concern, Cox's blog post qualifies.

The December 25 post alleged that Padrick, a court-appointed trustee, committed tax fraud while administering the assets of a company in a Chapter 11 reorganization, and called for the "IRS and the Oregon Department of Revenue to look" into the matter. Public allegations that someone is involved in crime generally are speech on a matter of public concern. This court has held that even consumer complaints of non-criminal conduct by a business can constitute matters of public concern.

Cox's allegations in this case are similarly a matter of public concern. Padrick was appointed by a United States Bankruptcy Court as the Chapter 11 trustee of a company that had defrauded its investors through a Ponzi scheme. That company retained him and Obsidian to advise it shortly before it filed for bankruptcy. The allegations against Padrick and his company raised questions about whether they were failing to protect the defrauded investors because they were in league with their original clients. Unlike the speech at issue in *Dun & Bradstreet* that the Court found to be a matter only of private concern, Cox's December 25 blog post was not "solely in the individual interest of the speaker and its specific business audience." 472 U.S. at 762 (plurality opinion). The post was published to the public at large, not simply made "available to only five subscribers, who, under the terms of the subscription agreement, could not disseminate it further. . . ." *Id.*

Because Cox's blog post addressed a matter of public concern, even assuming that *Gertz* is limited to such speech, the district court should have instructed the jury that it could not find Cox liable for defamation unless it found that she acted negligently. *See Gertz*, 418 U.S. at 350. The court also should have instructed the jury that it could not award presumed damages unless it found that Cox acted with actual malice. *Id.* at 349.

Cox also argues that Padrick and Obsidian are "tantamount to public officials," because Padrick was a court-appointed bankruptcy trustee. (She [unsuccessfully] argued in her pretrial memorandum that Padrick and Obsidian were public figures, but . . . raises only the public official argument on appeal.) Cox contends that the jury therefore should have been instructed that, under the *New York Times* standard, it could impose liability for defamation only if she acted with actual malice. We disagree.

Although bankruptcy trustees are an integral part of the judicial process, neither Padrick nor Obsidian became a public official simply by virtue of Padrick's appointment. Padrick was neither elected nor appointed to a government position, and he did not exercise "substantial . . . control over the conduct of governmental affairs." *Rosenblatt v. Baer*, 383 U.S. 75, 85 (1966). A Chapter 11 trustee can be appointed by the bankruptcy court [but] an appointed trustee simply substitutes for, and largely exercises the powers of, a debtor-in-possession. No one would contend that a debtor-in-possession has become a public official simply by virtue of seeking Chapter 11 protection, and we can reach no different conclusion as to the trustee who substitutes for the debtor in administering a Chapter 11 estate.

Padrick and Obsidian argue on cross-appeal that the district court erred in granting Cox summary judgment as to her other blog posts. Among other things, those posts accuse Padrick and Obsidian of engaging in "illegal activity," including "corruption," "fraud," "deceit on the government," "money laundering," "defamation," "harassment," "tax crimes," and "fraud against the government." Cox also claimed that Obsidian paid off "media" and "politicians" and may have hired a hit man to kill her.

In *Milkovich v. Lorain Journal Co.*, the Supreme Court refused to create a blanket defamation exemption for "anything that might be labeled 'opinion.'" 497 U.S. 1, 18 (1990). This court has held that "while 'pure' opinions are protected by the First Amendment, a statement that 'may . . . imply a false assertion of fact' is actionable." [citation omitted.] *Partington v. Bugliosi*, 56 F.3d 1147, 1153 (9th Cir. 1995) (quoting *Milkovich*, 497 U.S. at 19). We have developed a three-part test to determine whether a statement contains an assertion of objective fact. See *Unelko Corp. v. Rooney*, 912 F.2d 1049, 1053 (9th Cir. 1990). The test considers (1) whether the general tenor of the entire work negates the impression that the defendant was asserting an objective fact, (2) whether the defendant used figurative or hyperbolic language that negates that impression, and (3) whether the statement in question is susceptible of being proved true or false.

As to the first factor, the general tenor of Cox's blog posts negates the impression that she was asserting objective facts. The statements were posted on obsidianfinancesucks.com, a website name that leads "the reader of the statements [to be] predisposed to view them with a certain amount of skepticism and with an understanding that they will likely present one-sided viewpoints rather than assertions of provable facts" [(quoting the district court's decision)]. The district judge correctly concluded that the "occasional and somewhat run-on[,] almost 'stream of consciousness'-like sentences read more like a journal or diary entry revealing [Cox's] feelings rather than assertions of fact."

As to the second factor, Cox's consistent use of extreme language negates the impression that the blog posts assert objective facts. Cox regularly employed hyperbolic language in the posts, including terms such as "immoral," "really bad," "thugs," and "evil-doers." Cox's assertions that "Padrick hired a 'hit man' to kill her" or "that the entire bankruptcy court system is corrupt" similarly dispel any reasonable expectation that the statements assert facts. And, as to the third factor, the district court correctly found that, in the context of a non-professional website containing consistently hyperbolic language, Cox's blog posts are "not sufficiently factual to be proved true or false." We find no error in the court's application of the *Unelko* test and reject the cross-appeal.

District court judgment based on jury verdict in favor of plaintiffs reversed; case remanded for new trial on December 25 blog post; district court decision in favor of Cox on other blog posts affirmed.

Figure 6.1 Constitutional Aspects of Defamation—Fault Requirements and Rules on Damages*			
	Public Official Plaintiff or Public Figure Plaintiff	**Private Figure Plaintiff and Subject of Public Concern**	**Private Figure Plaintiff and Subject of Private Concern**
What Plaintiff Must Prove to Win Case	Actual malice, by clear and convincing evidence	Fault—at least negligence	Perhaps (probably?) fault—at least negligence
Damages Recoverable If Plaintiff Wins Case	Damages for proven actual injury and/or presumed damages, as well as punitive damages	Damages for proven actual injury, if plaintiff proves only negligence. For presumed and punitive damages, plaintiff must prove actual malice, by clear and convincing evidence.	Damages for proven actual injury and/or presumed damages, as well as punitive damages

*These requirements and rules apply at least in defamation cases against a media defendant. Although the Supreme Court has left some uncertainty on this point, the requirements and rules set forth here probably apply in all defamation cases, regardless of the defendant's media or nonmedia status.

Invasion of Privacy

LO6-10 Distinguish among the four types of invasion of privacy.

In tort law, the term *invasion of privacy* refers to four distinct torts. Each involves a different sense of the term *privacy*.

Intrusion on Solitude or Seclusion Any intentional intrusion on the solitude or seclusion of another constitutes an invasion of privacy if that intrusion would be highly offensive to a reasonable individual. The intrusion in question may be physical, such as an illegal search of a person's home or body or the opening of his mail. It may also be a nonphysical intrusion such as tapping another's telephone, examining her bank account, or subjecting her to harassing telephone calls. However, the tort applies only where there is a reasonable expectation of privacy. As a general rule, therefore, there is no liability for examining public records concerning a person, or for observing or photographing him in a public place.

Public Disclosure of Private Facts Publicizing facts concerning someone's private life can be an invasion of privacy if the publicity would be highly offensive to a reasonable person. The idea is that the public has no legitimate right to know certain aspects of a person's private life. Thus, publicity concerning someone's failure to pay his debts, humiliating illnesses he has suffered, or information about his sex life may constitute an invasion of privacy. Truth is *not* a defense to this type of invasion of privacy because the essence of the

tort is giving unjustified publicity to purely private matters. Here, in further contrast to defamation, publicity means a *widespread* communication of private details. For example, publication on the Internet would suffice.

As does defamation, this form of invasion of privacy potentially conflicts with the First Amendment. Courts have attempted to resolve this conflict in two major ways. First, no liability ordinarily attaches to publicity concerning matters of public record or legitimate public interest. Second, public figures and public officials have no right of privacy concerning information that is reasonably related to their public lives.

False Light Publicity Publicity that places a person in a false light in the public eye can be an invasion of privacy if that false light would be highly offensive to a reasonable person. What is required is unreasonable and highly objectionable publicity attributing to a person characteristics that she does not possess or beliefs that she does not hold. Examples include signing a person's name to a public letter that violates her deeply held beliefs or attributing authorship of an inferior scholarly or artistic work to her. As in defamation cases, truth is a defense to liability. It is not necessary, however, that a person be defamed by the false light in which he is placed. For instance, signing a gun rights advocate's name to a petition urging adoption of gun-control measures could create liability for false light publicity but probably not for defamation.

In view of the overlap between false light publicity and defamation, and the obvious First Amendment issues at stake, defendants in false light cases enjoy constitutional protections matching those enjoyed by defamation defendants.

Ethics and Compliance in Action

In *Hernandez v. Hillsides, Inc.*, 211 P.3d 1063 (Cal. 2009), the Supreme Court of California considered an invasion of privacy case arising out of the defendants' installation of a video surveillance system in an office shared by the plaintiffs. The defendants were the director of a residential facility for abused children and the two companies that operated the facility. The two plaintiffs were employees at the facility.

The defendant director had the video surveillance system installed in the plaintiffs' office without their knowledge because of reports from the defendants' computer technician that someone—evidently neither of the plaintiffs—had been accessing pornographic websites at night from one of the computers in the plaintiffs' office. The defendants activated the surveillance system only at night and after the plaintiffs' regular work hours had ended for the day. The plaintiffs were not depicted in any of the video generated. Although no individual was identified as the person who accessed pornographic websites, such accessing appeared to cease within roughly a month of the surveillance system's installation. The defendants therefore stopped using the system.

After the plaintiffs learned of the system's existence and operation, the director apologized for not having informed them and explained his rationale for using the system. The apology and explanation did not satisfy the plaintiffs, who sued on the theory that the facts constituted an unlawful intrusion on solitude. The trial court granted summary judgment in favor of the defendants, but the California Court of Appeal reversed, holding that the plaintiffs had a reasonable expectation of privacy in their office and that the defendants' actions would have been highly offensive to a reasonable person. The Supreme Court of California, however, reversed and directed that summary judgment be entered in favor of the defendants.

Although the Supreme Court recognized that the plaintiffs possessed a privacy interest in regard to their office, the court concluded that under the circumstances, the intrusion at issue would not have been highly offensive to reasonable persons. The surveillance was conducted for a limited period of time and only at night, and thus was suitably tailored to important rationales: finding out who was misusing the computers; and protecting minors at the facility against someone who might pose a danger to them.

The fact that courts at different levels of the review process in *Hernandez* disagreed on the appropriate analysis indicates the sensitive interests at stake when privacy interests and countervailing considerations come into conflict in an employment setting. Now consider relevant ethical questions that go beyond the pure legal issues facing the courts in *Hernandez* and similar cases. Give some thought, for instance, to these questions:

- When employers seek to monitor employees' actions through a video surveillance system, are there ethical obligations that constrain—or should constrain—employers? If so, what are those obligations, and how are they satisfied? Does it matter whether the employers have reason to suspect wrongdoing on the part of employees? Does it matter why the employers decide to use such a system?
- In the situation that led to the plaintiffs' lawsuit in *Hernandez*, did the defendants act ethically in not informing the plaintiffs about the video surveillance system? If the defendants had informed the plaintiffs of the plan to install the system but the plaintiffs objected, would it have been ethical for the defendants to proceed with the installation of the system anyway?
- If an employer owns the computers in employees' offices and the employer operates the network or system of which those machines are a part, is it ethical for the employer to engage in secret monitoring of employees' use of the computers? Is it ethical for the employer to monitor employees' e-mail?

Be prepared to discuss the above questions and the reasons for the conclusions you draw.

Commercial Appropriation of Name or Likeness

LO6-11 Identify circumstances in which a celebrity's right of publicity is implicated.

Liability for invasion of privacy can exist when, without that person's consent, the defendant commercially uses someone's name or likeness, normally to imply her endorsement of a product or service or a nonexistent connection with the defendant's business.

This form of invasion of privacy also draws on the personal property right connected with a person's identity and her exclusive right to control it. In recent decades, recognition of this property right has given rise to a separate legal doctrine known as the *right of publicity*, under which public figures, celebrities, and entertainers have a cause of action against defendants who, without consent, use the right holders' names, likenesses, or identities for commercial purposes. Protected attributes of a celebrity's identity may include such things as a distinctive singing voice. Use of a celebrity's name or a "soundalike" of her in an advertisement for a product would be a classic example of a commercial use, as would use of an entertainer's picture as a commercially sold poster. Not all uses are commercial in nature, however, even if there is an underlying profit motive at stake. For example, though the cases are not entirely consistent on this point, a television show or movie that uses a celebrity's name, likeness, or identity is likely to be classified as noncommercial and thus not a violation of the right of publicity. Some uses are close to the line and require courts to make difficult determinations regarding the use's commercial or noncommercial nature.

As the foregoing examples suggest, First Amendment interests may arise in right of publicity cases. Courts tend to hold that the intermediate level of First Amendment protection extended to commercial speech does not insulate a defendant against liability for having used the plaintiff's name, likeness, or identity in the context of commercial speech. (Discussion of the distinction between commercial speech and noncommercial speech appears in Chapter 3.) If, on the other hand, the defendant's speech was noncommercial, the First Amendment could come to the defendant's rescue. Whether it does so depends upon the case's particular facts and upon which one of various possible tests the court chooses to apply in balancing the plaintiff's property interest against the defendant's speech interest.

In *Jordan v. Jewel Food Stores*, which follows shortly, the Seventh Circuit Court of Appeals must decide the appropriate speech classification for a grocery chain's advertisement congratulating Michael Jordan on his induction into a basketball hall of fame. Is it commercial speech that potentially violates Jordan's right of publicity, or, instead, is it noncommercial speech that the First Amendment may shield? (For discussion of whether college athletes should be entitled to the right of publicity, see Figure 6.2, which appears after the *Jordan* case.)

States that recognize the right of publicity usually consider it inheritable—meaning that it may survive the death of the celebrity who held the right during his or her lifetime. There is little agreement among the states, however, on how long the right persists after the celebrity's death.

Jordan v. Jewel Food Stores, Inc.   743 F.3d 509 (7th Cir. 2014)

Jewel Food Stores, Inc. operates 175 Jewel-Osco supermarkets in and around Chicago. Basketball legend Michael Jordan, who spent most of his playing career in Chicago, is exceedingly well known and is widely regarded as one of the greatest players in history. On the occasion of Jordan's September 2009 induction into the Naismith Memorial Basketball Hall of Fame, Time Inc., the publisher of Sports Illustrated *magazine, produced a special commemorative issue devoted exclusively to Jordan's remarkable career. The commemorative issue was sold in stores and at newsstands from late October 2009 until late January 2010.*

Approximately a month prior to the scheduled publication of the commemorative issue, a Time sales representative contacted Jewel to offer free advertising space in the issue in return for Jewel's promise to stock and sell the magazines in its stores. Jewel agreed to the proposal and had its marketing department design a full-page color ad. The ad combined textual, photographic, and graphic elements and prominently included the Jewel-Osco logo as well as the supermarket chain's marketing slogan, "Good things are just around the corner." The logo and slogan were positioned in the middle of the page, above a photo of a pair of basketball shoes. Each shoe bore Jordan's familiar jersey number, 23. The ad's text read as follows:

A Shoe In! After six NBA championships, scores of rewritten record books and numerous buzzer beaters, Michael Jordan's elevation in the Basketball Hall of Fame was never in doubt! Jewel-Osco salutes #23 on his many accomplishments as we honor a fellow Chicagoan who was "just around the corner" for so many years.

Time accepted Jewel's ad and placed it on the inside back cover of the commemorative issue. Besides featuring Sports Illustrated *editorial content and photographs from the magazine's prior coverage of Jordan's career, the commemorative issue featured congratulatory ads from various parties.*

Soon after the commemorative issue was released, Jordan sued Jewel for allegedly violating his right of publicity. (Jordan also invoked various other legal theories, but the right of publicity claim receives the bulk of the attention here.) Jewel later sought summary judgment, raising the First Amendment as a defense against liability and arguing that its ad was noncommercial speech entitled to full First Amendment protection. (For discussion of the First Amendment distinction between commercial speech and noncommercial speech, see Chapter 3.) Jordan also sought summary judgment, arguing that Jewel's ad was a commercial use of his identity and therefore a potential violation of his right of publicity. The federal district court held that the ad was noncommercial speech and granted summary judgment in favor of Jewel. Jordan appealed to the U.S. Court of Appeals for the Seventh Circuit.

Sykes, Circuit Judge

Jewel maintains that its ad is noncommercial speech and thus has full First Amendment protection. Jordan insists that the ad is garden-variety commercial speech, which gets reduced constitutional protection and may give rise to liability for the private wrongs he alleges in this case. As the case comes to us, the commercial/noncommercial distinction is potentially dispositive. If the ad is properly classified as commercial speech, then it may be regulated, normal liability rules apply (statutory and common law), and the battle moves to the merits of Jordan's claims. If, on the other hand, the ad is fully protected expression, then Jordan agrees with Jewel that the First Amendment provides a complete defense and his claims cannot proceed.

The First Amendment prohibits the government from "abridging the freedom of speech." U.S. Const. amend. I. Because "not all speech is of equal First Amendment importance," [citation omitted], certain categories of speech receive a lesser degree of constitutional protection. Commercial speech was initially viewed as being outside the ambit of the First Amendment altogether. Current doctrine holds that commercial speech is constitutionally protected but governmental burdens on this category of speech are scrutinized more leniently than burdens on fully protected noncommercial speech.

To determine whether speech falls on the commercial or noncommercial side of the constitutional line, the Court has provided this basic definition: Commercial speech is "speech that proposes a commercial transaction." *Board of Trustees v. Fox*, 492 U.S. 469, 482 (1989). It is important to recognize, however, that [the basic definition] is just a starting point. Speech that does *no more than* propose a commercial transaction "fall[s] within the core notion of commercial speech," *Bolger v. Youngs Drug Products Corp.*, 463 U.S. 60, 66 (1983), but other communications also may "constitute commercial speech notwithstanding the fact that they contain discussions of important public issues." *Fox*, 492 U.S. at 475 (quoting *Bolger*, 463 U.S. at 67–68).

Indeed, the Supreme Court has "made clear that advertising which links a product to a current public debate is not thereby entitled to the constitutional protection afforded noncommercial speech." *Zauderer v. Office of Disciplinary Counsel*, 471 U.S. 626, 637 n.7 (1985) (quoting *Bolger*, 463 U.S. at 68). Although commercial-speech cases generally rely on the distinction between speech that proposes a commercial transaction and other varieties of speech, it is a mistake to assume that the boundaries of the commercial-speech category are marked exclusively by this "core" definition. To the contrary, there is a "commonsense distinction" between commercial speech and other varieties of speech, and we are to give effect to that distinction. [Citation omitted.]

The Supreme Court's decision in *Bolger* is instructive on this point. *Bolger* dealt with the question of how to classify speech

with both noncommercial and commercial elements. There, a prophylactics manufacturer published informational pamphlets providing general factual information about prophylactics but also containing information about the manufacturer's products in particular. *Bolger*, 463 U.S. at 62. The manufacturer brought a pre-enforcement challenge to a federal statute that prohibited the unsolicited mailing of advertisements about contraceptives. The Supreme Court held that although the pamphlets did not expressly propose a commercial transaction, they were nonetheless properly classified as commercial speech based on the following attributes: the pamphlets were a form of advertising, they referred to specific commercial products, and they were distributed by the manufacturer for economic purposes. *Id.* at 66–67.

We have read *Bolger* as suggesting certain guideposts for classifying speech that contains both commercial and noncommercial elements; relevant considerations include "whether: (1) the speech is an advertisement; (2) the speech refers to a specific product; and (3) the speaker has an economic motivation for the speech." [Citation omitted.] This is just a general framework, however; no one factor is sufficient, and *Bolger* strongly implied that all are not necessary.

Jewel argues that its ad doesn't propose a commercial transaction and therefore flunks the leading test for commercial speech. As we have explained, the commercial-speech category is not limited to speech that directly or indirectly proposes a commercial transaction. Jewel nonetheless places substantial weight on this test, and the district judge did as well, . . . so we will start there.

It is clear that the textual focus of Jewel's ad is a congratulatory salute to Jordan on his induction into the Hall of Fame. If the literal import of the words were all that mattered, this celebratory tribute would be noncommercial. But evaluating the text requires consideration of its context, and this truism has special force when applying the commercial-speech doctrine. Modern commercial advertising is enormously varied in form and style.

We know from common experience that commercial advertising occupies diverse media, draws on a limitless array of imaginative techniques, and is often supported by sophisticated marketing research. It is highly creative, sometimes abstract, and frequently relies on subtle cues. The notion that an advertisement counts as "commercial" only if it makes an appeal to purchase a particular product makes no sense today, and we doubt that it ever did. An advertisement is no less "commercial" because it promotes brand awareness or loyalty rather than explicitly proposing a transaction in a specific product or service. Applying the "core" definition of commercial speech too rigidly ignores this reality. Very often the commercial message is general and implicit rather than specific and explicit.

Jewel's ad served two functions: congratulating Jordan on his induction into the Hall of Fame and promoting Jewel's supermarkets. The first is explicit and readily apparent. The ad contains a congratulatory message remarking on Jordan's record-breaking career and celebrating his rightful place in the Basketball Hall of Fame. Jewel points to its longstanding corporate practice of commending local community groups on notable achievements, giving as examples two public-service ads celebrating the work of Chicago's Hispanocare and South Side Community Services. The suggestion seems to be that the Jordan ad belongs in this "civic booster" category: A praiseworthy "fellow Chicagoan" was receiving an important honor, and Jewel took the opportunity to join in the applause.

But considered in context, and without the rose-colored glasses, Jewel's ad has an unmistakable commercial function: enhancing the Jewel-Osco brand in the minds of consumers. This commercial message is implicit but easily inferred, and is the dominant one. [A] point that should be obvious . . . seems lost on Jewel: There is a world of difference between an ad congratulating a local community group and an ad congratulating a famous athlete. Both ads will generate goodwill for the advertiser. But an ad congratulating a famous athlete can only be understood as a promotional device for the advertiser. Unlike a community group, the athlete needs no gratuitous promotion and his identity has commercial value. Jewel's ad cannot be construed as a benevolent act of good corporate citizenship.

As for the other elements of the ad, Jewel-Osco's graphic logo and slogan appear just below the textual salute to Jordan. The bold red logo is prominently featured in the center of the ad and in a font size larger than any other on the page. Both the logo and the slogan are styled in their trademarked ways. Their style, size, and color set them off from the congratulatory text, drawing attention to Jewel-Osco's sponsorship of the tribute. Apart from the basketball shoes, the Jewel-Osco brand-name is the center of visual attention on the page. And the congratulatory message specifically incorporates Jewel's slogan: "as we honor a fellow Chicagoan who was 'just around the corner' for so many years." The ad is plainly aimed at fostering goodwill for the Jewel brand among the targeted consumer group—"fellow Chicagoans" and fans of Michael Jordan—for the purpose of increasing patronage at Jewel-Osco stores.

The district judge nonetheless concluded that the ad was not commercial speech based in part on his view that "readers would be at a loss to explain what they have been invited to buy," a reference to the fact that the ad features only the tribute to Jordan, the Jewel-Osco logo and slogan, and a pair of basketball shoes. Granted, Jewel does not sell basketball shoes; it is a chain of grocery stores, and this ad contains not a single word about the specific products that Jewel-Osco sells, nor any product-specific art or photography. The Supreme Court has said that the failure to reference a specific product is a relevant consideration in the commercial-speech determination. *See*

Bolger, 463 U.S. at 66-67. But it is far from dispositive, especially where "image" or brand advertising rather than product advertising is concerned.

Image advertising is ubiquitous in all media. Jewel's ad is an example of a neighborly form of general brand promotion by a large urban supermarket chain. What does it invite readers to buy? Whatever they need from a grocery store—a loaf of bread, a gallon of milk, perhaps the next edition of *Sports Illustrated*—from *Jewel-Osco*, where "good things are just around the corner." The ad implicitly encourages readers to patronize their local Jewel-Osco store. That it doesn't mention a specific product means only that this is a different genre of advertising. It promotes brand loyalty rather than a specific product, but that doesn't mean it is noncommercial.

The district judge was not inclined to put much stock in the ad's use of Jewel-Osco's slogan and graphic logo. Specifically, he considered the logo as little more than a convenient method of identifying the speaker and characterized the slogan as simply a means of ensuring "that the congratulatory message *sounded* like it was coming from Jewel." Dismissing the logo and slogan as mere nametags overlooks their value as advertising tools. The slogan is attached to the Jewel-Osco graphic logo and is repeated in the congratulatory message itself, which describes Jordan as "a fellow Chicagoan who was 'just around the corner' for so many years." This linkage only makes sense if the aim is to promote shopping at Jewel-Osco stores. Indeed, Jewel's copywriter viewed the repetition of the slogan the same way we do; she thought it was "too selly" and "hitting too over the head."

In short, the ad's commercial nature is readily apparent. It may be generic and implicit, but it is nonetheless clear. The ad is a form of image advertising aimed at promoting goodwill for the Jewel-Osco brand by exploiting public affection for Jordan at an auspicious moment in his career.

Our conclusion is confirmed by application of the *Bolger* framework, which applies to speech that contains both commercial and noncommercial elements. Again, the *Bolger* inquiry asks whether the speech in question is in the form of an advertisement, refers to a specific product, and has an economic motive. Jewel's ad certainly qualifies as an advertisement in form. Although the text is congratulatory, the page nonetheless promotes something to potential buyers: Jewel-Osco supermarkets. [T]he ad obviously isn't part of the editorial coverage of Jordan's career. It isn't an article, a column, or a news photograph or illustration. It looks like, and is, an advertisement.

We can make quick work of the second and third *Bolger* factors. As we have explained, although no *specific* product or service is offered, the ad promotes patronage at Jewel-Osco stores more generally. And there is no question that the ad serves an economic purpose: to burnish the Jewel-Osco brand name and enhance consumer goodwill. The record reflects that Jewel received Time's offer of free advertising space enthusiastically; its marketing representatives said it was a "great offer" and it "would be good for us to have our logo in *Sports Illustrated*" because "having your logo in any location where people see it is going to help your company." Indeed, Jewel gave Time valuable consideration—floor space in Jewel-Osco grocery stores—in exchange for the full-page ad in the magazine, suggesting that it expected valuable brand-enhancement benefit from it. We don't doubt that Jewel's tribute was in a certain sense public-spirited. We only recognize the obvious: that Jewel had something to gain by conspicuously joining the chorus of congratulations on the much-anticipated occasion of Jordan's induction into the Basketball Hall of Fame. Jewel's ad is commercial speech.

A contrary holding would have sweeping and troublesome implications for athletes, actors, celebrities, and trademark holders seeking to protect the use of their identities or marks. Image advertising is commonplace in our society. [F]or illustrative purposes, think of the television spots by the corporate sponsors of the Olympics. Many of these ads consist entirely of images of the American athletes coupled with the advertiser's logo or brand name and an expression of support for the U.S. Olympic team; nothing is explicitly offered for sale. Jewel's ad in the commemorative issue belongs in this genre. It portrays Jewel-Osco in a positive light without mentioning a specific product or service—in this case, by invoking a superstar athlete and a celebratory message with particular salience to Jewel's customer base. To say that the ad is noncommercial because it lacks an outright sales pitch is to artificially distinguish between product advertising and image advertising. Classifying this kind of advertising as constitutionally immune noncommercial speech would permit advertisers to misappropriate the identity of athletes and other celebrities with impunity.

Nothing we say here is meant to suggest that a company cannot use its graphic logo or slogan in an otherwise noncommercial way without thereby transforming the communication into commercial speech. Our holding is tied to the particular content and context of Jewel's ad as it appeared in the commemorative issue of *Sport Illustrated Presents*.

[Our holding] that Jewel's ad in the commemorative issue qualifies as commercial speech . . . defeats Jewel's constitutional defense, permitting Jordan's case to go forward. The substance of Jordan's case remains untested, however, [because] the district court's First Amendment ruling halted further consideration of the merits. We [therefore] remand for further proceedings.

District court's grant of summary judgment in favor of Jewel reversed; case remanded for further proceedings on Jordan's right of publicity claim and other claims.

Figure 6.2 College Athletes and the Right of Publicity?

Although college athletes who become well known might seem to be among those who would qualify for the right of publicity, the traditional assumption has been that the amateur status requirement under which they must operate not only distinguishes them from professional athletes but makes them ineligible for the right of publicity. That traditional assumption has been challenged in recent years, as current and former college athletes have filed right of publicity lawsuits against video game producers and against the National Collegiate Athletics Association (NCAA), the governing body that sets rules under which many schools' athletic programs operate.

NCAA rules require that college athletes maintain amateur status and prohibit those athletes from garnering financial benefits of the sort that would come from exercising a right of publicity if one were to be recognized. For instance, NCAA rules bar a college athlete from receiving compensation associated with sales of jerseys bearing his familiar number, whereas a professional athlete could utilize his right of publicity to derive a financial benefit from such activity insofar as it was connected with his professional exploits (as opposed to his college career). Universities themselves, however, may earn significant sums from those jersey sales, from other memorabilia sales, and from licensing other parties to make uses that arguably draw upon players' identities. Moreover, universities presumably have been free to do so without compensating their athletes despite the key role the athletes play in enhancing the value of such items and the value of the licensing right. Some universities have demonstrated sensitivity to such concerns by opting to have jersey and memorabilia sales draw upon the school or team generally, as opposed to invoking the identities of particular athletes. Clearly, however, not all universities have made such a change in their jersey and memorabilia sales practices. With current and former college athletes having instituted litigation in an effort to seek recognition of a full-fledged right of publicity (and with a settlement having taken place in one major case, as noted below), the relevant litigation and regulatory landscape has shown signs of shifting.

Another part of that landscape was an important case in which former college athletes employed other legal grounds to challenge the NCAA rules that restrict athletes from receiving right-of-publicity-like compensation and other financial benefits. The plaintiffs in the *O'Bannon* case (so named because the lead plaintiff was former UCLA basketball star Ed O'Bannon) attacked the pertinent NCAA rules and universities' agreement to abide by them as unreasonable restraints of trade in violation of a major antitrust statute, § 1 of the Sherman Act. (Antitrust law is the subject of Chapters 49 and 50.) A federal district court agreed with the plaintiffs' argument that § 1 was violated. The district court held that as a remedy, NCAA member schools should be permitted to compensate scholarship athletes up to the full cost of attendance. (At that time, NCAA rules on full scholarships left a gap between what the scholarship covered and the full cost of attendance, and barred member schools from financially covering that gap for the athletes.) In addition, the district court concluded that an appropriate remedy was to permit universities to set up accounts for athletes in amounts up to $5,000 in recognition of the use of their identities, with the monies to be paid to the athletes once their college playing eligibility was exhausted. In the judgment of the court, that remedy for the antitrust violation recognized the athletes' interests in their identities without unduly compromising the NCAA's (and universities') interests in promoting amateurism and furthering related educational concerns.

On appeal, however, the U.S. Court of Appeals for the Ninth Circuit only partially agreed with the district court's decision. The Ninth Circuit held that there was indeed an antitrust violation, but that the district court's remedy of permitting payments up to $5,000 was inappropriate. *O'Bannon v. National Collegiate Athletic Association*, 802 F.3d 1049 (9th Cir. 2015). Instead, the Ninth Circuit reasoned that the appropriate remedy was to permit NCAA member institutions to pay scholarship athletes amounts equal to the full cost of attendance—something that the NCAA had very recently changed its rules to allow member schools to do. The Ninth Circuit's decision in *O'Bannon* was thus a mixed bag for college athletes. Whether the decision leads to other changes in the status quo for college athletes will certainly bear watching.

The previously mentioned right of publicity actions against a video game maker have borne some fruit for former college athletes. Two federal courts of appeal have held that the First Amendment did not furnish a defense to Electronic Arts, whose college football video game arguably invoked the college identities of former players (though not their names). The alleged uses of the players' identities occurred without their consent but with the permission of a licensing organization that is affiliated with the NCAA and represents many universities. The two cases are *Hart v. Electronic Arts, Inc.*, 717 F.3d 141 (3d Cir. 2013), and *Keller v. NCAA*, 724 F.3d 1268 (9th Cir. 2013).

Although the Supreme Court has held in another context that video games have significant expressive content and therefore may merit substantial First Amendment protection (see the discussion of *Brown v. Entertainment Merchants Association* in Chapter 3), the courts in Hart and Keller focused on what was, and was not, present in the video game at issue. Both courts stressed that the First Amendment should not protect Electronic Arts because the defendants' video game appeared merely to use the payers' identities without being transformative in the sense of adding significant new creative or expressive content. The rejection of the First Amendment defense cleared the way for the plaintiffs' cases to proceed—prompting Electronic Arts to enter into a financial settlement with the plaintiffs and to announce that it would cease making a college football game of the sort it had produced. The NCAA also reached a financial settlement with the former college players regarding the NCAA's alleged role in granting the video game maker permission to use aspects of the players' identities.

Misuse of Legal Proceedings

Three intentional torts protect people against the harm that can result from wrongfully instituted legal proceedings. **Malicious prosecution** affords a remedy for the wrongful institution of criminal proceedings. Recovery for malicious prosecution requires proof that (1) the defendant caused the criminal proceedings to be initiated against the plaintiff without probable cause to believe that an offense had been committed, (2) the defendant did so for an improper purpose, and (3) the criminal proceedings eventually were terminated in the plaintiff's favor. **Wrongful use of civil proceedings** is designed to protect people from wrongfully instituted civil suits. Its elements are very similar to those for malicious prosecution.

Abuse of process imposes liability on those who initiate legal proceedings, whether criminal or civil, for a primary purpose other than the one for which the proceedings were designed. Abuse of process cases tend to involve situations in which the legal proceedings compel the other person to take some action unrelated to the subject of the suit. For example, Rogers wishes to buy Herbert's property, but Herbert refuses to sell. To pressure him into selling, Rogers files a private nuisance suit against Herbert, contending that Herbert's activities on his land interfere with Rogers's use and enjoyment of his adjoining property. Rogers may be liable to Herbert for abuse of process even if Rogers otherwise had reason to file the case.

The Global Business Environment

Does the right of publicity apply in a case brought in a court in the United States if the activities about which the plaintiff complains occurred outside the United States and in a nation that does not recognize the right of publicity as a part of its law? In *Love v. Associated Newspapers, Ltd.*, 611 F.3d 601 (2010), the U.S. Court of Appeals for the Ninth Circuit provided a "no" answer.

With some original members of the famous musical group known as The Beach Boys having died and others having gone their separate ways, the group no longer exists in its original form. As part of a settlement of earlier litigation, Mike Love, a founding member of the group, acquired the right to use The Beach Boys name in live performances. Love regularly tours with a varying lineup of musicians and uses The Beach Boys name in those appearances. Love sued former Beach Boy Brian Wilson and various other defendants—including British firms—in federal district court in California on the basis of the facts set forth here.

Wilson, also a founding member of The Beach Boys, wrote or co-wrote most of the group's hits before leaving the group many years ago. In 2004, Wilson released a solo album titled *Smile*. He and a backup band embarked on a tour to promote the album. As part of the promotional efforts for Wilson's *Smile*-themed tour, the British newspaper *Mail on Sunday* distributed a CD with approximately 2.6 million copies of an edition of the newspaper. The CD, titled *Good Vibrations*, consisted of Wilson's solo version of Beach Boys songs and other solo work by him. The editions of *Mail on Sunday*, complete with the CD, were distributed in the United Kingdom. Roughly 425 copies of the paper were distributed in the United States (including 18 in California), but without the CD. The front page of the *Mail on Sunday* edition prominently advertised the *Good Vibrations* CD and included an image of the CD's cover, which featured a photo of Wilson and three smaller photos of The Beach Boys. Love appeared in the photos of the group.

Because Love appeared in the pictures on the CD's cover, the right of publicity (as recognized under statute and common law in California) was among the various legal theories Love relied on in his lawsuit. Love later reached a settlement with Wilson. The federal district court dismissed various defendants from the case, some because they had nothing to do with the promotion of Wilson's tour and others for lack of in personam jurisdiction. (For discussion of in personam jurisdiction, see Chapter 2.) The British company that published *Mail on Sunday* remained as a defendant concerning the right of publicity claim.

The district court dismissed Love's right of publicity claim after holding that English law, which does not recognize the right of publicity, controlled the case. (The court also dismissed Love's various other legal claims.) Love appealed to the U.S. Court of Appeals for the Ninth Circuit, but fared no better there. The Ninth Circuit concluded that although California recognizes the right of publicity, the state "has no interest in applying its law to the conduct in question." The court stressed that the remaining defendant in the right of publicity component of the case was a British firm, that the allegedly wrongful behavior Love complained about "occurred almost exclusively" in the United Kingdom, and that "[a]t most, de minimis conduct occurred in California when a handful of copies of [*Mail on Sunday*] were delivered without the CD and a handful of copies of *Good Vibrations* were sent to Wilson's attorney in California." In addition, the Ninth Circuit emphasized that "England's interests would be . . . greatly impaired by a failure to apply English law." Firmly rejecting Love's attempt to invoke the right of publicity, the court stated:

> Even if California has an interest in protecting the right of an entertainer with economic ties to the state to exploit his image overseas, that interest is not nearly as significant as England's interest in (not) regulating the distribution of millions of copies of a newspaper and millions of compact discs by a British paper primarily in the United Kingdom.

Deceit (Fraud) Deceit (or fraud) is the formal name for the tort claim that is available to victims of knowing misrepresentations. Liability for fraud usually requires proof of a false statement of material fact that was knowingly or recklessly made by the defendant with the intent to deceive the plaintiff, along with actual, justifiable, and detrimental reliance on the part of the plaintiff. Because most fraud actions arise in a contractual setting, and because a tort action is only one of the remedies available to a victim of fraud, a more complete discussion of this topic is deferred until Chapter 13.

Interference with Property Rights

 LO6-12 Explain the difference between trespass to land and private nuisance.

Trespass to Land Trespass to land may be defined as any unauthorized or unprivileged intentional intrusion upon another's real property. Such intrusions include (1) physically entering the plaintiff's land, (2) causing another to do so (e.g., by chasing someone onto the land), (3) remaining on the land after one's right to remain has ceased (e.g., staying past the term of a lease), (4) failing to remove from the land anything one has a duty to remove, (5) causing an object or other thing to enter the land (although some overlap with nuisance exists here), and (6) invading the airspace above the land or the subsurface beneath it (if property law and federal, state, and local regulations give the plaintiff rights to the airspace or subsurface and do not allow the defendant to intrude).

The intent required for trespass liability is simply the intent to be on the land or to cause it to be invaded. A person, therefore, may be liable for trespass even though the trespass resulted from his mistaken belief that his entry was legally justified. Where the trespass was specifically intended, no actual harm to the land is required for liability, but actual harm is required for reckless or negligent trespasses.

Private Nuisance

In general, a private nuisance involves some interference with the plaintiff's use and enjoyment of her land. Unlike trespass to land, nuisance usually does not involve any physical invasion of the plaintiff's property. Trespass normally requires an invasion of tangible matter, whereas nuisance involves other interferences. Examples of such other interferences include odors, noise, smoke, light, and vibration. For nuisance liability to exist, however, the interference must be *substantial* and *unreasonable.* The defendant, moreover, must intend the interference.

Nuisance law distinguishes between *private nuisances* and *public nuisances.* In a private nuisance case, the plaintiff landowner has sustained a particular harm of the sort described above—one that pertains to his, her, or its own property and is not a harm common to the public generally. If the only harm a plaintiff landowner can demonstrate is the same one that the public in general has sustained as a result of the defendant's supposed nuisance, the plaintiff cannot prove what is necessary to win a private nuisance case. Any nuisance present in such an instance would likely be a public nuisance. As a general rule, the government is the appropriate party to seek abatement (i.e., elimination) of a public nuisance.

The *Toyo Tire* case, which follows, illustrates private nuisance and trespass principles and explores issues concerning recoverable damages.

Toyo Tire North America Manufacturing, Inc. v. Davis
787 S.E.2d (Ga. 2016)

Lynn and Duron Davis owned and resided in a house located on four acres adjacent to a highway in Bartow County, Georgia. As of 1995, the year the Davises began residing in the house, the general area was zoned for low-density residential or agricultural use. In 2004, however, the property located across the highway from the Davises' property was rezoned for heavy industrial use. That same year, Toyo Tire North America Manufacturing, Inc. began building a manufacturing and distribution facility on approximately 260 acres across the road from the Davises' home.

During the roughly five-year period after operations began at the Toyo Tire facility in January 2006, the facility underwent three expansions. In these expansions, the number of employees working at the facility went from 400 in 2006 to 570 in 2008 to 1,000 in mid-2011, and the number of tires produced per day went from 3,000 in 2006 to 4,500 in 2008 to 13,500 in mid-2011. In March 2014, with the litigation described below being under way, the facility was undergoing a fourth expansion. That expansion was expected to increase the number of employees to 1,450 and the number of tires per day to approximately 19,200. With employees working 12-hour shifts, the Toyo Tire facility operated around the clock every day.

In late 2007, the Davises sent a letter to Toyo Tire through their counsel, alluding to possible trespass and nuisance claims and requesting that Toyo Tire purchase their home (as it had done with the two properties next door to the Davises' property). Toyo Tire declined. In early 2013, the Davises sued Toyo Tire in a Georgia court. They alleged that the noise, lights, odors, black dust, and increased traffic from the facility constituted a nuisance. They also alleged that the black dust emitted by the facility constituted a trespass.

During the discovery phase of the case, Toyo Tire took the Davises' depositions. In those depositions, the Davises explained how Toyo Tire's operations—including the loud noises, bright lights, odors, and black dust emissions from the facility; its equipment; and frequent truck deliveries, as well as the increased traffic from both trucks and employees—interfered with their use and enjoyment of the property and with their daily lives. They testified, for example, that their sleep was interrupted by the light and noise from the facility. They also testified that they wore masks when they went outside and that they could no longer use their large yard for family gatherings because of the odors emitted from the facility, the danger from the increased traffic, and the black dust that settled in their yard.

Bruce Penn, a real estate appraisal expert hired by the Davises, was also deposed. He testified that the value of the Davises' property would be $280,000 if not for the presence and effects of the Toyo Tire plant. Penn also testified about his depreciation analysis, which led him to conclude that the nuisance of the Toyo Tire facility had decreased the value of the Davises' property by about 35 to 40%, with the black dust as a trespass decreasing the value by an additional 10 to 15%.

After the completion of discovery, Toyo Tire moved for summary judgment, arguing that the Davises failed to prove that the specific interferences they alleged had caused their property value to decrease and that, under Georgia law, the Davises could not recover both for diminution of property value and for discomfort and annoyance caused by a nuisance. Toyo Tire did not argue that Penn's expert testimony was inadmissible. The trial court denied Toyo Tire's summary judgment motion, concluding that material issues of fact existed. Toyo Tire appealed, but the Georgia Court of Appeals affirmed the denial of the summary judgment motion. Toyo Tire appealed further to the Supreme Court of Georgia, which agreed to decide the case.

Nahmias, Justice

First, we consider Toyo Tire's argument that the Davises presented insufficient evidence, at the summary judgment stage of the case, to show that the decrease in their property value was proximately caused by the alleged nuisance and trespass. Second, we consider Toyo Tire's argument that even if the Davises can establish causation, they cannot recover damages both for their discomfort and annoyance and for the diminution in their property value, because that would constitute an impermissible double recovery.

Toyo Tire [bases its above-noted first argument on the notion that] the Davises' appraisal expert, Bruce Penn, did not consider the specific interferences alleged by the Davises but rather looked at depreciation caused by industries in general. In his deposition, Penn explained that he had over 30 years of experience as a real estate appraiser, had done several hundred appraisals in the Bartow County area, and was certified in the top tier of licensing for appraising in Georgia. He testified that in his expert opinion, the Toyo Tire facility and its black dust emissions caused the Davises' property value to decrease by 50%—35 to 40% due to the nuisance and 10 to 15% due to the black dust trespass. Penn arrived at this conclusion primarily by conducting a "paired sales" analysis, in which he compared the sales prices of three pairs of houses. One house in each pair was very close to an industrial facility in the vicinity of Bartow County, and the other was far away but still in the same general market area; the houses in each pair were otherwise similar. The three industrial facilities used were the Dobbins Air Reserve base, the Shaw carpet plant, and the Budweiser beer plant. He based the additional decrease in value resulting from the black dust trespass on research he previously conducted to determine the decrease in the value of homes affected by concrete dust from a concrete recycling plant in west Atlanta. He also relied generally on other work he had done during his career examining the effects of industrial sites on residential property values.

The dissent in the Court of Appeals focused on several aspects of Penn's methodology that [might] call into genuine question its validity and reliability, including Penn's admission that he did not gather any evidence about the specific invasions involved here or conduct any analysis of whether the other industrial sites in his paired sales analysis involved similar situations. It is appropriate to question why an expert of this type did not actually visit the industrial facilities and residential properties that he was comparing to better determine whether the interferences caused by an Air Force base, a carpet factory, and a beer-brewing facility are really similar in type and degree to the interferences allegedly caused by a tire manufacturing and distribution facility. The flaw in the dissent's analysis, however, is that these potential deficiencies in Penn's methodology relate to whether his testimony should be admissible as expert opinion (and if so, what weight the factfinder should give his testimony), not to whether his opinions provide the evidence necessary on a motion for summary judgment to show causation. At this point in the case, only the latter question is properly presented for decision. Toyo Tire has not challenged the admissibility of Penn's expert testimony in the trial court, and that court therefore has not considered whether Penn's methodology [is sufficiently sound to warrant permitting him to testify as an expert]. An appellate court should not conduct the analysis of Penn's methodology in the first instance. "Whether the opinions of the experts are admissible . . . is something that must be determined in the first instance by the [trial] court. . . ." [Citation omitted.] Consequently, we will consider only whether the record as we now find it—including the opinions of the expert—is enough to get the Davises past summary judgment.

Toyo Tire maintains that even if Penn's testimony is admissible, the Davises have failed to show causation. We disagree. Although Penn acknowledged in his deposition that he had not visited the Davises' property or considered separately each specific claim of interference the Davises have made, he also testified that he was made generally aware of the characteristics of the Toyo Tire facility, including its "round-the-clock shifts" and the "middle of the night traffic," and interferences resulting from those characteristics, such as increased traffic, lights, noise, and emissions. He explained his belief that these are common byproducts of industry. Viewed in its full context, Penn's conclusion was not that Toyo Tire's mere presence near the Davises' property was a nuisance, but that the facility's industrial operations (which he would expect to include things such as odors, light, noise, and traffic) caused the value of the Davises' adjacent property to diminish.

The testimony from the Davises amply described the alleged nuisance and the specific interferences coming from it, so this is not a case where there is no evidence that the alleged nuisance has interfered with the plaintiffs' property. The Davises also testified about the black dust coming across the road from the tire factory onto their property, and Penn factored that alleged trespass into his diminution of value calculations. In sum, although it might not convince a jury at trial, the combined testimony of Penn and the Davises suffices to defeat Toyo Tire's challenge to causation on motion for summary judgment. Accordingly, the Court of Appeals did not err in affirming the trial court's denial of Toyo Tire's summary judgment motion on this issue.

We turn now to the second question presented—whether allowing the Davises to seek to recover both for their discomfort and annoyance caused by the alleged nuisance and for the diminution in their property value would permit a double recovery. Georgia courts have made it clear in nuisance and trespass cases . . . that a plaintiff cannot recover twice for the same injury. [In this case, however,] the alleged discomfort and annoyance experienced by the Davises and the alleged diminution in their property's fair market value are two separate injuries that cannot be fixed by one recovery. Recovery for their discomfort and annoyance is designed to compensate them for what they have already experienced as residents of the property due to the Toyo Tire factory. [C]ompensation for past discomfort and annoyance will not eliminate the discomfort and annoyance that will be experienced by future residents of the Davises' property. That future discomfort and annoyance is reflected in the diminished fair market value of the property. This ongoing diminution

in property value is therefore a second injury, which should be separately compensated (assuming it is proved at trial).

The distinction between these injuries may be more easily grasped where non-owner residents of the property suffer the discomfort and annoyance caused by a nuisance, and non-resident owners suffer the diminution in the value of their property. Both groups have been injured, and both can seek recovery under a theory of nuisance; when, as here, the residents and owners are the same, they can recover for both kinds of injuries. The distinction between the two kinds of damages is also clear in the timing of the harms each is meant to address.

The discomfort and annoyance damages would compensate the Davises for the interference with the use and enjoyment of their property that they have allegedly endured while living on the property. See *Restatement (Second) of Torts* § 929 (1)(c) (1979) (explaining that damages for harm to land resulting from a past invasion include "discomfort and annoyance to [the plaintiff] as an occupant"). The prospective damages available to the Davises as owners, on the other hand, are measured not through speculation about how much discomfort and annoyance they (or other occupants) may suffer in the future, but rather by how much the market value of their property has diminished based on the expectation of such continued discomfort and annoyance. See *Restatement (Second) of Torts* § 930(3) (explaining that the prospective damages for continuing invasions include "either the decrease in the value of the land caused by the prospect of the continuance of the invasion . . . or the reasonable cost to the plaintiff of avoiding future invasions").

For these reasons, the Davises can potentially recover for their past discomfort and annoyance as well as the diminution in their property value.

Judgment of Court of Appeals affirmed; Toyo Tire's motion for summary judgment correctly denied.

Conversion

Conversion Conversion is the defendant's intentional exercise of dominion or control over the plaintiff's personal property without the plaintiff's consent. Usually, the personal property in question is the plaintiff's goods. This can happen through the defendant's (1) *acquisition* of the plaintiff's property (e.g., theft, fraud, and even the purchase of stolen property), (2) *removal* of the plaintiff's property (e.g., taking that property to the dump or moving the plaintiff's car), (3) *transfer* of the plaintiff's property (e.g., selling stolen goods or misdelivering property), (4) *withholding possession* of the plaintiff's property (e.g., refusing to return a car one was to repair), (5) *destruction or alteration* of the plaintiff's property, or (6) *using* the plaintiff's property (e.g., driving a car left by its owner for storage purposes only).

In each case, the necessary intent is merely the intent to exercise dominion or control over the property. It is therefore possible for the defendant to be liable if she buys or sells stolen property in good faith. However, conversion is limited to *serious* interferences with the plaintiff's property rights.

If there is a serious interference and conversion, the defendant is liable for the *full value* of the property. What happens when the interference is nonserious? Although it has largely been superseded by conversion and its elements are hazy, a tort called trespass to personal property may come into play here. Suppose that Richards goes to Metzger Motors and asks to test-drive a new Corvette. If Richards either wrecks the car, causing major damage, or drives it across the United States, he is probably liable for conversion and obligated to pay Metzger the reasonable value of the car. On the other hand, if Richards is merely involved in a fender-bender, or keeps the car for eight hours, he is probably liable only for trespass. Therefore, he is obligated to pay only damages to compensate Metzger for the loss in value of the car or for its loss of use of the car.

A very different attempted application of trespass principles was unsuccessful in the *Intel* case, which is discussed in the nearby Cyberlaw in Action box.

Other Examples of Intentional Tort Liability

Chapter 8 discusses three additional intentional torts that protect various economic interests and often involve unfair competition: *injurious falsehood* (a type of business "defamation"), *intentional interference with contractual relations*, and *interference with prospective advantage.* Chapter 51 examines an intentional tortlike recovery for wrongful discharge called the *public policy* exception to employment at will.

CYBERLAW IN ACTION

If a person uses a corporation's e-mail system to distribute unsolicited e-mails to large numbers of the corporation's employees and does so without the consent of the corporation, has the distributor committed the tort of trespass to personal property? That was the issue addressed by the Supreme Court of California in a 2003 decision.

After being fired from his job at Intel, Kourosh Hamidi obtained the company's e-mail address list without breaching Intel's computer security system; instead, an anonymous source sent the list to Hamidi on a computer disk. Over a period of approximately two years, Hamidi sent six e-mails to each of at least 8,000, and perhaps as many as 35,000, Intel employees. Hamidi's e-mails discussed his grievances against Intel and criticized the company's employment practices. A number of Intel employees complained to their employer about having received Hamidi's e-mails. Hamidi offered, however, to remove from his distribution list the addresses of Intel employees who requested that their addresses be removed. When employees so requested, Hamidi followed through on his removal offer.

After Intel's attempts to block Hamidi's e-mails proved largely unsuccessful and Hamidi ignored Intel's demands that he cease sending messages to the firm's employees, Intel sued Hamidi. Intel alleged that it owned the e-mail system, that the system was intended primarily for business use by Intel employees, that the address list was confidential, and that Hamidi had continued his mass e-mailings despite demands from Intel that he stop. Contending that Hamidi's actions amounted to trespass to chattels (i.e., trespass to personal property), Intel asked the court for an injunction barring Hamidi from sending further e-mails to Intel employees at their Intel addresses. A California trial court later granted summary judgment in favor of Intel and issued the requested injunction.

Hamidi appealed to the California Court of Appeal, which affirmed the lower court's decision. The appellate court concluded that injunctive relief was appropriate in view of the disruption to Intel's business that resulted from Hamidi's intentional interference with the company's e-mail system. This interference, the court

reasoned, brought the case within the ownership and possession-related interests protected by the legal theory of trespass to personal property.

Again Hamidi appealed, this time to the Supreme Court of California. In *Intel Corp. v. Hamidi*, 71 P.3d 296 (Cal. 2003), the Supreme Court reversed the lower courts' decisions. The court observed that Hamidi's e-mails neither physically damaged nor functionally disrupted Intel's computers and did not prevent Intel from using its computers. These key facts caused the court to regard trespass to personal property as an ill-fitting theory. The court held that the trespass theory

> does not encompass, and should not be extended to encompass, an electronic communication that neither damages the recipient computer system nor impairs its functioning. Such an electronic communication does not constitute an actionable trespass to personal property, i.e., the computer system, because it does not interfere with the possessor's use or possession of, or any other legally protected interest in, the personal property itself.

Although Intel argued that it had suffered harm in the form of lost productivity resulting from the fact that employees read and reacted to Hamidi's messages, the Supreme Court noted that any such harm did not help Intel establish the necessary elements of a trespass claim. Such supposed harm was "not an injury to the company's interest in its computers—which worked as intended and were unharmed by the communications—any more than the personal distress caused by reading an unpleasant letter would be an injury to the recipient's mailbox. . . ." Intel's real concern, the court concluded, pertained to the content of Hamidi's messages. The court was unwilling to allow the trespass to personal property theory, whether in traditional or modified form, to be employed as a means of squelching speech that Intel found objectionable. Although the court only briefly touched on the potential First Amendment implications of a contrary holding, the decision appeared to have been influenced by the free speech arguments of organizations that had filed *amicus curiae* (friend-of-the-court) briefs in the case.

In rejecting Intel's attempt to employ the trespass to personal property theory to the facts at hand, the Supreme Court emphasized that its holding would not prohibit Internet service providers (ISPs) from invoking trespass principles as a basis for legal relief against senders of "unsolicited commercial bulk e-mail, also known as 'spam.'" Citing cases in which spammers had been held liable to ISPs, the court noted that in those cases, the trespass to personal property theory was applicable because "the extraordinary quantity of [spam] impaired the [relevant] computer system's functioning." The supposed injury in *Intel v. Hamidi*, by contrast, took the form of "the disruption or distraction caused to recipients by the *contents* of the e-mail messages, an injury . . . not directly affecting the possession or value of personal property."

Problems and Problem Cases

1. Betty England worked at a Dairy Queen restaurant owned by S&M Foods in Tallulah, Louisiana. One day while she was at work, her manager, Larry Garley, became upset when several incorrectly prepared hamburgers were returned by a customer. Garley expressed his dissatisfaction by throwing a hamburger that hit England on the leg. Assume that while Garley was not trying to hit England with the hamburger, he was aware that she was substantially certain to be hit as a result of his action. Also, assume that England was not harmed by the hamburger. England sued Garley for battery. Did Garley have the necessary intent for battery liability? Does England's not suffering harm defeat her battery claim?

2. On January 9, 2009, Lyshell Wilson filed suit against Jocelyn Howard in a Mississippi court. Wilson's complaint stated as follows:

   > On December 22, 2007, Plaintiff Lyshell Wilson . . . entered Citi Trends located [in] Jackson, Mississippi, for the purpose of shopping for clothing. While shopping on the premises of Citi Trends, Lyshell Wilson was brutally injured when an employee of Citi Trends, Jocelyn Howard, maliciously, recklessly, negligently, and violently attacked Lyshell Wilson with a pair of scissors.

   Howard filed a motion to dismiss, contending that Wilson had failed to file her complaint within the one-year statute of limitations set forth by a Mississippi statute, which provides that "all actions for assault, assault and battery . . . shall be commenced within one (1) year next after the cause of such action accrued, and not after." (Different statutes of limitation apply to different types of claims. When a lawsuit raising a given claim has not been filed with an appropriate court prior to the expiration of the period specified in the relevant statute of limitations, the claim can no longer be pursued and is subject to dismissal.) Wilson responded to Howard's motion by denying that she was filing a battery claim. Instead, Wilson insisted that the claim set forth in her complaint was a negligence claim. The Mississippi statute of limitations pertaining to negligence claims set forth a longer limitations period than the period specified by the statute applicable to assault and battery claims, and would not have expired by the time Wilson initiated her lawsuit. The trial court denied Howard's motion to dismiss. On appeal, Howard made two arguments. First, she argued that the claim made in Wilson's complaint was for battery—meaning that the complaint was not filed within the applicable one-year statute of limitations. Second, Howard argued that Wilson's attempt to characterize the incident as an act of negligence was simply an attempt to circumvent the relevant statute of limitations. Was Howard correct? How did the appellate court rule?

3. Rex Moats sought election to the Nebraska Legislature in 2008. During the run-up to the election, the Nebraska Republican Party paid for and distributed publications in opposition to Moats's candidacy. Moats filed a defamation lawsuit against the Republican Party on the basis of 10 statements in the publications. He listed the following statements in his complaint:

   Publication No. 1: "Trial attorney Rex Moats is a registered Democratic [sic] and the Democrat [sic] Party is supporting him!"

   Publication No. 2: "Moats received a $50,000 trust fund from the directors of National Warranty."

   Publication No. 3: "Would you put a shady insurance company based in the Cayman Islands ahead of Nebraska's consumers? You wouldn't. But trial attorney Rex Moats would. . . ." The same publication further stated: "How did Rex Moats mislead creditors and the public? Rex Moats claimed in an affidavit that National Warranty was doing financially well."

   Publication No. 4 (a mock letter purportedly sent by Moats from the Cayman Islands to Nebraskans): "Greetings from the Cayman Islands. From insurance company trial lawyer extraordinaire Rex Moats." The "letter" also stated, in relevant part:

> I have a fantastic job working for a shady insurance company that is incorporated right here in the Cayman Islands. The tax benefits sure are great out here! Unfortunately my company, National Warranty, has gone bankrupt and is unable to pay off numerous claims for thousands of Nebraskans. Also, it looks like I have made misleading statements in an affidavit. Evidently, I claimed that my company is doing "just fine," but then declared bankruptcy two weeks later.

Publication No. 5: "Rex Moats and National Warranty went down as a result of the same irresponsibility we see on Wall Street."

Publication No. 6: "Rex Moats cannot be trusted with your money." This publication further stated that Moats was a "trial attorney" and that "National Warranty's directors set aside $50,000 for Rex Moats."

Publication No. 7: This publication asserted that Moats was sued but the publication failed, according to the complaint, to disclose that the litigation against him was dismissed without a trial.

Publication No. 8: "Rex Moats received a $50,000 golden parachute even though 150 Nebraskans lost their jobs." This publication also stated: "Rex Moats misled creditors and the public about the solvency of National Warranty. Even worse, right before the company folded, Moats received $50,000 from the directors of National Warranty."

Publication No. 9: "[A]ccording to his own letter to the editor of a local newspaper, Rex Moats supports using your tax dollars to fund abortions."

Publication No. 10 (listed as No. 11 in Moats's complaint): "Rex Moats was legal counsel for a now bankrupt insurance company that cost Nebraskans their jobs but rewarded Rex with a $50,000 trust," and "Rex Moats supports using tax dollars to fund abortions."

In his complaint, Moats claimed that all of the above statements were false and defamatory and that the Republican Party made the statements with actual malice. The Republican Party filed a motion to dismiss, contending that Moats's complaint failed to state a claim on which relief could be granted. The trial court granted the motion, and Moats appealed. Was the trial court correct in granting the motion to dismiss?

4. Nicky Pope filed a false imprisonment lawsuit against the Rostraver Shop 'n Save store (Shop 'n Save) and its manager, Howard Russell, on the basis of the incident described below. Pope and Russell each provided deposition testimony during the discovery phase of the case. The incident, which took place in a Pennsylvania city, began when Pope entered the Shop 'n Save store, stopped at the bakery counter, and purchased a cup of coffee and a piece of cake to eat while in the store. She then browsed through the store. After being notified that Pope was walking back and forth without much in her shopping cart, Russell began watching her. Russell observed that she was wearing a long-sleeved, unbuttoned flannel shirt over a T-shirt. He testified in his deposition that he saw Pope's hand going "underneath and back into the . . . flannel shirt," followed by a "movement made down, possibly into the pants." Thereafter, her "arm came back out." Russell further observed what appeared to be a "protrusion from the left area of [Pope's] back, at about the belt area." Finally, Russell testified that "because of Pope's shirt as well as her movement and the way she was positioned with her cart," he could not see whether Pope had actually concealed any item. After Pope proceeded to the checkout stand and paid for the items, Russell stopped her in the store's vestibule area and asked to see her receipt. Russell verified that Pope's bakery receipt and store receipt matched her purchased items. He then asked Pope to lift up her outer shirt so that he could see whether she had concealed any items. Pope refused. As Pope acknowledged in her deposition, Russell did not touch her and did not create any physical barrier to prevent her from exiting the store. During their in-store exchange, however, Pope became upset at being accused of shoplifting. Pope told Russell that she believed she was being stopped because she was Black and that she intended to sue. Russell informed Pope that he was calling the police and that she should not leave the premises.

According to her deposition testimony, Pope believed that because the police had been called, she was not free to leave. During the 5 to 10 minutes it took for a police officer to arrive, Pope neither asked to leave the store premises nor made any attempt to leave. She also stated in her deposition that she decided to wait for the police. Upon his arrival at the Shop 'n Save, the police officer observed Russell waiting for him outside the store and Pope waiting alone in the vestibule area. Russell informed the officer of what he had observed. Pope exited the store and approached the officer, who questioned her but did not arrest her. Pope, who was never charged with shoplifting, testified in her deposition that since the incident, she had suffered from panic attacks and lack of sleep.

Pennsylvania has a statute providing that if a merchant or the merchant's employee has probable cause to believe that a customer was engaged in shoplifting, the merchant or employee may detain the customer in order to investigate. The statute further provides that if the detention is conducted for a reasonable time and in a reasonable manner, the detaining merchant or employee is protected against false imprisonment liability even if the customer did not shoplift. After the completion of the discovery phase in Pope's case, Pope moved for summary judgment in her favor and the defendants moved for summary judgment in their favor. How did the court rule? Why did the court rule that way?

5. "The Mating Habits of the Suburban High School Teenager" served as the headline for a *Boston* magazine article that addressed sexuality and promiscuity among teenagers in the Boston area. An accompanying subheading, which appeared in lettering smaller than that used for the headline, read this way: "They hook up online. They hook up in real life. With prom season looming, meet your kids—they might know more about sex than you do." According to the article, sexual experimentation had become increasingly common among high school students in recent years, with today's teenagers being both "sexually advanced" and "sexually daring." The author wrote that it had become common for "single boys and girls with nothing to do [to] go in a group to a friend's house . . . drink or smoke pot, then pair off and engage in no-strings hookups." Concerning the supposed prevalence of sexual promiscuity, the author quoted a teenager as saying that "everybody's having casual sex and pretty much everybody's doing it with multiple partners." Throughout the article, the author included excerpts from her interviews with Boston-area students about their sexual experiences and views on sexuality.

A large photograph accompanied the beginning portion of the article. The photograph, which took up a full page plus part of a facing page, showed five formally attired students standing near an exit door at a high school prom. Three students were smoking cigarettes, and a fourth was drinking from a plastic cup. The fifth student, Stacey Stanton, was looking in the direction of the camera with an apparently friendly expression. Her face and a portion of her body were readily visible. She wore a formal dress and was neither smoking nor drinking. Beneath the headlines and the article's opening text, and on the same page as the large photograph, there appeared the following caption and disclaimer: "*The photos on these pages are from an award-winning five-year project on teen sexuality by photojournalist Dan*

Habib. The individuals pictured are unrelated to the people or events described in this story. The names of the teenagers interviewed for the story have been changed." Of the type sizes used on the page, the one used for the caption and disclaimer was the smallest. Other pictures that did not depict Stanton accompanied later portions of the article.

Stanton, who was not named in the article, neither consented to the use of the large photograph nor participated in Habib's "project on teen sexuality." She sued Metro Corporation, the publisher of *Boston* magazine. According to her complaint, the juxtaposition of the large photograph and the article created the false impression that she was a person engaged in the activities described in the article. Therefore, Stanton contended that she had been the victim of defamation. Moreover, Stanton contended that the publication of the photograph amounted to an invasion of her privacy. The federal district court, however, ruled that Stanton had stated neither a valid defamation claim nor a valid invasion of privacy claim. Therefore, the court dismissed Stanton's complaint. Stanton appealed. Did the district court rule correctly?

6. Irma White, a churchgoing woman in her late forties, was employed at a Monsanto refinery. While working in the canning department, she and three other employees were told to transfer a corrosive and hazardous chemical from a larger container into smaller containers. After they asked for rubber gloves and goggles, a supervisor sent for the equipment. In the meantime, White began cleaning up the work area and one of the other employees went to another area to do some work. The other two employees sat around waiting for the safety equipment, contrary to a work rule requiring employees to busy themselves in such situations.

After learning that the group was idle, Gary McDermott, the canning department foreman, went to the work station. Once there, he launched into a profane one-minute tirade directed at White and the other two workers present, calling them "motherf—s," accusing them of sitting on their "f—g asses," and threatening to "show them to the gate." At this, White became upset and began to experience pain in her chest, pounding in her head, and difficulty in breathing. Her family physician met her at the hospital, where he admitted her, fearing that she was having a heart attack. She was later diagnosed as having had an acute anxiety reaction.

White later sued Monsanto for intentional infliction of emotional distress. Was her distress sufficiently severe for liability? Was McDermott's behavior sufficiently outrageous for liability?

7. Dr. David Kipper filed a defamation lawsuit in a New York trial court against NYP Holdings Co. (NYP), the owner and publisher of the *New York Post*. Kipper based his case on an article in the December 7, 2003, edition of the *Post*. The article was an 8-paragraph "rewrite" of a 98-paragraph article taken from the wire service of the *Los Angeles Times* (LAT). The LAT article described rock musician Ozzy Osbourne's allegations that his former physician, Kipper, had overprescribed various medications to him during the time that Osbourne starred in a television reality series. In addition, the LAT article accurately stated that the California Medical Board had "moved to revoke" Kipper's license because of his alleged gross negligence in the treatment of other patients. However, the *Post* article, which appeared under the inaccurate headline "Ozzy's Rx Doc's License Pulled," contained an error. Despite clearly indicating that it was based upon LAT reports, the *Post* rewrite incorrectly stated that "the state medical board revoked Kipper's license." NYP later conceded that this statement was false and defamatory, and published a "Correction" in response to a retraction demand from Kipper's attorney.

The circumstances surrounding the erroneous statement in the December 7 article were not entirely clear. During the evening of December 6, a *Post* editor assigned the task of rewriting the wire service story to a reporter, Lyle Hasani Gittens. Gittens testified at a deposition that he did not recall writing—and did not think he wrote—that Kipper's license was revoked. Gittens speculated that the error might have occurred during the editing process. After Gittens prepared the rewrite, he transmitted it to an electronic "basket" where it was reviewed by an editor. Gittens was aware that editors sometimes made stylistic changes to the text of articles. He denied having any knowledge that *Post* editors deliberately changed the facts of stories. The editor responsible for editing Gittens's rewrite testified at his deposition that he would "never deliberately" falsify information pertaining to a doctor's licensure, but that he could not offer any specific details pertaining to his review of the rewrite. Following the editor's review, the article then went to the copy desk, where, among other things, the story's headline was written.

The sole source material for Gittens's rewrite was the LAT wire service story. Gittens testified that the *Post* sometimes reprints stories disseminated on reputable wire services (such as that of the LAT) verbatim, and that additional research regarding the factual accuracy of such stories is not generally undertaken. Regarding the LAT wire service dispatch relevant to Kipper's case, the editor testified that "this is not the kind of story that [the *Post*] would have expected a reporter to do additional research [on]." Upon completion of the discovery phase in Kipper's defamation lawsuit against NYP, the defendant moved for summary judgment. Assume that Kipper is a public figure. What First Amendment–based fault requirement must be proved in order for Kipper to win the case? In light of the facts, which party should win the case? How would the analysis change if Kipper were a private figure?

8. The late Evel Knievel, a motorcycle daredevil, acquired considerable fame as a result of his widely publicized and dangerous stunts during a career that began in the mid-1960s. Knievel's exploits have been featured in several books and movies and in a Smithsonian Museum exhibit. Prior to his death in 2007, Knievel served as an advertising spokesman for various well-known corporations. He also devoted considerable time to the promotion of antidrug and motorcycle safety programs. In 2001, ESPN held its Action Sports and Music Awards ceremony. Celebrities from the field of "extreme" sports attended, as did famous rap and heavy-metal musicians. Knievel, sometimes known as the "father of extreme sports," attended along with his wife, Krystal. In one of the many photographs ESPN arranged to have taken at the ceremony, Knievel was pictured with his right arm around his wife and his left arm around an unidentified woman. Knievel was wearing rose-tinted sunglasses and a motorcycle jacket. The photograph of the Knievels and the unidentified woman was one of 17 photographs that ESPN published on the Green Carpet Gallery section of its EXPN.com website. That site featured information and photographs concerning motorcycle racing and various other "extreme" sports. The Green Carpet Gallery section was devoted to pictures of celebrity attendees of the Action Sports and Music Awards ceremony. A viewer who clicked on the Green Carpet Gallery icon was first directed to a photograph of two men grasping hands, with an accompanying caption stating that "Colin McKay and Cary Hart share the love." By clicking on the "next" icon, the viewer could scroll through the remaining photographs and corresponding captions. A photograph of a woman in a black dress had this caption: "Tara Dakides lookin' sexy, even though we all know she is hardcore." Another photograph showed a sunglasses-wearing man, with a caption stating that "Ben Hinkley rocks the shades so the ladies can't see him scoping." The photograph of the Knievels was the tenth in the sequence and could not be viewed without first viewing the photographs that preceded it. Its caption read this way: "Evel Knievel proves that you're never too old to be a pimp."

Evel and Krystal Knievel sued ESPN for defamation, contending that the caption, as used in connection with the photograph, falsely charged them with "immoral and improper behavior" and otherwise harmed their reputations. In particular, they alleged that after the publication of the photograph and caption, several of the corporations for which Evel had done product endorsements no longer wanted him associated with their products. ESPN moved to dismiss the Knievels' complaint for failure to state a claim on which relief could be granted. According to the defendant, defamation could not have occurred because reasonable persons would not have interpreted the caption as an allegation that Evel was a criminal "pimp" or that Krystal was a prostitute. The federal district court granted the motion to dismiss. The Knievels appealed. Did the district court rule correctly?

9. Victoria Dauzat and Phyllis Jeansonne were shopping at a Dollar General store. Security cameras were in operation at the store that day. A Dollar General employee, Amanda Poarch, commenced observation of security camera footage in the store's office at 11:56 A.M. Eight minutes later, Poarch called the police to report an alleged "theft in progress" at the store. Poarch stated in this call that she was presently watching Dauzat and Jeansonne steal several items from the store. Police officers arrived at the store at 12:09 P.M. Acting on an identification provided by Poarch, the officers directed Dauzat and Jeansonne to leave the checkout line. The officers then provided the *Miranda* warnings to Dauzat and Jeansonne. Other shoppers in the Dollar General store at the time included members of the same church Dauzat attended. Following the removal of Dauzat and Jeansonne from the checkout line, questioning of them took place in an office at the back of the store for more than an hour. The two maintained their innocence. Moreover, the video from the security cameras did not reveal evidence of apparent shoplifting.

Dauzat and Jeansonne, who ultimately were not criminally prosecuted, sued Poarch and Dollar General for false imprisonment and defamation. They based their false imprisonment claim on the detention that occurred following Poarch's identification of them to the police officers. They based their defamation

claim on the theory that false accusations of shoplifting would have been heard by other shoppers at the store and by other members of the tight-knit community on their in-home police scanner radios. The defendants argued that applicable state law included a shopkeepers' statute of the sort discussed in the text and that the statute should protect them against false imprisonment liability. The defendants also contended that a conditional privilege should apply to Poarch's report to the police and that they therefore should not be held liable for defamation. The trial court ruled in favor of the plaintiffs on both claims. The defendants appealed. How did the appellate court rule on the false imprisonment claim? How did the appellate court rule on the defamation claim?

10. In December 2000, a group of 18 plaintiffs sued James Pillen and various other defendants, seeking injunctive relief and damages on the theory that the defendants' hog confinement operation constituted a private nuisance. The plaintiffs alleged that the hog confinement operation, which was conducted at four facilities in two Nebraska counties, had been a nuisance since 1997. In addition, the plaintiffs alleged that they had been deprived of the normal use and enjoyment of their property, and that the defendants had been notified of the plaintiffs' concerns but had failed to take corrective action. At a 2002 bench trial in a state district court, Pillen testified about the relevant facilities, each of which was classified as a "5,000 sow unit." The first of the four facilities was put into operation in 1996. The most recent facility was added in 1999. Pillen testified that he knew in May 1997 of a complaint from Nebraska's Department of Environmental Quality (DEQ) concerning "the odor from [an] incinerator" at one of the facilities. Pillen believed that the DEQ complaint resulted from a complaint made to the DEQ by one of the plaintiffs. In addition, Pillen testified that he had discussed an odor problem with some of the plaintiffs prior to the end of September 1997.

All 18 plaintiffs testified concerning how the hog confinement operation had affected their lives and the use and enjoyment of their property. The testimony generally concerned the impact of odors. The plaintiffs described the odors from the defendants' facilities as "unbearable," as "overwhelmingly a suffocating stench," as a "musty hog [excrement] smell," as a "sewage odor," as a "gas[-like] smell," and as an odor that "chokes you." Various plaintiffs said the smell was so bad that they had to keep their houses closed up at all times. The odor problem prevented them from spending time in their yards or gardens, from hanging laundry on outdoor clotheslines, and from participating in outside activities with children and grandchildren. One plaintiff testified that she was a "prisoner" in her own home. According to Pillen's testimony, the defendants had tried various procedures to diminish the odors emanating from the facilities and waste lagoons located there. These measures included the use of food additives, waste additives, and lagoon treatments. Pillen further testified that he did not think the hog confinement operation had changed the plaintiff's quality of life or would ever disrupt their daily activities to such an extent that the operation should be changed.

The trial court ruled in favor of the plaintiffs and held that the defendants' four-facility operation constituted a nuisance. The court ordered the defendants to explore the utility of processes to mitigate the odors and to implement such processes. In addition, the court ordered that the defendants must, within 12 months, "abate the nuisance or cease operating" their hog confinement facilities. Although the court found that the plaintiffs had suffered at least "some damage" as a result of the nuisance, the court noted that "none of the plaintiffs [was] able to quantify any request for damages" and that the plaintiffs "had not adduced any evidence sufficient for the court to award them specific damages." As a result, the court awarded no monetary recovery to any of the plaintiffs. On appeal to the Nebraska Court of Appeals, the defendants challenged the trial court's conclusion that the hog confinement operation constituted a nuisance. The plaintiffs challenged the trial court's failure to award damages. How did the court of appeals rule on the parties' respective arguments?

11. At the time of the events described below, California's statute dealing with a deceased celebrity's right of publicity read as follows: "Any person who uses a deceased personality's name, voice, signature, photograph, and likeness, in any manner, on or in products, merchandise, or goods, or for purposes of advertising or selling, or soliciting purchases of products, merchandise, goods, or services, without prior consent from [the legal owner of the deceased personality's right of publicity] shall be liable" to the right of publicity owner. The statute also set forth exemptions from the consent requirement for uses in news, public affairs, or sports broadcasts; in plays, books, magazines, newspapers, musical compositions, or film, television, or radio programs; or in other works of political or news-related value. There was also an exemption for "single and original works of fine art."

Comedy III Production Inc. owns the rights of publicity of the deceased celebrities who, through their comedy act and films, had become familiar to the public as "The Three Stooges." Relying on the statute quoted above, Comedy III brought a right of publicity action against artist Gary Saderup and the corporation of which he was a principal. Without Comedy III's consent, the defendants (referred to here collectively as "Saderup") had produced and profited from the sale of lithographs and T-shirts bearing a depiction of The Three Stooges. The depiction had been reproduced from Saderup's charcoal drawing, which featured an accurate and easily recognizable image of the Stooges. The trial court awarded damages to Comedy III after concluding that Saderup had violated the right of publicity statute and that neither the exemptions set forth in statute nor the First Amendment furnished a defense. When the California Court of Appeals affirmed, Saderup appealed to the Supreme Court of California. Were the lower courts correct in ruling in favor of Comedy III?

12. Ann Bogie attended a comedy performance by Joan Rivers. During the performance, Rivers told a joke about the legendary Helen Keller, who was deaf and blind. This joke offended an audience member who had a deaf son. The audience member heckled Rivers, and the two had a brief but sharp exchange that was captured on film. Immediately after the show, Rivers exited to a backstage area closed to the general public. Bogie gained entry to this backstage area and asked Rivers to sign a copy of her book. Bogie engaged Rivers in a brief conversation during which Bogie expressed frustration with the heckler and sympathy for Rivers. Rivers responded with an expression of sympathy for the heckler. The conversation went as follows:

Bogie: Thank you. You are so . . . I never laughed so hard in my life.

Rivers: Oh, you're a good laugher and that makes such a difference.

Bogie: Oh, I know. And that rotten guy. . . .

Rivers: Oh, I'm sorry for him.

Bogie: I was ready to get up and say . . . tell him to leave.

Rivers: He has a, he has a deaf son.

Bogie: I know.

Rivers: That's tough.

Bogie: But he's gotta realize that this is comedy.

Rivers: Comedy.

Bogie: Right.

Unbeknownst to Bogie, her conversation with Rivers was captured on film. The film showed that at least three other persons were present during this exchange (a uniformed security guard and two other men who appeared to work for Rivers). They were all within a few feet of both Bogie and Rivers.

The film of the exchange between Rivers and the heckler and the film of Bogie's interaction with Rivers were included in a nationally distributed documentary titled *Joan Rivers: A Piece of Work.* Bogie's conversation with Rivers accounted for 16 seconds in the 82-minute documentary. Bogie sued Rivers and other defendants, contending that the filming of her conversation with Rivers and the inclusion of the interaction in the documentary constituted invasion of privacy. In her complaint, Bogie alleged (among other things) that she was portrayed in the documentary as having approved of condescending and disparaging remarks by Rivers toward the heckler. A federal district court granted the defendants' motion to dismiss Bogie's complaint for failure to state a claim on which relief could be granted. Was the district court correct in so ruling? (In deciding on your answer, consider each of the types of invasion of privacy discussed in the chapter.)

13. Mark Chanko was brought into the emergency room of New York and Presbyterian Hospital (the Hospital). He had been hit by a vehicle but was alert and responding to questions. Dr. Sebastian Schubl was the Hospital's chief surgical resident and was responsible for Chanko's treatment. While Chanko was being treated, employees of ABC News, a division of American Broadcasting Companies Inc. (ABC), were in the Hospital. With the Hospital's knowledge and permission, the ABC employees were filming a documentary series (*NY Med*) about medical trauma and the professionals who attend to

the patients suffering from such trauma. No one informed Chanko, his wife (who was at the Hospital), or members of his family (who were also there) that a camera crew was present and filming. Nor was their consent obtained for filming or for the crew's presence. Less than an hour after Chanko arrived at the Hospital, Dr. Schubl declared him dead. That declaration was filmed by ABC. Chanko's prior treatment was apparently filmed as well. Dr. Schubl then informed the family of Chanko's death. That moment was also recorded without their knowledge.

Sixteen months later, Chanko's widow, Anita Chanko, watched an episode of *NY Med* on her television at home. She recognized the scene, heard her late husband's voice as he asked about her, saw him pictured on a stretcher, heard him moaning, and watched the video depiction of him as he died. In addition, she saw, and relived, the scene in which Dr. Schubl informed the family of his death. She then told the other family members, who also watched the episode. This was the first time she and the family members became aware that decedent's medical treatment and death had been recorded. Anita Chanko and other family members later filed a lawsuit against ABC, the Hospital, and Dr. Schubl. They brought various claims, including one for intentional infliction of emotional distress (IIED). The defendants moved to dismiss the IIED claim. How did the court rule?

14. Mann was the attorney for the Town of Rye, a New York community. He filed a defamation lawsuit against a newspaper that served the Rye area and against the writer of that newspaper's Town Crier column. Mann based his case on statements that appeared in the column. The writer of the column referred to Mann as a "political hatchet man" and as "one of the biggest powers behind the throne in local government." The writer also asserted that "Mann pulls the strings" and raised the question whether Mann was "leading the Town of Rye to destruction." What arguments should the defendants make in an effort to avoid defamation liability? Should Mann win his case?

Negligence and Strict Liability

TNT Well Service Inc. hired Melvin Clyde as a rig operator. Clyde's duties called for him to travel to various well sites within approximately 100 miles of Gillette, Wyoming. TNT provided Clyde with a company-owned pickup, which he used for work-related purposes and for travel to and from his home. Although TNT had a general policy of drug-testing prospective employees, TNT did not drug-test Clyde before hiring him and furnishing him with the pickup. Neither did TNT look into whether Clyde had any history of impaired driving or illegal drug use. Had TNT done such checking, it would have discovered that during roughly the preceding eight years, Clyde had been convicted twice for driving under the influence of alcohol and once for possession of a controlled substance.

Late one afternoon approximately a year after he began working for TNT, Clyde was driving the TNT pickup when it crossed the highway's center line and collided head-on with a tractor-trailer driven by Rodney Shafer (the tractor-trailer's owner). Clyde died in the accident. A post-accident blood test revealed the presence of controlled substances in his blood. Shafer sustained serious injuries in the collision, and his tractor-trailer was damaged beyond repair.

Shafer and his wife sued TNT in a Wyoming court. In seeking to have TNT held liable, the Shafers were unable to rely on a frequently involved legal basis for imposing liability on employers. Under the doctrine of *respondeat superior*, an employer is liable for its employee's tort if the tort was committed within the scope of employment. *Respondeat superior* would not apply in this case, however, for either of two reasons: First, evidence offered by TNT indicated that Clyde had been fired from his job earlier in the afternoon of the accident (meaning that he would not have been TNT's employee at the time of the accident); second, even if Clyde was still TNT's employee at the time of the accident, he was outside the scope of employment because he was driving in an area that was outside TNT's business territory. (In this chapter, you will read other cases in which the *respondeat superior* theory is applicable.)

However, *respondeat superior*'s inapplicability would not necessarily bar the Shafers from succeeding in their case against TNT. Whereas *respondeat superior* provides a basis for an employer to be held liable for an *employee's* tort, an employer may sometimes be held liable for the *employer's own* tort. Look back over the facts set forth above and consider these questions as you study Chapter 7:

- Are there things that TNT failed to do, but probably should have done? If so, what? Why those things?
- Are there things that TNT did, but probably should not have done? If so, what? Why those things?
- How do the things you have identified relate to the above-described accident and to the Shafers' attempt to have TNT held legally liable?
- On what legal basis would the Shafers be relying in their lawsuit against TNT?

LEARNING OBJECTIVES

After studying this chapter, you should be able to:

7-1 Identify the elements necessary for a valid negligence claim to exist (duty, breach of duty, and causation of injury).

7-2 Explain what the reasonable care standard contemplates.

7-3 Explain the role of foreseeability in determining whether a defendant owed the plaintiff a duty of reasonable care.

7-4 Explain what goes into a determination of whether a defendant breached the duty of reasonable care.

7-5 Explain the differences among the respective duties of care owed by owners or possessors of property to invitees, licensees, and trespassers.

7-6 Explain what the doctrine of negligence per se does and when it applies.

7-7 Identify the types of injuries or harms for which a plaintiff may recover compensatory damages in a negligence case.

7-8 Explain the difference between actual cause and proximate cause.

7-9 Explain what an intervening cause is and what effect it produces.

7-10 Explain the difference between traditional contributory negligence and the comparative negligence doctrine now followed by almost all states.

7-11 Explain the difference in operation between pure comparative negligence and mixed comparative negligence.

7-12 Identify circumstances in which strict liability principles, rather than those of negligence, control a case.

THE INDUSTRIAL REVOLUTION THAT changed the face of 19th-century America created serious strains on tort law. Railroads, factories, machinery, and new technologies meant increased injuries to persons and harm to their property. These injuries did not fit within the intentional torts framework because most were unintended. In response, courts created the law of **negligence**.

Negligence law initially was not kind to injured plaintiffs. One reason was the fear that if infant industries were held responsible for all the harms they caused, the country's industrial development would be seriously restricted. As a viable industrial economy emerged in the 20th century, this concern began to fade. Also fading over the same period was the 19th-century belief that there should be no tort liability without genuine fault on the defendant's part. More and more, the injuries addressed by tort law have come to be seen as the inevitable consequences of life in a high-speed, technologically advanced society. Although 21st-century negligence rules have not eliminated the fault feature, they sometimes seem consistent with a goal of imposing tort liability on the party better positioned to bear the financial costs of these consequences. That party often is the defendant. However, it is important to remember that even though negligence law may seem to have become more pro-plaintiff in recent decades, statistics indicate that defendants win negligence cases at least as often as plaintiffs do.

Because most tort cases that do not involve intentional torts are governed by the law of negligence, the bulk of

this chapter will deal with negligence principles. In a narrow range of cases, however, courts dispense with the fault requirement of negligence and impose **strict liability** on defendants. Strict liability's more limited application will be addressed during the latter part of this chapter. The chapter will conclude with discussion of recent decades' tort reform movement, whose primary aims are to reduce plaintiffs' ability to prevail in tort cases and limit the amounts of damages they may receive when they win such cases.

Negligence

 LO7-1 Identify the elements necessary for a valid negligence claim to exist (duty, breach of duty, and causation of injury).

The previous chapter characterized negligence as conduct that falls below the level reasonably necessary to protect others against significant risks of harm. The elements of a negligence claim are that (1) the defendant owed a duty of care to the plaintiff, (2) the defendant committed a breach of this duty, and (3) this breach was the actual and proximate cause of injury experienced by the plaintiff. In order to win a negligence case, the plaintiff must prove each of these elements, which will be examined in the following pages. Later in the chapter, *defenses* to negligence liability will be considered.

Duty and Breach of Duty

Duty of Reasonable Care

 LO7-2 Explain what the reasonable care standard contemplates.

Negligence law rests on the premise that members of society normally should behave in ways that avoid the creation of unreasonable risks of harm to others. As a general rule, therefore, negligence law contemplates that each person must act as a *reasonable person of ordinary prudence* would have acted under the same or similar circumstances. This standard for assessing conduct is often called either the "reasonable person" test or the "reasonable care" standard. In most cases, the duty to exercise reasonable care serves as the relevant duty for purposes of a negligence claim's first element. The second element—breach of duty—requires the plaintiff to establish that the defendant failed to act as a reasonable person would have acted. Negligence law's focus on reasonableness of behavior leads to a broad range of applications in everyday personal life (e.g., a person's negligent driving of a car) and in business and professional contexts (e.g., an employer's negligent hiring of a certain employee or an accountant's, attorney's, or physician's negligent performance of professional obligations).

Recent years have witnessed attempts to extend negligence principles to contexts not previously explored in litigation. For instance, numerous former National Football League (NFL) players sued the NFL for alleged failures to disclose the full extent of the long-term health risks posed by concussions (particularly of the repeated variety) and for alleged failures to develop appropriate protocols that would guard against players being put back on the field too soon after a head injury. Negligence was among the legal theories being invoked by the plaintiffs. The players and the NFL eventually agreed to a settlement in which the NFL would, among other things, set up a very large fund against which the ex-players could make claims.

Was the Duty Owed?

 LO7-3 Explain the role of foreseeability in determining whether a defendant owed the plaintiff a duty of reasonable care.

Of course, there could not have been a breach of duty if the defendant did not owe the plaintiff a duty in the first place. It therefore becomes important, before we look further at how the reasonable person test is applied, to consider the ways in which courts determine whether the defendant owed the plaintiff a duty of reasonable care.

Courts typically hold that the defendant owed the plaintiff a duty of reasonable care if the plaintiff was among those who would foreseeably be at risk of harm stemming from the defendant's activities or conduct, or if a special relationship logically calling for such a duty existed between the parties. Most courts today broadly define the group of foreseeable "victims" of a defendant's activities or conduct. As a result, a duty of reasonable care is held to run from the defendant to the plaintiff in a high percentage of negligence cases—meaning that the outcome of the case will hinge on whether the defendant breached the duty or on whether the requisite causation link between the defendant's breach and the plaintiff's injury is established.

In *Magri v. Jazz Casino Co.*, which follows, the court considers whether the defendant casino owed and breached a duty of reasonable care to the plaintiff customer whose foot was injured while he was playing blackjack.

Magri v. Jazz Casino Co., LLC	275 So. 3d 352 (La. Ct. App. 2019)

On January 18, 2012, Mr. Magri went to Harrah's Casino [owned by Defendant Jazz Casino Company, LLC] to celebrate his birthday. Mr. Magri was seated on a high stool at the blackjack table, with an empty stool situated to Mr. Magri's immediate left. Because Mr. Magri recently had undergone a left knee replacement, he rested his left leg and ankle on the bottom of the empty stool and faced the dealer. While Mr. Magri was playing blackjack, the pit boss called for an employee to empty a trash can in the area. When the employee, Nakeisha McCormick, attempted to empty the trash can, she moved the stool upon which Mr. Magri's left foot was resting. Mr. Magri claims that she yanked the stool, twisting his left foot and ankle. After the incident, Harrah's employees applied ice and wrapping to Mr. Magri's left foot.

On January 15, 2013, Mr. Magri filed suit against Harrah's and others alleging various theories of negligence, including failure to exercise reasonable care, failure to warn of an unsafe condition, and failure to properly train employees. After a two-day bench trial, on October 17, 2018, the trial court rendered a judgment in favor of Mr. Magri and against Harrah's in the amount of $601,689.31, after reducing the amount of the original judgment by 30%, based on Mr. Magri's comparative fault.

Harrah's timely appealed.

Sandra Cabrina Jenkins, Judge

Defendant Jazz Casino Company, LLC, the owner of Harrah's New Orleans Casino ("Harrah's"), appeals the trial court's October 17, 2018 judgment awarding $601,689.31 in damages to plaintiff Irvin Magri, Jr., following a two-day bench trial. The suit arises from personal injuries sustained by Mr. Magri when a Harrah's employee abruptly moved a stool on which Mr. Magri was resting his foot while sitting at a blackjack table. Harrah's challenges the trial court's findings on three of the five legal elements of negligence.

For the reasons that follow, we find that Harrah's owed a duty of reasonable care to Mr. Magri, Harrah's breached that duty, and the particular harm sustained by Mr. Magri fell within the scope of Harrah's duty to exercise reasonable care. We also find that the trial court was not clearly wrong in apportioning 70% of fault to Harrah's, and 30% to Mr. Magri. Accordingly, we affirm the trial court's judgment.

Harrah's raises four assignments of error: (1) Harrah's owed no duty to protect or warn Mr. Magri because the risk that the empty stool could be moved was open and obvious to everyone who encountered it; (2) The trial court erred in finding that Harrah's breached its legal duty because a reasonably prudent person observing an empty stool would not have inspected underneath the stool before moving it; (3) The trial court erred in finding legal causation because the risk that a patron sitting on one stool would put his foot on an adjacent stool, and that his foot would be injured when the stool was moved, is not within the scope of a Harrah's duty to exercise reasonable care; and (4) The trial court erred in allocating only 30% of the fault to Mr. Magri since he placed his foot on an empty stool knowing that the stool could be moved at any time.

Mr. Magri testified that he had been to Harrah's four to ten times before the incident, and during these prior visits he saw "more people than he could count" sitting with their feet on adjacent stools. At the time of the accident, he was sitting at a blackjack table to the left of the dealer, with his left foot on the bottom rung of the empty stool next to him. Mr. Magri described his left foot as "intertwined" in the stool, with his foot inserted over the rung and then underneath it. He stated that he was facing the dealer with the majority of his body facing forward, while his left leg was on the rung of the adjacent stool. According to Mr. Magri, because he had a left knee replacement surgery on August 2, 2011, he was stretching his left leg out on the rung of the adjacent stool to relieve stiffness.

Mr. Magri testified that while he was playing blackjack, the pit boss called for environmental services to empty a trash can. Mr. Magri said that when a female employee arrived, she and the pit boss got involved in a heated argument that lasted thirty seconds or less. Mr. Magri said that after the argument, the employee "yanked" the stool two or three times, and after each time she yanked the stool, he yelled for her to stop. He said that when the employee pulled the empty stool out, his foot and ankle were tangled in it. Mr. Magri stated that after the third pull, the employee

stopped yanking the stool. He stated that he felt a sharp pain in his surgically repaired left knee and ankle.

Mr. Magri testified that before the accident, he did not ask any casino personnel if he could put his foot on the adjacent stool. He said that he was aware as a matter of "common sense" that another casino patron or employee could move the empty stool at any time, and he acknowledged that he did not need a sign to tell him that. He stated that he saw Ms. McCormick put her hands on the stool, but did not warn her that his foot was entwined in the stool.

After the accident, Mr. Magri completed a Guest Accident Report stating that the Harrah's employee "pulled the chair next to me (behind me) completely out with (unfortunately) my left foot attached causing me to almost fall." Mr. Magri also completed a handwritten form on February 8, 2012, stating that the Harrah's employee "basically yanked the high stool away from me with my left ankle and leg entangled in same."

Ms. McCormick testified that she has worked as a cleaning specialist at Harrah's for ten years. She said that on the night of the accident, she was assigned to work in the Smuggler's restroom, which is near the blackjack table. According to Ms. McCormick, she received a call on the radio stating that a trash can in Pit 3 needed to be emptied, but the employee who normally emptied the trash can did not respond, so Ms. McCormick volunteered to pick up the trash. Ms. McCormick testified that she was not upset about picking up the trash, as it was part of her job. She denied that she had an argument with the pit boss that night. Ms. McCormick stated that because the blackjack tables are located next to one another, she had to go between two tables to empty the trash can. She described the space between the blackjack tables as "narrow." She said that as she approached Pit 3 to empty the trash can, an empty stool at the blackjack table blocked her path. When she saw Mr. Magri, he was seated to the right of the empty stool, and was facing the dealer. She said that in order to get past the empty stool, she pushed it toward the blackjack table one time. She stated that she did not see Mr. Magri's feet and did not realize that his left foot was on the footrest of the empty stool before she pushed. She stated that she had no reason to believe that Mr. Magri's foot would be on the empty stool. According to Ms. McCormick, when she pushed the stool, Mr. Magri screamed "my foot, my leg." She stated that she did not move the stool again after Mr. Magri yelled. She said that she asked Mr. Magri if he was okay, and he responded that he was fine. Ms. McCormick stated that she retrieved the trash can, emptied it, and then departed.

Duty/Risk Analysis

The duty/risk analysis is the standard negligence analysis employed in determining whether to impose liability under [Louisiana statute and case law]. Under the duty/risk analysis, the plaintiff must prove five elements: (1) the defendant had a duty to conform his conduct to a specific standard (the duty element); (2) the defendant's conduct failed to conform to the appropriate standard (the breach element); (3) the defendant's substandard conduct was a cause-in-fact of the plaintiff's injuries (the cause-in-fact element); (4) the defendant's substandard conduct was a legal cause of the plaintiff's injuries (the scope of liability or scope of protection element); and (5) actual damages (the damages element). "A negative answer to any of the inquiries of the duty-risk analysis results in a determination of no liability." [Citation omitted] Harrah's challenges only the first, second, and fourth elements of the duty/risk analysis.

Legal Duty

"The threshold issue in any negligence action is whether the defendant owed the plaintiff a duty." [Citations omitted for all quoted legal principles] Whether a duty is owed is a question of law for the court to decide, subject to *de novo* review. "There is an almost universal duty on the part of the defendant in a negligence action to use reasonable care to avoid injury to another." "In general, the duty owed by a business owner to its customers is that of reasonable care." "This duty extends to keeping the premises safe from unreasonable risks of harm or warning persons of known dangers." "[T]he basic standard is that the defendant must exercise the degree of care that we might expect from an ordinarily prudent person under the same or similar circumstance." A reasonably prudent person will avoid creating an unreasonable risk of harm.

Harrah's relies on the "open and obvious" doctrine in support of its contention that it owed no legal duty to Mr. Magri. "[A] defendant generally does not have a duty to protect against that which is obvious and apparent." [Citations omitted] "In order for an alleged hazard to be considered obvious and apparent [the supreme] court has consistently stated the hazard should be one that is open and obvious to everyone who may potentially encounter it." Ms. McCormick testified that she did not see Mr. Magri's feet and did not realize that his left foot was on the footrest before she pushed the stool. She also testified that she had no reason to believe that Mr. Magri's foot would be on the empty stool. Mr. Magri testified that he did not inform anyone at the blackjack table that he was resting his foot on the adjacent high stool.

Under the circumstances, we find that the risk that a Harrah's employee would move a chair with a patron's foot entangled in it was not an open and obvious risk of harm, given the showing in the record that Ms. McCormick was the only person who knew Ms. McCormick was going to move the stool. As the "open and obvious" doctrine does not apply, we conclude that Harrah's, at a minimum, owed a legal duty to Mr. Magri to keep the casino safe from unreasonable risks of harm.

Breach of Duty

The second element, breach of duty, is a question of fact, or a mixed question of law and fact, and the reviewing court must accord great deference to the facts found and the inferences drawn by the fact-finder. [Citation omitted] Factual findings regarding breach of duty are subject to the manifest error standard of review. [Citation omitted] This Court has described the breach of duty standard as follows:

[T]o find that the defendant's conduct is substandard, you must find that an ordinarily prudent person under all of the surrounding circumstances would reasonably have foreseen that as a result of its conduct, some such injury as the plaintiff suffered would occur, and that defendant failed to do what an ordinarily prudent person would have done. You may find it helpful to ask yourself, "How would an ordinary prudent person have acted or what precautions would they have taken if faced with similar conditions or circumstances?" [Citation omitted]

Mr. Magri testified that it was common to see people resting their feet on an adjacent stool. Ms. McCormick testified that she did not look to see whether there was any impediment to moving the stool in the narrow space between the tables. A reasonably prudent person—particularly an employee working on the floor of a busy casino—moving a chair in a cramped space would have examined the stool prior to moving it to ensure that a customer would not be harmed. The trial court apparently found Mr. Magri's testimony that Ms. McCormick "yanked" on the stool several times, even after he screamed, to be credible. We find that the trial court was not clearly wrong in finding that Harrah's breached its duty to protect Mr. Magri from unreasonable harm.

Legal Cause

The fourth element of the duty/risk analysis is "legal cause" or "scope of protection." "[This] inquiry assumes that a legal duty exists and questions whether the injury suffered by the plaintiff is one of the risks encompassed by the rule of law that imposed the duty." [Citations omitted] "The extent of protection owed to a particular plaintiff is determined on a case-by-case basis to avoid making a defendant an insurer of all persons against all harms." This Court has described the "legal cause" or "scope of duty" inquiry as follows:

In determining the limitation to be placed on liability for a defendant's substandard conduct, the proper inquiry is often how easily the risk of injury to the plaintiff can be associated with the duty sought to be enforced. [Citations omitted] Thus, a risk may be found not within the scope of a duty where the circumstances of that injury to the plaintiff could not reasonably be foreseen or anticipated, because there was no ease of association between the risk of injury and the legal duty. [Citations omitted]

Under the circumstances presented here, it was foreseeable that a patron sitting at a blackjack table would have comfortably rested his foot and leg on an adjacent empty stool. We find an ease of association between the risk that a seated patron's foot would be injured when an adjacent stool is "yanked" three or four times, and Harrah's legal duty to protect Mr. Magri from unreasonable harm.

Assessment of Fault

Harrah's contends that the trial court should have allocated more than 30% fault to Mr. Magri. A trial court's findings regarding percentages of fault are factual, and will not be disturbed on appeal unless clearly wrong. [Citations omitted]

An appellate court's determination of whether the trial court was clearly wrong in its allocation of fault is guided by the factors set forth in *Watson v. State Farm Fire and Cas. Ins. Co.*, 469 So. 2d 967 (La. 1985). In *Watson*, the Supreme Court said that "various factors may influence the degree of fault assigned, including: (1) whether the conduct resulted from inadvertence or involved an awareness of the danger; (2) how great a risk was created by the conduct; (3) the significance of what was sought by the conduct; (4) the capacities of the actor, whether superior or inferior; and (5) any extenuating circumstances which might require the actor to proceed in haste, without proper thought." *Watson*, 469 So. 2d at 974. These same factors guide the appellate court's determination as to the highest or lowest percentage of fault that could reasonably be assessed.

The trial court found that the evidence showed that Harrah's negligence arose from Ms. McCormick's inadvertence. Ms. McCormick created a substantial risk of harm when she knowingly moved the chair without warning Mr. Magri or examining the area. The risk could have been avoided by Ms. McCormick by examining the stool beforehand to determine if anyone could be injured as a result of moving the stool.

The trial court also found that Mr. Magri's negligence arose from his own inadvertence, and that he had some comparative fault for placing his left foot on the adjacent empty chair. The trial court found that Mr. Magri should have expected that someone would attempt to move or utilize the adjacent empty chair. The trial court also considered that Mr. Magri did not ask permission to prop his foot on the chair, and did not inform anyone at the blackjack table that he was resting his foot on the high stool.

We find that a reasonable interpretation of the facts supports the trial court's finding that Harrah's, through Ms. McCormick, bears 70% of the fault. Accordingly, the trial court's assessment of 30% fault to Mr. Magri and 70% fault to Harrah's was not manifestly erroneous, and should be upheld.

Based on the foregoing we affirm the trial court's October 17, 2018 judgment, in favor of Mr. Magri and against Harrah's, in the amount of $601,689.31.

AFFIRMED.

Was the Duty Breached?

Explain the role of foreseeability in determining whether a defendant owed the plaintiff a duty of reasonable care.

Explain what goes into a determination of whether a defendant breached the duty of reasonable care.

Assuming that the defendant owed the plaintiff a duty of reasonable care, whether the defendant satisfied or instead breached that duty depends upon the application of the reasonable person test. This test is *objective* in two senses. First, it compares the defendant's actions with those that a hypothetical person with ordinary prudence and sensibilities would have taken (or not taken) under the circumstances. Second, the test focuses on the defendant's behavior rather than on the defendant's *subjective* mental state. The reasonable person test has another noteworthy characteristic: flexibility. In contemplating that courts consider all of the relevant facts and circumstances, the test allows courts to tailor their decisions to the facts of the particular case being decided.

When applying this objective yet flexible standard to specific cases, courts consider and balance various factors. The most important such factor is the *reasonable foreseeability* of harm. This factor does double duty, helping to determine not only whether the defendant owed the plaintiff a duty (as noted above) but also what the defendant's duty of reasonable care entailed in the case at hand. Suppose that Donald falls asleep at the wheel and causes a car accident in which another motorist, Peter, is injured. Falling asleep at the wheel involves a foreseeable risk of harm to others, so a reasonable person would remain awake while driving. Because Donald's conduct fell short of this behavioral standard, he has breached a duty to Peter. However, this probably would not be true if Donald's loss of awareness resulted from a sudden, severe, and unforeseeable blackout. On the other hand, there probably would be a breach of duty if Donald was driving and had a blackout to which a doctor had warned him he was subject.

Negligence law does not require that we protect others against all foreseeable risks of harm. Instead, the risk created by the defendant's conduct need only be an *unreasonable* one. In determining the reasonableness of the risk, courts consider other factors besides the foreseeability of harm. One such factor is the *seriousness* or *magnitude* of the foreseeable harm. As the seriousness of the harm increases, so does the need to take action to avoid it. Another factor is the *social utility* of the defendant's conduct. The more valuable that conduct, the less likely that it will be regarded as a breach of duty. A further consideration is the *ease or difficulty of avoiding the risk*. Negligence law normally does not require that defendants make superhuman efforts to avoid harm to others.

To a limited extent, negligence law also considers the *personal characteristics* of the defendant. For example, children are generally required to act as would a reasonable person of similar age, intelligence, and experience. A person who is physically disabled must act as would a reasonable person with the same disability. Mental deficiencies, however, ordinarily do not relieve a person from the duty to conform to the usual reasonable person standard. The same is true of voluntary and negligent intoxication.

Finally, negligence law is sensitive to the *context* in which the defendant acted. For example, someone confronted with an emergency requiring rapid decisions and action need not employ the same level of caution and deliberation as someone in circumstances allowing for calm reflection and deliberate action.

The *Currie* case, which follows, focuses mainly on the duty and breach of duty elements of a negligence claim. It also furnishes an introduction to concepts dealt with more fully later in the chapter.

Currie v. Chevron U.S.A., Inc.   266 F. App'x 857 (11th Cir. 2008)

Acting in her own right and as personal representative of the estate of her deceased daughter (Nodiana Antoine), Tracye Currie sued Chevron U.S.A., Inc. and Chevron Stations Inc. (collectively, "Chevron") on the theory that Chevron negligently caused Antoine's death. The facts giving rise to the case are summarized here.

For approximately two years, Antoine and Anjail Muhammad had had a close personal relationship. The relationship between the two women was a stormy one, with Muhammad sometimes threatening to inflict physical harm on Antoine. One morning in 2003, Muhammad and Antoine were in Muhammad's car, which Muhammad had parked in a restaurant parking lot in Marietta, Georgia. According to a statement Muhammad later made to the police, Muhammad and Antoine became involved in an argument, during which Antoine said that she wanted to end their relationship. Muhammad also said in her statement that Antoine left the car and started walking toward a Chevron gas station across the street to call her family. Muhammad followed her, and the women continued arguing as they walked across the street.

Pamela Robinson, a customer at the Chevron station, testified at the trial in Currie's case that when she pulled into the station, she saw Muhammad and Antoine approach the station. Muhammad was pulling on Antoine's neck or the collar of her clothing and essentially dragging Antoine. Robinson also stated that Muhammad appeared to tighten her grip when Antoine tried to pull away. Robinson, who watched the two women move in the direction of gas pump number one, went inside the station when she realized that the pump she was seeking to use had to be activated by a Chevron cashier before it would work. Jyotika Shukla was the cashier at the station on that day. Robinson testified that she entered the station and "told [Shukla] immediately that there was something going on with the two young ladies out here and that she needed to contact the police immediately." Robinson explained that she then pointed out the two women to Shukla.

Shukla testified at the trial that she did not know there was anything wrong outside until Robinson came into the station and told her, though an earlier statement by Shukla to the police indicated that Shukla saw the women before Robinson came into the station. Regardless of when she first saw the women, Shukla said that she did see the two women "verbally fighting" and that one woman was holding the other by her shirt. Shukla did not call the police because, according to her testimony, she thought the two women were or would be leaving the Chevron property.

Evidence adduced at the trial indicated that when customers at the Chevron station sought to use a gas pump, they had to lift a lever on the pump. A beeping sound inside the station would then inform the cashier that a customer had lifted the lever. In order for the customer to receive gas through the pump, the cashier would then have to hit the "authorize pump" button. After the pump was authorized, the beeping sound would stop.

The evidence established that Shukla authorized gas pump number one by pushing the appropriate button inside the station. This authorization of the pump enabled Muhammad to use it, even though Muhammad did not have a car on the premises. Shukla testified at trial that she authorized pump number one before Robinson came into the station and before she (Shukla) saw the women fighting, but Shukla's deposition testimony and an earlier statement given to the police indicated that she could not remember whether she knew about or had seen the fighting before she authorized the pump.

Robinson's testimony suggested that Shukla authorized a pump after Robinson told Shukla about the two women fighting. Based on her prior experience of working at a gas station, Robinson recognized that a beeping sound informed the cashier that a gas pump needed to be activated. Robinson testified that she heard a beeping sound when she entered the Chevron station. She also testified that the beeping sound stopped "right after" she told Shukla to call the police. Robinson also stated that she did not ask Shukla to authorize her gas pump until after she talked to Shukla about the two women fighting outside and showed Shukla where they were standing—by gas pump number one. Moreover, there were no other customers waiting for other pumps to be authorized.

Shukla's testimony was inconsistent about whether she looked at gas pump number one before authorizing it. She first testified that she did not remember whether she had looked at pump number one before authorizing it, but later she said "[m]aybe yes." In her statement to the police, Muhammad said that Shukla looked at pump number one before authorizing it. Muhammad stated that "[e]verybody was really helpful like the lady . . . in the store. . . . [S]he just turned the pump on." When a police detective asked, "Even though ya'll didn't have a car?" Muhammad responded, "Didn't even have a car right next to it, she just turned it on, she looked at us and just turned the pump on."

After Shukla authorized pump number one, Muhammad sprayed 65 cents worth of gasoline on Antoine. Robinson testified that she exited the station to return to her car to pump gas and immediately saw the two women "in the same position with [Muhammad] holding [Antoine]." Before Robinson got to her car, Muhammad asked Robinson whether she had a cigarette lighter. Robinson said she did not. She then watched the two women as they left the Chevron station, with Muhammad still pulling Antoine by her shirt.

According to Muhammad's statement to the police, she and Antoine left the Chevron station and went back to Muhammad's car. Muhammad then found a cigarette lighter in the car and used the lighter to set Antoine on fire. Antoine ran through the parking lot while on fire and tried to roll over in a grassy area in an effort to put out the flames. A passerby called 911, and Antoine was taken to the hospital. Several weeks later, Antoine died as a result of the burns she had suffered. Muhammad, who confessed to police that she set Antoine on fire, was later indicted on criminal charges of murder, aggravated battery, aggravated assault, and arson.

In Currie's wrongful death lawsuit against Chevron, Currie alleged that Shukla negligently authorized the gas pump used by Muhammad and that Antoine died as a result. Under the respondeat superior *principle discussed in Chapter 36 of this text, Chevron would be liable for any negligence on the part of its employee, Shukla, if that negligence occurred within the scope of Shukla's employment. A federal district court jury returned a $3,500,000 verdict in Currie's favor. The court issued a judgment against Chevron for $2,625,000, an amount that reflected a 25 percent reduction from $3,500,000 because of the jury's finding that Antoine's own negligence accounted for 25 percent of the reason why she was killed. (Later in this chapter, you will learn about the comparative negligence principle applied by the court in reducing the amount of damages awarded.) Chevron unsuccessfully moved for judgment as a matter of law or, in the alternative, a new trial. Chevron then appealed to the U.S. Court of Appeals for the Eleventh Circuit.*

Per Curiam

In this diversity case controlled by Georgia law, . . . Currie contended at trial that Chevron's Shukla negligently activated the gas pump for Muhammad only after: (1) Shukla saw Muhammad pulling Antoine around the Chevron station's property by her shirt and thought that something was wrong; (2) Shukla saw that Muhammad and Antoine did not have a vehicle; and (3) customer Pamela Robinson warned Shukla that there was a problem with the two women outside, asked Shukla to call the police, and showed Shukla where the two women were standing by gas pump number one. Currie claimed that, given this evidence, Shukla should have foreseen that Antoine would suffer some injury as a result of Shukla's activating the gas pump for Muhammad. On appeal, Chevron argues that . . . Muhammad's actions were not a reasonably foreseeable consequence of Shukla's negligence; [that] Antoine failed to exercise ordinary care to avoid the consequences of Shukla's negligence; [and that] Antoine's negligence was equal to or greater than Shukla's negligence.

A cause of action for negligence in Georgia must contain the following elements: (1) a legal duty to conform to a standard of conduct for the protection of others against unreasonable risks of harm; (2) a breach of this standard; (3) a legally attributable causal connection between the conduct and the resulting injury; and (4) some loss or damage resulting from the breach of the legal duty. In order to establish a breach of the applicable standard of conduct, there must be evidence that the alleged negligent act (or omission) created a foreseeable, unreasonable risk of harm. As to foreseeability of injury, Georgia courts have stated that "in order for a party to be held liable for negligence, it is not necessary that he should have been able to anticipate the particular consequences which ensued. It is sufficient if, in ordinary prudence, he might have foreseen that some injury would result from his act or omission, and that consequences of a generally injurious nature might result." [Citations omitted.]

In Georgia, questions of negligence, proximate cause, and foreseeability are generally for the jury. [After reviewing the record in this case, we] conclude that reasonable minds could differ as to whether Shukla was aware at the moment she authorized gas pump number one that her action would create a foreseeable risk of injury to Antoine. There was evidence from which the jury could have inferred that Shukla was aware that Muhammad and Antoine were involved in a serious fight on the Chevron station's property. In her statement to police on the day of the incident, Shukla said that she saw the two women walking on the station's property, that Muhammad had "grabbed" and "pulled" Antoine by the front of her shirt, and that Shukla "thought something was wrong." Shukla also testified at trial that she saw the women fighting on the Chevron station's property. Robinson's testimony confirmed Shukla's observation that the fight was serious. Robinson testified that [Muhammad tightened her grip on Antoine] when Antoine try to pull away from her. Robinson [also testified] that Muhammad then pulled Antoine "down to the ground like an animal."

There also was evidence from which the jury could have found that Shukla was aware that Muhammad and Antoine were involved in a serious fight at the Chevron station *before* she activated gas pump number one for Muhammad. [In addition,] there was evidence from which the jury could have concluded that Shukla looked at Muhammad before authorizing gas pump number one. Muhammad told police on the day of the incident that ". . . she looked at us and just turned the pump on. . . ." Based on Muhammad's statement and Shukla's own testimony, the jury could have found that Shukla looked at gas pump number one before she authorized it, saw Muhammad (whom Shukla had seen fighting with Antoine on the station's property and had recognized did not have a car), and nevertheless authorized gas pump number one for Muhammad.

[Considering] the totality of this evidence . . . , the jury could have found that the beeping sound that Robinson heard inside the Chevron station was Muhammad seeking authorization of gas pump number one and that Shukla looked at Muhammad and authorized gas pump number one for her (thus stopping the beeping sound) *after* Shukla's conversation with Robinson. The jury also could have found that Shukla was aware at the time she authorized gas pump number one for Muhammad that: (1) Muhammad had been pulling Antoine around the Chevron station's property by her shirt as they were fighting; (2) the fight was sufficiently serious that Shukla herself thought something was wrong and that Robinson came into the station to warn Shukla that something was going on with the two women outside and to ask her to call the police; (3) Muhammad and Antoine were fighting by gas pump number one; and (4) Muhammad and Antoine did not have a car on the station's property. Thus, we conclude that there was, at the very least, a substantial conflict in the evidence such that reasonable and fair-minded jurors might reach different conclusions as to whether Shukla was aware before she authorized gas pump number one that her negligent action would create a foreseeable risk of injury to Antoine.

Chevron presented expert testimony from Rosemary Erickson, Ph.D., a forensic sociologist, that it was not reasonably foreseeable to Shukla that Muhammad would douse Antoine with gas and set her on fire. Dr. Erickson based her opinion on a review of the depositions, the police records, the low crime rate in the area surrounding the Chevron station, the lack of previous violent crimes at this specific Chevron station, and the rarity of the particular crime that occurred here. In addition to Dr. Erickson's testimony, Shukla testified that she had never [witnessed] a crime or fire at the Chevron station before that day and never had to call the police. [The] former Chevron station manager testified that there had not been any criminal activity at the Chevron station in his eight to ten years working there before this incident.

However, in cross-examining Dr. Erickson, plaintiff's counsel asked, "You would agree with me . . . would you not, that if something is going on at a gas station and a clerk sees one person holding another at a gas pump and there's no car and no container, that it's foreseeable that the gas may be used inappropriately and harm can result. . . ." Dr. Erickson replied, "If all those factors were in evidence." Thus, even from Chevron's own witness, there was in effect testimony to support Currie's claim that Shukla should not have authorized the gas pump after Shukla saw Muhammad and Antoine fighting (or was told by Robinson they were fighting) and where Muhammad and Antoine had no car or gas container. [In addition, both the former station manager] and Robinson [, who had worked at a gas station,] testified that they would not activate a gas pump if they saw people at the gas pump without a car or gas can.

In arguing that this incident was not foreseeable, Chevron cites Georgia premises liability cases providing that property owners have a duty to exercise ordinary care to protect invitees from foreseeable third-party criminal attacks where there are prior similar criminal acts occurring on the premises that put the property owner on notice of the dangerous condition. Chevron argues that the criminal attack by Muhammad on Antoine was not foreseeable because this particular Chevron station was in a low crime area and had not been the site of any criminal activity in previous years, much less violent crime.

First, while Currie raised a premises liability theory at trial, her primary theory of liability was that given the particularly serious events unfolding before Shukla and given Robinson's warning, Shukla then committed her own affirmative negligent act in activating gas pump number one for Muhammad, not that Chevron breached its duty to Antoine to keep its premises safe generally. Second, the lack of prior criminal activity at this Chevron station does not wholly foreclose the foreseeability issue. Even in cases grounded solely on a premises liability theory, Georgia courts have stated that "a showing of prior similar incidents on a proprietor's premises is not always required to establish that a danger was reasonably foreseeable. An absolute requirement of this nature would create the equivalent of a one free bite rule for premises liability, even if the proprietor otherwise knew that the danger existed." [Citation omitted.] This Court applied this same reasoning in a premises liability case to conclude that there was a jury question of whether hostilities throughout the evening of which bowling alley employees were, or should have been, aware were sufficient to make it reasonably foreseeable to them that a fight would erupt, even though there had been no similar prior altercations on the premises. [Citation omitted.] Similarly, in this case, there was a sufficient conflict in the evidence for reasonable minds to differ as to whether the particular serious and exigent events unfolding right before Shukla at the Chevron station that morning, together along with Robinson's warning, should have put her on notice that activating the gas pump for Muhammad would

pose an unreasonable risk of harm to Antoine, even though there was no history of prior similar incidents at this specific Chevron station.

Therefore, we cannot say that the district court erred in denying Chevron's motion for judgment as a matter of law or a new trial.

[*Note:* In a later portion of the opinion not included here, the Eleventh Circuit concluded that the district judge had correctly instructed the jury on issues related to Antoine's own failure to use reasonable care, that the jury's assignment of a 25 percent degree of responsibility to Antoine was supported by the evidence, and that the court had therefore properly reduced the award of damages by 25 percent.]

Judgment in favor of Currie affirmed.

Ethics and Compliance in Action

Suppose that during regular work hours, an employee of XYZ Co. commits a sexual assault or other violent attack upon a member of the public. The employee, of course, is liable for the intentional tort of battery (about which you learned in Chapter 6), as well as a criminal offense. Although the doctrine of *respondeat superior* makes employers liable for their employees' torts when those torts are committed within the scope of employment, XYZ is quite unlikely to face *respondeat superior* liability for its employee's flagrantly wrongful act because a sexual assault or violent attack, even if committed during regular work hours, presumably would be outside the scope of employment.

However, as the principles explained in this chapter suggest, XYZ could be liable for its *own* tort if XYZ was negligent in hiring, supervising, or retaining the employee who committed the attack. A determination of whether XYZ was negligent would depend upon all of the relevant facts and circumstances.

Regardless of whether XYZ would or would not face legal liability, the scenario described above suggests related

ethical questions that may confront employers. Consider the following:

- Does an employer have an ethical obligation to take corrective or preventive action when the employer knows, or has reason to know, that the employee poses a danger to others?
- Does it matter whether the employer has irrefutable evidence that the employee poses a danger, or whether the employer has only a reasonable suspicion to that effect?
- If the employer has an ethical obligation to take corrective or preventive action, to whom does that obligation run and what should that obligation entail?
- Does the employer owe any ethical duty to the *employee* in such situations?

You may find it helpful to consider these questions through the frames of reference provided by the ethical theories discussed in Chapter 4 (e.g., utilitarianism, rights, virtue, shareholder, and justice theories). Then compare and contrast the results of the respective analyses.

Special Duties In some situations, courts have fashioned particular negligence duties to supplement the general reasonable person standard. When performing their professional duties, for example, professionals such as doctors, lawyers, and accountants generally must exercise the knowledge, skill, and care ordinarily possessed and employed by members of the profession.[1] Also, common carriers and (sometimes) innkeepers are held to an extremely high duty of care approaching strict liability

when they are sued for damaging or losing their customers' property. Many courts say that they also must exercise great caution to protect their passengers and lodgers against personal injury—especially against the foreseeable wrongful acts of third persons. This is true even though the law has long refused to recognize any general duty to aid and protect others from third-party wrongdoing unless the defendant's actions foreseeably increased the risk of such wrongdoing. Some recent decisions have imposed a duty on landlords to protect their tenants against the foreseeable criminal acts of others.

[1]Chapter 46 discusses professional liability in greater detail.

LO7-5 Explain the differences among the respective duties of care owed by owners or possessors of property to invitees, licensees, and trespassers.

Duties to Persons on Property Another important set of special duties runs from possessors of real estate (land and buildings) to those who enter that property. Negligence cases that address these duties are often called *premises liability* cases. Traditionally, the duty owed by the possessor has depended on the classification into which the entering party fits. The three classifications are:

1. *Invitees.* Invitees are of two general types, the first of which is the "business visitor" who is invited to enter the property for a purpose connected with the possessor's business. Examples include customers, patrons, and delivery persons. The second type of invitees consists of "public invitees" who are invited to enter property that is held open to the public. Examples include persons using government or municipal facilities such as parks, swimming pools, and public offices; attendees of free public lectures and church services; and people responding to advertisements that something will be given away. The entry, however, must be for the purpose for which the property is held open.

A possessor of property must exercise reasonable care for the safety of his invitees. In particular, he must take appropriate steps to protect an invitee against dangerous on-premises conditions that he knows about, or reasonably should discover, and that the invitee is unlikely to discover.

2. *Licensees.* A licensee enters the property for her own purposes, not for a purpose connected with the possessor's business. She does, however, enter with the possessor's consent. In some states, social guests are licensees, though today they are more commonly classified as invitees. Other examples of licensees are door-to-door salespeople, solicitors of money for charity, and sometimes persons taking a shortcut across the property. As these examples suggest, consent to enter the property is often implied. The possessor usually is obligated only to warn licensees of dangerous on-premises conditions that they are unlikely to discover.

3. *Trespassers.* A trespasser enters the land without its possessor's consent and without any other privilege. Traditionally, a possessor of land owed trespassers no duty to exercise reasonable care for their safety; instead, there was only a duty not to willfully and wantonly injure trespassers once their presence was known.

Recent years have seen some tendency to erode these traditional distinctions. Most notably, many courts no longer distinguish between licensees and invitees. These courts hold that the possessor owes a duty of reasonable care to persons regardless of whether they are licensees or invitees. Some courts have created additional duties that possessors owe to trespassers. For example, a higher level of care is often required as to trespassers who are known to regularly enter the land, and as to children known to be likely to trespass.

Traditionally, premises liability cases have focused on whether reasonable care was exercised to guard against or remedy potentially dangerous physical conditions such as slippery substances on the floor or poorly lighted staircases—the sorts of conditions that could cause an invitee to fall or experience a similar mishap resulting in physical injuries. (Hence, those premises liability cases are often referred to as "slip-and-fall" cases.) In recent years, courts have considered whether the duty of reasonable care should encompass measures to protect invitees against on-the-premises criminal acts of third parties. *Lord v. D & J Enterprises, Inc.*, which follows, is such a case.

Lord v. D & J Enterprises, Inc.   757 S.E.2d 695 (S.C. 2014)

D & J Enterprises, Inc. operates businesses involving check cashing, payday lending, and motor vehicle title lending. One of its businesses is Cash on the Spot, which is located in Rock Hill, South Carolina. For the protection of employees, Cash on the Spot is outfitted with iron bars on the windows of its building and bulletproof glass on its tellers' windows.

On February 14, 2008, Ida Lord went to Cash on the Spot to retrieve money that had been wired to her. As Lord approached a teller's window, a man seated at a nearby table stood up, reached under his clothing, pulled out a pistol, and shot Lord in the head and back. The man then demanded money as he slid his weapon through the opening in the teller's window. The store manager, who was stationed behind the bulletproof window and had access to a silent alarm, called 911. The man fled the premises but was soon arrested. He was later identified as Phillip Watts Jr.

After Watts was apprehended, he confessed to committing seven armed robberies in Rock Hill and elsewhere in York County (where Rock Hill is located). Those robberies, which began in October 2007 and primarily targeted small businesses, were the subject of significant media coverage. Two of the publicized robberies occurred within three weeks prior to the Cash on the Spot incident. In those robberies, Watts shot two store clerks and a bystander. Before the February 14, 2008, incident in which Lord was shot, D & J's president,

Darrell Starnes (who oversaw the corporation's day-to-day operations), warned his employees to be vigilant because "there is a madman on the loose." Watts ultimately pleaded guilty but mentally ill to criminal charges in connection with the Cash on the Spot incident and the other armed robberies.

Lord filed a negligence lawsuit against D & J in a South Carolina court in an effort to obtain damages for what she described as the "catastrophic brain injuries" she suffered in the shooting. She alleged that D & J breached its duty to use reasonable care to protect her while she was at Cash on the Spot. D & J later moved for summary judgment, arguing that it had no duty to protect Lord from the injuries directly caused by Watts. It was not foreseeable that Watts would shoot Lord, D & J contended, because Watts appeared to be a regular customer, because the incident lasted less than six seconds, and because there had not been prior instances of attempted armed robberies or acts of violence at Cash on the Spot. In opposing D & J's motion, Lord offered the deposition testimony of D & J officers and employees, an affidavit from a private security expert who opined that D & J should have had a security guard stationed at Cash on the Spot, and evidence of media coverage of the earlier robberies committed by Watts.

Concluding that D & J did not owe a duty to Lord, the trial court granted summary judgment in favor of D & J. After Lord appealed to the South Carolina Court of Appeals, the Supreme Court of South Carolina certified the case for resolution by that court rather than the Court of Appeals.

Beatty, Justice

In this premises liability case involving a third-party criminal act, Lord . . . asserts the court erred in granting summary judgment to D & J because she presented . . . evidence showing a genuine issue of material fact as to each element of her negligence claim. Specifically, Lord asserts that: (1) D & J owed a duty to her as she was a business invitee on the premises of Cash on the Spot; (2) the risk of harm to her was foreseeable because D & J's president admitted he knew before the shooting that "there was a madman on the loose" and reviewed procedures with D & J employees regarding a response to a potential armed robbery; (3) D & J failed to post a security guard at the entrance of Cash on the Spot despite the foreseen risk of a shooting; (4) the affidavit of private security expert Robert Clark established that the shooting of Lord "most probably would not have occurred if D & J had posted a security guard"; and (5) there is evidence that the shooting caused Lord to suffer profound neurological complications.

Bass v. Gopal, Inc., 716 S.E.2d 910 (S.C. 2011) (*Gopal II*) . . . is used to determine a business owner's duty to protect a patron based on the foreseeability of violent acts by third parties. *Gopal II* was a premises liability action that arose out of the shooting of Gerald Bass while he was a guest at the Super 8 Motel in Orangeburg, South Carolina. Gopal, Inc., a Super 8 franchisee, owned and operated the motel. [The shooter was someone who was at the motel for the apparent purpose of committing a robbery.] Bass filed a complaint alleging negligence [on the part of] Gopal, Inc. and Super 8. The defendants filed motions for summary judgment, which were granted by the circuit court. The South Carolina Court of Appeals affirmed. [Bass appealed to the Supreme Court of South Carolina.]

In [ruling on Bass's appeal in] *Gopal II*, we considered whether the Court of Appeals erred in upholding the circuit court's finding that Gopal, Inc., . . . did not have a duty to

protect Bass from the criminal act of a third party. [We] noted that the threshold question in any negligence action is whether the defendant owed a duty to the plaintiff. [We stated that although] "an innkeeper is not the insurer of [the] safety of its guests," an innkeeper "is under a duty to its guests to take reasonable action to protect them against unreasonable risk of physical harm." The court [further] explained in *Gopal II* that "a business owner has a duty to take a reasonable action to protect its invitees against the *foreseeable* risk of physical harm."*

In assessing the foreseeability issue, the *Gopal II* court [adopted] a balancing test, which . . . acknowledges that duty is a flexible concept, and seeks to balance the degree of foreseeability of harm against the burden of the duty imposed. The court explained that "the more foreseeable a crime, the more onerous is a business owner's burden of providing security." Accordingly, "[u]nder this test, the presence or absence of prior criminal incidents is a significant factor in determining the amount of security required of a business owner, but their absence does not foreclose the duty to provide some level of security if other factors support a heightened risk." The court found that "the balancing approach appropriately weighs both the economic concerns of businesses and the safety concerns of their patrons." By adopting this test, the court hoped to "encourage a reasonable response to the crime phenomenon without making unreasonable demands."

Applying the balancing approach to the facts of Bass's case, the court found the Court of Appeals correctly affirmed the grant of summary judgment in favor of Gopal, Inc. In reaching this decision, the court determined that Bass presented "at least some evidence the aggravated assault was foreseeable" because Bass produced a CRIMECAST report that showed . . . the risk of rape,

*Gerald BASS, Appellant, v. GOPAL, INC. and Super 8 Motels, Inc., Respondents. No. 4576.

robbery, and aggravated assaults at the Super 8 as compared to the national average risk, the state average risk, and the county average risk.

The court, however, found Bass did not provide any evidence that Gopal Inc.'s preventative measures were unreasonable given the risk of criminal activity on the property. Although Bass presented the deposition testimony of an expert who "concluded the addition of a closed circuit camera or some type of additional security personnel would have been reasonable in light of his perceived risk," the court found Bass "failed to provide any evidence that [Gopal, Inc.] should have expended more resources to curtail the risk of criminal activity that might have been probable." Instead, the court found determinative the expert's statement that "if . . . this is [the] first time [a criminal incident occurred], there wasn't enough data for [Gopal, Inc.] to say he really needed to spend a bunch of money on surveillance cameras, a bunch of money on a full-time security guard or part-time, or train his employees to do a guard tour."

[Gopal II provides controlling insights on] how to determine (1) if a crime is foreseeable, and (2) the economically feasible security measures that are required to prevent the foreseeable harm. Applying the Gopal II balancing test [to the case at hand], we hold the circuit court erred in granting summary judgment to D & J. Viewing the evidence in the light most favorable to Lord, we find she presented [enough] evidence to withstand the motion for summary judgment as to her negligence claim against D & J.

To prevail on a negligence claim, a plaintiff must establish duty, breach, causation, and damages. The key determination in the instant case is whether D & J breached its duty to take reasonable action to protect Lord, its business invitee, against the foreseeable risk of physical harm. Regarding the foreseeability prong of Gopal II, Lord presented the deposition testimony of Starnes (D & J's president) and Marsha Boyd, the manager of Cash on the Spot the day of the shooting. Starnes and Boyd testified they were aware of the prior robberies in York County because the local newspapers had covered the incidents. Prior to the shooting, Starnes discussed the robberies with his employees and warned them to "be on their toes to look out for suspicious people" because there was a "madman on the loose." Based on the foregoing, we find, as did the circuit court, that Lord produced at least some evidence that the shooting was foreseeable.

[T]he question [then] becomes whether D & J's preventative security measures were unreasonable given this risk. Lord primarily asserts that D & J should have posted a security guard at the entrance of Cash on the Spot. Although this court in Gopal II acknowledged the significant cost associated with hiring security guards absent evidence of prior crimes on the premises, we stated that a plaintiff may produce evidence of this prong through the testimony of an expert. Here, unlike the plaintiff in Gopal II, Lord presented expert testimony precisely on this point. Robert Clark, Lord's expert in private security, reviewed the media coverage of the prior armed robberies, reviewed the deposition testimonies of Starnes and Boyd, and conducted a field investigation of the security measures used at Cash on the Spot. Based on his investigation, Clark opined that D & J "had a duty, in the exercise of reasonable care, to post a security guard at the entrance" of Cash on the Spot in order to "provide reasonable protection for its employees and customers against the threat of a serial armed robber who had shot two store clerks and a bystander in two previous armed robberies of businesses that fit the profile of D & J's business." He further stated, "The armed robbery attempt during which Ida Lord was shot most probably would not have occurred if D & J had posted a security guard at the entrance of its check cashing location."

As we noted in Gopal II, "whether a business proprietor's security measures were reasonable in light of a risk will, at many times, be identified by an expert." Here, Lord presented such expert testimony. Under the specific facts presented in this case, we find the expert testimony was sufficient to create a question of fact for the jury.

[W]e conclude it is premature to deprive Lord of the opportunity to present her case to a jury. At this stage, it is not the role of the circuit court or this court to determine whether Lord will prevail on her negligence claim, but whether she presented [sufficient] evidence to withstand D & J's motion for summary judgment.

We emphasize that our decision should not be construed as requiring all merchants to hire costly security guards. Instead, we merely find that it is for a jury to decide whether D & J employed reasonable security measures to fulfill its duty to protect Lord from the foreseeable risk of a shooting. Clearly, D & J recognized that it was susceptible to an armed robbery at Cash on the Spot, as it had installed security cameras and placed bars on the office windows. It also sought to protect its employees by placing them behind bulletproof glass, equipping them with panic buttons, and providing them with immediate access to a silent alarm. The circumstances of this case, however, presented a heightened risk of danger beyond the ordinary operation of Cash on the Spot. As evidenced by Starnes's deposition testimony, there was a foreseeable risk of a shooting at Cash on the Spot given the rash of armed robberies that culminated in the shootings of store clerks and customers at nearby businesses. Under these unique facts, we cannot find that D & J was entitled to judgment as a matter of law on Lord's cause of action for negligence.

Circuit court's grant of summary judgment to D & J reversed; case remanded for trial regarding Lord's negligence claim.

LO7-6 Explain what the doctrine of negligence per se does and when it applies.

Negligence Per Se Courts sometimes use statutes, ordinances, and administrative regulations to determine how a reasonable person would behave. Under the doctrine of *negligence per se*, the defendant's violation of such laws may create a breach of duty and may allow the plaintiff to win the case if the plaintiff (1) was within the class of persons intended to be protected by the statute or other law and (2) suffered harm of a sort that the statute or other law was intended to protect against. In the *Winger* case, which follows, the plaintiffs' decedent fell to her death from an apartment balcony whose guardrail was shorter than the height mandated by a supposedly applicable municipal housing code provision. The court considers whether the negligence per se principle can be applied when the supposed violation was of a local ordinance rather than a state or federal law.

Winger v. CM Holdings, L.L.C.   881 N.W.2d 433 (Iowa 2016)

At 1:30 A.M. on July 23, 2011, 21-year-old Shannon Potts came to her friends' second-floor apartment at the Grand Stratford Apartments in Des Moines, Iowa. She arrived in a slightly intoxicated state and continued drinking until about 4:00 A.M., when her friends hid the alcohol. A conversation took place between Shannon and a friend while the two were on the apartment's balcony. When the conversation ended, the friend returned inside the apartment. A scream and a crash were then heard. Discovering that Shannon had fallen over the balcony's railing, the group of friends came to her aid and found her unresponsive. Shannon's injuries proved to be fatal. Toxicology tests indicated that she was intoxicated at the time of her fall and that she had marijuana and Xanax in her bloodstream.

Until roughly five months before Shannon's fatal fall, Mark Critelli solely owned the Grand Stratford Apartments (Apartments), which were located in buildings constructed in 1968. The Apartments were built to comply with the 1968 Des Moines housing code, which required balcony guardrails to be at least 30 inches in height. The original iron railings at the Apartments were 32 inches tall. They were still in place when Shannon fell to her death 43 years later. Amendments to the Des Moines housing code in 1979 and 2005 required that guardrails be at least 42 inches in height. However, these later versions of the housing code included a grandfather provision permitting previously installed guardrails that complied with the earlier version of the code to remain in use if they were in sound structural condition.

In 2009, Critelli attached a 48-inch-high white plastic lattice to the guardrails at the Apartments. He used zip ties to attach the lattice, which served as a privacy screen to shield each balcony from view. In February 2011, a Des Moines housing inspector visited the Apartments and found 106 violations, including the guardrail height. The inspector reasoned that Critelli's attachment of the lattice modified the guardrails and that this modification both eliminated the protection of the above-noted grandfather provision and triggered a duty to comply with the code provision requiring 42-inch-high guardrails.

Later in February 2011, CM Holdings, L.L.C. acquired controlling ownership interest in the Apartments. (Critelli retained a partial ownership interest.) CM undertook significant renovations and other actions to correct most of the problems identified in the list of 106 violations. During a July 5, 2011, visit to the property, the city housing inspector noted only six remaining violations, one of which was the guardrail-height violation. He imposed a penalty of $1,090 for that violation. CM, which had ordered new 42-inch guardrails but did not yet have them, did not appeal the finding that it had violated the guardrail-height requirement. Instead, CM requested that the Des Moines Housing Appeal Board (HAB) grant it a three-month extension to comply with the 42-inch height requirement and that the $1,090 penalty be suspended. In a decision issued on July 20, 2011, the HAB upheld the finding of a violation but granted CM's request for an extension of time to comply and a suspension of the penalty. Shannon Potts fell to her death three days later.

Acting in their personal capacities and as executors of Shannon's estate, Shannon's parents sued CM. They alleged that the 32-inch guardrails violated the housing code, that the code violation constituted negligence per se, and that a 42-inch-high guardrail would have prevented Shannon from falling. (During the eventual jury trial, the plaintiffs' expert witness offered such an opinion about the likely effect of a 42-inch guardrail.) The trial court ruled on a pretrial basis that the newer code provision (the one requiring 42-inch guardrails) applied as a matter of law. The court also rejected CM's arguments that the property was grandfathered out of the current code, that the 1968 code applied as a matter of law, and that, in any event, the HAB's extension of time to install higher railings excused tort liability. The court instructed the jury that CM's violation of the housing *code constituted negligence per se. The court also limited the jury to deciding causation, comparative fault on Shannon's part, and damages. The jury found CM 65 percent at fault and Shannon 35 percent at fault, and awarded damages of $1,750,000 ($1,137,500 after the necessary reduction for comparative fault).*

In a post-trial ruling, however, the trial court concluded that the doctrine of negligence per se did not apply after all and that a new trial was therefore warranted. Both sides appealed to the Iowa Court of Appeals, which affirmed the lower court's post-trial ruling and earlier rulings on other key issues. Both sides again appealed, this time to the Supreme Court of Iowa. The following edited version of that court's opinion notes various issues on which the court ruled but focuses on one key question: whether the negligence per se doctrine can apply when the defendant violated a municipal housing code provision (as opposed to a state statute).

Waterman, Justice

The central fighting issue on appeal is whether CM was negligent *as a matter of law* by failing to replace the 32-inch-high balcony guardrails with 42-inch-high guardrails. We must resolve several related questions. First, CM argues—and the court of appeals ultimately concluded—that only breach of a specific statewide statute or rule can constitute negligence per se, while the breach of a local ordinance cannot. [Analysis of this key issue appears below.]

Second, CM argues that its property was grandfathered out of the 42-inch-high guardrail requirement[, whereas] the plaintiffs argue that CM is bound by the HAB's determination that [the] 32-inch-high balcony guardrails with the attached lattice violated the code. We . . . hold that the HAB finding is not determinative in this tort action. Third, CM contends that the HAB's extension of time to install 42-inch-high railings excused its tort liability in the interim. We affirm the [trial] court's ruling rejecting that legal excuse. Finally, we conclude neither side was entitled to a directed verdict on the grandfather issue under the existing record. That issue must be litigated on remand. [Further discussion of the three issues noted in this paragraph is omitted.]

[Because the plaintiffs are seeking to rely on the negligence per se doctrine, we must resolve this threshold question:] *Can a violation of a city ordinance constitute negligence per se?* The court of appeals construed *Griglione v. Martin*, 525 N.W.2d 810 (Iowa 1994), [as holding] that only the breach of a statewide standard can constitute negligence per se and affirmed the order granting a new trial on that basis. The court of appeals understandably relied on this language from *Griglione*: "We believe rules of conduct that establish absolute standards of care, the violation of which is negligence per se, must be ordained by a state legislative body or an administrative agency regulating on a statewide basis under authority of the legislature."

The plaintiffs argued that [the quoted] language is dicta, but the court of appeals concluded that the language is controlling. We note that [the quoted] language was unnecessary to the decision and is not supported by the cited authorities. We resolve the issue by overruling *Griglione*.

Our court has long recognized that the violation of a municipal safety ordinance can be negligence per se. *See Hedges v. Conder*, 166 N.W.2d 844 (Iowa 1969) (holding that party could be negligent per se for failing to follow city ordinance requiring use of crosswalks); *Kisling v. Thierman*, 243 N.W. 552 (Iowa 1932) (adopting general rule that violation of rules of the road in statutes or ordinances constitutes negligence per se); *Tobey v. Burlington, Cedar Rapids & Northern Railway*, 62 N.W. 761 (Iowa 1895) (holding that violation of speech limit ordinance was negligence per se). However, the [trial] court and court of appeals questioned the viability of this line of cases based on what we [more] recently said in *Griglione*, a case that did not involve a municipal ordinance or code with the force of law.

The fighting issue in *Griglione* was whether the violation of a local police department's internal operating procedures constituted negligence per se. [In that case,] Paula Blythe had received threatening phone calls from Rodney Griglione. She called the Mt. Pleasant Police Department. The responding officer, while interviewing Blythe inside her trailer, heard someone yelling profanities outside. The officer stepped outside in the dark and looked around with his flashlight. He saw Griglione climbing over a fence with a large knife in his right hand. Griglione ran toward the officer, who drew his pistol and fired three times, fatally wounding Griglione.

Griglione's widow sued the officer, arguing that he was negligent per se [because he violated] his police department's operating procedures by using deadly force, by failing to call for backup before shooting, and by failing to identify himself as a police officer before shooting. The preamble to the operating procedures stated that the document provided "guidelines that are suggested" for handling situations and that they were not meant "to assist in assessing . . . possible liability after the fact."

We concluded in *Griglione* that violations of the police department's internal operating procedures were not negligence per se for two reasons. First, we held that the operating procedures "do not involve the delineation of that type of precise standard required to invoke the negligence per se doctrine." Second, we stated that only the violation of a rule applying "statewide" could constitute negligence per se. That statement was broader than necessary to decide the narrow issue of whether an officer's violation of his department's internal procedures is negligence per se. We could have answered "no" without addressing local ordinances that have the force of law.

In *Wiersgalla v. Garrett*, 486 N.W.2d 290 (Iowa 1992), we reiterated the governing standard as follows:

> [I]f a statute or regulation . . . provides a rule of conduct specifically designed for the safety and protection of a certain class of persons, and a person within that class receives injuries as a proximate result of a violation of the statute or regulation, the injuries "would be actionable, as . . . negligence per se." To be actionable as such, however, the harm for which the action is brought must be of the kind which the statute was intended to prevent; and the person injured, in order to recover, must be within the class which [the statute] was intended to protect.

Id. at 292 (internal citations omitted). We hold this standard applies equally to municipal ordinances.

The ordinance at issue here requires 42-inch-high guardrails on second-floor or higher balconies. The obvious purpose for requiring a 42-inch-high guardrail on balconies above ground level is to protect persons from getting killed or injured falling off the balcony. Shannon clearly was within the scope of persons intended to be protected from injury by the municipal ordinance. The requirement is sufficiently specific to prescribe a standard of care, the violation of which constitutes negligence per se. *See O'Neil v. Windshire Copeland Assocs., L.P.*, 197 F. Supp. 2d 507 (E.D. Va. 2002) (ruling that apartment owner was negligent per se for having balcony guardrail lower than required by city building code); *Heath v. La Mariana Apartments*, 180 P.3d 664 (N.M. 2008) (violation of guardrail spacing requirement in ordinance would be negligence per se if not for grandfather provision excusing landlord from obligation to upgrade railings to current code). [Compare the cases just cited with] *Brichacek v. Hiskey*, 401 N.W.2d 44 (Iowa 1987) (holding the Des Moines municipal code provision

requiring a "working lock" lacked the requisite specificity for negligence per se), and *Struve v. Payvandi*, 740 N.W.2d 436 (Iowa Ct. App. 2007) (holding statutory requirement to maintain heating appliances in a safe and working order was not specific enough to support negligence per se theory).

CM's argument that only a violation of a statewide law can be negligence per se conflicts with Iowa's public policy encouraging local control over residential housing for public health and safety. The legislature has specifically allowed local housing ordinances [that are] more stringent than statewide standards. *See* Iowa Code § 562A.15(1)(*a*) (requiring the landlord to follow greater duties imposed by local building or housing codes that materially affect health and safety). Our legislative enactments thus tolerate local variations in housing codes. Although building codes may differ on either side of a city's boundary, buildings are in fixed locations. Building owners will not have to deal with inconsistent local codes at a single location.

We see no good reason to limit application of the negligence per se doctrine to laws of statewide application. The negligence per se doctrine [can be applied regarding violations of] local ordinances. [Therefore, the trial court erred in its post-trial ruling that negligence per se was inapplicable, and the court of appeals erred in affirming that ruling. However, because the trial judge's instructions to the jury contemplated that the later code provision requiring 42-inch-high guardrails applied as a matter of law, the jury verdict in favor of the plaintiffs could not simply be reinstated. The record produced at trial was insufficient to allow a determination as a matter of law on the question whether the later code provision applied, or whether the 1968 code provision instead applied because of grandfathering. Hence, a remand for a new trial was necessary.]

Court of Appeals decision vacated; trial court's post-trial ruling on negligence per se issue reversed; other trial court orders affirmed in part and reversed in part; case remanded for new trial.

Causation of Injury
Proof that the defendant breached a duty does not guarantee that the plaintiff will win a negligence case. The plaintiff must also prove that the defendant's breach caused her to experience injury. We shall look briefly at the injury component of this *causation of injury* requirement before examining the necessary causation link in greater depth.

Types of Injury and Damages

 LO7-7 Identify the types of injuries or harms for which a plaintiff may recover compensatory damages in a negligence case.

Personal injury—also called "physical" or "bodily" injury—is harm to the plaintiff's body. It is the type of injury present in many negligence cases. Plaintiffs who experienced personal injury and have proven all elements of a negligence claim are entitled to recover compensatory damages. These damages may include not only amounts for losses such as medical expenses or lost wages but also sums for pain and suffering. Although the nature of the harm may make it difficult to assign a dollar value to pain and suffering, we ask judges and juries to determine the dollar value anyway. The rationale is that the plaintiff's pain and suffering is a distinct harm resulting from the defendant's failure to use reasonable care, and that merely totaling up the amounts of the plaintiff's medical bills and lost wages would not compensate the plaintiff for the full effects of the defendant's wrongful behavior.

Property damage—harm to the plaintiff's real estate or a personal property item such as a car—is another recognized type of injury for which compensatory damages are recoverable in negligence litigation. In other negligence cases, many of which arise in business or professional contexts, no personal injury or property damage is involved. Instead, the plaintiff's injury may take the form of *economic loss* such as out-of-pocket expenses, lost profits, or similar financial harms that resulted from the defendant's breach of duty but have no connection to personal injury or property damages. Compensatory damages are available for losses of this nature in appropriate cases.

Whatever the type of injury experienced by the plaintiff, the usual rule is that only compensatory damages are recoverable in a negligence case. As noted in Chapter 6, punitive damages tend to be reserved for cases involving flagrant wrongdoing. Negligence amounts to wrongdoing, but not of the more reprehensible sort typically necessary to trigger an assessment of punitive damages.

What if the plaintiff's claimed injury is *emotional* in nature? As you learned in Chapter 6, the law has long been reluctant to afford recovery for purely emotional harms. Until fairly recently, most courts would not allow a plaintiff to recover damages for emotional harms allegedly resulting from a defendant's negligence unless the plaintiff proved that she experienced a physical injury or at least some impact on or contact with her person. Growing numbers of courts have abandoned the physical injury and impact rules and allow recovery for foreseeable emotional harms that stand alone, but clearly not all have done so. Among courts that still require either physical injury or impact as a general rule when emotional distress damages are sought, many have recognized exceptions to that general rule in particular instances where emotional harm seems especially likely to occur and especially likely to be severe.

In *Philibert v. Kluser*, which follows, the court decides on the appropriate legal treatment of "bystander" emotional distress cases—those in which a person died as a result of the defendant's negligence and a member of the decedent's family witnessed the fatal injuries as they were being inflicted.

Philibert v. Kluser   385 P.3d 1038 (Ore. 2016)

Three brothers—ages 12, 8, and 7, respectively—were crossing a street together in an Oregon city. While the brothers were in the crosswalk with the stoplight's walk signal in their favor, Dennis Kluser drove his pickup truck through the crosswalk. The truck ran over the 7-year-old boy and narrowly missed the other two. The brother who was struck died at the scene. The other two boys witnessed their brother's death.

Acting in her capacity as guardian ad litem for the surviving brothers, Stacy Philibert brought a negligence lawsuit against Kluser. (Because Philibert brought the case for the benefit of the 12- and 8-year-old brothers, they will often be referred to as "the plaintiffs" in this statement of facts and in the edited version of the court's opinion.) The complaint alleged that as a result of witnessing their brother's death, the boys experienced severe emotional distress, depression, post-traumatic stress disorder, aggression, and severe anxiety. The defendant moved to dismiss the complaint for failure to state a claim upon which relief could be granted. He argued that because the plaintiffs were bystanders who had experienced neither a physical injury nor a physical impact in the accident, they could not recover for their emotional distress. The trial court granted the dismissal motion. The plaintiffs appealed to the Oregon Court of Appeals, which affirmed the trial court's ruling. The plaintiffs then appealed to the Supreme Court of Oregon.

Balmer, Chief Justice

This case requires us to consider the circumstances, if any, under which damages may be recovered by a bystander who suffers serious emotional distress as a result of observing the negligent physical injury of another person. Plaintiffs witnessed the death of a family member who was run over by a truck, but were not themselves physically injured. They sought recovery for their emotional distress. The trial court dismissed the action and the

Court of Appeals affirmed, both relying on the "impact rule." The impact rule allows a plaintiff to seek damages for negligently caused emotional distress only if the plaintiff can show some physical impact to himself or herself [. We must decide whether the rule applies here or whether, under the circumstances present here, the] plaintiffs should be able to pursue their claims notwithstanding the fact that they did not suffer physical injury [or a physical impact].

[In their decisions, the trial court and the Court of Appeals relied on *Saechao v. Matsakoun*, 717 P.2d 165 (Ore. Ct. App. 1986).] In *Saechao*, the Court of Appeals confronted a situation factually similar to the present case. A driver negligently drove a car onto a sidewalk, killing one child, striking a sibling, and leaving two additional siblings untouched. The three surviving children sued to recover for the emotional distress caused by witnessing their brother's death. The court recognized the case as presenting a question of first impression[:] "[whether, and if so, when] a person who witnesses the negligently caused injury or death of a member of the immediate family may recover damages for serious emotional distress resulting from witnessing the accident." A divided court adopted the impact rule, requiring that there be "a direct accompanying [physical] injury to the person who suffers the emotional distress as a prerequisite to its compensability." As a result, the child who was physically injured was permitted to seek emotional distress damages caused by witnessing his brother's death, but the claims by the two siblings who were not physically injured were dismissed. The Court of Appeals has continued to follow the impact rule in subsequent cases, as it did here. We directly address the bystander recovery issue [in this court] for the first time.

In *Norwest v. Presbyterian Intercommunity Hospital*, 652 P.2d 318 (Ore. 1982), we mapped the landscape of cases addressing claims for emotional distress damages. Oregon allows plaintiffs to recover damages for emotional distress when they are physically injured, and when the defendant acted intentionally. At issue here is a third basis recognized in *Norwest* for recovery of damages for emotional distress: when a defendant negligently causes foreseeable, serious emotional distress and also infringes some other legally protected interest. The plaintiff's claim in that circumstance partially resembles [other] negligence claims in that it rests on the concept of foreseeability. *Norwest* made clear, however, that the injury's foreseeability, standing alone, is insufficient to establish the defendant's liability: there must also be another legal source of liability for the plaintiff to recover emotional distress damages. Those two concepts identified in *Norwest*—foreseeability and the source of a legally protected interest—guide our analysis in this case.

Perhaps the simplest legally protected interest is that to be free from physical harm at the hands of another. Labeling freedom

from physical harm as a legally protected interest for purposes of recovering emotional distress damages under the third category outlined in *Norwest* is simply a different way of stating the general rule that emotional distress damages are available to a plaintiff who is physically injured.

In contrast to physical harms, emotional harms occur frequently. Any number of people may suffer emotional distress as the foreseeable result of a single negligent act. The *Restatement (Third) of Torts* provides an example: "[A] negligent airline that causes the death of a beloved celebrity can foresee genuine emotional harm to the celebrity's fans, but no court would permit recovery for emotional harm under these circumstances." *Restatement (Third)* § 48, comment g. For that reason, foreseeability, standing alone, is not a useful limit on the scope of liability for emotional injuries. Without some limiting principle in addition to foreseeability, permitting recovery for emotional injuries would create indeterminate and potentially unlimited liability.

Nevertheless, even where a plaintiff has not been physically harmed, recovery for foreseeable emotional damages is available when the defendant's conduct "infringed some legally protected interest apart from causing the claimed distress." *Norwest, supra.* In the context of emotional distress, a legally protected interest is "an independent basis of liability separate from the general duty to avoid foreseeable risk of harm." [Citation omitted.] The right to recovery for such injuries does not "arise from infringement of every kind of legally protected interest, but from only those that are of sufficient importance as a matter of public policy to merit protection from emotional impact." [Citation omitted.] *See, e.g., Hovis v. City of Burns*, 415 P.2d 29 (Ore 1966) (allowing claim for emotional damages on the basis of infringement of right of a surviving spouse to have the remains of a deceased spouse undisturbed). In contrast, this court has denied recovery to plaintiffs for emotional injuries resulting from a defendant's negligence when there is no independent legal source of liability. *See, e.g., Hammond v. Central Lane Communications Center*, 816 P.2d 593 (Ore. 1991) (denying recovery to wife who claimed emotional injury caused by watching husband die from heart attack while 911 system negligently delayed response because she had not "point[ed] to some legally protected interest of hers that defendants violated").

We now turn to the bystander's claim for negligently inflicted emotional distress. Plaintiffs assert a common law right of a bystander to avoid observing the physical injury of a close family member as [an important enough legal interest] to support their claims. This court has not had occasion to previously consider such a bystander claim. Our prior cases, however, have allowed claims for negligently inflicted emotional distress to proceed when the court has determined that an asserted common law interest is sufficiently important to support the imposition of liability. The negligent handling of a spouse's remains in *Hovis* [is an example].

In our view, the interest in avoiding being a witness to the negligently caused traumatic injury or death of a close family member is similarly important. Witnessing sudden physical injury or death is a palpable and distinct harm, different in kind even from the emotional distress that comes with the inevitable loss of our loved ones. Plaintiffs here watched as their younger brother was crushed by a pickup truck—a violation of their interest in not witnessing such a shocking and tragic event. And the resulting impact on them might be described as the emotional equivalent of a physical injury. We have no difficulty concluding that plaintiffs have alleged the violation of a legally protected common law interest to be free from the kind of emotional distress injury caused by defendant's negligence here.

Our remaining task is to frame the contours of that interest and identify the elements that will allow a bystander to recover for the negligent infliction of emotional distress, while also providing a limiting principle that will avoid potentially unlimited claims or damages. To do so, we consider three tests that courts commonly have used in similar cases: the impact test, the zone of danger test, and the *Restatement (Third)* approach.

The Impact Test

The impact rule allows a plaintiff to recover for emotional distress when he or she also has suffered a physical injury [or at least a physical impact]. The Court of Appeals in *Saechao* applied that general rule to bystander cases. Proponents of the impact rule claim that its merit lies in the bright line test for liability that it creates [and in the] "guarantee that the mental disturbance is genuine." [Citation omitted.]

The impact rule is problematic, however, because it sets a bar to recovery in bystander cases that can be both too high and too low. The bar is often too high because there is no principled reason to deny recovery for negligently caused emotional injury simply because the physical contact was with a third person rather than the plaintiff. The facts of this case illustrate that point. Plaintiffs witnessed the traumatic death of their brother, but under the impact rule were denied recovery because the truck did not touch them. Yet, their distress at witnessing the death of their brother is likely unrelated to the coincidental fact that the truck did not hit them also. To deny recovery because . . . the plaintiffs [were not] physically injured—when even a minor physical impact is sufficient under that test—seems arbitrary and fails to protect plaintiffs' interest in avoiding witnessing the negligently caused death of their brother. At the same time, the impact rule sets the bar too low in other circumstances,

because a minor injury unrelated to the emotional distress satisfies the impact requirement and permits the claim to proceed.

The impact rule bars plaintiffs who have suffered genuine serious emotional distress from recovering and fails to treat like cases alike. We therefore reject the impact rule as the test for a bystander's recovery of emotional distress resulting from injury to another.

The Zone of Danger Test

Plaintiffs suggest that we permit their recovery under the zone of danger test, which is used by some courts to allow recovery to a plaintiff who experiences "serious emotional distress due to witnessing a fatal injury to a third person only if the plaintiff was personally within the zone of danger of physical impact from the defendant's negligence." [Citation omitted.] Although the zone of danger test found some favor, California notably abandoned [it] in *Dillon v. Legg*, 441 P.2d 912 (Cal. 1968). In that case, a child's sister, standing close by, and her mother, standing down the block, observed a negligent driver kill the child. The court rejected the zone of danger rule and allowed both witnesses to proceed with their claims for emotional distress. The court explained that rejecting the zone of danger test logically follows rejecting the impact test. Neither test actually relates to the likelihood or severity of the emotional distress that can result from seeing a close family member suffer serious injury.

In practice, the zone of danger test results in unfairly denying recovery to plaintiffs who are located outside the zone of physical danger, but witness the physical injury to the third person just the same as if they had been in that zone, as the facts of *Dillon* demonstrate. We are persuaded by the reasoning of the California Supreme Court in *Dillon* and decline to adopt the zone of danger test.

The Restatement (Third) Rule

A number of authorities have attempted to articulate a test for bystander recovery that avoids the somewhat arbitrary aspects of the impact and zone of danger tests, while limiting the potential for indeterminate and excessive liability for emotional distress claims. Probably the most thoughtful recent formulation is found in the *Restatement (Third) of Torts* § 48, which builds on *Dillon* and similar cases. Under that approach, a defendant "who negligently causes sudden serious bodily injury to a third person is subject to liability for serious emotional harm caused thereby to a person who (a) perceives the event contemporaneously, and (b) is a close family member of the person suffering the bodily injury." *Restatement (Third)* § 48. In our view, that test hews closely to the interest that should be legally protected, while also recognizing necessary limits on potential liability and providing at least some guidance to courts and juries. Moreover, the *Restatement (Third)* test is generally consistent with this court's cases dealing with other aspects of claims for negligently caused serious emotional distress. We turn to a closer examination of the rule articulated in the *Restatement (Third)*.

The first element is that the bystander must witness a sudden, serious physical injury to a third person negligently caused by the defendant. *Hammond* presented a situation in which that element was not present. There, the plaintiff awoke to find her husband lying on the floor, apparently the victim of heart attack. The plaintiff sought to recover for her severe emotional distress, alleging that if the defendant 911 service had arrived in the "couple of minutes" that the 911 operator predicted, rather than after the 45 minutes that actually elapsed, she would not have suffered emotional distress. This court did not allow recovery. Although the defendant may have contributed to the death by failing to respond quickly enough, the defendant did not cause the actual physical injury—the heart attack.

Second, the plaintiff must have suffered serious emotional distress. It is a truism that emotional distress is an unavoidable and essential part of life. For that reason, our cases allow compensation for only serious emotional distress. A bystander who experiences emotional harm that does not rise to the level of serious emotional distress, therefore, cannot recover for that harm.

Third, in order to recover, the plaintiff must have perceived the events that caused injury to the third person as they occurred. This contemporaneous perception is at the core of the bystander's action for damages. Observation of the scene of an accident after it has happened, or perceiving a recently injured person, does not meet this requirement. This bright line rule is justified in part by the fact that the distressing life experience of learning about the death or injury of a loved one is unavoidable. In comparison, the visceral experience of witnessing the sudden death or injury of a loved one by a negligent driver, as here, is not a certain part of life and therefore presents a stronger basis for allowing recovery against the tortfeasor.

The final element of the claim is that the physically injured person be a close family member of the plaintiff. Witnessing the injury of a stranger or acquaintance, while likely distressing, is not sufficient to recover. The fraternal relationship of plaintiffs here to the person killed meets that requirement, but other cases may present closer questions as to the meaning of "close family member." *See Restatement (Third)* § 48 ("[A] grandparent who lives in the household may have a different status from a cousin who does not.").

We recognize that the bystander recovery rule outlined in the *Restatement (Third)* may give rise to the possibility of false or inflated claims and that aspects of the rule may seem arbitrary. For as long as courts have awarded damages for emotional injuries, there have been concerns about plaintiffs bringing false claims. Juries are charged with discerning truth from self-serving fiction when plaintiffs testify about their own injuries and are as competent to do this in claims for emotional injuries as they are in other cases. The *Restatement (Third)* rule [includes] elements that, on the basis of human experience, are objective indicators of possibly serious emotional injury. When the elements of the test are met, a plaintiff's claims of subjective emotional distress are more likely to be genuine.

The *Restatement (Third)* rule may have the effect of permitting some claims that would be rejected under other tests, and vice-versa. In this area of the law in particular, some arbitrariness cannot be avoided. But although the rule may be arbitrary in some circumstances, it "serve[s] a function and [is] neither random nor irrational." *Restatement (Third)* § 48, comment g. The undesirable arbitrary aspect of rules must be balanced against the need to provide *ex ante* understanding of liability and assistance in the orderly administration of justice.

We return to the facts of this case. Plaintiffs are two brothers who watched their brother die as a result of being hit by defendant's negligently driven pickup truck. They allege emotional injuries, including depression and severe emotional distress. Examined in the light of the *Restatement (Third)* test set forth above, plaintiffs here state a negligence claim for recovery of emotional distress damage.

Court of Appeals decision reversed; case remanded to trial court for further proceedings.

The Causation Link Even if the defendant has breached a duty and the plaintiff has suffered actual injury, there is no liability for negligence without the necessary causation link between breach and injury. The causation question involves three issues: (1) Was the breach an *actual cause* of the injury? (2) Was the breach a *proximate cause* of the injury? and (3) What was the effect of any *intervening cause* arising after the breach and helping to cause the injury? Both actual and proximate causes are necessary for a negligence recovery. Special rules dealing with intervening causes sometimes apply, depending on the facts of the case.

Actual Cause

 LO7-8 Explain the difference between actual cause and proximate cause.

Suppose that Dullard drove his car at an excessive speed on a crowded street and was therefore unable to stop the car in time to avoid striking and injuring Pence, who had lawfully entered the crosswalk. Dullard's conduct, being inconsistent with the behavior of a reasonable driver, was a breach of duty that served as the actual cause of Pence's injuries. To determine the existence of actual cause, courts often employ a "but-for" test. This test provides that the defendant's conduct is the actual cause of the plaintiff's injury when the plaintiff would not have been hurt but for (i.e., if not for) the defendant's breach of duty. In the example employed above, Pence clearly would not have been injured if not for Dullard's duty-breaching conduct.

In some cases, however, a person's negligent conduct may combine with another person's negligent conduct to cause a plaintiff's injury. Suppose that fires negligently started by Dustin and Dibble combine to burn down Potter's house. If each fire would have destroyed Potter's house on its own, the but-for test could absolve both Dustin and Dibble. In such cases, courts apply a different test by asking whether each defendant's conduct was a *substantial factor* in bringing about the plaintiff's injury. Under this test, both Dustin and Dibble are likely to be liable for Potter's loss.

Proximate Cause

 LO7-8 Explain the difference between actual cause and proximate cause.

The plaintiff who proves actual cause has not yet established the causation link necessary to enable her to win the case. She must also establish the existence of proximate cause—a task that sometimes, though clearly not always, is more difficult than proving actual cause.

Questions of proximate cause assume the existence of actual cause. Proximate cause concerns arise because it may sometimes seem unfair to hold a defendant liable for all the injuries actually caused by his breach—no matter how remote, bizarre, or unforeseeable they are. Thus, courts typically say that a negligent defendant is liable only for the *proximate* results of his breach. Proximate cause, then, concerns the required degree of proximity or closeness between the defendant's breach and the injury it actually caused.

Courts have not reached complete agreement on the appropriate test for resolving the proximate cause question. In reality, the question is one of social policy. When deciding which test to adopt, courts must recognize that negligent defendants may be exposed to catastrophic liability by a lenient test for proximate cause, but that a restrictive test prevents some innocent victims from recovering damages for their losses. Courts have responded in various ways to this difficult question.

A significant number of courts have adopted a test under which a defendant who has breached a duty of care is liable only for the "natural and probable consequences" of his actions. In many negligence cases, the injuries actually caused by the defendant's breach would easily qualify as natural and probable consequences because they are the sorts of harms that are both likely and logical effects of such a breach. The Dullard–Pence scenario discussed earlier would be an example. It is to be expected that a pedestrian struck by a car would sustain personal injury.

In other negligence cases, however, either the fact that the plaintiff was injured or the nature of his harms may seem unusual or in some sense remote from the defendant's breach, despite the existence of an actual causation link. The presence or absence of proximate cause becomes a more seriously contested issue in a case of that nature. A great deal will depend upon how narrowly or broadly the court defines the scope of what is natural and probable.

Other courts have limited a breaching defendant's liability for unforeseeable harms by stating that he is liable only to plaintiffs who were within the "scope of the foreseeable risk." This proximate cause test bears similarity to a key test for determining whether the *duty* element of a negligence claim exists. As earlier discussion noted, courts typically hold that a defendant owes no duty to those who are not foreseeable "victims" of his actions. The *Restatement (Second) of Torts* takes yet another approach to the proximate cause question. It suggests that a defendant's breach of duty is not the legal (i.e., proximate) cause of a plaintiff's injury if, looking back after the harm, it appears "highly extraordinary" to the court that the breach would have brought about the injury.

Further discussion of proximate cause issues can be found in the *Stahlecker* case, which appears in this chapter's later discussion of intervening causes. In *Black v. William Insulation Co.*, which follows, the court rests its decision on the duty element of a negligence claim but engages in considerable discussion of the proximate cause concept.

Black v. William Insulation Co.   141 P.3d 123 (Wyo. 2006)

William Insulation Co. (WIC) was a subcontractor on an expansion project at the Exxon/LaBarge Shute Creek Plant. The plant was located in a remote Wyoming area approximately 26 and 40 miles, respectively, from the nearest population centers, the towns of Green River and Kemmerer. Given the remoteness of the work site, WIC provided $30 per day in subsistence pay to each of its employees to defer part of the cost of a motel room or apartment in Green River or Kemmerer. WIC did not require its employees to spend the money on lodging. The employees were free to spend it—or not spend it—as they saw fit.

David Ibarra-Viernes, a WIC employee, was assigned to work on the above-described expansion project. Ibarra-Viernes received the $30 per day subsistence pay from WIC but elected to make the commute to the plant from his home in Evanston, Wyoming, which was 90 miles away. Ibarra-Viernes carpooled with a group of co-workers, who took turns driving. Ibarra-Viernes's work schedule was Monday through Friday, 7:00 A.M. to 5:30 P.M., with a half-hour lunch and no, or minimal, breaks. In addition to his employment with WIC, Ibarra-Viernes worked a second job at night, washing dishes at a restaurant.

Ibarra-Viernes completed his regular shift at the plant on a Tuesday and returned to Evanston at 8:30 P.M. He then worked his second job before going to bed around 11:00 P.M. Ibarra-Viernes rose at 4:00 A.M. on Wednesday to get his vehicle and collect his co-workers for the daily commute to the plant, where he worked his normal shift. The car pool, with Ibarra-Viernes driving, left the plant around 6:00 P.M. Shortly thereafter, Ibarra-Viernes fell asleep at the wheel. His vehicle crossed the centerline of the highway and collided head-on with a vehicle in which Richard Black was a passenger. Richard Black died in the accident. His widow, Peggy Ann Cook Black, acting in her own right and as personal representative of her late husband's estate, filed a negligence-based wrongful death action against WIC in a Wyoming state court.

In her lawsuit, Black claimed that WIC owed a duty of care to other travelers on the highway to prevent injury caused by employees who had become exhausted after being required to commute long distances and work long hours. She contended in her complaint that WIC breached its duty by "failing to take precautionary measures to prevent employees from becoming so exhausted that they pose a threat of harm to the traveling public and failing to provide alternative transportation to its exhausted employees or, in the alternative, failing to provide living quarters to its employees within a reasonable distance from the plant site." The district court granted WIC's motion for summary judgment, concluding that WIC did not owe a duty to the decedent. Black appealed to the Supreme Court of Wyoming.

Hill, Justice

Black sets out [this issue] on appeal: Did the trial court err in failing to recognize a duty of care from an employer to innocent third parties who are injured, or in this case, killed, by its employees who are exhausted due to the working conditions imposed by the employer and thus fall asleep at the wheel? WIC responds [by arguing that] Wyoming law does not, and should not, impose a legal duty of reasonable care on Wyoming employers to protect the motoring public from the negligence of their off-duty employees when those off-duty employees drive to and from their Wyoming worksites in their personal vehicles outside the scope of their employment.

"Whether a legal duty exists is a question of a law, and absent a duty, there is no liability." [Citation omitted.] A duty may arise by contract, statute, common law, "or when the relationship of the parties is such that the law imposes an obligation on the defendant to act reasonably for the protection of the plaintiff." [Citation omitted.]

In deciding whether to adopt a particular tort duty, a court's focus must be much broader than just the case at hand.

"The judge's function in a duty determination involves complex considerations of legal and social policies which will directly affect the essential determination of the limits to government protection. Consequently, . . . the imposition and scope of a legal duty is dependent not only on the factor of foreseeability but involves other considerations, including the magnitude of the risk involved in defendant's conduct, the burden of requiring defendant to guard against that risk, and the consequences of placing that burden upon the defendant." [Citations omitted.]

In *Gates v. Richardson*, 719 P.2d 193 (Wyo. 1986), we further detailed the factors to be considered:

(1) the foreseeability of harm to the plaintiff, (2) the closeness of the connection between the defendant's conduct and the injury suffered, (3) the degree of certainty that the plaintiff suffered injury, (4) the moral blame attached to the defendant's conduct, (5) the policy of preventing future harm, (6) the extent of the burden upon the defendant, (7) the consequences to the community and the court system, and (8) the availability, cost and prevalence of insurance for the risk involved. [Citations omitted.]

Before we can proceed to our analysis, we must identify the nature of the duty that Black seeks to impose on WIC. Black insists that she is not seeking . . . to establish a broad duty of care for an employer to control an off-duty employee's conduct. Instead, she argues that an employer has an obligation to ensure that the conditions of employment do not cause an employee to become fatigued and, to the extent that they do, the employer has a duty to take reasonable actions to protect the traveling public from the foreseeable consequences of those employees traveling from their worksite. Essentially, the question of duty that we must determine in this case is whether WIC's actions and/or inactions prior to the accident created a foreseeable risk of harm that the employer had a duty to guard against. In other words: whether or not Ibarra-Viernes's fatigue arose out of, and in the course of, his employment.

We turn to the first *Gates* factor: *The foreseeability of harm to the plaintiff.* We recently stated that this factor is essentially a consideration of proximate cause. Proximate cause [exists when] "the accident or injury [is] the natural and probable consequence of the act of negligence." [Citation omitted.] The ultimate test of proximate cause is foreseeability of injury. In order to qualify as a legal cause, the conduct must be a substantial factor in bringing about the plaintiff's injuries.

The question then is whether or not WIC's conduct was a substantial factor in bringing about the death of the decedent. Or more precisely, a showing of causation necessitates a showing that Ibarra-Viernes's work was a substantial contributing factor to his fatigue. This means that for an "employer to be liable for the actions of a fatigued employee on a theory of negligence, the fatigue must arise out of and in the course of employment . . . [because] . . . [t]o hold otherwise would charge an employer with knowledge of circumstances beyond his control." [Citation of quoted article omitted.]

Black contends that the accident was a foreseeable consequence of WIC's conduct. Specifically, she claims that . . . WIC required its employees to work long hours and make long commutes. She argues that workers who were commuting and working twelve to fourteen hours a day would not have sufficient time in the day to take care of life activities and still get sufficient sleep. Given these conditions, Black contends that without employer supplied alternatives such as bus transport, it was foreseeable that sleep-deprived workers would likely fall asleep and cause injury to other travelers on the roads.

The most obvious factor within the employer's control that could cause fatigue in an employee is the number of hours the employee is required to work. On the day of the accident and those preceding it, Ibarra-Viernes worked his normal shift of ten hours. A ten-hour shift within a twenty-four-hour period is not, on its face, an objectively unreasonable period of work when compared with those situations where an employer was held liable for the damages caused by a fatigued employee driving home from work. Compare *Robertson v. LeMaster*, 301 S.E.2d 563, 568–69 (W. Va. 1983) (employee required to work 32 consecutive hours) and *Faverty v. McDonald's Restaurants of Oregon,*

Inc., 892 P.2d 703, 705 (Ore. App. 1995) (18-year-old employee worked 12½ hours in a 17-hour period). Crucially, in both of those cases, the employers had actual knowledge of their employee's fatigued state. There is no evidence that WIC had notice that Ibarra-Viernes was fatigued on the day of the accident.

Black seeks to expand Ibarra-Viernes's hours of work to include the time of his commute, claiming that WIC "required" him to make the lengthy drive to and from the plant [by not providing alternative transportation such as a bus]. First, Black cites no authority for the proposition that WIC was required to provide its employees with alternatives, such as busing, to commuting. Furthermore, WIC did, in fact, provide an alternative to long-distance commuting for its employees: WIC provided its employees, including Ibarra-Viernes, with a daily $30 subsistence payment to partially offset the cost of taking lodging closer to the worksite. Ibarra-Viernes, however, elected to pocket that money and commute every day from his home in Evanston. That was a voluntary choice made by Ibarra-Viernes.

In making her argument, Black fails to address a significant factor: Ibarra-Viernes's decision to work a second job. After returning to Evanston upon completion of his work day for WIC, Ibarra-Viernes would go to a second job at a restaurant. On the night before the accident, Ibarra-Viernes stated that he returned home about 8:30 pm and then went to work [at] his second job. Ibarra-Viernes said he got to bed around 11:00 pm that night. Certainly, the second job had an effect on Ibarra-Viernes's ability to get rest, if not actual sleep. Ibarra-Viernes admitted that he normally got only about five to six hours of sleep a night. Nevertheless, Black neglects to discuss the consequences of the second job in her brief. Her failure to do so seriously undermines her argument.

Ibarra-Viernes had 13½ hours between shifts during the work week. The burden was on him to manage his own time to ensure that he was capable of performing his job. Ibarra-Viernes elected to expend a significant portion of his time making a lengthy commute and working a second job. These were voluntary decisions made by Ibarra-Viernes for which he is responsible. Under these circumstances, it cannot be said that his employment was the substantial factor in contributing to Ibarra-Viernes's fatigue.

We conclude that decedent's injuries were not the "natural and probable consequence of" any acts of negligence by WIC in the course of Ibarra-Viernes's employment; rather, the decisions and conduct of Ibarra-Viernes were the substantial factor that brought about the injuries. Since the harm to Black's decedent was not a foreseeable consequence of WIC's actions (or inactions), we decline to impose a duty under the circumstances. Given this conclusion, the remaining *Gates* factors are not persuasive, and we decline to discuss them.

Grant of summary judgment to WIC affirmed.

Later Acts, Forces, or Events In some cases, an act, force, or event occurring *after* a defendant's breach of duty may play a significant role in bringing about or worsening the plaintiff's injury. For example, suppose that after Davis negligently starts a fire, a high wind comes up and spreads the fire to Parker's home, or that after Davis negligently runs Parker down with his car, a thief steals Parker's wallet while he lies unconscious. If the later act, force, or event was *foreseeable*, it will not relieve the defendant of liability. So, if high winds are an occurrence that may reasonably be expected from time to time in the locality, Davis is liable for the damage to Parker's home even though his fire might not have spread that far under the wind conditions that existed when he started it. In the second example, Davis is liable not only for Parker's physical injuries but also for the theft of Parker's wallet if the theft was foreseeable, given the time and location of the accident. (The thief, of course, would also be liable for the theft.)

 LO7-9 Explain what an intervening cause is and what effect it produces.

Intervening Causes On the other hand, if the later act, force, or event that contributes to the plaintiff's injury was *unforeseeable*, most courts hold that it is an intervening cause, which absolves the defendant of liability for harms that resulted directly from the intervening cause. For example, Dalton negligently starts a fire that causes injury to several persons. The driver of an ambulance summoned to the scene has been drinking on duty and, as a result, loses control of his ambulance and runs up onto a sidewalk, injuring several pedestrians. Given the nature of the ambulance driver's position, his drinking while on duty is likely to make the ambulance crash an unforeseeable event and thus an intervening cause. Most courts, therefore, would not hold Dalton responsible for the pedestrians' injuries. The ambulance driver, of course, would be liable to those he injured.

An important exception to the liability-absolving effect of an intervening cause deals with unforeseeable later events that produce a foreseeable harm identical to the harm risked by the defendant's breach of duty. Why should the defendant escape liability on the basis that an easily foreseeable consequence of its conduct came about through unforeseeable means? For example, if the owners of a concert hall negligently fail to install the number of emergency exits required by law, the owners will not escape liability to those burned and trampled during a fire just because the fire was caused by an insane concertgoer who set himself ablaze.

As suggested by some of the examples used above, when a defendant's breach of duty is followed by a third party's criminal or other wrongful act, the later act may be either foreseeable or unforeseeable, depending on the facts and circumstances. This state of affairs reflects the prevailing modern approach, which differs sharply from the traditional view that third parties' criminal acts were unforeseeable as a matter of law and thus were always intervening causes serving to limit or eliminate the original defendant's negligence liability. Today, courts do not hesitate to classify a third party's criminal act as foreseeable if the time and place of its commission and other relevant facts point to such a conclusion.

Assume, for instance, that XYZ Inc. owns an apartment complex at which break-ins and prior instances of criminal activity had occurred. XYZ nevertheless fails to adopt the security-related measures that a reasonable apartment complex owner would adopt. As a result, a criminal intruder easily enters the complex. He then physically attacks a tenant. Because the intruder's act is likely to be seen as foreseeable—and thus not an intervening cause—XYZ faces negligence liability to the tenant for the injuries that the intruder directly inflicted on the tenant. (The intruder, of course, would face both criminal and civil liability for battery, but if his financial assets are limited, the injured tenant may find collecting a damages award from him either difficult or impossible.) Note that for purposes of the tenant's negligence claim, XYZ's breach of duty was a substantial factor in bringing about the plaintiff's injuries because the lack of reasonable security measures allowed the intruder to gain easy access to the premises. XYZ's breach thus would be considered the *actual cause* of the tenant's injuries under the previously discussed substantial factor test. It would also be considered the proximate cause under the various tests described earlier.

The *Stahlecker* case, which follows, illustrates the operation of intervening cause principles.

Stahlecker v. Ford Motor Co.   667 N.W.2d 244 (Neb. 2003)

During the early morning hours, Amy Stahlecker was driving a 1997 Ford Explorer equipped with Firestone Wilderness AT radial tires in a remote area of Nebraska. One of the tires failed, rendering the vehicle inoperable. Richard Cook encountered Amy while she was stranded as a result of the tire failure. Cook abducted Amy, sexually assaulted her, and then murdered her.

Susan and Dale Stahlecker, acting on behalf of themselves and as personal representatives of their daughter's estate, brought a wrongful death action in a Nebraska court against Cook, the Ford Motor Co. (manufacturer of the Explorer), and Bridgestone/Firestone Inc. (manufacturer of the tire that failed). The Stahleckers sought to make out negligence claims against Ford and Firestone. The plaintiffs alleged that Ford and Firestone knew of prior problems with the model of tire that was on the Explorer driven by Amy; knew those problems posed a greater-than-normal danger of tire failure; continued using a problematic model of Firestone tire on Explorers despite knowledge that tire failure would create a special risk of rollover and vehicle inoperability; failed to warn consumers of these dangers; and continued to advertise their tires and vehicles as suitable for uses of the sort Amy made immediately prior to the tire failure, even though they knew that drivers could become stranded in the event of tire failure. There was no allegation that the tire failure directly caused Amy to sustain physical harm prior to the obvious harm inflicted by Cook.

A state district court sustained demurrers filed by Ford and Firestone and dismissed the case as to those parties. The court concluded that the Stahleckers had not stated a valid cause of action against Ford and Firestone because Cook's criminal acts constituted an intervening cause that would relieve Ford and Firestone of any liability they might otherwise have had. The Stahleckers successfully petitioned to bypass the Nebraska Court of Appeals and pursue their appeal in the Supreme Court of Nebraska.

Stephan, Judge

In order to withstand a demurrer, a plaintiff must plead . . . "a narrative of events, acts, and things done or omitted which show a legal liability of the defendant to the plaintiff." [Citation omitted.] In determining whether a cause of action has been stated, a petition is to be construed liberally.

In order to prevail in a negligence action, a plaintiff must establish the defendant's duty to protect the plaintiff from injury, a failure to discharge that duty, and damages proximately caused by the failure to discharge that duty. The concept of "foreseeability" is a component of both duty and proximate cause, although its meaning is somewhat different in each context. We have noted this distinction in recent cases:

Foreseeability as a determinant of a [defendant's] duty of care . . . is to be distinguished from foreseeability as a determinant of whether a breach of duty is a proximate cause of an ultimate injury. Foreseeability as it impacts duty determinations refers to the knowledge of the risk of injury to be apprehended. The risk reasonably to be perceived defines the duty to be obeyed; it is the risk reasonably within the range of apprehension, of injury to another person, that is taken into account in determining the existence of the duty to exercise care. . . . Foreseeability that affects proximate cause, on the other hand, relates to the question of whether the specific act or omission of the defendant was such that the ultimate injury to the plaintiff reasonably flowed from defendant's breach of duty. . . . Foreseeability in the proximate cause context relates to remoteness rather than the existence of a duty.

[Citations omitted.]

[B]y alleging that Ford and Firestone failed to exercise reasonable care in designing and manufacturing their tires, and failed to warn users of potential tire defects, the Stahleckers have alleged the existence of a legal duty and a breach thereof by both Ford and Firestone. The remaining issue is whether the breach of this duty was the proximate cause of Amy's harm.

The proximate cause of an injury is "that cause which, in a natural and continuous sequence, without any efficient, intervening cause, produces the injury, and without which the injury would not have occurred." [Citation omitted.] Stated another way, a plaintiff must meet [these] basic requirements in establishing [causation]: (1) [the actual cause requirement] that without the negligent action, the injury would not have occurred, commonly known as the "but-for" rule; [and] (2) [the proximate cause requirement] that the injury was a natural and probable result of the negligence. [In addition, there cannot have been] an efficient intervening cause.

As to the first requirement, a defendant's conduct is the cause of the event if "the event would not have occurred but for that conduct; conversely, the defendant's conduct is not a cause of the event if the event would have occurred without it." [Citation omitted.] The petition alleges that Cook "found Amy alone and stranded as a direct result of the failure of the Firestone Wilderness AT Radial Tire and proceeded to abduct, terrorize, rape and murder Amy." Firestone concedes that under the factual allegations of the Stahleckers' petition—that "but for" the failure of its tire—Amy would not have been at the place where she was assaulted and murdered.

The [tests governing] proximate cause [and intervening cause] are somewhat interrelated. Was the criminal assault and murder the "natural and probable" result of the failure to warn of potential tire failure, or did the criminal acts constitute an effective intervening cause that would preclude any causal link between the failure to warn and the injuries and wrongful death for which damages are claimed in this action? An efficient intervening cause is a new, independent force intervening between the defendant's negligent act and the plaintiff's injury. This force may be the conduct of a third person who had full control of the situation, whose conduct the defendant could not anticipate or contemplate, and whose conduct resulted directly in the plaintiff's injury. An efficient intervening cause must break the causal connection between the original wrong and the injury.

In *Shelton v. Board of Regents*, 320 N.W.2d 748 (Neb. 1982), we considered whether criminal conduct constituted an intervening cause. *Shelton* involved wrongful death claims brought on behalf of persons who were poisoned by a former employee of the Eugene C. Eppley Institute for Research in Cancer and Allied Diseases (the Institute). In their actions against the Institute . . . , the plaintiffs alleged that [even though] the former employee had a prior criminal conviction involving an attempted homicide, the Institute hired him as a research technologist and gave him access to the poisonous substance which he subsequently used to commit the murders. The plaintiffs alleged that the Institute was negligent in hiring the employee, in allowing him to have access to the poisonous substance, and in failing to monitor its inventory of the substance. The plaintiffs further alleged that the Institute's negligence was the proximate cause of the injuries and deaths of the victims. The district court sustained a demurrer filed by the Institute and dismissed the actions. This court affirmed, holding . . . that the criminal acts of stealing the drug and administering it to the victims "were of such nature as to constitute an efficient intervening cause which destroys any claim that the alleged negligence of the [Institute] was the proximate cause of the appellants' injuries and damage." In reaching this conclusion, we relied upon *Restatement (Second) of Torts* § 448 (1965), which states the following rule:

The act of a third person in committing an intentional tort or crime is a superseding cause of harm to another resulting therefrom, although the actor's negligent conduct created a situation which afforded an opportunity to the third person to commit such a tort or crime, unless the actor at the time of his negligent conduct realized or should have realized the likelihood that such a situation might be created, and that a third person might avail himself of the opportunity to commit such a tort or crime.

We held [in *Shelton*] that the employee's criminal acts were the cause of the injuries for which damages were claimed and that "nothing which the [plaintiffs] claim the . . . Institute failed to do was in any manner related to those acts, nor could they have been reasonably contemplated by the . . . Institute."

We have, however, determined in certain premises liability cases and in cases involving negligent custodial entrustment that the criminal act of a third person does not constitute an efficient intervening cause. For example, in [one such case], a patron of a bar was seriously injured by another patron in the parking lot after the two were instructed by the bartender to take their argument "outside." The injured patron sued the owner of the bar,

alleging that the owner negligently failed to contact law enforcement, maintain proper security on the premises, and properly train his personnel. [R]evers[ing] a judgment on a jury verdict in favor of the owner, . . . [w]e reasoned that

because the harm resulting from a fight is precisely the harm against which [the owner] is alleged to have had a duty to protect [the patron], the "intervention" of [the other patron] cannot be said to be an independent act that would break the causal connection between [the owner's] negligence and [the patron's] injuries.

[Citation omitted.]

We employed similar reasoning in [two other cases that] involved negligent placement of juvenile wards of the state in foster homes without disclosure of their known histories of violent acts. In each of those cases, we held that criminal acts of foster children perpetrated upon members of the foster parents' households could not be asserted as intervening causes to defeat liability for the negligent placement. Similarly, we recently held that a psychiatric patient's criminal assault upon a nurse was not an intervening cause as to the negligence of a state agency which breached its duty to disclose the violent propensities of the patient at the time of his admission to the hospital where the assault occurred. These decisions were based upon the principle . . . that "once it is shown that a defendant had a duty to anticipate [a] criminal act and guard against it, the criminal act cannot supersede the defendant's liability." [Citation omitted.]

This principle requires that we determine whether the duty owed to Amy by Ford and Firestone, as manufacturers and sellers of the allegedly defective tires, included a duty to anticipate and guard against criminal acts perpetrated against the users of such tires. [As illustrated by the previously discussed cases dealing with juvenile wards and psychiatric patients,] we have recognized a duty to anticipate and protect another against criminal acts where the party charged with the duty has some right of control over the perpetrator of such acts or the physical premises upon which the crime occurs. [We have] recognized a duty on the part of the owner of business premises to protect invitees from criminal assault where there had been documented criminal activity in the immediate vicinity of the premises. [In addition, we have] held that a university had a duty to protect a student from physical hazing conducted in a fraternity house where similar incidents were known to have occurred previously[, and] that a university "owes a landowner-invitee duty to its students to take reasonable steps to protect against foreseeable acts of violence on its campus and the harm that naturally flows therefrom." [Citation omitted.] However, we have adopted *Restatement (Second) of Torts* § 315 (1965), which provides:

There is no duty so to control the conduct of a third person as to prevent him from causing physical harm to another unless . . . a special relation exists between the actor and the third person which imposes a duty upon the actor to control the third person's conduct, or . . . a special relation exists between the actor and the other which gives to the other a right to protection.

We have found no authority recognizing a duty on the part of the manufacturer of a product to protect a consumer from criminal activity at the scene of a product failure where no physical harm is caused by the product itself.

The Stahleckers argue that a duty to anticipate criminal acts associated with product failure arises from their allegations that Ford and Firestone knew or should have known of "the potential for similar dangerous situations arising as a result of a breakdown of a Ford Explorer and/or its tires." They also allege that Ford and Firestone had or should have had "knowledge, to include statistical information, regarding the likelihood of criminal conduct and/or sexual assault against auto and tire industry consumers as a result of unexpected auto and/or tire failures in general." Assuming the truth of these allegations, the most that can be inferred is that Ford and Firestone had general knowledge that criminal assaults can occur at the scene of a vehicular product failure. However, it is generally known that violent crime can and does occur in a variety of settings, including the relative safety of a victim's home. The facts alleged do not present the type of knowledge concerning a specific individual's criminal propensity, or right of control over premises known to have been the scene of prior criminal activity, upon which we have recognized a tort duty to protect another from criminal acts.

The Stahleckers have not alleged, and could not allege, any special relationship between Ford and Firestone and the criminal actor (Cook) or the victim of his crime (Amy) that would extend their duty, as manufacturers and sellers of products, to protect a consumer from harm caused by a criminal act perpetrated at the scene of a product failure. In the absence of such a duty, [we must] conclude as a matter of law that the criminal assault constituted an efficient intervening cause which precludes a determination that negligence on the part of Ford and Firestone was the proximate cause of the harm [to Amy].

[Therefore,] the district court did not err in sustaining the demurrers of Ford and Firestone . . . and in dismissing the action as to them.

District court's decision affirmed.

Special Rules Whatever test for proximate cause a court adopts, most courts agree on certain basic causation rules. In case of a conflict, these rules supersede the proximate cause and intervening cause rules stated earlier. One such rule is that persons who are negligent "take their victims as they find them." This means that a negligent defendant is liable for the full extent of her victim's injuries if those injuries are aggravated by some preexisting physical susceptibility of the victim—even though this susceptibility could not have been foreseen. Similarly, negligent defendants normally are liable for diseases contracted by their victims while in a weakened state caused by their injuries. Negligent defendants typically are jointly liable—along with medical personnel—for negligent medical care that their victims receive for their injuries.

Res Ipsa Loquitur
In some cases, negligence may be difficult to prove because the defendant has superior knowledge of the circumstances surrounding the plaintiff's injury. It may not be in the defendant's best interests to disclose those circumstances if they point to liability on his part. The classic example is an 1863 case, *Byrne v. Boadle*.

The plaintiff was a pedestrian who had been hit on the head by a barrel of flour that fell from a warehouse owned by the defendant. The plaintiff had no way of knowing what caused the barrel to fall; he merely knew he had been injured. The only people likely to have known the relevant facts were the owners of the warehouse and their employees, but they most likely were the ones responsible for the accident. After observing that "[a] barrel could not roll out of a warehouse without some negligence," the court required the defendant owner to show that he was not at fault.

Byrne v. Boadle eventually led to the doctrine of *res ipsa loquitur* ("the thing speaks for itself"). *Res ipsa* applies when (1) the defendant has exclusive control of the instrumentality of harm (and therefore probable knowledge of, and responsibility for, the cause of the harm); (2) the harm that occurred would not ordinarily occur in the absence of negligence; and (3) the plaintiff was in no way responsible for his own injury. Most courts hold that when these three elements are satisfied, a presumption of breach of duty and causation arises. The defendant then runs a significant risk of losing the case if he does not produce evidence to rebut this presumption.

CYBERLAW IN ACTION

Gentry v. eBay, Inc., 99 Cal. App. 4th 816 (2002), was a case brought by buyers of sports memorabilia that bore autographs later determined not to be genuine. The plaintiffs contended that eBay, an online marketplace on which the items were sold, should bear legal responsibility on various legal grounds, including negligence. According to the plaintiffs, eBay had been negligent (1) by maintaining an online forum that allowed any user, regardless of his or her purchase history, to give positive or negative feedback regarding dealers and (2) by endorsing certain dealers on the basis of this feedback and the dealers' sales volume. The plaintiffs contended that these actions by eBay created a false sense of confidence in the collectibles' authenticity because most, if not all, of the positive feedback about a dealer would be generated either by that dealer or by another cooperating dealer.

A California appellate court held in *Gentry* that § 230 of the federal Communications Decency Act provided eBay a meritorious defense against the plaintiffs' negligence claim. Section 230 states that "[n]o provider or user of an interactive computer service shall be treated as the publisher or speaker of any information provided by another information content provider." The court reasoned that eBay was a "provider . . . of an interactive computer service" and that the plaintiffs' negligence claim amounted, in substance, to an attempt to have eBay held liable for the effects of statements made by "another information content provider" or providers (i.e., those who, in the online forum, posted arguably misleading "feedback"). The court therefore regarded the plaintiffs' negligence claim as an effort to have eBay treated as the "publisher" of information provided by another party. Section 230, the court held, prohibited such treatment of eBay.

Negligence Defenses

The common law traditionally recognized two **defenses** to negligence: *contributory negligence* and *assumption of risk*. In many states, however, these traditional defenses have been superseded by new defenses called *comparative negligence* and *comparative fault*.

 LO7-10 Explain the difference between traditional contributory negligence and the comparative negligence doctrine now followed by almost all states.

Contributory Negligence Contributory negligence is the plaintiff's failure to exercise reasonable care for her own safety. In the very limited number of states where it still applies, contributory negligence is a complete defense for the defendant if it was a substantial factor in producing the plaintiff's injury. So, if Preston steps into the path of Doyle's speeding car without first checking to see whether any cars are coming, Preston would be denied any recovery against Doyle, in view of the clear causal relationship between Preston's injury and his failure to exercise reasonable care for his own safety.

 LO7-11 Explain the difference in operation between pure comparative negligence and mixed comparative negligence.

Comparative Negligence Traditionally, even a plaintiff's fairly minor failure to exercise reasonable care for his own safety—only a slight departure from the standard of reasonable self-protectiveness—gave the defendant a complete contributory negligence defense. This rule, which

probably stemmed from the 19th-century desire to protect railroads and infant manufacturing interests from negligence liability, came under increasing attack in the 20th century. The main reasons were the traditional rule's harsh impact on many plaintiffs. The rule frequently prevented slightly negligent plaintiffs from recovering any compensation for their losses, even though the defendants may have been much more at fault.

In response to such complaints, almost all states have adopted comparative negligence systems either by statute or by judicial decision. The details of these systems vary, but the principle underlying them is essentially the same: Courts seek to determine the relative negligence of the parties and award damages in proportion to the degrees of negligence determined. The formula is:

$$\text{Plaintiff's recovery} = \text{Defendant's percentage share of the negligence causing the injury} \times \text{Plaintiff's proven damages}$$

For example, assume that Dunne negligently injures Porter and that Porter suffers $100,000 in damages. A jury determines that Dunne was 80 percent at fault and Porter 20 percent at fault. Under comparative negligence, Porter would recover $80,000 from Dunne. What if Dunne's share of the negligence is determined to be 40 percent and Porter's 60 percent? Here, the results vary depending on whether the state in question has adopted a *pure* or a *mixed* comparative negligence system. Under a pure system, courts apply the preceding formula regardless of the plaintiff's and the defendant's percentage shares of the negligence. Porter therefore would recover

$40,000 in a pure comparative negligence state. Under a mixed system, the formula operates only when the defendant's share of the negligence is greater than (or, in some states, greater than or equal to) 50 percent. If the plaintiff's share of the negligence exceeds 50 percent, mixed systems provide that the defendant has a complete defense against liability. In such states, therefore, Porter would lose the case.

Currie v. Chevron USA, Inc., which appears earlier in the chapter, illustrates the operation of comparative negligence principles. In that wrongful death case arising out of a Chevron clerk's negligence in authorizing a gas pump, the court reduced the amount of damages awarded to the plaintiff because the plaintiff's decedent had been partially at fault (presumably through participating in a fight that, when it escalated, resulted in her death). The plaintiff still won a substantial damages award, but the amount was reduced in accordance with the percentage of fault attributed to her decedent.

Assumption of Risk Assumption of risk is the plaintiff's *voluntary* consent to a *known* danger. Voluntariness means that the plaintiff accepted the risk of her own free will; knowledge means that the plaintiff was aware of the nature and extent of the risk. Often, the plaintiff's knowledge and voluntariness are inferred from the facts. This type of assumption of risk is sometimes called implied assumption of risk. For example, Pilson voluntarily goes for a ride in Dudley's car, even though Dudley has told Pilson that her car's brakes frequently fail. Pilson probably has assumed the risk of injury from the car's defective brakes. (For a court decision on whether implied assumption of risk applies, see *Coomer v. Kansas City Royals Baseball Corp.*, a text case included in Chapter 1.)

A plaintiff can also expressly assume the risk of injury by entering into a contract that purports to relieve the defendant of a duty of care he would otherwise owe to the plaintiff. Such contract provisions are called *exculpatory clauses*. Chapter 15 discusses exculpatory clauses and the limitations that courts have imposed on their enforceability. The most important such limitations are that the plaintiff have knowledge of the exculpatory clause (which often boils down to a question of its conspicuousness) and that the plaintiff must accept it voluntarily (which does not happen when the defendant has greatly superior bargaining power).

What happens to assumption of risk in comparative negligence states? Some of these states maintain assumption of risk as a separate and complete defense. Most other states now incorporate implied assumption of risk within the state's comparative negligence scheme. In such states,

comparative negligence basically becomes **comparative fault**. Although the terms *comparative negligence* and *comparative fault* often are used interchangeably, technically the former involves only negligence and the latter involves all kinds of fault. In a comparative fault state, therefore, the fact-finder determines the plaintiff's and the defendant's relative shares of the fault—including assumption of risk—that caused the plaintiff's injury.

Strict Liability

 Identify circumstances in which strict liability principles, rather than those of negligence, control a case.

Strict liability is liability without fault or, perhaps more precisely, irrespective of fault. This means that in strict liability cases, the defendant is liable even though he did not intend to cause the harm and did not bring it about through recklessness or negligence.

The imposition of strict liability is a social policy decision that the risk associated with an activity should be borne by those who pursue it, rather than by innocent persons who are exposed to that risk. Such liability is premised on the defendant's voluntary decision to engage in a particularly risky activity. When the defendant is a corporation that has engaged in such an activity, the assumption is that the firm can pass the costs of liability on to consumers in the form of higher prices for goods or services. Through strict liability, therefore, the economic costs created by certain harms are "socialized" by being transferred from the victims to defendants to society at large.

Strict liability, however, does not apply to the vast majority of activities. It therefore becomes important to consider which activities do trigger the liability-without-fault approach. The owners of trespassing livestock and the keepers of naturally dangerous wild animals were among the first classes of defendants on whom the courts imposed strict liability. Today, the two most important activities subject to judicially imposed strict liability are abnormally dangerous (or ultrahazardous) activities and the manufacture or sale of defective and unreasonably dangerous products. We discuss the latter in Chapter 20 and the former immediately below.

Abnormally Dangerous Activities Abnormally dangerous (or ultrahazardous) activities are those necessarily involving a risk of harm that cannot be eliminated by the exercise of reasonable care. Among the activities

treated as abnormally dangerous are blasting, crop dusting, stunt flying, and, in one case, the transportation of large quantities of gasoline by truck. (Most courts, however, would be unlikely to label the latter as abnormally dangerous.) Traditionally, contributory negligence has not been a defense in ultrahazardous activity cases, but assumption of risk has been a defense. In the *Toms* case, which follows, the court considers the factors to be taken into account in deciding whether strict liability is appropriate.

Toms v. Calvary Assembly of God, Inc.   132 A.3d 866 (Md. Ct. App. 2016)

Andrew Toms operated a dairy farm in Maryland. He owned a herd of approximately 90 dairy cows. A party other than Toms owned a 40-acre tract of land that was adjacent to Toms's farm. With permission from the possessor of that tract of land, Calvary Assembly of God Inc. (a church) hosted a fireworks display on that property as part of a youth crusade. Calvary retained a professional fireworks company to handle the fireworks display. That company applied for and received the permit required by a Maryland statute. The fireworks company volunteered to have a 300-foot firing radius around the specific site at which the fireworks would be fired. The 300-foot radius exceeded the 250-foot minimum radius that state law required for the amount of fireworks to be discharged.

The fireworks display was open to the public. A deputy fire marshal was present to supervise the event. Approximately 250 shells were discharged over a 15-minute period, without any misfires. At the time of the event, Toms's cattle were inside the barn that was located on his property. The barn was located more than 300 feet—perhaps roughly 500 feet—from the firing location. Toms arrived at the barn a few minutes after the discharging of fireworks began. According to Toms, the explosions startled his dairy cows and caused them to stampede inside the barn. In the lawsuit referred to below, Toms contended that the stampede resulted in the deaths of four cows. In addition to the loss of the four cows, Toms sustained property damage to fences and gates, disposal costs, and lost milk revenue.

Toms sent a demand letter to Calvary outlining the damages he claimed, but Calvary and the fireworks company denied liability. Toms then filed a lawsuit in which he sought to have Calvary and the fireworks company held liable on two alternative theories: negligence and strict liability. After a bench trial, a Maryland district court held that the defendants were not negligent and that strict liability was inapplicable. Toms appealed to a Maryland circuit court, which affirmed. The Maryland Court of Appeals then granted Toms's request that it decide whether the lower courts ruled correctly on the strict liability question.

Greene, Judge

In this case, we address whether noise emanating from the discharge of a fireworks display constitutes an abnormally dangerous activity, which would warrant the imposition of strict liability.

Whether an activity constitutes an abnormally dangerous activity is a question of law. Maryland [recognizes] the doctrine of strict liability, which does not require a finding of fault in order to impose liability on a party. See *Yommer v. McKenzie*, 257 A.2d 138 (Md. 1969). The modern formulation of the strict liability doctrine is found in the *Restatement (Second) of Torts* §§ 519–520 (1977). This court adopted that formulation in *Yommer*, while the *Restatement (Second)* was still in its tentative draft. *Restatement (Second)* § 519 defines strict liability [this way]:

One who carries on an abnormally dangerous activity is subject to liability for harm to the person, land or chattels of another resulting from the activity, although he has exercised the utmost care to prevent the harm. . . . This strict liability is limited to the kind of harm, the possibility of which makes the activity abnormally dangerous.

To determine whether an activity is abnormally dangerous, a court uses six factors. These factors are:

a. existence of a high degree of risk of some harm to the person, land or chattels of others;
b. likelihood that the harm that results from it will be great;
c. inability to eliminate the risk by the exercise of reasonable care;
d. extent to which the activity is not a matter of common usage;
e. inappropriateness of the activity to the place where it is carried on; and
f. extent to which its value to the community is outweighed by its dangerous attributes.

Restatement (Second) § 520. As the *Restatement (Second)* reminds us:

Because of the interplay of these various factors, it is not possible to reduce abnormally dangerous activities to any definition. The essential question is whether the risk created is so unusual, either because of its magnitude or because of the circumstances surrounding it, as to justify the imposition of strict liability for the harm that results from it, even though it is carried on with all reasonable care.

Restatement (Second) § 520, comment f. The Reporter's Note for this section identifies typical abnormally dangerous activities, such as the storage of large quantities of water or explosives in dangerous locations, and conducting blasting operations in the middle of a city.

[W]e weigh each *Restatement* factor independently. [I]t is not necessary to have all six factors weigh in favor of a particular party. More emphasis is placed on the fifth factor: the appropriateness of the activity in relation to its location. In *Yommer*, the owners of a gasoline station were held strictly liable for damages resulting from gasoline contamination of the well water of an adjacent residential property. There, we applied the *Restatement* factors, and found the fifth factor to be the most persuasive factor:

> No one would deny that gasoline stations as a rule do not present any particular danger to the community. However, when the operation of such activity involves the placing of a large tank adjacent to a well from which a family must draw its water for drinking, bathing and laundry, at least that aspect of the activity is inappropriate to the locale, even when equated to the value of the activity.

Yommer, 257 A.2d at 139. "We accept the test of appropriateness as the proper one: that the unusual, the excessive, the extravagant, the bizarre are likely to be non-natural uses which lead to strict liability." *Id.*

Though the doctrine of strict liability has evolved . . . , the policy concerns in favor of limiting its application remain. [For example, in] *Gallagher v. H.V. Pierhomes, LLC*, 957 A.2d 628 (Md. Ct. Spec. App. 2008), the Court of Special Appeals held that pile-driving was not an abnormally dangerous activity. There, pile-driving operations at the Inner Harbor in Baltimore City caused minor damage in a 200-year-old residence located 325 feet away from the construction site. The intermediate appellate court found that the defendants had acted appropriately in obtaining the proper permits, conducting geotechnical studies, and carefully monitoring the vibrations produced by the pile driving operations. The court concluded that the risk of harm produced by pile driving operations "is not a high degree of risk which requires the application of strict liability" because that risk can be eliminated "through the exercise of ordinary care."

Whether fireworks discharge constitutes an abnormally dangerous activity is a case of first impression in Maryland. Some jurisdictions, however, have addressed the issue of whether fireworks are abnormally dangerous. Although fireworks liability cases often share similar facts, jurisdictions disagree on whether discharging fireworks is an abnormally dangerous activity.

The highest appellate court in Washington, for instance, held pyrotechnicians strictly liable when a shell exploded improperly and injured spectators at a public fireworks show. *Klein v. Pyrodyne Corp.*, 810 P.2d 917 (Wash. 1991). [The court] stated that *Restatement* factors (a) through (d) weighed in favor of imposing strict liability, because discharging fireworks creates a "high risk of serious bodily injury or property damage" due to the possibility of a malfunction or similar issue. *Id.* at 922. [The court added that] "[t]he dangerousness . . . is evidenced by the elaborate scheme of administrative regulations with which pyrotechnicians must comply[,]" including licensing and insurance requirements. *Id.* at 920. Under factor (d), [the court] further determined that discharging fireworks was not a matter of common usage, because the licensing scheme restricts the general public from engaging in that activity. In addition to the high risk discharging fireworks creates, the court determined that public policy and fairness warranted strict liability. Otherwise, the injured spectators would have been subject to the "problem of proof" because "all evidence was destroyed as to what caused the misfire of the shell that injured the [plaintiffs]." *Id.* at 921–22.

Other jurisdictions, however, have come to the opposite conclusion, and have held that the level of risk involved with a fireworks discharge does not warrant strict liability. In *Haddon v. Lotito*, 161 A.2d 160 (Pa. 1960), Pennsylvania's highest appellate court applied the ultrahazardous activity test, and determined that strict liability . . . did not apply in a case involving spectator injuries at a public fireworks display. Critically, that court distinguished lawful from unlawful fireworks displays:

> [A] public fireworks display, handled by a competent operator in a reasonably safe area and properly supervised (and there is no proof to the contrary herein), is not so dangerous an activity. . . . Where one discharges fireworks illegally or in such a manner as to amount to a nuisance and causes injury to another, some jurisdictions have held that liability follows without more. But the production of a public fireworks display, under the circumstances presented herein, is neither illegal nor a nuisance and, consequently, liability, if existing, must be predicated upon proof of negligence.

Id. at 162. Other courts have ruled similarly.

[We now consider] whether strict liability for an abnormally dangerous activity should be imposed on a . . . fireworks display [that was otherwise lawful under Maryland law]. [A Maryland statute] defines fireworks as "combustible, implosive or explosive compositions, substances, combinations of substances, or articles that are prepared to produce a visible or audible effect by combustion, explosion, implosion, deflagration, or detonation." We disagree with Toms that our analysis should be so narrow as to focus solely on the audible component—the noise produced—by a fireworks display. [T]he noise itself is a by-product of the activity of discharging fireworks. By definition, under [the relevant statute], fireworks "are prepared to produce a visible or audible effect. . . ." Therefore, when applying the multi-factor test from § 520 of the *Restatement (Second)*, we will consider all the characteristics and the nature of the risks associated with discharging fireworks. After all, we are also mindful that "[o]ne who carries on an abnormally dangerous activity is not under strict liability for every possible harm that may result from carrying it on." *Restatement (Second)* § 519, comment e. We [now] apply the *Restatement* factors to the instant case:

(a) existence of a high degree of risk of some harm to the person, land, or chattels of others. Special events requiring the use of large, professional "display fireworks" are heavily regulated in Maryland pursuant to [a statutory scheme that requires a detailed application for a permit, supervision by a qualified person, and both official inspection and approval of the site for the display. All of those steps took place here.] We hold that a lawful fireworks display does not pose a high degree of risk, because the statutory scheme in place is designed to significantly reduce the risks associated with fireworks, namely mishandling, misfires, and malfunctions. Furthermore, the required firing radius of 250 feet was voluntarily extended by [the professional fireworks company] to 300 feet. Critically, in enacting the [statutory scheme, the legislature] did not regulate the audible effects of display fireworks, which indicates that any risk associated with the decibel level of a fireworks discharge is minimal or non-existent.

Lawful fireworks displays do not pose a significant risk because [the Maryland Code provides that] "[a] person who possesses or discharges fireworks in violation" of the permitting process "is guilty of a misdemeanor and on conviction is subject to a fine not exceeding $250 for each offense." To impose a relatively light penalty for an unlawful fireworks display is telling. If an unlawful fireworks display is only a misdemeanor offense with no possibility of incarceration, why then should strict liability be imposed for risks associated with a lawful fireworks display?

(b) likelihood that the harm that results from it will be great. This factor also weighs in favor of not imposing strict liability, because the purpose of a 300-foot perimeter surrounding the firing location is to mitigate the likelihood of harm. The statutory scheme regulating the use of fireworks is specifically designed to reduce risk. Because Toms's dairy barn, and therefore his cows, were not located within the fallout zone, the likelihood of harm to the public and property was significantly reduced. The 300-foot firing radius was effective because no shells fired that night malfunctioned, and no debris littered Toms's property.

(c) inability to eliminate the risk by the exercise of reasonable care. We disagree with Toms that reasonable care cannot reduce the risk of harm to livestock to acceptable levels. [In the statutory scheme, the legislature] took care to implement

sufficient precautions so as to ensure that lawful fireworks displays can be a safe and enjoyable activity. This is evidenced by the active role the State Fire Marshal and authorities having jurisdiction have over the permitting process. Health and safety, therefore, are of paramount concern, and we are satisfied that the regulations sufficiently protect the public and property. Only qualified professional fireworks companies and their agents—authorized shooters—may apply for a permit. The requirements of mandatory insurance coverage, a physical site inspection, and event supervision is [sic] evidence of reasonable care that reduces the risk of harm. The site inspection and prior approval of an authority having jurisdiction ensures that the firing location is appropriate and that injury is unlikely. Importantly, additional measures are required if other properties are located within the fallout zone, including notice and permission from that property owner for their property to be used in the fallout zone.

The 300-foot firing radius is sufficient. Furthermore, notice to Toms was not necessary, because his dairy barn was located beyond the firing radius. In our view, the *Restatement* does not require the elimination of all risk, and because the risks inherent with a fireworks discharge can be reduced to acceptable levels, this factor does not support a conclusion of an abnormally dangerous activity.

(d) extent to which the activity is not a matter of common usage. [W]e define "common usage," as it pertains to this case, broadly to include not only the professionals who discharge fireworks, but also the spectators who partake in the fireworks display. Almost by definition, lawful fireworks displays involve two parties: the shooter and the audience. We conclude that lawful fireworks displays are a matter of common usage.

(e) inappropriateness of the activity to the place where it is carried on. When this court adopted the *Restatement (Second)*'s multi-factor test for abnormally dangerous activities, this particular factor was identified as being the most crucial. See *Yommer*, *supra*. Implicit in the granting of a permit to discharge fireworks is the lawfulness of that proposed fireworks display. At trial, two deputy fire marshals testified about the procedures entailed with the permitting process, that a physical site inspection showed that the proposed firing location was appropriate, that the event was supervised and properly executed, and that the defendants complied with all applicable laws. Furthermore, a deputy fire marshal testified that although the state required a perimeter of 250 feet from the firing location, the defendants voluntarily extended it to 300 feet. In sum, we agree that a lawful fireworks display does not fall within the context of "the unusual, the excessive, the extravagant, the bizarre . . . non-natural uses which lead to strict liability." *Yommer*, *supra*.

(f) extent to which its value to the community is outweighed by its dangerous attributes. Here, a church-sponsored fireworks display celebrated a youth crusade, and the event was open to the public. As a symbol of celebration, fireworks play an important role in our society, and are often met with much fanfare. The statutory scheme regulating its use minimizes the risk of accidents, thus reinforcing the popularity of these displays. [We] conclude that the social desirability of fireworks appears to outweigh their dangerous attributes.

Policy considerations. We are mindful that the doctrine of strict liability for abnormally dangerous activities is narrowly applied in order to avoid imposing "grievous burdens" on landowners and occupiers of land. [Citation omitted.] The use of fireworks, especially in public fireworks displays, is heavily regulated [by the state]. [According to the statute,] a permit to discharge fireworks cannot be obtained unless the State Fire Marshal determines that proposed fireworks display will "not

endanger health or safety or damage property. . . ." In light of this policy, the defendants cannot be held strictly liable, because they lawfully complied with the conditions of the permit as well as applicable laws.

At trial, Toms did not present any evidence concerning what noise levels should be appropriate for public fireworks display. Sufficient evidence was not presented to the trier of fact that a lawful fireworks display was abnormally dangerous to livestock. Lawful fireworks displays are not an abnormally dangerous activity, because the statutory scheme regulating the use of fireworks significantly reduces the risk of harm associated with the discharge of fireworks.

Circuit Court judgment affirmed.

Statutory Strict Liability Strict liability principles are also embodied in modern legislation. The most important examples are the workers' compensation acts passed by most states early in this century. Chapter 51 contains more detailed discussion of such statutes, which allow employees to recover statutorily limited amounts from their employers without any need to show fault on the employer's part and without any consideration of contributory fault on the employee's part. Employers participate in a compulsory liability insurance system and are expected to pass the costs of the system on to consumers, who then become the ultimate bearers of the human costs of industrial production. Other examples of statutory strict liability vary from state to state.

Tort Reform

The risk-spreading strategy of tort law has not been trouble-free. During roughly the past three decades, there has been considerable talk about a supposed crisis in the liability insurance system. From time to time over that period, the insurance system has been marked by refusals of coverage, reductions in coverage, and escalating premiums when coverage remains available. To some, this intermittent problem is largely the fault of the insurance industry. Among other things, such observers argue that insurers have manufactured the supposed crisis to obtain unjustified premium increases and to divert attention from insurer mismanagement of invested premium income.

To other observers, however, the reason for the supposed crisis is an explosion in tort liability. Examples cited

include the tendency toward somewhat greater imposition of strict liability, increases in the frequency and size of punitive damage awards, and similar increases in awards for noneconomic harms such as pain and suffering. The greater costs imposed on defendants, some observers say, operate to increase the price and diminish the availability of liability insurance. In some cases, therefore, businesses may be required to self-insure or go without insurance coverage. In others, they may be able to obtain insurance—but only at a price that cannot be completely passed on to consumers. Where the costs can be fully passed on, the argument continues, they depress the economy by diminishing consumers' purchasing power or adding to inflation, or both. In addition, the argument concludes, the liability explosion impedes the development of new products and technologies that might result in huge awards for injured plaintiffs.

These beliefs have fueled a movement for tort reform. By roughly 2000, many states had enacted some form of tort reform legislation. Such legislation typically follows one or both of two strategies: (1) limiting defendants' tort *liability* (plaintiffs' ability to obtain a judgment) and (2) limiting the *damages* plaintiffs can recover once they get a judgment.

The battle for tort reform has not ended, however. Proponents continue to seek additional reform measures. Tort reform opponents who lost the fight in the legislature have sometimes continued it in the courts. They have done so primarily by challenging tort reform measures on state constitutional grounds. Such challenges have succeeded in some states but have been rebuffed in others.

In recent years, there have been calls in some quarters for Congress to enact caps on dollar amounts of damages for pain and suffering and similar noneconomic harm in certain negligence cases, most notably those involving alleged medical malpractice. Critics argue that damage caps' major effect is a perverse one: limiting the rights of those who have experienced the worst and most long-lasting or debilitating injuries (and thus may be among the plaintiffs most deserving of recovery). Only those plaintiffs with quite severe injuries, the argument continues, have cases in which the potential damages would be likely to approach the ceiling set in the damage cap. As of the time this book went to press, no such federal measures had been enacted.

Problems and Problem Cases:

1. During the evening hours, Hen Horn, a truck driver employed by Ralphs Grocery Co. (Ralphs), was driving in California on Interstate 10 as part of his job duties. Horn stopped his tractor-trailer rig on a large dirt shoulder alongside the highway in order to eat a snack he had brought with him. He regularly stopped for a snack in that spot when driving in the vicinity. The dirt shoulder was part of a somewhat larger dirt area that sat between Interstate 10 and an intersecting highway. Near the spot where Horn parked, California's Department of Transportation had placed an "Emergency Parking Only" sign. Horn saw the sign from where he parked, approximately 16 feet from the outermost traffic lane of Interstate 10.

   That same evening, Adelelmo Cabral was driving home from work alone in his pickup truck on Interstate 10. Juan Perez was driving behind Cabral on that same highway. Perez saw Cabral's vehicle, which was traveling at 70 to 80 miles per hour, swerve within its lane, then change lanes rapidly, and then pass other vehicles. Cabral's pickup truck crossed the outermost lane of traffic, left the highway, and traveled parallel to the road along the adjacent dirt until it hit the rear of Horn's trailer. Perez saw no brake lights or other indications of an attempt on Cabral's part to slow down before the collision. A toxicology report on Cabral, who died at the scene, was negative. Because there was no evidence of intoxication, suicide, or mechanical defect in the pickup, it appeared that Cabral had either fallen asleep or had been victimized by an unknown medical condition.

   Cabral's widow, Maria Cabral, sued Ralphs for the allegedly wrongful death of her husband. She contended that Ralphs should be liable because its employee (Horn) had caused her husband's death through negligence in stopping for nonemergency reasons on the freeway shoulder. Ralphs responded by denying that Horn was negligent and by asserting that the decedent's own negligence was the real cause of the accident. A California jury concluded that both Cabral and Horn were negligent and that their respective negligent acts were substantial factors in causing Cabral's death. The jury returned a verdict in favor of Maria Cabral, but, as required by California law, the trial court reduced the amount of damages awarded by the jury in order to allow for the fact that the decedent's own negligence had partially accounted for his death. Ralphs appealed to the California Court of Appeal, which reversed the lower court's decision. The Court of Appeal held that there was no basis for holding Ralphs liable for negligence because neither Ralphs nor Horn owed the decedent a duty of reasonable care to prevent a collision with Horn's parked-off-the-roadway rig. Maria Cabral appealed to the Supreme Court of California.

   Was the Court of Appeal correct in its conclusion that neither Horn nor Ralphs owed a duty to the decedent? In any event, why would Ralphs even be at risk of liability? If there was negligence here, wasn't it Horn's? Why wouldn't the decedent's own negligence in falling asleep at the wheel bar Cabral from recovery, regardless of whether Horn or Ralphs was negligent?

2. Alvin and Gwendolyn Kallman retained All American Pest Control (AAPC) to treat and prevent pest infestation at their Virginia home on a quarterly basis. AAPC employee Patric Harrison performed one of the quarterly treatments. Three days before treating the Kaltmans' home, Harrison had treated a commercial establishment with Orthene pesticide. After applying Orthene at that business, Harrison did not thoroughly clean his pesticide application equipment. As a result, he ended up applying a diluted spray of Orthene to the baseboards and adjoining floor surfaces throughout the Kaltmans' home and to the concrete surfaces in the home's basement and garage. As the pesticide was being applied, the Kaltmans complained to Harrison about the unusual and extraordinarily pungent odor. Harrison told them that the smell would dissipate, but it did not. Later that day, the Kaltmans telephoned AAPC to report their concern about

the overwhelming stench. They were told that Harrison had applied an inappropriate pesticide that had a very strong and unpleasant odor.

The Kaltmans reported the incident to the Virginia Department of Agriculture and Consumer Services (VDACS). During the investigation by VDACS, Harrison admitted that he applied an Orthene dilution to the Kaltmans' home. Harrison also admitted that he falsified the pertinent work order by documenting that he applied different pesticides. Laboratory analyses performed by VDACS revealed concentrations of acephate—a toxic ingredient in Orthene PCO Pellets—in the Kaltmans' home. Exposure to acephate has been shown to cause nerve damage and cancer in laboratory animals. Orthene PCO Pellets are not licensed for residential use by VDACS. The Material Safety Data Sheet required by law for Orthene PCO Pellets states that the product "is not for indoor residential use," "is for use in places other than private homes," and should not be used on "unpainted masonry floors in poorly ventilated areas such as garages or basements . . . since persistent odor could develop." AAPC informed the Kaltmans that although the odor from Orthene was unpleasant, it did not represent a health hazard. The Kaltmans therefore made more than a dozen attempts to eradicate the odor by washing the treated surfaces. They also had their home professionally cleaned. However, high concentrations of acephate remained. Because of the noxious fumes, their home was rendered uninhabitable for a year.

The Kaltmans sued AAPC and Harrison on a negligence per se theory in an effort to recover damages for their physical and emotional harms and for expenses they incurred. The trial court granted the defendants' motion to have the "Pest Control Service Agreement" between the plaintiffs and AAPC made part of the pleadings. This agreement listed the pests to be controlled and stated that AAPC would "apply chemicals to control above-named pests in accordance with terms and conditions of this Service Agreement. All labors and materials will be furnished to provide the most efficient pest control and maximum safety required by federal, state and city regulations." AACP and Harrison then filed demurrers to the negligence per se claim (i.e., they asked the court to dismiss the Kaltmans' complaint for failure to state a valid course of action against them). The defendants argued that any duties they owed the plaintiffs stemmed from the parties' contract and that the plaintiffs therefore could not assert a negligence per se claim. The trial court sustained the defendants' demurrers. Was the trial

court correct in doing so? Were the Kaltmans entitled to proceed on a negligence per se theory?

3. Ludmila Hresil and her niece were shopping at a Sears retail store. There were few shoppers in the store at the time. Hresil spent about 10 minutes in the store's women's department, where she observed no other shoppers. After Hresil's niece completed a purchase in another part of the store, the two women began to walk through the women's department. Hresil, who was pushing a shopping cart, suddenly lost her balance and struggled to avoid a fall. As she did so, her right leg struck the shopping cart and began to swell. Hresil observed a "gob" on the floor where she had slipped. Later, a Sears employee said that "it looked like someone spat on the floor, like it was phlegm." Under the reasonable person standard, did Sears breach a duty to Hresil by not cleaning up the gob? *Hint:* Assume that Hresil could prove that the gob was on the floor only for the 10 minutes she spent in the women's department.

4. Five months after the September 11, 2001, hijackings of airplanes and less than two months after a passenger on a Paris to Miami flight attempted to detonate explosives hidden in his shoe, Bryan and Jennifer Cook took an Atlantic Coast Airlines flight from Indianapolis to New York City. While passengers waited to board, a man later identified as French national Frederic Girard ran toward the gate and abruptly stopped. Mr. Cook observed that the unaccompanied Girard had two tickets in his possession and that airline security had detained him at the boarding gate before allowing him to board. Mr. Cook further noticed that Girard's face was red and that his eyes were bloodshot and glassy. In boarding the 32-passenger plane, Girard ran up the steps and jumped inside. Rather than proceeding to his assigned seat, he attempted to sit in a seat nearest the cockpit. However, the flight attendant instructed him to sit in the back row. After taking a seat there, Girard repeatedly pressed the attendant call button and light switch above his head. Prior to takeoff, Mr. Cook approached the flight attendant and expressed concern that Girard was a possible security threat. The attendant acknowledged as much and explained that he had directed Girard to sit in the rear of the plane so he could keep an eye on him.

During takeoff, Girard ignored instructions to remain seated. He lit a cigarette, disregarding directives from the flight attendant that smoking onboard was prohibited. Despite this admonition, Girard was permitted to retain his lighter. Mr. Cook approached three male passengers and asked for their assistance in the event that Girard's behavior grew dangerous. Girard moved about the plane, sat in various empty seats, and finally walked up the aisle toward the cockpit. Mr. Cook blocked his path and instructed him to sit. Without any physical contact with Mr. Cook, Girard returned to his seat and lit another cigarette. The flight attendant again told him to extinguish the cigarette, and in response Girard stood and shouted, "Get back! Get back!" Mr. Cook and other passengers approached Girard and ordered him to sit down. Instead, Girard stomped his feet and shouted, mostly in French. The Cooks were able to discern the words "World Trade Center," "Americans," and "New York City." Eventually, a Delta employee convinced Girard to sit after speaking to him in French. The employee spent the remainder of the flight sitting across from Girard in the rear of the plane. The pilot diverted the flight to Cleveland, where police arrested Girard. The flight then continued to New York City.

Recalling the events of September 11th and reports of the shoe-bomber incident, the Cooks described their ordeal as one in which they "have never been so scared in their entire lives" (quoting a brief they filed in the litigation about to be described). They filed a small claims court action in Marion County, Indiana, naming Atlantic Coast as a defendant. The Cooks sought damages for negligent infliction of emotional distress. After the small claims court entered judgment against the Cooks, they appealed to the Marion County Superior Court, which denied Atlantic Coast's motion for summary judgment. The Indiana Court of Appeals upheld the Superior Court's denial of the summary judgment motion. Atlantic Coast then appealed to the Supreme Court of Indiana. Did the lower courts rule correctly in denying Atlantic Coast's motion for summary judgment?

5. Performance Plumbing and Heating (Performance) was in the business of installing water and sewer plumbing at Denver-area constitution sites. Unless assigned a company vehicle, Performance employees used their own vehicles to commute to and from work. Because employees were sometimes expected to drive for the company during the workday in order to transport job materials and company tools from Performance's construction trailers to job sites (and vice versa), Performance required employment applicants to hold a valid driver's license. However, Performance relied on the applicant's truthfulness in stating whether he held a valid license. Performance checked driver's licenses and driving records only as required by its insurance

company when it assigned an employee a company vehicle to drive.

Performance hired Cory Weese as an apprentice plumber. Weese had completed an employment application in which he stated that he had a valid driver's license and had not been cited for traffic violations. These statements were untrue. His license had been suspended because of numerous traffic violations, including careless driving and driving without a license. Because he would not be assigned a company vehicle, Performance hired Weese without checking to see whether his statements on the application were true. About a year after hiring Weese, Performance had his personal truck equipped with a rack for transporting pipe from construction trailers to work sites. Therefore, Performance intended that Weese drive during the day for the company, though it evidently did not check on his driving record at that time because he was not being assigned a company vehicle. (Weese's license apparently had been reinstated before Performance had the pipe rack installed on his truck, however.) On a later date, when Weese's work hours had ended and he was driving home, his truck collided with two cars. The collision resulted solely from Weese's negligence. Carolyn Raleigh and her son were severely injured in the collision. They sued Performance. (Weese was liable to the Raleighs, of course, but this question pertains to their claims against Performance.) The Raleighs alleged two theories of recovery against Performance: *respondeat superior* (the doctrine under which an employer is liable for a tort committed by its employee if the tort was committed within the scope of employment) and negligent hiring. Was Performance liable on *respondeat superior* grounds? Was Performance liable on negligent hiring grounds?

6. Neal Berberich entered into a contract with Naomi Jack to perform work on her South Carolina home. During the course of the project, a controversy arose regarding Jack's use of an automatic sprinkler system that came on periodically in various zones in the yard. In connection with an eventual lawsuit brought by Berberich against Jack, Berberich alleged that he asked Jack to shut off the sprinklers because he and his crew were having difficulty working with the sprinklers on. According to Berberich, Jack refused, told him to "make the best of the situation and work around it," and became upset when Berberich turned the sprinklers off on several occasions. Berberich also stated that Jack threatened to lock the controls if the sprinklers were turned off again. Jack denied this but admitted that she

did instruct one of Berberich's crew members that her sprinkler system was not to be shut off again.

At a time when Berberich was working alone on the exterior of Jack's home, he saw the sprinklers come on in an area of the yard. He noticed that the controls had been locked, so he could not turn the system off. Berberich then moved to the front of the house, away from the sprinklers, to work on the windows. He ascended an eight-foot ladder to reach the top of a tall bay window to clean some caulking. As he was working, the sprinklers came on in the zone where his ladder was located. While coming down the ladder, Berberich slipped on a wet rung and fell to the ground, injuring himself. Berberich stated that he told Jack he had fallen and that he asked her to call for an ambulance, but that she ignored his request. As he walked away from Jack's home, he collapsed in her driveway. Berberich used his cell phone to call for an ambulance, which arrived shortly after his call. He received medical treatment for his injuries, which included a lumbar strain and contusion, abrasions on his back and his left shoulder, and a swollen right ankle. Jack, in contrast, denied that Berberich told her he had fallen and that he had asked her to call an ambulance.

Berberich sued Jack in a South Carolina court, alleging that his injuries "were directly and proximately caused by [Jack's] negligence . . . and recklessness." His complaint sought recovery for medical expenses, lost wages, and other actual damages. At trial, Berberich contended that Jack's actions in locking the controls and refusing to turn off the sprinklers constituted reckless conduct (not merely negligence). He asked the trial judge to charge the jury on the definition of recklessness. He also asked for the jury to be instructed that ordinary negligence is not a defense to a heightened degree of wrongdoing (so that if there were ordinary negligence on his part, it could not be compared to Jack's allegedly reckless conduct). The trial judge denied the requests, concluding that the requested instructions were relevant only if punitive damages had been at issue (and they were not). The trial court instructed the jury on South Carolina's comparative negligence rule, but not in the way Berberich requested. The jury returned a verdict for the defense. The jury found Berberich 75 percent negligent and Jack 25 percent at fault in causing the accident, resulting in no recovery for Berberich because South Carolina utilizes a mixed comparative negligence approach. When the trial court denied Berberich's motions for a judgment notwithstanding the verdict and a new trial, Berberich

appealed to the Supreme Court of South Carolina. If Jack's fault consisted of negligence, was the jury verdict in favor of Jack correct in light of South Carolina's comparative negligence statute? If the trial judge should have given the requested instruction on recklessness and if a proper instruction in that regard could have caused the jury to conclude that Jack acted recklessly, was Berberich correct in his argument that any negligence on his part should not be compared with Jack's alleged recklessness?

7. LuAnn Plonski alleged that after shopping at a Kroger Co. grocery store in Indianapolis, Indiana, during afternoon hours, she proceeded to the store's parking lot (where her car was parked), placed her purse in the shopping cart she was using, opened the trunk of her car, and began loading her groceries into the trunk. She noticed that a man was walking toward her. He did not appear to be a Kroger employee (and, in fact, was not a Kroger employee). The man began running toward Plonski, who grabbed her purse and tried to run away but did not succeed. The man grabbed Plonski and her purse. He then picked her up, threw her in the trunk of the car, and began slamming the trunk lid on her legs. When the man looked away, Plonski jumped out of the trunk and ran into the Kroger store. The man then left the scene with Plonski's purse.

In an effort to collect damages for her injuries and the loss of her purse, Plonski filed a negligence lawsuit against Kroger in an Indiana court. After completion of discovery in the case, Kroger moved for summary judgment. Kroger argued that it owed no duty to Plonski and that even if it did owe a duty, there was no breach. In connection with its motion, Kroger provided affidavits from its risk manager and safety manager. Those affidavits asserted that the Kroger store in whose parking lot the incident occurred is located in a part of the city that has a reputation for low levels of criminal activity and that in the two-year period before the incident at issue, there had been only one report of criminal activity occurring on the store's premises. Plonski responded to Kroger's motion by citing her deposition testimony and other evidence. The trial court denied Kroger's summary judgment request, and the Indiana Court of Appeals affirmed. Kroger appealed to the Supreme Court of Indiana. How did that court rule on whether Kroger owed a duty to Plonski and on whether Kroger was entitled to summary judgment?

8. On August 24, William Garris III and David Billups flew from Raleigh, North Carolina, to Joplin, Missouri,

on a business trip for their employer, Carolina Forge Co. The trip was scheduled to take place from August 24 to August 27, in Joplin. The primary purpose of the trip was to participate in a golf outing at the invitation of F.A.G. Bearings, a Carolina Forge customer. In advance of the trip, Carolina Forge paid for the airline tickets for Garris and Billups and for their rental car. Carolina Forge also paid for hotel rooms for the men. In addition, Carolina Forge gave Garris and Billups $600 in cash to pay for expenses incurred during the trip. The $600 was intended to pay for entertaining customers and for gas in the rental car. Carolina Forge also had a policy of reimbursing employees for additional out-of-pocket expenses during business trips, including meals, snacks, and alcoholic beverages. Carolina Forge was aware that alcohol would likely be consumed on the particular business trip Garris and Billups would be taking.

Garris and Billups arrived in Joplin on the evening of August 24 and checked into their hotel. The next morning, they visited the F.A.G. Bearings headquarters. Next, Garris and Billups arrived at another F.A.G. facility, where they took a tour and then delivered a presentation to company representatives. Following the presentation, Garris and Billups toured another portion of the facility. Garris and Billups then took three F.A.G. Bearings representatives to lunch in Joplin. After lunch, Garris and Billups played golf with F.A.G. Bearings representatives at a course just outside Joplin. Later, Garris and Billups had dinner and drinks at a Joplin steakhouse. No F.A.G. Bearings representatives joined Garris and Billups for dinner. Garris and Billups then went to a casino located approximately 30 miles west of Joplin. No representatives from F.A.G. Bearings accompanied Garris and Billups to the casino. After spending several hours at the casino (where they used their own money for drinks and for gambling), Garris and Billups decided to return to their hotel in Joplin. Upon leaving the casino, Billups drove the rental car. Because Billups took the wrong appropriate ramp for the relevant interstate highway, he and Garris were going away from Joplin rather than toward it. When Billups attempted to turn around, he negligently caused the rental car to collide with a truck in which Charles and Jennifer Sheffer and their son were riding. All three Sheffers were injured in the collision, as was Garris. Billups died in the accident.

The Sheffers sued Carolina Forge on two theories: *respondeat superior*, under which an employer is liable for an employee's tort if it was committed within the scope of employment, and negligent entrustment of a vehicle (the rental car) to Billups and Garris. The trial court granted summary judgment in favor of Carolina Forge on both claims. Was the trial court correct in granting summary judgment to Carolina Forge on the *respondeat superior* claim? Was the trial court correct in granting summary judgment to Carolina Forge on the negligent entrustment claim?

9. On April 16, 1947, the SS *Grandchamp*, a cargo ship owned by the Republic of France and operated by the French Line, was loading a cargo of fertilizer grade ammonium nitrate (FGAN) at Texas City, Texas. A fire began on board the ship, apparently as a result of a longshoreman's having carelessly discarded a cigarette or match into one of the ship's holds. Despite attempts to put out the fire, it spread quickly. Approximately an hour after the fire was discovered, the *Grandchamp* exploded with tremendous force. Fire and burning debris spread throughout the waterfront, touching off further fires and explosions in other ships, refineries, gasoline storage tanks, and chemical plants. When the conflagration was over, 500 persons had been killed and more than 3,000 had been injured. The United States paid out considerable sums to victims of the disaster. The United States then sought to recoup these payments as damages in a negligence case against the Republic of France and the French Line. The evidence revealed that even though ammonium nitrate (which constituted approximately 95 percent of the FGAN) was known throughout the transportation industry as an oxidizing agent and a fire hazard, no one in charge on the *Grandchamp* had made any attempt to prohibit smoking in the ship's holds. The defendants argued that they should not be held liable because FGAN was not known to be capable of *exploding* (as opposed to simply being a fire hazard) under circumstances such as those giving rise to the disaster. Did the defendants succeed with this argument?

10. Vera Dyer and her sons owned a Maine home believed to be more than 70 years old. The home had a cement foundation and floor. A stand-alone garage with a cement floor was constructed in the 1980s. In September 2004, Maine Drilling & Blasting distributed a notice informing the Dyers that it would soon begin blasting rock near the home in connection with a construction project to replace a bridge and bridge access roads. The notice stated that Maine Drilling uses "the most advanced technologies available . . . to measure the seismic effect to the area" and assured the Dyers "that ground vibrations associated with the blasting [would] not exceed the established limits that could potentially

cause damage." As offered in the notice, Maine Drilling provided a pre-blast survey of the Dyer home. The survey report recorded the surveyor's observation of "some concrete deterioration to [the] west wall" and "cracking to [the] concrete floor," and a slight tilt to a retaining wall behind the garage.

Maine Drilling conducted more than 100 blasts between October 2004 and August 2005. The closest blast was approximately 100 feet from the Dyer home. Vera was inside the home for at least two of the blasts and felt the whole house shake. During other blasts, she was not in the home because Maine Drilling employees advised her to go outside. In the early spring of 2005, the Dyers observed several changes from the pre-blasting condition of the home and the garage: (1) the center of the basement floor had dropped as much as three inches; (2) the center beam in the basement that supported part of the first floor was sagging, and as a result, the first floor itself was noticeably un-level; (3) there was a new crack between the basement floor and the cement pad that formed the foundation of the chimney in the basement; (4) new or enlarged cracks radiated out across the basement floor from the chimney foundation; and (5) cracks that had previously existed in the garage floor were noticeably wider and more extensive. The Dyers also noticed that a flowerbed retaining wall that helped to support the rear wall of the garage had moved demonstrably.

The Dyers sued Maine Drilling in a Maine court. They alleged strict liability and negligence causes of action. Following completion of discovery, Maine Drilling moved for summary judgment. The court granted Maine Drilling summary judgment on the strict liability claim because Maine precedents indicated that blasting activities were to be governed by negligence principles rather than those of strict liability. The court also granted the defendant summary judgment on the negligence claim because, in the court's view, the Dyers had failed to establish the elements of a negligence claim. The Dyers appealed to the Supreme Judicial Court of Maine. Did the lower court rule correctly on which set of legal principles—those of negligence or, instead, those of strict liability—should control the case?

11. Appalachian Power Co. (APCO) owns the Philip Sporn power plant (Sporn), a coal-fired power plant that generates electricity by burning coal to create steam and then passing the steam through a turbine. The power plant's precipitators remove granular ash particles ("fly ash") from the gases produced by burning coal. Precipitators generate significant heat, which can cause corrosion to its exterior steel siding and result in fly ash leakage.

Industrial Contractors Inc. (ICI) was hired by APCO to perform general maintenance at Sporn. This included welding metal patches to the exterior of the precipitators to prevent fly ash leakage. Roger Hoschar was a boilermaker employed by ICI from March 2006 to March 2007. During that period, he worked exclusively at Sporn. One of his frequent assignments consisted of hanging from a suspended platform and welding steel patches over corroded portions of the ducts leading into and out of Sporn's Unit 5 precipitator. Before welding any steel patches, Hoschar and other workers had to remove debris that had built up in the steel channels. Because Unit 5 is an outdoor structure, pigeons sometimes perched on its steel channels and left their droppings behind. Therefore, the debris usually consisted of approximately three- to four-inch accumulations of bird manure and two-inch accumulations of fly ash. Hoschar removed the debris from the steel channels by hand, with a wire brush, or by using compressed air. When removing debris and while welding the steel patches, Hoschar wore a respirator over his face.

In March 2007, Hoschar's employment with ICI ended. A 2009 chest X-ray revealed the presence of a mass on his right lung. He was diagnosed with histoplasmosis, an infectious disease caused by inhaling the spores of a naturally occurring soil-based fungus called *Histoplasma capsulatum*. The *Histoplasma capsulatum* fungus is endemic in the Ohio Valley region, where Sporn is located, because it grows best in soils with high nitrogen content. Once an individual inhales the fungus, it colonizes the lungs. However, the vast majority of people infected by histoplasmosis do not experience any symptoms of infection or suffer any ill effects. While Hoschar was working at Sporn, the Occupational Safety and Health Administration website maintained a page titled "Respiratory Protection: Hazard Recognition." One of the reference documents found on that page was a publication by the National Institute for Occupational Safety and Health titled "Histoplasmosis: Protecting Workers at Risk." This publication explained that the *Histoplasma capsulatum* fungus "seems to grow best in soils having a high nitrogen content, especially those enriched with bird manure or bat droppings." It further noted that the fungus "can be carried on the wings, feet, and beaks of birds and infect soil under roosting sites or manure accumulations inside or outside buildings."

Hoschar and his wife sued APCO for negligence. They alleged that Hoschar contracted histoplasmosis while working at Sporn as a result of inhaling contaminated dust when he swept out the mixtures of bird manure and fly ash that had accumulated in Unit 5's steel channels. They also alleged APCO did not provide any written or verbal warnings concerning the presence of aged bird manure around Unit 5 or of the health risks associated with accumulations of bird manure, such as histoplasmosis. The court granted APCO's motion for summary judgment, reasoning that under the circumstances, APCO did not owe Hoschar a duty of reasonable care. Was the court correct in that ruling?

12. Betty Webb ventured out in the rain to shop at a Dick's Sporting Goods store. Upon her arrival, Webb noticed puddles in the parking lot and proceeded cautiously to the store's entrance. As she entered the store, she stepped onto floor mats that Dick's had placed in the entryway to soak up water tracked in by customers. Webb saw that the floor mats had shifted from their customary parallel formation into a "V" shape. A visible pool of water had formed in the center of the "V." According to Webb, the mats were wet and spongy. There were no signs at the front of the store to warn customers that the floor could be wet. A crowd of other customers entering the store at the same time surrounded Webb. In an attempt to avoid the visible pool of water in the "V," Webb stepped from one of the mats to a tile that appeared to her to be dry but was, in fact, wet. As she stepped onto the tile, she slipped and fell forward, injuring her knees, arms, and shoulders. A store employee witnessed the fall.

Webb later filed a negligence lawsuit against Dick's in a Kentucky trial court. In her deposition, she stated that there were a number of fellow customers entering the store at the same time, which made it difficult for her to avoid the pool without pausing and waiting for people to pass. Webb acknowledged that her shoes were wet and that the lighting in the store was bright. Webb also admitted that if Dick's had placed a sign near the entrance to warn of a wet floor, the warning probably would not have dissuaded her from entering the store.

Dick's moved for summary judgment, asserting that the wet floor was an open-and-obvious condition that eliminated any duty potentially owed to Webb. The trial court agreed and granted summary judgment in favor of Dick's. Webb appealed to the Kentucky Court of Appeals, which reversed the lower court's decision after concluding that according to a precedent decision from the Supreme Court of Kentucky, a property owner may still owe a duty of reasonable care to persons lawfully on the premises even when a danger on the property is open and obvious. The Court of Appeals held that Dick's had a duty to take reasonable steps to eliminate or reduce the open-and-obvious hazard and that whether Dick's satisfied its duty was a question for the jury. Dick's appealed to the Supreme Court of Kentucky. How did the Supreme Court rule? Did Dick's owe the duty identified by the Court of Appeals?

Intellectual Property
and Unfair Competition

The term *intellectual property* has received frequent mention in business circles in recent years, usually as part of a comment emphasizing the importance of protecting intellectual property rights. The names of key forms of intellectual property and the areas of law that apply to them—patent, copyright, trademark, and trade secret—are also often heard.

However, many people who find these names familiar lack a clear understanding of the differences among the forms of intellectual property and the respective legal treatments they receive. This chapter seeks to provide such an understanding, as well as an awareness of how to protect intellectual property and how to avoid violating others' rights in that regard. Study the chapter and you will understand that *patent, copyright,* and *trademark* are not interchangeable terms, even though they sometimes are used in such an erroneous fashion in media reports and ordinary conversation.

Let's begin with a pretest, of sorts. Each of the bullet-pointed items listed below could be the subject of intellectual property protection, though in some instances, more facts would be necessary in order to know for certain. *Before reading beyond this introductory exercise, jot down, for each listed item, the name of the potentially relevant area of intellectual property law* (patent, copyright, trademark, or trade secret). For most items, only one area of law would potentially apply, though in some instances there could be more than one.

Here is the list:

- A brand name for a product
- A new electronic device
- A TV commercial
- Computer software
- A three-word advertising slogan
- The formula for a beverage
- A logo regularly used by a business firm
- A pharmaceutical product
- A highly detailed customer list
- A song
- The recognizable shape of a beverage bottle

Keep in mind the above list of items as you read the chapter and learn about intellectual property concepts and principles. Then look back at the list when you complete the chapter and check the accuracy or inaccuracy of your initial impressions.

LO LEARNING OBJECTIVES

After studying this chapter, you should be able to:

8-1 List the categories of potentially patentable subject matter and explain what is contemplated by each of the requirements of patentability (novelty, nonobviousness, and utility).

8-2 Explain the rights a patent owner holds and the length of time those rights exist.

8-3 Explain what a patent owner must prove in order to establish that patent infringement occurred and identify defenses to a patent infringement claim.

8-4 List types of works that may carry copyright protection.

8-5 Explain how long copyrights last.

8-6 Explain the rights copyright owners hold and the relationship of those rights to claims for copyright infringement.

8-7 List the fair use factors and apply them to fact patterns in which the fair use defense to copyright infringement liability is invoked.

8-8 State what a trademark does and provide examples of potentially protectable trademarks.

8-9 Identify the key requirement for registration of a mark on the Principal Register (distinctiveness) and explain the role of secondary meaning when registration of a nondistinctive mark is sought.

8-10 Identify and apply the elements of trademark infringement.

8-11 Identify and apply the elements of trademark dilution.

8-12 Explain what a trade secret is and what the trade secret owner must prove in order to win a misappropriation case.

8-13 List the elements that a plaintiff must prove in order to win an injurious falsehood case.

8-14 Explain the elements of interference with contractual relations.

8-15 Identify key issues on which courts focus in false advertising cases brought under Lanham Act § 43(a).

THIS CHAPTER DISCUSSES LEGAL rules that allow civil recoveries for abuses of free competition. These abuses are (1) infringement of intellectual property rights protected by patent, copyright, and trademark law; (2) misappropriation of trade secrets; (3) the intentional torts of injurious falsehood, interference with contractual relations, and interference with prospective advantage; and (4) the various forms of unfair competition addressed by § 43(a) of the Lanham Act. Indeed, the term *unfair competition* describes the entire chapter. In general, competition is deemed unfair when (1) it discourages creative endeavor by robbing creative people of the fruits of their innovations or (2) it renders commercial life too uncivilized for the law to tolerate.

Protection of Intellectual Property

Patents   Patent law is exclusively federal in nature. In fact, Congress's authority to regulate patents is embedded in the U.S. Constitution under Article 1, Section 8. But while the source of Congress's power comes from the Constitution, the U.S.'s actual patent laws come from the patent statutes, particularly the Patent Act, which has been revised numerous times. As such, a patent may be viewed as an agreement between an inventor and the federal government. Under that agreement, the inventor obtains the exclusive right (for a limited time) to exclude others from making, using, or selling his invention in return for making the invention public by giving the government certain information about it. The patent holder's (or **patentee's**) monopoly encourages the creation and disclosure of inventions by stopping third parties from appropriating them once they become public.

Who is the "inventor," for purposes of the above discussion? Until a recent change, U.S. law has historically opted for a literal interpretation with a "first-to-invent" rule—meaning that only the true inventor would be eligible for a patent on his or her invention. Under that rule, a person who created an invention after the true inventor had already done so was not entitled to a patent even if she came up with her invention independently (without knowledge of what the true inventor had done) and filed a patent application before the true inventor did. The first-to-invent rule put U.S. law at odds with the patent laws in many nations, which contemplate a "first-to-file" approach that would allow the independent developer of an invention to obtain a patent if she filed a patent application before the earlier inventor did.

In a major change, the American Invents Act of 2011 (AIA) switched the United States from a first-to-invent system to a first-to-file system. Although the AIA was enacted in 2011, its provisions took effect in March 2013. Now, one who independently developed an invention after someone else did is considered an inventor entitled to a U.S. patent if he, she, or it files a patent application before the prior inventor does. Independent development is critical to this rule. One who had access to the prior inventor's work before supposedly inventing largely the same thing did not independently create and therefore would not be a qualifying inventor for purposes of the first-to-file rule.

The change from first-to-invent to first-to-file helps eliminate one set of potentially difficult issues when an inventor seeks patent protection in various nations under the country-by-country approach discussed in a Global Business Environment box that appears later in the chapter.

What Is Patentable?

List the categories of potentially patentable subject matter and explain what is contemplated by each of the requirements of patentability (novelty, nonobviousness, and utility).

Assuming that the novelty, nonobviousness, and utility requirements discussed later in the chapter are also satisfied, an inventor may obtain a patent on (1) a *process* (a mode of treatment of certain materials to produce a given result), (2) a *machine*, (3) a *manufacture* (here, a noun effectively meaning "product"), (4) a *composition of matter* (a combination of elements with qualities not present in the elements taken individually, such as a new chemical compound), or (5) an *improvement* of any of the above. Patents issued for any of these inventions are classified as *utility patents*. The Patent Act also permits different types of patents to be issued for ornamental designs for a product (often called *design patents*) and for plants produced by asexual reproduction. Our main focus in this chapter will be on utility patents.

The Patent Act section listing the above categories of inventions eligible for utility patents has long been interpreted by the courts as being subject to a rule that laws of nature and natural phenomena are ineligible for a patent. Therefore, one who discovers a wild plant whose existence was previously unknown has made a nice discovery but cannot obtain a patent on it. Recent years' advancements

and discoveries in medicine and other scientific fields have caused the U.S. Patent and Trademark Office (PTO) and the courts to struggle with difficult questions of patentability. For instance, think about a test that correlates the level of metabolites in the blood of a patient who has a certain disease with a drug dosage likely to be effective for that particular patient. Is this test a patentable process, or is it nonpatentable because of the law-of-nature prohibition? (Note, of course, that the drug itself may well have been a patentable composition of matter at some point, as many pharmaceutical products are.) In *Mayo Collaborative Services v. Prometheus Laboratories, Inc.*, 132 S. Ct. 1289 (2012), the Supreme Court held that the PTO erred in granting a patent on the drug-dosage correlation test and that the law-of-nature bar should have controlled. The Court noted that *applications* of laws of nature may sometimes be patentable, but that the test at issue was not such an application because it merely contemplated adding data-gathering and other conventional scientific activity to the metabolite-level information that was a law of nature.

The Supreme Court again addressed law-of-nature concerns in a 2013 decision. At issue in *Association for Molecular Pathology v. Myriad Genetics, Inc.*, 133 S. Ct. 2107 (2013), were patents pertaining to the discovery of the precise location and sequence of certain human genes that, in the event of mutations in a particular patient, would substantially increase the patient's risk of breast or ovarian cancer. The Court held that the patents should not have been granted because the genetic information and structure were naturally occurring phenomena and hence not patent-eligible.

Additionally, courts refuse to allow patents for abstract ideas, which can include anything from how to electronically track utility customers' energy use to electronic paywalls. However, distinguishing patentable inventions from abstract ideas has been a frequent challenge for courts. This is especially true in attempts to patent certain methods of doing business. For example in *Bilski v. Kappos*, 561 U.S. 593 (2010), the Supreme Court declined an opportunity to rule that business methods in general cannot be patented. The Court held that the business method at issue—a method for hedging risk in certain financial transactions—was merely an abstract idea and therefore nonpatentable. For discussion of *Bilski*, see *Alice Corporation Ltd. v. CLS Bank International*, which follows shortly. *Alice* also deals with computer software, another type of creative activity over which there has been uncertainty concerning patentability. The Court indicates in *Alice* that in order to be patentable, software and any business method to which it relates must go beyond expressing an abstract idea and using mathematical principles. Clearly, however, a computer program that forms part of an otherwise patentable process may be held protected and therefore not fair game for others to copy during the patent period.[1]

Even though an invention fits within one of the categories enumerated earlier, it is not patentable if it lacks novelty, is obvious, or has no utility.[2] The *novelty* requirement requires the invention to be new and truly different from what has gone before in the relevant field of inventive activity. This means an inventor cannot obtain a patent if any of the following occurred *before* the patent application for an invention was filed: the invention was already patented; the invention was already in public use, on sale, or otherwise available to the public; or the invention had already been described in a printed publication. However, in what may be described as the one-year window exception to the before-application test, an inventor who makes a public disclosure of the invention has one year from the making of the disclosure to file a patent application. Public disclosure is the nonconfidential sharing of information about the invention and can come in many forms such as "pitching" the

invention to investors without a nondisclosure agreement or selling the invention to the public. The inventor's filing of a patent application within one year after his, her, or its public disclosure leaves the inventor still able to pass the novelty requirement and obtain a patent, but the filing of an application outside the one-year window will be too late.

Just because someone has never filed a patent application for an invention does not make it patentable. While it may satisfy the *novelty* requirement, the Patent Act also requires inventions to be nonobvious. This *nonobviousness* requirement means that if an invention could have been easily made by someone skilled in the relevant field and familiar with the subject matter of the invention, then it is not worthy of a patent. An example of nonobviousness can be seen in the *ZUP, LLC v. Nash Manufacturing, Inc.* case. There, the federal circuit court found that a wakeboard design that allowed a user to pull him or herself up using foot bindings and handles was obvious in light of prior wakeboard designs.

A final requirement for patentability is utility. The *utility* requirement requires that the invention have some qualitative benefit. Therefore, if an invention is illegal or immoral, it cannot be patented. Similarly, if an invention such as a drug has no demonstrated usefulness, it cannot be patented.

---

[1] As discussed later in this chapter, computer programs may obtain copyright and trade secret protection.

[2] Plant and design patents are subject to requirements that are slightly different from those stated here.

Alice Corporation Ltd. v. CLS Bank International
134 S. Ct. 2347 (2014)

Alice Corporation is the assignee of several patents that disclose a method for mitigating settlement risk (the risk that only one party to an agreed-upon financial exchange will satisfy its obligation). The patent claims are designed to facilitate the exchange of financial obligations between two parties by using a computer system as a third-party intermediary.

Under the method contemplated by the patents, the intermediary creates "shadow" credit and debit records (i.e., account ledgers) that mirror the balances in the parties' real-world accounts at "exchange institutions" (e.g., banks). The intermediary updates the shadow records in real time as transactions are entered, allowing only those transactions for which the parties' updated shadow records indicate sufficient resources to satisfy their mutual obligations. At the end of the day, the intermediary instructs the relevant financial institutions to carry out the "permitted" transactions in accordance with the updated shadow records, thus mitigating the risk that only one party will perform the agreed-upon exchange. The claimed method requires the use of a computer and involves a computer-readable medium containing program code for performing the method of exchanging obligations.

CLS Bank International and an affiliated entity (referred to collectively as CLS Bank) operate a global network that facilitates currency transactions. CLS Bank sued Alice, seeking a declaration that Alice's patents were invalid. A federal district court and the U.S. Court of Appeals for the Federal Circuit held that the patents were invalid because they applied to merely an abstract idea. The U.S. Supreme Court granted Alice's petition for a writ of certiorari. (In the following edited version of the Supreme Court's decision, Alice is sometimes referred to as the petitioner.*)*

Thomas, Justice

The patents at issue in this case disclose a computer-implemented scheme for mitigating settlement risk by using a third-party intermediary. The question presented is whether these claims are patent-eligible under 35 U.S.C. § 101, or are instead drawn to a patent-ineligible abstract idea.

Section 101 of the Patent Act defines the subject matter eligible for patent protection. It provides: "Whoever invents or discovers any new and useful process, machine, manufacture, or composition of matter, or any new and useful improvement thereof, may obtain a patent therefor, subject to the conditions and requirements of this title." "We have long held that this provision contains an important implicit exception: Laws of nature, natural phenomena, and abstract ideas are not patentable." *Association for Molecular Pathology v. Myriad Genetics, Inc.*, 133 S. Ct. 2107 (2013). We have interpreted § 101 and its predecessors in light of this exception for more than 150 years.

We have described the concern that drives this exclusionary principle as one of pre-emption. See, e.g., *Bilski v. Kappos*, 561 U.S. 593 (2010) (upholding the patent [at issue there] "would pre-empt use of this approach in all fields, and would effectively grant a monopoly over an abstract idea"). Laws of nature, natural phenomena, and abstract ideas are "the basic tools of scientific and technological work." *Myriad, supra.* "[M]onopolization of those tools through the grant of a patent might tend to impede innovation more than it would tend to promote it," thereby thwarting the primary object of the patent laws. *Mayo Collaborative Services v. Prometheus Laboratories, Inc.*, 132 S. Ct. 1289 (2012). See U.S. Const., Art. I, § 8, cl. 8 (Congress "shall have Power . . . To promote the Progress of Science and useful Arts"). We have "repeatedly emphasized this . . . concern that patent law not inhibit further discovery by improperly tying up the future use" of these building blocks of human ingenuity. *Mayo, supra.*

At the same time, we tread carefully in construing this exclusionary principle lest it swallow all of patent law. At some level, "all inventions . . . embody, use, reflect, rest upon, or apply laws of nature, natural phenomena, or abstract ideas." *Id.* Thus, an invention is not rendered ineligible for patent simply because it involves an abstract concept. See *Diamond v. Diehr*, 450 U.S. 175 (1981). "[A]pplication[s]" of such concepts "'to a new and useful end,'" we have said, remain eligible for patent protection. *Gottschalk v. Benson*, 409 U.S. 63 (1972).

In *Mayo*, we set forth a framework for distinguishing patents that claim laws of nature, natural phenomena, and abstract ideas from those that claim patent-eligible applications of those concepts. First, we determine whether the claims at issue are directed to one of those patent-ineligible concepts. If so, we then ask, "[w]hat else is there in the claims before us?" [S]tep two of this analysis [is] a search for an "inventive concept"—*i.e.*, an element or combination of elements that is "sufficient to ensure that the patent in practice amounts to significantly more than a patent upon the [ineligible concept] itself." *Mayo, supra.*

We must first determine whether the claims at issue are directed to a patent-ineligible concept. We conclude that they are: These claims are drawn to the abstract idea of intermediated settlement.

The "abstract ideas" category embodies "the longstanding rule that an idea of itself is not patentable." *Gottschalk v. Benson, supra.* In *Benson*, for example, this Court rejected as ineligible patent claims involving an algorithm for converting binary-coded decimal numerals into pure binary form, holding that the claimed patent was "in practical effect . . . a patent on the algorithm itself." And in *Parker v. Flook*, 437 U.S. 584 (1978), we held that a mathematical

formula for computing "alarm limits" in a catalytic conversion process was also a patent-ineligible abstract idea.

We most recently addressed the category of abstract ideas in *Bilski v. Kappos*, 561 U.S. 593 (2010). The claims at issue in *Bilski* described a method for hedging against the financial risk of price fluctuations. Claim 1 recited a series of steps for hedging risk, including: (1) initiating a series of financial transactions between providers and consumers of a commodity; (2) identifying market participants that have a counterrisk for the same commodity; and (3) initiating a series of transactions between those market participants and the commodity provider to balance the risk position of the first series of consumer transactions. Claim 4 "pu[t] the concept articulated in claim 1 into a simple mathematical formula." The remaining claims were drawn to examples of hedging in commodities and energy markets.

All members of the Court agreed that the patent at issue in *Bilski* claimed an "abstract idea." Specifically, the claims described "the basic concept of hedging, or protecting against risk." The Court explained that "[h]edging is a fundamental economic practice long prevalent in our system of commerce and taught in any introductory finance class." The concept of hedging as recited by the claims in suit was therefore a patent-ineligible "abstract idea, just like the algorithms at issue in *Benson* and *Flook*."

It follows from our prior cases, and *Bilski* in particular, that the claims at issue here are directed to an abstract idea. On their face, the claims before us are drawn to the concept of intermediated settlement, *i.e.*, the use of a third party to mitigate settlement risk. Like the risk hedging in *Bilski*, the concept of intermediated settlement is "a fundamental economic practice long prevalent in our system of commerce." *Bilski, supra.* The use of a third-party intermediary (or "clearing house") is also a building block of the modern economy. [Citations omitted.] Thus, intermediated settlement, like hedging, is an "abstract idea" beyond the scope of § 101.

Because the claims at issue are directed to the abstract idea of intermediated settlement, we turn to the second step in *Mayo*'s framework. [W]e must examine the elements of the claim to determine whether it contains an "'inventive concept'" sufficient to "transform" the claimed abstract idea into a patent-eligible application. A claim that recites an abstract idea must include "additional features" to ensure "that the [claim] is more than a drafting effort designed to monopolize the [abstract idea]." *Mayo, supra. Mayo* made clear that transformation into a patent-eligible application requires "more than simply stat[ing] the [abstract idea] while adding the words 'apply it.'" *Id.*

Mayo itself is instructive. The patents at issue in *Mayo* claimed a method for measuring metabolites in the bloodstream in order to calibrate the appropriate dosage of thiopurine drugs in the treatment of autoimmune diseases. The respondent in that case contended that the claimed method was a patent-eligible application of natural laws that describe the relationship between the concentration of certain metabolites and the likelihood that the drug dosage will be harmful or ineffective. But methods for determining metabolite levels were already "well known in the art," and the process at issue amounted to "nothing significantly more than an instruction to doctors to apply the applicable laws when treating their patients." *Mayo, supra.* "Simply appending conventional steps, specified at a high level of generality," was not "*enough*" to supply an "'inventive concept.'" *Id.*

The introduction of a computer into the claims does not alter the analysis at *Mayo* step two. In *Benson*, for example, we considered a patent that claimed an algorithm implemented on a general-purpose digital computer. Because the algorithm was an abstract idea, the claim had to supply a new and useful application of the idea in order to be patent-eligible. But the computer implementation did not supply the necessary inventive concept; the process could be "carried out in existing computers long in use." *Benson, supra.* We accordingly "held that simply implementing a mathematical principle on a physical machine, namely a computer, [i]s not a patentable application of that principle." *Mayo, supra* (discussing *Benson*).

Flook is to the same effect. There, we examined a computerized method for using a mathematical formula to adjust alarm limits for certain operating conditions (e.g., temperature and pressure) that could signal inefficiency or danger in a catalytic conversion process. Once again, the formula itself was an abstract idea, and the computer implementation was purely conventional. Thus, "*Flook* stands for the proposition that the prohibition against patenting abstract ideas cannot be circumvented by attempting to limit the use of [the idea] to a particular technological environment." *Bilski, supra.*

In *Diehr*, 450 U.S. 175, by contrast, we held that a computer-implemented process for curing rubber was patent-eligible, but not because it involved a computer. The claim employed a well-known mathematical equation, but it used that equation in a process designed to solve a technological problem in "conventional industry practice." The invention in *Diehr* used a "thermocouple" to record constant temperature measurements inside the rubber mold—something "the industry ha[d] not been able to obtain." The temperature measurements were then fed into a computer, which repeatedly recalculated the remaining cure time by using the mathematical equation. These additional steps, we recently explained, "transformed the process into an inventive application of the formula." *Mayo, supra* (discussing *Diehr*). In other words, the claims in *Diehr* were patent-eligible because they improved an existing technological process, not because they were implemented on a computer.

These cases demonstrate that the mere recitation of a generic computer cannot transform a patent-ineligible abstract idea into a patent-eligible invention. Stating an abstract idea "while adding the words 'apply it'" is not enough for patent eligibility. *Mayo, supra.* Nor is limiting the use of an abstract idea "to a particular technological environment." *Bilski, supra.* Stating an abstract idea while adding the words "apply it with a computer" simply combines those two steps, with the same deficient result. Thus, if a patent's recitation of a computer amounts to a mere instruction to "implemen[t]" an abstract idea "on . . . a computer," *Mayo, supra*, that addition cannot impart patent eligibility. This conclusion accords with the pre-emption concern that undergirds our § 101 jurisprudence. Given the ubiquity of computers, wholly generic computer implementation is not generally the sort of additional feature that provides any "practical assurance that the process is more than a drafting effort designed to monopolize the [abstract idea] itself." *Mayo, supra.*

In light of the foregoing, the relevant question is whether the claims [in the patents held by Alice] do more than simply instruct the practitioner to implement the abstract idea of intermediated settlement on a generic computer. They do not.

Taking the claim elements separately, the function performed by the computer at each step of the process is "[p]urely conventional." *Mayo, supra.* Using a computer to create and maintain "shadow" accounts amounts to electronic recordkeeping—one of the most basic functions of a computer. The same is true with respect to the use of a computer to obtain data, adjust account balances, and issue automated instructions; all of these computer functions are well-understood, routine, conventional activities previously known to the industry. In short, each step does no more than require a generic computer to perform generic computer functions.

Considered "as an ordered combination," the computer components of petitioner's method "ad[d] nothing . . . that is not already present when the steps are considered separately." *Id.* Viewed as a whole, petitioner's method claims simply recite the concept of intermediated settlement as performed by a generic computer. The method claims do not, for example, purport to improve the functioning of the computer itself. Nor do they effect an improvement in any other technology or technical field. Instead, the claims at issue amount to nothing significantly more than an instruction to apply the abstract idea of intermediated settlement using some unspecified, generic computer. Under our precedents, that is not enough to transform an abstract idea into a patent-eligible invention.

Federal Circuit decision affirmed; patents held invalid.

ZUP, LLC v. Nash Manufacturing, Inc.
896 F.3d 1365 (Fed. Cir. 2018)

ZUP, LLC (ZUP) is the inventor of the "ZUP Board," which it brought to market in 2012. ZUP's U.S. Patent 8,292,681 (the '681 Patent) covered the board and method for riding the board, where a rider can use handles and foot bindings to achieve a standing position while riding.

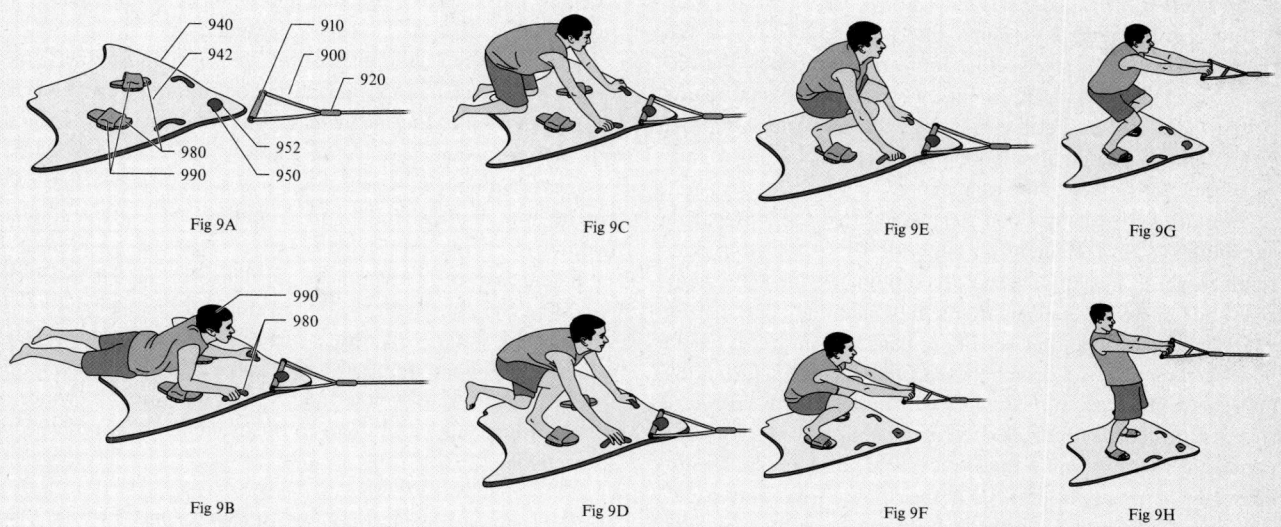

Fig 9A   Fig 9C   Fig 9E   Fig 9G

Fig 9B   Fig 9D   Fig 9F   Fig 9H

ZUP's competitor, Nash Manufacturing, Inc (Nash) brought a similar board to market in 2014, the "Versa Board." Like the ZUP Board, the Versa Board has a tow hook on the front section of the board. Unlike the ZUP Board, however, the Versa Board has several holes on the top surface of the board that allow users to attach handles or foot bindings in various configurations. Although Nash warns against having the handles attached to the board while standing, a user could theoretically ignore Nash's warnings and attach the handles and foot bindings in a configuration that mirrors the configuration of the ZUP Board.

ZUP filed a lawsuit in the U.S. District Court for the Eastern District of Virginia and alleged (1) contributory infringement of the '681 patent, (2) induced infringement of the '681 patent, (3) trade secret misappropriation under the Virginia Uniform Trade Secrets Act, and (4) breach of contract. Nash counterclaimed, seeking declaratory relief as to noninfringement and invalidity. The district court granted Nash's summary judgment motion with respect to invalidity, thus rendering the infringement claims moot. Specifically, the district court held that certain claims in ZUP's '681 patent were obvious in light of a combination of prior patents involving water boards, and therefore the patent was invalid.

Prost, Chief Judge

The primary issue in this case is whether claims 1 and 9 of the '681 patent are invalid as obvious under 35 U.S.C. § 103(a). Although the "ultimate judgment of obviousness is a legal determination," it is based on underlying factual inquiries, including (1) the scope and content of the prior art; (2) the differences between the claims and the prior art; (3) the level of ordinary skill in the pertinent art; and (4) any secondary considerations of non-obviousness. *Graham v. John Deere Co.*, 383 U.S. 1, 17–18 (1966). Likewise, whether one of skill in the art would have had a motivation to combine pieces of prior art in the way claimed by the patent is also a factual determination.

Here, there appears to be no dispute with respect to the content of the prior art or the differences between the prior art and the '681 patent. And, the parties agree that the relevant level of skill in the art is "a person with at least 3–5 years' experience in the design and manufacture of water recreational devices or [who has] a bachelor's degree in mechanical engineering." The only issues raised on appeal pertain to (1) whether a person of ordinary skill in the art would have been motivated to combine the prior art references in the way claimed in the '681 patent, and (2) whether the district court properly evaluated ZUP's evidence of secondary considerations.

A "motivation to combine may be found explicitly or implicitly in market forces; design incentives; the 'interrelated teachings of multiple patents'; 'any need or problem known in the field of endeavor at the time of invention and addressed by the patent'; and the background knowledge, creativity, and common sense of the person of ordinary skill." *Plantronics, Inc. v. Aliph, Inc.,* 724 F.3d 1343, 1354 (Fed. Cir. 2013).

The district court first found that all the elements of the claimed invention existed in the prior art. Specifically, the district court pointed to earlier patents on water recreational boards that included the same elements used in the '681 patent: a riding board, a tow hook, handles, foot bindings, and a plurality of rails on the bottom surface of the riding board.

From this, the district court explained that the '681 patent "identifie[s] known elements in the prior art that aided in rider stability while engaging a water recreational device and simply combined them in one apparatus and method." The district court then concluded that one of ordinary skill in the art would have been motivated to combine the various elements from the prior art references, noting that such motivation would have stemmed from a desire "to aid in rider stability, to allow a wide variety of users to enjoy the device, and to aid users in maneuvering between positions on a water board"—all motivations that were "a driving force throughout the prior art and have been shared by many inventors in the water recreational device industry."

The record evidence supports the district court's analysis. Although ZUP contends that a person of skill in the art would have been focused on achieving rider stability in a predetermined riding position, the evidence contradicts this assertion. Helping riders switch between riding positions had long been a goal of the prior art. . . .

The prior art accomplished this goal of helping riders maneuver between positions by focusing on rider stability. Indeed, ZUP even admits that achieving rider stability is an "age-old motivation in this field." Such stability was enhanced in the prior art through the same components employed in the '681 patent: tow hooks, handles, foot bindings, and other similar features.

In the face of the significant evidence presented by Nash regarding the consistent desire for riders to change positions while riding water recreational boards (and the need to maintain stability while doing so), and given that the elements of the '681 patent were used in the prior art for this very purpose, there is no genuine dispute as to the existence of a motivation to combine.

District court decision affirmed; patent held invalid.

Obtaining a Patent   The U.S. Patent and Trademark Office handles patent applications. The application must include both a *specification* and *claims*. A specification must describe the invention with sufficient detail and clarity to enable a person skilled in the relevant field to make and use the invention.

The claims in a patent application must show how the invention satisfies the various requirements of patentability—novelty, nonobviousness, and utility. The application must also contain a drawing when necessary for understanding the subject matter to be patented. The PTO then determines whether the invention meets the various tests for patentability. If the application is rejected, the applicant may resubmit it. Once any of the applicant's claims have been rejected twice, the applicant may appeal to the Patent and Trademark Appeals Board (PTAB). Subsequent appeals are also possible, but they can only be made to the U.S. District Court for the District of Columbia or the U.S. Court of Appeals for the Federal Circuit.

Ownership and Transfer of Patent Rights

 LO8-2   Explain the rights a patent owner holds and the length of time those rights exist.

Until a change in federal law during the mid-1990s, a patent normally gave the patentee exclusive rights regarding the patented invention for 17 years from the date the patent was granted. In order to bring the United States into compliance with the General Agreement on Tariffs and Trade (an international agreement commonly known as GATT), Congress amended the patent law to provide that the patentee's exclusive rights to exclude others from making, using, or selling the patented invention generally exist until the expiration of 20 years from the date the patent application was filed. This duration rule applies to utility patents. (A design patent, however, exists for 14 years from the date it was granted.) A 1999 enactment of Congress allowed for the possible extension of a patent's duration if the Patent

Office delayed an unreasonably long time in acting on and approving the patentee's application.

The patentee may transfer ownership of the patent by making a written *assignment* of it to another party. Alternatively, the patentee may retain ownership and license others to make, use, or sell the patented invention. The terms of the licensing agreement are normally whatever the parties agree upon, subject to the rule that even if the agreement does not specify an ending date for the licensee's duty to pay royalties to the patent owner, the licensee has no obligation to continue paying royalties once the 20-year patent period expires.

As the Supreme Court made clear in *Quanta Computer v. LG Electronics*, 553 U.S. 617 (2008), once the patent owner or licensee sells an item embodying the patented invention, the sale of the item exhausts the patent owner's rights regarding that item. For instance, if A licenses B to produce and sell an item that requires use of A's patent, B's production and sale of the item entitles A, of course, to payment of the licensing fee called for by the agreement between A and B. However, A is not entitled to enforce its patent against C in the event that B sells the licensed item to C. B's sale of the item to C—a sale contemplated by the license A granted B—exhausted A's patent rights in regard to the item purchased by C.

LOG ON

The applications of successful patents are by their nature publicly available. You can easily search complete applications, including those for international patents, through Google's Patent search, found at **patents.google.com.**

Employers and Employees As we have seen, the Patent Act contemplates that the creator of an invention is entitled to obtain a patent if the necessary requirements are met. What happens, however, when the creator of the invention is an employee and her employer seeks rights in the invention? If the invention was developed by an employee *hired to do inventive or creative work*, she must use the invention solely for the employer's benefit and must assign any patents she obtains to the employer. (Prior to the America Invents Act (AIA), the patent in such a situation had to be issued in the name of the employee, who would then be obligated to assign the patent to the employer. The AIA now would permit the patent to be issued in the name of the employer in such an instance, if proper procedures are followed.)

If the employee was hired for purposes other than invention or creation, however, she owns any patent she acquires. Finally, regardless of the purpose for which the employee was hired, the *shop right* doctrine gives the employer a nonexclusive, royalty-free *license* to use the employee's invention

if it was created on company time and through the use of company facilities. Any patent the employee might retain is still effective against parties other than the employer.

Patent Infringement

 Explain what a patent owner must prove in order to establish that patent infringement occurred and identify defenses to a patent infringement claim.

Patent infringement occurs when a defendant, without authorization from the patentee, usurps the patentee's rights by making, using, or selling the patented invention. Because the Patent Act does not have an extraterritorial reach, the allegedly infringing activities must have occurred within the United States in order for a valid infringement claim to be triggered. The making of an item that would infringe a U.S. patent if the item were made within the United States will not constitute infringement if the item is made, for instance, in China. However, a provision of the Patent Act potentially allows infringement liability to be imposed on a party who ships "all or a substantial portion" of the components of the patented invention from the United States with the intended result that the components are assembled, in another country, to produce an item covered by the terms of the patent. In *Life Technologies Corp. v. Promega Corp.*, 137 S. Ct. 734 (2017), the Supreme Court held that the provision just noted did not give rise to liability when the defendant supplied, to an overseas assembler, only a single component of the plaintiff's patented, multicomponent invention. The Court reasoned that if an invention has multiple components, a single component is not a "substantial portion" for purposes of the statute.

Direct infringement may be established under principles of *literal* infringement or under a judicially developed approach known as the *doctrine of equivalents*. Infringement is literal in nature when the subject matter made, used, or sold by the defendant clearly falls within the stated terms of the claims of invention set forth in the patentee's application. Under the doctrine of equivalents, a defendant may be held liable for infringement even though the subject matter he made, used, or sold contained elements that were not identical to those described in the patentee's claims of invention, if the elements of the defendant's subject matter nonetheless may be seen as equivalent to those of the patented invention. A traditional formulation of the test posed by the doctrine of equivalents is whether the alleged infringer's subject matter performs substantially the same function as the protected invention in substantially the same way, in order to obtain the same result.

During the 1990s, an alleged infringer sought to convince the Supreme Court to abolish the doctrine of equivalents on the ground that it effectively allows patentees to extend the scope of patent protection beyond the stated terms approved by the PTO when it issued the patent. In *Warner-Jenkinson Co. v. Hilton Davis Chemical Co.*, 520 U.S. 17 (1997), however, the Court rejected this attack on the doctrine. The Court observed that in view of courts' longstanding use of the doctrine (use in which Congress seemingly acquiesced by not legislatively prohibiting it), arguments for abolishing the doctrine would be better addressed to Congress.

The forms of direct infringement discussed above are regarded as strict liability violations of the patent owner's rights because they do not require proof that the defendant intended to infringe and because a defendant's good-faith beliefs do not constitute a defense. In addition to the forms of direct infringement, the Patent Act sets forth further bases on which a defendant may be held liable for infringement. The statute provides that one who "actively induces" another party's infringement of a patent "shall be liable as an infringer." The Supreme Court has held in recent decisions that inducement liability cannot exist in the absence of proven direct infringement and in the absence of proof that the alleged inducer knew of the infringing nature of the induced acts. In an inducement case, is it a defense to liability if the defendant had a good-faith—though erroneous—belief that the plaintiff's patent was invalid? The Supreme Court answered "no" in *Commil USA, LLC v. Cisco Systems, Inc.*, 135 S. Ct. 1920 (2015).

Another section of the Patent Act provides that one may be held liable for contributory infringement if he sells a direct patent infringer a component of the patented invention, or something useful in employing a patented process, and does so with knowledge not only of the patent's existence, but also of the component's or other item's role in an infringing use. The thing sold must be a material part of the invention and must not be a staple article of commerce with some other significant use. For example, suppose that Irving directly infringes Potter's patent on a certain electronic device by selling essentially identical electronic devices. If Davis sells Irving sophisticated circuitry with knowledge of Potter's patent and of the circuitry's role in Irving's infringing use, Davis may be liable for contributory infringement (assuming that the circuitry is an important component of the electronic devices at issue and does not have other significant uses). Presumably the previously noted *Commil* rule—that a good-faith, but erroneous, belief in the supposed invalidity of the patent is not a defense to inducement liability—also applies in the contributory infringement setting.

The basic recovery for patent infringement is damages adequate to compensate for the infringement plus court costs and interest. The damages cannot be less than a reasonable royalty for the use made of the invention by the infringer. The court may in its discretion award damages of up to three times those actually suffered. Injunctive relief is also available, and attorney fees may be awarded in exceptional cases.

Because injunctions have so frequently been issued against defendants held liable for patent infringement, some courts had concluded that injunctions were effectively a mandatory remedy. However, in *eBay, Inc. v. MercExchange, LLC*, 547 U.S. 388 (2006), the Supreme Court ruled that courts are not required to issue an injunction against a defendant who committed patent infringement, if damages would be an adequate remedy and the public interest would not be served by the granting of an injunction.

Defenses to Patent Infringement

LO8-3 Explain what a patent owner must prove in order to establish that patent infringement occurred and identify defenses to a patent infringement claim.

Defendants in patent infringement cases cannot expect to avoid liability by pointing to their good-faith, but erroneous, belief that the plaintiff's patent was invalid. However, if the defendant establishes the *invalidity* of the patent, the defendant has a good defense against liability. Sometimes the patent's invalidity stems from the supposed invention's failure to fall within a patentable category or from its effectively amounting to a law of nature or an abstract idea. See the previous discussion of such issues, as well as the *Alice* decision that appears earlier in the chapter.

Often, the patent invalidity defense rests on the argument that the invention was not sufficiently novel or was obvious, and thus did not merit a patent. Despite the fact that the patent was issued by the PTO, courts have the ability to second-guess the PTO and order the cancellation of a patent on the ground of invalidity. Challenges to the validity of patents prove to be successful with reasonable frequency. In *Microsoft Corp. v. i4i Ltd. Partnership*, 131 S. Ct. 2238 (2011), the Supreme Court held that a party challenging a patent on the ground of invalidity must prove the facts underlying the invalidity contention by clear and convincing evidence rather than a mere preponderance of the evidence.

Furthermore, one may also challenge a patent's validity without first being sued for infringement by filing a declaratory judgment action that seeks a court ruling of invalidity.

In appropriate cases, the defendant can assert that the patentee has committed *patent misuse*. This is behavior that unjustifiably exploits the patent monopoly. For example, the patentee may require the purchaser of a license on his patent to buy his unpatented goods, or may tie the obtaining of a license on one of his patented inventions to the purchase of a license on another. One who refuses the patentee's terms and later infringes the patent may attempt to escape liability by arguing that the patentee misused his monopoly position.

Other Changes Resulting from the America Invents Act Probably the most significant change brought about by the AIA was the previously discussed switch to the first-to-file approach. Other AIA provisions that made important changes to the Patent Act included the following:

- An expansion of the ability of other parties to pursue, within the PTO, post-patent-issuance review of a patent's validity.
- Creation of an opportunity for third parties, during the patent application review process, to provide the PTO with relevant information bearing upon whether the applied-for patent should be granted.
- Expansion of the independent discovery defense to patent infringement so that the defense may be invoked not only as to business method patents, but also as to patents on processes or machines that have been used by a business for more than one year prior to another party's filing of a patent application.

Although controversy continues over whether business methods should be patentable, the AIA did not address that set of issues. Also left out of the AIA were measures directly restricting damage awards in patent infringement cases, despite calls in some quarters for such measures. Neither did the AIA deal with another subject of controversy in recent years: the emergence of the so-called patent trolls—parties that acquire patents from others, not for the purpose of producing the patented items themselves, but solely to exercise licensing leverage against users of the invention. However, recent Supreme Court decisions appear to contemplate greater ability on the part of courts to assess attorney fees against an apparent troll that loses an arguably frivolous patent infringement case.

LOG ON

U.S. government websites contain a wealth of information on patent, copyright, and trademark law and procedures. For information on patents and trademarks, visit the site of the U.S. Patent and Trademark Office, at **www.uspto.gov**. Information on copyrights may be found at **www.copyright.gov**, the site of the U.S. Copyright Office.

Copyrights Copyright law gives certain exclusive rights to creators of *original works of authorship*. It prevents others from using their work, gives them an incentive to innovate, and thereby benefits society. Yet copyright law also tries to balance these purposes against the equally compelling public interest in the free movement of ideas, information, and commerce. It does so mainly by limiting what a copyright on a work protects and by allowing the fair use defense described later.

Coverage

LO8-4 List types of works that may carry copyright protection.

The federal Copyright Act protects a wide range of works of authorship, including books, periodical articles, dramatic and musical compositions, works of art ("pictorial, graphic, and sculptural works"), motion pictures and other audiovisual works, sound recordings, lectures, computer programs, and architectural plans. To merit copyright protection, such works must be *fixed*—set out in a tangible medium of expression from which they can be perceived, reproduced, or communicated. They also must be *original* (the author's own work) and *creative* (reflecting exercise of the creator's judgment). Unlike the inventions protected by patent law, however, copyrightable works need not satisfy a novelty requirement.

Copyright protection does not extend to ideas, facts, procedures, processes, systems, methods of operation, concepts, principles, or discoveries. Instead, it protects the *ways in which such things are expressed*. For instance, an author's phrasing of a descriptive passage in a novel or the story line of a play would be expression protected by the copyright on the novel or play, but the ideas, themes, or messages underlying the work would not be protected. Similarly, the expression in nonfiction works and compilations of facts would be protected by the copyright on such works, even though the facts present in them would be fair game for all to use.

Computer programs involve their own special problems. It is fairly well settled that copyright law protects a program's *object code* (program instructions that are machine-readable but not intelligible to humans) and *source code* (instructions intelligible to humans). There is less agreement, however, about the copyrightability of a program's nonliteral elements such as its organization, its structure, and its presentation of information on the screen. Most courts that have considered the issue hold that nonliteral elements may sometimes be protected by copyright law, but courts differ about the extent of this protection.

Copyright protection does not extend to utilitarian objects, which the Copyright Act refers to as "useful articles." However, works of art that are incorporated into useful articles may sometimes be protected by copyright. In the *Star Athletica* case, which follows, the Supreme Court addresses such issues with regard to the design of cheerleading uniforms.

Star Athletica, LLC v. Varsity Brands, Inc.
137 S. Ct. 1002 (2017)

The Copyright Act of 1976, in 17 U.S.C. § 102(a), lists categories of copyrightable "works of authorship." One category, noted in § 102(a) (5), is "pictorial, graphic, and sculptural works." The following definition of "pictorial, graphic, and sculptural works" appears in § 101 of the statute:

> "Pictorial, graphic, and sculptural works" include two-dimensional and three-dimensional works of fine, graphic, and applied art, photographs, prints and art reproductions, maps, globes, charts, diagrams, models, and technical drawings, including architectural plans. Such works shall include works of artistic craftsmanship insofar as their form but not their mechanical or utilitarian aspects are concerned; the design of a useful article, as defined in this section, shall be considered a pictorial, graphic, or sculptural work only if, and only to the extent that, such design incorporates pictorial, graphic, or sculptural features that can be identified separately from, and are capable of existing independently of, the utilitarian aspects of the article.

Section 101 goes on to define "useful article" as "an article having an intrinsic utilitarian function that is not merely to portray the appearance of the article or to convey information. An article that is normally a part of a useful article is considered a 'useful article.'"

Varsity Brands, Inc.; Varsity Spirit Corporation; and Varsity Spirit Fashions & Supplies Inc. design, make, and sell cheerleading uniforms. The Varsity entities have obtained or acquired more than 200 U.S. copyright registrations for two-dimensional designs appearing on the surface of their uniforms and other garments. These designs, as described in their applications for copyright registrations, are primarily "combinations, positionings, and arrangements of elements" that include "chevrons . . . , lines, curves, stripes, angles, diagonals, inverted [chevrons], coloring, and shapes."

Star Athletica, LLC (referred to here as Star or as petitioner) also markets and sells cheerleading uniforms. The Varsity entities sued Star for infringing their copyrights in five designs. The federal district court entered summary judgment for Star, reasoning that the designs did not qualify as copyrightable pictorial, graphic, or sculptural works under the Copyright Act provisions quoted above. The district court concluded that the designs served the useful, or "utilitarian," function of identifying the garments as cheerleading uniforms and therefore could not satisfy the § 101 requirement of being separable from the uniform's utilitarian aspects.

The Varsity entities appealed to the U.S. Court of Appeals for the Sixth Circuit, which reversed the district court's decision. In the Sixth Circuit's view, the designs were separately identifiable from, and capable of existing independently of, the uniform for purposes of § 101. The U.S. Supreme Court granted Star's petition for certiorari.

Thomas, Justice

Congress has provided copyright protection for original works of art, but not for industrial designs. The line between art and industrial design, however, is often difficult to draw. This is particularly true when an industrial design incorporates artistic elements. Congress has afforded limited protection for these artistic elements by providing that "pictorial, graphic, or sculptural features" of the "design of a useful article" are eligible for copyright protection as artistic works if those features "can be identified separately from, and are capable of existing independently of, the utilitarian aspects of the article." 17 U.S.C. § 101. We granted certiorari to [identify] the proper test for implementing § 101's separate identification and independent-existence requirements.

The Copyright Act of 1976 defines copyrightable subject matter as "original works of authorship fixed in any tangible medium of expression." 17 U.S.C. § 102(a). "Works of authorship" include "pictorial, graphic, and sculptural works," § 102(a)(5), which the statute defines [in § 101] to include "two-dimensional and three-dimensional works of fine, graphic, and applied art, photographs,

prints and art reproductions, maps, globes, charts, diagrams, models, and technical drawings, including architectural plans."

The Copyright Act also establishes a special rule for copyrighting a pictorial, graphic, or sculptural work incorporated into a "useful article," which is defined as "an article having an intrinsic utilitarian function that is not merely to portray the appearance of the article or to convey information." § 101. The statute does not protect useful articles as such. Rather, "the design of a useful article" is "considered a pictorial, graphical, or sculptural work only if, and only to the extent that, such design incorporates pictorial, graphic, or sculptural features that can be identified separately from, and are capable of existing independently of, the utilitarian aspects of the article." *Id.*

Courts, the Copyright Office, and commentators have described the analysis undertaken to determine whether a feature can be separately identified from, and exist independently of, a useful article as "separability." In this case, our task is to determine whether the arrangements of lines, chevrons, and colorful shapes appearing on the surface of respondents' cheerleading

uniforms are eligible for copyright protection as separable features of the design of those cheerleading uniforms.

This is not a free-ranging search for the best copyright policy, but
rather "depends solely on statutory interpretation." *Mazer* v. *Stein*,
347 U.S. 201, 214 (1954). The statute provides that a "pictorial,
graphic, or sculptural featur[e]" incorporated into the "design of
a useful article" is eligible for copyright protection if it (1) "can
be identified separately from," and (2) is "capable of existing independently of, the utilitarian aspects of the article." § 101. The
first requirement—separate identification—is not onerous. The decisionmaker need only be able to look at the useful article and
spot some two- or three-dimensional element that appears to have
pictorial, graphic, or sculptural qualities.

The independent-existence requirement is ordinarily more difficult to satisfy. The decisionmaker must determine that the separately identified feature has the capacity to exist apart from the
utilitarian aspects of the article. In other words, the feature must
be able to exist as its own pictorial, graphic, or sculptural work as
defined in § 101 once it is imagined apart from the useful article.
If the feature is not capable of existing as a pictorial, graphic, or
sculptural work once separated from the useful article, then it was
not a pictorial, graphic, or sculptural feature of that article, but
rather one of its utilitarian aspects.

Of course, to qualify as a pictorial, graphic, or sculptural
work on its own, the feature cannot itself be a useful article or
"[a]n article that is normally a part of a useful article" (which
is itself considered a useful article). § 101. Nor could someone
claim a copyright in a useful article merely by creating a replica
of that article in some other medium—for example, a cardboard
model of a car. Although the replica could itself be copyrightable, it would not give rise to any rights in the useful article
that inspired it.

The statute as a whole confirms our interpretation. The Copyright Act provides "the owner of [a] copyright" with the "exclusive righ[t] . . . to reproduce the copyrighted work in copies."
§ 106(1). The statute clarifies that this right "includes the right
to reproduce the [copyrighted] work in or on any kind of article,
whether useful or otherwise." § 113(a). Section 101 is, in essence,
the mirror image of § 113(a). Whereas § 113(a) protects a work of
authorship first fixed in some tangible medium other than a useful
article and subsequently applied to a useful article, § 101 protects
art first fixed in the medium of a useful article. The two provisions
make clear that copyright protection extends to pictorial, graphic,
and sculptural works regardless of whether they were created as
freestanding art or as features of useful articles. The ultimate separability question, then, is whether the feature for which copyright
protection is claimed would have been eligible for copyright protection as a pictorial, graphic, or sculptural work had it originally
been fixed in some tangible medium other than a useful article
before being applied to a useful article.

This interpretation is also consistent with the history of
the Copyright Act. In *Mazer*, a case decided under the 1909
Copyright Act, the respondents copyrighted a statuette depicting
a dancer. The statuette was intended for use as a lamp base, with
electric wiring, sockets and lamp shades attached. Copies of the
statuette were sold both as lamp bases and separately as statu-
ettes. The petitioners copied the statuette and sold lamps with
the statuette as the base. They defended against the respondents'
infringement suit by arguing that the respondents did not have a
copyright in a statuette intended for use as a lamp base.

Two of *Mazer*'s holdings are relevant here. First, the Court
held that the respondents owned a copyright in the statuette even
though it was intended for use as a lamp base. 347 U.S. at 214.
In doing so, the Court approved the Copyright Office's regulation extending copyright protection to works of art that might
also serve a useful purpose. Second, the Court held that it was
irrelevant to the copyright inquiry whether the statuette was initially created as a freestanding sculpture or as a lamp base. *Id.* at
218-19. *Mazer* thus interpreted the 1909 Act consistently with the
rule discussed above: If a design would have been copyrightable
as a standalone pictorial, graphic, or sculptural work, it is copyrightable if created first as part of a useful article.

Shortly thereafter, the Copyright Office enacted a regulation
implementing the holdings of *Mazer*. The regulation introduced
the modern separability test to copyright law. Congress [later] essentially lifted the language governing protection for the design of
a useful article directly from the post-*Mazer* regulation and placed
it into § 101 of the 1976 Act. Consistent with *Mazer*, the approach
we outline today interprets §§ 101 and 113 in a way that would
afford copyright protection to the statuette in *Mazer* regardless
of whether it was first created as a standalone sculptural work
or as the base of the lamp. In sum, a feature of the design of a
useful article is eligible for copyright if, when identified and imagined apart from the useful article, it would qualify as a pictorial,
graphic, or sculptural work either on its own or when fixed in
some other tangible medium.

Applying this test to the surface decorations on the cheerleading uniforms is straightforward. First, one can identify the decorations as features having pictorial, graphic, or sculptural qualities.
Second, if the arrangement of colors, shapes, stripes, and chevrons on the surface of the cheerleading uniforms were separated
from the uniform and applied in another medium—for example,
on a painter's canvas—they would qualify as "two-dimensional . . .
works of . . . art" [for purposes of] § 101. And imaginatively removing the surface decorations from the uniforms and applying them
in another medium would not replicate the uniform itself. Indeed,
respondents have applied the designs in this case to other media
of expression—different types of clothing—without replicating the
uniform. The decorations are therefore separable from the uniforms and eligible for copyright protection. (We do not today hold,

however, that the surface decorations *are* copyrightable. [We hold only that they are *eligible* for copyright protection.] We express no opinion on whether these works are sufficiently original to qualify for copyright protection, or on whether any other prerequisite of a valid copyright has been satisfied.)

The dissent argues that the designs are not separable because imaginatively removing them from the uniforms and placing them in some other medium of expression—a canvas, for example—would create "pictures of cheerleader uniforms." Petitioner similarly argues that the decorations cannot be copyrighted because, even when extracted from the useful article, they retain the outline of a cheerleading uniform.

This is not a bar to copyright. Just as two-dimensional fine art corresponds to the shape of the canvas on which it is painted, two-dimensional applied art correlates to the contours of the article on which it is applied. A fresco painted on a wall, ceiling panel, or dome would not lose copyright protection, for example, simply because it was designed to track the dimensions of the surface on which it was painted. Or consider, for example, a design etched or painted on the surface of a guitar. If that entire design is imaginatively removed from the guitar's surface and placed on an album cover, it would still resemble the shape of a guitar. But the image on the cover does not "replicate" the guitar as a useful article. Rather, the design is a two-dimensional work of art that corresponds to the shape of the useful article to which it was applied. The statute protects that work of art whether it is first drawn on the album cover and then applied to the guitar's surface, or vice versa. Failing to protect that art would create an anomaly: It would extend protection to two-dimensional designs that cover a part of a useful article but would not protect the same design if it covered the entire article. The statute does not support that distinction.

To be clear, the only feature of the cheerleading uniform eligible for a copyright in this case is the two-dimensional work of art fixed in the tangible medium of the uniform fabric. Even if respondents ultimately succeed in establishing a valid copyright in the surface decorations at issue here, respondents have no right to prohibit any person from manufacturing a cheerleading uniform of identical shape, cut, and dimensions to the ones on which the decorations in this case appear. They may prohibit only the reproduction of the surface designs in any tangible medium of expression—a uniform or otherwise.

Petitioner argues that allowing the surface decorations to qualify as a "work of authorship" is inconsistent with congressional intent to entirely exclude industrial design from copyright. Petitioner notes that Congress refused to pass a provision that would have provided limited copyright protection for industrial designs, including clothing, when it enacted the 1976 Act, and that it has enacted laws protecting designs for specific useful articles—semiconductor chips and boat hulls—while declining to enact other industrial design statutes. From this history of failed legislation, petitioner reasons that Congress intends to channel intellectual property claims for industrial design into design patents. It therefore urges us to approach this question with a presumption against copyrightability.

We do not share petitioner's concern. As an initial matter, "[c]ongressional inaction lacks persuasive significance" in most circumstances. [Citation omitted.] Moreover, we have long held that design patent and copyright are not mutually exclusive. *See Mazer*, 347 U.S. at 217. Congress has provided for limited copyright protection for certain features of industrial design, and approaching the statute with presumptive hostility toward protection for industrial design would undermine Congress's choice. In any event, as explained above, our test does not render the shape, cut, and physical dimensions of the cheerleading uniforms eligible for copyright protection.

We hold that an artistic feature of the design of a useful article is eligible for copyright protection if the feature (1) can be perceived as a two- or three-dimensional work of art separate from the useful article and (2) would qualify as a protectable pictorial, graphic, or sculptural work either on its own or in some other medium if imagined separately from the useful article. Because the designs on the surface of respondents' cheerleading uniforms in this case satisfy these requirements, the [designs are eligible for copyright protection.]

Sixth Circuit's decision affirmed.

Creation and Notice A copyright comes into existence upon the creation and fixing of a protected work. Although a copyright owner may register the copyright with the U.S. Copyright Office, registration is not necessary for the copyright to exist. However, registration normally is a procedural prerequisite to filing a suit for copyright infringement. Even though it is not required, copyright owners often provide *notice* of the copyright. Federal law authorizes a basic form of notice for use with most copyrighted works. A book, for example, might include the term *Copyright* (or the abbreviation *Copr.* or the symbol ©), the year of its first publication, and the name of the copyright owner in a location likely to give reasonable notice to readers.

Duration

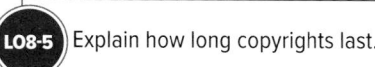

LO8-5 Explain how long copyrights last.

The U.S. Constitution's Copyright and Patents Clause (Article I, § 8) empowers Congress to "promote the Progress of Science and useful Arts" by enacting copyright and patent laws that "secur[e] for limited Times to Authors and Inventors the exclusive Right to their respective Writings and Discoveries." Thus, copyrights and patents cannot last forever. Even so, the history of copyright protection in the United States has featured various significant lengthenings of the "limited time" a copyright endures. When a copyright's duration ends, the underlying work enters the public domain and becomes available for any uses other parties wish to make of it. The former copyright owner, therefore, loses control over the work and forfeits what had been valuable legal rights.

With the enactment of the Sonny Bono Copyright Term Extension Act (hereinafter CTEA) in 1998, Congress conferred a substantial benefit on copyright owners. The CTEA added 20 years to the duration of copyrights, not only for works created after the CTEA's enactment, *but also for any preexisting work that was still under valid copyright protection* as of the CTEA's 1998 effective date. Copyright owners—especially some high-profile corporations whose copyrights on older works would soon have expired if not for the enactment of the CTEA—mounted a significant lobbying effort in favor of the term extension provided by the CTEA.

The CTEA's effect cannot be understood without discussion of the copyright duration rules that existed immediately before the CTEA's enactment. One set of rules applied to works created in 1978 or thereafter; another set applied to pre-1978 works. The copyright on pre-1978 works was good for a term of 28 years from first publication of the work, plus a renewal term of 47 years. (The renewal term had been only 28 years until Congress changed the law in 1976 and added 19 more years to the renewal term for any work then under valid copyright protection.) As a result, 75 years of protection was available for pre-1978 works.

For works created in 1978 or thereafter, Congress scrapped the initial-term-plus-renewal-term approach, opting instead for a normally applicable rule that the copyright lasts for the life of the author/creator plus 50 years. This basic duration rule did not apply, however, if the copyrighted work, though created in 1978 or thereafter, was a work-for-hire. (The two types of work-for-hire will be explained below.) In a work-for-hire situation, the copyright would exist for 75 years from first publication of the work or 100 years from creation of it, whichever came first.

The CTEA tacked on 20 years to the durations contemplated by the rules discussed in the preceding two paragraphs. A pre-1978 work that was still under valid copyright protection as of 1998 (when the CTEA took effect) now has a total protection period of 95 years from first publication—a 28-year initial term plus a renewal term that has been lengthened from 47 to 67 years. The copyright on Disney's "Steamboat Willie" cartoon—best known for its introduction of the famous Mickey Mouse character—serves as an example. The protection period for the Steamboat Willie copyright began to run in the late 1920s, when the cartoon was released and distributed (i.e., published, for purposes of copyright law). Given the rule that existed immediately before the CTEA's enactment (an initial term of 28 years plus a renewal term of 47 years), the Steamboat Willie copyright would have expired within the first few years of the current century. The CTEA, however, gave Disney an additional 20 years of rights over the Steamboat Willie cartoon before it would pass into the public domain.

With the enactment of the CTEA, the basic duration rule for works created in 1978 or thereafter is now life of the author/creator plus 70 years (up from 50). The duration rule for a work-for-hire is now 95 years from first publication (up from 75) or 120 years from creation (up from 100), whichever comes first.

Critics of the CTEA mounted a constitutional challenge to the statute in *Eldred v. Ashcroft*, a case that made its way to the Supreme Court. Those challenging the CTEA argued that the statute violated the purpose of the "limited Times" provision in the Constitution's Copyright Clause by making copyright protection so lengthy in duration. They also contended that the Copyright Clause's language empowering Congress to enact copyright laws to "promote the Progress of Science and useful Arts" served as an *incentive-to-create* limitation on the exercise of that power, and that the CTEA—at least insofar as it applied to works already created as of 1998—unconstitutionally violated the incentive-to-create limitation. In its 2003 decision in *Eldred*, 537 U.S. 186, the Supreme Court rejected the constitutional challenge to the CTEA. The Court concluded that the CTEA may have been an unwise enactment as a matter of public policy, but that it fell within the authority extended to Congress by the Copyright Clause.

Works-for-Hire A work-for-hire exists when (1) an employee, in the course of her regular employment duties, prepares a copyrightable work or (2) an individual or corporation and an independent contractor (i.e., nonemployee) enter into a written agreement under which the independent contractor is to prepare, for the retaining individual or corporation, one of several types of copyrightable works designated in the Copyright Act. In the first situation, the employer is legally classified as the work's author and copyright owner. In the second situation, the party who (or which) retained the independent contractor is considered the resulting work's author and copyright owner.

Ownership Rights

 LO8-6 Explain the rights copyright owners hold and the relationship of those rights to claims for copyright infringement.

A copyright owner has exclusive rights to reproduce the copyrighted work, prepare derivative works based on it (e.g., a movie version of a novel), and distribute copies of the work by sale or otherwise. With certain copyrighted works, the copyright owner also obtains the exclusive right to perform the work or display it publicly.

Copyright ownership initially resides in the creator of the copyrighted work, but the copyright may be transferred to another party. Also, the owner may individually transfer any of her ownership rights, or a portion of each, without losing ownership of the remaining rights. Most transfers of copyright ownership require a writing signed by the owner or his agent. The owner may also retain ownership while licensing the copyrighted work or a portion of it.

First Sale Doctrine An earlier discussion in this chapter dealt with patent law's first sale doctrine. Copyright law recognizes such a doctrine as well. As in patent law, copyright law's first sale doctrine extinguishes a copyright owner's rights regarding a particular copy of the copyrighted work once that copy has been lawfully sold.

For example, this book is a copyrighted work. Once the publishing company (the copyright owner in this instance) sells a copy of the book to, say, a bookstore, the copyright owner cannot control the further distribution of that copy of the book. The bookstore can sell it to you, you can sell or give that copy to someone else, and so on.

Copies of the textbook in the above example were published in the United States. Does the first sale doctrine apply when the relevant copies were produced outside the United States? In *Kirtsaeng v. John Wiley & Sons*, which follows, the Supreme Court addresses that question. The Court also considers the relationship between the first sale doctrine and a separate federal law providing that a copyright owner's right to distribute copies of the work is violated when copies of the work are acquired overseas and imported into the United States without the copyright owner's authorization.

Kirtsaeng v. John Wiley & Sons, Inc.　568 U.S. 519 (2013)

The Copyright Act grants certain "exclusive rights" to copyright owners. See 17 U.S.C. § 106. Among those rights is the right "to distribute copies" of the copyrighted work. Id. § 106(3). However, the copyright owner's rights are qualified by limitations set out in §§ 107 through 122, including the "first sale" doctrine. This doctrine, as set forth in § 109(a), provides that "the owner of a particular copy or phonorecord lawfully made under this title . . . is entitled, without the authority of the copyright owner, to sell or otherwise dispose of the possession of that copy or phonorecord."

A separate provision in federal law, § 602(a)(1), states that "[i]mportation into the United States, without the authority of the owner of copyright under this title, of copies . . . of a work that have been acquired outside the United States is an infringement of the exclusive right to distribute copies . . . under section 106." In Quality King Distributors v. L'anza Research Int'l, *523 U.S. 135, 145 (1998), the Supreme Court held that § 602(a)(1)'s reference to § 106(3) incorporates the §§ 107 through 122 limitations on copyright owners' rights, including § 109(a)'s first sale doctrine. The importer in* Quality King *therefore was held entitled to invoke the first sale doctrine as a defense. The imported copy at issue in that case was initially manufactured in the United States and then sent abroad and sold.*

John Wiley & Sons Inc. (Wiley), an academic textbook publisher, often assigns to its wholly owned foreign subsidiary (Wiley Asia) rights to publish, print, and sell foreign editions of Wiley's English-language textbooks abroad. As a result, there are often two essentially equivalent versions of a Wiley textbook (with each version being manufactured and sold with Wiley's permission): (1) an American version printed and sold in the United States and (2) a foreign version manufactured and sold abroad. The books produced and sold by Wiley Asia contain notices stating that they are to be sold only in certain designated nations other than the United States or in certain designated regions of the world outside the United States and that they are not to be taken into the United States without Wiley's permission.

Supap Kirtsaeng, a citizen of Thailand, was a student in the United States. He asked friends and family to buy foreign edition English-language Wiley textbooks in Thai book shops, where they sold at low prices, and to mail them to him in the United States They did so. Kirtsaeng then sold the books, reimbursed his family and friends, and kept the profits.

Wiley sued Kirtsaeng, claiming that his unauthorized importation and resale of the books infringed Wiley's § 106(3) right to distribute and § 602(a)(1)'s import prohibition. Kirtsaeng argued that because the books were "lawfully made" and acquired legitimately, § 109(a)'s first sale doctrine permitted importation and resale without Wiley's further permission. A federal district court held that the first sale doctrine does not apply to copies produced outside the United States and that Kirtsaeng therefore could not assert this defense. The jury found that Kirtsaeng had willfully infringed Wiley's copyrights and that Wiley was entitled to recover statutory damages totaling $600,000. The U.S. Court of Appeals for the Second Circuit affirmed, concluding that § 109(a)'s "lawfully made under this title" language does not sweep in copies of American copyrighted works manufactured abroad. With other federal courts having ruled differently on whether the first sale doctrine applies only when the copies were produced in the United States, the Supreme Court agreed to decide the case in order to resolve the split among the lower courts.

Breyer, Justice

[E]ven though § 106(3) forbids distribution of a copy of [a] copyrighted novel [work] without the copyright owner's permission, § 109(a) adds that, once a copy of [the work] has been lawfully sold (or its ownership otherwise lawfully transferred), the buyer of *that copy* and subsequent owners are free to dispose of it as they wish. In copyright jargon, the "first sale" has "exhausted" the copyright owner's § 106(3) exclusive distribution right [as to that copy].

What, however, if the copy of [the work] was printed abroad and then initially sold with the copyright owner's permission? Does the first sale doctrine still apply? Is the buyer, like the buyer of a domestically manufactured copy, free to bring the copy into the United States and dispose of it as he or she wishes?

To put the matter technically, an "importation" provision, § 602(a)(1), says that "[i]mportation into the United States, without the authority of the owner of copyright under this title, of copies . . . of a work that have been acquired outside the United States is an infringement of the exclusive right to distribute copies . . . under section 106." Thus § 602(a)(1) makes clear that importing a copy without permission violates the owner's exclusive distribution right. But in doing so, § 602(a)(1) refers explicitly to the § 106(3) exclusive distribution right. [Section] 106 is by its terms "[s]ubject to" the various doctrines and principles contained in §§ 107 through 122, including § 109(a)'s first sale limitation. Do those same modifications apply—in particular, does the first sale modification apply—when considering whether § 602(a)(1) prohibits importing a copy?

In *Quality King Distributors v. L'anza Research Int'l*, 523 U.S. 135, 145 (1998), we held that § 602(a)(1)'s reference to § 106(3)'s exclusive distribution right incorporates the later subsections' limitations, including, in particular, the first sale doctrine of § 109. Thus, it might seem that, § 602(a)(1) notwithstanding, one who buys a copy abroad can freely import that copy into the United States and dispose of it, just as he could had he bought the copy in the United States.

But *Quality King* considered an instance in which the copy, though purchased abroad, was initially manufactured in the United States (and then sent abroad and sold). This case is like *Quality King* but for one important fact. The copies at issue here were manufactured abroad. That fact is important because

§ 109(a) says that the first sale doctrine applies to "a particular copy or phonorecord *lawfully made under this title*." And we must decide here whether the five words, "lawfully made under this title," make a critical legal difference.

Putting section numbers to the side, we ask whether the first sale doctrine applies to protect a buyer or other lawful owner of a copy (of a copyrighted work) lawfully manufactured abroad. Can that buyer bring that copy into the United States (and sell it or give it away) without obtaining permission to do so from the copyright owner? Can, for example, someone who purchases, say at a used bookstore, a book printed abroad subsequently resell it without the copyright owner's permission?

We must decide whether the words "lawfully made under this title" restrict the scope of § 109(a)'s first sale doctrine geographically. The Second Circuit, the Ninth Circuit, Wiley, and the Solicitor General (as *amicus*) all read those words as imposing a form of *geographical* limitation. The Second Circuit held that they limit the first sale doctrine to particular copies "made in territories *in which the Copyright Act is law*," which (the Circuit says) are copies "manufactured domestically," not "outside of the United States." [Citation omitted.] [The Ninth Circuit has reached the same conclusion through similar reasoning. Wiley and the Solicitor General make essentially the same argument.]

Under [such a] geographical interpretation, § 109(a)'s first sale doctrine would not apply to the Wiley Asia books at issue here. And, despite an American copyright owner's permission to *make* copies abroad, one who *buys* a copy of any such book or other copyrighted work—whether at a retail store, over the Internet, or at a library sale—could not resell (or otherwise dispose of) that particular copy without further permission.

Kirtsaeng, however, reads the words "lawfully made under this title" as imposing a *non*-geographical limitation. He says that they mean made "in accordance with" or "in compliance with" the Copyright Act. Brief for Petitioner. [Under that interpretation], § 109(a)'s first sale doctrine would apply to copyrighted works as long as their manufacture met the requirements of American copyright law. In particular, the doctrine would apply where, as here, copies are manufactured abroad with the permission of the copyright owner. See § 106 (referring to the owner's right to authorize [the making of copies]).

In our view, § 109(a)'s language, its context, and the common-law history of the first sale doctrine, taken together, favor a *non-geographical* interpretation. [*Authors' note*: The Court engaged in extensive explanation of the linguistic difficulties and potentially complex questions that a geographical interpretation would involve and stressed the relative simplicity and easier-to-apply nature of the nongeographical interpretation. In addition, the Court explained at length why a legislative history approach also favored a nongeographic interpretation, chiefly because a previous version of the statutory section outlining the first sale doctrine did not include a geographic limitation and because the language inserted in the current statutory section did not seem to add a geographic qualifier. The Court also explained that the common law version of the first sale doctrine (which existed before the doctrine was placed in statutory form) did not contemplate a geographic limitation. Details of the Court's statutory language, legislative history, and common law discussions are omitted.]

We also doubt that Congress would have intended to create the practical copyright-related harms with which a geographical interpretation would threaten ordinary scholarly, artistic, commercial, and consumer activities. Associations of libraries, used-book dealers, technology companies, consumer-goods retailers, and museums point to various ways in which a geographical interpretation would fail to further basic constitutional copyright objectives, in particular "promot[ing] the Progress of Science and useful Arts." U.S. Const., Art. I, § 8, cl. 8. The American Library Association tells us that library collections contain at least 200 million books published abroad (presumably, many were first published in one of the nearly 180 copyright-treaty nations and enjoy American copyright protection under 17 U.S.C. § 104); that many others were first published in the United States but printed abroad because of lower costs; and that a geographical interpretation will likely require the libraries to obtain permission (or at least create significant uncertainty) before circulating or otherwise distributing these books. Brief for American Library Association et al. as *Amici Curiae*.

How, the American Library Association asks, are the libraries to obtain permission to distribute these millions of books? How can they find, say, the copyright owner of a foreign book, perhaps written decades ago? They may not know the copyright holder's present address. And, even where addresses can be found, the costs of finding them, contacting owners, and negotiating may be high indeed. Are the libraries to stop circulating or distributing or displaying the millions of books in their collections that were printed abroad?

Used-book dealers tell us that, from the time when Benjamin Franklin and Thomas Jefferson built commercial and personal libraries of foreign books, American readers have bought used books published and printed abroad. Brief for Powell's Books Inc. et al. as *Amici Curiae*. The dealers say that they have "operat[ed] . . .

for centuries" under the assumption that the "first sale" doctrine applies. But under a geographical interpretation a contemporary tourist who buys, say, at Shakespeare and Co. (in Paris), a dozen copies of a foreign book for American friends might find that she had violated the copyright law. The used-book dealers cannot easily predict what the foreign copyright holder may think about a reader's effort to sell a used copy of a novel. And they believe that a geographical interpretation will injure a large portion of the used-book business.

Technology companies tell us that "automobiles, microwaves, calculators, mobile phones, tablets, and personal computers" contain copyrightable software programs or packaging. Brief for Public Knowledge et al. as *Amici Curiae*. Many of these items are made abroad with the American copyright holder's permission and then sold and imported (with that permission) to the United States. A geographical interpretation would prevent the resale of, say, a car, without the permission of the holder of each copyright on each piece of copyrighted automobile software. Yet there is no reason to believe that foreign auto manufacturers regularly obtain this kind of permission from their software component suppliers. Without that permission, a foreign car owner [presumably] could not [lawfully] sell his or her used car [if the geographical interpretation were adopted].

Retailers tell us that over $2.3 trillion worth of foreign goods were imported in 2011. Brief for Retail Litigation Center. American retailers buy many of these goods after a first sale abroad. And, many of these items bear, carry, or contain copyrighted "packaging, logos, labels, and product inserts and instructions for [the use of] everyday packaged goods from floor cleaners and health and beauty products to breakfast cereals." The retailers add that American sales of more traditional copyrighted works, "such as books, recorded music, motion pictures, and magazines," likely amount to over $220 billion. A geographical interpretation would subject many, if not all, of them to the disruptive impact of the threat of infringement suits.

Art museum directors ask us to consider their efforts to display foreign-produced works by, say, Cy Twombly, Rene Magritte, Henri Matisse, Pablo Picasso, and others. A geographical interpretation, they say, would require the museums to obtain permission from the copyright owners before they could display the work—even if the copyright owner has already sold or donated the work to a foreign museum. Brief for Association of Art Museum Directors et al. as *Amici Curiae*. What are the museums to do, they ask, if the artist retained the copyright, if the artist cannot be found, or if a group of heirs is arguing about who owns which copyright?

[R]eliance upon the first sale doctrine is deeply embedded in the practices of those, such as booksellers, libraries, museums, and retailers, who have long relied upon its protection. [W]e believe that the practical problems that Kirtsaeng and his *amici* have described are too serious, too extensive, and too likely to come about for us to dismiss them as insignificant—particularly in light of the ever-growing importance of foreign trade to America. The upshot is that copyright-related consequences along with language, context, and interpretive canons argue strongly against a geographical interpretation of § 109(a).

Wiley [also argues] that our *Quality King* decision strongly supports [the] geographical interpretation [that Wiley favors]. [In that case,] an American copyright owner authorized the first sale and export of hair care products with copyrighted labels made in the United States, and [an overseas] buyer sought to import them back into the United States without the copyright owner's permission. We held that the importation provision [§ 602(a)] did *not* prohibit sending the products back into the United States without the copyright owner's permission. We pointed out that [the importation section made] importation an infringement of the "exclusive right to distribute . . . under § 106." We noted that § 109(a)'s first sale doctrine limits the scope of the § 106 exclusive distribution right. We took as given the fact that the products at issue had at least once been sold. And we held that consequently, importation of the copyrighted labels did not violate [the importation section].

[Although the products at issue in *Quality King* had been produced in the United States before being sent overseas and then reimported, as opposed to being produced overseas, the *Quality King* holding did not depend on that fact. Any statement seeming to suggest that production in the United States was a key fact on which that decision depended—or that *Quality King* was adopting a geographical limitation on the first-sale doctrine—was dictum and therefore not binding here.]

[The nongeographical interpretation adopted here does not] make § 602(a)(1) pointless. Section 602(a)(1) would still [generally] forbid importing (without permission . . .) copies lawfully made abroad, for example, where (1) a foreign publisher operating as the licensee of an American publisher prints copies of a book overseas but, prior to any authorized sale, seeks to send them to the United States; (2) a foreign printer or other manufacturer (if not the "owner" for purposes of § 109(a), e.g., before an authorized sale) sought to send copyrighted goods to the United States; (3) a book publisher transports copies to a wholesaler and the wholesaler (not yet the owner) sends them to the United States; or (4) a foreign film distributor, having leased films for distribution, or any other licensee, consignee, or bailee sought to send them to the United States. These examples show that § 602(a)(1) retains significance.

For [the foregoing] reasons we conclude that the considerations supporting Kirtsaeng's nongeographical interpretation of the words "lawfully made under this title" are the more persuasive.

Second Circuit decision reversed; Kirtsaeng held entitled to invoke first sale doctrine; case remanded for further proceedings.

Infringement

 LO8-6 Explain the rights copyright owners hold and the relationship of those rights to claims for copyright infringement.

Those who violate any of the copyright owner's exclusive rights may be liable for copyright infringement. Infringement is fairly easily proven when direct evidence of significant copying exists; verbatim copying of protected material is an example. Usually, however, proof of infringement involves establishing that (1) the defendant had *access* to the copyrighted work; (2) the defendant engaged in enough *copying*—either deliberately or subconsciously—that the resemblance between the allegedly infringing work and the copyrighted work does not seem coincidental; and (3) there is *substantial similarity* between the two works.

Access may be proven circumstantially, such as by showing that the copyrighted work was widely circulated. The copying and substantial similarity elements, which closely relate to each other, necessarily involve discretionary case-by-case determinations. Of course, the copying and

substantial similarity must exist with regard to the copyrighted work's protected expression. Copying of general ideas, facts, themes, and the like (i.e., copying of unprotected matter) is not infringement. The defendant's having paraphrased protected expression does not constitute a defense to what otherwise appears to be infringement. Neither does the defendant's having credited the copyrighted work as the source from which the defendant borrowed.

Recent years' explosion in Internet usage has led to difficult copyright questions. For instance, unlicensed services such as Napster, Grokster, and StreamCast allowed easy and free-of-charge access to musical recordings in digital files. Owners of copyrights on songs and recordings resorted to litigation against such providers on the theory that they materially contributed to or induced copyright infringement by their users. In the *Grokster* decision, the Supreme Court focused on the inducement basis for imposing liability. For discussion of that case, see the nearby Cyberlaw in Action box.

The basic recovery for copyright infringement is the owner's actual damages plus the attributable profits received by the infringer. In lieu of the basic remedy, however, the plaintiff may usually elect to receive *statutory*

CYBERLAW IN ACTION

Grokster Ltd. and StreamCast Networks Inc. distributed free software products allowing computer users to share electronic files through peer-to-peer networks in which users' computers communicated directly with each other rather than through central servers. Although the networks these persons enjoyed through using the Grokster and StreamCast software could be employed for the sharing of any type of digital file, most users employed the networks in order to share copyrighted music and video files without authorization. Numerous copyright owners—including motion picture studios, recording companies, songwriters, and music publishers, but referred to here as MGM for convenience—filed separate lawsuits against Grokster and StreamCast in an effort to have them held liable for their users' copyright infringements.

The various cases were consolidated into one case in a federal district court. Evidence produced in the district court proceedings indicated that users who downloaded the Grokster and StreamCast software received the protocol to send requests for files directly to the computers of others using compatible software. If the requested file was found, the requesting user could download it directly from the computer where it was located. As this description indicates, Grokster and StreamCast used no servers to intercept the content of the search requests or to mediate the file transfers conducted by users of their software. Although Grokster and StreamCast therefore did not know when particular files were copied, searches using their software revealed what was available on the networks the software reached. A study by a statistician for MGM showed that nearly 90 percent of the files available for download by Grokster and StreamCast users were copyrighted works. Grokster and StreamCast disputed this figure, argued that free copying of copyrighted works is sometimes authorized by the copyright holders and asserted that potential noninfringing uses of its software were significant. Some musical performers, the defendants noted, had gained new audiences by distributing their copyrighted works for free across peer-to-peer networks, and some distributors of public domain content (e.g., Shakespeare's plays) had used peer-to-peer networks to disseminate files. MGM provided evidence tending to indicate, however, that the vast majority of users' downloads were acts of infringement.

The district court granted summary judgment in favor of Grokster and StreamCast because the fact that no files passed through servers they owned or controlled meant that they did not have knowledge of particular acts of infringement (even if they knew of infringing uses in general) and that they therefore had neither a duty nor the ability to police how their systems were being used. Therefore, the court reasoned, the defendants could not be held liable for contributory or vicarious infringement. After a federal court of appeals affirmed, the Supreme Court granted MGM's request that it hear the case.

The Supreme Court went in another direction, holding that Grokster and StreamCast could be held liable for infringement on the basis of *inducement*. For the Court, it was highly significant that the record produced at the district court level revealed considerable evidence of the defendants' loud and public voicing—through electronic newsletters, electronic advertisements, and other means—of the objective that recipients of the Grokster and StreamCast software use it to download copyrighted works. MGM presented further evidence suggesting that after a successful lawsuit by copyright owners effectively shut down the Napster file-sharing service (which had routed files through Napster's servers), Grokster and StreamCast sought to promote their software as devices by which former Napster users could obtain easy access to desired files. Although Grokster and StreamCast distributed their software free of charge, they made money by selling advertising space and streaming the advertising to users of the software.

The Court observed that "[t]he question is under what circumstances the distributor of a product capable of both lawful and unlawful use is liable for acts of copyright infringement by third parties using the product." Confirming that the inducement basis of liability exists as part of copyright law, the Court held that "one who distributes a device with the object of promoting its use to infringe copyright, as shown by clear expression or other affirmative steps taken to foster infringement, is liable for the resulting acts of infringement by third parties." Under the Court's reasoning, the fact that the Grokster and StreamCast systems could have been used for significant noninfringing purposes probably would have insulated the defendants against liability if they had not actively promoted the infringing uses to which their systems could be put.

damages. The statutory damages set by the trial judge or jury must fall within the range of $750 to $30,000 unless the infringement was willful, in which event the maximum rises to $150,000. These limits do not apply if the plaintiff elects the basic remedy, however. Injunctive relief and awards of costs and attorney fees are possible in appropriate cases. Although it seldom does so, the federal government may pursue a criminal copyright infringement prosecution if the infringement was willful and for purposes of commercial advantage or private financial gain.

Fair Use

List the fair use factors and apply them to fact patterns in which the fair use defense to copyright infringement liability is invoked.

The fair use doctrine recognizes that the social purposes present in certain uses of copyrighted works may be important enough to excuse defendants' uses of the works without permission. When a court concludes that the defendant is entitled to the protection of the fair use defense, the defendant avoids liability for what otherwise would have been copyright infringement. In many infringement cases, there is little or no dispute over whether the defendant's actions would be infringing if the fair use defense did not apply. Therefore, whether the defendant's use was or was not fair use frequently demands much of the court's attention.

In the Copyright Act, Congress singled out these uses as good candidates for fair use protection: criticism or comment; news reporting; and teaching, scholarship, or research. The words *good candidates* are important here because even a use that falls within the list just noted could be held not to be fair use once the court engages in the necessary weighing and balancing of relevant factors specified by Congress. Those factors are (1) the purpose and character of the use; (2) the nature of the copyrighted work; (3) the amount and substantiality of the portion used in relation to the copyrighted work as a whole; and (4) the effect, if any, of the use on the potential markets for, or value of, the copyrighted work. The case-by-case nature of the inquiry makes fair use determinations highly fact-specific.

Two leading Supreme Court decisions serve as useful examples. In *Harper & Row, Publishers v. Nation Enterprises*, 471 U.S. 539 (1985), the Court applied the factors noted above and concluded that the fair use defense did not protect a magazine against copyright infringement liability for using, in a magazine article, 300 to 400 words from an unpublished book manuscript (the memoirs of former President Gerald Ford). The Court held that fair use was not present even though the magazine argued that it was engaging in news reporting and an educational endeavor.

In *Campbell v. Acuff-Rose Music, Inc.*, 510 U.S. 569 (1994), the Court ruled that use of portions of a copyrighted work for purposes of parody (a form of criticism or comment) will often have a strong claim to fair use protection. By stating that the fair use factors—especially the first but also the third and fourth—take into account whether the defendant's use was "transformative" in nature, the Court enunciated a principle that has since received great emphasis when courts apply the fair use factors. *Bouchat v. Baltimore Ravens Limited Partnership*, which appears shortly, considers what makes a use transformative.

Although Congress has specified that the factors listed earlier must be applied when courts decide fair use questions, courts are free to consider additional factors such as the public interest. The public interest consideration played a role in a court decision sustaining, as fair use, Google's book search project (in which Google displays snippets from other parties' copyrighted works in a program that enables persons to search for and within huge numbers of books). Similarly, the public interest consideration appears to have been a factor in a court decision holding that the fair use doctrine justified Google's display of search results in the form of thumbnail-sized images of another party's copyrighted pictures.

The *Bouchat* case, which follows, is the fifth installment in a series of cases dealing with a copyrighted drawing whose expressive content served for a time as the basis of a professional football team's logo. Besides applying the fair use factors in order to determine whether the uses at issue were fair use, the *Bouchat* court comments on the fair use determinations in the earlier cases in the series.

Bouchat v. Baltimore Ravens Limited Partnership
737 F.3d 932 (4th Cir. 2013)

In the latest chapter of extensive litigation dealing with uses of the "Flying B" logo, Frederick Bouchat sued the Baltimore Ravens Limited Partnership (hereinafter, Ravens) and the National Football League (hereinafter, NFL) for copyright infringement. Bouchat's lawsuit was the fifth in a series of Flying B logo–related cases. Background on the earlier cases is useful to an understanding of the facts and issues in the fifth case (which led to the Fourth Circuit decision that appears in edited form below).

In June 1996, two months before the beginning of the team's first season, the Ravens unveiled the Flying B logo as its symbol. Bouchat noticed that the logo bore a strong resemblance to one he had previously created and provided (in the form of drawings) to the Maryland Stadium Authority's chairperson, who was to pass it along to the Ravens franchise. Bouchat expected to be compensated if the Ravens decided to use the logo.

In May 1997, after the team's first season, Bouchat filed his first copyright infringement lawsuit against the Ravens and an NFL subsidiary. He contended that the Flying B logo infringed the copyrights on his drawings. After a jury concluded that the defendants infringed the copyright on one of Bouchat's drawings, the U.S. Court of Appeals for the Fourth Circuit refused to set aside the verdict. See Bouchat v. Baltimore Ravens, Inc., 241 F.3d 350 (4th Cir. 2000) (Bouchat I).

After the 1998 season, the Ravens adopted a new logo and no longer featured the Flying B on their uniforms and merchandise. The Fourth Circuit subsequently issued three more decisions in lawsuits brought by Bouchat regarding the Flying B logo: Bouchat v.

Baltimore Ravens Football Club, Inc., 346 F.3d 514 (4th Cir. 2003) (Bouchat II) *(affirming a jury award of zero dollars for the original infringement);* Bouchat v. Bon-Ton Dep't Stores, Inc., *506 F.3d 315 (4th Cir. 2007)* (Bouchat III) *(affirming a number of judgments in favor of NFL licensees that had used the Flying B logo because Bouchat was precluded from obtaining actual damages against them); and* Bouchat v. Baltimore Ravens Limited Partnership, *619 F.3d 301 (4th Cir. 2010)* (Bouchat IV) *(holding that footage of the Flying B logo in season highlight films and in a short video shown on the large screen during Ravens home games was not fair use, but that the Ravens' display of the logo in images in its corporate lobby was fair use).*

Bouchat commenced the case dealt with here in 2012. His claim against the NFL pertained to the league's use of the Flying B logo in three videos featured on its television network and various websites (videos that were not at issue in Bouchat IV*). His claim against the Ravens pertained to the team's display of images that showed the logo in the context of historical exhibits in the "Club Level" seating area of the Ravens' stadium. A federal district court granted summary judgment in favor of the defendants, ruling that they were entitled to the protection of the fair use defense. Bouchat appealed to the Fourth Circuit. Further pertinent facts appear in the following edited version of the Fourth Circuit's decision.*

Wilkinson, Circuit Judge

The power over patent and copyright granted to Congress in Article I, Section 8 of the Constitution "is intended to motivate the creative activity of authors and inventors by the provision of a special reward, and to allow the public access to the products of their genius after the limited period of exclusive control has expired." *Sony Corp. of America v. Universal City Studios, Inc.*, 464 U.S. 417, 429 (1984). To effectuate this public benefit, § 106 of the Copyright Act grants [various rights to the copyright owner, including the rights to make and distribute copies of the work and the right to display the work]. In order to vindicate the same "constitutional policy of promoting the progress of science and the useful arts" that underlies the Patent and Copyright Clause, . . . the doctrine of fair use [has been recognized in order to foster] new creation and innovation by limiting [, in appropriate cases,] the ability of writers and authors to control the use of their works. *Harper & Row Publishers, Inc. v. Nation Enterprises*, 471 U.S. 539, 549 (1985).

[T]he fair use doctrine [serves] as "an equitable rule of reason, for which no generally applicable definition is possible." [Citation omitted.] Nonetheless, Congress [has provided, in 17 U.S.C. § 107,] a list of four factors that guide the determination of whether a particular use is a fair use. These factors [, which are listed and applied in the discussion that follows,] cannot be treated in isolation from one another, but instead must be "weighed together, in light of the purposes of copyright." *Campbell v. Acuff-Rose Music, Inc.*, 510 U.S. 569, 578 (1994). This balancing necessitates a "case-by-case analysis" in any fair use inquiry. *Id.* at 577. [We now consider whether the fair use doctrine protects the defendants against Bouchat's claims of copyright infringement.]

Uses of Flying B Logo in Videos

The three videos Bouchat challenges were produced by the NFL for display on the NFL network, and were also featured on websites including NFL.com and Hulu.com. Two of the videos were part of the film series *Top Ten*, each episode of which features a countdown of ten memorable players, coaches, or events in NFL

history. The third video is part of the *Sound FX* series, which provides viewers with an inside look at the sights and sounds of the NFL.

Top Ten: Draft Classes recounts and analyzes in short segments the ten best NFL draft classes of all time. The video features a four-minute segment on the Ravens' 1996 draft class, rated number six by the show. It contains interviews with players, journalists, and Ravens front office personnel [and] shows historical footage from the day of the draft. These interviews and voiceovers make up the vast majority of the video. In two spots, however, the Flying B logo is visible for less than one second: once on a banner and a helmet at the opening of the segment, and again on the side of a helmet during game footage toward the end of the segment.

The second video, *Top Ten: Draft Busts*, begins with narration explaining that the episode will showcase the least successful draft picks. It then features short segments on each unsuccessful pick or set of picks, including the number eight "bust" Lawrence Phillips, who was selected by the St. Louis Rams in 1996. The segment recounts Phillips's promise as a football player and the [personal and legal] problems that prevented him from fulfilling it. At the end of the segment, a defensive player tackles Phillips, and . . . the Flying B logo on the [tackler's] helmet [is visible] for [a] fraction of a second.

The final video, *Sound FX: Ray Lewis*, features a collection of footage and audio of Ray Lewis throughout his career. The 24-minute video is split into eight sections, [one of which] focuses on Ray Lewis at training camp and lasts for roughly two minutes. During an eight-second period in the training camp segment, the Flying B logo is visible on some of the Ravens players' helmets. And twice in other segments of the show, as Lewis makes a tackle, the Flying B logo is partially visible for less than one second. Otherwise, [a logo the Ravens used after dropping the Flying B as the team symbol] is the only logo visible throughout *Sound FX: Ray Lewis*.

The first fair use factor focuses on "the purpose and character of the use, including whether such use is of a commercial nature or is for nonprofit educational purposes." 17 U.S.C. § 107(1). The preamble to § 107 lists examples of uses that are [good candidates for fair use treatment]: "criticism, comment, news reporting, teaching . . . scholarship, or research." These examples serve as a guide for analysis under the first factor. The essential inquiry under the first factor can be separated into two parts: whether the new work is transformative, and the extent to which the use serves a commercial purpose.

"A 'transformative' use is one that 'employ[s] the quoted matter in a different manner or for a different purpose from the original,' thus transforming it." [Citations omitted.] Transformative works rarely violate copyright protections because "the goal of copyright, to promote science and the arts, is generally furthered by the creation of transformative works. Such works thus lie at the heart of the fair use doctrine's guarantee of breathing space within the confines of copyright." *Campbell*, 510 U.S. at 579. Importantly, a transformative use is one that "adds something new" to the original purpose of the copyrighted work. *Id.*; *Bouchat IV*, 619 F.3d at 314.

Each of the videos in this case is intended to present a narrative about some aspect of Ravens or NFL history. [Although the Flying B logo is visible in the videos, the instances of visibility are limited in number and of brief duration.] The use of the Flying B logo in each of these videos differs from its original purpose. [The logo] initially served as the brand symbol for the team, its on-field identifier, and the principal thrust of its promotional efforts. None of the videos use the logo to serve the same purpose it once did. Instead, like the historical displays featuring the Flying B logo in the lobby of the Ravens' headquarters in *Bouchat IV*, these videos used the Flying B as part of the historical record to tell stories of past drafts, major events in Ravens history, and player careers. *See Bouchat IV*, 619 F.3d at 314; *see also Bill Graham Archives v. Dorling Kindersley Ltd.*, 448 F.3d 605, 609–10 (2d Cir. 2006) (noting that Grateful Dead posters reproduced in a biographical text served as "historical artifacts" that helped readers to understand the text). The logo, then, is being used "not for its expressive content, but rather for its . . . factual content," and in such a manner that no doubt "adds something new." *Bouchat IV*, 619 F.3d at 314. And contrary to Bouchat's claims, it does not matter that the Flying B logo is unchanged in the videos, for "[t]he use of a copyrighted work need not alter or augment the work to be transformative in nature." [Citation omitted.]

Bouchat argues that the uses of the Flying B logo in the videos in this case are indistinguishable from those adjudicated in *Bouchat IV*. Both, he says, act to identify the team. In reality, however, the uses are strikingly different. In the season highlight films from *Bouchat IV*, the logo was shown again and again, always as a brand identifier for the Ravens organization and its players. As we found, the logo simply replicated its original function when footage of the seasons was shot, condensed, and reproduced in a summary film. But the current use, as noted above, differs in

two important respects from the *Bouchat IV* videos. We found in that case that the season highlight videos did not change the way in which viewers experienced the logo, making the use non-transformative. Here, however, because the videos used the historical footage to tell new stories and not simply rehash the seasons, it used the Flying B logo for its "factual content" and was transformative.

This finding of transformative use is reinforced by the exceptionally insubstantial presence of the Flying B logo in these videos. In the vast majority of its appearances, it is present for fractions of a second, and can be perceived only by someone who is looking for it. "The extent to which unlicensed material is used in the challenged work can be a factor in determining whether a . . . use of original materials has been sufficiently transformative to constitute fair use." *Bill Graham Archives*, 448 F.3d at 611. The Flying B logo cannot be said to serve its original function of identifying the Ravens players and organization if it is all but imperceptible to those viewing the videos. It serves no expressive function at all, but instead acts simply as a historical guidepost—to those who even detect it—within videos that construct new narratives about the history of the Ravens and the NFL.

The first factor also requires an inquiry into the commercial nature of the use at issue. While a commercial purpose "may weigh against a finding of fair use," *Campbell*, 510 U.S. at 579, the Supreme Court has warned us not to over-emphasize its impact: "If, indeed, commerciality carried presumptive force against a finding of fairness, the presumption would swallow nearly all of the illustrative uses listed in the preamble paragraph of § 107, including news reporting, comment, criticism, teaching, scholarship, and research, since these activities are generally conducted for profit in this country." *Id.* at 584. Vast numbers of fair uses occur in the course of commercial ventures. An overbroad reading of the commercial sub-prong would thus eviscerate the concept of fair use. Instead, the commerciality inquiry is most significant when the allegedly infringing use acts as a direct substitute for the copyrighted work. *Id.* at 591. Meanwhile, "the more transformative the new work, the less will be the significance of other factors, like commercialism, that may weigh against a finding of fair use." *Id.* at 579.

In this case, there is no doubt . . . that the NFL has produced and distributed these videos for commercial gain. But as the district court . . . noted, the substantially transformative nature of the use renders its commercial nature largely insignificant. [Further], the limited nature of the uses counsels against placing significant weight on their commercial nature. The key inquiry is the extent to which the Flying B logo itself—and not the videos as a whole—provides commercial gain to the NFL. The uses of the Flying B logo in these three videos can only properly be described as incidental to the larger commercial enterprise of creating historical videos for profit [and as therefore playing] an unquestionably minimal role in facilitating that gain.

The fleeting and transformative use of the Flying B logo in the videos means that the first factor in § 107 counsels strongly in favor of fair use. The remaining criteria do nothing to undermine this conclusion. The second factor concerns "the nature of the copyrighted work." 17 U.S.C. § 107(2). The logo is a creative work, and therefore "closer to the core of works protected by the Copyright Act." *Bouchat IV*, 619 F.3d at 311. Nonetheless, "if the disputed use of the copyrighted work is not related to its mode of expression but rather to its historical facts, then the creative nature of the work" matters much less than it otherwise would. [Citation omitted.] Indeed, as we noted in *Bouchat IV*, "the second factor may be of limited usefulness where the creative work of art is being used for a transformative purpose." 619 F.3d at 315 (quoting *Bill Graham Archives*, 448 F.3d at 612) (internal quotation marks omitted). Thus, . . . the NFL's transformative use lessens the importance of the Flying B logo's creativity. Consequently, this factor is largely neutral.

The third factor is "the amount and substantiality of the portion used in relation to the copyrighted work as a whole." 17 U.S.C. § 107(3). The Flying B is reproduced in full in at least some of its appearances in the videos, [but] "the extent of permissible copying varies with the purpose and character of the use." *Campbell*, 510 U.S. at 586–87. Here, the NFL had no choice but to film the whole logo in order to fulfill its legitimate transformative purpose of creating the historical videos at issue. [T]he transformativeness of the use and the character of Bouchat's work lead us to give very little weight to this factor. It would be senseless to permit the NFL to use the Flying B logo for factual, historical purposes, but permit it to show only a half, or two-thirds of it.

The fourth factor is "the effect of the use upon the potential market for or value of the copyrighted work." 17 U.S.C. § 107(4). We are required to "determine whether the defendants' [use of the logo] would materially impair the marketability of the work and whether it would act as a market substitute for it." [Citation omitted.] A transformative use renders market substitution less likely and market harm more difficult to infer. *Campbell*, 510 U.S. at 591. The transient and fleeting use of the Flying B logo, as well as its use for its factual, and not its expressive, content, leads us to conclude that it serves a different purpose in the videos than it does standing alone. As a result, the new, transformative use is unlikely to supplant any market for the original.

The four § 107 factors indicate that the NFL's fleeting and insubstantial use of the Flying B logo in these videos qualifies as fair use. The first factor . . . counsels strongly in favor of fair use. The remaining fair use factors are largely neutral, providing compelling arguments neither for nor against fair use. Consequently, in the aggregate, the four factors point in favor of a fair use finding.

Our analysis under § 107 is confirmed by the Supreme Court's explication of the underlying interests that inform copyright law and its relationship to the First Amendment. Congress has attempted over the years to balance the importance of encouraging authors and inventors by granting them control over their work with "society's competing interest in the free flow of ideas, information and commerce." Absent any protection for fair use, subsequent writers and artists would be unable to build and expand upon original works, frustrating the very aims of copyright policy. *Campbell*, 510 U.S. at 575–76. For creation itself is a cumulative process; those who come after will inevitably make some modest use of the good labors of those who came before.

Fair use, then, is crucial to the exchange of opinions and ideas. It protects filmmakers and documentarians from the inevitable chilling effects of allowing an artist too much control over the dissemination of his or her work for historical purposes. Copyright law has the potential to constrict speech, and fair use serves as a necessary "First Amendment safeguard[]" against this danger. *Eldred v. Ashcroft*, 537 U.S. 186, 219 (2003).

Top Ten: Draft Classes, *Top Ten: Draft Busts*, and *Sound FX: Ray Lewis* share the qualities of other historical documentaries. Were we to require those wishing to produce films and documentaries to receive permission from copyright holders for fleeting factual uses of their works, we would allow those copyright holders to exert enormous influence over new depictions of historical subjects and events. Such a rule would encourage bargaining over the depiction of history by granting copyright holders substantial leverage over select historical facts. It would force those wishing to create videos and documentaries to receive approval and endorsement from their subjects, who could "simply choose to prohibit unflattering or disfavored depictions." [Citation omitted.] Social commentary as well as historical narrative could be affected if, for example, companies facing unwelcome inquiries could ban all depiction of their logos. This would align incentives in exactly the wrong manner, diminishing accuracy and increasing transaction costs, all the while discouraging the creation of new expressive works. This regime, the logical outgrowth of Bouchat's fair use position, would chill the very artistic creation that copyright law attempts to nurture.

Uses of Flying B Logo in Stadium Display

Bouchat next challenges the incidental use of the Flying B logo in certain historical displays located on the Club Level of the Baltimore Ravens' stadium. The Club Level . . . provides a host of amenities, including, among other things, spacious seating, carpeted floors, refuge from the elements, attractive décor, specialty concessions, and enhanced customer service. [It] is accessible only to those who purchase Club Level tickets, [which] are priced between $175 and $355 per game.

The three displays challenged by Bouchat—a timeline, a highlight reel, and a significant plays exhibit—are all located on the Club Level. Considered together, they cover an impressive span of

Baltimore football history. The Flying B logo plays an incidental role in only a fraction of the historical depictions featured in the displays. Overall, the exhibits document more than one hundred years of history preceding the advent of the Flying B logo and many significant historical events post-dating it.

The timeline, which begins with the year 1881, covers those individual years that illustrate important events in the Baltimore football story. With respect to Bouchat's challenge, the segment for [1996] includes, among other things, blown-up reproductions of the inaugural 1996 game-day program and ticket, each of which necessarily bears the Flying B logo. No other year in the extensive timeline display . . . includes even an incidental depiction of the logo. [The highlight reel and the important plays exhibit include instances in which the Flying B logo is very briefly displayed on a player's helmet.] As with the timeline, both the highlight reel and the important plays exhibit . . . feature many significant historical depictions where the logo does not appear at all.

The district court rejected Bouchat's challenge to the Club Level displays, finding each display of the Flying B justified under the fair use doctrine. Its analysis rested in significant part on this court's decision in *Bouchat IV*, which rejected an infringement challenge to a historical display located in the lobby of the Ravens' corporate headquarters. That display, like the one at issue here, contained incidental reproductions of the Flying B logo.

[M]uch of our analysis regarding the [challenge to] the documentaries discussed earlier is also applicable to Bouchat's [Club Level] display challenge. [*Authors' note*: In extensive analysis summarized here, the Fourth Circuit applied the fair use factors to the Club Level display in a manner similar to the way it applied those factors to the documentaries. The court concluded that the

images of the Flying B logo were displayed on the Club Level for historical purposes and were thus transformative. Moreover, the logo was displayed only briefly or otherwise in an incidental manner. Any commercial motivation was only indirect, in the sense that the historical display was a "fringe benefit of club membership" and not the primary reason why a fan would purchase a Club Level ticket to watch a Ravens game. Thus, the court concluded, the first fair use factor weighed strongly in favor of fair use. For reasons essentially the same as those expressed in the portion of the opinion dealing with the documentaries, the court concluded that the second and third fair use factors neither helped Bouchat nor caused a problem for the Ravens. As for the fourth fair use factor, the court noted that the transformative nature of the Ravens' use probably meant that harm to any markets for Bouchat's drawing was minimal or nonexistent. The court therefore held that the Club Level display was fair use.]

Our rejection of Bouchat's challenge to the incidental uses of the Flying B logo provides no support for a fair use defense where the alleged infringer exploits a protected work for profit based on its intrinsic expressive value. That scenario, however, is simply not presented on the facts before us. The uses here were not only transformative, but also—take your pick—fleeting, incidental, de minimis, innocuous. If these uses failed to qualify as fair, a host of perfectly benign and valuable expressive works would be subject to lawsuits. That in turn would discourage the makers of all sorts of historical documentaries and displays, and would deplete society's fund of informative speech.

District court's decision affirmed; defendants held entitled for protection of fair use defense.

Trademarks
Trademarks help purchasers identify favored products and services. For this reason, they also give sellers and manufacturers an incentive to innovate and strive for quality. However, both these ends would be defeated if competitors were free to appropriate each other's trademarks. Thus, the federal Lanham Act protects trademark owners against certain uses of their marks by third parties.[3]

 LO8-8 State what a trademark does and provide examples of potentially protectable trademarks.

_____
[3]In addition, the owner of a trademark may enjoy legal protection under common law trademark doctrines and state trademark statutes.

Protected Marks The Lanham Act recognizes four kinds of marks. It defines a **trademark** as any word, name, symbol, device, or combination thereof used by a manufacturer or seller to identify its products and distinguish them from the products of competitors. Although trademarks consisting of single words or names are most commonly encountered, federal trademark protection has sometimes been extended to colors, pictures, label and package designs, slogans, sounds, arrangements of numbers and/or letters (e.g., "7-Eleven"), and shapes of goods or their containers (e.g., Coca-Cola bottles).

Service marks resemble trademarks but identify and distinguish services. Certification marks certify the origin, materials, quality, method of manufacture, and other aspects of goods and services. Here, the user of the mark and its owner are distinct parties. A retailer, for example, may sell products bearing the Good Housekeeping Seal of Approval. Collective marks are trademarks or service marks used by organizations to identify themselves as the source of goods or services. Trade union and trade association marks fall into this category. Although all four kinds of marks receive federal protection, this chapter focuses on trademarks and service marks, using the terms *mark* or *trademark* to refer to both.

Distinctiveness

> **LO8-9** Identify the key requirement for registration of a mark on the Principal Register (distinctiveness) and explain the role of secondary meaning when registration of a nondistinctive mark is sought.

Because their purpose is to help consumers identify products and services, trademarks must be *distinctive* to merit maximum Lanham Act protection. Marks fall into five general categories of distinctiveness (or nondistinctiveness):

1. *Arbitrary or fanciful marks.* These marks are the most distinctive—and the most likely to be protected—because they do not describe the qualities of the product or service they identify. The "Exxon" trademark is an example.

2. *Suggestive marks.* These marks convey the nature of a product or service only through imagination, thought, and perception. They do not actually describe the underlying product or service. The "Dietene" trademark for a dietary food supplement is an example. Although not as clearly distinctive as arbitrary or fanciful marks, suggestive marks are nonetheless classified as distinctive. Hence, they are good candidates for protection.

3. *Descriptive marks.* These marks directly describe the product or service they identify (e.g., "Realemon," for bottled lemon juice). Descriptive marks are not protected unless they acquire *secondary meaning.* This occurs when their identification with a particular source of goods or services has become firmly established in the minds of a substantial number of buyers. "Realemon," of course, now has secondary meaning. Among the factors considered in secondary-meaning determinations are the length of time the mark has been used, the volume of sales associated with that use, and the nature of the advertising employing the mark. When applied to a package delivery service, for instance, the term *overnight* is usually descriptive and thus not protectible. It may come to deserve trademark protection, however, through long use by a single firm that advertised it extensively and made many sales while doing so. As will be seen, the same approach is taken concerning deceptively misdescriptive and geographically descriptive marks.

4. *Marks that are not inherently distinctive.* Although these marks are not distinctive in the usual senses of arbitrary nature, fanciful quality, or suggestiveness, proof of secondary meaning effectively makes these marks distinctive. They are therefore protectible if secondary meaning exists. The Supreme Court has held that under appropriate circumstances, product color is a potentially protectible trademark of this type.

5. *Generic terms.* Generic terms (e.g., *diamond* or *truck*) simply refer to the general class of which the particular product or service is one example. Because any seller has the right to call a product or service by its common name, generic terms are ineligible for trademark protection.

CYBERLAW IN ACTION

In the Digital Millennium Copyright Act of 1998 (DMCA), Congress addressed selected copyright issues as to which special rules seemed appropriate, in view of recent years' technological advances and explosion in Internet usage. One such issue was how narrowly or broadly to define the class of parties potentially liable for copyright infringement in an Internet context. If, without Osborne's consent, Jennings posts Osborne's copyrighted material in an online context made available by Devaney (an Internet service provider), is only Jennings liable to Osborne, or is Devaney also liable? In the DMCA, Congress enacted "safe harbor" provisions designed to protect many service providers such as Devaney from

liability for the actions of direct infringers who posted or transmitted copyrighted material.

The DMCA also addressed the actions of persons who seek to circumvent technological measures (e.g., encryption, password-protection measures, and the like) that control access to or copying of a copyrighted work. With certain narrowly defined exceptions of very limited applicability, Congress outlawed both (1) the circumvention of such technological measures and (2) the activity of trafficking in programs or other devices meant to accomplish such circumvention.

In *Universal City Studios, Inc. v. Corley*, 273 F.3d 429 (2d Cir. 2001), the U.S. Court of Appeals for the Second Circuit rejected the arguments of an individual (Corley) who had been held liable to various movie studios for violating the antitrafficking provisions of the DMCA. Corley had written an article about the decryption program known as "DeCSS" and had posted the article on his website, along with a copy of the DeCSS program itself and links to other sites where DeCSS could be found. DeCSS had been developed by parties other than Corley as a means of decrypting the "CSS" encryption technology that movie studios place on copyrighted DVDs of their movies. If it is not circumvented, CSS prevents the copying of the movie that appears on the DVD. A federal district court, holding that Corley had violated the DMCA's antitrafficking provisions, issued an injunction barring Corley from posting DeCSS on his website and from posting links to other sites where DeCSS could be found.

On appeal, Corley argued that his publication of the DeCSS program's codes was speech protected by the First Amendment and that the application of the DMCA to him was thus unconstitutional. The Second Circuit concluded that Corley was to some extent engaged in speech but that his actions also had a substantial nonspeech component. In any event, the Second Circuit reasoned, the DMCA's antitrafficking provisions served a substantial government interest in protecting the rights of intellectual property owners and were content-neutral restrictions unrelated to the suppression of free expression. The court therefore held that the antitrafficking provisions did not violate the First Amendment.

Some critics of the DMCA's anticircumvention and antitrafficking provisions have asserted that those provisions may operate to restrict users' ability to make fair use of copyrighted materials. Evidently attempting to convert this policy-based objection about what Congress enacted into a constitutional objection on which the court might be more inclined to rule, Corley argued that the fair use doctrine was required by the First Amendment and that the DMCA, insofar as it limited users' ability to rely on the fair use doctrine, was unconstitutional. The Second Circuit called it "extravagant" to assert that the fair use doctrine was constitutionally required, for there was no substantial authority to support such a contention. Moreover, the court reasoned that even if Corley's contention were not otherwise questionable, "[f]air use has never been held to be a guarantee of access to copyrighted material in order to copy it by the fair user's preferred technique or in the format of the original."

Federal Registration Once the seller of a product or service uses a mark in commerce or forms a bona fide intention to do so very soon, she may apply to register the mark with the U.S. Patent and Trademark Office (PTO). The office reviews applications for distinctiveness. Its decision to deny or grant the application may be contested by the applicant or by a party who feels that he would be injured by registration of the mark. Such challenges may eventually reach the federal courts.

Trademarks of sufficient distinctiveness are placed on the Principal Register of the Patent and Trademark Office. A mark's inclusion in the Principal Register (1) is prima facie evidence of the mark's ownership, validity, and registration (which is useful in trademark infringement suits); (2) gives nationwide constructive notice of the owner's claim of ownership (thus eliminating the need to show that the defendant in an infringement suit had notice of the mark); (3) entitles the mark owner to assistance from the Bureau of Customs in stopping the importation of certain goods that, without the consent of the mark owner, bear a likeness of the mark; and (4) means that the mark will be incontestable after five years of registered status (as described later).

Even though they are not distinctive, certain other marks may merit placement on the Principal Register if they have acquired secondary meaning. These include (1) marks that are *not inherently distinctive* (as discussed earlier), (2) *descriptive marks* (as discussed earlier), (3) some *deceptively misdescriptive* marks (such as "Dura-Skin," for plastic gloves), (4) *geographically descriptive* marks (such as "Indiana-Made"), and (5) marks that are *primarily a surname* (because as a matter of general policy, persons who have a certain last name should be fairly free to use that name in connection with their businesses). Once a mark in one of these classifications achieves registered status, the mark's owner obtains the legal benefits described in the previous paragraph.

Regardless of their distinctiveness, however, some kinds of marks are denied placement on the Principal Register. These include marks that (1) consist of the flags or other insignia of governments; (2) consist of the name, portrait, or signature of a living person who has not given consent to the trademark use; (3) are immoral, deceptive, or scandalous; or (4) are likely to cause confusion because they resemble a mark previously registered or used in the United States.

Until a key Supreme Court decision in 2017, the previous list of types of marks that may be denied placement on the Principal Register included another category: marks that are disparaging to individuals or groups (a denial basis commonly referred to as the "disparagement clause"). However, in *Matal v. Tam*, 137 S. Ct. 1744 (2017), the Supreme Court held that the disparagement clause violated the First Amendment's freedom of speech guarantee. The case arose after the PTO used the disparagement clause as the reason to deny registered status to "The Slants," the name of a band whose members were Asian Americans. The PTO noted that the name has been used as a derogatory term regarding Asian Americans and thus was disparaging. In holding the disparagement clause unconstitutional, the Supreme Court noted that the clause led to impermissible viewpoint discrimination in violation of the First Amendment. The Court also emphasized that the First Amendment's protection extends to speech that many may find offensive.

Although *Matal v. Tam* dealt only with the disparagement clause, the Court's analysis could have significance if a First Amendment–based challenge were brought regarding another Lanham Act provision noted earlier: the provision allowing the PTO to deny registration to marks that are immoral or scandalous. As this book went to press, no such challenge had yet been brought. (Because *Matal v. Tam* is a major First Amendment case, an edited version of the decision is included in Chapter 3. You may wish to review that edited version.)

Transfer of Rights Because of the purposes underlying trademark law, transferring trademark rights is more difficult than transferring copyright or patent interests. A trademark owner may license the use of the mark, but only if the owner reserves control over the nature and quality of the goods or services as to which the licensee will use the mark. An uncontrolled "naked license" would allow the sale of goods or services bearing the mark but lacking the qualities formerly associated with it, and could confuse purchasers. Trademark rights may also be assigned or sold, but only along with the sale of the goodwill of the business originally using the mark.

Losing Federal Trademark Protection Federal registration of a trademark lasts for 10 years, with renewals for additional 10-year periods possible. However, trademark protection may be lost before the period expires. The government must cancel a registration six years after its date unless the registrant files with the Patent and Trademark Office, within the fifth and sixth years following the registration date, an affidavit detailing that the mark is in use or explaining its nonuse.

Any person who believes that he has been or will be damaged by a mark's registration may petition the PTO to cancel that registration. Normally, the petition must be filed within five years of the mark's registration on the Principal Register because the mark becomes *incontestable* regarding goods or services with which it has continuously been used for five consecutive years after the registration. A mark's incontestability means that the permissible grounds for canceling its registration are limited.

Even an incontestable mark, however, may be canceled *at any time* if, among other things, it was obtained by fraud, has been abandoned, or has become the generic name for the goods or services it identifies. *Abandonment* may occur through an express statement or agreement to abandon, through the mark's losing its significance as an indication

of origin, or through the owner's failure to use it. A mark acquires a *generic meaning* when it comes to refer to a class of products or services rather than a particular source's product or service. For example, this has happened to such once-protected marks as aspirin, escalator, and thermos. Loss of registered status because the mark is generic occurs only if the PTO or a court rules, in an appropriate legal proceeding, that the mark indeed has become generic.

Another longstanding exception to the protections afforded by incontestability status has recently fallen by the wayside for First Amendment reasons. Earlier discussion noted that until the Supreme Court's 2017 decision in *Matal v. Tam*, the PTO could refuse to register a trademark if the mark was disparaging to individuals or groups. That same ground had also been available to the PTO as a basis for cancelling the registration of a mark. However, *Tam*'s First Amendment–based nullification of the disparagement clause as a basis for denying registration in the first place logically means that the disparagement clause cannot be used as a basis for cancelling a registration after the fact. *Tam* was no doubt good news for the owner of the Washington Redskins football team, whose registration of the Redskins trademark was canceled by the PTO in 2014 after many years on the Principal Register. The cancellation decision was being appealed at the time *Tam* was handed down. After *Tam*, the Redskins mark will continue to hold registered status.

Trademark Infringement

 LO8-10 Identify and apply the elements of trademark infringement.

A trademark is infringed when, without the owner's consent, another party uses a substantially similar mark in connection with the sale of goods or services and this use is likely to cause confusion concerning their source or concerning whether there is an endorsement relationship or other affiliation between the mark's owner and the other party. Most of the court's attention in a trademark infringement case tends to go toward determining whether the requisite likelihood of confusion is present in the facts. Because the likelihood of confusion determination is critical to resolution of trademark infringement cases, courts have had plenty of occasions to make such determinations. In the process, they have identified lists of factors that are weighed and balanced as part of the likelihood of confusion inquiry. The *Kibler* case, which appears later in the chapter, outlines such a list of factors. Although the relative weight assigned to a particular factor may vary from one case to another because the likelihood of confusion determination

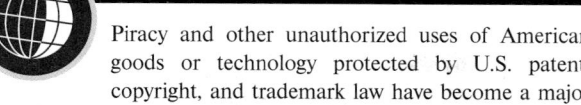

The Global Business Environment

Piracy and other unauthorized uses of American goods or technology protected by U.S. patent, copyright, and trademark law have become a major problem of American businesses. For example, foreign jeans manufacturers may without authorization place the Levi's label on their jeans, thereby damaging the business of Levi Strauss & Co. by depriving it of some of the jeans' market and damaging the value of the Levi trademark, especially if the imported jeans are of inferior quality. This is an example of counterfeit goods—goods that copy or otherwise purport to be those of the trademark owner whose mark has been unlawfully used on the nongenuine goods. Counterfeit goods may also unlawfully appropriate patented technology or copyrighted material. Assume, for example, that a foreign music recording company pirates the latest Katy Perry album and works with another party to import thousands of copies of it into the United States without the copyright owner's permission.

American firms harmed by the importation of counterfeit goods may obtain injunctions and damages under the Tariff Act of 1930, the Lanham Act, the Copyright Act, and the patent statute. In addition, the Trademark Counterfeiting Act of 1984 establishes civil and criminal penalties for counterfeiting goods. It also allows an American firm to recover from a counterfeiter three times its damages or three times the counterfeiter's profits (whichever is greater).

Patent, copyright, and trademark piracy is increasing in many parts of the world, especially in developing nations. Some developing nations believe that technology should be transferred freely to foster their economic growth. Consequently, they either encourage piracy or choose not to oppose it.

Gray market goods are goods lawfully bearing trademarks or using patents and copyrighted material but entering the American market without authorization. For example, Parker Pen Co. may authorize a Japanese manufacturer to make and sell Parker pens only in Japan. When an American firm imports the Japanese-made Parker pens into the United States, the goods become gray market goods.

While importing gray market goods may violate the contract between the American firm and its foreign licensee, it is not clear in what contexts it violates U.S. importation, trademark, patent, or copyright law. Some courts find a Lanham Act or Tariff Act violation, but other courts do not. The Trademark Counterfeiting Act of 1984 specifically excludes gray market goods from its coverage. The Copyright Act deals with gray market goods in a provision barring the "[i]mportation into the United States, without the authority of the owner of the copyright . . . of copies or phonorecords of a work that has been acquired outside the United States." Whether the items may lawfully enter the United States depends, therefore, on whether the copyright owner has provided "authority" for this to occur. Note, too, that the first sale doctrine discussed earlier in the chapter may also have a role to play. See the *Kirtsaeng* case, which appears earlier.

is highly fact-specific, courts often assign fairly significant weight to such factors as the degree of similarity between the plaintiff's mark and the defendant's version and the degree of similarity (or dissimilarity) between the parties' underlying products or services. The general assumption underlying those factors is this: the greater the degree of similarity, the greater the danger of consumer confusion.

Yet courts look very closely at the context in which the defendant's use of a substantially similar mark takes place. If, for instance, the defendant's use involves poking fun at the plaintiff's mark, the court could conclude that likelihood of confusion is lacking because reasonable consumers would not think the trademark owner would criticize or otherwise make fun of its own mark. A court so ruled in a case in which Jordache Inc., which used the Jordache name on its designer jeans, sued a company that began using the name Lardashe on its large-size designer jeans. The court held that even though both parties produced and sold jeans, the obvious parody present in the defendant's choice of the Lardashe name would cause consumers to recognize that the defendant's jeans were neither produced by Jordache nor licensed by that company. Hence, there was no likelihood of confusion.

A trademark owner who wins an infringement suit may obtain an injunction against uses of the mark that are likely to cause confusion. In addition, the owner may obtain money damages for provable injury resulting from the infringement, and sometimes the attributable profits realized by the infringing defendant.

Trademark Dilution

 Identify and apply the elements of trademark dilution.

Although trademark infringement is the traditional legal theory employed when a mark owner seeks legal relief against one who used the mark without the owner's consent, trademark dilution sometimes serves as an alternative to the standard claim of infringement. Roughly half the states have had laws recognizing the dilution doctrine for many years. Because of the geographic limitations inherent in state laws and because not all states have dilution statutes, trademark owners had long advocated enactment of a federal law recognizing dilution as a trademark rights theory. Congress finally obliged with the Federal Trademark Dilution Act of 1996 (FTDA), which was placed in the Lanham Act as § 43(c). However, a 2003 Supreme Court decision interpreting the FTDA made the statute less useful to trademark owners than it initially appeared to be. The Court concluded that in view of the FTDA's wording, proof of a § 43(c) violation required a showing of actual dilution of the plaintiff's mark rather than the likelihood of dilution required by state dilution laws. For trademark owners, the proof-of-actual-dilution requirement enhanced the difficulty of winning dilution cases under the federal statute.

Congress responded to the 2003 Supreme Court decision by enacting the Trademark Dilution Revision Act of 2006 (TDRA), which amended § 43(c) to state explicitly that a showing of likelihood of dilution was sufficient. Under the TDRA, one who makes a commercial use of a "famous mark" without the mark owner's consent faces liability if the use is "likely to cause dilution by blurring or dilution by tarnishment of the famous mark." The TDRA thus makes clear that there are two types of dilution (to be explained below): "dilution by blurring" and "dilution by tarnishment." In so providing, the TDRA responded to an expression of skepticism in the same 2003 Supreme Court decision over whether the tarnishment variety of dilution was contemplated by the federal law. Proof of a likelihood of either type of dilution satisfies the TDRA, assuming that the famous mark and commercial use elements are also met. Likelihood of confusion—the critical element in a trademark infringement case—need not be proven in a dilution case. Proof of competition between the plaintiff and the defendant is likewise unnecessary in a dilution case, as is proof of actual economic injury resulting from the defendant's actions.

According to the TDRA, a mark is "famous" if it is "widely recognized by the general consuming public." (The *Kibler* case, which appears later, explores this requirement.) The TDRA goes on to define "dilution by blurring" as an "association arising from the similarity between a mark or trade name and a famous mark that impairs the distinctiveness of the famous mark." Also recognized by the FTDA (the TDRA's predecessor) and the patchwork quilt of state dilution laws, this type of dilution takes place when the defendant's use of the plaintiff's mark causes, or is likely to cause, the public to cease associating the mark solely with the plaintiff and instead to associate it with both the plaintiff and the defendant. When this occurs or appears likely to occur, the mark's distinctiveness as a clear identifier of the plaintiff is in danger of being blurred or whittled away—in other words, diluted—even if the public recognizes that the plaintiff and defendant are not affiliated and that

they provide very different products or services. Consider a classic example: the dilution claim won by Polaroid (the camera company) against a small heating and air conditioning business whose chosen name, Polaraid, presented the danger of blurring the source-identification image conjured up by the Polaroid name. Clearly, however, dilution by blurring does not occur in every instance in which the plaintiff's mark and the defendant's version are quite similar, as Mead Data Central found out when it unsuccessfully sought to prove that its LEXIS mark (for legal research services) was diluted by Toyota's use of LEXUS (for a luxury car model and division).

The TDRA defines "dilution by tarnishment," the other type of dilution it recognizes, as an "association arising from the similarity between a mark or trade name and a famous mark that harms the reputation of the famous mark." This form of tarnishment is also recognized in state dilution laws. Although courts do not agree completely on what is necessary for likely tarnishment of a mark, various courts have concluded that the defendant's use of the plaintiff's mark in an unwholesome context—normally one suggesting illicit sexual or drug-related associations—may dilute a mark by tarnishing its reputation.

Presumably to guard against overuse of the dilution theory, the TDRA states that certain uses cannot constitute dilution by blurring or dilution by tarnishment. The TDRA lists noncommercial uses and uses amounting to "news reporting and news commentary" in the protected category. In addition, the TDRA's exclusions from dilution liability apply to "[a]ny fair use" of a famous mark to identify or describe that mark or its owner, as opposed to a defendant's use of a version of the plaintiff's mark "as a designation of source for the [defendant's] own goods or services." These fair uses may include a defendant's references to the plaintiff's mark in the context of comparative advertising of the parties' respective goods or services, as well as a defendant's references to the plaintiff's mark in the course of "identifying and parodying, criticizing, or commenting upon the famous mark owner or the goods or services of the mark owner."

When the mark owner makes out a TDRA-based dilution claim, the standard (and normally sole) remedy is an injunction against the defendant's continued use of the diluting version of the plaintiff's mark. The same is true of successful dilution cases brought under state laws. The TDRA allows the prospect of recovering damages and the defendant's attributable profits only if the evidence reveals that the defendant willfully sought to harm the mark's reputation or to trade on the recognition associated with the mark.

Kibler v. Hall   843 F.3d 1068 (6th Cir. 2016)

Disc jockey Lee Jason Kibler uses turntables and other performers' vocals to produce music containing jazz and funk elements. Since 1999, he has performed and released several albums under the name "DJ Logic." At the time of the litigation described here, however, he did not have a record deal. Kibler registered DJ LOGIC as a trademark in 2000, allowed the registration to lapse in 2003, and re-registered the name in 2013. He has also been known as simply "Logic."

Robert Bryson Hall II, a rapper, has performed under the name "Logic" since 2009. Three Oh One Productions and Visionary Music Group are companies owned by, or professionally connected with, Hall. He had a recording contract with UMG Recording d/b/a Def Jam Recordings (Def Jam) at times pertinent to the case described here. William Morris Endeavor Entertainment (WME) is Hall's booking agent.

In September 2012, Kibler's attorney sent Visionary Music Group and WME an e-mail ordering them to stop using the name Logic and to recall any product or advertisement that did. The attorney maintained that such use infringed on Kibler's DJ LOGIC mark. In January 2014, Kibler filed suit in the U.S. District Court for the Eastern District of Michigan against Hall and the firms noted above. Kibler alleged claims for trademark infringement and trademark dilution in violation of the federal Lanham Act. In March 2014, the defendants delayed Hall's tour and first album release because of ongoing settlement negotiations that ultimately collapsed. Def Jam proceeded to release the album in October of that year. The album sold more than 170,000 copies.

In May 2015, the defendants moved for summary judgment on each of Kibler's claims. After a hearing, the district court granted the defendants' motion.

Cole, Chief Judge

[Kibler's appeal requires] us to answer two questions. First, [regarding the trademark infringement claim,] has Kibler provided evidence sufficient to find that relevant consumers are likely to confuse the sources of his and Hall's products? Second, has Kibler provided evidence sufficient to find that Hall has diluted Kibler's mark?

Trademark Infringement

This court considers whether trademark infringement has occurred using a two-step test. First, we determine whether plaintiff's mark is protectable. Then, we assess whether relevant consumers are likely to confuse the sources of the parties' products. The relevant consumers are potential buyers of defendant's products. Here, the parties agree Kibler's mark is protectable. So we focus on the likelihood that potential buyers of rap would believe Kibler's music is Hall's, or vice-versa.

In assessing the likelihood of confusion, we take into account the following eight *Frisch* factors: 1) strength of the plaintiff's mark; 2) relatedness of the products; 3) similarity of the marks; 4) evidence of actual confusion; 5) parties' marketing channels; 6) likely degree of purchaser care; 7) defendant's intent in selecting the mark; and 8) probability that the product lines will expand. *CFE Racing Products, Inc. v. BMF Wheels, Inc.*, 793 F.3d 571, 592 (6th Cir. 2015) (citing *Frisch's Restaurants, Inc. v. Shoney's Inc.*, 759 F.2d 1261, 1264 (6th Cir. 1985)).

Plaintiff need not establish each factor to prevail. Each case is unique, so not all of the factors will be helpful. Further, there is no designated balancing formula for the factors. *CFE Racing*, 793 F.3d at 592. "The[ir] enumeration is meant 'merely to indicate the need for weighted evaluation of the pertinent facts in arriving

at the legal conclusion of confusion.'" *Id.* (quoting *Frisch*, 759 F.2d at 1264).

1. Strength of Plaintiff's Mark

The stronger a mark is, the greater the risk of confusion. *Homeowners Group, Inc. v. Home Marketing Specialists, Inc.*, 931 F.2d 1100, 1107 (6th Cir. 1991). A mark cannot be strong unless it is both conceptually and commercially strong. *Maker's Mark Distillery, Inc. v. Diageo North America, Inc.*, 679 F.3d 410, 419 (6th Cir. 2012). And it cannot be conceptually strong unless it is inherently distinctive. *Id.* Arbitrary marks, which convey something unrelated to the product they announce, *e.g.*, the "Apple" in "Apple computers," are distinctive. *Therma-Scan, Inc. v. Thermoscan, Inc.*, 295 F.3d 623, 631 (6th Cir. 2002). Descriptive marks, which describe the product they announce, are usually indistinctive. *See, e.g., Therma-Scan*, 295 F.3d at 632 (finding "Therma-scan," which describes the services plaintiff performs, indistinctive, and hence conceptually weak).

Further, courts presume that an incontestable mark is conceptually strong. *Daddy's Junky Music Stores, Inc. v. Big Daddy's Family Music Center*, 109 F.3d 275, 282 (6th Cir. 1997). A mark is incontestable when it has not been successfully challenged within five years of its registration. *Id.* In this case, the district court found that DJ LOGIC is moderately strong conceptually. The court reasoned that while "DJ" describes Kibler's craft, "LOGIC" is not even "suggestive of the characteristics of [his] music." Defendants concede this. Kibler contends only that the court erred in not considering the mark's incontestability. We need not address this argument because we agree with the district court's assessment, which renders DJ LOGIC at least as conceptually strong as a finding of incontestability would.

But a mark can be conceptually strong without being commercially strong, and thus weak under *Frisch*. A mark's commercial strength depends on public recognition, the extent to which people associate the mark with the product it announces. *Maker's Mark*, 679 F.3d at 419.

Survey evidence is not a prerequisite for establishing public recognition, but it is the most persuasive evidence of it. *See, e.g., id.* at 421. Proof of marketing is not a prerequisite either. *Therma-Scan*, 295 F.3d at 632. But plaintiffs lacking such proof must provide other evidence of "broad public recognition." *Id.*

Here, the district court concluded that DJ LOGIC is commercially weak. The court cited Kibler's lack of survey or marketing evidence and limited commercial success. [The court noted Kibler's] sale of fewer than 300 albums [during the previous] three years and fewer than 60,000 albums [during the] past sixteen years, [his] current lack of a recording contract, and [his] inability ever to secure a recording contract with a major label.

Kibler admits he offered no survey evidence, but . . . argues he provided marketing evidence. First is a sworn declaration that he advertises in print and online, including on MySpace, Twitter, and Facebook. Second are a 2006 *Downbeat* article featuring him, a 2001 *New York Times* review mentioning him, and a 1999 *Gig* article featuring him. Third is a sworn declaration that he has appeared on television shows such as *The Tonight Show Starring Jimmy Fallon*, *The Today Show*, and *Good Morning America*. Kibler also points to his tours and online music sales as proof of marketing. Additionally, Kibler insists he is commercially successful, noting that there is no fixed number of album sales establishing commercial success.

Defendants . . . argue that Kibler's failure to provide the number of his Facebook "likes" or Twitter followers creates an adverse inference, dismiss the publications as obscure and out-of-print, and question the number of people who have attended Kibler's concerts. [Defendants] also highlight Kibler's deposition testimony that he appeared on the television shows to support other, headlining artists.

Promotion on platforms such as Twitter and Facebook not only constitutes marketing, but is among the most popular and effective advertising strategies today. And whether publicity like magazine interviews and television appearances constitutes marketing or a separate form of evidence, it speaks to commercial strength.

But *some* proof is not enough. Kibler must offer evidence that would permit a reasonable jury to determine that wide segments of the public recognize DJ LOGIC as an emblem of his music. This means "extensive" marketing and "widespread" publicity around the music and mark. *Maker's Mark*, 679 F.3d at 421. Kibler's evidence . . . lacks the information jurors would need to find such awareness. For instance, how many and what kind of Twitter followers does Kibler have? A large number of

followers, or celebrities likely to re-tweet Kibler's messages to their large number of followers, for example, would suggest that many types of people know his work and mark. We can say the same of the number and kind of Kibler's Facebook fans, likes, posts, and re-posts.

Similarly, Kibler fails to provide the circulations or target audiences of *Downbeat* and *Gig*, which appear to be niche publications. Further, the *New York Times* review focuses on two other artists, placing "DJ Logic" in a series of supporting musicians. This leaves a slim chance that readers noticed and recalled Kibler.

Kibler has neither refuted nor explained his deposition testimony that he appeared on television shows to support other, headlining artists. For instance, he testified that Carly Simon, "the main act," introduced "the guests she had playing with her" on the Fallon show. We do not know how many guests there were, if Simon introduced them individually, if she said anything other than their names, etc. Kibler did not need to address each of these considerations. But they indicate the sort of information a jury would need to assess the extent to which the public affiliates DJ LOGIC with Kibler's music.

The district court rightly found that Kibler has enjoyed limited commercial success and that this implies that DJ LOGIC is not broadly familiar. But the court's analysis was incomplete. Album sales and even recording contracts are less critical markers of success than before because of widespread internet use. As a result, a plaintiff with low album sales or no representation could nevertheless show commercial success suggesting broad recognition of his mark using web-based indicators of popularity, *e.g.*, YouTube views. Because Kibler has not done that, we have only his low album sales, current lack of a recording contract, and inability ever to secure a recording contract with a major label. Kibler declares that he has participated "in hundreds of live performances held in at least 46 states," but he does not indicate the number of people who attended, the number of other artists involved, and whether he ever received top billing. Kibler's silence on his popularity online and general statement about his performances do not allow for a finding that most people will be familiar with DJ LOGIC.

DJ LOGIC lacks commercial strength. Because the record reflects that DJ LOGIC is moderately strong conceptually, but weak commercially, the first *Frisch* factor favors defendants.

2. Relatedness of Products

This court uses the following test to decide whether relatedness favors either party: 1) if the parties' products compete directly with each other, consumer confusion is likely if the parties' marks are sufficiently similar; 2) if the products are somewhat related, but do not compete directly, the likelihood of confusion will depend on other factors; 3) if the products are completely unrelated, confusion is unlikely. *Daddy's*, 109 F.3d at 282.

Products belonging to the same industry are not necessarily related. To be related, they must be marketed and consumed in ways that lead buyers to believe they come from the same source. The district court found the relatedness factor neutral insofar as the parties' products are somewhat related, but not directly competitive. The court reasoned that while both Kibler and Hall perform and sell music, only Hall uses his vocals. Kibler maintains that the factor favors him based on proof that he and Hall both sell hip-hop incorporating turntables and rap. Kibler refers to print and online media about Hall, much of which affiliates him with hip-hop and all of which describes him as a rapper.

The district court correctly found this factor neutral because the record supports that the parties' products are somewhat related, but not directly competitive. The most relevant evidence is a booking notice describing Hall as a "hot upcoming rapper" and two online ads featuring Hall holding a microphone. They indicate that while both are musicians and perhaps hip-hop artists, Hall markets himself as a rapper and Kibler a disc jockey. Incidental overlap of their customers [would] not sustain a finding of direct competition at trial. Accordingly, the factor is neutral.

3. Similarity of Marks

The more similar the marks are, the more likely it is that relevant consumers will confuse their sources. We determine the similarity of marks by considering whether either mark would confuse a consumer who did not have both marks before her and had only a vague impression of the other mark. We consider the marks' pronunciation, appearance, and verbal translation. The anti-dissection rule requires us not to dwell on the prominent features of a mark and instead consider it as a whole. *See Little Caesar Enterprises, Inc. v. Pizza Caesar, Inc.*, 834 F.2d 568, 571–72 (6th Cir. 1987) (finding differences in sound, appearance, and syllables distinguish "Little Caesar" from "Pizza Caesar USA" despite the prominent word they share).

The district court concluded that this factor favors defendants based on the anti-dissection rule. The court acknowledged that both marks include the prominent word "logic." Then it noted that the "'DJ' portion not only changes the look and sound of the mark but also describes or suggests certain characteristics of [Kibler's] music." The district court . . . correctly appl[ied] the anti-dissection rule [by] examining DJ LOGIC as a whole, including its appearance, sound, language, and impression. Kibler's call [in his brief] for this court to "focus on the dominant features of each mark and disregard the non-dominant features" is precisely what the anti-dissection rule forbids. Thus, the anti-dissection rule requires the similarity of marks factor to favor defendants here.

4. Evidence of Actual Confusion

Evidence of actual confusion is the strongest proof of likely confusion. *Frisch*, 759 F.2d at 1267. But the weight we give that evidence depends on the amount and type of confusion. On one end of the spectrum are persistent mistakes and confusion by actual customers. On the other are relatively few instances of confusion and inquiries rather than purchases. The analysis is, above all, contextual. In *Therma-Scan*, for example, the court found that six email inquiries implying that plaintiff manufactured the defendant's products provided only weak support for the conclusion that relevant consumers were likely to confuse the two. 295 F.3d at 635–36. The court considered the number of emails against the [very large] scale of defendant's operations. *Id.*

Kibler offers evidence of at most ten instances of actual confusion. These include tweets and webpages advertising a performance by "DJ Logic," but meaning Hall; an email offering to book "DJ Logic," but meaning Hall; and inquiries about whether Kibler would be performing somewhere advertising "logic" and referring to Hall. The district court concluded that the evidence of actual confusion favors Kibler only slightly. The court suggested that the ten instances paled in comparison to Hall's 170,000 album sales and popularity on YouTube, Facebook, and Twitter. The court also indicated that computer rather than human error caused the confusion on the webpages.

Because past confusion is the best proof of future confusion, any evidence at all favors the plaintiff. Kibler has offered some proof, but it is scant. If "Logic" really threatened to confuse consumers about the distinctions between Hall and Kibler, one would see much more than ten incidents throughout 170,000 album sales, 1.7 million album downloads, and 58 million YouTube views. The fact that none of the incidents were purchases would further prevent a jury from finding that this factor significantly helps Kibler. In sum, Kibler has not presented the quantity or type of proof that would tilt the actual confusion factor substantially in his favor.

5. Marketing Channels

The marketing channels factor requires us to compare both how the parties market their products and their main customers. The more channels and buyers overlap, the greater the likelihood that relevant consumers will confuse the sources of the parties' products. The reverse is true too.

Here, the district court found the marketing channels factor favors neither party. Kibler maintains that he has offered proof that would allow a reasonable jury to find the factor favorable to him. This includes deposition testimony 1) that he advertises on a personal website, MySpace, Twitter, and Facebook; 2) that he sells his music on Amazon and iTunes; and 3) that the parties have played fifteen of the same venues. It also includes tweets promoting Hall's album and performances and screenshots of Hall's Facebook page. Defendants [highlight] Kibler's deposition testimony that thousands of artists have played two of the fifteen venues and [note] that Hall has never appeared in *Downbeat* or *Gig*.

[Defendants also urge] us to discount the parties' online advertising, reasoning that such a pervasive channel as the Internet cannot clarify the likelihood of confusion.

The district court correctly concluded that this factor is neutral, but underestimated the impact of widespread Internet use. Kibler has shown that the parties market their products on the same websites, Twitter and Facebook, and target the same customers, users of Amazon or iTunes. At first glance, this overlap is compelling. But we must assess the likelihood of confusion in the real-life circumstances of the market. Most musical artists use those websites to advertise and sell their products today. At the same time, the popularity of these channels makes it that much less likely that consumers will confuse the sources of the parties' products. There are just too many other contenders. For these reasons, shared use of the above websites does not help us determine the likelihood of confusion.

Though evidence of the parties' common venues comes closest, it would not permit a reasonable jury to find that Kibler's and Hall's customers substantially overlap. Kibler himself admitted that thousands of artists have played two of the fifteen venues. The more artists there are, the fewer the chances of any one attendee encountering both Kibler's and Hall's songs, let alone confusing their sources. Proof of the remaining venues carries minimal weight without information about their traditional line-ups or patrons, for example.

The marketing channels factor is neutral because there is minimal evidence that the parties' advertising methods or targeted customers substantially overlap beyond shared use of congested websites like Facebook and iTunes.

6. Likely Degree of Purchaser Care

When consumers are more likely to exercise caution in purchasing items, they are less likely to confuse their origins. This happens when consumers have expertise in the items and when the items are particularly expensive. In this case, the district court found this factor unhelpful because the degree of care exercised by music consumers varies greatly by consumer and transaction. [T]he district court's analysis was sound and the factor is insignificant here.

7. Intent in Selecting the Mark

This court may infer a likelihood of confusion from evidence that defendant chose its mark to confuse consumers about the source of the parties' products. *Therma-Scan*, 295 F.3d at 638. The standard assumes that defendant itself believed that using the mark would divert business from plaintiff. *Daddy's*, 109 F.3d at 286. Circumstantial evidence of intent is sufficient when direct evidence is unavailable (as it often is). *Therma-Scan*, 295 F.3d at 638-39. And evidence that defendant knew of plaintiff's

trademark while using its mark constitutes such circumstantial evidence. *Daddy's*, 109 F.3d at 286-87.

Having found no evidence of intent, the district court concluded that the factor is neutral in this case. Kibler asserts that two pieces of evidence create a triable issue. One is his sworn declaration that a Google or YouTube search for "logic music" or "logic musician" yielded DJ LOGIC and Kibler's picture or music before Hall adopted LOGIC. The other is Hall's deposition testimony that he ran Google, Facebook, and Twitter searches for "any other rappers" using LOGIC before adopting it. Hall testified that he ran the search "[t]o see if [any rapper] with this name was already at a level where it wouldn't make sense for two people to coexist with the same name."

The district court properly found the factor neutral because the record prevents a reasonable jury from inferring intent. Here, we have no proof that Hall searched for "logic music" or "logic musician," no reason to believe he had to, and thus no evidence he knew of DJ LOGIC before adopting LOGIC. Hall's testimony shows, to the contrary, that he avoided choosing a mark that might lead consumers to confuse his product with that of another musician. The factor is therefore neutral.

8. Likelihood of Expansion

A strong possibility that either party will expand its business to compete with the other's increases the likelihood of consumers confusing the sources of the parties' products. As with intent, a finding that neither party will expand its business is irrelevant in determining the likelihood of confusion.

The district court concluded that this factor is neutral after finding it "unlikely that the parties will expand their markets to put them in competition." Kibler identifies book excerpts, press clippings, and deposition testimony describing his experimentation with different musical genres as proof he will expand his reach. He adds [in his brief that] there is "no evidence that [Hall] will not continue to expand his musical reach as well." Kibler stresses that the parties' mutual use of hip-hop predisposes them to expansion.

The district court rightly concluded that this factor is neutral. All we can conclude is that Kibler offered no proof that the parties will expand their businesses. Kibler's supposed evidence says nothing of the potential for competition with Hall, whether Kibler anticipates rapping or working closely with a rapper, for example. With no sign of any future overlap in the market, the parties' mutual use of hip-hop is irrelevant. Thus, the factor is neutral.

9. Balance of Factors

We note that evidence of actual confusion favors Kibler only marginally and that both the strength of plaintiff's mark and similarity of the marks favor defendants. Though the *Frisch* inquiry is flexible and contextual, these are the "most important factors." *Maker's Mark*, 679 F.3d at 424. Further, the remaining factors are either neutral or insignificant here. Because no reasonable jury could find a likelihood of confusion based solely on a few instances of actual confusion, defendants are entitled to judgment as a matter of law on Kibler's trademark infringement claim.

Trademark Dilution

Kibler also alleges trademark dilution in violation of the Lanham Act. The Act entitles "the owner of a famous mark that is distinctive" to an injunction against someone who "commences use of a mark . . . in commerce that is likely to cause dilution . . . of the famous mark" "any time after the owner's mark has become famous." 15 U.S.C. § 1125(c)(1).

The Act specifies that a mark is famous when it is "widely recognized by the general consuming public of the United States as a designation of source of the goods or services of the mark's owner." § 1125(c)(2)(A). In evaluating whether a mark is sufficiently recognized, courts may consider the duration, extent, and reach of advertising and publicity around the mark; amount, volume, and extent of product sales; and actual recognition of the mark. *Id.*

Courts have interpreted the Act to require the mark to be a "household name." *Coach Services, Inc. v. Triumph Learning LLC*, 668 F.3d 1356, 1373 (Fed. Cir. 2012). That is, "when the general public encounters the mark in almost any context, it associates the term, at least initially, with the mark's owner." *Id. See, e.g., Audi AG v. D'Amato*, 469 F.3d 534, 547 (6th Cir. 2006) (finding AUDI marks [are] famous under Lanham Act because Audi had spent millions of dollars on them and they are known globally); *Starbucks Corp. v. Wolfe's Borough Coffee, Inc.*, 588 F.3d 97, 105 (2d Cir. 2009) (finding that STARBUCKS marks are famous under the Lanham Act); *Louis Vuitton Malletier S.A. v. Haute Diggity Dog, LLC*, 507 F.3d 252, 257, 265 (4th Cir. 2007) (finding that LOUIS VUITTON marks are famous under the Lanham Act). It is difficult to establish fame under the Act sufficient to show trademark dilution. *Coach*, 668 F.3d at 1373.

The district court concluded that summary judgment was appropriate because no reasonable jury could find DJ LOGIC is famous under the Lanham Act. The court cited its finding that Kibler failed to show the mark is commercially strong for trademark infringement purposes. Indeed, it is easier to show public recognition under *Frisch* than it is under the Lanham Act['s dilution provision].

Kibler contends that the district court erred in discounting proof of his fame. He cites his sworn declaration describing his experience in the music industry and his deposition testimony that he was a guest contributor on a Grammy-winning album. Kibler's evidence clearly falls short of the high threshold for fame under the Lanham Act. DJ LOGIC is simply in a different league from the marks that have met this threshold. Indeed, having failed to show that his mark is commercially strong for even trademark infringement purposes, Kibler cannot point to a triable issue here. Thus, we do not address Kibler's remaining arguments on his trademark dilution claim.

Kibler has not provided evidence that would allow a reasonable jury to find relevant consumers are likely to confuse the sources of his and Hall's products, or that Hall's mark has diluted his. [Therefore, the district court did not err in granting summary judgment to defendants on Kibler's trademark infringement and trademark dilution claims.]

District Court's grant of summary judgment for defendants affirmed.

Trade Secrets

The law provides two partially overlapping means of protecting creative inventions. Owners of such inventions may go public and obtain monopoly patent rights. As an alternative, they may sometimes keep the invention secret and rely on trade secrets law to protect it.

The policies underlying patent protection and trade secrets protection differ. The general aim of patent law is to encourage the creation and disclosure of inventions by granting the patentee a temporary monopoly in the patented invention in exchange for his making it public. Trade secrets, however, are nonpublic by definition. Although protecting trade secrets may stimulate creative activity, it also keeps the information from becoming public knowledge. Thus, the main justification for trade secrets protection is simply to preserve certain standards of commercial morality.

State law historically served as the primary source of legal protection for trade secrets and as the only source of civil liability for the violation of another party's trade secret rights. Although a federal statute (the Economic Espionage Act of 1996) contemplated criminal liability in some instances of trade secret violations, federal law did not recognize a civil cause of action for misappropriation of trade secrets until very recently. That state of affairs changed with the enactment of a 2016 federal law, the Defend Trade Secrets Act (DTSA). The DTSA defines trade secrets and the elements of a misappropriation claim in ways that are very similar to state laws' customary treatment of

The Global Business Environment

An American firm may enter the world market by licensing its product or service to a foreign manufacturer. In exchange for granting a license to the foreign licensee, the American licensor will receive royalties from the sale of the licensed product or service. Usually, the licensed product or service or the name under which it is sold will be protected by American intellectual property law, such as patent, trade secret, copyright, or trademark law. Because American intellectual property law does not protect the property outside the boundaries of the United States, a licensor needs to take steps to ensure that its intellectual property will acquire protection in the foreign nation. Otherwise, the licensor risks that a competitor may appropriate the intellectual property without penalty.

The World Trade Organization has attempted to increase the protection of intellectual property through passage of the Agreement on Trade-Related Aspects of Intellectual Property Rights (TRIPS). Effective in 1995, TRIPS covers patents, trade secrets, copyrights, and trademarks. It sets out minimum standards of intellectual property protection to be provided by each member nation. Some signatory nations, such as the United States, provide greater protection of intellectual property.

Patents and Trade Secrets A patent filing must be made in each nation in which protection is desired. It is not especially difficult for a firm to acquire parallel patents in each of the major countries maintaining a patent system because many countries (including the United States) are parties to the Paris Convention for the Protection of Industrial Property. This convention recognizes the date of the first filing in any nation as the filing date for all, but only if subsequent filings are in fact made within a year of the first filing.

When technology is not patented, either because it is not patentable or because a firm makes a business decision not to patent it, a licensor may control its use abroad under **trade secret** law. For example, an American firm can license its manufacturing know-how to a foreign manufacturer for use in a defined territory in return for promises to pay royalties and to keep the trade secret confidential.

Copyright An American firm may license a foreign manufacturer to produce literary, artistic, or musical materials for which the firm holds an American copyright. For example, a computer software development firm may grant a license to a foreign manufacturer of software, or the American owner of copyrights protecting cartoon characters from the television program *The Simpsons* may license a Chinese firm to manufacture Homer, Marge, and Bart dolls.

There is no international copyright that automatically protects a copyrighted work everywhere in the world. Instead, copyright protection for a work must be secured under the laws of the individual nations in which protection is sought. International agreements, however, may smooth the way to copyright acquisition in many countries. The most notable is the Berne Convention, to which the United States and approximately 150 other nations subscribe. The Berne Convention guarantees that a work eligible for copyright in any signatory nation will be eligible for protection in all signatory nations. Although the Berne Convention does not completely standardize the copyright laws of the member nations, it does require each country's copyright laws to contain certain minimum guarantees of rights.

Another key aspect of the Berne Convention is its principle of *national treatment*, under which each signatory nation agrees to treat copyright owners from other subscribing countries according to the same rules it applies to copyright owners who are its own residents or citizens. Other international agreements to which the United States is a party operate in generally similar fashion. These include the Universal Copyright Convention and the World Intellectual Property Organization Copyright Treaty.

Trademarks The holder of an American trademark may license the use of its trademark in a foreign nation. For example, McDonald's may license a French firm to use the McDonald's name and golden arches at a restaurant on the Champs-Élysées, or the holder of the Calvin Klein trademark may license a South Korean firm to manufacture Calvin Klein jeans.

An American trademark's owner, when licensing its product or services abroad, runs the risk of experiencing unwanted and largely uncontrollable uses of its trademark in a foreign market unless it has acquired trademark rights in that nation.

Trademark registrations normally must be made in each nation in which protection is desired. Parallel trademark registrations, however, may be made in compliance with the Paris Convention for the Protection of Industrial Property. Under the Paris Convention, the date of the first filing in any nation is the filing date for all nations, if the subsequent filings are made within six months of the first filing.

The European Union allows a single filing to be effective in all EU nations. An agreement known as the Madrid Protocol also permits a firm to seek registration or a trademark in all its signatory nations simultaneously by filing an application for registration in any signatory nation and with the World Intellectual Property Organization (WIPO) in Geneva. The United States joined the Madrid Protocol in 2003.

such matters. Because the DTSA does not preempt state trade secrets law, state law remains an important player in the trade secrets realm. Those whose trade secret rights have arguably been violated are likely to have considerable freedom to decide whether to pursue litigation under the DTSA or, instead, under applicable state law. The following discussion focuses on key principles that typical state laws and the DTSA share.

Definition of a Trade Secret

 Explain what a trade secret is and what the trade secret owner must prove in order to win a misappropriation case.

A **trade secret** can be defined as any secret formula, pattern, process, program, device, method, technique, or compilation of information used in the owner's business, if it gives its owner an advantage over competitors who do not know it or use it.[4] Examples include chemical formulas, computer software, manufacturing processes, designs for machines, and certain detailed customer lists. To be protectible, a trade secret must usually have sufficient value or originality to provide an actual or potential competitive advantage. It need not possess the novelty required for patent protection, however.

Courts examine various factors when determining whether a trade secret exists. As common sense suggests, a trade secret must actually be *secret* if it is to be legally protected. A substantial measure of secrecy is necessary, but it need not be absolute. Thus, information that becomes public knowledge or becomes generally known in the industry cannot be a trade secret. Similarly, information that is reasonably discoverable by proper means may not be protected. "Proper means" include independent invention of the secret, observation of a publicly displayed product, the owner's advertising, published literature, product analysis, and reverse engineering (starting with a legitimately acquired product and working backward to discover how it was developed).

---

[4]This definition comes mainly from *Restatement (Third) of Unfair Competition* § 39 (1995), with some additions from Uniform Trade Secrets Act § 1(4) (1985). Many states have adopted the Uniform Trade Secrets Act (UTSA) in some form. The discussion in this chapter is a composite of the *Restatement*'s and the UTSA's rules.

CYBERLAW IN ACTION

Trademark infringement principles sometimes govern conflicts between one party's claim of trademark rights and another's claim of rights over a World Wide Web domain name. Such disputes sometimes raise dilution issues as well.

In a 1999 enactment, Congress paid special attention to the trademark rights–domain name rights conflict by enacting the Anticybersquatting Consumer Protection Act (ACPA). The ACPA authorizes a civil action in favor of a trademark owner against any person who, having a "bad faith intent to profit" from the owner's mark, registers, sells, purchases, licenses, or otherwise uses a domain name that is identical or confusingly similar to the owner's mark (or would dilute the mark, if it is famous). Among the factors listed in the ACPA as relevant to the existence of bad-faith intent to profit are a defendant's intent to divert consumers from the mark owner's online location to a site that could harm the mark's goodwill and a defendant's offer to sell the domain name to the mark owner without having used, or intended to use, the domain name in the offering of goods or services.

If the trademark owner wins a cybersquatting action, the court may order the forfeiture or cancellation of the domain name or may order that it be transferred to the mark owner. The successful trademark owner may also recover actual damages as well as the cybersquatter's attributable profits. Borrowing the statutory damages concept from the Copyright Act, the ACPA provides that in lieu of actual damages plus profits, the trademark owner may elect to recover statutory damages falling within a range of $1,000 to $100,000 per domain name, "as the court considers just."

Many cases in which a trademark owner complains about another party's registration of a domain name have been submitted to arbitration, rather than to a court, in recent years. When a party registers an Internet address with the Internet Corporation for Assigned Names and Numbers, the registrant must agree to submit to arbitration in the event that a trademark owner claims a right to the domain name. The World Intellectual Property Organization is a leading provider of arbitrators for this process.

In addition, a firm claiming a trade secret must usually show that it took *reasonable measures to ensure secrecy*. Examples include advising employees about the secret's secrecy, limiting access to the secret on a need-to-know basis, requiring those given access to sign a nondisclosure agreement, disclosing the secret only on a confidential basis, and controlling access to an office or plant. Computer software licensing agreements commonly forbid the licensee to copy the program except for backup and archival purposes, require the licensee and its employees to sign confidentiality agreements, call for those employees to use the program only in the course of their jobs, and require the licensee to use the program only in a central processing unit. Because the owner must make only *reasonable* efforts to ensure secrecy, however, she need not adopt extreme measures to block every ingenious form of industrial espionage.

Ownership and Transfer of Trade Secrets

The owner of a trade secret is usually the person who developed it or the business under whose auspices it was generated. Establishing the ownership of a trade secret can pose problems, however, when an employee develops a secret in the course of her employment. In such cases, courts often find the *employer* to be the owner if (1) the employee was hired to do creative work related to the secret, (2) the employee agreed not to divulge or use trade secrets, or (3) other employees contributed to the development of the secret. Even when the employee owns the secret, the employer still may obtain a royalty-free license to use it through the shop right doctrine discussed in the section on patents.

The owner of a trade secret may transfer rights in the secret to third parties. This may occur by assignment (in which case the owner loses title) or by license (in which case the owner retains title but allows the transferee certain uses of the secret).

Misappropriation of Trade Secrets

 LO8-12 Explain what a trade secret is and what the trade secret owner must prove in order to win a misappropriation case.

Misappropriation of a trade secret can occur in various ways, most of which involve *disclosure* or *use* of the secret. For example, misappropriation liability occurs when the secret is disclosed or used by one who did one of the following:

1. Acquired it by *improper means*. Improper means include theft, trespass, wiretapping, spying, bugging, bribery, fraud, impersonation, and eavesdropping.

2. Acquired it from a party who *is known or should be known* to have obtained it by improper means. For example, a freelance industrial spy might obtain one firm's trade secrets by improper means and sell them to the firm's competitors. If those competitors know or have reason to know that the spy obtained the secrets by improper means, they are liable for misappropriation along with the spy.

3. *Breached a duty of confidentiality regarding the secret.* If an employer owns a trade secret, for example, an employee is generally bound not to use or disclose it during his employment or thereafter.[5] As indicated in the *Coleman* case, which follows shortly, this rule applies to a former employee of the trade secret owner regardless of whether that ex-employee agreed in a written contract to respect the employer's trade secrets after the employment relationship ceased.

Remedies for misappropriation of a trade secret include damages, which may involve both the actual loss caused by the misappropriation and the defendant's unjust enrichment. In some states, punitive damages are awarded for willful and malicious misappropriations. Also, an injunction may be issued against actual or threatened misappropriations.

Noncompetition Agreements Once an employment relationship ends, the ex-employee is normally free to compete with her former employer on the basis of general knowledge and skills obtained and developed during the employment relationship (as opposed to *trade secrets* learned during the relationship). However, employers fairly often attempt to restrict such otherwise allowable postemployment relationship competition by having their employees enter into a written *noncompetition agreement* in which the employees agree not to compete with the employer (or accept employment with a competitor of the employer) for some period of time after the employment relationship ends. Often, these noncompetition agreements go well beyond the clearly important and legally recognized interest in preserving trade secrets. To the extent that they extend beyond trade secret protection and restrict postemployment competition more generally, such agreements are disfavored in the law because they may interfere unduly with individuals' important interests in working and making a living. Accordingly, courts tend to enforce noncompetition agreements that extend beyond trade secret protection only if their provisions restricting competition are narrowly defined in terms of duration, geographic area, and relationship to legitimate interests of the employer. Noncompetition agreements that strike the court as too broad may be ruled unenforceable.

The *Coleman* case, which follows, addresses not only misappropriation of trade secret issues, but also issues regarding enforceability of noncompetition agreements.

---

[5]This is an application of the agent's duty of loyalty, which is discussed in Chapter 35.

Coleman v. Retina Consultants, P.C.   687 S.E.2d 457 (Ga. 2009)

Retina Consultants, P.C. does business under the name The Retina Eye Center (TREC) and will be referred to here as TREC. As its name indicates, TREC is a medical practice specializing in retina surgery. In 2000, TREC hired Brendan Coleman as a software engineer. Prior to his employment by TREC, Coleman wrote and marketed a medical billing program called Clinex. While employed by TREC, Coleman, with the assistance of the doctors who worked for TREC, modified the Clinex program to suit TREC's specific business and developed an integrated retinal practice computer application called Clinex-RE. Clinex-RE is a software program that integrates electronic medical records and image storage with a billing software component. Clinex and Clinex-RE are different programs, and Clinex-RE works only in conjunction with Clinex. In order to develop Clinex-RE, Coleman incorporated into his Clinex program certain proprietary information and trade secrets of TREC.

In 2003, Coleman and TREC entered into a Software Agreement that allocated the rights to Clinex and Clinex-RE between TREC and Coleman. Although the Software Agreement stated that Coleman owns Clinex and that TREC had only a nonexclusive license to use and sell Clinex, Paragraph 8 of the agreement provided that "Coleman will not distribute, vend or license to any ophthalmologist or optometrist the Clinex software or any computer application competitive with the Clinex-RE software without the written consent of TREC."

Prior to ending his employment relationship with TREC in 2008, Coleman developed encryption keys that were required for the installation of the Clinex-RE package (i.e., Clinex as integrated with Clinex-RE) on any computer in TREC's office and that were necessary for the program to work properly. After the parties' employment relationship ended, TREC sued Coleman in a Georgia court for breach of the Software Agreement and for misappropriation of trade secrets. TREC alleged—and the trial court later found—that, after his resignation, Coleman removed all applicable encryption keys and source and access codes along with any manual/installation instructions; attempted to distribute, vend, or license to other ophthalmologists the Clinex and Clinex-RE software; refused to disclose to TREC the passwords required to read and revise copies of the Clinex and Clinex-RE software; refused to provide copies to TREC of all documentation in his possession and control relating to the programming and use of the software; refused to return to TREC copies of the Clinex-RE software; and used or attempted to use TREC's proprietary information and trade secrets to compete with TREC.

The trial court issued an injunction in favor of TREC and against Coleman. The injunction purported to enforce the Software Agreement and in particular the noncompetition provision in its Paragraph 8. The injunction further prohibited Coleman from "continuing to retain and use any applicable encryption keys, access codes, source codes and the multiple copies of manual/installation instructions," from "retaining any passwords required to read and to revise copies of the Clinex and Clinex-RE software," and from "retaining copies of all documentation in his possession or control relating to the programming and use of the Clinex and Clinex-RE software." Coleman appealed to the Supreme Court of Georgia.

Melton, Justice

Coleman claims that the non-compete clause in [Paragraph 8 of] the Software Agreement is unenforceable as a matter of law. A contract "which may have the effect of or which is intended to have the effect of defeating or lessening competition, or encouraging a monopoly, [is] unlawful and void." [Citation omitted.] However, "a restrictive covenant contained in an employment contract . . . will be upheld if the restraint imposed is not unreasonable, is founded on a valuable consideration, and is reasonably necessary to protect the interest of the party in whose favor it is imposed, and does not unduly prejudice the interests of the public." [Citation omitted.]

A useful tool in examining the reasonableness of a [noncompetition clause] consists of a "three-element test of duration, territorial coverage, and scope of activity." [Citation omitted.] Even if only a portion of a non-compete clause in an employment contract would be unenforceable, the entire covenant must fail.

We agree with Coleman that the non-compete clause at issue is unenforceable as a matter of law. [Paragraph 8 of] [t]he Software Agreement states that "Coleman will not distribute, vend or license to any ophthalmologist or optometrist the Clinex software or any computer applications competitive with the Clinex-RE software without the written consent of TREC." On its face, the agreement contains no time limitation, as the contract purports to limit Coleman's actions in perpetuity. A non-compete clause, such as the one at issue here, is invalid where it "contain[s] no limitation regarding duration." [Citation omitted.] Furthermore, "[t]he covenant which we are asked to consider in this case, as it is written, has no territorial limitation. The absence of such a limitation renders it void." [Citation omitted.] Indeed, the non-compete clause here would prohibit Coleman from marketing Clinex and any other competitive software to *any* ophthalmologist or optometrist, regardless of whether or not they are or ever were customers of TREC and regardless of where they are located. Such a restrictive covenant is overbroad and unenforceable.

For the foregoing reasons, we find that the non-compete clause of the Software Agreement is unreasonable and that the trial court therefore erred to the extent that the injunction enforces the clause against Coleman. Thus, the non-compete clause, in and of itself, cannot operate to prevent Coleman from marketing Clinex and Clinex-RE to ophthalmologists and optometrists.

However, this does not end our inquiry. Even without an express restrictive covenant, TREC could still prohibit Coleman from marketing the Clinex-RE package, that is, Clinex as integrated with Clinex-RE. Indeed, [according to a Georgia statute], "[i]n no event shall a contract be required in order to maintain an action or to obtain injunctive relief for misappropriation of a trade secret." *See also Thomas v. Best Mfg. Corp.*, 218 S.E.2d 68 (Ga. 1975) ("Even without an express restrictive covenant, one of the implied terms of a contract of employment is that the employee will not disclose a trade secret learned during his employment, to a competitor of his former employer. It is not relevant whether or not a valid express written contract or restrictive covenant was entered into.").

The trial court found that the Clinex-RE package is a trade secret belonging to TREC. Paragraph (c) of the injunction [issued by the trial court] correctly prohibits Coleman "from using, communicating, revealing or otherwise making available confidential information and trade secrets belonging to [TREC]." Therefore, regardless of the fact that the non-compete clause in the Software Agreement is unenforceable, Coleman would nevertheless be prohibited from using the Clinex-RE package to compete with TREC to the extent that the Clinex-RE package contains TREC's confidential information and trade secrets. Coleman would not, however, be restricted from using and marketing his own version of Clinex, which is undisputably his own property, to the extent that it does not contain any of TREC's confidential information or trade secrets.

Coleman claims that the trial court erred by enjoining him from retaining copies of the Clinex program and accompanying software. Specifically, the Software Agreement states that "the Clinex software is valuable commercial property of Coleman," and only requires Coleman to "*disclose* [to TREC] any passwords required to read and to revise . . . copies of the Clinex . . . software, and [to] provide *copies* of all documentation in his possession or control relating to the programming and use of the Clinex . . . software." The injunction, on the other hand, purports to enjoin Coleman from "continuing to *retain* . . . *any* . . . applicable encryption keys, access codes, source codes and . . . copies of manual/installation instructions [for Clinex]" and further enjoins him "from *retaining any* passwords required to read and revise copies of the Clinex . . . software and from *retaining* copies of all documentation in his possession or control relating to the programming and use of the Clinex . . . software."

By prohibiting Coleman from retaining any and all information and documentation related to Clinex, the plain language of the injunction [erroneously] goes beyond the scope of that which is required of Coleman pursuant to the terms of the Software Agreement [and beyond what misappropriation of trade secrets principles permit. It is Clinex-RE that contains TREC's trade secrets, not Clinex, which is Coleman's property under the terms of the Software Agreement].

Trial court's judgment affirmed in part and reversed in part; terms of injunction to be modified accordingly.

Commercial Torts

In addition to the intentional torts discussed in Chapter 6, other intentional torts involve business or commercial competition. These torts may help promote innovation by protecting creative businesses against certain competitive abuses. Their main aim, however, is simply to uphold certain minimum standards of commercial morality.

Injurious Falsehood

Injurious falsehood also goes by names such as product disparagement, slander of title, and trade libel. This tort involves the publication of false statements that disparage another's business, property, or title to property, and thus harm her economic interests. One common kind of injurious falsehood involves false statements that disparage either a person's *property rights* in land, things, or intangibles or their *quality*. The property rights in question include legally protected property interests that can be sold; examples include leases, mineral rights, trademarks, copyrights, and corporate stock. Injurious falsehood also includes false statements that harm another's economic interests even though they do not disparage property or property rights as such. For example, the seller of a bodybuilding program was held to have stated a valid claim for injurious falsehood against a book publisher regarding a false statement that the plaintiff's program was isometric in nature. The harm to the plaintiff's economic interest in the sale of its bodybuilding program stemmed from the juxtaposition of the untrue statement about the program with a statement concerning supposed dangers of isometric exercise programs.

Elements and Damages

List the elements that a plaintiff must prove in order to win an injurious falsehood case.

In injurious falsehood cases, the plaintiff must prove that the defendant made a false statement of the sort just described, and that the statement was communicated to a third party. The degree of fault required for liability is unclear. Sources often say that the standard is malice, but formulations of this differ. The *Restatement* requires either knowledge that the statement is false or reckless disregard as to its truth or falsity. There is usually no liability for false statements that are made negligently and in good faith.

The plaintiff must also prove that the false statement played a substantial part in causing him to suffer *special damages*. These may include losses resulting from the diminished value of disparaged property; the expense of measures for counteracting the false statement (e.g., advertising or litigation expenses); losses resulting from the breach of an existing contract by a third party; and the loss of prospective business. In cases involving the loss of prospective business, the plaintiff is usually required to show that some specific person or persons refused to buy because of the disparagement. This rule is often relaxed, however, where these losses are difficult to prove.

The special damages that the plaintiff is required to prove are his usual—and typically his only—remedy in injurious falsehood cases. Damages for personal injury or emotional distress, for instance, are generally not recoverable. However, punitive damages and injunctive relief are sometimes obtainable.

Injurious Falsehood and Defamation Injurious falsehood may or may not overlap with the tort of defamation discussed in Chapter 6. Statements impugning a businessperson's character or conduct are probably defamatory. If, on the other hand, the false statement is limited to the plaintiff's business, property, or economic interests, his normal claim is for injurious falsehood. Both claims are possible when the injurious falsehood implies something about the plaintiff's character and affects his overall reputation. An example would be a defendant's false allegation that the plaintiff company knew the children's products it sold contained dangerously high levels of lead. As in defamation cases, statements of pure opinion (as opposed to false statements of supposed fact) do not give rise to injurious falsehood liability.

Defamation law's absolute and conditional privileges generally apply in injurious falsehood cases.[6] Certain other privileges protect defendants who are sued for injurious falsehood. For example, a rival claimant may in good faith disparage another's property rights by asserting his own competing rights. Similarly, one may make a good-faith allegation that a competitor is infringing one's patent, copyright, or trademark. Finally, a person may sometimes make unfavorable comparisons between her product and that of a competitor. This privilege is generally limited to sales talk asserting the superiority of one's own product and does not cover unfavorable statements about a competitor's product.

Interference with Contractual Relations

Explain the elements of interference with contractual relations.

In a lawsuit for intentional interference with contractual relations, one party to a contract claims that the defendant's interference with the other party's performance of the contract wrongly caused the plaintiff to lose the benefit of that performance. One can interfere with the performance of a contract by causing a party to repudiate it or by wholly or partly preventing that party's performance. The means of interference can range from mere persuasion to threatened or actual violence. The agreement whose performance is impeded, however, must be an *existing* contract. This includes contracts that are voidable, unenforceable, or subject to contract defenses but *not* void bargains, contracts that are illegal on public policy grounds, or contracts to marry. Finally, the defendant must have *intended* to cause the breach; there is usually no liability for negligent contract interferences.

Even if the plaintiff proves these threshold requirements, the defendant is liable only if his behavior was *improper*. Despite the flexible, case-by-case nature of such determinations, a few generalizations about improper interference are possible.

1. If the contract's performance was blocked by such clearly improper means as threats of physical violence, misrepresentations, defamatory statements, bribery, harassment, or bad-faith civil or criminal actions, the defendant usually is liable. Liability is also likely where the interference was motivated *solely* by malice, spite, or a simple desire to meddle.

2. If his means and motives are legitimate, a defendant generally escapes liability when his contract interference is in the *public interest*—for example, when he informs an airport that an air traffic controller habitually uses hallucinogenic drugs. The same is true when the defendant acts

<hr>

[6]Chapter 6 discusses those privileges.

to *protect a person for whose welfare she is responsible*—for example, when a mother induces a private school to discharge a diseased student who could infect her children.

3. A contract interference resulting from the defendant's good-faith effort to protect her own *existing* legal or economic interests usually does not create liability so long as appropriate means are used. For example, a landowner can probably induce his tenant to breach a sublease to a party whose business detracts from the land's value. However, business parties generally cannot interfere with existing contract rights merely to further some *prospective* competitive advantage. For example, a seller cannot entice its competitors' customers to break existing contracts with those competitors.

4. Finally, defendants are sometimes less likely to be held liable when the contracts they allegedly interfered with were terminable at will. The reason is that in such cases, the plaintiff had only a desire or hope that the contract would continue but not an enforceable expectation in that regard. Accordingly, those who hire away their competitors' at-will employees may have a credible argument for avoiding liability, though the cases are highly fact-specific and the argument is not a guaranteed winner.

The basic measure of damages for intentional interference with contractual relations is the value of the lost contract performance. Some courts also award compensatory damages reasonably linked to the interference (including emotional distress and damage to reputation). Sometimes the plaintiff may obtain an injunction prohibiting further interferences.

The *Lewis-Gale Medical Center* case, which follows shortly, discusses issues arising in interference with contractual relations cases, including the improper behavior element and the effect when the contract interfered with was terminable at will.

Interference with Prospective Advantage

The rules and remedies for intentional interference with prospective advantage parallel those for interference with contractual relations. The main difference is that the former tort involves interferences with *prospective* relations rather than existing contracts. The protected future relations are mainly potential contractual relations of a business or commercial sort. Liability for interference with such relations requires intent; negligence does not suffice.

The "improper interference" factors weighed in interference-with-contract cases generally apply to interference with prospective advantage as well. One difference, however, is that interference with prospective advantage can be justified if (1) the plaintiff and the defendant are in competition for the prospective relation with which the defendant interferes; (2) the defendant's purpose is at least partly competitive; (3) the defendant does not use such improper means as physical threats, misrepresentations, and bad-faith lawsuits; and (4) the defendant's behavior does not create an unlawful restraint of trade under the antitrust laws or other regulations. Thus, a competitor ordinarily can win customers by offering lower prices and attract suppliers by offering higher prices. Unless this is otherwise illegal, he can also refuse to deal with suppliers or buyers who also deal with his competitors.

Lewis-Gale Medical Center, LLC v. Alldredge
710 S.E.2d 716 (Va. 2011)

Southwest Emergency Physicians Inc. (SWEP) and Lewis-Gale Medical Center entered into a 2005 contract under which SWEP's physician-employees exclusively staffed Lewis-Gale's Emergency Department. Dr. Karen Alldredge, an emergency room physician, was under contract with SWEP from 2005 until the termination of her employment in 2008. Her contract provided for a 12-month term of employment with SWEP and included an automatic renewal provision. However, the contract further provided that it could be terminated by either party without cause, subject to a 90-day written notice of the intent to do so. During her time as a SWEP employee, Dr. Alldredge worked in the Lewis-Gale emergency room.

In 2008, Dr. Alldredge attended an informal dinner with some of the emergency room nursing staff who were employees of Lewis-Gale. During the dinner, these nurses discussed and signed a letter addressed to the Lewis-Gale administration voicing certain work-related concerns. Dr. Alldredge was the only physician present. She did not sign the letter and later explained to one of the nurses that she did not sign the letter because it related to "a nursing issue, not a physician issue." Dr. Alldredge subsequently conceded that she did not sign the letter because she also knew that SWEP did not want its physicians involving themselves in Lewis-Gale's personnel issues.

Candi Carroll, Lewis-Gale's chief nursing officer, received a copy of the letter. Carroll subsequently became aware of Dr. Alldredge's involvement with the signatories to the letter. By e-mail, Carroll contacted Dr. Robert Dowling, SWEP's president, who also served as medical director for the emergency department at Lewis-Gale. Carroll informed him of her belief that Dr. Alldredge had supported the staff members who had sent the letter. She inquired "what the plan of [SWEP] is to deal with Doctor Alldredge." Carroll and Dr. Dowling exchanged several e-mails addressing Carroll's concerns. Carroll also advised her superiors of the situation.

After learning that Dr. Alldredge had attended the dinner referred to above, Charlotte Tyson, chief operating officer of Lewis-Gale, was concerned that Dr. Alldredge had become involved in the hospital's personnel matters. Tyson contacted Dr. Jeffrey Preuss, another SWEP physician. He later testified in the litigation referred to below that Tyson had "brought to [SWEP] the fact that there was a perceived issue with Doctor Alldredge's behavior and had asked that [SWEP] do something to take care of that issue, resolve it one way or another."

Later in 2008, at SWEP's request, Tyson and Carroll met with members of SWEP's executive board. During the meeting, Tyson described Dr. Alldredge's behavior as that of an "organizational terrorist," and told SWEP's executive board that when a business has someone like Dr. Alldredge, "they had to go." Although the representatives of SWEP repeatedly asked Tyson how Lewis-Gale wanted the situation addressed, Tyson later maintained that she never expressly told SWEP that Lewis-Gale's administration wanted Dr. Alldredge's employment to be terminated. Nonetheless, shortly after the meeting Dr. Dowling informed Tyson in an e-mail that he planned to recommend the termination of Dr. Alldredge's employment at an upcoming meeting of the SWEP board.

The minutes of SWEP's board meeting cited additional concerns about Dr. Alldredge's "treatment of other partners and group members" and "her behavior over the years." The board was of the opinion that "the situation had come to a crisis point" and that Dr. Alldredge "was not likely to improve her behavior long-term." Nonetheless, the principal concern cited by the board was that not terminating Dr. Alldredge's employment could jeopardize SWEP's contract with Lewis-Gale. Dr. Alldredge, who was present for part of the meeting, defended herself and expressed frustration and sadness at being called an "organizational terrorist." SWEP terminated Dr. Alldredge's employment in accordance with the provision of her contract by providing her with a 90-day notice period.

Dr. Alldredge then sued Lewis-Gale in a Virginia court, alleging tortious interference with her contract of employment with SWEP. The case eventually proceeded to a jury trial. At the close of Dr. Alldredge's evidence, Lewis-Gale sought a directed verdict in its favor. The trial court, however, submitted the case to the jury and instructed it that Dr. Alldredge had the burden of proving that Lewis-Gale "use[d] improper methods to interfere with the contractual relationship or expectancy" between Dr. Alldredge and SWEP. The jury returned a verdict for Dr. Alldredge, awarding her $900,000 in compensatory damages. Lewis-Gale appealed to the Supreme Court of Virginia.

Koontz, Senior Justice

The dispositive issue we consider is whether Dr. Alldredge presented sufficient evidence to permit the jury to find that Lewis-Gale employed improper methods to induce SWEP to terminate her employment.

Intentional interference with performance of a contract by a third party is a permissible cause of action in Virginia. "The elements required for a prima facie showing of the tort are: (i) the existence of a valid contractual relationship or business expectancy; (ii) knowledge of the relationship or expectancy on the part of the interferor; (iii) intentional interference inducing or causing a breach or termination of the relationship or expectancy; and (iv) resultant damage to the party whose relationship or expectancy has been disrupted." [Citation omitted.] "Additionally, when a contract is terminable at will, a plaintiff, in order to present a prima facie case of tortious interference, must allege and prove not only an intentional interference that caused the termination of the at-will contract, but also that the defendant employed improper methods." *Dunn, McCormack & MacPherson v. Connolly*, 708 S.E.2d 867 (Va. 2011).

An employment contract is terminable at will if the plain terms of the contract provide that the employer may terminate the contract prior to the designated period of time of the employment without being required to establish a just cause for doing so. Although such a contract may place conditions of notice and timing of the termination, when the employer complies with these conditions the termination does not constitute a breach of the employment contract.

In the present case, regardless of any expectancy that Dr. Alldredge may have had with regard to her continued employment by SWEP, because her contract provided for termination by SWEP after giving 90 days notice, Dr. Alldredge's contract was for employment at will. Accordingly, Dr. Alldredge was required to prove not only that Lewis-Gale intentionally interfered with her contract relationship with SWEP, but also that in doing so Lewis-Gale employed "improper methods."

The thrust of Lewis-Gale's assertions is that when Dr. Alldredge's evidence adduced at trial is viewed in its totality, it was insufficient as a matter of law to permit the jury to find that Lewis-Gale's dealings with SWEP with regard to its employment of Dr. Alldredge constituted improper methods that would sustain her cause of action for interference with her at-will employment contract. Thus, Lewis-Gale contends that the court erred in . . . submitting the case to the jury. We agree.

Our recent decision in *Dunn, McCormack & MacPherson* reiterated the contours of what constitutes the types of "improper methods" that a third party may not undertake when it intends for those actions to result in the termination of an at-will contract between others. Quoting from [an earlier case], we said:

Methods of interference considered improper are those means that are illegal or independently tortious, such as violations of statutes, regulations, or recognized common-law rules. Improper methods may include violence, threats or intimidation, bribery, unfounded litigation, fraud, misrepresentation or deceit, defamation, duress, undue influence, misuse of inside or confidential information, or breach of a fiduciary relationship. . . . Methods also may be improper because they violate an established standard of a trade or profession, or involve unethical conduct [even if not otherwise tortious]. Sharp dealing, overreaching, or unfair competition may also constitute improper methods.

We declined, however, to expand the parameters of "improper methods" to include "actions solely motivated by spite, ill will and malice" toward the plaintiff [even though some states have done so].

Dr. Alldredge did not allege or present any evidence tending to prove that Lewis-Gale's actions were illegal or independently tortious. Nor was there any fiduciary duty owed to Dr. Alldredge that Lewis-Gale could have violated. Dr. Alldredge did not assert that Lewis-Gale's motivation in seeking to have SWEP terminate her employment involved a desire to gain some competitive advantage, violated an established standard of the dealings between hospitals and their independent medical contractors, or involved unethical conduct in the form of sharp dealing, overreaching, or unfair competition.

Rather, Dr. Alldredge maintains that Lewis-Gale's actions were improper in that it used intimidation, duress, and undue influence based upon Lewis-Gale's ability to bring "financial ruin" on SWEP by canceling its contract to provide emergency room services to Lewis-Gale, which was SWEP's principal source of revenue. However, while the evidence supported the inference that SWEP was concerned about the continuation of its contract with Lewis-Gale, the at-will contract between Lewis-Gale and SWEP allowed termination of the contract upon due notice and without cause at any time. This status required that SWEP be continually sensitive to the possibility of termination for any reason or no reason, regardless of any specific action or comment made by Lewis-Gale officers or personnel. Thus, the inherent intimidation or duress experienced as a result of the very nature of this at-will contract cannot rise to the level of improper methods necessary to establish a cause of action for tortious interference with contract expectancy. Furthermore, in this case neither Dr. Alldredge's allegations nor her evidence demonstrated a specific threat or other action by Lewis-Gale that it was going to cancel its contract with SWEP if SWEP did not terminate Dr. Alldredge's employment.

We also reject Dr. Alldredge's allegations that Tyson's statements, such as her use of the term "organizational terrorist" to describe Dr. Alldredge, were independently tortious and therefore rose to improper methods. These statements were certainly unwise, unprofessional hyperbole, and may even indicate a personal animus toward Dr. Alldredge. In the context of Tyson's discussions with SWEP, however, the statements did not rise to the level of fraud, misrepresentation, deceit, or defamation that could constitute improper methods of interference with the contract between Dr. Alldredge and SWEP.

We disagree with Dr. Alldredge that the actions of Lewis-Gale's administrators, particularly Tyson, which Lewis-Gale's counsel concedes were "unsavory," "careless," and "harsh," rose to the level of the "improper methods" required to prove Lewis-Gale's actions exceeded that permissible in normal business relations in order to give rise to a cause of action in tort. In [an earlier case,] we noted that where the defendant has its own contractual or commercial relationship with the other party to the plaintiff's contract, a balance must "be struck between the social desirability of protecting the business relationship [of the plaintiff and the other party], on one hand, and the interferor's freedom of action [with the other party] on the other." [W]e addressed this observation to the availability of an affirmative defense of privilege or justification, but we are of the opinion that it applies with equal force to determining what the law will deem to be an improper method by the interferor when there is an existing commercial relationship between it and the other party to the contract with the plaintiff.

Under Virginia law, a threat to perform an act one is legally entitled to perform is not a wrongful act. As we have previously observed, "the law will not provide relief to every disgruntled player in the rough-and-tumble world comprising the competitive marketplace." [Citation omitted.] The fact that Virginia recognizes the existence of the tort of intentional interference with a contract does not mean that every contract relationship which is terminated or disrupted through the interference of a third party promoting its own interests will result in tort liability for that party. Rather, the law provides a remedy in tort only where the plaintiff can prove that the third party's actions were illegal or fell so far outside the accepted practice of that "rough-and-tumble world" as to constitute improper methods.

In sum, Lewis-Gale's actions in this case involving at-will contracts did not rise as a matter of law to the level of the "improper methods" required for Dr. Alldredge to prove that Lewis-Gale's purposeful interference in her contract relationship with SWEP was tortious. Accordingly, we hold that the circuit court erred in not [granting a directed verdict] to Lewis-Gale.

Trial court's judgment in favor of Alldredge reversed.

Lanham Act § 43(a)

 LO8-15 Identify key issues on which courts focus in false advertising cases brought under Lanham Act § 43(a).

Section 43(a) of the Lanham Act basically creates a federal law of unfair competition. Section 43(a) is not a consumer remedy; it is normally available only to commercial parties, which usually are the defendant's competitors. The section creates civil liability for a wide range of false, misleading, confusing, or deceptive representations made in connection with goods or services. Section 43(a)'s many applications include:

1. *Tort claims for "palming off" or "passing off."* This tort involves false representations that are likely to induce third parties to believe that the defendant's goods or services are those of the plaintiff. Such representations include imitations of the plaintiff's trademarks, trade names, packages, labels, containers, employee uniforms, and place of business.

2. *Trade dress infringement claims.* These claims resemble passing-off claims. A product's trade dress is its overall appearance and sales image. Section 43(a) prohibits a party from passing off its goods or services as those of a competitor by employing a substantially similar trade dress that is likely to confuse consumers as to the source of its products or services. For example, a competitor that sells antifreeze in jugs that are similar in size, shape, and color to a well-known competitor's jugs may face § 43(a) liability.

3. *Claims for infringement of both registered and unregistered trademarks.*

4. *Commercial appropriation of name or likeness claims and right of publicity claims* (discussed in Chapter 6).

5. *False advertising claims.* This important application of § 43(a) includes ads that misrepresent the nature, qualities, or characteristics of either the *advertiser's* products and services or a *competitor's* products and services. Section 43(a) applies to ads that are likely to mislead buyers even if they are not clearly false on their face, and to ads with certain deceptive *omissions*. Ordinary consumers are not regarded as appropriate plaintiffs in false advertising cases under § 43(a) (though they sometimes may sue under state laws dealing with deceptive trade practices). Rather, an appropriate plaintiff in a § 43(a) case has a commercial interest that goes beyond the interest a consumer typically has. This generally means that the plaintiff will be a competitor, either direct or indirect, of the defendant.

The *POM Wonderful* case, which follows, illustrates the types of allegations that may violate § 43(a) of the Lanham Act if they are proven. In *POM Wonderful*, the Supreme Court also addresses the interaction between § 43(a) and regulatory authority granted to the Food and Drug Administration under the federal Food, Drug, and Cosmetic Act.

POM Wonderful LLC v. Coca-Cola Co.   134 S. Ct. 2228 (2014)

POM Wonderful LLC (POM) produces, markets, and sells, under its POM Wonderful brand, a variety of pomegranate products, including a pomegranate-blueberry juice blend. POM competes in the pomegranate-blueberry juice market with Coca-Cola Co. Using its Minute Maid brand, Coca-Cola created and sold a juice blend containing 99.4 percent apple and grape juices, 0.3 percent pomegranate juice, 0.2 percent blueberry juice, and 0.1 percent raspberry juice. Despite the small amount of pomegranate and blueberry juices in the blend, the front label of the Coca-Cola product displayed the words "pomegranate blueberry" in all capital letters, on two separate lines. Below those words, Coca-Cola placed the phrase "flavored blend of 5 juices" in much smaller type. Below that phrase, in still smaller type, were the words "from concentrate with added ingredients and other natural flavors." The product's front label also displayed a vignette of blueberries, grapes, and raspberries in front of a halved pomegranate and a halved apple.

Claiming that Coca-Cola's label deceived consumers and thereby harmed POM as a competitor, POM sued Coca-Cola under § 43(a) of the federal Lanham Act. POM alleged that the name, label, marketing, and advertising of Coca-Cola's juice blend would mislead consumers into believing that the product consisted predominantly of pomegranate and blueberry juice when it, in fact, consisted predominantly of less-expensive apple and grape juices. That confusion, POM complained, caused it to lose sales and made its sought-after remedies of damages and injunctive relief appropriate.

A federal district court rejected POM's Lanham Act claim and granted summary judgment to Coca-Cola after concluding that Congress had entrusted matters of food and beverage labeling, including misleading labeling, to the Food and Drug Administration (FDA) under the federal Food, Drug, and Cosmetic Act (FDCA). Therefore, the district court reasoned, the plaintiff's

§ 43(a) cause of action was precluded. POM appealed to the U.S. Court of Appeals for the Ninth Circuit, which affirmed the district court's grant of summary judgment to Coca-Cola. The U.S. Supreme Court granted POM's petition for certiorari. (Further discussion of § 43(a) of the Lanham Act, the FDCA, and relevant FDA regulations will appear in the following edited version of the Supreme Court's decision.)

Kennedy, Justice

This case concerns the intersection and complementarity of . . . two federal laws[, the Lanham Act and the FDCA]. A proper beginning point is a description of the statutes.

Congress enacted the Lanham Act nearly seven decades ago [and included a provision that makes the statute's purposes clear.] Section 45 provides:

> The intent of this chapter is to regulate commerce within the control of Congress by making actionable the deceptive and misleading use of marks in such commerce; to protect registered marks used in such commerce from interference by State, or territorial legislation; to protect persons engaged in such commerce against unfair competition; [and] to prevent fraud and deception in such commerce by the use of reproductions, copies, counterfeits, or colorable imitations of registered marks. . . .

The Lanham Act's trademark provisions are the primary means of achieving these ends. But the Act also creates a federal remedy that goes beyond trademark protection. The broader remedy is at issue here.

[Section 43(a) of the] Lanham Act creates a cause of action for unfair competition through misleading advertising or labeling. Though in the end consumers also benefit from the Act's proper enforcement, the cause of action is for competitors, not consumers. The petitioner here (POM) asserts injury as a competitor.

The cause of action [created in § 43(a)] imposes civil liability on any person who "uses in commerce any word, term, name, symbol, or device, or any combination thereof, or any false designation of origin, false or misleading description of fact, or false or misleading representation of fact, which . . . in commercial advertising or promotion, misrepresents the nature, characteristics, qualities, or geographic origin of his or her or another person's goods, services, or commercial activities." The private remedy may be invoked only by those who "allege an injury to a commercial interest in reputation or sales. A consumer who is hoodwinked into purchasing a disappointing product may well have an injury-in-fact cognizable [on other legal grounds], but he cannot invoke the protection of the Lanham Act." *Lexmark International v. Static Control Components,* 134 S. Ct. 1377 (2014). POM's cause of action [under § 43(a)] would be straightforward enough but for Coca-Cola's contention that a separate federal statutory regime, the FDCA, allows it to use the label in question and in fact precludes the Lanham Act claim.

So the FDCA is the second statute to be discussed. The FDCA statutory regime is designed primarily to protect the health and safety of the public at large. The FDCA prohibits the misbranding of food and drink. 21 U.S.C. §§ 321(f), 331. A food or drink is deemed misbranded if, *inter alia*, "its labeling is false or misleading," § 343(a), information required to appear on its label "is not prominently placed thereon," § 343(f), or the label does not bear "the common or usual name of the food, if any there be." § 343(i). To implement these provisions, the Food and Drug Administration (FDA) promulgated regulations regarding food and beverage labeling, including the labeling of mixes of different types of juice into one juice blend. *See* 21 CFR § 102.33 (2013). One provision of those regulations is particularly relevant to this case: If a juice blend does not name all the juices it contains and mentions only juices that are not predominant in the blend, then it must either declare the percentage content of the named juice or "[i]ndicate that the named juice is present as a flavor or flavoring," *e.g.,* "raspberry and cranberry flavored juice drink." § 102.33(d). The Government represents that the FDA does not preapprove juice labels under these regulations. That contrasts with the FDA's regulation of other types of labels, such as drug labels, and is consistent with the less extensive role the FDA plays in the regulation of food than in the regulation of drugs.

Unlike the Lanham Act, which relies in substantial part for its enforcement on private suits brought by injured competitors, the FDCA and its regulations provide the United States with nearly exclusive enforcement authority, including the authority to seek criminal sanctions in some circumstances. 21 U.S.C. §§ 333(a), 337. Private parties may not bring enforcement suits. § 337. Also unlike the Lanham Act, the FDCA contains a provision pre-empting certain state laws on misbranding. That provision forecloses a "State or political subdivision of a State" from establishing requirements that are of the type but "not identical to" the requirements in some of the misbranding provisions of the FDCA. 21 U.S.C. § 343-1(a). It does not address, or refer to, other federal statutes or the preclusion thereof.

[In the case before us, the district court] granted summary judgment to Coca-Cola on POM's Lanham Act claim, ruling that the FDCA and its regulations preclude challenges to the name and label of Coca-Cola's juice blend. The district court reasoned that in the juice blend regulations, the "FDA has directly spoken on the issues that form the basis of POM's Lanham Act claim against the naming and labeling" of Coca-Cola's product, but has not prohibited any, and indeed expressly has permitted some, aspects of Coca-Cola's label. The Court of Appeals for the Ninth Circuit affirmed, [reasoning] that Congress decided "to entrust matters of juice beverage labeling to the FDA"; [that] the FDA has promulgated "comprehensive regulation of that labeling"; and [that] the FDA "apparently" has not imposed the requirements on Coca-Cola's label that are sought by POM. [The Ninth Circuit further noted that] "for a court to act when the FDA has not—despite regulating extensively in this area—would risk undercutting the FDA's expert judgments and authority." For these reasons, and "[o]ut of respect for the statutory and regulatory scheme," the Court of Appeals barred POM's Lanham Act claim.

This Court granted certiorari to consider whether a private party may bring a Lanham Act claim challenging a food label that is regulated by the FDCA. The answer to that question is based on the following premises.

First, this is not a pre-emption case. In pre-emption cases, the question is whether state law is pre-empted by a federal statute, or in some instances, a federal agency action. This case, however, concerns the alleged preclusion of a cause of action under one federal statute by the provisions of another federal statute. So the state-federal balance does not frame the inquiry.

Second, this is a statutory interpretation case and the Court relies on traditional rules of statutory interpretation. That does not change because the case involves multiple federal statutes. Nor does it change because an agency is involved. Analysis of the statutory text, aided by established principles of interpretation, controls.

Beginning with the text of the two statutes, it must be observed that neither the Lanham Act nor the FDCA, in express terms, forbids or limits Lanham Act claims challenging labels that are regulated by the FDCA. By its terms, § 43(a) of the Lanham Act subjects to suit any person who "misrepresents the nature, characteristics, qualities, or geographic origin" of goods or services. This comprehensive imposition of liability extends, by its own terms, to misrepresentations on labels, including food and beverage labels. No other provision in the Lanham Act limits that understanding or purports to govern the relevant interaction between the Lanham Act and the FDCA. And the FDCA, by its terms, does not preclude Lanham Act suits. In consequence, food and beverage labels regulated by the FDCA are not, under the terms of either statute, off limits to Lanham Act claims [such as POM's].

This absence is of special significance because the Lanham Act and the FDCA have coexisted since the passage of the Lanham Act in 1946. If Congress had concluded, in light of experience, that Lanham Act suits could interfere with the FDCA, it might well have enacted a provision addressing the issue during these 70 years. Congress enacted amendments to the FDCA and the Lanham Act, including an amendment that added to the FDCA an express pre-emption provision with respect to state laws addressing food and beverage misbranding. Yet Congress did not enact a provision addressing the preclusion of other federal laws that might bear on food and beverage labeling. This is powerful evidence that Congress did not intend FDA oversight to be the exclusive means of ensuring proper food and beverage labeling.

Perhaps the closest the statutes come to addressing the preclusion of the Lanham Act claim at issue here is the pre-emption provision added to the FDCA in 1990. But, far from expressly precluding suits arising under other federal laws, the provision if anything suggests that Lanham Act suits are not precluded. This pre-emption provision forbids a "State or political subdivision of a State" from imposing requirements that are of the type but "not identical to" corresponding FDCA requirements for food and beverage labeling. It is significant that . . . the provision does not refer to requirements imposed by other sources of law, such as federal statutes. Pre-emption of some state requirements does not suggest an intent to preclude federal claims.

The structures of the FDCA and the Lanham Act reinforce the conclusion drawn from the text. When two statutes complement each other, it would show disregard for the congressional design to hold that Congress nonetheless intended one federal statute to preclude the operation of the other. The Lanham Act and the FDCA complement each other in major respects, for each has its own scope and purpose. Although both statutes touch on food and beverage labeling, the Lanham Act protects commercial interests against unfair competition, while the FDCA protects public health and safety.

The two statutes complement each other with respect to remedies in a more fundamental respect. Enforcement of the FDCA and the detailed prescriptions of its implementing regulations is largely committed to the FDA. The FDA, however, does not have the same perspective or expertise in assessing market dynamics that day-to-day competitors possess. Competitors who manufacture or distribute products have detailed knowledge regarding how consumers rely upon certain sales and marketing strategies. Their awareness of unfair competition practices may be far more immediate and accurate than that of agency rulemakers and regulators. Lanham Act suits draw upon this market expertise by empowering private parties to sue competitors to protect their interests on a case-by-case basis. Allowing Lanham Act suits takes advantage of synergies among multiple methods of regulation. This is quite consistent with the congressional design to enact two different statutes, each with its own mechanisms to enhance the protection of competitors and consumers.

A holding that the FDCA precludes Lanham Act claims challenging food and beverage labels would not only ignore the distinct functional aspects of the FDCA and the Lanham Act but also would lead to a result that Congress likely did not intend. Unlike other types of labels regulated by the FDA, such as drug labels, it would appear the FDA does not preapprove food and beverage labels under its regulations and instead relies on enforcement actions, warning letters, and other measures. Because the FDA acknowledges that it does not necessarily pursue enforcement measures regarding all objectionable labels, if Lanham Act claims were to be precluded then commercial interests—and indirectly the public—could be left with less effective protection in the food and beverage labeling realm than in other, less regulated industries. It is unlikely that Congress intended the FDCA's protection of health and safety to result in less policing of misleading food and beverage labels than in competitive markets for other products.

The [lower courts'] ruling that POM's Lanham Act cause of action is precluded by the FDCA was incorrect. There is no statutory text or established interpretive principle to support the contention that the FDCA precludes Lanham Act suits like the one brought by POM in this case. Nothing in the text, history, or structure of the FDCA or the Lanham Act shows the congressional purpose or design to forbid these suits. Quite to the contrary, the FDCA and the Lanham Act complement each other in the federal regulation of misleading food and beverage labels. Competitors, in their own interest, may bring Lanham Act claims like POM's that challenge food and beverage labels that are regulated by the FDCA.

Ninth Circuit's judgment reversed; case remanded for further proceedings.

Problems and Problem Cases

1. In car engines without computer-controlled throttles, the accelerator pedal interacts with the throttle via a cable or other mechanical link. The traditional mechanical design of an accelerator pedal permitted the pedal to be pushed down or released, but the position in the footwell area of the car could not be adjusted by sliding the pedal forward or back. As a result, a driver who wished to be closer to or farther from the pedal had to reposition himself in the driver's seat or move the seat in some way. These were imperfect solutions for drivers of smaller stature who had cars with deep footwells. Inventors therefore designed pedals that could be adjusted to change their location in the footwell. Patents were issued for some of these inventions, which relied on a mechanical link. Steven Engelgau later invented an adjustable pedal with an electronic sensor mounted on a fixed pivot point. He received a patent on his invention. Engelgau's invention was the first adjustable pedal to employ an electronic sensor on a fixed pivot point. Of course, electronic sensors and computerized systems are used in various ways elsewhere in vehicles. Engelgau granted Teleflex Inc. an exclusive license to exercise his rights under the patent. Later, when Teleflex sued another party for alleged infringement of the patent, the defendant argued that the patent was invalid—and therefore should not have been issued—because Engelgau's invention was obvious. Was the defendant correct in this argument? Was Engelgau's invention obvious even though no other inventor in the field had utilized an electronic sensor mounted on a fixed pivot point?

2. Visual artist Jeff Koons created a painting called *Niagara*. The painting consisted of fragmentary images collaged against the backdrop of a landscape. It depicted four pairs of women's feet and lower legs dangling prominently over images of confections—a large chocolate fudge brownie topped with ice cream, a tray of donuts, and a tray of apple danish pastries—with a grassy field and Niagara Falls in the background. The images of the legs were placed side by side, each pair pointing vertically downward. Koons drew the images in *Niagara* from fashion magazines and advertisements. One of the pairs of legs in the painting was adapted from a copyrighted photograph taken by Andrea Blanch, an accomplished professional fashion and portrait photographer. The Blanch photograph used by Koons in *Niagara* was titled *Silk Sandals*. It appeared in the August 2000 issue of *Allure* magazine. While working on *Niagara* and other paintings, Koons saw *Silk Sandals* in *Allure*. In an affidavit submitted in the litigation referred to below, Koons stated that "certain physical features of the legs [in the photograph] represented for me a particular type of woman frequently presented in advertising." He considered this typicality to further his purpose of commenting on the "commercial images . . . in our consumer culture." Koons scanned the image of *Silk Sandals* into his computer and incorporated a version of the scanned image into *Niagara*. He omitted certain aspects of the scanned image from his painting and modified certain other aspects of the image, such as by making the woman's legs angle downward rather than upward (the opposite of how they had appeared in Blanch's photograph). Koons did not seek permission from Blanch before using her photograph. He later earned approximately $125,000 from financial exploitation of *Niagara*. When Blanch sued Koons for copyright infringement, what defense would Koons have attempted to establish? Did Koons succeed with that defense?

3. Monsanto Co. invented a genetic modification that enables soybean plants to survive exposure to glyphosate,

the active ingredient in many herbicides (including Monsanto's own Roundup product). Monsanto markets soybean seed containing this altered genetic material as Roundup Ready seed. Farmers planting that seed can use a glyphosate-based herbicide to kill weeds without damaging their crops. Two patents issued to Monsanto cover various aspects of its Roundup Ready technology, including a seed incorporating the genetic alteration. Monsanto sells, and allows other companies to sell, Roundup Ready soybean seeds to growers who assent to a special licensing agreement. That agreement permits a grower to plant the purchased seeds in one—and only one—season. The grower can then consume the resulting crop or sell it as a commodity, usually to a grain elevator or agricultural processor. Under the agreement, the farmer may not save any of the harvested soybeans for replanting, nor may he supply them to anyone else for that purpose. These restrictions reflect the ease of producing new generations of Roundup Ready seed. Because glyphosate resistance comes from the seed's genetic material, that trait is passed on from the planted seed to the harvested soybeans. A single Roundup Ready seed can grow a plant containing dozens of genetically identical beans, each of which, if replanted, can grow another such plant—and so on. The agreement's terms thus prevent the farmer from producing his own Roundup Ready seeds from season to season, forcing him instead to buy from Monsanto each season.

Vernon Bowman is an Indiana farmer. Each year, he purchased Roundup Ready seed from a company affiliated with Monsanto for his first crop of the season. In accordance with the agreement just described, he used all of that seed for planting and sold his entire crop to a grain elevator (which typically would resell it to an agricultural processor for human or animal consumption). For his second crop of each season, Bowman devised a different approach. Because he thought such late-season planting risky and because Monsanto charges a premium price for Roundup Ready seed, he went to a grain elevator, purchased commodity soybeans intended for human or animal consumption, and planted them in his fields. Those soybeans came from prior harvests of other local farmers. Because most of those farmers also used Roundup Ready seed, Bowman could anticipate that many of the soybeans he purchased from the grain elevator would contain Monsanto's patented technology. After he applied a glyphosate-based herbicide to his fields, a significant proportion of the new plants survived the treatment and produced a new crop of soybeans with the Roundup Ready trait. Bowman saved seed from that crop to use in his late-season planting the next year. He continued this pattern for the next several years—planting saved seed from the year before, spraying his fields with glyphosate to kill weeds, and yielding a new crop of glyphosate-resistant—that is, Roundup Ready—soybeans.

After discovering this practice, Monsanto sued Bowman for infringing its patents on Roundup Ready seed. Bowman raised patent exhaustion as a defense, arguing that Monsanto could not control his use of the soybeans because they were the subject of a prior authorized sale (from local farmers to the grain elevator). The federal district court rejected Bowman's argument and awarded damages of $84,456 to Monsanto. The U.S. Court of Appeals for the Federal Circuit affirmed. The U.S. Supreme Court agreed to decide the case. How did the Supreme Court rule? Did the patent exhaustion defense apply here to protect Bowman against liability?

4. Qualitex Co. produces pads that dry-cleaning firms use on their presses. Since the 1950s, Qualitex has colored its press pads a shade of green-gold. In 1989, Jabcobson Products Co. began producing press pads for sale to dry-cleaning firms. Jacobson colored its pads a green-gold resembling the shade used by Qualitex. Later in 1989, the U.S. Patent and Trademark Office granted Qualitex a trademark registration for the green-gold color (as used on press pads). Qualitex then added a trademark infringement claim to an unfair competition lawsuit it had previously filed against Jacobson. Qualitex won the case, but the Ninth Circuit Court of Appeals set aside the judgment on the trademark infringement claim. In the Ninth Circuit's view, the Lanham Act did not allow any party to have color alone registered as a trademark. The Supreme Court granted certiorari. How did the Supreme Court rule on the question whether color is a registrable trademark?

5. Starbucks Corp., a company primarily engaged in the sale of coffee products, was founded in Seattle in 1971. Starbucks has grown to more than 8,700 retail locations in the United States, Canada, and foreign countries and territories. In addition to operating its retail stores, Starbucks supplies its coffees to hundreds of restaurants, supermarkets, airlines, sport and entertainment venues, motion picture theaters, hotels, and cruise ship lines. Starbucks prominently displays its federally registered "Starbucks" marks (the "Starbucks Marks") in all of its commercial activities and spends large sums of money on advertising and promotional activities that feature the Starbucks Marks. Those marks include the "Starbucks" name and the company's logo, which is circular and contains a graphic mermaid-like siren and the phrase

"Starbucks Coffee." Starbucks has approximately 60 U.S. trademark registrations and trademark registrations in 130 countries. The company devotes substantial effort to policing the marketplace for possible violations of its trademark rights.

Wolfe's Borough Coffee Inc., which does business under the Black Bear name (and which will be referred to here by that name), also sells coffee products. Black Bear, whose principal place of business is New Hampshire, is a small, family-run business that produces and sells roasted coffee beans and related goods via mail order and Internet order as well as at a limited number of New England supermarkets. In addition, Black Bear sold coffee products from a single retail outlet. In April 1997, Black Bear began selling a "dark roasted blend" of coffee called "Charbucks Blend" and later "Mister Charbucks" (together, the "Charbucks Marks"). Charbucks Blend was sold in a packaging that showed a picture of a black bear above the following large-print words: "BLACK BEAR MICRO ROASTERY." The package informed consumers that the coffee was roasted and "Air Quenched" in New Hampshire and stated, in a fairly large font, that "You wanted it dark . . . You've got it dark!" Mister Charbucks was sold in a packaging that showed a picture of a man walking above the large font "Mister Charbucks." The package also informed consumers that the coffee was roasted in New Hampshire by "The Black Bear Micro Roastery" and that the coffee was "ROASTED TO THE EXTREME . . . FOR THOSE WHO LIKE THE EXTREME."

Not long after Black Bear made its first sale of Charbucks Blend, Starbucks demanded that Black Bear cease use of the Charbucks Marks. When Black Bear did not comply with this demand, Starbucks sued Black Bear in a federal district court. Starbucks alleged that Black Bear should be held liable for trademark infringement and trademark dilution under federal law. Did Black Bear commit trademark infringement? What about trademark dilution?

6. North Atlantic Instruments Inc. manufactured electronic equipment used on ships, tanks, and aircraft. In August 1994, North Atlantic acquired Transmagnetics Inc. (TMI), which designed, manufactured, and sold customized electronic devices to a limited number of engineers in the aerospace and high-tech industries. At the time North Atlantic acquired TMI, Fred Haber was a one-third owner of TMI, as well as its president and head of sales. This position allowed Haber to develop extensive client contacts. North Atlantic conditioned its agreement to acquire TMI on Haber's continuing to work for North Atlantic in a role similar to the role he had played at TMI.

The specialized nature of TMI's business made the identity of the relatively small number of engineers who required its products especially crucial to its business success. Even in companies employing thousands of engineers, a very small number of those engineers—sometimes only two—might need the technology produced by TMI. The identity and needs of that small number of engineers (i.e., TMI's client contacts) would have been very difficult for any company to derive on its own. TMI's list of client contacts was among the intangible assets for which North Atlantic paid when it acquired TMI. North Atlantic retained Haber as president of its new TMI division. An employment agreement between North Atlantic and Haber ran until July 31, 1997. Its terms obligated Haber not to disclose North Atlantic's customer lists, trade secrets, or other confidential information, either during his employment by North Atlantic or after that employment ceased. As president of the TMI division, Haber had access through desktop and laptop computers to information about North Atlantic's technology and customer bases, including lists of clients and information about their individual product needs and purchases.

In July 1997, Haber left North Atlantic to join Apex Signal Corp., which manufactured products targeted toward the same niche market as North Atlantic's TMI division. According to North Atlantic, Apex began targeting North Atlantic's customer base, with Haber allegedly asking clients he had dealt with at North Atlantic and TMI to do business with Apex. North Atlantic also contended that Haber had taken its confidential client information with him when he joined Apex. North Atlantic sued Haber and Apex for misappropriation of trade secrets and requested a preliminary injunction. The federal district court later preliminarily enjoined Haber and Apex from using the individual client contacts Haber had developed at North Atlantic and TMI. Haber and Apex appealed. Was the court correct in issuing the preliminary injunction?

7. Two persons who worked together to develop a business method applied for a patent. The invention for which they sought a patent explained how buyers and sellers of commodities in the energy market could protect, or hedge, against the risk of price changes. The key claims were claims 1 and 4. Claim 1 described a series of steps that amounted to instructions on how to hedge risk. Claim 4 put the concept articulated in claim 1 into a simple mathematical formula.

The remaining claims explained how claims 1 and 4 could be applied to allow energy suppliers and consumers to minimize the risks resulting from fluctuations in market demand for energy. Some of those claims also suggested familiar statistical approaches to determine the inputs to use in claim 4's equation. Are business methods potentially patentable? Should a patent be awarded for this particular claimed invention?

8. Louis Vuitton Malletier (Vuitton) is a well-known manufacturer of luxury luggage, leather goods, handbags, and accessories. Vuitton has a number of trademarks that it regularly uses in connection with its products. Among them are the LOUIS VUITTON name and the LV mark. The company's products are expensively priced and sold in department stores and boutique stores. Vuitton filed a trademark infringement and trademark dilution lawsuit against Haute Diggity Dog LLC, a firm that produced and sold, primarily through pet stores, inexpensive dog chew toys under the Chewy Vuitton brand name and various other brand names consisting of humorous versions of other companies' actual trademarks. The dog chew toys had the Chewy Vuitton name on them, along with a CV mark. Should Vuitton win its trademark infringement claim? What about its trademark dilution claim?

9. Carey Station Village Inc. (referred to below as the developer) purchased real estate near a Georgia lake in 1987. The developer planned to create a large residential subdivision known as Carey Station Village. Although the developer continued to own a number of the lots in the subdivision, it relinquished control of the subdivision to Carey Station Village Homeowners Association, Inc. (referred to below as the association) in 1994. In 1999, the developer began to sell off some of the lots whose ownership it had retained. These lots had been improved with double-wide, modular homes. The developer provided owner financing for a number of the purchases. Within the first three months of advertising the lots for sale, the developer had sold more than one-half of the lots. Later, however, the developer was required to foreclose on 16 of the 21 parcels of property it had sold.

The association brought suit against the developer in 2001 to recover dues and assessments it claimed were owed by the developer in regard to the developer's remaining lots. The developer and the association had been involved in an earlier lawsuit that resulted in a settlement in which the developer forgave a promissory note from the association, and in exchange, the association released the developer from any liability for association dues or assessments through the year 1999. The developer paid all dues and assessments owing in 2000 but did not make any payments during the subsequent years.

The developer filed a counterclaim asserting that the association committed the tort of interference with contractual relations. According to the developer, actions by the association caused a number of purchasers of the developer's lots to default on their promissory notes. In addition, the developer contended that the association's actions adversely affected the developer's ability to sell its remaining lots at market value. The developer sought to recover damages resulting from the foreclosures referred to above, as well as damages allegedly incurred when the developer's remaining 27 lots were sold at a price below market value.

The case was tried to a jury in a Georgia court. The trial judge denied the association's motion for a directed verdict on the developer's interference with contractual relations counterclaim. The jury found in favor of the association on its claim for unpaid dues and assessments and awarded it $40,527.09. The jury also found in favor of the developer on its counterclaim and awarded it $211,250. The trial judge entered a judgment in favor of the developer in the amount of $170,722.91, the net amount once the damages awarded to the association were offset against the greater amount of damages awarded to the developer. The association appealed. Should the association have been held liable on the developer's counterclaim?

10. Google Inc. operates a search engine that accesses many thousands of websites and indexes them in a database stored on Google's computers. Google generates revenue through an advertising program associated with its search engine. The search results that Google provides through its Google Image Search are provided in the form of small images called "thumbnails." The thumbnails are stored on Google's servers. Perfect 10 Inc., which markets and sells copyrighted images of nude models, operates a subscription website. For a fee, Perfect 10 subscribers can access a password-protected section of Perfect's 10 website. There, these subscribers have access to the photos Perfect 10 makes available. Perfect 10 has also done a limited amount of licensing of reduced-sized images of its copyrighted images for downloading and use on cell phones. Some of Perfect 10's copyrighted images ended up appearing in thumbnail-sized form in Google search results (probably because the Perfect 10 photos had been posted by others without Perfect 10's permission on websites that the Google search engine then picked up). Because Perfect 10 did not consent to Google's display of the thumbnail images, Perfect 10 sued Google for copyright infringement. What defense

should Google attempt to invoke? Should Google succeed with that defense?

11. In the late 1980s, SEB S.A., a French firm, invented a "cool-touch" deep fryer—a home-use appliance with external surfaces that remain cool during the frying process. SEB obtained a U.S. patent for its design in 1991. SEB later began manufacturing the cool-touch fryer and selling it in the United States. Presumably because it was superior to other products in the American market at the time, SEB's fryer was a commercial success.

In 1997, Sunbeam Products Inc., a competitor of SEB, asked Pentalpha Enterprises Ltd. to supply it with deep fryers meeting certain specifications. Pentalpha, a Hong Kong maker of home appliances, is a wholly owned subsidiary of Global-Tech Appliances Inc. In order to develop a deep fryer for Sunbeam, Pentalpha purchased an SEB fryer in Hong Kong and copied all but its cosmetic features. Because the SEB fryer bought in Hong Kong was made for sale in a foreign market, it bore no U.S. patent markings. After copying SEB's design, Pentalpha retained an attorney to conduct a right-to-use study. However, Pentalpha did not tell the attorney that its design was copied directly from SEB's.

The attorney failed to locate SEB's patent. In August 1997, he issued an opinion letter stating that Pentalpha's deep fryer did not infringe any of the patents he had found. Pentalpha then started selling its deep fryers to Sunbeam, which resold them in the United States under its trademarks. By obtaining its product from a manufacturer with lower production costs, Sunbeam was able to undercut SEB in the U.S. market. After SEB's customers started defecting to Sunbeam, SEB sued Sunbeam for patent infringement in March 1998. Sunbeam notified Pentalpha of the lawsuit the following month. Nevertheless, Pentalpha went on to sell deep fryers to Fingerhut Corp. and Montgomery Ward & Co., both of which resold them in the United States under their respective trademarks.

SEB settled the lawsuit with Sunbeam and then sued Pentalpha and Global-Tech on the theory that they had violated the Patent Act by actively inducing Sunbeam, Fingerhut, and Montgomery Ward to sell or to offer to sell the defendants' deep fryers in violation of SEB's patent rights. Are the defendants liable for inducing patent infringement? For purposes of that possible basis of liability, does it matter whether the defendants knew of SEB's patent?

12. Aereo Inc. sells a service that allows its paying subscribers to watch television programs over the Internet at about the same time as the programs are broadcast over the air. Most of these programs are copyrighted works. Aereo neither owns the copyrights in those works nor holds a relevant license from the copyright owners.

When an Aereo subscriber wants to watch a show that is currently airing, he selects the show from a menu on Aereo's website. Aereo's system, which consists of thousands of dime-sized antennas and other equipment housed in a centralized warehouse, responds roughly as follows: A server tunes an antenna to the broadcast carrying the selected show. Each antenna is dedicated to the use of a single subscriber. A transcoder translates the signals received by the antenna into data that can be transmitted over the Internet. A server saves the data in a subscriber-specific folder on Aereo's hard drive and, once several seconds of programming have been saved, begins streaming the show to the subscriber's screen (personal computer, tablet, smartphone, Internet-connected television, or other Internet-connected device). The streaming continues, a few seconds behind the over-the-air broadcast, until the subscriber has received the entire show. The data that Aereo's system streams to each subscriber are the data from that subscriber's own personal copy, made from the broadcast signals received by the particular antenna allotted to him. Aereo's system does not transmit data saved in one subscriber's folder to any other subscriber. When two subscribers wish to watch the same program, Aereo's system activates two separate antennas and saves two separate copies of the program in two separate folders. It then streams the show to the subscribers through two separate transmissions—each from the subscriber's personal copy.

Various television producers, marketers, distributors, and broadcasters that own the copyrights in programs that Aereo streams sued Aereo for copyright infringement. They sought a preliminary injunction, arguing that Aereo was infringing their right to perform their copyrighted works publicly. A federal district court denied the preliminary injunction, and the U.S. Court of Appeals for the Second Circuit affirmed. The U.S. Supreme Court granted the copyright owners' petition for a writ of certiorari. How did the Supreme Court rule? Did Aereo's actions amount to *performances* of the copyrighted works?

Contracts

Introduction to Contracts

The 2019 catalog that Gigantic State University (GSU) sent to prospective students described a merit-based scholarship called the "Eagle Scholarship." The catalog stated that GSU offers the Eagle Scholarship to all incoming students who are in the top 10 percent of their high school classes and have SAT scores of 1350 or above. Paul, a prospective student, read the 2019 catalog that GSU sent to him. Money was tight for Paul, so he paid particular attention to the part of the catalog that described financial aid. He read about the Eagle Scholarship and realized that he qualified for it. Paul picked GSU over other schools in large part because of the Eagle Scholarship. He applied to GSU and GSU admitted him. Before his freshman orientation, Paul called GSU and checked to be sure that he met the requirements of the Eagle Scholarship. A GSU representative informed him that he did. When Paul arrived at GSU for freshman orientation, however, he received a copy of the 2020 catalog and learned that the qualifications for the Eagle Scholarship had changed and that he no longer qualified.

- Was there a contract between GSU and Paul for the Eagle Scholarship?
- If so, what kind of contract was it?
- What body of legal rules would apply to the contract?
- If it wasn't a contract, is there any other basis for a legal obligation on the part of GSU?
- Would it be ethical for GSU not to honor its promise to Paul?

LO LEARNING OBJECTIVES

After studying this chapter, you should be able to:

9-1 Explain what a contract is and why contracts are useful.

9-2 Define the terms used to describe contracts and apply those terms to actual contracts.

9-3 Distinguish the applicability of the common law of contracts and Article 2 of the Uniform Commercial Code and identify which one governs a given contract.

9-4 Identify the circumstances under which quasi-contract or promissory estoppel can afford a remedy even though no contract exists.

The Nature of Contracts

 LO9-1 Explain what a contract is and why contracts are useful.

The law of contracts deals with the enforcement of promises. It is important to realize from the outset of your study of contracts that *not every promise is legally enforceable.* (If every promise were enforceable, this chapter could end here!) We have all made and broken promises without fear of being sued. If you promise to take a friend out to dinner and then fail to do so, you would be shocked to be sued for breach of contract. What separates such promises from legally enforceable contracts? The law of contracts sorts out what promises are enforceable, to what extent, and how they will be enforced.

A **contract** is a *legally enforceable* promise or set of promises. In other words, when promises have the status of *contract*, the contracting party harmed by a breach of the contract is entitled to obtain legal remedies against the breaching party.

The Functions of Contracts

Contracts give us the ability to enter into agreements with others with confidence that we may call on the *law*—not merely the good faith of the other party—to make sure that those agreements will be honored. Within limitations that you will study later, *contracting lets us create a type of private law*—the terms of the agreements we make—that governs our dealings with others.

Contracts facilitate the planning that is necessary in a modern, industrialized society. Who would invest in a business if she could not rely on the fact that the builders and suppliers of the facilities and equipment, the suppliers of the raw materials necessary to manufacture products, and the customers who agree to purchase those products would all honor their commitments? How could we make loans, sell goods on credit, or rent property unless loan agreements, conditional sales agreements, and leases were backed by the force of the law? Contract, then, is necessary to the world as we know it. Like that world, its particulars tend to change over time, while its general characteristics remain largely stable.

The Evolution of Contract Law

The idea of contract is ancient. Thousands of years ago, Egyptians and Mesopotamians recognized devices resembling contracts; by the 15th century, the common law courts of England had developed a variety of theories to justify enforcing certain promises. Contract law did not, however, assume major importance in our legal system until the 19th century, when the Industrial Revolution created the necessity for greater private planning and certainty in commercial transactions.

The central principle of contract law that emerged from this period was *freedom of contract*. Freedom of contract is the idea that contracts should be enforced because they are the products of the free wills of their creators, who should, within broad limits, be free to determine the extent of their obligations. The proper role of the courts in such a system of contract was to enforce these freely made bargains but otherwise to adopt a hands-off stance. The freedom to make good deals carried with it the risk of making bad deals. As long as a person voluntarily entered a contract, it would generally be enforced against him, even if the result was grossly unfair. And because equal bargaining power tended to be assumed, the courts were usually unwilling to hear defenses based on unequal bargaining power. This judicial posture allowed the courts to create a pure contract law consisting of precise, clear, and technical rules that were capable of general, almost mechanical, application. Such a law of contract met the needs of the marketplace by affording the predictable and consistent results necessary to facilitate private planning.

The emergence of large business organizations after the Civil War produced obvious disparities of bargaining power in many contract situations, however. These large organizations found it more efficient to standardize their numerous transactions by employing standard form contracts, which also could be used to exploit their greater bargaining power by dictating the terms of their agreements.

Contract law evolved to reflect these changes in social reality. During the 20th century, there was a dramatic increase in government regulation of private contractual relationships. Think of all the statutes governing the terms of what were once purely private contractual relationships. Legislatures commonly dictate many of the basic terms of insurance contracts. Employment contracts are governed by a host of laws concerning maximum hours worked, minimum wages paid, employer liability for on-the-job injuries, unemployment compensation, and retirement benefits. The purpose of much of this regulation has been to protect persons who lack sufficient bargaining power to protect themselves.

Courts also became increasingly concerned with creating contract rules that produce fair results. The precise, technical rules that characterized traditional common law gave way to permit some broader, imprecise standards such as good faith, injustice, reasonableness, and unconscionability. Despite the increased attention to fairness in contract law, the agreement between the parties is still the heart of every contract.

The Methods of Contracting

Many students reading about contract law for the first time may have the idea that contracts must be in writing to be enforceable. Generally speaking, that is not true. There are some situations in which the law requires certain kinds of contracts to be evidenced by a writing to be enforced. The most common examples of those situations are covered in Chapter 16. Unless the law specifically requires a certain kind of contract to be in writing, an oral contract that can be proven is as legally enforceable as a written one. (Of course, having a written contract may often be desirable even when a writing is not mandatory.)

Contracts can be and are made in many ways. When most of us imagine a contract, we envision two parties bargaining for a deal, drafting a contract on paper, and signing it or shaking hands. Some contracts are negotiated and formed in that way. Far more common today, both online and offline, is the use of standardized form contracts. Such contracts are preprinted by one party and presented to the other party for signing. In most situations, the party who drafts and presents the standardized contract is the one with greater bargaining power and/or sophistication in the transaction. Frequently, the terms of standardized contracts are nonnegotiable. Such contracts have the advantage of providing an efficient method of standardizing common transactions. On the other hand, they present the dangers that the party who signs the contract will not know what he is agreeing to and that the party who drafts and presents the contract will take advantage of her bargaining power to include terms that are oppressive or abnormal in that kind of transaction.

Basic Elements of a Contract

 LO9-1 Explain what a contract is and why contracts are useful.

Over the years, the law has developed a number of requirements that a set of promises must meet before they are treated as a contract. To qualify as a contract, a set of promises must be based on a voluntary agreement, which is made up of an **offer** and an **acceptance** of that offer. In addition, there usually must be **consideration** to support each party's promise. The contract must be between parties who have **capacity** to contract, and the objective and performance of the contract must be **legal**. (See Figure 9.1.) Each of the

Figure 9.1   Getting to Contract

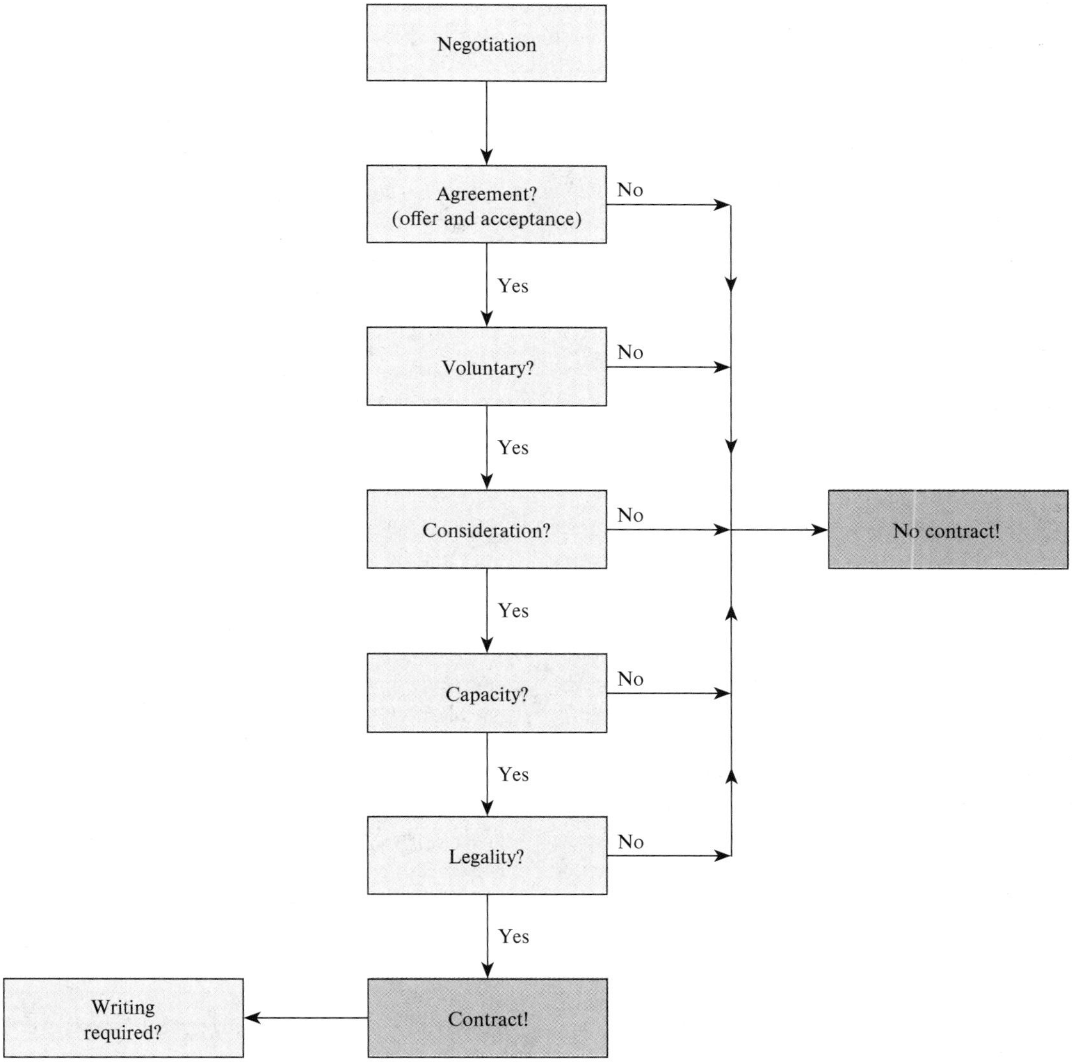

```
                    ┌─────────────────┐
                    │   Negotiation   │
                    └────────┬────────┘
                             │
                             ▼
                    ┌─────────────────┐     No
                    │   Agreement?    │──────────────────────►
                    │(offer and acceptance)│
                    └────────┬────────┘
                          Yes │
                             ▼
                    ┌─────────────────┐     No
                    │   Voluntary?    │──────────────────────►
                    └────────┬────────┘
                          Yes │
                             ▼
                    ┌─────────────────┐     No              ┌──────────────┐
                    │  Consideration? │──────────────────► │ No contract! │
                    └────────┬────────┘                     └──────────────┘
                          Yes │
                             ▼
                    ┌─────────────────┐     No
                    │    Capacity?    │──────────────────────►
                    └────────┬────────┘
                          Yes │
                             ▼
                    ┌─────────────────┐     No
                    │    Legality?    │──────────────────────►
                    └────────┬────────┘
                          Yes │
                             ▼
┌──────────────┐    ┌─────────────────┐
│   Writing    │◄───│    Contract!    │
│  required?   │    └─────────────────┘
└──────────────┘
```

elements of a contract will be discussed individually in subsequent chapters.

The elements of a contract can be found in all kinds of settings, from commercial dealings between strangers to agreements between family members to repeated interactions between businesses. In determining whether a contract exists, courts scrutinize the parties' communications and conduct in light of the context in which the parties interacted and their prior dealings. This process is illustrated by *Trapani Construction Co. v. Elliot Group, Inc.*, which follows.

Trapani Construction Co. v. Elliot Group, Inc.   64 N.E.3d 132 (Ill. App. Ct. 2016)

Trapani Construction Co. is a general contractor that had worked with the Elliot Group on a number of occasions. Over the years, Trapani had done more than $18 million in business with Elliot. Typically, Trapani would provide Elliot with a "contract" document, which called for signature but was never signed.

In July 2007, Trapani and Elliot were engaged in planning for a project known as the "Arlington Market Site Work." It included the project at issue in this case as well as a separate building project on the same site.

Consistent with their past practices, Trapani sent Elliot a draft contract document describing the services it would perform on the Arlington Market Site. It listed Elliot as the project owner. Through the first couple of weeks of July 2007, the parties engaged in a back-and-forth discussion about the terms of the project, both in person and by written correspondence. During that process, Trapani actually began work on the project and requested the first payment from Elliot.

Although Elliot never signed the draft contract document, it made payments to Trapani in the amount of $2,042,846.50. Those payments were made in response to requests prepared by a Trapani employee. The president of Elliot would "meticulously review" the requests and often require changes to them before paying. In addition, Trapani hired subcontractors for work on the project, obtained insurance (which named Elliot as an additional insured party), and sent to Elliot 16 change orders for the work. Elliot was aware of each.

Upon completing the project, Trapani claimed that Elliot still owed Trapani a balance of $257,764.70. Elliot refused to pay it.

Trapani sued Elliot claiming, among other things, a breach of contract. The trial court found in favor of Trapani. Elliot appealed, claiming that it never accepted Trapani's offer to provide construction services and that the unsigned draft contract document required signature to be enforceable.

Reyes, Justice

Defendant asserts there was no contract implied in fact between plaintiff and defendant because (1) defendant never accepted plaintiff's offer, (2) no consideration was provided to defendant, and (3) there was no meeting of the minds or mutual assent.

Even in the absence of an express contract, an implied contract can be created as a result of the parties' actions. In Illinois, two types of implied contracts are recognized, those implied in fact and those implied in law. Contracts implied in law are "equitable in nature, predicated on the fundamental principle that no one should unjustly enrich himself at another's expense." *In re Estate of Milborn*, 461 N.E.2d 1075 (Ill. App. Ct. 1984). Contracts implied in fact, as aforementioned, arise from a promissory expression that may be inferred from the facts and circumstances that demonstrate the parties' intent to be bound. Thus, "[t]he only difference between an express contract and an implied contract in the proper sense is, that in the former the parties arrive at an agreement by words, either verbal or written, while in the latter the agreement is arrived at by a consideration of their acts and conduct." *Litow v. Aurora Beacon News*, 209 N.E.2d 668 (Ill. App. Ct. 1965).

A contract implied in fact, which applies here, is a true contract. The elements of a contract are an offer, acceptance, and consideration. Thus, a contract implied in fact contains all of the elements of a contract, including a meeting of the minds.

Generally, for a contract to be valid, an acceptance must be objectively manifested; if it is not, there is no meeting of the minds. Acceptance of a contract implied in fact, however, can be proven by circumstances demonstrating that the parties intended to contract and by the general course of dealing between the parties. Similarly, mutual intent to contract can be established by the ordinary course of dealing and the common understanding of persons.

Based on our review of the record, we conclude the trial court's finding that a contract implied in fact existed between the parties was not against the manifest weight of the evidence for the following reasons.

In the instant case, plaintiff was paid in excess of $18 million by defendant for its work on other construction projects that was performed under similar circumstances, *i.e.,* under unsigned draft contracts. Plaintiff was also paid *in full* by defendant for its work on another building that was part of this particular project, also under an unsigned draft contract. For the work at issue, plaintiff submitted a proposal to defendant and performed pursuant to the terms and specifications in the draft contract dated July 5, 2007. To obtain payment for the work at issue, plaintiff submitted payment requests to defendant which defendant "meticulously review[ed]" before paying $2,041,846.50 to plaintiff in accordance with the draft contract. Further, defendant approved 16 written contract change orders that allowed plaintiff to continue to work on the project. In addition to these facts, defendant never corrected the subcontracts, certificates of insurance, change orders, weekly construction progress reports, contract activity reports, and documents for payment requests sent by plaintiff that identified defendant as the project owner. Moreover, defendant did not reject plaintiff's work or instruct plaintiff to cease work at any time. In light of this evidence, we find the circumstances and behaviors of the parties demonstrated a general course of dealing and a mutual intent to contract. Accordingly, we find there is ample evidence to support the trial court's ruling that a contract implied in fact existed between the parties.

* * *

Defendant [also] contends the draft contract dated July 5, 2007, "required acceptance by signature." Plaintiff . . . argues the draft contract did not require a signature to establish defendant's acceptance. Plaintiff also claims plaintiff's performance pursuant to the requirements of the draft contract, the progress payments made to plaintiff, and defendant's "conduct and silence" established that defendant had properly accepted plaintiff's offer. . . .

[T]he circumstances and behaviors of the parties demonstrated a general course of dealing and a mutual intent to contract. We thus conclude the trial court's finding that a contract implied in fact existed between the parties was not against the manifest weight of the evidence.

* * *

For the reasons stated above, we affirm the judgment of the circuit court of Cook County.

Affirmed.

CYBERLAW IN ACTION

Standardized contracts are common online as well as in the physical world. You have probably entered into online standardized contracts when you downloaded software from the Internet, joined an online service, initialized an e-mail account, or purchased goods online. The terms of standardized contracts online are sometimes presented in a manner that requires the viewer to click on an icon indicating agreement before he can proceed in the program. Standardized online contracts presented in this way are often called clickwrap contracts. Sometimes the terms of such contracts are included as a hyperlink on a page, and rather than requiring the user to click an icon, the indication of agreement is purportedly the use of the product or service. These types of standardized agreements are called browse-wrap contracts. In the past, though, consumers often purchased mass-marketed software in the form of a package of CD-ROM discs, which were typically bundled in a sealed package with a notice that stated that the consumer was agreeing to the terms of a proposed standardized license agreement when he or she broke the seal on the packaging. These are called shrinkwrap contracts or shrinkwrap licenses, a name that refers to that practice of using shrinkwrapped packaging. The enforceability of clickwraps, browse-wraps, and shrinkwraps, which has been a controversial topic, depends in large part on concepts addressed in Chapters 10 and 11.

Basic Contract Concepts and Types

 LO9-2 Define the terms used to describe contracts and apply those terms to actual contracts.

Bilateral and Unilateral Contracts Contracts traditionally have been classified as unilateral or bilateral, depending upon whether one party has made a promise or both parties have done so. In **unilateral contracts**, only one party makes a promise in exchange for something specific. For example, Perks Café issues "frequent buyer" cards to its customers, and stamps the cards each time a customer buys a cup of coffee. Perks promises to give any customer a free cup of coffee if the customer buys 10 cups of coffee and has his "frequent buyer" card stamped 10 times. In this case, Perks has made an offer for a unilateral contract, a contract that will be created with a customer only if and when the customer buys 10 cups of coffee and has his card stamped 10 times. In a **bilateral contract**, by contrast, *both* parties exchange promises and the contract is formed as soon as the promises are exchanged. For example, if Perks Café promises to pay Willowtown Mall $1,000 a month if Willowtown Mall will promise to lease a kiosk in the mall to Perks for the holiday season, Perks has made an offer for a bilateral contract because it is offering a promise in exchange for a promise. If Willowtown Mall makes the requested promise, a bilateral contract is formed at that point—even before the parties begin performing any of the acts that they have promised to do.

Valid, Unenforceable, Voidable, and Void Contracts

A valid contract is one that meets all of the legal requirements for a binding contract. Contracts must be valid to be enforceable in court. Some otherwise valid contracts, though, are not enforceable. An unenforceable contract is one that meets the basic legal requirements for a contract but may not be enforceable because of some other legal rule. You will learn about an example of this in Chapter 16, which discusses the statute of frauds, a rule that requires certain kinds of contracts to be evidenced by a writing. If a contract is one of those for which the statute of frauds requires a writing, but no writing is made, the contract is said to be unenforceable. Another example of an unenforceable contract is an otherwise valid contract whose enforcement is barred by the applicable contract statute of limitations.

Voidable contracts are those in which harmed parties have the legal right to cancel their obligations under the contract. For example, a contract that is induced by fraud or duress is voidable (cancelable) at the election of the victimized party. Other situations in which contracts are voidable are discussed in Chapters 13 and 14. The important feature of a voidable contract is that the injured party has the *right* to cancel the contract *if he chooses*. That right belongs only to the harmed party, and if he does not cancel the contract, it can be enforced by either party.

Void contracts are agreements that create no legal obligations and for which no remedy will be given. Contracts to commit crimes, such as "hit" contracts, are classic examples of void contracts. Illegal contracts are discussed in Chapter 15.

Express and Implied Contracts In an express contract, the parties have directly stated the terms of their contract orally or in writing at the time the contract was formed. However, as you read in the *Trapani Construction* case earlier in this chapter, the mutual agreement necessary to create a contract may also be demonstrated by the conduct of the parties. When the surrounding facts and circumstances indicate that an agreement has in fact been reached, an implied contract (also called a contract implied in fact) has been created.

If you are rushed to the emergency room for medical treatment following an accident, for example, you and the hospital do not ordinarily expressly state the terms of your agreement in advance, although it is clear that you do, in fact, have an agreement. A court would infer a promise by the hospital that its medical personnel will use reasonable care and skill in treating you and a return promise on your part to pay a reasonable fee for the treatment you receive. For further discussion of implied contracts, see *PWS Environmental v. All Clear*, which appears later in the chapter.

Executed and Executory Contracts A contract is executed when all of the parties have fully performed their contractual duties. It is **executory** until such duties have been fully performed.

Any contract may be described using one or more of the above terms. For example, Eurocars Inc. orders five new Mercedes-Maybach S 650 Sedans from Mercedes-Benz. Mercedes-Benz sends Eurocars its standard acknowledgment form accepting the order. The parties have a *valid, express, bilateral* contract that will be *executory* until Mercedes-Benz delivers the cars and Eurocars pays for them.

CYBERLAW IN ACTION

Currently, many courts are using the Uniform Commercial Code in cases involving disputes over software and other information contracts. However, the UCC was designed to deal with sales of goods and may not sufficiently address the concerns that parties have when making contracts to create or distribute information. During the 1990s, contract scholars, representatives of the affected information industries, consumer groups, and others worked as a drafting committee of the National Conference of Commissioners on Uniform State Laws to draft a uniform law that would be tailored to "information contracts." Internet access contracts and software licenses are two familiar examples of information contracts. These efforts resulted in a proposed statute called the Uniform Computer Information Transactions Act, or UCITA. Several UCITA positions—notably those dealing with shrinkwrap and clickwrap licenses—have been quite controversial. Only two states—Virginia and Maryland—have adopted UCITA, albeit with some modifications. Meanwhile, other states—including Iowa, North Carolina, West Virginia, and Vermont—have passed anti-UCITA legislation.

Sources of Law Governing Contracts

Two bodies of law—Article 2 of the Uniform Commercial Code and the common law of contracts—govern contracts today. The Uniform Commercial Code, or UCC, is statutory law in every state. The common law of contracts is court-made law that, like all court-made law, is in a constant state of evolution. Determining what body of law applies to a contract problem is a very important first step in analyzing that problem.

 LO9-3 Distinguish the applicability of the common law of contracts and Article 2 of the Uniform Commercial Code and identify which one governs a given contract.

The Uniform Commercial Code: Origin and Purposes
The UCC was created by the American Law Institute and the National Conference of Commissioners on Uniform State Laws. All of the states have adopted it except Louisiana, which has adopted only part of the UCC. The drafters of the UCC had several purposes in mind, the most obvious of which was to establish a uniform set of rules to govern commercial transactions, which are often conducted across state lines.[1]

In addition to promoting uniformity, the drafters of the UCC sought to create a body of rules that would realistically and fairly solve the common problems occurring in everyday commercial transactions. Finally, the drafters tried to formulate rules that would promote fair dealing and higher standards in the marketplace.

The UCC contains nine articles, most of which are discussed in detail in Parts 4, 6, and 7 of this book. The most important UCC article for our present purposes is Article 2, which deals with the sale of goods.

The UCC has changed and is in the process of continuing to change in response to changes in technology and business transactions. In some instances, the creation of new bodies of uniform law have been thought necessary to govern transactions that are similar to but different in significant ways from the sale of goods. For example, as leasing became a more common way of executing and financing transactions in goods, a separate UCC article, Article 2A, was developed to govern the *lease* of goods. Roughly one-third of the states have adopted Article 2A.

Application of Article 2
Article 2 expressly applies only to *contracts for the sale of goods* [2-102] (the numbers in brackets refer to specific UCC sections). The essence of the definition of goods in the UCC [1-105] is that *goods are tangible, movable personal property.* So, contracts for the sale of such items as motor vehicles, books, appliances, and clothing are covered by Article 2.

Application of the Common Law of Contracts
Article 2 of the UCC applies to contracts for the sale of goods, but it does *not* apply to contracts for the sale of real estate or intangibles such as stocks and bonds because those kinds of property do not constitute goods. Article 2 also does not apply to *service* contracts. Contracts for the sale of real estate, services, and intangibles are governed by the common law of contracts.

Law Governing "Hybrid" Contracts
Many contracts involve a hybrid of both goods and nongoods. As indicated in *Grimes v. Young Life, Inc.,* which follows, courts normally determine whether Article 2 applies to such a contract by asking which aspect—in *Grimes,* goods or services—*predominates* in the contract. For example, is the major purpose or thrust of the agreement the rendering of a service, or is it the sale of goods, with any services involved being merely incidental to that sale? This means that contracts calling for services that involve significant elements of personal skill or judgment in addition to goods probably are not governed by Article 2.

Relationship of the UCC and the Common Law of Contracts
Two important qualifications must be made concerning the application of UCC contract principles. First, the UCC does not change *all* of the traditional contract rules. Where no specific UCC rule exists, traditional contract law rules apply to contracts for the sale of goods (see Figure 9.2). Second, and ultimately far more important, courts have demonstrated a significant tendency to apply UCC contract concepts by analogy to some contracts that are not technically covered by Article 2. For example, the UCC concepts of good faith dealing and unconscionability have enjoyed wide application in cases that are technically outside the scope of Article 2. Thus, the UCC is an important influence in shaping the evolution of contract law in general.

---

[1]Despite the UCC's almost national adoption, however, complete uniformity has not been achieved. Many states have varied or amended the UCC's language in specific instances, and some UCC provisions were drafted in alternative ways, giving the states more than one version of particular UCC provisions to choose from. Also, the various state courts have reached different conclusions about the meaning of particular UCC sections.

Figure 9.2   When the Uniform Commercial Code Applies

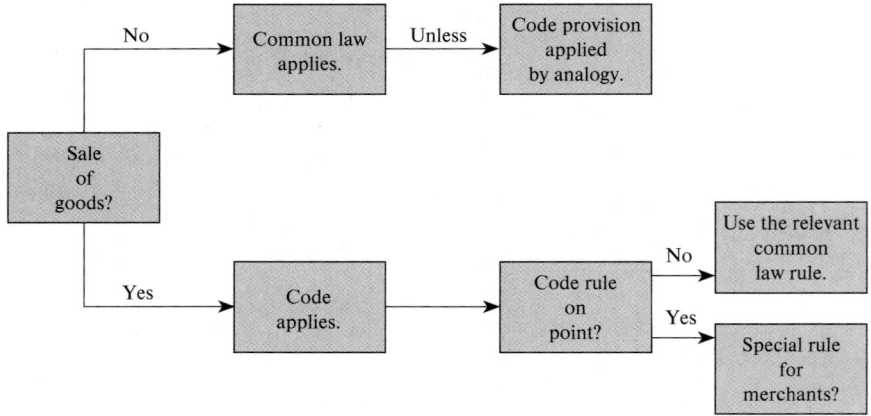

| Grimes v. Young Life, Inc. | 2017 WL 5634239 (D.S.C. 2017) |

In July 2015, Olivia Grimes died when she fell from a three-person giant swing at the Carolina Point camp facility owned by Young Life.

Phillip Wade Grimes, as personal representative of Olivia's estate, sued Young Life, as well as Inner Quest, the company that provided the materials and built the giant swing for Young Life. Inner Quest filed a crossclaim against Young Life, arguing that Young Life should indemnify it against any judgment.

Young Life and Inner Quest entered a contract for the construction of the swing, which included an indemnification clause. Whether that indemnification clause would apply and what effect it would have on the relationship between Young Life and Inner Quest depended on whether the common law or the state UCC applied to it.

Inner Quest and Young Life each filed motions for summary judgment on Inner Quest's crossclaim for indemnity. To determine the merits of the motions, the court had to determine what law applied to the hybrid contract between the parties for the construction of the swing.

Henry M. Herlong Jr., Senior United States District Judge

[T]he parties disagree about whether the indemnity clause is enforceable. Young Life argues that the purpose of the contract was as a services contract primarily for the design and construction of the swing and, therefore, common law [applies]. . . .

In contrast, Inner Quest argues that the contract was primarily for the sale of goods delivered in South Carolina and, therefore, the South Carolina Uniform Commercial Code's ("UCC") [applies]. . . .

Thus, as an initial matter the court must consider whether the contract at issue is predominately a contract for services or the sale of goods to determine whether the UCC or South Carolina common law applies in this case. Where a contract is for the mixed sale of goods and services, South Carolina courts apply the predominant factor test to determine whether the UCC applies. Factors that the court may consider in determining whether a contract is for services or the sale of goods include "(1) the language of the contract, (2) the nature of the business of the supplier, and (3) the intrinsic worth of the materials involved." *Coakley & Williams, Inc. v. Shatterproof Glass Corp.,* 706 F.2d 456, 460 (4th Cir. 1983).

Contracts which contain language primarily associated with the sale of goods, such as "buyer," "seller," "terms of sale," "customer," and "sales representative," are evidence that a contract is for the sale of goods. However, the court should consider the terminology in the context of the contract as a whole, rather than narrowly focusing on individual words. Additionally, the court may consider whether the contract was for a fixed price, the time and detail used to describe the goods and services to be provided, and the variety of services to be offered in the contract.

In the instant case, the contract is predominately for construction services. The contract does not use terms such as sale, buyer, or seller, but instead uses "project," "construction," "client," and "installation" to describe the work to be done. Similarly, the contract provides only a summary list of materials to be provided, while providing in-depth descriptions of the services offered and provided. Additionally, while the contract contains a single price, the price is listed as an estimate and provides for possible adjustments based upon the cost of obtaining necessary parts for the swing. As a result, the terms of the contract reveal that the primary purpose of the contract was for construction services, rather than the sale of goods.

This finding is also supported by the nature of Inner Quest's business. Inner Quest's corporate representative stated that Inner Quest has two divisions: "[o]ne is responsible for design, installation, training [and] inspection . . . services vended to owners and operators of challenge courses," and "the other division is a programming division where we market and operate adventure-based challenge courses . . . on contract for schools and other businesses. . . ." By its own admission, Inner Quest's primary business focus is to provide services related to the design, construction, and operation of challenge courses, rather than to sell equipment.

Lastly, the intrinsic value of the materials does not demonstrate that the contract is for the sale of goods. Both parties submit conflicting figures about the value of materials. Young Life argues that the cost of the swing's materials is no more than $12,000.00 of the approximately $36,000.00 total price. In contrast, Inner Quest argues that an additional $11,900.00 in costs should be factored in to account for the cost of the support poles and swing bar which support the swing. However, the cost of the support poles is composed of "both pole cost and installation." Because Inner Quest has not provided any further breakdown of the component and labor costs for the support poles and swing bar, the court can only speculate as to the intrinsic value of these components. Based on the foregoing, the contract in dispute is primarily for a services contract with the incidental sale of goods necessary only for the performance of those services. As a result, the UCC is not applicable to this case.

* * *

It is therefore

ORDERED that Young Life's motion for summary judgment . . . is granted. It is further

ORDERED Inner Quest's motion for summary judgment . . . is denied.

The Global Business Environment

Dealing with Contract Disputes in International Transactions

The United Nations Convention on Contracts for the International Sale of Goods, or CISG, is an international body of contract rules that harmonizes contract principles from many legal systems. Approximately 80 countries, including the United States and Canada, have adopted the CISG to date. The CISG is intended to provide a uniform code for international commercial contracts in much the same way as the UCC provides uniformity for transactions among contracting parties in different states in the United States. Like the UCC, though, the CISG does not have provisions to cover every contract problem that might occur. It applies to sales of goods, not services. Unlike the UCC, however, it applies only to commercial parties (whereas the UCC applies to such parties and to consumers). When there is a contract for the sale of goods between commercial parties whose relevant places of business are located in two different countries that have agreed to the CISG, the CISG applies by default unless the parties have opted out of the CISG in their contract. Because the CISG emphasizes freedom of contract, it does permit the parties to agree to exclude or vary any of the CISG rules or to opt out of the CISG completely by stating in their contract that some other body of law (such as the UCC) will apply to their contract.

Companies entering international transactions often protect themselves from disputes over what body of laws applies to their disputes by including a choice of law clause in their contracts. This is a provision stating the parties' agreement that a particular country or state's law will apply to their contract. (Of course, choice of law clauses are used extensively in domestic transactions as well.) In addition, it is very common for parties in international transactions to include an arbitration clause in their contracts, providing that future disputes between them will be resolved by arbitration.[2] Using arbitration gives the parties a relatively speedy and affordable dispute resolution process. An added benefit is that there are several international treaties that will enforce arbitration awards.

[2]Arbitration is discussed in more detail in Chapter 2.

Basic Differences in the Nature of Article 2 and the Common Law of Contracts
Many of the provisions of Article 2 differ from traditional common law rules in important ways. The UCC is more concerned with rewarding people's legitimate expectations than with technical rules, so it is generally more flexible than the common law of contracts. A court that applies the UCC is more likely to find that the parties had a contract than is a court that applies the common law of contracts [2-204]. In some cases, the UCC gives less

weight to technical requirements such as consideration [2–205 and 2–209].

The drafters of the UCC sought to create practical rules to deal with what people actually do in today's marketplace. We live in the day of the form contract, so some of the UCC's rules try to deal fairly with that fact [2–205, 2–207, 2–209(2), and 2–302]. The words *reasonable, commercially reasonable,* and *seasonably* (within a reasonable time) are found throughout the UCC. This reasonableness standard is different from the hypothetical reasonable person standard in tort law. A court that tries to decide what is reasonable under the UCC is more likely to be concerned with what people really do in the marketplace than with what a hypothetical reasonable person would do.

The drafters of the UCC also wanted to promote fair dealing and higher standards in the marketplace, so they imposed a duty of good faith [1–203] in the performance and enforcement of every contract under the UCC. Good faith means "honesty in fact," which is required of all parties to sales contracts [1–201(19)]. In addition, merchants are required to observe "reasonable commercial standards of fair dealing" [2–103(1)(b)]. The parties cannot alter this duty of good faith by agreement [1–102(3)]. Finally, the UCC expressly recognizes the concept of an **unconscionable** contract, one that is grossly unfair or one-sided, and it gives the courts broad discretionary powers to deal fairly with such contracts [2–302].[3]

The UCC also recognizes that buyers tend to place more reliance on professional sellers and that professionals are generally more knowledgeable and better able to protect themselves than nonprofessionals. So, the UCC distinguishes between **merchants** and nonmerchants by holding merchants to a higher standard in some cases [2–201(2), 2–205, and 2–207(2)]. The UCC defines the term *merchant* [2–104(1)] on a case-by-case basis. Contracting parties who regularly deal in the kind of goods being sold in a contract, who hold themselves out to have some special knowledge about goods being sold in a contact, or who have employed an agent in the sale of goods by contract who fits either of the preceding two descriptions are merchants for the purposes of the contract in question. So, if you buy a used car

from a used-car dealer, the dealer is a merchant for the purposes of your contract. But if you buy a refrigerator from a used-car dealer, the dealer is not a merchant.

Influence of *Restatement (Second) of Contracts*

In 1932, the American Law Institute published the first *Restatement of Contracts*,[4] an attempt to codify and systematize the soundest principles of contract law gleaned from thousands of often-conflicting judicial decisions. As the product of a private organization, the *Restatement* did not have the force of law, but as the considered judgment of some of the leading scholars of the legal profession, it was highly influential in shaping the evolution of contract law. The *Restatement (Second) of Contracts*, issued in 1979, is an attempt to reflect the significant changes that have occurred in contract law in the years following the birth of the first *Restatement*. The *Restatement (Second)* reflects the "shift from rules to standards" in modern contract law—the shift from precise, technical rules to broader, discretionary principles that produce just results.[5]

In fact, many *Restatement (Second)* provisions are virtually identical to their UCC analogues. For example, the *Restatement (Second)* has explicitly embraced the UCC concepts of *good faith*[6] and *unconscionability*.[7]

The *Restatement (Second)* does *not* have the force of law. Nonetheless, it can be and has been influential in shaping the evolution of contract law because courts have the option of adopting a *Restatement (Second)* approach to the contract issues presented in the cases that come before them. Particular approaches suggested by the *Restatement (Second)* will be mentioned in some of the following chapters.

LO9-4 Identify the circumstances under which quasi-contract or promissory estoppel can afford a remedy even though no contract exists.

"Noncontract" Obligations

Before we proceed to the following chapters' discussion of the individual elements of contract law, there is one more group of introductory concepts to be considered. Although contract obligations normally require mutual agreement and an exchange of value, there are some circumstances in which the law enforces an obligation to pay for certain losses or benefits even in the absence of mutual agreement

---

[3]Chapter 15 discusses unconscionability in detail.

[4]See Chapter 1 for a general discussion of the *Restatement* phenomenon.

[5]Richard E. Speidel, "Restatement Second: Omitted Terms and Contract Method," 67 *Cornell L. Rev.* 785, 786 (1982).

[6]*Restatement (Second) of Contracts* § 205 (1981).

[7]*Restatement (Second) of Contracts* § 208 (1981).

and exchange of value. We will refer to these circumstances as "noncontract" obligations because they impose the duty on a person to pay for a loss or benefit despite the absence of the requirements for formation of a contract. These non-contract doctrines give a person who cannot establish the existence of a contract a chance to obtain compensation.

Quasi-Contract Requiring all the elements of a binding contract before a contractual obligation is imposed can cause injustice in some cases. One person may have provided goods or services to another person who benefited from them but has no contractual obligation to pay for them because no facts exist that would justify a court in implying a promise to pay for them. Such a situation can also arise in cases where the parties contemplated entering into a binding contract, but some legal defense prevents the enforcement of the agreement. Consider the following examples:

1. Jones paints Smith's house by mistake, thinking it belongs to Reed. Smith knows that Jones is painting his house but does not inform him of his error. There are no facts from which a court can infer that Jones and Smith have a contract because the parties have had no prior discussions or dealings.

2. Thomas Products fraudulently induces Perkins to buy a household products franchise by grossly misstating the average revenues of its franchisees. Perkins discovers the misrepresentation after he has resold some products that he has received but before he has paid Thomas for them. Perkins elects to rescind (cancel) the franchise contract on the basis of the fraud.

In the preceding examples, both Smith and Perkins have good defenses to contract liability; however, enabling Smith to get a free paint job and Perkins to avoid paying for the goods he resold would *unjustly enrich* them at the expense of Jones and Thomas. To deal with such cases and to prevent such unjust enrichment, the courts imply *as a matter of law* a promise by the benefited party to pay the *reasonable value* of the benefits he received. This idea is called **quasi-contract** (also called unjust enrichment or contract implied in law) because it represents an obligation imposed by law to avoid injustice, not a contractual obligation created by voluntary consent. Quasi-contract liability has been imposed in situations too numerous and varied to detail. In general, however, quasi-contract liability is imposed when one party *confers a benefit* on another who *knowingly accepts it* and *retains it* under circumstances that make it *unjust* to do so without paying for it. So, if Jones painted Smith's house while Smith was away on vacation, Smith would probably not be liable for the reasonable value of the paint

job because he did *not* knowingly accept it and because he has no way to return it to Jones. In *PWS Environmental v. All Clear,* which follows, the court considers whether an implied contract existed and, if not, whether the plaintiff can invoke unjust enrichment principles. In addition, the case touches on promissory estoppel, another noncontract doctrine to be discussed later in the chapter.

Promissory Estoppel

 LO9-4 Identify the circumstances under which quasi-contract or promissory estoppel can afford a remedy even though no contract exists.

Another very important idea that courts have developed to deal with the unfairness that would sometimes result from the strict application of traditional contract principles is the doctrine of **promissory estoppel**. In certain situations, one person might rely on a promise made by another even though the promise and the relevant circumstances are not sufficient to justify the conclusion that a contract exists. To allow the person who made such a promise (the promisor) to argue that no contract was created could sometimes work an injustice on the person who relied on the promise (the promisee).

For example, in *Ricketts v. Scothorn*, a grandfather's promise to pay his granddaughter interest on a demand note he gave her so that she would not have to work was enforced against him after she had quit her job in reliance on his promise.[8] The Nebraska Supreme Court acknowledged that such promises were traditionally unenforceable because they were gratuitous and not supported by any consideration, but held that the granddaughter's reliance prevented her grandfather from raising his lack of consideration defense. In the early decades of this century, many courts began to extend similar protection to relying promisees. They said that persons who made promises that produced such reliance were *estopped*, or equitably prevented, from raising any defense they had to the enforcement of their promise. Out of such cases grew the doctrine of promissory estoppel. Section 90 of the *Restatement (Second) of Contracts* states:

> A promise which the promisor should reasonably expect to induce action or forbearance on the part of the promisee or a third person and which does induce such action or forbearance is binding if injustice can be avoided only by enforcement of the promise. The remedy granted for breach may be limited as justice requires.

---

[8]57 Neb. 51, 77 N.W. 365 (1898).

PWS Environmental, Inc. v. All Clear Restoration and Remediation, LLC
2018 WL 3139736 (M.D. Fla. 2018)

On September 16, 2017, All Clear Restoration and Remediation, LLC (All Clear) contacted PWS Environmental, Inc. (PWS) asking if PWS was available to provide pressure washing services to several condominium properties in the wake of Hurricane Irma, which struck west central and southwestern Florida the previous week. At the time PWS was performing pressure washing services in Texas as part of the Hurricane Harvey clean-up but decided to decline additional jobs in Texas in favor of moving the equipment to Florida for the business opportunities presented by All Clear there.

On September 18, 2017, PWS e-mailed a proposal to All Clear to provide services to 14 residential properties for whom All Clear was acting as agent in the Hurricane Irma clean up process. The e-mail asked All Clear to sign and return the proposal or acknowledge it by a return e-mail, which a representative of All Clear did, stating, "Thanks. I am fine with attachment. Please proceed."

Through the rest of September and October, PWS worked on pressure washing the condominiums and sent invoices to All Clear seeking payment for that work. All Clear failed to pay for any of the work. While PWS sued All Clear for breach of the contract it claims the parties entered, it also sued the condominium associations that owned the properties PWS power washed (the "condo defendants") for breach of implied contract (i.e., quasi-contract), seeking damages for the value of the work it performed.

The condo defendants moved to dismiss PWS's claims against them.

John E. Steele, Senior United States District Judge

A claim for breach of a contract implied in law is also known as "unjust enrichment" [or "quasi-contract."] "In Florida, a claim for unjust enrichment is an equitable claim based on a legal fiction which implies a contract as a matter of law even though the parties to such an implied contract never indicated by deed or word that an agreement existed between them." *14th & Heinberg, LLC v. Terhaar & Cronley Gen. Contractors, Inc.*, 43 So. 3d 877, 880 (Fla. Ct. App. 2010). . . . A claim of unjust enrichment requires PWS to show by at least a preponderance of the evidence that: (1) PWS conferred a direct benefit on the condo defendants, (2) the condo defendants had knowledge of the benefit, (3) the condo defendants accepted or retained the conferred benefit, and (4) the benefit was conferred under circumstances which make it inequitable for the condo defendants to retain the benefit without paying its fair value. Unjust enrichment "acknowledges an obligation which is imposed by law regardless of the intent of the parties." *Circle Fin. Co. v. Peacock*, 399 So. 2d 81, 84 (Fla. Ct. App. 1981). A plaintiff must directly confer the benefit upon defendant. *Peoples Nat'l Bank of Commerce v. First Union Nat'l Bank of Fla.*, 667 So. 2d 876, 879 (Fla. Ct. App. 1996). . . .

PWS has plausibly alleged the elements of an unjust enrichment claim in order to avoid dismissal. PWS alleges that it directly conferred the benefit of its pressure washing services on each of the condominiums. PWS serviced each of the condominiums for multiple days at a time, while regularly communicating with the condo defendants' agent, All Clear, about the progress. Plaintiff does not specifically allege that the condo defendants had knowledge of the benefit, but plaintiff does state that All Clear, as the condo defendants' agent, had knowledge of the benefit. In Florida, an agent may bind his or her principal based on real or actual authority. . . . The Court accepts at this stage in the proceedings the allegations that the condo defendants had knowledge of the benefit through its agent, as well as a reasonable inference that the condo defendants could have had personal knowledge based on the allegations that the pressure washing often went on for days at each property. Finally, the condo defendants, by the very nature of the services conferred upon them, retained the pressure washing benefits. These circumstances could result in inequity if the condominiums were able to retain these benefits without conferring just compensation upon PWS. . . .

For the foregoing reasons, the condo defendants' Motion to Dismiss is **denied**.

Thus, the elements of promissory estoppel are a *promise* that the *promisor should foresee is likely to induce reliance*, *reliance* on the promise by the promisee, and *injustice* as a result of that reliance. (See Figure 9.3.) If the plaintiff accomplishes the difficult task of establishing each of these elements, the plaintiff will obtain appropriate legal relief despite the lack of an enforceable contract. *Thomas v. Archer*, which follows, provides an example of promissory estoppel's operation.

When you consider the elements noted above, it becomes obvious that promissory estoppel is fundamentally

Figure 9.3   Contract and Noncontract Theories of Recovery

Theory	Key Concept	Remedy
Contract	Voluntary agreement	Enforce promise
Quasi-contract	Unjust enrichment	Reasonable value of services
Promissory estoppel	Foreseeable reliance	Enforce promise or recover reliance losses

different from traditional contract principles. Contract is traditionally thought of as protecting *agreements* or bargains. Promissory estoppel, on the other hand, protects *reliance*. Early promissory estoppel cases applied the doctrine only to gift promises such as the one made by the grandfather in the earlier example. As subsequent chapters demonstrate, however, promissory estoppel is now used by courts, in appropriate cases, to prevent offerors from revoking their offers, to enforce indefinite promises, and to enforce oral promises that would ordinarily have to be in writing.

Thomas v. Archer	384 P.3d 791 (Alaska 2016)

Rachel Thomas was admitted to the emergency room at Ketchikan General Hospital in Alaska in October 2008 for pregnancy-related complications. Her attending physician, Sarah B. Archer, determined that Rachel was at risk of premature delivery and needed an immediate transfer via medivac to a medical facility better equipped to handle her condition. Due to weather conditions in Anchorage, Alaska, which made transfer to a hospital there untenable, Archer recommended transferring Rachel to Swedish Medical Center in Seattle.

Rachel and her husband, Steven, informed Dr. Archer that they needed preauthorization from the Ketchikan Indian Corporation Tribal Health Clinic (KIC) and the Alaska Native Medical Center (ANMC) in order to be insured for treatment outside of ANMC's Anchorage facilities. According to the Thomases, Dr. Archer told them that she would contact KIC, that they should not worry, that everything would be taken care of, and that if KIC failed to cover the costs of the medivac, "we" will. The Thomases understood "we" to mean the hospital.

While the hospital was arranging Rachel's transfer, Steven signed a form titled "Acknowledgment of Financial Responsibility," which noted that the medivac by Guardian Flight could be very costly. While the form named KIC as the "Payment Source," Steven's signature indicated that he agreed to be personally responsible for any unpaid charges from the flight and to "save and hold the hospital harmless therefrom."

The Thomases eventually received bills totaling more than $23,000 from Swedish Medical Center and more than $69,000 by Guardian Flight. When they sought payment from KIC and ANMC under their insurance plan, they were denied for several reasons, the most relevant being that the Thomases failed to request preauthorization within 72 hours of beginning treatment or of Rachel's admission to Swedish Medical Center.

While the Thomases admitted that arranging preauthorization was ultimately their responsibility, they claimed that they boarded the medivac flight based on Dr. Archer's representation that someone else would arrange for the preauthorization requirements. Although Dr. Archer ultimately did write to KIC and ANMC to explain her decision to have Rachel transported to Seattle, she did not do so until more than six months later.

When the hospital and Dr. Archer would not pay the balances for which the Thomases were billed, the Thomases sued under a number of theories, including promissory estoppel. That claim was based on Dr. Archer's alleged promise to contact KIC and ANMC to ensure coverage of the expenses related to Rachel's transfer to Swedish Medical Center and treatment there.

The trial court granted summary judgment to the hospital and Dr. Archer. The Thomases appealed.

Maassen, Justice

The Thomases argue . . . that the superior court erred by rejecting promissory estoppel as a basis for enforcement of Dr. Archer's alleged promise to the Thomases.

* * *

C. It Was Error To Grant Summary Judgment On The Thomases' Promissory Estoppel Claim.

The Thomases . . . argue that the superior court erred when it rejected their claim that "[i]f the parties did not create a binding contract, their agreement is nevertheless enforceable by the doctrine of promissory estoppel." They argue that Dr. Archer's alleged promise induced them to leave the hospital immediately with-out their insurer's preauthorization, that this was a foreseeable response to the promise, that because they left the hospital without preauthorization they incurred substantial medical expenses, and that the interest of justice is served by enforcing Dr. Archer's promise. They argue that, at a minimum, a jury should have decided this claim.

"The doctrine of promissory estoppel allows the enforcement of contract-like promises despite a technical defect or defense that would otherwise make the promise unenforceable." [*Kiernan v. Creech*, 268 P.3d 312, 315 (Alaska 2012).]

Promissory estoppel has these elements: "1) [t]he action induced amounts to a substantial change of position; 2) it was either actually foreseen or reasonably foreseeable by the promisor; 3) an actual promise was made and itself induced the action or forbearance in reliance thereon; and 4) enforcement is necessary in the interest of justice." [*Simpson v. Murkowski*, 129 P.3d 435, 440 (Alaska 2006) (quoting *Zeman v. Lufthansa German Airlines*, 699 P.2d 1274, 1284 (Alaska 1985)).] The superior court, relying primarily on *Sea Hawk Seafoods, Inc. v. City of Valdez*, [282 P.3d 359 (Alaska 2012),] held that Dr. Archer's "alleged promise [was] not 'definitive,' 'clear,' or 'precise'" enough to constitute an "actual promise." The court discussed what it perceived to be "the lack of clarity in the alleged oral promises and the lack of unequivocal acceptance," noting "[Steven's] signature on the Acknowledgment of Financial Responsibility and [Rachel's] deposition testimony that . . . she would have taken the flight to Swedish even if it was not covered." The court concluded that even if all other elements of promissory estoppel were met, the Thomases "fail to show a substantial change in position" because of Rachel's testimony that she "would have gone to Swedish even if she knew the [medivac] would not be covered."

We conclude that there are genuine issues of material fact about whether the elements of the doctrine were met. It was therefore error to grant summary judgment on the Thomases' promissory estoppel claim.

1. Whether there was a substantial change of position

"Whether particular actions represent substantial changes [in position] is a question of all the circumstances and is not determinable by reference to a set formula." [*Zeman*, 699 P.2d at 1284 (citing 1A A. Corbin, Corbin on Contracts § 200, at 216 (1963)).] Courts tend to "look for evidence of actual and substantial economic loss." [*Id.*]

In deciding that the "substantial change in position" element was not met, the superior court relied on the Thomases' concession that they would have followed Dr. Archer's advice regardless of whether they had insurance coverage. Rachel testified at her deposition that "[a]t this point, [she] would have gone anywhere to save [her unborn] son's life." She continued:

"I mean, had [Dr. Archer] said you need to go to Anchorage, I would have gone to Anchorage. She said, you need to go to Seattle, so I am going to Seattle." When asked whether she would have agreed to be transported to Seattle "if [she] felt that it would have saved [her] son's life" even if there was no insurance coverage for it, she responded, "Again, my concern was not billing at that time. It was immediate health." This testimony, the superior court concluded, demonstrated that the Thomases did not substantially change their position based on Dr. Archer's alleged promise.

But while there is no dispute that the Thomases would have flown to Seattle regardless of insurance coverage, questions of fact remain because of their assertions that they would have called their insurance providers for preauthorization had they not believed that Dr. Archer was going to do so. A reasonable person could conclude that the Thomases substantially changed their position in reliance upon Dr. Archer's alleged promise by failing to do what they otherwise would have done.

2. Whether the change in position was foreseeable

"According to Corbin on Contracts, '[f]oreseeability of reliance raises a question of fact for court and jury.' " *Simpson*, 129 P.3d at 441 (alteration in original) (quoting Corbin on Contracts, at 216). The superior court did not address the foreseeability prong in its order on summary judgment, nor does the hospital address it on appeal, focusing its analysis instead on the elements of changed position and actual promise. We conclude that a reasonable person, when viewing the circumstances of Dr. Archer's alleged promise—including that it was made by a treating physician in the context of a medical emergency—could find it was reasonably foreseeable that the Thomases would rely on the promise and not seek preauthorization themselves.

3. Whether there was an actual promise

The superior court's rejection of the Thomases' promissory estoppel claim rested primarily on its conclusion that there was no "actual promise" on which the Thomases were entitled to rely. "When a promissory estoppel claim is made in conjunction with a breach of contract claim, the 'actual promise' element of promissory estoppel is 'analytically identical to' the '"acceptance" required for a contract.' " [*Valdez Fisheries Dev. Ass'n v. Alyeska Pipeline Serv. Co.*, 45 P.3d 657, 668 (Alaska 2002) (quoting *Brady v. State*, 965 P.2d 1, 11 (Alaska 1998)).] "Were it otherwise, promissory estoppel . . . would become a device by which parties could be held to contracts they did not accept." [*Id.*] "An 'actual promise' is one that is 'definitive, . . . very clear, . . . and must use precise language.' " [*Safar v. Wells Fargo Bank, N.A.*, 254 P.3d 1112, 1119 (Alaska 2011) (alterations in original) (quoting *Alaska Trademark Shellfish, LLC v. State, Dep't of Fish & Game*, 172 P.3d 764, 767 (Alaska 2007)).] "[A] promise . . .

must 'manifest an unequivocal intent to be bound.' " [*Id.* (quoting *Alaska Trademark Shellfish*, 172 P.3d at 767).]

The superior court, in deciding that there was no actual promise, relied on *Sea Hawk Seafoods, Inc. v. City of Valdez*, in which we reversed the trial court's denial of summary judgment to Valdez on Sea Hawk's promissory estoppel claim. Valdez had made oral promises to Sea Hawk that it would submit a grant application for funds, which it would then turn over to Sea Hawk to pay for the conversion of one of Sea Hawk's processing facilities. Valdez confirmed these promises in a letter, indicating that it was in the process of finalizing the application but that a number of issues remained to be resolved before it would accept the grant. After the grant application was tentatively approved, Valdez sent Sea Hawk another letter reiterating that it would not accept the grant until it had reached an agreement with Sea Hawk. The parties could not agree and Valdez did not accept the grant, prompting Sea Hawk's suit.

The superior court in this case noted our holding in *Sea Hawk* that Valdez's "alleged oral promises were not sufficiently 'definitive,' 'clear,' and 'precise' to constitute an actual promise, particularly when considered in conjunction with [Valdez's] letter." [282 P.3d at 367.] The court reasoned that because "[t]he language of [Valdez's] alleged promises [in *Sea Hawk*] . . . was more certain than in the present case," Dr. Archer's alleged promises could not be considered precise enough to constitute an actual promise.

We do not consider *Sea Hawk* controlling. Valdez's oral offer in *Sea Hawk* identified "three conditions prior to submitting the Sea Hawk grant application," and its later confirming letter again noted those "conditions, informing Sea Hawk these issues would need to be resolved before Valdez accepted the grant funds, and stating the parties would need to enter [into] an agreement once the State decided whether to award Valdez the grant." [*Id.* at 366.] We therefore held that "even assuming [Valdez] made such promises, [it] alerted [Sea Hawk] that Valdez would not accept the grant *unconditionally* and then specifically outlined those conditions in the [confirming] letter." [*Id.* at 366–67 (emphasis added).] The promises in that case instead "demonstrate[d] [that] Valdez contemplated entering into a future agreement with Sea Hawk addressing various issues." [*Id.*at 365.]

The alleged promise at issue in this case, unlike the promises in *Sea Hawk*, was not expressly conditional. As the Thomases describe Dr. Archer's promise, it gave no indication that it depended on the outcome of future negotiations. The alleged promise defined Dr. Archer's role—she would contact the insurers if the Thomases boarded the medivac plane immediately—and it defined the Thomases' role—they would board the plane without taking time to contact their insurers. Because the evidence could support a conclusion that the Thomases unequivocally accepted a clear offer, a reasonable person could conclude that there was an "actual promise."

4. Whether enforcement of the promise is necessary in the interest of justice

"The fourth requirement, that enforcement is necessary in the interest of justice, presents fact questions that ordinarily should not be decided on summary judgment." *Reeves v. Alyeska Pipeline Serv. Co.*, 926 P.2d 1130, 1142 (Alaska 1996) (citing *State v. First Nat'l Bank of Ketchikan*, 629 P.2d 78, 82 n.4 (Alaska 1981)). This is a fact-intensive analysis in which reasonable people could reach different conclusions.

Because the Thomases identified issues of fact that precluded summary judgment, it was error to grant the hospital's motion on the Thomases' promissory estoppel claim.

Conclusion

We **REVERSE** the superior court's grant of summary judgment on the Thomases' promissory estoppel claim and **REMAND** for further proceedings consistent with this opinion.

Ethics and Compliance in Action

The idea that contracts should be enforced because they are voluntary agreements can obviously be justified on ethical grounds. But what about quasi-contracts and promissory estoppel? What ethical justifications can you give for departing from the notion of voluntary agreement in quasi-contract and promissory estoppel cases?

From a compliance point of view, what sorts of controls and practices should an organization have in place to ensure that it only makes contractual commitments it intends to enter and does not end up committed by noncontract obligations like quasi-contract or promissory estoppel?

Problems and Problem Cases

1. Clarence Jackson went to the Snack Plus convenience store in Hamden, Connecticut, and bought a Connecticut Lotto "Quick Pick" ticket for the drawing of October 13, 1995. On the back of the ticket were various provisions, including the admonition that "Prize must be claimed within one year from the drawing date. Determination of winners subject to DOSR rules and regulations." It also stated instructions for claiming the prize by presentment to any online agent or to "Lottery Claims" in Newington, Connecticut. The drawing was held on October 13, and the winning six-number combination was announced. One of the six-number combinations on Jackson's Lotto ticket matched the six-number combination drawn in the October 13 drawing, for a prize of $5.8 million. Jackson learned of the match only 15 minutes before the one-year deadline. Instead of claiming his prize online, Jackson waited several more days until after the Columbus Day holiday to present his ticket in person at the Lottery Claims Center because he was under the impression that it had to be presented there. The Connecticut Lottery Corporation (CLC) denied Jackson's claim because the one-year presentment period had elapsed. Did contract law give Jackson the right to claim the prize under these circumstances?

2. Donald Lambert and Don Barron were friends. They had a longstanding professional relationship based on their service together on the Louisiana State Board of Licensed Contractors. Lambert was a specialist in resolving construction disputes. Barron was a commercial construction contractor, whose business was experiencing difficulty in part due to five projects that were mired in various kinds of difficulty. Lambert became concerned about his friend when he heard about Barron's struggles and witnessed Barron's depressed mental state. As a result, Lambert flew to Barron's hometown to meet with Barron. Prior to the flight, one of Barron's employees sent Lambert copies of various contracts and correspondence related to the troubled projects. After the visit, as Lambert prepared to board his flight back home, he claimed that he and Barron contracted for Lambert to provide consulting services for Barron, at his customary rate of $3,100 per month for the minimum term of one year. Then, after a year passed, Lambert billed Barron for $34,000 on the alleged oral contract. Barron professed to be shocked by the bill and disclaimed any contract for extended consulting services. Rather, his business paid the first monthly invoice of $3,100, assuming that was the fee for the one-time visit and document review services. Barron claimed that Lambert had done no additional work throughout the year, and he denied ever agreeing to any additional work. The record showed that their only contact throughout the year had been initiated by Lambert. Nonetheless, Lambert sued Barron for breach of contract. Did he win?

3. Stephen Gall and his family became ill after drinking contaminated water supplied to their home by the McKeesport Municipal Water Authority. They filed suit against the utility, arguing, among other things, that the utility had breached the UCC implied warranty of merchantability when it sold them contaminated water. Arguing that water was not "goods" and that the UCC therefore should not apply, the utility moved to dismiss the Galls' complaint. How did the court rule?

4. Piece of America (POA) hired Gray Loon Marketing to design and publish its website. Gray Loon finished the site in December 2003 at a final cost of about $8,500. Once the website was running to POA's satisfaction, it paid Gray Loon in full during the first quarter of 2004. In April 2004, POA requested that Gray Loon make several changes, some of which required major programming work. Gray Loon immediately began the requested alterations. Gray Loon subsequently sent POA a bill for $5,224.50. POA's representative stated he did not have any issues with the invoice, but POA needed time to obtain additional funds. During this period, Gray Loon was also charging POA $75 a month for hosting the site. Once Gray Loon published the modified website, it remained available from July to September 2004. Gray Loon filed suit against POA and its principals for nonpayment. Did the UCC apply to this contract?

5. LandTech Co. entered an "Outsourcing Agreement" with Ohio Fresh Eggs, LLC, and Trillium Farm Holdings, LLC, pursuant to which LandTech would obtain the right to remove chicken manure from the egg-laying facilities Ohio Fresh and Trillium operated in Hardin County, Ohio. LandTech sought to act as a "manure broker," removing the manure produced at the Hardin County facilities and selling it for use as fertilizer. The relationship broke down before any manure changed hands. LandTech sued. At trial, the parties argued whether the Agreement stated a specific quantity of manure that Ohio Fresh and Trillium were obligated to provide to LandTech. The nature of the quantity term

was vital to determine whether the parties were subject to a contractual obligation or they had just entered an "agreement to make an agreement." And that, in turn, depended on which of the UCC or the common law of contracts applied to this situation. Applying the predominant purpose or factor test, does the UCC or the common law apply?

6. Over the course of six years, David Hix, on behalf of his company HAD Enterprises, repeatedly asked Wanda Galloway, who owned the property adjacent to Hix's, to allow him to fill in the pond on her property and to regrade her property to avoid flooding and mosquito problems that plagued both properties. Galloway finally agreed to let Hix do the work on her land. Hix claimed that, in exchange for his labor, he requested to be allowed to use the improved land for parking, either for himself or for HAD Enterprises. Galloway recalled no such agreement. After roughly two years of extensive work by Hix on both his and Galloway's land (during which time Galloway apparently expressed concern several times to Hix about the unexpectedly large scope of the work he was doing), Galloway instructed Hix to stop. Even after all that time, the pond was only partially filled. Nonetheless, Hix submitted to Galloway a bill totaling $14,972 for the work he had done to her land. Galloway refused to pay, saying she had never agreed to pay Hix anything for the work and had agreed to allow him to commence the work only because it seemed so important to him. Hix sued Galloway for the cost of his work on the land. If he claims Galloway has breached a contract between them, will he succeed on that theory? Even if there is no contract between the two, could he recover under the doctrine of quasi-contract?

7. On March 21, 2003, Robert Palese bought five Delaware State Lottery tickets from a Delaware liquor store. To select his numbers for the game, Palese used a "play slip" that contained five game panels. Each panel had a selection grid bearing numbers 1 through 38. Palese chose six numbers from each grid by manually filling in the grids. After purchasing the tickets, Palese placed them in his pants pocket and returned home. Several days later, he learned that someone had won the March 21 lottery but that the winner had not yet come forward. Palese searched for his tickets to see whether he had chosen the winning numbers, but he was unable to find the tickets. Eventually, he remembered that he had done laundry the same evening he purchased the tickets. He then concluded that the tickets, which had been left in his pants pocket, had probably been destroyed in the wash. Although the tickets were gone, Palese still had the play slip he used when he purchased the tickets. He checked the numbers on the play slip and discovered that the numbers he selected on the play slip's fifth game panel were the winning numbers for the March 21 lottery. Reasoning that the play slip should be sufficient to satisfy the state's Lottery Office that he had selected the winning numbers, Palese informed the office of his predicament. The Lottery Office ultimately took the position that the state's lottery regulations and any contract arising from the purchase of the ticket required that the winning ticket itself be produced in order for the winner to claim the jackpot. Therefore, the Lottery Office denied Palese's claim and transferred the jackpot to the state's General Fund. Palese then sued the Lottery Office on a quasi-contract (unjust enrichment) theory. Did Palese win the case and collect the jackpot amount?

8. In 1994, Schumacher and his wife along with their two daughters moved to Finland, Minnesota, to operate a bar and restaurant called the Trestle Inn, which was owned by his parents. Schumacher claimed that his parents induced him to leave his previous job and to make the move by orally agreeing to (1) provide him a job managing the inn for life and (2) leave the business and a large parcel of land to him when his first parent died. Schumacher was given free reign in managing the inn and was allowed to retain all profits of the business, but he was not given any salary or wage. While he was operating the inn, Schumacher used his own funds to build a home for his family on his parents' land, install a well, buy equipment for the business, and develop various marketing tools for the business. In 1998, Schumacher suspected that his parents were about to sell the inn and the adjoining property. He brought suit for a restraining order to prevent them from doing so, claiming breach of contract and unjust enrichment, among other claims. In October 1998, the parents notified Schumacher that his employment at the inn and his right to possess the adjoining property were terminated. The parents moved for summary judgment. The trial court held that Schumacher's oral contract claim was invalid because the contract needed to be in writing under applicable Minnesota law. However, did Schumacher have a valid claim for unjust enrichment?

9. In 2006, Claudia Aceves obtained from her bank a loan in the amount of $845,000 to buy a house. The loan had an initial interest rate of 6.35 percent. After two years, the rate became adjustable and increased significantly. She could no longer afford the monthly payments on the loan. In March 2008, she received a notice that the bank was going to foreclose on her house. She filed for bankruptcy protection, which posed an automatic stay (i.e., "froze") on the foreclosure proceedings. Aceves contacted the bank and was told that once her loan was out of bankruptcy, the bank "would work with her on a mortgage reinstatement and loan modification." Relying on this representation, Aceves decided to forgo a legal process in the bankruptcy court that would have allowed her to reinstate the loan and repay the past due portion over time, while retaining her home. At the same time, the bank requested the bankruptcy court to remove the stay, so it could proceed with the foreclosure. Aceves did not object to that request, assuming that she and the bank were going to resolve things outside the court. The bank, however, scheduled Aceves's home for public auction before the end of 2008 without allowing Aceves to discuss reinstatement and modification of the loan. When a "negotiator" for the bank did finally contact her on the day before the public auction was scheduled, he told her that the new balance on the loan was nearly $1 million, that the new monthly payment would be nearly twice what it was before she declared bankruptcy, and that she needed to send a $6,500 deposit immediately to avoid the sale. When the negotiator refused to put any of those terms in writing, Aceves rejected the offer. Her house was sold the next day to the bank, which served her a three-day notice to vacate and instituted eviction proceedings against her. Aceves filed suit against the bank, claiming that to her detriment she relied on the promise by the bank that it would work with her. Did she succeed?

10. The Weitz Company, a general contractor, received an invitation to bid on a planned nursing facility. H & S Plumbing and Heating submitted a bid to Weitz for the plumbing work, as well as the heating, ventilation, and air conditioning parts of the job. Weitz's bid to the project owner incorporated the amount of H & S's bid. Because the bid was speculative, there was no contract formed between Weitz and H & S at that point. After the owner awarded the project to Weitz, H & S refused to honor its bid. Weitz completed the project with different subcontractors at greater expense. Does Weitz have any recourse against H & S to recover the lower profit margin that resulted from H & S's refusal to honor its bid?

CHAPTER 10

The Agreement: Offer

O n March 4, 2004, the "The Buzz" section of *Louisville Scene*, an online service of the *Louisville Courier-Journal*, ran the following report:

How much would you pay for Hollywood hunk George Clooney to wash your car in a toga?

The star of such films as "Ocean's Eleven" and "The Perfect Storm" is hoping to raise money for father Nick Clooney's congressional campaign.

According to the *New York Post*, Clooney, 42, made the oddball offer in a handwritten appeal to potential donors, who were invited to a fund-raiser at his home in Studio City, Calif.

The letter begins: "OK, this is a little tricky. I'll start with a warning: I'm asking for money so you might want to stop reading and pretend you never got this letter. My father, Nick, is running for the U.S. House of Representatives in Kentucky's 4th District. He's the Democratic candidate . . . There's a limit to what anyone can donate to a campaign. If I was allowed, I'd pay for the whole thing (and cover a few Father's Days), but I can't. So I'm writing you in hopes of scaring up some cash for his Congressional bid.

"If you can't or don't want to, I understand. However, if you can . . . I'm having a cocktail party at my house on Saturday March 6, at 7 P.M. It's a benefit so there will be entertainment, hors d'oeurves and booze. *And I'll wash your car every week till it's paid off and Armor-all the tires . . . in a toga*. Hope to see you there, George."

The former "ER" hunk notes the minimum contribution is $500 and the maximum $4,000. And who wouldn't pay top dollar to have him rub his hands all over your car?

- Is Clooney's handwritten note an offer that could bind him to wash cars (in a toga) if accepted?
- One can imagine, if Clooney were asked whether he intended to be making a formal offer to contract, he would likely respond something to the effect, "I certainly did not mean to commit myself to toga-clad car washing. I was joking!" What legal significance does this subjective intent have on whether the letter constitutes an offer to contract?
- How would the determination of whether Clooney was joking be made as a legal matter? Is it relevant to whether the letter is an offer?
- Assuming for the sake of argument that it is not a joke, is the letter specific enough to be an offer?

LO LEARNING OBJECTIVES

After studying this chapter, you should be able to:

10-1 Explain the elements of an offer under both the Uniform Commercial Code (UCC) and common law.

10-2 Determine whether a given proposal is likely to be considered to be an offer.

10-3 Distinguish advertisements that are considered to be offers from those that are merely invitations to negotiate.

10-4 Describe the circumstances that terminate an offer and determine whether a given offer remains "on the table."

THE CONCEPT OF MUTUAL agreement lies at the heart of traditional contract law. Courts faced with deciding whether two or more persons entered into a contract look first for an *agreement* between the parties. Because the formation of an agreement is normally a two-step process by which one party makes a proposal and the other responds to the proposal, it is customary to analyze the agreement in two parts: *offer* and *acceptance*. This chapter, which concerns itself with the offer, and the next chapter, which covers acceptance, focus on the tools used by courts to determine whether the parties have reached the kind of agreement that becomes the foundation of a contract.

Requirements for an Offer

 LO10-1 Explain the elements of an offer under both the Uniform Commercial Code (UCC) and common law.

An **offer** is the critically important first step in the contract formation process. An offer says, in effect, "This is it—if you agree to these terms, we have a contract." The person who makes an offer (the **offeror**) gives the person to whom the offer is made (the **offeree**) the power to bind the offeror to a contract simply by accepting the offer.

Not every proposal qualifies as an offer. Some proposals are vague, for example, or made in jest, or thrown out merely as a way of opening negotiations. To distinguish an offer, courts look for three requirements. First, they look for some objective indication of a *present intent to contract* on the part of the offeror. Second, they look for specificity, or *definiteness*, in the terms of the alleged offer. Third, they look to see whether the alleged offer has been *communicated to the offeree*.

Chapter 9 discussed the fact that contracts for the sale of goods are governed by Article 2 of the Uniform Commercial Code (UCC) whereas contracts for services, real estate, and intangibles are generally governed by the common law of contracts. Common law and UCC standards for contract formation have a great deal in common, but they also differ somewhat. This chapter will point out those areas in which an offer for the sale of goods would be treated somewhat differently from an offer for services, real estate, and intangibles.

Intent to Contract

 LO10-2 Determine whether a given proposal is likely to be considered to be an offer.

For a proposal to be considered an offer, the offeror must indicate *present intent to contract*. Present intent means the

intent to enter the contract upon acceptance. It signifies that the offeror is not joking, haggling, or equivocating. It makes sense that intent on the part of the offeror would be required for an offer—otherwise, an unwilling person might wrongly be bound to a contract. But what is meant by intent? Should courts try to divine what the offeror was actually thinking at the time by searching the offeror's mind (that is, determine *subjective* intent)? Or should the offeror's intent be judged by the impression that the offeror has given to the rest of the world through the offeror's words and acts, as well as the circumstances under which those words and acts occurred (that is, determine *objective* intent)?

The Objective Standard of Intent   Early American courts took a subjective approach to contract formation, asking whether there was truly a "meeting of the minds" between the parties. This subjective standard, however, created uncertainty in the enforcement of contracts because it left every contract vulnerable to disputes about actual intent. The desire to meet the needs of the marketplace by affording predictable and consistent results in contracts cases dictated a shift toward an *objective theory of contracts*. By the middle of the 19th century, the objective approach to contract formation, which judges agreement by looking at the parties' outward manifestations of intent, was firmly established in American law. Judge Learned Hand once described the effect of the objective contract theory as follows:

> A contract has, strictly speaking, nothing to do with the personal, or individual, intent of the parties. A contract is an obligation attached by the mere force of law to certain acts of the parties, usually words, which ordinarily accompany and represent a known intent. If however, it were proved by 20 bishops that either party when he used the words intended something else than the usual meaning which the law imposes on them, he would still be held, unless there were mutual mistake or something else of that sort.[1]

Following the objective theory of contracts, then, an offeror's intent will be judged by an objective standard—that is, what the offeror's words, acts, and the circumstances signify about the offeror's intent. If a reasonable person familiar with all the circumstances would be justified in believing that the offeror intended to contract, a court would find that the intent requirement of an offer was satisfied even if the offeror claims not to have intended to contract.

Definiteness of Terms   If Smith says to Ford, "I'd like to buy your house," and Ford responds, "You've got a deal," has a contract been formed? An obvious problem here is lack of specificity. A proposal that fails to state

---

[1] *Hotchkiss v. National City Bank*, 200 F. 287, 293 (S.D.N.Y. 1911).

specifically what the offeror is willing to do and what the offeror asks in return for performance is unlikely to be considered an offer. One reason for the requirement of definiteness is that definiteness and specificity in an offer tend to indicate an intent to contract, whereas indefiniteness and lack of specificity tend to indicate that the parties are still negotiating and have not yet reached agreement. In the conversation between Smith and Ford, Smith's statement that he'd like to buy Ford's house is merely an invitation to offer or an invitation to negotiate. It indicates a willingness to contract in the future if the parties can reach agreement on mutually acceptable terms, but not a present intent to contract. If, however, Smith sends Ford a detailed and specific written document stating all of the material terms and conditions on which he is willing to buy the house and Ford writes back agreeing to Smith's terms, the parties' intent to contract would be objectively indicated and a contract probably would be created.

A second reason definiteness is important is that courts need to know the terms on which the parties agreed in order to determine if a breach of contract has occurred and calculate a remedy if it has. Keep in mind that the offer often contains all the terms of the parties' contract. This is so because all that an offeree is allowed to do in most cases is to accept or reject the terms of the offer. If an agreement is too indefinite, a court would not have a basis for giving a remedy if one of the parties alleged that the "contract" was breached.

Definiteness Standards under the Common Law
Classical contract law took the position that courts are contract enforcers, not contract makers. The prospect of enforcing an agreement in which the parties had omitted terms or left terms open for later agreement was unthinkable to courts that took a traditional, hands-off approach to contracts. Traditionally, contract law required a relatively high standard of definiteness for offers, requiring that all the essential terms of a proposed contract be stated in the offer. The traditional insistence on definiteness can serve useful ends. It can prevent a person from being held to an agreement when none was reached or from being bound by a contract term to which that person never assented. Often, however, it can operate to frustrate the expectations of parties who intend to contract but, for whatever reason, fail to procure an agreement that specifies all the terms of the contract. The definiteness standard, like much of contract law, is constantly evolving. The trend of modern contract law is to tolerate a lower degree of specificity in agreements than classical contract law would have tolerated, although it is still unlikely that an agreement that leaves open important aspects of a transaction will be enforced. The following *Domingo v. Mitchell* case discusses the elements of an offer, including the objective standard of intent and the requirement of definiteness. It is an example of the modern contract law to allow for some particularly important terms, like price, to be implied when the circumstances warrant.

Domingo v. Mitchell   257 S.W.3d 34 (Tex. Ct. App. 2008)

Coworkers Betty Domingo and Brenda Mitchell often played the Texas Lottery together. Their arrangement included an agreement to pool their money to purchase tickets and split their winnings equally. From time to time, Mitchell would purchase the lottery tickets prior to getting Domingo's money, and Domingo would promptly reimburse Mitchell, win or lose.

On March 9, 2006, Cindy Skidmore sent an e-mail to Mitchell asking if Mitchell was interested in joining a lottery group. Skidmore had formed LGroup, a Texas Limited Partnership, for the purpose of pooling money to play the lottery. On March 23, she sent a follow-up e-mail to members of the group, including Mitchell, notifying them of a meeting the next week at a local restaurant, during which members would pay their share into the pool and select numbers for the April 2006 lottery drawings. The e-mail also provided, "[i]f there is someone else you want to invite (& you feel pretty sure they won't drop out) let me know." Mitchell did not ask Skidmore if Domingo could participate in the April 2006 drawings.

According to Domingo, sometime after the March 23 e-mail, Mitchell invited her to participate in the LGroup for April 2006, specifically to play Lotto Texas and Mega Millions. When Domingo asked how much her contribution would have to be, Mitchell offered to cover for her and be reimbursed at a later time.

On March 30, Mitchell and other members of the group met at a restaurant to pay their share for the April 2006 tickets and contribute their numbers. Domingo was not present at this meeting. Mitchell paid her $17 contribution, but she did not contribute for Domingo's share. According to Mitchell's deposition testimony, she did not have enough money to cover Domingo's payment.

On April 29, 2006, one of the tickets purchased by LGroup was a winner in the amount of $20,925,315.23. Domingo was excluded from any share of the winnings. As a result, she sued Mitchell for breach of contract. Mitchell filed a motion for summary judgment, alleging among other things, that she had never made a valid offer to Domingo, so they could not have entered into a contractual relationship. The trial court granted summary judgment for Mitchell, and Domingo appealed.

Pirtle, Justice

The threshold question is whether Mitchell and Domingo entered into a contract. . . . In determining the existence of an oral contract, courts look at the communications between the parties and the acts and circumstances surrounding those communications. . . . To determine whether there was an offer and acceptance, and therefore a "meeting of the minds," courts use an objective standard, considering what the parties did and said, not their subjective states of mind. . . .

To prove that an offer was made, a party must show (1) the offeror intended to make an offer, (2) the terms of the offer were clear and definite, and (3) the offeror communicated the essential terms of the offer to the offeree. . . .

Mitchell alleges she did not make an offer to Domingo, but if she did, some of the material terms of the offer were lacking, making the contract invalid. She argues that price had not been agreed to and that Domingo failed to submit numbers for the drawings, which was an essential element of the agreement. In response, Domingo asserts that a reasonable price can be implied. She also asserts that submitting numbers was not an essential term of the agreement. We agree with Domingo.

When all other elements of a contract have been met, a court may imply a reasonable price. According to Domingo's affidavit, she was an experienced lottery player and estimated that playing Lotto Texas and Mega Millions for the month of April 2006 would have cost approximately $20 to $25. According to the evidence, Mega Millions was played every Tuesday and Friday and Lotto Texas was played every Wednesday and Saturday. Looking at a calendar for April 2006 at $1 per ticket, there were eight drawings for Mega Millions and nine drawings for Lotto Texas, for a total cost of $17 per participant. Thus, a reasonable price could have been implied.

Whether a term forms an essential element of a contract depends primarily upon the intent of the parties. The question is whether the parties regarded the term as a vitally important ingredient of their bargain.

Mitchell contends that submitting numbers was an essential term of the agreement and that without Domingo complying, there was no valid contract. However, the evidence suggests that submitting numbers for the April drawings was not an essential element of the contract. Copies of e-mails established that different numbers were selected on the day after the LGroup met for dinner to decide on a price and submit numbers. Members of the LGroup were also notified by e-mail and given a deadline of noon on April 1st in which to pick different numbers. Thus, any numbers submitted at the meeting on March 30th were an uncertainty as they were subject to being changed and thus, could not have been regarded by the parties as an essential element of the contract.

According to Domingo, she and Mitchell frequently participated in lottery pools with co-workers. They occasionally covered for each other and when Mitchell would advance Domingo's share, Domingo would promptly reimburse her. Shondra Stewart and Ellen Clemons, co-workers of Domingo and Mitchell, both gave deposition testimony that Cindy Ruff, another co-worker, claimed she was present when Mitchell agreed to cover for Domingo's share of the April 2006 lottery tickets.

* * *

This summary judgment evidence, coupled with Mitchell and Domingo's conduct and course of prior dealings with one another, is sufficient to raise a genuine issue of material fact concerning the offer . . . element[] of the alleged contract between Mitchell and Domingo.

* * *

Accordingly, the trial court's judgment is **reversed** and the cause is **remanded** to the trial court for further proceedings.

Definiteness Standards under the UCC The UCC, with its increased emphasis on furthering people's justifiable expectations and its encouragement of a hands-on approach by the courts, often creates contractual liability in situations where no contract would have resulted at common law. Perhaps no part of the UCC better illustrates this basic difference between the UCC and classical common law than does the basic UCC section on contract formation [2-204]. This section says that sales contracts under Article 2 can be created "in any manner sufficient to show agreement, including conduct which recognizes the existence of a contract" [2-204(1)]. So, if the parties are acting as though they have a contract by delivering or accepting goods or payment, for example, this may be enough to create a binding contract, even if it is impossible to point to a particular moment in time when the contract was created [2-204(2)].

An important difference between UCC and classical common law standards for definiteness is that under the UCC, the fact that the parties left open one or more terms of their agreement does not necessarily mean that their agreement is too indefinite to enforce. A sales contract is created if the court finds that the parties intended to make a contract and that their agreement is complete enough to allow the court to reach a fair settlement of their dispute ("a reasonably certain basis for giving an appropriate remedy" [2-204(3)]). If a term is left open in a contract that meets these two standards, that open term or "gap" can be "filled" by inserting a presumption found in the UCC's "gap-filling" rules. The gap-filling rules allow courts to fill contract terms left open on matters of price [2-305], quantity [2-306], delivery [2-307, 2-308, and 2-309(1)], and time for payment [2-310] when such terms have been left open by the parties.[2] Of course, if a term was left out because the parties were *unable* to reach agreement about it, this would indicate that the intent to contract was absent and no contract would result, even under the UCC's more liberal rules. *Intention is still at the heart of these modern contract rules*; the difference is that courts applying UCC

principles seek to further the parties' *underlying* intent to contract even though the parties have failed to express their intention about specific aspects of their agreement.

The following *J.D. Fields & Company, Inc. v. United States Steel International, Inc.* case illustrates the UCC approach to determining whether an offer has been made. Note how the elements of intent, definiteness, and communication are intertwined in the court's evaluation of whether the price quotes were offers. The case also highlights the general rule that price quotes are invitations to offer rather than offers (as well as when that general rule does not apply). Issues related to that general rule are discussed shortly after the case in the section "Special Offer Problem Areas."

---

[2] Chapter 19 discusses these UCC provisions in detail.

J.D. Fields & Company, Inc. v. United States Steel International, Inc.
426 Fed. App'x 271 (5th Cir. 2011)

United States Steel International (USSI) sells and markets steel products manufactured at U.S.-based steel mills for sale on the international market. J.D. Fields & Company, Inc. (J.D. Fields) distributes steel products from producers to consumers. USSI and J.D. Fields were repeat contracting partners on at least 30 occasions over the prior five years. The typical course of their dealings was that J.D. Fields requested a price quotation from USSI, USSI provided J.D. Fields that quote, J.D. Fields sent USSI a purchase order, USSI sent J.D. Fields an order acknowledgment, and USSI shipped the product along with an invoice.

The present case resulted from a dispute over two e-mail-based transactions. The first transaction involved a type of seamless carbon steel pipe for which J.D. Fields requested a price quote on February 6, 2008. USSI's representative provided the quote for 800 feet, but clearly indicated that USSI could not manufacture that particular type of pipe without an order for at least 100 tons.

On February 11, 2008, J.D. Fields sent a purchase order (PO 45850) to USSI for 880 feet of the pipe; however, 880 feet would constitute only 60 tons. On February 14, 2008, J.D. Fields inquired about the order, and USSI responded that it could not run less than 100 tons of the pipe. Thus, USSI requested a revised purchase order, which J.D. Fields never sent. USSI likewise never issued an order acknowledgment for PO 45840.

On March 6, 2008, J.D. Fields contacted USSI for a quote on two other types of pipe. USSI responded with a quote for the price, timing, delivery location, and other details. That same day, J.D. Fields sent a second purchase order (PO 46110) matching the details of the quote.

On March 26, 2008, J.D. Fields followed up on the status of PO 45850, particularly inquiring whether USSI had found any other takers for the same size pipe to fill out the 100-ton required allotment. J.D. Fields also requested an order acknowledgment on PO 45850. USSI responded that it had "not found any other order to piggyback on," so J.D. Fields would need to order the 100-ton minimum. USSI requested instructions for how to proceed. J.D. Fields responded that it could not afford to keep its customers waiting and risk losing their business and indicated that it would "look[] into" increasing the order to hit the 100-ton minimum. Shortly thereafter, J.D. Fields's representative and the USSI representative spoke on the phone, during which J.D. Fields's representative claims he made a more concrete commitment to order 100 tons "if need be." Even after these exchanges, J.D. Fields never sent a revision of PO 45850 for 100 tons or more.

On April 24, 2008, J.D. Fields inquired with USSI about the status of both purchase orders. That inquiry prompted a series of increasingly contentious communications between the companies. USSI argued that J.D. Fields had never actually ordered the required 100 tons on PO 45850 and that, in any event, it was not taking new orders during the relevant time frame due to an impending price increase. As to PO 46110, USSI admitted that it may have "fallen through the cracks." PO 46110 was never processed by USSI. Ultimately, USSI concluded that the purchase orders had not been entered into its systems, that USSI never sent J.D. Fields order acknowledgments on either purchase order, and that USSI did not plan to fill the orders.

J.D. Fields filed suit against USSI for breach of contract (and other claims not relevant here) on the basis of both purchase orders. The district court granted USSI's motion for summary judgment on the breach of contract claims. J.D. Fields appealed.

Aycock, Judge

The first issue on appeal is whether the district court properly granted summary judgment on J.D. Fields's breach of contract claims when it concluded that USSI's price quotations could not reasonably be construed as offers as a matter of law. . . . When parties enter into a contract for the sale of goods, the Uniform Commercial Code ("UCC") controls the conduct of the parties. There is no dispute that Article 2 of the UCC governs this transaction, as the contracts at issue concern the sale of steel. Steel qualifies as a "thing[] . . . which [is] movable at the time of identification to the contract for sale," and therefore it is considered a "good." Tex. Bus. & Com. Code Ann. § 2.105(a). Where the UCC applies, it displaces all common law rules of law regarding breach of contract and substitutes instead those rules of law and procedures set forth in the UCC. However, common law principles of law and equity continue to supplement its provisions.

In Texas, the essential elements of a breach of contract claim are: (1) the existence of a valid contract; (2) performance or tendered performance by the plaintiff; (3) breach of the contract by the defendant; and (4) damages sustained by the plaintiff as a result of the breach. The central dispute in this action revolves around the first element: whether the parties ever formed a valid contract as to [the two purchase orders]. Contract formation hinges on the existence of an acceptable offer. The UCC, however, provides no guidance as to what an offer is. Although the UCC does not define the term "offer," we have held that "[a]n offer is an act that leads the offeree reasonably to believe that assent (i.e., acceptance) will conclude the deal." *Axelson, Inc. v. McEvoy-Willis*, 7 F.3d 1230, 1232 (5th Cir. 1993).

A contract for the sale of goods may be made in any manner sufficient to show agreement, including conduct by both parties which recognizes the existence of such a contract. Tex. Bus. & Com. Code Ann. §§ 2.201–.210. Generally, a price quotation, such as one appearing in a brochure or on a flyer, is not considered an offer; rather, it is typically viewed as an invitation to offer. Despite this general rule, a price quotation, if detailed enough, can constitute an offer capable of acceptance. However, to do so, it must reasonably appear from the price quote that assent to the quote is all that is needed to ripen the offer into a contract.

Purchase Order 45850

The first e-mailed price quotation was sent from USSI to J.D. Fields on February 6, 2008. The price quotation contained the following: (i) a specified price per ton, (ii) specified payment term, (iii) a general delivery time, (iv) a validity period ("valid for 14 days"), (v) specified rolling/manufacturing time frame, (vi) product specification, (vii) the quantity (800 feet), and (viii) that the price quote was subject to heat lot accumulation of 100 tons. The price quote did not contain the specific shipping location, the mode of shipping, or the legal terms and conditions. Five days after receiving this price quote, J.D. Fields faxed USSI Purchase Order 45850.

Purchase Order 45850 contained a different quantity than the initial inquiry. That is, the purchase order requested 880 feet, whereas the price quote was for 800 feet. Importantly, neither a quantity of 800 feet nor 880 feet was enough to meet the 100-ton minimum expressly required by USSI. J.D. Fields, while conceding that its quantity specifications failed to meet this 100-ton minimum, asserts that it told USSI it would increase its order. On March 26, 2008, J.D. Fields's representative . . . e-mailed USSI's representative . . . stating that J.D. Fields was "looking into increasing [the] order to . . . the minimum 100 tons." Similarly, [J.D. Fields] alleged . . . that [its representative] also discussed this order with [the USSI representative] on the phone and stated that, "if need be, we will go up to 100 tons."

The exchange . . . at most establishes that J.D. Fields was considering—or "looking into"—increasing its order to reach the 100-ton minimum. There is no evidence that J.D. Fields in fact did increase its order or that the parties ever reached an agreement as to a quantity term meeting the 100-ton minimum. The quote contained a 14-day validity period. By the time the March 2008 exchange occurred, the validity period for the price quote had long lapsed. Further, [another] USSI representative repeatedly informed [J.D. Fields] that it would need a revised purchase order. J.D. Fields concedes that it never submitted such a revised order. As such, the district court did not err in finding that it was unreasonable as a matter of law for J.D. Fields to believe that the price quotation was an offer. Thus, we **affirm** the grant of summary judgment as to Purchase Order 45850.

Purchase Order 46110

Purchase Order 46110 falls on different footing than Purchase Order 45850. While the general rule is that a price quote is not an offer, we have held that a price quote, if detailed enough, can constitute an offer capable of acceptance. In *Tubelite, Inc. v. Risica & Sons, Inc.*, 819 S.W.2d 801, 803 (Tex. 1991), the Texas Supreme Court found a price quotation sufficiently detailed to constitute an offer under the Texas UCC when the quote stated it was valid for 60 days, was signed by Tubelite's authorized agent, and did not limit acceptance to a specified manner. In [a similar prior case], the lower court had noted that the price quote contained product specifications, service options, and an itemized price breakdown. The price quote . . . likewise contained no language of approval, or any other indicia suggesting that an order would be subject to approval before it was accepted.

Here, the price quotation preceding Purchase Order 46110 was considerably detailed. It was also only transmitted to J.D. Fields. *See Restatement (Second) of Contracts* § 26, cmt c (stating that a "relevant factor" for "determining whether an offer is made" is the "number of persons to whom a communication is addressed"). The quote contained the following information: (i) a specified price, (ii) delivery time, (iii) a validity period ("valid for 14 days"), (iv) specified rolling/manufacturing time frame,

(v) product specification, (vi) a reference to the quantity listed in J.D. Fields's e-mail, and (vii) a delivery location. Further, unlike some of the previous price quotations sent to J.D. Fields from USSI, this particular price quote was devoid of any language which would condition the formation of a contract on some further step. . . . Specifically, J.D. Fields provided evidence that previous e-mailed price quotes were explicitly conditioned on "mill and steel availability" or were "subject to prior sale." [The J.D. Fields representative] testified via sworn affidavit that it was his understanding that when a quote from USSI gave a validity period without further condition on mill approval, it meant that the representative presenting the quote had already checked with the mill regarding the availability of the steel needed to meet the request. J.D. Fields transmitted Purchase Order 46110 five days after receiving USSI's price quote, and the purchase order mirrored the terms contained in the price quotation.

[The district court relied on industry custom and the parties' course of dealing to determine that the price quotes could not be offers.] While the district court's conclusions regarding industry custom and course of dealing in this case are relevant to the issue

of reasonableness, the UCC never informs that industry custom and course of dealing are alone determinative of the issue of contract *formation*. As such, industry custom and course of dealing do not compel the conclusion that a price quotation cannot be construed as an offer as a matter of law.

Contract formation is a question of fact under Texas law and, here, the price quotation was detailed, transmitted only to J.D. Fields, void of any conditional language, sent in direct response to an inquiry from J.D. Fields's representative, did not limit acceptance to a specified manner, and contained a validity period. Viewing the evidence in the light most favorable to the nonmovant, there are questions of material fact present as to whether J.D. Fields could reasonably construe the price quote relating to Purchase Order 46110 as an offer. At the summary judgment stage, we may not weigh or decide factual disputes or make credibility determinations. Although we find that summary judgment was not appropriate, we express no view on the ultimate merits of J.D. Fields's breach of contract claim.

Accordingly, the grant of summary judgment as to Purchase Order 46110 is **reversed** and **remanded** for further proceedings as the district court may deem appropriate.

The Global Business Environment

Under the United Nations Convention on Contracts for the International Sale of Goods (CISG), a proposal will be considered an offer to contract if it is addressed to one or more specific persons, is sufficiently definite, and indicates the intent of the offeror to be bound in case of acceptance. Unlike the UCC, the CISG does not consider an offer to be sufficiently definite when the price term for goods is left open. The CISG states that the offer must indicate the goods and either expressly or impliedly make a provision for determining the quantity and price.

Communication to Offeree When an offeror communicates the terms of an offer to an offeree, he objectively indicates an intent to be bound by those terms. The fact that an offer has *not* been communicated, on the other hand, may be evidence that the offeror has not yet decided to enter into a binding agreement. For example, assume that Stevens and Meyer have been negotiating over the sale of Meyer's restaurant. Stevens confides in his friend Reilly that he plans to offer Meyer $150,000 for the restaurant. Reilly goes to Meyer and tells Meyer that Stevens has decided to offer him $150,000 for the restaurant and has drawn up a written offer to that effect. After learning the details of the offer from Reilly, Meyer telephones Stevens and says, "I accept your offer." Is Stevens now contractually obligated to buy the restaurant? No. Because *Stevens did not communicate the proposal to Meyer*, there was no offer for Meyer to accept.

Special Offer Problem Areas

Advertisements

 Distinguish advertisements that are considered to be offers from those that are merely invitations to negotiate.

Generally speaking, advertisements for the sale of goods at specified prices are *not* considered to be offers. Rather, they are treated as being invitations to offer or negotiate. The same rule is generally applied to signs, handbills, catalogs, price lists, and price quotations (as described in the previous *J.D. Fields* case). This rule is based on the presumed intent of the sellers involved. It is not reasonable to conclude that a seller who has a limited number of items to sell intends to give every person who sees her ad, sign, or catalog the power to bind her to contract. Thus, if Customer sees Retailer's advertisement of Fantastitab tablet computers for $650 and goes to Retailer's store indicating his intent to buy the tablet, Customer is making an offer, which Retailer is free to accept or reject. This is so because *Customer* is manifesting a present intent to contract on the definite terms of the ad.

In some cases, however, particular ads have been held to amount to offers. Such ads limit the power of acceptance to one offeree or a small number of offerees, are highly specific about the nature and number of items offered for sale and what is requested in return, and leave nothing further to be negotiated. This specificity precludes the possibility that the offeror could become contractually bound to an infinite number of offerees. In addition, many of the ads treated as offers have required some special performance by would-be buyers or have in some other way clearly indicated that immediate action by the buyer creates a binding agreement.

For example, in one classic case,[3] a newspaper advertisement that stated, "Saturday 9 A.M. . . . 1 Black Lapin Stole Beautiful, worth $139.50 . . . $1.00 First Come First Served" was held to be an offer. The ad was clear and specific about what was being offered and asked for in exchange—one had to be the first one to appear at the seller's place of business

_____
[3]*Lefkowitz v. Great Minneapolis Surplus Store*, 86 N.W.2d 689 (Minn. 1957).

and pay $1.00—and there were no terms left open for further discussion or negotiation. Moreover, the "first come first served" language limits the number of people who would have the power of acceptance. The potential for unfairness to those who attempt to accept such ads and their fundamental difference from ordinary ads justify treating them as offers.

Rewards Advertisements offering rewards for lost property, for information, or for the capture of criminals are generally treated as offers for unilateral contracts. To accept the offer and be entitled to the stated reward, offerees must perform the requested act—return the lost property, supply the requested information, or capture the wanted criminal. Some courts have held that only offerees who started performance with knowledge of the offer are entitled to the reward. Other courts, however, have indicated the only requirement is that the offeree know of the reward before completing performance. In reality, the result in most such cases probably reflects the court's perception of what is fairer given the facts involved in the particular case at hand.

In any event, a reward offer must meet the basic requirements of an offer of any kind to be binding. The following *Kolodziej* case grapples with whether a purported reward offer made on the NBC television news program *Dateline* manifested the requisite intent and definiteness. While the lower court focused on issues specific to reward offers (like whether the offeree knew of the reward terms prior to performing), the appeals court targets the validity of the offer itself.

Kolodziej v. Mason — 774 F.3d 736 (11th Cir. 2014)

In 2006, James Cheney Mason, through his law firm J. Cheney Mason, P.A., represented Nelson Serrano in a Florida murder trial in which Serrano was accused of murdering four people on December 3, 1997, about 60 miles outside of Orlando, Florida.

During Serrano's highly publicized capital murder trial, Mason participated in an interview with NBC News, which aired on the primetime television show Dateline, *in which he focused on the seeming implausibility of the prosecution's theory of the case. Indeed, his client ostensibly had an alibi—on the day of the murders, Serrano claimed to be on a business trip in an entirely different state, several hundred miles away from the scene of the crimes in central Florida. Hotel surveillance video confirmed that Serrano was at an Atlanta, Georgia, La Quinta Inn, several hours before and after the murders occurred in Bartow, Florida.*

Nevertheless, the prosecution maintained that Serrano committed the murders in an approximately ten-hour span between the times that he was seen on the security camera. According to the prosecution, after being recorded by the hotel security camera in the early afternoon, Serrano slipped out of the hotel and, traveling under several aliases, flew from Atlanta to Orlando, where he rented a car, drove to Bartow, and committed the murders. From there, Serrano allegedly drove to the Tampa International Airport, flew back to Atlanta, and drove from the Atlanta International Airport to the La Quinta, to make an appearance on the hotel's security footage once again that evening.

Mason argued that it was impossible for his client to have committed the murders in accordance with this timeline; for instance, for the last leg of the journey, Serrano would have had to get off a flight in Atlanta's busy airport, travel to the La Quinta several miles away, and arrive in that hotel lobby in only 28 minutes. After extensively describing the delays that would take place to render that 28-minute timeline even more unlikely, Mason stated in his Dateline *interview, "I challenge anybody to show me, and guess what? Did they bring in any evidence to say that somebody made that route, did so? State's burden of proof. If they can do it, I'll challenge 'em. I'll pay them a million dollars if they can do it."*

Dustin Kolodziej, then a law student at the South Texas College of Law, had been following the Serrano case and saw the edited version of Mason's interview, which aired on Dateline. *Kolodziej understood the statement as a serious challenge, open to anyone, to "make it off the plane and back to the hotel within [28] minutes"—that is, in the prosecution's timeline—in return for $1 million.*

Kolodziej subsequently ordered and studied the Dateline *transcript of the edited interview, interpreting it as an offer to form a unilateral contract—an offer he decided to accept by performing the challenge. In December 2007, Kolodziej recorded himself retracing Serrano's alleged route, traveling from a flight at the Atlanta airport to what he believed was the former location of the now-defunct La Quinta within 28 minutes. Kolodziej then sent Mason a copy of the recording of his journey and a letter stating that Kolodziej had performed the challenge and requested payment. Mason responded with a letter in which he refused payment and denied that he made a serious offer in the interview. Kolodziej again demanded payment, and Mason again refused.*

Kolodziej sued in Texas, but that lawsuit was dismissed for lack of personal jurisdiction over Mason. Thereafter, Kolodziej discovered the existence of Mason's unedited interview with NBC and learned that Dateline *had independently edited the interview before it aired. (Mason was unaware of that editing, or that the interview in any form had aired, until he received the demand of payment from Kolodziej.) Kolodziej subsequently filed suit in the U.S. District Court for the Northern District of Georgia. That suit was transferred to the Middle District of Florida, where Mason moved for summary judgment.*

The district court granted summary judgment on two grounds: First, Kolodziej was unaware of the unedited Mason interview at the time he attempted to perform the challenge, and thus he could not accept an offer he did not know existed; second, the challenge in the unedited interview was unambiguously directed to the prosecution only, and thus Kolodziej could not accept an offer not open to him. The district court declined to address the arguments that Mason's challenge was not a serious offer and that, in any event, Kolodziej did not adequately perform the challenge. This appeal ensued.

Wilson, Circuit Judge

We do not find that Mason's statements were such that a reasonable, objective person would have understood them to be an invitation to contract, regardless of whether we look to the unedited interview or the edited television broadcast seen by Kolodziej. Neither the content of Mason's statements, nor the circumstances in which he made them, nor the conduct of the parties reflects the assent necessary to establish an actionable offer—which is, of course, essential to the creation of a contract.

As a threshold matter, the "spoken words" of Mason's purported challenge do not indicate a willingness to enter into a contract. Even removed from its surrounding context, the edited sentence that Kolodziej claims creates Mason's obligation to pay (that is, "I challenge anybody to show me—I'll pay them a million dollars if they can do it") appears colloquial. The exaggerated amount of "a million dollars"—the common choice of movie villains and schoolyard wagerers alike—indicates that this was hyperbole. As the district court noted, "courts have viewed such indicia of jest or hyperbole as providing a reason for an individual to doubt that an 'offer' was serious." *See Kolodziej v. Mason*, 996 F. Supp. 2d 1237, 1252 (M.D. Fla. 2014) (discussing, in dicta, a laughter-eliciting joke made by Mason's co-counsel during the interview). Thus, the very content of Mason's spoken words "would have given any reasonable person pause, considering all of the attendant circumstances in this case." *See id.*

Those attendant circumstances are further notable when we place Mason's statements in context. As Judge Learned Hand once noted, "the circumstances in which the words are used is always relevant and usually indispensable." *N.Y. Trust Co. v. Island Oil & Transp. Corp.*, 34 F.2d 655, 656 (2d Cir. 1929). . . . Here, Mason made the comments in the course of representing a criminal defendant accused of quadruple homicide and did so during an interview solely related to that representation. Such circumstances would lead a reasonable person to question whether the requisite assent and actionable offer giving rise to contractual liability existed. Certainly, Mason's statements—made as a defense attorney in response to the prosecution's theory against his client—were far more likely to be a descriptive illustration of what that attorney saw as serious holes in the prosecution's theory instead of a serious offer to enter into a contract.

Nor can a valid contract be inferred in whole or in part from the parties' conduct in this case. By way of comparison, consider *Lucy v. Zehmer*, 196 Va. 493, 84 S.E.2d 516 (1954), the classic case describing and applying what we now know as the objective standard of assent. That court held that statements allegedly made "in jest" *could* result in an offer binding the parties to a contract, since "the law imputes to a person an intention corresponding to the reasonable meaning of his words and acts." *Id.* at 522. Therefore, "a person cannot set up that he was merely jesting when his conduct and words would warrant a reasonable person in believing that he intended a real agreement." *Id.*

In so holding, the *Lucy* court considered that the offeror wrote, prepared, and executed a writing for sale; the parties engaged in extensive, serious discussion prior to preparing the writing; the offeror prepared a second written agreement, having changed the content of the writing in response to the offeree's request; the offeror had his wife separately sign the writing; and the offeror allowed the offeree to leave with the signed writing without ever indicating that it was in jest. *Id.* at 519-22. Given that these "words and acts, judged by a reasonable standard, manifest[ed] an intention to agree," the offeror's "unexpressed state of . . . mind" was immaterial. *Id.* at 522. Under the objective standard of assent, the *Lucy* court found that the parties had formed a contract. *See id.*

Applying the objective standard here leads us to the real million-dollar question: "What did the party say and do?" Here, it is what both parties did not say and did not do that clearly distinguishes this case from those cases where an enforceable contract was formed. Mason did not engage in any discussion regarding his statements to NBC with Kolodziej, and, prior to Kolodziej demanding payment, there was no contact or communication between the parties. Mason neither confirmed that he made an offer nor asserted that the offer was serious. Mason did not have the payment set aside in escrow; nor had he ever declared that he had money set aside in case someone proved him wrong. Mason had not made his career out of the contention that the prosecution's case was implausible; nor did he make the statements in a commercial context for the "obvious purpose of advertising or promoting [his] goods or business." He did not create or promote the video that included his statement, nor did he increase the amount at issue. He did not, nor did the show include, any information to contact Mason about the challenge. Simply put, Mason's conduct lacks any indicia of assent to contract.

In fact, none of Mason's surrounding commentary—either in the unedited original interview or in the edited television broadcast—gave the slightest indication that his statement was anything other than a figure of speech. In the course of representing his client, Mason merely used a rhetorical expression to raise questions as to the prosecution's case. We could just as easily substitute a comparable idiom such as "I'll eat my hat" or "I'll be a monkey's uncle" into Mason's interview in the place of "I'll pay them a million dollars," and the outcome would be the same. We would not be inclined to make him either consume his headwear or assume a simian relationship were he to be proven wrong; nor will we make him pay one million dollars here.

Additionally, an enforceable contract requires mutual assent as to sufficiently definite essential terms. . . . Here, even the proper starting and ending points for Mason's purported challenge were unspecified and indefinite; Kolodziej had to speculate and decide for himself what constituted the essential terms of the challenge. For instance, in the prosecution's theory of the case, Serrano, using an alias, was seated in the coach section of an aircraft loaded with over one hundred other passengers. Kolodziej, however, purchased a front row aisle seat in first class and started the twenty-eight-minute countdown from that prime location. Comparably, Kolodziej did not finish his performance in the La Quinta lobby; rather, Kolodziej ended the challenge at an EconoLodge, which, based on anecdotal information, he believed was the former location of the La Quinta in which Serrano stayed.

We highlight these differences not to comment as to whether Kolodziej adequately performed the challenge—which the parties dispute for a multitude of additional reasons—but instead to illustrate the lack of definiteness and specificity in any purported offer (and absence of mutual assent thereto). It is challenging to point to anything Mason said or did that evinces a "display of willingness to enter into a contract on specified terms, made in a way that would lead a reasonable person to understand that an acceptance, having been sought, will result in a binding contract." *See Black's Law Dictionary* 1189 (9th ed. 2009) (defining "offer" in contract law). Therefore, we conclude that Mason did not manifest the requisite willingness to contract through his words or conduct, and no amount of subsequent effort by Kolodziej could turn Mason's statements into an actionable offer.

* * *

Just as people are free to contract, they are also free *from* contract, and we find it neither prudent nor permissible to impose contractual liability for offhand remarks or grandstanding. Nor would it be advisable to scrutinize a defense attorney's hyperbolic commentary for a hidden contractual agenda, particularly when that commentary concerns the substantial protections in place for criminal defendants. Having considered the content of Mason's statements, the context in which they were made, and the conduct of the parties, we do not find it reasonable to conclude that Mason assented to enter into a contract with anyone for one million dollars. We affirm the district court's judgment in favor of Mason. . . .

AFFIRMED.

Auctions Sellers at auctions are generally treated as making an invitation to offer. Those who bid on offered goods are, therefore, treated as making offers that the owner of the goods may accept or reject. Acceptance occurs only when the auctioneer strikes the goods off to the highest bidder; the auctioneer may withdraw the goods at any time before acceptance. However, when an auction is advertised as being "without reserve," the seller is treated as having made an offer to sell the goods to the highest bidder and the goods cannot be withdrawn after a call for bids has been made unless no bids are made within a reasonable time.[4]

---

[4]These rules and others concerned with the sale of goods by auction are contained in section 2-328 of the UCC.

CYBERLAW IN ACTION

On April 27, 2020, the Twitter account for the streaming service Disney+ posted a thread of tweets including the following:

- "Celebrate the Saga! Reply with your favorite #StarWars memory and you may see it somewhere special on #MayThe4th."
- "By sharing your message with us using #MayThe4th, you agree to our use of the message and your account name in all media and our terms of use. . . ."

The latter tweet included a link to The Walt Disney Company Terms of Use.   After around five hours and numerous replies and retweets criticizing the notion that Disney might claim rights in tweets that used the hashtag MayThe4th, the thread was updated with the following: "The above legal language applies ONLY to replies to this tweet using #MayThe4th and mentioning @DisneyPlus. These replies may appear in something special on May the 4th!"

According to the legal rules and principles discussed in this chapter (and particularly in light of the analysis in the *Cordas* case below), would you expect that the original Twitter thread is an offer for a unilateral contract that would bind anyone tweeting with #MayThe4th to grant Disney rights in their tweet and subject them to the Terms of Use? Does the follow-up tweet clarifying that only replies to the original tweet and mentioning @DisneyPlus change the analysis at all?

Bids The bidding process is a fertile source of contract disputes. Advertisements for bids are generally treated as invitations to offer. Those who submit bids are treated as offerors. According to general contract principles, bidders can withdraw their bids at any time prior to acceptance by the offeree inviting the bids, and the offeree is free to accept or reject any bid. The previously announced terms of the bidding may alter these rules, however. For example, if the advertisement for bids unconditionally states that the contract will be awarded to the lowest responsible bidder, this will be treated as an offer that is accepted by the lowest bidder. Only proof by the offeror that the lowest bidder is not responsible can prevent the formation of a contract. Also, under some circumstances discussed later in this chapter, promissory estoppel may operate to prevent bidders from withdrawing their bids.

Bids for governmental contracts are generally covered by specific statutes rather than by general contract principles. Such statutes ordinarily establish the rules governing the bidding process, often require that the contract be awarded to the lowest bidder, and frequently establish special rules or penalties governing the withdrawal of bids.

Which Terms Are Included in the Offer?

After making a determination that an offer existed, a court must decide which terms were included in the offer so that it can determine the terms of the parties' contract. Put another way, which terms of the offer are binding on the offeree who accepts it? Should offerees, for example, be bound by fine-print clauses or by clauses on the back of the contract? Originally, the courts tended to hold that offerees were bound by all the terms of the offer on the theory that every person had a duty to protect himself by reading agreements carefully before signing them.

In today's world of lengthy, complex form contracts, however, people often sign agreements that they have not fully read or do not fully understand. Modern courts tend to recognize this fact by saying that offerees are bound only by terms of which they had actual or reasonable notice. If the offeree actually read the term in question, or if a reasonable person should have been aware of it, it will probably become part of the parties' contract. A fine-print provision on the back of a theater ticket would probably not be binding on a theater patron, however, because a reasonable person would not normally expect such a ticket to contain contractual terms. By contrast, the terms printed on a multipage airline ticket might well be considered binding on the purchaser if such documents would be expected to contain terms of the contract.

In the following *Cordas* case, the court applies these principles in a thoroughly modern context—terms and conditions of a ride-sharing app.

Cordas v. Uber Technologies, Inc.
228 F. Supp. 3d 985 (N.D. Cal. 2017)

In July 2015, Michael Cordas downloaded the Uber ride-sharing app and attempted to request a ride in New York City. His requested ride did not appear after the estimated 10-minute arrival time elapsed, and Cordas was unsuccessful in his attempts to contact the driver. Cordas received a notification from Uber that he would be charged $10 for canceling his ride, but he denies ever canceling. Cordas later experienced similar incidents in Toronto and Irvine, California. Cordas sued Uber on behalf of himself and a similarly situated class of Uber users, alleging that Uber purposely was generating millions of dollars in cancellation fees through deceptive, false, misleading, and illusory business policies and practices.

According to the testimony of the Uber engineer manager responsible for overseeing the rider sign-up and registration process, which was given during a pretrial hearing, no Uber account could be created unless the user navigated through the screen containing a notice stating, "By creating an Uber account, you agree to the Terms & Conditions and Privacy Policy." The same screen required the new registrant to click "DONE" in order to create an account. The phrase "Terms & Conditions and Privacy Policy" was displayed in a clickable box that linked a user to the pages containing the then-current terms and conditions and privacy policies. The Terms & Conditions included the following provision:

> ARBITRATION. You agree that any dispute, claim or controversy arising out of or relating to these Terms or the breach, termination, enforcement, interpretation or validity thereof or the use of the Services (collectively, "Disputes") will be settled by binding arbitration between you and Uber, except that each party retains the right to bring an individual action in small claims court and the right to seek injunctive or other equitable relief in a court of competent jurisdiction to prevent the actual or threatened infringement, misappropriation or violation of a party's copyrights, trademarks, trade secrets, patents or other intellectual property rights. You acknowledge and agree that you and Uber are each waiving the right to a trial by jury or to participate as a plaintiff or class in any purported class or representative proceeding. Further, unless both you and Uber otherwise agree in writing, the arbitrator may not consolidate more than one person's claims, and may not otherwise preside over any form of any class or representative proceeding.

The Uber engineer manager presented evidence showing that Cordas had registered and clicked "DONE," indicating his agreement to the Terms & Conditions. Thus, Uber filed a motion to compel arbitration.

Seeborg, District Judge

Cordas raises a number of arguments for why Uber's motion to compel arbitration should be denied. They are all unavailing.

* * *

Cordas . . . argues Uber's terms and conditions amount to an unenforceable "browsewrap" agreement. "[A] browsewrap agreement does not require the user to manifest assent to the terms and conditions expressly . . . [a] party instead gives his assent simply by using the website." *Nguyen v. Barnes & Noble Inc.*, 763 F.3d 1171, 1176 (9th Cir. 2014). "Thus, by visiting the website—something that the user has already done—the user agrees to the Terms of Use. . . ." *Id.* "Because no affirmative action is required by the website user to agree to the terms of a contract other than his or her use of the website, the determination of the validity of the browsewrap contract depends on whether the user has actual or constructive knowledge of a website's terms and conditions." *Id.* "Courts have . . . been more willing to find the requisite notice for constructive assent where the browsewrap agreement resembles a clickwrap agreement—that is, where the user is required to affirmatively acknowledge the agreement before proceeding with use of the website." *Id.* (citing *Fteja v. Facebook, Inc.*, 841 F. Supp.

2d 829, 838 (S.D.N.Y. 2012) (finding user assented by clicking "Sign Up" after being presented with notice stating: "By clicking Sign Up, you are indicating that you have read and agree to the Terms of Service.")).

The agreement at issue is not a browsewrap agreement; an Uber user is not told he has assented to Uber's terms and conditions simply by passively viewing one screen of the Uber app. Instead, he must affirmatively assent to Uber's terms and conditions by clicking "DONE" to complete his sign-up process on a page clearly displaying the notice: "By creating an Uber account, you agree to the Terms & Conditions and Privacy Policy." Only by clicking "DONE" does the user assent. If he does not create an account, he does not agree to Uber's terms and conditions. By creating an account on the Uber app, Cordas "affirmatively acknowledge[d] the agreement" and is bound by its terms. Thus, the parties agreed to arbitrate. . . .

* * *

CONCLUSION

Uber's motion to compel arbitration is **granted**, and the case is hereby **stayed**, pending completion of the arbitration. . . .

IT IS SO ORDERED.

Ethics and Compliance in Action

Jerry, who was in the process of opening a new small business in Connecticut, ordered an expensive new computer system from ABC Computing. As part of this transaction, ABC presented Jerry with a contract of sale. The contract was written on lightweight paper that was difficult to read. The signature line was on the bottom of the first page, but there were more contract terms on the reverse side of the page. On the reverse side, under the heading "Warranty Service," was a provision that disclaimed all implied warranties and stated that any dispute that might arise between the parties would be resolved by arbitration in California (where ABC is headquartered). Jerry signed the contract without reading the reverse side. The computer system was defective and never worked correctly. Jerry wants to sue ABC Computing but cannot afford to go to California to do so. Is it ethical for businesses who deal with consumers and other less-sophisticated parties to "hide" contract terms under misleading headings, in small print, deep in a website, or on the reverse side of the contract? If not, what sort(s) of organizational checks need to be in place at companies like ABC Computing to avoid putting consumers or less-sophisticated parties in that position?

Termination of Offers

LO10-4 Describe the circumstances that terminate an offer and determine whether a given offer remains "on the table."

After a court has determined the existence and content of an offer, it must determine the duration of the offer. Was the offer still in existence when the offeree attempted to accept it? If not, no contract was created and the offeree is treated as having made an offer that the original offeror is free to accept or reject. This is so because, by attempting to accept an offer that has terminated, the offeree has indicated a present intent to contract on the terms of the original offer though he lacks the power to bind the offeror to a contract due to the original offer's termination.

Terms of the Offer The offeror is often said to be "the master of the offer." This means that offerors have the power to determine the terms and conditions under which they are bound to a contract. An offeror may include terms in the offer that limit its effective life. These may be specific terms, such as "you must accept by December 5, 2010," or "this offer is good for five days," or more general terms such as "for immediate acceptance," "prompt wire acceptance," or "by return mail." General time-limitation language in an offer can raise difficult problems of interpretation for courts trying to decide whether an offeree accepted before the offer terminated. Even more specific language, such as "this offer is good for five days," can cause problems if the offer does not specify whether the five-day period begins when the offer is sent or when the offeree receives it. Not all courts agree on such questions, so wise offerors should be as specific as possible in stating when their offers terminate.

Lapse of Time Offers that fail to provide a specific time for acceptance are valid for a reasonable time. What constitutes a reasonable time depends on the circumstances surrounding the offer. How long would a reasonable person in the offeree's position believe the offer is open and subject to acceptance? Offers involving things subject to rapid fluctuations in value, such as stocks, bonds, or commodities futures, have a very brief duration. The same is true for offers involving goods that may spoil, such as produce.

The context of the parties' negotiations is another factor relevant to determining the duration of an offer. For example, most courts hold that when parties bargain face-to-face or over the telephone, the normal time for acceptance does not extend past the conclusion of their conversation unless the offeror indicates a contrary intention. Where negotiations are carried out by mail or other time-delayed forms of communication, the time for acceptance would ordinarily include at least the normal time for communicating the offer and a prompt response by the offeree. Finally, in cases where the parties have dealt with each other on a regular basis in the past, the timing of their prior transactions would be highly relevant in measuring the reasonable time for acceptance.

Revocation

General Rule: Offers Are Revocable As the masters of their offers, offerors can give offerees the power to bind them to contracts by making offers. They can also terminate that power by revoking their offers. The general common law rule on revocations is that offerors may revoke their offers at any time prior to acceptance, *even if they have promised to hold the offer open for a stated period of time.*

Exceptions to the General Rule In the following situations (summarized in Figure 10.1), however, offerors are *not* free to revoke their offers:

Figure 10.1	When Offerors Cannot Revoke
Options	Offeror has promised to hold offer open and has received consideration for that promise.
Unilateral Contract Offers	Offeree has started to perform requested act before offeror revokes.
Promissory Estoppel	Offeree foreseeably and reasonably relies on offer being held open, and will suffer injustice if it is revoked.
Firm Offers	Merchant offeror makes written offer to buy or sell goods, giving assurances that the offer will be held open. [Maximum duration is three months or the amount of time in the assurance, whichever is shorter.]

1. *Options.* An **option** is a separate contract in which an offeror agrees not to revoke the offer for a stated time in exchange for some valuable consideration. You can think of it as a contract in which an offeror sells to the offeree the right the offeror usually retains to revoke the offer. For example, Jones, in exchange for $5,000, agrees to give Dewey Development Co. a six-month option to purchase her farm for $550,000. In this situation, Jones would not be free to revoke the offer during the six-month period of the option. The offeree, Dewey Development, has no obligation to accept Jones's offer. In effect, it has merely purchased the right to consider the offer for the stated time without fear that Jones will revoke it.

2. *Offers for unilateral contracts.* Suppose Franklin makes the following offer for a unilateral contract to Waters: "If you mow my lawn, I'll pay you $25." Given that an offeree in a unilateral contract must fully perform the requested act to accept the offer, can Franklin wait until Waters is almost finished mowing the lawn and then say "I revoke!"? Obviously, the application of the general rule that offerors can revoke at any time before acceptance creates the potential for injustice when applied to offers for unilateral contracts because it would allow an offeror to revoke after the offeree has begun performance but before the offeree has had a chance to complete it. To prevent injustice to offerees who rely on such offers by beginning performance, two basic approaches are available to modern courts.

Some courts have held that once the offeree has begun to perform, the offeror's power to revoke is suspended for the amount of time reasonably necessary for the offeree to complete performance. Another approach to the unilateral contract dilemma is to hold that a bilateral contract is created once the offeree begins performance.

3. *Promissory estoppel.* In some cases in which the offeree *relies* on the offer being kept open, the doctrine of promissory estoppel can operate to prevent offerors from revoking their offers prior to acceptance. Section 87(2) of the *Restatement (Second)* says:

An offer which the offeror should reasonably expect to induce action or forbearance of a substantial character on the part of the offeree before acceptance and which does induce such action or forbearance is binding as an option contract to the extent necessary to avoid injustice.

Many of the cases in which promissory estoppel has been used successfully to prevent revocation of offers involve the bidding process. For example, Gigantic General Contractor seeks to get the general contract to build a new high school gymnasium for Shadyside School District. It receives bids from subcontractors. Liny Electric submits the lowest bid to perform the electrical work on the job, and Gigantic uses Liny's bid in preparing its bid for the general contract. Here, Liny has made an offer to Gigantic, but Gigantic cannot accept that offer until it knows whether it has gotten the general contract. The school district awards the general contract to Gigantic. Before Gigantic can accept Liny's offer, however, Liny attempts to revoke it. In this situation, a court could use the doctrine of promissory estoppel to hold that the offer could not be revoked.

4. *Firm offers for the sale of goods [Note: This applies to offers for the sale of goods ONLY!].* The UCC makes a major change in the common law rules governing the revocability of offers by recognizing the concept of a **firm offer** [2-205]. Like an option, a firm offer is irrevocable for a period of time. In contrast to an option, however, a firm offer does not require consideration to be given in exchange for the offeror's promise to keep the offer open. Not all offers to buy or sell goods qualify as firm offers, however. To be a firm offer, an offer must:

• Be made by an offeror who is a *merchant.*
• Be contained in a signed writing.[5]
• Give assurances that the offer will be kept open.

An offer to buy or sell goods that fails to satisfy these three requirements is governed by the general common law rule and is revocable at any time prior to acceptance. If an offer *does* meet the requirements of a firm offer, however, it will be irrevocable for the time stated in the offer. If no specific time is stated in the offer, it will be irrevocable

---

[5]Under the UCC [1-201(39)], the word *signed* includes any symbol that a person makes or adopts with the intent to authenticate a writing.

What Terminates Offers?

- Their own terms
- Lapse of time
- Revocation
- Rejection
- Death or insanity of offeror or offeree
- Destruction of subject matter
- Intervening illegality

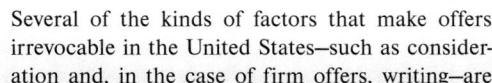

The Global Business Environment

Several of the kinds of factors that make offers irrevocable in the United States—such as consideration and, in the case of firm offers, writing—are not required to make offers irrevocable under the CISG. The CISG states that an offer cannot be revoked if it indicates that it is irrevocable or if it was reasonable for the offeree to rely on the offer as being irrevocable and the offeree has acted in reliance on the offer. However, even when an offer is irrevocable, the CISG allows it to be revoked if the revocation reaches the offeree before or at the same time as the offer.

for a *reasonable* time. Regardless of the terms of the firm offer, the outer limit on a firm offer's irrevocability is *three months*. For example, if Worldwide Widget makes an offer in a signed writing in which it proposes to sell a quantity of its XL Turbo Widget to Howell Hardware and gives assurances that the offer will be kept open for a year, the offer is a firm offer, but it can be revoked after three months if Howell Hardware has not yet accepted it.

In some cases, however, offerees are the true originators of an assurance term in an offer. When offerees have effective control of the terms of the offer by providing their customers with preprinted purchase order forms or order blanks, they may be tempted to take advantage of their merchant customers by placing an assurance term in their order forms. This would allow offerees to await market developments before deciding whether to fill the order, while their merchant customers, who may have signed the order without reading all of its terms, would be powerless to revoke. To prevent such unfairness, the UCC requires that assurance terms on forms provided by offerees be separately signed by the offeror to effect a firm offer. For example, if Fashionable Mfg. Co. supplies its customer, Retailer, with preprinted order forms that contain a fine-print provision giving assurances that the customer's offer to purchase goods will be held open for one month, the purported promise to keep the offer open would not be enforceable unless Retailer separately signed that provision.

Time of Effectiveness of Revocations The question of *when* a revocation is effective to terminate an offer is often a critical issue in the contract formation process. For example, Davis offers to landscape Winter's property for $1,500. Two days after making the offer, Davis changes his mind and mails Winter a letter revoking the offer. The next day, Winter, who has not received Davis's letter, telephones Davis and attempts to accept. Contract? Yes. The general rule on this point is that revocations are effective only when they are actually *received* by the offeree.

The only major exception to the general rule on effectiveness of revocations concerns offers to the general public. Because it would be impossible in most cases to reach every offeree with a revocation, it is generally held that a revocation made in the same manner as the offer is effective when published, without proof of communication to the offeree.

Rejection An offeree may expressly reject an offer by indicating that the offeree is unwilling to accept it. The offeree may also impliedly reject it by making a counteroffer, an offer to contract on terms materially different from the terms of the offer. As a general rule, either form of rejection by the offeree terminates the offeree's power to accept the offer. This is so because an offeror who receives a rejection may rely on the offeree's expressed desire not to accept the offer by making another offer to a different offeree.

Identifying whether a response is a counteroffer and, thus, a rejection is not always straightforward. The following *D'Agostino* case engages in that analysis with regard to a potential agreement settling a disputed legal claim.

One exception to the general rule that rejections terminate offers concerns offers that are the subject of an option contract. Some courts hold that a rejection does not terminate an option contract and that the offeree who rejects still has the power to accept the offer later, so long as the acceptance is effective within the option period.

D'Agostino v. Federal Insurance Company
969 F. Supp. 2d 116 (D. Mass. 2013)

Miia C. D'Agostino was the sole beneficiary of the Bruno D'Agostino Trust. (A trust is a relationship created by one person, the settlor, in which a trustee holds or manages the settlor's property solely for the benefit of one or more others, the beneficiaries.) The D'Agostino Trust owned a multifamily residential property located in Cambridge, Massachusetts. The property was substantially damaged in a fire on December 9, 2008. It was insured by Federal Insurance Company under a policy issued to Bank of America, which acted as trustee for the D'Agostino Trust.

Federal and D'Agostino disputed the amount of money to which D'Agostino was entitled to compensate for her losses. D'Agostino filed this lawsuit against Federal, claiming breach of contract and charging that Federal engaged in unfair and deceptive practices under Massachusetts law.

Nonetheless, D'Agostino's attorney, Richard Goren, and Federal's attorneys continued to engage in negotiations to settle the claims. D'Agostino's conditions for settlement included an amount of money in exchange for a full release of any claims against Federal, while clearly maintaining her right to sue Bank of America. Federal had been generally agreeable but wanted D'Agostino to guarantee that she would indemnify Federal against any claims Bank of America might press against Federal. (To indemnify another party means to reimburse or promise to reimburse them from a loss or to otherwise act as security or protection against that loss.)

On February 6, 2009, Goren sent a settlement offer to Federal's attorneys demanding a monetary settlement of $1.15 million, releasing the claims against Federal, and reserving D'Agostino's right to sue Bank of America. Goren, however, explicitly and definitively rejected the notion that D'Agostino might indemnify Federal against Bank of America's potential claims.

Eventually, Federal's attorneys formally responded to Goren's settlement offer with a seven-page "Confidential Release and Settlement Agreement." Among the Release's 18 paragraphs was an agreement to pay D'Agostino $1.15 million in return for a release of her claims against Federal (though not against Bank of America). In addition, the Release included clauses addressing choice of law, termination of the litigation, nondisparagement, confidentiality, and indemnification. Some of these were boilerplate; others were more substantive.

D'Agostino purported to reject the Release and continued to litigate the case against Federal. In response, Federal filed an "Emergency Motion to Enforce Settlement Agreement" with the court, arguing that the Release was an acceptance of D'Agostino's settlement offer.

Dein, U.S. Magistrate Judge

The critical issue raised by Federal's motion[] is whether the parties reached an enforceable settlement agreement. The court has "an inherent power to supervise and enforce settlement agreements entered into by parties to an action pending before the court." *Dankese v. Defense Logistics Agency*, 693 F.2d 13, 16 (1st Cir. 1982). . . . In order to form a contract under Massachusetts law, "[a]n offer must be matched by an acceptance. A counteroffer proposing a term that is materially different from that contained in the original offer constitutes a rejection of the offer and negates any agreement." *Kennedy v. JPMorgan Chase Nat'l Corp.*, No. 10-CV-11324-RGS, 2011 U.S. Dist. LEXIS 44664, at *2 (D. Mass. Apr. 26, 2011) (internal citation omitted). [W]hile "[i]t is not required that all terms of the agreement be precisely specified, and the presence of undefined or unspecified terms will not necessarily preclude the formation of a binding contract[,]" in order for an enforceable contract to exist, the parties must have reached an agreement on all of the essential terms. *Situation Mgmt. Sys., Inc. v. Malouf, Inc.*, 724 N.E.2d 699, 703 (Mass. 2000). As described below, although the parties agreed on certain essential matters, they

failed to reach agreement on all the material terms of a settlement. Therefore, this court concludes that . . . the defendant's motion[] should be denied.

Failure to Reach an Enforceable Settlement Agreement

Federal contends that an enforceable settlement agreement was created on February 6, 2013, when its counsel sent Attorney Goren the Release for his client's execution. In particular, the defendant argues that because the Release contained an agreement by Federal to pay D'Agostino $1.15 million, and provided for the release of the plaintiff's claims against Federal, it constituted an acceptance of the plaintiff's settlement offer and resulted in a binding contract. D'Agostino denies that any binding agreement occurred on February 6 or at any other time during the course of the parties' communications. According to D'Agostino . . . the Release was a counteroffer rather than an acceptance because it contained significant additional terms beyond those set forth in D'Agostino's proposal. . . . For the reasons that follow, this court finds . . . that Federal's response to the offer was timely. However, because this court also finds the response was a counteroffer, which was never accepted in full by the plaintiff, this court concludes that there is no enforceable settlement agreement.

Nature of Federal's Response

D'Agostino . . . argues that to the extent there was an offer, there was no agreement by the parties because Federal never accepted the offer. Instead, according to D'Agostino, Federal's transmittal of a Release containing different terms constituted a counteroffer and thereby terminated the defendant's power to accept the original offer. This court agrees that the defendant's decision to send a Release containing additional material terms rendered its response a counteroffer, which could only become binding upon the plaintiff's acceptance. It is undisputed that on February 6, 2013, Federal replied to D'Agostino's settlement offer by sending her a seven-page Release, along with an e-mail requesting that the plaintiff "execute the release as soon as possible[.]" Although the Release was consistent with the plaintiff's offer to the extent it provided for a $1.15 million payment to D'Agostino and the release of the plaintiff's claims against Federal, it contained numerous additional terms beyond those set forth in the plaintiff's settlement offer. "A reply to an offer which purports to accept it but is conditional on the offeror's assent to terms additional to or different from those offered is not an acceptance but is a counter-offer." *Restatement (Second) of Contracts* § 59 (1981). By asking D'Agostino to sign a document that was conditional upon D'Agostino's assent to numerous additional terms, Federal rejected the plaintiff's offer and created a counteroffer.

Federal acknowledges that the Release contained various additional terms. Nevertheless, it argues that the Release constituted an acceptance because it expressed Federal's agreement on the only two material terms that had been articulated by the plaintiff, and all other matters were merely subsidiary. This argument is not persuasive. Where the parties have reached agreement on all material matters, the existence of unresolved subsidiary matters will not preclude enforcement of the contract. Here, however, the Release contained certain additional terms that were essential to a settlement and could not be characterized as "subsidiary." Therefore, Federal's response to D'Agostino's offer did not create a binding agreement.

[T]he Release was not limited to standard, boilerplate provisions. It also contained provisions which had not been included in the original offer, and which sought to impose significant obligations upon the plaintiff. For example, the Release contained a lengthy confidentiality provision that imposed strict requirements on the plaintiff, including an obligation to forfeit the entire amount of the $1.15 [million] settlement payment if she were to violate its terms, even absent evidence of any harm to the defendant. Moreover, as set forth in the Release, the plaintiff's "representations and promises of strict confidentiality . . . go to the essence

of and form a valuable part of the consideration for [Federal] to make the Settlement Payment and enter into this Agreement[.]" Accordingly, the express language of the document demonstrates that the confidentiality provision was an "essential and inducing feature of the contract" and was therefore material to a settlement agreement.

This court also finds that Federal's inclusion of an indemnity provision introduced a material term which rendered the Release a counteroffer. . . . [T]he indemnity provision would have required D'Agostino to indemnify Federal against claims relating to the December 9, 2008, fire at the Property. Therefore, as the plaintiff argues, "[i]f the Bank were to make a claim against [Federal] as a result of plaintiff's claims against the Bank, under the Draft Release [Federal] would be entitled to indemnification from plaintiff." However, Attorney Goren had made it clear at the time he conveyed the plaintiff's settlement offer on January 17, 2013, that D'Agostino was unwilling to enter into an agreement which would require her to indemnify Federal for any claims which Bank of America might assert against [Federal] or any obligations that Federal might have to the Bank. He reiterated this position following his receipt of the Release, in a letter to Federal's counsel dated February 22, 2013. As Attorney Goren wrote in his letter, "[i]n previous communications I believe I made clear, and I repeat herein, there will be no separate settlement with [Federal] pursuant to which Ms. D'Agostino will hold [Federal] harmless from any claims or liabilities from third parties." Thus, the proposed Release varied materially from D'Agostino's original offer, thereby making it a counteroffer.

To the extent Federal now contends that it did not consider these matters essential to a settlement with the plaintiff and would have been willing to dispense with them in order to reach an agreement, its argument is insufficient to support enforcement of a settlement agreement. . . . If Federal actually believed at the time it sent the Release that the additional terms contained therein were immaterial, it could have conveyed that information to the plaintiff or simply accepted the offer on the terms set forth in Attorney Goren's January 17, 2013, e-mail correspondence. Instead, Federal sent the Release to D'Agostino's counsel and asked that the plaintiff "execute the release as soon as possible[.]" Because the Release contained material matters beyond those addressed in D'Agostino's offer, Federal effectively rejected the offer and terminated its power to accept it.

CONCLUSION

For . . . the reasons described herein, this court recommends to the District Judge to whom this case is assigned that "Defendant Federal Insurance Company's Emergency Motion to Enforce Settlement Agreement" be **DENIED**.

Time of Effectiveness of Rejections As a general rule, rejections, like revocations, are effective only when actually received by the offeror. Therefore, an offeree who has mailed a rejection could still change her mind and accept if she communicates the acceptance before the offeror receives the rejection.[6]

Death or Mental Incapacity of Either Party
If either party to an offer dies or becomes mentally incapacitated (sometimes referred to in cases and other texts as being "insane"), the offer is automatically terminated without notice. Agreement between the parties is clearly impossible when one of them is dead or no longer has the mental capacity to contract.[7]

Destruction of Subject Matter
If, prior to acceptance of an offer, the subject matter of a proposed contract is destroyed without the knowledge or fault of either party, the offer is terminated.[8] So, if Marks offers to sell Wiggins his lakeside cottage and the cottage is destroyed by fire before Wiggins accepts, the offer was terminated on the destruction of the cottage. Subsequent acceptance by Wiggins would not create a contract.

Intervening Illegality
An offer is terminated if the performance of the contract it proposes becomes *illegal* before the offer is accepted. So, if a computer manufacturer offered to sell sophisticated computer equipment to another country, but two days later, before the offer was accepted, Congress placed an embargo on all sales to this country, the offer was terminated by the embargo.[9]

---

[6]Chapter 11 discusses this subject in detail.

[7]Even after the formation of a contract, a party who is obligated by it to perform personal services can be excused from that performance based on death or mental incapacity. Chapter 18 discusses this in more detail.

[8]In some circumstances, destruction of subject matter can also serve as a legal excuse for a party's failure to perform obligations under an existing contract. Chapter 18 discusses this subject.

[9]In some circumstances, intervening illegality can also serve as a legal excuse for a party's failure to perform obligations under an existing contract. Chapter 18 discusses this subject.

Problems and Problem Cases

1. Armstrong and Pottle worked as ceramic grinders at Morton International's Spencer facility. When the Rohm & Haas Co. (R&H) acquired Morton, it gave employees a month to decide whether to quit and receive a severance payment or transfer to another facility and receive a larger incentive payment. Armstrong and Pottle wanted to keep their jobs, but the plant manager told them that they would make more money if they would resign and start their own business handling R&H's outsourced grinding work. He stated that R&H would give Armstrong and Pottle's new business all the outsourced work they could handle and that the company would like to give them all its outsourced work. Armstrong and Pottle followed this advice, and their business failed. In addition, R&H continued giving outsourced work to another firm. Armstrong and Pottle asserted the formation of an oral contract and claimed that R&H breached it. Were they correct?

2. Frank Meram attended a presentation by Robert MacDonald, who was promoting his new book, *Cheat to Win*. MacDonald was a multimillionaire who had started as an insurance agent and built his company, LifeUSA, to a worth of more than a billion dollars at the time of the presentation. Meram attended along with approximately 100 other people. At the beginning of the presentation, MacDonald announced that one of the attendees would leave that day with $1 million. All that was required was to place a business card in the basket that he passed around and to stay until the end of the presentation. MacDonald pulled Meram's business card from the basket. He congratulated Meram and then explained "how this works." MacDonald said Meram would receive one dollar per year for a million years. He gave Meram $100 in cash for the first 100 years. According to MacDonald, all Meram had to do was attend a presentation once a year to claim the rest of the million dollars. MacDonald laughed and thanked everyone for coming. Meram, on the other hand, filed suit against MacDonald and his company's parent, Allianz Sales, seeking the remainder of the promised $1 million. Did MacDonald make a valid offer that Meram accepted by placing his business card in the basket and staying until the end of the presentation?

3. Rodziewicz was driving a 1999 Volvo conventional tractor-trailer on I-90 in Lake County, Indiana, when he struck a concrete barrier. His truck was stuck on top of the barrier, and the state police contacted Waffco Heavy Duty Towing to help in the recovery. Before Waffco began working, Rodziewicz asked how much it would cost to tow the truck. He was told that the fee would be $275, and there was no discussion of labor or other costs. Rodziewicz instructed Waffco to take his truck to a Volvo dealership. After a few minutes of work, Waffco pulled Rodziewicz's truck off the barrier and towed the truck to its towing yard a few miles away.

Subsequently, Waffco notified Rodziewicz that, in addition to the $275 towing fee, he would have to pay $4,070 in labor costs. Waffco calculated its labor charges as $.11 cents per pound. Waffco would not release the truck until payment was made, so Rodziewicz paid the total amount. Was Rodziewicz contractually obligated to pay Waffco the $4,070 labor fee?

4. Comedian Bill Maher appeared on the January 7, 2013, episode of *The Tonight Show with Jay Leno*. In an interview largely focused on poking fun at politicians, Maher turned his attention to then-real-estate-mogul and reality-television-star Donald Trump, who had recently offered to pay $5 million to the charity of President Barak Obama's choice, if Obama released his college and passport records and applications. Maher began by noting that an orangutan's hair was the only thing in nature that matched the color of Trump's hair. Maher further stated that he would donate $5 million to Trump, which Trump would then donate to a charity of his choice, if Trump would provide evidence that he was not "the spawn of his mother having sex with an orangutan." Maher suggested Trump might choose the "Hair Club for Men" or the "Institute for Incorrigible Douchebaggery" as his charities. On January 8, Scott Balber, one of Trump's attorneys, sent a letter to Maher, which stated, "I write on [Donald Trump's] behalf to accept your offer (made during the Jay Leno Show on January 7, 2013) that Mr. Trump prove he is not 'the spawn of his mother having sex with an orangutan.'" Balber enclosed with the letter a copy of Trump's birth certificate, indicating that it showed Trump's father to be "Fred Trump, not an orangutan" and demanding that Maher "remit $5 million to Mr. Trump immediately." The letter indicated that Trump would allocate the money in equal shares to four charities. When Maher ignored the letter and a subsequent demand, Trump's attorneys filed a lawsuit against Maher for breach of contract. Was Maher's statement on *The Tonight Show* an offer that created a contractual obligation once Trump accepted by providing evidence of his actual, non-orangutan parentage?

5. Leonard saw a "Pepsi Stuff" commercial encouraging consumers to collect "Pepsi Points" from specially marked packages of Pepsi or Diet Pepsi and redeem these points for merchandise featuring the Pepsi logo. The commercial depicts a teenager preparing to leave for school, dressed in a shirt emblazoned with the Pepsi logo. The drumroll sounds as the subtitle "T-SHIRT 75 PEPSI POINTS" scrolled across the screen. The teenager strides down the hallway wearing a leather jacket, and the subtitle "LEATHER JACKET 1450 PEPSI POINTS" appears. The teenager opens the door of his house and puts on a pair of sunglasses. The drum roll then accompanies the subtitle "SHADES 175 PEPSI POINTS." A voiceover then intones, "Introducing the new Pepsi Stuff catalog." The scene then shifts to three young boys sitting in front of a high school building. The boy in the middle is intent on his Pepsi Stuff catalog, while the boys on either side are drinking Pepsi. The three boys gaze in awe at an object approaching overhead. The military music swelled, and the viewer senses the presence of a mighty plane as the extreme winds generated by its flight create a paper maelstrom in a classroom devoted to an otherwise dull physics lesson. Finally, a Harrier jet swings into view and lands by the side of the school building, next to a bicycle rack. Several students run for cover, and the velocity of the wind strips one faculty member down to his underwear. The voiceover announces, "Now the more Pepsi you drink, the more great stuff you're gonna get." The teenager opens the cockpit of the fighter and can be seen, holding a Pepsi. "Sure beats the bus," he says. The military drum roll swells a final time and the following words appear: "HARRIER FIGHTER 7,000,000 PEPSI POINTS." Inspired by the commercial, Leonard set out to get a Harrier jet. He consulted the Pepsi Stuff catalog, but it did not contain any entry or description of the Harrier jet. The amount of Pepsi Points necessary to get the listed merchandise ranged from 15 for a "jacket tattoo" to 3,300 for a mountain bike. The rear foldout pages of the catalog contained directions for redeeming Pepsi Points for merchandise. These directions note that merchandise may be ordered "only" with the original Order Form. The catalog notes that in the event that a consumer lacks enough Pepsi Points to obtain a desired item, additional Pepsi Points may be purchased for 10 cents each; however, at least 15 original Pepsi Points must accompany each order. Leonard initially set out to collect 7,000,000 Pepsi Points by consuming Pepsi products, but then switched to buying Pepsi Points. Leonard ultimately raised about $700,000. In March 1996, Leonard submitted an Order Form, 15 original Pepsi Points, and a check for $700,008.50. At the bottom of the Order Form, Leonard wrote in "1 Harrier Jet" in the "Item" column and "7,000,000" in the "Total Points" column. In a letter accompanying his submission, he stated that the check was to purchase additional Pepsi Points for obtaining a new Harrier jet as advertised in the Pepsi Stuff commercial. Several months later, Pepsico's fulfillment house rejected Leonard's submission and returned the check, explaining that the item he requested was not part of the Pepsi Stuff collection, and only catalog merchandise could be redeemed under this program. It also stated, "The Harrier jet in the Pepsi commercial is fanciful and is simply included to create a humorous and entertaining ad." Leonard sued Pepsico for breach of contract. Will he win?

6. Pernal owned a parcel of real estate adjacent to property owned by St. Nicholas Greek Orthodox Church. Pernal sent a letter to the church indicating that he was offering it for sale for "$825,000 cash/mortgage, 'as is,' with no conditions, no contingencies related to zoning and 120 days post closing occupancy for the present tenants." This offer was dated June 3, 2003, and expressly provided that it would remain open for a two-week period. On the same day, Pernal also sent the same offer to sell the property on the same terms to another prospective purchaser, White Chapel Memorial Association Park Perpetual Care Trust. On June 4, the church sent a letter indicating that it accepted the terms of the offer that Pernal had set forth in his letter. However, the church's letter also referenced an attached purchase agreement. The purchase agreement agreed with Pernal's purchase price and the close occupancy period, but contrary to the offer, it contained additional terms. The church's president signed this attached purchase agreement, but defendant did not sign it. The offer by letter dated June 3, 2003, did not reference other potential purchasers. On June 10, White Chapel, by letter, offered to pay $900,000 cash for the property, with no conditions or contingencies related to zoning and 180 days post closing occupancy rent free. On that same date (June 10), Pernal sent a letter to both potential purchasers. This letter indicated that "amended offers" had been received. The letter further provided that the offer would remain open for two weeks' time as provided in the initial offering letter. On June 13, the church sent a letter to Pernal, stating that the offer had been accepted on June 4, and that an enforceable contract was formed. The church sued Pernal for breach of contract. Will it win?

7. Michael Freeman and Cindy Hazen listed an auction on eBay for their historic home, which was once owned by Elvis Presley. A partnership formed to participate in the auction for the home and used partner Peter Gleason's eBay account to do so. eBay's terms and conditions state, "eBay Real Estate's auctions-style advertisements of real property do not involve legally binding offers to buy and sell. Instead, eBay Real Estate's auctions are simply a way for sellers to advertise their real estate and meet potential buyers." The sellers' real estate broker, however, contradicted that language on the home's eBay auction site, stating the following: "Please note that bidding on eBay is a legally binding contract in which the winner commits to following through on the purchase." The broker included that language to deter frivolous bids. During the bidding process, Mike Curb offered to buy the house immediately and stop the auction; however, he was not willing to meet the sellers' $1.3 million ask. So, the auction continued. When the bidding officially ended, an eBay automated message informed the Gleason partnership that they had submitted the winning bid of just over $900,000. Two days later, the partnership's real estate agent sent the sellers a "proposed sale contract," about which they had further discussion. A few days later, Curb renewed his offer to purchase the house, this time for $1 million. The sellers and Curb signed a contract for the sale of the house later that week and refused to sell to the Gleason partnership. The partnership sued for breach of contract arguing that the language the sellers' broker appended to the listing overrode the eBay terms and conditions and created a binding contract upon their bid being declared a winner. Are the Gleason partners correct?

8. Family Video made a written offer to buy out Home Folks' lease because it wanted to purchase and open a video store on the property on which Home Folks operated a restaurant. Over four months went by and Home Folks' operators did not sign the offer. The property was destroyed by fire and then Home Folks signed the offer and attempted to accept. Did Home Folks and Family Video have an enforceable contract?

9. Cynthia Hines purchased a vacuum cleaner online from Overstock.com, believing that she was buying an unused product. When the vacuum cleaner was delivered, however, Hines discovered that it was not new but rather had been "refurbished." Hines returned the vacuum, and Overstock credited her with the purchase price less a $30 "restocking fee." Hines brought suit against Overstock on behalf of a class of customers who had been charged such fees. Overstock moved to dismiss the case or stay the action in favor of arbitration, arguing that the "Terms and Conditions" of its website contained an arbitration clause, and therefore, the parties had an agreement to arbitrate the dispute. Overstock presented no evidence, however, that Hines had actually had the opportunity to see or read the Terms and Conditions prior to allegedly "accepting" them simply by using the website. Should the parties be forced to arbitrate?

10. Jeff visited a car dealership and test-drove a used car. After discussing the price with the salesman, Jake, and learning that he could purchase the car for $500 less than the sticker price, Jeff asked Jake to hold the car for him until 8:00 that evening so that he could bring his wife back to see the car. Jake agreed, writing out a note promising not to sell the car before 8:00 P.M. The note was written on dealership stationery, but Jake did not sign his name. The dealership broke its promise and sold the car to Jones before 8:00 P.M. Was it free to revoke its offer to Jeff? Jones, the new purchaser of the car (and a nonmerchant), later offered in a signed writing to sell the car to Jill and to hold the car for her until she returned with her husband. Could Jones revoke this offer?

The Agreement: Acceptance

First Texas Savings Association promoted a "$5,000 Scoreboard Challenge" contest. Contestants who completed an entry form and deposited it with First Texas were eligible for a random drawing. The winner was to receive an $80 savings account with First Texas, plus four tickets to a Dallas Mavericks home basketball game chosen by First Texas. If the Mavericks held their opponent in the chosen game to 89 or fewer points, the winner was to receive an additional $5,000 money market certificate. In October 1982, Jergins deposited a completed entry form with First Texas. On November 1, 1982, First Texas tried to amend the contest rules by posting a notice at its branches that the Mavericks would have to hold their opponent to *85* or fewer points before the contest winner would receive the $5,000. In late December, Jergins was notified that she had won the $80 savings account and tickets to the January 22, 1983, game against the Utah Jazz. The notice contained the revised contest terms. The Mavericks held the Jazz to 88 points at that game.

- Did Jergins accept First Texas's offer?
- If so, when was the acceptance effective?
- Did First Texas have the right to revoke its original offer?
- Does Jergins have the right to collect the $5,000 money market certificate?

LO LEARNING OBJECTIVES

After studying this chapter, you should be able to:

11-1 Explain the elements of an acceptance under both common law and the Uniform Commercial Code (UCC).

11-2 Determine how acceptance can be communicated in a given scenario and analyze the time at which acceptance is likely to be effective.

11-3 Identify the circumstances under which silence is acceptance.

11-4 Determine whether an oral acceptance is effective in a situation in which the parties anticipate putting their contract in writing.

CHAPTER 10 DISCUSSED the circumstances under which a proposal will constitute the first stage of an agreement: the offer. This chapter focuses on the final stage of forming an agreement: the acceptance. The acceptance is vitally important because it is with the acceptance that the contract is formed. This chapter discusses the requirements for making a valid acceptance as well as the rules concerning the time at which a contract comes into being.

What Is an Acceptance?

 LO11-1 Explain the elements of an acceptance under both common law and the UCC.

An **acceptance** is "a manifestation of assent to the terms [of the offer] made by the offeree in the manner invited or required by the offer."[1] In determining if an offeree accepted an

---
[1]*Restatement (Second) of Contracts* § 50(1) (1981).

offer and created a contract, a court will look for evidence of three factors: (1) the offeree intended to enter the contract, (2) the offeree accepted on the terms proposed by the offeror, and (3) the offeree communicated acceptance to the offeror.

Intention to Accept In determining whether an offeree accepted an offer, the court is looking for the same *present intent to contract* on the part of the offeree that it found on the part of the offeror. And, as is true of intent to make an offer, intent to accept is judged by an objective standard. The difference is that the offeree must objectively indicate a present intent to contract on the terms of the

offer for a contract to result. As the master of the offer, the offeror may specify in detail what behavior is required of the offeree to bind the offeree to a contract. If the offeror does so, the offeree must ordinarily comply with all the terms of the offer before a contract results.

Intent to accept is objectively demonstrated by words or conduct or a combination of the two. The following *Long* case illustrates how these longstanding, general rules endure even in the face of changes wrought by the increasing incidence of commerce on the Internet. Note how an Internet user's assent to contract terms is determined by an objective standard.

Long v. Provide Commerce, Inc.   245 Cal. App. 4th 855 (2016)

Provide Commerce, Inc. (Provide) is an online retailer that operates several websites, including ProFlowers.com, through which it advertises and sells a variety of floral products. Brett Long purchased a floral arrangement on ProFlowers.com, which he claimed had been depicted on the website as an assembled bouquet, but which arrived as a "do-it-yourself kit" requiring assembly by the buyer.

Long sued Provide on behalf of himself and a class of California consumers who purchased similarly depicted floral arrangements on ProFlowers.com. Long relied on a claim pursuant to California's Consumers Legal Remedies Act and Unfair Competition Law.

Provide filed a motion in that case requesting the court to compel arbitration, arguing that Long was bound by the Terms of Use for ProFlowers.com, which included a dispute resolution provision requiring mandatory arbitration of any disputes. According to a series of screenshots of the ProFlowers.com site, which Provide submitted as evidence along with the motion to compel arbitration, the Terms of Use were accessible via a capitalized and underlined hyperlink titled "TERMS OF USE" located at the bottom of each page on the ProFlowers.com site. Each page was lime green in color and the hyperlinked typeface was light green in color. The hyperlink for the Terms of Use was situated alongside 14 other capitalized and underlined hyperlinks of the same color, font, and size. Provide's evidence also showed that, to complete his order, Plaintiff was required to input information and click through a multipage "checkout flow." The checkout flow screenshots showed the customer information fields and click-through buttons displayed in a bright white box set against the website's lime green background. At the bottom of the white box was a notice indicating "Your order is safe and secure," displayed next to a "VeriSign Secured" logo. Below the white box was a dark green bar with a hyperlink titled "SITE FEEDBACK" displayed in light green typeface. Finally, below the dark green bar, at the bottom of each checkout flow page, were two hyperlinks titled "PRIVACY POLICY" and "TERMS OF USE," displayed in the same light green typeface on the site's lime green background.

Following Long's purchase, he also received a confirmatory e-mail message. That message also included a link to the Terms of Use, along with a litany of other links. The link for the Terms of Use was near the bottom of the message and was in the same gray typeface as pro forma information about customer service contact information and Provide's corporate address.

Long objected to Provide's motion to compel arbitration because he "did not notice a reference of any kind to ProFlowers 'Terms and Conditions' nor a hyperlink to ProFlowers 'Terms of Use" when he purchased the flowers. Thus, he argued he could not have assented to the Terms of Use and could not be bound by them.

The trial court agreed with Long, concluding the hyperlinks were too inconspicuous to put a reasonably prudent consumer on notice. Provide appealed.

Jones, Judge

DISCUSSION

A. *Legal Principles; Arbitration and Browsewrap Agreements*

"Under 'both federal and state law, the threshold question presented by a petition to compel arbitration is whether there is an agreement to arbitrate.'" *Cruise v. Kroger Co.*, 233 Cal. App. 4th 390,

396 (Cal. Ct. App. 2015). . . . As our Supreme Court has observed, "[t]here is indeed a strong policy in favor of enforcing agreements to arbitrate, but there is no policy compelling persons to accept arbitration of controversies which they have not agreed to arbitrate." *Freeman v. State Farm Mut. Auto. Ins. Co.*, 535 P.2d 341 (Cal. Sup. Ct. 1975).

This requirement applies with equal force to arbitration provisions contained in contracts purportedly formed over the Internet. While Internet commerce has exposed courts to many new situations, it has not fundamentally changed the requirement that "[m]utual manifestation of assent, whether by written or spoken word or by conduct, is the touchstone of contract." *Nguyen v. Barnes & Noble Inc.*, 763 F.3d 1171, 1175 (9th Cir. 2014). Mutual assent is determined under an objective standard applied to the outward manifestations or expressions of the parties, i.e., the reasonable meaning of their words and acts, and not their unexpressed intentions or understandings. In applying this objective standard, outward manifestations of a party's supposed assent are to be judged with due regard for the context in which they arise. California law is clear—"an offeree, regardless of apparent manifestation of his consent, is not bound by inconspicuous contractual provisions of which he was unaware, contained in a document whose contractual nature is not obvious." *Windsor Mills, Inc. v. Collins & Aikman Corp.*, 25 Cal. App. 3d 987, 993 (Cal. Ct. App. 1972).

"Contracts formed on the Internet come primarily in two flavors: 'clickwrap' (or 'click-through') agreements, in which Web site users are required to click on an 'I agree' box after being presented with a list of terms and conditions of use; and 'browsewrap' agreements, where a Web site's terms and conditions of use are generally posted on the Web site via a hyperlink at the bottom of the screen." *Nguyen, supra*, 763 F.3d at 1175–1176. The parties agree that the subject Terms of Use for the ProFlowers.com Web site falls into the browsewrap category.

Unlike a clickwrap agreement, a browsewrap agreement does not require the user to manifest assent to the terms and conditions expressly . . . [a] party instead gives his assent simply by using the Web site. Indeed, "in a pure-form browsewrap agreement, the Web site will contain a notice that—by merely using the services of, obtaining information from, or initiating applications within the Web site—the user is agreeing to and is bound by the site's terms of service." Thus, by visiting the Web site—something that the user has already done—the user agrees to the Terms of Use not listed on the site itself but available only by clicking a hyperlink. The defining feature of browsewrap agreements is that the user can continue to use the Web site or its services without visiting the page hosting the browsewrap agreement or even knowing that such a Web page exists. Because no affirmative action is required by the Web site user to agree to the terms of a contract other than his or her use of the Web site, the determination of the validity of the browsewrap contract depends on whether the user has actual or constructive knowledge of a Web site's terms and conditions. *Nguyen, supra*, 763 F.3d at 1176 (internal citations and quotes omitted). More to the point here, absent actual notice, "the validity of [a] browsewrap agreement turns on whether the Web site puts a reasonably prudent user on inquiry notice of the terms of the contract." *Id.* at p. 1177.

With these foundational legal principles in place, we turn our focus to the specifics of the browsewrap agreement in the instant case, and whether the design of Provide's Web site and order confirmation e-mail were sufficient to conclude [Long] agreed to be bound by the Terms of Use and arbitration provision contained therein simply by placing his order on ProFlowers.com.

B. *The "Terms of Use" Hyperlinks Are Not Sufficiently Conspicuous to Put a Reasonably Prudent Internet Consumer on Inquiry Notice; Plaintiff Did Not Manifest His Unambiguous Assent to Be Bound by the Terms of Use*

Provide does not dispute Plaintiff's testimony that he had no actual knowledge of the Terms of Use when he placed his order on ProFlowers.com. Accordingly, we must decide whether the design of the ProFlowers.com Web site and/or the conspicuousness of the hyperlinks to the Terms of Use were sufficient to put a reasonably prudent Internet consumer on inquiry notice of the browsewrap agreement's existence and contents.

It appears that no California appellate court has yet addressed what sort of Web site design elements would be necessary or sufficient to deem a browsewrap agreement valid in the absence of actual notice. Accordingly, in addition to the general contract principles discussed above, our analysis is largely guided by two federal cases from the Second and Ninth Circuit Courts of Appeals, each of which considered the enforceability of a browsewrap agreement applying the objective manifestation of assent analysis dictated by California law. *See Specht v. Netscape Communs. Corp.*, 306 F.3d 17, 30 fn. 13 (2d Cir. 2002); *Nguyen*, 763 F.3d at p. 1175. In keeping with the principles articulated in these authorities, we conclude the design of the ProFlowers.com Web site, even when coupled with the hyperlink contained in the confirmation e-mail, was insufficient to put Plaintiff on inquiry notice of the subject Terms of Use.

In *Specht*, the Second Circuit declined to enforce an arbitration provision contained in a software licensing browsewrap agreement where the hyperlink to the agreement appeared on "a submerged screen" below the Download button that the plaintiffs clicked to initiate the software download. After reviewing California contract law, the *Specht* court acknowledged that a user's act of clicking a download button, combined with circumstances sufficient to put a prudent man upon inquiry as to the existence of licensing terms, would constitute a sufficient manifestation of assent to be bound. However, the court was quick to point out that the opposite must also be true—that "a consumer's clicking on a download button does not communicate assent to contractual terms if the offer did not make clear to the consumer that clicking on the download button would signify assent to those terms." *Specht*, 306 F.3d at 29–30. The design of the defendant's Web site, the *Specht* court concluded, exemplified the latter circumstance.

Though the Web site advised users to "Please review and agree to the terms of the . . . software license agreement before downloading and using the software," the *Specht* court emphasized that users would have encountered this advisement only if they scrolled down to the screen below the Web site's invitation to download the software by clicking the download button. This meant that when the plaintiffs clicked the download button, they "were responding to an offer that did not carry an immediately visible notice of the existence of license terms or require unambiguous manifestation of assent to those terms." *Specht*, 306 F.3d at 31. The fact that users might have noticed from the position of the scroll bar that an unexplored portion of the Web page remained below the download button did not change the reasonableness calculation. Under the circumstances presented, "where consumers [were] urged to download free software at the immediate click of a button," the *Specht* court concluded placing the notice of licensing terms on a submerged page "tended to conceal the fact that [downloading the software] was an express acceptance of [the defendant's] rules and regulations." *Id.* at p. 32. Thus, notwithstanding what the plaintiffs might have found had they taken as much time as they needed to scroll through multiple screens on a Web page, the *Specht* court held that "a reasonably prudent offeree in plaintiffs' position would not have known or learned . . . of the reference to [the software's] license terms hidden below the 'Download' button on the next screen." *Id.* at p. 35.

More than a decade after the Second Circuit decided *Specht*, the Ninth Circuit in *Nguyen* considered whether the conspicuous placement of a "Terms of Use" hyperlink, standing alone, would be sufficient to put an Internet consumer on inquiry notice. Unlike in *Specht*, the hyperlink in *Nguyen* was visible "without scrolling" on some of the Web site's pages, while on others "the hyperlink [was] close enough to the 'Proceed with Checkout' button that a user would have to bring the link within his field of vision" to complete an online order. *Nguyen, supra,* 763 F.3d at 1178. These differences with *Specht* notwithstanding, the *Nguyen* court concluded the plaintiff's act of placing an order did not constitute an unambiguous manifestation of assent to be bound by the browsewrap agreement, holding "proximity or conspicuousness of the hyperlink alone is not enough to give rise to constructive notice" *Id.* The court reasoned that *Specht* had only identified a circumstance that was *not sufficient* to impart inquiry notice—where the only reference to license terms appeared on a submerged screen. But in cases where courts had "relied on the proximity of the hyperlink *to enforce* a browsewrap agreement," the *Nguyen* court explained, those Web sites had "also included something more to capture the user's attention and secure her assent." *Id.* at 1178, fn. 1 (emphasis added). Typically that "something more" had taken the form of an explicit textual notice warning users to "Review terms" or admonishing users that by clicking a button to complete the transaction "you agree to the terms and conditions in the agreement." *Id.* From those cases, the *Nguyen* court derived the following bright line rule for determining the validity of browsewrap agreements: "[W]here a Web site makes its terms of use available via a conspicuous hyperlink on every page of the Web site but otherwise provides no notice to users nor prompts them to take any affirmative action to demonstrate assent, even close proximity of the hyperlink to relevant buttons users must click on—without more—is insufficient to give rise to constructive notice." *Id.* at 1178-1179.

Provide argues we should disregard *Nguyen* as an outlier case, and follow *Specht* to the extent it suggests a conspicuous hyperlink that provides "immediately visible notice" of a browsewrap agreement is sufficient, standing alone, to put a reasonably prudent Internet consumer on inquiry notice of the agreement's terms. . . . Provide argues the Terms of Use hyperlink on ProFlowers.com "is immediately visible on the checkout flow, is viewable without scrolling, and located next to several fields that the Web site user is required to fill out and the buttons he must click to complete an order." Given this distinction, Provide argues the hyperlink was sufficiently conspicuous to "put a reasonable user on notice of the Terms of Use." We disagree.

Though it may be that an especially observant Internet consumer could spot the Terms of Use hyperlinks on some checkout flow pages without scrolling, that quality alone cannot be all that is required to establish the existence of an enforceable browsewrap agreement. Rather, as the *Specht* court observed, "[r]easonably conspicuous notice of the existence of contract terms and unambiguous manifestation of assent to those terms by consumers are essential if electronic bargaining is to have integrity and credibility." *Specht*, 306 F.3d at 35. Here, the Terms of Use hyperlinks—their placement, color, size and other qualities relative to the ProFlowers.com Web site's overall design—are simply too inconspicuous to meet that standard.

Indeed, our review of the screenshots reveals how difficult it is to find the Terms of Use hyperlinks in the checkout flow *even when one is looking for them.* This of course is to say nothing of how observant an Internet consumer must be to discover the hyperlinks in the usual circumstance of using ProFlowers.com *to purchase flowers*, without any forewarning that he or she should also be on the lookout for a reference to "Terms of Use" somewhere on the Web site's various pages. Contrary to Provide's characterization, the subject hyperlinks in the checkout flow are not "located next to" the fields and buttons a consumer must interact with to complete his order. Those fields and buttons are contained in a separate bright white box in the center of the page that contrasts sharply with the Web site's lime green background. To find a Terms of Use hyperlink in the checkout flow, a consumer placing an order must (1) remove attention from the fields in which he or she is asked to enter his information; (2) look below the buttons he must click to proceed with the order; (3) look even further below a "VeriSign Secured" logo and notification advising that his or her **order is safe and secure,** which itself includes a hyperlink to ***Click here*** for more details; (4) look still further below a thick dark green bar with a hyperlink for "SITE FEEDBACK"; and (5) finally find the "*TERMS OF USE*" hyperlink situated to the right of another hyperlink for the Web site's "*PRIVACY POLICY*," both of which appear in the same font and light green typeface that, to the unwary flower purchaser, could blend in with the Web site's lime green background. True, on a handful of these pages no scrolling is required to complete the hunt. But that, in our assessment, does not change the practical reality that the checkout flow is laid out "in such a manner that it tended to conceal the fact that [placing an order] was an express acceptance of [Provide's] rules and regulations." *Specht*, 306 F.3d at 32.

As for Provide's contention that the subsequent order confirmation e-mail somehow provides the notice that was missing from the checkout flow, again, we disagree. Unlike the hyperlink on some checkout flow pages, the screenshots suggest the hyperlink

in the e-mail is located on a submerged page, requiring the customer to scroll below layers of order summary details, advertisement banners, hyperlinks to "convenient account management services," several logos for Provide's "Family of Brands," and customer service contact information to finally find a reference to "*Terms*" printed in grey typeface on a white background. This is not the sort of conspicuous alert that can be expected to put a reasonably prudent Internet consumer on notice to investigate whether disputes related to his or her order will be subject to binding arbitration.

* * *

DISPOSITION

The order is affirmed.

Intent and Acceptance on the Offeror's Terms

Common Law: Traditional "Mirror Image" Rule The traditional contract law rule is that an acceptance must be the *mirror image* of the offer. Attempts by offerees to change the terms of the offer or to add new terms to it are treated as counteroffers because they impliedly indicate an intent by the offeree to reject the offer instead of being bound by its terms. However, recent years have witnessed a judicial tendency to apply the mirror image rule in a more liberal fashion by holding that only *material* (important) variances between an offer and a purported acceptance result in an implied rejection of the offer.

Even under the mirror image rule, no rejection is implied if an offeree merely asks about the terms of the offer without indicating its rejection (an *inquiry regarding terms*), or accepts the offer's terms while complaining about them (a *grumbling acceptance*). Distinguishing among a counteroffer, an inquiry regarding terms, and a grumbling acceptance is often a difficult task. The fundamental issue, however, remains the same: Did the offeree objectively indicate a present intent to be bound by the terms of the offer? You will see an application of the traditional mirror image rule in the following *Pena* case.

Pena v. Fox	198 So. 3d 61 (Fla. Ct. App. 2015)

Diana Pena and Matthew Fox were in an automobile accident on July 4, 2013. Pena allegedly suffered injuries as a result. Pena's attorney worked with Fox's insurance company, USAA Casualty Insurance, toward settling her claims against Fox. Pena's attorney delivered to USAA a settlement offer, the terms of which included money up to Fox's USAA policy limits. In return, Pena agreed to release all claims against Fox relating to the accident. The settlement offer also contemplated that USAA would provide a proposed release form for Pena to sign. Pena's attorney, however, explained that certain conditions applied as to the type of release that would be acceptable to Pena. In the offer letter, Pena's attorney described those conditions as follows:

If USAA provides us all the information and funds requested above my [client] will sign a general release releasing all claims. . . . [M]y clients will sign a general release releasing all claims of my clients only. My clients will not accept, nor will they sign, a release containing a hold harmless nor an indemnity agreement, *nor will my client release any claim other than your insured's claim*; nor will my client release anyone's claim other than my client's claims. Therefore, *any attempt to provide a release* which contains a hold harmless or indemnity agreement, *which releases anyone other than your insured*, or which releases any claim other than my client's claim *will act as a rejection of this good faith offer*.

(emphasis added).

After receiving the offer letter from Pena's attorney, USAA responded with a settlement check along with a proposed release. The release included an introductory paragraph stating that, by signing, Pena would acknowledge the settlement funds and would "release, acquit, and forever discharge Matthew R. Fox, his/her heirs, executors and assigns, from any liability." In addition, the release included the following term:

> I/We further state that while I/we hereby release all claims against Releasee(s), its agents, and employees, the payment hereunder does not satisfy all of my/our damages resulting from the accident. . . . I/We further reserve my/our right to pursue and recover all unpaid damages from any person, firm, or organization who may be responsible for payment of such damages, including first party health and automobile insurance coverage, but such reservation does not include the Releasee(s), its agents, and employees. . . .

Pena considered the release to be a rejection of her offer, because she considered the language "Releasee(s), its agents, and employees" an attempt to expand the release to include USAA. Thus, she filed a lawsuit against Fox.

Fox responded to Pena's suit by filing a Motion to Enforce Settlement on the theory that the settlement agreement was complete and barred the suit. The trial court agreed with Fox, finding that Pena's claim against him had been settled. The court held that the language in question related only to Fox and that the rest of the release's language was clear. Finally, it held that there was no "nefarious inclusion" of USAA in the release. As a result, the court dismissed Pena's complaint.

Pena appealed.

Lucas, Judge

I.

This case invokes a [textbook] tenet of contract law: the symmetry needed between an offer and an acceptance to establish an enforceable agreement. . . .

II.

Settlement agreements are governed by contract law. . . . Like any contract, a settlement agreement is formed when there is mutual assent and a "meeting of the minds" between the parties—a condition that requires an offer and an acceptance supported by valid consideration. . . . Florida law further requires that "an acceptance of an offer must be absolute and unconditional, identical with the terms of the offer." *Ribich v. Evergreen Sales & Serv., Inc.*, 784 So. 2d 1201, 1202 (Fla. Ct. App. 2001) (citing *Sullivan v. Econ. Research Props.*, 455 So. 2d 630, 631 (Fla. Ct. App. 1984)). That is, the acceptance must be a "mirror image" of the offer in all material respects, or else it will be considered a counteroffer that rejects the original offer. . . . An attempted acceptance can become a counteroffer "either by adding additional terms or not meeting the terms of the original offer." *Grant v. Lyons*, 17 So. 3d 708, 711 (Fla. Ct. App. 2009).

The release USAA delivered appears to have done both: it added parties beyond those Ms. Pena proposed to release in her original offer, and it materially deviated from the limitation Ms. Pena's offer clearly expressed. The proposed release specifically releases Mr. Fox, his heirs, executors, and assigns in its first paragraph but then in another inexplicably shifts its reference to "Releasee(s)," a term that is nowhere defined within the document. Assuming, as the parties have, that Mr. Fox, his heirs, executors, and assigns, and "Releasees" are all one and the same, USAA's release goes on to expand the latter term to include Mr. Fox's "agents and employees," who are also left undefined and otherwise unidentified within the release. Presumably, the release's inclusion of "agents and employees" meant someone other than the "Releasee(s)" or Matthew R. Fox. . . . Although the incongruity in terms may have been nothing more than boilerplate migrating across computer-generated files, nevertheless, "agents and employees" was a new term, and it was a part of USAA's response to Ms. Pena's offer. And that offer had been explicit: Ms. Pena would not agree to release any party other than Mr. Fox.

While we share the circuit court's view that the inclusion of Mr. Fox's agents and employees within the release was not the product of nefarious motives, USAA's intention when it drafted this document, whatever it might have been, was irrelevant to the issue at hand. . . . The words are what matter because they will control who will, or will not, be released. . . . Mr. Fox's proposed acceptance would release additional parties, Mr. Fox's agents and employees, which Ms. Pena's offer would not. His acceptance did not mirror her offer.

III.

Reading Ms. Pena's offer and Mr. Fox's acceptance together, we conclude there was no meeting of the minds between these parties, and, thus, there was no settlement agreement that barred Ms. Pena's claims. . . . Accordingly, we reverse the order dismissing the complaint and remand this case for further proceedings.

Reversed and remanded.

UCC Standard for Acceptance on the Offeror's Terms: The "Battle of the Forms" Strictly applying the mirror image rule to modern commercial transactions, most of which are carried out by using preprinted form contracts, would often result in frustrating the parties' true intent. Offerors use standard order forms prepared by their lawyers, and offerees use standard acceptance or acknowledgment forms drafted by their counsel. The odds that these forms will agree in every detail are slight, as are the odds that the parties will read each other's forms in their entirety. Instead, the parties to such transactions are likely to read only crucial provisions concerning the goods ordered, the price, and the delivery date called for, and if these terms are agreeable, believe that they have a contract.

If a dispute arose before the parties started to perform, a court strictly applying the mirror image rule would hold that no contract resulted because the offer and acceptance forms did not match exactly. If a dispute arose after performance had commenced, the court would probably hold that the offeror had impliedly accepted the offeree's counteroffer and was bound by its terms.

Because neither of these results is very satisfactory, the UCC, in a very controversial provision often called the "Battle of the Forms" section [2-207] (see Figure 11.1), has changed the mirror image rule for contracts involving the sale of goods. UCC section 2-207 allows the formation of a contract even when there is some variance between the terms of the offer and the terms of the acceptance. It also makes it possible, under *some* circumstances, for a term contained in the acceptance form to become part of the contract. The UCC provides that a *definite and timely expression of acceptance* creates a contract, even if it includes terms that are *different from those stated in the offer* or even if it states *additional terms* that the offer did not address [2-207(1)]. An attempted acceptance that *was expressly conditioned* on the offeror's agreement to the offeree's terms would *not* be a valid acceptance, however [2-207(1)].

What are the terms of a contract created by the exchange of standardized forms? The *additional* terms contained in the offeree's form are treated as "proposals for addition to the contract." If the parties are both *merchants*, the additional terms become part of the contract *unless:*

1. The offer *expressly limited acceptance* to its own terms,

2. The new terms would *materially alter* the offer, or

3. The offeror gives notice of objection to the new terms within a reasonable time after receiving the acceptance [2-207(2)].

In the following *Duro* case, the court evaluates whether a forum selection clause included in a merchant offeree's response is part of the contract.

When the offeree has made his acceptance expressly conditional on the offeror's agreement to the new terms

Figure 11.1   The "Battle of the Forms"—A Section 2-207 Flowchart

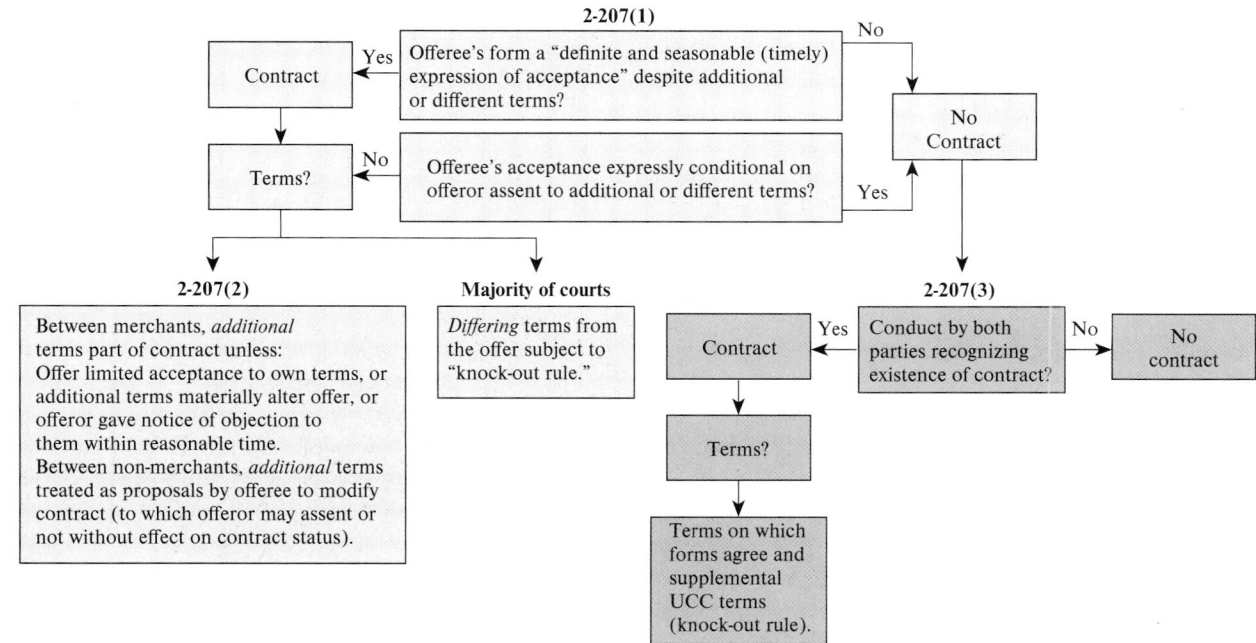

or when the offeree's response to the offer is clearly not "an expression of acceptance" (e.g., an express rejection), no contract is created under section 2-207(1). A contract will result in such cases only if the parties engage in conduct that "recognizes the existence of a contract," such as an exchange of performance. Unlike the offeror's counterpart under traditional contract principles, however, the offeror who accepts performance in the face of an express rejection or expressly conditional acceptance is not thereby bound to all of the terms contained in the offeree's response. Instead, the UCC provides that the

terms of a contract created by such performance are those on which the parties' writings agree, supplemented by appropriate gap-filling provisions from the UCC [2-207(3)]. Courts and litigants often refer to this as the knock-out rule.

The knock-out rule is also used by the majority of courts when there is an acceptance that contains terms that are *different* from (not merely additional to) the terms of the offer. That is, the contract will consist of those terms on which the parties' writings agree *plus* any appropriate gap-filling presumptions of the UCC.

Duro Textiles, LLC v. Sunbelt Corporation　　　12 F. Supp. 3d 221 (D. Mass. 2014)

Duro Textiles produces and distributes textile products. In November 2011, Duro ordered and received a large amount of blue dye from defendant Sunbelt Corporation. Duro alleges that when it used Sunbelt's dye in its production process, random blue spots appeared on its product. As a result, Duro claimed, it sustained losses totaling more than $550,000. Duro sued Sunbelt for breach of contract, breach of the implied covenant of good faith and fair dealing, and negligent misrepresentation.

Sunbelt moved to dismiss. It asserted that an invoice that it sent to Duro included a forum selection clause that granted exclusive jurisdiction for any dispute under the contract to South Carolina courts. Sunbelt sent the invoice to Duro along with Sunbelt's shipment of dye and also, separately, by U.S. Mail. Sunbelt claimed that the forum selection clause was part of the contract under UCC 2-207, the "battle of the forms."

Duro opposed the motion to dismiss, arguing that the forum selection clause was not part of the parties' contract because it "materially altered" the terms of the contract.

Wolf, District Judge

II. Analysis

Forum selection clauses are "*prima facie* valid and should be enforced unless enforcement is shown by the resisting party to be 'unreasonable' under the circumstances." *The Bremen v. Zapata Off Shore Co.*, 407 U.S. 1, 10 (1971).

Duro's position is not that the forum selection clause on which Sunbelt relies is "unreasonable," however, but that this clause is not part of the contract between the parties. . . . Under Massachusetts law, where a contractual provision is presented to a buyer in a seller's invoice, the analysis of whether that provision becomes part of the sales contract is governed by § 2-207. This section provides, in part, that if a seller's "written confirmation . . . is sent within a reasonable time," a contract is formed, and "[t]he additional or different terms are to be construed as proposals for addition to the contract." § 2-207(1). Between "merchants," these additional or different terms:

become part of the contract unless:

(a) the offer expressly limits acceptance to the terms of the offer;

(b) they materially alter it; or

(c) notification of objection to them has already been given or is given within a reasonable time after notice of them is received.

§ 2-207(2). Duro and Sunbelt tacitly agree that they are each a "merchant," namely "a person who deals in goods of the kind or otherwise by his occupation holds himself out as having knowledge or skill peculiar to the practices or goods involved in the transaction. . . ." Mass. Gen. Laws ch. 106, § 2-104(1).

Duro's primary argument is that Sunbelt's forum selection clause "materially altered" the contract and, therefore, was not incorporated into it. The official comments to § 2-207 "advise that a new term proposed by the seller is a 'material alteration' where it would 'result in [unreasonable] surprise or hardship [to the buyer] if incorporated without [the buyer's] express awareness.' . . . Ultimately, whether a term is material should be judged in the specific context of all relevant facts and circumstances. Thus, what is appropriate is a fact specific, case-by-case analysis." *Sibcoimtrex, Inc. v. Am. Foods Grp., Inc.*, 241 F. Supp. 2d 104, 109 (D. Mass. 2003).

The parties have not cited, and the court has not identified, any binding precedent that examines, under Massachusetts law, whether a forum selection clause materially alters a contract. In general, however, courts have considered forum selection clauses to be material. The Southern District of New York has explained that:

[T]he [forum selection] clause proposes that defendant is required to give up the right it would otherwise enjoy, to [sue or] be sued where it is doing business, or in the state of its principal office, and consent to [sue or] be sued in an adjoining state. A reasonable merchant would probably regard this as a material alteration.

There are still subtle differences between the courts in various states. Certainly the jurors are selected from different economic, political and social backgrounds, which may affect their attitudes even in commercial matters. Counsel other than the party's regular attorney may be needed, at additional expense. The bench and bar has always regarded choice of forum as a significant right. . . . [A] party, by agreeing to such a change, "waives in large part many of his normal rights under the procedural and substantive law of the state, and it would be unfair to infer such a significant waiver on the basis of anything less than a clear indication of intent."

Gen. Instr. Corp. v. Tie Mfg., Inc., 517 F. Supp. 1231, 1235 (S.D.N.Y. 1981) (quoting *Nat'l Mach. Exch., Inc. v. Peninsular Equip. Corp.*, 431 N.Y.S.2d 948 (Sup. Ct. N.Y. 1980)). The conclusion that a forum selection clause materially alters a contract has also been reached by various other courts under the laws of various other jurisdictions[, including Michigan, Indiana, Oklahoma, Pennsylvania, and Washington]. While a fact specific, case-by-case analysis is appropriate, the reasoning followed by other courts in other fact patterns is applicable to the instant case. Duro asserts, and Sunbelt does not dispute, that Duro's principal place of business is in Fall River, Massachusetts, and that Sunbelt's principal place of business is in Rock Hill, South Carolina. The forum selection clause in question would require Duro to litigate any disputes in Sunbelt's home state, in a forum far from Duro's own principal place of business and state of incorporation. Enforcement of the forum selection clause would entail "[s]ubtle differences in courts, jurors and law . . . and considerations of litigation expense . . . [that] most merchants would consider important." The court, therefore, finds that Sunbelt's forum selection clause is a material alteration to the contract within the meaning of § 2-207(2)(b). Consequently, this provision is not part of the contract between the parties. **Sunbelt's motion to dismiss is being denied on the foregoing grounds. . . .**

Communication of Acceptance

To accept an offer for a bilateral contract, the offeree must make the promise requested by the offer. In Chapter 10, you learned that an offeror must communicate the terms of his proposal to the offeree before an offer results. This is so because communication is a necessary component of the present intent to contract required for the creation of an offer. For similar reasons, it is generally held that an offeree must communicate his intent to be bound by the offer before a contract can be created. To accept an offer for a unilateral contract, however, the offeree must perform the requested act. The traditional contract law rule on this point assumes that the offeror will learn of the offeree's performance and holds that no further notice from the offeree is necessary to create a contract unless the offeror specifically requests notice.

Manner of Communication The offeror, as the master of the offer, has the power to specify the precise time, place, and manner in which acceptance must be communicated. This is called a *stipulation*. If the offeror stipulates a particular manner of acceptance, the offeree must respond in this way to form a valid acceptance. Suppose Prompt Printing makes an offer to Jackson and the offer states that Jackson must respond by certified mail. If Jackson deviates from the offer's instructions in any significant way, no contract results unless Prompt Printing indicates a willingness to be bound by the deviating acceptance. If, however, the offer merely *suggests* a method or place of communication or is *silent* on such matters, the offeree may accept within a *reasonable time* by *any reasonable means* of communication. So, if Prompt Printing's offer did not *require* any particular manner of accepting the offer, Jackson could accept the offer by any reasonable manner of communication within a reasonable time.

When Is Acceptance Communicated?

 LO11-2 Determine how acceptance can be communicated in a given scenario and analyze the time at which acceptance is likely to be effective.

Acceptances by Instantaneous Forms of Communication

When the parties are dealing face-to-face, by telephone, or by other means of communication that are virtually instantaneous, there are few problems determining when the acceptance was communicated. As soon as the offeree says, "I accept," or words to that effect, a contract is created, assuming that the offer is still in existence.

Acceptances by Noninstantaneous Forms of Communication

Suppose the circumstances under which the offer was made reasonably led the offeree to believe that acceptance by some noninstantaneous form of communication is acceptable, and the offeree responds by using postal mail or some other means of communication that creates a time lag between the dispatching of the acceptance and its actual receipt by the offeror. The practical problems involving the timing of acceptance multiply in such transactions. The offeror may be attempting to revoke the offer while the offeree is attempting to accept it. An acceptance may get lost and never be received by the offeror. The time limit for accepting the offer may be rapidly approaching. Was the offer accepted before a revocation was received or before the offer expired? Does a lost acceptance create a contract when it is dispatched, or is it totally ineffective?

Under the so-called *mailbox rule*, properly addressed and dispatched acceptances can become effective when they are *dispatched*, even if they are lost and never received by the offeror. The mailbox rule, which is discussed further in the following *Wilson* case, protects the offeree's reasonable belief that a binding contract was created when the acceptance was dispatched. By the same token, it exposes the offeror to the risk of being bound by an acceptance that the offeror has never received. The offeror, however, has the ability to minimize this risk by stipulating in the offer that the offeror must actually receive the acceptance for it to be effective. Offerors who do this maximize the time that they have to revoke their offers and ensure that they will never be bound by an acceptance that they have not received.

Operation of the Mailbox Rule: Common Law of Contracts As traditionally applied by the common law of contracts, the mailbox rule would make acceptances effective upon dispatch when the offeree used a manner of communication that was expressly or impliedly authorized (invited) by the offeror. Any manner of communication *suggested* by the offeror (e.g., "You may respond by mail") would be expressly authorized, resulting in an acceptance sent by the suggested means being effective on dispatch. Unless circumstances indicated to the contrary, a manner of communication *used by the offeror in making the offer* would be impliedly authorized (e.g., an offer sent by mail would impliedly authorize an acceptance by mail), as would a manner of communication common in the parties' trade or business (e.g., a trade usage in the parties' business that offers are made by mail and accepted by telegram would authorize an acceptance by telegram). Conversely, an improperly dispatched acceptance or one that was sent by some means of communication that was *nonauthorized* would be effective when *received*, assuming that the offer was still open at that time. This placed on the offeree the risk of the offer being revoked or the acceptance being lost.

The mailbox rule is often applied more liberally by courts today. A modern version of the mailbox rule that is sanctioned by the *Restatement (Second)* holds that an offer that does not indicate otherwise is considered to invite acceptance by *any reasonable means* of communication, and a properly dispatched acceptance sent by a reasonable means of communication within a reasonable time is effective on dispatch.

United States Life Insurance Company in the City of New York v. Wilson
18 A.3d 110 (Md. Ct. App. 2011)

On November 15, 1998, Dr. John G. Griffith purchased a life insurance policy underwritten by United States Life Insurance Company in the City of New York (US Life) through the AMA Insurance Agency Inc. (AMAIA). The policy was for a 10-year term, and Dr. Griffith was obligated to make premium payments every six months. If he missed a payment, the policy included a 31-day grace period, during which he could remit the missed payment and continue coverage. The policy further stated that US Life could extend the grace period by written notice. If, however, Dr. Griffith failed to make a premium payment even within the grace period, the policy could be reinstated within 90 days of the due date of the first missed premium by making all outstanding premium payments and by receiving written approval from US Life that he remained insurable. However, if the reinstatement payment was received within 31 days of the end of the grace period, then written approval and evidence of insurability was not required.

*Dr. Griffith made timely premium payments through 2006. He did not timely pay his May 15, 2007, premium, though. AMAIA sent Dr. Griffith a **REMINDER NOTICE**, stating: "To assure active coverage, full payment of the premium must be received no later than 60 days from the due date." Sometime shortly after June 15, 2007, AMAIA sent Dr. Griffith a **LAPSE NOTICE**, which informed him that his coverage had lapsed and that if he wished to continue it he needed to reinstate the policy.*

On July 23, 2007, Dr. Griffith logged on his online Bank of America account and directed that the missing premium payment be made. Bank of America sent a check to AMAIA on July 25, 2007. On August 2, 2007, AMAIA rejected the payment and returned the check with a letter stating that Dr. Griffith's payment was received more than 30 days after the end of the grace period and, therefore, he had to present evidence of insurability in order to reinstate the policy.

Meanwhile, on Saturday, July 28, 2007, Dr. Griffith was killed while riding his bicycle. His wife, Elizabeth Wilson, who was the sole beneficiary of the life insurance policy, subsequently submitted a claim on the policy. AMAIA denied the claim, indicating that the policy lapsed on May 15, 2007.

Ms. Wilson sued US Life and AMAIA for breach of contract. The parties filed competing motions for summary judgment. The trial court denied the defendants' motions and granted Ms. Wilson's motion, entering a judgment in her favor for the full amount of the policy plus costs and prejudgment interest.

US Life and AMAIA appealed.

*In portions of the opinion not reproduced here, the court determined that the **"REMINDER NOTICE"** acted as a written extension of the grace period as provided in the policy. As a result, it found that the policy lapsed on July 15, 2007. Nonetheless, the policy allowed for reinstatement for up to 90 days after the first missed premium payment. Because of the extended grace period, the court found that Dr. Griffith could reinstate the policy without written permission or evidence of insurability. Thus, the question for the court was whether Dr. Griffith had reinstated the policy by payment of the unpaid premium prior to his death on July 28, 2007.*

Deborah S. Eyler, Judge

Insurance contracts initially are formed when an insurer unconditionally accepts an insured's application, which constitutes an offer, for coverage. From then on, the life insurance policy operates as a unilateral contract, . . . *i.e.,* one that is formed by performance. "The periodic payment of premiums is the mechanism by which the insured opts to keep the insurance policy in force." 29 APPLEMAN ON INSURANCE 2d § 179.0-3, at 230 (2006). Failure to pay the premiums will result in coverage lapsing.

Life insurance policies have standard non-forfeiture clauses that allow for reinstatement after a lapse in coverage. The **"REINSTATEMENT"** clause in the Policy in this case is such a standard non-forfeiture clause. . . . Under the policy, when the relevant time frame for reinstatement is "within 31 days after the end of the Grace Period" (as it is here), the **"REINSTATEMENT"** clause is a promise by the insurer to reinstate coverage upon performance by the insured of a single act—payment of the overdue premium. In that situation, the insurer is not being asked to consider and either accept or reject an offer by the insured to enter into a life insurance contract. Thus, the plain language of the **"REINSTATEMENT"** clause of the Policy establishes that, upon payment by the insured of the overdue premium within 31 days after the end of the grace period, the Policy is revived. In other words, in that situation, the **"REINSTATEMENT"** clause is an offer of a unilateral contract to revive the Policy, with the insurer promising that revival will take place upon the insured's performing by paying the overdue premium.

It is within the context of Dr. Griffith's acceptance by performance (that is, by payment of the overdue premium) of US Life's offer to revive the Policy that we must determine *when* payment took place. At common law, what is often called the "mailbox rule," the "dispatch rule," or sometimes the "postal acceptance rule" is the widely adopted convention for pinpointing the time that an offer is accepted and a contract is formed. [The state law at issue here] recognizes the rule, by which the mailed acceptance of an offer is effective when mailed, not when received or acknowledged.

Section 63(a) of the RESTATEMENT (SECOND) OF CONTRACTS (1979), while not using any of the familiar mailbox rule nomenclature, recognizes with respect to the time that acceptance of an offer takes effect that, unless an offer states otherwise, "an acceptance made in a manner and by a medium invited by the offer is operative and completes the manifestation of mutual assent as soon as put out of the offeree's possession, without regard to whether it ever reaches the offeror." The rationale for the rule . . . is, essentially, certainty and predictability. [E]ven though it may be possible under United States postal regulations for a sender to stop delivery and reclaim a letter, it remains the case that one to whom an offer has been made "needs a dependable basis for his decision whether to accept," and has such a basis when he knows that, once properly dispatched, his acceptance is binding and the offer cannot be revoked. *Id.*

In 2 WILLISTON ON CONTRACTS § 6:32 (4th ed. Richard A. Lord, 2007) ("WILLISTON"), the author explains that the "dispatch rule" applies equally to bilateral and unilateral contracts. If an offer for a unilateral contract calls for the performance of an act by the offeree that can be accomplished by sending money through the mail, including in the form of a check, "as soon as the money is sent it would become the property of the offeror, and the offeror would become bound to perform its promise for which the money was the consideration." *Id.* at 441–42 (footnote omitted). The offeror must have authorized the use of the particular medium . . . as a means of acceptance, and the acceptance must have been properly dispatched.

In addressing with particularity when acceptance is dispatched, WILLISTON states: "An acceptance is dispatched within the meaning of the rule under consideration when it is put out of the possession of the offeree and within the control of the postal authorities, telegraph operator, or other third party authorized to receive it." § 6:37, at 484. However, "mere delivery of an acceptance to a messenger with directions to mail it amounts to no acceptance until the messenger actually deposits it in the mail." *Id.* The treatise continues:

> The private delivery service, under the modern view, would have to be independent of the offeree, reliable both in terms of its delivery obligations and record keeping, and of a type that would customarily be used to communicate messages of this sort. Such agencies as the United Parcel Service, Federal Express, or even private messenger services in urban areas would qualify, and as soon as the communication leaves the offeree's possession and is placed with an authorized recipient of the instrumentality, an effective dispatch will be deemed to have occurred.

WILLISTON § 6:37, at 486–87 (emphasis added) (footnote omitted).

We conclude that the long-recognized mailbox rule governing the time of formation of a contract by written acceptance applies in the case at bar to control the time the Policy was reinstated, that is, when coverage under the Policy was revived. The transaction at issue here is not wholly traditional, that is, one in which a paper document, whether a check or otherwise, is mailed by the offeree to the offeror, in that it began electronically, as an online banking directive by Dr. Griffith on July 23, 2007. The Bank of America documents in the summary judgment record show, however, that the directive was acted upon by preparation of a paper check drawn on a JPMorgan Chase Bank, N.A. account under Dr. Griffith's name, and bearing his "Authorized Signature"; and that the paper check then was "sent" to AMAIA on July 25, 2007, coming into AMAIA's physical possession on July 30, 2007.

The transaction thus resembles a traditional acceptance by writing mailed to the offeror, in that a writing (the check) was "sent" to AMAIA, even though its creation was directed electronically and it was created not by the offeree but by his bank. A writing thus was generated by actions taken by Dr. Griffith; the writing complied with that which was necessary to accept the reinstatement offer; and the writing was "sent," which was a permissible mode of acceptance, and subsequently was delivered to AMAIA, the proper recipient. The nature of the transaction, involving the sending of a written acceptance, is such that, just like a transaction in which a written acceptance is prepared in writing and mailed, or a written acceptance is prepared by telegram and sent, the mailbox rule is a necessary tool to establish the time that the new agreement—here, one to revive a prior contract—was formed. The nature of the transaction is not akin to those that have been determined to be outside the sphere of the dispatch rule[, like telephones or teletypes.]

Application of the mailbox rule to the undisputed material facts in this case produces the legal conclusion that the date of payment of the overdue premium was July 25, 2007. On July 23, 2007, Dr. Griffith electronically instructed Bank of America, as his agent, to make payment to AMAIA. The evidence viewed most favorably to the appellants supports a reasonable inference that Dr. Griffith could have reinstructed Bank of America not to make the payment; therefore, as of July 23, 2007, he had set in motion the means to accept the offer of reinstatement but still had the power to reverse course. On July 25, 2007, however, Bank of America remitted payment to AMAIA by *sending* it a check, drawn on the JPMorgan Chase Bank, N.A. account, for $369.46. At that point, the permissible means for acceptance was in motion and, so far as is established by the common law mailbox rule, was beyond Dr. Griffith's power to stop. This would be true whether Bank of America sent the check through the U.S. Postal Service, a courier service, or otherwise.

* * *

Judgment in favor of Elizabeth Wilson against the United States Life Insurance Company in the City of New York affirmed.

Operation of the Mailbox Rule: UCC The UCC, like the *Restatement (Second)*, provides that an offer that does not specify a particular means of acceptance is considered to invite acceptance by *any reasonable means* of communication. It also provides that a properly dispatched acceptance sent by a reasonable means of communication within a reasonable time is effective on dispatch. What is reasonable depends on the circumstances in which the offer was made. These include the speed and reliability of the means used by the offeree, the nature of the transaction (e.g., does the agreement involve goods subject to rapid price fluctuations?), the existence of any trade usage governing the transaction, and the existence of prior dealings between the parties (e.g., has the offeree previously used the mail to accept telegraphed offers from the offeror?). So, under proper circumstances, a mailed response to a telegraphed offer or a telegraphed response to a mailed offer might be considered reasonable and therefore effective on dispatch.

What if an offeree attempts to accept the offer by some means that is *unreasonable* under the circumstances or if the acceptance is not properly addressed or dispatched (e.g., misaddressed or accompanied by insufficient postage)? The UCC rejects the traditional rule that such acceptances cannot be effective until received. It provides that an acceptance sent by an unreasonable means would be effective on dispatch *if* it is received within the time that an acceptance by a reasonable means would normally have arrived.

Stipulated Means of Communication

As discussed earlier, an offer may stipulate the means of communication that the offeree must use to accept by saying, in effect: "You must accept by mail." An acceptance by the stipulated means of communication is effective on dispatch, just like an acceptance by any other reasonable or authorized means of communication (see Figure 11.2). The difference is that an acceptance by other than the stipulated means does not create a contract because it is an acceptance at variance with the terms of the offer.

Special Acceptance Problem Areas

Acceptance in Unilateral Contracts

A unilateral contract involves the exchange of a promise for a requested act. To accept an offer to enter such a contract, the offeree must perform the requested act. As you learned in Chapter 10, however, courts applying modern contract rules may prevent an offeror from revoking such an offer once the offeree has begun performance. This is achieved by holding either that a bilateral contract is created by the beginning of performance or that the offeror's power to revoke is suspended for the period of time reasonably necessary for the offeree to complete performance.

Acceptance in Bilateral Contracts

A bilateral contract involves the exchange of a promise for a promise of some requested performance in return. As a general rule, to accept an offer to enter such a contract, an offeree must *make the promise requested by the offer.* This may be done in a variety of ways. For example, Wallace sends Stevens a detailed offer for the purchase of Stevens's business. Within the time period prescribed by the offer, Stevens sends Wallace a letter that says, "I accept your offer." Stevens has *expressly* accepted Wallace's offer, creating a contract on the terms of the offer. Acceptance, however, can be *implied* as well as expressed. Offerees who take action that objectively indicates agreement risk the formation of a contract. For example, offerees who act in a manner that is inconsistent with an offeror's ownership of offered property are commonly held to have accepted the offeror's terms. So, if Arnold, a farmer, leaves 10 bushels of corn with Porter, the owner of a grocery store, saying, "Look this corn over. If you want it, it's $5 a bushel," and Porter sells the corn, he has impliedly accepted Arnold's offer. But what if Porter just let the corn sit and, when Arnold returned a week later, Porter told Arnold that he did not want it? Could Porter's failure to act ever amount to an acceptance?

Figure 11.2   Time of Acceptance

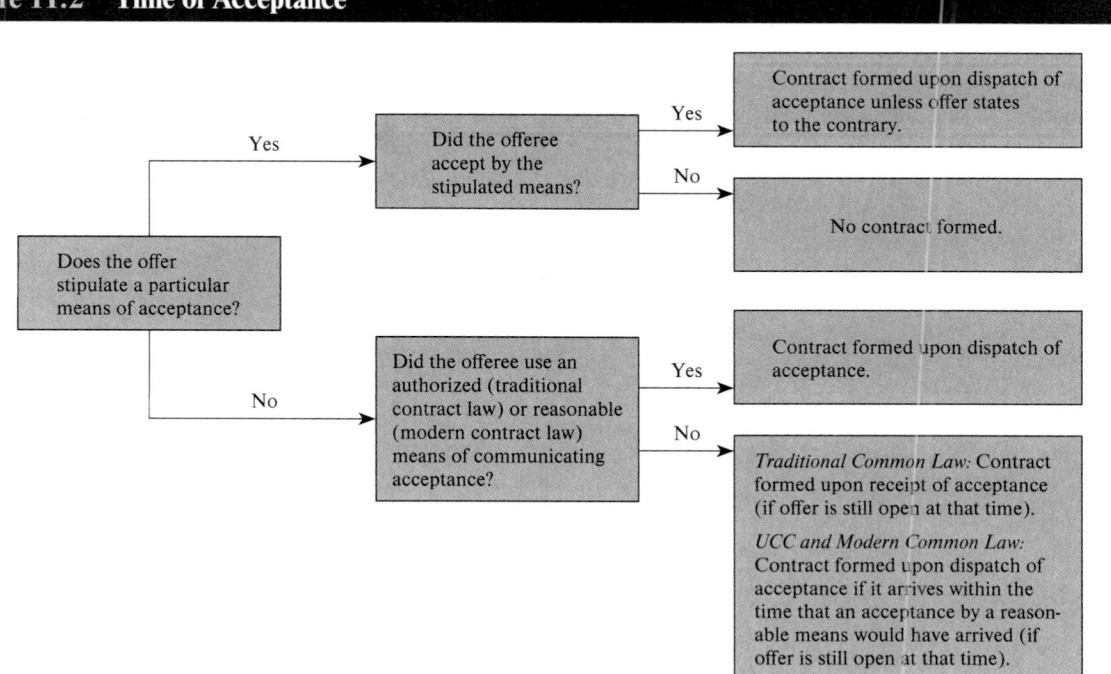

Silence as Acceptance

LO11-3 Identify the circumstances under which silence is acceptance.

Because contract law generally requires some objective indication that an offeree intends to contract, the general rule is that an offeree's silence, without more, is *not* an acceptance. In general, an offeror cannot impose on the offeree a duty to respond to the offer. So, even if Arnold made an offer to sell corn to Porter and said, "If I don't hear from you in three days, I'll assume you're buying the corn," Porter's silence would still not amount to acceptance.

On the other hand, the circumstances of a case sometimes impose a duty on the offeree to reject the offer affirmatively or be bound by its terms. These are cases in which the offeree's silence objectively indicates an intent to accept. Customary trade practice or prior dealings between the parties may indicate that silence signals acceptance. So, if Arnold and Porter had dealt with each other on numerous occasions and Porter had always promptly returned items that he did not want, Porter's silent retention of the goods for a week would probably constitute an acceptance. Likewise, an offeree's silence can also operate as an acceptance if the offeree has indicated that it will. For example, Porter (the *offeree*) tells Arnold, "If you don't hear from me in three days, I accept." In *Bauer v. Qwest Communications Company*, which follows, the court has to determine whether the prior dealings of the parties are such that one party's silence is an objective manifestation of intent to accept.

Finally, it is generally held that offerees who accept an offeror's performance knowing what the offeror expects in return for his performance have impliedly accepted the offeror's terms. So, if Apex Paving Corporation offers to do the paving work on a new subdivision being developed by Majestic Homes Corporation, and Majestic fails to respond to Apex's offer but allows Apex to do the work, most courts would hold that Majestic is bound by the terms of Apex's offer.

Bauer v. Qwest Communications Company, LLC   743 F.3d 221 (7th Cir. 2014)

For more than 13 years, trial lawyers across the United States challenged the installation of fiber-optic cable on property without the landowners' consent. Following a long process of complex litigation in a number of state courts, these challenges began to settle on a state-by-state basis. As a result, the numerous lawyers who worked on the cases were left to sort out the allocation of attorney fees that were being held by a disinterested third-party while the attorneys tried to resolve the share of that money each was entitled to get.

The lawyers had informally split among three factions for purposes of the fee-allocation dispute. Arthur Susman and his colleagues made up one group (Susman). A former collaborator and now rival of Susman, William Gotfryd, represented another faction (Gotfryd). The final faction consisted of a coalition of 48 law firms (the 48-Firm Group).

The parties engaged in court-mandated mediation; however, they were not able to quickly resolve their disputes. The mediators made a "final effort" at resolution by offering a final "Mediator's Proposal," which awarded each faction a certain percentage of the nationwide fees. The proposal was "blind" in that each lawyer or group of lawyers knew only the percentage allocation he or it would receive. Thereby, parties would be forced to focus only on the adequacy of their own absolute percentage, rather than worry about the amount of their awards relative to others. The proposal was take-it-or-leave-it, meaning that each party could respond only with "Accept" or "Reject." Everyone accepted the proposal.

The mediators notified the parties that the proposal was unanimously accepted and the lawyers set about memorializing it in a written agreement. A representative of the 48-Firm Group drafted an agreement and distributed it. Susman quickly responded with two minor points to be clarified. Others sought some changes as well. Based on that feedback, a couple of additional drafts were produced, until the final version was distributed for signature. After the initial draft, Susman never objected to any of the versions or the final version, despite having around two weeks to do so.

Nonetheless, after everyone else had signed, Susman refused to sign the final agreement. He formally objected to terms dealing with enforcement of the agreement through arbitration; however, the others suspected he truly objected to the percentage allocation he received in the settlement, which was about half of Gotfryd's percentage allocation.

The other lawyers asked the court to enforce the agreement, despite Susman's refusal to sign. The judge held that Susman was bound by the final written agreement. Susman appealed.

Sykes, Circuit Judge

On appeal Susman acknowledges that he approved the mediators' fee-allocation proposal but insists that he never agreed to the additional terms that appeared in the final written agreement. More specifically, he objects to . . . the enforcement provisions empowering the mediators to arbitrate future disputes and "forfeit" the fees of attorneys who do not cooperate in implementing the agreement in state-by-state settlements. Susman relies heavily on the fact that he did not sign the agreement. Illinois contract law applies.

"Under Illinois contract law, a binding agreement requires a meeting of the minds or mutual assent as to all material terms." *Abbott Lab. v. Alpha Therapeutic Corp.*, 164 F.3d 385, 387 (7th Cir. 1999). "Whether the parties had a 'meeting of the minds' is determined not by their actual subjective intent," [*id.*], but rather based an [sic] "objective theory of intent," *Newkirk v. Village of Steger*, 536 F.3d 771, 774 (7th Cir. 2008). To determine whether a party assented, the court "look[s] first to the written records, not to mental processes." [*Id.*] . . .

The critical question here is a factual one: Did Susman objectively manifest assent to be bound even though he did not sign the agreement? The district court answered that question "yes," and we review that determination deferentially.

"Generally, one of the acts forming the execution of a written contract is its signing. Nevertheless, 'a party named in a contract may, by his acts and conduct, indicate his assent to its terms and become bound by its provisions even though he has not signed it.'" *Carlton at the Lake, Inc. v. Barber*, 401 Ill. App. 3d 528, 928 N.E.2d 1266, 1270, 340 Ill. Dec. 669 (Ill. Ct. App. 2010) (citation omitted) (quoting *Landmark Props., Inc. v. Architects Int'l–Chi.*, 172 Ill. App. 3d 379, 526 N.E.2d 603, 606, 122 Ill. Dec. 344 (Ill. 1988)). Silence reasonably may be interpreted as acceptance of a contract in certain limited circumstances.

Silence may be construed as acceptance where "because of previous dealings or otherwise, it is reasonable that the offeree should notify the offeror if he does not intend to accept." RESTATEMENT (SECOND) OF CONTRACTS § 69(1)(c) (1981). In this situation, "the offeree's silence is acceptance, regardless of his actual intent, unless both parties understand that no acceptance is intended." RESTATEMENT (SECOND) OF CONTRACTS § 69 cmt. d (1981).

The district court found that under the circumstances here, Susman's silence should be interpreted as assent to the written agreement. That was a reasonable determination. The parties had worked on the fiber-optic-cable class actions for more than a decade, whether as cocounsel or in clear awareness of the parallel litigation activity in multiple states. They had recently worked out a system for settling the litigation on a state-by-state basis, and they were close to the end of a long and contentious fight over fees. Susman in particular had been a holdout on that front, having rejected [an earlier attempt to resolve the dispute]; he admits that he had a history of promptly speaking up when he found something objectionable. True to form, in this case Susman raised two minor points to the initial draft of the agreement within hours of its circulation. His suggestions were immediately addressed and incorporated into a subsequent draft.

Tellingly, he did *not* object to any of the terms he now complains of. . . . As to these terms, he remained silent for two weeks.

By this time the lawyers were a sort of community of interest, working together toward a final resolution of the fee dispute and an end to the litigation. They accepted the mediators' fee-division proposal with the understanding that it was a final effort to get "the entire fee fight settled" once and for all—to achieve "global peace," as Gotfryd put it at oral argument. The declarations submitted to the district court by Gotfryd and various members of the 48-Firm Group indicate that they accepted the mediators' proposal largely because they understood it to put an end to uncertainty and bring about an expeditious distribution of attorney's fees with no further threat of litigation. Indeed, it's hard to imagine that their acceptance of the fee-allocation proposal could be understood in any other way. The unanimous approval of the mediators' proposal included the agreed-upon division of fees but also plainly contemplated an enforcement mechanism that would foreclose future litigation.

Consistent with this understanding, the written agreement provided for enforcement by arbitration if necessary. Needless to say, alternative dispute resolution is commonplace in this context, and under the particular circumstances here, the arbitration provisions could not have been unexpected. As the district court noted, it would be "remarkable . . . that you would work out this kind of arrangement and it wouldn't include some kind of arbitration or other dispute resolution mechanism in light of the fact that there are several other states that are out there."

Susman's past hostility toward arbitration isn't incongruous with construing his silence as a lack of objection rather than a lack of assent. His previous rejection of arbitration pertained to the substantive fee-division issue, but that issue was now resolved. The arbitration provisions he now finds objectionable cover future disagreements that may arise in the implementation of the fee-allocation agreement. Susman cannot rely on his past objection to arbitration to explain his two-week silence in the face of a sense of urgency and a need for repose that was known to all. The parties had settled their substantive dispute, and the written agreement memorializing that settlement unsurprisingly contained an enforcement mechanism ensuring that the implementation would proceed without the threat of litigation. In short, it was reasonable for the other lawyers to expect Susman to promptly raise his objections to the written agreement and to construe his two-week silence as assent. . . .

Given the parties' lengthy relationship and course of dealings, the district court reasonably construed Susman's silence as an assent to be bound.

Affirmed.

Acceptance When a Writing Is Anticipated

 LO11-4 Determine whether an oral acceptance is effective in a situation in which the parties anticipate putting their contract in writing.

Frequently, the parties to a contract intend to prepare a written draft of their agreement for both parties to sign. This is a good idea not only because the law requires written evidence of some contracts,[2] but also because it provides written evidence of the terms of the agreement if a dispute arises at a later date. If a dispute arises before such a writing has been prepared or signed, however, a question may arise concerning whether the signing of the agreement was a necessary condition to the creation of a contract. A party to the

[2]Chapter 16 discusses this subject in detail.

agreement who now wants out of the deal may argue that the parties did not intend to be bound until both parties signed the writing. A clear expression of such an intent by the parties during the negotiation process prevents the formation of a contract until both parties have signed. However, in the absence of such a clear expression of intent, the courts ask whether a reasonable person familiar with all the circumstances of the parties' negotiations would conclude that the parties intended to be bound only when a formal agreement was signed. If it appears that the parties had concluded their negotiations and reached agreement on all the essential aspects of the transaction, most courts would probably find a contract at the time agreement was reached, even though no formal agreement had been signed.

The following *Cabot Oil* case requires the court to determine whether a formal written agreement was necessary to create a binding contract. The court notes six factors to be considered.

Cabot Oil & Gas Corporation v. Daugherty Petroleum, Inc.
479 F. App'x 524 (4th Cir. 2012)

Cabot Oil issued a solicitation for bids to purchase several oil and gas leases it owned in West Virginia. The solicitation letter invited recipients to submit a "preliminary bid or proposal" and stated that "those submitting such proposals, if any, will be notified for further discussion and negotiation." Daugherty Petroleum received the solicitation and responded with a letter that it called alternatively a "bid" and an "offer." Daugherty Petroleum proposed a purchase price and indicated its ability to close on the deal within 75 days of Cabot Oil's acceptance. The Daugherty Petroleum letter emphasized, however, that it was "contingent and conditioned" on the negotiation of various terms, including form of payment, due diligence issues, and a requirement that Cabot Oil take the leases off the market for 60 days to allow the due diligence process to be completed. The parties referred to the latter as the "exclusivity period." Finally, Daugherty Petroleum indicated that, during the due diligence process, the parties would "negotiate the terms and conditions of an asset purchase agreement."

Eventually, after some delay when the parties communicated informally and Cabot Oil executives contemplated the bid, Cabot Oil sent Daugherty Petroleum a letter in which it agreed to the purchase price and the proposed form of payment. Cabot Oil indicated that it preferred to move directly into hammering out a purchase and sale agreement (PSA), during which Daugherty Petroleum could perform whatever due diligence it deemed necessary. To that end, Cabot Oil indicated that it would begin drafting the PSA immediately. Cabot Oil's letter omitted any reference to the exclusivity period.

Around six weeks later, after numerous failed attempts to communicate with Daugherty Petroleum and hearing nothing, Cabot Oil sent a letter indicating that it had accepted Daugherty Petroleum's offer to purchase the leases and threatening to pursue legal action. Daugherty Petroleum responded that their bid was conditioned on the negotiation of a PSA and the completion of due diligence. Shortly thereafter, Cabot Oil sent Daugherty Petroleum a 12-page draft PSA. The terms differed in certain respects from Daughtery Petroleum's letter, including terms governing form and timing of payment. It also included additional terms not previously contemplated in their communications.

Daugherty Petroleum never responded to the PSA despite Cabot Oil's numerous attempts to make contact.

Cabot Oil sued Daugherty Petroleum in West Virginia for breach of contract, seeking more than $2 million in damages. Both companies moved for summary judgment. The district court granted Daugherty Petroleum's motion and denied Cabot Oil's motion, finding that the correspondence between the parties did not create a binding contract. Cabot Oil appealed.

Per Curiam

A.

The fundamental elements of a binding, enforceable contract are competent parties, legal subject-matter, valuable consideration, and mutual assent. Mutuality of assent, in turn, generally requires an offer by one party and acceptance by the other. Offer and acceptance may be manifested through word, act, or conduct that evinces the intention of the parties to contract. . . .

Parties may form binding contracts through correspondence. Yet courts must be careful not to construe correspondence as constituting a binding agreement if the parties intended for it to serve merely as preliminary negotiations. If the correspondence reflects that the parties intended to reduce an agreement to a formal written contract, a presumption arises under West Virginia law that the correspondence does not constitute a binding contract, but instead only preliminary negotiations. Strong evidence is necessary to rebut this presumption.

In considering whether a party has rebutted this presumption, the overarching goal is to discern whether the parties intended for a final written document to be merely a "convenient memorial" of their agreement or the "consummation of the negotiation." The Supreme Court of West Virginia has recognized six factors to guide courts in making this determination: (1) "whether the contract is of that class . . . usually found to be in writing"; (2) "whether it is of such nature as to need a formal writing for its full expression"; (3) "whether it has few or many details"; (4) "whether the amount involved is large or small"; (5) "whether it is a common or unusual contract"; and (6) "whether the negotiations themselves indicate that a written draft is contemplated as a final conclusion of the negotiations." *Blair v. Dickinson*, 133 W. Va. 38, 54 S.E.2d 828, 844 (W. Va. 1949) (quoting *Elkhorn-Hazard Coal Co. v. Ky. River Coal Corp.*, 20 F.2d 67, 70 (6th Cir. 1927)) (internal quotation marks omitted).

Moreover, "[i]f a written draft is proposed, suggested or referred to, during the negotiations, it is some evidence that the parties intended it to be the final closing of the contract." *Id.* (quoting *Elkhorn-Hazard*, 20 F.2d at 70) (internal quotation marks omitted). And if "the parties to an agreement make its reduction to writing and signing a condition precedent to its completion, it will not be a contract until this is done, although all of the terms of the contract have been agreed upon." *Id.* at 843 (quoting *Brown v. W. Md. Ry. Co.*, 114 S.E. 457, 457 (W. Va. 1922)) (internal quotation marks omitted).

B.

We begin by recognizing that from the start the parties manifested their intention to reduce any agreement into a final purchase and sale agreement. Daugherty Petroleum's . . . letter proposing a purchase price made the negotiation of such an agreement a condition to its bid. Likewise, Cabot Oil's purported acceptance of Daugherty Petroleum's proposed purchase price reflected an understanding that the parties needed to negotiate a [PSA]. Barr's response to Cabot Oil's follow-up e-mail and letter again emphasized that Daugherty Petroleum conditioned its offer on the execution of a mutually agreeable [PSA]. Most emblematic of the parties' mutual understanding that they would negotiate a formal contract, however, is the [draft PSA] that Cabot Oil composed and sent to Daugherty Petroleum. Hence, because the parties manifested their mutual intention to memorialize any agreement in a formal written contract, we begin with the presumption that their correspondence did not create a binding agreement in the absence of such a formal contract.

Using the factors recognized by the Supreme Court of West Virginia, we next conclude that Cabot Oil has not offered strong evidence to overcome this presumption. Even accepting as true Cabot Oil's suggestion that these types of lease contracts are not unusual, we find that the other five factors reinforce that an executed [PSA] was necessary to form a binding contract. We address these five factors in turn.

First, as the district court noted and Cabot Oil acknowledged at oral argument, representatives from both parties indicated in depositions that formal [PSAs] are customary for these types of lease transactions. Second, a formal contract appears to have been necessary to fully express the parties' agreement. Although the parties' correspondence contained a number of essential terms of an agreement, such as a proposed price term, general information about the leases, and so forth, it left many terms for the parties to negotiate later. Third, the numerous details that the parties still needed to negotiate after their initial correspondence are evidenced by the [draft PSA], which spans twelve pages in length and includes a multitude of terms that either conflicted with or were additional to Daugherty Petroleum's letter. Fourth, the amount involved in the transaction—over $2,600,000—is large. Finally, the parties' correspondence not only reveals that a final [PSA] was contemplated as a conclusion to their negotiations, but, as reflected in Daugherty Petroleum's initial proposal, it was a condition to the bid. Because these factors militate in Daugherty Petroleum's favor, Cabot Oil has failed to rebut the presumption that a formal [PSA] was necessary to form a binding contract.

We therefore agree with the district court that the undisputed facts indicate that the parties merely engaged in preliminary negotiations and there was no mutual assent. From the start, the parties' correspondence reflected that the execution of a mutually agreeable [PSA] was necessary to consummate their negotiations and would not merely be a convenient memorial of a preexisting agreement. And, furthermore, such a [PSA] was a condition precedent to the formation of a binding agreement. In the absence of an executed [PSA], we agree with the district court that under West Virginia law no binding contract exists between the parties. As a result, Daugherty Petroleum's decision to abandon the negotiations and not to purchase the leases does not constitute a breach of contract.

For these reasons, we affirm the district court's grant of summary judgment.

Acceptance of Ambiguous Offers

Although offerors have the power to specify the manner in which their offers can be accepted by requiring that the offeree make a return promise (a bilateral contract) or perform a specific act (a unilateral contract), often an offer is unclear about which form of acceptance is necessary to create a contract. In such a case, the offer may be accepted in any manner that is *reasonable* in light of the circumstances surrounding the offer. Thus, either a promise to perform or performance, if reasonable, creates a contract.

Acceptance by Shipment The UCC specifically elaborates on the rule stated in the preceding section by stating that an order requesting prompt or current shipment of goods may be accepted either by a *prompt promise to ship* or by a *prompt or current shipment* of the goods [2-206(1)(b)]. So, if Ampex Corporation orders 500 Apple iPads from Marks Office Supply, to be shipped immediately, Marks could accept either by promptly promising to ship the goods or by promptly shipping them. If Marks accepts by shipping, any subsequent attempt by Ampex to revoke the order will be ineffective.

What if Marks did not have 500 iPads in stock and Marks knew that Ampex desperately needed the goods? Marks might be tempted to ship another brand of tablet (that is, *nonconforming goods*—goods different from what the buyer ordered), hoping that Ampex would be forced by its circumstances to accept them because by the time they arrived it would be too late to get the correct goods elsewhere. Marks would argue that by shipping the wrong goods it had made a counteroffer because it had not performed the act requested by Ampex's order. If Ampex accepts the goods, Marks could argue that Ampex has impliedly accepted the counteroffer. If Ampex rejects the goods, Marks would arguably have no liability because it did not accept the order.

The UCC prevents such a result by providing that prompt shipment of either conforming goods (what the order asked for) or nonconforming goods (something else) operates as an acceptance of the order [2-206(1)(b)]. This protects buyers such as Ampex because sellers who ship the wrong goods have simultaneously accepted their offers and breached the contract by sending the wrong merchandise.[3]

---

[3]Chapter 19 discusses the rights and responsibilities of the buyer and seller following the shipment of nonconforming goods.

Ethics and Compliance in Action

Marble Publications is a publisher of various magazines and newsletters. Samantha has a subscription to one of Marble's publications, *Parent's World*. In 2018, Marble sends Samantha a complimentary copy of another of its publications, *Gardens Unlimited*, along with a letter that states that Samantha will receive *Gardens Unlimited* free of charge for three months, but if she does not want to receive any further copies of *Gardens Unlimited*, she must contact Marble and cancel. The letter states that if Samantha fails to contact Marble, she will be subscribed for one year at a cost of $24.95. Samantha does not read the letter carefully and never contacts Marble. After three months, she receives a bill for $24.95. Is this an ethical way of marketing *Gardens Unlimited*? What ethical problems might arise if silence were generally considered to constitute acceptance?

The Global Business Environment

Under the United Nations Convention on Contracts for the International Sale of Goods (CISG), as under U.S. law, statements or other conduct by the offeree that shows assent is an acceptance, and silence alone generally does not suffice as acceptance. And, as is true under U.S. law, a contract is concluded when an acceptance of an offer becomes effective. There are several notable differences between acceptance doctrines under U.S. law and the CISG, however. For one, the "battle of the forms," as it is formulated under the Uniform Commercial Code, does not exist under the CISG. Rather, under the CISG, a reply to an offer that purports to be an acceptance but in fact contains new or different terms or limitations that are *material* is a rejection and *not* an acceptance. Examples of terms that would be considered material are terms relating to price, payment, quality, the extent of a party's liability, and settlement of disputes (such as arbitration clauses). However, a reply purporting to be an acceptance that contains *nonmaterial* new or different terms can be an acceptance. Another major difference between U.S. law and the CISG is that, unlike the U.S. "mailbox rule," the CISG generally holds acceptances to be effective when they are received.

But what if Marks is an honest seller merely trying to help out a customer that has placed a rush order? Must Marks expose itself to liability for breach of contract in the process? The UCC prevents such a result by providing that no contract is created if the seller notifies the buyer within a reasonable time that the shipment of nonconforming goods is intended as an accommodation (an attempt to help the buyer) [2-206(1)(b)]. In this case, the shipment is merely a counteroffer that the buyer is free to accept or reject and the seller's notification gives the buyer the opportunity to seek the goods he needs elsewhere.

Who Can Accept an Offer? As the masters of their offers, offerors have the right to determine who can bind them to a contract. So, the only person with the legal power to accept an offer and create a contract is the *original offeree*. An attempt to accept by anyone other than the offeree is treated as an offer because the party attempting to accept is indicating a present intent to contract on the original offer's terms. For example, Price offers to sell his car to Waterhouse for $5,000. Anderson learns of the offer, calls Price, and attempts to accept. Anderson has made an offer that Price is free to accept or reject.

Problems and Problem Cases

1. In December 1999, Wilson applied for a Citibank credit card and signed an acceptance certificate in which she agreed to be bound by the terms and conditions of the credit card agreement. Citibank then issued a credit card to her, which Wilson began using. In July 2001, Citibank mailed Wilson her credit card statement, which informed her that it was modifying the terms of the original agreement. This revised agreement was enclosed with the credit card statement. After the July 2001 statement was made to her, Wilson continued using her credit card and made monthly payments on her account balance. Wilson made her last payment to Citibank in March 2002 and failed to make payments thereafter. Citibank then filed suit against her to collect her overdue balance, which was $12,272.84. In this action, Citibank attempted to enforce the revised agreement rather than the original agreement. Wilson argued that she never accepted the revised agreement. Is this a good argument?

2. 23andMe Inc. sold its Personal Genome Service (PGS) product on the Internet. The PGS consists of a DNA saliva collection kit and DNA test results with certain information gleaned from saliva samples that customers submit using the DNA kit. The PGS transaction is structured as a two-step process. First, a customer purchases the DNA kit, which 23andMe ships along with a pre-addressed return box. The customer collects the saliva with the kit and returns the collected saliva to 23andMe, which sends the saliva to a certified laboratory for analysis. When the laboratory returns results, 23andMe posts the results online to the customer's personal genome profile and sends an e-mail to the customer notifying him or her that the results are available. The customer must then log on to the profile to access the information.

23andMe's Terms of Service (TOS) are accessible by a hyperlink at the bottom of its homepage and many, though not all, of its other pages. The web page upon which a customer purchases a DNA kit is one such page with no reference to the TOS. Thus, the first step of the PGS transaction does not require the customer to view or otherwise agree to the TOS. The second step, however, requires the customer to create an account on the 23andMe site and register the DNA kit. The account creation page requires customers to check a box next to the line, "Yes, I have read and agree to the Terms of Service and Privacy Statement." The TOS and Privacy Statement appear in blue font and are hyperlinks to the full terms. Similarly, during the registration process, customers must view a page with the title "To continue, accept our terms of service" written in large font at the top of the page. The registration page provides a hyperlink to the full TOS next to the line: "When you sign up for 23andMe's service you agree to our Terms of Service. Click here to read our full Terms of Service." Customers must then click a large blue icon that reads, "I ACCEPT THE TERMS OF SERVICE," before finishing the registration process and receiving their DNA information. The TOS state that customers who use 23andMe services have manifested acceptance of the TOS by their conduct, regardless of whether they ever read the TOS. Are PGS customers bound by the TOS? What about customers who purchase the PGS as a gift for another person and that person is the one who collects the saliva sample and sets up his or her own account?

3. Belden was AEC's longtime supplier of wire, which it used in its sensors, including the sensors that it sold to Chrysler for inclusion in its cars. In 2003, Belden began using a nonconforming insulation in its wire. Belden's order acknowledgment, sent in response to AEC's purchase order, contained a limitation of remedy that

was not in the offer. It also stated that its acceptance was expressly conditioned on AEC's agreement to its terms. The sensors that AEC sold to Chrysler failed, due to the nonconforming wiring, and Chrysler had to recall cars in which it had been installed. AEC had to reimburse Chrysler for its losses caused by the recall. AEC sued Belden to recover the amount of money AEC paid to reimburse Chrysler, and Belden claimed that the limitation of remedies in its acknowledgment protected it from liability for these damages. Is Belden correct?

4. Standard Bent Glass wanted to buy a machine for its factory that would produce cut glass. In March 1998, it started negotiations with Glassrobots Oy, a Finnish corporation. By February 1999, negotiations had reached a critical juncture. On February 1, Standard Bent Glass faxed an offer to purchase a glass fabricating system from Glassrobots. The offer sheet began, "Please find below our terms and conditions related to ORDER #DKH2199," and defined the items to be purchased; the quantity; the price of $1.1 million; the payment terms; and installation specifics, instructions, and warranties. The letter concluded, "Please sign this ORDER and fax to us if it is agreeable." On February 2, Glassrobots responded with a cover letter, invoice, and standard sales agreement. The cover letter recited: "Attached you'll find our standard sales agreement. Please read it through and let me know if there is anything you want to change. If not, I'll send 2 originals, which will be signed." The contract included an arbitration clause and several references to arbitration. Glassrobots did not return, nor refer to, Standard Bent Glass's order. Later that day, Standard Bent Glass faxed a return letter that began, "Please find our changes to the Sales Agreement," by which it meant Glassrobots's standard sales agreement. This letter apparently accepted Glassrobots's standard sales agreement as a template and requested five specific changes. The letter closed, "Please call me if the above is not agreeable. If it is we will start the wire today." On February 4, Standard Bent Glass wired the down payment to Glassrobots, and on February 8, the wire transfer cleared Glassrobots's bank account. On February 5, Glassrobots sent Standard Bent Glass a revised sales agreement that incorporated almost all of the requested changes. Glassrobots's cover letter stated, "Attached you'll find the revised sales agreement. . . . Please return one signed to us; the other one is for your files." A provision of this agreement stated that "this Agreement shall come into force when signed by both parties." Standard Bent Glass never signed the agreement.

On February 9, Standard Bent Glass sent another fax to Glassrobots in which it stated, "Just noticed on our sales agreement that the power is 440 ± 5. We must have 480 ± 5 on both pieces of equipment." There was no further written correspondence after February 9 and no contract was ever signed by both parties. Nevertheless, both parties continued to perform. Glassrobots installed the glass fabricating system and Standard Bent Glass made its final payment to Glassrobots. Standard Bent Glass noticed defects in the equipment, and the parties disputed the cause of the defects. Standard Bent Glass sued Glassrobots. Glassrobots claimed that the contract between the parties included an arbitration clause under an appendix to the standard sales agreement. Did it?

5. Richard Davis, a South Carolina real estate broker who buys underpriced properties to renovate and sell (i.e., "flipping" homes), conceived of and developed a pilot episode of a television show documenting the flipping process. He shopped the pilot to a number of television networks, including to A & E, where he worked with the director of lifestyle programming, Charles Nordlander. Davis and Nordlander discussed turning the show into a series for A & E. Davis proposed that he would assume all of the financial risk relating to the purchase and resale of the real estate but that they would otherwise split the revenues of the show. According to Davis, Nordlander responded, "Okay, okay, I get it." Thereafter, Nordlander arranged for Davis to meet with various A & E representatives and with a production company, Departure Films, all the while reiterating the terms Davis outlined; however, they never reduced the terms to writing. With Departure Films on board, filming began, and A & E's senior vice president notified Davis that "the board approved the money for our series," *Flip This House*. They filmed 13 episodes of the series, and the show was a commercial success. Unfortunately, there was a dispute over Davis's compensation. A & E offered to pay Davis an appearance fee per episode and a 5 percent share of incremental revenue attributable to the show. Davis rejected that arrangement and signed a talent agreement with another network. A & E went on to produce three more seasons of *Flip This House* without Davis and never paid him any money, let alone half of the series' net revenue as required by the terms Davis and Nordlander discussed. Davis sued for breach of contract, but A & E denied ever entering into a contract with Davis. Does A & E owe Davis half the net revenues for *Flip This House*'s first season?

6. In the summer of 2002, after several South Louisiana women had been murdered, the Multi-Agency

Homicide Task Force was established to investigate these murders, believed to have been committed by an individual referred to as the "South Louisiana Serial Killer." In April 2003, the Baton Rouge Crime Stoppers (BRCS) began publicizing a reward offer in newspapers, television stations, and billboards around the Baton Rouge area regarding the South Louisiana Serial Killer. The offer read, in part:

> A $100,000 reward will be given for information leading to the arrest and indictment of the South Louisiana Serial Killer. Call today and help make Baton Rouge a safer place for you and your family. All calls remain anonymous. 334-STOP or 1-877-723-7867. Reward expires August 1, 2003.

A short time later, Lafayette Crime Stoppers (LCS) also publicized a reward offer. It stated in part:

> In order to qualify for the reward, the tipster must provide information which leads to the arrest, DNA match, and the formal filing of charges against a suspect through grand jury indictment. . . . In addition, the qualifying tip must be received prior to midnight, August 1, 2003. . . . Tips can be submitted 24 hours a day at 232-TIPS or toll free at 1-800-TIPS.

On July 9, 2002, Alexander was attacked in her home in St. Martin Parish, Louisiana. Alexander's son arrived home during the attack and chased the attacker from the property. Alexander reported the attack to local police and later, she and her son described the attacker to the Lafayette Sheriff's Department. Her report led investigators to suspect that her attacker could be the South Louisiana Serial Killer. In May 2003, Alexander was interviewed by an FBI agent assisting the task force. Based on the interview, a composite sketch was drawn and released to the public. On May 25, 2003, a photo lineup was prepared and presented to Alexander, and she identified her attacker. On or about August 14, 2003, Alexander contacted LCS and sought to collect the advertised award. However, LCS informed her she was ineligible to receive the award because she did not contact LCS via the tipster hotline and did not conform to the conditions of the offer. Alexander and her son filed suit against LCS and BRCS. Assuming that the information they provided led to the arrest and prosecution of the serial killer, did they accept the offers for the rewards?

7. Cantu was hired as a special education teacher by the San Benito Consolidated Independent School District under a one-year contract for the 1990–91 school year. On August 18, 1990, shortly before the start of the school year, Cantu hand-delivered to her supervisor a letter of resignation, effective August 17, 1990. In this letter, Cantu requested that her final paycheck be forwarded to an address in McAllen, Texas, some 50 miles from the San Benito office where she tendered the resignation. The San Benito superintendent of schools, the only official authorized to accept resignations on behalf of the school district, received Cantu's resignation on Monday, August 20. The superintendent wrote a letter accepting Cantu's resignation the same day and deposited the letter, properly stamped and addressed, in the mail at approximately 5:15 P.M. that afternoon. At about 8:00 A.M. the next morning, August 21, Cantu hand-delivered to the superintendent's office a letter withdrawing her resignation. This letter contained a San Benito return address. In response, the superintendent hand-delivered that same day a copy of his letter mailed the previous day to inform Cantu that her resignation had been accepted and could not be withdrawn. The dispute was taken to the state commissioner of education, who concluded that the school district's refusal to honor Cantu's contract was lawful because the school district's acceptance of Cantu's resignation was effective when mailed, which resulted in the formation of an agreement to rescind Cantu's employment contract. Cantu argued that the mailbox rule should not apply because her offer was made in person and the superintendent was not authorized to accept by using mail. Is this a good argument?

8. Andrew and Joyce Kay Pride owned a house in Nodaway County, Missouri, which they placed for sale in 2002. The Prides moved to a farm, so the house sat empty for some time while it was on the market. To avoid that, the Prides found a tenant to rent the house for $450 per month until such time the house sold. Larry Lewis made an offer to purchase the house for $55,000, sending the Prides and their Realtor a signed purchase agreement on April 9, 2003. The agreement indicated a closing date of May 13. The Prides changed that date on the agreement, crossing out May 13 and replacing it with June 1. They then signed the agreement on April 9 and initialed the change to the closing date. They informed their tenant that she would have to vacate by June 1. When June rolled around, though, there was a problem with closing. While the Prides and their Realtor appeared and were prepared to close, neither Lewis nor his wife nor Lewis's Realtor showed up. The Prides' real estate agent contacted Lewis's Realtor and was informed that Lewis had not responded to phone calls or otherwise communicated with his Realtor. The

Prides thereafter sent Lewis a letter notifying him of his default and re-listed the house. They eventually sold the house the following June for $40,000. Moreover, the Prides were unable to find a new tenant after their initial tenant vacated as directed prior to the failed closing with Lewis. Do the Prides and Lewis have a contract pursuant to which the Prides could sue for breach of contract and recover the difference between the $55,000 contract price with Lewis and the $40,000 for which the house actually sold?

9. In 1985, State Farm Mutual Insurance issued Casto an automobile insurance policy on her Jaguar. Casto also insured a second car, a Porsche, with State Farm. Some time in September or early October 1987, Casto received two renewal notices for her policy on the Jaguar, indicating that the next premium was due on October 10, 1987. State Farm sent a notice of cancellation on October 15, indicating that the policy would be canceled on October 29. Casto denied having received this notice. On October 20, Casto placed two checks, one for the Jaguar and one for the Porsche, in two pre-addressed envelopes that had been supplied by State Farm. She gave these envelopes to Donald Dick, who mailed them on the same day. The envelope containing the Porsche payment was timely delivered to State Farm, but State Farm never received the Jaguar payment, and that policy was canceled. Casto was involved in an accident on November 20 while driving the Jaguar. When she made a claim with State Farm, she learned that the policy had been canceled. After the accident, the envelope containing the Jaguar payment was returned to her stamped, "Returned for postage." The envelope did not bear any postage when returned to Casto. Casto brought a declaratory judgment action seeking a declaration that her insurance policy was in effect as of the date of the accident. Was it?

10. McGurn entered into negotiations to begin work at Bell Microproducts as a regional vice president. McGurn was eager for any employment agreement to include a termination clause that would entitle him to six months' pay and half his commissions if he were to be fired. Bell Microproducts at first balked and presented McGurn with an agreement absent any termination clause. In response, McGurn indicated he would be satisfied with a termination clause that covered only the first two years of his employment. Bell Microproducts sent him a revised employment agreement with a termination clause; however, as written, the clause covered only the first 12 months of McGurn's employment. McGurn signed and dated this agreement, but he also crossed out "twelve months" as the term of the termination clause and replaced it with a hand-written "twenty-four months." He initialed that alteration, which appeared in the middle of a two-page document about five inches above his signature. No one from Bell Microproducts noticed McGurn's edit to the agreement until McGurn's supervisor decided to fire him for poor performance 13 months after McGurn's start date. Did Bell Microproducts accept McGurn's counteroffer of a 24-month termination clause based on its silence on the subject for over a year?

Consideration

The Valley Area Anti-Smoking Foundation (VAAF) offered to pay any Valley Area residents $500 each if they would refrain from smoking for one year. Chad, a Valley Area resident, decided to accept this offer. He quit smoking immediately and did not smoke for a whole year. When Chad contacted VAAF to inform it of his success and collect his $500, VAAF informed him that it was able to pay only $250 because so many Valley Area residents had taken advantage of its offer. Chad reluctantly agreed to accept $250 instead of $500.

- Was VAAF contractually obligated to pay Chad for refraining from smoking?
- Was there consideration to support its promise to pay $500?
- Are there other facts you need to know to make that determination?
- Is Chad entitled to receive the entire $500 or only $250?
- Was VAAF ethically required to pay the entire $500?

LO — LEARNING OBJECTIVES

After studying this chapter, you should be able to:

12-1 Define the concept of consideration and describe its significance in the formation of a valid contract.

12-2 Explain the elements of consideration.

12-3 Explain why illusory promises, past consideration, and promises to perform preexisting obligations are not consideration.

12-4 Determine what is required to create a valid modification of a contract under both the common law of contracts and the UCC.

ONE OF THE THINGS that separates a contract from an unenforceable social promise is that a contract requires voluntary agreement by two or more parties. Not all agreements, however, are enforceable contracts. At a fairly early point in the development of classical contract law, the common law courts decided not to enforce gratuitous (free) promises. Instead, only promises supported by consideration were enforceable in a court of law. This was consistent with the notion that the purpose of contract law was to enforce freely made bargains. As one 19th-century work on contracts put it: "The common law . . . gives effect only to contracts that are founded on the mutual exigencies of men, and does not compel the performance of any merely gratuitous

agreements."[1] The concept of consideration distinguishes agreements that the law will enforce from gratuitous promises, which are normally unenforceable. This chapter focuses on the concept of consideration.

 LO12-1 Define the concept of consideration and describe its significance in the formation of a valid contract.

LO12-2 Explain the elements of consideration.

---

[1] T. Metcalf, *Principles of the Law of Contracts* (1874), p. 161.

Elements of Consideration

A common definition of **consideration** is *legal value, bargained for and given in exchange for an act or a promise.* Thus, a promise generally cannot be enforced against the person who made it (the *promisor*) unless the person to whom the promise was made (the *promisee*) has given up something of legal value in exchange for the promise. In effect, the requirement of consideration means that a promisee must pay the price that the promisor asked to gain the right to enforce the promisor's promise. So, if the promisor did not ask for anything in exchange for making a promise or if what the promisor asked for did not have legal value (e.g., because it was something to which she was already entitled), the promise is not enforceable against the promisor because it is not supported by consideration.

Consider the early case of *Thorne v. Deas*, in which the part owner of a sailing ship named the *Sea Nymph* promised his co-owners that he would insure the ship for an upcoming voyage.[2] He failed to do so, and when the ship was lost at sea, the court found that he was not liable to his co-owners for breaching his promise to insure the ship. Why? Because his promise was purely gratuitous; he had neither asked for nor received anything in exchange for making it. Therefore, it was unenforceable because it was not supported by consideration.

This early example illustrates two important aspects of the consideration requirement. First, the requirement *tended to limit the scope of a promisor's liability for his promises* by insulating him from liability for gratuitous promises and by protecting him against liability for reliance on such promises. Second, the mechanical application of the requirement *often produced unfair results.* This potential for unfairness has produced considerable dissatisfaction with the consideration concept. As the rest of this chapter indicates, the relative importance of consideration in modern contract law has been somewhat eroded by numerous exceptions to the consideration requirement and by judicial applications of consideration principles designed to produce fair results.

Legal Value   Consideration can be an act in the case of a unilateral contract or a promise in the case of a bilateral contract. An act or a promise can have legal value in one of two ways. If, in exchange for the promisor's promise, the promisee does, or agrees to do, something he had no prior legal duty to do, that provides legal value. If, in exchange for the promisor's promise, the promisee refrains from doing, or agrees not to do, something she has a legal right to do, that also provides legal value. This form of consideration is known as "forbearance." Though valid consideration can result from forbearance from all sorts of otherwise legal activities, later in this chapter we discuss a specific type of forbearance common in commercial settings, namely, forbearance to sue someone else when you have a good-faith belief that you have a valid claim to do so.

Note that this definition does not require that an act or a promise have monetary (economic) value to amount to consideration. Thus, in a famous 19th-century case, *Hamer v. Sidway,*[3] an uncle's promise to pay his nephew $5,000 if he refrained from using tobacco, drinking, swearing, and playing cards or billiards for money until his 21st birthday was held to be supported by consideration. Indeed, the nephew had refrained from doing any of these acts, even though he may have benefited from so refraining. He had a legal right to indulge in such activities, yet he had refrained from doing so at his uncle's request and in exchange for his uncle's promise. This was all that was required for consideration.

Adequacy of Consideration   The point that the legal value requirement is not concerned with actual value is further borne out by the fact that the courts generally will not concern themselves with questions regarding the adequacy of the consideration that the promisee gave. This means that as long as the promisee's act or promise satisfies the legal value test, the courts do not ask whether that act or promise was worth what the promisor gave, or promised to give, in return for it. This rule on adequacy of consideration reflects the laissez-faire assumptions underlying classical contract law. Freedom of contract includes the freedom to make bad bargains as well as good ones, so promisors' promises are enforceable if they got what they asked for in exchange for making their promises, even if what they asked for was not nearly so valuable in worldly terms as what they promised in return. Also, a court taking a hands-off stance concerning private contracts would be reluctant to step in and second-guess the parties by setting aside a transaction that both parties at one time considered satisfactory. Finally, the rule against judging the adequacy of consideration can promote certainty and predictability in commercial transactions by denying legal effect to what would otherwise be a possible basis for challenging the enforceability of a contract—the inequality of the exchange.

Several qualifications must be made concerning the general rule on adequacy of consideration. First, if the inadequacy of consideration is apparent on the face of the agreement, most courts conclude that the agreement was a disguised gift rather than an enforceable bargain. Thus, an agreement calling for an unequal exchange of money (e.g., $500 for $1,000) or identical goods

---

[2] 4 Johns. 84 (N.Y. 1809).

[3] 27 N.E. 256 (N.Y. Ct. App. 1891).

(20 business law textbooks for 40 identical business law textbooks) and containing no other terms would probably be unenforceable. Gross inadequacy of consideration may also give rise to an inference of fraud, duress,[4] lack of capacity,[5] unconscionability,[6] or some other independent basis for setting aside a contract. However, inadequacy of consideration, standing alone, is never sufficient to prove lack of true consent or contractual capacity. Although gross inadequacy of consideration is not, by itself, ordinarily a sufficient reason to set aside a contract, the courts may refuse to grant specific performance or other equitable remedies to persons seeking to enforce unfair bargains.

Finally, some agreements recite "$1," or "$1 and other valuable consideration," or some other small amount as consideration for a promise. If no other consideration is actually exchanged, this is called *nominal consideration.* Often, such agreements are attempts to make gratuitous promises look like true bargains by reciting a nonexistent consideration. Most courts refuse to enforce such agreements unless they find that the stated consideration was truly bargained for.

Bargained-For Exchange

Up to this point, we have focused on the legal value component of our consideration definition. But the fact that a promisee's act or promise provides legal value is not, in itself, a sufficient basis for finding that it amounted to consideration. In addition, the promisee's act or promise must have been bargained for and given in exchange for the promisor's promise. In effect, it must be the price that the promisor asked for in exchange for making his promise. Over a hundred years ago, Oliver Wendell Holmes, one of our most renowned jurists, expressed this idea when he said, "It is the essence of a consideration that, by the terms of the agreement, it is given and accepted as the motive or inducement of the promise."[7]

The following *Steinberg* case illustrates the concept of bargained-for legal value.

---

[4]Fraud and duress are discussed in Chapter 13.
[5]Lack of capacity is discussed in Chapter 14.
[6]Chapter 15 discusses unconscionability in detail.

[7]O. W. Holmes, *The Common Law* (1881), p. 239.

Steinberg v. United States	**90 Fed. Cl. 435 (2009)**

In preparation for the January 20, 2009, inauguration ceremony for President-Elect Barack Obama, the Joint Congressional Committee on Inaugural Ceremonies (JCCIC) announced that it would distribute approximately 240,000 complimentary tickets to the general public to view the inauguration ceremonies. The tickets were available at no charge, and interested parties could obtain them by contacting the office of their congressional representatives.

Michael Steinberg obtained two of the tickets from his congressman, Gus Bilirakis. Steinberg and a guest traveled to Washington, D.C., from his home in Florida and arrived several hours before the start of the ceremony at the viewing area indicated on his tickets. Eventually, however, Steinberg and his guest were refused admittance, and they were unable to view the inauguration.

Steinberg claimed that the JCCIC never told ticketholders that they might not be admitted to the designated viewing section, despite the fact that they anticipated some would be turned away. He was particularly upset about incurring travel expenses without being able to accurately weigh the risk of nonadmittance, about which the JCCIC easily could have notified him.

Steinberg filed a lawsuit against the United States for, among other things, breach of contract for the JCCIC's failure to notify him about the risk of being turned away and for failing to honor the ticket.

The United States moved to dismiss the claim.

Hewitt, Chief Judge

To recover for a breach of contract, a party must allege and establish: (1) a valid contract between the parties, (2) an obligation or duty arising under the contract, (3) a breach of that duty, and (4) damages caused by the breach. . . . To establish a valid contract with the government, a party must allege and establish: (1) mutuality of intent, (2) consideration, (3) lack of ambiguity in the offer and acceptance, and (4) that the government official whose conduct the contractor relies upon has actual authority to bind the government in contract. . . . An implied-in-fact contract has the same requirements as an express contract, but an implied-in-fact contract is founded upon the meeting of the minds and the mutual understanding of the parties. . . .

Valid contract formation also requires consideration. "[A]ny performance which is bargained for is consideration." [Restatement (Second) of Contracts (Restatement) § 72 (1981). "To constitute consideration, a performance or a return promise must be bargained for." *Id.* § 71(1). "A performance or return promise is bargained for if it is sought by the promisor in exchange for his promise and is given by the promisee in exchange for that promise." *Id.* § 71(2).

* * *

Mr. Steinberg asserts that "those persons offered tickets would have to personally pick up the tickets from his or her Congressperson's office." More specifically, in plaintiff's Motion, he asserts that "pick[ing] up the ticket in person was mandatory and thus acted as consideration in order to receive the ticket." In rendering a decision on a motion to dismiss, the court must presume that undisputed factual allegations in the complaint are true. . . . Here, however, the factual allegation supporting plaintiff's claim that such "consideration" was required is contradicted by plaintiff himself. Even if a requirement of "pick[ing] up the ticket" in person could somehow be viewed as consideration, the "mandatory" requirement on which Mr. Steinberg relies does not exist. Attached as an exhibit to the Amended Complaint was an e-mail that Mr. Steinberg received from Cristin Datch, Staff Assistant to Congressman Bilirakis, which states that "*if someone will be picking up tickets on your behalf, we must have his/her name and telephone number in order to verify his/her information when he/she arrives in our office. Therefore, if that is the case, please respond to this email with his/her contact information.*" Mr. Steinberg was not required to pick up his free ticket in person. Picking up the tickets in person could not serve as consideration necessary to establish a contract.

Nor does the court find that Mr. Steinberg's traveling expenses constitute consideration. Plaintiff defines consideration as "a detriment to the promisee or a benefit to the promisor," and asserts that the cost of traveling to DC was a detriment to him and therefore constitutes consideration. A detriment to one party may serve as consideration, but only if such detriment is bargained for. *See* Restatement § 72. Plaintiff fails to assert that his detriment, the cost of travel, was bargained for or sought by the government in any way.

Plaintiff also suggests that his attendance at the inauguration ceremonies is analogous to the activities of a plaintiff who participated in the promotion of a casino. ("The process was similar to a contest, with winners being selected.") (citing *Gottlieb v. Tropicana Hotel & Casino*, 109 F. Supp. 2d 324 (E.D. Pa. 2000)). In *Gottlieb*, the plaintiff was required to report information about her gambling habits to the casino and became "a part of the entertainment" at the casino. The court in *Gottlieb* concluded that the casino "offered the promotion in order to generate patronage of and excitement within the casino." *Id.* at 330. The plaintiff in *Gottlieb* established bargained-for consideration and survived a motion for summary judgment.

The court [is unconvinced by] plaintiff's comparison of a presidential inauguration to a casino's business effort to attract customers in an attempt to turn a profit. Throngs of people traveled to Washington for the inauguration. Plaintiff notes that "[p]ersons who desired the tickets exceeded the number available." A message on plaintiff's tickets warned the holders to "arrive early due to large crowds." Unlike the proprietor of the casino in *Gottlieb*, the government did not bargain for Mr. Steinberg's attendance. The United States did not receive a bargained-for benefit from the spectators who attended the inauguration ceremonies.

Plaintiff asserts that "the JCCIC received an intangible benefit of promoting the Inauguration by means of the complimentary tickets offered through the various mediums." Plaintiff does not explain what such an intangible benefit might be. The government did not attempt to make money from the inauguration, nor did it need to attract participants as the casino in *Gottlieb* did. In determining whether there was consideration, the question is not whether one party received a benefit (tangible or otherwise), but whether the benefit was bargained for. *See* Restatement § 71. If the benefit was not bargained for, and here it was not, it cannot constitute consideration necessary to support a contract. The government did not bargain for the attendance of plaintiff or others at the inauguration ceremonies. Because the inauguration is unlike the business in *Gottlieb*, the court finds that there was no bargained-for benefit, tangible or intangible, that could serve as consideration.

* * *

For the reasons set forth above, the court **GRANTS** defendant's Motion. Because defendant's Motion is **GRANTED**, the case is **DISMISSED**. . . .

IT IS SO ORDERED.

Exchanges That Fail to Meet Consideration Requirements

 LO12-3 Explain why illusory promises, past consideration, and promises to perform preexisting obligations are not consideration.

Illusory Promises For a promise to serve as consideration in a bilateral contract, the promisee must have promised to do, or to refrain from doing, something at the promisor's request. It seems obvious, therefore, that if the promisee's promise is illusory because it really does not bind the promisee to do or refrain from doing anything, such a promise could not serve as consideration. Such agreements are often said to lack the mutuality of obligation required for an agreement to be enforceable. So, a promisee's promise to buy "all the sugar that I want" or to "paint your house if I feel like it" would not be sufficient consideration for a promisor's return promise to sell sugar or hire a painter. In neither case has the promisee given the promisor anything of legal value in exchange for the promisor's promise. Remember, though: So long as the promisee has given legal value, the agreement will be enforceable even though what the promisee gave is worth substantially less than what the promisor promised in return.

Effect of Cancellation or Termination Clauses The fact that an agreement allows one or both of the parties to cancel or terminate their contractual obligations does not necessarily mean that the party (or parties) with the power to cancel has given an illusory promise. Such provisions are a common and necessary part of many business relationships. The central issue in such cases concerns whether a promise subject to cancellation or termination actually represents a binding obligation. A right to cancel or terminate at any time, for any reason, and without any notice would clearly render illusory any other promise by the party possessing such a right. However, limits on the circumstances under which cancellation may occur (such as a dealer's failure to live up to dealership obligations), or the time in which cancellation may occur (such as no cancellations for the first 90 days), or a requirement of advance notice of cancellation (such as a 30-day notice requirement) would all effectively remove a promise from the illusory category. This is so because in each case the party making such a promise has bound himself to do *something* in exchange for the other party's promise. A party's duty of good faith and fair dealing can also limit the right to terminate and prevent its promise from being considered illusory.

The court in *Day v. Fortune Hi-Tech Marketing, Inc.*, which follows, addresses the effect of a clause in a contract that gave one party the option to modify it at will.

Day v. Fortune Hi-Tech Marketing, Inc.   536 F. App'x 600 (6th Cir. 2013)

Fortune Hi-Tech Marketing Inc. (FHTM) is a multilevel marketing company and acts as a third-party marketing firm that sells services from companies to consumers. Yvonne Day and a number of other individuals paid an enrollment fee to serve as Independent Representatives (IRs) of FHTM. They sold the services of various companies on behalf of FHTM, for which they would receive commissions. IRs also received bonuses of $100 for each new IR they recruited.

When enrolling an IR, an individual completed an application and agreement that indicated he or she had read and agreed to the FHTM Policies and Procedures, which were incorporated into the agreement between the company and the IR. The FHTM Policies and Procedures included a requirement that any claim brought under the agreement would be arbitrated. Another clause in the Policies and Procedures indicated that FHTM could modify the agreement at any time without notice.

Eventually, Day and others filed suit against FHTM in a federal district court in Kentucky under various federal and Kentucky state consumer protection and antiracketeering laws. They alleged that FHTM was running an illegal pyramid scheme. The plaintiffs alleged that the only way to recoup their enrollment fees and/or to make additional money was to recruit new IRs because doing that was far more lucrative than selling services on behalf of FHTM.

FHTM filed a motion with the court to compel arbitration of the claims based on the arbitration clause in the Policies and Procedures. Initially, the district court found that the plaintiffs had agreed to arbitrate their claims. However, the plaintiffs moved the court to reconsider its ruling. Upon reconsideration, the district court determined that the arbitration agreement was invalid and ordered the claims to proceed to trial.

Although appeals to the circuit court must usually await a final resolution of the case at the district-court level, certain issues are subject to interlocutory appeal prior to final resolution of the case. A ruling on the validity of an arbitration clause is typically one such issue, and FHTM was allowed to file an interlocutory appeal of the district court's denial of its motion to compel arbitration.

Clay, Circuit Judge

There is a general presumption in favor of arbitration. . . . Even if courts are meant to favor a finding that parties have agreed to submit their claims to arbitration, parties must still have a valid and enforceable agreement to resolve their claims in arbitration. Although it is a basic principle of contract law that every contract requires mutuality and consideration, an arbitration clause does not require independent consideration; so long as the contract as a whole is adequately supported by consideration, each clause is valid unless there is some other deficiency in the contract's validity.

The district court found that the arbitration clause was unenforceable because the contract between Plaintiffs and Defendant was not supported by adequate consideration, and we agree. Because Defendant retained the ability to modify any term of the contract, at any time, its promises were illusory. Defendant was not bound by any particular provision of the contract because at any point, including immediately after acceptance, Defendant could have changed any clause without any recourse sounding in contract law available to Plaintiffs. The only notice provision made changes effective upon their issuance, rather than after a fixed period of time. Had the contract permitted unilateral alteration upon thirty days' notice, for example, there might have been consideration, because the altering party would still have been bound to the original terms for the thirty day period. *See* Restatement (Second) of Contracts § 77 cmt. b, illus. 5 (1981). But in this case, in effect, Defendant promised to do certain things unless it decided not to, and that is by definition illusory. While some states may permit enforcement of a contract that requires only notice, rather than advance notice, for alteration of its terms, Kentucky is not one of those states. Accordingly, because the contract lacked consideration, the entire contract, including the arbitration clause, is void and unenforceable. . . .

Defendant raises [several] arguments as to why the agreement was supported by consideration, or why, even if there was no consideration, the contract is still enforceable. First, [it argues that] there was no modification of the arbitration clause at any point during the relevant time period here. . . . [T]hat argument confuses performance of the terms with an obligation to perform under the contract. The fact that Defendant voluntarily continued to maintain the terms of their promise is irrelevant; the question is whether it had a legally binding obligation to continue to do so. Nothing bound Defendant to continue its agreement, or even to maintain the same terms. As the district court pointed out, Defendant could have, through any one of the various notice devices it included, changed the contract immediately upon receipt of a signed copy from any one of the Plaintiffs. Without a binding obligation, a promise is illusory, and therefore not enforceable as a contract. . . .

For the foregoing reasons, the judgment of the district court is AFFIRMED.

Effect of Output and Requirements Contracts Contracts in which one party to the agreement agrees to buy all of the other party's production of a particular commodity (*output* contracts) or to supply all of another party's needs for a particular commodity (*requirements* contracts) are common business transactions that serve legitimate business purposes. They can reduce a seller's selling costs and provide buyers with a secure source of supply. Prior to the enactment of the UCC, however, many common law courts refused to enforce such agreements on the ground that their failure to specify the quantity of goods to be produced or purchased rendered them illusory. The courts also feared that a party to such an agreement might be tempted to exploit the other party. For example, subsequent market conditions could make it profitable for the seller in an output contract or the buyer in a requirements contract to demand that the other party buy or provide more of the particular commodity than the other party had actually intended to buy or sell. The UCC legitimizes requirements and output contracts. It addresses the concern about the potential for exploitation by limiting a party's demands to those quantity needs that occur in *good faith* and are not unreasonably disproportionate to any quantity estimate contained in the contract, or to any normal prior output or requirements if no estimate is stated [2-306(1)]. Chapter 19 discusses this subject in greater detail.

As the following *Mid-American Salt* case shows, however, parties must be careful to clearly indicate the nature of the contract is one of output or requirements. Otherwise, no obligations are contemplated, and there is no consideration to support the agreement, even under the UCC.

Effect of Exclusive Dealing Contracts When a manufacturer of goods enters an agreement giving a distributor the exclusive right to sell the manufacturer's products in a particular territory, does such an agreement impose sufficient obligations on both parties to meet the legal value test? Put another way, does the distributor have any duty to sell the manufacturer's products and does the manufacturer have any duty to supply any particular number of products? Such agreements are commonly encountered in today's business world, and they can serve the legitimate interests of both parties. The UCC recognizes this fact by providing that, unless the parties agree to the contrary, an exclusive dealing contract imposes a duty on the distributor to use her best efforts to sell the goods and imposes a reciprocal duty on the manufacturer to use his best efforts to supply the goods [2-306(2)].

Mid-American Salt, LLC v. Morris County Cooperative Pricing Council   964 F.3d 218 (3d Cir. 2020)

Through a competitive bidding process, Mid-American Salt, LLC (Mid-American) agreed with the Morris County Cooperative Pricing Council (Council), a group of more than 200 New Jersey counties, municipalities, police departments, and school districts, to supply the Council with rock salt during the 2016–2017 winter. The bid specifications anticipated that the Council would require 115,000 tons of rock salt that season, and Mid-American offered to provide the salt at a particular price. The specifications, which were incorporated into the agreement between Mid-American and the Council, further stated:

> This is an Open-Ended contract, meaning all items are specified with an estimated quantity. There is no obligation to purchase that quantity during the contract period, and the actual quantity purchased by members of the [Council] may vary.
>
> All quantities may be more or less than estimated. No minimum order requirements are allowed, unless stated otherwise elsewhere.

The only quantities stated in the contract were clearly estimates, not obligations.

Following the execution of the agreement, Mid-American undertook several complex and costly steps to source from Morocco, transport by boat and tug, and properly store at a New Jersey port a quantity of rock salt sufficient to meet the estimated requirements of the Council members. During the winter, however, Council members purchased only 5% of the inventory of rock salt Mid-American acquired. Moreover, Mid-American alleged that several members purchased salt from one of its competitors at a below-market rate.

In June 2017, Mid-American sued the Council and a number of its members for, among other things, breach of contract. The defendants moved to dismiss the breach of contract claim for lack of consideration. The district court granted the dismissal, finding no requirements contract existed. Mid-American appealed.

Hardiman, Circuit Judge

At issue in this case is a "requirements contract." Under New Jersey law, such a contract measures quantity through "the requirements of the buyer," instead of through a fixed number stated in the contract. N.J. Stat. Ann. § 12A:2-306(1). Requirements contracts do not need a minimum or maximum order set forth therein, but instead rely on "such actual . . . requirements as may occur in good faith, except that no quantity unreasonably disproportionate to any stated estimate . . . may be tendered or demanded." *Id.* The official comment to this section further explains:

> If an estimate of output or requirements is included in the agreement, no quantity unreasonably disproportionate to it may be tendered or demanded. Any minimum or maximum set by the agreement shows a clear limit on the intended elasticity. In similar fashion, the agreed estimate is to be regarded as a center around which the parties intend the variation to occur.

N.J. Stat. Ann. § 12A:2-306, Comment 3.

Mid-American relies heavily on [a] case in New Jersey that involved a cooperative pricing agreement for asphalt paving materials signed by the Council. . . . The Council responds . . . with a contrary administrative law decision. Because [those two cases] cannot be reconciled and they include some dissimilar facts to this appeal, New Jersey caselaw does not answer the question presented.

The Council members argue they entered into a valid, binding contract with Mid-American. Under the contract terms, Mid-American was required to provide bulk road salt to the members as needed. Yet the Council members claim no corresponding requirement existed for any of them to purchase a single pound of salt from Mid-American. In their view, the agreement is essentially an options contract.

Mid-American counters that the contract must be read to require Council members who submitted estimates to purchase all their salt needs from Mid-American. On this reading, the contract's final quantity-variation provision relieves a member with no salt needs of any obligation to purchase. But that does not mean, Mid-American says, that members remain free to purchase salt from Mid-American's competitors at discounted prices.

Neither the general terms of the contract nor the specific provision Mid-American relies on support its position. Found in bold in the bid specifications, the quantity-variation provision reads: "**There is no obligation to purchase that quantity** [referring to the estimates] **during the contract period, and the actual quantity purchased by members of the [Council] may vary.**" Citing the explicit statement "that defendants had 'no obligation to purchase' during the contract period," the District Court observed that "[Mid-American's] own pleadings and the unambiguous language of the contract" contradicted Mid-American's contention that there was an implicit promise to purchase certain amounts of salt. We agree.

[The] contract does not clearly state that it is for "requirements." Nor does it mention the word "exclusive," which is another hallmark of a requirements contract. *See* N.J. Stat. Ann. § 12A:2-306. The absence of these fundamental attributes of a requirements contract, when combined with the Council members' promise to buy salt in such quantities "as may be desired" or as they "may want," compels us to hold that the contract is illusory.

* * *

Finally, we note these are sophisticated parties capable of entering into precisely the kind of contract they desire. It would have been easy to, for example, insert a simple provision stating, "This is a contract for rock salt requirements and the Council covenants to purchase (and pay for) its rock salt requirements from the Contractor." Even merely titling this a "Requirements Contract" would have indicated to us that a requirements contract was, in fact, being formed. But that is not the contract we have before us and we will not rewrite the bargain for the parties.

In sum, neither the Council nor its members ever promised to purchase from Mid-American all the rock salt they required.

And their promise to pay for any rock salt they might have purchased—a rather obvious proposition—does not oblige them to actually purchase anything. Nor can the implied covenant of good faith and fair dealing . . . supply a promise that was never made. Because Mid-American promised to supply rock salt requirements to the Council and its members without obtaining a corresponding promise in return, we hold that the contract is illusory.

* * *

In sum, no valid requirements contract for bulk rock salt existed here because the contract was illusory. **We will affirm the orders of the District Court.**

Preexisting Duties

The legal value component of our consideration definition requires that promisees do, or promise to do, something that they had no prior legal duty to do in exchange for a promisor's promise. Thus, as a general rule, performing or agreeing to perform a preexisting duty is not consideration. This seems fair because the promisor in such a case has effectively made a gratuitous promise because she was already entitled to the promisee's performance.

Preexisting Public Duties Every member of society has a duty to obey the law and refrain from committing crimes or torts. Therefore, a promisee's promise not to commit such an act can never be consideration. So, Thomas's promise to pay Brown $100 a year in exchange for Brown's promise not to burn Thomas's barn would not be enforceable against Thomas. Because Brown has a preexisting duty not to burn Thomas's barn, his promise lacks legal value.

Similarly, public officials, by virtue of their offices, have a preexisting legal duty to perform their public responsibilities. For example, Smith, the owner of a liquor store, promises to pay Fawcett, a police officer whose beat includes Smith's store, $50 a week to keep an eye on the store while walking her beat. Smith's promise is unenforceable because Fawcett has agreed to do something that she already has a duty to do.

Preexisting Contractual Duties and Modifications of Contracts under the Common Law

 Determine what is required to create a valid modification of a contract under both the common law of contracts and the UCC.

The most important preexisting duty cases are those involving preexisting *contractual* duties. These cases generally occur when the parties to an existing contract agree to *modify* that contract. The general common law rule on contract modifications holds that an agreement to modify an existing contract requires *some new (independent) consideration* to be binding.

For example, Turner enters into a contract with Acme Construction Company for the construction of a new office building for $3,500,000. When the construction is partially completed, Acme tells Turner that due to rising labor and materials costs it will stop construction unless Turner agrees to pay an extra $500,000. Turner, having already entered into contracts to lease office space in the new building, promises to pay the extra amount. When the construction is finished, Turner refuses to pay more than $3,500,000. Is Turner's promise to pay the extra $500,000 enforceable against him? No. All Acme has done in exchange for Turner's promise to pay more is build the building, something that Acme had a preexisting contractual duty to do. Therefore, Acme's performance is not consideration for Turner's promise to pay more.

Although the result in the preceding example seems fair (why should Turner have to pay $4,000,000 for something he had a right to receive for $3,500,000?) and is consistent with consideration theory, the application of the preexisting duty rule to contract modifications has generated a great deal of criticism. Plainly, the rule can protect a party to a contract such as Turner from being pressured into paying more because the other party to the contract is trying to take advantage of his situation by demanding an additional amount for performance. However, mechanical application of the rule could also produce unfair results when the parties have freely agreed to a fair modification of their contract. Some critics argue that the purpose of contract modification law should be to enforce freely made modifications of existing contracts and to deny enforcement to coerced modifications. Such critics commonly suggest that general principles such as good faith and unconscionability, rather than technical consideration rules, should be used to police contract modifications.

Other observers argue that most courts in fact apply the preexisting duty rule in a manner calculated to reach fair results because several exceptions to the rule can be used to enforce a fair modification agreement. For example, any new consideration furnished by the promisee provides sufficient consideration to support a promise to modify an existing contract. So, if Acme had promised to finish construction a week before the completion date called for in the original contract, or had promised to make some change in the original contract specifications such as to install a better grade of carpet, Acme would have done something that it had no legal duty to do in exchange for Turner's new promise. Turner's promise to pay more would then be enforceable because it would be supported by new consideration.

Many courts also enforce an agreement to modify an existing contract if the modification resulted from *unforeseen*

circumstances that a party could not reasonably be expected to have foreseen and that made that party's performance far more difficult than the parties originally anticipated. For example, if Acme had requested the extra payment because abnormal subsurface rock formations made excavation on the construction site far more costly and time-consuming than could have been reasonably expected, many courts would enforce Turner's promise to pay more.

Courts can also enforce fair modification agreements by holding that the parties mutually agreed to terminate their original contract and then entered a new one. Because contracts are created by the will of the parties, they can be terminated in the same fashion. Each party agrees to release the other party from his contractual obligations in exchange for the other party's promise to do the same. Because such a mutual agreement terminates all duties owed under the original agreement, any subsequent agreement by the parties would not be subject to the preexisting duty rule. A court is likely to take this approach, however, only when it is convinced that the modification agreement was fair and free from coercion. The following *Welsh* case illustrates the common law approach to modification of contracts.

Welsh v. Lithia Vaudm, Inc.   895 N.W.2d 487 (Iowa Ct. App. 2016)

On January 14, 2015, Kent and Julie Welsh took their 2008 Volkswagen Toureg to Lithia Volkswagen of Des Moines for evaluation of possible mechanical problems, specifically complaining that the vehicle's "oil pressure" light was activated. After Lithia evaluated the car, an employee called Kent to recommend repairs amounting to $4,336. Kent agreed. Lithia proceeded to repair the car. At no time in person or on the phone did Welsh or any representative of Lithia discuss arbitration.

Lithia completed the repair, including some unanticipated work when the "check engine" light subsequently activated, but it invoiced that work at no charge to the Welshes. Julie, Kent's spouse, picked up the car at Lithia after the repairs were completed, on March 16, 2015. She paid the expected charge of $4,336 and signed a three-page document titled "INVOICE." Immediately above Julie's signature, the invoice provided for the arbitration of disputes "pursuant to the Federal Arbitration Act." Julie took the vehicle home.

A few days later, however, the Welshes returned the car to Lithia, noting the "check engine" light was activated. After evaluations, Lithia proposed a costly repair, which the Welshes declined to authorize.

Subsequently, the Welshes sued Lithia for damages arising from the Lithia's alleged failure to repair the car. Lithia moved to compel arbitration in response, stating, "On or about March 16, 2015, [the parties] entered into a contractual Agreement . . . for certain repairs to the vehicle." Based on that purported Agreement, Lithia argued that Julie had committed the Welshes to submit any disputes to arbitration. The Welshes responded that their contract was formed shortly after January 14, 2015, when Kent authorized Lithia to do the repairs during the telephone conversation with the Lithia employee.

The trial court found that the arbitration clause was not part of the parties' contract. Lithia appealed.

Tabor, Judge

Lithia . . . argues the district court's ruling failed to recognize the basic principle that written agreements such as the invoice are presumed to be supported by consideration. . . . Lithia asserts: "Lithia's work in replacing the oil pump and the timing chains and adjustors, and [the Welshes'] act of paying money and

waiting for those repairs to be completed," constituted "independent consideration." We are not persuaded.

General principles of contract law determine the validity of an arbitration agreement. For a contract to be valid in Iowa, it must contain three elements—offer, acceptance, and consideration. The consideration element supports the fact "contract law exists to enforce mutual bargains, not gratuitous promises." [*Margeson v. Artis*, 776 N.W.2d 652, 655 (Iowa 2009).] Generally, "when the parties modify a contract, a new contract arises." *Iowa Arboretum, Inc. v. Iowa 4-H Found.*, 886 N.W.2d 695, 706 (Iowa 2016). But where "the parties to a contract modify the terms, there must be some new and valid consideration." *Id.* The party asserting a lack of consideration, here Welsh, must establish the defense.

We look for the element of consideration in the language of the contract and by "what the parties contemplated at the time the instrument was executed." *Margeson*, 776 N.W.2d at 657 (citation omitted). A promise to perform a preexisting duty generally does not constitute additional consideration. Specifically,

> a promise made by one party to a contract normally cannot be enforced by the other party to the contract unless the party to whom the promise was made provided some promise or performance in exchange for the promise sought to be enforced. In other words, if the promisor did not seek anything in exchange for the promise made, . . . the promise made by the promisor is unenforceable due to the absence of consideration.

Margeson, Id. 776 N.W.2d at 655–56.

Applying these principles, we conclude the district court was correct in its analysis. The document containing the arbitration language was not signed when Welsh brought his vehicle to Lithia to be repaired. After the repairs were completed, Julie did not seek anything in exchange for the promise to arbitrate; Lithia already had completed its work at the set price, making her promise to arbitrate unenforceable due to the absence of consideration. In other words, no additional consideration existed where Lithia, the promisee, had a preexisting duty under the oral contract to evaluate and repair the car for a set price, and it did so. Lithia's alleged modification was nothing more than a *post-performance*, unilateral demand by it to submit any future disputes to arbitration. *After* Lithia completed the repairs, it asked the Welshes to give up their right to litigate in court in return for the same performance by Lithia—repairing the car at the set price. . . .

Thus, Lithia cannot enforce the promise to arbitrate because there is no evidence Lithia "promised to do something more than [it] had promised to do under the [oral] agreement." *Margeson, Id.* 776 N.W.2d at 658. Accordingly, we affirm the district court's denial of Lithia's motion to compel arbitration.

AFFIRMED.

Preexisting Duty and Contract Modification under the UCC

 LO12-4 Determine what is required to create a valid modification of a contract under both the common law of contracts and the UCC.

The drafters of the UCC sought to avoid many of the problems caused by the consideration requirement by dispensing with it in two important situations: As discussed in Chapter 10, the UCC does not require consideration for firm offers [2-205]. The UCC also provides that an agreement to modify a contract for the sale of goods needs *no consideration* to be binding [2-209(1)]. For example, Electronics World orders 200 XYZ televisions at $150 per unit from XYZ Corp. Electronics World later seeks to cancel its order, but XYZ refuses to agree to cancellation. Instead, XYZ seeks to mollify a valued customer by offering to reduce the price to $100 per unit. Electronics World agrees, but when the televisions arrive, XYZ bills Electronics World for $150 per unit. Under classical contract principles, XYZ's promise to reduce the price of the goods would not be enforceable because Electronics World has furnished no new consideration in exchange for XYZ's promise. Under the UCC,

no new consideration is necessary, and the agreement to modify the contract is enforceable.

Several things should be made clear about the operation of this UCC rule. First, XYZ had no duty to agree to a modification and could have insisted on payment of $150 per unit. Second, modification agreements under the UCC are still subject to scrutiny under the general UCC principles of good faith and unconscionability, so unfair agreements or agreements that are the product of coercion are unlikely to be enforced. Finally, the UCC contains two provisions to protect people from fictitious claims that an agreement has been modified. If the original agreement requires any modification to be in writing, an oral modification is unenforceable [2-209(2)]. Regardless of what the original agreement says, if the price of the goods in the modified contract is $500 or more, the modification is unenforceable unless the requirements of the UCC's statute of frauds section [2-201] are satisfied [2-209(3)].[8]

Preexisting Duty and Agreements to Settle Debts One special variant of the preexisting duty rule that causes considerable confusion occurs when a debtor offers to pay a creditor a sum less than the creditor is demanding in

---

[8]Chapter 16 discusses § 2-201 of the UCC in detail.

exchange for the creditor's promise to accept the part payment as full payment of the debt. If the creditor later sues for the balance of the debt, is the creditor's promise to take less enforceable? The answer depends on the nature of the debt and on the circumstances of the debtor's payment.

Liquidated Debts A **liquidated debt** is a debt that is both due and certain; that is, the parties have no good-faith dispute about either the existence or the amount of the original debt. If a debtor does nothing more than pay less than an amount he clearly owes, how could this be consideration for a creditor's promise to take less? Such a debtor has actually done less than he had a preexisting legal duty to do—namely, to pay the full amount of the debt. For this reason, the creditor's promise to discharge a liquidated debt for part payment of the debt at or after its due date is *unenforceable* for lack of consideration.

For example, Connor borrows $10,000 from Friendly Finance Company, payable in one year. On the day payment is due, Connor sends Friendly a check for $9,000 marked: "Payment in full for all claims Friendly Finance has against me." Friendly cashes Connor's check, thus impliedly promising to accept it as full payment by cashing it, and later sues Connor for $1,000. Friendly is entitled to the $1,000 because Connor has given no consideration to support Friendly's implied promise to accept $9,000 as full payment.

However, had Connor done something he had no preexisting duty to do in exchange for Friendly's promise to settle for part payment, he could enforce Friendly's promise and avoid paying the $1,000. For example, if Connor had paid early, before the loan contract called for payment, or in a different medium of exchange from that called for in the loan contract (such as $4,000 in cash and a car worth $5,000), he would have given consideration for Friendly's promise to accept early or different payment as full payment.

Unliquidated Debts A good-faith dispute about either the existence or the amount of a debt makes the debt an *unliquidated debt*. The settlement of an unliquidated debt is called an **accord and satisfaction**.[9] When an accord and satisfaction has occurred, the creditor cannot maintain an action to recover the remainder of the debt that he alleges is due. For example, Computer Corner, a retailer, orders 50 laptop computers and associated software from Computech for $75,000. After receiving the goods, Computer Corner refuses to pay Computech the full $75,000, arguing that some of the computers were defective and that some of the software it received did not conform to its order. Computer Corner sends Computech a check for $60,000

marked: "Payment in full for all goods received from Computech." A creditor in Computech's position obviously faces a real dilemma. If Computech cashes Computer Corner's check, it will be held to have impliedly promised to accept $60,000 as full payment. Computech's promise to accept part payment as full payment would be enforceable because Computer Corner has given consideration to support it: Computer Corner has given up its right to have a court determine the amount it owes Computech. This is something that Computer Corner had no duty to do; by giving up this right and the $60,000 in exchange for Computech's implied promise, the consideration requirement is satisfied. The result in this case is supported not only by consideration theory but also by a strong public policy in favor of encouraging parties to settle their disputes out of court. Who would bother to settle disputed claims out of court if settlement agreements were unenforceable?

Computech could refuse to accept Computer Corner's settlement offer and sue for the full $75,000, but doing so involves several risks. A court may decide that Computer Corner's arguments are valid and award Computech less than $60,000. Even if Computech is successful, it may take years to resolve the case in the courts through the expensive and time-consuming litigation process. In addition, there is always the chance that Computer Corner may file for bankruptcy before any judgment can be collected. Faced with such risks, Computech may feel that it has no practical alternative other than to cash Computer Corner's check.[10]

Composition Agreements Composition agreements are agreements between a debtor and two or more creditors who agree to accept as full payment a stated percentage of their liquidated claims against the debtor at or after the date on which those claims are payable. Composition agreements are generally enforced by the courts despite the fact that enforcement appears to be contrary to the general rule on part payment of liquidated debts. Many courts have justified enforcing composition agreements on the ground that the creditors' mutual agreement to accept less than the amount due them provides the necessary consideration. The main reason why creditors agree to compositions is that they fear that their failure to do so may force the debtor into bankruptcy proceedings, in which case they might ultimately recover a smaller percentage of their claims than that agreed to in the composition.

---

[9]Accord and satisfaction is also discussed in Chapter 18.

[10]A provision of Article 3 of the Uniform Commercial Code, section 3-311, covers accord and satisfaction by use of an instrument such as a "full payment" check. With a few exceptions, the basic provisions of section 3-311 parallel the common law rules regarding accord and satisfaction that are described in this chapter and Chapter 18.

The Global Business Environment

Like the UCC, the CISG does not require new consideration to modify a contract. The CISG states that contracts can be modified by the "mere agreement" of the parties. Another similarity between the UCC and

CISG is that under the CISG, a term in a written contract stating that modifications of that contract can only be made in writing will generally preclude oral modifications.

Ethics and Compliance in Action

Rex Roofing contracted with the O'Neills to install a new roof on their house for $2,500. Rex began the work and soon realized that he had underbid the job. He informed the O'Neills that he would not do the job for $2,500 after all, but that he would complete the work for $3,200. The O'Neills promised to pay him $3,200. Assuming

that there were no unforeseen conditions that affected the roof and no obvious mistakes in the bid calculations, was it ethical for Rex Roofing to refuse to do the job at the agreed-upon price? Because the O'Neills agreed to pay the higher price, are they ethically obligated to do so, even if the law does not require them to pay more than the originally agreed-upon price?

Forbearance to Sue An agreement by a promisee to refrain, or forbear, from pursuing a legal claim against a promisor can be valid consideration to support a return promise—usually to pay a sum of money—by a promisor. The promisee has agreed not to file suit, something that she has a legal right to do, in exchange for the promisor's promise. The courts do not wish to sanction extortion by allowing people to threaten to file spurious claims against others in the hope that those threatened will agree to some payment to avoid the expense or embarrassment associated with defending a lawsuit. On the other hand, we have a strong public policy favoring private settlement of disputes. Therefore, it is generally said that the promisee must have a good-faith belief in the validity of his or her claim before forbearance amounts to consideration.

Past Consideration
Past consideration—despite its name—is not consideration at all. Past consideration is an act or other benefit given in the past that was *not* given in exchange for the promise in question. Because the past act was not given in exchange for the present promise, it cannot be consideration. Consider again the facts of the famous case of *Hamer v. Sidway*, discussed earlier in this chapter. There, an uncle's promise to pay his nephew $5,000 for refraining from smoking, drinking, swearing, and other delightful pastimes until his 21st birthday was supported by consideration because the nephew had given legal value by refraining from participating in the prohibited activities. However, what if the uncle had said to his nephew on the eve of his

21st birthday: "Your mother tells me you've been a good lad and abstained from tobacco, hard drink, foul language, and gambling. Such goodness should be rewarded. Tomorrow, I'll give you a check for $5,000." Should the uncle's promise be enforceable against him? Clearly not, because although his nephew's behavior still passes the legal value test, in this case it was not bargained for and given in exchange for the uncle's promise.

Moral Obligation As a general rule, promises made to satisfy a preexisting moral obligation are unenforceable for lack of consideration. The fact that a promisor or some member of the promisor's family, for example, has received some benefit from the promisee in the past (e.g., food and lodging, or emergency care) would not constitute consideration for a promisor's promise to pay for that benefit, due to the absence of the bargain element. Some courts find this result distressing and enforce such promises despite the absence of consideration. In addition, a few states have passed statutes making promises to pay for past benefits enforceable if such a promise is contained in a writing that clearly expresses the promisor's intent to be bound.

In the following *Doe* case, the court finds that even an organization like the Roman Catholic Church has no legal obligation to fulfill its moral obligations. Note, however, that had the Archdiocese's commitment to pay for Doe's therapy been negotiated to avoid the Does otherwise filing a valid lawsuit against it, the outcome likely would have been different.

Doe v. Roman Catholic Archdiocese of Indianapolis
958 N.E.2d 472 (Ind. Ct. App. 2011)

Jane Doe reported that she was sexually abused by a Roman Catholic priest when she was a teenager. In 1999, Doe's husband met with officials of the Roman Catholic Archdiocese of Indianapolis to discuss the abuse. Initially, the Does demanded a lump-sum payment from the Archdiocese as compensation for the abuse. The Archdiocese denied any legal liability to Doe and declined to make any direct payment to Doe in relation to her claim. Doe's husband pressed on, hiring an attorney and sending a letter in August 2000 indicating that, even though the Archdiocese had "no legal responsibility at this time," it had a moral responsibility to Doe.

Consistent with its policy on dealing with victims of childhood sexual abuse by church officials, the Archdiocese offered to pay for Doe's therapy and counseling. The Does accepted that arrangement, and the Archdiocese began paying the fees in 2001. In 2006, the Archdiocese's chancellor became concerned that Doe's therapy was producing no signs of recovery despite more than $100,000 it had paid for Doe's care. In consultation with multiple health professionals (though allegedly against the advice of Doe's psychiatrist and therapist), the chancellor concluded that the Archdiocese would reduce its commitment to pay for Doe's psychotherapy from two sessions weekly to one session per month. Doe had no insurance. If the Archdiocese did not pay for her therapy, she had to pay for it out of pocket.

Doe sued the Archdiocese for breach of contract. The trial court granted the Archdiocese's motion for summary judgment, finding that it had no legal responsibility to continue paying all of Doe's continuing therapy costs.

Doe appealed.

Baker, Judge

Doe argues that the trial court erred in granting the Archdiocese's motion for summary judgment primarily because the Archdiocese breached its obligation to continue paying for all of her therapist and counseling fees. Doe contends that the Archdiocese should have continued to pay because it was both legally and morally responsible for it to do so.

At the outset, we note that the Archdiocesan "Policy on Care of Victims Sexual Misconduct" (Policy) provides for "the general courses of action that may be taken by the chancellor." And one course of action described in the policy includes offering victims and/or the family "appropriate counseling and spiritual direction, as needed." However, a portion of the Policy makes it clear that

4. This statement of policy does not constitute a contractual undertaking of any nature of the payment of any amount to any person, but is an exoteric statement for guidance of the resource team of the Archdiocese. In all cases, the Archdiocese expressly reserves the right to withhold or change the terms of any benefits payable pursuant to this statement of policy or any other arrangement with victims, in the sole discretion of the Archdiocese.

And, as mentioned above, Doe's husband expressly acknowledged in his letter of August 11, 2000, that the Archdiocese's response was based upon its moral obligation. More specifically, a portion of that letter acknowledges that Doe understood that "the archdiocese has no legal responsibility at this time, but it seems to me that when the loss due to the actions of a representative of the archdiocese is so evident and measureable, a moral responsibility remains to compensate for that loss."

As the Archdiocese points out, a promise must be predicated upon adequate consideration before it can command performance. And a moral obligation to perform an agreement does not provide sufficient consideration to support the enforcement of an agreement nor does it create an enforceable contract.

In this case, while the letters that the Archdiocese sent to the Does express an intent to assist them with counseling costs, that correspondence does not amount to a contract to provide them unlimited care and treatment at its expense. Therefore, the designated evidence establishes that there was no enforceable contract in this instance, and Doe's claim fails on this basis.

The judgment of the trial court is affirmed.

Exceptions to the Consideration Requirement

The consideration requirement is a classic example of a traditional contract law rule. It is precise, abstract, and capable of almost mechanical application. It can also, in some instances, result in significant injustice. Modern courts and legislatures have responded to this potential for injustice by carving out numerous exceptions to the requirement of consideration. Some of these exceptions (for example, the UCC firm offer and contract modification rules) have already been discussed in this and preceding chapters. In the remaining portion of this chapter, we focus on several other important exceptions to the consideration requirement.

Consideration

Consideration*	Not Consideration
Doing something you had no preexisting duty to do	Doing something you had a preexisting duty to do
Promising to do something you had no preexisting duty to do	Promising to do something you had a preexisting duty to do
Paying part of a liquidated debt prior to the date the debt is due	Nominal consideration (unless actually bargained for)
Paying a liquidated debt in a different medium of exchange than originally agreed to	Paying part of a liquidated debt at or after the date the debt is due
Agreeing to settle an unliquidated debt	Making an illusory promise
Agreeing not to file suit when you have a good-faith belief in your claim's validity	Past consideration
	Preexisting moral obligation

*Assuming bargained for.

Promissory Estoppel As discussed in Chapter 9, the doctrine of promissory estoppel first emerged from attempts by courts around the turn of this century to reach just results in donative (gift) promise cases. Classical contract consideration principles did not recognize a promisee's reliance on a donative promise as a sufficient basis for enforcing the promise against the promisor. Instead, donative promises were unenforceable because they were not supported by consideration. In fact, the essence of a donative promise is that it does not seek or require any bargained-for exchange. Yet people continued to act in reliance on donative promises, often to their considerable disadvantage.

Refer to the facts of *Thorne v. Deas*, discussed earlier in this chapter. The co-owners of the *Sea Nymph* clearly relied on their fellow co-owner's promise to get insurance for the ship. Some courts in the early 1900s began to protect such relying promisees by *estopping* promisors from raising the defense that their promises were not supported by consideration. In a wide variety of cases involving gratuitous agency promises (as in *Thorne v. Deas*), promises of bonuses or pensions made to employees, and promises of gifts of land, courts began to use a promisee's detrimental (harmful) reliance on a donative promise as, in effect, a *substitute* for consideration.

In 1932, the first *Restatement of Contracts* legitimized these cases by expressly recognizing promissory estoppel in section 90. The elements of promissory estoppel were then essentially the same as they are today: a *promise* that the promisor should reasonably expect to induce reliance, *reliance* on the promise by the promisee, and *injustice* to the promisee as a result of that reliance. Promissory estoppel is now widely used as a consideration substitute, not only in donative promise cases but also in cases involving commercial promises contemplating a bargained-for exchange. The construction contract bid cases discussed in Chapter 10 are another example of this expansion of promissory estoppel's reach. In fact, promissory estoppel has expanded far beyond its initial role as a consideration substitute into other areas of contract law.

In *McLellan v. Charly*, the parties dispute whether there was sufficient consideration to support an option contract.[11] In the absence of such consideration, the court must decide whether promissory estoppel applies to a promise made by an offeree to keep an offer open for a given period of time.

---

[11]Option contracts are discussed in detail in Chapter 10.

McLellan v. Charly   758 N.W.2d 94 (Wis. Ct. App. 2008)

Roger Charly owned a parcel of land in Madison, Wisconsin, that is situated between the University of Wisconsin's Harlow Primate Psychology Laboratory and the Wisconsin National Primate Research Center. The University indicated an interest in buying the land in 2003 but balked at Charly's $1 million asking price.

In 2004, Rick Bogle, an animal rights activist, met with Charly to discuss purchasing the land. Bogle wanted to house the National Primate Research Center Exhibition Hall on it as a protest against the activities at the two neighboring facilities. Charly indicated he would sell the property to Bogle for $750,000, if Bogle could raise the money.

Bogle accomplished the fundraising through Dr. Richard McLellan. Bogle and McLellan agreed that McLellan would borrow funds to purchase the property and Bogle would make the payments on the loan.

In October 2004, Bogle notified Charly that he had the money. Bogle's attorney drafted an agreement titled "Option to Purchase," which Charly and McLellan signed on May 10, 2005. It indicated that McLellan could purchase the property for $675,000 within 180 days, with an opportunity to extend that option for another 90-day period. The agreement contained detailed provisions on the terms of the sale.

In June 2005, Bogle held a rally at the property and posted a sign reading "Future Home of the National Primate Research Exhibition Hall," which depicted a monkey with a device screwed into its skull. Someone from the University apparently noticed the rally and sign because, shortly thereafter, a University representative called Charly to express its consternation with the exhibition hall plan and to once again offer to buy the property. Charly maintained his million-dollar purchase price demand from the University.

Around this same time, Charly took the "Option to Purchase" document to a different attorney for evaluation. The attorney concluded that the option was "voidable and void due to lack of consideration," sending a letter to McLellan to that effect and offering to enter into an enforceable option contract with different terms. McLellan declined.

On August 1, Charly received an offer from the University to purchase the property for $1 million. McLellan, then, attempted to exercise his supposed option by letter dated August 12. The letter was returned to McLellan unopened, and Charly's attorney personally informed McLellan that there was no enforceable option and that Charly would not sell the property to him.

McLellan, Bogle, and the Primate Freedom Protect (an organization formed by Bogle) sued Charly stating theories of breach of contract and promissory estoppel. The trial court found in favor of the plaintiffs on the breach of contract theory, determining that the option was supported by valid consideration. It ordered the remedy of specific performance. The trial court held, in the alternative, that there was no basis for promissory estoppel liability and dismissed the plaintiff's promissory estoppel claims.

Charly appealed the trial court's determination that he breached the contract. The plaintiffs argued that, even if the court determined there was no breach of contract, they were entitled to relief under the promissory estoppel theory.

On appeal, the appellate court first determined that a valid option contract requires consideration that is distinct from the consideration that supports the underlying contract. In this case, that means McLellan had to give something of legal value for which Charly bargained in exchange for the 180-day option that was different from and in addition to the value Charly sought for the sale of the property.

Vergeront, Judge

II. Existence of Separate Consideration for this Option

Charly contends there is no evidence of consideration for the option separate from the consideration for the sale. In particular, he asserts that the only consideration the circuit court found were for the sale, not for the option. The plaintiffs disagree and also assert the court erred in rejecting three additional bases for consideration. We discuss each of the four potential bases for consideration.

The leaseback and repurchase provisions, like all the other terms for the sale of the property, apply only if McLellan exercises the option within the prescribed period of time. If McLellan does not do so, there is no contract for sale and thus no benefit to Charly from these provisions. The plaintiffs argue that [two particular terms in the Option to Purchase] led to Charly's decision to agree to the option. [E]ven if it were these two particular provisions that led Charly to agree to the option, like all the bargained-for terms of the sale that benefit the seller, these two provisions are a benefit to the seller only if the option is timely exercised and a sale occurs. In other words, they are consideration for the sale contract, but not separate consideration for the option contract. . . .

Second, the plaintiffs contend there is evidence of intent to be bound by the option contract and . . . intent to be bound is sufficient in itself to constitute consideration. We [find] that it is not sufficient. . . .

Third, the plaintiffs argue that the evidence of Charly's personal satisfaction at "tweaking" the University constituted separate consideration for the option. The plaintiffs emphasize . . . that this satisfaction was not entirely dependent upon a sale taking place, and thus it constitutes consideration separate from that for the sale. This is so, according to the plaintiffs, because the "tweaking" occurred at least in part when the prospective sale was made public at the rally and because this publicity resulted in a higher offer from the University, which is what Charly wanted.

The [trial] court found that Charly "took personal satisfaction in selling the building to Bogle for use as a primate museum . . . [either] because he was insulted by a previous offer the UW made . . . or because he didn't like . . . the animal research facilities in that location." In concluding this did not constitute consideration, the court reasoned that it was not bargained for: Charly did not request it and there was no requirement in the written agreement between the parties that the property be used for a museum.

[W]e confine our analysis to the benefit the plaintiffs assert Charly obtained independent from the sale—Charly's personal satisfaction at "tweaking" the University through the announcement of the prospective sale and the resulting higher offer from the University. We conclude that neither constitutes consideration for the option because neither was bargained for.

As for the satisfaction Charly derived from "tweaking" the University with the public announcement of the prospective sale, there is no evidence he requested that the option be publicized or that a rally be held. As for the higher offer the University made after the publicity, that offer—to state the obvious—cannot logically be the subject of bargaining between the parties to the option. . . .

Fourth, the plaintiffs contend that their efforts to obtain financing constitute consideration for the option, given the evidence that Charly knew they needed to raise money in order to purchase the property. . . .

Focusing our attention on separate consideration for the option, we, like the circuit court, reject the plaintiffs' argument. The written agreement is silent on financing. There is no evidence that Charly requested that anything be done with respect to financing and the evidence is that McLellan did nothing.

The plaintiffs provide no authority for the proposition that Bogle's efforts to raise money to repay McLellan could constitute consideration for the option Charly gave McLellan simply because Charly knew Bogle was going to do that. [I]n certain circumstances the optionee's efforts to obtain financing may constitute the requisite separate consideration for an option contract, [but there is no support for the notion] that the efforts of a person in Bogle's situation might do so. . . .

In summary, . . . there is no evidence of consideration for the option that is separate from the consideration for the sale. Therefore, the option was not a binding and irrevocable contract and

could be withdrawn at any time before it was exercised within the prescribed time period.

III. Promissory Estoppel

The plaintiffs assert that, if the option is unenforceable because of lack of consideration, they are entitled to an order conveying the property based on the doctrine of promissory estoppel. They seek to enforce with this doctrine the oral promise Charly made to Bogle to sell the property to him for $750,000. They contend that, in reliance on this promise, Bogle took various actions of which Charly was aware, which included efforts to find financing, which he was ultimately able to arrange with McLellan, moving to Madison with his wife instead of continuing to look for teaching jobs, public fundraising after the agreement between McLellan and Charly was signed, which cost him approximately $15,000 for the initial mailing, and holding the rally.

[T]he plaintiffs . . . tended to merge the promise Charly made to Bogle with the promise expressed in the option. We view the two promises as separate bases for two distinct theories for relief under the promissory estoppel doctrine. Accordingly, we analyze them separately. . . .

A party is entitled to prevail on a claim of promissory estoppel if (1) the promise is one that the promisor should reasonably expect to induce action or forbearance of a definite and substantial character on the part of the promisee; (2) the promise induced such action or forbearance; and (3) injustice can be avoided only by enforcement of the promise. . . .

In deciding that the doctrine of promissory estoppel did not support enforcement of Charly's promise to Bogle, the court . . . found that Bogle moved to Madison and started fundraising after having only a couple brief conversations with Charly and it was not reasonable to rely on a promise "obtained by walking into a store and having a brief conversation with a stranger about a real estate transaction of three quarters of a million dollars." Thus, the court found, Charly could not reasonably anticipate that his promise would "induce action or [inaction] of a definite and substantial character" on the part of Bogle. The court also found that the evidence did not show that Bogle's move to Madison and fundraising efforts were to his detriment. It further found that, because of Bogle's role in the negotiation of the agreement between McLellan and Charly, Bogle "could not possibly have believed that he still had a valid offer to sell the property to him." Finally, the court found that the promise Charly initially made to Bogle was of a preliminary nature and was never intended as the final agreement; instead, it was the beginning of negotiations for a more formal written agreement, for which Bogle obtained an attorney. The court reasoned that the doctrine of promissory estoppel was not intended to convert contract negotiations into an enforceable promise.

We accept the circuit court's findings because they are not clearly erroneous, and we agree with the court's policy decision that justice does not require enforcement of Charly's promise to Bogle. The evidence supports a finding that, when Charly offered to sell the property for $750,000, both he and Bogle understood that they would negotiate the specific terms of the sale, and they did so. The written agreement that resulted was between Charly and McLellan, with Bogle's involvement, agreement, and consultation with counsel. The steps Bogle took that he claims were to his detriment before the written agreement between McLellan and Charly was executed—moving to Madison and attempting to obtain financing—were in furtherance of the anticipated written agreement that did in fact occur. The steps he took after that—public fundraising and the rally—were not in reliance on Charly's promise to him, but on the written agreement between McLellan and Charly. . . . As a policy matter, in these circumstances justice does not require the enforcement of Charly's initial promise to sell the property to Bogle for $750,000. It is fair not to, in effect, revive that initial promise to Bogle when he was involved with and approved of the written agreement that evolved from that.

We next consider the option as the promise potentially affording relief—specifically, Charly's written promise to McLellan that he would not revoke the offer to sell the property on the specified terms to McLellan for 180 days plus an additional ninety days if McLellan chose. We have already concluded that Charly's promise not to revoke the offer was not supported by consideration separate from that for the sale. We agree with the plaintiffs that this failure of consideration does not in itself bar enforcement of the promise under the doctrine of promissory estoppel. In adopting the doctrine in *Hoffman*, the court explained:

> Originally the doctrine of promissory estoppel was invoked as a substitute for consideration rendering a gratuitous promise enforceable as a contract. *In other words, the acts of reliance by the promisee to his detriment provided a substitute for consideration. . . . However, § 90 of Restatement [First of] Contracts [which the court adopted], does not impose the requirement that the promise giving rise to the cause of action must be so comprehensive in scope as to meet the requirements of an offer that would ripen into a contract if accepted by the promisee.*

Hoffman v. Red Owl Stores, Inc., 26 Wis. 2d 683, 697–98 (1965) (citation omitted) (emphasis added). . . .

We turn, then, to the question whether Charly's promise of the option induced McLellan to take any action or forbearance of a definite and substantial character. The circuit court, in the context of its findings on consideration, accepted McLellan's testimony that he did nothing in connection with the project between mailing the option back and receiving notification that the option was being declared void. The plaintiffs point to McLellan's efforts to negotiate the agreement with Charly—his consultation with real estate attorneys, his flying to Madison to meet with Charly, his "work[ing] through several versions of the parties' written agreement," and his signing and having the contract notarized while he was in Europe. However, these efforts—all typical steps in negotiating an agreement—*preceded* Charly's promise, embodied in the option provisions of the written agreement, that he would not revoke the offer to sell on the specified terms for at least 180 days. Based on the circuit court's findings, we conclude McLellan is not entitled to enforcement of the option under the doctrine of promissory estoppel. . . .

CONCLUSION

[W]e affirm the circuit court in part, reverse in part, and remand with instructions to dismiss the complaint.

Promises to Pay Debts Barred by Statutes of Limitations

Statutes of limitations set an express statutory time limit on a person's ability to pursue any legal claim. A creditor who fails to file suit to collect a debt within the time prescribed by the appropriate statute of limitations loses the right to collect it. Many states, however, enforce a new promise by a debtor to pay such a debt, even though technically such promises are not supported by consideration because the creditor has given nothing in exchange for the new promise. Most states afford debtors some protection in such cases, however, by requiring that the new promise be in writing to be enforceable.

Promises to Pay Debts Barred by Bankruptcy Discharge

Once a bankrupt debtor is granted a discharge,[12] creditors no longer have the legal right to collect discharged debts. Most states enforce a new promise by the debtor to pay (reaffirm) the debt regardless of whether the creditor has given any consideration to support it. To reduce creditor attempts to pressure debtors to reaffirm, the Bankruptcy Reform Act of 1978 made it much more difficult for debtors to reaffirm debts discharged in bankruptcy proceedings. The act requires that a reaffirmation promise be made prior to the date of the discharge and gives the debtor the right to revoke his promise within 30 days after it becomes enforceable. This act also requires the Bankruptcy Court to counsel individual (as opposed to corporate) debtors about the legal effects of reaffirmation

---

[12]Chapter 30 discusses bankruptcy in detail.

and requires Bankruptcy Court approval of reaffirmations by individual debtors. In addition, a few states require reaffirmation promises to be in writing to be enforceable.

Charitable Subscriptions

Promises to make gifts for charitable or educational purposes are often enforced, despite the absence of consideration, when the institution or organization to which the promise was made has acted in reliance on the promised gift. This result is usually justified on the basis of either promissory estoppel or public policy.

Problems and Problem Cases

1. William Skebba was a top sales executive for M.W. Kasch Co. The company was failing financially, and Skebba received another job offer. Jeffrey Kasch, one of the owners of the company, persuaded Skebba not to take the job and agreed to pay Skebba $250,000 if the company were sold while Skebba was still employed there. Though Skebba repeatedly asked for a written memorialization of the agreement, Kasch never provided one. The company was sold for $5.1 million; however, Kasch refused to pay Skebba the promised amount, denying ever having made the agreement. Assuming that there is no enforceable contract here, can Skebba recover by claiming promissory estoppel? What would be his recovery?

2. Rena Gottlieb was a member of the "Diamond Club" at the Tropicana casino in Atlantic City, New Jersey. To become a Diamond Club member, an individual must visit a promotional booth in the casino, obtain and fill out an application form, and show identification. There was no charge. The application form required a prospective member to list her name, address, telephone number, and e-mail address. Tropicana entered that information in the casino's customer database. Members received a Diamond Club card with a unique identification number, which the member swiped each time she gambled on a machine. Tropicana then tracked the gambling habits of its members and used that information for marketing purposes. The card entitled members to one free spin per day on the Fun House Million Dollar Wheel Promotion, which offered participants a chance to win a grand prize of $1 million. On July 24, Gottlieb presented her Diamond Club card at the Million Dollar Wheel, a casino operator swiped it and pressed a button to activate the wheel, and the wheel began spinning. According to Gottlieb and several witnesses, the wheel landed on the $1 million grand prize. But, when it did so, the casino attendant immediately swiped another card, reactivated the wheel, and the wheel landed on a lesser prize. Despite Gottlieb's protests, Tropicana refused to recognize that she won the grand prize. She sued for breach of contract. Though Tropicana denied that its operator intervened, it also defended by claiming that no valid contract existed between it and Gottlieb because she had provided no consideration to support any supposed agreement. Is Tropicana correct?

3. John and Jennifer Margeson entered into a contract to sell a weight-loss franchise business called "Inches-a-Weigh" to Theresa Artis. The parties signed a written "Asset Purchase Agreement" on October 1, 2004. The purchase price was $125,000, payable at closing. Later, on October 7, 2004, the parties signed a second document entitled "Sales Agreement Addendum" This addendum set the price of the business at $155,000, with $135,000 payable at closing. Of that $135,000, $125,000 was to be paid from the proceeds of a loan secured by Artis from First Bank, and $10,000 was to be paid in cash. The remaining $20,000 of the purchase price was to be paid to the Margesons in monthly installments based on sales. The closing was set for October 18. On that date, Artis tendered the $125,000 from the First Bank loan, together with $10,000 from two personal checks drawn on Artis's bank account. Thereafter, the relationship between the Margesons and Artis soured. Artis stopped payment on one of the personal checks she presented at closing, and she stopped making the monthly payments in March 2005. The Margesons sued Artis for breach of the Addendum. Artis claimed that the Addendum was not enforceable because it was not supported by consideration. Who is correct?

4. Patricia Contreras borrowed $5,000 from Kyung-Hu Kim so that she could buy a badly needed used car. She had previously gotten around on an old Vespa scooter, but she recently learned she was pregnant and did not want to take the risk of riding the scooter while she was pregnant. Furthermore, she knew she would need a car once the baby arrived. Patricia was supposed to have paid Kyung-Hu back on October 30, 2013. At that point, Patricia only had about $3,000. She asked Kyung-Hu if he would be willing to take that amount plus her Vespa in satisfaction

of the debt she owed him. The Vespa was worth about $2,500 when Patricia bought it, but it was dated and now worth around $800. Kyung-Hu agreed to Patricia's proposal. The next day, Patricia paid Kyung-Hu the $3,000 and delivered the scooter to his house. The next month Patricia's grandmother died and left her $125,000 in her will. Kyung-Hu learned of Patricia's inheritance and approached her requesting that Patricia make good on the balance of her $5,000 debt. He said he was willing to take $1,200 (i.e., the difference between the value of the scooter and the $2,000 in cash Patricia never paid). Will Kyung-Hu have any recourse if Patricia rebuffs his proposal?

5. Approximately four years before his death, Dr. Martin Luther King Jr. gave Boston University possession of some of his correspondence, manuscripts, and other papers. He did this pursuant to a letter, which read as follows:

> On this 16th day of July, 1964, I name the Boston University Library the Repository of my correspondence, manuscripts, and other papers, along with a few of my awards and other material which may come to be of interest in historical and other research.
>
> In accordance with this action I have authorized the removal of most of the above-mentioned papers and other objects to Boston University, including most correspondence through 1961, at once. It is my intention that after the end of each calendar year, similar files of materials for an additional year should be sent to Boston University.
>
> All papers and other objects which thus pass into the custody of Boston University remain my legal property until otherwise indicated, according to the statements below. However, if, despite scrupulous care, any such materials are damaged or lost while in custody of Boston University, I absolve Boston University of responsibility to me for such damage or loss.
>
> I intend each year to indicate a portion of the materials deposited with Boston University to become the absolute property of Boston University as an outright gift from me, until all shall have been thus given to the University. In the event of my death, all such materials deposited with the University shall become from that date the absolute property of Boston University.
>
> Sincerely,
> Martin Luther King, Jr.

Acting in her capacity as administrator of Dr. King's estate, his widow, Coretta Scott King, sued Boston University, alleging that the King Estate, not BU, owned the papers that had been housed in the BU Library's special collection since the 1964 delivery of them. BU contended that it owned them because Dr. King had made an enforceable charitable pledge to give them to BU. Was Dr. King's promise to give ownership of his papers to BU enforceable?

6. In 1999, American Golf Corporation (AGC) hired Heye for a job in the pro shop at the Paradise Hills Golf Course, a club that it managed. AGC gave Heye a number of documents, including the Co-Worker Alliance Handbook. On page 20 of the handbook was a reference to arbitration that essentially stated that binding arbitration would be the exclusive means of resolving all disputes about unlawful harassment, discrimination, wrongful discharge, and other causes of action and that the employee was agreeing to waive her right to pursue such claims in court. Page 23 of the handbook contained the following acknowledgment:

> My signature below indicates that I have read this AGC Co-Worker Alliance agreement and handbook and promise and agree to abide by its terms and conditions. I further understand that the Company reserves the right to amend, supplement, rescind or revise any policy, practice, or benefit described in this handbook—other than employment at-will provisions—as it deems appropriate. I acknowledge that my employment is at-will, which means that either the Company or I have the absolute right to end the employment relationship at any time with or without notice or reason. I further understand that the president of American Golf Corporation is the only authorized representative of the Company who can modify this at-will employment relationship and the contents of this handbook, and that any such modifications must be made in writing. I further acknowledge that I have read and agree to be bound by the arbitration policy set forth on page 20 of this handbook.

Heye signed the acknowledgment. Heye worked for AGC until January 2000. She later sued AGC on a variety of grounds, including sex discrimination and sexual harassment. AGC moved to compel arbitration under the acknowledgment form that Heye signed. Was the arbitration agreement supported by consideration?

7. Dr. James Taylor was employed as president of the University of the Cumberlands for 35 years beginning in August 1980. Over the course of a decade, the university entered into and reaffirmed a commitment to an agreement to provide Dr. Taylor and his wife, Dinah Taylor, with compensation for life following Dr. Taylor's retirement from the position of president. The university further agreed to provide a number of retirement benefits to Dr. and Mrs. Taylor after his retirement from the presidency, including health insurance benefits, and the university agreed to provide the Taylors with a residence or apartment in Williamsburg, Kentucky, where the university is located. The agreement

indicated that Dr. Taylor would serve in the newly created position of chancellor for as long as he pleased and Mrs. Taylor would continue to serve as "ambassador" for the university. They had been prolific fundraisers for the university, and they agreed to continue with those efforts even after Dr. Taylor's retirement. When Dr. Taylor retired, the Trustees reaffirmed their commitment to the agreement, but after a while they tried to reduce the amount of benefits owed to Dr. and Mrs. Taylor by offering Dr. Taylor a one-year renewable contract that provided for a reduced salary that was significantly less than had been provided for in the disputed agreement. Dr. Taylor refused, claiming that the university was contractually bound to the agreement to provide the benefits and pay to him and Mrs. Taylor for life. The university countered that the agreement was not enforceable as a contract because the Taylors provided no legal value for it. According to the university, the agreement was entered into solely based upon the plaintiffs' past performance, which could not serve as valid consideration. They pointed to language in the agreement and resolution that "The University of the Cumberlands and the Board of Trustees agree that the compensation and benefits contained in this agreement is/are for the past decades of duties and/or work performed by Dr. and Mrs. Taylor all for the benefit of The University of the Cumberlands." Was the university correct to argue that it had no contractual obligation to the Taylors due to a lack of consideration?

8. Bob Acres entered into a written contract to buy 25 acres of land from Schumacher Farms for $70,000. The contract recited that Bob Acres had paid $500 earnest money, but it never did pay this money. The deal fell through when Schumacher refused to close. Bob Acres sued for breach of contract, and Schumacher asserted that the contract was not supported by consideration because Bob Acres had not paid the $500 earnest money. Did the false recital of acknowledgment of receipt of the earnest money cause the contract to be unenforceable because of lack of consideration?

9. Perry Rowan worked at Salomon North America Inc. as a glide tester for snow skis. Glide testing determines which ski waxes and structures of the ski bottom run the fastest on the snow located at the venue where the testing is being determined. Rowan was a national-caliber ski racer with international racing experience.

On December 1, 1994, he was killed while glide testing skis on a ski run located in Vail, Colorado, which was owned by Beaver Creek Associates. When completing a glide test, Rowan lost control and slid into unpadded support beams on a picnic deck that Beaver Creek Associates had built. The fatal run occurred on the third day of a three-day testing period on the course. On the third day, just prior to his death, Beaver Creek Associates asked Rowan to sign a form releasing it of any liability for injuries, including death, that he might suffer while engaging in the testing. Rowan's parents as representatives of his estate sued, among others, Beaver Creek Associates for wrongful death, asserting they were negligent in constructing, placing, and failing to pad the deck. Beaver Creek Associates defended by arguing that the release was valid. Rowan's parents countered that the release was nonbinding because it lacked consideration (i.e., Beaver Creek Associates gave nothing additional of value to change the relationship between it and Rowan on that third day of testing). Was the release valid?

10. Susannah Baxter's mother Betty married Bazel Winstead in 1998. Susannah grew up with Betty and Bazel, and Bazel raised her as his daughter. Susannah's siblings—John, Stephen, and Lanie—were older and not as close to Bazel. Following Betty's death, Bazel updated his estate plan, including taking out a life insurance policy for which he named Susannah as the sole beneficiary. Bazel explained to Susannah that his will designated his estate to be divided in four equal parts going to Susannah and her siblings. In a telephone conversation, Bazel told Susannah about the life insurance policy and told her to "just share some with your brothers and sister." When Bazel died, Susannah received the proceeds from the life insurance policy, totaling more than $200,000. Susannah purportedly told her siblings that she would share some of the proceeds, but her siblings believed that she should pay each of them a quarter of the total. Susannah, on the other hand, believed that the proceeds were hers and that Bazel's instructions to her were to "share some" as she chose. Accordingly, when Susannah refused to commit to a particular amount to be shared with her siblings, her brother John sued. Was Susannah under a specific obligation to split the life insurance proceeds in quarters to be distributed among her and her siblings?

Reality of Consent

I n August 2019, Duncan went to Smith Motors to look for a used car to buy. He test-drove a 2014 Corvette with an odometer reading of 52,000. Duncan assumed that the heater worked, but he did not turn it on to test it because it was so hot outside. The salesperson assured him that the car was in "mint condition." Duncan purchased the car. He later learned that the heater was broken, that the radio would not work, that the car would not start when the temperature dropped below 30 degrees, and that the car really had 152,000—not 52,000—miles on it.

- Can Duncan get out of this contract and get his money back?
- Did Smith Motors have a duty to disclose the defects in the car?
- Was the statement that the car was in "mint condition" a misrepresentation?
- Did Duncan have the obligation to investigate the car more thoroughly?
- What are the ethical concerns involved in this situation?

LO LEARNING OBJECTIVES

After studying this chapter, you should be able to:

13-1 Explain what a party who claims misrepresentation, fraud, mistake, duress, or undue influence is required to do in order to rescind a contract.

13-2 Identify the conditions under which a contract can be rescinded on the basis of misrepresentation and fraud.

13-3 Explain the elements of mistake and determine when mistake makes a contract voidable.

13-4 Explain the circumstances under which duress makes a contract voidable.

13-5 Distinguish undue influence from duress and explain the circumstances under which undue influence makes a contract voidable.

IN A COMPLEX ECONOMY that depends on planning for the future, it is crucial that the law can be counted on to enforce contracts. In some situations, however, there are compelling reasons for permitting people to escape or *avoid* their contracts. An agreement obtained by force, trickery, unfair persuasion, or error is not the product of mutual and voluntary consent. A person who has made an agreement under these circumstances will be able to avoid it because his consent was not *real*.

This chapter discusses five doctrines that permit people to avoid their contracts because of the absence of real consent: misrepresentation, fraud, mistake, duress, and undue influence. Doctrines that involve similar considerations will be discussed in Chapter 14, Capacity to Contract, and Chapter 15, Illegality.

Effect of Doctrines Discussed in This Chapter

Contracts induced by misrepresentation, fraud, mistake, duress, or undue influence are generally considered to be **voidable**. This means that the person whose consent was not real has the power to **rescind** (cancel) the contract. A person who rescinds a contract is entitled to the return of anything he gave the other party. By the same token, he must offer to return anything he has received from the other party.

LO13-1 Explain what a party who claims misrepresentation, fraud, mistake, duress, or undue influence is required to do in order to rescind a contract.

Necessity for Prompt and Unequivocal Rescission

Suppose Johnson, who recently bought a car from Sims Motors, learns that Sims Motors made fraudulent statements to her to induce her to buy the car. She believes the contract was induced by fraud and wants to rescind it. How does she act to protect her rights? To rescind a contract based on fraud or any of the other doctrines discussed in this chapter, she must act promptly and unequivocally. She must object promptly upon learning the facts that give her the right to rescind and must clearly express her intent to cancel the contract. She must also avoid any behavior that would suggest that she affirms or ratifies the contract. (**Ratification** of a voidable contract means that a person who had the right to rescind has elected not to do so. Ratification ends the right to rescind.) This means that she should avoid unreasonable delay in notifying the other party of her rescission because unreasonable delay communicates that she has ratified the contract. She should also avoid any conduct that would send a "mixed message," such as continuing to accept benefits from the other party or behaving in any other way that is inconsistent with her expressed intent to rescind.

Misrepresentation and Fraud

LO13-2 Identify the conditions under which a contract can be rescinded on the basis of misrepresentation and fraud.

Relationship between Misrepresentation and Fraud

A misrepresentation is an assertion that is not in accord with the truth. When a person enters a contract because of his justifiable reliance on a misrepresentation about some important fact, the contract is voidable.

It is not necessary that the misrepresentation be intentionally deceptive. Misrepresentations can be either "innocent" (not intentionally deceptive) or "fraudulent" (made with knowledge of falsity and intent to deceive). A contract may be voidable even if the person making the misrepresentation believes in good faith that what he says is true. Either innocent misrepresentation or fraud gives the complaining party the right to rescind a contract.

Fraud is the type of misrepresentation that is committed knowingly, with the intent to deceive. The legal term for this knowledge of falsity, which distinguishes fraud from innocent misrepresentation, is **scienter**. A person making a misrepresentation would be considered to do so "knowingly" if she knew that her statement was false, if she knew that she did not have a basis for making the statement, or even if she just made the statement without being confident that it was true. The intent to deceive can be inferred from the fact that the defendant knowingly made a misstatement of fact to a person who was likely to rely on it.

As is true for innocent misrepresentation, the contract remedy for fraudulent misrepresentation is rescission. The tort liability of a person who commits fraud is different from that of a person who commits innocent misrepresentation, however. A person who commits fraud may be liable for damages, possibly including punitive damages, for the tort of **deceit**.[1] As you will learn in the following sections, innocent misrepresentation and fraud share a common core of elements.

Election of Remedies In some states, a person injured by fraud cannot rescind the contract *and* sue for damages for deceit; he must elect (choose) between these remedies. In other states, however, an injured party may pursue both rescission and damage remedies and does not have to elect between them.[2]

Requirements for Rescission on the Ground of Misrepresentation

The fact that one of the parties has made an untrue assertion does not in itself make the contract voidable. Courts do not want to permit people who have exercised poor business judgment or poor common sense to avoid their contractual obligations, nor do they want to grant rescission of a contract when there have been only minor and unintentional misstatements of relatively unimportant details. A drastic remedy such as rescission should be used only when a person has been seriously misled

---

[1]The tort of deceit is discussed in Chapter 6.

[2]Under every state's law, however, a person injured by fraud in a contract for the *sale of goods* can both rescind the contract and sue for damages. This is made clear by Section 2-721 of the Uniform Commercial Code, which specifically states that no election of remedies is required in contracts for the sale of goods.

about a fact important to the contract by someone he had the right to rely on. A person seeking to rescind a contract on the ground of innocent or fraudulent misrepresentation must be able to establish each of the following elements:

1. An untrue assertion of fact was made.
2. The fact asserted was material *or* the assertion was fraudulent.
3. The complaining party entered the contract because of his reliance on the assertion.
4. The reliance of the complaining party was reasonable.

In addition, as noted earlier, establishing fraud necessitates proof that the untrue assertion was made with *scienter*.

In tort actions in which the plaintiff is seeking to recover damages for deceit, the plaintiff would have to establish another element: injury. He would have to prove that he had suffered actual economic injury because of his reliance on the fraudulent assertion. In cases in which the injured person seeks only rescission of the contract, however, proof of economic injury usually is not required.

Untrue Assertion of Fact To have misrepresentation or fraud, one of the parties must have made an untrue assertion of fact or engaged in some conduct that is the equivalent of an untrue assertion of fact. The fact asserted must be a *past or existing fact*, as distinguished from an opinion or a promise or prediction about some future happening.

Consider, for instance, a contract under which a franchisor, Able, issues a franchise for a children's daycare business to a franchisee, Baker. During the negotiations leading up to the contract, Able provides Baker an income and earnings statement purportedly based on the actual incomes and expenses of others who had acquired daycare franchises from Able and had operated their businesses for at least three years. According to the statement, a new daycare franchisee would have approximately $260,000 in net income after one year of operation of the business and approximately $440,000 in net income after each of the next two years of operation. Baker enters into the contract for acquisition of the daycare franchise, opens the daycare business, loses money the first year, and makes very little income the second year. Would the income and earnings statement provided by Able to Baker during the negotiations phase be merely a prediction about a possible future happening (and thus not the sort of thing on which Baker could base a misrepresentation or fraud claim)? Instead, would the numbers in the income and earnings

statement furnish a potential basis on which Baker could obtain legal relief? Assuming that the numbers are not consistent with the actual experience of other franchisees even though Able represented them as such, an untrue assertion of past or existing fact would be present. Baker, therefore, could seek an appropriate remedy on misrepresentation grounds and possibly on fraud grounds.[3]

The **concealment** of a fact through some active conduct intended to prevent the other party from discovering the fact is considered to be the equivalent of an assertion. Like a false statement of fact, concealment can be the basis for a claim of misrepresentation or fraud. For example, if Summers is offering her house for sale and paints the ceilings to conceal the fact that the roof leaks, her active concealment may be considered an assertion of fact.

Nondisclosure can also be the equivalent of an assertion of fact. Nondisclosure differs from concealment in that concealment involves the active hiding of a fact, whereas nondisclosure is the failure to volunteer information. Disclosure of a fact—even a fact that will harm the speaker's bargaining position—is required in a number of situations, such as when the person has already offered *some* information, but further information is needed to give the other party an accurate picture, or when there is a relationship of trust and confidence between the parties. In recent years, courts and legislatures have tended to impose a duty to disclose when a party has access to information that is not readily available to the other party. This is consistent with modern contract law's emphasis on influencing ethical standards of conduct and achieving fair results. Transactions involving the sale of real estate are among the most common situations in which this duty to disclose arises. Most states now hold that a seller who knows about a latent (hidden) defect that materially affects the value of the property he is selling has the obligation to speak up about this defect.

In *Stephen A. Wheat Trust v. Sparks*, which follows, the court addresses nondisclosure and concealment issues in ruling on the plaintiffs' claim that the defendants committed fraud in connection with their sale of real estate to the plaintiffs.

Materiality If the misrepresentation was innocent, the person seeking to rescind the contract must establish that the fact asserted was **material**. A fact will be considered

---

[3]This illustration was drawn from *Legacy Academy v. Mamilove, LLC*, 761 S.E.2d 880 (Ga. App. 2014), which was ultimately reversed by the Georgia Supreme Court in *Legacy Academy v. Mamilove, LLC*, 771 S.E.2d 868 (Ga. 2015), due to a merger clause. Merger clauses are discussed in more detail in Chapter 16.

Stephen A. Wheat Trust v. Sparks   754 S.E.2d 640 (Ga. Ct. App. 2014)

Robert and Louise Sparks (the Sparkses) sold a house in Decatur, Georgia, to Stephen A. Wheat and Teresa M. McCrerey-Wheat (the Wheats). The parties' contract, dated August 14, 2009, incorporated a Seller's Property Disclosure Statement (Disclosure) dated March 5, 2009. The Sparkses conveyed the property to the Wheats at a September 14, 2009, closing of the transaction. At the closing, the Sparkses also signed an Owners' Affidavit. Upon taking title to the house, Mr. Wheat deeded his interest in the property to Ms. McCrerey-Wheat and the Stephen A. Wheat Trust (Wheat Trust), which had just been created.

In the Disclosure, the Sparkses represented that there were no "encroachments (known or recorded), leases, unrecorded easements, or boundary line disputes" regarding the property. In an addendum attached to the Disclosure, the Sparkses stated that the "[e]xterior sewer line [was] replaced with PVC in 2005. All waterlines, including service line, were replaced with copper plumbing in 2006." The Owners' Affidavit reiterated that "there are no disputes . . . concerning the encroachment of any improvements including fences, drive-ways, structures, [etc.] onto the property of neighbors or vice versa."

Approximately 18 months after taking possession of the property, the Wheats experienced a problem with the sewer lateral servicing the property. (A sewer lateral is an underground pipe that connects a house or business to a city or county sewer line.) During the process of repairing the problem, they learned that the sewer lateral extended approximately 133 feet beyond the property and included a portion that lay under both the property of their neighbors (the Gransdens) and a piece of heavily wooded land owned by the City of Decatur. The Wheats contacted the Sparkses' real estate agent about the sewer problem. In response, she forwarded the Wheats an e-mail from Robert Sparks regarding the Sparkses' past troubles with the sewer lateral. The e-mail stated that the "only small hurdle in making the replacement was the fact that the lateral crosses the Grandsen's [sic] property." In other e-mails to the real estate agent, Robert Sparks noted that one of the sewer line's "clean-outs" is on "the back corner of the Gransden property (quite near the city's tap)" and confirmed that when the Sparkses replaced the sewer lateral line in 2005, they "had to get permission from the next-door neighbor, Joe Gransden, to trench across the corner of his yard." The Wheats eventually reached an easement agreement with the Gransdens and the city to resolve the encroachments between the property and the public sewer connection.

In another section of the Disclosure, the Sparkses affirmed that there had been water leakage, water accumulation, or damp-ness within the house's basement. The addendum attached to the Disclosure further explained, "During very heavy rains the front corner of the basement occasionally became damp. Installed French drains down sides of house to draw water downhill and away from house." Evidence adduced in the litigation referred to below indicated that the Sparkses became aware of three major leaks and a minor leak that occurred during the months after they completed their Disclosure (while the property was on the market). During that time, Louise Sparks set up fans (including some that were borrowed) in the basement to dry the leaks before showing the property. Although their real estate agent advised the Sparkses to update their Disclosure to acknowledge the continued leaks, they did not do so.

On April 2, 2009, Ms. Sparks stated in an e-mail to the agent:

I think Rob or my parents mentioned the leak in the basement—we have a piece of masonry missing in the basement, causing water to come in the front right corner, Rob has found someone to fix on Monday. We've had a water issue in the basement too, near the window facing the driveway, water is coming in off the deck. Rob has asked someone else to come over on Saturday to address—hopefully we'll have this one done before the open house, and it doesn't rain any time soon! Thanks again for your fans (I set them up this A.M. at 6:30).

However, Ms. Sparks later stated in a deposition that she did not believe they ultimately made any repairs to correct the leaks identified in her e-mail. The Wheats visited the property during an open house in April 2009 and viewed the basement after it had been dried by the fans. After purchasing the property, the Wheats experienced water leaks in the basement, which they undertook to repair.

Subsequently, the Wheats, the Wheat Trust, and Stephen A. Wheat in his role as trustee filed suit against the Sparkses. The plaintiffs asserted a fraud claim based on false representations about the sewer lateral and misleading failures to disclose impor-tant particulars regarding the lateral. In addition, they asserted a fraud claim based on misleading nondisclosure, or active con-cealment, of the water intrusions in the basement. The plaintiffs sought compensatory and punitive damages. Following discovery, the Sparkses filed a motion for summary judgment, which the trial court granted. The plaintiffs (referred to collectively, for ease-of-reference purposes, as "the Wheats" except where clarity dictates otherwise) appealed.

McMillian, Judge

Summary judgment is proper when there is no genuine issue of material fact and the movant is entitled to judgment as a matter of law. [In reviewing a grant of summary judgment], we view the evidence, and all reasonable conclusions and inferences drawn from it, in the light most favorable to the nonmovant.

A purchaser claiming he was fraudulently induced to enter into a sales contract has an election of remedies: (1) promptly after discovering the fraud he may rescind the contract . . . ; or (2) he may affirm the contract and sue for damages resulting from the fraud. The Wheats have elected to [pursue] the second [option].

Fraud requires proof of five elements: (i) false representation made by the defendant, (ii) knowledge by the defendant that the representation was false when made, (iii) intent to induce the plaintiff to act or refrain from acting, (iv) justifiable reliance by the plaintiff, and (v) damage to the plaintiff. "Fraud in the sale of real estate may be predicated upon a willful misrepresentation, i.e., the seller tells a lie." [Citation omitted.] In addition, fraudulent inducement of a sale may be based on claims of fraudulent concealment where the seller, who knows of the defect, either (1) takes active steps to conceal it and prevent the buyer from discovering it or (2) passively conceals the defect by simply keeping quiet about it. Here, the Wheats assert fraud [mainly] on the latter theory—that the Sparkses concealed the fact that the sewer lateral servicing the property encroached onto the neighboring property and the fact that the basement had multiple, continued leaks.

As evidence of fraud regarding the encroachment of the sewer lateral, the Wheats point to the Sparkses' statement in the Disclosure that there were no known encroachments, their reiteration of this fact in their Owners' Affidavit, and their silence as to the subterranean encroachment. The Sparkses, on the other hand, although not disputing that the sewer lateral does run underneath the neighboring properties for approximately 133 feet, argue that because they made their disclosures based upon their understanding and personal knowledge, there was no actionable misrepresentation. Moreover, Mr. Sparks [stated in his deposition] that he did not disclose the encroachment to the Wheats because he "did not believe it to be material."

Based on our review of the record, we find that whether the Sparkses had knowledge as to the falsity of their representation and their intention to induce the Wheats to purchase the property are issues of fact best left to a jury. We have frequently cautioned that "[q]uestions of fraud, the truth and materiality of representations made by a seller, and whether the buyer could have protected himself by the exercise of proper diligence are, except in plain and indisputable cases, questions for the jury." [Citation omitted.]

In support of their motion for summary judgment, Mr. Sparks submitted an affidavit showing that when the Sparkses purchased the property in 2004 from the previous owners, the seller's disclosure statement likewise did not disclose any encroachment. However, we are not persuaded that the Sparkses' knowledge in 2004 regarding the sewer lateral encroachment is relevant to whether they knowingly made a false representation at the time that they induced the Wheats to purchase the property in 2009. "For purposes of summary judgment, scienter and intent to deceive are determined on the basis of the seller's knowledge of the falsity of his representations at the time made to the prospective purchaser." [Citation omitted.] More significantly, there is evidence in the record to support the Wheats' assertion that the Sparkses did in fact know of the encroachment as early as 2005, including admissions from Mr. Sparks that when they replaced the sewer lateral line in 2005, they had to get permission from their neighbors to trench across the corner of their yard.

The Sparkses also argue that the Wheats were put on notice as to the previous problems with the sewer system, yet failed to exercise due diligence and therefore cannot prove justifiable reliance. The Wheats, however, point out that the sewer line servicing the property was subterranean and the encroachment of that line onto the neighboring properties was not something that they could have discovered through their own investigation until they were forced to excavate in 2011. Because the Wheats have established that genuine issues of material fact remain with respect to their fraud claim regarding the sewer lateral encroachment, the trial court erred in granting summary judgment to the Sparkses on that claim.

We likewise find that genuine issues of material fact exist regarding the Wheats' fraud claim based on the basement water intrusion. The Sparkses argue [in their brief] that they satisfied their duty of disclosure by acknowledging the past problem and disclosing "an attempted repair to the water leaks they experienced," and that the Wheats were therefore on notice of the defect and cannot show justifiable reliance. We disagree with the Sparkses' characterization of the additional information provided in the addendum to their Disclosure. A jury would be authorized to find that the Sparkses' explanation—that "[d]uring very heavy rains the front corner of the basement occasionally became damp. Installed French drains down sides of house to draw water downhill and away from house"—was stated in such a way as to induce a purchaser to believe that the problem was in the past and had been resolved, not that it was an "attempted" repair. Moreover, there is evidence, namely the e-mail communications between the Sparkses and their real estate agent, that the Sparkses were experiencing additional leaks at the time they were marketing the property and that those current leaks were never disclosed.

In this case, although the conclusion that the Wheats should have realized there may be additional water-related defects was *authorized* by the evidence, this conclusion was not *demanded* by the evidence. As discussed above, questions of fraud, including materiality of representations made by a seller and whether the buyer could have protected himself by the exercise of proper diligence, are generally questions for the jury. Because the Wheats have established a genuine issue of material fact as to their fraud claim regarding the basement water intrusions, the trial court erred in granting summary judgment to the Sparkses on that claim.

The Wheats further assert that the trial court erred in ruling that the Wheat Trust did not have standing [to bring a claim for fraud]. In order for a fraud claim to be actionable, the fraud must be based upon a misrepresentation made *to* a defrauded party and relied upon *by* the defrauded party. Here, as the Sparkses have noted, the Wheat Trust was not even in existence at the time the alleged misrepresentations (or fraudulent concealments) were made. Therefore, no evidence exists that the Wheat Trust relied on the alleged misstatements. Accordingly, we find that the trial court did not err in granting summary judgment as to the claims made by the Wheat Trust.

The Wheats (Stephen Wheat individually and Teresa McCrerey-Wheat) next challenge the trial court's holding that Mr. Wheat was not damaged. [T]he trial court [concluded] that because Mr. Wheat conveyed his interest in the property to the Wheat Trust, he was no longer an owner of the property, and therefore, was not damaged by any alleged fraud. The Wheats, however, each averred that they individually expended time and money in securing an easement from the neighbors and the City of Decatur. They further averred that they each individually spent time and money in making the necessary repairs to the basement to prevent further leaks. Mr. Wheat also averred that the money expended in solving these two problems was paid for out of the Wheats' joint checking account.

"General damages awarded on a fraud claim may cover a broader range of damages than those awarded on contract claims." [Citation omitted.] Because there is sufficient evidence in the record to allow a jury to find that Mr. Wheat was individually damaged, we find that the trial court incorrectly held that Mr. Wheat's lack of ownership in the property precluded his proof of damages. [In addition, the trial court erred in ruling that the Wheats could not seek punitive damages.] Fraud is an intentional tort for which punitive damages may be awarded.

Grant of summary judgment to the Sparkses reversed in favor of the Wheats individually; case remanded for further proceedings.

to be material if it is likely to play a significant role in inducing a reasonable person to enter the contract or if the person asserting the fact knows that the other person is likely to rely on the fact. For example, Rogers, who is trying to sell his car to Ferguson and knows that Ferguson idolizes professional bowlers, tells Ferguson that a professional bowler once rode in the car. Relying on that representation, Ferguson buys the car. Although the fact Rogers asserted might not be important to most people, it would be material here because Rogers knew that his representation would be likely to induce Ferguson to enter the contract.

Even if the fact asserted was not material, the contract may be rescinded if the misrepresentation was *fraudulent*. The rationale for this rule is that a person who fraudulently misrepresents a fact, even one that is not material under the standards previously discussed, should not be able to profit from his intentionally deceptive conduct.

Actual Reliance   Reliance means that a person pursues some course of action because of his faith in an assertion made to him. For misrepresentation for fraud to exist, there must have been a causal connection between the assertion and the complaining party's decision to enter the contract. If the complaining party knew that the assertion was false or was not aware that an assertion had been made, there has been no reliance.

Justifiable Reliance   Courts also scrutinize the reasonableness of the behavior of the complaining party by requiring that his reliance be *justifiable*. A person does not act justifiably if he relies on an assertion that is obviously false or not to be taken seriously.

One problem involving the justifiable reliance element is determining the extent to which the relying party is responsible for investigating the accuracy of the statement on which he relies. Classical contract law held that a person who did not attempt to discover readily discoverable facts generally was not justified in relying on the other party's statements about them. For example, under traditional law, a person would not be entitled to rely on the other party's assertions about facts that are a matter of public record or that could be discovered through a reasonable inspection of available documents or records. The extent of the responsibility placed on a relying party to conduct an independent investigation has declined in modern contract law, however. Today, a court might be more likely to follow the approach of section 172 of the *Restatement*, which provides that a relying party's failure to discover facts before entering the contract does not make his reliance unjustifiable unless the degree of his fault was so extreme as to amount to a failure to act in good faith and in accordance with reasonable standards of fair dealing. Thus, today's courts tend to place a greater degree of accountability on the person who makes the assertion than on the person who relies on the assertion.

You will see an example of this approach to justifiable reliance in the *Timothy* case, which follows.

Timothy v. Keetch   251 P.3d 848 (Utah Ct. App. 2011)

Teri and Thomas Keetch wanted to establish a therapeutic horse ranch as a business venture. Their concept for the ranch was that it would be a place where children who were victims of abuse could ride and care for horses as a means of healing. The Keetches lacked sufficient funds to start the ranch, however. In the summer of 2000, they sought to buy a stallion for breeding purposes, and they turned to MSF Properties for financing. The Keetches eventually borrowed $102,000 from MSF and pledged the stallion—a quarterhorse named Hesa Son of a Dun—as collateral for the loan. This transaction was memorialized in a security agreement. A financing statement was filed with Utah's Division of Corporations and Commercial Code, which maintains an online database for Uniform Commercial Code filings.

A month or two later, Rebecca Mendenhall, a broker representing the Keetches, contacted Paul and Janice Timothy and suggested that they make a "bridge loan" (a short-term loan used as a means of interim financing) to the Keetches for funding the therapeutic horse ranch. The Keetches and the Timothys met at a fast-food restaurant to discuss the transaction. The Keetches offered to pledge Hesa Son of a Dun as security for the loan. Following the meeting, Teri showed the horse to Paul. Teri said that she owned the horse and that it was worth between $125,000 and $175,000. Paul asked Teri if the horse was encumbered in any way—that is, if ownership of the horse was subject to any debts or obligations—and Teri responded that the horse was not encumbered.

In September 2001, Paul met with Thomas and asked several questions about his financial status. Thomas gave false answers to a number of questions, including the purposes for the loan and whether the Keetches owned the horse "free and clear." After the meeting, Paul asked the horse's trainer if the horse was encumbered. He also inquired of the American Quarter Horse Association, which maintains ownership, lien, and breeding records for quarterhorses. Neither had any knowledge of any prior encumbrances. The Timothys did not check Uniform Commercial Code filings to see if a financing statement had been filed on the horse. Had they done so, they would have discovered that, contrary to the Keetches' representations, the horse was already serving as collateral on the loan MSF made to the Keetches.

Oblivious to the horse's true status, the Timothys made the bridge loan to the Keetches, secured—or so they thought—by the full value of the horse. The Keetches defaulted on their loan from MSF, and MSF seized the horse in October 2001. The Keetches later defaulted on the bridge loan from the Timothys as well. At this point, the Timothys learned that their collateral had been lost to MSF.

The Timothys sued the Keetches for breach of contract and fraud, among other claims. A bench trial was held and the court found in favor of the Timothys. The Keetches appealed.

Orme, Judge

In general, Utah law does not require one to inspect the public record to verify the truthfulness of statements made to him or her. In *Christiansen v. Commonwealth Land Title Ins. Co.*, 666 P.2d 302, 307 (Utah 1983), an escrow company represented that a land development company held an interest in property that it actually did not have. The injured party sued because the escrow company's representations that certain properties held in escrow had unencumbered equity values available as security for the plaintiff were not true. On appeal, the Utah Supreme Court held in favor of the plaintiff, noting that a defendant who makes misrepresentations, even negligently, can be held liable. As to reasonable reliance, the Court differentiated between available documents that are part of a transaction and documents contained in public records, and stated that "failure to examine public records does not defeat an action for a false representation because in most cases there is no duty to make such an examination."

We considered the doctrine of reasonable reliance in *Conder v. A. L. Williams & Associates, Inc.*, 739 P.2d 634 (Utah Ct. App. 1987), and held that a plaintiff may justifiably rely on positive assertions of fact without independent investigation. It is only where, under the circumstances, the facts should make it apparent to one of his knowledge and intelligence, or he has discovered something which should serve as a warning that he is being deceived, that a plaintiff is required to make his own investigation. Applying these principles to the facts, the Timothys were not required to check for prior UCC filings on the horse. The Keetches unqualifiedly represented that they owned the horse free of prior encumbrances. Nothing in the transaction, in the Keetches' representations, in Paul's visit to the ranch, or in the inquiries the Timothys made suggested anything that would "serve as a warning" that they were being deceived.

Affirmed in favor of the Timothys.

CONCEPT REVIEW

Misrepresentation and Fraud

	Innocent Misrepresentation	Fraud
Remedy Elements	Rescission 1. Untrue assertion of fact (or equivalent) 2. Assertion relates to material fact 3. Actual reliance 4. Justifiable reliance	Rescission *and/or* tort action for damages 1. Untrue assertion of fact (or equivalent) 2. Assertion made with knowledge of falsity (scienter) and intent to deceive 3. Justifiable reliance 4. Economic loss (in a tort action for damages)

LOG ON

A number of useful sites provide information about the nature of Internet fraud and how to reduce the chances of being victimized. Some even provide a method of reporting Internet fraud. An example is the National Fraud Information Center, **www.fraud.org/**. For a good resource on identity theft and identity fraud, see the U.S. Department of Justice's web page on the topic at **www.usdoj.gov/criminal/fraud/websites/idtheft.html**.

Mistake

Nature of Mistake

LO13-3 Explain the elements of mistake and determine when mistake makes a contract voidable.

Anyone who enters into a contract does so on the basis of her understanding of the facts that are relevant to the contract. Her decision about what she is willing to exchange with the other party is based on this understanding. If the parties are wrong about an important fact, the exchange that they make is likely to be quite different from what they contemplated when they entered into the contract. This difference is due to simple error rather than to any external events such as an increase in market price. For example, Fox contracts to sell to Ward a half-carat stone, which both believe to be a tourmaline, at a price of $65. If they are wrong and the stone is actually a diamond worth at least $2,500, Fox will have suffered an unexpected loss and Ward will have reaped an unexpected gain. The contract would not have been made at a price of $65 if the parties' belief about the nature of the stone had been in accord with the facts. In such cases, the person adversely affected

by the mistake can avoid the contract under the doctrine of mistake. The purpose of the doctrine of mistake is to prevent unexpected and unbargained for losses that result when the parties are mistaken about a fact central to their contract.

What Is a Mistake? In ordinary conversation, we may use the term *mistake* to mean an error in judgment or an unfortunate act. In contract law, however, a mistake is a *belief* about a fact that is *not in accord with the truth*.[4] The mistake must relate to facts as they exist at the time the contract is created. An erroneous belief or prediction about facts that might occur in the future would not qualify as a mistake.

As in misrepresentation cases, the complaining party in a mistake case enters into a contract because of a belief that is at variance with the actual facts. Mistake is unlike misrepresentation, however, in that the erroneous belief is not the result of the other party's untrue statements.

Mistakes of Law A number of the older mistake cases state that mistake about a principle of law will not justify rescission. The rationale for this view was that everyone was presumed to know the law. More modern cases, however, have granted relief even when the mistake is an erroneous belief about some aspect of law.

Negligence and the Right to Avoid for Mistake Although courts sometimes state that relief will not be granted when a person's mistake was caused by his own negligence, they often have granted rescission even when the mistaken party was somewhat negligent. Section 157 of the *Restatement (Second) of Contracts* focuses on the *degree* of a party's negligence in making

---

[4]*Restatement (Second) of Contracts* § 151.

the mistake. It states that a person's fault in failing to know or discover facts before entering the contract will not bar relief unless his fault amounted to a failure to act in good faith.

Effect of Mistake The mere fact that the contracting parties have made a mistake is not, standing alone, a sufficient ground for avoidance of the contract. The right to avoid a contract because of mistake depends on several factors that are discussed in later sections. One important factor that affects the right to avoid is whether the mistake was made by just one of the parties (unilateral mistake) or by both parties (mutual mistake).

Mutual Mistakes in Drafting Writings Sometimes, mutual mistake takes the form of erroneous *expression* of an agreement, frequently caused by a clerical error in drafting or typing a contract, deed, or other document. In such cases, the remedy is *reformation* of the writing rather than avoidance of the contract. Reformation means modification of the written instrument to express the agreement that the parties made but failed to express correctly. Suppose Arnold agrees to sell Barber a vacant lot next to Arnold's home. The vacant lot is "Lot 3, block 1"; Arnold's home is on "Lot 2, block 1." The person typing the contract strikes the wrong key, and the contract reads, "Lot 2, block 1." Neither Arnold nor Barber notices this error when reading and signing the contract, yet clearly they did not intend to have Arnold sell the lot on which his house stands. In such a case, a court will reform the contract to conform to Arnold and Baker's true agreement.

Requirements for Mutual Mistake A mutual mistake exists when both parties to the contract have erroneous assumptions about the same fact. When *both* parties are mistaken, the resulting contract can be avoided if the three following elements are present:

1. The mistake relates to a basic assumption on which the contract was made.
2. The mistake has a material effect on the agreed-upon exchange.
3. The party adversely affected by the mistake does not bear the risk of the mistake.[5]

Mistake about a Basic Assumption Even if the mistake is mutual, the adversely affected party will not have the right to avoid the contract unless the mistake concerns a basic assumption on which the contract was based.

Assumptions about the identity, existence, quality, or quantity of the subject matter of the contract are among the basic assumptions on which contracts typically are founded. It is not necessary that the parties be consciously aware of the assumption; an assumption may be so basic that they take it for granted. For example, if Peterson contracts to buy a house from Tharp, it is likely that both of them assume at the time of contracting that the house is in existence and that it is legally permissible for the house to be used as a residence.

An assumption would not be considered a basic assumption if it concerns a matter that bears an indirect or collateral relationship to the subject matter of the contract. For example, mistakes about matters such as a party's financial ability or market conditions usually would not give rise to avoidance of the contract.

Material Effect on Agreed-Upon Exchange It is not enough for a person claiming mistake to show that the exchange is something different from what he expected. He must show that the imbalance caused by the mistake is so severe that it would be unfair for the law to require him to perform the contract. He will have a better chance of establishing this element if he can show not only that the contract is less desirable for him because of the mistake but also that the other party has received an unbargained-for advantage.

Party Harmed by Mistake Did Not Bear the Risk of Mistake Even if the first two elements are present, the person who is harmed by the mistake cannot avoid the contract if he is considered to bear the risk of mistake.[6] Courts have the power to allocate the risk of a mistake to the adversely affected person whenever it is reasonable under the circumstances to do so.

One situation in which an adversely affected person would bear the risk of mistake is when he has expressly contracted to do so. For example, if Buyer contracted to accept property "as is," he may be considered to have accepted the risk that his assumption about the quality of the property may be erroneous.

The adversely affected party also bears the risk of mistake when he contracts with *conscious awareness* that he is ignorant or has limited information about a fact—in other words, he *knows that he does not know* the true state of affairs about a particular fact, but he binds himself to perform anyway. Suppose someone gives you an old, locked safe. Without trying to open it, you sell it and "all of its contents" to one of your friends for $25. When your friend succeeds in opening

---

[5]*Restatement (Second) of Contracts* § 152.

[6]*Restatement (Second) of Contracts* § 154.

the safe, he finds $10,000 in cash. In this case, you would not be able to rescind the contract because, in essence, you gambled on your limited knowledge—and lost.

Hicks v. Sparks, which follows, illustrates the mutual mistake issues discussed above, including whether the party seeking relief bore the risk of mistake.

Hicks v. Sparks	**2014 Del. LEXIS 142 (Del. Mar. 25, 2014)**

In March 2011, 72-year-old Patricia Hicks was a passenger in a motor vehicle that was rear-ended by a car driven by Debra Sparks. Hicks went to the local hospital's emergency room and followed up with her family physician a few days later with complaints of neck pain and headaches. During approximately 15 visits, she received medical treatment and physical therapy for neck pain and headaches.

In April 2011, Hicks presented a claim regarding her injuries to Progressive Northern Insurance Co., Sparks's liability carrier. Adjuster Sharon O'Connell handled the claim. Hicks spoke with O'Connell, explaining that she had stopped physical therapy. She also told O'Connell that she was still having some problems but was satisfied with her progress and was ready to negotiate a settlement. O'Connell offered Hicks $2,000 in resolution of the claim, but Hicks did not accept. Hicks spoke with O'Connell a second time in May 2011 and told O'Connell that she was still having headaches. Hicks made a settlement demand of $7,000. O'Connell countered with a $2,500 offer. Hicks stated that she wanted more time to consider the counteroffer.

More than three months after the accident, Hicks contacted O'Connell again. Hicks made a settlement demand for $5,000. She explained that two attorneys to whom she had spoken had advised her to wait at least a year before settling, in order to ensure that her injuries were resolved. O'Connell explained that she respected Hicks's right to wait for settlement but offered her $3,000. In October 2011, Hicks reiterated her demand of $5,000. O'Connell responded with an offer of $4,000, which Hicks accepted. She later went to the Progressive office, obtained a settlement check, and executed a full and final release (the Release).

Nearly a year after the accident, Hicks began to experience pain in both of her arms and tingling and numbness in her hands. An MRI revealed a cervical disc herniation. She later underwent disc surgery. In 2013, Hicks filed suit in the Delaware Superior Court, alleging that Sparks's negligence had caused the March 2011 accident and Hicks's resulting injuries. The court granted Sparks's motion for summary judgment, largely because of the above-referred-to Release. Hicks appealed to the Delaware Supreme Court.

Ridgely, Justice

Hicks contends that . . . a mutual mistake of fact between the parties . . . should have allowed for rescission of the Release. [She alleges that her] post-Release injuries are materially different from those contemplated in the Release, [thus] amounting to a mistake of fact, [that she] did not assume the risk of mistake, [and that] the Superior Court therefore erred by granting Sparks's motion for summary judgment.

A release is a device by which parties seek to control the risk of the potential outcomes of litigation. Releases are executed to resolve the claims the parties know about as well as those that are unknown or uncertain. Because litigation is inherently risky, a general release avoids the uncertainty, expenses, and delay of a potential trial. Delaware courts will generally uphold a release and will only set aside a clear and unambiguous release where it was the product of fraud, duress, coercion, or mutual mistake.

To establish a mutual mistake of fact, the plaintiff must show by clear and convincing evidence that (1) both parties were mistaken as to a basic assumption, (2) the mistake materially affects the agreed-upon exchange of performances, and (3) the party adversely affected did not assume the risk of the mistake. Under principles of contract law, a contract is voidable on the grounds of mutual mistake existing at the time of contract formation. But the mutual mistake "must relate to a past or present fact material to the contract and not to an opinion respecting future conditions as a result of present facts." [Citation omitted.] Nevertheless, mutuality of mistake in the insurance context can "exist[] only where neither the claimant nor the insurance carrier is aware of the existence of personal injuries." [Citation omitted.]

A release will bar suit for a plaintiff's subsequently discovered injuries unless the injuries are materially different from the parties' expectations at the time the release was signed. Mutual mistake will invalidate the release where both parties are mistaken as to the presence or extent of the plaintiff's injuries at the time they executed the release. If the plaintiff knew that "an *indicia* of injuries exist[ed] at the time [she] signed the release," the release will bar suit and a court will not invalidate it by mutual mistake. [Citation omitted.] Even though the plaintiff might be unaware of "the exact degree of injuries with medical certainty," knowledge of the existence of an injury will preclude a finding of mutual mistake. [Citation omitted.]

Finally, mutual mistake does not exist if the party adversely affected assumed the risk of the mistake. As the *Restatement (Second) of Contracts* explains in § 154(a–b), a party assumes the risk of a mistake where the contract assigns the risk to the party or where the mistaken party consciously performed under a contract aware of his or her limited knowledge with respect to the facts to which the mistake relates.

Hicks argues that the Release is voidable by mutual mistake because her injuries are materially different from the injuries that both parties believed she sustained at the time the Release was signed. Hicks explains that she and O'Connell were aware that Hicks suffered a cervical sprain requiring treatment before signing the Release. Hicks contends that surgery for a herniated disc is materially different from the minor head and neck injuries contemplated at the time of release. Hicks further argues that this mistake adversely affected the parties' agreed-upon performance because the herniated disc was a new, undiscovered injury for which Hicks did not assume the risk of mistake.

The record shows that Hicks has failed to demonstrate a mutual mistake of fact held by both parties at the time of the release. Hicks concedes that she told O'Connell that she had not made a full recovery and continued to experience headaches and neck pain. Although Hicks may have been mistaken as to the future effect of her injury, both parties were aware that Hicks

injured her neck in the accident. This can reasonably be considered an "indicia of injuries" existing at the time of the Release. Hicks had ample opportunity to consult additional physicians and obtain further diagnoses to discover the herniated disc. Her later diagnosis is not a materially different fact but an injury of which Hicks and O'Connell had some awareness. Therefore, there was no mutual mistake.

The record also shows that Hicks assumed the risk of mistake. She executed a clear and unambiguous Release in exchange for a settlement payment. This release specifically provided that Hicks "declares and represents that the injuries are or may be permanent and that recovery therefrom is uncertain and indefinite." Hicks assumed the risk of mistake when she signed the Release without obtaining a more thorough medical examination to fully discover the extent of her injuries related to her neck pain. She assumed the risk that her injuries were more serious than she believed and that her symptoms could worsen and require further treatment. Because Hicks assumed this risk, she cannot now claim mutual mistake.

Grant of summary judgment to Sparks affirmed.

Requirements for Unilateral Mistake

A unilateral mistake exists when only one of the parties makes a mistake about a basic assumption on which he made the contract. For example, Plummer contracts to buy 25 shares of Worthwright Enterprises Inc. from Taylor, mistakenly believing that he is buying 25 shares of the much more valuable Worthwrite Industries. Taylor knows that the contract is for the sale of shares of Worthwright. Taylor (the "nonmistaken party") is correct in his belief about the identity of the stock he is selling; only Plummer (the "mistaken party") is mistaken in his assumption about the identity of the stock. Does Plummer's unilateral mistake give him the right to avoid the contract? Courts are more likely to allow avoidance of a contract when both parties are mistaken than when only one is mistaken. The rationale for this tendency is that in cases of unilateral mistake, at least one party's assumption about the facts was correct, and allowing avoidance disappoints the reasonable expectations of that nonmistaken party.

It is possible to avoid contracts for unilateral mistake, but to do so, proving the elements necessary for mutual mistake is just a starting point. *In addition to* proving the elements of mistake discussed earlier, a person trying to

avoid on the ground of unilateral mistake must show *either* one of the following:

1. *The nonmistaken party caused or had reason to know of the mistake.* Courts permit avoidance in cases of unilateral mistake if the nonmistaken party caused or knew of the mistake, or if the mistake was so obvious that the nonmistaken party had reason to realize that a mistake had been made.[7] For example, Ace Electrical Company makes an error when preparing a bid that it submits to Gorge General Contracting. If the mistake in Ace's bid was so obvious that Gorge knew about it when it accepted Ace's offer, Ace could avoid the contract even though Ace is the only *mistaken* party. The reasoning behind this rule is that the nonmistaken person could have prevented the loss by acting in good faith and informing the person in error that he had made a mistake. It also reflects the judgment that people should not take advantage of the mistakes of others.

Or

2. *It would be unconscionable to enforce the contract.* A court could also permit avoidance because of unilateral

---

[7]*Restatement (Second) of Contracts* § 153.

mistake when the effect of the mistake was such that it would be unconscionable to enforce the contract. To show unconscionability in this context, the mistaken party would have to convince the court that the consequences of the mistake would be severe enough to make the contract unreasonably harsh or oppressive if it were enforced.[8] In the example above, Ace Electrical Company made an error when preparing a bid that it submits

to Gorge General Contracting. Suppose that Gorge had no reason to realize that a mistake had been made, and accepted the bid. Ace might show that it would be unconscionable to enforce the contract by showing that not only will its profit margin not be what Ace contemplated when it made its offer, but also that it would suffer a grave loss by having to perform at the mistaken price.

The *Patterson* case, which follows, deals with a situation in which a party is unable to bind a unilaterally mistaken party to a contractual obligation.

---

[8]The concept of unconscionability is developed more fully in Chapter 15.

Patterson v. CitiMortgage, Inc.   820 F.3d 1273 (11th Cir. 2016)

In 2008, Toby Breedlove fell behind on his mortgage payments to CitiMortgage. Hoping to avoid foreclosure, he sought to sell his home to Victor Patterson through a short sale. (A short sale occurs when the mortgage company will not recoup all the money that it is owed by the mortgagor through a sale of the house but agrees to the sale nonetheless because it likely nets the mortgage company more than a foreclosure sale would. In a short sale, the mortgagor is released from his debt to the mortgage company.)

Patterson communicated directly with CitiMortgage to negotiate the sale. During those negotiations, CitiMortgage emphasized that it would not agree to a deal unless the short sale would generate a net payout greater than the expected proceeds from a foreclosure sale. In pursuit of a deal, Patterson made a series of escalating offers to CitiMortgage over the course of several months. In succession, Patterson offered $371,000, $412,000, and $444,000. CitiMortgage rejected the first two offers outright, as the net payout for each would have been insufficient, namely, $350,000 and $391,940, respectively. As to the third offer, CitiMortgage decided to accept it on the condition that Patterson reduce certain fees associated with the sale so that the net payout would be $423,940.

CitiMortgage intended to convey that counteroffer in a letter dated September 19, 2008, which it sent to Patterson. Due to a clerical error, however, the letter actually indicated that CitiMortgage sought a net payout amount of $113,968.45. The letter set a closing deadline for October 24, 2008. CitiMortgage faxed the letter to Patterson with a subject line reading, "Toby Breedlove Shortsale approval."

Patterson received the letter and immediately notified CitiMortgage that he wanted to move forward with the short sale. The parties, though, never explicitly discussed the payoff amount. Thereafter, Patterson scheduled a closing, revised the sale agreement to reflect a sale price that would produce a net payout amount to CitiMortgage of $113,968.45, and obtained a $130,000 loan to finance the purchase of Breedlove's house.

On October 23, 2008—the date of the closing—the closing attorney sent the payout funds to CitiMortgage by wire transfer. Only then did CitiMortgage realize its mistake and immediately attempted to contact the closing attorney to let him know that it would be rejecting the funds. CitiMortgage left a voicemail message for the closing attorney and faxed a letter to him explaining that the net payout amount was based on a clerical error in the September 19 letter and that the "corrected" amount was $423,940.

The next day CitiMortgage received a letter from Patterson demanding that it accept the $113,968.45 payment. He insisted that was the amount CitiMortgage had agreed to accept for the house and that they had a binding contract.

Eventually, CitiMortgage commenced foreclosure proceedings on the Breedlove property, which prompted Patterson to file a complaint in state court against CitiMortgage for breach of contract. CitiMortgage removed the case to federal court based on diversity and filed a motion for summary judgment, based in part on the theory that the contract for the sale of Breedlove's house to Patterson was voidable due to unilateral mistake. The district court granted the motion. Patterson appealed.

Carnes, Chief Judge

The dispositive issue is whether CitiMortgage's unilateral mistake, the clerical error in its September 19, 2008 letter about the amount of the net payout it was seeking, prevented the parties from forming a valid contract. . . .

[Patterson] argue[s] that, under Georgia law, a court may not rescind a contract based on a unilateral mistake.

It is true that Georgia courts will often refuse to save contracting parties from their own unilateral mistakes that could have been avoided through the exercise of due diligence. But it is equally true, if not more so, that Georgia courts will not permit a party to take unfair advantage of an offer that contains an *obvious*, unilateral mistake. As the Georgia Supreme Court explained more than a century ago, "There is no disposition in the law to let one 'snap up' another, or take an advantage of mistakes." *Singer v. Grand Rapids Match Co.*, 43 S.E. 755, 757 (Ga. 1903). Georgia courts will rescind or refuse to enforce a contract when "one of the parties has, without gross fault . . . on his part, made a mistake," the mistake "was known, or ought to have been known, to the opposite party," and "the mistake can be relieved against without injustice." *Id.* Under those circumstances, a unilateral mistake "may be a ground for rescinding a contract, or for refusing to enforce its specific performance." *Werner v. Rawson*, 15 S.E. 813, 814 (Ga. 1892).

If Patterson was unaware that CitiMortgage's September 19 offer was a mistake, then CitiMortgage should suffer the loss. "On the other hand if [CitiMortgage] inadvertently (though negligently) made an obvious mistake and this mistake was apparent on the face of the offer and was known to [Patterson], then relief should [be] granted to [CitiMortgage]. . . ." [*Frazier Assocs. Mfrs. Representatives, Inc. v. Dabbs & Stewart*, 325 S.E.2d 914, 916 (Ga. 1985).]

Given the parties' negotiations and Patterson's series of escalating offers, CitiMortgage's mistake was obvious and Patterson knew or should have known it was a mistake. Patterson made successive offers of $371,000 and $412,000, which would have generated net payouts to CitiMortgage in the amounts of $350,000 and $391,940, respectively. CitiMortgage rejected both of those offers without making a counteroffer. Then Patterson offered $444,000, which would have generated a net payout of $412,620. In response to that highest offer from Patterson, CitiMortgage sent the September 19 letter counteroffering for a net payout to it of $113,968.45. No rational person would believe that was anything but a mistake because rational persons and mortgage companies do not counteroffer for less—in this case nearly $300,000 less—than the latest and highest and still outstanding offer.

Patterson . . . will not suffer an injustice under Georgia law because [he] will only be deprived of what Georgia law does not allow [him] to have—the opportunity to take advantage of another's obvious unilateral mistake. . . .

* * *

AFFIRMED.

CONCEPT REVIEW

Avoidance on the Ground of Mistake

	Mutual Mistake	Unilateral Mistake
Description Needed for Avoidance of Contract	Both parties mistaken about same fact Elements of mistake: 1. Mistake about basic assumption on which contract was made 2. Material effect on agreed exchange 3. Person adversely affected by mistake does not bear the risk of the mistake	Only one party mistaken about a fact Same elements as mutual mistake *Plus* a. Nonmistaken party caused mistake or had reason to know of mistake *Or* b. Effect of mistake is to make it unconscionable to enforce contract

---

Duress

Nature of Duress
Duress is wrongful coercion that induces a person to enter or modify a contract. One kind of duress is physical compulsion to enter a contract. For example, Thorp overpowers Grimes, grasps his hand, and forces him to sign a contract. This kind of duress is rare, but when it occurs, a court would find that the contract was void. A far more common type of duress occurs when a person is induced to enter a contract by a *threat* of physical, emotional, or economic harm. In these cases, the contract is considered *voidable* at the option of the victimized person. This is the form of duress addressed in this chapter.

The elements of duress have undergone dramatic changes. Classical contract law took a very narrow view of the type of coercion that constituted duress, limiting duress to threats of imprisonment or serious physical harm. Today, however, courts take a much broader view of the types of coercion that will constitute duress. For example, modern courts recognize that threats to a person's economic interests can be duress under some circumstances.

Requirements for Duress

 LO13-4 Explain the circumstances under which duress makes a contract voidable.

To rescind a contract because of duress, one must be able to establish both of the following elements:

1. The contract was induced by an improper threat.
2. The victim had no reasonable alternative but to enter into the contract.

Improper Threat It would not be desirable for courts to hold that every kind of threat constituted duress. If they did, the enforceability of contracts in general would be in question because every contract negotiation involves at least the implied threat that a person will not enter into the transaction unless her demands are met. What degree of wrongfulness, then, is required for a threat to constitute duress? Traditionally, a person would have to threaten to do something she was not legally entitled to do—such as threaten to commit a crime or a tort—for that threat to be duress. Some courts still follow that rule. Other courts today

follow the *Restatement* position that, to be duress, the threat need not be wrongful or illegal but must be *improper*—that is, improper to use as leverage to induce a contract.

Under some circumstances, threats to institute legal actions can be considered improper threats that will constitute duress. A threat to file either a civil or a criminal suit without a legal basis for doing so would clearly be improper. What of a threat to file a well-founded lawsuit or prosecution? Generally, if there is a good-faith dispute over a matter, a person's threat to file a lawsuit to resolve that dispute is *not* considered to be improper. Otherwise, every person who settled a case out of court could later claim duress. However, if the threat to sue is made in bad faith and for a purpose unrelated to the issues in the lawsuit, the threat can be considered improper. In one case, for example, duress was found when a husband who was in the process of divorcing his wife threatened to sue for custody of their children—something he had the right to do—unless the wife transferred to him stock that she owned in his company.[9]

Victim Had No Reasonable Alternative The person complaining of duress must be able to prove that the coercive nature of the improper threat was such that he had no reasonable alternative but to enter or modify the contract. Classical contract law applied an objective standard of coercion, which required that the degree of coercion

[9]*Link v. Link*, 179 S.E.2d 697 (N.C. 1971).

CYBERLAW IN ACTION

Pricing Glitches on the Web: Legal, Ethical, and Marketing Issues

The accidental advertisement of a mistaken price for a product or service occurs sometimes in bricks-and-mortar businesses. But when e-tailers make price glitches, the impact is likely to be far greater because news of extremely low prices travels fast on the web through various bargain hunter websites and online bulletin boards. By the time the company learns of and repairs the error, it may have confirmed hundreds of orders for the product or service. Amazon.com, United Airlines, and Staples.com are a few of the e-commerce leaders that have experienced pricing glitches. In one widely reported incident, for example, United Airlines's website accidentally listed mistaken fares to Paris and various other cities—$24.98 for a flight from San Francisco to Paris—for five hours on one day. In that time, more than 140 people had booked trips based on the mistaken fares.[10]

Legally, the doctrine of mistake presents at least a possible avenue for avoidance of contracts that are formed based on a

mistaken price, but this would depend on factors such as the size and obviousness of the discrepancy between the mistaken price and the intended price. Of equal or greater concern to the e-tailer is likely to be the issue of how to maintain good customer relations. Should it sell the product at the advertised price and absorb the loss? Refuse to honor the mistaken deal and perhaps offer the customer something else of value to preserve goodwill? Some commercial websites have a provision in their "Terms and Conditions" link that notifies customers of the possibility of pricing mistakes and purports to protect the company in cases of price glitches.

Ethical issues are also present in these situations. Is it ethical for an e-tailer to refuse to honor a contract that is based on a mistaken price? Is it ethical for a customer to insist on a contract that is based on a mistaken price?

[10]Frank Hayes, "A Deal's a Deal: Should Pricing Glitches Be Honored?," *Computerworld*, February 26, 2001, www.itworld.com /Tech/2403/CWSTO58053.

Ethics and Compliance in Action

Ashton Development's general contractor, Britton, hired Rich & Whillock to do grading and excavation on one of Ashton's construction projects for $112,990. After a month's work, Rich & Whillock encountered rock on the project site. Ashton and Britton agreed that the rock would have to be blasted and that this would involve extra costs because the original contract between Ashton and Rich & Whillock specified that any rock encountered would be considered an extra. Britton directed Rich & Whillock to go ahead with the blasting and bill for the extra cost. Rich & Whillock did so, submitting separate invoices for the regular contract work and the extra blasting work and receiving payment every two weeks. After completing the work and receiving payments totaling over $190,000, Rich & Whillock submitted a final billing for an additional $72,286.45. This time, Britton refused to pay, stating that he and Ashton had no money left to pay the final billing. In response to Whillock's statement that Rich & Whillock would "go broke" without this final payment because it was a new business with rented equipment and numerous subcontractors waiting to be paid, Britton stated that he and Ashton would pay $50,000 or nothing, and Rich & Whillock could sue for the full amount if they were not satisfied with this compromise. Ultimately, Rich & Whillock signed a compromise agreement and took the $50,000. What is your legal and ethical analysis of this situation?

exercised had to be sufficient to overcome the will of a person of ordinary courage. The more modern standard for coercion focuses on the alternatives open to the complaining party. For example, Barry, a traveling salesman, takes his car to Cheatum Motors for repair. Barry pays Cheatum the full amount previously agreed upon for the repair, but Cheatum refuses to return Barry's car to him unless Barry agrees to pay substantially more than the contract price for the repairs. Because of his urgent need for the return of his car, Barry agrees to do this. In this case, Barry technically had the alternative of filing a legal action to recover his car. However, this would not be a *reasonable alternative* for someone who needs the car urgently because the time, expense, and uncertainty involved in pursuing a lawsuit would be considerable. Thus, Barry could avoid his agreement to pay more money under a theory of duress.

The following *Olmsted* case illustrates that the class of threats that can give rise to a valid claim of duress is quite limited and that what might constitute a reasonable alternative is not necessarily what one might consider a "good" alternative.

Olmsted v. Saint Paul Public Schools	830 F.3d 824 (8th Cir. 2016)

Timothy Olmsted worked for the Saint Paul Public School District ("District") from 1995 until his resignation in 2012. During the 2011 school year, families of several students alleged that Olmsted racially discriminated against certain students and acted inappropriately toward students. The District commenced an investigation and, on January 12, 2012, placed Olmsted on paid administrative leave "pending further investigation of allegations of serious misconduct."

Olmsted contacted Margaret Luger-Nikoli (Luger), a union attorney, and asked her to represent him in the investigation and any subsequent proceedings. Thus, Luger corresponded with the District on his behalf, primarily communicating with Jeff Lalla, the District's attorney.

On March 8, 2012, Lalla informed Luger that the District "would propose termination [of Olmsted's employment] at a school board meeting." When Luger asked Lalla for the basis for that decision, Lalla reported that the investigation had uncovered "additional issues" and provided some examples from the District's written investigation report. He did not detail specific charges the District would bring, but he did tell Luger that he had begun drafting formal charges to present to the school board and the Minnesota Board of Teaching. Lalla suggested to Luger that if Olmsted resigned, the District would not issue the report or present the charges. Luger requested that Lalla delay drafting the formal charges until she had the chance to discuss the situation with Olmsted.

Luger relayed the information to Olmsted and outlined three possible responses Olmsted could pursue: (1) acquiesce in the termination, (2) negotiate a separation or severance, or (3) go to a hearing. Later, Olmsted testified that he only "vaguely" remembered Luger going through these options with him, but he did remember Luger telling him that he had a statutory right to a hearing if the District brought termination charges against him. Olmsted did not feel like he was left with a real choice; instead, he felt like the District had a "gun to [his] head" forcing him to resign.

On March 11, 2012, Olmsted e-mailed Luger a draft resignation letter, which requested that the District allow him to exhaust his sick days, leave him with a "clean file," provide a letter of recommendation, and allow him to continue to teach driver's education. Luger relayed Olmsted's terms to Lalla, and the District agreed to permit him to exhaust his accumulated sick days. It would not allow him to continue to teach driver's education, though.

When Luger conveyed the District's counteroffer to Olmsted, he agreed to go on sick leave and resign in October 2012, when his bank of sick days would run out. Thus, on March 16, 2012, Olmsted submitted his notice of resignation to the District, with an effective date of October 8, 2012. The school board accepted and approved Olmsted's offer of resignation and never pursued termination charges nor initiated any disciplinary action against him.

Three months after submitting his resignation, on June 12, 2012, Olmsted wrote the District purporting to rescind his resignation and requesting to resume his duties as a driver's education teacher. The District sent him a letter, dated June 18, 2012, declining to accept Olmsted's withdrawal of his resignation or to grant his request to resume his teaching duties.

Olmsted sued the District for, among other things, breach of his employment contract. The District moved for summary judgment, which the district court granted over Olmsted's claims that his resignation was voidable due to duress. Olmsted appealed.

Smith, Circuit Judge

On appeal, Olmsted argues that the district court erred in granting summary judgment on his breach-of-contract claim. Olmsted contends that his resignation was revocable because when he resigned he . . . was under duress.

Olmsted asserts that the District threatened to file termination charges against him when it had no intention or grounds to do so. Olmsted further asserts that in light of Minnesota law that requires "[a] school board [to] report to the Board of Teaching . . . when a teacher or administrator is suspended or resigns while an investigation is pending," the District illegally promised not to report him if he resigned. According to Olmsted, this threat and promise placed him under legal duress and compelled him to resign. As such, Olmsted argues that his resignation is revocable.

Under Minnesota law, it is "undisputed that duress is coercion by means of physical force or unlawful threats which destroys the victim's free will and compels him to comply with some demand of the party exerting the coercion." *Wise v. Midtown Motors*, 42 N.W.2d 404, 407 (Minn. 1950). "As a rule, duress will not prevail to invalidate a contract entered into with full knowledge of all the facts, with ample time and opportunity for investigation, consideration, consultation and reflection." *Am. Nat'l. Bank of Lake Crystal v. Helling*, 202 N.W. 20, 23 (Minn. 1925). . . .

Olmsted cannot demonstrate that his free will was overcome. No evidence supports the allegation that the District made an unlawful threat. Olmsted claims that the District unlawfully threatened him "[b]y pitting [his] property interest in his job against his property interest in his [teaching] license." Olmsted avers that the District had no grounds to file termination charges against him, thus it used its investigation only to intimidate. The District initiated an investigation of the claims made against Olmsted.

Olmsted's resignation obviated the need for the District to seek his termination. The District's decision not to pursue termination charges against Olmsted after his resignation did not mean it lacked grounds to do so. When Olmsted learned of the District's proposed intention to file termination charges, he had already been placed on administrative leave "pending further investigation of allegations of serious misconduct," and he knew the nature of the allegations against him. Olmsted has not pointed to any evidence to support his contention that the District had no grounds to file termination charges against him.

Instead, Olmsted posits that the District has a statutory duty to report teachers that are under investigation. Assuming this statutory duty, Olmsted infers that the District had no basis to file any charges against him because it did not report him to the Board of Teaching. But the District presented evidence that it did not make a report every time a teacher was suspended, so the absence of a report neither proves nor disproves the validity of any charges under investigation at time of his resignation. Olmsted has not pointed to any record evidence that would support his claim that the District unlawfully threatened him.

Even if Olmsted could demonstrate that the District unlawfully threatened him, the threat was cured. . . . Olmsted had full knowledge of all the facts, advice from an attorney, and ample time for reflection. Olmsted did not know the specific charges, if any, that the District planned to bring against him, but he was aware of the nature of the allegations against him based on his conversations with the District's investigative team. Olmsted claims that he felt like the District had a gun to his head, but he also "vaguely" remembers Luger informing him of his options. Further, the record demonstrates that throughout the investigation and his separation from the District, Olmsted was represented by and received counsel from Luger, a union attorney skilled in the relevant matters. Finally, approximately eight days elapsed between the time that Olmsted first learned of the District's plan and when Olmsted ultimately, without prompting by the District, submitted his notice of resignation. This period of time provided Olmsted with ample opportunity to reflect on his options.

* * *

Accordingly, we affirm the judgment of the district court.

Economic Duress Today, the doctrine of duress is often applied in a business context. *Economic duress*, or *business compulsion*, are terms commonly used to describe situations in which one person induces the formation or modification of a contract by threatening another person's economic interests. A common coercive strategy is to threaten to breach the contract unless the other party agrees to modify its terms. For example, Moore, who has contracted to sell goods to Stephens, knows that Stephens needs timely delivery of the goods. Moore threatens to withhold delivery unless Stephens agrees to pay a higher price. Another common situation involving economic duress occurs when one of the parties offers a disproportionately small amount of money in settlement of a debt and refuses to pay more. Such a strategy can exert great economic pressure on a creditor who is in a desperate financial situation to accept the settlement because he cannot afford the time and expense of bringing a lawsuit.

Undue Influence

 LO13-5 Distinguish undue influence from duress and explain the circumstances under which undue influence makes a contract voidable.

Nature of Undue Influence
Undue influence is unfair persuasion. Like duress, undue influence involves wrongful pressure exerted on a person during the bargaining process. In undue influence, however, the pressure is exerted through *persuasion* rather than through coercion. The doctrine of undue influence was developed to give relief to persons who are unfairly persuaded to enter into a contract while in a position of weakness that makes them particularly vulnerable to being preyed upon by those they trust or fear. A large proportion of undue influence cases arise after the death of the person who has been the subject of undue influence, when her relatives seek to set aside that person's contracts or wills.

Determining Undue Influence
All contracts are based on persuasion. There is no precise dividing line between permissible persuasion and impermissible persuasion. Nevertheless, several hallmarks of undue influence cases can be identified. Undue influence cases normally involve both of the following elements:

1. The relationship between the parties is either one of trust and confidence or one in which the person exercising the persuasion dominates the person being persuaded.
2. The persuasion is unfair.[11]

Relation between the Parties Undue influence cases involve people who, though they have capacity to enter a contract, are in a position of particular vulnerability in relationship to the other party to the contract. This relationship can be one of trust and confidence, in which the person being influenced justifiably believes that the other party is looking out for his interests, or at least that he would not do anything contrary to his welfare. Examples of such relationships would include parent and child, husband and wife, or lawyer and client.

The relationship also can be one in which one of the parties holds dominant psychological power that is not derived from a confidential relationship. For example, Royce, an elderly man, is dependent on his housekeeper, Smith, to care for him. Smith persuades Royce to withdraw most of his life savings from the bank and make an interest-free loan to her. If the persuasion Smith used was unfair, the transaction could be voided because of undue influence.

Unfair Persuasion The mere existence of a close or dependent relationship between the parties that results in economic advantage to one of them is not sufficient for undue influence. It must also appear that the weaker person entered into the contract because he was subjected to unfair methods of persuasion. In determining this, a court will look at all of the surrounding facts and circumstances.

---
[11]*Restatement (Second) of Contracts* § 177.

Was the person isolated and rushed into the contract, or did he have access to outsiders for advice and time to consider his alternatives? Was the contract discussed and consummated in the usual time and place that would be expected for such a transaction, or was it discussed or consummated at an unusual time or in an unusual place? Was the contract a reasonably fair one that a person might have entered into voluntarily, or was it so lopsided and unfair that one could infer that he probably would not have "agreed" to it unless he had been unduly influenced by the other party? The answers to these and similar questions help determine whether the line between permissible and impermissible persuasion has been crossed.

CONCEPT REVIEW

Wrongful Pressure in the Bargaining Process

	Duress	Undue Influence
Nature of Pressure Elements	Coercion 1. Contract induced by improper threat 2. Threat leaves party no reasonable alternative but to enter or modify contract	Unfair persuasion of susceptible individual 1. Relationship of trust and confidence or dominance 2. Unfair persuasion

---

Problems and Problem Cases

1. Nelson died in 1996 and Newman and Franz were appointed co-personal representatives of her estate. Newman and Franz hired McKenzie-Larson to appraise the estate's personal property in preparation for an estate sale. McKenzie-Larson told them that she did not appraise fine art, and that if she saw any, they would need to hire an additional appraiser. McKenzie-Larson did not report finding any fine art, and relying on her silence and her appraisal, Newman and Franz priced the personal property and held an estate sale. Rice responded to the newspaper advertisement for the sale and attended it. At the sale, Rice bought two oil paintings for $60. Rice had bought and sold some art, but he was no expert. He had never made more than $55 on any single piece, and he had bought many that turned out to be frauds, forgeries, or the work of lesser artists. He assumed that the paintings at the estate sale were not originals, given their price and the fact that the sale was being managed by professionals. Subsequently, Rice learned that the paintings were original works of Martin Johnson Heade. Rice sold the paintings on consignment at Christie's in New York for $1,072,000. After subtracting the buyer's premium and the commission, Rice realized $911,780 from the sale. Newman and Franz sued Rice, claiming that the sale contract should be rescinded on the basis of mistake. Will Newman and Franz win?

2. In November 2006, Lopez was working for The G-Man Inc. as a "thrower" on one of its garbage trucks. Lopez was injured when a garbage can fell on his left hand. Lopez was treated for his injuries; spent approximately eight days in the hospital; and, ultimately, had a majority of his left ring finger amputated. Lopez returned to work in February 2007. At about this time, Lopez and The G-Man began a series of negotiations about compensation for Lopez's injury and the resulting medical treatment. During the period of negotiations, a number of people assisted Lopez with translation and interpretation of the proposed agreement because Lopez could not read or understand English. Following the parties' first meeting, Lopez was provided with a copy of the proposed agreement for his further review. The parties later reconvened, but parted ways without reaching an agreement. Lopez again took the proposed release agreement with him. Upon the parties' third meeting, Lopez was assisted by a certified interpreter who translated the agreement for Lopez from English to Spanish and sought to assure that Lopez understood the terms of the agreement. Thereafter, in May 2007, Lopez signed the agreement. Under the terms of the agreement, The G-Man agreed to pay Lopez $5,000 in $100 monthly increments. The parties further agreed to "carve out" of the release Lopez's past medical expenses and reasonable and necessary future medical expenses. In exchange, Lopez agreed to release The G-Man from all claims, including claims

for negligence and gross negligence. The G-Man terminated Lopez's employment in July 2007. Lopez then sued The G-Man, alleging that it was liable for his previous injury under theories of negligence and negligence per se. The G-Man claimed that Lopez had validly released it from all liability, but Lopez asserted that he signed the release under duress. He claimed that Hawley, the owner of The G-Man, had told him at some time during the three-month period after he returned to work that he would not be permitted to return to work or to go on vacation until he signed the agreement. The interpreter testified that no statement of any kind was made to indicate that Lopez's job was in jeopardy if he did not sign the agreement. Was the release voidable because of duress?

3. Rodi was recruited to the defendant law school, which had provisional accreditation, by statements indicating that accreditation would be forthcoming. (However, the school's catalog, which was sent to Rodi, stated that it made no representations about accreditation.) After his first year, the school was still unaccredited and he considered transfer. Accreditation was essential for him to sit for the New Jersey bar. The acting dean of the school learned of Rodi's intentions and wrote him that there was "no cause for pessimism" about accreditation. In fact, however, the school had strayed farther away from accreditation standards. The school was not accredited by the time Rodi graduated, and he was unable to sit for the New Jersey bar. He sued the acting dean and the law school for fraud. Should his complaint be dismissed?

4. A group of golf caddies for professional golfers on the PGA Tour sued the Tour for violations of their right of publicity, as well as antitrust and trademark violations. Their claim was based on a requirement that caddies wear "bibs" during golf tournaments sponsored by the Tour. These bibs display the name of the golf tournament; the name of the golfer for whom the caddie works (on the back); and, often, corporate logos. The caddies are not compensated for the publicity they provided or the advertising revenues generated by the logos on the bibs, and because of the bibs they are not able to seek endorsements from companies who might otherwise pay them to wear patches or the like on their shirts. The caddies, however, have been required to wear the bibs for decades by the contracts they all sign with the Tour. Part of the caddies' suit was on a claim that the contracts were voidable due to duress. They alleged that the Tour "threatened to and attempted to interfere with [the caddies'] business relationships with their respective players and individual sponsors" if they would not agree to wear the bibs. The Tour also allegedly "threatened to or did in fact preclude caddies from working for their golfers [at Tour events] if they refused to" wear the bibs. The caddies assert that, because they "lack viable alternative employment," they had no choice but to agree to wear the bibs at the Tour's insistence. Should the caddies be able to avoid the contractual requirement to wear the bibs?

5. In February 2005, Dandey Corporation and Nick's Hideaway Inc. entered into a 10-year lease of property for use as a restaurant. The property had been operated as a restaurant for decades and had a certificate of occupancy as an existing nonconforming use. Immediately after signing the lease, Nick's began extensive renovations of the premises, without first seeking a permit for such work. Nick's later submitted an application for a permit. During the town's review of that application, it was discovered that, approximately 20 years earlier, Dandey had expanded the original building, in violation of a zoning rule that a nonconforming use may not be enlarged, and that the extensions did not have a certificate of occupancy. Upon discovering that the premises could not be used as intended, Nick's stopped paying rent. In January 2007, Dandey sued Nick's for nonpayment of rent. Nick's seeks rescission of the lease. Will it win?

6. Boskett, a part-time coin dealer, paid $450 for a dime purportedly minted in 1916 and two additional coins of relatively small value. After carefully examining the dime, Beachcomber Coins, a retail coin dealer, bought the coin from Boskett for $500. Beachcomber then received an offer from a third party to purchase the dime for $700, subject to certification of its genuineness from the American Numismatic Society. The organization labeled the coin a counterfeit. Can Beachcomber rescind the contract with Boskett on the ground of mistake?

7. Retailer opened a baseball card store in vacant premises next to an existing store. The card shop was very busy on opening day, so Retailer got a clerk from the adjacent store to help out. The clerk knew nothing about baseball cards. A boy who had a large baseball card collection asked to see an Ernie Banks rookie card, which was in a plastic case with an adhesive dot attached that read "1200." The boy asked the salesclerk, "Is it really worth $12?" The salesclerk responded, "I guess so," or "I'm sure it is." The boy bought the card for $12. In fact, the true price intended by Retailer was $1,200. Can Retailer get the card back from the boy?

8. Keith contracted to build a house for Radford. Shortly before the closing, he met with Radford, accused her of fraud, and threatened to prevent the deal from closing. During the meeting, Keith's associate stood outside the door for two hours to prevent her from leaving. He gave her the choice of signing a Note and Deed of Trust promising to pay him more money or of going to court to settle the matter. Radford signed the agreement, but later sought to rescind it. Should she be able to rescind the agreement?

9. In February 2006, Konstantinos Koumboulis shot and killed his wife and himself inside his house in a Pennsylvania community. The murder/suicide was highly publicized in the local media and on the Internet. At a September 2006 auction, Kathleen and Joseph Jacono purchased the property from the Koumboulis estate for $450,000. After completing renovations of the home, the Jaconos listed the property for sale in June 2007. They informed their listing real estate agents about the murder/suicide. They also consulted their attorney, their agents, and representatives of the Pennsylvania Real Estate Commission, asking whether the murder/suicide was a "material defect" requiring disclosure under Pennsylvania's Real Estate Seller Disclosure Law (RESDL). The persons consulted informed the Jaconos that they did not consider the murder/suicide a material defect for purposes of the RESDL because it would not adversely affect the value of the property. Although the real estate agents did not think that disclosure of the murder/suicide was required by the statute, they suggested that disclosure would be a good idea "just to get it out there" (quoting the deposition of one of the agents). The Jaconos replied that they had investigated the issue and did not wish to disclose the murder/suicide.

Thereafter, the Jaconos signed a Seller's Property Disclosure Statement of the sort called for by the RESDL. Their statement contained numerous specific disclosures concerning the property, indicated when the house was last occupied, and showed that the Jaconos had owned the property for seven months. However, the statement did not disclose the murder/suicide. Later in June 2007, Janet Milliken, who lived in California, viewed the property and received a copy of the disclosure statement. Milliken then entered into a contract to purchase the house from the Jaconos for $610,000. After the closing took place and Milliken moved into the house, she learned of the murder/suicide from her neighbor. Contending that she would not have gone ahead with the purchase of the house if she had known about the murder/suicide prior to closing, Milliken sued the Jaconos over the nondisclosure. She brought her case on common law misrepresentation and common law fraud grounds (rather than on the theory that the RESDL had been violated). Did the Jaconos have a duty, under common law principles, to disclose the murder/suicide? In not disclosing this information, did they commit either misrepresentation or fraud?

10. Stambovky, a resident of New York City, contracted to buy a house in the Village of Nyack, New York, from Ackley. The house was widely reputed to be possessed by poltergeists, which Ackley and members of her family had reportedly seen and reported to both *Reader's Digest* and the local press. In 1989, the house was included in a five-home walking tour of Nyack and described in a newspaper article as a "riverfront Victorian (with ghost)." Ackley did not tell Stambovsky about the poltergeists before he bought the house. When Stambovsky learned of the house's reputation, however, he promptly sued for rescission. Will he be successful?

Capacity to Contract

In a state in which the age of majority for contracting purposes is 18, 17-year-old Daniel was married, employed, and living with his wife in their own apartment. Daniel and his wife went to Mattox Motors, a used car dealership, and purchased a used car for $500 cash. After driving the car for several months, Daniel was involved in a serious collision and damaged the car. He was one week over the age of 18 at this time. The next day, Daniel sent a letter to Mattox Motors stating that he was disaffirming the sales contract because he was underage at the time he entered the contract and that he wanted his money back.

- Does Daniel have the right to get out of his contract?
- Does Mattox Motors have to give him his money back?
- Would it make a difference if Daniel had used the car to earn a living?
- If, instead of being a minor at the time the contract was made, Daniel had been mentally disabled or intoxicated, would he have the right to get out of the contract?
- Is it ethical for Daniel to disaffirm the contract after having wrecked the car?

LO LEARNING OBJECTIVES

After studying this chapter, you should be able to:

14-1 Explain the concept of capacity to contract.

14-2 List and describe the categories of persons who lack capacity to contract.

14-3 Describe the effect of lack of capacity to contract.

14-4 Explain the rights and duties of the parties to a contract when there has been disaffirmance because of lack of capacity.

ONE OF THE MAJOR justifications for enforcing a contract is that the parties voluntarily consented to be bound by it. It follows, then, that a person must have the *ability* to give consent before he can be legally bound to a contract. This ability to give consent must involve more than the mere physical ability to say yes, shake hands, sign one's name. Rather, the person's maturity and mental ability must be such that it is fair to presume that he is capable of representing his own interests effectively. This concept is embodied in the legal term *capacity*.

What Is Capacity?

 LO14-1 Explain the concept of capacity to contract.

Capacity means the ability to incur legal obligations and acquire legal rights. Today, the primary classes of people who are considered to lack capacity are minors (who, in legal terms, are often seen as *infants*), persons suffering from mental illnesses or defects, and intoxicated persons.[1] Contract law gives them the right to *avoid* (escape the legal consequences of) contracts that they enter during incapacity. This rule provides a means of protecting people who, because of mental impairment, intoxication, or youth and inexperience, are disadvantaged in the normal give-and-take of the bargaining process.

 LO14-2 List and describe the categories of persons who lack capacity to contract.

Usually, lack of capacity to contract comes up in court in one of two ways. In some cases, it is asserted by a plaintiff as the basis of a lawsuit for the money or other benefits that he gave the other party under their contract. In others, it arises as a defense to the enforcement of a contract when the defendant is the party who lacked capacity. The responsibility for alleging and proving incapacity is placed on the person who bases his claim or defense on his lack of capacity.

Effect of Lack of Capacity

 LO14-3 Describe the effect of lack of capacity to contract.

Normally, a contract in which one or both parties lack capacity because of infancy, mental impairment, or intoxication is considered to be voidable. People whose capacity is impaired in any of these ways are able to enter a contract and enforce it if they wish, but they also have the right to

---

[1] In times past, married women, convicts, and aliens were also among the classes of persons who lacked capacity to contract. These limitations on capacity have been removed by statute and court rule, however.

avoid the contract. There are, however, some individuals whose capacity is so impaired that they do not have the ability to form even a voidable contract. A bargain is considered to be void if, at the time of formation of the bargain, a court had already **adjudicated** (adjudged or decreed) one or more of the parties to be mentally incompetent or one or more of the parties was so impaired that he could not even manifest assent (e.g., he was comatose or unconscious).

Capacity of Minors

Minors' Right to Disaffirm
Courts have long recognized that minors are in a vulnerable position in their dealings with adults. As a result, minors are considered to lack capacity to contract. You will see the implications of this principle in the following *J.T. ex rel. Thode v. Monster Mountain* case. Minors have the right to avoid contracts as a means of protecting against their own improvidence and against overreaching by adults. The exercise of this right to avoid a contract is called **disaffirmance**. The right to disaffirm is personal to the minor. That is, only the minor or a legal representative such as a guardian may disaffirm the contract. No formal act or written statement is required to make a valid disaffirmance. Any words or acts that effectively communicate the minor's desire to cancel the contract can constitute disaffirmance.

If, on the other hand, the minor wishes to enforce the contract instead of disaffirming it, the adult party must perform. You can see that the minor's right to disaffirm puts any adult contracting with a minor in an undesirable position: She is bound on the contract unless it is to the minor's advantage to disaffirm it. The right to disaffirm has the effect of discouraging adults from dealing with minors.

J.T. *ex rel.* Thode v. Monster Mountain, LLC
754 F. Supp. 2d 1323 (M.D. Ala. 2010)

In late January of 2009, J.T.—a minor from Indiana and a competitive motocross rider—traveled to Monster Mountain MX Park in Alabama. Prior to departing, J.T.'s parents signed a notarized authorization for James Thompson (J.T.'s coach) to act as their son's legal guardian for the purpose of signing all release of liability and registration forms.

To ride at Monster Mountain, all riders are required to pay an entry fee and execute a "Release and Waiver of Liability and Indemnity Agreement" (the "Release") that reads:

IN CONSIDERATION of being permitted to enter . . . EACH OF THE UNDERSIGNED, for himself, his personal representatives, heirs, and next of kin, acknowledges, agrees, and represents that he has or will immediately upon entering . . . [inspect the premises] . . . [and] HEREBY RELEASES, WAIVES, DISCHARGES, AND COVENANTS NOT TO SUE the . . . track operator [or] track owner . . . from all liability to the undersigned, his personal representatives, assigns, heirs, and next of kin for any and all loss or damage . . . whether caused by the negligence of the releasees or otherwise while the undersigned is in or upon the restricted area . . . [and] HEREBY AGREES TO INDEMNIFY AND SAVE AND HOLD HARMLESS the releasees and each of them from any loss, liability, damage, or cost they may incur due to the presence of the undersigned in or upon the restricted area . . . [and] HEREBY ASSUMES FULL RESPONSIBILITY FOR AND RISK OF BODILY INJURY, DEATH OR PROPERTY DAMAGE due to the negligence of releasees or otherwise. . . . THE UNDERSIGNED HAS READ AND VOLUNTARILY SIGNS THE RELEASE AND WAIVER . . . and further agrees that no oral representations, statements or inducements apart from the foregoing written agreement have been made.

Each day that J.T. rode the track at Monster Mountain, J.T. and Thompson signed the Release on J.T.'s behalf and paid J.T.'s entry fee. During his first three days of riding, J.T. rode without incident, but on the morning of February 1, 2009, J.T. rode over a blind jump, became airborne, and crashed into a tractor on the track that he did not see until he was airborne.

J.T. sued Monster Mountain alleging negligence, premises liability, and wantonness for its failure to remove the tractor from the track. Monster Mountain moved for summary judgment on the basis that the Release barred J.T.'s claim.

Albritton, Senior District Judge

The issue before the court is whether J.T.'s negligence claims against the Monster Mountain Defendants are barred by the Release. The Monster Mountain Defendants contend that they are entitled to summary judgment because J.T. signed the Release and Thompson "signed [the Release] on [J.T.'s] behalf," thus binding J.T. to a contract that exculpates the Monster Mountain Defendants from liability for J.T.'s injuries.

J.T. responds that, under Alabama law, a contract made with a minor is voidable. [Case citation omitted] J.T. argues that because the Release is effectively a contract with a minor, whether signed on his behalf or not, the Release is not binding on him.

The Monster Mountain Defendants concede that J.T.'s signature on the contract cannot make it binding, due to the rule that a contract with a minor is voidable. However, they attempt to overcome J.T.'s argument by asserting that Thompson, an adult who was acting on behalf of J.T.'s parents, signed the Release on J.T.'s behalf. Thus, the Monster Mountain Defendants contend that if a child's parents, acting through an agent, sign an exculpatory contract on their child's behalf, the contract is binding on the child and not voidable.

As the following discussion indicates, the court agrees with J.T., and therefore, summary judgment is due to be denied.

A. Alabama Law

The parties agree that Alabama law applies in this case. They also agree that Alabama courts have not addressed the specific factual situation presented by this case. However, Alabama courts have dealt with three relevant legal principles.

First, Alabama, like virtually all jurisdictions, applies the long-standing common law rule that, except for a contract for necessaries, "a minor is not liable on any contract he makes and that he may disaffirm the same." [Case citation omitted] This rule exists to protect minors from being taken advantage of by others due to minors' "improvidence and incapacity." [Case citation omitted] This rule is firmly entrenched in the common law and has existed at least since the year 1292. [Citation omitted]

Second, while Alabama courts have noted an exception to this rule, that exception is narrow. [Discussion of the narrow exception in Alabama pertaining to medical insurance and public policy considerations]

Third, Alabama courts have restricted the right of a parent or guardian to release a minor's post-injury claims. [Case citation omitted] Specifically, a parent or guardian cannot bind a minor to a settlement that releases the minor's post-injury claims without express court approval. The rationale behind the need for express court approval, similar to the voidable contract rule for minors, is to protect the minor's "best interest[s]."

The teaching of these cases is that, in Alabama, the default rule is that contracts with minors are voidable. . . .

B. Law from Other Jurisdictions

Because no Alabama case or statute directly addresses the issue of the case at bar, the court turns to the law of other jurisdictions for persuasive guidance. There are three important conclusions to be drawn from the law of other jurisdictions.

First, the majority rule in the United States is that parents may not bind their children to pre-injury liability waivers by signing the waivers on their children's behalf. *See, e.g., Galloway v. Iowa*, 790 N.W.2d 252, 256 (Iowa 2010) (listing cases and stating that "the majority of state courts who have examined the issue . . . have concluded public policy precludes enforcement of a parent's preinjury waiver of her child's cause of action for injuries caused by negligence"); *Kirton v. Fields*, 997 So. 2d 349, 356 (Fla. 2008) (listing cases, and stating that "[i]n holding that preinjury releases executed by parents on behalf of minor children are unenforceable for participation in commercial activities, we are in agreement with the majority of other jurisdictions.").

Second, many courts rejecting parents' right to bind children to pre-injury releases have relied on legal principles recognized by Alabama, as discussed above. For example, courts have relied in part on the principle that parents may not bind a child to a settlement releasing post-injury claims without court approval. *Galloway*, 790 N.W.2d at 257 ("As the Washington Supreme Court has noted, if a parent lacks authority without court approval to compromise and settle her minor child's personal injury claim after an injury has occurred, 'it makes little, if any, sense to conclude a parent has the authority to release a child's cause of action prior to an injury.'") [Additional case citations omitted] Courts have also relied on the policy, also recognized in Alabama, of the state's role of protecting minors from harm. [Case citations omitted]

Third, the only published decisions from other jurisdictions that have bound children to pre-injury releases executed by a parent or guardian on the child's behalf have done so in the context of a "minor's participation in school-run or community-sponsored activities." [Case citations omitted] By contrast, this court is not aware of a single case, that has not been overturned, that has held these clauses to be binding in the context of a for-profit activity.

C. Application to the Case at Bar

The court concludes, based on the law of Alabama as well as persuasive authority from other jurisdictions, that the Release signed by Thompson on J.T.'s behalf is not binding on J.T.

Children tend to be vulnerable in such situations, however, in ways adults are not. The parent who reads, understands, and executes a waiver of liability for her child is not the person who will participate in the activity.

First, J.T. is a minor, so the applicable default rule under Alabama law is that any contract made with J.T. is voidable.

Second, there is no exception under current Alabama law that requires that this court apply a different rule under the facts of this case. . . .

Third, under Alabama law, a parent may not bind a child to a settlement releasing the child's post-injury claims without express court approval. This court agrees with the rationale of other jurisdictions that it would be completely illogical if, despite this rule, a parent could bind a child, before any injury occurs, to an exculpatory clause releasing parties from any liability for injuries which might be caused in the future, simply by signing a contract on the child's behalf.

Fourth, the weight of authority in other jurisdictions suggests that the release in this case is not binding. The majority rule in jurisdictions throughout the United States is that a parent may not bind a child to a liability waiver. Moreover, and more significantly, no published decision that has not been overturned holds that a parent may bind a child to a liability waiver in favor of a *for-profit* entity, such as the Monster Mountain Defendants in this case. The few cases that have upheld a pre-injury waiver have made a point of emphasizing that the policy reasons for doing so are based on the fact of the defendant being a non-profit sponsor of the activity involved, such as with school extra-curriculars.

Based on all of the above considerations, the court concludes that, under Alabama law, a parent may not bind a child to a pre-injury liability waiver in favor of a for-profit activity sponsor by signing the liability waiver on the child's behalf. Accordingly, the Release Thompson signed on J.T.'s behalf, based on authority given by J.T.'s parents, does not bar J.T. from asserting a negligence claim against the Monster Mountain Defendants. Summary judgment on this issue in favor of the Monster Mountain Defendants, therefore, is due to be **DENIED**.

Ethics and Compliance in Action

Joseph Dodson, age 16, bought a 1984 Chevrolet truck from Burns and Mary Shrader, owners of Shrader's Auto Sales, for $4,900 cash. At the time, Burns Shrader, believing Dodson to be 18 or 19, did not ask Dodson's age and Dodson did not volunteer it. Dodson drove the truck for about eight months, when he learned from an auto mechanic that there was a burned valve in the engine. Dodson did not have the money for the repairs, so he continued to drive the truck without repair for another month until the engine "blew up" and stopped operating. He parked the car in the front yard of his parents' house. He then contacted the Shraders, rescinding the purchase of the truck and requesting a full refund. The Shraders refused to accept the truck or to give Dodson a refund. Dodson then filed an action seeking to rescind the contract and recover the amount paid for the truck. Before the court could hear the case, a hit-and-run driver struck Dodson's parked truck, damaging its left front fender. At the time of the circuit court trial, the truck was worth only $500. The Shraders argued that Dodson should be responsible for paying the difference between the present value of the truck and the $4,900 purchase price. The trial court found in Dodson's favor, ordering the Shraders to refund the $4,900 purchase price upon delivery of the truck.

- What ethical issues are raised in this case?
- What is your ethical analysis of Dodson's conduct, Shrader's conduct, and the trial court's decision?
- If you were the parent of a child in Dodson's situation, how would you advise him or her and why?

Exceptions to the Minor's Right to Disaffirm Not every contract involving a minor is voidable, however. State law often creates statutory exceptions to the minor's right to disaffirm. These statutes prevent minors from disaffirming such transactions as marriage, agreements to support their children, educational loans, life and medical insurance contracts, contracts for transportation by common carriers, and certain types of contracts approved by a court (such as contracts to employ a child actor).

Period of Minority
At common law, the age of majority was 21. However, the ratification in 1971 of the Twenty-Sixth Amendment to the Constitution giving 18-year-olds the right to vote stimulated a trend toward reducing the age of majority. The age of majority has been lowered by 49 states. In almost all of these states, the age of majority for contracting purposes is now 18.

Emancipation
Emancipation is the termination of a parent's right to control a child and receive services and wages from him. There are no formal requirements for emancipation. It can occur by the parent's express or implied consent or by the occurrence of some events such as the marriage of the child. In most states, the mere fact that a minor is emancipated does *not* give him capacity to contract. A person younger than the legal age of majority is generally held to lack capacity to enter a contract, even if he is married and employed full time.

Time of Disaffirmance
Contracts entered during minority that affect title to *real estate* cannot be disaffirmed until majority. This rule is apparently based on the special importance of real estate and on the need to protect a minor from improvidently disaffirming a transaction (such as a mortgage or conveyance) involving real estate. All other contracts entered during minority may be disaffirmed as soon as the contract is formed. The minor's power to avoid her contracts does not end on the day she reaches the age of majority. It continues for a period of time after she reaches majority.

How long after reaching majority does a person retain the right to disaffirm the contracts she made while a minor? A few states have statutes that prescribe a definite time limit on the power of avoidance. In Oklahoma, for example, a person who wishes to disaffirm a contract must do so within one year after reaching majority.[2] In most states, however, there is no set limit on the time during which a person may disaffirm after reaching majority. In determining whether a person has the right to disaffirm, a major factor that courts consider is whether the adult has rendered performance under the contract or relied on the contract. If the adult has relied on the contract or has given something of value to the minor, the minor must disaffirm within a reasonable time after reaching majority. If she delays longer than a period of time that is considered to be reasonable under the circumstances, she will run the risk of *ratifying* (affirming) the contract. (The concept and consequences of ratification are discussed in the next section.) If the adult has neither performed nor relied on the contract, however, the former minor is likely to be accorded a longer period of time in which to disaffirm, sometimes even years after she has reached majority.

Ratification
Though a person has the right to disaffirm contracts made during minority, this right can be given up after the person reaches the age of majority. When a person who has reached majority indicates that he intends to be bound by a contract that he made while still a minor, he surrenders his right to disaffirm. This act of affirming the contract and surrendering the right to avoid the contract is known as **ratification**. Ratification makes a contract valid from its inception. Because ratification represents the former minor's election to be bound by the contract, he cannot later disaffirm. Ratification can be done effectively only after the minor reaches majority. Otherwise, it would be as voidable as the initial contract.

There are no formal requirements for ratification. Any of the former minor's words or acts after reaching majority that indicate with reasonable clarity his intent to be bound by the contract are sufficient. Ratification can be *expressed* in an oral or written statement, or, as is more often the case, it can be *implied* by conduct on the part of the former minor. Naturally, ratification is clearest when the former minor has made some express statement of his intent to be bound. Predicting whether a court will determine that a contract has been ratified is a bit more difficult when the only evidence of the alleged ratification is the conduct of the minor. A former minor's acceptance or retention of benefits given by the other party for an unreasonable time after he has reached majority can constitute implied ratification. Also, a former minor's continued performance of his part of the contract after reaching majority has been held to imply his intent to ratify the contract.

[2]Okla. Stat. Ann. tit. 15, § 18 (1983).

Duties upon Disaffirmance

LO14-4 Explain the rights and duties of the parties to a contract when there has been disaffirmance because of lack of capacity.

Duty to Return Consideration If neither party has performed her part of the contract, the parties' relationship will simply be canceled by the disaffirmance. Because neither party has given anything to the other party, no further adjustments are necessary. But what about the situation where, as is often the case, the minor has paid money to the adult and the adult has given property to the minor? Upon disaffirmance, each party has the duty to return to the other any consideration that the other has given. This means that the minor must return any consideration given to her by the adult that remains in her possession. However, if the minor is unable to return the consideration, most states will still permit her to disaffirm the contract.

The duty to return consideration also means that the minor has the right to recover any consideration she has given to the adult party. She even has the right to recover some property that has been transferred to third parties. One exception to the minor's right to recover property from third parties is found in section 2-403 of the Uniform Commercial Code, however. Under this section, a minor cannot recover *goods* that have been transferred to a **good-faith purchaser**. For example, Simpson, a minor, sells a used Ford to Mort's Car Lot. Mort's then sells the car to Vane, a good-faith purchaser. If Simpson disaffirmed the contract with Mort's, he would *not* have the right to recover the Ford from Vane.

Must the Disaffirming Minor Make Restitution? A Split of Authority If the consideration given by the adult party has been lost, damaged, or destroyed, or simply has depreciated in value, is the minor required to make restitution to the adult for the loss? The traditional rule is that the minor who cannot fully return the consideration that was given to her is *not* obligated to pay the adult for the benefits she has received or to compensate the adult for loss or depreciation of the consideration. Some states still follow this traditional rule. (As you will read in the next section, however, a minor's misrepresentation of age can, even in some of these states, make her responsible for reimbursing the other party upon disaffirmance.) The rule that restitution is not required is designed to protect minors by discouraging adults from dealing with them. After all, if an adult knew that he might be able to demand

the return of anything that he transferred to a minor, he would have little incentive to refrain from entering into contracts with minors.

The traditional rule, however, can work harsh results for innocent adults who have dealt fairly with minors. It strikes many people as unprincipled that a doctrine intended to protect against unfair exploitation of one class of people can be used to unfairly exploit another class of people. As courts sometimes say, the minor's right to disaffirm was designed to be used as a "shield rather than as a sword." For these reasons, a growing number of states have rejected the traditional rule. The courts and legislatures of these states have adopted rules that require minors who disaffirm their contracts and seek refunds of purchase price to reimburse adults for the use or depreciation of their property.

Minors' Obligation to Pay Reasonable Value of Necessaries Though the law regarding minors' contracts is designed to discourage adults from dealing with (and possibly taking advantage of) minors, it would be undesirable for the law to discourage adults from selling minors the items that they need for basic survival. For this reason, disaffirming minors are required to pay the reasonable value of items that have been furnished to them that are classified as **necessaries**. A necessary is something that is essential for the minor's continued existence and general welfare that has not been provided by the minor's parents or guardian. Examples of necessaries include food, clothing, shelter, medical care, tools of the minor's trade, and basic educational or vocational training.

A minor's liability for necessaries supplied to him is **quasi-contractual**. That is, the minor is liable for the *reasonable value* of the necessaries that she actually receives. She is not liable for the entire price agreed on if that price exceeds the actual value of the necessaries, and she is not liable for necessaries that she contracted for but did not receive. For example, Joy Jones, a minor, signs a one-year lease for an apartment in Mountain Park at a rent of $300 per month. After living in the apartment for three months, Joy breaks her lease and moves out. Because she is a minor, Joy has the right to disaffirm the lease. If shelter is a necessary in this case, however, she must pay the reasonable value of what she has actually received—three months' rent. If she can establish that the actual value of what she has received is less than $300 per month, she will be bound to pay only that lesser amount. Furthermore, she will not be obligated to pay for the remaining nine months' rent because she has not received any benefits from the remainder of the lease.

Whether a given item is considered a necessary depends on the facts of a particular case. The minor's age, station in life, and personal circumstances are all relevant to this issue. An item sold to a minor is not considered a necessary if the minor's parent or guardian has already supplied him with similar items. For this reason, the range of items that will be considered necessaries is broader for married minors and other emancipated minors than it is for unemancipated minors.

The following *Zelnick* case involves a situation in which the court is challenged to determine whether a minor has been provided with a necessary.

Zelnick v. Adams   606 S.E.2d 843 (Va. 2005)

The trust beneficiary filed a bill of complaint against his attorney for a declaration that the contract for legal services, entered into when beneficiary was a minor, was void. The Circuit Court, Prince William County, Thomas A. Fortkort, J., granted summary judgment voiding the contract, but the court awarded quantum meruit damages to the attorney. Both parties appealed.

Agee, Justice

"A contract with an infant is not void, only voidable by the infant upon attaining the age of majority." [*Zelnick v. Adams*, 263 Va. 601,] at 608, 561 S.E.2d [711,] at 715 [(2002)]. When a plea of infancy is timely raised, as in this case, the trial court makes a mixed inquiry of law and fact to ascertain whether the defense applies to the case at hand. As we described in *Zelnick I*, the initial inquiry of the trial court is a matter of law: "whether the 'things supplied' to the infant under a contract may fall within the general class of necessaries." *Id.* If this first query is answered in the affirmative, then the trial court proceeds to a second inquiry on a matter of fact: "whether there is sufficient evidence to allow the finder of fact to determine whether the things supplied were in fact necessary in the instant case." *Id.*

Should this second inquiry also be answered in the affirmative, then the trial court must resolve a third query, also one of fact, which is "whether the 'things supplied' were actually necessary to the 'position and condition' of the infant"? *Id.* Should all three inquiries be answered in the affirmative, then the plea of infancy is defeated and the infant is bound "under an implied contract to pay what the goods or services furnished were reasonably worth." *Id.*

In *Zelnick I*, the trial court erroneously answered the first inquiry in the negative because "a contract for legal services is within the 'general classes of necessaries' that may defeat a plea of infancy." *Id.* at 611, 561 S.E.2d at 717. Although our decision definitively answered the first inquiry as a matter of law, the prior record was without evidence upon which the trial court could answer the remaining questions of fact. *See Id.* at 612, 561 S.E.2d at 717–18. We, therefore, remanded the case for the taking of such evidence as necessary to answer those questions. *Id.*, 561 S.E.2d at 718.

Upon remand, Jonathan Ray Adams (Jonathan) contended the legal services provided for him by Robert J. Zelnick (Zelnick), under the contract executed for Jonathan by his mother, Mildred A. Adams (Adams) were not "in fact necessary." Alternatively, even if Zelnick's legal services were necessary, Jonathan argued they were not "actually necessary to the 'position and condition of the infant'" at the time rendered.

Jonathan introduced evidence that he was living a comfortable lifestyle in a middle class home and was not "necessitous." He further argued that the suit filed by Zelnick was not necessary because his status as issue for purposes of distributions from the trusts of Jonathan's grandfather, Cecil D. Hylton, Sr. (Mr. Hylton) was settled by a Florida court's paternity order establishing Cecil D. Hylton, Jr. (Sonny) as his biological father.

In addition, Jonathan contended no legal action was necessary during his minority because distributions under the trusts would not be made until 2014 and 2021, long after he was an adult. Accordingly, Jonathan averred no prejudice could have occurred to him had Zelnick waited until Jonathan was 18 and obtained his consent before proceeding with legal action against the trusts. Further, Jonathan testified the legal proceedings prosecuted by Zelnick had harmed Jonathan because it exacerbated tensions between Adams and Sonny thus adversely affecting him.

In response, Zelnick contended the Florida court's paternity order was not determinative of Jonathan's status under the trusts. Moreover, Zelnick directed the trial court's attention to the fact that Mr. Hylton's will placed the decision as to Jonathan's status as issue for purposes of trust distributions within the purview of the trustees. Adams also communicated to Zelnick that she feared payments were being made to some of Mr. Hylton's grandchildren through the trusts.

The trial court found that Zelnick's legal services were "in fact necessary" because Jonathan's status as issue of Mr. Hylton for purposes of trust distributions would not have been resolved without legal proceedings to compel a resolution. Our inquiry, therefore, goes only to the final question of whether Zelnick's legal services were "actually necessary" to Jonathan's "position and condition." As we indicated in *Zelnick I*, the answer to this inquiry "must be determined by consideration of the circumstances at the time of rendering the services or providing the things in issue." *Zelnick I*, 263 Va. at 611, 561 S.E.2d at 717.

The record amply supports the trial court's determination. Zelnick filed suit on Jonathan's behalf on May 15, 1997, when

Jonathan was less than a year from attaining status as an adult. The consent decree establishing Jonathan as Mr. Hylton's grandchild and issue was entered on January 23, 1998, less than three months before Jonathan's eighteenth birthday.

Before Zelnick executed the retainer agreement, he obtained a copy of Mr. Hylton's probated will and reviewed the trust accountings. Zelnick knew that the distribution dates for the grandchildren's trusts would be in 2014 and 2021. Zelnick testified that he "read the will over many times" in order to "make sure [he] had a full understanding of the terms and conditions and how the will would work." Even though any interest Jonathan might have had in the trusts would not be realized for at least 17 years, Zelnick began writing to the trustees, asking them to acknowledge Jonathan as Mr. Hylton's grandson and issue for the purposes of trust distributions.

However, trustees' counsel did confirm by letter of December 13, 1996, that the triggering events for any distributions from Mr. Hylton's trust were "many years in the future." Trustees' counsel also informed Zelnick that the trustees had been advised to "carefully evaluate the merits of [Jonathan's] claim" "as soon as any amount is to be paid to Mr. Hylton's grandchildren. . . ." Trustees' counsel also confirmed distributions of the trusts would be made in 2014 and 2021 respectively. On February 19, 1997, trustees' counsel

again replied to Zelnick indicating that the trust was "still in the process of conducting a due diligence analysis of [Jonathan's] claim." Nonetheless, Zelnick filed suit on Jonathan's behalf on May 15, 1997, 11 months before Jonathan became an adult.

"By consideration of the circumstances at the time of rendering the services," *Zelnick I*, 263 Va. at 611, 561 S.E.2d at 717, we agree with the trial court's judgment that delaying the suit until Jonathan became 18 "would not have compromised Jonathan's position." The record does not reflect any advantage to the legal proceedings before Jonathan turned 18 or that he would have been disadvantaged by waiting.

Zelnick's legal action on Jonathan's behalf was not a necessity to his "position and condition" at the time this service was rendered. The trial court thus did not err in so finding because its decision is supported by the record.

We find sufficient support in the record for the trial court's judgment that Zelnick's legal services were not necessary for Jonathan's position and condition under all the circumstances. The trial court was thus correct in sustaining Jonathan's plea of infancy and denying any fee award to Zelnick. We will accordingly affirm the judgment of the trial court.

Affirmed.

Effect of Misrepresentation of Age

It is not unheard of for a minor to occasionally pretend to be older than he is. The normal rules dealing with the minor's right to disaffirm and his duties upon disaffirmance can be affected by a minor's misrepresentation of his age.[3] Suppose, for example, that Jones, age 17, wants to lease a car from Acme Auto Rentals but knows that Acme rents only to people who are at least 18. Jones induces Acme to lease a car to him by showing a false identification that represents his age to be 18. Acme relies on the misrepresentation. Jones wrecks the car, attempts to disaffirm the contract, and asks for the return of his money. What is the effect of Jones's misrepresentation? State law is not uniform on this point.

The traditional rule was that a minor's misrepresentation about his age did not affect his right to disaffirm and did not create any obligation to reimburse the adult for damages or pay for benefits received. The theory behind this rule is that one who lacks capacity cannot acquire it merely by claiming to be of legal age. As you can imagine, this traditional approach does not "sit well" with modern

courts—at least in those cases in which the adult has dealt with the minor fairly and in good faith—because it creates severe hardship for innocent adults who have relied on minors' misrepresentations of age.

State law today is fairly evenly divided among those states that take the position that the minor who misrepresents his age will be *estopped* (prevented) from asserting his infancy as a defense and those states that will allow a minor to disaffirm regardless of his misrepresentation of age. Among the states that allow disaffirmance despite the minor's misrepresentation, most hold the disaffirming minor responsible for the losses suffered by the adult, either by allowing the adult to counterclaim against the minor for the tort of deceit or by requiring the minor to reimburse the adult for use or depreciation of his property.

Capacity of Mentally Impaired Persons

Theory of Incapacity

Like minors, people who suffer from a mental illness or defect are at a disadvantage in their ability to protect their own interests in the bargaining process. Contract law makes their contracts either void

---

[3]You might want to refer back to Chapter 13 to review the elements of misrepresentation.

or voidable to protect them from the results of their own impaired perceptions and judgment and also from others who might take advantage of them.

Test for Mental Incapacity
Incapacity on grounds of mental illness or defect, which is often referred to in cases and texts as "insanity," encompasses a broad range of causes of impaired mental functioning, such as mental illness, brain damage, mental retardation, or senility. The mere fact that a person suffers from some mental illness or defect does not necessarily mean that she lacks capacity to contract, however. She could still have full capacity unless the defect or illness affects the particular transaction in question.

The usual test for mental incapacity is a *cognitive* one; that is, courts ask whether the person had sufficient mental capacity to understand the nature and effect of the contract. Some courts have criticized the traditional test as unscientific because it does not take into account the fact that a person suffering from a mental illness or defect might be unable to *control* her conduct. Section 15 of the *Restatement (Second) of Contracts* provides that a person's contracts are voidable if she is unable to *act* in a reasonable manner in relation to the transaction and the other party has reason to know of her condition. Where the other party has reason to know of the condition of the mentally impaired person, the *Restatement (Second)* standard would provide protection to people who understood the transaction but, because of some mental defect or illness, were unable to exercise appropriate judgment or to control their conduct effectively.

The Effect of Incapacity Caused by Mental Impairment
The contracts of people who are suffering from a mental defect at the time of contracting are usually considered to be *voidable*. In some situations, however, severe mental or physical impairment may prevent a person from even being able to manifest consent. In such a case, no contract could be formed.

As mentioned at the beginning of this chapter, contract law makes a distinction between a contract involving a person who has been *adjudicated* (judged by a court) incompetent at the time the contract was made and a contract involving a person who was suffering from some mental impairment at the time the contract was entered but whose incompetency was not established until *after* the contract was formed. If a person is under guardianship at the time the contract is formed—that is, if a court has found a person mentally incompetent after holding a hearing on his mental competency and has appointed a guardian for him—the contract is considered *void*. You will see an example of this in the following *Rogers* case. On the other hand, if *after* a contract has been formed, a court finds that the person who manifested consent lacked capacity on grounds of mental illness or defect, the contract is usually considered *voidable* at the election of the party who lacked capacity (or her guardian or personal representative).

Rogers v. Household Life Insurance Co.
2011 Idaho LEXIS 53 (Idaho Mar. 18, 2011)

Alan Rogers was diagnosed with Alzheimer's and dementia in 2003. Soon after, Alan's son, Jason, sought an adjudication that Alan was incapacitated. An order to that effect was entered in 2004. The letters appointing Jason as guardian and conservator for his father did not place any limitations on Jason's powers. On May 15, 2007, Jason helped his father complete and submit an online application for life insurance offered by Household Life Insurance Company (HLIC). The application requested information regarding Alan's health but did not specifically inquire as to whether Alan suffered from Alzheimer's or dementia. The completed application did not reveal that Alan had been adjudicated to be incapacitated, nor did it reveal that Jason had been appointed as his father's guardian and conservator. That day, HLIC approved the application, the initial $447.20 premium was paid, and Alan Rogers's term life insurance policy with a face value of $250,000 took effect. Jason was the sole beneficiary of the policy.

Alan passed away on June 7, 2007. His death certificate lists the sole cause of his death as "dementia of the Alzheimer's type." Jason submitted a notice of claim to HLIC, seeking the $250,000 policy proceeds. HLIC conducted a medical-history verification, a routine procedure for claims arising within two years of a policy's inception. Several months later, HLIC informed Jason that, because Alan had been adjudicated mentally incompetent prior to the May 15, 2007, application and effective date, the policy was void from its inception.

Jason brought suit against HLIC, alleging breach of contract and bad faith. HLIC moved for summary judgment on the grounds that Alan Rogers was adjudicated mentally incapacitated prior to entering into the insurance contract and therefore the contract was void. Jason took the position that the contract was merely voidable at the election of the incompetent's guardian, and that a guardian may ratify such a contract. The district court granted HLIC's motion for summary judgment and dismissed Jason's complaint. Jason appealed.

Horton, Justice

Idaho Code § 32-108 provides as follows:

> After his incapacity has been judicially determined, a person of unsound mind can make no conveyance or other contract, nor delegate any power or waive any right until his restoration to capacity. . . .

Jason asserts that the statute's language that one adjudicated to be incapacitated "can make no conveyance or other contract" means that although such a person should not contract, if he or she does, the contract is merely voidable. HLIC responds that under the statute's plain language, the contracts of one who is adjudicated incompetent are void because the individual lacks all capacity to contract. The language of I.C. § 32-108 does not, upon preliminary consideration, support Jason's position. Effectively, Jason argues that the statutory language that a person adjudicated to be incapacitated "can make no . . . contract" means that such a person may enter into a contract, while simultaneously retaining the ability to avoid the obligations imposed by the agreement. Nevertheless, when considering Jason's claim that the insurance contract in this case was merely voidable, rather than void *ab initio*, we consider the statutory framework relating to persons who suffer from impaired capacity and their ability to make decisions regarding the conduct of their lives.

Idaho Code §§ 32-106 through 32-108 address the enforceability of contracts involving persons of unsound mind. If a person is "entirely without understanding," he "has no power to make a contract of any kind, but he is liable for the reasonable value of things furnished to him necessary for his support or the support of his family." I.C. § 32-106. A contract involving a party who is "not entirely without understanding" and has not been adjudicated to be incapacitated "is subject to rescission." I.C. § 32-107.

In other words, prior to a judicial determination of incapacity, such contracts are voidable. However, after a judicial determination of incapacity, "a person of unsound mind can make no conveyance or other contract, nor delegate any power or waive any right until his restoration to capacity." Comparing I.C. § 32-107 and I.C. § 32-108, it is evident that the legislature intended that contracts involving persons not adjudicated to be incapacitated are to be voidable and to declare that a person adjudicated to be incompetent is without the legal capacity to contract until that person has been "restored to reason."

Guardianship proceedings fall directly within the scope of those the legislature intended to be conclusive judicial determinations of incapacity. In a guardianship proceeding, the trial court assesses whether an individual's acts and statements during the twelve preceding months strongly indicate the inability to maintain his or her self or property. If the individual has some ability to care for himself or herself, the court may craft a guardianship that corresponds with his or her capacity. This "limited guardianship" is accomplished by noting limitations within the letters of guardianship. A finding that one is incapacitated and a grant of unrestricted guardianship powers represents [sic] a finding that the ward lacks all capacity to make decisions and take actions that protect his or her well-being. Thus, we conclude that the appointment of a guardian with full powers represents a finding that the ward lacks the capacity to contract as a matter of law. According to the plain language of Idaho Code § 32-108, an adjudication that one is incapacitated is a determination that one lacks the capacity to contract as a matter of law. Thus, agreements entered into by such a person do not give rise to enforceable contracts.

Affirmed in favor of HLIC.

The Right to Disaffirm If a contract is found to be voidable on the ground of mental impairment, the person who lacked capacity at the time the contract was made has the right to disaffirm the contract. A person formerly incapacitated by mental impairment can ratify a contract if he regains his capacity. Thus, if he regains capacity, he must disaffirm the contract unequivocally within a reasonable time, or he will be deemed to have ratified it.

As is true of a disaffirming minor, a person disaffirming on the ground of mental impairment must return any consideration given by the other party that remains in his possession. A person under this type of mental incapacity is liable for the reasonable value of necessaries in the same manner as are minors. Must the incapacitated party reimburse the other party for loss, damage, or depreciation of non-necessaries given to him? Generally, this depends on whether the contract was basically fair and on whether the other party had reason to be aware of his impairment. If the contract is fair and was bargained for in good faith, and the other party had no reasonable cause to know of the incapacity, the contract cannot be disaffirmed unless the other party is placed in *status quo* (the position she was in before the creation of the contract). However, if the other party had reason to know of the incapacity, the incapacitated party is allowed to disaffirm without placing the other party in status quo. This distinction discourages people from attempting to take advantage of mentally impaired people, but it spares those who are dealing in good faith and have no such intent.

Contracts of Intoxicated Persons

Intoxication and Capacity Intoxication (either from alcohol or the use of drugs) can deprive a person of capacity to contract. The mere fact that a party to a contract had been drinking when the contract was formed would *not* normally affect his or her capacity to contract, however. Intoxication is a ground for lack of capacity only when it is so extreme that the person is unable to understand the nature of the business at hand. Section 16 of the

Restatement (Second) of Contracts further provides that intoxication is a ground for lack of capacity only if *the other party has reason to know* that the affected person is so intoxicated that he or she cannot understand or act reasonably in relation to the transaction.

The rules governing the capacity of intoxicated persons are very similar to those applied to the capacity of people who are mentally impaired. The basic right to disaffirm contracts made during incapacity, the duties upon disaffirmance, and the possibility of ratification upon regaining capacity are the same for an intoxicated person as for a person under a mental impairment. In practice, however, courts traditionally have been less sympathetic with a person who was intoxicated at the time of contracting than with minors or those suffering from a mental impairment. It is rare for a person to actually escape his contractual obligations on the ground of intoxication. A person incapacitated by intoxication at the time of contracting might nevertheless be bound to his or her contract if he or she fails to disaffirm in a timely manner.

Problems and Problem Cases

1. Williams was 18 years old when she was admitted to Baptist Health Systems for treatment of serious health conditions. The age of majority for contracting in Williams's state was 19. Williams was hospitalized for two days, during which she had a variety of medical procedures and tests. At this time, Williams had been admitted to college and was awaiting enrollment, did not work, had no source of income, and was dependent on her mother to provide support. According to her, she believed that she was covered by her mother's health insurance, and that is what she told the hospital, but in fact, she was not covered. Williams's mother was listed in the hospital records as "guarantor." The hospital bill was $12,144. Williams's mother did not pay the bill. The hospital sued both Williams and her mother for the principal amount plus interest. Was Williams legally obligated to pay the bill, despite the fact that she was a minor when the contract was formed?

2. Robertson, while a minor, contracted to borrow money from his father for a college education. His father mortgaged his home and took out loans against his life insurance policies to get some of the money he lent to Robertson, who ultimately graduated from dental school. Two years after Robertson's graduation,

his father asked him to begin paying back the amount of $30,000 at $400 per month. Robertson agreed to pay $24,000 at $100 per month. He did this for three years before stopping the payments. His father sued for the balance of the debt. Could Robertson disaffirm the contract?

3. In the fall of 2001, Kim Young, who at the time was 18 years old and had been living with her parents all of her life, decided that she "wanted to move out and get away from [her] parents and be on [her] own." Young and a friend, Ashley Springer, also a minor at the time, signed a contract for the lease of an apartment with Phillip Weaver on September 20, 2001. No adult signed the lease as a guarantor. Young was employed on a full-time basis at a Lowe's hardware store at the time she entered into the lease agreement. Young paid a security deposit in the amount of $300; the rent for the apartment was $550 per month, and the lease was set to expire on July 31, 2002. Young and Springer moved into the apartment in late September and, together, paid rent at the agreed-upon rate for the portion of that month in which they lived in the apartment. Young and Springer continued to live in the apartment during October and most of November 2001. Young moved out near the end of November and returned to live with her parents. Young paid the full amount of her portion of the rent for October and November, but she

stopped making any rent payments after she moved out of the apartment. Young had a dog that stayed in the apartment, and the dog damaged part of the floor and the bathroom door in the apartment, causing $270 in damage. Young did not pay for this damage before vacating the apartment. Weaver managed to rent the apartment to someone else in June 2002. Weaver filed a claim against Young in Small Claims, seeking damages for the unpaid rent and the damage done by Young's dog to the apartment. The court ruled in favor of Weaver and awarded $1,370 in damages. Young appealed the decision to the Tuscaloosa Circuit Court, which tried the case and also entered a judgment in favor of Weaver and awarded him $1,095, the amount of Young's share of the unpaid rent for December 2001 and January and February 2002, as well as the $270 in damage caused by Young's dog. Young appealed. How did the appellate court rule?

4. In 2002, the State charged Bishop, who was 16 at the time, with a misdemeanor DUI. Bishop entered into a diversion agreement with the State to avoid prosecution. In 2004, the City of Pratt charged Bishop with another DUI and disobeying a stop sign. Again, Bishop entered into a diversion agreement with the City to avoid prosecution for the charges. In 2007, Bishop was again arrested under suspicion of driving under the influence. Her blood alcohol test revealed a blood alcohol concentration of .24 gram per 100 milliliters, in excess of the legal limit. The State charged Bishop in the alternative with driving under the influence of alcohol to a degree that rendered her incapable of safely driving a vehicle (third offense), and with driving under the influence of alcohol while having a blood alcohol content greater than .08 (third offense). A third DUI is a felony. Bishop moved to dismiss the charges, asserting it was not her third offense. She claimed that the State could not rely on the 2002 diversion agreement as a prior conviction because Bishop was 16 when she entered into it and, therefore, it was not a legally binding contract due to her lack of capacity to contract. Is this a good argument under these facts?

5. At a time when the age of majority in Ohio was 21, Lee, age 20, contracted to buy a 1964 Plymouth Fury for $1,552 from Haydocy Pontiac. Lee represented herself to be 21 when entering the contract. She paid for the car by trading in another car worth $150 and financing the balance. Immediately following delivery of the car to her, Lee permitted one John Roberts to take possession of it. Roberts delivered the car to someone else, and it was never recovered. Lee failed to make payments on the car, and Haydocy Pontiac sued her to recover the car or the amount due on the contract. Lee repudiated the contract on the ground that she was a minor at the time of purchase. Can Lee disaffirm the contract without reimbursing Haydocy Pontiac for the value of the car?

6. Five-year-old Trent Woodman's parents had his birthday party at Bounce Party, which is operated by Kera LLC. Bounce Party is an indoor play area that contains inflatable play equipment. Before the party, Trent's father, Jeffrey Woodman, signed a liability waiver on Trent's behalf. The waiver provided that the undersigned acknowledged the risk and waived claims against Bounce Party.

> THE UNDERSIGNED, by his/her signature herein affixed does acknowledge that any physical activities involve some element of personal risk and that, accordingly, in consideration for the undersigned waiving his/her claim against BOUNCE PARTY, and their agents, the undersigned will be allowed to participate in any of the physical activities. By engaging in this activity, the undersigned acknowledges that he/she assumes the element of inherent risk, in consideration for being allowed to engage in the activity, agrees to indemnify and hold BOUNCE PARTY, and their agents, harmless from any liability. Further, the undersigned agrees to indemnify and hold BOUNCE PARTY, and their agents, harmless from any and all costs incurred including, but not limited to, actual attorney's fees that BOUNCE PARTY, and their agents, may suffer by an action or claim brought against it by anyone as a result of the undersigned's use of such facility.

During the party, Trent Woodman jumped off a slide and broke his leg. Trent's mother filed suit on Trent's behalf. Kera filed a motion for summary judgment, arguing that Trent's claims were barred by the liability waiver. The Woodmans filed a cross-motion for summary judgment, arguing that the waiver was invalid as a matter of law. The trial court ruled that the waiver barred Trent's negligence claim but not his gross negligence claim. Both parties appealed. The court of appeals reversed and held that the waiver was invalid to bar the negligence claim. Kera appealed.

A parental preinjury waiver is a contract. Mr. Woodman purportedly signed the contract on behalf of his son. Consequently, Kera necessarily asserts that the contract is enforceable against Trent because Mr. Woodman had authority to bind his son to the contract. The well-established Michigan common law rule is that a minor lacks the capacity to contract.

It is undisputed that if five-year-old Trent had signed the waiver, defendant could not enforce the waiver against him unless Trent confirmed it after he reached the age of majority. Can a parent bind his child by contract if the child could not otherwise be bound?

7. David Denison is a developmentally disabled young man who has been under the legal guardianship of his parents since 1999, when he turned 18. In October 2002, David was living in his own apartment, but his parents strictly controlled his finances. They visited him at least once each week to make sure he had a clean and safe place to live and was budgeting his food money properly. They also visited him socially several times every week and spoke with him nearly every day. The Denisons first learned that David wanted to buy a car when David called his father, Michael, from Kenai Chrysler and asked him to cosign for a used car; Michael refused. The next day, David again tried to purchase a car from Kenai Chrysler. This time, he was trying to buy a new car, which he could finance without a cosigner. David called his mother, Dorothy, to ask for money for a down payment. Dorothy refused and told him not to buy a car. She assumed her word would be final because she did not realize that David could obtain any appreciable amount of money with his debit card. David used his debit card and bought a Dodge Neon. Kenai Chrysler charged a total price of $17,802, including taxes, fees, and extended service plan. One or two days after David signed the contract, Dorothy came to Kenai Chrysler with David and informed the salesman who had sold the car to David and a Kenai Chrysler manager that David was under the legal guardianship of his parents and had no legal authority to enter into a contract to buy the Neon. Dorothy showed the manager David's guardianship papers and asked him to take back the car. The manager refused; according to Dorothy, he told her that Kenai Chrysler would not take back the car and that the company sold cars to "a lot of people who aren't very smart." Dorothy insisted that the contract was void, but the Kenai Chrysler manager ignored her and handed the keys to David over Dorothy's objection. David drove off in the new car. Dorothy contacted Bannock, the general manager of Kenai Chrysler, the next day; he told her that he had seen the guardianship papers, but he still thought that the contract was valid and that David was bound by it. Is the general manager correct?

8. In October 1995, Mitchell, a 17-year-old married minor, was injured in an auto accident while riding in a car owned by her father and driven by her husband. Subsequently, while Mitchell was still 17, she signed a release with State Farm Mutual Automobile Insurance Co. to settle her bodily injury claims for $2,500. No guardian or conservator was appointed at the time Mitchell signed this release. Mitchell then claimed that the release was voidable because she lacked capacity at the time she signed it. State Farm argued that the release was enforceable because she was married at the time she signed it. Will Mitchell be able to disaffirm the contract?

9. A boy bought an Ernie Banks rookie card for $12 from an inexperienced clerk in a baseball card store owned by Johnson. The card had been marked "1200," and Johnson, who had been away from the store at the time of the sale, had intended the card to be sold for $1,200, not $12. Can Johnson get the card back by asserting the boy's lack of capacity?

10. Fourteen-year-old Taneia Galloway attended a field trip to Milwaukee with Upward Bound, a youth outreach program. On the field trip, Galloway was injured when she was struck by a car as she attempted to cross the street. Before going on the field trip, her mother signed two documents titled "Field Trip Permission Form" and "Release and Medical Authorization." If Galloway sues Upward Bound, will she prevail or will the release signed by her mother protect Upward Bound from liability?

Illegality

Wilson had been licensed to practice architecture in Hawaii, but his license lapsed in 1971 because he had failed to pay a required $15 renewal fee. A Hawaii statute provides that any person who practices architecture without having been registered and "without having a valid unexpired certificate of registration . . . shall be fined not more than $500 or imprisoned not more than one year, or both." In 1972, Wilson performed architectural and engineering services for Kealakekua Ranch and billed the Ranch more than $33,000 for the work.

- Is this a legal contract?
- Would it matter if Wilson had never met the licensing requirements to be licensed in Hawaii?
- Is Kealakekua Ranch required to pay Wilson anything for his work?
- Is it ethical for the Ranch to refuse to pay Wilson, even if he is unlicensed?

LO LEARNING OBJECTIVES

After studying this chapter, you should be able to:

15-1 Explain the concept of illegality as it is used in contract law.

15-2 Determine when a contract that violates the language or policy of a statute is likely to be illegal.

15-3 Analyze whether a given noncompete clause is likely to be enforceable.

15-4 Analyze whether a given exculpatory clause is likely to be enforceable.

15-5 Explain the concept of unconscionability and identify the circumstances that make a contract unconscionable.

15-6 Determine the effect of illegality in a given scenario.

ALTHOUGH THE PUBLIC INTEREST normally favors the enforcement of contracts, there are times when the interests that usually favor the enforcement of an agreement are subordinated to conflicting social concerns. As you read in Chapter 13, Reality of Consent, and Chapter 14, Capacity to Contract, for example, people who did not truly consent to a contract or who lacked the capacity to contract have the power to cancel their contracts. In these situations, concerns about protecting disadvantaged persons and preserving the integrity of the bargaining process outweigh the usual public interest in enforcing private agreements. Similarly, when an agreement involves an act or promise that violates some legislative or court-made rule, the public interests threatened by the agreement outweigh the interests that favor its enforcement. Such an agreement will not be enforced on the ground of *illegality*, even if there is voluntary consent between two parties who have capacity to contract.

Meaning of Illegality

 LO15-1 Explain the concept of illegality as it is used in contract law.

When a court says that an agreement is illegal, it does not necessarily mean that the agreement violates a criminal law, although an agreement to commit a crime is one type of illegal agreement. Rather, an agreement is illegal either because the legislature has declared that particular type of contract to be unenforceable or void or because the agreement violates a public policy that has been developed by courts or that has been manifested in constitutions, statutes, administrative regulations, or other sources of law.

The term *public policy* is impossible to define precisely. Generally, it is taken to mean a widely shared view about what ideas, interests, institutions, or freedoms promote public welfare. For example, in our society there are strong public policies favoring the protection of human life and health, free competition, and private property. Judicial and legislative perceptions of desirable public policy influence the decisions they make about the resolution of cases or the enactment of statutes. Public policy may be based on a prevailing moral code, on an economic philosophy, or on the need to protect a valued social institution such as the family or the judicial system. If the enforcement of an agreement would create a threat to a public policy, a court may determine that it is illegal.

Determining Whether an Agreement Is Illegal

If a statute states that a particular type of agreement is unenforceable or void, courts will apply the statute and refuse to enforce the agreement. Relatively few such statutes exist, however. More frequently, a legislature will forbid certain conduct but will not address the enforceability of contracts that involve the forbidden conduct. In such cases, courts must determine whether the importance of the public policy that underlies the statute in question and the degree of interference with that policy are sufficiently great to outweigh any interests that favor enforcement of the agreement.

In some cases, it is relatively easy to predict that an agreement will be held to be illegal. For example, an agreement to commit a serious crime is certain to be illegal. However, the many laws enacted by legislatures are of differing degrees of importance to the public welfare. The determination of illegality would not be so clear if the agreement violated a statute that was of relatively small importance to the public welfare. For example, in one Illinois case,[1] a seller of fertilizer failed to comply with an Illinois statute requiring that a descriptive statement accompany the delivery of the fertilizer. The sellers prepared the statements and offered them to the buyers but did not give them to the buyers at the time of delivery. The court enforced the contract despite the sellers' technical violation of the law because the contract was not seriously injurious to public welfare.

Similarly, the public policies developed by courts are rarely absolute; they, too, depend on a balancing of several factors. In determining whether to hold an agreement illegal, a court will consider the importance of the public policy involved and the extent to which enforcement of the agreement would interfere with that policy. They will also consider the seriousness of any wrongdoing involved in the agreement and how directly that wrongdoing was connected with the agreement.

For purposes of our discussion, illegal agreements will be classified into three main categories: (1) agreements that violate statutes, (2) agreements that violate public policy developed by courts, and (3) unconscionable agreements and contracts of adhesion.

You will see the court grapple with conflicting public policies in deciding the following *Coma Corporation* case.

---

[1]*Amoco Oil Co. v. Toppert*, 56 Ill. App. 3d 1294 (1978).

Coma Corporation v. Kansas Department of Labor
154 P.3d 1080 (Kan. 2007)

Cesar Martinez Corral was an undocumented worker who was not legally permitted to work in the United States. He was nevertheless employed by Coma Corporation, which did business as Burrito Express. Corral stated that Coma's manager, Luis Calderon, had agreed to pay him $6 per hour, with payment made weekly. Corral maintained that he worked 50 to 60 hours per week, 6 or 7 days per week, but that he was paid "$50 or $60 bucks a week."

Coma fired Corral, and Corral filed a claim with the Kansas Department of Labor for earned but unpaid wages under the Kansas Wage Payment Act. He was awarded a total of $7,657 against Coma and its president. Coma filed a petition for judicial review of final order. The district court held that the employment contract was illegal due to Corral's status as an undocumented worker and remanded to the Kansas Department of Labor for recalculation at the applicable minimum wage. The Kansas Department of Labor appealed.

Nuss, Judge

Coma argues that Corral's employment contract was illegal and unenforceable because he is an illegal alien. Intertwined with this argument is another: Coma claims that federal immigration law preempts the Kansas Wage Payment Act. Coma's purported trumping argument is based upon [The Immigration Reform and Control Act (IRCA)], which makes employment of unauthorized aliens illegal. Preemption, however is not presumed. It is well established that the states enjoy broad authority under their police powers to regulate employment relationships to protect workers within the state. Minimum and other wage laws and workmen's compensation law are only a few examples of the exercise of this broad authority. We conclude that under this case's facts, Coma has not overridden the presumption against federal preemption.

Finally, we agree with the rationale set forth in *Flores v. Amigon,* 233 F. Supp. 2d 462 (E.D.N.Y. 2002), where the court granted Fair Labor Standards Act protections to an undocumented worker and determined that payment of unpaid wages for work actually performed furthers the federal immigration policy:

> Indeed, it is arguable that enforcing the FLSA's provisions requiring employers to pay proper wages to undocumented aliens when the work had been performed actually furthers the goal of the IRCA, which requires the employer to discharge any worker upon discovery of the worker's undocumented alien status. If employers know that they will not only be subject to civil penalties when they hire illegal aliens, but they will also be required to pay them at the same rates as legal workers for work actually performed, there are virtually no incentives left for an employer to hire an undocumented alien in the first instance. Whatever benefit an employer might have gained by paying less than the minimum wage is eliminated and the employer's incentive would be to investigate and obtain proper documentation from each of his workers.

Coma also asserts that Corral's employment contract is illegal under state law. Specifically, it argues that Kansas Department of Labor regulations require that a contract of employment contain lawful provisions in order to be enforceable. Coma reasons that because Corral does not have a legal right to be or to work in the United States, his contract violates IRCA and is unenforceable under Kansas Department of Labor regulations and state law.

Prior to IRCA's enactment, the Alaska Supreme Court confronted the issue of whether a contract of employment entered into by a Canadian alien was barred by illegality. *Gates v. Rivers Construction Co., Inc.,* 515 P.3d 1020 (Alaska 1973). The court first discussed the nature of illegal contracts:

> Generally, a party to an illegal contract cannot recover damages for its breach. But as in the case of many such simplifications, the exceptions and qualifications to the general rule are numerous and complex. Thus, when a statute imposes sanctions but does not specifically declare a contract to be invalid, it is

necessary to ascertain whether the legislature intended to make unenforceable contracts entered into in violation of the statute.

The *Gates* court then concluded that enforcement of the employment contract with the Canadian alien was not barred. It looked at the statutory language:

> [I]t is clear that the contract involved here should be enforced. First, it is apparent that the statute itself does not specifically declare the labor or service contracts of aliens seeking to enter the United States for the purpose of performing such labor or services to be void. The statute only specifies that aliens who enter this country for such purpose, without having received the necessary certification, "shall be ineligible to receive visas and shall be excluded from admission into the United States."

The court next advanced the concept of equity and fairness to the employee:

> Second, that the employer, who knowingly participated in an illegal transaction, should be permitted to profit thereby at the expense of the employee is a harsh and undesirable consequence of the doctrine that illegal contracts are not to be enforced. This result, so contrary to general considerations of equity and fairness, should be countenanced only when clearly demonstrated to have been intended by the legislature.

Finally, in a general foreshadowing of the benefit described in *Flores*, that is, of reducing employer incentives to violate the law, the *Gates* court stated:

> Third, since the purpose of this section would appear to be the safeguarding of American labor from unwanted competition, the appellant's contract should be enforced, because such an objective would not be furthered by permitting employers knowingly to employ excludable aliens and then, with impunity, to refuse to pay them for their services. *Indeed, to so hold could well have the opposite effect from the one intended, by encouraging employers to enter into the very type of contracts sought to be prevented.*

We agree with Kansas Department of Labor's position concerning the strong and longtime Kansas public policy of protecting wages and wage earners. As we stated in *Burriss v. Northern Assurance Co. of America,* 236 Kan. 326 (1984): "[t]hroughout the history of this state, the protection of wages and wage earners has been a principal objective of many of our laws in order that they and the families dependent upon them are not destitute." Accordingly, we conclude that to deny or to dilute an action for wages earned but not paid on the ground that such employment contracts are "illegal," would thus directly contravene the public policy of the State of Kansas. We hold for the above reasons that the district court erred in concluding that Corral's employment contract was illegal and therefore not enforceable.

Reversed in favor of Kansas Department of Labor.

Agreements in Violation of Statute

LO15-2 Determine when a contract that violates the language or policy of a statute is likely to be illegal.

Agreements Declared Illegal by Statute

State legislatures occasionally enact statutes that declare certain types of agreements unenforceable, void, or voidable. In a case in which a legislature has specifically stated that a particular type of contract is void, a court need only interpret and apply the statute. These statutes differ from state to state. Some are relatively uncommon. For example, an Indiana statute declares surrogate birth contracts to be void.[2] Others are common, such as statutes setting limits on the amount of interest that can be charged for a loan or forbearance (usury statutes) and statutes prohibiting or regulating wagering or gambling.

Agreements That Violate the Public Policy of a Statute

As stated earlier, an agreement can be illegal even if no statute specifically states that that particular sort of agreement is illegal. Legislatures enact statutes in an effort to resolve some particular problem. If courts enforced agreements that involve the violation of a statute, they would frustrate the purpose for which the legislature passed the statute. They would also promote disobedience of the law and disrespect for the courts.

Agreements to Commit a Crime For the reasons stated above, contracts that require the violation of a criminal statute are illegal. If Grimes promises to pay Judge John Doe a bribe of $5,000 to dismiss a criminal case against Grimes, for example, the agreement is illegal. Sometimes the very formation of a certain type of contract is a crime, even if the acts agreed on are never carried out. An example of this is an agreement to murder another person. Naturally, such agreements are considered illegal under contract law as well as under criminal law.

Agreements That Promote Violations of Statutes Sometimes a contract of a type that is usually perfectly legal—say, a contract to sell goods—is deemed to be illegal under the circumstances of the case because it promotes or facilitates the violation of a statute. Suppose Davis sells Sims goods on credit. Sims uses the goods in some illegal manner and then refuses to pay Davis for the goods. Can Davis recover the price of the goods from Sims? The answer depends on whether Davis knew of the illegal purpose and whether he intended the sale to further that illegal purpose. Generally speaking, such agreements will be legal unless there is a direct connection between the illegal conduct and the agreement in the form of active, intentional participation in or facilitation of the illegal act. Knowledge of the other party's illegal purpose, standing alone, is generally not sufficient to render an agreement illegal. When a person is aware of the other's illegal purpose *and* actively helps to accomplish that purpose, an otherwise legal agreement—such as a sale of goods—might be labeled illegal.

Licensing Laws: Agreement to Perform an Act for Which a Party Is Not Properly Licensed Congress and the state legislatures have enacted a variety of statutes that regulate professions and businesses. A common type of regulatory statute is one that requires a person to obtain a license, permit, or registration before engaging in a certain business or profession. For example, state statutes require lawyers, physicians, dentists, teachers, and other professionals to be licensed to practice their professions. In order to obtain the required license, they must meet specified requirements such as attaining a certain educational degree and passing an examination. Real estate brokers, stockbrokers, insurance agents, sellers of liquor and tobacco, pawnbrokers, electricians, barbers, and others too numerous to mention are also often required by state statute to meet licensing requirements to perform services or sell regulated commodities to members of the public.

What is the status of an agreement in which one of the parties agrees to perform an act regulated by state law for which she is not properly licensed? This will often be determined by looking at the purpose of the legislation that the unlicensed party has violated. If the statute is regulatory—that is, the purpose of the legislation is to protect the public against dishonest or incompetent practitioners—an agreement by an unlicensed person is generally held to be unenforceable. For example, if Spencer, a first-year law student, agrees to draft a will for Rowen for a fee of $150, Spencer could not enforce the agreement and collect a fee from Rowen for drafting the will because she is not licensed to practice law. This result makes sense, even though it imposes a hardship on Spencer. The public interest in ensuring that people on whose legal advice others rely have an appropriate educational background and proficiency in the subject matter outweighs any interest in seeing that Spencer receives what she bargained for.

On the other hand, where the licensing statute was intended primarily as a revenue-raising measure—that is, as a means of collecting money rather than as a means of protecting the public—an agreement to pay a person for performing an act for which she is not licensed will

---

[2]Ind. Code §§31-20-1-1 and 31-20-1-2.

generally be enforced. For example, suppose that in the example used above, Spencer is a lawyer who is licensed to practice law in her state and who met all of her state's educational, testing, and character requirements but neglected to pay her annual registration fee. In this situation, there is no compelling public interest that would justify the harsh measure of refusing enforcement and possibly inflicting forfeiture on the unlicensed person.

Whether a statute is a regulatory statute or a revenue-raising statute depends on the intent of the legislature, which may not always be expressed clearly. Generally, statutes that require proof of character and skill and impose penalties for violation are considered to be regulatory in nature. Their requirements indicate that they were intended for the protection of the public. Those that impose a significant license fee and allow anyone who pays the fee to obtain a license are usually classified as revenue raising. The fact that no requirement other than the payment of the fee is imposed indicates that the purpose of the law is to raise money rather than to protect the public. Because such a statute is not designed for the protection of the public, a violation of the statute is not as threatening to the public interest as is a violation of a regulatory statute.

It would be misleading to imply that cases involving unlicensed parties always follow such a mechanical test. In some cases, courts may grant recovery to an unlicensed party even where a regulatory statute is violated. If the public policy promoted by the statute is relatively trivial in relation to the amount that would be forfeited by the unlicensed person and the unlicensed person is neither dishonest nor incompetent, a court may conclude that the statutory penalty for violation of the regulatory statute is sufficient to protect the public interest and that enforcement of the agreement is appropriate.

Agreements That May Be in Violation of Public Policy Articulated by Courts

Courts have broad discretion to articulate public policy and to decline to lend their powers of enforcement to an agreement that would contravene what they deem to be in the best interests of society. There is no simple rule for determining when a particular agreement is contrary to public policy. Public policy may change with the times; changing social and economic conditions may make behavior that was acceptable in an earlier time unacceptable today, or vice versa. The following are examples of agreements that are frequently considered vulnerable to attack on public policy grounds.

Agreements in Restraint of Competition

 LO15-3 Analyze whether a given noncompete clause is likely to be enforceable.

The policy against restrictions on competition is one of the oldest public policies declared by the common law. This same policy is also the basis of federal and state antitrust statutes. The policy against restraints on competition is based on the economic judgment that the public interest is best served by free competition. Nevertheless, courts have long recognized that some contractual restrictions on competition serve legitimate business interests and should be enforced. Therefore, agreements that limit competition are scrutinized very closely by the courts to determine whether the restraint imposed is in violation of public policy.

If the *sole* purpose of an agreement is to restrain competition, it violates public policy and is illegal. For example, if Martin and Bloom, who own competing businesses, enter an agreement whereby each agrees not to solicit or sell to the other's customers, such an agreement would be unenforceable. Where the restriction on competition was part of (*ancillary to*) an otherwise legal contract, the result may be different because the parties may have a legitimate interest to be protected by the restriction on competition.

For example, if Martin had *purchased* Bloom's business, the goodwill of the business was part of what she paid for. She has a legitimate interest in making sure that Bloom does not open a competing business soon after the sale and attract away the very customers whose goodwill she paid for. Or suppose that Martin hired Walker to work as a salesperson in her business. She wants to assure herself that she does not disclose trade secrets, confidential information, or lists of regular customers to Walker only to have Walker quit and enter a competing business.

To protect herself, the buyer or the employer in the above examples might bargain for a contractual clause that would provide that the seller or employee agrees not to engage in a particular competing activity in a specified *geographic area* for a specified *time* after the sale of the business or the termination of employment. This type of clause is called an **ancillary covenant not to compete**, or, as it is more commonly known, a noncompetition clause or "noncompete." Such clauses most frequently appear in *employment contracts*, *contracts for the sale of a business*, *partnership agreements*, and *small-business buy–sell agreements*. In an employment contract, the noncompetition clause might be the only part of the contract that the parties put in writing.

Enforceability of Noncompetition Clauses Although noncompetition clauses restrict competition and thereby affect the public policy favoring free competition, courts enforce them if they meet the following three criteria:

1. *Clause must serve a legitimate business purpose.* This means that the person protected by the clause must have some justifiable interest—such as an interest in protecting goodwill or trade secrets—that is to be protected by the noncompetition clause. It also means that the clause must be *ancillary* to, or part of, an otherwise valid contract. For example, a noncompetition clause that is one term of an existing employment contract would be ancillary to that contract. By contrast, a promise not to compete would not be enforced if the employee made the promise *after* he had already resigned his job because the promise not to compete was not ancillary to any existing contract.

2. *The restriction on competition must be reasonable in time, geographic area, and scope.* Another way of stating this is that the restrictions must not be any greater than necessary to protect a legitimate interest. It would be unreasonable for an employer or buyer of a business to restrain the other party from engaging in some activity that is not a competing activity or from doing business in a territory in which the employer or buyer does not do business because this would not threaten his legitimate interests.

3. *The noncompetition clause should not impose an undue hardship.* A court will not enforce a noncompetition clause if its restraints are unduly burdensome either on the public or on the party whose ability to compete would be restrained. In one case, for example, the court refused to enforce a noncompetition clause against a gastroenterologist because of evidence that the restriction would have imposed a hardship on patients and other physicians requiring his services.[3] Noncompetition clauses in employment contracts that have the practical effect of preventing the restrained person from earning a livelihood are unlikely to be enforced as well. This is discussed further in the next section.

Noncompetition Clauses in Employment Contracts
In employment contracts, noncompetition clauses are one form of agreement that places restrictions on an employee's conduct after the employment is over. Other restrictions on employees' postemployment conduct can include confidentiality or nondisclosure agreements, which constrain the employee from divulging or using certain information gained during his employment, and nonsolicitation agreements, which forbid an employee from soliciting the employer's employees, clients, or customers. In many cases, employees sign all these forms of postemployment restrictions. In others, the postemployment restriction may reflect just one or two of these forms of restraints.

Restrictions on competition work a greater hardship on an employee than on a person who has sold a business. For this reason, courts tend to judge noncompetition clauses contained in employment contracts by a stricter standard than they judge similar clauses contained in contracts for the sale of a business. In some states, statutes limit or even prohibit noncompetition clauses in employment contracts. In others, there is a trend toward refusing enforcement of these clauses in employment contracts unless the employer can bring forth very good evidence that he has a protectible interest that compels enforcement of the clause. The employer can do this by showing that he has entrusted the employee with trade secrets or confidential information, or that his goodwill with "near-permanent" customers is threatened. In the absence of this kind of proof, a court might conclude that the employer is just trying to avoid competition with a more efficient competitor and refuse enforcement because there is no legitimate business interest that requires protection.

Furthermore, many courts refuse to enforce noncompetition clauses if they restrict employees from engaging in a "common calling." A common calling is an occupation that does not require extensive or highly sophisticated training but instead involves relatively simple, repetitive tasks. Under this common calling restriction, various courts have refused to enforce noncompetition clauses against salespersons, a barber, and an auto trim repairperson.

In the following *Clark's* case, the court determines whether to enjoin employees from violating their noncompete agreement.

The Effect of Overly Broad Noncompetition Clauses
The courts of different states treat unreasonably broad noncompetition clauses in different ways. Some courts will strike the entire restriction if they find it to be unreasonable and will refuse to grant the buyer or employer any protection. Others will refuse to enforce the restraint as written, but will adjust the clause and impose such restraints as would be reasonable. In case of breach of an enforceable noncompetition clause, the person benefited by the clause may seek damages or an injunction (a court order preventing the promisor from violating the covenant).

[3]*Iredell Digestive Disease Clinic, P.A. v. Petrozza*, 373 S.E.2d 449 (N.C. Ct. App. 1988).

Clark's Sales and Service, Inc. v. Smith   4 N.E.3d 772 (Ind. Ct. App. 2014)

Smith worked for HH Gregg Appliances and Electronics ("Gregg") for four years prior to commencing employment with Clark's in 1998. While working for Gregg, Smith became familiar with and sold high-end appliances. Clark's, a family-owned business since it was founded in 1913, is involved in builder-distributor appliance sales and service in Indiana and concentrates its efforts in high-end appliance sales. Clark's generated approximately $750,000 in sales in 1986, when Bob Clark purchased the business from his parents, and he grew the business to a peak of $28 million in sales during the first decade of the 2000s. Clark's seeks to hire sales consultants with prior appliance experience but does not consider its business to be similar to that of Sears, Lowe's, or Gregg, which do business in a traditional retail setting offering low-end, mid-range, and high-end appliances. Smith acquired knowledge, skill, and information in connection with his employment as an appliance sales representative with Clark's.

In 2004, one of Clark's high-level managers left to join Gregg in a position that Clark's viewed to be a competitive role. As a result, in September 2004, Clark's asked Smith and other employees to sign a written employment agreement, which contained both a nondisclosure clause and a restrictive covenant. The restrictive covenant provides in relevant part as follows:

During the term of Employee's employment and this Agreement and for a period of two (2) years following the termination of Employee's employment, Employee agrees not to, directly or indirectly, for any other individual, partnership, firm, corporation, company or other entity, engage in the following prohibited activities:

(C) Solicit or provide, or offer to solicit or provide, services competitive to those offered by Employer, or to any business or customer of Employer during the term of Employee's employment within the 12-month period preceding the termination [of] Employee's employment or about whom Employee obtained Confidential Information;

(D) Work in a competitive capacity for HH Gregg's in Indianapolis, Indiana, within the State of Indiana, or in any state or municipal corporation, city [,] town, village, township, county or other governmental association in which HH Gregg's does business, or for an individual partnership, firm, corporation, company or other entity providing services similar to those offered by Employer or within any county in Indiana in which Employer provided services or has at least one customer or client, the State of Indiana, or within a 50 mile radius of Employee's principal office with Employer.

(E) Otherwise attempt to interfere with Employer's business.

Smith signed the employment agreement.

Smith was made an assistant store manager in 2009 at Clark's Castleton showroom.

After approximately 14 years working for Clark's, Smith tendered his resignation on April 13, 2012. Prior to tendering his resignation, Smith e-mailed copies of Clark's 2010 and 2011 monthly and quarterly sales bonus reports for all of Clark's sales personnel to his personal e-mail account from his company e-mail address, even though he was not authorized to do so. The reports contained information about all of the sales made by each of Clark's salespeople and included customer and builder contact information, the price of the materials sold, Clark's costs on those items, and Clark's profit margin on each sale. Smith provided this information to his attorney, but to no third parties. On April 18, 2012, Smith accepted an offer of employment with Ferguson.

Ferguson was also in the business of high-end appliance sales and service, although it was principally engaged in the plumbing and lighting business. Smith currently works for Ferguson at its builder and designer showroom in Carmel as an appliance manager. The showroom is within a 50-mile radius of Smith's former principal office with Clark's. Smith's employment does not involve direct sales but does include training sales employees; coordinating with vendors; and assisting with service, installation, and delivery. Smith's position is salaried, and he is compensated for the overall growth of the department.

Clark Cutshaw, Ferguson's sales manager for the Indianapolis area, testified that the information contained in Clark's sales reports is of no value to Ferguson because Ferguson's corporate office dictates cost and pricing. He further testified that Smith had no direct selling responsibilities. Hoover, Ferguson's general manager for the central Indiana area and Cutshaw's boss, testified that appliances constituted only 1 percent of Ferguson's sales to customers and that he was trying to increase those sales. Smith was expected to convince builders, remodelers, and kitchen designers who had not previously done so to purchase appliances from Ferguson.

On June 1, 2012, Clark's filed an amended verified complaint for preliminary and permanent injunctive relief and compensatory damages against Smith and Ferguson based upon Smith's alleged violation of the nondisclosure provision and the restrictive covenant in the employment agreement. The trial court's denial of the preliminary injunction regarding the restrictive covenant was based on its conclusion that the provision was not supported by adequate consideration.

Clark's appeals the trial court's denial of its motion for preliminary injunction. We review the trial court's denial of a request for a preliminary injunction for an abuse of discretion. [Citation omitted.]

Crone, Judge

Enforceability of the Restrictive Covenant

The parties raise several issues that bear on Clark's first hurdle to obtain a preliminary injunction, the reasonable likelihood of Clark's success at trial. The dispositive issues are: (1) whether the restrictive covenant protects a legitimate interest; and (2) whether the restrictive covenant is reasonable in scope as to the time, activity, and geographic area restricted.

"Covenants not to compete are contractual provisions which might be described as step-children of the law." [Citation omitted.] Our supreme court has long held that noncompetition covenants in employment contracts are disfavored in the law, and we will construe these covenants strictly against the employer and will not enforce an unreasonable restriction. [Citation omitted.] Indeed, "[p]ost-employment restraints are scrutinized with particular care because they are often the product of unequal bargaining power and because the employee is likely to give scant attention to the hardship he may later suffer through loss of his livelihood." *Restatement (Second) of Contracts*, § 188 cmt. G (1981). In order for a noncompetition agreement to be enforceable it must be reasonable, and such reasonableness is a question of law. [Citation omitted.] In arguing the reasonableness of a noncompetition agreement, the employer must first show that it has a legitimate interest to be protected by the agreement. Second, the employer bears the burden to show that the agreement is reasonable in scope as to the time, activities, and geographic area restricted.

Section 1—Legitimate Interest

As to the first factor of reasonableness, in order "[t]o demonstrate a legitimate protectable interest, 'an employer must show some reason why it would be unfair to allow the employee to compete with the former employer.'" [Citation omitted.] Indeed, "the employee should only be enjoined if he has gained some advantage at the employer's expense which would not be available to the general public." [Citation omitted.] Our courts have held that "the advantageous familiarity and personal contact which employees derive from dealing with an employer's customers are elements of an employer's 'good will' and are a protectible interest which may justify a restraint. . . ." [Citation omitted.] "Goodwill includes secret or confidential information such as the names and addresses of customers and the advantage acquired through representative contact." [Citation omitted.] In addition, "in industries where personal contact between the employee and the customer is especially important due to the similarity in product offered by the competitors, the advantage acquired through the employee's representative contact with the customer is part of the employer's good will, regardless of whether the employee has access to confidential information." [Citation omitted.]

Regarding this factor, the evidence supports the trial court's finding that Clark's established that, during Smith's fourteen-year employment with Clark's, Smith had the advantage of having been part of Clark's efforts to build goodwill with its business accounts and referral network of home builders, remodelers, and kitchen designers, and that such advantage is not available to a person in the general public. We agree with Clark's and the trial court that such goodwill is a legitimate protectable interest.

Section 2—Reasonableness of Restrictions

Next, Clark's has the burden to establish that the restrictive covenant is reasonable in scope as to the time, activities, and geographic area restricted. The parties agree that the two-year time restriction in the covenant is reasonable and valid. The parties disagree, however, as to the reasonableness of the noncompetition covenant as to scope of activities and geographic area restricted. We find the covenant unreasonable as to both.

Section 2.1—Scope of Activities

Paragraph 7(C) of the restrictive covenant prohibits Smith from providing "services competitive to those offered by [Clark's], or those provided by [Smith] on behalf of [Clark's]" to anyone who was a customer of Clark's during the term of Smith's employment.

This Court has held that although present customers are a protectable interest of an employer, a contract prohibiting contact with any past or prospective customers, no matter how much time has elapsed since their patronage ceased, was vague and too broad. *Seach [v. Richards, Dieterle & Co.]*, 439 N.E.2d [208,] at 214[(Ind. Ct. App. 1982)]. We agree with the trial court's conclusion that Clark's attempt to protect a customer base spanning the entire term of Smith's employment is overly broad and unreasonable.

For example, although Smith was an inside appliance salesman for Clark's, he would be prohibited from performing maintenance, repair, delivery, ordering, or pricing services, to name just a few, to anyone who was a customer of Clark's during his fourteen-year employment, because those services are competitive to services offered by Clark's. Presumably, assuming arguendo that Clark's sold snacks or beverages within its showroom, Smith would be prohibited from selling snacks or beverages for a new employer because that would be a service competitive to a service offered by Clark's. A covenant that restricts the employee from competing with portions of the business with which he was never associated is invalid.

As noted by the trial court, whether a geographic scope is reasonable depends on the interest of the employer that the restriction serves. *See [Cent. Indiana Podiatry, P.C. v.] Krueger*, 882 N.E.2d [723,] at 730 [(Ind. 2008)]. The trial court found that "[a]s one of the largest 'high end' appliance stores in the area, with over $1 million in sales each month, it is reasonable for individuals in the community to travel up to 50 miles to visit Clark's."

Appellant's App. at 15. While we agree with the implication of the trial court's finding that a fifty-mile geographic restriction would have been reasonable due to Clark's prominence in the high-end appliance business, as written, the fifty-mile radius is in addition to, and not a limitation of, the much more expansive geographic restriction of this provision, which includes any state in which Gregg does business, the entirety of Indiana and any county in which Clark's has at least one customer. It is unquestionable that the expansive geographic scope referenced in paragraph 7(D) is unreasonable as written.

Even assuming that the restrictive covenant is overly broad and unreasonable as written, Clark's urges this Court to do what the trial court determined it could not: make the covenant reasonable and enforceable by applying Indiana's "blue pencil" doctrine. "When reviewing covenants not to compete, Indiana courts have historically enforced reasonable restrictions, but struck unreasonable restrictions, granted they are divisible." [Citation omitted.] This principle is known as the blue pencil doctrine. If a court finds that portions of a noncompetition agreement are unreasonable, it may not create a reasonable restriction under the guise of interpretation, since this would subject the parties to an agreement that they have not made. [Citation omitted.] But, if the noncompetition agreement is divisible into parts, and some parts are reasonable while others are unreasonable, a court may enforce the reasonable portions only. When blue-penciling, a court must not add terms that were not originally part of the agreement but may only strike unreasonable restraints or offensive clauses to give effect to the parties' intentions. [Citation omitted.]

Clark's proposes blue pencil modification for paragraph 7(C).

The restriction provided by paragraph 7(C) is written as an indiscrete whole. There is no clear separation of terms or clauses that were or could be intended to be excised from the whole without changing the entire meaning and import of the passage. Paragraph 7(C) is indivisible and unreasonable as a whole, and the blue pencil doctrine is inapplicable.

Moreover, even were we to blue-pencil paragraph 7(C) as proposed by Clark's, such modification does nothing to remedy the overbreadth of the scope of activities prohibited. Smith would still be prohibited from providing "services competitive to those offered by [Clark's]" irrespective of what services Smith actually provided to Clark's during the term of his employment.

Clark's also suggests the following blue pencil modification for paragraph 7(D):

Work in a competitive capacity ~~for HH Gregg's in Indianapolis, Indiana, within the State of Indiana, or in an state or municipal corporation, city town, village, township, county or other governmental association in which HH Gregg's does business, or~~ for an individual, partnership, firm, corporation, company, or other entity providing services similar or competitive to those offered by Employer to the residential or commercial builder and remodeling business sectors during the term of Employee's employment with Employer, including but not limited to providing those services performed by Employee while employed by or working for Employer, within Marion County, Indiana, any county contiguous to Marion County, Indiana (including Hamilton County, Hancock County, Shelby County, Johnson County, Morgan County, Hendricks County, and Boone County), any county in Indiana in which Employer provided services or has at least one customer or client, the State of Indiana, or within a 50 mile radius of Employee's principal office with Employer.

As we concluded with the proposed modification for the preceding paragraph, this blue-penciling, which merely removes the reference to Gregg, also fails to adequately address the grossly overbroad restrictions. The mere removal of the reference to Gregg does not cure the remaining expansive geographic restriction of the covenant. In sum, the restrictions contained in paragraphs 7(C) and (D) are not clearly separated into divisible parts.

Clark's proposed redactions do not adequately solve the overbreadth of the restrictions, and we would be required to do additional redaction and engage in substantial interpretation to render the restrictions reasonable. This is not the purpose of the blue pencil doctrine as we see it.

We remind Clark's that "Indiana law strongly discourages employers' attempts to draft unreasonably broad and oppressive covenants." [Citation omitted.]

The overly broad and unenforceable covenant that Clark's did draft is not clearly separated into divisible parts or severable in terms such that we can mechanically strike unreasonable restrictions and enforce reasonable ones.

The trial court's denial of Clark's motion for preliminary injunction is affirmed.

Exculpatory Clauses

 LO15-4 Analyze whether a given exculpatory clause is likely to be enforceable.

An **exculpatory clause** (often called a "release" or "liability waiver") is a provision in a contract that purports to relieve one of the parties from tort liability. Exculpatory clauses are suspect on public policy grounds for two reasons. First, courts are concerned that a party who can contract away his liability for negligence will not have the incentive to use care to avoid hurting others. Second, courts are concerned that an agreement that accords one party such a powerful advantage might have been the result of the abuse of superior bargaining power rather than truly voluntary choice. Although exculpatory agreements are often said to be "disfavored" in the law, courts do not want to prevent parties who are dealing on a fair and voluntary basis from determining how the risks of their transaction shall be borne if their agreement does not threaten public health or safety.

Courts enforce exculpatory clauses in some cases and refuse to enforce them in others, depending on the circumstances of the case, the identity and relationship of the parties, and the language of the agreement. A few ground rules can be stated. First, an exculpatory clause cannot protect a party from liability for any wrongdoing greater than negligence. One that purports to relieve a person from liability for fraud or some other willful tort will be considered to be against public policy. In some states, in fact, exculpatory clauses have been invalidated on this ground because of broad language stating that one of the parties was relieved of "all liability." Second, exculpatory clauses will not be effective to exclude tort liability on the part of a party who owes a duty to the public (such as an airline) because this would present an obvious threat to the public health and safety.

A third possible limitation on the enforceability of exculpatory clauses arises from the increasing array of statutes and common law rules that impose certain obligations on one party to a contract for the benefit of the other party to the contract. Workers' compensation statutes and laws requiring landlords to maintain leased property in a habitable condition are examples of such laws. Sometimes the person on whom such an obligation is placed will attempt

to escape it by inserting an exculpatory or waiver provision in a contract. Such clauses are often—though not always—found to be against public policy because, if enforced, they would frustrate the very purpose of imposing the duty in question. For example, an employee's agreement to relieve her employer from workers' compensation liability is likely to be held illegal as a violation of public policy.

Even if a clause is not against public policy on any of the above three grounds, a court may still refuse to enforce it if a court finds that the clause was *unconscionable*, a *contract of adhesion*, or some other product of abuse of superior bargaining power. (Unconscionability and contracts of adhesion are discussed later in this chapter.) This determination depends on all of the facts of the case. Facts that tend to show that the exculpatory clause was not the product of *knowing* consent increase the likelihood that the clause will not be enforced. A clause that is written in clear language and conspicuous print is more likely to be enforced than one written in "legalese" and presented in fine print. Facts that tend to show that the exculpatory clause was the product of *voluntary* consent increase the likelihood of enforcement of the clause. For example, a clause contained in a contract for a frivolous or unnecessary activity is more likely to be enforced than is an exculpatory clause contained in a contract for a necessary activity such as medical care.

In the following *Walters* case, the court is asked to decide the effectiveness of an exculpatory clause used in the context of a fitness center.

Walters v. YMCA   437 N.J. Super. 111 (App. Div. 2014)

Plaintiff James F. Walters badly injured his knee when he slipped on steps leading to the YMCA indoor pool in Newark, New Jersey. Mr. Walters was not engaged in any physical exercise when he slipped and fell on the steps. A photograph produced at trial revealed that all of the stair treads incorporated slip-resistant rubber, except for the bottom stair where the rubber had been removed due to wear.

At the time the accident occurred, Mr. Walters had been a member of this YMCA for more than three years. The continuous health membership agreement he signed contained the following exculpatory provision, using all capital letters:

I AGREE THAT THE YMCA WILL NOT BE RESPONSIBLE FOR ANY PERSONAL INJURIES OR LOSSES SUSTAINED BY ME WHILE ON ANY YMCA PREMISES OR AS A RESULT OF YMCA SPONSORED ACTIVITIES. I FURTHER AGREE TO INDEMNIFY AND SAVE HARMLESS THE YMCA FROM ANY CLAIMS OR DEMANDS ARISING OUT OF ANY SUCH INJURIES OR LOSSES.

Defendant YMCA argued that the "hold harmless" provision in the membership agreement that was voluntarily signed by Plaintiff Walters is a reasonable condition imposed on anyone engaging in sports and related physical activities. Furthermore, the YMCA argued that Mr. Walters's accident and resulting injuries were entirely foreseeable consequences given the nature of the activities and facilities offered, including the swimming pool. The trial court, relying on New Jersey Supreme Court precedent in Stelluti v. Casapenn Enters., *agreed with Defendant YMCA and granted the motion for summary judgment based on the membership agreement's exculpatory clause. Although the Plaintiff was not engaged in any physical exercise when he slipped and fell on the steps that led to the indoor pool, the trial judge found the pool area was "just another type of equipment that is being offered by the health club."*

Now on appeal, Plaintiff Walters argues that the trial court erred in construing the exculpatory clause as a bar to his cause of action because his accident was caused by a negligently maintained stair tread. Additionally, the plaintiff argues that the basis of his cause of action is predicated on the ordinary common law duty of care owed by all business operators to its invitees, and thus it is completely unrelated to the inherent risky nature of the activities offered by health clubs.

Fuentes, Judge

. . . We disagree with the motion judge and reverse. A close reading of [New Jersey Supreme Court] Justice LaVecchia's analysis in *Stelluti* [v. *Casapenn Enters.*, 203 N.J. 286 (2010),] reveals that the Court's holding was grounded on the recognition that health clubs, like defendant YMCA, are engaged in a business that offers its members the use of physical fitness equipment and a place to engage in strenuous physical activities that involve an inherent risk of injury. The Court upheld the defendant's limited exculpatory clause in *Stelluti* because the injury sustained [when handlebars of a stationary bike dislodged, causing plaintiff to fall off the bike] was foreseeable as an inherent aspect of the nature of the [inherently risky physical activity] of health clubs.

As Justice LaVecchia clearly explained on behalf of a majority of the Court:

In sum, the standard we apply here places in fair and proper balance the respective public-policy interests in permitting parties to freely contract in this context (i.e., private fitness center memberships) and requires private gyms and fitness centers to adhere to a standard of conduct in respect of their businesses. Specifically, *we hold such business owners to a standard of care congruent with the nature of their business, which is to make available the specialized equipment and facility to their invitees who are there to exercise, train, and to push their physical limits. That is, we impose a duty not to engage in reckless or gross negligence.* We glean such prohibition as a fair sharing of risk in this setting, which is also consistent with the analogous assumption-of-risk approach used by the Legislature to allocate risks in other recreational settings with limited retained-liability imposed on operators. [Citation omitted.]

Indeed, the legal question presented by this case, whether a fitness center or health club can insulate itself through an exculpatory clause from the ordinary common law duty of care owed by all businesses to its invitees, was specifically not addressed or decided by the Court in *Stelluti*. We again quote directly Justice LaVecchia's emphatic, cautionary language addressing this issue:

In the instant matter . . . we feel no obligation to reach and discuss the validity of other aspects of the agreement not squarely presented by the facts of Stelluti's case. Thus, we need not address the validity of the agreement's disclaimer of liability for injuries that occur on the club's sidewalks or parking lot that are common to any commercial enterprise that has business invitees. With respect to its agreement and

its limitation of liability to the persons who use its facility and exercise equipment for the unique purpose of the business, we hold that it is not contrary to the public interest, or to a legal duty owed, to enforce [the defendant]'s agreement limiting its liability for injuries sustained as a matter of negligence that results from a patron's voluntary use of equipment and participation in instructed activity. *As a result, we find the exculpatory agreement between [the defendant] and Stelluti enforceable as to the injury Stelluti sustained when riding the spin bike.* [Citation omitted.]

. . . The plaintiff in *Stelluti* was injured when the handlebars of her stationary bike dislodged and caused her to fall during a spinning class at a private fitness center. [Citation omitted.] The inherently risky nature of this type of physical activity was the key consideration the Court found to justify enforcing the exculpatory clause at issue. [Citation omitted.]

Here, Mr. Walters's accident and resulting injuries occurred when he slipped on a step and fell, as he walked to defendant YMCA's indoor pool. Plaintiff Walters did not injure himself while swimming in the pool or using any physical fitness equipment. The type of accident involved here could have occurred in any business setting. The inherently risky nature of defendant's activities as a physical fitness club was immaterial to this accident. Stated in the vernacular of the personal injury bar, this is a "garden variety slip and fall case."

Under these circumstances, plaintiff Walters argues here, as he did at the trial level, that defendant YMCA should be held liable to compensate him for his injuries pursuant to the common law duty all business owners owe to their invitees. Our colleague Judge Sabatino aptly described that duty of care in the Appellate Division's decision in *Stelluti v. Casapenn Enters.*:

In general, "[b]usiness owners owe to invitees a duty of reasonable or due care to provide a safe environment for doing that which is in the scope of the invitation. [Citation omitted.] This duty of care flows from the notion that "business owners 'are in the best position to control the risk of harm.'" [Citations omitted.]

We are thus compelled to address and answer the question the [New Jersey] Supreme Court intentionally left unanswered in *Stelluti*, to wit: whether an exculpatory clause that insulates a physical fitness club, like defendant YMCA, from liability "for any personal injuries or losses sustained by [a member] while on any [of the club's] premises" is enforceable when the accident and resulting injuries sustained by the member/invitee was not caused by or related to an inherently risky physical fitness activity. In answering this question, we will apply the same standards the Supreme Court applied in *Stelluti*.

An exculpatory agreement "is enforceable only if: (1) it does not adversely affect the public interest; (2) the exculpated party is not under a legal duty to perform; (3) it does not involve a public utility or common carrier; or (4) the contract does not grow out of unequal bargaining power or is otherwise unconscionable." [Citations omitted.]

. . . We will examine the provisions of this exculpatory clause in defendant's agreement giving due deference to the freedom to contract and to the right of competent adults to bind themselves as they see fit. [Citations omitted.] However, we are mindful that exculpatory agreements "have historically been disfavored in law and thus have been subjected to close judicial scrutiny." [Citations omitted.] Any ambiguities in language about the scope of an exculpatory agreement's coverage, or doubts about its enforceability, should be resolved in favor of holding a tortfeasor accountable. "The law does not favor exculpatory agreements because they encourage a lack of care." [Citations omitted.]

Judge Sabatino noted in the Appellate Division version of *Stelluti* that an exculpatory clause construed "to its outermost limits of protection . . . [would preclude] literally any and all claims or causes of action[.] [Such a prospect] threatens an adverse impact upon the public interest. As we have already noted, business establishments in New Jersey have well-established duties of care to patrons that come upon their premises. An unbounded waiver of liability unjustifiably eviscerates those protections for business invitees." [Citations omitted.]

Given the expansive scope of the exculpatory clause here, we hold that if applied literally, it would eviscerate the common law duty of care owed by defendant to its invitees, regardless of the nature of the business activity involved. Such a prospect would be inimical to the public interest because it would transfer the redress of civil wrongs from the responsible tortfeasor to either the innocent injured party or to society at large, in the form of taxpayer-supported institutions. . . .

The "Waiver and Release Form" in *Stelluti* included a relatively lengthy narrative explanation of the inherent risk of being seriously injured while engaging in strenuous physical exercise. Here, the exculpatory clause, although far more brief in language, is considerably more legally expansive in the scope of activity defendant YMCA sought to insulate from civil liability. By signing the membership agreement, plaintiff Walters purportedly agreed to hold defendant YMCA harmless "for any personal injuries or losses sustained by me while on any YMCA premises *or* as a result of a YMCA sponsored activities [sic]." The key word here is the disjunction "or," which expands the scope of the exculpatory clause to include injuries resulting "while on the premises" *or* as a result of participating in defendant's "sponsored activities."

We reasonably assume the agreement, especially the exculpatory clause, signed by plaintiff Walters is a contract of adhesion. . . . As the Court did in *Stelluti*, we recognize that "[w]hen a party enters into a signed, written contract, that party is presumed to understand and assent to its terms, unless fraudulent conduct is suspected." [Citations omitted.] However, all contracts are subject to judicial scrutiny to determine their enforceability. Here, defendant YMCA seeks to shield itself from all civil liability, based on a one-sided contractual arrangement that offers no countervailing or redeeming societal value. Such a contract must be declared unenforceable as against public policy.

Finally, defendant YMCA also argues that swimming in the pool is a "sponsored activity," and therefore an accident resulting from slipping on the steps leading into the pool is also covered under the "activities" part of the clause. Such an interpretation ignores the cause of this accident. Plaintiff Walters was not injured using the pool. Thus, based on the record before us, we conclude the language in defendant's exculpatory clause is void and unenforceable as against public policy for the reasons expressed here. . . .

Reversed and remanded.

Family Relationships and Public Policy

In view of the central position of the family as a valued social institution, it is not surprising that an agreement that unreasonably tends to interfere with family relationships will be considered illegal. Examples of this type of contract include agreements whereby one of the parties agrees to divorce a spouse or agrees not to marry.

In recent years, courts have been presented with an increasing number of agreements between unmarried cohabitants that purport to agree upon the manner in which the parties' property will be shared or divided upon separation.

It used to be widely held that contracts between unmarried cohabitants were against public policy because they were based on an immoral relationship. As unmarried cohabitation has become more widespread, however, the law concerning the enforceability of agreements between unmarried couples has changed. For example, in the 1976 case of *Marvin v. Marvin*, the California Supreme Court held that an agreement between an unmarried couple to pool income and share property could be enforceable.[4]

[4]134 Cal. Rptr. 815 (1976).

Today, most courts hold that agreements between unmarried couples are not against public policy unless they are explicitly based on illegal sexual relations as the consideration for the contract or unless one or more of the parties is married to someone else.

Unfairness in Agreements: Contracts of Adhesion and Unconscionable Contracts

LO15-5 Explain the concept of unconscionability and identify the circumstances that make a contract unconscionable.

Under classical contract law, courts were reluctant to inquire into the fairness of an agreement. Because the prevailing social attitudes and economic philosophy strongly favored freedom of contract, American courts took the position that so long as there had been no fraud, duress, misrepresentation, mistake, or undue influence in the bargaining process, unfairness in an agreement entered into by competent adults did not render it unenforceable.

As the changing nature of our society produced many contract situations in which the bargaining positions of the parties were grossly unequal, the classical contract assumption that each party was capable of protecting himself was no longer persuasive. The increasing use of standardized contracts (preprinted contracts) enabled parties with superior bargaining power and business sophistication to virtually dictate contract terms to weaker and less sophisticated parties.

Legislatures responded to this problem by enacting a variety of statutory measures to protect individuals against the abuse of superior bargaining power in specific situations. Examples of such legislation include minimum wage laws and rent control ordinances. Courts became more sensitive to the fact that superior bargaining power often led to **contracts of adhesion** (contracts in which a stronger party is able to determine the terms of a contract, leaving the weaker party no practical choice but to "adhere" to the terms). Some courts responded by borrowing a doctrine that had been developed and used for a long time in courts of equity,[5] the doctrine of **unconscionability**. Under this doctrine, courts would refuse to grant the equitable remedy of specific performance for breach of a contract if they found the contract to be oppressively unfair. Courts today can use the concepts of unconscionability or adhesion to analyze contracts that are alleged to be so unfair that they should not be enforced.

Unconscionability One of the most far-reaching efforts to correct abuses of superior bargaining power was the enactment of section 2-302 of the Uniform Commercial Code, which gives courts the power to refuse to enforce all or part of a contract for the sale of goods or to modify such a contract if it is found to be unconscionable. By virtue of its inclusion in Article 2 of the Uniform Commercial Code, the prohibition against unconscionable terms applies to every contract for the sale of goods. The concept of unconscionability is not confined to contracts for the sale of goods, however. Section 208 of the *Restatement (Second) of Contracts*, which closely resembles the unconscionability section of the UCC, provides that courts may decline to enforce unconscionable terms or contracts. The prohibition of unconscionability has been adopted as part of the public policy of many states by courts in cases that did not involve the sale of goods, such as banking transactions and contracts for the sale or rental of real estate. It is therefore fair to state that the concept of unconscionability has become part of the general body of contract law.

Consequences of Unconscionability The UCC and the *Restatement (Second)* sections on unconscionability give courts the power to manipulate a contract containing an unconscionable provision so as to reach a just result. If a court finds that a contract or a term in a contract is unconscionable, it can do one of three things: It can refuse to enforce the entire agreement, it can refuse to enforce the unconscionable provision but enforce the rest of the contract, or it can "limit the application of the unconscionable clause so as to avoid any unconscionable result." This last alternative has been taken by courts to mean that they can make adjustments in the terms of the contract.

Meaning of Unconscionability Neither the UCC nor the *Restatement (Second) of Contracts* attempts to define the term *unconscionability*. Though the concept is impossible to define with precision, unconscionability is generally taken to mean the *absence of meaningful choice* together with *terms unreasonably advantageous* to one of the parties.

The facts of each individual case are crucial to determining whether a contract term is unconscionable. Courts will scrutinize the process by which the contract was reached to see if the agreement was reached by fair methods and whether it can fairly be said to be the product of knowing and voluntary consent.

[5]Chapter 1 discusses courts of equity.

Procedural Unconscionability Courts and writers often refer to unfairness in the bargaining process as *procedural unconscionability*. Some facts that may point to procedural unconscionability include the use of fine print or inconspicuously placed terms; complex, legalistic language; and high-pressure sales tactics. One of the most significant facts pointing to procedural unconscionability is the lack of voluntariness as shown by a marked imbalance in the parties' bargaining positions, particularly where the weaker party is unable to negotiate more favorable terms because of economic need, lack of time, or market factors. In fact, in most contracts that have been found to be unconscionable, there has been a serious inequality of bargaining power between the parties. It is important to note, however, that the mere existence of unequal bargaining power does not make a contract unconscionable. If it did, every consumer's contract with the telephone company or the electric company would be unenforceable. Rather, in an unconscionable contract, the party with the stronger bargaining power *exploits* that power by driving a bargain containing a term or terms that are so unfair that they "shock the conscience of the court."

Substantive Unconscionability In addition to looking at facts that might indicate procedural unconscionability, courts will scrutinize the contract terms themselves to determine whether they are oppressive, unreasonably one-sided, or unjustifiably harsh. This aspect of unconscionability is often referred to as *substantive unconscionability*. Examples include situations in which a party to the contract bears a disproportionate amount of the risk or other negative aspects of the transaction and situations in which a party is deprived of a remedy for the other party's breach. In some cases, unconscionability has been found in situations in which the contract provides for a price that is greatly in excess of the usual market price.

There is no mechanical test for determining whether a clause is unconscionable. Generally, in cases in which courts have found a contract term to be unconscionable, there are elements of *both* procedural and substantive unconscionability. Though courts have broad discretion to determine what contracts will be deemed to be unconscionable, it must be remembered that the doctrine of unconscionability is designed to prevent oppression and unfair surprise—not to relieve people of the effects of bad bargains.

The cases concerning unconscionability are quite diverse. Some courts have found unconscionability in contracts involving grossly unfair sales prices. Although the doctrine of unconscionability has been raised primarily by victimized consumers, there have been cases in which businesspeople in an inherently weak bargaining position have been successful in asserting unconscionability.

You will see an example of the unconscionability analysis in the following *Singh* case.

Singh v. Uber Technologies Inc.   235 F. Supp. 3d 656 (D.N.J. 2017)

Uber is a technology company that serves as a conduit between riders looking for transportation and drivers seeking riders. Uber provides this technology through its smartphone application that allows riders and drivers to connect based on their geographic location. Raiser LLC is a wholly owned subsidiary of Uber and operates as a technology service provider.

Plaintiff Jaswinder Singh, an Uber driver, registered with the Uber App in order to use its "uberX" platform, which provided him with the option to accept ride requests from prospective passengers and transport them for a fare. In doing so, Plaintiff was required to electronically accept the applicable Raiser Software License and Online Services Agreement ("Raiser Agreement") dated June 21, 2014. When Plaintiff logged on to the Uber App with his unique user name and password, he was given the opportunity to review the Raiser Agreement by clicking a hyperlink to the Raiser Agreement within the Uber App. To advance past the screen with the hyperlink and actively use the Uber App, Plaintiff had to confirm that he had first reviewed and accepted the Raiser Agreement by clicking "YES, I AGREE." After clicking "YES, I AGREE," he was prompted to confirm that he reviewed and accepted the Raiser Agreement for a second time.

Plaintiff was permitted to spend as much time as he found necessary in reviewing the Raiser Agreement on his smartphone or other electronic devices before accepting it. In fact, Plaintiff accepted the Raiser Agreement approximately three months after it was made available for his review. After Plaintiff confirmed his acceptance for a second time through the Uber App, the Raiser Agreement was uploaded to Plaintiff's "driver portal," where he could access the Agreement at his own leisure, either online or by printing out a hard copy.

The first page of the Raiser Agreement contains a paragraph, written in large bold and capital text, indicating that a voluntary arbitration agreement ("Arbitration Provision") is contained therein and that Plaintiff should review the Raiser Agreement with an attorney before agreeing to its terms and conditions:

IMPORTANT: PLEASE NOTE THAT TO USE THE UBER SERVICES, YOU MUST AGREE TO THE TERMS AND CONDITIONS SET FORTH BELOW. PLEASE REVIEW THE ARBITRATION PROVISION SET FORTH BELOW CAREFULLY, AS IT WILL REQUIRE YOU TO RESOLVE DISPUTES WITH THE COMPANY ON AN INDIVIDUAL BASIS THROUGH FINAL AND BINDING ARBITRATION UNLESS YOU CHOOSE TO OPT OUT OF THE ARBITRATION PROVISION. BY VIRTUE OF YOUR ELECTRONIC EXECUTION OF THIS AGREEMENT, YOU WILL BE ACKNOWLEDGING THAT YOU HAVE READ AND UNDERSTOOD ALL OF THE TERMS OF THIS AGREEMENT (INCLUDING THE ARBITRATION PROVISION) AND HAVE TAKEN TIME TO CONSIDER THE CONSEQUENCES OF THIS IMPORTANT BUSINESS DECISION. IF YOU DO NOT WISH TO BE SUBJECT TO ARBITRATION, YOU MAY OPT OUT OF THE ARBITRATION PROVISION BY FOLLOWING THE INSTRUCTIONS PROVIDED IN THE ARBITRATION PROVISION BELOW.

A similar paragraph, also written in large bold and capital text, appears within the text of the arbitration provision itself, stating:

WHETHER TO AGREE TO ARBITRATION IS AN IMPORTANT BUSINESS DECISION. IT IS YOUR DECISION TO MAKE, AND YOU SHOULD NOT RELY SOLELY UPON THE INFORMATION PROVIDED IN THIS AGREEMENT AS IT IS NOT INTENDED TO CONTAIN A COMPLETE EXPLANATION OF THE CONSEQUENCES OF ARBITRATION. YOU SHOULD TAKE REASONABLE STEPS TO CONDUCT FURTHER RESEARCH AND TO CONSULT WITH OTHERS–INCLUDING BUT NOT LIMITED TO AN ATTORNEY–REGARDING THE CONSEQUENCES OF YOUR DECISION, JUST AS YOU WOULD WHEN MAKING ANY OTHER IMPORTANT BUSINESS DECISION OR LIFE DECISION.

The Arbitration Provision requires transportation drivers–if they do not opt out–to individually arbitrate all disputes arising out of, or relating to, the Raiser Agreement, or their relationship with Uber, including disputes alleging breach of contract, wages and hours, and compensation claims. The Arbitration Provision, in pertinent part, reads as follows:

IMPORTANT: This Arbitration Provision will require you to resolve any claim that you may have against the Company or Uber on an individual basis pursuant to the terms of the Raiser Agreement unless you choose to opt out of the Arbitration Provision. This provision will preclude you from bringing any class, collective, or representative action against Uber.

It further provides:

Except as it otherwise provides, this Arbitration Provision is intended to apply to the resolution of disputes that otherwise would be resolved in a court of law or before a forum other than arbitration. This Arbitration Provision requires all such disputes to be resolved only by an arbitrator through final and binding arbitration on an individual basis only and not by way of court or jury trial, or by way of class, collective, or representative action.

Notably, after Plaintiff confirmed that he had reviewed and accepted the Raiser Agreement, along with the Arbitration Provision, Plaintiff was provided with an additional 30 days to optout of the Arbitration Provision:

<u>Your Right to Opt Out of Arbitration.</u>

Arbitration is not a mandatory condition of your contractual relationship with Uber. If you do not want to be subject to this Arbitration Provision, you may opt out of this Arbitration by notifying Uber in writing of your desire to opt out of this Arbitration Provision, either by (1) sending, within 30 days of the date this Raiser Agreement is executed by you, electronic mail to optout@uber.com, stating your name and intent to opt out of the Arbitration Provision or (2) by sending a letter by U.S. Mail, or by any nationally recognized delivery service (e.g., UPS, Federal Express, etc.), or by hand delivery to [Raiser's legal department].

Despite these terms of his contract with Uber, Singh filed his Complaint in federal court, alleging that Uber (1) misclassified him and other Uber drivers as independent contractors, as opposed to employees; (2) failed to pay overtime compensation; and (3) required the drivers to pay for significant business expenses that were incurred for the benefit of Uber.

Defendant Uber moved to dismiss the Complaint and compel arbitration, arguing that Plaintiff is bound by the Arbitration Provision in the Raiser Agreement. Plaintiff Singh, attempting to keep his lawsuit in federal court, argued that the Arbitration Provision is unenforceable for multiple reasons, including his claim that it is unconscionable. Only the portion of the court's analysis addressing the unconscionability claim is included below.

Wolfson, District Judge

. . . Lastly, Plaintiff contends that the Arbitration Provision is unconscionable and cannot be enforced. In support of this contention, Plaintiff primarily attacks the Arbitration Provision on two separate grounds. First, Plaintiff takes issue with the parties' purported grossly unequal bargaining power. Plaintiff maintains that Uber capitalized on this imbalance by providing him with "a standardized mass contract," without the opportunity to bargain for, or negotiate any of its terms, thereby making it a contract of adhesion, despite its opt-out provision. Second, Plaintiff points to the language of the Arbitration Provision's cost-sharing provision, which "requires [Plaintiff] to pay for half the costs of arbitration," and posits that this cost-sharing provision renders the Arbitration Provision unconscionable because it prevents him from vindicating his statutory rights. However, the Court finds both of these arguments meritless.

A contract in New Jersey will be enforceable unless there are indicia of both procedural and substantive unconscionability. "Procedural unconscionability pertains to the process by which an agreement is reached and the form of an agreement, including the use therein of fine print and convoluted or unclear language." [Citation omitted.] This element of the unconscionability analysis may be satisfied if the agreement constitutes a contract of adhesion. Such agreements are typically prepared by a party with excessive bargaining power, and signed by a weaker party on a "take-it-or-leave-it" basis.

However, a disparity in bargaining power alone will not render an agreement unconscionable. The party challenging the agreement must also establish that it is substantively unconscionable. "This element refers to the terms that unreasonably favor one party to which the disfavored party does not truly assent." [Citation omitted.] Indeed "gross inequality of bargaining power, together with terms unreasonably favorable to the stronger party . . . may show that the weaker party had no meaningful choice, no real alternative, or did not in fact assent or appear to assent to the unfair terms." [Citation omitted.] Thus, unconscionability "requires a two-fold determination: that the contractual terms are unreasonably favorable to the drafter and that there

is no meaningful choice on the part of the other party regarding acceptance of the provisions." [Citation omitted.]

Here, the agreement between the parties was not a contract of adhesion. Plaintiff contends that "[t]here was and is absolutely no ability for [Uber drivers] to bargain or negotiate the terms [of the Raiser Agreement] with Defendant." However, this assertion is baseless, as Plaintiff was presented with the choice of either arbitrating or litigating his disputes against Uber. Indeed, arbitration between the parties is not required; Plaintiff was afforded a 30-day period to opt-out. Nor was Plaintiff coerced or pressured into accepting arbitration as a means of resolving his claims with Uber. Accordingly, Plaintiff was free to decline the Raiser Agreement's Arbitration Provision—without any consequences. Therefore, the contract between the parties cannot be construed as a contract of adhesion. [Citations omitted.]

Furthermore, the Arbitration Provision's cost-sharing provision is not substantively unconscionable. "[W]here, as here, a party seeks to invalidate an arbitration agreement on the ground that arbitration would be prohibitively expensive, that party bears the burden of showing the likelihood of incurring such costs." [Citation omitted.] The Raiser Agreement's Arbitration Provision contains a cost-sharing provision:

> In all cases where required by law, [Uber] will pay the Arbitrator's and arbitration fees. If under applicable law [Uber] is not required to pay all of the Arbitrator's and/or arbitration fees, such fee(s) will be apportioned equally between the Parties or as otherwise required by applicable law.

Significantly, Plaintiff does not adequately allege any facts indicating that the arbitration fees would be prohibitively expensive. Rather, Plaintiff merely summarizes the terms of the cost-sharing provision and then asserts, in a conclusory fashion, that "the cost-sharing language precludes [Plaintiff] from vindicating his statutory rights." Therefore, Plaintiff does not establish a likelihood of incurring prohibitively expensive costs, and there can be no finding of substantive unconscionability based on this reason.

The Court dismisses the case in favor of arbitration.

Contracts of Adhesion

A contract of adhesion is a contract, usually on a standardized form, offered by a party who is in a superior bargaining position on a "take-it-or-leave-it" basis. The person presented with such a contract has no opportunity to negotiate the terms of the contract; they are imposed on him if he wants to receive the goods or services offered by the stronger party. In addition to not having a "say" about the terms of the contract, the person who signs a standardized

contract of adhesion may not even know or understand the terms of the contract that he is signing. When these factors are present, the objective theory of contracts and the normal duty to read contracts before signing them may be modified. These factors may be viewed as a form of procedural unconscionability. A court may use the word *adhesion* to describe procedural unconscionability.

All of us have probably entered contracts of adhesion at one time or another. The mere fact that a contract is a contract of adhesion does not, in and of itself, mean that the contract is unenforceable. Courts will not refuse enforcement to such a contract unless the term complained of either is substantively unconscionable or is a term that the adhering party could not reasonably expect to be included in the form that he was signing.

Unenforceable contracts of adhesion can take different forms. The first is seen when the contract of adhesion contains a term that is harsh or oppressive. In this kind of case, the party offering the contract of adhesion has used his superior bargaining power to dictate unfair terms. In the second situation in which contracts of adhesion are refused, enforcement occurs when a contract of adhesion contains a term that, while it may not be harsh or oppressive, is a term that the adhering party could *not* be expected to have been aware that he was agreeing to. This type of case relates to the fundamental concept of agreement in an era in which lengthy, complex, standardized contracts are common. If a consumer presented with a contract of adhesion has no opportunity to negotiate terms and signs the contract without knowing or fully understanding what he is signing, is it fair to conclude that he has consented to the terms? It is reasonable to conclude that he has consented at least to the terms that he could have expected to be in the contract, but *not* to any terms that he could not have expected to be contained in the contract.

Effect of Illegality

LO15-6 Determine the effect of illegality in a given scenario.

General Rule: No Remedy for Breach of Illegal Agreements
As a general rule, courts will refuse to give any remedy for the breach of an illegal agreement. A court will refuse to enforce an illegal agreement and will also refuse to permit a party who has fully or partially performed her part of the agreement to recover what she has parted with. The reason for this rule is to serve the public interest, not to punish the parties.

In some cases, the public interest is best served by allowing some recovery to one or both of the parties. Such cases constitute exceptions to the "hands-off" rule. The following discussion concerns the most common situations in which courts will grant some remedy even though they find the agreement to be illegal.

Exceptions

Excusable Ignorance of Facts or Legislation Though it is often said that ignorance of the law is no excuse, courts will, under certain circumstances, permit a party to an illegal agreement who was excusably ignorant of facts or legislation that rendered the agreement illegal to recover damages for breach of the agreement. This exception is used where only *one* of the parties acted in ignorance of the illegality of the agreement and the other party was aware that the agreement was illegal. For this exception to apply, the facts or legislation of which the person claiming damages was ignorant must be of a relatively minor character—that is, it must not involve an immoral act or a serious threat to the public welfare. Finally, the person who is claiming damages cannot recover damages

Ethics and Compliance in Action

Murphy, a welfare recipient with four minor children, saw an advertisement in the local newspaper that had been placed by McNamara, a television and stereo dealer. It stated:

Why buy when you can rent? Color TV and stereos. *Rent to own!* Use our Rent-to-own plan and let TV Rentals deliver either of these models to your home. *We feature*—Never a repair bill—No deposit—No credit needed—No long term obligation—Weekly or monthly rates available—Order by phone—Call today—Watch color TV tonight.

As a result of the advertisement, Murphy leased a 25-inch Philco color console TV set from McNamara under the "Rent to Own" plan. The lease agreement provided that Murphy would pay a $20 delivery charge and 78 weekly payments of $16. At the end of the period, Murphy would own the set. The agreement also

provided that the customer could return the set at any time and terminate the lease as long as all rental payments had been made up to the return date. Murphy entered the lease because she believed that she could acquire ownership of a TV set without first establishing credit as was stressed in McNamara's ads. At no time did McNamara inform Murphy that the terms of the lease required her to pay a total of $1,268 for the TV. The retail sales price for the same TV was $499. After making $436 in payments over a period of about six months, Murphy read a newspaper article criticizing the lease plan and realized the amount that the agreement required her to pay. She stopped making payments and McNamara sought to repossess the TV. Murphy argued that the agreement was unconscionable. Was it ethical to market the Rent to Own plan? Was McNamara ethically required to inform Murphy that the total price of the TV would be $1,268 under the Rent to Own plan?

for anything that he does after learning of the illegality. For example, Warren enters a contract to perform in a play at Craig's theater. Warren does not know that Craig does not have the license to operate a theater as required by statute. Warren can recover the wages agreed on in the parties' contract for work that he performed before learning of the illegality.

When *both* of the parties are ignorant of facts or legislation of a relatively minor character, courts will not permit them to enforce the agreement and receive what they had bargained for, but they will permit the parties to recover what they have parted with.

Rights of Parties Not Equally in the Wrong The courts will often permit a party who is not equally in the wrong (in technical legal terms, not in *pari delicto*) to recover what she has parted with under an illegal agreement. One of the most common situations in which this exception is used involves the rights of "protected parties"—people who were intended to be protected by a regulatory statute—who contract with parties who are not properly licensed under that statute. Most regulatory statutes are intended to protect the public. As a general rule, if a person guilty of violating a regulatory statute enters into an agreement with another person for whose protection the statute was adopted, the agreement will be enforceable by the party whom the legislature intended to protect.

Another common situation in which courts will grant a remedy to a party who is not equally in the wrong is one in which the less guilty party has been induced to enter the agreement by misrepresentation, fraud, duress, or undue influence. The following *Gamboa* case illustrates how courts analyze the doctrine of in pari delicto to protect victims of fraud in an otherwise criminal contract.

Gamboa v. Alvarado 941 N.E.2d 1012 (Ill. Ct. App. 2011)

On December 7, 2009, plaintiffs (individually referred to as Gamboa, Nava, and Lopez) filed a five-count complaint against defendants alleging (count I) violations of the Consumer Fraud Act, (count II) common law fraud, (count III) unjust enrichment, (count IV) civil conspiracy, and (count V) intentional infliction of emotional distress. In early 2006, Alvarado told plaintiffs he could obtain "authentic citizenship documents" for plaintiffs through a contact at the U.S. Consulate office in Ciudad Juarez, Mexico, and plaintiffs would be able to use the documents to obtain Social Security numbers. He stated his contact could influence both American and Mexican immigration officials to expedite the application process but would need to pay employees in the different departments to obtain the necessary releases. The cost for adjustments to legal permanent residency status would be $12,000 per person and to obtain U.S. citizenship would add an additional $3,000 per person.

Alvarado stated he and his brother were obtaining their citizenship documents through the contact and invited plaintiffs to join their group. He explained that once the contact obtained the necessary documents, the group would travel across the Mexican border and pick up the documents at the consulate office after having photos and fingerprints taken and a short interview. If plaintiffs could get their money to him by the end of June 2006, they could have their documents by October. Otherwise, there would be a six-month delay.

Plaintiffs each made payments totaling $15,000 to Alvarado over a period of months and received receipts from Marco's Digital Photography in return for their payments. Alvarado explained he was providing receipts from his business to assure plaintiffs that the process was legitimate. Gamboa made some of his payments at Alvarado's home and at Marco's Digital Photography. Nava and Lopez alleged Alvarado used "high-pressure tactics" to get the payments by the June deadline, calling them weekly until they had paid in full. Nava did not make his final payment until October 2006. Alvarado informed plaintiffs that, because the deadline had not been met, there would be a delay and plaintiffs would not receive their documents until December 2006.

In February 2007, Alvarado told Gamboa that Gamboa's documents were ready and Gamboa needed to make plane reservations to fly to El Paso in order to cross the border and get the documents. Gamboa went to Marco's Digital Photography where Alvarado "purchased" the reservations for $500 plus a $25 credit card fee. Shortly before Gamboa was to leave, Alvarado told him his Mexican contact would not be able to get the documents and the trip was canceled. Alvarado refunded Gamboa's $500 but not the $25 fee.

Plaintiffs regularly called Alvarado inquiring about the status of their documents. Alvarado avoided plaintiffs. After repeated calls from plaintiffs, he told them that his contact had suffered a heart attack, which would delay obtaining the documents. He gave Lopez his contact's phone number in Mexico. Lopez spoke to the contact, "Jose de Jesus Castellanos," who confirmed Alvarado's version of heart attack-induced delay. At some later point, Alvarado stated the delays were due to problems in Phoenix and El Paso, which "Castellanos" confirmed when Gamboa called him.

In March 2009, Alvarado met with plaintiffs and told them that there was nothing he could do for them. He stated they had all been swindled by Castellanos and it was necessary to bring legal action in Mexico. He requested plaintiffs each pay him $200 to hire a Mexican lawyer and sign a power of attorney. Lopez and Nava paid and signed the power of attorney. Gamboa refused and demanded his money back. Alvarado subsequently called Nava and Lopez, asking if they knew what Gamboa was planning and threatened them that if Alvarado "fell, they would all fall."

Plaintiffs pressed Alvarado to return their money. In September 2009, Alvarado told Nava and Lopez the lawsuit was no longer a viable option and explained his new plan was to hire thugs in Mexico to kidnap Castellanos and get the money back from Castellanos in return for Castellanos's release. If Castellanos did not return the money, Alvarado implied the kidnappers would kill Castellanos. Nava and Lopez told Alvarado they were opposed to the violence and did not want to be part of the kidnapping scheme. On October 29, 2009, Alvarado told Nava and Lopez the kidnapping was on hold.

Plaintiffs' complaint alleged defendants engaged in numerous instances of unfair and deceptive practices in the conduct of trade or commerce in violation of section 2AA of the Consumer Fraud Act (815 Ill. Comp. Stat. 505/2AA (West 2008)), which governs private providers of immigration assistance services. Plaintiffs also alleged defendants committed common law fraud by inducing plaintiffs to rely on their misrepresentations; defendants were unjustly enriched by the monies plaintiffs paid them; defendants engaged in a civil conspiracy to defraud plaintiffs; and defendants intended to inflict emotional distress on plaintiffs by making the malicious statements that if Alvarado fell, they would all fall. Plaintiffs requested the court enjoin defendants from engaging in conduct relating to the provision of immigration services or in any of the deceptive practices charged and payment of assorted damages, including $45,000 to each plaintiff as the civil penalty provided for by section 2AA(m) (815 Ill. Comp. Stat. 505/2AA(m) (West 2008)).

Defendants filed a motion to dismiss pursuant to section 2-619 of the Illinois Code of Civil Procedure (735 Ill. Comp. Stat. 5/2-619 et seq. (West 2008)). They asserted the entire complaint should be dismissed pursuant to section 2-619(a)(9) because the agreement between the parties was an illegal contract that violated the law and public policy and courts refuse to enforce a contract when the purpose of the contract violates the law.

The court granted defendants' motion to dismiss on all counts, ruling that the plaintiffs and defendants entered into a contract that violated the law and public policy. It declared the order final and appealable. The plaintiffs appealed to Illinois Court of Appeals.

Karnezis, Judge

Taking the well-pleaded facts in plaintiffs' complaint as true, there is no question that the verbal contract between defendants and plaintiffs was illegal. Indeed, defendants admit that the parties entered into a contract that violates Illinois and Federal law and public policy. They correctly describe the parties' agreement as a "scheme" wherein the five members of the group agreed to obtain their residency or citizenship documents "by circumventing the normal, legal process that the public follows in obtaining such documents" such as by paying bribes and paying off government officials in violation of assorted criminal codes. Courts will not enforce an illegal contract, a contract that expressly contravenes either Illinois or Federal law and thus violates public policy. *Kim v. Citigroup, Inc.*, 368 Ill. App. 3d 298, 307, 856 N.E.2d 639, 305 Ill. Dec. 834 (2006). Illegality of contract is, therefore, a defense to actions seeking enforcement of a contract. *Kim*, 368 Ill. App. 3d at 307. Arguably, therefore, the illegality of the contract between plaintiffs and defendants would be a defense to plaintiffs' enforcement of the contract.

But plaintiffs are not seeking to enforce the contract. Rather, they are seeking to be reimbursed for the monies they paid defendants on the basis of the apparently fraudulent contract, costs they incurred as a result of the contract and assorted punitive damages including those provided for by section 2AA of the Consumer Fraud Act. As the basis for plaintiffs' claimed relief,

they are asserting (1) violations of section 2AA of the Consumer Fraud Act; (2) common law fraud; (3) unjust enrichment; (4) civil conspiracy; and (5) intentional infliction of emotional distress. They do not, in any of these counts, seek enforcement of the agreement they had with defendants or assert a breach of contract claim. Illegality of contract, therefore, would not be a valid defense to plaintiffs' claims.

We do not find, notwithstanding defendants' argument to the contrary, that allowing plaintiffs to proceed with their claims would be tantamount to allowing them to enforce an illegal contact. On the contrary, allowing plaintiffs' claims to proceed will send a message to those unscrupulous individuals who mislead and prey on others by promising them immigration services they cannot deliver that there are ramifications for this antisocial behavior. These individuals cannot be allowed to use the very illegality of their agreement as a way to avoid the consequences of their actions.

Granted, generally, "parties to a void contract will be left where they have placed themselves with no recovery of the money paid for illegal services." *Ransburg v. Haase*, 224 Ill. App. 3d 681, 686, 586 N.E.2d 1295, 167 Ill. Dec. 23 (1992). However, exceptions to this rule have been recognized where (1) the person who paid for the services was not in pari delicto ("in equal fault" with the offender) and (2) the law in question was passed for the protection of the person who paid for the services and the purpose of the law would be better served by granting relief than by denying it. *Ransburg*, 224 Ill. App. 3d at 686.

On the facts as they stand now, it appears plaintiffs were not in pari delicto with defendants: plaintiffs spoke little English, did not know defendants were lying/unable to deliver on their promises and would not necessarily know the agreement was illegal or that, as will be described below, they had recourse under section 2AA. Further, section 2AA was clearly passed for the protection of persons such as plaintiffs and would be best served if plaintiffs are allowed to proceed with their claims.

Section 2AA was created to deter the abuses allegedly committed by defendants here. In section 2AA, the General Assembly, given the substantial effect on the public interest of private individuals providing or offering to provide immigration assistance services, established rules of practice and conduct for such individuals in order to promote honesty and fair dealing with Illinois residents and preserve public confidence. 815 ILCS 505/2AA(a-1), (a-5) (West 2008).

Any person performing any of the authorized services must register with the Illinois Attorney General and submit verification of malpractice insurance or a surety bond (815 ILCS 505/2AA(c) (West 2008)); provide the customer with a written contract explaining the services and costs in English and in the customer's native language before performing any services (815 ILCS 505/2AA(d), (f) (West 2008)); and post a sign, a separate sign for each language in which he offers immigration assistance services at his place of business stating he is not an attorney licensed to practice law and disclosing his fee schedule and assorted other information. 815 ILCS 505/2AA(e) (West 2008).

Persons violating section 2AA shall be guilty of a Class A misdemeanor for a first offense and Class 3 felony for second or subsequent offenses. 815 ILCS 505/2AA(m) (West 2008). If the Attorney General or State's Attorney fails to file an action under this section, any person may file a civil action to enforce the provisions of the section and maintain an action for injunctive relief, compensatory damages to recover prohibited fees. 815 ILCS 505/2AA(m) (West 2008). A prevailing plaintiff may be awarded three times the prohibited fees. 815 ILCS 505/2AA(m) (West 2008). Plaintiffs filed such a civil action here, seeking triple the amount they paid defendants pursuant to section 2AA(m).

Again taking the well-pleaded facts in plaintiffs' complaint as true, there is no question that defendants were providers of immigration assistance services. There is also no question that they, as plaintiffs asserted in their complaint, violated section 2AA when they (1) failed to provide plaintiffs with a written contract explaining services to be performed and compensation to be charged in violation of section 2AA(d); (2) failed to provide plaintiffs with a written contract in English and Spanish, the language spoken by plaintiffs, in violation of section 2AA(f); (3) failed to post signs with the mandated disclosures at Marco's Digital Photography in violation of section 2AA(e); (4) retained plaintiffs' money after failing to obtain the promised documents, misrepresented to plaintiffs they could assist them in obtaining immigration documents and misrepresented that Castellanos was employed by the United States Consulate in Juarez, Mexico, in violation of section 2AA(j); and (5) failed to file the required registration statement or verification of malpractice statement or surety bond in violation of section 2AA(c).

Trial court's order of dismissal reversed, and case remanded for further proceedings.

Rescission before Performance of Illegal Act Obviously, public policy is best served by any rule that encourages people not to commit illegal acts. People who have fully or partially performed their part of an illegal contract have little incentive to raise the question of illegality if they know that they will be unable to recover what they have given because of the courts' hands-off approach to illegal agreements. To encourage people to cancel illegal contracts, courts will allow a person who rescinds such a contract before any illegal act has been performed to recover any consideration that he has given. For example, Dixon, the owner of a restaurant, pays O'Leary, an employee of a competitor's restaurant, $1,000 to obtain some of the competitor's recipes. If Dixon has second thoughts and tells O'Leary the deal is off before receiving any recipes, he can recover the $1,000 he paid O'Leary.

Divisible Contracts If part of an agreement is legal and part is illegal, the courts will enforce the legal part so long as it is possible to separate the two parts. A contract is said to be *divisible*—that is, the legal part can be separated from the illegal part—if the contract consists of several promises or acts by one party, each of which corresponds with an act or a promise by the other party. In other words, there must be a separate consideration for each promise or act for a contract to be considered divisible.

Where no separate consideration is exchanged for the legal and illegal parts of an agreement, the agreement is said to be *indivisible*. As a general rule, an indivisible contract that contains an illegal part will be entirely unenforceable unless it comes within one of the exceptions discussed above. However, if the major portion of a contract is legal but the contract contains an illegal provision that does not affect the primary, legal portion, courts will often enforce the legal part of the agreement and simply decline to enforce the illegal part. For example, suppose Alberts sells his barbershop to Bates. The contract of sale provides that Alberts will not engage in barbering anywhere in the world for the rest of his life. The major portion of the contract—the sale of the business—is perfectly legal. A provision of the contract—the ancillary covenant not to compete—is overly restrictive, and thus illegal. A court would enforce the sale of the business but modify or refuse to enforce the restraint provision. See Figure 15.1.

Figure 15.1   Effect of Illegality

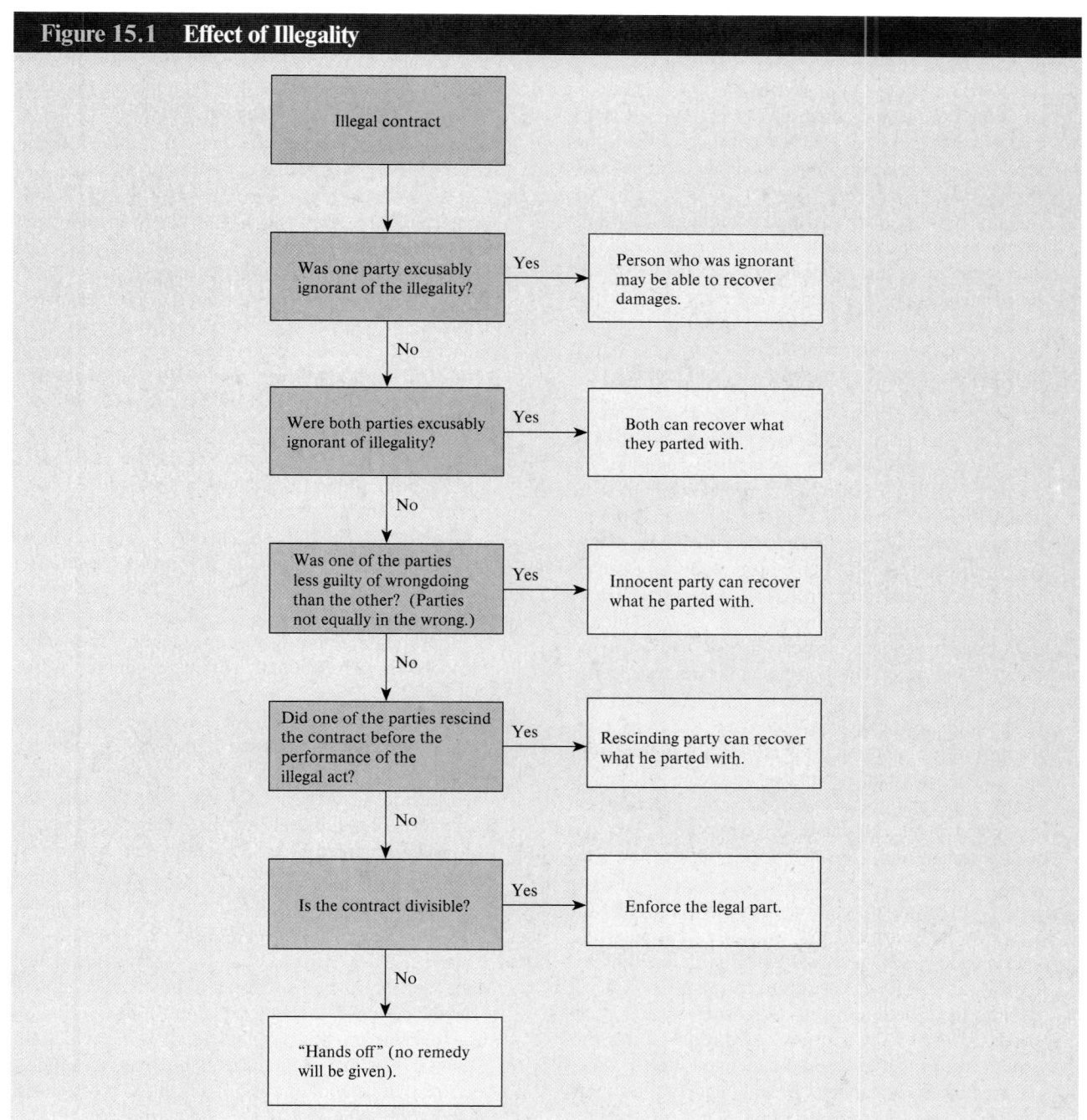

Problems and Problem Cases

1. Defendants who are citizens of the United Kingdom and have played, taught, coached, and worked in the soccer industry most of their lives were hired by plaintiffs to provide soccer camp services to roughly 185 soccer clubs in the past year, accounting for approximately $1.5 million in annual revenue. Each of the defendants entered into an employment contract that included clauses of noncompete, not to solicit, and not to disclose. After several months, defendants all wished to distance themselves from Russell, MLS Camps's owner, because of alleged mistreatment, deception, bullying, and abuse. Defendants attained new employment.

   Plaintiffs alleged that, since defendants left their employment with plaintiffs, plaintiffs experienced an immediate drop in customers in the New York–New Jersey area. They sought injunctive relief to bar defendants from working. After balancing the equities in public interest of noncompetition clauses as well as the basic need for employment, who will prevail?

2. Broemmer, age 21, was unmarried and 16 or 17 weeks pregnant. She was a high school graduate earning less than $100 a week and had no medical benefits. Broemmer was in considerable turmoil and confusion. The father-to-be insisted that she have an abortion, but her parents advised against it. Broemmer went to Abortion Services with her mother and was escorted into an adjoining room and asked to complete three forms: a consent to treatment form, a questionnaire asking for a detailed medical history, and an agreement to arbitrate. The agreement to arbitrate stated that "any dispute arising between the Parties as a result of the fees and/or services would be settled by binding arbitration" and that "any arbitrators appointed by the AAA [American Arbitration Association] shall be licensed medical doctors who specialize in obstetrics/gynecology." No one made any effort to explain this to Broemmer, and she was not provided with a copy of the agreement. She completed all three forms in less than five minutes. After Broemmer returned the forms to the front desk, she was taken into an examination room where preoperation procedures were performed. She was then instructed to return at 7:00 A.M. the next day. She returned the following day and a physician performed the abortion. As a result of this procedure, Broemmer suffered a punctured uterus, which required medical treatment. Broemmer later filed a malpractice lawsuit against Abortion Services. Abortion Services moved to dismiss the suit on the ground that arbitration was required under the agreement. Should the arbitration clause be enforced in this situation?

3. Piatek had served a 10-year term in San Quentin State Prison for assault with a deadly weapon with great bodily injury. His criminal background prevented him from acquiring the license to sell insurance that was required by state law. Nevertheless, he sold insurance for American Income Life Insurance Company under several false names. He then sued American Income Life Insurance to recover commissions on the sales that he had made. Will he be successful?

4. Strickland attempted to bribe Judge Sylvania Woods to show leniency toward one of Strickland's friends who had a case pending before the judge. Judge Woods immediately reported this to the state's attorney and was asked to play along with Strickland until the actual payment of money occurred. Strickland gave $2,500 to the judge, who promptly turned it over to the state's attorney's office. Strickland was indicted for bribery, pled guilty, and was sentenced to a four-year prison term. Three months after the criminal trial, Strickland filed a motion for the return of his $2,500. Will the court order the return of his money?

5. Steamatic of Kansas City Inc. specialized in cleaning and restoring property damaged by fire, smoke, water, or other elements. It employed Rhea as a marketing representative. His duties included soliciting customers, preparing cost estimates, supervising restoration work, and conducting seminars. At the time of his employment, Rhea signed a noncompetition agreement prohibiting him from entering into a business in competition with Steamatic within six counties of the Kansas City area for a period of two years after the termination of his employment with Steamatic. Late in 1987, Rhea decided to leave Steamatic. In contemplation of the move, he secretly extracted the agreement restricting his postemployment activity from the company's files and destroyed it. Steamatic learned of this and discharged Rhea. Steamatic filed suit against Rhea to enforce the noncompetition agreement when it learned that he was entering a competing business. Will the noncompetition agreement be enforced?

6. Plaintiff filed a lawsuit after discovering that defendant allegedly had engaged in a fraudulent accounting scheme designed to reduce plaintiff's compensation by expensing monies, which defendant received from Centegra Health Systems, directly to her. Plaintiff also learned that defendant was not a licensed professional corporation, even though she had given plaintiff prior

assurances that she was properly registered. According to plaintiff, to induce her to join its medical practice, defendant expressly represented in writing that the "Corporation [was] registered to practice medicine in the State of Illinois."

Can the defendant's failure to comply with the act's certificate of registration requirement render the employment agreement void?

7. Pinnacle Market Development constructed and sold condominiums in downtown San Diego known as the Pinnacle Museum Tower Project. In connection with this project, Pinnacle recorded a declaration of covenants, conditions, and restrictions (CC&R) forming the Pinnacle Museum Tower Association ("Association") to manage and govern the project's common areas. Each condo buyer became a part-owner of the Association. The CC&R stated a mandatory arbitration procedure for resolution of construction disputes. When condo buyers signed the paperwork to purchase their units, they were presented with a document that waived their right to trial by jury and stated that they were bound by the terms of the CC&R, which would be recorded in the official records of San Diego County. Is the jury waiver provision unconscionable?

8. Marcinczyk, a security officer at University of Medicine and Dentistry of New Jersey (UMDNJ), received a promotion to the position of police officer conditioned upon his attendance at a police academy for training. In order to attend the Academy, all other recruits were required to execute an exculpatory agreement accepting possible risk of physical or psychological harm.

In training, Marcinczyk was designated as one of two "lunch recruits. . . ." He slipped on "some kind of substance" on the steps and fell, suffering severe and disabling back injuries. Can Marcinczyk argue that the exculpatory agreement violated public policy?

9. Mantor began working for Circuit City in August 1992. When Circuit City hired Mantor, it had no arbitration program. In 1995, Circuit City instituted an arbitration program called the "Associate Issue Resolution Program" (AIRP). Circuit City emphasized to managers the importance of full participation in the AIRP, claiming that the company had been losing money because of lawsuits filed by employees. Circuit City management stressed that employees had little choice in this matter. They suggested that employees should sign the agreement or prepare to be terminated. Although Circuit City circulated the forms regarding the AIRP in 1995, Mantor was able to avoid either signing up or openly refused to

participate in the AIRP for three years. In 1998, two Circuit City managers arranged a meeting with Mantor to discuss his participation in the AIRP. During this meeting, Mantor asked the two Circuit City managers what would happen should he decline to participate in the arbitration program. They responded to the effect that he would have no future with Circuit City. In February 1998, Mantor agreed to participate in the AIRP, acknowledging in writing his receipt of (1) an "Associate Issue Resolution Handbook," (2) the "Circuit City Dispute Resolution Rules and Procedures," and (3) a "Circuit City Arbitration Opt-Out Form." Under its arbitration program, Circuit City requires an employee to pay a $75 filing fee to initiate an arbitration proceeding. There is a provision for waiving this fee at Circuit City's discretion. In October 2000, Circuit City terminated Mantor's employment. A year later, Mantor brought a civil action in state court, alleging 12 causes of action. Circuit City petitioned the district court to compel arbitration, and the district court granted Circuit City's motion to compel arbitration. Mantor appealed, arguing that the arbitration agreement was unenforceable because it was unconscionable. Was it unconscionable?

10. Gianni Sport was a New York manufacturer and distributor of women's clothing. Gantos was a clothing retailer headquartered in Grand Rapids, Michigan. In 1980, Gantos's sales total was 20 times greater than Gianni Sport's, and in this industry, buyers were "in the driver's seat." In June 1980, Gantos submitted to Gianni Sport a purchase order for women's holiday clothing to be delivered on October 10, 1980. The purchase order contained the following clause:

> Buyer reserves the right to terminate by notice to Seller all or any part of this Purchase Order with respect to Goods that have not actually been shipped by Seller or as to Goods which are not timely delivered for any reason whatsoever.

Gianni Sport made the goods in question especially for Gantos. This holiday order comprised 20 to 22 percent of Gianni Sport's business. In late September 1980, before the goods were shipped, Gantos canceled the order. Was the cancellation clause unconscionable?

11. During a prenatal appointment for her high-risk pregnancy, Monica Moore was told to complete a series of forms related to medical treatment, privacy rights, and payment of services. Neither the office receptionist who gave her the forms nor her OBGYN specialist physician (to whom she had been referred) brought her attention to the fact that among the

forms she was signing was also included a four-page-long arbitration agreement. The title of the top page, however, was in boldface type and capitalized letters: **"ARBITRATION AGREEMENT FOR CLAIMS ARISING OUT OF OR RELATED TO MEDICAL CARE AND TREATMENT."** The arbitration agreement purported to be binding on Monica, her husband, and their unborn child; required that all future claims against any medical provider in the practice would be arbitrated (if the medical provider elected to be involved in arbitration); stated that Monica's, her husband's, and her unborn child's constitutional rights to jury trial or trial by judge were being waived; noted that the patient acknowledged her right to consult with an attorney prior to signing the contract; and provided Monica with 15 days in which to rescind the agreement after she signed it, although she was not provided with a copy of the arbitration agreement. Monica later filed a medical malpractice action in state court, and the trial judge granted the defendant medical provider's motion to compel arbitration. Monica appealed on the grounds that the arbitration agreement is a contract of adhesion with both procedural and substantive unconscionability. Is this arbitration agreement enforceable?

Writing

Moore went to First National Bank and requested that the president of the bank allow his adult sons, Rocky and Mike, to open an account in the name of Texas Continental Express Inc. Moore promised to bring his own business to the bank and orally agreed to make good any losses that the bank might incur from receiving dishonored checks from Texas Continental. The bank then furnished a regular checking account and bank draft services to Texas Continental. Several years later, Texas Continental wrote checks that were returned for insufficient funds. The amounts of those checks totaled $448,942.05. Texas Continental did not cover the checks, and the bank turned to Moore for payment.

- Was Moore's oral promise to pay Texas Continental's dishonored checks enforceable?
- If not, what would have been required in the nature of a writing to make the promise enforceable?
- Suppose there had been a written agreement between Moore and the bank. Would the bank have been able to enforce an oral promise made by Moore that was not stated in the written contract?
- Would it be ethical of Moore not to pay the bank?

LO LEARNING OBJECTIVES

After studying this chapter, you should be able to:

16-1 List the contracts that must be evidenced by a writing under the statute of frauds.

16-2 Explain the exceptions to the statute of frauds.

16-3 Explain how to satisfy the statute of frauds under both the common law and UCC.

16-4 Explain the parol evidence rule and the exceptions to the rule.

YOUR STUDY OF CONTRACT law so far has focused on the requirements for the formation of a valid contract. You should be aware, however, that even when all the elements of a valid contract exist, the enforceability of the contract and the nature of the parties' obligations can be greatly affected by the *form* in which the contract is set out and by the *language* that is used to express the agreement. This chapter discusses such issues.

The Significance of Writing in Contract Law

Purposes of Writing Despite what many people believe, there is no general requirement that contracts be in writing. In most situations, oral contracts are legally enforceable, assuming that they can be proven. Still, oral contracts are less desirable than written contracts in many ways. They are more easily misunderstood or forgotten than written contracts tend to be. They are also more subject to the danger that a person might fabricate terms or fraudulently claim to have made an oral contract when none exists.

Writing is important in contract law and practice for a number of reasons. When people memorialize their contracts in a writing, they are enhancing their chances of proving that an obligation was undertaken and making it harder for the other party to deny making the promise. A person's signature on a written contract provides a basis for the contract to be authenticated, or proved to be genuinely the contract of the signer. In addition, signing a writing also communicates the seriousness of the occasion to the signer. Occasionally there are problems with proving the genuineness of the writing, and often there are disagreements about the interpretation of language in a contract, but the written form is still very useful in increasing the chances that you will be able to depend on the enforcement of your contracts.

Writing and Contract Enforcement In contract law, there are certain situations in which a promise that is not in writing can be denied enforcement. In such situations, an otherwise valid contract can become unenforceable if it does not comply with the formalities required by state law. These situations are controlled by a type of statute called the statute of frauds.

Overview of the Statute of Frauds

History and Purposes In 17th-century England, the dangers inherent in oral contracts were exacerbated by a legal rule that prohibited parties to a lawsuit from testifying in their own cases. Because the parties to an oral contract could not give testimony, the only way they could prove the existence of the contract was through the testimony of third parties. As you might expect, third parties were sometimes persuaded to offer false testimony about the existence of contracts. In an attempt to stop the widespread fraud and perjury that resulted, Parliament enacted the Statute of Frauds in 1677. It required written evidence before certain classes of contracts would be enforced. Although the possibility of fraud exists in every contract, the statute focused on contracts in which the potential for fraud was great or the consequences of fraud were thought to be especially serious. The legislatures of American states adopted very similar statutes, also known as statutes of frauds. These statutes, which require certain kinds of contracts to be evidenced by a signed writing, are exceptions to the previously noted general rule that oral contracts are enforceable.

Statutes of frauds have produced a great deal of litigation, due in part to the public's ignorance of their provisions. It is difficult to imagine an aspect of contract law that is more practical for businesspeople to know about than the circumstances under which an oral contract will not suffice.

Effect of Violating the Statute of Frauds
The statute of frauds applies only to executory contracts. If an oral contract has been completely performed by both parties, the fact that it did not comply with the statute of frauds would not be a ground for rescission of the contract.

What happens if an executory contract is within the statute of frauds but has not been evidenced by the type of writing required by the statute? It is not treated as an illegal contract because the statute of frauds is more of a formal rule than a rule of substantive law. Rather, the contract that fails to comply with the statute of frauds is *unenforceable*. Although the contract will not be enforced, a person who has conferred some benefit on the other party pursuant to the contract may be able to recover the reasonable value of his performance in an action based on *quasi-contract*.

Contracts Covered by the Statute of Frauds

 List the contracts that must be evidenced by a writing under the statute of frauds.

A contract is said to be "within" (covered by) the statute of frauds if the statute requires that sort of contract to be evidenced by a writing. In almost all states, the following types of contracts are *within* the statute of frauds:

1. Collateral contracts in which a person promises to perform the obligation of another person.
2. Contracts for the sale of an interest in real estate.
3. Bilateral contracts that cannot be performed within a year from the date of their formation.
4. Contracts for the sale of goods for a price of $500 or more.
5. Contracts in which an executor or administrator promises to be personally liable for the debt of an estate.
6. Contracts in which marriage is the consideration.

Of this list, the first four sorts of contracts have the most significance today, and our discussion will focus primarily on them.

The statutes of frauds of the various states are not uniform. Some states require written evidence of other contracts in addition to those listed above. For example, a number of states require written evidence of contracts to pay a commission for the sale of real estate. Others require written evidence of ratifications of infants' promises or promises to pay debts that have been barred by the statute of limitations or discharged by bankruptcy.

The following discussion examines in greater detail the sorts of contracts that are within most states' statute of frauds.

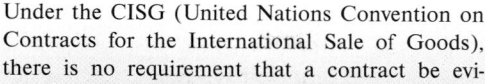

The Global Business Environment

Under the CISG (United Nations Convention on Contracts for the International Sale of Goods), there is no requirement that a contract be evidenced by a writing. A contract need not take any particular form, and can be proven by any means. The CISG does permit parties to a written contract to require that any modifications of the contract be in writing, however.

Collateral Contracts A collateral contract is one in which one person (the *guarantor*) agrees to pay the debt or obligation that a second person (the *principal debtor*) owes to a third person (the *obligee*) if the principal debtor fails to perform. For example, Cohn, who wants to help Davis establish a business, promises First Bank that he will repay the loan that First Bank makes to Davis if Davis fails to pay it. Here, Cohn is the guarantor, Davis is the principal debtor, and First Bank is the obligee. Cohn's promise to First Bank must be in writing to be enforceable.

Figure 16.1 shows that a collateral contract involves at least three parties and at least two promises to perform (a promise by the principal debtor to pay the obligee and a promise by the guarantor to pay the obligee). In a collateral contract, the guarantor promises to pay *only if the principal debtor fails to do so*. The essence of the collateral contract is that the debt or obligation is owed primarily by the principal debtor and the guarantor's debt is *secondary*. Thus, not all three-party transactions are collateral contracts. The *Dynegy* case, which follows shortly, focuses on whether an obligation was primary or collateral and, therefore, on whether the oral contract at issue was subject to the statute of frauds.

When a person undertakes an obligation that is *not* conditioned on the default of another person, and the debt is his own rather than that of another person, his obligation is said to be *original*, not collateral. For example, when Timmons calls Johnson Florist Company and says, "Send flowers to Elrod," Timmons is undertaking an obligation to pay *her own*—not someone else's—debt.

When a contract is determined to be collateral, however, it will be unenforceable unless it is evidenced by a writing.

Exception: Main Purpose or Leading Object Rule

LO16-2 Explain the exceptions to the statute of frauds.

There are some situations in which a contract that is technically collateral is treated as if it were an original contract. Under the main purpose or leading object rule, no writing is required where the guarantor makes a collateral promise for the main purpose of obtaining some personal economic advantage. When the consideration given in exchange for the collateral promise is something the guarantor seeks primarily for his own benefit rather than for the benefit of the primary debtor, the contract is outside the statute of frauds. Suppose, for example, that Penn is a major creditor of Widgetmart, a retailer. To help keep Widgetmart afloat and increase the chances that Widgetmart will repay the debt it owes him, Penn orally promises Rex Industries, one of Widgetmart's suppliers, that he will guarantee Widgetmart's payment for goods that Rex sells to Widgetmart. In this situation, Penn's oral agreement could be enforced under the main purpose rule if the court finds that Penn was acting for his own personal financial benefit.

In the *Dynegy* case, which follows, the court not only explores the primary-versus-collateral distinction but also considers whether the main purpose exception applies and renders an oral contract of a collateral nature enforceable.

Interest in Land Any contract that creates or transfers an interest in land is within the statute of frauds. The inclusion of real estate contracts in the statute of frauds reflects the values of an earlier, agrarian society in which land was the primary basis of wealth. Our legal system historically has treated land as being more important than

Figure 16.1   Collateral Contract

Obligee — Primary contract (Principal debtor) — Collateral contract (Guarantor)

Guarantor's promise must be evidenced by a writing.

other forms of property. Courts have interpreted the land provision of the statute of frauds broadly to require written evidence of any transaction that will affect the ownership of an interest in land. Thus, a contract to sell or mortgage real estate must be evidenced by a writing, as must an option to purchase real estate or a contract to grant an easement or permit the mining and removal of minerals on land. A lease is also a transfer of an interest in land, but most states' statutes of frauds do not require leases to be in writing unless they are long-term leases, usually those for one year or more. On the other hand, a contract to construct or insure a building would not be within the real estate provision of the statute of frauds because such contracts do not involve the transfer of interests in land.[1]

---

[1]Note, however, that a writing might be required under state insurance statutes.

Dynegy, Inc. v. Yates	422 S.W.3d 638 (Tex. 2013)

A grand jury indicted James Olis, a former officer of Dynegy, Inc., on multiple counts of securities fraud, mail and wire fraud, and conspiracy arising out of work he performed while at Dynegy. Dynegy's board of directors passed a resolution authorizing the advancement of attorney fees for Olis's defense, provided that Olis acted in good faith, in Dynegy's best interests, and in compliance with applicable law.

Olis hired attorney Terry Yates to defend him in the criminal investigation and an ongoing civil investigation conducted by the Securities and Exchange Commission. Olis told Yates and Mark Clark, Yates's associate, that Dynegy would be paying his legal fees. Clark telephoned Cristin Cracraft, an attorney in Dynegy's legal department, who confirmed during the conversation that Dynegy would pay Olis's legal fees. Clark testified in the litigation referred to below that Cracraft stated, "The Board has passed a resolution, so, yes, we are paying Jamie Olis's fees," and instructed Clark that the bills should be submitted to her. Cracraft's later testimony was similar to Clark's version of the conversation.

In Olis's written fee agreement with Yates, Olis acknowledged that he was responsible for payment of his legal fees. The contract stated that "all fees are due when billed unless other specific arrangements have been made." Yates later testified that despite the written fee agreement, he and Olis had a separate agreement under which Yates would not look to Olis for payment of fees, but instead would look to Dynegy for payment. Yates also testified that he spoke to Cracraft after faxing his fee agreement and hourly rate to Dynegy and that Cracraft told him Dynegy would pay Olis's legal fees through his criminal trial. Cracraft's testimony contradicted Yates's testimony about the phone call, however. Cracraft testified that she spoke only to Clark and never to Yates as of the date of the trial.

After the communications noted above, Dynegy hand-delivered a letter notifying Yates that it would pay him directly for Olis's legal fees through August 17, 2003, but that the remaining fees incurred were to be paid into escrow pursuant to a board resolution. Dynegy paid Yates's initial invoice for $15,000. Yates submitted a further bill for $105,176 in August, but Dynegy did not pay it until after Olis's trial in November. Olis was ultimately convicted of securities fraud, mail and wire fraud, and conspiracy. Yates submitted a third and final invoice for $448,556, representing all work performed from August 2003 through April 2004, including the November 2003 trial. Dynegy initially escrowed that amount pursuant to the board resolution, but later refused to release the escrowed funds after concluding that Olis did not meet the "good faith" standard for indemnification set forth in the board's resolution.

Alleging that Dynegy orally promised that it would pay Yates's fees through Olis's trial, Yates sued Dynegy for breach of contract. A Texas jury returned a verdict in favor of Yates. Dynegy moved for judgment notwithstanding the verdict on the theory that the statute of frauds should have been held to bar Yates's claim, but the trial court denied the motion. Dynegy appealed to the Texas Court of Civil Appeals. In affirming the lower court's judgment in favor of Yates, the appellate court concluded that the statute of frauds did not apply because Dynegy's promise amounted to a primary obligation rather than a promise to pay the debt of another. Dynegy appealed to the Supreme Court of Texas.

Green, Justice

The statute of frauds' suretyship provision provides that an oral promise "by one person to answer for the debt, default, or miscarriage of another person" is generally unenforceable. Tex. Bus. & Com. Code § 26.01(a), (b)(2). Dynegy contends that this provision bars the current suit [because the] breach of contract claim against it is based on an oral promise to pay the attorney's fees incurred by one of Dynegy's former officers.

The statute of frauds generally renders a contract that falls within its purview unenforceable. The party pleading the statute of frauds bears the initial burden of establishing its applicability. Once that party meets its initial burden, the burden shifts to the opposing party to establish an exception that would take the verbal contract out of the statute of frauds. One recognized exception to the statute of frauds' suretyship provision is the main purpose doctrine [(described below)].

Here, Dynegy pleaded the statute of frauds as an affirmative defense and thus had the initial burden to establish that the alleged promise fell within the statute of frauds. Yates argues that the suretyship provision does not apply to the oral agreement in this case because there is not a preexisting debt. On the contrary, the suretyship provision applies regardless of "whether [the debt was] already incurred or to be incurred in the future." *Restatement (Second) of Contracts* § 112 cmt. b (1981).

The record indicates that Olis hired Yates to represent him in the criminal proceedings. Olis signed a fee agreement with Yates, in which Dynegy was not mentioned. Yates agreed to defend Olis, and Olis agreed in exchange that fees were due when billed unless other arrangements were made. Both Clark and Yates testified that Cracraft orally promised that Dynegy would be paying Olis's fees through trial, and it is undisputed that this agreement was never reduced to writing. These facts establish one conclusion: Dynegy orally promised to pay attorney's fees associated with Olis's defense that, under the fee agreement, were Olis's obligation (i.e., Olis's debt). We hold that Dynegy established as a matter of law that the statute of frauds' suretyship provision initially applied to bar the claims against it. The court of appeals erred when it held otherwise.

At this point, the burden shifted to Yates to establish an exception that would take the verbal contract out of the statute of frauds—namely, the main purpose doctrine. The main purpose doctrine required Yates to prove: (1) Dynegy intended to create primary responsibility in itself to pay the debt; (2) there was consideration for the promise; and (3) the consideration given for the promise was primarily for Dynegy's own use and benefit—that is, the benefit it received was Dynegy's main purpose for making the promise. We have noted that the question of intent to be primarily responsible for the debt is a question for the finder of fact, taking into account all the facts and circumstances of the case. Thus, the burden was on Yates to secure favorable findings [from the trial court] on the main purpose doctrine. [Yates did not do so, however.] Yates failed to plead and prove the [intent and] consideration elements of the main purpose exception. [In its written objection to the jury instructions approved by the trial judge.] Dynegy even

pointed out to the trial court and Yates the omission of any jury questions related to an exception to the statute of frauds. [Because Yates did not carry his burden to prove the elements of the main purpose doctrine, the trial court and the court of appeals erred in holding that the statute of frauds did not apply.]

Based on the preceding analysis, we hold that the statute of frauds renders the oral agreement between Dynegy and Yates unenforceable.

Court of Appeals decision reversed in favor of Dynegy; Yates's case dismissed.

Devine, Justice, dissenting

The statute of frauds "is a two-edged sword. It . . . may be used to perpetrate frauds as well as to prevent them. Under it a person may obtain an oral promise to pay the debt of a third person and then resist payment on the ground that this promise is oral and therefore unenforceable under the statute of frauds. Because of this and other dangers, the courts of England and this country have sought to keep the statute within its intended purpose." [Citation omitted.]

The dispute in this case is not about whether Dynegy agreed to pay Yates; it clearly did. The dispute instead is about the extent of Dynegy's promise. Dynegy contends that its promise to Yates was conditioned by the [good faith provision in] the board resolution. Yates contends that Dynegy's promise to pay for Olis' defense through trial was unconditional and, as to Yates, primarily the company's responsibility.

The dispute was submitted to a jury, which was asked to determine the extent of Dynegy's agreement with Yates. The charge instructed the jury that an essential term of the asserted agreement was whether Dynegy agreed to pay Yates for his legal services to Olis through trial. In closing argument, Dynegy argued that the jury should not find it in breach of the agreement unless it believed Dynegy made an unconditional promise to pay Yates through trial. The jury found Dynegy in breach of its agreement to pay Yates and awarded damages.

The court concludes, however, that the written fee agreement between Yates and Olis conclusively establishes Olis as the primary obligor, making Dynegy merely the surety of that obligation. Because Dynegy never intended to act as a guarantor of Olis' debt, however, the statute of frauds' suretyship provision should not apply as a matter of law. I therefore disagree with the court's conclusion, but even if I agreed with it, I would nevertheless hold that the main purpose exception takes Dynegy's promise to Yates out of the statute.

Exception: Full Performance by the Vendor

 LO16-2 Explain the exceptions to the statute of frauds.

An oral contract for the sale of land that has been completely performed by the vendor (seller) is "taken out of the statute of frauds"–that is, is enforceable without a writing. For example, Peterson and Lincoln enter into an oral contract for the sale of Peterson's farm at an agreed-on price and Peterson, the vendor, delivers a deed to the farm to Lincoln. In this situation, the vendor has completely performed, making the contract enforceable despite its oral nature.

Exception: Part Performance (Action in Reliance) by the Vendee

 LO16-2 Explain the exceptions to the statute of frauds.

When the vendee (purchaser of land) acts in clear reliance on an oral contract for the sale of land, an equitable doctrine commonly known as the "part performance doctrine" permits the vendee to enforce the contract notwithstanding the fact that it was oral. The doctrine recognizes that a person's conduct can "speak louder than words" and can indicate the existence of a contract almost as well as a writing can. The part performance doctrine is also based on the desire to avoid the injustice that would otherwise result if the contract were repudiated after the vendee's reliance.

Under § 129 of the *Restatement (Second) of Contracts*, a contract for the transfer of an interest in land can be enforced even without a writing if the person seeking enforcement:

1. Has *reasonably relied* on the contract and on the other party's assent.

2. Has changed his position to such an extent that *enforcement of the contract is the only way to prevent injustice.*

In other words, the vendee must have acted in reliance on the contract and the nature of the action must be such that restitution (returning his money) would not be an adequate remedy. The part performance doctrine will not permit the vendee to collect damages for breach of contract, but it will permit him to obtain the equitable remedy of **specific performance**, a remedy whereby the court orders the breaching party to perform his contract.[2]

A vendee's reliance on an oral contract could be shown in many ways. Traditionally, many states have required that the vendee pay part or all of the purchase price and either make substantial improvements on the property or take possession of it. For example, Contreras and Miller orally enter into a contract for the sale of Contreras's land. If Miller pays Contreras a substantial part of the purchase price and either takes possession of the land or begins to make improvements on it, the contract would be enforceable without a writing under the part performance doctrine. These are not the only sorts of acts in reliance that would make an oral contract enforceable, however. Under the *Restatement (Second)* approach, if the promise to transfer land is clearly proven or is admitted by the breaching party, it is not necessary that the act of reliance include making payment, taking possession, or making improvements.[3] It still is necessary, however, that the reliance be such that restitution would not be an adequate remedy. For this reason, a vendee's payment of the purchase price, standing alone, is usually *not* sufficient for the part performance doctrine.

Contracts That Cannot Be Performed within One Year

A bilateral, executory contract that, according to its terms, cannot be performed within one year from the day on which it comes into existence is within the statute of frauds and must be evidenced by a writing. The apparent purpose of this provision is to guard against the risk of faulty or willfully inaccurate recollection of long-term contracts. Courts have tended to construe it very narrowly.

One aspect of this narrow construction is that most states hold that a contract that has been fully performed by *one* of the parties is "taken out of the statute of frauds" and is enforceable without a writing. For example, Nash enters into an oral contract to perform services for Thomas for 13 months. If Nash has already fully performed his part of the contract, Thomas will be required to pay him the contract price.

In addition, this provision of the statute has been held to apply only when the terms of the contract make it impossible for the contract to be completed within one year. If the contract is for an indefinite period of time, it is not within the statute of frauds. This is true even if, in retrospect, the contract was not completed within a year. Thus, Weinberg's agreement to work for Wolf for an indefinite period of time would not have to be evidenced by a writing, even if Weinberg eventually works for Wolf for many years. The mere fact that performance is unlikely to be completed in one year does not bring the contract within the statute of frauds. *Browning v. Poirier*, which follows shortly, provides an illustration of the principles noted above.

---

[2]Specific performance is discussed in more detail in Chapter 18.

[3]*Restatement (Second) of Contracts* § 129, comment d.

In most states, a contract "for life" is not within the statute of frauds because it is possible—because death is an uncertain event—for the contract to be performed within a year. In a few states, contracts for life are within the statute of frauds.

Computing Time In determining whether a contract is within the one-year provision, courts begin counting time on the day when the contract comes into existence. If, under the terms of the contract, it is possible to perform it within one year from this date, the contract does not fall within the statute of frauds and does not have to be in writing. If, however, the terms of the contract make it impossible to complete performance of the contract (without breaching it) within one year from the date on which the contract came into existence, the contract falls within the statute and must meet its writing requirement to be enforceable. Thus, if Hammer Co. and McCrea orally agree on August 1, 2020, that McCrea will work for Hammer Co. for one year, beginning October 1, 2020, the terms of the contract dictate that it is not possible to complete performance until October 1, 2021. Because that date is more than one year from the date on which the contract came into existence, the contract falls within the statute of frauds and must be evidenced by a writing to be enforceable.

Browning v. Poirier	**113 So. 3d 976 (Fla. Dist. Ct. App. 2013)**

Beginning in 1991, Howard Browning and Lynn Anne Poirier lived together in a romantic relationship. In approximately 1993, the parties entered into an oral agreement in which they agreed to purchase lottery tickets on a regular basis and to share equally in the proceeds of any winning tickets. While the two were still co-habitating, Poirier purchased a winning lottery ticket on June 2, 2007, and won $1,000,000, minus deductions for taxes. Poirier refused to share.

When Browning requested half of the proceeds and Poirier refused, he sued her for breach of contract. Browning alleged their agreement was to apply whether the tickets were purchased "together, separately, in different locations, or at different times. . . ." Browning's breach of contract claim further alleged that "[t]his agreement was capable of being performed within one (1) year" and that the agreement had been "reaffirmed and/or ratified several times orally and by the parties' conduct since 1993."

At trial, Browning testified that he and Poirier would go in and buy lottery tickets together, play together, and that if either were to win, "we would split the money." He claimed that Poirier had purchased the $1 million winning ticket when they had stopped at the convenience store together to buy more tickets for the upcoming lottery drawing on July 4, 2007. He claimed to have given Poirier $20 with which to purchase the ticket and that they had both purchased tickets that night.

Browning conceded that their agreement was to be effective only as long as they were in a romantic relationship, and he had friendships with other women.

At the close of Browning's case, prior to any findings by the trier of fact, the trial court granted a directed verdict for Poirier, holding that the breach of oral contract action was barred as a matter of law by the statute of frauds because it was not in writing as required for a contract "not to be performed within the space of 1 year from the making thereof . . ." (citing Fla. Stat. section 725.01).

Browning appealed the directed verdict.

Jacobus, Judge

The threshold issue presented by this case is whether Browning's action [for breach of contract] is barred by the statute of frauds. We hold that it is not. The statute provides in relevant part that:

> No action shall be brought . . . upon any agreement that is not to be performed within the space of 1 year from the making thereof . . . unless the agreement or promise upon which such action shall be brought, or some note or memorandum thereof, shall be in writing and signed by the party to be charged therewith or by some other person by her or him thereunto lawfully authorized.

The general rule is that the statute of frauds bars enforcement of oral contracts which by their terms are not to be performed within a year. *Yates v. Ball*, 132 Fla. 132, 181 So. 341, 344 (1937).

The fact that a contract may not be performed within a year does not bring it within the statute. "In other words, to make a parol contract void, it must be apparent that it was the understanding of the parties that it was not to be performed within a year from the time it was made." *Id.*

Contracts for an indefinite period generally do not fall within the statute of frauds. *Id.*; *Restatement (Second) of Contracts* § 130 cmt. (a) (1981) ("Contracts of uncertain duration are simply excluded; the provision covers only those contracts whose performance cannot possibly be completed within a year."). As the court explained in *Yates*:

> When, as in this case, no definite time was fixed by the parties for the performance of their agreement, and there is nothing in its terms to show that it could not be performed within a year

according to its intent and the understanding of the parties, it should not be construed as being within the statute of frauds.

Id. . . . In arguing that enforcement of the contract was barred by statute, Poirier . . . contends that the parties did not intend for the agreement to be fully performed within one year as it was a "perpetual" agreement with no termination date. The flaw in her argument is the assumption that the agreement was intended to be "perpetual." It was simply an agreement for an indefinite term which, according to Browning's testimony, was to continue as long as the parties were involved in a romantic relationship. Although the parties contemplated that the relationship would last more than one year, there was nothing in the agreement, which was terminable at will, to show that it could not be performed within one year, or which required performance for a period of time exceeding one year. Hence, Browning's suit for breach of contract is not barred by the statute (citations omitted). . . .

Reversed and remanded.

Sawaya, Judge, concurring in part, dissenting in part

This case involves two romantically involved individuals who allegedly agreed to split the proceeds of any lottery tickets they purchased, only to have the eventual winning ticket split their romance. The purchaser of the winning ticket is Lynn Anne Poirier, the Appellee. The claimant of half of the proceeds is Howard Browning, the Appellant. Browning testified at trial that he and Poirier became romantically involved in 1991 and started living together that year. He further testified that in 1993, they entered into an oral agreement to split the proceeds of any lottery tickets they may purchase and that this agreement was to last as long as they remained romantically involved. Some fourteen years after the alleged agreement was made and while the parties were still romantically involved and living together, Poirier purchased the winning ticket, collected one million dollars, and refused Browning's request for half of the proceeds. The displeased and disgruntled Browning then filed the underlying suit for breach of contract and unjust enrichment seeking half of the proceeds. Poirier denied the existence of any oral agreement to split future lottery proceeds and interposed the defense of the statute of frauds. The trial court directed a verdict in favor of Poirier concluding that if there was an oral agreement, Browning's claim is barred because the parties intended it to last for far longer than one year. Browning appeals, arguing that factual issues remain that should be resolved by a jury and asks us to reverse the judgment in favor of Poirier and remand this case for a new trial.

The majority holds that the alleged oral contract to share lottery winnings is not barred by the statute of frauds and remands for a new trial only on the issue of whether the oral agreement was entered into by the parties. That holding is based on reasoning that it was possible that the alleged oral contract could have

been performed within the statutory one-year performance period and, therefore, the statute does not apply to bar the claim for breach of the agreement. I believe the key factor to determine the applicability of the statute to this alleged oral contract which, as the majority concedes, is for an indefinite period of time, is whether the parties intended that the contract extend beyond the one-year statutory period. What the parties intended is a question that should be left to the jury to resolve.

. . . The courts have consistently applied the rule that when an alleged oral contract is for an indefinite period of time, the determining factor is whether the parties intended the contract to extend beyond the one year statutory period (citations omitted).

The courts have construed the statutory language found in section 725.01 "not to be performed within the space of one year" to refer to the express intent of the parties at the time they make the oral contract (citations omitted).

Therefore, when an oral contract is for an indefinite period, the court must determine whether it was the intent of the parties that the contract be fully performed within one year. The district courts have consistently followed this rule (citations omitted). The intent of the parties is a fact question that should be resolved by the finder of fact (citations omitted). The object to be accomplished was to win the lottery. The circumstances surrounding the alleged oral agreement was that it would last for as long as the parties remained romantically involved. The record reveals that the romantic relationship lasted many years after the date the agreement was allegedly made and that is a factor that can be considered in determining what the parties intended at the time the agreement was made (citations omitted).

The majority applies the "possible" principle reasoning that it was possible that one of the parties would win the lottery and they would end their relationship within the year performance period. Appellant goes so far as to argue that it was possible that the agreement "could have been completed within 1 year based on the fact that either party could have died during the year. . . ." In *Hesston Corp. v. Roche*, 599 So. 2d 148, 153 (Fla. 5th DCA 1992), this court explained that even if it is possible to perform an alleged oral contract within one year, it must be shown that the parties intended and expected performance within the year. . . .

Hence, if it was possible to perform the alleged oral agreement in one year, there is no evidence that the parties intended or expected that. To the contrary, it does not take an advanced degree in statistics or mathematics to know that the odds of winning the lottery are very slim and the odds of winning it within a year period are even slimmer. I think it stretches the "possible" principle too far to suggest that two people would enter into an agreement to split lottery winnings intending that they would both win and end their relationship either voluntarily or by death within the year period. At least death is an eventual certainty and the only question is when it will happen. I believe that applying the "possible" principle to this case offends the admonition enunciated in *Yates* and many other cases that "[t]he statute should be strictly construed to prevent the fraud it was designed to correct, and so long as it can be made to effectuate this purpose, courts should be reluctant to take cases from its protection." *Yates*, 181 So. 2d at 344.

The majority remands this case for trial so the jury can decide whether the parties entered into the alleged oral agreement. I think that in order to determine whether the alleged oral agreement was made, the jury will have to determine the terms and conditions of the alleged agreement, including what the parties intended the duration of the agreement to be. Unlike the majority, I believe those findings should determine whether the statute of frauds applies in the instant case. Finally, I would note that even Appellant requests remand for trial so the jury can decide whether the agreement was entered into and whether the parties intended it to extend beyond the year period.

I, therefore, concur in the decision to reverse the judgment in favor of Poirier and to remand this case for a new trial. Regarding the part of the majority opinion that declares the statute of frauds inapplicable, I respectfully dissent because I believe that is an issue for the trier of fact to decide.

This case ultimately came before the Florida Supreme Court to resolve the question of whether a terminable-at-will agreement to pool lottery winnings is unenforceable in the absence of an express agreement to continue the agreement for a period of time exceeding one year, when full performance of the agreement is possible within one year from the inception of the agreement. The Court answered this question in the negative, upholding the majority opinion authored by Judge Jacobus and reiterating that because the oral agreement between Browning and Poirier was of indefinite duration and could have possibly been performed within one year, it falls outside the statute of frauds. Relying on its interpretation of Yates, *the Court explained that if Browning or Poirier had purchased a winning lottery ticket and split the proceeds before the expiration of one year, the agreement would have been fully performed before the expiration of one year. Alternatively, either Browning or Poirier could have ended the agreement at any time. Thus, judging from the time the oral contract was made, nothing in the terms of their contract demonstrated that it could not be performed within one year.*

The original English Statute of Frauds required a writing for contracts for the sale of goods for a price of 10 pounds sterling or more. In the United States today, the writing requirement for the sale of goods is governed by § 2-201 of the Uniform Commercial Code. This section provides that contracts for the sale of goods for the price of $500 or more are not enforceable without a writing or other specified evidence that a contract was made. There are a number of alternative ways of satisfying the requirements of § 2-201. These will be explained later in this chapter.

Modifications of Existing Sales Contracts Just as some contracts to extend the time for performance fall within the one-year provision of the statute of frauds, agreements to modify existing sales contracts can fall within the statute of frauds if the contract as modified is for a price of $500 or more.[4] UCC § 2-209(3) provides that the requirements of the statute of frauds must be satisfied if the contract as modified is within its provisions. For example, if Carroll and Kestler enter into a contract for the sale of goods at a price of $490, the original contract does *not* fall within the statute of frauds. However, if they later modify the contract by increasing the contract price to $510, the modification falls within the statute of frauds and must meet its requirements to be enforceable.

Promise of Executor or Administrator to Pay a Decedent's Debt Personally
When a person dies, a personal representative is appointed to administer his estate. One of the important tasks of this personal representative, called an executor if the person dies leaving a will or an administrator if the person dies without a will, is to pay the debts owed by the decedent. No writing is required when an executor or administrator—acting in her representative capacity—promises to pay the decedent's debts from the funds of the decedent's estate. The statute of frauds requires a writing, however, if the executor, acting in her capacity as a private individual rather than in her representative capacity, promises to pay one of the decedent's debts out of her own (the executor's) funds. For example, Anne, who has been appointed executor of her Uncle Max's estate, is presented with a bill for $10,500 for medical services rendered to Uncle Max during his last illness by the family physician, Dr. Friend. Feeling bad that there are not adequate funds in the estate to compensate Dr. Friend for his services, Anne

---

[4]See UCC §2-209(3). Modifications of sales contracts are discussed in greater detail in Chapter 12.

Contracts within the Statute of Frauds

Provision	Description	Exceptions (Situations in Which Contract Does Not Require a Writing)
Marriage	Contracts, other than mutual promises to marry, where marriage is the consideration	–
Year	Bilateral contracts that, *by their terms*, cannot be performed within one year from the date on which the contract was formed	Full (complete) performance by one of the parties
Land	Contracts that create or transfer an ownership interest in real property	1. Full performance by vendor (vendor deeds property to vendees) or 2. "Part performance" doctrine: Vendee relies on oral contract—for example, by: a. Paying substantial part of purchase price and b. Taking possession or making improvements
Executor's promise	Executor promises to pay estate's debt out of his own funds	–
Sale of goods at price of $500 or more (UCC § 2-201)	Contracts for the sale of goods for a contract price of $500 or more; also applies to modifications of contracts for goods where price as modified is $500 or more	See alternative ways of satisfying statute of frauds under UCC
Collateral contracts guaranty	Contracts where promisor promises to pay the debt of another if the primary debtor fails to pay	"Main purpose" or "leading object" exception: Guarantor makes promise primarily for her own economic benefit

promises to pay Dr. Friend from her own funds. Anne's promise would have to be evidenced by a writing to be enforceable.

Contract in Which Marriage Is the Consideration

The statute of frauds also requires a writing when marriage is the consideration to support a contract. The marriage provision has been interpreted to be inapplicable to agreements that involve only mutual promises to marry. It can apply to any other contract in which one party's promise is given in exchange for marriage or the promise to marry on the part of the other party. This is true whether the promisor is one of the parties to the marriage or a third party. For example, if Hank promises to deed his ranch to Edna in exchange for Edna's agreement to marry Hank's son, Edna could not enforce Hank's promise without written evidence of the promise.

Prenuptial (or antenuptial) agreements present a common contemporary application of the marriage provision of the statute of frauds. These are agreements between couples who contemplate marriage. They usually involve such matters as transfers of property, division of property upon divorce or death, and various lifestyle issues. Assuming that marriage or the promise to marry is the consideration supporting these agreements, they are within the statute of frauds and must be evidenced by a writing.[5]

---

[5]Note, however, that "nonmarital" agreements between unmarried cohabitants who do not plan marriage are not within the marriage provision of the statute of frauds, even though the agreement may pertain to the same sorts of matters that are typically covered in a prenuptial agreement.

Meeting the Requirements of the Statute of Frauds

 LO16-3 Explain how to satisfy the statute of frauds under both the common law and UCC.

Nature of the Writing Required The statutes of frauds of the various states are not uniform in their formal requirements. However, most states require only a *memorandum* of the parties' agreement; they do not require that the entire contract be in writing. Essential terms of the contract must be stated in the writing. The memorandum must provide written evidence that a contract was made, but it need not have been created with the intent that the memorandum itself would be binding. In fact, in some cases, written offers that were accepted orally have been held sufficient to satisfy the writing requirement. Typical examples include letters, e-mails, telegrams, receipts, or any other writing indicating that the parties had a contract. The memorandum need not be made at the same time the contract comes into being; in fact, the memorandum may be made at any time before suit is filed. If a memorandum of the parties' agreement is lost, its loss and its contents may be proven by oral testimony.

Contents of the Memorandum Although there is a general trend away from requiring complete writings to satisfy the statute of frauds, an adequate memorandum must still contain several things. The essential terms of the contract generally must be indicated in the memorandum. States differ in their requirements concerning how specifically the terms must be stated, however. The identity of the parties must be indicated in some way, and the subject matter of the contract must be identified with reasonable certainty. This last requirement causes particular problems in contracts for the sale of land because many statutes require a detailed description of the property to be sold.

Contents of Memorandum under the UCC The standard for determining the sufficiency of the contents of a memorandum is more flexible in cases concerning contracts for the sale of goods. This looser standard is created by UCC § 2-201, which states that the writing must be sufficient to indicate that a contract for sale has been made between the parties, but that a writing can be sufficient even if it omits or incorrectly states a term agreed on. However, the memorandum is not enforceable for more than the quantity of goods stated in the memorandum. Thus, a writing that does not indicate the *quantity* of goods to be sold would not satisfy the Code's writing requirement.

Signature Requirement The memorandum must be signed by the *party to be charged* or his authorized agent. (The party to be charged is the person using the statute of frauds as a defense—generally the defendant unless the statute of frauds is asserted as a defense to a counterclaim.) This means that it is not necessary for purposes of meeting the statute of frauds for both parties' signatures to appear on the document. It is, however, in the best interests of both parties for both signatures to appear on the writing; otherwise, the contract evidenced by the writing is enforceable only against the signing party. Unless the statute expressly provides that the memorandum or contract must be signed at the end, the signature may appear anywhere on the memorandum. Any writing, mark, initials, stamp, engraving, electronic signature, or other symbol placed or printed on a memorandum will suffice as a signature, as long as the party to be charged intended it to authenticate (indicate the genuineness of) the writing.

Memorandum Consisting of Several Writings In many situations, the elements required for a memorandum are divided among several documents. For example, Wayman and Allen enter into a contract for the sale of real estate, intending to memorialize their agreement in a formal written document later. While final drafts of a written contract are being prepared, Wayman repudiates the contract. Allen has a copy of an unsigned preliminary draft of the contract that identifies the parties and contains all of the material terms of the parties' agreement, an unsigned note written by Wayman that contains the legal description of the property, and a letter signed by Wayman that refers to the contract and to the other two documents. None of these documents, standing alone, would be sufficient to satisfy the statute of frauds. However, Allen can combine them to meet the requirements of the statute, provided that they all relate to the same agreement. This can be shown by physical attachment, as where the documents are stapled or bound together, or by references in the documents indicating that they all apply to the same transaction. In some cases, it has also been shown by the fact that the various documents were executed at the same time.

 LO16-3 Explain how to satisfy the statute of frauds under both the common law and UCC.

 **LOG ON**

You can learn more about e-signatures in this article: Ennis & Green, *Electronic Signatures: Not So Fast,* **www.americanbar.org/groups/litigation/ committees/commercial-business/practice/2019/ electronic-signatures-contracts-agreements/**

UCC: Alternative Means of Satisfying the Statute of Frauds in Sale of Goods Contracts

As you have learned, the basic requirement of the UCC statute of frauds [2-201] is that a contract for the sale of goods for the purchase price of $500 or more must be evidenced by a written memorandum that indicates the existence of the contract, states the quantity of goods to be sold, and is signed by the party to be charged. Recognizing that the underlying purpose of the statute of frauds is to provide more evidence of the existence of a contract than the mere oral testimony of one of the parties, however, the Code also permits the statute of frauds to be satisfied by any of four other types of evidence. These different methods of satisfying the UCC statute of frauds are depicted in Figure 6.2. Under the UCC, then, a contract for the sale of goods for a purchase price of $500 or more is enforceable even in the absence of a suitable written memorandum, if the evidence makes applicable any of the following alternative ways of satisfying the statute of frauds:

1. *Confirmatory memorandum between merchants.* Suppose Gardner and Roth enter into a contract over the telephone for the sale of goods at a price of $5,000. Gardner then sends a memorandum to Roth confirming the deal they made orally. If Roth receives the memo and does not object to it, it would be fair to say that the parties' conduct provides some evidence that a contract exists. Under some circumstances, the UCC permits such confirmatory memoranda to satisfy the statute of frauds even though the writing is signed by the party who is seeking to enforce the contract rather than the party against whom enforcement is sought [2-201(2)]. This exception applies only when *both* of the parties to a contract are *merchants.* Furthermore, the memo must be sent within a reasonable time after the contract is made and must be sufficient to bind the person who sent it if enforcement were sought against him (that is, it must indicate that a contract was made, state a quantity, and be signed by the sender). If the party against whom enforcement is sought receives the memo, has reason to know its contents, and yet fails to give written notice of objection to the contents of the memo within 10 days after receiving it, the memo can be introduced to meet the requirements of the statute of frauds.

2. *Part payment or part delivery.* Suppose Rice and Cooper enter into a contract for the sale of 1,000 units of goods at $1 each. After Rice has paid $600, Cooper refuses to deliver the goods and asserts the statute of frauds as a defense to enforcement of the contract. The Code permits part payment or part delivery to satisfy the statute of frauds, but only for the quantity of goods that have been delivered or paid for [2-201(3)(c)]. Thus, Cooper would be required to deliver only 600 units rather than the 1,000 units Rice alleges that he agreed to sell.

3. *Admission in pleadings or court.* Another situation in which the UCC statute of frauds can be satisfied without a writing occurs when the party being sued admits the existence of the oral contract in his trial testimony or in any document that he files with the court. For example, Nelson refuses to perform an oral contract he made with Smith for the sale of $2,000 worth of goods, and Smith sues him. If Nelson admits the existence of the oral contract in pleadings or in court proceedings, his admission is sufficient to meet the statute of frauds. This exception is justified by the strong evidence that such an admission provides. After all, what better evidence of a contract can there be than is provided when the party being sued admits under penalty of perjury that a contract exists? When such an admission is made, the statute of frauds is satisfied as to the quantity of goods admitted [2-201(3)(b)]. For example, if Nelson admits contracting only for $1,000 worth of goods, the contract is enforceable only to that extent.

4. *Specially manufactured goods.* Finally, an oral contract within the UCC statute of frauds can be enforced without a writing in some situations involving the sale of specially manufactured goods. This exception to the writing requirement will apply only if the nature of the specially manufactured goods is such that they are not suitable for sale in the ordinary course of the seller's business. Completely executory oral contracts are not enforceable under this exception. The seller must have made a substantial beginning in manufacturing the goods for the buyer, or must have made commitments for their procurement, before receiving notice that the buyer was repudiating the sale [2-201(3)(a)]. For example, Bennett Co. has an oral contract with Stevenson for the sale of $2,500 worth of calendars imprinted with Bennett Co.'s name and address. If Bennett Co. repudiates the contract before Stevenson has made a substantial beginning in manufacturing the calendars, the contract will be unenforceable under the statute of frauds. If, however, Bennett Co. repudiated the contract after Stevenson had made a substantial beginning, the oral contract would be enforceable. The specially manufactured goods provision is based both on the evidentiary value of the seller's conduct and on the need to avoid the injustice that would otherwise result from the seller's reliance. The *Green Garden* case, which follows shortly, deals with whether the statute of frauds has been satisfied in regard to an oral contract for the sale of goods for at least $500.

Figure 16.2   Satisfying the Statute of Frauds through a Contract for the Sale of Goods with a Price of $500 or More

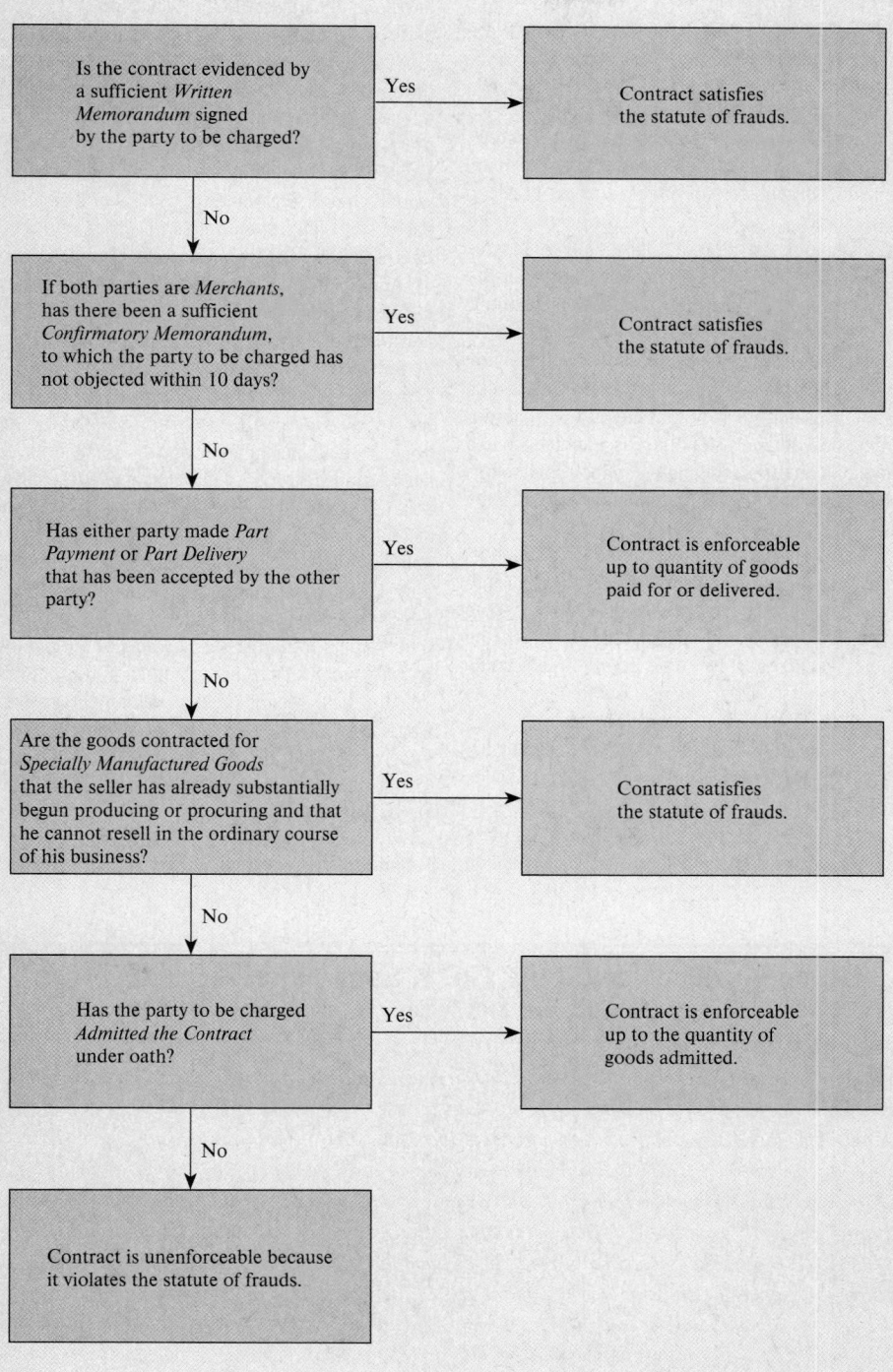

CYBERLAW IN ACTION

E-Signatures and the Statute of Frauds

The necessity of being able to prove the existence of a contract is as great online as it is in offline transactions. When we communicate or transact business online, we cannot depend on the traditional means of authenticating a contract—reading a person's distinctive signature, seeing the face, or hearing the voice of the other party, for example. Practical questions flow from this state of affairs, such as how can we be sure that a transmission arrives in the same condition as it left the sender and that it has not been altered or forged? Technologies to increase security online have been developed and new ones are emerging all the time. One method of increasing security in electronic transmissions is the use of digital signatures. A digital signature is an electronic identifier that tells a person receiving the document whether it is genuinely from the sender and whether it has been altered in any way. It is important to note that a digital signature is not an electronic image of a person's signature or a person's name typed out. Rather, digital signatures employ encryption technology to create a unique identifier for a sender that can be verified by the receiver.

The absence of traditional authentication methods raises legal questions as well, such as whether a contract formed electronically, through e-mail or on an e-tailer's website, satisfies the statute of frauds. Few courts have dealt with this issue. However, the vast majority of states have enacted some form of legislation to accommodate formal legal requirements to the realities of e-commerce. The trouble is that this legislation has not been uniform. Some states' legislation has been tied to a particular technology, such as recognizing only digital signatures as satisfying legal requirements.

The Uniform Electronic Transactions Act (UETA) takes a different approach. It is a proposed uniform state law that was designed to "remove barriers to electronic commerce by validating and effectuating electronic records and signatures."[6] It is not tied to any particular technology. The UETA states that an "electronic signature" (defined as an "electronic sound, symbol, or process attached to or logically associated with an electronic record and executed or adopted by a person with the intent to sign the electronic record") satisfies any law requiring a signature. Thus, digital signatures, which are one form of electronic signature, would satisfy the UETA, but so would a more commonplace symbol or event such as a typewritten name at the end of an e-mail or a click of a mouse. The UETA has been enacted in nearly all states and the District of Columbia.

Against the background of lack of uniformity in state law, the federal government enacted the Electronic Signatures in Global and National Commerce Act (E-Sign) in 2000. E-Sign provides that in transactions that are in or affecting interstate commerce, "a signature, contract, or other record relating to such transaction may not be denied legal effect, validity, or enforceability solely because it is in electronic form," nor can "a contract relating to such a transaction be denied legal effect, validity, or enforceability solely because an electronic signature or electronic record was used in its formation." As does the UETA, E-Sign broadly interprets the concept of electronic signature—using, in fact, the same statutory definition of electronic signature as that which is used in the UETA. E-Sign overrides any state law that is inconsistent with the UETA, thus helping to harmonize U.S. law about the interaction of formal requirements such as the statute of frauds and electronic contracts.

The most recent legal development in this area occurred in December 2018 at the federal level with passage of the 21st Century Integrated Digital Experience Act (IDEA), which required the head of each executive federal agency to accelerate use of electronic signatures under E-Sign.

[6]Uniform Electronic Transactions Act, Prefatory Note (1999).

Green Garden Packaging Co. v. Schoenmann Produce Co.
2010 Tex. App. LEXIS 8887 (Tex. Ct. App. Nov. 4, 2010)

Green Garden Packaging Co. is a wholesale producer of fresh-cut vegetables, fruits, and ready-made products, including salad kits. It develops and owns equipment, recipes, and manufacturing processes for use in producing these items. Schoenmann Produce Co. distributes fresh and packaged food items and produce to various clients, including the Houston Independent School District (HISD). In order to fulfill a produce contract it had with HISD, Schoenmann began purchasing food items from Green Garden in 2005.

In the spring of 2007, HISD was compiling competitive bids on the produce contract. According to Green Garden, Schoenmann asked Green Garden to provide its items "exclusively" to Schoenmann in exchange for Schoenmann's agreement to use Green Garden as the supplier of these items if HISD accepted Schoenmann's bid. Based upon this agreement, Green Garden provided Schoenmann detailed written information on its products for use in preparing a bid to HISD. Green Garden prepared a confidentiality notice, which provided that Green Garden's information and product specifications were "confidential" and "proprietary," and then gave samples of its products to Schoenmann. Schoenmann submitted the confidentiality notice and the samples to HISD. Schoenmann was the only distributor to submit a compliant bid, and Schoenmann won the HISD contract for a one-year term beginning in August 2007. However, Schoenmann *did not purchase food items from Green Garden to fulfill the HISD contract, and it shared Green Garden's specifications and confidential information with other suppliers.*

Green Garden sued Schoenmann, claiming that Schoenmann had breached its contract to purchase Green Garden products after using its trade secrets, samples, and other information in submitting the bid to HISD. Schoenmann filed a motion for partial summary judgment on Green Garden's breach of contract claim, arguing that it was barred as a matter of law by the statute of frauds. The trial court granted Schoenmann's summary judgment motion and Green Garden appealed.

Jennings, Justice

Schoenmann sought summary judgment under the statute of frauds for a contract for the sale of goods for the price of $500 or more. Section 2-201, which applies to a sale of goods, provides,

(a) Except as otherwise provided in this section a contract for the sale of goods for the price of $500 or more is not enforceable by way of action or defense unless there is some writing sufficient to indicate that a contract for sale has been made between the parties and signed by the party against whom enforcement is sought or by his authorized agent or broker. . . .

Here, it is undisputed that there is no writing evidencing the alleged agreement between Green Garden and Schoenmann. Moreover, the summary judgment evidence conclusively establishes that the alleged agreement that Green Garden seeks to enforce against Schoenmann was for a sale of goods that exceeded $500. Thus, § 2-201 applies to bar Green Garden's breach of contract claim, unless an exception applies.

Section 2-201 provides several statutory exceptions to the application of the statute of frauds. A contract for a sale of goods of $500 or more that does not satisfy the requirements of subsection (a) of section 2-201 but is valid in other respects is enforceable,

(1) if the goods are to be specially manufactured for the buyer and are not suitable for sale to others in the ordinary course of the seller's business and the seller, before notice of repudiation is received and under circumstances which reasonably indicate that the goods are for the buyer, has made either a substantial beginning of their manufacture or commitments for their procurement; or

(2) if the party against whom enforcement is sought admits in his pleading, testimony or otherwise in court that a contract for sale was made, but the contract is not enforceable under this provision beyond the quantity of goods admitted; or

(3) with respect to goods for which payment has been made and accepted or which have been received and accepted.

However, none of these exceptions apply in this case. Green Garden did not specially manufacture any food items, Schoenmann has not admitted that a contract for sale of these food items was ever made, and there is no evidence that any payments were made or accepted or that any food items were received or accepted by Schoenmann.

Green Garden asserts that it partially performed the contract; that "the essence of the agreement" was "the proprietary information, forms, and samples" it provided to Schoenmann during the bidding process; and that in its attempt to recover the lost profits from the produce contract, the "valuable consideration" it provided "could not possibly be separated apart from the goods that were then to be supplied if the HISD contract was obtained." However, the agreement on which Green Garden seeks recovery is, at its core, an agreement that would have required Schoenmann to purchase food items, valued well in excess of $500, from Green Garden for a minimum of a one-year term. Although Green Garden has presented evidence that it exclusively provided Schoenmann with information and samples of its products in the course of the bidding process, and although Green Garden asserts that it did this pursuant to an agreement with Schoenmann, the only consideration Green Garden sought under its alleged agreement was Schoenmann's purchase of goods from Green Garden. Such a contract plainly falls within § 2-201(a), and, without a writing to evidence the agreement, it is unenforceable under the statute of frauds. Accordingly, we hold that the trial court did not err in granting summary judgment on Green Garden's breach of contract claim.

Affirmed in favor of Schoenmann.

Promissory Estoppel and the Statute of Frauds

The statute of frauds, which was created to prevent fraud and perjury, has often been criticized because it can create unjust results. While the statute exists to defeat fictitious agreements, its harsh requirements present the possibility that it can be used to defeat a contract that was actually made. As you have seen, courts and legislatures have created several exceptions to the statute of frauds that reduce the statute's potential for creating unfair results. In recent years, courts in some states have allowed the use of the doctrine of **promissory estoppel**[7] to enable some parties to recover under oral contracts that the statute of frauds would ordinarily render unenforceable.

Courts in these states hold that, when one of the parties would suffer serious losses because of her reliance on an oral contract, the other party is estopped from raising the statute of frauds as a defense. This position has been approved in the *Restatement (Second) of Contracts*. According to § 139 of the *Restatement (Second)*, a promise that induces action or forbearance can be enforceable notwithstanding the statute of frauds if the reliance was foreseeable to the person making the promise and if injustice can be avoided only by enforcing the promise. The idea behind this section and the cases employing promissory estoppel is that the statute of frauds, which is designed to prevent injustice, should not be allowed to work an injustice. Section 139 and these cases also impliedly recognize the fact that the reliance required by promissory estoppel to some extent provides evidence of the existence of a contract between the parties because it is unlikely that a person would materially rely on a non-existent promise.

The use of promissory estoppel as a means of circumventing the statute of frauds is still controversial, however. Many courts fear that enforcing oral contracts on the basis of a party's reliance will essentially negate the statute. In cases involving the UCC statute of frauds, an additional source of concern involves the interpretation of § 2-201. Some courts have construed the provisions listing specific alternative methods of satisfying § 2-201's formal requirements to be *exclusive*, precluding the creation of any further exceptions by courts.

The Parol Evidence Rule

 LO16-4 Explain the parol evidence rule and the exceptions to the rule.

Explanation of the Rule In many situations, contracting parties prefer to express their agreements in writing even when they are not required to do so by the statute of frauds. Written contracts rarely come into being without some prior discussions or negotiations between the parties, however. Various promises, proposals, or representations are often made by one or both of the parties

before the execution of a written contract. What happens when one of those prior promises, proposals, or representations is not included in the terms of the written contract? For example, suppose that Jackson wants to buy Stone's house. During the course of negotiations, Stone states that he will pay for any major repairs that the house needs for the first year that Jackson owns it. The written contract that the parties ultimately sign, however, does not say anything about Stone paying for repairs, and, in fact, states that Jackson will take the house "as is." The furnace breaks down three months after the sale, and Stone refuses to pay for its repair. What is the status of Stone's promise to pay for repairs? The basic problem is one of defining the boundaries of the parties' agreement. Are all the promises made in the process of negotiation part of the contract, or do the terms of the written document that the parties signed supersede any preliminary agreements?

The **parol evidence** rule provides the answer to this question. The term *parol evidence* means written or spoken statements that are *not contained in the written contract*. The parol evidence rule provides that, when parties enter into a *written contract* that they intend as a complete integration (a complete and final statement of their agreement), a court will not permit the use of evidence of *prior* or *contemporaneous* statements to add to, alter, or contradict the terms of the written contract. This rule is based on the presumption that when people enter into a written contract, the best evidence of their agreement is the written contract itself. It also reflects the idea that later expressions of intent are presumed to prevail over earlier expressions of intent. In the hypothetical case involving Stone and Jackson, assuming that they intended the written contract to be the final integration of their agreement, Jackson would not be able to introduce evidence of Stone's promise to pay for repairs. The effect of excluding preliminary promises or statements from consideration is, of course, to confine the parties' contract to the terms of the written agreement. The lesson to be learned from this example is that people who put their agreements in writing should make sure that all the terms of their agreement are included in the writing. The *Yung-Kai Lu* case, which follows shortly, illustrates the application of the parol evidence rule.

Scope of the Parol Evidence Rule The parol evidence rule is relevant only in cases in which the parties have expressed their agreement in a written contract. Thus, it would not apply to a case involving an oral contract or to a case in which writings existed that were not intended to embody the final statement of

---
[7]The doctrine of promissory estoppel is discussed in Chapters 9 and 12.

at least part of the parties' contract. The parol evidence rule has been made a part of the law of sales in the Uniform Commercial Code [2-202], so it is applicable to contracts for the sale of goods as well as to contracts governed by the common law of contracts. Furthermore, the rule excludes only evidence of statements made *prior to* or *during* the signing of the written contract. It does not apply to statements made after the signing of the contract. Thus, evidence of subsequent statements is freely admissible.

 LO16-4 Explain the parol evidence rule and the exceptions to the rule.

Admissible Parol Evidence

In some situations, evidence of statements made outside the written contract is admissible notwithstanding the parol evidence rule. Parol evidence is permitted in the situations discussed below either because the writing is not the best evidence of the contract or because the evidence is offered, not to contradict the terms of the writing, but to explain the writing or to challenge the underlying contractual obligation that the writing represents.

1. *Additional terms in partially integrated contracts.* In many instances, parties will desire to introduce evidence of statements or agreements that would supplement rather than contradict the written contract. Whether they can do this depends on whether the written contract is characterized as *completely integrated* or *partially integrated*. A completely integrated contract is one that the parties intend as a *complete and exclusive statement* of their entire agreement. A partially integrated contract is one that expresses the parties' final agreement as to some but not all of the terms of their contract. When a contract is only partially integrated, the parties are permitted to use parol evidence to prove the *additional* terms of their agreement. Such evidence cannot, however, be used to contradict the written terms of the contract.

To determine whether a contract is completely or partially integrated, a court must determine the parties' intent. A court judges intent by looking at the language of the contract, the apparent completeness of the writing, and all the surrounding circumstances. It will also consider whether the contract contains a **merger clause** (also known as an integration clause). These clauses, which are very common in form contracts and commercial contracts, provide that the written contract is the complete integration of the parties' agreement. They are designed to prevent a party from giving testimony about prior statements or agreements and are generally effective

in indicating that the writing was a complete integration. However, even if a contract contains a merger clause, parol evidence could be admissible when one of the following exceptions applies.

2. *Explaining ambiguities.* Parol evidence can be offered to explain an ambiguity in the written contract. Suppose a written contract between Lowen and Matthews provides that Lowen will buy "Matthews's truck," but Matthews has two trucks. The parties could offer evidence of negotiations, statements, and other circumstances preceding the creation of the written contract to identify the truck to which the writing refers. Used in this way, parol evidence helps the court interpret the contract. It does not contradict the written contract.

3. *Circumstances invalidating contract.* Any circumstances that would be relevant to show that a contract is not valid can be proven by parol evidence. For example, evidence that Holden pointed a gun at Dickson and said, "Sign this contract, or I'll kill you," would be admissible to show that the contract was voidable because of duress. Likewise, parol evidence would be admissible to show that a contract was illegal or was induced by fraud, misrepresentation, undue influence, or mistake.

4. *Existence of condition.* It is also permissible to use parol evidence to show that a writing was executed with the understanding that it was *not to take effect until the occurrence of a condition* (a future, uncertain event that creates a duty to perform). Suppose Farnsworth signs a contract to purchase a car with the agreement that the contract is not to be effective unless and until Farnsworth gets a new job. If the written contract is silent about any conditions that must occur before it becomes effective, Farnsworth could introduce parol evidence to prove the existence of the condition. Such proof merely elaborates on, but does not contradict, the terms of the writing.

5. *Subsequent agreements.* As you read earlier, the parol evidence rule does not forbid parties to introduce proof of *subsequent agreements.* This is true even if the terms of the later agreement cancel, subtract from, or add to the obligations stated in the written contract. The idea here is that when a writing is followed by a later statement or agreement, the writing is no longer the best evidence of the agreement. You should be aware, however, that subsequent modifications of contracts may sometimes be unenforceable because of lack of consideration or failure to comply with the statute of frauds. In addition, contracts sometimes expressly provide that modifications must be written. In this situation, an oral modification would be unenforceable.

Parol Evidence Rule

Parol Evidence Rule	Applies when:	Provides that:
	Parties create a writing intended as a final and complete integration of at least part of the parties' contract.	Evidence of statements of promises made before or during the creation of the writing cannot be used to supplement, change, or contradict the terms of the written contract.
But parol evidence *can* be used to	1. Prove consistent, additional terms when the contract is *partially integrated*. 2. Explain an ambiguity in the written contract. 3. Prove that the contract is void, voidable, or unenforceable. 4. Prove that the contract was subject to a condition. 5. Prove that the parties subsequently modified the contract or made a new agreement.	

Yung-Kai Lu v. University of Utah   660 Fed. App'x. 573 (10th Cir. 2016)

The University of Utah entered into a written agreement with Yung-Kai Lu, a citizen of Taiwan, in May 2010, agreeing to give him a doctoral-studies scholarship in return for Lu's agreement to be a teaching assistant (the "contract"). The contract specified that scholarships and teaching assistant appointments are limited to "one academic year at a time" and that Lu's appointment was "a nine-month appointment beginning August 16, 2010, and ending May 15, 2011." Despite this limitation, Lu alleged that University Assistant Music Director Donn Schaefer verbally promised him that as long as he maintained a 3.00 GPA, the assistantship and scholarship would be renewed for the full three years Lu planned to study for his doctorate.

In April 2011, Schaefer told Lu the contract wouldn't be renewed because the university lacked sufficient funding. According to Lu, however, he was told the contract wouldn't be renewed because of a report to university officials that he had been rude. Lu didn't re-enroll for the next academic term, and his failure to enroll was reported to immigration officials. As a result, Lu's visa wasn't extended and he was deported to Taiwan.

Lu's complaint against the university and university officials in their official capacities alleged they breached the contract and verbal promises, in addition to tort claims for slander, false statements, providing inaccurate information to immigration officials, and violations of the Taiwan Relations Act and International Covenant on Economic, Social and Cultural Rights.

The defendants moved to dismiss the suit on the basis that Lu's complaint failed to state any plausible claim as a matter of law.

The trial court granted defendants' motion, finding Lu lacked any plausible claim under international treaties and his tort claims were barred under the Eleventh Amendment and the Utah Governmental Immunity Act. Further, the court concluded that Lu failed to allege any plausible breach of contract claims given the contract's unambiguous language as to the term of the contract. Additionally, the court reasoned that Utah's parol evidence rule and statute of frauds barred any verbal promise to extend Lu's appointment for three years.

Lu made his appeal to the 10th Circuit Court of Appeals pro se.

Moritz, Judge

To survive a motion to dismiss, a complaint must contain sufficient factual matter, accepted as true, "to state a claim to relief that is plausible on its face" (citations omitted). . . . Because Lu proceeds pro se, we construe his complaint liberally, but pro se parties are "not relieved of the burden of alleging sufficient facts on which a recognized legal claim could be based" (citations omitted).

[The court dispensed with all ancillary legal allegations and then considered Lu's contract-based claims.]

Lu challenges the dismissal of his breach of contract claims. He argues Utah's parol evidence rule doesn't apply because the contract was an incomplete integrated contract. Contrary to Lu's suggestion, the contract contained a complete, final expression as to the length of Lu's scholarship and teaching assistant appointment. *See Tangren Family Tr. v. Tangren*, 182 P.3d 326, 330 (Utah 2008) (defining an integrated agreement as "a writing . . . constituting a final expression of one or more terms of an agreement" and holding that an agreement reduced to writing is "conclusively presumed" to contain "the whole of the agreement between the parties"). Thus, the district court correctly ruled Utah's parol evidence rule would bar admission of any pre-contract verbal agreement to extend the appointment past May 15, 2011.

Citing language in the contract limiting doctoral students to three-year teaching assistant appointments, Lu argues the district court erred in applying the statute of frauds to bar his breach of contract claim. But the language Lu relies on does not bind the parties to renewing the appointment for three years; instead, it simply states the outside limit on such reappointments. Thus, the district court correctly ruled that evidence of a verbal agreement to renew his appointment for two years after the May 2011 termination date would be barred by Utah's statute of frauds. . . .

Having found no error in the district court's dismissal of Lu's complaint, we affirm the dismissal for substantially the reasons stated by the district court in its order dated October 7, 2015.

Judgment affirmed.

Interpretation of Contracts

Once a court has decided what promises are included in a contract, it is faced with *interpreting* the contract to determine the meaning and legal effect of the terms used by the parties. Courts have adopted broad, basic standards of interpretation that guide them in the interpretation process.

The court will first attempt to determine the parties' *principal objective*. Every clause will then be determined in the light of this principal objective. Ordinary words will be given their usual meaning and technical words (such as those that have a special meaning in the parties' trade or business) will be given their technical meaning, unless a different meaning was clearly intended.

Guidelines grounded in common sense are also used to determine the relationship of the various terms of the contract. Specific terms that follow general terms are presumed to qualify those general terms. Suppose that a provision that states that the subject of the contract is "guaranteed for one year" is followed by a provision describing the "one-year guarantee against defects in workmanship." Here, it is fair to conclude that the more specific term qualifies the more general term and that the guarantee described in the contract is a guarantee of workmanship only, and not of parts and materials.

Sometimes, there is internal conflict in the terms of an agreement and courts must determine which term should prevail. When the parties use a form contract or some other type of contract that is partially printed and partially handwritten, the handwritten provisions will prevail. If the contract was drafted by one of the parties, any ambiguities will be resolved against the party who drafted the contract.

If both parties to the contract are members of a trade, profession, or community in which certain words are commonly given a particular meaning (this is called a *usage*), the courts will presume that the parties intended the meaning that the usage gives to the terms they use. For example, if the word *dozen* in the bakery business means 13 rather than 12, a contract between two bakers for the purchase of 10 dozen loaves of bread will be presumed to mean 130 loaves of bread rather than 120. Usages can also add provisions to the parties' agreement. If the court finds that a certain practice is a matter of common usage in the parties' trade, it will assume that the parties intended to include that practice in their agreement. If contracting parties are members of the same trade, business, or community but do not intend to be bound by usage, they should specifically say so in their agreement.

Ethics and Compliance in Action

For those who draft and present standardized form contracts to the other contracting party, the parol evidence rule can be a powerful ally because it has the effect of limiting the scope of an integrated, written contract to the terms of the writing. Although statements and promises made to a person before she signs a contract might be highly influential in persuading her to enter the contract, the parol evidence rule effectively prevents these precontract communications from being legally enforceable. Consider also that standardized form contracts are usually drafted by, and for the benefit of, the more sophisticated and powerful party in a contract (e.g., the landlord rather than the tenant, the bank rather than the customer). Considering all of this, do you believe that the parol evidence rule promotes ethical behavior?

Problems and Problem Cases

1. In August 2003, R.F. Cunningham & Co., a farm products dealer, and Driscoll, a farmer in Cayuga County, entered into an oral contract for the sale of 4,000 bushels of soybeans at a price of $5.50 per bushel, to be picked up after harvest time. Immediately afterward, Cunningham sent to Driscoll a "purchase confirmation," and Driscoll did not object to its contents. In October 2003, with his attorney asserting that he had no legal obligation to perform, Driscoll refused to sell his soybeans to Cunningham. As a result, Cunningham was forced to purchase replacement soybeans at the then-prevailing market price of $7.74 per bushel. Cunningham suffered a financial loss of $8,960.00, which was the difference between the contract price and Cunningham's costs to obtain the replacement soybeans. Cunningham sued Driscoll for breach of contract. Driscoll moved for summary judgment on the ground that the contract did not satisfy the statute of frauds. Did he win?

2. In July 2008, the Fuglebergs agreed to purchase from Triangle Ag 352.5 tons of urea fertilizer at a cost of $660 per ton and 135 tons of MES-15 fertilizer at a cost of $1,100 per ton. No terms of the contract were put in writing. The Fuglebergs prepaid the $381,150 purchase amount. The Fuglebergs later contended that Triangle's agents told them at the time they agreed to the purchase that they could rescind the contract at any time by remitting $50 for each ton of undelivered fertilizer plus payment of accrued interest. In November 2008, the Fuglebergs attempted to rescind the contract with Triangle, but Triangle refused to cancel the contract, stating that it had already ordered the fertilizer. The Fuglebergs filed suit against Triangle for rescission and other claims. Both parties admitted the existence of the contract in court. One of Triangle's defenses was that the statute of frauds barred the Fuglebergs' contract claims. Did it?

3. On two occasions in 1980, Hodge met with Tilley, president and chief operating officer of Evans Financial Corporation, to discuss Hodge's possible employment by Evans. Hodge was 54 years old at that time and was assistant counsel and assistant secretary of Mellon National Corporation and Mellon Bank of Pittsburgh. During these discussions, Tilley asked Hodge what his conditions were for accepting employment with Evans, and Hodge replied, "Number 1, the job must be permanent. Because of my age, I have a great fear about going back into the marketplace again. I want to be here until I retire." Tilley allegedly responded, "I accept that condition." Regarding his retirement plans, Hodge later testified, "I really questioned whether I was going to go much beyond 65." Hodge later accepted Evans's offer of employment as vice president and general counsel. He moved from Pittsburgh to Washington, D.C., in September 1980 and worked for Evans from that time until he was fired by Tilley on May 7, 1981. Hodge brought a breach of contract lawsuit against Evans. Evans argued that the oral contract was unenforceable because of the statute of frauds. Was Evans correct?

4. Wintersport Ltd. contacted Millionaire.com Inc. to offer advertising, production, and printing services for Millionaire.com's magazine, *Opulence*. Wintersport and Millionaire.com entered into a $170,000 contract for the printing of one monthly issue in October 2000. They performed that contract and launched negotiations to print the next month's issue. Strong, senior vice president of Millionaire.com, and Leiter, president of Wintersport, handled most of the negotiations and communications. Due to financial difficulties, Millionaire.com reduced the size of its order for the second issue and requested payment terms on the reduced price of $80,000. Concerned about Millionaire.com's creditworthiness, Leiter told Strong that Wintersport would extend credit to Millionaire.com only if Millionaire.com paid a $10,000 down payment and Millionaire.com's CEO (White) personally guaranteed the balance due. During a phone call between their respective offices in Washington and South Carolina, Leiter requested and received White's oral agreement to the personal guaranty. Leiter then sent a confirming fax to White's office, and White express mailed to Wintersport a $10,000 check drawn on Millionaire.com's account. When Millionaire.com failed to pay the amount due on the contract, Wintersport filed suit against White and others. White argued that the action should have been dismissed because the statute of frauds prevented the enforcement of his oral guaranty. Was he correct?

5. Carrow owned a farm and Arnold and Mitchell, who were partners in a real estate partnership, were interested in buying it. In mid-April 2003, they met with Carrow at his farm. At this meeting, Carrow expressed reservations about selling the farm. Arnold offered Carrow $1.2 million for the farm, but Carrow declined. During their discussions, Arnold told Carrow that if he sold Arnold the farm, he could continue to live on the farm and till the land as long as Arnold owned it. Approximately a week later, Arnold and Mitchell returned to the farm and negotiated with Carrow over the terms and conditions of a sale. During these negotiations,

Carrow again expressed reservations about selling the farm because he did not want to leave it. Carrow testified that Arnold assured him that "Nothing would ever change for you, nothing. . . ." and that Carrow could "go right on farming this farm the rest of your life. . . ." Carrow claimed that Arnold assured him that he wanted to buy the land to use strictly as a hunting farm. He understood this to mean that Arnold did not intend to develop the property or to transfer it any time in the near future. Carrow later testified that he would not have sold the farm without these representations. Arnold admitted that during various stages of the negotiations he assured Carrow that Carrow could continue to live on and farm the land and that he would never develop it. He also agreed that he told Carrow that he wanted the land for hunting purposes. According to Arnold, however, in making this and other assurances to Carrow, he always included the qualifier "as long as I own it."

After some bargaining, Carrow agreed to sell the farm to Arnold for $1.4 million, not including the farm equipment. Arnold returned to the farm and left a draft of a written contract with Carrow. Carrow put the contract on a shelf and did not discuss it with anyone for approximately one week. Although he saw provisions in the draft agreement that he did not like, he did not pay too much attention to it and did not "look at [the agreement] like I should have." Carrow did not seek the advice of an attorney or tell his adult children that he was selling the farm. He instead sought the assistance of his accountant. In late April, Carrow and Arnold met in the accountant's office to discuss the proposed contract. Carrow expressed reservations about certain provisions in the contract, and the parties changed those provisions in response to Carrow's concerns. At the conclusion of the meeting, the parties signed the Agreement and Arnold gave Carrow a $200,000 deposit. Within days of executing the Agreement, Arnold and Mitchell began to have the land surveyed for subdivision. Mitchell submitted plans to county officials to have the land approved for residential development. Arnold and Mitchell testified that they never had any intention to develop the land, but submitted the plans to the county because the land would be more valuable if approved for residential development. By early May, Carrow was having reservations about selling his farm, so he called Arnold and told him that he wanted to return the deposit. Arnold replied that Carrow could not back out of the deal. Carrow asserted that he did not know Arnold and Mitchell were professional real estate developers and that he began to reconsider the

agreement after he saw surveyors on various parts of the property. Carrow sued Arnold and Mitchell based on the representations made to him before the contract was signed. Was he successful?

6. According to the Chavezes, they entered into a May 1998 verbal agreement with Bravo to purchase a home located in Alamo, Texas, for $65,000, payable through a $2,000 down payment and monthly installments of $500. The Chavezes moved into the home and made monthly payments to Bravo from June 1998 until December 2005. They also made a number of repairs. When Bravo died, his widow sold the Alamo home to Cantu. After obtaining ownership of the home, Cantu gave the Chavezes notice to vacate the premises. Cantu and Mrs. Bravo claimed that the monthly payments from the Chavezes were rent and that no contract of sale was ever consummated. The Chavezes filed suit against Mrs. Bravo and Cantu, seeking a determination that they had an enforceable contract with Bravo and were wrongfully evicted. Cantu and Mrs. Bravo asserted that the statute of frauds barred enforcement of any contract. The Chavezes claimed that they provided partial performance, making the oral contract valid. Did the Chavezes win?

7. John Jacobs, the owner of Sataria Distribution and Packaging, met with Mark Hinkel in August 2005 to discuss the possibility that Hinkel might go to work for Sataria instead of continuing to work for the two companies that employed him. Although Jacobs offered Hinkel a job with Sataria, Hinkel had reservations. According to Hinkel, Jacobs told him, "Mark, are you worried that I'll f*** you? If so, and things don't work, I'll pay you one year's salary and cover your insurance for one year as well. But let me make it clear, should you decide this is not for you, and you terminate your own employment, then the agreement is off." Jacobs later sent Hinkel the following written job offer:

> Dear Mark,
>
> This is written as an offer of employment. The terms are as described below:
>
> 1. Annual Compensation: $120,000
> 2. Work Location: Belmont Facility
> 3. Initial Position: Supervisor Receiving Team
> 4. Start Date: 08/19/2005
> 5. Paid Vacation: To be determined
> 6. Health Insurance: Coverage begins 09/01/2005 pending proper enrollment submission
>
> Please sign and return.

Hinkel signed the offer, returned it to Jacobs, and resigned from his two other jobs. He began working at Sataria in September 2005. Hinkel claimed in the lawsuit referred to later that Jacobs reiterated the above-noted severance promise in November 2005. Sataria terminated Hinkel's employment on January 23, 2006. Thereafter, Sataria paid Hinkel six weeks of severance compensation. Hinkel sued Sataria for breach of contract, claiming that Sataria owed him the full severance package that Jacobs promised him in August and again in November. The trial court granted Sataria's motion for summary judgment. Was the court correct in doing so?

8. In July 2004, the Harrises entered into a contract with the Hallbergs to purchase the Hallbergs' home in Waccabuc, New York, for the sum of $1.9 million. Later, the Harrises had second thoughts about the purchase. In November 2004, the Harrises and the Hallbergs signed an agreement that provided that, upon the forfeiture of the Harrises' down payment, "all contractual obligations" that the parties owed each other under the contract of sale would be terminated and each party would "have no further obligation" toward the other. The release was consistent with the terms of the contract of sale, which had specified the Hallbergs' remedy in the event of a default by the Harrises. Both parties were represented by independent counsel during the transaction. Mr. Harris was a lawyer. Later, the Harrises alleged that prior to signing the release, the parties entered into an oral agreement whereby the Hallbergs agreed that if they could sell the property for more than $1.9 million, they would return all or part of the Harrises' down payment. The Harrises alleged that the Hallbergs sold the property for $2.4 million but had refused to return any part of the down payment. Did the Harrises have the legal right to enforce the alleged oral agreement for the return of the down payment?

9. Roose hired the law firm of Gallagher, Langlas, and Gallagher P.C. to represent her in her divorce. Langlas, an attorney in the firm, signed an attorney fee contract and gave it to Roose to sign and return. He also requested a $2,000 retainer fee. Roose never signed or returned the contract and did not pay the retainer fee in full. The firm represented Roose even though she did not sign the contract or pay the retainer fee in full. In April 1995, the Gallagher attorneys met with Roose and her father, Burco. The attorneys told Burco that the expense of his daughter's child custody trial would be approximately $1,000 per day. The firm would not guarantee Burco

that the trial would last for only two or three days. The firm later contended that during the meeting, Burco gave the firm a check for $1,000 to pay the outstanding balance on Roose's account and said he would pay for future services. Before the trial, an attorney with the firm contacted Burco and requested an additional retainer to secure fees to be incurred. Burco told her, "My word as a gentleman should be enough . . . I told Mr. Langlas I would pay and I will pay." Roose failed to pay her legal fees. In July 1995, the attorneys sent Burco a letter requesting either $5,000 for Roose's legal fees or the signing of a promissory note. At the end of July 1995, they sent Burco another letter asking him to sign a promissory note for $10,000. Neither Roose nor Burco paid the fees or signed the note. The firm represented Roose in the July 1995 trial. Burco took an active part in the trial by testifying and participating in conferences with counsel during recesses. After trial, Burco returned the second letter and promissory note with a notation stating that he was not responsible for his daughter's attorney fees. The firm sued Roose and Burco for the unpaid fees. Was Burco legally responsible for the fees?

10. Rosenfeld, an art dealer, claimed that Jean-Michel Basquiat, an acclaimed neoexpressionist artist, had agreed to sell her three paintings titled *Separation of the "K," Atlas*, and *Untitled Head*. She claimed that she went to Basquiat's apartment on October 25, 1982; that while she was there he agreed to sell her three paintings for $4,000 each; and that she picked out the three works. According to Rosenfeld, Basquiat asked for a cash deposit of 10 percent. She left his loft and later returned with $1,000 in cash, which she paid him. When she asked for a receipt, he insisted on drawing up a "contract," and got down on the floor and wrote it out in crayon on a large piece of paper, remarking that "some day this contract will be worth money." She identified a handwritten document listing the three paintings, bearing her signature and that of Basquiat, which stated: "$12,000–$1,000 DEPOSIT–OCT 25 82." Was this writing sufficient to satisfy the statute of frauds?

11. St. Jude Medical S.C. is a medical device manufacturer. In July 2001, Jennifer Schaadt began working as a product manager in St. Jude's Cardiac Rhythm Management Division. By all accounts, she performed well. Eventually, however, she became frustrated by what she regarded as sexual harassment and other sex discrimination within her division, so she applied for and obtained a position in St. Jude's

U.S. Sales Division (USD). Schaadt began working in USD as a field marketing manager in May 2004. Shortly after she started her new position, upper management in USD asked Schaadt and all other field marketing managers to sign a written contract containing nonsolicitation and confidentiality provisions. In return for agreeing to those provisions, the field marketing managers—who otherwise would have been employees at will—were to be given one-year terms of employment. The contract required St. Jude to employ Schaadt for a minimum of one year and prohibited Schaadt from soliciting St. Jude's employees for one year after the termination of her employment with St. Jude. USD provided the agreement to Schaadt and asked her to sign it. Schaadt alleged in the litigation referred to below that she signed the agreement, but there was no proof that any representative of St. Jude signed it.

After Schaadt had conflicts with her supervisor in USD, she began looking for another job. Before Schaadt could obtain other employment, however, she was fired. The firing occurred less than one year from the time of the agreement referred to above. Schaadt sued St. Jude for breach of contract. St. Jude moved for summary judgment on the ground that Schaadt's breach of contract claim was barred by the statute of frauds. How did the court rule?

12. In July 2002, attorneys Linscott, Shasteen, and Brock formed a law firm and two years later drafted a proposed shareholder agreement specifying how attorney fees would be divided if any of the three left the firm. The proposed agreement contemplated that the departing attorney would receive a one-third share of all fees collected from existing in-process, open cases and that the firm would receive two-thirds. The proposed agreement was never executed, and in 2004 Linscott left the firm at the request of Shasteen and Brock, who offered to honor the proposed agreement for distribution of fees. From September 17, 2004, through January 10, 2005, Linscott sent 42 fee checks to Shasteen and Brock. Likewise, starting on September 20, 2004, and continuing through December 28, 2004, Shasteen and Brock sent 26 fee checks to Linscott. According to Brock, the exchange of fees was done without his knowledge, and when he learned of the arrangement, he ordered it to stop. Shasteen and Brock ceased sending checks on December 28, 2004, and Linscott filed a breach of contract lawsuit. In court, Shasteen and Brock argued that any implied contract was void under the statute of frauds as the time period from the break-up of the firm until the time of trial was over seven years. Based on these facts, was there an implied contract and could it have been performed within one year?

13. HVAC Inc., a contractor that installs and services air handling equipment, was sued by Jacco & Associates for breach of contract after HVAC canceled an order and refused to pay the $23,000 cancelation fee. In court, HVAC argued that certain delivery obligations (not specified in the original contract) had not been met by Jacco, and thus, HVAC had a valid defense for canceling the order and refusing to pay Jacco's fee. Jacco argued that HVAC's claims regarding failure to deliver by a certain date constituted parol evidence not permissible in light of the contract's "Terms and Conditions for Sale" provision, which stated: "The terms and conditions stated herein constitute the full understanding between Jacco & Associates and the buyer, and no terms, conditions, understanding or agreement purporting to modify or vary these terms shall be binding unless hereafter made in writing by Jacco and the buyer." Furthermore, the contract also included a provision that "Jacco & Associates does not guarantee a particular date of shipment or delivery." If Jacco is successful in court, what will be the court's rationale?

Rights of Third Parties

Peterson was employed by Post-Network as a newscaster-anchor on station WTOP-TV Channel 9 under a three-year employment contract with two additional one-year terms at the option of Post-Network. During the first year of Peterson's employment, Post-Network sold its operation license to Evening News in a sale that provided for the assignment of all contracts, including Peterson's employment contract. Peterson continued working for the station for more than a year after the change of ownership but then found a job at a competing station and resigned. Evening News sued Peterson for breach of the employment contract.

- Can a person who was not an original party to a contract sue to enforce it?
- Was the assignment of Peterson's employment contract a valid transfer, or does Peterson have a right not to have his employment transferred to another employer?
- Does Peterson have any right to enforce the contract between Post-Network and Evening News?
- Would it be ethical for Evening News to prevent Peterson from changing jobs and working for a competing station?

LO LEARNING OBJECTIVES

After studying this chapter, you should be able to:

17-1 Explain the concept of assignment and the consequences of an assignment.

17-2 Explain the concept of delegation and the consequences of a delegation.

17-3 Explain the concept of third-party beneficiary and distinguish among the three kinds of third-party beneficiaries.

IN PRECEDING CHAPTERS, WE have emphasized the way in which an agreement between two or more people creates legal rights and duties *on the part of the contracting parties.* Because a contract is founded on the consent of the contracting parties, it might seem to follow that they are the only ones who have rights and duties under the contract. Although this is generally true, there are two situations in which people who were not parties to a contract have legally enforceable rights under it: when a contract has been *assigned* (transferred) to a third party and when a contract is *intended to benefit a third person* (a *third-party beneficiary*). This chapter discusses the circumstances in which third parties have rights under a contract.

Assignment of Contracts

 L017-1 Explain the concept of assignment and the consequences of an assignment.

Contracts give people both rights and duties. If Murphy buys Wagner's motorcycle and promises to pay him $1,000 for it, Wagner has the *right* to receive Murphy's promised performance (the payment of the $1,000), and Murphy has the *duty* to perform the promise by paying $1,000. In most situations, contract rights can be transferred to a third person and contract duties can be delegated to a third person.

The transfer of a *right* under a contract is called an **assignment**. The appointment of another person to perform a *duty* under a contract is called a **delegation**.

Nature of Assignment of Rights

A person who owes a duty to perform under a contract is called an **obligor**. The person to whom he owes the duty is called the **obligee**. For example, Samson borrows $500 from Jordan, promising to repay Jordan in six months. Samson, who owes the duty to pay the money, is the obligor, and Jordan, who has the right to receive the money, is the obligee. An assignment occurs when the obligee transfers his right to receive the obligor's performance to a third person. When there has been an assignment, the person making the assignment—the original obligee—is then called the **assignor**. The person to whom the right has been transferred is called the **assignee**. Figure 17.1 summarizes these key terms.

Suppose that Jordan, the obligee in the example above, assigns his right to receive Samson's payment to Kane. Here, Jordan is the assignor and Kane is the assignee. The relationship between the three parties is represented in Figure 17.2. Notice that the assignment is a separate transaction: It occurs after the formation of the original contract.

The effect of the assignment is to extinguish the assignor's right to receive performance and to transfer that right to the assignee. In the above example, Kane now owns the right to collect payment from Samson. If Samson fails to pay, Kane, as an assignee, now has the right to file suit against Samson to collect the debt.

People assign rights for a variety of reasons. A person might assign a right to a third party to satisfy a debt that he owes. For example, Jordan, the assignor in the above example, owes money to Kane, so he assigns to Kane the right to receive the $500 that Samson owes him. A person might also sell or pledge the rights owed to him to obtain financing. In the case of a business, the money owed to the business by customers and clients is called *accounts receivable*. A business's accounts receivable are an asset to the business that can be used to raise money in several ways. For example, the business may pledge its accounts receivable as collateral for a loan. Suppose Ace Tree Trimming Co. wants to borrow money from First Bank and gives First Bank a security interest (an interest in the debtor's property that secures the debtor's performance of an obligation) in its accounts receivable.[1] If Ace defaults in its payments to First Bank, First Bank will acquire Ace's rights to collect the accounts receivable. A person might also make an assignment of a contract right as a gift. For example, Lansing owes $2,000 to Father. Father assigns the right to receive Lansing's performance to Son as a graduation gift.

Evolution of the Law Regarding Assignments Contract rights have not always been transferable. Early common law refused to permit assignment or delegation because debts were considered to be too personal to transfer. A debtor who failed to pay an honest debt was subject to severe penalties, including imprisonment, because such a failure to pay was viewed as the equivalent of theft.

Figure 17.1 Assignment: Key Terms

Obligor	Obligee	Assignment	Assignor	Assignee
Person who owes the duty to perform	Person who has the right to receive obligor's performance	Transfer of the right to receive obligor's performance	Obligee who transfers the right to receive obligor's performance	Person to whom the right to receive obligor's performance is transferred

Figure 17.2 Assignment

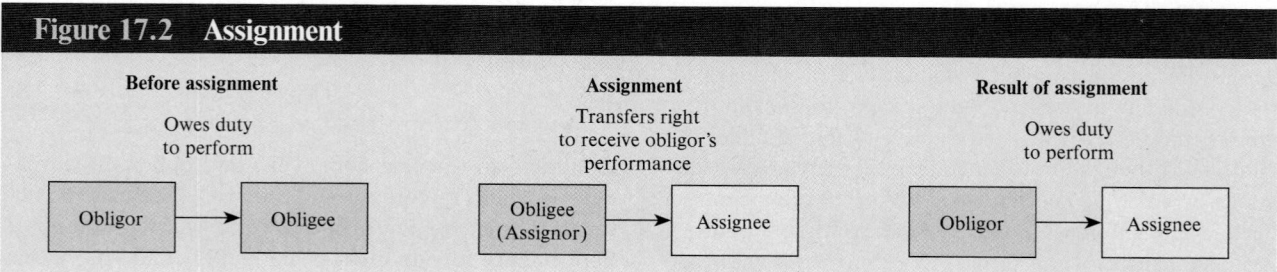

Before assignment	Assignment	Result of assignment
Owes duty to perform	Transfers right to receive obligor's performance	Owes duty to perform
Obligor → Obligee	Obligee (Assignor) → Assignee	Obligor → Assignee

[1]Security interests in accounts and other property are discussed in Chapter 29.

The identity of the creditor was of great importance to the debtor because one creditor might be more lenient than another. Courts also feared that the assignment of debts would stir up unwanted litigation. In an economy that was primarily land-based, the extension of credit was of relatively small importance. As trade increased and became more complex, however, the practice of extending credit became more common. The needs of an increasingly commercial society demanded that people be able to trade freely in intangible assets such as debts. Consequently, the rules of law regarding the assignment of contracts gradually became more liberal. Today, public policy favors free assignability of contracts.

Sources of Assignment Law Today Legal principles regarding assignment are found not only in the common law of contracts but also in Articles 2 and 9 of the Uniform Commercial Code. Section 2-210 of Article 2 contains principles applicable to assignments of rights under a contract for the sale of *goods*. Article 9 governs security interests in accounts and other contract rights as well as the outright sale of accounts. Article 9's treatment of assignments will be discussed in more detail in Chapter 29, Security Interests in Personal Property, but some provisions of Article 9 relating to assignments will be discussed in this chapter.

Creating an Assignment
An assignment can be made in any way that is sufficient to show the assignor's intent to assign. No formal language is required, and a writing is not necessary unless required by a provision of the statute of frauds or some other statute. Many states do have statutes requiring certain types of assignments to be evidenced by a writing, however. Additionally, an assignment for the purposes of security must meet Article 9's formal requirements for security interests.[2]

It is not necessary that the assignee give any consideration to the assignor in exchange for the assignment. Gratuitous assignments (those for which the assignee gives no value) are generally revocable until such time as the obligor satisfies the obligation, however. They can be revoked by the assignor's death or incapacity or by notification of revocation given by the assignor to the assignee.

Assignability of Rights
Most, but not all, contract rights are assignable. Although the free assignability of contract rights performs a valuable function in our modern credit-based economy, assignment is undesirable if it would adversely affect some important public policy or if it would materially vary the bargained-for expectations of the parties. There are several basic limitations on the assignability of contract rights.

First, an assignment will not be effective if it is *contrary to public policy*. For example, most states have enacted statutes that prohibit or regulate a wage earner's assignment of future wages. These statutes are designed to protect people against unwisely impoverishing themselves by signing away their future incomes. State law may prohibit assignment of lottery prizes or certain kinds of lawsuits on grounds of public policy. The court in the following *Sogeti USA* case considers if an assignment of a noncompete agreement to a successor employer violates public policy when the employee never agreed to the assignment.

----
[2]These requirements are discussed in Chapter 29.

Sogeti USA LLC v. Scariano   606 F. Supp. 2d 1080 (D. Ariz. 2009)

Christian Martinez was originally employed by Software Architects Inc. (SARK), with whom he signed an employment agreement containing a noncompetition provision (restrictive covenant). The provision said nothing about assignability. Sogeti acquired SARK in March 2007. Martinez became Sogeti's employee at that time. While Sogeti was not a party to the employment agreement between SARK and Martinez, it alleges that SARK's rights under the restrictive covenant were assigned to Sogeti as part of the acquisition.

Martinez resigned his employment with Sogeti in 2008 and went to work for Neudesic LLC a few days afterward. Sogeti sued Martinez and others, alleging that Martinez violated the restrictive covenant by working for Neudesic and recruiting Sogeti's employees to do the same. The defendants filed a motion to dismiss for failure to state a claim, arguing that Martinez's express consent was required for a valid assignment of his employment contract.

Silver, U.S. District Judge

Whether an employee's express consent is required before an employment contract can be assigned to a successor company employer is a question of first impression in Arizona. Under Arizona law, contractual rights are generally assignable unless the assignment is precluded by the contract, is forbidden by public policy, or materially alters the duties of the obligor. Moreover, an obligor's assent is not necessary to make an assignment effective.

Jurisdictions outside Arizona disagree on whether an employee must consent to the assignment of a restrictive covenant prior to enforcement by a successor company.

a. Jurisdictions Requiring Express Consent

Some jurisdictions require express consent because a restrictive covenant contained in an employment agreement is "personal" to the employee. The jurisdictions do not explicitly define "personal" as used in this context. However, the term appears to refer to a contract in which the promisor (employee) agrees to limit a right so fundamental to his liberty that the law presumes the promisor only agreed to bind himself in that way because the promisor knows and trusts the identity of the promisee (employer). Addressing the issue as a matter of first impression, the Supreme Court of Nevada held a restrictive covenant is "unassignable absent an express clause permitting assignment." A similar conclusion was reached in Pennsylvania, where the court held that, because restrictive covenants are "personal" to the employee, they are not assignable absent employee consent.

b. Jurisdictions Not Requiring Express Consent

Other jurisdictions support the enforcement of restrictive covenants in employment contracts by successor companies even when the contract is silent as to assignability. In these jurisdictions, contractual rights are generally assignable, the "personal" nature of an employment contract ends following termination, and restrictive covenants are scrutinized to ensure reasonableness in scope or duration. In an Illinois case, for example, a successor company could enforce restrictive covenants against several employees who left to work for a competitor even though the employment contracts were silent on assignability. The same reasoning was applied in a case involving stylists at a hair salon who challenged the ability of a successor company to enforce restrictive covenants. Analyzing the dispute in a context supportive of the general assignability of contractual rights, the court rejected

authority requiring express consent, stating such a position is based on "certain quaint notions of employment contracts" requiring the employee to know "the character and personality of his master" before agreeing to a restrictive covenant. Additional jurisdictions allow a successor company to enforce a restrictive covenant in personal services contracts following a merger or acquisition, because a mere change in the nature of the business is not enough to prevent enforcement of a restrictive covenant by a successor company even when the contract is silent on assignability.

Arizona law is most consistent with the jurisdictions that allow successor companies to enforce restrictive covenants, even when the contract is silent regarding assignability and the employee has not consented. Like those jurisdictions, Arizona law favors the enforcement and assignment of contractual rights, does not disfavor restrictive covenants in employment agreements, and allows such restrictive covenants to be assigned. Arizona courts treat restrictive covenants in employment agreements as assignable assets enforceable by successor companies, not as highly personalized arrangements between employee and employer. Arizona law has a distinct focus, less concerned with the personal relationship between employer and employee and more concerned with protecting employees from overreaching or other unconscionable arrangements, scrutinizing restrictive covenants for whether they are "unreasonable . . . demonstrate bad faith, or contravene public policy." The Court agrees with the holding of the Northern District of Illinois which found, in the absence of "precedent holding that restrictive covenants may never be assigned without consent . . . new public policy restrictions on contractual rights" should not be created. As such, absent a contrary ruling by an Arizona court, express consent of an employee is not required before an employer's contractual rights can be assigned to, and enforced by, a successor company.

Defendants' motion to dismiss denied in favor of Sogeti.

Second, an assignment will not be effective if it *adversely affects the obligor* in some significant way. An assignment is ineffective if it materially changes the obligor's duty or increases the burden or risk on the obligor. Naturally, any assignment will change an obligor's duty to some extent. The obligor will have to pay money or deliver goods or render some other performance to one party instead of to another. These changes are not considered to be sufficiently material to render an assignment ineffective. Thus, a right to receive money or goods or land is generally assignable. In addition, covenants not to compete are generally considered to be assignable to buyers of businesses. For example, Jefferson sells RX Drugstore

to Waldman, including in the contract of sale a covenant whereby Jefferson promises not to operate a competing drugstore within a 30-mile radius of RX for 10 years after the sale. Waldman later sells RX to Tharp. Here, Tharp could enforce the covenant not to compete against Jefferson. The reason for permitting assignment of covenants not to compete is that the purpose of such covenants is to protect an asset of the business—goodwill—for which the buyer has paid.

An assignment could be ineffective because of its variation of the obligor's duty, however, if the contract right involved a *personal relationship* or an element of *personal skill*, *judgment*, or *character*. For this reason, contracts of employment in which an employee works under the direct and personal supervision of an employer cannot be assigned to a new employer. An employer could assign a contract of employment, however, if the assignee-employer could perform the contract without adversely affecting the interests of the employee, such as would be the case when an employment relationship does not involve personal supervision by an individual employer.

A purported assignment is ineffective if it significantly increases the burden of the obligor's performance. For example, if Walker contracts to sell Dwyer all of its requirements of wheat, a purported assignment of Dwyer's rights to a corporation that has much greater requirements of wheat would probably be ineffective because it would significantly increase the burden on Walker.

Contract Clauses Prohibiting Assignment A contract right may also be nonassignable because the original contract expressly forbids assignment. For example, leases often contain provisions forbidding assignment or requiring the tenant to obtain the landlord's permission for assignment.[3]

Antiassignment clauses in contracts are generally enforceable. Because of the strong public policy favoring assignability, however, such clauses are often interpreted

_____
[3]The assignment of leases is discussed further in Chapter 25.

narrowly. For example, a court might view an assignment made in violation of an antiassignment clause as a breach of contract for which damages may be recovered but not as an invalidation of the assignment. Another tactic is to interpret a contractual ban on assignment as prohibiting only the delegation of duties.

The UCC takes this latter position. Under section 2-210(2), general language prohibiting assignment of "the contract" or "all my rights under the contract" is interpreted as forbidding only the delegation of duties, unless the circumstances indicate to the contrary. Section 2-210 also states that a right to damages for breach of a whole sales contract or a right arising out of the assignor's performance of his entire obligation may be assigned even if a provision of the original sales contract prohibited assignment. In addition, UCC section 9-318(4) invalidates contract terms that prohibit (or require the debtor's consent to) an assignment of an account or creation of a security interest in a right to receive money that is now due or that will become due. As the following *Filer* case illustrates, however, specific enough antiassignment language will bar a purported assignee from exercising rights under a contract. And much rides on whether a purported assignment of accounts receivable is for a security interest or simply for purposes of collection on the account.

Filer, Inc. v. Staples, Inc.   766 F. Supp. 2d 314 (D. Mass. 2011)

In 2006, Staples Inc., the office supplies retailer, entered into two manufacturing and purchase agreements with Hwa Fuh Plastics Co., Ltd. (HFP), whose president held the patent on a particular style of file folders. The agreements set out the terms and conditions for the sale of products and manufacturing services from HFP to Staples. Each agreement included a choice of law clause, providing that Massachusetts law would govern the agreement. The following year, however, the relationship between HFP and Staples deteriorated. Staples alleged that HFP unilaterally demanded an increase in the sales price for the file folders in contravention of the procedures outlined in the agreements and that HFP delayed and withheld shipments of file folders, which disrupted Staples's supply chain and caused product shortages. As a result, Staples purchased substitute products from an alternative supplier.

In November 2009, HFP purportedly assigned its rights under the agreements with Staples to Filer Inc.

On June 11, 2010, Filer filed a complaint against Staples for breach of contract in the U.S. District Court for the Central District of California. Staples moved for a transfer of venue to the District of Massachusetts, pursuant to the choice of law clause, which the California court granted. In the Massachusetts court, Staples filed counterclaims against both Filer and HFP and moved for summary judgment of Filer's breach of contract claim, arguing that Filer had no rights under the contract because the purported assignment of HFPs rights to Filer was prohibited by the agreements' provisions regarding assignments.

Stearns, District Judge

The parties do not dispute that the Agreements contain provisions governing assignments. In the first agreement, the assignment clause states: "Staples may assign in whole or in part its rights and obligations hereunder to any other entity. Without

the prior written consent of Staples, Manufacturer [HFP] shall not transfer or assign this Agreement or any rights or obligations thereunder." Similarly, the assignment clause in the second agreement reads: "Staples may assign in whole or in part its rights and obligations hereunder to any other entity without Company's

[HFP's] consent. Without the prior written consent of Staples, Company [HFP] shall not transfer or assign this Agreement or any rights or obligations thereunder." It is undisputed that Staples has not consented to the assignment of HFP's rights or obligations under the Agreements.

Staples contends that these clauses governing assignment (or non-assignment, with respect to HFP) are valid and enforceable. . . . Staples argues that because the Agreements bar any assignment from HFP to Filer, Filer holds no legal rights under either of the Agreements and therefore cannot maintain a breach of contract claim.

Filer, for its part, argues that the non-assignment clauses are rendered unenforceable by Uniform Commercial Code (U.C.C.) § 9-406(d), which is entitled, "Term restricting assignment generally ineffective." However, as Staples points out, Article 9 of the U.C.C. applies to secured transactions (obligations the payment of which is guaranteed by the borrower's pledge of collateral), while HFP's assignment of rights to Filer involved a transfer of "certain accounts receivable" from HFP to Filer. An assignment of an account exclusively for the purpose of collection is not governed by Article 9 of the U.C.C. *See* Mass. Gen. Laws Ann. ch. 106, § 9-109(d) ("This article shall not apply to: . . . an assignment of accounts, chattel paper, payment intangibles, or promissory notes which is for the purpose of collection only."); *see also In re Gull Air, Inc.*, 90 B.R. 10, 14 n.4 (Bankr. D. Mass. 1988) ("An assignment of an account which is for the purpose of collection only or a transfer of an account to an assignee in whole or partial satisfaction of a pre-existing indebtedness is not subject to Article 9 of the Uniform Commercial Code."). Because the HFP assignment to Filer is for the purpose of collection, in satisfaction of a pre-existing indebtedness, it is not subject to Article 9 of the U.C.C. Moreover, as the non-assignment clauses in the Agreements are valid and enforceable, Filer holds no legal rights under either of the Agreements and cannot maintain a breach of contract claim.

* * *

ORDER

For the foregoing reasons, Staples's motion for summary judgment . . . is *ALLOWED*. . . .

SO ORDERED.

Nature of Assignee's Rights

When an assignment occurs, the assignee is said to "step into the shoes of his assignor." This means that the assignee acquires all of the rights that his assignor had under the contract. The assignee has the right to receive the obligor's performance, and if performance is not forthcoming, the assignee has the right to sue in his own name for breach of the obligation. By the same token, the assignee acquires no greater rights than those possessed by the assignor.

Because the assignee has no greater rights than did the assignor, the obligor may assert any defense or claim against the assignee that he could have asserted against the assignor, subject to certain time limitations discussed below. A contract that is void, voidable, or unenforceable as between the original parties does not become enforceable just because it has been assigned to a third party. For example, if Richards induces Dillman's consent to a contract by duress and subsequently assigns his rights under the contract to Keith, Dillman can assert the doctrine of duress against Keith as a ground for avoiding the contract.

Importance of Notifying the Obligor An assignee should promptly notify the obligor of the assignment. Although notification of the obligor is not necessary for the assignment to be valid, such notice is of great practical importance. One reason notice is important is that an obligor who does not have reason to know of the assignment could render performance to the assignor and claim that his obligation had been discharged by performance. An obligor who renders performance to the assignor without notice of the assignment has no further liability under the contract. For example, McKay borrows $500 from Goodheart, promising to repay the debt by June 1. Goodheart assigns the debt to Rogers, but no one informs McKay of the assignment, and McKay pays the $500 to Goodheart, the assignor. In this case, McKay is not liable for any further payment. But if Rogers had immediately notified McKay of the assignment and, after receiving notice, McKay had mistakenly paid the debt to Goodheart, McKay would still have the legal obligation to pay $500 to Rogers. Having been given adequate notice of the assignment, he may remain liable to the assignee even if he later renders performance to the assignor.

An assignor who accepts performance from the obligor after the assignment holds any benefits that he receives as a trustee for the assignee. If the assignor fails to pay those benefits to the assignee, however, an obligor who has been notified of the assignment and renders performance to the wrong person may have to pay the same debt twice.

An obligor who receives notice of an assignment from the assignee will want to assure himself that the assignment has in fact occurred. He may ask for written evidence of the assignment or contact the assignee and ask for verification of the assignment. Under UCC section 9-318(3), a notification of assignment is ineffective unless it reasonably identifies the rights assigned. If requested by the account debtor (an obligor who owes money for goods sold or leased or services rendered), the assignee must furnish reasonable proof that the assignment has been made, and, unless he does so, the account debtor may disregard the notice and pay the assignor.

Defenses against the Assignee An assignee's rights in an assignment are subject to the defenses that the obligor could have asserted against the assignor. Keep in mind that the assignee's rights are limited by the terms of the underlying contract between the assignor and the obligor. When defenses arise from the terms or performance of that contract, they can be asserted against the assignee even if they arise after the obligor receives notice of the assignment. For example, on June 1, Worldwide Widgets assigns to First Bank its rights under a contract with Widgetech, Inc. This contract obligates Worldwide Widgets to deliver a quantity of widgets to Widgetech by September 1, in return for which Widgetech is obligated to pay a stated purchase price. First Bank gives prompt notice of the assignment to Widgetech. Worldwide Widget fails to deliver the widgets and Widgetech refuses to pay. If First Bank brought an action against Widgetech to recover the purchase price of the widgets, Widgetech could assert Worldwide Widget's breach as a defense, even though the breach occurred after Widgetech received notice of the assignment.[4]

In determining what other defenses can be asserted against the assignee, the time of notification plays an important role. After notification, as we discussed earlier, payment by the obligor to the assignor will not discharge the obligor.

Subsequent Assignments
An assignee may "reassign" a right to a third party, who would be called a subassignee. The subassignee then acquires the rights held by the prior assignee. He should give the obligor prompt notice of the subsequent assignment because he takes his interest subject to the same principles discussed above

regarding the claims and defenses that can be asserted against him.

Successive Assignments
Notice to the obligor may be important in one other situation. If an assignor assigns the same right to two assignees in succession, both of whom pay for the assignment, a question of priority results. An assignor who assigns the same right to different people will be held liable to the assignee who acquires no rights against the obligor, but which assignee is entitled to the obligor's performance? Which assignee will have recourse only against the assignor? There are several views on this point.

In states that follow the "American rule," the first assignee has the better right. This view is based on the rule of property law that a person cannot transfer greater rights in property than he owns. In states that follow the "English rule," however, the assignee who first gives notice of the assignment to the obligor, without knowledge of the other assignee's claim, has the better right. The *Restatement (Second) of Contracts* takes a third position. Section 342 of the *Restatement (Second)* provides that the first assignee has priority unless the subsequent assignee gives value (pays for the assignment) and, without having reason to know of the other assignee's claim, does one of the following: obtains payment of the obligation, gets a judgment against the obligor, obtains a new contract with the obligor by novation, or possesses a writing of a type customarily accepted as a symbol or evidence of the right assigned (such as a passbook for a savings account).

Assignor's Warranty Liability to Assignee
Suppose that Ross, a 16-year-old boy, contracts to buy a used car for $2,000 from Donaldson. Ross pays Donaldson $500 as a down payment and agrees to pay the balance in equal monthly installments. Donaldson assigns his right to receive the balance of the purchase price to Beckman, who pays $1,000 in cash for the assignment. When Beckman later attempts to enforce the contract, however, Ross disaffirms the contract on grounds of lack of capacity. Thus, Beckman has paid $1,000 for a worthless claim. Does Beckman have any recourse against Donaldson? When an assignor is paid for making an assignment, the assignor is held to have made certain implied warranties about the claim assigned.

The assignor impliedly warrants that the claim assigned is valid. This means that the obligor has capacity to contract, the contract is not illegal, the contract is not voidable for any other reason known to the assignor (such as fraud or duress), and the contract has not been discharged prior to assignment. The assignor also warrants that he has good

---

[4]Similarly, if the assignor's rights were subject to discharge because of other factors such as the nonoccurrence of a condition, impossibility, impracticability, or public policy, this can be asserted as a defense against the assignee even if the event occurs after the obligor receives notice of assignment. See *Restatement (Second) of Contracts* § 336(3). The doctrines relating to discharge from performance are explained in Chapter 18.

title to the rights assigned and that any written instrument representing the assigned claim is genuine. In addition, the assignor impliedly agrees that he will not do anything to impair the value of the assignment. These guarantees are imposed by law unless the assignment agreement clearly indicates to the contrary. One important aspect of the assigned right that the assignor does not impliedly warrant, however, is that the obligor is solvent.

Delegation of Duties

LO17-2 Explain the concept of delegation and the consequences of a delegation.

Nature of Delegation A **delegation** of duties occurs when an obligor indicates his intent to appoint another person to perform his duties under a contract. For example, White owns a furniture store. He has numerous existing contracts to deliver furniture to customers, including a contract to deliver a sofa to Coombs. White is the *obligor* of the duty to deliver the sofa and Coombs is the *obligee*. White decides to sell his business to Rosen. As a part of the sale of the business, White assigns the rights in the existing contracts to Rosen and delegates to him the performance of those contracts, including the duty to deliver the sofa to Coombs. Here, White is the *delegator* and Rosen is the *delegatee*. White

is appointing Rosen to carry out his duties to the obligee, Coombs. Figure 17.3 summarizes the key terms regarding delegation.

In contrast to an assignment of a right, which extinguishes the assignor's right and transfers it to the assignee, the delegation of a *duty* does *not* extinguish the duty owed by the delegator. The delegator remains liable to the obligee unless the obligee agrees to substitute the delegatee's promise for that of the delegator (this is called a *novation* and will be discussed in greater detail later in this chapter). This makes sense because, if it were possible for a person to escape his duties under a contract by merely delegating them to another, any party to a contract could avoid liability by delegating duties to an insolvent acquaintance. The significance of an effective delegation is that performance by the delegatee will discharge the delegator. In addition, if the duty is a delegable one, the obligee cannot insist on performance by the delegator; he must accept the performance of the delegatee. The relationship between the parties in a delegation is shown in Figure 17.4.

Delegable Duties A duty that can be performed fully by a number of different persons is delegable. Not all duties are delegable, however. The grounds for finding a duty to be nondelegable resemble closely the grounds for finding a right to be nonassignable. A duty is nondelegable if delegation would violate public policy or if the

Figure 17.3   Delegation: Key Terms

Obligor	Obligee	Delegation	Delegator	Delegatee
Person who owes the duty to perform	Person who has the right to receive the obligor's performance	Appointment of another person to perform the obligor's duty to the obligee	Obligor who appoints another to perform his duty to the obligee	Person who is appointed to perform the obligor's duty to the obligee

Figure 17.4   Delegation

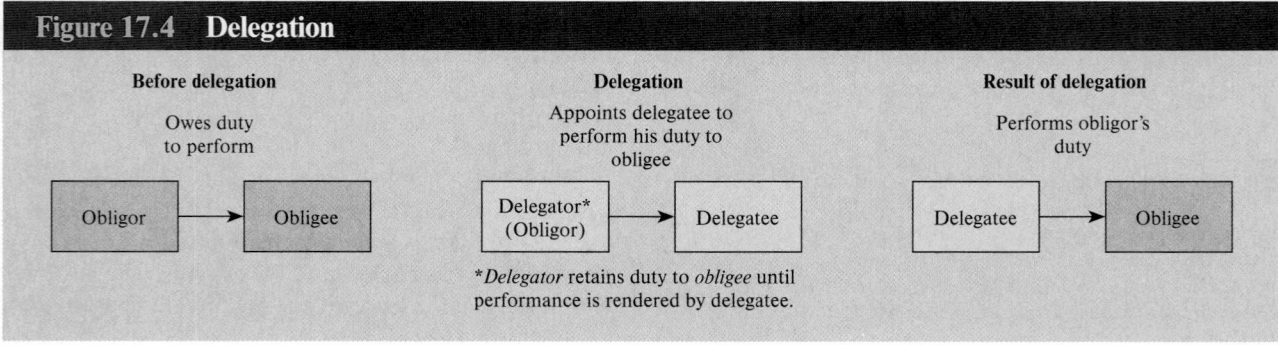

original contract between the parties forbids delegation. In addition, both section 2-210(1) of the UCC and section 318(2) of the *Restatement (Second) of Contracts* take the position that a party to a contract may delegate his duty to perform to another person unless the parties have agreed to the contrary or unless the other party has a *substantial interest* in having the original obligor perform the acts required by the contract. The key factor used in determining whether the obligee has such a substantial interest is the degree to which performance is dependent on the individual traits, skill, or judgment of the person who owes the duty to perform. For example, if Jansen hires Skelton, an artist, to paint her portrait, Skelton could not effectively delegate the duty to paint the portrait to another artist. Similarly, an employee could not normally delegate her duties under an employment contract to some third person because employment contracts are made with the understanding that the person the employer hires will perform the work. The situation in which a person hires a general contractor to perform specific work is distinguishable, however. In that situation, the person hiring the general contractor would normally understand that at least part of the work would be delegated to subcontractors.

In the *Johnson* case, which appears below, the court must decide whether a contractual duty was delegable.

Johnson v. Bank of America, N.A.
2010 U.S. Dist. LEXIS 38080 (D.S.C. Apr. 16, 2010)

Carl Johnson was a customer of Bank of America's (BofA) retail banking services. BofA's Online Service Agreement, to which customers must agree in order to use BofA's online banking services, allows an account holder to use its "Bill Pay" service. The Agreement grants BofA the option to complete a Bill Pay request by one of three means: (1) an electronic transmission, (2) a corporate check, or (3) a personal check. BofA deducts electronic transmissions and corporate checks from the customer's checking account on the scheduled day of delivery. A personal check, though, results in a debit from the customer's account when the payee presents the check for payment. In other words, if a personal check is issued, the customer retains the funds in his or her account for a few extra days during which those funds can accrue interest. BofA has contracted with a vendor, Fiserv, to handle Bill Pay transactions.

Johnson claims that he requested Bill Pays to several retail shops in Columbia, South Carolina. These shops were not equipped to receive electronic transmissions. BofA debited the account for those purchases on the day that the checks were scheduled for delivery, even though the payees did not present them until between 3 and 10 days later. Thus, Fiserv issued a corporate check rather than a personal check and deprived Johnson of the benefit of holding the funds in his checking account for those extra days.

Johnson filed a class action lawsuit against BofA alleging that delegating the discretion to select the payment method, combined with Fiserv's financial motive to deprive customers of interest, constitutes breach of contract. BofA filed a motion to dismiss Johnson's complaint.

Joseph F. Anderson Jr., Judge

Johnson alleges that BofA's assignment of rights and delegation of duties to Fiserv effects a breach of the implied duty of good faith and fair dealing implicit in every contract. Specifically, Johnson argues that Fiserv improperly caused Johnson to incur losses when it prematurely debited his account. As an initial matter, the court notes that an assignee or delegatee stands in the shoes of the assignor or delegator. Accordingly, if the agreement allows or requires BofA to act or not act in a certain way, it also allows or requires Fiserv to conduct itself in the same manner.

The Agreement provides [BofA], incident to its Bill Pay services, the discretion to effect payment through one of three methods. The contract states:

You authorize us to make payments in the manner we select from the following methods:

- Electronic transmission. Most payments are made by electronic transmission.
- Corporate check. This is a check drawn on our account or the account of our vendor. If a Payee on a corporate check fails to negotiate the check within 90 days, we will stop payment on the check and recredit your account for the amount of the payment.
- Personal check. This is a check drawn on your account based on your authorization under this Agreement.

The Agreement further provides that:

For payments made by electronic transmission or corporate check, the payment amount will be debited from, or charged to the account you designate on the scheduled delivery date. . . . For payments made by personal check, the account you designate will be debited when the check is presented to us for payment.

Johnson alleges that the Agreement governs the relationship between the parties. He does not allege that the Agreement is somehow invalid or that some other agreement defines the relationship of the parties. In his complaint, Johnson alleges that BofA's vendor, Fiserv, issued a corporate check to satisfy Johnson's outstanding accounts at several Columbia, South Carolina, establishments that have not elected to receive electronic transmissions. Johnson alleges that by issuing a corporate check on Fiserv's account, and at Johnson's behest, BofA deprived Johnson of interest he is entitled to.

The plain language of the Agreement states that BofA has the discretion to choose between three methods of payment. The agreement also indicates that a corporate check may be drawn on the account of its vendor and sets forth the relative dates on which a customer should expect his account to be charged for payments he requests BofA fulfill on his behalf. The court finds that the complaint alleges that BofA, through its assignee or delegatee Fiserv, "has done what provisions of the [Agreement] expressly gave [it] the right to do." *Adams v. G.J. Creel and Sons, Inc.*, 465 S.E.2d 84 (S.C. 1995). Further, Johnson fails to adequately allege how BofA's actions run afoul of reasonable commercial standards, or how BofA's conduct contravenes the plain language of the Agreement.

Johnson also alleges that BofA's assignment of the right to choose payment methods breaches the implied covenant of good faith and fair dealing because the assignment materially alters the contractual arrangement between Johnson and BofA. In South Carolina, executory contracts, those that have not been fully performed, are assignable, . . . and "[a]n assignee stands in the shoes of its assignor." *Moore v. Weinberg*, 373 S.C. 209, 644 S.E.2d 740 (S.C. App. 2007). That is to say that the assignee has the same rights and privileges under the contract as the assignor. However, rights arising out of a contract cannot be transferred if they are coupled with liabilities or with contracts for personal services, or if they involve a relationship of personal credit and confidence. . . . Similarly, contract duties are generally delegable, unless prohibited by statute, public policy, the terms of the contract, or

if they involve the personal qualities or skills of the obligor. 29 Richard A. Lord, *Williston on Contracts*, § 74:27 (4th ed. 2009); *Restatement (Second) of Contracts* § 318. To the extent that Johnson asserts that BofA's assignment and delegation to Fiserv was improper, his argument lacks merit. As noted above, assignments and delegations are generally valid unless prohibited by law or the terms of the contract, or where the effect of the assignment effects a change in the terms of the contract, as can the case in a contract for personal services. Johnson cites to no statute or case that suggests BofA's assignment and delegation violates the law of South Carolina. Instead, Johnson argues in his response to BofA's motion to dismiss that the assignment and delegation changes the underlying basis of the bargain between BofA and Johnson because, Johnson argues, Fiserv has an improper financial motive to maximize the period in which it can earn interest. However, argument of the existence of an improper motive in a response to a motion to dismiss is a different animal than an allegation in a complaint that Fiserv acts on this motive. Simply stating that an American corporation is motivated by a desire to make money does little more than restate a bedrock principle of capitalism.

Both BofA and Fiserv could reasonably be expected to make an attempt to turn a profit in providing banking services. If BofA, rather than Fiserv, executed the Bill Pay requests it would have exactly the same motivations as Fiserv: to minimize the risk incurring loss due to insufficient funds, to lower transactions cost, and to accrue interest from money in its possession. Johnson's argument to the contrary fails to show how his complaint sufficiently alleges that there is any difference between BofA and Fiserv in the execution the Bill Pay requests. Such failure proves fatal to Johnson's argument at the motion to dismiss stage.

In sum, Johnson fails to adequately allege how the assignment and delegation materially changes the benefit of the bargain under the contract or that Johnson has any interest in BofA, rather than Fiserv, performing the contract. Accordingly, the court finds that BofA's assignment and delegation to Fiserv valid, and that Fiserv stands in the shoes of BofA with respect to the rights and duties created by the Agreement. Because the court finds that neither BofA nor Fiserv, as BofA's assignee, violated the terms of the contract or breached the implied duty of good faith and fair dealing, the court **GRANTS** BofA's motion to dismiss.

Language Creating a Delegation

No special, formal language is necessary to create an effective delegation of duties. In fact, because parties frequently confuse the terms *assignment* and *delegation*, one of the problems frequently presented to courts is determining whether the parties intended an assignment only or both an assignment and a delegation. Unless the agreement indicates a contrary intent, courts tend to interpret assignments as including a delegation of the assignor's duties. Both the UCC §2-210(4) and section 328 of the *Restatement (Second) of Contracts* provide that, unless the language or the circumstances indicate to the contrary, general language of assignment such as language indicating an assignment of "the contract" or of "all my rights under the contract" is to be interpreted as creating *both* an assignment and a delegation.

Assumption of Duties by Delegatee

A delegation gives the delegatee the right to perform the duties of the delegator. The mere fact that duties have been delegated does not always place legal responsibility on the delegatee to perform. The delegatee who fails to perform will not be liable to either the delegator or the obligee unless the delegatee has assumed the duty by expressly or impliedly undertaking the obligation to perform. However, both section 2-210(4) of the UCC and section 328 of the *Restatement (Second)* provide that an assignee's acceptance of an assignment is to be construed as a promise by her to perform the duties under the contract, unless the language of the assignment or the circumstances indicate to the contrary. Frequently, a term of the contract between the delegator and the delegatee provides that the delegatee assumes responsibility for performance. A common example of this is the assumption of an existing mortgage debt by a purchaser of real estate. Suppose Morgan buys a house from Friedman, agreeing to assume the outstanding mortgage on the property held by First Bank. By this assumption, Morgan undertakes personal liability to both Friedman and First Bank. If Morgan fails to make the mortgage payments, First Bank has a cause of action against Morgan personally. An assumption does *not* release the delegator from liability, however. Rather, it creates a situation in which both the delegator and the assuming delegatee owe duties to the obligee. If the assuming delegatee fails to pay, the delegator can be held liable. Thus, in the example described above, if Morgan fails to make mortgage payments and First Bank is unable to collect the debt from Morgan, Friedman would have secondary liability. Friedman, of course, would have an action against Morgan for breach of their contract. This resolution makes sense because Friedman was the one who introduced Morgan into the relationship. Therefore, she ought to be the one who ultimately bears the risk of Morgan's nonperformance.

Discharge of Delegator by Novation

As you have seen, the mere delegation of duties—even when the delegatee assumes those duties—does not release the delegator from his legal obligation to the obligee. A delegator can, however, be discharged from performance by **novation**.

A novation is a particular type of substituted contract in which the obligee agrees to discharge the original obligor and to substitute a new obligor in his place. The effects of a novation are that the original obligor has no further obligation under the contract and the obligee has the right to look to the new obligor for fulfillment of the contract. A novation requires more than the obligee's consent to having the delegatee perform the duties. In the example used above, the mere fact that First Bank accepted mortgage payments from Morgan would not create a novation. Rather, there must be some evidence that the obligee agrees to discharge the old obligor and substitute a new obligor. As you will see in the following *Russell* case, the Alabama Supreme Court strictly adheres to this principle.

The Industrial Development Board of the City of Montgomery v. Russell
124 So. 3d 127 (Ala. 2013)

In September 2001, various state and local officials, including officials from the City of Montgomery (the City), the City's Industrial Development Board (IDB), the Montgomery County Commission (the County), and the Montgomery Area Chamber of Commerce, worked to secure the options to purchase property in the Montgomery, Alabama, area for the purpose of creating an incentive package to persuade Hyundai Motor Manufacturing to build a vehicle assembly plant there. An essential part of the incentive package included a large parcel of "free" land upon which Hyundai could build the plant. Although the funds to purchase the land would be provided by the City and the County, the IDB was the contracting party to all of the options because that was necessary for the deals to comply with laws governing tax breaks and industry incentives.

The IDB secured options to purchase 328 acres from the Russells, 54 acres from the McLemore group, 320 acres from Southdale LLC, and 807 acres from Wheeler/Phillips. The options were identical, providing for a period of 120 days and setting a purchase price floor of $4,500 per acre. Moreover, the options included a "most-favored-nation" or "price-escalation" clause whereby it guaranteed that no landowner would be paid a lower price per acre than that "paid to any other landowner included in the project planned for the Property."

Joy Shelton was also approached about selling her land as part of the project, but she refused. The IDB and the State sent the incentive package to Hyundai without including the Shelton property, having determined that the Shelton property was unnecessary. However, in response to the package, Hyundai indicated that it needed to secure rail access to the site, which would require acquiring the Shelton property after all.

The now-increased urgency of acquiring the Shelton property would likely drive up the cost of all properties due to the most-favored-nation clauses if the IDB were to try to secure it. In that case, the project cost would increase by roughly $10 million. Therefore, the parties considered a number of approaches that did not involve the IDB, including having rail company CSX Transportation try to secure the option to purchase the Shelton property.

Thereafter, the IDB provided notice to the Russell, McLemore, Southdale, and Wheeler/Phillips property owners that it would exercise its options on those properties and assigned the options to the City and County. The City and County purchased the properties for $4,500 per acre.

CSX entered a real estate purchase agreement with Shelton on the property for $12,000 per acre. CSX assigned that agreement to Hyundai, and the State provided Hyundai with the funds to pay for the Shelton property, rather than Hyundai financing the purchase on its own.

The various property owners each filed separate breach-of-contract actions in the Montgomery Circuit Court against the IDB and Hyundai, as well as other parties, alleging that the IDB and Hyundai had violated the most-favored-nation clauses by not paying them $12,000 per acre for their properties. Even though IDB was not a party to the option or purchase of the Shelton property, the other property owners argued that Shelton was "a landowner included in the project," thus triggering the most-favored-nation clause.

Throughout the proceedings, the IDB contended that it was an improper party to the litigation and moved for summary judgment. After a complicated procedural history during which a number of the claims involving various parties were consolidated for consideration on appeal and remanded to the trial court for reconsideration, IDB sought an interlocutory appeal to the Alabama Supreme Court to answer the following question: "Were the obligations under the option contracts signed by the Plaintiffs and the IDB assumed by the City of Montgomery and Montgomery County, thus barring any claims for breach of contract against the IDB?" If the Supreme Court answered that question in the affirmative, the IDB would be entitled to summary judgment on the claims against it.

Murdock, Justice

The IDB bases its argument that its assignment of the option agreements to the City relieved it of any liability under those agreements on the following portion of [a prior opinion dealing with these claims]:

The City first argues that the City was not a party to the option agreements executed by the IDB and therefore was not liable for breach of contract because, it argues, the IDB was not acting as the City's agent. Under such circumstances, the City says, it is not liable under any breach-of-contract theory. We disagree. Pursuant to Resolution No. 111-2002, adopted by the City in June 2002 in conjunction with the Hyundai project, "the IDB did exercise the purchase options, but assigned its rights to purchase thereunder to the City and Montgomery County (the 'County'), and the City and County each have issued debt to provide the necessary funds and have acquired the Parcels." *As the IDB's assignee, the City assumed the obligations and liabilities of the assigned contracts. Meighan v. Watts Constr. Co.*, 475 So. 2d 829, 834–35 (Ala. 1985).

[Emphasis added.] In its principal brief, the IDB argues:

Because the City of Montgomery assumed all of the obligations under the option contracts, there can be no liability for breach of contract on the part of the IDB. To establish a breach of contract, [the Plaintiffs] must show

(1) the existence of a valid contract binding the parties to the action, (2) [their] own performance under the contract, (3) the defendant's nonperformance, and (4) damages.

Congress Life Ins. Co. v. Barstow, 799 So. 2d 931, 937 (Ala. 2001). . . . [The Plaintiffs] cannot prove the first required element—the existence of a valid contract binding the parties to this action. This is because the City of Montgomery assumed all of the obligations under the options. The IDB no longer has any duties, obligations, rights or remedies under the option contracts.

The IDB essentially argues that, because this Court stated in [the prior opinion] that the City, as the assignee of the option agreements, is potentially liable for breach of contract, the Court impliedly held that the IDB is not liable. We reject this argument for several reasons.

First, the portion of the [prior] opinion relied upon by the IDB addressed the City's potential liability for breach of contract; it did not address, much less determine, the IDB's potential liability for breach of contract.

[T]he IDB cites no authority for its proposition that the assignment of rights under a contract relieves the assignor of any potential for liability for duties not performed under the assigned contract. Moreover, the law provides no support for such a proposition and, indeed, supports the contrary proposition. In a dissent in *DuPont v. Yellow Cab Co. of Birmingham, Inc.*, 565 So. 2d 190, 193 (Ala. 1990), Justice Jones explained the distinction between assignment and delegation:

In the instant case, there exist both an assignment of rights and a delegation of duties. The assignment-delegation distinction is relatively straightforward: rights are assigned; duties are delegated. When a party to a contract transfers his rights under the contract to a third party, he has made an assignment. If a party to the contract appoints a third party to render performance under the contract, he has made a delegation. Generally speaking, upon assignment of a right, the assignor's interest in that right is extinguished; however, upon the delegation of a contractual duty, the delegating party remains liable under the contract, unless the contract provides otherwise or there is a novation. Calamari and Perillo's *Hornbook on Contracts,* § 18-25 (3d ed. 1987). Professor Knapp analogizes the assignment-delegation distinction thusly: "If assigning a right is like passing a football, then delegating a duty resembles more the dissemination of a catchy tune or a communicable disease: Passing it on is not the same as getting rid of it." C. Knapp, *Problems in Contract Law* 1161 (1976).

(Footnote omitted.) *See also Restatement (Second) of Contracts* § 318 (1981).

[T]he IDB assigned to the City and the County its rights under the option agreements. Assuming that this assignment of rights carried with it a delegation of the duties owed by the IDB under the agreements, the IDB nonetheless also would have had to demonstrate either (1) that the terms of the contracts allowed the IDB to relieve itself of contractual liability by way of such a delegation or (2) that the parties had entered into novations pursuant to which [the Plaintiffs] agreed that the IDB's obligations had changed. *See generally, e.g., Marvin's, Inc. v. Robertson,* 608 So. 2d 391, 393 (Ala. 1992) (explaining that "[a] novation is the substitution of one contract for another, which extinguishes the pre-existing obligation and releases those bound thereunder. . . . In addition, the party alleging a novation has the burden of proving that such was the intention of the parties." (quoting *Pilalas v. Baldwin County Sav. & Loan Ass'n,* 549 So. 2d 92, 94–95 (Ala. 1989) (emphasis omitted))). The IDB does not assert or demonstrate either condition. Accordingly, the trial court's denial of the IDB's motion for a summary judgment is not due to be reversed on this ground.

Conclusion

The trial court's order denying the IDB's motion for a summary judgment, in which the trial court rejected the IDB's arguments that the IDB should be relieved from liability based on its assignment of [its] rights under the option agreements . . . is due to be **affirmed**.

Third-Party Beneficiaries

 Explain the concept of third-party beneficiary and distinguish among the three kinds of third-party beneficiaries.

There are many situations in which the performance of a contract would constitute some benefit to a person who was not a party to the contract. Despite the fact that a nonparty may expect to derive advantage from the performance of a contract, the general rule is that no one but the parties to a contract or their assignees can enforce it. In some situations, however, parties contract for the purpose of benefiting some third person. In such cases, the benefit to the third person is an essential part of the contract, not just an incidental result of a contract that was really designed to benefit the parties. Where the parties to a contract *intended* to benefit a third party, courts will give effect to their intent and permit the third party to enforce the contract. Such third parties are called **third-party beneficiaries**.

Intended Beneficiaries versus Incidental Beneficiaries

For a third person (other than an assignee) to have the right to enforce a contract, she must be able to establish that the contract was made with the intent to benefit her. A few courts have required that both parties must have intended to benefit the third party. Most courts, however, have found it to be sufficient if the person to whom the promise to perform was made (the *promisee*) intended to benefit the third party. In ascertaining intent to benefit the third party, a court will look at the language used by the parties and all the surrounding circumstances. One factor that is frequently important in determining intent to benefit is whether the party making the promise to perform (the *promisor*) was to render performance directly to the third party. For example, if Allison contracts with Jones Florist to deliver flowers to Kirsch, the fact that performance was to be rendered to Kirsch would be good evidence that the parties intended to benefit Kirsch. This factor is not conclusive, however. There are some cases in which intent to benefit a third party has been found even though performance was to be rendered to the promisee rather than to the third party. Intended beneficiaries are often classified as either *creditor* or *donee beneficiaries*. These classifications are discussed in greater detail below.

A third party who is unable to establish that the contract was made with the intent to benefit her is called an *incidental beneficiary*. A third party is classified as an incidental beneficiary when the benefit derived by that third party was merely an unintended by-product of a contract that was created for the benefit of those who were parties to it. Incidental beneficiaries acquire no rights under a contract. For example, Hutton contracts with Long Construction Company to build a valuable structure on his land. The performance of the contract would constitute a benefit to Keller, Hutton's next-door neighbor, by increasing the value of Keller's land. The contract between Hutton and Long was made for the purpose of benefiting themselves, however. Any advantage derived by Keller is purely incidental to their primary purpose. Thus, Keller could not sue and recover damages if either Hutton or Long breaches the contract.

As a general rule, members of the public are held to be incidental beneficiaries of contracts entered into by their municipalities or other governmental units in the regular course of carrying on governmental functions. A member of the public cannot recover a judgment in a suit against a promisor of such a contract, even though all taxpayers will suffer some injury from nonperformance. A different result may be reached, however, if a party contracting with a governmental unit agrees to reimburse members of the public for damages or if the party undertakes to perform some duty for individual members of the public. In the following *Wallis* case, the court explores whether a member of the public is a third-party beneficiary of a contract as a result of that kind of public duty analysis.

Wallis v. Brainerd Baptist Church 509 S.W.3d 886 (Tenn. 2016)

Brainerd Baptist Church (the Church) owned and operated a fitness and recreation facility, Brainerd Crossroads or BX (BX). Sandra and Jerry Wallis were members of BX. On August 20, 2011, Mr. Wallis participated in an indoor cycling class at BX. After exiting the cycling room, Mr. Wallis collapsed. The instructor of the class, Kelly Casey, as well as two off-duty police officers, attended to Mr. Wallis while awaiting the arrival of an ambulance and paramedics. When Casey observed Mr. Wallis, he was lying on the floor on his side, his body rigid, his eyes open, and his head lifted off the floor. Casey heard him breathing and saw his chest rising and falling, and after checking his wrist, she determined that he had a pulse. Based on those observations, Casey believed Mr. Wallis was having a seizure, and she placed towels beneath his head for support. The off-duty police officers asked Casey if BX had an automated external defibrillator device (an AED), which Casey retrieved. However, no one used the AED on Mr. Wallis, apparently because they did not believe he was having a coronary event. Eventually, the ambulance and paramedics arrived and transported Mr. Wallis to the hospital, where he later died.

Mrs. Wallis ultimately sued the Church, claiming Mr. Wallis's death was the result of negligence. In addition, Mrs. Wallis sued ExtendLife Inc., the seller of BX's AED device, claiming in part that Mr. Wallis was a third-party beneficiary of the contract between the Church and ExtendLife. Mrs. Wallis alleged that the contract obligated ExtendLife to ensure that the Church complied with all federal, state, and local regulations regarding AEDs and to ensure that the Church's employees and agents were properly trained in the use of AEDs. She asserted that ExtendLife had failed to perform these contractual obligations, that Mr. Wallis was a third-party beneficiary of the contract, and that ExtendLife's breach of contract caused Mr. Wallis's death. Indeed, although ExtendLife had provided several training classes for the Church and BX personnel in 2009, no one who attended those trainings was present on the day Mr. Wallis collapsed.

ExtendLife moved for summary judgment on Mrs. Wallis's third-party beneficiary claim; however, the trial court denied that motion. ExtendLife was granted permission to seek an interlocutory appeal of that ruling. The intermediate appellate court refused to hear the interlocutory appeal, but the Supreme Court of Tennessee took up the appeal.

Cornelia A. Clark, Justice

B. Plaintiff's Third-Party Beneficiary Claim

"A contract is an agreement between two or more persons that creates obligations that are legally enforceable by the contracting parties." *West v. Shelby Cnty. Healthcare Corp.*, 459 S.W.3d 33, 46 (Tenn. 2014). A contract is presumed to be executed for the benefit of the contracting parties and not for the benefit of third parties. *Id.*; *Owner-Operator Indep. Drivers Ass'n v. Concord EFS, Inc.*, 59 S.W.3d 63, 68 (Tenn. 2001) [hereinafter *Owner-Operator*]. Nevertheless, a third party may seek to recover under a contract, but the third party bears the burden of proving, from the terms of the contract or the circumstances surrounding its execution, that, *at the time of contracting*, he was an intended third-party beneficiary of the contract. If the contractual benefits flowing to the third party are merely incidental, rather than intended, the third party may not recover under the contract.

Determining whether a contract was intended to benefit a third party is a matter of contract construction. Thus, the usual rules of contract interpretation apply, including the cardinal principle of ascertaining and effectuating the intent of the parties to the contract. Consistent with these general rules, a nonparty may be deemed "an intended third-party beneficiary of a contract . . . entitled to enforce the contract's terms," if:

(1) The parties to the contract have not otherwise agreed;

(2) Recognition of a right to performance in the [third party] is appropriate to effectuate the intention of the parties; and

(3) The terms of the contract or the circumstances surrounding performance indicate that either:

(a) the performance of the promise will satisfy an obligation or discharge a duty owed by the promisee to the [third party]; or

(b) the promisee intends to give the [third party] the benefit of the promised performance.

Owner-Operator, 59 S.W.3d at 70. Part (1) of the foregoing test "honor[s] any expression of intent by the parties to reserve to themselves the benefits of the contract." *Id.* Part (2) "ensures that third-party beneficiaries will be allowed to enforce the contract only when enforcement would further the parties' objectives in making the agreement." *Id.* In applying part (2), courts must "look to what the parties intended to accomplish by their agreement" and refuse to grant a nonparty intended third-party beneficiary status if doing so "would undermine the parties' purposes." *Id.* at 70–71. Part (3) "provides guidance for differentiating between intended and incidental beneficiaries" by "focus[ing] upon the promisee's intent, and not the promisor's." *Id.* at 71. Subsection (a) of part (3) "focuses upon the promisee's intent to 'discharge a duty . . . to the beneficiary[,]" and may be applied "even though the duty [the promisee] owed to the beneficiary is not easily convertible into money." *Id.* As this Court explained in *Owner-Operator*:

contracting parties in [part (3),] subsection (a) cases will not necessarily express a direct desire to confer a benefit upon the third party, for the promisee often may be motivated by a self-interested *intent to discharge the duty owed to the third party.* As noted in one California case, "in contracts of [this] type the main purpose of the promisee is not to confer a benefit on the third[-]party beneficiary, but to secure the discharge of his debt or performance of his duty to the third party." Regardless of self-interest, however, a clear expression of intent to discharge a duty owed by the promisee to the third party will satisfy subsection (a).

Under [part (3),] subsection (b), the analysis more directly centers upon whether the promisee actually intends to confer a benefit upon the third party. Part [(3), subsection] (b) analysis will encompass those [nonparty] beneficiaries who . . . *clearly were intended by the parties to receive the primary benefit of the contract.*

Id. at 71 (emphases added) (citations omitted). Evidence of the promisee's intent to discharge a duty to, or confer a benefit upon, the third party must be clear and direct before the third party

may avail himself of the exceptional remedy of recovering on an agreement to which he was not a party. To be deemed an intended third-party beneficiary, all three parts of the foregoing analysis must be satisfied.

Here, part (1) is satisfied because the parties did not expressly exclude third parties from the benefits of the contract. We need not consider whether part (2) is satisfied in these circumstances, because the undisputed facts fail to establish satisfaction of part (3). At the time of contracting, when third-party status is determined, the undisputed material facts fail to establish that ExtendLife's contractual obligations to the Church were intended to "satisfy an obligation or discharge a duty" the Church owed to Mr. Wallis.

1. Statutory Duties

Like many states, Tennessee has adopted statutes intended to increase the availability of AEDs . . . and the aim of these statutes is "[to] minimize the number of deaths from sudden cardiac arrest," *Hudson v. Town of Jasper*, No. M2013-00620-COA-R9CV, 2013 WL 5762224, at *4 (Tenn. Ct. App. Oct. 22, 2013). Importantly for purposes of the issue in this appeal, however, Tennessee's AED statutes only *encourage* businesses and other entities to acquire and make AEDs available for use in emergency situations. They do not impose any mandatory duty on businesses to do so, nor do they mandate that businesses use AEDs after they are acquired. To the contrary, after an AED is acquired, statutory prerequisites must be satisfied "[i]n order for [the] entity to use or allow the use of [the AED]." Tenn. Code Ann. § 68-140-404. These post-acquisition statutory prerequisites relate to training, maintenance, registration, and program development, all of which must be accomplished in compliance with rules adopted by the Tennessee Department of Health. . . . In summary, while Tennessee statutes encourage entities to acquire AEDs and make them available for use, these statutes do not impose any affirmative or mandatory duty on businesses to do so, nor do these statutes mandate use of AEDs that are acquired. Furthermore, businesses that acquire AEDs, comply with statutory prerequisites, and use AEDs receive immunity from liability for negligence. Accordingly, at the time of contracting, the Church had no statutory duty to Mr. Wallis to acquire and make an AED available for use, nor did the Church have a statutory duty to use the AED it had already acquired.

2. Common Law Duties

We next consider whether, under the common law, the Church owed Mr. Wallis a duty to acquire and make an AED available for use at BX or to use the AED it had acquired. To answer this question, we begin with the well-established principle, that, "[w]hile individuals have an obligation to refrain from acting in a way that *creates* an unreasonable risk of harm to others, the law generally does not impose on individuals an affirmative duty to aid or protect others." *Downs ex rel. Downs v. Bush*, 263 S.W.3d

812, 819 (Tenn. 2008) (emphasis added) (citations omitted). "As a means of mitigating the harshness of the common law rule, exceptions have been created for circumstances in which the defendant has a special relationship with either the individual who is the source of the danger or the person who is at risk." *Giggers v. Memphis Hous. Auth.*, 277 S.W.3d 359, 364 (Tenn. 2009). One of these "long-recognized special relationship[s] . . . is that between a business owner and patron." *Cullum v. McCool*, 432 S.W.3d 829, 833 (Tenn. 2013). Tennessee courts have turned to section 314A of the *Restatement (Second) of Torts* and decisions from other jurisdictions to define the scope of the duty to render aid created by such special relationships. Generally, this duty requires a business entity to take reasonable action to protect or aid a patron who sustains injury or becomes ill on business premises. [A business entity] is not required to give aid to one whom he has no reason to know to be ill. [A business entity] will seldom be required to do more than give such first aid as [it] reasonably can, and take reasonable steps to turn the sick person over to a doctor or to those who will look after him until one can be brought. And business entities "are not required to give aid to persons whom they have no reason to know to be ill or injured or whose illness or injury does not appear to be serious or life-threatening." *McCammon v. Gifford*, No. M2001-01357-COA-R3-CV, 2002 WL 732272, at *4 (Tenn. Ct. App. 2002). Furthermore, a business entity's "duty to render aid does not extend to providing all medical care that a business could reasonably foresee might be needed by its patrons or to provide the sort of aid that requires special training to administer." *Id.*

In this case, Mrs. Wallis seeks to recover based on a theory that the Church's duty to render aid to her husband included utilizing an AED. We agree that the special relationship exception applies here, because Mr. Wallis was a patron of BX. However, no Tennessee court has previously considered whether a business entity's duty to aid and protect its patrons requires it to acquire and make an AED available for use or to use an AED that has already been acquired. . . .

The law in other jurisdictions concerning the duty of business entities to render aid and the acquisition and use of AEDs is still developing. Although our research has revealed no other case in which a lawsuit has been brought against the seller of an AED, we note that every state appellate court to consider the issue has held that the common law duty a business entity owes to patrons does not require a business to acquire and make an AED available for use. . . . Furthermore, research reveals that a majority of appellate courts, and particularly those in jurisdictions that, like Tennessee, apply section 314A of the *Restatement (Second) of Torts*, have held that even after a business acquires an AED, the business's common law duty to render aid to patrons does not include use of the AED.

These decisions are consistent with current Tennessee law and the law of this State at the time of the 2008 contract. . . . Accordingly, we hold that the Church had no common law duty to Mr. Wallis to acquire an AED or to make it available for use, or to use it. Accordingly, the Church did not, by its contract with ExtendLife, intend to discharge a duty it owed to Mr. Wallis. And, in the absence of any such duty on the part of the Church, which the contract was intended to satisfy, Mrs. Wallis cannot prevail on her claim that Mr. Wallis was an intended third-party beneficiary of the contract between ExtendLife and the Church. ExtendLife, therefore, is entitled to summary judgment on Mrs. Wallis's second amended complaint.

* * *

Conclusion

For the reasons stated herein, we **reverse** the judgment of the trial court and **remand** the case to the trial court for entry of summary judgment in favor of ExtendLife. . . .

Creditor Beneficiaries If the promisor's performance is intended to satisfy a legal duty that the promisee owes to a third party, the third party is a creditor beneficiary. The creditor beneficiary has rights against both the promisee (because of the original obligation) and the promisor. For example, Smith buys a car on credit from Jones Auto Sales. Smith later sells the car to Carmichael, who agrees to pay the balance due on the car to Jones Auto Sales. (Note that Smith is delegating his duty to pay to *Carmichael*, and Carmichael is assuming the personal obligation to do so.) In this case, Jones Auto Sales is a creditor beneficiary of the contract between Smith and Carmichael. It has rights against both Carmichael and Smith if Carmichael does not perform.

Donee Beneficiaries If the promisee's primary purpose in contracting is to make a gift of the agreed-on performance to a third party, that third party is classified as a *donee beneficiary*. If the contract is breached, the donee beneficiary will have a cause of action against the promisor, but not against the promisee (donor). For example, Miller contracts with Perpetual Life Insurance Company, agreeing to pay premiums in return for which Perpetual agrees to pay $100,000 to

Third-Party Beneficiaries

Type of Third-Party Beneficiary	Distinguishing Feature	Can Enforce Contract Against
Incidental beneficiary	Contract was *not* made with the intent to benefit him/her	Neither promisor nor promisee
Donee beneficiary	Contract was made with the intent to benefit him/her and performance was intended to be a gift	Promisor only
Creditor beneficiary	Contract was made with the intent to benefit him/her and performance was intended to satisfy a legal obligation that the promisee owes to him/her	Both promisor and promisee

Miller's husband when Miller dies. Miller's husband is a donee beneficiary and can bring suit and recover judgment against Perpetual if Miller dies and Perpetual does not pay.

Vesting of Beneficiary's Rights

Another possible threat to the interests of the third-party beneficiary is that the promisor and the promisee might modify or discharge their contract so as to extinguish or alter the beneficiary's rights. For example, Gates, who owes $500 to Sorenson, enters into a contract with Connor whereby Connor agrees to pay the $500 to Sorenson. What happens if, before Sorenson is paid, Connor pays the money to Gates and Gates accepts it or Connor and Gates otherwise modify the contract? Courts have held that there is a point at which the rights of the beneficiary vest—that is, the beneficiary's rights cannot be lost by modification or discharge. A modification or discharge that occurs after the beneficiary's

rights have vested cannot be asserted as a defense to a suit brought by the beneficiary. The exact time at which the beneficiary's rights vest differs from jurisdiction to jurisdiction. Some courts have held that vesting occurs when the contract is formed, while others hold that vesting does not occur until the beneficiary learns of the contract and consents to it or does some act in reliance on the promise.

The contracting parties' ability to vary the rights of the third-party beneficiary can also be affected by the terms of their agreement. A provision of the contract between the promisor and the promisee stating that the duty to the beneficiary cannot be modified would be effective to prevent modification. Likewise, a contract provision in which the parties specifically reserved the right to change beneficiaries or modify the duty to the beneficiary would be enforced. For example, provisions reserving the right to change beneficiaries are very common in insurance contracts.

Ethics and Compliance in Action

Westendorf bought her friend an Apple iPad, which, at her request, Apple delivered directly to her friend Myers. Several months later, Myers made a similar generous gift by purchasing an Apple iPad, which he requested be delivered directly to Westendorf. Westendorf received and kept that iPad. In the shipment, Apple included its Standard Terms and Conditions Agreement, which contains an arbitration clause. Westendorf allegedly began experiencing numerous and serious difficulties when attempting to use the Siri voice-activated components of the iPad. She brought a class action against Apple. Westendorf argues that she is not bound by the arbitration clause because as a nonpurchasing user of the iPad, she never expressly agreed to arbitration. Is it ethical to obligate a donee beneficiary such as Westendorf to the arbitration clause that was part of the contract between Myers, who gave her the iPad, and Apple?

Problems and Problem Cases

1. Schauer and Erstad went shopping for an engagement ring on August 15, 1999. After looking at diamonds in premier jewelry establishments such as Tiffany and Company and Cartier, they went to Mandarin Gem's store, where they found a ring that salesperson Joy said featured a 3.01 carat diamond with a clarity grading of "SI1." Erstad bought the ring the same day for $43,121.55. The following month, for insurance purposes, Mandarin Gem provided Erstad a written appraisal verifying the ring had certain characteristics, including an SI1 clarity rating and an average replacement value of $45,500. Lam, a graduate gemologist with the European Gemological Laboratory (EGL), signed the appraisal. The couple's subsequent short-term marriage was dissolved in a North Dakota judgment awarding each party "the exclusive right, title and possession of all personal property . . . which such party now owns, possesses, holds or hereafter acquires." Schauer's personal property included the engagement ring given to her by Erstad. On June 3, 2002, after the divorce, Schauer had the ring evaluated by the Gem Trade Laboratory, which gave the diamond a rating of "SI2" quality, an appraisal with which other unidentified jewelers, including one at Mandarin Gem's store, agreed. Schauer alleged that the true clarity of the diamond and its actual worth are some $23,000 less than what Erstad paid for it. Schauer sued Mandarin Gems on several theories, alleging that she was a third-party beneficiary of Erstad's contract with Mandarin Gems. Is she correct?

2. In March 2004, White was stopped in her van when Berkenheuer, driving a Penske truck in the course of his job with Taylor Distributing Company, hit her, causing her serious injury. White settled a first-party action with her no-fault insurer, Amex Insurance, which provided:

   > IN CONSIDERATION of the payment to the undersigned, . . . [plaintiff] does hereby release and forever discharge AMEX INSURANCE COMPANY, and their officers, employees, principals, shareholders, executors, administrators, agents, successors, insurers and assigns of and from any and all actions, causes of action, claims, demands, damages, costs, loss of services, expenses and/or compensation on account of, or in any way growing out of, any and all known and unknown personal injuries and property damage resulting or to result from an accident that occurred on or about March 15, 2004.

   > IT IS expressly agreed that this Release also refers to any and all (past, present and future) claims/benefits arising or that may arise from the March 15, 2004 accident.

   This release identified Amex and its agents in great detail, but made no mention of Berkenheuer, Taylor, and Penske. In a later lawsuit by White against Berkenheuer, Taylor, and Penske, the defendants claimed that they were third-party beneficiaries to this release and that they "stood in the shoes of the promisee (Amex)." Is this a good argument?

3. Ramirez loaned Regalado $75,000. In return, Regalado assigned $65,000 of his eventual recovery in a workers' compensation matter on which Bloom represented him. Bloom signed the assignment along with Ramirez and Regalado, agreeing "to disburse the proceeds of the aforementioned settlement, award or judgment in accordance with the terms" of the assignment. When the matter settled, however, Bloom paid the proceeds to Regalado despite the terms of the assignment because a relevant state law expressly prohibited the assignment of funds due or received from a workers' compensation claim. Regalado never turned the funds over to Ramirez. Ramirez sued Bloom and Regalado for breach of contract, arguing (as the claims related to Bloom) that the policy is in favor of free assignability. Is this argument correct?

4. In February 1980, Mary Pratt entered into a contract to buy a Dairy Queen restaurant from Harold and Gladys Rosenberg. The terms of the contract for the franchise, inventory, and equipment were a purchase price totaling $62,000, a $10,000 down payment, and $52,000 due in quarterly payments at 10 percent interest over a 15-year period. The sales contract also contained a provision denying the buyer a right of prepayment for the first five years of the contract. In October 1982, Pratt assigned her rights and delegated her duties under this contract to Son Inc. The assignment between Pratt and Son contained a "Consent to Assignment" clause, which was signed by the Rosenbergs. It also contained a "save harmless" clause, in which Son promised to indemnify Pratt for any claims, demands, or actions that might result from Son's failure to perform the agreement. After this transaction, Pratt moved to Arizona and had no further knowledge of or involvement with the Dairy Queen business. Also following the assignment, the Dairy Queen was moved from the mall to a different location. Son assigned the contract to Merit Corporation in June 1984. This assignment did not include a consent clause, but the Rosenbergs knew of the assignment and

apparently acquiesced in it. They accepted a large pre-payment from Merit, reducing the principal balance to $25,000. After the assignment, Merit pledged the inventory and equipment of the Dairy Queen as collateral for a loan from Valley Bank and Trust. Payments from Merit to the Rosenbergs continued until June 1988, at which time the payments ceased, leaving an unpaid principal balance of $17,326.24 plus interest. The Rosenbergs attempted to collect the balance from Merit, but Merit filed bankruptcy. The business assets pledged as collateral for the loan from Valley Bank and Trust were repossessed. The Rosenbergs brought an action for collection of the outstanding debt against Son and Pratt, claiming that they were still obligated on the contract and that there was no novation in either case. Are Son and/or Pratt liable to the Rosenbergs given Merit's breach or was either or both released by the assignments and subsequent circumstances?

5. Jones paid Sullivan, the chief of the Addison Police Department, $6,400 in exchange for Sullivan's cooperation in allowing Jones and others to bring marijuana by airplane into the Addison airport without police intervention. Instead of performing the requested service, Sullivan arrested Jones. The $6,400 was turned over to the district attorney's office and was introduced into evidence in the subsequent trial in which Jones was tried for and convicted of bribery. After his conviction, Jones assigned his alleged claim to the $6,400 to Melvyn Bruder. Based on the assignment, Bruder brought suit against the state of Texas to obtain possession of the money. Will he be successful?

6. Locke, a physical education teacher, served as an umpire for high school baseball games for a number of years. He was a member of the Southeast Alabama Umpires Association (SAUA), which provides officials to athletic events sponsored by the Alabama High School Athletic Association (AHSAA). In March 1999, Locke was serving as the head umpire in a baseball game between Carroll High School and George W. Long High School. The game was being played at Carroll High School, and the principal and the athletic director of Carroll High School were in attendance; however, Carroll High School did not provide police protection or other security personnel for the game. After the baseball game, the parent of one of the baseball players for Carroll High School attacked Locke, punching him three times in the face—in his right eye, on the right side of his face, and on the left side of his neck. As a result, Locke sustained physical injuries to his neck and face that caused him pain, discomfort, scarring, and blurred vision. Locke sued the Ozark City Board of Education, alleging breach of contract. Locke specifically alleged that because Carroll High School, through the Board, is a member of the AHSAA, it is therefore required to follow the rules and regulations of the AHSAA. According to Locke, the AHSAA Directory provides that all school principals have the duty to "insure good game administration and supervision by providing for . . . adequate police protection" at athletic events. Locke alleged that, by not fulfilling its duty under the Directory, the Board breached its contract with the AHSAA by failing to provide police protection at the baseball game, that he was an intended third-party beneficiary of the contract, and that he was injured as a result of the Board's breach of the contract. Is this a good argument?

7. Alegent, the owner of a hospital, staffed its emergency room by contracting with Premier Health, which supplied ER physicians from New Century Physicians of Nebraska, each as independent contractors. Though the New Century ER physicians were "seamlessly integrated" in the Alegent health care system and, by all appearances (including their employee ID tags), looked to be part of Alegent, the agreement between Alegent and Premier Health was clear that the parties were independent entities contracting solely for the purposes of the agreed services and that "[n]either of the parties . . . shall have the authority to bind the other or shall be deemed or construed to be the agent, employee or representative of the other." Podraza's appendix ruptured after treatment in Alegent's ER, and Podraza and her husband began talks with Alegent about compensation. Premier Health and New Century did not participate in the settlement negotiations. Alegent and the Podrazas reached a settlement involving forgiveness of the hospital bill and payment of additional money in exchange for which the Podrazas released "the said Released Parties, and all others directly or indirectly liable or claimed to be liable" from all claims and demands. The Podrazas later sued New Century, and New Century moved for summary judgment on the ground that they were protected by the release as third-party beneficiaries. Was New Century correct?

8. Eagle Mountain City entered into a contract with Cedar Valley Water Association to share in any recovery from a legal malpractice action against the City's attorneys, Parsons Kinghorn & Harris P.C. Parsons Kinghorn represented the City in the negotiation and management of an agreement with Cedar Valley for the

purchase of a well. That deal fell apart, largely because Parsons Kinghorn (allegedly negligently) advised the City that certain conditions that were a prerequisite to the City's performance failed to occur. Cedar Valley sued the City for breach of the well contract. Now represented by other legal counsel, the City agreed to settle the claim with Cedar Valley. The settlement agreement included the assignment to Cedar Valley of its interest in the malpractice action against Parsons Kinghorn. In response, Parsons Kinghorn argued that the assignment was ineffective because it was contrary to a strong public policy against voluntary assignment of legal malpractice claims because of concerns about commoditizing or merchandising such claims, the effect such assignments would have on the sanctity of the attorney–client relationship, and the possibility that such assignments would create an incentive for parties to collude against the losing party's attorney (by agreeing to artificially inflated damages in return for the right to collect on the subsequent malpractice claim). Were these concerns sufficient to overcome the strong presumption in favor of assignability?

9. The Flomers were divorced in 2001. At the time of their divorce, they negotiated a settlement agreement containing the following postminority-educational-support provision for the benefit of their then minor daughter, Jessica:

> For the support and maintenance of the [daughter], [the father] shall pay and be responsible for all reasonable costs of her post-secondary education. The [parents] agree to make reasonable efforts to obtain grants and/or scholarships for the [daughter].

The parents' agreement was incorporated into the divorce judgment entered by the court. In 2006, in a custody modification/contempt proceeding involving the Flomers' other minor child, the court entered a judgment that stated in part, "Father shall continue to pay for the daughter's . . . college tuition, books and fees." Jessica began her college studies at Auburn University in Montgomery in 2003. She completed the prerequisites for pharmacy school and then transferred to pharmacy school at Auburn University in 2004. She graduated from pharmacy school in 2008. In 2008, Jessica sent her father a letter informing him that her student loans were about to come due and seeking $62,000 plus interest for tuition that had not been covered by scholarships or grants. Jessica ultimately filed a petition in court to have her father held in contempt for his failure to comply with the postminority-educational-support provision of her parents' divorce judgment. Was Jessica entitled to enforce that provision against her father?

10. The Wattses contracted to sell real estate to MW Development in a contract that specified July 31 as the date for the closing. MW paid the Wattses a down payment and contracted to pay them 8 percent interest on the balance if it failed to close on time. Simpson was not a party to the real estate contract between the Wattses and MW, but he had loaned MW the money for the down payment. As security for this loan, MW executed a promissory note and assignment pursuant to which MW assigned all of its interest in the real estate it was buying from the Wattses. When Simpson saw this note, he realized that it did not become due until August 4 and, in addition, provided for a 10-day grace period before he could enforce his rights against MW. This left Simpson vulnerable to losing the deposit money. As a result, Simpson entered an agreement with the Wattses in which the Wattses agreed to a 14-day period during which Simpson would have the exclusive right to purchase the property on the same terms of MW, including credit for the down payment, should MW default. MW failed to buy the property, and the Wattses sued MW, Simpson, and others. In their claim against Simpson, the Wattses argued that the assignment contract between MW and Simpson obligated Simpson to perform the promises set forth in the real estate contract between the Wattses and MW. Given these facts, did Simpson assume the duties MW owed to the Wattses by becoming MW's assignee such that he was obligated to buy the Wattses property upon MW's default?

CHAPTER 18

Performance and Remedies

The Warrens hired Denison, a building contractor, to build a house on their property for $73,400. Denison's construction deviated somewhat from the project's specifications. These deviations were presumably unintentional, and the cost of repairing them was $1,941.50. The finished house had a market value somewhat higher than the market value would have been without the deviations. The Warrens refused to pay the $48,400 balance due under the contract, alleging that Denison had used poor workmanship in building the house and they were under no obligation to perform further duties under the contract.

- Do the Warrens have the right to withhold all further payment?
- What are the consequences of Denison's breach of contract?
- What are the appropriate remedies for Denison's breach of contract?
- Are the Warrens under an ethical duty to pay Denison?

LO · LEARNING OBJECTIVES

After studying this chapter, you should be able to:

18-1 Explain the effect of conditions on the duty to perform a contract and identify contract language that is likely to be considered an express condition.

18-2 Distinguish strict performance and substantial performance standards and determine which is likely to be applied to a given contract duty.

18-3 Explain the possible effects of breach of contract.

18-4 List and explain the circumstances that can excuse performance of a contract.

18-5 Distinguish the various remedies for breach of contract and identify the circumstances under which each remedy is appropriate.

CONTRACTS ARE GENERALLY FORMED before either of the parties renders any actual performance to the other. A person may be content to bargain for and receive the other person's promise at the formation stage of a contract because this permits him to plan for the future. Ultimately, however, all parties bargain for the *performance* of the promises that have been made to them.

In most contracts, the parties carry out their promises and are *discharged* (released from any other contractual obligations) when their performances are complete.

Sometimes, however, a party fails to perform or performs in an unsatisfactory manner. In such cases, courts often must determine the parties' respective rights and duties. This frequently involves deciding such questions as whether performance was due, whether the contract was breached, to what extent it was breached, and whether performance was excused. This task is made more difficult by the fact that contracts often fail to specify the consequences of nonperformance or defective performance. In deciding questions involving the performance of contracts and remedies for breach of contract, courts draw on a variety of legal principles that attempt to do justice, prevent forfeiture and unjust enrichment, and effectuate the parties' presumed intent.

This chapter presents an overview of the legal concepts that courts use to resolve disputes arising in the performance stage of contracting. It describes how courts determine whether performance is due and what kind of performance is due, the consequences of contract breach, and the excuses for a party's failure to perform. It also includes a discussion of the remedies that courts use when a contract has been breached.

Conditions

 LO18-1 Explain the effect of conditions on the duty to perform a contract and identify contract language that is likely to be considered an express condition.

Nature of Conditions
One issue that frequently arises in the performance stage of a contract is whether a party has the duty to perform. Some duties are *unconditional* or *absolute*—that is, the duty to perform does not depend on the occurrence of any further event other than the passage of time. For example, if Root promises to pay Downing $100, Root's duty is unconditional. When a party's duty is unconditional, he has the duty to perform unless his performance is excused. (The various excuses for nonperformance will be discussed later in this chapter.) When a duty is unconditional, the promisor's failure to perform constitutes a *breach of contract*.

In many situations, however, a promisor's duty to perform depends on the occurrence of some event that is called a **condition**. A condition is an uncertain, future event that affects a party's duty to perform. For example, if Melman contracts to buy Lance's house on condition that First Bank approve Melman's application for a mortgage loan by January 10, Melman's duty to buy Lance's house is *conditioned* on the bank's approving his loan application by January 10. When a promisor's duty is conditional, his duty to perform is affected by the occurrence of the condition. In this case, if the condition does not occur, Melman has no duty to buy the house. His failure to buy it because of the nonoccurrence of the condition will *not* constitute a breach of contract. Rather, he is discharged from further obligation under the contract.

Almost any event can be a condition. Some conditions are beyond the control of either party, such as when Morehead promises to buy Pratt's business if the prime rate drops by a specified amount. Others are within the control of a party,

such as when one party's performance of a duty under the contract is a condition of the other party's duty to perform.

Types of Conditions
There are two ways of classifying conditions. One way of classifying conditions focuses on the effect of the condition on the duty to perform. The other way focuses on the way in which the condition is created.

Classifications of Conditions Based on Their Effect on the Duty to Perform As Figure 18.1 illustrates, conditions vary in their effects on the duty to perform.

1. *Condition precedent.* A **condition precedent** is a future, uncertain event that creates the duty to perform. If the condition does not occur, performance does not become due. If the condition does occur, the duty to perform arises. In the *Killian* case, which appears shortly, you will see an example of a condition precedent.

2. *Concurrent condition.* When the contract calls for the parties to perform at the same time, each person's performance is conditioned on the performance or tender of performance (offer of performance) by the other. Such conditions are called **concurrent** conditions. For example, if Martin promises to buy Johnson's car for $5,000, the parties' respective duties to perform are subject to a concurrent condition. Martin does not have the duty to perform unless Johnson tenders his performance, and vice versa.

3. *Condition subsequent.* A **condition subsequent** is a future, uncertain event that **discharges** the duty to perform. When a duty is subject to a condition subsequent, the duty to perform arises but is discharged if the future, uncertain event occurs. For example, Wilkinson and Jones agree that Wilkinson will begin paying Jones $2,000 per month, but that if XYZ Corporation dissolves, Wilkinson's obligation to pay will cease. In this case, Wilkinson's duty to pay is subject to being discharged by a condition subsequent. The major significance of the distinction between conditions precedent and conditions subsequent is that the plaintiff bears the burden of proving the occurrence of a condition precedent, while the defendant bears the burden of proving the occurrence of a condition subsequent.

Classifications of Conditions Based on the Way in Which They Were Created Another way of classifying conditions is to focus on the means by which the condition was created.

1. *Express condition.* An express condition is a condition that is specified in the language of the parties' contract. For example, if Grant promises to sell his regular season

Figure 18.1   Effect of Conditions

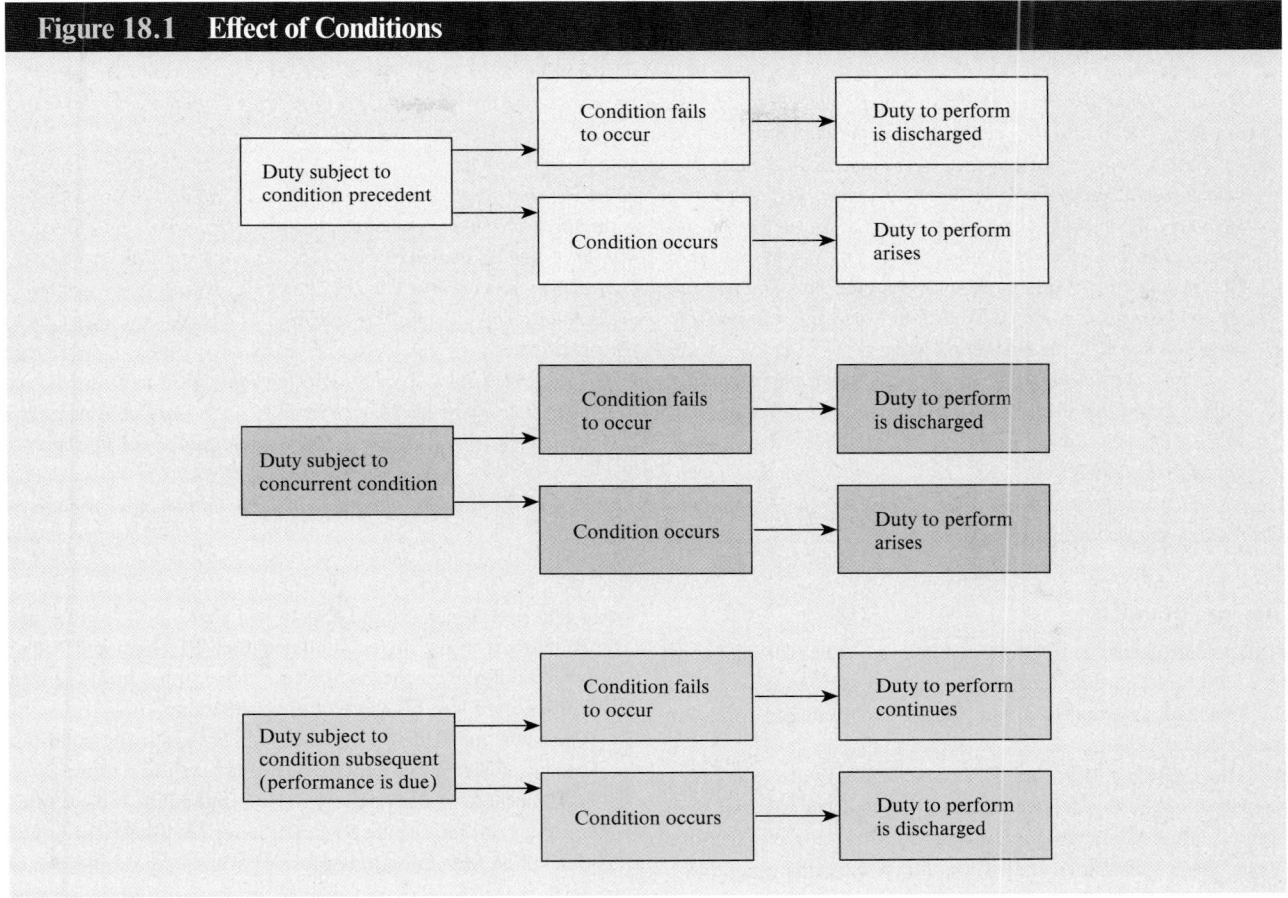

Killian v. Ricchetti	**2016 WL 6471245 (E.D. Pa. Oct. 31, 2016)**

David J. Killian and Christopher Ricchetti became friends in 2011, based on their shared interest in real estate development. Each owned a property in Philadelphia that, together, they believed they could leverage to co-develop a mixed-used condominium and retail project. From September 2011 into early 2012, they exchanged ideas on how they could use Killian's condo on Pine Street to generate cash income to use for construction loans to develop the condo/retail project on a vacant lot Ricchetti owned at 2nd and Brown Street. In order to move forward, the 2nd and Brown Street property needed to be rezoned for mixed commercial use, and a number of other permits and construction arrangements needed to be made. With regard to the Pine Street condo, the idea was that Ricchetti would buy a senior mortgage on the condo and foreclose on it to give Killian the cash to participate in the 2nd and Brown Street development.

On February 6 and 8, 2012, the two exchanged e-mails setting out much of these plans in detail. However, that e-mail exchange left several important terms unresolved, and the messages were best characterized as an offer and counteroffer. No acceptance took place.

Following that, on February 19, Ricchetti initiated a different e-mail chain by asking Killian four questions about the Pine Street condo mortgage, namely, how the loan would be split, the value of the mortgage, legal review of the mortgage, and the timing of the Pine Street condo sale.

Ricchetti proposed, "when the Pine is clear title we form an LLC with an equal partnership of 50% and [w]e do so only [to] develop that property as planned with 10 or more units, 6 floors and retail bottom. We both agree that we have no [other] plans but to develop that property this year, and cost are equal for us, as well as profit when we agree to sell. We both have rights to see and obtain all cost information records related to 2nd and [B]rown. If one of us is found and proven stealing from the other or the business the[y] [l]ose their half of the property." On February 20, Killian responded, *"OF COURSE"* to Ricchetti's proposal. Killian also answered Ricchetti's questions about the Pine Street condo mortgage and told Ricchetti he was waiting for Prudential's attorney, the lender for Pine Street, to get back to him so they could close on the Pine Street condo mortgage.

Thereafter, both Richetti and Killian undertook a number of steps to move their plans forward, including working with the Philadelphia Streets Department for approval of a curb cut and discussing the zoning code parking requirements for the 2nd and Brown Street location. They worked to get the rezoning approval. They secured an architect for the development. They organized a civic meeting to get neighborhood support for the project. And they moved forward with the purchase and sale of the Pine Street condo. Ricchetti paid Prudential $100,000 to assign its mortgage to him, and he instituted foreclosure proceedings. Ricchetti never successfully foreclosed on the condo, however, because Wells Fargo, which held a junior lien on the condo, was "adamant" in asserting its position, and Ricchetti decided not to fight the legal battle necessary to overcome Wells Fargo's position.

Despite the substantial progress the two made on the plans for the 2nd and Brown Street development (including ultimately securing Zoning Board approval for the mixed-use building) and despite holding themselves out to everyone as partners on the project, Ricchetti sold the 2nd and Brown Street property as a vacant lot for $740,000 several months after the Zoning Board approval. He did not share any of the proceeds from the sale of 2nd and Brown Street with Killian.

Killian sued Richetti for breach of contract, alleging damages in excess of $50,000. Ricchetti moved for summary judgment arguing that no contract existed as a matter of law.

Kearney, District Judge

The e-mails exchanged between Killian and Ricchetti on February 19th and February 20th do form a contract but it could not be breached, as a matter of law, because the required condition never occurred. . . .

The February 19th and February 20th e-mails evidence a "meeting of the minds" but because the contract is based on a condition precedent which never occurs, the contract never matures. "It is well settled that if a contract contains a condition precedent, the condition precedent must occur before a duty to perform under the contract arises."

The February 19th and February 20th e-mails evidence a meeting of the minds on the defined terms. Ricchetti and Killian agree they will have a deal when Ricchetti receives clear title to Killian's Pine Street condo. Once Ricchetti receives clear title, Ricchetti and Killian agree they will form a partnership shared fifty/fifty to develop 2nd and Brown Street. They agree developing 2nd and Brown Street is the only project for their partnership this

year and both Ricchetti and Killian will share profits, costs, and an equal right to see financial information. Ricchetti and Killian also agreed if one partner is proven to have stolen from the partnership, he will lose his share of the partnership.

Ricchetti and Killian's agreement is based on the condition precedent of Ricchetti receiving clear title on Killian's Pine Street condo. Ricchetti's offer opens with, "when the Pine is clear title." The parties do not dispute Ricchetti never received clear title to Killian's Pine Street condo because of Wells Fargo's unexpected intransigence. There is no evidence either party interfered with performing the condition precedent. Because the condition precedent never occurred, the contract never matured and the parties' duty to perform under the contract never arose.

* * *

Conclusion

We grant Ricchetti's motion for summary judgment as to Killian's breach of contract claim as a matter of law.

---

football tickets to Carson on condition that Indiana University wins the Rose Bowl, Indiana's winning the Rose Bowl is an express condition of Grant's duty to sell the tickets.

When the contract expressly provides that a party's duty is subject to a condition, courts take it very seriously. When a duty is subject to an express condition, that condition

must be strictly complied with in order to give rise to the duty to perform. The *Macomb Mechanical* case that follows this discussion provides an example of a harsh application of a particular type of express condition, a "pay if paid" clause. The case also illustrates that courts will limit the operation of the condition to only those duties under the contract to which they apply.

2. *Implied-in-fact condition.* An implied-in-fact condition is one that is not specifically stated by the parties but is *implied* by the nature of the parties' promises. For example, if Summers promises to unload cargo from Knight's ship, the ship's arrival in port would be an implied-in-fact condition of Summer's duty to unload the cargo.

3. *Constructive condition.* Constructive conditions (also known as *implied-in-law conditions*) are conditions that are imposed by law rather than by the agreement of the parties. The law imposes constructive conditions to do

justice between the parties. In contracts in which one of the parties is expected to perform before the other, the law normally infers that performance is a constructive condition of the other party's duty to perform. For example, if Thomas promises to build a house for King, and the parties' understanding is that King will pay Thomas an agreed-on price when the house is built, King's duty to pay is subject to the constructive condition that Thomas complete the house. Without such a constructive condition, a person who did not receive the performance promised him would still have to render his own performance.

Macomb Mechanical, Inc. v. LaSalle Group, Inc.
2015 WL 1880189 (Mich. Ct. App. Apr. 23, 2015)

As a subcontractor hired by general contractor LaSalle Group, Inc., Macomb Mechanical, Inc. performed plumbing and mechanical work on a dining facility construction project at Fort Sill in Oklahoma. The U.S. Army Corps of Engineers (USACE) owned the project, and Veterans Enterprise Technology Services (VETS) oversaw it as the prime contractor.

Macomb's work was originally scheduled to take about six months, but complications caused Macomb's work to extend for 15 months. In addition, Macomb alleged that the project's scope changed after it entered the subcontract. Though Macomb performed the work associated with the change in scope, LaSalle refused to sign change orders related to it.

LaSalle failed to pay Macomb for some of the work clearly described in the subcontract, as well as the extra work Macomb claimed to have done.

Macomb sued LaSalle for breach of contract, but LaSalle argued that it was excused from paying Macomb because a condition precedent to its duty to perform on the subcontract had not occurred, namely, LaSalle had not yet been paid by USACE or VETS. LaSalle pointed to a series of "pay if paid" clauses in the subcontract to establish that payment to LaSalle was a condition precedent to its duty to pay Macomb. The particular clauses included the following:

2.1 Subje\ct to approval by Contractor, and approval as required by the Subcontract Documents, Contractor will pay Subcontractor monthly progress payments provided as a condition precedent that Owner has paid Contractor.

2.7 Contractor will use Owner funds to pay Subcontractor within ten (10) days after receipt and Contractor shall have no obligation to pay Subcontractor for the Subcontract work, or any claims related thereto, unless and until Owner pays Contractor for the same. Receipt of funds by payment from Owner for specific payment to the subcontractor, shall be a condition precedent to Contractor's obligation to pay Subcontractor.

2.9 Conditioned upon precedent payment by Owner, Contractor will pay to Subcontractor the final payment for the Subcontract work within ten (10) days after receipt thereof from the Owner.

The trial court agreed with LaSalle and summarily dismissed Macomb's claims. Macomb appealed.

PER CURIAM

Pay-if-Paid Clauses

Macomb . . . challenges the [trial court's] dismissal of its claim for $21,589.20 remaining due for work indisputably covered by the subcontract, and $172,049 for allegedly extracontractual work for which Macomb had requested change orders and additional work related to alleged discrepancies in project drawings. We

agree that summary disposition was improper with respect to the second category of charges because genuine issues of material fact exist concerning those claims. But the [trial court] properly granted summary disposition to defendants with respect to the amount owed on the subcontract itself because the "pay if paid" clauses bar recovery for that amount until the USACE or VETS compensates LaSalle.

As noted, several contractual provisions indicate that LaSalle's duty to pay Macomb for subcontract work is conditioned on the USACE's or VETS's payment to LaSalle for that work. LaSalle Chief Executive Officer Steve Palermo submitted an affidavit stating that LaSalle had not been paid by VETS for the monies sought by Macomb for work performed on the project or for Macomb's requested extra compensation. According to Palermo, LaSalle had submitted a claim to VETS, which incorporated various payment requests, including those made by Macomb, into a final billing for the USACE. Palermo indicated that VETS filed suit against the USACE, which is apparently still pending, in federal court regarding payment for the project.

This Court has upheld the applicability of pay-if-paid clauses. In *Berkel & Co. Contractors v. Christman Co.*, 533 N.W.2d 838 (Mich. Ct. App. 1995), this Court found no ambiguity in a contractual clause providing that "all payments to the subcontractor [were] to be made only from equivalent payments received by" the general contractor from the project owner. This Court continued:

> Berkel next argues that even if considered operative, a "pay when paid" clause is merely a provision that postpones payment for a reasonable amount of time, not indefinitely. Again, we disagree. As indicated earlier, the trial court quite properly found that Christman was not required to pay Berkel until it received payment from the owner. Failure to satisfy a condition precedent prevents a cause of action for failure of performance. . . . The contract contains no language limiting the condition precedent to any "reasonable time."

Although such clauses are valid, there is a limit. A contracting party who prevents or renders impossible the satisfaction of a condition precedent may not rely on that condition to defeat liability.

The subcontract unambiguously provides that the owner's payment to LaSalle is a condition precedent to Macomb's right to receive payment from LaSalle. Palermo has sworn that neither the USACE nor VETS has paid LaSalle any of the monies sought by Macomb in this case. There is no evidence that LaSalle has taken any action to prevent satisfaction of the condition precedent. There is no evidence contradicting that VETS has filed a federal lawsuit against the USACE for payments, and that if VETS is successful, part of the judgment would benefit Macomb. Therefore, Macomb is not entitled to recover from LaSalle the amount indisputably owed under the subcontract.

Yet Macomb created a genuine issue of material fact that $172,049 of its requested compensation fell outside the parameters of the subcontract. If this fact is ultimately proven, the subcontract would not apply to those amounts, including the pay-if-paid clauses. This allegedly extracontractual work was documented in Macomb's requested change orders. . . . LaSalle refused to issue those change orders and therefore did not submit them to VETS or the USACE for payment. Macomb asserts that changes in the project drawings and specifications after Macomb submitted its bid caused it to incur additional costs that were not part of the subcontract, prompting it to present the change orders to LaSalle. Had LaSalle issued the change orders, Macomb concedes that the work would have become part of the subcontract. The failure to do so, according to Macomb, means this work was never incorporated into the parties' agreement. If the work is not governed by the subcontract's pay-if-paid clause, then any payment owed to Macomb would have been due within a reasonable time.

LaSalle, of course, disagrees with Macomb's position. LaSalle denied Macomb's proposed change orders . . . , claiming that the underlying work was part of the base subcontract, negating Macomb's claim for extra compensation. LaSalle argues that there is no evidence that the parties entered into a separate contract with respect to the alleged extracontractual work. Therefore, LaSalle contends, its refusal to issue the change orders does not prevent the application of the subcontract's pay-if-paid clause.

Macomb presented evidence creating a genuine issue of material fact that proposed change orders . . . covered extracontractual work. Macomb's project manager, Morris, described at his deposition that LaSalle failed to follow the "chain of command" and directly ordered Macomb's foremen to engage in work under the guise of the subcontract. Macomb management only learned of the work after it was underway and was forced to belatedly draft change orders. . . .

Overall, the evidence is conflicting regarding the extent to which the project drawings changed after Macomb bid on the project and the amount of additional work and costs necessitated by those changes. Therefore, a genuine issue of material fact exists regarding Macomb's claim that it was not provided updated drawings, thereby requiring Macomb to provide additional work and incur further expenses. Because no change order was issued with respect to the additional work and costs allegedly necessitated by the drawing discrepancies, the additional work and costs may reasonably be found to fall outside the scope of the subcontract and therefore not be subject to the subcontract's pay-if-paid clause. LaSalle would then be required to pay Macomb within a reasonable time.

* * *

We affirm in part, reverse in part, and remand for further proceedings consistent with this opinion.

Creation of Express Conditions

Although no particular language is required to create an express condition, the conditional nature of promises is usually indicated by such words as *provided that, subject to, on condition that, if, when, while, after,* and *as soon as.* The process of determining the meaning of conditions is not a mechanical one. Courts look at the parties' overall intent as indicated in language of the entire contract.

The following discussion explores two common types of express conditions.

Example of Express Condition: Satisfaction of Third Parties It is common for building and construction contracts to provide that the property owner's duty to pay is conditioned on the builder's production of certificates to be issued by a specific architect or engineer. These certificates indicate the satisfaction of the architect or engineer with the builder's work. They are often issued at each stage of completion, after the architect or engineer has inspected the work done.

The standard usually used to determine whether the condition has occurred is a *good-faith* standard. As a general rule, if the architect or engineer is acting honestly and has some good-faith reason for withholding a certificate, the builder cannot recover payments due. In legal terms, the condition that will create the owner's duty to pay has not occurred.

If the builder can prove that the withholding of the certificate was fraudulent or done in bad faith (as a result of collusion with the owner, for example), the court may order that payment be made despite the absence of the certificate. In addition, production of the certificate may be excused by the death, insanity, or incapacitating illness of the named architect or engineer.

Example of Express Condition: Personal Satisfaction Contracts sometimes provide that a promisor's duty to perform is conditioned on his personal satisfaction with the promisee's performance. For example, Moore commissions Allen to paint a portrait of Moore's wife, but the contract provides that Moore's duty to pay is conditioned on his personal satisfaction with the portrait.

In determining which standard of satisfaction to apply, courts distinguish between cases in which the performance bargained for involves personal taste and comfort and cases that involve mechanical fitness or suitability for a particular purpose. If personal taste and comfort are involved, as they would be in the hypothetical case described above, a promisor who is honestly dissatisfied with the promisee's performance has the right to reject the performance without being liable to the promisee. If, however, the performance involves mechanical fitness or suitability, the court will apply a reasonable person test. If the court finds that a reasonable person would be satisfied with the performance, the condition of personal satisfaction has been met and the promisor must accept the performance and pay the contract price.

Excuse of Conditions

In most situations involving conditional duties, the promisor does not have the duty to perform unless and until the condition occurs. There are, however, a variety of situations in which the occurrence of a condition will be excused. In such a case, the person whose duty is conditional will have to perform even though the condition has not occurred.

One ground for excusing a condition is that the party benefiting from the condition *prevented* or *hindered* the occurrence of the condition. For example, Connor hires Ingle to construct a garage on Connor's land, but when Ingle attempts to begin construction, Connor refuses to allow Ingle access to the land. In this case, Connor's duty to pay would normally be subject to a constructive condition that Ingle build the garage. However, because Connor prevented the occurrence of the condition, the condition will be excused, and Ingle can sue Connor for damages for breach of contract even though the condition has not occurred.

Other grounds for excuse of a condition include **waiver** and **estoppel**. When a person whose duty is conditional voluntarily gives up his right to the occurrence of the condition (waiver), the condition will be excused. Suppose that Buchman contracts to sell his car to Fox on condition that Fox pay him $2,000 by June 14. Fox fails to pay on June 14, but, when he tenders payment on June 20, Buchman accepts and cashes the check without reservation. Buchman has thereby *waived* the condition of payment by June 14.

When a person whose duty is conditional leads the other party to rely on his noninsistence on the condition, the condition will be excused because of estoppel. For example, McDonald agrees to sell his business to Brown on condition that Brown provide a credit report and personal financial statement by July 17. On July 5, McDonald tells Brown that he can have until the end of the month to provide the necessary documents. Relying on McDonald's assurances, Brown does not provide the credit report and financial statement until July 29. In this case, McDonald would be *estopped* (precluded) from claiming that the condition did not occur.

A condition may also be excused when performance of the act that constitutes the condition becomes *impossible.* For example, if a building contract provides that the owner's duty to pay is conditioned on the production of a certificate from a named architect, the condition would be excused if the named architect died or became incapacitated before issuing the certificate.

Performance of Contracts

 LO18-2 Distinguish strict performance and substantial performance standards and determine which is likely to be applied to a given contract duty.

When a promisor has performed his duties under a contract, he is discharged. Because one party's performance constitutes the occurrence of a constructive condition, the other party's duty to perform is also triggered, and the person who has performed has the right to receive the other party's performance. In determining whether a promisor is discharged by performance and whether the constructive condition of performance has been fulfilled, courts must consider the standard of performance they expect.

Level of Performance Expected of the Promisor
In some situations, no deviation from the promisor's promised performance is tolerated; in others, less-than-perfect performance will be sufficient to discharge the promisor and trigger the right to recover under the contract.

Strict Performance Standard A strict performance standard requires virtually perfect compliance with the contract terms. Remember that when a party's duty is subject to an express condition, that condition must be strictly and completely complied with in order to give rise to a duty of performance. Thus, when a promisor's performance is an express condition of the promisee's duty to perform, that performance must strictly and completely comply with the contract in order to give rise to the other promisee's duty to perform. For example, if McMillan agrees to pay Jester $500 for painting his house "on condition that" Jester finish the job no later than June 1, 2020, a standard of strict or complete performance would be applied to Jester's performance. If Jester does not finish the job by June 1, his breach will have several consequences. First, because the condition precedent to McMillan's duty to pay has not occurred, McMillan does not have a duty to pay the contract price. Second, because it is now too late for the condition to occur, McMillan is discharged. Third, McMillan can sue Jester for breach of contract. The law's commitment to freedom of contract justifies such results in cases in which

the parties have expressly bargained for strict compliance with the terms of the contract.

The strict performance standard is also applied to contractual obligations that can be performed either exactly or to a high degree of perfection. Examples of this type of obligation include promises to pay money, deliver deeds, and, generally, deliver goods. A promisor who performs such promises completely and in strict compliance with the contract is entitled to receive the entire contract price. The promisor whose performance deviates from perfection is not entitled to receive the other party's performance if he does not render perfect performance within an appropriate time. He may, however, be able to recover the value of any benefits that he has conferred on the other party under a theory of quasi-contract.

Substantial Performance Standard A substantial performance standard is a somewhat lower standard of performance that applies to duties that are difficult to perform without some deviation from perfection *if* performance of those duties is *not* an express condition. A common example of this type of obligation is a promise to erect a building. Other examples include promises to construct roads, to cultivate crops, and to render some types of personal or professional services. Substantial performance is performance that falls short of complete performance in minor respects. It does not apply when a contracting party has been deprived of a material part of the consideration that party bargained for. When a substantial performance standard is applied, the promisor who has substantially performed is discharged. The promisor's substantial performance triggers the other party's duty to pay the contract price less any damages resulting from the defects in the promisor's performance. The obvious purpose behind the doctrine of substantial performance is to prevent forfeiture by a promisor who has given the injured party most of what was bargained for. Substantial performance is generally held to be inapplicable to a situation in which the breach of contract has been *willful*, however.

The *Harrison* case, which appears shortly, involves a project for which substantial performance is the applicable standard.

Good-Faith Performance
One of the most significant trends in modern contract law is that courts and legislatures have created a duty to perform in good faith in an expanding range of contracts.[1] The Uniform

---

[1]This trend is discussed in Chapter 9.

Substantial Performance

Definition	Application	Effects	Limitation
Performance that falls short of complete performance in some minor respect but that does not deprive the other party of a material part of the consideration for which the party bargained	Applies to performance that (1) is *not* an express condition of the other party's duty to perform and (2) is difficult to do perfectly	Triggers other party's duty to perform; requires other party to pay the contract price minus any damages caused by defects in performance	Breach cannot have been willful

Commercial Code specifically imposes a duty of good faith in every contract within the scope of any of the articles of the UCC [1-203]. A growing number of courts have applied the duty to use good faith in transactions between lenders and their customers as well as insurance contracts, employment contracts, and contracts for the sale of real property.

This obligation to carry out a contract in good faith is usually called the implied covenant of good faith and fair dealing. It is a broad and flexible duty that is imposed by law rather than by the agreement of the parties. It generally means that neither party to a contract will do anything to prevent the other from obtaining the expected benefits from the parties' agreement or their contractual relationship. The law's purpose in imposing such a term in contracts is to prevent abuses of power and encourage ethical behavior.

Breach of the implied covenant of good faith gives rise to a contract remedy. In some states, it can also constitute a tort, depending on the severity of the breach. A court is more likely to recognize a tort action for breach of the implied covenant of good faith when a contract involves a special relationship of dependency and trust between the parties or where the public interest is adversely affected by a contracting party's practices. Numerous cases exist, for example, in which insurance companies' bad-faith refusal to settle claims or perform duties to their insured and lenders' failure to exercise good faith in their dealings with their customers have led to large damage verdicts. Likewise, in states in which the implied duty of good faith has been held applicable to contracts of employment, employers who discharge employees in bad faith have been held liable for damages.[2]

---

[2]This is discussed in Chapter 51.

Breach of Contract

LO18-3 Explain the possible effects of breach of contract.

When a person's performance is due, any failure to perform that is not excused is a breach of contract. Not all breaches of contract are of equal seriousness, however. Some are relatively minor deviations, whereas others are so extreme that they deprive the promisee of the essence of what he bargained for. The legal consequences of a given breach depend on the extent of the breach.

At a minimum, a party's breach of contract gives the nonbreaching party the right to sue and recover for any damages caused by that breach. When the breach is serious enough to be called a material breach, further legal consequences ensue.

Effect of Material Breach A material breach occurs when the promisor's performance fails to reach the level of performance that the promisee is justified in expecting under the circumstances. In a situation in which the promisor's performance is judged by a substantial performance standard, a claim that the promisor failed to give substantial performance is equivalent to a claim that the promisor materially breached the contract.

The party injured by a material breach has the right to withhold performance, is discharged from further obligations under the contract, and may cancel the contract. The nonbreaching party also has the right to sue for damages for total breach of contract.

Effect of Nonmaterial Breach By contrast, when the breach is not serious enough to be material, the nonbreaching party may sue for only those damages caused by the particular breach. The nonbreaching party does not have the right to cancel the contract. Rather, a nonmaterial breach gives the nonbreaching party the right to suspend performance until the breach is remedied. Once the breach is remedied, however, the nonbreaching party must go ahead and render performance, minus any damages caused by the breach.

Determining the Materiality of the Breach

The standard for determining materiality is a flexible one that takes into account the facts of each individual case. The key question is whether the breach deprives the injured party of the benefits that the party reasonably expected. For example, Norman, who is running for mayor, orders campaign literature from Prompt Press, to be delivered in September. Prompt Press's failure to deliver the literature until after the election in November deprives Norman of the essence of what he bargained for and would be considered a material breach.

In determining materiality, courts take into account the extent to which the breaching party will suffer forfeiture if the breach is held to be material. They also consider the magnitude (amount) of the breach and the breaching party's willfulness or good faith. The timing of the breach can also be important. A breach that occurs early on in the parties' relationship is more likely to be viewed as material than is one that occurs after an extended period of performance. Courts also consider the extent to which the injured party can be adequately compensated by the payment of damages.

Time for Performance A party's failure to perform on time is a breach of contract that may be serious enough to constitute a material breach, or it may be relatively trivial under the circumstances.

At the outset, it is necessary to determine when performance is due. Some contracts specifically state the time for performance, which makes it easy to determine the time for performance. In some contracts that do not specifically state the time for performance, such a time can be inferred from the circumstances surrounding the contract. In the Norman and Prompt Press campaign literature example, the circumstances surrounding the contract probably would have implied that the time for performance was some time before the election, even if the parties had not specified the time for performance. In still other contracts, no time for performance is either stated or implied. When no time for performance is stated or implied, performance must be completed within a "reasonable time," as judged by the circumstances of each case. In the following *Harrison* case, the court addresses whether it can determine if a reasonable time has passed as a matter of law in response to a motion for summary judgment.

Harrison v. Family Home Builders, LLC   84 So. 3d 879 (Ala. Ct. App. 2011)

Gary and Patsy Harrison hired Family Home Builders, LLC (FHB) to remodel their house. The Harrisons planned remodeling and additions of bedrooms and bathrooms, an addition of an outdoor kitchen, an outdoor pavilion, and the installation of a concrete pad. Kyle Gean, a subcontractor of FHB who was employed to supervise the work at the Harrisons', met with them prior to commencing the work and estimated that the project would take around four months and cost approximately $109,000.

FHB entered a contract with the Harrisons for the remodel. The contract stated no specific date for completion of the work and did not indicate that time was of the essence. Moreover, the contract did not include a total price, but rather required the Harrisons to pay all of the costs of the work to be done plus a 13 percent contractor's fee to FHB on all such costs. Finally, it required FHB to follow the plans and specifications provided by the Harrisons and to comply with applicable local building codes.

According to the Harrisons, almost every aspect of the project was botched by FHB. In their eventual responses to FHB's discovery requests, the Harrisons outlined a number of these problems. The concrete slab was not level and allowed water to stand on it, was excessively cracked, and had an uneven and splotchy color, among other problems. The brickwork outside was faulty. The framing of bedrooms, bathrooms, the outdoor pavilion, and windows in many rooms was done incorrectly. Improper or incorrect materials were ordered and installed. They further claimed that Gean was often absent, failed to order materials in a timely manner, scheduled subcontractors prior to when the work could be done, and ignored the plans and directions provided by decorator Madelyn Hereford and architect Robert Weber.

FHB disputed the Harrisons' claims. In contrast, FHB claimed that the Harrisons and Hereford made significant changes to the original plans during the project, including those that changed the sizes of various features, added elements to the job, and modified others. According to FHB, those changes required additional time and increased costs. FHB argued that it was entitled to a reasonable amount of time to complete the work, which the Harrisons refused to provide.

By mid-April (three months into the project), the total cost of the project was between $135,000 and $145,000, and Gary Harrison asked FHB to commit to a May 18 completion date. When FHB refused, the Harrisons terminated the contract and hired Coffman Custom Homes to correct, repair, and complete the work. All parties agree the work was about half done at that point.

Derrick Coffman, owner of Coffman Custom Homes, testified at a deposition that FHB's work did not conform to any known building code's standards of good workmanship. He testified that the cost of repairing FHB's poor work was $151,411.55. He admitted, though, that changes in plans and specifications cause delays in projects and that his estimation was that the Harrisons' remodel was a "one year project at minimum."

In July (six months after the remodel had commenced), the Harrisons filed a lawsuit claiming FHB breached the contract, as well as committed negligence and fraud. As to the breach of contract claim, the Harrisons alleged that FHB failed to complete the work in accordance with the plans and specifications, failed to complete some of the work, and did not comply with applicable building codes, among other claims.

After discovery, FHB moved the trial court for summary judgment on all claims, which the trial court granted. The Harrisons appealed.

Bryan, Judge

The Harrisons argue that the trial court erred in granting the summary-judgment motion with respect to their breach-of-contract claim insofar as that claim is based on (1) the allegation that FHB failed to perform the work in accordance with the plans and specifications provided by the Harrisons, (2) the allegation that FHB failed to perform the work in a workmanlike manner, and (3) the allegation that FHB failed to complete the work.

"[N]ot every partial failure to comply with the terms of a contract by one party . . . will entitle the other party to abandon the contract at once." *Birmingham News Co. v. Fitzgerald*, 133 So. 31, 32 (Ala. 1931) [(internal quotations omitted)]. In the case now before us, in order for the Harrisons to establish that they had the right to unilaterally terminate the contract on May 4, 2007, they bore the burden of proving that FHB had committed a breach of the contract that was "of so material and substantial a nature as would constitute a defense to an action brought by [FHB] for [the Harrisons'] refusal to proceed with the contract." *Id.* (quoting 3 *Williston on Contracts* § 1467). . . .

In order for FHB's breach of the contract to constitute a defense to an action brought by FHB based on the Harrisons' refusal to proceed with the contract, the breach must be sufficient to establish that FHB had not rendered substantial performance of the contract. *See* John D. Calamari & Joseph M. Perillo, *The Law of Contracts* § 11.18(b) (4th ed. 1998) ("Substantial performance is the antithesis of material breach. If a breach is material, it follows that substantial performance has not been rendered."). "Substantial performance of a contract does not contemplate exact performance of every detail but performance of all important parts." *Mac Pon Co. v. Vinsant Painting & Decorating Co.*, 423 So. 2d 216, 218 (Ala. 1982).

The Harrisons' [discovery responses], the testimony regarding defects in the concrete contained in Coffman's affidavit, and the testimony regarding defects in the concrete and the framing contained in Coffman's deposition testimony constituted substantial evidence tending to prove that FHB had failed to perform some of its work in a workmanlike manner. We conclude that the question whether that evidence indicates that FHB committed a material breach of the contract that entitled the Harrisons to terminate the contract unilaterally is a question of fact to be determined by a jury. [Citation omitted.] Therefore, we reverse the summary judgment with respect to the breach-of-contract claim insofar as that claim is based on the allegation that FHB failed to perform the work in a workmanlike manner.

Insofar as their breach-of-contract claim is based on the allegation that FHB failed to perform the work in accordance with the plans and specifications, the Harrisons argue that the trial court erred in granting the summary-judgment motion because, they say, (1) Madelyn Hereford, their decorator, testified that FHB installed plumbing pipes and electrical wiring in the wall to the left of a sliding pocket door instead of to the right as specified by the plans, which required that those pipes and wires be torn out and reinstalled, and (2) Gary Harrison testified in his affidavit that "Mr. Gean did not follow the drawings, plans and directions of Madelyn Hereford, our interior decorator, and Robert Weber, our architect." That testimony of Gary Harrison is a mere conclusory statement that cannot be considered in ruling upon a summary-judgment motion. [Citation and quotes omitted.] Hereford's testimony tended to prove one instance of FHB's failure to follow the plans and specifications. However, in order for that one instance of FHB's failure to follow the plans and specifications to constitute a material breach of the contract, it would have to be sufficient to establish that FHB had failed to render substantial performance of the contract. We conclude that that one instance alone is not sufficient to establish that FHB failed to render substantial performance of the contract. Therefore, we affirm the summary judgment with respect to the breach-of-contract claim insofar as that claim is based on the allegation that FHB failed to follow the plans and specifications.

Insofar as their breach-of-contract claim is based on the allegation that FHB failed to complete the work, the Harrisons argue that the trial court erred in granting the summary-judgment motion because, they say, (1) Gean testified that, before the contract was signed, he had estimated that it would take three to four months to complete the work; (2) Gary Harrison testified that FHB could have completed the work by mid-April 2007 if it had performed the work properly; and (3) Hereford testified as follows:

[By FHB's attorney] Q. In your judgment, with all the changes that were made—and it goes up—in your notes, up until April the 1st, between April 1st and 6th. Due to those changes, this job couldn't be completed by March or April of 2007; is that fair?

A. Yes—no—wait a minute. Is it fair that it was not completed by March or April?

Q. Due to the changes?

A. I see no reason that it could not have been completed.

Q. Okay. Even changes that were still made in March and April, huh?

A. Well, look at the changes that were made. We changed from a jetted tub to spa. That—I believe that is—the space was already there. The framing could have been done.

Because the contract neither specified a date for completion of the work nor stated that time was of the essence, FHB was entitled to a reasonable time to perform the contract. . . . Although Coffman, who testified as an expert witness on behalf of the Harrisons, testified in his deposition that it would take a minimum of a year to perform the work, the Harrisons submitted sufficient evidence to establish a genuine issue of material fact regarding whether the Harrisons afforded FHB a reasonable time to perform the work before terminating the contract on May 4, 2007. . . . Moreover, we conclude that, if a jury should find that the Harrisons afforded FHB a reasonable time to complete the work, it would also be a jury question whether FHB's failure to complete the work by May 4, 2007, constituted a material breach of the contract that would entitle the Harrisons to terminate the contract unilaterally. [Citation omitted.] Therefore, we reverse the summary judgment with respect to the breach-of-contract claim insofar as that claim is based on the allegation that FHB failed to complete the work.

Affirmed in Part; Reversed in Part; and Remanded.

[Note: In a portion of the opinion not reproduced here, the court addressed the negligence and fraud claims, reversing summary judgment on the negligence claim on several theories and affirming the summary judgment on the fraud claim.]

Consequences of Late Performance After a court determines when performance was due, it must determine the consequences of late performance. In some contracts, the parties expressly state that "time is of the essence" or that timely performance is "vital." This means that each party's timely performance by a specific date is an express condition of the other party's duty to perform. Thus, in a contract that contains a time is of the essence provision, any delay by either party normally constitutes a material breach. Sometimes, courts will imply such a term even when the language of the contract does not state that time is of the essence. A court would be likely to do this if late performance is of little or no value to the promisee. For example, Schrader contracts with the local newspaper to run an advertisement for Christmas trees from December 15, 2010, to December 24, 2010, but the newspaper does not run the ad until December 26, 2010. In this case, the time for performance is an essential part of the contract and the newspaper has committed a material breach.

When a contract does not contain language indicating that time is of the essence and a court determines that the time for performance is not a particularly important part of the contract, the promisee must accept late performance rendered within a reasonable time after performance was due. The promisee is then entitled to deduct or set off from the contract price any losses caused by the delay. Late performance is not a material breach in such cases unless it is unreasonably late.

Anticipatory Repudiation
One type of breach of contract occurs when the promisor indicates before the time for performance an unwillingness or inability to carry

Time for Performance

Contract Language	Time for Performance	Consequences of Late Performance
"Time is of the essence" or similar language	The time stated in the contract	Material breach
Specific time is stated in or implied by the contract and later performance would have little or no value	The time stated in or implied by the contract	Material breach
Specific time is stated in or implied by the contract, but the time for performance is a relatively unimportant part of the contract	The time stated in or implied by the contract	Not a material breach unless performance is unreasonably late
No time for performance is stated in or implied by the contract	Within a reasonable time	Not material breach unless performance is unreasonably late

out the contract. This is called anticipatory repudiation or **anticipatory breach**. Anticipatory breach generally constitutes a material breach of contract that discharges the promisee from all further obligation under the contract.

In determining what constitutes anticipatory repudiation, courts look for some unequivocal statement or voluntary act that clearly indicates that the promisor cannot or will not perform. This may take the form of an express statement by the promisor. The promisor's intent not to perform could also be implied from the promisor's actions. For example, if Ross, who is obligated to convey real estate to Davis, conveys the property to some third person instead, Ross has repudiated the contract.

When anticipatory repudiation occurs, the promisee is faced with several choices. For example, Marsh and Davis enter a contract in which Davis agrees to deliver a quantity of bricks to Marsh on September 1, 2014, and Marsh agrees to pay Davis a sum of money in two installments. The agreement specifies that Marsh will pay 50 percent of the purchase price on July 15, 2014, and 50 percent of the purchase price within 30 days after delivery. On July 1, 2014, Davis writes Marsh and unequivocally states that he will not deliver the bricks. Must Marsh go ahead and send the payment that is due on July 15? Must he wait until September 1 to bring suit for total breach of contract? The answer to both questions is no.

When anticipatory repudiation occurs, the nonbreaching party is justified in withholding performance and suing for damages right away, without waiting for the time for performance to arrive.[3] A nonbreaching party who was ready, willing, and able to perform can recover damages for total breach of the contract. The nonbreaching party is not obligated to do this, but may instead wait until the time for performance in case the other party decides to perform.

Recovery by a Party Who Has Committed Material Breach

A party who has materially breached the contract (i.e., has not substantially performed) does not have the right to recover the contract price. If a promisor who has given some performance to the promisee cannot recover under the contract, however, the promisor will face forfeiture and the promisee will have obtained an unearned gain. There are two possible avenues for a party who has committed material breach to obtain some compensation for the performance conferred on the nonbreaching party.

1. *Quasi-contract.* A party who has materially breached a contract might recover the reasonable value of any benefits conferred on the promisee by bringing an action under quasi-contract.[4] This would enable the promisor to obtain

[3]Uniform Commercial Code rules regarding anticipatory repudiation in contracts for the sale of goods are discussed in Chapter 21.

[4]Quasi-contract is discussed in Chapter 9. It involves the use of the remedy of restitution, which is discussed later in this chapter.

Ethics and Compliance in Action

Marsh, a contractor, enters into a contract with Needmore Tree Farm to build a structure on Needmore's property that Needmore plans to use as a sales office for selling Christmas trees to the public. The contract provides that Needmore will pay Marsh $110,000 for the structure, with 50 percent of the payment in advance and 50 percent upon completion. It also provides that Marsh will complete the construction and have the structure ready for occupation by December 1. With regard to this last provision, the contract states, "time is of the essence." The December 1 date is significant to Needmore because it wanted to be sure to have the sales office ready for Christmas season. On December 1, the construction has progressed substantially, but the structure is not going to be ready for occupation for several more weeks. Needmore fires Marsh and refuses to pay him the remaining 50 percent due under the contract. Assuming that Marsh has materially breached the contract, does Needmore have an ethical duty to pay Marsh for the benefit that Marsh has conferred on it?

---

compensation for the value of any performance that has benefited the nonbreaching party. Some courts take the position that a person in material breach should not be able to recover for benefits conferred, however.

2. *Partial performance of a divisible contract.* Some contracts are divisible; that is, each party's performance can be divided in two or more parts and each part is exchanged for some corresponding consideration from the other party. For example, if Johnson agrees to mow Peterson's lawn for $20 and clean Peterson's gutters for $50, the contract is divisible. A promisor who performs one part of the contract but materially breaches another part can recover at the contract price for the part the promisor did perform. For example, if Johnson breached his duty to clean the gutters but fully performed his obligation to mow the lawn, he could recover at the contract price for the lawn-mowing part of the contract.

Excuses for Nonperformance

 LO18-4 List and explain the circumstances that can excuse performance of a contract.

Although nonperformance of a duty that has become due will ordinarily be a breach of contract, there are some situations in which nonperformance is excused because of factors that arise after the formation of the contract. When this occurs, the person whose performance is made impossible or impracticable by these factors is discharged from further obligation under the contract. The following discussion concerns the most common grounds for excuse of nonperformance.

Impossibility When performance of a contractual duty becomes impossible after the formation of the contract, the duty will be discharged on grounds of **impossibility**. This does not mean that a person can be discharged merely because of an inability to perform on the contract or because doing so will cause hardship or difficulty. Impossibility in the legal sense of the word means "it cannot be done by anyone" rather than "I cannot do it." Thus, promisors who find that they have agreed to perform duties that are beyond their capabilities or that turn out to be unprofitable or burdensome are generally not excused from performance of their duties. This principle is illustrated in the *World of Boxing* case, which follows and which involves a promise that famous boxing promoter Don King was unable to perform. Impossibility will provide an excuse for nonperformance, however, when some unexpected event arises after the formation of the contract and renders performance objectively impossible. The event that causes the impossibility need not have been entirely unforeseeable. But normally the event will be one that the parties would not have reasonably thought of as a real possibility that would affect performance.

There are a variety of situations in which a person's duty to perform may be discharged on grounds of impossibility. The three most common situations involve illness or death of the promisor, supervening illegality, and destruction of the subject matter of the contract.

Illness or Death of Promisor Incapacitating illness or death of the promisor excuses nonperformance when the promisor has contracted to perform personal services. For example, if Pauling, a college professor who has a contract with State University to teach for an academic year, dies

World of Boxing LLC v. King   56 F. Supp. 3d 507 (S.D.N.Y. 2014)

On May 17, 2013, professional boxers Guillermo Jones and Denis Lebedev fought in a Cruiserweight Title Fight in Moscow, sanctioned by the World Boxing Association (WBA), which Jones won by knockout in the 11th round. After the bout, however, Jones's urine tested positive for furosemide, prompting an investigation by the WBA. On October 17, 2013, the WBA found Jones guilty of using a banned substance, stripped him of the Cruiserweight title, and suspended him from WBA-sanctioned bouts for six months.

On January 28, 2014, Vladimir Hrunov and Andrey Ryabinskiy, doing business as World of Boxing LLC (WOB), and Don King— the representatives of Lebedev and Jones, respectively—finalized terms for a second administration of the Cruiserweight Title match between Lebedev and Jones. In the Agreement, King represented that he "holds the exclusive promotional rights for Jones," and he promised to "cause Jones . . . to participate" in the rematch. The Agreement also imposed the following restrictions on Jones:

> Jones must arrive in Moscow a minimum of 7 days before the Event and shall remain in Moscow until the Event. Jones also undertakes to be subjected to drug testing before and after the fight, in compliance with the rules of the WBA and the [2013 WBA Resolution].

The purpose of these provisions, as King has explained by affidavit, was to "preclude another . . . positive drug test."

The rematch was set for April 25, 2014. On April 23, 2014, urine samples were collected from both Jones and Lebedev and submitted for testing. On April 25, 2014—the day the bout was supposed to take place—a report was issued, finding that Lebedev's sample was clean but that Jones's sample tested positive for furosemide. When WOB and Lebedev learned of this news, Lebedev withdrew from the bout. On April 28, 2014, the WBA issued a letter deeming Lebedev's withdrawal "justifiabl[e]" on the basis that "[t]he WBA would not, and could not, sanction a championship bout when it was aware of Jones' positive test as this would violate WBA rules, may cause unnecessary harm to [Lebedev], and would otherwise compromise the nature of WBA world title bouts." On May 23, 2014, after reviewing the test results more carefully, the WBA issued a resolution (1) affirming the finding that Jones's urine contained furosemide, (2) suspending Jones from WBA-sanctioned bouts for two years, and (3) naming Lebedev Cruiserweight champion.

WOB sued King for breach of contract for failing to "cause Jones . . . to participate" in the bout. In response to WOB's motion for summary judgment on the issue of King's liability for breach of contract, King responded by pleading that he did not breach the contract and, even if he did, his nonperformance was excused by the doctrine of impossibility.

Shira A. Scheindlin, District Judge

DISCUSSION

A. King Breached the Contract

The Agreement required King to "cause [Jones] to participate in a 12 Round WBA Cruiserweight World Title match [against Lebedev]." King argues that this clause is ambiguous, and that its meaning depends on unresolved factual questions, making summary judgment inappropriate.

But the relevant facts are not in dispute. Under WBA rules— which the Agreement incorporates by reference—any boxer who tests positive for a banned, performance-enhancing substance is disqualified from WBA-sponsored bouts for no less than six months. Both parties agree that Jones ingested furosemide, and there is no question that having tested positive for furosemide, Jones could not participate in the bout. This ends the inquiry. If Jones could not participate in the bout, it follows *a fortiori* that King could not have *caused* Jones to participate in the bout. Therefore, King breached the Agreement.

King protests that this interpretation of the Agreement yields "unreasonable and illogical" results. It would require of King

"nothing less than . . . personal supervision of Jones's every action between the execution of [the Agreement] and the scheduled date of the [bout against Lebedev]." Indeed, in order to avoid liability, King avers that he would have had "to *imprison* Jones to prevent him from having any access to a banned substance"— clearly an untenable outcome.

While these arguments might have force, they are addressed to the wrong issue. King could be right: under the circumstances, it is possible that his contractual obligations *were* too onerous to be enforceable. But that question goes to whether King's failure to perform may be excused, not to whether King in fact failed to perform. As to the latter, Jones's disqualification plainly put King in breach.

B. Impossibility Does Not Excuse King's Breach

In general, "contract liability is strict liability." Nevertheless, failure to perform can be excused if "destruction of . . . the means of performance makes performance objectively impossible." In this vein, King likens his plight to that of a singing troupe manager who signed a contract with a theater owner, promising that the troupe would play for two weeks, only to have the lead singer fall ill on the eve of the first show. When the theater owner sued for breach, the New York Court of Appeals excused the manager's non-performance on the grounds that "[c]ontracts for personal services"—contracts that require action by a specific person—"are subject to [the] implied condition that . . . if [the person] dies, or without fault on the part of the covenantor becomes disabled, the obligation to perform is extinguished." Likewise here, argues King: by ingesting furosemide, Jones "disabled" himself from participating in a WBA-sponsored bout, thereby "extinguishing" King's obligation to perform.

New York law is very clear, however, that an impossibility defense is only available if the frustration of performance was "produced by an unanticipated event that could not have been foreseen or guarded against in the contract." In this case, two key facts compel the conclusion that Jones's ingestion of furosemide was not "unanticipated"—*i.e.*, that King should have foreseen the possibility of Jones testing positive and guarded against it in the contract. *First*, Jones had a history of doping. The result of the first Cruiserweight Title match between Jones and Lebedev—in May 2013—had to be vacated because Jones tested positive for furosemide after the fact. *Second*, the Agreement provided for mandatory pre-bout drug testing, as required by the 2013 WBA Resolution.

King tries to turn these facts around. Noting how "stunned" and "shocked" he was to learn of the positive drug test on April 25, 2014, King reports that "it defie[d] belief, that Jones, aware that he would be subjected to pre-bout drug testing due to his previous positive result, *would again test positive* for the same banned substance." Put otherwise, King "believed that the mandatory drug testing provision . . . would preclude another potential positive drug test, because [Jones] knew that [he] would be subject to random testing." Therefore, in King's view, he should not be punished for failing to foresee such a "plainly remote and unlikely event."

While King's dismay is understandable—it *is* stunning that Jones was foolish enough to test positive for the same drug twice—his argument misconstrues the term "unanticipated event." King casts the question in terms of probability: an event is "unanticipated," in his view, if it is unlikely to occur. What the case law has in mind, however, are not improbable events, but events that fall outside the sphere of what a reasonable person would plan for. Even assuming that King is right about the likelihood of a second positive test, it strains credibility to call the event "unanticipated."

King's own testimony proves the point. By way of explaining why the Agreement was silent about what to do in the event of a second positive test, King admits that he thought the "mandatory drug testing provision" would "preclude" Jones from ingesting furosemide. No doubt he did. From this testimony, however, no one could reasonably conclude that King had not anticipated the possibility of a second positive test. Rather, the inescapable conclusion is that King *had* anticipated such a possibility—and having anticipated it, he believed the threat of a mandatory drug test would ward it off. That King's belief turned out to be mistaken is no basis for relieving him of his contract obligations.

In essence, King argues that he should not be held liable because Jones's decision to take furosemide was outside of King's control: short of "imprison[ing] Jones," there was no way for him to perform. But this argument ignores what *was* in King's control: the decision not to bargain for more protective contract terms.

* * *

CONCLUSION

For the foregoing reasons, WOB's partial motion for summary judgment as to liability is GRANTED.

---

before the completion of the contract, her estate will not be liable for breach of contract. The promisor's death or illness does not, however, excuse the nonperformance of duties that can be delegated to another, such as the duty to deliver goods, pay money, or convey real estate. For example, if Odell had contracted to convey real estate to Ruskin and died before the closing date, Ruskin could enforce the contract against Odell's estate.

Supervening Illegality If a statute or governmental regulation enacted after the creation of a contract makes performance of a party's duties illegal, the promisor is excused from performing. Statutes or regulations that merely make performance more difficult or less profitable do not, however, excuse nonperformance.

Destruction of the Subject Matter of the Contract If something that is essential to the promisor's performance is destroyed after the formation of the contract through no fault of the promisor, the promisor is excused from performing. For example, Woolridge contracts to sell his car to Rivkin. If an explosion destroys the car after the contract has been formed but before Woolridge has made delivery, Woolridge's nonperformance will be excused.

The destruction of nonessential items that the promisor intended to use in performing does not excuse nonperformance if substitutes are available, even though securing them makes performance more difficult or less profitable. Suppose that Ace Construction Company had planned to use a particular piece of machinery in fulfilling a contract to build a building for Worldwide Widgets Company. If the piece of machinery is destroyed but substitutes are available, destruction of the machinery before the contract is performed would *not* give Ace an excuse for failing to perform.

Commercial Impracticability
Section 2-615 of the Uniform Commercial Code has extended the scope of the common law doctrine of impossibility to cases in which unforeseen developments make performance by the promisor highly impracticable, unreasonably expensive, or of little value to the promisee. Rather than using a standard of impossibility, then, the UCC uses the more relaxed standard of impracticability. Despite the less stringent standard applied, cases actually excusing nonperformance on grounds of impracticability are relatively rare. To be successful in claiming excuse based on impracticability, a promisor must be able to establish that the event that makes performance impracticable occurred without the promisor's fault and that the contract was made with the basic assumption that this event would not occur. This basically means that the event was beyond the scope of the risks that the parties contemplated at the time of contracting and that the promisor did not expressly or impliedly assume the risk that the event would occur.

Case law and official comments to UCC section 2-615 indicate that neither increased cost nor collapse of a market for particular goods is sufficient to excuse nonperformance because those are the types of business risks that every promisor assumes. However, drastic price increases or severe shortages of goods resulting from unforeseen circumstances such as wars and crop failures can give rise to impracticability.

If the event causing impracticability affects only a part of the seller's capacity to perform, the seller must allocate production and deliveries among customers in a "fair and reasonable" manner and must notify them of any delay or any limited allocation of the goods. You can read more about commercial impracticability in Chapter 21, Performance of Sales Contracts.

Other Grounds for Discharge

Earlier in this chapter, you learned about several situations in which a party's duty to perform could be discharged even though that party had not performed. These include the nonoccurrence of a condition precedent or concurrent condition; the occurrence of a condition subsequent; material breach by the other party; and excuse from performance by impossibility, impracticability, or frustration. The following discussion deals with additional ways in which a discharge can occur.

Discharge by Mutual Agreement Just as contracts are created by mutual agreement, they can also be discharged by *mutual agreement*. An agreement to discharge a contract must be supported by consideration to be enforceable.

Discharge by Accord and Satisfaction An accord is an agreement whereby a promisee who has an existing claim agrees with the promisor to accept some performance different from that which was originally agreed on. When the promisor performs the accord, that is called a satisfaction.[5] When an **accord and satisfaction** occurs, the parties are discharged. For example, Root contracts with May to build a garage on May's property for $30,000. After Root has performed his part of the bargain, the parties then agree that instead of paying money, May will transfer a one-year-old Porsche to Root. When this is done, both parties are discharged.

Discharge by Waiver A party to a contract may voluntarily relinquish any right he has under a contract, including the right to receive return performance. Such a relinquishment of rights is known as a **waiver**. If one party tenders an incomplete or defective performance and the other party accepts that performance without objection, knowing that the defects will not be remedied, the party to whom performance was due has waived the right to enforce complete or perfect performance. For example, a real estate lease requires Long, the tenant, to pay a $5 late charge for late payments of rent. Long pays his rent late each month for five months, but the landlord accepts it without objection and without assessing the late charge. In this situation, the landlord has probably waived his right to collect the late charge.

To avoid waiving rights, a person who has received defective performance should give the other party prompt notice that she expects complete performance and will seek damages if the defects are not corrected.

Discharge by Alteration If the contract is represented by a *written* instrument, and one of the parties

---

[5]Accord and satisfaction is also discussed in Chapter 12.

intentionally makes a material alteration in the instrument without the other's consent, the alteration acts as a discharge of the other party. If the other party consents to the alteration or does not object to it when he learns of it, he is not discharged. Alteration by a third party without the knowledge or consent of the contracting parties does not affect the parties' rights.

Discharge by Statute of Limitations

Courts have long refused to grant a remedy to a person who delays bringing a lawsuit for an unreasonable time. All of the states have enacted statutes known as **statutes of limitations**, which specify the period of time in which a person can bring a lawsuit.

The time period for bringing a contract action varies from state to state, and many states have shorter periods for cases involving oral contracts than those for cases concerning written contracts. Section 2-725 of the Uniform Commercial Code provides for a four-year statute of limitations for contracts involving the sale of goods.

The statutory period ordinarily begins to run from the date of the breach. It may be delayed if the party who has the right to sue is under some incapacity at that time (such as minority or insanity) or if the breaching party is beyond the jurisdiction of the state. If the nonbreaching party chooses not to bring a lawsuit before the statutory period runs out, the party who breached the contract will not be liable.

Discharge by Decree of Bankruptcy

The contractual obligations of a debtor are generally discharged by a decree of bankruptcy. Bankruptcy is discussed in Chapter 30.

Remedies for Breach of Contract

 LO18-5 Distinguish the various remedies for breach of contract and identify the circumstances under which each remedy is appropriate.

Our discussion of the performance stage of contracts so far has focused on the circumstances under which a party has the duty to perform or is excused from performing. In situations in which a person is injured by a breach of contract and is unable to obtain compensation by a settlement out of court, a further important issue remains: What remedy will a court fashion to compensate for breach of contract?

Contract law seeks to encourage people to rely on the promises made to them by others. Contract remedies focus on the economic loss caused by breach of contract, not on the moral obligation to perform a promise. The objective of granting a remedy in a case of breach of contract is simply to compensate the injured party.

Types of Contract Remedies

There are a variety of ways in which an injured party can be compensated. The basic categories of contract remedies include:

1. Legal remedies (money damages).
2. Equitable remedies.
3. Restitution.

The usual remedy is an award of money damages that will compensate for the losses suffered by the injured party. This is called a legal remedy or remedy at law because the imposition of money damages in our legal system originated in courts of law. Less frequently used but still important are equitable remedies such as specific performance. Equitable remedies are those remedies that had their origins in courts of equity rather than in courts of law.[6] Today, they are available at the discretion of the judge. A final possible remedy is **restitution**, which requires the defendant to pay the value of the benefits that the plaintiff has provided to the defendant.

Interests Protected by Contract Remedies

Remedies for breach of contract protect one or more of the following interests that a promisee may have:[7]

1. *Expectation interest.* The expectation interest is the objective or opportunity for gain that the promisee bargained for and "expected" from the contract. Courts attempt to protect this interest by formulating a remedy that will place the promisee in the position he would have been in if the contract had been performed as promised.

2. *Reliance interest.* The reliance interest is a promisee's interest in being compensated for losses suffered as a result of relying on the other party's promise. In some cases, such as when a promise is unable to prove the value of the expectation interest with reasonable certainty, the promisee may seek reliance damages rather than expectation damages.

3. *Restitution interest.* The restitution interest represents the amount by which the breaching party was enriched or benefited. Both the reliance and restitution interests

---

[6]The nature of equitable remedies is also discussed in Chapter 1.

[7]*Restatement (Second) of Contracts* § 344.

involve promisees who have changed their position. The difference between the two is that the reliance interest involves a loss to the promisee that does not benefit the promisor, whereas the restitution interest involves a loss to the promisee that does constitute an unjust enrichment to the promisor. A remedy based on restitution enables a party who has performed or partially performed and has benefited the other party to obtain compensation for the value of the benefits conferred on the other party.

Legal Remedies (Damages)

Limitations on Recovery of Damages in Contract Cases
An injured party's ability to recover damages in a contract action is limited by three principles:

1. *A party can recover damages only for those losses proven with reasonable certainty.* Losses that are purely speculative are not recoverable. Thus, if Jones Publishing Company breaches a contract to publish Powell's memoirs, Powell may not be able to recover damages for lost royalties (her expectation interest) because she may be unable to establish, beyond speculation, how much money she would have earned in royalties if the book had been published. (Note, however, that Powell's reliance interest might be protected here; she could be allowed to recover provable losses incurred in reliance on the contract.)

2. *A breaching party is responsible for paying only those losses that were foreseeable to the breaching party at the time of contracting.* A loss is foreseeable if it would ordinarily be expected to result from a breach or if the breaching party had reason to know of particular circumstances that would make the loss likely. For example, if Prince Manufacturing Company renders late performance in a contract to deliver parts to Cheatum Motors without knowing that Cheatum is shut down waiting for the parts, Prince will not have to pay the business losses that result from Cheatum's having to close its operation.

3. *Plaintiffs injured by a breach of contract have the duty to mitigate (avoid or minimize) damages.* A party cannot recover for losses that could have been avoided without undue risk, burden, or humiliation. For example, an employee who has been wrongfully fired would be entitled to damages equal to his wages for the remainder of the employment period. The employee, however, has the duty to minimize the damages by making reasonable efforts to seek a similar job elsewhere.

Compensatory Damages Subject to the limitations discussed above, a person who has been injured by a breach of contract is entitled to recover **compensatory damages**. In calculating the compensatory remedy, a court will attempt to protect the expectation interest of the injured party by giving him the "benefit of his bargain" (placing him in the position he would have been in *had the contract been performed as promised*). To do this, the court must compensate the injured person for the provable losses he has suffered as well as for the provable gains that he has been prevented from realizing by the breach of contract. Normally, compensatory damages include one or more of three possible items: loss in value, any allowable consequential damages, and any allowable incidental damages.

1. *Loss in value.* The starting point in calculating compensatory damages is to determine the loss in value of the performance that the plaintiff had the right to expect. This is a way of measuring the expectation interest. The calculation of the loss in value experienced by an injured party differs according to the sort of contract involved and the circumstances of the breach. In contracts involving nonperformance of the sale of real estate, for example, courts normally measure loss in value by the difference between the contract price and the market price of the property. Thus, if Willis repudiates a contract with Renfrew whereby Renfrew was to purchase land worth $20,000 from Willis for $10,000, Renfrew's loss in value was $10,000.[8] Where a seller has failed to perform a contract for the sale of goods, courts may measure loss in value by the difference between the contract price and the price that the buyer had to pay to procure substitute goods.[9] In cases in which a party breaches by rendering defective performance—say, by breaching a warranty in the sale of goods—the loss in value would be measured by the difference between the value of the goods if they had been in the condition warranted by the seller and the value of the goods in their defective condition.[10]

2. *Consequential damages.* **Consequential damages** (also called **special damages**) compensate for losses that occur as a consequence of the breach of contract. Consequential losses occur because of some special or unusual circumstances of the particular contractual relationship of the parties. For example, Apex Trucking Company buys a computer system from ABC Computers. The system fails

---

[8]In this example, Renfrew may also be able to seek specific performance as a remedy. Specific performance is discussed later in this chapter.

[9]Remedies under Article 2 of the Uniform Commercial Code are discussed in detail in Chapter 22.

[10]See Chapter 20 for further discussion of the damages for breach of warranty in the sale of goods.

to operate properly, and Apex is forced to pay its employees to perform the tasks manually, spending $10,000 in overtime pay. In this situation, Apex might seek to recover the $10,000 in overtime pay in addition to the loss of value that it has experienced.

Lost profits flowing from a breach of contract can be recovered as consequential damages if they are foreseeable and can be proven with reasonable certainty. It is important to remember, however, that the recovery of consequential damages is subject to the limitations on damage recovery discussed earlier.

The following *George* case involves the requirements for consequential damages.

3. *Incidental damages.* **Incidental damages** compensate for reasonable costs that the injured party incurs after the breach in an effort to avoid further loss. For example, if Smith Construction Company breaches an employment contract with Brice, Brice could recover as incidental damages those reasonable expenses he must incur in attempting to procure substitute employment, such as the reasonable cost of travel to his interviews for other jobs.

George v. Al Hoyt & Sons, Inc.   27 A.3d 697 (N.H. 2011)

Adelaide George, doing business as Homes by George, was the developer of a residential real estate development known as Esther's Estates. Esther's Estates was financed by loans from EML Builders, which were secured by a mortgage on the property. In December 2001, George's son, Rick, entered into a written contract on behalf of Homes by George to hire Al Hoyt & Sons to perform work on the development, including the building of a road. The agreed contract price was $79,278.31. In January and February 2002, Hoyt began doing the work on Esther's Estates. On February 15, Homes by George paid Hoyt $10,500 as a deposit for a bridge that was necessary to complete the road, and ultimately the development of Esther's Estates. Homes by George had a wetlands permit that required the bridge to be installed by July 2002. In June 2002, a disagreement arose between the parties as to whether the contract required Hoyt to construct and install the bridge as part of the road construction. That same month, Hoyt informed Homes by George that it would not construct and install the bridge. Shortly thereafter, Homes by George entered into a contract with another company to provide the bridge for $21,140, but learned that it would take three months for the bridge to be built.

As a result of the delay in installation of the bridge, Homes by George was forced to return deposits to two prospective purchasers of homes to be built in Esther's Estates and to void their respective purchase and sale agreements. Homes by George had planned to use the profits from these sales to pay down the mortgage with EML Builders and continue with the project. However, EML Builders learned that the bridge would not be installed in July and "called the note" because "performance wasn't being done." Consequently, on August 22, Homes by George transferred Esther's Estates to EML Builders via a deed in lieu of foreclosure for the amount of $300,000.

Homes by George sued Hoyt for breach of contract, among other claims. A jury ultimately awarded Homes by George $500,000 on its breach of contract claim. The trial court set aside the award and instead awarded Homes by George $56,580 on its other claims. Homes by George appealed.

Hicks, Judge

Homes by George argues that the failure to build the bridge was a breach of the contract between the parties, and, therefore, they "were entitled not only to the return of the deposit, but the cost of the . . . bridge in addition to consequential damages flowing from the breach." They contend "that there was competent evidence from [them] on the issue of consequential damages," including evidence of the cost of the bridge deposit, the total bridge cost, lost profits and the value of the development at the time they deeded the property to EML Builders in lieu of foreclosure.

We have held that consequential damages that could have been reasonably anticipated by the parties as likely to be caused by the defendant's breach are properly awarded to the non-breaching

party in a contract action. The requirement of reasonable foreseeability may be satisfied in either of two ways: (1) as a matter of law if the damages follow the breach in the ordinary course of events; or (2) by the claimant specifically proving that the breaching party had reason to know the facts and to foresee injury. The goal of damages in actions for breach of contract is to put the non-breaching party in the same position it would have been if the contract had been fully performed.

In this case, George testified that, after Hoyt informed Homes by George that it would not install the bridge, Homes by George lost the sales and hence the profit from two houses that were to be built on lots in Esther's Estates. She presented uncontroverted testimony that Hoyt knew from the start that Homes by George had those two lots under contract and that Homes by George "had to have the bridge in in June." Thus, Hoyt should have realized that the failure to install the bridge in a timely manner could result in lost profits for Homes by George.

The trial court found that the jury's verdict was unreasonable, in part, because "there was no testimony as to how much lost profit specifically was applicable to the two lots that were the subject of this award." New Hampshire law, however, does not require that damages be calculated with mathematical certainty, and the method used to compute them need not be more than an approximation. We will uphold an award of damages for lost profits if sufficient data existed indicating that profits were reasonably certain to result.

Here, George testified that the two purchase and sale contracts were for $277,900 and $276,900 and that the expected profit on each of the two houses was between $100,000 and $125,000 but no less than $100,000. She further testified that Homes by George had already built thirteen houses in the earlier phases of Esther's Estates and that the profit margin for those houses was at least $100,000. Based upon this evidence, we find that HBG's lost profits on these two houses were reasonably certain.

There is evidence in the record from which a reasonable jury could have found lost profit damages between $200,000 to $250,000. However, the jury's $500,000 verdict is unsustainable unless Homes by George proved that they were entitled to damages for the value of the property Homes by George lost on the deed transfer. The trial court's ruling with respect to this portion of damages is unclear. We remand on this issue for a determination whether the record supports an award of damages beyond the lost profits on the lost home sales.

Vacated and remanded in favor of Homes by George.

Alternative Measures of Damages The foregoing discussion has focused on the most common formulation of damage remedies in contracts cases. The normal measure of compensatory damages is not appropriate in every case, however. When it is not appropriate, a court may use an alternative measure of damages. For example, a party who has suffered losses by performing or preparing to perform might seek damages based on *reliance interest* instead of expectation interest. In such a case, the party would be compensated for the provable losses suffered by relying on the other party's promise. This measure of damages is often used in cases in which a promise is enforceable under promissory estoppel.[11]

Nominal Damages **Nominal damages** are very small damage awards that are given when a technical breach of contract has occurred without causing any actual or provable economic loss. The sums awarded as nominal damages typically vary from 2 cents to a dollar.

Liquidated Damages The parties to a contract may expressly provide in their contract that a specific sum shall be recoverable if the contract is breached. Such provisions are called **liquidated damages** provisions. For example, Murchison rents space in a shopping mall in which she plans to operate a retail clothing store. She must make improvements in the space before opening the store, and it is very important to her to have the store opened for the Christmas shopping season. She hires Ace Construction Company to construct the improvements. The parties agree to include in the contract a liquidated damages provision stating that, if Ace is late in completing the construction, Murchison will be able to recover a specified sum for each day of delay. Such a provision is highly desirable from Murchison's point of view because, without a liquidated damages provision, she would have a difficult time establishing the precise losses that would result from delay. Courts scrutinize these agreed-on damages carefully, however.

If the amount specified in a liquidated damages provision is reasonable and if the nature of the contract is such that actual damages would be difficult to determine, a court will enforce the provision. When liquidated damages provisions are enforced, the amount of damages agreed on will be the injured party's exclusive damage remedy. If the amount specified is unreasonably great in relation to the probable loss or injury, however, or if the amount of damages could be readily determined in the event of breach, the courts will declare the provision a penalty and refuse to enforce it.

In the *Garden Ridge* case, the court explains and applies the UCC test for differentiating an enforceable liquidated damages clause from an unenforceable penalty clause.

---

[11]Promissory estoppel is discussed in Chapters 9 and 12.

Garden Ridge, L.P. v. Advance International, Inc.
403 S.W.3d 432 (Tex. Ct. App. 2013)

Garden Ridge is a Houston-based chain of housewares and home décor stores. Advance International is one of Garden Ridge's vendors. In 2009, Advance sent Garden Ridge quote sheets for lighted inflatable holiday snowmen, which included a color photo of each item and described its cost, weight, dimensions, and packaging. The two snowmen on the quote sheets each wore a scarf, held a broom that stated "Merry Christmas" on it, and waved; one stood eight feet tall, and the other stood nine feet tall. Advance then sent two sample snowmen to Garden Ridge; one of the samples did not match its quote sheet. The sample eight-foot snowman wore a Santa-type hat and held a "Merry Christmas" banner. Garden Ridge sent Advance two purchase orders, one for approximately 950 nine-foot waving snowmen (PO '721), and the other for approximately 3,500 eight-foot waving snowmen (PO '743), based on the quote sheets.

Five days before Thanksgiving, Garden Ridge realized that the eight-foot snowmen that Advance sent were not waving snowmen, but instead were banner snowmen. The nine-foot snowmen that Advance sent were waving snowmen. There were no customer complaints, and both the eight-foot banner snowmen and the nine-foot waving snowmen sold well. Garden Ridge made approximately $113,000 in profit on the snowmen it received from Advance and made all the money it would have made if the snowmen were delivered exactly as ordered.

Nonetheless, based on liquidated-damages provisions in the parties' contract, Garden Ridge assessed chargebacks against Advance for its alleged noncompliance violations. For Advance's "purchase order" violation—that is, sending the eight-foot banner snowman instead of the waving snowman—Garden Ridge charged back the entire merchandise cost plus the cost of freight on PO '743 as an "unauthorized substitution" chargeback, which totaled $49,176.00. In addition to paying nothing for the eight-foot banner snowmen, Garden Ridge paid nothing for the nine-foot waving snowmen despite the fact that those snowmen complied with PO '721. Garden Ridge charged back the entire merchandise cost plus the cost of freight on the nine-foot waving snowmen as a "merchant initiated" chargeback, which totaled $29,178.00.

Advance demanded payment for its snowmen. The parties filed claims and counterclaims against each other for breach of contract. Of particular importance here, Advance argued that Garden Ridge's claims were barred because the chargeback provisions were unenforceable penalty clauses.

A jury found that Garden Ridge violated the contract and assessed damages despite Garden Ridge's argument that Advance had first breached the contract and excused Garden Ridge from performance. Garden Ridge appealed.

Tracy Christopher, Judge

The parties agree that this case is governed by the Uniform Commercial Code, as adopted by Texas, which applies to transactions involving goods. TEX. BUS. & COM. CODE ANN. § 2.102 (West 2009). The parties agree that section 2.718(a) of the UCC, on liquidation of damages, governs the enforceability of the chargeback provisions in this case. Section 2.718(a) provides:

(a) Damages for breach by either party may be liquidated in the agreement but only at an amount which is reasonable in the light of the anticipated or actual harm caused by the breach, the difficulties of proof of loss, and the inconvenience or non-feasibility of otherwise obtaining an adequate remedy. A term fixing unreasonably large liquidated damages is void as a penalty.

Id. § 2.718(a). The parties also agree that if the chargeback provisions governing Advance's noncompliance violations at issue are unenforceable as penalties, Garden Ridge no longer has any basis to argue that Advance committed any prior material breach. But what the parties do not agree on is the proper analysis by which courts determine the legal question of whether a liquidated-damages provision is unenforceable as a penalty.

a. Determining whether a liquidated-damages provision constitutes a penalty

"Liquidated damages" ordinarily refers to an acceptable measure of damages that parties stipulate in advance will be assessed in the event of a contract breach. "The common law and the Uniform Commercial Code have long recognized a distinction between liquidated damages and penalties." *Flores v. Millennium Interests, Ltd.*, 185 S.W.3d 427, 431 (Tex. 2005). Section 2.718(a) codified the common-law distinction between liquidated damages and penalties as part of Texas' adoption of the UCC's article on sales. *Id.* at 432.

In *Phillips v. Phillips*, the Texas Supreme Court restated the common-law test for determining whether to enforce a liquidated-damages provision. "In order to enforce a liquidated damages clause, the court must find: (1) that the harm caused by the breach is incapable or difficult of estimation, and (2) that the amount of liquidated damages called for is a reasonable forecast of just compensation." *Phillips v. Phillips*, 820 S.W.2d 785, 788 (Tex. 1991). The *Phillips* court explained that one way a party can "show that a liquidated damages provision is unreasonable" is by showing that "the actual damages incurred were much less than the amount contracted for," which requires the party "to prove what those actual damages were." *Id.* . . .

The common-law test as described in *Phillips* closely tracks the language of section 2.718(a) of the UCC. . . . We therefore conclude that the common-law test as described in *Phillips* and the UCC test as outlined in 2.718(a) reflect the same essential factors and the same type of reasonableness test.

b. Do actual damages matter

Garden Ridge argues that the test is conducted entirely on an *ex ante* basis. That is, if, at the time the contract is formed, actual damages are difficult to estimate and the amount specified in the contract is a reasonable forecast of just compensation, a liquidated-damages term is enforceable. Garden Ridge contends that the test contains no *ex post* actual-harm assessment to determine reasonableness. Thus, according to Garden Ridge, Advance could only show that the chargeback provisions were unenforceable as penalties if, *ex ante*, actual damages are easy to estimate or the liquidated damages are based on an unreasonable forecast. Garden Ridge asserts that Advance did not meet its burden because Garden Ridge's CFO, Bill Uhrig, testified that the chargeback schedule was created because actual damages from noncompliance violations are difficult to calculate, and that the schedule was based on computations and estimations by Garden Ridge's executive and purchasing staff. . . .

This court also has recognized that actual harm factors into the test to determine whether a liquidated-damages provision is an enforceable penalty. In *Chan v. Montebello Development Co.*, we described the *Phillips* test as follows: "The test for determining whether a provision is valid and enforceable as liquidated damages is (1) if the damages for the prospective breach of the contract are difficult to measure; and (2) the stipulated damages are a reasonable estimate of actual damages." *Chan v. Montebello Dev. Co.*, 2008 Tex. App. LEXIS 5980, at *3 (Tex. App. July 31, 2008). Further, we stated:

> In order to meet this burden, the party asserting the defense is required to prove the amount of the other parties' actual damages, if any, to show that the liquidated damages are not an approximation of the stipulated sum. If the liquidated damages are shown to be disproportionate to the actual damages, then the liquidated damages must be declared a penalty. . . .

Id. at *3–4 (citations omitted).

Most importantly, the UCC reasonableness test explicitly refers to actual harm, providing that one way a liquidated-damages provision can be invalidated is where the stipulated amount proves unreasonable in light of "the anticipated or *actual* harm caused by the breach." TEX. BUS. & COM. CODE ANN. § 2.718(a) (emphasis added). In addition, the UCC expressly provides that "[a] term fixing unreasonably large liquidated damages is void as a penalty." *Id.* In order to determine whether a term fixes unreasonably large liquidated damages, it follows that courts would need to consider what actual harm, if any, was caused by the breach and then compare it to the stipulated amount of liquidated damages.

Thus, both the common law and the UCC allow for courts to determine the reasonableness of a liquidated-damages clause by considering whether the defendant has shown that the stipulated amount was "unreasonably large" compared to the actual damages. [Citations omitted.]

c. Comparing the amount of the chargebacks to Garden Ridge's actual damages

Advance argues that it proved that the harm anticipated from its alleged noncompliance was not difficult to estimate, that Garden Ridge did not even attempt to determine a chargeback amount that was reasonable in light of the anticipated or actual harm, and that the liquidated damages Garden Ridge assessed are disproportionate to its actual damages. We conclude Advance met its burden to show that the chargeback amounts constituted a disproportionate estimation of Garden Ridge's actual damages; therefore, the chargeback provisions are void as penalties under the UCC.

Advance elicited evidence from Garden Ridge employees . . . sufficient to prove that Garden Ridge suffered no actual damages as a result of Advance's substitution of the eight-foot banner snowmen. The trial court also determined that Garden Ridge suffered no actual damages from any of Advance's noncompliance violations when the court directed a verdict against Garden Ridge on its breach-of-contract claim; Garden Ridge does not challenge that ruling. And Garden Ridge itself acknowledges it argued no amount of actual damages other than zero and the record shows that Garden Ridge suffered no actual damages resulting from Advance's noncompliance violations.

Thus, Advance has shown that the chargebacks assessed by Garden Ridge for Advance's "unauthorized substitution" and "merchant initiated" noncompliance violations—100% of the invoiced merchandise cost plus freight for the eight-foot banner snowmen and the nine-foot waving snowmen, for a total of $79,457.00—were unreasonably large when compared to Garden Ridge's actual damages of zero. . . . Therefore, as a matter of law, we conclude that, under these circumstances, the chargeback amounts were unreasonable, and that the chargeback provisions are unenforceable as penalties under the UCC because they fixed unreasonably large liquidated damages.

Accordingly, we . . . affirm the trial court's judgment.

Punitive Damages **Punitive damages** are damages awarded in addition to the compensatory remedy that are designed to punish a defendant for particularly reprehensible behavior and to deter the defendant and others from committing similar behavior in the future. The traditional rule is that punitive damages are not recoverable in contracts cases unless a specific statutory provision (such as some consumer protection statutes) allows them or the defendant has committed *fraud* or some other independent tort. A few states will permit the use of punitive damages in contracts cases in which the defendant's conduct, though not technically a tort, was malicious, oppressive, or tortious in nature.

Punitive damages have also been awarded in many of the cases involving breach of the implied covenant of good faith. In such cases, courts usually circumvent the traditional rule against awarding punitive damages in contracts cases by holding that breach of the duty of good faith is an independent tort. The availability of punitive damages in such cases operates to deter a contracting party from deliberately disregarding the other party's rights. Insurance companies have been the most frequent target for punitive damages awards in bad-faith cases, but employers and banks have also been subjected to punitive damages verdicts.

Equitable Remedies

In exceptional cases in which money damages alone are not adequate to fully compensate for a party's injuries, a court may grant an equitable remedy either alone or in combination with a legal remedy. Equitable relief is subject to several limitations, however, and will be granted only when justice is served by doing so. The primary equitable remedies for breach of contract are specific performance and injunction.[12]

Specific Performance **Specific performance** is an equitable remedy whereby the court orders the breaching party to perform contractual duties as promised. For example, if Barnes breached a contract to sell a tract of land to Metzger and a court granted specific performance of the contract, the court would require Barnes to deed the land to Metzger. (Metzger, of course, must pay the purchase price.) This remedy can be advantageous to the injured party because he is not faced with

the complexities of proving damages, he does not have to worry about whether he can actually collect the damages, and he gets exactly what he bargained for. However, the availability of this remedy is subject to the limitations discussed below.

The Availability of Specific Performance Specific performance, like other equitable remedies, is available only when the injured party has no adequate remedy at law—in other words, when money damages do not adequately compensate the injured party. This generally requires a showing that the subject of the contract is unique or at least that no substitutes are available. Even if this requirement is met, a court will withhold specific performance if the injured party has acted in bad faith, if he unreasonably delayed in asserting his rights, or if specific performance would require an excessive amount of supervision by the court.

Contracts for the sale of real estate are the most common subjects of specific performance decrees because every tract of real estate is presumed to be unique. Specific performance is rarely granted for breach of a contract for the sale of goods because the injured party can usually procure substitute goods. However, there are situations involving sales of goods contracts in which specific performance is given. These cases involve goods that are unique or goods for which no substitute can be found. Examples include antiques, heirlooms, works of art, and objects of purely sentimental value.[13] What about a pet? That question is raised in the following *Houseman* case. Specific performance is not available for the breach of a promise to perform a personal service (such as a contract for employment, artistic performance, or consulting services). A decree requiring a person to specifically perform a personal-services contract would probably be ineffective in giving the injured party what he bargained for. It would also require a great deal of supervision by the court. In addition, an application of specific performance in such cases would amount to a form of involuntary servitude.

Injunction Injunction is an equitable remedy used in many different contexts, sometimes as a remedy for breach of contract. An **injunction** is a court order requiring a person to do something (mandatory injunction) or ordering a person to refrain from doing something (negative injunction). Unlike legal remedies that apply only when the breach has already occurred, the equitable remedy of injunction can be invoked when a breach has merely been *threatened*.

---

[12]Another equitable remedy, *reformation*, allows a court to reform or "rewrite" a written contract when the parties have made an error in expressing their agreement. Reformation is discussed, along with the doctrine of mistake, in Chapter 13.

[13]Specific performance under § 2-716(1) of the UCC is discussed in Chapter 22.

Houseman v. Dare   966 A.2d 24 (N.J. Super. Ct. 2009)

Doreen Houseman and Eric Dare had been in a relationship for 13 years. In 1999, they bought a residence together, and in 2000, they became engaged. In 2003, they purchased a pedigree dog for $1,500, which they registered with the American Kennel Club, reporting that they both owned the dog. In May 2006, Dare decided to end the relationship. At that time, Dare wanted to stay in the house and buy Houseman's interest in the property, so Houseman signed a deed transferring her interest in the house to Dare for $45,000. When she vacated the home, she took the dog and its paraphernalia with her. She left one of the dog's jerseys and some photographs behind as mementos for Dare.

According to Houseman, "from the minute [Dare] told [her they] were breaking up, he told [her she] could have" the dog. She and Dare agreed that she would get the dog and one-half the value of the house. Although she admitted that she would not have wanted more than one-half the value of their house if she were not taking the dog, she asserted that her primary concern during her negotiations with Dare was possession of their dog, and she accepted his representations that her share of the equity in the house was $45,000. Dare and Houseman did not have a written agreement about the dog, but after Houseman left the residence, she allowed him to take the dog for visits, after which he returned the pet to her. According to Houseman, when she asked Dare to put their agreement about the dog in a writing, he told her she could trust him and he would not keep the dog from her. In late February 2007, Houseman left the dog with Dare when she went on vacation. On March 4, 2007, she asked Dare for the dog, but the pet was not returned. Houseman sued Dare for breach of an oral contract and sought specific performance of the agreement. Prior to trial, Dare sold the residence and received equity in an amount greater than $90,000.

The trial court determined that pets are personal property and lack the unique value essential to an award of specific performance. Houseman appealed.

Grall, Judge, Appellate Division

At the conclusion of trial, the court found Houseman's testimony to be "extremely" and "particularly credible." The court noted that Houseman testified "without guile," "was truthful" and answered even the "hard questions . . . in a way that would not have been advantageous to her." On those grounds, the court accepted her testimony. In contrast, the court concluded that Dare took unfair advantage of Houseman by giving her only $45,000 for her interest in their residence.

The court made the following findings relevant to the dog:

I'm more than satisfied, hearing Ms. Houseman testify, that the dog was in no way related to the sale of the house. They may have an understanding about the dog. She thought she was getting the dog. He picked the dog up later. He has the dog. We know what the value of the dog is. The dog is worth $1,500. I believe it's now in Mr. Dare's possession. He'll pay Ms. Houseman $1,500 [the full value stipulated by the parties] for the dog.

The foregoing passage suggests that the court found that Houseman established an oral agreement under which she was to obtain possession and ownership of the dog. Despite that finding and solely on the ground that Dare had possession of the dog at that time, the court awarded Dare possession and Houseman the dog's stipulated value.

The court's conclusion that specific performance is not, as a matter of law, available to remedy a breach of an oral agreement about possession of a dog reached by its joint owners is

not sustainable. The remedy of specific performance can be invoked to address a breach of an enforceable agreement when money damages are not adequate to protect the expectation interest of the injured party and an order requiring performance of the contract will not result in inequity to the offending party, reward the recipient for unfair dealing or conflict with public policy.

Specific performance is generally recognized as the appropriate remedy when an agreement concerns possession of property such as heirlooms, family treasures, and works of art that induce a strong sentimental attachment. That is so because money damages cannot compensate the injured party for the special subjective benefits he or she derives from possession. The special subjective value of personal property worthy of recognition by a court of equity is sentiment explained by facts and circumstances—such as the party's relationship with the donor or prior associations with the property—that give rise to the special affection. In a different context, this court has recognized that pets have special "subjective value" to their owners. Courts of other jurisdictions have considered the special subjective value of pets in resolving questions about possession.

There is no reason for a court of equity to be more wary in resolving competing claims for possession of a pet based on one party's sincere affection for and attachment to it than in resolving competing claims based on one party's sincere sentiment for an inanimate object based upon a relationship with the donor. In both types of cases, a court of equity must consider the interests of the parties pressing competing claims for possession and public policies that may be implicated by an award of possession.

In those fortunately rare cases when a separating couple is unable to agree about who will keep jointly held property with special subjective value, our courts are equipped to determine whether the assertion of a special interest in possession is sincere and grounded in facts and circumstances which endow the chattel with a special value or based upon a sentiment assumed for the purpose of litigation out of greed, or other sentiment or motive similarly unworthy of protection in a court of equity. We are less confident that there are judicially discoverable and manageable standards for resolving questions of possession from the perspective of a pet, at least apart from cases involving abuse or neglect contrary to public policies expressed in laws designed to protect animals.

Houseman's evidence was adequate to require the trial court to consider the oral agreement and the remedy of specific performance. The special subjective value of the dog to Houseman can be inferred from her testimony about its importance to her and her prompt effort to enforce her right of possession when Dare took action adverse to her enjoyment of that right. And, Dare did not establish that an order awarding specific performance would be harsh or oppressive to him, reward Houseman for unfair conduct or violate public policy. To the contrary, assuming an oral agreement that Dare breached by keeping the dog after a visit, an order awarding him possession because he had the dog at the time of trial would reward him for his breach.

Reversed and remanded in favor of Houseman.

Injunctions are available only when the breach or threatened breach is likely to cause *irreparable injury*.

In the contract context, specific performance is a form of mandatory injunction. Negative injunctions are appropriately used in several situations, such as contract cases in which a party whose duty under the contract is forbearance threatens to breach the contract. For example, Norris sells his restaurant in Gas City, Indiana, to Ford. A term of the contract of sale provides that Norris agrees not to own, operate, or be employed in any restaurant within 30 miles of Gas City for a period of two years after the sale.[14] If Norris threatens to open a new restaurant in Gas City several months after the sale is consummated, a court could *enjoin* Norris from opening the new restaurant.

Restitution Restitution is a remedy that can be obtained either at law or in equity. Restitution applies when one party's performance or reliance has conferred a benefit on the other. A party's restitution interest is protected by providing compensation for the value of benefits conferred on the other person. This can be done through specific restitution, in which the defendant is required to return the exact property conferred by the plaintiff, or substitutionary

restitution, in which a court awards the plaintiff a sum of money that reflects the amount by which the plaintiff benefited the defendant. In an action for damages based on quasi-contract, substitutionary restitution would be the remedy.[15]

Restitution can be used in a number of circumstances. Sometimes, parties injured by breach of contract seek restitution as an alternative remedy instead of damages that focus on their expectation interest. In other situations, a *breaching party* who has partially performed seeks restitution for the value of benefits he conferred in excess of the losses he caused. In addition, restitution often applies in cases in which a person rescinds a contract on the grounds of lack of capacity, misrepresentation, fraud, duress, undue influence, or mistake. Upon rescission, each party who has been benefited by the other's performance must compensate the other for the value of the benefit conferred. Another application of restitution occurs when a party to a contract that violates the statute of frauds confers a benefit on the other party. For example, Boyer gives Blake a $10,000 down payment on an oral contract for the sale of a farm. Although the contract is unenforceable (i.e., Boyer could not get compensation for his expectation interest), the court would give Boyer restitution of his down payment.

---

[14]Ancillary covenants not to compete, or noncompetition agreements, are discussed in detail in Chapter 15.

[15]Quasi-contract is discussed in detail in Chapter 9.

Problems and Problem Cases

1. The Grondas, who owned a party store along with land, fixtures, equipment, and a liquor license, entered into a contract to sell their liquor license and fixtures to Harbor Park Market in an agreement that was expressly conditioned on approval by the Grondas' attorney. The Grondas submitted the contract to their attorney, but before the attorney had approved it, they received a second, better offer and submitted that contract to the attorney as well. The attorney reviewed both agreements and approved the second one. Harbor Park Market sued the Grondas for breach of contract. Will their suit succeed?

2. The Ewells bought a home in Seaford, Delaware. They planned to renovate it and reside in it later. The Ewells insured the house with an insurance company, Lloyd's of London. Shortly after purchasing the house, the Ewells notified the insurance company that they intended to renovate the house. The insurance company thereupon issued a Special Use Form Policy that contained a single-page "Course of Construction/Renovation Endorsement." The Fire Provision of the Endorsement stated:

   > In the event of any construction or renovation work at the premises described in the Declarations the following conditions shall apply:
   >> You must ensure that visible and accessible fire extinguishers be placed on each level of the dwelling. Failure to comply with this provision will render this insurance null and void.

   The Ewells did not place any fire extinguishers in the house. The work on the house proceeded with the removal of plaster and gutting of the kitchen and another room. In the early morning hours of January 20, 2009, the house and its contents were destroyed by fire. At the time of the fire, the Ewells were sleeping in a shed that they had built in the back yard rather than in the house. They were awakened by the arrival of fire trucks. The Ewells informed the insurance company of the fire, and it assigned an adjuster to investigate the loss. The insurance company ultimately denied the claim because the Ewells had not complied with the condition requiring them to place fire extinguishers on each floor of the house, as required by the Endorsement. The Ewells sued the insurance company for breach of contract. They argued that the fire extinguisher provision was meaningless because no one was in the house at the time of the fire, so no one could have used a fire extinguisher if there had been one present. They also argue that the condition was not triggered because the work

that they were in the process of doing was demolition and they had not yet begun renovation. Will they win?

3. Smith and his coworkers signed an at-will employment agreement that promised a deferred salary of $15,000 "[i]n the event that Employee remains employed . . . for two years." The agreement also provided that if the employees left before that date or were terminated for cause, the employees would forfeit the incentive payment and were responsible for paying the costs of returning to their home locations. The employees were terminated after the eight-week orientation period but within two years, when the project they had been hired to work on was withdrawn. They claimed the right to the $15,000 on the ground that they had not resigned and had not been terminated for cause. Were the employees entitled to the $15,000 deferred salary?

4. In 2006, M. Jay Carter hired Robert "Casey" Jones, a real estate agent at The Janet Jones Company, to represent him in a real estate transaction with Ernie and Karen Cline. Carter intended to purchase residential property located at 8 Longfellow Place in Little Rock, Arkansas. The real estate contract was signed on June 11, 2006. It contained a provision setting the purchase price for the property at $1,037,500, "subject to Buyer's ability to obtain financing." The contract also included a handwritten provision under this same subsection that the buyer was required to "provide a letter of approval within 10 business days." On June 21, 2006, Pulaski Mortgage Company approved a loan for Carter to purchase the Longfellow property. The approval letter was conditioned upon, among other things, there being no material change in Carter's financial condition that might adversely affect his current level of creditworthiness, credit score, debt, or income. Pursuant to this conditional approval, Carter was required to submit to Pulaski Mortgage prior to closing an employment certification providing evidence that his employment and income situation had not changed since his conditional approval. This approval letter from Pulaski Mortgage was submitted to Janet Jones Company within 10 business days as required by the contract, and closing was set for September 22, 2006. According to Carter and the documentation submitted to Pulaski Mortgage, Carter's income began declining in July 2006. On September 8, 2006, Carter orally informed Pulaski Mortgage of his decline in income, and the company requested that Carter provide it with a year-to-date profit-and-loss statement and balance sheet. Carter also contacted Casey Jones on September 8, 2006, and told him that he had a decline in his third-quarter

income and that he had informed Pulaski Mortgage of his current financial situation. On September 11, 2006, Carter submitted to Pulaski Mortgage additional documentation. On September 11, 2006, Pulaski Mortgage sent a notice of adverse action to Carter advising him that his "recent application for an extension or renewal of credit has been denied." The company informed him that "the decision to deny your application was based on the following reasons: . . . Excessive obligations . . . Insufficient income . . . Add[itional] current income information furnished by applicant." On September 11, 2006, Casey Jones informed Shannon Treece, an independent contractor at Janet Jones Company and the Clines' agent, that Carter would not be able to close the real estate transaction on the Longfellow property because he had lost his financing approval from Pulaski Mortgage. She then informed the Clines that Carter would be unable to close on their property. The Clines sued Carter for breach of contract. Should they succeed?

5. Arnhold and Argoudelis agreed to sell their farm to Ocean Atlantic with a closing date originally set for November 1997. After delay in satisfying conditions precedent and several postponements of the closing date over almost four years, the parties finally entered into a settlement agreement, which identified January 25, 2001, as a "drop dead" date. The closing did not occur by that time, and Arnhold and Argoudelis gave notice that the contract was terminated. Ocean Atlantic sued for specific performance. Was the failure to close on the drop dead date a material breach?

6. The Bassos contracted with Dierberg to purchase her property for $1,310,000. One term of the contract stated, "[t]he sale under this contract shall be closed . . . at the office of Community Title Company . . . on May 16, 1988 at 10:00 AM. . . . Time is of the essence of this contract." After forming the contract, the Bassos assigned their right to purchase Dierberg's property to Miceli and Slonim Development Corp. At 10:00 AM on May 16, 1988, Dierberg appeared at Community Title for closing. No representative of Miceli and Slonim was there, nor did anyone from Miceli and Slonim inform Dierberg that there would be any delay in the closing. At 10:20 AM, Dierberg declared the contract null and void because the closing did not take place as agreed, and she left the title company office shortly thereafter. Dierberg had intended to use the purchase money to close another contract to purchase real estate later in the day. At about 10:30 AM, a representative of Miceli and Slonim appeared at Community Title to begin the closing, but the representative did not have the funds

for payment until 1:30 PM. Dierberg refused to return to the title company, stating that Miceli and Slonim had breached the contract by failing to tender payment on time. She had already made alternative arrangements to finance her purchase of other real estate to meet her obligation under that contract. Miceli and Slonim sued Dierberg, claiming that the contract did not require closing exactly at 10:00 AM, but rather some time on the day of May 16. Will they prevail?

7. In 1992, White and J.M. Brown Amusement Co. entered into a contract giving Brown exclusive rights to place "certain coin-operated amusement machines" in 13 of White's stores, all in Oconee and Anderson counties in South Carolina. The contract was for a term of 15 years. Under the contract, White agreed "not to allow other machines on the premises without the express written consent of [Brown]." Brown placed the machines in White's stores as the contract provided. In 1993, the state legislature enacted a local option law as part of the Video Game Machines Act, permitting counties to hold an individual referendum to determine whether cash payouts for video gaming should remain legal. As a result of local referenda held in November 1994, 12 counties, including Oconee and Anderson, voted to ban cash payouts. The South Carolina Department of Revenue revoked the licenses required to operate the machines Brown had placed in White's stores, effective July 1, 1995, as required by the act. Consequently, Brown removed the video poker machines from White's stores. Brown did not replace the machines with any other coin-operated amusement machines. In November 1996, the South Carolina Supreme Court struck down the local option law contained in the act as unconstitutional. Given this court's ruling, Brown planned to return the video poker machines to White's stores, but White informed Brown that the contract was no longer valid. White then filed suit seeking to have the contract declared void and unenforceable so that he would be free to sign a contract with another provider of legal video and amusement machines. Approximately one month after filing suit, White entered into an agreement with Hughes Entertainment, Inc. giving Hughes exclusive rights to place "all video game terminals and all coin operated music and amusement machines" in 12 of the same stores listed in the Brown contract. Was White's duty to perform the contract with Brown excused?

8. East Capitol hired Robinson on a one-year contract that stated that her continued employment would be based on her performance but said nothing about her

employment being based on funding. East Capitol discharged Robinson before the one-year term was over because it lost grant funding, without which it had insufficient funds to pay her. Robinson sued for breach of contract, and East Capitol claimed the defense of impossibility. Was East Capitol entitled to be excused from performance on the contract?

9. Einstein Moomjy Inc. is a large retail distributor of carpets. In August 1999, at an annual clearance sale held by Einstein Moomjy, Furst purchased five remnant carpets for his home for $10,139.68. One of these carpets was the "Mystery Ivory" carpet. Attached to the Mystery Ivory carpet at the time of its sale was a tag containing the following information:

> The Back Yd.
>
> Einstein Moomjy, The Carpet Department Store
>
> REMNANT
>
> REDUCED FOR CLEARANCE
>
> SIZE: 11'4" × 31'
>
> REGULAR PRICE $5,775–
>
> SALE PRICE
>
> $1,499–
>
> QUALITY: Mystery
>
> COLOR: Ivory
>
> Fibre: Wool
>
> Sale
>
> 1,199

When the Mystery Ivory carpet was delivered to his home, Furst noticed that the carpet was damaged and smaller than the size indicated on the sales invoice. He complained about the condition and size of the carpet to Einstein Moomjy, who offered either a refund of the sale price of $1,199.00 or a similar carpet at an additional price. Einstein Moomjy claimed that the Mystery Ivory carpet was a high-quality "Ireloom" white wool carpet that had been tagged mistakenly with the wrong sale price. Furst demanded that Einstein Moomjy comply with the warranty on the back of the sales invoice. The invoice promised that if the carpets purchased were not delivered by the scheduled delivery date, Furst had the choice of canceling the "order with a prompt full refund" or "accepting delivery at a specific later date." Furst insisted on delivery of an undamaged Ireloom carpet at the size he ordered and at

the price he paid. When Einstein Moomjy refused to replace the Ireloom carpet at that price, Furst sued Einstein Moomjy. The court determined that Furst's "ascertainable loss" was the fair market or replacement value of the carpet, but it would not permit him to introduce evidence of the price tag to prove replacement value. The trial court excluded the use of the unmarked-down regular price on the sales tag as evidence of the market value of the Ireloom carpet. The court also barred testimony from Furst's interior decorator regarding her investigation of market prices and testimony from defendant Moomjy regarding the market value of the Ireloom carpet. Because Furst could not prove replacement value, the court awarded him the purchase price. Was this ruling correct?

10. Diamond Aircraft announced that it would build a single-engine light jet aircraft referred to as the "D-JET," noting that it would select a powerplant and other equipment for the plane in the future and identifying a "projected price" of under $1 million. In April 2003, Diamond issued a press release in which it projected that the D-JET's first flight would be scheduled in 2004, with initial deliveries to customers in 2006. In 2004, Barnes signed a "Reservation Agreement" with Diamond. The agreement made it clear that there was no existing aircraft to consider for purchase yet, and there were no specifications of the aircraft provided except for general descriptions such as "premium interior" and "glass cockpit." It listed the "Manufacturer's Suggested" price of $850,000 and provided that Barnes would be required to pay a 10 percent deposit within 30 days of "JAA IFR certification" in order to "keep the order position secured." The parties also agreed to limit their liability to the return or forfeiture of the deposit in the event of breach. Barnes paid a deposit of $20,000 to reserve a place in line to purchase a D-JET, and Diamond assigned her the 52nd North American delivery position. Later, Diamond reconfigured the D-JET entirely and announced the new configuration and new pricing in 2006. It sent Barnes and other deposit holders a letter explaining that upgrades in the aircraft would cause it to be priced at $1.38 million. It gave deposit holders the choice of maintaining their delivery positions for a D-JET priced at $1.38 million or recovering their deposits and relinquishing their delivery positions. Barnes filed suit against Diamond, alleging breach of contract and seeking specific performance or money damages. Will she win?

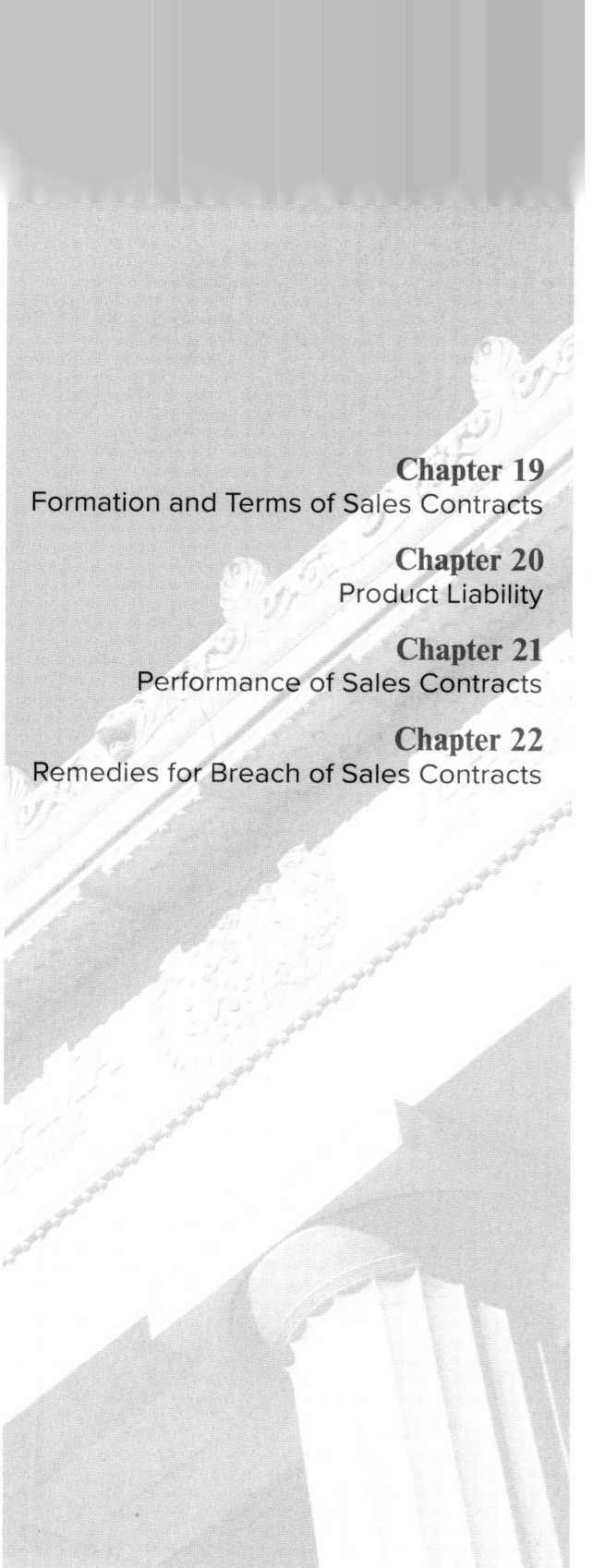

Sales

Pixtal/AGE Fotostock

Formation and Terms
of Sales Contracts

Paul Reynolds used the Trek website to purchase a racing bike with a frame utilizing a newly developed high-strength but lightweight alloy. He selected the model he wanted and provided the company with the necessary information to place the $2,200 purchase price and $75 shipping costs on his Visa card. The bicycle was damaged during shipment when the box was punctured by a forklift truck that was loading other boxes onto the carrier's truck. Paul took the damaged bicycle to a local bicycle dealer to have it repaired. After the bicycle was repaired, but before Paul could pick it up, a clerk in the store, by mistake, sold the bicycle for $1,500 to Melissa Stevenson, who bought it as a birthday gift for her boyfriend. This situation raises a number of legal issues that, among others, will be covered in this chapter, including:

- Can a legally enforceable contract for the sale of goods be formed electronically?
- Between Paul and Trek, who had the risk of loss or damage to the bicycle during the time it was under shipment to him?
- Would Paul be entitled to recover possession of the bicycle from Melissa and her boyfriend?
- Even if Melissa and her boyfriend are not legally required to return the bicycle to Paul, would returning it be the ethical thing to do?

LO   LEARNING OBJECTIVES

After studying this chapter, you should be able to:

19-1 Analyze whether a transaction involves the sale of goods to which the Uniform Commercial Code (UCC) applies or whether common law principles apply to the transaction.

19-2 Recall the major provisions of the UCC that are applicable to the formation of contracts for the sale of goods, including the "gap fillers" that the UCC deems part of the contract when the parties omit critical terms or state them in an unclear manner.

19-3 Explain when title to goods passes from the seller to the buyer.

19-4 Explain what is meant by a *voidable title* and explain when a buyer can obtain better title to goods than the seller had.

19-5 Apply the UCC rules concerning risk of loss to determine who had the risk of loss in a given transaction where the goods that were the subject of a contract were lost or damaged before the buyer took possession.

19-6 Distinguish between sale or return and sales on approval and explain the ramifications those distinctions have for the rights of buyers and sellers.

IN PART 3, CONTRACTS, we introduced the common law rules that govern the creation and performance of contracts generally. Throughout much of history, special rules, known as the law merchant, were developed to control mercantile transactions in goods. Because transactions in goods commonly involve buyers and sellers located in different states—and even different countries—a common body of law to control these transactions can facilitate the smooth flow of commerce. To address this need, the Uniform Commercial Code (UCC) was prepared to simplify and modernize the rules of law governing commercial transactions.

In 2003, the American Law Institute adopted a series of proposed amendments to Article 2 (Sales) of the UCC that are intended to further modernize and clarify some of its provisions. The amendments are not effective until they have been adopted by a state and incorporated into its version of Article 2. However, there has been controversy concerning the proposed amendments, and because at the time this book went to press they had not been adopted by any state, they are not incorporated in the discussion of Article 2 that follows.

This chapter reviews some rules that govern the formation of sales contracts previously discussed. It also covers some key terms in sales contracts, such as delivery terms, title, and risk of loss. Finally, it discusses the rules governing sales on trial, such as sales on approval and consignments.

Sale of Goods

 LO19-1 Analyze whether a transaction involves the sale of goods to which the Uniform Commercial Code (UCC) applies or whether common law principles apply to the transaction.

The **sale of goods** is the transfer of ownership to tangible personal property in exchange for money, other goods, or the performance of services. The law of sales of goods is codified in Article 2 of the UCC. While the law of sales is based on the fundamental principles of contract and personal property, it has been modified to accommodate current practices of merchants. In large measure, the UCC discarded many technical requirements of earlier law that did not serve any useful purpose in the marketplace and replaced them with rules that are consistent with commercial expectations.

Article 2 of the UCC applies only to *transactions in goods*. Thus, it does not cover contracts to provide services or to sell real property. However, some courts have applied the principles set out in the UCC to such transactions. When a contract appears to call for the furnishing of both goods and services, a question may arise as to whether the UCC applies. For example, the operator of a hair salon may use a commercial solution intended to be used safely on humans that causes injury to a person's head. The injured person then might bring a lawsuit claiming that there was a breach of the UCC's warranty of the suitability of the solution. In such cases, the courts commonly ask whether the sale of goods is the *predominant* part of the transaction or merely an *incidental* part; where the sale of goods predominates, courts normally apply Article 2. The *Janke v. Brooks* case, which follows, illustrates the type of analysis courts use to determine whether a particular contract should be governed by the UCC.

Thus, the first question you should ask when faced with a contracts problem is this: Is this a contract for the sale of goods? If it is not, then the principles of common law that were discussed in Part 3, Contracts, apply. If the contract is one for the sale of goods, then the UCC applies. This analysis is illustrated in Figure 19.1.

Choice of Law

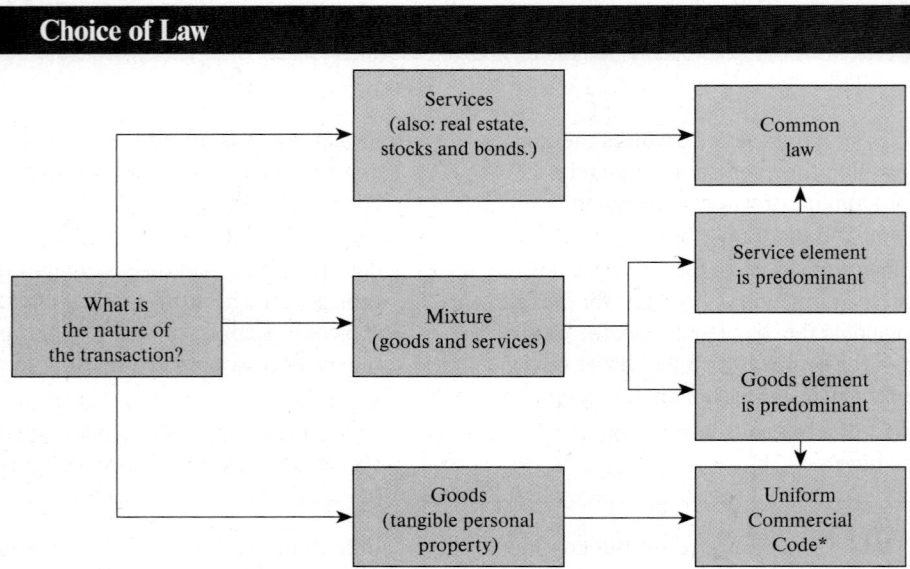

*If there is no specific Uniform Commercial Code provision governing the transaction, use the common law.

Janke v. Brooks   77 UCC Rep. 2d 352 (D. Colo. 2012)

Janke was the owner of a classic, 1957 Chevrolet Nomad. After seeing a feature on the ESPN program On The Block, *he contacted Donald and Normandy Brooks about restoring the car. He traveled to the Brooks' shop in Sparks, Nevada, to discuss the project.*

He received an estimate that included a series of price quotes and list sheets that contemplated the installation and/or repair of a number of parts as well as a number of items that were to be fabricated by the Brooks' mechanic. If the items could have been fabricated or installed by any competent mechanic, there would not have been any need to ship the prized car to a specialty shop to remodel the vehicle. The parts and materials constituted slightly more than half of the quoted price, which was somewhat skewed by the fact there was a 50 percent markup on the price of new parts and materials.

Janke then forwarded a deposit and had the Nomad shipped from his home in Wheatridge, Colorado, in September 2008. He informed the Brookses that he wanted the car to be ready in time to be entered in and displayed at the "Hot August Nights" classic car show in Reno, Nevada, in early August 2010. Despite assurances, when he arrived in Nevada on July 28, 2010, he learned that the car was not finished. Subsequently, he was advised that the car's engine block was cracked and would have to be replaced. Donald Brooks assured Janke that the car would be fixed and shipped to him in Colorado.

On November 17, 2010, the car was delivered to Janke in Wheatridge. The car broke down several times in the first 25 miles, after which Janke hired another mechanic to inspect and evaluate the build. He discovered a number of defects in the car, that the Brookses' design strategy was unreasonable, that the car was not built consistently with the build sheet, and that the defects in the car could not have been corrected simply by replacing the defective parts.

Janke brought an action against the Brookses for breach of contract as well as for breach of implied warranties under the Uniform Commercial Code.

Blackburn, District Judge

By its express terms, the Uniform Commercial Code applies only to "transactions in goods," and contracts "relating to the present or future sale of goods."

Moreover, and more relevant here, when the contract contemplates both the sale of goods and the performance of services, the controlling criterion should be the primary purpose of the contract:

> The test for inclusion or exclusion is not whether goods and services are mixed, but granting that they are mixed, whether their predominant factor, their thrust, their purpose, reasonably stated, is the rendition of service with goods incidentally involved (e.g., contract with artist for painting) or is a transaction of sale, with labor incidentally involved (e.g., installation of a water heater in a bathroom).

Factors that may bear on this determination include (1) the language of the contract; (2) whether the contract lists a unitary price or bills discretely for goods and labor; (3) the ratio between the cost of goods and the overall contract price; and (4) whether the purchaser has a reasonable expectation of acquiring a property interest in the goods.

The contract at issue here was just such a mixed contract. Considering these relevant factors, as well as case law from other jurisdictions and the overall thrust of the contract, I find and conclude that it was predominantly a contract for services. Thus, the warranties implied under the UCC are inapplicable.

The language of the series of price quotes and list sheets that constitute the contract in this case contemplates the installation and/or repair of a number of parts, while other items were to be fabricated by the Brooks' mechanic himself. Nevertheless, the enumeration of these parts and materials was not an end unto itself, but rather a necessary prerequisite towards the ultimate end of restoring the car. If these items could have been fabricated by any competent mechanic, there would have been little reason for Janke to ship his prized car to a specialty provider far distant from his home. Although technically Janke acquired a property interest in all the parts and materials incorporated into the car, such was merely incidental to the overarching purpose to craft a wholly remodeled car. In other words, in this case, the sum was greater than the parts.

Janke sought out the Brooks specifically for their expertise in rebuilding and customizing classic cars. Janke did not buy a car from the Brooks—he held title to the Chevy at all times relevant to this action. Nor did he simply contract for the Brooks to acquire the various parts listed in the quotes, which the Brooks did not manufacture or sell in any event, despite the fact that the purchase of such parts was a necessary prerequisite to the build. Instead, what the contract primarily contemplated was that the Brooks would bring their specialized knowledge and experience to bear in selecting and installing appropriate parts, repairing existing components, and generally refurbishing the car in such a way as to restore it to a show-worthy condition. Indeed, the primary shortcoming of the build as identified by Janke's expert is that the Brooks "design strategy was unreasonable." The application of skills necessary to create such a design strategy is undoubtedly a service.

I, thus, conclude that the contract at issue in this case predominantly was one for services. The furnishing of such goods as were necessary to complete the remodel was merely incidental to the provision of such services.

Summary Judgment for the Brooks as to Janke's claims for breach of implied warranties under the UCC.

Leases

A lease of goods is a transfer of the right to possess and use goods belonging to another. Although the rights of one who leases goods (a lessee) do not constitute ownership of the goods, leasing is mentioned here because it can be an important way of acquiring the use of many kinds of goods, from automobiles to farm equipment. In most states, Article 2 and Article 9 of the UCC are applied to such leases by analogy. However, rules contained in these articles sometimes are inadequate to resolve special problems presented by leasing. For this reason, a new article of the UCC dealing exclusively with leases of goods, Article 2A, was written in 1987 and has been adopted by 49 states and the District of Columbia. You can access the UCC by visiting www.law.cornell.edu/ucc.

Higher Standards for Merchants

The UCC recognized that buyers tend to place more reliance on professional sellers and that professionals are generally more knowledgeable and better able to protect themselves than nonprofessionals. Therefore, the UCC distinguishes between merchants and nonmerchants by holding merchants to a higher standard in some cases [Sections 2–201(2), 2–205, 2–207(2), and 2–314].[1]

The UCC defines **merchant** [2–104(1)] on a case-by-case basis.[2] If a person regularly deals in the kind of goods being sold, or purports to have some special knowledge about the goods, or employs an agent in the sale who fits either of these two descriptions, that person is a merchant for the purposes of the contract in question. So, if you buy a used car from a used-car dealer, the dealer is a merchant for the purposes of your contract. But if you buy a refrigerator from a used-car dealer, the dealer is probably not considered to be a merchant for purposes of that sale.

UCC Requirements

 LO19-2 Recall the major provisions of the UCC that are applicable to the formation of contracts for the sale of goods, including the "gap fillers" that the UCC deems part of the contract when the parties omit critical terms or state them in an unclear manner.

The UCC requires that parties to sales contracts act in good faith and in a commercially reasonable manner. Further, when a contract contains an unfair or unconscionable clause, or the contract as a whole is unconscionable, the courts have the right to refuse to enforce the unconscionable clause or contract [2–302]. The UCC's treatment of unconscionability is discussed in detail in Chapter 15, Illegality.

A number of the UCC provisions concerning the sale of goods were discussed in the chapters on contracts. The Concept Review (on the next page) lists some of the important provisions discussed earlier, together with the chapters in the text where the discussion can be found.

Terms of Sales Contracts

Gap Fillers The UCC recognizes the fact that parties to sales contracts frequently omit terms from their agreements or state terms in an indefinite or unclear manner. The UCC deals with these situations by filling in the blanks with common trade practices, or by giving commonly used terms a specific meaning that is applied unless the parties' agreement clearly indicates a contrary intent.

---

[1]The numbers in brackets refer to sections of the Uniform Commercial Code.

[2]Under the UCC, a "merchant" is defined as a "person who deals in goods of the kind or otherwise by his occupation holds himself out as having knowledge or skill peculiar to the practices or goods involved in the transaction or to whom such knowledge or skill may be attributed by his employment of an agent or broker or other intermediary who by his occupation holds himself out as having such knowledge or skill" [2–104(1)].

Formation of Contracts

Offer and Acceptance (Chapters 10 and 11)	1. A contract can be formed in any manner sufficient to show agreement, including conduct by both parties that recognizes the existence of a contract.
	2. The fact that the parties did not agree on all the terms of their contract does not prevent the formation of a contract.
	3. A firm written offer by a merchant that contains assurances it will be held open is irrevocable for a period of up to three months.
	4. Acceptance of an offer may be made by any reasonable manner and is effective on dispatch.
	5. A timely expression of acceptance creates a contract even if it contains terms different from the offer or states additional terms *unless* the attempted acceptance is expressly conditioned on the offeror's agreement to the terms of the acceptance.
	6. An offer inviting a prompt shipment may be accepted either by a prompt promise to ship or a prompt shipment of the goods.
Consideration (Chapter 12)	1. Consideration is not required to make a firm offer in writing by a merchant irrevocable for a period of up to three months.
	2. Consideration is not required to support a modification of a contract for the sale of goods.
Statute of Frauds (Chapter 16)	1. Subject to several exceptions, all contracts for the sale of goods for $500 or more must be evidenced by a writing signed by the party against whom enforcement of the contract is sought. It is effective only as to the quantity of goods stated in the writing.
	2. A signed writing is not required if the party against whom enforcement is sought is a merchant, received a written memorandum from the other party, and did not object in writing within 10 days of his receipt of it.
	3. An exception to the statute of frauds is made for specially manufactured goods not suitable for sale to others on which the seller has made a substantial beginning in manufacturing or has entered into a binding contract to acquire.
	4. An exception to the statute of frauds is made for contracts that a party admits the existence of in court testimony or pleadings.
	5. If a party accepts goods or payment for goods, the statute of frauds is satisfied to the extent of the payment made or the goods accepted.
Unconscionability (Chapter 15)	If a court finds a contract for the sale of goods to be unconscionable, it can refuse to enforce it entirely, enforce it without any unconscionable clause, or enforce it in a way that avoids an unconscionable result.

Price Terms A fixed price is not essential to the creation of a binding sales contract. Of course, if price has been the subject of a dispute between the parties that has never been resolved, no contract is created because a "meeting of the minds" never occurred. However, if the parties omitted a price term or left the price to be determined at a future date or by some external means, the UCC supplies a price term [2–305]. Under the common law, such contracts would have failed due to "indefiniteness." If a price term is simply omitted, or if the parties agreed that the price would be set by some external agency (like a particular market or trade journal) that fails to set the price, the UCC says the price is a *reasonable price at the time for delivery* [2–305(1)]. If the agreement gives either party the power to fix the price, that party must do so in *good faith* [2–305(2)]. If the surrounding circumstances clearly indicate that the parties did not intend to be bound in the event a price was not determined in the agreed-upon manner, no contract results [2–305(4)].

Quantity Terms

In some cases, the parties may state the quantity of goods covered by their sales contract in an indefinite way. Contracts that obligate a buyer to purchase a seller's *output* of a certain item or all of the buyer's *requirements* of a certain item are commonly encountered. These contracts caused frequent problems under the common law because of the indefiniteness of the parties' obligations. If the seller decided to double its output, did the buyer have to accept the entire amount? If the market price of the item soared much higher than the contract price, could the buyer double or triple its demands?

Output and Needs Contracts

In an "output" contract, one party is bound to sell its entire output of particular goods and the other party is bound to buy that output. In a "needs" or "requirements" contract, the quantity of goods is based on the needs of the buyer. In determining the quantity of goods to be produced or taken pursuant to an output or needs contract, the rule of *good faith* applies. Thus, no quantity can be demanded or taken that is unreasonably disproportionate to any stated estimate in the contract or to "normal" prior output or requirements if no estimate is stated [2–306(2)].

For example, assume the Manhattan Ice Company enters into a five-year agreement with the Madison Square Garden Corporation to provide at a fixed, specified price all the ice required for the concession stands at Madison Square Garden. Manhattan Ice expands its capacity to make ice to fulfill the anticipated requirements and during the first two years of the contract delivers between 1.25 and 1.5 million pounds of ice to the Garden. If in the third year of the agreement, Madison Square Garden wants Manhattan Ice to deliver approximately twice that much ice so that it can be used at other arenas owned by the corporation, Manhattan Ice would not be obligated to provide the additional ice. Similarly, Madison Square Garden would not be able to reduce its request to 100,000 pounds of ice because it decides to make its own ice on the premises. In the latter case, it is obligated to continue to acquire all of its requirements for ice from Manhattan Ice.

In the *Noble Roman's* case that follows, the court looked to the contract and to the parties' course of performance to conclude that the contract was a "requirements" contract and not an order for a specified number of pizza boxes.

Exclusive Dealing Contracts

The UCC takes a similar approach to *exclusive dealing contracts*. Under the common law, these contracts were sources of difficulty due to the indefinite nature of the parties' duties. Did the dealer have to make any effort to sell the manufacturer's products, and did the manufacturer have any duty to supply the dealer? The UCC says that unless the parties agree to the contrary, sellers have an obligation to use their *best efforts* to supply the goods to the buyer and the buyers are obligated to use their *best efforts* to promote their sale [2–306(2)].

CYBERLAW IN ACTION

Electronic Writings and the Statute of Frauds

The Electronic Signatures in Global and National Commerce Act (the "E-Sign" act) was enacted by Congress and became effective in the United States on October 1, 2000. The E-Sign law covers many everyday transactions including sales transactions, even where the law of the state involved still has a version of Article 2 that requires a "signed writing" or another means of satisfying the Article 2 statute of frauds found in Section 2–201. Federal laws "preempt"—that is, displace—state laws if the two sets of laws are in conflict. If state law requires a signed writing or another indicator that the purported buyer and

seller actually intended to form a contract, E-Sign allows the parties to use electronic authentications instead of signed writings. E-mail messages and online orders sent by the buyer would suffice. States that have adopted the Uniform Electronic Transactions Act (UETA) also allow online communications to satisfy the Section 2–201 statute of frauds requirement.

The hypothetical scenario at the beginning of this chapter poses the situation where a person uses a manufacturer's website to purchase a bicycle and asks whether an enforceable contract for the sale of goods can be formed electronically. Given the preceding information, how would you answer the question?

| Noble Roman's v. Pizza Boxes | 57 UCC Rep. 2d 901 (Ind. Ct. App. 2005) |

Noble Roman's is a franchisor of pizza restaurants, but the company does not own or operate any restaurants. Noble Roman's franchisees order supplies approved by Noble Roman's. Pizza Boxes is a broker that acts as an intermediary for vendors who manufacture pizza boxes.

In 2002 William Gilbert, director of R&D and distribution for Noble Roman's, e-mailed Michael Rosenberg, vice president of Pizza Boxes, regarding Noble Roman's interest in "clamshell" boxes for use in a new "pizza-by-the-slice" program. Gilbert stated that the estimated usage at this stage is from 400,000 to a million units per year to start. After Noble Roman's approved the box design, the parties worked out the details for the purchase. Gilbert explained that the pizza-by-the-slice program was just getting started at one of its franchise locations, but he anticipated that other locations would implement the program over time. The two agreed that 2.5 million boxes would be needed annually; that Multifoods, Noble Roman's distributor, would submit orders for the boxes and pay the invoices; and that Multifoods would pick up the boxes after the orders were filled.

On November 1, 2002, Rosenberg sent Gilbert a confirming letter, that stated:

Dear Bill:

Please sign in the space below to confirm the following order:

Item: 18/6 Slice Box 220/case

Quantity: 2,500,000

Print: Two colors

Price: $101.45/M

FOB: Bakersfield or Stockton, Ca. (in trailer load quantity—approx. 230,000 per load)

To be picked up by Multifoods. PBI remits invoice Multifoods.

Extras for printing preps are included at $4,500 ($1.80/M) and amortized over the entire order. In the event that the total of 2.5 million boxes are not manufactured, Noble Roman's is responsible for any portion of the prep charge remaining.

Gilbert signed and dated the letter and returned it to Rosenberg. On its own initiative, Pizza Boxes, through its vendor, Dopaco Inc., manufactured 519,200 boxes in anticipation of Multifoods's future orders. Multifoods submitted an initial purchase order to Pizza Boxes for six cases (12,000 boxes), and Multifoods paid Pizza Boxes for that order. However, after the initial order, Multifoods did not order any more boxes. When Rosenberg called Multifoods to inquire why it had not ordered more boxes, he was told that the franchisees were "not using this product."

Pizza Boxes then asked Noble Roman's to pay for approximately 500,000 boxes that Pizza Boxes had made but Multifoods had not ordered. Noble Roman's responded that it was a franchisor and not an operator of restaurants that specifies and arranges for the manufacture of products and supplies sold by its franchisees, and that Noble Roman's does not purchase any supplies or products. Once Noble Roman's includes products or supplies in its specifications, then any purchase order is signed by the distributor who buys all of the supplies and distributes them to the franchisees who sign purchase orders with the distributor.

Pizza Boxes then filed suit against Noble Roman's alleging breach of contract, seeking $54,901.44 for the unpaid inventory and tooling charges. The trial court entered summary judgment in favor of Pizza Boxes and Noble Roman's appealed.

Najam, Judge

Noble Roman's contends that the trial court erred when it entered summary judgment in favor of Pizza Boxes. In particular, Noble Roman's maintains that its only obligation under the November 1, 2002, letter was to pay the "printing prep" charges remaining in the event Pizza Boxes did not manufacture the 2.5 million boxes. We agree.

Initially, we note that Pizza Boxes's complaint suggests that the November 1, 2002, letter is a purchase order, that is, "[a] document authorizing a seller to deliver goods with payment to be made later." But the plain and ordinary meaning of the letter shows that it is a requirements contract. See UCC 2–306. The letter is not an order for 2.5 million boxes but, on its face, contemplates the possibility that not all 2.5 million boxes would be manufactured. Thus, it is not a purchase order. And, despite the inclusion in the letter of a specific estimate of quantity, it is clear that there was no meeting of the minds on how many boxes Pizza Boxes would ultimately produce under the requirements contract.

Noble Roman's contends, and we agree, that the letter is unambiguous and provides that it is only responsible for the unpaid "printing prep" charges "in the event that the total of 2.5 million boxes are not manufactured." In interpreting an unambiguous contract, a court gives effect to the parties' intentions as expressed in the four corners of the instrument, and clear, plain and unambiguous terms are conclusive of that intent. Particular words and phrases cannot be read alone, and the parties' intentions must be determined by reading the contract as a whole.

The terms of the November 1 letter show that: (1) Multifoods would pick up the boxes; (2) Pizza Boxes would remit the invoices to Multifoods; and (3) Noble Roman's was responsible for "any portion of the [printing] prep charges remaining in the event that not all 2.5 million boxes were manufactured." While the terms regarding quantity and price might, at first glance, suggest the letter is a purchase order from Noble Roman's for 2.5 million boxes, when the letter is read as a whole it shows that it is a requirements contract under which Multifoods, not Noble Roman's, is the purchaser. In effect, Multifoods is a third-party beneficiary of the contract, in that Noble Roman's established the specifications for the manufacture, and negotiated the price of the boxes for the benefit of Multifoods.

In addition, the parties' course of performance shows that Pizza Boxes did not expect that Noble Roman's would be responsible for paying for the boxes. Indiana Code Section 2-208 provides in relevant part:

Where the contract for sale involves repeated occasions for performance by either party with knowledge of the nature of the performance and opportunity for objection to it by the other, any course of performance accepted or acquiesced in without objection shall be relevant to determine the meaning of the agreement.

Indiana Code Section 2-202 provides in relevant part:

Terms with respect to which the confirmatory memoranda of the parties agree or which are otherwise set forth in a writing intended by the parties as a final expression of their agreement with respect to such terms as are included therein may not be contradicted by evidence of any prior agreement or a contemporaneous oral agreement but *may be explained or supplemented:*

(a) by course of dealing or usage of trade (1-205) or *by course of performance* (2-208).

Here, the requirements contract involved "repeated occasions for performance" in that not all 2.5 million boxes would be ordered, manufactured, and purchased at once.

Multifoods submitted a purchase order for sixty cases to Pizza Boxes; Pizza Boxes submitted an invoice to Multifoods; and Multifoods paid Pizza Boxes for the boxes. When Multifoods did not submit any subsequent orders, Rosenberg looked to Multifoods for an explanation and telephoned its buyer to ask why no other orders had been submitted. The conduct of Multifoods in submitting the order to Pizza Boxes and paying Pizza Boxes, and Pizza Boxes in submitting the invoice to Multifoods and contacting Multifoods to inquire about additional orders, establish a course of performance between them, consistent with the terms of the letter, all of which shows that Multifoods is the purchaser. Pizza Boxes did not suggest that the November 1, 2002, letter obligated Noble Roman's until it realized that Multifoods was not going to submit any additional purchase orders.

Noble Roman's did not order the boxes in dispute and is entitled to summary judgment on Pizza Boxes's breach of contract claim for the cost of the boxes as a matter of law. However, under the terms of contract, Noble Roman's is liable to Pizza Boxes for the portion of the prep charges still owed for the boxes that were not manufactured.

Judgment reversed in favor of Noble Roman's and remanded with instructions.

Time for Performance The UCC takes the same position as the common law when the parties' contract is silent about the time for performance. Performance in such cases must be tendered within a *reasonable time* [2-309(1)]. If the parties' contract calls for a number of performances over an indefinite period of time (e.g., an open-ended requirements contract), the contract is valid for a *reasonable time* but may be terminated at any time by either party after giving *reasonable notice* [2-309(2) and (3)]. For example, Farmer Jack agrees to sell his entire output of peaches each fall to a cannery at the then-current market price. If the contract does not contain a provision spelling out how and when the contract can be terminated, Farmer Jack can terminate it if he gives the cannery a reasonable time to make arrangements to acquire peaches from someone else. Finally, the UCC also provides for the time and place of payment. Unless the parties agreed on some other payment terms, payment for the goods is due at the "time and place at which the buyer is to receive the goods" [2-310(a)].

Delivery Terms   Unless the parties agree to the contrary, the UCC says that the goods ordered are to be delivered in a *single-lot shipment* [2-307]. If the contract is silent about the place for delivery, the goods are to be delivered at the *seller's place of business* [2-308(a)]. The only exception to this rule is in the case of contracts dealing with identified goods that both parties at the time of contracting know are located someplace other than the seller's place of business. In such a case, the *site of the goods* is the place for delivery [2-308(b)].

Standardized shipping terms that through commercial practice have come to have a specific meaning are customarily used in sales contracts. The terms **FOB (free on board)** and **FAS (free alongside ship)** are basic delivery terms. If the delivery term of the contract is FOB or FAS the place at which the goods originate, the seller is obligated to deliver to the carrier goods that *conform to the contract* and *are properly prepared for shipment* to the buyer, and the seller must make a *reasonable contract for transportation of the goods* on behalf of the buyer. Under such delivery terms, the goods are at the risk of the buyer during transit and he must pay the shipping charges. If the term is *FOB destination,* the seller must deliver the goods to the designated destination and they are at the seller's risk and expense during transit. These terms will be discussed in more detail later in this chapter.

Title

 Explain when title to goods passes from the seller to the buyer.

UCC Changes   The UCC also deals with many important questions about the ownership (title) of the goods in sales contracts. This is important for several reasons. If the goods are lost, stolen, damaged, or destroyed, who must bear the risk of loss, the seller or the buyer? Whose creditors (the seller's or the buyer's) have the legal right to seize the goods to satisfy their claims? What are the rights of those who buy goods that are subject to the claims of third parties (e.g., their rightful owner or secured creditors)? Who has the insurable interest that the law requires before a party can purchase insurance protection for the goods?

Under the common law, most problems concerning risk of loss, insurable interest, and the rights of various third parties to the goods were answered by determining who had title to the goods. The UCC, to clarify these questions, has specific rules that generally do not depend on who has title.

General Title Rule

Physical Delivery   The UCC does have a general title section. It provides that title passes to the buyer when the seller has completely performed his or her duties concerning *physical delivery* of the goods [2-401(2)]. So, if the contract merely requires the seller to *ship* the goods, title passes to the buyer when the seller delivers the goods to the carrier. If the contract requires *delivery* of the goods by the seller, title passes to the buyer when the goods are delivered and tendered to the buyer.

Delivery without Moving the Goods   If delivery is to be made without moving the goods, title passes at the *time and place of contracting* if the goods have been identified to the contract. Identification occurs when the surrounding circumstances make it clear that the goods are those "to which the contract refers" [2-501]. This may result from the contract description of the goods (if they are distinct from other goods in the seller's possession) or from actions of the seller, such as setting aside or marking the goods.

Negotiable Document of Title   Sometimes when the goods are being shipped by a professional carrier, the parties will use a negotiable document of title. For instance, a seller may ship the goods to the buyer with payment due on delivery. The document of title (a negotiable bill of lading) serves as the contract between the seller and the shipper as well as identifies who has title and control of the goods. The document of title (signifying the right to control the goods) will not be surrendered to the buyer until she pays for the goods. If the contract calls for the seller to deliver a negotiable document of title to the goods (like a warehouse receipt or a bill of lading) to the buyer, title passes when the document of title is delivered.

Buyer's Rejection   In some instances, the buyer will reject the goods, perhaps because he does not believe that they conform to the contractual specifications. Whatever the reason, if the buyer rejects tender of the goods, title will automatically be revested in the seller.

The *National Music Museum: America's Shrine to Music* case, which follows, illustrates the application of these rules concerning passage of title. In this case, the court held that title to a guitar never passed to the buyer despite the fact he had entered into a contract to purchase it because the seller never delivered the guitar to the buyer and he had never possessed it.

CYBERLAW IN ACTION

Buying Beer on the Internet

While his parents were away from home on vacation, Hunter Butler, a minor, used a credit card in his name to order 12 bottles of beer through Beer Across America's website. When his mother, Lynda Butler, returned home, she found several bottles from the shipment of beer remaining in the refrigerator. Lynda Butler then filed a civil lawsuit against Beer Across America seeking damages under Section 6–5–70 of the Alabama Civil Damages Act. The Civil Damages Act provides for a civil action by the parent or guardian of a minor against anyone who knowingly sells or furnishes liquor to the minor. A threshold issue in the lawsuit was whether the sale of the beer had taken place in Alabama so that a court in Alabama would have personal jurisdiction over Beer Across America.

Beer Across America was an Illinois corporation involved in the marketing and sale of alcoholic beverages and other merchandise.

The beer was brought by carrier from Illinois to Alabama. The sales invoice and shipping documents provided that the sale was FOB the seller, with the carrier acting as the buyer's agent. Moreover, the invoice included a charge for sales tax but no charge for beer tax; Alabama law requires that sales tax be collected for out-of-state sale of goods that are then shipped to Alabama but requires beer tax be collected only on sales within Alabama.

The court held that the sale arranged over the Internet took place in Illinois. The court noted that under the versions of the Uniform Commercial Code in effect in both Illinois and Alabama, a sale consists in the passing of title from the seller to the buyer. Title to goods passes at the time and place of the shipment when the contract does not require the seller to make delivery at the destination. Accordingly, ownership to the beer passed to Hunter Butler upon tender of the beer to the carrier. The court then transferred the case to the U.S. District Court for the Northern District of Illinois. *Butler v. Beer Across America,* 40 UCC Rep. 2d 1008 (N.D. Ala. 2000).

National Music Museum: America's Shrine to Music v. Johnson
904 F.3d 598 (8th Cir. 2018)

Robert Johnson and Larry Moss had known each other for 35 years and shared an interest in historic memorabilia. Whenever Johnson came across pieces he thought Moss would enjoy, he contacted him, and during that time, Moss had purchased 15–20 pieces of memorabilia.

In the summer of 2007, Johnson contacted Moss about acquiring three guitars once owned by Elvis Presley, including a Martin D-35 guitar. Subsequent discussions finally led to an agreement on February 12, 2008, in which Moss agreed to pay Johnson $120,000 for four guitars, three of which were connected to Elvis. A written contract organized the transaction into two parts. Part one involved Moss paying Johnson $70,000 and taking immediate possession of two guitars. Part two required Johnson to deliver the two remaining guitars—one of which was the Martin D-35—by April 12, 2009. Upon delivery, Moss would pay Johnson $50,000.

Moss was unable to take possession at the time the arrangement was finalized because the Martin D-35 guitar was on display at the Rock n' Soul Museum in Memphis, Tennessee, under an agreement Johnson made to leave it there until January 2009. Moss promised Johnson he would not retrieve the guitar from Rock n' Soul. Thus, the only way Moss could have taken possession of the Martin D-35 was by having Johnson deliver it to him. Moss expected Johnson to physically deliver the guitar.

Toward the end of 2008, Johnson took the D-35 from Rock n' Soul. Over the next five years, the parties corresponded by e-mail about the guitar, but Moss never asked Johnson to bring it to him or claimed he was the owner. Subsequently, in February 2013, Johnson entered into an agreement with the National Music Museum whereby it would pay Johnson $250,000 for a John Entwistle Gibson Korina Explorer guitar and would also receive seven enumerated donations from Johnson, one of which was the Martin D-35 guitar. On December 10, 2013, Moss contacted the National Music Museum and claimed he owned the Martin D-35 that had been donated to it.

The National Music Museum brought suit against Moss and Johnson seeking a declaratory judgment that it was the legal owner of Martin D-35 previously owned by Elvis Pressley. The federal district court held that because the guitar had never been delivered to Moss, he never acquired title to it. Johnson still had title to the Martin D-35 when he transferred it to the Museum and, consequently, the Museum became the owner. Moss then appealed the district court decision to the U.S. Court of Appeals.

Wollman, Circuit Judge.

Moss argues that title to the Martin D-35 guitar passed to him when he entered into the contract with Johnson on February 12, 2008. Moss claims that constructive delivery of the guitar was sufficient to pass title because the guitar was on display at the Rock n' Soul Museum and Moss assured Johnson that he would allow it to remain there.

Under Tennessee law, "unless otherwise explicitly agreed title passes to the buyer at the time and place at which the seller completes performance with reference to the physical delivery of the goods." Section 2-401(2). "Where delivery is to be made without moving the goods," however, title passes at the time of contracting "if the goods have been identified and no documents of title are to be delivered." Section 2-401(3)(B).

The February 12, 2008, contract between Moss and Johnson provided that Moss would pay $50,000 "upon delivery" of the Martin D-35 and Sonny Burgess guitars. The contract further stated that "Johnson guarantees he will deliver to Moss both items . . . on or before April 12, 2008; and Moss guarantees that he will pay the balance of $50,000 when that delivery occurs." Even assuming that Moss verbally agreed to the Martin D-35's continued display at the Rock n' Roll Museum, the contract required physical delivery of the guitar. Nothing in the contract indicated that delivery was to be made without physically moving the guitar. Because Johnson never delivered the Martin D-35 guitar to Moss, Moss never acquired title to it. Accordingly, we uphold the district court's determination that Johnson had title to the Martin D-35 guitar when he transferred the guitar to the Museum and that the Museum owns the Martin D-35 guitar.

The judgment is affirmed.

Title and Third Parties

 Explain what is meant by a *voidable title* and explain when a buyer can obtain better title to goods than the seller had.

Obtaining Good Title A fundamental rule of property law is that a buyer cannot receive better title to goods than the seller had. If Thief steals an iPad from Adler and sells it to Brown, Brown does not get good title to the iPad because Thief had no title to it. Adler would have the right to recover the iPad from Brown. Similarly, if Brown sold the iPad to Carroll, Carroll could get no better title to it than Brown had. Adler would have the right to recover the iPad from Carroll.

Under the UCC, however, there are several exceptions to the general rule that a buyer cannot get better title to goods than his seller had. The most important exceptions include the following: (1) A person who has a voidable title to goods can pass good title to a bona fide purchaser for value, (2) a person who buys goods in the regular course of a retailer's business usually takes free of any interests in the goods that the retailer has given to others, and (3) a person who buys goods in the ordinary course of a dealer's business takes free of any claim of a person who entrusted those goods to the dealer.

Transfers of Voidable Title A seller who has a **voidable title** has the power to pass good title to a *good-faith* *purchaser for value* [2-403(1)]. A seller has a voidable title to goods if he has obtained his title through fraudulent representations. For example, a person would have a voidable title if he obtained goods by impersonating another person or by paying for them with a bad check or if he obtained goods without paying the agreed purchase price when it was agreed that the transaction was to be a cash sale. Under the UCC, **good faith** means "honesty in fact in the conduct or transaction concerned" [1-201(19)] and a buyer has given **value** if he has given any consideration sufficient to support a simple contract [1-201(44)].

For example, Jones goes to the ABC Appliance Store; convinces the clerk that he is really Clark, who is a good customer of ABC; and leaves with a Sony TV charged to Clark's account. If Jones sells the Sony TV to Davis, who gives Jones value for it and has no knowledge of the fraud that Jones perpetrated on ABC, Davis gets good title to the Sony TV. ABC cannot recover the Sony TV from Davis; instead, it must look for Jones, the person who deceived it. In this situation, both ABC and Davis were innocent of wrongdoing, but the law considers Davis to be the more worthy of its protection because ABC was in a better position to have prevented the wrongdoing by Jones and because Davis bought the goods in good faith and for value.

The same result would be reached if Jones had given ABC a check that later bounced and then sold the Sony TV to Davis, who was a good-faith purchaser for value. Davis would have good title to the Sony TV, and ABC would have to pursue its right against Jones on the bounced check. The primary reason for this exception is to place the burden of loss on the party who had the best opportunity to avoid the harm. Good-faith purchasers can do nothing to avoid injury. However, the rightful owners of goods at least have the opportunity to protect themselves by taking steps to assure themselves of the buyer's identity, accepting only cash or certified checks, refusing to part with the goods until they have cash in hand, or taking steps to discover fraud before parting with the goods. In view of their greater relative fault, the UCC requires the original owners of the goods to bear the burden of collecting from their fraudulent buyers.

Buyers in the Ordinary Course of Business

The second exception made by the UCC concerns **buyers in the ordinary course of business**. A buyer in ordinary course is a person who in good faith and without knowledge that the sale to him is in violation of the ownership rights of a third party buys goods in the ordinary course of business of a person selling goods of that kind, other than a pawnbroker [1–201(9)]. Under the UCC, buyers in the ordinary course take goods free of any security interest in the goods that their seller may have given a third party [9–307].

For example, Brown Buick may borrow money from Bank in order to finance its inventory of new Buicks; in turn, Bank may take a security interest in the inventory to secure repayment of the loan. If Carter buys a new Buick from Brown Buick, he gets good title to the Buick free and clear of the bank's security interest if he is a buyer in the ordinary course of business and without knowledge that the sale is in violation of a security interest. The basic purpose of this exception is to protect those who innocently buy from merchants and thereby to promote confidence in

such commercial transactions. The exception also reflects the fact that the bank is more interested in the proceeds from the sale than in the inventory. Security interests and the rights of buyers in the ordinary course of business are discussed in more detail in Chapter 29, Security Interests in Personal Property.

Entrusting of Goods

A third exception to the general rule is that if goods are entrusted to a merchant who deals in goods of that kind, the merchant has the power to transfer all rights of the entruster to a buyer in the ordinary course of business [2–403(2)]. In the scenario presented at the beginning of this chapter, Paul takes his damaged bicycle for repair to a shop that sells and repairs bicycles. By mistake, a clerk in the bicycle shop sells the bicycle to Melissa. The bicycle shop can pass good title to Melissa, a buyer in the ordinary course of business. In such a case, Paul would have to sue the bicycle shop for damages for conversion of the bicycle; he could not get it back from Melissa. The purpose behind this rule is to protect commerce by giving confidence to buyers that they will get good title to the goods they buy from merchants in the ordinary course of business. However, a merchant-seller cannot pass good title to stolen goods even if the buyer is a buyer in the ordinary course of business. This is because the original owner did nothing to facilitate the transfer.

In the case that follows, *Zaretsky v. William Goldberg Diamond Corp.*, where the owner of a diamond consigned it to a well-known celebrity fashion consultant who sold it rather than returning it, the court rejected the argument that the fashion consultant was a merchant with voidable title who had the power to transfer all rights of the original owner to a subsequent buyer in the ordinary course of business.

Zaretsky v. William Goldberg Diamond Corp.
89 UCC Rep. 2d 623 (2d Cir. 2016)

The William Goldberg Diamond Corp. (WGDC) was the owner of a 7.44-carat pear-shaped diamond. In February 2003, WGDC consigned the diamond, along with other items, to Derek Khan, a well-known celebrity fashion stylist. The purpose of the consignment—which reflected an ongoing arrangement between Khan and WGBC and between Khan and other established jewelers—was for Khan to adorn his celebrity clients with high-end jewelry in preparation for special events and fashion shoots.

The arrangement was governed by a Consignment Agreement, which made clear that Khan had no freestanding authority to "sell, pledge, hypothecate, or otherwise dispose of the diamond," but that he could sell the diamond "if and when he…received from WGDC a separate invoice." In other words, Khan was authorized to sell the diamond only if WGDC approved the sale and set out specific terms, prior to any sale.

Typically, after WGDC consigned a piece of jewelry to Khan, he would return the jewelry to WGDC within a few days of the celebrity event. After the February 2003 consignment, however, Khan failed to return the diamond in a timely manner, prompting WGDC to become suspicious and, eventually, to file a police report.

On March 17, 2003, the diamond surfaced in the legitimate market, when Louis Newman—a New York diamond merchant—submitted the diamond to the Gemological Institute of America (GIA) for certification, which was issued on March 25, 2003. In late 2003, the diamond was purchased by Stanley & Sons—another New York diamond merchant—on behalf of Frank and Donna Walsh. In August 2012, Donna Walsh gave the diamond to her daughter and son-in-law, Suzanne and Steven Zaretsky. Steven Zaretsky authorized another jeweler to appraise the diamond for insurance purposes. On December 10, 2012, that jeweler submitted the diamond to the GIA for certification. Soon thereafter, the GIA informed the Zaretskys that the diamond appeared to have been stolen from WGDC in 2003. The GIA retained possession pending a final resolution of its rightful owner.

When WGDC finally traced the diamond to the Zaretskys, it filed an action seeking a declaratory judgment that it was the rightful owner of the diamond. WGDC contended that because Khan stole the diamond, he could neither hold title in the diamond—nor transfer title to it—as a matter of law.

On the other hand, the Zaretskys argued that Khan was not a thief, but rather an entrusted merchant who held "voidable title" in the diamond—and therefore was capable of transferring title—under the Uniform Commercial Code. As a result, when the Walshes purchased the diamond in 2003, they acquired good title to the diamond, which was subsequently transferred to the Zaretskys. Accordingly, they contended that WGDC was no longer the owner of the diamond as a matter of law.

The trial court held that Khan had the power to transfer WGDC's rights to the diamond under Section 2-403(2), which provides that "any entrusting of possession of goods to a merchant who deals in goods of that kind gives him power to transfer all rights of the entruster to a buyer in ordinary course of business." The court concluded that Khan had the power to transfer WGDC's rights to the diamond under Section 2-403(2) because Kahn fell within the definition of a "merchant" in Section 2-104(1) because, by his occupation, he held "himself out as having knowledge or skill peculiar to the practices or goods involved in the transaction." The trial court then granted summary judgment in favor of the Zaretskys and entered a final order adjudging the Zaretskys to be the rightful owners of the diamond. WGDC then filed an appeal of the decision and order.

Sack, Circuit Judge

As the district court noted, two provisions of the NYUCC are relevant to the parties' competing claims to the diamond. The first is section 2-104(1) which provides three alternative definitions for the stand-alone term "merchant" under the code:

(1) a person who deals in goods of the kind *or*
(2) otherwise by his occupation holds himself out as having knowledge or skill peculiar to the practices or goods involved in the transaction *or*
(3) to whom such knowledge or skill may be attributed by his employment of an agent or broker or other intermediary who by his occupation holds himself out as having such knowledge or skill.

The second relevant provision is section 2-403(2) which states that "[a]ny entrusting of possession of goods to a merchant *who deals in goods of that kind* gives him the power to transfer all rights of the entruster to a buyer in the ordinary course of business."

In concluding that the Zaretskys are the rightful owners of the diamond, the district court construed section 2-403(2) as empowering anyone who qualifies as a "merchant" under section 2-104(1) with the ability to pass title to an entrusted good. The court then decided that Khan by holding himself out as having the knowledge or skill peculiar to jewelry, was a "merchant" under the second definition contained in section 2-401(1), and that the entrustment provision under 2-403(2) therefore enabled him to transfer all rights to the diamond to others.

We disagree with the district court's construction of 2-403(2) of the NYUCC. Section 2-403(2) enables a merchant to transfer rights to an entrusted good only if the person is a "merchant" who "deals in goods of that kind," in this case diamonds or other high-end jewelry. The entrustment provision, therefore applies to a person who is a merchant under section 2-104(1)'s first definition, which includes the requirement that the person be one who "deals in" the relevant good. But it does not necessarily apply to the person who is a "merchant" under the second or third definition. Even if, as the district court has determined, Khan was a "merchant" under section 2-104(1)'s second definition, the court was also required to find that Khan dealt in goods like the diamond in order for him to have transferred rights to it under section 2-403(2).

This appeal turns on whether Khan regularly sold the kind of goods at issue in this case: diamonds or other high-end jewelry. The entrustee must be a person who deals in goods of the kind entrusted to him or her. Because the Zaretsky's have submitted no evidence that Khan regularly conducted such sale, we conclude that WGDC is entitled to summary judgment.

The record supports WGDC's contention that Khan never sold any of the diamonds WGDC consigned to him. The terms of the Consignment Agreement denied Khan any independent authority to sell the diamond and specified that a sale could only occur if he received a written invoice from WGDC, which WDGC did not provide to him. There is also no record evidence of Khan's participation in any specific sale of WGDC's jewelry. The only evidence bearing on Khan's potential involvement in selling other diamonds or other high-end jewelry is his own declaration, which

WGDC urges us to ignore because it was "made by a convicted felon and habitual liar who has fled to Dubai (and whom the WGDC has no ability to depose)."

We note that our conclusion is consistent with the New York Court of Appeals' assessment of the underlying purpose of section 2-403(2). It is, the court tells us, "designed to enhance the reliability of commercial sales by merchants (who deal with the kind of goods sold on a regular basis) while shifting the risk of loss through fraudulent transfer to the owner of the goods, who can select the merchant to whom he entrusts his property." It would be inappropriate in light of that principle, we think, to shift the risk of loss to WGDC here. Absent evidence that Khan regularly sold diamonds or other high-end jewelry, WGDC had little reason to suspect that he would do so once the company entrusted the diamond to him.

Case remanded to district court with instructions to enter summary judgment for WGDC.

Ethics and Compliance in Action

Perils of Entrusting Goods

Suppose you are the owner of a small jewelry store that sells new and antique jewelry. A customer leaves a family heirloom—an elaborate diamond ring—with you for cleaning and resetting. By mistake, a clerk in your store sells it to another customer. What would you do? If you were the buyer of the ring and had given it to your fiancée as a gift and then were informed of the circumstances, what would you do?

CONCEPT REVIEW

Title and Third Parties

General Rule	A seller cannot pass better title to goods than he has.
Exceptions to General Rule	1. A person who has voidable title to goods can pass good title to a bona fide purchaser for value.
	2. A buyer in the ordinary course of a retailer's business usually takes free of any interests in the goods that the retailer has given to others.
	3. A person who buys goods in the ordinary course of a dealer's business takes free of any claims of a person who entrusted those goods to the dealer.

Risk of Loss

 LO19-5 Apply the UCC rules concerning risk of loss to determine who had the risk of loss in a given transaction where the goods that were the subject of a contract were lost or damaged before the buyer took possession.

The transportation of goods from sellers to buyers can be a risky business. The carrier of the goods may lose, damage, or destroy them; floods, hurricanes, and other natural catastrophes may take their toll; thieves may steal all or part of the goods. If neither party is at fault for the loss, who should bear the risk? If the buyer has the risk when the goods are damaged or lost, the buyer is liable for the contract price. If the seller has the risk, he is liable for damages unless substitute performance can be tendered.

The common law placed the risk on the party who had technical title at the time of the loss. The UCC rejects this approach and provides specific rules governing risk of loss that are designed to provide certainty and to place the risk on the party best able to protect against loss and most likely to be insured against it. Risk of loss under the UCC depends on the terms of the parties' agreement, on the moment the loss occurs, and on whether one of the parties was in breach of contract when the loss occurred.

Terms of the Agreement The contracting parties, subject to the rule of good faith, may specify who has the risk of loss in their agreement [2-509(4)]. This they may do directly or by using certain commonly accepted shipping terms in their contract. In addition, the UCC has certain general rules on risk of loss that amplify specific shipping terms and control risk of loss in cases where specific terms are not used [2-509].

Shipment Contracts

If the contract requires the seller to ship the goods by carrier but does not require their delivery to a specific destination, the risk passes to the buyer when the seller delivers the goods to the carrier [2-509(1)(a)]. Shipment contracts are considered to be the normal contract where the seller is required to send goods to the buyer but is not required to guarantee delivery at a particular location.

The following are commonly used shipping terms that create shipment contracts:

1. *FOB (free on board) point of origin.* This term calls for the seller to deliver the goods free of expense and at the seller's risk at the place designated. For example, a contract between a seller located in Chicago and a buyer in New York calls for delivery FOB Chicago. The seller must deliver the goods at his expense and at his risk to a carrier in the place designated in the contract—namely, Chicago—and arrange for their carriage. Because the shipment term in this example is FOB Chicago, the seller bears the risk and expense of delivering the goods to the carrier, but the seller is not responsible for delivering the goods to a specific destination. If the term is "FOB vessel, car, or other vehicle," the seller must load the goods on board at his own risk and expense [2-319(1)].

2. *FAS (free alongside ship).* This term is commonly used in maritime contracts and is normally accompanied by the name of a specific vessel and port—for example, "FAS Calgary [the ship], Chicago Port Authority." The seller must deliver the goods alongside the vessel *Calgary* at the Chicago Port Authority at his own risk and expense [2-319(2)].

3. *CIF (cost, insurance, and freight).* This term means that the price of the goods includes the cost of shipping and insuring them. The seller bears this expense and the risk of loading the goods [2-320].

4. *C & F.* This term is the same as CIF, except that the seller is not obligated to insure the goods [2-320].

Destination Contracts

If the contract requires the seller to deliver the goods to a specific destination, the seller bears the risk and expense of delivery to that destination [2-509(1)(b)]. The following are commonly used shipping terms that create destination contracts:

1. *FOB destination.* An FOB term coupled with the place of destination of the goods puts the expense and risk of delivering the goods to that destination on the seller [2-319(1)(b)]. For example, a contract between a seller in Chicago and a buyer in Phoenix might call for shipment FOB Phoenix. The seller must ship the goods to Phoenix at her own expense, and she also retains the risk of delivery of the goods to Phoenix.

2. *Ex-ship.* This term does not specify a particular ship, but it places the expense and risk on the seller until the goods are unloaded from whatever ship is used [2-322].

3. *No arrival, no sale.* This term places the expense and risk during shipment on the seller. If the goods fail to arrive through no fault of the seller, the seller has no further liability to the buyer [2-324].

For example, a Chicago-based seller contracts to sell a quantity of Weber grills to a buyer FOB Phoenix, the buyer's place of business. The grills are destroyed en route when the truck carrying the grills is involved in an accident. The risk of the loss of the grills is on the seller, and the buyer is not obligated to pay for them. The seller may have the right to recover from the trucking company, but between the seller and the buyer, the seller has the risk of loss. If the contract had called for delivery FOB the seller's manufacturing plant, then the risk of loss would have been on the buyer. The buyer would have had to pay for the grills and then pursue any claims that he had against the trucking company.

Goods in the Possession of Third Parties

If the goods are in the possession of a third-party bailee (like a carrier or warehouse) and are to be delivered without being moved, the risk of loss passes to the buyer upon delivery to him of a negotiable document of title for the goods; if no negotiable document of title has been used, the risk of loss passes when the bailee indicates to the buyer that the buyer has the right to the possession of the goods [2-509(2)]. For example, if Farmer sells Miller a quantity of grain currently stored at Grain Elevator, the risk of loss of the grain will shift from Farmer to Miller (1) when a negotiable warehouse receipt for the grain is delivered to Miller or (2) when Grain Elevator notifies Miller that it is holding the grain for Miller.

Risk Generally

If none of the special rules that have just been discussed applies, the risk passes to the buyer on receipt of the goods if the seller is a merchant. If the seller is not a merchant, the risk passes to the buyer when the seller tenders (offers) delivery of the goods [2-509(3)]. For example, Frank offers to sell Susan a car, and Susan sends an e-mail accepting Frank's offer. When he receives the e-mail, Frank calls Susan and tells her she can "pick up the car any time." That night, the car is destroyed when a tree falls on it during a storm. If Frank is a used-car salesman, he must bear the loss. If Frank is an accountant, Susan must bear the loss.

The case that follows, *Capshaw v. Hickman,* illustrates another critical issue—that is, whether the seller in fact tendered delivery to the buyer.

Capshaw v. Hickman   64 UCC Rep. 2d 543 (Ohio Ct. App. 2007)

Charles Capshaw entered into a written contract with Rachel Hickman to purchase Hickman's 1996 Honda Civic EX for $5,025. The contract provided, among other things, that "the title will be surrendered upon the new owner's check clearing." Capshaw made a down payment of $80 in cash and gave Hickman a personal check for the balance. She provided Capshaw with the keys to the vehicle and also complied with his request to sign the certificate of title over to his father and placed the certificate in the vehicle's glovebox. They agreed the vehicle was to remain parked in Hickman's driveway until the check cleared.

Unfortunately, before Hickman was notified by her bank that the check had cleared, a hailstorm heavily damaged the vehicle. Due to the damage, Capshaw decided that he no longer wanted the vehicle and asked Hickman to return his money. Hickman refused, believing that the transaction was complete and that the vehicle belonged to Capshaw. She also requested that it be removed from her driveway. Capshaw brought suit against Hickman, alleging, among other things, conversion, breach of contract, and "quasi-contract and unjust enrichment—promissory estoppel." Capshaw contended that the risk of loss remained with Hickman until the check cleared; because it had not cleared at the time the hail damaged the car, Hickman sustained the loss. Hickman maintained that the risk of loss for a nonmerchant seller like her passes to the buyer after the seller tenders delivery to the buyer.

The trial court found that the parties agreed the transfer of title and delivery of the vehicle would occur only after the successful transfer of funds. Because neither had occurred at the time of the hailstorm, the court concluded that the risk of loss remained with the seller. Hickman appealed, arguing that the risk of loss in this instance should depend on whether there had been a tender of delivery and not on whether or not title had passed.

Bryant, Judge

Where a motor vehicle identified to a purchase contract is damaged, lost, or destroyed prior to the issuance of a certificate of title in the buyer's name, the risk of such damage, loss or destruction lies with either the seller or buyer as determined under section 1302.53. In relevant part section 1302.53 states "the risk of loss passes to the buyer on his receipt of the goods if the seller is a merchant; otherwise the risk passes to the buyer on tender of delivery." The parties here agree that defendant is not a merchant. Thus, if Hickman tendered delivery, Capshaw bore the risk of loss; if Hickman did not tender delivery, the risk of loss remained with her.

Although the trial court concluded Hickman did not tender delivery, it incorrectly focused on ownership and legal title in reaching its decision. Title is no longer of any importance in determining whether a buyer or seller bears the risk of loss. Rather, tender of delivery "requires that the seller put and hold conforming goods at the buyer's deposition and give the buyer any notification reasonably necessary to enable him to take delivery." In this context, disposition means "doing with as one wishes: discretionary control."

When tendering delivery, the seller must not limit the buyer's disposition of the goods. When, however, limitations upon a buyer's disposition of personal property do not result from the seller's activity, then the requirements for tender of delivery are met.

Hickman contends she fulfilled the statutory requirements for tendering delivery by turning over the keys to the vehicle and, after signing the certificate of title over to Capshaw's father per Capshaw's request, by placing the certificate of title in the vehicle's glove box. She asserts Capshaw chose to leave the vehicle at her residence in order to induce her to take a personal check. Hickman argues that "for all intents and purposes" Capshaw "possessed and controlled the vehicle when the keys were given to him." She thus claims not only that she tendered delivery of the vehicle, but that Capshaw was in actual possession of the vehicle at the time it was damaged. Describing the fact that the vehicle remained parked in her driveway as a "red herring," Hickman asserts she could have done "absolutely nothing else" to complete her performance with respect to the physical delivery of the vehicle.

The vehicle's continued presence in Hickman's driveway is not a red herring. Under Ohio law, a purchaser's performance under a contract generally is completed when the purchaser tenders the check. Section 1302.55(B) states "tender of payment is sufficient when made by any means or in any manner current in the ordinary course of business unless the seller demands payment in legal tender and gives any extension of time reasonably necessary to procure it." Thus upon tendering the check, Capshaw ordinarily would be free to drive away in the vehicle. Understanding why the car remained in the driveway is central to determining whether Hickman tendered delivery.

The difficulty in applying the law to this case lies in determining why the car remained on Hickman's property as the pleadings do not disclose that information. If Capshaw paid by check but Hickman refused to consider payment made until the check cleared, then Capshaw was not free to remove the vehicle from Hickman's driveway until the check cleared. Under those circumstances Hickman did not tender delivery under section 1302.47, as Capshaw lacked the discretionary control over the vehicle. As a result, the risk of loss would not have passed to Capshaw.

By contrast, if to induce Hickman to accept payment by check Capshaw offered to allow the vehicle to remain on Hickman's driveway until the check cleared, then the risk of loss passed to Capshaw who in his discretion volunteered to leave the car on

Hickman's driveway in order to pay in tender most convenient to him. Because the pleadings do not reveal the underlying reasons for leaving the car in the driveway until Capshaw's check cleared, judgment on the pleadings is inappropriate.

Accordingly . . . we reverse the judgment of the trial court granting judgment on the pleadings to Capshaw, and we remand for further proceedings in accordance with this opinion.

Effect of Breach on Risk of Loss The UCC follows the trend set by earlier law of placing the risk of loss on a party who is in breach of contract. There is no necessary reason why a party in breach should bear the risk, however. In fact, shifting the risk to parties in breach sometimes produces results contrary to some of the basic policies underlying the UCC's general rules on risk by placing the risk on the party who does not have possession or control of the goods. When the seller tenders goods that the buyer could lawfully reject because they do not conform to the contract description, the risk of loss remains on the seller until the defect is cured or the buyer accepts the goods [2–510(1)]. When a buyer rightfully revokes acceptance of the goods, the risk of loss is on the seller from the beginning to the extent that it is not covered by the buyer's insurance [2–510(2)].

Buyers who repudiate a contract for identified, conforming goods before risk of loss has passed to them are liable for a commercially reasonable time for any damage to the goods that is not covered by the seller's insurance [2–510(3)]. For example, Trendy Shoe Stores contracts to buy 1,000 pairs of shoes from Acme Shoe Manufacturing Company. Acme crates the shoes and stores them in its warehouse pending delivery to Trendy. Trendy then tells Acme it will not honor its contract for the shoes, and they are destroyed by a fire in Acme's warehouse shortly thereafter. If Acme's insurance covers only part of the loss, Trendy is liable for the balance.

Insurable Interest The UCC rules that govern risk of loss are supplemented by rules that give the parties an **insurable interest** in the goods, which allows them to insure themselves against most of the risks they must bear. Buyers may protect their interest in goods before they obtain title to them because they have an insurable interest in goods at the moment the goods are *identified to the contract* [2–501(1)]. Sellers have an insurable interest in their goods as long as they have title to the goods or a security interest in them [2–501(2)].

Sales on Trial

There are several common commercial situations in which a seller entrusts goods to another person. This may be done to give a potential buyer the chance to decide whether or not to buy the goods or to give the other party a chance to sell the goods to a third party. These cases present difficult questions about who has the risk of loss of the goods and whose creditors may attach the goods. The UCC provides specific rules to answer these questions depending on the nature of the parties' agreement.

 LO19-6 Distinguish between sale or return and sales on approval and explain the ramifications those distinctions have for the rights of buyers and sellers.

Sale or Return In a **sale or return** contract, the goods are delivered to the buyer *primarily for resale* with the understanding that the buyer has the right to return them [2–326(1)(b)]. Unless the parties agreed to the contrary, title and risk of loss rest with the buyer. Return of the goods is at the buyer's risk and expense [2–327(2)(b)], and the buyer's creditors can attach the goods while they are in the buyer's possession [2–326(2)]. Placing the risk on the buyer in these cases recognizes the fact that sale or return contracts are generally *commercial* transactions.

Sale on Approval In a **sale on approval**, the goods are delivered to the buyer *primarily for the buyer's use* [2–326(1)(a)]. The buyer is given the opportunity to examine or try the goods so as to decide whether to accept them. Risk of loss and title to the goods do not pass to the buyer until the buyer accepts the goods [2–327(1)(a)]. Any use of the goods that is consistent with a trial of the goods is not an acceptance, but the buyer who fails to give reasonable notice of an intent to return the goods may be held to have accepted them [2–327(1)(b)].

The buyer's creditors cannot reach goods held on approval [2–326(2)], and return of the goods is at the seller's risk and expense [2–327(1)(c)]. These provisions recognize the fact that sales on approval are primarily *consumer* transactions.

Risk of Loss

The point at which the risk of loss or damage to goods identified to a contract passes to the buyer is as follows:

1. If there is an agreement between the parties, the risk of loss passes to the buyer at the time they have agreed to.
2. If the contract requires the seller to ship the goods by carrier but does not require that the seller guarantee their delivery to a specific destination (shipment contract), the risk of loss passes to the buyer when the seller has delivered the goods to the carrier and made an appropriate contract for their carriage.
3. If the contract requires the seller to guarantee delivery of the goods to a specific destination (destination contract), the risk of loss passes to the buyer when the seller delivers the goods to the designated destination.
4. If the goods are in the hands of a third person and the contract calls for delivery without moving the goods, the risk of loss passes to the buyer when the buyer has the power to take possession of the goods—for example, when he receives a document of title.
5. In any situation other than those noted above where the seller is a merchant, the risk of loss passes to the buyer on his receipt of the goods.
6. In any situation other than those noted above where the seller is not a merchant, the risk of loss passes to the buyer on the tender of delivery to the buyer by the seller.
7. When a seller tenders goods that the buyer lawfully could reject because they do not conform to the contract description, the risk of loss stays on the seller until the defect is cured or the buyer accepts them.
8. When a buyer rightfully revokes acceptance of goods, the risk of loss is on the seller from the beginning to the extent it is not covered by the buyer's insurance.
9. If a buyer repudiates a contract for identified, conforming goods before risk of loss has passed to the buyer, the buyer is liable for a commercially reasonable time for any loss or damage to the goods that is not covered by the seller's insurance.

The Global Business Environment

Risk of Loss in International Sales

Risk of loss is an important concept in the sale of goods—and takes on additional significance in international sales because of the substantial distances and multiple modes of transportation that may be involved. Between the time a contract is formed and the time the obligations of the parties are completed, the goods that are the subject of the contract may be lost, damaged, or stolen. Both the UCC and the Convention on Contracts for International Sale of Goods (CISG) explicitly address risk of loss in four different situations: (1) where goods are being held by the seller, (2) where goods are being held by a third person or bailee, (3) where goods are in transit, and (4) where goods are in the control of the buyer. Moreover, the CISG deals with risk of loss where goods have been sold or resold while in transit. Under both the UCC and the CISG, breach by a party may alter the basic rules regarding risk of loss.

Before discussing the CISG provisions, it is important to note that the definitions of some terms in the UCC differ from the meaning those terms may have in international trade. The International Chamber of Commerce has compiled a list of widely accepted international shipping terms in a document known as "INCOTERMS." The most recent version, INCOTERMS 2000, includes 13 different terms that are placed in four different categories, depending on the seller's responsibilities concerning the goods.

Under the first category (known as Group "E"), the seller's obligation is only to make the goods available to the buyer at the seller's place of business. This is referred to as an EXW, or EX Works, term. Risk passes from the seller to the buyer when the goods are placed at the buyer's disposal. Under the second category (known as Group "F"), the seller is required to deliver the goods to a carrier designated by the buyer. This category includes terms like "F.O.B." (Free on Board) and "F.A.S." (Free Along Side Ship). Passage of risk varies with the term.

Terms in the third category (Group "C") require the seller to contract for carriage of the goods but not to assume the risk of loss after shipment. Terms in the fourth category (Group "D") impose on the seller the costs and risks of bringing the goods to the country of destination. Under one such term, "D.A.F." (Delivered at Frontier), the seller must pay for the carriage of goods to some defined point after that where goods have been cleared for export in the country of origin but before the customs boundary of another identified, usually adjoining, country.

The CISG, like the UCC, provides a set of default rules governing risk of loss where the parties do not explicitly address risk of loss in their contract. However, it also permits parties to contract out of those rules. Parties to international agreements commonly utilize the INCOTERMS and incorporate them into contracts otherwise governed by the CISG. Thus, the INCOTERMS are used to define when risk of loss passes, and CISG, in turn, provides the legal consequences of the passage of the risk of loss in a particular case.

Problems and Problem Cases

1. Star Coach LLC is in the business of converting sport-utility vehicles and pickup trucks into custom vehicles. Star Coach performs the labor involved in installing parts supplied by other companies onto vehicles owned by dealers. Heart of Texas Dodge purchased a new Dodge Durango from Chrysler Motors and entered into an agreement with Star Coach, whereby Star Coach would convert the Durango to a Shelby 360 custom performance vehicle and then return the converted vehicle to Heart of Texas Dodge. The manufacturer delivered the dealer's Durango to Star Coach and, over a period of several months, Star Coach converted the vehicle using parts supplied by another company, Performance West. Several months later, Star Coach delivered the vehicle to Heart of Texas Dodge, and Heart of Texas Dodge paid Star Coach the contract price of $15,768 without inspecting the vehicle. Two days later, Heart of Texas Dodge inspected the vehicle and concluded that the workmanship was faulty. It stopped payment on the check, and Star Coach filed suit against Heart of Texas Dodge. One of the issues in the litigation was whether the UCC applied to the contract in this case. Does the UCC apply to a contract for the conversion of a van that involves both goods and services?

2. Keith Russell, a boat dealer, contracted to sell a 19-foot Kindsvater boat to Robert Clouser for $8,500. The agreement stipulated that Clouser was to make a down payment of $1,700, with the balance due when he took possession of the boat. According to the contract, Russell was to retain possession of the boat in order to install a new engine and drivetrain. While the boat was still in Russell's possession, it was completely destroyed when it struck a seawall. Transamerica, Russell's insurance company, refused to honor Russell's claim for the damages to the boat.

The insurance policy between Transamerica and Russell covered only watercraft under 26 feet in length that were not owned by Russell. Transamerica argued that the boat was not covered by the policy because Russell still owned it at the time of the accident. Did Russell have title to the boat at the time of the accident?

3. Kenneth West agreed to sell his car, a 1975 Corvette, to a man representing himself as Robert Wilson. In exchange for a cashier's check, West signed over the Corvette's title to Wilson. Ten days later, when West learned that the cashier's check was a forgery, he filed a stolen vehicle report with the police. However, the police did not locate Wilson or the Corvette, and the case grew cold. Nearly two and a half years later, West asked the police to run a check on the Corvette's vehicle identification number. The check revealed the name and address of Tammy Roberts. Roberts, who held the certificate of title, had purchased it from her brother, who in turn had purchased it in response to a newspaper ad. West filed suit against Roberts to establish legal ownership of the Corvette. Is West entitled to regain possession and title to the Corvette from Roberts?

4. Club Pro Golf Products was a distributor of golf products. It employed salespeople who called on customers to take orders for merchandise. The merchandise was sent by Club Pro directly to the purchaser, and payment was made by the purchaser directly to Club Pro. A salesman for Club Pro, Carl Gude, transmitted orders for certain merchandise to Club Pro for delivery to several fictitious purchasers. Club Pro sent the merchandise to the fictitious purchasers at the fictitious addresses, where it was picked up by Gude. Gude then sold the merchandise, worth approximately $19,000, directly to Simpson, a golf pro at a golf club. Gude then retained the proceeds of sale for himself. Club Pro discovered the fraud and brought suit against Simpson to recover the merchandise. Did Simpson

get good title to the merchandise he purchased from Gude even though Gude had obtained it by fraud?

5. In December, Arlene Bradley entered Alsafi Oriental Rugs and advised the owner that she was an interior decorator and that she was interested in selling some of his rugs to one of her customers. Alsafi did not know Bradley and had never done business with her. However, he allowed her to take three rugs out on consignment with the understanding that she would return them if her customer was not interested. In fact, however, Bradley was not obtaining the rugs for a "customer" but was, instead, working for another individual, Walid Salaam, a rug dealer.

   A friend of Bradley's had introduced her to Salaam earlier. Salaam had advised the two women that he was the owner of a recently closed oriental rug store that he was attempting to reopen. He offered to teach them how to become decorators and told them that when his store reopened, they could operate out of the store. Salaam advised them that until he got his store restocked, however, he wanted them to "check out" rugs on approval from other rug dealers in town. As they had no experience with oriental rugs, Salaam instructed them which rugs to look for. He then instructed them to go to rug dealers in Memphis and advise them that they were interior decorators with customers that wanted to purchase oriental rugs.

   After Bradley obtained possession of the three rugs from Alsafi, she turned them over to Salaam, who in turn took them to a pawnshop operated by the American Loan Company. There, Salaam pawned the rugs, obtaining approximately $5,000 after filling out the required paperwork. Salaam failed to redeem the rugs. Following the default, the pawnshop gave the appropriate notice that it intended to dispose of them.

   In April of the following year, Alsafi learned that his rugs were at the pawnshop. After visiting the pawnshop and identifying the three rugs as his, he brought suit to recover possession of them. Was Alsafi entitled to recover the rugs from the pawnshop?

6. Legendary Homes, a home builder, purchased various appliances from Ron Mead T.V. & Appliance, a retail merchant selling home appliances. They were intended to be installed in one of Legendary Homes's houses and were to be delivered on February 1. At 5 o'clock on that day, the appliances had not been delivered. Legendary Homes's employees closed the home and left. Sometime between 5 and 6:30, Mead delivered the appliances. No one was at the home so the delivery-person put the appliances in the garage. During the night, someone stole the appliances. Legendary Homes denied it was responsible for the loss and refused to pay Mead for the appliances. Mead then brought suit for the purchase price. Did Legendary Homes have the risk of loss of the appliances?

7. In June, Ramos entered into a contract to buy a motorcycle from Big Wheel Sports Center. He paid the purchase price of $893 and was given the papers necessary to register the cycle and get insurance on it. Ramos registered the cycle but had not attached the license plates to it. He left on vacation and told the salesperson for Big Wheel Sports Center that he would pick up the cycle on his return. While Ramos was on vacation, there was an electric power blackout in New York City and the cycle was stolen by looters. Ramos then sued Big Wheel Sports Center to get back his $893. Did Big Wheel Sports Center have the risk of loss of the motorcycle?

8. Richard Burnett agreed to purchase a mobile home with a shed from Betty Jean Putrell, executrix of the estate of Lena Holland. On Saturday, March 3, Burnett paid Putrell $6,500 and was given the certificate of title to the mobile home as well as a key to it, but no keys to the shed. At the time the certificate of title was transferred, the following items remained in the mobile home: the washer and dryer, mattress and box springs, two chairs, items in the refrigerator, and the entire contents of the shed. These items were to be retained by Putrell and removed by her. To facilitate removal she retained one key to the mobile home and the only keys to the shed. On Sunday, March 4, the mobile home was destroyed by fire through the fault of neither party. At the time of the fire, Putrell still had a key to the mobile home as well as the keys to the shed and she had not removed the contents of the mobile home or of the shed. The contents of the shed were not destroyed and were subsequently removed by Putrell. Burnett brought suit against Putrell to recover the $6,500 he had paid for the mobile home and shed. Did the seller, Putrell, have the risk of loss of the mobile home?

Product Liability

In February 2017, as a high school junior and a minor child, Matthew Divello first tried JUUL e-cigarettes, the pods of which contain high levels of nicotine intentionally designed to taste like candy. Despite measures taken by Matthew's mother to get him to quit JUULing and his personal desire to quit, Matthew is intensely addicted to nicotine and cannot stop. He experiences intense withdrawal symptoms if he does not JUUL, including headaches.

At the time Matthew began using the JUUL products, there were no warnings about the existence of nicotine or the risks of nicotine addiction anywhere on the JUUL products or packaging. He visited JUUL.com, which promoted JUUL use as safe and offered $30.00 gift cards for taking surveys. After prolonged use, he lost 10–12 pounds and was hospitalized on August 4, 2019, for 3 days with high fever, nausea, and vomiting blood. Moreover, his behavior was impacted by the addiction as he became withdrawn, anxious, highly irritable, and prone to angry outbursts. His GPA also dropped during his senior year of high school.

Arguing that JUUL was responsible for his nicotine addiction, at-risk status for life-long health problems, and economic losses flowing from his need to sustain his addiction, in August 2019, as an 18-year-old, Matthew filed a lawsuit in New Jersey, his place of residence, against JUUL Labs, a Delaware corporation with its principal place of business in San Francisco.

In his complaint, Matthew alleged that JUUL e-cigarettes are different from competing e-cigarettes because of a patented nicotine formulation derived from decades of research and created to foster addiction using a combination of nicotine salts and benzoic acid. Moreover, the lawsuit noted the explosive growth of JUUL among social media platforms aimed at teenagers, and the variety of flavors available, including mango, "cool" cucumber, fruit medley, cool mint, and crème brulee.

Noted in the complaint were media reports finding that in one Connecticut high school, "you go to the bathroom . . . there's a 50-50 chance that there's five guys JUULing," and a Kentucky high school student capturing the appeal to children with this comment: "In my opinion it looks like the coolest thing ever. Almost futuristic . . . It's so small, so easy to hide in the palm of your hand. And they're rechargeable! I've lost track of the number of people I have found charging their JUULs in class through their laptops."

Matthew's lawsuit also dispelled the fiction that JUUL e-cigarettes were created as a safer alternative to cigarettes or a strategy to wean addicts off of cigarettes. On the contrary, given the increased levels of nicotine distributed into the bloodstream, JUUL use is likely to worsen nicotine addictions. Furthermore, a 2016 report of the U.S. Surgeon General found that the nicotine in JUULs and other e-cigarettes negatively influences brain development in adolescents, specifically impairing cognitive, attention, and memory processes and increasing the risk of anxiety disorders and depression. [Although not a part of Matthew's original lawsuit filed in August 2019, the U.S. Food and Drug Administration released a report in April 2020 that suggested vaping also increased the risks to lung and heart function and could make one more susceptible to severe complications of COVID-19.]

As you read this chapter, consider the following questions:

- Will Matthew be successful in his products liability lawsuit if he can prove that his nicotine addiction and adverse health conditions were a result of a defective manufacturing process or the way in which JUUL products are designed?

- Will Matthew be successful in this litigation if he can prove that JUUL was aware of its product's potential risks but failed to adequately warn or inform him?
- What is the difference between a product liability lawsuit brought on a negligence theory versus a lawsuit based on strict liability?
- Is Matthew only eligible for compensatory damages, or is he also eligible for a punitive award? What is the difference?
- How would you analyze JUUL's business practices—as alleged by Matthew in his complaint—according to the various ethical theories discussed in Chapter 4?

LEARNING OBJECTIVES

After studying this chapter, you should be able to:

20-1 Explain what is necessary under the UCC for creation of an express warranty regarding goods.

20-2 Identify circumstances in which an implied warranty of merchantability becomes part of a contract for the sale of goods.

20-3 Explain what is meant by the *merchantability* concept.

20-4 Identify the elements necessary for creation of the implied warranty of fitness for a particular purpose and explain how that warranty differs from the implied warranty of merchantability.

20-5 Identify the major categories into which negligence-based product liability claims fall (negligent manufacture, negligent inspection, negligent failure to provide adequate warnings, and negligent design).

20-6 Explain the factors courts consider and the test they frequently use in determining whether a manufacturer is vulnerable to a negligent design claim.

20-7 Identify the elements of a strict liability claim under *Restatement (Second)* § 402A and explain how strict liability differs from liability for negligence.

20-8 Describe the *Restatement (Third)*'s proposed framework of product liability rules.

20-9 Identify the types of compensatory damages available in product liability cases based on tort theories and in cases based on warranty theories.

20-10 Explain what is normally necessary in order for punitive damages to be awarded in a product liability case.

20-11 Explain the privity doctrine's lack of role in tort cases and its partial role in warranty-based cases.

20-12 Explain what is necessary for effective disclaimers of the respective implied warranties.

20-13 Describe the role of comparative negligence and comparative fault principles in cases in which fault on the part of the defendant and on the part of the plaintiff led to the harm experienced by the plaintiff.

20-14 Identify the circumstances in which a court may conclude that a federal law preempts a state law-based product liability claim and thus furnishes the defendant a defense against liability.

SUPPOSE YOU HOLD AN executive position in a firm that makes products for sale to the public. One of your concerns would be the company's exposure to civil liability for defects in those products. In particular, you might worry about legal developments that make such liability more likely or more expensive. In other situations, however, such developments might appeal to you—especially if *you* are harmed by defective products you purchase as a consumer. You might also appreciate certain liability-imposing legal theories if your firm wants to sue a supplier that has sold it defective products.

Each of these situations involves the law of *product liability*, the body of legal rules governing civil lawsuits for losses and harms resulting from a defendant's furnishing of defective goods. After sketching product liability law's historical evolution, this chapter discusses the most important *theories of product liability* on which plaintiffs rely. The second part of the chapter considers certain legal problems that may be resolved differently under different theories of recovery.

The Evolution of Product Liability Law

The 19th Century
A century or so ago, the rules governing suits for defective goods were very much to manufacturers' and other sellers' advantage. This was the era of *caveat emptor* (let the buyer beware). In contract cases involving defective goods, there usually was no liability unless the seller had made an express promise to the buyer and the goods did not conform to that promise. In negligence cases, the "no liability without fault" principle was widely accepted, and plaintiffs often had difficulty proving negligence because the necessary evidence was under the defendant's control. In both contract and negligence cases, finally, the doctrine of "no liability outside privity of contract"—that is, no liability without a direct contractual relationship between plaintiff and defendant—often prevented plaintiffs from recovering against parties with whom they had not directly dealt.

The laissez-faire approach that influenced public policy and the law helped lead to such prodefendant rules. A key factor limiting manufacturers' liability for defective products was the perceived importance of promoting industrialization by preventing potentially crippling damage recoveries against infant industries. Even though the 19th century's approach to product liability was prodefendant, some commentators maintain that most plaintiffs were not especially disadvantaged by the applicable legal rules. Goods tended to be simple, so buyers often could inspect them for defects. Before the emergence of large corporations late in the 19th century, moreover, sellers and buyers often were of relatively equal size, sophistication, and bargaining power. Thus, they could deal on relatively equal footing.

The 20th and 21st Centuries
Today, laissez-faire values, while still influential, do not pack the weight they once did. With the development of a viable industrial economy, there is less perceived need to protect manufacturers from liability for defective goods. The emergence of long chains of distribution has meant that consumers often do not deal directly with the parties responsible for defects in the products they buy. Because large corporations tend to dominate the economy, consumers are less able to bargain freely with the corporate sellers with which they deal. Finally, the growing complexity of goods has made buyers' inspections of the goods more difficult.

In response to these changes, product liability law has moved from its earlier *caveat emptor* emphasis to a stance that sometimes resembles *caveat venditor* (let the seller beware). To protect consumers, modern courts and legislatures effectively intervene in private contracts for the sale of goods and, in certain instances, impose liability regardless of fault. As a result, sellers and manufacturers face potentially greater liability for defects in their products than they once did. Underlying the shift toward *caveat venditor* is the belief that sellers, manufacturers, and their insurers are better able to bear the economic costs associated with product defects, and that they usually can pass on these costs through higher prices. Thus, the economic risk associated with defective products can be spread throughout society, or "socialized."

The Current Debate over Product Liability Law
Modern product liability law and its socialization-of-risk rationale have come under increasing attack over the past three decades. Such attacks often focus on the increased costs sellers and manufacturers sometimes encounter in obtaining product liability insurance. Some observers blame insurance industry practices for these developments, whereas others trace them to the increased liability prospect noted earlier. Whatever their origin, these problems have, at times, put sellers and manufacturers in a difficult spot. Businesses unwilling or unable to buy expensive product liability insurance run the risk of being crippled by large damage awards unless they self-insure, which can be an expensive option. Firms that purchase insurance, on the other hand, often must pay higher prices for it. In either case, the resulting costs may be difficult to pass on to consumers. Those costs may also deter the development and marketing of innovative new products.

For reasons including those identified earlier, calls have been made in some quarters for a reining-in of the proplaintiff aspects of product liability law. This is one aspect of the tort reform movement discussed in Chapter 7. Opponents of reform point out, however, that plaintiffs tend to win product liability cases no more often—or even less frequently—than defendants do and that average amounts of damage awards when plaintiffs do win have not been on the rise in recent years. Proponents of reform have periodically urged Congress to federalize certain aspects of product liability law (which historically has been state law) by enacting such measures as caps on damages, but such federal measures neither had been enacted nor had appeared on the horizon as this book went to press in 2020. However, as we note later in this chapter, tort reform measures have been enacted in some states.

Theories of Product Liability Recovery

Some theories of product liability recovery are contractual and some are tort-based. The contract theories involve a product **warranty**—an express or implied promise about the nature of the product sold. In warranty cases, plaintiffs claim that the product failed to live up to the seller's promise. In tort cases, on the other hand, plaintiffs contend that the defendant was negligent or that strict liability should apply.

 Explain what is necessary under the UCC for creation of an express warranty regarding goods.

Express Warranty

Creation of an Express Warranty UCC § 2-313(1) states that an **express warranty** may be created in any of three ways.

1. *If an affirmation of fact or promise* regarding the goods becomes part of the basis of the bargain (a requirement to be discussed shortly), there is an express warranty that the goods will conform to the affirmation or promise. For instance, if a computer manufacturer's website says that a computer has a certain amount of memory, this statement may create an express warranty to that effect.

2. Any *description* of the goods that becomes part of the basis of the bargain creates an express warranty that the goods will conform to the description. Descriptions include (a) statements that goods are of a certain brand, type, or model (e.g., a Hewlett-Packard laser printer); (b) adjectives that characterize the product (e.g., shatter-proof glass); and (c) drawings, blueprints, and technical specifications. A description that gives rise to an express warranty under which the goods must be as described does not, without more, amount to an express warranty regarding quality or duration of the goods' future performance.

3. Assuming it becomes part of the basis of the bargain, a *sample* or *model* of goods to be sold creates an express warranty that the goods will conform to the sample or model. A sample is an object drawn from an actual collection of goods to be sold, whereas a model is a replica offered for the buyer's inspection when the goods themselves are unavailable. Moreover, any seller—professional or not—may make an express warranty. When an express warranty has been breached (because the goods were not as warranted), the plaintiff who demonstrates resulting losses is entitled to compensatory damages. Damages issues receive further attention later in this chapter.

The first two types of express warranties may often overlap; also, each may be either written or oral. "Magic" words such as *warrant* or *guarantee* are not necessary for creation of an express warranty.

Value, Opinion, and Sales Talk Statements of *value* ("This chair would bring you $2,000 at an auction") or *opinion* ("I think this chair might be an antique") do not create an express warranty. The same is true of statements that amount to *sales talk* or *puffery* ("This chair is a good buy"). No sharp line separates such statements from express warranties. In close cases, a statement is more likely to be an express warranty if it is specific rather than indefinite, if it is stated in the sales contract rather than elsewhere,[1] or if it is unequivocal rather than hedged or qualified. The relative knowledge possessed by the seller and the buyer also matters. For instance, a car salesperson's statement about a used car may be more likely to be an express warranty where the buyer knows little about cars than where the buyer is another car dealer.

The Basis-of-the-Bargain Requirement Under pre-UCC law, there was no recovery for breach of an express warranty unless the buyer significantly relied on that warranty in making the purchase. The UCC, however, requires—though ambiguously—that the affirmation, promise, description, or sample or model has become *part of the basis of the bargain* in order for an express warranty to be created. Although some courts read the UCC's basis-of-the-bargain test as saying that significant reliance still is necessary, most courts require only that the seller's warranty has been a *contributing factor* in the buyer's decision to purchase.

Advertisements Statements made in advertisements, catalogs, or brochures may be express warranties. However, such sources often are filled with sales talk. Basis-of-the-bargain problems may arise if it is unclear whether or to what degree the statement induced the buyer to make the purchase. For example, suppose that the buyer read an advertisement containing a supposed express warranty one month before actually purchasing the product. In such an instance, there may be a dispute over whether the advertisement's content contributed to the buyer's decision to buy.

Multiple Express Warranties What happens when a seller gives two or more express warranties and those warranties arguably conflict? UCC § 2-317 says that such warranties should be read as consistent with each other and as cumulative if this is reasonable. If not, the parties' intention controls. In determining that intention, (1) exact or technical specifications defeat a sample, a model, or general descriptive language and (2) a sample defeats general descriptive language.

---

[1] Parol evidence rule problems may arise in express warranty cases. For example, a seller who used a written contract may argue that the rule excludes an alleged oral warranty. On the parol evidence rule, see Chapter 16.

Implied Warranty of Merchantability

 Identify circumstances in which an implied warranty of merchantability becomes part of a contract for the sale of goods.

 Explain what is meant by the *merchantability* concept.

An **implied warranty** is a warranty created by operation of law rather than the seller's express statements. UCC § 2-314(1) creates the UCC's implied warranty of merchantability with this language: "[A] warranty that the goods shall be merchantable is implied in a contract for their sale if the seller is a merchant with respect to goods of that kind." This is a clear example of the modern tendency of legislatures to intervene in private contracts to protect consumers.

In an implied warranty of merchantability case, the plaintiff argues that the seller breached the warranty by selling unmerchantable goods and that the plaintiff should therefore recover compensatory damages. Under § 2-314, such claims can succeed only where the seller is a *merchant with respect to goods of the kind sold.*[2] An accounting professor's sale of homemade preserves and a grocery store owner's sale of a used car, for example, would not trigger the implied warranty of merchantability.

UCC § 2-314(2) states that, to be merchantable, goods must at least (1) pass without objection in the trade; (2) be fit for the ordinary purposes for which such goods are used; (3) be of even kind, quality, and quantity within each unit (case, package, or carton); (4) be adequately contained, packaged, and labeled; (5) conform to any promises or statements of fact made on the container or label; and (6) in the case of fungible goods, be of fair average quality. The most important of these requirements is that the goods must be *fit for the ordinary purposes for which such goods are used.* (In the *Moss* case, which appears later in the chapter, the implied warranty of merchantability was made but was not breached because the relevant goods were suitable for ordinary purposes.) The goods need not be perfect to be fit for their ordinary purposes. Rather, they need only meet the reasonable expectations of the average consumer.

This broad, flexible test of merchantability is almost inevitable given the wide range of products sold in the United States today and the varied defects they may pre-

sent. Still, a few generalizations about merchantability determinations are possible. Goods that fail to function properly or that have harmful side effects normally are not merchantable. A computer that fails to work properly or that destroys the owner's programs, for example, is not fit for the ordinary purposes for which computers are used. In cases involving allergic reactions to drugs or other products, courts may find the defendant liable if it was reasonably foreseeable that an appreciable number of consumers would suffer the reaction.

When food products have been alleged to be unmerchantable because they contained harmful objects or substances, courts have developed two tests for determining whether the implied warranty of merchantability was violated. The traditional test, still employed by some courts, asks whether the object or substance in the food product is "foreign" or, instead, "natural" to the product. Under this test, the food product is unmerchantable if the harm-causing object or substance is "foreign" to the food product but not if it is "natural" to it. The trend among courts, however, has been to replace the foreign–natural test with the reasonable expectations test. Under the latter test, a food product containing a harmful object or substance is deemed unmerchantable if consumers would not reasonably have expected to encounter such an object or substance in the food product. Although the cases are highly fact-specific, the reasonable expectations test holds the potential for being more pro-plaintiff in nature than the foreign–natural test. Sometimes, however, either test might lead to the same outcome in a given case. *Bissinger v. New Country Buffet*, which follows, serves as an example.

Implied Warranty of Fitness

 Identify the elements necessary for creation of the implied warranty of fitness for a particular purpose and explain how that warranty differs from the implied warranty of merchantability.

UCC § 2-315's implied warranty of fitness for a particular purpose arises where (1) the seller has reason to know a particular purpose for which the buyer requires the goods, (2) the seller has reason to know that the buyer is relying on the seller's skill or judgment for the selection of suitable goods, and (3) the buyer actually relies on the seller's skill or judgment in purchasing the goods. If these tests are met, there is an implied warranty that the goods will be fit for the buyer's *particular* purpose. Any seller—merchant or nonmerchant—may make this implied warranty, the

---

[2]The term *merchant* is defined in Chapter 9.

Bissinger v. New Country Buffet   2014 Tenn. App. LEXIS 331 (June 6, 2014)

At a New Country Buffet Restaurant in Nashville, Tennessee, customer Randall Bissinger ordered an "All You Can Eat" buffet meal. He selected three raw oysters from the buffet table. Soon after consuming the oysters, Bissinger began to experience severe symptoms and illness. His brother took him to a hospital, where he was diagnosed with Vibrio vulnificus septicemia, a serious blood infection. Vibrio vulnificus is a naturally occurring bacterium found in shellfish that absorb it from their environment.

Approximately three months later, Bissinger filed a lawsuit in a Tennessee court against New Country Buffet and its owner (hereinafter "New Country Buffet" or "the restaurant"). Bissinger alleged that the oysters he consumed were contaminated and that they caused his injuries. Several weeks after Bissinger filed the case, he died. His nephew, the executor of his estate, was substituted as the plaintiff.

In an amended complaint, the nephew named as defendants not only New Country Buffet, but also three companies that supplied oysters (hereinafter "the Suppliers") to the restaurant. He pleaded causes of action for negligence and breach of the implied warranty of merchantability. The plaintiff asserted that his uncle's illness and death resulted from his ingestion of Vibrio vulnificus. He also alleged that his uncle suffered from hepatitis C and cirrhosis of the liver, was unaware of the dangers of severe injury or death associated with consuming raw oysters, and was unaware that people with liver disease or weakened immune systems were at increased risk of those dangers. In addition, the plaintiff alleged that not long before Bissinger's visit to New Country Buffet, the restaurant had been cited by the Nashville Public Health Department for health and safety violations, including storing seafood (though not necessarily raw oysters) and other food at improper temperatures.

There was no dispute that the oysters Bissinger ate contained Vibrio vulnificus, although there was no proof regarding the level of the bacteria in the oysters. New Country Buffet and the Suppliers moved for summary judgment. A Tennessee trial court granted the Suppliers' motion and dismissed the negligence and breach of implied warranty of merchantability claims against them. The court denied New Country Buffet's motion, however. The plaintiff and the restaurant appealed to the Tennessee Court of Appeals, which affirmed the trial court's grant of summary judgment to the Suppliers on the plaintiff's negligence claim. The following edited version of the Court of Appeals opinion focuses on that court's treatment of the breach of implied warranty of merchantability claims against the restaurant and the Suppliers.

Cottrell, Judge

The standards for decision on a motion for summary judgment are well-known. The trial court may only grant such a motion if the filings supporting the motion show that there is no genuine issue of material fact and that the moving party is entitled to judgment as a matter of law.

The undisputed expert testimony was that *Vibrio vulnificus* is a naturally occurring, salt-loving bacteria [sic] found mainly in warmer marine environments all over the world. Some level of *Vibrio* is present in almost all oysters. The bacteria has no taste and no odor, and it cannot be detected by any method that does not also require killing the oyster. There was also undisputed testimony that *Vibrio vulnificus* can be lethal when large enough quantities are ingested. There was no evidence regarding the concentration of the bacteria in the oysters consumed by Bissinger or those on the buffet. [However, the] absolute numbers [of deaths] are relatively small. [T]he vast majority of those who become infected with *Vibrio* also suffer from predisposing conditions such as liver disease and diabetes.

In fact, the presence of *Vibrio vulnificus* in oysters is not seriously harmful to the general public. While otherwise healthy individuals may suffer temporary gastrointestinal illness, they do not contract the serious blood infection involved in this case. The only danger of serious illness from the bacteria is to those individuals with immune disorders, liver conditions, or stomach disorders.

A certified food safety professional testified that *Vibrio vulnificus* proliferates in warm water, which is the reason for the widespread recognition that it can be dangerous to eat raw oysters in the summer. Because *Vibrio* can continue to multiply in raw oysters after they are harvested, federal and state regulations govern the manner in which such oysters are handled, in order to prevent such proliferation by always keeping them at a temperature below 45 degrees Fahrenheit and preferably between 37 degrees and 40 degrees.

[Authors' note: In a portion of the opinion not excerpted here, the Court of Appeals held that the trial court had properly rejected the plaintiffs' negligence claim against the Suppliers. The court then turned to the implied warranty of merchantability claim against the Suppliers.]

The plaintiff alleged that Suppliers breached an implied warranty that the oysters were merchantable. Tennessee Code Annotated § 47-2-314, part of the Sales Chapter of the Uniform Commercial Code, states that a contract of sale between a merchant and a customer implies a warranty that the goods sold are "merchantable." To be merchantable, goods must, among other things, be "fit for the ordinary purposes for which such goods are used." § 47-2-314(2)(c). That statute specifically includes the sale of food and drink for consumption either on the premises or else-where as subject to the implied warranty. To be "fit for ordinary purposes" and thus merchantable, food must be safe to eat.

[W]arranty claims sound in contract rather than in tort. [T]o prevail on a warranty theory, it is not necessary to show negligence, but only breach of the implied warranty that the prod-uct is wholesome and fit for human consumption. There are no Tennessee cases that specify the standards a court should apply to determine whether food is merchantable under § 47-2-314. How-ever, one undisputed principle is that regardless of the type of product involved, to recover for breach of an implied warranty, the plaintiff must establish that the alleged defect or unfitness was present when the product left the defendant's control.

Suppliers argue that, as a matter of law, the presence of *Vibrio vulnificus* could not be deemed a breach of the warranty that their oysters were wholesome and fit for human consumption, because the microorganism is natural to shellfish and is found in almost all oysters. The plaintiff offered no proof of the concentration of *Vibrio* in the oysters consumed by his uncle or the concentration when the oysters left the control of Suppliers. Thus, the plaintiff would have us hold that any amount of the bacteria would make an oyster unmerchantable.

As Suppliers have explained, although Tennessee has not established a standard for analyzing the merchantability of food, other states have adopted the "foreign natural test" or the "rea-sonable expectation test." Under the foreign natural test, food is unfit for the purpose for which it is sold if an object found in the food does not naturally occur in that food. Under the reason-able expectation test, "liability will lie for injuries caused by a sub-stance where the consumer of the product would not reasonably have expected to find the substance in the product." [Citation omitted.]

Factors relevant to the reasonable expectation analysis, i.e., what a consumer might reasonably expect, include the "natural-ness" of the substance causing the injury and the amount of pro-cessing the food may have gone through since its harvesting and its sale. As one court explained, "A consumer, by seeking to eat clams raw, wishes the clams to be such. Thus a consumer should expect substances that are indigenous to the organism in its natural state to be present when he or she receives it." [Citation omitted.] Because *Vibrio vulnificus* is naturally occurring, appears in most shellfish and almost all oysters to some degree, and can reasonably be expected to be found in live raw oysters, the oysters supplied herein were merchantable under both tests. We find the tests used in other states to be a reasonable way to analyze the issue of merchantability of food products.

Since the consumption of raw summer oysters can be danger-ous to consumers who suffer from certain medical conditions, it follows that the sale of such oysters without adequate warn-ing of the dangers of ingesting them could indeed render them unmerchantable and make their sale a breach of the implied warranty. Suppliers acknowledge that they have a duty to warn such individuals of the danger of consuming raw oysters. Sup-pliers contend, however, that, even if there were a question of merchantability as to certain individuals, they have rendered their product merchantable by furnishing specific warnings directed toward people whose medical condition places them at risk. They also insist that they had no reason to believe that such individuals would be so foolish as to ignore those warnings.

The proof in this case showed that in accordance with fed-eral regulations, [Suppliers] fastened harvesting tags to each bag of oysters they sold. The information on the tags included the harvest date, the state where the oysters were harvested, and the instruction that the product should not be consumed raw after 14 days from the date of harvest, but should be thoroughly cooked. The tags contained the following warning:

> Consumer Information: *There is a risk associated with consum-ing raw oysters or any raw animal protein. If you have chronic illness of the liver, stomach, or blood or have immune disorders, you are at greater risk of serious illness from raw oysters. You may, however, eat your oysters fully cooked. If unsure of your risk you should consult your physician. Please share this information with your customers.*

These warnings were adequate to put a susceptible individual on notice and to put a restaurant on notice that it should pass the warning on to customers. The plaintiff argued that the notice was not sufficient because it did not mention death as a potential risk. It is not entirely clear if the plaintiff's failure-to-warn claim was brought as a separate, negligence-based claim or whether it was part of its lack of merchantability argument. Despite the plaintiff's insistence, we hold that the warnings provided by Suppliers were sufficient to meet the reasonable care standard and to satisfy the implied warranty of merchantability. Additionally, because Sup-pliers had no ability to directly warn customers of restaurants that bought oysters from them, they cannot be held to have breached a duty to warn the eventual consumer of its products.

Accordingly, we [affirm the grant of] summary judgment to Suppliers on the claim of breach of implied warranty of merchantability.

[Authors' note: The Court then addressed the plaintiff's claims against the restaurant. Because it identified factual disputes in regard to New Country Buffet's handling and storage of foods and in regard to whether the restaurant passed along the Suppliers' warnings to its customers, the court concluded that the restau-rant was not entitled to summary judgment on the plaintiff's neg-ligence claim against it. Next, the court addressed the breach of implied warranty of merchantability claim against the restaurant.]

The plaintiff also claimed that New Country Buffet violated the implied warranty of merchantability "by serving oysters that were contaminated with *Vibrio vulnificus* and were therefore unmerchantable and unfit for human consumption" [quoting the plaintiff's brief]. New Country Buffet asserts on appeal "that it should have been granted summary judgment on this claim as the raw oysters in question were merchantable, wholesome and fit for human consumption" [quoting the restaurant's brief]. Based upon the same authorities and standards that we discussed with regard to Suppliers, the restaurant argues that because *Vibrio vulnificus* is natural to shellfish, their oysters should be deemed to have passed the two tests that are normally applied to determine whether food is suitable for sale and consumption.

Under the foreign-natural test, food is considered unfit for ordinary purposes if an object is found in the food that does not occur naturally. There are no allegations in the record that such an object made the oysters unfit. Under the reasonable expectations test, food is considered unfit for ordinary purposes if it contains substances which cause injury and which the consumer would not reasonably expect to find in the product, even if those substances are natural. Such substances might include a chicken bone found in a chicken enchilada or a walnut shell in walnut ice cream.

New Country Buffet argues that because *Vibrio vulnificus* occurs naturally, the restaurant cannot be found liable under the foreign-natural test, and that since the proof shows that *Vibrio* is found in virtually all oysters, a consumer cannot reasonably expect to receive an oyster free from the bacteria. For these or similar reasons, we hold that Suppliers could not be held liable under [the] implied warranty of merchantability. The same basic legal principles apply to New Country Buffet. However, if New Country was, in fact, negligent in its handling of the oysters, its conduct may have allowed the bacteria to proliferate. Thus, actions of the restaurant may have rendered the oysters unfit for consumption. [Tennessee law] defines adulterated food as including shellfish capable of supporting rapid and progressive growth of infectious or toxigenic micro-organisms, unless the shellfish is stored or offered for sale at a temperature greater than forty-five degrees Fahrenheit (45°F).

Because of testimony on the temperature findings of inspectors [from the Health Department], it may be possible for the plaintiff to establish that the oysters consumed by his uncle were adulterated and, thus, unfit for consumption. At present, there is no proof of the concentration of *Vibrio* when the oysters were delivered to the restaurant or the concentration when the oysters were served. However, while it may be difficult for the plaintiff to establish an increase, that question is not before us at this time.

The trial court did not err in declining to grant New Country Buffet summary judgment [on the] breach of implied warranty of merchantability [claim].

Trial court's grant of summary judgment in favor of Suppliers affirmed; trial court's denial of summary judgment to restaurant affirmed.

breach of which will give rise to liability for compensatory damages.

In many fitness warranty cases, buyers effectively put themselves in the seller's hands by making their needs known and by saying that they are relying on the seller to select goods that will satisfy those needs. This may happen, for example, when a seller sells a computer system specially manufactured or customized for a buyer's particular needs. Sellers also may be liable when the circumstances reasonably indicate that the buyer has a particular purpose and is relying on the seller to satisfy that purpose, even though the buyer fails to make either explicit. However, buyers may have trouble recovering if they are more expert than the seller, submit specifications for the goods they wish to buy, inspect the goods, actually select them, or insist on a particular brand.

As indicated in *Moss v. Batesville Casket Co.*, which follows, the implied warranty of fitness differs from the implied warranty of merchantability. The tests for the creation of each warranty plainly are different. Under § 2-315, moreover, sellers warrant only that the goods are fit for the buyer's *particular* purposes, not the *ordinary* purposes for which such goods are used. If a 400-pound man asks a department store for a hammock that will support his weight but is sold a hammock that can support only average-sized people, there is a breach of the implied warranty of fitness but no breach of the implied warranty of merchantability. Depending on the facts of the case, therefore, one of the implied warranties may be breached but the other is satisfied, both implied warranties may be breached, or, as in *Moss*, neither ends up being breached.

Moss v. Batesville Casket Co.	935 So. 2d 393 (Miss. 2006)

Nancy Moss Minton, a Mississippi resident, died on March 7, 1999. Her four adult children became the plaintiffs in the lawsuit described below and will be referred to as "the plaintiffs" during this summary of the facts. The plaintiffs engaged Ott & Lee Funeral Home, a Mississippi firm, to handle the arrangements for their mother's burial. From the models on Ott & Lee's showroom floor, the plaintiffs selected a cherry wood casket manufactured by Batesville Casket Co. According to the deposition testimony later provided by each of the plaintiffs, aesthetic reasons played a key role in the choice of the cherry wood casket. The casket "looked like" their mother and "suited her" because all the furniture in her home was cherry wood. The plaintiffs contended that Ott & Lee told them the casket was "top of the line."

At the time the wooden casket was selected, Ott & Lee informed the plaintiffs that unlike a metal casket, a wooden casket could not be sealed. The plaintiffs testified in their depositions that Ott & Lee so informed them and that at Ott & Lee's suggestion, they chose to use a concrete vault with the wooden casket. According to the plaintiffs, Ott & Lee said the vault would keep the pressure of the dirt off the casket and would prevent water from reaching the casket. Ott & Lee made no representations to the plaintiffs about the ability of a wooden casket to preserve the remains contained inside it. The plaintiffs made no inquiry about whether the casket could or would preserve the remains.

The wooden casket chosen by the plaintiffs carried Batesville's written limited warranty, which specified that Batesville would replace the casket if, "at any time prior to the interment of this casket," defects in materials or workmanship were discovered. Thus, Batesville expressly warranted the casket until the time of Ms. Minton's burial, which took place on March 9, 1999. Later, believing that a medical malpractice claim may have existed against Ms. Minton's medical care providers, the plaintiffs had their mother's body exhumed for an autopsy on August 10, 2001. When the casket was exhumed, the plaintiffs observed visible cracks and separation in the casket. As the casket was removed, it began to break apart. The body remained in the casket, and none of the plaintiffs saw the body.

After the exhumation, the plaintiffs filed suit against Ott & Lee and Batesville in a Mississippi court. The plaintiffs claimed that given the casket's cracked, separated, and partially dismantled condition, as revealed during the exhumation, the defendants had breached the implied warranties of merchantability and fitness for particular purpose. Ott & Lee and Batesville each moved for summary judgment. The plaintiffs presented affidavits from expert witnesses whose specialties were wood rot and adhesives, as opposed to caskets per se. These experts opined that the casket appeared as it did during the exhumation because of a probable failure of the adhesives used when it was manufactured. There was no evidence that Ms. Minton's body had not been properly preserved or that there was any damage to the body because of the cracks and separation in the casket. After the Mississippi circuit court granted the defendants' motions for summary judgment, the plaintiffs appealed to the Supreme Court of Mississippi.

Easley, Justice

Miss. Code Ann. § 75-2-315 establishes the foundation for the concept of an implied warranty for fitness for a particular purpose. The statute provides in pertinent part [that] "where the seller at the time of contracting has reason to know any particular purpose for which the goods are required and that the buyer is relying on the seller's skill or judgment to select or furnish suitable goods, there is an implied warranty that the goods shall be fit for such purpose." The warranty of fitness for a particular purpose does not arise unless there is reliance on the seller by the buyer, and the seller selects goods which are unfit for the particular purpose.

During discovery, depositions were taken from the plaintiffs. These depositions, which were provided to the trial court [in connection with] the motion for summary judgment, demonstrate that the plaintiffs purchased the wooden casket for its aesthetic value. [One plaintiff] testified:

We spotted the cherry wood casket. [An Ott & Lee employee] walked us over there to it and we all decided, standing there— us four—that it looked like our mother. That's—I mean—she

had everything in her house was cherry wood. I mean, it just looked like her. We asked . . . about the casket. I mean, I'm not stupid. I know a casket won't seal—a wood casket.

[Another plaintiff] testified: "We were looking at the different caskets, and when we saw the wood casket, we knew that we wanted this one for Mother because it looked just like her—a wood cherry casket. And we were just all [in] agreement with it." [A third plaintiff] testified that the reason he chose this casket was because his mother "just liked cherry wood furniture." He further stated [that] "[i]t just suited her."

In [its] conclusions of law, the trial court stated: "The court is convinced from the deposition testimony that the plaintiffs were well aware of the characteristic differences between a wooden casket as compared to a metal one, but that the former was selected because of their mother's love of cherry wood." The trial court found that "the fitness-purpose aspect was served during the time the decedent's body was placed in the casket and viewed by family members, loved ones, and friends at the funeral home."

Here, the evidence did not justify the submission of this case to a jury on the [implied] warranty of fitness for a particular purpose [claim]. Nothing in the record provides that the plaintiffs identified any particular purpose to the defendants when the casket was selected. Furthermore, assuming arguendo that the plaintiffs sought to preserve their mother's remains for some unspecified, indefinite period of time in the wooden casket, the record is completely devoid of any proof that the body had been damaged in any way by the alleged problems with the casket. As such, the burial had preserved the remains until the plaintiffs had their mother's remains unearthed and the autopsy performed. [T]he trial court did not err in granting summary judgment [in favor of the defendants on this implied warranty claim].

Miss. Code Ann. § 75-2-314 establishes the statutory foundation for the concept of an implied warranty of merchantability. [The statute] provides in pertinent part: "[A] warranty that the goods shall be merchantable is implied in a contract for their sale if the seller is a merchant with respect to goods of that kind." [The statute also states that in order for goods to be merchantable, they must be] "fit for the ordinary purposes for which such goods are used."

The plaintiffs argue that, as reasonable consumers, they expected the casket to preserve the remains for an indefinite period of time. The defendants contend that even if the plaintiffs' theory that the ordinary purpose of the casket was to preserve the remains for an indefinite or some unknown period of time is accepted as true, there is no evidence in the record which indicates the remains were not in fact properly preserved for an indefinite or unknown period of time. When the remains were exhumed by the plaintiffs approximately two and one-half years after burial, the record reflects the remains were preserved. The plaintiffs present no claim that the remains had been damaged in any way by the cracks and separations. As such, the defendants assert the plaintiffs' alleged ordinary purpose of the casket was satisfied.

In *Craigmiles v. Giles*, 110 F. Supp. 2d 658, 662 (E.D. Tenn. 2000), the district court stated:

> A casket is nothing more than a container for human remains. Caskets are normally constructed of metal or wood, but can be made of other materials. Some have "protective seals," but those seals do not prevent air and bacteria from exiting. All caskets leak sooner or later, and all caskets, like their contents, eventually decompose.

Likewise, Batesville contends that the ordinary purpose of a wooden casket is to house the remains of the departed until interment. Batesville argues that the ordinary purpose includes uses which the manufacturer intended and those which are reasonably foreseeable. Accordingly, Batesville asserts that it would not be reasonably foreseeable that any customer would expect a wooden casket to preserve the remains for an indefinite period of time, as claimed by the plaintiffs.

[T]he record does not indicate that the plaintiffs ever stated a specified period of time that they, as reasonable customers, would have reasonably expected the wooden casket to last. The plaintiffs contend that they reasonably expected the casket to protect the remains for an indefinite period of time. *Indefinite* is defined as "without fixed boundaries or distinguishing characteristics; not definite, determinate, or precise." *Black's Law Dictionary* 393 (5th ed. 1983). [Under the circumstances, the] trial court [appropriately] found that the ordinary purpose for which the casket was designed ceased once the pallbearers bore the casket from the hearse to the grave site for burial. [In any event,] [a]s previously stated, the record also fails to demonstrate that the remains were damaged in any way from the alleged cracks and separation when the casket and body were exhumed.

Accordingly, [we reject] the plaintiffs' assignment of error [concerning the lower court's grant of summary judgment in favor of the defendants on the breach of implied warranty of merchantability claim].

Summary judgment in favor of defendants affirmed.

Negligence

 LO20-5 Identify the major categories into which negligence-based product liability claims fall (negligent manufacture, negligent inspection, negligent failure to provide adequate warnings, and negligent design).

Product liability lawsuits brought on the **negligence** theory discussed in Chapter 7 usually allege that the seller or manufacturer breached a duty to the plaintiff by failing to eliminate a reasonably foreseeable risk of harm associated with the product. Such cases typically involve one or more of the following claims: (1) negligent *manufacture* of the goods (including improper materials and packaging), (2) negligent *inspection*, (3) negligent failure to provide *adequate warnings*, and (4) negligent *design*.

Negligent Manufacture Negligence claims alleging the manufacturer's improper assembly, materials, or packaging often encounter obstacles because the evidence needed to prove a breach of duty is under the defendant's control. However, modern discovery rules and the doctrine of *res ipsa loquitur* may help plaintiffs establish a breach in such situations.[3]

Negligent Inspection Manufacturers have a duty to inspect their products for defects that create a reasonably foreseeable risk of harm, if such an inspection would be practicable and effective. As noted above, *res ipsa loquitur* and modern discovery rules may help plaintiffs prove their case against the manufacturer.

Most courts have held that intermediaries such as retailers and wholesalers have a duty to inspect the goods they sell only when they have actual knowledge or reason to know of a defect. In addition, such parties generally have no duty to inspect if inspection would be unduly difficult, burdensome, or time-consuming. Unless the product defect is obvious, for example, middlemen usually are not liable for failing to inspect goods sold in the manufacturer's original packages or containers.

On the other hand, sellers that prepare, install, or repair the goods they sell ordinarily have a duty to inspect those goods. Examples include restaurants, automobile dealers, and installers of household products. In general, the scope of the inspection need only be consistent with the preparation, installation, or repair work performed. It is unlikely, therefore, that such sellers must unearth hidden or latent defects.

If there is a duty to inspect and the inspection reveals a defect, further duties may arise. For example, a manufacturer or other seller may be required not to sell the product in its defective state, or at least to give a suitable warning. The *Wilke* case, which appears in this chapter's later section on implied warranty disclaimers, also deals with a seller's presale duty to inspect goods (in that case, a used car) and potential negligence liability for a breach of that duty.

Negligent Failure to Warn Sellers and manufacturers often have a duty to give an appropriate warning when their products pose a reasonably foreseeable risk of harm. In determining whether there was a duty to warn and whether the defendant's warning was adequate, however, courts often consider other factors besides the reasonable foreseeability of the risk. These include the *magnitude or severity* of the likely harm, the *ease or difficulty of providing an appropriate warning*, and the likely *effectiveness of a warning*. Many courts, moreover, hold there is no duty to warn if the risk is *open and obvious*.

Negligent Design

 LO20-6 Explain the factors courts consider and the test they frequently use in determining whether a manufacturer is vulnerable to a negligent design claim.

Manufacturers have a duty to design their products so as to avoid reasonably foreseeable risks of harm. As in failure-to-warn cases, however, design defect cases frequently involve other factors such as the *magnitude or severity* of the foreseeable harm. Three other factors are *industry practices* at the time the product was manufactured, the *state of the art* (the state of existing scientific and technical knowledge) at that time, and the product's compliance or noncompliance with *government safety regulations*.

When determining whether a manufacturer was negligent in adopting a particular design, courts frequently supplement the above factors with an analysis known as the *risk-utility test*. In that analysis, three other factors—the design's social utility, the *availability and effectiveness of alternative designs*, and the *cost of safer designs*—assume considerable importance.

Special considerations may attend the negligent design determination regarding certain products. Consider, for instance, a motor vehicle. Because vehicle accidents occur on a very frequent basis and are thus to be expected, is the manufacturer obligated to use due care to design a "crashworthy" vehicle? Courts have fairly often, but not always, furnished a "yes" answer. Given the foreseeability of traffic accidents—even ones resulting from driver error—some courts have concluded that vehicle manufacturers must adopt designs that furnish reasonable protection to vehicle occupants in the event of typical crashes. Of course, this crashworthiness doctrine does not make vehicle manufacturers liable every time a vehicle occupant is injured in a traffic accident. Instead, as a specialized application of the due care standard, the crashworthiness doctrine recognizes that foreseeable harm-causing scenarios require relevant and reasonable steps on the part of the manufacturer. The *Green* case, which appears in the chapter's later section on comparative fault issues, contains a useful discussion of the crashworthiness doctrine.

As indicated earlier, however, not all courts recognize the crashworthiness doctrine. *Holiday Motor Corp. v. Walters*, which follows, serves as an example. The decision also explores various issues that arise in cases brought on a negligent design theory.

---

[3]Chapter 2 discusses discovery. Chapter 7 discusses *res ipsa loquitur*.

Holiday Motor Corp. v. Walters   790 S.E.2d 447 (Va. 2016)

In June 2006, Shannon Walters was driving her 1995 Mazda Miata convertible along a two-lane highway in Virginia. The Miata was equipped with a soft top that could be folded and stowed for open-air driving. The soft top also could be unfolded and closed by engaging latches located on each side of the vehicle in order to connect the top to the windshield header (the curved steel bar running across the top of the windshield). Walters was operating the Miata in the closed-top configuration with the latches engaged.

As she later testified at the trial of the case described below, she saw a large object—one that "basically covered [her] whole lane of travel"—coming toward her from the back of a pickup truck she was following. (The object that fell from the truck was later determined to be a swimming pool. The driver of the truck did not return to the scene and was not apprehended.) Seeing no traffic in the oncoming lane, Walters veered left across the road, off the highway, and up a slight grassy incline. The vehicle overturned and landed on its top, with the driver's side pushed up against a tree.

Michael Evans, who was also driving on the same highway, came upon the same object in the road, hit his brakes, steered left, and pulled his vehicle onto the grass. As he later testified, he saw Walters's vehicle and noted that it was "inverted, on its top, up against the tree," which "was against the driver's side." Because the vehicle was "resting on a slope," the driver's side "was closer to the ground than the passenger side." Evans testified that the "back of the convertible bows," or the beams across the top, "appeared to be holding the vehicle up, but the front of the hood and windshield . . . were flat on the ground." Because Evans could not enter the vehicle through the driver's side, he broke the glass out of the passenger's side window, reached through the window, and opened the passenger's side door. He then crawled into the vehicle and turned off the ignition. At that time, he noticed that the windshield header was separated from the soft top in such a way that the top "was actually underneath of the windshield." Evans cut Walters's seat belt and lowered her to a reclining position. He observed that Walters had a head injury and was bleeding. Because Walters told Evans she could not feel her legs, he was reluctant to move her. Evans remained with Walters until emergency medical personnel arrived on the scene.

Walters, who sustained a serious cervical spine injury in the accident, later sued three defendants: Mazda Motor Corp., which designed and manufactured her Miata; Mazda Motor of America Inc., which distributed the vehicle; and Holiday Motor Corp., which sold her the vehicle. (Hereinafter, the three defendants will be referred to collectively as "Mazda.") She contended that her injuries in the rollover accident stemmed from the fact that the windshield header disconnected from the Miata's top and collapsed into the occupant compartment. In particular, she claimed that Mazda was negligent in failing to design the latches connecting the windshield header to the top in a way that would keep the latches engaged during a foreseeable rollover crash.

An automotive engineer testified as an expert witness for Walters at the trial. He offered an opinion that supported the negligent design argument referred to above. A physician who specialized in sports medicine offered the opinion that the plaintiff's spine injury resulted from her being hit on the top of the head—probably by the collapsing windshield header—during the rollover accident. Mazda argued that it had no duty to design or supply a soft top that provided occupant protection in a rollover crash. After the jury returned a $20 million verdict in favor of Walters, Mazda appealed to the Supreme Court of Virginia.

McClanahan, Justice

Mazda argues that it owed no legal duty to design the soft top or the latches to provide occupant rollover protection because it is not the intended or foreseeable purpose of a convertible soft top, including the latching system, to provide such protection. Mazda points out that there was no evidence that Mazda or any car manufacturer designs soft tops or latches to provide occupant rollover protection, that consumers expect a soft top to provide occupant rollover protection, or that there exists any industry standard or custom to design soft tops or their latches to provide such protection.

Walters contends that Mazda sold a dual-purpose product. According to Walters, when the top was in use, it was a foreseeable purpose of the top and latching mechanism to provide the same occupant rollover protection as a sedan with a permanent roof structure. Walters specifically asserts [in her brief] that it was "a fundamental and intended purpose" of the latches to

"keep any part of the structure from intruding into the occupant compartment and creating a hazardous environment." Thus, she argues, "the latches failed their intended safety purpose of keeping the structures connected and thus away from the occupant."

The issue of whether a manufacturer of a soft top convertible owes a legally recognized duty to design or supply a soft top or its latching system to provide occupant rollover protection is a threshold question that we determine as a matter of law. Walters does not claim that a defect in the Miata caused the rollover crash; rather, Walters seeks to hold Mazda liable for failing to design the soft top latching system to provide occupant protection during the rollover crash. In Virginia, [unlike in some states,] there is no duty on the part of vehicle manufacturers to design or supply a crashworthy vehicle. *See Slone v. General Motors Corp.,* 457 S.E.2d 51, 53–54 (Va. 1995) (expressly rejecting the "crashworthiness" doctrine). Therefore, if a duty to design convertible soft tops to provide occupant rollover protection exists, it must be found within the scope of a vehicle manufacturer's duty to exercise reasonable care to design a product that is reasonably safe for the purpose for which it is intended. *See id.* (stating that instead of injecting the doctrine of "crashworthiness" into our well-settled jurisprudence, we will apply the product liability principles articulated in our precedent).

Our well-settled jurisprudence establishes that the manufacturer of a product is only under a duty "to exercise ordinary care to design a product that is reasonably safe for the purpose for which it is intended." [Citation omitted.] The determination of whether a vehicle manufacturer owes a duty to design a convertible soft top to provide occupant rollover protection, therefore, requires that we consider whether such protection is the intended or reasonably foreseeable use, given the inherent characteristics, market purposes, and utility of a convertible soft top. "After all, it is a commonplace that utility of design and attractiveness of the style of the car are elements which car manufacturers seek after and by which buyers are influenced in their selections." *Dreisonstok v. Volkswagenwerk, A.G.*, 489 F.2d 1066, 1072 (4th Cir. 1974). "Foreseeability [of harm], it has been many times repeated, is not to be equated with duty." *Id.* at 1070. Accordingly, while the possibility that a convertible may be involved in a rollover accident is undoubtedly foreseeable, "[c]ommon knowledge of a danger from the foreseeable misuse of a product does not alone give rise to a duty to safeguard against the danger of that misuse." [Citation omitted.] "To the contrary, the purpose of making the finding of a legal duty as a prerequisite to a finding of negligence . . . is to avoid the extension of liability for every conceivably foreseeable accident, without regard to common sense or good policy." [Citation omitted.]

Existence of duty is an issue that is separate and distinct from its breach. To sustain a claim for negligent design, a plaintiff must show that the manufacturer failed to meet objective safety standards prevailing at the time the product was made. "When deciding whether a product's design meets those standards, a court should consider whether the product fails to satisfy applicable industry standards, applicable government standards, or reasonable consumer expectations." [Citation omitted.]

In contrast to vehicles with a permanent roof structure, soft top convertibles provide the owner with a roof that can, with relative ease, be retracted and stowed for an open-air driving experience or closed to protect the occupants from the outside elements such as wind and rain. The absence of a permanent roof structure necessarily diminishes the level of occupant rollover protection. Not only is this characteristic of a convertible "readily discernible to anyone using the vehicle," it is "the unique feature of the vehicle." *Dreisonstok*, 489 F.2d at 1074 (noting that the unique design of the Volkswagen microbus reduced the space between the front of the vehicle and driver's compartment so as

to provide the maximum amount of cargo or passenger space). "If a person purchases a convertible . . . he cannot expect—and the Court may not impose on the manufacturer the duty to provide him with—the exact kind of protection in a roll-over accident as in the standard American passenger car." *Id.* at 1075.

In connection with examining the duty of a vehicle manufacturer to design a convertible soft top to provide rollover protection, we note that when the Mazda Miata was manufactured in 1995, there were no government or automotive industry safety standards in existence requiring that convertible soft tops provide protection from intrusion of the roof system into the occupant compartment during a rollover crash. While the National Highway Transportation Safety Administration (NHTSA) established strength requirements for the passenger compartment roof of specified vehicles, it expressly excluded convertibles from such requirements. *See* Federal Motor Vehicle Safety Standard (FMVSS) No. 216, 49 C.F.R. § 571.216(S3)(c). The stated purpose of FMVSS No. 216 "is to reduce deaths and injuries due to the crushing of the roof into the occupant compartment in rollover crashes." The roof over the front seat area specifically includes the windshield header.

In 2009, NHTSA upgraded its safety standard on roof crush resistance "[a]s part of a comprehensive plan for reducing the risk of rollover crashes and the risk of death and serious injury in those crashes." 74 Fed. Reg. 22,348. NHTSA continued to exclude convertibles, including retractable hard top convertibles, from the FMVSS No. 216 requirements. Explaining its reason for excluding convertibles from the roof crush resistance standard, NHTSA stated:

> We believe that to establish a roof crush requirement on vehicles that do not have a permanent roof structure would not be practical from a countermeasure perspective. A convertible roof would have to be strong enough to pass the quasi-static test, yet flexible enough to fold into the vehicle. Since we are not aware of any such designs, we do not agree with Advocates [who objected to excluding convertibles from FMVSS No. 216] on this point. We also note that new rollover and ejection requirements for convertibles are outside the scope of this rulemaking.

74 Fed. Reg. at 22,375. Even as to folding hardtops and removable hardtops, NHTSA noted that "[t]hese roof systems are not intended as significant structural elements but are designed primarily to provide protection from inclement weather, improve theft protection and are generally offered as a luxury item." *Id.* Furthermore, NHTSA expressed its belief that "consumers readily recognize that [these roof systems] will afford occupants limited protection in a rollover." *Id.* Accordingly, there continues to be no government or automotive industry safety standards requiring convertible soft tops to provide occupant rollover protection.

Walters argues that consideration of FMVSS No. 216, and in particular the exclusion of convertibles from its roof crush requirements, is inappropriate because this case is about defective latches, not a defective roof. Walters' argument is a non sequitur. It is the absence of a permanent roof structure that requires use of latches to connect the top to the windshield. And it is this inherent feature of a convertible—the absence of a fixed, rigid structural member to connect the . . . frame [for] the vehicle's windshield to the . . . frame [for] the vehicle's rear window—that makes roof crush requirements impractical for convertibles. Furthermore, Walters' effort to make a distinction between the roof and the latches is unavailing since the basis of her claims for negligence . . . is that the Miata "would not provide reasonable occupant protection in a foreseeable rollover while being used in its closed top configuration" [quoting her brief]. Occupant protection in a rollover crash is the precise issue addressed by FMVSS No. 216.

In short, we believe that imposing a duty upon manufacturers of convertible soft tops to provide occupant rollover protection defies both "common sense" and "good policy." [Citation omitted.] There are no safety standards in existence, promulgated either by the government or the automotive industry, that require convertible soft tops, including their latching mechanisms, to provide occupant rollover protection. Indeed, NHTSA has expressly excepted convertibles from the roof crush standard because it is unaware of any convertible top that could meet such a standard. There is certainly no evidence that Mazda or any other manufacturer of convertibles in fact designs or markets soft tops to provide occupant rollover protection or that consumers reasonably expect such protection. To the contrary, the marketable feature of the soft top convertible is the absence of a permanent roof structure. The absence of this structural component is not only obvious but chosen by consumers who desire the flexibility of a soft top that can be easily detached, folded, and stowed for an open-air driving experience, or closed and latched to the windshield header for a quieter ride without exposure to the outside elements. The use of a convertible soft top, including its latches, for occupant rollover protection is neither its purpose nor an intended or reasonably foreseeable use.

For these reasons, we hold that no duty extended to Mazda to design the soft top, including its latches, so that it would provide occupant rollover protection. Therefore, we reverse the judgment of the circuit court and enter final judgment in favor of Mazda.

Jury verdict in favor of Walters vacated; lower court decision reversed; judgment entered in favor of Mazda.

Strict Liability

 LO20-7 Identify the elements of a strict liability claim under *Restatement (Second)* § 402A and explain how strict liability differs from liability for negligence.

Strict liability for certain defective products has been a feature of the legal landscape since the mid-20th century. The movement toward imposing strict liability received a critical boost when the American Law Institute promulgated § 402A of the *Restatement (Second) of Torts* in 1965. By now, the vast majority of the states have adopted some form of strict liability, either by statute or under the common law. The most important reason is the socialization-of-risk strategy discussed earlier. By not requiring plaintiffs to prove a breach of duty, strict liability makes it easier for them to recover; sellers then may pass on the costs of this liability through higher prices. Another justification for strict liability is that it stimulates manufacturers to design and build safer products.

Section 402A's Requirements Because it is the most common version of strict liability in the products context, we limit our discussion of the subject to § 402A. It provides that a "seller . . . engaged in the business of selling" a product is liable for physical harm or property damage suffered by the ultimate user or consumer of that product, if the product was "in a defective condition unreasonably dangerous to the user or consumer or to his property." This rule applies even though "the seller has exercised all possible care in the preparation and sale of his product." Thus, § 402A states a strict liability rule, which does not require plaintiffs to prove a breach of duty.

Each element required by § 402A must be present in order for strict liability to be imposed.

1. The seller must be *engaged in the business of selling the product that harmed the plaintiff.* Thus, § 402A binds only parties who resemble UCC merchants because they regularly sell the product at issue. For example, the section does not apply to a plumber's sale of a used car.

2. The product must be in a *defective condition* when sold and must also be *unreasonably dangerous* because of that condition. The reasonable-expectations-of-the-consumer test normally governs the determination of whether a product is in a defective condition. Determining whether a product is unreasonably dangerous can vary depending upon what supposedly makes the product possess that level of dangerousness. Where the apparent problem was manufacturing-oriented, the test tends to be whether the product is dangerous to an extent beyond the reasonable contemplation of the average consumer. For instance, good whiskey is not unreasonably dangerous even though it can cause harm, but whiskey contaminated with a poisonous substance would be considered unreasonably dangerous. Where the question is whether the design adopted for a product made it unreasonably dangerous, courts today often employ a version of the *risk-utility* test noted earlier in the discussion of negligence-based cases. The *Branham* case, which appears shortly, discusses the role of the risk-utility test in strict liability cases involving allegedly defective designs.

Section 402A's requirement of unreasonable dangerousness means that strict liability applies to a smaller range of product defects than does the implied warranty of merchantability. For example, a power mower that fails to operate shortly after a merchant's sale of it would be unmerchantable and evidently defective (satisfying one element of a § 402A claim) but would not be unreasonably dangerous (failing the remaining § 402A element). Therefore, the merchant seller could be liable for a breach of the implied warranty of merchantability but would not be held strictly liable under § 402A.

3. Finally, defendants may avoid § 402A liability where the product was *substantially modified* by the plaintiff or another party after the sale, and the modification contributed to the plaintiff's injury or other loss.

Applications of § 402A   As the preceding discussion suggests, manufacturing-defect and design-defect cases can be brought under § 402A. The same is true of failure-to-warn cases. Even though § 402A sets forth a strict liability rule, the factors considered and tests employed in § 402A cases resemble those applied in the negligence cases discussed in the chapter's previous section. The conceptual difference between negligence-based cases and strict liability cases is that the former consider the defendant's conduct as it contributed to the product's condition, whereas in strict liability cases the focus is solely on the product's condition (not on whether the defendant's conduct was blameworthy). Nevertheless, given that similar factors and tests apply in each type of case and the further fact that plaintiffs often argue in the alternative by bringing negligence and strict liability claims in the same case, courts sometimes encounter difficulty in keeping the two claims analytically distinct.

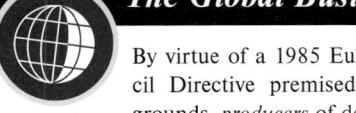

The Global Business Environment

By virtue of a 1985 European Union (EU) Council Directive premised on consumer protection grounds, *producers* of defective products face strict liability for the personal injuries and property damage those products cause. The 1985 Directive defined *product* as

> all movables, with the exception of primary agricultural products and game, even though incorporated into another movable or into an immovable. "Primary agricultural products" means the products of the soil, of stock-farming and of fisheries, excluding products which have undergone initial processing. "Product" includes electricity.

A 1999 amendment, however, broadened the Directive's definition of *product* and coverage of the strict liability regime by eliminating the original version's exclusion of agricultural products. After the 1999 amendment, *product* includes "all movables even if incorporated into another movable or into an immovable." The 1999 amendment also retained the original version's inclusion of "electricity" within the definition of *product*.

The Directive states that a product is considered *defective* when it does not provide the safety which a person is entitled to expect, taking all circumstances into account, including: (a) the presentation of the product; (b) the use to which it could reasonably be expected that the product would be put; [and] (c) the time when the product was put into circulation.

Because the Directive contemplates strict liability, the harmed consumer need not show a failure to use reasonable care on the part of the producer. The typical tendency among the states of the United States is to require, in a strict liability case, proof that the product was both defective and unreasonably dangerous. The Directive, however, takes a different approach to strict liability. Although the consumer must demonstrate personal injury or property damage resulting from use of the product, the Directive's definition of *defective* does not contemplate a separate showing that the harm-causing product was defective to the point of being unreasonably dangerous. Only limited possible defenses against liability are provided for producers in the Directive.

[As will be seen, the *Restatement (Third) of Torts* borrows features of negligence and strict liability without using either of those labels and then combines those features in a proposed set of rules that emphasizes differences among types of product defects.]

Because it applies to professional sellers, § 402A covers retailers and other middlemen who market goods containing defects that they did not create and may not have been able to discover. Even though such parties often escape negligence liability, courts have held them liable under § 402A's strict liability rule. Some states, however, have given middlemen protection against § 402A liability or have required the manufacturer or other responsible party to indemnify them.

What about products, such as some medications, that have great social utility but pose serious and unavoidable risks? Imposing strict liability regarding such "unavoidably unsafe" products might deter manufacturers from developing and marketing them. When products of this kind cause harm and a lawsuit follows, many courts follow Comment k to § 402A. Comment k says that unavoidably unsafe products are neither defective nor unreasonably dangerous if they are properly prepared and accompanied by proper directions and a proper warning. For this rule to apply, the product must be genuinely incapable of being made safer.

The *Restatement (Third)*

> **LO20-8** Describe the *Restatement (Third)*'s proposed framework of product liability rules.

In 1998, the American Law Institute published its *Restatement (Third) of Torts: Product Liability*. The *Restatement (Third)*'s proposed approach to the tort aspects of product liability calls for different analyses for different types of defects. It borrows to some extent from both negligence and strict liability in doing so (though without using those terms). Although its approach has not yet been adopted by enough states to make it a majority rule, the *Restatement (Third)* may signal the likely evolution of product liability law in coming years. As evidenced by the *Branham* case, which appears shortly, the *Restatement (Third)* can be influential even when courts continue to adhere to the traditional theories of negligence and strict liability.

Basic Provisions The *Restatement (Third)*'s basic product liability rule states: "One engaged in the business of selling or otherwise distributing products who sells or distributes a defective product is subject to liability for harm to persons or property caused by the defect." As does § 402A, this rule covers only those who are engaged in the

business of selling the kind of product that injured the plaintiff. The rule also resembles § 402A in covering not only manufacturers but also other sellers down the product's chain of distribution. Unlike § 402A, however, the *Restatement (Third)* does not require that the product be unreasonably dangerous.

Specific Rules The *Restatement (Third)* states special rules governing the sale of product components, prescription drugs, medical devices, food products, and used goods. More importantly, it adds substance to the basic rule set forth above by describing three kinds of product defects.

1. *Manufacturing defects.* A manufacturing defect occurs when the product does not conform to its intended design at the time it leaves the manufacturer's hands. This includes products that are incorrectly assembled, physically flawed, or damaged.

2. *Inadequate instructions or warnings.* Although the *Restatement (Third)* applies strict liability to manufacturing defects, liability for inadequate instructions or warnings resembles negligence more than strict liability. [The *Restatement (Third)* rules regarding failures to warn do not use the term *negligence*, however.] This liability exists when reasonable instructions or warnings could have reduced the product's foreseeable risk of harm, but the seller did not provide such instructions or warnings and the product thus was not reasonably safe. Manufacturers and sellers are liable only for failing to instruct or warn about *reasonably foreseeable* harms, and not about every conceivable risk their products might present. As with negligence and § 402A, moreover, they need not warn about obvious and generally known risks. The other failure-to-warn factors discussed earlier probably apply under the new *Restatement* as well.

3. *Design defects.* The *Restatement (Third)* calls for liability for design defects to be determined under principles resembling those of negligence [though the *Restatement (Third)* rule for such cases avoids using the term *negligence*]. According to the *Restatement (Third)*, courts should employ a risk-utility test of the sort discussed earlier and plaintiffs must prove that the use of a reasonable alternative design would have reduced or avoided foreseeable risks of harm.

The *Branham* case, which follows, presents a plaintiff's attempt to have strict liability imposed for a design defect. Although the court regards § 402A as controlling, it points to the *Restatement (Third)* in support of its conclusions that the risk-utility test should guide the unreasonable dangerousness inquiry and that the plaintiff had to demonstrate the existence of a reasonable alternative design. The court also addresses the question whether evidence of a manufacturer's decisions and actions after the harm-causing product's distribution should be permitted in a design defect case.

Branham v. Ford Motor Co.   701 S.E.2d 5 (S.C. 2010)

Cheryl Hale purchased a 1987 Ford Bronco II (Bronco) in 1999. The Bronco had been manufactured by Ford Motor Co. in 1986. In 2001, Hale was driving the Bronco on a South Carolina road. She was transporting several children to her home. Among them was Jesse Branham. Hale momentarily took her eyes off the road and turned to the backseat to ask the children to quiet down. When she did so, the Bronco veered to the right. Its right rear wheel then went off the roadway. Realizing what was happening, Hale responded by over-correcting to the left. The vehicle began to shake and then rolled over. Branham was thrown from the vehicle and was seriously injured.

Branham (through his parents, acting on his behalf) sued Ford and Hale in a South Carolina court. The case against Ford presented a "handling and stability" design defect claim related to the Bronco's supposed tendency to roll over. Branham pursued this claim on the alternative grounds of negligence and strict liability. Ford denied liability and asserted that Hale's negligence caused the accident. The jury found both Ford and Hale liable. It awarded Branham $16,000,000 in compensatory damages and $15,000,000 in punitive damages. Ford appealed to the Supreme Court of South Carolina. (Further relevant facts appear below, in the edited version of the state supreme court's opinion.)

Kittredge, Justice

The "handling and stability" design defect claim (strict liability and negligence) is the gravamen of Branham's case [against Ford]. Ford appeals from the denial of its motions to dismiss the strict liability and negligence causes of action.

For a plaintiff to successfully advance a [strict liability-based] design defect claim, he must show that the design of the product caused it to be unreasonably dangerous. In South Carolina, we have traditionally employed two tests to determine whether a product was unreasonably dangerous as a result of a design defect: (1) the consumer expectations test; and (2) the risk-utility test.

In [an earlier decision], this Court phrased the consumer expectations test as follows: "The test . . . is whether the product is unreasonably dangerous to the consumer or user given the conditions and circumstances that foreseeably attend use of the product." [In the same decision, we] articulated the risk-utility test in the following manner: "[N]umerous factors must be considered [when determining whether a product is unreasonably dangerous], including the usefulness and desirability of the product, the cost involved for added safety, the likelihood and potential seriousness of injury, and the obviousness of danger." Later, . . . our court of appeals phrased the risk-utility test as follows: "[A] product is unreasonably dangerous and defective if the danger associated with the use of the product outweighs the utility of the product." [Citation omitted.]

Ford contends Branham failed to present evidence of a feasible alternative design. Implicit in Ford's argument is the contention that a product may only be shown to be defective and unreasonably dangerous by way of a risk-utility test, for by its very nature, the risk-utility test requires a showing of a reasonable alternative design. Branham counters, arguing that under [our prior decisions] he may prove a design defect by resort to the consumer expectations test or the risk-utility test. Branham also argues that regardless of which test is required, he has met both, including evidence of a feasible alternative design. We agree

with Branham's contention that he produced evidence of a feasible alternative design.

As discussed above, Branham challenged the design of the Ford Bronco II by pointing to the MacPherson suspension as a reasonable alternative design. A former Ford vice-president (Feaheny) testified that the MacPherson suspension system would have significantly increased the handling and stability of the Bronco II, making it less prone to rollovers. Dr. Richardson also noted that the MacPherson suspension system would have enhanced vehicle stability by lowering the vehicle center of gravity. There was further evidence that the desired sport utility features of the Bronco II would not have been compromised by using the MacPherson suspension. Moreover, there is evidence that use of the MacPherson suspension would not have increased costs. Whether this evidence satisfies the risk-utility test is ultimately a jury question. But it is evidence of a feasible alternative design, sufficient to survive [Ford's] directed verdict motion.

While the consumer expectations test fits well in manufacturing defect cases, we agree with Ford that the test is ill-suited in design defect cases. We hold today that the exclusive test in a product liability design defect case is the risk-utility test with its requirement of showing a feasible alternative design. In doing so, we recognize our legislature's presence in the area of strict liability for products liability.

In 1974, our legislature adopted the *Restatement (Second) of Torts* § 402A (1965), and identified its comments as legislative intent. The comments [regarding] § 402A are pointed to as the basis for the consumer expectations test. Since the adoption of § 402A, the American Law Institute published the *Restatement (Third) of Torts: Products Liability* (1998). The third edition effectively moved away from the consumer expectations test for design defects, and toward a risk-utility test. We believe the legislature's foresight in looking to the American Law Institute for guidance in this area is instructive.

The legislature has expressed no intention to foreclose court consideration of developments in product liability law. For example, this Court's approval of the risk-utility test in [a previous case] yielded no legislative response. We thus believe the adoption of the risk-utility test in design defect cases in no manner infringes on the legislature's presence in this area.

Some form of a risk-utility test is employed by an overwhelming majority of the jurisdictions in this country. Some of these jurisdictions exclusively employ a risk-utility test, while others do so with a hybrid of the risk-utility and the consumer expectations test, or an explicit either-or option. States that exclusively employ the consumer expectations test are a decided minority.

We believe that in design defect cases the risk-utility test provides the best means for analyzing whether a product is designed defectively. Unlike the consumer expectations test, the focus of a risk-utility test centers upon the alleged defectively designed product. The risk-utility test provides objective factors for a trier of fact to analyze when presented with a challenge to a manufacturer's design. Conversely, we find the consumer expectations test and its focus on the consumer ill-suited to determine whether a product's design is unreasonably dangerous. The consumer expectations test is best suited for a manufacturing defect claim. [Our adoption of the risk-utility test as the exclusive test in design defect cases is also] in accord with the current edition of the *Restatement (Third) of Torts*:

A product . . . is defective in design when the foreseeable risks of harm posed by the product could have been reduced or avoided by the adoption of a reasonable alternative design by the seller or other distributor, or a predecessor in the commercial chain of distribution, and the omission of the alternative design renders the product not reasonably safe.

In sum, in a product liability design defect action, the plaintiff must present evidence of a reasonable alternative design. The plaintiff will be required to point to a design flaw in the product and show how his alternative design would have prevented the product from being unreasonably dangerous. This presentation of an alternative design must include consideration of the costs, safety, and functionality associated with the alternative design. The analysis asks the trier of fact to determine whether the potential increased price of the product (if any), the potential decrease in the functioning (or utility) of the product (if any), and the potential increase in other safety concerns (if any) associated with the proffered alternative design are worth the benefits that will inhere in the proposed alternative design. On retrial, [which is necessary for the reasons set forth below], Branham's design defect claim will proceed pursuant to the risk-utility test and not the consumer expectations test.

Post-Distribution Evidence

Notwithstanding the existence of ample evidence to withstand a directed verdict motion on the handling and stability design defect claim, we reverse and remand for a new trial. [T]his case implicates [an important] evidentiary rule related to product liability

cases. The rule provides that whether a product is defective must be measured against information known at the time the product was placed into the stream of commerce. When a claim is asserted against a manufacturer, post-manufacture evidence is generally not admissible. Evidence was introduced that violated [this] rule.

[T]o prove his case in a product liability action, [the plaintiff] must show that the "product was in a defective condition at the time that it left the hands of the particular seller . . . and unless evidence can be produced which will support the conclusion that it was *then* defective, the burden is not sustained." [Citation omitted.] Because the claim here is against the manufacturer, the "time of distribution" is the time of manufacture.

While we find Branham presented sufficient evidence to create a jury question on his design defect claim, we further find Ford was prejudiced by Branham's unrelenting pursuit of post-distribution evidence on the issue of liability. Given the extent of the improper post-distribution evidence introduced, the error cannot be considered harmless.

Simply defined, post-distribution evidence is evidence of facts neither known nor available at the time of distribution. When assessing liability in a design defect claim against a manufacturer, the judgment and ultimate decision of the manufacturer must be evaluated based on what was known or reasonably attainable at the time of manufacture. The use of post-distribution evidence to evaluate a product's design through the lens of hindsight is improper.

Hale's Ford Bronco II 4x2 was manufactured in 1986. The following is a sampling of the post-manufacture (or post-distribution) evidence.

Branham introduced a memorandum dated April 14, 1989, dealing with a meeting that three Ford engineers had with "six people from Consumers Report." The memorandum stated that:

Our objective was to "give it our best shot" at diffusing a very negative story on the Bronco II in the June issue. . . . The magazine has done a comparative test of the Chevy S-10 Blazer, Geo Tracker, Dodge Raider and Bronco II. As the result of several calls from a Consumer Report writer, we were led to believe that the story could be nearly as negative as last summer's Suzuki Samurai story. Plus, NHTSA is currently conducting an engineering analysis of the Bronco II which creates a negative cloud. And, FARS [Fatal Analysis Reporting System] data shows Bronco II to have a higher fatal rollover rate relative to certain competitors.

The memorandum went on to note the following: "Our data are not terribly favorable. Our rollover rate is three times higher than the Chevy S-10 Blazer." This evidence of the Bronco II's rollover rate is post-manufacture evidence.

Through Branham's expert, Dr. Richardson, a 1989 film was introduced. [T]his film, taped in 1989, compared the S-10 Blazer and the Bronco II. [It] revealed that the 1989 Bronco II did not handle as well as the S-10 Blazer. Dr. Richardson also testified regarding a document . . . referencing post-manufacture evidence that compared a 1989 Bronco II to the [supposedly safer] UN46 prototype, now known as the Ford Explorer. This document shows the additional evidence of the rollover tendency of the Bronco II that came to light after 1986. Yet another example of post-distribution evidence is found in a memorandum addressing [a 1989 Bronco II rollover] accident caused while Ford was testing a prototype anti-lock braking system.

There are other examples of post-manufacture evidence, but the few examples cited illustrate the inherent prejudice that flows from post-distribution evidence. It is good when a manufacturer continues to test and evaluate its product after initial manufacture. As additional information is learned, changes may be made that improve product safety and function. As a matter of policy, the law should encourage the design and manufacture of safe, functional products. In holding manufacturers accountable

for unreasonably dangerous products pursuant to a fair system, product liability law serves that goal. Moreover, the law should encourage manufacturers to continue to improve their products in terms of utility and safety free from prior design decisions judged through the lens of hindsight.

Whether the 1987 Ford Bronco II was defectively designed and in a defective condition unreasonably dangerous must be determined as of the 1986 manufacture date of the vehicle. Ford's 1986 design and manufacture decision should be assessed on the evidence available at that time, not the increased evidence of additional rollover data that came to light after 1986.

Trial court's judgment in favor of Branham affirmed in part and reversed in part; case remanded for new trial.

CYBERLAW IN ACTION

When Amazon sells defective products via third-party sellers on Amazon's Marketplace, can Amazon be held liable? As this text goes to press in 2020, the answer is not clear, but a variety of cases in recent years are worth noting, especially because third-party vendors accounted for half of all sales on Amazon, or approximately $160 billion, in 2018.

As for official Amazon policy, the company claims to have no responsibility for flawed or defective items sold by third-party merchants, and many courts have agreed. For examples, see the 2018 decisions in *Allstate New Jersey Insurance Co. v. Amazon.com* and *Eberhart v. Amazon.com*.

However, in *Oberdorf v. Amazon.com, Inc.,* decided in July 2019, the U.S. Court of Appeals for the Third Circuit became the first court to reject Amazon's claim that it cannot be considered a "seller" of products offered by third parties.

In this case, Heather Oberdorf bought a retractable leash dog collar on Amazon.com. While out for a walk with her dog Sadie, the animal lunged forward, causing the collar to break and the retractable leash to recoil and hit Ms. Oberdorf in the face and eyeglasses. As a result, she was rendered permanently blind in her left eye.

Unable to locate the third-party seller of the leash, Ms. Oberdorf sued Amazon.com on claims of strict products liability and negligence. At trial, the district court found that under Pennsylvania law, Amazon was not liable for Oberdorf's injuries. The district court emphasized that a third-party vendor—not Amazon—had listed the collar on Amazon's online marketplace and shipped the collar directly to Oberdorf. Based on these facts, the court first found Amazon was not a "seller" under Pennsylvania law, and then concluded that the Communications Decency Act (CDA) barred Oberdorf's claims that Amazon was liable for its role as the online publisher of third-party content.

On appeal, the Third Circuit Court of Appeals disagreed with the trial court and found that Amazon.com was indeed a "seller" and not merely an online marketplace for other sellers. The appellate court's analysis focused on Amazon's practice of neither ensuring that its third-party vendors are in good legal standing in their country of registration nor vetting that these vendors are amenable to the legal process. Moreover, the appellate court concluded that by virtue of its strong position as a gatekeeper to permitting third-party vendors access to the Amazon online marketplace, Amazon was fully capable of removing unsafe products from its website and incentivized to do so. Judge Jane Richards Roth, writing for the court, noted summarized majority opinion: "We do not believe that Pennsylvania law shields a company from strict liability simply because it adheres to a business model that fails to prioritize consumer safety."

While Amazon is currently appealing the appellate court's decision, some commentators noted that consumers would be left with little recourse against sellers of defective products if the decision was overturned by future proceedings. Still, e-commerce advocates warned that this decision could hurt the expansion of online commerce and harm the U.S. economy.

Even while the fate of the *Oberdorf* decision is not settled, its impact has already been felt in other jurisdictions. A district court in New Jersey, following the logic in *Oberdorf*, concluded in *Papataros v. Amazon.com*, a case involving a defective scooter, that Amazon is a "seller" for purposes of New Jersey strict products liability law. In Wisconsin, a district court similarly found that Amazon bears responsibility for putting a defective bathtub faucet adapter (which caused a house to be flooded) into the stream of commerce in that state, and Amazon was best positioned to allocate among itself and its third-party sellers the risks that products sold on Amazon.com would be defective.

Other Theories of Recovery

The Magnuson-Moss Act The relevant civil-recovery provisions of the federal Magnuson-Moss Warranty Act apply to sales of *consumer products* costing more than *$10 per item*. A consumer product is tangible personal property normally used for personal, family, or household purposes. If a seller gives a *written warranty* for such a product to a *consumer*, the warranty must be designated as full or limited. A seller who gives a full warranty promises to (1) *remedy* any defects in the product and (2) *replace* the product or *refund* its purchase price if, after a reasonable number of attempts, it cannot be repaired.[4] A seller who gives a limited warranty is bound to whatever promises it actually makes. However, neither warranty applies if the seller simply declines to give a written warranty.

Misrepresentation Product liability law has long allowed recoveries for misrepresentations made by sellers of goods. The *Restatement (Third)* does likewise. Its rule applies to merchantlike sellers engaged in the business of selling the product in question. The rule includes fraudulent, negligent, or innocent misrepresentations made by such sellers. The misrepresentation must involve a *material fact* about the product—a fact that would matter to a reasonable buyer. This means that sellers are not liable for inconsequential misstatements, sales talk, and statements of opinion. However, the product need not be defective. Unlike past law, moreover, the misrepresentation need not be made to the public, and the plaintiff need not have justifiably relied upon it. However, it must have made the plaintiff suffer personal injury or property damage.

Industrywide Liability The legal theory we call industrywide liability is a way for plaintiffs to bypass problems of causation that exist where several firms within an industry have manufactured a harmful standardized product, and it is impossible for the plaintiff to prove which firm produced the product that injured her. The main reasons for these proof problems are the number of firms producing the product and the time lag between exposure to the product

and the appearance of the injury. Most of the cases presenting such problems have involved DES (an antimiscarriage drug that produced various ailments in daughters of the women to whom it was administered) or diseases resulting from long-term exposure to asbestos. In such cases, each manufacturer of the product can argue that the plaintiff should lose because she cannot show that its product harmed her.

How do courts handle these cases? Most of the time, they continue to deny recovery under traditional causation rules because the special circumstances necessary to trigger application of industrywide liability are found not to be present. However, using various approaches whose many details are beyond the scope of this text, other courts have made it easier for plaintiffs to recover in appropriate cases. Where recovery is allowed, some of these courts have apportioned damages among the firms that might have produced the harm-causing product. Such an apportionment is typically based on market share at some chosen time.

Time Limitations

We now turn to several problems that are common to each major product liability theory but that may be resolved differently from theory to theory. One such problem is the time within which the plaintiff must sue or else lose the case. Traditionally, the main time limits on product liability suits have been the applicable contract and tort **statutes of limitations**. The usual UCC statute of limitations for express and implied warranty claims is four years after the seller offers the defective goods to the buyer (usually, four years after the sale). In tort cases, the applicable statute of limitations may be shorter, depending upon applicable state law. It begins to run, however, only when the defect was or should have been discovered—often, the time of the injury.

In part because of tort reform, some states now impose various other limitations on the time within which product liability suits must be brought. Among these additional time limitations are (1) special statutes of limitations for product liability cases involving death, personal injury, or property damage (e.g., from one to three years after the time the death or injury occurred or should have been discovered); (2) special time limits for "delayed manifestation" injuries such as those resulting from exposure to asbestos; (3) useful safe life defenses (which prevent plaintiffs from suing once the product's "useful safe life" has passed); and (4) statutes of repose (whose aim is similar). Statutes of repose usually run for a 10- to 12-year period

---

[4]Also, many states have enacted so-called lemon laws that may apply only to motor vehicles or to various other consumer products as well. The versions applying to motor vehicles generally require the manufacturer to replace the vehicle or refund its purchase price once certain conditions are met. These conditions may include the following: a serious defect covered by warranty, a certain number of unsuccessful attempts at repair or a certain amount of downtime because of attempted repairs, and the manufacturer's failure to show that the defect is curable.

Ethics and Compliance in Action

Litigation against tobacco companies has proliferated in recent years. Many cases have been brought by cigarette smokers or the estates of deceased smokers in an effort to obtain damages for the adverse health effects resulting from their years of smoking cigarettes. Sometimes, class action suits brought by groups of smokers or persons exposed to secondhand smoke have been instituted. The federal government and many state governments have also sued tobacco companies in an effort to recoup health care costs incurred by those governments in regard to citizens whose health problems allegedly resulted from smoking.

The cases against tobacco firms—particularly those brought by private parties—have been pursued on a wide variety of legal theories that initially included breach of express or implied warranty, negligent design, negligent failure to warn, and strict liability. Results have been mixed, with tobacco companies frequently prevailing but plaintiffs occasionally receiving jury verdicts for very large amounts of damages (some of which have been subject to reduction or outright elimination by the trial judge or an appellate court). During the past several years, plaintiffs had greater success in cases against tobacco companies than they once did, in large part because plaintiffs acquired access to old tobacco industry documents they previously did not have. Some of these documents helped plaintiffs augment the traditional product liability claims referred to above with claims for fraudulent concealment of, and conspiracy to conceal, the full extent of the health risks of smoking during a time when tobacco firms' public pronouncements allegedly minimized or soft-pedaled those risks. Although plaintiffs' cases against tobacco companies remain far from surefire winners, there is no doubt that plaintiffs' chances of winning such cases are somewhat better today than they were roughly 20 years ago.

In addition to the many legal issues spawned by cases against tobacco companies, various ethical issues come to mind. Consider, for instance, the questions set forth below. Some of them pertain to tobacco litigation, whereas others pertain to related issues for business and society. In considering these questions, you may wish to employ the ethical theories outlined in Chapter 4, as well as that chapter's suggested process for making decisions that carry potential ethical implications.

- Given what is now known about the dangers of tobacco use, are the production and sale of tobacco products ethically justifiable business activities? What are the arguments each way? Does it make a difference whether the health hazards of smoking have, or have not, been fully disclosed by the tobacco companies?

- Would the federal government be acting ethically if it took the step of outlawing the production and sale of tobacco products? Why or why not?

- If a company that produces a product—whether tobacco or another product—acquires information indicating that its product may be or is harmful to users of it, does the company owe an ethical duty to disclose this actual or potential danger? If so, at what point? What considerations should be taken into account?

- If a manufacturer's product—whether tobacco or another product—is well received by users but poses a significant risk of harm when used as intended by the manufacturer, does the manufacturer owe an ethical duty to take steps to redesign the product so as to lessen the risk or severity of the harm? Justify your conclusion, noting the considerations you have taken into account.

- When tobacco companies comply with federal law by placing the mandated health warnings on packages of their cigarettes and in their cigarette advertisements, have they simultaneously taken care of any ethical obligations they may have regarding disclosure of health risks? Why or why not?

- Are smokers' (or smokers' estates') lawsuits against tobacco companies ethically justifiable? If so, is this true of all of them or only some of them, and why? If only some are ethically justifiable, which ones, and why? If you believe that such lawsuits are not ethically justifiable, why do you hold that view?

- Some critics have taken the position that health care cost-recouping litigation brought by the federal government and state governments against tobacco companies reflects hypocrisy because our governments extend support to tobacco farmers and collect considerable tax revenue from parties involved in tobacco growing, tobacco product manufacturing, and tobacco product sales. How do you weigh in on this issue? Are there ethical dimensions here? If our federal and state governments are "in bed" with the tobacco industry, did our governments act unethically in pursuing this litigation, or would our governments have been acting unethically if they had not pursued this litigation? Be prepared to justify your conclusions.

that begins when the product is sold to the first buyer not purchasing for resale—usually an ordinary consumer. In a state with a 10-year statute of repose, for example, such parties cannot recover for injuries that occur more than 10 years after they purchased the product causing the harm. This is true even when the suit is begun quickly enough to satisfy the applicable statute of limitations.

Damages in Product Liability Cases

 LO20-9 Identify the types of compensatory damages available in product liability cases based on tort theories and in cases based on warranty theories.

The damages obtainable under each theory of product liability recovery strongly influence a plaintiff's strategy. Here, we describe the major kinds of damages awarded in product liability cases, along with the theories under which each can be recovered. One lawsuit may involve claims for all these sorts of damages.

 LO20-10 Explain what is normally necessary in order for punitive damages to be awarded in a product liability case.

1. *Basis-of-the-bargain damages.* Buyers of defective goods have not received full value for the goods' purchase price. The resulting loss, usually called basis-of-the-bargain damages or direct economic loss, is the value of the goods as promised under the contract, minus the value of the goods as received. (For an example, see the *Lincoln Composites* case, which appears later in the chapter.)

Basis-of-the-bargain damages are almost never awarded in tort cases. In express and implied warranty cases, however, basis-of-the-bargain damages are recoverable where there was *privity of contract* (a direct contractual relation) between the plaintiff and the defendant. As discussed in the next section, however, only occasionally will a warranty plaintiff who lacks privity with the defendant obtain basis-of-the-bargain damages. Such recoveries most often occur where an express warranty was made to a remote plaintiff through advertising, brochures, or labels.

2. *Consequential damages.* Consequential damages include personal injury, property damage (harm to the plaintiff's property other than the product at issue), and indirect economic loss (e.g., lost profits or diminished business reputation) resulting from a product defect. Consequential damages also include noneconomic loss—for example, pain and suffering, physical impairment, mental distress, loss of enjoyment of life, loss of companionship or consortium, inconvenience, and disfigurement (as opposed to more readily quantifiable damages such as the dollar amounts of medical bills). As the just-noted examples suggest, noneconomic loss usually is part of a plaintiff's personal injury claim. In recent years, some states have limited noneconomic loss recoveries by placing a dollar cap on them.

The tort theories of recovery—negligence and strict liability—permit claims for personal injury and property damage. The type of harm experienced by the plaintiff can be a factor in the determination of whether the case can proceed on a tort theory.

Plaintiffs in tort cases normally can recover for personal injury and property damage. Recoveries for foreseeable indirect economic loss sometimes are allowed.

In express and implied warranty cases where *privity exists* between the plaintiff and the defendant, the plaintiff can recover for (1) personal injury and property damage, if either proximately resulted from the breach of warranty, and (2) indirect economic loss, if the defendant had reason to know that this was likely. As discussed in the next section, a UCC plaintiff who *lacks privity* with the defendant has a reasonably good chance of recovering for personal injury or property damage. Recovery for indirect economic loss is rare because remote sellers usually cannot foresee such losses.

3. *Punitive damages.* Unlike the compensatory damages discussed above, punitive damages are not designed to compensate the plaintiff for harms suffered (even though the plaintiff typically becomes entitled to collect any punitive damages assessed against the defendant). Punitive damages are intended to punish defendants who have acted in an especially outrageous fashion, and to deter them and others from so acting in the future. Of the various standards for awarding punitive damages, probably the most common is the defendant's conscious or reckless disregard for the safety of those likely to be affected by the goods. Examples include concealment of known product hazards, knowing violation of government or industry product safety standards, failure to correct known dangerous defects, and grossly inadequate product testing or quality control procedures.

In view of their perceived frequency, size, and effect on business and the economy, punitive damages were targeted for some states' tort reform efforts during the 1980s and 1990s. The approaches taken by the resulting statutes vary. Some set the standards for punitive damage assessment and the plaintiff's burden of proof; some articulate factors courts should consider when ruling on punitive damage awards; and some create special procedures for punitive damage determinations. A number of states have also limited the size of punitive damage recoveries, usually by restricting them to some multiple of the plaintiff's compensatory damages or by putting a flat dollar cap on them. Moreover, decisions of the U.S. Supreme Court have revealed that constitutional concerns may be implicated by a punitive damages award that does not bear a reasonable relation to the amount of compensatory damages awarded.

Assuming that the standards just described have been met, punitive damages are recoverable in tort cases. Because of the traditional rule that punitive damages are not available in contract cases, they seldom are awarded in express and implied warranty cases.

However, in recent years enormous punitive damages have been awarded by some juries. A Philadelphia jury ordered Johnson & Johnson to pay $8 billion in punitive damages when it found that the company failed to warn males that taking the drug Risperdal could result in the development of female breast tissue. This award was later reduced by the judge to $6.8 million. In another blockbuster punitive damages award, a jury in Oakland, California, ordered Monsanto to pay a couple more than $2 billion in damages after concluding that its Roundup week killer had caused the couple to develop non-Hodgkin's lymphoma.

The No-Privity Defense

 LO20-11 Explain the privity doctrine's lack of role in tort cases and its partial role in warranty-based cases.

Today, defective products often move through long chains of distribution before reaching the person they harm. This means that a product liability plaintiff often has not dealt directly with the party ultimately responsible for her losses. For example, in a chain of distribution involving defective component parts, the parts may move *vertically* from their manufacturer to the manufacturer of a product in which those parts are used, and then to a wholesaler and a retailer before reaching the eventual buyer. The defect's consequences may move *horizontally* as well, affecting members of the buyer's family, guests in her home, and even bystanders. If the buyer or one of these parties suffers loss because of the defect in the component parts, may she successfully sue the component parts manufacturer or any other party in the vertical chain of distribution with whom she did not directly deal?

Such cases were unlikely to succeed under 19th-century law. At that time, there was no recovery for defective goods without privity of contract between the plaintiff and the defendant. In many such cases, a buyer would have been required to sue his dealer. If the buyer was successful, the retailer might have sued the wholesaler, and so on up the chain. For various reasons, the party ultimately responsible for the defect often escaped liability.

Tort Cases By now, the old no-liability-outside-privity rule effectively has been eliminated in tort cases. It has no effect in strict liability cases, where even bystanders can recover against remote manufacturers. In negligence cases, a plaintiff generally recovers against a remote defendant if the plaintiff's loss was a reasonably foreseeable consequence of the defect. Depending on the circumstances, therefore, bystanders and other distant parties may recover in a negligence case against a manufacturer. The *Restatement (Third)* suggests that tort principles should govern the privity determination. This should mean a test of reasonable foreseeability in most instances.

Warranty Cases The no-privity defense retains some vitality in UCC cases. Unfortunately, the law on this subject is complex and confusing. Under the UCC, the privity question is formally governed by § 2-318, which comes in three alternative versions. Section 2-318's language, however, is a less-than-reliable guide to the courts' actual behavior in UCC privity cases.

UCC § 2-318 Alternative A to § 2-318 states that a seller's express or implied warranty runs to natural persons in the family or household of *his* (the seller's) buyer and to guests in his buyer's home, if they suffer personal injury and if it was reasonable to expect that they might use, consume, or be affected by the goods sold. On its face, Alternative A does little to undermine the traditional no-privity defense.

Alternatives B and C go much further. Alternative B extends the seller's express or implied warranty to any natural person who has suffered personal injury, if it was reasonable to expect that this person would use, consume, or be affected by the goods. Alternative C is much the same, but it extends the warranty to any person (not just natural persons) and to those suffering injury in general (not just personal injury). If the reasonable-to-expect test is met, these two provisions should extend the warranty to many remote parties, including bystanders.

Departures from § 2-318 For various reasons, § 2-318's literal language sometimes has little relevance in UCC privity cases. Some states have adopted privity statutes that differ from any version of § 2-318. One of the comments to § 2-318, moreover, allows courts to extend liability beyond what the section expressly permits. Finally, versions B and C are fairly open-ended as written. The plaintiff's ability to recover outside privity in warranty cases thus varies from state to state and situation to situation. The most important factors affecting resolution of this question are:

1. Whether it is *reasonably foreseeable* that a party such as the plaintiff would be harmed by the product defect in question.

2. The *status of the plaintiff*. On average, consumers and other natural persons fare better outside privity than do corporations and other business concerns.

3. The *type of damages* the plaintiff has suffered. In general, remote plaintiffs are (*a*) most likely to recover for personal injury, (*b*) somewhat less likely to recover for property damage, (*c*) occasionally able to obtain basis-of-the-bargain damages, and (*d*) seldom able to recover for indirect economic loss. Recall from the previous section that a remote plaintiff is most likely to receive basis-of-the-bargain damages where an express warranty was made to her through advertising, brochures, or labels.

Disclaimers and Remedy Limitations

 Explain what is necessary for effective disclaimers of the respective implied warranties.

A product liability **disclaimer** is a clause in the sales contract whereby the seller attempts to eliminate *liability* it might otherwise have under the theories of recovery described earlier in the chapter. A remedy limitation is a clause attempting to block recovery of certain *damages*. If a disclaimer is effective, no damages of any sort are recoverable under the legal theory attacked by the disclaimer. A successful remedy limitation prevents the plaintiff from recovering certain types of damages but does not attack the plaintiff's theory of recovery. Damages not excluded still may be recovered because the theory is left intact.

The main justification for enforcing disclaimers and remedy limitations is freedom of contract. Why, however, would any rational contracting party freely accept a disclaimer or remedy limitation? Because sellers need not insure against lawsuits for defective goods accompanied by an effective disclaimer or remedy limitation, they should be able to sell those goods more cheaply. Thus, enforcing such clauses allows buyers to obtain a lower price by accepting the economic risk of

a product defect. For purchases by ordinary consumers and other unsophisticated buyers, however, this argument often is illusory. Sellers normally present the disclaimer or remedy limitation in a standardized, take-it-or-leave-it fashion. It is also doubtful whether many consumers read disclaimers and remedy limitations at the time of purchase, or would comprehend them if they did read them. As a result, there is little or no genuine bargaining over disclaimers or remedy limitations in consumer situations. Instead, they are effectively dictated by a seller with superior size and organization. These observations, however, are less valid when the buyer is a business entity with the capability to engage in genuine bargaining with sellers.

Because the realities surrounding the sale differ from situation to situation, and because some theories of recovery are more hospitable to contractual limitation than others, the law on product liability disclaimers and remedy limitations is complicated. We begin by discussing implied warranty disclaimers. Then we examine disclaimers of express warranty liability, negligence liability, strict liability, and liability under the *Restatement (Third)*, before considering remedy limitations separately.

Implied Warranty Disclaimers

The Basic Tests of UCC § 2-316(2) UCC § 2-316(2) makes it relatively easy for sellers to disclaim the implied warranties of merchantability and fitness for a particular purpose. The section states that to exclude or modify the implied warranty of merchantability, a seller must (1) use the word *merchantability* and (2) make the disclaimer conspicuous if it is written. To exclude or modify the implied warranty of fitness, a seller must (1) use a writing and (2) make the disclaimer conspicuous. A disclaimer is conspicuous if it is written so that a reasonable person ought to have noticed it. Capital letters, larger type, contrasting type, and contrasting colors usually suffice.

Unlike the fitness warranty disclaimer, a disclaimer of the implied warranty of merchantability can be oral. Although disclaimers of the latter warranty must use the word *merchantability*, no special language is needed to disclaim the implied warranty of fitness. For example, a conspicuous written statement that "THERE ARE NO WARRANTIES THAT EXTEND BEYOND THE DESCRIPTION ON THE FACE HEREOF" disclaims the implied warranty of fitness but not the implied warranty of merchantability.

Other Ways to Disclaim Implied Warranties: § 2-316(3) According to UCC § 2-316(3)(a), sellers may also disclaim either implied warranty by using such terms as "with all faults," "as is," and "as they stand." Some courts have held that these terms must be conspicuous to be effective as disclaimers. Other courts have allowed such terms to be effective disclaimers only in sales of used goods. The *Wilke* case, which follows, illustrates the application of an "as is" disclaimer.

UCC § 2-316(3)(b) describes two situations in which the buyer's *inspection* of the goods or her *refusal to inspect* may operate as a disclaimer. If a buyer examines the goods before the sale and fails to discover a defect that should have been reasonably apparent to her, there can be no implied warranty claim based on that defect. Also, if a seller requests that the buyer examine the goods and the buyer refuses, the buyer cannot base an implied warranty claim on a defect that would have been reasonably apparent had she made the inspection. The definition of a reasonably apparent defect varies with the buyer's expertise. Unless the defect is blatantly obvious, ordinary consumers have little to fear from § 2-316(3)(b).

Finally, UCC § 2-316(3)(c) says that an implied warranty may be excluded or modified by *course of dealing* (the parties' previous conduct), *course of performance* (the parties' previous conduct under the same contract), or *usage of trade* (any practice regularly observed in the trade). For example, if it is accepted in the local cattle trade that buyers who inspect the seller's cattle and reject certain animals must accept all defects in the cattle actually purchased, such buyers cannot mount an implied warranty claim regarding those defects.

Unconscionable Disclaimers From the previous discussion, it seems that any seller who retains a competent attorney can escape implied warranty liability at will. A seller's ability to disclaim implied warranties sometimes is restricted, however, by the doctrine of **unconscionability** established by UCC § 2-302 and discussed in Chapter 15. In appropriate instances, courts may apply § 2-302's unconscionability standards to implied warranty disclaimers even though those disclaimers satisfy UCC § 2-316(2). Despite a growing willingness to protect smaller firms that deal with corporate giants, however, courts still tend to reject unconscionability claims where business parties have contracted in a commercial context. Implied warranty disclaimers are more likely to be declared unconscionable in personal injury cases brought by ordinary consumers.

In the *Wilke* case, the court upholds an implied warranty disclaimer and declines to hold that the disclaimer violated public policy even though one of the plaintiffs suffered personal injury. The court emphasizes, however, that the implied warranty disclaimer would not protect the defendant against possible liability for negligent failure to inspect the product (there, a van) before selling it to the plaintiffs.

Wilke v. Woodhouse Ford, Inc.   774 N.W.2d 370 (Neb. 2009)

Elizabeth and Mark Wilke purchased a used 2002 Ford Econoline cargo van from Woodhouse Ford, Inc. in 2004. Besides stating that the van was used, the parties' purchase agreement stated in bold type that the van was being sold "AS IS" and "WITHOUT ANY WARRANTY." The agreement further provided, in a smaller font, that "DEALER HEREBY EXPRESSLY DISCLAIMS ALL WARRANTIES, EXPRESS OR IMPLIED, INCLUDING ANY IMPLIED WARRANTIES OF MERCHANTABILITY OR FITNESS FOR A PARTICULAR PURPOSE." Woodhouse made no affirmative representations to the Wilkes regarding the condition or quality of the van.

Immediately after purchasing the van, the Wilkes drove to the home of a friend. Mark parked the van in the friend's driveway, which was slightly sloped. Mark did not apply the emergency brake after he parked the van. [In a deposition provided in connection with the litigation described below,] he testified that after parking the van, he took the key out of the ignition and put the key in his pocket. Elizabeth testified in her deposition that she did not hear any chimes or buzzers indicating that the key had been left in the ignition.

After Mark parked the van, the Wilkes began showing it to their friend. Mark opened the driver's-side door and the two doors in the back of the van. Elizabeth testified in her deposition that as they were talking to their friend, she saw their daughter climbing into the driver's seat. Elizabeth immediately screamed for her daughter to get down and ran to the driver's side of the van.

Elizabeth testified that as she approached the side of the van, she saw her daughter with her left hand on the steering wheel and her right hand on the gearshift. Elizabeth heard a "clunk," and then the van started rolling backward. As the van rolled backward, Elizabeth was hit by the open door. The force caused her to fall backward. Her head struck the pavement and the van's left front tire rolled over her right foot and thigh. Mark managed to stop the van from rolling by entering the van through the open back doors, diving for the brake pedal, and depressing it with his hand. Elizabeth was taken by ambulance to a hospital. Mark testified in his deposition that he did not know which gear the van was in as it rolled over Elizabeth, but that he knew the gearshift was not "aligned with the P" [for "park"].

A deputy sheriff who responded to a call regarding the accident filed a report stating that "Vehicle was discovered to have a defective shift lever that was able to be shifted out of park mode without depressing brake pedal." Donald Jeffers, an automotive engineering consultant and the Wilkes's expert witness, conducted an investigation of the accident and prepared a report on his findings. According to the Federal Motor Vehicle Safety Standards relied upon by Jeffers, vehicles that have an automatic transmission with a "park" position must "'prevent removal of the key unless the transmission or transmission shift lever is locked in "park" as the direct result of removing the key.'" The purpose of this feature is "'to reduce the incidence of crashes resulting from the rollaway of parked vehicles with automatic transmissions as a result of children moving the shift mechanism out of the "park" position.'"

After the accident, Elizabeth's father took the van to Woodhouse for the first of two repairs. Woodhouse adjusted the linkage on the gearshift in case it was not going into "park" completely. A Woodhouse employee involved in the repair testified in his deposition that there was excessive play in the gearshift. He stated that "[y]ou could move the lever up and down excessively but not actually physically get it out of gear." He further testified that although there was free play in the gearshift, the transmission would not shift from park to reverse without the key in the ignition.

According to Mark, the transmission continued to shift out of park without the key in the ignition after the first Woodhouse repair. He therefore returned the van to Woodhouse for further repair. Even though Woodhouse employees reportedly could not duplicate the complained-about problem of being able to shift the van out of park without the key in the ignition and the brake depressed, they replaced the bushings and adjusted the shifter cable. Mark testified that after the second repair, he could not get the gearshift to come out of park without the key in the ignition and the brake pedal depressed. The gearshift on the van thus seemed to work properly after the second repair.

Based on his review and investigation, Jeffers concluded that "[t]hree separate failure modes caused and contributed" to the accident. According to his report, the brake shift interlock system failed, the transmission shift cable was misadjusted, and the key shift interlock failed or malfunctioned.

It was undisputed that the van was not inspected by Woodhouse employees prior to the Wilkes's purchase. Woodhouse employees explained in deposition testimony that because of the high volume of vehicles traded in, there are times when the service department does not inspect used vehicles before they are resold.

The Wilkes sued Woodhouse in a Nebraska district court in an effort to obtain suitable compensatory damages, including damages for Elizabeth's injuries. They pleaded two theories: that the van was unmerchantable and that Woodhouse therefore breached the UCC's implied warranty of merchantability; and that Woodhouse negligently failed to inspect the van prior to selling it. Woodhouse sought summary judgment, maintaining that it had effectively disclaimed the implied warranty of merchantability and that the plaintiff's negligence claim was without merit. The district court granted Woodhouse summary judgment, and the Wilkes appealed. The Supreme Court of Nebraska moved the case to its docket from that of the state's intermediate court of appeals pursuant to statutory authority permitting the Supreme Court to do so in order to regulate the caseload of the intermediate appellate court.

McCormack, Judge

This case presents two issues: (1) whether a car dealer can exclude through the use of an "as is" clause the implied warranty of merchantability, and (2) whether a car dealer has a duty to inspect used vehicles for safety defects prior to selling the vehicle.

Implied Warranty of Merchantability Claim

The Wilkes' breach of warranty claim arises from the law of sales as codified in the Uniform Commercial Code (UCC). Under the UCC, warranties relating to goods sold can be either express or implied. Under UCC § 2-314:

(1) Unless excluded or modified (section 2-316), a warranty that the goods shall be merchantable is implied in a contract for their sale if the seller is a merchant with respect to goods of that kind. . . .

(2) Goods to be merchantable must be at least such as. . . .

(c) are fit for the ordinary purposes for which such goods are used[.]

The Wilkes contend that Woodhouse breached [the implied] warranty of merchantability with respect to the van it sold to them.

As noted in the statutory language defining an implied warranty of merchantability, it exists "unless excluded or modified." Section 2-316(3)(a) provides: "[U]nless the circumstances indicate otherwise, all implied warranties are excluded by expressions like 'as is,' 'with all faults' or other language which in common understanding calls the buyer's attention to the exclusion of warranties and makes plain that there is no implied warranty." The purchase agreement evidencing the sale of the van from Woodhouse to the Wilkes included a conspicuous statement that it was sold "as is," "without any warranty either expressed or implied," and further stated that Woodhouse was disclaiming any implied warranty of merchantability. This language met the requirements of § 2-316(2) and (3)(a) for excluding an implied warranty of merchantability.

The Wilkes argue, however, that exclusion of an implied warranty of merchantability with respect to a safety defect would violate public policy and therefore should not be enforced by a court. In support of their argument, the Wilkes cite to general propositions defining public policy as restrictions on the freedom to contract in order to prevent acts injurious to the public. But we have also explained that it is the function of the legislature, through the enactment of statutes, to declare what is the law and public policy of this state. And our legislature has provided, in § 2-316, that the implied warranty of merchantability may be disclaimed or excluded.

The provisions of the UCC which permit a seller to exclude warranties make no exception for warranties relating to the safety of the product. We conclude that the use of an "as is" clause to exclude the implied warranty of merchantability cannot be against the public policy of this state when it mirrors the statutory requirements specifically allowing for such exclusion. Section 2-316 is the legislature's clear expression of the public policy of this state. Therefore, the purchase agreement effectively disclaimed and excluded any implied warranties for the vehicle. As such, the district court properly entered summary judgment in favor of Woodhouse on the Wilkes' cause of action for breach of the implied warranty of merchantability.

Negligence Claim

The Wilkes also alleged a theory of recovery based on negligence. A negligence claim focuses on the seller's conduct. A common law duty exists to use due care so as not to negligently injure another person. The absence of implied warranties [from the parties' transaction] does not absolve Woodhouse from any potential liability resulting from its failure to exercise reasonable care. In other words, nothing in the statutes dealing with exclusion of implied warranties allows for the exclusion of tort liability.

The Wilkes alleged that Woodhouse was negligent because it failed to reasonably inspect the van for safety defects prior to its sale and that but for such negligence, Elizabeth would not have sustained her injuries by being run over by the van. Ordinary negligence is defined as the doing of something that a reasonably careful person would not do under similar circumstances, or the failing to do something that a reasonably careful person would do under similar circumstances. In order to prevail in a negligence action, there must be a legal duty on the part of the defendant to protect the plaintiff from injury, a failure to discharge that duty, and damage proximately caused by the failure to discharge that duty.

Woodhouse first maintains that it had no duty to inspect the van prior to its sale. When determining whether a legal duty exists, a court employs a risk-utility test concerning (1) the magnitude of the risk, (2) the relationship of the parties, (3) the nature of the attendant risk, (4) the opportunity and ability to exercise care, (5) the foreseeability of the harm, and (6) the policy interest in the proposed solution.

The existence of a duty and the identification of the applicable standard of care are questions of law, but the ultimate determination of whether a party deviated from the standard of care and was therefore negligent is a question of fact. To resolve the issue, a finder of fact must determine what conduct the standard of care would require under the particular circumstances presented by the evidence and whether the conduct of the alleged tortfeasor conformed with the standard.

We have never before addressed whether a used-car dealer has a duty to its customers to inspect vehicles for safety defects before they are sold. Most courts which have considered the issue have recognized a limited duty on the part of the dealer to inspect for patent safety defects existing at the time of sale. For example, Minnesota courts have held that the seller of a used vehicle intended for use upon the public highways has a duty to the public using such highways to exercise reasonable care in supplying the purchaser with a vehicle which will not constitute a menace or source of danger, so that liability attaches to the seller for injuries which are the result of patent defects in the vehicle, or defects which could have been discovered in the exercise of reasonable care. Ohio courts have held that even when a dealer sells a used vehicle "as is," the dealer has a duty to exercise reasonable care in examining the vehicle to discover defects which would make the vehicle dangerous to users or those who might come in contact with them, and upon discovery, to correct those defects or at least give warning to the purchaser. The Montana Supreme Court has held that a used-car dealer had a duty to inspect a vehicle for safety defects prior to sale, notwithstanding the fact that the vehicle was sold "as is." The court reasoned:

> When the ordinary person purchases a car "as is," he expects to have to perform certain repairs to keep the car in good condition. He does not expect to purchase a death trap. Public policy requires a used car dealer to inspect the cars he sells and to make sure they are in safe, working condition. This duty cannot be waived by the use of a magic talisman in the form of an "as is" provision.

But courts which have recognized a duty on the part of used car dealers to inspect for safety defects prior to sale have also emphasized that the duty is limited. Courts have stated that used-car dealers are not insurers and therefore are not liable for latent defects in the vehicle. Courts have limited the duty to inspect for patent defects affecting the minimum essentials for safe operation of the vehicle. Dealers are not required to disassemble the vehicle to inspect for latent defects, and they are not responsible for the continuing safety of the vehicles they sell.

Applying our risk-utility test for the existence of a legal duty to use reasonable care, we conclude that there is a relatively great magnitude of risk of injury in the circumstance where an unknowing buyer drives off the dealer's lot in a used vehicle which has a patent safety defect, such as defective brakes or steering. The dealer is better equipped than the purchaser to perceive such a defect before it causes harm. The nature of the risk is such that personal injury or death could result not only with respect to the purchaser of the defective vehicle, but to other members of the motoring public. The dealer has the earliest opportunity to discover and repair a patent safety defect in a used vehicle. An unknown safety defect existing at the time of sale poses foreseeable harm to the purchaser and the general public, and there exists a policy interest in requiring reasonable conduct on the part of the dealer to prevent such harm.

We, therefore, hold that a commercial dealer of used vehicles intended for use on public streets and highways has a duty to conduct a reasonable inspection of the vehicle prior to sale in order to determine whether there are any patent defects existing at the time of sale which would make the vehicle unsafe for ordinary operation and, upon discovery of such a defect, to either repair it or warn a prospective purchaser of its existence. The dealer has no duty to disassemble the vehicle to discover latent defects or to anticipate the future development of safety defects which do not exist at the time of sale. The tort duty we recognize today is not affected by a valid disclaimer or exclusion of UCC warranties, because such contractual provisions do not absolve a seller from exercising reasonable care to prevent foreseeable harm. Tort liability is not based upon representations or warranties. Rather, it is based upon a duty imposed by the law upon one who may foresee that his or her actions or failure to act may result in injury to others.

That being the case, whether or not the court properly entered summary judgment in favor of Woodhouse depends upon whether Woodhouse breached this duty. It is undisputed that Woodhouse did not inspect the van prior to selling it. However, that alone does not rise to the level of a breach of the applicable standard of care, because its duty extends only to patent, not to latent, defects. Thus, a breach of duty occurred if a reasonable inspection would have revealed the alleged defect in the gearshift. This is a question of fact that must be decided by the fact finder. The record presents conflicting testimony as to whether the gearshift malfunctioned occasionally or regularly. As such, there is a genuine issue of material fact (and thus a jury question as to) whether a reasonable inspection of the van would have revealed any alleged defect.

Woodhouse argues that even if there is a duty that was breached, there is no material issue of fact that Woodhouse was not the proximate cause of the accident. Determination of causation is, ordinarily, a matter for the trier of fact. To establish proximate cause, the plaintiff must meet three basic requirements:

(1) Without the negligent action, the injury would not have occurred, commonly known as the "but for" rule; (2) the injury was a natural and probable result of the negligence; and (3) there was no efficient intervening cause.

Assuming that Woodhouse breached its duty to reasonably inspect, Woodhouse proximately caused the vehicle to be placed into the hands of the Wilkes with a defect that could have been discovered by a reasonable inspection. This defect undoubtedly existed at the time of sale. And it is undisputed that the van was not altered in any way prior to the incident. But Woodhouse first argues that Mark's failure to set the parking brake was the proximate cause of the accident. In doing so, however, Woodhouse confuses the concepts of proximate causation and contributory negligence. Woodhouse is really arguing that Mark was contributorily negligent by not using the parking brake. Whether or not the Wilkes were contributorily negligent to the point where recovery is precluded is a question for the trier of fact, and Woodhouse's allegations regarding Mark's failure to implement the parking brake are insufficient to warrant summary judgment in Woodhouse's favor.

Second, Woodhouse argues that the Wilkes' daughter was the proximate cause of the accident because she manipulated the gearshift, causing the accident. Essentially, Woodhouse is arguing that viewing the facts in the light most favorable to the Wilkes, the daughter's actions constituted an efficient intervening cause, warranting judgment as a matter of law in its favor. An efficient intervening cause is new and independent conduct of a third person, which itself is a proximate cause of the injury in question and breaks the causal connection between the original conduct and the injury. But if a third party's negligence is reasonably foreseeable, then the third party's negligence is not an efficient intervening cause as a matter of law. A jury could find that it is foreseeable that an accident could occur if a young child was able to take the vehicle out of park without the key in the ignition and the brake pedal depressed.

We conclude that Woodhouse effectively disclaimed all implied warranties, including the warranty of merchantability. But we also conclude that commercial dealers of used vehicles have a duty to exercise reasonable care to discover any existing safety defects that are patent or discoverable in the exercise of reasonable care or through reasonable inspection. Because there are genuine issues of material fact as to whether Woodhouse breached its duty of care and, if so, whether Woodhouse's breach was the proximate cause of Elizabeth's injuries, we conclude that the district court incorrectly granted summary judgment in favor of Woodhouse on the Wilkes' negligence claim.

District court's grant of summary judgment in favor of Woodhouse affirmed as to breach of implied warranty of merchantability claim but reversed as to negligence claim; case remanded for further proceedings.

The Impact of Magnuson-Moss The Magnuson-Moss Act also limits a seller's ability to disclaim implied warranties. If a seller gives a consumer a full warranty on consumer goods whose price exceeds $10, the seller may not disclaim, modify, or limit the duration of any implied warranty. If a limited warranty is given, the seller may not disclaim or modify any implied warranty but may limit its duration to the duration of the limited warranty if this is done conspicuously and if the limitation is not unconscionable. These are significant limitations on a seller's power to disclaim implied warranties. Presumably, however, a seller still can disclaim by refusing to give a written warranty while placing the disclaimer on some other writing.

Express Warranty Disclaimers UCC § 2-316(1) says that an express warranty and a disclaimer should be read consistently if possible, but that the disclaimer must yield if such a reading is unreasonable. Because it normally is unreasonable for a seller to exclude with one hand what he has freely and openly promised with the other, it is quite difficult to disclaim an express warranty.

Disclaimers of Tort Liability Disclaimers of negligence liability and strict liability are usually ineffective in cases involving ordinary consumers. However, some courts enforce such disclaimers where both parties are business entities that (1) dealt in a commercial setting, (2) had relatively equal bargaining power, (3) bargained over the product's specifications, and (4) negotiated the risk of loss from product defects (e.g., the disclaimer itself). Even though it has a provision that seems to bar all disclaimers, the same should be true under the *Restatement (Third)*.

Limitation of Remedies In view of the expense they can create for sellers, consequential damages are the usual target of remedy limitations. When a limitation of consequential damages succeeds, buyers of the product may suffer. For example, suppose that Dillman buys a computer system for $20,000 under a contract that excludes consequential damages and limits the buyer's remedies to the repair or replacement of defective parts. Suppose also that the system never works properly, causing Dillman to suffer $10,000 in lost profits. If the remedy limitation is enforceable, Dillman could only have the system replaced or repaired by the seller and could not recover his $10,000 in consequential damages.

In tort cases, the tests for the enforceability of remedy limitations resemble the previous tests for tort liability disclaimers. Under the UCC, however, the standards for remedy limitations differ from those for disclaimers. UCC § 2-719 allows the limitation of consequential damages in express and implied warranty cases unless the limitation of remedy "fails of its essential purpose" or is unconscionable. The section adds that a limitation of consequential damages is very likely to be unconscionable where the sale is for *consumer goods* and the plaintiff has suffered *personal injury*. Where the loss is "commercial," however, the limitation may or may not be unconscionable.

Whether a limitation of remedy "fails of its essential purpose" depends on all of the relevant facts and circumstances. For instance, a court concluded that a limitation of remedy in a contract for the sale of a motor home failed of its essential purpose when a collection of problems caused the motor home to be out of service for 162 days during the first year after the buyer purchased it.[5]

In the *Lincoln Composites* case, which follows, the court considers whether a limited remedy provision calling for repair or replacement of fire-detection tubing failed of its essential purpose and therefore entitled the plaintiff to pursue damages remedies.

Defenses

Various matters—for example, the absence of privity or a valid disclaimer—can be considered defenses to a product liability suit. Here, however, our initial concern is with product liability defenses that involve the plaintiff's behavior. Although the *Restatement (Third)* has a "comparative responsibility" provision that apportions liability among the plaintiff, the seller, and distributors, and various states have similar rules, the following discussion is limited to two-party situations.

The Traditional Defenses Traditionally, the three main defenses in a product liability suit have been the overlapping trio of product misuse, assumption of risk, and contributory negligence. Product misuse (or abnormal use) occurs when the plaintiff uses the product in some unusual, unforeseeable way, and this causes the loss for which he sues. Examples include ignoring the manufacturer's instructions, mishandling the product, and using the product for purposes for which it was not intended. If, however, the defendant had reason to foresee the misuse and failed to take reasonable precautions against it, there is no defense. Product misuse traditionally has been a defense in warranty, negligence, and strict liability cases.

---

[5]*Pack v. Damon Corp.*, 2006 U.S. App. LEXIS 2303 (6th Cir. Jan.5, 2006).

CYBERLAW IN ACTION

In earlier chapters, you learned about shrinkwrap and clickwrap contracts, which are often used in sales of computer hardware and licenses of software and in establishing terms of use for access to networks and websites. It is extremely common for these shrinkwrap or clickwrap contracts to contain warranty disclaimers and limitation of remedy clauses. For some examples of how these disclaimers and limitations of remedy look, see *Warranty and Liability Disclaimer Clauses in Current Shrinkwrap and Clickwrap Contracts,* **www.cptech.org/ecom/ucita/licenses/liability.html**.

The courts that have considered the enforceability of clickwrap or shrinkwrap warranty disclaimers or limitations of remedy have upheld them. For example, in *M. A. Mortenson Company, Inc. v. Timberline Software Corp.*, 998 P.2d 305 (Wash. 2000), Mortenson, a general contractor, purchased Timberline's licensed software and used it to prepare a construction bid. Mortenson later discovered that its bid was $1.95 million too low because of a malfunction of the software. When Mortenson sued Timberline and others for breach of warranty, Timberline asserted that the limitation of remedies clause contained in the software license, which limited Mortenson's remedies to the purchase price of the software, prevented Mortenson from recovering any consequential damages caused by a defect in the software. Although Mortenson contended that it never saw or agreed to the terms of the license agreement, the Washington Supreme Court held that the terms of the license became part of the parties' contract. The terms were set forth or referenced in various places, such as the shrinkwrap packaging for the program disks, the software manuals, and the protection devices for the software. Applying the principle that limitations of remedy are generally enforceable unless they are unconscionable, the court found the limitation of remedies clause to be enforceable.

Lincoln Composites, Inc. v. Firetrace USA, LLC   825 F.3d 453 (8th Cir. 2016)

Lincoln Composites, Inc. manufactures composite tanks for the storage and transport of natural gas in places where pipelines are unavailable. Firetrace USA, LLC makes custom-designed fire suppression systems that detect and suppress fires. In a series of transactions, Lincoln purchased fire-detection tubing from Firetrace. Lincoln then installed this tubing in its Titan Module tanks. There was no dispute that through these transactions, the parties entered into a contract for the purchase and delivery of Firetrace's tubing. Some of the tubing later proved to be defective. Despite Firetrace's repeated attempts to fix the defect, the tubing failed, resulting in natural gas being vented into the air when there was not a fire. After 18 months, Lincoln decided that it could no longer use the Firetrace tubing and demanded that Firetrace refund the purchase price. Firetrace refused, contending that the contract was governed by Firetrace's written terms and conditions, which limited remedies to repair or replacement of the tubing.

Lincoln then sued Firetrace in Nebraska state court on various grounds, including breach of express warranty. Firetrace removed the case to federal court. At the conclusion of the trial in the U.S. District Court for the District of Nebraska, the jury returned a verdict in favor of Lincoln. Having concluded that Firetrace breached an express warranty to Lincoln, the jury awarded damages in the amount of $920,227.76. Firetrace moved for a new trial on the merits and either a new trial on damages or a remittitur on damages (i.e., a reduction in the damages amount). When the federal district court denied Firetrace's post-trial motions, Firetrace appealed to the U.S. Court of Appeals for the Eighth Circuit.

Kelly, Circuit Judge

Firetrace first asserts it is entitled to a new trial because the jury's finding that it breached an express warranty to Lincoln is against the weight of the evidence. "When the basis of the motion for a new trial is that the jury's verdict is against the weight of the evidence, the district court's denial of the motion is virtually unassailable on appeal." [Citation omitted.] Because this is a diversity action, we apply the substantive law of the forum state, in this case, Nebraska. Under Nebraska law, the existence and scope of an express warranty is one of fact. [The jury resolved this question by determining that an express warranty was both made and breached. Moreover, the district court's denial of the new trial motion suggests that the court regarded the jury's conclusions as supported by the evidentiary record. On appeal, the Eighth Circuit will not second-guess that conclusion.]

[Although Firetrace does not agree that it breached an express warranty, Firetrace agrees that its written contract terms] provided an express warranty. [Firetrace stresses, however, that] upon a breach of the express warranty, Firetrace's terms limited

Lincoln's remedies to repair or replacement of any defective tubing. [Therefore, Firetrace contends, Lincoln should not have been awarded damages.]

[Despite their disagreements over the outcome in the district court], the parties agree that by finding that Firetrace breached an express warranty to Lincoln and awarding damages to Lincoln, the jury must have decided . . . that the exclusive repair or replace remedy failed of its essential purpose, making a remedy of damages available. Firetrace argues that [the jury] erroneously concluded that Firetrace's limited remedy of repair or replace failed of its essential purpose. Nebraska law allows a seller to establish exclusive limited warranties, as well as to limit the availability of damages. *See* Neb. UCC § 2-719. But, "[w]here circumstances cause an exclusive or limited remedy to fail of its essential purpose, remedy may be had as provided in this act." *Id.* As explained in the comments to § 2-719, "where an apparently fair and reasonable clause because of circumstances fails in its purpose or operates to deprive either party of the substantial value of the bargain, it must give way to the general remedy provisions of this article." *Id.* cmt. 1. "Where a seller is given a reasonable chance to correct defects and the equipment still fails to function properly, the limited remedy of repair or replacement of defective products fails of its essential purpose." *Id.* If this happens, the buyer may invoke any remedies available under the UCC, including damages. *Id.*

The district court concluded that a reasonable jury could find that Firetrace's limited remedy of repair or replacement failed of its essential purpose when Firetrace was not able to repair the tubing properly within a reasonable time. Don Baldwin, Lincoln's engineering director, testified that he worked on the Titan Modules beginning in 2008. Baldwin described the repeated failures of the tubing and Firetrace's multiple unsuccessful attempts, over the course of a year and a half, to provide tubing that did not fail. An expert in engineering and plastics testified about how and why the tubing failed. He testified that the failures were the result of manufacturing defects [and] that the Firetrace tubing still in Titan Modules out in the field also would fail at some point.

Whether Lincoln was deprived of the substantial value of its contract by Firetrace's limited remedy of repairing and replacing the tubing was a question for the jury. The district court did not abuse its discretion when it denied Firetrace's motion for a new trial because there was sufficient evidence for a reasonable jury to find that Firetrace's limited repair or replace remedy failed of its essential purpose.

Firetrace argues that it is entitled to a new trial because the district court erred in . . . its instructions to the jury. We generally review a district court's jury instructions for an abuse of discretion. Our review is limited to determining "whether the instructions, taken as a whole and viewed in the light of the evidence and applicable law, fairly and accurately submitted the issues to the jury." [Citation omitted.]

At the final instruction conference, the district court informed the parties it would instruct the jury as follows:

To show that the limited remedy of repair and replacement has failed of its essential purpose, Lincoln Composites must prove all of the following elements by the greater weight of the evidence:

1. That Lincoln Composites provided Firetrace with a reasonable opportunity to fix the defects in the tubing;

2. That despite Firetrace's attempts to fix the defects or provide replacement tubing, the tubing still failed to function properly; and

3. That this deprived Lincoln Composites of the substantial value of its contract with Firetrace.

It is for you to decide how many attempts were needed, and what was a reasonable time frame in which to remedy the defect, before the remedy would fail of its essential purpose, if it did.

[In deciding to give the above instruction, the court rejected Firetrace's proposed jury instruction. Firetrace's proposed instruction matched the above instruction in its introductory language and in itemized points 1, 2, and 3, but offered this different concluding sentence:]

The mere fact that a defect is not properly remedied after the first attempt, or even multiple attempts to repair or replace it does not mean the warranty failed its essential purpose. Additionally, if Defendant stands ready to perform, there is no failure of essential purpose, even though the buyer remains highly unsatisfied with the results obtained by the limited remedy. Finally, a repair or replace remedy does not fail of its essential purpose so long as repairs are made each time a defect arises.

Firetrace asserts that its proposed instruction more closely follows the law of Nebraska. We disagree. Although Nebraska law allows a seller to limit a buyer's remedies to repair and replacement, the Nebraska Supreme Court has stated that "[t]he purpose of an exclusive remedy of 'repair or replacement' from a buyer's viewpoint is to give him goods which conform to the contract within a reasonable time after a defect is discovered." *John Deere Co. v. Hand*, 319 N.W.2d 434, 437 (Neb. 1982). "Where the seller is given a reasonable chance to correct defects and the equipment still fails to function properly, the limited remedy of repair or replacement of defective parts fails of its essential purpose." *Id.*

The court's jury instruction was a correct statement of Nebraska law and recognized that the key issue for the jury to decide was whether Firetrace was given a reasonable amount of time in which to correct defects in the tubing. Accordingly, we conclude that the district court did not plainly err in not giving Firetrace's proposed instruction.

Firetrace argues that the district court erred by not granting its motion for a remittitur or new trial on damages, alleging Lincoln did not present sufficient evidence to support the amount of damages awarded by the jury. Under the Nebraska UCC, the measure of direct damages for the breach of an express warranty "is the difference at the time and place of acceptance between the value of the goods accepted and the value they would have had if they had been as warranted. . . ." Neb. UCC § 2-714(2). "The measure set forth in § 2-714 is the equivalent of what is known as the diminished value rule." *T.O. Haas Tire Co., Inc. v. Futura Coatings, Inc.*, 507 N.W.2d 297, 304 (Neb. Ct. App. 1993). A buyer asserting a breach of warranty under the UCC has the burden to prove damages. "[The buyer does not have to] prove damages with mathematical certainty, but the evidence must be sufficient to allow the trier of fact to estimate the actual damages with reasonable certainty." [Citation omitted.]

The jury found that the value of the tubing as warranted was $857,334.48 and that the value of the tubing as received was zero. Firetrace does not dispute the jury's conclusion of the value of the tubing as warranted, but argues Lincoln failed to prove that the tubing as received had no value. Firetrace claims the only evidence Lincoln offered to support its claim was the testimony of its President and CEO, John Schimenti. Schimenti testified that the tubing had no value to Lincoln. Firetrace argues that this evidence, by itself, was insufficient to support the jury's award. But Schimenti also testified that the [already installed tubing] had to be removed and that Lincoln would not charge customers for the removal.

Don Baldwin, an engineering director at Lincoln, also testified the tubing had no value to Lincoln because of "inadvertent releases"—that is, random releases of large amounts of natural gas into the atmosphere due to the tubing falsely "detecting" a fire that . . . would require evacuations of neighborhoods. Baldwin testified that Lincoln felt obligated to replace all the previously installed Firetrace tubing before it failed because of this risk. In addition, Lincoln's expert [witness] testified that he believed all of the remaining tubing would fail at some point.

Firetrace concedes that this testimony might demonstrate there was a latent defect in the tubing but asserts that it did not address the value of the tubing. Firetrace contends that it presented evidence from which a reasonable jury could find that most of the tubing had not failed, giving the tubing at least some

salvage value, and points out that Lincoln passed on the cost of the Firetrace tubing to its buyers. As the district court noted, however, the determination of whether even a low risk of failure rendered the tubing worthless to Lincoln was a question for the jury. "In determining whether to grant a new trial, a district judge is not free to reweigh the evidence and set aside the jury verdict merely because the jury could have drawn different inferences or conclusions or because judges feel that other results are more reasonable." [Citation omitted.] Firetrace's arguments to the jury may have been compelling, but the jury's verdict is not so against the great weight of the evidence as to rise to the level of a miscarriage of justice or so excessive as to shock the judicial conscience. Under the circumstances, the district court did not abuse its discretion in denying Firetrace's motion for remittitur or new trial.

Firetrace also challenges the jury's award of $62,893.29 in consequential damages because at least some of the award was for future replacement of tubing that Firetrace asserts was no longer under warranty, calling into question whether Lincoln would continue to replace that tubing. Lincoln presented evidence through two of its engineers . . . about travel and labor expenses Lincoln had already incurred in replacing tubing previously installed in Titan Modules. [One engineer] estimated that Lincoln would incur an additional $57,140.00 in future costs to replace the remaining tubing, based on Lincoln's estimate that it would take four trips of 7–10 days each to replace the tubing in all the modules located in Vietnam and a separate trip of 7–10 days to replace the tubing in 5 modules in Peru.

Lincoln presented sufficient evidence as to the cost of travel and labor expenses it has incurred and will incur in the future to replace the Firetrace tubing to support the consequential damages awarded by the jury. Under Nebraska law, damages need not be proved with mathematical certainty. It was the jury's responsibility to weigh the evidence and determine whether Lincoln would ultimately replace the tubing in all these modules and at what cost. Firetrace's challenge to the estimate of Lincoln's future consequential damages is in essence an attack on the jury's credibility determinations. Firetrace asks us to make a factual finding that, despite its witnesses' testimony to the contrary, Lincoln did not intend to replace the Firetrace tubing still remaining in Titan Modules. We decline to second-guess the jury's credibility determinations, and the district court did not abuse its discretion in denying Firetrace's motion for remittitur or a new trial on the award of consequential damages.

Jury verdict and district court judgment in favor of Lincoln affirmed.

Assumption of risk, discussed in Chapter 7, is the plaintiff's voluntary consent to a known danger. It can occur anytime the plaintiff willingly exposes herself to a known product hazard—for example, by consuming obviously adulterated food. As with product misuse, assumption of risk ordinarily has been a defense in warranty, negligence, and strict liability cases.

Contributory negligence, also discussed in Chapter 7, is the plaintiff's failure to act reasonably and prudently. In the product liability context, perhaps the most common example is the simple failure to notice a hazardous product defect. Contributory negligence is a defense in a negligence case (if state law has not replaced the contributory negligence defense with the comparative rules discussed below), but courts have disagreed about whether or when it should be a defense in warranty and strict liability cases.

Comparative Principles

> **LO20-13** Describe the role of comparative negligence and comparative fault principles in cases in which fault on the part of the defendant and on the part of the plaintiff led to the harm experienced by the plaintiff.

Where they are allowed and proven, the three traditional product liability defenses completely absolve the defendant from liability. Dissatisfaction with this all-or-nothing situation has spurred the increasing use of comparative principles in product liability cases.[6] Rather than letting the traditional defenses completely absolve the defendant, nearly all states now require apportionment of damages on the basis of relative fault. They do so by requiring that the fact-finder establish the plaintiff's and the defendant's percentage shares of the total fault for the injury and then award the plaintiff his total provable damages times the defendant's percentage share of the fault.

Unsettled questions persist among the states that have adopted comparative principles. First, it is not always clear what kinds of fault will reduce the plaintiff's recovery. Some state comparative negligence statutes, however, have been read as embracing assumption of risk and product misuse, and state comparative fault statutes usually define fault broadly. Second, comparative principles may assume either the *pure* or the *mixed* forms described in Chapter 7. In "mixed" states, for example, the defendant has a complete defense when the plaintiff was more at fault than the defendant. There is also some uncertainty about the theories of recovery and the types of damage claims to which comparative principles apply.

In *Green v. Ford Motor Co.*, which follows, the plaintiff claimed that the vehicle manufactured by the defendant was not "crashworthy." (The crashworthiness doctrine receives discussion earlier in the chapter.) The plaintiff further contended that the defendant's alleged breach of the crashworthiness obligation caused the plaintiff to experience enhanced injuries when an accident occurred—in other words, more extensive injuries than he would have suffered in the accident if the vehicle had been crashworthy. The defendant asserted, however, that the plaintiff's own fault caused, or played a key role in causing, the accident in which the plaintiff was injured. The court therefore had to decide whether, under the state's comparative fault system, evidence of the plaintiff's role in causing the accident should be taken into account even though the plaintiff's claim was for enhanced injury damages.

---

[6]Comparative negligence and comparative fault are discussed in Chapter 7. Although courts and commentators often use the terms *comparative fault* and *comparative negligence* interchangeably, comparative fault usually includes forms of blameworthiness other than negligence.

Green v. Ford Motor Co.   **942 N.E.2d 791 (Ind. 2011)**

Nicholas Green sued Ford Motor Co. in the U.S. District Court for the Southern District of Indiana. Relying on the Indiana Product Liability Act, Green claimed that his Ford Explorer vehicle was defective and unreasonably dangerous and that Ford was negligent in its design of the vehicle's restraint system. In particular, Green alleged that Ford failed to fulfill its obligation to produce a "crashworthy" vehicle.

The case arose from a 2006 accident in which the Explorer left the road, struck a guardrail, rolled down an embankment, and came to rest upside down in a ditch. Green, who was driving the Explorer at the time of the accident, sustained severe injuries and was rendered a quadriplegic. He claimed that his injuries were substantially enhanced because of the alleged defects in the vehicle's restraint system.

Green filed a motion in limine in which he asked the court to exclude any evidence of his alleged negligence in operating the vehicle because, in his view, any conduct by him in causing the vehicle to leave the road and strike the guardrail was not relevant to whether Ford's negligent design of the restraint system caused him to suffer more extensive injuries than he otherwise would have suffered. Ford responded by asserting that Green's product liability lawsuit was subject to Indiana's statutory comparative fault principles, which require the jury to consider the fault of Green in causing or contributing to the physical harm he suffered. The federal district court concluded that the question presented by Green's motion and Ford's response was not clearly answered by Indiana legislation and case law. At Green's request, the district court utilized a procedure in which it certified the issue to the Supreme Court of Indiana for its analysis and resolution. The following is an edited version of the opinion issued by the Supreme Court of Indiana.

Dickson, Justice

The U.S. District Court for the Southern District of Indiana has certified for our resolution the following issue of Indiana state law: "Whether, in a crashworthiness case alleging enhanced injuries under the Indiana Product Liability Act, the finder of fact shall apportion fault to the person suffering physical harm when that alleged fault relates to the cause of the underlying accident." As explained more fully below, subject to certain qualifications that require modification of the question, our answer is in the affirmative.

The "crashworthiness" doctrine[, on which Green relies in this case,] was enunciated by the Eighth Circuit Court of Appeals in *Larsen v. General Motors Corp.*, 391 F.2d 495, 502 (8th Cir. 1968). *Larsen* recognized that, in light of the statistical inevitability of collisions, a vehicle manufacturer must use reasonable care in designing a vehicle to avoid subjecting the user to an unreasonable risk of injury in the event of a collision. The court explained that "the manufacturer should be liable for that portion of the damage or injury caused by the defective design over and above the damage or injury that probably would have occurred as a result of the impact or collision absent the defective design." [The court added that] "[t]he normal risk of driving must be accepted by the user but there is no need to further penalize the user by subjecting him to an unreasonable risk of injury due to negligence in design."

In *Miller v. Todd*, 551 N.E.2d 1139 (Ind. 1990), this Court expressly recognized the theory of crashworthiness presented in *Larsen*, noting that "the doctrine of crashworthiness merely expands the proximate cause requirement to include enhanced injuries." We reasoned that, because it is foreseeable that a vehicle may be involved in collisions, for purposes of product liability law, such occurrences are included in the concept of expected use of a vehicle.

[In Indiana cases decided since *Miller*], claims for enhanced injuries based on alleged uncrashworthiness have been viewed as separate and distinct from the circumstances relating to the initial collision or event. [The focus has been on] the "second collision" involving a manufacturer's failure to exercise reasonable care in the design of a product to protect its users in light of the likelihood that the product could be involved in an accident. Thus, a claimant could recover only for the enhanced injuries caused by the lack of reasonable care in designing a crashworthy product. And the fact that the initial collision was not caused by the product's uncrashworthy design did not preclude such a claim for enhanced injuries. We acknowledge the logical appeal to extend this analysis so as to view any negligence of a claimant in causing the initial collision as therefore irrelevant to determining liability for the "second collision." But two considerations lead to a contrary conclusion.

First, most of the early crashworthiness decisions arose under common law or statutory product liability law that imposed strict liability for which a plaintiff's contributory negligence was not available as a defense, making it irrelevant in those cases to consider a plaintiff's contributory negligence. Second, and more important, product liability claims in Indiana are governed by the Indiana Product Liability Act, which, since 1995, has expressly required liability to be determined in accordance with the principles of comparative fault. We find the statutory language to be significant in resolving the question.

The appropriate considerations in determining comparative fault are primarily established by statute. The statutory definition of "fault" provides:

(a) "Fault," for purposes of [the Indiana Product Liability Act], means an act or omission that is negligent, willful, wanton, reckless, or intentional toward the person or property of others. The term includes the following:

(1) Unreasonable failure to avoid an injury or to mitigate damages.

(2) A finding under IC 34-20-2 . . . that a person is subject to liability for physical harm caused by a product, notwithstanding the lack of negligence or willful, wanton, or reckless conduct by the manufacturer or seller.

(b) "Fault," for purposes of [the Indiana Comparative Fault Act,] includes any act or omission that is negligent, willful, wanton, reckless, or intentional toward the person or property of others. The term also includes unreasonable assumption of risk not constituting an enforceable express consent, incurred risk, and unreasonable failure to avoid an injury or to mitigate damages.

Ind. Code § 34-6-2-45. In evaluating and allocating comparative fault, a jury may also consider "the relative degree of causation attributable among the responsible actors." [Citation omitted.] Our statutory scheme thus allows a diverse array of factors to be considered in the allocation of comparative fault.

In both the Product Liability Act and the Comparative Fault Act, the [Indiana] legislature employed expansive language to describe the breadth of causative conduct that may be considered in determining and allocating fault. Both enactments require consideration of the fault of all persons "who caused or contributed to cause" the harm. Ind. Code §§ 34-20-8-1(a), 34-51-2-7(b)(1), 34-51-2-8(b)(1). We note that in prescribing the scope of such initial consideration, the legislature employed the phrase "caused or contributed to cause" instead of "proximately caused." The Comparative Fault Act, however, further specifies that, in comparative fault actions, the "legal requirements of causal relation apply." Ind. Code § 34-51-2-3. This requirement of proximate cause to establish liability was preserved in the Indiana comparative fault scheme. The legislature has thus directed that a broad range of potentially causative conduct initially may be considered by the fact-finder but that the jury may allocate comparative fault only to those actors whose fault was a proximate cause of the claimed injury.

We conclude that, in a crashworthiness case alleging enhanced injuries under the Indiana Product Liability Act, it is the function of the fact-finder to consider and evaluate the conduct of all relevant actors who are alleged to have caused or contributed to cause the harm for which the plaintiff seeks damages. An assertion that a plaintiff is limiting his claim to "enhanced injuries" caused by only the "second collision" does not preclude the fact-finder from considering evidence of all relevant conduct of the plaintiff reasonably alleged to have contributed to cause the injuries. From that evidence, the jury must then, following argument of counsel and proper instructions from the court, determine whether such conduct satisfies the requirement of proximate cause. The

fact-finder may allocate as comparative fault only such fault that it finds to have been a proximate cause of the claimed injuries. And if the fault of more than one actor is found to have been a proximate cause of the claimed injuries, the fact-finder, in its allocation of comparative fault, may consider the relative degree of proximate causation attributable to each of the responsible actors. Thus, while a jury in a crashworthiness case may receive evidence of the plaintiff's conduct alleged to have contributed to cause the claimed injuries, the issue of whether such conduct constitutes proximate cause of the injuries for which damages are sought is a matter for the jury to determine in its evaluation of comparative fault.

As presented, the certified question asks whether the fact-finder shall apportion fault to the person suffering physical harm when the alleged fault of the injured person "relates to" the "underlying accident." As explained above, the fact-finder shall apportion fault to the injured person only if the fact-finder concludes that the fault of the injured person is *a proximate cause of* (not merely "relates to") the injuries *for which damages are sought* (not merely the "underlying accident"). Otherwise, any alleged fault of the injured person is not fault for the purposes of the Product Liability or Comparative Fault Acts and shall not be apportioned.

With these qualifications, we revise and restate the certified question as follows: "Whether, in a crashworthiness case alleging enhanced injuries under the Indiana Product Liability Act, the finder of fact shall apportion fault to the person suffering physical harm when that alleged fault is a proximate cause of the harm for which damages are being sought." We answer this question in the affirmative.

Certified question, as revised and restated, answered affirmatively.

Preemption and Regulatory Compliance

Identify the circumstances in which a court may conclude that a federal law preempts a state law–based product liability claim and thus furnishes the defendant a defense against liability.

What if Congress—or an administrative agency acting within the scope of power delegated to it by Congress—enacts legislation or promulgates regulations dealing with safety standards for a certain type of product, and the

product's manufacturer has met those standards? Does the manufacturer's compliance with the federal standards serve as a defense when a plaintiff brings state law claims such as negligence, strict liability, or breach of implied warranty in an effort to hold the manufacturer liable for supposed defects in product? The answer: *Sometimes*. The questions just posed, and the indefinite answer just offered, pertain to two potential defenses: the *preemption* defense and the *regulatory compliance* defense.

The preemption defense rests on a federal supremacy premise—the notion that federal law overrides state law when the two conflict or when state law stands in the way of the objectives underlying federal law. Sometimes a federal statute dealing with a certain type of product may contain a provision that calls for preemption of state law–based claims under circumstances specified in the federal law's preemption provision. In that event, courts must determine whether the plaintiff's state law–based claim (e.g., negligence, strict liability, or breach of implied warranty) is preempted. Such a determination depends heavily upon the language used in the statute and the specific nature of the plaintiff's claim. When preemption occurs, the federal law controls and the state law–based claim cannot serve as a basis for relief—meaning that the plaintiff loses. For instance, in *Riegel v. Medtronic, Inc.*, a 2008 decision that follows shortly, the Supreme Court interpreted a preemption provision in the federal statute dealing with medical devices as barring the plaintiffs' state law–based claims against the manufacturer of an allegedly defective medical device.

Even when a federal law dealing with product safety does not contain a preemption section, it is conceivable that courts could interpret the statute as having a pre-emptive effect if the federal law sets up a highly specific regulatory regime that the court believes would be undermined by allowance of liability claims brought under state law. The absence of a specific preemption section from the relevant federal statute, however, makes it less likely that a court would consider a plaintiff's state law–based claims to be preempted.

For example, there is no preemption provision in the federal statute requiring Food and Drug Administration (FDA) approval of new drugs and of their labels before they go into the marketplace (in contrast with the medical device approval statute interpreted in *Riegel*). In *Wyeth v. Levine*, 555 U.S. 555 (2009), the Supreme Court relied on the absence of a preemption provision in concluding that the federal law requiring FDA approval of drugs and their labels did not preempt a state law–based product liability claim in which the plaintiff asserted that a stronger warning than what appeared on a medication's FDA-approved label would have prevented the harm she suffered. The Court also concluded that allowing such a product liability claim would not undermine the federal regulatory regime regarding drug and drug label approval, given that the federal statute also contained a provision permitting drug manufacturers to employ labels containing stronger warnings than those on the FDA-approved labels if information indicating the probable need for such stronger warnings came to the manufacturers' attention. In such a situation, the manufacturer could begin using the enhanced label and then request FDA approval of that label. Allowance of the state law–based product liability claim of the sort at issue in *Levine* thus seemed generally consistent with the purpose of the enhanced-label provision in the federal law.

Two years after *Levine*, the Supreme Court decided *Pliva, Inc. v. Mensing*, 131 S. Ct. 2567 (2011). There, a five-justice majority held that federal law preempted a state law–based product liability claim that was premised on the need for a stronger warning than what was on the federally approved label for the drug at issue. The Court explained that *Levine*'s reasoning did not control the decision in *Mensing* because the drug at issue in *Mensing* was a generic version of a brand-name drug. The court concluded that federal law required generics to have exactly the same label as the corresponding brand-name drugs—meaning that the maker of the generic in *Mensing* could not have adopted a label with a stronger warning on its own and that permitting the plaintiff's state law–based claim would undermine the purposes of the federal regulatory regime. For the dissenters in *Mensing*, the Court's resolution of the case amounted to little more than an attempt to cut back on the effect of *Levine*. The close vote in *Mensing* and the divergent views expressed there by the justices illustrate the difficulty of predicting the outcome in a case in which the preemption defense is raised.

Regulatory compliance is the other potential defense connected with the questions asked earlier. Even if outright preemption of the plaintiff's negligence, strict liability, or breach-of-warranty claim is not appropriate, defendants in product liability cases have become increasingly likely in recent years to argue that their products complied with applicable federal safety standards and that this compliance should shield them from liability. This defense becomes highly fact-specific, with its potential for success depending upon the particular product and product defect at issue and the specific content of the federal standards.

In some cases, courts may not treat regulatory compliance as a full-fledged defense, but may still allow it to be considered as a factor in determining whether the defendant should be held liable. For instance, in a negligence case, the court may regard the defendant's compliance with federal standards as being among the relevant factors in a determination of whether the defendant failed to use reasonable care in the design or manufacturing of the product or in not issuing a warning about a supposed danger presented by the product. *Holiday Motor Corp. v. Walters*, which appears earlier in the chapter, serves as an example. Similarly, in a strict liability case, the court may decide to take the defendant's compliance with federal standards into account in determining whether the product was both defective and unreasonably dangerous.

Riegel v. Medtronic, Inc.   552 U.S. 312 (2008)

The case referred to below centered around an allegedly defective medical device—a balloon catheter—that was produced by Medtronic, Inc. and was inserted into Charles Riegel's right coronary artery during an angioplasty procedure. Before further discussion of the case's facts and identification of the key issues presented, explanation of the federal regulatory process regarding medical devices is necessary.

A federal statute, the Food, Drug, and Cosmetic Act, has long required Food and Drug Administration (FDA) approval prior to the introduction of new drugs into the marketplace. Until the Medical Device Amendments of 1976 (MDA), however, the introduction of new medical devices was left largely for the states to supervise as they saw fit. The regulatory landscape changed in the 1960s and 1970s, as complex devices proliferated and some failed. In the absence of federal regulation, several states adopted regulatory measures requiring premarket approval of medical devices. In 1976, Congress federalized the medical device approval requirement by enacting the MDA, 21 U.S.C. § 360(c) et seq., which imposed a regime of detailed federal oversight of medical devices.

The new regulatory regime established by the MDA set differing levels of oversight for medical devices, depending on the risks they present. Class I, which includes such devices as elastic bandages and examination gloves, is subject to the lowest level of oversight: "general controls" such as labeling requirements. Class II, which includes such devices as powered wheelchairs and surgical drapes, is subject in addition to "special controls" such as performance standards and postmarket surveillance measures. Class III devices receive the most federal oversight. That class includes such devices as replacement heart valves, implanted cerebella stimulators, and pacemaker pulse generators. In general, a device is assigned to Class III if it cannot be established that a less stringent classification would provide reasonable assurance of safety and effectiveness, and the device is "purported or represented to be for a use in supporting or sustaining human life or for a use which is of substantial importance in preventing impairment of human health," or the device "presents a potential unreasonable risk of illness or injury." 21 U.S.C. § 360c(a)(1)(C)(ii).

Although the MDA established a rigorous regime of premarket approval for new Class III devices, it grandfathered many that were already on the market. Devices sold before the MDA's effective date may remain on the market until the FDA promulgates a regulation requiring premarket approval. A related provision seeks to limit the competitive advantage grandfathered devices thus would appear to receive. According to that provision, a new device need not undergo premarket approval if the FDA finds it is "substantially equivalent" to another device exempt from premarket approval. The FDA's review of devices for substantial equivalence is known as the § 510(k) process, named after the section of the MDA describing the review. Most new Class III devices enter the market through § 510(k). In 2005, for example, the FDA authorized the marketing of 3,148 devices under § 510(k) and granted premarket approval to just 32 devices.

Premarket approval is a rigorous process involving the device manufacturer's submission of a multivolume application; detailed explanations of the device's components, ingredients, and properties; and detailed reports regarding studies and investigations into the device's safety and effectiveness. Before deciding whether to approve the application, the FDA may refer it to a panel of outside experts and may request additional data from the manufacturer. The FDA spends an average of 1,200 hours reviewing each application for premarket approval (as opposed to roughly 20 hours for the typical § 510(k) substantial equivalence application). The premarket approval process also includes review of the device's proposed labeling. The FDA evaluates safety and effectiveness under the conditions of use set forth on the label, and must determine that the proposed labeling is neither false nor misleading.

After completing its review, the FDA may grant or deny premarket approval, or may also condition approval on adherence to performance standards or other specific conditions or requirements. Premarket approval is to be granted only if the FDA concludes there is a "reasonable assurance" of the device's "safety and effectiveness." § 360e(d). The agency must "weigh[] any probable benefit to health from the use of the device against any probable risk of injury or illness from such use." § 360c(a)(2)(C).

The MDA includes an express preemption provision, § 360k(a), which states, in pertinent part:

[N]o State or political subdivision of a State may establish or continue in effect with respect to a device intended for human use any requirement—

(1) which is different from, or in addition to, any requirement applicable under this chapter to the device, and

(2) which relates to the safety or effectiveness of the device or to any other matter included in a requirement applicable to the device under this chapter.

Inclusion of the preemption provision causes the MDA to differ from the Food, Drug, and Cosmetic Act's sections requiring FDA approval prior to the introduction of new drugs into the marketplace. No such preemption provision appears in the drug approval sections of the Food, Drug, and Cosmetic Act.

Medtronic's Evergreen Balloon Catheter Company Profile is a Class III device that received premarket approval from the FDA in 1994. Changes to its label received supplemental approvals in 1995 and 1996. Charles Riegel underwent coronary angioplasty in

1996, shortly after suffering a myocardial infarction. His right coronary artery was diffusely diseased and heavily calcified. Riegel's doctor inserted the Evergreen Balloon Catheter into his patient's coronary artery in an attempt to dilate the artery, even though the device's labeling stated that use was contraindicated for patients with diffuse or calcified stenoses. The label also warned that the catheter should not be inflated beyond its rated burst pressure of eight atmospheres. Riegel's doctor inflated the catheter five times, to a pressure of 10 atmospheres. On its fifth inflation, the catheter ruptured. Riegel developed a heart block, was placed on life support, and underwent emergency coronary bypass surgery.

In 1999, Riegel and his wife, Donna, sued Medtronic in the U.S. District Court for the Northern District of New York. Their complaint raised various claims centering around the allegations that Medtronic's catheter was designed, labeled, and manufactured in a manner that violated New York common law, and that these defects caused Riegel to suffer severe and permanent injuries. The district court held that the MDA preempted the Riegels' claims of strict liability, breach of implied warranty, and negligence in the design, testing, manufacturing, inspection, distribution, labeling, marketing, and sale of the catheter. After the U.S. Court of Appeals for the Second Circuit affirmed, the U.S. Supreme Court granted the Riegels' petition for a writ of certiorari.

Scalia, Justice

We consider whether the pre-emption clause enacted in the MDA, 21 U.S.C. § 360k, bars common-law claims challenging the safety and effectiveness of a medical device given premarket approval by the Food and Drug Administration (FDA). Since the MDA expressly pre-empts only state requirements "different from, or in addition to, any requirement applicable . . . to the device" under federal law, § 360k(a)(1), we must determine whether the federal government has established requirements applicable to Medtronic's catheter. If so, we must then determine whether the Riegels' common-law claims are based upon New York requirements with respect to the device that are "different from, or in addition to" the federal ones, and that relate to safety and effectiveness. § 360k(a).

We turn to the first question. In *Medtronic, Inc. v. Lohr*, 518 U.S. 470 (1996), . . . this Court interpreted the MDA's pre-emption provision [and] concluded that federal manufacturing and labeling requirements applicable across the board to almost all medical devices did not pre-empt the common-law claims of negligence and strict liability at issue in [the case]. The federal requirements, we said, were not requirements specific to the device in question—they reflected "entirely generic concerns about device regulation generally." While we disclaimed a conclusion that general federal requirements could never pre-empt, or [that] general state duties [could] never be pre-empted, we held that no pre-emption occurred in the case at hand based on a careful comparison between the state and federal duties at issue.

Even though substantial-equivalence review under § 510(k) is device specific, *Lohr* also rejected the manufacturer's contention that § 510(k) approval [(which the device at issue in the case had received)] imposed device-specific "requirements." We regarded the fact that products entering the market through § 510(k) may be marketed only so long as they remain substantial equivalents of

the relevant pre-1976 devices as a qualification for an exemption rather than a requirement.

Premarket approval, in contrast, imposes "requirements" under the MDA as we interpreted it in *Lohr*. Unlike general labeling duties, premarket approval is specific to individual devices. And it is in no sense an exemption from federal safety review—it is federal safety review. Thus, the attributes that *Lohr* found lacking in § 510(k) review are present here. While § 510(k) is "focused on equivalence, not safety" (quoting *Lohr*), premarket approval is focused on safety, not equivalence. While devices that enter the market through § 510(k) have "never been formally reviewed under the MDA for safety or efficacy" (quoting *Lohr*), the FDA may grant premarket approval only after it determines that a device offers a reasonable assurance of safety and effectiveness. § 360e(d). And while the FDA does not require that a device allowed to enter the market as a substantial equivalent "take any particular form for any particular reason" (quoting *Lohr*), the FDA requires a device that has received premarket approval to be made with almost no deviations from the specifications in its approval application, for the reason that the FDA has determined that the approved form provides a reasonable assurance of safety and effectiveness.

We turn, then, to the second question: whether the Riegels' common-law claims rely upon "any requirement" of New York law applicable to the catheter that is "different from, or in addition to" federal requirements and that "relates to the safety or effectiveness of the device or to any other matter included in a requirement applicable to the device." § 360k(a). Safety and effectiveness are the very subjects of the Riegels' common-law claims, so the critical issue is whether New York's tort duties constitute "requirements" under the MDA.

In *Lohr*, five Justices [expressed the view] that common-law causes of action for negligence and strict liability do impose "requirement[s]" and would be pre-empted by federal requirements specific to a medical device [if such device-specific requirements, not present in *Lohr*, were present in an appropriate case]. We adhere to that view. In interpreting two other statutes we have likewise held that a provision pre-empting state "requirements" pre-empted common-law duties. *Bates v. Dow Agrosciences LLC*, 544 U.S. 431 (2005), found common-law actions to be pre-empted by a provision of the Federal Insecticide, Fungicide, and Rodenticide Act that said certain states "shall not impose or continue in effect any requirements for labeling or packaging in addition to or different from those required under this subchapter." *Cipollone v. Liggett Group, Inc.*, 505 U.S. 504 (1992), held [certain] common-law [claims] pre-empted by a provision of the Public Health Cigarette Smoking Act of 1969, which said that "[n]o requirement or prohibition based on smoking and health shall be imposed under state law with respect to the advertising or promotion of any cigarettes" whose packages were labeled in accordance with federal law.

Congress is entitled to know what meaning this Court will assign to terms regularly used in its enactments. Absent other indication, reference to a state's "requirements" includes its common-law duties. As the plurality opinion said in *Cipollone*, common-law liability is "premised on the existence of a legal duty," and a tort judgment therefore establishes that the defendant has violated a state-law obligation. And while the common-law remedy is limited to damages, a liability award[, as noted in *Cipollone*,] "can be, indeed is designed to be, a potent method of governing conduct and controlling policy."

In the present case, there is nothing to contradict this normal meaning. To the contrary, in the context of this legislation excluding common-law duties from the scope of pre-emption would make little sense. State tort law that requires a manufacturer's catheters to be safer, but hence less effective, than the model the FDA has approved disrupts the federal scheme no less than state regulatory law to the same effect. Indeed, one would think that tort law, applied by juries under a negligence or strict-liability standard, is less deserving of preservation. A state statute, or a regulation adopted by a state agency, could at least be expected to apply cost-benefit analysis similar to that applied by the experts at the FDA: How many more lives will be saved by a device which, along with its greater effectiveness, brings a greater risk of harm? A jury, on the other hand, sees only the cost of a more dangerous design, and is not concerned with its benefits; the patients who reaped those benefits are not represented in court. As Justice Breyer explained in [his concurring opinion in] *Lohr*, it is

implausible that the MDA was meant to "grant greater power (to set state standards different from, or in addition to, federal standards) to a single state jury than to state officials acting through state administrative or legislative lawmaking processes." That perverse distinction is not required or even suggested by the broad language Congress chose in the MDA, and we will not turn somersaults to create it.

The dissent would narrow the pre-emptive scope of the term "requirement" on the ground that it is "difficult to believe that Congress would, without comment, remove all means of judicial recourse" for consumers injured by FDA-approved devices (quoting Justice Ginsburg's dissent). But, as we have explained, this is exactly what a pre-emption clause for medical devices does by its terms. It is not our job to speculate upon congressional motives. If we were to do so, however, the only indication available—the text of the statute—suggests that the solicitude for those injured by FDA-approved devices, which the dissent finds controlling, was overcome in Congress's estimation by solicitude for those who would suffer without new medical devices if juries were allowed to apply the tort law of 50 states to all innovations.

The Riegels contend that the duties underlying negligence, strict-liability, and implied-warranty claims are not pre-empted even if they impose "requirements," because general common-law duties are not requirements maintained "'with respect to devices.'" Again, a majority of [the justices] suggested otherwise in *Lohr*. And with good reason. The language of the statute does not bear the Riegels' reading. The MDA provides that no state "may establish or continue in effect with respect to a device . . . any requirement" relating to safety or effectiveness that is different from, or in addition to, federal requirements. § 360k(a). The Riegels' suit depends upon New York's "continu[ing] in effect" general tort duties "with respect to" Medtronic's catheter. Nothing in the statutory text suggests that the pre-empted state requirement must apply only to the relevant device, or only to medical devices and not to all products and all actions in general.

State requirements are pre-empted under the MDA only to the extent that they are "different from, or in addition to" the requirements imposed by federal law. § 360k(a)(1). Thus, § 360k does not prevent a state from providing a damages remedy for claims premised on a violation of FDA regulations; the state duties in such a case parallel, rather than add to, federal requirements.

Court of Appeals judgment in favor of Medtronic affirmed.

Problems and Problem Cases

1. Brian Felley went to the home of Thomas and Cheryl Singleton to look at a used car that the Singletons had offered for sale. The car, a six-year-old Ford Taurus, had approximately 126,000 miles on it. Felley test-drove the car and discussed its condition with the Singletons. The Singletons told him that the car was in "good mechanical condition" and that they had experienced no brake problems. This was a primary consideration for Felley, who purchased the car from the Singletons for $5,800. Felley soon began experiencing problems with the car. On the second day after he bought it, he noticed a problem with the clutch. Over the next few days, the clutch problem worsened to the point where he was unable to shift the gears, no matter how far he pushed in the clutch pedal. He had to pay $942.76 for the removal and repair of the clutch. Within the first month that Felley owned the car, it developed serious brake problems, the repairs of which cost Felley more than $1,400. Felley brought a small claims action against the Singletons, claiming that they had made and breached an express warranty to him. At trial, an expert witness testified that based on his examination of the car and discussion with Felley about the car and other factors, it was his opinion that the car's brake and clutch problems probably existed when Felley bought the car. The trial court ruled in Felley's favor and ordered the Singletons to pay him $2,343.03. On appeal, the Singletons argued that what they said to Felley about the car did not constitute an express warranty and that they therefore should not have been held liable. Were they correct?

2. Hilda Forbes was the driver in an accident in which the front end of her car struck another vehicle. The driver's airbag did not deploy, and she sustained serious injuries. She later filed suit against the car's manufacturer because of the failure of the airbag to deploy. The owner's manual for the car—a manual prepared by the manufacturer—contained a statement that if a front-end collision was "hard enough," the air bag would deploy. Although Forbes did not read the manual before buying the car, she told the salesman with whom she negotiated the purchase that a working air bag was important to her. The salesman informed Forbes of the gist of what the owner's manual said about a functioning air bag. In her lawsuit, Forbes presented the testimony of an expert witness who offered the opinion that the collision in which she was involved was severe enough to cause a properly functioning airbag to deploy. Under the circumstances, did the owner's manual's "hard enough" statement constitute an express warranty concerning the airbag. If so, why? If not, why not? If the "hard enough" statement constituted an express warranty, was the warranty breached?

3. In October 2002, Tina and Thad Crowe purchased a 1999 Dodge Durango automobile from CarMax Auto Superstores, Inc. They received a 30-day/1,000-mile express warranty from CarMax. In addition, the Crowes purchased an 18-month/18,000-mile "Mechanical Repair Agreement" (MRA). The obligated party on this extended warranty was a corporation other than CarMax. Over the course of the next year, the Crowes brought the vehicle to CarMax and other repair facilities numerous times for a variety of repairs. All repairs within the original and extended warranty periods were done at little or no cost to the Crowes. However, the Crowes lost confidence in the vehicle because of the numerous times repairs had been necessary. In May 2003, the Crowes sued CarMax, contending that CarMax had breached the implied warranty of merchantability. After the trial court granted summary judgment in favor of CarMax, the Crowes appealed to the Georgia Court of Appeals. Should the Crowes win the summary judgment?

4. Yong Cha Hong bought take-out fried chicken from a Roy Rogers Family Restaurant owned by the Marriott Corporation. While eating a chicken wing from her order, she bit into an object that she perceived to be a worm. Claiming permanent injuries and great physical and emotional upset from this incident, Hong sued Marriott in federal district court. She claimed that Marriott had breached the implied warranty of merchantability. After introducing an expert's report opining that the object in the chicken wing was not a worm but was instead the chicken's aorta or trachea, Marriott moved for summary judgment. What two alternative tests might the court have applied in deciding whether the chicken wing was merchantable? Which of the two alternative tests did the court decide to apply? Under that test, was Marriott entitled to summary judgment?

5. In 1994, David and Corrine Bako signed a contract with Don Walter Kitchen Distributors (DW) for the purchase and installation of cabinets in their new home. DW ordered the cabinets from a manufacturer, Crystal Cabinet Works. Crystal shipped the cabinets to DW, which installed them in the Bakos' residence. Soon after the installation, Corrine Bako contacted a DW employee, Neil Mann, and asked whether DW could provide a stain to match the kitchen cabinets. She informed Mann that the stain would be applied to

the wood trim primarily on the first floor of the house. Mann ordered two one-gallon cans of stain from Crystal, which shipped the stain to DW in unmarked cans. There were no labels, instructions, or warnings regarding improper use or application of the stain. The cans arrived at DW's store in unmarked cardboard boxes and were delivered to the Bakos in this manner. The stain in the cans turned out to be lacquer-based. Shortly thereafter, Corrine Bako again contacted Mann about purchasing additional stain in a slightly different color to apply to a hardwood floor. At Mann's suggestion, she contacted Crystal's paint lab and spoke with a Crystal employee. The Crystal employee shipped the Bakos a series of samples from which Corrine ordered two gallons of stain. This stain was also a lacquer-based stain and was shipped directly from Crystal to the Bakos in unmarked cans. Once again, there were no instructions for use, no warning regarding improper use or application of the product, no label indicating that it was a lacquer-based stain, and no label indicating that a special topcoat was required because it was a lacquer-based stain. The Bakos applied the stain to their floor.

The Bakos then obtained a polyurethane topcoat sealant and applied it to the wood surfaces they had stained with the stain purchased from DW and Crystal. Following this application of the sealant, all of the stained and sealed areas suffered severe and permanent damage as a result of the nonadherence of the polyurethane sealant to the lacquer-based stain. Evidence adduced at the trial of the case referred to below established that lacquer-based stains are incompatible with the polyurethane topcoat that the Bakos applied to their home's wood surfaces. In October 1996, the Bakos filed suit against Crystal and DW for breach of the implied warranty of merchantability and breach of the implied warranty of fitness for a particular purpose. They also claimed that the defendants had been negligent. An Ohio trial court found for the Bakos and held the defendants liable for approximately $25,000 in compensatory damages. Contending that the Bakos should not have prevailed on any of their claims, Crystal appealed to the Court of Appeals of Ohio. How did the appellate court rule on the Bakos' two breach of implied warranty claims?

6. Connie Daniell attempted to commit suicide by locking herself inside the trunk of her Ford LTD. She remained in the trunk for nine days but survived after finally being rescued. Later, Daniell brought a negligence action against Ford in an effort to recover for her resulting physical and psychological injuries. She contended that the LTD was defectively designed

because its trunk did not have an internal release or opening mechanism. She also argued that Ford was liable for negligently failing to warn her that the trunk could not be unlocked from within. Was Ford liable for negligent design and/or negligent failure to warn?

7. In 2001, Donald Malen purchased a Yard-Man riding mower at a Home Depot store. The mower was manufactured by MTD Products in 1998 and was advertised as "Reconditioned Power Equipment" with a "Full Manufacturer's Warranty." The mower was designed with a safety interlock system. One component of that system was the Operator Presence Control, or OPC, a device that kills the engine if the operator rises from the seat without first disengaging the cutting blade and setting the parking brake. A second component was the "no cut in reverse" switch, or NCR, which kills the engine if the operator shifts into reverse without first disengaging the blade. The American National Standards Institute ("ANSI"), a voluntary organization that develops nationwide consensus standards for a variety of devices and procedures, did not make an NCR compulsory until 2003, but by 1996 the organization had mandated that riding mowers had to have an OPC that would stop the engine and fully arrest the blade within five seconds of being triggered. Before Malen purchased the mower, he tested it under the supervision of a Home Depot sales employee. During that test ride, Malen never rose from the seat with the engine running. A label on the mower in front of the seat warned the operator with these statements:

DO NOT OPERATE THE UNIT WHERE IT COULD SLIP OR TIP. BE SURE BLADE(S) AND ENGINE ARE STOPPED BEFORE PLACING HANDS OR FEET NEAR BLADE(S). BEFORE LEAVING THE OPERATOR'S POSITION, DISENGAGE BLADE(S), PLACE THE SHIFT LEVER IN NEUTRAL, ENGAGE THE PARKING BRAKE, SHUT OFF AND REMOVE KEY.

Between 2001 and 2004, Malen operated the mower 30 to 50 times without incident. But in October 2004 he was mulching leaves with the mower and wedged the right front tire over a curb. He tried without success to free the machine by rocking his weight in the seat and shifting gears between forward and reverse. At that point Malen raised the cutting deck, removed his foot from the pedal which engages the blade, and started to dismount. But he did not turn off the engine or listen to confirm whether the blade had stopped spinning. It had not. As Malen rose from the seat and stepped off the mower, his left foot slipped under the cutting deck and was struck by the rotating blade. The lacerations to the sole of his foot were severe, and he permanently lost full use of his foot. Neither the OPC nor the NCR functioned when the accident occurred.

Malen sued MTD Products and Home Depot on strict liability and negligence grounds. He contended that the mower was negligently manufactured and unreasonably dangerous because its OPC was not connected and thus inoperable. He also contended that the mower was negligently designed because MTD Products had shunned a "fail safe" system that would have made the cutting blade unusable even without the OPC connected. The court granted summary judgment in favor of the defendants, concluding that Malen's own actions were the sole proximate cause of his injury. Was the court correct in granting summary judgment to the defendants?

8. Chefik Simo, an 18-year-old first-year student on the varsity soccer team at Furman University, was a passenger in a 2000 Mitsubishi P45 Montero Sport, a sport-utility vehicle designed, manufactured, and sold by Mitsubishi Motors Corp. and Mitsubishi Motors North America (collectively referred to here as "Mitsubishi"). Simo suffered severe injuries when the Montero Sport rolled over on an interstate highway after the driver suddenly steered left to avoid another vehicle and then attempted to correct his course by quickly turning back to the right. While the vehicle was on its side, it was struck by a Federal Express truck. In the litigation referred to below, Simo presented testimony that he was the top soccer recruit in the country the year he entered college and was among the best players on the United States' "Under-20" national team. Simo had intended to begin his professional career in Europe following the conclusion of the soccer season at Furman. Many European teams, including some at the top levels, had expressed interest in signing Simo when he became available.

Simo's injuries from the accident included a fractured shoulder blade, a fractured pelvis, a dislocated shoulder, a ruptured small intestine, a broken wrist, a knee dislocation in his left leg involving a complete separation of the thigh bone from the shin bone, and tears of three of the four major ligaments in the knee. He suffered irreparable nerve damage that resulted in a "drop foot." As a result of these injuries, Simo underwent a number of surgeries and incurred more than $277,000 in medical bills. He engaged in arduous rehabilitation efforts in an attempt to resume his soccer career. When he returned to the field, however, he ended up overcompensating for his injuries to his left side, leading to painful stress fractures that forced him to terminate his comeback. Simo filed a strict liability lawsuit against Mitsubishi. Based on what you have studied in Chapter 20, what elements would Simo need to prove in order to win his strict liability case? What test would the court be likely to apply in determining whether strict liability should apply? What types of damages would Simo be entitled to obtain if he establishes liability on the part of Mitsubishi? Would the lost career opportunity in soccer be something accounted for in any award of damages to Simo?

9. Sandra Goodin purchased a new Hyundai Sonata automobile in November 2000 from an Evansville, Indiana, dealer. The Sonata's manufacturer, Hyundai Motor America, provided a written express warranty of a limited nature, but the dealer did not furnish an express warranty. The contract of sale between the dealer and Goodin contained the dealer's disclaimer of the implied warranty of merchantability. Because Hyundai provided a written warranty, the federal Magnuson-Moss Warranty Act prohibited Hyundai from disclaiming the implied warranty of merchantability. For a two-year period that ran essentially from the time of purchase, Goodin complained that the car vibrated excessively and that its brakes groaned, squeaked, and made a grinding noise when applied. Various repairs were performed by the dealer that sold Goodin the car and by another Hyundai dealer. Hyundai Motor America's limited warranty covered most of these repairs. Goodin incurred the cost of other repairs conducted after the expiration of Hyundai's limited warranty. None of the repairs, however, completely took care of the problems Goodin had consistently pointed out.

In April 2002, Goodin's attorney retained an expert to examine the car. The expert noted the brake-related problems and the excessive vibration and expressed the view that the car was "defective and unmerchantable at the time of manufacture and unfit for operation on public roadways." In October 2002, a district service manager for Hyundai inspected and test-drove Goodin's car. Although he did not notice excessive vibration or the brake-related noises about which Goodin complained, he heard "a droning noise" that probably resulted from a failed wheel bearing. The district service manager said he regarded the wheel bearing problem as a serious one that should have been covered by Hyundai's limited warranty. Goodin later sued Hyundai in an Indiana court for breach of express warranty and breach of the implied warranty of merchantability. Over Hyundai's objection, the trial judge's instructions to the jury on the implied warranty of merchantability claim made no mention of any privity requirement. The jury returned a verdict for Hyundai on Goodin's breach of express warranty claim, but awarded Goodin $3,000 on her claim for breach of the implied warranty of merchantability.

Did the court rule correctly when it did so?

10. Matthew Kovach, a nine-year-old child, was admitted to Surgicare LLC (Surgicare) to undergo a scheduled adenoidectomy. While he recovered in the ambulatory surgery center, a nurse administered Capital of Codeine, an opiate, to him. To administer the drug, the nurse used a graduated medicine cup (the Cup), manufactured and/or sold by various parties that later became defendants in the case described below. (Those defendants will be referred to here as the Cup Defendants.) The Cup is made of flexible translucent plastic that is not completely clear and denotes various volume measurement graduation markings, including milliliters (ml), drams, ounces, teaspoons, tablespoons, and cubic centimeters. These measurement markers are located on the interior surface of the Cup and have a similar translucency as the Cup. The vertical distance between the ml volume graduation markings varies: the smallest volume of ml measurement for the graduations between empty and 10 ml is 2.5 ml; while the smallest volume of ml measurement for the graduations between 10 ml and 30 ml is 15 ml. The Cup holds 30 ml or more of medicine when full. Matthew was prescribed 15 ml, or one-half of the Cup's volume, of Capital of Codeine. Although the nurse stated that she gave Matthew only 15 ml of Codeine, Matthew's father, Jim Kovach, who was in the room at the time, testified that the Cup was completely full. Matthew drank all of the medicine in the Cup. After being discharged from Surgicare and arriving home, Matthew went into respiratory arrest. He was transported to a hospital, where he was pronounced dead of asphyxia due to an opiate overdose. The autopsy revealed that Matthew's blood contained between 280 and 344 nanograms per ml of codeine, more than double the recommended therapeutic level of the drug.

Jim and Jill Kovach (Matthew's mother) filed suit in an Indiana trial court against the Cup Defendants, asserting claims for (1) breach of the implied warranty of merchantability, (2) breach of the implied warranty of fitness for a particular purpose, (3) negligent design, and (4) strict liability. Their claims centered around contentions that the design of the Cup was defective,

largely because its translucency and lack of clear, easily distinguishable measurement markings led to a danger of measurement errors, and because the Cup Defendants issued no warning to the effect that the Cup should not be used when a precise measurement of medication quantity was important. By way of affidavit, the Kovaches' expert witness, a pharmacy professor with many years of experience, offered an opinion consistent with the above contentions regarding the Cup's design and lack of warning. The trial court granted the Cup Defendants' motion for summary judgment on each of the claims filed against them by the Kovaches. Did the trial court rule correctly in doing so? In your answer, consider each of the four claims brought by the plaintiffs.

11. Duane Martin, a small farmer, placed an order for cabbage seed with the Joseph Harris Company, a large national producer and distributor of seed. Harris's order form included the following language:

> NOTICE TO BUYER: Joseph Harris Company, Inc. warrants that seeds and plants it sells conform to the label descriptions as required by Federal and State seed laws. IT MAKES NO OTHER WARRANTIES, EXPRESS OR IMPLIED, OF MERCHANTABILITY, FITNESS FOR PURPOSE, OR OTHERWISE, AND IN ANY EVENT ITS LIABILITY FOR BREACH OF ANY WARRANTY OR CONTRACT WITH RESPECT TO SUCH SEEDS OR PLANTS IS LIMITED TO THE PURCHASE PRICE OF SUCH SEEDS OR PLANTS.

All of Harris's competitors used similar clauses in their contracts.

After Martin placed his order, and unknown to Martin, Harris stopped using a cabbage seed treatment that had been effective in preventing a certain cabbage fungus. Later, Martin planted the seed he had ordered from Harris, but a large portion of the resulting crop was destroyed by fungus because the seed did not contain the treatment Harris had previously used. Martin sued Harris for his losses under the implied warranty of merchantability.

Which portion of the notice quoted above is an attempted disclaimer of implied warranty liability, and which is an attempted limitation of remedies? Will the disclaimer language disclaim the implied warranty of merchantability under UCC § 2-316(2)? If Martin had sued under the implied warranty of fitness for a particular purpose, would the disclaimer language disclaim that implied warranty as well? Assuming that the disclaimer and the remedy limitation contained the correct legal boilerplate needed to make them effective, what argument could Martin still make to block their operation? What are his chances of success with this argument?

12. William Croskey was seriously injured in July 2000 when his girlfriend's 1992 BMW automobile overheated and he opened the hood to add fluid. Because the plastic neck on the car's radiator failed, scalding radiator fluid spewed out and came in contact with Croskey, severely burning him. Relying on diversity of citizenship jurisdiction, Croskey filed suit in the U.S. District Court for the Eastern District of Michigan against the car's manufacturer, Bayerische Motoren Werk Aktiengesellschaft (BMW AG), and the North American distributor of BMW vehicles, BMW of North America (BMW NA). Croskey pleaded two alternative claims: (1) negligent design on the part of BMW AG and (2) negligent failure to warn on the part of BMW AG and BMW NA. Deciding an evidentiary question prior to trial, the district court ruled that Croskey could use evidence of substantially similar incidents of plastic neck failure if those incidents came to the attention of the defendants and if the incidents occurred between 1991 and the date Croskey was injured. However, the court allowed this evidence to be used only in regard to the negligent failure to warn claim, and prohibited its use in regard to the negligent design claim. The court also ruled that concerning the negligent failure to warn claim, the defendants could introduce evidence of the number of BMWs sold with plastic-necked radiators between 1994 (when the defendants first learned of a neck failure) and the date of the Croskey incident. The purpose of such evidence was to show the likelihood—or lack of likelihood—of a neck failure. The case proceeded to trial. Rejecting Croskey's negligent design and negligent failure to warn claims, the jury returned a verdict in favor of the defendants. Croskey appealed to the U.S. Court of Appeals for the Sixth Circuit. Should the court of appeals reverse the district court's decision?

13. Richard Jimenez was injured when a disc for the handheld electric disc grinder he had purchased from Sears Roebuck shattered while he used the grinder to smooth down a steel weld. When Jimenez brought a strict liability lawsuit against Sears, the defendant argued that he had misused the grinder and that this misuse caused his injury. Assuming that Sears was right, what effect would this have in a state that has not adopted comparative negligence or comparative fault? What effect would it have in a comparative fault state?

14. Standard Candy Co., a Tennessee firm, produces candy bars, including one known as the "Goo Goo Cluster." The Goo Goo Cluster candy bar contains peanuts provided to Standard Candy by an outside supplier. When James Newton II purchased a Goo Goo Cluster and bit into it, he encountered what he claimed to be an undeveloped peanut. Newton maintained that biting the undeveloped peanut caused him to experience a damaged tooth as well as recurring jaw-locking and hearing-loss problems. Newton sued Standard Candy and pleaded the following alternative claims: breach of the implied warranty of merchantability, negligent manufacture, negligent failure to warn, and strict liability. Concerning the breach of implied warranty of merchantability claim, what two tests might the court choose from in determining whether the Goo Goo Cluster Newton purchased was unmerchantable? Was the Goo Goo Cluster unmerchantable under either or both of these tests? What would Newton need to establish in order to win on the other three claims (the two negligence claims and the strict liability claim)? On which of those three claims would Newton stand the best chance of succeeding?

15. James Bainbridge and Daniel Fingarette formulated a plan for a three-dimensional photography business through four independent companies. In January 1988, Bainbridge met with officials of the Minnesota Mining & Manufacturing Company (3M) to seek assistance with the three-dimensional film development process. In mid-1989, 3M formulated a new emulsion that it claimed would work well with the film development process. 3M apparently understood that this emulsion would be used in combination with a backcoat sauce that 3M had also developed. In December 1989, 3M began selling the new emulsion and backcoat sauce to two of the claimants' four companies, but not to the two others. After Bainbridge and Fingarette began using 3M's new emulsion, they encountered a problem with the film development process: The photographs faded, losing their three-dimensional effect. By early 1990, the claimants experienced a significant decline in camera sales. 3M eventually solved the problem, but the claimants' business ultimately failed.

The four companies established by Bainbridge and Fingarette sued 3M in a Texas trial court for breach of express and implied warranties. They argued that the photographic fading was caused by the incompatibility of 3M's new emulsion and its old backcoat sauce. The jury concluded that 3M breached an express warranty for the emulsion and implied warranties for the emulsion and the backcoat sauce. Applying Minnesota law, the trial court awarded the four firms $29,873,599 in lost profits. An intermediate appellate court upheld this award. The Supreme Court of Texas withheld final judgment and certified the following question to the Supreme Court of Minnesota: "For breach of warranty under [Minnesota's version of UCC section 2-318], is a seller liable to a person who never acquired any goods from the seller, directly or indirectly, for pure economic damages (e.g., lost profits), unaccompanied by any injury to the person or the person's property?" This question arose because two of the plaintiff companies, while suffering losses due to 3M's breaches of warranty, had not dealt directly with 3M. How did the Supreme Court of Minnesota answer the certified question?

16. Steven Taterka purchased a new Ford Mustang from a Ford dealer. More than two years later, after Taterka had put 75,000 miles on the car and Ford's express warranty had expired, he discovered that the taillight assembly gaskets on his Mustang had been installed in such a way that water was permitted to enter the taillight assembly, causing rust to form. Even though the rusting problem was a recurrent one of which Ford was aware, Ford did nothing for Taterka. Was Ford liable to Taterka under the implied warranty of merchantability?

17. On February 28, 2005, David Dobrovolny purchased a 2005 F-350 pickup truck, which had been manufactured by Ford Motor Co. The truck caught fire in Dobrovolny's driveway on April 16, 2006. No one was physically injured, and no property other than the truck was damaged. The truck was completely destroyed. Dobrovolny filed suit against Ford on May 20, 2009. In his complaint, Dobrovolny alleged that the defective nature of the truck caused it to catch fire. He pleaded three alternative claims—breach of the implied warranty of merchantability, negligence, and strict liability—in an effort to recover damages for the loss he sustained as a result of purchasing a defective truck. Ford filed a motion to dismiss each of the claims. On what basis would Ford have argued that the breach of implied warranty of merchantability claim should be dismissed? On what basis would Ford have argued that the negligence and strict liability claims should be dismissed? How did the court rule on Ford's motion to dismiss?

18. Iowa residents Robert and DeAnn Wright sued various cigarette manufacturers in a federal district court in an effort to obtain damages for harms allegedly resulting from Robert's cigarette smoking. The plaintiffs pleaded a number of alternative claims, including strict liability. The defendants filed a motion to dismiss, but the federal court largely overruled it. Thereafter, the defendants asked the federal court to certify questions of law to the Iowa Supreme Court, in accordance with an Iowa statute. Concluding that the case presented potentially determinative state law questions as to which there was either no controlling precedent or ambiguous precedent, the federal court certified questions to the Iowa Supreme Court regarding the use of strict liability principles in design defect cases. In answering the certified questions, the Iowa Supreme Court adopted the design defect rules proposed in the *Restatement (Third) of Torts: Product Liability*. Therefore, what controlling rules did that court identify in answering the certified questions? What test did it say courts should apply in design defect cases? What did it say a plaintiff in a design defect case must prove?

19. A General Motors pickup truck driven by Paul Babcock went off the road and struck a tree. The accident rendered Mr. Babcock a paraplegic. Roughly a year later, he died as a result of complications from his injuries. The executor of his estate, Frances Babcock, sued General Motors (GM) on behalf of the estate and herself. According to the plaintiff's version of the facts, Mr. Babcock was wearing his seat belt prior to the accident but as soon as pressure was exerted on it, the belt unbuckled and released because of a condition known as "false latching." The plaintiff claimed that the false-latching condition existed because of negligent design and/or mechanism and that the resulting failure of the seat belt in Mr. Babcock's pickup was a substantial factor in causing Mr. Babcock's severe—and ultimately fatal—injuries.

In addition to various witnesses who testified that Mr. Babcock always wore his seat belt when he was driving, Dr. Malcolm Newman testified as an expert witness for the plaintiff. He was a structural and mechanical engineering specialist with significant involvement in accident reconstruction and analysis of automobile restraint systems. Employing a method used by accident reconstruction specialists, Dr. Newman reviewed photos and other materials given to him and formed opinions as to how fast Mr. Babcock's pickup was traveling when it left the highway and hit the tree. He testified that in his opinion, the "impact" speed was between 20 and 25 miles per hour and the Babcock truck had been traveling at 35 to 45 miles per hour at the time it left the highway. Dr. Newman also opined that the normal wear and tear associated with continued use of the buckle would increase the danger of false latching. Using a Volvo seat belt buckle, he demonstrated that the Volvo design eliminated the risk that false latching would occur. Dr. Newman noted that the buckle on the GM truck evidently had been tested pursuant to the Federal Motor Vehicle Safety Standards. He offered the view that any testing done by GM had not included testing for false latching. After the jury returned a verdict holding GM liable on the plaintiff's negligence claim, GM appealed. Could GM properly have been held liable even though nothing it did or failed to do caused Mr. Babcock's truck to leave the highway and strike a tree? Did the plaintiff sufficiently prove what was necessary to establish negligent design and/or negligent testing on the part of GM?

20. Rita Emeterio bought disposable butane lighters for use at her bar. Her daughter, Gloria Hernandez, took lighters from the bar time to time for her personal use. Hernandez's five-year-old daughter, Daphne, took a lighter from her mother's purse on the top shelf of a closet in her grandparents' home. Using the lighter, Daphne started a fire in which her two-year-old brother, Ruben, was severely burned. On Ruben's behalf, Hernandez sued the manufacturers and distributors of the lighter, Tokai Corporation and Scripto-Tokai Corporation (collectively, "Tokai"), in the U.S. District Court for the Western District of Texas. Asserting a strict liability claim, Hernandez alleged that the lighter was defectively designed and unreasonably dangerous because it did not have a child-resistant safety mechanism that would have prevented or substantially reduced the

likelihood of a child's using it to start a fire. Tokai moved for summary judgment, contending that a disposable lighter is a simple household tool intended for adult use only, and that a manufacturer has no duty to incorporate child-resistant features into a lighter's design to protect unintended users—children—from obvious and inherent dangers. Tokai also noted that adequate warnings against access by children were provided with its lighters, even though that danger was obvious and commonly known. In response to Tokai's motion, Hernandez argued that because an alternative design in existence at the time the lighter at issue was manufactured and distributed would have made the lighter safer in the hands of children, it remained for the jury to decide whether the lighter was defective under Texas's common-law risk-utility test. The federal district court granted summary judgment for Tokai. Hernandez appealed to the U.S. Court of Appeals for the Fifth Circuit. The Fifth Circuit then certified the following question of state law to the Supreme Court of Texas:

Under the Texas Products Liability Act of 1993, can the legal representative of a minor child injured as a result of the misuse of a product by another minor child maintain a defective-design products liability claim against the product's manufacturer where the product was intended to be used only by adults, the risk that children might misuse the product was obvious to the product's manufacturer and to its intended users, and a safer alternative design was available?

How did the Supreme Court of Texas answer the certified question?

Performance of Sales Contracts

Sarah Saunders was interested in purchasing a new hybrid-fueled vehicle. Using the web page of a large-volume dealer in a nearby city, she provided the dealer with the make, model, color, and primary options for the vehicle she was seeking. The dealer indicated that he could obtain a vehicle meeting Sarah's specifications, quoted her a very favorable price, and offered to deliver the vehicle to her at the apartment house where she lived. Sarah accepted the offer and wired a deposit to the dealer. When the vehicle arrived, the truck driver refused to unload it from the car carrier or let Sarah inspect it until she had given him a certified check for the balance due. Then he gave her the title to the vehicle, unloaded it, and drove away. Sarah subsequently discovered a number of scratches in the paint and that some of the options she had bargained for—such as a sunroof—were not on the vehicle. When she complained to the dealer, he offered her a monetary "allowance" to cover the defects. She also discovered that the vehicle had a tendency to stall and have to be restarted when she stopped at intersections. Despite repeated trips to the nearby city to have the dealer remedy the problem, those efforts have been unavailing. Sarah has indicated that she wants to return the vehicle to the dealer and get a vehicle that performs properly, but the dealer insists that she has to give him additional time to try to fix it. This situation raises a number of legal questions that, among others, will be discussed in this chapter, including:

- Did Sarah have the right to inspect the vehicle before she paid the balance of the purchase price?
- When Sarah discovered the scratches on the vehicle and that it did not conform to the contract specifications, could she have refused to accept the car and required the dealer to provide one that met the contract?
- Does Sarah have the right to return the defective vehicle to the dealer and obtain either a new vehicle or her money back, or must she give the dealer the opportunities he wants to try to remedy the defect?
- If the dealer knew the vehicle he was delivering to Sarah did not conform to the contract and was damaged, was it ethical for him to deliver it anyway?

LO LEARNING OBJECTIVES

After studying this chapter, you should be able to:

21-1 Explain what is meant by the terms *good faith*, *course of dealing*, and *usage of trade* as they pertain to the performance of sales contracts.

21-2 List the basic obligations and rights of the buyer and seller concerning the delivery of and payment for goods.

21-3 Explain when acceptance of goods occurs, what the effect of accepting goods is, and when a buyer who has accepted goods has the right to revoke such acceptance.

21-4 Discuss the buyer's rights and duties on improper delivery of goods as well as the seller's right to cure a defective delivery.

21-5 Indicate when a party to a contract has the right to seek assurances from the other party that it will perform its obligations.

21-6 Evaluate when a party will have its performance excused on the grounds of commercial impracticability.

IN THE TWO PREVIOUS chapters, we discussed the formation and terms of sales contracts, including those terms concerning express and implied warranties. In this chapter, the focus is on the legal rules that govern the performance of contracts. Among the topics covered are the basic obligations of the buyer and seller with respect to delivery and payment, the rights of the parties when the goods delivered do not conform to the contract, and the circumstances that may excuse the performance of a party's contractual obligations.

General Rules

The parties to a contract for the sale of goods are obligated to perform the contract according to its terms. The Uniform Commercial Code (UCC) gives the parties great flexibility in deciding between themselves how they will perform a contract. The practices in the trade or business as well as any past dealings between the parties may supplement or explain the contract. The UCC gives both the buyer and the seller certain rights, and it also sets out what is expected of them on points that they did not deal with in their contract. It should be kept in mind that the UCC changes basic contract law in a number of respects.

Good Faith

 **LO21-1** Explain what is meant by the terms *good faith*, *course of dealing*, and *usage of trade* as they pertain to the performance of sales contracts.

The buyer and seller must act in good faith in the performance of a sales contract [1-203].[1] Good faith is defined to mean "honesty in fact" in performing the duties assumed in

---

[1]The numbers in brackets refer to sections of the Uniform Commercial Code.

the contract or in carrying out the transaction [1-201(19)]. And, in the case of a merchant, **good faith** means honesty in fact as well as the observance of reasonable commercial standards of fair dealing in the trade [2-103(1)(b)]. Thus, if the contract requires the seller to select an assortment of goods for the buyer, the selection must be made in good faith; the seller should pick out a reasonable assortment [2-311]. It would not, for example, be good faith to include only unusual sizes or colors.

Course of Dealing
The terms in the contract between the parties are the primary means for determining the obligations of the buyer and seller. The meaning of those terms may be explained by looking at any performance that has already taken place. For example, a contract may call for periodic deliveries of goods. If the seller has made a number of deliveries without objection by the buyer, the way the deliveries were made shows how the parties intended them to be made. Similarly, if there were any past contracts between the parties, the way the parties interpreted those contracts is relevant to the interpretation of the present contract. If there is a conflict between the express terms of the contract and the past course of dealing between the parties, the express terms of the contract prevail [1-205(4)].

In the case below, *Grace Label, Inc. v. Kliff*, the court looked to the prior dealing between the parties to explain or supplement the terms of a current contract between the parties.

Usage of Trade
In many kinds of businesses, there are customs and practices of the trade that are known by people in the business and that are usually assumed by parties to a contract for goods of that type. Under the UCC, the parties and courts may use these trade customs and practices—known as usage of trade—in interpreting a contract [2-202, 1-205]. If there is a conflict between the express terms of the contract and trade usage, the express terms prevail [1-205(4)].

Ethics and Compliance in Action

What Should You Do When the Price Rises—or Falls?

When goods that are the subject of a contract are in significantly shorter supply than when the agreement was made and the price has risen, the seller may be tempted to look for an excuse so that he can sell to someone else and realize a greater profit. This situation often arises in the sale of commodities, such as crops, fuel oil, gasoline, and natural gas. Similarly, if goods are in significantly more plentiful supply than when a contract was made, a buyer might be tempted to create an excuse to cancel so that she could buy elsewhere at a lower price. When, if ever, is a seller or buyer ethically justified in trying to find a way out of a contractual obligation because the supply or market conditions have so changed that he or she can make a much better deal elsewhere? Concomitantly, are there circumstances under which the other party, acting in an ethically responsible manner, should voluntarily release the disadvantaged party from his or her contractual commitment?

An example of usage of trade comes from the building supply business where one common lumber item is referred to as a "two-by-four" and might be assumed to measure two inches by four inches by someone not familiar with trade practice. If you were to buy two-by-fours of varying lengths from your local lumberyard or building supply store, you would find that they in fact measure 1⅞ inches by 3¼ inches.

Grace Label, Inc. v. Kliff   355 F. Supp. 2d 965 (S.D. Iowa 2005)

Steve Kliff, a citizen of California, is a sole proprietor in the business of brokering printing projects. On May 24, 2002, Barcel S.A. de C.V. (Barcel), a Mexican company, by purchase order contracted with Kliff for at least 47,250,000 foil trading cards bearing the likeness of Britney Spears. Barcel is a large, multinational corporation that sells a variety of food products. It indicated that the cards would be placed in snack-food packaging and would come in direct contact with the food contents.

On May 30, Kliff by purchase order contracted with Grace Label to produce the Spears cards. Grace is an Iowa corporation engaged in the business of manufacturing pressure-sensitive labels and flexible packaging. The purchase order described the product as a "Foil Trading Card (Direct Food Contact Compatible)." It also specified the printing process was to use "FDA Varnish," which Grace Label understood it was to use to accomplish the food contact compatibility requirement. Grace Label did not have any direct communication with Barcel because Kliff did not want it to be in touch with his customer.

The Spears job was the third or fourth Barcel job Grace Label had worked on with Kliff in about a year's time. Two of the jobs were arranged while Kliff was employed by Chromium Graphics; together, they involved 58,000,000 "scratch off" game piece cards, where customers rubbed off a coating to determine if they had won a prize. In February 2002, Kliff arranged for Grace Label to do the "Ponte Sobre Ruedas Job," which involved printing about 42,000,000 "peel apart" game piece cards, whereby consumers peeled off a top layer to see if they had won a prize. The Spears card was simply a trading card with no "scratch off" or "peel apart" feature. The Spears card was varnished on both sides; the others were varnished on one side. The "direct food compatible" description appeared only in the Spears card purchase order. All of the cards manufactured by Grace Label for the various Barcel projects were inserted in packages of Barcel's snack-food products. On several occasions, Kliff advised Grace Label that he wanted the same materials used for the Spears cards as had been used on the prior jobs.

The adhesive used on the Chromium Graphics cards was Rad-Cure 12PSFLV, as specified by Chromium Graphics. This particular adhesive is not listed on the Rad-Cure website as being among Rad-Cure's FDA (Food & Drug Administration) food-grade adhesives—but Grace Label was unaware of this. Other than ordering the FDA-approved varnish, Grace Label did nothing to determine if the other materials used to produce the Spears cards were compatible for direct contact with food items. Before its work for Barcel, Grace Label had not produced a product intended to be in direct contact with food—and it assumed that the materials it was told to use had been approved by Chromium Graphics or Barcel.

Grace Label produced prototype cards, using leftover materials from the past Barcel jobs (except for the foil, which has no odor), and submitted them to Barcel, through Kliff, for approval. Grace Label understood that Barcel was interested in the size and weight of the cards to make sure they would fit in the Barcel dispensing units. Kliff was on the Grace Label premises during the first week of production and had many boxes of cards brought to him for inspection. He raised no issues concerning the cards.

On June 28, 2002, Grace Label shipped 17,138,000 production cards directly to Barcel. An additional 7,500,000 cards were shipped to Barcel on July 5, 2002. After receipt of the production cards, Barcel complained to Kliff that the cards emitted a foul odor and were not fit for use in the potato chip bags for which they were intended. Grace Label suggested they be aired out to eliminate the odor. Barcel attempted to do this—but the odor persisted despite Grace Label's contention that the Spears production cards smelled the same as the cards for the other Barcel jobs that Grace Label had printed and that had been accepted by Kliff and Barcel.

Barcel rejected the cards under its contract with Kliff before the final production of cards was shipped from Grace Label. Kliff thereupon canceled the remaining order with Grace Label. Beyond a $90,000 down payment, Kliff did not pay Grace Label the contract amount for the cards. Grace Label then brought suit against Kliff for breach of contract. Kliff contended that the cards smelled bad and that the smell was caused by a chemical (beta-phenoxyethyl acrylate [BPA]) in the adhesive, which was not direct food compatible. Kliff's expert stated that the BPA was undetectable in the prototype cards but that in the production cards, the concentration of BPA far exceeded that in uncured or cured Rad-Cure. Grace Label's response was that Kliff specified and approved of the material components of the cards and it relied on Kliff and Barcel to select appropriate material as it had no expertise in the area. This argument would require the court to consider the course of dealing between the parties; Kliff objected to the introduction of this evidence.

Walters, Chief United States Magistrate Judge

The parol evidence rule does not bar the course of dealing between the parties. The UCC codifies a commercial version of the rule:

> Terms with respect to which the confirmatory memoranda of the parties agree or which are otherwise set forth in a writing intended as a final expression of their agreement with respect to such terms as are included therein and may not be contradicted by evidence of any prior agreement or of a contemporaneous oral agreement but may be explained or supplemented (a) by a course of dealing or usage of trade . . . or by course of performance.

[2-202(a)]. "Course of dealing" is a defined term meaning "a sequence of previous conduct between the parties to a particular transaction which is fairly to be regarded as establishing a common basis for interpreting their expressions and other conduct." [1-205(3)]. A course of dealing "gives particular meaning to and supplements or qualifies terms of an agreement." [1-205(3)].

"Whenever reasonable" express terms and the course of dealing are to be construed consistent with each other. The rule incorporated in the UCC reflects the commonsense assumption that the course of prior dealings between the parties and usages of trade were taken for granted when the contract document was phrased.

[Author's note: The court then held that the written contract could be explained or supplemented by "course of dealing" between the parties. Such evidence would be intended not to change or vary the contract terms, but rather to explain what the parties meant by them. At the same time, the court concluded that there were genuine issues of material fact that precluded giving summary judgment at this time. These included (1) whether the parties intended, on the basis of successful use of adhesive and other material on prior jobs, that the trading cards made with the same materials would be "direct food compatible" within the meaning of the contract and (2) whether the odor on the cards was worse than what had been accepted before.]

Motion for summary judgment denied.

Modification

Under the UCC, consideration is not required to support a modification or rescission of a contract for the sale of goods. However, the parties may specify in their agreement that modification or rescission must be in writing, in which case a signed writing is necessary for enforcement of any modification to the contract or its rescission [2-209].

Waiver

In a contract that entails a number of instances of partial performance (such as deliveries or payments) by one party, the other party must be careful to object to any late deliveries or payments. If the other party does not object, it may waive its rights to cancel the contract if other deliveries or payments are late [2-208(3), 2-209(4)]. For example, a contract calls for a fish wholesaler to deliver fish to a supermarket every Thursday and for the supermarket to pay on delivery. If the fish wholesaler regularly delivers the fish on Friday and the supermarket does not object, the supermarket will be unable to cancel the contract for that reason. Similarly, if the supermarket does not pay cash but sends a check the following week, then unless the fish wholesaler objects, it will not be able to assert the late payments as grounds for later canceling the contract. A party that has waived rights to a portion of the contract not yet performed may retract the waiver by giving reasonable notice to the other party that strict performance will be required. The retraction of the waiver is effective unless it would be unjust because of a material change of position by the other party in reliance on the waiver [2-209(5)].

CYBERLAW IN ACTION

The Internet and E-Commerce Facilitate Contract Modifications

Buyers and sellers sometimes change parts of their contracts after formation. For example, the buyer may need the goods slightly sooner or somewhat later than originally planned. Or the seller may be able to supply only yellow life jackets instead of the buyer's preferred blue and red mix of life jackets. So long as the parties agree to change the particulars of the performance contracted for, an event that Article 2 calls a "modification," they may change their contract. Modifications are quite common in deals between two merchants and are not uncommon in sales in which one lay buyer and one merchant participate.

Let's assume that the buyer decides that her customers like the first shipment of goods under a contract so much that she should order more. To change the quantity in her office, she can do several things—call the seller, or send a revised contract for the seller to sign and return.

E-commerce makes this easier—the buyer can send an e-mail asking the seller to send more of the same goods, preferably by specifying the number above that provided in the earlier agreement that the buyer now wishes to buy. If the buyer bought three $60 life jackets for her own use, Article 2 allows a court to enforce the seller's commitment to sell three at $60 each even without worrying about the statute of frauds in Section 2-201. However, if the buyer wanted to increase her order from 3 to 15 life jackets, the dollar amount of the purchase would rise above $500—and courts would not enforce the larger purchase unless the deal met the statute of frauds.

How does the Internet help buyers and sellers who want to be able to enforce their agreements in court if the other party does not perform? Using either the federal E-Sign law or state-enacted versions of the Uniform Electronic Transactions Act (UETA), the party seeking to enforce the larger quantity could send an e-mail or message using a click-through form provided by a seller's website, and could use that e-mail or other electronically revised order to show the fact of the revision to the "order" and, as applicable, the existence of a reply message from the seller confirming the seller's agreement to the change.

As a further example of how e-mail and the Internet assist sales transactions, sellers now routinely send or post confirmations that shipment has occurred. These messages help buyers plan for the arrival of goods, otherwise keep track of delays in orders that they may need to act upon, and also check that their insurance is effective for a particular purchase or that their warehouse is ready to receive the goods sent.

Assignment Under the UCC, the buyer and/or the seller may delegate their duties to someone else. If there is a strong reason for having the original party perform the duties, perhaps because the quality of the performance might differ otherwise, the parties may not delegate their duties. Also, they may not delegate their duties if the parties agree in the contract that there is to be no assignment of duties. However, they may assign rights to receive performance—for example, the right to receive goods or payment [2-210].

Delivery

 List the basic obligations and rights of the buyer and seller concerning the delivery of and payment for goods.

Basic Obligation The basic duty of the seller is to deliver the goods called for by the contract. The basic duty of the buyer is to accept and pay for the goods if they conform to the contract [2-301]. The buyer and seller may agree that the goods are to be delivered in several lots or installments. If there is no such agreement, then a single delivery of all the goods must be made. Where delivery is to be made in lots, the seller may demand the price of each lot upon delivery unless there has been an agreement for the extension of credit [2-307].

Place of Delivery The buyer and seller may agree on the place where the goods will be delivered. If no such agreement is made, then the goods are to be delivered at the seller's place of business. If the seller does not have a place of business, then delivery is to be made at his home. If the goods are located elsewhere than the seller's place of business or home, the place of delivery is the place where the goods are located [2-308].

Seller's Duty of Delivery The seller's basic obligation is to tender delivery of goods that conform to the contract with the buyer. Tender of delivery means that the seller must make the goods available to the buyer. This must be done during reasonable hours and for a reasonable period of time, so that the buyer can take possession of the goods [2-503]. The contract of sale may require the seller merely to ship the goods to the buyer but not to deliver the goods to the buyer's place of business. If this is the case, the seller must put the goods into the possession of a carrier, such as a trucking company or a railroad. The seller must also make a reasonable contract with the carrier to take the goods to the buyer. Then, the seller must notify the buyer that the goods have been shipped [2-504]. Shipment terms were discussed in Chapter 19, Formation and Terms of Sales Contracts.

If the seller does not make a reasonable contract for delivery or notify the buyer and a material delay or loss results, the buyer has the right to reject the shipment. Suppose the goods are perishable, such as fresh produce, and the seller does not ship them in a refrigerated truck or railroad car. If the produce deteriorates in transit, the buyer can reject the produce on the ground that the seller did not make a reasonable contract for shipping it.

In some situations, the goods sold may be in the possession of a bailee such as a warehouse. If the goods are covered by a negotiable warehouse receipt, the seller must endorse the receipt and give it to the buyer [2-503(4)(a)]. This enables the buyer to obtain the goods from the warehouse. Such a situation exists when grain being sold is stored at a grain elevator. The law of negotiable documents of title, including warehouse receipts, is discussed in Chapter 23, Personal Property and Bailments.

If the goods in the possession of a bailee are not covered by a negotiable warehouse receipt, then the seller must notify the bailee that it has sold the goods to the buyer and must obtain the bailee's consent to hold the goods for delivery to the buyer or release the goods to the buyer. The risk of loss as to the goods remains with the seller until the bailee agrees to hold them for the buyer [2-503(4)(b)].

Inspection and Payment

Buyer's Right of Inspection Normally, the buyer has the right to inspect the goods before he accepts or pays for them. The buyer and seller may agree on the time, place, and manner in which the buyer will inspect the goods. If no agreement is made, then the buyer may inspect the goods at any reasonable time and place and in any reasonable manner [2-513(1)].

If the shipping terms are cash on delivery (COD), then the buyer must pay for the goods before inspecting them unless they are marked "Inspection Allowed." However, if it is obvious even without inspection that the goods do not conform to the contract, the buyer may reject them without paying for them first [2-512(1)(a)]. For example, if a farmer contracted to buy a bull and the seller delivered a cow, the farmer would not have to pay for it. The fact that a buyer may have to pay for goods before inspecting them does not deprive the buyer of remedies against the seller if the goods do not conform to the contract [2-512(2)].

If the goods conform to the contract, the buyer must pay the expenses of inspection. However, if the goods are nonconforming, he may recover his inspection expenses from the seller [2-513(2), 2-715(1)].

Payment The buyer and seller may agree in their contract that the price of the goods is to be paid in money or in other goods, services, or real property. If all or part of the price of goods is payable in real property, then only the transfer of goods is covered by the law of sales of goods. The transfer of the real property is covered by the law of real property [2-304].

The contract may provide that the goods are sold on credit to the buyer and that the buyer has a period of time to pay for them. If there is no agreement for extending credit to the buyer, the buyer must pay for them upon delivery. The buyer usually can inspect goods before payment except where the goods are shipped COD, in which case the buyer must pay for them before inspecting them.

Unless the seller demands cash, the buyer may pay for the goods by personal check or by any other method used in the ordinary course of business. If the seller demands cash, the seller must give the buyer a reasonable amount of time to obtain it. If payment is made by check, the payment is conditional on the check's being honored by the bank when it is presented for payment [2-511(3)]. If the bank refuses to pay the check, the buyer has not satisfied the duty to pay for the goods. In that case, the buyer does not have the right to retain the goods and must give them back to the seller.

Acceptance, Revocation, and Rejection

LO21-3 Explain when acceptance of goods occurs, what the effect of accepting goods is, and when a buyer who has accepted goods has the right to revoke such acceptance.

Acceptance **Acceptance** of goods occurs when a buyer, after having a reasonable opportunity to inspect them, either indicates that he will take them or fails to reject them. To **reject** goods, the buyer must notify the seller of the rejection and specify the defect or nonconformity. If a buyer treats the goods as if he owns them, the buyer is considered to have accepted them [2-606].

For example, Ace Appliance delivers a new large flat-screen television set to Baldwin. Baldwin has accepted the set if, after trying it and finding it to be in working order, she says nothing to Ace or tells Ace that she will keep it. Even if the set is defective, Baldwin is considered to have accepted it if she does not give Ace timely notice that she does not want to keep it because it is not in working order. If she takes the set to her vacation home even though she knows that it does not work properly, this is also an acceptance. In the latter case, her use of the television set would be inconsistent with its rejection and the return of ownership to the seller.

The Global Business Environment

Assurance of Payment

Perhaps the most important provisions in the international sales contract cover the manner by which the buyer pays the seller. Frequently, a foreign buyer's contractual promise to pay when the goods arrive does not provide the seller with sufficient assurance of payment. The seller may not know the overseas buyer well enough to determine the buyer's financial condition or inclination to refuse payment if the buyer no longer wants the goods when they arrive. When the buyer fails to make payment, the seller will find it difficult and expensive to pursue its legal rights under the contract. Even if the seller is assured that the buyer will pay for the goods on arrival, the time required for shipping the goods often means that payment is not received until months after shipment.

To solve these problems, the seller often insists on receiving an **irrevocable letter of credit**. The buyer obtains a letter of credit from a bank in the buyer's country. The letter of credit obligates the buyer's bank to pay the amount of the sales contract to the seller. To obtain payment, the seller must produce a negotiable **bill of lading** and other documents proving that it shipped the goods required by the sales contract in conformity with the terms of the letter of credit.* A letter of credit is irrevocable when the buyer's bank cannot withdraw its obligation to pay without the consent of the seller and the buyer.

Letters of credit may be confirmed or advised. Under a **confirmed letter of credit**, the seller's bank agrees to assume liability on the letter of credit. Typically, under a confirmed letter of credit, the buyer's bank issues a letter of credit to the seller; the seller's bank confirms the letter of credit; the seller delivers the goods to a carrier; the carrier issues a negotiable bill of lading to the seller; the seller delivers the bill of lading to the seller's bank and presents a draft** drawn on the buyer demanding payment for the goods; the seller's bank pays the seller for the goods; the buyer's bank reimburses the seller's bank; and the buyer reimburses its bank.

With an **advised letter of credit**, the seller's bank merely acts as an agent for collection of the amount owed to the seller. The seller's bank acts as agent for the seller by collecting from the buyer's bank and giving the payment to the seller. The buyer's bank is reimbursed by the buyer.

The confirmed letter of credit is the least risky payment method for sellers. The confirmation is needed because the seller, unlike the confirming bank, may not know any more about the financial integrity of the issuing bank than it knows about that of the buyer. The seller has a promise of immediate payment from an entity it knows to be financially solvent—the confirming bank. If the draft drawn pursuant to the letter of credit is not paid, the seller may sue the confirming bank, which is a bank in his home country.

Under the confirmed letter of credit, payment is made to the seller well before the goods arrive. Thus, the buyer cannot claim that the goods are defective and refuse to pay for them. When the goods are truly defective on arrival, however, the customer can commence an action for damages against the seller based on their original sales contract.

Figure 21.1 summarizes the confirmed letter of credit transaction.

Conforming and Nonconforming Documents

In a letter of credit transaction, the promises made by the buyer's and seller's banks are independent of the underlying sales contract between the seller and the buyer. Therefore, when the seller presents a bill of lading and other documents that *conform* to the terms of the letter of credit, the issuing bank and the confirming bank are required to pay, even if the buyer refuses to pay its bank or even, generally, if the buyer claims to know that the goods are defective. However, if the bill of lading or other required documents do not conform to the terms of the letter of credit, a bank may properly refuse to pay. A bill of lading is *nonconforming* when, for example, it indicates the wrong goods were shipped, states the wrong person to receive the goods, or states a buyer's address differently than the letter of credit.

---

*A bill of lading is a document issued by a carrier acknowledging that the seller has delivered particular goods to it and entitling the holder of the bill of lading to receive these goods at the place of destination. Bills of lading are discussed in Chapter 23.

**A draft is a negotiable instrument by which the drawer (in this case, the seller) orders the drawee (the buyer) to pay the payee (the seller). Drafts are discussed in Chapter 31.

If a buyer accepts any part of a **commercial unit** of goods, he is considered to have accepted the whole unit [2-606(2)]. A commercial unit is any unit of goods that is treated by commercial usage as a single whole. It can be a single article (such as a machine), a set or quantity of articles (such as a dozen, bale, gross, or carload), or any other unit treated as a single whole [2-105(6)]. Thus, if a bushel of apples is a commercial unit, then a buyer purchasing 10 bushels of apples who accepts 8½ bushels is considered to have accepted 9 bushels.

In the *Weil v. Murray* case, which follows, the buyer was considered to have accepted goods that it had handled inconsistently with a claim of rejection and return of ownership of the goods to the seller.

Figure 21.1 Confirmed Letter of Credit Transaction

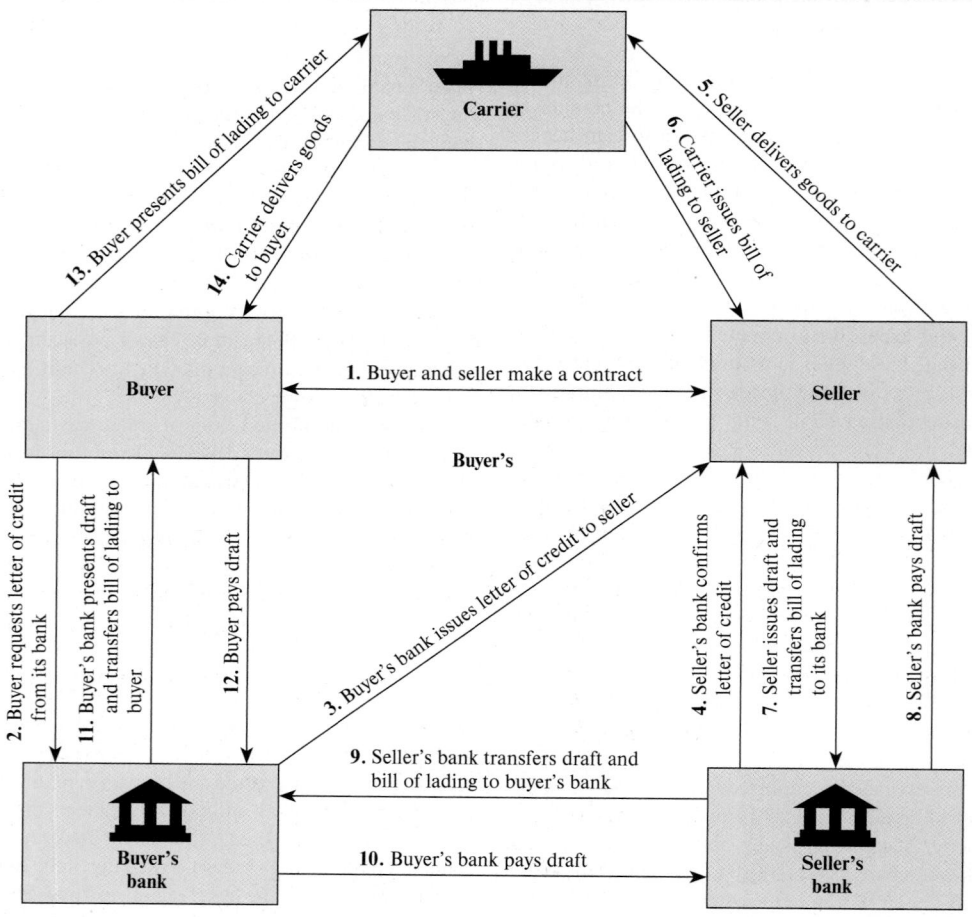

Weil v. Murray	**161 F. Supp. 2d 250 (S.D.N.Y. 2001)**

On October 19, 1997, Mark Murray, a New York art dealer and gallery owner, traveled to Montgomery, Alabama, to view various paintings in the art collection owned by Robert Weil. Murray examined one of the paintings under ultraviolet light—a painting by Edgar Degas titled Aux Courses. *Murray discussed the Degas with Ian Peck, another art dealer, who indicated an interest in buying it and asked Murray to arrange to have it brought to New York.*

Murray and Weil executed an agreement that provided for consignment of the Degas to Murray's gallery "for a private inspection in New York for a period of a week from November 3" to be extended only with the express permission of the consignor. The director of Murray's Gallery picked up the painting, which was subsequently shown by Murray to Peck. Peck agreed to purchase the painting for $1,225,000 with Murray acting as a broker. On November 8, Murray advised Weil that he had a buyer for the Degas, and they orally agreed to the sale. Subsequently, they entered into a written agreement for the sale of the painting for $1 million that indicated, among other things, that if Weil did not receive full payment by December 8, Murray would disclose the name of the undisclosed principal on whose behalf he was acting.

Neither Murray nor anyone else ever paid Weil the $1 million. Nonetheless, Murray maintained possession of the Degas from November 3, 1997, through March 25, 1998, when Weil requested its return. At some point in mid-November, Weil and Peck took the

Degas to an art conservator. A condition report prepared by the conservator and dated December 3, 1997, showed that the conservator had cleaned the painting and sought to correct some deterioration. Weil brought an action to recover the price of the painting from Murray.

Mukasey, District Judge

The undisputed facts establish also that Murray accepted the Degas. "Goods that a buyer has in its possession necessarily are accepted or rejected by the time a reasonable opportunity for inspecting them passes." Murray first inspected the Degas under an ultraviolet light when he viewed it at the Weils' home in late October. Murray had the opportunity to further examine the Degas at his gallery in New York pursuant to the consignment agreement and his continued possession of the painting following the expiration of the consignment agreement. It is also undisputed that Murray was present when Simon Parkes assessed the condition of the painting sometime between November 3 and November 19, 1997. Not only did Murray have a reasonable time to inspect the goods, but also it is undisputed that he actually did inspect the Degas. There is no evidence that Murray found the painting unsatisfactory or nonconforming. *See Integrated Circuits Unltd. v. E. F. Johnson Co.*, 875 F.2d 1040, 1042 (2d Cir. 1989) (discussing acceptance as the failure to make an effective rejection after a reasonable time to inspect). Although the question of whether the buyer has had a reasonable time to inspect is generally a question for the trier of fact, no reasonable jury could

find that Murray did not accept the Degas in light of the undisputed facts that he inspected the Degas on at least two occasions, signed the written agreement, and continued to retain possession of the Degas. See *Sessa v. Riegle*, 427 F. Supp. 760, 767 (D.C. Pa. 1977) (finding acceptance when buyer was permitted unlimited inspection of a horse and then indicated that he would buy the horse).

Moreover, it is undisputed that, without Weil's consent, Murray, at a minimum, permitted the painting to be cleaned and restored in late November or early December. Murray's participation in the alteration of the painting, regardless of whether such alteration increased its value, was an act inconsistent with Weils' ownership. *See In re Fran Char Press, Inc.*, 55 B.R. 55, 57 (Bankr. E.D.N.Y. 1985) (finding that buyer had accepted posters by taking possession of them and mounting them on cardboard); *Industria De Calcados Martini Ltd. v. Maxwell Shoe Co.*, 630 N.E.2d 299 (Mass. App. Ct. 1994) (finding acceptance where buyer had shoes refinished). The Weils have established that Murray agreed to purchase the Degas, accepted it, and nonetheless failed to pay the purchase price.

Summary judgment granted in favor of the Weils.

Effect of Acceptance Once a buyer has accepted goods, he cannot later reject them unless, at the time they were accepted, the buyer had reason to believe that the nonconformity would be cured. By accepting goods, the buyer does not forfeit or waive all remedies against the seller for any nonconformities in the goods. However, if the buyer wishes to hold the seller responsible, he must give the seller timely notice that the goods are nonconforming.

The buyer is obligated to pay for goods that are accepted. If the buyer accepts all of the goods sold, she is, of course, responsible for the full purchase price. If the buyer accepts only part of the goods, she must pay for that part at the contract rate [2-607(1)].

Explain when acceptance of goods occurs, what the effect of accepting goods is, and when a buyer who has accepted goods has the right to revoke such acceptance.

Revocation of Acceptance Under certain circumstances, a buyer may revoke or undo the acceptance. A buyer may revoke acceptance of nonconforming goods where (1) the nonconformity substantially impairs

the value of the goods and (2) the buyer accepted them without knowledge of the nonconformity because of the difficulty of discovering the nonconformity or the buyer accepted the goods because of the seller's assurances that it would cure the defect [2-608(1)].

The buyer must exercise her right to revoke acceptance within a reasonable time after the buyer discovers or should have discovered the nonconformity. Revocation is not effective until the buyer notifies the seller of the intention to revoke acceptance. After a buyer revokes acceptance, her rights are the same as they would have been if the goods had been rejected when delivery was offered [2-608]. The *Pittman v. Henry Moncure Motors* case, which follows, illustrates some of the considerations involved in determining whether a buyer acted reasonably to revoke acceptance.

The right to revoke acceptance could arise, for example, where Arnold buys a new car from Dealer. While driving the car home, Arnold discovers that it has a seriously defective transmission. When she returns the car to Dealer, Dealer promises to repair it, so Arnold decides to keep the car. If Dealer does not fix the transmission after repeated efforts to fix it, Arnold could revoke her acceptance on the grounds that the nonconformity substantially impairs the value of the car, that she took delivery of the car without knowledge of the nonconformity, and that her acceptance was based on Dealer's assurances that he would fix the car. Similarly, revocation of acceptance might be involved where a serious problem with the car not discoverable by inspection shows up in the first month's use.

Revocation must occur prior to any substantial change in the goods, however, such as serious damage in an accident or wear and tear from using them for a period of time. What constitutes a "substantial impairment in value" and when there has been a "substantial change in the goods" are questions that courts frequently have to decide when an attempted revocation of acceptance results in a lawsuit.

Pittman v. Henry Moncure Motors
87 UCC Rep. 2d 619 (N.C. Ct. App. 2015)

On January 10, 2003, Ashley Keith Pittman and DeAnna Pittman entered into a contract with Moncure Motors for the sale, delivery, and setup of a manufactured home for a total price of $92,135. That price included $15,000 in "optional equipment," $9,500 of which was for a brick foundation. The Pittmans intended it to be their primary residence.

At Moncure's request, Ashley Pittman contracted with a mason to build a foundation for the home and with a contractor to perform the rest of the setup of the home. This entailed lifting the walls and the roof, including putting braces on the rafters, attaching plywood to the roof, and nailing extra shingles.

The home was manufactured by Crestline Homes, a company that subsequently filed for bankruptcy. It was delivered to the Pittmans' lot in two sections wrapped in plastic wrap seal in May 2003. In transit, wind and rain ripped the plastic of one of the sections all the way down its side, causing water to enter into it. After both sections were delivered, more rain fell and entered into the exposed section. Prior to the setup, Ashley Pittman and Philip Moncure, the president and general manager of Moncure Motors, together saw that one of the sections had suffered water damage from the leakage.

After the foundation was built and the home was lifted onto the foundation by crane, the contractor erected the roof. However, he improperly installed the roof.

Although Ashley Pittman told Moncure that "this is not what I paid for" and to "take the home back," Moncure assured him that he would address the problems with the home. Part of the home was gutted, cleaned of mold, and rebuilt. In September 2003, the Pittmans moved into the house; subsequently, they experienced severe water leakage through the roof as well as a number of other problems with the interior and exterior of the home. Moncure unsuccessfully attempted to address these problems over the next year and, in September 2004, the Pittmans, through their attorney, demanded a replacement home from Moncure Motors and Crestline.

Following the September 2004 letter, the parties agreed that Crestline would be given a further opportunity to cure the defects in the home, and Moncure Motors would be financially responsible for the repairs covered by warranty. While over the next two years the roof, vinyl siding, and electrical circuit breakers were replaced, many defects, including problems with the electrical system, persisted.

The Pittmans then brought suit against Moncure Motors and Crestline alleging breach of warranty and seeking a refund of the full purchase price as buyers who had justifiably revoked their acceptance of the purchase price. The trial court awarded the Pittmans damages for breach of warranty in the amount of $92,135 plus interest at the legal rate from September 1, 2004, the date the trial court found that the Pittmans had made it unequivocally clear they had rescinded the contract. The trial court further specified that upon Moncure Motors's payment of the damages, it would be entitled to recover the manufactured home from the Pittmans' property upon no less than six months' notice. Moncure and Crestline Homes appealed.

Geer, Judge

The UCC's warranty of implied merchantability guarantees, among other things, that goods are fit for the ordinary purposes for which such goods are used. Implicit to a home's fitness for use as a dwelling is that it be free of major defects. The evidence presented at trial overwhelmingly supports the conclusion that the home was not fit for use as a dwelling unit.

We next address the trial court's determination that the Pittmans "elected to rescind" the purchase of the manufactured home by their "words and conduct." Although "rescission" is not a remedy available under the UCC, section 2-608 provides for the similar remedy of revocation of acceptance. After accepting goods from a seller,

1. The buyer may revoke his acceptance of a lot or commercial unit whose nonconformity substantially impairs its value to him if he accepted it
   (a) On the reasonable assumption that its nonconformity would be cured and it has not been seasonably cured; or
   (b) Without discovery of such nonconformity if his acceptance was reasonably induced either by the difficulty of discovery before acceptance or by the seller's assurances.

A buyer who revokes has the same rights and duties with respect to the goods as if he had rejected them. Section 2-608(3). Formal notice that acceptance is being revoked is not necessary; any conduct by the buyer manifesting to the seller that he is seriously dissatisfied with the goods and expects redress or satisfaction is sufficient.

Although the trial court referred to the remedy of rescission, our appellate courts have concluded that references to the remedy of rescission should be treated as revocations of acceptance. Accordingly, we must determine whether the trial court's findings are sufficient to support the conclusion that the Pittmans revoked their acceptance.

After making findings regarding the substantial defects in the manufactured home, the trial court determined that the Pittmans by "words and conduct" elected to rescind the purchase of the dwelling. The court found that a reasonable person in the same or similar circumstances would consider the breach a substantial deprivation of the material benefit of the purchase of the dwelling.

After the Pittmans gave Moncure Motors notice of the breach, Moncure Motors "attempted to repair and correct the water damage and the workmanlike setup of the dwelling in a reasonable and timely manner, but failed to be successful in doing so." Based on these findings, the trial court concluded that the Pittmans "justifiably rescinded the sale/purchase of the manufactured mobile home." We hold that the record contains ample evidence to support the findings regarding the defects, notice of those defects to Moncure Motors, the Pittmans's attempts to reject acceptance of the manufactured home by demanding replacement of the home, and Moncure Motors' inability to repair and correct the defects. The evidence is sufficient to support a determination that the Pittmans initially revoked acceptance of the purchase of their home.

Nonetheless, the defendants contend that the Pittmans's uninterrupted residence in the home, for at least 11 years, should ultimately be read as the Pittmans's acceptance of the home and its nonconformities.

The reasonableness of continued use of defective goods after revocation may depend on whether "(1) the seller tendered instructions concerning return of the rejected goods upon notice of the revocation; (2) business needs or personal circumstances compelled the buyer's continued use; (3) the seller continued to offer assurances that the nonconformities would be cured or that the buyer would be recompensed for dissatisfaction and inconvenience during the period of continued use; (4) the seller acted in good faith; and (5) the seller suffered undue prejudice as a result of the continued use." [Citation omitted.]

Here, pursuant to Crestline's promise to make further repairs following the September 2004 letter, numerous attempts were made to address continued defects in the home, including, among other things, replacing the roof, vinyl siding, and electric circuit breakers. Yet, despite these attempted repairs, the record and transcript are replete with references to problems that had not been repaired at the time of trial. Further, Mr. Pittman testified that he has been continuously dissatisfied with the home: "[I]t is steady stuff wrong. It has never been right. . . . And, I feel like when I paid that money—I can understand a few things being wrong, but I think it went overboard." Mr. Pittman testified that he would have returned the home to Moncure Motors, but Moncure Motors would not allow that. He also testified that he and his family would have walked away from the home if they were not indebted on it and the home were not on their family's land. Nothing in the record suggests that the Pittmans ever indicated to the defendants that they were even remotely satisfied with the home.

Contrary to defendants' contention that the Pittmans ultimately accepted the egregiously defective home, the evidence shows that if the Pittmans at all waived revocation of acceptance after giving notice via the September 2004 letter, such waiver was made on the condition that the repairs would be made to the Pittmans's satisfaction. The evidence was uncontradicted that the Pittmans would have walked away from the home but for the facts that Moncure Motors refused tender of the home; the home was placed on the Pittmans's family land; the Pittmans were indebted on it; after giving notice of revocation of acceptance, the Pittmans agreed to allow Moncure Motors and Crestline more time to attempt repairs; and the subsequent numerous attempts to address the defects in the home were unsuccessful.

Based on that evidence, the conditions necessary for the Pittmans to waive their revocation of acceptance failed to materialize. We also note that there is no evidence that the defendants were prejudiced by the continued use: Mr. Moncure testified that it cost less to attempt repairs than to replace the home, and Moncure Motors acquiesced in Crestline's decision to attempt further repairs.

Judgment for the Pittmans affirmed.

Buyer's Rights on Improper Delivery

If the goods delivered by the seller do not conform to the contract, the buyer has several options. The buyer can (1) reject all of the goods, (2) accept all of them, or (3) accept any commercial units and reject the rest [2-601]. The buyer, however, cannot accept only part of a commercial unit and reject the rest. The buyer must pay for the units accepted at the price per unit provided in the contract.

Where the contract calls for delivery of the goods in separate installments, the buyer's options are more limited. The buyer may reject an installment delivery only if the nonconformity *substantially affects the value* of that delivery and *cannot be corrected* by the seller in a timely fashion. If the nonconformity is relatively minor, the buyer must accept the installment. The seller may offer to replace the defective goods or give the buyer an allowance in the price to make up for the nonconformity [2-612].

For example, a produce wholesaler agrees to provide a grocer with 10 crates of lettuce each week for the next year. This would be an installment contract. If one week about half the lettuce in one of the crates has rotted, the buyer likely would have to accept the shipment and settle for an adjustment in the price for that crate. If six of the crates contained rotten lettuce, the seller would either have to promptly remedy the nonconforming delivery and send six replacement crates, or the buyer would be able to reject the entire shipment on the grounds that the nonconformity (the six crates of rotten lettuce) substantially affected the value of the entire delivery that week.

Where the nonconformity or defect in one installment impairs the value of the whole contract, the buyer may treat it as a breach of the whole contract but must proceed carefully so as not to reinstate the remainder of the contract [2-612(3)].

Rejection

If a buyer has a basis for rejecting a delivery of goods, the buyer must act within a *reasonable time* after delivery. The buyer must also give the seller *notice* of the rejection, preferably in writing [2-602]. The buyer should be careful to state all of the defects on which he is basing the rejection, including all of the defects that a reasonable inspection would disclose. This is particularly important if these are defects that the seller might cure (remedy) and the time for delivery has not expired. In that case, the seller may notify the buyer that he intends to redeliver conforming goods.

If the buyer fails to state in connection with his rejection a particular defect that is ascertainable by reasonable inspection, he cannot use the defect to justify his rejection if the seller could have cured the defect had he been given reasonable notice of it. In a transaction taking place between merchants, the seller has, after rejection, a right to a written statement of all the defects in the goods on which the buyer bases his right to reject, and the buyer may not later assert defects not listed in justification of his rejection [2-605].

If the buyer wrongfully rejects goods, she is liable to the seller for breach of the sales contract [2-602(3)].

In the case that follows, *Hillerich & Bradsby v. Charles Products*, the court addressed the question of whether a buyer had acted in a timely fashion to notify the seller of a defect in products it had delivered to it for sale in a museum store.

CYBERLAW IN ACTION

Providing Notice

Sections 2-602 and 2-607 require that the buyer notify the seller if the buyer wishes to reject goods the seller has tendered to the buyer, or if the buyer decides to revoke acceptance of goods that the seller has promised to repair or replace and has neither repaired nor replaced the goods as promised—or where the buyer gets goods that have a latent (hard-to-find) defect. "Notice" does not have to be in writing to be effective under 2-602 or 2-607, but many buyers prefer to have a record that they gave notice to the seller and the time of the notice

given. This reduces the risk that a court will find that the buyer's failure to give notice deprives the buyer of her right to a remedy [see Section 2-607(3)(a)]. Electronic commerce tools, including e-mail, allow buyers to provide speedy and reliable information to sellers in cases such as these. Buyers whose e-mail systems provide confirmation that the seller recipient actually has received the message about the buyer's concerns about the goods, or who show the time and date that the intended recipient opened the e-mail, should make providing notice easier and less expensive than using traditional means of communication.

Hillerich & Bradsby Co. v. Charles Products   88 UCC Rep. 2d 178 (W.D. Ky. 2015)

On November 29, 2010, Charles Products entered into an agreement to provide Hillerich & Bradsby with a variety of products to be sold in Hillerich & Bradsby's Louisville Slugger Museum Store. The products included ball and cup sets, baseball piggy banks, batter ducks, stress balls, "Bunny H2O cups," "Kids Pop-Up Water Bottles," "Bunny Sippy Cups," and lunchboxes.

Under the Consumer Products Safety Improvement Act of 2008 (CPSIA), manufacturers generally must provide accompanying a shipment of goods designed to be sold to children a certificate of compliance that identifies "the manufacturer or private labeler issuing the certificate and any third-party conformity assessment body on whose testing the certificate depends." CPSIA also requires manufacturers to place permanent, distinguishing marks on children's products and packaging. The markings are intended to enable the manufacturer as well as the ultimate purchaser to ascertain the location and date of production of the product and cohort information (including the batch, run number, or other identifying characteristic). CPSIA also mandates that children's products generally must not contain more than 100 parts per million of total lead content.

Charles Products began tendering the items about February 15, 2011. After two months of selling the items, the director of retail for the museum sent an e-mail to the regional sales representative for Charles Products, asking whether they were sure the paint on the "ball and cup" set was not lead based and whether it complied with the CPSIA regulations. In November, some nine months after Charles Products began to tender products to Hillerich & Bradsby, the director of retail again contacted the Charles representative indicating that she needed the certificates for the products they had that were intended for youth under 12. Subsequently, she also asked for test documentation that they were in compliance with the CPSIA guidelines. Further e-mail exchanges between the parties in February 2012 focused on the lack of documentation for the products.

In April 2012, Charles Products was informed that one of its products—a rubber die cut mug—was tested for lead content and found to exceed the CPSIA lead limit. The following month, two other products—the baseball piggy bank and the lunchbox—were similarly found to be nonconforming due to excess lead. Hillerich & Bradsby then had to pull those items from the sales floor and sought to return them for a full refund of the purchase price. In August, after consulting with the Consumer Products Safety Commission concerning items with noncompliant tracking labels, Hillerich & Bradsby informed Charles Products it would be returning all noncompliant items.

Hillerich & Bradsby had sold a substantial number of some items. For example, it sent back only 107 of 1,514 "timers" it had received, 34 of 748 "batter ducks," 1,394 out of 4,4452 "stress balls," and 263 of 1,001 "Big Rig Trailers." On the other hand, it had only sold a small fraction of the amount of some other items received from Charles Products; for example, it returned 1,338 of 1,443 "Bunny H20 cups," 1,236 out of 1,438 "Kids Pop Up Water bottles," and 2,321 of 2,472 "#@1 Bunny Sippy Cups." However, over a period of a year and a half, Hillerich & Bradsby had sold hundreds of products it subsequently alleged were nonconforming.

Charles Products picked up the remaining products on September 14, 2012, and then hired a division of Underwriters Laboratory to review the disputed products to determine whether or not any products were noncompliant with the CPSIA and, if so, how to bring them into compliance. Charles Products advised Hillerich & Bradsby of the results on November 9.

Hillerich & Bradsby then filed a breach of contract claim against Charles Products alleging noncompliance with the CPSIA, and it, in turn, filed a counterclaim for breach of contract.

Simpson, Senior Judge.

Both parties move for summary judgment on Hillerich & Brasby's claim for breach of contract. The Court will grant Hillerich & Bradsby's motion for summary judgment on its breach of contract claim relating to the baseball piggy bank and rubber die cut mug products. The court will grant Charles Products' motion for summary judgment with respect to all other items except relating to the lunchbox.

a. Timely Revocation of Tendered Goods

Under Kentucky law governing the revocation of tendered goods, "where a tender has been accepted (a) the buyer must *within a reasonable time* after he discovers or should have discovered any breach, notify the seller of breach or be barred from any remedy. . . ." [2-607 (emphasis added)]. Whether an action is

taken within a reasonable time "depends on the nature, purpose, and circumstances." [1-205]. While this is generally a question for the trier of fact, "there simply are situations in which a buyer has delayed so excessively that his actions become untimely as a matter of law." *Chernick v. Casares*, 759 S.W.2d 832, 834 (Ky. Ct. App. 1988).

Beginning about February 15, 2011, Charles Products tendered to Hillerich & Bradsby the relevant products. Hillerich & Bradsby accepted those products and began to sell them in the museum store. While lead content in products is not readily identifiable, the lack of a certificate of compliance within a shipment or failure to properly label a product is immediately ascertainable upon delivery.

Hillerich & Bradsby's representative, Laura Ginnebaugh, knew CPSIA regulations applied to these products. Yet neither

Ginnebaugh nor anyone at Hillerich & Bradsby contacted Charles Products concerning certificates of compliance until at the earliest November 16, 2011—approximately nine months after the initial non-conforming tender. Indeed, Ginnebaugh's email to Doug Miller at Charles Products shows that Hillerich & Bradsby knew it should have addressed the issue earlier than nine months after it began receiving shipments. *See* November 18, 2011, Ginnebaugh email informing Miller that Ginnebaugh's "quality assurance manager is asking for test documentation that we are in compliance with CPSIA guidelines. . . . I knew this was going to catch up to me."

Further, Ginnebaugh did not contact Miller about the lack of tracking labels on Charles Products' products until February 10, 2012: "I will HAVE to have some sort of identifying number on these products. . . . I have a REALLY bad feeling about this." (emphasis in original document). During the time of these email conservations, Hillerich & Bradsby continued selling Charles Products' products. Hillerich & Bradsby did not remove these items from the museum store shelves until May 22, 2012, and did not inform Charles Products it was revoking acceptance of the goods until August 14, 2012—approximately a year and a half after the initial non-conforming tender.

This is a situation where a buyer has delayed so excessively that his actions become untimely as a matter of law. *See Knapp Shoes v. Sylvania Shoe Mfg. Corp.,* 72 F. 3d 190, 201 (1st Cir. 1995) (noting that under the UCC a buyer cannot "accept deliveries of a vast number of items over a period of a year and a half and then suddenly revoke the acceptance of all of them based on defects whose presence was known or suspected during the entire period").

Hillerich & Bradsby should have discovered the failure to include certificates of compliance and proper product labeling a short period after receipt, if not immediately. Instead, Hillerich & Bradsby sold hundreds of these products for approximately a year and a half. Accepting deliveries for nine months without mentioning readily identifiable defects and waiting one and a half years to revoke bars Hillerich & Bradsby from now properly revoking its contract. Whatever the reasonable amount of time to raise such issues and subsequently timely revoke a contract, no reasonable trier of fact could find that obvious and immediately ascertainable defects were timely revoked after this unreasonable, substantial delay.

As an impermissible lead content is not an obvious breach, however, Hillerich & Bradsby did reasonably revoke the contract after relying on Charles Products' assurances pertaining to the three products—baseball piggy bank, lunchbox and rubber die cut mug—containing an impermissible amount of lead.

The Court will grant Charles Products' motion for summary judgment as it pertains to Hillerich & Bradsby's breach of contract claim for Charles Products' failure to provide certificates of compliance and proper labeling.

b. Meaningful Opportunity to Seasonally Cure the Defects

Under Kentucky law, a "buyer may revoke his acceptance of a lot or commercial unit whose nonconformity substantially impairs its value to him if he has accepted it (a) on the reasonable assumption that its nonconformity would be cured and it has not been seasonably cured. . . ." [2-608(1)].

Both parties agree Charles Products advised Hillerich & Bradsby that any defective products would be brought into conformance. The only question is whether Charles Products had reasonable time to cure the remaining defective products. As Charles Products admits the piggy bank and rubber die cup were not curable, this affirmative defense does not apply to that aspect of Hillerich & Bradsby's claim.

On May 22, 2012, a Hillerich & Bradsby representative emailed Charles Products indicating that the lunchboxes were nonconforming. Emails prior to that date inquiring whether the products were generally conforming did not give Charles Products sufficient notice that the lunchboxes did not conform. General inquiry emails are not the same as demanding specific products to be cured or an affirmative statement of non-compliance.

After receiving Hillerich & Bradsby's test reports on the lead content of the lunchboxes, Charles Products emailed Hillerich & Bradsby saying that it was looking at curing the defect by switching the handles on the lunchbox with a compliant part. Approximately three weeks later, Hillerich & Bradsby informed Charles Products that it was revoking the acceptance of goods.

The facts suggest that Charles Products would have had difficulties in contacting its overseas manufacturer to replace the defective handles in a short period of time. While a trier of fact could find that Charles Products was given a reasonable amount of time to cure the defect, there remains a genuine issue of material fact on whether Hillerich & Bradsby allowed Charles Products a meaningful opportunity to cure the defects.

The Court will deny both parties' motion for summary judgment as it pertains to Hillerich & Bradsby's breach of contract claim based on Charles Products' supplying lunchboxes with an impermissible lead content.

c. Baseball Piggy Bank and Rubber Die Cut Mug

The parties agree the baseball piggy bank and rubber die cut mug contained impermissible amounts of lead under the CPSIA. Charles Products "has conceded liability on these products and agreed to provide [Hillerich & Bradsby] a credit when the parties still had a commercial relationship."

The Court will grant Hillerich & Bradsby's motion for summary judgment in part for breach of contract due to the baseball piggy bank and rubber die cut mug containing impermissible amounts of lead.

Right to Cure

If the seller has some reason to believe that the buyer would accept nonconforming goods, then the seller can take a reasonable time to reship conforming goods. The seller has this opportunity even if the original time for delivery has expired. For example, Ace Manufacturing contracts to sell 200 red, white, and blue soccer balls to Sam's Sporting Goods, with delivery to be made by April 1. On March 1, Sam's receives a package from Ace containing 200 all-white soccer balls and refuses to accept them. Ace can notify Sam's that it intends to cure the improper delivery by supplying 200 red, white, and blue soccer balls, and it has until April 1 to deliver the correct balls to Sam's. If Ace thought that Sam's would accept the all-white soccer balls because on past shipments Sam's did not object to the substitution of white balls for red, white, and blue balls, then Ace has a reasonable time even after April 1 to deliver the red, white, and blue soccer balls [2-508].

Buyer's Duties after Rejection

If the buyer is a merchant, then the buyer owes certain duties concerning the goods that he rejects. First, the buyer must follow any reasonable instructions that the seller gives concerning disposition of the goods. The seller, for example, might request that the rejected goods be shipped back to the seller. If the goods are perishable or may deteriorate rapidly, then the buyer must make a reasonable effort to sell the goods. The seller must reimburse the buyer for any expenses that the buyer incurs in carrying out the seller's instructions or in trying to resell perishable goods. In reselling goods, the buyer must act reasonably and in good faith [2-603(2) and (3)].

If the rejected goods are not perishable or if the seller does not give the buyer instructions, then the buyer has several options. First, the buyer can store the goods for the seller. Second, the buyer can reship them to the seller. Third, the buyer can resell them for the seller's benefit. If the buyer resells the goods, the buyer may keep his expenses and a reasonable commission on the sale. If the buyer stores the goods, the buyer should exercise care in handling them. The buyer also must give the seller a reasonable time to remove the goods [2-604].

If the buyer is not a merchant, then her obligation after rejection is to hold the goods with reasonable care for a sufficient time to give the seller an opportunity to remove them. The buyer is not obligated to ship the goods back to the seller [2-602].

CONCEPT REVIEW

Acceptance, Revocation, and Rejection

Acceptance	1. Occurs when buyer, having had a reasonable opportunity to inspect goods, either (a) indicates he will take them or (b) fails to reject them.
	2. If buyer accepts any part of a commercial unit, he is considered to have accepted the whole unit.
	3. If buyer accepts goods, he cannot later reject them *unless* at the time they were accepted the buyer had reason to believe that the nonconformity would be cured.
	4. Buyer is obligated to pay for goods that are accepted.
Revocation	1. Buyer may revoke acceptance of nonconforming goods where (a) the nonconformity *substantially impairs the value* of the goods and (b) buyer accepted the goods without knowledge of the nonconformity because of the difficulty of discovering the nonconformity *or* buyer accepted because of assurances by the seller.
	2. Right to revoke must be exercised within a *reasonable* time after buyer discovers or should have discovered the nonconformity.
	3. Revocation must be invoked before there is any *substantial* change in the goods.
	4. Revocation is not effective until buyer notifies seller of his intent to revoke acceptance.
Rejection	1. Where the goods delivered do not conform to the contract, buyer may (a) reject all of the goods, (b) accept all of the goods, or (c) accept any commercial unit and reject the rest. Buyer must pay for goods accepted.
	2. Where the goods are to be delivered in installments, an installment delivery may be rejected *only if* the nonconformity substantially affects the value of that delivery and cannot be corrected by the seller.
	3. Buyer must act within a reasonable time after delivery.

Assurance, Repudiation, and Excuse

 LO21-5 Indicate when a party to a contract has the right to seek assurances from the other party that it will perform its obligations.

Assurance The buyer or seller may become concerned that the other party may not be able to perform his contract obligations. If there is a reasonable basis for that concern, the buyer or seller can demand **assurance** from the other party that the contract will be performed. If such assurances are not given within a reasonable time not exceeding 30 days, the party is considered to have repudiated the contract [2-609].

Anticipatory Repudiation

Sometimes, one of the parties to a contract repudiates the contract by advising the other party that he does not intend to perform his obligations. When one party repudiates the contract, the other party may suspend his performance. In addition, he may either await performance for a reasonable time or use the remedies for breach of contract that are discussed in Chapter 22 [2-610].

Suppose the party who repudiated the contract changes his mind. Repudiation can be withdrawn by clearly indicating that the person intends to perform his obligations. The repudiating party must do this before the other party has canceled the contract or has materially changed position, for example, by buying the goods elsewhere [2-611].

Excuse

LO21-6 Evaluate when a party will have its performance excused on the grounds of commercial impracticability.

Unforeseen events may make it difficult or impossible for a person to perform his contractual obligations. The UCC rules for determining when a person is excused from performing are similar to the general contract rules. General contract law uses the test of **impossibility**. In most situations, however, the UCC uses the test of **commercial impracticability**.

The UCC attempts to differentiate events that are unforeseeable or uncontrollable from events that were part of the risk borne by a party. If the goods required for the performance of a contract are destroyed without fault of either party prior to the time that the risk of loss passed to the buyer, the contract is voided [2-613]. Suppose Jones agrees to sell and deliver an antique table to Brown. The table is damaged when Jones's antiques store is struck by lightning and catches fire. The specific table covered by the contract was damaged without fault of either party prior to the time that the risk of loss was to pass to Brown. Under the UCC, Brown has the option of either canceling the contract or accepting the table with an allowance in the purchase price to compensate for the damaged condition [2-613].

The Global Business Environment

Insecurity in International Transactions

The Convention on Contracts for the International Sale of Goods (CISG) has provisions concerning insecurity, assurance, and anticipatory repudiation that parallel those in the UCC. Under Article 71 of CISG, a party may suspend performance of his obligations if, after the contract is entered, it "becomes apparent that the other party will not perform a substantial part of his obligations as a result of: (a) a serious deficiency in his ability to perform or his creditworthiness; or (b) his conduct in preparing to perform or in performing the contact." The party suspending performance must immediately give notice to the other party and must continue with performance if the other party provides adequate assurance of its performance.

Under Article 72 of CISG, if prior to the date of performance of a contract, it is clear that one of the parties will "commit a fundamental breach of contract," the other party may declare the contract avoided. If time allows, the party intending to declare the contract avoided must give reasonable notice to the other party in order to permit him to provide adequate assurance of his performance. However, such notice need not be provided if the other party has declared that he will not perform the contract.

A German court* upheld an Italian shoe manufacturer's decision to avoid a contract and awarded damages against the German buyer. The German company had ordered 140 pairs of winter shoes from the Italian manufacturer. After the shoes were manufactured, the Italian seller demanded security for the sales price as the buyer had other accounts payable to the seller still outstanding. When the buyer neither paid nor provided security, the seller declared the contract avoided and resold the shoes to other retailers. The court allowed the seller to recover the difference between the contract price and the price it obtained in the substitute transactions.

---

*Oberlandesgericht Dusseldorf, 17 U 146/93, Jan. 14, 1994 (Germany), 1 UNILEX D. 1994-1 (M. J. Bonnell, ed.)

If unforeseen conditions cause a delay or the inability to make delivery of the goods and thus make performance impracticable, the seller is excused from making delivery. However, if a seller's capacity to deliver is only partially affected, the seller must allocate production in any fair and reasonable manner among his customers. The seller has the option of including any regular customer not then under contract in his allocation scheme. When the seller allocates production, he must notify the buyers [2-615]. When a buyer receives this notice, the buyer may either terminate the contract or agree to accept the allocation [2-616].

For example, United Nuclear contracts to sell certain quantities of fuel rods for nuclear power plants to a number of electric utilities. If the federal government limits the amount of uranium that United has access to, so that United is unable to fill all of its contracts, United is excused from full performance on the grounds of commercial impracticability. However, United may allocate its production of fuel rods among its customers by reducing each customer's share by a certain percentage and giving the customers notice of the allocation. Then, each utility can decide whether to cancel the contract or accept the partial allocation of fuel rods.

In the absence of compelling circumstances, courts do not readily excuse parties from their contractual obligations, particularly where it is clear that the parties anticipated a problem and sought to provide for it in the contract.

In the case that follows, *Rochester Gas and Electric Corporation v. Delta Star*, a court rejected a seller's contention that a significant increase in its cost of materials created a commercial impracticability, excusing it from its obligation to perform the contract at the agreed-upon price.

Rochester Gas and Electric Corporation. v. Delta Star
68 UCC Rep. 2d 130 (W.D.N.Y. 2009)

On June 15, 2005, Delta Star agreed to sell Rochester Gas and Electric (RG&E) eight electrical transformers as specified in subsequent purchase orders issued by RG&E. The agreement provided, among other things, that "prices stated on the face of the Purchase Order shall be considered firm, unless otherwise noted, and Delta Star warrants that said prices do not exceed the prices allowed by any federal, state or local law, regulation, or order." In July, Delta Star received RG&E's purchase orders for the purchase of eight transformers at a price of $616,780 per unit and a total price of $5,586,664.

The agreement also contained a force majeure clause that read as follows:

> Force Majeure. Any delay or failure in the performance by either Party hereunder shall be excused if and to the extent caused by the occurrence of a Force Majeure. For purposes of this Agreement, Force Majeure shall mean a cause or event that is not reasonably foreseeable or otherwise caused by or under the control of the Party claiming Force Majeure, including acts of God, fires, floods, explosions, riots, wars, hurricane, sabotage terrorism, vandalism, accident, restraint of government, governmental acts, injunctions, labor strikes, other than those of Seller or its suppliers, that prevent Seller from furnishing the materials or equipment, and other like events that are beyond the reasonable expectation and control of the Party affected thereby, despite such Party's reasonable efforts to prevent, avoid, delay, or mitigate the effect of such acts, events or occurrences, and which . . . are not attributable to a Party's failure to perform its obligations under this Agreement.

During the fall of 2005, the demand for the type of steel used in the transformers outstripped the supply as buyers in China and India began paying a premium over other markets for such steel. On December 21, 2005, Delta Star sent a letter to its customers stating, among other things:

> Delta Star received notification from our sole electrical steel supplier, AK Steel, Butler, PA, that they will not guarantee any core steel production as of December 7. Delta Star has relied upon this relationship for roughly forty years but now must quickly look to other suppliers. . . . Another factor that has definitely had an effect is the increase in distribution transformer demand due to the hurricanes hitting off the gulf coast. . . .
>
> The predictable result of this is dramatically overall higher prices and some designs requiring modification to accommodate other grades of steel. . . .
>
> The grave reality of the situation is that Delta Star has no choice but to submit these increased prices to its customers. This is a force majeure condition impossible for us to predict and impossible for us to deal with in any other way. . . .

The letter further stated that Delta Star anticipated the per unit increase in price for RG&E's transformers to be $67,183, for a total increase of $537,464.

RG&E advised Delta Star that it appeared to be rejecting its obligation to deliver the transformers for the price specified in the Agreement and asked Delta Star "to provide adequate assurance that it will perform the Agreement in accordance with its terms." When following discussions between the parties, assurances satisfactory to RG&E were not forthcoming, it notified Delta Star on February 7, 2006, that it considered its actions as a repudiation of the Agreement, and thus it was terminating the Agreement effective immediately.

RG&E brought suit against Delta Star for breach of contract. Delta Star then asserted affirmative defenses, including the doctrine of commercial impracticability, force majeure, and failure of presupposed conditions. Experts for both parties stated that the desired steel was available, albeit at much higher prices, and one noted that while the steel was very difficult to obtain, Delta Star was able to secure a new supplier at such higher price. A March 2005 magazine article admitted into evidence indicated that from December 20, 2004, steel prices were increasing, dropping, rebounding, and dropping and suggested the need for clear provisions in contracts indicating which party is to assume the risk of a change in material prices.

Siragusa, District Judge

The defense of commercial impracticability implicates the Uniform Commercial Code. Section 2-615 of the UCC, Excuse by Failure of Presupposed Conditions, states in relevant part:

> Except so far as a seller may have assumed a greater obligation and subject to the preceding section on substituted performance:
>
> (a) Delay in delivery in or non-delivery in whole or in part by a seller who complies with paragraphs (b) and (c) is not a breach of his duty under a contract for sale if performance as agreed has been made impracticable by the occurrence of a contingency the non-occurrence of which was a basic assumption on which the contract was made or by compliance in good faith with any applicable foreign or domestic governmental regulation or order whether or not it later proves to be invalid.

N.Y. U.C.C. Section 2-615(a) (2004). Official Comment four under this section states:

> 4. Increased cost alone does not excuse performance unless the rise in cost is due to some unforeseen contingency which alters the essential nature of the performance. Neither is a rise or a collapse in the market in itself a justification, for that is exactly the type of business risk which business contracts made at fixed prices are intended to cover. But a severe shortage of raw materials or of supplies due to a contingency such as war, embargo, local crop failure, unforeseen shutdown of major sources of supply or the like, which either causes a marked increase in cost or altogether prevents the seller from securing supplies necessary to his performance is within the contemplation of this section.

U.C.C. Section 2-615 Comment 4.

A New York court addressed the application of this section in *Maple Farms, Inc. v. City School District of the City of Elmira*, 352 N.Y.S.2d 784 (1974). There, the plaintiff sought to be relieved from a fixed price contract for supplying milk to the school district in the face of ever-rising milk prices which would have caused a substantial loss on the contract. The New York court found that, "the contingency causing the increase in the price of raw milk was not totally unexpected." Consequently, the court concluded that,

> [t]here is no precise point, though such could conceivably be reached, at which an increase in cost of raw goods above the norm would be so disproportionate to the risk assumed as to as to amount to "impracticability" in a commercial sense. However, we cannot say on these facts that the increase here has reached the point of "impracticality" in performance of this contract in light of the risks that we find were assumed by the plaintiff.

Section 2-615 also addresses governmental interference, by stating in an official comment that, "[h]owever, governmental interference cannot excuse unless it truly 'supervenes' in such a manner as to be beyond the seller's assumption of risk."

In *Maple Farms*, the governmental action was setting the price of milk, subsidizing it for the school district, and selling grain to Russia. Here, the allegation is that government-run companies in China are buying up the M3 steel, causing the subsequent shortage in this country. However, as Delta Star pointed out in its letter to RG&E, a suitable replacement steel, M4, was available, albeit at a higher price. The March 2005 magazine article indicates that from December 20, 2004, headlines showed that steel prices were increasing, dropping, rebounding, and dropping. One of the suggestions contained in the article is the "need for clear bid documents specifying which party is to assume the risk of a change in material prices."

Here, both affiants stated that M4 steel was available, albeit at a much higher price. "While it was also very difficult to obtain, ultimately Delta Star was able to secure a new supplier, albeit at a much higher price." To paraphrase the Second Circuit, "the mere fact that this undertaking may have become burdensome, as a result of subsequent, perhaps unanticipated developments, does not operate to relieve [Delta Star] of its obligation."

For the foregoing reasons, RG&E's application to strike Delta Star's defense of the doctrine of commercial impracticability . . . is granted.

Problems and Problem Cases

1. Cavenish Farms owns a potato processing facility. Mathiason Farms and Valley View Farms ("the Growers") are in the business of raising potatoes. In 2005, Cavenish and the Growers entered into contracts whereby each of the Growers agreed to grow 25,000 hundredweight of russet Burbank potatoes on certain designated fields and sell them to Cavenish. The contracts specified that they were for "crop year 2005," and Cavenish agreed to pay a base price of $4.70 per hundredweight for "usable potatoes." The Growers could not sell potatoes grown on the designated fields unless Cavenish first rejected or released them.

   In November 2005, Cavenish made advance payments to the Growers as required by the contracts. It thereafter became apparent that there were problems with the quality of the potatoes, and the Growers attempted to recondition the potatoes by warming the piles. Cavenish refused to make the next scheduled advance payments due on February 15, 2006. Cavenish inspected two loads of potatoes in late February 2006 and determined that they were not acceptable. On March 31, 2006, Cavenish e-mailed the Growers that it was rejecting the potatoes and sent a formal letter of rejection on April 3, 2006. By that time the potatoes had deteriorated and were unmarketable.

   Cavenish sued the Growers, seeking return of the advance payments as well as damages for failure to deliver potatoes as promised. The Growers counterclaimed, arguing, among other things, that Cavenish had breached the implied covenant of good faith and acted in bad faith by delaying its notice of rejection of the 2005 crop, thereby precluding the Growers from selling the potatoes to another buyer before they totally deteriorated. Cavenish took the position that it had the right under the contract to accept or reject the potatoes at any time up until July 31, 2006, without breaching the contract. Should the court find that Cavenish acted in bad faith in delaying its notice of rejection for more than a month after it had decided to reject the potatoes?

2. Harold Ledford agreed to purchase three used Mustang automobiles (a 1966 Mustang coupe, a 1965 fastback, and a 1966 convertible) from J. L. Cowan for $3,000. Ledford gave Cowan a cashier's check for $1,500 when he took possession of the coupe, with the understanding he would pay the remaining $1,500 on the delivery of the fastback and the convertible. Cowan arranged for Charles Canterberry to deliver the remaining vehicles to Ledford. Canterberry dropped the convertible off at a lot owned by Ledford and proceeded to Ledford's residence to deliver the fastback. He refused to unload it until Ledford paid him $1,500. Ledford refused to make the payment until he had an opportunity to inspect the convertible, which he suspected was not in the same condition that it had been in when he purchased it. Canterberry refused this request and returned both the fastback and the convertible to Cowan. Cowan then brought suit against Ledford to recover the balance of the purchase price. Was Ledford entitled to inspect the car before he paid the balance due on it?

3. Spada, an Oregon corporation, agreed to sell Belson, who operated a business in Chicago, Illinois, two carloads of potatoes at "$4.40 per sack, FOB Oregon shipping point." Spada had the potatoes put aboard the railroad cars; however, he did not have floor racks used in the cars under the potatoes as is customary during winter months. As a result, there was no warm air circulating and the potatoes were frozen while in transit. Spada claims that his obligations ended with the delivery to the carrier and that the risk of loss was on Belson. What argument would you make for Belson?

4. In April, Reginald Bell contracted to sell potatoes to Red Ball Potato Company for fall delivery. The contract specified that the potatoes were to be "85 percent U.S. 1's." In Red Ball's dealing with Bell and other farmers, potatoes were delivered and paid for in truckload quantities. In the fall, Bell delivered several truckloads of potatoes. Samples of each load were taken for testing, and most of the loads were determined to be below 85 percent U.S. No. 1. What options are open to Red Ball?

5. James Shelton is an experienced musician who operates the University Music Center in Seattle, Washington. On Saturday, Barbara Farkas and her 22-year-old daughter, Penny, went to Shelton's store to look at violins. Penny had been studying violin in college for approximately nine months. Mrs. Farkas and Penny advised Shelton of the price range in which they were interested, and Penny told him she was relying on his expertise. He selected a violin for $368.90, including case and sales tax. Shelton claimed that the instrument was originally priced at $465 but that he discounted it because Mrs. Farkas was willing to take it on an "as is" basis. Mrs. Farkas and Penny alleged that Shelton represented that the violin was "the best" and "a perfect violin for you" and that it was of high quality. Mrs. Farkas paid for it by check. On the following Monday, Penny took the violin to her college music teacher, who immediately told her that it had poor tone and a crack in the body and that it was not the right instrument for her. Mrs. Farkas telephoned Shelton and asked for a refund. He refused, saying that she had purchased and accepted the violin

on an "as is" basis. Had Farkas "accepted" the violin so that it was too late for her to "reject" it?

6. Maxwell Shoe Co., a wholesale shoe distributor, ordered a quantity of shoes from Martini Industries. When Maxwell Shoe received the shipment, it discovered that all of the shoes were cracked and peeling. Maxwell Shoe contacted Martini Industries and stated that it was rejecting the shipment because the shoes were defective. Maxwell Shoe wanted to ship the shoes back to Martini Industries but received no communication from Martini Industries regarding what was to be done with the shipment. Maxwell Shoe did not pay the remainder owed for the shipment and stopped payment on the check that had been initially issued for the order. Subsequently, Maxwell Shoe had the shoes refinished by another company and distributed and sold the shoes. Martini Industries sued for the value of the shipment. Did Maxwell Shoe accept the shipment of shoes and owe Martini Industries for the goods?

7. On May 23, Deborah McCullough, a secretary, purchased a Chrysler LeBaron from Bill Swad Chrysler-Plymouth. The automobile was covered by both a limited warranty and a vehicle service contract (extended warranty). Following delivery, McCullough advised the salesperson that she had noted problems with the brakes, transmission, air conditioning, paint job, and seat panels, as well as the absence of rust-proofing. The next day, the brakes failed and the car was returned to the dealer for the necessary repairs. When the car was returned, McCullough discovered that the brakes had not been properly repaired and that none of the cosmetic work had been done. The car was returned several times to the dealer to correct these problems and others that developed subsequently. On June 26, the car was again returned to the dealer, who kept it for three weeks. Many of the defects were not corrected, however, and new problems with the horn and brakes arose. While McCullough was on a shopping trip, the engine abruptly shut off and the car had to be towed to the dealer. Then, while she was on her honeymoon, the brakes again failed. The car was taken back to the dealer with a list of 32 defects that needed correction. After repeated efforts to repair the car were unsuccessful, McCullough sent a letter to the dealer calling for rescission of the purchase, requesting return of the purchase price, and offering to return the car on receipt of shipping instructions. She received no answer and continued to drive it. McCullough then filed suit. In the following May, the dealer refused to do any further work on the car, claiming that it was in satisfactory condition.

By the time of the trial, in June of the next year, it had been driven 35,000 miles, approximately 23,000 of which had been logged after McCullough mailed her notice of revocation. By continuing to operate the vehicle after notifying the seller of her intent to rescind the sale, did McCullough waive her right to revoke her original acceptance?

8. Walters, a grower of Christmas trees, contracted to supply Traynor with "top-quality trees." When the shipment arrived and was inspected, Traynor discovered that some of the trees were not top quality. Within 24 hours, Traynor notified Walters that he was rejecting the trees that were not top quality. Walters did not have a place of business or an agent in the town where Traynor was. Christmas was only a short time away. The trees were perishable and would decline in value to zero by Christmas Eve. Walters did not give Traynor any instructions, so Traynor sold the trees for Walters's account. Traynor then tried to recover from Walters the expenses he incurred in caring for and selling the trees. Did the buyer act properly in rejecting the trees and reselling them for the seller?

9. Haralambos Fekkos purchased from Lykins Sales & Service a Yammar Model 165D, 16-horsepower diesel tractor and various implements. On Saturday, April 27, Fekkos gave Lykins a check for the agreed-on purchase price, less trade-in of $6,596, and the items were delivered to his residence. The next day, while attempting to use the tractor for the first time, Fekkos discovered it was defective. The defects included a dead battery requiring jump starts, overheating while pulling either the mower or tiller, missing safety shields over the muffler and the power takeoff, and a missing water pump. On Monday, Fekkos contacted Lykins's sales representative, who believed his claims to be true and agreed to have the tractor picked up from Fekkos's residence; Fekkos also stopped payment on his check. Fekkos placed the tractor with the tiller attached in his front yard as near as possible to the front door without driving it onto the landscaped area closest to the house. Fekkos left the tractor on the lawn because his driveway was broken up for renovation and his garage was inaccessible and because the tractor would have to be jump-started by Lykins's employees when they picked it up. On Tuesday, Fekkos went back to Lykins's store to purchase an Allis-Chalmers tractor and reminded Lykins's employees that the Yammar tractor had not been picked up and remained on his lawn. On Wednesday, May 1, at 6:00 A.M., Fekkos discovered that the tractor was missing although the tiller had been unhitched and remained in the yard. Later that day, Lykins

picked up the remaining implements. The theft was reported to the police. On several occasions, Fekkos was assured that Lykins's insurance would cover the stolen tractor, that it was Lykins's fault for not picking it up, and that Fekkos had nothing to worry about. However, Lykins subsequently brought suit against Fekkos to recover the purchase price of the Yammar tractor. Was Fekkos liable for the purchase price of the tractor that had been rejected and was stolen while awaiting pickup by the seller?

10. Creusot-Loire, a French manufacturing and engineering concern, was the project engineer to construct ammonia plants in Yugoslavia and Syria. The design process engineer for the two plants—as well as a plant being constructed in Sri Lanka—specified burners manufactured by Coppus Engineering Corporation. After the burner specifications were provided to Coppus, it sent technical and service information to Creusot-Loire.

Coppus expressly warranted that the burners were capable of continuous operation using heavy fuel oil with combustion air preheated to 260 degrees Celsius. The warranty extended for one year from the start-up of the plant but not exceeding three years from the date of shipment. In January 1989, Creusot-Loire ordered the burners for the Yugoslavia plant and paid for them; in November 1989, the burners were shipped to Yugoslavia. Due to construction delays, the plant was not to become operational until the end of 1993. In 1991, however, Creusot-Loire became aware that there had been operational difficulties with the Coppus burners at the Sri Lanka and Syria plants and that efforts to modify the burners had been futile. Creusot-Loire wrote to Coppus expressing concern that the burners purchased for the Yugoslavia plant, like those in the other plants, would prove unsatisfactory and asking for proof that the burners would meet contract specifications. When subsequent discussions failed to satisfy Creusot-Loire, it requested that Coppus take back the burners and refund the purchase price. Coppus refused. Finally, Creusot-Loire indicated that it would accept the burners only if Coppus extended its contractual guarantee to cover the delay in the start-up of the Yugoslavia plant and if Coppus posted an irrevocable letter of credit for the purchase price of the burners. When Coppus refused, Creusot-Loire brought an action for breach of contract, seeking a return of the purchase price. Coppus claimed that Creusot-Loire's request for assurance was unreasonable. How should the court rule?

Remedies For Breach of Sales Contracts

Kathy is engaged to be married. She contracts with the Bridal Shop for a custom-designed bridal gown in size 6 with delivery to be made by the weekend before the wedding. Kathy makes a $1,500 deposit against the contract price of $4,500. If the dress is completed in conformance with the specifications and on time, then Kathy is obligated to pay the balance of the agreed-on price. But what happens if either Kathy or the Bridal Shop breaches the contract? For example:

- If Kathy breaks her engagement and tells the Bridal Shop that she is no longer interested in having the dress before the shop has completed making it, what options are open to the Bridal Shop? Can it complete the dress or should it stop work on it?
- If the Bridal Shop completes the dress but Kathy does not like it and refuses to accept it, what can the Bridal Shop do? Can it collect the balance of the contract price from Kathy, or must it first try to sell the dress to someone else?
- If the Bridal Shop advises Kathy that it will be unable to complete the dress in time for the wedding, what options are open to Kathy? If she has another dress made by someone else, or purchases a ready-made one, what, if any, damages can she collect from the Bridal Shop?
- If the Bridal Shop completes the dress but advises Kathy it plans to sell it to someone else who is willing to pay more money for it, does Kathy have any recourse?
- Would it be ethical for the Bridal Shop to sell the dress to someone else who offers more money for it?

LO LEARNING OBJECTIVES

After studying this chapter, you should be able to:

22-1 Recall the basic objective of the remedies provided for by the UCC for a breach of a contract for the sale of goods.

22-2 Explain what is meant by the term *liquidated damages* and discuss when the UCC allows the enforcement of a liquidated damages clause in a contract for the sale of goods.

22-3 Recall the statute of limitation provided in the UCC that is applicable to lawsuits alleging breach of a contract for the sale of goods.

22-4 List and describe the remedies that the UCC makes available to an injured seller.

22-5 List and describe the remedies that the UCC makes available to an aggrieved buyer.

22-6 Explain what is meant by the term *cover* in the context of a contract for the sale of goods.

22-7 Explain what is meant by the terms *incidental damages* and *consequential damages* and indicate when an injured buyer is able to recover consequential damages.

22-8 Discuss when an aggrieved buyer has a right to specific performance of a contract for the sale of goods.

LO22-1 Recall the basic objective of the remedies provided for by the UCC for a breach of a contract for the sale of goods.

USUALLY, BOTH PARTIES TO a contract for the sale of goods perform the obligations that they assumed in the contract. Occasionally, however, one of the parties to a contract fails to perform his obligations. When this happens, the Uniform Commercial Code (UCC) provides the injured party with a variety of remedies for breach of contract. This chapter will set forth and explain the remedies available to an injured party, as well as the UCC's rules that govern buyer–seller agreements as to remedies and the UCC's statute of limitations. The *objective* of the UCC remedies is to put the injured person in the *same position* that he would have been in *if the contract had been performed*. Under the UCC, an injured party may not recover consequential or punitive damages unless such damages are specifically provided for in the UCC or in another statute [1-106].[1]

Agreements as to Remedies

LO22-2 Explain what is meant by the term *liquidated damages* and discuss when the UCC allows the enforcement of a liquidated damages clause in a contract for the sale of goods.

The buyer and seller may provide their own remedies in the contract, to be applied in the event that one of the parties fails to perform. They may also limit either the remedies that the law makes available or the damages that can be covered [2-719(1)]. If the parties agree on the amount of damages that will be paid to the injured party, this amount is known as **liquidated damages**. An agreement for liquidated damages is enforced if the amount is reasonable and if actual damages would be difficult to prove in the event of a breach of the contract. The amount is considered reasonable if it is not so large as to be a penalty or so small as to be unconscionable [2-718(1)].

---

[1]The numbers in brackets refer to sections of the Uniform Commercial Code.

For example, Carl Carpenter contracts to build and sell a display booth for $5,000 to Hank Hawker for Hawker to use at the state fair. Delivery is to be made to Hawker by September 1. If the booth is not delivered on time, Hawker will not be able to sell his wares at the fair. Carpenter and Hawker might agree that if delivery is not made by September 1, Carpenter will pay Hawker $2,750 as liquidated damages. The actual sales that Hawker might lose without a booth would be very hard to prove, so Hawker and Carpenter can provide some certainty through the liquidated damages agreement. Carpenter then knows what he will be liable for if he does not perform his obligation. Similarly, Hawker knows what he can recover if the booth is not delivered on time. The $2,750 amount is probably reasonable. If the amount were $500,000, it likely would be void as a penalty because it is way out of line with the damages that Hawker would reasonably be expected to sustain. And if the amount were too small, say $10, it might be considered unconscionable and therefore not enforceable.

If a liquidated damages clause is not enforceable because it is a penalty or unconscionable, the injured party can recover the actual damages that he suffered.

Liability for consequential damages resulting from a breach of contract (such as lost profits or damage to property) may also be limited or excluded by agreement. The limitation or exclusion is not enforced if it would be unconscionable. Any attempt to limit consequential damages for injury caused to a person by consumer goods is considered prima facie unconscionable [2-719(3)].

Suppose an automobile manufacturer makes a warranty as to the quality of an automobile that is purchased as a consumer good. It then tries to disclaim responsibility for any person injured if the car does not conform to the warranty and to limit its liability to replacing any defective parts. The disclaimer of consequential injuries in this case would be unconscionable and therefore would not be enforced. Exclusion of or limitation on consequential damages is permitted where the loss is commercial, as long as the exclusion or limitation is not unconscionable. Where circumstances cause a limited remedy agreed to by the parties to fail in its essential purpose, the limited remedy is not enforced, and the general UCC remedies are available to the injured party.

These principles are illustrated in the following case, *Helena Chemical Co. v. Williamson*.

Helena Chemical Co. v. Williamson   86 UCC Rep. 2d 180 (W.D. La. 2015)

Lavelle Williamson began farming in 2010. Prior to that time, he had marked timber and worked in the oilfield industry and as a painter. He had a tenth-grade education.

Until 2010, Williamson had never purchased seeds or chemicals for farming purposes. During his first year of farming, he sought to purchase goods and services from Helena Chemical Company. Helena presented him with a Credit Sales and Services Agreement, which he signed. The terms were not discussed or explained to him. Between 2010 and 2013, Williamson purchased seed, fertilizer, and chemicals from Helena under the Agreement. The Agreement was not superseded or canceled at any time.

For the 2013 crop, Helena provided certain goods and services to Williamson, including corn seed and soybeans and related products, for a total price of $79,188.50. After Helena's delivery, Williamson had difficulty getting the corn seed out of Helena's tender. He contacted Helena's sales representative to complain about the issue but proceeded with planting the corn seed.

Williamson's corn seed failed to germinate, and a sufficient stand of corn was not realized for the 2013 crop year. He contended that the corn seed was wet when it was delivered to him in Helena's tender, and as a result, the wet corn seed absorbed more chemicals than it normally would, resulting in a loss of at least 80 bushels of corn per acre. Helena contended that Williamson's corn crop failure was a result of his own improper application of fertilizer.

Williamson made one payment to Helena, but then made no further payments. Helena brought suit to recover the balance of the amount owing to it. Williamson filed a counterclaim based on negligence, claiming that he suffered damages in the amount of $148,964.15 for decreased corn production, $64,439.16 for loss of a higher contract price, and $13,491.50 for increased farming expenses for the 2013 crop year.

Helena moved for summary judgment on the counterclaim, arguing that as a matter of law, the clear and unambiguous language in the Agreement prevented Williamson from recovering consequential damages. Williamson opposed the motion and argued that the exclusion/limitation of remedies provision in the Agreement was unenforceable under Tennessee law.

The Agreement provided, in pertinent part:

THE EXCLUSIVE REMEDY FOR ANY CAUSE OF ACTION BY OR ON BEHALF OF PURCHASER UNDER THIS STATEMENT AND RELATED TRANSACTION(S) IS A CLAIM FOR DAMAGES AND IN NO EVENT SHALL DAMAGES OR ANY OTHER RECOVERY OF ANY KIND . . . EXCEED THE PRICE OF THE SPECIFIC GOODS OR SERVICES WHICH CAUSE THE ALLEGED LOSS, DAMAGE, INJURY OR OTHER CLAIM. NEITHER SHALL HELENA . . . BE LIABLE, AND ANY AND ALL CLAIMS AGAINST HELENA . . . ARE WAIVED FOR SPECIAL, DIRECT OR CONSEQUENTIAL DAMAGES, OR EXPENSES, OF ANY NATURE, INCLUDING, BUT NOT LIMITED TO, LOSS OF PROFITS OR INCOME, CROP OR PROPERTY LOSS OR DAMAGE, LABOR CHARGES AND FREIGHT CHARGES, WHETHER OR NOT BASED ON HELENA'S, ITS OFFICERS', DIRECTORS', EMPLOYEES' AND/OR AFFLIATES' NEGLIGENCE, BREACH OF WARRANTY, STRICT LIABILITY IN TORT, OR ANY OTHER CAUSE OF ACTION.

THE FOREGOING CONDITIONS OF SALE AND LIMITATIONS OF WARRANTY LIABILITY MAY BE VARIED OR WAIVED ONLY BY AGREEMENT IN WRITING SIGNED BY A DULY AUTHORIZED REPRESENTATIVE OF HELENA.

James, District Judge

Tennessee Code Annotated 2-719 provides:

(1) Subject to the provisions of subsections (2) and (3) of this section and of the preceding section on liquidation and limitation of damages:

   (*a*) The agreement may provide for remedies in addition or in substitution for those provided in this chapter and **may limit or alter the measure of damages recoverable under this chapter, as by limiting the buyer's remedies to return of the goods and repayment of the price** or to repair and replacement of nonconforming goods or parts; and

   (*b*) Resort to a remedy as provided is optional unless the remedy is agreed to be exclusive, in which case it is the sole remedy.

(2) **Where circumstances cause an exclusive or limited remedy to fail of its essential purpose, remedy may be had as provided in chapters 1–9 of this title.**

(3) Consequential damages may be limited or excluded **unless the limitation is unconscionable**. Limitation of consequential damages for injury to the person in the case of consumer goods is prima facie unconscionable but limitation of damages where the loss is commercial is not.

[emphasis added]

The comments following the statute explain:

1. Under this section parties are left free to shape their remedies to their particular requirements and reasonable agreements limiting or modifying remedies are to be given effect.

   However, it is of the essence of a sales contract that at least minimum adequate remedies be available. If the parties intend to conclude a contract for sale within this Article they must accept the legal consequence that there be at least a fair quantum of remedy for breach of the obligations or duties outlined in the contract. Thus, any clause purporting to modify or limit the remedial provisions of this Article in an unconscionable manner is subject to deletion and in that event, the remedies made available by this Article are applicable as if the stricken clause had never existed. Similarly, under subsection (2), where an apparently fair and reasonable clause because of circumstances fails in its purpose or operates to deprive either party of the substantial value of the bargain, it must give way to the general remedy provisions of this Article.

. . .

2. Subsection (3) recognizes the validity of clauses limiting or excluding consequential damages but makes it clear that they may not operate in an unconscionable manner. Actually such terms are merely an allocation of unknown or undeterminable risks. The seller in all cases is free to disclaim warranties in the manner provided in 2-316.

Thus, Tennessee permits the limitation of remedies unless circumstances cause the remedy to fail of its essential purpose. Specifically, commercial parties may limit or exclude consequential damages unless the limitation or exclusion is unconscionable.

In this case at the time the Agreement was entered, Williamson was a first time farmer with a tenth grade education and no apparent experience in the agricultural industry. He needed the goods and services Helena provided to begin his farming career. Helena then presented him with an agreement which had to be signed if he wished to purchase from Helena. Although the Agreement was not *prima facie* unconscionable under Tennessee law and commercial parties are presumed to have engaged in permissible dealings, this simply was not a commercial contract between two parties on equal footing. Williamson was in no position to bargain and thus signed an Agreement which left him without recourse, even if Helena's action resulted in substantial damages to him. Under these circumstances, and finding the decisions of every other court to consider this issue persuasive, the Court finds that the exclusion/limitations of remedies provision is unconscionable and unenforceable.

Further, even if the provision survived an unconscionability review, the Court also finds that the remedy provision fails of its essential purpose. Failure of essential purpose as codified in the Tennessee Code Annotated section 2-719 is concerned with the essential purpose of the remedy chosen by the parties, and in contrast to the unconscionability provisions, this code provision is concerned only with novel circumstances not contemplated by the parties. The most frequent application of 2-719(2) occurs when under a limited "repair and replacement" remedy, the seller is unwilling or unable to repair the defective goods within a reasonable period of time. Thus the remedy fails of its essential purpose, i.e., fails to cure the defect.

In this case, a repair or replace remedy was not included in the Agreement and obviously would have served no purpose. The Agreement does not use the word "refund" but does provide that damages or any other recovery of any kind against Helena "may not exceed the price of the specific goods or services which cause the alleged loss, damage, injury or other claim." Thus, under the Agreement, Williamson can recover the cost of the corn seed which allegedly caused the loss, i.e., a refund. Typically, under Tennessee law, a refund is a minimum adequate remedy.

However, in this case, the refund of the purchase price is a totally inadequate remedy in the agricultural context. The true value of the seeds only comes from the crop yielded which is preceded by considerable time and cost expended by the farmer. A farmer's lost growing season and the accompanying loss of expected profits due to the defective seeds clearly is not compensated by simply replacing or refunding the price of the defective seeds. Williamson suffered the loss, not of corn seed, but of his corn crop. Thus, this court, like the other courts who have considered the issue, finds that the exclusion/limitations of remedies provision in the Agreement fails of its essential purpose. If he can prove Helena's negligence at trial, then Williamson is not prevented by the Agreement from seeking consequential damages.

Statute of Limitations

 LO22-3 Recall the statute of limitation provided in the UCC that is applicable to lawsuits alleging breach of a contract for the sale of goods.

The UCC provides that a lawsuit for breach of a sales contract must be filed within four years after the breach occurs. The parties to a contract may shorten this period to one year, but they may not extend it for longer than four years [2-725]. Normally, a breach of warranty is considered to have occurred when the goods are delivered to the buyer. However, if the warranty covers future performance of goods (e.g., a warranty on a tire for four years or 40,000 miles), then the breach occurs at the time the buyer should have discovered the defect in the product. If, for example, the buyer of the tire discovers the defect after driving 25,000 miles on the tire over a three-year period, he would have four years from that time to bring any lawsuit to remedy the breach.

Seller's Remedies

 LO22-4 List and describe the remedies that the UCC makes available to an injured seller.

Remedies Available to an Injured Seller
A buyer may breach a contract in a number of ways. The most common are (1) by wrongfully refusing to accept goods, (2) by wrongfully returning goods, (3) by failing to pay for goods when payment is due, and (4) by indicating an unwillingness to go ahead with the contract. When a buyer breaches a contract, the seller has a number of remedies under the UCC, including the right to:

- Cancel the contract [2-703(f)].
- Withhold delivery of undelivered goods [2-703(a)].
- Complete manufacture of unfinished goods and identify them as to the contract or cease manufacture and sell for scrap [2-704].
- Resell the goods covered by the contract and recover damages from the buyer [2-706].
- Recover from the buyer the profit that the seller would have made on the sale or the damages that the seller sustained [2-708].
- Recover the purchase price of goods delivered to or accepted by the buyer [2-709].

In addition, a buyer may become insolvent and thus unable to pay the seller for goods already delivered or for goods that the seller is obligated to deliver. When a seller learns of a buyer's insolvency, the seller has a number of remedies, including the right to:

- Withhold delivery of undelivered goods [2-703(a)].
- Recover goods from a buyer upon the buyer's insolvency [2-702].
- Stop delivery of goods that are in the possession of a carrier or other bailee before they reach the buyer [2-705].

Cancellation and Withholding of Delivery
When a buyer breaches a contract, the seller has the right to cancel the contract and to hold up her own performance of the contract. The seller may then set aside any goods that were intended to fill her obligations under the contract [2-704].

If the seller is in the process of manufacturing the goods, she has two choices. She may complete manufacture of the goods, or she may stop manufacturing and sell the uncompleted goods for their scrap or salvage value. In choosing between these alternatives, the seller should select the alternative that will minimize the loss [2-704(2)]. Thus, a seller would be justified in completing the manufacture of goods that could be resold readily at the contract price. However, a seller would not be justified in completing specially manufactured goods that could not be sold to anyone other than the buyer who ordered them. The purpose of this rule is to permit the seller to follow a reasonable course of action to mitigate (minimize) the damages.

The hypothetical case at the beginning of the chapter posits a customer who contracts with the Bridal Shop for the creation of a custom-designed bridal gown in size 6 and then seeks to cancel the order before the Bridal Shop has completed it. What options are open to the Bridal Shop? Can it complete the dress and recover the full contract price from the customer, or should it stop work on it? What facts would be important to your decision? As you reflect on these questions, you might consider the facts set out in problem case 4 at the end of this chapter, where a manufacturer of pool tables stopped work on some customized pool tables. What considerations does it suggest that the Bridal Shop might be advised to take into account in deciding whether or not to continue work on the bridal gown?

Resale of Goods
If the seller sets aside goods intended for the contract or completes the manufacture of such goods, he is not obligated to try to resell the goods to someone else. However, he may resell them and recover damages. The seller must make any resale in good faith and in a commercially reasonable manner. If the seller does so, he is entitled to recover from the buyer as damages the difference between the resale price and the price the buyer agreed to pay in the contract [2-706].

If the seller resells, he may also recover incidental damages, but the seller must give the buyer credit for any expenses that the seller saved because of the buyer's breach of contract. Incidental damages include storage charges and sales commissions paid when the goods were resold [2-710]. Expenses saved might be the cost of packaging the goods and/or shipping them to the buyer.

If the buyer and seller have agreed as to the manner in which the resale is to be made, the courts will enforce the agreement unless it is found to be unconscionable [2-302]. If the parties have not entered into an agreement as to the resale of the goods, they may be resold at public or private sale, but in all events, the resale must be made in good faith and in a commercially reasonable manner. The seller should make it clear that the goods he is selling are those related to the broken contract.

If the goods are resold at a private sale, the seller must give the buyer reasonable notification of his intention to resell [2-706(3)]. If the resale is a public sale, such as an auction, the seller must give the buyer notice of the time and place of the sale unless the goods are perishable or threaten to decline in value rapidly. The sale must be made at a usual place or market for public sales if one is reasonably available; if the goods are not within the view of those attending the sale, the notification of the sale must state the place where the goods are located and provide for reasonable inspection by prospective bidders. The seller may bid at a public sale [2-706(4)].

The purchaser at a public sale who buys in good faith takes free from any rights of the original buyer even though the seller has failed to conduct the sale in compliance with the rules set out in the UCC [2-706(5)]. The seller is not accountable to the buyer for any profit that the seller makes on a resale [2-706(6)].

Recovery of the Purchase Price
In the normal performance of a contract, the seller delivers conforming goods (goods that meet the contract specifications) to the buyer. The buyer accepts the goods and pays for them. The seller is entitled to the purchase price of all goods accepted by the buyer. She also is entitled to the purchase price of all goods that conformed to the contract and were lost or damaged after the buyer assumed the risk for their loss [2-709].

The case below, *Beau Townsend Ford Lincoln v. Don Hinds Ford,* illustrates the principle that a buyer is liable for the purchase price of goods that have been received and accepted and is not relieved of that obligation where he erroneously makes payment to someone other than the seller with whom he is contractually obligated to pay.

For example, a contract calls for Frank, a farmer, to ship 1,000 dozen eggs to Sutton, a grocer, with shipment "FOB Frank's Farm." If the eggs are lost or damaged while on their way to Sutton, she is responsible for paying Frank for them. Risk of loss is discussed in Chapter 19, Formation and Terms of Sales Contracts.

In one other situation, the seller may recover the purchase or contract price from the buyer. This is where the seller has made an honest effort to resell the goods and was unsuccessful or where it is apparent that any such effort to resell would be unsuccessful. This might happen where the seller manufactured goods especially for the buyer and the goods are not usable by anyone else. Assume that Sarton's Supermarket sponsors a bowling team. Sarton's orders six green-and-red bowling shirts to be embroidered with "Sarton's Supermarket" on the back and the names of the team members on the pocket. After the shirts are completed, Sarton's wrongfully refuses to accept them. The seller will be able to recover the agreed purchase price if it cannot sell the shirts to someone else.

If the seller sues the buyer for the contract price of the goods, she must hold the goods for the buyer. Then, the seller must turn the goods over to the buyer if the buyer pays for them. However, if resale becomes possible before the buyer pays for the goods, the seller may resell them. Then, the seller must give the buyer credit for the proceeds of the resale [2-709(2)].

Beau Townsend Ford Lincoln v. Don Hinds Ford   93 UCC Rep. 2d 1052 (S.D. Ohio 2017)

In September 2015, Beau Townsend Ford Lincoln entered into a fleet deal with a customer for seventy-five Ford Explorers. That deal, however, fell through, and Beau Townsend Ford's Commercial Sales Manager sold some of the vehicles to retail customers and then reached out to other Ford dealers in the region to ascertain their interest in buying some of the vehicles.

Don Hinds Ford agreed to pay Beau Townsend Ford $736,225.40 to purchase 20 Ford Explorers. Beau Townsend Ford was obligated to deliver the vehicles to Don Hinds Ford. Past vehicle trades between the two dealers had been for one or two vehicles at a time and had typically been paid through a check, delivered at the same time the vehicles were picked up. In this instance, the arrangement was worked out through e-mail exchanges, and there was no formal written contract.

At the time the Commercial Account Manager at Don Hinds Ford inquired about receiving invoices and titles for the vehicles, he indicated that Don Hinds Ford would be paying by check. This was the first time there was any reference to the manner of payment. A short time later, he received an e-mail from the Commercial Sales Manager's account at Beau Townsend Ford indicating that Beau Townsend Ford would prefer a wire transfer, and attached some wiring instructions. The attachment indicated that the purchase monies for the 20 Explorers were to be sent by wire transfer to a Bank of America Account in Missouri City, Texas, for the benefit of "K.B. KEY LOGISTICS LLC."

Don Hinds Ford made the requested wire transfers over a three-day period (because of daily transfer limits on its bank account) and began picking up the vehicles from Beau Townsend Ford's dealership in Vandalia, Ohio, and transporting them to its location in Fishers, Indiana. On October 7, 2015, the day the last vehicles were picked up, it received an e-mail confirming the receipt of the final installment of the wired funds. The money received in the account was either withdrawn or transferred out of the account, with the last withdrawal occurring on October 13, 2015.

For nearly a week thereafter, Don Hinds Ford believed the story was over. It had been given the titles to the vehicles (in this case, the Manufacturer's Certificates of Origin), was allowed to drive all of the Explorers back to Indiana, and had wired over $730,000.

On October 13, Don Hinds Ford received from an e-mail from Beau Townsend Ford stating it had not been paid and inquiring when it should expect to receive payment (by check). Don Hinds Ford communicated that it had already sent payment pursuant to the wiring instructions it had received. A subsequent investigation discovered that the Commercial Sales Manager's e-mail account had been compromised. A filter had been set up that removed all of the Commercial Sales Manager's e-mails in his inbox and forwarded them to a third party, who then sent replies back to the original sender in a way that appeared to come from the Commercial Sales Manager's account. Beau Townsend Ford utilized a third-party "webmail" interface that allowed the users to set up certain rules for forwarding their e-mail to other e-mail addresses. The Commercial Sales Manager indicated he was not aware of the forwarding rules that had been put in place on his account. A subsequent investigation indicated that on September 28, 2015, someone in Nigeria had created a new e-mail address in the name of the Commercial Sales Manager on Google's Gmail service.

Beau Townsend Ford demanded that Don Hinds Ford immediately return the 20 Ford Explorers on the grounds that it had not received payment and had the right to reclaim the vehicles. Don Hinds Ford responded to the demand, noting that payment had been made in accordance with the wiring instructions from Beau Townsend Ford's Commercial Sales Manager. It also indicated that its position was that it had no knowledge of any false or misleading statements and as such was a good-faith purchaser for value.

Beau Townsend Ford then filed suit against Don Hinds Ford seeking the agreed-upon purchase price of the 20 vehicles for which it had not received payment.

Rose, United States District Judge.

The instant case provides a reminder that on the internet, no one knows you're a dog. Quite possibly no one figures out you're a Nigerian swindler. The swindler having made off with a princely sum, the Court must determine which party shall be paupered.

In Ohio, the essential elements of a breach of contract claim are: (1) a binding contract or agreement was formed; (2) the non-breaching party performed its contractual obligations; (3) the other party failed to fulfill its contractual obligations without legal excuse; and (4) the non-breaching party suffered damages as a result of the breach. Damages are not awarded for mere breach alone. Rather the damages that can be awarded for breach of contract are those which are the natural or probable consequence of the breach of contract or damages that were within the contemplation of both parties at the time of making the contract.

To prove the first element of a breach of contract claim, that a binding contract or agreement was formed, a party must establish the essential elements of a contract: (1) an offer; (2) an acceptance; (3) a meeting of the minds; (4) exchange of consideration; and (5) certainty as to the essential terms of the contract. A contract is formed when there is mutual consent and consideration.

Don Hinds Ford and Beau Townsend Ford agreed that Beau Townsend Ford would sell to Don Hinds Ford 20 Ford Explorers and that Don Hinds Ford would pay Beau Townsend Ford the amount of $736,225.40. Don Hinds Ford asserts that the parties modified this contract to include a term concerning payment, that payment was to be made by wire transfer. That Don Hinds received an email from Beau Townsend Ford's email account does not make this amendment a contractual term, what is required is a meeting of the minds, agreement in fact.

In order to constitute a valid contract there must be a "meeting of the minds" of the parties which is achieved by both an offer and acceptance of the contract's provisions. See *Grant v. DeGryse,* 1991 WL 254211 (Ohio App. 1991) (finding terms to which the parties had not agreed to be unenforceable).

Ohio Revised Code lists a seller's principal remedies upon a buyer's breach. When a buyer fails to pay the price as it becomes due, the seller may recover the price of goods accepted. When a buyer accepts goods, the buyer must pay for such goods. Don Hinds Ford accepted the 20 Ford Explorers from Beau Townsend Ford. Therefore, Beau Townsend Ford is entitled to be paid by Don Hinds Ford. Accordingly, summary judgment will be granted in favor of Beau Townsend Ford and against Don Hinds Ford.

While Don Hinds Ford claims the result is unjust in light of the fact it wired funds to the Bank of America account based on the instructions that appeared to come from Beau Townsend Ford, that transfer does not satisfy its obligation to Beau Townsend Ford. Here there was no meeting of minds to a contractual provision that payment is to be made by wire transfer.

The Court notes that Don Hines Ford is not a "good faith purchaser for value" by virtue of having wired money to the Bank of America account of K.B. KEY LIOGISTICS in Missouri City, Texas. A "good faith purchaser for value" purchases from a seller that obtained "voidable" title from a previous seller. The subsequent purchaser acquires "good title" despite irregularities in the transaction by which the seller obtained the property. Neither is the "good faith purchaser" doctrine implicated as between the original seller and the subsequent seller, Beau Townsend Ford and Don Hinds Ford. While parties that purchased the 20 Ford Explorers from Don Hinds Ford might qualify as "good faith purchasers for value" such that Beau Townsend Ford cannot seek relief from such subsequent purchasers, the subsequent sales do not extinguish Don Hinds Ford's original obligation to Beau Townsend Ford. Accordingly, the "good faith purchaser" doctrine has no application and Don Hinds Ford owes Beau Townsend Ford $736,225.40.

Don Hinds Ford's defense of equitable estoppel also is unprevailing. Under the doctrine of equitable estoppel, relief is precluded where one party induces another to believe certain facts are true and the other party changes his position in reasonable reliance to his detriment. Equitable estoppel requires that the proponent prove four elements: (1) that the adverse party made a factual misrepresentation; (2) that the misrepresentation was misleading; (3) that the misrepresentation induced actual reliance which was reasonable and in good faith; and (4) the proponent suffered detriment due to the reliance.

As to the first element, a showing of fraud is necessary. It was not Beau Townsend Ford that instructed Don Hinds Ford to send funds to "K.B. KEY LOGISTICS, L.L.C." in Missouri City, Texas. Beau Townsend Ford made no representation to Don Hinds Ford regarding such "wire instructions," much less any misrepresentation that would satisfy the first element of equitable estoppel. Since there were no misrepresentations, Don Hinds Ford's equitable estoppel defense fails.

Both parties would each have the Court find that the other was in the best position to avoid the misfortune that occurred in this case. If there is a policy inherent in the UCC rules for the allocation of losses due to fraud, it surely is that the loss be placed on the party in the best position to prevent it.

Beau Townsend Ford asserts Don Hinds Ford was in the best position to prevent the loss, pointing out "red flags" that it believes should have alerted Don Hinds Ford that the wiring instructions were likely sent by an "imposter." Beau Townsend points to the fact that the parties' previous transactions, involving one or two vehicles at a time, were handled by way of checks; that the beneficiary of the fraudulent wiring instructions was "K.B. KEY LOGISTICS LLC," not Beau Townsend Ford; that the wiring instructions were sent in substandard English; and that the wiring instructions provided that the funds should be sent to an account in Missouri City, Texas, whereas Beau Townsend Ford is located in Vandalia, Ohio. Don Hines Ford points to Beau Townsend Ford's unsecured email and to the slow response to signs that something was amiss.

Here, both parties were negligent in their business practices. It cannot be said that either was obviously in the best position to protect their own interest. Beau Townsend Ford should have maintained a more secure email system and taken quicker action upon learning it had been compromised. Don Hinds Ford should have ascertained that an actual agent of Beau Townsend Ford was requesting that it send money by wire transfer.

Additionally, Ohio courts have held that the doctrine of equitable estoppel will not be used to benefit parties who were negligent in their business transactions, and who obviously were in the best position to protect their own interest. Again, because both parties were capable of preventing the loss, this principle does not apply.

Summary Judgment for Beau Townsend Ford on its breach of contract claim and Don Hinds Ford is ordered to pay Beau Townsend Ford the sum of $736,225.40.

Damages for Rejection or Repudiation

When the buyer refuses to accept goods that conform to the contract or repudiates the contract, the seller does not have to resell the goods. The seller has two other ways of determining the damages that the buyer is liable for because of the breach of contract: (1) the difference between the contract price and the market price at which the goods are currently selling and (2) the "profit" that the seller lost when the buyer did not go through with the contract [2-708].

The seller may recover as damages the difference between the contract price and the market price at the time and place the goods were to be delivered to the buyer. The seller also may recover any incidental damages but must give the buyer credit for any expenses that the seller has saved [2-708(1)]. This measure of damages most commonly is sought by a seller when the market price of the goods dropped substantially between the time the contract was made and the time the buyer repudiated the contract.

The Global Business Environment

Seller's Remedies in International Transactions

Under the Convention on Contracts for the International Sale of Goods (CISG), an aggrieved seller has five potential remedies when the buyer breaches the contract: (1) suspension of the seller's performance, (2) "avoidance" of the contract, (3) reclamation of the goods in the buyer's possession, (4) an action for the price, and (5) an action for damages. The last two remedies can be pursued only in a judicial proceeding.

As noted in Chapter 21 (see The Global Business Environment box titled "Insecurity"), the seller may "suspend its performance" when it is apparent the other party to the contract will not be performing its obligations, for example, if the buyer was insolvent and unable to pay for any goods delivered to it.

Avoidance of a contract—which, under the CISG, essentially means canceling the contract—is a remedy most commonly utilized by buyers because the initial performance called for in contracts typically rests with the seller—for example, to deliver specified goods. When a seller has not been paid for goods, it may "avoid" the contract and seek their return from the buyer. If the buyer has possession of the goods when the contract is avoided, he must take reasonable steps to preserve them. Where the goods are perishable, the buyer might try to sell them for the seller's account but is not required to follow a seller's instructions to resell.

Where the seller has performed its obligations, the seller has the right to require the buyer to pay the contract price unless the seller has pursued an inconsistent remedy—such as reclaiming the goods. An aggrieved seller may also pursue an action for damages based on either (1) the difference between the contract price and the resale price (where the seller resold the goods) or (2) the difference between the contract price and the market price at the time the contract was avoided. The CISG also permits a measure of damages based on lost profits. Thus, in a number of respects, the UCC and CISG offer similar remedies to sellers.

For example, on October 1, Wan Ho Manufacturing contracts with Sports Properties to sell the company 100,000 New England Patriot bobble heads at $6.50 each with delivery to be made in Boston on December 1. By December 1, the market for New England Patriot bobble heads has softened considerably because a competitor flooded the market with them first and the bobble heads are selling for $3.00 each in Boston. If Sports Properties repudiates the contract on December 1 and refuses to accept delivery of the 100,000 bobble heads, Wan Ho is entitled to the difference between the contract price of $650,000 and the December 1 market price in Boston of $300,000. Thus, Wan Ho could recover $350,000 in damages plus any incidental expenses, but less any expenses saved by it not having to ship the bobble heads to Sports Properties (such as packaging and transportation costs).

If getting the difference between the contract price and the market price would not put the seller in as good a financial position as the seller would have been in if the contract had been performed, the seller may choose an alternative measure of damages based on the lost profit and overhead that the seller would have made if the sale had gone through. The seller can recover this lost profit and overhead plus any incidental expenses. However, the seller must give the buyer credit for any expenses saved as a result of the buyer's breach of contract [2-708(2)].

Using the bobble head example, assume that the direct labor and material costs to Wan Ho Manufacturing of making the bobble heads was $2.75 each. Wan Ho could recover as damages from Sports Properties the profit Wan Ho lost when Sports Properties defaulted on the contract. Wan Ho would be entitled to the difference between the contract price of $650,000 and its direct cost of $275,000. Thus, Wan Ho could recover $375,000 plus any incidental expenses and less any expenses saved, such as the shipping costs to Boston.

Seller's Remedies Where Buyer Is Insolvent If the seller has not agreed to extend credit to the buyer for the purchase price of goods, the buyer must make payment on delivery of the goods. If the seller tenders delivery of the goods, he may withhold delivery unless the agreed payment is made. Where the seller has agreed to extend credit to the buyer for the purchase price of the goods, but discovers before delivery that the buyer is insolvent, the seller may refuse delivery unless the buyer pays cash for the goods together with the unpaid balance for all goods previously delivered under the contract [2-702(1)].

At common law, a seller had the right to rescind a sales contract induced by fraud and to recover the goods unless they had been resold to a bona fide purchaser for value. Based on this general legal principle, the UCC provides that where the seller discovers that the buyer has received goods while insolvent, the seller may reclaim the goods upon demand made within 10 days after their receipt. This right granted to the seller is based on constructive deceit on the part of the buyer. Receiving goods while insolvent is equivalent to a false representation of solvency. To protect his rights, all the seller must do is to make a demand within the 10-day period; he need not actually repossess the goods.

If the buyer has misrepresented his solvency to this particular seller in writing within three months before the delivery of the goods, the 10-day limitation on the seller's right to reclaim the goods does not apply. However, the seller's right to reclaim the goods is subject to the rights of prior purchasers in the ordinary course of the buyer's business, good-faith purchasers for value, creditors with a perfected lien on the buyer's inventory [2-702(2) and (3)], and a trustee in bankruptcy. The relative rights of creditors to their debtor's collateral are discussed in Chapter 29, Security Interests in Personal Property.

CONCEPT REVIEW

Problem	Seller's Remedy

Buyer Refuses to Go Ahead with Contract and Seller Has Goods	1. Seller may cancel contract, suspend performance, and set aside goods intended to fill the contract.
	
	   a. If seller is in the process of manufacturing, he may complete manufacture or stop and sell for scrap, picking an alternative that, in his judgment at the time, will minimize the seller's loss.
	
	   b. Seller can resell goods covered by contract and recover difference between contract price and proceeds of resale.
	
	   c. Seller may recover purchase price where resale is not possible.
	
	   d. Seller may recover damages for breach based on difference between contract price and market price, or in some cases based on lost profits.

Goods Are in Buyer's Possession	1. Seller may recover purchase price. 2. Seller may reclaim goods in possession of insolvent buyer by making a demand within 10 days after their receipt. If the buyer represented solvency to the seller in writing within three months before delivery, the 10-day limitation does not apply.
Goods Are in Transit	1. Seller may stop any size shipment if buyer is insolvent. 2. Seller may stop carload, truckload, planeload, or other large shipment for reasons other than buyer's insolvency.

Seller's Right to Stop Delivery

If the seller discovers that the buyer is insolvent, he has the right to stop the delivery of any goods that he has shipped to the buyer, regardless of the size of the shipment. If a buyer repudiates a sales contract or fails to make a payment due before delivery, the seller has the right to stop delivery of any large shipment of goods, such as a carload, a truckload, or a planeload [2-705].

To stop delivery, the seller must notify the carrier or other bailee in time for the bailee to prevent delivery of the goods. After receiving notice to stop delivery, the carrier or other bailee owes a duty to hold the goods and deliver them as directed by the seller. The seller is liable to the carrier or other bailee for expenses incurred or damages resulting from compliance with his order to stop delivery. If a nonnegotiable document of title has been issued for the goods, the carrier or other bailee does not have a duty to obey a stop-delivery order issued by any person other than the person who consigned the goods to him [2-705(3)].

Liquidated Damages

If the seller has justifiably withheld delivery of the goods because of the buyer's breach, the buyer may recover any money or goods he has delivered to the seller over and above the agreed amount of liquidated damages. If there is no such agreement, the seller may not retain an amount in excess of $500 or 20 percent of the value of the total performance for which the buyer is obligated under the contract, whichever is smaller. This right of restitution is subject to the seller's right to recover damages under other provisions of the UCC and to recover the amount of value of benefits received by the buyer directly or indirectly by reason of the contract [2-718].

Buyer's Remedies

 LO22-5 List and describe the remedies that the UCC makes available to an aggrieved buyer.

Buyer's Remedies in General

A seller may breach a contract in a number of ways. The most common are (1) failing to make an agreed delivery, (2) delivering goods that do not conform to the contract, and (3) indicating that she does not intend to fulfill the obligations under the contract.

CYBERLAW IN ACTION

E-Commerce Aids Buyers

Electronic commerce helps solve two of the most important concerns for buyers of goods in enforcing their rights under Article 2. The first of these relates to means by which the buyer may learn—from the seller or otherwise—of a recall that affects the goods purchased. For example, sellers could notify merchant buyers that it is notifying consumer buyers that they will need to take their cars into a dealership to have a seatbelt replaced. This early e-mail or posting on the seller's website can alert the merchant buyer to the need to train personnel how to handle recall questions from the buyers and also how to make the needed replacement. Buyers also may be able to determine in advance of their purchases whether the goods they plan to buy have been the subject of a recall and whether the recall was voluntary (a problem found by the seller) or required by the federal government. For example, information about earlier recalls may be especially helpful to buyers of used goods, such as cars and trucks, baby items, and anything where personal safety is critically important.

The second involves the buyer's duty to give the seller "notice" if the buyer needs a remedy from the seller. As noted in Chapter 21, Sections 2-602 and 2-607 require that the buyer notify the seller if the buyer wishes to reject goods the seller has tendered, or if the buyer decides to revoke acceptance of goods that the seller has promised to repair or replace and has neither repaired nor replaced the goods as promised—or where the buyer gets goods that have a latent defect. "Notice" does not have to be in writing to be effective, but it usually is preferable to have a record that the buyer gave notice to the seller and the time of the notice given. This reduces the risk that a court will find that the buyer's failure to give notice deprives the buyer of her right to a remedy [see Section 2-607(3)(a)]. Electronic commerce tools, including e-mail, allow buyers to provide speedy and reliable information to sellers in cases such as these. Buyers whose e-mail systems provide confirmation that the seller recipient actually has received the message about the buyer's concerns about the goods, or who show the time and date that the intended recipient opened the e-mail, make providing notice easier and easier to document than using traditional methods of communication.

A buyer whose seller breaks the contract is given a number of alternative remedies. These include:

- Buying other goods (covering) and recovering damages from the seller based on any additional expense that the buyer incurs in obtaining the goods [2-712].
- Recovering damages based on the difference between the contract price and the current market price of the goods [2-713].
- Recovering damages for any nonconforming goods accepted by the buyer based on the difference in value between what the buyer got and what she should have gotten [2-714].
- Obtaining specific performance of the contract where the goods are unique and cannot be obtained elsewhere [2-716].

In addition, the buyer can, in some cases, recover consequential damages (such as lost profits) and incidental damages (such as expenses incurred in buying substitute goods).

Buyer's Right to Damages Where a buyer has rightfully rejected goods or has justifiably revoked acceptance of goods, the buyer may cancel the contract, recover as much of the purchase price as has been paid, and recover damages. Thus, while the UCC does not explicitly use the common law term *rescission* (discussed in Chapter 17), it does incorporate the concept. This is illustrated in the case that follows, *Beer v. Bennett*.

Beer v. Bennett	71 UCC Rep. 2d 507 (N.H. 2010)

Bennett was a registered automobile dealer in New Hampshire doing business under the name The Nickled Stork. He posted an advertisement on his Internet website offering the following for sale:

1958 Fiat Osca Spyder 1.5 liter DOHC engine 4 speed trans. Engine and trans are out of the car, but we have most of a spare engine that comes with the car. Body is in very good condition, recently painted robin's egg blue. Top bows will need new top added and some other upholstery work required, but quite rare PinninFarina coachwork, pretty vigorous performance from a well designed DOHC Italian Motor.

Beer restored old cars as a hobby and had been searching for some time for a car like the one Bennett advertised. He contacted him and, after some negotiation, purchased the advertised vehicle for $6,000. He also arranged to have the car shipped to him at a cost of $1,298.

On receipt of the car, Beer discovered that it was missing a number of the parts necessary to make it operable, including "a bell housing starter, generator, distributor, engine mounts, fan, exhaust manifold, and the entire hand-brake mechanism." He contacted Bennett, but they could not resolve the issue, and Beer brought suit against Bennett.

The trial court awarded damages to Beer that included a refund of the purchase price and shipping costs plus certain other costs. The court also ordered Beer to return the Fiat to Bennett upon payment of the judgment and the cost of the return shipment. If Bennett failed to make payment and arrangements for return within 60 days, he would forfeit ownership of the Fiat.

Bennett appealed, claiming that the trial court failed to apply the correct measure of damages. He claimed they should have been based on the difference between what Beer paid and the value of what he received. Bennett further argued that since Beer failed to prove the value of what he received, he was not entitled to recover any damages.

Hicks, Justice

The terms of the remedy awarded make it clear it was not intended to be an award of actual damages. The remedy is clearly one of rescission. Specifically, we conclude that the remedy is sustainable as enforcement of a revocation of acceptance under the Uniform Commercial Code.

Section 2-608 provides for revocation of acceptance of nonconforming goods by a buyer under certain circumstances. Once a valid revocation of acceptance has been made, the proper measure of damages is found in section 2-711. That section provides that a buyer who justifiably revokes acceptance may recover so much of the price as has been paid. It also provides, in part, that the buyer has a security interest in goods in his possession or control for any payments made on their price, and any expenses reasonably incurred in their inspection, receipt, transportation, care, and custody.

The UCC also states that a buyer who justifiably revokes acceptance has the same rights and duties with regard to the goods involved as if he had rejected them. Section 2-608(3). Therefore, where the buyer has physical possession of the goods, and after the seller has repaid the purchase price, the nonmerchant's only duty with respect to the goods is to hold them with reasonable care at the seller's disposition for a time sufficient to permit the seller to remove them. Section 2-602(2)(b). The remedy order here—return of the purchase price to Beer and return of the Fiat to Bennett upon his payment of the judgment and his arrangements for return shipment and payment for the same—is entirely proper under the UCC.

Judgment affirmed for Beer.

Buyer's Right to Cover

 Explain what is meant by the term *cover* in the context of a contract for the sale of goods.

If the seller fails or refuses to deliver the goods called for in the contract, the buyer can purchase substitute goods; this is known as **cover**. If the buyer does purchase substitute goods, the buyer can recover as damages from the seller the difference between the contract price and the cost of the substitute goods [2-712]. For example, Frank Farmer agrees to sell Ann's Cider Mill 1,000 bushels of apples at $10 a bushel. Farmer then refuses to deliver the apples. Cider Mill can purchase 1,000 bushels of similar apples, and if it has to pay $15 a bushel, it can recover the difference ($5 a bushel) between what it paid ($15) and the contract price ($10). Thus, Cider Mill could recover $5,000 from Farmer.

The buyer can also recover any incidental damages sustained but must give the seller credit for any expenses saved. In addition, she may be able to obtain consequential damages. The buyer is not required to cover, however. If she does not cover, the other remedies under the UCC are still available [2-712].

Incidental Damages

 Explain what is meant by the terms *incidental damages* and *consequential damages* and indicate when an injured buyer is able to recover consequential damages.

Incidental damages include expenses that the buyer incurs in receiving, inspecting, transporting, and storing goods shipped by the seller that do not conform to those called for in the contract. Incidental damages also include any reasonable expenses or charges that the buyer has to pay in obtaining substitute goods [2-715(1)].

Consequential Damages
In certain situations, an injured buyer is able to recover consequential damages, such as the buyer's lost profits caused by the seller's breach of contract. The buyer must be able to show that the seller knew or should have known at the time the contract was made that the buyer would suffer special damages if the seller did not perform his obligations. In case of commercial loss, the buyer must also show that she could not have prevented the damage by obtaining substitute goods [2-715(2)(a)].

Suppose Knitting Mill promises to deliver 15,000 yards of a special fabric to Dorsey by September 1. Knitting Mill knows that Dorsey wants to acquire the material to make garments suitable for the Christmas season. Knitting Mill also knows that in reliance on the contract with it, Dorsey will enter into contracts with stores to deliver the finished garments by October 1. If Knitting Mill fails to deliver the fabric or delivers the fabric after September 1, it may be liable to Dorsey for any consequential damages that she sustains if she is unable to acquire the same material elsewhere in time to fulfill her October 1 contracts.

Consequential damages can also include an injury to a person or property caused by a breach of warranty [2-715(2)(b)]. For example, an electric saw is defective. Hanson purchases the saw, and while he is using it, the blade comes off and severely cuts his arm. The injury to Hanson is consequential damage resulting from a nonconforming or defective product.

In the hypothetical case presented at the beginning of this chapter, a customer contracts with Bridal Shop to make a custom-designed bridal gown in size 6 in time for her wedding. The case posits the Bridal Shop advising the customer that it will not be able to complete the production of the gown in time for the wedding. If the customer "covers" by buying a gown from another wedding shop, what is the measure of damages that the customer would be entitled to? Can you think of "incidental damages" or "consequential damages" that might be incurred in this situation and that might be claimed?

Damages for Nondelivery
If the seller fails or refuses to deliver the goods called for by the contract, the buyer has the option of recovering damages for the nondelivery. Thus, instead of covering, the buyer can get the difference between the contract price of the goods and their market price at the time she learns of the seller's breach. In addition, the buyer may recover any incidental damages and consequential damages but must give the seller credit for any expenses saved [2-713].

Suppose Biddle agreed on June 1 to sell and deliver 1,500 bushels of wheat to a grain elevator on September 1 for $7 per bushel and then refused to deliver on September 1 because the market price was then $10 per bushel. The grain elevator could recover $4,500 damages from Biddle, plus incidental damages that could not have been prevented by cover.

The case that follows, *Green Wood Industrial Company v. Forceman International Development Group*, involves an award of damages in connection with a contract to sell scrap metal to a buyer in China where the goods were never shipped even though the seller fraudulently represented they had been shipped.

Green Wood Industrial Company v. Forceman International Development Group
64 UCC Rep. 2d 378 (Cal. Ct. App. 2007)

Green Wood, a sole proprietorship owned and operated by Joseph Li in Hong Kong, is primarily in the business of buying scrap from sellers in the United States for resale to buyers in China. Richshine Metals Inc. (Richshine), owned and operated by its president, Christine Fan, was in the business in California of selling scrap metal for export. In the summer of 2003, Green Wood purchased approximately 680 metric tons of scrap plate metal from Richshine. Green Wood sold the scrap plate to a buyer in China. Green Wood's buyer was very pleased with the material supplied by Richshine and wanted more.

In November 2003, Green Wood placed a purchase order with Richshine to acquire 2,100 metric tons of scrap plate metal and 10,650 metric tons of scrap iron for a total purchase price of $1.89 million. Richshine was to deliver the goods directly to Green Wood's buyer at Guangxi Port in southern China by the end of November. Green Wood was to pay a $200,000 deposit, $340,000 cash on delivery, and the balance by letter of credit.

By the beginning of January 2004, Richshine had not shipped the goods. During this time frame, the price of scrap metal was rising in the world market. Li and Green Wood's buyer were concerned that Richshine might have sold the goods to another buyer at a higher price. They agreed to make some changes in the shipping terms and to wire additional money to Richshine's account. Green Wood *ultimately paid Richshine $1,074,548 in advance toward the purchase price of the goods. Green Wood's Chinese buyer funded $862,500 of that amount.*

Thereafter, Richshine provided packing lists, invoices, and bills of lading as well as certain certificates required by the Chinese government that the goods had been inspected (China Certification and Inspection Corporation, or CCIC, certificates). The certificates had been obtained by Forceman International Development Group Inc. (Forceman) and purported to represent they had been issued by CCIC South America and indicated that the containers with the scrap had been inspected in Tijuana, Mexico. The goods allegedly were awaiting shipment to China.

Unbeknownst to Li, the packing lists provided by Richshine with respect to the purchase order were fake, the CN Link bills of lading were forgeries, and the CCIC certificates were obtained fraudulently. The goods that Richshine had purported to ship pursuant to the purchase order never existed.

When the goods did not arrive, Li mounted an investigation to track down Fan and her confederates. They were eventually found in Nevada, where they had moved and were doing business under the name of Moundhouse Metals. When Li confronted Fan, telling her that if the goods did not arrive soon, Li would sue Fan, she, in essence, dared Li to do so.

When further investigation made it clear the goods had never existed, Li brought suit against Richline, Fan, and Forceman for fraud and negligence. Li sought to recover, as out-of-pocket damages, $1,074,548 paid to Richline and Fan; $159,000 in lost profits that Green Wood lost as a result of the nondelivery of the goods; and $274,868 for a claim Green Wood's buyer had made against Green Wood, apparently for its lost profits, which Green Wood had agreed to pay but had not yet paid. A jury awarded Green Wood compensatory damages of $1,508,416 plus punitive damages of $5,000, and the defendants appealed.

Mosk, Judge

The fraud in this case is related to the purchase order. The purchase order was a contract for the sale of goods subject to Article 2 of the Uniform Commercial Code. Accordingly, the damages available to Green Wood from the fraud are governed by UCC section 2-721, which provides for recovery on a basis-of-the-bargain basis. That section provides: "Remedies for material misrepresentation or fraud include all remedies available under this section for nonfraudulent breach. Neither rescission or a claim for rescission of the contract for sale nor rejection or return of the goods shall bar or be deemed inconsistent with a claim for damage or other remedy." Section 2-721 represents an exception to the general rule in California that a plaintiff defrauded in the purchase or sale of property may recover only out-of-pocket loss.

Where, as here, a seller fails to deliver goods pursuant to a contract governed by the UCC and the buyer does not cover, the buyer's remedy is set forth in section 2-713(1). That section provides, in pertinent part, "the measure of damages for nondelivery or repudiation by the seller is the difference between the market price at the time when the buyer learned of the breach and the contract price *together with any incidental and consequential damages provided in this division* (2-715), but less expenses saved in consequence of the seller's breach" [italics added]. Green Wood did not seek damages based on the difference between contract price and market price, but rather sought its out-of-pocket damages and consequential damages based on its lost profits. Pursuant to section 2-715(2)(a), a buyer of goods for resale may generally recover its lost profits as consequential damages, provided such damage "could not reasonably be prevented by cover or otherwise. . . ."

In this case, none of the defendants offered evidence that Green Wood had failed to mitigate its consequential damages. Green Wood, however, introduced substantial evidence to sustain an award of lost profits. Green Wood presented evidence of its purchase price from Richshine, which included the cost of shipping the goods to China. Li of Green Wood testified that Green Wood sold the plate scrap to its buyer for $25 per ton more than Green Wood paid, and sold the scrap iron at $10 per ton more than Green Wood paid. Forceman had a full and fair opportunity to test Green Wood's damage calculation through cross-examination or rebuttal. On appeal, Forceman does not identify any specific manner in which Li's calculation was erroneous, and Forceman provides no argument or authority that the amount of lost profits awarded was excessive. Accordingly, substantial evidence supports the $159,000 award for Green Wood's lost profits.

Forceman asserts that the trial court erred in awarding Green Wood $274,868 for a claim made against Green Wood by its Chinese buyer, or an obligation of Green Wood to that buyer, for damages suffered by that buyer resulting from Green Wood's failure to deliver the goods. We agree that as to this item, the damage award was improper. A plaintiff may not recover damages for unpaid liabilities to a third party, unless the plaintiff proves to a reasonable certainty that the liability could and would be enforced by the third party against the plaintiff or that the plaintiff otherwise could and would satisfy the obligation.

Under California law, a plaintiff—whether the plaintiff's claim sounds in contract or tort—generally cannot recover damages alleged to arise from a third-party claim against the plaintiff when caused by the defendant's misconduct. It is clear that the mere possibility, or even probability, that an event causing damage will result from a wrongful act, does not render the act actionable. Accordingly, the existence of a mere liability is not the equivalent of actual damage. This is because the *fact* of damage is inherently uncertain in such circumstances. The facts that a third party has demanded payment by the plaintiff of a particular liability and plaintiff has admitted such liability are not, by themselves, sufficient to support an award of damages for that liability, because that third party may never attempt to force the plaintiff to satisfy the alleged obligation, and plaintiff may never pay the obligation.

California law does, however, recognize that a plaintiff in a tort action may recover for a "loss reasonably certain to occur in the future." A similar concept has been recognized by some authorities in the context of contract damages. For example, an authority states, "Indeed, in a resale situation, the buyer has been permitted to claim as consequential damages from the seller the amount of the buyer's potential liability to its customer; if the buyer establishes the probability that the buyer will be sued by the customer, it is immaterial that the buyer has not yet been sued and made to bear the loss, and recovery is measured by the probable liability of the buyer to the customer." Other authorities note that a plaintiff may recover for future losses if there is an appropriate showing that those losses will in fact be incurred in the future.

It may be that existing California authorities generally require payment of the liability in order to include the liability as damages. But even if a liability to a third party might be included as damages without actual payment, more certainty is required than just evidence of an obligation to pay a third party.

In this case, the evidence established that, at the time of trial, Green Wood has not paid any portion of its Chinese buyer's $274,868 claim. Although there is evidence that Green Wood had, in effect, settled the claim by agreeing to pay it, Green Wood presented no evidence that any such agreement would be enforceable in China, or that the liability could and would be enforced by the buyer in the United States or elsewhere, or that the claim will otherwise be paid. There was no evidence from which the jury could conclude that it was reasonably certain that Green Wood would ever have to pay the money.

Furthermore, it appears that the Chinese buyer's claim against Green Wood was for the buyer's own lost profits. The only evidence regarding the Chinese buyer's business, however, was that the buyer is a manufacturer of some kind, not a reseller. Green Wood presented no evidence to establish the fact or amount of the Chinese buyer's lost profits other than the Chinese buyer's mere claim. This illustrates another problem with allowing damages based on a third-party claim. If a defendant is liable for any sum a plaintiff *agreed* to pay a third party, that sum could be subject to unfair manipulation.

Accordingly, the evidence is insufficient to sustain the award of $274,868 for the Chinese buyer's claim.

Damages for Defective Goods

If a buyer accepts defective goods and wants to hold the seller liable, the buyer must give the seller notice of the defect within a reasonable time after the buyer discovers the defect [2-607(3)]. Where goods are defective or not as warranted and the buyer gives the required notice, she can recover damages. The buyer is entitled to recover the difference between the value of the goods received and the value the goods would have had if they had been as warranted. She may also be entitled to incidental and consequential damages [2-714].

For example, Al's Auto Store sells Anders an automobile tire, warranting it to be four-ply construction. The tire goes flat when it is punctured by a nail, and Anders discovers that the tire is really only two-ply. If Anders gives the store prompt notice of the breach, she can keep the tire and recover from Al's the difference in value between a two-ply and a four-ply tire.

This remedy is illustrated in the following case, *Cahaba Disaster Recovery v. Rogers.*

Cahaba Disaster Recovery v. Rogers   **76 UCC Rep. 2d 624 (S.D. Ala. 2012)**

On April 20, 2010, the Deepwater Horizon *drilling rig exploded in the Gulf of Mexico. The resultant oil spill threatened coastal communities from Louisiana to Florida. In an effort to protect their beaches and marshlands, certain of these communities hired emergency response companies to deploy and service offshore "boom"–floating barriers designed to arrest the movement of oil-contaminated water. Among those companies was DRC Emergency Services, an Alabama-based limited liability company that in turn engaged Cahaba Disaster Recovery to locate and procure oil boom to be used for DRC's projects.*

In April 2010, Cahaba made its first-ever purchases of small quantities of oil-containment boom and oil-absorbent boom. "Oil-containment" boom is designed to keep oil-contaminated water in place, whereas "oil-absorbent" boom is meant to extract and retain oil while repelling water. The purchases had to conform to certain specifications in DRC's contracts. With respect to containment boom, those specifications were quite detailed. Conversely, the absorbent boom that Cahaba was instructed to order simply had to be either five or eight inches in diameter.

After a telephone exchange with Lenny Rogers, the Managing Partner of International Lining LLC on May 1, in which Cahaba's interest in acquiring absorbent boom were made clear, Cahaba entered into a contract with International Lining for the purchase of 150,000 feet of what it believed would be "eight-inch absorbent boom" at a contract price of $200,000 plus $8,100 in freight charges for a total of $208,100.

Cahaba wired the purchase price to International Lining. When the product was delivered to Cahaba on May 7, part of the delivery was accompanied by a shipping statement that referred to 13,000 lineal feet of "FOC 8" boom product. When Cahaba's employees could not identify the type of product that Cahaba had received, they contacted Rogers. He explained that the delivered product, labeled as "Rapid Oil Containment Barrier," but occasionally referred to by International Lining as "Fast Oil containment" or "FOC," was a revolutionary product that could both absorb and contain oil. During a subsequent telephone conversation, Rogers assured Cahaba that the FOC boom was, in fact, absorbent boom.

Cahaba then attempted, without success, to employ the FOC boom to satisfy its contracts with DRC and also to sell the boom to others responding to the Deepwater Horizon spill.

Six weeks later, on June 15, 2010, Cahaba advised Rogers that the FOC boom did not meet Cahaba's needs and that it wished to return the boom. Rogers quickly responded that International Lining would not accept any return. Subsequently, Cahaba conducted a field test of the FOC boom off the coast of Escambia, Florida—and determined that the FOC boom effectively contained, but did not absorb, oil. When Rogers was advised of the test results, he confirmed that the boom acted like a containment boom but also asserted that it also acted like an absorbent boom because oil is "almost magnetized" to the material and "I promise you that it works." However, he did not offer to, or attempt to, replace Cahaba's stock of FOC boom with absorbent boom. Three months later, Cahaba filed suit against Rogers and International Lining, alleging breach of contract and fraud for delivering containment boom rather than absorbent boom.

In its defense, International Lining contended that it did everything it was required to do under the contract. Moreover, as an affirmative defense, International Lining asserted that under the Alabama UCC, a buyer's acceptance of nonconforming goods precludes its right to return the goods to the seller.

DuBose, District Judge

The court's factual finding that the parties contracted for 150,000 feet of absorbent boo[m] and International Lining's admission that the boo[m] delivered to Cahaba was not absorbent undermine its position entirely. Quite simply, International Lining's tender of FOC boom did not conform to the terms of its contract with Cahaba and therefore constitutes nonperformance on the part of International Lining.

International Lining's delivery of non-absorbent boo[m] also constitutes a breach of International Lining's express warranty that the boom would absorb. Alabama law provides that any description of goods which is made part of the basis of the bargain creates an express warranty that the goods shall conform to the description.

In support of their affirmative defenses, International Lining relies on a provision of the Alabama Uniform Commercial Code (Section 2-607(2)) that sets forth that a buyer's acceptance of nonconforming goods precludes its right to return the goods to the seller. While the record establishes that Cahaba accepted the FOC boom by relying on the manufacturer's

representations that it would absorb oil and by waiting nearly seven weeks from the date of delivery to assess the validity of that assurance, the code section relied upon by International Lining also notes that a buyer who accepts nonconforming goods does not forfeit its right to otherwise recover for a seller's breach. Section 2-607(2) states, "Acceptance does not of itself impair any other remedy provided by this article for nonconformity."

To preserve its right to recover damages, a buyer who has accepted nonconforming goods must timely notify the seller of the breach. Cahaba's June 24, 2010 e-mail which was sent immediately after Cahaba discovered that the FOC boom was not absorbent satisfies the notice requirement. The e-mail clearly informed International Lining that testing by Cahaba revealed the FOC boom "is not an absorbent but a containment boom" and thereby presented International Lining with an unrealized opportunity to cure the nonconformity or otherwise settle with Cahaba. Accordingly, Cahaba has preserved its right to recover damages for International Lining's established breaches.

The measure of damages for breach of warranty in regard to accepted goods is governed by Code Section 2-714, which provides in pertinent part:

The measure of damages for breach of warranty is the difference at the time and place of acceptance between the value of the goods accepted and the value they would have had if they had been as warranted, unless special circumstances show proximate damages of a different amount.

International Lining is liable for the $208,100 purchase price, less the value of the FOC boom as accepted by Cahaba. The FOC boom had no value to Cahaba because it could not be deployed as absorbent boom and does not satisfy any of DRC's specifications for containment boom. Accordingly, the difference between the value of the goods as warranted and the value at the time and place of acceptance is $208,100.

Judgment for Cahaba.

Ethics and Compliance in Action

Should the Buyer Get an Honest Answer?

Problem case 8 at the end of this chapter is based on the following situation: Barr purchased from Crow's Nest Yacht Sales a 31-foot Tiara pleasure yacht manufactured by S-2 Yachts. He had gone to Crow's Nest knowing the style and type of yacht he wanted. He was told that the retail price was $102,000 but that he could purchase the model it had for $80,000. When he asked about the reduction in price, he was told that Crow's Nest had to move it because there was a change in the model and it had new ones coming in. He was assured that the yacht was new, that there was nothing wrong with it, and there were only 20 hours on the engine. When Barr began to use the boat, he experienced tremendous difficulties with equipment malfunctions. On examination by an expert, it was determined that the yacht had earlier been sunk in saltwater, resulting in significant rusting and deterioration in the engine, equipment, and fixtures. How would you assess the ethicality of the representations made by the salesperson in response to his question? In a case like this, should it be incumbent on the buyer to ask the "right" question in order to protect himself or herself, or should there be an ethical obligation on the seller to disclose voluntarily material facts that may be relevant to the buyer making an informed decision?

The Global Business Environment

Buyer's Remedies in International Transactions

Under the Convention on Contracts for the International Sale of Goods (CISG), an aggrieved buyer has four potential types of remedies against a seller who has breached the contract: (1) "avoidance" of the contract, (2) an adjustment in the price, (3) specific performance, and (4) an action for damages. The first two remedies can be pursued without involving a court, and the last two require the buyer to initiate a judicial proceeding.

As noted in Chapter 21 (see The Global Business Environment box titled "Insecurity"), a buyer has the right to suspend its performance and/or to "avoid" a contract where the seller appears unable to perform its obligations and does not provide adequate assurances that it can and will perform. A buyer may also "avoid" the contract—which, under the CISG, essentially means "cancel" the contract—and refuse to accept and pay for goods that are so defective or nonconforming as to constitute a "fundamental breach" of the contract.

Aggrieved buyers who receive nonconforming goods "may reduce the price" paid to the seller. The CISG provides a formula for calculating the reduction that involves comparing the value of the goods actually delivered at the time they were delivered to the value that conforming goods would have had at the time of delivery.

The CISG gives the aggrieved buyer a right to "require performance" by the seller. This follows the civil law principle that the best relief to the buyer is not damages but rather having the seller perform as promised. Thus, the CISG does not require that the goods must be "unique"—as the UCC does—in order for the buyer to be entitled to specific performance.

While the buyer has the right to seek specific performance with the assistance of a court, the buyer also has the option of seeking damages, including consequential damages. Such damages can be based on either (1) the difference between the cost of cover and the contract price or (2) the difference between the market price and the contract price. However, unlike the UCC, the CISG requires the buyer to use the "cover" formula for calculating damages if the buyer does cover by obtaining substitute goods.

Buyer's Remedies (on breach by seller)

Problems	Buyer's Remedy
Seller Fails to Deliver Goods or Delivers Nonconforming Goods That Buyer Rightfully Rejects or Justifiably Revokes Acceptance of	1. Buyer may cancel the contract and recover damages. 2. Buyer may "cover" by obtaining substitute goods and recover difference between contract price and cost of cover. 3. Buyer may recover damages for breach based on difference between contract price and market price.
Seller Delivers Nonconforming Goods That Are Accepted by Buyer	Buyer may recover damages based on difference between value of goods received and value of goods if they had been as warranted.
Seller Has the Goods but Refuses to Deliver Them and Buyer Wants Them	Buyer may seek specific performance if goods are unique and cannot be obtained elsewhere, or buyer may replevy (obtain from the seller) goods identified to contract if buyer cannot obtain cover.

Buyer's Right to Specific Performance

 Discuss when an aggrieved buyer has a right to specific performance of a contract for the sale of goods.

LO22-8

Sometimes, the goods covered by a contract are unique and it is not possible for a buyer to obtain substitute goods. When this is the case, the buyer is entitled to specific performance of the contract.

Specific performance means that the buyer can require the seller to give the buyer the goods covered by the contract [2-716]. Thus, the buyer of an antique automobile, such as a 1910 Ford, might have a court order for the seller to deliver the specific automobile to the buyer if it was unique or one of a kind. On the other hand, the buyer of grain in a particular storage bin could not get specific performance if she could buy the same kind of grain elsewhere.

Buyer and Seller Agreements as to Remedies

As mentioned earlier in this chapter, the parties to a contract may provide remedies in addition to or as substitution for those expressly provided in the UCC [2-719]. For example, the buyer's remedies may be limited by the contract to the return of the goods and the repayment of the price or to the replacement of nonconforming goods or parts. However, a court looks to see whether such a limitation was freely agreed to or whether it is unconscionable. In the latter case, the court does not enforce the limitation and the buyer has all the rights given to an injured buyer by the UCC.

Problems and Problem Cases

1. International Record Syndicate (IRS) hired Jeff Baker to take photographs of the musical group Timbuk-3. Baker mailed 37 "chromes" (negatives) to IRS via the business agent of Timbuk-3. When the chromes were returned to Baker, holes had been punched in 34 of them. Baker brought an action for breach of contract to recover for the damage done to the chromes.

   A provision printed on Baker's invoice to IRS stated: "[r]eimbursement for loss or damage shall be determined by a photograph's reasonable value which shall be no less than $1,500 per transparency." Baker testified that he had been paid as much as $14,000 for a photo session, which resulted in 24 photographs, and that several of them had already been resold. He also had received as little as $125 for a single photograph. He once sold a photograph taken in 1986 for $500 and sold several reproductions of it later for a total income of $1,500. Was the liquidated damages provision enforceable by Baker?

2. Lobianco contracted with Property Protection for the installation of a burglar alarm system. The contract provided in part:

Alarm system equipment installed by Property Protection is guaranteed against improper function due to manufacturing defects of workmanship for a period of 12 months. The installation of the above equipment carries a 90-day warranty. The liability of Property Protection is limited to repair or replacement of security alarm equipment and does not include loss or damage to possessions, persons, or property.

As installed, the alarm system included a standby battery source of power in the event that the regular source of power failed. During the 90-day warranty period, burglars broke into Lobianco's house and stole $35,815 worth of jewelry. First, they destroyed the electric meter so that there was no electric source to operate the system, and then they entered the house. The batteries in the standby system were dead, and thus the standby system failed to operate. Accordingly, no outside siren was activated and a telephone call that was supposed to be triggered was not made. Lobianco brought suit, claiming damage in the amount of her stolen jewelry because of the failure of the alarm system to work properly. Did the disclaimer effectively eliminate any liability on the alarm company's part for consequential damages?

3. On July 1, 2005, Gary Woods purchased a Maytag 30-inch gas range oven from Plesser's, a department store in Babylon, New York. The gas oven came with a warranty that provided as follows:

> Full One Year Warranty—Parts and Labor
>
> For one (1) year from the original retail purchase date, any part which fails in normal home use will be repaired or replaced free of charge.
>
> . . .
>
> The specific warranties expressed above are the **ONLY** warranties provided by the manufacturer. This warranty gives you specific legal rights, and you may also have other rights that vary from state to state.

On February 29, 2008, when Woods attempted to use the oven, a malfunction occurred that caused the oven to explode. Woods attributed the explosion to an alleged defect in the starter mechanism in the oven that "causes the gas valve to open in such a manner that the open valve causes the oven to fill with gas but not ignite." On December 10, 2009, Woods brought suit against Maytag claiming, among other things, breach of express warranty. Maytag moved to dismiss the count, contending that it was barred by the four-year statute of limitations in the UCC. Woods contended that the warranty came within an exception to the four-year rule because it related to future performance. Should the court view the warranty as one relating to future performance?

4. Murrey & Sons Company (Murrey) was engaged in the business of manufacturing and selling pool tables. Erik Madsen was working on an idea to develop a pool table that, through the use of electronic devices installed in the rails of the table, would produce lighting and sound effects in a fashion similar to a pinball machine. Murrey and Madsen entered into a written contract whereby Murrey agreed to manufacture 100 of its M1 4-foot by 8-foot six-pocket coin-operated pool tables with customized rails capable of incorporating the electronic lighting and sound effects desired by Madsen. Under the agreement, Madsen would design the rails and provide the drawings to Murrey, which would manufacture them to Madsen's specifications. Madsen was to design, manufacture, and install the electronic components for the tables. Madsen agreed to pay $550 per table or a total of $55,000 for the 100 tables and made a $42,500 deposit on the contract.

Murrey began the manufacture of the tables while Madsen continued to work on the design of the rails and electronics. Madsen encountered significant difficulties and notified Murrey that he would be unable to take delivery of the 100 tables. Madsen then brought suit to recover the $42,500 he had paid Murrey.

Following Madsen's repudiation of the contract, Murrey dismantled the pool tables and used salvageable materials to manufacture other pool tables. A good portion of the material was simply used as firewood. Murrey made no attempt to market the 100 pool tables at a discount or at any other price in order to mitigate its damages. It claimed the salvage value of the materials it reused was $7,488. There was evidence that if Murrey had completed the tables, they would have had a value of at least $21,250 and could have been sold for at least that much and that the changes made in the frame to accommodate the electrical wiring would not have adversely affected the quality or marketability of the pool tables. Murrey said it had not completed manufacture because its reputation for quality might be hurt if it dealt in "seconds" and that the changes in the frame might weaken it and subject it to potential liability. Was Murrey justified in not completing manufacture of the pool tables?

5. Catherine Baker purchased a fake fur coat from the Burlington Coat Factory Warehouse store in Scarsdale, New York, paying $127.99 in cash. The coat began shedding profusely, rendering the coat unwearable. The shedding was so severe that Baker's allergies were exacerbated, necessitating a visit to her doctor and to the drugstore for a prescription.

   She returned the coat to the store after two days and demanded that Burlington refund her $127.99 cash payment. Burlington refused, indicating that it would give her a store credit or a new coat of equal value, but no cash refund. Baker searched the store for a fake fur of equal value and found none. She refused the store credit, repeated her demand for a cash refund, and brought a lawsuit against Burlington when it refused to make a cash refund.

   In its store, Burlington displayed several large signs that state, in part:

   WAREHOUSE POLICY

   Merchandise in New Condition May Be Exchanged Within 7 Days for Store Credit and Must Be Accompanied by a Ticket and Receipt. No Cash Refunds or Charge Credits.

   On the front of Baker's sales receipt was the following language:

   Holiday Purchases May Be Exchanged Through January 11th, 1998. In House Store Credit Only. No Cash Refunds or Charge Card Credits.

   On the back of the sales receipt was the following language:

   We Will Be Happy to Exchange Merchandise in New Condition Within 7 Days When Accompanied By Ticket and Receipt. However, Because of Our Unusually Low Prices: No Cash Refunds or Charge Card Credits Will Be Issued. In House Store Credit Only.

   At the trial, Baker claimed that she had not read the language on the receipt and was unaware of Burlington's no-cash-refunds policy. The court found that Burlington had breached the implied warranty of merchantability when it sold the defective coat to Baker. Where the seller breaches the implied warranty of merchantability and the buyer returns the defective goods, is the buyer entitled to a refund of the purchase price paid for the goods?

6. Dubrow, a widower, was engaged to be married. In October, he placed a large order with a furniture store for delivery the following January. The order included rugs cut to special sizes for the prospective couple's new house and many pieces of furniture for various rooms in the house. One week later, Dubrow died. When the order was delivered, his only heir, his daughter, refused to take the furniture and carpeting. The furniture store then sued his estate to recover the full purchase price. It had not tried to resell the furniture and carpeting to anyone else. Under the circumstances, was the seller entitled to recover the purchase price of the goods?

7. Cohn advertised a 30-foot sailboat for sale in *The New York Times.* Fisher saw the ad, inspected the sailboat, and offered Cohn $4,650 for the boat. Cohn accepted the offer. Fisher gave Cohn a check for $2,535 as a deposit on the boat. He wrote on the check, "Deposit on aux sloop, D'arc Wind, full amount $4,650." Fisher later refused to go through with the purchase and stopped payment on the deposit check. Cohn readvertised the boat and sold it for the highest offer he received, which was $3,000. Cohn then sued Fisher for breach of contract. He asked for damages of $1,679.50. This represented the $1,650 difference between the contract price and the sale price plus $29.50 in incidental expenses in reselling the boat. Is Cohn entitled to this measure of damages?

8. Barr purchased from Crow's Nest Yacht Sales a 31-foot Tiara pleasure yacht manufactured by S-2 Yachts. He had gone to Crow's Nest knowing the style and type of yacht he wanted. He was told that the retail price was $102,000 but that he could purchase the model it had for $80,000. When he asked about the reduction in price, he was told that Crow's Nest had to move it because there was a change in the model and it had new ones coming in. He was assured that the yacht was new, that there was nothing wrong with it, and that it had only 20 hours on the engines. Barr installed a considerable amount of electronic equipment on the boat. When he began to use it, he experienced tremendous difficulties with equipment malfunctions. On examination by a marine expert, it was determined that the yacht had earlier been sunk in saltwater, resulting in significant rusting and deterioration in the engine, equipment, and fixtures. Other experts concluded that significant replacement and repair were required; that the engines would have only 25 percent of their normal expected life; and that following its sinking, the yacht would have only half of its original value. Barr then brought suit against Crow's Nest and S-2 Yachts for breach of warranty. To what measure of damages is Barr entitled to recover for breach of warranty?

9. De La Hoya bought a used handgun for $140 from Slim's Gun Shop, a licensed firearms dealer. At the time, neither De La Hoya nor Slim's knew that the gun had been stolen prior to the time Slim's bought it. While De La Hoya was using the gun for target shooting, he was questioned by a police officer. The officer traced the serial number on the gun, determined that it had been stolen, and arrested De La Hoya. De La Hoya had to hire an attorney to defend himself against the criminal charges. De La Hoya then brought a lawsuit against Slim's Gun Shop for breach of warranty of title. He sought to recover the purchase price of the gun plus $8,000, the amount of his attorney's fees, as "consequential damages." Can a buyer who does not get good title to the goods he purchased recover from the seller consequential damages caused by the breach of warranty of title?

10. Schweber contracted to purchase a certain black Rolls-Royce Corniche automobile from Rallye Motors. He made a $3,500 deposit on the car. Rallye later returned his deposit to him and told him that the car was not available. However, Schweber learned that the automobile was available to the dealer and was being sold to another customer. The dealer then offered to sell Schweber a similar car, but with a different interior design. Schweber brought a lawsuit against the dealer to prevent it from selling the Rolls-Royce Corniche to anyone else and to require that it be sold to him. Rallye Motors claimed that he could get only damages and not specific performance. Approximately 100 Rolls-Royce Corniches were being sold each year in the United States, but none of the others would have the specific features and detail of this one. Is the remedy of specific performance available to Schweber?

Property

Personal Property And Bailments

Claudio is a skilled craftsman employed by the Goldcasters Jewelry to make handcrafted jewelry. Working after his normal working hours and using materials he paid for himself, Claudio crafts a fine ring by skillfully weaving together strands of gold wire. He presents the ring to his fiancé, Cheryl, as an engagement ring in anticipation of their forthcoming marriage. While visiting the restroom in a steak and ribs restaurant, Cheryl removes the ring so she can wash some barbecue sauce from her hands. In her haste to get back to her table, she leaves the ring on the washstand when she exits the restroom. Sandra, a part-time janitor for the restaurant, finds the ring and slips it into her purse. When Cheryl realizes she is missing the ring and returns to the restroom to look for it, neither the ring nor Sandra is still there. Later that evening, Sandra sells the ring to her cousin, Gloria, who gives her $200 for it. Several days later, Cheryl breaks her engagement to Claudio, telling him that she no longer loves him. Claudio asks Cheryl to return the ring, indicating that he intended for her to have it only if their engagement led to marriage. This situation raises a number of questions concerning rights and interests in personal property that will be discussed in this chapter. They include:

- Between Claudio and Goldcasters, who was the owner of the ring at the time Claudio created it?
- Did Claudio make an effective gift of the ring to Cheryl? Or was it a conditional gift that he could revoke when Cheryl decided to call off the marriage?
- What was Sandra's responsibility when she found the ring? Between Sandra and the restaurant, who had the better right to the ring?
- Did Gloria become the owner of the ring when she paid the $200 to Sandra? Does Cheryl have the right to recover the ring from Gloria if she finds that Gloria has it?
- Was it ethical for Claudio to use his employer's tools and facilities for a personal project?

LEARNING OBJECTIVES

After studying this chapter, you should be able to:

23-1 Understand the concept of ownership of property as a bundle of rights that the law recognizes.

23-2 Differentiate personal property from real property.

23-3 List the primary ways to acquire ownership of personal property.

23-4 Explain how the rights of finders of abandoned, lost, and mislaid property differ.

23-5 List and discuss the elements that are necessary for making a valid gift of property.

23-6 List the three essential elements of a bailment.

23-7 List and compare the three different types of bailments.

23-8 Explain the basic duties of the bailee and the bailor of personal property.

23-9 Discuss the special rules applicable for bailments to common carriers and hotelkeepers.

23-10 Discuss the special rules applicable to bailments covered by negotiable documents of title, including warehouse receipts and bills of lading.

Nature of Property

LO23-1 Understand the concept of ownership of property as a bundle of rights that the law recognizes.

The concept of property is central to the organization of society. The essential nature of a particular society is often reflected in the way it views property, including the degree to which property ownership is concentrated in the state, the extent to which it permits individual ownership of property, and the rules that govern such ownership. History is replete with wars and revolutions that arose out of conflicting claims to, or views concerning, property. Significant documents in our Anglo-American legal tradition, such as the Magna Carta and the Constitution, deal explicitly with property rights.

The word **property** is used to refer to something that is capable of being owned. It is also used to refer to a right or interest that allows a person to exercise dominion over a thing that may be owned or possessed.

When we talk about property ownership, we are speaking of a *bundle of rights* that the law recognizes and enforces. For example, ownership of a building includes the exclusive right to use, enjoy, sell, mortgage, or rent the building. If someone else tries to use the property without the owner's consent, the owner may use the courts and legal procedures to eject that person. Ownership of a patent includes the rights to produce, use, and sell the patented item and to license others to do those things.

In the United States, private ownership of property is protected by the Constitution, which provides that the government shall deprive no person of "life, liberty, or property, without due process of law." We recognize and encourage the rights of individuals to acquire, enjoy, and use property. These rights, however, are not unlimited. For example, a person cannot use property in an unreasonable manner that injures others. Also, the state has **police power** through which it can impose reasonable regulations on the use of property, tax it, and take it for public use by paying the owner compensation for it.

Property is divided into a number of categories based on its characteristics. The same piece of property may fall into more than one class. The following discussion explores the meaning of **personal property** and the numerous ways of classifying property.

Classifications of Property

LO23-2 Differentiate personal property from real property.

Personal Property versus Real Property

Personal property is defined by process of exclusion. The term *personal property* is used in contrast to *real property*. Real property is the earth's crust and all things firmly attached to it.[1] For example, land, office buildings, and houses are considered to be real property. All other objects and rights that may be owned are personal property. Clothing, books, and stock in a corporation are examples of personal property.

Real property may be turned into personal property if it is detached from the earth. Personal property, if attached to the earth, becomes real property. For example, marble in the ground is real property. When the marble is quarried, it becomes personal property, but if it is used in constructing a building, it becomes real property again. Perennial vegetation that does not have to be seeded every year, such as trees, shrubs, and grass, is usually treated as part of the real property on which it is growing. When trees and shrubs are severed from the land, they become personal property. Crops that must be planted each year, such as corn, oats, and potatoes, are usually treated as personal property. However, if the real property on which they are growing is sold, the new owner of the real property also becomes the owner of the crops.

When personal property is attached to, or used in conjunction with, real property in such a way as to be treated as part of the real property, it is known as a **fixture**. The law concerning fixtures is discussed in Chapter 24.

Tangible versus Intangible Personal Property

Personal property may be either tangible or intangible. Tangible property has a physical existence. Cars, animals, and computers are examples. Property that has no physical existence is called intangible property. For example, rights under a patent, copyright, or trademark would be intangible property.[2]

The distinction between tangible and intangible property is important primarily for tax and estate planning purposes. Generally, tangible property is subject to tax in the state in which it is located, whereas intangible property is usually taxable in the state where its owner lives.

Public and Private Property

Property is also classified as public or private, based on the ownership of the property. If the property is owned by the government or a governmental unit, it is public property. If it is owned

---

[1]The law of real property is treated in Chapter 24.
[2]These important types of intangible property are discussed in Chapter 8.

by an individual, a group of individuals, a corporation, or some other business organization, it is private property.

Acquiring Ownership of Personal Property

 LO23-3 List the primary ways to acquire ownership of personal property.

Production or Purchase The most common ways of obtaining ownership of property are by producing it or purchasing it. A person owns the property that she makes unless the person has agreed to do the work for another party. In that case, the other party is the owner of the product of the work. For example, a person who creates a painting, knits a sweater, or develops a computer program is the owner unless she has been retained by someone to create the painting, knit the sweater, or develop the program.

Another major way of acquiring property is by purchase. The law regarding the purchase of tangible personal property (i.e., sale of goods) is discussed in Chapter 19.

The scenario set out at the start of this chapter posits that Claudio, a skilled craftsman employed by Goldcasters to make handcrafted jewelry, works after his normal working hours and uses materials he paid for himself to make a gold ring. Who should be considered to be the owner of the ring at the time Claudio created it, Claudio or Goldcasters? What are the critical factors that lead you to this conclusion?

Possession of Unowned Property In very early times, the most common way of obtaining ownership of personal property was simply by taking possession of unowned property. For example, the first person to take possession of a wild animal became its owner. Today, one may still acquire ownership of personal property by possessing it if the property is unowned. The two major examples of unowned property that may be acquired by possession are wild animals and abandoned property. Abandoned property will be discussed in the next section, which focuses on the rights of finders.

The first person to take possession of a wild animal normally becomes the owner.[3] To acquire ownership of a wild animal by taking possession, a person must obtain enough control over it to deprive it of its freedom. If a person fatally wounds a wild animal, the person becomes the owner. Wild animals caught in a trap or fish caught in a net are usually considered to be the property of the person who set the trap or net. If a captured wild animal escapes and is caught by another person, that person generally becomes the owner. However, if that person knows that the animal is an escaped animal and that the prior owner is chasing it to recapture it, then he does not become the owner.

Rights of Finders of Lost, Mislaid, and Abandoned Property

 LO23-4 Explain how the rights of finders of abandoned, lost, and mislaid property differ.

The old saying "finders keepers, losers weepers" is not a reliable way of predicting the legal rights of those who find personal property that originally belonged—or still belongs—to another. The rights of the finder will be determined according to whether the property he finds is classified as abandoned, lost, or mislaid.

1. *Abandoned property.* Property is considered to be abandoned if the owner intentionally placed the property out of his possession with the intent to relinquish ownership of it. For example, Norris takes his TV set to the city dump and leaves it there. The finder who takes possession of abandoned property with intent to claim ownership becomes the owner of the property. This means he acquires better rights to the property than anyone else in the world, including the original owner. For example, if Fox finds the TV set, puts it in his car, and takes it home, Fox becomes the owner of the TV set.

2. *Lost property.* Property is considered to be lost when the owner did not intend to part with possession of the property. For example, if Barber's iPhone fell out of her handbag while she was walking down the street, it would be considered lost property. The person who finds lost property does not acquire ownership of it, but he acquires better rights to the lost property than anyone other than the true owner. For example, suppose Lawrence finds Barber's iPhone in the grass where it fell. Jones then steals the iPhone from Lawrence's bookbag. Under these facts, Barber is still the owner of the iPhone. She has the right to have it returned to her if she discovers where it is—or if Lawrence knows that it belongs to Barber. As the finder of lost property, however, Lawrence has a better right to the iPhone than anyone else except Barber. This means that Lawrence has the right to require Jones to return it to him if he finds out that Jones has it.

If the finder does not know who the true owner is or cannot easily find out, the finder must still return the

---

[3]As wildlife is increasingly protected by law, however, some wild animals cannot be owned because it is illegal to capture them (e.g., endangered species).

property when the real owner shows up and asks for the property. If the finder of lost property knows who the owner is and refuses to return it, the finder is guilty of **conversion** and must pay the owner the fair value of the property.[4] A finder who sells the property that he has found can pass to the purchaser only those rights that he has; he cannot pass any better title to the property than he himself has. Thus, the true owner could recover the property from the purchaser.

3. *Mislaid property.* Property is considered to be mislaid if the owner intentionally placed the property somewhere and accidentally left it there, not intending to relinquish ownership of the property. For example, Fields places her backpack on a coatrack at Campus Bookstore while shopping for textbooks. Forgetting the backpack, Fields leaves the store and goes home. The backpack would be considered mislaid rather than lost because Fields intentionally and voluntarily placed it on the coatrack. If property is classified as mislaid, the finder acquires no rights to the property. Rather, the person in possession of the real property on which the personal property was mislaid has the right to hold the property for the true owner and has better rights to the property than anyone other than the true owner. For example, if Stevens found Fields's backpack in Campus Bookstore, Campus Bookstore would have the right to hold the mislaid property for Fields. Stevens would acquire neither possession nor ownership of the backpack.

The rationale for this rule is that it increases the chances that the property will be returned to its real owner. A person who knowingly placed the property somewhere but forgot to pick it up might well remember later where she left the property and return for it.

In the case that follows, *Grande v. Jennings,* the court held that money secreted in a wall of a home belonged to the estate of the person who had placed the money there rather than the current owner of the property when the money was found.

In the scenario set out at the start of this chapter, Cheryl visits the restroom in a steak and ribs restaurant in order to wash some barbecue sauce from her hands. She removes her engagement ring and places it on the washstand, but in her haste to get back to her table, she leaves the ring on the washstand when she exits the washroom. Sandra, a part-time janitor for the restaurant, finds the ring, slips it in her purse, and later sells the ring to her cousin, Gloria, for $200. When Cheryl returns to the restroom to look for the ring, neither the ring nor Sandra is still there.

At the time Sandra discovers the ring, should it be considered abandoned, lost, or mislaid property? What factors lead you to this conclusion? What should Sandra do with the ring at that point? Between Sandra and the owner of the restaurant, who has the best claim to the ring? Among the restaurant owner, Sandra, and Cheryl, who has the best claim to it? Why? If Cheryl discovers that Gloria has the ring, does she have the right to recover it from her? Why?

Some states have a statute that allows finders of property to clear their title to the property. The statutes, known as estray statutes, generally provide that the person must give public notice of the fact that the property has been found, perhaps by putting an ad in a local newspaper. All states have statutes of limitations that require the true owner of property to claim it or bring a legal action to recover possession of it within a certain number of years. A person who keeps possession of lost or unclaimed property for longer than that period of time will become its owner.

Legal Responsibilities of Finders
Some states go further and make it a criminal offense for a person who comes into control of property that he knows or learns has been lost or mislaid to appropriate the property to his own use without first taking reasonable measures to restore the property to the owner. For example, under the Georgia Code, "A person commits the offense of theft of lost or mislaid property that he knows or learns to have been lost or mislaid property when he comes into control of property that he knows or learns to have been lost or mislaid and appropriates the property to his own use without first taking reasonable measures to restore the property to the owner" (Ga. Code Ann. § 16-8-6).

In a case[5] under that statute, an individual was convicted of the offense when she found a bank deposit bag containing checks, deposit slips, and more than $500 in cash and subsequently attempted to cash one of the checks at a local check cashing business. The deposit bag had been misplaced while the victim was transporting it from her business located in a shopping mall to a car parked outside the mall. Some of the checks contained the victim's phone number and address, and the finder admitted that she never contacted the victim to restore the property to her.

[4]The tort of conversion is discussed in Chapter 6.

[5]*Shannon v. The State*, 574 S.E.2d 889 (Ga. Ct. App. 2002).

Rights of Finders of Personal Property

Character of Property	Description	Rights of Finder	Rights of Original Owner
Lost	Owner unintentionally parted with possession	Rights superior to everyone except the owner	Retains ownership; has the right to the return of the property
Mislaid	Owner intentionally put property in a place but unintentionally left it there	None; person in possession of real property on which mislaid property was found holds it for the owner, and has rights superior to everyone except owner	Retains ownership; has the right to the return of the property
Abandoned	Owner intentionally placed property out of his possession with intent to relinquish ownership of it	Finder who takes possession with intent to claim ownership acquires ownership of property	None

Grande v. Jennings   278 P.3d 1287 (Ariz. Ct. App. 2012)

When Robert Spann passed away in 2001, his daughter, Karen Spann Grande, became the personal representative of the estate. She and her sister took charge of the house, which Spann owned and resided in for many years. They made some repairs to the house and also looked for valuables their father might have left or hidden. They knew from experience that he had hidden gold, cash, and other valuables in unusual places in other homes. Over the course of seven years, they found stocks and bonds, as well as hundreds of military-style ammunition cans hidden throughout the house, some of which contained gold or cash.

The house was sold "as is" to Sarina Jennings and Clinton McCallum in September 2008. They hired Randy Bueghly and his company, Trinidad Builders, to remodel the dilapidated house. Shortly after the work began, Rafael Cuen, a Trinidad employee, discovered two ammunition cans full of cash in a kitchen wall, went looking, and found two more cash-filled ammunition cans inside the framing of an upstairs bathroom.

After Cuen reported the find to his boss, Bueghly took the four ammo cans—but did not tell the new owners about the find—and tried to secret the cans. Cuen, however, eventually told the new owners about the discovery and the police were called. The police ultimately took control of $500,000, which Bueghly had kept in a floor safe in his home.

Jennings/McCallum sued Bueghly for conversion and a declaration that Bueghly had no right to the money, and Bueghly later filed a counterclaim for a declaration that he was entitled to the found funds. In the meantime, Grande filed a petition in probate court on behalf of the estate to recover the money. The two cases were consolidated in June 2009. Jennings/McCallum argued that the money belonged to them because it was found on their property. Bueghly argued that the money had been abandoned and that as the first to reduce it to his possession, he was entitled to it. Grande contended that the money had been mislaid by her father and that the estate should be recognized as the true owner.

Portley, Judge

Although elementary school children like to say "finders keepers," the common law generally characterizes found property in one of four ways. Found property can be mislaid, lost, abandoned, or treasure trove. Property is "mislaid" if the owner intentionally places it in a certain place and forgets about it. "Lost" property includes property the owner unintentionally parts with through either carelessness or neglect. "Abandoned" property has been thrown away or

was voluntarily forsaken by its owner. Property is considered "treasure trove" if it is verifiably antiquated and has been concealed for so long as to indicate that the owner is probably dead or unknown.

A finder's rights depend on how a court classifies the found property. In characterizing the property, a court should consider all of the particular facts and circumstances of the case. Under the common law, the finder of lost or abandoned property and treasure trove acquires a right to possess the property against the entire world but the rightful owner regardless of the place of finding. A finder of mislaid property, however, must turn the property over to the premises owner who has the duty to safeguard the property for the true owner.

Significantly, among the various categories of found property, only lost property necessarily involves an element of involuntariness. The remaining categories entail intentional and voluntary acts by the rightful owner in depositing property in a place where someone else eventually discovers it. For example, the Iowa Supreme Court has stated that "mislaid property is voluntarily put in a certain place by the owner who then overlooks or forgets where the property is" and that one who finds mislaid property does not necessarily attain any rights to it because possession belongs to the owner of the premises upon which the property is found, absent a claim by the true owner. In *Benjamin v. Linder Aviation*, 534 N.W.2d 400, 406 (Iowa 1995), the court determined that packets of money found in a sealed panel of a wing during an inspection of a repossessed airplane were mislaid property because the money was intentionally placed there by one of two prior owners.

Arizona follows the common law. In *Strawberry Water Co. v. Paulsen*, 207 P.3d 654, 661 (Ariz. Ct. App. 2008), we stated that in order to abandon personal property, one must voluntarily and intentionally give up a known right. Abandonment is a virtual throwing away of property without regard as to who may take over or carry on.

Here, it is undisputed that Spann placed the cash in the ammunition cans and then hid those cans in the recesses of the house. He did not, however, tell his daughters where he had hidden the cans before he passed away. His daughters looked for and found many of the ammo cans, but not the last four. In fact, it was not until the wall-mounted toaster oven and bathroom drywall were removed, that Cuen found the remaining cash-filled cans. As a result, and as the trial court found, the funds are, as a matter of law, mislaid funds that belong to the true owner, Spann's estate.

Other state courts have also characterized found money as mislaid funds. For example, in *Hill v. Shrunk*, the Oregon Supreme Court held that cash, which was wrapped in oiled paper, placed in waterproof containers, and found lodged in the bottom of a natural water pool on decedent's property, belonged to him at death, and was mislaid, rather than abandoned, lost, or treasure trove. Similarly, the Arkansas Supreme Court affirmed the trial court's finding that a dusty cardboard box containing $38,000 and found in the ceiling of a motel room during renovation was mislaid property because the money was found where it was placed for its security, in order to shield it from unwelcome eyes.

As a result, the court affirmed the determination that the motel owner's rights to the funds were superior to those of the whole world except the true owner.

Jennings/McCallum assert, however, that the mislaid funds were abandoned because Grande consciously ignored the fact that neither she nor her sister had found all of the money that their father had withdrawn from his bank account, and did not do more to find it. We disagree.

The fact that the trial court correctly determined that the funds were mislaid precludes the funds from being considered abandoned. Moreover, abandonment is generally not presumed, but must be proven. Here the facts are undisputed that the estate did not know that the money was mislaid, and did not intend to abandon the funds. In fact, the evidence is to the contrary; once Grande learned of the discovery, she filed a probate petition to recover the property. Her action as the personal representative undermines the argument that the sisters abandoned the money through conscious ignorance.

Jennings/McCallum cite *Michael v. First Chicago Corp.* to support their argument that Grande had "constructive knowledge" of the cash hidden within the house and, therefore, abandoned the money when the house was sold. There the bank sold several filing cabinets "as is" to a used furniture dealer. Some of the cabinets were locked and, to the bank's surprise, one of the locked cabinets contained several certificates of deposit worth approximately $6.6 million. There was evidence that the certificates were supposed to be transferred to another storage area, but bank employees overlooked the task. The court held that the relinquishment of possession, under the circumstances, without a showing of an intention to permanently give up all right to the certificates of deposit was not enough to show abandonment.

Despite the argument that Grande had constructive knowledge that money and valuables had been hidden, and therefore abandoned the money when the house was sold, *Michael* demonstrates that the fact that neither party knew of the existence of additional ammo cans filled with cash and secreted inside the walls of the house is exactly why we cannot conclude that Grande abandoned the funds.

Based on the evidence before the trial court, there were no facts from which we could begin to infer that the estate intended to relinquish any valuable items that may have been secreted within the home. In fact, the evidence is to the contrary.

Accordingly, summary judgment was appropriately granted.

Leasing A lease of personal property is a transfer of the right to possess and use personal property belonging to another.[6] Although the rights of one who leases personal property (a lessee) do not constitute ownership of personal property, leasing is mentioned here because it is an important way of acquiring the use of many kinds of personal property, from automobiles to farm equipment.

---

[6]A lease of personal property is a form of bailment, a "bailment for hire." Bailments are discussed later in this chapter.

Articles 2 and 9 of the UCC may sometimes be applied to personal-property leases by analogy. However, rules contained in these articles are sometimes inadequate to resolve special problems presented by leasing. For this reason, a new article of the UCC dealing exclusively with leases of goods, Article 2A, was written in 1987. Forty-nine states (all except Louisiana), the District of Columbia, and the Virgin Islands have adopted Article 2A.

> **LO23-5** List and discuss the elements that are necessary for making a valid gift of property.

Gifts   Title to personal property may be obtained by **gift**. A gift is a voluntary transfer of property to the **donee** (the person who receives a gift), for which the **donor** (the person who gives the gift) gets no consideration in return. To have a valid gift, all three of the following elements are necessary:

1. The donor must *intend* to make a gift.

2. The donor must make *delivery* of the gift.

3. The donee must *accept* the gift.

The most critical requirement is delivery. The donor must actually give up possession and control of the property either to the donee or to a third person who is to hold it for the donee. Delivery is important because it makes clear to the donor that he is voluntarily giving up ownership without getting something in exchange. A promise to make a gift is usually not enforceable;[7] the person must actually part with the property. In some cases, the delivery may be symbolic or constructive. For example, handing over the key to a strongbox may be symbolic delivery of the property in the strongbox.

There are two kinds of gifts: gifts *inter vivos* and gifts *causa mortis*. A gift *inter vivos* is a gift between two living persons. For example, when Melissa's parents give her a car for her 21st birthday, that is a gift *inter vivos*. A gift *causa mortis* is a gift made in contemplation of death. For example, Uncle Earl, who is about to undergo a serious heart operation, gives his watch to his nephew, Bart, and says that he wants Bart to have it if he does not survive the operation.

A gift *causa mortis* is a conditional gift and is effective unless any of the following occurs:

1. The donor recovers from the peril or sickness under fear of which the gift was made, or

2. The donor revokes or withdraws the gift before he dies, or

3. The donee dies before the donor.

If one of these events takes place, ownership of the property goes back to the donor.

Conditional Gifts   Sometimes a gift is made on condition that the donee comply with certain restrictions or perform certain actions. A conditional gift is not a completed gift. It may be revoked by the donor before the donee complies with the conditions. Gifts in contemplation of marriage, such as engagement rings, are a primary example of a conditional gift. Such gifts are generally considered to have been made on an implied condition that marriage between the donor and donee will take place. The traditional rule applied in many states provides that if the donee breaks the engagement without legal justification or the engagement is broken by mutual consent, the donor will be able to recover the ring or other engagement gift. However, if the engagement is unjustifiably broken by the donor, the traditional rule generally bars the donor from recovering gifts made in contemplation of marriage. As illustrated by the *Lindh* case, which follows shortly, many courts have rejected the traditional approach and its focus on fault. Some states have enacted legislation prescribing the rules applicable to the return of engagement presents.

In the scenario set out at the beginning of this chapter, Claudio gave the ring to Cheryl as an engagement ring in anticipation of their forthcoming marriage. Later, Cheryl breaks off the engagement, telling Claudio that she no longer loves him. Claudio then asks Cheryl to return the ring to him.

What argument would Claudio make to support his claim that he has the legal right to have the ring returned to him? What argument might Cheryl make to support her contention that she should have the legal right to retain the ring? If Claudio and Cheryl lived in Pennsylvania, where the *Lindh v. Surman* case was decided, would Claudio be entitled to recover the ring from Cheryl? Why or why not? Would it make a difference if they lived in a state that used a fault-based approach concerning gifts given in anticipation of marriage?

Uniform Transfers to Minors Act   The Uniform Transfers to Minors Act, which has been adopted in one form or another in every state, provides a fairly simple and flexible method for making gifts and other transfers of property to minors.[8] As defined in this act, a minor is anyone under the age of 21. Under the act, an adult may transfer money, securities, real property, insurance policies, and

---

[7]The idea is discussed in Chapter 12.

[8]This statute was formerly called, and is still called in some states, the Uniform Gift to Minors Act.

Lindh v. Surman   742 A.2d 643 (Pa. 1999)

In August 1993, Rodger Lindh (Rodger) proposed marriage to Janis Surman (Janis). Rodger presented her with a diamond engagement ring that he had purchased for $17,400. Janis accepted the marriage proposal and the ring. Two months later, Rodger broke the engagement and asked Janis to return the ring. She did so. Rodger and Janis later reconciled, with Rodger again proposing marriage and again presenting Janis with the engagement ring. Janis accepted the proposal and the ring. In March 1994, Rodger again broke the engagement and asked Janis to return the ring. This time, however, she refused. Rodger sued her, seeking recovery of the ring or a judgment for its value. The trial court held in Rodger's favor and awarded him damages in the amount of the ring's value. When Janis appealed, the Pennsylvania Superior Court affirmed the award of damages and held that when an engagement is broken, the engagement ring must be returned even if the donor broke the engagement. Janis appealed to the Supreme Court of Pennsylvania.

Newman, Justice

We are asked to decide whether a donee of an engagement ring must return the ring or its equivalent value when the donor breaks the engagement. We begin our analysis with the only principle on which the parties agree: that Pennsylvania law treats the giving of an engagement ring as a conditional gift. In *Pavlicic v. Vogtsberger*, 136 A.2d 127 (Pa. 1957), the plaintiff supplied his ostensible fiancée with numerous gifts, including money for the purchase of engagement and wedding rings, with the understanding that they were given on the condition that she marry him. When the defendant left him for another man, the plaintiff sued her for recovery of these gifts. Justice Musmanno explained the conditional gift principle:

> A gift given by a man to a woman on condition that she embark on the sea of matrimony with him is no different from a gift based on the condition that the donee sail on any other sea. If, after receiving the provisional gift, the donee refuses to leave the harbor—if the anchor of contractual performance sticks in the sands of irresolution and procrastination—the gift must be restored to the donor.

The parties disagree, however, over whether fault [on the part of the donor] is relevant to determining return of the ring.

Janis contends that Pennsylvania law . . . has never recognized a right of recovery in a donor who severs the engagement. She maintains that if the condition of the gift is performance of the marriage ceremony, [a rule allowing a recovery of the ring] would reward a donor who prevents the occurrence of the condition, which the donee was ready, willing, and eagerly waiting to perform. Janis's argument that . . . the donor should not be allowed to recover the ring where the donor terminates the engagement has some basis in [decisions from Pennsylvania's lower courts and in treatises]. This Court, however, has not decided the question of whether the donor is entitled to return of the ring where the donor admittedly ended the engagement.

The issue we must resolve is whether we will follow the fault-based theory argued by Janis, or the no-fault rule advocated by Rodger. Under a fault-based analysis, return of the rings depends on an assessment of who broke the engagement, which necessarily entails a determination of why that person broke the engagement. A no-fault approach, however, involves no investigation into the motives or reasons for the cessation of the engagement and requires the return of the engagement ring simply upon the nonoccurrence of the marriage.

The rule concerning the return of a ring founded on fault principles has superficial appeal because, in the most outrageous instances of unfair behavior, it appeals to our sense of equity. Where one of the formerly engaged persons has truly "wronged" the other, justice appears to dictate that the wronged individual should be allowed to keep the ring or have it returned, depending on whether the wronged person was the donor . . . or the donee. However, the process of determining who is "wrong" and who is "right," when most modern relationships are complex circumstances, makes the fault-based approach less desirable. A thorough fault-based inquiry would not . . . end with the question of who terminated the engagement, but would also examine that person's reasons. In some instances the person who terminated the engagement may have been entirely justified in his or her actions. This kind of inquiry would invite the parties to stage the most bitter and unpleasant accusations against those whom they nearly made their spouse. A ring-return rule based on fault principles will inevitably invite acrimony and encourage parties to portray their ex-fiancées in the worst possible light. Furthermore, it is unlikely that trial courts would be presented with situations where fault was clear and easily ascertained.

The approach that has been described as the modern trend is to apply a no-fault rule to engagement ring cases. Courts that have applied this rule have borrowed from the policies of their respective legislatures that have moved away from the notion of fault in their divorce statutes. All fifty states have adopted some form of no-fault divorce. We agree with those jurisdictions that have looked toward the development of no-fault divorce law for a principle to decide engagement ring cases. In addition, the inherent weaknesses in any fault-based system lead us to adopt a no-fault approach to resolution of engagement ring disputes.

Decision of Superior Court in favor of Rodger Lindh affirmed.

Cappy, Justice, dissenting

The majority urges adoption of the no-fault rule to relieve trial courts from having the onerous task of sifting through the debris of the broken engagement in order to ascertain who is truly at fault. Are broken engagements truly more disturbing than cases where we ask judges and juries to discern possible abuses in nursing homes, day care centers, dependency proceedings involving abused children, and criminal cases involving horrific, irrational injuries to innocent victims? The subject matter our able trial courts address on a daily basis is certainly of equal sordidness as any fact pattern they may need to address in a simple case of who broke the engagement and why.

I can envision a scenario whereby the prospective bride and her family have expended thousands of dollars in preparation for the culminating event of matrimony and she is, through no fault of her own, left standing at the altar holding the caterer's bill. To add insult to injury, the majority would also strip her of her engagement ring. Why the majority feels compelled to modernize this relatively simple and ancient legal concept is beyond the understanding of this poor man. As I see no valid reason to forgo the fault-based rule for determining possession of the engagement ring under the simple concept of conditional gift law, I cannot endorse the modern trend advocated by the majority.

other property. The specific ways of doing this vary according to the type of property transferred. In general, however, the transferor (the person who gives or otherwise transfers the property) delivers, pays, or assigns the property to, or registers the property with, a custodian who acts for the benefit of the minor "under the Uniform Transfers to Minors Act." The custodian is given fairly broad discretion to use the gift for the minor's benefit and may not use it for the custodian's personal benefit. The custodian may be the transferor himself, another adult, or a trust company, again depending on the type of property transferred. If the donor or other transferor fully complies with the Uniform Transfers to Minors Act, the transfer is considered to be irrevocable.

Will or Inheritance

Ownership of personal property may also be transferred upon the death of the former owner. The property may pass under the terms of a will if the will was validly executed. If there is no valid will, the property is transferred to the heirs of the owner according to state laws. Transfer of property at the death of the owner will be discussed in Chapter 26.

Confusion

Title to personal property may be obtained by **confusion**. Confusion is the intermixing of different owners' goods in such a way that they cannot later be separated. For example, suppose wheat belonging to several different people is mixed in a grain elevator. If the mixing was by agreement or if it resulted from an accident without negligence on anyone's part, each person owns his proportionate share of the entire quantity of wheat. However, a different result would be reached if the wheat was wrongfully or negligently mixed. Suppose a thief steals a truckload of Grade #1 wheat worth $8.50 a bushel from a farmer. The thief dumps the wheat into his storage bin, which contains a lower-grade

wheat worth $4.50 a bushel, with the result that the mixture is worth only $4.50 a bushel. The farmer has first claim against the entire mixture to recover the value of the higher-grade wheat that was mixed with the lower-grade wheat. The thief, or any other person whose intentional or negligent act results in confusion of goods, must bear any loss caused by the confusion.

Accession

Ownership of personal property may also be acquired by **accession**. Accession means increasing the value of property by adding materials, labor, or both. As a general rule, the owner of the original property becomes the owner of the improvements. This is particularly likely to be true if the improvement was done with the permission of the owner. For example, Hudson takes his automobile to a shop that replaces the engine with a larger engine and puts in a new four-speed transmission. Hudson is still the owner of the automobile as well as the owner of the parts added by the auto shop.

Problems may arise if materials are added or work is performed on personal property without the consent of the owner. If property is stolen from one person and improved by the thief, the original owner can get it back and does not have to reimburse the thief for the work done or the materials used in improving it. For example, a thief steals Rourke's used car, puts a new engine in it, replaces the tires, and repairs the brakes. Rourke is entitled to get his car back from the thief and does not have to pay him for the engine, tires, and brakes.

The result is less easy to predict, however, if property is mistakenly improved in good faith by someone who believes that he owns the property. In such a case, a court must weigh the respective interests of two innocent parties: the original owner and the improver.

For example, Johnson, a stonecarver, finds a block of limestone by the side of the road. Assuming that it has been abandoned, he takes it home and carves it into a sculpture. In fact, the block was owned by Hayes. Having fallen off a flatbed truck during transportation, the block is merely lost property, which Hayes ordinarily could recover from the finder. In a case such as this, a court could decide the case in either of two ways. The first alternative would be to give the original owner (Hayes) ownership of the improved property, but to allow the person who has improved the property in good faith (Johnson) to recover the cost of the improvements. The second alternative would be to hold that the improver, Johnson, has acquired ownership of the sculpture, but that he is required to pay the original owner the value of the property as of the time he obtained it. The greater the extent to which the improvements have increased the value of the property, the more likely it is that the court will choose the second alternative and permit the improver to acquire ownership of the improved property.

Bailments

 List the three essential elements of a bailment.

Nature of Bailments
A **bailment** is the delivery of personal property by its owner or someone holding the right to possess it (the **bailor**) to another person (the **bailee**) who accepts it and is under an express or implied agreement to return it to the bailor or to someone designated by the bailor. Only personal property can be the subject of bailments.

Although the legal terminology used to describe bailments might be unfamiliar to most people, everyone is familiar with transactions that constitute bailments. For example, Lincoln takes his car to a parking garage where the attendant gives Lincoln a claim check and then drives the car down the ramp to park it. Charles borrows his neighbor's lawn mower to cut his grass. Tara, who lives next door to Kyle, agrees to take care of Kyle's cat while Kyle goes on a vacation. These are just a few of the everyday situations that involve bailments.

Elements of a Bailment
The essential elements of a bailment are:

1. The bailor owns personal property or holds the right to possess it.

2. The bailor delivers exclusive possession of and control over the personal property to the bailee.

3. The bailee knowingly accepts the personal property with the understanding that he owes a duty to return the property, or to dispose of it, as directed by the bailor.

Creation of a Bailment A bailment is created by an express or implied contract. Whether the elements of a bailment have been fulfilled is determined by examining all the facts and circumstances of the particular situation. For example, a patron goes into a restaurant and hangs his hat and coat on an unattended rack. It is unlikely that this created a bailment because the restaurant owner never assumed exclusive control over the hat and coat. However, if there is a checkroom and the hat and coat are checked with the attendant, a bailment will arise.

If a customer parks her car in a parking lot, keeps the keys, and may drive the car out herself whenever she wishes, a bailment has not been created. The courts treat this situation as a lease of space. Suppose, however, that she takes her car to a parking garage where an attendant, after giving her a claim check, parks the car. There is a bailment of the car because the parking garage has accepted delivery and possession of the car. However, a distinction is made between the car and packages locked in the trunk. If the parking garage was not aware of the packages, it probably would not be a bailee of them as it did not knowingly accept possession of them. The creation of a bailment is illustrated in the Concept Review box.

Types of Bailments

 List and compare the three different types of bailment.

Bailments are commonly divided into three different categories:

1. Bailments for the sole benefit of the bailor.

2. Bailments for the sole benefit of the bailee.

3. Bailments for mutual benefit.

The type of bailment involved in a case can be important in determining the liability of the bailee for loss of or damage to the property. As will be discussed later, however, some courts no longer rely on these distinctions when they determine whether the bailee is liable.

Bailments for Benefit of Bailor A bailment for the sole benefit of the bailor is one in which the bailee renders some service but does not receive a benefit in return.

Creation of a Bailment

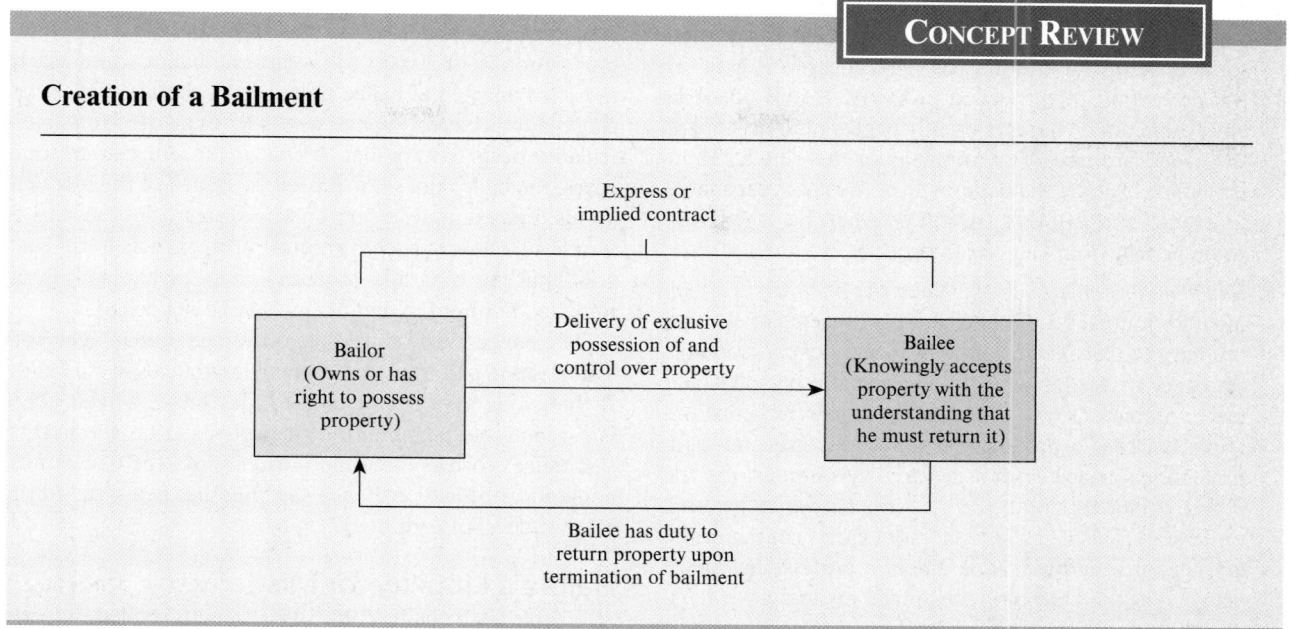

Express or implied contract

Bailor
(Owns or has right to possess property)

Delivery of exclusive possession of and control over property

Bailee
(Knowingly accepts property with the understanding that he must return it)

Bailee has duty to return property upon termination of bailment

For example, Brown allows his neighbor, Reston, to park her car in Brown's garage while she is on vacation. Brown does not ask for any compensation. Here, Reston, the bailor, has received a benefit from the bailee, Brown, but Brown has not received a benefit in return.

Bailments for Benefit of Bailee A bailment for the sole benefit of the bailee is one in which the owner of the goods allows someone else to use them free of charge. For example, Anderson lends a lawn mower to her neighbor, Moss, so he can cut his grass.

Bailments for Mutual Benefit If both the bailee and the bailor receive benefits from the bailment, it is a bailment for mutual benefit. For example, Sutton rents china for his daughter's wedding from E-Z Party Supplies for an agreed-on price. Sutton, the bailee, benefits by being able to use the china; E-Z benefits from his payment of the rental charge. On some occasions, the benefit to the bailee is less tangible. For example, a customer checks a coat at an attended coatroom at a restaurant. Even if no charge is made for the service, it is likely to be treated as a bailment for mutual benefit because the restaurant is benefiting from the customer's patronage.

Special Bailments Certain professional bailees, such as innkeepers and common carriers, are treated somewhat differently by the law and are held to a higher level of responsibility than is the ordinary bailee. The rules applicable to common carriers and innkeepers are detailed later in this chapter.

Duties of the Bailee

 Explain the basic duties of the bailee and the bailor of personal property.

The bailee has two basic duties:

1. To take care of the property that has been entrusted to her.
2. To return the property at the termination of the bailment.

The following discussion examines the scope of these duties.

Duty of Bailee to Take Care of Property

The bailee is responsible for taking steps to protect the property during the time she has possession of it. If the bailee does not exercise proper care and the property is lost or damaged, the bailee is liable for negligence. The bailee would then be required to reimburse the bailor for the amount of loss or damage. If the property is lost or damaged without the fault or negligence of the bailee, however, the bailee is not liable to the bailor. The degree of care required of the bailee traditionally has depended in large part on the type of bailment involved.

1. *Bailment for the benefit of the bailor.* If the bailment is solely for the benefit of the bailor, the bailee is expected to exercise only a minimal, or slight, degree of care for the protection of the bailed property. He would be liable, then, only if he were grossly negligent in his care of the bailed property. The rationale for this rule is that if the bailee is doing the bailor a favor, it is not reasonable to expect him to be as careful as when he is deriving some benefit from keeping the goods.

2. *Bailment for mutual benefit.* When the bailment is a bailment for mutual benefit, the bailee is expected to exercise ordinary or reasonable care. This degree of care requires the bailee to use the same care a reasonable person would use to protect his own property in the relevant situation. If the bailee is a professional that holds itself out as a professional bailee, such as a warehouse, it must use the degree of care that would be used by a person in the same profession. This is likely to be more care than the ordinary person would use. In addition, a professional bailee usually has the obligation to explain any loss of or damage to property—that is, to show it was not negligent. If it cannot do so, it will be liable to the bailor.

3. *Bailment for the benefit of the bailee.* If the bailment is solely for the benefit of the bailee, the bailee is expected to exercise a high degree of care. For instance, a person who lends a sailboat to a neighbor would probably expect the neighbor to be even more careful with the sailboat than the owner might be. In such a case, the bailee would be liable for damage to the property if his action reflected a relatively small degree of negligence.

A number of courts today view the type of bailment involved in a case as just one factor to be considered in determining whether the bailee should be liable for loss of or damage to bailed goods. The modern trend appears to be moving in the direction of imposing a duty of reasonable care on bailees, regardless of the type of bailment. This flexible standard of care permits courts to take into account a variety of factors such as the nature and value of the property, the provisions of the parties' agreement, the payment of consideration for the bailment, and the experience of the bailee. In addition, the bailee is required to use the property only as was agreed between the parties. For example, Jones borrows Morrow's lawn mower to mow his lawn. If Jones uses the mower to cut the weeds on a trash-filled vacant lot and the mower is damaged, he would be liable because he was exceeding the agreed purpose of the bailment—to cut his lawn.

Bailee's Duty to Return the Property

An essential element of a bailment is the duty of the bailee to return the property at the termination of the bailment. If the bailed property is taken from the bailee by legal process, the bailee should notify the bailor and must take whatever action is necessary to protect the bailor's interest. In most instances, the bailee must return the identical property that was bailed. A person who lends a 2015 Honda to a friend expects to have that particular car returned. In some cases, the bailor does not expect the return of the identical goods. For example, a farmer who stores 1,500 bushels of Grade #1 wheat at a local grain elevator expects to get back 1,500 bushels of Grade #1 wheat when the bailment is terminated, but not the identical wheat he deposited.

The bailee must return the goods in an undamaged condition to the bailor or to someone designated by the bailor. If the goods have been damaged, destroyed, or lost, there is a rebuttable presumption of negligence on the part of the bailee. To overcome the presumption, the bailee must come forward with evidence showing that he exercised the relevant level of care.

Bailee's Liability for Misdelivery

The bailee is also liable to the bailor if he misdelivers the bailed property at the termination of the bailment. The property must be returned to the bailor or to someone specified by the bailor.

The bailee is in a dilemma if a third person, claiming to have rights superior to those of the bailor, demands possession of the bailed property. If the bailee refuses to deliver the bailed property to the third-party claimant and the claimant is entitled to possession, the bailee is liable to the claimant. If the bailee delivers the bailed property to the third-party claimant and the claimant is not entitled to possession, the bailee is liable to the bailor. The circumstances may be such that the conflicting claims of the bailor and the third-party claimant can be determined only by judicial decision. In some cases, the bailee may protect himself by bringing the third-party claimant into a lawsuit along with the bailor so that all the competing claims can be adjudicated by the court before the bailee releases the property. This remedy is not always available, however.

Limits on Liability

Bailees may try to limit or relieve themselves of liability for the bailed property. Some examples include the storage receipts purporting to limit liability to a fixed amount such as $100, signs near checkrooms such as "Not responsible for loss of or damage to checked property," and disclaimers on claim checks such as "Goods left at owner's risk." The standards used to determine whether such limitations and disclaimers are enforceable are discussed in Chapter 15.

Any attempt by the bailee to be relieved of liability for intentional wrongful acts is against public policy and will not be enforced. A bailee's ability to be relieved of liability for negligence is also limited. Courts look to see whether the disclaimer or limitation of liability was communicated to the bailor at the time of the bailment. When the customer handed her coat to the checkroom attendant, did the attendant point out the "not responsible for loss or damage" sign? Did the parking lot attendant call the car owner's attention to the disclaimer on the back of the claim check?

If not, the court may hold that the disclaimer was not communicated to the bailor and did not become part of the bailment contract. Even if the bailor was aware of the disclaimer, it still may not be enforced on the ground that it is contrary to public policy.

If the disclaimer was offered on a take-it-or-leave-it basis and was not the subject of arm's-length bargaining, it is less likely to be enforced than if it was negotiated and voluntarily agreed to by the parties. A bailee may be able to limit liability to a certain amount or to relieve himself of liability for certain perils. Ideally, the bailee will give the

bailor a chance to declare a higher value and to pay an additional charge in order to be protected up to the declared value of the goods. Common carriers, such as railroads and trucking companies, often take this approach. Courts do not look with favor on efforts by a person to be relieved of liability for negligence. For this reason, terms limiting the liability of a bailee stand a better chance of being enforced than do terms completely relieving the bailee of liability.

An implied agreement as to the bailee's duties may arise from a prior course of dealing between the bailor and the bailee, or from the bailor's knowledge of the bailee's facilities or method of doing business. The bailee may, if he wishes, assume all risks incident to the bailment and contract to return the bailed property undamaged or to pay for any damage to or loss of the property.

In the case that follows, *Weissman v. City of New York*, the court concluded that an exculpatory clause was too vague to shield a bailor from liability for its negligence.

Weissman v. City of New York   860 N.Y.S.2d 393 (N.Y. Civ. Ct. 2009)

In 2005, Ken Weissman rented storage space at the West 79th Street Boat Basin, which is owned and operated by the City of New York Parks & Recreation Department. The written agreement contained an exculpatory clause that stated:

I understand that the City of New York Parks & Recreation Department will not be responsible for any damages incurred to my vessel while at the dinghy dock or while in the facility at the 79th Street Boat Basin, and that I store my vessel at my own risk.

The policy and practice at the facility was that users would store their vessels in an enclosed cage-like structure that had storage bins. Each user had a key to the storage area and had unrestricted access. Within the cage, users could further secure their vessels to the bin with their own devices such as chain and lock.

In 2007, Weissman had two brand-new kayaks stolen from the caged area. The lock to the caged area was intact but his kayaks and locks were missing. Weissman reported this theft to the police, staff, and management. He indicated to the Boat Basin that he was no longer going to use the facility because of the theft. The manager of the facility spoke to him and urged him to continue to use the facility because they were changing their practice and policy by adding more security measures. Only West 79th Street Boat Basin employees would have keys to the caged storage area. Users no longer had unrestricted access and would have to get an employee to escort them, open the lock, and admit them to the storage area. Security cameras were going to be installed.

The Boat Basin posted a notice with the new changes, which said:

Attention Kayak Owners

Please see marina staff to gain access to kayak storage area. We have had a security issue and have temporarily changed the locks. We will be adding security cameras to the area shortly. We apologize for any inconvenience in the meantime.

Based on the assurances by the manager that the security would be better, Weissman purchased two used kayaks and again stored them in the caged area. He and the others no longer had keys to the area and had to be admitted and escorted by an employee to access the vessels in the storage area. On or about July 23, 2007, a week after the first two kayaks were stolen, one of Weissman's replacement kayaks, which cost $1,400, was missing from the storage area. He filed a notice of claim and then brought suit against the City of New York, seeking the value of the missing kayak and a refund of the unused portion of the storage fee.

Martino, Judge

The general rule is that a marina is not liable for negligence for loss of a vessel not due to the condition of the docking facility. The privilege of keeping a vessel in a marina without an agreement to keep daily or continuous guard over the vessel or without the marina taking over or assuming custody of the vessel does not constitute a bailment. This was initially the situation under the original arrangement between Weissman and the Boat Basin. Weissman had exclusive custody of his vessels and unrestricted access because he had a key to the storage area. He had the privilege of storing his kayaks there but Boat Basin was not an insurer.

However, the arrangement between the parties changed when Boat Basin took custody of the kayaks by retaining the key and controlling access to the kayaks, notifying users that this was the new temporary policy, promising better security, and urging Weissman to keep his kayaks there because of the new security measures. Under these facts, a bailment was established.

A bailment gives rise to the duty of exercising ordinary care in keeping and safeguarding property. In the instant case, Weissman has made out a prima facie case of breach of that duty by establishing that Boat Basin had exclusive possession of the kayak under lock and key and that the kayak is now missing. It then becomes the obligation of the Boat Basin to come forward with evidence to rebut the presumption of negligence. Here, Boat Basin did not come forward with any evidence and argues that it had no duty of care. However, when Boat Basin took exclusive possession of Weissman's kayak and urged him to continue using the facility because of its improved security, it created the duty of ordinary care in safeguarding the property.

Boat Basin argues that it cannot be held liable for negligence because of the exculpatory clause in the original 2005 contract, which Weissman concedes was subsequently renewed by his yearly payments. Although exculpatory clauses are enforceable, they are strictly construed against the party seeking exemption from liability. Unless the intention of the parties to insulate one of them from liability for its own negligence is expressed in unequivocal terms, the clause will not operate to have such an effect.

The exculpatory clause in this case is vague and does not suggest an intent to shield Boat Basin from its own negligence in carrying out its duty to care for Weissman's kayak. This makes perfect sense because the City did not initially have any duty to safeguard Weissman's vessel. There was no bailment. Weissman had the key to the storage cage and retained custody and control of his kayak. He stored the vessel at his own risk and the Boat Basin would not be responsible for any damages. This was the intent of the exculpatory clause.

However, the relationship changed when Boat Basin took it upon itself to secure and take control of Weissman's vessel. Boat Basin now had the only key and assured Weissman that his kayaks would be safer under Boat Basin's custody because of the heightened security. The initial contract could not have been meant to cover this new arrangement. The court holds that under the facts of this case, a bailment was created and Boat Basin was negligent by breaching its duty of care. The exculpatory clause in the original contract is too vague to shield Boat Basin from liability for its own negligence.

Judgment in favor of Weissman for $1,400, the value of the missing kayak.

Right to Compensation

The express or implied contract creating the bailment controls whether the bailee has the right to receive compensation for keeping the property or must pay for having the right to use it. If the bailment is made as a favor, then the bailee is not entitled to compensation even though the bailment is for the bailor's sole benefit. If the bailment involves the rental of property, the bailee must pay the agreed rental rate. If the bailment is for the storage or repair of property, the bailee is entitled to the contract price for the storage or repair services. When no specific price was agreed on but compensation was contemplated by the parties, the bailee is entitled to the reasonable value of the services provided.

In many instances, the bailee will have a lien (a charge against property to secure the payment of a debt) on the bailed property for the reasonable value of the services. For example, Silver takes a chair to Ace Upholstery to have it recovered. When the chair has been recovered, Ace has the right to keep it until the agreed price—or, if no price was set, the reasonable value of the work—is paid. This is an example of an **artisan's lien**, which is discussed in Chapter 29.

Bailor's Liability for Defects in the Bailed Property

When personal property is rented or loaned, the bailor makes an implied warranty that the property has no hidden defects that make it unsafe for use. If the bailment is for the bailee's sole benefit, the bailor is liable for injuries that result from defects in the bailed property only if the bailor knew about the defects and did not tell the bailee. For example, Price lends his car, which he knows has bad brakes, to Sloan. If Price does not tell Sloan about the bad brakes and Sloan is injured in an accident because the brakes fail, Price is liable for Sloan's injuries.

If the bailment is a bailment for mutual benefit, the bailor has a greater obligation. The bailor must use reasonable care in inspecting the property and seeing that it is safe for the purpose for which it is intended. The bailor is liable for injuries suffered by the bailee because of defects that the bailor either knew about or should have discovered through reasonable inspection. For example, Acme Rent-All, which rents trailers, does not inspect the trailers after they are returned. A wheel has come loose on a trailer that Acme rents to Hirsch. If the wheel comes off while Hirsch is using the trailer and the goods Hirsch is carrying in it are damaged, Acme is liable to Hirsch.

In addition, product liability doctrines that apply a higher standard of legal responsibility have been applied to bailors who are commercial lessors of personal property.[9] Express or implied warranties of quality under either Article 2 or Article 2A of the UCC may apply. Liability under these warranties does not depend on whether the bailor knew about or should have discovered the defect. The only question is whether the property's condition complied with the warranty. Some courts have also imposed strict liability on the commercial lessor-bailor of defective, unreasonably dangerous goods that cause personal injury or property damage to the lessee-bailee. This liability is imposed regardless of whether the lessor was negligent.

Special Bailments

 LO23-9 Discuss the special rules applicable for bailments to common carriers and hotelkeepers.

Common Carriers   Bailees that are common carriers are held to a higher level of responsibility than are bailees that are private carriers. Common carriers are licensed by governmental agencies to carry the property of anyone who requests the service. Private contract carriers carry goods only for persons selected by the carrier.

Both common carriers and private contract carriers are bailees. However, the law makes the common carrier a near-absolute insurer of the goods it carries. The common carrier is responsible for virtually any loss of or damage to the entrusted goods, unless the common carrier shows that the loss or damage was caused by one of the following:

1. An act of God.
2. An act of a public enemy.
3. An act or order of the government.
4. An act of the person who shipped the goods.
5. The nature of the goods themselves.

Therefore, the common carrier is liable if goods entrusted to it are stolen by some unknown person, but not if the goods are destroyed when the warehouse is damaged by a hurricane.

If goods are damaged because the shipper improperly packaged or crated them, the carrier is not liable. Similarly, if perishable goods are not in suitable condition to be shipped and therefore deteriorate in the course of shipment, the carrier is not liable so long as it used reasonable care in handling them.

Common carriers are usually permitted to limit their liability to a stated value unless the bailor declares a higher value for the property and pays an additional fee.

Hotelkeepers   Hotelkeepers are engaged in the business of offering food and/or lodging to transient persons. They hold themselves out to serve the public and are obligated to do so. As is the common carrier, the hotelkeeper is held to a higher standard of care than that of the ordinary bailee. The hotelkeeper, however, is not a bailee in the strict sense of the word. The guest does not usually surrender the exclusive possession of his property to the hotelkeeper. Even so, the hotelkeeper is treated as the virtual insurer of the guest's property. The hotelkeeper is not liable for loss of or damage to property if she shows that it was caused by one of the following:

1. An act of God.
2. An act of a public enemy.
3. An act of a governmental authority.
4. The fault of a member of the guest's party.
5. The nature of the goods.

Most states have passed laws that limit the hotelkeeper's liability, however. Commonly, the law requires the hotel owner to post a notice advising guests that any valuables should be checked into the hotel vault. The hotelkeeper's liability is then limited, usually to a fixed amount, for valuables that are not so checked.

Safe-Deposit Boxes   If a person rents a safe-deposit box at a local bank and places property in the box, the box and the property are in the physical possession of the bank. However, it takes both the renter's key and the key held by the bank to open the box. In most cases, the bank does not know the nature, amount, or value of the goods in the box. Although a few courts have held that the rental of a safe-deposit box does not create a bailment, most courts have concluded that the renter of the box is a bailor and the bank is a bailee. As such, the bank is not an insurer of the contents of the box. It is obligated, however, to use due care and to come forward and explain loss of or damage to the property entrusted to it.

---

[9]Product liability doctrines are discussed in Chapter 20.

Duties of Bailees and Bailors

Type of Bailment	Duties of Bailee	Duties of Bailor
Sole Benefit of Bailee	1. Must use great care; liable for even slight negligence. 2. Must return goods to bailor or dispose of them at his direction. 3. May have duty to compensate bailor.	1. Must notify the bailee of any known defects.
Mutual Benefit	1. Must use reasonable care; liable for ordinary negligence. 2. Must return goods to bailor or dispose of them at his direction. 3. May have duty to compensate bailor.	1. Must notify bailee of all known defects and any defects that could be discovered on reasonable inspection. 2. Commercial lessors may be subject to warranties of quality and/or strict liability in tort. 3. May have duty to compensate bailee.
Sole Benefit of Bailor	1. Must use at least slight care; liable for gross negligence. 2. Must return goods to bailor or dispose of them at his direction.	1. Must notify bailee of all known defects and any hidden defects that are known or could be discovered on reasonable inspection. 2. May have duty to compensate bailee.

Involuntary Bailments Suppose a person owns a cottage on a beach. After a violent storm, a sailboat washed up on his beach. As the finder of lost or misplaced property, he may be considered the involuntary bailee or constructive bailee of the sailboat. This relationship may arise when a person finds himself in possession of someone else's property without having agreed to accept possession.

The duties of the involuntary bailee are not well defined. The involuntary bailee does not have the right to destroy or use the property. If the true owner shows up, the property must be returned to him. Under some circumstances, the involuntary bailee may be under an obligation to assume control of the property or to take some minimal steps to ascertain the owner's identity, or both.

Documents of Title

 Discuss the special rules applicable to bailments covered by negotiable documents of title, including warehouse receipts and bills of lading.

Storing or shipping goods, giving a warehouse receipt or bill of lading representing the goods, and transferring such a receipt or bill of lading as representing the goods are practices of ancient origin. The warehouseman or the common carrier is a bailee of the goods who contracts to store or transport the goods and to deliver them to the owner or to act otherwise in accordance with the lawful directions of the owner. The warehouse receipt or the bill of lading may be either negotiable or nonnegotiable. To be negotiable, a warehouse receipt, bill of lading, or other document of title must provide that the goods are to be delivered to the bearer or to the order of a named person [7-104(1)]. The primary differences between the law of negotiable instruments and the law of negotiable documents of title are based on the differences between the obligation to pay money and the obligation to deliver specific goods.

Warehouse Receipts A warehouse receipt, to be valid, need not be in any particular form, but if it does not embody within its written or printed form each of the following, the warehouseman is liable for damages caused by the omission to a person injured as a result of it: (1) the location of the warehouse where the goods are stored; (2) the date of issue; (3) the consecutive number of the receipt; (4) whether the goods are to be delivered to the bearer or to the order of a named person; (5) the rate of storage and handling charges; (6) a description of the goods or of the packages containing them; (7) the signature of the warehouseman or his agent; (8) whether the warehouseman is the owner of the goods, solely, jointly, or in common with others; and (9) a statement of the amount of the advances made and of the liabilities incurred for which the warehouseman claims a lien or security interest. Other terms may be inserted [7-202].

A warehouseman is liable to a purchaser for value in good faith of a warehouse receipt for nonreceipt or misdescription of goods. The receipt may conspicuously qualify the description by a statement such as "contents, condition, and quantity unknown" [7-203].

Because a warehouseman is a bailee of the goods, he owes to the holder of the warehouse receipt the duties of a mutual benefit bailee and must exercise reasonable care [7-204]. The warehouseman may terminate the relation by notification where, for example, the goods are about to deteriorate or where they constitute a threat to other goods in the

warehouse [7-206]. Unless the warehouse receipt provides otherwise, the warehouseman must keep separate the goods covered by each receipt; however, different lots of fungible goods such as grain may be mingled [7-207].

A warehouseman has a lien against the bailor on the goods covered by his receipt for his storage and other charges incurred in handling the goods [7-209]. The Code sets out a detailed procedure for enforcing this lien [7-210].

Bills of Lading In many respects, the rights and 'iabilities of the parties to a negotiable bill of lading are the same as the rights and liabilities of the parties to a negotiable warehouse receipt. The contract of the issuer of a bill of lading is to transport goods, whereas the contract of the issuer of a warehouse receipt is to store goods. Like the issuer of a warehouse receipt, the issuer of a bill of lading

The Global Business Environment

Liability of Carriers of Goods

When an American firm ships goods to a foreign buyer, the goods may be shipped by ground, air, or water carrier. The duties and extent of liability of these various carriers is largely determined by domestic statutes and international law.

Ground Carriers American trucking and railroad companies are regulated by the Interstate Commerce Act. American carriers are liable for any loss or damage to the goods with few exceptions—for example, damage caused by acts of God and acts of the shipper (usually the seller of the goods), such as poorly packaging the goods. An American carrier may limit its liability by contract, provided it allows the shipper to obtain full liability by paying a higher shipping charge.

Most European trucking companies and railroads are covered by EU rules, which place liability on carriers for damages to goods they carry with few exceptions—for example, defective packaging by the shipper and circumstances beyond the carrier's control. EU rules also limit a carrier's liability unless the shipper agrees to pay for greater liability.

Air Carriers The Warsaw Convention governs the liability of international air carriers. Most nations have ratified the Warsaw Convention in its original or amended form. Under the Convention, an air carrier is liable to the shipper for damages to goods with few exceptions, including that it was impossible for the carrier to prevent the loss or that the damage was caused by the negligence of the shipper. The Warsaw Convention limits a carrier's liability to a stated amount per pound, unless the shipper pays for greater liability.

Water Carriers The Hague Rules govern the liability of international water carriers. The Hague Rules were amended in Visby, Sweden, in 1968. The United States codified the Hague Rules in

the Carriage of Goods by Sea Act (COGSA) but has not ratified the Visby amendments, which do not substantially change the liability of international water carriers.

The Hague–Visby Rules and the COGSA impose on international water carriers the duties to (1) furnish a seaworthy ship and (2) stow the cargo carefully to prevent it from breaking loose during storms at sea. When these duties are met, a water carrier will not usually be liable for damages to cargo. Water carriers have no liability for damages caused by circumstances beyond their control—such as poor packaging, piracy, or acts of war. Under COGSA, liability is limited to $500 per package, unless the shipper agrees to pay a higher shipping fee. Under the Hague–Visby Rules, liability will be the value of the goods declared by the shipper. Sometimes a carrier will attempt to reduce or eliminate its liability in the shipping contract. However, COGSA does not permit a carrier to eliminate its liability for loss or damages to goods resulting from the carrier's negligence or other fault.

Under COGSA or the Hague–Visby Rules, the owner of cargo will be liable for damage his cargo does to other cargo. Also, under the ancient maritime doctrine of general average, when a carrier sacrifices an owner's cargo, such as throwing it overboard in order to save the ship and the other cargo, the other owners have liability to the owner whose cargo was sacrificed; liability is prorated to each owner according to the value of each owner's goods in relation to the value of the voyage (the value of the ship plus the value of the other owners' goods plus the carrier's total shipping fees).

The doctrine of general average is commonly expanded by the contract between the carrier and cargo owners in New Jason clauses. Typically, a New Jason clause provides that in *all* cases when goods are damaged and the carrier is not liable under COGSA, the goods owner is entitled to general average contributions from all other cargo owners. The doctrine of general average, bolstered by a New Jason clause, also requires cargo owners to pay for damages to the ship when not the result of the carrier's fault.

is liable for nonreceipt or misdescription of the goods, but he may protect himself from liability where he does not know the contents of packages by marking the bill of lading "contents or condition of packages unknown" or similar language. Such terms are ineffective when the goods are loaded by an issuer who is a common carrier unless the goods are concealed by packages [7-301].

Duty of Care   A carrier who issues a bill of lading, or a warehouse operator who issues a warehouse receipt, must exercise the same degree of care in relation to the goods as

a reasonably careful person would exercise under similar circumstances. Liability for damages not caused by the negligence of the carrier may be imposed on him by a special law or rule of law. Under tariff rules, a common carrier may limit her liability to a shipper's declaration of value, provided that the rates are dependent on value [7-309].

In the case that follows, *Gyamfoah v. EG&G Dynatrend*, a warehouseman who was unable to return goods that had been entrusted to it for safekeeping or to account for their disappearance was held liable to the bailor for the value of the goods.

Gyamfoah v. EG&G Dynatrend (now EG&G Technical Services)
51 U.C.C. Rep. 2d 805 (E.D. Pa. 2003)

On May 7, 1999, Yaa Gyamfoah, a citizen of Ghana, arrived at JFK International Airport with two suitcases containing a number of watches she had purchased in Hong Kong. The suitcases were seized by U.S. Customs because it suspected the watches were counterfeit. Gyamfoah was given a receipt for 3,520 watches. The watches were transported to a warehouse operated by EG&G Dynatrend (EG&G), now known as EG&G Technical Services, under contract with the U.S. Department of Treasury to provide seized management services for all agencies of the department. The warehouse accepted and signed for the watches on June 2, 1999.

On October 13, U.S. Customs advised Gyamfoah's agent that the nonviolative (ones that were not counterfeit) portion of the seizure (2,940 watches) would be released upon payment of $1,470. On November 18, a Customs agent, observed by EG&G's warehouse supervisor, separated the watches into a group of 580 "violative" watches, which were placed in a carton, and 2,940 "nonviolative" watches, which were placed back in the suitcases. The carton and the suitcases were then returned to the custody of EG&G. When the Customs agent returned on November 24 to again, under the observation of the warehouse supervisor, examine the watches, there were only 1,002 watches in the carton and suitcases; some 2,518 were missing.

Gyamfoah subsequently brought suit against the United States and EG&G. The claim against the United States was dismissed, and the case went to trial on the claim against EG&G.

O'Neil, Jr., Judge

The duties of a warehouseman that existed under New Jersey common law have now been codified in N.J.S.A. 12A: 7-101. EG&G is a warehouseman under the definition in the statute: "a person engaged in the business of storing goods for hire." New Jersey requires that a warehouseman exercise reasonable care when storing bailed items. The statute imposes the following liability, in a provision adopted from the Uniform Commercial Code:

> A warehouseman is liable for damages for loss of or injury to the goods caused by his failure to exercise such care in regard to them as a reasonably careful man would exercise under like circumstances but unless otherwise agreed he is not liable for damages which could not have been avoided by the exercise of such care.

N.J.S.A. 12A: 7-204(1).

The warehouseman's statute has been interpreted to involve a burden-shifting scheme that reflects that common law of bailment. The bailor must present a *prima facie* case of conversion by proving (1) delivery of the bailed goods to the bailee; (2) demand for return of the bailed goods from the bailee; and (3) failure of

the bailee to return the bailed goods. Once the bailee has proved these three points, the burden shifts to the bailee to show how the bailed goods were lost. If the bailee cannot prove how the bailed goods were lost it is liable under the New Jersey statute for conversion. Although the burden of proof regarding how the goods were lost shifts to the defendant, the burden of proving conversion rests at all times on the bailor as plaintiff.

The tort of conversion that can be proved under the statute is not necessarily an intentional tort. In this instance "[a] conversion can occur even when a bailee has not stolen the merchandise but has acted negligently in permitting the loss of the merchandise from its premises." In other words, if a bailor establishes that the bailed goods had disappeared while in the care of the bailee, there is a rebuttable presumption of conversion based either on the bailee's negligent conduct in permitting third parties to steal the goods, or by the negligent or intentional conduct of the bailee's employees or agents.

As established earlier, I find that Gyamfoah showed by a preponderance of the evidence that: (1) 3,520 watches were delivered to EG&G's warehouse; (2) when Gyamfoah's agent presented the papers entitling Gyamfoah to return of the watches, 2,518 watches were missing; and (3) the U.S. Customs officers who manipulated the watches did not remove the missing watches.

Therefore, Gyamfoah has established delivery to EG&G and EG&G's failure to redeliver all of the items on Gyamfoah's demand. Under New Jersey law this creates a rebuttable presumption of conversion by EG&G.

EG&G produced evidence at trial of reasonable precautions against loss. Mr. Wenzcel testified that the watches were shrink-wrapped to a pallet and stored in a secured area on a high shelf that required a forklift to be reached. Paul Hehir, the EG&G district manager who oversaw operations in the New York district of the company, also testified about security. He testified that the area in which the watches were stored was alarmed and within a gated area that only EG&G employees could enter.

EG&G does not provide any evidence, however, regarding what happened to the missing watches. EG&G mentions the possibility that the missing watches were never delivered to the warehouse. This possibility is refuted, however, by evidence that U.S. Customs officers left the warehouse on November 18 thinking that there were 3,520 watches in storage. As I stated earlier, I find that Gyamfoah has proved by a preponderance of the evidence that there were 3,520 watches in the suitcases when the suitcases were delivered to EG&G's warehouse. There is no explanation for the disappearance of the watches other than EG&G's negligence. In fact, when asked "so it's fair to say that sitting here

today, EG&G can offer no explanation of the loss of the majority of the contents of those two suitcases?" EG&G employee Mr. Herir testified "I cannot offer any explanation, no."

EG&G has not met its burden to rebut the presumption of negligence created by plaintiff's case. Gyamfoah has met her burden of proving by a preponderance of the evidence that EG&G is liable to her under New Jersey's law of bailment, as found in Section 7-204(1) and the common law. EG&G is liable for the value of the lost watches.

Gyamfoah has proved by a preponderance of the evidence that EG&G is liable for the loss of 2,518 watches. For negligence, the measure of damages is the value of the lost goods.

The only evidence presented at trial regarding the value of the missing watches is a receipt from Andex Trading Limited. The receipt lists ten models of watches, the quantity bought by Gyamfoah, the unit price and the amount paid for the number of watches of each model bought. Because Gyamfoah has not shown which models the 2,518 missing watches were, I will calculate damages as if the least expensive 2,518 watches are missing.

The cost of the least expensive 2,518 watches is $3,781.30. That includes 300 watches at $0.90 each, 100 watches at $1.40 each, 350 watches at $1.55 each and 1,768 watches at $1.60 each.

Judgment in favor of Yaa Gyamfoah and against EG&G Dynatrend in the amount of $3,781.30.

Negotiation of Document of Title

A negotiable document of title and a negotiable instrument are negotiated in substantially the same manner. If the document of title provides for the delivery of the goods to bearer, it may be negotiated by delivery. If it provides for delivery of the goods to the order of a named person, it must be endorsed by that person and delivered. If an order document of title is endorsed in blank, it may be negotiated by delivery unless it bears a special endorsement following the blank endorsement, in which event it must be endorsed by the special endorsee and delivered [7-501].

A person taking a negotiable document of title takes as a bona fide holder if she takes in good faith and in the regular course of business. The bona fide holder of a negotiable document of title has substantially the same advantages over a holder who is not a bona fide holder or over a holder of a nonnegotiable document of title as does a holder in due course of a negotiable instrument over a holder who is not a holder in due course or over a holder of a nonnegotiable instrument.

Rights Acquired by Negotiation

A person who acquires a negotiable document of title by due negotiation acquires (1) title to the document, (2) title to the goods, (3) the right to the goods delivered to the bailee after the issuance of the document, and (4) the direct obligation of the issuer to hold or deliver the goods according to the terms of the document [7-502(1)].

Under the broad general principle that a person cannot transfer title to goods he does not own, a thief—or the owner of goods subject to a perfected security interest—cannot, by warehousing or shipping the goods on a negotiable document of title and then negotiating the document of title, transfer to the purchaser of the document of title a better title than he has [7-503].

Warranties of Transferor of Document of Title

The transferor of a negotiable document of title warrants to his immediate transferee, in addition to any warranty of goods, only that the document is genuine, that he has no knowledge of any facts that would impair its validity or worth, and that his negotiation or transfer is rightful and fully effective with respect to the title to the document and the goods it represents [7-507].

Problems and Problem Cases

1. Jann Wenner hired Anderson Asphalt Paving to construct a driveway on his ranch. Larry Anderson, the owner of Anderson Asphalt Paving, and his employee, Gregory Corliss, were excavating soil for the driveway when they unearthed a glass jar containing paper-wrapped rolls of gold coins. Anderson and Corliss collected, cleaned, and inventoried the gold pieces dating from 1857 to 1914.

   The 96 coins weighed about 4 pounds. Initially, Anderson and Corliss agreed to split the coins between themselves, with Anderson retaining possession of all the coins. Subsequently, Anderson and Corliss argued over ownership of the coins, and Anderson fired Corliss. Anderson later gave possession of the coins to Wenner in exchange for indemnification on any claim Corliss might have against him regarding the coins.

   Corliss sued Anderson and Wenner for possession of some or all of the coins. Corliss contended that the coins should be considered "treasure trove" and awarded to him pursuant to the "finders-keepers" rule of treasure trove. Wenner, defending both himself and Anderson, contended that he had the better right to possession of the gold coins. Does the finder of the buried gold coins have a better right to the coins than the owner of the property on which they were found?

2. Michael Preston was shopping in a Walmart in Tumwater, Washington, when he found a diamond ring on the floor. Video surveillance footage showed him picking up the ring and pausing before walking out of the store. The next day he took the ring to a pawn shop and used the ring to secure a loan for $175. Preston said that the ring belonged to his girlfriend who lived in Texas.

   The ring, which belonged to Nicole Amacker, was a wedding band with three diamonds that had a retail value of $3,200. Amacker had taken the ring off in the parking lot while assisting a man who had locked his keys in the car, but forgot to put the ring back on. She went inside the store and returned home, where she discovered the ring was missing. Amacker later viewed the store's surveillance video, which showed that the ring had been stuck to her sweater while she was in the store and that she had been in the area where Preston found the ring. The video showed that Preston picked up the ring approximately 12 minutes after Amacker was in the area.

   Amacker posted an advertisement on Craigslist offering a reward for the lost ring. Through the advertisement, Amacker came into contact with Preston. He said that he had found the ring and had pawned it. Amacker told him that she needed him to be present to get the ring back from the pawn shop. She said that she would pay the amount needed to obtain the ring, but that the payment would come out of the reward. Preston then became uncooperative and would not assist Amacker in retrieving the ring from the pawn shop. When Preston was contacted by the police, Preston admitted he had found the ring but believed Amacker no longer owned it because he had found it.

   Under State of Washington law, a person is guilty of second degree theft if he or she commits theft of property that exceeds $750 in value but does not exceed $5,000 in value. The definition of theft includes "to appropriate lost . . . property . . . of another, or the value thereof, with intent to deprive him or her of such property. . . ." The phrase "appropriate lost . . . property" is further defined as "obtaining or exerting control over the property . . . of another which the actor knows to have been lost or mislaid."

   The State charged Preston with second degree theft. On these facts, should a jury conclude that the ring was lost—rather than abandoned—property?

3. Rick Kenyon purchased a painting by a noted Western artist, Bill Gollings, valued between $8,000 and $15,000 for $25 at a Salvation Army thrift store. Claude Abel filed suit against Kenyon seeking the return of the painting, which had belonged to his late aunt. Abel claimed that the Salvation Army mistakenly took the painting from his aunt's house when the box in which it was packed was mixed with items being donated to the thrift store. Abel's aunt, Billie Taylor, was a friend of the artist whose works were known for their accurate portrayal of the Old West. Sometime before his death in 1932, Gollings gave a painting to Taylor depicting a Native American on a white horse in the foreground with several other Native Americans on horses in the background traveling through a traditional Western prairie landscape. The painting remained in Taylor's possession at her home in Sheridan, Wyoming, until her death on August 31, 1999. After Taylor's death, Abel traveled from his home in Idaho to Sheridan for the funeral and to settle the estate. Abel was the sole heir of Taylor's estate, so he inherited all of her personal belongings, including the Gollings painting. Abel and his wife sorted through Taylor's belongings, selecting various items they would keep

for themselves. Abel and his wife, with the help of a local moving company, packed those items into boxes marked for delivery to their home in Idaho. Items not being retained by Abel were either packed for donation to the Salvation Army or, if they had sufficient value, were taken by an antiques dealer for auction. The scene at the house was one of some confusion as Abel tried to vacate the residence as quickly as possible while attempting to make sure all of the items went to their designated destinations. The painting was packed by Abel's wife in a box marked for delivery to Idaho. However, in the confusion and unbeknown to Abel, the box containing Gollings's painting was inadvertently picked up with the donated items by the Salvation Army. It was priced at $25 in its thrift store and sold to Kenyon. After returning to Idaho, Abel discovered that the box containing the painting was not among those delivered by the moving company. He also learned that the painting had gone to the Salvation Army and had been sold to Kenyon. When Kenyon refused to acknowledge he had the painting, Abel brought suit seeking its return. Kenyon claimed that he was a good-faith purchaser of the painting that had been given to the Salvation Army. Was Abel entitled to have the painting returned to him on the grounds that not having made a gift of the painting, he was still the owner, and that its sale by the Salvation Army was a conversion of his property?

4. Charles Miller and Nicolette Chiaia met each other through work in 2007 and began a relationship. In October 2008, Miller moved into Chiaia's home, where she lived with her minor children from a prior marriage. Miller had also been married and was recently divorced. The parties' living arrangement was predicated on a mutual belief that they would become engaged and would marry. In early November 2008, the parties took a trip to Italy during which Miller proposed and presented Chiaia with a ring. She accepted the proposal and the ring. Subsequently, she asked Miller where he had purchased the ring, was disappointed with the answer, and gave it back to him. When they got back from Italy, Miller took the ring back to the seller and received a full refund of the amount he had paid, $5,000. Chiaia suggested the style of a different ring she would like and Miller purchased one like it from a jeweler for $12,000. Miller then "reproposed" and presented Chiaia with the second ring.

Over the next few months, Miller, who was self-employed, had business difficulties that caused friction between the parties, and the relationship soured. In February 2009, Miller moved out of Chiaia's house and the parties never reconciled. Miller asked for the ring back, but Chiaia refused. Miller then brought a lawsuit, seeking replevin of the ring. Chiaia contended that there had been a completed gift and that she owned the ring. Miller claimed that it was a conditional gift given at the time of the engagement and in contemplation of marriage. Is Miller entitled to recover the ring from Chiaia?

5. Faith Ballard's Corvette was substantially damaged in an accident and was being stored in her garage. Her son, Tyrone Ballard, told her that he would take the vehicle and have it restored. Instead, he sold it to Lambert Auto Parts. Johnny Wetzel purchased the Corvette "hull" for $900 from Lambert, whose regular business is selling parts. Wetzel obtained a receipt documenting the purchase of the parts. He also checked the VIN numbers through the county clerk's office to make sure the parts were not stolen. Wetzel spent approximately $5,000 and 100 hours of labor restoring the vehicle. When completed, the restoration had a market value of $7,950. George Martin, an employee of Lambert, testified that he purchased only a "hull" of a car—rather than a whole vehicle—from Tyrone Ballard. Martin also testified that he usually received a title when he bought a "whole" vehicle but had not received one in this case where he had purchased only part of one. Under Tennessee law, a certificate of title is not required to pass ownership of a motor vehicle, but any owner dismantling a registered vehicle is to send the certificate of title back to the state. Faith Ballard brought suit against Wetzel to recover possession of the Corvette. Wetzel contended that he was a good-faith purchaser for value and had become the owner of the restored auto hull by accession. Did Wetzel become the owner of the Corvette by accession?

6. R. B. Bewley and his family drove to Kansas City to attend a weeklong church convention. When they arrived at the hotel where they had reservations, they were unable to park their car and unload their luggage because of a long line of cars. They then drove to a nearby parking lot where they took a ticket, causing the gate arm to open, and drove in 15 or 20 feet. A parking attendant told them that the lot was full, that they should leave the keys with him, and that he would park the car. They told the attendant that they had reservations at a nearby hotel and that after they checked in they would come back for their luggage.

Subsequently, someone broke into the Bewleys' car and stole their personal property from the car and its trunk. Was the parking lot a bailee of the property?

7. On September 2, Deborah Jones signed a Storage Rental Agreement with Econo-Self Storage owned by Ernie Hanna. Jones needed to store her personal belongings and furniture because of the flooding of her apartment. The self-storage agreement was written as a lease and designated the parties as landlord and tenant. The warehouse space leased by Jones was 10 feet by 10 feet, on a monthly term of $45. The agreement provided in part: "All property kept, stored, or maintained within the premises by Tenant shall be at Tenant's sole risk."

   On May 2, Jones learned that the lock to her storage unit had been cut and virtually all of her possessions were stolen. The circumstances of the theft were not known. The storage units, 180 in all, were protected by a 6-foot fence and a locked gate. The tenants placed their own locks on the units. No security dogs or watchmen were provided. Access could be made to the units between 6 A.M. and 9 P.M. daily. No inventory was made of the goods by the facility owner, and the goods were never placed in his hands, nor did he know what was stored. Jones brought suit to recover damages for the loss of her property. Was Econo-Self Storage the bailee of Jones's goods?

8. On March 27, 2001, Felice Jasphy brought three fur coats to Illana Osinsky's establishment trading as Cedar Lane Furs in Teaneck, New Jersey, for storage and cleaning. The three coats included a ranch mink coat, a shearling, and a blush mink. In addition to storage of the three coats, Jasphy also sought cleaning of the ranch mink. In 1997, the ranch mink had been appraised for $11,500; the shearling for $3,500; and the blush mink for $3,995. Jasphy signed a written agreement, labeled "fur storage sales receipt," which included Jasphy's name and address, and the price of the storage and cleaning. On the back of the receipt, the following preprinted provision limiting Cedar Lane Furs's liability read:

   This receipt is a storage contract, articles listed are accepted for storage until December 31, of dated year, subject to the terms and conditions hereof, in accepting this receipt, the depositor agrees to be bound by all its terms and conditions and acknowledges that this receipt is the entire agreement with the furrier, which cannot be changed except by endorsement herein signed by the

furrier. If no value is specified, or if no separate insurance covering the garment is declared at the time of issuance of this receipt, insurance in the amount of $1.00 will be placed on the garment.

Immediately above the location on the receipt for a customer's signature, the following was printed: "I understand and agree that Cedar Lane Furs's liability for loss or damage from any cause whatsoever, including their own negligence or that of employees and others, is limited to the declared valuation." Jasphy did not state the value of the coats or declare whether she had separate insurance coverage when the receipt was issued. There is no identifiable room provided on the receipt to specify such information. The limitation of the furrier's liability was not brought to Jasphy's attention, nor was she asked to furnish the value of her coats for storage. The following day, March 28, 2001, a fire swept through Cedar Lane Furs, causing Jasphy's furs to be completely destroyed. A hot iron, which Cedar Lane Furs's employees apparently forgot to unplug overnight, caused the fire. Jasphy subsequently learned that her furs had not been placed in the fur vault before the fire and were destroyed in the fire. Jasphy filed a claim form with Cedar Lane Furs's insurance company but never received any reimbursement. She then brought suit against Osinsky and Cedar Lane Furs. They contended that their liability was limited by the contract provision to $1 per garment. Should the court enforce the contractual provision limiting the furrier's liability to $1 per garment?

9. Marie Wallinga was staying at the Commodore Hotel. She had her son take her two diamond rings to the hotel clerk for safekeeping. The rings were shown to the clerk and then placed in a "safe-deposit envelope," which was sealed. The son received a depositor's check stub, which had a number corresponding to the number on the envelope. He also signed his name on the safe-deposit envelope. Both the stub and his signature were necessary to get the envelope back. The envelopes were kept in a safe located in the hotel's front office, which was 4 or 5 feet behind the reception desk. The safe was used to keep cash for use in the hotel as well as the valuables of guests. The safe was equipped with a combination lock, but for many years it had never been locked. A clerk was always on duty at the reception desk. One morning, at 3:30 A.M., the hotel was robbed by two armed men, and Wallinga's rings were taken. She sued the hotel for the value of

the rings. The hotel claimed that the robbery relieved it of liability for them. Was the hotelkeeper liable for the theft of property left with it for safekeeping?

10. Griswold and Bateman Warehouse Company stored 337 cases of Chivas Regal Scotch Whiskey for Joseph H. Reinfeld Inc. in its bonded warehouse. The warehouse receipt issued to Reinfeld limited Griswold and Bateman's liability for negligence to 250 times the monthly storage rate, a total of $1,925. When Reinfeld sent its truck to pick up the whiskey, 40 cases were missing. Reinfeld then brought suit seeking the wholesale market value of the whiskey, $6,417.60. Reinfeld presented evidence of the delivery of the whiskey, the demand for its return, and the failure of Griswold and Bateman to return it. Reinfeld claimed that the burden was on Griswold and Bateman to explain the disappearance of the whiskey. Griswold and Bateman admitted that it had been negligent, but sought to limit its liability to $1,925. Is Griswold and Bateman's liability limited to $1,925?

Real Property

Joyce and John, a married couple with two young children, are in the process of buying a house. They made an offer on a single-family house in Greenwood, a new subdivision. The house has four bedrooms, one with custom-built bunk beds in it; four bathrooms; a swimming pool; and a large basement. There is a well-equipped kitchen and a large dining room with a vintage Tiffany lamp over the dining room table. The basement is perfect for Joyce, who plans to operate a small daycare center in the house. Joyce and John notice that the next-door neighbors, the Fieldings, have been dumping their garden refuse in a ravine at the back of the property that they have offered to buy, but they assume that they will be able to stop that practice once they move in.

- Are the bunk beds and Tiffany lamp considered to be part of the real property that Joyce and John have offered to buy?
- If their offer is accepted, how will Joyce and John share ownership of the property? What form of ownership will they have?
- What are the steps involved in purchasing this property?
- What rights might others, such as the Fieldings, have in the property?
- What liability might John and Joyce have to others who are injured on their property?
- What controls does the legal system place on the use of property?
- Is it ethical for the Fieldings to dump their garden refuse on this property?

LO LEARNING OBJECTIVES

After studying this chapter, you should be able to:

24-1 Define *real property* and explain what is included in the concept of real property.

24-2 Provide several examples of property that would be considered to be a fixture and explain the significance of classifying an item of property as a fixture.

24-3 Explain and distinguish among the various forms of ownership of real property.

24-4 Explain the legal effects of easements and restrictive covenants as well as the duties of property owners toward third persons.

24-5 Distinguish the various ways in which ownership of real property is transferred and how title to property can be assured.

24-6 Distinguish the different types of deeds, explain the purposes of recording deeds, and describe how state law determines priorities among those who claim competing rights in a parcel of real property.

24-7 Explain governmental powers to control and purchase private land and the constitutional limits on those powers.

LAND'S SPECIAL IMPORTANCE IN the law has long been recognized. In the agrarian society of previous eras, land served as the basic measure and source of wealth. In today's society, land functions not only as a source of food, clothing, and shelter but also as an instrument of commercial and industrial development. It is not surprising, then, that a complex body of law—the law of *real property*—exists regarding the ownership, acquisition, and use of land.

This chapter discusses the scope of real property and the various legal interests in it. In addition, the chapter examines the ways in which real property is transferred and the controls society places on an owner's use of real property.

Scope of Real Property

Define *real property* and explain what is included in the concept of real property.

Real property includes not only land, but also things firmly attached to or embedded in land. Buildings and other permanent structures thus are considered real property. The owner of a tract of real property also owns the air above it, the minerals below its surface, and any trees or other vegetation growing on the property.[1]

Unlike readily movable personal property, real property is immovable or attached to something immovable. Distinguishing between real and personal property is important because rules of law governing real property transactions such as sale, taxation, and inheritance are frequently different from those applied to personal property transactions.

Fixtures

Provide several examples of property that would be considered to be a fixture and explain the significance of classifying an item of property as a fixture.

An item of personal property may, however, be attached to or used in conjunction with real property in such a way that it ceases being personal property and instead becomes part of the real property. This type of property is called a **fixture**.

Fixtures belong to the owner of the real property. One who provides or attaches fixtures to real property without a request to that effect from the owner of the real property

is normally not entitled to compensation from the owner. A conveyance (transfer of ownership) of real property also transfers the fixtures associated with that property, even if the fixtures are not specifically mentioned.

People commonly install items of personal property on the real property they own or rent. Disputes may arise regarding rights to such property. Suppose that Jacobsen buys an elaborate ceiling fan and installs it in his home. When he sells the house to Orr, may Jacobsen remove the ceiling fan, or is it part of the home Orr has bought? Suppose that Luther, a commercial tenant, installs showcases and tracklights in the store she leases from Nelson. May Luther remove the showcases and the lights when her lease expires, or do the items now belong to Nelson? If the parties' contracts are silent on these matters, courts will resolve the cases by applying the law of fixtures. As later discussion will reveal, Jacobsen probably cannot remove the ceiling fan because it is likely to be considered part of the real property purchased by Orr. Luther, on the other hand, may be entitled to remove the showcases and the lights under the special rules governing trade fixtures.

Factors Indicating Whether an Item Is a Fixture There is no mechanical formula for determining whether an item has become a fixture. Courts tend to consider these factors:

1. *Attachment.* One factor helping to indicate whether an item is a fixture is the degree to which the item is attached or annexed to real property. If firmly attached to real property so that it cannot be removed without damaging the property, the item is likely to be considered a fixture. An item of personal property that may be removed with little or no injury to the property is less likely to be considered a fixture.

Actual physical attachment to real property is not necessary, however. A close physical connection between an item of personal property and certain real property may enable a court to conclude that the item is constructively annexed. For example, heavy machinery or remote control devices for automatic garage doors may be considered fixtures even though they are not physically attached to real property.

2. *Adaptation.* Another factor to be considered is adaptation—the degree to which the item's use is necessary or beneficial to the use of the real property. Adaptation is a particularly relevant factor when the item is not physically attached to the real property or is only slightly attached. When an item would be of little value except for use with certain real property, the item is likely to be considered a fixture even if it is unattached or could easily be removed. For example, keys and custom-sized window screens and storm windows have been held to be fixtures.

---

[1]Ownership of air above one's property is not an unlimited interest, however. Courts have held that the flight of aircraft above property does not violate the property owner's rights, so long as it does not unduly interfere with the owner's enjoyment of her land.

3. *Intent.* The third factor to be considered is the intent of the person who installed the item. Intent is judged not by what that person subjectively intended, but by what the circumstances indicate he intended. To a great extent, intent is indicated by the annexation and adaptation factors. An owner of real property who improves it by attaching items of personal property presumably intended those items to become part of the real estate. If the owner does not want an attached item to be considered a fixture, he must specifically reserve the right to keep the item. For instance, if a seller of a house wants to keep an antique chandelier that has been installed in the house, the seller should either replace the chandelier before the house is shown to prospective purchasers or specify in the contract of sale that the chandelier will be excluded from the sale.

Express Agreement If the parties to an express agreement have clearly stated their intent about whether a particular item is to be considered a fixture, a court will generally enforce that agreement. For example, the buyer and seller of a house might agree to permit the seller to remove a fence or shrubbery that would otherwise be considered a fixture.

Trade Fixtures An exception to the usual fixture rules is recognized when a tenant attaches personal property to leased premises for the purpose of carrying on her trade or business. Such fixtures, called **trade fixtures**, remain the tenant's personal property and may normally be removed at the termination of the lease. This trade fixtures exception encourages commerce and industry. It recognizes that the commercial tenant who affixed the item of personal property did not intend a permanent improvement of the leased premises.

The tenant's right to remove trade fixtures is subject to two limitations. First, the tenant cannot remove the fixtures if doing so would cause substantial damage to the landlord's realty. Second, the tenant must remove the fixtures by the end of the lease if the lease is for a definite period. If the lease is for an indefinite period, the tenant usually has a reasonable time after the expiration of the lease to remove the fixtures. Trade fixtures not removed within the appropriate time become the landlord's property.

Leases may contain terms expressly addressing the parties' rights in any fixtures. A lease might give the tenant the right to attach items or make other improvements and to remove them later. The reverse may also be true. The lease could state that any improvements made or fixtures

---

CONCEPT REVIEW

Fixtures

Concept	A *fixture* is an item of personal property attached to or used in conjunction with real property in such a way that it is treated as being part of the real property.
Significance	A transfer of the real property will also convey the fixtures on that property.
Factors Considered in Determining Whether Property Is a Fixture	1. Attachment: Is the item physically attached or closely connected to the real property? 2. Adaptation: How necessary or beneficial is the item to the use of the real property? 3. Intent: Did the person who installed the item manifest intent for the property to become part of the real property?
Express Agreement	Express agreements clearly stating intent about whether property is a fixture are generally enforceable.
Trade Fixtures (Tenants' Fixtures)	Definition of *trade fixture:* personal property attached to leased real property by a tenant for the purpose of carrying on the tenant's trade or business. Trade fixtures can be removed and retained by the tenant at the termination of the lease except when any of the following applies: 1. Removal would cause substantial damage to the landlord's real property. 2. The tenant fails to remove the fixtures by the end of the lease (or within a reasonable time, if the lease is for an indefinite period of time). 3. An express agreement between the landlord and tenant provides otherwise.

attached will become the landlord's property at the termination of the lease. Courts generally enforce parties' agreements on fixture ownership.

In *Mogilevsky v. Rubicon Technology, Inc.*, the court analyzes whether components of a complex electrical and cooling system are removable trade fixtures, even when other components of it (e.g., those buried beneath the floor of the building) clearly are not. Also note how the court does not find that damage resulting from removal of the components automatically makes them permanent fixtures. Rather, that damage is handled through remedies for breach of the lease.

Mogilevsky v. Rubicon Technology, Inc.
(2014 IL App (1st) 132702-U 2014)

In 1999, Dr. Radion Mogilevsky and his wife Nanette bought an empty two-story industrial warehouse-style building in Franklin Park, Illinois. They leased the building to S & R Rubicon Inc., a company they largely controlled.

S & R manufactured sapphire crystals for use in various commercial applications such as LED lighting. To make the building usable for that purpose, it purchased and installed a 2,000-amp electrical system and components of a cooling system to support the furnaces used in sapphire crystal manufacturing. The particular furnaces S & R used were of sufficiently large capacity to allow S & R to manufacture crystals of much larger size than its competitors' crystals.

The cooling system included components inside, outside, and underneath the building, including a rooftop water tower and above-ground pipe loop that ran the water to the tower. A second pipe loop ran coolant water under the concrete floor of the building.

Although Dr. Mogilevsky designed the system, Christopher Moffitt loaned S & R more than half a million dollars to purchase the furnaces, electrical, and cooling systems. As a result, Moffitt eventually became a 20 percent owner of S & R. Moffitt testified that he never intended that the systems would permanently remain on the premises because S & R had funded their purchase. In contrast, the Mogilevskys expected that the systems would remain permanently affixed to the premises because they had arranged for S & R to pay for the systems only for tax reasons.

In 2000, the Mogilevskys and Moffitt organized Rubicon Technology LLC (the LLC) to succeed S & R and to facilitate outside investment in anticipation of eventually converting it to a publicly held corporation. The Mogilevskys entered into a new lease with the LLC for the warehouse. Neither the sale documents nor the lease mentioned the components of the cooling system or the furnaces, but the sale document did state in the preface that S & R intended to transfer "all assets of or used in the business."

In January 2001, Rubicon Technology, Inc. (Rubicon) became the successor to the LLC. In 2005, the Mogilevskys and Rubicon entered into a five-year lease for the warehouse. The lease provided that at the conclusion of the lease, Rubicon would "at once surrender the Premises to Landlord, broom clean, in good order, condition, and repair, reasonable wear and tear excepted."

At the end of the lease term in 2010, Rubicon surrendered the premises and abandoned the underground components of the cooling system, but removed the major components. The removal left holes in the walls and floors, which required patching. Also, the 2,000-amp electrical service had been removed, leaving a 1,200-amp service only. Dr. Mogilevsky had planned to continue to use the building and the electrical and cooling systems for a new company he had created to produce high-purity densified alumina, which is used as a raw material to produce sapphire crystals. Thus, the Mogilevskys faced significant repair and replacement costs.

The Mogilevskys filed a lawsuit against Rubicon, seeking $950,000 in damages for breach of the lease and conversion. A jury awarded the Mogilevskys only $22,000 on the breach of contract claim for their cost to repair the holes. It found against them on the conversion claim, essentially determining that the system components were removable trade fixtures that belonged to Rubicon. The Mogilevskys moved for a judgment notwithstanding the verdict, which the court denied. They appealed.

Delort, Judge

We begin with the well-recognized principle that there are essentially two kinds of fixtures attached to real estate: permanent fixtures and trade fixtures. A tenant may not remove "permanent fixtures" from leased property, as they become part of the real estate. A permanent fixture is "a former chattel which, while retaining its separate physical identity, is so connected with the reality [sic] that a disinterested observer would consider it a part thereof." *St. Louis v. Rockwell Graphic Systems, Inc.*, 605 N.E.2d 555 (1992). . . . To determine whether an item is a tenant's personal property and not part of the realty, courts consider three factors: (1) the nature of its attachment to the realty; (2) its adaptation to and necessity for the purpose for which the premises are devoted; and (3) whether it was intended that the item in question be considered part of the realty. [Citations omitted.] Intent is the "preeminent factor; the other considerations are primarily evidence of intent." *A & A Market, Inc. v. Pekin Insurance Co.*, [306 Ill. App. 3d 485, 488 (1999)]. . . .

A "trade fixture" is also affixed to the real estate, but differs from a "permanent fixture" in two respects: (1) it must be personal property of the tenant; and (2) it is affixed to the realty for purposes of carrying on the tenant's business. [Citation omitted.] There is a rebuttable presumption that items installed by a tenant for the purpose of carrying on a trade are trade fixtures. The test to determine whether a fixture is a trade fixture is essentially identical to the test used for permanent fixtures. [Citation omitted.] A trade fixture is the tenant's property and may be removed by the tenant if the removal does not damage the real estate. . . .

The jury did hear evidence regarding the manner in which the system was attached to the building and the necessity of the system for Rubicon's manufacturing process. The jury also learned that the property began as an empty warehouse which, as a "white shell," could be converted to any number of uses. Rubicon's predecessor corporation had paid for the equipment in the first place, and the equipment was specially made for and required by manufacturers of sapphire crystals. Some key evidence, though, was clearly disputed. On the critical element of intent, Dr. Mogilevsky and Moffitt had sharply differing opinions regarding the intent of the parties at the time of installation. That intent was never memorialized in writing, so the jury was only able to ascertain intent through the testimony of the witnesses for each party. As the trier of fact, the jury was entitled to determine which witness's testimony was more credible, and we cannot disturb that finding. . . . The fact that the tenant paid for the installation is quite relevant to the issue of intent. [Citation omitted.] The property began as an empty warehouse and was returned to that condition, with the exceptions of $22,000 in damage caused by the removal of the system and the presence of installed underground lines which would not have affected the usability of the building for other purposes. Based on all this evidence, the jury was entitled to determine that the system was a removable trade fixture, and that Rubicon was not liable for conversion. In sum, neither the verdict on the breach of contract count nor the verdict on the conversion count was against the manifest weight of the evidence.

For these reasons, we affirm the judgment of the circuit court.

Affirmed.

Security Interests in Fixtures Special rules apply to personal property subject to a lien or security interest at the time it is attached to real property. Assume, for example, that a person buys a dishwasher on a time-payment plan from an appliance store and has it installed in the person's kitchen. To protect itself, the appliance store takes a security interest in the dishwasher and perfects that interest by filing a financing statement in the appropriate real estate records office within the period of time specified by the Uniform Commercial Code. The appliance store then is able to remove the dishwasher if the buyer defaults. The store could be liable, however, to third parties such as prior real estate mortgagees for any damage removal of the dishwasher caused to the real estate. The rules governing security interests in personal property that will become fixtures are explained more fully in Chapter 29.

Rights and Interests in Real Property

 LO24-3 Explain and distinguish among the various forms of ownership of real property.

When we think of real property ownership, we normally envision one person owning all of the rights in a particular piece of land. Real property, however, involves a bundle of rights subject to ownership—sometimes by different people. This discussion examines the most common forms of present *possessory interests* (rights to exclusive possession of real property): *fee simple absolute* and *life estate*. It also explores the ways in which two or more persons may share ownership of a possessory interest. Finally, it discusses the interests and rights one may have in another person's real property, such as the right to use the property or restrict the way the owner uses it.

Estates in Land The term **estate** is used to describe the nature of a person's ownership interest in real property. Estates in land are classified as either freehold estates or nonfreehold estates. Nonfreehold (or leasehold) estates are those held by persons who lease real property. They will be discussed in Chapter 25, which deals with landlord–tenant law. Freehold estates are ownership interests of uncertain duration. The most common types of freehold estates are fee simple absolute and life estates.

Fee Simple Absolute The **fee simple absolute** is what we normally think of as "full ownership" of land. One who owns real property in fee simple absolute has the right to possess and use the property, and exclude others from using and possessing the property, for an unlimited period of time, subject only to governmental regulations or private restrictions. A fee simple absolute owner also has the unconditional power to dispose of the property during the owner's lifetime or upon death. A person who owns land in fee simple absolute may grant many rights to others without giving up ownership. For example, the owner may grant a mortgage on the property to a party who has loaned the owner money, lease the property to a tenant, or grant rights such as those to be discussed later in this section.

Life Estate The property interest known as a **life estate** gives a person exclusive rights to possess and use property for a time measured by that or another person's lifetime. For example, if Haney has a life estate (measured by his life) in a tract of land known as Greenacre, he has the right to use Greenacre for the remainder of his life. At Haney's death, the property will revert to the person who conveyed the estate to him or will pass to some other designated person. Although a life tenant has the right to use the property, he is obligated not to commit acts that would result in permanent injury to the property.

Co-ownership of Real Property
Co-ownership of real property exists when two or more persons share the same ownership interest in certain property. The co-owners do not have separate rights to any portion of the real property; each has a share in the whole property. Seven types of co-ownership are recognized in the United States.

Tenancy in Common Persons who own property under a **tenancy in common** have undivided interests in the property and equal rights to possess it. When property is transferred to two or more persons without specification of their co-ownership form, it is presumed that they acquire the property as tenants in common. The respective ownership interests of tenants in common may be, but need not be, equal. One tenant, for example, could have a two-thirds ownership interest in the property, with the other tenant having a one-third interest.

Each tenant in common has the right to possess and use the property. Individual tenants, however, cannot exclude the other tenants in common from also possessing and using the property. If the property is rented or otherwise produces income, each tenant is entitled to share in the income in proportion to that tenant's ownership share. Similarly, each tenant must pay *contribution* (that is, the tenant's proportionate share of property taxes and necessary maintenance and repair costs). If a tenant in sole possession of the property receives no rents or profits from the property, that tenant is not required to pay rent to a cotenant unless the possession is adverse or inconsistent with the cotenant's property interests.

A tenant in common may dispose of an interest in the property during life and at death. Similarly, the tenant in common's interest is subject to that tenant's creditors' claims. Upon a tenant's death, the interest in the property passes to the tenant's heirs or to the person or persons specified as the beneficiaries in the tenant's will. Suppose Peterson and Sievers own Blackacre as tenants in common. Sievers dies, having executed a valid will in which he leaves his Blackacre interest to Johanns. In this situation, Peterson and Johanns become tenants in common.

Tenants in common may sever the cotenancy by agreeing to divide the property or, if they are unable to agree, by petitioning a court for *partition*. The court will physically divide the property if that is feasible, so that each tenant receives his or her proportionate share. If physical division is not feasible, the court will order that the property be sold and that the proceeds be appropriately divided.

Joint Tenancy A **joint tenancy** is created when equal interests in real property are conveyed to two or more persons by means of a document clearly specifying that they are to own the property as joint tenants. The rights of use, possession, contribution, and partition are the same for a joint tenancy as for a tenancy in common. The *Ballard* case, which follows shortly, addresses partition issues in the context of a joint tenancy.

The joint tenancy's distinguishing feature is that it gives the owners the **right of survivorship**, which means that upon the death of a joint tenant, the deceased tenant's interest automatically passes to the surviving joint tenant(s). The right of survivorship makes it easy for a person to transfer property at death without the need for a will. For example, Devaney and Osborne purchase Redacre and take title as joint tenants. At Devaney's death, his Redacre interest will pass to Osborne even if Devaney did not have a will setting forth such an intent. Moreover, even if Devaney had a will that purported to leave his Redacre interest to someone other than Osborne, the will's Redacre provision would be ineffective.

When the document of conveyance contains ambiguous language, a court may be faced with determining whether persons acquired ownership of real property as joint tenants or, instead, as tenants in common.

A joint tenant may mortgage, sell, or give away her interest in the property during her lifetime. Her interest in the property is subject to her creditors' claims. When a joint tenant transfers her interest, the joint tenancy is severed and a tenancy in common is created as to the share affected by the transaction. For example, when a joint tenant sells her interest to a third person, the purchaser becomes a tenant in common with the remaining joint tenant(s).

Ballard v. Dornic   140 A.3d 1147 (D.C. Ct. App. 2016)

Matthew Dornic and Glenn Ballard owned, as cotenants, two properties in the District of Columbia. One was a single-family home in which Ballard resided. The other was a condominium.

Their relationship apparently having deteriorated, Dornic filed a complaint for partition-by-sale of the properties. The trial court granted Dornic's motion. Ballard appealed, arguing that Dornic had voluntarily limited his right to partition by failing to pay his fair share of the mortgages and other expenses associated with each of the properties and that the trial judge erred in holding that only tenants by the entirety are limited in their ability to seek partition. An issue on appeal was also whether partition-by-sale was appropriate, instead of dividing the properties.

Thompson, Associate Judge

I.

Our case law recognizes that a cotenant's unilateral "right to partition, while normally an integral part of the cotenancy form of ownership, is like most property rights subject to possible limitation by voluntary act of the parties[,]" *Carter v. Carter*, 516 A.2d 917, 921 (D.C. 1986), such as through the cotenants' agreement that one of the cotenants is to have exclusive use and possession of the property for some limited time period. We therefore agree with Mr. Ballard that the fact that an estate is not a tenancy by the entireties does not negate the possibility that one of the cotenants has, by a voluntarily act, restricted his right to seek partition. But our agreement on this point does not help Mr. Ballard's cause, because he cites no authority, and we know of none, for his novel argument that a joint tenant voluntarily restricts his right to partition by virtue of the fact—as Mr. Ballard avers is the case with Mr. Dornic—that he has paid a less-than-equal or relatively small share of the expenses related to the property. Nor does the summary judgment record reveal any evidence that either of the parties "expressed their intent *not* to partition." We therefore conclude that Judge Campbell did not err in rejecting Mr. Ballard's theory that Mr. Dornic limited his right to partition by a voluntary act.

II.

As his basis for granting partial summary judgment to Mr. Dornic, [the trial judge] determined that a partition-by-sale is appropriate because it "appears that the propert[ies] cannot be divided without loss or injury to the parties interested[.]" Mr. Ballard argues that [the judge] erred in finding, on disputed facts and on an incomplete factual record, that the property cannot be divided without loss or injury to the parties, and by concluding without analysis that a partition-by-sale is necessary.

Actions for partition are governed by D.C. Code § 16-2901(a), which provides that "when it appears that the property cannot be divided without loss or injury to the parties interested, the court may decree a sale thereof and a division of the money arising from the sale among the parties, according to their respective rights." The general test of whether a partition-in-kind—a physical division of the property according to the cotenants' shares—would

result in loss or injury to the owners is whether the property can be divided "without materially impairing its value or the value of an owner's interest in it."

In this case, no one contests that the properties in question—a single family home and condominium—cannot be physically divided without diminishing their value. Mr. Ballard contends, however, that a partition-in-kind does not necessarily require that a property be physically severed into separate parts. He argues that each of the properties can and should be partitioned in kind by awarding each in its totality to him. Mr. Ballard appears to be correct that if a property is subject to partition, "*a fortiorari* it can be awarded in part, or in its totality, to one tenant depending upon the facts, evidence, etc., in the case." *Hipp v. Hipp*, 191 F. Supp. 299, 301 (D.D.C. 1960). But again, the principle on which Mr. Ballard relies does not help him, because the summary judgment record does not support an award of the properties to Mr. Ballard alone. That is so even if we take as true the factual allegations to which Mr. Ballard swore. . . .

"[I]n a suit for partition, the court must first determine the respective shares which the parties hold in the property, before the property can be divided." *Sebold v. Sebold*, 444 F.2d 864, 872 (D.C. Cir. 1971). "[A] presumption arises that upon dissolution of [a] joint tenancy during the lives of the cotenants, each is entitled to an equal share of the proceeds." *Id.* However, that presumption "is subject to rebuttal . . . and does not prevent proof from being introduced that the respective holdings and interests of the parties are unequal." *Id.* at 872. The presumption that joint tenants own an equal share of a property can be rebutted by "evidence showing the source of the actual cash outlay at the time of acquisition, the intent of the cotenant creating the joint tenancy to make a gift of the half-interest to the other cotenant, unequal contribution by way of money or services, unequal expenditures in improving the property or freeing it from encumbrances and clouds, or other evidence raising inferences contrary to the idea of equal interest in the joint estate." *Id.*

The foregoing case law addresses the effect the trial court may give to cotenants' unequal contributions when determining their respective shares in a property upon partition. In addition, the partition statute prescribes the effect that may be given to cotenants' unequal receipt of rents from a jointly owned property. Specifically, D.C. Code § 16-2901(c) addresses the situation "[i]n a case of partition, when a tenant in common has received the rents and profits of the property to his own use[.]" It provides that such a cotenant "may be required to account to his cotenants for their respective shares of the rents and profits" and that "[a]mounts found to be due on the accounting may be charged against the share of the party owing them in the property, or its proceeds in case of sale."

Mr. Ballard's opposition to Mr. Dornic's motion for partial summary judgment [was based in part on] Mr. Ballard's allegation that Mr. Dornic paid a total of only $17,225.53 toward the purchase price and mortgage service for first and second mortgages on the [property where Ballard lives], while Mr. Ballard paid a total of over $586,662. Regarding the condominium, Mr. Ballard [alleged] that he has made mortgage payments totaling about $147,000, while Mr. Dornic has made payments totaling about $177,000. He also averred that Mr. Dornic has collected rents of $210,000 from the [condominium] and not shared them with Mr. Ballard. As to each of the properties, Mr. Ballard contends that the amount Mr. Dornic owes him in order to equalize mortgage-payment contributions and/or to pay him his share of the rents collected is more than Mr. Dornic would realize from his half of the proceeds of a sale of the property. For that reason, Mr. Ballard contends, a sale of the property would leave Mr. Dornic with accrued liabilities to Mr. Ballard still hanging over his head, while a partition-in-kind, awarding 100% of the property to Mr. Ballard (upon Mr. Ballard's agreement to refinance the existing mortgages so that they are solely his responsibility) would at least arguably leave Mr. Dornic *better off* than he is now (meaning, Mr. Ballard implies, that it is a partition-by-sale, not a partition-in-kind, that would cause "loss or injury to the parties interested").

There are, to be sure, issues of fact regarding the parties' relative financial contributions; Mr. Dornic's answer to Mr. Ballard's counterclaims denies most of the relevant allegations about uneven contributions. We nonetheless are satisfied that [the trial judge] was presented with no issues of *material* fact that precluded partial summary judgment. Even if Mr. Ballard's averments are taken as

true, and it also is assumed that Mr. Dornic made no non-monetary contributions and received no gifts from Mr. Ballard that entitle him to a larger share of the property, it seems clear that Mr. Dornic holds whatever ownership share in the [single-family home] his $17,000 investment in the property represents and whatever ownership share in the [condominium] his $177,000 investment represents. If the parties' relative contributions are as Mr. Ballard avers, Mr. Ballard's proportionately larger contributions and Mr. Dornic's accrued liability to Mr. Ballard for [the condominium] rents collected may warrant adjustments to the parties' otherwise presumed equal shares in the properties, and may mean that Mr. Ballard has a greater-than-50% share in each property. That is because, per the case law and the partition statute discussed above, the parties' disproportionate contributions and accrued liabilities are to be considered in determining "the respective holdings and interests of the parties," *Sebold*, 444 F.2d at 872, and, for purposes of a partition-in-kind, are to be "charged against the share of the party owing them[.]" D.C. Code § 16-2901(c). But the summary judgment record provided no basis for [the trial judge] to conclude that Mr. Dornic owns *no* share or interest in the properties such that Mr. Ballard is entitled to sole ownership of one or both properties as the result of a partition-in-kind.

* * *

Because the record does not support a finding that Mr. Dornic voluntarily limited his right to partition; because there is no dispute that the properties cannot be physically divided without injury or loss; and because, even according to Mr. Ballard's calculations, Mr. Dornic owns a more-than-nominal share of each of the properties, which the court may not require him to sell to Mr. Ballard, [the court below] did not err in granting partial summary judgment to Mr. Dornic on his claim for partition-by-sale. . . . Accordingly, the judgment of the Superior Court is

Affirmed.

Tenancy by the Entirety Approximately half of the states permit married couples to own real property under a **tenancy by the entirety**. This tenancy is essentially a joint tenancy with the added requirement that the owners be married. As does the joint tenancy, the tenancy by the entirety features the right of survivorship. Neither spouse can transfer the property by will if the other is still living. Upon the death of the husband or wife, the property passes automatically to the surviving spouse.[2]

A tenancy by the entirety cannot be severed by the act of only one of the parties. Neither spouse can transfer the property unless the other also signs the deed. Thus, a creditor of one tenant cannot claim an interest in that person's share of property held in tenancy by the entirety. Divorce, however, severs a tenancy by the entirety and transforms it into a tenancy in common. Figure 24.1 compares the features of tenancy in common, joint tenancy, and tenancy by the entirety.

Community Property A number of western and southern states recognize the community property system of co-ownership of property by married couples. This type of co-ownership assumes that marriage is a partnership

---

[2]In states that do not recognize the tenancy by the entirety, married couples often own real property in joint tenancy, but they are not required to elect that co-ownership form.

Figure 24.1   Tenancy in Common, Joint Tenancy, and Tenancy by the Entirety

	Tenancy in Common	Joint Tenancy	Tenancy by the Entirety
Equal Possession and Use?	Yes	Yes	Yes
Share Income?	Yes	Yes	Presumably
Contribution Requirement?	Generally	Generally	Generally
Free Conveyance of Interest?	Yes; transferee becomes tenant in common	Yes, but joint tenancy is severed on conveyance and reverts to tenancy in common	Both must agree; divorce severs tenancy
Effect of Death?	Interest transferable at death by will or inheritance	Right of survivorship; surviving joint tenant takes decedent's share	Right of survivorship; surviving spouse takes decedent's share

in which each spouse contributes to the family's property base. Property acquired during the marriage through a spouse's industry or efforts is classified as *community* property. Each spouse has an equal interest in such property regardless of who produced or earned the property. Because each spouse has an equal share in community property, neither can convey community property without the other spouse also joining in the transaction. Various community property states permit the parties to dispose of their interests in community property at death. The details of each state's community property system vary, depending on the specific provisions of that state's statutes.

Not all property owned by a married person is community property, however. Property a spouse owned before marriage or acquired during marriage by gift or inheritance is *separate* property. Neither spouse owns a legal interest in the other's separate property. Property exchanged for separate property also remains separately owned.

Tenancy in Partnership When a partnership takes title to property in the partnership's name, the co-ownership form is called **tenancy in partnership**. This form of co-ownership is discussed in Chapter 37.

Condominium Ownership Under condominium ownership, a purchaser takes title to an individual unit and becomes a tenant in common with other unit owners in shared facilities such as hallways, elevators, swimming pools, and parking areas. The condominium owner pays property taxes on the individual unit and makes a monthly payment for the maintenance of the common areas. The owner may generally mortgage or sell the unit without the other unit owners' approval. Federal income tax laws treat the condominium owner the same as an owner of a single-family home, allowing deduction of property taxes and mortgage interest expenses.

Cooperative Ownership In a cooperative, a building is owned by a corporation or group of persons. One who wants to buy an apartment in the building purchases stock in the corporation and holds the apartment under a long-term, renewable lease called a *proprietary lease*. Frequently, the cooperative owner must obtain the other owners' approval to sell or sublease the unit.

Interests in Real Property Owned by Others

LO24-4 Explain the legal effects of easements and restrictive covenants as well as the duties of property owners toward third persons.

In various situations, a person may hold a legally protected interest in someone else's real property. Such interests, to be discussed below, are not possessory because they do not give their holder the right to complete dominion over the land. Rather, they give the person the right to use another person's property or to limit the way in which the owner uses the property.

Easements An **easement** is the right to make certain uses of another person's property (*affirmative easement*) or the right to prevent another person from making certain uses of the property (*negative easement*). The right to run a sewer line across someone else's property would be an affirmative easement. Suppose an easement prevents Rogers from erecting, on his land, a structure that would block his neighbor McFeely's solar collector. Such an easement would be negative in nature.

If an easement qualifies as an easement appurtenant, it will pass with the land. This means that if the owner of the land benefited by an easement appurtenant sells or otherwise conveys the property, the new owner also acquires the right contemplated by the easement. An easement appurtenant is primarily designed to benefit a certain tract of land, rather than merely giving an individual a personal right. For example, Agnew and Nixon are next-door neighbors. They share a common driveway that runs along the borderline of their respective properties. Each has an easement in the portion of the driveway that lies on the other's property. If Agnew sells his property to Ford, Ford also obtains the easement in the driveway portion on Nixon's land. Nixon, of course, still has an easement in the driveway portion on Ford's land.

Creation of Easements
Easements may be acquired in the following ways:

1. *By grant.* When an owner of property expressly provides an easement to another while retaining ownership of the property, the owner is said to grant an easement. For example, Monroe may sell or give Madison, who owns adjoining property, the right to go across Monroe's land to reach an alley behind that land.

2. *By reservation.* When an owner transfers ownership of land but retains the right to use it for some specified purpose, the owner is said to reserve an easement in the land. For example, Smythe sells land to Jones but reserves the mineral rights to the property as well as an easement to enter the land to remove the minerals.

3. *By prescription.* An easement by prescription is created when one person uses another's land openly, continuously, and in a manner adverse to the owner's rights for a period of time specified by state statute. The necessary period of time varies from state to state. In such a situation, the property owner presumably is on notice that someone else is acting as if they possess rights to use the property. If the property owner does not take action during the statutory period to stop the other person from making use of the property, the owner may lose the right to stop that use. Suppose, for instance, that State X allows easements by prescription to be obtained through 15 years of prescriptive use. Tara, who lives in State X, uses the driveway of her next-door neighbor, Kyle. Tara does this openly, on a daily basis, and without Kyle's permission. If this use by Tara continues for the 15-year period established by statute and Kyle takes no action to stop Tara within that time span, Tara will obtain an easement by prescription. In that event, Tara will have the right to use the driveway not only while Kyle owns the property,

but also when Kyle sells the property to another party. Easements by prescription resemble *adverse possession*, a concept discussed later in this chapter.

4. *By implication.* Sometimes, easements are implied by the nature of the transaction rather than created by express agreement of the parties. Such easements, called easements by implication, take either of two forms: easements by prior use and easements by necessity.

An *easement by prior use* may be created when land is subdivided and a path, road, or other apparent and beneficial use exists as of the time that a portion of the land is conveyed to another person. In this situation, the new owner of the conveyed portion of the land has an easement to continue using the path, road, or other prior use running across the nonconveyed portion of the land. Assume, for example, that a private road runs through Greenacre from north to south, linking the house located on Greenacre's northern portion to the public highway that lies south of Greenacre. Douglas, the owner of Greenacre, sells the northern portion to Kimball. On these facts, Kimball has an easement by implication to continue using the private road even where it runs across the portion of Greenacre retained by Douglas. To prevent such an easement from arising, Douglas and Kimball would need to have specified in their contract of sale that the easement would not exist.

An *easement by necessity* is created when real property once held in common ownership is subdivided in such a fashion that the only reasonable way a new owner can gain access to her land is through passage over another's land that was once part of the same tract. Such an easement is based on the necessity of obtaining access to property. Assume, for instance, that Tinker, the owner of Blackacre, sells Blackacre's northern 25 acres to Evers and its southern 25 acres to Chance. In order to have any reasonable access to her property, Chance must use a public road that runs alongside and just beyond the northern border of the land now owned by Evers; Chance must then go across Evers's property to reach hers. On these facts, Chance is entitled to an easement by necessity to cross Evers's land in order to go to and from her property.

In the *Francini* case, which follows, the Appellate Court of Connecticut had to determine whether an easement by necessity could be granted for something other than physical access to the land. Note how the court relies on the same justifications for the traditional easement by necessity to extend the doctrine to include access to utilities (namely, electricity) for a property that was landlocked from them.

Francini v. Goodspeed Airport, LLC   134 A.3d 1278 (Conn. App. Ct. 2016)

William Francini owned a parcel of land in East Haddam, Connecticut. The only access from Francini's land to a public highway was over an abutting property owned by Goodspeed Airport, LLC. Goodspeed acquired its land in 1999 under a warranty deed subject to a right-of-way easement for Francini, as well as several of Francini's neighbors, each of whom also owned land abutting Goodspeed's property.

In 2001, Goodspeed entered into an agreement with several of Francini's neighbors, who also shared the right-of-way across defendant's property, to allow them to improve the right-of-way by installing and maintaining a utility distribution system under the existing easement. As a result, a commercial utility system was constructed under the existing right-of-way, which was used to provide electricity to Francini's neighbors. Each of the neighbors paid Goodspeed $7,500 for the addition of the utility easement to the right-of-way. Francini likewise offered to pay Goodspeed $7,500 for use of the utility easement, but Goodspeed demanded that Francini not only pay $7,500, but also that he grant it the authority to move the location of the easement at will. (It is not clear from the facts presented in the opinion why Goodspeed treated Francini differently from his neighbors or why Goodspeed would desire to retain the right to move the location of the easement, but Goodspeed did both.) Francini refused the additional terms, and he and Goodspeed never reached an agreement.

Without the utility easement, Francini's property was unable to connect to commercial electric service. Instead, a generator powered his house. The generator was insufficient, though, to run and maintain some of Francini's basic requirements, like powering security devices and running a refrigerator. Moreover, the generator was not equipped to turn on automatically in the event of a flood.

In 2011, Francini sued Goodspeed seeking an easement by necessity for access to commercial utilities across the same right-of-way that he already owned and that already provided his neighbors with commercial electric power. Goodspeed filed a motion for summary judgment, arguing that easements by necessity could not be granted for anything other than physical access to landlocked parcels.

The trial court granted Goodspeed's motion. Francini appealed. The question of whether an easement by necessity could be granted for access to utility services rather than physical access had not yet been addressed by any Connecticut appellate court.

Lavery, Judge

The common-law easement by necessity creates an implied servitude that burdens one piece of property, the servient estate, for the benefit of another, the dominant estate, to enable the normal "use and enjoyment of the [benefited] property." In the classic example, "an easement by necessity will be imposed where a conveyance by the grantor leaves the grantee with a parcel inaccessible save over the lands of the grantor, or where the grantor retains an adjoining parcel which he can reach only through the lands conveyed to the grantee." *Hollywyle Assn., Inc. v. Hollister*, 324 A.2d 247 (Conn. 1973). In such cases, the element of necessity lies in the grantee's inability to use his property beneficially because he lacks physical access to it, "[f]or the law will not presume, that it was the intention of the parties, that one should convey land to the other, in such manner that the grantee could derive no benefit from the conveyance; nor that he should so convey a portion as to deprive himself of the enjoyment of the remainder." *Robinson v. Clapp*, 32 A. 939 (Conn. 1895). In other words, "the necessity does not create the way, but merely furnishes evidence as to the real intention of the parties"; *id.*; because courts ascribe to the parties a fictitious intent—presumably, if the parties actually intended there to be an easement, they would have said so in the written grant—based on "the public policy that no land should be left inaccessible or incapable of being put to profitable use." *Thomas v. Primus*, 84 A.3d 916 (Conn. App. Ct. 2014). Accordingly, the easement is based on the beliefs that parties do not intend to effectuate

a conveyance that would render the land useless . . . and that parties naturally intend to convey whatever rights are necessary for the use and enjoyment of the land conveyed. . . . Therefore, the imposition of an easement by necessity upon the burdened estate is justified by two partnering rationales, the presumed intent of the parties to the conveyance and general public policy.

Today, we conclude that easements by necessity may provide not only physical access to landlocked property, but a property landlocked from commercial utilities may likewise receive an easement by necessity to access utility services. Easements by necessity are not artifacts of a more ancient era and must serve their intended purpose, to render land useful, in the present day as the beneficial use of land conforms to modern innovations and needs. This follows from the general rule that the need constituting the necessity that implies an easement by necessity may change over time. In fact, in the context of a granted right-of-way, the easement's owner may use the easement for all purposes consistent with the reasonable use of the benefited land and is not limited to using the easement for only those purposes that existed at the time the benefited and burdened properties were created. We therefore reject the defendant's argument that easements by necessity may be granted only for physical access to landlocked property simply because no such easement has yet been recognized. To "deny [property owners] such right would be to stop to some extent the wheels of progress, and invention, and finally make residence in the country more and more undesirable and less endurable." *Dowgiel v. Reid*, 59 A.2d 115 (Pa. 1948).

In our view, the legal justifications underlying easements by necessity, intent and public policy, support extending the doctrine to include access to utilities for properties landlocked from them. Utilities are so obviously necessary for the reasonable use and enjoyment of all types of property that the law will assume that parties to a land conveyance intend to convey whatever is necessary to ensure a property's access to utilities in the same way that the law presumes the parties intended to convey an easement for physical access. Accordingly, we conclude that access to utilities is reasonably necessary to the reasonable use and enjoyment of property, especially, as is the case here, residential property. . . . To deny a residence access to utilities would, practically speaking, deny use of that property as a residence.

As further support, under the approach adopted by the Restatement (Third) of Property, Servitudes, a property that is landlocked from commercial electricity enjoys an implied easement by necessity for utility services. The Restatement (Third), itself adopted eighteen years ago, explains that "the increasing dependence in recent years on electricity and telephone service, delivered through overland cables, justify the conclusion that implied servitudes by necessity will be recognized for those purposes." By including access to commercial electricity within the easement by necessity, the Restatement (Third) recognizes that "'[n]ecessary' rights are not limited to those essential to enjoyment of the property, but include those which are reasonably required to make effective use of the property." Therefore, because electricity is essential to daily life and is reasonably required to make effective use of property, the easement by necessity includes not only physical access to landlocked property, but also access to utilities for properties landlocked from utilities. This decision honors both the principles underlying the easement by necessity and the fundamental actualities of modern life.

* * *

The judgment is reversed and the case is remanded with direction to deny the defendant's motion for summary judgment and for further proceedings according to law.

Note: In 2018, the Connecticut Supreme Court affirmed the Connecticut Appellate Court's decision in this case. See Francini v. Goodspeed Airport, LLC, 174 A.3d 779 (Conn. 2018).

Easements and the Statute of Frauds As interests in land, easements are potentially within the coverage of the statute of frauds. To be enforceable, an express agreement granting or reserving an easement must be evidenced by a suitable writing signed by the party to be charged.[3] An express grant of an easement normally must be executed with the same formalities observed in executing the grant of a fee simple interest. However, easements not granted expressly (such as easements by prior use, necessity, or prescription) are enforceable despite the lack of a writing.

Profits
A **profit** is a right to enter another person's land and remove some product or part of the land. Timber, gravel, minerals, and oil are among the products and parts frequently made the subject of profits. Generally governed by the same rules applicable to easements, profits are sometimes called *easements with a profit.*

Licenses
A **license** is a temporary right to enter another's land for a specific purpose. Ordinarily, licenses are more informal than easements. Licenses may be created orally or in any other manner indicating the landowner's permission for the licensee to enter the property. Because licenses are considered to be personal rights, they are not true interests in land. The licensor normally may revoke a license at will. Exceptions to this general rule of revocability arise when the license is coupled with an interest (such as the licensee's ownership of personal property located on the licensor's land) or when the licensee has paid money or provided something else of value either for the license or in reliance on its existence. For example, Branch pays Leif $900 for certain trees on Leif's land. Branch is to dig up the trees and haul them to her own property for transplanting. Branch has an irrevocable license to enter Leif's land to dig up and haul away the trees.

Restrictive Covenants
Within certain limitations, real estate owners may create enforceable agreements that restrict the use of real property. These private agreements are called **restrictive covenants**. For example, Grant owns two adjacent lots. She sells one to Foster subject to the parties' agreement that Foster will not operate any liquor-selling business on the property. This use restriction appears in the deed Grant furnishes Foster. As another illustration, a subdivision developer sells lots in the subdivision and places a provision in each lot's deed regarding the minimum size of house to be built on the property.

[3]Chapter 16 discusses the statute of frauds and compliance with the writing requirement it imposes when it is applicable.

The validity and enforceability of such private restrictions on the use of real property depend on the purpose, nature, and scope of the restrictions. A restraint that violates a statute or other expression of public policy will not be enforced. For example, the federal Fair Housing Act (discussed later in this chapter) would make unlawful an attempt by a seller or lessor of residential property to refuse to sell or rent to certain persons because of an existing restrictive covenant that purports to disqualify those prospective buyers or renters on the basis of their race, color, religion, sex, disability, familial status, or national origin.

Public policy generally favors the unlimited use and transfer of land. A restrictive covenant, therefore, is unenforceable if it effectively prevents the sale or transfer of the property. Similarly, ambiguous language in a restrictive covenant is construed in favor of the less restrictive interpretation. A restraint is enforceable, however, if it is clearly expressed and neither unduly restrictive of the use and transfer of the property nor otherwise violative of public policy. Restrictions usually held enforceable include those relating to minimum lot size, building design and size, and maintenance of an area as a residential community.

An important and frequently arising question is whether subsequent owners of property are bound by a restrictive covenant even though they were not parties to the original agreement that established the covenant. Under certain circumstances, restrictive covenants are said to "run with the land" (or, in legal jargon, are "appurtenant") and thus bind subsequent owners of the restricted property. For a covenant to run with the land, it must have been *binding* on the original parties to it, and those parties must have *intended that the covenant bind their successors*. The covenant must also "*touch and concern*" the restricted land. This means that the covenant must involve the use, value, or character of the land, rather than being merely a personal obligation of one of the original parties. The legal jargon for the latter is that such restrictive covenants are "in gross." The *Wykeham Rise* case, which follows, involves the analysis of whether a restrictive covenant runs with the land. In addition, a covenant will typically bind a subsequent purchaser who had notice of the covenant's existence when taking the interest. This notice would commonly be provided by the recording of the deed (a subject discussed later in this chapter) or other document containing the covenant.

Restrictive covenants may be enforced by the parties to them, by persons meant to benefit from them, and—if the covenants run with the land—by successors of the original parties to them. If restrictive covenants amounting to a general building scheme are contained in a subdivision plat (recorded description of a subdivision), property owners in the subdivision may be able to enforce them against noncomplying property owners.

The following *Wykeham Rise* case considers whether a subsequent purchaser retains the ability to enforce the benefit of restrictive covenants, along with whether the burden of the covenants runs with the land.

Wykeham Rise, LLC v. Federer   52 A.3d 702 (Conn. 2012)

A parcel of land that was owned by the Wykeham Rise School abutted an adjacent property owned by Bertram Read, who was a member of the school's board of trustees and past chairman of the board. In 1990, the school sold the property to a limited liability corporation subject to a set of restrictive covenants, one of which provides that the grantee "will not construct any buildings or other structures or any parking lots on that area of the above described premises lying within 300 feet, more or less, at all points . . . [of the] area now commonly known as 'the Playing Field.'" The deed further provides that "[t]he foregoing covenants and agreements shall be binding upon the [g]rantee, its successors and assigns, shall inure to the benefit of the [g]rantor, its successors and assigns, and shall run with the land." The covenant said nothing explicitly about third parties.

Also in 1990, the school was administratively dissolved by the Connecticut Secretary of State. Over the next 17 years, the school property changed hands a couple of times, first to another LLC and then to Wykeham Rise, the plaintiff in this case, in 2008. The deed conveyed to Wykeham Rise expressly referenced the restrictive covenants.

Around 1995, during the time that the second LLC owned the property (i.e., the one prior to the plaintiff), Read sold his land to his daughter and son-in-law, Wendy and Eric Federer. In 2005, Wendy Federer and the chairman of the now-defunct school's board of trustees executed a document purporting to assign the school's rights under the restrictive covenants to Wendy Federer in exchange for consideration of $500. Several years later, Wendy Federer also executed and recorded a "Declaration of Beneficial Ownership" claiming the right, along with Eric Federer and their heirs and assigns, to the benefit of the covenants as owners of the adjacent property.

After purchasing the school property, Wykeham Rise sought permits to develop it in a manner inconsistent with the terms of the restrictive covenants. The Federers objected to the issuance of the permits and brought an administrative appeal after one such permit was issued. Wykeham Rise then filed a suit seeking a declaratory judgment that the covenants "are null and void, are of no legal effect, and are accordingly unenforceable as to [Wykeham Rise], it's successors, and assigns. . . ." The Federers counterclaimed, seeking to have the covenants declared enforceable and, thereby, to enjoin Wykeham Rise from violating them.

Wykeham Rise moved for summary judgment on both its declaratory judgment action and on the Federers' counterclaims, arguing that the restrictive covenants were invalid and regardless were neither enforceable by the Federers nor applicable to Wykeham Rise because the covenants did not run with the land.

On the basis of the pleadings and affidavits submitted by both parties, the trial court ruled in favor of Wykeham Rise. The court concluded that "the restrictive covenants are null, void and of no legal effect because they were void at the time they were first conveyed in 1990." The court further concluded that the facts did not establish that the covenants were intended to benefit the Federers' property and that the covenants were of a personal nature that did not run with the land. The defendants' appeal followed.

Harper, Justice

I

The threshold question presented by this case—whether the trial court properly concluded, as a matter of law, that the covenants were not properly created—can be answered in relatively straightforward fashion. First, because the covenants were created as part of a conveyance of land, they are subject to the formal writing and recording requirements set forth in [Connecticut statutory enactments]. To be valid, covenants also must not violate the public interest. [Citations omitted.]

In the present case, no formal or public policy defects in the formation of the covenants at issue have been alleged, nor are any such invalidating features apparent on the face of the covenants. It is therefore clear that summary judgment could not properly have been rendered on the ground that the covenants are inherently invalid. . . .

II

Having determined that summary judgment could not properly have been granted on the ground that the covenants are inherently invalid, we address the possibility that summary judgment was nonetheless appropriate on the ground that the covenants are unenforceable. More precisely, we consider whether the covenants, presumably enforceable as between the original covenanting parties, remain effective as between the parties in the present case, who are both strangers to that initial agreement. For purposes of clarity, we divide our analysis of enforceability into two parallel inquiries, outlining on the one hand the considerations governing whether the *burdens* of the covenants pass to [Wykeham Rise], and on the other hand whether the covenants' *benefits* pass to the [Federers].

A

The first question, whether the plaintiff can properly be burdened by the covenants at issue, implicates both principles of law and considerations of equity. Our inquiry begins with consideration of whether the burdens are to be characterized as "running with the land" (appurtenant) or as personal (in gross)—that is, whether they apply to the burdened property itself or rather to the person of the initial grantee. As we later explain, in the present case the covenants may be enforced at law only if they run with the land such that the plaintiff acquired the school property subject to the covenants. Even if the covenants do not run with the land, however, we also must consider whether the plaintiff may nonetheless be subject to them as a matter of equity. We conclude that the covenant burdens in the present case are likely enforceable against the plaintiff both at law and in equity.

1

Whether the covenants' burdens run with the land is, primarily, a question of the parties' intent. [Citations omitted.] The presence or absence of express words of succession—such as "heirs" or "assigns"—offers strong, though not conclusive, evidence of whether the parties intended to bind future owners of the land. . . .

The intent of the parties, however, is not dispositive, insofar as obligations that are inherently personal cannot be made appurtenant to the land. Thus, "[t]he use of words of succession binding the 'heirs and assigns' of the grantee of restricted land does not in itself cause the burden to run if the nature of the restriction is not one which could run with the land. . . . It is well settled that a covenant personal in its nature and relating to something collateral to the land cannot be made to run with the land so as to charge the assignee by the fact that the covenantor covenanted on behalf of himself and his assigns." *Pulver v. Mascolo*, 155 Conn. 644, 650–51 (1967). On the other hand, "[i]f [a promise] touches the land involved to the extent that it materially affects the value of that land, it is generally to be interpreted as a covenant which runs with the land." *Carlson v. Libby*, 137 Conn. 362, 367 (1950). With respect to the relative strength of these competing considerations, moreover, this court has long held that a restrictive covenant "will not be inferred to be personal when it can fairly be construed to be appurtenant to the land. . . ." *Bauby v. Krasow*, 107 Conn. 109, 114 (1927).

In addition to these considerations, one final formal requirement also potentially bears on the question of whether a covenant's burdens may be said to run with the land so as to bind a stranger to the covenant. Common-law doctrine dictates that covenants may run with the land only if they are conveyed along with some other interest in land. As this court previously has held, relying on an earlier Restatement of Property, "[t]he burden of a covenant will run with land only when the transaction of which the covenant is a part includes a transfer of an interest in land which is either benefited or burdened thereby. . . ." *Carlson v. Libby*, 137 Conn. [at] 368.

2

Alongside the legal rules governing whether the restrictive covenants in the present case run with the land, long-standing equitable principles applicable to restrictive covenants provide an important, and independent, framework for determining whether the covenants' burdens may be enforced as a matter of equity. This court has long recognized that "[t]he question whether [a restrictive] covenant runs with the land is material in equity only on the question of notice. If it runs with the land, it binds the owner whether he had knowledge of it or not. If it does not run with the land, the owner is bound only if he has taken the land with notice of it. . . . The question is, not whether the covenant runs with the land, but whether a party shall be permitted to use the land in a manner inconsistent with the contract entered into by his vendor, and with notice of which he purchased. The decisions proceed upon the principle of preventing one having knowledge of the just rights of another from defeating such rights, and not upon the theory that the covenants enforced create easements or are of a nature to run with the land." *Bauby v. Krasow*, 107 Conn. [at] 112 [(internal citation and quotes omitted)]. Therefore, under the rules of equity, if the plaintiff took the property in question with notice that it is burdened by restrictive covenants, it may be bound in equity to those burdens, regardless of whether the burdens run with the land.

3

Turning to the summary judgment rendered in the plaintiff's favor in the present case, we cannot say as a matter of law that the burdens of the covenants at issue in this case do not run with the land. Indeed, there is strong evidence to the contrary: the covenants were formally created as part of a transfer of land; they explicitly provide that they are "binding upon the [g]rantee, its successors and assigns, shall inure to the benefit of the [g]rantor, its successors and assigns, and shall run with the land"; and they appear on their face to relate to the land and not to impose any conceivable burden on the initial grantee independent of its ownership of the land. We recognize that circumstantial facts may emerge casting doubt on the apparent intent of the covenanting parties to create burdens appurtenant to the land; however, such determinations are for the finder of fact to make with the benefit of evidence introduced at trial.

Even if the covenants did not meet all the requirements at law for the burden to run with the land, the issue of enforceability also turns on the possibility of an equitable remedy. In the present case, there is uncontested evidence indicating that the covenants at issue restrict [Wykeham Rise] from using the land in certain ways, rather than requiring affirmative action by [Wykeham Rise], a burden that could not be enforced in equity. There is also uncontested evidence that [it] knew of these covenants at the time of purchase. Although further facts may be uncovered that preclude [Wykeham Rise] from being burdened by the covenants, at this point it cannot be said as a matter of law that those burdens do not apply to [it], either at law or in equity.

B

Looking to the other side of the equation, we now outline the conditions that must be met in order for the [Federers] to potentially enforce the covenants against [Wykeham Rise], such that summary judgment could not have been rendered on this basis. The [Federers] claim the right to enforce the covenants as the successors or assigns of the covenants' original beneficiary or beneficiaries. We must therefore consider the covenants' benefits at two points in time: first, looking to the time of the covenants' creation, we determine the intended beneficiary or beneficiaries and the type of benefit or benefits created; second, looking to the present time, we determine whether the [Federers] could obtain the right to those benefits by way of assignment or devolution. . . . [T]he trial court decided that it was not necessary to reach [Wykeham Rise]'s claim that the rights to enforce the covenants had not been validly assigned to the [Federers]. We conclude that the [Federers] are not precluded from enforcing the covenants as a matter of law and that material questions of fact exist regarding whether they may enforce the covenants here.

As with covenant burdens, covenant benefits may be appurtenant (directly benefiting the land) or in gross (accruing to a person independent of ownership of land) and may be held by the signatory to the covenant as well as third parties that the parties to the covenant intended to so benefit. The covenant benefits in the present case, at the time of their creation, thus may conceptually be described in one or more of four ways: (1) the benefits inured to the school as the owner of a piece of land; (2) the benefits inured to the school independent of its ownership of land; (3) the benefits inured to Read, Wendy Federer's father, a third party beneficiary, as owner of the land adjacent to the school; and (4) the benefits inured to Read independent of his ownership of land. Under the circumstances of this case, we focus on scenarios two and three, leaving the relatively implausible scenarios represented by one and four to the side. We consider each in turn along with the related question of whether the defendants properly could have obtained those benefits.

1

We consider first whether the benefits of the covenants inured to the school in a manner that is independent of its ownership of a particular parcel of land. It is clear that these benefits in gross may validly be created. [Citation omitted.] A further question potentially arises regarding whether the right to such benefits may be transferred or assigned.

Although this court previously has not addressed this specific question, related case law indicates that such assignments properly can be made, if consistent with the covenanting parties' intent. Assignability of rights is clearly favored with respect to contracts generally. [Citations omitted.] We find this approach generally appropriate to covenant rights held in gross; however, recognizing that the burdens of covenants typically endure far longer than those of contracts, we add the important caveat that covenant benefits (or burdens) in gross may not be transferred if doing so would be inconsistent with the intent of the parties. . . . Accordingly, under this rubric, if the benefits were intended to benefit the school, and the parties did not intend them to be non-assignable, the school could validly assign those benefits to the [Federers].

2

Turning to the alternative plausible interpretation of the covenants in the present case, we next consider whether the [Federers] may enforce the covenants on the theory that Read, as the owner of the land adjacent to the school property, was the intended third party beneficiary of the covenant between the school and the initial buyer of the school property and that, by virtue of their purchasing the benefited parcel of land, the right to enforce the covenants [passed on] to the defendants.

The third party beneficiary doctrine provides that "[a] third party beneficiary may enforce a contractual obligation without being in privity with the actual parties to the contract. . . . Therefore, a third party beneficiary who is not a named obligee in a given contract may sue the obligor for breach." *Wilcox v. Webster Ins., Inc.*, 294 Conn. 206, 217 (2009). Although the third party beneficiary doctrine was originally developed in the law of contracts, this court has recognized that third party beneficiaries may enforce covenants in land.

Under the third party beneficiary doctrine, "[t]he ultimate test to be applied [in determining whether a person has a right of action as a third party beneficiary] is whether the intent of the parties to the contract was that the promisor should assume a direct obligation to the third party [beneficiary]. . . . [T]hat intent is to be determined from the terms of the contract read in the light of the circumstances attending its making, including the motives and purposes of the parties. . . . [I]t is not in all instances necessary that there be express language in the contract creating a direct obligation to the claimed third party beneficiary. . . ." *Dow & Condon, Inc. v. Brookfield Development Corp.*, 266 Conn. 572, 580 (2003).

3

With this framework in mind, we now look to the undisputed facts of the present case relating to covenant benefits and the intent of the covenanting parties that may be discerned from those facts. First, it is possible to conclude that the covenants at issue created a transferable benefit in gross that inured to the school independent of its ownership of land. Specifically, the deed provides that the covenant benefits "shall inure to the benefit of the [g]rantor, its successors and assigns, and shall run with the land." This language makes clear that the parties intended to create an enduring benefit that would survive the school, but because the school retained no land following the sale, any benefits conferred on the school cannot possibly be appurtenant to the land and therefore must be construed to be in gross.

The possibility that the covenants at issue created a transferable benefit in gross in the school sets up a potentially dispositive question regarding whether the school has transferred that right to Wendy Federer. It appears that the school and Wendy Federer attempted to accomplish such a transfer, but that the putative transfer occurred after the school had been dissolved by administrative order. . . . In the present case, the trial court concluded that the covenants are void and therefore made no determination whether there are material questions of fact regarding whether the school's attempted transfer of its rights under the covenant qualified as [permissible under the Connecticut statute that allows dissolved organizations to "wind up" their affairs].

With respect to the question of whether the defendants could enforce the covenants in the present case as third party beneficiaries, the trial court concluded that "the present deed expresses a clear intent to benefit the grantor, the school, not the defendants' property, and the surrounding circumstances do not contradict that intent." After a review of the record, we conclude that the trial court improperly determined that there are no issues of material fact regarding whether the parties to the original contract intended that the covenants would provide an appurtenant benefit to Read as owner of the adjacent property now owned by the defendants. Although the covenants do not specifically mention the adjacent property or Read, the circumstances surrounding the transaction at the very least create an ambiguity as to whether the covenants were intended to confer such a benefit. Although the school may enjoy some personal benefits from the covenants notwithstanding the fact that it retained no land, the most obvious and direct benefits of the covenants flowed to Read as the owner of the adjacent land. The clear aesthetic—and likely financial—benefits conferred on Read's property from not having the school property commercially developed, considered along with the relationship between Read and the school and the fact that, as attested to by the chairman of the school's board of trustees, Read's request prompted the creation of the covenants, could provide a factual basis for concluding that the original covenanting parties intended the covenants to be enforceable by the owner of the defendants' land. Faced with uncertainty in the factual record on this issue, the trial court could not properly have rendered summary judgment on the ground that the defendants are not entitled to enforce the covenants.

We thus conclude that the enforceability of the covenants in the present case cannot be foreclosed as a matter of law. Further proceedings are necessary to determine both whether the plaintiff is bound by the covenants' burdens, as a matter of law or equity, and whether the defendants may enforce the covenants as assignees of the school's interest or, alternatively, as third party beneficiaries to whom Read's third party interest [passed]. Additionally, it may be necessary to determine whether, even if valid at the time of creation and properly passed down to the parties here, the covenants continue to serve "a legal and useful purpose" and thus remain enforceable burdens on the plaintiff's land. *Gangemi v. Zoning Board of Appeals*, 255 Conn. 143, 151 (2001). . . .

The judgment is reversed and the case is remanded for further proceedings.

Termination of Restrictive Covenants Restrictive covenants may be terminated in a variety of ways, including voluntary relinquishment or *waiver*. They may also be terminated *by their own terms* (such as when the covenant specifies that it is to exist for a certain length of time) or *by dramatically changed circumstances*. If Oldcodger's property is subject, for instance, to a restrictive covenant allowing only residential use, the fact that all of the surrounding property has come to be used for industrial purposes may operate to terminate the covenant. When a restrictive covenant has been terminated or held invalid, the deed containing the restriction remains a valid instrument of transfer but is treated as if the restriction had been removed from the document.

Ethics and Compliance in Action

Joel Misita is a folk artist who creates and sells custom pieces of large metal sculptures from scrap. He lives on a 10-acre plot of scenic land in Adams County, Mississippi, just off of Highway 61. He originally owned seven acres, upon which he built a large three-story house in which his metalwork studio takes up the ground floor, several outbuildings, and sheds. He also stores several trailers, sculptures, and the metal raw materials for his sculptures. Kevin and Rebecca Wilson agreed to sell Misita a three-acre plot that abuts Misita's original land and fronts Highway 61. The plot is in direct line of the scenic view of the area from the Wilson's property. The deed to the plot includes a restrictive covenant "that no structures are to be erected on the property" because the Wilsons were otherwise concerned that Misita might clutter the land like his existing property or build another large structure on it.

The Wilsons subsequently sold their land to Roy and Mitzi Conn. The restrictive covenant played a major role in the Conn's decision to purchase the property, as it prevented the three-acre frontage portion of Misita's property from becoming "junked-up" like the rest of it.

After the Conns moved in, though, Misita built and stored on the plot a "sign" in the shape of a triangular prism, which is intended to advertise his art. The design of the "sign" is such that its interior is big enough to serve as a showroom for his art as well. The sign/showroom has a hitch at one vertex of the prism's base and wheels on the other two vertices. The sign/showroom sat in the area subject to the "no-structure" restrictive plot for months without being moved.

The Conns complained that the "sign" violates the restrictive covenant. Misita insisted that it is not a structure within the meaning of the covenant because it is movable. Regardless of whether Misita's argument would withstand legal scrutiny, does he have any ethical obligation to honor the spirit of the restrictive covenant and remove the "sign"?

Acquisition of Real Property

 LO24-5 Distinguish the various ways in which ownership of real property is transferred and how title to property can be assured.

Title to real property may be obtained in various ways, including purchase, gift, will or inheritance, tax sale, and adverse possession. Original title to land in the United States was acquired either from the federal government or from a country that held the land prior to its acquisition by the United States. The land in the 13 original colonies had been granted by the king of England either to the colonies or to certain individuals. The states ceded the land in the Northwest Territory to the federal government, which in turn issued grants or patents of land. Original ownership of much of the land in Florida and the Southwest came by grants from Spain's rulers.

Acquisition by Purchase
Selling one's real property is a basic ownership right. Unreasonable restrictions on an owner's right to sell her property are considered unenforceable because they violate public policy. Most owners of real property acquired title by purchasing the property. Each state sets the requirements for proper conveyances of real property located in that state. The various elements of selling and buying real property are discussed later in this chapter.

Acquisition by Gift
Real property ownership may be acquired by gift. For a gift of real property to be valid, the donor must deliver a properly executed deed to the donee or to some third person who is to hold it for the donee. Neither the donee nor the third person needs to take actual possession of the property. Intent to make a gift is required. The gift's essential element is delivery of the deed. Suppose that Fields executes a deed to the family farm and leaves it in his safe-deposit box for delivery to his daughter (the intended donee) when he dies. The attempted gift will not be valid because Fields did not deliver the gift during his lifetime.

Acquisition by Will or Inheritance
The owner of real property generally has the right to dispose of the property by will. The requirements for a valid will are discussed in Chapter 26. If the owner of real property dies without a valid will, the property passes to the owner's heirs as determined under the laws of the state in which the property is located.

Acquisition by Tax Sale
If taxes assessed on real property are not paid when due, they become a *lien* on the property. This lien has priority over other claims to the land. If the taxes remain unpaid, the government may sell the land at a tax sale. Although the purchaser at the tax sale acquires title to the property, a number of states have statutes giving the original owner a limited time (such as a year) within which to buy the property from the tax sale purchaser for the price paid by the purchaser, plus interest.

Acquisition by Adverse Possession
Each state has a statute of limitations that gives an owner of land a specific number of years within which to bring suit to regain possession of her land from someone who is trespassing on it. This period varies from state to state, generally ranging from 5 to 20 years. If someone wrongfully possesses land and acts as if he were the owner, the actual owner must take steps to have the possessor ejected from the land. If the owner fails to do this within the statutory period, the owner loses the right to eject the possessor.

Assume, for example, that Titus owns a vacant lot next to Holdeman's house. Holdeman frequently uses the vacant lot for a variety of activities and appears to be the property's only user. In addition, Holdeman regularly mows and otherwise maintains the vacant lot. He has also placed a fence around it. By continuing such actions and thus staying in possession of Titus's property for the statutory period (and by meeting each other requirement about to be discussed), Holdeman may position himself to acquire title to the land by **adverse possession**.

To acquire title by adverse possession, one must possess land in a manner that puts the true owner on notice of the owner's cause of action against the possessor. The adverse possessor's acts of possession must be (1) *open* and *notorious*, (2) *actual*, (3) *continuous*, (4) *exclusive*, and (5) *hostile* (or adverse) *to the owner's rights*. The hostility element is not a matter of subjective intent. Rather, it means that the adverse possessor's acts of possession must be inconsistent with the owner's rights. If a person is in possession of another's property under a lease, as a cotenant, or with the permission of the owner, that person's possession is not hostile. In some states, the possessor of land must also pay the property taxes in order to gain title by adverse possession.

It is not necessary that the same person occupy the land for the statutory period. The periods of possession of several adverse possessors may be "tacked" together when calculating the period of possession if each possessor claimed rights from another possessor. The possession must, however, be continuous for the requisite time.

The following *Stratford* case considers a claim of adverse possession, focusing on what it means to actually, openly, and notoriously possess land.

Stratford v. Long	430 S.W.3d 921 (Mo. Ct. App. 2014)

Robert and Dora Stratford and Roger and Pamela Long own abutting parcels of land in Douglas County, Missouri. They disagreed about the ownership of a strip of land running the length of their shared boundary. It also includes a natural spring and waterfall that flows from the spring. A good portion of the disputed area of land is rugged.

The Stratfords purchased their land in 1976 and moved onto the property in 1985. When they moved onto the land, there was an existing fence on the northwest corner of the property that bent west around the upper ledge of the waterfall. The Stratfords wrongly assumed that the fence marked the boundary line between the two properties.

The Stratfords undertook a number of projects that reflected their mistaken belief that the disputed strip of land was within their purchased plot. Sometime after 1985—but well before 2005, when the Longs purchased the neighboring parcel—the Stratfords installed a 1,500-foot coil that ran from their home's geothermal heat pump through the disputed land to the spring. They also constructed a berm, 374 feet in length, that separated a smaller stream from the larger spring on the property. The berm extended from the Stratfords' property into the disputed area as well. In 1997, they constructed a fence on what they understood to be their west boundary line, beginning in the southwest corner of their property and connecting to the existing fence around the waterfall on the northwest corner. The Stratfords told Russell Doran, who was the owner of what eventually became the Longs' property, that the fence was on the survey line. The Stratfords intended to establish a boundary line with the fence. The new fence ran through a pasture and was clearly visible. Doran used his property as a cattle pasture, allowing the cattle to graze up to the fence but not beyond it. Finally, the Stratfords mowed and cleared brush from the land in the disputed area at least once per year and allowed their bees to use the area to pollinate.

The Longs purchased the neighboring property in 2005. Based on their own survey of the property boundary, they concluded that the Stratfords' fence and other developments encroached on their land. When they could not work out a compromise, the Stratfords filed a petition with the court to quiet title, which is an action asking the court to determine the true owner of a piece of land and to remove or "quiet" any challenges or claims to title in the land. They claimed that they had acquired title to the land through adverse possession. The Longs responded with a counterclaim seeking a declaratory judgment that the legal description in their deed marked the proper boundary of their land.

Following a bench trial, the judge found in favor of the Longs, concluding that the Stratfords had not proven their adverse possession claim because their possession of the disputed area had not been actual, open, and notorious. The Stratfords appealed, so they are referred to as "Appellants" in the opinion below. The Longs are referred to as "Respondents."

Jeffrey W. Bates, Judge

In Appellants' first two points, they contend the trial court misapplied the law by concluding that Appellants failed to prove their adverse possession claim. Appellants argue that the facts found by the court were sufficient to prove that Appellants' possession of the disputed area was actual, open and notorious. We agree.

A party who seeks to establish title to real property by adverse possession must prove that he possessed the land, and that his possession was: (1) hostile and under a claim of right; (2) actual; (3) open and notorious; (4) exclusive; and (5) continuous for a period of ten years. *Conduff v. Stone*, 968 S.W.2d 200, 203 (Mo. App. 1998). The claimant's failure to prove even one of the elements of adverse possession will defeat his claim. . . .

The Actual Possession Element

"Actual possession is the present ability to control the land and the intent to exclude others from such control." *Eime v. Bradford*, 185 S.W.3d 233, 236 (Mo. App. 2006). "A mere mental enclosure of land does not constitute the requisite actual possession." [*Harris v. Lynch*, 940 S.W.2d 42, 45 (Mo. App. 1997)]. "Rather,

there must be continual acts of occupying, clearing, cultivating, pasturing, erecting fences or other improvements and paying taxes on the land." *Id.*

The trial court cited [prior case law] for the proposition that, to prove the element of actual possession, Appellants were required to show they used the entire disputed area. The trial court concluded that:

> The credible evidence in this case showed, as to the entire contested area, the [Appellants] made no use of the entire contested parcel. There was no evidence that [Appellants] used the entire parcel for any use. Part of this parcel was a low-lying natural spring area, another quite small part was pasture, while much of the land was unimproved, rough and hilly timbered land. The [Appellants'] evidence was devoid of facts that would show that the "entire" area was used for anything. Accordingly, the Court finds that the [Appellants] have failed to prove actual possession of the entire parcel.

We agree with Appellants that the trial court misapplied the law to its factual findings in reaching this legal conclusion.

The trial court failed to account for the densely wooded and rugged nature of much of the disputed area. "The 'actual possession' element of adverse possession is less strict for wild, undeveloped land than it is for developed land, because the nature, location, and possible uses for the property may restrict the type of affirmative acts of ownership that may be appropriate for the land." [*Luttrell v. Stokes*, 77 S.W.3d 745, 749 (Mo. App. 2002).]

The trial court's own factual findings demonstrate that Appellants ran a long geothermal coil from their home to the spring and constructed a large 374-foot berm in part on the disputed area. Appellants also used the wooded part of the disputed area to allow their bees to pollinate. "[T]he nature of the property determines the kinds of acts which constitute possession." *Cunningham v. Hughes*, 889 S.W.2d 864, 867 (Mo. App. 1994). Given the "rough and hilly" quality of most of the disputed area, these acts are sufficient to establish Appellants' actual possession of the disputed area.

Appellants also constructed a fence through the open, pasture part of the disputed area. By constructing the fence through the pasture, Appellants established a boundary and limited use of the pasture by Respondents' predecessors' cattle. . . . Appellants also maintained the land on their side of the fence by cutting the brush and clearing the pasture. Again, the acts of possession undertaken by Appellants, considered together, are sufficient to satisfy the actual possession element in light of the character and location of the disputed area.

The Open and Notorious Possession Element

In the judgment, the trial court [held] that Appellants had to prove their occupancy was "conspicuous, widely recognized and commonly known" in order to satisfy the open and notorious possession element of their adverse possession claim. The trial court concluded that Appellants failed to prove this element because they did not install "No Trespassing" signs. Appellants argue that the trial court misapplied the law in concluding that the facts it found were insufficient to prove open and notorious possession. Once again, we agree.

The requirement that the occupancy be "conspicuous, widely recognized, and commonly known" exists to make sure that "the legal owner had cause to know of the adverse claim of ownership by another." *Bowles v. McKeon*, 217 S.W.3d 400, 405 (Mo. App. 2007). . . . "The open and notorious requirement of adverse possession can be met by showing the defendant's actual knowledge of a plaintiff's claim." *Dobbs v. Knoll*, 92 S.W.3d 176, 183 (Mo. App. 2002). Knowledge or notice has been held to mean "knowledge of all that would be learned by reasonable inquiry." *Id.* . . .

The trial court found that: (1) Doran was told by Appellants that they were constructing a boundary fence through the open pasture; and (2) once the fence was installed, Doran's cattle used the pasture only up to Appellants' fence line. Therefore, Doran had actual knowledge of Appellants' possession of the disputed area and their intention to claim all of the land inside the fence as their own. Thereafter, Doran accepted the fence as the boundary line, and the cattle he pastured in the field were not able to cross the fence line to graze on the disputed area any longer. None of Respondents' predecessors in title challenged Appellants' use of the disputed property at any time during the statutory period. The court also found that Appellants' 374-foot berm, which took three years to construct, was visible from the county road, despite the rugged and wooded nature of the land in that area. The foregoing factual findings were sufficient to prove that Appellants' use of the disputed area was open and notorious. Taking into account the character of the disputed area and Doran's actual knowledge of Appellants' use of the land, their possession of the property was sufficiently conspicuous to satisfy the open and notorious requirement.

The trial court's judgment in favor of Respondents is reversed. The cause is remanded for further proceedings consistent with this opinion.

Transfer by Sale

Steps in a Sale
The major steps normally involved in the sale of real property are:

1. Contracting with a real estate broker to locate a buyer.
2. Negotiating and signing a contract of sale.
3. Arranging for the financing of the purchase and satisfying other requirements, such as having a survey conducted or acquiring title insurance.
4. Closing the sale, which involves payment of the purchase price and transfer of the deed, as well as other matters.
5. Recording the deed.

LOG ON

For a variety of articles about practical aspects of buying, selling, or owning real estate, see Nolo Real Estate Law Center at **www.nolo.com/legal-encyclopedia/buying-house/**.

Contracting with a Real Estate Broker

Although engaging a real estate broker is not a legal requirement for the sale of real property, it is common for one who wishes to sell his property to "list" the property with a broker. A listing contract empowers the broker to act as the seller's agent in procuring a ready, willing, and able buyer and in managing details of the property transfer. A number of states' statutes of frauds require listing contracts to be evidenced by a writing and signed by the party to be charged.

Real estate brokers are regulated by state and federal law. They owe *fiduciary duties* (duties of trust and confidence) to their clients. Chapter 35 contains additional information regarding the duties imposed on such agents.

Types of Listing Contracts   Listing contracts specify such matters as the listing period's duration, the terms on which the seller will sell, and the amount and terms of the broker's commission. There are different types of listing contracts.

1. *Open listing.* Under an open listing contract, the broker receives a *nonexclusive* right to sell the property. This means that the seller and third parties (e.g., other brokers) also are entitled to find a buyer for the property. The broker operating under an open listing is entitled to a commission only if he was the first to find a ready, willing, and able buyer.

2. *Exclusive agency listing.* Under an exclusive agency listing, the broker earns a commission if he *or any other agent* finds a ready, willing, and able buyer during the period of time specified in the contract. Thus, the broker operating under such a listing would have the right to a commission even if another broker actually procured the buyer. Under the exclusive agency listing, however, the seller has the right to sell the property himself without being obligated to pay the broker a commission.

3. *Exclusive right to sell.* An exclusive right to sell contract provides the broker the exclusive right to sell the property for a specified period of time and entitles her to a commission no matter who procured the buyer. Under this type of listing, a seller must pay the broker her commission even if it was the seller or some third party who found the buyer during the duration of the listing contract.

Contract of Sale

The contract formation, performance, assignment, and remedies principles about which you read in earlier chapters apply to real estate sales contracts. Such contracts identify the parties and subject property, and set forth the purchase price, the type of deed the purchaser will receive, the items of personal property (if any) included in the sale, and other important aspects of the parties' transaction. Real estate sales contracts often make the closing of the sale contingent on the buyer's obtaining financing at a specified rate of interest, on the seller's procurement of a survey and title insurance, and on the property's passing various inspections. Because they are within the statute of frauds, real estate sales contracts must be evidenced by a suitable writing signed by the party to be charged in order to be enforceable.

Financing the Purchase   The various arrangements for financing the purchase of real property—such as mortgages, land contracts, and deeds of trust—are discussed in Chapter 28.

Fair Housing Act

The Fair Housing Act, enacted by Congress in 1968 and substantially revised in 1988, is designed to prevent discrimination in the housing market. Its provisions apply to real estate brokers, sellers (other than those selling their own single-family dwellings without the use of a broker), lenders, lessors, and appraisers. Originally, the act prohibited discrimination on the basis of race, color, religion, sex, and national origin. The 1988 amendments added "handicap" and "familial status" to this list. The familial status category was intended to prevent discrimination in the housing market against pregnant women and families with children.[4] "Adult" or "senior citizen" communities restricting residents' age do not violate the Fair Housing Act even though they exclude families with children, so long as the housing meets the requirements of the act's "housing for older persons" exemption.[5]

The act prohibits discrimination on the above-listed bases in a wide range of matters relating to the sale or rental of housing. These matters include refusals to sell or rent, representations that housing is not available for sale or rental when in fact it is, and discriminatory actions regarding terms, conditions, or privileges of sale or rental or regarding the provision of services and facilities involved in sale or rental.[6] The act also prohibits discrimination in connection with brokerage services, appraisals, and financing of dwellings.

---

[4]"Familial status" is defined as an individual or individuals under the age of 18 who is/are domiciled with a parent, some other person who has custody over him/her/them, or the designee of the parent or custodial individual. The familial status classification also applies to one who is pregnant or in the process of attempting to secure custody of a child or children under the age of 18.

[5]The Fair Housing Act defines "housing for older persons" as housing provided under any state or federal program found by the Secretary of HUD to be specifically designed to assist elderly persons, housing intended for and solely occupied by persons 62 years old or older, or housing that meets the requirements of federal regulations and is intended for occupancy by at least one person 55 years old or older.

[6]Chapter 25 discusses the Fair Housing Act's application to rentals of residential property.

CYBERLAW IN ACTION

How does the Fair Housing Act apply to websites that permit users to post advertisements about the sale or rental of real estate? Advertisements about property for sale or lease that are posted by individuals sometimes make statements indicating a "preference, limitation, or discrimination, or an intention to make a preference, limitation, or discrimination, on the basis of race, color, national origin, disability, sex, religion, and familial status" that could violate the Fair Housing Act if the statements were made offline. For example, in *Chicago Lawyers' Committee for Civil Rights under the Law, Inc. v. Craigslist, Inc.*, 519 F.3d 666 (7th Cir. 2008), the plaintiff alleged that Craigslist.com posted notices in violation of the Fair Housing Act such as "Apt. too small for families with small children," "NO MINORITIES," and "Christian single straight female needed." The content of advertisements on the website is created by Craigslist.com users, not by Craigslist Inc. This is a legally significant point because a federal statute, § 230 of the Communications Decency Act, states that "No provider or user of an interactive computer service shall be treated as the publisher or speaker of any information provided by another information content provider." This statute has been interpreted in many cases to immunize websites, ISPs, and other interactive computer services for liability for third-party content. In the *Craigslist* case, the Seventh Circuit held that under § 230 of the Communications Decency Act, Craigslist could not be treated as the publisher of information provided by others and, therefore, that § 230 shielded Craigslist from liability.

In *Fair Housing Council of San Fernando Valley v. Roommates. com, LLC*, 521 F.3d 1157 (9th Cir. 2008), however, the Ninth Circuit held that § 230 of the Communications Decency Act immunized Roommates.com for some but not all of its activities. Roommates. com operates a roommate-matching website. Prior to searching or posting listings, subscribers were required to disclose their sex and sexual orientation, and to indicate whether children would live with them. Subscribers also described their preferences in roommates with regard to the same three criteria and were encouraged to provide additional comments. Roommates.com would then compile information provided in the questionnaires into a profile for each user, which would be used to match subscribers with listings and which could be viewed by other subscribers. The plaintiffs alleged that these practices constituted Fair Housing Act violations. The Ninth Circuit emphasized that § 230 provides a shield for an interactive computer service for content created by third parties, but not for content developed by the interactive computer service itself. It characterized Roommates.com's creation and required use of the questionnaires as being "entirely its own" and the profiles created and displayed from the information provided in the questionnaire as information developed by Roommates.com. Because these practices involved content developed by Roommates.com and not a third party, they were not shielded from potential Fair Housing Act liability. However, § 230 did immunize Roommates.com liability for discriminatory content authored by subscribers in the open-ended "additional comments" section of the questionnaire.

In 2015, the Supreme Court clarified that the Fair Housing Act incorporates disparate impact claims of discrimination, as well as claims of disparate treatment.[7]

Prohibited discrimination on the basis of disability includes refusals to permit a person with a disability to make (at that person's own expense) reasonable modifications to the property. It also includes refusals to make reasonable accommodations in property-related rules, policies, practices, or services when such modifications or accommodations are necessary to afford the person with a disability full enjoyment of the property. The act also outlaws the building of multifamily housing that is inaccessible to persons with disabilities.

A violation of the Fair Housing Act may result in a civil action brought by the government or the aggrieved individual. If the aggrieved individual sues and prevails, the court may issue injunctions, award actual and punitive damages,

assess attorney fees and costs, and grant other appropriate relief. Finally, the Fair Housing Act invalidates any state or municipal law requiring or permitting an action that would be a discriminatory housing practice under federal law.

Deeds

LO24-6 Distinguish the different types of deeds, explain the purposes of recording deeds, and describe how state law determines priorities among those who claim competing rights in a parcel of real property.

Each state's statutes set out the formalities necessary to accomplish a valid conveyance of land. As a general rule, a valid conveyance is brought about by the execution and delivery of a **deed**, a written instrument that transfers title from one person (the grantor) to another (the grantee). Three types of deeds are in general use in the United States: *quitclaim deeds*, *warranty deeds*, and *deeds of bargain and sale* (also called *grant deeds*). The precise rights contemplated by a deed depend on the type of deed the parties have used.

---

[7]*Texas Dep't of Hous. & Cmty. Affairs v. The Inclusive Cmtys. Project*, 576 U.S. 519 (2015). Chapter 51 discusses disparate impact and disparate treatment theories of discrimination in detail in the context of employment.

Quitclaim Deeds A **quitclaim deed** conveys whatever title the grantor has at the time he executes the deed. It does not, however, contain warranties of title. The grantor who executes a quitclaim deed does not claim to have good title—or any title, for that matter. The grantee has no action against the grantor under a quitclaim deed if the grantee does not acquire good title. Quitclaim deeds are frequently used to cure technical defects in the chain of title to property.

Warranty Deeds A **warranty deed**, unlike a quitclaim deed, contains covenants of warranty. Besides conveying title to the property, the grantor who executes a warranty deed guarantees the title that is conveyed. There are two types of warranty deeds.

1. *General warranty deed.* Under a general warranty deed, the grantor warrants against (and agrees to defend against) all title defects and encumbrances (such as liens and easements), including those that arose before the grantor received title.

2. *Special warranty deed.* Under a special warranty deed, the grantor warrants against (and agrees to defend against) title defects and encumbrances that arose after the grantor acquired the property. If the property conveyed is subject to an encumbrance such as a mortgage, a long-term lease, or an easement, the grantor frequently provides a special warranty deed that contains a provision excepting those specific encumbrances from the warranty.

Deeds of Bargain and Sale In a deed of bargain and sale (also known as a grant deed), the grantor makes no covenants. The grantor uses language such as "I grant" or "I bargain and sell" or "I convey" property. Such a deed does contain, however, the grantor's implicit representation that he owns the land and has not previously encumbered it or conveyed it to another party.

Form and Execution of Deed

Some states' statutes suggest a form for deeds. Although the requirements for execution of deeds are not uniform, they do follow a similar pattern. As a general rule, a deed states the *name of the grantee*, contains a *recitation of consideration and a description of the property conveyed*, and is *signed by the grantor*. Most states require that the deed be notarized (acknowledged by the grantor before a notary public or other authorized officer) in order to be eligible for recording in public records.

No technical words of conveyance are necessary for a valid deed. Any language is sufficient if it indicates with reasonable certainty the grantor's intent to transfer ownership of the property. The phrases "grant, bargain, and sell" and "convey and warrant" are commonly used. Deeds contain recitations of consideration primarily for historical reasons. The consideration recited is not necessarily the purchase price of the property. Deeds often state that the consideration for the conveyance is "one dollar and other valuable consideration."

The property conveyed must be described in such a manner that it can be identified. This usually means that the legal description of the property must be used. Several methods of legal description are used in the United States. In urban areas, descriptions are usually by lot, block, and plat. In rural areas where the land has been surveyed by the government, property is usually described by reference to the government survey. It may also be described by a metes and bounds description that specifies the boundaries of the tract of land.

Recording Deeds

Delivery of a valid deed conveys title from a grantor to a grantee. Even so, the grantee should promptly record the deed in order to prevent the interest from being defeated by third parties who may claim interests in the property. The grantee must pay a fee to have the deed recorded, a process that involves depositing and indexing the deed in the files of a government office designated by state law. A recorded deed operates to provide the public at large with notice of the grantee's property interest.

Recording Statutes Each state has a recording statute that establishes a system for the recording of all transactions affecting real property ownership. These statutes are not uniform in their provisions. In general, however, they provide for the recording of all deeds, mortgages, land contracts, and similar documents.

Types of Recording Statutes State recording statutes also provide for priority among competing claimants to rights in real property, in case conflicting rights or interests in property should be deeded to (or otherwise claimed by) more than one person. (Obviously, a grantor has no right to issue two different grantees separate deeds to the same property, but if this should occur, recording statutes provide rules to decide which grantee has superior title.) These priority rules apply only to grantees who have given value for their deeds or other interest-creating documents (primarily purchasers and lenders), and not to donees. A given state's recording law will set up one of three basic types of priority systems: race statutes, notice statutes, and race-notice statutes. Figure 24.2 explains these priority systems. Although the examples used

Figure 24.2	Three Basic Types of Priority Systems for Recording Deeds
Race Statutes	Under a race statute—so named because the person who wins the race to the courthouse wins the property ownership "competition"—the first grantee who records a deed to a tract of land has superior title. For example, if Grantor deeds Blackacre to Kerr on March 1 and to Templin on April 1, Templin will have superior title to Blackacre if she records her deed before Kerr's is recorded. Race statutes are relatively uncommon today.
Notice Statutes	Under a notice system of priority, a later grantee of property has superior title if that later grantee acquired the interest without notice of an earlier grantee's claim to the property under an unrecorded deed. For example, Grantor deeds Greenacre to Jonson on June 1, but Jonson does not record his deed. On July 1, Marlowe purchases Greenacre without knowledge of Jonson's competing claim. Grantor executes and delivers a deed to Marlowe. In this situation, Marlowe would have superior rights to Greenacre even if Jonson ultimately records his deed before Marlowe's is recorded.
Race-Notice Statutes	The race-notice priority system combines elements of the systems just discussed. Under race-notice statutes, the grantee having priority is the one who both *takes interest without notice* of any prior unrecorded claim and *records first.* For example, Grantor deeds Redacre to Frazier on September 1. On October 1 (at which time Frazier has not yet recorded his deed), Grantor deeds Redacre to Gill, who is then unaware of any claim by Frazier to Redacre. If Gill records his deed before Frazier's is recorded, Gill has superior rights to Redacre.

in Figure 24.2 deal with recorded and unrecorded deeds, recording statutes apply to other documents that create interests in real estate. Chapter 28 discusses the recording of mortgages, as well as the adverse security interest–related consequences a mortgagee may experience if its mortgage goes unrecorded.

Methods of Assuring Title In purchasing real property, the buyer is really acquiring the seller's ownership interests. Because the buyer does not want to pay a large sum of money for something that proves to be of little or no value, it is important for the buyer to obtain assurance that the seller has good title to the property. This is commonly done in one of three ways:

1. *Title opinion.* In some states, it is customary to have an attorney examine an **abstract of title**. An abstract of title is a history of what the public records show regarding the passage of title to, and other interests in, a parcel of real property. It is not a guarantee of good title. After examining the abstract, the attorney renders an opinion about whether the grantor has marketable title, which is title free from defects or reasonable doubt about its validity. If the grantor's title is defective, the nature of the defects will be stated in the attorney's title opinion.

2. *Torrens system.* A method of title assurance available in a few states is the Torrens system of title registration. Under this system, one who owns land in fee simple obtains a certificate of title. When the property is sold, the grantor delivers a deed and a certificate of title to the grantee. All liens and encumbrances against the title are noted on the

certificate, thus assuring the purchaser that the title is good except as to the liens and encumbrances noted on the certificate. However, some claims or encumbrances, such as those arising from adverse possession, do not appear on the records and must be discovered through an inspection of the property. In some Torrens states, encumbrances such as tax liens, short-term leases, and highway rights are valid against the purchaser even though they do not appear on the certificate.

3. *Title insurance.* Purchasing a policy of title insurance provides the preferred and most common means of protecting title to real property. Title insurance obligates the insurer to reimburse the insured grantee for loss if the title proves to be defective. In addition, title insurance covers litigation costs if the insured grantee must go to court in a title dispute. Lenders commonly require that a separate policy of title insurance be obtained for the lender's protection. Title insurance may be obtained in combination with the other previously discussed methods of ensuring title.

Seller's Responsibilities Regarding the Quality of Residential Property

Buyers of real estate normally consider it important that any structures on the property be in good condition. This factor becomes especially significant if the buyer intends to use the property for residential purposes. The rule of caveat emptor (let the buyer beware) traditionally applied to the sale of real property unless the seller committed misrepresentation or fraud or made express warranties about the property's condition. In addition, sellers had no duty to disclose hidden defects in the property. Over the decades, however, the legal environment for sellers—especially real estate professionals such as developers and builder-vendors of residential property—has changed substantially. This section examines two important sources of liability for sellers of real property.

Implied Warranty of Habitability
Historically, sellers of residential property were not regarded as making any **implied warranty** that the property was habitable or suitable for the buyer's use. The law's attitude toward the buyer–seller relationship in residential property sales began to shift, however, as product liability law underwent rapid change in the late 1960s. Courts began to see that the same policies favoring the creation of implied warranties in the sale of goods applied with equal force to the sale of residential real estate.[8] Both goods and housing are frequently mass produced. The disparity of knowledge and bargaining power often existing between a buyer of goods and a professional seller is also likely to exist between a buyer of a house and a builder-vendor (one who builds and sells houses). Moreover, many defects in houses are not readily discoverable during a buyer's inspection. This creates the possibility of serious loss because the purchase of a home is often the largest single investment a person ever makes.

For these reasons, courts in most states now hold that builders, builder-vendors, and developers make an implied warranty of habitability when they build or sell real property for residential purposes. An ordinary owner who sells her house—in other words, a seller who was neither the builder nor the developer of the residential property—does not make an implied warranty of habitability.

The implied warranty of habitability amounts to a guarantee that the house is free of latent (hidden) defects that would render it unsafe or unsuitable for human habitation. A breach of this warranty subjects the defendant to liability for damages, measured by either the cost of repairs or the loss in value of the house.[9]

A related issue that has led to considerable litigation is whether the implied warranty of habitability extends to subsequent purchasers of the house. For example, PDQ Development Co. builds a house and sells it to Johnson, who later sells the house to McClure. May McClure

successfully sue PDQ for breach of warranty if a serious defect renders the house uninhabitable? Although some courts have rejected implied warranty actions brought by subsequent purchasers, many courts today hold that an implied warranty made by a builder-vendor or developer would extend to a subsequent purchaser.

May the implied warranty of habitability be *disclaimed* or *limited* in the contract of sale? It appears at least possible to disclaim or limit the warranty through a contract provision, subject to limitations imposed by the unconscionability doctrine, public policy concerns, and contract interpretation principles.[10] Courts construe attempted disclaimers very strictly against the builder-vendor or developer, and often reject disclaimers that are not specific regarding rights supposedly waived by the purchaser.

Duty to Disclose Hidden Defects
Traditional contract law provided that a seller had no duty to disclose to the buyer defects in the property being sold, even if the seller knew about the defects and the buyer could not reasonably find out about them. The seller's failure to volunteer information, therefore, could not constitute misrepresentation or fraud. This traditional rule of nondisclosure was another expression of the prevailing *caveat emptor* notion. Although the nondisclosure rule was subject to certain exceptions,[11] the exceptions seldom applied. Thus, there was no duty to disclose in most sales of real property.

Today, courts in many jurisdictions have substantially eroded the traditional nondisclosure rule and have placed a duty on the seller to disclose any known defect that materially affects the property's value and is not reasonably observable by the buyer. The seller's failure to disclose such defects effectively amounts to an assertion that the defects do not exist—an assertion on which a judicial finding of misrepresentation or fraud may be based.[12]

Other Property Condition–Related Obligations of Real Property Owners and Possessors

In recent years, the law has increasingly required real property owners and possessors to take steps to further the safety of persons on the property and to make the property

---

[8]See Chapter 20 for a discussion of the development of similar doctrines in the law of product liability.

[9]Measures of damages are discussed in Chapter 18.

[10]The unconscionability doctrine and public policy concerns are discussed in Chapter 15. Chapter 16 addresses contract interpretation.

[11]These exceptions are discussed in Chapter 13.

[12]Misrepresentation and fraud are discussed in Chapter 13.

more accessible to persons who are disabled. This section discusses two legal developments along these lines: the trend toward expansion of *premises liability* and the inclusion of property-related provisions in the *Americans with Disabilities Act*.

Expansion of Premises Liability

Premises liability is the name sometimes used for negligence cases in which property owners or possessors (such as business operators leasing commercial real estate) are held liable to persons injured while on the property. As explained in Chapter 7, property owners and possessors face liability when their *failures to exercise reasonable care* to keep their property reasonably safe result in injuries to persons lawfully on the property.[13] The traditional premises liability case was one in which a property owner's or possessor's negligence led to the existence of a potentially hazardous condition on the property (e.g., a dangerously slick floor or similar physical condition at a business premises), and a person justifiably on the premises (e.g., a business customer) sustained personal injury upon encountering that unexpected condition (e.g., by slipping and falling).

Security Precautions against Foreseeable Criminal Acts Recent years have witnessed a judicial inclination to expand premises liability to cover other situations in addition to the traditional scenario. A key component of this expansion has been many courts' willingness to reconsider the once-customary holding that a property owner or possessor had no legal obligation to implement security measures to protect persons on the property from the wrongful acts of third parties lacking any connection with the owner or possessor. Today, courts frequently hold that a property owner's or possessor's duty to exercise reasonable care includes the obligation to take *reasonable security precautions* designed to protect persons lawfully on the premises from *foreseeable* wrongful (including criminal) acts by third parties.

This expansion has caused hotel, apartment building, and convenience store owners and operators to be among the defendants held liable—sometimes in very large damage amounts—to guests, tenants, and customers on whom third-party attackers inflicted severe physical injuries. In such cases, the property owners' or possessors' negligent failures to take security precautions restricting such wrongdoers' access to the premises served as at least a *substantial factor* leading to the plaintiffs' injuries.[14] The security lapses amounting to a lack of reasonable care in a particular case may have been, for instance, failures to install deadbolt locks, provide adequate locking devices on sliding glass doors, maintain sufficient lighting, or employ security guards.

Determining Foreseeability The security precautions component of the reasonable care duty is triggered only when criminal activity on the premises is foreseeable. It therefore becomes important to determine whether the foreseeability standard has been met. In making this determination, courts look at such factors as whether previous crimes had occurred on or near the subject property (and if so, the nature and frequency of those crimes), whether the property owner or possessor knew or should have known of those prior occurrences, and whether the property was located in a high-crime area. The fact-specific nature of the foreseeability and reasonable care determinations makes the outcome of a given premises liability case difficult to predict in advance. Nevertheless, there is no doubt that the current premises liability climate gives property owners and possessors more reason than ever before to be concerned about security measures.

Americans with Disabilities Act

In 1990, Congress enacted the broad-ranging Americans with Disabilities Act (ADA). This statute was designed to eliminate long-standing patterns of discrimination against persons who are disabled in matters such as employment, access to public services, and access to business establishments and similar facilities open to the public. The ADA's Title III focuses on places of *public accommodation*.[15] It imposes on certain property owners and possessors the obligation to take reasonable steps to make their property accessible to persons who are disabled (individuals with a physical or mental impairment that substantially limits one or more major life activities).

Places of Public Accommodation Title III of the ADA classifies numerous businesses and nonbusiness enterprises as places of **public accommodation**. These include hotels, restaurants, bars, theaters, concert halls, auditoriums, stadiums, shopping centers, stores at which goods are sold or rented, service-oriented businesses (running

---

[13]Chapter 7 explains the law's traditional view that real property owners and possessors owe persons who come on the property certain duties that vary depending on those persons' invitee, licensee, or trespasser status. It also discusses courts' increasing tendency to merge the traditional invitee and licensee classifications and to hold that property owners and possessors owe invitees and licensees the duty to exercise reasonable care to keep the premises reasonably safe.

[14]See Chapter 7's discussion of the *causation* element of a negligence claim.

[15]42 U.S.C. §§ 12181–12189. These sections examine only Title III of the ADA. Chapter 51 discusses the employment-related provisions set forth elsewhere in the statute.

the gamut from gas stations to law firm offices), museums, parks, schools, social services establishments (daycare centers, senior citizen centers, homeless shelters, and the like), places of recreation, and various other enterprises, facilities, and establishments. Private clubs and religious organizations, however, are not treated as places of public accommodation for purposes of the statute.

Modifications of Property Under the ADA, the owner or operator of a place of public accommodation cannot exclude people with disabilities from the premises or otherwise discriminate against them in terms of their ability to enjoy the public accommodation. Avoiding such exclusion or other discrimination may require alteration of the business or nonbusiness enterprise's practices, policies, and procedures. Moreover, using language contemplating the possible need for physical modifications of property serving as a place of public accommodation, the ADA includes within prohibited discrimination the property owner's or possessor's "failure to take such steps as may be necessary to ensure that no individual with a disability is excluded" or otherwise discriminated against in terms of access to what nondisabled persons are provided. The failure to take these steps does not violate the ADA, however, if the property owner or possessor demonstrates that implementing such steps would "fundamentally alter the nature" of the enterprise or would "result in an undue burden."

Prohibited discrimination may also include the "failure to remove architectural barriers and communication barriers that are structural in nature," if removal is "readily achievable." When the removal of such a barrier is not readily achievable, the property owner or possessor nonetheless engages in prohibited discrimination if he, she, or it does not adopt "alternative methods" to ensure access to the premises and what it has to offer (assuming that the alternative methods are themselves readily achievable). The ADA defines *readily achievable* as "easily accomplishable and able to be carried out without much difficulty or expense." The determination of whether an action is readily achievable involves consideration of factors such as the action's nature and cost, the nature of the enterprise conducted on the property, the financial resources of the affected property owner or possessor, and the effect the action would have on expenses and resources of the property owner or possessor.

New Construction Newly constructed buildings on property used as a place of public accommodation must contain physical features making the buildings *readily accessible* to people with disabilities. The same is true of additions built on to previous structures. The ADA is supplemented by federal regulations setting forth property accessibility guidelines designed to lend substance and specificity to the broad legal standards stated in the statute. In addition, the federal government has issued technical assistance manuals and materials in an effort to educate public accommodation owners and operators regarding their obligations under the ADA.

Remedies A person subjected to disability-based discrimination in any of the respects discussed above may bring a civil suit for injunctive relief. An injunction issued by a court must include "an order to alter facilities" to make the facilities "readily accessible to and usable by individuals with disabilities to the extent required" by the ADA. The court has discretion to award attorney fees to the prevailing party. The U.S. Attorney General also has the legal authority to institute a civil action alleging a violation of Title III of the ADA. In such a case, the court may choose to grant injunctive and other appropriate equitable relief, award compensatory damages to aggrieved persons (when the Attorney General so requests), and assess civil penalties (up to $75,000 for a first violation and up to $150,000 for any subsequent violation) "to vindicate the public interest." When determining the amount of any such penalty, the court is to give consideration to any good-faith effort by the property owner or possessor to comply with the law. The court must also consider whether the owner or possessor could reasonably have anticipated the need to accommodate people with disabilities.

Land Use Control

 LO24-7 Explain governmental powers to control and purchase private land and the constitutional limits on those powers.

Although a real property owner generally has the right to use the property as the owner desires, society has placed certain limitations on this right. This section examines the property use limitations imposed by nuisance law and by zoning and subdivision ordinances. It also discusses the ultimate land use restriction—the eminent domain power—which enables the government to deprive property owners of their land.

Nuisance Law One's enjoyment of her land depends to a great extent on the uses her neighbors make of their land. When the uses of neighboring landowners conflict, the aggrieved party sometimes institutes litigation to resolve the conflict. A property use that unreasonably interferes with another person's ability to use or enjoy her own property may lead to an action for **nuisance** against the landowner or possessor engaging in the objectionable use.

The term *nuisance* has no set definition. It is often regarded, however, as encompassing any property-related use or activity that unreasonably interferes with the rights of others. Property uses potentially constituting nuisances include uses that are inappropriate to the neighborhood (such as using a vacant lot in a residential neighborhood as a garbage dump), bothersome to neighbors (such as keeping a pack of barking dogs in one's backyard), dangerous to others (such as storing large quantities of gasoline in 50-gallon drums in one's garage), or of questionable morality (such as operating a house of prostitution). To amount to a nuisance, a use need not be illegal. The fact that relevant zoning laws allow a given use does not mean that the use cannot be a nuisance. The use's having been in existence before complaining neighbors acquired their property does not mean that the use cannot be a nuisance, though it does lessen the likelihood that the use would be held a nuisance.

The test for determining the presence or absence of a nuisance is necessarily flexible and highly dependent on the individual case's facts. Courts balance a number of factors, such as the social importance of the parties' respective uses, the extent and duration of harm experienced by the aggrieved party, and the feasibility of abating (stopping) the nuisance.

Nuisances may be private or public. To bring a *private nuisance* action, the plaintiff must be a landowner or occupier whose enjoyment of her own land is substantially lessened by the alleged nuisance. The remedies for private nuisance include damages and injunctive relief designed to stop the offending use. A *public nuisance* occurs when a nuisance harms members of the public, who need not be injured in their use of property. For example, if a power plant creates noise and emissions posing a health hazard to pedestrians and workers in nearby buildings, a public nuisance may exist even though the nature of the harm has nothing to do with any loss of enjoyment of property. Public nuisances involve a broader class of affected parties than do private nuisances. The action to abate a public nuisance must usually be brought by the government. Remedies generally include injunctive relief and civil penalties that resemble fines. On occasion, constitutional issues may arise in public nuisance cases brought by the government. Private parties may sue for abatement of a public nuisance or for damages caused by one only when they suffered unique harm different from that experienced by the general public.

Eminent Domain

The Fifth Amendment to the Constitution provides that private property shall not be taken for public use without "just compensation." Implicit in this provision is the principle that the government has the power to take property for public use if it pays "just compensation" to the owner of the property. This power, called the power of **eminent domain**, makes it possible for the government to acquire private property for highways, water control projects, municipal and civic centers, public housing, urban renewal, and other public uses. Governmental units may delegate their eminent domain power to private corporations such as railroads and utility companies.

Although the eminent domain power is a useful tool of efficient government, there are problems inherent in its use. Determining when the power can be properly exercised presents an initial problem. When the governmental unit itself uses the property taken, as would be the case with property acquired for construction of a municipal building or a public highway, the exercise of the power is proper. The use of eminent domain is controversial, however, when the government acquires the property and transfers it to a private developer.[16] In the *Kelo* case, which follows shortly, the U.S. Supreme Court grappled with this issue.[17]

Determining *just compensation* in a given case poses a second and frequently encountered eminent domain problem. The property owner is entitled to receive the "fair market value" of the property. Critics assert, however, that this measure of compensation falls short of adequately compensating the owner for the loss because *fair market value* does not cover such matters as the lost goodwill of a business or one's emotional attachment to one's home.

A third problem sometimes encountered is determining when there has been a "taking" that triggers the government's just compensation obligation. The answer is easy when the government institutes a formal legal action to exercise the eminent domain power (often called an action to *condemn* property). In some instances, however, the government causes or permits a serious physical invasion of a landowner's property without having instituted formal condemnation proceedings. For example, the government's dam-building project results in persistent flooding of a private party's land. Courts have recognized the right of property owners in such cases to institute litigation seeking compensation from the governmental unit whose actions effectively amounted to a physical taking of their land. In these so-called inverse condemnation cases, the property owner sends the message that "you have taken my land; now pay for it."

---

[16]This issue is discussed further in Chapter 3, as are other issues relating to eminent domain.

[17]As you read the *Kelo* opinion, keep in mind that the decision was controversial. In fact, in response to the decision, a substantial majority of the states have subsequently passed legislation intended to limit the types of takings allowed by *Kelo*, where the justification is economic development (though some of those enactments allow such takings when the goal is to eliminate "blight").

Kelo v. City of New London   545 U.S. 469 (2005)

The city of New London, Connecticut, had experienced decades of economic decline. In 1990, a state agency designated the city a "distressed municipality." In 1996, the federal government closed a U.S. naval facility in the Fort Trumbull area of the city that had employed more than 1,500 people. In 1998, the city's unemployment rate was nearly double that of the rest of the state and its population of just under 24,000 residents was at its lowest since 1920. These conditions prompted state and local officials to target New London, and particularly its Fort Trumbull area, for economic revitalization.

To this end, New London Development Corporation (NLDC), a private nonprofit entity established some years earlier to assist the city in planning economic development, was reactivated. In January 1998, the state authorized a $5.35 million bond issue to support the NLDC's planning activities. In February, the pharmaceutical company Pfizer Inc. announced that it would build a $300 million research facility on a site immediately adjacent to Fort Trumbull; local planners hoped that Pfizer would draw new business to the area, thereby serving as a catalyst to the area's rejuvenation. In May, the city council authorized the NLDC to formally submit its plans to the relevant state agencies for review. Upon obtaining state-level approval, the NLDC finalized an integrated development plan focused on 90 acres of the Fort Trumbull area, which comprises approximately 115 privately owned properties, as well as the 32 acres of land formerly occupied by the naval facility.

The development plan called for the creation of restaurants, shops, marinas for both recreational and commercial uses, a pedestrian "riverwalk," 80 new residences, a new U.S. Coast Guard Museum, research and development office space, and parking. The NLDC intended the development plan to capitalize on the arrival of the Pfizer facility and the new commerce it was expected to attract. In addition to creating jobs, generating tax revenue, and helping to build momentum for the revitalization of downtown New London, the plan was also designed to make the city more attractive and to create leisure and recreational opportunities on the waterfront and in the park. The city council approved the plan in January 2000 and designated the NLDC as its development agent in charge of implementation. The city council also authorized the NLDC to purchase property or to acquire property by exercising eminent domain in the city's name.

The NLDC successfully negotiated the purchase of most of the real estate in the 90-acre area, but its negotiations with nine property owners, including the petitioners Susette Kelo, Wilhelmina Dery, and Charles Dery, failed. As a result, in November 2000, the NLDC initiated condemnation proceedings. Kelo had lived in the Fort Trumbull area since 1997. She had made extensive improvements to her house, which she prizes for its water view. Wilhelmina Dery was born in her Fort Trumbull house in 1918 and had lived there her entire life. Her husband, Charles, had lived in the house since they married some 60 years prior. In all, the nine petitioners owned 15 properties in Fort Trumbull. There was no allegation that any of these properties were blighted or otherwise in poor condition; rather, they were condemned only because they happened to be located in the development area.

In December 2000, the petitioners brought this action claiming, among other things, that the taking of their properties would violate the "public use" restriction in the Fifth Amendment. The trial court granted a permanent restraining order prohibiting the taking of properties in one area of Fort Trumbull, but denied the order for properties in another area. Both sides appealed to the Supreme Court of Connecticut. That court held that all of the city's proposed takings were valid. The petitioners then appealed to the U.S. Supreme Court.

Stevens, Justice

Two polar propositions are perfectly clear. On the one hand, it has long been accepted that the sovereign may not take the property of *A* for the sole purpose of transferring it to another private party *B*, even though *A* is paid just compensation. On the other hand, it is equally clear that a State may transfer property from one private party to another if future "use by the public" is the purpose of the taking; the condemnation of land for a railroad with common-carrier duties is a familiar example. Neither of these propositions, however, determines the disposition of this case.

As for the first proposition, the City would no doubt be forbidden from taking petitioners' land for the purpose of conferring a private benefit on a particular private party. Nor would the City be allowed to take property under the mere pretext of a public purpose, when its actual purpose was to bestow a private benefit. The takings before us, however, would be executed pursuant to a carefully considered development plan. The trial judge and all the members of the Supreme Court of Connecticut agreed that there was no evidence of an illegitimate purpose in this case. On the other hand, this is not a case in which the City is planning to open the condemned land—at least not in its entirety—to use by the general public. Nor will the private lessees of the land in any sense be required to operate like common carriers, making their services available to all comers. But although such a projected use would be sufficient to satisfy the public use requirement, this Court long ago rejected any literal requirement that condemned property be put into use for the general public. Indeed, while many state courts in the mid-19th century endorsed "use by the public" as the proper definition of public use, that narrow view steadily eroded over time. Not only was the "use by the public" test difficult to administer (e.g., what proportion of the public need have access to the property? at what price?), but it proved to be impractical given the diverse and always evolving needs of society. Accordingly, when this Court began applying the Fifth Amendment to the States at the close of the 19th century, it embraced the broader and more natural interpretation of public use as "public purpose." The disposition of this case therefore turns on the question whether the City's development plan serves a "public purpose."

Without exception, our cases have defined that concept broadly, reflecting our long-standing policy of deference to legislative judgments in this field. Viewed as a whole, our jurisprudence has recognized that the needs of society have varied between different parts of the Nation, just as they have evolved over time in response to changed circumstances. For more than a century, our public use jurisprudence has wisely eschewed rigid formulas and intrusive scrutiny in favor of affording legislatures broad latitude in determining what public needs justify the use of the takings power.

Those who govern the City were not confronted with the need to remove blight in the Fort Trumbull area, but their determination that the area was sufficiently distressed to justify a program of economic rejuvenation is entitled to our deference. The City has carefully formulated an economic development plan that it believes will provide appreciable benefits to the community, including—but by no means limited to—new jobs and increased tax revenue. As with other exercises in urban planning and development, the City is endeavoring to coordinate a variety of commercial, residential, and recreational uses of land, with the hope that they will form a whole greater than the sum of its parts. To effectuate this plan, the City has invoked a state statute that specifically authorizes the use of eminent domain to promote economic development. Given the comprehensive character of the plan, the thorough deliberation that preceded its adoption, and the limited scope of our review, it is appropriate for us to resolve the challenges of the individual owners, not on a piecemeal basis, but rather in light of the entire plan. Because that plan unquestionably serves a public purpose, the takings challenged here satisfy the public use requirement of the Fifth Amendment.

To avoid this result, petitioners urge us to adopt a new bright-line rule that economic development does not qualify as a public use. Putting aside the unpersuasive suggestion that the City's plan will provide only purely economic benefits, neither precedent nor logic supports petitioners' proposal. Promoting economic development is a traditional and long-accepted function of government. There is, moreover, no principled way of distinguishing

economic development from the other public purposes that we have recognized. In our cases upholding takings that facilitated agriculture and mining, for example, we emphasized the importance of those industries to the welfare of the States in question. It would be incongruous to hold that the City's interest in the economic benefits to be derived from the development of the Fort Trumbull area has less of a public character than any of those other interests. Clearly, there is no basis for exempting economic development from our traditionally broad understanding of public purpose.

Petitioners contend that using eminent domain for economic development impermissibly blurs the boundary between public and private takings. Again, our cases foreclose this objection. Quite simply, the government's pursuit of a public purpose will often benefit individual private parties. It is further argued that without a bright-line rule nothing would stop a city from transferring citizen A's property to citizen B for the sole reason that citizen B will put the property to a more productive use and thus pay more taxes. Such a one-to-one transfer of property, executed outside the confines of an integrated development plan, is not presented in this case. While such an unusual exercise of government power would certainly raise a suspicion that a private purpose was afoot, the hypothetical cases posited by petitioners can be confronted if and when they arise. They do not warrant the crafting of an artificial restriction on the concept of public use.

Alternatively, petitioners maintain that for takings of this kind we should require a "reasonable certainty" that the expected public benefits will actually accrue. Such a rule, however, would represent an even greater departure from our precedent. The disadvantages of a heightened form of review are especially pronounced in this type of case. Orderly implementation of a comprehensive redevelopment plan obviously requires that the legal rights of all interested parties be established before new construction can be commenced. A constitutional rule that required postponement of the judicial approval of every condemnation until the likelihood of success of the plan had been assured would unquestionably impose a significant impediment to the successful consummation of many such plans.

Just as we decline to second-guess the City's considered judgments about the efficacy of its development plan, we also decline to second-guess the City's determinations as to what lands it needs to acquire in order to effectuate the project. In affirming the City's authority to take petitioners' properties, we do not minimize the hardship that condemnations may entail, notwithstanding the payment of just compensation. We emphasize that nothing in our opinion precludes any State from placing further restrictions on its exercise of the takings power. Indeed, many States already impose "public use" requirements that are stricter than the federal baseline. Some of these requirements have been established as a matter of state constitutional law, while others are expressed in state eminent domain statutes that carefully limit the grounds upon which takings may be exercised. As the submissions of the parties make clear, the necessity and wisdom of using eminent domain to promote economic development are certainly matters of legitimate public debate. This Court's authority, however, extends only to determining whether the City's proposed condemnations are for a "public use" within the meaning of the Fifth Amendment to the Federal Constitution.

Affirmed in favor of the City.

Zoning and Subdivision Laws

State legislatures commonly delegate to cities and other political subdivisions the power to impose reasonable regulations designed to promote the public health, safety, and welfare (often called the *police power*). Zoning ordinances, which regulate real property use, stem from the exercise of the police power. Normally, zoning ordinances divide a city or town into various districts and specify or limit the uses to which property in those districts may be put. They also contain requirements and restrictions regarding improvements built on the land.

Zoning ordinances frequently contain direct restrictions on land use, such as by limiting property use in a given area to single-family or high-density residential uses, or to commercial, light industrial, or heavy industrial uses. Other sorts of use-related provisions commonly found in zoning ordinances include restrictions on building height, limitations on the portion of a lot that can be covered by a building, and specifications of the distance buildings must be from lot lines (usually called *setback* requirements). Zoning ordinances also commonly restrict property use by establishing population density limitations. Such restrictions specify the maximum number of persons who can be housed on property in a given area and dictate the amount of living space that must be provided for each person occupying residential property. In addition, zoning ordinances often establish restrictions designed to maintain or create a certain aesthetic character in the community. Examples of this type of restriction include specifications of buildings' architectural style, limitations on billboard and sign use, and designations of special zones for historic buildings.

Many local governments also have ordinances dealing with proposed subdivisions. These ordinances often require the subdivision developer to meet certain requirements regarding lot size, street and sidewalk layout, and sanitary facilities. They also require that the city or town approve the proposed development. Such ordinances are designed to further general community interests and to protect prospective buyers of property in the subdivision by ensuring that the developer meets minimum standards of suitability.

Nonconforming Uses A zoning ordinance has *prospective* effect. This means that the uses and buildings already existing when the ordinance is passed (nonconforming uses) are permitted to continue. The ordinance may provide, however, for the gradual phasing out of nonconforming uses and buildings that do not fit the general zoning plan.

Relief from Zoning Ordinances A property owner who wishes to use the property in a manner prohibited by a zoning ordinance has more than one potential avenue of relief from the ordinance. The owner may, for instance, seek to have the ordinance amended--in other words, attempt to get the law changed—on the ground that the proposed amendment is consistent with the essence of the overall zoning plan.

A different approach would be to seek permission from the city or political subdivision to deviate from the zoning law. This permission is called a variance. A person seeking a variance usually claims that the ordinance works an undue hardship on her by denying her the opportunity to make reasonable use of her land. Examples of typical variance requests include a property owner's seeking permission to make a commercial use of her property even though it is located in an area zoned for residential purposes, or permission to deviate from normal setback or building size requirements.

Attempts to obtain variances and zoning ordinance amendments frequently clash with the interests of other owners of property in the same area—owners who have a vested interest in maintaining the status quo. As a result, variance and amendment requests often produce heated battles before local zoning authorities.

Challenges to the Validity of the Zoning Ordinance A disgruntled property owner might also attack the zoning ordinance's validity on constitutional grounds. Litigation challenging zoning ordinances has become frequent in recent years, as cities and towns have used their zoning power to achieve social control. For example, assume that a city creates special zoning requirements for adult bookstores or other uses considered moral threats to the community. Such uses of the zoning power have been challenged as unconstitutional restrictions on freedom of speech. In *City of Renton v. Playtime Theatres, Inc.*,[18] however, the Supreme Court upheld a zoning ordinance that prohibited the operation of adult bookstores within 1,000 feet of specified uses such as residential areas and schools. The Court established that the First Amendment rights of operators of adult businesses would not be violated by such an ordinance so long as the city provided them a "reasonable opportunity to open and operate" their businesses within the city.

Other litigation has stemmed from ordinances by which municipalities have attempted to "zone out" residential facilities such as group homes for developmentally disabled adults. In a leading case, the Supreme Court held that the Constitution's Equal Protection Clause was violated by a zoning ordinance that required a special use permit for such a group home.[19] The Fair Housing Act, which forbids discrimination on the basis of disability and familial status, has also been used as a basis for challenging decisions that zone out group homes. Such a challenge has a chance of success when the plaintiff demonstrates that the zoning board's actions were a mere pretext for discrimination.[20] Certain applications of zoning ordinances that establish single-family residential areas may also raise Fair Housing Act–based claims of disability discrimination.

Many cities and towns have attempted to restrict single-family residential zones to living units of traditional families related by blood or marriage. In enacting ordinances along those lines, municipalities have sought to prevent the presence of groups of unrelated students, commune members, or religious cult adherents by specifically defining the term *family* in a way that excludes these groups. In *Belle Terre v. Boraas*,[21] the Supreme Court upheld such an ordinance as applied to a group of unrelated students. The Court later held, however, that an ordinance defining *family* so as to prohibit a grandmother from living with her grandsons was an unconstitutional intrusion on personal freedom regarding family life.[22] Restrictive definitions of *family* have been held unconstitutional under state constitutions in some cases but narrowly construed by courts in other cases.

Land Use Regulation and Taking

Another type of litigation seen with increasing frequency in recent years centers around zoning laws and other land use regulations that impose burdens or diminish properties' values by restricting their permissible uses.[23] Affected property owners have challenged the application of such regulations as unconstitutional takings of property without just compensation, even though these cases do not involve the actual physical invasions present in the inverse condemnation cases discussed earlier in this chapter.

States normally have broad discretion to use their police power for the public benefit, even when that means interfering to some extent with an owner's right to develop the property as the owner desires. Some regulations, however, may interfere with an owner's use of the property to such an extent that they constitute a taking.

For instance, in *Nollan v. California Coastal Commission*,[24] the owners of a beachfront lot (the Nollans) wished to tear down a small house on the lot and replace that structure with a larger house. The California Coastal Commission conditioned the grant of the necessary coastal development permit on the Nollans' agreeing to allow the public an easement across their property. This easement would have allowed the public to reach certain nearby public beaches more easily. The Nollans challenged the validity of the Coastal Commission's action.

Ultimately, the Supreme Court concluded that the Coastal Commission's placing the easement condition on the issuance of the permit amounted to an impermissible regulatory taking of the Nollans' property. In reaching this conclusion, the Court held that the state could not avoid paying compensation to the Nollans by choosing to do by way of the regulatory route what it would have had to pay for if it had followed the formal eminent domain route.

Regulations Denying Economically Beneficial Uses What about a land use regulation that allows the property owner no *economically beneficial use* of the property? *Lucas v. South Carolina Coastal Commission*[25] was brought by a property owner, Lucas, who had paid nearly $1 million for two residential beachfront lots before South Carolina enacted a coastal protection statute. This statute's effect was to bar Lucas from building any permanent habitable structures on the lots. The trial court held that the statute rendered Lucas's property "valueless" and that an unconstitutional taking had occurred, but the South Carolina

[18]475 U.S. 41 (1986).

[19]*City of Cleburne v. Cleburne Living Centers*, 473 U.S. 432 (1985).

[20]See, for example, *Baxter v. City of Belleville*, 720 F. Supp. 720 (S.D. Ill. 1989), which involves a challenge by a hospice for AIDS patients to a city's denial of a special use permit.

[21]416 U.S. 1 (1974).

[22]*Moore v. City of East Cleveland*, 431 U.S. 494 (1977).

[23]This issue is also discussed in Chapter 3.

[24]483 U.S. 825 (1987).

[25]505 U.S. 1003 (1992).

Supreme Court reversed. The U.S. Supreme Court, however, held that when a land use regulation denies "all economically beneficial use" of property, there normally has been a taking for which just compensation must be paid. The exception to this rule, according to the Court, would be when the economically productive use being prohibited by the land use regulation was already disallowed by nuisance law or other comparable property law principles. The Court therefore reversed and remanded the case for determination of whether there had been a taking under the rule crafted by the Court, or instead an instance in which the "nuisance" exception applied. On remand, the South Carolina Supreme Court concluded that a taking calling for compensation had occurred (and, necessarily, that the nuisance exception did not apply to Lucas's intended residential use).[26]

The mere fact that a land use regulation deprives the owner of the *highest and most profitable use* of the property does not mean, however, that there has been a taking. If the regulation still allows a use that is economically beneficial in a meaningful sense—even though not the most profitable use—the *Lucas* analysis would seem to indicate

---

[26]*Lucas v. South Carolina Coastal Council*, 424 S.E.2d 484 (S.C. 1992).

that an unconstitutional taking probably did not occur. At the same time, *Lucas* offered hints that less-than-total takings (in terms of restrictions on economically beneficial uses) may sometimes trigger a right of compensation on the landowner's part. Thus, it appears that even as to land use regulations that restrict some but not all economically beneficial uses, property owners are likely to continue arguing (as they have in recent years) that the regulations go "too far" and amount to a taking.

There is no set formula for determining whether a regulation has gone too far. Courts look at the relevant facts and circumstances and weigh a variety of factors, such as the economic impact of the regulation, the degree to which the regulation interferes with the property owner's reasonable expectations, and the character of the government's invasion. The weighing of these factors occurs against the backdrop of a general presumption that state and local governments should have reasonably broad discretion to develop land use restrictions pursuant to the police power. As a result, the outcome of a case in which *regulatory taking* allegations are made is less certain than when a *physical taking* (either in the traditional sense or when there is a physical invasion of the sort addressed in the earlier discussion of inverse condemnation cases) appears to have occurred.

Problems and Problem Cases

1. In 2003, Hall acquired a sculpture by Anselm Kiefer, a German artist, and placed it on the lawn of his property fronting Harbor Road in the Southport Historic District, which is one of three historic districts in Fairfield, Connecticut. The sculpture is approximately 80 feet long and weighs more than six tons. It was placed on a specially prepared trench filled with more than 21 tons of gravel and stone. The Fairfield Historic District Commission regulates the use of historic property under a Connecticut statute that states, "No building or structure shall be erected or altered within an historic district until after an application for a certificate of appropriateness as to exterior architectural features has been submitted to the historic district commission and approved by said commission." Hall initially filed an application for a "certificate of appropriateness" with the Commission, but withdrew it before the Commission acted on it and went ahead and installed the sculpture. The Commission filed an action against Hall, seeking to force Hall to remove the sculpture or file an application for a certification of appropriateness within 30 days. Hall claims that the sculpture is not a "structure" because it is not affixed to the land by direct physical attachment nor embedded in the ground, and therefore, the Commission has no jurisdiction over the placement of the sculpture. Is the sculpture likely to be considered a "structure"?

2. Chevron U.S.A. Inc. and Sheikhpour had entered into a settlement agreement that would require Sheikhpour to complete reconstruction work on his gas station. When Sheikhpour did not do the work, Chevron sued to enforce the settlement agreement. Sheikhpour requested continued access to the property for 14 days to allow him to remove his "personal property." The parties then entered a Release and Indemnification Agreement, which allowed Sheikhpour to access the property for the sole purpose of removing his personal property. Sheikhpour informed Chevron that he intended to dig up and remove the fuel storage tanks. The tanks, which are valued at about $120,000, sit in a "tank pit area" and are covered with gravel. Are the tanks personal property or fixtures, and what difference does that make?

3. In May 1994, the Hubers rented a house to Lois Olbekson, who was the daughter of their friends, Loren and

Alice May Olbekson. Lois hoped to be able to purchase the house from the Hubers one day. The primary source of heat for the rental house was a wood furnace located in the basement. Lois was not happy with the wood furnace. In the fall of 1995, she persuaded her parents to buy an oil furnace to replace the wood furnace in the rental house. During the process of installing the new oil furnace, the old wood furnace was removed from the rental house at the Olbeksons' direction and hauled to the landfill. Installation of the oil furnace required wiring in a thermostat and drilling a hole in the wall to accommodate the fuel line from the outside oil tank, and the Olbeksons had to widen an existing doorway into the basement in order to accommodate the new oil furnace. The Olbeksons paid $2,525 to have the new oil furnace installed. The Hubers acquiesced in the installation of the new furnace but would not have done so if they had believed that they would be required to purchase it. During the time that Lois lived in the Hubers' rental house, the Hubers spent approximately $28,000 remodeling it, yet collected only $175 per month in rent. Lois admitted that before the remodeling was complete, the reasonable rental value of the house was probably $250 per month. In order to placate her husband about the rent, Emelia prepared an agreement that purported to tie the low rent to compensation for the cost of the furnace. The agreement, which Emelia and Lois signed, stated as follows:

> During October 1995, a fuel furnace for $2,525.00 was installed at 317 W. Lincoln and paid for by Loren and Alice May Olbekson. To compensate for the expense of this heating device, rent on this residence will remain at $175.00 per month thru the duration of Nov. 1st, 1995 thru Dec. 31st 1997.

Lois continued to rent the house until September 2000. Even though the written agreement provided that Lois would enjoy reduced rent only until December 31, 1997, the Hubers did not raise the rent at any time prior to the termination of the tenancy. At the end of Lois's tenancy, the Olbeksons removed the outside oil tank. Do they have the right to remove the oil furnace as well?

4. Janet and Frank Mandeville were married in 1975 and remained married until Janet died in 2002, after a battle with breast cancer. The Mandevilles acquired two properties during their marriage, their home in Macomb County and a parcel of property in Ogamaw County. They owned both properties as tenants by the entirety. Accordingly, by the right of survivorship inherent in a tenancy by the entirety, both properties passed to Frank upon Janet's death.

In the last decade of their marriage, Frank was often out of the country for extended periods. Specifically, he was absent for the 18 months preceding Janet's death. During this period, he did not try to call Janet or otherwise communicate with her, even though he knew she was seriously ill. He did not attend her funeral. In Frank's absence, Janet maintained the properties and was responsible for paying the taxes, insurance, and mortgage. She was cared for by her sister, Susan Tkachik.

In the months before she died, Janet executed a trust and will that stated her intent to disinherit her husband and leave everything to her mother. She tried to defeat the right of survivorship in the real estate by transferring her interest in them to her mother by a quitclaim deed.

In November 2003, Tkachik filed suit on behalf of the estate to effectuate Janet's intent to disinherit Frank. She claimed the Mandevilles should be considered tenants in common with regard to their real property and Frank should not obtain full ownership of the properties. Tkachik later amended her petition to seek contribution from Frank for the expenses Janet incurred in maintaining the property before her death. What is Frank's ownership interest in the properties, if any? Is he liable for contribution?

5. Aidinoff purchased land in 1979. It is adjacent to Sterling City Road but can only be reached by crossing land formerly owned by Rand. Other routes of access are impossible because of wetlands and a brook. A gravel driveway crosses the Rand land to Aidinoff's land. The person from whom Aidinoff purchased her land used the driveway for access to her land, and Aidinoff used the driveway from 1979 until 2003. She drove vehicles, walked, and brought animals across the driveway. She also used the power coming in over utility lines serving the property. After Aidinoff had begun using the driveway, she and Rand had had a conversation about the driveway, and Rand had told her that he owned it and he had no problem with her using it, but it was not "an open way for everybody to go through." In 2003, Rand sold his property to the Lathrops. After buying the property, the Lathrops blocked the driveway and prevented Aidinoff from using it to access her property. Aidinoff claimed that she had the right to use the driveway because she had acquired an easement by prescription and an easement by necessity. Did she?

6. William Jefferys's parents transferred parcels of their land to the Gardners with a deed that contained a restrictive covenant that required that a specified part of the property be kept open and free of all structures, with

certain exceptions. The deed indicated that the restrictive covenants were to be enforced by the grantors, their heirs and assigns. The Jefferys also conveyed a parcel of land above the Gardners to Souminen, who then conveyed that parcel to the Soules, who built a house on their land. The Jefferys deeded the remainder of their land to their son, William, and his wife. The Gardners wanted to build a structure on the restricted land and sought permission of William Jefferys. The Soules claimed that they were interested parties as assigns of the elder Jefferys. The Gardners began planting white pines directly in the Soules' view. The Gardners filed a declaratory judgment action about this and the Soules counterclaimed. Do the benefits and the burdens of the restrictive covenant still affect the relationship between the landowners who were not parties to it originally? And does planting the trees violate the restrictive covenant if it is still effective?

7. Schlichtling had lived on her property since 1979 and had a friendly relationship with her then-neighbors, the Nitsos. The boundary between the two parcels had never been surveyed, and the parties had a vague understanding of where the boundary lay. Schlichtling continuously and exclusively gardened, mowed, and otherwise cared for land that she thought was hers. The Nitsos sold their property to the Cotters in 2005, and the Cotters claimed that Schlichtling was encroaching on their land. The Cotters cut down trees on the disputed parcel, removed part of a stone wall, dug up the lawn, cut up a driveway that crossed the land, erected a fence, and otherwise disturbed the property. Schlichtling applied for a temporary injunction against the Cotters to stop them from entering and altering the land and to direct them to return the property to the state in which Schlichtling had maintained it. The court's decision, of course, depended on who was the rightful owner of the disputed parcel of land. During the legal proceedings, surveys showed that the land had originally been part of the Nitsos' property, but they and Schlichtling had mutually mistook the proper boundary. As such, does Schlichtling have any claim to the land?

8. The Buzby Landfill was operated from 1966 to 1978. Although it was not licensed to receive liquid industrial or chemical wastes, large amounts of hazardous materials and chemicals were dumped there. Toxic wastes began to escape from the landfill because it had no liner or cap. Tests performed by a state environmental protection agency revealed ground water contamination caused by hazardous waste seepage from the landfill. The federal Environmental Protection Agency investigated the situation and recommended that the Buzby Landfill site be considered for cleanup under the federal Superfund law, but the cleanup did not take place. During the 1980s, Canetic Corp. and Canuso Management Corp. developed a housing subdivision near the closed Buzby Landfill. Some of the homes in the subdivision were within half a mile of the old landfill. Some of the homeowners filed a class action lawsuit alleging that Canetic and Canuso had substantial information about the dangers of placing a subdivision near the landfill, but they had not disclosed to buyers the fact that the subdivision was located near a hazardous waste dump. The defendants claimed that they did not have the duty to disclose conditions that happened on someone else's property. Will the defendants win?

9. Angel Castelan and Marvin Huezo are friends who enjoy visiting the Universal Studios theme park. They were each denied access to one of their favorite rides, The Mummy, because they did not satisfy the rider requirements in the manufacturer recommendations. In particular, Castelan was turned away because the requirements indicate that each rider must have at least "one functioning arm [and] hand." Huezo was denied access to the ride because the rider requirements state that each rider must have at least one leg that may be placed behind the shin pad. Castelan's forearms were amputated due to an electrical accident when he was a child. Huezo's legs were amputated after he was hit by a car during an attempt to assist another motorist. After being turned away from The Mummy on a couple of occasions, Castelan and Huezo filed a lawsuit under Title III of the Americans with Disabilities Act for failure to design a ride that does not require rider eligibility criteria that excludes patrons with disabilities. Will their claim succeed?

10. Voyeur Dorm operates an Internet-based website that provides a 24-hour-a-day Internet transmission portraying the lives of the residents of 2312 West Farwell Drive, Tampa, Florida. Throughout its existence, Voyeur Dorm has employed 25 to 30 different women, most of whom entered into a contract that specifies, among other things, that they are "employees," on a "stage and filming location," with "no reasonable expectation of privacy," for "entertainment purposes." Subscribers to voyeurdorm.com pay a subscription fee of $34.95 a month to watch the women employed at the premises and pay an added fee of $16.00 per month to "chat" with the women. At a zoning hearing, Voyeur Dorm's counsel conceded that five women live in the house; that there are cameras in the corners of

all the rooms of the house; that for a fee a person can join a membership to a website wherein a member can view the women 24 hours a day, seven days a week; that a member, at times, can see someone disrobed; that the women receive free room and board; and that the women are paid as part of a business enterprise. From August 1998 to June 2000, Voyeur Dorm generated subscriptions and sales totaling $3,166,551.35.

Section 27-523 of Tampa's City Code defines adult entertainment establishments as:

> any premises . . . on which is offered to members of the public or any person, for a consideration, entertainment featuring or in any way including specified sexual activities . . . or entertainment featuring the displaying or depicting of specified anatomical areas . . . ; "entertainment" as used in this definition shall include, but not be limited to, books, magazines, films, newspapers, photographs, paintings, drawings, sketches or other publications or graphic media, filmed or live plays, dances or other performances either by single individuals or groups, distinguished by their display or depiction of specified anatomical areas or specified sexual activities.

The City of Tampa argues that Voyeur Dorm is an adult use business pursuant to the express and unambiguous language of section 27-523 and, as such, cannot operate in a residential neighborhood. Is the city correct?

Landlord and Tenant

Frank Johnson and Sonia Miller, along with several other friends, were looking to rent a house near campus for the following school year. In June, they orally agreed with a landlord on a one-year lease to begin the following August 15 with a monthly rent of $1,750 and provided a $2,000 security deposit. When they arrived at school in August, the current tenants were still in possession and did not move out until September 1, leaving the house a mess. The landlord told Frank and Sonia to move in and that he would clean it up later; however, he never did so despite repeated requests. They complained to the city housing department, which conducted an inspection and found numerous violations of the city's housing code. The city gave the landlord 15 days to make the necessary repairs. Before any of the repairs were made, a friend who was visiting was injured when she fell through some rotten floorboards on the porch. At the end of September, Frank, Sonia and the other tenants moved out, but the landlord refused to return their security deposit.

Among the legal issues raised by this scenario are:

- Did the oral agreement create an enforceable lease?
- Were the tenants' rights violated when they were unable to take possession on August 15?
- Does the landlord have any liability to the injured friend?
- Are the tenants entitled to terminate the lease on the grounds the house is not habitable and obtain the return of their security deposit?
- If the landlord never intended to clean up the house, was it ethical for him to tell the tenants he would do so?

LO · LEARNING OBJECTIVES

After studying this chapter, you should be able to:

25-1 Recognize that the legal principles applicable to landlord–tenant relationships are drawn from property law, contract law, and the law of negligence and that they incorporate the common law as well as legislative enactments.

25-2 Describe and differentiate the four main types of tenancies.

25-3 Understand the importance of a carefully drafted lease that makes clear the parties' rights and obligations and complies with any applicable provisions of state law, including the statute of frauds.

25-4 List and discuss the primary rights, duties, and liabilities of the landlord.

25-5 List and discuss the primary rights, duties, and liabilities of the tenant.

25-6 Describe the different ways that a lease may be terminated and identify the legal principles that apply to each method of termination.

LANDLORD-TENANT LAW HAS undergone dramatic change, owing in large part to the changing nature of the relationship between landlords and tenants. In England and in early America, farms were the usual subjects of leases. The tenant sought to lease land on which to grow crops or graze cattle. Accordingly, traditional landlord-tenant law viewed the lease as primarily a conveyance of land and paid relatively little attention to its contractual aspects.

In today's society, however, the landlord–tenant relationship is typified by the lease of property for residential or commercial purposes. A residential tenant commonly occupies only a small portion of the total property. He bargains primarily for the use of structures on the land rather than for the land itself. He is likely to have signed a landlord-provided form lease, the terms of which he may have had little or no opportunity to negotiate. In areas with a shortage of affordable housing, a residential tenant's ability to bargain for favorable lease provisions is further hampered. Because the typical landlord–tenant relationship can no longer fairly be characterized as one in which the parties have equal knowledge and bargaining power, it is not always realistic to presume that tenants are capable of negotiating to protect their own interests.

> **LO25-1** Recognize that the legal principles applicable to landlord–tenant relationships are drawn from property law, contract law, and the law of negligence and that they incorporate the common law as well as legislative enactments.

Although it was initially slow to recognize the changing nature of the landlord–tenant relationship, the law now places greater emphasis than it once did on the contract components of the relationship. As a result, modern contract doctrines such as unconscionability, constructive conditions, the duty to mitigate damages, and implied warranties are commonly applied to leases. Such doctrines may operate to compensate for tenants' lack of bargaining power. In addition, state legislatures and city councils have enacted statutes and ordinances that regulate leased property and the landlord–tenant relationship.

This chapter's discussion of landlord–tenant law will focus on the nature of leasehold interests, the traditional rights and duties of landlords and tenants, and recent statutory and judicial developments affecting those rights and duties.

Leases and Tenancies

Nature of Leases
A **lease** is a contract under which an owner of property, the landlord (also called the *lessor*), conveys to the tenant (also called the *lessee*) the exclusive right to possess property for a period of time. The property interest conveyed to the tenant is called a leasehold estate.

Types of Tenancies

 LO25-2 Describe and differentiate the four main types of tenancies.

The duration of the tenant's possessory right depends upon the type of **tenancy** established by or resulting from the lease. There are four main types of tenancies.

1. *Tenancy for a term.* In a **tenancy for a term** (also called a *tenancy for years*), the landlord and tenant have agreed on a specific duration of the lease and have fixed the date on which the tenancy will terminate. For example, if Dudley, a college student, leases an apartment for the academic year ending May 25, 2021, a tenancy for a term will have been created. The tenant's right to possess the property ends on the date agreed upon without any further notice, unless the lease contains a provision permitting extension.

2. *Periodic tenancy.* A **periodic tenancy** is created when the parties agree that rent will be paid in regular successive intervals until notice to terminate is given, but do not agree on a specific lease duration. If the tenant pays rent monthly, the tenancy is from month to month; if the tenant pays yearly, as is sometimes done under agricultural leases, the tenancy is from year to year. (Periodic tenancies therefore are sometimes called *tenancies from month to month* or *tenancies from year to year*.) To terminate a periodic tenancy, either party must give advance notice to the other. The precise amount of notice required is often defined by state statutes. For example, to terminate a tenancy from month to month, most states require that the notice be given at least one month in advance.

3. *Tenancy at will.* A **tenancy at will** occurs when property is leased for an indefinite period of time and either party may choose to conclude the tenancy at any time. Generally, tenancies at will involve situations in which the tenant either does not pay rent or does not pay it at regular intervals. For example, Landon allows her friend Trumbull to live in the apartment over her garage. Although this tenancy's name indicates that it is terminable "at [the] will" of either party, most states require that the landlord give reasonable advance notice to the tenant before exercising the right to terminate the tenancy.

4. *Tenancy at sufferance.* A **tenancy at sufferance** occurs when a tenant remains in possession of the property (holds over) after a lease has expired. In this situation, the landlord has two options: (a) treating the holdover tenant as a trespasser and bringing an action to eject him or (b) continuing to treat him as a tenant and collecting rent from him. Until the landlord makes her election, the tenant is a tenant at sufferance.

Types of Tenancies

Type of Lease	Characteristics	Termination
Tenancy for a term	Landlord and tenant agree on a specific duration of the lease and fix the date on which the tenancy will end.	Ends automatically on the date agreed upon; no additional notice necessary.
Periodic tenancy	Landlord and tenant agree that tenant will pay rent at regular, successive intervals (e.g., month to month).	Either party may terminate by giving the amount of advance notice required by state law.
Tenancy at will	Landlord and tenant agree that tenant may possess property for an indefinite amount of time, with no agreement to pay rent at regular, successive intervals.	May be terminated "at will" by either party, but state law requires advance notice.
Tenancy at sufferance	Tenant remains in possession after the termination of one of the leaseholds described above, until landlord brings ejectment action against tenant or collects rent from him.	Landlord has choice of: 1. Treating tenant as a trespasser and bringing ejectment action against him or 2. Accepting rent from tenant, thus creating a new leasehold.

Suppose that Templeton has leased an apartment for one year from Larson. At the end of the year, Templeton holds over and does not move out. Templeton is a tenant at sufferance. Larson may have him ejected or may continue treating him as a tenant. If Larson elects the latter alternative, a new tenancy is created. The new tenancy will be either a tenancy for a term or a periodic tenancy, depending on the facts of the case and any presumptions established by state law. Thus, a tenant who holds over for even a few days runs the risk of creating a new tenancy he might not want.

Execution of a Lease

 LO25-3 Understand the importance of a carefully drafted lease that makes clear the parties' rights and obligations and complies with any applicable provisions of state law, including the statute of frauds.

As transfers of interests in land, leases may be covered by the statute of frauds. In most states, a lease for a term of more than one year from the date it is made is unenforceable unless it is evidenced by a suitable writing signed by the party to be charged. A few states, however, require leases to be evidenced by a writing only when they are for a term of more than three years.

The vignette at the start of this chapter poses a situation with an oral lease entered into in June that will run for a year beginning on August 15. This lease would not be enforceable in a state where the statute of frauds requires a lease for more than a year from the date it is made to be in writing. However, it would be enforceable in a state where an oral lease for a period of less than three years is allowed.

Good business practice demands that leases be carefully drafted to make clear the parties' respective rights and obligations. Care in drafting leases is especially important in cases of long-term and commercial leases. Lease provisions normally cover such essential matters as the term of the lease, the rent to be paid, the uses the tenant may make of the property, the circumstances under which the landlord may enter the property, the parties' respective obligations regarding the condition of the property, and the responsibility (as between landlord and tenant) for making repairs. In addition, leases often contain provisions allowing a possible extension of the term of the lease and purporting to limit the parties' rights to assign the lease or sublet the property. State or local law often regulates lease terms. For example, the Uniform Residential Landlord and Tenant Act (URLTA) has been enacted in a substantial minority of states. The URLTA prohibits the inclusion of certain lease provisions, such as a clause by which the tenant supposedly agrees to pay the landlord's attorney's fees in an action to enforce the lease. In states that have not enacted the URLTA, lease terms are likely to be regulated at least to a moderate degree by some combination of state statutes, common law principles, and local housing codes.

Rights, Duties, and Liabilities of the Landlord

 LO25-4 List and discuss the primary rights, duties, and liabilities of the landlord.

Landlord's Rights The landlord is entitled to receive the *agreed rent* for the term of the lease. Upon expiration of the lease, the landlord has the right to the *return of the property in as good a condition as it was when leased*, except for normal wear and tear and any destruction caused by an act of God.

Security Deposits Landlords commonly require tenants to make security deposits or advance payments of rent. Such deposits operate to protect the landlord's right to receive rent as well as her right to reversion of the property in good condition. In recent years, many cities and states have enacted statutes or ordinances designed to prevent landlord abuse of security deposits. These laws typically limit the amount a landlord may demand and require that the security deposit be refundable, except for portions withheld by the landlord because of the tenant's nonpayment of rent or tenant-caused property damage beyond ordinary wear and tear. Some statutes or ordinances also require the landlord to place the funds in interest-bearing accounts when the lease is for more than a minimal period of time. As a general rule, these laws require landlords to provide tenants a written accounting regarding their security deposits and any portions being withheld. Such an accounting normally must be provided within a specified period of time (30 days, for example) after the termination of the lease. The landlord's failure to comply with statutes and ordinances regarding security deposits may cause the landlord to experience adverse consequences that vary state by state.

Landlord's Duties

Fair Housing Act As explained in Chapter 24, the Fair Housing Act prohibits housing discrimination on the basis of race, color, sex, religion, national origin, disability, and familial status.[1] The Fair Housing Act prohibits discriminatory practices in various transactions affecting housing, including the rental of dwellings.[2] Included within the act's prohibited instances of discrimination against a protected person are refusals to rent property to such a person; discrimination against him or her in the terms, conditions, or privileges of rental; publication of any advertisement or statement indicating any preference, limitation, or discrimination operating to the disadvantage of a protected person; and representations that a dwelling is not available for rental to such a person when, in fact, it is available.

The act also makes it a discriminatory practice for a landlord to refuse to permit a tenant with a disability to make—at his own expense—reasonable modifications to leased property. The landlord may, however, make this permission conditional on the tenant's agreement to restore the property to its previous condition upon termination of the lease, reasonable wear and tear excepted. In addition, landlords are prohibited from refusing to make reasonable accommodations in rules, policies, practices, or services if such accommodations are necessary to afford a disabled tenant equal opportunity to use and enjoy the leased premises. When constructing certain types of multifamily housing for first occupancy, property owners and developers risk violating the act if they fail to make the housing accessible to persons with disabilities.

Because of a perceived increase in the frequency with which landlords refused to rent to families with children, the act prohibits landlords from excluding families with children. If, however, the dwelling falls within the act's "housing for older persons" exception, this prohibition does not apply.[3]

Implied Warranty of Possession Landlords have certain obligations that are imposed by law whenever property is leased. One of these obligations stems from the landlord's implied warranty of possession. This warranty guarantees the tenant's right to possess the property for the term of the lease. Suppose that Turner rents an apartment from Long for a term to begin on September 1, 2021, and to end on August 31, 2022. When Turner attempts to move in on September 1, 2021, she

---

[1]Familial status is defined in Chapter 24.

[2]The act provides an exemption for certain persons who own and rent single-family houses. To qualify for this exemption, owners must not use a real estate broker or an illegal advertisement and cannot own more than three such houses at one time. It also exempts owners who rent rooms or units in dwellings in which they themselves reside, if those dwellings house no more than four families.

[3]The "housing for older persons" exception is described in Chapter 24.

finds that Carlson, the previous tenant, is still in possession of the property. In this case, Long has breached the implied warranty of possession.

Implied Warranty of Quiet Enjoyment By leasing property, the landlord also makes an implied warranty of quiet enjoyment (or *covenant of quiet enjoyment*). This covenant guarantees that the tenant's possession will not be interfered with as a result of the landlord's act or omission. In the absence of a contrary provision in the lease, allowance by state or local law, or an emergency that threatens the property, the landlord may not enter the leased property during the term of the lease. If he does, he will be liable for trespass. In some cases, courts have held that the covenant of quiet enjoyment was violated when the landlord failed to stop third parties, such as trespassers or other tenants who make excessive noise, from interfering with the tenant's enjoyment of the leased premises.

Constructive Eviction The doctrine of **constructive eviction** may aid a tenant when property becomes unsuitable for the purposes for which it was leased because of the landlord's act or omission, such as the breach of a duty to repair or the covenant of quiet enjoyment. Under this doctrine, which applies to both residential and commercial property, the tenant may terminate the lease because she has effectively been evicted as a result of the poor condition or the objectionable circumstances there. Constructive eviction gives a tenant the right to vacate the property without further rent obligation if she does so *promptly* after giving the landlord reasonable notice and an opportunity to correct the problem. Because constructive eviction requires the tenant to vacate the leased premises, it is an unattractive option, however, for tenants who cannot afford to move or do not have a suitable alternative place to live.

Landlord's Responsibility for Condition of Leased Property

The common law historically held that landlords made no implied warranties regarding the *condition* or *quality* of leased premises. As an adjunct to the landlord's right to receive the leased property in good condition at the termination of the lease, the common law imposed on the *tenant* the duty to make repairs. Even when the lease contained a landlord's express warranty or express promise to make repairs, a tenant was not entitled to withhold rent if the landlord failed to carry out his obligations. This was because a fundamental contract performance principle—that a party is not obligated to perform if the other party fails to perform—was considered inapplicable to leases. However, changing views of the landlord–tenant relationship

have resulted in dramatically increased legal responsibility on the part of landlords for the condition of leased residential property.

Implied Warranty of Habitability The legal principle that landlords made no implied warranty regarding the condition of leased property arose during an era when tenants used land primarily for agricultural purposes. Buildings existing on the property were frequently of secondary importance. They also tended to be simple structures, lacking modern conveniences such as plumbing and wiring. These buildings were fairly easily inspected and repaired by the tenant, who was generally more self-sufficient than today's typical tenant. In view of the relative simplicity of the structures, landlord and tenant were considered to have equal knowledge of the property's condition upon commencement of the lease. Thus, a rule requiring the tenant to make repairs seemed reasonable.

The position of modern residential tenants differs greatly from that of an earlier era's agricultural tenants. The modern residential tenant bargains not for the use of the ground itself but for the use of a building (or portion thereof) as a dwelling. The structures on land today are complex, frequently involving systems (such as plumbing and electrical systems) to which the tenant does not have physical access. Besides decreasing the likelihood of perceiving defects during inspection, this complexity compounds the difficulty of making repairs—something at which today's tenant already tends to be less adept than his grandparents were. Moreover, placing a duty on tenants to negotiate for express warranties and duties to repair is no longer feasible. Residential leases are now routinely executed on standard forms provided by landlords.

For these reasons, statutes or judicial decisions in most states now impose an **implied warranty of habitability** on many landlords who lease residential property. According to the vast majority of cases, this warranty is applicable only to *residential* property and not to property leased for commercial uses. The implied warranty of habitability's content in lease settings is basically the same as in the sale of real estate: The property must be safe and suitable for human habitation. In lease settings, however, the landlord not only must deliver a habitable dwelling at the beginning of the lease but also must *maintain* the property in a habitable condition during the term of the lease. Various statutes and judicial decisions provide that the warranty includes an obligation that the leased property comply with any applicable housing codes.

In the scenario set out at the start of this chapter, the tenants who arrived on the date when the lease was to begin and found that the property was not in suitable condition for habitation, including violations of the city's housing code, would have an arguable claim against the landlord for breach of implied warranty of habitability.

Remedies for Breach of Implied Warranty of Habitability From a tenant's point of view, the implied warranty of habitability is superior to constructive eviction because a tenant does not have to vacate the leased premises in order to seek a remedy for breach of the warranty. The particular remedies for breach of the implied warranty of habitability differ from state to state. Some of the remedies a tenant may pursue include:

1. *Action for damages.* The breach of the implied warranty of habitability violates the lease and renders the landlord liable for damages. The damages generally are measured by the diminished value of the leasehold. The landlord's breach of the implied warranty of habitability may also be asserted by the tenant as a counterclaim and defense in the landlord's action for eviction and/or non-payment of rent.

2. *Termination of lease.* In extreme cases, the landlord's breach of the implied warranty of habitability may justify the tenant's termination of the lease. For this remedy to be appropriate, the landlord's breach must have been substantial enough to constitute a material breach.

3. *Rent abatement.* Some states permit rent abatement, a remedy under which the tenant withholds part of the rent for the period during which the landlord was in breach of the implied warranty of habitability. Where authorized by law, this approach allows the tenant to pay a reduced rent that reflects the *actual* value of the leasehold in its defective condition. There are different ways of computing this value. State law determines the amount by which the rent will be reduced.

4. *Repair-and-deduct.* A number of states have statutes that permit the tenant to have defects repaired and to deduct the repair costs from her rent. The repairs authorized in these statutes are usually limited to essential services such as electricity and plumbing. They also require that the tenant give the landlord notice of the defect and an adequate opportunity to make the repairs himself.

Housing Codes Many cities and states have enacted housing codes that impose duties on property owners with respect to the condition of leased property. Typical of these provisions is Section 14-400.3 of the District of Columbia Municipal Regulations, which provides: "No person shall rent or offer to rent any habitation, or the furnishings of a habitation, unless such habitation and its furnishings are in a clean, safe, and sanitary condition, in repair, and free from rodents or vermin." Such codes commonly call for the provision and maintenance of necessary services such as heat, water, and electricity, as well as suitable bathroom and kitchen facilities. Housing codes also tend to require that specified minimum space-per-tenant standards be met; that windows, doors, floors, and screens be kept in repair; that the property be painted and free of lead paint; that keys and locks meet certain specifications; and that the landlord issue written receipts for rent payments. A landlord's failure to comply with an applicable housing code may result in a fine or in liability for injuries resulting from the property's disrepair. The noncompliance may also result in the landlord's losing part or all of his claim to the agreed-upon rent. Some housing codes establish that tenants have the right to withhold rent until necessary repairs have been made and the right to move out in cases of particularly egregious violations of housing code requirements.

In the case that follows, *Brooks v. Lewin Realty III, Inc.,* the court held that a landlord could be liable for injuries to a child that were caused by the landlord's failure to comply with the city's housing code.

Brooks v. Lewin Realty III, Inc.   **835 A.2d 616 (Md. Ct. App. 2003)**

In August 1988, Shirley Parker rented a house in Baltimore City. Fresh paint was applied to the interior of the house at the beginning of the tenancy. Sharon Parker, Shirley's daughter, moved into the house shortly after her mother rented it. On December 6, 1989, Sharon gave birth to Sean, who then also lived there. Early in 1991, when Sean was slightly more than a year old, Lewin Realty purchased the house at an auction. Before the purchase, one of the owners of Lewin Realty walked through the house accompanied by Sharon as he inspected it. At the time of the walk-through, there was peeling, chipping, and flaking paint present in numerous areas of the interior of the house, including in Sean's bedroom. After Lewin Realty purchased the house, it entered into a new lease with Shirley but did not paint its interior at that time.

In February 1992, Sean was diagnosed with an elevated blood lead level. In May 1992, the house was inspected and found to contain 56 areas of peeling, chipping, and flaking lead paint, and the Baltimore City Health Department (BCHD) issued a lead paint violation notice to Lewin Realty.

Section 702(a) of the Baltimore City Housing Code requires that a dwelling be kept in "good repair" and "safe condition" and prohibits a landlord from leasing a dwelling that violates the Housing Code. The Housing Code further provides that maintaining a dwelling in good repair and safe condition includes keeping all interior walls, ceilings, woodwork, doors, and windows clean and free of any flaking, loose, or peeling paint. It also mandates the removal of loose and peeling paint from interior surfaces and requires that any new paint be free of lead. The Housing Code also grants the landlord the right of access to rental dwellings at reasonable times for purpose of making inspections and such repairs as are necessary to comply with the Code.

Sharon Parker brought a lawsuit on behalf of her son, alleging, among other things, negligence. The negligence claim was founded on several grounds, including (1) Lewin Realty's violation of the Baltimore City Code; (2) Sean's exposure to an unreasonable risk of harm from the lead-based paint while Lewin Realty knew that its dangerous properties were not known to Sean and not discoverable in the exercise of reasonable care; (3) Lewin Realty's failure to exercise reasonable care in properly maintaining the walls, doors, and ceilings after Lewin Realty had actual and constructive knowledge of the flaking paint condition; and (4) Lewin Realty's failure to exercise reasonable care to inspect the dwelling's paint when a reasonable inspection would have revealed the flaking paint condition.

One of the questions in the litigation was whether the tenants were required to show that the landlord had notice of the violation in order to establish a prima facie case of negligence. Lewin Realty argued that because the tenant had control over the property and neither the common law nor any statute expressly required inspections during the tenancy, the court should not impose such a duty. Lewin Realty further argued it should not be held liable unless it had actual knowledge of the violation and that landlords who do not perform periodic inspections should not be charged with knowledge of what such inspections would reveal.

Eldridge, Justice

As the parties point out, under the common law and in the absence of a statute, a landlord ordinarily has no duty to keep rental premises in repair, or to inspect the rental premises either at the inception of the lease or during the lease term. There are, however, exceptions to this general rule.

Moreover, where there is an applicable statutory scheme designed to protect a class of persons which includes the plaintiff, another well-settled Maryland common law rule has long been applied by this Court in negligence actions. That rule states that the defendant's duty ordinarily "is prescribed by the statute" or ordinance and that the violation of the statute or ordinance is itself evidence of negligence.

Under this principle, in order to make out a *prima facie* case in a negligence action, all that a plaintiff must show is: (a) the violation of a statute or ordinance designed to protect a specific class of persons which includes the plaintiff, and (b) that the violation proximately caused the injury complained of. "Proximate cause is established by determining whether the plaintiff is within the class of persons sought to be protected, and the harm suffered is of a kind which the drafters intended the statute to prevent. . . . It is the existence of this cause and effect relationship that makes the violation of a statute *prima facie* evidence of negligence."

We stress that none of the cases we cite impose upon the plaintiff the additional burden of proving that the defendant was aware that he or she was violating the statute or ordinance. Depending upon the statute and the particular sanction involved, knowledge, and the type thereof, may or may not be pertinent in establishing whether or not there was a statutory violation. Nevertheless, once it is established that there was a statutory violation, the tort defendant's knowledge that he or she violated the statute is not part of the tort plaintiff's burden of proof. It is the violation of the statute or ordinance alone which is evidence of negligence.

This rule has been stated in the context of landlords and tenants in the *Restatement (Second) of Property, Landlord and Tenant* Section 17.6 (1977), and cited with approval by this Court in lead paint premises liability cases. Section 17.6 of the *Restatement (Second) of Property* provides (emphasis added):

A landlord is subject to liability for physical harm caused to the tenant . . . by a dangerous condition existing before or arising after the tenant has taken possession, if he has failed to exercise reasonable care to repair the condition and the existence of the condition is in violation of:

(1) an implied warranty of habitability; or

(2) *a duty created by statute or administrative regulation.*

In the instant case, the Housing Code, Baltimore City Code imposes numerous duties and obligations upon landlords who rent residential property to tenants. The plaintiffs are obviously within a class of persons which the Housing Code was designed to protect. *Brown v. Dermer*, 357 Md. 344, 367 (2000) ("Patently, by enacting Sections 702 and 703 of the Housing Code, the City Council sought to protect children from lead paint poisoning by putting landlords on notice of conditions which could enhance the risk of such injuries"). Under the established principles of Maryland tort law set forth in the previously cited cases, if the plaintiffs can establish a violation of the Housing Code which proximately caused Sean's injuries, then the plaintiffs are entitled to have count one of their complaint submitted to the trier of facts. Under the above-cited cases, the plaintiffs need not prove that Lewin Realty had notice of the Housing Code violation.

* * *

Thus, under the plain meaning of the Code's language, it is clear that the Mayor and City Council of Baltimore mandated a *continuing* duty to keep the dwelling free of flaking, loose, or peeling paint, *at all times* "while [the dwelling is] in use," in order for the landlord to remain in compliance with the Housing Code. The nature of the landlord's duty is continuous. The Housing Code does not limit the landlord's duty to keep the premises free of flaking paint to a one-time duty at the inception of the lease. The landlord must take whatever measures are necessary during the pendency of the lease to ensure the dwelling's continued compliance with the Code.

To facilitate such continuous maintenance of the leased premises, Section 909 explicitly grants a right of entry to the landlord to ensure that he or she can "make such inspections and such repairs as are necessary" to comply with the Housing Code. It states:

> Every occupant of a dwelling . . . shall give the owner thereof . . . access to any part of such dwelling . . . at all reasonable times for the purpose of making such inspection and such repairs or alterations as are necessary to effect compliance with the provisions of this Code. . . .

Although this section may not explicitly require the landlord to perform periodic inspections, it grants such right to the landlord and shows that the City anticipated that periodic inspections might be necessary to comply with the Code.

Lewin Realty urges that "during a tenancy . . . the landlord surrenders control of the property and, in doing so, surrenders the ability, at least in some respects, to prevent a violation of the housing code during the tenancy." Lewin Realty's principal argument is that the landlord has no ability to control the condition of the interior surfaces of the premises during the tenancy. We disagree. Contrary to Lewin Realty's argument, Section 909 vests the landlord with sufficient control of the leased premises during the tenancy to inspect and to rectify a condition of flaking, loose, or peeling paint.

Furthermore, contrary to Lewin Realty's statements in its brief, our holding in the instant case does not impose a strict liability regime upon landlords. Whether Lewin Realty is held liable for an injury to a child, based on lead paint poisoning, will depend on the jury's evaluation of the reasonableness of Lewin Realty's actions under all the circumstances.

Lewin Realty also contends that "the imposition of a duty to inspect during [the] tenancy would create a minefield of difficulties." The respondent's concerns that a landlord will be required to "inspect the property every day, three times a week, twice a week, twice a month, once a month . . ." are without basis. The nature of the defective condition in question—a flaking, loose, or peeling paint condition—is a slow, prolonged process which is easily detected in the course of reasonable periodic inspections. As Lewin Realty concedes, "we know that paint in a property will chip—it is just a matter of time." It does not occur overnight.

In addition, Lewin Realty raises doubts about the ability to quantify the dangerousness of a lead paint condition: "Is one area in a far corner of a property a 'dangerous condition'? . . . Is the presence of lead-based paint in the eighth layer of paint, covered by seven non-leaded layers of paint, a hazardous condition when present on a windowsill as opposed to the upper far corner of a wall?" In a negligence case, such as the case at bar, the simple answer to these questions is that it will be the duty of the trier of fact to determine whether the steps taken by the landlord to ensure continued compliance with the Code, i.e., the frequency and thoroughness of inspections, and the maintenance of the interior surfaces of the dwelling, were reasonable under all the circumstances. The test is what a reasonable and prudent landlord would have done under the same circumstances.

Finally, Lewin Realty suggests that a tenant might object to the landlord's need to inspect the premises. That concern is allayed by the fact that the Housing Code *requires* the tenant to give the owner access to the premises "at all reasonable times for the purpose of making such inspections . . . as are necessary to effect compliance with the provisions of this Code." Section 909.

JUDGMENT OF THE COURT OF SPECIAL APPEALS AFFIRMED.

Raker, Judge, dissenting

I respectfully dissent. The majority explicitly overrules *Richwind v. Brunson*, 335 Md. 661 (1994)—a case that, until today, had never had any doubt cast upon it by this Court or any other—and holds that by enacting the Baltimore City Housing Code, the City Council intended to abolish the element of notice in a common law negligence action for injuries resulting from flaking, loose or peeling paint. In the process of overruling *Richwind*, the majority also reads into the Code an ongoing, affirmative duty by landlords to inspect periodically each of their housing units for loose or flaking paint for as long as they retain ownership of the premises. I disagree with the majority's conclusion that the ordinance does away with the traditional, common law notice requirement to the landlord as a precursor to liability for negligence.

It is helpful to understand first what the majority's holding actually means and its implications for landlords and tenants in Baltimore. A violation of Baltimore's Housing Code occurs when the landlord does not comply with Section 703, which mandates, in relevant part, that "all walls, ceilings, woodwork, doors and windows shall be kept clean and free of any flaking, loose or peeling paint. . . ." The majority asserts that "if the plaintiffs can establish a violation of the Housing Code which proximately caused [their] injuries, then the plaintiffs are entitled to have . . . their complaint submitted to the trier of facts." Read together, the result of the majority's holding is astounding: *Any* flaking, loose or peeling paint in a leased premises, combined with an injury from lead paint, automatically gives rise to a cognizable action, worthy of a jury trial. The majority admits as much in summarizing its holding:

> In sum, the presence of flaking, loose, or peeling paint is a violation of the Housing Code. As earlier pointed out, certain provisions of the Housing Code were clearly enacted to

prevent lead poisoning in children. Therefore, the plaintiff Sean is in the class of people intended to be protected by the Housing Code, and his injury, lead poisoning, is the kind of injury intended to be prevented by the Code. *This is all the plaintiffs must show to establish a* prima facie *case sounding in negligence.*

The majority's new rule means that the landlord will be forced to defend the case in court even if the plaintiff concedes that the landlord behaved reasonably in not knowing about a Code violation. Without any express instruction, the majority reads into the statute the dramatic institution of a wholly new regulatory scheme that essentially imposes strict liability upon landlords and makes landlords the insurers of litigants for injuries sustained by a minor plaintiff due to exposure to lead-based paint. Furthermore, the majority's new rule means that plaintiff tenants will no longer be required to notify landlords of hazards in their dwelling home, hazards that they, not the landlord, are in the best position to identify.

The common law used to deal with such unfairness by providing that a landlord who had a valid excuse, such as lack of notice, for not remedying the violation would not be held liable, *see Restatement (Second) of Torts* Section 288A(2)(b) (1965) (excusing liability for violation of a legislative enactment or administrative regulation when defendant neither knows nor should know of the occasion for compliance). But under the majority's new rule, no such excuse is relevant.

Americans with Disabilities Act Landlords leasing property constituting a *place of public accommodation* (primarily commercial property as opposed to private residential property) must pay heed to Title III of the Americans with Disabilities Act. Under Title III, owners and possessors of real property that is a place of public accommodation may be expected to make reasonable accommodations, including physical modifications of the property, in order to allow people with disabilities to have access to the property. Chapter 24 contains a detailed discussion of Title III's provisions.

Landlord's Tort Liability

Traditional No-Liability Rule There were two major effects of the traditional rule that a landlord had no legal responsibility for the condition of the leased property. The first effect—that the uninhabitability of the premises traditionally did not give a tenant the right to withhold rent, assert a defense to nonpayment, or terminate a lease—has already been discussed. The second effect was that landlords normally could not be held liable in tort for injuries

suffered by tenants on leased property. This state of affairs stemmed from the notion that the tenant had the ability and responsibility to inspect the property for defects before leasing it. By leasing the property, the tenant was presumed to take it as it was, with any existing defects. As to any defects that might arise during the term of the lease, the landlord's tort immunity was seen as justified by his lack of control over the leased property once he had surrendered it to the tenant.

Traditional Exceptions to No-Liability Rule Even before the current era's protenant legal developments, however, courts created exceptions to the no-liability rule. In the following situations, landlords have traditionally owed the tenant (or an appropriate third party) a duty the breach of which could constitute a tort:

1. *Duty to maintain common areas.* Landlords have a duty to use reasonable care to *maintain the common areas* (such as stairways, parking lots, and elevators) over which they retain control. If a tenant or a tenant's guest sustains injury as a result of the landlord's negligent maintenance of a common area, the landlord is liable.

2. *Duty to disclose hidden defects.* Landlords have the duty to disclose hidden defects about which they know, if the defects are not reasonably discoverable by the tenant. The landlord is liable if a tenant or appropriate third party suffers injury because of a hidden danger that was known to the landlord but went undisclosed.

3. *Duty to use reasonable care in performing repairs.* If a landlord repairs leased property, he must *exercise reasonable care in making the repairs.* The landlord may be liable for the consequences stemming from negligently performed repairs, even if he was not obligated to perform them.

4. *Duty to maintain property leased for admission to the public.* The landlord has a duty to suitably maintain property that is leased for *admission to the public.* A theater would be an example.

5. *Duty to maintain furnished dwellings.* The landlord who rents a *fully furnished dwelling* for a short time impliedly warrants that the premises are safe and habitable.

Except for the above circumstances, the landlord traditionally was not liable for injuries suffered by the tenant on leased property. Note that none of these exceptions would apply to one of the most common injury scenarios—when the tenant was injured by a defect in her own apartment and the defect resulted from the landlord's failure to repair, rather than from negligently performed repairs.

Current Trends in Landlord's Tort Liability Today, the traditional rule of landlord tort immunity has largely been abolished. The proliferation of housing codes and the development of the implied warranty of habitability have persuaded a majority of courts to impose on landlords the duty to use *reasonable care* in their maintenance of the leased property. As discussed earlier, a landlord's duty to keep the property in repair may be based on an express clause in the lease, the implied warranty of

habitability, or provisions of a housing code or statute. The landlord now may be liable if injury results from her negligent failure to carry out her duty to make repairs. As a general rule, a landlord will not be liable unless she had *notice* of the defect and a reasonable opportunity to make repairs.

Applying these principles to the vignette at the beginning of this chapter, a landlord who was on notice of a significant defect in property he had leased, namely rotten floorboards in a porch, and who failed to make repairs in a timely fashion probably would be liable for injuries sustained by an invitee of the tenants.

The duty of care landlords owe tenants has been held to include the duty to take reasonable steps to protect tenants from substantial risks of harm created by other tenants. Courts have held landlords liable for tenants' injuries resulting from dangerous conditions (such as vicious animals) maintained by other tenants when the landlord knew or had reason to know of the danger.

It is not unusual for landlords to attempt to insulate themselves from negligence liability to tenants by including an *exculpatory clause* in the standard form leases they expect tenants to sign. An exculpatory clause purports to relieve the landlord from legal responsibility that the landlord could otherwise face (on negligence or other grounds) in certain instances of premises-related injuries suffered by tenants. In recent years, a number of state legislatures and courts have frowned upon exculpatory clauses when they are included in leases of residential property. There has been an increasing judicial tendency to limit the effect of exculpatory clauses or declare them unenforceable on public policy grounds when they appear in residential leases.

In the case that follows, *Wendzel v. Feldstein*, the Court of Appeals of Michigan considers what sorts of lease terms might act as a disfavored exculpatory clause. A Michigan statute prohibits such clauses; however, as the court notes, that does not mean the landlord will inevitably bear the risk of actually paying the damages caused by its own negligence.

| **Wendzel v. Feldstein** | **2015 WL 7288057 (Mich. Ct. App. Nov. 17, 2015)** |

Susan Feldstein leased an apartment at Whethersfield Apartments in Bloomfield Hills, Michigan. Though the lease prohibited dogs "in the Apartment or common areas," Feldstein adopted and brought home to her apartment an eight- or nine-year-old German Shepherd named Dreidel. Due to the developments addressed below, DeAnna Bruzos, Whethersfield's manager, learned that Feldstein was keeping Dreidel in her apartment. Bruzos delivered to Feldstein Whethersfield's standard "dog pet addendum" to the lease. The addendum permitted the lessee to keep one dog in her apartment as long as the lessee agreed to the terms of the addendum and paid a refundable $200 pet deposit. The addendum included the following language in paragraph 6: "Resident *agrees to indemnify and hold Landlord harmless from any and all claims arising out of the presence of said pet. Resident also affirms that renters insurance will be in force for the duration of the lease."*

Feldstein signed the addendum and paid the deposit. She and Whethersfield agree that the terms of the addendum applied retroactively to the date she signed her lease. She never secured renters insurance.

Prior to moving to Whethersfield and adopting Dreidel, Feldstein had fostered the dog. Dreidel's previous owner kept him in the basement most of the time. As a result, Dreidel had serious problems with socialization. During the seven months that Dreidel lived with Feldstein at Whethersfield, he bit three people in the apartment complex's common areas. Dreidel's first victim was a drunken neighbor who allegedly ignored Feldstein's order to stay back while she walked Dreidel on a leash. No one notified Whethersfield of this incident. The second victim was Peter Lee, a young boy who was riding his bicycle near the edge of Feldstein's back patio in the complex's courtyard. Dreidel broke free from a 12-foot steel cable attached to a stake just outside Feldstein's door and bit Peter's ankle. Peter's parent told Bruzos about this episode, which was what prompted her to deliver the addendum to Feldstein. Bruzos and Feldstein also discussed plans for keeping Dreidel leashed and muzzled in any of the common areas.

Nonetheless, a little over a month later, Feldstein's neighbor, Carold Wendzel, was walking on a path through the middle of the courtyard when Dreidel emerged from behind the patio privacy wall of Feldstein's apartment and bit her leg, knocking her to the ground and breaking her ankle. Dreidel apparently broke free once again from a 12-foot tether with a reinforced collar.

Animal control seized Dreidel, and after a 10-day quarantine period, Feldstein had Dreidel euthanized.

Wendzel filed suit against Feldstein and Whethersfield, claiming strict liability and negligence against Feldstein and negligence against Whethersfield. Whethersfield filed a cross-complaint against Feldstein seeking indemnification under the pet addendum.

Wendzel and Whethersfield settled for $30,000, after which the court granted Whethersfield's motion for summary judgment against Feldstein, reasoning that the language of paragraph 6 of the pet addendum clearly and unambiguously obligated Feldstein to indemnify Whethersfield for losses related to Wendzel's injury, which were due to the presence of Feldstein's dog.

Feldstein appealed.

Per Curiam

Feldstein first contends that the indemnification clause in paragraph 6 of the pet addendum violates public policy because it conflicts with . . . Michigan's Truth in Renting Act, [which] provides in relevant part:

A rental agreement shall not include a provision that does 1 or more of the following: . . .

(e) Exculpates the lessor from liability for the lessor's failure to perform, or negligent performance of, a duty imposed by law. . . .

Feldstein argues that the indemnification requirement illegally exculpated Whethersfield from liability for Whethersfield's breach of its nondelegable duty to maintain the common areas "fit for the use intended by the parties," thereby free from Dreidel's attacks. . . .

The language of the indemnification agreement is plain, unambiguous, and broad in scope. It requires Feldstein to indemnify Whethersfield from "any and all claims arising out of the presence of" Dreidel in the apartment complex. Feldstein does not dispute the meaning of this provision.

Landlords have "a duty of care to keep the premises within their control reasonably safe from physical hazard," and to generally keep common areas "reasonably safe." *Bailey v. Schaaf*, 835 N.W.2d 413 (Mich. 2013). According to Feldstein, this includes protecting tenants "from foreseeable activities in the common areas where for example the presence of a 'vicious'

dog might be found." By transferring this duty to Feldstein through the indemnification clause in the pet addendum, Feldstein contends, Whethersfield "effectively exculpated itself from liability arising from violation of the duty imposed by law." We [disagree], as the indemnification agreement did not "exculpate" Whethersfield.

Exculpatory clauses in residential leases that negate a landlord's statutory duties are unenforceable because they violate public policy[; however, w]e are unpersuaded that the indemnification provision in Feldstein's lease amounts to an illegal exculpation clause. First, nothing in paragraph 6 (or the balance of the lease) absolves Whethersfield of its own liability for breaches of its standard of care. Assuming that Whethersfield bore a statutory duty to keep the common areas safe from "vicious dogs," the indemnification agreement simply did not delegate that duty to Feldstein. . . . [N]othing in the lease or the addendum released Whethersfield from the obligation to keep the premises safe from physical or other hazards. As stated by the Supreme Court of Colorado in a somewhat analogous case:

An agreement to indemnify against liability for the breach of a duty is clearly not the equivalent of delegating that duty to another. An agreement to indemnify in no way purports to relieve the indemnitee of a duty owed to someone else, whether that duty is considered delegable or not. As in this case, an indemnitee remains liable to another for injury resulting from its breach of a duty owed to the injured party, and its indemnitor merely agrees to hold the indemnitee harmless from such loss or damage as may be specified in their contract. Significantly, an agreement to indemnify, by definition, does not (and could not, without becoming something more than an agreement to indemnify) purport to substitute an indemnitor for an indemnitee, or in any way diminish the indemnitee's obligation to a party it has injured, whether the indemnitor ultimately fulfills its agreement or not. [*Constable v. Northglenn, LLC*, 248 P.3d 714, 718 (Colo. 2011).]

Rather than immunizing Whethersfield from its statutory duties, paragraph 6 identified the tenant as the party bearing ultimate financial responsibility when a tenant's dog causes injuries or damage on the premises. As articulated in *Constable*, "It is often the case that such an allocation of the risk of injury, without regard to fault, serves as a constituent component of the consideration demanded for entering into a lease agreement." *Id.* Unlike [a true exculpatory] provision . . . , the language of paragraph 6 merely allocates financial responsibility for loss incurred by the landlord that was occasioned by an act or omission of the tenant.

Nor do we find objectionable the fact that the provision serves in part to reimburse Whethersfield for its own failure to take more aggressive actions against Feldstein and Dreidel after the Peter Lee incident. This Court has held that an indemnification agreement may be upheld despite that it indemnifies an indemnitee for its own negligence:

Michigan courts have discarded the additional rule of construction that indemnity contracts will not be construed to provide indemnification for the indemnitee's own negligence unless such an intent is expressed clearly and unequivocally in the contract. Instead, broad indemnity language may be interpreted to protect the indemnitee against its own negligence if this intent can be ascertained from "other language in the contract, surrounding circumstances, or from the purpose sought to be accomplished by the parties." [*Sherman v. DeMaria Bldg Co, Inc.*, 513 N.W.2d 187 (Mich. Ct. App. 1994).]

Thus, the clear and unequivocal language of the agreement does not collide with any public policy considerations.

* * *

We affirm.

Ethics and Compliance in Action

Disclosing Possible Hazards to Tenants

Suppose you own an older home that in the past was painted with lead-based paint. You rent it to a family with three small children. A state law forbids using lead-based paint on residential property after the effective date of the statute, but it does not require owners of property with residues of lead-based paint to remove it. Should you disclose the presence of the lead-based paint to your tenants? What legal liability might you incur if you do not do so?

Landlord's Liability for Injuries Resulting from Others' Criminal Conduct Another aspect of the trend toward increasing landlords' legal accountability is that many courts have imposed on landlords the duty to take reasonable steps to protect tenants and others on their property from foreseeable criminal conduct.[4] Although landlords are not insurers of the safety of persons on their property, an increasing number of courts have found them liable for injuries sustained by individuals who were criminally attacked on the landlord's property if the attack was facilitated by the landlord's failure to comply with housing codes or maintain reasonable security. This liability has been imposed on residential and commercial landlords (such as shopping mall owners). Some courts have held that the implied warranty of habitability includes the obligation to provide reasonable security. In most states that have imposed this type of liability, however, principles of negligence or negligence per se furnish the controlling rationale.[5]

In the case that follows, *Tan v. Arnel Management Company*, a California court applied negligence principles in holding that a landlord violated its duty of care to a tenant who was rendered a quadriplegic when shot in the course of an attempted carjacking on a common area of an apartment complex.

---

[4]Chapter 24 contains a more extensive discussion of courts' recent inclination to impose this duty on owners and possessors of property.

[5]The law of negligence is covered in detail in Chapter 7.

Tan v. Arnel Management Company   170 Cal. App. 4th 1087 (2009)

Arnel Management Company manages the Pheasant Ridge Apartments, a 620-unit, multibuilding apartment complex with more than 1,000 residents situated on 20.59 acres in Rowland Heights, California. The entrance road bisects the property. The beginning of the entrance road has a grassy median and is bordered on both sides by tennis courts. A little farther up the road lie two open parking lots. One is a visitor lot, located on one side of the entrance road, and the other is the parking lot for the leasing office, located on the other side of the road. Just before the two parking lots, in the middle of the entrance road, sits a "guard shack." Continuing past the two parking lots to the back of the property, the entrance road fans out into a circle by which vehicles can turn left or right through two security gates. The apartments are located beyond the security gates. The gates are remote-control operated. Most of the property's parking spaces lie behind these gates by the apartments.

Yu Fang Tan, his wife Chun Kuei Chang, and their son moved into Pheasant Ridge in July 2002 and received one assigned parking space. Tenants could pay an additional fee for a garage, but Tan and his family chose not to rent one. At the time they leased the apartment, they learned that if they had a second car, they could park it in unassigned parking spaces throughout the complex or in one of the two lots for visitors and the leasing office, as long as the car was removed from the leasing office lot before 7:00 A.M.

At around 11:30 P.M. on December 28, 2002, Tan arrived home and drove around the property looking for an open parking space because his wife had parked the family's other car in their assigned space. Unable to locate an available space, Tan parked in the leasing office parking lot outside the gated area.

As Tan was parking his car, an unidentified man approached him and asked for help. When Tan opened his window, the man pointed a gun at Tan and told him to get out of the car because the man wanted it. Tan responded, "Okay. Let me park my car first." But the car rolled a little, at which point the assailant shot the plaintiff in the neck. The incident rendered Tan a quadriplegic.

Tan and his wife brought suit against Arnel Management alleging, among other things, negligence and loss of consortium. Arnel Management sought and obtained a pretrial hearing to ascertain whether Tan's proposed evidence of prior similar criminal conduct was sufficiently similar to make the assault on Tan foreseeable.

Tan's expert, a UCLA sociology professor, looked at police reports, complaints to the police, property management reports, and records of Pheasant Ridge's security services. After excluding from his analysis those prior incidents involving attacks by acquaintances, he found 10 incidents he viewed as being "particularly significant warning signs," of which three involved "prior violent incidents." All of the incidents involved a sudden attack without warning late at night by a stranger who was on the ungated portion of the premises. Tan also presented nearly 80 examples of thefts from garages or cars or thefts of cars occurring on the Pheasant Ridge property, but the trial court excluded the evidence because the incidents did not involve robberies or violent attacks on people.

In response to a question from the court as to what additional security measures Tan was contending fell within the apartment manager's duty to have in place in order to prevent the harm he sustained, Tan's counsel indicated they wanted gates installed on the entrance roadway before the leasing office and visitor parking lots, rather than at the back of the entrance road. The purpose would be to effectively deter escape and to reduce the probability of a carjack occurring. He also indicated that Tan was not asking that any measure be undertaken that would require ongoing surveillance or monitoring or necessitate the expenditure of funds. The expert presented evidence that when gates were installed in crime areas, the rate of violence went down as potential offenders want to anticipate an easy escape. Moreover, gates deter strangers who must explain their presence on the property.

The trial court ruled that Tan had failed to demonstrate that enclosing the entire complex, moving the gates, and installing some system or a guard that would let invited guests enter the complex at night, as Tan proposed, would be any less burdensome than providing full-time security guards at night. Therefore, the court observed that in order to impose a duty on the apartment manager, Tan would have to demonstrate a high degree of foreseeability of the crime committed against Tan based upon prior similar incidents of violent crime at Pheasant Ridge. However, the court ruled that none of the prior incidents referenced by Tan's expert involved a prior attempted carjacking, or of an attempted murder, or of anyone being shot, or shot at. Therefore, the trial court held that Arnel Management had no duty to take the additional security measures proposed by Tan to enhance the security in the common areas, including the leasing office parking lot where the crime occurred. Tan appealed.

Aldrich, Judge

b. The duty of landlords to prevent third-party criminal acts on their premises

To succeed in a negligence action, the plaintiff must show that (1) the defendant owed the plaintiff a legal duty, (2) the defendant breached the duty, and (3) the breach proximately or legally caused (4) the plaintiff's damages or injuries.

Our Supreme Court has clearly articulated the scope of a landowner's duty to provide protection from foreseeable third-party criminal acts. It is determined in part by balancing the foreseeability of the harm against the burden of the duty to be imposed. In cases where the burden of preventing future harm is great, a high degree of foreseeability may be required. On the other hand, in cases where there are strong policy reasons for preventing the harm, or the harm can be prevented by simple means, a lesser degree of foreseeability may be required. Duty in such circumstances is determined by a balancing of foreseeability of the criminal acts against the burdensomeness, vagueness and efficacy of the proposed security measures. The higher the burden to be imposed on the landowner, the higher the degree of foreseeability is required.

The appropriate analytical approach was confirmed by the Supreme Court in *Castaneda v. Olsher,* 41 Cal. 4th 1205 (2007). First, the court must determine the specific measures the defendant should have taken to prevent the harm. This frames the issue for the court's determination by defining the scope of the duty under consideration. Second, the court must analyze how financially and socially burdensome these proposed measures would be to a landlord, which measures could range from minimally burdensome to significantly burdensome under the facts of the case. Third, the court must identify the nature of the third-party conduct that the plaintiff claims could have been prevented had the landlord taken the proposed measures and assess how foreseeable (on a continuum from a mere possibility to a reasonable probability) it was that this conduct would occur. Once the burden and foreseeability have been independently assessed, they can be compared in determining the scope of the duty the court imposes on a given defendant. The more certain the likelihood of harm, the higher the burden a court will impose on a landlord; the less foreseeable the harm, the lower the burden a court will impose on a landlord.

c. The trial court erred in finding defendants owed no duty.

Referring to the first step of the analysis, i.e., the specific security measures that plaintiffs proposed defendants should have taken, the record shows that plaintiff requested minimal changes. Professor Katz recommended (1) moving the existing security gates from the back of the access road, or (2) installing very similar gates before the visitor and leasing office parking lots. Any gate could remain open during the day to allow business in the leasing office. Plaintiffs clearly stated they were *not* asking for the hiring of a guard or for any form of ongoing surveillance or monitoring.

Furthermore, existing fencing extends around almost the entire perimeter of the property, only a "very minor" extension over a "very small area" would be necessary to close the fencing gap.

The second issue requires the court to analyze how financially and socially onerous the proposed measures would be to the landlord. The evidence adduced at the hearing was that the cost to defendants to install the two security gates barricading the two roads at the back of the property was about $13,500. And plaintiffs suggested using the same gates for the front of the property. Although plaintiffs presented no evidence about the cost of extending the fence, notably Professor Katz testified that would necessitate only a "minor extension" because the property is already almost completely surrounded by walls *and could even involve merely mounding dirt.* As plaintiffs observed, their proposed security measures involved a one-time expenditure and did not require ongoing surveillance of any kind, or the expenditure of significant funds. We disagree with the trial court that the proposed security measures were onerous.

Turning to the heart of the case, the third element of foreseeability, the plaintiffs demonstrated three prior incidents of sudden, unprovoked, increasingly violent assaults on people in *ungated parking* areas on the Pheasant [R]idge premises by a stranger in the middle of the night, causing great bodily injury. We conclude that plaintiffs presented substantial evidence of prior similar incidents or other indications of a reasonably foreseeable risk of violent criminal assaults on the property so as to impose on defendants a duty to provide the comparatively minimal security measures plaintiffs described.

The court here required a heightened showing of foreseeability necessitating nearly identical prior crimes, in part, because the court perceived the proposed security to be onerous. We have already concluded that the actual measures sought were not especially burdensome under the facts of this case. Thus, the court's ruling is erroneous that where none of these incidents involved guns, shootings, attempted carjacking, or attempted murder, the incidents were not sufficiently similar to meet the heightened standard of foreseeability.

Perfect identity of prior crimes to the attack on plaintiff is not necessary. Under the Supreme Court's "sliding scale balancing formula," heightened foreseeability is required to impose a high burden whereas some showing of a lesser degree of foreseeability is sufficient where a minimum burden is sought to be imposed on defendants. Because plaintiffs have only asked for relatively minimal security measures—ones already taken by defendants in another portion of the property—the degree of foreseeability here is not especially high. As a matter of law, therefore, the three prior incidents cited are sufficiently similar to make the assault on plaintiff foreseeable and to place a duty of care on defendants. Accordingly, the trial court erred in ruling defendants had no duty of care in this case.

Judgment in favor of Arnel Management Company reversed.

Rights, Duties, and Liabilities of the Tenant

 LO25-5 List and discuss the primary rights, duties, and liabilities of the tenant.

Rights of the Tenant The tenant has the right to *exclusive possession* and *quiet enjoyment* of the property during the term of the lease. The landlord is not entitled to enter the leased property without the tenant's consent, unless an emergency threatens the property or the landlord is acting under an express lease provision or a state or local law giving her the right to enter. The tenant may use the leased premises for any lawful purpose that is reasonable and appropriate, unless the purpose for which it may be used is expressly limited in the lease. Furthermore, the tenant has both the right to receive leased residential property in a habitable condition at the beginning of the lease and the right to have the property maintained in a habitable condition for the duration of the lease.

The *Miller* case that appears at the end of the chapter discusses the tenant's rights of exclusive possession and quiet enjoyment.

Duty to Pay Rent The tenant, of course, has the duty to pay rent in the agreed amount and at the agreed times. If two or more persons are cotenants on the same lease, their liability under the lease is generally *joint and several*. This means that each cotenant has complete responsibility—not just partial responsibility—for performing the tenants' duties under the lease. For example, Alberts and Baker rent an apartment from Caldwell, with both Alberts and Baker signing a one-year lease. If Alberts moves out after three months, Caldwell may hold Baker responsible for the entire rent, not just half of it. Naturally, Alberts remains liable on the lease—as well as to Baker under any rent-sharing agreement the two of them had—but Caldwell is free to proceed against Baker solely if Caldwell so chooses.

Duty Not to Commit Waste The tenant also has the duty not to commit **waste** on the property. This means that the tenant is responsible for the routine care and upkeep of the property and that he has the duty not to commit any act that would harm the property. In the past, fulfillment of this duty required that the tenant perform necessary repairs. Today, the duty to make repairs has generally been shifted to the landlord by court ruling, statute, or lease provision. The tenant now has no duty to make major repairs unless the relevant damage was caused by his own negligence. When damage exists through no fault of the tenant and the tenant

therefore is not obligated to make the actual repairs, the tenant nonetheless has the duty to take reasonable interim steps to prevent further damage from the elements. This duty would include, but not necessarily be limited to, informing the landlord of the problem. The duty would be triggered, for instance, when a window breaks or the roof leaks.

Assignment and Subleasing As with rights and duties under most other types of contracts, the rights and duties under a lease may generally be assigned and delegated to third parties. **Assignment** occurs when the landlord or the tenant transfers all of her remaining rights under the lease to another person. For example, a landlord may sell an apartment building and assign the relevant leases to the buyer, who will then become the new landlord. A tenant may assign the remainder of her lease to someone else, who then acquires whatever rights the original tenant had under the lease (including, of course, the right to exclusive possession of the leased premises).

Subleasing occurs when the tenant transfers to another person some, but not all, of his remaining right to possess the property. The relationship of tenant to sublessee then becomes one of landlord and tenant. For example, Dorfman, a college student whose 18-month lease on an apartment is to terminate on December 31, 2021, sublets his apartment to Wembley for the summer months of 2021. This is a sublease rather than an assignment because Dorfman has not transferred all of his remaining rights under the lease.

The significance of the assignment–sublease distinction is that an assignee acquires rights and duties under the lease between the landlord and the original tenant, but a sublessee does not. An assignee steps into the shoes of the original tenant and acquires any rights she had under the lease.[6] For example, if the lease contained an option to renew, the assignee would have the right to exercise this option. The assignee, of course, becomes personally liable to the landlord for the payment of rent.

Unless otherwise stated in the original lease, under both an assignment and a sublease, the original tenant remains liable to the landlord for the commitments made in the lease. If the assignee or sublessee fails to pay rent, for example, the tenant has the legal obligation to pay it. The Concept Review box compares the characteristics of assignments and subleases.

Lease Provisions Limiting Assignment Leases commonly contain limitations on assignment and subleasing. This is especially true of commercial leases. Such provisions typically require the landlord's consent to any assignment or sublease, or purport to prohibit such a transfer of the tenant's interests.

---

[6]Assignment is discussed in detail in Chapter 17.

Comparison of Assignment and Sublease	Sublease	Assignment
Does the tenant transfer to the third party *all* his remaining rights under the lease?	No	Yes
Does the tenant remain liable on the lease?	Yes	Yes
Does the third party (assignee or sublessee) acquire rights and duties under the tenant's lease with the landlord?	No	Yes

Provisions requiring the landlord's consent are upheld by the courts, although some courts hold that the landlord cannot withhold consent unreasonably. Total prohibitions against subleasing or assignment may be enforced as well, but they are disfavored in the law. Courts usually construe them narrowly, resolving ambiguities against the landlord. Additionally, in recent years, many state and local laws invalidate lease terms prohibiting subleasing or assignment.

Tenant's Liability for Injuries to Third Persons

The tenant is normally liable to persons who suffer harm while on the portion of the property over which the tenant has control, *if the injuries resulted from the tenant's negligence.*

Termination of the Leasehold

 LO25-6 Describe the different ways that a lease may be terminated and identify the legal principles that apply to each method of termination.

A leasehold typically terminates because the lease term has expired. Sometimes, however, the lease is terminated early because of a party's material breach of the lease or because of mutual agreement.

Eviction

If a tenant breaches the lease (most commonly, by nonpayment of rent), the landlord may take action to **evict** the tenant. State statutes usually establish a relatively speedy eviction procedure. The landlord who desires to evict a tenant must be careful to comply with any applicable state or city regulations governing evictions. These regulations usually forbid self-help measures on the landlord's part, such as forcible entry to change locks. At common law, a landlord had a lien on the tenant's personal property. The landlord therefore could remove and hold such property as security for the rent obligation. This lien has been abolished in many states. Where the lien still exists, it is subject to

constitutional limitations requiring that the tenant be given notice of the lien, as well as an opportunity to defend and protect his belongings before they can be sold to satisfy the rent obligation.

Agreement to Surrender

A lease may terminate prematurely by mutual agreement between landlord and tenant to surrender the lease (i.e., return the property to the landlord prior to the end of the lease). A valid surrender discharges the tenant from further liability under the lease.

Abandonment

Abandonment occurs when the tenant unjustifiably and permanently vacates the leased premises before the end of the lease term, and defaults in the payment of rent. If a tenant abandons the leased property, he is making an offer to surrender the leasehold. As shown in the Concept Review box, the landlord must make a decision at this point. If the landlord's conduct shows acceptance of the tenant's offer of surrender, the tenant is relieved of the obligation to pay rent for the remaining period of the lease. If the landlord does not accept the surrender, she may sue the tenant for the rent due until such time as she rents the property to someone else, or, if she cannot find a new tenant, for the rent due for the remainder of the term.

At common law, the landlord had no obligation to mitigate (decrease) the damages caused by the abandonment by attempting to rent the leased property to a new tenant. In fact, taking possession of the property for the purpose of trying to rent it to someone else was a risky move for the landlord—her retaking of possession might be construed as acceptance of the surrender. Historically, a nonbreaching landlord had no duty to mitigate damages in most jurisdictions. Today, however, all but six of the states impose a duty on landlords to mitigate damages, usually by making a reasonable effort to rerent the property. Most of these states also hold that the landlord's retaking of possession for the purpose of rerenting does not constitute a waiver of her right to pursue an action to collect unpaid rent.

The following *Miller* case explores the notion of abandonment and the landlord's duty to mitigate damages.

Miller v. Burnett	397 P.3d 448 (Kan. Ct. App. 2017)

William Burnett rented 35 acres of pastureland to Linda Miller, pursuant to an oral lease agreement under which Miller agreed to pay $1,000 per year for a period of roughly six years. Miller and her husband used the land to grow and harvest brome grass for grazing their cattle.

Burnett claimed that Miller failed to pay the $1,000 rent for 2015. Because of that, he permitted his neighbor's four horses to graze on the rented pastureland in late summer and then denied Miller access to the pastureland from December 2015 through February 2016.

At that point, Miller sued Burnett in small-claims court for violation of the lease and sought half the cost of fertilizing the pastureland, half the rent, the cost of feeding their cattle instead of grazing them, and an unspecified amount for being denied access to the property. Burnett filed a counterclaim against Miller for the unpaid rent as well as other alleged wrongdoing by Miller not relevant to the issue presented here.

The small-claims court denied Miller's claims and granted Burnett's claim for rent. Miller appealed that decision to the district court. The district court also denied Miller's claims and ordered her to pay Burnett $1,000 for the unpaid rent. The district court reasoned that Burnett had not breached the lease by allowing the horses to graze and cutting off Miller's access to the land because he was "obligated upon [Miller]'s breach to mitigate his damages."

Miller appealed.

Leben, Judge

In a landlord-tenant context, only a minority of states recognize a duty to mitigate damages. The majority rule is that if a tenant abandons the lease, the landlord doesn't have to try to find a new tenant; the landlord can just sue the abandoning tenant for the full amount of rent owed under the lease. But Kansas follows the minority rule: If a tenant abandons a lease, the landlord has a duty to try to find a new tenant rather than just suing the original tenant for any remaining rent. But the duty to mitigate damages doesn't arise *until* a tenant abandons the lease. And there's no suggestion before us that Miller abandoned the lease.

Even so, the district court concluded that Burnett had to mitigate his damages without considering whether Miller had abandoned the lease—its conclusion was based solely on Miller's nonpayment of rent. We can find no caselaw suggesting that the duty to mitigate damages arises or applies in cases that don't involve either abandonment or termination of the lease. On the contrary, the Kansas Supreme Court has described it this way: "Kansas follows the minority position, imposing upon a landlord the duty to make reasonable effort to secure a new tenant *if a tenant surrenders possession of leased property*." (Emphasis added.) *In re Estate of Sauder*, 156 P.3d 1204, 1205 (Kan. 2007). And though the Restatement (Second) of Property follows the majority, no-duty rule, it nonetheless phrases the duty to mitigate as one that could arise only when a tenant abandons the property: "[*I*]*f the tenant abandons the leased property*, the landlord is under no duty to attempt to relet the leased property for the balance of the term of the lease to mitigate the tenant's liability under the lease." (Emphasis added.) Restatement (Second) of Property, Landlord and Tenant § 12.1(3). In sum, the district court wrongly concluded that Burnett had a duty to mitigate damages based solely on a nonpayment of rent and without any consideration of whether Miller had abandoned the lease. Nothing in the record available to us suggests that Miller had abandoned the lease.

An additional problem with the district court's conclusion is that it would allow a landlord to interfere with the tenant's possession of the rented property. When a landlord leases property to a tenant, the tenant has exclusive right of possession. The tenant's right to exclusive possession is encapsulated in what lawyers call the "implied covenant of quiet enjoyment," which exists in every Kansas lease, including oral farm leases. . . . If a landlord were required to mitigate damages caused by the nonpayment of rent when a tenant has not abandoned the property, then the landlord would be required to violate the implied covenant of quiet enjoyment and the tenant's right to exclusive possession without the landlord's interference. . . . The duty to mitigate damages has its limits. It isn't a license for landlords to interfere with a current tenant's use of the rented property.

Saying that a landlord can't interfere with the tenant's exclusive use of the property merely due to nonpayment of rent doesn't leave the landlord without recourse: The landlord has other remedies available when a tenant fails to pay rent but doesn't abandon the leased property. For example, if a tenant fails to pay rent when it's due, the landlord can give the tenant notice that the lease will be terminated if rent isn't paid within 10 days. And specifically related to farm leases, a landlord can enforce a lien (a legal interest in someone else's property) on the crops growing on the farmland. . . . Either of these options protects the landlord's right to receive rent without interfering with the tenant's possessory rights.

[I]t's clear to us that the district court's judgment was based in part on a legal error—its conclusion that Burnett's duty to mitigate damages authorized him to allow others to graze their horses on the rented pastureland. Because the district court's judgment is based in part on a legal error, we reverse it. We remand the case for the district court to reconsider application of the law to the facts as it found them in a manner consistent with this opinion.

The district court's judgment is reversed, and this case is remanded for further proceedings consistent with this opinion.

Termination of a Leasehold by Abandonment

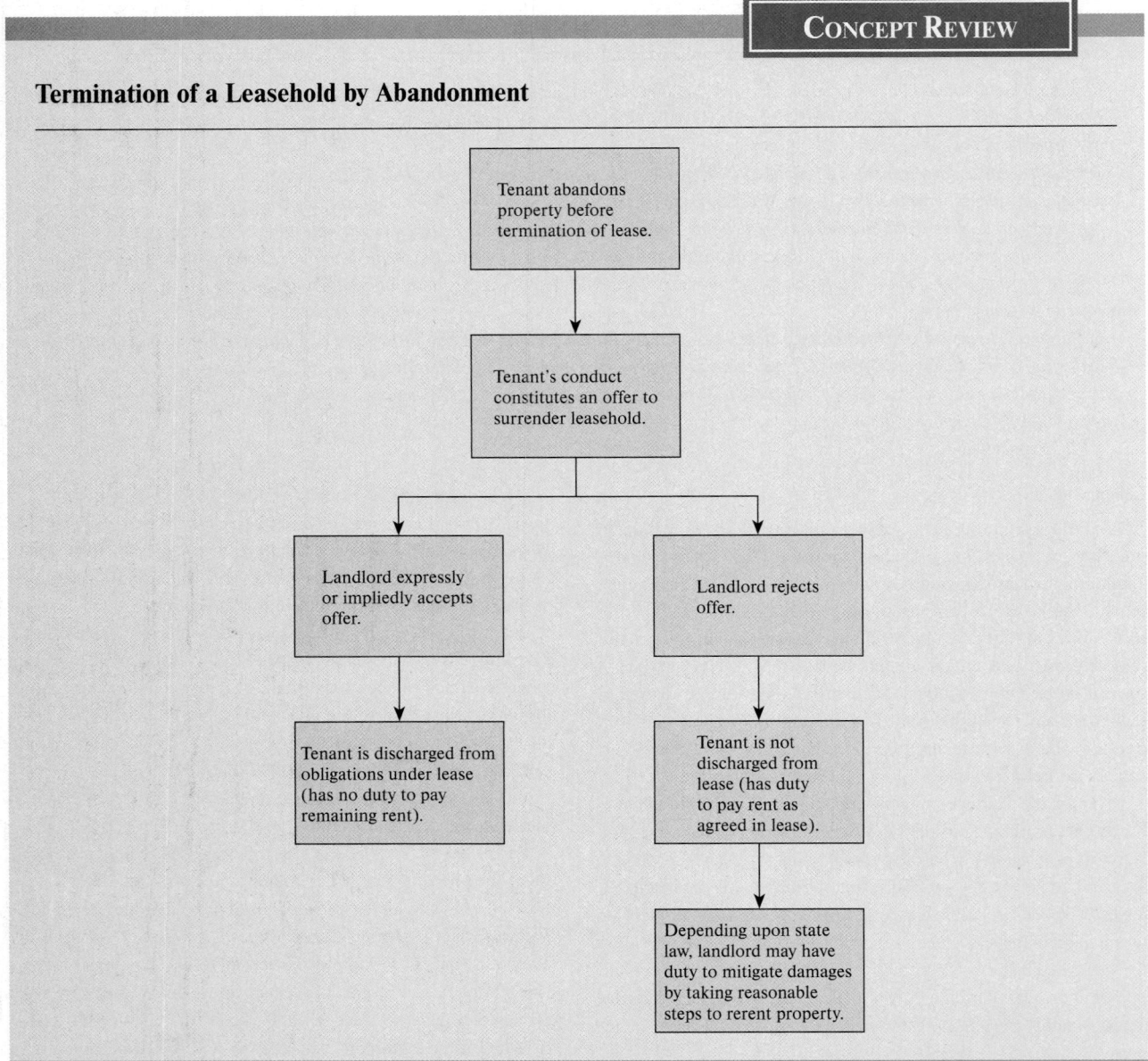

Problems and Problem Cases

1. A tenant rented an apartment from the landlord pursuant to a lease that required her to surrender the premises in "as good a state and condition as reasonable use and wear and tear will permit," and also required her to make a refundable security deposit. After the lease was executed, the landlord notified the tenants in the building that no tenant was to shampoo the wall-to-wall carpet on surrender of the lease because the landlord had retained a professional carpet cleaner to do it. The cost of the carpet cleaner's services was to be automatically deducted from the security deposit. When the tenant left the building, a portion of her security deposit was withheld to cover carpet cleaning, and she sued for a refund of the full deposit. Is the tenant entitled to a refund?

2. Mary Ajayi and Wemi Alakija were tenants in an apartment complex managed for the landlord by Lloyd Management. Neighboring tenants complained on various occasions to Lloyd about repeated disturbances that continued late into the night and included yelling and loud noises coming from the apartment shared by Ajayi and Alakija. The sound of running could also be heard during those disturbances. Neighbors whose apartment walls adjoined those of the Ajayi–Alakija apartment also complained that items were knocked off their walls as a result of banging and jarring coming from that apartment. Do Lloyd and the landlord have any obligations to take responsive action? If so, why? What course(s) of action might they pursue?

3. On August 2, Dan Maltbie and John Burke, students at Indiana University, entered into a one-year written lease with Breezewood Management Company for the rental of an apartment in an older house in Bloomington, Indiana. When they moved in, they discovered numerous defects: rotting porch floorboards, broken and loose windows, an inoperable front door lock, leaks in the plumbing, a back door that would not close, a missing bathroom door, inadequate water pressure, falling plaster, exposed wiring, and a malfunctioning toilet. Later they discovered a leaking roof, cockroach infestation, the absence of heat and hot water, more leaks in the plumbing, and pigeons in the attic. The City of Bloomington had a minimum housing code in effect at that time. Code enforcement officers inspected the apartment and found more than 50 violations, 11 of which were "life safety" violations, defined as conditions that might be severely "hazardous to the health of the occupant." These conditions remained largely uncorrected after notice by the code officers and further complaints by Maltbie and Burke. On May 3 of the following year, Maltbie vacated the apartment, notified Breezewood, and refused to pay any further rent. Breezewood agreed to let Burke remain and pay half the rate of the originally agreed-upon rent. Breezewood then filed suit against Maltbie and Burke for the balance due under the original rental contract plus a number of additional charges. Maltbie and Burke each filed counterclaims against Breezewood, claiming damages and abatement of the rent for breach of the implied warranty of habitability. Was there an implied warranty of habitability in the lease of the property that was breached?

4. On February 14, Don Weingarden entered into a written rental agreement with Eagle Ridge Condominiums for an apartment in Maumee, Ohio. Weingarden paid $150 as a security deposit with a monthly rental rate of $750 payable on the first of each month; the month of March was rent free. The parties also agreed that the landlord would replace the bedroom door, repair the electrical outlet in the bedroom, and replace the boards in the basement.

Weingarden took possession on March 1. On March 23, he notified the apartment manager in writing that the basement of the apartment would leak when snow melted and also after a rain. The leak would saturate the carpeting in the basement and render the basement useless. When wet, the carpet would become mildewed and odorous. Weingarden also indicated that the stairway in the unit was not in compliance with the Ohio Basic Building Code and that he had fallen as a result and, further, that the door in the bedroom had not been repaired and/or replaced and that the frame on the master bedroom door was cracked. Weingarden indicated that as a result he would vacate the premises on or before July 1.

The landlord attempted to remedy the basement leak by applying cement to the interior basement walls; however, the basement continued to leak and soak the carpet. On April 1, the landlord replied to Weingarden that it would not release him from his obligations under the lease agreement. On June 16, Weingarden surrendered his keys to the apartment and indicated in writing that his deposit should be forwarded to the address in Michigan that was on the application he had submitted for the lease.

The landlord did not return any security deposit to Weingarden and did not send any itemization of disbursements to him. The landlord spent the security deposit on a water bill of $27.11 and for the cost of carpet cleaning, with the balance being applied to unpaid rent pursuant to the terms of the lease.

Weingarden brought suit against the landlord to recover the balance of his security deposit and damages of $250 per month for the diminution of value of the rental unit because of the inability to utilize the basement, which constituted one-third of the apartment. The landlord counterclaimed for the unpaid rent due for the balance of the lease term. One of the issues in the case was whether the conditions in the basement amounted to a constructive eviction of Weingarden. Did the wet conditions in the basement substantially affect the habitability of the apartment and amount to a constructive eviction of the tenant?

5. Linda Schiernbeck rented a house from Clark and Rosa Davis. Approximately one month after she moved in,

Schiernbeck noticed a discolored area on one of the walls. There was a screw in the middle of this area. Schiernbeck determined that a smoke detector had been attached to the wall, but no smoke detector was present during the time she lived there. Schiernbeck later contended that she had notified the Davises about the missing smoke detector, but the Davises denied this. About 15 months after Schiernbeck's occupancy began, a fire broke out in the house. Schiernbeck and her daughter were severely injured. Contending that the Davises should have installed a smoke detector, Schiernbeck sued them for negligence and breach of contract. Did the Davises owe Schiernbeck a duty to install a smoke detector?

6. DeEtte Junker leased an apartment from F. L. Cappaert in the Pecan Ridge Apartment Complex, which consisted of six buildings, each with 12 apartments. Junker's apartment was upstairs, and she and the tenants in two other apartments used a common stairway for access to their apartments. Junker slipped on the stairway and was injured. She sued Cappaert for damages on the grounds that he had been negligent in maintaining the stairway. Junker's lease contained an exculpatory clause in which Cappaert disclaimed any liability for injury due to his negligence. Did the exculpatory clause immunize the landlord against damages caused by his own negligence in maintaining a common area in leased residential property?

7. Kevin Allen was the owner and manager of an apartment building in Chicago, Illinois. Marybeth Duncavage, a second-year medical student, entered into an agreement with Allen for the rental of Apartment 1-W. She moved into the apartment on August 1. About 3 A.M. on August 4, Tommy Lee Jackson came into the rear yard adjacent to Apartment 1-W and concealed himself in an unlighted area and in the tall weeds. Using a ladder that Allen had stored adjacent to Duncavage's apartment, Jackson climbed the building wall and entered Apartment 1-W through a window that was incapable of being locked. Once inside the apartment, Jackson tied up Duncavage, repeatedly raped and sodomized her, and then strangled her to death. Allen was aware that the ladder had been used on an earlier occasion to burglarize the same apartment through the same unlockable window and that it was still accessible to unauthorized persons on the property. Marybeth Duncavage's father, as the administrator of her estate, brought an action for negligence against Allen. Under the circumstances, did Allen owe Duncavage a duty to protect her against the criminal conduct that resulted in her death?

8. On March 1, Sharon Fitzgerald entered into an oral lease of a house owned by Parkin. The lease was on a month-to-month basis, and the rent was set at $290 per month. Parkin also agreed to make certain repairs to the house. On July 1, Fitzgerald notified Parkin by mail of the repairs that needed to be made. These included repairs of leaky pipes, the kitchen ceiling, and the back porch. Fitzgerald also said she would withhold the rent if the repairs were not made within 30 days. On July 13, Fitzgerald had the premises inspected by a city housing inspector, who found eight violations of the city code. Parkin was given notice of these violations. On July 29, Parkin served Fitzgerald with a formally correct notice to vacate the premises within 30 days. In September, he brought a lawsuit to have Fitzgerald evicted. A Minnesota statute gives a tenant a defense to an eviction action if the eviction is in retaliation for the reporting of a housing violation in good faith to city officials. Could the landlord evict the tenant from the house under these circumstances?

9. Kridel entered into a lease with Sommer, owner of the Pierre Apartments, to lease apartment 6-L for two years. Kridel, who was to be married in June, planned to move into the apartment in May. His parents and future parents-in-law had agreed to assume responsibility for the rent because Kridel was a full-time student who had no funds of his own. Shortly before Kridel was to have moved in, his engagement was broken. He wrote Sommer a letter explaining his situation and stating that he could not take the apartment. Sommer did not answer the letter. When another party inquired about renting apartment 6-L, the person in charge told her that the apartment was already rented to Kridel.

Sommer did not enter the apartment or show it to anyone until he rented apartment 6-L to someone else when there were approximately eight months left on Kridel's lease. He sued Kridel for the full rent for the period of approximately 16 months before the new tenant's lease took effect. Kridel argued that Sommer should not be able to collect rent for the first 16 months of the lease because he did not take reasonable steps to rerent the apartment. Was Sommer entitled to collect the rent he sought?

Estates and Trusts

George, an elderly widower, has no children of his own but enjoys a very close relationship with his two stepdaughters, his late wife's children by her first marriage. George's only living blood relative is his brother, from whom he has been estranged for many years. George has a substantial amount of property—his home, two cars, stocks and bonds, rental property, bank accounts, and a valuable collection of baseball cards. Though retired, George is an active volunteer for, and supporter of, several community charities and organizations. Presently, George does not have a will, but he is considering writing one.

- What will happen to George's property upon his death if he does not have a will at that time?
- What are the requirements for executing a valid will?
- What can cause a will to be invalid?
- After George's death, how would his estate be probated?
- If George decided to create a trust to benefit his stepdaughters, what is required to create a trust, and what are the legal duties of a trustee? What are the *ethical* duties of a trustee?

LO LEARNING OBJECTIVES

After studying this chapter, you should be able to:

26-1 List and explain the requirements for a valid will.

26-2 Explain how wills can be changed and revoked.

26-3 Identify and explain the legal tools ("advance directives") available for planning for possible future incapacity.

26-4 Explain and provide examples of how property is disposed of when a person dies without leaving a will.

26-5 Identify the steps in the process of administering an estate and explain the responsibilities of the personal representative for the estate.

26-6 Explain the concept of *trust*, identify various types of trusts, and explain the powers and responsibilities of a trustee.

26-7 List the requirements for the formation of a trust and describe how trusts can be revoked or modified.

ONE OF THE BASIC features of the ownership of property is the right to dispose of the property during life and at death. You have already learned about the ways in which property is transferred during the owner's life. The owner's death is another major event for the transfer of property. Most people want to be able to choose who will get their property when they die. There are a variety of ways to control the ultimate disposition of one's property, including taking title to the property in a form of joint ownership that gives co-owners a right of survivorship; creating a trust and transfering property to it to be used for the benefit of a spouse, child, elderly parent, or other beneficiary; or executing a will that directs real and personal property be distributed to persons named in the will. If, however, a person makes no provision for the disposition of property at death, the property will be distributed to the person's heirs as defined by state law. This chapter focuses on the transfer of property at death and on the use of trusts for the transfer and management of property, both during life and at death.

The Law of Estates and Trusts

Each state has its own statutes and common law regulating the distribution of property upon death. Legal requirements and procedures may vary from state to state, but many general principles can be stated. The Uniform Probate Code (UPC) is a comprehensive, uniform law that has been enacted in 19 states. In the remaining states, the law has been profoundly influenced by the UPC and many have adopted portions of it. Several relevant UPC provisions will be discussed in this chapter.

Estate Planning   A person's **estate** is all of the property owned by that person. Estate planning is the popular name for the complicated process of planning for the transfer of a person's estate in later life and at death. Estate planning also concerns planning for the possibility of prolonged illness or disability. An attorney who is creating an estate plan will take an inventory of the client's assets, learn the client's objectives, and draft the instruments necessary to carry out the plan. This plan is normally guided by the desire to provide for the orderly disposition of the estate, minimize lawsuits, and decrease tax liability.

Wills

Right of Disposition by Will   The right to control the disposition of property at death has not always existed. In the English feudal system, the king owned all land. The lords and knights had only the right to use land for their lifetime. A landholder's rights in land terminated upon death, and no rights descended to heirs. In 1215, the king granted the nobility the right to pass their interest in the land they held to their heirs. Later, that right was extended to all property owners. In the United States, each state has enacted statutes that establish the requirements for a valid will, including the formalities that must be met to pass property by will.

 LO26-1 List and explain the requirements for a valid will.

Nature of a Will   A **will** is a document executed with specific legal formalities by a **testator** (person making a will) that contains her instructions about the way her property will be disposed of at her death. A will can dispose only of property belonging to the testator at the time of her death. Furthermore, wills do not control property that

goes to others through other planning devices (such as life insurance policies) or by operation of law (such as by right of survivorship). For example, property held in joint tenancy or tenancy by the entirety is not controlled by a will because the property passes automatically to the surviving cotenant by right of survivorship. In addition, life insurance proceeds are controlled by the insured's designation of beneficiaries, not by any provision of a will. (Because joint tenancy and life insurance are ways of directing the disposition of property, they are sometimes referred to as "will substitutes.")

Common Will Terminology   Some legal terms commonly used in wills include the following:

1. *Bequest.* A **bequest** (also called **legacy**) is a gift of personal property or money. For example, a will might provide for a bequest of a special piece of jewelry to the testator's daughter.

2. *Devise.* A **devise** is a gift of real property. For example, the testator might devise his family farm to his grandson. However, the terms *devise* and *bequest* are often used interchangeably.

3. *Residuary.* The **residuary** estate is the balance of the estate that is left after specific devises and bequests are made by the will. After providing for the disposition of specific personal and real property, a testator might provide that the residuary estate is to go to his spouse or be divided among his descendants.

4. *Issue.* A person's **issue** are his lineal descendants (children, grandchildren, great-grandchildren, and so forth). This category of persons includes adopted children.

5. *Representation.* When one of several children has died before the decedent, leaving descendants, all states provide for the dead child's descendants to *represent* him or her and divide that child's share.

6. *Per stirpes.* The oldest system of representation is **per stirpes**. When a gift is given to the testator's issue or descendants *per stirpes* each surviving descendant divides the share that his or her parent would have taken if the parent had survived. For example, Grandmother dies, leaving a will providing that her residuary estate is to go to her issue or descendants *per stirpes*. Grandmother had two children, Terese and Marshawn. Terese had two children, Tyrone and Sue. Marshawn had one child, Aneesa. Terese and Marshawn die before Grandmother (in legal terms, *predecease* her), but all three of Grandmother's grandchildren are living at the time of her death. In this case, Aneesa would take one-half of the residuary estate,

while Tyrone and Sue would take one-quarter each (that is, they would divide the share that would have gone to their mother).

7. *Per capita.* The more modern system of representation is **per capita**, which means that each of the group of persons share in the gift equally. In the preceding example, if Grandmother's will had stated that the residuary estate is to go to her issue or descendants *per capita,* Tyrone, Sue, and Aneesa would each take one-third of the residuary.

Testamentary Capacity

The capacity to make a valid will is called testamentary capacity. To have testamentary capacity, a person must be *of sound mind* and *of legal age,* which is 18 in most states. A person does not have to be in perfect mental health to have testamentary capacity. Because people often delay executing wills until they are weak and in ill health, the standard for mental capacity to make a will is fairly low. To be of "sound mind," a person need only be sufficiently rational to be capable of understanding the nature and character of her property, of realizing that she is making a will, and of knowing the persons who would normally be the beneficiaries of her affection. A person could move in and out of periods of lucidity and still have testamentary capacity if she executed her will during a lucid period.

Lack of testamentary capacity and *undue influence* are the most common grounds upon which wills are challenged by persons who were excluded from a will. *Fraud, duress,* and *tortious interference* with an expectancy are also grounds for challenging the validity of a will.[1]

---

[1]Fraud and undue influence are discussed in detail in Chapter 13.

Hutchison v. Kaforey   67 N.E.3d 121 (Ohio Ct. App. 2016)

Michael Hutchison died in 2012 from a heroin overdose. He was not married and did not have any children. His estate consisted of substantial sums of money received from the settlement of a lawsuit alleging sexual abuse by a priest to which Michael was subjected as a child.

Prior to his death, Michael was under guardianship because he was incapable of managing his own finances, health care, and living arrangements. He suffered from schizophrenia and post-traumatic stress disorder. He had a low IQ and no more than a seventh-grade education. Michael was a frequent drug user, particularly of cocaine and heroin. He was hospitalized on multiple occasions and had run-ins with the criminal justice system.

Mary Hutchison Barnes, Michael's mother, had served as Michael's guardian prior to 2005, when she moved out of state to pursue a relationship and relinquished her guardianship. At that point, Ellen Kaforey was named Michael's guardian. Kaforey was a public health nurse for a number of years before devoting herself to the full-time practice of law. As a nurse, she gained experience caring for patients with mental illnesses and substance abuse problems, which she applied in her work as guardian for hundreds of wards over the years, including Michael.

Kaforey drafted wills for Michael in 2006, 2007, and 2008. The 2008 will was similar to the others, except that it added beneficiaries including the "Altoona Childrens' Services Board" of Pennsylvania and "St. Jude's Children's Cancer Hospital," as well as Michael's father, three of his brothers, his nephew, and his girlfriend (who had passed away between the time Michael executed the 2008 will and his own death). As with his prior wills, Barnes was not named in the will, nor was Michael's sister.

Upon Michael's death, his 2008 will was admitted to probate. Barnes contested the will. She claimed it was invalid because Michael lacked testamentary capacity and was subject to undue influence by Kaforey, who was appointed executrix of Michael's estate in the will. Barnes claimed that Kaforey had admitted to Michael's brother Mark that Michael was not competent to draft or execute a will and that she only helped him because she was scared of him.

The trial court granted summary judgment against Barnes, and she appealed.

Whitmore, Judge

I.

Barnes claims that the trial court erroneously concluded that the evidence does not give rise to a genuine issue of material fact regarding Michael's testamentary capacity. We agree.

The parties that moved for summary judgment included Kaforey as executrix of the 2008 will and multiple other beneficiaries of the 2008 will who were named as defendants in the will contest. The movants claimed that there was no triable issue of fact regarding whether Michael lacked testamentary capacity and whether he was unduly influenced.

The law recognizes that a testator whose mind is impaired "by disease or otherwise" can still have capacity to make a will. Testamentary capacity exists when the testator has sufficient mind to: (1) understand the nature of the business in which he is engaged;

(2) comprehend generally the nature and extent of the property which constitutes his estate; (3) hold in his mind the names and identity of those who have natural claims on his bounty; and (4) appreciate his relation to the members of his family. The general rule is that "[t]he mental condition of the testator at the time of making a will determines the testamentary capacity of the testator." *Oehlke v. Marks*, 207 N.E.2d 676 (Ohio Ct. App. 1964), quoting *Kennedy v. Walcutt*, 161 N.E. 336 (Ohio 1928). Evidence of the testator's condition "within a reasonable time before and after the making of the will is admissible as throwing light on his mental condition at the time of the execution of the will in question." *Id.* What constitutes a "reasonable time" depends on the circumstances of the particular case. The burden of proof in determining testamentary capacity is on the party contesting the will.

A rebuttable presumption exists that a person under guardianship lacks the testamentary capacity to write a valid will. The degree of proof necessary to rebut this presumption is not high. Instead, the degrees of proof necessary to both rebut the presumption of incompetency and establish capacity are [the same.]

Kaforey testified in her capacity as a nurse and lawyer that Michael possessed testamentary capacity to make the 2008 will. She had been Michael's guardian for about three years when she drafted the 2008 will. Kaforey stated that Michael was compliant with his medications and was not under the influence of drugs when he executed the 2008 will. She testified that she was familiar with signs that Michael was not compliant with his medications for schizophrenia or on drugs. When Michael was not taking his medications properly he suffered from, and would react to, auditory hallucinations. He would also be dirty or unkempt and agitated. Kaforey testified that there were times during her guardianship of Michael when he was not competent to execute a will because he was not taking his medications or was using drugs. However, she testified that Michael did not exhibit any of the signs of noncompliance with his medications or of being under the influence of drugs when he made the 2008 will.

Kaforey also testified that Michael wanted to make the will. She explained that she met with Michael on multiple occasions and discussed with him at length who the beneficiaries of the will would be. Michael specifically requested to add his girlfriend as a beneficiary of the 2008 will. He also requested to add St. Jude's Hospital as a beneficiary because he wanted to contribute to the hospital's care for children. Kaforey testified that she discussed with Michael that he did not want Barnes to take under the will because Barnes was already financially stable.

Kaforey further testified that she specifically assessed Michael's capacity to make the 2008 will on the day he executed the will. She had no doubt that he possessed testamentary capacity. She testified that Michael was of sufficient mind and memory to understand the nature of what he was doing and the nature or extent of his property. According to Kaforey, Michael knew the identities of those he wanted to name as beneficiaries, and also

understood and appreciated his relationship to family members. Having concluded that Michael possessed testamentary capacity to make the 2008 will, Kaforey permitted Michael to execute the will in the presence of two witnesses.

Based upon Kaforey's testimony, we conclude that the movants successfully rebutted the presumption that Michael lacked testamentary capacity because he was under guardianship. . . .

In response to the motions for summary judgment, Barnes argues that a question of fact exists as to whether Michael lacked capacity to execute the 2008 will (and the 2007 and 2006 wills). She argues . . . that Michael's extensive medical records show that Michael could not have possessed testamentary capacity at the time he made the will. However, the medical records to which Barnes refers apparently were never placed in the record. Moreover, Barnes does not discuss the contents of the medical records with any particularity, nor did she testify regarding any specific facts in those records that would show that Michael lacked testamentary capacity at the time he made the 2008 will. Accordingly, there is no basis to conclude that the medical records created an issue of fact sufficient to overcome summary judgment.

Barnes also points to evaluations of Michael by his psychiatrist to establish that Michael lacked testamentary capacity. However, while the psychiatrist opined that Michael should remain under guardianship because he had chronic mental illness and poor insight and judgment, the psychiatrist did not address any of the criteria necessary to determine testamentary capacity. . . . Accordingly, the psychiatric evaluations upon which Barnes relies do not create a triable issue of fact regarding Michael's testamentary capacity.

Barnes further argues that the fact that Michael remained under guardianship is evidence sufficient to overcome summary judgment. Her reliance on Michael's status as a ward under guardianship is misplaced, however. The presumption that a person under guardianship lacks testamentary capacity is a rebuttable one. . . . Once evidence is produced sufficient to rebut the presumption, the presumption disappears. . . . As already discussed, we conclude that the movants presented sufficient evidence to rebut the presumption that Michael lacked testamentary capacity because he was under guardianship.

Barnes also relies on her roles as Michael's mother and former guardian to support her contention that Michael could not have had testamentary capacity to make a will. Barnes is required to present evidence of Michael's condition "within a reasonable time before and after the making of the will" in order to create an issue of fact regarding Michael's testamentary capacity at the time he executed the 2008 will. However, Barnes testified in her deposition that she could not recall the last time that she had either seen Michael or spent significant time with him before he executed the 2008 will, or when she next saw him after he signed the will. Barnes admitted in her deposition that Kaforey was in a better position than she was to evaluate Michael's testamentary capacity when he signed the 2008 will. Neither Barnes nor [Michael's brother] Mark observed

Michael's condition at the time he signed the 2008 will. Accordingly, Barnes has not pointed to any evidence that anyone other than Kaforey had personal knowledge of Michael's condition "within a reasonable time before or after the making of the will" that would give rise to an issue of fact as to Michael's testamentary capacity when he signed the 2008 will.

Barnes further argues that summary judgment is inappropriate because Kaforey admitted to her and to Mark that Michael was incompetent to write a will. Barnes and Mark both testified that Kaforey specifically discussed with them Michael's testamentary capacity and told them that Michael could never make a will. Barnes testified that Kaforey told her before Michael's death that the 2007 will was invalid. Mark testified that he and his mother met with Kaforey after Michael's death and Kaforey informed them that Michael's 2008 will was invalid "[b]ecause Michael was incompetent. . . ." Kaforey allegedly told them that a court would not uphold any will that Michael executed and that Michael's entire estate would revert to the family. According to Mark, Kaforey told them that submitting the will to the probate court was "a matter of process that she had to go through." He testified that Kaforey advised them to file a will contest and referred them to legal counsel.

Kaforey denied ever stating that Michael lacked testamentary capacity when he executed the 2008 will. She also denied telling Barnes and Mark that Michael's entire estate would revert to the family.

Despite the testimony of Barnes and Mark that Kaforey told them that Michael lacked testamentary capacity, the trial court found that "the only evidence as to [Michael's] testamentary capacity in the relevant time period is the testimony of Kaforey that [Michael] had sufficient testamentary capacity when he signed the [2008 will]." In so holding, the court emphasized that "Kaforey is an experienced probate attorney with a medical background who has repeatedly dealt with clients with mental health and/or substance abuse issues." The court did not address the assertions that Kaforey told Michael's family members that he was not competent to make a will, but rather disregarded that testimony.

We find that the trial court improperly weighed the credibility of testimony in disregarding the assertions of Barnes and Mark that Kaforey told them that Michael was incompetent. [I]f Kaforey did tell Barnes and Mark that she believed that Michael lacked testamentary capacity, her statement was an admission that would support Barnes' claim that Michael was not competent to make the 2008 will. Thus, it would constitute evidence that Michael lacked testamentary capacity. The trial court was not entitled to ignore such evidence, even if the court felt that it was contrived or that Kaforey's testimony was more credible. . . .

Barnes' first assignment of error is sustained. . . .

II.

In her second assignment of error, Barnes argues that the trial court improperly granted summary judgment on her claim that Michael's 2008 will was the product of undue influence. We disagree.

A will that has been admitted to probate is presumed to have been made free from restraint. The contestants have the burden to prove undue influence.

To invalidate a will, undue influence "must so overpower and subjugate the mind of the testator as to destroy his free agency and make him express the will of another rather than his own, and the mere presence of influence is not sufficient." *West v. Henry*, 184 N.E.2d 200 (Ohio 1962). In addition, the "[u]ndue influence must be present or operative at the time of the execution of the will resulting in dispositions which the testator would not otherwise have made." *Id.* Proof of undue influence requires: (1) a susceptible testator; (2) another's opportunity to exert influence on the testator; (3) the fact of improper influence exerted or attempted; and (4) a result showing the effect of such influence. *Id.*

Barnes . . . asserts that Kaforey unduly influenced Michael with respect to the making of his will. On appeal, Barnes argues that a presumption of undue influence arises because "Kaforey was a guardian and acted as the ward's attorney while naming herself [e]xecutrix in the contested will."

Barnes contends that a presumption of undue influence arises because Kaforey and Michael had a confidential relationship, and Kaforey will benefit from her position as executrix of the will. We are not persuaded by Barnes' argument. In the cases that Barnes cites where a confidential relationship gave rise to a presumption of undue influence, the confidential relationship existed between the decedent and a beneficiary of the will. . . . Here, Kaforey was not a beneficiary of Michael's will. The mere fact that Kaforey is executrix of the will does not, by itself, give rise to a presumption of undue influence. . . .

In response, Barnes fails to point to any fact that could give rise to a reasonable inference that Kaforey exerted or attempted improper influence in relation to Michael's 2008 will. In fact, Barnes argues that Kaforey was frightened of Michael, and that she drafted the 2008 will without regard for Michael's testamentary capacity because she was intimidated by him. Rather than demonstrate that Michael was either unduly influenced or the target of undue influence by Kaforey, these alleged facts, if true, would tend to show that Kaforey drafted the 2008 will under some degree of duress from Michael.

We find that the probate court properly granted summary judgment to the movants on Barnes' claim that Michael suffered undue influence in making the 2008 will. On this basis, Barnes' second assignment of error is overruled.

* * *

III.

Judgment affirmed in part and reversed in part.

In *Hutchison v. Kaforey*, which follows, the Ohio Court of Appeals considers whether someone with serious enough mental illness and addiction issues to be under legal guardianship had testamentary capacity. Moreover, because the testator's guardian was also his attorney and the executor of his estate, the court explores whether the will was invalid because of undue influence.

Execution of a Will

Except in states that allow for harmless error, a will is not valid unless it is executed with the formalities required by state law. The courts are strict in interpreting statutes concerning the execution of wills. If a will is declared invalid, the property of the deceased person will be distributed according to the provisions of state laws that will be discussed later.

The formalities required for a valid will differ from state to state. For that reason, it is vital to consult state law before making a will. If an individual has executed a will and then moves to another state, that individual should consult with a lawyer to determine whether a new will needs to be executed in order to meet the requirements of the state where the person now lives. Despite that state-by-state variability, there are three core formalities:

1. All states require that a will be *in writing*.
2. State laws also require that a formal will be *witnessed*, generally by two or three *disinterested* witnesses (in other words, persons who do not stand to inherit any property under the will).
3. Most states require that the testator sign the will in the presence and the sight of the witnesses and that the witnesses sign in the presence and the sight of each other.

As a general rule, an attestation clause, which states the formalities that have been followed in the execution of the will, is written following the testator's signature. Sometimes a testator is also required to *publish* the will—that is, declare or indicate at the time of signing that the instrument is, in fact, the testator's will. These detailed formalities are designed to prevent fraud. Section 2-502 of the UPC requires that a will must be in writing, signed by the testator (or in the testator's name by some other individual in the testator's conscious presence and by the testator's direction), and signed by at least two individuals, each of whom signed within a reasonable time after he witnessed either the signing of the will or the testator's acknowledgment of that signature or will. Also, under the UPC, any individual who is generally competent to be a witness may witness a will, and the fact that the witness is an interested party does not invalidate the will [2-505]. In lieu of signature by two witnesses, the UPC also allows for a will to be witnessed by a notary. Finally, the UPC incorporates the "harmless error" rule. When a testator has made a technical error in executing a will, the UPC permits the document to be treated as if it had been executed properly if it can be proven by clear and convincing evidence that the testator intended the document to constitute a will [2-503]. The following *Zimmerman* case provides an example of how courts deal with situations in which it is unclear if a document is, in fact, a will.

Zimmerman v. Allen   250 P.3d 558 (Ariz. Ct. App. 2011)

Gloria Waterloo belonged to a congregation of which Jack Zimmerman is the senior rabbi. In April 2008, Zimmerman and his wife, Sandie, visited Waterloo in a hospice facility. Because handwriting was difficult for Waterloo, she dictated to Sandie a document that stated:

To Whom It Concerns: April 11, 08

My name is Gloria Anne Waterloo. I live at [address]. The reason for this letter is so that my wishes are carried out by Jack Howard Zimmerman Also known as Rabbi Jack. He lives at [address].

1. I want Him Jack Zimmerman to have full guardianship of My Health Decisions along with Myself.
2. Also as far as my finances, and realestate transaction I want Jack Zimmerman to have full guardianship along with Myself.
3. Properties are in CCA As of 2003, I have properties in many countries in CCA.
4. After I am deceased Jack has full instructions frome me. Attached is a list of final instructions I want to leave Jack Howard Zimmerman A sum of $3,000,000 or more Three Million dollars, or More. He has full & final guardianship of my finances & realestate properties.
5. As far as a Memorial Service I want Rabbi Jack to organize All of it. I am to be buryed next to my husband Dale Bec Waterloo at Sunny Slope Memorial in Sunny Slope, Phoenix.

In the presence of the Zimmermans, Waterloo reviewed the one-page document, initialed each of the five numbered paragraphs, and dated and signed the document at the bottom. Notwithstanding the document's reference to an "attached list of final instructions," Waterloo dictated no such list and no such list ever was attached to the instrument. About an hour after Waterloo dictated the document, another couple from the congregation arrived to visit her. One of them read the document aloud to Waterloo and confirmed with her that it represented her wishes.

Waterloo died less than a month later. After first petitioning for a declaration that Waterloo died intestate (i.e., without a valid will), Zimmerman petitioned the court to probate the document as a will.

Waterloo's heirs then moved for partial summary judgment, arguing that the document could not be admitted to probate because it was incomplete. They contended that because it referenced a "list of final instructions" that did not exist, the document failed as a will because it did not represent Waterloo's full testamentary intent. The court granted the heirs' motion, ruling it could not ascertain Waterloo's "complete intent . . . without knowing what was to be contained in the list of instructions." Zimmerman appealed.

Johnsen, Judge

A will is a "legal declaration of one's intentions, which he wills to be performed after death. It is not necessary that the testator use the word 'will' in his last testament. No particular words need be used, it being sufficient if it appears that the maker intended to dispose of his property after his death. . . . A letter written and signed by the author may serve as his last will where it contains testamentary language indicating that it was so intended." *In re Miller's Estate*, 92 P.2d 335 (Ariz. 1939).

To be treated as a will, an instrument that satisfies the requirement of testamentary intent must be properly executed. A nonholographic will must be signed by the testator or in the testator's name by some other individual in the testator's conscious presence and by the testator's direction, and must be signed by two witnesses. An instrument that demonstrates testamentary intent and complies with the statutory execution requisites should be admitted to probate as a will even though all of its terms are not capable of being enforced. The only issue in a will contest is whether the will is valid.

There is no question that Waterloo signed the document at issue (she even initialed each of the five numbered paragraphs that make up the substance of the document). As for the statutory witness requirement, Waterloo's heirs did not cross-appeal from the superior court's decision accepting the affidavits of the Zimmermans and the other couple for that purpose. Thus, the only issue before the court in the contested will proceeding was whether the letter Waterloo dictated contained her testamentary intent.

The heirs correctly do not dispute that the document Waterloo dictated contains testamentary language indicating it was intended to constitute a will. Waterloo gave burial instructions in the letter and made provisions for what was to happen "[a]fter I am deceased." The use of certain formal phrases and the care that Waterloo took to initial the sections of substance and to sign and date the instrument also demonstrate testamentary intent. The superior court, however, refused to admit the will to probate based on its conclusion that the absence of the "list of final instructions" referenced in Waterloo's letter made it impossible to determine her "complete intent." On appeal, the heirs argue that we should affirm because the absence of the "list of final instructions" means that, as a matter of law, Waterloo lacked testamentary intent when she signed the letter.

In considering this argument, we are mindful that, as a general matter, an instrument will be admitted to probate even if it is vague or incomplete in some respects, as long as "there is a single portion of the instrument which is certain in its character." *In re Harris' Estate*, 296 P. 267 (Ariz. 1931). Therefore, if some of an instrument's testamentary terms are clear, a court may not decline to admit the will to probate simply because other terms are indefinite.

Although this rule normally will doom the argument that an instrument that demonstrates testamentary intent is too ambiguous to admit to probate, we understand the heirs to argue not that the instrument is fatally ambiguous but that the omission of the "list of final instructions" necessarily means that Waterloo lacked testamentary intent when she created the letter. For the reasons set forth below, however, we conclude that the absence of the list does not disprove the presumption we are required to apply in favor of testacy.

Significantly, Waterloo executed the instrument knowing that she had not created the list. Waterloo placed the date and her signature at the bottom of the single page that contained what she had dictated. From that we conclude she was satisfied with what she had dictated and that she believed that the instrument she executed adequately expressed her testamentary intent even though it lacked the "list" that she apparently had once intended to create.

The heirs argue, however, that public policy requires us to affirm the order denying probate. They argue that a contrary ruling would encourage the filing of partial wills for probate, with petitioners submitting "only pages of a will that are advantageous to them, while withholding pages that are not in their favor." But the heirs do not allege any fraud on Zimmerman's part, and the situation the heirs posit is not present here, when the evidence is undisputed that the "missing" document never existed.

Zimmerman asks that beyond ordering that the letter be admitted to probate, we construe the instrument to contain a bequest to him of "$3,000,000 or more." The heirs argue that, at most, the letter is a direction that Zimmerman be appointed "guardian" of Waterloo's estate. We decline both sides' suggestions to construe the will and instead remand the matter to the superior court to conduct all further proceedings that may be required to determine the meaning of the instrument's various terms.

Vacated and remanded with instructions to admit Waterloo's will to probate.

Incorporation by Reference

In some situations, a testator might want her will to refer to and incorporate an existing writing. For example, the testator may have created a list of specific gifts of personal property that she wants to incorporate in the will. A writing such as this is called an extrinsic document—that is, a writing apart from the will. In most states, the contents of extrinsic documents can be essentially incorporated into the will when the circumstances satisfy rules that have been designed to ensure that the document is genuine and that it was intended by the testator to be incorporated in the will. This is called incorporation by reference. For an extrinsic document to be incorporated by reference, it must have been *in existence at the time the will was executed*. In addition, the writing and the will must refer to each other so that the extrinsic document can be identified and so that it is clear that the testator intended the extrinsic document to be incorporated in the will. Under the UPC, incorporation by reference is allowed when the extrinsic document was in existence when the will was executed, the language of the will manifests the intent to incorporate the writing, and the will describes the writing sufficiently to identify it [2-510].

Informal Wills

Some states recognize certain types of wills that are not executed with these formalities. These are:

1. *Nuncupative wills.* A nuncupative will is an oral will. Such wills are recognized as valid in some states, but only under limited circumstances and to a limited extent. In a number of states, for example, nuncupative wills are valid only when made by soldiers in military service and sailors at sea, and even then they will be effective only to dispose of personal property that was in the actual possession of the person at the time the oral will was made. Other states place low dollar limits on the amount of property that can be passed by a nuncupative will.

2. *Holographic wills.* **Holographic wills** are wills that are written and signed in the testator's handwriting; therefore, they do not need to be attested by witnesses. They are recognized in about half of the states and by Section 2-502(b) of the UPC, even though they are not executed with the formalities usually required of valid wills. For a holographic will to be valid in the states that recognize them, it must evidence testamentary intent and must actually be *handwritten* by the testator. A typed holographic will would be invalid. Some states require that the holographic will be *entirely* handwritten, and some also require that the will be dated. The UPC, however, only requires that the signature and the material portions of the will be handwritten by the testator [2-502(b)].

Joint and Mutual Wills

In some circumstances, two or more people—a married couple, for example—decide together on a plan for the disposition of their property at death. To carry out this plan, they may execute a joint will (a single instrument that constitutes the will of both or all of the testators and is executed by both or all) or they may execute mutual wills (joint or separate, individual wills that reflect the common plan of distribution).

Underlying a joint or mutual will is an agreement on a common plan. This common plan often includes an express or implied contract (a contract to make a will or not to revoke the will). One issue that sometimes arises is whether a testator who has made a joint or mutual will can later change the will. Whether joint and mutual wills are revocable depends on the language of the will, on state law, and on the timing of the revocation. For example, a testator who made a joint will with his spouse may be able to revoke his will during the life of his spouse because the spouse still has a chance to change her own will, but he may be unable to revoke or change the will after the death of his spouse. The UPC provides that the mere fact that a joint or mutual will has been executed does *not* create the presumption of a contract not to revoke the will or wills [2-514].

Because of these problems, attorneys generally advise against joint and mutual wills.

Construction of Wills

Even in carefully drafted wills, questions sometimes arise as to the meaning or legal effect of a term or provision. Disputes about the meaning of the will are even more likely to occur in wills drafted by the testator himself, such as holographic wills. To interpret a will, a court will examine the entire instrument in an attempt to determine the testator's intent.

Limitations on Disposition by Will

A person who takes property by will takes it subject to all outstanding claims against the property. For example, if real property is subject to a mortgage or other lien, the beneficiary who takes the property gets it subject to the mortgage or lien. In addition, the rights of the testator's creditors are superior to the rights of beneficiaries under her will. Thus, if the testator was insolvent (her debts exceeded her assets), persons named as beneficiaries do not receive any property by virtue of the will.

Under the laws of most states, the surviving spouse of the testator has statutory rights in property owned solely by the testator that cannot be defeated by a contrary will provision. This means that one spouse cannot effectively disinherit the other. Even if the will provides for the surviving spouse, the survivor can elect to take the elective share of the decedent's estate that would be provided by state law rather than the amount specified in the will. In some states, personal property, such as furniture, passes automatically to the surviving spouse.

At common law, a widow had the right to a life estate in one-third of the lands owned by her husband during their marriage. This was known as a widow's **dower right**. A similar right for a widower was known as **curtesy**. A number of states have changed the right by statute to give a surviving spouse a one-half to one-third interest in fee simple in the real and personal property owned by the deceased spouse at the time of death. (Naturally, a testator can leave the spouse more, if desired.) Under UPC 2-201, the surviving spouse's elective share varies depending on the length of the surviving spouse's marriage to the testator—the elective share increases with the length of marriage.

As a general rule, a surviving spouse is given the right to use the family home for a stated period as well as a portion of the deceased spouse's estate. In community property states, each spouse has a one-half interest in community property that cannot be defeated by a contrary will provision. (Note that the surviving spouse will obtain *full* ownership of any property owned by the testator and the surviving spouse as joint tenants or tenants by the entirety.)

While not technically a limitation on disposition, the law does provide for **preterimitted** children—that is, children of the testator who were born or adopted after the will was executed. There is a presumption that the testator intended to provide for such a child, unless there is evidence to the contrary. State law gives pretermitted children the right to a share of the testator's estate. For example, under Section 2-302 of the Uniform Probate Code, a pretermitted child has the right to receive the share he would have received under the state intestacy statute unless it appears that the omission of this child was intentional, the testator gave

substantially all of his estate to the child's other parent, or the testator provided for the child outside of the will.

Revocation of Wills

 LO26-2 Explain how wills can be changed and revoked.

One important feature of a will is that it is *revocable* until the moment of the testator's death. For this reason, a will confers *no present interest* in the testator's property. A person is free to revoke a prior will and to make a new will. Wills can be revoked in a variety of ways. Physical destruction and mutilation done with intent to revoke a will constitute revocation, as do other acts such as crossing out the will or creating a writing that expressly cancels the will.

In addition, a will is revoked if the testator later executes a valid will that expressly revokes the earlier will. A later will that does not *expressly* revoke an earlier will operates to revoke only those portions of the earlier will that are inconsistent with the later will. Under the UPC, a later will that does not expressly revoke a prior will operates to revoke it by inconsistency if the testator intended the subsequent will to *replace* rather than *supplement* the prior will [2-507(b)]. Furthermore, the UPC presumes that the testator intended the subsequent will to replace rather than supplement the prior will if the subsequent one makes a complete disposition of her estate, but it presumes that the testator intended merely to supplement and not replace the prior will if the subsequent will disposes of only part of her estate [2-507(c), (d)]. In some states, a will is presumed to have been revoked if it cannot be located after the testator's death, although this presumption can be rebutted with contrary evidence.

Wills can also be revoked by operation of law without any act on the part of the testator signifying revocation. State

---

⚖ Ethics and Compliance in Action

Dr. Coggins died in 1963. In his last will, Dr. Coggins gave the residue of his estate to the Mercantile–Safe Deposit & Trust Company, to be held by it as trustee under the will. The trust provided for monthly payments to four income beneficiaries until the death of the last of them. The last of these annuitants was Dr. Coggins's widow, who died in 1998. A provision of the will stated that, upon the death of the survivor of the four annuitants, the trust would terminate and the assets and all unpaid income shall be paid over "free of trust unto the Keswick Home, formerly Home for Incurables of Baltimore City, with the request that said Home use the estate and property thus passing to it for the acquisition or

construction of a new building to provide additional housing accommodations to be known as the 'Coggins Building,' to house white patients who need physical rehabilitation. If not acceptable to the Keswick Home, then this bequest shall go to the University of Maryland Hospital to be used for physical rehabilitation." What are the major ethical considerations involved in determining whether this will provision should be enforced?

In addition or in parallel to those ethical considerations, what are the related compliance responsibilities of the trustee? Consider a situation in which Coggins's widow died but her cousin, who had cared for her in her last days, was still cashing the checks from the trust.

statutes provide that certain changes in relationships operate as revocations of a will. In some states, marriage will operate to revoke a will that was made when the testator was single. Similarly, a divorce may revoke provisions in a will made during marriage that leave property to the divorced spouse. Under the laws of a few states, the birth of a child after the execution of a will may operate as a partial revocation of the will.

Codicils   A **codicil** is an amendment of a will. A person who wants to change a provision of a will without making an entirely new will, may amend the will by executing a codicil. One may *not* amend a will by merely striking out objectionable provisions and inserting new provisions. The same formalities are required for the creation of a valid codicil as for the creation of a valid will. Similarly, where the harmless error rule applies to wills, it will also apply to codicils.

Advance Directives: Planning for Incapacity

 LO26-3   Identify and explain the legal tools ("advance directives") available for planning for possible future incapacity.

Advances in medical technology have increased life expectancy. A person can be kept alive by artificial means, even in many cases in which there is no hope of the person being able to function without life support. Many people are opposed to their lives being prolonged with no chance of recovery. In response to these concerns, almost all states have enacted statutes permitting individuals to manage their property and to state their choices about the medical procedures that should be administered or withheld if they should become incapacitated in the future and cannot recover. Collectively, the written medical instructions are called **advance directives**. An advance directive is a written document (such as a living will or durable power of attorney for health care) that directs others how future health care decisions should be made in the event that the individual becomes incapacitated. Increasingly, these matters are handled by attorneys specializing in elder law.

Durable Power of Attorney   A **durable power of attorney** allows for incapacitated individuals to have their property managed by a trusted person or professional.

A *power of attorney* is an express statement in which one person (the **principal**) gives another person (the **attorney in fact**) the authority to do an act or series of acts on the principal's behalf. For example, Andrews enters into a contract to sell his house to Willis, but he must be out of state on the date of the real estate closing. He gives Paulsen a power of

attorney to attend the closing and execute the deed on his behalf. Ordinary powers of attorney terminate upon the principal's incapacity. By contrast, the *durable power of attorney* is not affected if the principal becomes incompetent.

A durable power of attorney permits a person to give someone else extremely broad powers to make decisions and enter transactions such as those involving real and personal property, bank accounts, and health care, and to specify that those powers will not terminate upon incapacity. The durable power of attorney is an extremely important planning device. For example, a durable power of attorney executed by an elderly parent to an adult child at a time in which the parent is competent would permit the child to take care of matters such as investments, property, bank accounts, and hospital admission. Without the durable power of attorney, the child would be forced to apply to a court for a guardianship, which is a more expensive and often less efficient manner in which to handle personal and business affairs.

Living Wills   **Living wills** are documents in which a person states in advance an intention to forgo or obtain certain life-prolonging medical procedures. Almost all states have enacted statutes recognizing living wills. These statutes also establish the elements and formalities required to create a valid living will and describe the legal effect of living wills. Currently, the law concerning living wills is primarily a matter of state law and differs from state to state. Living wills are typically included with a patient's medical records. Many states require physicians and other health care providers to follow the provisions of a valid living will. Because living wills are created by statute, it is important that all terms and conditions of one's state statute be followed. Figure 26.1 shows an example of a living will form.

Durable Power of Attorney for Health Care   The majority of states have enacted statutes specifically providing for **durable powers of attorney for health care** (sometimes called **health care representatives**). This is a type of advance directive in which the principal specifically gives the attorney in fact the authority to make certain health care decisions for him if the principal should become incompetent. Depending on state law and the instructions given by the principal to the attorney in fact, this could include decisions such as consenting or withholding consent to surgery, admitting the principal to a nursing home, and possibly withdrawing or prolonging life support. Note that the durable power of attorney becomes relevant only in the event that the principal becomes incompetent. So long as the principal is competent, he retains the ability to make health care decisions. This power of attorney is also revocable at the will of the principal. The precise requirements for creation of the

Figure 26.1   Living Will

LIVING WILL DECLARATION*

Declaration made this _____ day of _____ (month, year). I, _____, being at least eighteen (18) years of age and of sound mind, willfully and voluntarily make known my desires that my dying shall not be artificially prolonged under the circumstances set forth below, and I declare:

If at any time my attending physician certifies in writing that: (1) I have an incurable injury, disease, or illness; (2) my death will occur within a short time; and (3) the use of life prolonging procedures would serve only to artificially prolong the dying process, I direct that such procedures be withheld or withdrawn, and that I be permitted to die naturally with only the performance or provision of any medical procedure or medication necessary to provide me with comfort care or to alleviate pain, and, if I have so indicated below, the provision of artificially supplied nutrition and hydration. (Indicate your choice by initialing or making your mark before signing this declaration):

___ I wish to receive artificially supplied nutrition and hydration, even if the effort to sustain life is futile or excessively burdensome to me.

___ I do not wish to receive artificially supplied nutrition and hydration, if the effort to sustain life is futile or excessively burdensome to me.

___ I intentionally make no decision concerning artificially supplied nutrition and hydration, leaving the decision to my health care representative appointed under IC 16-36-1-7 or my attorney in fact with health care powers under IC 30-5-5.

In the absence of my ability to give directions regarding the use of life prolonging procedures, it is my intention that this declaration be honored by my family and physician as the final expression of my legal right to refuse medical or surgical treatment and accept the consequences of the refusal.

I understand the full import of this declaration.

Signed: _____

City, County, and State of Residence _____

The declarant has been personally known to me, and I believe (him/her) to be of sound mind. I did not sign the declarant's signature above for or at the direction of the declarant. I am not a parent, spouse, or child of the declarant. I am not entitled to any part of the declarant's estate or directly financially responsible for the declarant's medical care. I am competent and at least eighteen (18) years of age.

Witness _____   Date _____

Witness _____   Date _____

*From Ind. Code § 16-36-4-10 (2017).

durable power of attorney differ from state to state, but all states require a written and signed document executed with specified formalities, such as witnessing by disinterested witnesses.

Federal Law and Advance Directives

A federal statute, the Patient Self-Determination Act,[2] requires health care providers to take active steps to educate people about the opportunity to make advance decisions about medical care and the prolonging of life and to record the choices that they make. This statute, which became effective in 1991, requires health care providers such as hospitals, nursing homes, hospices, and home health agencies to provide written information to adults receiving medical care about their rights concerning the ability to accept or refuse medical or surgical treatment, the health care provider's policies concerning those rights, and their right to formulate advance directives. The act also requires the provider to document in the patient's medical record whether the patient has executed an advance directive, and it forbids discrimination against the patient based on the individual's choice regarding an advance directive. In addition, the provider is required to ensure compliance with the requirements of state law concerning advance directives and to educate its staff and the community on issues concerning advance directives.

[2]42 U.S.C. § 1395cc (1990).

Intestacy

 LO26-4 Explain and provide examples of how property is disposed of when a person dies without leaving a will.

If a person dies without making a will, or makes a will that is declared invalid, that person has died **intestate**. When that occurs, that person's property will be distributed to the persons designated as the intestate's heirs under the appropriate state's intestacy or intestate succession statute. The intestate's real property will be distributed according to the intestacy statute of the state in which the property is located. Personal property will be distributed according to the intestacy statute of the state of **domicile** at the time of death. A domicile is a person's permanent home. A person can have only one domicile at a time. Determinations of a person's domicile turn on facts that tend to show that person's intent to make a specific state a permanent home.

Partial intestacy is possible when only a portion of a will is declared invalid or when a valid will does not dispose of the entire estate.

Characteristics of Intestacy Statutes The

provisions of intestacy statutes are not uniform. Their purpose, however, is to distribute property in a way that reflects the *presumed intent* of the deceased—that is, to carry out the probable intent of the typical testator. Most people prefer that their property is given to their closest relatives. In general, such statutes first provide for the distribution

of most or all of a person's estate to her surviving spouse, children, or grandchildren. If no such survivors exist, the statutes typically provide for the distribution of the estate to parents, siblings, or nieces and nephews. If no relatives at this level are living, the property may be distributed to surviving grandparents, uncles, aunts, or cousins. Generally, persons with the same degree of relationship to the deceased person take equal shares. If the deceased had no surviving relatives, the property **escheats** (goes) to the state.

Figure 26.2 shows an example of a distribution scheme under an intestacy statute.

Special Rules Under intestacy statutes, a person

must have a relationship to the deceased person through blood or marriage in order to inherit any part of the deceased person's property. State law includes adopted children within the definition of "children" and treats adopted children in the same way as it treats biological children. Normally adopted children inherit from their adoptive families and not from their biological families, although some states' laws may allow them to inherit from both. The following *Hill v. Nakai* case illustrates how, in the interest of efficiency and predictability, intestacy rules in probate codes have displaced many older common law rules and doctrines that once governed the distribution of a decedent's estate. In *Hill*, the doctrine of equitable adoption is found to be preempted by the state probate code, which the court interprets strictly to allow inheritance only by biological and legally adopted children.

Figure 26.2   Example of a Distribution Scheme under an Intestacy Statute

Person Dying Intestate Is Survived By	Result
1. Spouse* and child or issue of a deceased child	Spouse ½, Child ½
2. Spouse and parent(s) but no issue	Spouse ¾, Parent ¼
3. Spouse but no parent or issue	All of the estate to spouse
4. Issue but no spouse	Estate is divided among issue
5. Parent(s), brothers, sisters, and/or issue of deceased brothers and sisters but no spouse or issue	Estate is divided among parent(s), brothers, sisters, and issue of deceased brothers and sisters
6. Issue of brothers and sisters but no spouse, issue, parents, brothers, and sisters	Estate is divided among issue of deceased brothers and sisters
7. Grandparents, but no spouse, issue, parents, brothers, sisters, or issue of deceased brothers and sisters	All of the estate goes to grandparents
8. None of the above	Estate goes to the state

*Note, however, second and subsequent spouses who had no children by the decedent may be assigned a smaller share.

Hill v. Nakai (*In re* Estate of Hannifin)   311 P.3d 1016 (Utah 2013)

In the summer of 1958, Father William J. Hannifin, an Episcopal priest, visited the Navajo Reservation near Aneth, Utah, where Willis Nakai and his biological family were living. Following a conversation with Nakai's mother and maternal grandparents, Hannifin agreed to raise Nakai as his own child, even though they were neither biologically nor legally related. From that point forward, Hannifin provided Nakai an allowance, food, clothing, medical care, transportation, and emotional support. He monitored Nakai's schoolwork and generally provided for Nakai's health and welfare. Nakai visited his biological family yearly during his childhood, but his biological parents did not assert parental control over him and did not support him financially.

Even into adulthood Nakai referred to Hannifin as his father, and Hannifin referred to Nakai as his son. Hannifin also treated Nakai's children and grandchildren as his own grandchildren and great-grandchildren.

Upon Hannifin's death, he had arranged for many of his assets, including his life insurance policy, bank accounts, and investment accounts to be transferred to Nakai. However, Hannifin did not execute a valid will and, therefore, died intestate. He had no spouse and no biological heirs.

Nakai sought to be appointed Personal Representative of Hannifin's estate, alleging that he and his family were Hannifin's only known heirs and devisees. The court granted the petition.

Max Hill, acting on behalf of himself and 19 other collateral relatives of Hannifin, petitioned the court to be appointed Special Administrator of Hannifin's estate for the limited purpose of contesting Nakai's claim to the estate. The court granted Hill's petition and, following a bench trial, held that under the doctrine of equitable adoption, Nakai was entitled "to inherit from Father Hannifin's estate as though he were his legally adopted son."

Hill appealed, arguing that Utah's enactment of the Probate Code preempted the common law doctrine of equitable adoption.

Justice Lee, opinion of the Court

We have long recognized the axiom that our precedent must yield when it conflicts with a validly enacted statute. Statutes may preempt the common law either by governing an area in so pervasive a manner that it displaces the common law (field preemption) or by directly conflicting with the common law (conflict preemption). Preemption may be indicated expressly, by a stated intent to preempt the common law. More often, however, explicit preemption language does not appear, or does not directly answer the question. In that event, courts must consider whether the . . . statute's structure and purpose or nonspecific statutory language nonetheless reveal a clear, but implicit, preemptive intent. [Citations and quotation marks omitted throughout paragraph.]

[F]ield preemption occurs when the scope of a statute indicates that the legislature intended a statute to occupy a field in such a way as to make reasonable the inference that the legislature left no room for the common law to supplement it. Conflict preemption, on the other hand, occurs where it is impossible . . . to comply with both the common law and a statute, or where the common law stands as an obstacle to the accomplishment and execution of the full purposes and objectives of the legislature. [Citations and quotation marks omitted throughout paragraph.]

This notion of conflict preemption is reiterated in the Probate Code. Though the Code provides that "principles of . . . equity supplement its provisions," Utah Code § 75-1-103, it also contains an express caveat that principles of equity may not be invoked where they are "displaced by the particular provisions of th[e]

code." *Id.* A judge-made doctrine that conflicts with a statute is certainly "displaced" by it.

We find the Code to displace the doctrine of equitable adoption recognized in *Williams' Estates*. In that case, a couple took a child into their home, agreeing with the birth mother that they would adopt the child and "raise, care for and treat [her] in all respects as their own child." *In re Williams' Estates*, 348 P.2d 683, 685 (Utah 1960). Though they never formally adopted the child, they did raise her as their own. *Id.* at 684. And when the couple died intestate, the child claimed that "she should be awarded the same share of the Williamses['] estate as she would have been entitled to had they . . . fulfilled their agreement to adopt." *Id.* We agreed that a child in that situation could possibly inherit through intestacy. . . .

Though we have not had occasion to opine on this doctrine since it was recognized, most other jurisdictions employing the doctrine have followed the same path, requiring claimants to prove the existence of an agreement to adopt. Most also limit use of the doctrine to situations that benefit the equitably adopted child, meaning, for example, that the doctrine does not prevent the equitably adopted child from inheriting from natural parents, and typically cannot be used by an adoptive parent to inherit from the equitably adopted child. Courts deem these and other similar restrictions proper since equitable adoption is only an equitable remedy to enforce a contract right, is not intended or applied to create the legal relationship of parent and child, with all the legal consequences of such relationship, [and] is [not] meant to create a legal adoption. [Citations and quotation marks omitted.]

The Probate Code, enacted fifteen years after we embraced equitable adoption in *Williams' Estates*, is in direct conflict with the doctrine in three principal respects: (A) Equitable adoption allows children who cannot satisfy the Probate Code's definition of "Child" to nonetheless participate in intestate succession as if they had. (B) Equitably adopted children can take by succession from both natural and adoptive parents—despite the Code's clear mandate to the contrary. (C) The doctrine adds confusion and complexity to our law's intestate succession scheme, in contravention of the Code's stated purpose of streamlining and clarifying the distribution of a decedent's estate.

In light of these conflicts, the equitable adoption doctrine cannot be squared with the Probate Code; it is impossible to satisfy both the requirements of the Probate Code and the elements of equitable adoption. This is a doctrine in conflict with the Code, which we therefore repudiate as preempted by statute.

A

At the time of our decision in *Williams' Estates*, our intestate succession statutes did not define the terms "child" or "parent." *See* UTAH CODE § 74-4-1 to -24 (1953). They did not distinguish classes of children that could take by succession (such as natural and adopted children) from those that could not (like foster children, stepchildren, and grandchildren). The Probate Code changed the landscape by providing precise definitions of parties legally entitled to take by intestate succession. These provisions displaced the open-ended system within which *Williams' Estates* was situated.

The Probate Code provides that "[a]ny part of a decedent's estate not effectively disposed of by will passes by intestate succession to the decedent's heirs as provided in" the Code. Utah Code § 75-2-101(1). Thus, the Code establishes a detailed scheme that governs the priority by which certain classes of heirs are entitled to succeed to the decedent's estate. Under the Code, "[a]ny part of the intestate estate" that does not pass to the decedent's spouse (because, for example, the decedent's spouse did not survive him) passes "to the decedent's descendants per capita at each generation," . . . and if no surviving descendants exist, then to the decedent's parent(s). . . . And if neither parent survived the decedent, the estate goes to the parents' descendants, if any, and then, if none exist, to the decedent's grandparents or the grandparents' descendants. . . .

The second group of takers, "the decedent's descendants," generally includes a decedent's children, "with the relationship of parent and child . . . being determined by the definition of child and parent contained in [the Probate Code]." *Id.* § 75-1-201(9). And according to the Code, a "Child" is "any individual entitled to take as a child under this code by intestate succession from the parent whose relationship is involved and excludes any person who is only a stepchild, a foster child, a grandchild, or any

more remote descendant." *Id.* § 75-1-201(5). "Parent" similarly "includes any person entitled to take, or who would be entitled to take if the child died without a will, as a parent under this code by intestate succession from the child whose relationship is in question and excludes any person who is only a stepparent, foster parent, or grandparent." *Id.* § 75-1-201(33). And "for purposes of intestate succession by, through, or from a person, an individual is the child of the individual's natural parents" and "[a]n adopted individual is the child of the adopting parent or parents and not of the natural parents." *Id.* § 75-2-114(1), (2).

By enacting a Probate Code with a specific definition of "child" that excludes those "equitably" adopted, the legislature preempted common law doctrines that are in conflict with the results those definitions require. . . . Under this scheme and according to these definitions, the only methods of determining who is a child for intestate succession purposes are legal adoption and natural parentage. And Nakai is neither Hannifin's legally adopted nor his natural child. The closest Nakai comes to any of the relations delineated in the Probate Code is to a foster child, which is a category specifically excluded from taking intestate. Yet he falls short even there. A foster child/parent relationship is one marked by legal rights and responsibilities, neither of which existed in this case. Nakai thus can have no claim under the Probate Code to a distribution through intestate succession.

It is thus impossible to comply with both the Probate Code and with the principles of equitable adoption. Because Hannifin had neither a spouse nor children, the Probate Code requires that his estate pass to his parents or, if neither survived him, to his parents' descendants. Utah Code § 75-2-103(1)(a)–(c). If no takers exist in those categories, then his estate must past to his grandparents or, if none survived him, to their descendants. The statutory scheme makes this chain of distribution both clear and mandatory. And Hill and his fellow relatives qualify as takers in that chain. In contrast, equitable adoption requires that the estate pass to Nakai, a legal stranger to Hannifin, leaving nothing for Hill and the others. There is no way to reconcile the two different sets of requirements.

B

Another intractable conflict between the Probate Code and equitable adoption stems from section 75-2-114(1)–(2), which states that "for purposes of intestate succession . . . [a]n adopted individual is the child of the adopting parent . . . and not of the natural parents." This section operates to prohibit adopted children from taking by intestacy from both their natural parents and their adoptive parents. This is in direct contravention of the doctrine of equitable adoption, which is purely beneficial to the child and in no way alters the legal relationship between the claimant and the decedent or between the claimant and the biological parents. . . .

[W]hen our legislature enacted the Probate Code . . . , it expressly foreclosed [the] possibility [of dual succession]. It did so by enacting section 114, which prevents a child from inheriting from two sets of parents. *See* Utah Code § 75-2-114(1)–(2) ("[F]or purposes of intestate succession . . . [a]n adopted individual is the child of the adopting parent . . . and not of the natural parents."). That is a significant legislative development in our law in the Probate Code and one that is in direct conflict with equitable adoption. . . .

Dual succession is an inherent element of equitable adoption. Yet dual succession is expressly foreclosed by statute. The conflict is palpable and explicit. Again, it is impossible to comply with both the Probate Code and with the judge-made doctrine of equitable adoption, as the former prohibits what the latter requires. And in light of this conflict, our only option is to abandon the doctrine of equitable adoption.

Such abandonment is the only way to maintain fidelity to the objectives expressly detailed in the Probate Code. As the Code indicates, its detailed intestate succession scheme is designed:

(a) To simplify and clarify the law concerning the affairs of decedents, missing persons . . . ;

(b) To discover and make effective the intent of a decedent in distribution of his property;

(c) To promote a speedy and efficient system for administering the estate of the decedent and making distribution to his successors;

(d) To facilitate use and enforcement of certain trusts; and

(e) To make uniform the law among the various jurisdictions.

Id. § 75-1-102(2).

The doctrine of equitable adoption undermines these objectives by introducing uncertainty, complexity, and inefficiency—the very evils the Probate Code was designed to avoid.

Though the equitable adoption doctrine has been on the books for more than fifty years, neither we nor any other Utah court has given it any dimension. This boundary-less quality is another point of incompatibility with the Probate Code, which values predictability and stability. Were we to retain the doctrine, we would have to provide predictable definition to the otherwise vague standard announced in *Williams' Estates.* For instance, in future cases we would surely be called on to decide questions along the following lines: Must both biological parents be party to the agreement to adopt? What kind of evidence is required to prove the existence of an agreement to adopt? How long must the adoptive parents treat the child as their own before the child qualifies for intestate succession? Just how limited must the child's relationship with his biological family be? How completely must the natural parents relinquish all their rights to the child?

In working to populate these fields, we would only compound the problem we identify today. With each new contour added to the standard, we would inevitably substitute our own policy choice for that expressed by the legislature when it enacted the Probate Code. We cannot condone such substitution. In the Code the legislature decided, as a policy matter, that efficiency and predictability are best served by distributing the estates of those that die intestate in accordance with a prediction as to the preference of the average intestate decedent. And that prediction follows biological and legal relationship lines. . . .

We accordingly jettison the doctrine of equitable adoption as a vestige of a common-law friendly intestacy regime that has been overtaken by statute. Thus, we hold that the administration of Hannifin's estate is subject to the express terms of the Probate Code, including terms governing matters of distribution and representation. **We reverse and remand for further proceedings consistent with this opinion.**

Half brothers and half sisters are usually treated in the same way as brothers and sisters related by whole blood. An illegitimate child may inherit from his mother, but as a general rule, illegitimate children do not inherit from their fathers unless paternity has been either acknowledged or established in a legal proceeding.

A person must be alive at the time the decedent dies to claim a share of the decedent's estate. An exception may be made for children or other descendants who are born *after* the decedent's death. If a person who is entitled to a share of the decedent's estate survives the decedent but dies before receiving that share, it becomes part of the person's own estate.

Simultaneous Death Prior to the advent of automobiles and airplanes, the prospect of spouses dying in a common accident or tragedy was rare enough that there was typically not a special legal rule to determine how estates would be distributed in such instances. If one spouse survived the other, even for just a short time, the predeceased spouse's estate passed to the surviving spouse. Particularly as automobile accidents made it marginally more likely that spouses could die simultaneously (or at least under circumstances where it was very difficult to determine which of the two died first), a need arose to craft a legal doctrine to deal with the uncertainty that created. Moreover, modern courts were less willing to allow a decedent's estate to pass to a spouse who died shortly thereafter without getting the benefit of the estate's distribution, particularly because that situation could result in disinheriting the predeceased spouse's heirs on a mere formality. As a result, a statute known as the Uniform Simultaneous Death Act provides that where two persons who would inherit from each other (such as husband and wife) die under circumstances that make it difficult or impossible to determine who died first, each person's property is to be distributed as though he or she survived. This means, for example, that the husband's property will go to his relatives and the wife's property to her relatives. Jointly owned property is typically distributed in equal shares to the heirs of each of the husband and wife.

Many states that have enacted the Uniform Simultaneous Death Act treat deaths that are within 120 hours (or five days) of one another as simultaneous. Most of those states also allow for a testator's will to opt out of the simultaneous death provisions either by explicit reference or by creating contingencies and bequests that are inconsistent with the provisions of the Simultaneous Death Act.

Administration of Estates

Identify the steps in the process of administering an estate and explain the responsibilities of the personal representative for the estate.

When a person dies, an orderly procedure is needed to collect property, settle debts, and distribute any remaining property to those who will inherit it under the will or by intestate succession. This process occurs under the supervision of a probate court and is known as the administration process or the probate process. Summary (simple) procedures are sometimes available when an estate is relatively small—for example, when it has assets of less than $7,500.

The Probate Estate
The probate process operates only on the decedent's property that is considered to be part of the probate estate. The probate estate is that property that passes under the decedent's will or by intestacy. Assets that pass by operation of law and assets that are transferred by other devices such as trusts or life insurance policies do not pass through probate.

Note that the decedent's probate estate and *taxable estate* for purposes of federal estate tax are two different concepts. The taxable estate is broader and includes all property owned or controlled by the decedent at the time of death. For example, if a person purchased a $1 million life insurance policy made payable to his spouse or

children, the policy would be included in his taxable estate, but not in his probate estate.

Determining the Existence of a Will
The first step in the probate process is to determine whether the deceased left a will. This may require a search of the deceased person's personal papers and safe-deposit box. If a will is found, it must be *proved* to be admitted to probate. This involves the testimony of the persons who witnessed the will, if they are still alive. If the witnesses are no longer alive, the signatures of the witnesses and the testator will have to be established in some other way. In the vast majority of states and under UPC Section 2-504, a will may be proved by an affidavit (declaration under oath) sworn to and signed by the testator and the witnesses at the time the will was executed. This is called a self-proving affidavit. If a will is located and proved, it will be admitted to probate and govern many of the decisions that must be made in the administration of the estate.

Selecting a Personal Representative
Another early step in the administration of an estate is the selection of a personal representative to administer the estate. If the deceased left a will, it is likely that he designated his personal representative in the will. The personal representative under a will is also known as the **executor**. Almost anyone could serve as an executor. The testator may have chosen, for example, his spouse, a grown child, a close friend, an attorney, or the trust department of a bank.

If the decedent died intestate, or if the personal representative named in a will is unable to serve, the probate court will name a personal representative to administer the estate. In the case of an intestate estate, the personal representative is called an **administrator**. A preference is usually accorded to a surviving spouse, child, or other close relative. If no relative is available and qualified to serve, a creditor, bank, or other person may be appointed by the court.

Most states require that the personal representative *post a bond* in an amount in excess of the estimated value of the estate to ensure that her duties will be properly and faithfully performed. A person making a will often directs that the executor may serve without posting a bond, and this exemption may be accepted by the court.

Responsibilities of the Personal Representative
The personal representative has a number of important tasks in the administration of the estate, including ensuring that an inventory is taken of the estate's assets and that the assets are appraised. Notice must then be given to creditors or potential claimants against the estate so that they can file and prove their claims within a specified time,

normally two to six months. As a general rule, the surviving spouse of the deceased person is entitled to be paid an allowance during the time the estate is being settled. This allowance has priority over other debts of the estate. The personal representative must see that any properly payable funeral or burial expenses are paid and that the creditors' claims are satisfied.

Both federal and some state governments impose estate or inheritance taxes on estates of a certain size. The personal representative is responsible for filing estate tax returns. The federal tax is a tax on the deceased's estate, with provisions for deducting items such as debts, expenses of administration, and charitable gifts. In addition, an amount equal to the amount left to the surviving spouse may be deducted from the gross estate before the tax is computed. State inheritance taxes are imposed on the person who receives a gift or statutory share from an estate. It is common, however, for wills to provide that the estate will pay all taxes, including inheritance taxes, so that the beneficiaries will not have to do so. The personal representative must also make provisions for filing an income tax return and for paying any income tax due for the partial year prior to the decedent's death.

When the debts, expenses, and taxes have been taken care of, the remaining assets of the estate are distributed to the decedent's heirs (if there was no will) or to the beneficiaries of the decedent's will. Special rules apply when the estate is too small to satisfy all of the bequests made in a will or when some or all of the designated beneficiaries are no longer living.

When the personal representative has completed all of these duties, the probate court will close the estate and discharge the personal representative.

Trusts

LO26-6 Explain the concept of *trust*, identify various types of trusts, and explain the powers and responsibilities of a trustee.

Nature of a Trust
A **trust** is a legal relationship in which a person who has legal title to property has the duty to hold it for the use or benefit of another person. The person benefited by a trust is considered to have equitable or beneficial title to the property because it is being maintained for her benefit. This means that she is the real owner even though the trustee has the legal title in the trustee's name. A trust can be created in a number of ways. An owner of property may *declare* that he is holding certain property in trust. For example, a mother might state that she is holding 100 shares of General Motors stock in trust

for her daughter. A trust may also arise *by operation of law.* For example, when a lawyer representing a client injured in an automobile accident receives a settlement payment from an insurance company, the lawyer holds the settlement payment as trustee for the client. Most commonly, however, trusts are created through *express instruments* or deed of trust whereby an owner of property transfers title to the property to a trustee who is to hold, manage, and invest the property for the benefit of either the original owner or a third person. For example, Long transfers certain stock to First Trust Bank with instructions to pay the income to his daughter during her lifetime and to distribute the stock to her children after her death.

Trust Terminology
A person who creates a trust is known as a **settlor**, grantor, or trustor. The person who holds the property for the benefit of another person is called the **trustee**. The person for whose benefit the property is held in trust is the **beneficiary**. Figure 26.3 illustrates the relationship among these parties. A single person may occupy more than one of these positions; however, if there is only one beneficiary, he cannot be the sole trustee. The property held in trust is called the corpus or **res**. A distinction is made between the property in trust, which is the principal, and the income that is produced by the principal.

A trust that is established and effective during the settlor's lifetime is known as an ***inter vivos*** trust. A trust can also be established in a person's will. Such trusts take effect only at the death of the settlor. They are called testamentary trusts.

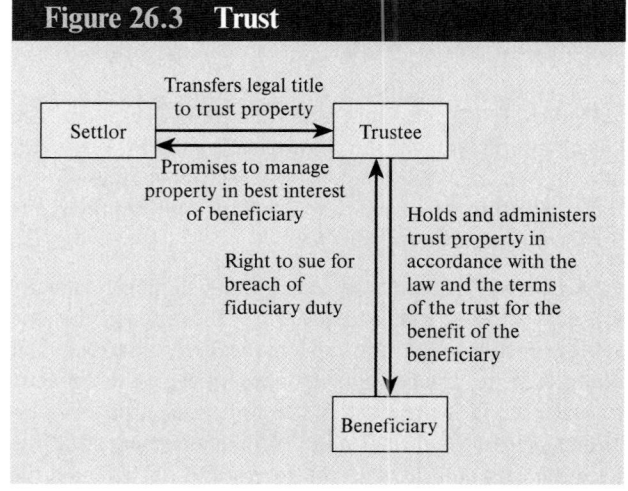

Figure 26.3   Trust

Why People Create Trusts

Bennett owns a portfolio of valuable stock. Her husband has predeceased her. She has two children and an elderly father for whom she would like to provide. Why might it be advantageous to Bennett to transfer the stock to a trust for the benefit of the members of her family?

First, there may be income tax or estate tax planning advantages in doing so, depending on the type of trust she establishes and the provisions of that trust. For example, she can establish an irrevocable trust for her children and remove the property transferred to her trust from her estate so that it is not taxable at her death. In addition, the trust property can be used for the benefit of others and may even pass to others after the settlor's death without the necessity of having a will. Many people prefer to pass their property by trust rather than by will because trusts afford more privacy. Unlike a probated will, they do not become items of public record. Trusts also afford greater opportunity for postgift management than do outright gifts and bequests. If Bennett wants her children to enjoy the income of the trust property during their young adulthood without distributing unfettered ownership of the property to them before she considers them able to manage it properly, she can accomplish this through a trust provision. A trust can prevent the property from being squandered or spent too quickly. Trusts can be set up so that a beneficiary's interest cannot be reached by creditors in many situations. Such trusts, called spendthrift trusts, will be discussed later.

Placing property in trust can operate to increase the amount of property held for the beneficiaries if the trustee makes good investment decisions. Another important consideration is that a trust can be used to provide for the needs of disabled beneficiaries who are not capable of managing funds. Ultimately, the advantage of a trust lies in its flexibility. The relationship among the three parties can be structured in myriad ways.

Creation of Express Trusts

There are five basic requirements for the creation of a valid express trust, although special and somewhat less restrictive rules govern the establishment of charitable trusts. The requirements for forming an express trust are:

1. *Capacity.* The settlor must have had the legal capacity to convey the property to the trust. This means that the settlor must have had the capacity needed to make a valid contract if the trust is an *inter vivos* trust or the capacity to make a will if the trust is a testamentary trust. For example, a trust would fail under this requirement if, at the time the trust was created, the settlor had not attained the age required by state law for the creation of valid wills and contracts (age 18 in most states).

2. *Intent and formalities.* The settlor must *intend* to create a trust at the present time. To impose enforceable duties on the trustee, the settlor must meet certain formalities. Under the laws of most states, for example, the trustee must accept the trust by signing the trust instrument. In the case of a trust of land, the trust must be in writing so as to meet the statute of frauds. If the trust is a testamentary trust, it must satisfy the formal requirements for wills.

3. *Conveyance of specific property.* The settlor must convey *specific property* to the trust. The property conveyed must be property that the settlor has the *right to convey*. This need not be a substantial sum. It can be a penny or any interest.

4. *Proper purpose.* The trust must be created for a *proper purpose.* It cannot be created for a reason that is contrary to public policy, such as the commission of a crime.

5. *Identity of the beneficiaries.* The *beneficiaries* of the trust must be described clearly enough so that their identities can be ascertained. Sometimes, beneficiaries may be members of a specific class, such as "my children."

Charitable Trusts

A distinction is made between private trusts and trusts created for charitable purposes. In a private trust, property is devoted to the benefit of specific persons, whereas in a charitable trust, property is devoted to a charitable organization or to some other purposes beneficial to society. While some of the rules governing private and charitable trusts are the same, a number of these rules are different. For example, when a private trust is created, the beneficiary must be known at the time or ascertainable within a certain time (established by a legal rule known as the rule against perpetuities). However, a charitable trust is valid even though no definitely ascertainable beneficiary is named and even though it is to continue for an indefinite or unlimited period.

Doctrine of Cy Pres A doctrine known as *cy pres* is applicable to charitable trusts when property is given in trust to be applied to a particular charitable purpose that becomes impossible, impracticable, or illegal to carry out. Under the doctrine of *cy pres*, the trust will not fail if the settlor indicated a general intention to devote the property to charitable purposes. If the settlor has not specifically provided for a substitute beneficiary, the court will direct the application of the property to some charitable purpose that falls within the settlor's general charitable intention.

In the following *Citizens National Bank* case, the court grapples with the issue of effectuating the donor's intent in a charitable trust.

Citizens National Bank of Paris v. Kids Hope United, Inc.
922 N.E.2d 1093 (Ill. 2009)

La Fern Blackman died in 1967. Her will provided that, after the death of her sister, Citizens National Bank of Paris would hold her farmland in trust and pay 75 percent of the income from the land to the Edgar County Children's Home (ECCH) and the other 25 percent to the trustees of the Embarrass Cemetery. The will further provided,

> In the event either of the aforesaid organizations shall cease to exist, then said bank as trustee is to distribute said portion or portions of said net income to such charitable organization or organizations as it deems worthy of said money.

Blackman's sister, Etoile Davis, died in 1971. Her will directed the bank to hold her farmland in trust and give 75 percent of the net income to ECCH and the other 25 percent to the trustees of the Embarrass Cemetery. The will further provided,

> In the event either of the aforesaid organizations shall cease to function in its present capacity, then the part of the trust fund which would have gone to this organization shall be divided equally between the FIRST METHODIST CHURCH OF PARIS MEMORIAL FOUNDATION, INC., THE EDGAR COUNTY CHAPTER OF THE AMERICAN CANCER SOCIETY, and THE EDGAR COUNTY HEART ASSOCIATION.

ECCH was incorporated in Illinois in 1803. Its charter stated that it was formed to "establish an institution for the education of dependent children of Edgar County, Illinois, and for the custody and maintenance of such children and to provide permanent homes for them in approved private families." In 1900, it erected a Children's Home facility on Eads Avenue to serve that purpose. In 1980, ECCH amended its articles of incorporation to allow it to become a residential placement resource for children throughout Illinois and to receive state funding. As a result of the amendment, ECCH's objective was to:

> provide services to children and youth in the fields of health, welfare and education in the State of Illinois, including multi-treatment and educational programs for emotionally handicapped boys and girls of all races in residential treatment centers, day treatment services, counseling services to family, and such other related and auxiliary services as are necessary or desirable from time to time to accomplish these purposes; and to own or lease property, establish and maintain residential treatment centers, homes, schools and other facilities required.

In 2003, ECCH merged with the Hudelson Baptist Children's Home, and ECCH dissolved as an entity and merged all its assets and programs into Hudelson. The Children's Home facility owned by ECCH was also transferred to Hudelson. In the merger agreement between ECCH and Hudelson, Hudelson "guaranteed that ECCH's mission of working with children in Edgar and the surrounding counties will be continued for as long as it is financially feasible to do so." In 2005, Hudelson changed its name to Kids Hope. The Children's Home that ECCH had built in 1900 closed and later was sold to a school district.

The bank, as trustee for the Blackman and Davis trusts, filed a petition in court stating that it believed that ECCH "had ceased to exist," and asked the court to determine whether this was true and, if so, to approve the distribution of 75 percent of the trust's net income to the alternate beneficiaries named in the Davis will. The bank and Kids Hope both filed motions for summary judgment. The trial court granted the bank's motion and found that ECCH had ceased to exist and directed the distribution of trust income to other beneficiaries. Kids Hope appealed, and the appellate court reversed. The bank appealed.

Freeman, Justice

In interpreting trusts, the goal is to determine the settlor's intent, which the court will effectuate if it is not contrary to law or public policy. Charitable gifts are viewed with peculiar favor by the courts, and every presumption consistent with the language contained in the instruments of gift will be employed in order to sustain them.

In the case at bar, it is true that ECCH ceased to exist as a separate corporate entity following its merger with Kids Hope. However, the important question here is not whether ECCH ceased to exist as a separate entity. Rather, in interpreting the restrictive condition to determine the testator's intent, the important question is whether the new corporation with which the original charitable organization merged was no longer suited to carry out the purposes of the bequest. If Kids Hope is not suited to carry out the purposes of Blackman's bequest, ECCH will have ceased to operate or exist within the meaning of Blackman's restrictive condition, and the gift to ECCH would lapse. If, however, Kids Hope *is* suited to carry out the purposes of the bequest, then in our view ECCH did not cease to operate or exist, as Blackman meant those words, even if it did cease to exist as a separate corporate entity.

We note that there is nothing in the language of Blackman's restrictive condition that would indicate that she meant "cease to operate or exist" to refer to ECCH's separate corporate existence.

In the 2003 merger agreement, Hudelson "guaranteed that ECCH's mission of working with children in Edgar and the surrounding counties will be continued for as long as it is financially feasible to do so." Moreover, part of the object for which ECCH was established was to "provide permanent homes for the dependent children of Edgar County in approved private families." According to the parties' agreed statement of facts, Kids Hope currently "has families in Edgar County who serve as approved foster homes." We agree with the appellate court that "the merger did not hinder Kids Hope's ability to carry out the purposes of Blackman's original bequest." Kids Hope is suited to carry out these purposes, and ECCH did not cease to operate or exist as Blackman intended those words.

Affirmed in favor of Kids Hope.

Totten Trusts A Totten trust is a deposit of money in a bank or other financial institution in the name of the depositor *as trustee* for a named beneficiary. For example, Bliss deposits money in First Bank in trust for his daughter, Bessie. The Totten trust creates a revocable living trust. At Bliss's death, if he has not revoked this trust, the money in the account will belong to Bessie. The UPC has abolished the Totten trust as a formal category and instead treats them as payment-on-death accounts.

Powers and Duties of the Trustee In most express trusts, the settlor names a specific person to act as trustee. If the settlor does not name a trustee, the court will appoint one. Similarly, a court will replace a trustee who resigns, is incompetent, or refuses to act.

The trust codes of most states contain provisions giving trustees broad management powers over trust property. These provisions can be limited or expanded by express provisions in the trust instrument. The trustee has a duty of prudence, which means the trustee must use a *reasonable degree of skill, judgment, and care.* A trustee who claims to have a greater degree of skill will be held to that higher standard. Section 7-302 of the UPC provides that the trustee is held to the standard of a prudent person dealing with the property of another, and if the trustee has special skills or is named trustee based on a representation of special skills, that level of skill is required. The trustee *may not commingle* the property held in trust with the trustee's own property or with that of another trust.

A trustee owes a *duty of loyalty* (fiduciary duty) to the beneficiaries. This means that the trustee must administer the trust for the benefit of the beneficiaries and avoid any conflict between personal interests and the interest of the trust. For example, a trustee cannot do business with a trust that she administers without express permission in the trust agreement. She must not prefer one beneficiary's interest to another's, and she must account to the beneficiaries for all transactions. Unless the trust agreement provides otherwise, the trustee must make the trust productive. The trustee may not delegate the performance of discretionary duties (such as the duty to select investments) to another but may delegate the performance of ministerial duties (such as the preparation of statements of account).

A trust may give the trustee discretion as to the amount of principal or income paid to a beneficiary. In such a case, the beneficiary cannot require the trustee to exercise her discretion in the manner desired by the beneficiary.

One of the duties of the trustee is to distribute the principal and income of the trust in accordance with the terms of the trust instrument. Suppose Wheeler's will created a testamentary trust providing that his wife was to receive the income from the trust for life, and at her death, the trust property was to be distributed to his children. During the duration of the trust, the trust earns profits, such as interest or rents, and has expenses, such as taxes or repairs. How should the trustee allocate these items as between Wheeler's surviving spouse, who is an income beneficiary, and his children, who are **remaindermen**?

The terms of the trust and state law bind the trustee in making this determination, via a duty of impartiality. As a general rule, ordinary profits received from the investment of trust property are allocated to income. For example, interest on trust property or rents earned from leasing real property held in trust would be allocated to income. Ordinary expenses such as insurance premiums, the cost of ordinary maintenance and repairs of trust property, and property taxes, would be chargeable to income. The principal of the trust includes the trust property itself and any extraordinary receipts, such as proceeds or gains derived from the sale of trust property. Modern trust codes give trustees the power to adjust among these categories and allow for the use of unitrusts, which provide a formula or percentage of returns that are treated as income.

Liability of Trustee

A trustee who breaches any of the duties of a trustee or whose conduct falls below the standard of care applicable to trustees may incur personal liability. For example, if the trustee invests unwisely and imprudently, the trustee may be personally liable to reimburse the trust estate for the shortfall. The language of the trust affects the trustee's liability and the level of care owed by the trustee. A settlor might, for example, include language lowering the trustee's duty of care or relieving the trustee of some liability that he might otherwise incur.

The trustee can also have liability to third persons who are injured by the operation of the trust. Because a trust is not in itself a legal entity that can be sued, a third party who has a claim (such as a tort claim or a claim for breach of contract) must file that claim against the trustee of the trust. The trustee's actual personal liability to a third party depends on the language of the trust and of any contracts entered on behalf of the trust as well as the extent to which the injury complained of by the third party was a result of the personal fault or omission of the trustee.

Spendthrift Trusts

Generally, the beneficiary of a trust may voluntarily assign rights to the principal or income of the trust to another person. In addition, any distributions to the beneficiary are subject to the claims of creditors. Sometimes, however, trusts contain provisions known as spendthrift clauses, which restrict the voluntary or involuntary transfer of a beneficiary's interest. Such clauses are generally enforced, and they preclude assignees or creditors from compelling a trustee to recognize their claims to the trust. The enforceability of such clauses is usually subject to four exceptions, however:

1. For the most part, a person cannot put property beyond the claims of creditors. Thus, a spendthrift clause is not effective in a trust when the settlor and the beneficiary are the same person.
2. Divorced spouses and minor children of the beneficiary can usually compel payment for alimony and child support.

3. In some states, creditors of the beneficiary who have furnished necessaries can compel payment.
4. Once the trustee distributes property to a beneficiary, it can be subject to valid claims of others.

 List the requirements for the formation of a trust and describe how trusts can be revoked or modified.

Termination and Modification of a Trust

Normally, a settlor cannot revoke or modify a trust unless he reserves the power to do so at the time he establishes the trust. However, a trust may be modified or terminated with the consent of the settlor and all of the beneficiaries. When the settlor is dead or otherwise unable to consent, a trust can be modified or terminated by consent of all the persons with a beneficial interest, but only when this would not frustrate a material purpose of the trust. Because trusts are under the supervisory jurisdiction of a court, the court can permit a deviation from the terms of a trust when unanticipated changes in circumstances threaten accomplishment of the settlor's purpose.

Implied and Constructive Trusts

Under exceptional circumstances in which the creation of a trust is necessary to effectuate a settlor's intent or avoid unjust enrichment, the law *implies* or imposes a trust even though no express trust exists or an express trust exists but has failed. One trust of this type is a resulting trust, which arises when there has been an incomplete disposition of trust property. For example, if Hess transferred property to Wickes as trustee to provide for the needs of Hess's grandfather and the grandfather died before the trust funds were exhausted, Wickes will be deemed to hold the property in a resulting trust for Hess or Hess's heirs. Similarly, if Hess had transferred the property to Wickes as trustee and the trust had failed because Hess did not meet one of the requirements of a valid trust, Wickes would not be permitted to keep the trust property as his own. A resulting trust would be implied.

A constructive trust is a trust created by operation of law to avoid fraud, injustice, or unjust enrichment. This type of trust imposes on the constructive trustee a duty to convey property he holds to another person on the ground that the constructive trustee would be unjustly enriched if he were allowed to retain it. For example, when a person procures the transfer of property by means of fraud or duress, he becomes a constructive trustee and is under the sole obligation to return the property to its original owner.

Problems and Problem Cases

1. John Irvine and Deana Dodge married in 1979. At the time of their marriage, Deana had a son from a previous marriage, Michael Dodge. During their marriage, John and Deana had no children together, nor did they adopt any children. John did not adopt Dodge. In 1983, John and Deana executed wills. The lawyer who drafted the wills retained the wills in his file. When he retired, the law firm that took over his practice retained the files. Deana died in 2008 and John in 2009. At the time of John's death, he was survived by his stepson, Dodge; his brother, William; and his mother, Va Va. Under the laws of intestacy, Va Va stood to inherit all of John's property if John left no will. One week after John died, William—who believed his brother had died without a will—sought to be appointed personal representative of his brother's estate. Later, however, while going through John's belongings, William found a copy of John's will. He also obtained the original signed will from the law firm. The will purported to pass all of John's property to Dodge if Deana predeceased him. There was no indication that John had made another will or had destroyed the will or otherwise attempted to revoke it. Va Va filed an objection to the probate of John's will, challenging its validity. Will she win?

2. In 2003, Grubbs transferred his individual retirement account (IRA) to Raymond James and Associates Inc., naming Nunnenman as the beneficiary to receive the residue in the event of his death. Grubbs was hospitalized in 2005. He summoned an attorney to the hospital, where he made and executed a last will and testament that did not mention the IRA account. The will left Grubbs's entire estate to his mother, Shervena, who was also named as executrix. Months after Grubbs's death, Shervena stated that she found a handwritten note in Grubbs's Bible that stated:

   May 2005

   My Will

   I Donnie Grubbs want all of my estate All IRA and any SBC Telco and all other assets and worldly goods to go to my Mother Shervena Grubbs. Being of sound mind.

   Donnie Grubbs

   In her capacity as executrix, Shervena filed an action for an injunction freezing the assets of the IRA account based on the handwritten note, which she claimed indicated the intent to make her the beneficiary of the account. Will she win?

3. Roy and Icie Johnson established two revocable *inter vivos* trusts in 1966. The trusts provided that upon Roy's and Icie's deaths, income from the trusts was to be paid in equal shares to their two sons, James and Robert, for life. Upon the death of the survivor of the sons, the trust was to be "*divided equally between all of my grandchildren, per stirpes.*" James had two daughters, Barbara and Elizabeth. Robert had four children, David, Rosalyn, Catherine, and Elizabeth. James and Robert disclaimed their interest in the trust in 1979, and a dispute arose about how the trust should be distributed to the grandchildren. The trustee filed an action seeking instructions on how the trusts should be distributed. What should the court hold?

4. Elma Ward died in 2008. Frazier petitioned the court to probate a holographic will made by Ward. The document contains two typewritten sections, separated by one handwritten section. The document reads:

   [Typewritten section] October 14, 1987

   All of our worl[d]ly things, which we owne [sic] will not be sold, given away, borrowed or otherwise disposed of, until one year after either of our death. The one that is left can do what they think is best for them. This includes house, land, trucks, cars, boats, shop & all contents, and contents of the house.

   [A signature, purporting to be that of Elma Ward is located here]

   [Handwritten section] To whom it's [sic] concern[ed]:

   Everything we own will be sold at both our death[s]. Patricia B. Smith—leave to her $1,000 in cash. She has been a dear daughter to her stepdad and me. Jimmy Buchanan [$]200. Diane Buchanan Moorehead $200. The rest of the cash from the sale be divided between Sheila Willis, Teresa L. Ward Frazier, Robert E. Ward.

   [A notary seal, with the signature of Jimmy Wells, is located here. The date "2/2/99" is handwritten above Mr. Wells's signature, and the date "4/18/2001" is handwritten below Mr. Wells's signature.]

   [Typewritten section, identical to that above, is included a second time at this place in the document]

   [Following the typewritten section, the document contains the signature of Edward Ward and a second signature purported to be that of Elma K. Ward. A second notary seal follows these signatures, which seal is signed by Jimmy Wells with the handwritten dates of 2/12/99, and 4/18/2001.]

Two individuals familiar with Ward's handwriting provided affidavits that the signature on the alleged will was genuine. Ward's son objected to the probate of this document, arguing that it does not meet the statutory requirements for a will because his mother's signature was not directly below the handwritten portion of the will. Tennessee law provides that "No witness to a holographic will is necessary, but the signature and all its material provisions must be in the handwriting of the testator and the testator's handwriting must be proved by two (2) witnesses." Was this a valid will?

5. Troy and Marie McDonald had a rocky marriage marked by domestic disturbances and substance abuse. They filed for divorce and a judge had issued a final order of dissolution to be effective in October 2005. In the interim, however, Marie and Troy were working toward reconciliation and were contemplating asking the court to withdraw the dissolution order. Tragically, Troy died in a motorcycle accident during the reconciliation period, after the order was filed but before it was officially effective. Troy's mother claimed that she and Troy's father should inherit his entire intestate estate because Marie was not a surviving spouse within the meaning of California Law. Marie opposed this. The Probate Code states that "surviving spouse" does not include "[a] person who was a party to a valid proceeding concluded by an order purporting to terminate all marital property rights." Marie argued that they were getting back together and the divorce was not finalized. Who was correct?

6. Vencie Beard shot and killed his wife, Melba, on April 16, 2011. The death certificate states that the time of her death was 8:59 P.M. Vencie shot himself at the same time, but he did not immediately die from his injuries. Rather, he died later that same night at 10:55 P.M. They each had wills that were identical in structure. Paragraph 2.02 of each will provided for specific cash bequests to nine named individuals if both Vencie and Melba died in a common disaster or under circumstances making it impossible to determine which died first. Paragraph 2.03 of each will provided that if the spouse did not survive the testator by 90 days, Janet Lea Hopkins would receive a portion of a tract of land the Beards co-owned. Paragraph 2.04 of each will provided that if the spouse did not survive the testator by 90 days, Matthew C. Hopkins would receive the remaining portion of that tract of land. In paragraph 2.05 of each will, Vencie and Melba gave "the rest and residue" of their estates to their respective spouses. That paragraph further provided that if the spouse did not survive the testator by 90 days, Beverly Kaye Gilmore and Janet Lea Hopkins would receive the residuary estate. The executrix of both estates sought a declaratory judgment from the court to determine whether they died in a common disaster and whether, if so, the Simultaneous Death Act applied to the wills (or only to certain of the paragraphs and not others). What should the court decide?

7. Before 1985, Franklin Timmons and his wife, Kathryn, owned property that included a marina called the "Boatyard," where Timmons operated the family business. Timmons's primary income was derived from the Boatyard, and according to him, the business ran at a loss. In 1980, a court awarded a judgment against Timmons in a case involving the Boatyard. Timmons never paid the judgment. In 1985, with the judgment still outstanding and no improvement in their financial conditions, the Timmonses established a Joint Irrevocable Living Trust. They conveyed to the Trust the farm and the Boatyard, which comprised all the real property that they owned and the only significant assets that were capable of responding to a creditor judgment. Under the terms of the Trust, the Timmonses and their son, Jimmy, were named as trustees. The Trust instrument gave trustees discretion to invade the trust principal and to sell the land for their own benefit. Although his property was held by the Trust, Timmons never viewed the Trust as limiting his ability to use the land for himself or to rent it to others. Timmons believed that he could continue to live on the land, operate his business on it, and use the land as his own, as he had done in the past. In 1985, six months after the Trust was created, Kulp, Timmons's employee, was severely injured while working at the Boatyard. Timmons did not carry workers' compensation insurance, and he did not reimburse any of Kulp's medical expenses. Kulp filed a petition for compensation due with the Industrial Accident Board (IAB), and the IAB ordered Timmons to post a $150,000 bond and to pay Kulp's medical expenses and other benefits. Timmons did not comply with the IAB order, and several years of litigation ensued. Timmons's son, Jimmy, died in October 1994, and Timmons's wife, Kathryn, died two years later. As a consequence, Timmons became the sole settlor, trustee, and lifetime beneficiary of the Trust. Kulp's IAB award still remained unpaid. In 1997, the Superior Court entered a money judgment in favor of Kulp, doubling the initial IAB award to $194,316.74 to compensate Kulp for the delay in payment. Kulp brought an action seeking a determination that the Trust was invalid and that its assets were subject to execution process. Less than one month after this action was filed, Timmons conveyed all his personal property

to his daughter-in-law, Beverly, and his granddaughter, Brandi. Thereafter, Beverly and Brandi conveyed a life estate in the conveyed property to Timmons. Timmons argued that as a consequence of that conveyance, and the transfer of his (and his wife's) assets to the Trust in 1985, he has no assets from which to satisfy the judgment. Can Kulp reach the trust assets to collect his judgment?

8. Almost a century ago, Henry and Martha Kolb started a family-owned floral business in Storm Lake, Iowa. Both the business and the family grew into prominence. After their grandson, Robert, was tragically killed in a hunting accident, the Kolbs established an agreement with the City of Storm Lake to establish a flower garden in the memory of Robert. The agreement provided for the "establishment, installation and maintenance of a formal flower garden" at a specific location within the city park on the north shore of Storm Lake. The agreement made it clear that the garden was a gift to the city, and that the agreement was to "continue during the period of the trust as created in [Henry's] Will . . . providing for the continued maintenance of said formal flower garden." The trust was later supplemented for the addition of a water fountain in the garden. The Robert James Kolb Memorial Trust Fund was finally established in 1970. Henry and Martha established the trust by deeding a quarter section of farmland they owned to their sons "Robert H. Kolb and Norman J. Kolb, as Trustees for the use and benefit of the City of Storm Lake." The warranty deed stated in pertinent part:

> It is the purpose of the grantors to hereby establish the Robert James Kolb Memorial Trust Fund out of the real estate above described and the proceeds derived from the sale thereof and/or the income derived therefrom, or any investments created by said trust fund. . . .

> The said trust fund shall be used in connection with improvements needed for the planting and upkeep of flower beds, such as annuals and perennials of all kinds, also flowering bulbs and rose bushes as may be put upon the tract of real estate hereinafter described.

In 1973, Henry and Martha deeded another quarter section of their farmland to their sons, Robert and Norman, as trustees, "for the use and benefit of the City of Storm Lake" to become a "part of the Robert James Kolb Memorial Trust Fund established by the grantors in the year 1970, in order that this trust and the previously established trust may be handled as a single trust." Neither warranty deed stated when the trust terminated. The trust operated without much trouble or question for over 30 years under the direction of Robert and Norman as trustees. The reports indicated the income produced from the farmland was more than enough to pay for the trust expenses. The trust disbursements mainly consisted of farm, garden, and fountain expenses, which often equaled $20,000–$30,000. On one occasion, however, the trustees used surplus trust funds to help the Storm Lake School District purchase additional school property. This transaction was memorialized in a 1980 agreement between Norman and the school district.

Henry died intestate in 1978 and Martha died a short time later. Despite their deaths, the garden and fountain survived for many years with the help of the city's maintenance and funds provided by the trust. It was a cherished location in Storm Lake, and often provided an ideal spot for weddings and celebrations. In 2003, however, the existence of the garden and fountain was placed in jeopardy. At this time the city was developing plans for an economic revitalization project called "Project Awaysis," funded with Vision Iowa grant money. The plans sought to turn the city's park on the north shore of Storm Lake and surrounding areas into a Midwest vacation destination. Among other things, the project was to provide a new public beach, a lighthouse, a family playground, a lodge, and an indoor/outdoor water park. Most importantly, the plans called for relocating the memorial gardens and fountain within the city's park. The project was viewed by its planners, and others, as a vital and necessary move for the city to grow and compete for jobs and residents in the future. Norman, as trustee of the Kolb trust, filed a petition for an injunction preventing the removal of the garden and fountain. The trial court ruled against Norman on the injunction and the city began the removal of the garden and fountain. After a later trial, however, the court found that the trust's purpose had been destroyed and that it therefore became a resulting trust to benefit the Kolbs' successors. Was this ruling correct?

Insurance Law

Hurricane Katrina struck Louisiana, Mississippi, and Alabama with overwhelming force in late August 2005. For many weeks thereafter, media coverage focused on the tragic personal consequences produced by Katrina and the tremendous devastation the storm inflicted on the Gulf Coast. Billions of dollars of property damage resulted from the hurricane and the flooding it spawned. Large numbers of homeowners simply did not have a property insurance policy. To their dismay, homeowners and commercial property owners who did have property insurance policies discovered that their particular losses may not have been covered by their policies. This was so even though damage from wind is a typical covered peril in a property insurance policy.

Coverage disputes between property owners and insurance companies began to spring up with frequency not long after the extensive damage stemming from Hurricane Katrina became apparent. Property owners filed numerous cases against their insurers in an effort to convince courts to rule that typical property insurance policies' coverage of wind damage would cover a broad range of Katrina-related losses, including those directly related to post-hurricane flooding. In general, however, the plaintiffs had little success. As you read this chapter, consider the hurricane aftermath and think about the following questions:

- If wind is a typical covered peril in property insurance policies, how is it possible that losses stemming from Hurricane Katrina might not be covered under such policies?
- Is there a typical exclusion from coverage that property insurers could credibly argue as a basis for denying coverage of certain Katrina-connected losses?
- Why might a policyholder whose home or building was flattened by the powerful storm be in a stronger position to collect under her insurance policy than, say, a New Orleans insured whose home was destroyed or rendered uninhabitable by the flooding that engulfed the city when the powerful hurricane caused the city's levee system to fail?

Think, too, about these broader questions:

- What is the nature of the relationship between an insurer and the insured? Is it collaborative, adversarial, or some of each?
- What legal obligations does an insurer owe to an insured? Do ethical obligations also attend the insurer–insured relationship?
- When a disaster of Hurricane Katrina's magnitude strikes, should the terms of an insurance policy be interpreted any differently from how they would have been interpreted in the event of more ordinary losses?
- What role do courts play in resolving insurance policy disputes?
- Should legislatures and government agencies regulate the terms of insurance policies, or should the content of policies be left to the market?

(See Figure 27.1, which appears later in the chapter.)

LEARNING OBJECTIVES

After studying this chapter, you should be able to:

27-1 Explain the contractual nature of the relationship between an insurer and an insured.

27-2 Describe the effect an insured's misrepresentation may have on the enforceability of an insurance policy.

27-3 Explain the approach courts normally take to interpretation of an ambiguous provision in an insurance policy.

27-4 Identify circumstances in which an insurer's breach of a coverage obligation in its policy could subject the insurer to liability beyond the dollar limits set forth in the policy.

27-5 Explain what an insurable interest is and what role it plays in property insurance.

27-6 Identify perils typically covered in and excluded from property insurance policies.

27-7 Explain the difference between a valued policy of property insurance and an open policy of property insurance.

27-8 Describe how coinsurance and pro rata clauses apply in property insurance policies.

27-9 Explain what is meant by an insurer's right of subrogation.

27-10 Identify the major types of liability insurance policies and the types of liabilities they typically cover.

27-11 Explain the difference between a liability insurer's duty to defend and its duty to pay sums owed by the insured.

27-12 Describe the types of circumstances in which an insurer may face bad-faith liability.

INSURANCE SERVES AS a frequent topic of discussion in various contexts in today's society. Advertisements for companies offering life, automobile, and property insurance appear daily on television and in the print media. Journalists report on issues of health insurance coverage (or lack thereof) and on legal developments concerning such issues. Persons engaged in business lament the excessive (from their perspective) costs of obtaining liability insurance. Insurance companies and insurance industry critics offer differing explanations for why those costs have reached their present levels.

Despite the frequency with which insurance matters receive public discussion and the perceived importance of insurance coverage, major legal aspects of insurance relationships remain unfamiliar to many persons. This chapter, therefore, examines important components of insurance law. We begin by discussing the nature of insurance relationships and exploring contract law's application to insurance policies in general. We then discuss other legal concepts and issues associated with specific types of insurance, most notably property insurance and liability insurance. Although health insurance issues are largely beyond the scope of this chapter, we briefly address recent years' public debate over such issues. (See Figure 27.1, which appears later in the chapter.) The chapter concludes with an examination of an important judicial trend: allowing insurers to be held liable for compensatory and punitive damages if they refuse in bad faith to perform their policy obligations.

Nature and Benefits of Insurance Relationships

 LO27-1 Explain the contractual nature of the relationship between an insurer and an insured.

Insurance relationships arise from an agreement under which a risk of loss that one party (normally the insured) otherwise would have to bear is shifted to another party (the insurer). The ability to obtain insurance enables the insured to lessen or avoid the adverse financial effects that would be likely if certain happenings were to take place. In return for the insured's payment of necessary consideration (the premium), the insurer agrees to shoulder the financial consequences stemming from particular risks if those risks materialize in the form of actual events.

Each party benefits from the insurance relationship. The insured obtains a promise of coverage for losses that, if they occur, could easily exceed the amounts of the premiums paid. Along with this promise, the insured acquires the "peace of mind" that insurance companies and agents like to emphasize. By collecting premiums from many insureds over a substantial period of time, the insurer stands to profit despite its obligation to make payments covering financial losses that stem from insured-against risks. The insured-against risks, after all, are just that—risks.

In some instances, events triggering the insurer's payment obligation to a particular insured may never occur (e.g., the insured's property never sustains damage from a cause contemplated by the property insurance policy). The insurer nonetheless remains entitled to the premiums collected during the policy period. Other times, events that call the insurer's payment obligation into play in a given situation may occur infrequently (e.g., a particular insured under an automobile insurance policy has an accident only every few years) or only after many years of premium collection (e.g., an insured paid premiums on his life insurance policy for 35 years prior to his death).

Insurance Policies as Contracts

Interested Parties   Regardless of the type of insurance involved, the insurance relationship is contractual. This relationship involves at least two—and frequently more than two—interested parties. As noted earlier, the insurer, in exchange for the payment of consideration (the premium), agrees to pay for losses caused by specific events (sometimes called *perils*). The insured is the person who acquires insurance on real or personal property or insurance against liability, or, in the case of life or health insurance, the person whose life or health is the focus of the policy. The person to whom the insurance proceeds are payable is the **beneficiary**. Except in the case of life insurance, the insured and the beneficiary will often be the same person. In most but not all instances, the insured will also be the policy's owner (the person entitled to exercise the contract rights set out in the insurance policy and in applicable law). In view of the contractual nature of the insurance relationship, insurance policies must satisfy all of the elements required for a binding contract.

Offer, Acceptance, and Consideration

The insurance industry's standard practice is to have the potential insured make an offer for an insurance contract by completing and submitting an application (provided by the insurer's agent), along with the appropriate premium, to the insurer. The insurer may then either accept or reject this offer. If the insurer accepts, the parties have an insurance contract under which the insured's initial premium payment and future premium payments furnish consideration for the insurer's promises of coverage for designated risks, and vice versa.

What constitutes acceptance of the offer set forth in the application may vary somewhat, depending on the type of insurance requested and the language of the application. As a general rule, however, acceptance occurs when the insurer (or agent, if authorized to do so) indicates to the insured an intent to accept the application. It is important to know the precise time when acceptance occurs because the insurer's contractual obligations to the insured do not commence until acceptance has taken place. If the insured sustains losses after the submission of the application (the making of the offer) but prior to acceptance by the insurer, those losses normally must be borne by the insured rather than the insurer.

With property insurance and sometimes other types of insurance, the application may be worded so that insurance coverage begins when the insured signs the application. This arrangement provides temporary coverage until the insurer either accepts or rejects the offer contained in the application. The same result may also be achieved by the use of a *binder*, an agreement for temporary insurance pending the insurer's decision to accept or reject the risk. The *Stuart* case, which follows, deals with interpretation of a property insurance binder issued shortly before an ice storm damaged the property.

Stuart v. Pittman	**255 P.3d 482 (Ore. 2011)**

John Stuart decided to build a new house on a small farm in Yamhill County. In March 2003, Stuart met with Ronald Pittman, a Country Mutual Insurance Co. agent, and told him that he wanted course-of-construction insurance to cover the house while it was being built. Stuart was unfamiliar with the form and content of traditional course-of-construction policies. However, Pittman had been an insurance agent for 19 years and was experienced regarding such policies. During their meeting, Stuart and Pittman discussed, at length, the scope of coverage that the policy would provide—coverage from the start of construction to its finish and coverage beyond what normally would be covered in a homeowner's policy. Stuart told Pittman he wanted coverage that would provide "safety net," or "catch basin," coverage "in all instances that something goes wrong during construction." Stuart wanted coverage that would include loss resulting from weather, injury, faulty work, and the builder's failure to perform. Pittman agreed to provide coverage and did not communicate to Stuart any coverage limitations. Relying on Pittman's oral assurance of coverage, Stuart did not require the builder to carry a performance bond or liability insurance, which Stuart could have required of the builder under the provisions of the construction contract.

In August 2003, Stuart met with Pittman and notified him that he had signed a construction contract and that course-of-construction insurance needed to be in effect at the beginning of September 2003. Pittman agreed to provide course-of-construction insurance effective September 1, 2003. The builder started construction later that month. In October 2003, Stuart notified Pittman that he had not received the written policy and Pittman told Stuart that he would receive the policy soon. By December 2003, however, Stuart had received only a premium statement from Country Mutual.

An ice storm struck the Willamette Valley in January 2004. Because the builder had left the partially completed house open to the weather, snow, ice, and water accumulated inside the house. As a result, the interior sheathing split, water accumulated in the crawl space, and mold grew.

Shortly thereafter, Stuart contacted Pittman to inform him of the damage and to initiate an insurance claim. Pittman told Stuart that damage caused by wind, rain, flood, and water would be covered and that mold damage also might be covered. Stuart still had not received his written policy. In March 2004, Stuart received a declaration page from Country Mutual showing that coverage for a "dwelling under construction" had been added to his existing policy. Pittman told Stuart that the addition provided the coverage for the new construction previously discussed.

However, the policy that Country Mutual issued contained provisions requiring direct physical loss, as well as exclusions for the perils of faulty workmanship, mold, and damage caused by water backup from sewer drains. Country Mutual later denied Stuart's insurance claim based on those exclusions.

Stuart brought an action against Country Mutual for breach of the oral binder and, alternatively, for failing to deliver a copy of the written policy within a reasonable time. At the conclusion of the trial's evidentiary phase, Country Mutual moved for a directed verdict, arguing that Stuart had failed to establish that the oral binder provided coverage beyond that expressed in the written policy and that Stuart had failed to establish that he had been damaged by Country Mutual's failure to deliver the policy in a timely manner. The trial court denied Country Mutual's motion. A jury subsequently returned a verdict finding that Pittman had entered into an oral contract of insurance on behalf of Country Mutual that eliminated both the requirement for direct physical loss and the exclusions for mold, water damage, and damage by faulty workmanship or construction and further finding that defendant had failed to deliver the written policy within a reasonable period of time. The jury awarded Stuart damages in the amount of $268,417. The trial court entered a supplemental judgment awarding Stuart attorney fees and costs.

On appeal, Country Mutual raised multiple assignments of error. The court of appeals, however, reached only Country Mutual's challenge to the trial court's denial of Country Mutual's motion for directed verdict on Stuart's contract claims under the oral binder and for Country Mutual's failure to provide a written policy within a reasonable period of time. On the first issue, the court of appeals concluded that there was no evidence from which a jury could have found that Pittman agreed to terms that clearly and expressly waived or superseded the usual policy terms or exclusions. The court reasoned that, even assuming that Pittman agreed to provide "safety net" or "catch basin" coverage "in all instances that something goes wrong during construction," those terms were too vague to satisfy a relevant Oregon statute, which provides that an oral binder is deemed to include "all the usual terms of the policy except as superseded by the clear and express terms of the binder." As to Stuart's claim that Country Mutual had failed to provide a written policy within a reasonable time, the court of appeals concluded that there was no evidence from which a jury could have found that Stuart had been damaged because Country Mutual had failed to deliver the written policy in a reasonable time. Based on the foregoing, the court of appeals reversed the trial court's judgment.

De Muniz, Chief Justice

On review, Stuart argues that the Court of Appeals incorrectly construed ORS 742.043(1) by requiring Stuart to show that the usual exclusions of the written policy had been "definitely, explicitly, and unambiguously" superseded by the binder. Stuart further argues that the Court of Appeals erred in concluding that he had not proven that he was damaged by Country Mutual's failure to timely deliver the written policy. For its part, Country Mutual maintains that (1) the Court of Appeals correctly held that the "usual terms of the policy" are superseded only when the parties have agreed to "clear and express" terms—definite,

express, and unambiguous—that are different from the usual policy terms; and (2) there was no evidence Stuart was damaged by Country Mutual's failure to timely deliver the policy. According to Country Mutual, the trial court erred in denying its motion for directed verdict and in submitting the case to the jury.

At the outset, we observe that Country Mutual concedes that Pittman entered into an oral binder for course-of-construction insurance covering Stuart's new residence, and that the binder remained in place at all times relevant to this litigation. Because the jury rendered a verdict in Stuart's favor, "we do not weigh the evidence; we consider the evidence, including inferences, in the light most favorable to plaintiff." [Citation omitted.] A jury verdict can be set aside only if this court concludes that there was no evidence from which the jury could have found for the plaintiff. Furthermore, this court reviews a trial court's denial of a motion for directed verdict for any evidence to support the verdict in plaintiff's favor. The answer to the parties' contentions regarding the trial court's denial of defendant's directed verdict motion turns on the proper interpretation of ORS 742.043(1).

ORS 742.043 provides, in part:

(1) Binders or other contracts for temporary insurance may be made orally or in writing, and shall be deemed to include all the usual terms of the policy as to which the binder was given together with such applicable indorsements as are designated in the binder, except as superseded by the clear and express terms of the binder.

(2) Except as provided in subsection (3) of this section and ORS 746.195, within 90 days after issue of a binder a policy shall be issued in lieu thereof, including within its terms the identical insurance bound under the binder and the premium therefor.

In interpreting a statute, our paramount goal is to discern the legislature's intent, and the statute's own words are the most persuasive evidence of that intent. The text of ORS 742.043(1) provides that the binder "shall be deemed to include all the usual terms of the policy, except as superseded by the clear and express terms of the binder." That highlighted text modifies "all the usual terms of the policy" and makes the binder's clear and express terms controlling over those contained in the usual policy. That reading of the statute also gives effect to the text in subsection (2), which provides that the written policy issued as a result must "include within its terms the identical terms bound under the binder."

The question remains, however, what the legislature meant by the terms "clear and express." The Court of Appeals concluded that the terms "clear and express" meant that the oral binder terms must "definitely, explicitly, and unambiguously supersede the terms [in the written policy]." The Court of Appeals assumed, because of the jury verdict in Stuart's favor, that Pittman had agreed to

provide Stuart with a "safety net" of coverage "in all instances that something goes wrong" and that he even agreed that Country Mutual could provide some type of coverage in the event of "faulty work[.]"

Nevertheless, the Court of Appeals concluded that the terms "safety net" and coverage "in all instances that something goes wrong" were too vague and obscure to satisfy the "clear and

express" requirements of ORS 742.043(1). For the reasons that follow, we disagree.

Words of common usage, such as "clear" and "express," should be given their plain and ordinary meaning. We agree with the Court of Appeals that, as used in the statute, the term "clear" means "easily understood" and the term "express" means "directly and distinctly stated, rather than implied or left to inference." Those definitions lead to the unremarkable conclusion that the "clear and express" requirement in ORS 742.043(1) means that those binder terms that are easily understood and expressed, as opposed to implied, will ordinarily be sufficient to supersede the usual or contrary terms in a policy.

As noted above, there is evidence that Stuart requested insurance that provided "catch basin" or "safety net" coverage in "all instances that something goes wrong during construction," in essence an "all risk" policy. Those words were expressed by Stuart to Pittman, not implied, and the request for coverage "in all instances [where] something goes wrong during construction" is easily understood as meaning exactly what it says. Further, Pittman was aware that Stuart wanted a policy that covered perils beyond those usually covered by a traditional homeowner's policy—the policy needed to cover loss resulting from weather, injury, faulty work, and builder's failure to perform. Pittman subsequently indicated that Country Mutual's policy "covered those things." Pittman's promise, which contained no exception or qualifications, left no room for an exclusion for faulty work or water- or mold-caused damage. Moreover, after the damage to Stuart's house, Pittman told Stuart that damage caused by wind, rain, flood, water, and mold would likely be covered.

Contrary to the Court of Appeals, we conclude that the terms "safety net" or "catch basin" or coverage "in all instances that something goes wrong during construction" were not vague or obscure. Rather, those terms, in the context in which they were used, were easily understood and were not implied or left to inference, and thus were sufficient under the "clear and express" requirement in ORS 742.043(1). Accordingly, there was evidence in the record from which the jury reasonably could conclude that Pittman agreed to coverage that was different from that expressed in the written policy—eliminating the requirement for direct physical loss and the exclusions for mold, water damage, and faulty workmanship or construction. Under Article VII (Amended), section 3, of the Oregon Constitution, we are required to sustain the jury's verdict on plaintiff's claim. The Court of Appeals erred in reaching a contrary conclusion.

Decision of the Court of Appeals reversed; jury verdict in favor of Stuart reinstated.

Insurer's Delay in Acting on Application A common insurance law problem is the effect of the insurer's delay in acting on the application. If the applicant suffers a loss after applying but before a delaying insurer formally accepts, who must bear the loss? As a general rule, the insurer's delay does not constitute acceptance. Some states, however, have held that an insurer's retention of the premium for an unreasonable time constitutes acceptance and hence obligates the insurer to cover the insured's loss.

Other states have allowed negligence suits against insurers for delaying unreasonably in acting on an application. The theory of these cases is that insurance companies have a public duty to insure qualified applicants and that an unreasonable delay prevents applicants from obtaining insurance protection from another source. A few states have enacted statutes establishing that insurers are bound to the insurance contract unless they reject the prospective insured's application within a specified period of time.

Effect of Insured's Misrepresentation

 LO27-2 Describe the effect an insured's misrepresentation may have on the enforceability of an insurance policy.

Applicants for insurance have a duty to reveal to insurers all the material (significant) facts about the nature of the risk so that the insurer may make an intelligent decision about whether to accept the risk. When an application for property, liability, or health insurance includes an insured's false statement regarding a material matter, the insured's misrepresentation, if relied on by the insurer, has the same effect produced by misrepresentation in connection with other contracts—the contract becomes voidable at the election of the insurer. This means that the insurer may avoid its obligations under the policy. The same result is possible if the insured failed, in the application, to disclose known material facts to the insurer, which issued a policy it would not have issued if the disclosures had been made. However, special rules applicable to misrepresentations in life insurance applications may sometimes limit the life insurer's ability to use the insured's misrepresentation as a way of avoiding all obligations under the policy.

Warranty/Representation Distinction It sometimes becomes important to distinguish between **warranties** and representations that the insured makes (usually in the application) to induce the insurer to issue an insurance policy. Warranties are *express terms in the insurance policy*. They are intended to operate as conditions on which the insurer's liability is based. The insured's breach of warranty terminates the insurer's duty to perform under the policy.

For example, a property insurance policy on a commercial office building specifies that the insured must install and maintain a working sprinkler system in the building, but the insured never installs the sprinkler system. The sprinkler system requirement is a warranty, which the insured breached by failing to install the system. This means that the insurer may not be obligated to perform its obligations under the policy.

Traditionally, an insured's breach of warranty has been seen as terminating the insurer's duty to perform *regardless of whether the condition set forth in the breached warranty was actually material to the insurer's risk* (unlike the treatment given to the insured's misrepresentations, which do not make the insurance policy voidable unless they pertained to a material matter). In view of the potential harshness of the traditional rule concerning the effect of a breach of warranty, some states have refused to allow insurers to escape liability on breach of warranty grounds unless the condition contemplated by the breached warranty was indeed material.

Legality The law distinguishes between unlawful wagering contracts and valid insurance contracts. A wagering contract creates a new risk that did not previously exist. Such a contract is contrary to public policy and therefore illegal. An insurance contract, however, *transfers existing risks*—a permissible, even desirable, economic activity. A major means by which insurance law separates insurance contracts from wagering contracts is the typical requirement that the party who purchases a policy of property or life insurance must possess an **insurable interest** in the property or life being insured. Specific discussion of the insurable interest requirement appears later in the chapter.

Form and Content of Insurance Contracts

Writing State law governs whether insurance contracts are within the statute of frauds and must be evidenced by a writing. Some states require specific types of insurance contracts to be in writing. Contracts for property insurance are not usually within the statute of frauds, meaning that they may be either written or oral unless they come within some general provision of the statute of frauds—for example, the "one-year" provision.[1] Even when a writing is not legally required, however, wisdom dictates that the parties reduce their agreement to written form whenever possible.

Reformation of Written Policy As one would expect, insurance companies' customary practice is to issue written policies of insurance regardless of whether the applicable

---

[1]The usual provisions of the statute of frauds are discussed in detail in Chapter 16.

statute of frauds requires a writing. An argument some-times raised by insureds is that the written policy issued by the insurer did not accurately reflect the content of the par-ties' actual agreement. For instance, after the occurrence of a loss for which the insured thought there was coverage under the insurance contract, the insured learns that the loss-causing event was excluded from coverage by the terms expressly stated in the written policy. In such a situation, the insured may be inclined to argue that the written policy should be judicially reformed, so as to make it conform to the parties' supposed actual agreement.

Although reformation is available in appropriate cases, courts normally presume that the written policy of insur-ance should be treated as the embodiment of the parties' actual agreement. Courts consider reformation an extreme remedy. Hence, they usually refuse to grant reformation unless either of two circumstances is present. The first reformation-triggering circumstance exists when the insured and the insurer, through its agent or agents, were *mutually mistaken* about a supposedly covered event or other sup-posed contract term (i.e., both parties believed an event was covered by, or some other term was part of, the parties' insurance agreement, but the written policy indicated oth-erwise). The alternative route to reformation calls for proof that the insurer committed fraud as to the terms contained in the policy or otherwise engaged in inequitable conduct.

Interpretation of Insurance Contracts

 LO27-3 Explain the approach courts normally take to interpretation of an ambiguous provision in an insurance policy.

Modern courts realize that many persons who buy insurance do not have the training or background to fully understand the technical language often contained in insurance policies. As a result, courts interpret insurance policy provisions as they would be understood by an average person. In addition, courts construe ambiguities in an insurance contract against the insurer, the drafter of the contract (and hence the user of the ambiguous language). This rule of construction means that if a word or phrase used in an insurance policy is equally subject to two possible interpretations, one of which favors the insurer and the other of which favors the insured, the court will adopt the interpretation that favors the insured.

A number of states purport to follow the *reasonable expectations of the insured* approach to interpretation of insurance policies. Analysis of judicial decisions reveals, however, that this approach's content and effect vary among the states ostensibly subscribing to it. Some states do little more than attach the reasonable expectations

label to the familiar principles of interpretation set forth in the preceding paragraph. A few states give the reason-able expectations approach a much more significant effect by allowing courts to effectively read clauses into or out of an insurance policy, depending on whether reasonable persons in the position of the insured would have expected such clauses to be in a policy of the sort at issue. When applied in the latter manner, the reasonable expectations approach tends to resemble reformation in its effect.

Clauses Required by Law The insurance business is highly regulated by the states, which recognize the import-ance of the interests protected by insurance and the differ-ence in bargaining power that often exists between insurers and their insureds. In an attempt to remedy this imbalance, many states' statutes and insurance regulations require the inclusion of certain standard clauses in insurance pol-icies. Many states also regulate such matters as the size and style of the print used in insurance policies. Laws in a growing number of states encourage or require the use of plain, straightforward language—rather than insurance jargon and legal terms of art—whenever such language is possible to use.

Notice and Proof of Loss-Causing Event The insured (or, in the case of life insurance, the beneficiary) who seeks to obtain the benefits or protection provided by an insur-ance policy must notify the insurer that an event covered by the policy has occurred. In addition, the insured (or the beneficiary) must furnish reasonable proof of the loss-causing event. Property insurance policies, for instance, ordinarily require the insured to furnish a sworn statement (called a *proof of loss*) in which the covered event and the resulting damage to the insured's property are described. Under life insurance policies, the beneficiary is usually expected to provide suitable documentation of the fact that the insured person has died. Liability insurance policies call for the insured to give the insurer copies of liability claims made against the insured.

Time Limits Insurance policies commonly specify that notice and proof of loss must be given within a speci-fied time. Policies sometimes state that compliance with these requirements is a condition of the insured's recovery and that failure to comply terminates the insurer's obliga-tion. Other times, policies merely provide that failure to comply suspends the insurer's duty to pay until compli-ance occurs. Some courts require the insurer to prove it was harmed by the insured's failure to give notice before allowing the insurer to avoid liability on the ground of tardy notice.

Cancellation and Lapse When a party with the power to terminate an insurance policy (extinguish all rights under the policy) exercises that power, **cancellation** has occurred. Lapse occurs at the end of the term specified in a policy written for a stated duration, unless the parties take action to renew the policy for an additional period of time. Alternatively, lapse may occur as a result of the insured's failure to pay premiums or some other significant default on the part of the insured.

Performance and Breach by Insurer

 LO27-4 Identify circumstances in which an insurer's breach of a coverage obligation in its policy could subject the insurer to liability beyond the dollar limits set forth in the policy.

The insurer performs its obligations by paying out the sums (and taking other related actions) contemplated by the policy's terms within a reasonable time after the occurrence of an event that triggers the duty to perform. If the insurer fails or refuses to pay despite the occurrence of such an event, the insured may sue the insurer for breach of contract. By proving that the insurer's denial of the insured's claim for payment constituted a breach, the insured becomes entitled to recover compensatory damages in at least the amount that the insurer would have had to pay under the policy if the insurer had not breached.

What if the insurer's breach caused the insured to incur consequential damages that, when added to the amount due under the policy, would lead to a damages claim exceeding the dollar limits set forth in the policy? Assume that XYZ Computer Sales's store building is covered by a property insurance policy with Secure Insurance Co., that the building is destroyed by an accidental fire (a covered peril), and that the extent of the destruction makes the full $500,000 policy limit due from Secure to XYZ. Secure, however, denies payment because it believes—erroneously—that XYZ officials committed arson (a cause, if it had been the actual one, that would have relieved Secure from any duty to pay). Because it needs to rebuild and take other related steps to stay in business but is short on available funds as a result of Secure's denial of its claim, XYZ borrows the necessary funds from a bank. XYZ thereby incurs substantial interest costs, which are consequential damages XYZ would not have incurred if Secure had performed its obligation under the policy. Assuming that XYZ's consequential damages would have been foreseeable to Secure, most states would allow XYZ to recover the consequential damages in addition to the amount due from

Secure under the policy.[2] This is so even though the addition of the consequential damages would cause XYZ's damages recovery to exceed the dollar limit set forth in the parties' insurance policy. The breaching insurer's liability may exceed the policy limits despite the insurer's good-faith (though incorrect) basis for denying the claim because a good-faith but erroneous refusal to pay is nonetheless a breach of contract. If the insurer could point to the policy limits as a maximum recovery in this type of situation, it would have an all-too-convenient means of avoiding responsibility for harms that logically flowed from its breach of contract.

Many states' laws provide that if an insured successfully sues her insurer for amounts due under the policy, the insured may recover interest on those amounts (amounts that, after all, should have been paid by the insurer much sooner and without litigation). Some states also have statutes providing that insureds who successfully sue insurers are entitled to awards of attorney fees. Punitive damages are *not* allowed, however, when the insurer's breach of contract consisted of a *good-faith (though erroneous) denial* of the insured's claim. Later in this chapter, we will explore the trend toward allowing punitive damages when the insurer's breach was in *bad faith* and thus amounted to the tort of bad-faith breach of contract.

Property Insurance

Owners of residential and commercial property always face the possibility that their property might be damaged or destroyed by causes beyond their control. These causes include, to name a few notable ones, fire, lightning, hail, and wind. Although property owners may not be able to prevent harm to their property, they can secure some protection against resulting financial loss by contracting for property insurance and thereby transferring certain risks of loss to the insurer. Persons holding property interests that fall short of ownership may likewise seek to benefit, as will be seen, from the risk-shifting feature of property insurance.

---

[2]Even though the terms of the insurance policy almost certainly would state that Secure's payment obligation is limited to costs of repair or replacement or to the property's actual cash value—that is, without any coverage for consequential harms experienced by the insured—Secure cannot invoke this policy language as a defense. If Secure had performed its contract obligation, its payment obligation would have been restricted to what the policy provided in that regard. Having breached the insurance contract, however, Secure stands potentially liable for consequential damages to the full extent provided for by general contract law. For additional discussion of damages for breach of contract, see Chapter 18.

The Insurable Interest Requirement

 LO27-5 Explain what an insurable interest is and what role it plays in property insurance.

As noted earlier in this chapter, in order for a property insurance contract not to be considered an illegal wagering contract, the person who purchases the policy (the policy owner) must have an **insurable interest** in the property being insured. One has an insurable interest if he, she, or it possesses a legal or equitable interest in the property and that interest translates into an economic stake in the continued existence of the property and the preservation of its condition. In other words, a person has an insurable interest if he would suffer a financial loss in the event of harm to the subject property. If no insurable interest is present, the policy is void.

Examples of Insurable Interest The legal owner of the insured property would obviously have an insurable interest. So might other parties whose legal or equitable interests in the property do not rise to the level of an ownership interest. For example, mortgagees and other lienholders would have insurable interests in the property on which they hold liens. A nonexhaustive list of other examples would also include holders of life estates in real property, buyers under as-yet unperformed contracts for the sale of real property, and lessees of real estate.[3] In the types of situations just noted, the interested party stands to lose financially if the property is damaged or destroyed.

Timing and Extent of Insurable Interest A sensible and important corollary of the insurable interest principle is that the requisite insurable interest must exist *at the time of the loss* (i.e., at the time the subject property was damaged). If an insurable interest existed when the holder thereof purchased the property insurance but the interest was no longer present when the loss occurred, the policy owner is not entitled to payment for the loss. This would mean, for example, that a property owner who purchased property insurance would not be entitled to collect from the insurer for property damage that occurred after she had transferred ownership to someone else. Similarly, a lienholder who purchased property insurance could not collect

under the policy if the loss took place after his lien had been extinguished by payment of the underlying debt or by another means.[4]

The extent of a person's insurable interest in property is limited to the value of that interest. For example, Fidelity Savings & Loan extends Williams a $250,000 loan to purchase a home and takes a mortgage on the home as security. In order to protect this investment, Fidelity obtains a $250,000 insurance policy on the property. Several years later, the house is destroyed by fire, a cause triggering the insurer's payment obligation. At the time of the fire, the balance due on the loan is $220,000. Fidelity's recovery under the insurance policy is limited to $220,000 because that amount is the full extent of its insurable interest. (An alternative way by which mortgagees protect their interest is to insist that the property owner list the mortgagee as the *loss payee* under the property owner's policy. This means that if the property is destroyed, the insurer will pay the policy proceeds to the mortgagee. Once again, however, the mortgagee's entitlement to payment under this approach would be limited to the dollar value of its insurable interest, with surplus proceeds going to the insured property owner.)

Covered and Excluded Perils

 LO27-6 Identify perils typically covered in and excluded from property insurance policies.

Property insurers usually do not undertake to provide coverage for losses stemming from any and all causes of harm to property. Instead, property insurers tend to either specify certain causes (covered perils) as to which the insured *will* receive payment for resulting losses—meaning that there is no coverage regarding a peril not specified—or set forth a seemingly broad statement of coverage but then specify certain perils concerning which there will be *no* payment for losses (excluded perils). Sometimes, property insurers employ a combination of these two approaches

---

[3]Chapter 28 contains a detailed discussion of security interests in real property. Chapter 29 addresses security interests in personal property. Chapter 24 contains a discussion of life estates and an examination of contracts for the sale of real property. Leases of real estate are explored in Chapter 25.

[4]In the life insurance context, the requisite insurable interest *must exist at the time the policy was issued* but need not exist at the time of the insured's death. Persons who stand to suffer a financial loss in the event of the insured's death have the insurable interest necessary to support the purchase of a life insurance policy on the insured. The insured and his or her spouse, parents, children, and other dependents thus possess an insurable interest in the insured's life. In addition, the business associates of the insured may also have an insurable interest in his or her life. Such persons would include the insured's employer, business partners, or shareholders in a closely held corporation with which the insured is connected. Creditors of the insured also have an insurable interest, but only to the extent of the debt owed by the insured.

The Global Business Environment

A California statute, the Holocaust Victim Insurance Relief Act of 1999 (HVIRA), provided that if an insurer doing business in California sold insurance policies to persons in Europe between 1920 and 1945 (Holocaust-era policies), the insurer was to file certain information about those policies with the California insurance commissioner. The reporting requirement also applied to insurance companies that did business in California and were "related" to a company that sold Holocaust-era policies, even if the relationship arose after the policies were issued. A "related company" was defined as any "parent, subsidiary, reinsurer, successor in interest, managing general agent, or affiliate company of the insurer."

Insurance companies subject to HVIRA were expected to provide this information: (1) the number of Holocaust-era insurance policies; (2) the holder, beneficiary, and current status of each such policy; and (3) the city of origin, domicile, or address for each policyholder listed in the policies. In addition, HVIRA required the insurers to certify whichever one of the following was accurate: (1) that the proceeds of the policies were paid; (2) that the beneficiaries or heirs could not, after diligent search, be located, and the proceeds were distributed to Holocaust survivors or charities; (3) that a court of law had certified a plan for the distribution of the proceeds; or (4) that the proceeds had not been distributed. HVIRA instructed the California insurance commissioner to store the information disclosed under the statute in a Holocaust Era Insurance Registry, which was available to the public. In addition, HVIRA required the insurance commissioner to "suspend the certificate of authority to conduct insurance business in the state of any insurer that fails to comply" with HVIRA's reporting requirements.

Various U.S.-based, German, and Italian insurance companies filed suit in a federal district court in an effort to have HVIRA invalidated on constitutional grounds. The district court held the statute unconstitutional on various grounds, but the U.S. Court of Appeals for the Ninth Circuit reversed. Seeing no constitutional obstacle, the Ninth Circuit regarded HVIRA as legitimate, state-related legislative action that fit within the customary authority of states to regulate regarding insurance-related matters. The U.S. Supreme Court granted the insurers' petition for certiorari.

In *American Insurance Association v. Garamendi*, 539 U.S. 396 (2003), the Supreme Court identified Article II of the U.S. Constitution as the key constitutional provision at issue in the case. Article II reserves to the federal executive branch the power to conduct foreign policy.

Pointing to relevant history as necessary background, the Court observed that after a 1990 treaty lifted a previous moratorium on certain claims related to the Holocaust, various class action lawsuits were filed in U.S. courts against non-U.S. firms that allegedly had done business in Germany during the Nazi era. These cases drew protests from the defendant firms and from various foreign governments. Following these protests, the executive branch of the U.S. government entered into agreements with the governments of Germany, Austria, and France during 2000 and 2001. The agreements outlined a Holocaust-related claims resolution process under which the foreign governments were to create foundations that would be funded by those governments and certain foreign firms. Foundation funds would satisfy valid Holocaust-related claims. The claims to be covered by the agreements included insurance claims the resolution of which was to be eased by agreement provisions calling for the foundations to negotiate with European insurers. The agreements stated that the claims resolution process was in the foreign policy interest of the United States. In addition, the federal government agreed to use its "best efforts" to have Holocaust-related claims go through the process rather than through the courts or other mechanisms set up by state and local governments.

After taking into account the history, purposes, and content of the 2000 and 2001 agreements entered into by the executive branch and the governments of Germany, Austria, and France, the Court concluded that HVIRA posed a significant obstacle to, if not an outright conflict with, the foreign policy objectives articulated in the agreements. This meant that the federal government's Article II foreign policy power must preempt—that is, take precedence over—HVIRA. Therefore, the Court reversed the Ninth Circuit's decision and held HVIRA unconstitutional.

---

by specifying certain covered perils and certain excluded perils. For an example, see the *Michigan Battery Equipment* case, which follows shortly.

Typical Covered Perils The effects of these approaches are essentially the same, as most property insurers tend to provide coverage for the same sorts of causes of harm to property. The perils concerning which property insurance

policies typically provide benefits include fire, lightning, hail, and wind. In addition, property insurance policies often cover harms to property resulting from causes such as the impact of an automobile or aircraft (e.g., an automobile or aircraft crashes into an insured building), vandalism, certain collapses of buildings, and certain accidental discharges or overflows from pipes or heating and air-conditioning systems.

Michigan Battery Equipment, Inc. v. Emcasco Insurance Co.
892 N.W.2d 456 (Mich. Ct. App. 2016)

Emcasco Insurance Co. (EMC) was the insurer and Michigan Battery Equipment, Inc. was the insured under a property insurance policy that applied to Michigan Battery's warehouse building. Because of prolonged water infiltration through deteriorated rubber grommets in the building's roof, the roof trusses of the warehouse rotted. When snow and ice accumulated on the roof, the rotted trusses split, cracked, and partially collapsed. Michigan Battery submitted a claim to EMC regarding the roof damage, but EMC denied the claim on the ground that an exclusion in the insurance policy applied. Regarding the coverage denial as unjustified, Michigan Battery sued EMC in a Michigan court. The court granted summary judgment in favor of EMC, ruling that the roof damage resulted from wet rot—a risk excluded by a provision in the insurance policy. Michigan Battery appealed to the Michigan Court of Appeals. (Further information about the insurance policy's terms appears in the following edited version of the Court of Appeals opinion.)

Saad, Judge

The question on appeal is whether EMC's insurance policy covers the damage to Michigan Battery's roof. To resolve this dispute, we must examine the terms of the insurance policy and determine whether the damage is excluded from coverage under any exclusion.

Insurance policies must be enforced in accordance with their terms. "The language of insurance contracts should be read as a whole and must be construed to give effect to every word, clause, and phrase." [Citation omitted.] To determine the intent of the parties, a court must first ascertain whether the policy provides coverage to the insured. Then, it must determine whether that coverage is negated by an exclusion. Where a contract provision is ambiguous, the contract is construed in favor of the insured. However, "[a] court should not create ambiguity in an insurance policy where the terms of the contract are clear and precise." *Henderson v. State Farm Fire & Casualty Co.*, 596 N.W.2d 190 (Mich. Sup. Ct. 1999). Instead, contract terms should be interpreted using their plan and ordinary meanings. *Id.*

Michigan Battery insured its property with an "all-risk" policy issued by EMC on its warehouse and attached offices. "Notwithstanding the presence of an 'all-risks' provision in an insurance policy, the loss will not be covered if it comes within any specific exclusion contained in the policy." 10A *Couch, Insurance*, 3d § 148.68. Here, the policy provides for various exclusions, of which two were the focus of the arguments at the trial court: (1) the exclusion for damage caused by collapse; and (2) the exclusion for damage caused by fungus, wet rot, dry rot, and bacteria. Such exclusionary clauses are strictly construed in favor of the insured. However, "[c]lear and specific exclusions must be given effect," and "coverage under a policy is lost if any exclusion within the policy applies to an insured's particular claims." *Auto-Owners Insurance Co. v. Churchman*, 489 N.W.2d 431 (Mich. Sup. Ct. 1992).

Because the language of the policy is controlling, we turn our attention to the rot exclusion in the policy, which provides in pertinent part:

B. Exclusions

1. We will not pay for loss or damage caused directly or indirectly by any of the following. Such loss or damage is excluded regardless of any other cause or event that contributes concurrently or in any sequence to the loss.

[Exclusions (a) through (g) omitted];

h. "Fungus," Wet Rot, Dry Rot And Bacteria

Presence, growth, proliferation, spread or any activity of "fungus," wet or dry rot or bacteria.

But if "fungus," wet or dry rot or bacteria results in a "specified cause of loss," we will pay for the loss or damage caused by that "specified cause of loss."

This exclusion does not apply:

1. When "fungus," wet or dry rot or bacteria results from fire or lightning; or

2. To the extent that coverage is provided in the Additional Coverage—Limited Coverage For "Fungus," Wet Rot, Dry Rot And Bacteria with respect to loss or damage by a cause of loss other than fire or lightning.

Exclusions B.1.a. through B.1.h. apply whether or not the loss event results in widespread damage or affects a substantial area.

As the trial court properly held, the plain language of the above-quoted insurance policy provisions excludes from coverage damage caused by fungus, wet rot, dry rot, and bacteria. However, this exclusion has exceptions: (1) when the fungus, wet rot, dry rot, or bacteria results from fire or lightning; (2) to the extent that coverage is provided in the "Additional Coverage" provision; and (3) where the fungus, rot, or bacteria "results in a 'specified cause of loss.'" As a result, because there is no question that wet rot caused the damage at issue, we must determine if any of the exceptions to the rot exclusion applies.

The first exception does not apply because there is nothing on the record to show, and the parties do not argue, that the wet rot here was the result from fire or lightning. Indeed, the record shows that the wet rot was caused by water leakage through grommets located in the roof.

Additionally, the second exception related to the rot being covered under the "Additional Coverage" does not apply. Under this "Additional Coverage," damage from fungus, rot, and bacteria is covered where the fungus, rot, or bacteria is the result of (1) "a specified cause of loss" other than fire or lightning or (2) flood. The term "specified causes of loss" is defined as meaning

> fire; lightning; explosion; windstorm or hail; smoke; aircraft or vehicles; riot or civil commotion; vandalism; leakage from fire-extinguishing equipment; sinkhole collapse; volcanic action; falling objects; weight of snow, ice or sleet; water damage.

And "water damage" is further defined as

> accidental discharge or leakage of water or steam as the direct result of the breaking apart or cracking of a plumbing, heating, air conditioning or other system or appliance (other than a sump system including its related equipment and parts), that is located on the described premises and contains water or steam.

Here, there is nothing on the record to establish, and the parties do not argue, that the wet rot in the warehouse was the result of or caused by a specified cause of loss. Likewise, there is nothing in the record to support that the damage was caused by flood. As already noted, the wet rot damage was caused by water intrusion through deteriorated rubber grommets in the roof. Accordingly,

because the wet rot was not the result of a "specified cause of loss" and was not the result of flood, the "Additional Coverage" provision simply does not apply.

Similarly, the third exception is not implicated. The rot in the trusses resulted in the roof and trusses to fall down a [few] feet, which, importantly, is not one of the enumerated specified causes of loss.

Therefore, the wet rot and resulting damage is not covered under the policy because it is excluded under the general exclusion in section B.1.h and none of the exclusion's exceptions applies. In brief, the policy plainly identifies the risks that EMC was willing to [cover] and did contract to cover. [U]nfortunately for Michigan Battery, wet rot is not one of those risks. Indeed, this risk was specifically excluded from coverage, and had Michigan Battery desired to obtain coverage, it could have purchased a rider for this specific loss. Consequently, because EMC identified wet rot as a particular type of risk that it was unwilling to insure, Michigan Battery cannot recover under the policy.

Trial court's grant of summary judgment in favor of EMC affirmed.

Fire as a Covered Peril Historically, the importance of coverage against the peril of fire made *fire insurance* a commonly used term. Various insurance companies incorporated the term into their official firm name; the policies these companies issued came to be called *fire insurance policies* even when they covered perils in addition to fire (as policies increasingly have done in this century). As a result, judges, commentators, and persons affiliated with the insurance industry will sometimes refer to today's policies as fire insurance policies despite the usual property insurer's tendency to cover not only fire but also some combination of the other perils mentioned in the preceding paragraph. Whether the term used is *property insurance* (generally employed in this chapter) or *fire insurance*, reference is being made to the same type of policy.

Fire-related losses covered by property insurance policies are those resulting from accidental fires. An accidental fire is one other than a fire deliberately set by, or at the direction of, the insured for the purpose of damaging the property. In other words, the insured obtains no coverage for losses stemming from the insured's act of arson. This commonsense restriction on an insurer's duty to pay for losses also applies to other harms the insured deliberately caused to his property.

For purposes of fire coverage, insurance contracts sometimes distinguish between *friendly fires*, which are those contained in a place intended for a fire (such as fires in a woodstove or fireplace), and *hostile fires*, which burn where no fire is intended to be (such as fires caused by lightning, outside sources, or electrical shorts, or those that began as friendly fires but escaped their boundaries). Losses caused by hostile fires are covered; those stemming from friendly fires may not be (depending, of course, upon the language of the policy at issue). As a general rule, covered fire losses may extend beyond direct damage caused by the fire. Indirect damage caused by smoke and heat is usually covered, as is damage caused by firefighters in their attempts to put out the fire.

Typical Excluded Perils Although flood-related harm to property may seem similar to harm stemming from some of the weather-related causes listed earlier among the typical covered perils, it does not usually receive the same treatment. Property insurance policies frequently exclude coverage for flood damage. On this point, however, as with other questions regarding perils covered or excluded, the actual language of the policy at issue must always be consulted before a coverage issue is resolved in any given case.[5] Other typical exclusions include earthquake damage and harm to property stemming from war or nuclear reaction, radiation, or contamination. As previously indicated, property insurance policies exclude coverage for losses caused by the insured's deliberate actions that were intended to cause harm to the property.

Additional Coverages Even as to perils for which there may not be coverage in the typical property insurance policy, the property owner may sometimes be able to purchase a specialized policy (e.g., a flood insurance policy) that does afford coverage for such perils. Other times, even if coverage for a given peril is not provided by the terms of most standard property insurance policies, it may nonetheless be possible for the property owner to have coverage for that peril added to the policy by paying an additional premium. This is sometimes done, for example, by policy owners who desire earthquake coverage.

Personal Property Insurance Although the broad term *property insurance* is what has been employed, the discussion so far in this section has centered around policies providing coverage for harm to *real* property. Items of *personal* property are, of course, insurable as well. Property insurance policies commonly known as homeowners' policies—because the real property serving as the policy's primary subject is the insured's dwelling—cover not only harm to the dwelling but also to personal property located inside the dwelling or otherwise on the subject real property. (Sometimes, depending on the policy language, there may be coverage even when the item of personal property was not located at the designated real property when the item was damaged.) Property insurance policies covering office buildings and other commercial real estate often provide some level of personal property coverage as well. When personal property coverage is included in a policy primarily concerned with real property coverage, the perils insured against in the personal property coverage tend to be largely the same as, though not necessarily identical to, those applicable to the real property coverage.

Lessees of residential or commercial real estate may obtain insurance policies to cover their items of personal property that are on the leased premises. Such policies are highly advisable because the apartment or office building owner's insurance policy on the real property is likely to furnish little or no coverage for the tenant's personal property.

Automobile insurance policies are in part personal property insurance policies because they provide coverage (under what are usually called the *comprehensive* and *collision* sections) for car damage resulting from such causes as fire, wind, hail, vandalism, or collision with an animal or tree. As will be seen, automobile insurance policies also contain significant features of another major type of insurance policy to be discussed later—liability insurance. Other specialized types of personal property insurance are also available. For example, many farmers purchase crop insurance in order to guard against the adverse financial effects that would result if a hailstorm or other covered peril severely damaged a season's crop.

Nature and Extent of Insurer's Payment Obligation
Property insurance policies are indemnity contracts. This means that the insurer is obligated to reimburse the insured for his actual losses associated with a covered harm to the insured property. The insured's recovery under the policy thus cannot exceed the extent of the loss sustained. Neither may it exceed the extent of the insured's insurable interest or the amount of coverage that the insured purchased (the policy limits).[6]

Policy provisions other than the policy limits also help define the extent of the insurer's obligation to pay. When covered real property is damaged but not destroyed, the cost of repair is normally the relevant measure. Many policies provide that when covered real property is destroyed, the insurer must pay the actual cash value (or *fair market value*) of the property. Some policies, however, establish cost of replacement as the payment obligation in this situation. The policies that call for payment of the actual cash value frequently give the insurer the option to pay the cost of replacement, however, if that amount would be less than the actual cash value. As to covered personal property, the controlling standard is typically the least of the following: cost of repair, cost of replacement, or actual cash value.[7]

---

[5]It may be that a type of peril frequently excluded in property insurance policies is in fact a covered peril under the language of the policy at issue. Alternatively, losses that at first glance appear to have resulted from an excluded peril may sometimes be characterized as having resulted, at least in part, from a covered peril. In the latter event, there may be some coverage for the losses.

[6]Some insurers, however, provide, in exchange for a more substantial premium than would be charged for a policy without this feature, a homeowner's policy under which the insurer could become obligated to pay *more* than the policy limits if the insured's home was destroyed and the cost to replace it would actually exceed the policy limits.

[7]Concerning certain designated items of personal property such as furs or jewelry, policies often set forth a maximum insurer payout (such as $1,000) that is less than the general policy limits applicable to personal property. Such a payout limitation would operate as a further restriction on the extent of the insurer's obligation.

Many property insurance policies supplement the above provisions by obligating the insurer to pay the insured's reasonable costs of temporarily living elsewhere if the insured property was her residence and the damage to the residence made it uninhabitable pending completion of repairs or replacement. Comparable benefits may sometimes be provided in policies covering business property. Lost profits and similar consequential losses resulting from harm to or destruction of one's insured property, however, do not normally fall within the insurer's payment obligation unless a specific provision obligates the insurer along those lines.[8] Regardless of whether the damaged or destroyed property is real or personal in nature, the particular language of the policy at issue must always be consulted before a definite determination can be made concerning what is and is not within the insurer's duty to pay.

Valued and Open Policies

 Explain the difference between a valued policy of property insurance and an open policy of property insurance.

When insured real property is destroyed as a result of fire or another covered peril, the amount to be paid by the insurer may be further influenced by the type of policy involved. Some property insurance contracts are valued policies. If real property insured under a valued policy is destroyed, the insured is entitled to recover the face amount of the policy regardless of the property's fair market value. For example, in 1985, Douglas purchased a home with a fair market value of $90,000. Douglas also purchased a valued policy with a face amount of $90,000 to insure the house against various risks, including fire. The home's fair market value decreased in later years because of deterioration in the surrounding neighborhood. In 2017, when the home had a fair market value of only $75,000, it was destroyed by fire. Douglas is entitled to $90,000 (the face amount of the valued policy) despite the reduction in the home's fair market value.

Most property insurance policies, however, are open policies. Open policies allow the insured to recover the fair market value (actual cash value) of the property at the time it was destroyed, up to the limits stated in the policy. Thus, if Douglas had had an open policy in the example presented in the previous paragraph, he would have been

entitled to only $75,000 when the home was destroyed by fire. Suppose instead that Douglas's home had increased in value, so that at the time of the fire its fair market value was $200,000. In that event, it would not matter what type of policy (valued or open) Douglas had. Under either type of policy, his recovery would be limited to the $90,000 face amount of the policy.

Coinsurance Clause

 Describe how coinsurance and pro rata clauses apply in property insurance policies.

Some property insurance policies contain a coinsurance clause, which may operate as a further limit on the insurer's payment obligation and the insured's right to recovery. A coinsurance clause provides that in order for the insured to be able to recover the full cost of partial losses, the insured must obtain insurance on the property in an amount equal to a specified percentage (often 80 percent) of the property's fair market value.

For example, PDQ Corporation has a fire insurance policy on its warehouse with Cooperative Mutual Insurance Group. The policy has an 80 percent coinsurance clause. The warehouse had a fair market value of $400,000, meaning that PDQ was required to carry at least $320,000 of insurance on the building. PDQ, however, purchased a policy with a face amount of only $240,000. A fire partially destroyed the warehouse, causing $200,000 worth of damage to the structure. Because of the coinsurance clause, PDQ will recover only $150,000 from Cooperative. This figure was arrived at by taking the amount of insurance carried ($240,000) divided by the amount of insurance required ($320,000) times the loss ($200,000).

The coinsurance formula for recovery for partial losses is stated as follows:

$$\frac{\text{Amount of insurance carried}}{\text{Coinsurance percent}} \times \text{Fair market value} \times \text{Loss} = \text{Recovery}$$

Remember that the coinsurance formula applies only to *partial* losses (i.e., damage to, but not complete destruction of, property). If PDQ's warehouse had been totally destroyed by the fire, the formula would not have been used. PDQ would have recovered $240,000—the face amount of the policy—for the total loss. If the formula had been used, it would have indicated that Cooperative owed PDQ $300,000—more than the face amount of the policy. This result would be neither logical nor in keeping with

---

[8]Recall, however, that if the insurer violates its payment obligation by wrongfully failing or refusing to pay what the policy contemplates, the insurer has committed a breach of contract. As noted in this chapter's earlier discussion of insurance policies as contracts, fundamental breach of contract principles dictate that the breaching insurer is potentially liable for consequential damages.

the parties' insurance contract. Whether the loss is total or partial, the insured is not entitled to recover more than the face amount of the policy.

Pro Rata Clause With the limited exception of the valued policy (discussed above), the insured cannot recover more than the amount of the actual loss. A rule allowing the insured to recover more than the actual loss could encourage unscrupulous persons to purchase policies from more than one insurer on the same property—thus substantially overinsuring it—and then intentionally destroy the property in a way that appeared to be a covered peril (e.g., committing arson but making the fire look accidental). In order to make certain that the insured does not obtain a recovery that exceeds the actual loss, property insurance policies commonly contain a *pro rata clause*, which applies when the insured has purchased insurance policies from more than one insurer. The effect of the pro rata clause is to apportion the loss among the insurance companies. (Applicable state law sometimes contains a rule having this same effect.)

Under the pro rata clause, the amount any particular insurer must pay the insured depends on the percentage of total insurance coverage represented by that insurer's policy. For example, Mumford purchases two insurance policies to cover his home against fire and other risks. His policy from Security Mutual Insurance Corp. has a face amount of $50,000; his policy from Reliable Insurance Co. is for $100,000. Mumford's home is partially destroyed by an accidental fire, with a resulting loss of $30,000. Security Mutual must pay Mumford $10,000, with Reliable having to pay the remaining $20,000 of the loss.

The formula for determining each insurer's liability under a pro rata clause is stated as follows:

$$\frac{\text{Amount of insurance policy}}{\text{Total coverage by all insurers}} \times \text{Loss} = \text{Liability of insurer}$$

Thus, Security Mutual's payment amount was calculated as follows:

$$\frac{\$50{,}000 \ (\text{Security Mutual's policy})}{\$150{,}000 \ (\text{Total of both policies})} \times \$30{,}000 \ (\text{Loss}) = \$10{,}000$$

Reliable's payment amount could be similarly calculated by substituting $100,000 (Reliable's policy amount) for the $50,000 (Security Mutual's policy amount) in the numerator of the equation. This formula may be used for both partial and total losses. However, each company's payment obligation is limited by the face amount of its policy. Thus, Security Mutual could never be liable for more than $50,000. Similarly, Reliable's liability is limited to a maximum of $100,000.

Right of Subrogation

LO27-9 Explain what is meant by an insurer's right of subrogation.

The insurer may be able in some instances to exercise a right of subrogation if it is required to pay for a loss under a property insurance contract. Under the right of subrogation, the insurer obtains all of the insured's rights to pursue legal remedies against anyone who negligently or intentionally caused the harm to the property. For example, Arnett purchased a property insurance policy on her home from Benevolent Insurance Company. Arnett's home was completely destroyed by a fire that spread to her property when her neighbor, Clifton, was burning leaves and negligently failed to control the fire. After Benevolent pays Arnett for her loss, Benevolent's right of subrogation entitles it to sue Clifton to recover the amount Benevolent paid Arnett. Arnett will be obligated to cooperate with Benevolent and furnish assistance to it in connection with the subrogation claim.

If the insured provides the liable third party a general release from liability, the insurer will be released from his payment obligation to the insured. Suppose that in the above scenario, Clifton persuaded Arnett to sign an agreement releasing him from liability for the fire. Because this action by Arnett would interfere with Benevolent's right of subrogation, Benevolent would not have to pay Arnett for the loss. A partial release of Clifton by Arnett would relieve Benevolent of responsibility to Arnett to the extent of her release.

Duration and Cancellation of Policy

Property insurance policies are usually effective for a designated period such as six months or a year. They are then extended for consecutive periods of like duration if the insured continues to pay the necessary premium and neither the insured nor the insurer elects to cancel the policy. The insured is normally entitled to cancel the policy at any time by providing the insurer written notice to that effect or by surrendering the policy to the insurer. Although property insurers usually have some right to cancel policies, terms of the policies themselves and/or governing law typically limit the grounds on which property insurers may do so. Permitted grounds for cancellation include the insured's nonpayment of the premium and, as a general rule, the insured's misrepresentation or fraud (see this chapter's discussion of contract law's applicability to insurance policies). Policy provisions and/or applicable law typically provide that if the property insurer intends to cancel the policy, the insured must be given meaningful advance written notice (often 30 days) of this intent before cancellation takes effect.

Another cancellation basis exists by virtue of the increase of hazard clauses that appear in many property insurance policies. An increase of hazard clause provides that the insurer's liability will be terminated if the insured takes any action materially increasing the insurer's risk. Some increase-of-hazard provisions also specify certain types of behavior that will cause termination. Common examples of such behavior include keeping highly explosive material on the property and allowing the premises to remain vacant for a lengthy period of time.

Figure 27.1   The Health Insurance Debate

The seemingly ever-rising costs of health care services pose a major problem for those who lack health insurance. Even those who have such insurance may find themselves obligated to pay very substantial medical bills associated with serious illnesses or injuries because health insurance policies do not cover the full cost of health care services. Most Americans who have health insurance receive their coverage through a group policy, in which an insurer agrees to furnish coverage of persons who belong to a particular group. The most common group consists of employees of a particular firm that has chosen to work with an insurer to set up a policy for its employees. Group policies tend to be less expensive, premium-wise, for insured persons than individual policies would be.

However, many millions of Americans do not have health insurance, typically because they have no access (or no affordable access) to a group policy and cannot afford an individual policy. Movements for health insurance reform have come and gone over the past decades, with legislation enacted prior to 2010 usually nibbling around the edges of the access-to-health-insurance problem or being restricted to a particular segment of the population. (The laws establishing the Medicare program of health coverage for persons 65 years of age or older would be an example of the latter.)

In 2010, however, Congress enacted the Patient Protection and Affordable Care Act (hereinafter, "Affordable Care Act" or "ACA")—easily the most sweeping health insurance reform to become law as of that time. The complex Affordable Care Act cannot be fully summarized here. It is fair to say, however, that the single ACA provision triggering the most public attention and debate was a provision that took effect in 2014: the requirement that every person have health insurance in force or pay a penalty for not having obtained such coverage. Proponents of the ACA maintained that the everyone-must-have-insurance provision (often known as the *individual mandate*) took direct aim at the problem of so many millions being uninsured and that the measure was critical to the statute's health care cost-containment goals. Critics of the law vowed to seek repeal of the statute and complained in particular about the individual mandate.

Certain objectors to the ACA went further, singling out the individual mandate as the target of constitutional challenges initiated in court. After mixed results in the federal district courts and circuit courts of appeal, the U.S. Supreme Court issued a 2012 decision that upheld the have-insurance-or-pay-a-penalty provision as a valid exercise of the Taxing Power extended to Congress by the U.S. Constitution. (See *National Federation of Independent Business v. Sebelius*, which is excerpted and discussed in Chapter 3.)

Other provisions in the ACA included, among others: elimination of health insurers' ability to deny coverage on the basis of a would-be insured's preexisting health condition; elimination of insurers' caps on lifetime benefits paid out to an insured; a provision permitting adult children to remain insured under their parents' health policies until the age of 26; requirements that health insurance policies cover certain essential benefits; directions to states to establish health benefit exchanges in order to help individuals and small employers obtain coverage; tax credits for persons of certain incomes in order to help defer some of the costs of obtaining health insurance; a tax increase on high-income earners, in order to help fund ACA-related expenditures; a requirement that employers with more than 200 employees automatically enroll full-time employees in health coverage; and provisions regarding an expansion of the existing Medicaid program (which provides health coverage for low-income persons).

Since the ACA's enactment, critics of the law vowed that they would "repeal and replace" it if they acquired the political means to do so. The repeal-and-replace movement went into high gear in early 2017, with the same political party having assumed control of the White House, the House of Representatives, and the Senate. In May 2017, the House passed a bill that, if it were enacted, would replace the ACA with a statutory program that its proponents claimed would control health care costs better and without a mandate that everyone have insurance. Critics charged that if the bill became law, it would not control costs effectively and would cause millions of persons who obtained insurance under the ACA to lose their coverage or find it far more expensive (particularly if they had a preexisting condition). As this book went to press, the Senate was considering whether to accept or modify the House bill or to develop a new bill. In dramatic fashion, the movement to repeal and replace the ACA failed in July 2017 when the Senate failed to pass the proposed legislation. As this text goes to press, legal challenges continue. Whatever the outcome of the legislative moves, the health insurance debate seems destined to continue for years to come.

CYBERLAW IN ACTION

As this text goes to press in 2020, cyber attacks continue to dominate media reports around the world, as hackers seem to have proven that their illicit business models are effective. Concerns about data security and malicious online activities have given rise to an emerging market for cyber coverage, and the cyber insurance market is projected to grow to $20 billion by 2025.

A 2019 survey of 1,200 business leaders found that cyber risks now top the list of concerns on the mind of policyholders, followed by rising medical costs, employee benefit costs, the ability to attract and retain talent, and exposure to legal liability. This is not surprising, given the average cost to a U.S. company of $230 per compromised record, and more for certain industries like health care, where specific additional fines exist.

The types of coverage most often desired are for cyber fraud (e.g., phishing scams and business e-mail compromise) and ransomware. In 2019, the incidence of ransomware attacks rose by 105%, with a particular focus on IT vendors and their customers. To release data, hackers requested an average payment of $224,871. Several high-profile attacks were launched against municipal governments, schools, and health-care organizations, with some victims paying six- or seven-figure ransom extortion payments. Those who refused often incurred costs 5 to 10 times greater as they were forced to recreate data and the systems by which it is stored.

Additionally, property damage and bodily injury flowing from technology failures are beginning to be included in some policies, as concerns begin to emerge with an increasing use of self-driving cars and other Internet-connected technologies.

In terms of emerging statutory trends, California's Consumer Privacy Act (CCPA) went into effect on January 1, 2020, and is expected to be a model for data privacy laws in the United States. As it pertains to cyber insurance, the CCPA is expected to have a big impact on businesses because of the provision permitting them to be fined by the government for CCPA violations and sued by individuals in situations involving data breaches. Cyber insurance policies are likely to follow this trend and cover violations under the CCPA.

Liability Insurance

LO27-10 Identify the major types of liability insurance policies and the types of liabilities they typically cover.

As its name suggests, liability insurance provides the insured the ability to transfer liability risks to the insurer. Under policies of liability insurance, the insurer agrees, among other things, to pay sums the insured becomes legally obligated to pay to another party. This enables the insured to minimize the troublesome or even devastating financial effects that he could experience in the event of his liability to someone else.

Types of Liability Insurance Policies

Liability insurance policies come in various types. These include, but are not limited to, personal liability policies designed to cover a range of liabilities an individual person could face; business liability policies (sometimes called *comprehensive general liability policies*) meant to apply to various liabilities that sole proprietors, partnerships, and corporations might encounter in their business operations; professional liability policies (sometimes called *malpractice insurance policies*) that cover physicians, attorneys, accountants, and members of other professions against liabilities to clients and sometimes other persons; and workers' compensation policies under which insurers agree to cover employers' statutorily required obligation to pay benefits to injured workers.

Some policies combine property insurance features with liability insurance components. Automobile insurance policies, for instance, afford property insurance when they cover designated automobiles owned by the insured against perils such as vandalism, hail, and collisions with animals, telephone poles, and the like. Other sections of automobile insurance policies provide liability insurance to the insured (the policy owner), members of her household, and sometimes other authorized drivers when their use of a covered automobile leads to an accident in which they face liability to another party. Typical homeowners' policies also combine property and liability insurance features. Besides covering the insured's home and contents against perils of the types discussed earlier in this chapter, these policies normally provide the insured coverage for a range of liabilities he may face as an individual.

Liabilities Insured Against

Although the different types of liability insurance policies discussed above contain different terms setting forth the liabilities covered and not covered, liability policies commonly afford coverage against the insured's liability for negligence but not against the insured's liability stemming from deliberate wrongful acts (most intentional torts and most behavior constituting a crime). Liability policies tend to reach this common ground in the same sorts of ways property insurance policies define the scope of coverage—by listing particular liabilities that are covered and stating that an unlisted liability is not covered, by setting forth a seemingly broad statement of coverage and then specifying exclusions from coverage, or by employing a combination of the previous approaches (e.g., specifying certain covered liabilities and certain excluded liabilities). The *World Harvest Church* case, which follows shortly, helps to illustrate this point.

Personal Liability and Homeowners' Policies Personal liability policies and the liability sections of homeowners' policies often state that coverage is restricted to instances of "bodily injury" and "property damage" experienced by a third party as a result of an "occurrence" for which the insured faces liability. These sorts of policies normally define *occurrence* as an "accident" resulting in bodily injury or property damage. The provisions just noted often lead to the conclusion that intentional torts and most criminal behavior, if committed or engaged in by the insured, would fall outside the coverage of the policy at issue because they are not accidents (whereas instances of the insured's negligence would be). This conclusion is underscored by typical clauses purporting to exclude coverage for bodily injury or property damage the insured intended to cause.

The occurrence, bodily injury, and property damage references in liability policies also indicate that harms stemming from, for example, breach of contract would not be covered either (no accident, no bodily injury, no property damage). In addition, personal liability policies and liability sections of homeowners' policies tend to specify that if bodily injury or property damage results from the insured's business or professional pursuits, it is not covered.

---

[9]The *respondeat superior* doctrine is discussed in Chapter 36. Although the insured's own intentional torts would not normally be covered, business liability policies sometimes provide that if the insured is liable on *respondeat superior* grounds for an employee's intentional tort such as battery, the insured will be covered unless the insured directed the employee to commit the intentional tort.

Business Liability Policies Business liability policies also feature coverage for bodily injury and property damage stemming from the insured's actions. The relevant range of actions, of course, is broadened to include the insured's business pursuits or "conduct of business." A major focus remains on unintentional wrongful conduct (usually negligence) of the insured, with the insured's deliberate wrongful acts normally being specifically excluded from coverage. Another typical exclusion is the pollution exclusion, which deprives the insured of coverage for actions that lead to pollution of other parties' property, unless the pollution occurs suddenly and accidentally.

Business liability policies also tend to provide the insured coverage in instances where the insured would be liable for certain torts of his employees (normally under the *respondeat superior* doctrine).[9] In addition, business liability policies sometimes afford coverage broader than instances of tortious conduct producing physical injury or property damage. Some policies, for instance, contain a clause that contemplates coverage for the insured's defamation of another person or invasion of that person's privacy (though other policies specifically exclude coverage for those same torts). Furthermore, the broad "conduct of business" language in certain policies, as well as specialized clauses (in some policies) referring to liability stemming from advertising or unfair competition, may contemplate coverage for the insured's legal wrongs that cause others to experience economic harm. In the end, the particular liabilities covered by a business liability policy cannot be determined without a close examination of the provisions in the policy at issue. It may become necessary for a court to interpret a policy provision whose meaning is unclear or scope is uncertain.

World Harvest Church v. Grange Mutual Casualty Co.
68 N.E.3d 738 (Ohio 2016)

World Harvest Church (WHC) operated a preschool in an Ohio city. A.F., the two-and-one-half-year-old son of Michael and Lacey Faieta, attended the preschool. On one school day, WHC employee Richard Vaughan filled in for A.F.'s regular teacher. When Mr. Faieta picked up A.F. from the preschool that day, A.F. seemed anxious and upset, his eyes were red, and he clung to his father's side as his belongings were gathered. On the way home, A.F. said that Vaughan had "spanked" him. A.F. also complained of pain. After the Faietas noticed numerous bright red marks and abrasions on A.F.'s back, buttocks, and upper thigh areas, they learned from A.F. that what he had referred to as spanking consisted of Vaughan's striking him repeatedly with a ruler.

The Faietas spoke with their pediatrician and the police, who advised the Faietas to take A.F. to the hospital. Emergency room personnel at the hospital found A.F.'s injuries to be consistent with physical abuse. When the Faietas complained to WHC's preschool headmaster, they were told not to come to WHC and were threatened with the filing of trespass charges if they did so.

On behalf of A.F., the Faietas sued WHC and Vaughan. They asserted claims for assault and battery against Vaughan, claims for negligence and intentional infliction of emotional distress against Vaughan and WHC, and claims for negligent hiring and supervision and respondeat superior *against WHC. (Negligent hiring and supervision, if established, would be bases of direct liability.* Respondeat superior, *under which an employer is liable for an employee's tort if the employee was acting within the scope of employment, is a form of vicarious liability.) WHC admitted in response to the complaint that Vaughan was an employee of WHC and that at all relevant times, he had acted within the scope of his employment. WHC denied, however, that any acts by Vaughan were unlawful or otherwise actionable.*

An Ohio jury returned a verdict in favor of the Faietas for more than $5 million in compensatory damages, punitive damages, and attorney fees. Vaughan was held liable for part of that award, but WHC was held liable for the bulk of it. Most of WHC's liability stemmed from the direct liability grounds noted above, but a portion of it was based on WHC's vicarious liability under the respondeat superior *doctrine for Vaughan's torts. Later, the Faietas and WHC settled the case for approximately $3.1 million.*

At the time of the incident that gave rise to the Faietas' lawsuit, WHC was insured under a commercial liability policy issued by Grange Mutual Casualty Co. (Grange). When the Faietas filed their complaint in the case referred to above, WHC submitted a claim under the Grange policy and asked Grange to defend WHC in the lawsuit. Grange agreed to defend the matter and retained a law firm to do so but also expressly reserved its right to deny coverage and refuse payment of any claim.

After the jury ruled in favor of the Faietas, WHC demanded that Grange cover the damage award assessed against WHC. Grange refused, taking the position that a policy provision excluding coverage for abuse or molestation applied. WHC then sued Grange, contending that Grange had unjustifiably denied coverage under the liability policy. An Ohio trial court ruled that Grange must indemnify WHC for the compensatory damages and attorney fees awarded to the Faietas, but not for the punitive damages. Grange appealed to the Ohio Court of Appeals, which concluded that Grange must indemnify WHC for the attorney fees awarded to the Faietas and for the portion of the compensatory damages attributable to WHC's vicarious liability under respondeat superior, *but not for the other compensatory damages and the punitive damages.*

Grange and WHC both asked the Supreme Court of Ohio to grant review of the court of appeals decision. The state supreme court granted Grange's petition for review but denied WHC's. (Further discussion of the relevant provisions of the insurance policy at issue will appear in the following edited version of the state supreme court's opinion.)

O'Connor, Chief Justice

In this appeal, we address whether an abuse or molestation exclusion in a commercial liability insurance policy excludes coverage for an award of damages based on the insured's vicarious liability for a claim arising from its employee's physical abuse of a child in the insured's care and custody.

In its commercial general liability policy, Grange agreed to pay those sums that WHC, the insured, would become legally obligated to pay as damages because of "bodily injury" or "property damage" as those terms were defined in the policy. The policy applied only to "bodily injury" caused by an "occurrence," which the policy defined as an "accident." But the policy excluded from coverage "bodily injury" that was "expected or intended from the standpoint of the insured."

Two endorsements further modified the coverage for bodily injury. An endorsement regarding corporal punishment stated that the exclusion for bodily injury did not apply if the injury resulted from "corporal punishment to [WHC's] student administered by or at the direction" of the insured. A second endorsement, titled the "Abuse or Molestation Exclusion" ("the abuse exclusion"), further modified the coverage for "bodily injury" and stated:

This insurance does not apply to "bodily injury," "property damage" or "personal and advertising injury" arising out of:
1. The actual or threatened abuse or molestation by anyone of any person while in the care, custody or control of any insured, or
2. The negligent:
a. Employment;
b. Investigation;

c. Supervision;
d. Reporting to the proper authorities, or failure to so report; or
e. Retention;
of a person for whom any insured is or ever was legally responsible and whose conduct would be excluded by Paragraph 1 above.

We accepted Grange's discretionary appeal but denied WHC's cross-appeal. The [key] issue presented is whether the abuse exclusion [quoted above] bars coverage under the policy for the sum awarded based on WHC's vicarious liability for claims arising from its employee's physical abuse of a child.

Grange contends that all damages arising out of the abuse are excluded from coverage regardless of the cause of action asserted against WHC. WHC counters that only those damages awarded because of the direct liability of a bad actor and the direct liability of the employer would be excluded from coverage, not those damages based on the employer's vicarious liability for its employee's abuse. Central to WHC's claim is its assertion that the exclusion contains no language excluding damages awarded based on the insured's vicarious liability.

WHC also contends that (1) Vaughan's actions constituted "excessive corporal punishment" rather than abuse and are therefore covered by the policy, and (2) the abuse exclusion is intended to exclude only sexual abuse, not physical abuse, from coverage. Although presented as counterarguments, these contentions raise issues that we declined to address when we denied discretionary review of WHC's cross-appeal. Because we did not accept the cross-appeal, these arguments are outside the scope of this appeal. Indeed, the appellate court squarely addressed these arguments when it concluded that the exclusion unambiguously applied to physical abuse and not just sexual abuse. [According to the appellate court,] "[t]he plain and ordinary meaning of the word 'abuse,' which is not defined in the [Grange] policies, is, as pertinent here, physical maltreatment" [and that] "WHC's narrow construction of the term 'abuse' as only 'sexual abuse' is [inconsistent with common definitions] which define the term more broadly to include physical abuse." Additionally, [as the Court of Appeals noted], "it was conclusively determined in the [Faietas'] personal-injury case that Vaughan's battery constituted abuse of the Faietas' minor child."

The appellate court similarly rejected WHC's argument that the corporal-punishment endorsement permitted coverage. [Therefore, the court] concluded that "the . . . corporal punishment endorsement does not change the fact that claims concerning Vaughan's battery and WHC's negligent supervision are excluded under the policy's abuse or molestation exclusion." These conclusions are not before this court on Grange's appeal, and therefore, we do not review them.

The scope of this appeal is limited to whether the abuse exclusion eliminates coverage for damages awarded for WHC's vicarious liability for abuse. The appellate court concluded that "unless corporate management committed the intentionally wrongful conduct, the corporate insured will not be denied coverage on the basis of an employee's intentional tort," and that "WHC's corporate management did not commit Vaughan's intentionally wrongful conduct." In other words, as the appellate court later clarified, even if Vaughan acted intentionally, and thus his conduct was excluded from coverage because it was not accidental and thus not an "occurrence," coverage turned on whether Vaughan's act was intentional from the perspective of WHC, the entity seeking coverage. And because WHC did not intend the act, Grange could not deny coverage.

The effect of the abuse exclusion on the issue of coverage is central to the inquiry and the basis of this appeal. Insurance contracts are construed by the same rules used to construe contracts. [O]ur task when interpreting an insurance policy is to "examine the insurance contract as a whole and presume that the intent of the parties is reflected in the language used in the policy." [Citation omitted.] Moreover, "[w]e look to the plain and ordinary meaning of the language used in the policy unless another meaning is clearly apparent from the contents of the policy." [Citation omitted.] An exclusion in an insurance policy will be interpreted as applying only to that which is clearly intended to be excluded. Ambiguity in the policy language is construed against the insurer and liberally in favor of the insured, particularly when the ambiguity exists in a provision that purports to limit or qualify coverage under the insurance policy.

With these principles in mind, we turn to the policy language in this case. The language of the abuse exclusion is broad. It excludes from coverage "'bodily injury' . . . arising out of . . . [t]he actual or threatened abuse or molestation by anyone of any person while in the care, custody, or control of any insured." It excludes from coverage actual or threatened abuse or molestation. And it covers actual or threatened abuse or molestation by anyone. The victim, however, must be in the care, custody, or control of an insured. Additionally, the abuse exclusion eliminates coverage for damages awarded for claims of bodily injury arising from the insured's negligence in employing, investigating, supervising, or retaining the bad actor, as well as from negligence in reporting, or failing to report, the abuse or molestation to the authorities.

We do not find any language in the abuse exclusion that limits its application to damages awarded for an insured's direct liability. The failure to include an express denial of coverage for claims of vicarious liability does not support the interpretation advanced by WHC, i.e., that the policy must therefore cover vicarious liability. Nor does it render the exclusion ambiguous.

The exclusion covers a narrow category of conduct—actual or threatened abuse by anyone. But construing the exclusion to apply only to that which is clearly excluded, as we must, its plain wording states that there is no coverage as long as the claim is for bodily injury that arises out of the abuse by anyone of any person while in the care, custody, or control of the insured.

We find that the abuse exclusion simply does not limit the exclusion to claims for bodily injury arising from direct liability, while failing to exclude claims for bodily injury arising from vicarious liability, for the same conduct. Indeed, the language in the exclusion is simple and unambiguous: there is no coverage for any injury arising from abuse or molestation. To hold otherwise, we would have to insert language into the exclusion. We may not do so, particularly when the terms of the policy are clear and unambiguous. "Where a written agreement is plain and unambiguous, it does not become ambiguous by reason of the fact that in its operation it will work a hardship on one of the parties thereto and corresponding advantage to the other." [Citation omitted.] To hold that the exclusion applies to claims of direct liability but not to vicarious liability would require rewriting the policy language.

Here, WHC's vicarious liability arose from its admission that Vaughan acted within the scope of his employment when he committed the abusive acts while A.F. was in WHC's care, custody, and control. And those acts gave rise to the damages awarded. Thus, the language of the abuse exclusion encompasses WHC's vicarious liability.

For the foregoing reasons, we conclude that the language of Grange's abuse exclusion bars coverage for an award of damages based on WHC's vicarious liability for [torts] arising from Vaughan's abuse of A.F. while in WHC's care and custody. Because we hold that coverage is excluded, and there are no remaining covered claims for damages awarded in the Faietas' lawsuit, we also conclude that the policy does not provide coverage for an award of attorney fees. Accordingly, we reverse the judgment of the court of appeals.

Court of Appeals judgment in favor of WHC reversed; final judgment entered in favor of Grange.

Other Liability Policies Professional liability policies also afford coverage for the insured's tortious conduct, this time in the practice of his or her profession. Negligent professional conduct producing harm to a third party (normally bodily injury in the medical malpractice setting but usually economic harm in the legal or other professional malpractice context) would be a covered liability. Wrongful professional conduct of an intentional nature typically would not be covered.

Automobile liability policies cover liability for physical injury and property damage stemming from the insured's (and certain other drivers') negligent driving. Once again, however, there is no coverage for liability arising from the insured's (or another driver's) deliberate vehicle operation acts of a wrongful nature.

Workers' compensation policies tend to approach coverage questions somewhat differently, primarily because injured employees need not prove negligence on the part of their employer in order to be entitled to benefits. Therefore, the insurer's obligation under a workers' compensation policy is phrased in terms of the liability the insured employer would face under state law.

Insurer's Obligations

 LO27-11 Explain the difference between a liability insurer's duty to defend and its duty to pay sums owed by the insured.

Duty to Defend When another party makes a legal claim against the insured and the nature and allegations of the claim are such that the insurer would be obligated to cover the insured's liability if the claim were proven, the insurer has a duty to defend the insured. A commonsense precondition of this duty's being triggered is that the insured must notify the insurer that the claim has been made against her. The duty to defend means that the insurer must furnish, at its expense, an attorney to represent the insured in litigation resulting from the claim against her. If the insurer fails to perform its duty to defend in an instance where the duty arose, the insurer has breached the insurance contract. Depending on the facts, the breaching insurer would at least be liable for compensatory damages (as indicated

in this chapter's earlier discussion of insurance policies as contracts)[10] and potentially for punitive damages as well under the *bad-faith* doctrine examined later in this chapter.

Sometimes it is quite clear that the insurer's duty to defend applies or does not apply, given the nature of the claim made against the insured. Other times, however, there may be uncertainty as to whether the claim alleged against the insured would fall within the scope of the liability insurance policy. Such uncertainty, of course, means that it is not clear whether the insurer has a duty to defend. Insurers tend to take one of two approaches in an effort to resolve this uncertainty. Under the first approach, the insurer files a declaratory judgment action against the insured. In this suit, the insurer asks the court to determine whether the insurer owes obligations to the insured under the policy in connection with the particular liability claim made against the insured by the injured third party. The other option insurers often pursue when it is unclear whether the liability policy applies is to retain an attorney to represent the insured in the litigation filed by the third party—thus fulfilling any duty to defend that may be owed—but to do so under a *reservation of rights* notice. By providing the reservation of rights notice to the insured, the insurer indicates that it reserves the right, upon acquisition of additional information, to conclude (or seek a later judicial determination) that it does not have the obligation to pay any damages that may be assessed against the insured as a result of the third party's claim. The insurer's reservation of rights also serves to eliminate an argument that by proceeding to defend the insured, the insurer waived the ability to argue that any actual liability would not be covered.

The *Medmarc* case, which follows, illustrates issues that courts encounter in deciding whether an insurer had the duty to defend.

---

[10]The compensatory damages in such an instance would normally be the reasonable costs incurred by the insured in retaining an attorney and paying him to represent her. Of course, if the insured ended up being held liable in the third party's suit and the insurer wrongfully refused to pay the damages assessed against the insured in that case, the insured's compensatory damages claim against the breaching insurer would be increased substantially.

Medmarc Casualty Insurance Co. v. Avent America, Inc.
612 F.3d 607 (7th Cir. 2010)

Consumers initiated class action litigation against Avent America, Inc. for not having informed them of the health risks associated with the potential leaching of Bisphenol-A ("BPA"), which Avent used in certain plastic products it manufactured and sold. These products included bottles and "sippy cups" used by infants and young children. The plaintiffs were parents who purchased Avent's products for their children and did not know of the potential health dangers associated with BPA exposure (including, according to lab animal studies the plaintiffs cited, early sexual maturation in females, increased obesity, and increased neuron-behavioral problems such as ADD/HD and autism). The plaintiffs alleged that Avent was aware of a large body of research indicating that BPA, even at low levels, is harmful to humans and is particularly harmful to children; that despite this knowledge, Avent marketed its products as superior in safety to other products for infants and toddlers; that the plaintiffs would not have purchased Avent's products if they had known that using products containing BPA could be harmful to their children; that upon learning of the safety problems associated with products containing BPA, the plaintiffs stopped using the products; and that they therefore did not receive the full benefit of their purchases.

The plaintiffs' complaint alleged various legal claims that emphasized the prevailing consensus regarding a need to be concerned about exposure to BPA for humans. Their complaint, however, did not allege that any of the negative health effects had manifested themselves in their children. Moreover, the plaintiffs did not allege that they or their children ever used the products or were actually exposed to the BPA. Instead, they alleged an economic harm stemming from their purchases of an unusable product. The federal district court eventually dismissed some of the legal claims pleaded by the plaintiffs but permitted the case to go forward on the theory that Avent had been unjustly enriched.

Various insurers, including Medmarc Casualty Insurance Co., provided Avent with liability insurance during the time period contemplated by the plaintiffs' complaint. Avent informed its insurers of the class action litigation and requested that they defend the case and cover amounts Avent would be required to pay if it lost the case. Because the relevant insurers' polices all read essentially the same way in the portions important to this case, the insurers will be referred to collectively as "Medmarc." The relevant policy language stated as follows:

> We will pay those sums that the insured becomes legally obligated to pay as damages because of "bodily injury" or "property damage" included within the "products-completed operations hazard" to which this insurance applies. We will have the right and duty to defend the insured against any "suit" seeking those damages. However, we will have no duty to defend the insured against any "suit" seeking damages for "bodily injury" or "property damage" to which this insurance does not apply.

The policies defined "bodily injury" as "bodily injury, sickness or disease sustained by a person, including death resulting from any of these at any time."

Medmarc declined to furnish Avent a defense in the class action case and further denied that its policy would cover Avent if Avent lost the case. Avent and Medmarc then became involved in litigation over the duty-to-defend and coverage issues. The federal district court considering that case ruled that Medmarc had no duty to defend and no coverage obligation because, in the court's view, the class action case against Avent did allege "bodily injury" and thus did not come within Medmarc's policy language. The court therefore granted summary judgment in favor of Medmarc. Avent appealed to the U.S. Court of Appeals for the Seventh Circuit.

Flaum, Circuit Judge

The plaintiffs in the underlying [class action case against Avent] are parents who bought Avent products containing BPA and then refused to use the products once they learned of the dangers of BPA. The case at hand hinges on whether the underlying lawsuit states claims for damages "because of bodily injury," and is therefore covered by the insurance policies. Avent argues that the underlying suit's claims that the plaintiffs will not use the products out of fear of bodily injury sufficiently state claims for damages "because of bodily injury." Medmarc argues that the underlying suit is not covered by the policies because the claims are limited to economic damages due to the purchase of unusable products and these damages are not "because of bodily injury."

In assessing whether the district court correctly [ruled in favor of] Medmarc we must begin our analysis with a review of the general standard for duty to defend under Illinois law. An insurer must provide its insured with a defense when "the allegations in the complaint are even potentially within the scope of

the policy's coverage." [Citation omitted.] "If the underlying complaints allege facts within or potentially within policy coverage, the insurer is obligated to defend its insured even if the allegations are groundless, false, or fraudulent." [Citation omitted.]

When considering whether an insurance company has a duty to defend, the court "should not simply look to the particular legal theories pursued by the claimant, but must focus on the allegedly tortious conduct on which the lawsuit is based." [Citation omitted.] Although we focus on factual allegations above legal theories, factual allegations are only important insofar as they point to a theory of recovery. Therefore, based on these standards, we must consider whether the allegations in the complaint point to a theory of recovery that falls within the insurance contract: Do the allegations amount to a claim for damages "because of bodily injury"?

Avent characterizes the complaint as alleging: (1) the underlying plaintiffs purchased BPA-containing products manufactured, sold, and/or distributed by Avent and that BPA migrates from those products; (2) BPA potentially causes a wide variety of adverse health problems that may not manifest for years; and (3) Avent somehow violated a standard of care by manufacturing, selling, and/or distributing BPA-containing baby products that allegedly cause these injuries. Based on this chain of allegations, Avent argues that the complaints state claims for damages because of bodily injury and therefore fall within the policy coverage. [Medmarc argues, however, that it does not] owe Avent a defense because there are no allegations in the complaint that the products caused bodily injury. Rather, the complaints allege that, due to the risk of potential bodily harm from BPA exposure, the plaintiffs did not receive the full benefit of their bargain (because they now will not use the product) and therefore incurred purely economic damages unrelated to bodily injury. We agree with Medmarc's assessment of the complaints.

The problem with Avent's argument is that, even if the underlying plaintiffs proved every factual allegation in the underlying complaint, the plaintiffs could not collect for bodily injury because the complaints do not allege any bodily injury occurred. Additionally, the complaint does not allege that the underlying plaintiffs now have an increased risk of bodily injury for which they should be compensated. The closest the complaint comes to alleging bodily injury is [its contention] that Avent was aware of a large body of scientific research that BPA exposure can cause physical harm. Proving such allegations would not entitle the plaintiffs to recover for bodily injury or for damages flowing from bodily injury because these allegations lack the essential element of actual physical harm to the plaintiffs.

Avent recognizes this gap in the underlying complaints, but rebuts it with the argument that the plaintiffs left these claims out to make it easier to be certified as a class. Avent argues [in its brief] that "[i]t is precisely these 'whims' that are not, under Illinois law, supposed to change whether or not particular factual allegations are sufficient to trigger coverage under general liability insurance policies." Although Illinois courts have recognized that a duty to defend should not be at the mercy of the drafting whims of plaintiffs' attorneys, these omissions were not mere whims. In the underlying case, the plaintiffs' attorneys have limited their claims solely to economic damages that resulted from the plaintiffs purchasing a product from which they cannot receive a full benefit because they were falsely led to believe that it was safe. This is not a drafting whim (or mistake) on the part of the plaintiffs' attorneys, but rather a serious strategic decision to pursue only this limited claim. The strategic intention behind this decision is clear from the plaintiffs' concession in the underlying suit that they are seeking only economic damages and do not claim any bodily injury. The district court in the underlying suit also acknowledged this strategic decision when it found that the complaint does validly set out a claim for economic damages but not damages for physical harm.

Avent relies heavily on *Ace Am. Ins. Co. v. RC2 Corp.*, 568 F. Supp. 2d 946 (N.D. Ill. 2008) to support its argument that this complaint could be construed to make claims for damages because of bodily injury. The underlying complaint in *RC2* dealt with children exposed to lead paint in toys. In coming to the conclusion that the insurers in *RC2* had a duty to defend, the district court found that exposure to lead paint constituted a bodily injury. Avent characterizes the underlying complaint in *RC2* in much the same way it characterizes the underlying complaints in this case. However, the complaint in *RC2* is not as similar to the complaint in this case as Avent claims. In *RC2*, the underlying complaint specifically alleged that the named plaintiffs and the class members "suffered an increased risk of serious health problems making periodic examinations reasonable and necessary." Such allegations are absent from the complaint in this case. Avent claims that the district court placed too much weight on this distinction, but this distinction is exactly what the district court should have focused on. In *RC2*, the complaint alleged that the product caused bodily injury, albeit in the form of an increased risk of future harm. In this case, there is no claim of bodily injury in any form.

The theory of relief in the underlying complaint is that the plaintiffs would not have purchased the products had Avent made certain information known to the consumers and therefore the plaintiffs have been economically injured. The theory of the relief is not that a bodily injury occurred and the damages sought flow from that bodily injury. [Medmarc therefore owed Avent] no duty to defend.

District court's decision in favor of Medmarc affirmed.

Duty to Pay Sums Owed by Insured If a third party's claim against the insured falls within the liabilities covered by the policy, the insurer is obligated to pay the compensatory damages held by a judge or jury to be due and owing from the insured to the third party. In addition, the insured's obligation to pay such expenses as court costs would also be covered. These payment obligations are subject, of course, to the policy limits of the insurance contract involved. For example, if the insured is held liable for compensatory damages and court costs totaling $150,000, but the policy limits of the relevant liability policy are $100,000, the insurer's contractual obligation to pay sums owed by the insured is restricted to $100,000.

CYBERLAW IN ACTION

So-called bugs in Version 5.0 of America Online, Inc.'s Internet access software ("AOL 5.0") drew the ire of large numbers of disgruntled customers. In numerous cases that were later consolidated, these customers sued AOL. Relying on a variety of legal theories, the plaintiffs contended that AOL 5.0 was defective and that, as a result, their computers crashed or they experienced other loss of use of their computers, computer systems, and computer software and data.

AOL called upon its liability insurer, St. Paul Mercury Insurance Co., to defend it against the customers' claims. St. Paul refused, contending that the claims did not fall within the coverage obligations St. Paul had assumed. AOL retained legal counsel to defend it against the customers' claims and then sued St. Paul for an alleged breach of the contract of insurance. Concluding that the claims against AOL were not covered by the policy St. Paul issued, a federal district court granted summary judgment in favor of St. Paul. AOL appealed.

In *America Online, Inc. v. St. Paul Mercury Insurance Co.*, 347 F.3d 89 (4th Cir. 2003), the U.S. Court of Appeals for the Fourth Circuit considered AOL's appeal. The court began its analysis by noting basic rules applicable to insurance policy interpretation and determinations of whether a liability insurer must defend its policyholder against third parties' claims. First, if the language of the policy is unambiguous, the court will "give the words their ordinary meaning and enforce the policy as written." Second, "if the language of the policy is subject to different interpretations, [the court] will construe it in favor of coverage." Third, the insurer's "obligation to defend arises whenever the complaint against the insured alleges facts and circumstances, some of which, if proved, would fall within the risk covered by the policy."

The St. Paul policy at issue included a coverage provision stating that St. Paul would "pay amounts [AOL] is legally required to pay as damages for covered bodily injury, property damage, or premises damage." The policy defined *property damage* as "physical damage to tangible property of others, including all resulting loss of use of that property . . . or loss of use of tangible property of others that isn't physically damaged."

In addition, the St. Paul policy excluded certain events or harms from coverage. Among these exclusions was a provision stating that St. Paul would not cover "property damage to impaired property, or to property which isn't physically damaged, that results from [AOL's] faulty or dangerous products or completed work [or from] a delay or failure in fulfilling the terms of a contract or agreement." The policy defined *impaired property* as "tangible property, other than [AOL's] products or completed work, that can be restored to use by nothing more than . . . an adjustment, repair, replacement, or removal of [AOL's] products or completed work which forms a part of it, [or AOL's] fulfilling the terms of a contract or agreement."

Proceeding to interpret the St. Paul policy in light of the rules noted earlier, the court paid careful attention to the types of damages sought by the AOL customers. The court reasoned that claims seeking damages from AOL for harm to or loss of use of computer systems or computer software or data were not covered claims because systems, software, and data are not "tangible" because they are not "'capable of being touched [and] able to be perceived as materially existent . . . by the sense of touch'" [quoting definition of "tangible" in *Webster's New Third International Dictionary of the English Language* (1993)]. Systems, software, and data thus would not appear to be "tangible property" for purposes of St. Paul's policy. The Fourth Circuit also noted that computer systems, software, and data are customarily classified by courts as *intangible* property. In view of the St. Paul policy's *property damage* definition (quoted above) and its references to "tangible property," the court held that any harm to or loss of use of computer data, software, and systems would not be covered by the policy.

The claims brought against AOL, however, also alleged loss of use of the customers' computers. The court concluded that the computers themselves would be tangible property under the definition set forth above and that the claims alleging loss of use of computers might therefore appear, at first glance, to be covered by the policy. However, the Fourth Circuit noted, the AOL customers were not actually alleging that their computers were physically harmed. Instead, the AOL customers were contending that AOL 5.0 interfered with the proper operation of their computers and that loss of use of the computers resulted. The claimants' allegations that their computers crashed were substantively allegations of system failure rather than of physical harm to the computers themselves. The absence of a claim of physical damage to the computers meant that harm consisting of loss of use would not be covered by the portion of the *property damage* definition that referred to "physical damage to tangible property of others, including all resulting loss of use of that property."

Still potentially applicable, though again at first glance only, was the portion of the *property damage* definition that appeared to cover "loss of use of tangible property of others that isn't physically damaged." That possible avenue to coverage was blocked, according to the court, by the St. Paul policy's "impaired property" exclusion. The plaintiffs, after all, premised their claim on the notion that AOL 5.0 was defective and that as a result, their computers were rendered inoperable. The court observed that "the straightforward meaning of [the impaired property] exclusion bars coverage for loss of use of tangible property of others that is not physically damaged by the insured's defective product." The Fourth Circuit stressed that even though AOL 5.0 allegedly "caused damage to other software, including operating systems[, . . .] there has been no demonstration or claim that the physical or tangible components of any computer were damaged. In the absence of property that is physically damaged, AOL's arguments for covering loss of use must be rejected."

Having concluded that none of the customers' claims against AOL came within the terms of the St. Paul policy, the Fourth Circuit affirmed the district court's grant of summary judgment to St. Paul and held that the insurer owed AOL no duty to defend it against those claims.

Is the insurer also obligated to pay any *punitive damages* assessed against the insured as a result of a covered claim? As a general rule, the insurer will have no such obligation, either because of an insurance contract provision to that effect or because of judicial decisions holding that notions of public policy forbid arrangements by which one could transfer his punitive damages liability to an insurer. Not all courts facing this issue have so held, however, meaning that in occasional instances the insured's punitive damages liability may also be covered if the insurance policy's terms specifically contemplate such a result.

The liability insurer need not wait until litigation has been concluded to attempt to dispose of a liability claim made against the insured.

Insurance policy provisions, consistent with our legal system's tendency to encourage voluntary settlements of claims, allow insurers to negotiate settlements with third parties who have made liability claims against the insured. These settlements involve payment of an agreed sum of money to the third party, in exchange for the third party's giving up her legal right to proceed with litigation against the insured. Settlements may occur regardless of whether litigation has been formally instituted by the third party or whether the claim against the insured consists of the third party's prelitigation demand for payment by the insured. If settlements are reached—and they are reached much more often than not—the substantial costs involved in taking a case all the way to trial may be avoided. The same is also true, from the insurer's perspective, of the damages that might have been assessed against the insured if the case had been tried. Note, however, that even if the defendant (the insured) wins a suit that does proceed to trial, the costs to the insurer are still substantial even though there is no award of damages to pay. Those costs include a considerable amount for attorney fees for the insured (the insurer's obligation regardless of the outcome of the case) as well as other substantial expenses associated with protracted litigation. Accordingly, even when the insurer thinks that the insured probably would prevail if the case went to trial, the insurer may be interested in pursuing a settlement with the third-party claimant if a reasonable amount—an amount less than what it would cost the insurer to defend the case—can be agreed upon.

Is There a Liability Insurance Crisis?

In recent decades, the necessary premiums for liability insurance policies of various types (particularly business and professional liability policies) have risen considerably. Sometimes, the premiums charged by liability insurers have become so substantial that would-be insureds have concluded that they cannot afford liability insurance and

therefore must go without it despite its importance. In addition, some insurers have ceased offering certain types of liability policies and/or have become much more restrictive in their decisions about which persons or firms to insure.

Insurance companies tend to blame the above state of affairs on what they see as a tort law regime under which plaintiffs win lawsuits too frequently and recover very large damage awards too often. As a result, insurers have been among the most outspoken parties calling for tort reform, a subject discussed in earlier chapters in this book. Plaintiffs' attorneys and critics of the insurance industry blame rising liability insurance premiums on, primarily, another alleged cause: questionable investment practices and other unsound business practices supposedly engaged in by insurance companies. The parties making these assertions thus oppose tort reform efforts as being unnecessary and unwise.

Liability insurance premiums in general may not be increasing as rapidly today as they once did, but they remain substantial in amount. So long as liability insurance remains unaffordable or otherwise difficult to obtain, there is a "crisis," given the adverse financial consequences that could beset an uninsured person. This is so regardless of which of the competing explanations set forth above bears greater legitimacy.

Bad-Faith Breach of Insurance Contract

 LO27-12 Describe the types of circumstances in which an insurer may face bad-faith liability.

Earlier in this chapter, we discussed the liability that an insurer will face if it breaches its policy obligations by means of a good-faith but erroneous denial of coverage. That liability is for compensatory damages—damages designed to compensate the insured for the losses stemming from the insurer's breach—just as in breach of contract cases outside the insurance setting. Punitive damages are not available, however, when the insurer's wrongful failure or refusal to perform stemmed from a good-faith (though erroneous) coverage denial. What if the insurer's failure or refusal to perform exhibited a lack of good faith? In this section, we examine the recent judicial tendency to go beyond the conventional remedy of compensatory damages and to assess punitive damages against the insurer when the insurer's refusal to perform its policy obligations amounted to the tort of bad-faith breach of contract.

The special nature of the insurer–insured relationship tends to involve a "we'll take care of you" message

Ethics and Compliance in Action

With the costs of medical treatment, hospitalization, and medications having increased dramatically in recent years, health insurance has become a critical means by which insured persons minimize the adverse financial consequences associated with illness and injury. The costs of serious illness or injury may be financially crippling unless insurance coverage exists for a person or family—and sometimes even when it does exist. As noted in Figure 27.1, which appears earlier in the chapter, coverage for health care expenses often comes in the form of a group policy that is made available to employees of a certain company or to persons affiliated with a particular organization. Subject to certain exclusions and other contractual restrictions, group policies tend to cover a significant portion of the costs of obtaining medical services.

Although a very large percentage of the U.S. population has some form of health insurance, many millions of U.S. residents do not. Public policy questions regarding health insurance availability and costs have been debated extensively in political arenas during recent decades. Until very recently, Congress opted for measures that were important but limited in effect. For example, the Health Insurance Portability and Accountability Act of 1996 allows most employees who had health insurance in connection with their employment to change jobs without fear of losing health coverage. That statute followed the lead of the earlier COBRA statute, under which persons who end an employment status that had entitled them to group policy coverage may continue that coverage for a limited time. In 2010, however, Congress changed course and enacted the far-more-sweeping Affordable Care Act (ACA). Figure 27.1 contains discussion of that legislation and of the 2017 legislative efforts of ACA opponents to replace the law with a significantly different statutory approach.

There is an ethical flavor to much of the debate over whether health insurance "reform" is desirable and over what form it should take. For instance, consider the questions set forth below. In doing so, you may wish to employ ethical theories discussed in Chapter 4.

- Is there a "right," in an ethical sense, to health insurance coverage? If so, why? If not, why not?
- Do *employers* have an ethical obligation to make group health insurance available to their employees? If so, why? If so, does this obligation always exist, or does it exist only under certain circumstances? If employers do not have such an obligation, why don't they?
- Would Congress be acting ethically if it enacted a law requiring *all* employers in the United States to make health insurance available to their employees? Be prepared to justify your position.
- Does the *U.S. government* have an ethical duty to furnish health coverage to *all* U.S. residents? Be prepared to justify your position.

that insurers communicate to insureds—at least at the outset of the relationship. Recognizing this, courts have displayed little tolerance in recent years for insurers' unjustifiable refusals to take care of insureds when taking care of them is clearly called for by the relevant policy's terms. When an insurer refuses to perform obvious policy obligations without a plausible, legitimate explanation for the refusal, the insurer risks more than being held liable for compensatory damages. If the facts and circumstances indicate that the insurer's refusal to perform stemmed not from a reasonable argument over coverage but from an intent to "stonewall," deny or unreasonably delay paying a meritorious claim, or otherwise create hardship for the insured, the insurer's breach may be of the bad-faith variety. Because bad-faith breach is considered an independent tort of a flagrantly wrongful nature, punitive damages—in addition to compensatory damages—have been held to be appropriate. The purposes of punitive damages in this context are the same as in other types of cases that call for punitive damages: to punish the flagrant wrongdoer and to deter the

wrongdoer (as well as other potential wrongdoers) from repeating such an action.

The past 30-some years have witnessed bad-faith cases in which many millions of dollars in punitive damages have been assessed against insurers. The types of situations in which bad-faith liability has been found have included a liability insurer's unjustifiable refusal to defend its insured and/or pay damages awarded against the insured in litigation that clearly triggered the policy obligations. Various cases involving very large punitive damages assessments for bad-faith liability have stemmed from property insurers' refusals to pay for the insured's destroyed property when the cause was clearly a covered peril and the insurer had no plausible rationale for denying coverage. Still other bad-faith cases in which liability was held to exist have included malpractice or other liability insurers' refusals to settle certain meritorious claims against the insured within the policy limits. Bad-faith liability in these cases tends to involve a situation in which the insured is held legally liable to a plaintiff for an amount well in excess of the dollar limits of the liability policy (meaning that the insured would be personally responsible for the amount of the judgment in excess of the policy limits), after the liability insurer, without reasonable justification, refused the plaintiff's offer to settle the case for an amount less than or equal to the policy limits.

Whether bad-faith liability exists in a given case depends, of course, on all of the relevant facts and circumstances. Although bad-faith liability is not established in every case in which insureds allege it, cases raising a bad-faith claim are of particular concern to insurers.

Problems and Problem Cases

1. Prior to the September 11, 2001, attacks that destroyed the World Trade Center (WTC) towers, 22 insurance companies had issued property insurance binders covering the WTC complex. These binders were issued to Silverstein Properties, the holder of a 99-year lease of the WTC complex under an agreement with the Port Authority of New York and New Jersey. A binder is a temporary contract of insurance that is in force until a formal insurance policy is issued by the insurer. The 22 insurers intended to issue formal insurance policies to Silverstein, but very few had done so as of 9/11. Therefore, the binders established and limited their obligations to pay Silverstein after the destruction of the WTC complex. Property insurance binders and policies often provide that the insurer's obligation to pay is triggered when a covered "occurrence" results in damage to or destruction of the relevant real estate. Binders and policies also have policy limits, which are both the amount of insurance coverage purchased and the maximum sum that the insurer can be obligated to pay for a covered claim. The policy limits in a property insurance binder or policy typically apply on a per-occurrence basis. For example, if the policy limits are $200,000, the insurer may become obligated to pay up to a maximum of $200,000 for losses resulting from one occurrence and up to another $200,000 on losses stemming from a separate occurrence. Various ones of the 22 insurers that had issued binders regarding the WTC complex prior to 9/11 became involved in litigation with Silverstein over the amounts they were obligated to pay after the events of 9/11. Three of the insurers that were parties to the litigation—Hartford Fire Insurance Company, Royal Indemnity Company, and St. Paul Fire and Marine Insurance Company— had issued binders whose combined policy limits totaled approximately $112 million, out of a total of approximately $3.5 billion in insurance coverage contemplated by the binders and policies issued by all 22 insurers. Another party to the litigation was Travelers Indemnity Co., which also promised millions of dollars of coverage under a binder that differed in a key respect from the Hartford, Royal, and St. Paul binders. The estimated cost of rebuilding the complex was $5 billion or more. In the litigation referred to above, a federal court agreed with an argument made by Hartford, Royal, and St. Paul: that their binders should be interpreted as containing the terms set forth in a form binder known as the "WilProp form," which had been circulated among many of the various insurers. The WilProp form made the insurance coverage applicable on a per-occurrence basis and contained a specific definition of occurrence. (The form defined *occurrence* as "all losses or damages that are attributable directly or indirectly to one cause or to one series of similar causes," and went on to state that "[a]ll such losses will be added together and the total amount of such losses will be treated as one occurrence.") The court then addressed the critical issue: whether, for purposes of the binders at issue, the two plane attacks that destroyed the WTC towers on 9/11 were one occurrence or, instead, two occurrences. If, as argued by Hartford, Royal, and St. Paul, the two plane attacks were one occurrence, those three insurers would be obligated to pay Silverstein a total of $112 million. If, as argued by Silverstein, the two plane attacks were two occurrences, the three insurers would be obligated to pay Silverstein a total of $224 million. Although most of the remaining insurers were not parties to the case, a determination of the extent of their liabilities to Silverstein was likely to be heavily influenced by the court's decision because it seemed reasonably likely that various ones of the other insurers would be viewed as having agreed to the same form binder terms to which Hartford, Royal, and St. Paul had agreed. Thus, although the actual amount in controversy under the Hartford, Royal, and St. Paul binders ranged from a minimum of $112 million to a maximum of $224 million, the practical economic stakes appeared to be much higher. Ruling on a motion for partial summary judgment filed by Hartford, Royal, and St. Paul, the district court held that in view of the WilProp form's definition of

occurrence, the two plane attacks on the WTC were one occurrence for purposes of those companies' binders. Travelers, however, had issued a binder that differed from the form binder employed by Hartford, Royal, and St. Paul. The Travelers binder called for coverage on a per-occurrence basis but did not contain a definition of occurrence. Silverstein moved for partial summary judgment, asking the court to rule that under the Travelers binder, the two plane attacks constituted two occurrences. Concluding that there were genuine issues of material fact to be resolved by a jury in regard to the plane attacks on the WTC, the district court denied Silverstein's motion. Appealing to the U.S. Court of Appeals for the Second Circuit, Silverstein asked the appellate court to overturn the district court's grant of partial summary judgment to Hartford, Royal, and St. Paul. Silverstein also appealed the district court's denial of its (Silverstein's) motion for partial summary judgment against Travelers.

Should the court affirm the grant of summary judgment for Hartford, Royal, and St. Paul and should it affirm the denial of Silverstein's motion for summary judgment against Travelers?

2. Don Davis owned a lumber mill that was subject to a $248,000 mortgage held by Diversified Financial Systems. Early in 1995, Aaron Harber became interested in forming a partnership with Davis for ownership and operation of the mill. Harber and Davis orally agreed upon the terms of a partnership. Harber contended that these terms included a purchase by Harber of Diversified's interest in the mortgage on the mill. Davis later informed Harber that he (Davis) would not proceed with the partnership. Nevertheless, Harber purchased Diversified's mortgage interest in April 1995. Harber did this in reliance on the oral partnership agreement with Davis—an agreement Harber intended to enforce despite Davis's refusal to proceed.

During Harber's negotiations with Davis concerning their supposed partnership and with Diversified for purchase of its mortgage interest, Harber discovered that the mill was not covered by property insurance. Harber therefore purchased a policy from Underwriters at Lloyd's of London (Lloyd's). The policy, whose one-year term began in late May 1995, named Harber and U.S.A. Properties, a corporation set up and wholly owned by Harber, as insureds.

In mid-June 1995, one of the buildings at the mill was destroyed by fire. Approximately two weeks later, in an effort to prompt negotiations in the dispute with

Davis over whether a partnership existed or would be pursued, Harber filed suit to foreclose the Diversified mortgage. The mortgage was in default at that time. Harber and Davis soon entered into a settlement agreement that provided in part for the transfer of the mill property to Harber, in exchange for Harber's giving up all of his claims against Davis. The agreement also conveyed, to Harber, whatever interest Davis had in insurance proceeds related to the building that had been destroyed by fire.

Harber and U.S.A. Properties submitted a claim to Lloyd's concerning the destroyed building. After Lloyd's denied the claim, Harber and U.S.A. Properties sued Lloyd's for payment according to the terms of the policy. A federal district court held that the plaintiffs lacked an insurable interest and that Lloyd's was therefore entitled to summary judgment. Harber and U.S.A. Properties appealed. Was the district court's holding correct?

3. Property Owners Insurance Co. (POI) was the insurer and Thomas Cope was the insured under a liability policy that excluded liability except in cases of liability "with respect to the conduct of a business" owned by Cope. Cope's business was a roofing company. While the policy was in force, Cope traveled to Montana with Edward Urbanski, a person with whom Cope did significant business. While on the trip, Cope snowmobiled with a group of persons that included Gregory Johnson, who died in a snowmobiling accident. Johnson's estate brought a wrongful death lawsuit against Cope. After Cope notified POI of the case brought against him, POI filed a declaratory judgment action against Cope and Johnson's estate. In the declaratory judgment action, POI sought a judicial determination that it had no obligations to Cope and Johnson's estate under the liability policy. POI took the position that Cope's trip to Montana was a personal trip for recreation purposes and that it therefore was not a trip "with respect to the conduct of [Cope's] business." Cope maintained that even if the trip was largely recreational, it was at least incidental to his business because Urbanski, who also was on the trip, was a business associate of Cope's. POI moved for summary judgment. Was POI entitled to summary judgment?

4. In a class action suit against Aamco Transmissions, consumers Joseph R. Tracy and Joseph P. Tracy claimed that Aamco and its network of franchisees used deceptive advertising that inaccurately described Aamco's services and lured many consumer purchasers of transmission services into

paying excessively and for unnecessary repairs. The Tracys asserted that Aamco was liable under the Pennsylvania Unfair Trade Practices and Consumer Protection Law. Aamco was the insured under a comprehensive general liability insurance policy issued by Granite State Insurance Co. This policy provided liability coverage to Aamco "for personal injury or advertising injury . . . arising out of the conduct of" Aamco's business. The policy defined *advertising injury* as "injury arising . . . in the course of [Aamco's] advertising activities, if such injury arises out of libel, slander, defamation, violation of right of privacy, piracy, unfair competition, or infringement of copyright, title or slogan."

Contending that it had coverage under the "unfair competition" category of the advertising injury coverage, Aamco demanded that Granite defend and indemnify it in connection with the consumer class action case described above. When Granite declined to do so, Aamco settled the case on its own. Granite then brought a declaratory judgment action against Aamco in federal district court. Granite sought a ruling that it was not obligated to provide coverage for Aamco in the class action case brought by the Tracys. A federal district court concluded that the *unfair competition* term in the policy contemplated coverage only for common law–based claims against Aamco, not for any claims based on a state or federal statute. Because the Tracys' class action case was based on a supposed violation of a Pennsylvania statute, the district court held that Granite's policy did not furnish coverage to Aamco. In addition, the court held that the term *unfair competition* was not ambiguous and that Aamco could not have had a reasonable expectation that consumers' claims against it would be covered. Aamco appealed. Did Aamco win its appeal?

5. Shelter Mutual Insurance Co. brought a declaratory judgment action against Tommy and Bessie Maples (referred to collectively as "Maples") in the U.S. District Court for the Western District of Arkansas. Shelter asked the court to declare that Shelter had no obligation to pay a claim made by Maples under a homeowner's insurance policy issued by Shelter. The facts set forth here were as stipulated (i.e., as agreed to) by the parties. While residing in Saudi Arabia, Maples contracted for the construction of a single-family retirement home in Arkansas. Maples purchased homeowner's insurance from Shelter, whose policy, issued in November 2000, was in full effect at

all times relevant to the case. The two-story residence, which had a wooden frame and a basement made of concrete, was largely complete as of November 2000. Maples, who remained in Saudi Arabia, took reasonable precautions for winter weather by leaving a key with the contractor and asking him to winterize the residence. At some unknown time, a water pipe froze and burst. As a result, between four and six inches of water stood continuously in the basement until the contractor discovered the problem in April 2001. The standing water caused only minimal structural damage to the basement, but the humidity from the standing water caused mold to form on all of the interior surfaces of the residence. As a result of the mold, the residence became uninhabitable and had to be demolished. Maples reported the loss to Shelter, which instituted the declaratory judgment action referred to above. After the federal district court granted summary judgment in favor of Shelter, Maples appealed to the U.S. Court of Appeals for the Eighth Circuit. Should the district court's grant of summary judgment in favor of Shelter be reversed?

6. Brandy Harvey, age 16, and Toby Gearheart, age 19, were at a Wabash River boat ramp one evening. When a disagreement arose, Brandy moved toward Gearheart and pushed him toward the water more than once. When she again approached Gearheart, he put his hands on her shoulders and pushed her. Brandy lost her balance and fell off the boat ramp, down a rocky embankment, and into the river, where she drowned. In a criminal proceeding concerning the incident, Gearheart pleaded guilty to involuntary manslaughter. Acting as co-personal representatives of Brandy's estate, her parents, Jon Harvey and Misty Johnson, filed a wrongful death action against Gearheart in an Indiana trial court. They contended in their complaint that Gearheart's "negligence and recklessness" had caused Brandy's death. Harvey and Johnson also named Auto-Owners Insurance Co. as a defendant on the theory that because of the liability insurance portion of a homeowners' insurance policy issued to Gearheart's parents, Auto-Owners would be obligated to pay any judgment entered against Gearheart (who still lived in his parents' home and was therefore an insured person under the policy). The insurance policy at issue stated that Auto-Owners "will pay all sums any insured becomes legally obligated to pay as damages because of or arising out of bodily injury or property damage caused by an occurrence to which this coverage applies." The policy also defined

"occurrence" to mean "an accident that results in bodily injury or property damage and includes, as one occurrence, all continuous or repeated exposure to substantially the same generally harmful conditions." The word "accident" was not defined in the policy. In addition, an exclusion set forth in the policy indicated that there was no coverage for "bodily injury or property damage reasonably expected or intended by the insured."

Auto-Owners moved for summary judgment, asserting that in view of the facts and the above-quoted provisions, the policy furnished no coverage in regard to Gearheart's actions. The trial court denied Auto-Owners' motion, but the Court of Appeals of Indiana reversed. Harvey and Johnson appealed to the Supreme Court of Indiana.

Should the appellate court's decision be reversed?

7. In August 1982, a hog confinement building owned by Charles Ridenour collapsed and was rendered a total loss. Some of Ridenour's hogs were killed as a further result of the collapse. Ridenour made a claim for these losses with his property insurer, Farm Bureau Insurance Company, whose Country Squire policy had been issued on Ridenour's property in July 1977 and had been renewed on a yearly basis after that. Farm Bureau denied the claim because the policy did not provide coverage for the collapse of farm buildings such as the hog confinement structure. Moreover, though the policy provided coverage for hog deaths resulting from certain designated causes, collapse of a building was not among the causes listed. Asserting that the parties' insurance contract was to have covered the peril of building collapse notwithstanding the terms of the written policy, Ridenour sued Farm Bureau. He asked the court to order reformation of the written policy so that it would conform to the parties' supposed agreement regarding coverage. At trial, Ridenour testified about a February 1982 meeting in which he, his wife, and their son discussed insurance coverage with Farm Bureau agent Tim Moomey. Ridenour testified that he wanted to be certain there was insurance coverage if the hog confinement building collapsed because he had heard about the collapse of a similar structure owned by someone else. Therefore, he asked Moomey whether the Country Squire policy then in force provided such coverage. According to Ridenour, Moomey said that it did. Ridenour's wife, Thelma, testified that she asked Moomey (during the same meeting) whether there would be coverage if the floor slats of the hog confinement building collapsed and caused hogs to fall into the pit below the building. According

to her testimony, Moomey responded affirmatively. The Ridenours' son, Tom, testified to the same effect. Mr. and Mrs. Ridenour both testified that they had not completely read the Country Squire policy and that because they did not understand the wording, they relied on Moomey to interpret the policy for them.

Moomey, who had ended his relationship with Farm Bureau by the time the case came to trial, testified that at no time did the Ridenours request that the hogs and the confinement building be insured so as to provide coverage for losses resulting from collapse of the building. Moomey knew that collapse coverage was not available from Farm Bureau for hog confinement buildings. In addition, Moomey testified that he met with Ridenour in April 1982 and conducted a "farm review" in which he discussed a coverage checklist and the Country Squire policy's declarations pages (which set forth the policy limits). This checklist, which Ridenour signed after Moomey reviewed it with him, made no reference to coverage for collapse losses. (Ridenour admitted in his testimony that he had signed the checklist after Moomey read off the listed items to him.) When Moomey was contacted by the Ridenours on the day the building collapsed, he had his secretary prepare a notice of loss report for submission to Farm Bureau. He also assigned an adjuster to inspect the property. Moomey and the adjuster discussed the fact that the Country Squire policy did not provide coverage for Ridenour's losses. Ridenour further testified that the day after the collapse occurred, Moomey told him he was sorry but that Farm Bureau's home office had said there was no coverage.

The trial court granted reformation, as Ridenour had requested. Farm Bureau appealed. Was the trial court's decision correct?

8. Enterprise Financial Group provided financing and credit life insurance to consumers who bought automobiles from a certain Oklahoma dealership. If purchased by a car buyer, the credit life insurance would pay off the customer's car loan in the event of his death. In March 1992, Milford Vining (Milford) purchased a Jeep from the dealership. An Enterprise employee whose office was at the dealership sold a credit life insurance policy to Milford when he purchased the jeep. In late May 1993, Milford suffered a fatal heart attack. His surviving spouse, Billie Vining (Vining), filed a claim with Enterprise for death benefits of approximately $10,000 under Milford's credit life policy. Enterprise refused to pay the claim and rescinded the policy on the supposed ground that Milford had misrepresented his health history in his

application for the credit life policy. After unsuccessfully contesting the rescission, Vining sued Enterprise for breach of contract and for rescinding the policy in bad faith. In defense, Enterprise maintained that it had a legitimate basis for contesting the claim and that Milford had made material misrepresentations in his application for the credit life policy.

The evidence adduced at trial showed that in 1983, Milford suffered from coronary artery disease and underwent a triple bypass operation. After the surgery and follow-up tests, Milford began taking heart maintenance medication to prevent the occurrence of angina. From the time immediately following the 1983 surgery until the time of his death, Milford led an active life. He did not complain of chest pain or related symptoms. In February 1992, Milford visited Dr. Michael Sullivan. This visit took place because Milford, who had recently moved, wanted to find a doctor closer to home. Milford's visit to Dr. Sullivan was not brought on by illness or physical symptoms. At the general time of this visit, Milford suffered from little, if any, angina. Dr. Sullivan continued Milford on his heart maintenance medications as a preventive measure. When Milford applied for the credit life policy in March 1992, he signed an application that contained the following statement:

> I hereby certify that I am in good health as of the effective date above. I further certify that I do not presently have, nor have I ever had, nor have I been told I have, nor have I been treated within the preceding 12 months for, any of the following: any heart disease, or other cardiovascular diseases.

The parties to the case agreed that Milford did not intend to misstate any facts when he signed the application. At trial, Vining presented evidence designed to show that Enterprise routinely rescinded credit life policies after insureds' deaths and that the rescission of Milford's policy fit into this pattern. If Vining were to win the case, what sorts of damages would she be entitled to receive? Should Vining win the case?

9. Jeffrey Lane was employed by Memtek (a corporation) at its Arby's Restaurant. He was being trained as a cook. After 11:00 one evening, Lane finished work and clocked out. He remained in the restaurant's lobby, however, because he was waiting for the manager to complete her duties. As Lane waited, friends of other restaurant employees came to a door of the restaurant. Lane and the other employees became involved in a conversation with these persons, who

included John Taylor. Lane told Taylor that he could not enter the restaurant because it was closed. Taylor did not attempt to force his way into the restaurant. Instead, he "dared" Lane to come outside. Lane left the restaurant "of [his] own will" (according to Lane's deposition) for what he assumed would be a fight with Taylor. In the fight that transpired, Lane broke Taylor's nose and knocked out three of his teeth. Lane later pleaded guilty to a criminal battery charge. Taylor filed a civil suit against Lane and Memtek in an effort to collect damages stemming from the altercation with Lane. American Family Mutual Insurance Company provided liability insurance for Memtek in connection with its restaurant. The policy stated that for purposes of American Family's duties to defend and indemnify, "the insured" included not only Memtek but also Memtek's "employees, . . . but only for acts within the scope of their employment." American Family filed a declaratory judgment action in which it asked the court to determine that it owed Lane neither a duty to defend nor a duty to indemnify in connection with the incident giving rise to Taylor's lawsuit. American Family's theory was that for purposes of that incident, Lane was not an insured within the above-quoted policy provision. Was American Family correct?

10. Earl and Vonette Crowell owned a farm in Minnesota. In 1980, they mortgaged the farm to Farm Credit Services and purchased a property insurance policy on the farm (including the farmhouse) from Delafield Farmers Mutual Insurance Co. Fire was among the perils covered by this policy, which ran from October 1985 to October 1988. When the Crowells fell behind on their mortgage payments, Farm Credit began foreclosure proceedings. Upon foreclosure, mortgagors such as the Crowells have a right of redemption for a specified time. The right of redemption allows the defaulting mortgagors to buy back their property after it has been sold to someone else in the foreclosure proceedings. In November 1987, the Crowells' right of redemption expired. Minnesota law provides, however, that farmers who lose their farms to corporate lenders are given an additional opportunity to repurchase their farms under a "right of first refusal." This right meant that Farm Credit was forbidden to sell the farm to anyone else before offering it to the Crowells at a price no higher than the highest price offered by a third party. Farm Credit allowed the Crowells to remain on the farm while they attempted to secure financing to buy the property under their right of first refusal. In November 1987, a fire substantially damaged the

farmhouse. The Crowells filed a claim for the loss with Delafield. Although Delafield paid the claim concerning the Crowells' personal effects that were located inside the farmhouse and were destroyed in the fire, it denied the claim on the farmhouse itself. Delafield took the position that because the time period for the Crowells' right of redemption had expired, they no longer had an insurable interest in the farmhouse. The Crowells therefore sued Delafield. Concluding that the Crowells had an insurable interest in the farmhouse, the trial court granted summary judgment in their favor. Was the trial court correct?

Credit

Pixtal/AGE Fotostock

Introduction to Credit and Secured Transactions

Eric Richards decided to go into the commercial laundry and dry-cleaning business. He began by agreeing to buy the land, building, and equipment of a small dry cleaner. Richards agreed to pay the owner $300,000 in cash and "to assume" a $150,000 existing mortgage on the property. He next entered into a contract with a local contractor to build, within five months, an addition to the building for $250,000 with $40,000 payable with the signing of the contract and the balance to be paid in periodic installments as the construction progressed. Because Richards had heard some horror stories from friends in the local Chamber of Commerce about contractors who walked away from jobs without completing them, he asked the contractor to post a security bond or provide a surety to ensure the contract would be completed in a timely manner. Richards also had some of the existing dry-cleaning equipment picked up for repair and refurbishment. When the work was completed, the repairman refused to redeliver it until Richards paid in full for the work, claiming he had a lien on the equipment until he was paid.

Among the questions that will be addressed in this chapter are:

- What legal rights and obligations accompany the "assumption" of a mortgage?

- Would Richards risk losing any of his rights to recover against the surety if he granted the contractor additional time to complete the construction?

- If the contractor does not pay subcontractors or companies who provide construction material for the job, would they be able to assert a lien against the property until they are paid?

- Would the person who repaired and refurbished the dry-cleaning equipment be able to assert a lien until Richards paid for it? Would it make a difference if the repair work had been done on site?

- Would it be ethical for a person who has sold a parcel of real property on a land contract to declare a default of the contract when there is a minor default in making the payments called for in the contract and to reclaim possession of the property with the purchaser losing all the equity he might have built up in the property?

LO LEARNING OBJECTIVES

After studying this chapter, you should be able to:

28-1 Explain the difference between unsecured credit and secured credit.

28-2 Recall the definition of a surety, relate how the principal and surety relationship is created, and explain the defenses that may be available to a surety as well as the duties that a creditor owes to a surety.

28-3 Describe common law liens and how they are created and recall the rights that they provide to artisans and others who hold such a lien.

> **28-4** Compare and contrast mortgages, deeds of trust, and land contracts as mechanisms for holding a security interest in real property.
>
> **28-5** List the formalities necessary for the creation of a legally enforceable mortgage and explain
>
> what is meant by *foreclosure* and the *right of redemption*.
>
> **28-6** Describe mechanic's and materialman's liens created by state law and explain how they are obtained and what rights they give the lienholder.

IN THE UNITED STATES, a substantial portion of business transactions involves the extension of credit. The term *credit* has many meanings. In this chapter, it will be used to mean transactions in which goods are sold, services are rendered, or money is loaned in exchange for a promise to repay the debt at some future date.

In some of these transactions, a creditor is willing to rely on the debtor's promise to pay at a later time; in others, the creditor wants some further assurance or security that the debtor will make good on her promise to pay. This chapter will discuss the differences between secured and unsecured credit and will detail various mechanisms that are available to the creditor who wants to obtain security. These mechanisms include obtaining liens or security interests in personal or real property, sureties, and guarantors. Security interests in real property, sureties and guarantors, and common law liens on personal property will be covered in this chapter, and the Uniform Commercial Code (UCC) rules concerning security interests in personal property will be covered in Chapter 29, Security Interests in Personal Property. The last chapter in Part 6 deals with bankruptcy law, which may come into play when a debtor is unable to fulfill his obligation to pay his debts when they are due.

Credit

 Explain the difference between unsecured credit and secured credit.

Unsecured Credit Many common transactions are based on unsecured credit. For example, a person may have a charge account at a department store or a MasterCard account. If the person buys a sweater and charges it to his charge account or MasterCard account, unsecured credit has been extended to him. He has received goods in return for his promise to pay for them later. Similarly, if a person goes to a dentist to have a cavity in a tooth filled and the dentist sends her a bill payable by the end

of the month, services have been rendered on the basis of unsecured credit. Consumers are not the only people who use unsecured credit. Many transactions between businesspeople utilize it; for example, a retailer buys merchandise or a manufacturer buys raw materials, promising to pay for the merchandise or materials within 30 days after receipt.

Unsecured credit transactions involve a maximum of risk to the creditor—the person who extends the credit. When goods are delivered, services are rendered, or money is loaned on unsecured credit, the creditor gives up all rights in the goods, services, or money. In return, the creditor gets a promise by the debtor to pay or to perform the promised act. If the debtor does not pay or keep the promise, the creditor's options are more limited than if he had obtained security to ensure the debtor's performance. One course of action is to bring a lawsuit against the debtor and obtain a judgment. The creditor might then have the sheriff execute the judgment on any property owned by the debtor that is subject to execution. The creditor might also try to garnish the wages or other moneys to which the debtor is entitled. However, the debtor might be judgment-proof; that is, the debtor may not have any property subject to execution or may not have a steady job. Under these circumstances, execution or garnishment would be of little aid to the creditor in collecting the judgment.

A businessperson may obtain credit insurance to stabilize the credit risk of doing business on an unsecured credit basis. However, he passes the costs of the insurance to the business, or of the unsecured credit losses that the business sustains, on to the consumer. The consumer pays a higher price for goods or services purchased, or a higher interest rate on any money borrowed, from a business that has high credit losses.

Secured Credit To minimize his credit risk, a creditor may contract for security. The creditor may require the debtor to convey to the creditor a security interest or lien on the debtor's property. Suppose a person borrows $3,000 from a credit union. The credit union might require her to put up her car as security for the loan or might ask that some other person agree to be liable if she defaults. For example, if a student who does not have a regular job goes to a bank to borrow money, the bank might ask that the student's father or mother cosign the note for the loan.

When the creditor has security for the credit he extends and the debtor defaults, the creditor can go against the security to collect the obligation. Assume that a person borrows $18,000 from a bank to buy a new car and that the bank takes a security interest (lien) on the car. If the person fails to make his monthly payments, the bank has the right to repossess the car and have it sold so that it can recover its money. Similarly, if the borrower's father cosigned for the car loan and the borrower defaults, the bank can sue the father to collect the balance due on the loan.

Development of Security
Various types of security devices have been developed as social and economic need for them has arisen. The rights and liabilities of the parties to a secured transaction depend on the nature of the security—that is, on whether (1) the security pledged is the promise of another person to pay if the debtor does not or (2) a security interest in goods, intangibles, or real estate is conveyed as security for the payment of a debt or obligation.

If personal credit is pledged, the other person may guarantee the payment of the debt—that is, become a guarantor—or the other person may join the debtor in the debtor's promise to pay, in which case the other person would become surety for the debt.

The oldest and simplest security device was the pledge. To have a pledge valid against third persons with an interest in the goods, such as subsequent purchasers or creditors, it was necessary that the property used as security be delivered to the pledgee or a pledge holder. Upon default by the pledger, the pledgee had the right to sell the property and apply the proceeds to the payment of the debt.

Situations arose in which it was desirable to leave the property used as security in the possession of the debtor. To accomplish this objective, the debtor would give the creditor a bill of sale to the property, thus passing title to the creditor. The bill of sale would provide that if the debtor performed his promise, the bill of sale would become null and void, thus revesting title to the property in the debtor. A secret lien on the goods was created by this device, and the early courts held that such a transaction was a fraud on third-party claimants and void as to them. An undisclosed or secret lien is unfair to creditors who might extend credit to the debtor on the strength of property that they see in the debtor's possession but that in fact is subject to the prior claim of another creditor. Statutes were enacted providing for the recording or filing of the bill of sale, which

was later designated as a chattel mortgage. These statutes were not uniform in their provisions. Most of them set up formal requirements for the execution of the chattel mortgage and also stated the effect of recording or filing on the rights of third-party claimants.

To avoid the requirements for the execution and filing of the chattel mortgage, sellers of goods would sell the goods on a "conditional sales contract" under which the seller retained title to the goods until their purchase price had been paid in full. Upon default by the buyer, the seller could (1) repossess the goods or (2) pass title and recover a judgment for the unpaid balance of the purchase price. Abuses of this security device gave rise to some regulatory statutes. About one-half of the states enacted statutes providing that the conditional sales contract was void as to third parties unless it was filed or recorded.

No satisfactory device was developed whereby inventory could be used as security. The inherent difficulty is that inventory is intended to be sold and turned into cash and the creditor is interested in protecting his interest in the cash rather than in maintaining a lien on the sold goods. Field warehousing was used under the pledge, and an after-acquired property clause in a chattel mortgage on a stock of goods held for resale partially fulfilled this need. One of the devices used was the trust receipt. This short-term marketing security arrangement had its origin in the export–import trade. It was later used extensively as a means of financing retailers of consumer goods having a high unit value.

Security Interests in Personal Property
Chapter 29, Security Interests in Personal Property, will discuss how a creditor can obtain a security interest in the personal property or fixtures of a debtor. It will also explain the rights to the debtor's property of the creditor, the debtor, and other creditors of the debtor. These security interests are covered by Article 9 of the Uniform Commercial Code, which sets out a comprehensive scheme for regulating security interests in personal property and fixtures. The Code abolishes the old formal distinctions between different types of security devices used to create security interests in personal property.

Security Interests in Real Property
Three types of contractual security devices have been developed by which real estate may be used as security: (1) the real estate mortgage, (2) the trust deed, and (3) the land contract. In addition to these contract security devices, all of the states have enacted statutes granting the right to mechanic's liens on real estate. Security interests in real property are covered later in this chapter.

Suretyship and Guaranty

LO28-2 Recall the definition of a surety, relate how the principal and surety relationship is created, and explain the defenses that may be available to a surety as well as the duties that a creditor owes to a surety.

Sureties and Guarantors

As a condition of making a loan, granting credit, or employing someone (particularly as a fiduciary), a creditor may demand that the debtor, contractor, or employee provide as security for his performance the liability of a third person as surety or guarantor. The purpose of the contract of suretyship or guaranty is to provide the creditor with additional protection against loss in the event of default by the debtor, contractor, or employee.

A **surety** is a person who is *liable for the payment of another person's debt or for the performance of another person's duty.* The surety joins with the person primarily liable in promising to make the payment or to perform the duty. For example, Kathleen Kelly, who is 17 years old, buys a used car on credit from Harry's Used Cars. She signs a promissory note, agreeing to pay $200 a month on the note until the note is paid in full. Harry's has Kathleen's father cosign the note; thus, her father is a surety. Similarly, the city of Chicago hires the B&B Construction Company to build a new sewage treatment plant. The city will probably require B&B to have a surety agree to be liable for B&B's performance of its contract. There are insurance companies that, for a fee, will agree to be a surety on the contract of a company such as B&B.

The surety is *primarily liable* for the debtor's obligation, and the debtor can demand performance from the surety at the time the debt is due. The creditor does not need to establish a default by the debtor or proceed first against the debtor on his obligation.

A guaranty contract is similar to a suretyship contract in that the promisor agrees to answer for the obligation of another. However, a guarantor does not join the principal in making a promise; rather, a guarantor makes a separate promise and agrees to be liable upon the happening of a certain event. For example, a father tells a merchant, "I will guarantee payment of my daughter Rachel's debt to you if she does not pay it," or "If Rachel becomes bankrupt, I will guarantee payment of her debt to you." While a surety is *primarily liable*, a guarantor is *secondarily liable* and can be held to his guarantee *only after* the principal defaults and cannot be held to his promise or payment. Generally, a guarantor's promise must be made in writing to be enforceable under the statute of frauds.

Most commercial contracts and promissory notes today that are to be signed by multiple parties provide for the parties to be "jointly and severally" liable, thus making the surety relationship the predominate one.

In the case that follows, *Columbia Realty Ventures v. Dang*, the court concluded that a document that purported to establish the signator as a guarantor actually created a suretyship and held that under the circumstances of the case, it would be unconscionable to enforce the guaranty.

Columbia Realty Ventures v. Dang
2011 Va. Cir. LEXIS 115 (Aug. 16, 2011)

Dong Dang and his wife, Hao Dang, attended a settlement with Columbia Realty for Mr. Dang to execute a commercial lease agreement in Mr. Dang's sole name for a nail salon in the District of Columbia. During the course of the settlement, Mrs. Dang was handed a document titled "Guaranty" and told that she had to sign the document or her husband would not be able to obtain the lease. While both Mr. Dang and Columbia Realty's representative urged Mrs. Dang to sign the document, no explanation was given as to the document's contents, no explanation was given as to the terms of the underlying commercial lease, and at no time was she advised that she was signing a document that made her individually liable to a greater degree than Mr. Dang would be on the commercial lease.

Mr. Dang was in default on the lease, and Columbia Realty brought suit against the Dangs and, among other things, sought to hold Mrs. Dang liable on the Guaranty she had signed. At the trial, Mrs. Dang raised concerns about the validity of the Guaranty due to its failure to name the property involved and the person whose obligation it required Mrs. Dang to guarantee. At the conclusion of the evidence, Mrs. Dang moved to strike the claims against her based on her contention that the Guaranty was invalid and unenforceable against her. In essence, she contended that the contract of guarantee was unenforceable against her because it was unconscionable.

Nordlund, Judge

A guaranty is a collateral undertaking by one person to be answerable for the payment of some debt or the performance of some duty if another person defaults on his payment or performance. A guaranty must be in writing and supported by adequate consideration. The law deems a guaranty absolute unless its terms import some condition precedent to the liability of the guarantor. If a guaranty is conditional, however, the creditor must satisfy those conditions before proceeding against the guarantor. In Virginia, the distinction between guaranty and suretyship is that guaranty is a secondary obligation while suretyship is a primary one. The Supreme Court of Virginia elaborated on this distinction, stating:

> The contract of the guarantor is his own separate undertaking, in which the principal does not join. The guarantor contracts to pay, if, by the use of due diligence, the debt cannot be made out of the principal debtor, while the surety undertakes directly for the payment, and so is responsible at once if the principal debtor makes default; or, in other words, guaranty is an undertaking that the debtor shall pay; suretyship, that the debt shall be paid.

The document at issue in this case states in pertinent part:

> Guarantors further covenant that (1) the liability of the Guarantors is primary, shall not be subject to deduction for any claim of offset, counterclaim or defense which Tenant or Guarantors may have against Landlord, and Landlord may proceed against Guarantors separately or jointly, before, after or simultaneously with any proceeding against Tenant for default . . . (4) this Guaranty shall be absolute and unconditional . . .

Even Columbia's counsel had to acknowledge, during the June 30, 2011 hearing, that the "Guaranty" in this case did indeed operate as a suretyship and not a guaranty, making Mrs. Dang primarily obligated to Columbia should the current tenant default on his contractual duties to Columbia. Consistent with the above stated principles, the Court finds that Mrs. Dang signed what amounts to a primary obligation and an absolute guaranty, which is therefore a suretyship, not a guaranty.

When construing a suretyship contract, the Court must apply the same rules as it would to the construction of any other contract, the relevant inquiry being: "What was the intention of the parties as disclosed by the instrument in the light of the surrounding circumstances?"

Virginia law has several well settled principles regarding the liability of sureties. At its most basic level, a surety's liability to the creditor is the same as that of the principal. Accordingly, the creditor's right of recovery against the surety does not extend beyond that against the principal, nor will a surety be liable where the creditor could not assert that liability against the principal.

Moreover, a creditor must demonstrate that he has performed his obligations under the contract before he can recover against the debtor's surety. If the creditor demonstrates a prima facie case for liability against the principal, the surety may assert the same defenses as the principal because the surety and principal are in privity.

A surety who receives no payment for his contract is a favored debtor under Virginia law because she receives no benefit for her obligation. In the case, the "Guaranty" contains no explicit statement about consideration, nor could the Court reasonably imply one from its terms. Therefore, Mrs. Dang is a gratuitous surety.

In *Southern Cross Coal Corp.*, the Supreme Court described the obligation of a gratuitous, or accommodation surety, as follows: "Accommodation sureties are entitled to the benefit of the *strictissimi juris* rule: they are discharged by any change in the obligation." *Strictissimi juris* is usually defined as "most strictly according to the law." Additionally, if a creditor and a principal debtor make a positive contract to extend the time of the debtor's obligation without the surety's consent, the surety is thereby discharged.

Despite these well settled principles, the "Guaranty" in this case requires Mrs. Dang to forfeit multiple rights she otherwise would have as a gratuitous surety. Specifically, the Guarantor covenants that:

(1) the liability of the Guarantors [sic] is primary, *shall not be subject to deduction for any claim of offset, counterclaim or defense which Tenant . . . may have against Landlord;*

(2) this Guaranty shall not be terminated or impaired in any manner whatsoever by reason of the assertion by Landlord against Tenant of any of the rights or remedies reserved to Landlord pursuant to the provisions of such Lease, by reason of summary or other proceedings against Tenant . . . *or by reason of any extension of time or indulgence granted by Landlord to Tenant or any other defense available to guarantors or sureties. . . .*

(4) the Guaranty shall be absolute and unconditional and shall remain and *continue in full force and effect as to any renewal, extension, amendment, additions, assignments, sublease, transfer or other modification of the Lease, whether or not currently expressed in the Lease and whether or not the Guarantors have notice thereof;*

(emphasis added). These sections of the "Guaranty" stand in direct opposition to Mrs. Dang's rights to bring any defenses that her husband might have against the landlord, be discharged because of an extension of time or modification of the underlying obligation without her notice, and "any other defense available to guarantors or sureties." Because the "Guaranty" essentially requires Mrs. Dang to give up all rights she would normally be entitled to under Virginia law, the Court finds it necessary to determine whether this forfeiture makes the "Guaranty" unconscionable and unenforceable against Mrs. Dang.

Virginia law sets a high burden for declaring a contract unconscionable.

While the jurisdiction undoubtedly exists in the courts to avoid a contract on the ground that it makes an unconscionable bargain, nevertheless an inequitable and unconscionable bargain has been defined to be "one that no man in his senses and not under a delusion would make, on the one hand and as no fair man would accept, on the other." The inequality must be so gross as to shock the conscience.

Applying the law to the evidence from the trial in this case, it appears that a corporate party told an individual that she needed to sign the Guaranty or her husband would not be allowed to lease the property. The evidence from trial therefore indicates that no bargaining over the terms of the "Guaranty" took place. Even Columbia admits that Mr. Dang simply instructed Mrs. Dang to sign the "Guaranty" so that Columbia would lease him the property, without offering her the opportunity to discuss or negotiate the terms of either document.

Looking then to the substance of the "Guaranty," it appears to convert Mrs. Dang from a guarantor, with a conditional and secondary obligation, to a gratuitous surety with a primary obligation. In addition, the terms of the "Guaranty" then attempt to take away many of the rights Mrs. Dang would otherwise have as a gratuitous surety under Virginia law. Even putting many of them aside, Mrs. Dang's signature on the "Guaranty" made her primarily liable for the obligation of the Tenant, regardless of whether the Tenant continued to be her husband or not, and regardless of how much Columbia and the Tenant decided to change the underlying obligation, all without ever notifying Mrs. Dang. Additionally, despite any modifications to that underlying obligation, Mrs. Dang would be liable and utterly defenseless in a trial for the collection of that obligation and could potentially be forced to pay Columbia more than a Tenant owed.

Columbia has argued that the Court should not find the "Guaranty" unconscionable because it chose not to enforce the more problematic terms against Mrs. Dang during the trial of this case. Specifically, Columbia notes that it allowed Mrs. Dang to present defenses at trial, including defenses available to the Tenant. But it is well settled in this Commonwealth, that when the terms of a contract are clear and unambiguous, as they are here, the contract needs no interpretation, and the intention of the parties must be determined only from the terms themselves. The Court finds the terms of the "Guaranty" in this case clear and unambiguous. Therefore, the Court cannot and will not interpret the "Guaranty" based upon Columbia's representation that it did not enforce certain terms at the trial and perhaps never intended to enforce them.

The Court further finds that Mrs. Dang was given no opportunity to review or understand the "Guaranty" or to negotiate over its terms, and thereby had unequal bargaining power with Columbia at the time of her signature. Additionally, the Court finds that Mrs. Dang was a gratuitous surety, as she primarily obligated herself to Columbia under the Lease, for no consideration, and therefore is a favored debtor. In addition, despite that the laws governing suretyships allow a surety to assert the same defense as the principal, the "Guaranty" purports to waive and deny Mrs. Dang the right to assert any rights or defenses the Tenant would have under the Lease, (including any right of set-off), regardless of how severely Columbia and the Tenant may have modified the Lease from its form at the time of her signature. Most importantly, by definition, a surety is only liable for the underlying obligation of the primary debtor, and by waiving Mrs. Dang's right to assert the same defenses as the Tenant, the "Guaranty" opens her up to potentially be liable for more than the underlying obligation.

For the reasons stated herein, the Court concludes that the circumstances surrounding Mrs. Dang's execution of the "Guaranty," combined with the terms of the "Guaranty" itself, constitute an inequality "so gross as to shock the conscience."

Accordingly, the Court finds that the "Guaranty" is unconscionable and unenforceable against Mrs. Dang, and hereby grants her Motion to Strike the claims against her.

Creation of Principal and Surety Relation
The relationship of principal and surety, or that of principal and guarantor, is created by contract. The basic rules of contract law apply in determining the existence and nature of the relationship as well as the rights and duties of the parties.

Defenses of a Surety
Suppose Jeffrey's mother agrees to be a surety for Jeffrey on his purchase of a motorcycle. If the motorcycle was defectively made and Jeffrey refuses to make further payments on it, the dealer might try to collect the balance due from Jeffrey's mother. As a surety, Jeffrey's mother can use any defenses against the dealer that Jeffrey has if they go to the merits of the primary contract. Thus, if Jeffrey has a valid defense of breach of warranty against the dealer, his mother can use it as a basis for not paying the dealer.

Other defenses that go to the merits include (1) lack or failure of consideration, (2) inducement of the contract by fraud or duress, and (3) breach of contract by the other party. Certain defenses of the principal cannot be used by the surety. These defenses include lack of capacity, such as minority or insanity, and bankruptcy. Thus, if Jeffrey is only 17 years old, the fact that he is a minor cannot be used by Jeffrey's mother to defend against the dealer. This defense of Jeffrey's lack of capacity to contract does not go to the merits of the contract between Jeffrey and the dealer and cannot be used by Jeffrey's mother.

A surety contracts to be responsible for the performance of the principal's obligation. If the principal and the creditor change that obligation by agreement, the surety is relieved of responsibility unless the surety agrees to the change. This is because the surety's obligation cannot be changed without his consent.

For example, Fredericks cosigns a note for his friend Kato, which she has given to Credit Union to secure a loan. Suppose the note was originally for $2,500 and payable in 12 months with interest at 11 percent a year. Credit Union and Kato later agree that Kato will have 24 months to repay the note but that the interest will be 13 percent per year. Unless Fredericks consents to this change, he is discharged from his responsibility as surety. The obligation he agreed to assume was altered by the changes in the repayment period and the interest rate.

The most common kind of change affecting a surety is an extension of time to perform the contract. If the creditor merely allows the principal more time without the surety's consent, this does not relieve the surety of responsibility. The surety's consent is required only where there is an actual binding agreement between the creditor and the principal as to the extension of time.

In addition, the courts usually make a distinction between accommodation sureties and compensated sureties. An accommodation surety is a person who acts as a surety without compensation, such as a friend who cosigns a note as a favor. A compensated surety is a person, usually a professional such as a bonding company, who is paid for serving as a surety.

The courts are more protective of accommodation sureties than of compensated sureties. Accommodation sureties are relieved of liability unless they consent to an extension of time. Compensated sureties, on the other hand, must show that they will be harmed by an extension of time before they are relieved of responsibility because of a binding extension without their consent. A compensated surety must show that a change in the contract was both material and prejudicial to him if he is to be relieved of his obligation as surety.

Creditor's Duties to Surety

The creditor is required to disclose any material facts about the risk involved to the surety. If he does not do so, the surety is relieved of liability. For example, a bank (creditor) knows that an employee, Arthur, has been guilty of criminal conduct in the past. If the bank applies to a bonding company to obtain a bond on Arthur, the bank must disclose this information about Arthur. Similarly, suppose the bank has an employee, Alison, covered by a bond and discovers that Alison is embezzling money. If the bank agrees to give Alison another chance but does not report her actions to the bonding company, the bonding company is relieved of responsibility for further wrongful acts by Alison.

If the debtor posts security for the performance of an obligation, the creditor must not surrender the security without the consent of the surety. If the creditor does so, the surety is relieved of liability to the extent of the value surrendered.

Subrogation, Reimbursement, and Contribution

If the surety has to perform or pay the principal's obligation, then the surety acquires all of the rights that the creditor had against the principal. This is known as the surety's **right of subrogation**. The rights acquired could include the right to any collateral in the possession of the creditor, any judgment right the creditor had against the principal on the obligation, and the rights of a creditor in bankruptcy proceedings.

If the surety performs or pays the principal's obligation, she is entitled to recover her costs from the principal; this is known as the surety's **right to reimbursement**. For example, Amado cosigns a promissory note for $2,500 at the credit union for her friend Anders. Anders defaults on the note, and the credit union collects $2,500 from Amado on her suretyship obligation. Amado then not only gets the credit union's rights against Anders under the right of subrogation, but also the right to collect $2,500 from Anders under the right of reimbursement.

Suppose several persons (Tom, Dick, and Harry) are cosureties of their friend Sam. When Sam defaults, Tom pays the whole obligation. Tom is entitled to collect one-third from both Dick and Harry because he paid more than his prorated share. This is known as the cosurety's **right to contribution**. The relative shares of cosureties, as well as any limitations on their liability, are normally set out in the contract of suretyship.

A surety also has what is known as a **right of exoneration**, which is the right of the surety or guarantor to require the debtor to make good on his commitment to the creditor when he (1) is able to do so and (2) does not have a valid defense against payment. The right is exercised when the creditor is pursuing the surety or guarantor to make good on their liability. The surety or guarantor then sues the debtor to force him to pay the creditor, automatically staying the creditor's action against the surety or guarantor. The surety or guarantor uses this right to prevent its having to pay the creditor (which may require liquidation of some of the surety's or guarantor's assets) and then having to sue the debtor under the right of subrogation or reimbursement.

Liens on Personal Property

 LO28-3 Describe common law liens and how they are created and recall the rights that they provide to artisans and others who hold such a lien.

Security Interests in Personal Property and Fixtures under the Uniform Commercial Code Chapter 29 will discuss how a creditor can obtain a security interest in the personal property or fixtures of a debtor. It will also explain the rights of the creditor, the debtor, and other creditors of the debtors to the property. These security interests are covered by Article 9 of the Uniform Commercial Code, which sets out a comprehensive scheme for regulating security interests in personal property and fixtures. Article 9 does not deal with the liens that landlords, artisans, and materialmen are given by statute or with security interests in real estate. These security interests will be covered in this chapter.

Common Law Liens Under the common—or judge-made—law, artisans, innkeepers, and common carriers (such as airlines and trucking companies) were entitled to liens to secure the reasonable value of the services they performed. An artisan such as a furniture upholsterer or an auto mechanic uses his labor or materials to improve

personal property that belongs to someone else. The improvement becomes part of the property and belongs to the owner of the property. Therefore, the artisan who made the improvement is given a **lien** on the property until he is paid.

For example, the upholsterer who recovers a sofa for a customer is entitled to a lien on the sofa. The innkeeper and common carrier are in business to serve the public and are required by law to do so. Under the common law, the innkeeper, to secure payment for his reasonable charges for food and lodging, was allowed to claim a lien on the property that the guest brought to the hotel or inn. Similarly, the common carrier, such as a trucking company, was allowed to claim a lien on the goods carried for the reasonable charges for the service. The justification for such liens was that the innkeeper and common carrier were entitled to the protection of a lien because they were required by law to provide the service to anyone seeking it.

Statutory Liens While common law liens are still generally recognized today, many states have incorporated this concept into statutes. Some of the state statutes have created additional liens, while others have modified the common law liens to some extent. The statutes commonly provide a procedure for foreclosing the lien. Foreclosure is the method by which the rights of the property owner are cut off so that the lienholder can realize her security interest. Typically, the statutes provide for a court to authorize the sale of the personal property subject to the lien so that the creditor can obtain the money to which she is entitled.

Carriers' liens and warehousemen's liens are provided for in Article 7, Documents of Title, of the Uniform Commercial Code. They are covered in Chapter 23, Personal Property and Bailments.

Characteristics of Liens The common law lien and most of the statutory liens are known as possessory liens. They give the artisan or other lienholder the right to keep possession of the debtor's property until the

Ethics and Compliance in Action

What Is the Ethical Thing to Do?

Suppose you own and operate a small loan business. A young man applies for a $1,000 loan. When you run a credit check on him, you find that he has had difficulty holding a job and has a terrible credit record. You conclude that he is a poor credit risk and inform him that you are willing to make the requested loan only if he can find

someone who has a good credit rating to cosign a promissory note with him. The next day he comes by the office with a young woman who meets your criteria for a good credit rating and who indicates she is willing to cosign the note. Do you have any ethical obligation to share with the young woman the information you have about the young man's employment and credit history?

reasonable charges for services have been paid. For the lien to come into play, possession of the goods must have been entrusted to the artisan. Suppose a person takes a chair to an upholsterer to have it repaired. The upholsterer can keep possession of the chair until the person pays the reasonable value of the repair work. However, if the upholsterer comes to the person's home to make the repair, the upholsterer would not have a lien on the chair as the person did not give up possession of it.

The two essential elements of the lien are (1) possession by the improver or the provider of services and (2) a debt created by the improvement or the provision of services concerning the goods. If the artisan or other lienholder gives up the goods voluntarily, he loses the lien. For example, if a person has a new engine put in his car and the mechanic gives the car back to him before he pays for the engine, the mechanic loses the lien on the car to secure the person's payment for the work and materials. However, if the person uses a spare set of keys to regain possession, or does so by fraud or another illegal act, the lien is not lost. Once the debt has been paid, the lien is terminated and the artisan or other lienholder no longer has the right to retain the goods. If the artisan keeps the goods after the debt has been paid, or keeps the goods without the right to a lien, he is liable for conversion or unlawful detention of goods.

Another important aspect of common law liens is that the work or service must have been performed at the request of the owner of the property. If the work or service is performed without the consent of the owner, no lien is created.

In the case that follows, *Allstate Lien & Recovery Corporation v. Stansbury*, the court concluded that a lienholder had sought to include charges within its lien that it was not authorized under the statute to include and awarded damages to the owner of a vehicle that was sold at auction to satisfy the unlawful lien.

Allstate Lien & Recovery Corporation v. Stansbury
101 A.3d 520 (Md. Ct. Spec. App. 2014)

In December 2010, Cedric Stansbury brought his two-year-old vehicle to Russel Auto Imports for an oil change. Although the vehicle had been running great before the oil change, a week after the oil change, the engine cut off in the middle of the street during rush hour traffic and he could not get it started again. As the car sat in the middle of the roadway, in the snow, another car ran into the back of his car. Stansbury had it towed to Russel Auto.

On May 18, 2011, Russel contacted Stansbury to tell him his vehicle was ready to be picked up. The same day, at approximately 5:30 P.M., Stansbury went to Russel, and he was told that he owed $6,330.67. He began to write a check for that amount, but was told he would have to return the next day to talk to Jeremy Martin. Stansbury did not have $6,330.37 in his account when he wrote the check, but he stated that he intended to immediately deposit the funds into the account after leaving Russel Auto. The following day, Stansbury called Martin to tell him he would try to get to Russel Auto to pick up his vehicle, but by the time he arrived after work, the shop was closed. He made three or four attempts to get to Russel before it closed, but was unable to do so.

In the beginning of June, Stansbury received a Lien Notice stating that there was a lien on his vehicle in the amount of $7,630.37. The Lien Notice stated that Allstate Lien & Recovery would sell Stansbury's vehicle at public auction on June 23 unless he paid "repair costs" of $6,630.37 plus "costs of the process" of $1,000 in full within 10 days. The "repair cost" figure included $300 that Allstate had suggested Russel Auto include as "storage charges," even though Stansbury had never agreed to pay any storage charges.

He called Martin and asked why there was a lien on his car. Martin responded that Stansbury did not pay for the repairs "in time," and that he would have to contact Allstate Lien & Recovery to ask the company not to put the car up for auction. Stansbury attempted to call Allstate, but his calls were not answered.

During the week of June 8, Stansbury went to Allstate where the office manager was "nasty" and not "very agreeable or cooperative." She told him his car would be put up for auction. She said the vehicle was not his and that if he wanted it, he would have to bid for it at auction. Between June 8 and June 23, Stansbury repeatedly tried calling Allstate, but no one would answer or return his vehicle. At that point, Stansbury had $6,300 to recover his vehicle, but did not have $7,600.

The car was sold at auction for $7,730. Of that amount, Russel Auto received $6,630 plus $522 that it had paid to Allstate to process the lien. Allstate kept the balance of the $1,000 processing fee, and Stansbury was entitled to receive $99.60. At the time of the auction, Stansbury believed that it was worth at least $25,000. He had paid more than $31,000 for it two years prior to the time it was auctioned for sale.

Maryland law provides:

(a) Motor vehicle lien
    (1) any person who, with the consent of the owner, has custody of a motor vehicle and who, at the request of the owner, provides a service to or materials for the motor vehicle, has a lien on the motor vehicle for any charge incurred for any:
        i. Repair or rebuilding;
        ii. Storage; or
        iii. Tires or other parts or accessories.
    (2) A lien is created under this subsection when any charges set out under paragraph (1) of this subsection giving rise to the lien are incurred.

While the lien statute does provide that the "costs of process" may be recovered from the proceeds of the sale, it does not include them within the lien itself. Stansbury brought suit against Russel Auto, Martin (its owner), and Allstate Lien & Recovery, alleging that they violated Maryland's Consumer Protection Act and Consumer Debt Collection Act by, among other things, including a "processing fee" of $1,000 as part of the lien that Stansbury was required to pay to redeem his vehicle.

The trial court ruled as a matter of law that the processing fee was not part of a garageman's lien, and a jury found that there had been violations of the Maryland Consumer Protection Act and the Debt Collection Act by enforcing a right that did not exist. The jury awarded Stansbury $16,500 in compensatory damages plus attorneys's fees. The defendants appealed the court's ruling.

Graeff, Justice

This case involves a garageman's lien, a lien created on behalf of someone who conducted work on a vehicle but was not paid for the service by the owner of the vehicle. Appellants contend that the circuit court erred in its interpretation of CL section 16-202, the garageman's lien statute. The issue presented is what is encompassed in the lien created when a person requests repairs to be done to a motor vehicle and then does not pay for those repairs. Appellants argue that the court erred in determining and instructing the jury that the $1,000 processing fee "was not an appropriate part of the lien, that it should not have been an upfront cost added to the lien in advance."

It is well settled in Maryland that the goal of statutory interpretation is to ascertain and implement, to the extent possible, the legislative intent. In doing so, we look first to the statute's plain language, giving words their natural and ordinary meaning. If the language is clear and unambiguous on its face, our inquiry ends.

If the language of the statute is ambiguous, the courts consider not only the literal or usual meaning of the words, but their meaning and effect in light of the setting, the objectives and purposes of the enactment under consideration.

Appellants acknowledge that the plain language of the statute does not include processing fees as part of the lien on the motor vehicle. They argue, however, that a review of the statutory scheme as a whole shows that an illogical result would occur if the processing fees are not included in the amount necessary to redeem the vehicle.

Mr. Stansbury argues that a plain reading of the statute prohibits front loading the $1,000 cost of process and making it part of the lien. He asserts that the statutory scheme as a whole

provides that "costs of process" be recovered from the proceeds of the sale, not made part of the lien itself. He further argues that, even if processing costs could be deemed part of the lien, the costs here were improper because they were not actual costs incurred by Russel.

The plain language of CL section 16-202 is clear and unambiguous. A person who provides a service to, or materials for, a vehicle has a "motor vehicle lien" only for those charges incurred for repair or rebuilding, storage, or tires or other parts or accessories. A processing fee is not included as part of the lien.

A review of the statutory scheme as a whole does not, as appellants argue, suggest a different conclusion. Although processing fees may be recovered if the vehicle is sold or if judicial proceedings are instituted, the statutory scheme does not suggest that processing fees constitute a part of the lien that may be included as a part of the amount the consumer must pay to redeem the vehicle.

Having determined that the inclusion of the "processing fees" in the lien amount was improper, the next issue presented by appellants is whether its action in doing so, violated the Maryland Consumer Debt Collection Act (MCDCA) which provides that a debt collector may not "claim, attempt, or threaten to enforce a right with knowledge that the right does not exist." Although appellants are correct that they had the right to enforce the garageman's lien, as we have explained, the plain language of the statute makes clear that "costs of process" are not part of the lien amount. In requiring Mr. Stansbury to pay the $1,000 "costs of process" to redeem the vehicle, appellants were attempting to enforce a right they did not have. Accordingly, the jury properly found the appellants were liable for a violation of the MCDCA.

Judgment affirmed for Stansbury.

Foreclosure of Lien

The right of a lienholder to possess goods does not automatically give the lienholder the right to sell the goods or to claim ownership if his charges are not paid. Commonly, there is a procedure provided by statute for selling property once it has been held for a certain period of time. The lienholder is required to give notice to the debtor and to advertise the proposed sale by posting or publishing notices. If there is no statutory procedure, the lienholder must first bring a lawsuit against the debtor. After obtaining a judgment for his charges, the lienholder can have the sheriff seize the property and have it sold at a judicial sale.

Security Interests in Real Property

LO28-4 Compare and contrast mortgages, deeds of trust, and land contracts as mechanisms for holding a security interest in real property.

There are three basic contract devices for using real estate as security for an obligation: (1) the real estate mortgage, (2) the deed of trust, and (3) the land contract. In addition, the states have enacted statutes giving mechanics, such as carpenters and plumbers, and materialmen, such as lumberyards, a right to a lien on real property into which their labor or materials have been incorporated.

Historical Developments of Mortgages

A **mortgage** is a security interest in real property or a deed to real property that is given by the owner (the **mortgagor**) as security for a debt owed to the creditor (the **mortgagee**). The real estate mortgage was used as a form of security in England as early as the middle of the 12th century, but our present-day mortgage law developed from the common law mortgage of the 15th century. The common law mortgage was a deed that conveyed the land to the mortgagee, with the title to the land to return to the mortgagor upon payment of the debt secured by the mortgage. If the mortgagor defaulted on the debt, the mortgagee's title to the land became absolute. The land was forfeited as a penalty, but the forfeiture did not discharge the debt. In addition to keeping the land, the mortgagee could sue on the debt, recover a judgment, and seek to collect the debt.

The early equity courts did not favor the imposition of penalties and would relieve mortgagors from such forfeitures, provided that the mortgagor's default was minor and was due to causes beyond his control. Gradually, the courts became more lenient in permitting redemptions and allowed the mortgagor to redeem (reclaim his property) if he tendered performance without unreasonable delay. Finally, the courts of equity recognized the mortgagor's right to redeem as an absolute right that would continue until the mortgagee asked the court of equity to decree that the mortgagor's right to redeem be foreclosed and cut off. Our present law regarding the foreclosure of mortgages developed from this practice.

Today, the mortgage is generally viewed as a lien on land rather than a conveyance of title to the land. There are still some states where the mortgagor goes through the process of giving the mortgagee some sort of legal title to the property. Even in these states, however, the mortgagee's title is minimal, and the real ownership of the property remains in the mortgagor.

LO28-5 List the formalities necessary for the creation of a legally enforceable mortgage and explain what is meant by *foreclosure* and the *right of redemption*.

Form, Execution, and Recording

Because the real estate mortgage conveys an interest in real property, it must be executed with the same formality as a deed. As a general rule, the mortgage must contain the name of the secured party, the legal description of the property, and the terms and conditions of the security interest in the property—and it must be signed by the debtor/owner of record of the property. In addition, most states require a mortgage to be notarized—that is, acknowledged by the debtor/owner before a notary public or other authorized officer. Unless it is executed with the required formalities, it will not be eligible for recording in the local land records. Recordation of the mortgage does not affect its validity as between the mortgagor and the mortgagee. However, if it is not recorded, it will not be effective against subsequent purchasers of the property or creditors, including other mortgagees, who have no notice of the earlier mortgage. It is important to the mortgagee that the mortgage be recorded so that the world will be on notice of the mortgagee's interest in the property.

Rights and Liabilities

The owner (mortgagor) of property subject to a mortgage can sell the interest in the property without the consent of the mortgagee. However, the sale does not affect the mortgagee's interest in the property or the mortgagee's claim against the mortgagor. In some cases, the mortgage may provide that if the property is sold, then any remaining balance becomes immediately due and payable. This is known as a "due on sale" clause.

Suppose Erica Smith owns a lot on a lake. She wants to build a cottage on the land, so she borrows $155,000 from First National Bank. She signs a note for $155,000 and gives the bank a $155,000 mortgage on the land and cottage as security for her repayment of the loan. Several years later, Smith sells her land and cottage to Melinda Mason. The mortgage she gave First National might make the unpaid balance due on the mortgage payable on sale. If it does not, Smith can sell the property with the mortgage on it. If Mason defaults on making the mortgage payments, the bank can foreclose on the mortgage. If at the foreclosure sale the property does not bring enough money to cover the costs, interest, and balance due on the mortgage, First National is entitled to a deficiency judgment against Smith. However, some courts are reluctant to give deficiency judgments where real property is used as security for a debt. If on foreclosure the property sells for more than the debt, Mason is entitled to the surplus.

A purchaser of mortgaged property may buy it subject to the mortgage or may assume the mortgage. If she buys subject to the mortgage and there is a default and foreclosure, the purchaser is not personally liable for any deficiency. The property is liable for the mortgage debt and can be sold to satisfy it in case of default; in addition, the original mortgagor remains liable for its payment. If the buyer assumes the mortgage, then she becomes personally liable for the debt and for any deficiency on default and foreclosure.

The creditor (mortgagee) may assign his interest in the mortgaged property. To do this, the mortgagee must assign the mortgage as well as the debt for which the mortgage is security. In most jurisdictions, the negotiation of the note carries with it the right to the security and the holder of the note is entitled to the benefits of the mortgage.

Foreclosure

Foreclosure is the process by which any rights of the mortgagor or the current property owner are cut off. Foreclosure proceedings are regulated by statute in the state in which the property is located. In many states, two or more alternative methods of foreclosure are available to the mortgagee or his assignee. The methods in common use today are (1) strict foreclosure, (2) action and sale, and (3) power of sale.

A small number of states permit what is called *strict foreclosure*. The creditor keeps the property in satisfaction of the debt, and the owner's rights are cut off. This means that the creditor has no right to a deficiency and the debtor has no right to any surplus. Strict foreclosure is normally limited to situations where the amount of the debt exceeds the value of the property.

Foreclosure by *action and sale* is permitted in all states, and it is the only method of foreclosure permitted in some states. Although the state statutes are not uniform, they are alike in their basic requirements. In a foreclosure by action and sale, suit is brought in a court having jurisdiction. Any party having a property interest that would be cut off by the foreclosure must be made a defendant, and if any such party has a defense, he must enter his appearance and set up his defense. After the case is tried, a judgment is entered and a sale of the property ordered. The proceeds of the sale are applied to the payment of the mortgage debt, and any surplus is paid over to the mortgagor. If there is a deficiency, a deficiency judgment is, as a general rule, entered against the mortgagor and such other persons as are liable on the debt. Deficiency judgments are generally not permitted where the property sold is the residence of the debtor.

The right to foreclose under a *power of sale* must be expressly conferred on the mortgagee by the terms of the mortgage. If the procedure for the exercise of the power is set out in the mortgage, that procedure must be followed. Several states have enacted statutes that set out the procedure to be followed in the exercise of a power of sale. No court action is required. As a general rule, notice of the default and sale must be given to the mortgagor. After the statutory period, the sale may be held. The sale must be advertised, and it must be at auction. The sale must be conducted fairly, and an effort must be made to sell the property at the highest price obtainable. The proceeds of the sale are applied to the payment of costs, interest, and the principal of the debt. Any surplus must be paid to the mortgagor. If there is a deficiency and the mortgagee wishes to recover a judgment for the deficiency, she must bring suit on the debt.

Right of Redemption

At common law and under existing statutes, the mortgagor or an assignee of the mortgagor has what is called an **equity of redemption** in the mortgaged real estate. This means that he has the absolute right to discharge the mortgage when due and to have title to the mortgaged property restored free and clear of the mortgage debt. Under the statutes of all states, the mortgagor or any party having an interest in the mortgaged property that will be cut off by the foreclosure may redeem the property after default and before the mortgagee forecloses the mortgage. In several states, the mortgagor or any other party in interest is given by statute what is known as a redemption period (usually six months or one year, beginning either after the foreclosure proceedings are started or after a foreclosure sale of the mortgaged property has been made) in which to pay the mortgaged debt, costs, and interest and to redeem the property.

As a general rule, if a party in interest wishes to redeem, he must, if the redemption period runs after the foreclosure sale, pay to the purchaser at the foreclosure sale the amount that the purchaser has paid plus interest up to the time of redemption. If the redemption period runs before the sale, the party in interest must pay the amount of the debt plus the costs and interest. The person who wishes to redeem from a mortgage foreclosure sale must redeem the entire mortgage interest; he cannot redeem a partial interest by paying a proportionate amount of the debt or by paying a proportionate amount of the price bid at the foreclosure sale.

Recent Development Concerning Foreclosures

As the subprime lending crisis unfolded during 2007, the number of defaults and foreclosure actions on both subprime and conventional mortgages increased significantly, and the trend continued into 2008 and beyond. In 2010, there were 3.8 million foreclosure filings in the country, an increase of about 800,000 over the number filed the previous year. Historically, mortgage lenders were local banks that lent money to a homeowner who then paid the money back to the bank. If the loan was in difficulty, the borrower and his local lender would work through the matter directly. Over time, local lenders began to resell or assign the loans they originated to others. And the practice of bundling loans together as mortgage-backed securities became commonplace.

Securitization takes the role of the lender and breaks it down into different components. The loan is sold to a third party, the issuer, that bundles the loan into a security and then sells it to investors who are entitled to a share of the cash paid by the borrowers on their mortgages. Another party—the trustee—is created to represent the interests of the investors. And, another party—the servicer—collects the payments, distributes them to the issuer, and also deals with any delinquencies on the part of borrowers.

Thus, these arrangements involving bundles of hundreds or thousands of mortgages are much more complex than the simple assignment of a single mortgage, and concomitantly, the paperwork involved is much more complicated—and the documentation sometimes incomplete when there was/is pressure to get deals done.

As some of the collateralized loans fell into default and the owners of the securities—often large banks—brought foreclosure actions, judges began to scrutinize the cases to make sure that the parties bringing the foreclosure actions actually were the legal holders of the mortgage obligation and to dismiss the cases where that showing had not been made. The opinion that follows by Judge Boyko in *In re Foreclosure Cases* generated a lot of attention in the media and in the financial and legal communities when it was issued in October 2007 and served as a warning to would-be foreclosers that they needed to have their paperwork in order before they sought to put a homeowner out of his house.

These same issues continue to arise in cases in the decade beginning in 2010 and continuing today.

In re Foreclosure Cases   **2007 U.S. Dist. LEXIS 84011 (N.D. Ohio 2007)**

Boyko, U.S. District Judge

On October 10, 2007, this court issued an Order requiring Plaintiff-Lenders in a number of pending foreclosure cases to file a copy of the executed Assignment demonstrating Plaintiff was the holder and owner of the Note and Mortgage *as of the date the Complaint was filed*, or the Court would order a dismissal. After considering the submissions along with all the documents filed of record, the Court dismisses the captioned cases without prejudice.

To satisfy the requirements of Article III of the United States Constitution, the plaintiff must show he has personally suffered some actual injury as a result of the illegal conduct of the defendant.

In each of the ... Complaints, the named Plaintiff alleges that it is the holder and owner of the Note and Mortgage. However, the attached Note and Mortgage identify the mortgagee and promisee as the original lending institution—one other than the named Plaintiff. Further the Preliminary Judicial Report attached as an exhibit to the complaint makes no reference to the named Plaintiff in the recorded chain of title/interest. The Court's Amended General Order requires Plaintiff to submit an affidavit along with the complaint, which identifies Plaintiff either as the original mortgage holder, or as an assignee, trustee, or successor-in-interest. Once again, the affidavits submitted in all these cases recite the averment that Plaintiff is the owner of the Note and Mortgage, without any mention of an assignment or trust or successor interest. Consequently, the very filings and submissions of the Plaintiff create a conflict. In every instance, then, Plaintiff has not satisfied its burden of demonstrating standing at the time of the filing of the Complaint.

Understandably, the Court requested clarification by requiring each Plaintiff to submit a copy of the Assignment of the Note and Mortgage, executed as of the date of the Foreclosure Complaint. In the above-captioned cases, *none* of the Assignments show the named Plaintiff to be the owner of the rights, title, and interest under the Mortgage at issue as of the date of the Foreclosure

Complaint. The Assignments, in every instance, express a present intent to convey all rights, title and interest in the Mortgage and the accompanying Note to the Plaintiff named in the Foreclosure Complaint upon receipt of sufficient consideration on the date the Assignment was signed and notarized. Those preferred documents belie Plaintiffs' assertion they own the Note and Mortgage by means of a purchase which pre-dated the Complaint by days, months or years.

This Court is obligated to carefully scrutinize all filings and pleadings in foreclosure actions, since the unique nature of real property requires contracts and transactions concerning real property to be in writing. Ohio law holds that when a mortgage is assigned, moreover, the assignment is subject to the recording requirements. "Thus, with regards to real property, before an entity assigned an interest in that property would be entitled to receive a distribution from the sale of the property, their interest therein must have been recorded in accordance with Ohio law."

This Court acknowledges the right of banks, holding valid mortgages, to receive timely payments. And, if they do not receive timely payments, banks have the right to properly file actions on the defaulted notes—seeking foreclosure on the property securing the notes. Yet, this Court possesses the independent obligations to preserve the judicial integrity of the federal court and to jealously guard federal jurisdiction. Neither the fluidity of the secondary mortgage market, nor monetary or economic considerations of the parties, nor the convenience of the litigants supersede those obligations.

Despite Plaintiffs' counsel's belief that "there appears to be some level of disagreement and/or misunderstanding amongst professionals, borrowers, attorneys and members of the judiciary," the Court does not require instruction and is not operating under any misapprehension.

Plaintiff's, "Judge, you just don't understand how things work," argument reveals a condescending mindset and quasi-monopolistic system where financial institutions have traditionally controlled, and still control, the foreclosure process. Typically, the homeowner who finds himself/herself in financial straits, fails to make the required mortgage payments and faces

a foreclosure suit, is not interested in testing state or federal jurisdictional requirements, either *pro se* or through counsel. Their focus is either, "how do I save my home," or "if I have to give it up, I'll simply leave and find somewhere else to live."

In the meantime, the financial institutions or successors/assignees rush to foreclose, obtain a default judgment and then sit on the deed, avoiding responsibility for maintaining the property while reaping the financial benefits of interest running on a judgment. The financial institutions know the law charges the one with title (still the homeowner) with maintaining the property.

There is no doubt every decision made by a financial institution in the foreclosure process is driven by money. And the legal work which flows from winning the financial institution's favor is highly lucrative. There is nothing improper or wrong with financial institutions or law firms making a profit—to the contrary, they should be rewarded for sound business and legal practices. However, unchallenged by underfinanced opponents, the institutions worry less about jurisdictional requirements and more about maximizing returns. Unlike the focus of financial institutions, the federal courts must act as gatekeepers, assuring that only those who meet diversity and standing requirements are allowed to pass through. Counsel for the institutions are not without legal argument to support their position, but their arguments fall woefully short of justifying their premature filings, and utterly fail to satisfy their standing and jurisdictional burdens. The institutions seem to adopt the attitude that since they have been doing this for so long, unchallenged, this practice equates with legal compliance. Finally put to the test, their weak legal arguments compel the Court to stop them at the gate.

The Court will illustrate in simple terms its decision: "Fluidity of the market"—"X" dollars, "contractual arrangements between institutions and counsel"—"X" dollars, "purchasing mortgages in bulk and securitizing"—"X" dollars, "rush to file, slow to record after judgment"—"X" dollars, "the jurisdictional integrity of United States District Court"—"Priceless."

For all the foregoing reasons, the above-captioned Foreclosure Complaints are dismissed without prejudice.

Deed of Trust States typically use either the mortgage or the **deed of trust** as the primary mechanism for holding a security interest in real property. There are three parties to a deed of trust: (1) the owner of the property who borrows the money (the debtor), (2) the trustee who holds legal title to the property put up as security, and (3) the lender who is the beneficiary of the trust. The trustee serves as a fiduciary for both the creditor and the debtor. The purpose of the deed of trust is to make it easy

for the security to be liquidated. However, most states treat the deed of trust like a mortgage in giving the borrower a relatively long period of time to redeem the property, thereby defeating this rationale for the arrangement.

In a deed of trust transaction, the borrower deeds to the trustee the property that is to be put up as security. The trust agreement usually gives the trustee the right to foreclose or sell the property if the debtor fails to make a required payment on the debt. Normally, the trustee does not sell the property until the lender notifies him that the borrower is in default and demands that the property be sold. The trustee must notify the debtor that he is in default and that the land will be sold. The trustee advertises the property for sale. After the statutory period, the trustee will sell the property at a public or private sale. The proceeds are applied to the costs of the foreclosure, interest, and debt. If there is a surplus, it is paid to the borrower. If there is a deficiency, the lender has to sue the borrower on the debt and recover a judgment.

Land Contracts

The **land contract** is a device for securing the balance due the seller on the purchase price of real estate. Essentially, it is an installment contract for the purchase of land. The buyer agrees to pay the purchase price over a period of time. The seller agrees to convey

---

Ethics and Compliance in Action

Who Was Ethical?

During the first half of the decade beginning in 2000, housing prices in many areas of the country escalated, creating a bubble in the housing market. At the same time, lenders began relaxing their standards for making loans to prospective homebuyers. In prior years, a purchaser would have to make a significant down payment on a house, putting up 10 or 20 percent of the purchase price. As banks and other mortgage originators increasingly sold the mortgages in packages to investors, they became less demanding about down payments and were willing to accept 5 percent or even nothing down. They also made loans that appeared very attractive to borrowers, with low interest rates and required monthly payments for the first few years of the loan—but then provided that both interest rates and monthly payments could escalate dramatically in a few years. Some borrowers entered into the loan agreements knowing they were a stretch but counting on prices continuing to rise, and they assumed they could always refinance into a more viable arrangement. Others experienced a change in their employment circumstances and no longer had the ability to make their payments. And others may not have understood the financial ramifications of what they had agreed to do or entered into the mortgage arrangements after making fraudulent statements about their financial circumstances and income. Do you find any of these actions to be unethical? Why?

CONCEPT REVIEW

Security Interests in Real Property

Type of Security Instrument	Parties	Features
Mortgage	1. Mortgagor (property owner/debtor) 2. Mortgagee (creditor)	1. Mortgagee holds a security interest (and in some states, title) in real property as security for a debt. 2. If mortgagor defaults on her obligation, mortgagee must *foreclose on* property to realize his security interest. 3. Mortgagor has a limited time after foreclosure to *redeem* her interest.
Deed of Trust	1. Owner/debtor 2. Lender/creditor 3. Trustee	1. Trustee holds legal title to the real property put up as security. 2. If debt is satisfied, the trustee conveys property back to owner/debtor. 3. If debt is not paid as agreed, creditor notifies trustee to sell the property. 4. While intended to make foreclosure easier, most states treat it like a mortgage for purposes of foreclosure.
Land Contract	1. Buyer 2. Seller	1. Seller agrees to convey title when full price is paid. 2. Buyer usually takes possession, pays property taxes and insurance, and maintains the property. 3. If buyer defaults, seller may declare a forfeiture and retake possession (most states) after buyer has limited time to redeem; some states require foreclosure

title to the property to the buyer when the full price is paid. Usually, the buyer takes possession of the property, pays the taxes, insures the property, and assumes the other obligations of an owner. However, the seller keeps legal title and does not turn over the deed until the purchase price is paid.

If the buyer defaults, the seller usually has the right to declare a forfeiture and take over possession of the property. The buyer's rights to the property are cut off at that point. Most states give the buyer on a land contract a limited period of time to redeem his interest. Moreover, some states require the seller to go through a foreclosure proceeding. Generally, the procedure for declaring a forfeiture and recovering property sold on a land contract is simpler and less time-consuming than foreclosure of a mortgage. In most states, the procedure in case of default is set out by statute. If the buyer, after default, voluntarily surrenders possession to the seller, no court procedure is necessary; the seller's title will become absolute, and the buyer's equity will be cut off.

Purchases of farm property are commonly financed through the use of land contracts. As an interest in real estate, a land contract should be in writing and recorded in the local land records so as to protect the interests of both parties.

However, some courts have invoked the equitable doctrine against forfeitures and have required that the seller on a land contract must foreclose on the property in order to avoid injustice to a defaulting buyer.

Mechanic's and Materialman's Liens

LO28-6 Describe mechanic's and materialman's liens and explain how they are obtained and what rights they give the lienholder.

Each state has a statute that permits persons who contract to furnish labor or materials to improve real estate to claim a lien on the property until they are paid. There are many differences among states as to exactly who can claim such a lien and the requirements that must be met to do so.

Rights of Subcontractors and Materialmen   A general contractor is a person who has contracted with the owner to build, remodel, or improve real property. A subcontractor is a person who has contracted with the general contractor to perform a stipulated portion of the general contract. A materialman is a person who has

contracted to furnish certain materials needed to perform a designated general contract.

Two distinct systems—the New York system and the Pennsylvania system—are followed by the states in allowing mechanic's liens on real estate to subcontractors and materialmen. The New York system is based on the theory of subrogation, and the subcontractors or materialmen cannot recover more than is owed to the contractor at the time they file a lien or give notice of a lien to the owner. Under the Pennsylvania system, the subcontractors or materialmen have direct liens and are entitled to liens for the value of labor and materials furnished, irrespective of the amount due from the owner to the contractor. Under the New York system, the general contractor's failure to perform his contract or his abandonment of the work has a direct effect on the lien rights of subcontractors and materialmen, whereas under the Pennsylvania system, such breach or abandonment by the general contractor does not directly affect the lien rights of subcontractors and materialmen.

Basis for Mechanic's or Materialman's Lien   Some state statutes provide that no lien shall be claimed unless the contract for the improvement is in writing and embodies a statement of the materials to be furnished and a description of the land on which the improvement is to take place and of the work to be done. Other states permit the contract to be oral, but in no state is a licensee or volunteer entitled to a lien. No lien can be claimed unless the work is done or the materials are furnished in the performance of a contract to improve specific real property. A sale of materials without reference to the improvement of specific real property does not entitle the person furnishing the materials to a lien on real property that is, in fact, improved by the use of the materials at some time after the sale.

Unless the state statute specifically includes submaterialmen, they are not entitled to a lien. For example, if a lumber dealer contracts to furnish the lumber for the erection of a specific building and orders from a sawmill a carload of lumber that is needed to fulfill the contract, the sawmill will not be entitled to a lien on the building in which the lumber is used unless the state statute expressly provides that submaterialmen are entitled to a lien.

At times, the question has arisen as to whether materials have been furnished. Some courts have held that the materialman must prove that the material furnished was actually incorporated into the structure. Under this ruling, if material delivered on the job is diverted by the general contractor or others and not incorporated into the structure, the materialman will not be entitled to a lien. Other courts have held that the materialman is entitled to a lien if he can provide proof that the material was delivered on the job under a contract to furnish the material.

Requirements for Obtaining a Lien

The requirements for obtaining a mechanic's or materialman's lien must be complied with strictly. Although there is no uniformity in the statutes as to the requirements for obtaining a lien, the statutes generally require the filing of a notice of lien with a county official such as the register of deeds or the county clerk, which notice sets forth the amount claimed, the name of the owner, the names of the contractor and the claimant, and a description of the property. Frequently, the notice of lien must be verified by an affidavit of the claimant. In some states, a copy of the notice must be served on the owner or be posted on the property.

The notice of lien must be filed within a stipulated time. The time varies from 30 to 90 days, but the favored time is 60 days after the last work performed or after the last materials furnished. Some statutes distinguish among labor claims, materialmen's claims, and claims of general contractors as to time of filing. The lien, when filed, must be foreclosed within a specified time, which generally varies from six months to two years.

Priorities and Foreclosure

The provisions for priorities vary widely, but most of the statutes provide that a mechanic's lien has priority over all liens attaching after the first work is performed or after the first materials are furnished. This statutory provision creates a hidden lien on the property, in that a mechanic's lien, filed within the allotted period of time after completion of the work, attaches as of the time the first work is done or the first material is furnished, but no notice of lien need be filed during this period. And if no notice of lien is filed during this period, third persons would have no means of knowing of the existence of a lien. There are no priorities among lien claimants under the majority of the statutes.

The case that follows, *Trump Endeavor 12 LLC v. Fernich, Inc. d/b/a The Paint Spot*, illustrates a situation where a subcontractor was able to enforce a lien on property to which it had provided materials but had not been paid by the owner of the property.

The procedure followed in the foreclosure of a mechanic's lien on real estate follows closely the procedure followed in a court foreclosure of a real estate mortgage. The rights acquired by the filing of a lien and the extent of the property covered by the lien are set out in some of the mechanic's lien statutes. In general, the lien attaches only to the interest that the person has in the property that has been improved at the time the notice is filed. Some statutes provide that the lien attaches to the building and to the city lot on which the building stands, or if the improvement is to farm property, the lien attaches to a specified amount of land.

Waiver of Lien

The question often arises as to the effect of an express provision in a contract for the improvement of real estate that no lien shall attach to the property for the cost of the improvement. In some states, there is a statute requiring the recording or filing of the contract and making such a provision ineffective if the statute is not complied with. In other states, courts have held that such a provision is effective against everyone; in other states, courts have held that the provision is ineffective against everyone except the contractor; and in still other states, courts have held that such a provision is ineffective as to subcontractors, materialmen, and laborers. Whether the parties to the contract have notice of the waiver of lien provision plays an important part in several states in determining their right to a lien.

It is common practice that before a person who is having improvements made to his property makes final payment, he requires the contractor to sign an affidavit that all materialmen and subcontractors have been paid and to supply him with a release of lien signed by the subcontractors and materialmen.

Trump Endeavor 12 LLC v. Fernich, Inc. d/b/a The Paint Spot
216 So. 3d 704 (Fla. Dist. Ct. App. 2017)

On October 21, 2014, The Paint Spot (Paint Spot) recorded a claim of lien against the Trump National Doral Miami owned by Trump Endeavor 12 (Trump). When Trump failed to pay $32,535.87 owed to Paint Spot for paint and related materials, Paint Spot filed a complaint to foreclose its claim of lien. Trump asserted that the claim of lien was invalid because it identified the wrong contractor on the project and did not comply with the Florida Construction Lien Law. The trial court entered final judgment of foreclosure of the lien, as well as an award of attorney fees and costs, to Paint Spot. Trump appealed.

The project at the Trump National Doral Miami consisted of two parts: renovations to the property's 10 lodges (the Lodge Project) and renovations to the clubhouse (the Clubhouse Project). Both the Lodge Project and the Clubhouse Project share the same property address: 4400 NW 87 Avenue, Miami, Florida.

Trump hired a different general contractor for each of the two projects: Straticon, LLC for the Lodge Project and T & G Constructors for the Clubhouse Project. Straticon hired M&P Reynolds (M&P) to furnish paint and labor for the Lodge Project, which in turn contracted with the Paint Spot to supply paint and related materials. Paint Spot negotiated pricing with M&P, which M&P submitted to Straticon. Trump approved M&P's price quotations. Trump recorded multiple notices of commencement (NOC) for the Lodge Project, and later recorded an NOC naming T&G as the general contractor for the Clubhouse Project. All the NOCs disclosed the same address for both projects: 4400 NW 87 Avenue, Miami, Florida.

Prior to supplying materials to the Lodge Project, the Paint Spot's president visited the project site for the purpose of obtaining a copy of the NOC so that Paint Spot could prepare its statutory NTO. He made it a habit to obtain the NOC from the owner of the project, rather than the general contractor, to ensure his NTO contained the correct information. When he asked for the NOC from Trump's Director of Construction, Frank Sanzo, Sanzo mistakenly gave him the T&G NOC instead of the Straticon NOC. At this point, Paint Spot's president was unaware that there was a different general contractor for each of the two projects.

Using the T&G NOC, Paint Spot prepared and timely served its NTO on Trump and T&G by certified mail in November 2013 and began supplying materials to the Lodge Project that month. Later that month, Straticon learned that the Paint Spot had listed T&G in error on the NTO; however, it also knew that Paint Spot was supplying paint materials to the Lodge Project and knew that Paint Spot was M&P's only paint supplier for the project. Paint Spot attended meetings with Straticon regarding the Lodge Project, and Paint Spot signed partial waivers of lien to M&P as a precondition to receiving payment for the paint materials. Straticon would not pay M&P without M&P submitting partial waivers from its suppliers.

Paint Spot continued supplying materials to the Lodge Project through September of 2014, at which time M&P stopped working on the project because it was not being paid by Straticon. At the time M&P left the Lodge Project, $32,535.87 worth of paint and supplies delivered by Paint Spot that had not been paid for remained at the Lodge Project. Trump used those materials to finish the painting work, but Paint Spot was never paid for those items, resulting it filing the action to foreclose the lien.

Emas, Judge.

Chapter 713 of the Florida Statutes, entitled "Construction Lien Law," establishes a statutory framework for establishment and enforcement of construction liens by subcontractors, laborers and materialmen. The fundamental purpose of the Construction Lien Law is to protect those who have provided labor and materials for the improvement of real property. It is to be construed favorably so as to give laborers and suppliers the greatest protection compatible with justice and equity. The mechanics lien law was enacted to protect the interests of subcontractors and materialmen who remain unpaid while the owner pays the contractor directly.

Section 713.06(2)(a) provides [in pertinent part]:

All liens under this section, except laborers, as a prerequisite to perfecting a lien under this chapter and recording a claim of lien, *must serve a notice on the owner setting forth the lienor's name and address, a description sufficient for identification of the real property and the nature of the services or materials furnished, or to be furnished.* A sub- subcontractor or a materialman to a subcontractor *must serve a copy of the notice on the contractor as a prerequisite to perfecting a lien under this chapter and recording a claim of lien.* ***

The notice must be served before commencing, or not later than 45 days after commencing, to furnish his or her labor, services, or materials . . . .

(Emphasis added.)

Under section 713.06(2)(f):

If a lienor has substantially complied with the provisions of paragraphs (a), (b), and (c), errors and omissions do not prevent the enforcement of a claim against a person who has not been adversely affected by such omission or error. *However, a lienor must strictly comply with the time requirements of paragraph (a).*

In the instant case, Trump and Straticon had actual, express and timely notice that: Paint Spot mistakenly named the wrong contractor in its NTO; M&P (whose name was properly listed on the NTO) was Straticon's own subcontractor for the Lodge Project; Paint Spot was supplying materials to the Lodge Project under M&P; and Paint Spot intended to lien the property if payment was not timely made.

Further, the evidence established that Straticon treated Paint Spot as a potential lienor for the duration of the Lodge Project. For example, Paint Spot attended meetings with Straticon, and Straticon received partial lien waivers from M&P, which included partial lien waivers from Paint Spot for materials provided for the Lodge Project. Straticon even attempted to assist Paint Spot in obtaining payment from Trump for the remaining Paint Spot materials left at the Lodge Project, which materials were later used to complete M&P's work.

Trump has failed to carry its burden of demonstrating that it was adversely affected by Paint Spot's erroneous listing of T&G as the contractor. Notably, there is no evidence that, as a result of this error, Trump paid T&G for the paint supplies, and was thus at risk of paying twice for the same materials. Rather, the evidence at trial established that the painting subcontractor (who replaced M&P when it left the job) used Paint Spot's materials to finish the Lodge Project, and that Paint Spot was never fully paid for those materials. At trial, Straticon's project manager admitted the reason for not paying Paint Spot the amounts due:

> [T]he decision not to pay Paint Spot had nothing to do with a defective Notice to Owner. . . . They weren't paid because Mr. Trump had already paid M&P a decent amount of money of the contract . . . and there was still a lot of work that needed to be completed, so we used the money, M&P's remaining balance, plus additional funds to get the work done.

"The purpose of the NTO is to protect an owner from the possibility of paying over to his contractor sums which ought to go to a subcontractor who remains unpaid."

Accordingly, we hold that the trial court correctly determined that Paint Spot substantially complied with the time requirements of subsection (2)(a). We also hold that Trump failed to establish that it was adversely affected by the error contained in the NTO. We also affirm the final judgment awarding attorney's fees.

Affirmed.

Problems and Problem Cases

1. Rusty Jones, a used car dealer, applied to First Financial Federal Savings and Loan Association for a $50,000 line of credit to purchase an inventory of used cars. First Financial refused to make the loan to Jones alone but agreed to do so if Worth Camp, an attorney and friend of Jones, would cosign the note. Camp agreed to cosign as an accommodation maker or surety. The expectation of the parties was that the loans cosigned by Camp would be repaid from the proceeds of the car inventory. The original note for $25,000 was signed on August 2, 1994; renewals were executed on January 25, 1995, September 11, 1995, and March 15, 1996; and the amount was eventually increased to $50,000. In August 1995, as Camp was considering whether to sign the September renewal note, he was advised by First Financial's loan officer that the interest on the loan had not been paid. In fact, interest payments were four months delinquent. In addition, unknown to Camp, as the $50,000 credit limit was approached, First Financial began making side, or personal, loans to Jones totaling about $25,000, which were also payable out of the used car inventory. Camp knew nothing of these loans and thought that Jones's used car business was making payments only on the loans he had cosigned. Jones defaulted on the $50,000 note cosigned by Camp, and First Financial brought suit against Camp on his obligation as surety on the note. Was Camp relieved of his obligation as surety by First Financial's failure to disclose material facts to him?

2. Mr. and Mrs. Marshall went to Beneficial Finance to borrow money but were deemed by Beneficial's office manager, Puckett, to be bad credit risks. The Marshalls stated that their friend Garren would be willing to cosign a note for them if necessary. Puckett advised Garren not to cosign because the Marshalls were bad credit risks. This did not dissuade Garren from cosigning a note for $480, but it prompted him to ask Beneficial to take a lien or security interest in Mr. Marshall's custom-built Harley-Davidson motorcycle, then worth more than $1,000. Beneficial took and perfected a security interest in the motorcycle. Marshall defaulted on the first payment. Beneficial gave notice of the default to Garren and advised him that it was looking to him for payment. Garren then discovered that Beneficial and Marshall had reached an agreement whereby Marshall would sell his motorcycle for $700; he was to receive $345 immediately, which was to be applied to the loan, and he promised to pay the balance of the loan from his pocket. Marshall paid Beneficial $89.50 and left town without giving the proceeds of the sale to Beneficial. Because Beneficial was unable to get the proceeds from Marshall, it brought suit against Garren on his obligation as surety. When Beneficial released the security for the loan (the motorcycle) without Garren's consent, was Garren relieved of his obligation as surety for repayment of the loan?

3. Krista Babcock cosigned an automobile loan agreement that enabled her friend, Horne, to obtain a $5,000 loan to acquire an automobile from a third party. Horne defaulted on the loan after making a number of payments, and Babcock paid $2,000 to the

lending institution to pay off the remaining balance on the loan. Babcock then brought suit against Horne to recover the $2,000. Is she entitled to recover the $2,000?

4. Wieslaw Wik was the owner of a truck tractor on which Navistar Financial Corporation held a lien to secure a purchase loan agreement. On February 21, Wik was driving his truck tractor and pulling a trailer owned by the V. Seng Teaming Company. The tractor/trailer unit overturned in a ditch. Allen's Corner Garage and Towing Service was called by the Illinois State Police. Its crew removed the cargo from the trailer and hoisted the tractor and trailer out of the ditch and onto the highway. They then took the truck, trailer, and cargo to Allen's garage for storage. The uprighting and towing of semitrailer trucks is an intricate process and involves a good deal of specialized equipment. Allen's was licensed by the Interstate Commerce Commission and the Illinois Commerce Commission as a common carrier and owned more than 50 specialized trucks and trailers for such operations. Wik defaulted on his loan agreement with Navistar and the right to possession passed to Navistar. One of its employees contacted Allen's and offered to pay the towing plus storage charges on the truck in exchange for possession of it. Allen's refused, saying it would not release the truck unless the charges for the truck, trailer, and cargo were all paid. Navistar then brought suit against Allen's to recover possession of the truck.

Subsequently, V. Seng Teaming Company paid $13,000 in towing and storage charges on the trailer and cargo and took possession of them. Navistar then reiterated its willingness to pay the towing charges but refused to pay any storage charges accruing after its initial offer. Was Allen's entitled to a common law lien for its towing and storage charges?

5. Philip and Edith Beh purchased some property from Alfred M. Gromer and his wife. Sometime earlier, the Gromers had borrowed money from City Mortgage. They had signed a note and had given City Mortgage a second deed of trust on the property. There was also a first deed of trust on the property at the time the Behs purchased it. In the contract of sale between the Behs and the Gromers, the Behs promised to "assume" the second deed of trust of approximately $5,000 at 6 percent interest. The Behs later defaulted on the first deed of trust. Foreclosure was held on the first deed of trust, but the proceeds of the sale left nothing for City Mortgage on its second deed of trust. City Mortgage then brought a lawsuit against

the Behs to collect the balance due on the second deed of trust. When the Behs "assumed" the second deed of trust, did they become personally liable for it?

6. Pope agreed to sell certain land to Pelz and retained a mortgage on the property to secure payment of the purchase price. The mortgage contained a clause providing that if Pelz defaulted, Pope had the "right to enter upon the above-described premises and sell the same at public sale" to pay the balance of the purchase price, accounting to Pelz for any surplus realized on the sale. What type of foreclosure does this provision contemplate: (1) strict foreclosure, (2) action and sale, or (3) private power of sale?

7. In October 1992, Verda Miller sold her 107-acre farm for $30,000 to Donald Kimball, who was acting on behalf of his own closely held corporation, American Wonderlands. Under the agreement, Miller retained title, and Kimball was given possession pending full payment of all installments of the purchase price. The contract provided that Kimball was to pay all real estate taxes. If he did not pay them, Miller could discharge them and either add the amounts to the unpaid principal or demand immediate payment of the delinquencies plus interest. Miller also had the right to declare a forfeiture of the contract and regain possession if the terms of the agreement were not met. In 1995, Miller had to pay the real estate taxes on the property in the amount of $672.78. She demanded payment of this amount plus interest from Kimball. She also served a notice of forfeiture on him that he had 30 days to pay. Kimball paid the taxes but refused to pay interest of $10.48. Miller made continued demands on Kimball for 2 months, then filed notice of forfeiture with the county recorder in August 1995. She also advised Kimball of this. Was Miller justified in declaring a forfeiture and taking back possession of the land?

8. Bowen-Rodgers Hardware Company was engaged in the business of furnishing materials for the construction of buildings. It delivered a quantity of materials to property owned by Ronald and Carol Collins. The materials were for the use of a contractor who was building a home for the Collinses as well as several other houses in the area. The hardware company was not paid for the materials by the contractor, and it sought to obtain a mechanic's lien against the Collinses' property. The Collinses claimed that even though the materials were delivered to their home, they were actually used to build other houses in the area. Was the Collinses' property subject to a mechanic's lien because payment had not been made for materials delivered to it?

Security Interests
in Personal Property

Emily Morales purchased a used Honda Civic from her local Honda dealer. She paid $500 down, and the dealer helped her arrange financing of the $4,500 balance through a local bank that placed a lien on the car to secure the loan. She fell behind in her payments when she was temporarily laid off from her job. Then the car was damaged by vandals one night while parked in the parking lot of the apartment complex where she rented an apartment. She took it to an automobile repair shop to have the damaged windshield and broken mirrors and headlamps replaced and portions of it repainted. When she went to pick it up, the repair shop refused to release it to her until she paid $950 cash for the repairs. Emily borrowed the money from her mother and was able to reclaim the car. However, several weeks later, she awoke one evening to see a flashing yellow light outside her apartment. She looked out the window and saw a tow truck was in the process of picking up her car by its rear end. She raced outside and confronted the driver as to what he was doing with her car. A loud shouting match ensued, during which the driver indicated he had been instructed by the bank to repossess the car because she was behind on her payments. Eventually, the truck driver got in his truck and drove away with the car towed behind, leaving Emily and a number of her neighbors, who had gathered to see what the commotion was about, cursing at the driver.

Among the issues posed by this hypothetical are these:

- What did the bank have to do to protect its interest in the Honda until Emily paid off the loan?
- If the bank had learned that the car was at the repair shop and sought to repossess it then, would the bank's lien or the repair shop's artisan's lien have the first priority?
- Was the bank within its rights in repossessing the car in the manner it did? If it was not, does Emily have any recourse?

LEARNING OBJECTIVES

After studying this chapter, you should be able to:

29-1 Recognize and describe the different classes or types of collateral that can be used as collateral to secure a security interest under Article 9 of the Uniform Commercial Code (UCC).

29-2 List and explain the three requirements for creating a security interest in a debtor's property that will be enforceable against a debtor.

29-3 Explain why it is important that the creditor perfect his security interest and list the three main ways of perfecting a security interest.

29-4 Recall the general priority rules that the UCC sets out for determining which of any conflicting security interests take precedence over other security interests or liens.

29-5 Explain what is meant by a purchase money security interest and discuss why the UCC accords it preferential treatment.

29-6 Describe the steps a creditor can take when there is a default on the part of the debtor.

IN MANY CREDIT TRANSACTIONS, the creditor, in order to protect his right to payment or performance of the underlying obligation, takes a security interest, or lien, in personal property belonging to the debtor. The law covering security interests in personal property is set forth in Article 9 of the Uniform Commercial Code. Article 9, titled Secured Transactions, applies to situations that consumers and businesspeople commonly face; for example, the financing of an automobile, the purchase of a refrigerator on a time-payment plan, or the financing of business inventory.

Article 9

If a creditor wants to obtain a security interest in the personal property of the debtor, he also wants to be sure that his interest is superior to the claims of other creditors. To do so, the creditor must carefully comply with Article 9. In Part 4 of this text, Sales, we pointed out that businesspersons sometimes leave out important terms in a contract or insert vague terms to be worked out later. Such looseness is a luxury that is not permitted in secured transactions. If a debtor gets into financial difficulties and cannot meet her obligations, even a minor noncompliance with Article 9 may cause the creditor to lose his preferred claim to the personal property of the debtor. A creditor who loses his secured interest is only a general creditor if the debtor is declared bankrupt. As a general creditor in bankruptcy proceedings, he may have little chance of recovering the money owed by the debtor because of the relatively low priority of such claims. Chapter 30, Bankruptcy, covers this in detail.

In 1998, the National Conference on Uniform State Laws adopted a "Revised Article 9" that has now been adopted by all 50 states with effective dates ranging from 2001 to 2002. Then in 2010, additional amendments to Article 9 were drafted to respond to filing issues and other matters that have arisen in practice following a decade of experience with the 1998 revision. The 2010 amendments were designed to go into effect simultaneously on July 1, 2013. Because Article 9 has not been adopted in exactly the same form in every state, the law must be examined very carefully to determine the procedure in a particular state for obtaining a security interest and for ascertaining the rights of the creditors and debtors. However, the general concepts are the same in each state and will be the basis of our discussion in this chapter.

Security Interests under the Code

Security Interests
Basic to a discussion of secured consumer and commercial transactions is the term **security interest**. A security interest is an interest in personal property or fixtures a creditor obtains from a debtor to secure payment or performance of an obligation [1-201(37)].[1] For example, when a person borrows money from a bank to buy a new car, the bank takes a security interest in, or puts a lien on, the car until the loan is repaid. If the person defaults on the loan, the bank can repossess the car and have it sold to cover the unpaid balance. A security interest is a property interest in the collateral.

 LO29-1 Recognize and describe the different classes or types of collateral that can be used as collateral to secure a security interest under Article 9 of the Uniform Commercial Code (UCC).

Types of Collateral
Goods—tangible items such as automobiles and business computers—are commonly used as collateral for loans. Article 9 of the Uniform Commercial Code also covers security interests in a much broader range of personal property. The UCC breaks down personal property into a number of different classifications, which are important in determining how a creditor obtains—and perfects—an enforceable security interest in a particular kind of collateral.

The UCC classifications include:

1. *Accounts.* This includes the rights to payment of a monetary obligation for goods sold or leased or for services rendered that are not evidenced by instruments or chattel paper but are carried on open accounts, including lottery winnings and health care insurance receivables. Items in the "accounts" category include such rights to payment whether or not the rights have been earned by performance [9-102(a)(2)].

2. *Chattel paper.* This includes written documents that evidence both an obligation to pay money and a security interest in specific goods [9-102(a)(11)]. A typical example of chattel paper is what is commonly known as a *conditional sales contract.* This is the type of contract that a consumer might sign when she buys a large appliance such as a refrigerator on a time-payment plan.

3. *Deposit accounts.* This includes demand, time, savings, passbook, and similar accounts maintained with a bank [9-102(a)(29)].

4. *Documents of title.* This includes bills of lading, dock warrants, dock receipts, and warehouse receipts [9-102(a)(30)].

5. *General intangibles.* This is a catchall category that includes, among other things, patents, copyrights, software, and franchises [9-102(a)(42)].

---

[1]The numbers in brackets refer to sections of the Uniform Commercial Code.

6. *Goods.* Goods [9-102(a)(44)] are divided into several classes; the same item of collateral may fall into different classes at different times, depending on its use:

   a. *Consumer goods.* Goods used or bought primarily for personal, family, or household use, such as automobiles, furniture, and appliances [9-102(a)[23]].

   b. *Equipment.* Goods other than inventory, farm products, or consumer goods [9-102(a)(33)].

   c. *Farm products.* Crops, livestock, or supplies used or produced in farming operations as long as they are still in the possession of a debtor who is engaged in farming [9-102(a)(34)].

   d. *Inventory.* Goods held for sale or lease or to be used under contracts of service, as well as raw materials, work in process, or materials used or consumed in a business [9-102(a)(48)].

   e. *Fixtures.* Goods that will be so affixed to real property that they are considered a part of the real property [9-102(a)(41)].

7. *Instruments.* This includes checks, notes, drafts, and certificates of deposit [9-102(a)(47)].

8. *Investment property.* This includes securities such as stocks, bonds, and commodity contracts [9-102(a)(49)].

It is important to note that an item such as a stove could, in different situations, be classified as inventory, equipment, or consumer goods. In the hands of the manufacturer or an appliance store, the stove is *inventory.* If it is being used in a restaurant, it is *equipment.* In a home, it is classified as *consumer goods.*

Obtaining a Security Interest
The goal of a creditor is to obtain a security interest in certain personal property that will be good against (1) the debtor, (2) other creditors of the debtor, and (3) a person who might purchase the property from the debtor. In case the debtor defaults on the debt, the creditor wants to have a better right to claim the property than anyone else. Obtaining an enforceable security interest is a two-step process—**attachment** and **perfection**.

Attachment of the Security Interest

> **LO29-2** List and explain the three requirements for creating a security interest in a debtor's property that will be enforceable against a debtor.

Attachment
A security interest is not legally enforceable against a debtor until it is attached to a particular item or items of the debtor's property. The *attachment of the security interest* takes place in a legal sense rather than in a physical sense. There are three basic requirements for a security interest to be attached to the goods of a debtor [9-203]. First, either there must be an *agreement* by the debtor granting the creditor a security interest in particular property (*collateral*) or the secured party must have possession of the property. Second, the creditor must give something of value to the debtor. The creditor must, for example, loan money or advance goods on credit to the debtor. Third, the debtor must have rights in the collateral or the owner of the collateral must agree to allow its use as collateral. Unless the debtor owes a *debt* to the creditor or an unfulfilled promise to perform, there can be no security interest. The purpose of obtaining the security interest is to secure a debt or performance.

The Security Agreement
The agreement in which a debtor grants a creditor a security interest in the debtor's property must generally be authenticated by the debtor. An authenticated agreement is required in all cases except where the creditor has possession or control of the collateral [9-203]. Suppose Cole borrows $50 from Fox and gives Fox her wristwatch as a security for the loan. The agreement whereby Cole put up her watch as collateral does not have to be authenticated by Cole to be enforceable. Because the creditor (Fox) is in possession of the collateral, an oral agreement is sufficient.

The security agreement must reasonably describe the collateral so that it can readily be identified. For example, it should list the year, make, and serial number of an automobile. Accuracy in the description is important: It allows the creditor to prove, for example, which of the watches the debtor owns is the debtor's collateral.

The security agreement usually spells out the terms of the arrangement between the creditor and the debtor. Also, it normally contains a promise by the debtor to pay certain amounts of money in a certain way. The agreement specifies which events, such as nonpayment by the buyer, constitute a default. In addition, it may contain provisions that the creditor feels are necessary to protect his security interest. For example, the debtor may be required to keep the collateral insured, not to move it without the creditor's consent, or to periodically report sales of secured inventory goods. In the case that follows, *Palmatier v. Wells Fargo Financial National Bank,* the court found that the information contained in a sales ticket met the requirements for a security agreement.

Purchase Money Security Interests
When the seller of goods retains a security interest in goods until

Palmatier v. Wells Fargo Financial National Bank
79 UCC Rep. 2d 236 (N.D.N.Y. 2010)

On June 13, 2007, Palmatier and his wife purchased furniture from a local retailer, Raymour & Flanigan, for the sum of $2,969.89. Included in the total amount paid was $249.95 for a "Platinum Protection Plan."

On December 7, 2007, the Palmatiers filed a Chapter 13 bankruptcy petition. The petition listed Wells Fargo as having an unsecured claim to the purchase money for the furniture. Wells Fargo subsequently filed a secured proof of claim for the remaining amount of money owed for the furniture, $2,852.89. The Palmatiers objected to the proof of a secured claim.

In support of its proof of claim, Wells Fargo submitted three documents provided to the Palmatiers at the time of purchase: (1) a sales order ticket signed by Mr. Palmatier, (2) a signature page also bearing his signature, and (3) an unsigned credit card agreement. The sales order ticket provided, in pertinent part:

SECURITY INTEREST. You agree to give the applicable party (WFFNB or Raymour & Flanigan Furniture) a purchase money security interest in goods purchased in this transaction to the extent provided by law.

The signature page signed by Mr. Palmatier read, in pertinent part:

Signature. Your signature means that you have read and agree to the terms of our Credit Card Account Agreement and our Authorization Agreement. You give us and we will retain a purchase money security interest in goods purchased under this agreement.

Forwarding applications. If we do not approve your application for credit, you agree to allow us to forward your application to Raymour & Flanigan Furniture for consideration of credit approval. Raymour & Flanigan Furniture will independently investigate, verify and consider your application.

The credit card agreement bore the title "Raymour & Flanigan Credit Card Account Agreement General Terms." It read, in pertinent part:

To the extent permitted by applicable law, you hereby grant to us and we are retaining a purchase money security interest under the Uniform Commercial Code in the merchandise purchased on your account until such merchandise is paid for in full. You agree to assist us in executing any document necessary to perfect our security interest. If you do not make a minimum payment due on your card by the date on which it is due, we may repossess any merchandise that has not been paid for in full.

Hurd, District Judge

Debtors contend that there is insufficient documentation to support creditor's secured proof of claim. On appeal, the only argument debtors assert as to this issue is that creditor has not conclusively established that the signature page attached to its proof of claim correlates to the credit card agreement.

Regardless of any ambiguity as to whether the signature page reflects Mr. Palmatier's consent to the terms in the attached credit card agreement, the bankruptcy court properly concluded creditor has a validly perfected purchase money security interest in the debtor's furniture as set forth in the sales order ticket attached to the proof of claim.

Under New York law, a "security interest attaches to collateral when it becomes enforceable against the debtor with respect to the collateral." N.Y. U.C.C. Section 9-203(a). The security interest becomes enforceable so long as "(1) value has been given; (2) the debtor has rights in the collateral or the power to transfer

rights in the collateral to a secured party; and (3) . . . the debtor has authenticated a security agreement that provides a description of the collateral. . . . " Section 9-203(b).

The sales order ticket submitted in support of creditor's proof of claim describes the furniture purchased and the debtors' agreement to give creditor a purchase money security interest in the purchased goods. The same document incorporates either the terms of the credit card agreement with creditor, or alternatively, the terms of the credit card agreement with Raymour & Flanigan in the event creditor rejects the transaction. It is particularly telling that debtors decline to expressly argue that any of the requirements of Section 9-203(b) are not met.

For all of these reasons, the bankruptcy court's decision that creditor has a validly perfected purchase money security interest in debtor's furniture as set forth in the sales order ticket will be affirmed.

they are paid for, or when money is loaned for the purpose of acquiring certain goods and the lender takes a security interest in those goods, the security interest that is created and attached to the goods is known as a **purchase money security**

interest (PMSI). Creditors who hold PMSIs are considered important creditors because they help the economy by financing the purchase of property and are given certain advantages vis-à-vis other creditors. These advantages are discussed later in this chapter in the sections concerning perfection of security interests and priorities.

Future Advances

A security agreement may stipulate that it covers advances of credit to be made at some time in the future [9-204(3)]. Such later extensions of credit are known as **future advances**. Future advances would be involved where, for example, a bank grants a business a line of credit for $100,000 but initially advances only $20,000. When the business draws further against its line of credit, it has received a future advance and the bank is considered to have given additional "value" at that time. The security interest that the creditor obtained earlier expands to cover these later advances of money.

By covering future advances in the security agreement, the creditor can use the collateral to protect his interest in repayment of the money advanced to the debtor at a later time. The creditor also saves transaction expense; the creditor does not need a new agreement for each future advance.

After-Acquired Property

A security agreement under Article 9 may be drafted to grant a creditor a security interest in the **after-acquired property** of the debtor. After-acquired property is property that the debtor does not currently own or have rights in but that he may acquire in the future. However, the security interest does not attach until the debtor actually obtains some rights to the new property [9-203(b)(2)].[2] For example, Dan's Diner borrows $25,000 from the bank and gives it a security interest in all of its present restaurant equipment as well as all of the restaurant equipment that it may "hereafter acquire." If Dan's owns only a stove at the time, then the bank has a security interest only in the stove. However, if a month later Dan's buys a refrigerator, the bank's security interest would "attach" to the refrigerator when Dan's acquires some rights to it.

A security interest in after-acquired property may not have priority over certain other creditors if the debtor acquires his new property subject to a *purchase money security interest.* Later in this chapter, the section titled "Priority Rules" discusses the rights of the holder of a purchase money security interest versus the rights of another creditor who filed earlier on after-acquired property of the debtor.

Proceeds

The creditor is commonly interested in having his security interest cover not only the collateral described in the agreement but also the **proceeds** on the disposal of the collateral by the debtor. For example, if a bank lends money to Dealer to enable Dealer to finance its inventory of new automobiles and the bank takes a security interest in the inventory, the bank wants its interest to continue in any cash proceeds obtained by Dealer when the automobiles are sold to customers. Under the 1998 amendments to Article 9, these proceeds are automatically covered as of the time the security interest attaches to the collateral [9-203(f)].

---

[2]The UCC imposes an additional requirement as to security interests in after-acquired consumer goods. Security interests do not attach to consumer goods other than "accessions" unless the consumer acquires them within 10 days after the secured party gave value [9-203(b)].

CONCEPT REVIEW

Attachment

A security interest is not legally enforceable against a debtor until it is attached to one or more particular items of the debtor's property; the attachment takes place in a legal, rather than physical, sense.

There are three requirements for a security interest to attach to the goods of the debtor:

1. There must be an agreement in which the debtor grants the creditor a security interest in the debtor's property.

2. The debtor must have rights in the collateral.

3. The creditor must give value to the debtor, for example, by lending him money or advancing goods on credit.

Future Advances. A security may provide for the advance of credit to a debtor at some time in the future. At the time the debtor actually draws on the future extension of credit, the creditor is considered to have given additional value for purposes of attachment of a security interest.

After-Acquired Property. A security agreement may be drafted to grant a creditor a security interest in property that the debtor does not currently own but that she may acquire at some time in the future. However, the security interest does not attach until the debtor actually obtains some rights in the new property.

Proceeds. Proceeds on the sale or other disposition of collateral to which a security interest has been attached are automatically covered as of the time the security interest attaches to the collateral.

Perfecting the Security Interest

LO29-3 Explain why it is important that the creditor perfect his security interest and list the three main ways of perfecting a security interest.

Perfection While attachment of a security interest to collateral owned by the debtor gives the creditor rights vis-à-vis the debtor, a creditor is also concerned about making sure that she has a better right to the collateral than any other creditor if the debtor defaults. In addition, a creditor may be concerned about protecting her interest in the collateral if the debtor sells it to someone else. The creditor gets protection against other creditors or purchasers of the collateral by perfecting her security interest. Perfection is not effective without an attachment of the security interest [9-308(a)].

Under the UCC, there are three main ways of perfecting a security interest:

1. By filing a public notice of the security interest.
2. By the creditor's taking possession or control of the collateral.
3. In certain transactions, by mere attachment of the security interest; this is known as automatic perfection.

Perfection by Public Filing The most common way of perfecting a security interest is to file a **financing statement** in the appropriate public office. The financing statement serves as constructive notice to the world that the creditor claims an interest in collateral that belongs to a certain named debtor. The financing statement usually consists of a multicopy form that is available from the office of the secretary of state (see Figure 29-1), often called a UCC-1. However, the security agreement can be filed as the financing statement if it contains the required information and has been signed by the debtor. Most states now allow creditors to file financing statements electronically.

To be sufficient, the financing statement must (1) contain the names of the debtor, (2) give the name of the secured party, and (3) contain a statement indicating or describing the collateral covered by the financing statement. If the financing statement covers goods that are to become fixtures, a description of the real estate must be included.

As noted earlier in this chapter, the 2010 Amendments to Article 9 that became effective in 2013 modify the earlier version of Article 9 to address problems that had arisen under it. Of most importance, the 2010 Amendments provide greater guidance as to the name of an individual debtor to be listed on a financing statement. The amendments offer two alternatives to Section 9-503[b] to each state:

- Alternative A provides that, if the debtor holds an unexpired driver's license from the state where the financing statement is filed, the debtor's name as it appears on the driver's license is the name required to be used on the financing statement. If the debtor does not have such a driver's license, either the debtor's actual name or the debtor's surname and first personal name may be used on the financing statement.

- Alternative B provides that the debtor's driver's license name, the debtor's actual name, or the debtor's surname and first personal name may be used on the financing statement.

CYBERLAW IN ACTION

Revised Article 9 Is E-Commerce Friendly

The revision to Article 9 that became effective in most states on July 1, 2001, is friendlier to e-commerce than the version it replaced. It no longer requires that the debtor "sign" a "security agreement" to create an enforceable interest in the collateral that supports the loan or performance obligation. Instead, it allows an "authenticated record"—one produced by the consumer online—to substitute for the signed "writing" of the earlier versions of Article 9 and the earlier state laws that Article 9 replaced. This is very advantageous for the buyer who wants to finance, for example, the purchase of an expensive computer or camera without using a credit card to pay for the purchase. The buyer will be able to complete the purchase transaction using an Internet seller of the type of merchandise desired and also finalize the secured transaction at the same time and using the same Internet-based system provided on the seller's website. If the seller is providing financing, in a "purchase-money" transaction, the seller can obtain an enforceable sales contract and an enforceable security agreement, and get the goods heading toward the consumer from the seller's warehouse without delay. The seller in many states also will be able to file an "authenticated record" in substitution for a paper "financing statement" and can complete the filing (and perhaps even pay the filing fee) using e-commerce applications.

Like the "click-through" method of forming a contract described in Chapter 9, click-through secured transactions give the buyer and seller the time- and money-saving advantages of other online transactions. They have similar risks to those present in the pure sales portion of the transaction—of unscrupulous persons trying to take advantage of either the buyer or seller, or both. But the speed and convenience are likely to outweigh the risks for many consumers and many sellers as well.

Figure 29.1   A Financing Statement

UCC FINANCING STATEMENT
FOLLOW INSTRUCTIONS (front and back) CAREFULLY

A. NAME & TELEPHONE OF CONTACT AT FILER (optional)

B. SEND ACKNOWLEDGMENT TO: (Name and Address)

THE ABOVE SPACE IS FOR FILING OFFICE USE ONLY

1. DEBTOR'S EXACT FULL LEGAL NAME -insert only one debtor name (1a or 1b) - do not abbreviate or combine names

1a ORGANIZATION'S NAME					
OR 1b INDIVIDUAL'S LAST NAME		FIRST NAME	MIDDLE NAME		SUFFIX
1c MAILING ADDRESS		CITY	STATE	POSTAL CODE	COUNTRY
1d TAX ID SSN OR EIN	ADD'L INFO RE ORGANIZATION DEBTOR	1e TYPE OF ORGANIZATION	1f JURISDICTION OF ORGANIZATION	1g ORGANIZATIONAL ID #, if any	□ NONE

2. ADDITIONAL DEBTOR'S EXACT FULL LEGAL NAME - insert only one debtor name (2a or 2b) - do not abbreviate or combine names

2a ORGANIZATION'S NAME					
OR 2b INDIVIDUAL'S LAST NAME		FIRST NAME	MIDDLE NAME		SUFFIX
2c MAILING ADDRESS		CITY	STATE	POSTAL CODE	COUNTRY
2d TAX ID SSN OR EIN	ADD'L INFO RE ORGANIZATION DEBTOR	2e TYPE OF ORGANIZATION	2f JURISDICTION OF ORGANIZATION	2g ORGANIZATIONAL ID #, if any	□ NONE

3. SECURED PARTY'S NAME (or NAME of TOTAL ASSIGNEE of ASSIGNOR S/P) - insert only one secured party name (3a or 3b)

3a ORGANIZATION'S NAME				
OR 3b INDIVIDUAL'S LAST NAME	FIRST NAME	MIDDLE NAME		SUFFIX
3c MAILING ADDRESS	CITY	STATE	POSTAL CODE	COUNTRY

4. This FINANCING STATEMENT covers the following collateral

5. ALTERNATIVE DESIGNATION (if applicable) ☐ LESEE/LESSOR ☐ CONSIGNEE/CONSIGNOR ☐ BAILEE/BAILOR ☐ SELLER/BUYER ☐ AG LIEN ☐ NON-UCC FILING

6. ☐ This FINANCING STATEMENT is to be filed (for record)(or recorded) in the REAL ESTATE RECORDS   Attach Addendum   If applicable | 7. Check to REQUEST SEARCH REPORT(S) on Debtor(s) [ADDITIONAL FEE]   (optional)   ☐ ALL DEBTORS ☐ DEBTOR 1 ☐ DEBTOR 2

8. OPTIONAL FILER REFERENCE DATA

FILING OFFICE COPY–NATIONAL UCC FINANCING STATEMENT (FORM UCC1) (REV. 07/29/98)

Figure 29.1   A Financing Statement (continued)

UCC FINANCING STATEMENT **ADDENDUM**
FOLLOW INSTRUCTIONS (front and back) CAREFULLY

9. NAME OF FIRST DEBTOR (1a or 1b) ON RELATED FINANCING STATEMENT

	9a ORGANIZATION'S NAME		
OR	9b INDIVIDUAL'S LAST NAME	FIRST NAME	MIDDLE NAME SUFFIX

10. MISCELLANEOUS:

THE ABOVE SPACE IS FOR FILING OFFICE USE ONLY

11. ADDITIONAL DEBTOR'S EXACT LEGAL NAME -insert only one name (11a or 11b) - do no abbreviate or combine names

	11a ORGANIZATION'S NAME			
OR	11b INDIVIDUAL'S LAST NAME	FIRST NAME	MIDDLE NAME	SUFFIX

11c MAILING ADDRESS	CITY	STATE	POSTAL CODE	COUNTRY

11d TAX ID SSN OR EIN	ADD'L INFO RE ORGANIZATION DEBTOR	11e TYPE OF ORGANIZATION	11f JURISDICTION OF ORGANIZATION	11g ORGANIZATIONAL ID #, if any
				☐ NONE

12. ☐ ADDITIONAL SECURED PARTY'S or ☐ ASSIGNOR S/P'S   NAME -insert only <u>one</u> name (12a or 12b)

	12a ORGANIZATION'S NAME			
OR	12b INDIVIDUAL'S LAST NAME	FIRST NAME	MIDDLE NAME	SUFFIX

12c MAILING ADDRESS	CITY	STATE	POSTAL CODE	COUNTRY

13. This FINANCING STATEMENT covers ☐ timber to be cut or ☐ as extracted collateral, or is filed as a ☐ future filing.

14. Description of real estate

15. Name and address of a RECORD OWNER of above-described real estate (if Debtor does not have a record interest):

16. Additional collateral description

17. Check <u>only</u> if applicable and Check <u>only</u> one box

Debtor is a ☐ Trust or ☐ Trustee acting with respect to property held in trust or ☐ Decedent's estate

18. Check <u>only</u> if applicable and check <u>only</u> one box.
☐ Debtor is a TRANSMITTING UTILITY
☐ Filed in connection with a Manufacturing-Home Transaction–effective 30 years
☐ Filed in connection with a Public Finance Transaction–effective 30 years

FILING OFFICE COPY–NATIONAL UCC FINANCING STATEMENT ADDENDUM (FORM UCC1Ad) (REV. 07/29/98)

The amendments further improve the filing system for the filing of financing statements. More detailed guidance is provided for the debtor's name on a financing statement when the debtor is a corporation, a limited liability company, or limited partnership or when the collateral is held in a statutory or common law trust or in a decedent's estate.

Each state specifies by statute where the financing statement has to be filed. In all states, a financing statement that covers fixtures must be filed in the office where a mortgage on real estate would be filed [9-501]. To obtain maximum security, the secured party acquiring a security interest in property that is a fixture or is to become a fixture should double file—that is, file the security interest as a fixture and as a nonfixture.

In regard to collateral other than fixtures, most states require only central filing, usually in the office of the secretary of state. However, if you are a creditor taking a security interest, it is important to check the law in your state to determine whether to file the financing statement in the central office or locally (for example, in a county office) [9-501].

A financing statement is effective for a period of five years from the date of filing, and it lapses then unless a continuation statement has been filed before that time. An exception is made for real estate mortgages that are effective as fixture filings—they are effective until the mortgage is released or terminates [9-515].

A **continuation statement** may be filed within six months before the five-year expiration date. The continuation statement must be signed by the secured party, identify the original statement by file number, and state that the original statement is still effective. Successive continuation statements may be filed [9-403(3)].

When a consumer debtor completely fulfills all debts and obligations secured by a **financing statement**, she is entitled to a termination statement signed by the secured party or an assignee of record [9-513].

Possession by Secured Party as Public Notice

Public filing of a security interest is intended to put any interested members of the public on notice of the security interest. A potential creditor of the debtor, or a potential buyer of the collateral, can check the records to see whether anyone else claims an interest in the debtor's collateral. The same objective can be reached if the debtor gives up possession of the collateral to the creditor or to an independent third person who holds the collateral for the creditor. If a debtor does not have possession of collateral that he claims to own, then a potential creditor or debtor is on notice that someone else may claim an interest in it. Thus, a security interest is perfected by change of possession of collateral from the debtor to the creditor/secured party or his agent [9-313(a)]. For example, Simpson borrows $150 from a pawnbroker and leaves his guitar as collateral for the loan.

The pawnbroker's security interest in the guitar is perfected by virtue of her possession of the guitar.

Change of possession is not a common or convenient way for perfecting most security interests in consumer goods. It is more practicable for perfecting security interests in commercial collateral. In fact, possession is the only way to perfect a security interest in money [9-312(b)].

Possession of collateral by the creditor is often the best way to perfect a security interest in chattel paper and negotiable documents of title. Possession is also a possible way of perfecting a security interest in inventory. This is sometimes achieved through a **field warehousing arrangement**. For example, a finance company makes a large loan to a peanut warehouse to enable it to buy peanuts from local farmers. The finance company takes a security interest in the inventory of peanuts. It sets up a field warehousing arrangement under which a representative of the finance company takes physical control over the peanuts. This representative might actually fence off the peanut storage area and control access to it. When the peanut warehouse wants to sell part of the inventory to a food processor, it must make a payment to the finance company. Then the finance company's representative will allow the peanut warehouse to take some of the peanuts out of the fenced-off area and deliver them to the processor. In this way, the finance company controls the collateral in which it has a security interest until the loan is repaid.

Possession by the creditor is usually not a practicable way of perfecting a security interest in equipment or farm products. In the case of equipment, the debtor needs to use it in the business. For example, if a creditor kept possession of a stove that was sold on credit to a restaurant, it would defeat the purpose for which the restaurant was buying the stove, that is, to use it in its business. Filing a financial statement is the best perfection method for equipment and farm products.

The person to whom the collateral is delivered holds it as bailee, and he owes the duties of a bailee to the parties in interest [9-207].

Control

A secured party can provide a similar form of public notice by controlling the collateral [9-314]. Control is the only perfection method if the collateral is a deposit account [9-312(b)(1)]. A secured party obtains control by one of three means: (1) the secured party is the bank with which the deposit account is maintained; (2) the debtor, secured party, and the bank have agreed that the bank will comply with the secured party's instructions regarding funds in the account; or (3) the secured party becomes the bank's customer for the deposit account.

Perfection by Attachment/Automatic Perfection

Perfection by mere attachment of the security interest, sometimes known as automatic perfection, is the only form of perfection that occurs without the giving of public notice. It occurs automatically when all the requirements of attachment are complete. This form of perfection is limited to certain classes of collateral; in addition, it may be only a temporary perfection in some situations.

A creditor who sells goods to a consumer on credit, or who lends money to enable a consumer to buy goods, can obtain limited perfection of a security interest merely by attaching the security interest to the goods. A creditor under these circumstances has what is called a *purchase money security interest in consumer goods*. For example, an appliance store sells a flat screen TV to Margaret Morse on a conditional sales contract, or time-payment plan. The store does not have to file its purchase money security interest (PMSI) in the TV. The security interest is considered perfected just by virtue of its attachment to the TV in the hands of the consumer.

Exceptions to Perfection by Attachment: Consumer Goods
Perfection by attachment is

not effective if the consumer goods are motor vehicles for which the state issues certificates of title and has only limited effectiveness if the goods are fixtures [9-303]. A later section of this chapter discusses the special rules covering these kinds of collateral.

There are also major limitations to the perfection by attachment principle. As discussed later in the "Priority Rules" section of this chapter, relying on attachment for perfection does not, in some instances, provide as much protection to the creditor as does public filing.

One potential concern for a creditor is that the use of the collateral will change from that anticipated when the security interest was obtained. It is important that the creditor properly perfect the security interest initially so that it will not be adversely affected by a subsequent change in use and will continue to have the benefit of its initial perfection.

Automatic perfection by attachment of the security interest is illustrated in the following case, *In re* Lance.

In re Lance   59 UCC Rep. 2d 632 (Bankr. W.D. Mo. 2006)

On February 15, 2005, Lance purchased a 2004 Arctic Cat Snowmobile using money borrowed from the NW Preferred Federal Credit Union and, in the loan documents, granted the Credit Union a purchase money security interest in the snowmobile. At the time, the Credit Union did not file a UCC-1 financing form with the state.

On October 6, 2005, Lance filed a voluntary Chapter 7 bankruptcy petition in which he listed the snowmobile with a value of $4,000 and a secured claim of $4,152 held by the Credit Union. In his bankruptcy filing, he indicated that he intended to keep the snowmobile and to reaffirm his debt to the Credit Union.

The Chapter 7 Bankruptcy Trustee sought to have the snowmobile turned over to him as an asset of the bankruptcy estate, contending that the Credit Union's security interest was unperfected because it had failed to file a financing statement. The Credit Union asserted that the snowmobile was a "consumer good" under the Uniform Commercial Code and, therefore, perfection occurred when the security interest attached and that no filing was necessary.

Federman, Bankruptcy Judge

Under Missouri law, certain types of collateral require the filing of a financing statement in order to perfect a security interest in them. The Credit Union asserts that the snowmobile is a "consumer good," and therefore is exempted from the filing requirements. Goods are classified as "consumer goods" if they are "goods that are used or bought for use primarily for personal, family or household purposes." The determinative factor is the principal use to which the property is put.

There is no dispute that the Debtor [Lance] uses the snowmobile for recreational purposes when he visits his brother in Minnesota. Hence, I find that the Debtor uses the snowmobile primarily for personal purposes and is therefore a "consumer good" under the UCC.

The UCC provides for the automatic perfection of purchase money security interests taken in consumer goods, other than goods covered under Missouri's motor vehicle laws. Because the snowmobile is a "consumer good" and is not a motor vehicle

subject to registration and licensing laws,[*] the Credit Union's purchase money security interest was perfected when it attached. The Credit Union was not required to file a financing statement in order to perfect its security interest.

Accordingly, because NW Preferred Credit Union has a perfected security interest in the 2004 Arctic Cat Snowmobile and there is no equity in it, the trustee's motion to compel turnover is denied.

---

[*]In Missouri, motor vehicles are covered by certificates of title and are subject to different rules governing the perfection of security interests. The Missouri Attorney General has issued an opinion indicating that "because a snowmobile does not have wheels, nor is it used on highways, it is not a 'motor vehicle' within the language of the statute." While Missouri law also requires certain all-terrain vehicles to be covered by a certificate of title, the only vehicles covered are those designed exclusively for off-highway use. . . traveling on three, four or more low pressure tires. The court held that because the snowmobile does not have tires, it would not be an "all-terrain vehicle" within the statute.

Motor Vehicles If state law requires a certificate of title for motor vehicles, then a creditor who takes a security interest in a motor vehicle (other than a creditor holding a security interest in inventory held for sale by a person in the business of selling goods of that kind) must have the security interest noted on the title [9-302].

Suppose a credit union lends Carlson money to buy a new car in a state that requires certificates of title for cars. The credit union cannot rely on filing or on attachment of its security interest in the car to perfect that interest; rather, it must have its security interest noted on the certificate of title.

CONCEPT REVIEW

Perfection

Perfection is the mechanism by which a creditor who has attached his security interest to collateral obtains protection for his interest in the collateral against other creditors or against purchasers of the collateral from the debtor. As will be seen in the section "Priorities," the amount of protection obtained by perfection can vary depending on the nature of any competing security interests, whether and how the security interests were perfected, and the nature of the buyer.

The primary ways of perfecting a security interest are:

1. Perfection by public filing of a financing statement with the appropriate government office.

   - To be sufficient, a financing statement must:

     a. Contain the name(s) of the debtor.

     b. Provide the name of the secured party.

     c. Contain a statement describing the collateral covered by the financing statement.

     d. If the financing statement covers goods that are to become fixtures, a description of the real estate must be included.

   - Filing a financing statement can be used to perfect a security interest in most kinds of collateral except for (1) money, (2) noninventory motor vehicles where the security interest must be noted on the title, and (3) letters of credit.
   - Filing a financing statement is the only way to perfect a security interest in accounts receivable and general intangibles.

2. Perfection by the secured party taking possession of the collateral.

   - Possession works for most kinds of collateral except for accounts receivable and general intangibles.
   - Possession is the only way to perfect a security interest in money.

3. Perfection by the secured party taking control of the security.

   - Taking control works for security interests in securities (such as stocks), letter of credit rights, and electronic chattel paper.
   - Taking control is the only way for letter of credit rights.
   - There are two ways for a creditor to take control of a security entitlement:

     a. The security intermediary lists the creditor/secured party as a beneficial owner of the security.

     b. The security intermediary agrees to act on the instructions of the creditor/secured party.

4. Attachment of the security interest/automatic perfection.

   - This method of perfection, whereby the security interest is perfected automatically when it attaches to the collateral, is available only for purchase money security interests in consumer goods (other than motor vehicles for which the state issues titles).

5. Notation of the security interest on Certificate of Title of Motor Vehicles.

   - This method is appropriate only for motor vehicles for which the state issues titles.

This requirement protects the would-be buyer of the car or another creditor who might extend credit based on Carlson's ownership of the car. By checking the certificate of title to Carlson's car, a potential buyer or creditor would learn about the credit union's security interest in the car. If no security interest is noted on the certificate of title, the buyer usually can buy—or the creditor can extend credit—with confidence that there are no undisclosed security interests that would be effective against him.

Fixtures The UCC also provides special rules for perfecting security interests in consumer goods that become fixtures by virtue of their attachment to or use with real property. A creditor with a security interest in consumer goods (including consumer goods that will become fixtures) obtains perfection merely by attachment of her security interest to a consumer good. However, as discussed in the "Priority Rules" section of this chapter, a creditor who relies on attachment for perfection will not, in some instances, prevail against other creditors who hold an interest in the real estate to which the consumer good is attached unless a special financing statement known as a fixture filing is filed with the real estate records to perfect the security interest [9-102(40), 9-334].

Priority Rules

 LO29-4 Recall the general priority rules that the UCC sets out for determining which of any conflicting security interests take precedence over other security interests or liens.

Importance of Determining Priority
Because several creditors may claim a security interest in the same collateral of a debtor, the UCC establishes a set of rules for determining which of the conflicting security interests has **priority**. Determining which creditor has priority or the best claim takes on particular importance in bankruptcy situations, where, unless a creditor has a perfected secured interest in collateral that fully protects the obligation owed to him, the creditor may realize nothing or only a few cents on every dollar owed to him.

General Priority Rules The basic rule established by the UCC is that when more than one security interest in the same collateral has been filed (or otherwise perfected), the first security interest to be filed (or perfected) has priority over any that is filed (or perfected) later [9-322(a)(1)]. If only one security interest has been perfected, for example, by filing, then that security

interest has priority. However, if none of the conflicting security interests has been perfected, then the first security interest to be *attached* to the collateral has priority [9-322(a)(3)].

Thus, if Bank A filed a financing statement covering a retailer's inventory on February 1, 2021, and Bank B filed a financing statement on March 1, 2021, covering that same inventory, Bank A would have priority over Bank B. This is true even though Bank B might have made its loan and attached its security interest to the inventory prior to the time that Bank A did so. However, if Bank A neglected to perfect its security interest by filing and Bank B did perfect, then Bank B would prevail, as it has the only perfected security interest in the inventory.

If both creditors neglected to perfect their security interest, then the first security interest that attached would have priority [9-322(a)(3)]. For example, if Loan Company Y has a security agreement covering a dealer's equipment dated June 1, 2021, and advances money to the dealer on that date, whereas Bank Z does not obtain a security agreement covering that equipment or advance money to the dealer until July 1, 2021, then Loan Company Y has priority over Bank Z. In connection with the last situation, it is important to note that unperfected secured creditors do not enjoy a preferred position in bankruptcy proceedings, thus giving additional importance to filing or otherwise perfecting a security interest.

Purchase Money Security Interest in Inventory

 LO29-5 Explain what is meant by a purchase money security interest and discuss why the UCC accords it preferential treatment.

There are several very important exceptions to the general priority rules. First, a *perfected purchase money security interest in inventory* has priority over a conflicting security interest in the same inventory *if* all four of these requirements are met: (1) the purchase money security interest is perfected at the time the debtor receives possession of the inventory, (2) the purchase money secured party gives notification in writing to the prior secured creditor before the debtor receives the inventory, (3) the holder of the competing security interest received notification within five years before the debtor receives the inventory, and (4) the notification states that the person expects to acquire a purchase money security interest in inventory of the debtor and describes the inventory [9-324(b)].

Assume that Bank A takes and perfects a security interest in "all present and after-acquired inventory" of a debtor. Then the debtor acquires some additional inventory from a wholesaler, which retains a security interest in the inventory until the debtor pays for it. The wholesaler perfects this security interest. The wholesaler has a *purchase money security interest* in inventory goods and will have priority over the prior secured creditor (Bank A) if the wholesaler has perfected the security interest by the time the collateral reaches the debtor and if the wholesaler sends notice of its purchase money security interest to Bank A before the wholesaler ships the goods.

Thus, to protect itself, the wholesaler must check the public records to see whether any of the debtor's creditors are claiming an interest in the debtor's inventory. When it discovers that some are claiming an interest, it should file its own security interest and give notice of that security interest to the existing creditors [9-324(b) and (c)].

In the case that follows, *Woven Treasures v. Hudson Capital*, the court held that a perfected security interest in the inventory of a furniture store had priority over the unperfected security interest of a consignor whose rugs were included in the inventory.

Woven Treasures v. Hudson Capital
70 UCC Rep. 2d 603 (Ala. Sup. Ct. 2009)

In January 2001, Woven Treasures, a seller of oriental rugs, consigned a number of oriental rugs to Reproduction Galleries, a furniture store owned by Richard Clarke. The agreement provided:

Woven Treasures herewith engages Reproduction Galleries, Inc. to provide space for the sale of inventory provided by Woven Treasures on an individual consignment basis in exchange for a commission amount set and agreed upon by both parties and in accordance to each rug sold by Reproduction Galleries, Inc. Such individual consignments of rugs will be made by separate documents which are subject to the terms herein, and those separate documents shall contain specific references to the selling price, commission, delivery and identification of each individual rug.

* * *

Once the item(s) have been sold to a customer by Reproduction Galleries, Inc., Woven Treasures shall be entitled to the purchase price agreed upon by the Parties whether or not the customer has paid in full. Woven Treasures shall be entitled to receive the purchase price agreed upon by the Parties hereto, less the commission amount for Reproduction Galleries, Inc., within ten (10) days of each sale, whether or not the customer has paid Reproduction Galleries in full.

Pursuant to this agreement, Woven Treasures executed nine consignment slips that each listed 4 to 11 rugs.

Approximately two years after the consignment agreement was executed, Reproduction Galleries went out of business. Clarke advised Woven Treasures that he was opening a new furniture store owned by TSR Imports, of which he was the sole owner, and operating under the name Old Mobile Furniture. Clarke and Woven Treasures agreed that the remaining consigned rugs at Reproduction Galleries would be moved to the new store.

After the consigned rugs were moved to the new location, TSR Imports defaulted on its loan to Compass Bank and the bank, which held a security interest in TSR's inventory, sought to sell its interest in the inventory. It, in concert with TSR Imports, reached an agreement with a liquidator, Hudson Capital, whereby Hudson acquired the inventory in the Old Mobile Furniture store for the purpose of selling it at a "Going Out of Business" sale—and with ownership of any unsold merchandise remaining after the sale, free and clear of "any liens, claims or encumbrances." On August 26, 2005, Hudson Capital and TSR Imports also entered into a security agreement whereby TSR Imports granted Hudson Capital a "security interest in and to (i) all of the Merchandise in the Store, (ii) all Proceeds, and (iii) all proceeds arising therefrom . . . ." The agreement expressly authorized Hudson Capital to file a UCC financing statement describing the merchandise in order to perfect the lien granted to it by TSR Imports.

Prior to signing the agreement, an attorney for Hudson Capital conducted a UCC search for TSR Imports and Old Mobile furniture to ensure the inventory was not claimed by someone else because, as one of its offers testified, "when you deal with people in distress, you never know if they are telling the truth." The search found no financing statements filed on behalf of Woven Treasures that named TSR Imports or Old Mobile Furniture as a debtor.

In August, Hudson Capital commenced a week liquidation sale. At the conclusion, Hudson Capital perfected its security interest in the merchandise of Old Mobile Furniture and the proceeds arising from the sale by filing a financing statement with the Alabama Secretary of State.

Woven Treasures requested that Hudson Capital tender a sum equal to the fair market value of the rugs it had originally consigned to Reproduction Galleries. Hudson Capital refused. In January, Woven Treasures sued Hudson Capital, alleging that Hudson Capital improperly possessed and sold consigned rugs in which it maintained an unperfected security interest.

Hudson Capital moved for summary judgment on several grounds, including that (1) Hudson Capital properly obtained and perfected a security interest in the rugs and (2) Hudson Capital obtained title to the rugs as a good-faith purchaser for value. The trial court granted the motion for summary judgment.

Smith, Justice

Hudson Capital argues that the trial court did not err in entering summary judgment in its favor because, it contends, its perfected security interest in the consigned rugs is senior to Woven Treasures' unperfected security interest. We agree. Stated another way, TSR granted Hudson Capital a security interest in all the merchandise displayed at Old Mobile Furniture (including the consigned rugs) and Hudson Capital perfected this interest, while Woven Treasures never filed a financing statement asserting their interest in the rugs.

In analyzing whether Hudson Capital obtained a security interest in the rugs, we begin by examining TSR Imports' ability to grant a security interest in the consigned rugs. TSR Imports displayed the rugs at the Old Mobile Furniture Store on a consignment basis. Consequently, TSR was a consignee as to the rugs. As a consignee of the rugs, TSR Imports obtained the rights and title to the rugs identical to those of Woven Treasures under section 9-319(a). Section 9-319(a) provides as follows:

> Consignee has consignor's rights. Except as otherwise provided . . . , for purposes of determining the rights of creditors of, and purchasers for value of goods from, a consignee, while the goods are in the possession of the consignee, the consignee is deemed to have the rights and title to the goods identical to those the consignor had or had power to transfer.

Thus Hudson Capital, as a creditor of TSR Imports—by way of Compass Bank—acquired a security interest in the consigned rugs under the security agreement it had entered into with TSR Imports.

The following example from the Official comment to section 9-319 explains the operation of the statute and closely corresponds to the facts of this case:

> Example 1: SP-1 delivers goods to Debtor in a transaction constituting a "consignment" as defined in section 9-102. SP-1 does not file a financing statement. Debtor then grants a security interest in the goods to SP-2. SP-2 files a proper financing statement. Assuming Debtor is a mere bailee, as in a "true" consignment, Debtor would not have any rights in the collateral (beyond those of a bailee) so as to permit SP-2's security interest to attach to any greater rights. Nevertheless, under this section, for purposes of determining the rights of Debtor's creditors, Debtor is deemed to acquire SP-1's rights. Accordingly, SP-2's security interest attached, is perfected by the filing, and, under section 9-322 is senior to SP-1's interests.

Here, SP-1 is Woven Treasures, the Debtor is Reproduction Galleries/TSR Imports, and SP-2 is Hudson Capital. Following the example, Woven Treasures executed a consignment agreement with Reproduction Galleries. Reproduction Galleries then went out of business, and Woven Galleries permitted the rugs that had been consigned to Reproduction Galleries to be moved to Old Mobile Furniture in a transaction constituting another consignment.

When Hudson Capital perfected its security interest in the rugs, it also perfected its security interest in any proceeds from the sale of the rugs, and the fact remains that Woven Treasures never filed a financing statement reflecting their security interest in the rugs. Hudson Capital has a superior security interest in the consigned rugs.

We affirm the trial court's summary judgment in favor of Hudson Capital.

Purchase Money Security Interest in Noninventory Collateral The second exception to the general priority rule is that a purchase money security interest in collateral other than inventory has priority over a conflicting security interest in the same collateral if the purchase money security interest is perfected at the time the debtor receives the collateral or within 20 days afterward [9-324(a)].

Assume that Bank B takes and perfects a security interest in all the present and after-acquired equipment belonging to a debtor. Then, a supplier sells some equipment to the debtor, reserving a security interest in the equipment until it is paid for. If the supplier perfects the purchase money security interest by filing at the time the debtor obtains the collateral or within 20 days thereafter, it has priority over Bank B. This is because its purchase money security interest in noninventory collateral prevails over a prior perfected security interest if the purchase money security interest is perfected at the time the debtor takes possession or within 20 days afterward.

Rationale for Protecting Purchase Money Security Interests

The preference given to purchase money security interests, provided that their holders comply with the statutory procedure in a timely manner, serves several ends. First, it prevents a single creditor from closing off all other sources of credit to a particular debtor and thus possibly preventing the debtor from obtaining additional inventory or equipment needed to maintain his business. Second, the preference makes it possible for a supplier to have first claim on inventory or equipment until it is paid for, at which time it may become subject to the after-acquired property clause of another creditor's security agreement. By requiring that the first perfected creditor be given notice of a purchase money security interest at the time the new inventory comes into the debtor's inventory, the UCC serves to alert the first creditor to the fact that some of the inventory on which it may be relying for security is subject to a prior secured interest until the inventory is paid for.

Buyers in the Ordinary Course of Business

 LO29-4 Recall the general priority rules that the UCC sets out for determining which of any conflicting security interests take precedence over other security interests or liens.

A third exception to the general priority rule is that a **buyer in the ordinary course of business** (other than a person buying farm products from a person engaged in farming operations) takes free from a security interest created by his seller even though the security interest is perfected and even though the buyer knows of its existence [9-320(a)]. For example, a bank loans money to a dealership to finance that dealership's inventory of new automobiles and takes a security interest in the inventory, which it perfects by filing. Then, the dealership sells an automobile out of inventory to a customer. The customer takes the automobile free of the bank's security interest even though the dealership may be in default on its loan agreement and even if the customer knows about the bank's interest. As long as the customer is a buyer in the ordinary course of business, she is protected. The reasons for this rule are that a bank really expects to be paid from the proceeds of the dealership's automobile sales and that the rule is necessary to the smooth conduct of commerce. Customers would be very reluctant to buy goods if they could not be sure they were getting clear title to them from the merchants from whom they buy.

Artisan's and Mechanic's Liens

The UCC also provides that certain liens arising by operation of law (such as an artisan's lien, or as provided by separate statutes) have priority over a perfected security interest in the collateral [9-333]. For example, Marshall takes her automobile, on which a credit union has a perfected security interest, to Frank's Garage to have it repaired. Under common or statutory law, Frank's Garage may have a lien on the car to secure payment for the repair work; such a lien permits Frank's to keep the car until it receives payment. If Marshall defaults on her loan to the credit union, she refuses to pay Frank's Garage for the repair work, and the car is sold to satisfy the liens, Frank's Garage is entitled to its share of the proceeds before the credit union gets anything.

In the case that follows, *In re Borden*, the court had to decide whether an artisan lost its priority claim to some farming equipment it had repaired when the owner of the equipment removed it from the artisan without permission and without paying for it.

In re **Borden**   361 B.R. 489 (B.A.P. 8th Cir. 2007)

On June 25, 2002, Michael Borden and his wife granted the Genoa National Bank a blanket security interest on all of their personal property, including machinery and equipment then owned and thereafter acquired. The lender perfected its security interest by filing a UCC financing statement with the Nebraska Secretary of State on June 26, 2002.

On separate occasions in late 2004, Borden took a cornhead and a tractor to Bellamy's for repairs. Bellamy's performed the repairs and, in February 2005, sent the Bordens a bill in the amount of $3,811.46 for the work performed on the cornhead and, in March 2005, sent a bill in the amount of $1,281.34 for the work performed on the tractor. Borden did not have the money to pay for the repairs, and Bellamy's refused to release the tractor and cornhead to Borden without payment, so they remained in Bellamy's possession.

On April 1, Borden and his wife filed a voluntary petition for relief under Chapter 12 of the Bankruptcy Code. [Bankruptcy is discussed in Chapter 30.] On this date the tractor and cornhead were in Bellamy's possession. In June 2005, Borden took the tractor from Bellamy's lot without permission and used it in connection with his farming operation. Bellamy's discovered the tractor was missing and contacted Borden to inquire if he had it in his possession. Borden admitted he had taken the tractor, explained that he needed it for his farming operation, and agreed to return it to Bellamy's as soon as he was finished using it. The tractor broke down while he was using it, and he returned it to Bellamy's in the fall of 2005.

In September 2005, Borden took the cornhead from Bellamy's without permission. Bellamy's became aware that the cornhead was missing and contacted Borden. He admitted that he had taken the cornhead, explained that he needed it to harvest corn, and agreed to return it as soon as he completed harvesting the crop. Borden returned the cornhead to Bellamy's in November 2005.

In 2006, Genoa National Bank filed a motion with the bankruptcy court to determine the priority of the respective liens claimed by it and by Bellamy's. The bankruptcy court determined that no controlling authority existed in Nebraska concerning the situation of competing liens where an artisan loses possession of the personal property through action of the property owner. The bankruptcy court looked to other jurisdictions for guidance and found that other courts faced with the issue had reached conflicting results. The bankruptcy court decided that Genoa National Bank's lien had priority over the lien asserted by the artisan, Bellamy's. In reaching its decision, the bankruptcy court concluded that continuous possession is required to maintain an artisan's lien. Bellamy's appealed.

Schermer, Bankruptcy Judge

Nebraska law provides a lien to any person who repairs a vehicle, machinery, or a farm implement while in such person's possession for the reasonable or agreed charges for the work done or materials furnished on or to such vehicle, machinery, or farm implement and authorizes the artisan to retain possession of the property until the charges are paid. Such a lien is referred to as an artisan's lien. Nebraska law also recognizes a possessory lien as an interest, other than a security interest or an agricultural lien, which secures payment or performance of an obligation for services or materials furnished with respect to goods by a person in the ordinary course of such person's business which is created by statute or rule in favor of the person and whose effectiveness depends on the person's possession of the goods. An artisan's lien falls within this definition of possessory lien under Nebraska law. A possessory lien on goods, such as an artisan's lien, has priority over a security interest in the goods unless the possessory lien is created by a statute that expressly provides otherwise. The artisan's lien statute does not provide otherwise; accordingly, an artisan's lien has priority over a previously perfected security interest in the same goods.

In order to determine the respective rights of the Lender and the Artisan in the Equipment, we must determine if the Artisan has an artisan's lien in the Equipment under Nebraska law. If the Artisan does, its lien has priority over the Lender's security interest in the Equipment. In making this determination, we must answer the difficult question of whether the Artisan has a possessory lien where it involuntarily lost and later regained possession of the Equipment without court authority following the Debtor's bankruptcy filing. The statute is silent on this situation and no Nebraska court has addressed this situation other than the trial court below.

Courts from other jurisdictions have addressed various situations where artisans have lost possession of the personal property to which they provided services yet asserted a lien thereon either without possession or after regaining possession. Some general rules can be gleaned from the case law. First, possession is generally required for a possessory lien. If an artisan surrenders possession, the artisan no longer has a possessory lien with priority over pre-existing security interests. Some courts recognize a continuing lien as between the artisan and the owner after return of possession to the owner; however, such lien lacks priority over pre-existing security interests. Other courts relegate the lien to a state of suspended animation upon release of the goods to the owner; the artisan cannot enforce the lien while it is in a state of suspended animation. In this situation, if the artisan regains possession lawfully, the ability to enforce the artisan's lien is once again available to the artisan.

Where the artisan loses possession involuntarily, the artisan does not necessarily lose the artisan's lien. Likewise, a conditional release of goods does not necessarily defeat the artisan's lien. This result follows at least with respect to holders of prior security interests who are not impaired by the conditional release. Some courts hold that an artisan's lien lost when possession is lost is revived upon resumption of possession. Such a lien retains its priority as before the release except that the lien is subordinate to the interests of a bona fide purchaser or a creditor who attached or levied on the property while it was in the possession of the owner.

We conclude that the Artisan did not lose its artisan's lien in the Equipment when the Debtor took the Equipment without the Artisan's knowledge or consent. Such involuntary loss of possession does not defeat the Artisan's lien. Furthermore, even if the Artisan's failure to take action to regain possession of the Equipment can be deemed consent to the Debtor's prior wrongful taking of the Equipment, such after-the-fact consent could not have been more than a conditional consent to the Debtor's temporary use of the Equipment with an agreement to return it to the Artisan. A conditional consent to a prior wrongful taking likewise does not defeat the Artisan's lien.

This result is consistent with the policy underlying the creation and priority of security interests. A lien or security interest must be perfected. The purpose of perfection is to give the world notice of the lien or security interest. Notice is generally accomplished in one of three ways: by registering the lien with an agency (usually a local government entity or a secretary of state's office), by noting the lien on the title, or by possession. Third parties can learn of any liens or security interests in any particular property by searching the records of the appropriate authority or by viewing the title. If no lien or security interest is disclosed, the third party may rely on the assumption that the property is owned free and clear of any liens if the property is in the owner's possession.

An artisan's lien does not require registration with any entity. Therefore, in order to give notice of the lien, the artisan is permitted to retain the property until receiving payment for the services provided to the property. Upon payment the lien is satisfied and the artisan releases the property. A third party interested in the property can easily learn that the property is not in the owner's possession and is then put on inquiry notice to determine why the owner does not have possession of the property. If the owner cannot produce the property, the third party has notice that another entity, including an artisan, may assert an interest in such property. A third party who continues to deal with the property owner after learning the owner lacks possession of the property does so at his or her peril.

With respect to competing holders of liens or security interests in the same property, notice of the various liens and security interests allows each interested party to know where he or she falls in the pecking order. With respect to recorded interests, the general rule is that first in time has priority. However, artisan's liens are not recorded and invariably are created after security interests have been granted. Courts and legislatures generally recognize that a party who provides labor and materials to property enhances the value of the property. Therefore, the principles of natural justice and commercial necessity dictate that the entity who enhances the value of property should be entitled to payment for such services and may retain the property until receipt of payment therefore. Indeed, the Nebraska statute at issue in this case provides exactly that. Artisan's lien laws are to be liberally construed to accomplish their equitable purpose of aiding materialmen and laborers to obtain compensation for materials used and services bestowed upon property of another which thereby enhances the value of such property.

A lender who advances funds to acquire certain property or who loans money secured by existing property does so on the basis of the property at the time of the loan. The lender generally assumes the owner will maintain the property after the loan is made and often mandates such maintenance in the loan documentation. If the property later breaks or is in need of maintenance, the owner takes the property to an artisan for repair or maintenance. Such repair or maintenance enhances the value of the property, thus enhancing the value of the lender's collateral. The lender thus benefits from the repair.

This was the case with the Equipment. The Lender took the security interest in the Equipment long before the Artisan performed the repairs to it. Immediately prior to the repairs, the Equipment was not working properly and therefore its value was diminished. By performing the repairs, the Artisan enhanced the value of the Equipment, thus benefitting the Lender by increasing the value of its collateral. Recognizing the superiority of the Artisan's lien over the Lender's security interest is consistent with the policy underlying artisan lien law.

The bankruptcy court was troubled by the lack of certainty where an artisan is permitted to retain a lien without maintaining possession of the property. By requiring continuous possession in order to maintain an artisan's lien, the court limited uncertainty. While certainty is a valid goal in statutory interpretation, it should not come at the expense of the purpose behind the statute. Artisan's liens are designed to be equitable in nature and to protect the rights of artisans. If the artisan voluntarily surrenders possession, the artisan loses its lien. However, if the artisan loses possession through no action of his or her own, the artisan should not be punished. This is especially true where the Lender benefited from the repairs to its collateral and its interests in the Equipment were in no way impaired when the Debtor took the Equipment from the Artisan nor when he later returned the Equipment to the Artisan.

Conclusion

The Artisan had an artisan's lien in the Equipment on the date the Debtor filed bankruptcy which had priority over the Lender's security interest under Nebraska law. The Artisan did not lose its artisan's lien nor its priority over the Lender's security interest when the Debtor took the Equipment from the Artisan's possession postpetition without authority. **Accordingly, under these circumstances we REVERSE the bankruptcy court's order determining that the Lender's security interest in the Equipment takes priority over the Artisan's lien therein.**

Kressel, Chief Judge, dissenting

The majority has done an admirable job of reviewing the split of authority on the issue presented here, none of which admittedly is binding, and picking the line of cases which it feels provides the fair result for this case. I concede that the result reached is appealing. I think that in reaching it, the majority has departed from well-established principles of interpretation and, as a result, has essentially engaged in the legislative process.

Since I think the Nebraska statute unequivocally provides for a first priority possessory lien only until possession is lost, I would hold that the bankruptcy court correctly held that Genoa National Bank's perfected security interest has priority over Bellamy's lien and would affirm.

Liens on Consumer Goods Perfected Only by Attachment/Automatic Perfection

A retailer of consumer goods who relies on attachment of a security interest to perfect it prevails over other creditors of the debtor-buyer. However, the retailer does not prevail over someone who buys the collateral from the debtor if the buyer (1) has no knowledge of the security interest; (2) gives value for the goods; and (3) buys the goods for his personal, family, or household use [9-320(b)]. The retailer does not have priority over such a **bona fide purchaser** unless it filed its security interest.

For example, an appliance store sells a television set to Arthur for $750 on a conditional sales contract, reserving a security interest in the set until Arthur has paid for it. The store does not file a financing statement, but relies on attachment for perfection. Arthur later borrows money from a credit union and gives it a security interest in the television set. When Arthur defaults on his loans and the credit union tries to claim the set, the appliance store has a better claim to the set than does the credit union. The credit union then has the rights of an unsecured creditor against Arthur. The first to attach has priority if neither security interest is perfected [9-322(a)(2)].

Now, suppose Arthur sells the television set for $500 to his neighbor Andrews. Andrews is not aware that Arthur still owes money on the set to the appliance store. Andrews buys it to use in her home. If Arthur defaults on his obligation to the store, it cannot recover the television set from Andrews. To be protected against such a purchaser from its debtor, the appliance store must file a financing statement rather than relying on attachment for perfection [9-320(b)].

Fixtures

A separate set of problems is raised when the collateral is goods that become fixtures by being so related to particular real estate that an interest in them arises under real estate law. Determining the priorities among a secured party with an interest in the fixtures, subsequent purchasers of the real estate, and those persons who have a secured interest such as a mortgage on the real property, can involve both real estate law and the UCC.

The general rule is that the interest of an encumbrancer of real estate (such as a mortgagor) or the interest of the owner of real estate (other than the debtor) has priority over a security interest in fixtures [9-334(c)]. However, a perfected security interest in fixtures has priority over the conflicting interest of an encumbrancer or owner of the real property if (1) the debtor has an interest of record in the real property or is in possession of it, (2) the security interest is a purchase money security interest, (3) the interest of the encumbrancer arose before the goods became fixtures, and (4) the fixtures' security interest is perfected by a "fixtures filing" either before the goods became fixtures or within 20 days after the goods became fixtures [9-334(d)].

For example, Restaurant Supply sells Arnie's Diner a new stove on a conditional sales contract, reserving a security interest until Arnie's pays for it. The stove is to be installed in a restaurant where Arnie's is in possession under a 10-year lease. Restaurant Supply can ensure that its purchase money security interest in the stove will have priority over a conflicting claim to the stove by the owner of the restaurant and anyone holding a mortgage on the restaurant if Restaurant Supply (1) enters into a security agreement with Arnie's prior to the time the stove is delivered to him and (2) perfects its security interest by fixture filing before the stove is hooked up by a plumber or within 20 days of that time.

The UCC contains several other rules concerning the relative priority of a security interest in fixtures [9-334(e)–(h)]. For example, the secured party whose interest in fixtures is perfected will have priority where (1) the fixtures are removable factory or office machines or readily removable replacements of domestic appliances that are consumer goods and (2) the security interest is perfected *prior* to the time the goods become fixtures. Suppose Harriet's dishwasher breaks and she contracts with an appliance store to buy a new one on a time-payment plan. The mortgage on Harriet's house provides that it covers the real property along with all kitchen appliances or their replacements. The appliance store's security interest will have priority on the dishwasher over the interest of the mortgagee if the appliance store perfects its security interest prior to the time the new dishwasher is installed in Harriet's home [9-334(e)(2)]. Perfection in consumer goods can, of course, be obtained merely by attaching the security interest through the signing of a valid security agreement.

Note that a creditor holding a security interest in consumer goods that become fixtures who relies on attachment for perfection prevails over other creditors with an interest in the real property *only* where the consumer goods are "readily removable replacements for domestic appliances."

Suppose a hardware store takes a security interest in some storm windows. Because the storm windows are likely to become fixtures through their use with the homeowner's home, the hardware store cannot rely merely on attachment to protect its security interest. It should file a financing statement to protect that security interest against other creditors of the homeowner with an interest in his home. This rule helps protect a person interested in buying the real property or a person considering lending money based on the real property. By checking the real estate records, the potential buyer or creditor would learn of the hardware store's security interest in the storm windows.

Once a secured party has filed his security interest as a fixture filing, he has priority over purchasers or encumbrances whose interests are filed after that of the secured party [9-334(e)(1)].

Where the secured party has priority over all owners and encumbrancers of the real estate, he generally has the right on default to remove the collateral from the real estate. However, he must make reimbursement for the cost of any physical injury caused to the property by the removal.

CONCEPT REVIEW

Priority Rules

Priority between Two or More Secured Creditors Claiming an Interest in the Same Collateral
General rule. The first creditor to file or to perfect his security interests has priority over other creditors who filed or perfected later. If no secured creditor has perfected, then the first security interest to attach has priority.
Exceptions to the general rule. These secured creditors have higher priorities:

- A *purchase money security interest* (*PMSI*) in inventory has priority over a conflicting security interest if the PMSI in inventory is perfected and written notice is given to the conflicting secured creditor no later than when the collateral is delivered to the debtor.
- A *PMSI in noninventory* collateral has priority over a conflicting security interest if the PMSI in noninventory collateral is perfected not later than 20 days after the collateral is delivered to the debtor.
- A *PMSI in fixtures* has priority over a security interest in the real property to which the fixtures are affixed if the PMSI in fixtures is perfected not later than 20 days after the time the goods are attached to the real property.
- A *security interest in fixtures that are removable equipment or readily removable replacements of domestic appliance consumer goods* has priority over a security interest in the real property if the security interest in such fixtures is perfected prior to the time the fixtures are attached to the real property.
- A *security interest in securities perfected by possession or control* has priority over a security interest in the securities perfected by filing.
- *Artisan's liens*—and other possessory liens arising by operation of law—generally have priority over other security interests.

Between Secured Creditors and a Buyer of the Collateral from the Debtor
General rule. Buyer has priority over an unperfected security interest that is unknown to the buyer.
Exceptions to the general rule. These buyers have higher priorities:

- A *buyer in the ordinary course of business (BITOCOB) of his seller* has priority over any security interest created by his seller.
- A *bona fide purchaser of consumer goods for value* has priority over an unfiled, unknown *PMSI in consumer goods.*
- A *bona fide purchaser of a negotiable instrument* has a priority over a secured interest in the negotiable instrument perfected other than by possession if the bona fide purchaser takes possession of the negotiable instrument.

Default and Foreclosure

 LO29-6 Describe the steps a creditor can take when there is a default on the part of the debtor.

Default

Default The UCC does not define what constitutes default. Usually, the creditor and debtor state in their agreement what events constitute a default by the buyer, subject to the UCC requirement that the parties act in "good faith" in declaring defaults. If the debtor defaults, the secured creditor has several options:

1. Forget the collateral, and sue the debtor on his note or promise to pay.
2. Repossess the collateral, and use strict foreclosure—in some cases—to keep the collateral in satisfaction of the remaining debt.
3. Repossess and sell the collateral, and then, depending on the circumstances, either sue for any deficiency or return the surplus to the debtor.

Right to Possession

Right to Possession The agreement between the creditor and the debtor may authorize the creditor to repossess the collateral in case of default. If the debtor does default, the creditor is entitled under the UCC to possession of the collateral. If through self-help the creditor can obtain possession peaceably, he may do so. However, if the collateral is in the possession of the debtor and cannot be obtained without disturbing the peace, then the creditor must take court action to repossess the collateral [9-609]. See the *Hyman v. Capital One Auto Finance* case, which follows shortly, for a discussion of what constitutes repossession without breach of the peace.

If the collateral is intangible, such as accounts, chattel paper, instruments, or documents, *and performance has been rendered to the debtor*, the secured party may give notice and have payments made or performance rendered to her [9-607].

Sale of the Collateral

Sale of the Collateral The secured party may dispose of the collateral by sale or lease or in any manner calculated to produce the greatest benefit to all parties concerned. However, the method of disposal must be commercially reasonable [9-610, 9-627]. Notice of the time and place of a public sale must be given to the debtor, as must notice of a private sale. If the creditor decides to sell the collateral at a public sale such as an auction, then the creditor must give the debtor accurate advance notice of the time and place of the public sale. Similarly, if the creditor

proposes to make a private sale of the collateral, notice must be given to the debtor. This gives the debtor a chance to object to the proposed private sale if she considers it not to be commercially reasonable or to otherwise protect her interests [9-613].

Until the collateral is actually disposed of by the creditor, the buyer has the right to *redeem* it. This means that if the buyer tenders fulfillment of all obligations secured by the collateral as well as any reasonable expenses incurred by the secured party in retaking, holding, and preparing the collateral for disposition, she can recover the collateral from the creditor [9-623].

Consumer Goods

Consumer Goods If the creditor has a security interest in consumer goods and the debtor has paid 60 percent or more of the purchase price or debt (and has not agreed in writing to a strict foreclosure), the creditor must sell the repossessed collateral [9-620(e)]. If less than 60 percent of the purchase price or debt related to consumer goods has been paid, and as to any other security interest, the creditor may propose to the debtor that the seller keep the collateral in satisfaction of the debt. The consumer-debtor has 20 days to object in writing. If the consumer objects, the creditor must sell the collateral. Otherwise, the creditor may keep the collateral in satisfaction of the debt [9-610(b)].

Distribution of Proceeds

Distribution of Proceeds The UCC sets out the order in which any proceeds are to be distributed after the sale of collateral by the creditor [9-615]. First, any expenses of repossessing, storing, and selling the collateral, including reasonable attorney fees, are paid. Second, the proceeds are used to satisfy the debt of the creditor who conducts the sale. Third, any junior interests or liens are paid. Finally, if any proceeds remain (called a surplus), the debtor is entitled to them. If the proceeds are not sufficient to satisfy the debt, then the creditor is usually entitled to a deficiency judgment. This means that the debtor remains personally liable for any debt remaining after the sale of the collateral [9-615(d)(2)].

For example, suppose a loan company lends Christy $5,000 to purchase a car and takes a security interest. After making several payments and reducing the debt to $4,800, Christy defaults. The loan company pays $50 to have the car repossessed and then has it sold at an auction, where it brings $4,500, thus incurring a sales commission of 10 percent ($450) and attorney fees of $150. The repossession charges, sales commission, and attorney fees, totaling $650, are paid first from the $4,500 proceeds. The remaining $3,850 is applied to the $4,800 debt, leaving a balance due of $950. Christy remains liable to the loan company for the $950 unless Christy challenges the amount of the deficiency claimed [9-626(a)].

Liability of Creditor
A creditor who holds a security interest in collateral must be careful to comply with the provisions of Article 9 of the Code. A creditor acting improperly in repossessing collateral or in its foreclosure and sale is liable to the parties injured. Thus, a creditor can be liable to a debtor if she acts improperly in repossessing or selling collateral [9-625, 9-627].

In the case that follows, *Hyman v. Capital One Auto Finance* the court held that the plaintiff had stated a case for breach of the peace in connection with a repossession.

Hyman v. Capital One Auto Finance   94 UCC Rep. 2d 900 (W.D. Pa. 2018)

In 2014, Hyman [first name unknown] purchased a new Toyota Corolla. Capital One Auto Finance financed the purchase and obtained a security interest in the vehicle. In 2016, Hyman became ill and was hospitalized and requested that Capital One defer her auto payments. Capital One considered the request but never informed her whether it would approve it. Ultimately, Capital One "ordered" Commonwealth Recovery to repossess Hyman's automobile.

The repossession occurred the evening of October 5, 2016. Hyman and her partner, Shyree, heard a truck pulling up to Hyman's house. When they peered out the window, they saw a "repo man" in the driveway attempting to repossess Hyman's car. The driveway is part of Hyman's property.

Hyman went outside and told the repo man to get off her property. Shyree believed the "repo man" was about to illegally repossess Hyman's vehicle and, in an attempt to keep him from succeeding, got into Hyman's car and closed the door. Hyman repeatedly demanded that the "repo man" vacate her property and told him he was "trespassing." Despite these demands, he remained on the property.

At some point the "repo man" called the Pennsylvania State Police. Shortly thereafter, multiple state troopers arrived at Hyman's residence and assisted the "repo man" in repossessing the vehicle even though they knew that neither Capital One nor the "repo man" had received a court order authorizing them to seize the vehicle; in fact, no such legal determination had been sought. Nonetheless, one of the troopers informed Hyman that the "repo man" had the right to repossess the vehicle.

At this point, while Shyree was still in the car, Hyman called her daughter Makiba, a law student, for advice. Makiba told the troopers politely that their actions were a violation of the law, that this was a civil matter, and that the police were inappropriately taking sides between two parties in a civil contract dispute. Their response was that she could file a complaint against them later.

After continued discussion between Makiba and the troopers in which she told them she was recording them, they told Makiba that was OK but Shyree was going to be removed and arrested for disorderly conduct and the car would be repossessed. A trooper then said that he was not going to wait all day; she had 30 seconds to get out, or he was going to break the window and remove her from the car.

Shyree complied with the trooper's command and exited the vehicle. Once she had done so, the trooper directed Hyman to surrender her vehicle to the "repo man."

Hyman subsequently brought suit against Capital One, Commonwealth Recovery, and the state troopers alleging, among other things, that Capital One violated the Pennsylvania Uniform Commercial Code in the manner it repossessed the vehicle, including breach of the peace. The other counts in the complaint included claims for conversion and trespass against Capital One and Commonwealth, violation of the Fair Debt Collection Practices Act by Commonwealth Recovery, and civil rights violations by the troopers. She also sought punitive damages.

The defendants filed motions to dismiss some, but not all, of the counts. One of the issues addressed by the court in denying the motions to dismiss was whether the property had been taken without legal justification.

Gibson, United States District Court Judge.

A plaintiff has a cause of action in conversion if he or she had actual or constructive possession of a chattel at the time of the alleged conversion. As this Court recently stated, "Under Pennsylvania law, conversion is (1) the deprivation of another's right in, or use or possession of property, (2) without the owner's consent, and (3) without lawful justification."

In regards to the third element—that the property is taken "without lawful justification"—the Court turns to 13 Pa. C.S.A. section 9609, which deals with a secured party's right to take possession after a default. Under section 9609(a)-(b), a secured party may "take possession of the collateral . . . without judicial process if it proceeds without breach of the peace."

Pennsylvania courts have not specifically defined what actions constitute a breach of the peace and there is very little case-law interpreting a breach of the peace in the repossession context. However, the Superior Court of Pennsylvania has recognized, albeit in dicta, a line of authority that says use of law enforcement agents in repossessions itself creates a constructive breach of the peace. Moreover, Comment 3 of the Pennsylvania Uniform Commercial Code specifically provides that section 9609(a)–(b) "*does not* authorize a secured party who repossesses without judicial process to utilize the assistance of a law-enforcement officer." Section 9609, Comment 3 (emphasis added).

The Court finds that Hyman has alleged sufficient facts to plausibly satisfy all three elements of conversion. Hyman alleges (1) that Capital One and Commonwealth, through their agent the "repo man," deprived Hyman of her possessory right to her automobile when he repossessed it; (2) that the "repo man" interfered with her possessory right without her consent; and in fact, despite her repeated instructions to "get off her property"; and (3) that the "repo man" obtained the affirmative assistance of multiple State Police Troopers which, if true, could have constituted a breach of the peace—in fact, Hyman claims that "repo man" summoned the State Troopers specifically to help him repossess Hyman's car after Hyman's repeated demands that "repo man" vacate her property. Accordingly, Hyman has pleaded a plausible conversion claim against Capitol One and Commonwealth Recovery.

In conclusion, the Court will deny Capitol One and Commonwealth Recovery's motion to dismiss Hyman's conversion claim.

Ethics and Compliance in Action

What Is the Ethical Thing to Do?

Suppose you own an appliance business in a working-class neighborhood that makes most of its sales on credit. What considerations would you take into account in determining whether and when to foreclose or repossess items on which customers have fallen behind in making their payments?

Should you be swayed by the personal circumstances of your debtors or look only to protecting your financial interests? For example, would you consider the value of the item to the debtor—such as whether it is a necessity for her life, like a refrigerator, or a luxury? Would you consider the reason the person had fallen behind—that is, whether she had been ill or recently lost her job?

Problems and Problem Cases

1. Symons, a full-time insurance salesperson, bought a set of drums and cymbals from Grinnel Brothers. A security agreement was executed between them but was never filed. Symons purchased the drums to supplement his income by playing with a band. He had done this before, and his income from his two jobs was about equal. He also played several other instruments. Symons became bankrupt, and the trustee tried to acquire the drums and cymbals as part of his bankruptcy estate. Grinnel claimed that the drums and cymbals were consumer goods and thus it had a perfected security interest merely by attachment of the security interest. Were the drums and cymbals consumer goods?

2. Richard Silch purchased a camcorder at Sears by charging it to his Sears charge account. Printed on the face of the sales ticket made at that time was the following:

   This credit purchase is subject to the terms of my Sears Charge Agreement which is incorporated herein by reference and identified by the above account number. I grant Sears a security interest or lien in this merchandise, unless prohibited by law, until paid in full.

   Silch's signature appeared immediately below that language on the sales ticket. The ticket also contained the brand name of the camcorder and a stock number.

   Silch subsequently filed a Chapter 7 bankruptcy proceeding and was eventually discharged. Sears filed a petition to recover the camcorder from Silch, contending that it had a valid and enforceable security interest in the camcorder. Silch, in turn, contended that the sales ticket did not constitute a valid and enforceable security agreement. Does the sales ticket constitute a valid security agreement?

3. Nicolosi bought a diamond ring on credit from Rike-Kumber as an engagement present for his fiancée. He signed a purchase money security agreement giving Rike-Kumber a security interest in the ring until

it was paid for. Rike-Kumber did not file a financial statement covering its security interest. Nicolosi filed for bankruptcy. The bankruptcy trustee claimed that the diamond ring was part of the bankruptcy estate because Rike-Kumber did not perfect its security interest. Rike-Kumber claimed that it had a perfected security interest in the ring. Did Rike-Kumber have to file a financing statement to perfect its security interest in the diamond ring?

4. Jacob Phillips and his wife, Charlene, jointly owned the Village Variety 5 & 10 Store in Bluefield, Virginia. In addition, Mrs. Phillips was a computer science teacher at the Wytheville Community College. On December 1, 1984, Mrs. Phillips entered into a retail installment sales contract with Holdren's Inc. for the purchase of a computer and a color printer. The contract, which was also a security agreement, provided for a total payment of $3,175.68, with monthly payments of $132.32 to begin on March 5, 1985. On December 1, 1984, Holdren's assigned the contract to Creditway of America. At the time of purchase, Mrs. Phillips advised Holdren's that she was purchasing the computer for professional use in her teaching assignments as well as for use in the variety store. One of the software programs purchased was a practical accounting program for business transactions. Mrs. Phillips also received a special discount price given by Holdren's to state instructors buying for their teaching use. She used the computer in the Village Variety 5 & 10 Store until it closed in April 1985. In June, the Phillipses filed a petition under Chapter 7 of the Bankruptcy Act. At the time, they owed $2,597.79 on the computer. No financing statement was ever filed. Creditway filed a motion in the bankruptcy proceeding, claiming that it had a valid lien on the computer and seeking to be permitted to repossess it. Does Creditway have a perfected security interest in the computer?

5. Ronald Allegretti purchased a bedroom set valued at $900 and a television set valued at $350 from Goldblatt Brothers, a furniture and appliance store, on a revolving credit account. Under the terms of the revolving credit agreement and the credit slip that was signed at the time of each purchase, Goldblatt's reserved a security interest in all goods sold on credit to Allegretti. Goldblatt's then assigned its interest in the extended credit agreement to General Electric Credit Corporation. Neither filed a financing statement. Allegretti subsequently filed a voluntary petition in bankruptcy, and one of the questions in the bankruptcy action was whether Goldblatt's, and in turn General Electric Credit Corporation, held a perfected security interest in the bedroom set and the television. Did the creditors hold a perfected security interest in the bedroom set and the television set?

6. On November 18, Firestone & Company made a loan to Edmund Carroll, doing business as Kozy Kitchen. To secure the loan, a security agreement was executed, which listed the items of property included, and concluded as follows: "together with all property and articles now, and which may hereafter be, used or mixed with, added or attached to, and/or substituted for any of the described property." A financing statement that included all the items listed in the security agreement was filed with the town clerk on November 18 and with the secretary of state on November 22. On November 25, National Cash Register Company delivered a cash register to Carroll on a conditional sales contract. National Cash Register filed a financing statement on the cash register with the town clerk on December 20 and with the secretary of state on December 21. Carroll defaulted in his payments to both Firestone and National Cash Register. Firestone repossessed all of Carroll's fixtures and equipment covered by its security agreement, including the cash register, and then sold the cash register. National Cash Register claimed that it was the title owner of the cash register and brought suit against Firestone for conversion. Did Firestone or National Cash Register have the better right to the cash register?

7. Grimes purchased a new Dodge car from Hornish, a franchised Dodge dealer. The sale was made in the ordinary course of Hornish's business. Grimes paid Hornish the purchase price of the car at the time of the sale. Hornish had borrowed money from Sterling Acceptance and had given it a perfected security interest in its inventory, including the car Grimes bought. Hornish defaulted on its loan to Sterling and Sterling then tried to recover the Dodge from Grimes. Was the car Grimes bought from Hornish still subject to Sterling Acceptance's security interest?

8. Benson purchased a new Ford Thunderbird automobile. She traded in her old automobile and financed the balance of $4,326 through the Magnavox Employees Credit Union, which took a security interest in the Thunderbird. Several months later, the Thunderbird was involved in two accidents and sustained major damage. It was taken to ACM for repairs, which took seven months and resulted in charges of $2,139.54. Benson was unable to pay the charges, and ACM claimed a garageman's lien. Does Magnavox Credit Union's lien or ACM's lien have priority?

9. In August, Norma Wade purchased a Ford Thunderbird automobile and gave Ford Motor Credit a security interest in it to secure her payment of the $7,000 balance of the purchase price. When Wade fell behind on her monthly payments, Ford engaged the Kansas Recovery Bureau to repossess the car. On the following February 10, an employee of the Recovery Bureau located the car in Wade's driveway, unlocked the door, got in, and started it. He then noticed a discrepancy between the serial number of the car and the number listed in his papers. He shut off the engine, got out, and locked the car. When Wade appeared at the door to her house, he advised her that he had been sent by Ford to repossess the car but would not do so until he had straightened out the serial number. She said that she had been making payments, that he was not going to take the car, and that she had a gun, which she would use. He suggested that Wade contact Ford to straighten out the problem. She called Ford and advised its representative that if she caught anybody on her property again trying to take her car, she would use her gun to "leave him laying right where I saw him." Wade made several more payments, but Ford again contracted to have the car repossessed. At 2:00 A.M. on March 5, the employee of the Kansas Recovery Bureau successfully took the car from Wade's driveway. She said that she heard a car burning rubber, looked out of her window, and saw that her car was missing. There was no confrontation between Wade and the employee because he had safely left the area before she discovered that the car had been taken. Wade then brought a lawsuit against Ford claiming that the car had been wrongfully repossessed. She sought actual and punitive damages, plus attorney fees. Should Ford be held liable for wrongful repossession?

10. Gibson, a collector of rare old Indian jewelry, took two of his pieces to Hagberg, a pawnbroker. The two pieces, a silver belt and a silver necklace, were worth $500 each. Hagberg loaned only $45 on the belt and $50 on the necklace. Gibson defaulted on both loans, and immediately and without notice, the necklace was sold for $240. A short time later, the belt was sold for $80. At the time of their sale, Gibson owed interest on the loans of $22. Gibson sued Hagberg to recover damages for improperly disposing of the collateral. Is Gibson entitled to damages because of Hagberg's actions in disposing of the collateral?

Bankruptcy

Bob and Sue Brown are a young couple with two small children. When they were students, they borrowed about $120,000 to finance their undergraduate educations, as well as an MBA for Bob and a teaching certificate for Sue. Within the past three years, they stretched themselves further financially in the course of acquiring and furnishing their first home and starting their family. Recently, Bob was laid off from his job managing computer technology operations for a telecom company. Then, Sue was injured in an automobile accident and has been unable to continue substitute teaching. Bob's unemployment benefits are insufficient to provide for the ordinary family expenses, much less meet the heavy financial obligations the family has taken on. The bank has filed a notice of intent to foreclose the mortgage on their home, and other creditors have sent letters threatening to repossess their car and furnishings. A friend has suggested that Bob and Sue consult with an attorney who specializes in bankruptcy matters who may be able to get them some relief from their creditors and gain a new start financially.

This situation raises a number of questions that will be addressed in this chapter. They include:

- If the Browns file a petition in bankruptcy, what assets would they be able to retain as exempt from the claims of their creditors?
- Which of their debts could be discharged in a bankruptcy proceeding?
- What advantages and disadvantages would the Browns have if they filed under Chapter 7 (liquidation) as opposed to filing under Chapter 13 (consumer debt adjustment), which would require them to continue to make payments on their debts?

LO · LEARNING OBJECTIVES

After studying this chapter, you should be able to:

30-1 Explain the purpose of the Bankruptcy Code.

30-2 List and describe the major types of bankruptcy proceedings.

30-3 Explain the procedure by which Chapter 7 (liquidation) proceedings are begun and the roles the court and the bankruptcy trustee play in managing the bankruptcy process.

30-4 Understand what assets are included in the bankruptcy estate and the nature of exemptions.

30-5 Understand when the trustee can avoid prior transactions made by the debtor to reclaim assets for the bankruptcy estate.

30-6 Distinguish among claims, allowable claims, secured claims, and priority claims of creditors.

30-7 Describe the process by which the property in a debtor's estate is distributed to creditors and the debtor is granted a discharge in bankruptcy.

30-8 List the kinds of debts that are not dischargeable.

30-9 Explain the purpose and basic procedure of Chapter 11 reorganizations.

30-10 Explain the purpose and basic procedure of Chapter 13 consumer debt adjustments.

30-11 Compare the major types of bankruptcy proceedings.

WHEN AN INDIVIDUAL, a partnership, or a corporation is unable to pay its debts to creditors, problems can arise. Some creditors may demand security for past debts or start court actions on their claims in an effort to protect themselves. Such actions may adversely affect other creditors by depriving them of their fair share of the debtor's assets. Also, quick depletion of the debtor's assets may effectively prevent the debtor who needs additional time to pay off his debts from having an opportunity to do so.

At the same time, creditors need to be protected against the actions a debtor in financial difficulty might be tempted to take to their detriment. For example, the debtor might run off with his remaining assets or might use them to pay certain favored creditors, leaving nothing for the other creditors. Finally, a means is needed by which a debtor can get a fresh start financially and not continue to be saddled with debts beyond his ability to pay. This chapter focuses on the body of law and procedure that has developed to deal with the competing interests when a debtor is unable to pay his debts in a timely manner.

The Bankruptcy Code

LO30-1 Explain the purpose of the Bankruptcy Code.

The Bankruptcy Code is a federal law that provides an organized procedure under the supervision of a federal court for dealing with insolvent debtors. Debtors are considered insolvent if they are unable or fail to pay their debts as they become due. The power of Congress to enact bankruptcy legislation is provided in the Constitution. Through the years, there have been many amendments to the Bankruptcy Code. Congress completely revised the code in 1978 and then passed significant amendments to it in 1984, 1986, and 1994. On April 20, 2005, President Bush signed the Bankruptcy Abuse, Prevention and Consumer Protection Act of 2005, the most substantial revision of the bankruptcy law since the 1978 Bankruptcy Code was adopted.

The Bankruptcy Code has several major purposes. One is to ensure that the debtor's property is fairly distributed to the creditors and that some creditors do not obtain unfair advantage over the others. At the same time, the code protects all of the creditors against actions by the debtor that would unreasonably diminish the debtor's assets to which they are entitled. The code also provides the honest debtor with a measure of protection against the demands for payment by his creditors. Under some circumstances, the debtor is given additional time to pay the creditors, freeing him of those pressures creditors might otherwise exert. If the debtor makes a full and honest accounting of his assets and liabilities and deals fairly with his creditors, the debtor may have most—if not all—of the debts discharged so as to have a fresh start.

At one time, **bankruptcy** carried a strong stigma for the debtors who became involved in it. Today, this is less true. It is still desirable that a person conduct her financial affairs in a responsible manner. However, there is a greater understanding that such events as accidents, natural disasters, illness, divorce, and severe economic dislocations are often beyond the ability of individuals to control and may lead to financial difficulty and bankruptcy.

Bankruptcy Proceedings

LO30-2 List and describe the major types of bankruptcy proceedings.

The Bankruptcy Code covers a number of bankruptcy proceedings. In this chapter, our focus will be on:

1. Straight bankruptcy (liquidations).
2. Reorganizations.
3. Family farms and commercial fishing operations.
4. Consumer debt adjustments.

The Bankruptcy Code also contains provisions regarding municipal bankruptcies, which are not covered in this chapter.

Liquidations A liquidation proceeding, traditionally called straight bankruptcy, is brought under Chapter 7 of the Bankruptcy Code. Individuals, as well as businesses, may file under Chapter 7. The debtor must disclose all of the property she owns and surrender this bankruptcy estate to the bankruptcy trustee. The trustee separates out certain property that the debtor is permitted to keep and then administers, liquidates, and distributes the remainder of the bankrupt debtor's estate. There is a mechanism for determining the relative rights of the creditors, for recovering any preferential payments made to creditors, and for disallowing any preferential liens obtained by creditors. If the bankrupt person has been honest in her business transactions and in the bankruptcy proceedings, she is usually given a **discharge** (relieved) of her debts.

Reorganizations Chapter 11 of the Bankruptcy Code provides a proceeding whereby a debtor can work out a plan to solve its financial problems under the supervision of a federal court. A reorganization plan is essentially a contract between a debtor and its creditors. The proceeding is intended for debtors, particularly businesses, whose financial problems may be solvable if they are given some time and guidance and if they are relieved of some pressure from creditors.

Family Farms Historically, farmers have been accorded special attention in the Bankruptcy Code. Chapter 12 of the Bankruptcy Code provides a special proceeding whereby a debtor involved in a family farming operation or a family-owned commercial fishing operation can develop a plan to work out his financial difficulties. Generally, the debtor remains in possession of the farm or fishing operations and continues to operate it while the plan is developed and implemented.

Consumer Debt Adjustments Under Chapter 13 of the Bankruptcy Code, individuals with regular incomes who are in financial difficulty can develop plans under court supervision to satisfy their creditors. Chapter 13 permits compositions (reductions) of debts and/or extensions of time to pay debts out of the debtor's future earnings.

The Bankruptcy Courts Bankruptcy cases and proceedings are filed in federal district courts. The district courts have the authority to refer the cases and proceedings to bankruptcy judges, who are considered to be units of the district court. If a dispute falls within what is known as a core proceeding, the bankruptcy judge can hear and determine the controversy. Core proceedings include a broad list of matters related to the administration of a bankruptcy estate. However, if a dispute is not a core proceeding but rather involves a state law claim, then the bankruptcy judge can only hear the case and prepare draft findings and conclusions for review by the district court judge.

Certain proceedings affecting interstate commerce have to be heard by the district court judge if any party requests that this be done. Moreover, the district courts are precluded from deciding certain state law claims that could not normally be brought in federal court, even if those claims are related to the bankruptcy matter. Bankruptcy judges are appointed by the president for terms of 14 years.

Chapter 7: Liquidation Proceedings

 LO30-3 Explain the procedure by which Chapter 7 (liquidation) proceedings are begun and the roles the court and the bankruptcy trustee play in managing the bankruptcy process.

Petitions All bankruptcy proceedings, including liquidation proceedings, are begun by the filing of a petition. The petition may be either a voluntary petition filed by the debtor or an involuntary petition filed by a creditor or creditors of the debtor. A voluntary petition in bankruptcy may be filed by an individual, a partnership, or a corporation. However, municipal, railroad, insurance, and banking corporations and savings or building and loan associations are not permitted to file for straight bankruptcy proceedings. A person filing a voluntary petition need not be insolvent—that is, her debts need not be greater than her assets. However, the person must be able to allege that she has debts. The primary purpose for filing a voluntary petition is to obtain a discharge from some or all of the debts.

The 2005 revisions establish a new "means test" for consumer debtors to be eligible for relief under Chapter 7. The purpose of the test is to ensure that individuals who will have income in the future that might be used to pay off at least a portion of their debts must pursue relief under Chapter 13 as opposed to pursuing relief and a discharge of liabilities through the liquidation provisions of Chapter 7. In general, debtors who earn more than the median income in their state and who can repay at least $8,175 of their debt over five years are required to use Chapter 13. This means test is discussed in detail later in this section under the subsection titled "Dismissal for Substantial Abuse."

Involuntary Petitions An involuntary petition is a petition filed by creditors of a debtor. By filing it, they seek to have the debtor declared bankrupt and his assets distributed to the creditors. Involuntary petitions may be filed against many debtors. However, involuntary petitions in straight bankruptcy cannot be filed against (1) farmers; (2) ranchers; (3) nonprofit organizations; (4) municipal, railroad, insurance, and banking corporations; (5) credit unions; and (6) savings or building and loan associations.

If a debtor has 12 or more creditors, an involuntary petition to declare him bankrupt must be signed by at least three creditors. If there are fewer than 12 creditors, then an involuntary petition can be filed by a single creditor. The creditor or creditors must have valid claims against the debtor exceeding the value of any security they hold by $16,750 or more. To be forced into involuntary bankruptcy, the debtor must be generally not paying his debts as they become due—or have had a custodian for his property appointed within the previous 120 days.

If an involuntary petition is filed against a debtor engaged in business, the debtor may be permitted to continue to operate the business. However, the court may appoint an interim trustee if this is necessary to preserve the bankruptcy estate or to prevent loss of the estate. A creditor who suspects that a debtor may dismantle her business or dispose of its assets at less than fair value may apply to the court for protection.

Requirement for Credit Counseling and Debtor Education Under the 2005 revisions, individuals are ineligible for relief under any chapter of the code unless within 180 days preceding their bankruptcy filing they received individual or group credit counseling from an approved nonprofit budget and credit counseling agency or obtain an exemption from the requirement. The required briefing, which may take place by telephone or on the Internet, must "outline" the opportunities for credit counseling and assist the debtor in performing a budget analysis. The debtor is required to file a certificate from the credit counseling agency that describes the services that were provided to the debtor and also to file any debt repayment plan developed by the agency. Because individuals who have not received the required briefing are not eligible for relief under the Bankruptcy Code, it is difficult for a creditor to force an individual debtor into bankruptcy by filing an involuntary petition against the debtor.

Attorney Certification The 2005 act increased the legal responsibilities for an attorney who signs a bankruptcy petition. The attorney's signature constitutes a certification that the attorney, after inquiry, has no knowledge that the information contained in the schedules filed by the debtor is incorrect. In addition, the attorney's signature on a petition, motion, or other written pleading constitutes a certification that the attorney, after inquiry, has determined that the pleading is well grounded in fact and is either warranted by existing law or is based on a good faith argument for extending existing law. In cases where the trustee files a motion to dismiss a case for substantial abuse, the court may order the debtor's attorney to reimburse the trustee for the reasonable costs, including attorney fees, for prosecuting the motion and may also order the attorney to pay a civil penalty to the trustee or the U.S. Trustee.

These provisions have raised concerns that bankruptcy practice will be less attractive to bankruptcy attorneys who handle a large volume of cases because the provisions will increase their costs and risks—and they operate on relatively thin margins.

Automatic Stay Provisions The filing of a bankruptcy petition operates as an **automatic stay**, holding in abeyance various forms of creditor action against a debtor or her property. These actions include (1) beginning or continuing judicial proceedings against the debtor; (2) actions to obtain possession of the debtor's property; (3) actions to create, perfect, or enforce a lien against the debtor's property; and (4) setoff of indebtedness owed to the debtor before commencement of the bankruptcy proceeding. A court may give a creditor relief from the stay if the creditor can show that the stay does not give her "adequate protection" and jeopardizes her interest in certain property. The relief to the creditor might take the form of periodic cash payments or the granting of a replacement lien or an additional lien on property.

Concerned that debtors were taking advantage of the automatic stay provisions to the substantial detriment of some creditors, such as creditors whose claims were secured by an interest in a single real estate asset, in 1994 Congress provided specific relief from the automatic stay for such creditors. Debtors must either file a plan of reorganization that has a reasonable chance of being confirmed within a reasonable time or must be making monthly payments to each such secured creditor that are in an amount equal to interest at a current fair market rate on the value of the creditor's interest in the real estate.

The automatic stay provisions are not applicable to actions to establish paternity, to establish or modify orders for domestic support obligations, for the collection of domestic support obligations from property that is not the property of the bankruptcy estate, or to withhold, suspend, or restrict a driver's license or professional, occupational, or recreational license.

In 2005, Congress added two additional exceptions from the automatic stay provisions for the benefit of landlords seeking to evict tenants. First, any eviction proceedings in which the landlord obtained a judgment of possession prior to the filing of the bankruptcy petition can be continued. Second, in cases where the landlord's claim for eviction is based on the use of illegal substances on the property or "endangerment" of the property, the eviction proceedings are exempt from the stay even if they are initiated after the bankruptcy proceeding was filed so long as the endangerment or illegal use occurred within 30 days before the filing. Debtors are able to keep the stay in effect by filing certifications that certain nonbankruptcy laws allow the lease to remain in effect and that they have cured any defaults within 30 days of the bankruptcy filing.

Order of Relief

Order of Relief Once a bankruptcy petition has been filed, the first step is a court determination that relief should be ordered. If a voluntary petition is filed by the debtor, or if the debtor does not contest an involuntary petition, this step is automatic. If the debtor contests an involuntary petition, then a trial is held on the question of whether the court should order relief. The court orders relief only (1) if the debtor is generally not paying his debts as they become due or (2) if, within 120 days of the filing of the petition, a custodian was appointed or took possession of the debtor's property. The court also appoints an interim trustee pending election of a trustee by the creditors.

Meeting of Creditors and Election of Trustee

Meeting of Creditors and Election of Trustee The bankrupt person is required to file a list of her assets, liabilities, and creditors and a statement of her financial affairs. The 2005 revisions imposed a number of new production requirements on debtors. Now, individual debtors must file, along with their schedules of assets and liabilities:

- A certificate that they have received and/or have read the notice from the Clerk of the Bankruptcy Court that they must receive credit counseling to be eligible for relief under the Bankruptcy Code;
- Copies of all payment advices and other evidence of payments they have received from any employer within 60 days before the filing of the petition;
- A statement of the amount of monthly net income, itemized to show how the amount is calculated; and
- A statement showing any anticipated increase in income or expenditures over the 12-month period following the date of filing the petition.

Should an individual debtor in a voluntary Chapter 7 case or in a Chapter 13 case fail to file the required information within 45 days of the filing of the petition, the case is to be automatically dismissed. A court, upon finding that an extension is justified, can extend the time period to file for up to an additional 45 days.

Individual debtors also must provide copies of their most recent tax returns to the trustee and to creditors making a timely request; failure to do so can result in dismissal of the case. Debtors also must, at the request of the judge or a party in interest, file at the same time they file with the IRS copies of federal tax returns due while the bankruptcy case is pending and also file copies of tax returns (including any amended returns) for tax years that ended within the three years before the bankruptcy petition was filed.

Once the court receives the bankruptcy filing and the required schedules and certifications, the U.S. Trustee calls a meeting of the creditors. At the meeting, the U.S. Trustee is required to examine the debtor to make sure she is aware of (1) the potential consequences of seeking a discharge in bankruptcy, including the effects on credit history; (2) the debtor's ability to file a petition under other chapters (such as 11, 12, or 13) of the Bankruptcy Code; (3) the effect of receiving a discharge of debts; and (4) the effect of reaffirming a debt (discussed later in this chapter).

The creditors also elect a **trustee** who, if approved by the judge, takes over administration of the bankrupt's estate. The trustee represents the creditors in handling the estate. At the meeting, the creditors have a chance to ask the debtor questions about her assets, liabilities, and financial difficulties. These questions commonly focus on whether the debtor has concealed or improperly disposed of assets.

Duties of the Trustee

Duties of the Trustee The trustee takes possession of the debtor's property and has it appraised. The debtor must also turn over her records to the trustee. For a time, the trustee may operate the debtor's business. The trustee sets aside the items of property that a debtor is permitted to keep under state exemption statutes or federal law.

The 2005 act places restrictions on the authority of the trustee to sell personally identifiable information about individuals to persons who are not affiliated with the debtor. Congress was concerned about situations where individuals had provided information to persons and entities on the understanding and commitment that the information would remain in confidence with the recipient. These data files often are a valuable asset of a debtor involved in bankruptcy proceedings, but Congress concluded it was not reasonable to allow that information to be sold to a third party that was not in their contemplation when the individuals provided the information to the debtor under a promise of confidentiality.

The trustee examines the claims filed by various creditors and objects to those that are improper in any way. The trustee separates the unsecured property from the secured and otherwise exempt property. He also sells the bankrupt's nonexempt property as soon as possible, consistent with the best interest of the creditors.

The trustee is required to keep an accurate account of all the property and money he receives and to promptly deposit moneys into the estate's accounts. The trustee files a final report with the court, with notice to all creditors who then may file objections to the report.

Health Care Businesses The 2005 revisions reflected Congress's concern with what happens if a petition for bankruptcy is filed by a health care business and contain a number of provisions concerning that possibility. First, the trustee is instructed to use his reasonable best efforts to transfer patients in a health care business that is in the process of being closed to an appropriate health care business in the vicinity of the one being closed that offers similar services and maintains a reasonable quality of care. Second, the actual, necessary costs of closing a health care business are considered administrative expenses entitled to priority. Third, the automatic stay provisions do not apply to actions by the Secretary of Health and Human Services to exclude the debtor from participating in Medicare and other federal health care programs. Finally, the act sets out requirements for the disposal of patient records where there are insufficient funds to continue to store them as required by law. The requirements include giving notice to the affected patients and specifying the manner of disposal for unclaimed records.

Liquidation of Financial Firms The Bankruptcy Code contains special provisions for the liquidation of stockbrokers, commodity brokers, and clearing banks that are designed to protect the interests of customers of the entities who have assets on deposit with the bankrupt debtor. These responsibilities are overseen by the trustee.

LO30-4 Understand what assets are included in the bankruptcy estate and the nature of exemptions.

The Bankruptcy Estate
The commencement of a Chapter 7 bankruptcy case by the filing of a voluntary or involuntary petition creates a bankruptcy estate. The estate is composed of all of the debtor's legal and equitable interests in property, including certain community property. Certain property is exempted (see "Exemptions" section below). The estate also includes:

1. Profits, royalties, rents, and revenue, along with the proceeds from the debtor's estate, received during the Chapter 7 proceeding.

2. Property received by the debtor in any of the following ways within 180 days of the filing of the Chapter 7 petition: (*a*) by bequest or inheritance, (*b*) as a settlement with a divorced spouse or as a result of a divorce decree, or (*c*) as proceeds of a life insurance policy.

3. Property recovered by the bankruptcy trustee because (*a*) creditor of the debtor received a voidable preferential transfer or (*b*) the debtor made a fraudulent transfer of her assets to another person. Preferential and fraudulent transfers are discussed later in this chapter.

Exemptions
Even in a liquidation proceeding, the bankrupt is generally not required to give up all of his property; he is permitted to **exempt** certain items of property. Under the Bankruptcy Code, the debtor may choose to keep certain items or property either exempted by state law or exempt under federal law, unless state law specifically forbids use of the federal exemptions. However, any such property concealed or fraudulently transferred by the debtor may not be retained.

The 2005 revisions specify that the state or local law governing the debtor's exemptions is the law of the place where the debtor was domiciled for 730 days before filing. If the debtor did not maintain a domicile in a single state for that period, then the law governing the exemptions is the law of the place of the debtor's domicile for the majority of the 180-day period preceding the filing of the petition that is between two and two and one-half years before the filing. For example, on January 1, 2019, Alex Smith was living in Florida. In March 2019, he moved to Georgia and in November 2019, he moved again and took up residence in Alabama. On July 1, 2021, Smith filed a petition in bankruptcy. Because Smith had not lived in Alabama for the two years (730 days) before he filed, he would not be able to claim the exemptions that Alabama provides. Rather, he would be entitled to claim the exemptions provided by Georgia, where he lived for the majority of the 180 days between January 1, 2019, and July 1, 2019.

The debtor must elect to use *either* the set of exemptions provided by the state or the set provided by the federal bankruptcy law; she may not pick and choose between them. A husband and wife involved in bankruptcy proceedings must both elect either the federal or the state exemptions; where they cannot agree, the federal exemptions are deemed elected.

The **exemptions** permit the bankrupt person to retain a minimum amount of the assets considered necessary to life and to his ability to continue to earn a living. They are part of the fresh-start philosophy that is one of the purposes of the Bankruptcy Code. The general effect of the federal exemptions is to make at least a minimum exemption available to debtors in all states. States that wish to be more generous to debtors can provide more liberal exemptions.

The specific items that are exempt under state statutes vary from state to state. Some states provide fairly liberal exemptions and are considered "debtors' havens." For example, in Florida, none of the equity in the debtor's homestead can be used to pay off unsecured creditors, thus allowing even relatively well-off individuals to shield significant assets from creditors. Items that are commonly made exempt from sale to pay debts owed creditors include the family Bible; tools or books of the trade; life insurance policies; health aids, such as wheelchairs and hearing aids; personal and household goods; and jewelry, furniture, and motor vehicles worth up to a certain amount.

In the case that follows, *In re Rogers*, the court concluded that a debtor was entitled to claim a homestead exemption in property that she acquired more than 1,215 days before filing for bankruptcy but that she began to use as her homestead within that period.

In re Rogers (Wallace v. Rogers)   513 F.3d 212 (5th Cir. 2008)

On January 17, 1994, Sarah Rogers inherited a 72.5-acre tract of real property in Forney, Texas. Rogers was single at the time she inherited the property from her mother. Subsequently, Rogers married George Rogers and they purchased a 5.1-acre property in Rockwall, Texas, and built a residence on it, which they claimed as their homestead.

In January 2004, Rogers separated from her husband, moved into a mobile home on the Forney property, and claimed it as her homestead. On April 6, Rogers and her husband divorced. Pursuant to the divorce decree, she gave up all right, title, and interest in the property in Rockwall, and no equity from that property was rolled into the property in Forney. The divorce decree awarded the Forney property to Sarah Rogers, reflecting the fact that it was her separate property, having inherited it from her mother before her marriage.

Prior to 2004, Rogers and her husband had borrowed money from Jack Wallace to embark on an ultimately unsuccessful business venture. Wallace sued to recover the unpaid balance on the loan and on April 19, 2004, he obtained a judgment against both Sarah Rogers and her then ex-husband for $316,180.95. On September 28, 2005, Sarah Rogers filed for relief under Chapter 7 of the Bankruptcy Code. She elected state law exemptions and claimed her homestead exemption on the Forney property in the amount of $359,000.

Wallace objected to the claimed homestead exemption, arguing that the Bankruptcy Code capped the exemption at the federal statutory amount of $125,000 because the debtor acquired her homestead interest in the Forney property within the 1,215-day period preceding the filing of her bankruptcy petition. Both the bankruptcy court and the district court held that Sarah Rogers was entitled to the homestead exemption but gave different reasons for their holding. Wallace appealed the matter to the Fifth Circuit.

DeMoss, Circuit Judge

The bankruptcy estate is comprised of "all legal or equitable interests of the debtor in property as of the commencement of the case." Rogers elected to exempt the Forney property as her homestead under Texas state law. An exemption is an interest withdrawn from the estate (and hence from the creditors) for the benefit of the debtor.

Enacted as part of the Bankruptcy Abuse Prevention and Consumer Protection Act of 2005 (BAPCA), 11 U.S.C. section 522(p)(1) limits the state law homestead exemption under certain circumstances. Section 522(p)(1) prevents the debtor from exempting certain interests from the bankruptcy estate if they were acquired by the debtor during the statutory period and their aggregate value exceeds a certain dollar threshold. The statute reads, in pertinent part:

> As a result of electing . . . to exempt property under State or local law, a debtor may not exempt any amount of interest that was acquired by the debtor during the 1,215-day period preceding the date of the filing of the petition that exceeds in the aggregate [$125,000][a] in value in real or personal property that the debtor or dependent of the debtor claims as a homestead.

The statute further states that "any amount of such interest does not include any interest transferred from a debtor's previous principal residence (which was acquired prior to the beginning of such 1,215-day period) into the debtor's principal residence if the debtor's previous and current residences are located in the same state."

Based on the legislative history, the bankruptcy court concluded that the purpose of the statute was to close the "mansion loophole" and prevent debtors from moving to states with more generous homestead exemptions on the eve of bankruptcy in order to avail themselves of those exemptions. After observing that Rogers did not move to Texas in anticipation of bankruptcy and that her homestead designation of the Forney property was precipitated by divorce, the bankruptcy judge overruled Wallace's objection and held that Rogers may exempt the entirety of her homestead from the bankruptcy estate.

* * *

The legislative history indicates that Congress was concerned with the acquisition of vested economic interests in property during the statutory period.

On March 10, Senator Carper stated the following:

> Today, under current law, a wealthy individual in a state such as Florida or Texas can go out, if they are a millionaire, and take those millions of dollars and invest the money in real estate, a huge house, and land in the State, file for bankruptcy,

---

[a]In 2007, the Judicial Conference of the United States adjusted the dollar amount from $125,000 to $136,875. At the time the bankruptcy petition was filed in this case, the relevant dollar amount was $125,000.

and basically protect all of their assets which they own because of a provision in Florida or Texas law.

With the legislation we have before us, someone has to figure out that 2-1/2 years ahead of time people are going to want to file for bankruptcy and be smart enough to put the money into a home, or an estate, or into a trust—not something you can do today—and file for bankruptcy tomorrow. . . .

151 Cong. Rec. S2415-02, at S2415-16 (daily ed. March 10, 2005).

Senator Carper's statement is also supported by language in the House Report which states that "the bill also restricts the so-called mansion loophole." Under current bankruptcy law, debtors living in certain states can shield from their creditors virtually all of the equity in their homes. In light of this, some debtors actually relocate to those states just to take advantage of their mansion loophole laws. In this case, it is undisputed that Rogers did not move to Texas to exploit the so-called mansion loophole.

According to Wallace, BAPCPA was intended to address fraudulent transfers in general, including conversions of nonexempt assets into exempt assets within the statutory period. We concur that Congress could have defined all the debtors exemptions to be whatever they would have been 1,215 days before the filing of the petition. Instead, Congress defined the cap more narrowly. We do not believe that Congress was concerned with the timing of the establishment of the homestead when it enacted section 522(p)(1). The statutory text and legislative history indicate that the term "interest" refers to vested economic interests that were acquired by the debtor within the 1,215-day period preceding the filing of the petition. If Congress enacted into law something different from what it intended, then it should amend the statute to conform to its intent.

We hold that Rogers is entitled to her full homestead exemption.

Limits on State Homestead Exemptions Concerns that very generous homestead exemptions in a number of states were leading to abuses by debtors who transferred assets into large homes in those states and then filed for bankruptcy led Congress in 2005 to place some limits on state homestead exemptions. These limits include:

- The value of the debtor's homestead for purposes of a state homestead exemption is reduced to the extent that it reflects an increase in value on account of the disposition of nonexempt property by the debtor during the 10 years prior to the filing with the intent to hinder, delay, or defraud creditors.
- Any value in excess of $170,350—irrespective of the debtor's intent—that is added to the value of a homestead during the 1,215 days (about three years, four months) preceding the bankruptcy filing may not be included in a state homestead exemption unless it was transferred from another homestead in the same state or the homestead is the principal residence of a family farmer.
- An absolute $170,350 homestead cap applies if either (*a*) the bankruptcy court determines that the debtor has been convicted of a felony demonstrating that the filing of the case was an abuse of the provisions of the Bankruptcy Code or (*b*) the debtor owes a debt arising from a violation of federal or state securities laws, fiduciary fraud, racketeering, or crimes or intentional torts that caused serious injury or death in the preceding five

years. In certain cases, a discharge of a debtor under Chapter 7, 11, or 13 may be delayed where the debtor is subject to a proceeding that might lead to a limitation of a homestead exemption.

Federal Exemptions Twelve categories of property are exempt under the federal exemptions, which the debtor may elect in lieu of the state exemptions. The federal exemptions include:

1. The debtor's interest (not to exceed $25,150 in value) in real or personal property that the debtor or a dependent of the debtor uses as a residence.
2. The debtor's interest (not to exceed $4,000 in value) in one motor vehicle.
3. The debtor's interest (not to exceed $750 in value for any particular item) up to a total of $13,650 in household furnishings, household goods, wearing apparel, appliances, books, animals, crops, or musical instruments that are held primarily for the personal, family, or household use of the debtor or a dependent of the debtor.
4. The debtor's aggregate interest (not to exceed $1,700 in value) in jewelry held primarily for the personal, family, or household use of the debtor or a dependent of the debtor.
5. $1,325 in value of any other property of the debtor's choosing, plus up to $12,575 of any unused homestead exemption.

6. The debtor's aggregate interest (not to exceed $2,525 in value) in any implements, professional books, or tools of the trade.

7. Life insurance contracts.

8. Interest up to $13,400 in specified kinds of dividends or interest in certain kinds of life insurance policies.

9. Professionally prescribed health aids.

10. Social Security, disability, alimony, and other benefits reasonably necessary for the support of the debtor or his dependents.

11. The debtor's right to receive certain insurance and liability payments.

12. Retirement funds that are in a fund or account that is exempt from taxation under the Internal Revenue Code. For certain individual retirement accounts, the aggregate amount exempted is limited to $1,362,800. Also protected are some contributions to certain education and college savings accounts made more than one year prior to bankruptcy.

The term **value** means "fair market value as of the date of the filing of the petition." In determining the debtor's interest in property, the amount of any liens against the property must be deducted.

Avoidance of Liens

The debtor is also permitted to **void** certain liens against exempt properties that impair her exemptions. Liens that can be voided on this basis are judicial liens or nonpossessionary, nonpurchase money security interests in (1) household furnishings, household goods, wearing apparel, appliances, books, animals, crops, musical instruments, or jewelry that are held primarily for the personal, family, or household use of the debtor or a dependent of the debtor; (2) implements, professional books, or tools of the trade of the debtor or a dependent of the debtor; and (3) professionally prescribed health aids for the debtor or a dependent of the debtor.

Under the 2005 revisions, the "household goods" as to which a nonpossessory, nonpurchase–money security interest can be avoided have been limited. The new definition limits electronic equipment to one radio, one television, one VCR, and one computer with related equipment. Specifically excluded are works of art other than those created by the debtor or family member, jewelry worth more than $675 (except wedding rings), and motor vehicles (including lawn tractors, motorized vehicles such as ORVs [off-road vehicles]), watercraft, and aircraft.

Redemptions

Debtors are also permitted to redeem exempt personal property from secured creditors by paying

them the full value of the collateral at the time the property is redeemed. Then, the creditor is an unsecured creditor as to any remaining debt owed by the debtor. Under the 2005 revisions, the value of personal property securing a claim of an individual debtor in a Chapter 7 proceeding is based on the cost to the debtor of replacing the property—without deduction for costs of sale or marketing—and if the property was acquired for personal, family, or household purposes, the replacement cost will be the retail price for property of similar age and condition. The debtor is not permitted to retain collateral without redemption or reaffirmation of the debt (discussed later in this chapter) by just continuing to make the payments on the secured debt.

 LO30-5 Understand when the trustee can avoid prior transactions made by the debtor to reclaim assets for the bankruptcy estate.

Preferences (Preferential Payments or Liens)

A major purpose of the Bankruptcy Code is to ensure equal treatment for creditors of an insolvent debtor. The code also seeks to prevent a debtor from distributing her assets to a few favored creditors to the detriment of other creditors.

A "preference" is a preferential payment made or a lien ("security interest") granted by a debtor within 90 days before filing the petition for bankruptcy relief that allows a creditor to obtain a greater percentage of a preexisting debt than other creditors of the debtor. (These payments or liens are also referred to as "transfers.") It is irrelevant whether the recipient creditor knows that the debtor was insolvent at the time of the payment or security-interest grant. The code presumes that all debtors are insolvent on and during the 90 days immediately preceding the filing of the petition for relief. To maintain equal treatment, the code gives the trustee the right to recover for the benefit of the estate preferential payments made or liens granted by the debtor in advance of the petition filing.

In the case of an individual debtor whose debts are primarily consumer debts, the trustee may not avoid preferences unless the aggregate value of the property involved is $725 or more. In the case of a corporate debtor, a transfer of less than $6,825 in the aggregate is not subject to avoidance.

If the favored creditor is an insider—a relative of an individual debtor or an officer, director, or related party of the debtor company—who had reasonable cause to believe the debtor was insolvent at the time the transfer was made, then the trustee can recover a preferential transfer made to that creditor up to one year prior to the filing date of the petition.

The 1994 amendments to the Bankruptcy Code provided that the trustee may not recover as preferential payments any bona fide payments of debts to a spouse, former spouse, or child of the debtor for alimony, maintenance, or support pursuant to a separation agreement, divorce decree, or other court order.

Preferential Liens
Preferential liens are treated in a similar manner. A creditor might try to obtain an advantage over other creditors by obtaining a lien on the debtor's property to secure an existing debt. The creditor might seek to get the debtor's consent to a lien or to obtain a lien by legal process. Such liens are considered *preferential* and are invalid if they are obtained on property of an insolvent debtor within 90 days before the filing of a bankruptcy petition and if their purpose is to secure a preexisting debt. A preferential lien obtained by an insider up to one year prior to the filing of the bankruptcy petition can be avoided.

Transactions in the Ordinary Course of Business
The Bankruptcy Code provides several exceptions to the trustee's avoiding power that are designed to allow a debtor and his creditors to engage in ordinary business transactions. The exceptions include (1) transfers that are intended by the debtor and creditor to be a contemporaneous exchange for new value or (2) the creation of a security interest in new property where new value was given by the secured party to enable the debtor to obtain the property and where the new value was in fact used by the debtor to obtain the property and perfected within 20 days after the debtor took possession of the collateral.

For example, George Grocer is insolvent. He is permitted to purchase and pay cash for new inventory, such as produce or meat, without the payment being considered preferential. His assets have not been reduced. He has simply traded money for goods to be sold in his business. Similarly, he could buy a new display counter and give the seller a security interest in the counter until he has paid for it. This would not be considered a preferential lien. The seller of the counter has not gained an unfair advantage over other creditors, and Grocer's assets have not been reduced by the transaction. The unfair advantage comes where an existing creditor tries to take a lien or obtain a payment of more than his share of the debtor's assets. Then, the creditor has obtained a preference over other creditors, which is what the trustee is allowed to avoid.

The Bankruptcy Code also provides an exception for transfers made in payment of a debt incurred in the ordinary course of the business or financial affairs of the debtor and the transferee (1) made in the ordinary course of business or (2) made according to ordinary business terms. Thus,

for example, a consumer could pay her monthly utility bills in a timely fashion without the creditor/utility being vulnerable to having the transfer of funds avoided by a trustee. The purpose of this exception is to leave undisturbed normal financial relations, and it is consistent with the general policy of the preference section of the code to discourage *unusual action* by either a debtor or her creditors when the debtor is moving toward bankruptcy.

Exceptions to the trustee's avoidance power are also made for certain statutory liens; certain other perfected security interests; cases filed by individual debtors, whose debts are primarily consumer debts and the aggregate value of all property affected by the transfer is less than $725; and cases filed by a debtor, where debts are not primarily consumer debts and the aggregate value of all property affected by the transfer is less than $6,825.

Fraudulent Transfers
If a debtor transfers property or incurs an obligation with *intent to hinder, delay, or defraud creditors*, the transfer is *voidable* by the trustee. Transfers of property for less than reasonable value are similarly voidable. Suppose Kasper is in financial difficulty. She "sells" her $15,000 car to her mother for $100 so that her creditors cannot claim it. Kasper did not receive fair consideration for this transfer. The transfer could be declared void by a trustee if it was made within two years before the filing of a bankruptcy petition against Kasper.

Some states provide longer periods of time; for example, New York allows trustees to avoid fraudulent transfers made in a six-year period before the bankruptcy filing.

Avoidance of Certain "Retention Bonuses" The 2005 revisions also explicitly authorize the trustee to avoid two types of transfers as fraudulent. First, he may avoid transfers to or for the benefit of an insider under an employment contract and not in the ordinary course of business. Specifically addressed are "retention bonuses," which Congress believed had been abused in some recent high-profile corporate bankruptcies. Retention bonuses can be paid to insiders only where they are made in response to bona fide outside offers, the individual's services are essential to the survival of the business, and the amount of the bonus is not more than 10 times the mean of similar bonuses paid to nonmanagement employees during the year.

Avoidance of Transfers to Certain Asset Protection Trusts The second type of transfer that the trustee was explicitly authorized to avoid as fraudulent is transfers to a self-settled trust made within 10 years of the filing by a debtor where the debtor is a beneficiary and the transfer

Ethics and Compliance in Action

Should the Homestead Exemption Be Limited?

As of June 2002, six states, including Florida and Texas, provided an unlimited household exemption that allows bankrupt debtors to shield unlimited amounts of equity in a residential estate. The unlimited exemption has come under increased scrutiny in recent years as a number of public figures as well as noted wrongdoers have taken advantage of the unlimited exemption to shield significant amounts of wealth from creditors. For example, a prominent actor who was declared bankrupt in 1996 was allowed to keep a $2.5 million estate located in Hobe Sound, Florida, and a corporate executive convicted of securities fraud kept his Tampa, Florida, mansion from the claims of his creditors in bankruptcy, including federal regulators seeking to collect civil fines. When the Enron and WorldCom corporate scandals broke in 2001 and 2002, the media called attention to a $15 million mansion under construction in Boca Raton, Florida, for the former CFO of WorldCom and to a $7 million penthouse owned by the former CEO of Enron as well as to the fact that the liberal exemption laws in Florida and Texas might be utilized by them to protect a significant amount of their wealth against claims from creditors and regulators.

As noted previously, in the 2005 act, Congress took some steps to limit the ability of debtors to shift assets into an expensive home in a state with an unlimited household exemption shortly before filing for bankruptcy and also to limit the

exemption for debtors convicted of violations of the federal securities laws. While the act was pending in the conference committee, a group of about 80 law professors who teach bankruptcy and commercial law wrote to the committee urging that it adopt a hard cap on the homestead exemption contained in the Senate version of the bill. They pointed out the fundamental unfairness created when residents of one state can protect in a supposedly "uniform" federal bankruptcy proceeding an asset worth millions, while residents in other states face sharp limitations on what they can protect. As an example, they noted that a wealthy investor in Texas could keep an unencumbered home worth $10 million, while a factory worker in Virginia puts at risk anything over $10,000 in equity.

The law professors described various ways that the formulation the conference committee had adopted could be gamed. They also asserted that the provisions to limit the homestead exemption for those who violate securities laws, who commit fraud while in a fiduciary capacity, or who commit certain felonies or intentional torts were too tightly drawn and would create a "playground of loopholes for wealthy individuals and clever lawyers." They noted, for example, that the provisions "would not cap the homestead exemption for someone who finds a dozen ways to bilk the elderly out of their money, someone who takes advantage of first-time home buyers, or someone who deceives people trying to set up college funds for their children."

Should Congress adopt a uniform cap on the homestead exemption?

was made with actual intent to hinder or delay. There is a particular focus on transfers made in anticipation of any money judgment, settlement, civil penalty, equitable order, or criminal fine that the debtor believed would be incurred through any violation of federal or state securities laws or fraud, through deceit or manipulation in a fiduciary capacity, or in connection with the purchase or sale of securities registered under the federal securities acts.

The provisions of law concerning fraudulent transfers are designed to prevent a debtor from concealing or disposing of his property in fraud of creditors. Such transfers may

also subject the debtor to criminal penalties and prevent discharge of the debtor's unpaid liabilities.[1]

The case that follows, *In re Bernard L. Madoff Investment Securities*, a Trustee, exercising powers under the Bankruptcy Code, sought to avoid monies paid out to certain investors pursuant to a Ponzi scheme as preferential and fraudulent transfers.

---

[1]Bulk sales of a debtor's materials, supplies, merchandise, or other inventory of the business in bulk and not in the ordinary course of business have the potential to defraud creditors.

In re Bernard L. Madoff Investment Securities
445 B.R. 206 (Bankr. S.D.N.Y. 2011)

For decades, Bernard L. Madoff operated a Ponzi scheme through his investment company, Bernard L. Madoff Investment Securities (BLMIS). It was a fraud of unparalleled magnitude in which the only assets were other people's money or assets derived from such funds. During the course of the fraud, there were approximately 90,000 disbursements of fictitious profits to Madoff investors *totaling $18.8 billion. Due to the longstanding nature of the Ponzi scheme, many of the customer accounts presented multiple generational investments, requiring the Trustee for the Liquidation of BLMIS, Irving Picard, to conduct a full forensic analysis of all of BLMIS's books and records dating back to at least the early 1980s. As of February 18, 2011, the Trustee had determined 16,267 claims under the Securities Investor Protection Act (SIPA), denied 2,740 claims (and 10,731 third-party claims), and allowed claims in the amount of $6,854,549.81.*

As part of his effort to recoup monies that could be used to reimburse those who had been defrauded by Madoff, the Trustee brought suit against Stanley Chais, a sophisticated investment advisor who had been closely associated with Madoff since the 1970s, as well as against those who held accounts directed and controlled by Chais, including members of his family and related entitles. The Trustee sought to recover more than $1 billion as constituting preferential payments or fraudulent transfers under the Bankruptcy Code.

Prior to Madoff's arrest, Stanley Chais invested in BLMIS for over three decades through more than 60 entity or personal accounts. The Trustee alleged that from his investments with BLMIS, Chais withdrew hundreds of millions of dollars of other investors' money, funneling much of it to his children and their spouses, his grandchildren, and various entities he created for the benefit of his family. He served as the settlor and trustee for numerous trusts as well as the general partner and investment advisor to a number of companies.

As the general partner of Chais Funds, which invested heavily in BLMIS, Chais collected management fees equal to 25 percent of each of Chais Funds's entire net profit for every calendar year in which profits exceeded 10 percent, which occurred every calendar year since at least 1996. The Trustee asserted that by virtue of his close and personal relationship with Madoff and expertise as an investment advisor, Stanley Chais knew or should have known that BLMIS was predicated on fraud.

The Trustee also asserted that the other defendants, whether independently or through Stanley Chais, knew or should have known that BLMIS was predicated on fraud and failed to exercise reasonable due diligence into BLMIS. In support of this allegation, the Trustee alleged the following indicia of irregularity and fraud: (1) their accounts, directed and controlled by Stanley Chais, received fantastical rates of return from 1996 through 2007, including 125 instances of returns exceeding 50 percent, more than 35 instances of returns exceeding 100 percent, and one instance of returns exceeding 300 percent; (2) losses were manufactured after the dates when various transactions took place, including a purchase and sale of 125,000 shares of Micron Technology Inc. for a loss of more than $1 million appearing for the first time 150 days after the purported purchase; (3) purported losses were generally remedied in subsequent periods with monumental rates of return that far outpaced the market, including a return in one defendant's account from negative 89 percent returns in 2003 to positive 165 percent returns the following year; (4) financial industry press reports questioned the legitimacy of BLMIS and Madoff and their ability to achieve promised returns, and many banks and advisors refused to deal with BLMIS and Madoff; (5) BLMIS lacked transparency to investors, regulars, and other outside parties by failing to provide customers with real-time online access to their accounts and excluding an independent custodian of securities; and (6) BLMIS, one of the world's largest hedge funds, was supposedly audited by Friehling & Horowitz, an accounting firm with only three employees, one of whom was semiretired, with offices in a strip mall.

Chais and a number of the family and related-party defendants filed a motion to dismiss the complaint filed by the Trustee for failure to state a claim on which relief can be granted. In considering such a motion, the court is required to accept all factual allegations in the complaint as true and draw all reasonable inferences in the plaintiff's [the Trustee's] favor.

Lifland, Bankruptcy Judge

The Trustee has sufficiently pled Count Three of the Complaint pursuant to sections 548(a)(1)(A), 550, and 551 of the [Bankruptcy] Code to avoid and recover fraudulent transfers.

Under the Code, "the trustee may avoid any transfer . . . of an interest of the debtor in property . . . made or incurred on or within 2 years before the date of the filing of the petition, if the debtor . . . made such transfer . . . with actual intent to hinder, delay, or defraud." To do this, the complaint must allege "(1) the property subject to

the transfer, (2) the timing and, if applicable, frequency of the transfer, and (3) the consideration paid with respect thereto." In contrast, fraudulent intent may be pled generally, and under the Code, the Trustee must show such intent on the part of the debtor-transferor.

Exhibit B to the Complaint specifically identifies the date, account number, transferor, transferee, method of transfer, and amount of each of the Transfers that the Trustee has thus far identified. In addition, the Trustee alleges that the Transfers represent redemptions of both principal and fictitious profits. The Six

Year Transfers total $804 million, the Two Year Transfers total $377 million, and the Ninety Day Transfers total $46 million. Therefore, the Trustee's allegations sufficiently identify the specific Transfers sought to be avoided.

The Defendants do not dispute that the Trustee has sufficiently alleged the intent of the transferor, BLMIS, for purposes of section 548(a)(1)(A) of the Code. It is now well recognized that the existence of a Ponzi scheme establishes that transfers were made with the intent to hinder, delay, and defraud creditors. The breadth and notoriety of the Madoff Ponzi scheme leave no basis for disputing the application of the Ponzi scheme presumption to the facts of this case, particularly in light of Madoff's criminal admission. Accordingly, BLMIS's fraudulent intent is established as a matter of law for purposes of the Trustee's Code-based actual fraudulent claims.

The trustee has sufficiently pled actual fraud under the Code, and the motion to dismiss is denied.

[At the same time, the Bankruptcy judge ruled, among other things, that the Trustee had (1) adequately alleged fraudulent intent on the part of the defendant and (2) sufficiently pled that transfers challenged as constructively fraudulent under the code were not made in exchange for reasonably equivalent value.]

 LO30-6 Distinguish among claims, allowable claims, secured claims, and priority claims of creditors.

Claims

If creditors wish to participate in the estate of a bankrupt debtor, they must file a proof of claim in the estate within a certain time, usually 90 days after the first meeting of creditors. Only unsecured creditors are required to file proofs of claims. However, a secured creditor whose secured claim exceeds the value of the collateral is an unsecured creditor to the extent of the deficiency. That creditor must file a proof of claim to support the recovery of the deficiency.

Allowable Claims

The fact that a proof of claim is filed does not ensure that a creditor can participate in the distribution of the assets of the bankruptcy estate. The claim must also be allowed. If the trustee has a valid defense to the claim, he can use the defense to disallow or reduce it. For example, if the claim is based on goods sold to the debtor and the seller breached a warranty, the trustee can assert the breach as a defense. All of the defenses available to the bankrupt person are available to the trustee.

Under the 2005 revisions, the court is authorized to reduce claims based on unsecured consumer debt by 20 percent on motion by the debtor and a showing that the creditor refused to negotiate a reasonable alternative repayment schedule proposed on behalf of the debtor by an approved nonprofit budget and credit counseling agency. The offer had to have been made at least 60 days before filing of the petition and to have provided for the payment of at least 60 percent of the debt over a period not to exceed the original period of the loan or a reasonable extension of the time.

Secured Claims

The trustee must also determine whether a creditor has a lien or secured interest to secure an allowable claim. If the debtor's property is subject to a secured claim of a creditor, that creditor has first claim to it. The property is available to satisfy claims of other creditors only to the extent that its value exceeds the amount of the debt secured.

Priority Claims

The Bankruptcy Code declares certain claims to have priority over other claims. The 10 classes of priority claims are:

1. Domestic support obligations of the debtor, including (*a*) claims for debts to a spouse, former spouse, or child for alimony to, maintenance for, or support of such spouse or child in connection with a separation agreement, divorce decree, or other court order (but not if assigned to someone else other than a governmental unit); (*b*) expenses of a trustee in administering assets that might otherwise be used to pay the support obligations have priority before the support obligations themselves; and (*c*) support obligations owed directly to, or recoverable by, spouses and children have priority over support obligations that have been assigned to or are owed directly to a governmental unit.

2. Expenses and fees incurred in administering the bankruptcy estate.

3. Unsecured claims in involuntary cases that arise in the ordinary course of the debtor's business after the filing of the petition but before the appointment of a trustee or the order of relief.

4. Unsecured claims of up to $13,650 per individual (including vacation, severance, and sick pay) for

employee's wages earned within 180 days before the petition was filed or the debtor's business ceased.

5. Contributions to employee benefit plans up to $13,650 per person (moreover, the claim for wages plus pension contribution is limited to $13,650 per person).

6. Unsecured claims up to $6,725 (*a*) for grain or the proceeds of grain against a debtor who owns or operates a grain storage facility or (*b*) by a U.S. fisherman against a debtor who operates a fish produce storage or processing facility and who has acquired fish or fish produce from the fisherman.

7. Claims of up to $3,025 each by individuals for deposits made in connection with the purchase, lease, or rental of property or the purchase of goods or services for personal use that were not delivered or provided.

8. Certain taxes owed to governmental units.

9. Allowed unsecured claims based on a commitment by the debtor to a federal depository institution regulatory agency (such as the FDIC).

10. Allowed claims for liability for death or personal injury resulting from operation of a motor vehicle where the operator was unlawfully intoxicated from alcohol, drugs, or other substances.

The 2005 act adds as a category of administrative expenses (see priority 2 above) "the value of any goods received by a debtor within 20 days before the petition date in which the goods have been sold to the debtor in the ordinary course of the debtor's business." The expectation is that a very significant percentage of claims arising from goods sold and received will qualify as administrative expenses. The 2005 revisions also extend the right of vendors to reclaim goods shipped before the petition. Any goods sold in the ordinary course of business and received by a debtor while insolvent may be reclaimed by the seller provided that the seller demands reclamation in writing not later than 45 days after the receipt of the goods or, if the debtor filed its petition during the 45 days, then not later than 20 days after the commencement of the bankruptcy case.

Distribution of the Debtor's Estate

 LO30-7 Describe the process by which the property in a debtor's estate is distributed to creditors and the debtor is granted a discharge in bankruptcy.

The priority claims are paid *after* secured creditors realize on their collateral but *before* other unsecured creditors are paid. Payments are made to the 10 priority classes, in order, to the extent there are funds available. Each class must be paid in full before the next class is entitled to receive anything. To the extent there are insufficient funds to satisfy all the creditors within a class, each class member receives a pro rata share of his claim.

Unsecured creditors include (1) those creditors who had not taken any collateral to secure the debt owed to them, (2) secured creditors to the extent their debt was not satisfied by the collateral they held, and (3) priority claimholders to the extent their claims exceed the limits set for priority claims.

Unsecured creditors, to the extent any funds are available for them, share in proportion to their claims. Unsecured creditors frequently receive little or nothing on their claims. Secured claims, trustee's fees, and other priority claims often consume a large part of the bankruptcy estate.

Special rules are set out in the Bankruptcy Code for distribution of the property of a bankrupt stockbroker or commodities broker.

Discharge in Bankruptcy

LO30-8 List the kinds of debts that are not dischargeable.

Discharge A bankrupt person who has not been guilty of certain dishonest acts and has fulfilled his duties as a bankrupt is entitled to a discharge in bankruptcy. A discharge relieves the bankrupt person of further responsibility for dischargeable debts and gives him a fresh start. A corporation or a partnership is not eligible for a discharge in bankruptcy. A bankrupt person may file a written waiver of his right to a discharge. An individual may not be granted a discharge if she obtained one within the previous eight years.

Objections to Discharge After the bankrupt has paid all of the required fees, the court gives creditors and others a chance to file objections to the discharge of the bankrupt. Objections may be filed by the trustee, a creditor, or the U.S. attorney. If objections are filed, the court holds a hearing to listen to them. At the hearing, the court must determine whether the bankrupt person has committed any act that is a bar to discharge. If the bankrupt has not committed such an act, the court grants the discharge. If the bankrupt has committed an act that is a bar to discharge, the discharge is denied. The discharge is also denied if the bankrupt fails to appear at the hearing on objections or if he refused earlier to submit to the questioning of the creditors.

Distribution of Debtor's Estate (Chapter 7)

Secured creditors proceed directly against the collateral. If debt is fully satisfied, they have no further interest; if debt is only partially satisfied, they are treated as general creditors for the balance.

↓

Debtor's Estate Is Liquidated and Distributed

↓

Priority Creditors (10 classes)

1. Domestic support obligations of the debtor and expenses of administration of assets used to pay support obligations.
2. Costs and expenses of administration.
3. If involuntary proceeding, expenses incurred in the ordinary course of business after petition filed but before appointment of trustee.
4. Claims for wages, salaries, and commissions earned within 180 days of petition; limited to $13,650 per person.
5. Contributions to employee benefit plans arising out of services performed within 180 days of petition; limit of $13,650 (including claims for wages, salaries, and commissions) per person.
6. Unsecured claims (a) for grain or the proceeds of grain against a debtor who owns or operates a grain storage facility or (b) up to $6,725 by a U.S. fisherman against a debtor who operates a fish produce or processing facility and who has acquired fish or fish produce from the fisherman.
7. Claims of individuals, up to $3,025 per person, for deposits made on consumer goods or services that were not received.
8. Government claims for certain taxes.
9. Allowed unsecured claims based on a commitment by the debtor to a federal depository institution regulatory agency.
10. Allowed claims for liability for death or personal injury resulting from operation of a motor vehicle where the operator was intoxicated.

A. Distribution is made to 10 classes of priority claims in order.
B. Each class must be fully paid before next class receives anything.
C. If funds are not sufficient to satisfy everyone in a class, then each member of the class receives same proportion of claim.

↓

General Creditors

1. General unsecured creditors.
2. Secured creditors for the portion of their debt that was not satisfied by collateral.
3. Priority creditors for amounts beyond priority limits.

If funds are not sufficient to satisfy all general creditors, then each receives the same proportion of their claims.

↓

Debtor

Debtor receives any remaining funds.

Acts That Bar Discharge

Discharges in bankruptcy are intended for honest debtors. Therefore, the following acts bar a debtor from being discharged: (1) the unjustified falsifying, concealing, or destroying of records; (2) making false statements, presenting false claims, or withholding recorded information relating to the debtor's property or financial affairs; (3) transferring, removing, or concealing property in order to hinder, delay, or defraud creditors; (4) failing to account satisfactorily for any loss or deficiency of assets; and (5) failing to obey court orders or to answer questions approved by the court.

Nondischargeable Debts

Certain debts are not affected by the discharge of a bankrupt debtor. The Bankruptcy Code provides that a discharge in bankruptcy releases a debtor from all provable debts except for certain specified debts. These include, among others, debts that:

1. Are due as a tax or fine to the United States or any state or local unit of government.

2. Result from liabilities for obtaining money by false pretenses or false representations.

3. Were incurred by the debtor's purchase of more than $725 in luxury goods or services on credit from a single creditor within 90 days of filing a petition (presumed to be nondischargeable).

4. Are cash advances in excess of $1,000 obtained by use of a credit card or a revolving line of credit at a credit union and obtained within 70 days of filing a bankruptcy petition (presumed to be nondischargeable).

5. Were not scheduled in time for proof and allowance because the creditor holding the debt did not have notification of the proceeding even though the debtor was aware that he owed money to that creditor.

6. Were created by the debtor's larceny or embezzlement or by the debtor's fraud while acting in a fiduciary capacity.

7. Were for a domestic support obligation (unless excepting it from discharge would impose an undue hardship on the debtor's dependents).

8. Are due for willful or malicious injury to a person or his property.

9. Are educational loans.

10. Are judgments arising out of a debtor's operation of a motor vehicle while legally intoxicated.

11. Are debts incurred to pay a tax to the United States that would not be dischargeable.

12. Are property settlements arising from divorce or separation proceedings *other than* support provisions that are priority claims.

All of these nondischargeable debts are provable debts. The creditor who owns these claims can participate in the distribution of the bankrupt's estate. However, the creditor has an additional advantage: His right to recover the unpaid balance is not cut off by the bankrupt's discharge. All other provable debts are dischargeable; that is, the right to recover them is cut off by the bankrupt's discharge.

In the case that follows, *Rosenberg v. N.Y. State Higher Education Services Corp.*, the bankruptcy court granted a discharge of student loans on the grounds that their repayment would constitute an undue hardship.

Rosenberg v. N.Y. State Higher Education Services Corp.
610 B.R. 454 (Bankr. S.D.N.Y 2020)

On March 12, 2018, Kevin Jared Rosenberg filed a petition for relief under Chapter 7 of the Bankruptcy Code and received a discharge of his debts, exclusive of his student loans, on July 26, 2019. In the interim, Rosenberg filed an adversary proceeding to have his student loan debt declared dischargeable: Student loans are normally not dischargeable under the normal discharge rules unless it would impose an "undue hardship" on the debtor not to grant the discharge. Historically, the bankruptcy courts have not looked favorably on efforts to discharge student loans.

Rosenberg began borrowing money to fund his education in August 1993, and from 1993 to 1996 he borrowed money to pay for his undergraduate education at the University of Arizona. After obtaining a Bachelor of Arts degree in history, he served in the U.S. Navy on active duty for five years. After completing his tour of duty, Rosenberg attended Cardoza Law School at Yeshiva University, where he applied for and received additional student loans to cover his tuition and board from 2001 through 2004. After graduating from law school, Rosenberg consolidated his student loan on April 22, 2005, in the original principal amount of $116,464.75. The total outstanding balance of the student loan as of November 19, 2019, was $221,385.49 with an interest rate of 3.38% per annum.

Rosenberg filed a motion for summary against asking that the debt owed to Educational Credit Management Corporation ECMC, the holder of the debt, be discharged.

Morris, Chief U.S. Bankruptcy Judge

Dischargeability of Student Loans under U.S.C. § 523(a)(8)

Section 523(a)(8) states:

A discharge under section 727 . . . of this title does not discharge an individual debtor from any debt—unless excepting such debt from discharge under this paragraph would impose an undue hardship on the debtor and the debtor's dependents, for—

(A)

    (i) an educational benefit, overpayment, or loan made, insured, or guaranteed by a governmental unit, or made under any program funded in whole or in part by a governmental unit or nonprofit institution; or

    (ii) an obligation to repay funds received as an educational benefit, scholarship, or stipend; or

(B) any other educational loan that is a qualified education loan, as defined in section 221(d)(1) of the Internal Revenue Code of 1986, incurred by a debtor who is an individual.

Both Rosenberg and ECMC agree that the proper test to be applied in this instance is *Brunner v. N.Y. State Higher Educ. Servs. Corp. (In re Brunner)* (2d Cir. 1987). The test set forth in *Brunner* is

(1) that the debtor cannot maintain, based on current income and expenses, a "minimal" standard of living for herself and her dependents if forced to repay the loans;

(2) that additional circumstances exist indicating that this state of affairs is likely to persist for a significant portion of the repayment period of the student loans; and

(3) that the debtor has made good faith efforts to repay the loans.

Brunner has received a lot of criticism for creating too high of a burden for most bankruptcy petitioners to meet. For petitioners like Brunner, who filed for bankruptcy approximately seven months after receiving a degree, the *Brunner* test is difficult to meet. However, for a multitude of petitioners like Mr. Rosenberg, who have been out of school and struggling with student loan debt for many years, the test itself is fairly straight-forward and simple.

The harsh results that are often associated with *Brunner* are actually the result of cases interpreting *Brunner.* Over the past 32 years, many cases have pinned on *Brunner* punitive standards that are not contained therein. *See Briscoe v. Bank of N.Y. (In re Briscoe)* (Bankr. S.D.N.Y. 1981) (coining the infamous and oft-repeated term "certainty of hopelessness" but not applying the *Brunner* test, which was established six years later). These retributive dicta were then applied and reapplied so frequently in the context of *Brunner* that they have subsumed the actual language of the *Brunner* test. They have become a quasi-standard of mythic proportions so much that most people (bankruptcy professionals as well as lay individuals) believe it is impossible to discharge student loans.

To this end, some courts have even called it "bad faith" when someone struggling with repaying a student loan attempts to discharge that debt in bankruptcy court.

This Court will not participate in perpetuating these myths. Rather, this Court will apply the *Brunner* test as it was originally intended.

Brunner Test

1. Whether the Petitioner cannot maintain, based on current income and expenses, a "minimal" standard of living for himself and his dependents if forced to repay the loans?

Under the first prong of the test, the Court must determine that the debtor cannot maintain, based on current income and expenses, a "minimal" standard of living for [him]self and h[is]dependents if forced to repay the loans.

Section 707(b)(2) codifies the "means test," which is a formula that calculates a bankruptcy petitioner's average monthly disposable income over a 60-month period by deducting statutorily allowable expenses, secured debt payments, and priority debt payments from current monthly income.

Here, Rosenberg's means test lists his monthly income as $3,136.24 and his annual income as $37,634.88. He lists his income and expenses on schedules I & J as $2,456.24 (income) and $4,005.00 (expenses), leaving Rosenberg with a monthly income of −$1,548.74 at the time of filing. Thus, he has declared under penalty of perjury that he has negative income each month. Neither ECMC nor any other party in interest has objected to Rosenberg's schedules or means test, and he has received a discharge. Therefore, the Court accepts Rosenberg's income and expenses as undisputed.

As of the filing of this bankruptcy case, Rosenberg's Student Loan is currently in default. As such, his Student Loan is currently due and payable in the full amount of $221,385.49 plus interest and costs. Rosenberg has successfully proven that he cannot immediately pay his Student Loan in full on his current income.

As Rosenberg has a negative income each month, he has no money available to repay his Student Loan and maintain a "minimal" standard of living. This prong of the test is met.

2. Whether additional circumstances exist indicating that this state of affairs is likely to persist for a significant period of the repayment period of the student loans?

Next, the Court must consider whether additional circumstances exist indicating that this state of affairs is likely to persist for a significant portion of the repayment period of the student loans. Here, the repayment period has ended. Rosenberg is in default and his loan was accelerated. As of November 19, 2019, he is responsible for the full amount of $221,385.49. His circumstances will certainly exist for the remainder of the repayment period as the repayment period has ended and the loan is due and payable in the full amount. The second prong of the *Brunner* test is, therefore, satisfied.

3. Whether the debtor has made good faith efforts to repay the loans?

Turning to the third and final prong, the Court must determine whether the debtor has made good faith efforts to repay the loans. The *Brunner* test asks the Court to look at whether Rosenberg has made good faith efforts to repay the loan, which indicates that the Court should only consider Rosenberg's past (pre petition) behavior in repaying the loans. It is therefore inappropriate to consider: Rosenberg's reasons for filing bankruptcy; how much debt he has; or whether Rosenberg rejected repayment options.

Based on the loan history provided by ECMC, Rosenberg missed only 16 payments in the almost 13 years since this Student Loan originated in April 2005. He made 10 payments, in varying amounts, during the 26 months he was responsible for making payments, which is approximately a 40% rate of payment over a thirteen-year period. Additionally, Rosenberg did not sit back for 20 years but made a good faith effort to repay his Student Loan. He actively called and requested forbearance on at least five separate occasions, all of which were granted by the servicer.

Rosenberg has demonstrated a good faith effort to repay the loan and has satisfied the "undue hardship" standard of 11 U.S.C § 523(a)(8).

Conclusion

For the foregoing reasons, Rosenberg has satisfied the *Brunner* test. **Based on the foregoing, it is hereby ORDERED that the Student Loan imposes an undue hardship on Rosenberg and is discharged.**

Reaffirmation Agreements

Sometimes, creditors put pressure on debtors to reaffirm, or to agree to pay, debts that have been discharged in bankruptcy. When the 1978 amendments to the Bankruptcy Code were under consideration, some individuals urged Congress to prohibit such agreements. They argued that reaffirmation agreements were inconsistent with the fresh start philosophy of the Bankruptcy Code. Congress did not agree to a total prohibition; instead, it set up a rather elaborate procedure for a creditor to go through to get a debt reaffirmed. Essentially, the agreement must be made *before* the discharge is granted and the debtor must receive certain specified disclosures at or before the time he signs the reaffirmation agreement. These disclosures include the "amount reaffirmed," the annual percentage rate of interest, the total of fees and costs accrued to date, that the agreement may be rescinded at any time prior to discharge or within 60 days after filing with the court, and a clear and conspicuous statement advising the debtor that the reaffirmation agreement is not required by the bankruptcy law or any other law.

The agreement must be filed with the court—and if the debtor is represented by an attorney, the agreement must be accompanied by a certification from the debtor's attorney that (1) it represents a voluntary agreement by the debtor, (2) it does not impose an undue hardship on the debtor or any dependent of the debtor, and (3) the debtor was fully advised about the legal consequences of signing the agreement. Where the debtor is not represented by an attorney during the negotiation of the reaffirmation agreement, it is not effective unless approved by the court.

Until 60 days after a reaffirmation agreement is filed with the court, there is a presumption that the agreement will work an undue hardship on the debtor if the debtor's income less the monthly expenses as shown on the schedule she filed is less than the scheduled payments on the reaffirmed debt. The debtor has the opportunity to rebut the presumption, but where the debtor does not do so, the court may disapprove the reaffirmation agreement.

Dismissal for Substantial Abuse

In 1984, Congress, concerned that too many individuals with an ability to pay their debts over time pursuant to a Chapter 13 plan were filing petitions to obtain Chapter 7 discharges of liability, authorized the bankruptcy courts to dismiss cases that they determined were a substantial abuse of the bankruptcy process. The courts used this power to dismiss cases where it determined the debtor had acted in bad faith or had the present or future ability to pay a significant portion of her current debts. In the 2005 amendments, Congress reduced the standard for dismissal from "substantial abuse" to just "abuse."

Means Testing In the 2005 act, Congress amended the Bankruptcy Code to provide for the dismissal of Chapter 7 cases—or with the debtor's consent their conversion to Chapter 13 cases—on a finding of abuse by an individual debtor with primarily consumer debts. The abuse can be established in two ways: (1) through an unrebutted finding of abuse based on a new "means test" that is included in the code or (2) on general grounds of abuse, including bad faith, determined under the totality of the circumstances.

The means test is designed to determine the debtor's ability to repay general unsecured claims. It has three elements: (1) a definition of "current monthly income," which is the total income a debtor is presumed to have available; (2) a list of allowed deductions from the current monthly income for the purpose of supporting the debtor and his family and for repayment of higher priority debts; and (3) defined "trigger points" at which the income remaining after the allowed deductions would trigger the presumption of abuse. For example, if the debtor's current monthly income after the defined deductions is more than $166.66, the presumption of abuse arises irrespective of the amount of debt; and if the debtor has at least $100 per month of current monthly income after the allowed deductions (which would amount to $6,000 over five years), then abuse is presumed if that income would be sufficient to pay at least 25 percent of the debtor's unsecured debts

over five years. To rebut the presumption of abuse, the debtor must show "special circumstances" that would decrease the income or increase expected expenses so as to bring the debtor's income below the trigger points.

Debtors have to file a statement of their calculations under the means test as part of their schedule of current income and expenditures. If the presumption of abuse arises, then the court has to notify the creditors of this situation. While any party in interest generally has the right to bring a motion seeking dismissal of a Chapter 7 case for abuse, only the U.S. Trustee or bankruptcy administrator can bring the motion if the debtor's income is below the median income in the state. Moreover, the means test presumption is inapplicable to debtors whose income is below that state median and also to certain disabled veterans.

In the case that follows, *In re Siegenberg*, the court dismissed a Chapter 7 case on the grounds it was filed in bad faith.

In re **Siegenberg**	2007 Bankr. LEXIS 2538 (C.D. Cal. July 31, 2007)

Commencing in 2000, when she was hired by Mariah Carey, a prominent entertainer, Nicole Siegenberg worked as a costumer in the entertainment business. Her duties were to buy clothes for and costume her employer. In 2004, she lost her job with Carey and began looking for other similar employment in the entertainment industry. In order to do that, she had to build a portfolio, which required purchases of clothing stock totaling $9,273 in 2004. Siegenberg's statement of financial affairs indicates that she earned $10,000 in 2004.

Since 2004, Siegenberg was employed only sporadically on temporary jobs such as television pilots. When employed, she earned about $2,000 per week. Unfortunately, since 2004 she was usually unemployed. Thus, in 2005 she earned $12,648, and in 2006 she earned $35,253.

Siegenberg lived with her parents in her parents' condominium in Pacific Palisades. During the 2004 to 2006 period, she incurred debts to, among other things, assist her parents with a property they had bought as an investment to provide income when her father was unable to continue his job; assist a boyfriend who was a Realtor with expenses on properties he was seeking to market; travel with her boyfriend and her mother to South Africa to visit her sick grandmother; assist her mother with medical expenses; and provide living expenses for herself. Some of the expenses were reimbursed to her, while others were not.

Siegenberg filed a Chapter 7 bankruptcy on November 29, 2006. Siegenberg owed $82,597.12 in unsecured debt and $27,664 in secured debt on her car and her boyfriend's car (a 2001 BMW and a 1999 Cadillac Escalade, respectively). The U.S. Trustee (UST) filed a motion to dismiss Siegenberg's Chapter 7 petition as filed in bad faith and sought a one-year bar against refiling.

Donovan, U.S. Bankruptcy Judge

In considering whether a Chapter 7 case should be dismissed because granting relief would be an abuse of the provisions of Chapter 7, courts may consider (a) whether the debtor filed the petition in bad faith; or (b) whether the totality of the circumstances of the debtor's financial situation demonstrates abuse.

A. Dismissal for Bad Faith under 707(b)(3)(A)

Section 707(b)(3) was added to the Bankruptcy Code by the Bankruptcy Abuse Prevention and Consumer Protection Act of 2005 (BAPCPA). Since BAPCPA, the Ninth Circuit has not

established a standard for determining a finding of "bad faith" in Chapter 7 cases under § 707(b)(3)(A). However, a few bankruptcy courts have addressed the issue. The court in *In re Mitchell*, a Chapter 7 case, used a nine-part test borrowing both from the Ninth Circuit's pre-BAPCPA "substantial abuse" test and from Chapters 11 and 13 bad faith cases. The court in *Mitchell* considered the following nine factors in determining whether "the debtor's intention in filing bankruptcy is inconsistent with the Chapter 7 goals of providing a 'fresh start' to debtors and maximizing return to creditors" and whether the case should thus be dismissed under § 707(b)(3)(A):

1. Whether the Chapter 7 debtor has a likelihood of sufficient future income to fund a Chapter 11, 12, or 13 plan which would pay a substantial portion of the unsecured claims;
2. Whether debtor's petition was filed as a consequence of illness, disability, unemployment, or other calamity;
3. Whether debtor obtained cash advances and consumer goods on credit exceeding his or her ability to repay;
4. Whether debtor's proposed family budget is excessive or extravagant;
5. Whether debtor's statement of income and expenses misrepresents debtor's financial condition;
6. Whether debtor made eve of bankruptcy purchases;
7. Whether debtor has a history of bankruptcy petition filings and dismissals;
8. Whether debtor has invoked the automatic stay for improper purposes, such as to delay or defeat state court litigation;
9. Whether egregious behavior is present.

1. Likelihood that the Chapter 7 debtor will have sufficient future income to fund a Chapter 11 or 13 plan. Siegenberg does not currently have income to fund a chapter 11 or 13 plan. According to the pleadings, such future income is not foreseeable. This fact supports Siegenberg's position.

2. Consequence of illness, disability, unemployment or other calamity. Siegenberg claims, in part, that the bankruptcy petition was filed as a consequence of the disability of her father. His disability and surgery in April 2006 caused financial panic in her family, in response to which her parents bought a house in the hope of remodeling it and selling it quickly at a profit. Siegenberg contributed $35,000 to remodel that investment property under an agreement that promised her 50 percent of the profit. However, her parents sold the home at a loss and Siegenberg received no money in return for her investment.

Siegenberg did not experience an illness, disability, new unemployment, or other calamity. On the contrary, she provides evidence of only modest improvement in her employment status for the year 2006, not enough to match her greater expenditures. There was no change in her health status after 2004.

Further Siegenberg incurred thousands of dollars of new credit card debt on plane tickets, a car for her boyfriend, hotel stays, and other consumer items that are not convincingly attributable to any reasonably, potentially revenue-producing activities during May 2006, the month after her father's surgery and the month during which her parents purchased a house as an investment property, the alleged period of financial distress.

3. Obtaining cash advances and consumer goods on credit exceeding Siegenberg's ability to repay. Much of the argument between the two parties revolves around the question of consumer spending. The UST argues that Siegenberg purchased luxury consumer items on credit beyond her ability to repay at the expense of her creditors. Siegenberg urges in response that various expenditures were either for business purposes or were repaid.

Siegenberg asserts that she spent approximately $35,000 on her parent's residential investment; she repaid pre-bankruptcy almost two-thirds of the cost of the plane tickets to South Africa ($5,500); her parents wrote a check that she forwarded to her credit card company to repay $12,500 for the credit card charges for her mother's surgery; her expenditures on clothing were (a) a legitimate business expense and (b) some of the clothing was returned for credit; and she traveled to Mexico for the purpose of attaining a job.

On the other hand, Siegenberg provides no detail to explain $42,775 in cash advances she received on her credit card accounts between May 2005 and October 2006. She does not provide evidence of contractor payments she claims to have made that exceeded $19,607. She does not provide corroborating detailed evidence that during the period covered by the UST's motion she used the clothing she bought for demonstrable business purposes. Regarding her Mexican expenditures, it appears that she incurred credit card debt of more than $6,000 before July 2006, but only about $2,000 between July and October 2006, the period during which she claims she was interviewing for employment in Mexico. The pre-July Mexican expenditures appear to be for consumer items such as plane tickets, hotels, and restaurants for the personal pleasure of Siegenberg and her boyfriend, and Siegenberg offers no convincing evidence to persuade me otherwise.

Similarly, Siegenberg does not persuasively explain the reasonable business purpose of about $5,500 in car-related credit card debt creating expenditures (including $2,500 on her boyfriend's Cadillac down payment), as well as $2,129 on restaurants, and about $900 on hotels in Southern California, among other consumer items.

The sum of Siegenberg's justified business or personal expenditures, including contractor expenses, reimbursed tickets to South Africa, her mother's surgery, returned clothing, and spending to pursue employment in Mexico is about $59,000. On the other hand, the sum of her unexplained and unjustified cash advances, and other credit card debt for Mexican travel spending prior to her Mexican job interviews, on cars, Southern California hotels, and unexplained clothing expenditures is about $58,000. Further, if only the $19,607 in contractor charges are included in her explained expenditures, instead of her uncorroborated claim that she incurred $35,000 for such contractor charges, then her adequately explained expenditures are about $44,000 while her unexplained expenditures would appear to be about $73,000.

Whatever Siegenberg's business-oriented goals, her very substantial credit card charges for consumer goods and cash advances were incurred without any reasonable or foreseeable ability to repay them. I conclude, on balance, that such charges, under the circumstances, are evidence of Siegenberg's bad faith.

4. Excessive or extravagant proposed family budget. Siegenberg's budget appears to be excessive. In Schedules I and J, she claims average monthly income of $2,466.58 and average monthly expenditures of $5,368.60, including $1,824 to support her parents and $560.43 for car payments, as well as $652 in regular business operating expenses. In light of the thousands of dollars Siegenberg charged on her credit cards monthly during 2006, as well as minimal credit card payments she was required to make, the gap between her monthly income and budget appears excessive and is suggestive of a lack of good faith on her part.

5. Statement of income and expenses misrepresenting financial condition. The UST has not alleged any misrepresentation in Siegenberg's statement of financial condition.

6. Eve of bankruptcy purchases. Siegenberg claims that in fact she made an eve of bankruptcy payment rather than purchases, $12,500 toward her mother's surgery, militating in favor of a finding of good faith.

On the other hand, according to her Schedule F, Siegenberg opened at least three of her 11 credit cards in 2006, one in January and two in July. She owes $7,670 on the one opened in January, $10,925 on one opened in July, and $6,522 on the other opened in July. Thus, in under four months of use, Siegenberg became indebted for $17,447 on two cards that she opened within five months of filing. Also, she charged at least $6,759 in September and October 2006, within about two months of her bankruptcy petition. These are instances of eve of bankruptcy purchases that suggest a lack of good faith under the circumstances, regardless of alleged business purpose, given the wide gaps between her earnings and her new credit card debt.

7. Bankruptcy history. Siegenberg does not have a history of bankruptcy petition filing and dismissals.

8. Improper purpose for automatic stay: state litigation. There is no evidence that Siegenberg has invoked the automatic stay for an improper purpose, such as to defeat state court litigation.

9. Egregious behavior. Siegenberg argues that rather than exhibiting egregious behavior, the facts illustrate bad financial luck. She points to the fact that she has had a hard time finding a job in the entertainment industry, though she has spent a lot of money trying; her family's real estate investment flopped; and the interviews for a job selling Mexican time shares turned out to be a waste of time. In the end, she claims that despite her honest efforts to improve her income, she has been unlucky and, thus, is unable to pay off her debts.

Even assuming all of what Siegenberg says is true, those factors do not justify the spending detailed above. In light of her low rate of income over a three-year period preceding bankruptcy, her sizeable consumer-oriented expenditures and unexplained cash

advance debt appear to be egregious under the circumstances, rather than legitimate startup business expenses.

Thus, analysis pursuant to five of nine *Mitchell* factors, factors 2, 3, 4, 6, and 9, supports a finding of a lack of good faith.

B. Dismissal under 707(b)(3)(B): Totality of the Circumstances

Additionally, dismissal would appear to be appropriate under § 707(b)(3)(B), considering the "totality of the circumstances" presented by the evidence. Bankruptcy courts that have addressed § 707(b)(3) since the enactment of BAPCPA have found that the "totality of the circumstances" tests that were applicable under the former § 707(b) remain applicable under BAPCPA. BAPCPA made changes, however, making it easier for the UST to prove a case for abuse because (a) there is no longer a presumption in favor of granting relief to a debtor, and (b) the standard for dismissal is reduced from "substantial abuse" to mere "abuse." The *In re Price* "totality of the circumstances" test includes the following six factors:

1. Whether there is a likelihood of future income to fund debtor's Chapter 11, 12, or 13 plan;
2. Whether the petition was filed as a consequence of illness, disability, unemployment, or other calamity;
3. Whether the schedules suggest debtor obtained cash advances and consumer goods without the ability to repay;
4. Whether debtor's proposed family budget is excessive or extravagant;
5. Whether debtor's papers misrepresent his or her financial condition; and
6. Whether debtor engaged in eve of bankruptcy purchases.

Here, *Price* factors 2, 3, 4, and 6 are unfavorable to Siegenberg, indicating a lack of good faith and supporting a conclusion of abuse under § 707(b)(3)(B).

1. Future income to fund a Chapter 11 or 13 plan. The UST has failed to establish that Siegenberg has a foreseeable likelihood of future income to fund a Chapter 11 or 13.

2. Consequence of illness, disability, unemployment, or calamity. This factor is unfavorable to Siegenberg because she does not present evidence that she herself experienced a grave illness, change in employment status, disability, or any other calamity that might explain the excess of her debt over her income.

3. Cash advances and consumer goods without ability to repay. As discussed above, Siegenberg incurred substantial credit card debt that might be considered business related or which may have been incurred in the attempt to improve her financial situation. However, a large portion of her credit card debt was incurred to acquire consumer goods and services and cash advances whose business purposes remain unexplained. Thus, on balance, this factor weighs against her.

4. Excessive or extravagant family budget. As discussed above, Siegenberg's monthly income is less than half of her monthly spending, which includes $560.43 on cars payments and $1,824 in support of her parents. Considering her high rate of debt accumulation, her budget is excessive and suggestive of a lack of good faith.

5. Misrepresentation of financial condition. The UST has not alleged any misrepresentation in Siegenberg's papers as to her financial condition.

6. Eve of bankruptcy purchases. As discussed above, Siegenberg opened two credit cards in July of 2006. During the four months in which those cards were in use she charged $17,447 on those two cards alone. Further, Siegenberg purchased at least $6,759 on various cards in September and October 2006. These facts are suggestive of a lack of good faith in her bankruptcy filing.

C. Dismissal with a One-Year Bar against Refiling

A bankruptcy court may, for cause, dismiss a bankruptcy case with a bar against later discharge of debt. A finding of bad faith based on egregious behavior can justify dismissal with prejudice. The bankruptcy court should consider the following factors when considering barring later discharge for bad faith:

1. Whether debtor misrepresented facts in her petition, unfairly manipulated the bankruptcy code, or otherwise filed in an inequitable manner;
2. Debtor's filing history;
3. Whether debtor only intended to defeat state court litigation;
4. Whether egregious behavior is present.

Here, while egregious behavior is present, the other three factors are not. There are no allegations of misrepresentation; Siegenberg has no bankruptcy history; and there has been no mention of state court litigation. Under the egregious circumstances outlined, it would appear to be appropriate to bar Siegenberg from refiling a bankruptcy petition for at least one year, as the UST has requested.

Conclusion

Siegenberg has used her credit cards in various efforts to extricate herself and her family from financial difficulties. She also used her credit cards for tens of thousands of dollars in personal expenditures, the purchase of consumer goods and services, and to obtain unexplained cash advances. The record contains significant evidence of these ostensibly excessive expenditures and contains only patchy, incomplete, and unconvincing evidence that most of these expenditures were made to further Siegenberg's business efforts. **I believe it is appropriate to grant the UST's motion to dismiss Siegenberg's Chapter 7 petition, and to impose a one-year bar on future bankruptcy filings by or against Siegenberg.**

Chapter 11: Reorganizations

 LO30-9 Explain the purpose and basic procedure of Chapter 11 reorganizations.

Reorganization Proceeding Sometimes, creditors benefit more from the continuation of a bankrupt debtor's business than from the liquidation of the debtor's property. Chapter 11 of the Bankruptcy Code provides a proceeding whereby, under the supervision of the Bankruptcy Court, the debtor's financial affairs can be reorganized rather than liquidated. Chapter 11 proceedings are available to individuals and to virtually all business enterprises, including individual proprietorships, partnerships, and corporations (except banks, savings and loan associations, insurance companies, commodities brokers, and stockbrokers).

Chapter 11 cases for individuals look much like the Chapter 13 cases, which are discussed later in this chapter, but the amount of debt is usually much larger and is, most commonly, a predominance of nonconsumer debt. The 2005 act created a special subclass of "small business debtors" with less than $2,725,625 in debts and provides special rules for them, including expedited decision making.

Petitions for reorganization proceedings can be filed voluntarily by the debtor or involuntarily by its creditors. Once a petition for a reorganization proceeding is filed and relief is ordered, the court usually appoints (1) a committee of creditors holding unsecured claims and (2) a committee of equity security holders (shareholders). Normally, the debtor becomes the debtor in possession and has the responsibility for running the debtor's business. It is also usually responsible for developing a plan for handling the various claims of creditors and the various interests of persons such as shareholders.

The reorganization plan is essentially a contract between a debtor and its creditors. This contract may involve recapitalizing a debtor corporation and/or giving creditors some equity, or shares, in the corporation in exchange for part or all of the debt owed to them. The plan must (1) divide the creditors into classes; (2) set forth how each creditor will be satisfied; (3) state which claims, or classes of claims, are impaired or adversely affected by the plan; and (4) provide the same treatment to each creditor in a particular class, unless the creditors in that class consent to different treatment.

For example, when Kmart's Chapter 11 reorganization plan was accepted by its creditors and approved by the bankruptcy court in 2003, the plan called for its banks that held secured claims to receive about 40 cents on each dollar they were owed and for the holders of unsecured claims to receive new stock valued at 14.4 percent of their claim.

The Bankruptcy Code provides for an initial 120-day period after the petition is filed during which only the debtor can file a reorganization plan and a 180-day period within which only the debtor may solicit acceptances of the plan from creditors. The bankruptcy court, in its discretion, may extend these periods. The 2005 act limits the debtor's exclusive plan proposal period to 18 months and the exclusive solicitation period to 20 months. After the initial time periods pass, creditors are free to propose plans and seek acceptance of them by other creditors. In some cases, debtors develop what is known as a prepackaged plan, whereby the debtor solicits acceptances of the plan prior to filing for bankruptcy. The 2005 act contains a number of provisions designed to facilitate the use of such plans.

A reorganization plan must be confirmed by the court before it becomes effective. Plans can be confirmed either through the voluntary agreement of creditors or alternatively through what is known as a **cram down**, whereby the court forces dissenting creditors whose claims would be impaired by a proposed plan to accept the plan when the court can find that it is fair and equitable to the class of creditors whose claims are impaired. If the plan is confirmed, the debtor is responsible for carrying it out.

However, until a plan is confirmed, the bankruptcy court has no authority to distribute any portion of the bankruptcy assets to unsecured creditors.

Confirmation through Acceptance by Creditors A court must confirm a plan if the following requirements, among others, are met:

1. Each class of creditors or interests has either accepted the plan or such class is not impaired under the plan.

2. Each impaired class of claimants has either unanimously accepted the plan or will receive or retain under the plan property of a value not less than the holders of the claims would receive or retain if the debtor was liquidated under Chapter 7.

3. All secured creditors have either accepted the plan or their class of creditors is not impaired under the plan.

4. If any class of claims is impaired, then at least one class of impaired claims must have voted to accept the plan. A plan is deemed accepted by a class of creditors if more than one-half the number of creditors who vote to accept the plan represent at least two-thirds of the dollar amount of allowed claims in the class.

5. The plan must be feasible. The court must be able to conclude that confirmation of the plan is not likely to be followed by the liquidation or the need for further financial reorganization of the debtor or any successor to the debtor unless the reorganization is proposed in the plan.

In addition, where the debtor is an individual, the amount of property to be distributed under the plan must not be less than the projected disposable income of the individual to be received during the period for which payments are to be made or five years, whichever is longer. Also, the debtor must have paid all domestic support obligations that became payable after the filing of the petition.

In the case below, *In re Made In Detroit*, the court was unable to conclude that a proposed plan was feasible and therefore declined to confirm it.

Confirmation of a Plan by a Cram Down Where a class of creditors whose claims or interests are impaired does not accept the proposed plan, then the plan has not been accepted, but the court may still confirm the plan under a "cram down" if it concludes that the plan is fair and equitable to the impaired class. A plan is considered to be fair and equitable to an impaired class of *secured creditors* if the reorganization plan (1) allows the class to retain its liens securing the claims (even where the property is transferred to a third person) and each holder of a claim in the class receives deferred cash payments totaling at least the allowed amount of claim, of value of at least the value of the holder's interest in the bankruptcy estate's interest in the property; *or* (2) provides for the sale of any property subject to liens securing such claims free and clear of such liens with the liens to attach to the proceeds of the sale; *or* (3) provides for the realization by the holders of the "indubitable equivalent" of such claims.

A plan is considered to be fair and equitable to *a class of impaired claimants with unsecured claims* if (1) the plan provides that each holder of a claim will receive or retain on account of the claim property of a value equal to the allowed amount of such claim *or* (2) the holder of any claim that is junior to the claims of such class will not receive or retain any property on account of the junior claim or interest.

A plan is considered to be fair and equitable to a *class of interests* (such as equity holders) if (1) the plan provides that each holder of an interest in the class receives or retains property of a value equal to the greatest of the amount of any fixed liquidation preference to which the holder is entitled, any fixed redemption price to which the holder is entitled, or the value of such interest or (2) the holder of any interest that is junior to the interests of such class will not receive any property on account of such junior claim.

In re Made In Detroit   299 B.R. 170 (Bankr. E.D. Mich. 2003)

In 1997, Made In Detroit purchased approximately 410 acres of property for the purpose of development. The property is located on the Detroit River in Gibraltar and Trenton, Michigan, and is Made In Detroit's only significant asset. For the next five years, Made In Detroit attempted to develop the property. Due to problems obtaining permits, and because Made In Detroit was not generating income, it became delinquent to secured creditors. In 2002, the primary secured creditor, Standard Federal, commenced a foreclosure action against Made In Detroit. As a result, on October 23, 2002, Made In Detroit filed for bankruptcy protection under Chapter 11 of the Bankruptcy Code.

On July 15, 2003, Made In Detroit filed its Third Amended Combined Plan and Disclosure Statement (the "Debtor's Plan"). The Debtor's Plan provided that it would be funded with a $9 million loan from Kennedy Funding and that the Kennedy loan was contingent on certain conditions precedent, including the payment of a nonrefundable $270,000 commitment fee and an appraisal of the property that indicated it would have a "quick sale" value of at least $15 million. The Kennedy commitment also provided a condition of its part; namely, that it intended to bring participants into the transaction and if it was unable to do so, it would only be obligated to refund the commitment fee less compensation for its time and expenses. The Debtor's Plan provided that once the $9 million loan was obtained, the secured creditors and administrative claimants would be paid in full, the unsecured creditors would receive an initial distribution of $750,000 (with the balance of the claims to be paid from the sale of lots), and equity shareholders would retain their interest.

The Official Committee of Unsecured Creditors (the Committee) and the Wayne County Treasurer filed objections to confirmation of the Debtor's Plan. In addition, on July 9, 2003, the Committee filed its own plan of reorganization. The Committee's Plan provided that it would be financed by an "as is" immediate cash sale of the property to the Trust for Public Land for $4 million. Under the Plan, the Trust for Public Land would pay $4 million to the Debtor's Estate to settle all claims with respect to the real property and would receive title to the property free of all liens, claims, and other encumbrances. Under the terms of the Committee's Plan, the secured creditors would be paid in full, the unsecured creditors would receive a pro rata payment (after payment of the administrative claims and higher classes of claims), and the equity shareholders would not receive any distribution nor would they retain any property interest.

Made In Detroit objected to the Committee's Plan, and the Bankruptcy Court held a hearing on confirmation of both the Debtor's and the Committee's Plans.

McIvor, Bankruptcy Judge

Debtor's Plan fails to meet the requirement that a plan must be feasible. Feasibility is a mandatory requirement for confirmation. Section 1129(a)(11) of the Bankruptcy Code provides that a plan can be confirmed only if "confirmation of the plan is not likely to be followed by the liquidation, or the need for further organization, of the debtor or any successor to the debtor under the plan, unless such liquidation or reorganization is proposed in the plan."

Section 1129(a)(11) prevents confirmation of visionary schemes which promise creditors more than the debtor can possibly attain after confirmation. A plan that is submitted on a conditional basis is not considered feasible, and thus confirmation of such a plan must be denied.

The plan does not need to guarantee success, but it must present reasonable assurance of success. To provide such reasonable assurance, a plan must provide a realistic and workable framework for reorganization. The plan cannot be based on "visionary promises"; it must be doable.

> Sincerity, honesty and willingness are not sufficient to make the plan feasible, and neither are visionary promises. The test is whether the things which are to be done after confirmation can be done as a practical matter under the facts.

In re Hoffman, 52 B.R. 212, 215 (Bankr. D.N.D. 1985).

In *Hoffman*, the debtor's plan proposed to pay creditors within two years from the sale of real property. However, there was no potential purchaser and the plan did not set forth the terms of the proposed sale. The court found that the plan was not feasible because the proposed sale of the real estate was not "sufficiently concrete to assure either consummation within the two-years, or that even if sold within the two-year period the price obtained would be sufficient" to pay the secured creditor.

Similarly, in *In re Walker,* 165 B.R. 994 (E.D. Va. 1994), the court also found a plan based on funding through a speculative sale of real estate was not feasible. There, the district court reversed the bankruptcy court's confirmation of a plan because the plan was not feasible. The plan proposed to pay creditors from the sale of two parcels of real estate. However, the plan did not provide any time frame within which the properties would be sold, did not set forth the terms of the proposed sale, and did not set forth a plan for the liquidation of other properties if the proceeds from the sale of the two identified properties was insufficient to pay creditors. Based on these deficiencies, the court held that the proposed plan was not feasible.

Likewise, in *In re Thurmon,* 87 B.R. 190 (Bankr. M.D. Fla. 1988), the court found that a plan conditioned on a sale of property which in turn was conditioned on financing was not feasible. In *Thurmon*, the plan proposed that funding would be obtained through a lease-purchase agreement. The lease-purchase agreement provided that a buyer would lease property from the debtor and would then purchase 147 acres from the debtor. The closing of the land sale was conditioned on the buyer's ability to obtain financing on favorable terms. The buyer had not yet applied for the financing but testified that he would do so within 30 days. The court found that the plan was not feasible because it was not reasonably likely that the money to fund the plan would come from the buyer.

While Debtor in this case is sincere, honest, and willing, the Debtor's Plan of Reorganization is not realistic, as it does not provide a reasonable assurance of success. The Plan is based on "wishful thinking" and "visionary promises." As a practical matter, the Debtor's Plan is not sufficiently concrete as to be feasible because it is contingent on exit financing from Kennedy and there is no reasonable assurance that the Kennedy loan will ever close or that the property will be appraised at a value high enough to provide a $9 million loan. Like in *Hoffman*, *Walker*, and *Thurmon*, it is not reasonably likely that Debtor's Plan will be funded. The conditions precedent to Kennedy's funding of the loan were not satisfied as of the date of the confirmation hearing. Further, the evidence did not show that the satisfaction of such conditions was reasonably likely in the foreseeable future.

The $270,000 loan commitment fee was never put into an escrow account or paid to Kennedy Funding. Even if Debtor had paid the commitment fee, there still were substantial obstacles to closing on the proposed Kennedy loan. First and foremost, in order for Kennedy to fund the required $9 million loan, it would need to value the property on an "as is" quick sale basis at $15 million. The evidence did not provide any reasonable assurance that the property would be valued at this amount; in fact, the evidence showed that the property, if sold "as is," was only worth approximately $4.2 million.

The best evidence of the value of the property, what a reasonable buyer would pay a reasonable seller for the property, is the Trust for Public Land's offer to purchase the property "as is" for $4.8 million. Additional evidence that the "as is" value of the property is well below the $15 million value needed to obtain the Kennedy financing was provided by a current appraisal prepared by Integra Realty Resources.

The Integra appraisal report, dated on September 5, 2003, indicates that the "as is" market value of the property, if marketed from nine to twelve months, was $5,260,000. The report also stated the "disposition value" of the property, if only marketed for three to six months, was $4,210,000. The "as is" quick sale value as defined in the Kennedy commitment letter was based on a marketing period of "90 to 120 days," i.e., three to six months. Thus, for Kennedy to fund the $9 million loan proposed in Debtor's Plan, the "disposition value" of the property would have to be at least $15 million. The appraiser who prepared the Integra report, Kenneth Blondell, testified at the confirmation hearing. Blondell is a certified MAI appraiser, and he was qualified as an expert. The Integra report and Blondell's testimony provided a credible expert opinion that the disposition value of the property is only $4.2 million.

In summary, the Debtor failed to show at confirmation that it had exit financing to fund its plan. The proposed financing had so many contingencies that Debtor's Plan was conditional at best. Thus, the Debtor's Plan is not feasible under 1129(a)(11), and the Court must deny confirmation of Debtor's Plan.

The Court denied confirmation of Debtor's Plan.

Use of Chapter 11

Corporate bankruptcies and filings for reorganization often come in cycles with economic conditions, high levels of debt, changes in competition and consumer shopping preferences, and/or efforts to shred product liability, pensions, and collective bargaining agreements as major contributing factors.

During the 1980s, attempts by a number of corporations to seek refuge in Chapter 11 as a means of escaping problems they were facing received considerable public attention. Some of the most visible cases involved efforts to obtain some protection against massive product liability claims and judgments for damages for breach of contract and to escape from collective bargaining agreements. Thus, for example, Johns-Manville Corporation filed under Chapter 11 because of the claims against it arising out of its production and sale of asbestos years earlier, while A. H. Robins Company was concerned about a surfeit of claims arising out of its sale of the Dalkon Shield, an intrauterine birth control device. And, in 1987, Texaco, faced with a $10.3 billion judgment in favor of Pennzoil in a breach of contract action, filed a petition for reorganizational relief under Chapter 11. Companies such as LTV and Allegheny Industries sought changes in retirement and pension plans, and other companies such as Eastern Airlines sought refuge in Chapter 11 while embroiled in labor disputes.

In the 1990s, a number of companies that were the subject of highly leveraged buyouts (LBOs) financed with so-called junk bonds, including a number of retailers, resorted to Chapter 11 to seek restructuring and relief from their creditors. Similarly, companies such as Pan Am and TWA that were hurt by an economic slowdown and increase in fuel prices filed Chapter 11 petitions. In 2001, Enron and Kmart filed for reorganization under Chapter 11 as did WorldCom and USAirways in 2002.

The dramatic economic slowdown in 2008 saw firms like Lehman Brothers Holdings, Washington Mutual, Indy Mac Bancorp, Financial Corp. of America, and Thornburg Mortgage as well as automobile giants General Motors and Chrysler seek bankruptcy protection. In 2017, Westinghouse Electric filed for Chapter 11 as its nuclear business continued to decline.

In recent years, with the increased popularity of shopping online and other changes in consumer shopping preferences, iconic brands like Toys R Us filed for bankruptcy in 2017 and subsequently closed all of its stores. In 2018, Sears Holding, which owns both Sears and Kmart, filed for bankruptcy, seeking a reorganization, as did J. Crew in 2020.

Between 2004 and January 2020, 24 Catholic dioceses and religious orders sought bankruptcy protection during the sexual abuse crisis in the Catholic Church; and in 2020, the Boy Scouts of America filed for bankruptcy protection at a time when the organization faced hundreds of sexual abuse lawsuits. In 2019, Pacific Gas and Electric Company (PG&E) filed for bankruptcy protection at a time when it was facing billions of dollars in claims arising out of its alleged negligence that resulted in or contributed to massive forest fires in California.

Chapter 11 has been the subject of significant criticism and calls for its revision. Critics point out that many of the Chapter 11 cases are permitted to drag on for years, thus depleting the assets of the debtor through payments to trustees and lawyers involved in administration and diminishing the assets available to creditors. For example, *The Wall Street Journal* noted in a July 11, 2003, article, "The Chapter 11 restructuring of Enron, whose controversial collapse became a symbol of corporate malfeasance, has dragged on for 19 months, generating more than 11,000 court filings and nearly $500 million in professional fees." This took the case to the point where the company was about to file its proposed reorganization plan and seek acceptance from creditors and approval by the bankruptcy court.

In the 2005 act, Congress responded to some of these concerns by establishing tighter time frames and placing some limits or restrictions on the availability of extensions of time. Examples include the limitations on the time period in which the debtor has the exclusive right to develop a reorganization plan and special rules forcing debtors to make decisions as to whether to assume or reject unexpired leases of nonresidential property such as space in shopping centers and office buildings.

Special Rules for Nonresidential Real Property Lessors Under the pre-2005 act, courts were allowed to grant, and often granted, repeated extensions of the 60-day period that debtors in Chapter 11 proceedings have to either assume or reject unexpired leases of nonresidential real property. Under the 2005 revisions, debtors must assume or reject unexpired leases of nonresidential real property by the earlier of 120 days from the date the petition is filed or the date a plan is confirmed. Failure to do so in a timely way results in the lease being deemed rejected. Courts are permitted to extend the time for an additional 90 days on a showing of good cause, but any further extensions can be granted only if the lessor consents in writing. These provisions help protect landlords who have leased property to individuals or entities that subsequently filed for bankruptcy protection. They require the bankrupt to decide relatively quickly whether they will go forward with the lease and fulfill their obligation or whether they will surrender the property to the landlord so he can secure a new paying tenant.

Ethics and Compliance in Action

Using Bankruptcy to Manage Product Liability or to Change Labor Contracts

As noted above, a number of corporations have resorted to Chapter 11 to deal with their exposure to product liability claims or to seek changes in labor contracts. Is it ethical for a company like A. H. Robins Company that is faced with significant liability for birth-control devices it made and sold or for a company like Johns-Manville that faces multimillion-dollar claims from individuals who were exposed to asbestos it made to seek the protection accorded by the bankruptcy laws? Similarly, is it ethical for a company that believes it is hampered by a labor contract under which it incurs higher costs than some of its competitors to try to use a Chapter 11 proceeding to get out of the labor contract?

Collective Bargaining Agreements Collective bargaining contracts pose special problems. Prior to the 1984 amendments, there was concern that some companies would use Chapter 11 reorganizations as a vehicle to avoid executed collective bargaining agreements. The concern was heightened by the Supreme Court's 1984 decision in *NLRB v. Bildisco and Bildisco*. In that case, the Supreme Court held that a reorganizing debtor did not have to engage in collective bargaining before modifying or rejecting portions of a collective bargaining agreement and that such unilateral alterations by a debtor did not violate the National Labor Relations Act.

Congress then acted to try to prevent the misuse of bankruptcy proceedings for collective bargaining purposes. The act's 1984 amendments adopted a rigorous multistep process that must be complied with in determining whether a labor contract can be rejected or modified as part of a reorganization. Among other things that must be done before a debtor or trustee can seek to avoid a collective bargaining agreement is the submission of a proposal to the employees' representative that details the "necessary" modifications to the collective bargaining agreement and ensures that "all creditors, the debtor and all affected parties are fairly treated." Then, before the bankruptcy court can authorize a rejection of the original collective bargaining agreement, it must review the proposal and find that (1) the employees' representative refused to accept it without good cause and (2) the balance of equities clearly favors the rejection of the original collective bargaining agreement.

Pension plans are usually terminated in corporate reorganizations and always terminated in liquidation. At that point, a federal agency, the Pension Benefit Guaranty Corporation (PBGC), takes over the pension benefits. Operations of the PBGC, which currently guarantees basic pension benefits of some 44 million workers and retirees in over 29,000 defined benefit pension plans, are financed largely by insurance premiums paid by companies that sponsor pension plans and investment returns. There is a maximum annual payment, which rises with inflation, and employees with the largest pensions can receive less than they had expected under the employer's plan.

Small Business Reorganization Act of 2019 Chapter 11 is designed to allow businesses that are in financial difficulty because of the amount of debt they are carrying to restructure their finances so they can remain in business and not have to liquidate. At the same time, Chapter 11 provides creditors the opportunity to maximize their return and realize more than they would if the debtor liquidated. However, as noted earlier in this chapter, Chapter 11 bankruptcy can be complicated, time-consuming, and expensive. It also provides creditors with strong leverage against the debtor because the debtor, in order to have its proposed reorganization plan approved, must obtain the approval of classes of creditors whose interests are impaired.

Consequently, Chapter 11 has not provided a viable option for many small businesses and their owners. This has been problematic because the overwhelming percentage of businesses in the country are small businesses and close to half of the entire workforce is employed by them.

Responding to this situation, Congress passed the Small Business Reorganization Act of 2019, which became effective on February 19, 2020. The act establishes a new subchapter of Chapter 11, known as Subchapter V, to address the difficulties faced by small businesses and make reorganization more of a possibility. This timing may prove to be particularly fortuitous because of the devasting effect the Covid-19 pandemic is having on many small businesses who were forced to suspend their operation or to try to do business with restrictions that dramatically restricted the number of customers that could be served at any time.

The most significant features of Subchapter V include:

- It is available, on an opt-in basis, to companies and individuals who have no more than $2,725,625 of aggregate noncontingent liquidated and secured debt and whose debts, with a few exceptions, arose primarily from commercial or business activities. Subsequently, Congress temporarily raised the debt limit to $7.5M to help businesses deal with Covid-19-related downturns in their business.
- Only the debtor may file a plan, which generally must be filed within 90 days after the petition in bankruptcy is filed. Creditors may not file plans.
- A trustee with limited powers and duties is appointed. The role of the trustee is to facilitate the development of a plan and, in some cases, to make distributions under the plan.
- Generally, no committee of unsecured creditors is appointed.
- Normally, the debtor will remain as a "debtor in possession" to continue running the business while the matter is proceeding. The court, for cause, can order a different arrangement.
- The act modifies the "cram down" rules relative to unsecured creditors that are applicable in a regular Chapter 11 case by requiring that all of the disposable income of the debtor (called "net operating income") to be received in a period between three and five years must be applied to payments under the plan or the value of any property to be distributed must not be less than the projected disposable income.

Subchapter V of Chapter 11 also allows certain individual debtors to use its procedures rather than using Chapter 13. Subchapter V's features that may help individuals compared to proceeding under Chapter 13 (which is discussed later in this chapter) include:

- Less stringent debt limitations as only individual debtors with unsecured debts of less than $419,275 are eligible to file under Chapter 13. Thus, business owners with unsecured debts larger than that can file to reorganize as long as they are within the considerably higher Subchapter V limitations.
- The ability to repay debt over a longer period of time than is permissible under Chapter 13.
- The ability to obtain a discharge before the completion of plan payments.
- The ability to modify certain residential mortgages, provided that the loan was not used to acquire the residence and was used primarily in connection with the business.

Chapter 12: Family Farmers and Fishermen

Relief for Family Farmers and Fishermen

Historically, farmers have been accorded special treatment in the Bankruptcy Code. In the 1978 act, as in earlier versions, small farmers were exempted from involuntary proceedings. Thus, a small farmer who filed a voluntary Chapter 11 or 13 petition would not have the proceeding converted into a Chapter 7 liquidation over his objection so long as he complied with the code's requirements in a timely fashion. Additional protection was also accorded through the provision allowing states to opt out of the federal exemption scheme and to provide their own exemptions. A number of states used this flexibility to provide generous exemptions for farmers so they would be able to keep their tools and implements.

Despite these provisions, the serious stress on the agricultural sector in the mid-1980s led Congress in 1986 to further amend the Bankruptcy Code by adding a new Chapter 12 targeted to the financial problems of the family farm. During the 1970s and 1980s, farmland prices appreciated, and many farmers borrowed heavily to expand their productive capacity, thus creating a large debt load in the agricultural sector. When land values subsequently dropped and excess production in the world kept farm product prices low, many farmers faced extreme financial difficulty. In the 2005 act, Chapter 12 proceedings were made available to family fishermen.

Chapter 12 is modeled after Chapter 13, which is discussed next. It is available only for family farmers and fishermen with regular income. To qualify, a farmer and spouse must have not less than 80 percent of their total noncontingent, liquidated debts arising out of their farming operations. The aggregate debt must be less than $2,044,225, and at least 50 percent of an individual's or couple's income during the year preceding the filing of the petition must have come from the farming operation and at least 80 percent of the assets must be related to the farming operation. A corporation or partnership can also qualify, provided that more than 50 percent of the stock or equity is held by one family or its relatives and they conduct the farming operation. Again, 80 percent of the debt must arise from the farming operation; the aggregate debt ceiling is $10,000,000.

In the case of a family fisherman, the debtor and spouse engaged in a commercial fishing operation are eligible for relief under Chapter 12 if their aggregate debts do not exceed $2,044,225 and if not less than 80 percent of their aggregate noncontingent liquidated debts (excluding a debt for their principal residence) arise out of the commercial fishing operation. Again, a corporation or partnership can qualify so long as at least 50 percent is held by the family and relatives that conduct the fishing operation, its aggregate debts do not exceed $2,044,225, and at least 80 percent of the aggregate noncontingent liquidated debts arise out of a commercial fishing operation.

The debtor is usually permitted to remain in possession to operate the farm or fishing vessel. Although the debtor in possession has many of the rights of a Chapter 11 trustee, a trustee is appointed under Chapter 12, and the debtor is subject to his supervision. The trustee is permitted to sell unnecessary assets, including farmland and farming or fishing equipment, without the consent of secured creditors and before a plan is approved. However, the secured creditor's interest attaches to the proceeds of the sale.

The debtor is required to file a plan within 90 days of the filing of the Chapter 12 petition—although the bankruptcy court has the discretion to extend the time. A hearing is held on the proposed plan, and it can be confirmed over the objection of creditors. The debtor may release to any secured party the collateral that secures the claim to obtain confirmation without the acceptance by that creditor.

Unsecured creditors are required to receive at least liquidation value under the Chapter 12 plan. If an unsecured creditor or the trustee objects to the plan, the court may still confirm the plan despite the objection so long as it calls for full payment of the unsecured creditor's claim or it provides that the debtor's disposable income for the duration of the plan is applied to making payments on it. A debtor who fulfills his plan, or is excused from full performance because of subsequent hardship, is entitled to a discharge.

The Global Business Environment

Transnational Insolvency Proceedings

As the volume of international trade and the number of multinational corporations have grown, there has been a concomitant increase in transnational insolvency cases. When a company engaged in international business transactions becomes insolvent, commonly some kind of insolvency proceeding will be initiated in each country where the company does business. Different laws and different national interests can produce a challenging—if not difficult—situation for creditors of the insolvent enterprise. Where and how should the creditor go about protecting its interests? Should it seek to have its claim allowed in any one— or more—of the various proceedings? What rights will it be accorded in those proceedings, particularly the foreign forums?

Historically, two different approaches have been used to deal with transnational insolvencies. The first uses the principle of "territoriality," where each country takes control of the enterprise's assets within that country and administers them according to the law of that country, giving little attention to what may be happening in other forums or to foreign interests. A second approach, often referred to as "universalism," seeks a cooperative or coordinated approach to transnational insolvency. This might be achieved through the identification of a single forum or proceeding where all assets of a company would be administered and all claims and interests addressed. Another variant of this approach is to identify a primary proceeding that has

the lead in conjunction with a number of coordinated ancillary proceedings in other countries.

In an effort to encourage cooperation among countries and to try to harmonize the competing and conflicting schemes, the United Nations Commission on International Trade Law has adopted a Model Law on Cross-Border Insolvency. On a regional level, the European Union has adopted a "Convention on Insolvency Proceedings" to coordinate and harmonize such proceedings in EU countries. And the American Law Institute has a Transnational Insolvency Project to develop principles of cooperation in transnational insolvency cases among the members (United States, Canada, and Mexico) of the North American Free Trade Agreement (NAFTA).*

The 2005 Bankruptcy Act creates a new chapter of the Bankruptcy Code to deal with cross-border cases. The new sections incorporate the Model Code of Cross-Border Insolvency. The new chapter expands the scope of U.S. bankruptcy law and provides an explicit statutory mechanism for dealing with cross-border insolvency and for the U.S. courts, trustees, and debtors to cooperate with their foreign counterparts. It provides a framework for common cross-border situations such as providing access for foreign creditors to domestic cases and for the coordination of simultaneous domestic and foreign proceedings for the same debtor so that the relief afforded in different jurisdictions is consistent.

*In July 2020, NAFTA was replaced by the United States-Mexico-Canada Agreement which reflected some changes to the prior trade agreement.

Chapter 13: Consumer Debt Adjustments

LO30-10 Explain the purpose and basic procedure of Chapter 13 consumer debt adjustments.

Relief for Individuals Chapter 13 of the Bankruptcy Code, titled Adjustments of Debts for Individuals, gives individuals who want to avoid the stigma of a Chapter 7 bankruptcy an opportunity to pay their debts in installments under the protection of a federal court. Under Chapter 13, the debtor has this opportunity free of such problems as garnishments and attachments of her property by creditors. Only individuals with regular incomes (including sole proprietors of businesses) who owe individually (or with their spouse) liquidated, unsecured debts of less than $419,275 and secured debts of less than $1,257,850 are eligible to file under Chapter 13.

Procedure Chapter 13 proceedings are initiated only by the voluntary petition of a debtor filed in the Bankruptcy

Court. Creditors of the debtor may not file an involuntary petition for a Chapter 13 proceeding. Commonly, the debtor files at the same time a list of his creditors as well as a list of his assets, liabilities, and executory contracts. The court then appoints a trustee.

Following the filing of the petition, the trustee calls a meeting of creditors, at which time proofs of claims are received and allowed or disallowed. The debtor is examined, and she submits a plan of payment. If the court is satisfied that the plan is proposed in good faith, meets the legal requirements, and is in the interest of the creditors, the court approves the plan.

If the debtor's income is above the state median income for a family of the size of his family, then the plan must provide for payments over a period of five years unless all claims will be fully paid in a shorter period. In the case of a debtor whose income is less than the median income of the applicable state, the plan may not provide for payments over a period that is longer than three years unless the court, for cause, approves a longer period, which in no case can be more than five years.

The plan must provide that all of the debtor's disposable income during the applicable commitment period will be applied to make payments to unsecured creditors under the plan. Unsecured creditors must receive at least what they would receive under Chapter 7. All priority claims must be paid in full.

No plan may be approved if the trustee or an unsecured creditor objects, unless the plan provides for the objecting creditor to be paid the present value of what he is owed or provides for the debtor to commit all of his projected disposable income for the applicable period to pay his creditors.

In the case below, *In re Burt*, the court agreed with an objection raised by a creditor to confirmation of a proposed Chapter 13 plan that would cram down the creditor's secured interest.

A Chapter 13 debtor must begin making the installment payments proposed in her plan within 30 days after the plan is filed. The interim payments must continue to be made until the plan is confirmed or denied. If the plan is denied, the money, less any administrative expenses, is returned to the debtor by the trustee. The interim payments give the trustee an opportunity to observe the debtor's performance and thus to be in a better position to make a recommendation about whether the plan should be approved.

Once approved, a plan may be subsequently modified on petition of a debtor or a creditor where there is a material change in the debtor's circumstances.

In re Burt   378 B.R. 352 (Bankr. D. Utah 2007)

On December 31, 2005, Darin Burt purchased a 2006 Ford F-150, a pickup truck for his personal use, from LaPoint Automotive LLC. LaPoint financed the transaction through a Utah Simple Interest Retail Installment Contract. Under the contract, LaPoint retained a purchase money security interest (PMSI) in the truck. LaPoint later assigned its interest in the truck to Ford Motor Credit, which perfected its security interest by notation on the truck's title as required by the Utah Motor Vehicle Act.

The contract indicated that the cash price of the truck was $32,630 and the total amount financed was $45,628.14. The difference between the two amounts included charges of $2,425 for a service contract, $500 for gap insurance, $298 for document preparation fee, $1,149.46 for tax and license fees, and $11,021.68 to pay off the obligation owed on a trade-in vehicle (2004 Ford F-150). The negative equity rolled into the transaction, therefore, was the $11,021.68 payoff less Burt's down payment of $1,800 and the manufacturer's rebate of $3,000, yielding a net negative equity of $6,221. Because of Burt's marginal credit, he was required to trade in his 2004 Ford F-150 in order to qualify for financing on the new vehicle. The dealer would not have financed the purchase had Burt not agreed to all the terms of the contract, including the refinancing of negative equity.

On July 13, 2007, Burt filed a petition under Chapter 13. On August 30, 2007, Ford Motor Credit filed a proof of secured claim for its security interest in the truck in the amount of $42,941.64. Burt filed his Chapter 13 plan on July 25, 2007, which proposed to bifurcate Ford Motor Credit's claim into a secured portion in the amount of $28,000 and an unsecured portion in the amount of the negative equity paid off by the financing transaction. Ford Motor Credit objected to confirmation of the debtor's plan, arguing that its entire claim qualified for treatment as a secured claim and could not be bifurcated.

Thurman, U.S. Bankruptcy Judge

In order to obtain confirmation of a Chapter 13 plan, the debtor must comply with provisions of 11 U.S.C. § 1325(a). Prior to the enactment of the Bankruptcy Abuse Prevention and Consumer Protection Act of 2005 (BAPCPA), sections 506(a)(1) and 1325(a)(5)(B) allowed a Chapter 13 debtor to bifurcate an under-secured creditor's claim into secured and unsecured portions, with the result that a creditor's claim was allowed as secured only to the extent of the value of the collateral securing its debt. The portion of the creditor's claim allowed as secured would be paid in full with interest, whereas the unsecured portion of the claim would be paid pro-rata with all other general unsecured claims. This process of bifurcation is often referred to as "cram-down." BAPCPA, however, amended § 1325 to give special protection to creditors who finance automobile transactions that occur within 910 days prior to the debtors' filing for Chapter 13 relief.

Under BAPCPA, Congress added the "hanging paragraph" after § 1325(a)(9), which prevents the bifurcation of certain secured claims. It is commonly referred to as the "hanging paragraph" because it follows the numbered subsections of § 1325(a) but has no numerical designation of its own. Specifically, the hanging paragraph states:

For purposes of paragraph (5), section 506 shall not apply to a claim described in that paragraph if the creditor has a purchase money security interest securing the debt that is the subject of the claim, the debt was incurred within the 910-day [sic] preceding the date of the filing of the petition, and the collateral for that debt consists of a motor vehicle acquired for the personal use of the debtor, or if collateral for that debt consists of any other thing of value, if the debt was incurred during the 1-year period preceding that filing.

Thus, in order to avoid a cram-down, four conditions must be satisfied: (1) the creditor has a purchase money security interest (PMSI); (2) the debt was incurred within 910 days preceding the filing of the petition; (3) the collateral for the debt is a motor vehicle; and (4) the motor vehicle was acquired for the personal use of the debtor. If these requirements are satisfied, "then the creditor's claim is deemed fully secured" and cannot be bifurcated. The parties do not dispute that the collateral in this case was a motor vehicle, purchased within 910 days of the debtor's petition, or that it was acquired for personal use. The only requirement that is in dispute is whether Ford Motor Credit's debt is secured by a purchase money security interest. To determine this issue, the Court must first decide whether the negative equity from the trade-in vehicle that was rolled into the financing for the truck as well as the other costs associated with the purchase constitute a purchase money security interest as defined under Utah law.

In order to address the effect of the hanging paragraph, the Court must first determine the extent to which Ford Motor Credit's security interest is a purchase money security interest. The term "purchase money security interest," as used in the hanging paragraph, is not defined in the Bankruptcy Code. Therefore, courts uniformly refer to state law, and specifically to the state's version of the Uniform Commercial Code (UCC), to determine whether a creditor holds a purchase money security interest. The applicable statute in Utah is the Utah Code Annotated § 9a-103(2), which provides that "[a] security interest in goods is a purchase-money security interest . . . to the extent that the goods are a purchase-money collateral with respect to that security interest. . . ." "Purchase-money collateral" is defined as "goods . . . that secures [sic] a purchase-money obligation incurred with respect to that collateral," and "purchase-money obligation" is defined as "an obligation of an obligor incurred as all or part of the *price of the collateral* or for *value given to enable* the debtor to acquire rights in or the use of the collateral if the value is in fact so used."

Whether a PMSI exists in this case, then, "turns on whether the negative equity on the debtor's trade-in vehicle constitutes 'part of the price of the collateral,' *i.e.*, part of the price of the new vehicle, or whether it constitutes 'value given to enable the debtor to acquire rights in or the use of the collateral. . . .'" Although § 9a-103 does not define the terms "price" or "value given," Comment 3 to § 9a-103 states that "the 'price' of collateral or the 'value given to enable' includes obligations for expenses incurred in connection with acquiring rights in the collateral, sales, taxes, duties, finance charges, interest freight charges, costs of storage in transit, demurrage, administrative charges, expenses of collection and enforcement, attorney's fees, and other similar obligations."

The Court believes that this list is not exhaustive and the expenses identified in Comment 3 are merely examples or additional components of the "price of the collateral" or of "value given" by the debtor. Therefore, this Court cannot see how the refinancing of negative equity and the other transaction costs incurred in connection with the purchase of the debtor's new truck could not qualify as an "expense" within the meaning of Comment 3.

The debtor and the dealer in this case agreed that as part of the purchase of the truck and pursuant to the retail installment contract, the dealer would advance funds to payoff the lien on the debtor's trade-in vehicle and to cover tax, license, and document preparation fees. Essentially, this was a package deal. Ford Motor Credit later stepped into the purchase-money lender shoes of the dealer. The Court concludes that the agreement and the dealings between the debtor and the dealer/creditor demonstrate that the costs of satisfying these outstanding obligations of the debtor were clearly incurred in connection with the purchase of the new vehicle.

Additionally, Comment 3 states that "[t]he concept of 'purchase money security interest' requires a close nexus between the acquisition of the collateral and the secured obligation." The Court finds that in the present case, there is a very close connection between the negative equity and the financing of the debtor's new vehicle. As noted earlier, the financing transaction was a package deal where the negative equity in the trade-in was paid off by the dealer as part of its retail installment sale of the new vehicle and the related obligation was included in the Contract with the Debtor. All of the amounts financed in the contract, except the gap insurance and service contract, were directly connected to the Debtor's purchase of the new vehicle. In fact, the evidence before this Court shows that Ford Motor Credit would not have financed the total purchase price had the Debtor not agreed to all of the terms of the Contract including the negative equity and the add-on transaction costs. The Court, therefore, concludes that because of this close nexus between the negative equity and the financing of the Debtor's new vehicle, the entire transaction qualifies as a purchase money security interest.

Accordingly, Ford Motor Credit's entire claim including that portion of the claim attributable to the payoff of negative equity on the Debtor's trade-in vehicle and the other transaction costs, should be allowed as a fully secured claim that must be paid in full through the Debtor's Chapter 13 plan.

[Author's note—There is a significant split of authority concerning the issue in this case, and other courts have reached a different conclusion, allowing the claim to be bifurcated. *See, e.g., In re* Penrod, 392 B.R. 835 (9th Cir. BAP 2008) (negative equity not purchase money debt).]

Comparison of Major Forms of Bankruptcy Proceedings

Purpose	Chapter 7 Liquidation	Chapter 11 Reorganization	Chapter 12 Adjustments of Debts	Chapter 13 Adjustments of Debts
Eligible Debtors	Individuals, partnerships, and corporations *except* municipal corporations, railroads, insurance companies, banks, and savings and loan associations. Farmers and ranchers are eligible only if they petition voluntarily.	Generally, same as Chapter 7, except a railroad may be a debtor, and a stockbroker and commodity broker may not be a debtor under Chapter 11.	Family farmer with regular income, at least 50 percent of which comes from farming, and less than $10,000,000 in debts, at least 80 percent of which is farm related. Family fishermen with regular income whose aggregate debts do not exceed $2,044,275, at least 80 percent of which arose out of the fishing operation.	Individual with regular income with liquidated unsecured debts less than $419,275 and secured debts of less than $1,257,850.
Initiation of Proceeding	Petition by debtor (voluntary). Petition by creditors (involuntary).	Petition by debtor (voluntary). Petition by creditors (involuntary).	Petition by debtor.	Petition by debtor.
Basic Procedure	1. Appointment of trustee. 2. Debtor retains exempt property. 3. Nonexempt property is sold and proceeds distributed based on priority of claims. 4. Dischargeable debts are terminated.	1. Appointment of committees of creditors and equity security holders. 2. Debtor submits reorganization plan. 3. If plan is approved and implemented, debts are discharged.	1. Trustee is appointed, but debtor usually remains in possession. 2. Debtor submits a plan in which unsecured creditors must receive at least liquidation value. 3. If plan is approved and fulfilled, debtor is entitled to a discharge.	1. Trustee is appointed, but debtor usually remains in possession. 2. Debtor submits a plan in which unsecured creditors must receive at least liquidation value. 3. If plan is approved and fulfilled, debts covered by plan are discharged.
Advantages	After liquidation and distribution of assets, most or all debts may be discharged and debtor gets a fresh start.	Debtor remains in business and debts are liquidated through implementation of approved reorganization plan.	Debtor generally remains in possession and has opportunity to work out of financial difficulty over period of time (usually three years) through implementation of approved plan.	Debtor has opportunity to work out of financial difficulty over period of time (usually three to five years) through implementation of approved plan.

LO30-11 Compare the major types of bankruptcy proceedings.

Suppose Curtis Brown has a monthly take-home pay of $1,800 and a few assets. He owes $2,800 to the credit union, borrowed for the purchase of furniture; he is supposed to repay the credit union $150 per month. He owes $3,600 to the finance company on the purchase of a used car; he is supposed to repay the company $180 a month. He has also run up charges of $2,400 on a MasterCard account, primarily for emergency repairs to his car; he must pay $120 per month to MasterCard. His rent is $750 per month, and food and other living expenses run him another $675 per month.

Curtis was laid off from his job for a month and fell behind on his payments to his creditors. He then filed a Chapter 13 petition. In his plan, he might, for example, offer to repay the credit union $100 a month, the finance company $120 a month, and MasterCard $80 a month—with the payments spread over three years rather than the shorter time for which they are currently scheduled.

Discharge   As soon as practicable after the completion by the debtor of all payments under the plan, the court is required to grant the debtor a discharge of all debts provided for by the plan (or specifically disallowed) except:

- Debts covered by a waiver of discharge executed by the debtor and approved by the court;
- Debts that are for taxes required to be collected or paid and for which the debtor is liable;
- Certain debts that are not dischargeable under Chapter 7 such as those that result from liabilities for obtaining money by false pretenses or false representations (see page 30-16 for a more complete list);
- Debts for restitution or a criminal fine included in a sentence on the debtor's conviction of a crime; or
- Debts for restitution or damages awarded in a civil action against the debtor as a result of willful or malicious injury by the debtor that caused personal injury to an individual or the death of an individual.

A debtor who is subject to a judicial or administrative order, or, by statute, to pay a domestic support obligation, must, in addition to making the payments pursuant to his plan, certify that all amounts under the order or statute have been paid up to the date of certification in order to be entitled to a discharge.

As is the situation under Chapter 7, the court is also prohibited from granting a discharge where there is reason to believe there is a pending proceeding in which the debtor may be found guilty of a violation of the federal securities laws or is liable for a debt based on the violation of those laws.

Repeat Bankruptcies   The 2005 act prohibits a court from granting a discharge of the debts provided for in the plan (or disallowed) if the debtor received a discharge in a case filed under Chapter 7, 11, or 12 of the Bankruptcy Code in the four-year period preceding the date of the order for relief under Chapter 13—or in a case filed under Chapter 13 during the two-year period preceding the date of the order of relief in the current case.

Advantages of Chapter 13   A debtor may choose to file under Chapter 13 to avoid the stigma of bankruptcy or to retain more of his property than is exempt from bankruptcy under state or federal law. Nonexempt property would have to be surrendered to the trustee in a Chapter 7 liquidation proceeding. Chapter 13 can provide some financial discipline to a debtor as well as an opportunity to get his financial affairs back in good shape. It also gives him relief from the pressures of individual creditors so long as he makes the payments called for by the plan. The debtor's creditors may benefit by recovering a greater percentage of the debt owed to them than would be obtainable in straight bankruptcy.

Problems and Problem Cases

1. Gilbert and Kimberly Barnes filed a voluntary Chapter 7 petition in the U.S. Bankruptcy Court for the District of Maryland. Subsequently, they moved to avoid a non-purchase money lien held by ITT Financial Services on their exempt "household goods." Among the goods that the Barneses were claiming as "household goods" were a digital video disk (DVD) player, a 12-gauge pump shotgun, a 20-gauge shotgun, a 30-06 rifle, and a 22 pistol. ITT contended that the DVD player and the firearms were not household goods that could be exempt. Under Maryland law, household goods are items of personal property necessary for the day-to-day existence of people in the context of their homes. Should the court consider the DVD player and firearms to be "household goods"?

2. In 2008, Virgil Hurd was kicked out of his home by his ex-wife. At that time, he moved into his horse trailer (the "Trailer") to keep warm. The Trailer is 20 feet long and 6 feet wide. Virgil gets electricity for the Trailer from a socket and water from a barrel with a pump. He receives his mail at the land where the Trailer is parked. Since January 2010, Virgil spends approximately 70 percent of his time at his girlfriend's house. In addition to using the Trailer as a place to sleep, Virgil also uses it for transporting his horses and his girlfriend's horses. In April 2010, he filed a voluntary petition for relief under Chapter 7 in the U.S. Bankruptcy Court for the Western District of Missouri. In his schedule of exemptions, he

listed the entire $3,000 value of the Trailer as exempt under a Missouri statute, which exempts any *mobile home* used as the principal residence that does not exceed $5,000 in value. The term "mobile home" is not defined in that statute. The Chapter 7 trustee objects to Virgil's claim of a Missouri exemption in a horse trailer used as his living quarters. The trustee contends that the Trailer was not Virgil's principal residence during the 6- to 12-month period before filing his bankruptcy petition, and that the Trailer does not qualify as a "mobile home" under the Missouri statute. Should the Trailer be exempt from the bankruptcy estate?

3. William Kranich Jr. was the sole shareholder in the DuVal Finance Corporation (DFC). On November 10, Kranich filed a voluntary petition for relief under Chapter 7; on the following January 6, DFC also filed a voluntary petition under Chapter 7. Prior to the commencement of the Chapter 7 proceedings, Kranich conveyed his personal residence in Clearwater, Florida, to DFC. The transfer was wholly without consideration. Shortly thereafter, DFC transferred the property to William Kranich III and June Elizabeth Kranich, Kranich's son and daughter, as tenants in common. This transfer was also without consideration. The bankruptcy trustee brought suit to recover the property from the son and daughter on the grounds that the transfer was fraudulent. Could the trustee recover the property on the grounds that its transfer, without consideration, was fraudulent?

4. David Hott was a college graduate with a degree in business administration who was employed as an insurance agent. He and his wife graduated from college in 1996. At the time he graduated, Hott had outstanding student loans of $14,500, for which he was given a grace period before he had to repay them. Hott became unemployed. Bills began to accumulate, and a number of his outstanding bills were near the credit limits on his accounts. About that time, he received a promotional brochure by mail from Signal Consumer Discount Company, offering the opportunity to borrow several thousand dollars. The Hotts decided it appeared to be an attractive vehicle for them to use to consolidate their debts. Hott went to the Signal office and filled out a credit application. He did not list the student loan as a current debt. He later claimed that someone in the office told him he didn't have to list it if he owned an automobile, but there was significant doubt about the credibility of this claim. Had he listed it, he would not have met the debt–income ratio required by Signal, and it would not have made the loan.

As it was, Signal agreed to make the loan on the condition Hott pay off a car debt in order to reduce his debt–income ratio, and Hott agreed to do so. On March 30, 1997, Signal loaned the Hotts $3,458.01. On June 24, 1998, the Hotts filed for bankruptcy. Signal objected to discharge of the balance remaining on its loan on the ground it had been obtained through the use of a materially false financial statement. Was discharge of the debt barred on the ground it had been obtained through the use of a materially false financial statement?

5. Brian Scholz was involved in an automobile collision with a person insured by Travelers Insurance Company. At the time, Scholz was cited for, and pled no contest to, a criminal charge of driving under the influence of alcohol arising out of the accident. Travelers paid its insured $4,303.68 and was subrogated to the rights of its insured against Scholz. Subsequently, Travelers filed a civil action against Scholz to recover the amount it had paid, and a default judgment was entered against Scholz. Eleven months later, Scholz sought relief from the bankruptcy court by filing a voluntary petition under Chapter 7. One of the questions in the bankruptcy proceeding was whether the debt owing to Travelers was nondischargeable. Is the debt dischargeable?

6. Susan Krieger was 53 years old and lived with her mother, age 75, in a rural community where few jobs were available. Between mother and daughter, they had only a few hundred dollars a month from various government programs to live on. She was too poor to move in search of better employment prospects elsewhere, and her car, which was more than a decade old, needed repairs. She had no Internet access, which along with the lack of transportation hampered her search for work.

Krieger had not held a job since 1986, when she left the workforce to raise a family. She had not earned more than $12,000 a year in her working career between 1978 and 1986. In 1999, Krieger received an associate of arts degree in business accounting from St. Charles Community College. In 2000, she enrolled in Webster University in Webster Groves, Missouri, where she earned a paralegal certificate and graduated with a bachelor of arts in legal studies. She had a high GPA and received significant recognition for her academic achievements. Over the next decade, she applied for about 200 jobs but was unsuccessful in obtaining any of them.

In obtaining her education, Krieger had accumulated $17,000 in student loans, which, through years of nonpayment, had grown to $25,000. Faced with a situation with no job prospects, Krieger filed a petition for bankruptcy seeking a discharge, including discharge of the student loans that were her largest obligation. The Educational Credit Management Corporation, which acts on behalf of some federal loan guarantors, asked the bankruptcy judge to exempt her student loans from the discharge, citing a provision of the bankruptcy code that excludes educational loans "unless exempting such debt from discharge would impose an undue hardship on the debtor."

The bankruptcy judge concluded that she had satisfied the standard for obtaining a discharge of her educational loans, noting her thorough effort to find a job and her good faith in using a substantial portion of a divorce settlement to pay off as much of the educational loan as she could. The district court judge reversed and held that educational debt could not be discharged. The judge thought Krieger should have searched harder for work, especially in later years (when she conceded her applications had tapered off in light of the failure of the many earlier applications). And the judge thought that Krieger had failed the good-faith standard because she had not enrolled in a program that would have offered her a 25-year repayment schedule. Even if she could not pay even $1 a year now, the judge thought that accepting a deferred payment schedule would have shown good faith by committing to pay some of the debt should she become employed in the future. Krieger appealed the decision to the U.S. Court of Appeals for the Seventh Circuit. Should the court affirm the bankruptcy judge's grant of a discharge?

7. Doug Boyce works as a claims adjuster for GEICO. He makes $57,000 a year as a base salary plus several thousand more as part of a discretionary annual profit-sharing agreement. In 2008, he earned $67,961 from GEICO. GEICO also provides Boyce with a vehicle for his work and personal use. In 2007, Boyce took out a $16,000 loan from his 401(k) to purchase a house. He lives in the home and rents out some of the rooms for an additional rental income of approximately $5,800 a year. In October 2007, Boyce finalized his divorce and assumed responsibility for $34,000 in student loans and $16,000 in credit card debt. By October 2008, Boyce had added an additional $17,000 to his credit card debt. In March 2008, Boyce purchased a Ford F-350 with a $2,000 down payment and a monthly payment of $186. Boyce filed for bankruptcy protection under Chapter 7 on October 28, 2008. After filing for bankruptcy, Boyce surrendered his Ford F-350 and borrowed $14,750 from his 401(k) to purchase a Dodge Ram truck. He later sold the truck and purchased a Chevrolet truck and borrowed another $6,000 from his 401(k) to purchase a recreational camper. At the time of filing, Boyce did not disclose the money he earned from the profit-sharing agreement or his rental income, and his reported monthly income was short by $109. In addition, Boyce did not include the $34,000 student loan debt on his schedules. The U.S. Trustee commenced a contested proceeding against Boyce seeking dismissal of the Chapter 7. Should the court dismiss Boyce's Chapter 7 bankruptcy filing or alternatively force him into Chapter 13?

8. Paul Kelly was a graduate student at the University of Nebraska and had been working on his Ph.D. since 1991. He expected to complete it in 1999. He was also working as a clerk in a liquor store approximately 32 hours per week and earning $5.85 per hour. His monthly expenses were $743, and his monthly take-home pay was $761. Kelly borrowed money through student loans to enable him to pay tuition, fees, books, and other school-related expenses and expected to continue to do so until he finished his Ph.D. On July 26, 1994, the U.S. District Court in Minnesota entered a judgment in the amount of $30,000 against Kelly and in favor of Capitol Indemnity Corporation. The judgment was based on a misappropriation of funds by Kelly from a bank insured by Capitol. The court's order provided that the judgment was not dischargeable in bankruptcy.

Kelly filed a Chapter 13 petition. In his Chapter 13 plan, Kelly proposed to pay a total of $7,080 by paying off $118 per month, $100 of which would come from student loans. In the proceeding, Kelly testified that, among other things, he was currently qualified to teach at the college or university level and could earn about $20,000 but preferred to work part-time as a clerk while he completed his graduate school. Capitol objected to the proposed plan on the ground that it was not proposed in good faith. Capitol contended that Kelly should not be allowed to languish in graduate school, remain underemployed, and obtain the benefit of Chapter 13 discharge. Capitol asserted that Kelly was attempting to discharge a debt that was nondischargeable under Chapter 7, proposed to make payments primarily from his student loans, and would be paying a dividend to an unsecured creditor of only 8.5 percent. These factors, Capitol contended, demonstrated that the plan had not been proposed in good faith and that it should not be confirmed. Should confirmation of Kelly's plan be denied on the grounds that it was not proposed in good faith?

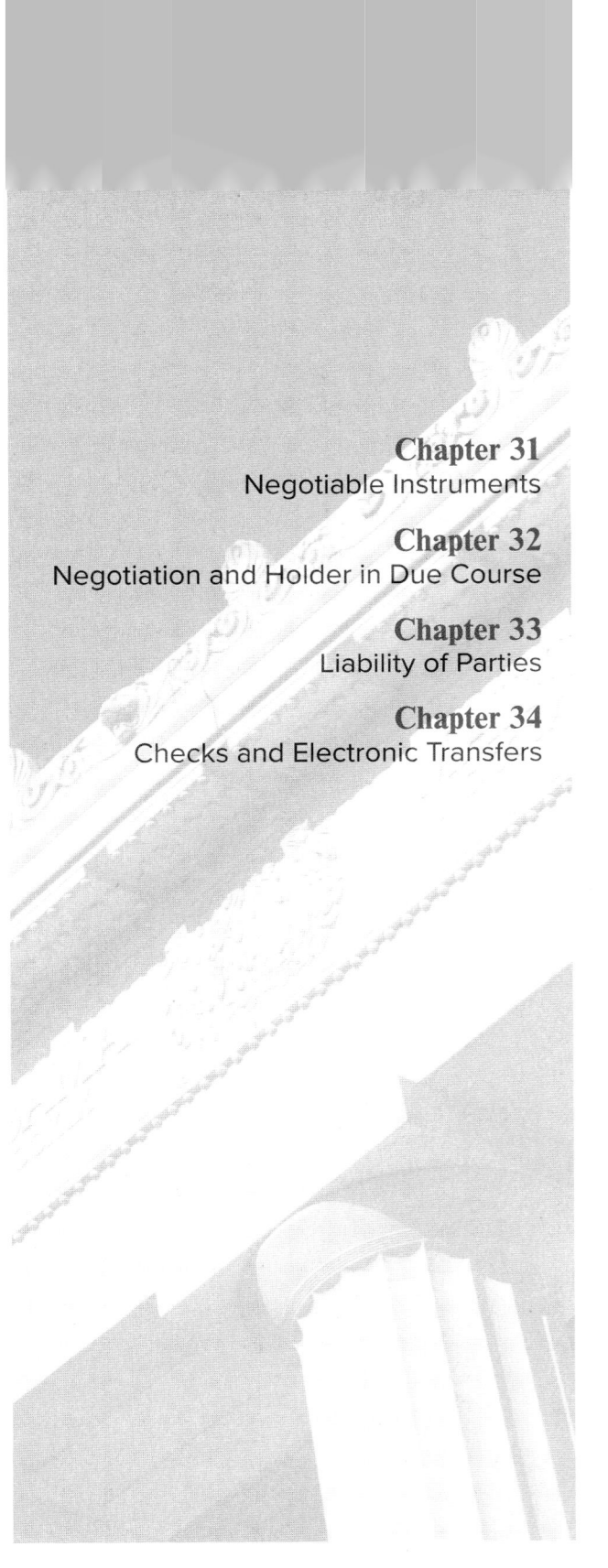

Commercial Paper

Negotiable Instruments

Chances are that you are using a variety of negotiable instruments in your everyday life, perhaps without realizing the special qualities that have led to their widespread use in commerce and the rules that govern them. If you have a job, your employer probably pays you by check, and you likely have a checking account that you use to make purchases and pay your bills. If you have accumulated some savings, you may have invested them in a certificate of deposit at a bank. And, if you have borrowed money, you very likely were asked to sign a promissory note acknowledging the debt and committing to repay it on specified terms. This chapter introduces the law of negotiable instruments, including:

- The special qualities and benefits of negotiable instruments.
- The basic types of commercial paper and their defining characteristics.
- The formal requirements that must be met for instruments such as checks, notes, and certificates of deposit to qualify as negotiable instruments.
- What happens if you write or receive a check in which there is a conflict between the amount set forth in figures and the amount set out in words.

LO LEARNING OBJECTIVES

After studying this chapter, you should be able to:

31-1 Explain the advantages of commercial paper that can qualify as a negotiable instrument.

31-2 Identify the different types of negotiable instruments and the key features of each type of instrument.

31-3 List and discuss the formal requirements that commercial paper must have to qualify as a negotiable instrument.

31-4 Apply the Uniform Commercial Code's (UCC's) rules that are applicable when the terms of an instrument conflict or are ambiguous.

AS COMMERCE AND TRADE developed, people moved beyond exclusive reliance on barter to the use of money and then to the use of substitutes for money. The term *commercial paper* encompasses substitutes in common usage today such as checks, promissory notes, and certificates of deposit.

This chapter and the three following chapters outline and discuss the body of law that governs commercial paper. Of particular interest are those kinds of commercial paper having the attribute of *negotiability*—that is, they can generally be transferred from party to party and accepted as a substitute

for money. This chapter discusses the nature and benefits of negotiable instruments and then outlines the requirements an instrument must meet to qualify as a negotiable instrument. Subsequent chapters discuss transfer and negotiation of instruments, the rights and liabilities of parties to negotiable instruments, and the special rules applicable to checks.

Over the past three decades, many new mechanisms have emerged for transferring money electronically without the need for paper money or the use of paper-based negotiable instruments such as checks. Financial institutions, merchants, and providers of service are encouraging customers to use these mechanisms in order to expedite the payment of money in a more cost-effective manner, to the benefit of all parties involved in financial transactions.

The electronic funds transfer (EFT) system utilized by consumers includes (1) automated teller machines (ATMs); (2) point-of-sale terminals that allow customers to use their EFT cards, such as cards and prepaid cards, as they would checks to transfer money from their checking account to the merchant; (3) preauthorized payments using the automated clearing house (ACH) system, such as automatic deposits of paychecks and government benefits or payments of mortgage, credit card, and utility bills; (4) telephone transfers between accounts or authorization to pay specific bills; (5) Internet payments, including payment processed directly by the account holder's bank or through intermediaries such as PayPal; and (6) mobile payment applications (apps), including payments processed directly by the account holder's bank or through intermediaries such as PayPal or Square and "remote deposit capture" offered by depositary institutions, including USAA. Remote deposit capture customers send images of checks payable to their order to their banks using special applications on smartphones. For large businesses, wire transfers of funds are commonly used to move large sums of money around the country or around the world. Wire transfers are not considered "commercial paper."

As newer electronic mechanisms have emerged and are increasingly supplanting the traditional methods for transferring money, they have required new legal constructs to deal with the issues and problems that do not fit well within the existing legal regimes such as Articles 3 (Negotiable Instruments) and 4 (Bank Deposits and Collections) of the Uniform Commercial Code (UCC). The mechanisms for transferring money, many of which you frequently use, will be discussed in detail in Chapter 34, Checks and Electronic Transfers.

But first, we need to discuss the legal regime applicable to paper-based negotiable instruments.

Nature of Negotiable Instruments

 Explain the advantages of commercial paper that can qualify as a negotiable instrument.

When a person buys a flat screen TV and gives the merchant a check drawn on his checking account, that person uses a form of negotiable commercial paper. Similarly, a person who goes to a bank or a credit union to borrow money might sign a promissory note agreeing to pay the money back in 90 days. Again, the bank and borrower use a form of negotiable commercial paper.

Commercial paper is basically a *contract for the payment of money.* It may serve as a substitute for money payable immediately, such as a check. Or it can be used as a means of extending credit. When a flat screen TV is bought by giving the merchant a check, the check is a substitute for money. If a credit union loans a borrower money now in exchange for the borrower's promise to repay it later, the promissory note signed by the borrower is a means of extending credit.

Uniform Commercial Code The law of commercial paper is covered in Article 3 (Negotiable Instruments) and Article 4 (Bank Deposits and Collections) of the Uniform Commercial Code. Other negotiable documents, such as investment securities and documents of title, are treated in other articles of the UCC. The original UCC Articles 3 and 4, adopted initially in the 1960s, generally followed the basic, centuries-old rules governing the use of commercial paper; but, at the same time, they adopted modern terminology and coordinated, clarified, and simplified the law. However, business practices continued to evolve, and new technological developments have changed the way that banks process checks. Accordingly, in 1990 a Revised Article 3, along with related amendments to Articles 1 and 4, were developed and have now been adopted by all states except New York. However, the reader should keep in mind that instruments may be interpreted under the version of the UCC that was in effect when the instruments were issued.

Negotiable Instruments The two basic types of negotiable instruments are *promises to pay money* and *orders to pay money.* Promissory notes and certificates of deposit issued by banks are promises to pay someone money. Checks and drafts are orders to another person to pay money to a third person. A check, which is a type of draft, is an order directed to a bank to pay money from a person's account to a third person.

Negotiability Negotiable instruments are a special kind of commercial paper that can pass readily through our financial system and often is accepted in place of money. This gives negotiable instruments many advantages.

For example, Searle, the owner of a clothing store in New York, contracts with Amado, a swimsuit manufacturer in Los Angeles, for $10,000 worth of swimsuits. If negotiable instruments did not exist, Searle would have to send or carry $10,000 across the country, which would be both inconvenient and risky. If someone stole the money along the way, Searle would lose the $10,000 unless he could locate the thief. By using a check in which Searle orders his bank to pay $10,000 from his account to Amado, or to someone designated by Amado, Searle makes the payment in a far more convenient manner. He sends only a single piece of paper to Amado. If the check is properly prepared and sent, sending the check is less risky than sending money. Even if someone steals the check along the way, Searle's bank may not pay it to anyone but Amado or someone authorized by Amado. And because the check gives Amado the right either to collect the $10,000 or to transfer the right to collect it to someone else, the check is a practical substitute for cash to Amado as well as to Searle.

In this chapter and in the three following chapters, we discuss the requirements necessary for a contract for the payment of money to qualify as a negotiable instrument. We also explain the features that not only distinguish a negotiable instrument from a simple contract but also led to the widespread use of negotiable instruments as a substitute for money.

Kinds of Negotiable Instruments

 LO31-2 Identify the different types of negotiable instruments and the key features of each type of instrument.

Promissory Notes The promissory note is the simplest form of commercial paper; it is simply a promise to pay money. A **promissory note** is a two-party instrument in which one person (known as the **maker**) makes an unconditional promise in writing to pay another person (the **payee**), a person

specified by that person, or the bearer of the instrument, a fixed amount of money, with or without interest, either on demand or at a specified, future time [3-104].[1]

The promissory note, shown in Figures 31.1 and 31.2, is a credit instrument; it is used in a wide variety of transactions in which credit is extended. For example, if a person purchases an automobile using money borrowed from a bank, the bank has the person sign a promissory note for the unpaid balance of the purchase price. Similarly, if a person borrows money to purchase a house, the lender who makes the loan and takes a mortgage on the house has the person sign a promissory note for the amount due on the loan. The note probably states that it is secured by a mortgage. The terms of payment on the note should correspond with the terms of the sales contract for the purchase of the house.

Certificates of Deposit The certificate of deposit given by a bank or a savings and loan association when a deposit of money is made is a type of note—namely, a note of a bank. A **certificate of deposit** is an instrument containing (1) an acknowledgment by a bank that it has received a deposit of money and (2) a promise by the bank to repay the sum of money [3-104(j)].

Most banks no longer issue certificates of deposit (CD) in paper form. Rather, the bank maintains an electronic deposit and provides the customer with a statement indicating the amount of principal held on a CD basis and the terms of the CD, such as the maturity and interest rate. In these instances, the certificate of deposit is not in negotiable instrument form.

---

[1]The numbers in brackets refer to the sections of the 1990 Revised Article 3 (and the conforming amendments to Articles 1 and 4) of the Uniform Commercial Code.

Figure 31.1   Promissory Note

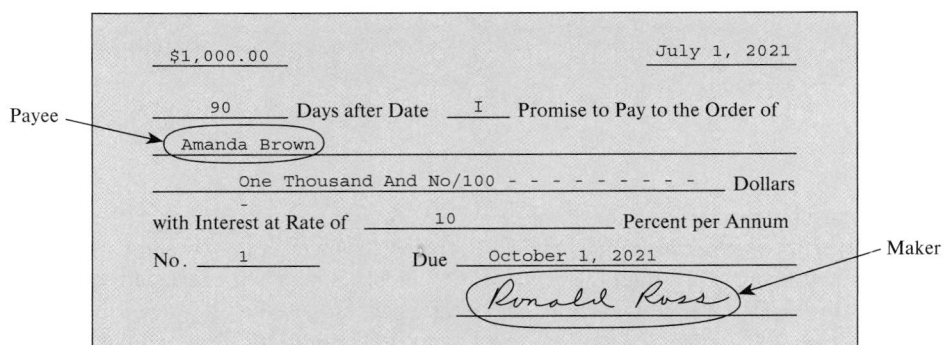

Figure 31.2   Promissory Note (Consumer Loan Note)

Figure 31.2   Promissory Note (Consumer Loan Note)

Drafts A **draft** is a form of commercial paper that involves an *order* to pay money rather than a promise to pay money [3-104(e)]. The most common example of a draft is a check. A draft has three parties to it: one person (known as the **drawer**) orders a second person (the **drawee**) to pay a certain sum of money to a third person (the **payee**), to a person specified by that person, or to bearer.

Drafts other than checks are used in a variety of commercial transactions. If Brown owes Ames money, Ames may draw a draft for the amount of the debt, naming Brown as drawee and herself or her bank as payee, and send the draft to Brown's bank for payment. Alternatively, Ames might send a draft providing for payment on a certain day in the future to Brown for "acceptance." Brown could "accept" the draft by signing his name to it, thereby obligating himself to pay the amount specified in the draft on that day in the future to Ames or to someone specified by Ames. Automobile dealers selling to each other, or selling cars at auctions, commonly use drafts, as do sellers and buyers of livestock.

In freight shipments in which the terms are "cash on delivery," the seller commonly ships the goods to the buyer on an "order bill of lading" consigned to himself at the place of delivery. The seller then endorses the bill of lading and attaches a draft naming the buyer as drawee. He then sends the bill of lading and the draft through banking channels to the buyer's bank. A bank in the buyer's locale presents the draft to the buyer's bank for payment and, when the former bank receives payment, delivers the bill of lading to the buyer. Through this commercial transaction, the buyer gets the goods and the seller gets his money.

When credit is extended, the same procedure is followed, but the seller uses a time draft—a draft payable at some future time (see Figure 31.3). In such a transaction, the buyer "accepts" the draft (instead of paying it) and obligates herself to pay the amount of the draft when due. In these cases, the *drawee* (now called the acceptor) should date her signature so that the date at which payment is due is clear to all [3-409(c)].

As a consumer, you are most likely to encounter drafts when your insurance company pays a claim—you'll see that often it is denoted as a "DRAFT" and indicates that it is payable through a particular bank. This notation means that the bank will pay the draft to you only after it has checked with the insurance company (the drawer) and the insurance company authorizes the bank to pay the instrument.

Checks   A **check** is a *draft payable on demand* and drawn on a bank (i.e., a bank is the drawee or person to whom the order to pay is addressed). Checks are the most widely used form of commercial paper. The issuer of a check orders the bank at which she maintains an account to pay a specified person, or someone designated by that person, a fixed amount of money from the account. For example, Elizabeth Brown has a checking account at First National Bank. She goes to Home Depot and agrees to buy a washing machine priced at $459.95. If she writes a check to pay for it, she is the drawer of the check, First National Bank is the drawee, and Home Depot is the payee. By writing the check, Elizabeth is ordering her bank to pay $459.95 from her account to Home Depot or to Home Depot's order—that is, to whomever Home Depot asks the bank to pay the money (see Figure 31.4 for an example of a check).

The UCC definition of a "check" includes a "cashier's check" and a "teller's check." A **cashier's check** is a draft on which the drawer and drawee are the same bank (or branches of the same bank); a teller's check is a draft drawn by a bank (as drawer) on another bank or payable at or through a bank [3-104(g) and (h)]. For example, a check drawn by a credit union on its account at a federally insured bank would be a teller's check.

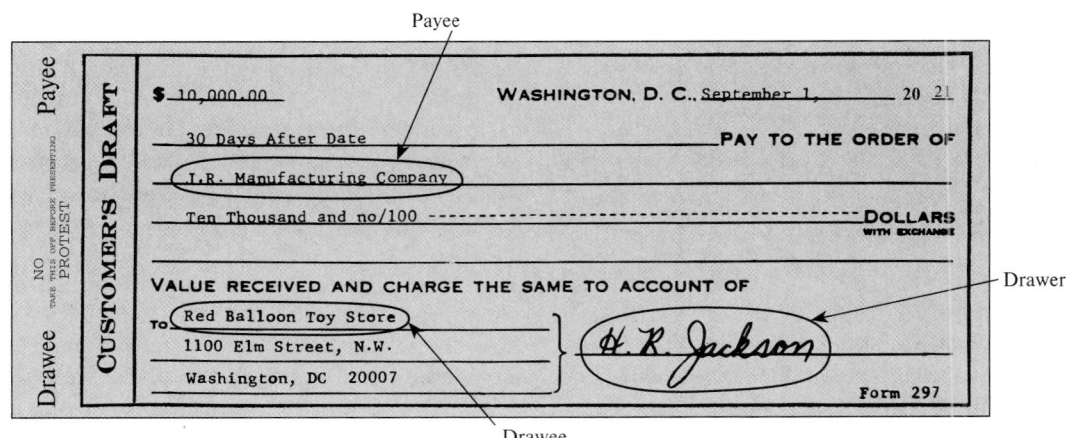

Figure 31.3   Draft

CYBERLAW IN ACTION

Check Conversion and Remotely Created Checks

In addition to electronic fund transfers consumers initiate through ATMs and point-of-sale readers, retailers increasingly transform paper checks they take from customers and process them electronically. The process, which is known as "check conversion," starts when a consumer gives a seller a paper check. The seller gathers information from the check, including the buyer's bank account number, the "routing number" that identifies the buyer's bank, and the serial number of the check. The seller hands the paper check back to the buyer and completes the payment transaction by adding the amount of the purchase to an electronic file. "Check conversion" saves the seller time and money it otherwise would spend collecting the paper through the buyer's bank manually.

In addition, consumers often pay using "telephone checks" (also called "remotely created checks") by giving the same pieces of information from a paper check to a seller over the phone. The seller uses the information to create a paper check, which it can deposit in the ordinary manner, or to create an electronic file of information that it can send to its depository bank. The legal rules concerning check conversion and remotely created checks are discussed in Chapter 34, Checks and Electronic Transfers.

Figure 31.4   Check

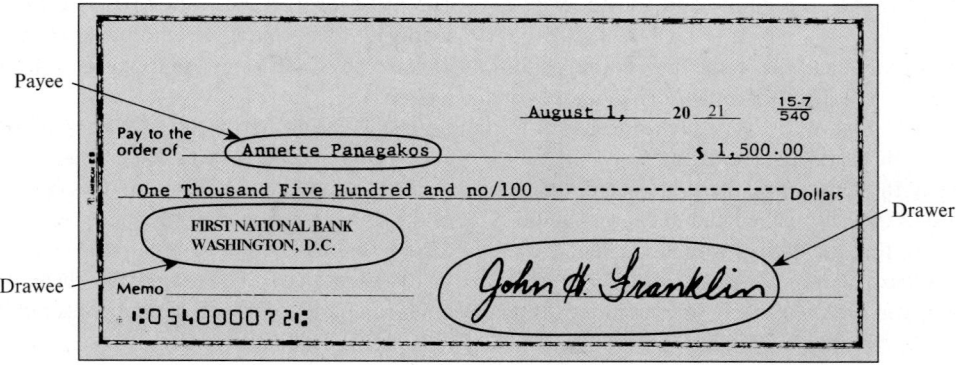

An instrument may qualify as a "check" and be governed by Article 3 even though it is described on its face by another term, such as "money order" or a "travelers check." The critical element is whether it is drawn on a bank and payable on demand.

Benefits of Negotiable Instruments

Rights of an Assignee of a Contract
As we noted in Chapter 17, Rights of Third Parties, the assignee of a contract can obtain no greater rights than the assignor had at the time of the assignment. For example, Browning Construction Company agrees to build an in-ground swimming pool pursuant to plans provided by Geraldo Garcia. At the time the contract is signed by the two parties on March 1, Garcia makes a down payment of $5,000 and agrees to pay the balance of $30,000 when Browning Construction completes the pool. If, on April 1, Browning Construction assigns its rights under the contract to First Bank—including the right to collect the money from Garcia—then First Bank will obtain whatever rights Browning Construction has at the time First Bank seeks to collect the balance due on the contract. If Browning Construction has completed its work consistent with the plans, then First Bank is entitled to be paid the $30,000. However, if the work has not been completed, or was not done consistent with the plans, then Garcia may have a valid defense or reason to avoid paying the full $30,000.

Taking an assignment of a contract involves assuming certain risks. The assignee (First Bank) may not be aware of the nature and extent of any defenses that the party liable on the contract (Garcia) might have against the assignor (Browning Construction). An assignee who does not know what rights he is getting, or which risks he is assuming, may be reluctant to take an assignment of the contract.

Rights of a Holder of a Negotiable Instrument

The object of a negotiable instrument is to have it accepted readily as a substitute for money. In order to accept it readily, a person must be able to take it free of many of the risks assumed by the assignee of a regular contract. Under the law of negotiable instruments, this is possible if two conditions are met: (1) The contract for the payment of money must meet the formal requirements to qualify as a negotiable instrument and (2) the person who acquires the instrument must qualify as a holder in due course. Basically, a *holder in due course* is a person who has good title to the instrument, paid value for it, acquired it in good faith, and had no notice of certain claims or defenses against payment at the time he first had possession of the instrument. In addition, the instrument cannot bear facial irregularities (evidence of forgery or alteration or questions concerning its authenticity).

The next section of this chapter discusses the formal requirements for a negotiable instrument. Chapter 32, Negotiation and Holder in Due Course, outlines the requirements that a person must meet to qualify as a holder in due course.

A holder in due course of a negotiable instrument takes the instrument free of all defenses and claims to the instrument except those that concern its validity. For example, a holder in due course of a note given in payment for goods may enforce the obligation in spite of the buyer's claim that the seller breached a warranty. However, if the maker of a note wrote it under duress, such as a threat of force, or was a minor, then even a holder in due course is subject to the defenses of duress or infancy to the extent other law (1) would nullify the obligation for duress or (2) would permit infancy as a defense to a simple contract. The person who holds the note could not obtain the payment from the maker but would have to recover from the person from whom he got the note.

The Federal Trade Commission (FTC) has adopted a regulation that alters the rights of a holder in due course in consumer purchase transactions. This regulation allows a consumer who gives a negotiable instrument, to finance an automobile, for example, to use additional defenses

(breach of warranty or fraudulent inducement) against payment of the instrument against even a holder in due course. Similarly, some states have enacted the Uniform Consumer Credit Code (UCCC), which produces a similar result. Chapter 32, Negotiation and Holder in Due Course, discusses the rights of a holder in due course, as well as the FTC rule.

Formal Requirements for Negotiability

LO31-3 List and discuss the formal requirements that commercial paper must have to qualify as a negotiable instrument.

Basic Requirements

An instrument such as a check or a note must meet certain formal requirements to be a negotiable instrument. If the instrument does not meet these requirements, it is nonnegotiable; that is, it is treated as a simple contract and not as a negotiable instrument. A primary purpose for these formal requirements is to ensure the willingness of prospective purchasers of the instrument—particularly, financial institutions such as banks—to accept it as a substitute for money.

For an instrument to be negotiable, it must:

1. Be in writing.

2. Be signed by the issuer (the *maker* in the case of a person undertaking to pay or the *drawer* in the case of a person giving an order or instruction to pay).

3. Contain an unconditional promise or order to pay a fixed amount of money, with or without interest or other charges described in the promise or order.

4. Be payable to order or to bearer.

5. Be payable on demand or at a definite time.

6. Not state any other undertaking or instruction by the person promising or ordering to do any act in addition to the payment of money [however, it may contain (*a*) an undertaking or promise relative to collateral to secure payment, (*b*) an authorization for confession of judgment, or (*c*) a waiver of benefit of any law intended for the advantage or protection of an obligor] [3-103, 3-104].

In addition, an instrument that otherwise qualifies as a check can be negotiable even if it is not explicitly payable to order or to bearer [3-104(c)]. As explained later, this means that a check that reads "pay John Doe" could be negotiable even though the normal form for a check is "pay to the order of _____."

A promise or order other than a check is not a negotiable instrument if at the time it is issued or first comes into the possession of a holder it contains a conspicuous statement that the promise or order is not negotiable or is not an instrument governed by Article 3 [3-104(d)]. For example, if a promissory note contained the legend "NONNEGOTIABLE," it would not qualify as a negotiable instrument even if it otherwise met the formal requirements for one.

Importance of Form   Whether or not an instrument satisfies these formal requirements is important for the purpose of determining whether an instrument is negotiable or nonnegotiable. Negotiability should not be confused with validity or collectibility. If an instrument is negotiable, the law of negotiable instruments in the UCC controls in determining the rights and liabilities of the parties to the instrument. If an instrument is nonnegotiable, the general rules of contract law control. The purpose of determining negotiability is to ascertain whether a possessor of the instrument can become a holder in due course.

An instrument that meets all of the formal requirements is a negotiable instrument even though it is void, voidable, unenforceable, or uncollectible for other reasons. Negotiability is a matter of form and nothing else. Suppose a person gives an instrument in payment of a gambling debt in a state that has a statute declaring that any instrument or promise given in payment of a gambling debt is void. The instrument is a negotiable instrument if it is negotiable in form even though it is void for separate public policy reasons. Also, an instrument that is negotiable in form is a negotiable instrument even though it is issued by a minor. The instrument is voidable at the option of the minor if state law makes infancy a defense to a simple contract, but it is negotiable.

In Writing

To be negotiable, an instrument must be in writing. An instrument that is handwritten, typed, or printed is considered to be in writing [1-201(46)]. The writing does not have to be on any particular material; all that is required is that the instrument be in writing. A person could create a negotiable instrument in pencil on a piece of wrapping paper. It would be poor business practice to do so, but the instrument would meet the statutory requirement that it be in writing.

Signed

To qualify as a negotiable instrument, an instrument in the form of a note must be signed by the person undertaking to pay (the maker) and an instrument in the form of a draft must be signed by the person giving the instruction to pay (the drawer) [3-103]. An instrument has been signed if the maker or drawer has put a name or other symbol on it with the intention of validating it [3-401(b)]. Normally, the maker or drawer signs an instrument by writing his name on it; however, this is not required. A person or company may authorize an agent to sign instruments for it. A typed or rubber-stamped signature is sufficient if it was put on the instrument to validate it. A person who cannot write her name might make an X or some other symbol and have it witnessed by someone else.

Unconditional Promise or Order

Requirement of a Promise or Order   If an instrument is promissory in nature, such as a note or a certificate of deposit, it must contain an unconditional promise to pay, or it cannot be negotiable. Merely acknowledging a debt is not sufficient [3-103(9)]. For example, the statement "I owe you $100" does not constitute a promise to pay. An IOU in this form is not a negotiable instrument.

If an instrument is an order to pay, such as a check or a draft, it must contain an unconditional order. A simple request to pay as a favor is not sufficient; however, a politely phrased demand, such as "please pay," can meet the requirement. Checks commonly use the language "Pay to the order of." This satisfies the requirement that the check contain an order to pay. The order is the word "pay," not the word "order." The word "order" has another function—that of designating the instrument as payable "to order" or "to bearer" for purposes of negotiability.

Promise or Order Must Be Unconditional

An instrument is not negotiable unless the promise or order is unconditional. For example, a note that provides "I promise to pay to the order of Karl Adams $2,500 if he replaces the roof on my garage" is not negotiable because it is payable on a condition.

To be negotiable, an instrument must be written so that a person can tell from reading the instrument alone what the obligations of the parties are. If a note contains the

CYBERLAW IN ACTION

E-Payments Compared to "Negotiable Instruments"

Article 3 has numerous requirements for the appearance and content of promises to pay (notes) and orders to pay (drafts/checks) if they are to qualify as negotiable instruments and be readily transferable. Two of these requirements contemplate paper-based transactions—the requirement that promises to pay and orders to pay be "in writing" (see [3-103]) and be "signed" (see [3-104]). For this reason, at present, it would be difficult to "electrify" negotiable instruments successfully.

In contrast, e-payments—more commonly substitutes for traditional "check" payments—are neither in writing nor "signed" by affixing a signature in ink to a sheet of paper. Instead, the transaction is documented electronically—such as by sending an e-mail message or fax to a bank to direct it to pay a third-party seller of goods or services (such as the purchase of an online information product).

The buyer and seller using e-payments have many of the same concerns as buyers and sellers using traditional payment methods: They want to be certain that they are dealing with each other honestly and that it will not be easier for the seller to double-charge the buyer's account or to get away with taking payment but not delivering the goods or services that the buyer seeks from the transaction. They want to guard against unscrupulous persons hacking into their records and stealing from either the buyer or seller. Different laws apply to different means of making payments. Payments made with a credit card and payments made with a debit or ATM card or through "check conversion" are subject to federal laws. Payments made with paper checks not converted into electronic files are subject to state laws and a different federal law than applies to purely electronic transmission of payment information. Consumers need to understand what laws apply to the payments they make and how they work so that they can take full advantage of the consumer protections those laws afford them.

---

statement "Payment is subject to the terms of a mortgage dated November 20, 2021," it is not negotiable. To determine the rights of the parties on the note, one would have to examine another document—the mortgage.

However, a reference to another document for a statement of rights with respect to collateral, prepayment, or acceleration does not destroy the negotiability of a note [3-106(b)]. For example, a note could contain this statement: "This note is secured by a mortgage dated August 30, 2021" without affecting its negotiability. In this case, the mortgage does not affect rights and duties of the parties to the note. It would not be necessary to examine the mortgage document to determine the rights of the parties to the note; the parties need only examine the note.

The negotiability of an instrument is not affected by a statement of the consideration for which the instrument was given or by a statement of the transaction that gave rise to the instrument. For example, a negotiable instrument may state that it was given in payment of last month's rent or that it was given in payment of the purchase price of goods. The statement does not affect the negotiability of the instrument.

A check may reference the account to be debited without making the check conditional and thus nonnegotiable. For example, a check could contain the notation "payroll account" or "petty cash." Similarly, the account number that appears on personal checks does not make the instrument payable only out of a specific fund. Under original Article 3, a check (other than a governmental check) that stated that it was payable only out of a specific fund or account was treated as a conditional order and thus was not negotiable. Revised Article 3 changed this rule so that limiting payment to a particular fund or source does not make the promise or order conditional [3-106(b)].

Revised Article 3 also addresses the negotiability of traveler's checks that commonly require, as a condition to payment, a countersignature of a person whose specimen signature appears on the draft. Under the revision, the condition does not prevent the instrument from meeting the "unconditional promise or order" requirement [3-106(c)]. However, if the person whose specimen signature appears on the instrument fails to countersign it, the failure to sign becomes a defense to the obligation of the issuer to pay. Defenses are discussed in the following chapter.

A conditional *indorsement* does not destroy the negotiability of an otherwise negotiable instrument. The UCC determines negotiability at *issuance*, so that indorsements do not affect the underlying negotiability of the instrument. We discuss conditional indorsements in Chapter 32, Negotiation and Holder in Due Course.

Fixed Amount of Money

Fixed Amount The promise or order in an instrument must be to pay a fixed amount of money, with or without interest or other charges described in the promise or order. The requirement of a "fixed amount" applies only to principal; the amount of any interest payable is that described in the instrument. Interest may be stated in an instrument as a fixed or variable amount of money or it may be expressed as a fixed or variable rate or rates. If a variable rate of interest is prescribed, the amount of interest is calculated by reference to the formula or index referenced in the instrument. For example, a note might provide for interest at "three percent (3.00%) over JPMorgan Chase Prime Rate to be adjusted monthly." If the description of interest in the instrument does not allow the amount of interest to be ascertained, then interest is payable at the judgment rate in effect at the place of payment at the time interest first accrues [3-112]. The judgment rate is the rate of interest courts impose on losing parties until they pay the winning parties.

Under the original version of Article 3, a promise or order had to be to pay a "sum certain." Generally, to meet this requirement, a person had to be able to compute from the information in the instrument the amount required to discharge—or pay off—the instrument at any given time. Among other things, this caused problems when applied to variable rate instruments that came into common commercial usage in the United States after the original Article 3 was drafted. Some state courts held that instruments providing for variable interest rates ascertainable through reference to indexes outside the instrument were not negotiable; other courts sought to interpret the UCC to accommodate this new commercial practice. As noted above, the negotiability of instruments that provide for variable interest rates has now been resolved in Revised Article 3.

In the case that follows, *Heritage Bank v. Bruha*, the court held that a promissory note that evidenced a revolving line of credit that was extended to a borrower was not a negotiable instrument.

Heritage Bank v. Bruha   76 UCC Rep. 2d 836 (Neb. 2012)

On four different occasions in 2008, Jerome Bruha signed promissory notes with Sherman County Bank securing lines of credit under which Bruha could borrow money from Sherman County Bank. Bruha invested the money he borrowed in a trading company that shared management with the bank. One of the notes, signed on December 16, 2008, evidenced a promise to pay "the principal amount of Seventy-five thousand & 00/000 Dollars ($75,000.00) or so much as may be outstanding, together with interest on the unpaid outstanding principal balance of each advance." The note also stated that it evidenced "a revolving line of credit."

The note contained a variable interest rate. The rate was subject to change every month and was calculated on an index maintained by Sherman County Bank. The interest rate on Bruha's note was 1 percentage point under the percentage on the index at any given time. The initial rate was 7.25 percent and was later adjusted to 6.75 percent. On default, the interest rate was to increase by 5 percentage points.

Bruha received three advancements on the note totaling $51,000. Sherman County Bank eventually failed, and its assets, including the note signed by Bruha, were assigned to Heritage Bank. Heritage Bank brought suit against Bruha on the note. Bruha admitted signing the note but claimed that Sherman County Bank had procured his signature "by fraud and/or misrepresentation." Bruha admitted that he had not paid the note but denied that he was obligated to do so.

A critical question in the case was whether the promissory note Bruha had signed was a "negotiable instrument" under Article 3. If it was, then Heritage Bank might qualify as a holder in due course* and be immune to certain defenses Bruha might assert against payment.

Connolly, Justice

We conclude that Heritage is not a holder in due course because the note was not "negotiable." And Article 3 of the Uniform Commercial Code does not apply to this case.

Nebraska U.C.C. Section 3-104(a) provides: "Except as provided in subsections (c) and (d), 'negotiable instrument'

means an unconditional promise or order to pay *a fixed amount of money*, with or without interest or other charges described in the promise or order. . . ." (Emphasis supplied.) Here, the note fails to meet the definition of a "negotiable instrument" because it was not a promise "to pay a fixed amount of money."

Although the Uniform Commercial Code allows notes to have a variable interest rate, under Section 3-104(a), the principal amount must be fixed. A fixed amount is an absolute requisite to

---

*The concept of a holder in due course is detailed in Chapter 32, Negotiation and Holder in Due Course.

negotiability. This is because unless a purchaser can determine how much it will be paid under the instrument, it will be unable to determine a fair price to pay for it, which defeats the basic purpose for negotiable instruments.

Here, the text of the note states that Bruha "promises to pay . . . the principal amount of Seventy-five Thousand & 00/000 dollars ($75,000.00) *or so much as may be outstanding. . . .*" (Emphasis supplied.) Further, the note states that it "evidences a revolving line of credit" and that Bruha could request advances under the obligation up to $75,000. This fails the "fixed amount of money" requirement of Section 3-104(a); one looking at the instrument itself cannot tell how much Bruha has been advanced at any given time. Simply stated, a note given to secure a line of credit under which the amount of the obligation varies, depending on the extent to which the line of credit is used, is not negotiable.

Payable in Money The amount specified in the instrument must be payable in money. *Money* is a medium of exchange authorized or adopted by a domestic or foreign government and includes a monetary unit of account established by an intergovernmental organization or by agreement between two or more nations [1-201(24)]. Unless the instrument otherwise provides, an instrument that states the amount payable in foreign money may be paid in the foreign money or in an equivalent dollar amount [3-107]. If the person obligated to pay off an instrument can do something other than pay money, the instrument is not negotiable. For example, if a note reads "I promise to pay to the order of Sarah Smith, at my option, $40 or five bushels of apples, John Jones," the note is not negotiable.

Payable on Demand or at a Definite Time

To be negotiable, the promise or order must be payable either "on demand" or at a specified time in the future. The reason for this requirement is that the time when the instrument is payable can be determined just by reading the instrument. An instrument that is payable on the happening of some uncertain event is not negotiable. Thus, a note payable "when my son graduates from college" is not negotiable, even though the son does graduate subsequently.

Payable on Demand A promise or order is "payable on demand" if (1) it states that it is payable on "demand" or "sight" or otherwise at the will of the holder of the instrument or (2) does not state any time for payment [3-108(a)]. For example, if the maker forgets to state when a note is payable, it is payable by the close of business on the day of demand to the holder of the note.

An instrument may be antedated (back-dated) or post-dated, but normally an instrument payable on demand is not payable before the date of the instrument [3-113(a)]. However, Revised Article 3 makes an important exception for checks: A payor bank (a bank that is the drawee of a draft) may pay a postdated check before the stated date *unless* the drawer has notified the bank of postdating pursuant to a procedure set out in the UCC [3-113(a), 4-401(c)] that is similar to the process involved in stopping payment on a check. (See Chapter 34.)

Payable at a Definite Time A promise or order is "payable at a definite time" if it is payable at a fixed date or dates or at a time or times readily ascertainable from the face of the instrument at the time the promise or order is issued [3-108(b)]. Thus, a note dated March 25, 2021, might be made payable at a fixed time after a stated date, such as "30 days after date."

Under the UCC, an instrument that names a fixed date or time for payment—without losing its negotiable character—also may contain a clause permitting the time for payment to be accelerated at the option of the maker. Similarly, an instrument may allow an extension of time at the option of the holder or allow a maker to extend payment to a further definite time. Or the due date of a note might be triggered by the happening of an event, such as the filing of a petition in bankruptcy against the maker. The UCC permits these clauses so long as one can determine the time for payment with certainty [3-108].

A promise or order also is "payable at a definite time" if it is payable on elapse of a definite period of time after "sight" or "acceptance." A draft payable at a specified time—such as "15 days after sight"—is, in effect, payable at a fixed time after the draft is presented to the drawee for acceptance.

If an instrument is undated, its "date" is the date it is issued by the maker or drawer [3-113(b)].

Payable to Order or Bearer

Except for checks, to be negotiable an instrument must be "payable to order or to bearer." A note that provides "I promise to pay to the order of Sarah Smith" or "I promise to pay to Sarah Smith or bearer" is negotiable. However, one that provides "I promise to pay to Sarah Smith" is not. The words "to the order of" or "to bearer" show that the drawer of a draft, or the maker of a note, intends to issue a negotiable instrument. The drawer or maker is not restricting payment of the instrument to just Sarah Smith but is willing to pay someone else designated by Sarah Smith. This is the essence of negotiability.

In the original version of Article 3, an order in the form of a check also had to be "payable to order or bearer" to qualify as a negotiable instrument. However, the drafters of Revised Article 3 created an exception for instruments that otherwise meet the requirements for a negotiable instrument as well as the definition of a check [3-104(c)]. Under the revised article, a check that reads "Pay John Doe" could qualify as a negotiable instrument. As a result, the UCC treats checks as negotiable instruments whether or not they contain the words "to the order of." The drafters explained that most checks are preprinted with these words but that occasionally the drawer may strike out the words before issuing the check and that a few check forms have been in use, most often in Canada or the northern United States, that do not contain these words. In these instances, the drafters preferred not to limit the rights of holders of such checks who may pay money or give credit for a check without being aware that it is not in the conventional form for a negotiable instrument.

A promise or order is considered to be payable "to order" if it is payable (1) to the order of an identified person or (2) to an identified person or that person's order [3-109(b)]. Examples would include: "Pay to the order of Sandy Smith" and "Pay to Sandy Smith or order." The most common forms of a promise or order being payable to bearer use the words "pay to bearer," "pay to the order of bearer," "pay to cash," or "pay to the order of cash" [3-109(a)]. A check sent with the payee line blank is payable to bearer. However, it is also considered an incomplete instrument. The rules concerning incomplete instrument will be discussed in the next two chapters.

The original payee of a draft or a note can transfer the right to receive payment to someone else. By making the instrument payable "to the order of" or "to bearer," the drawer or maker is giving the payee the chance to negotiate the instrument to another person and to cut off certain defenses that the drawer or maker may have against payment of the instrument.

An instrument that is payable to the order of a specific person is known as "order paper." Order paper can be negotiated or transferred only by indorsement. An instrument payable "to bearer" or "to cash" is known as "bearer paper"; it can be negotiated or transferred by delivery of possession without indorsement [3-201(b)]. The rules governing negotiation of instruments will be detailed in the next chapter.

An instrument can be made payable to two or more payees. For example, a check could be drawn payable "to the order of John Jones and Henry Smith." Then, both Jones and Smith have to be involved in negotiating it or enforcing its payment. An instrument also can be made payable to alternative persons—for example, "to the order of Susan Clark or Betsy Brown." In this case, either Clark or Brown could negotiate it or enforce its payment [3-110(d)].

A number of recent cases have addressed the question of whether checks should be interpreted as being payable jointly, or whether they are payable in the alternative. Some of those cases have addressed the use of the virgule (/) punctuation mark to separate the names of the payees. One recent case involved a check made payable to "International Livestock/Purina Mills." The court reasoned that a virgule is used to separate alternatives and concluded that the check required only the indorsement of either International Livestock or Purina Mills. The following case, *Pelican National Bank*, involves a check where the payees were listed in a stacked formation without any grammatical connector or punctuation. The court concluded that the check was ambiguous and applied the default rule that treated the document as if it was payable in the alternative.

Pelican National Bank v. Provident Bank of Maryland
849 A.2d 475 (Md. Ct. App. 2004)

Hartford Mutual Insurance Company issued a check drawn on Allfirst Bank in the amount of $60,150.00 to payees as follows:

Andrew Michael Bogdan, Jr., Crystal Bogdan
Oceanmark Bank FSB
Goodman-Gable-Gould Company

The check was in payment of a casualty claim made by Bogdan on an insurance policy issued by Hartford Mutual on commercial property owned by Bogdan and his wife and on which Oceanmark Bank (Pelican National Bank's predecessor) held a mortgage. Thus, the payees on the check were the property owners, the mortgage holder, and the insurance agent who adjusted the casualty claim. In addition to the payees, the front of the check listed in small print the insurance policy number, claim identification number, the "loss date," and a small notation that read "MEMO Fire—building."

The check, indorsed only by the Bogdans and the adjuster, was presented for payment to Provident Bank, which cashed it. Michael Bogdan deposited the proceeds to a commercial account he held at Provident Bank. When Oceanmark Bank was unable to obtain reimbursement from Provident Bank for negotiating the check without Oceanmark Bank's indorsement, it brought suit against Provident Bank for conversion of the check by paying it without having obtained a required indorsement.

The trial court held that the check was ambiguous as to whether it was payable jointly and thus negotiable only with the indorsement of all of the payees. Accordingly, the court held that it could be negotiated with the indorsement of any of the named payees. Oceanmark Bank appealed.

Bell, Chief Judge

The issue in this case is whether a check made payable to multiple payees, listed in stacked formation on its face, without any grammatical connector or punctuation, is ambiguous as to whether it is negotiable only jointly, thus, requiring the indorsement of all of the named payees, or alternatively, requiring the indorsement of any one of the named payees.

Enacted as part of the 1996 revision to the Maryland Uniform Commercial Code, Section 3-110(d) enunciates the rules for determining, objectively, the intent of a drawer with respect to an instrument made payable to multiple payees. Therefore, we must first examine Section 3-110(d) to determine whether the stacked payee format in this case is an ambiguous multiple payee designation as contemplated by the Maryland Legislature when it enacted the statute. Section 3-110(d) provides:

(d) If an instrument is payable to two or more persons alternatively, it is payable to any of them and may be negotiated, discharged, or enforced by any or all of them in possession of the instrument. If an instrument is payable to two or more persons not alternatively, it is payable to all of them and may be negotiated, discharged, or enforced only by all of them. If an instrument payable to two or more persons is ambiguous as to whether it is payable to the persons alternatively, the instrument is payable to the persons alternatively.

The Official Comment to that section provides further guidance regarding how to treat a check with multiple payees:

An instrument payable to X or Y is governed by the first sentence of subsection (d). An instrument payable to X and Y is governed by the second sentence of subsection (d). If an instrument is payable to X or Y, either is the payee and if either is in possession that person is the holder and the person entitled to enforce the instrument. . . . If an instrument is payable to X and Y, neither X nor Y acting alone is the person to whom the instrument is payable. . . . The instrument is "payable to an identified person." The "identified person" is X and Y acting jointly.

* * *

The third sentence of subsection (d) is directed to cases in which it is not clear whether an instrument is payable to multiple payees alternatively. In the case of ambiguity, persons dealing with the instrument should be able to rely on the indorsement of a single payee. For example, an instrument payable to X and/or Y is treated like an instrument payable to X or Y.

Thus, Section 3-110(d), confirmed by the explanation in the Official Comment, clearly and unambiguously enunciates the default rule, that, unless checks payable to multiple payees are specifically and clearly made payable jointly or in the alternative, they are ambiguous with respect to how they are to be paid and, therefore, are payable alternatively. Indeed, that is precisely what the last sentence of the section states.

Applying Section 3-110(d) and this default rule to the facts of this case produces a clear result. The subject check was drawn to the order of three payees, listed in stacked format, with no grammatical connector, punctuation or symbol indicating their relationship or how the check was intended to be paid. Therefore, the check was neither clearly payable in the alternative, the payees not being connected by "or" or its equivalent, nor clearly payable jointly, the payees not being joined by "and" or its equivalent. It was, consequently, we hold, "ambiguous as to whether it is payable to the persons alternatively." Accordingly, we further hold, it was proper for Provident Bank to have negotiated the check without the indorsement of Oceanmark. The indorsement of any one of the payees was sufficient.

Judgment for Provident Bank affirmed.

Requirements for Negotiability

Requirement	Basic Rules
Must Be in Writing	1. The instrument may be handwritten, typed, or printed.
Must Be Signed by the Maker or Drawer	1. Person issuing the instrument must sign with intent of validating his or her obligation. 2. Person issuing may affix the signature in a variety of ways—for example, by word, mark, or rubber stamp. 3. Agent or authorized representative may supply the "signature."
Must Contain a Promise or Order to Pay	1. Promise must be more than acknowledgment of a debt. 2. Order requirement is met if the drawer issues an instruction to "pay."
Promise or Order Must Be Unconditional	1. Entire obligation must be found in the instrument itself and not in another document or documents. 2. Payment cannot be conditioned on the occurrence of an event.
Must Call for Payment of a Fixed Amount of Money	1. Must be able to ascertain the principal from the face of the instrument. 2. May contain a clause providing for payment of interest or other charges such as collection or attorney fees.
Must Be Payable in Money	1. Obligation must be payable in a medium of exchange authorized or adopted by a government or by an international organization or agreement between two or more nations. 2. Maker or drawer cannot have the option to pay in something other than money.
Must Be Payable on Demand or at a Definite Time	1. Requirement is met if instrument says it is payable on demand or, if no time for payment is stated, it is payable on demand. 2. Requirement is met if it is payable on a stated date, at a fixed time after a stated date, or at a fixed time "after sight." 3. Instrument may contain an acceleration clause or a clause allowing maker or holder to extend the payment date to a further definite time.
Generally Must Be Payable to Bearer or to Order	1. Bearer requirement is met if instrument is payable "to bearer" or "to cash." 2. Order requirement is met if instrument is payable "to the order of" a specified person or persons. 3. Exception from requirement is made for instruments meeting both the definition of a check and all the other requirements for a negotiable instrument.
May Not State Any Other Undertaking or Instruction by the Person Promising or Ordering Payment to Do Any Act in Addition to the Payment of Money	1. However, it may contain (*a*) an undertaking or power to give, maintain, or protect collateral to secure payment; (*b*) an authorization or power to the holder to confess judgment or realize on or dispose of collateral; or (*c*) a waiver of the benefit of any law intended for the advantage or protection of an obligor on the instrument.

Special Terms

 LO31-4 Apply the Uniform Commercial Code's (UCC's) rules that are applicable when the terms of an instrument conflict or are ambiguous.

Additional Terms   Generally, if an instrument is to qualify as a negotiable instrument, the person promising or

ordering payment may not state undertakings or instructions in addition to the payment of money [3-104(a)(3)]. However, the instrument may include clauses concerning (1) giving, maintaining, or protecting collateral to secure payment; (2) an authorization to confess judgment or to realize on or dispose of collateral; and (3) waiving the benefit of any law intended for the protection or benefit of any person obligated on the instrument.

Thus, a term authorizing the confession of judgment on an instrument when it is due does not affect the negotiability of the instrument. A confession of judgment clause authorizes the creditor to go into court if the debtor defaults and, with the debtor's acquiescence, to have a judgment entered against the debtor. However, some states prohibit confessions of judgment.

Banks and other businesses often use forms of commercial paper that meet their particular needs. These forms may include certain other terms that do not affect the negotiability of an instrument. For example, a note may designate a place of payment without affecting the instrument's negotiability. Where the instrument does not specify a place of payment, the Code sets out rules for ascertaining where payment is to be made [3-111].

Ambiguous Terms

Occasionally, a person may write or receive a check on which the amount written in figures differs from the amount written in words. Or a note may have conflicting terms or an ambiguous term. Where a conflict or an ambiguous term exists, there are general rules of interpretation that are applied to resolve the conflict or ambiguity: Typewritten terms prevail over printed terms; handwritten terms prevail over printed and typewritten terms; and where words and numbers conflict, the words control the numbers [3-114].

Problems and Problem Cases

1. Is the following instrument a note, a check, or a draft? Why? If it is not a check, how would you have to change it to make it a check?

   To: Arthur Adams January 1, 2022
   TEN DAYS AFTER DATE PAY TO THE ORDER OF:
   Bernie Brown
   THE SUM OF: Ten thousand and no/100 DOLLARS
   SIGNED: Carl Clark

2. Frank agrees to build a garage for Sarah for $45,000. Sarah offers either to sign a contract showing her obligation to pay Frank $45,000 or to sign a negotiable promissory note for $45,000 payable to the order of Frank. Would you advise Frank to ask for the contract or the promissory note? Explain.

3. A handwritten note provided as follows:

   I, Robert Harrison, owe Peter Jacob $25,000 (twenty-five thousand dollars) as of 3/27/08 for the following:

   1) $15,000 for Caterpillar loader.
   2) $5,000 for a loan.
   3) $5,000 for a tag-a-long trailer.

   Would this instrument qualify as a negotiable instrument?

4. Holly Hill Acres Ltd. executed a promissory note and mortgage and delivered them to Rogers. The note contained the following stipulation:

   this note with interest is secured by a mortgage on real estate of even date herewith, made by the maker hereof in favor of the said payee, and shall be construed and enforced according to the laws of the State of Florida. The terms of said mortgage are by this reference made a part hereof.

   Does the note qualify as a negotiable instrument?

5. Holiday made out a promissory note to Anderson, leaving the date of payment of the note blank. Anderson filled in the words "on demand" in the blank without Holiday's knowledge. Does this alter the rights or obligations of the parties?

6. Gary Vaughn signed a document stating that Fred and Martha Smith were loaning him $9,900 to be "repaid when you can." Eighteen months later when Vaughn had not paid the note, the Smiths sued Vaughn, claiming he had defaulted on the note. They contended that the document was a negotiable instrument that should be construed to be "payable on demand." Does this document qualify as a negotiable instrument?

7. Sheri Zimmerman executed a "Promissory Note" dated March 20, 2007. The total amount on the note was $46,378 with a principal amount of $40,000 and $6,378 in interest. The promissory note stated as follows:

   FOR VALUE RECEIVED, the undersigned here by jointly and severally promises to pay to the order of _____

   _____,
   the sum of *forty six thousand three hundred seventy eight ($46,378.00)*, together with interest thereon at a rate of *six percent (6%)* per annum on the unpaid balance. Said sum shall be paid in the manner following: *See attached schedule.*

   The promissory note further stated that any payments under it had to be made to such address as may be designated by "any holder." It was signed by Zimmerman alone as "Borrower" and it appeared that she had signed in her individual capacity because she did not sign in any other capacity. No other borrowers signed the note and it was not witnessed or notarized. Attached to the promissory note was a loan amortization schedule showing a total of 60 payments (12 payments a year for five years) totaling $46,378 ($40,000 principal and $6,378 interest).

Sheri Zimmerman and Robert Scott, who had known each other for a long time, decided to go into a new business venture called Aggressive Suspensions involving the fabrication of race car components. Scott, a skilled welder and fabricator of race cars, was to do the fabrication, and Zimmerman was going to take care of the books. Scott borrowed $40,000 from his mother, issued two checks totaling $40,000 that went into the business venture, and received the note from Zimmerman who considered herself the 75 percent owner of the business.

On January 29, 2009, Scott filed suit against Zimmerman for breach of contract and unjust enrichment, alleging that he had never received any payment from her, despite multiple requests to her for payment. One of the issues in the case was whether the promissory note was a valid note. Did the absence of a named payee invalidate the note?

8. Darryl Young presented five photocopied checks to the Lynnwood Check-X-Change on five different days between June 13 and June 21. Lynnwood cashed the first four checks presented. The fifth check, which was presented on a Saturday, was drawn on a different account from the first four checks and was payable on the following Monday. Lynnwood's practice was to cash checks on Saturday that are dated the following Monday. Young was convicted of five counts of forgery. On appeal, Young argued that the postdated check was not a legal instrument for purposes of the forgery statute. The crime of forgery requires an instrument that, if genuine, may have legal effect or be the foundation of legal liability. Young argued that the postdated check did not meet this requirement "because the time for payment had not arrived and thus the check could not have created any legal liability on the part of any person at that time." If a check is postdated, can it qualify as a negotiable instrument and create legal liability?

Negotiation and Holder in Due Course

Rachel Allen purchases a used Honda from Friendly Fred's Used Cars, paying $1,500 down and signing a promissory note in which she promises to pay $3,000 to Fred or to his order 12 months from the date of the note with interest at 8.5 percent. Fred assures Rachel that the car is in good condition and has never been involved in an accident. Fred indorses (signs) his name on the back of the promissory note and discounts (assigns) the note to Factors Inc. Subsequently, Rachel discovers that, contrary to Fred's assurance, the Honda had in fact been involved in an accident that caused a front-end alignment problem. When Factors notifies her of the assignment to it of the note and asks for payment on the due date, Rachel wants to assert a defense of failure of consideration or breach of contract (warranty) against full payment of the note.

Among the legal issues raised in this scenario are:

- When Fred transferred the promissory note to Factors after signing his name to the back of it, what rights did Factors obtain?
- Will Rachel be able to assert a defense of failure of consideration or breach of contract against full payment of the note to Factors?
- If the promissory note contained the clause required by the Federal Trade Commission in consumer notes or installment sales contracts, would it change Rachel's rights?

LO LEARNING OBJECTIVES

After studying this chapter, you should be able to:

32-1 Explain how negotiable instruments are transferred from one person to another.

32-2 Describe how *order* paper and *bearer* paper are negotiated.

32-3 Distinguish among blank, special, restrictive, and qualified indorsements.

32-4 Explain the importance of being a holder in due course of a negotiable instrument.

32-5 Identify and apply the requirements for becoming a holder in due course.

32-6 Define *holder*.

32-7 Distinguish "real defenses" from "personal defenses."

32-8 Explain how the Federal Trade Commission has changed the holder in due course rule as it applies to some or many consumer credit transactions.

CHAPTER 31 DISCUSSED the nature and benefits of negotiable instruments. It also outlined the requirements an instrument must meet to qualify as a negotiable instrument and thus possess the qualities that allow it to be accepted as a substitute for money.

This chapter focuses on negotiation—the process by which rights to a negotiable instrument pass from one person to another. Commonly, this involves an indorsement and transfer of the instrument. This chapter also develops the requirements that a transferee of a negotiable instrument must meet to qualify as a holder in due course and thus attain special rights under negotiable instruments law. These rights, which put a holder in due course in an enhanced position compared to an assignee of a contract, are discussed in some detail.

In this chapter, you also will consider whether it would be ethical to incur a gambling debt, to issue a check or other negotiable instrument in satisfaction of the debt, and then assert the defense of illegality against payment of the instrument.

Negotiation

 Explain how negotiable instruments are transferred from one person to another.

Nature of Negotiation
Under Revised Article 3, **negotiation** is the transfer of possession (whether voluntary or involuntary) of a negotiable instrument by a person (other than the issuer) to another person who becomes its *holder* [3-201]. A person is a **holder** if she is in possession of an instrument (1) that is payable to bearer or (2) made payable to an identified person and she is that identified person [1-201(20)].[1]

For example, when an employer gives an employee, Susan Adams, a paycheck payable "to the order of Susan Adams," she is the holder of the check because she is in possession of an instrument payable to an identified person (Susan Adams) and she is that person. When she indorses (writes her name) on the back of the check and exchanges it for cash and merchandise at Ace Grocery, she has negotiated the check to the grocery store and the store is now the holder because it is in possession by transfer of a check and unless she specifies the grocery store by name, the check now is payable to bearer. Similarly, if Susan Adams indorsed the check "Pay to the Order of Ace Grocery, Susan Adams" and transferred it to the grocery store, it would be a holder through the negotiation of the order check to it. The grocery store would be in possession of an instrument payable to an identified person (Ace Grocery) and is the person identified in the check.

In certain circumstances, Revised Article 3 allows a person to become a holder by negotiation even though the transfer of possession is involuntary. For example, if a negotiable instrument is payable to bearer and is stolen

by Tom Thief or found by Fred Finder, Thief or Finder becomes the holder when he obtains possession. The involuntary transfer of possession of a bearer instrument results in a negotiation to Thief or Finder.

Formal Requirements for Negotiation

 Describe how *order* paper and *bearer* paper are negotiated.

The formal requirements for negotiation are very simple. If an instrument is payable to the order of a specific payee, it is called *order paper*, and it can be negotiated by transfer of possession of the instrument after indorsement by the person specified [3-201(b)].

For example, if Rachel's father gives her a check payable "to the order of Rachel Stern," then Rachel can negotiate the check by indorsing her name on the back of the check and giving it to the person to whom she wants to transfer it. Note that the check is order paper, not because the word *order* appears on the check but, rather, because it named a specific payee, Rachel Stern.

If an instrument is payable "to bearer" or "to cash," it is called *bearer paper*, and negotiating it is even simpler. An instrument payable to bearer may be negotiated by transfer of possession alone [3-201(b)]. Thus, if someone gives you a check that is made payable "to the order of cash," you can negotiate it simply by giving it to the person to whom you wish to transfer it. No indorsement is necessary to negotiate an instrument payable to bearer. However, the person who takes the instrument may ask for an indorsement for her protection. By indorsing the check, you agree to be liable for its payment to that person if it is not paid by the drawee bank when it is presented for payment. This liability will be discussed in Chapter 33, Liability of Parties.

Nature of Indorsement
An indorsement is made by adding the signature of the holder of the instrument to the instrument, usually on the back of it, either alone or with other words. **Indorsement** is defined to mean "a signature (other than that of a maker or drawer) that alone or accompanied by other words, is made on an instrument for purpose of (i) negotiating the instrument, (ii) restricting payment of the instrument, or (iii) incurring indorser's liability on the instrument" [3-204(a)]. The negotiation and restriction of payment aspects of indorsements will be discussed next; indorser's liability will be covered in the next chapter.

---

[1]The numbers in brackets refer to sections of the Uniform Commercial Code (UCC), which can be accessed at www.law.cornell.edu/ucc.

The signature constituting an indorsement can be supplied or written either by the holder or by someone who is authorized to sign on behalf of the holder. For example, a check payable to "H&H Meat Market" might be indorsed "H&H Meat Market by Jane Frank, President," if Jane is authorized to do this on behalf of the market.

Wrong or Misspelled Name

When indorsing an instrument, the holder should spell his name in the same way as it appears on the instrument. If the holder's name is misspelled or wrong, then legally the indorsement can be made either in his name or in the name that is on the instrument. However, any person who pays the instrument or otherwise gives value for it may require the indorser to sign both names [3-204(d)].

Suppose Joan Ash is issued a check payable to the order of "Joanne Ashe." She may indorse the check as either "Joan Ash" or "Joanne Ashe." However, if she takes the check to a bank to cash, the bank may require her to sign both "Joanne Ashe" and "Joan Ash."

Checks Deposited without Indorsement

Occasionally, when a customer deposits a check to her account with a bank, she may forget to indorse the check. It is common practice for depositary banks to receive unindorsed checks under what are known as "lockbox" arrangements with customers who receive a high volume of checks. Normally, a check payable to the order of an identified person would require the indorsement of that person in order for a negotiation to the depositary bank to take place and for it to become a holder. Under the original Article 3, the depositary bank, in most cases, had the right to supply the customer's indorsement. Instead of actually signing the customer's name to the check as the indorsement, the bank might just stamp on it that it was deposited by the customer or credited to her account. Banks did not have the right to put the customer's indorsement on a check that the customer has deposited if the check specifically required the payee's signature. Insurance and government checks commonly require the payee's signature.

The revision to Article 3 and the conforming amendments to Articles 1 and 4 address the situation where a check is deposited in a depositary bank without indorsement differently. The depositary bank becomes a holder of an item delivered to it for collection, whether or not it is indorsed by the customer, if the customer at the time of delivery qualified as a holder [4-205]. The depositary bank warrants to other collecting banks, the payor bank (drawee), and the drawer that it paid the amount of the item to the customer or deposited the amount to the customer's account.

Transfer of Order Instrument

Except for the special provisions concerning depositary banks, if an order instrument is transferred without indorsement, the instrument has not been negotiated and the transferee cannot qualify as a holder. For example, Sue Brown gives a check payable "to the order of Susan Brown" to a drugstore in payment for some cosmetics. Until Sue indorses the check, she has not "negotiated" it and the druggist could not qualify as a "holder" of the check.

Transfer of an instrument, whether or not the transfer is a negotiation, vests in the transferee, such as the drugstore, any right of Sue, the transferor, to enforce the instrument. However, the transferee cannot obtain the rights of a holder in due course (discussed later in this chapter) if he engaged in any fraud or illegality affecting the instrument. Unless otherwise agreed, if an instrument is transferred for value but without a required indorsement, the transferee has the right to obtain the unqualified indorsement of the transferor; however, the "negotiation" takes place only when the transferor applies her indorsement [3-203(c)].

The *Town of Freeport* case, which follows, illustrates these principles.

Town of Freeport v. Ring   727 A.2d 901 (Me. 1999)

Thornton Ring was the owner of real property located on Main Street in Freeport, Maine. In August 1994, the Town sent Ring a letter noting that his 1993–1994 real estate taxes were unpaid and notified him of the Town's intent to file a lien on the property if payment was not received within 30 days. The taxes remained unpaid and a tax lien was filed on the property. On January 26, 1996, because a portion of the taxes still remained unpaid, the Town sent a Notice of Impending Foreclosure of the Tax Lien Certificate to Ring by certified mail, advising him that the tax lien would be deemed to be foreclosed on February 27, 1996. Ring subsequently was in default for his 1994–1995 taxes and similar notices were sent.

In January 1997, Ring delivered to the Town a check in the amount of $11,347.09. The check was issued by Advest and made payable to the order of Thornton D. Ring. The back of the check was inscribed as follows:

Payable to Town of Freeport
Property Taxes
2 Main St[.]

The check was accompanied by a letter, signed by Ring and dated January 20, 1997, which reads, "I have paid $11,347.09 of real estate taxes and request the appropriate action to redeem the corresponding property." On February 3, 1997, Ring received a letter from the Town explaining that the Town was returning the check because the 1994 tax lien on the property had matured in 1996.

The Town filed suit seeking a declaratory judgment that it had good title to the Main Street property. One of the issues was whether the delivery of the check by Ring constituted payment of his outstanding taxes.

Clifford, Justice

With respect to a check that is made payable to the order of a specific person, negotiation occurs, and the person receiving the check becomes a holder of a negotiable instrument, if possession of the check is transferred and the check is indorsed by the transferor. An indorsement is a signature of someone other than the maker, or some other designation identifying the indorser, that is made on an instrument for the purpose of negotiating the instrument. *Kelly v. Central Bank & Trust Co.* (writing on back of check which reads "For deposit only" to an account other than the payee's and without payee's signature is not an effective indorsement). If negotiation occurs and the holder qualifies as a holder in due course, the holder can demand payment of the instrument subject only to real defenses.

The check Ring sent to the Town was issued by Advest payable to the order of Thornton D. Ring. Because it was payable to Ring's order, the check could only be negotiated by Ring through indorsement and transfer of possession. Ring's signature, however, does not appear on the back of the check. The words that do appear on the back of the check—"Payable to Town of Freeport[/]Property Taxes[/]2 Main St[.]"—do not identify Ring. The words only indicate to whom the instrument should have been payable had the check been properly indorsed. Thus, the writing is an incomplete attempt to create a special indorsement. A special indorsement is an indorsement that identifies a person to whom the indorser is making the check payable.

The statement included within the letter accompanying the check does not serve as a valid indorsement either. In determining whether an instrument is properly indorsed, any papers affixed to the instrument are considered part of the instrument. See section 3-204(1). This language specifically references only "affixed" documents. Courts interpreting this language have concluded that a signature on a separate, unattached piece of paper is not an indorsement of the instrument. Ring does not dispute

that there is no evidence on record to suggest that the letter was physically attached to the check.

Relying on sections 3-203(3) and 3-203(2), Ring also contends that even in the absence of an indorsement, the check should have been accepted as payment of his outstanding taxes because the Town (1) had a statutory right to demand an indorsement of the check or (2) was entitled to enforce the instrument without the indorsement. Section 3-203(3) provides that "if an instrument is transferred for value and the transferee does not become a holder because of lack of indorsement by the transferor, the transferee has a specifically enforceable right to the unqualified indorsement of the transferor. . . ." Section 3-203(2) provides "Transfer of an instrument, whether or not the transfer is a negotiation, vests in the transferee any right of the transferor to enforce the instrument."

Even if the Town could demand an indorsement pursuant to section 3-203(3), negotiation does not occur until the indorsement is made. See section 3-203(3). Thus, at the time the check was received, the Town had a right to demand an indorsement, but could not go to the bank to demand payment of the check. Pursuant to section 3-203(2), the bank also had the right to enforce the instrument as the transferee of an instrument from a holder. That right, however, could be enforced only through a judicial proceeding. Such contingent rights to receive payment are not sufficient to redeem property subject to a municipal tax lien. Checks are meant to be the functional equivalent of cash when they are properly issued and negotiated. If the Town has to institute a judicial proceeding to receive the cash equivalent of the check, the check has not served its purpose. The unindorsed check presented to the Town is not the type of payment the redemption option of the tax lien statute contemplates.

Judgment for Town affirmed.

Indorsements

LO32-3 Distinguish among blank, special, restrictive, and qualified indorsements.

Effects of an Indorsement

There are three functions to an indorsement. First, an indorsement is necessary in order for the negotiation of an instrument that is payable to the order of a specified person. Thus, if a check is payable "to the order of James Lee," James must indorse the check before it can be negotiated. Second, the form of the indorsement that the indorser uses also affects future attempts to negotiate the instrument. For example, if James indorses it "Pay to the order of Sarah Hill," Sarah must indorse it before it can be negotiated further.

Third, an indorsement generally makes a person liable on the instrument. By indorsing an instrument, a person incurs an obligation to pay the instrument if the person primarily liable on it (e.g., the maker of a note) does not pay it. We discuss the contractual liability of indorsers in Chapter 33. In this chapter, we discuss the effect of an indorsement on further negotiation of an instrument.

Kinds of Indorsements

There are three basic kinds of indorsements: (1) special, (2) blank, and (3) restrictive. In addition, an indorsement may be "qualified."

Special Indorsement A special indorsement contains the signature of the indorser along with words indicating to whom, or to whose order, the instrument is payable. For example, if a check is drawn "Pay to the Order of Marcia Morse" and Marcia indorses it "Pay to the Order of Sam Smith, Marcia Morse," or "Pay to Sam Smith, Marcia Morse," it has been indorsed with a special indorsement. An instrument that is indorsed with a special indorsement remains "order paper." It can be negotiated only with the indorsement of the person specified [3-205(a)]. In this example, Sam Smith must indorse the check before he can negotiate it to someone else.

Blank Indorsement If an indorser merely signs his name and does not specify to whom the instrument is payable, he has indorsed the instrument in blank. For example, if a check drawn "Pay to the Order of Natalie Owens" is indorsed "Natalie Owens" by Natalie, Natalie has indorsed it in blank. An instrument indorsed in blank is now payable to the bearer (person in possession of it) and from that act is "bearer paper." As such, the bearer negotiates it by transfer alone and no further indorsement is necessary for negotiation [3-205(b)].

If Natalie indorsed the check in blank and gave it to Kevin Foley, Kevin would have the right to convert the blank indorsement into a special indorsement [3-205(c)]. He could do this by writing the words "Pay to the Order of Kevin Foley" above Natalie's indorsement. Then Kevin would have to indorse the check before it could be further negotiated.

If Kevin took the check indorsed in blank to a bank and presented it for payment or for collection, the bank normally would ask him to indorse the check. It asks not because it needs his indorsement for the check to be negotiated to it; the check indorsed in blank can be negotiated merely by delivering it to the bank cashier. Rather, the bank asks for his indorsement because it wants to make him liable on the check if it is not paid when the bank sends it to the drawee bank for payment. Chapter 33, Liability of Parties, discusses the liability of indorsers.

Restrictive Indorsement A restrictive indorsement is one that specifies the purpose of the indorsement or specifies the use to be made of the instrument. Among the more common restrictive indorsements are:

1. Indorsements for deposit. For example, "For Deposit Only" or "For Deposit to My Account at First National Bank."
2. Indorsements for collection, which are commonly put on by banks involved in the collection process. For example, "Pay any bank, banker, or trust company" or "For collection only."
3. Indorsements indicating that the indorsement is for the benefit of someone other than the person to whom it is payable. For example, "Pay to Arthur Attorney in Trust for Mark Minor."

Generally, the person who takes an instrument with a restrictive indorsement must pay or apply any money or other value he gives for the instrument consistently with the indorsement. In the case of a check indorsed "for deposit" or "for collection," any person other than a bank who purchases the check is considered to have converted the check unless (1) the indorser received the amount paid for it or (2) the bank applied the amount of the check consistently with the indorsement (e.g., deposited it to the indorser's account). Similarly, a depositary bank (a bank that takes an item for collection) or payor bank (the drawee bank) that takes an instrument for deposit or for immediate payment over the counter that has been indorsed "for deposit" or "for collection" will be liable for conversion unless the indorser received the amount paid for the instrument or the proceeds or the bank applied the amount consistently with the indorsement [3-206(c)].

Lehigh Presbytery v. Merchants Bancorp
17 UCC Rep. 2d 163 (Pa. Super. Ct. 1991)

Mary Ann Hunsberger was hired by the Lehigh Presbytery as a secretary/bookkeeper. In this capacity, she was responsible for opening the Presbytery's mail, affixing a rubber-stamp indorsement to checks received by the Presbytery, and depositing the checks into the Presbytery's account at Merchants Bancorp. Over a period of more than five years, Hunsberger deposited into her own account 153 of these checks. Each check was indorsed: "For Deposit Only To The Credit of Presbytery of Lehigh, Ernest Hutcheson, Treas." The bank credited the checks to Hunsberger's account, despite the rubber-stamp restrictive indorsement because it relied solely on the account number handwritten on the deposit slips submitted by Hunsberger with the checks at the time of deposit. Hunsberger obtained the deposit slips in the lobby of the bank, wrote the proper account title, "Lehigh Presbytery," but inserted her own account number rather than the account number of her employer.

When Lehigh Presbytery discovered the diversionary scheme, it sued the bank to recover the funds credited to Hunsberger's account. The primary issue in the case was whether the bank was bound to follow the restrictive indorsements on the 153 checks that it instead had deposited to the personal account of Hunsberger. The trial court ruled in favor of the bank and Lehigh Presbytery appealed.

McEwen, Judge

UCC Section 3-205 provides:

An indorsement is restrictive which either:

. . .

(3) includes the words "for collection," "for deposit," "pay any bank," or like terms signifying a purpose of deposit or collection; or

. . .

It is undisputed that the indorsement stamped on each check by Ms. Hunsberger is a restrictive indorsement within the meaning of section 3-205.

Section 3-206 of the UCC addresses the effect of such an indorsement and provides, in pertinent part:

(c) Conditional or specified purpose indorsement—Except for an intermediary bank, any transferee under an indorsement which is conditional or includes the words "for collection," "for deposit," "Pay any bank," or like terms (section 3-205(1) and (3) relating to restrictive indorsements) must pay or apply

any value given by him for or on the security of the instrument consistently with the indorsement and to the extent he does he becomes a holder for value.

Thus, the UCC mandates application of the value of the checks consistently with the indorsement, that is, for deposit to Lehigh Presbytery's account.

Courts considering the significance of a restrictive indorsement have consistently concluded that the UCC imposes an unwaivable obligation upon the bank to follow the indorsement. New York State's highest court has held that "[t]he presence of a restriction imposes upon the depositary bank an obligation not to accept that item other than in accord with the restriction. By disregarding the restriction, it not only subjects itself to liability for any losses resulting from its actions, but it also passes up what may be the best opportunity to prevent the fraud."

Judgment reversed in favor of Lehigh Presbytery.

Note: Although this case was decided under the original version of Article 3, the same result would be expected under Revised Article 3.

By way of illustration, assume that Robert Franks has indorsed his paycheck "For Deposit to My Account No. 4068933 at First Bank." While on his way to the bank he loses the check, and Fred Finder finds it. If Finder tries to cash the check at a check-cashing service, the service must ensure that any value it gives for the check either is deposited to Franks's account at First Bank or is received by Franks. If the service gives the money to Finder, it will be liable to Franks for converting his check. This principle is illustrated in *Lehigh Presbytery*, which involves a bank

that failed to apply value given for checks consistently with restrictive indorsements on the checks.

Some indorsements indicate payment to the indorsee as an agent, trustee, or fiduciary. A person who takes an instrument containing such an indorsement from the indorsee may pay the proceeds to the indorsee without regard to whether the indorsee violates a fiduciary duty to the indorser *unless* he is on *notice* of any breach of fiduciary duty that the indorser may be committing [3-206(d)]. A person would have such notice if he took the instrument

The Global Business Environment

**Convention on International Bills
of Exchange and International Promissory
Notes**

In 1988 the Convention on International Bills of Exchange and International Promissory Notes was adopted by the United Nations. The Convention is applicable to drafts and notes but not to checks. Under the Convention, a bill of exchange is an order to pay money, while a promissory note is a promise to pay money. To be covered, they must have the attributes of negotiability. They also must be international in nature in that at least two of the places where their operations occur—such as the address of the drawer or promissory, the address of the payee, or the place of payment—must be in different countries. The Convention also requires that the parties must affirmatively elect to be covered by the Convention by placing a specified legend on the instrument.

In drafting the Convention, the drafters had to try to accommodate or harmonize differences between civil and common law countries concerning negotiable instruments. A major difference between the two systems is how they deal with forged indorsements. Under the common law and UCC Articles 3 and 4, a forged indorsement is not effective to negotiate an instrument to the indorsee, while under the civil law it is. Under the civil law, the indorsee takes title to the instrument and acquires the rights of a holder, and payment to the indorsee discharges makers and drawers. As discussed in this and the following chapter, under the UCC, an indorsee taking an instrument with a forged indorsement does not gain these rights, and a maker or drawer is not discharged by making payment to that indorsee. The resolution of these differences in the Convention is too complex to discuss in this textbook.

---

in any transaction that benefited the indorsee personally [3-307]. Suppose a person takes a check indorsed to "Arthur Attorney in Trust for Mark Minor." The money given for the check should be put in Mark Minor's trust account. A person would not be justified in taking the check in exchange for a television set that he knew Attorney was acquiring for his own—rather than Minor's—use.

There are two other kinds of indorsements that the original Article 3 treated as restrictive indorsements but that the Revised Article 3 no longer considers as restrictive indorsements. They are:

1. Indorsements purporting to prohibit further negotiation. For example, "Pay to Carl Clark Only."

2. Conditional indorsements, which indicate that they are effective only if the payee satisfies a certain condition. For example, "Pay to Bernard Builder Only If He Completes Construction on My House by November 1, 2022."

Under Revised Article 3, any indorsement that purports to limit payment to a particular person, or to prohibit further transfer or negotiation of the instrument, is not effective to prevent further transfer or negotiation [3-206(a)]. Thus, if a note is indorsed "Pay to Carl Clark Only" and given to Clark, he may negotiate the note to subsequent holders who may ignore the restriction on the indorsement.

Indorsements that state a condition to the right of the indorsee to receive payment do not affect the right of the indorsee to enforce the instrument. Any person who pays the instrument or takes it for value or for collection may disregard the condition. Moreover, the rights and liabilities

of the person are not affected by whether the condition has been fulfilled [3-206(b)].

Qualified Indorsement A qualified indorsement is one where the indorser disclaims her contractual liability to make the instrument good if the maker or drawer defaults on it. Words such as "Without Recourse" are used to qualify an indorsement. They can be used with either a blank indorsement or a special indorsement and thus make it a qualified blank indorsement or a qualified special indorsement. The use of a qualified indorsement does not change the negotiable nature of the instrument. Its effect is to eliminate the contractual liability of the particular indorser. Chapter 33, Liability of Parties, will discuss this liability in detail.

Rescission of Indorsement

Negotiation is effective to transfer an instrument even if the negotiation is (1) made by a minor, a corporation exceeding its powers, or any other person without contractual capacity; (2) obtained by fraud, duress, or mistake of any kind; (3) made in breach of duty; or (4) part of an illegal transaction. A negotiation made under the preceding circumstances is subject to rescission before the instrument has been negotiated to a transferee who can qualify as a holder in due course or a person paying the instrument in good faith and without knowledge of the factual basis for rescission or other remedy [3-202]. The situation in such instances is analogous to a sale of goods where the sale has been induced by fraud or misrepresentation. In such a case, the seller may rescind the

Indorsements (Assume a check is payable "To the Order of Mark Smith.")

Type	Example	Consequences
Blank	Mark Smith	1. Satisfies the indorsement requirement for the negotiation of order paper. 2. The instrument becomes bearer paper and can be negotiated by delivery alone. 3. The indorser becomes obligated on the instrument. (See Chapter 33, Liability of Parties.)
Special	Pay to the Order of Joan Brown, Mark Smith	1. Satisfies the indorsement requirement for the negotiation of order paper. 2. The instrument remains order paper and Joan Brown's indorsement is required for further negotiation. 3. The indorser becomes obligated on the instrument. (See Chapter 33.)
Restrictive	For deposit only to my account in First American Bank, Mark Smith	1. Satisfies the indorsement requirement for the negotiation of order paper. 2. The person who pays value for the instrument is obligated to pay it consistent with the indorsement (i.e., to pay it into Mark Smith's account at First American Bank). 3. The indorser becomes obligated on the instrument. (See Chapter 33.)
Qualified	Mark Smith (without recourse)	1. Satisfies the indorsement requirement for negotiation of order paper. 2. Eliminates the indorser's obligation. (See Chapter 33.)

sale and recover the goods, provided that the seller acts before the goods are resold to a bona fide purchaser for value.

Holder in Due Course

 Explain the importance of being a holder in due course of a negotiable instrument.

A person who qualifies as a holder in due course of a negotiable instrument gets special rights. Normally, the transferee of an instrument—like the assignee of a contract—gets only those rights in the instrument that are held by the person from whom he got the instrument. But a holder in due course can get better rights. A holder in due course takes a negotiable instrument free of all personal defenses, claims to the instrument, and claims in recoupment either of the obligor or of a third party. A holder in due course does not take free of the real defenses, which go to the validity of the instrument or of claims that develop after he becomes a holder. We develop the differences between "personal" and "real defenses" in more detail later in this chapter and also explain claims to the instrument and claims in recoupment. The following example illustrates the advantage that a holder in due course of a negotiable instrument may have.

Assume that Carl Carpenter contracts with Helen Hawkins to build her a garage for $38,500, payable on October 1 when he expects to complete the garage. Assume further that Carpenter assigns his right to the $38,500 to First National Bank in order to obtain money for materials. If the bank tries to collect the money from Hawkins on October 1 but Carpenter has not finished building the garage, then Hawkins may assert the fact that the garage is not complete as a defense to paying the bank. As assignee of a simple contract, the bank has only those rights that its assignor, Carpenter, has and is subject to all claims and defenses that Hawkins has against Carpenter.

Now assume that instead of simply signing a contract with Hawkins, Carpenter had Homeowner give him a negotiable promissory note in the amount of $38,500 payable to the order of Carpenter on October 1 and that Carpenter then negotiated the note to the bank. If the bank is able to qualify as a holder in due course, it may collect the $38,500 from Hawkins on October 1 even though she might have a personal defense against payment of the note because Carpenter had not completed the work on the garage. Hawkins cannot assert that personal defense against a holder in due course. She would have to pay the note to the bank and then independently seek to recover from Carpenter for breach of their agreement. The bank's improved position is due to its status as a holder in due course of a negotiable instrument. If the instrument in question was not negotiable, or if the bank could not qualify as a holder in due course, then it would be in the same position as the assignee of a simple contract and would be subject to Homeowner's personal defense.

We turn now to a discussion of the requirements that must be met for the possessor of a negotiable instrument to qualify as a holder in due course.

General Requirements

 LO32-5 Identify and apply the requirements for becoming a holder in due course.

In order to become a **holder in due course**, a person who takes a negotiable instrument must be a *holder* and take the instrument:

1. For *value*.
2. In *good faith*.
3. *Without notice* that it is *overdue* or has been *dishonored* or that there is any uncured default with respect to payment of another instrument issued as part of the same series.
4. *Without notice that the instrument contains an unauthorized signature or has been altered.*
5. *Without notice of any claim of a property or possessory interest in it.*
6. *Without notice* that any party has any *defense against it* or claim in *recoupment to it* (3-302[a][2]).

In addition, Revised Article 3 requires "that the instrument when issued or negotiated to the holder does not bear such *apparent evidence of forgery or alteration* or is not otherwise so *irregular* or *incomplete* as to call into question its authenticity" [3-302(a)(1)].

If a person who takes a negotiable instrument does not meet these requirements, he is not a holder in due course. Then the person is in the same position as an assignee of a contract.

Holder

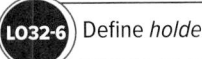 **LO32-6** Define *holder.*

To be a **holder** of a negotiable instrument, a person must have possession of an instrument that is either payable to "bearer" or that is payable to him. For example, if Teresa

Gonzales is given a check by her grandmother that is made payable "to the order of Teresa Gonzales," Teresa is a holder of the check because it is made out to her. If Teresa indorses the check "Pay to the order of Ames Hardware, Teresa Gonzales" and gives it to Ames Hardware in payment for some merchandise, then Ames Hardware is the holder of the check. Ames Hardware is a holder because it is in possession of a check that is indorsed to its order. If Ames Hardware indorses the check "Ames Hardware" and deposits it in its account at First National Bank, the bank becomes the holder. The bank is in possession of an instrument that is indorsed in blank and thus is payable to bearer.

It is important that all indorsements on the instrument at the time it is payable to the order of someone are *authorized indorsements.* With limited exceptions (discussed later), a forged indorsement is not an effective indorsement and prevents a person from becoming a holder.

To be a holder, a person must have a complete chain of authorized indorsements. Suppose the Internal Revenue Service mails to Robert Washington an income tax refund check payable to him. Tom Turner steals the check from Washington's mailbox, signs (indorses) "Robert Washington" on the back of the check, and cashes it at a shoe store. The shoe store is not a holder of the check because its transferor, Turner, was not a holder and because it needs Washington's signature to have a good chain of authorized indorsements. Robert Washington has to indorse the check in order for there to be a valid chain of indorsements. Turner's signature is not effective for this purpose because Washington did not authorize him to sign Washington's name to the check [1-201(20), 3-403(a), 3-416(a)(2)].

As a result of subprime home loans made during the 2000s to borrowers who were unable to meet their obligations, defaults on the loans and foreclosures became common in 2007 and the following years. In many instances, the loans had been securitized by being bundled together and sold to investors or institutions other than the originating banks. When foreclosure actions were brought, one of the issues was whether the party bringing the foreclosure action was a party entitled to enforce the promissory note that was part of the original transaction. In the case that follows, *Bank of America v. Inda,* a bank was successful in showing that it was the holder of a note and thus entitled to enforce it, even though it had transferred the beneficial interest to another entity and was acting only as the servicer of the loan. In some other cases, however, entities bringing foreclosure actions were not able to establish their right to bring a foreclosure action and collect on a note when their right to do so was challenged by the borrower.

Bank of America, N.A. v. Inda   80 UCC Rep. 2d 1 (Kan. Ct. App. 2013)

On March 30, 2007, Dennis Inda and his wife signed a promissory note promising to pay Pulaski Bank the principal sum of $244,000 plus interest in monthly installments. As security for the note, they signed a mortgage on their home in Olathe, Kansas. The mortgage defined the Mortgage Electronic Registration Systems (MERS), a separate corporation, and stated that MERS was acting "solely as nominee" for Pulaski and Pulaski's successors and assigns.

The note was indorsed by Pulaski to Countrywide Bank N.A., which in turn indorsed the note to Countrywide Home Loans. Countrywide Home Loans then indorsed the note "in blank," and the note was transferred to Bank of America. Meanwhile, the mortgage had been assigned to BAC Home Loans Servicing, which was subsequently merged into Bank of America. Bank of America then sold its beneficial interest to Freddie Mac but continued to serve as the servicer of the note and also continued to possess the note.

Inda defaulted on the note, and on January 25, 2010, Bank of America filed a foreclosure action on the mortgage. One of the issues in the lawsuit was whether Bank of America was a holder of the note and thus entitled to enforce the mortgage. The trial court granted summary judgment in favor of Bank of America.

Green, Judge

In Kansas, a note is a negotiable instrument which is subject to Article 3 of the Kansas Uniform Commercial Code. Under section 3-301 of the UCC, a person entitled to enforce an instrument can be any of the following:

(a) the holder of the instrument, (b) a non-holder in possession of the instrument who has the rights of a holder, or (c) a person not in possession of the instrument who is entitled to enforce the instrument under 3-309 or 3-418(d). A person may be a person entitled to enforce the instrument *even though the person is not the owner of the instrument* or is in wrongful possession of the instrument. (Emphasis added).

"Holder" means a "person in possession of a negotiable instrument that is payable either to bearer or to an identified person who is the person in possession." Section 1-201(21)(A).

A person who is a holder remains a holder although that person has made an assignment of a beneficial interest therein. *In re Martinez* (Bankr. D. Kan. 2011).

Further, under section 3-205(b), in a case like this, a note can be indorsed "in blank," which means that the instrument becomes payable to the bearer and may be negotiated by transfer of possession alone until specifically indorsed.

Based on these provisions of the UCC, Bank of America was entitled to enforce the note against Inda upon a showing (1) that the note was payable to Bank of America or was indorsed in blank and (2) that Bank of America remained in possession of the note.

[The court went on to hold that because the record established that Bank of America was the holder of the note executed by Inda, Bank of America was the successor on the mortgage and that because Inda was in default on the note, Bank of America was entitled to summary judgment on its mortgage foreclosure action as a matter of law.]

Judgment for Bank of America affirmed.

CYBERLAW IN ACTION

In Chapter 19, we noted that the Uniform Electronic Transactions Act adopted by many states and the federal Electronic Signatures in Global and National Commerce Act (the "E-Sign Act") covered many kinds of commercial transactions and authorized the use of electronic signatures and messages indicating approval where the state law requires a "signed writing." However, both UETA and the E-Sign Act explicitly exclude items governed by Article 3—Negotiable Instruments of the Uniform Commercial Code. Thus, one cannot scan a promissory note into an electronic note and have the electronic version qualify as a negotiable instrument.

As a result, investors who believed they had acquired bundles of mortgages and accompanying notes in the form of securitized investment vehicles in recent years have encountered problems trying to enforce the notes when the borrowers defaulted because the courts have refused to recognize serial electronic assignments of the notes where there is no clear chain of ownership of a given note. For example, in *In re* Wilhelm (Bankr. D. Idaho 2009), the court rejected the efforts of the assignees of mortgage obligations to enforce the obligations as holders. The court noted that to be a "holder," both one must possess the note and the note must be payable to the person in possession of the note or to bearer. In this instance, none of the notes were payable to the assignee seeking to enforce them and none of the notes had been indorsed, either in blank or specifically to the assignee.

Value To qualify as a holder in due course of a negotiable instrument, a person must give **value** for it. Value is not identical to simple consideration. Under the provisions of the Revised Article 3, a holder takes for value if (1) the agreed-upon promise of performance has been performed—for example, if the instrument was given in exchange for a promise to deliver a refrigerator and the refrigerator has been delivered; (2) he acquires a security interest in, or a lien on, the instrument; (3) he takes the instrument in payment of, or as security for, an antecedent claim; (4) he gives a negotiable instrument for it; or (5) he makes an irrevocable commitment to a third person [3-303]. Thus, a person who gets a check as a gift or merely makes an executory promise in return for a check has not given value for it and cannot qualify as a holder in due course.

A bank or any person who takes an instrument at a discount in the *regular course of trade* has given value for it. In this context, the discount essentially is a means for increasing the return or the rate of interest on the instrument. Likewise, if a loan is made and an instrument is pledged as security for the repayment of the loan, the secured party has given value for the instrument to the amount of the loan. If Axe, who owes Bell a past-due debt, indorses and delivers to Bell, in payment of the debt or as security for its repayment, an instrument issued to Axe, Bell has given value for the instrument. If a bank allows a customer to draw against a check deposited for collection, it has given value to the extent of the credit drawn against.

If the promise of performance that is the consideration for an instrument has been partially performed, the holder may assert rights as a holder in due course of the instrument only to the fraction of the amount payable under the instrument equal to the partial performance divided by the value of the promised performance [3-302(d)]. For example, Arthur Wells agrees to purchase a note payable to the order of Helda Parks. The note is for the sum of $5,000. Wells pays Parks $1,000 on the negotiation of the note to him and agrees to pay the balance of $4,000 in 10 days. Initially, Wells is a holder in due course for one-fifth of the amount of the note. If he later pays the $4,000 due, he may become a holder in due course for the full amount.

Good Faith To qualify as a holder in due course of a negotiable instrument, a person must take it in **good faith**, which means that the person obtained it honestly and in the observance of reasonable commercial standards of fair dealing [3-103(a)(4)]. If a person obtains a check by trickery or with knowledge that it has been stolen, the person has not obtained the check in good faith and cannot be a holder in due course. A person who pays too little for an instrument, perhaps because she suspects that something may be wrong with the way it was obtained, may have trouble meeting the good-faith test. Suppose a finance company works closely with a door-to-door sales company that engages in shoddy practices. If the finance company buys the consumers' notes from the sales company, it will not be able to meet the good-faith test and qualify as a holder in due course of the notes.

In the case that follows, *RR Maloan Investment v. New HGE*, the court concluded that a holder who had taken a postdated check had taken it in good faith and could qualify as a holder in due course.

RR Maloan Investment v. New HGE   **83 UCC Rep. 2d 311 (Tex. Ct. App. 2014)**

On September 23, 2011, Houston Gold Exchange issued a $3,500 check as payor to Shelly McKee as drawer to buy a purported Rolex watch from her. The check was postdated September 26, 2011. McKee endorsed the check and took it to a check-cashing service, RR Maloan, which cashed the check for her on September 24, 2011. Also on September 24, 2011, Houston Gold Exchange issued a stop-payment order based on information that the watch was counterfeit. When RR Maloan presented the check to Houston Gold Exchange's bank for payment, the bank refused to honor the check based on the stop-payment order.

RR Maloan sued Houston Gold Exchange, asserting that it was a holder in due course entitled to collect on the check. Among other things, Houston Gold Exchange took the position that the check was a not a negotiable instrument because it had been postdated. It also argued that RR Maloan should have investigated based on the fact the check was postdated and that its failure to do so meant it had not taken the check in good faith and could not qualify as a holder in due course.

Boyce, Justice

The holder of a negotiable instrument is a holder in due course if the holder takes the instrument: (1) for value; (2) in good faith; and (3) without notice of any claim or defense to the instrument. UCC Section 3-302. At trial, Houston Gold Exchange argued that the check at issue was not a negotiable instrument because it was post-dated. We reject this contention because the negotiability of a check is not affected by post-dating. UCC Section 3-113.

A holder is presumed to be a holder in due course unless there is evidence to the contrary. A holder in due course takes the instrument free from all claims and all defenses of any party to the instrument with whom he has not dealt unless a defense that bars recovery by a holder in due course applies.

The evidence adduced at trial conclusively establishes that RR Maloan was a holder in due course. Under section 3-302, a holder of an instrument is a holder in due course if "the instrument when issued or negotiated to the holder does not bear such apparent evidence of forgery or alteration or is not otherwise so irregular or incomplete as to call into question its authenticity. No evidence in this record suggests that the check was forged, altered, or not authentic.

There is no dispute on this record that RR Maloan took the check "for value" as required under section 3-302(a)(2)(A).

With respect to good faith under section 1-201(b)(20), in the UCC, "good faith" is defined as "honesty in fact and the observance of reasonable commercial standards of fair dealing." The record here conclusively establishes RR Maloan's good faith as that concept is defined for these purposes in the statute.

RR Maloan's owner had testified that the company is a check cashing business. The owner testified that an employee of the company took Houston Gold Exchange's check from McKee in exchange for cash in the normal course of business. The owner testified that at the time the check was taken, he did not have any knowledge that the purported Rolex watch was not authentic and did not have knowledge of any claim or defense to the check. The test for "good" faith is whether the purchaser had actual knowledge of facts and circumstances amounting to bad faith. No evidence was presented that the owner or any employee of RR Maloan had knowledge at the time the check was accepted that the watch was not authentic.

As for "reasonable commercial standards," Texas law holds that knowledge of post-dating by itself does not (1) give notice of a defense or claim; or (2) impose any duty to make any investigation to ascertain whether or not the maker had any defense which would have justified him refusing to pay the payee. Because the fact of post-dating did not impose a duty on RR Maloan to investigate the surrounding circumstances, Houston Gold Exchange cannot establish that RR Maloan failed to observe reasonable commercial standards of fair dealing by failing to investigate based on post-dating of the check.

In light of this record and the admitted validity of the signatures on the check, production of the check entitled RR Maloan to recover unless Houston Gold Exchange established a viable defense that would defeat holder in due course status. An assertion that the sale was conditioned on the watch's authenticity, even if true, does not bar recovery by RR Maloan; there is no evidence that it had knowledge of this asserted fact.

Judgment for RR Maloan.

Overdue or Dishonored

In order to qualify as a holder in due course, a person must take a negotiable instrument before he has notice that it either is **overdue** or has been **dishonored**. The reason for this is that one should perform obligations when they are due. If a negotiable instrument is not paid when it is due, the Code considers the person taking it to be on notice that there may be defenses to the payment of it.

Overdue Instruments If a negotiable instrument is payable on demand, it is overdue (1) the day after demand for payment has been made in a proper manner and form; (2) 90 days after its date if it is a check; and (3) if it is an instrument other than a check, when it has been outstanding for an unreasonably long period of time in light of the nature of the instrument and trade practice [3-304(a)]. Thus, a check becomes **stale** after 90 days. For other kinds of instruments, one must consider trade practices and the facts of the particular case. In a farming community, the normal period for loans to farmers may be six months. A demand note might be outstanding for six or seven months before it is considered overdue. On the other hand, a demand note issued in an industrial city where the normal period of such loans is 30 to 60 days would be considered overdue in a much shorter period of time.

If a negotiable instrument due on a certain date is not paid by that date, normally then it will be overdue at the beginning of the next day after the due date. For example, if a promissory note dated January 1 is payable "30 days after date," it is due on January 31. If it is not paid by January 31, it is overdue beginning on February 1 and can be enforced on that date.

As to instruments payable at a definite time, Revised Article 3 sets out the following rules: (1) if the principal is not payable in installments and the due date has not been accelerated, the instrument is overdue on the day after the due date; (2) if the principal is due in installments and a due date has not been accelerated, the instrument is overdue upon default for nonpayment of an installment and remains overdue until the default is cured; (3) if a due date for the principal has been accelerated, the instrument is overdue on the day after the accelerated due date; and (4) unless the due date of the principal has been accelerated, an instrument does not become overdue if there is a default in payment of interest but no default in payment of principal [3-304(b)].

Dishonored Instruments To be a holder in due course, a person not only must take a negotiable instrument before he has notice that it is overdue but also must take it before it has been dishonored. A negotiable instrument has been *dishonored* when the holder has *presented* it for payment (or acceptance) and payment (or acceptance) has been refused.

For example, Susan writes a check on her account at First National Bank that is payable "to the order of Sven Sorensen." Sven takes the check to First National Bank to cash it, but the bank refuses to pay it because Susan has insufficient funds in her account to cover it. The check has been dishonored. If Sven then takes Susan's check to Harry's Hardware and uses it to pay for some paint, Harry's cannot be a holder in due course of the check if it is on notice that the check has been dishonored. Harry's would have such notice if First National had stamped the check "Payment Refused NSF" (not sufficient funds).

Similarly, suppose Carol Carson signs a 30-day note payable to Ace Appliance for $500 and gives it to Ace as payment for a washing machine. When Ace asks Carol for payment, she refuses to pay because the washer does not work properly. If Ace negotiates the note to First National Bank, First National cannot be a holder in due course if it knows about Carol's refusal to pay.

Notice of Unauthorized Signature or Alteration

A holder who has notice that an instrument contains an unauthorized signature or has been altered cannot qualify as a holder in due course of the instrument. For example, Frank makes out a check in the amount of $5 payable to George Grocer and gives it to his daughter, Jane, to take to the grocery store to purchase some groceries. The groceries Frank wants cost $20, and Jane changes the check to read $25, giving it to Grocer in exchange for the groceries and $5 in cash. Grocer cannot qualify as a holder in due course if he sees Jane make the alteration to the check or otherwise is on notice of it. [See 3-302(a)(1).]

Notice of Claims

If a person taking a negotiable instrument is *on notice of an adverse claim* to the instrument by someone else (e.g., that a third person is the rightful owner of the instrument) or that someone earlier sought to rescind a prior negotiation of the instrument, the current holder cannot qualify as a holder in due course. For example, a U.S. Treasury check is payable to Susan Samuels. Samuels loses the check and it is found by Robert Burns. Burns takes the check to a hardware store, signs "Susan Samuels" on the back of the check in the view of a clerk, and seeks to use it in payment of merchandise. The hardware store cannot be a holder in due course because it is on notice of a potential claim to the instrument by Susan Samuels.

Notice of Breach of Fiduciary Duty One situation in which the Code considers a person to be on notice of a claim is if she is taking a negotiable instrument from a fiduciary, such as a trustee. If a negotiable instrument is payable to a person as a trustee or an attorney for someone, then any attempt by that person to negotiate it for his own behalf or for his use (or benefit) or to deposit it in an account other than that of the fiduciary puts the person on notice that the beneficiary of the trust may have a claim [3-307].

For example, a check is drawn "Pay to the order of Arthur Adams, Trustee for Mary Minor." Adams takes the check to Credit Union, indorses his name to it, and uses it to pay off the balance on a loan Adams had from Credit Union. Credit Union cannot be a holder in due course because it should know that the negotiation of the check is in violation of the fiduciary duty Adams owes to Mary Minor. Ace should know this because Adams is negotiating the check for his own benefit, not Mary's.

Notice of Defenses and Claims in Recoupment To qualify as a holder in due course, a person must also acquire a negotiable instrument without notice that any party to it has any defenses or claims in recoupment. Potential defenses include infancy, duress, fraud, and failure of consideration. Thus, if a person knows that a signature on the instrument was obtained by fraud, misrepresentation, or duress, the person cannot be a holder in due course.

A *claim in recoupment* is a claim of the person obligated on the instrument against the original payee of the instrument. The claim must arise from the transaction that gave rise to the instrument. An example of a claim in recoupment would be as follows: Buyer purchases a used automobile from Dealer for $8,000, giving Dealer a note for $8,000 payable in one year. Because the automobile is not as warranted, Buyer has a breach of warranty claim that could be asserted against Dealer as counterclaim or "claim in recoupment" to offset the amount owing on the note.

CONCEPT REVIEW

Requirements for a Holder in Due Course

Requirement	Rule
1. Must be a *holder*.	A holder is a person in possession of an instrument payable to bearer or payable to an identified person and he is that person.
2. Must take *for value*.	A holder has given value: a. To the extent the agreed-on consideration has been paid or performed. b. To the extent a security interest or lien has been obtained in the negotiable instrument. c. By taking the negotiable instrument in payment of—or as security for—an antecedent claim. d. By giving a negotiable instrument for it. e. By making an irrevocable commitment to a third person.
3. Must take in *good faith*.	Good faith means honesty in fact and the observance of reasonable commercial standards of fair dealing.
4. Must take *without notice* that the instrument is *overdue*.	• An instrument payable on demand is overdue the day after demand for payment has been duly made. • A check is overdue 90 days after its date. • If it is an instrument other than a check and payable on demand, then it is overdue when it has been outstanding for an unreasonably long period of time in light of nature of the instrument and trade practice. • If it is an instrument due on a certain date, then it is overdue at the beginning of the next day after the due date.
5. Must take *without notice* that the instrument has been *dishonored*.	An instrument has been dishonored when the holder has presented it for payment (or acceptance) and payment (or acceptance) has been refused.
6. Must take *without notice* of any *uncured default* with respect to payment of another instrument issued as part of the same series.	If there is a series of notes, holder must take without notice that there is an uncured default as to any other notes in the series.
7. Must take *without notice* that the instrument contains an *unauthorized signature* or has been *altered*.	Notice of unauthorized signature or alteration—that is, a change in a material term—prevents holder from obtaining holder in due course status.
8. Must take *without notice* of any *claim of a property* or possessory *interest* in it.	Claims of property or possessory interest include: a. Claim by someone that she is the rightful owner of the instrument. b. Person seeking to rescind a prior negotiation of the instrument. c. Claim by a beneficiary that a fiduciary negotiated the instrument for his own benefit.
9. Must take *without notice* that any party has a *defense* against it.	Defenses include real defenses that go to the validity of the instrument and personal defenses that commonly are defenses to a simple contract.
10. Must take *without notice* of a *claim in recoupment* to it.	A claim in recoupment is a claim of the obligor on the instrument against the original payee that arises from the transaction that gave rise to the instrument.
11. The instrument must not bear *apparent evidence of forgery or alteration* or be *irregular* or *incomplete*.	The instrument must not contain obvious reasons to question its authenticity.

Irregular and Incomplete Instruments

A person cannot be a holder in due course of a negotiable instrument if, when she takes it, the instrument is irregular or some important or material term is blank. If the negotiable instrument contains a facial irregularity, such as an obvious alteration in the amount, then it is considered to be irregular paper. If you take an irregular instrument, you are considered to be on notice of any possible defenses to it. For example, Kevin writes a check for "one dollar" payable to Karen. Karen inserts the word "hundred" in the amount, changes the figure "$1" to "$100," and gives the check to a druggist in exchange for a purchase of goods. If the alterations in the amount should be obvious to the druggist, perhaps because there are erasures, different handwritings, or different inks, then the druggist cannot be a holder in due course. She would have taken irregular paper and would be on notice that there might be defenses to it. These defenses include Kevin's defense that he is liable for only $1 because that is the amount for which he made the check.

Similarly, if someone receives a check that has been signed but the space where the amount of the check is to be written is blank, then the person cannot be a holder in due course of that check. The fact that a material term is blank means that the instrument is incomplete and should put the person on notice that the drawer may have a defense to payment of it. To be material, the omitted term must be one that affects the legal obligation of the parties to the negotiable instrument. Material terms include the amount of the instrument and the name of the payee. If a negotiable instrument is unauthorizedly completed after the obligor signed it but before a person acquires it, the person can qualify as a holder in due course if she had no notice about the unauthorized completion. A person has notice if she knows or should know of the unauthorized completion.

Shelter Rule

The transferee of an instrument—whether or not the transfer is a negotiation—obtains those rights that the transferor had, including (1) the transferor's right to enforce the instrument and (2) any right as a holder in due course [3-203(b)]. This means that any person who can trace his title to an instrument back to a holder in due course receives rights like those of a holder in due course even if he cannot meet the requirements himself. This is known as the shelter rule in Article 3. For example, Archer makes a note payable to Bryant. Bryant negotiates the note to Carlyle, who qualifies as a holder in due course. Carlyle then negotiates the note to Darby, who cannot qualify as a holder in due course because she knows the note is overdue. Because Darby can trace her title back to a holder in due course (Carlyle), Darby has rights like a holder in due course when she seeks payment of the note from Archer.

There is, however, a limitation on the shelter rule. A transferee who has himself been a party to any fraud or illegality affecting the instrument cannot improve his position by taking, directly or indirectly, from a later holder in due course [3-203(b)]. For example, Archer, through fraudulent representations, induced Bryant to execute a negotiable note payable to Archer and then negotiated the instrument to Carlyle, who took as a holder in due course. If Archer thereafter took the note for value from Carlyle, Archer could not acquire Carlyle's rights as a holder in due course. Archer was a party to the fraud that induced the note, and, accordingly, cannot improve his position by negotiating the instrument and then reacquiring it.

The case that follows, *Triffin v. Sinha*, provides an illustration of the operation of the shelter rule. In this case, the assignee of a check was held to be entitled to holder in due course status because the entity that assigned the check to him was a holder in due course.

Triffin v. Sinha   **93 UCC Rep. 2d 49 (N.J. Super. Ct. App. Div. 2017)**

Dr. Binod Sinha contracted with Cabanaman Pools & Spa to perform services for a contract price of $41,000. During the course of the work, Sinha had paid a total of $31,000. Then, on August 8, 2015, he issued a check to Cabanaman for $10,000. The memo line stated the check was for "pool renovation."

On the same day the check was issued, Cabanaman presented it to S & S Check Cashing, which cashed the check and paid Cabanaman $9,779. At that time, S & S had no knowledge of any defense, dishonor, or impediments with the check. Nothing on the face of the check indicated any contingencies for payment or raised any other facts or circumstances that might cast doubt upon the validity of the check.

Unknown to S & S at the time it cashed the check, Sinha had stopped payment on it. When S & S presented the check, it was dishonored as a result of Sinha's stop payment order. S & S assigned the dishonored check to Robert Triffin for $6,500. Triffin then brought a lawsuit against Sinha to enforce the check. The trial court granted summary judgment in favor of Triffin against Sinha for $10,081.60, inclusive of costs. Sinha appealed the decision of the trial court.

Per Curiam

In opposition to Triffin's summary judgment motion, Sinha argued that S & S was precluded from attaining holder in due course because the check was obviously a payment to a contractor performing home improvement work. Sinha argued that such contracts are subject to the stringent requirements of the Consumer Fraud Act (CFA), and therefore S & S had a duty to investigate that none of the many potential violations of the CFA or regulations had occurred. Sinha makes the same argument on appeal.

Judge Escandon rejected this argument. He found that, based on the undisputed facts, S & S was a holder in due course and Triffin, by virtue of the assignment, achieved the same status. The judge stated:

As to the good-faith requirement under the Uniform Commercial Code (UCC), this court recognizes that no language on the check in any way indicated that the payment was contingent on any condition requiring further inquiry or investigation. The memo line merely said "pool renovation." While the good faith standard imposed under the UCC could require some due diligence on the part of the Assignee, this Court is of the belief that the mere words "pool renovation" would not be sufficient to alert the check cashing entity or the assignee of any problem with the check issued by Defendant Dr. Sinha which would require further inspection.

The judge noted that any defenses Sinha might have against Cabanaman under the CFA could not be asserted against S & S or its assignee, Triffin. This is because there was no relationship between Sinha and either of those parties. Sinha's relationship was with Cabanaman.

The judge concluded:

This action seeks recovery upon a dishonored negotiable instrument, not upon an unperformed home improvement contract. It is well settled that a negotiable instrument, such as the check subject to this litigation, is defined as an unconditional promise or order to pay a fixed amount of money, if it: (1) is payable to the bearer, (2) is payable on demand, and (3) does not state any other undertaking or instruction by the person promising or ordering payment to do any act in addition to the payment of money. UCC section 3-104(a). Plaintiff Triffin has presented evidence to show that these criteria have been satisfied and that he is entitled to judgment. Defendant Dr. Sinha has failed to come forward with evidence creating a genuine issue as to a material fact dispute.

We agree with Judge Escandon that undisputed facts entitled Triffin to judgment as a matter of law.

Affirmed.

Rights of a Holder in Due Course

Claims and Defenses Generally

Revised Article 3 establishes four categories of claims and defenses. They are:

1. *Real defenses*—which go to the validity of the instrument.
2. *Personal defenses*—which generally arise out of the transaction that gave rise to the instrument.
3. *Claims to an instrument*—which generally concern property or possessory rights in an instrument or its proceeds.
4. *Claims in recoupment*—which also arise out of the transaction that gave rise to the instrument.

These defenses and claims are discussed in some detail in the following sections.

Importance of Being a Holder in Due Course

LO32-4 Explain the importance of being a holder in due course of a negotiable instrument.

In the preceding chapter, we explained that one advantage of negotiable instruments over other kinds of contracts is that they are accepted as substitutes for money. People are willing to accept them as substitutes for money because, generally, they can take them free of claims or defenses to payment between the original parties to the instrument. On the other hand, a person who takes an assignment of a simple contract gets only the same rights as the person had who assigned the contract.

There are two qualifications to the ability of a person who acquires a negotiable instrument to be free of claims or defenses between the original parties. First, the person in possession of a negotiable instrument must be a *person entitled to enforce the instrument* as well as a *holder in due course* (or must be a holder who has the rights of a holder in due course through the shelter rule). If the person is neither, then she is subject to all claims or defenses to payment that any party to it has. Second, the only claims or defenses that the holder in due course has to worry about are real defenses—those that affect the validity of the instrument—or claims that arose after she became a holder. For example, if the maker or drawer did not have legal capacity because she was a minor, the maker or drawer has a real defense. The holder in due course does not have to worry about other defenses and claims that do not go to the validity of the instrument—personal defenses.

Real Defenses

LO32-7 Distinguish "real defenses" from "personal defenses."

There are some claims and defenses to payment of an instrument that go to the validity of the instrument. These claims and defenses are known as real defenses. They can be used as reasons against payment of a negotiable instrument to any holder, including a holder in due course (or a person who has the rights of a holder in due course). Real defenses include:

1. *Minority or infancy* that under state law makes the instrument void or voidable. For example, if Mark Miller, age 17, signs a promissory note as maker, he can use his lack of capacity to contract as a defense against paying it even to a holder in due course if other state law allows.

2. *Incapacity* that under state law makes the instrument void. For example, if a person has been declared mentally incompetent by a court, or had a guardian appointed, then the person has a real defense if state law declares all contracts entered into by the person after the adjudication of incompetency to be void.

3. *Duress* that voids or nullifies the obligation of a party liable to pay the instrument. For example, if Harold points a gun at his grandmother and forces her to execute a promissory note, the grandmother can use duress as a defense against paying it even to a holder in due course.

4. *Illegality* that under state law renders the obligation void. For example, in some states, checks and notes given in payment of gambling debts are void.

5. *Fraud in the essence (or fraud in the factum).* This occurs where a person signs a negotiable instrument without knowing or having a reasonable opportunity to know that it is a negotiable instrument or of its essential terms. For example, Amy Jones is an illiterate person who lives alone. She signs a document that is actually a promissory note but is told that it is a grant of permission for a television set to be left in her house on a trial basis. Amy has a real defense against payment of the note even to a holder in due course. Fraud in the essence is distinguished from fraud in the inducement, discussed below, which is only a personal defense.

6. *Discharge in bankruptcy.* For example, if the maker of a promissory note has had the debt discharged in a bankruptcy proceeding, she no longer is liable on it and has a real defense against payment [3-305(a)(1)].

Real defenses can be asserted even against a holder in due course of a negotiable instrument because it is more desirable to protect people who have signed negotiable instruments in these situations than it is to protect persons who have taken negotiable instruments in the ordinary course of business.

In addition to the real defenses discussed above, there are several other reasons a person otherwise liable to pay an instrument would have a defense against payment that would be effective even against a holder in due course. They include:

1. *Forgery.* For example, if a maker's signature has been put on the instrument without his authorization and without his negligence, the maker has a defense against payment of the note.

2. *Alteration of a completed instrument.* This is a partial defense against a holder in due course (or a person having the rights of a holder in due course) and a complete defense against a nonholder in due course. A holder in due course can enforce an altered instrument against the maker or drawer according to its original tenor (terms).

3. *Discharge.* If a person takes an instrument with knowledge that the obligation of any party obligated on the instrument has been discharged, the person takes subject to the discharge even if the person is a holder in due course.

Ethics and Compliance in Action

Asserting the Defense of Illegality against Payment of a Gambling Debt

Assume that in the course of a vacation, you drop by the casino in the hotel where you were staying. You decide to play a few hands of blackjack. After winning your first few hands, you then go on a sustained losing streak. Believing your luck is about to change, you keep going until you have lost $10,000, much more than you intended or could readily afford. At the end of the evening, you write the casino a check. Later in the hotel bar, you tell your sad tale to a fellow drinker who is a local lawyer and who informs you that a state law makes gambling obligations void. Would it be ethical for you to stop payment on the check and then assert the defense of illegality against the holder of the check?

E & G Food Corp. v. Cumberland Farms
75 UCC Rep. 2d 571 (Mass. Dist. Ct., App. Div. 2011)

In December 2008, Cumberland Farms issued four payroll checks to four of its employees. Each check was drawn on its account at Bank of America. Each bore Cumberland Farms's name as well as an eight-digit check number, the employee's name, and an authorized stamp of the signature of the company's CEO. The checks were subsequently negotiated.

In February 2009, unidentified individuals presented four checks to E & G Food Corporation, which is in the business of cashing checks for its customers for a fee. The checks, totaling $2,809.70, were very similar to the four payroll checks issued by Cumberland Farms in December. They bore the same check numbers. But the names of the payees on the checks were different, and the named payees were not employed by Cumberland Farms. It had given Bank of America a list of its employees so that the bank could verify that every employee payroll check presented for payment listed the proper employee. E & G did not contact Bank of America to verify the authenticity of the checks.

Each payroll check issued by Cumberland Farms in December and each of the checks presented to E & G in February also bore a notation stating that the check "contains ultraviolet fibers, chemical reactive paper, void pantograph, microprint signature line, and an artificial watermark on the back." Prior to cashing the checks, E & G's employees examined them and scanned each check under a machine to detect alterations, but they found nothing improper. At the same time, those employees were unfamiliar with some of the enumerated security features of Cumberland Farms's actual payroll checks. Moreover, they did not have all of the equipment needed to verify that the checks presented had all of the listed safety features.

In addition, each of Cumberland Farms's actual payroll checks bore a three-digit number on the payee line. This number reflected the last three digits of the check number printed in the upper right corner of the check. The three-digit numbers on the four checks E & G received in February 2009, however, did not match the last three digits of the respective check numbers of the actual payroll checks. Despite these questionable circumstances, E & G cashed all four checks, only to be notified later by Bank of America that the checks would not be honored. Cumberland Farms refused E & G's subsequent demand that it make payment of the checks.

E & G then brought suit against Cumberland Farms, asserting that it was a holder in due course and that Cumberland Farms was obligated to make good on the checks. The trial court determined that the checks presented to E & G in February were counterfeits, that is, forged images of the true payroll checks previously issued to Cumberland Farms's employees. The checks had not been signed by any authorized representative or employee of Cumberland Farms; neither had they been produced from any misappropriated blank checks previously in its possession. Nonetheless, the trial court found Cumberland Farms legally responsible for E & G's loss based on E & G's status as a holder in due course. Cumberland Farms appealed, arguing that it had a defense to payment that could be asserted against even a holder in due course.

Hadley, Justice

Massachusetts law provides that the right to enforce an obligation of a party to pay an instrument is subject to a defense based on "illegality of the transaction which under other law nullifies the obligation of the obligor." Even the right of a holder in due course to enforce an obligation is subject to this defense.

In the instant case, the trial judge clearly found that the counterfeit checks in question were created by unknown third-party actors who were not in any way related to Cumberland Farms. The judge concluded that Cumberland Farms had no knowledge of the creation of the counterfeit checks. The creation of the checks and their presentment by the third-party actors constituted, therefore, criminal acts. In light of these facts, despite the trial judge's conclusion that E & G was a holder in due course, its right to enforce the obligation to pay on the four checks was subject to the defense of illegality set out in section 3-305(a)(1)(ii). As the illegality of the transaction was established at trial, judgment should have been entered for Cumberland Farms.

Judgment reversed and granted in favor of Cumberland Farms.

In the case above, *E & G Food Corp. v. Cumberland Farms*, the court held that a defense of forgery could be asserted against even a holder in due course of four checks.

Personal Defenses
Personal defenses are legal reasons for avoiding or reducing liability of a person who is liable on a negotiable instrument. Generally, personal defenses arise out of the transaction in which the negotiable instrument was issued or taken and are based on negotiable instruments law or contract law. A holder in due course of a negotiable instrument (or one who can claim the rights of one) is not subject to any personal defenses or claims that may exist between the original parties to the instrument. Personal defenses include:

1. *Lack or failure of consideration.* For example, a promissory note for $1,000 was given to someone without intent to make a gift and without receiving anything in return [3-303(b)].

2. *Breach of contract, including breach of warranty.* For example, a check was given in payment for repairs to an automobile, but the repair work was defective.

3. *Fraud in the inducement of any underlying contract.* For example, an art dealer sells a lithograph to Cheryl, telling her that it is a Picasso, and takes Cheryl's check for $500 in payment. The art dealer knows that the lithograph is not a genuine Picasso but a forgery. Cheryl has been induced to make the purchase and to give her check by the art dealer's fraudulent representation. Because of this fraud, Cheryl has a personal defense against having to honor her check to the art dealer.

4. *Incapacity to the extent that state law makes the obligation voidable, as opposed to void.* For example, where state law makes the contract of a person of limited mental capacity but who has not been adjudicated incompetent voidable, the person has a personal defense to payment.

5. *Illegality that makes a contract voidable, as opposed to void.* For example, where the payee of a check given for certain professional services was required to have a license from the state but did not have one.

6. *Duress, to the extent it is not so severe as to make the obligation void but rather only voidable.* For example, if the instrument was signed under a threat to prosecute the maker's son if it was not signed, the maker might have a personal defense.

7. *Unauthorized completion or alteration of the instrument.* For example, the instrument was completed in an unauthorized manner or was altered after it left the maker's or drawer's possession.

8. *Nonissuance of the instrument, conditional issuance, and issuance for a special purpose.* For example, the person in possession of the instrument obtained it by theft or by finding it, rather than through an intentional delivery of the instrument to him [3-105(b)].

9. *Failure to countersign a traveler's check* [3-106(c)].

10. *Modification of the obligation by a separate agreement of which the holder was not aware* [3-117].

11. *Payment that violates a restrictive indorsement* [3-206(f)].

The following example illustrates the limited extent to which a maker or drawer can use personal defenses as a reason for not paying a negotiable instrument he signed. Suppose Tucker Trucking bought a used truck from Honest Harry's and gave Harry a 60-day promissory note for $32,750 in payment for the truck. Honest Harry's "guaranteed" the truck to be in "good working condition," but, in fact, the truck had a cracked engine block. If Harry tries to collect the $32,750 from Tucker Trucking, Tucker Trucking could claim breach of warranty as a reason for not paying Harry the full $32,750 because Harry is not a holder in due course. However, if Harry negotiated the note to First National Bank and the bank was a holder in due course, the situation would be changed. If the bank tried to collect the $32,750 from Tucker Trucking, Tucker Trucking would have to pay the bank. Tucker Trucking cannot use its defense or claim of breach of warranty as a reason for not paying the bank, which qualified as a holder in due course. It is a personal defense. Tucker Trucking must pay the bank the $32,750 and then pursue its breach of warranty claim against Harry.

The rule that a holder in due course takes a negotiable instrument free of any personal defenses or claims to it has been modified to some extent, particularly in relation to certain instruments given by consumers. These modifications will be discussed in the next section of this chapter.

In the case that follows, *General Credit Corp. v. New York Linen*, the court held that a holder in due course of a check was not subject to the personal defense of failure of consideration that the drawer of the check had against the payee of the check.

General Credit Corp. v. New York Linen Co.
46 UCC Rep. 2d 1055 (N.Y. Civ. Ct., Kings Cty. 2002)

On February 25, 2001, New York Linen Co., a party rental company, agreed to purchase approximately 550 chairs from Elite Products, a company owned by Meir Schmeltzer. A deposit was given for the chairs, and upon their delivery, a final check dated February 27, 2001, was issued for $13,300. After a final count of the chairs was made, New York Linen discovered that the delivery was not complete. New York Linen then contacted its bank and asked that the bank stop payment of the check. A second check, dated February 28, 2001, for $11,275, was drafted and delivered to Meir Schmeltzer the next day. This check reflected the adjusted amount due for the chairs that had actually been delivered.

Unbeknownst to New York Linen, the original check for $13,300 was sold by Meir Schmeltzer to General Credit Corp., a company in the business of purchasing instruments from payees in exchange for immediate cash. When New York Linen's bank refused to pay the check to General Credit because of the stop-payment order that had been placed on it, General Credit Corp. brought suit against New York Linen to collect on the check.

Baily-Schiffman, Judge

Pursuant to UCC section 3-302 [pre-1990 version inasmuch as New York has not yet adopted Revised Article 3], General Credit is a holder in due course since it took the instrument for value and claims to have all the rights of a holder in due course. General Credit seeks to force New York Linen to pay on the check.

Pursuant to Article 3 of the Uniform Commercial Code, a holder in due course has significant rights vis-à-vis the negotiable instrument being held. A holder of an instrument becomes the holder in due course if the instrument is taken for value, in good faith, and without notice of defect or defense (UCC section 3-302). An indorsed check, as in this case, is a negotiable instrument as defined in this section of the UCC. In this case, pursuant to the applicable sections of Article 3 (sections 3-303 and 3-304), General Credit was a good faith purchaser without notice. As a holder in due course, General Credit is protected by section 3-305, taking the check free of all defenses and claims, except those enumerated by the section. Thus, any defense New York Linen had which related to its purchase of the chairs was not a defense against General Credit.

New York Linen contends that it would not have drafted a second check if it had known that Elite had already been paid by General Credit. While to the casual observer, the potential double payment by New York Linen may seem an unfair result, it is specifically mandated by the Uniform Commercial Code. New York Linen has offered no legal defense to General Credit's claim as a holder in due course pursuant to Article 3 of the UCC. By tradition the defenses from which a holder in due course takes free are called "personal defenses" and they include failure for lack of consideration, which is New York Linen's defense in this case.

Summary judgment granted in favor of General Credit on its claim against New York Linen.

———————

Note: While this case was decided under the pre-1990 version of Article 3 because New York is the one state that has not yet adopted Revised Article 3, the same result would occur from application of Revised Article 3 to the facts of this case.

Claims to the Instrument

For purposes of Revised Article 3, the term *claims to an instrument* can include:

1. A claim to ownership of the instrument by one who asserts that he is the owner and was wrongfully deprived of possession.

2. A claim of a lien on the instrument.

3. A claim for rescission of an indorsement.

A holder in due course takes free of claims that arose before he became a holder but is subject to those arising when or after she becomes a holder in due course. For example, if a holder impairs the collateral given for an obligation, he may be creating a defense for an obligor.

Claims in Recoupment

A *claim in recoupment* is not actually a defense to an instrument but rather an *offset to liability.* For example, Ann Adams purchases a new automobile from Dealer, giving it a note for the balance of the purchase price beyond her down payment. After accepting delivery, she discovers a breach of warranty that the dealer fails to remedy. If Dealer has sold the note to a bank that subsequently seeks payment on the note from Adams, she has a claim in recoupment for breach of warranty. If the bank is a holder in due course, the claim in recoupment cannot be asserted against it. However, if the bank is not a holder in due course, then Adams can assert the claim in recoupment to reduce the amount owing on the instrument at the time the action is brought against her on the note. Her claim could serve only to reduce the amount owing and not as a basis for a net recovery from the bank. However, if Dealer was the person bringing an action to collect the note, Adams could assert the breach of warranty claim as a counterclaim and potentially might recover from Dealer any difference between the claim and the damages due for breach of warranty.

The obligor may assert a claim up to the amount of the instrument if the holder is the original payee but cannot assert claims in recoupment against a holder in due course. In addition, the obligor may assert a claim against a transferee who does not qualify as a holder in due course, but only to reduce the amount owing on the instrument at the time it brought the claim in recoupment.

CONCEPT REVIEW

Claims and Defenses against Payment of Negotiable Instruments

Claim or Defense	Examples
Real Defense Valid against all holders, including holders in due course and holders who have the rights of holders in due course.	1. Minority that under state law makes the contract void or voidable. 2. Other lack of capacity that makes the contract void. 3. Duress that makes the contract void. 4. Illegality that makes the contract void. 5. Fraud in the essence (fraud in the factum). 6. Discharge in bankruptcy.
Personal Defense Valid against plain holders of instruments—but not against holders in due course or holders who have the rights of in due course holders through the shelter rule.	1. Lack or failure of consideration. 2. Breach of contract (including breach of warranty). 3. Fraud in the inducement. 4. Lack of capacity that makes the contract voidable (except minority). 5. Illegality that makes the contract voidable. 6. Duress that makes the contract voidable. 7. Unauthorized completion of an incomplete instrument, or material alteration of the instrument. 8. Nonissuance of the instrument. 9. Failure to countersign a traveler's check. 10. Modification of the obligation by a separate agreement. 11. Payment that violates a restrictive indorsement. 12. Breach of warranty when a draft is accepted.
Claim to an Instrument	1. Claim of ownership by someone who claims to be the owner and that he was wrongfully deprived of possession. 2. Claim of a lien on the instrument. 3. Claim for rescission of an indorsement.
Claims in Recoupment	1. Breach of warranty in the sale of goods for which the instrument was issued.

Changes in the Holder in Due Course Rule for Consumer Credit Transactions

Consumer Disadvantages The rule that a holder in due course of a negotiable instrument is not subject to personal defenses between the original parties to it makes negotiable instruments a readily accepted substitute for money. This rule can also result in serious disadvantages to consumers. Consumers sometimes buy goods or services on credit and give the seller a negotiable instrument such as a promissory note. They often do this without knowing the consequences of their signing a negotiable instrument. If the goods or services are defective or not delivered, the consumer would like to withhold payment of the note until the seller corrects the problem or makes the delivery. Where the note is still held by the seller, the consumer can do this because any defenses of breach of warranty or nonperformance are good against the seller.

However, the seller may have negotiated the note at a discount to a third party such as a bank. If the bank qualifies as a holder in due course, the consumer must pay the note in full to the bank. The consumer's personal defenses are not valid against a holder in due course. The consumer must pay the holder in due course and then try to get her money back from the seller. This may be difficult if the seller cannot be found or will not accept responsibility. The consumer would be in a much stronger position if she could just withhold payment, even against the bank, until the goods or services are delivered or the performance is corrected.

State Consumer Protection Legislation

Some state legislatures and courts have limited the holder in due course rule, particularly as it affects consumers. State legislation limiting the doctrine typically amended state laws dealing with consumer credit transactions. For example, some state laws prohibit a seller from taking a negotiable instrument other than a check from a consumer in payment for consumer goods and services. Other states require promissory notes given by consumers in payment for goods and services to carry the words *consumer paper.* Holders of instruments with the legend "consumer paper" are not eligible to be holders in due course[2] [3-106(d)].

Federal Trade Commission Regulation

 LO32-8 Explain how the Federal Trade Commission has changed the holder in due course rule as it applies to some or many consumer credit transactions.

The Federal Trade Commission (FTC) has promulgated a regulation designed to protect consumers against operation of the holder in due course rule. The FTC rule applies to persons who sell to consumers on credit and have the consumer sign a note or an installment sale contract or arrange third-party financing of the purchase. The seller must ensure that the note or the contract contains the following clause:

NOTICE: ANY HOLDER OF THIS CONSUMER CREDIT CONTRACT IS SUBJECT TO ALL CLAIMS AND DEFENSES WHICH THE DEBTOR COULD ASSERT AGAINST THE SELLER OF THE GOODS OR SERVICES

OBTAINED PURSUANT HERETO OR WITH THE PROCEEDS HEREOF. RECOVERY HEREUNDER BY THE DEBTOR SHALL NOT EXCEED AMOUNTS PAID BY THE DEBTOR HEREUNDER.

The effect of the notice is to make a potential holder of the note or contract subject to all claims and defenses of the consumer. This is illustrated in *Music Acceptance Corp.,* which follows.

In the hypothetical case set out at the start of this chapter, Rachel buys a used car and gives the seller a negotiable promissory note in which she promises to pay the balance in 12 months. The seller then negotiates the promissory note to a third party. When Rachel discovers that, contrary to the seller's assurances, the car had previously been involved in an accident, Rachel would like to assert a defense of failure of consideration or breach of contract (warranty) against payment. You know that normally, if the person to whom the note was assigned can qualify as a holder in due course, then the maker of a note will not be able to assert those particular defenses against payment because they are considered to be "personal defenses," and a holder in due course of an instrument takes the instrument free of such defenses against payment. However, the introductory hypothetical goes on to pose the question of whether it would make a difference if the promissory note contained the clause required by the Federal Trade Commission in consumer notes. You are now in a position to know that it would make a difference in Rachel's rights and that she would be able to assert such defenses against payment of the note to the current holder, even if he could qualify as holder in due course. If the note or contract does not include the clause required by the FTC rule, the consumer does not gain any rights that he would not otherwise have under state law, and a subsequent holder may qualify as a holder in due course. However, the FTC does have the right to seek a fine of as much as $10,000 against the seller who failed to include the clause.

---

[2]Revised Article 3 expressly deals with these state variations in section 3-106(d) and Official Comments 3 to 3-106 and Comments 3 to 3-305. Section 3-106(d) permits instruments containing legends or statements required by statutory or administrative law that preserve the obligator's right to assert claims or defenses against subsequent holders as within Article 3 except that no holder can be holder in due course.

Music Acceptance Corp. v. Lofing   39 Cal. Rptr. 159 (Cal. Ct. App. 1995)

Dan Lofing purchased a Steinway grand piano from Sherman Clay & Co., Steinway & Sons's Sacramento dealer, and received financing through Sherman Clay's finance company, Music Acceptance Corporation (MAC). The consumer note for $19,650.94 prepared by MAC and signed by Lofing included the following in boldface type:

NOTICE

ANY HOLDER OF THIS CONSUMER CREDIT CONTRACT IS SUBJECT TO ALL CLAIMS AND DEFENSES WHICH THE DEBTOR COULD ASSERT AGAINST THE SELLER OF GOODS OR SERVICES OBTAINED PURSUANT HEREIN OR WITH THE PROCEEDS HEREOF. RECOVERY HEREUNDER SHALL NOT EXCEED AMOUNTS PAID BY THE DEBTOR HEREUNDER.

Lofing received a warranty from Steinway that provided the company "will promptly repair or replace without charge any part of this piano which is found to have a defect in material or workmanship within five years" from the date of sale.

Lofing became disenchanted with the piano after experiencing a variety of problems with it. There was a significant deterioration in the action and tonal quality of the piano that the Sherman Clay piano technician was unable to remedy despite lengthy and repeated efforts. A Steinway representative who was called in to inspect the piano concluded that it was in "terrible condition" and expressed surprise that it had ever left the factory. He concluded that the piano would have to be completely rebuilt at the factory.

Because the piano was impossible to play and was ruining his technique, Lofing stopped making payments on the piano. To mitigate his damages, Lofing sold the piano for $7,000 and purchased a Kawai piano from another dealer. He brought suit against Sherman Clay, Steinway, and MAC for, among other things, breach of warranty. One of the issues in the litigation was whether the Notice in the note allowed him to assert the breach of warranty as a grounds for not continuing to pay off the note to MAC.

Sparks, Associate Justice

The FTC adopted a rule which makes it an unfair or deceptive act or practice for a seller to take or receive a consumer credit application which does not contain the following provision in large boldface type:

NOTICE

ANY HOLDER OF THIS CONSUMER CREDIT CONTRACT IS SUBJECT TO ALL CLAIMS AND DEFENSES WHICH THE DEBTOR COULD ASSERT AGAINST THE SELLER OF GOODS OR SERVICES OBTAINED PURSUANT HEREIN OR WITH THE PROCEEDS HEREOF. RECOVERY HEREUNDER SHALL NOT EXCEED AMOUNTS PAID BY THE DEBTOR HEREUNDER.

This notice is identical to that included in Lofing's sales contract.

The FTC enacted this rule because it believed it was "an unfair practice for a seller to employ procedures in the course of arranging the financing of a consumer deal which separate[d] the buyer's duty to pay for goods or services from the seller's reciprocal duty to perform as promised." The FTC explained: "Our primary concern . . . has been the distribution or allocation of costs occasioned by seller misconduct in credit sale transactions. These costs arise from breaches of contract, breaches of warranty, misrepresentation, and even fraud. The current commercial system which enables sellers and creditors to divorce a consumer's obligation to pay for goods and services from the seller's obligation to perform as promised, allocates all of these costs to the consumer/buyer."

In its "Guidelines on Trade Regulation Rule Concerning Preservation of Consumers' Claims and Defenses," the FTC explained further:

[The] dramatic increase in consumer credit over the past thirty years has caused certain problems. Evolving doctrines and principles of contract law have not kept pace with changing social needs. One such legal doctrine which has worked to deprive consumers of the protection needed in credit sales is the so-called "holder in due course doctrine." Under this doctrine, the obligation to pay for goods or services is not conditioned upon the seller's corresponding duty to keep his promises.

Typically, the circumstances are as follows: A consumer relying in good faith on what the seller has represented to be a product's characteristics, service warranty, etc., makes a purchase on credit terms. The consumer then finds the product unsatisfactory; it fails to measure up to the claims made on its behalf by the seller, or the seller refuses to provide promised maintenance. The consumer, therefore, seeks relief from his debt obligations only to find that no relief is possible. His debt obligation, he is told, is not to the seller but to a third party whose claim to payment is legally unrelated to any promise made about the product.

The seller may, prior to the sale, have arranged to have the debt instrument held by someone other than himself; he may have sold the debt instrument at a discount after the purchase.

From the consumer's point of view, the timing and means by which the transfer was effected are irrelevant. He has been left without ready recourse. He must pay the full amount of his obligation. He has a product that yields less than its promised value. And he has been robbed of the only realistic leverage he possessed that might have forced the seller to provide satisfaction—his power to withhold payment.

As one court noted, before this rule was adopted "[t]he reciprocal duties of the buyer and seller which were mutually dependent under ordinary contract law became independent of one another. Thus, the buyer's duty to pay the creditor was not excused upon the seller's failure to perform. In abrogating the holder in due course rule in consumer credit transactions, the FTC preserved the consumer's claims and defenses against the creditor-assignee. The FTC rule was therefore designed to reallocate the cost of seller misconduct to the creditor. The commission felt the creditor was in a better position to absorb the loss or recover the cost from the guilty party—the seller."

MAC contends the FTC rule is inapplicable here. MAC cites comments in the FTC guidelines discussing possible limitations on the rule. Specifically, the FTC points out that because the regulation's definition of "Financing a Sale" expressly refers to the Truth-in-Lending Act, it "thus incorporate[s] the limitations contained in these laws. As a result, even with respect to transactions involving a sale of consumer goods or services, a purchase involving an expenditure of more than $25,000 is not affected by the Rule." MAC argues that since the cash price of the piano, including sales tax, was $25,650.94, the transaction is exempt from these requirements.

MAC's argument is unavailing as it is based on the guideline's unfortunate use of the phrase "expenditure of more than $25,000." As Lofing points out, the exemption referred to in the Truth-in-Lending Act does not speak of expenditures of more than $25,000, but of transactions in which the "total amount financed exceeds $25,000." Here, because Lofing traded in his piano, the total amount financed was $19,650.94, well below the exemption level.

More importantly, it is irrelevant whether the FTC rule applies. Even if such a notice was not required to be given, the fact remains that it was: Lofing's contract included the precise language mandated by the FTC rule. Put simply, Lofing is in the same position whether we apply the FTC rule or the language of his particular contract. The jury's finding that Sherman Clay breached its warranties mandates that the judgment in favor of MAC and against Lofing be reversed.

Judgment in favor of Lofing.

The Transfer of Commercial Paper

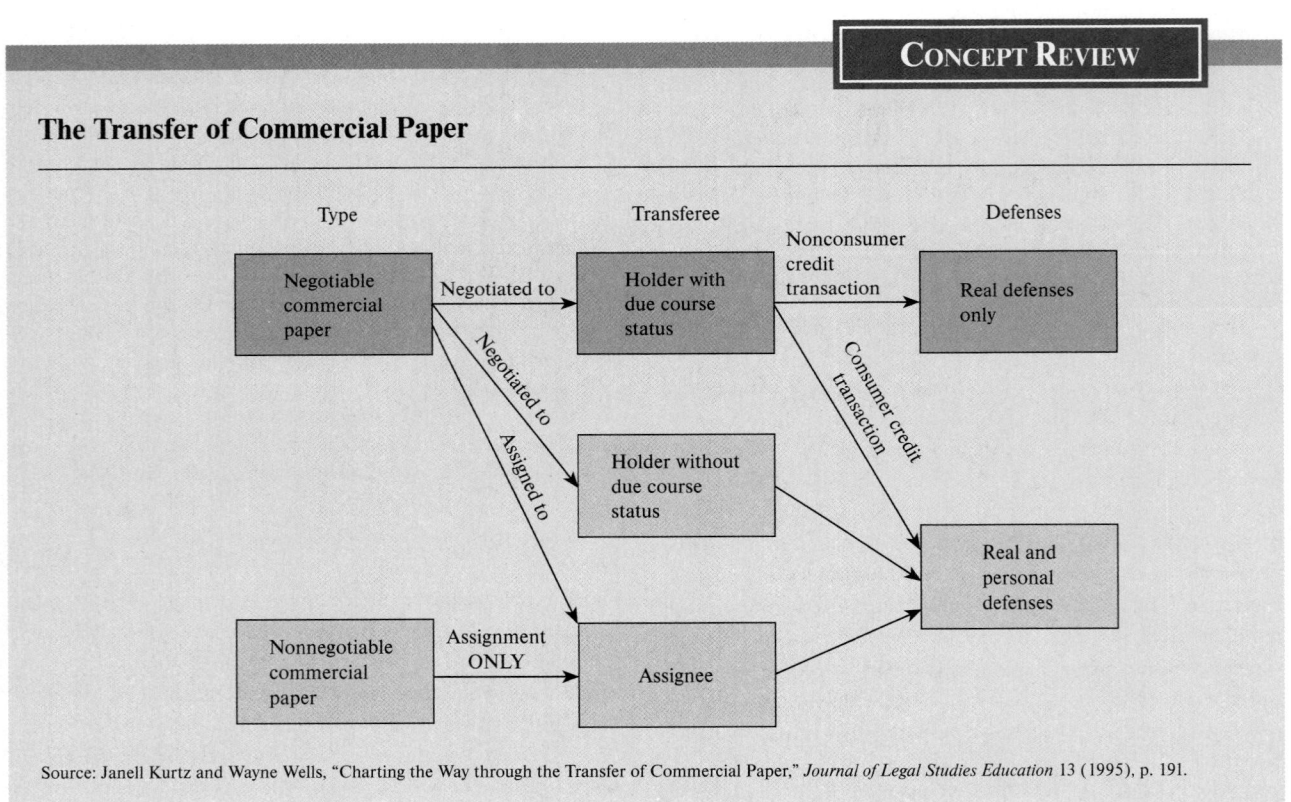

Source: Janell Kurtz and Wayne Wells, "Charting the Way through the Transfer of Commercial Paper," *Journal of Legal Studies Education* 13 (1995), p. 191.

Problems and Problem Cases

1. Nancy Gabbard, the office manager for the Golden Years Nursing Home, received at the nursing home Social Security checks drawn on the U.S. Treasury and made payable either to individual patients or to "Golden Years Nursing Home for [an individual patient]." Gabbard engaged in an embezzling scheme whereby she would have certain patients indorse their own checks in blank—each patient would sign his or her own name on the back of the check, placing no restrictions on the manner in which the check could subsequently be negotiated. Gabbard would then cash the checks and either keep the cash or deposit the

funds into her personal bank account. After Gabbard's scheme was discovered, Golden Years brought suit against Gabbard and against the Star Bank Corporation where the checks had been cashed. The patients had, in other documents, assigned their interests in the checks to Golden Years, and the claim against the bank alleged that it had converted Golden Year's property by cashing checks with forged indorsements. One of the issues in the lawsuit was whether the checks had been properly negotiated to Star Bank. Did Star Bank become a holder of the checks that had been indorsed in blank by the payees?

2. A bank cashed the checks of its customer, Dental Supply, presented to the bank by an employee of Dental Supply named Wilson. The checks were indorsed in blank with a rubber stamp of Dental Supply. Wilson had been stealing the checks by taking cash rather than depositing them to Dental Supply's account. What could Dental Supply have done to avoid this situation?

3. Reliable Janitorial Service maintained a bank account with AmSouth Bank. Rosa Pennington was employed by Reliable as a bookkeeper/office manager. She deposited checks made payable to Reliable but did not have the authority to write checks on Reliable's account. Beginning in January, Pennington obtained counter deposit slips from AmSouth. She wrote on the deposit slips that the depositor was "Reliable Janitorial Services Inc.," but in the space for the account number, Pennington wrote the account number for her own personal account with AmSouth. She stamped the checks that were made payable to "Reliable Janitorial Services Inc." with the indorsement "For Deposit Only, Reliable Carpet Cleaning Inc." Over an 11-month period, Pennington was able to deposit 169 checks so indorsed. AmSouth credited the deposits to Pennington, not Reliable. Pennington spent all the funds that she diverted to her account. When Reliable discovered the fraud, it brought suit against AmSouth for conversion and sought to have its account credited with the improperly paid checks. Was AmSouth Bank liable to Reliable for the value of the restrictively indorsed checks that it paid inconsistently with the indorsement?

4. Reggie Bluiett worked at the Silver Slipper Gambling Hall and Saloon. She received her weekly paycheck made out to her from the Silver Slipper. She indorsed the check in blank and left it on her dresser at home. Fred Watkins broke into Bluiett's house and stole the check. Watkins took the check to the local auto store, where he bought two tires at a cost of $71.21. He obtained the balance of the check in cash. Could the auto store qualify as a holder in due course?

5. Horton wrote a check for $20,000 to Axe, who in turn indorsed it to Halbert. In return, Halbert advanced $8,000 in cash to Axe and promised to cancel a $12,000 debt owed him by Axe. The check, when presented by Halbert to the bank, was not paid due to insufficient funds. Halbert thus never regarded the debt as canceled. To what extent can Halbert be a holder in due course of the check?

6. Liccardi Ford made out a check dated August 10, 2007, that was payable to one of its employees, Charles Stallone. Because Stallone was suspected of embezzlement, the company withheld the check from him. However, the check disappeared from the company offices, and when the disappearance was discovered, Liccardi immediately placed a stop-payment order on the check. On or before August 9, 2007, JCNB Check Cashing cashed the check for Stallone and deposited the check to its own checking account. However, the issuing bank refused to honor the check because of the stop-payment order that had been placed on it. On February 11, 2009, Robert Triffin acquired the dishonored payroll check from JCNB and sued Liccardi and Stallone for the amount of the check. One of the issues in the lawsuit against Liccardi was whether Triffin was a holder in due course, either in his own right, or because his transferor, JCNB, had the rights of a holder in due course. A New Jersey law, the Check Cashers Regulatory Act, prohibits a check-cashing service from cashing a postdated check. Is Triffin a holder in due course or an assignee of an entity that had the rights of a holder in due course?

7. Two smooth-talking salesmen for Rich Plan of New Orleans called on Leona and George Henne at their home. They sold the Hennes a home food plan. One of the salesmen suggested that the Hennes sign a blank promissory note. The Hennes refused. The salesman then wrote in ink "$100" as the amount and "4" as the number of installments in which the note was to be paid, and the Hennes signed the note. Several days later, the Hennes received a payment book from Nationwide Acceptance. The payment book showed that a total of $843.37 was due payable in 36 monthly installments. Rich Plan had erased the "$100" and "4" on the note and typed in the figures "$843.37" and "36." The erasures were cleverly done but were visible to the naked eye. Rich Plan then negotiated the Hennes' note to Nationwide Acceptance. The Hennes refused to pay the note. Nationwide claimed that it was a holder in

due course and was entitled to receive payment. Was Nationwide Acceptance a holder in due course?

8. A representative of Gracious Living called on the Hutchinsons and identified himself as a "demonstrator" of water-softening equipment. After explaining the cost of the equipment, he told the Hutchinsons that Gracious Living would install it for a four-month trial. In return, the Hutchinsons were to give him a list of their friends and neighbors and permit a demonstration in their house. They were to receive a bonus if sales were made to any of their friends and neighbors. The Hutchinsons claimed that the man "asked them to sign a form that he could show to his boss to prove that he had made the demonstration and also as a bond to cover the unit while it was on the Hutchinson's property." They signed the form. Later, the Hutchinsons received a payment book from the Reading Trust Company. They then realized that they had been tricked into signing a contract and a note. Hutchinson was a high school graduate, and his wife had completed her junior year in high school. Both could read and write the English language. Reading Trust had obtained the note from Gracious Living. It had no notice of Gracious Living's business practice and was a holder in due course. The Hutchinsons refused to pay the note, and Reading Trust sued them to collect on it. Did the Hutchinsons have a real defense that they could use against the Reading Trust Company even though it was a holder in due course?

9. Panlick, the owner of an apartment building, entered into a written contract with Bucci, a paving contractor, whereby Bucci was to install asphalt paving on the parking lot of the building. When Bucci finished the job, Panlick gave Bucci a check for $6,500 and a promissory note for $7,593 with interest at 10 percent due six months from its date. When the note came due, Panlick refused to pay it. Bucci brought suit to collect the note, and Panlick claimed that there had been a failure of consideration because the asphalt was defectively installed. Can Panlick assert this defense against Bucci?

10. Pedro and Paula de la Fuente were visited by a representative of Aluminum Industries, who was seeking to sell them aluminum siding for their home. They agreed to purchase the siding and signed a number of documents, including a retail installment contract and a promissory note for $9,137.24. The contract granted Aluminum Industries a first lien on the de la Fuentes' residence; this was in violation of the Texas Civil Code, which prohibited such provisions. The promissory note contained a notice in bold type as required by the Federal Trade Commission. It read in part:

> NOTICE: ANY HOLDER OF THIS CONSUMER CREDIT CONTRACT IS SUBJECT TO ALL CLAIMS AND DEFENSES WHICH THE DEBTOR COULD ASSERT AGAINST THE SELLER OF GOODS OR SERVICES OBTAINED PURSUANT HERETO WITH THE PROCEEDS THEREOF.

Aluminum Industries assigned the promissory note and first lien to Home Savings Association. Aluminum Industries subsequently went out of business. Home Savings brought suit against the de la Fuentes to collect the balance due on the note. Home Savings contended that it was a holder in due course and that the de la Fuentes could not assert any defense against it that they had against Aluminum Industries. Can an assignee of a consumer promissory note that includes the notice required by the FTC qualify as a holder in due course?

Liability of Parties

When you sign a promissory note, you expect that you will be liable for paying the note on the day it is due. Similarly, when you sign a check and mail it off to pay a bill, you expect that it will be paid by your bank out of your checking account and that if there are not sufficient funds in the account to cover it, you will have to make it good out of other funds you have. The liability of the maker of a note and of the drawer of a check is commonly understood.

However, there are other ways a person can become liable on a negotiable instrument. Moreover, some of the usual liability rules are modified when a party is negligent in issuing, receiving, or paying a negotiable instrument—or otherwise contributes to a potential loss.

The issues that will be discussed in this chapter include:

- Suppose you indorse a check that is payable to your order and "cash" it at a check-cashing service. What liability have you assumed by indorsing and transferring the check?
- Suppose you make out a check in such a way that someone is able to raise (change) the amount of the check from $10 to $110 and then obtain payment of the check from the drawee bank. Will your bank be entitled to charge your account for $110, or can you limit the charge to $10, the original amount of the check?
- Suppose one of your employees who has responsibility for writing checks makes some of them payable to people you normally do business with and then keeps the checks, indorses the checks in the name of the named payee, and obtains payment of the checks for her own purposes. Are you entitled to have your account recredited for the amount of the checks on the grounds they were paid over a forged indorsement?
- Whether, in some circumstances, it is ethical to use a qualified indorsement to avoid the contractual liability of an indorser.

LO LEARNING OBJECTIVES

After studying this chapter, you should be able to:

33-1 Explain the difference between primary and secondary liability on a negotiable instrument.

33-2 Recall the obligations of makers, drawees or acceptors, drawers, indorsers, and accommodation parties.

33-3 Explain when a person's signature on a negotiable instrument makes the person contractually liable on it.

33-4 Explain what is meant by *presentment* of a note or of a check or draft.

33-5 List the warranties made by persons who transfer negotiable instruments to someone else.

33-6 List the warranties made by persons who present negotiable instruments for payment or acceptance.

33-7 Discuss the three exceptions to the normal liability rules: negligence, the impostor rule, and the fictitious payee rule.

33-8 Explain how the liability of a party to pay an instrument is normally discharged.

THUS FAR IN PART 7, Commercial Paper, the focus has been on the nature of, and requirements for, negotiable instruments as well as the rights that an owner of an instrument can obtain and how to obtain them. Another important aspect to negotiable instruments concerns how a person becomes liable on a negotiable instrument and the nature of the liability incurred.

Liability in General

Liability on negotiable instruments flows from signatures on the instruments as well as actions taken concerning them. It can arise from the fact that a person has signed a negotiable instrument or has authorized someone else to sign it. The liability depends on the capacity in which the person signs the instrument. Liability also arises from (1) transfer or presentment of an instrument; (2) negligence relating to the issuance, alteration, or indorsement of the instrument; (3) improper payment; or (4) conversion of an instrument.

Contractual Liability

When a person signs a negotiable instrument, whether as maker, drawer, indorser, or acceptor, she generally becomes contractually liable on the instrument. As mentioned earlier, this contractual liability depends on the capacity in which the person signed the instrument. The terms of the contract of the parties to a negotiable instrument are not set out in the text of the instrument. Rather, Article 3 of the Uniform Commercial Code supplies the terms, which are as much a part of the instrument as they would be as part of its text.

Primary and Secondary Liability

 Explain the difference between primary and secondary liability on a negotiable instrument.

A party to a negotiable instrument may be either *primarily liable* or *secondarily liable* for payment of it. A person who is primarily liable has agreed to pay the negotiable instrument. For example, the maker of a promissory note is the person who is primarily liable on the note.

A person who is secondarily liable is like a guarantor on a contract; Article 3 requires a secondary party to pay the negotiable instrument only if a person who is primarily liable defaults on that obligation. Chapter 28, Introduction to Credit and Secured Transactions, discusses guarantors of contracts.

Secondary liability is a contingent liability. To trigger it, the instrument must be properly *presented* for payment or acceptance, the instrument must be *dishonored* (i.e., the payment or acceptance must be refused or not obtained within the prescribed time), and normally *notice of the dishonor* must be given to the person secondarily liable. The notice may be given in any reasonable manner—such as orally, in writing, or by e-mail—and must be given to any party other than a bank (which has a very limited time to provide the notice) within 30 days following the day of the dishonor.

 Recall the obligations of makers, drawees or acceptors, drawers, indorsers, and accommodation parties.

Obligation of a Maker The **maker** of a promissory note is primarily liable for payment of it. The maker makes an unconditional promise to pay a fixed amount of money and is responsible for making good on that promise. The obligation of the maker is to pay the negotiable instrument according to its terms at the time he issues it or, if it is not issued, then according to its terms at the time it first came into possession of a holder [3-412].[1] If the material terms of the note are not complete when the maker signs it, then the maker's obligation is to pay the note as it is completed, provided that the terms filled in are as authorized. If the instrument is incomplete when the maker signs it and it is completed in an unauthorized manner, then the maker's liability will depend on whether the person seeking to enforce the instrument can qualify as a holder in due course.

The obligation of the maker is owed to (1) a *person entitled to enforce the instrument* or (2) any indorser who paid the instrument pursuant to her indorser's liability (discussed shortly). A person entitled to enforce an instrument includes (1) the holder of the instrument; (2) a nonholder in possession of the instrument who has the rights of a holder; and (3) a person not in possession of the instrument who has the right to enforce the instrument under section 3-309, which deals with lost, destroyed, or stolen instruments.

Revised Article 3 provides that the *drawer of a cashier's check* has the same obligation as the maker or issuer of a note. Thus, it treats a draft drawn by a bank on itself as a drawer—a cashier's check—the same as a note for purposes of the issuer's liability rather than treating the issuer as a drawer of a draft [3-412].

---

[1]The numbers in brackets refer to sections of the Uniform Commercial Code (UCC), which can be accessed at www.law.cornell.edu/ucc.

Ethics and Compliance in Action

Would Qualifying an Indorsement Be Ethical?

Suppose you have taken a promissory note for $3,500 payable in 12 months with interest at 10 percent as payment for some carpentry work you did for a friend. You have some reason to believe the maker of the note is in financial difficulty and may not be able to pay the note when it is due. You discuss with an elderly neighbor the possibility of her buying the note from you as an investment, and she agrees to buy it from you for $3,000. Would it be ethical for you to indorse the note with a qualified indorsement ("without recourse")?

Obligation of a Drawee or an Acceptor

The acceptor of a draft is obligated to pay the draft according to the terms at the time of its acceptance. As was discussed in Chapter 31, acceptance is the drawee's signed engagement to honor the draft as presented—and it is commonly indicated by the signature of the acceptor on the instrument itself. The acceptor's obligation extends to (1) a person entitled to enforce the draft, (2) the drawer, and (3) an indorser who paid the instrument pursuant to her indorser's liability [3-413].

If the certification of a check or other acceptance of a draft states the amount certified or accepted, the obligation of the acceptor is that amount. If the certification or acceptance does not state an amount or if the amount of the instrument is subsequently raised and then the instrument is negotiated to a holder in due course, the obligation of the acceptor is the amount of the instrument at the time a holder in due course takes it [3-413(b)].

At the time a payee receives possession of a check or other draft, the payee gets the drawer's contract to pay the instrument if the drawee—bank or buyer of goods—does not pay. (This liability is discussed in the next section of this chapter.) *Issuance* of the check or draft, however, does not obligate the *drawee* to pay it. Like other Article 3 contracts discussed in this chapter, the drawee does not have liability on the instrument until it *signs* the instrument.

The drawer or a holder of the check may ask the drawee bank to accept or certify the check. The drawee bank certifies the check by signing its name to the check and, with that act, accepts liability as acceptor. The drawee bank debits, or takes the money out of, the drawer's account and holds the money to pay the check. If the drawee bank certifies the check, it becomes primarily, or absolutely, liable for paying the check as it reads at the time of its acceptance [3-413], and its acceptance discharges the drawer and indorsers who indorsed before the acceptance. Similarly, when a trade draft is presented for acceptance or payment, and the named drawee accepts it, then the drawee accepts the obligation set forth in the instrument and the drawer and earlier indorsers are discharged.

A drawee has no liability on a check or other draft unless it certifies or accepts the check or draft—that is, agrees to be liable on it. However, a drawee bank that refuses to pay a check when it is presented for payment may be liable to the drawer for wrongfully refusing payment, assuming the drawer had sufficient funds in his checking account to cover it. The next chapter discusses liability for wrongful dishonor by a drawee bank.

Obligation of a Drawer

The **drawer's** obligation is that if the drawee dishonors an unaccepted check (or draft), the drawer will pay the check (or draft) according to its terms at the time he issued it or, if it was not issued, according to its terms at the time it first came into possession of a holder. If the draft was not complete when issued but was completed as authorized, then the obligation is to pay it as completed. If any completion is not authorized, then the obligation will depend on whether the person seeking to enforce the instrument can qualify as a holder in due course. A person entitled to enforce the draft or an indorser who paid the draft pursuant to his indorser's liability may enforce the drawer's obligation [3-414(b)].

For example, Janis draws a check on her account at First National Bank payable to the order of Collbert. If First National does not pay the check when Collbert presents it for payment, then Janis is liable to Collbert on the basis of her drawer's obligation.

If a draft is accepted by a bank—for example, if the drawee bank certifies a check—the drawer is discharged of her drawer's obligation. If someone other than a bank accepts a draft, then the obligation of the drawer to pay the draft, if the draft is dishonored, is the same as an indorser (discussed next) [3-414(c) and (d)].

Obligation of an Indorser

A person who indorses a negotiable instrument usually is secondarily liable. An indorser is liable upon the *dishonor* by the maker (of a note), drawer (of an unaccepted draft) or the drawee (of an accepted draft), and the indorser's *receipt of notice of the dishonor*. Unless the indorser qualifies or otherwise disclaims liability, the indorser's obligation on dishonor of the instrument is to pay the amount due on the instrument according to its terms at the time he indorsed it or if he indorsed it when incomplete, then according to its terms when completed, provided that it is completed as authorized. The indorser owes the obligation to a person entitled to enforce the instrument or to any subsequent indorser who had to pay it [3-415].

In the vignette at the beginning of the chapter, the question is posed as to your liability if you indorse a check that is payable to your order and then cash it at a check-cashing service. If that check is not paid when it is presented to the drawee bank for payment, then you would be liable for repaying the amount of the check to the check-cashing service. It would then be up to you to locate—and try to recover from—the person from whom you took the check.

The indorser can avoid this contractual liability only by qualifying his indorsement, such as "without recourse," on the instrument when he indorses it [3-415(b)].

Indorsers are liable to each other in the chronological order in which they indorse, from the last indorser back to the first. For example, Mark Maker gives a promissory note to Paul Payee. Payee indorses it and negotiates it to Fred First, who indorses it and negotiates it to Shirley Second. If Maker does not pay the note when Second takes it to him for payment, then Second can require First to pay it to her. First is secondarily liable on the basis of his indorsement. First, in turn, can require Payee to pay him because Payee also became secondarily liable when he indorsed it. Then, Payee is left to try to collect the note from Maker. Second also could have skipped over First and proceeded directly against Payee on his indorsement. First has no liability to Payee, however, because First indorsed after Payee indorsed the note.

If a bank accepts a draft (e.g., by certifying a check) after an indorsement is made, the acceptance discharges the liability of the indorser [3-415(d)]. If notice of dishonor is required and proper notice is not given to the indorser, she is discharged of liability [3-415(c)]. And, where no one presents a check or gives it to a depositary bank for collection within 30 days after the date of an indorsement, the indorser's liability is discharged [3-415(e)].

Obligation of an Accommodation Party

An **accommodation party** is a person who signs a negotiable instrument for the purpose of lending her credit to another party to the instrument but is not a direct beneficiary of the value given for the instrument. For example, a bank might be reluctant to lend money to—and take a note from—Maker because of his shaky financial condition. However, the bank may be willing to lend money to Maker if he signs the note and has a relative or a friend also sign the note as an accommodation maker.

The obligation of an accommodation party depends on the capacity in which the party signs the instrument [3-419]. If Maker has his brother Sam sign a note as an accommodation maker, then Sam has the same contractual liability as a maker. Sam is primarily liable on the note. The bank may ask Sam to pay the note before asking Maker to pay. However, if Sam pays the note to the bank, he has the right to recover his payment from Maker, the person on whose behalf he signed.

Similarly, if a person signs a check as an accommodation indorser, his contractual liability is that of an indorser. If the accommodation indorser has to make good on that liability, he can collect in turn from the person on whose behalf he signed.

The obligation of a party who signs a note as an accommodation maker is illustrated in the case that follows, *National College Loan Trust 2004-1 v. Irizarry*.

National College Loan Trust 2004-1 v. Irizarry
86 UCC Rep. 2d 600 (Ohio Ct. App. 2015)

On April 28, 2004, Anis Algahmee cosigned a $10,000 promissory note enabling Louis Irizarry to obtain a student loan to attend Ohio State University. Both principal and interest were deferred so that payments would not begin until 2008. With a variable annual percentage rate beginning at 6.636 percent, the finance charge was disclosed as $12,168.80 over the life of the 20-year loan, for a total cost of $22,168.80.

Payments were commenced, but no payments were made after July 2010. On May 23, 2013, the National College Loan Trust filed a complaint against Irizarry and Algahmee, stating that they failed to pay the promissory note upon due demand. The note and the accompanying documents were attached to the complaint. The complaint listed the amount of $16,084.42 plus $1,584.68 in accrued interest.

On January 10, 2014, a consent judgment was approved by the court as to Irizarry only. Upon agreement of the parties, judgment was granted in favor of the Loan Trust against Irizarry for $16,084.42 plus interest, plus the costs of the action. The entry stated that, except for the filing of a judgment lien, no execution would be issued if Irizarry paid $100 a month for 12 months, at which time the account would be reviewed to ascertain if the amount should be increased. It also stated that if Irizarry failed to submit a payment on time, the Loan Trust would have the right to commence execution proceedings without further order of the court.

That same day, the Loan Trust filed a motion for summary judgment against Algahmee, stating that there were no material facts to be litigated as to Algahmee because he had admitted executing the note, the note had plain language as to his liability, and the damages were established by an affidavit showing the amount due to be $16,084.42 plus $1,584.68 in interest.

Algahmee opposed the motion for summary judgment, arguing that he received no money for himself, he received no student loans, he served only as a cosigner, the lender had entered into an accord and satisfaction with the student, and the lender had not shown the loan to the student was uncollectible. He also contended that he was entitled to a notice of dishonor or a notice of protest before the note holder could attempt to collect on the note upon Irizarry's default.

The note explicitly stated that the loan proceeds would be used only for educational expenses and that the cosigner would not receive any of the loan proceeds. It also stated, "It shall not be necessary for you to resort to or exhaust your remedies against other Borrower before calling upon any other borrower to make repayment." The signatories furthermore agreed that:

> Each Borrower intends to be treated as a principal on the Application/Promissory Note and not as a surety. To the extent the Borrower may be treated as a surety, such Borrower waives all notices to which such Borrower might otherwise be entitled by such law, and all suretyship defenses that might be available to such Borrower.

The trial court awarded summary judgment to the Loan Trust, and Algahmee appealed.

Robb, Judge

Algahmee's arguments are without effect. A party signs an instrument as an accommodation party where he signs for the purpose of incurring liability without being a direct beneficiary of the value, which is given to benefit another when the instrument is issued. An accommodation party may sign as a maker or indorser (or drawer or acceptor) and is obligated to be in the capacity in which he signs.

The note clearly states that Algahmee is primarily liable without regard to the student's (Irizarry's) ability to pay or the exhaustion of remedies against the student. The note also plainly states that Algahmee's responsibility for paying the loan is unaffected by the failure to notify him when a required payment is missed, that a separate notice to the cosigner is not required, and that notice to one borrower is notice to all borrowers. It further specifies: "You will not be obligated to make any demand upon me, send me any notice, present this Application/Promissory Note to me for payment or make any protest of non-payment to me before suing to collect on this application/Promissory Note if I am in default, and to the extent permitted by applicable law, I hereby waive any right I might otherwise have to require such actions."

In any event, the language of the note eliminated any factual dispute as to Algahmee's argument that the cosigner is not principally liable because he received no loan proceeds.

Algahmee acknowledged that as the cosigner he received no proceeds while promising to pay the debt *on the terms in the note.* The note reiterated that the promise was made by "each and every borrower and cosigner, individually and collectively." It was also explicitly agreed that Algahmee's responsibility for paying the loan was unaffected by the liability of any person to him.

Algahmee also agreed that the Loan Trust was not required to resort to remedies against the student before calling upon Algahmee to make payment. Exhaustion of remedies against the student was expressly not required. Algahmee contracted "to be treated as a principal on this Application/Promissory Note and not as a surety." Algahmee waived all notices and suretyship defenses.

Furthermore, Algahmee signed a notice to the cosigner which provided: "You may be sued for payment although the person who receives the education is able to pay."

Article 3 of the UCC provides that the discharge of an obligation of one party to pay an instrument does not discharge the obligation of the indorser or accommodation party having recourse against the discharged party. Thus the Loan Trust could discharge Irizarry without discharging the cosigner, Algahmee.

Judgment for National Student Loan Trust affirmed.

LO33-3 Explain when a person's signature on a negotiable instrument makes the person contractually liable on it.

Signing an Instrument

No person is contractually liable on a negotiable instrument unless she or her authorized agent has signed it and the signature is binding on the represented person. A signature can be any name, word, or mark used in place of a written signature [3-401]. As discussed earlier, the capacity in which a person signs an instrument determines his liability on the instrument.

Signature by an Authorized Agent

An authorized agent can sign a negotiable instrument. If Sandra Smith authorized her attorney to sign checks as her agent, then she is liable on any checks properly signed by the attorney as her agent. All negotiable instruments signed by corporations have to be signed by an agent of the corporation who is authorized to sign negotiable instruments.

If a person purporting to act as a representative signs an instrument by signing either the name of the represented person or the name of the signer, that signature binds the represented person to the same extent she would be bound if the signature were on a simple contract. If the represented person has authorized the signature of the representative, it is the "authorized signature of the represented person" and the represented person is liable on the instrument, whether or not identified in the instrument. This brings the UCC in line with the general principle of agency law that binds an undisclosed principal on a simple contract. For example, if Principal authorizes Agent to borrow money on Principal's behalf and Agent signs her name to a note without disclosing that the signature was on behalf of Principal, Agent is liable on the note. In addition, if the person entitled to enforce the note can show that Principal authorized Agent to sign on his behalf, then Principal is liable on the note as well.

When a representative signs an authorized signature to an instrument, then the representative is not bound provided the signature shows "unambiguously" that the signature was made on behalf of the represented person who is named in the instrument [3-402(b)(1)]. For example, if a note is signed "XYZ Inc. by Flanigan, Treasurer," Flanigan is not liable on the instrument in his own right, but XYZ Inc. is liable.

If an authorized representative signs his name as the representative of a drawer of a check without noting his representative status, but the check is payable from an account of the represented person who is identified on the check, the signer is not liable on the check as long as his signature was authorized [3-402(c)]. The rationale for this provision is that because most checks today identify the person on whose account the check is drawn, no one is deceived into thinking that the person signing the check is meant to be liable.

Except for the check situation noted above, a representative is personally liable to a holder in due course that took the instrument without notice that the representative was not intended to be liable if (1) the form of the signature does not show unambiguously that the signature was made in a representative capacity or (2) the instrument does not identify the represented person. As to persons other than a holder in due course without notice of the representative nature of the signature, the representative is liable *unless* she can prove that the original parties did not intend her to be liable on the instrument [3-402(b)(2)].

Thus, if an agent or a representative signs a negotiable instrument on behalf of someone else, the agent should indicate clearly that he is signing as the representative of someone else. For example, Kim Darby, the president of Swimwear Inc., is authorized to sign negotiable instruments for the company. If Swimwear borrows money from the bank and the bank asks her to sign a 90-day promissory note, Darby should sign it either "Swimwear Inc. by Kim Darby, President" or "Kim Darby, President, for Swimwear Inc." If Kim Darby signed the promissory note merely "Kim Darby," she could be personally liable on the note. Similarly, if Clara Carson authorizes Arthur Anderson, an attorney, to sign checks for her, Anderson should make sure either that the checks identify Clara Carson as the account involved or should sign them "Clara Carson by Arthur Anderson, Agent." Otherwise, he risks being personally liable on them.

This principle is illustrated in the *Marion T v. Northwest Metals Processors* case that follows. This case also indicates that the criminal law takes a different view of this issue.

Marion T v. Northwest Metals Processors
67 UCC Rep. 2d 379 (N.D. Ind. 2008)

Marion T contracted with Northwest Metals Processors to remove and salvage equipment and materials at Marion's facility located in Marion, Indiana. The company became in arrears on the payments it was to make on the salvaging contract, resulting in Troy Reed—the sole shareholder, board member, and officer of Northwest Metals—issuing two checks drawn on the company's account at Sky Bank and payable to Marion. Reed also issued a third check drawn on the account of Buckeye Industrial Sales & Service, a company in which, again, he was the sole shareholder.

The checks were returned to Marion by the bank where it had deposited them marked "NOT SUFFICIENT FUNDS." In each instance, Reed knew there were insufficient funds to satisfy the amount of the check. The checks were preprinted Sky Bank checks showing in the upper left corner the name of the corporation account holder (i.e., Northwest or Buckeye), and each listed the respective corporation's account number. Reed was authorized to sign checks for both Northwest Metals and Buckeye, and each check was signed simply "Troy Reed," without any notation or indication of his agency status.

Reed then became the subject of a criminal proceeding brought by the state of Indiana for check deception. Marion also brought a civil suit against the two companies and Reed. Among other things, Marion contended that Reed should be personally liable for the dishonored checks.

Cosby, U.S. Magistrate Judge

At the outset, it is undisputed that Marion's claims against Reed are based on three separate negotiable instruments (i.e., corporate checks), and thus it follows that Indiana's version of the U.C.C. applies.

This brings the Court to what is essentially the central issue in this case: whether Reed can be held personally liable for the check deception claim Marion asserts in its complaint in light of the language that now exists in Indiana Code section 3.1-402(c). That section provides:

If a representative [i.e., Reed] signs the name of the representative as drawer of a check without indication of the representative status and the check is payable from an account of the represented person who is identified on the check [i.e., Northwest or Buckeye], the signer is not liable on the check if the signature is an authorized signature of the represented party.

Applying the statute here, it is undisputed that Reed signed his name to each of the corporate checks on the Sky Bank accounts as the authorized signatory, but without indicating his representative capacity. Consequently, in the language of Indiana Code section 3.1-402(c), he is "not liable on the check(s)."

Of course, as Marion notes, Reed is the subject of a criminal proceeding in the state of Indiana for check deception under Indiana Code section 35-43-5-5, a Class A Misdemeanor, arising out of this incident. The difference between the criminal proceedings and the case here, however, is that in the civil context, agency principles govern and the drafters of the U.C.C. chose

to incorporate them into Indiana Code 3.1-402(c), favoring the agent in printed check cases. In the criminal realm, however, agency principles cannot be applied as a shield; thus a corporate officer who issues a worthless check in the corporate name may be held personally responsible under a criminal check deception scheme. The reasoning can be succinctly stated:

There is no language in the [check deception] statute which exempts from its operation a person who shall obtain money or property with fraudulent intent by means of a check which he draws or makes in a representative capacity. If he draws the check as the representative or officer of a corporation, he is none the less the maker or drawer within the contemplation of this statute, and the fraud which the statute is designed to prevent is personal to him. There is no doctrine of agency in the criminal law which will permit an officer of a corporation to shield himself from criminal responsibility for his own act on the ground that it was the act of the corporation and not his personal act.

Walker v. State, 467 N.E.2d 1278, 1250-51 (Ind. Ct. App. 1984).

Therefore, while there is no doctrine of agency in criminal law that can shield Reed if he, with fraudulent intent, was the drafter of a check that was later dishonored, the drafters of the U.C.C. have chosen not to expose agents to civil liability involving transactions where the obvious intent (such as in printed check cases) was to have the check bind the company even if an authorized agent signs his own name.

Summary judgment granted in favor of Reed.

Unauthorized Signature If someone signs a person's name to a negotiable instrument without that person's authorization or approval, the signature does not bind the person whose name appears. However, the signature is effective as the signature of the unauthorized signer in favor of any person who in good faith pays the instrument or takes it for value [3-403(a)]. For example,

if Tom Thorne steals Ben Brown's checkbook and signs Brown's name to a check, Brown is not liable on the check because Brown had not authorized Thorne to sign Brown's name. Thorne can be liable on the check, however, because he did sign it, even though he did not sign it in his own name. Thorne's forgery of Brown's signature operates as Thorne's signature. Thus, if Thorne cashed the check at the bank, Thorne would be liable to it, or if he negotiated it to a store for value, he would be liable to the store to make it good.

An exception to this rule may apply if Brown's negligence in managing checks contributed to the forgery (3-406[a][b]). Negligence is discussed later in this chapter. Even though a signature is not "authorized" when it is put on an instrument initially, it can be ratified later by the person represented [3-403(a)]. It also should be noted that if more than one person must sign to constitute the authorized signature of an organization, the signature of the organization is unauthorized if one of the required signatures is lacking [3-403(b)]. Corporate and other accounts sometimes require multiple signatures as a matter of maintaining sound financial control.

Contractual Liability in Operation

To bring the contractual liability of the various parties to a negotiable instrument into play, generally it is necessary that parties signed the instrument and the instrument is then *presented for payment*. In addition, to hold the parties that are secondarily liable on the instrument to their contractual liability, generally it is necessary that the instrument be *presented for payment* and *dishonored*.

 LO33-4 Explain what is meant by *presentment* of a note or of a check or draft.

Presentment of a Note
The maker of a note is primarily liable to pay it when it is due. Normally, the holder takes the note to the maker at the time it is due and asks the maker to pay it. Sometimes, the note may provide for payment to be made at a bank or the maker sends the payment to the holder at the due date. The party to whom the holder presents the instrument, without dishonoring the instrument, may (1) require the exhibition of the instrument, (2) ask for reasonable identification of the person making presentment, (3) ask for evidence of his authority to make it if he is making it for another person, or (4) return the instrument for lack of any necessary indorsement, (5) ask that a receipt be signed for any payment made, and (6) surrender the instrument if full payment is made [3-501]. These rights protect the party from paying someone not entitled to payment.

Dishonor of a note occurs (1) if the maker does not pay the amount due when it is presented in the case of (*a*) a demand note or (*b*) a note payable at or through a bank on a definite date that is presented on or after that date or (2) if it is not paid on the date payable in the case of a note payable on a

definite date but not payable at or through a bank [3-502]. If the maker or payor dishonors the note, the dishonor triggers the contracts and the holder can seek payment from any persons who indorsed the note before the holder took it. The basis for going after the indorsers is that they are secondarily liable. To hold the indorsers to their contractual obligation, the holder must give them notice of the dishonor. The notice can be either written or oral [3-503].

For example, Susan Strong borrows $1,000 from Jack Jones and gives him a promissory note for $1,000 at 9 percent annual interest payable in 90 days. Jones indorses the note "Pay to the order of Ralph Smith" and negotiates the note to Ralph Smith. At the end of the 90 days, Smith takes the note to Strong and presents it for payment. If Strong pays Smith the $1,000 and accrued interest, she can have Smith mark it "paid" and give it back to her. If Strong does not pay the note to Smith when he presents it for payment, then she has dishonored the note. Smith should give notice of the dishonor to Jones and advise him that he intends to hold Jones secondarily liable on his indorsement. Smith may collect payment of the note from Jones. Jones, after making the note good to Smith, can try to collect the note from Strong on the ground that she defaulted on the contract she made as maker of the note. Of course, Smith also could sue Strong directly on the basis of her maker's obligation.

Presentment of a Check or a Draft
The holder should present a check or draft to the drawee. The **presentment** can be either for payment or for acceptance (certification) of the check or draft. Under Revised Article 3, the presentment may be made by any commercially reasonable means, including a written, oral, or electronic communication [3-501]. The drawee is not obligated on a check or draft unless it accepts (certifies) it [3-408]. An acceptance of a draft is the drawee's signed commitment to honor the draft as presented. The acceptance must be written on the draft, and it may consist of the drawee's signature alone [3-409].

A drawer who writes a check issues an order to the drawee to pay a certain amount out of the drawer's account to the payee (or to someone authorized by the payee). This order is not an assignment of the funds in the drawer's account [3-408]. The drawee bank does not have an obligation to the payee to pay the check unless it certifies the check. However, the drawee bank usually does have a separate contractual obligation (apart from Article 3) to the drawer to pay any properly payable checks for which funds are available in the drawer's account.

For example, Janet Payne has $850 in a checking account at First National Bank and writes a check for $100 drawn on First National and payable to Ralph Smith.

Contract Liability Based on Signature on a Negotiable Instrument

Concept	Contractual Liability

Primary and Secondary Liability	Every party (other than an indorser who qualifies his/her indorsement) who *signs a negotiable instrument* is either primarily or secondarily liable for payment of the instrument when it comes due.
	1. *Primary liability*—Makers and acceptors (a drawee that promises to pay the instrument when it is presented for payment at a later time) are primarily liable.
	2. *Secondary liability*—Drawers and indorsers are secondarily liable. Parties who are secondarily liable on an instrument promise to pay the instrument only if the following events occur:
	  a. The instrument is properly presented for payment.
	  b. The instrument is dishonored.
	  c. Timely notice of the dishonor is given to the party who is secondarily liable.

Accommodation Parties	An accommodation party is one who signs an instrument for the purpose of lending his/her credit to another party to the instrument but is not a direct beneficiary of the value given for the instrument. The obligation of the accommodation party depends on the capacity in which the party signs the instrument. Thus, an accommodation maker has the same obligation as a maker and is primarily liable while an accommodation indorser is secondarily liable on the instrument.
Signature by Agent	An authorized agent can sign an instrument on behalf of the principal and create liability for the principal on the instrument. 1. If the represented person authorized the signature, then the represented person is liable on the instrument whether or not identified in the instrument. 2. If the agent signs an authorized signature to an instrument, the agent is not personally bound on the instrument provided the signature shows unambiguously that the signature was made on behalf of the represented person. 3. If the agent does not identify the represented party in the instrument, then the agent is liable as well unless the instrument is a check drawn on an account for which the agent is an authorized signature.
Unauthorized Signature	An unauthorized signature operates as the signature of the unauthorized signer in favor of a person who in good faith pays the instrument or takes it for value—but it is wholly inoperative as the signature of the person whose name is signed unless: 1. The person whose name is signed ratifies (affirms) the signature. 2. The person whose signature is signed is precluded from denying it.

The writing of the check is the issuance of an order by Payne to First National to pay $100 from her account to Smith or to whomever Smith requests it to be paid. First National owes no obligation to Smith to pay the $100 unless it has certified the check. However, if Smith presents the check for payment and First National refuses to pay it even though there are sufficient funds in Payne's account, then First National is liable to Payne for breaching its contractual obligation to her to pay items properly payable from existing funds in her account. Chapter 34, Checks and Electronic Transfers, discusses the liability of a bank for wrongful dishonor of checks in more detail.

If the drawee bank does not pay or certify a check when it is properly presented for payment or acceptance (certification), the drawee bank has dishonored the check [3-502]. Similarly, if a draft is not paid on the date it is due (or accepted by the drawee on the due date for acceptance), it has been dishonored. The holder of the draft or check then can proceed against either the drawer or any indorsers on their liability. To do so, the holder must give them notice of the dishonor [3-503]. Notice of dishonor, like presentment, can be by any commercially reasonable means, including oral, written, or electronic communication. Under certain circumstances, set out in

Section 3-504, presentment or notice of dishonor may be excused.

Suppose Matthews draws a check for $200 on her account at a bank payable to the order of Williams. Williams indorses the check "Pay to the order of Clark, Williams" and negotiates it to Clark. When Clark takes the check to the bank, it refuses to pay the check because there are insufficient funds in Matthews's account to cover the check. The check has been presented and dishonored. Clark has two options: He can proceed against Williams on Williams's secondary liability as an indorser (because by putting an unqualified indorsement on the check, Williams is obligated to make the check good if it was not honored by the drawee). Or he can proceed against Matthews on Matthews's obligation as drawer because in drawing the check, Matthews must pay any person entitled to enforce the check if it is dishonored. Because Clark dealt with Williams, Clark is probably more likely to return the check to Williams for payment. Williams then has to go against Matthews on Matthews's liability as drawer.

Time of Presentment

If an instrument is payable at a definite time, the holder should present it for payment on the due date. In the case of a demand instrument, the nature of the instrument, trade or bank usage, and the facts of the particular case determine a reasonable time for presentment for acceptance or payment. In a farming community, for example, a reasonable time to present a promissory note that is payable on demand may be six months or within a short time after the crops are ready for sale because the holder commonly expects payment from the proceeds of the crops. If the drawer does not pay a check or accepted draft by the close of business on the day of demand, the drawee has dishonored the check or demand draft [3-502(b)].

Warranty Liability

Whether or not a person signs a negotiable instrument, a person who transfers such an instrument or presents it for payment or acceptance may incur liability on the basis of certain implied warranties. These warranties are (1) transfer warranties, which persons who transfer negotiable instruments make to their transferees, and (2) presentment warranties, which persons who present negotiable instruments for payment or acceptance (certification), and prior transferors, make to those who pay or accept the instruments.

Transfer Warranties

 LO33-5 List the warranties made by persons who transfer negotiable instruments to someone else.

A person who transfers a negotiable instrument to someone else and for consideration makes five warranties to his

---

CONCEPT REVIEW

Transfer Warranties

The six transfer warranties made by a person who transfers a negotiable instrument to someone else for consideration are:

1. The warrantor is entitled to enforce the instrument.

2. All signatures on the instrument are authentic or authorized.

3. The instrument has not been altered.

4. The instrument is not subject to a defense or a claim in recoupment that any party can assert against the warrantor.

5. The warrantor has no knowledge of any insolvency proceedings commenced with respect to the maker or acceptor or, in the case of an unaccepted draft, the drawer.

6. With respect to a remotely created consumer item, the person on whose account the item is drawn authorized the issuance of the item in the amount for which the item is drawn. [Note: This warranty has been adopted in only 11 states and the District of Columbia.]

Who	What Warranties	To Whom
Nonindorsing Transferor	Makes all transfer warranties	To his immediate transferee only
Indorsing Transferor	Makes all transfer warranties	To all subsequent transferees

immediate transferee. If the transfer is by indorsement, the transferor makes these warranties to all subsequent transferees. The five transfer warranties are:

1. The warrantor is a person entitled to enforce the instrument. (In essence, the transferor warrants that there are no unauthorized or missing indorsements that prevent the transferor from making the transferee a holder or a person entitled to enforce the instrument.)

2. All signatures on the instrument are authentic or authorized.

3. The instrument has not been altered.

4. The instrument is not subject to a defense or a claim in recoupment that any party can assert against the warrantor.

5. The warrantor has no knowledge of any insolvency proceedings commenced with respect to the maker or acceptor or, in the case of an unaccepted draft, the drawer [3-416(a)]. Note that this is not a warranty against difficulty in collection or insolvency—the warranty stops with the warrantor's knowledge.

In 2003, a sixth transfer warranty was added to the uniform version of Article 3 to deal with unauthorized or repetitive "remotely created checks." These are sometimes called *telephone checks* because the person on whose account the check will be drawn is not present to sign it and provides information to the payee over the telephone. The payee then "creates" a paper check or an ACH file including the information the account owner provided about the account. These checks have been the vehicles for certain consumer frauds, including telemarketing frauds, but they also serve a valuable function for consumers who need to pay creditors on time. The new transfer warranty provides: "(6) with respect to a remotely created consumer item, that the person on whose account the item is drawn authorized the issuance of the item in the amount for which the item is drawn." As of the time this book went to press, this warranty had been adopted by 11 states and the District of Columbia.

Revised Article 3 provides that in the event of a breach of a transfer warranty, a beneficiary of the transfer warranties who took the instrument in good faith may recover from the warrantor an amount equal to the loss suffered as a result of the breach. However, the damages recoverable may not be more than the amount of the instrument plus expenses and loss of interest incurred as a result of the breach [3-416(b)].

Transferors of instruments other than checks may disclaim the transfer warranties. Unless the warrantor receives notice of a claim for breach of warranty within 30 days after the claimant has reason to know of the breach and the identity of the warrantor, the delay in giving notice of the claim may discharge the warrantor's liability to the extent of any loss the warrantor suffers from the delay, such as the opportunity to proceed against the transferor [3-416(c)].

Although contractual liability often furnishes a sufficient basis for suing a transferor when the party primarily obligated does not pay, warranties are still important. First, they may apply even when the transferor did not indorse. Second, unlike contractual liability, they do not depend on presentment, dishonor, and notice but may be utilized before presentment has been made or after the time for giving notice has expired. Third, a holder may find it easier to return the instrument to a transferor on the ground of breach of warranty than to prove her status as a holder in due course against a maker or drawer.

In the case that follows, *Huntington National Bank v. Guishard, Wilburn & Shorts*, an individual who deposited checks to a corporate account containing forged endorsements was held liable to the bank for breach of the transfer warranties he made by depositing the checks.

Huntington National Bank v. Guishard, Wilburn & Shorts
85 UCC Rep. 2d 364 (E.D. Ohio 2014)

In February 2012, Guishard, Wilburn & Shorts (GWS), a Delaware company with its principal place of business in Georgia, opened an account with Huntington National Bank and began depositing federal checks. Joseph Gray worked with the president of GWS, Allen Pendergrass, in depositing the checks into the GWS account. Gray had previously worked for Pendergrass from 1999 to 2001 at National Unclaimed Funds, an asset recovery business. In late April or early May 2012, Pendergrass asked Gray to deposit endorsed federal checks into the account. Gray, based on his previous experience at National Unclaimed Funds, believed that the transactions were legal and "within the bounds of legitimate asset recovery" and that GWS had the requisite documents and contracts necessary to obtain and deposit the checks.

Gray and Pendergrass agreed that Gray would deposit the checks into the GWS account, and in exchange, Pendergrass would receive 3 percent of the proceeds from the checks. Gray made numerous deposits and received $16,500 from the GWS account as payment for his work. Gray received the checks in envelopes and took the checks directly to Huntington Bank to deposit.

A total of 51 checks, each allegedly endorsed by the intended payee, were deposited in the GWS account. The checks totaled $806,358.51, and over a period of seven months, more than $460,000 was withdrawn from the account.

The U.S. Treasury Department began issuing reclamation claims on the checks several months after the initial deposit into the GWS account. In each reclamation claim, the original payee alleged that he or she did not authorize any other person to deposit the check and received no benefit from it. Reclamation is a process by which the federal government requests a bank to return funds received from the federal government. An individual who has not received a federal check submits a reclamation form to the IRS, and the government forwards the reclamation claim and a copy of the canceled check to the bank at which the federal check was deposited.

Huntington Bank notified GWS and Gray of the reclamation requests and obtained a preliminary injunction from a court enjoining them from "spending, using, dissipating or otherwise transferring" any funds related to the fraud. They were also ordered to immediately withdraw the remaining funds from the GWS account and deposit them with the Clerk of Courts.

Huntington Bank then filed a motion for summary judgment against Gray, seeking recovery of the $16,500 he received from the stolen checks, as damages sustained when he breached the transfer warranties he made to the Huntington Bank when he deposited the checks. *

Marberly, District Judge

The Ohio Revised Code provides that a person who obtains payment from a check warrants to the payor that: (1) he is entitled to enforce the check; (2) all signatures, including endorsements are authentic and authorized; (3) the instrument has not been altered; and (4) the check is not subject to any other defense or claim by any other party. It also provides that an entity that takes a check in good faith may recover as damages for breach of these warranties "an amount equal to the loss suffered as a result of the breach," including the amount of the check, expenses, and lost interest.

A party who negotiates a check with forged endorsements breaches a transfer warranty and is liable for the loss, irrespective of knowledge of the forgery.

In this case, Gray admits to depositing checks personally into the GWS account. He asserts, however, that he had no knowledge of or intent to commit theft or fraud, and that he was unaware the federal checks were stolen or had forged endorsements. Gray also argues that GWS should be responsible, as its name is on the deposit slip received by the bank. The Ohio Code states that any "person who transfers an instrument," makes the transfer warranties. It does not require that the depositor be listed on the deposit slip in order to be held liable, as Gray asserts. Further, when Gray personally deposited the checks, he made all the warranties described in the Ohio Code. Defendant Gray deposited at least $550,000 in the GWS account, which Huntington accepted in good faith. The fact that Gray had no knowledge of the forged indorsements is irrelevant. At the time of Huntington Bank's Motion, Huntington Bank had paid thirty-eight (38) reclamation requests, and the federal government has since indicted Allen Pendergrass, identifying the fifty-one (51) federal checks as stolen and containing forged endorsements. Thus, because the checks contained fraudulent endorsements, Gray breached the transfer warranty and is strictly liable under the Ohio Code.

Finally, although Gray claims that repayment of the $16,500 would be a burden, Huntington is entitled to recover the amounts of the stolen checks, expenses, and lost interest. Pursuant to the Ohio Code, Huntington is permitted to recover the "amount equal to the loss suffered" up to the "amount of the instrument plus expenses and loss of interest," regardless of how much he received personally. Thus, liability in the amount of $16,500 is appropriate in this instance.

---

*Subsequently, the federal government indicted Allen Pendergrass, identifying the 51 federal checks as having been stolen and containing forged endorsements.

Presentment Warranties

 LO33-6 List the warranties made by persons who present negotiable instruments for payment or acceptance.

Persons who present negotiable instruments for payment or drafts for acceptance also make warranties, but their warranties differ from those transferors make. If an unaccepted draft (such as a check) is presented to the drawee for payment or acceptance and the drawee pays or accepts the draft, then the person obtaining payment or acceptance warrants to the drawee making payment or accepting the draft in good faith that:

1. The warrantor is, or was, at the time the warrantor transferred the draft, a person entitled to enforce the draft or authorized to obtain payment or acceptance of the draft on behalf of a person entitled to enforce the draft.

2. The draft has not been altered.

3. The warrantor has no knowledge that the signature of the drawer of the draft has not been authorized [3-417(a)].

In 2003, a fourth presentment warranty was added to the uniform version of Article 3 to deal with unauthorized or repetitive remotely created checks (telephone checks). The new presentment warranty provides: "(4) with respect to any remotely created consumer item, that the person on whose account the item is drawn authorized the issuance of the item in the amount for which the item is drawn." The states and the District of Columbia that enacted the sixth transfer warranty also enacted the fourth presentment warranty.

These warranties also are made by any prior transferor of the instrument at the time the person transfers the instrument; the warranties run only to the drawee who makes payment or accepts the draft in good faith. Such a drawee would include a drawee bank paying a check presented to it for payment directly or through the bank collection process.

The effect of the third presentment warranty is to leave with the drawee the risk that the drawer's signature is unauthorized, unless the person presenting the draft for payment, or a prior transferor, had knowledge of any lack of authorization.

A drawee who makes payment may recover as damages for any breach of a presentment warranty an amount equal to the amount paid by the drawee less the amount the drawee received or is entitled to receive from the drawer because of the payment. In addition, the drawee is entitled to compensation for expenses and loss of interest resulting from the breach [3-417(b)]. The drawee's right to recover damages for breach of warranty is not affected by any failure on the part of the drawee to exercise ordinary care in making payment.

If a drawee asserts a claim for breach of a presentment warranty based on an unauthorized indorsement of the draft or an alteration of the draft, the warrantor may defend by showing that the indorsement is effective under the *impostor* or *fictitious payee* rules (discussed later in this chapter) or that the drawer's negligence precludes him from asserting against the drawee the unauthorized indorsement or alteration (also discussed shortly) [3-417(c)].

If (1) a *dishonored draft* is presented for payment to the drawer or an indorser or (2) any other instrument (such as a note) is presented for payment to a party obligated to pay the instrument and the presenter receives payment, the presenter makes the following single presentment warranty:

> The person obtaining payment is a person entitled to enforce the instrument or authorized to obtain payment on behalf of a person entitled to enforce the instrument [3-417(d)].

On breach of this warranty, the person making the payment may recover from the warrantor an amount equal to the amount paid plus expenses and loss of interest resulting from the breach.

With respect to checks, the party presenting the check for payment cannot disclaim the presentment warranties [3-417(e)]. Unless the payor or drawee provides notice of a claim for breach of a presentment warranty to the warrantor within 30 days after the claimant has reason to know of the breach and the identity of the warrantor, the warrantor is discharged to the extent of any loss caused by the delay in giving notice of the claim of breach.

Payment or Acceptance by Mistake

A long-standing general rule of negotiable instruments law is that payment or acceptance is final in favor of a holder in due course or payee who changes his position in reliance on the payment or acceptance. Revised Article 3 retains this concept by making payment final in favor of a person who took the instrument in good faith and for value or who in good faith changed position in reliance on the payment or acceptance [3-418(c)].

However, payment is not final and may be recovered from a person who does not meet these criteria where the drawee acted on the mistaken belief that (1) payment of a draft or check has not been stopped and (2) the signature of the purported drawer of the draft was authorized [3-418(a)]. In some jurisdictions, the drawee's mistaken belief that the account held available funds also could serve as a basis for recovery of the payment [3-418(b)].

As a result, this means that if the drawee bank mistakenly paid a check over a stop-payment order, paid a check with a forged or unauthorized drawer's signature on it, or paid despite the lack of sufficient funds in the drawer's account to cover the check, the bank cannot recover if it paid the check to a presenter who had taken the instrument in good faith and for value. In that case, the drawee bank would have to pursue someone else, such as the forger or unauthorized signer, or seller whose goods proved to be defective. On the other hand, if the presenter had not taken in good faith or for value, the bank could, in these enumerated instances, recover from the presenter the payment it made by mistake.

Operation of Warranties

Following are three scenarios that show how the transfer and presentment warranties shift the liability back to a wrongdoer or to the person who dealt immediately with a wrongdoer and thus was in the best position to avert the wrongdoing.

Scenario 1 Arthur makes a promissory note for $2,000 payable to the order of Betts. Carlson steals the note from

Betts, indorses her (Betts') name on the back, and gives it to Davidson in exchange for a television set. Davidson negotiates the note for value to Earle, who presents the note to Arthur for payment. Assume that Arthur refuses to pay the note because Betts has advised him that it has been stolen and that she is the person entitled to enforce the instrument. Earle then can proceed to recover the face amount of the note from Davidson on the grounds that as a transferor, Davidson has warranted that he is a person entitled to enforce the note and that all signatures were authentic. Davidson, in turn, can proceed against Carlson on the same basis—if he can find Carlson. If he cannot, then Davidson must bear the loss caused by Carlson's wrongdoing. Davidson was in the best position to ascertain whether Carlson was the owner of the note and whether the indorsement in the name of Betts was genuine. Of course, even though Arthur does not have to pay the note to Earle, Arthur remains liable for his underlying obligation to Betts.

Scenario 2 Anderson draws a check for $10 on her checking account at First Bank payable to the order of Brown. Brown cleverly raises the check to $110, indorses it, and negotiates it to Carroll. Carroll then presents the check for payment to First Bank, which pays her $110 and charges Anderson's account for $110. Anderson then asks the bank to recredit her account for the altered check, and it does so. The bank can proceed against Carroll for breach of the presentment warranty that the instrument had not been altered, which she made to the bank when she presented the check for payment. Carroll in turn can proceed against Brown for breach of her transfer warranty that the check had not been altered—if she can find her. Unless she was negligent in drawing the check, Article 3 limits Anderson's liability to $10 because her obligation is to pay the amount in the instrument at the time she issued it.

Scenario 3 Bates steals Albers's checkbook and forges Albers's signature to a check for $100 payable to "cash," which he uses to buy $100 worth of groceries from a grocer. The grocer presents the check to Albers's bank. The bank pays the amount of the check to the grocer and charges Albers's account. Albers then demands that the bank recredit his account. The bank can recover against the grocer only if the grocer knew that Albers's signature had been forged. Otherwise, the bank must look for Bates. The bank had the responsibility to recognize the true signature of its drawer, Albers, and not to pay the check that contained an unauthorized signature. The bank may be able to resist recrediting Albers's account if it can show he was negligent. The next section of this chapter discusses negligence.

CONCEPT REVIEW

Presentment Warranties

If an unaccepted draft (such as a check) is presented for payment or acceptance and the drawee pays or accepts the draft, then the person obtaining payment or acceptance and prior transferors warrant to the drawee that:

1. The warrantor is a person entitled to enforce payment or authorized to obtain payment or acceptance on behalf of a person entitled to enforce the draft.

2. The draft has not been altered.

3. The warrantor has no knowledge that the signature of the drawer of the draft has not been authorized.

4. With respect to any remotely created consumer item, the person on whose account the item is drawn authorized the issuance of the item in the amount for which the item is drawn. [Note: This warranty has been adopted in only 11 states and the District of Columbia.]

If (*a*) a dishonored draft is presented for payment to the drawer or indorser or (*b*) any other instrument (such as a note) is presented for payment to a party obligated to pay the instrument and the presenter receives payment, the presenter (as well as a prior transferor of the instrument) makes the following warranty to the person making payment in good faith:

The person obtaining payment is a person entitled to enforce the instrument or authorized to obtain payment on behalf of a person entitled to enforce the instrument.

Other Liability Rules

 LO33-7 Discuss the three exceptions to the normal liability rules: negligence, the imposter rule, and the fictitious payee rule.

Normally, a bank may not charge against (debit from) the drawer's account a check that has a forged payee's indorsement. Similarly, a maker does not have to pay a note to the person who currently possesses the note if the payee's signature has been forged. If a check or note has been altered—for example, by raising the amount—the drawer or maker usually is liable only for the instrument in the amount for which he originally issued it. However, there are a number of exceptions to these usual rules. These exceptions, as well as liability based on conversion of an instrument, are discussed in the following sections.

Negligence A person can be so negligent in writing or signing a negotiable instrument that she, in effect, invites an alteration or an unauthorized signature on it. If a person has been negligent, Article 3 precludes her from using the alteration or lack of authorization as a reason for not paying a person who, in good faith, pays the instrument or takes it for value [3-406(a)]. For example, Mary Maker makes out a note for $10 in such a way that someone could alter it to read $10,000. Someone alters the note and negotiates it to Katherine Smith, who can qualify as a holder in due course. Smith can collect $10,000 from Maker. Maker's negligence precludes her from claiming alteration as a defense to paying it. Maker then has to find the person who "raised" her note and try to collect the $9,990 from him.

Where the person asserting the preclusion failed to exercise ordinary care in taking or paying the instrument and that failure substantially contributed to the loss, Article 3 allocates the loss between the two parties based on their comparative negligence [3-406(b)]. Thus, if a drawer was so negligent in drafting a check that he made it possible for the check to be altered and the bank that paid the check, in the exercise of ordinary care, should have noticed the alteration, then any loss occasioned by the fact that the person who made the alteration could not be found would be split between the drawer and the bank based on their comparative fault.

Impostor Rule Article 3 establishes special rules for negotiable instruments made payable to impostors and fictitious persons. An **impostor** is a person who poses as someone else and convinces a drawer to make a check or note payable to the person being impersonated—or to an organization the person purports to be authorized to represent. When this happens, the UCC makes any indorsement "substantially similar" to that of the named payee effective [3-404(a) and (c)]. Where the impostor has impersonated a person authorized to act for a payee, such as claiming to be Jack Jones, the president of Jones Enterprises, the impostor has the power to negotiate a check drawn payable to Jones Enterprises.

An example of a situation involving the impostor rule would be the following: Arthur steals Paulsen's automobile and finds the certificate of title in the automobile. Then, representing himself as Paulsen, he sells the automobile to Berger Used Car Company. The car dealership draws its check payable to Paulsen for the agreed purchase price of the automobile and delivers the check to Arthur. Any person can negotiate the check by indorsing it in the name of Paulsen.

The rationale for the impostor rule is to put the responsibility for determining the true identity of the payee on the drawer or maker of a negotiable instrument. The drawer is in a better position to do this than some later holder of the check who may be entirely innocent. The impostor rule allows that later holder to have good title to the check by making the payee's signature valid although it is not the signature of the person with whom the drawer or maker thought he was dealing. It forces the drawer or maker to find the wrongdoer who tricked him into signing the negotiable instrument or to bear the loss himself.

Fictitious Payee Rule A **fictitious payee** commonly arises in one of the two following situations: (1) a dishonest employee makes a check payable to a "fictitious payee"—someone who does not exist or (2) the dishonest employee makes the check payable to a real person who does business with the employer—but the employee does not intend to send the check to that person. If the employee has the authority to sign checks, he may sign the check himself. Where the employee does not have the authority to sign checks for the employer, the dishonest employee gives the check with the fictitious payee to the employer for signature and represents to the employer that the employer owes money to the person named as the payee. The dishonest employee then takes the check, indorses it in the name of the payee, presents it for payment, and pockets the money. The employee may be in a position to cover up the wrongdoing by intercepting the canceled checks or juggling the company's books.

The UCC allows any indorsement in the name of the fictitious payee to be effective as the payee's indorsement in favor of any person that pays the instrument in good faith or takes it for value or for collection [3-404(b) and (c)].

For example, Anderson, an accountant in charge of accounts payable at Moore Corporation, prepares a false invoice naming Parks Inc., a supplier of Moore Corporation, as having supplied Moore Corporation with goods, and draws a check payable to Parks for the amount of the invoice. Anderson then presents the check to Temple, treasurer of Moore Corporation, together with other checks with invoices attached. Temple signs all of these checks and returns them to Anderson for mailing. Anderson then withdraws the check payable to Parks. Anyone, including Anderson, can negotiate the check by indorsing it in the name of Parks Inc.

The rationale for the fictitious payee rule is similar to that for the impostor rule. If someone has a dishonest employee or agent who is responsible for the forgery of some checks, the employer of the wrongdoer should bear the immediate loss of those checks rather than some other innocent party. In turn, the employer must locate the unfaithful employee or agent and try to recover from him. This outcome is consistent with other law referred to as "respondeat superior," under which principals bear responsibility for their agents.

Comparative Negligence Rule Concerning Impostors and Fictitious Payees

Revised Article 3 also establishes a comparative negligence rule if (1) the person, in a situation covered by the impostor or fictitious payee rule, pays the instrument or takes it for value or collection without exercising ordinary care in paying or taking the instrument and (2) that failure substantially contributes to the loss resulting from payment of the instrument. In these instances, the person initially bearing the loss may recover an allocable share of the loss from the person who did not exercise ordinary care [3-404(d)].

Fraudulent Indorsements by Employees

Revised Article 3 specifically addresses employer responsibility for **fraudulent indorsements** by employees and adopts the principle that the risk of loss for such indorsements by employees who are entrusted with responsibilities for handling or processing checks should fall on the employer rather than on the bank or other person that takes the check or pays it [3-405]. As to any person who in good faith pays an instrument or takes it for value, a fraudulent indorsement by a responsible employee is effective as the indorsement of the payee if it is made in the name of the payee or in a substantially similar name [3-405(b)]. This means that later takers get "good title" to the instrument. If the person taking or paying the instrument failed to exercise ordinary care and that failure substantially contributed to loss resulting from the fraud, the comparative negligence doctrine guides the allocation of the loss.

A fraudulent indorsement includes a forged indorsement purporting to be that of the employer on an instrument payable to the employer; it also includes a forged indorsement purporting to be that of the payee of an instrument on which the employer is drawer or maker [3-405(a)(2)]. "Responsibility" with respect to instruments means the authority to (1) sign or indorse instruments on behalf of the employer, (2) process instruments received by the employer, (3) prepare or process instruments for issue in the name of the employer, (4) control the disposition of instruments to be issued in the name of the employer, or (5) otherwise act with respect to instruments in a responsible capacity. "Responsibility" does not cover those who simply have access to instruments as they are stored or transported, or that are in incoming or outgoing mail [3-405(a)(3)].

In the case that follows, *Victory Clothing Co. v. Wachovia Bank, N.A.*, the court applied comparative negligence principles to split the loss between a company whose employee forged checks and a depositary bank that allowed the forger to deposit the checks to her own personal account in violation of its own rules. As you read the case and note the reasons the court gave for assigning 30 percent of the risk to the employer, you might ask yourself whether the answer would be different today when many banks no longer return copies of canceled checks—or even photocopies of them—regularly to the customer. You might also ask yourself what steps could be taken to prevent something like this from

Victory Clothing Co. v. Wachovia Bank, N.A.
59 UCC Rep. 2d 376 (Penn. Ct. Com. Pl. 2006)

Victory Clothing Company maintained a corporate checking account at Hudson Bank. Jeannette Lunny was employed by Victory as its office manager and bookkeeper for approximately 24 years until she resigned in May 2003. From August 2001 through May 2003, Lunny deposited approximately 200 checks drawn on Victory's corporate account totaling $188,273 into her personal checking account at Wachovia Bank.

Lunny's scheme involved double forgeries. She prepared checks in the company's computer system and made them payable to known vendors of Victory (e.g., Adidas) to whom no money was actually owed. The checks were for dollar amounts that were consistent with the

legitimate checks to those vendors. She then would forge the signature of Victory's owner, Mark Rosenfeld, as drawer on the front of the check and then forge the indorsement of the unintended payee (Victory's various vendors) on the reverse of the check. After forging the indorsement of the payee, Lunny either indorsed the check with her name followed by her account number or referenced her account number following the forged indorsement. She then deposited the checks into her personal account at Wachovia Bank.

At the time of the fraud by Lunny, Wachovia's policies and regulations regarding the acceptance of checks for deposit provided that "checks payable to a non-personal payee can be deposited ONLY into a non-personal account with the same name."

Rosenfeld reviewed the bank statements from Hudson Bank on a monthly basis. However, among other observable irregularities, he failed to detect that Lunny had forged his signature on approximately 200 checks. Nor did he have a procedure to match checks to invoices.

Victory brought suit against Wachovia pursuant to the Pennsylvania Commercial Code, claiming that Wachovia should be liable to it for the entire amount of the losses it sustained by virtue of Lunny's forgery scheme. Victory contended that Wachovia had failed to exercise ordinary care in taking the instruments that were payable to various businesses and allowing them to be deposited into Lunny's personal account. It asserted that this was commercially unreasonable, was contrary to Wachovia's own internal rules and regulations, and exhibited a lack of ordinary care, substantially contributing to the loss resulting from the fraud. Under section 3-405 of the Code, in such circumstances, the person bearing the loss can recover from the person failing to exercise ordinary care to the extent the failure to exercise ordinary care contributed to the loss.

Wachovia, in turn, argued that because Lunny made the fraudulent checks payable to actual vendors of Victory with the intention that the vendors not get paid, Victory's action against it should be barred by the fictitious payee rule set out in section 3-404. Because section 3-404 contains a comparative negligence provision, the court also needed to decide whether it should be applied in this case.

Abrahamson, Judge

In 1990, new revisions to Articles 3 and 4 of the UCC were implemented (the "revisions"). The new revisions made a major change in the area of double forgeries. Before the revisions, the case law was uniform in treating a double forgery case as a forged drawer's signature case, with the loss falling on the drawee bank. The revisions, however, changed this rule by shifting to a comparative fault approach. Under the revised version of the UCC, the loss in double forgery cases is allocated between the depositary and drawee banks based on the extent that each contributed to the loss. "By adopting a comparative fault approach, classification of the double forgery as either a forged signature or forged indorsement case is no longer necessarily determinative." Thus, under the revised Code, a depositary bank may not necessarily escape liability in double forgery situations, as they did under the prior law.

Specifically, revised § 3-405 of the UCC, entitled "Employer's Responsibility for Fraudulent Indorsement by Employee," introduced the concept of comparative fault as between the employer of the dishonest employee/embezzler and the bank(s). This is the section under which Victory sued Wachovia. Section 3-405(b) states, in relevant part:

If the person paying the instrument or taking it for value or for collection fails to exercise ordinary care in paying or taking the instrument and that failure substantially contributes to loss resulting from the fraud, the person bearing the loss may recover from the person failing to exercise ordinary care to the extent the failure to exercise ordinary care contributed to the loss.

The Fictitious Payee Rule

Lunny made the fraudulent checks payable to actual vendors of Victory with the intention that the vendors not get paid. Wachovia therefore argues that Victory's action against it should be barred by the fictitious payee rule under § 3-404. Section 3-404 states, in relevant part:

§ 3-404. Impostors; fictitious payees
(b) FICTITIOUS PAYEE.—If a person whose intent determines to whom an instrument is payable (section 3-110(a) or (b)) does not intend the person identified as payee to have any interest in the instrument or the person identified as payee of an instrument is a fictitious person, the following rules apply until the instrument is negotiated by special indorsement:
(1) Any person in possession of the instrument is its holder.
(2) An indorsement by any person in the name of the payee stated in the instrument is effective as the indorsement of the payee in favor of a person who, in good faith, pays the instrument or takes it for value or for collection.

The fictitious payee rule applies when a dishonest employee writes checks to a company's actual vendors, but intends that the vendors never receive the money; instead, the employee forges the names of the payees and deposits the checks at another bank. Under section 3-404(b) of the UCC, the indorsement is deemed to be "effective" since the employee did not intend for the payees to receive payment. The theory under the rule is that since the indorsement is "effective," the drawee bank was justified in debiting the company's account. Therefore, the loss should fall on the company whose employee committed the fraud.

Revised UCC § 3-404 changed the prior law by introducing a comparative fault principle. Subsection (d) of 3-404 provides that if the person taking the checks fails to exercise ordinary care, "the person bearing the loss may recover from the person failing to exercise ordinary care to the extent the failure to exercise ordinary care contributed to the loss." Therefore, "although the fictitious payee rule makes the indorsement 'effective,' the corporate drawer can shift the loss to any negligent bank, to the extent that the bank's negligence substantially contributed to the loss." Under the revised UCC, the drawer now has the right to sue the depositary bank directly based on the bank's negligence. Under the Old UCC, the fictitious payee rule was a "jackpot" defense for depositary banks because most courts held that the depositary bank's own negligence was irrelevant. However, under revised UCC §§ 3-404 and 3-405, the fictitious payee defense triggers principles of comparative fault, so a depositary bank's own negligence may be considered by the trier of fact. Therefore, based on the foregoing reasons, the fictitious payee defense does not help Wachovia in this case.

Allocation of Liability

As stated, comparative negligence applies in this case because of the revisions in the UCC. In determining the liability of the parties, the Court has considered, *inter alia*, the following factors:

- At the time of the fraud by Lunny, Wachovia's policies and regulations regarding the acceptance of checks for deposit provided that "checks payable to a non-personal payee can be deposited ONLY into a non-personal account with the same name."
- Approximately two hundred (200) checks drawn on Victory's corporate account were deposited into Lunny's personal account at Wachovia.
- The first twenty-three (23) fraudulent checks were made payable to entities that were not readily distinguishable as businesses, such as "Sean John." The check dated December 17, 2001, was the first fraudulent check made payable to a payee that was clearly a business, specifically "Beverly Hills Shoes, Inc."
- Lunny had been a bookkeeper for Victory from approximately 1982 until she resigned in May 2003. Rosenfeld never had any problems with Lunny's bookkeeping before she resigned.
- Lunny exercised primary control over Victory's bank accounts.
- Between 2001 and 2003, the checks that were generated to make payments to Victory's vendors were all computerized checks generated by Lunny. No other Victory employee, other than Lunny, knew how to generate the computerized checks, including Rosenfeld.

- The fraudulent checks were made payable to known vendors of Victory in amounts that were consistent with previous legitimate checks to those vendors.
- After forging the indorsement of the payee, Lunny either indorsed the check with her name followed by her account number, or referenced her account number following the forged indorsement. All of the checks that were misappropriated had the same exact account number, which was shown on the back side of the checks.
- About ten (10) out of approximately three hundred (300) checks each month were forged by Lunny and deposited into her personal account.
- Rosenfeld reviewed his bank statements from Hudson Bank on a monthly basis. Rosenfeld received copies of Victory's cancelled checks from Hudson Bank on a monthly basis. However, the copies of the cancelled checks were not in their normal size; instead, they were smaller, with six checks (front and back side) on each page.
- The forged indorsements were written out in longhand, i.e., Lunny's own handwriting, rather than a corporate stamped signature.
- Victory did not match its invoices for each check at the end of each month.
- An outside accounting firm performed quarterly reviews of Victory's bookkeeping records, and then met with Rosenfeld. This review was not designed to pick up fraud or misappropriation.

Based on the foregoing, the Court finds that Victory and Wachovia are comparatively negligent. With regard to Wachovia's negligence, it is clear that Wachovia was negligent in violating its own rules in repeatedly depositing corporate checks into Lunny's personal account at Wachovia. Standard commercial bank procedures dictate that a check made payable to a business be accepted only into a business checking account with the same title as the business. Had a single teller at Wachovia followed Wachovia's rules, the fraud would have been detected as early as December 17, 2001, when the first fraudulently created non-personal payee check was presented for deposit into Lunny's personal checking account. Instead, Wachovia permitted another one hundred and seventy-six (176) checks to be deposited into Lunny's account after December 17, 2001. The Court finds that Wachovia failed to exercise ordinary care, and that failure substantially contributed to Victory's loss resulting from the fraud. Therefore, the Court concludes that Wachovia is seventy (70) percent liable for Victory's loss.

Victory, on the other hand, was also negligent in its supervision of Lunny, and for not discovering the fraud for almost a two-year period. Rosenfeld received copies of the cancelled checks, albeit smaller in size, on a monthly basis from Hudson Bank. The copies of the checks displayed both the front and back of the checks. Rosenfeld was negligent in not recognizing his own forged signature on the front of the checks, as well as not spotting his own book-keeper's name and/or account number on the back of the checks (which appeared far too many times and on various "payees" checks to be seen as regular by a non-negligent business owner).

Further, there were inadequate checks and balances in Victory's record keeping process. For example, Victory could have ensured that it had an adequate segregation of duties, meaning that more than one person would be involved in any control activity. Here, Lunny exercised primary control over Victory's bank accounts. Another Victory employee, or Rosenfeld himself, could have reviewed Lunny's work. In addition, Victory could have increased the amount of authorization that was needed to perform certain transactions. For example, any check that was over a threshold monetary amount would have to be authorized by more than one individual. This would ensure an additional control on

checks that were larger in amounts. Furthermore, Victory did not match its invoices for each check at the end of each month. When any check was created by Victory's computer system, the value of the check was automatically assigned to a general ledger account before the check could be printed. The values in the general ledger account could have been reconciled at the end of each month with the actual checks and invoices. This would not have been overly burdensome or costly because Victory already had the computer system that could do this in place. Based on the foregoing, the Court concludes that Victory is also thirty (30) percent liable for the loss.

For all the foregoing reasons, the Court finds that Wachovia is 70 percent liable and Victory is 30 percent liable for the $188,273.00 loss. Therefore, Victory Clothing Company is awarded $131,791.10.

happening without you being aware of the fact an employee was forging checks on the company's account.

Conversion   Conversion of an instrument is an unauthorized assumption and exercise of ownership over it. A negotiable instrument can be converted in a number of ways. For example, it might be presented for payment or acceptance, and the person to whom it is presented might refuse to pay or might accept and refuse to return it. An instrument also is converted if a person pays an instrument to a person not entitled to payment—for example, if it contains a forged indorsement.

Revised Article 3 modifies and then expands the previous treatment of conversion and provides that the law applicable to conversion of personal property applies to instruments. It also specifically provides that conversion occurs if (1) an instrument lacks an indorsement necessary for negotiation and (2) it is (a) purchased, (b) taken for collection, or (c) paid by a drawee to a person not entitled to payment. An action for conversion may not be brought by (1) the maker, drawer, or acceptor of the instrument or (2) a payee or an indorsee who did not receive delivery of the instrument either directly or through delivery to an agent or copayee [3-420].

Thus, if a bank pays a check that contains a forged indorsement, the bank has converted the check by wrongfully paying it. The bank then becomes liable for the face amount of the check to the person whose indorsement was forged [3-420]. For example, Arthur Able draws a check for $500 on his account at First Bank, payable to the order of Bernard Barker. Carol Collins steals the check, forges Barker's indorsement on it, and cashes it at First Bank. First Bank has converted Barker's property because it had no right to pay the check without Barker's valid indorsement. First Bank must pay Barker $500, and then it can try to locate Collins to get the $500 back from her.

As is true under the original version of Article 3, if a check contains a restrictive indorsement (such as "for deposit" or "for collection") that shows a purpose of having the check collected for the benefit of a particular account, then any person who purchases the check or any depositary bank or payor bank that takes it for immediate payment converts the check unless the indorser receives the proceeds or the bank applies them consistent with the indorsement [3-206].

In the case that follows, *Jones v. Wells Fargo Bank*, the court concluded that a depositary bank was liable for conversion when it paid it to someone not entitled to enforce the check.

Jones v. Wells Fargo Bank, N.A.	**76 UCC Rep. 2d 529 (5th Cir. 2012)**

In September 2006, Adley Abdulwahab ("Wahab") opened a business cash management account on behalf of W Financial Group with Wells Fargo Bank, N.A. Wahab, along with Michael K. Wallens and Michael K. Wallens Jr., was an authorized signer on the account.

On January 29, 2007, Wahab withdrew $1,701,250 from W Financial's account at Wells Fargo Post Oak Branch in Houston. Wahab used the funds to buy a cashier's check payable to Lubna Lateef, Misba Lateef, Shahed Lateef, and Zahed Lateef (the "Lateefs"). Later *that same day, Wahab returned to a different Wells Fargo Branch in Spring, Texas. Wahab deposited the check into the Wells Fargo account of a separate entity, CA Houston Investment Center. Wahab was CA Houston's managing member and the only authorized signer on its account. The Lateefs never received or endorsed the cashier's check. Rather, Wells Fargo stamped the following on the back of the check: "CREDITED TO THE ACCOUNT OF WITHIN NAMED PAYEE LACK OF ENDORSEMENT GUARANTEED WELLS FARGO BANK, N.A." The account number for CA Houston was handwritten below the stamp.*

In March 2008, the Securities and Exchange Commission (SEC) brought an enforcement action against W Financial, alleging that it had engaged in the fraudulent sale of securities. The U.S. District Court for the Northern District of Texas, where that action was filed, entered an order appointing Vernon T. Jones as receiver for W Financial for the purpose of recovering the company's assets for the benefit of its investors. Pursuant to his responsibilities as receiver, Jones filed an action against Wells Fargo, asserting conversion and breach of contract based on the January 29, 2007, transaction. The district court granted summary judgment in favor of the Receiver on the conversion claim against Wells Fargo.

PER CURIAM. Under Texas law, which has adopted most provisions of the Uniform Commercial Code verbatim, a bank may be liable for conversion of a cashier's check if a bank makes or obtains payment with respect to the instrument for a person not entitled to enforce the instrument or receive payment.

In this case CA Houston (through Wahab as its agent), and not W Financial, is the entity that sought to enforce the instrument. As Wells Fargo states, "W Financial did not enforce the cashier's check as it is not the party that received payment." CA Houston was; thus, CA Houston enforced the cashier's check. The resolution of this case depends on whether CA Houston was entitled to enforce the cashier's check.

The UCC lists the following persons who are "entitled to enforce" an instrument: (1) the holder of the instrument, (2) a non-holder in possession of the instrument who has the rights of a holder, or (3) a person not in possession of the instrument who is entitled to enforce the instrument. A holder is defined as the person in possession of an instrument that is payable to bearer or to an identified person that is the person in possession. CA Houston was not a holder under the UCC because the check was payable to the Lateefs, not to Wahab, CA Houston or to "bearer." Furthermore, the parties agree that Wahab was in physical possession of the check, precluding him or CA Houston from

qualifying "as a person not in possession of the instrument who is entitled to enforce the instrument."

The only conceivable manner in which CA Houston could have acquired W Financial's enforcement rights in this case is through a transfer of the cashier's check from W Financial to CA Houston. There is, however, no evidence of a transfer. A transfer occurs only when an instrument is delivered by a person other than its issuer for the purpose of giving the person receiving the delivery the right to enforce the instrument. No such purpose is evident here. Because Wells Fargo made payment on the cashier's check to CA Houston, an entity that was not entitled to enforce the instrument, Wells Fargo is liable for conversion under section 3-420.

The district court also concluded that Wells Fargo is liable for conversion because it deposited the cashier's check without the necessary indorsement. We agree. The UCC places the burden on the first bank in the collection chain to ensure an indorsement's authenticity. Wells Fargo accepted and processed the cashier's check even though it had not been indorsed by the Lateefs. When Wahab deposited the cashier's check into CA Houston's account, Wells Fargo should have first required the Lateefs' indorsement.

Judgment affirmed.

Discharge of Contractual Liability on Negotiable Instruments

 LO33-8 Explain how the liability of a party to pay an instrument is normally discharged.

Discharge of Contractual Liability The obligation of a party to pay an instrument is discharged (1) if he meets the requirements set out in Revised Article 3 or (2) by any act or agreement that would discharge an obligation to pay money on a simple contract. Discharge of an obligation is not effective against a person who has the rights of a holder in due course of the instrument and took the instrument without notice of the discharge [3-601].

The most common ways that an obligor is discharged from her contract liability are:

1. Payment of the instrument.
2. Cancellation of the instrument.

3. Alteration of the instrument.

4. Modification of the principal's obligation that causes loss to a surety or impairs the collateral.

5. Unexcused delay in presentment or notice of dishonor with respect to a check (discussed earlier in this chapter).

6. Acceptance of a draft [3-414(c) or (d), 3-415(d)]; as noted earlier in the chapter, a drawer is discharged of liability of a draft that is accepted by a bank (e.g., if a check is certified by a bank) because at that point the holder is looking to the bank to make the instrument good.

Discharge by Payment Generally, payment in full discharges contractual liability on an instrument to the extent payment is (1) by or on behalf of a party obligated to pay the instrument and (2) to a person entitled to enforce the instrument. For example, Arthur makes a promissory note for $1,000 payable to the order of Bryan. Bryan indorses the note "Pay to the order of my account no. 16154 at First Bank, Bryan." Bryan then gives the note to his employee, Clark, to take to the bank. Clark takes the note to Arthur, who pays Clark the $1,000. Clark then runs off with the money. Arthur is not discharged of his primary liability on the note because he did not make his payment consistent with the restrictive indorsement. To be discharged, Arthur has to pay the $1,000 into Bryan's account at First Bank.

To the extent of payment, the obligation of a party to pay the instrument is discharged even though payment is made with knowledge of a claim to the instrument by some other person. However, the obligation is not discharged if (1) there is a claim enforceable against the person making payment and payment is made with knowledge of the fact that payment is prohibited by an injunction or similar legal process or (2) in the case of an instrument other than a cashier's, certified, or teller's check, the person making the payment had accepted from the person making the claim indemnity against loss for refusing to make payment to the person entitled to enforce payment. The obligation also is not discharged if he knows the instrument is a stolen instrument and pays someone he knows is in wrongful possession of the instrument [3-602].

Discharge by Cancellation A person entitled to enforce a negotiable instrument may discharge the liability of the parties to the instrument by canceling or renouncing it. If the holder mutilates or destroys a negotiable instrument with the intent that it no longer evidences an obligation to pay money, the holder has canceled it [3-604]. For example, a grandfather lends $5,000 to his grandson for college expenses. The grandson gives his grandfather a promissory note for $5,000. If the grandfather later tears up the note with the intent that the grandson no longer owes him $5,000, the grandfather has canceled the note.

An accidental destruction or mutilation of a negotiable instrument is not a cancellation and does not discharge the parties to it. If an instrument is lost, mutilated accidentally, or destroyed, the person entitled to enforce it still can enforce the instrument. In such a case, the person must prove that the instrument existed and that she was its holder when it was lost, mutilated, or destroyed.

Altered Instruments: Discharge by Alteration A person paying a fraudulently altered instrument, or taking it for value, in good faith and without notice of the alteration, may enforce the instrument (1) according to its original terms or (2) in the case of an incomplete instrument later completed in an unauthorized manner, according to its terms as completed [3-407(c)]. An alteration occurs if there is (1) an unauthorized change that modifies the obligation of a party to the instrument or (2) an unauthorized addition of words or numbers or other change to an incomplete instrument that changes the obligation of any party [3-407]. A change that does not affect the obligation of one of the parties, such as dotting an *i* or correcting the grammar, is not considered to be an alteration.

Two examples illustrate the situations in which Revised Article 3 allows fraudulently altered instruments to be enforced. First, assume the amount due on a note is fraudulently raised from $10 to $10,000. The contract of the maker has been changed: The maker promised to pay $10, but after the change has been made, he would be promising to pay much more. If the note is negotiated to or paid by a person who was without notice of the alteration, that person can enforce the note against the maker only according to its original terms. It would pursue the alterer or the person taking from the alterer for the balance on a presentment or transfer warranty [3-416, 3-417]. If the maker's negligence substantially contributed to the alteration, then the maker would be responsible for as much as the entire $10,000 [3-406, 3-407(c)].

Second, assume Swanson draws a check payable to Frank's Nursery, leaving the amount blank. He gives it to his gardener with instructions to purchase some fertilizer at Frank's and to fill in the purchase price of the fertilizer when it is known. The gardener fills in the check for $100 and gives it to Frank's in exchange for the fertilizer ($17.25) and the difference in cash ($82.75). The gardener then leaves town with the cash. If Frank's had no knowledge of the unauthorized completion, it could enforce the check for $100 against Swanson.

In any other case, a fraudulent alteration **discharges** any party whose obligation is affected by the alteration *unless* the party (1) assents or (2) is precluded from asserting the alteration (e.g., because of the party's negligence). Assume that Anderson signs a promissory note for $100 payable to Bond. Bond indorses the note "Pay to the order of Connolly, Bond" and negotiates it to Connolly. Connolly changes the $100 to read $100,000. Connolly's change is unauthorized and fraudulent. As a result, Anderson is discharged from her liability as maker of the note and Bond is discharged from her liability as indorser. Neither of them has to pay Connolly. The obligations of both Anderson and Bond were changed because the amount for which they are liable was altered.

No other alteration—that is, one that is not fraudulent—discharges any party and a holder may enforce the instrument according to its *original* terms. Thus, there would be no discharge if a blank is filled in the honest belief that it is authorized or if a change is made, without any fraudulent intent, to give the maker on a note the benefit of a lower interest rate.

Discharge of Indorsers and Accommodation Parties

If a person entitled to enforce an instrument agrees, with or without consideration, to a material modification of the obligation of a party to the instrument, including an extension of the due date, then any accommodation party or indorser who has a right of recourse against the person whose obligation is modified is discharged *to the extent the modification causes a loss to the indorser or accommodation party.* Similarly, if collateral secures the obligation of a party to an instrument and a person entitled to enforce the instrument impairs the value of the collateral, the obligation of the indorser or accommodation party having the right of recourse against the obligor is discharged to the extent of the impairment. These discharges are not effective unless the person agreeing to the modification or causing the impairment knows of the accommodation or has notice of it. Also, no discharge occurs if the obligor assented to the event or conduct, or if the obligor has waived the discharge [3-605].

For example, Frank goes to Credit Union to borrow $4,000 to purchase a used automobile. The credit union has Frank sign a promissory note and takes a security interest in the automobile (i.e., takes it as collateral for the loan). It also asks Frank's brother, Bob, to sign the note as an accommodation maker. Subsequently, Frank tells the credit union he wants to sell the automobile and the credit union releases its security interest. Because release of the collateral adversely affects Bob's obligation as accommodation maker, he is discharged from his obligation as accommodation maker in the amount of the value of the automobile.

Problems and Problem Cases

1. Thomas Kirkman was involved in the horse business and was a friend of John Roundtree, a loan officer for American Federal Bank. Kirkman and Roundtree conceived a business arrangement in which Kirkman would locate buyers for horses and the buyers could seek financing from American Federal. Roundtree gave Kirkman blank promissory notes and security agreements from American Federal. Kirkman was to locate the potential purchaser, take care of the paperwork, and bring the documents to the bank for approval of the purchaser's loan.

Kirkman entered into a purchase agreement with Gene Parker, a horse dealer, to copurchase for $35,000 a horse named Wills Hightime, which Kirkman represented he owned. Parker signed the American Federal promissory note in blank and executed in blank a security agreement that authorized the bank to disburse the funds to the seller of the collateral. Kirkman told Parker he would cosign the note and fill in the details of the transaction with the bank. Although Kirkman did not cosign the note, he did complete it for $85,000 rather than $35,000. Kirkman took the note with Parker's signature to Roundtree at American Federal and received two checks from the bank payable to him in the amounts of $35,000 and $50,000. Kirkman took the $35,000 and gave it to the real owner of the horse. Parker then received the horse.

Parker began making payment to the bank and called upon Kirkman to assist in making the payments pursuant to their agreement. However, Kirkman skipped town, taking the additional $50,000 with him. Parker repaid the $35,000 but refused to pay any more. He argued that he agreed to borrow only $35,000 and the other $50,000 was unauthorized by him.

Was Parker's liability on the note limited to the $35,000 he had authorized Kirkman to fill in?

2. Formica Construction Company was the general contractor in the renovation of a restaurant owned by Mossi Inn Inc. Mossi is a closely held corporation whose sole officers and shareholders are the parents of

Daniel Mills. Mills is an employee of Mossi, manages the restaurant, and served as the authorized agent of the company in dealing with Formica Construction. At the time the construction loan for the renovation was being converted into a mortgage on the property, the loan proceeds were insufficient to cover $37,000 Formica was owed for extras on the project. Mills signed a negotiable promissory note payable to the order of Formica in which he promised to pay the $37,000, but he did not indicate he was signing in a representative capacity on behalf of Mossi. When a portion of the note remained unpaid, Formica brought suit against Mills seeking payment of the balance. Mills claimed that he was only an employee of Mossi and had signed only as a representative. On these facts, is Mills personally liable for repayment of the note?

3. Clay Haynes was the bookkeeper for Johnstown Manufacturing Inc. He had express check-signing authority, and his signature was on the signature card for the account that Johnstown maintained at BancOhio National Bank. Haynes was also the bookkeeper of another corporation, Lynn Polymers Inc., which was operated by the same individuals that operated Johnstown. Over a period of a year, Haynes engaged in a check-cashing scheme from which he pocketed approximately $70,000. Haynes wrote 35 corporate checks to the order of BancOhio National Bank, and the bank, in return, gave the cash to Haynes. Johnstown brought suit against BancOhio to recover $300 for the one check written on the Johnstown account the bank paid to Haynes. Johnstown claimed that the check was written without the express authority of the corporation, and thus it contained an "unauthorized" signature. Was Haynes's signature on the check "unauthorized" as that term is used in the Uniform Commercial Code?

4. In November 2005, Michele Fehl, an administrative assistant recently hired by AFT Trucking, stole eight company checks from the company's offices. She made out the checks to herself in various amounts. Fehl was not authorized to sign checks on behalf of the company. Over the next three weeks, Fehl presented the checks at Money Stop, a check-cashing service, which gave her cash for the checks. Subsequently, the checks were dishonored by AFT Trucking. It fired Fehl, who was arrested and criminally prosecuted. Money Stop brought suit against AFT Trucking to recover the funds it had disbursed. AFT Trucking asserted that Money Stop's only recourse was against Fehl, the person who had signed the checks. Is Money Stop entitled to recover from AFT Trucking?

5. First National Bank certified Smith's check in the amount of $29. After certification, Smith altered the check so that it read $2,900. He presented the check to a merchant in payment for goods. The merchant then submitted the check to the bank for payment. The bank refused, saying it had certified the instrument for only $29. Can the merchant recover the $2,900 from the bank?

6. A check was drawn on First National Bank and made payable to Howard. It came into the possession of Carson, who forged Howard's indorsement and cashed it at Merchant's Bank. Merchant's Bank then indorsed it and collected payment from First National. Assuming that Carson is nowhere to be found, who bears the loss caused by Carson's forgery?

7. Mrs. Gordon Neely hired Louise Bradshaw as the bookkeeper for a Midas Muffler shop she and her husband owned and operated as a corporation, J. Gordon Neely Enterprises (Neely). Bradshaw's duties included preparing company checks for Mrs. Neely's signature and reconciling the checking account when the company received a bank statement and canceled checks each month. Bradshaw prepared several checks payable to herself and containing a large space to the left of the amount written on the designated line. When Mrs. Neely signed the checks, she was aware of the large gaps. Subsequently, Bradshaw altered the checks by adding a digit or two to the left of the original amount and then cashed them at American National Bank, the drawee bank. Several months later, Neely's hired a new accountant, who discovered the altered checks. Neely brought suit against American National Bank to have its account recredited for the altered checks, claiming American was liable for paying out on altered instruments. The bank contended that Neely's negligence substantially contributed to alterations of the instruments and thus Neely was precluded from asserting the alteration against the bank. Between Neely and American National Bank, who should bear the loss caused by Bradshaw's fraud?

8. Clarice Rich was employed by the New York City Board of Education as a clerk. It was her duty to prepare requisitions for checks to be issued by the board, to prepare the checks, to have them signed by authorized personnel, and to send the checks to the recipients. In some instances, however, she retained them. Also, on a number of occasions she prepared duplicate requisitions and checks, which, when signed, she likewise retained. She then forged the indorsement of the named payees on the checks she had retained and cashed the checks at Chemical Bank, where the Board of Education maintained

its account. After the board discovered the forgeries, it demanded that Chemical Bank credit its account for the forged checks. Is Chemical Bank required to credit the board's account as requested?

9. Stockton's housekeeper stole some of his checks, forged his name as drawer, and cashed them at Gristedes Supermarket, where Stockton maintained check-cashing privileges. The checks were presented to Stockton's bank and honored by it. Over the course of 18 months, the scheme netted the housekeeper in excess of $147,000 on approximately 285 forged checks. Stockton brought suit against Gristedes Supermarket for conversion, seeking to recover the value of the checks it accepted and for which it obtained payment from the drawee bank. Was Gristedes Supermarket liable to Stockton for conversion for accepting and obtaining payment of the stolen and forged checks?

Checks and Electronic Transfers

S usan Williams opened a checking account at the First National Bank. She made an initial deposit of $1,800, signed a signature card that indicated to the bank that she was the authorized signator on the account, and was given a supply of blank checks. She also received an ATM debit card that, when used along with an assigned PIN (personal identification number), allowed her to make deposits to her account and to obtain cash from it as well as to make purchases from merchants with the funds being transferred electronically from her account to the merchant. Each month, the bank sent her a statement reflecting the activity in the account during the previous month along with the canceled checks. Several months after she opened the account, the bank erroneously refused to pay a check she had written to a clothing store even though she had sufficient funds in her account. As a result, the store filed a complaint with the local prosecutor indicating she had written a "bad check." On one occasion, Susan called the bank to stop payment on a check she had written to cover repairs to her automobile because, while driving the car home, she discovered the requested repair had not been made. However, the bank paid the check later that day despite the stop-payment order she had given the bank. Another time, Susan's wallet fell out of her purse while she was shopping at a mall. She received a call the next morning indicating the wallet had been found, and she retrieved it at that time. However, when she received her next monthly statement from the bank, she discovered that someone had apparently used her ATM card to withdraw $200 from her account on the day her wallet had been lost. Susan's experiences raise a number of legal issues that will be covered in this chapter, including:

- What rights does Susan have against the bank for refusing to pay the check to the clothing store despite the fact she had sufficient funds on deposit to cover it?
- What rights does Susan have against the bank for failing to honor the stop-payment order she placed on the check she had written to the repair shop?
- What rights does Susan have against the bank because of the unauthorized use of her ATM card? What must she do to preserve those rights?
- If a repair shop refuses to release your automobile unless you pay it more than the repair shop had advised you it would charge you for the work, would it be ethical to give the repair shop a check for the larger amount knowing you intend to immediately go to your bank and stop payment on it?

LO   LEARNING OBJECTIVES

After studying this chapter, you should be able to:

34-1 Recall that the basic duty of a bank is to pay any properly drawn and payable check if there are sufficient funds in the customer's account.

34-2 Discuss the rules pertaining to postdated checks.

34-3 Explain what is meant by a stop-payment order and discuss the bank's duties and potential liabilities when it is given such an order.

34-4 Distinguish *certified checks* from *cashier's checks*.

34-5 Discuss the bank's obligations to its customer when it is presented with forged or altered checks.

34-6 Explain the customer's duty to report forgeries and alterations and the consequences for the customer if he or she does not do so in a timely manner.

34-7 Discuss the implications of Check 21 from the perspective of the customer of a bank.

34-8 Discuss the major features of the Electronic Fund Transfer Act as they relate to the rights, liabilities, and responsibilities of participants in electronic funds transfer systems.

FOR MOST PEOPLE, a checking account provides the majority of their contact with negotiable instruments. This chapter focuses on the relationship between the drawer with a checking account and the drawer's bank, known as the drawee bank.

The Drawer–Drawee Relationship

There are two main sources that govern the relationship between the depositor and the drawee bank: the deposit agreement (which is a contract) and Articles 3 and 4 of the UCC. Article 4, which governs bank deposits and collections, allows the depositor and drawee bank (which Article 4 calls the "payor bank") to vary Article 4's provisions with a few important exceptions. The deposit agreement cannot disclaim the bank's responsibility for its own lack of good faith or failure to exercise ordinary care or limit the measure of damages for the lack or failure; however, the parties may determine by agreement the standards by which to measure the bank's responsibility so long as the standards are not manifestly unreasonable [4-103].[1]

The deposit agreement establishes many important relationships between the depositor and drawee-payor bank. The first of these is their relationship as creditor and debtor, respectively, so that when a person deposits money in an account at the bank, the law no longer considers him the owner of the money. Instead, he is a creditor of the bank to the extent of his deposits, and the bank becomes his debtor. Also, when the depositor deposits a check to a checking account, the bank also becomes his agent for collection of the check. The bank as the person's agent owes a duty to him to follow his reasonable instructions concerning payment of checks and other items from his account and a duty of ordinary care in collecting checks and other items deposited to the account.

Bank's Duty to Pay

LO34-1 Recall that the basic duty of a bank is to pay any properly drawn and payable check if there are sufficient funds in the customer's account.

When a bank receives a properly drawn and payable check on a person's account and there are sufficient funds to cover the check, the bank is under a duty to pay it. If the person has sufficient funds in the account and the bank refuses to pay, or dishonors, the check, the bank is liable for the actual damages proximately caused by its wrongful dishonor as well as consequential damages [4-402]. Actual damages may include charges imposed by retailers for returned checks as well as damages for arrest or prosecution of the customer. Consequential damages include injury to the depositor's credit rating that results from the dishonor.

For example, Donald Dodson writes a check for $1,500 to Ames Auto Sales in payment for a used car. At the time that Ames Auto presents the check for payment at Dodson's bank, First National Bank, Dodson has $1,800 in his account. However, a teller mistakenly refuses to pay the check and stamps it NSF (not sufficient funds). Ames Auto then goes to the local prosecutor and signs a complaint against Dodson for writing a bad check. As a result, Dodson is arrested. Dodson can recover from First National the damages that he sustained because the bank wrongfully dishonored his check, including the damages involved in his arrest, such as his attorney fees.

Bank's Right to Charge to Customer's Account
The drawee bank has the right to charge any properly payable check to the account of the customer or drawer. The bank has this right even though payment of the check creates an overdraft in the account [4-401]. If an account is overdrawn, the customer owes the bank the amount of the overdraft, and the bank may take that amount out of the next deposit that the customer makes or from another account that the depositor maintains with the bank. Alternatively, the bank might seek to collect the amount directly from the customer. If there is more than one customer who can draw from an account, only those customers who sign the item or who benefit from the proceeds of an overdraft are liable for the overdraft.

Stale Checks The bank does not owe a duty to its customer to pay any checks out of the account that are more

---

[1]The numbers in brackets refer to sections of the Uniform Commercial Code.

CYBERLAW IN ACTION

Account Aggregation

"Account aggregation" is a financial management tool offered by banks and by third-party, Internet-based companies. Consumers who want to use this tool will allow a bank or third party to gather information from many accounts (checking, savings, pension funds, certificates of deposit, securities firms, and insurance companies) by giving the account aggregator key information such as the account numbers and passwords for the consumer's various accounts. The aggregator then gathers information from the websites of the different financial services firms (insurance companies, banks, investment planners, securities brokers, etc.) and makes it possible for the consumer to view all of this

information on one screen and, in some cases, to transfer funds between accounts.

Some consumer advocates argue that account aggregation—also known as "screen scraping"—is riskier for consumers than accessing each financial service provider's website separately. They worry that the possibility of hacking into such an information-heavy account increases the chance that a criminal could wipe out the entire holdings of one consumer or a group of consumers. Consumers like account aggregation because it gives them all of their financial accounts essentially on one "page" on their computer screens. Other consumers like it because account aggregation allows them to move funds between their various accounts quickly from their computers without waiting to speak to each specific financial services provider to complete transactions.

than six months old. Such checks are called stale checks. However, the bank, acting in good faith, may pay a check that is more than six months old and charge it to the drawer-depositor's account [4-404].

Altered and Incomplete Items If the bank in good faith pays a check drawn by the drawer-depositor but subsequently altered, it may charge the customer's account with the amount of the check as originally drawn. Also, if an incomplete check of a customer gets into circulation, is completed, and is presented to the drawee bank for payment, and the bank pays the check, the bank can charge the amount as completed to the customer's account even though it knows that the check has been completed, unless it has notice that the completion was improper [4-401(d)]. The respective rights, obligations, and liabilities of drawee banks and their drawer-customers concerning forged and altered checks are discussed in more detail later in this chapter.

Limitations on Bank's Right or Duty Article 4 recognizes that the bank's right or duty to pay a check or to charge the depositor's account for the check (including exercising its right to set off an amount due to it by the depositor) may be terminated, suspended, or modified by the depositor's order to stop payment (which is discussed in the next section of this chapter). In addition, the bank's right to pay may be stopped by events external to the relationship between the depositor and the bank. These external events include the filing of a bankruptcy petition by the depositor or by the depositor's creditors and the garnishment of the account by a creditor of the depositor. The bank must

receive the stop-payment order from its depositor or the notice of the bankruptcy filing or garnishment before the bank has certified the check, paid it in cash, settled with another bank for the amount of the item without a right to revoke the settlement, or otherwise become accountable for the amount of the check under Article 4 or before the cut-off hour on the banking day after the check is received if the bank established a cut-off hour [4-303]. These restrictions on the bank's right or duty to pay are discussed in later sections of this chapter.

Postdated Checks

 Discuss the rules pertaining to postdated checks.

Under original Articles 3 and 4, a postdated check was not properly payable by the drawee bank until the date on the check. The recent amendments to Article 4 change this. Under the revision, an otherwise properly payable postdated check that is presented for payment before the date on the check may be paid and charged to the customer's account *unless* the customer has given notice of it to the bank. To prevent early payment, the customer must give notice of the postdating in a way that describes the check with reasonable certainty. It is effective for the same time periods as Article 4 provides for stop-payment orders (discussed shortly). The customer must give notice to the bank at such time and in such a manner as to give the bank an opportunity to act on it before the bank takes any action with respect to paying the check. If the bank charges the customer's account for a postdated check before the date stated in the notice given to the bank, the bank is liable for damages for any loss that results. Such damages might include those associated with the dishonor of subsequent items [3-113(a), 4-401(c)].

There are a variety of reasons a person might want to postdate a check. For example, a person might have a mortgage payment due on the first of the month at a bank located in another state. To make sure that the check arrives on time, the customer may send the payment by mail several days before the due date. However, if the person is depending on a deposit of her next monthly paycheck on the first of the month to cover the mortgage payment, she might postdate the check to the first of the following month. Under the original version of Articles 3 and 4, the bank could not properly pay the check until the first of the month. However, under the revisions, it could be properly paid by the bank before that date if presented earlier. To avoid the risk that the bank would dishonor the check for insufficient funds if presented before the first, the customer should notify the drawee bank in a manner similar to that required for stop payment of checks.

Checks Not Properly Payable Whereas a bank has a duty to pay any check that is properly payable and to charge the customer's account, it lacks the authority to pay if the check is not properly payable. In the case that follows, *Forcht Bank v. Gribbins*, the court held that the bank was liable for cashing eight checks containing forged drawer's signatures and charging them against the customer's account.

Forcht Bank v. Gribbins   87 UCC Rep. 2d 31 (Ky. Ct. App. 2015)

Between July 18, 2010, and August 9, 2010, Forcht Bank honored and paid eight checks with forged drawer signatures from the checking account of Renee Gribbins, who was a depositor at the bank. All eight checks were made payable to Andy Akers and presented for payment at the Campbellsville, Kentucky, branch of Forcht Bank. Gribbins was the only signator on the account, and it was the only account she had with the bank. Forcht Bank was both the drawee and the collecting bank.

On August 12, 2010, a bank employee contacted Gribbins about the forged checks, which had completely depleted the funds in Gribbins's account. Upon learning about the forgeries, Gribbins went to the Campbellsville branch of the bank and completed affidavits of forgery for each check. Initially, she did not know who had forged the checks but learned from the bank that the checks had all been made payable to Akers and cashed by him.

On October 27, 2010, Gribbins filed a complaint against Forcht Bank, alleging that the bank had wrongfully honored and improperly paid eight forged checks to her account. In her complaint, she noted that the bank and she were in a contractual relationship, and the bank's payment was a breach of contract. Gribbins's signature was forged on each of the eight checks as the drawer's signature.

Gribbins testified that the checks were not signed by her, that she received no benefit from them, and that Akers did not have authority to write the checks. Although the memo line on the checks suggested that Akers had performed a variety of services for her, such as a kitchen remodel, Gribbins asserted that Akers never provided any such services.

Gribbins also testified that she had a romantic relationship with Akers and that, on occasion, he had stayed at her home. But as soon as she learned about the forgeries, she contacted the police. Ultimately, Akers was charged with eight counts of criminal possession of a forged instrument. He pled guilty and was ordered to pay restitution.

With respect to the checking account, Gribbins provided information that she consistently maintained a balance in excess of $5,000 and did not write checks often. In fact, the August 15 statement listed 12 canceled checks, of which Gribbins had authorized and signed four checks. By the time she received the bank statement, she had already submitted the affidavits of forgery. The bank had cashed the checks totaling $7,650 with signatures that clearly were not hers, allowing the funds in the checking account to be depleted in a matter of days.

Akers admitted to stealing the checks and forging Gribbins's signature. He testified that Gribbins was a victim and did not contribute to the forgery in any way. He said he had purposely concealed the theft of the blank checks from her, that she had received no benefit from them, and that he fabricated the information on the memo line of the checks.

The bank maintained that the comparative fault analysis provided in Kentucky 3-406 precluded Gribbins from asserting forgery against the bank. It asserted that Gribbins was careless in having a relationship with Akers, did not safeguard her checks, and thereby gave him access to her checks, which she denied.

The trial court granted Gribbins's motion for summary judgment and awarded her compensatory damages with interest. The bank appealed the judgment and order.

Clayton, Judge

The relationship between a customer and a bank is inherently contractual and thus it has been held that banks have a duty to act in good faith and to exercise ordinary care in dealing with their customers and accounts. Furthermore, sections 1-203 and 4-103 of the Uniform Commercial Code as adopted in Kentucky also impose a duty of good faith and fair dealing on banks.

Additionally, section 4-401 provides that "an item is properly payable if it is authorized by the customer and is in accordance with any agreement between the customer and the bank. Here, it is not disputed that Forcht Bank improperly made payment from Gribbins's account on eight forged checks. She established, under section 4-401 that she did not sign the eight checks, and, thus, did not authorize the payment of the instruments. However, despite the forgery and the lack of proper authorization, Forcht Bank paid the checks without hesitation. In doing so, it failed to use ordinary care in the disbursement of Gribbins's funds, resulting in harm to her by the depletion of the deposited funds in the account over the course of 21 days.

The next step in our analysis is to consider Gribbins's duties as a customer of the bank. The duties are found in section 4-406. Keep in mind, this statute applies only to claims based on checks with "unauthorized signatures." These duties are outlined in section 4-406(3), which elucidates that a customer has a duty to exercise reasonable promptness in examining the bank statement to ascertain whether any payment was unauthorized because of an alteration or forged signature. If such a discovery is made by a bank customer, the customer must promptly notify the bank of the relevant fact. In the case at bar, Gribbins actually completed the appropriate affidavits of forgery prior to even receiving the bank statement. Thus, she exercised ordinary care as delineated by the statute.

In sum, Forcht Bank failed its duty to exercise ordinary care to Gribbins when it honored eight forged checks drawn on her account. Under section 4-406(4), the bank bears the burden of presenting evidence that Gribbins's conduct contributed to its payment or injury from the payment of the forged checks. It cannot do so—Gribbins notified the bank about the forged checks even before the bank statement. Thus, the trial court properly granted summary judgment to Gribbins because there were no issues of material fact that would preclude it.

Forcht Bank attempts to persuade this Court that section 3-406(1) is applicable to the case at hand. This statute, found in Article 3 of the UCC, refers to a person whose own negligence contributes to the making of an unauthorized signature. If a person's actions substantially contributed to such action, under the statute he or she cannot assert the lack of authority against a holder in due course or a drawee or other payor who pays the instrument in good faith. We are not persuaded.

Gribbins brought this action against the bank for its failure contractually to honor the precepts of her relationship with the bank and only pay items with her signature. The signature on the checks is clearly not Gribbins's, and Forcht Bank does not establish that it made any efforts to ascertain whether the signature was authorized. Hence, Forcht Bank's reliance on section 3-406 to establish comparative negligence on Gribbins's part is inapposite since it breached its contract with Gribbins, and she exercised ordinary care.

Forcht Bank's other assertions that she did not exercise ordinary care were not supported by evidence. The depositions of Gribbins and Akers were uncontradicted. Gribbins established that she was unaware of the forgeries, took no part in them, did not benefit from them, and was unaware that checks had been stolen. Akers's deposition supported her rendition completely and implicated him solely for the forgeries. Consequently, the trial court's grant of summary judgment was proper.

 LO34-3 Explain what is meant by a stop-payment order and discuss the bank's duties and potential liabilities when it is given such an order.

Stop-Payment Order

Stop-Payment Order A stop-payment order is a request made by a customer of a drawee bank instructing it not to pay a specified check or to close the account. As the drawer's agent in the payment of checks, the drawee bank must follow the reasonable orders of the drawer-customer about payments made on the drawer's behalf. Any person authorized to draw a check may stop payment of it. Thus, any person authorized to sign a check on the account may stop payment even if she did not sign the check in question [4-403(a)].

To be effective, a payor bank must receive the stop-payment order in time to give the bank a reasonable opportunity to act on the order. This means that the bank must receive the stop-payment order before it has paid or certified the check. In addition, the stop-payment order must come soon enough to give the bank time to instruct its tellers and other employees that they should not pay or certify the check [4-403(a)]. The stop-payment order also must describe the check with "reasonable certainty" so as to provide the bank's employees the ability to recognize it as the check corresponding to the stop-payment order.

The customer may give a stop-payment order orally to the bank, but it is valid for only 14 days unless the customer confirms it in writing during that time. A written stop-payment order is valid for six months, and the customer

Figure 34.1   Stop-Payment Order

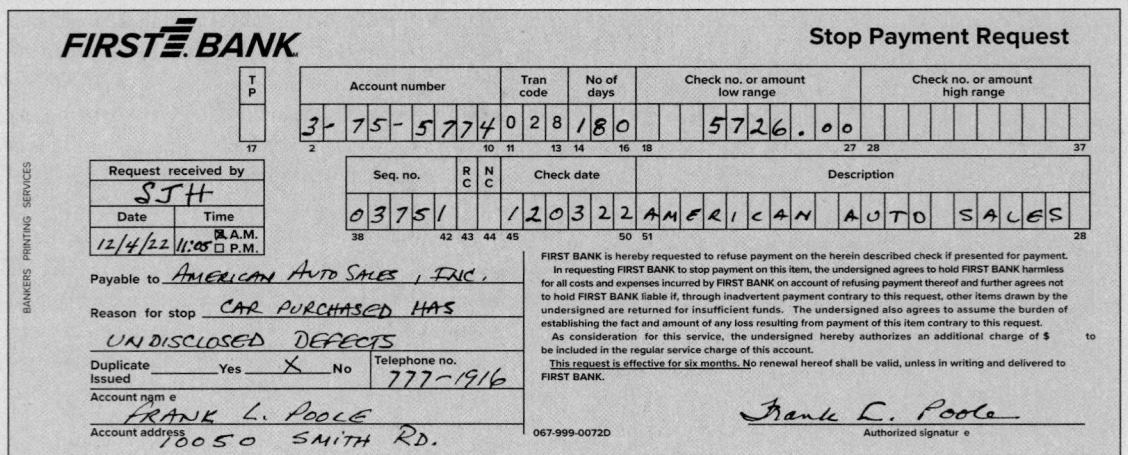

can extend it for additional six-month periods by giving the bank instructions in writing to continue the order [4-403(b)]. (See Figure 34.1.)

Sometimes, the information given the bank by the customer concerning the check on which payment is to be stopped is incorrect. For example, there may be an error in the payee's name, the amount of the check, or the number of the check. The question then arises whether the customer has accorded the bank a reasonable opportunity to act on his request. A common issue is whether the stop-payment order must have the dollar amount correct to the penny. Banks often take the position that the stop-payment order must be correct to the penny because they program and rely on computers to focus on the customer's account number and the amount of the check in question to avoid paying an item subject to

a stop-payment order. The amendments to Article 4 do not resolve this question. In the Official Comments, the drafters indicate that "in describing an item, the customer, in the absence of a contrary agreement, must meet the standard of what information allows the bank under the technology then existing to identify the check with reasonable certainty." In the stop-payment order in Figure 34.1, the bank takes a more lenient approach than some: It asks for the range of number or low and high dollar of the check the customer does not want the bank to pay.

In the case that follows, *Aliaga v. Harris Bank*, the court held that placing a notation "void after 90 days" on a check was not the legal equivalent of placing a stop-payment order, and the bank was not liable to the drawer for honoring a check containing that legend and charging it to the drawer's account.

Aliaga Medical Center v. Harris Bank   84 UCC Rep. 2d 579 (Ill. App. Ct. 2014)

In December 2003, Aliaga Medical Center opened a business checking account with Harris Bank. Concomitantly, it acknowledged receipt of a document titled "Agreement" that was to govern the account. The agreement required that if it wanted to stop payment on a check it had written, the following requirements would apply:

If you do not want us to pay a check you have written, you can order us to stop payment. You can notify us in person by Harris Telephone Banking (1-888-340-2265), by Harris online Banking, or by mail to: Harris, Attn.: Support, P.O. Box 94033, Palatine IL 60094-4033. For business accounts you can contact our Business Banking Service Center at 1-888-489-2265. Your stop payment order must include your account number, the number and date of the check, the name of the payee, and the amount. We must receive your stop payment order before our stop payment cut-off time which is 10 A.M. Central Time (C.T.) on the next business Day after the check is presented to us for payment. We will accept a stop payment order from any account owner regardless of who signed the check. Your stop payment order will be effective for six months. If you want the stop payment order to continue after six months, you must renew it. A stop payment order will not be effective on a check we have already paid or certified. There is a stop payment fee as shown in the Services Guide.

Furthermore, under the agreement, Harris Bank specifically "reserved its right to pay . . . a stale check."

The agreement contained a number of other relevant notification requirements. Including:

You must also notify us of any other account problem, including an erroneous statement . . . or improper charges within 60 days of the date we send or make your statement available to you.

We shall not be liable for error . . . unless you have given us the required notice. You agree that you will not commence any legal action or proceeding against any such error . . . unless you do so within one year of the date we send or make available to you the statement . . . in question.

On July 10, 2010, Dr. Federico Aliaga, the president of Aliaga Medical Center, issued a check in the amount of $50,000 payable to his wife, whom he was divorcing. The face of the check included the statement "void after 90 days" immediately above the signature line. Harris honored the check on December 30, 2010. Aliaga never placed a stop-payment order on the check, and, in fact, never communicated with Harris about the check anytime between July 10, 2010, and December 30, 2010.

In January 2011, Harris Bank sent and made available to Aliaga its December 2010 checking account statement, which showed Harris Bank had honored the check on December 30, 2010. Aliaga, however, did not notify Harris Bank of the improper check payment within the 60-day notification period delineated in the parties' agreement. Additionally, Aliaga did not initiate a lawsuit within one year of the date Harris Bank sent or made available the December 2010 statement. Instead, Aliaga waited until October 2012, nearly two years after the December 2010 statement, before disputing the check with Harris.

The trial court dismissed Aliaga's claim against Harris Bank for improperly honoring the check, and Aliaga appealed. One of the issues in the appeal was whether Harris Bank improperly honored the check that contained language saying it was "void after 90 days" and charged it against Aliaga's account.

Delort, Presiding Judge

Aliaga does not dispute the applicability of the various contractual provisions on which Harris relies, but argues that the use of the printed word "void" on the check and the passage of time somehow took it outside the scope of the account agreement. We disagree. Like the proverbial bird that is identified as a duck because of its distinctive characteristics, the document in question was a check. It was in the standard form of a check, contained standard check language, bore the bank's name, route number and the account number set in electronically readable magnetic ink character recognition (MICR) type and was otherwise presented, paid, and accounted for as a check in the normal course of the account's regular operation. We cannot agree with Aliaga's characterization, as it would create unworkable burdens on financial institutions in this era of ubiquitous electronic check processing. The agreement between the parties governs.

Harris Bank had the right to pay the check despite the "void after 90 days" language because Aliaga failed to properly stop payment of the check. Under the parties' agreement, if Aliaga did not want Harris Bank to pay a check it had written, then Aliaga must comply with certain requirements. In particular, Aliaga must order Harris Bank, either in person, online, or in writing to stop payment of a check by including an "account number, the number and date of the check, the name of the payee, and the amount" by a certain deadline and must also pay a stop-payment fee. Here, Aliaga acknowledges that it did not comply with the stop payment provisions of the agreement. Without the required stop payment order, Harris Bank maintained it right to honor the check. Therefore, the check's "void" language did not suffice to

stop payment because the agreement contains no exception for such language on checks.

Furthermore, the "void" notation was ineffective because it did not comply with section 4-403(a) of the UCC by providing notice "at a time and in a manner that affords the bank a reasonable opportunity to act on it." Here, Aliaga admitted that it did not provide the check bearing the language "void" directly to Harris Bank. Thus, Aliaga neither knew when the check would be received at Harris Bank nor the means by which it would be processed once it was received. This type of notation, alone, is not a reasonable means by which to direct a bank to stop payment on a check.

As commentators to the UCC have stated:

in light of the manner in which checks are processed, banks need to have the right to pay checks no matter how old the check is. This is because banks process checks by feeding the checks through a computer that reads only the MICR-encoded line. The only information the computer can use in determining whether or not to pay a check is the MICR-encoded information. The MICR-encoded information does not include the date the check was written. As a result, a prohibition on paying a check more than six months old would require that a bank visually inspect every check to determine whether a check is stale.

Accordingly, we do not view the "void" notation on the check as constituting a stop-payment order under 4-403(a).

Furthermore, under the parties' agreement, Harris Bank specifically "reserved the right to pay . . . a stale check."

Accordingly, we hold that under the terms of the stop-payment provision of the parties' agreement, Harris Bank appropriately paid the check.

Bank's Liability for Payment after Stop-Payment Order

While a stop-payment order is in effect, the drawee bank is liable to the drawer of a check that it pays for any loss that the drawer suffers by reason of such payment. However, the drawer-customer has the burden of establishing the fact and amount of the loss. To show a loss, the drawer must establish that the drawee bank paid a person against whom the drawer had a valid defense to payment. To the extent that the drawer has such a defense, he has suffered a loss due to the drawee's failure to honor the stop-payment order.

For example, Brown buys what is represented to be a new car from Foster Ford and gives Foster Ford his check for $16,280 drawn on First Bank. Brown then discovers that the car is, in fact, a used demonstrator model and calls First Bank, ordering it to stop payment on the check. If Foster Ford presents the check for payment the following day and First Bank pays the check despite the stop-payment order, Brown can require the bank to recredit his account. (The depositor-drawer bases her claim to recredit on the fact that the bank did not follow her final instruction—the instruction not to pay the check.) Brown had a valid defense of misrepresentation that she could have asserted against Foster Ford if it had sued her on the check. Foster Ford would have been required to sue on the check or on Brown's contractual obligation to pay for the car.

Assume, instead, that Foster Ford negotiated the check to Smith and that Smith qualified as a holder in due course. Then, if the bank paid the check to Smith over the stop-payment order, Brown would not be able to have her account recredited because Brown would not be able to show that she sustained any loss. If the bank had refused to pay the check, so that Smith came against Brown on her drawer's liability, Brown could not use her personal defense of misrepresentation of the prior use of the car as a reason for not paying Smith. Brown's only recourse would be to pursue Foster Ford on her misrepresentation claim.

The bank may ask the customer to sign a form in which the bank tries to disclaim or limit its liability for the stop-payment order, or, as in Figure 34.1, for damages if it fails to obey the stop-payment order. As explained at the beginning of this chapter, the bank cannot disclaim its responsibility for its failure to act in good faith or to exercise ordinary care in paying a check over a stop-payment order [4-103].

If a bank pays a check after it has received a stop-payment order and has to reimburse its customer for the improperly paid check, it acquires all the rights of its customer against the person to whom it originally made payment, including rights arising from the transaction on which the check was based [4-407]. In the previous example involving Brown and Foster Ford, assume that Brown was able to have her account recredited because First Bank had paid the check to Foster Ford over her stop-payment order. Then, the bank would have any rights that Brown had against Foster Ford for the misrepresentation.

If a person stops payment on a check and the bank honors the stop-payment order, the person may still be liable to the holder of the check. Suppose Peters writes a check for $450 to Ace Auto Repair in payment for repairs to her automobile. While driving the car home, she concludes that the car was not repaired properly. She calls her bank and stops payment on the check. Ace Auto negotiated the check to Sam's Auto Parts, which took the check as a holder in due course. When Sam's takes the check to Peters's bank, the bank refuses to pay because of the stop-payment order. Sam's then comes after Peters on her drawer's liability. All Peters has is a personal defense against payment, which is not good against a holder in due course. So, Peters must pay Sam's the $450 and pursue her claim separately against Ace. If Ace were still the holder of the check, however, the situation would be different. Peters could use her personal defense concerning the faulty work against Ace to reduce or possibly to cancel her obligation to pay the check.

Ethics and Compliance in Action

What Is the Ethical Thing to Do?

Suppose you take your car to a body shop to have it repainted. When you go to pick it up, you are not happy with the quality of the work, but the body shop refuses to release the car to you unless you pay in full for the work. You give the shop a check in the amount requested, and on your way home you stop at your bank and request that the bank stop payment on the check you have just written, an action you decided to take when you were writing the check. Have you acted ethically?

LO34-4 Distinguish *certified checks* from *cashier's checks*.

Certified Check Normally, a drawee bank is not obligated to certify a check. When a drawee bank does certify a check, it substitutes its undertaking (promise) to pay the check for the drawer's undertaking and becomes obligated to pay the check. At the time the bank certifies a check, the bank usually debits the customer's account for the amount of the certified check and shifts the money to a special account at the bank. It also adds its signature to the check to show that it has accepted primary liability for paying it. The bank's signature is an essential part of the certification: The bank's signature must appear on the check [3-409]. If the holder of a check chooses to have it

certified, rather than seeking to have it paid at that time, the holder has made a conscious decision to look to the certifying bank for payment and no longer may rely on the drawer or the indorsers to pay it. See Figure 34.2 for an example of a certified check.

If the drawee bank certifies a check, then the drawer and any persons who previously indorsed the check are discharged of their liability on the check [3-414(c), 3-415(d)].

Cashier's Check A cashier's check differs from a certified check. A check on which a bank is both the drawer and the drawee is a cashier's check. The bank is primarily liable on the cashier's check. See Figure 34.3 for an example of a cashier's check—also called an "official check." A *teller's check* is similar to a cashier's check. It is a check on which one bank is the drawer and another bank is the drawee. An

Figure 34.2   Certified Check

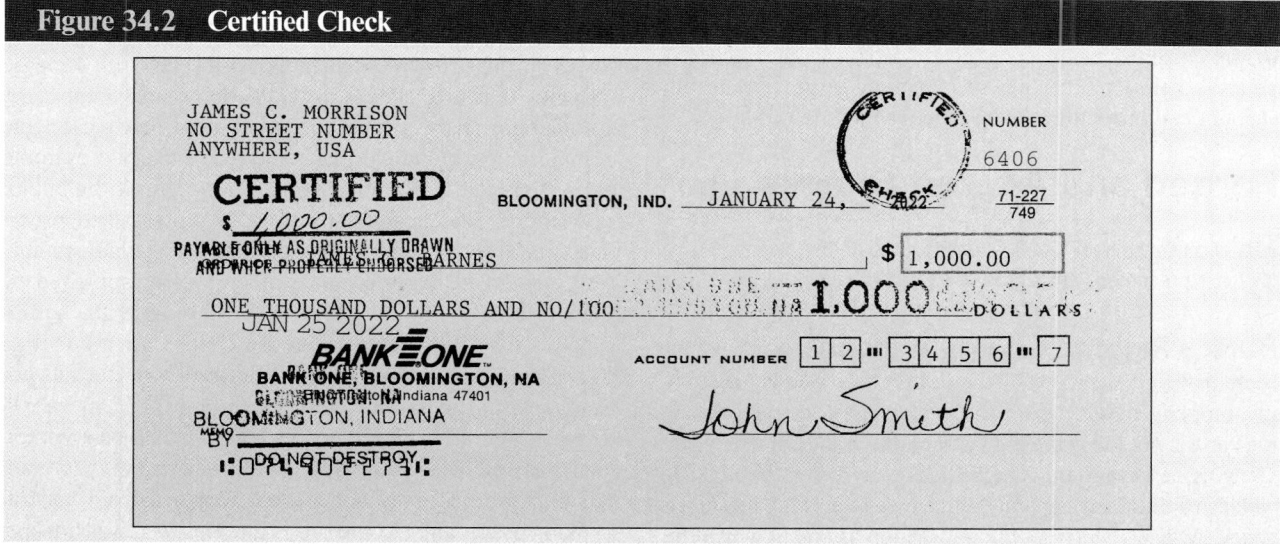

Figure 34.3   Cashier's Check

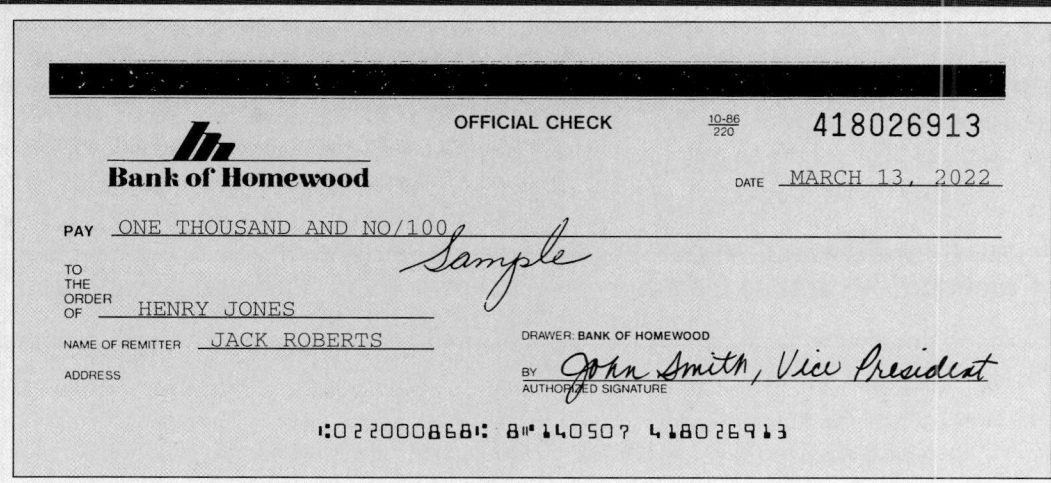

example of a teller's check is a check drawn by a credit union on its account at a bank.

Death or Incompetence of Customer
Under the general principles of agency law, the death or incompetence of the principal terminates the agent's authority to act for the principal. However, slightly different rules apply to the authority of a bank to pay checks out of the account of a deceased or incompetent person. The bank has the right to pay the checks of an incompetent person until it has notice that a court has determined that the person is incompetent. Once the bank learns of this fact, it loses its authority to pay that person's checks—because the depositor is not competent to issue instructions to pay.

Similarly, a bank has the right to pay the checks of a deceased customer until it has notice of the customer's death. Even if a bank knows of a customer's death, for a period of 10 days after the customer's death, it can pay checks written by the customer prior to his death. However, the deceased person's heirs or other persons claiming an interest in the account can order the bank to stop payment [4-405].

Forged and Altered Checks

 Discuss the bank's obligations to its customer when it is presented with forged or altered checks.

Bank's Right to Charge Account
A check that bears a forged signature of the drawer or payee is generally not properly payable from the customer's account because the bank is not following the instructions of the depositor precisely as he gave them. The bank is expected to be familiar with the authorized signature of its depositor. If it pays such a check, Article 4 will treat the transaction as one in which the bank paid out its own funds, rather than the depositor's funds.

Similarly, a check that was altered after the drawer made it out—for example, by increasing the amount of the check—is generally not properly payable from the customer's account. However, as noted earlier, if the drawer is negligent and contributes to the forgery or alteration, he may be barred from claiming it as the reason that a particular check should not be charged to his account.

For example, Barton makes a check for $100 in a way that makes it possible for someone to easily alter it to read $1,000, and it is so altered. If the drawee bank pays the check to a holder in good faith, it can charge the $1,000 to Barton's account if Barton's negligence contributed to the alteration. Similarly, if a company uses a mechanical check writer or a computer program to write checks, it must use reasonable care to see that unauthorized persons do not have access to blank checks and to the check writer.

If the alteration is obvious, the bank should note that fact and refuse to pay the check when it is presented for payment. Occasionally, the alteration is so skillful that the bank cannot detect it. In that case, the bank is allowed to charge to the account the amount for which the check originally was written.

The bank has a duty to exercise "ordinary care" in the processing of negotiable instruments; it must observe the reasonable commercial standards prevailing among other banks in the area in which it does business. In the case of banks that take checks for collection or payment using automated means, it is important to note that reasonable commercial standards do not require the bank to examine every item or the drawer's signature on them *if* the failure to examine does not violate the bank's prescribed procedures and those procedures do not vary unreasonably from general banking practice or are not disapproved by the UCC [3-107(a)(7), 4-103(c)]. For example, the bank's practice may be to examine those checks for more than $1,000 and a sample of smaller checks. Thus, if it did not examine a particular check in the amount of $250 for evidence of alteration or forgery, its action would be commercially reasonable so long as (1) it followed its own protocol, (2) that protocol was not a great variance from general banking usage, and (3) the procedure followed was not specifically disallowed in the UCC.

In a case where both a bank and its customer fail to use ordinary care, a comparative negligence standard is used [4-406(e)].

The effect of an agreement between a customer and the bank as to the degree of care a customer was expected to exercise is at issue in the case that follows, *Cincinnati Insurance Company v. Wachovia Bank National Association.*

Cincinnati Insurance Company v. Wachovia Bank National Association
72 UCC Rep. 2d 744 (D. Minn. 2010)

Schultz Foods maintained a commercial checking account with Wachovia. Over the course of its relationship with Wachovia, Schultz Foods was the victim of check fraud on four separate occasions. Wachovia and Schultz Foods were able to amicably resolve the first three instances of check fraud. On those three occasions, Schultz Foods closed the compromised account and opened a new account, and Wachovia absorbed the fraud-related loss. The fourth occasion gave rise to this lawsuit.

In late 2005, Schultz issued a check in the amount of $153,856.46 to Amerada Hess Corporation. The check was stolen before it could be deposited by the intended recipient. In what is known as a "washing" scam, thieves removed the name of the original payee and substituted the name of Kenneth Payton—who was an unwitting accomplice of the thieves. Payton then endorsed the check and deposited it into his account at TCF Bank. TCF presented the check to Wachovia, and Wachovia transferred $153,856.46 from Schultz's account at Wachovia to Payton's account at TCF. Following the instructions of the thieves, Payton then wired the money to a bank account in Singapore, and the thieves took the money and ran.

When the fraud came to light, Schultz Foods demanded that Wachovia recredit its account, claiming that Wachovia must bear the loss because it processed the altered check in violation of section 4-401(a) of the Uniform Commercial Code (UCC). Wachovia disagreed, citing the fact that Schultz Foods had declined to implement "Positive Pay," a check-fraud deterrence program that had been offered by Wachovia and that would have prevented the loss if Schultz had only implemented it. According to Wachovia, under the terms of the deposit agreement between Schultz Foods and Wachovia, the failure to implement Positive Pay made Schultz Foods liable for the loss.

Unless a customer implements a program such as Positive Pay, a bank has little chance of identifying a forged or altered check because the bank has no way of knowing whether a particular check was actually issued by a customer, whether a particular check was issued to the payee whose name appears on the check, or whether a particular check was issued in the account that appears on the check.

Positive Pay is a software program that enables a customer to transmit to its bank pertinent information about every check that the customer issues. For example, when a customer who uses Positive Pay issues check number 7394 to Acme Inc. in the amount of $15,286.25, the customer's bank is promptly informed that the customer has issued check number 7394 to Acme in the amount of $15,286.25. When a bearer then presents check number 7394 for payment, the bank's computer can compare the information on the check to the information that was transmitted by the customer. If the information does not match—if, for example, the name of the payee on check number 7394 is "Jane Smith" instead of "Acme Inc."—the bank can contact the customer before clearing the check. Had Schultz Foods implemented Positive Pay, Wachovia would not have paid the "Kenneth Payton" check, and the loss would not have occurred.

Wachovia did pay the check, though, and thus $153,856.46 was deducted from the account of Schultz Foods. After Wachovia refused to recredit the account, Schultz Foods filed a claim with its insurer, Cincinnati Insurance Company. Cincinnati paid the claim, and then filed a subrogation action against Wachovia.

Schiltz, District Court Judge

Bank deposits are governed by Article 4 of the UCC. Section 4-401(a) provides that "[a] bank may charge against the account of a customer an item that is properly payable from that account. . . . An item is properly payable if it is authorized by the customer and in accordance with any agreement between the customer and the bank." Ordinarily, if a bank charges a customer's account for a check that is not properly payable—for example a check that has been forged and therefore has not been authorized by the customer—the bank will be liable to the customer for the loss. But this is merely a default rule. Section 4-103(a) permits banks and their customers to agree to a different rule, except that an agreement between a bank and a customer "cannot disclaim the responsibility of a bank for its lack of good faith or failure to exercise ordinary care."

Schultz Foods did not issue a check to Kenneth Payton. Wachovia concedes that the altered check, as it was presented to the teller at Payton's bank, was not authorized by Schultz Foods. Thus the check was not "properly payable" under section 4-401(a), and absent an agreement to the contrary, Wachovia is liable to Schultz Foods for charging the unauthorized check against the company's account.

The problem for Schultz Foods is that there *is* an agreement to the contrary—a deposit agreement signed by Schultz Foods when it opened its commercial checking account at Wachovia. Section 12 of that agreement describes a variety of methods by which a customer can safeguard its account from fraud. The methods fall into two categories:

First, section 12 contains a non-exhaustive bullet-pointed list of "precautions" that customers "can and should take to decrease the risk of unauthorized transactions." "Precautions," as that word is used in section 12, are actions that any customer of the bank can take on its own to protect the security of its checking account. They include such common-sense measures as protecting the secrecy of passwords, promptly reviewing bank statements for unauthorized activities and immediately reporting suspicious activity to the bank.

Second, section 12 provides that "[i]n addition"—that is, in addition to the "precautions" that customers can take on their own—Wachovia itself may make available to its customers "certain products and services that are designed to detect and/or deter check fraud." Unlike the precautions, these "products and services" are developed by Wachovia (or purchased from vendors by Wachovia) and offered to customers. Obviously, these "products and services" will do nothing to prevent fraud unless a customer implements them.

After first describing the "precautions" that a customer may take on its own and then mentioning the "products and services" that Wachovia may offer, section 12 of the deposit agreement concludes with a conditional release of Wachovia's liability:

You agree that if you fail to implement any of these products or services, or you fail to follow these and other precautions reasonable for your particular circumstances, you will be precluded from asserting any claim against [Wachovia] for paying any unauthorized, altered, counterfeit or other fraudulent item that such product, service, or precaution was designed to detect or defer, and we will not be required to re-credit your account or otherwise have any liability for paying such items.

There appears to be no dispute that Positive Pay was a "product or service" for purposes of section 12. There also appears to be

no dispute that Positive Pay was made available to Schultz Foods, and that Schultz Foods chose not to implement it. Finally, there appears to be no dispute that Positive Pay was "designed to detect or deter" precisely the type of fraud that caused the $153,856.46 loss. On their face then, the releases appear to absolve Wachovia of any responsibility for that loss.

[The court went on to reject a number of arguments made by Cincinnati, including whether the releases were an unreasonable effort by the bank to disclaim responsibility for its lack of good faith or failure to exercise ordinary care.] The court finds that the relevant provisions of the deposit agreement are not "manifestly unreasonable" and are "reasonable under the circumstances."

Judgment dismissing Cincinnati's complaint with prejudice and on the merits.

Customer's Duty to Report Forgeries and Alterations

 LO34-6 Explain the customer's duty to report forgeries and alterations and the consequences for the customer if he or she does not do so in a timely manner.

A bank must send a monthly (or quarterly) statement listing the transactions in an account, and formerly it commonly returned the canceled checks to the customer. Revised Article 3 recognizes the modern bank practice of truncating (or retaining) checks and permits the bank to supply only a statement showing the item number, amount, and date of payment [4-406(a)]. When the bank does not return the paid items to the customer, the bank

must either retain the items or maintain the capacity to furnish legible copies of the items for seven years after their receipt. The customer may request an item and the bank has a reasonable time to provide either the item or a legible copy of it [4-406(b)].

If the bank sends or makes available a statement of account or items, the customer must exercise reasonable promptness to examine the statement or items to determine whether payment was not authorized because of an alteration of any item or because a signature of the customer was not authorized. If, based on the statement or items provided, the customer should discover the unauthorized payment, the customer must notify the bank of the relevant facts promptly [4-406(c)]. Failure to provide prompt notice may cost the customer a recredit for an unauthorized check [4-406(f)].

CONCEPT REVIEW

Liability for Multiple Forgeries or Alterations of Checks or Drafts by the Same Person

Date First Statement Disclosing an Altered or Forged Check Is Available to Customer	Date 30 Days Later	Date Customer Gives Notice of Alteration or Forgery
Customer is not liable for forged/altered checks paid during this period unless bank suffers a loss from customer's unreasonable delay in notifying bank of forgery or alteration.	Customer is liable for forged or altered checks paid during this period unless customer gives bank notice of forgery or alteration within a reasonable time after date the first statement containing a forged or altered check was available to customer.	Customer is not liable for forged or altered checks paid after this period.

Multiple Forgeries or Alterations   Revised Article 4 provides a special rule to govern the situation in which the same wrongdoer makes a series of unauthorized drawer's signatures or alterations. The customer generally cannot hold the bank responsible for paying, in good faith, any such checks after the statement of account or item that contained the first unauthorized customer's signature or an alteration was available to the customer for a reasonable period, not exceeding 30 calendar days. This rule holds if (1) the customer did not notify the bank of the unauthorized signature or alteration and (2) the bank proves it suffered a loss because of the customer's failure to examine his statement and notify the bank [4-406(d)]. Unless the customer has notified the bank about the forgeries or alterations that he should have discovered by reviewing the statement or item, the customer generally bears responsibility for any subsequent forgeries or alterations by the same wrongdoer.

Suppose that Allen employs Farnum as an accountant and that over a period of three months, Farnum forges Allen's signature to 10 checks and cashes them. One of the forged checks is included in the checks returned to Allen at the end of the first month. Within 30 calendar days after the return of these checks, Farnum forges two more checks and cashes them. Allen does not examine the returned checks until three months after the checks that included the first forged check were returned to her. The bank would be responsible for the first forged check and for the two checks forged and cashed within the 30-day period after it sent the first statement and the canceled checks (unless the bank proves that it suffered a loss because of the customer's failure to examine the checks and notify it more promptly). It would not be liable for the seven forged checks cashed after the expiration of the 30-day period.

Regardless of which party may have been negligent, a customer must discover and report to the bank any unauthorized customer's signature or any alteration within one year from the time after the statement or items are made available to him. If the customer does not do so, he cannot require the bank to recredit his account for such items. [4-406(f)].

These principles are illustrated in the case that follows, *Grodner & Associates v. Regions Bank*.

Grodner & Associates v. Regions Bank
98 UCC Rep. 2d 384 (5th Cir. 2019)

Grodner & Associates is a law firm based in Baton Rouge, Louisiana. It was defrauded by its bookkeeper, Anna Alford, who wrote checks and initiated Automated Clearing House transactions to herself from two accounts Grodner maintained at Regions Bank. The fraud began in March 2015 and remained undetected until June 2016, when Grodner's managing member bounced a personal check. Alford allegedly concealed her fraud by intercepting and photo-shopping the account statements Regions sent to Alford.

Grodner brought claims for conversion and negligence against Regions for the unauthorized payments initiated by Alford. The district court concluded that Grodner's claims were untimely because Grodner failed to notify Regions of the fraud until more than one year after first receiving a statement with an unauthorized payment to Alford. Grodner appealed.

PER CURIAM:

Alford initiated fraudulent payments from two accounts maintained with Regions: an "operating" account and a "trust" account. These account relationships were governed by a deposit agreement which required Grodner to make a prompt examination of account statements and notify Regions in writing of any unauthorized payments or other discrepancies.

The deposit agreement also provided that Grodner would "be precluded from asserting against Regions any unauthorized signature or alteration by the same wrongdoer on any item paid in good faith on or after 10 calendar days after the first statement describing the first altered or unauthorized items was sent or made available." This provision was explicitly "intended to define a reasonable time for the examination of bank statements for the purposes of the 'Repeater Rule,' or the 'Same Wrongdoer' rule as provided in Section 4-406(d) of the UCC."

The rule is statutorily codified in Louisiana as La. Stat. Ann. Section 10:4-406(d) (2018). It "imposes on the customer the risk of loss on all subsequent forgeries by the *same wrongdoer* after the customer had a reasonable time to detect an initial forgery if the bank has honored subsequent forgeries prior to notice."

During discovery, Grodner admitted that the first fraudulent transaction for both accounts occurred in March 2015. Grodner also admitted that in April 2015 Regions sent the account statements that included these unauthorized transactions. Finally, Grodner admitted that it did not notify Regions about Alford's fraud until June 2016, more than a year after Regions first sent account statements identifying unauthorized transactions initiated by Alford.

Grodner's failure to notify Regions of the first unauthorized payments within ten days of the April 2015 statement means that it is "precluded from asserting against the bank all subsequent forgeries by the same unauthorized signatory." Grodner's allegation that Alford tampered with the statements is irrelevant because the "same wrongdoer rule" only requires that Regions sent or made available the statements, not that Grodner received them intact.

There is a caveat in La. Stat. Ann. Section 10:4-406. Claims against the bank are precluded "only when the bank itself has acted reasonably in honoring the instrument in dispute." Grodner, though, failed to offer competent proof that that bank's practices failed to comport with ordinary care, or the observance of reasonable commercial standards, prevailing in the area in which Grodner is located, with respect to the business in which it is engaged.

The mere fact that a forgery of a signature on a check is not detected does not prove that a bank's signature verification procedures are in accordance with reasonable commercial standards of the banking industry. Grodner insists that Regions should have detected the fraud by comparing the unauthorized checks to the signature cards on file, but Louisiana law does not impose a duty upon a paying bank to inspect every check to verify signatures appearing thereon prior to processing the check for payment. In fact, Louisiana law explicitly provides that "sight examination by a payor bank" is not required if its procedure is reasonable and is commonly followed by other comparable banks in the area.

There are realities to modern banking that make signature verification impractical. Checks are processed through automation, meaning that "signature verification is a dinosaur." Signature cards are a "quaint historical relic" with little practical force in modern banking law. Reflecting these facts, the Regions deposit agreement explained the bank's "automated check processing precludes it from identifying items that require multiple signatures," authorizes Regions to "honor items signed in a different form from that set forth in the signature card," and disclaimed Regions' liability for any unauthorized use of a facsimile signature. [Author's note: The court of appeals noted in a footnote that the district court had observed that 64 of the 69 unauthorized checks employed facsimile signatures and thus could not have been detected by outdated signature card protocols even if they had been in place.]

Nothing in the record demonstrated a deviation either from the Bank's own procedures or local banking standards and practices, or from the terms of the parties' deposit agreement.

AFFIRMED.

Check Collection and Funds Availability

Historically, the process of collecting a check that has been deposited or presented for payment has been a fairly complicated and time-consuming one. While the process is simplified if the check happens to be presented for payment at the drawee bank on which it is written, commonly checks are deposited for collection at other banks, and later presented to the drawee bank where the drawer's account is maintained. The historical process is explained below.

Because the bank where a check has been deposited for collection needs some time to make sure that the item is valid and will be paid, banks typically put a "hold" on the depositor's ability to access some or all of the funds represented by the instrument until it "clears" through the system. The current rules established by the Federal Reserve to govern funds availability are discussed in the section following the check collection process.

In the past few years, developments in electronic technology allow payments to be processed much more rapidly and efficiently than the old paper-based systems and are rapidly changing the way that goods and services are paid for and that money is transferred from one entity to another. In 2003, Congress enacted a federal law, known as *Check 21*, that is designed to allow banks to handle more check collection electronically and provides a federal overlay to some of the law that has previously been state-based in the form of Articles 3 and 4 of the Uniform Commercial Code. Check 21, along with various electronic substitutes for checks, will be covered later in this chapter.

Check Collection As Chapter 31, Negotiable Instruments, describes, checks and other drafts collected through the banking system usually have at least three parties—the drawer, the drawee bank, and the payee. If the payee deposits the check at the same bank as the drawee bank, the latter will take a series of steps necessary to reflect the deposit as a credit to the payee's account and to decide whether to pay the check from the drawer's account. In connection with its handling of the deposit for the payee's benefit, it will make one ledger entry showing the deposit as a credit to the payee's account. In connection with its decision to pay, the bank's employees and computers will perform several steps commonly referred to as the process of "posting." These steps need not be taken in any particular order, but they customarily include determining whether there are sufficient funds to pay, debiting the drawer's account for the amount of the check, and placing the check into a folder or imaging it for later return to the drawer (to satisfy its obligations under the "bank statement" rule) [4-406]. Banks in New York, which is the only state that has not adopted the 1990 amendments to Article 4, usually will compare the drawer's signature on the check with that on the deposit agreement as part of this process.

If the payee deposits the check at a bank other than the drawee bank, the depositary bank, acting as the agent of the payee, will make the ledger entry showing the deposit as a credit to the payee's account. The next step of the collection process depends on where the depositary bank is located. If the drawee and depositary banks are in the same town or county, the depositary bank will indorse the check and present it to the drawee bank for payment. It may deliver it by courier or through a local association of banks known as a "clearing house" [4-104(1)(d)] or it may send data from the check or an image to the drawee bank. Under Article 4, the drawee-payor bank must settle for the check before midnight of the banking day of its receipt of the check, which means that it must give the depositary bank funds or a credit equal to the amount of the check. Once it settles for the check, the drawee-payor bank has until midnight of the banking day after the banking day of receipt to pay the check or to return the check or send notice of dishonor. This deadline for the drawee-payor bank's action on the check is known as the bank's "midnight deadline" [4-104(1)(h)]. The drawee-payor bank's failure to settle by midnight of the banking day of receipt, or its failure to pay, or return the check or send notice of dishonor, results in the drawee-payor bank's becoming "accountable" for the amount of the check, which means it must pay the amount of the check to the presenting bank [4-302(a)].

If the drawee and depositary banks are located in different counties, or in different states, the depositary bank will use an additional commercial bank, and one or more of the regional Federal Reserve Banks, in the collection of the check. In these cases, the depositary bank will send the check on to the drawee-payor bank through these "collecting banks." Each bank in the sequence must use ordinary care in presenting the check or sending it for presentment and in sending notice of dishonor or returning the check after learning that the check has not been paid [4-202(a)]. The depositary and collecting banks each has until its respective midnight deadline—or, in some cases, a further reasonable time—to take the action required of it in the sequence of collection steps.

If the drawee-payor bank dishonors the check prior to its midnight deadline or shortly after the midnight deadline under circumstances specified in Regulation CC of the Federal Reserve Board (described in the next section of this chapter), it will send the check back to the depositary bank.

Until September 1, 1988, the drawee-payor bank customarily sent the dishonored check back to the collecting bank from which it received the check, and the collecting bank sent it back to the bank from which it had received it, and through any other bank that handled the check in the "forward collection" process, until the check again reached the depositary bank. The provisions of Article 4 still describe this sequence as the "return collection" process.

Regulation CC imposes new responsibilities on the payor bank and on any other "returning bank." Each bank in the return sequence adjusts its accounts to reflect the return and has until its midnight deadline to send the check back to the bank from which it originally had received the check. After September 1, 1988, the drawee-payor bank may return the check directly to the depositary bank— skipping all of the collecting banks and the delay represented by the midnight deadlines that each bank otherwise would have had.

Direct return also increases the likelihood that the depositary bank will know whether the check has been dishonored by the day on which Regulation CC requires the depositary bank to allow the payee to write checks or otherwise make withdrawals against the deposit. The next section of this chapter discusses the "funds availability" aspect of Regulation CC in more detail.

On receipt of the dishonored check, the depositary bank will return the check or otherwise notify its depositor (the payee) of the dishonor and will debit or charge back her account for the check it did not collect. The depositary bank may charge back the deposit even if it previously had allowed the payee-depositor to withdraw against the credit given for the deposit.

When the depositor receives the notice of dishonor or a returned check, it will take one of several steps, depending on whether it received the check directly from the drawer or took it by indorsement from another person. If the depositor was not the original payee of the check, it usually will prefer to return the check—giving notice of dishonor unless already given by the drawee bank or another collecting bank—to the person who negotiated the check to her, the prior indorser.

Recall that an indorser is obligated to pay the check following dishonor and notice of dishonor [3-415].

If the depositor received the check directly from the drawer—for example, as payee—the depositor normally will demand payment from the drawer. Recall that the drawer is obligated to pay the check upon dishonor [3-414]; alternatively, the payee may seek to enforce the underlying obligation for which the drawer originally issued the check, such as the purchase of groceries or an automobile.

The case that follows, *Valley Bank of Ronan v. Hughes*, involves the question of a bank's right to charge back a depositor's account for the amount of checks he had received and deposited in the course of being the victim of a scam.

Valley Bank of Ronan v. Hughes	**61 UCC Rep. 2d 277 (Mont. 2006)**

Lured by the promise of quick wealth, Charles Hughes was conned by a "Nigerian scam." The swindlers promised Hughes a $3 million to $4.5 million commission for his aid in procuring agricultural equipment for import into Africa and then proceeded to bilk him for hundreds of thousands of dollars in advanced fees. Some of the funds that Hughes advanced were wired via the services of Valley Bank of Ronan, resulting in a dispute over which party should bear the loss from the flimflam.

On Friday, March 22, 2002, Hughes received four checks from one of the con-artists and deposited them into accounts Hughes held at Valley Bank. Two of them were "official" checks, and the other two were personal checks. One official check, for $1 million, was drawn on Colonial Bank. The other official check, for $500,000, was drawn on Firstar. The personal checks were for $62,000—drawn on the account of Maximilian H. Miltzlaff—and for $70,000—drawn on a CapitalOne credit card account held by Sarah Briscoe and Mary Bullard.

Prior to depositing the checks, Hughes requested that Nancy Smith, a cashier and officer of Valley Bank, verify the validity of the official checks. In his deposition, Hughes described his conversation with Smith:

Well, my question was, how long do you have to hold money to have—how long do you have to hold these checks before they're sufficient funds; I think the bank calls them collected funds. And she said, these are official checks, Chuck. These two big ones are official checks. You will be transferring these? And I said I will be transferring a large sum. We'll have to determine next week what it will be. And she says, official checks, same as cash. You can do whatever you want to do.

Smith also assured Hughes that official checks were "just like" cashier's checks. Milanna Shear, another bank employee, told Hughes to believe whatever Smith said regarding the validity of the checks. According to the deposition testimony of Hughes's wife, Barbara, Hughes had told her that "everybody at the bank assured him that the checks would be good."

On Tuesday, March 26, 2002, Hughes delivered a written request to Valley Bank to wire $800,000 to Ali dh. Abbas, an accountholder at the Housing Bank for Trade and Finance in Amman, Jordan. Valley Bank executed the transfer no later than 1:51 P.M. on the same day. The transfer proceeded through two intermediary banks, Wells Fargo, near Denver, Colorado, and Citibank in New York, before being sent to Amman. Upon receipt in Amman, the funds were promptly withdrawn, never to be seen again.

At about 2:00 P.M.—approximately 10 minutes after initiation of the transfer—Valley Bank and Hughes learned that one of the personal checks was being returned marked "nonsufficient funds." Hughes immediately requested the wire to be stopped. No later than 3:26 P.M. Valley Bank requested that Wells Fargo reverse the wire transfer. The record is unclear about what happened during the interim between Hughes's request for cancellation and Valley Bank's attempts to comply with the request. The efforts of the several banks involved in the transfer to reverse the transaction were unsuccessful, and the later discovery that the two official checks were counterfeit resulted in Hughes's account being overdrawn by $800,000.

Valley Bank subsequently exercised its right to charge back the account and collect the $800,000 from Hughes. Allen Buhr, Valley Bank's president, met with Hughes on March 29, 2002, to discuss Hughes's liability and suggested at that time that Hughes could be involved in a criminal prosecution for fraud. On April 11, 2002, Hughes deposited $607,838, which he had withdrawn from his retirement account, into the Valley Bank account. Also, on April 30, 2002, Hughes executed a promissory note to Valley Bank on behalf of his trust in the amount of $400,000, secured by mortgaged property. Of the $400,000 in proceeds generated by the secured note, $202,751.21 was used to pay off a previous loan against the mortgaged property, and the balance, $197,248.79, was applied to satisfy the charge-back liability in Hughes's account. Hughes was under the impression, given by Buhr, that the bank needed the note and loan agreement because it expected to be the subject of a government audit in the near future, and though Hughes thought that a new agreement might be reached after resolution of the *"fraud situation," he understood that the loan may not be forgiven. The trust subsequently made the first interest payment on the note on August 1, 2002, though it was one month late. The trust made no other payments on the note, and Valley Bank sent a notice of default and acceleration on October 15, 2002. Hughes requested that the bank forebear foreclosure until the end of the year, and the bank complied.*

However, when Hughes failed to make any more payments on the note, Valley Bank initiated an action for judicial foreclosure. Hughes asserted counterclaims of negligence, negligent misrepresentation, constructive fraud, unjust enrichment, breach of contract, breach of the implied covenant of good faith and fair dealing, promissory estoppel, and intentional infliction of emotional distress (which was later abandoned). The district court granted Valley Bank summary judgment on its claims regarding the promissory note. Hughes appealed.

Rice, Justice

A short introduction to the check settlement process will give context to our following legal analysis. When a customer deposits a check at a bank, the bank will sometimes (but not always) credit the customer's account immediately with the face amount of the check and permit the customer to draw on the deposited funds. This practice is known in Uniform Commercial Code parlance as "provisional settlement" because the bank has not yet presented the check to the drawee bank and received payment from the check maker's account (which would constitute "final settlement"). The depositary bank, however, may "charge back" the depositor's account in the event the check is subsequently dishonored by the drawee bank. Thus, the UCC encourages the provisional settlement process by protecting a depositary bank from fraudulent or otherwise unenforceable check deposits. With this overview of the check settlement process in mind, we turn now to the specifics of the case before us.

Hughes argues that the District Court erroneously concluded that the UCC preempts Hughes' equitable and common law claims. Hughes asserts that preemption does not occur because "[t]here *are* no regulations or UCC provisions which expressly regulate . . . promises and representations that bank personnel make to their customers." Further, Hughes contends that the "practical effect of the District Court's interpretation affords banks absolute immunity for negligence, fraud, misrepresentation and other acts which are not expressly addressed in the UCC. . . ."

The District Court rested its conclusion on its interpretation of § 1-103, MCA, which reads as follows:

Unless displaced by the particular provisions of this code, the principles of law and equity, including the law merchant and the law relative to capacity to contract, principal and agent, estoppel, fraud, misrepresentation, duress, coercion, mistake, bankruptcy, or other validating or invalidating cause shall supplement its provisions.

We disagree with the District Court's interpretation of § 1-103. A bank receiving checks from depositors must use "ordinary care"—as that term is defined and used in the UCC—in settling those checks. See §§ 4-103(3), 4-103(5), and 4-212, MCA. Section 3-102(1)(g) defines "ordinary care" as follows:

"Ordinary care" in the case of a person engaged in business means observance of reasonable commercial standards, prevailing in the area in which that person is located, with respect to

the business in which that person is engaged. In the case of a bank that takes an instrument for processing for collection or payment by automated means, reasonable commercial standards do not require the bank to examine the instrument if the failure to examine does not violate the bank's prescribed procedures and the bank's procedures do not vary unreasonably from general banking usage not disapproved by this chapter or chapter 4.

In its order, the District Court examined the meaning of "ordinary care" but did not distinguish the term's application to the two different actions at issue here: the settlement of the deposited checks and the alleged representations about the check settlement process. The second sentence of the definition of ordinary care specifically states that, subject to certain exceptions, a bank does not have a duty to examine instruments, in this case, checks. Pursuant to § 1-103 and UCC § 1-103, cmt. 2, such specificity preempts any common law concepts that might otherwise supplement the UCC. Thus, to the extent that Hughes' common law claims relate to Valley Bank's processing of the checks, they are preempted by the UCC.

Indeed, Hughes presents a claim directed toward the UCC-defined standard of ordinary care with respect to check processing. Hughes asserts that, by failing to comply with its own policies and the applicable federal regulations, Valley Bank inappropriately charged back his account after the dishonor of the deposited checks. However, § 4-212(4) states, "[t]he right to charge back is not affected by . . . failure by any bank to exercise ordinary care with respect to the item but any bank so failing remains liable." Official Comment 5 to § 4-212(4) expounds on this point, stating that "charge-back is permitted *even where nonpayment results from the depositary bank's own negligence.*" (Emphasis added.) Accordingly, in evaluating the propriety of Valley Bank's actions with regard to check processing, it is irrelevant whether Valley Bank exercised ordinary care in exercising its charge back rights, and the claims are preempted.

Note: The court went on to hold that Hughes could assert common law claims of negligence against the bank as to the communications the bank made to him about the process on which he claimed to have relied. Thus, while the bank had an absolute right to charge back the fraudulent checks to Hughes's account and he had the obligation to repay the bank, it nonetheless was possible for Hughes to obtain a judgment against the bank to compensate him for the charge-back debt.

Funds Availability When a bank takes a check for deposit to a customer's account, it typically places a hold on the funds represented by the deposited check because it runs a number of risks in allowing a customer to withdraw deposits that it has not collected from the drawee bank. The risks that the check may be returned include (1) there may be insufficient funds in the drawer's account or the account may have been closed; (2) the check may contain a forged drawer's or indorser's signature, or there may have been a material alteration of the check; (3) the possibility that the drawer is kiting checks or playing two accounts off against each other; or (4) the drawer has placed a stop-payment order against the check. These are real concerns to a depositary bank, and it has a significant interest in protecting itself against these possibilities.

Until 1988, the risks run by a depositary bank were complicated by a very slow process used by drawee-payor banks in returning a dishonored check or notifying the bank of the dishonor. Moreover, depositary banks frequently did not get direct notice from drawee-payor banks when they paid checks. Accordingly, banks often restricted the depositor's use of the deposit by placing relatively long holds on checks deposited with them for collection; holds sometimes ran 15 to 20 days for items drawn on other than local banks.

The extensive use of holds, and a growing public sentiment that they were excessive and often unfair, led to the passage by Congress in 1987 of the Expedited Funds Availability Act. In the act, Congress set out mandatory schedules limiting check holds and specifying when funds are to be made available to customers by depositary institutions. The act also delegated to the Federal Reserve Board the authority to speed up the check-processing system. The regulations adopted by the Board to speed up check processing supersede the provisions of Article 4 of the UCC (Bank Deposits and Collections) in a number of respects but will not be covered in this text.

The key elements of the mandatory funds availability are set out in Federal Reserve Board Regulation CC. Some examples include:

1. "Local checks" (those drawn on banks in the same Federal Reserve check region as the depositary bank) must be made available for the depositor to draw against by the second business day following deposit.

2. "Nonlocal checks" (those drawn on banks located in the United States but outside the Federal Reserve check-processing region in which the depositary bank is located) must be made available by the fifth business day following deposit.

3. Certain items must be made available by the next day after the day of deposit. These include:

   a. Cash deposits where the deposit is made in person to an employee of the depositary bank (i.e., not at an ATM).
   b. Electronic payments.
   c. Checks drawn on the U.S. Treasury and deposited to an account held by the payee of the check.
   d. U.S. Postal Service money orders deposited to an account held by the payee or in person to an employee of the bank.
   e. Checks drawn on a Federal Reserve Bank or Federal Home Loan Bank deposited to an account held by the payee.
   f. Checks drawn by a state or a unit of local government (under certain conditions).
   g. Cashier's, certified, or teller's checks deposited to an account held by the payee.
   h. Checks drawn on the depositary bank.
   i. The lesser of $100 or the aggregate deposit on any one banking day.

4. If the next-day items are not deposited in person with an employee of the depositary institution but rather are deposited in an ATM or by mail, then the deposit does not have to be made available for withdrawal until the second business day after deposit.

5. Generally, the depositary bank must begin accruing interest to a depositor's interest-bearing account from the day it receives credit for cash and check deposits to an interest-bearing account.

There are six major exceptions to the mandatory availability schedules set out above that are designed to safeguard depositary banks against higher-risk situations. The exceptions are:

1. *New account exception.* The depositary bank may suspend the availability rules for new accounts and can limit the next-day and second-day availability to the first $5,000 deposited on any banking day.

2. *Large deposit exception.* The hold periods can be extended to the extent the aggregate deposit on any banking day exceeds $5,000.

3. *Redeposited check exception.* Deposit availability can be extended where a check has been returned one or more times.

4. *Repeated overdraft exception.* The scheduled availability may be required for deposits to accounts that have been overdrawn repeatedly over the past six months.

5. *Reasonable cause exception.* The scheduled availability may be extended where the bank has reasonable cause to believe the check is uncollectible.

6. *Emergency conditions exception.* The scheduled availability may be extended under certain emergency conditions such as a communications interruption or a computer failure beyond the bank's control.

Banks are required to disclose their funds availability policy to all of their customers; they may provide different policies to different classes or categories of customers.

Check 21

LO34-7 Discuss the implications of Check 21 from the perspective of the customer of a bank.

The Check Clearing for the 21st Century Act, commonly known as "Check 21," a 2003 federal law that is designed to enable banks to collect more checks electronically, became effective on October 28, 2004. For many years banks had to physically move checks from the bank where they are deposited to the drawee bank that pays them—a time-consuming, inefficient, and costly process. And, for many years, banks then returned the canceled checks to their customers along with their monthly account statement. In recent years, many banks have stopped providing canceled checks to their customers. Instead, they provide images of the checks with multiple pictures of canceled checks appearing on pages of a paper or electronic bank statement or just a list of transactions with amounts and dates. If the drawee bank keeps the original checks, this is called *check truncation* (if the payee, such as a grocery store, or its depository bank, keeps the original check, this is called *radical truncation*). Credit unions and an increasing number of commercial banks have been truncating checks for quite a while or have allowed their retailer customers to do so.

For many years, banks have had the capacity to capture information from the **Magnetic Ink Character Recognition**[2] **(MICR)** line on the bottom fronts of checks, and to transmit that information electronically to collecting banks as well as the drawee bank if the banks later in the collection chain had electronic capabilities. But, in order for a bank to send only the electronic image forward (as opposed to the paper check drawn by the drawer of the check), each bank had to have an "electronic presentment agreement" with the other banks in

the collection chain. If one bank in the chain of collection or the drawee bank did not have electronic processing ability, then the use of electronic processing was ended. One bank could hold up the use of electronic innovations simply by refusing to take electronic items.

Check 21 authorizes banks to transform information they receive in electronic form back into a paper copy of the check. It grants legal status to paper copies that meet specific standards and so qualify as "**substitute checks**," that is, the equivalent as against all persons and for all purposes of the paper check drawn by the drawer. Check 21 thus added a new category of negotiable instruments. As a result, if a bank with electronic capacity encountered a drawee bank that did not have electronic capacity, the first bank could use its electronic information file to create a substitute check (assuming it met the standards) and to present that substitute check for payment. Similarly, if all the banks in a check collection chain used electronic presentment processing, but the payee or drawer needed a paper copy of the check to prove it had paid an obligation, its bank could create and deliver a substitute check to the payee or drawer. In both cases, the resulting substitute check is legally the same as the original check if it accurately represents the information on the original check and includes the following statement: "This is a legal copy of your check. You can use it the same way you would use the original check." The substitute check must also have been handled by a bank.

Banks are not required to keep your original check for any specific period of time. Existing federal law requires that banks retain a legible copy of checks for seven years, but neither federal nor state law requires that the copies returned to customers with statements be legible. Check 21 does not add any new retention requirements. Under Check 21, original checks are more likely to be destroyed. If you request your original check from your bank, your bank may provide you with the original check, a substitute check, or a paper or electronic copy of the check.

Articles 3 and 4 of the Uniform Commercial Code continue to provide protection against erroneous and unauthorized checks. In addition, Check 21 contains a number of new protections for customers. For example, Check 21 contains a special refund procedure, called expedited recredit, for a customer who suffers a loss because of a substitute check.

Because checks are now transmitted electronically from one bank to another, customers must make sure they have funds in their account to cover them and no longer anticipate a "float" based on the time it would take the check to be physically transmitted back to the drawee bank. Consumer groups warn consumers to be aware that

---
[2]Technology that can read special ink that is sensitive to magnetic fields.

there is an increased risk that a check will bounce if funds are not in the account when the check is written. At the same time, customers may not get access to the funds from checks that they deposit to their account any sooner because Check 21 does not shorten the check hold times set out in the Federal Expedited Funds Availability Act.

Electronic Transfers

The introduction of automated teller machines (ATMs) in the 1970s caused a significant expansion in the types of electronic payments available to consumers and businesses. Most of the new electronic payment options developed since 1970 have benefited consumers by making it easier to pay merchants remotely, faster to make payments in the merchants' stores, or easier to send funds to relatives and charities at a distance from their homes or places of business. The decreasing need to move paper money or coins and checks—and even paper-based credit card receivables—saves time and expense for merchants.

The electronic payments options available in the United States today include (1) automated teller machines; (2) point-of-sale terminals for ATM cards and prepaid access cards (including general-purpose prepaid cards to which consumers can send funds, payroll cards used by employers instead of checks, and gift cards); (3) preauthorized payments, using the **Automated Clearing House System (ACH)**, to receive paychecks and retirement or government benefits or to pay recurring obligations such as utility bills, home mortgages, insurance, or installment loans or one-time payments; (4) telephone or Internet transfers between bank or credit union accounts or to give authorization to make payments or deposits; (5) remote deposits of checks; (6) services such as PayPal that allow consumers to pay sellers they do not know from bank accounts or credit card accounts without revealing their account information to the seller; (7) mobile payment options including Google Wallet, Amazon, and Apple Pay; and (8) virtual currencies. Companies such as Western Union and MoneyGram, for example, also take funds from consumers in one location and send messages to their offices and agents in other locations; the latter disburse proceeds to the intended recipients, including recipients outside the United States. Finally, for larger-dollar funds transfers, some consumers and larger numbers of businesses and financial institutions use the "wire transfer" systems offered by banks.

The speed at which each of these options moves funds to the intended recipients varies considerably. Most of them at this time are less-than-real-time options, and some are far more expensive for consumers and businesses to use than others.

Each of these payments options has its own legal constructs to deal with the types of issues that may arise. The rules provided by Articles 3 (Negotiable Instruments) and 4 (Bank Deposits and Collections) of the Uniform Commercial Code, first enacted in the 1960s, quickly proved to be less optimal for some of these newer payment options. Congress enacted the Electronic Fund Transfer Act in 1978 (EFTA) to provide basic disclosures and consumer protections for ATM and debit card transfers. Article 4A of the Uniform Commercial Code, which became available for states' enactment in 1989, governs funds transfers, together with regulations adopted by the Federal Reserve Board of Governors and other system rules. ACH transfers operate under clearing house rules with some disclosures and consumer protections for consumer transactions from the Electronic Fund Transfer Act and the federal regulation that implements it— Regulation E. Regulation E also governs consumer issues in PayPal and Apple Pay transactions and telephone transfers between bank accounts or credit union accounts and, to a lesser extent, governs other mobile payments that move credits from a consumer's bank or credit union account to the merchant's account. For the moment, no federal law governs payments made in virtual currencies, and only a few states regulate providers of virtual currency payment options, and then only in limited ways. Many of the types of payments described in this section of the book also employ provider–customer contracts and follow system rules to allocate rights and duties among payment participants.

Electronic Fund Transfer Act

 LO34-8 Discuss the major features of the Electronic Fund Transfer Act as they relate to the rights, liabilities, and responsibilities of participants in electronic funds transfer systems.

The consumer who used electronic funds transfer systems (EFTs), the so-called cash machines or electronic tellers, in the early years often experienced problems in identifying and resolving mechanical errors resulting from malfunctioning EFTs. In response to these problems, Congress passed the Electronic Fund Transfer Act in 1978 to provide "a basic framework, establishing the rights, liabilities, and responsibilities of participants in electronic funds transfer systems" and especially to provide "individual consumer rights."

The basic EFT systems are *automated teller machines*; *point-of-sale terminals*, which allow consumers to use their EFT cards, including payroll and prepaid gift or general-purpose readable cards (like checks) at retail establishments;

preauthorized payments, such as automatic paycheck deposits or mortgage or utility payments; and *telephone transfers* between accounts or payment of specific bills by phone.

Similar to the Truth in Lending Act and the Fair Credit Billing Act (FCBA) discussed in Chapter 48, the EFTA requires disclosure of the terms and conditions of electronic funds transfers at the time the consumer contracts for the EFT service. Among the nine disclosures required are the following: the consumer's liability for unauthorized electronic funds transfers (those resulting from loss or theft), the nature of the EFT services under the consumer's account, any pertinent dollar or frequency limitations, any charges for the right to make EFTs, the consumer's right to stop payment of a preauthorized transfer, the financial institution's liability to the consumer for failure to make or stop payments, and the consumer's right to receive documentation of transfers both at the point or time of transfer and periodically. The act also requires 21 days' notice prior to the effective date of any change in the terms or conditions of the consumer's account that pertains to the required disclosures.

The EFTA differs from the Fair Credit Billing Act in a number of important respects. For example, under the EFTA, the operators of EFT systems have a maximum of 10 working days to investigate errors or provisionally recredit the consumer's account, whereas issuers of credit cards have a maximum of 60 days under the FCBA. The liability of the consumer also is different if an EFT card is lost or stolen than it is if a credit card is lost or stolen.

The *Kruser* case illustrates the application of the EFTA's provisions that require a customer to provide timely notification of any unauthorized use of his card in order to limit his liability for the unauthorized use of the card.

Kruser v. Bank of America NT & SA　　281 Cal. Rptr. 463 (Ct. App. 1991)

Lawrence and Georgene Kruser maintained a joint checking account with the Bank of America. The bank issued each of them a "Versatel" card and separate personal identification numbers that would allow access to funds in their account from automated teller machines. The Krusers also received with their cards a "Disclosure Booklet" that provided to the Krusers a summary of consumer liability, the bank's business hours, and the address and telephone number by which they could notify the bank in the event they believed an unauthorized transfer had been made.

The Krusers believed Mr. Kruser's card had been destroyed in September 1986. The December 1986 account statement mailed to the Krusers by the bank reflected a $20 unauthorized withdrawal of funds by someone using Mr. Kruser's card at an automated teller machine. The Krusers reported this unauthorized transaction to the bank when they discovered it in August or September 1987.

Mrs. Kruser underwent surgery in late 1986 or early 1987 and remained hospitalized for 11 days. She then spent a period of six or seven months recuperating at home. During this time, she reviewed the statements the Krusers received from the bank.

In September 1987, the Krusers received bank statements for July and August 1987 that reflected 47 unauthorized withdrawals totaling $9,020 made from an automated teller machine, again by someone using Mr. Kruser's card. They notified the bank of these withdrawals within a few days of receiving the statements. The bank refused to credit the Kruser's account with the amount of the unauthorized withdrawals. The Krusers sued the bank claiming damages for the unauthorized withdrawals from their account. The trial court ruled in favor of the bank on the grounds that the Krusers had failed to comply with the note and reporting requirements of the Electronic Fund Transfer Act (EFTA). The Krusers appealed.

Stone, Associate Justice

The ultimate issue we address is whether, as a matter of law, the unauthorized $20 withdrawal which appeared on the December 1986 statement barred the Krusers from recovery for the losses incurred in July and August 1987. Resolution of the issue requires the interpretation of the EFTA and section 205.6 of Regulation E, one of the regulations prescribed by the Board of Governors of the Federal Reserve System in order to carry out the EFTA.

Section 205.6 of Regulation E mirrors [the EFTA] and in particular provides:

(b) Limitations on the amount of liability. The amount of a consumer's liability for an unauthorized electronic fund transfer or a series of related unauthorized transfers shall not exceed $50 or the amount of unauthorized transfers that occur before notice to the financial institution . . . whichever is less, unless one of the following exceptions apply:

. . .

(2) If the consumer fails to report within 60 days of transmittal of the periodic statement any unauthorized electronic fund transfer that appears on the statement, the consumer's liability shall not exceed the sum of (i) The lesser of $50 or the amount of unauthorized electronic fund transfers that appear on the periodic statement during the 60-day period and (ii) The amount of unauthorized electronic fund transfers that occur after the close of the 60 days and before notice

to the financial institution and that the financial institution establishes would not have occurred but for the failure of the consumer to notify the financial institution within that time.

. . .

(4) If a delay in notifying the financial statements was due to extenuating circumstances, such as extended travel or hospitalization, the time periods specified above shall be extended to a reasonable time.

The trial court concluded the Bank was entitled to judgment as a matter of law because the unauthorized withdrawals of July and August 1987 occurred more than 60 days after the Krusers received a statement which reflected an unauthorized transfer in December 1986. The court relied upon section 205.6(b)(2) of Regulation E.

The Krusers contend the December withdrawal of $20 was so isolated in time and minimal in an amount that it cannot be considered in connection with the July and August withdrawals. They assert the court's interpretation of section 205.6(b)(2) of Regulation E would have absurd results which would be inconsistent with the primary objective of the EFTA—to protect the consumer. They argue that if a consumer receives a bank statement which reflects an unauthorized minimal electronic transfer and fails to report the transaction to the bank within 60 days of transmission of the bank statement, unauthorized transfers many years later, perhaps totaling thousands of dollars, would remain the responsibility of the consumer.

The result the Krusers fear is avoided by the requirement that the bank establish the subsequent unauthorized transfers could have been prevented had the consumer notified the bank of the first unauthorized transfer. Here, although the unauthorized transfer of $20 occurred approximately seven months before the unauthorized transfers totaling $9,020, it is undisputed that all transfers were made by using Mr. Kruser's card which the Krusers believed had been destroyed prior to December 1986. According to the declaration of Yvonne Maloon, the Bank's Versatel risk manager, the Bank could have and would have canceled Mr. Kruser's card had it been timely notified of the December unauthorized transfer. In that event Mr. Kruser's card could not have been used to accomplish the unauthorized transactions in July and August.

In the alternative, the Krusers contend the facts establish that Mrs. Kruser, who was solely responsible for reconciling the bank statements, was severely ill and was also caring for a terminally ill relative when the December withdrawal occurred. Therefore they claim they were entitled to an extension of time within which to notify the bank.

The evidence the Krusers rely upon indicates in late 1986 or early 1987 Mrs. Kruser underwent surgery and remained in the hospital for 11 days. She left her house infrequently during the first six or seven months of 1987 during which she was recuperating. Mrs. Kruser admits, however, she received and reviewed bank statements during her recuperation. Therefore, we need not consider whether Mrs. Kruser's illness created circumstances which might have excused her failure to notice the unauthorized withdrawal pursuant to the applicable sections. She in fact did review the statements in question.

Judgment for Bank of America affirmed.

Wire Transfers

Wire Transfers Two wire transfer systems operate in the United States—Fedwire and CHIPS. Fedwire is a domestic-only wire transfer payment system operated by Federal Reserve Banks. CHIPS is a global wire transfer payment system operated by The Clearing House (a consortium of large banks formerly called the New York Clearing House Association). These two wire transfers handle daily transfer volumes well in excess of $1 trillion.

Both of these wire transfer systems use highly automated processing once receiving the instruction to push funds from the sender or originator's account through one or more banks to the bank representing the beneficiary of the transfer. If no consumer account is involved, Article 4A of the Uniform Commercial Code governs, and for transfers made using the Federal Reserve System's Fedwire, Federal Reserve Board Regulation J applies. For consumer accounts, section 4A-108 and the Electronic Fund Transfer Act as implemented by Federal Reserve Board Regulation E provides that the EFTA governs.

In the Prefatory Note to Article 4A, the Uniform Law Commission notes that the typical transfer covered by the Article is not a complex transaction and provides the following example, which also illustrates the terminology used in wire transfers:

> X, a debtor, wants to pay an obligation owed to Y. Instead of delivering to Y a negotiable instrument such as a check or other writing such as a credit card slip that enables Y to obtain payment from a bank, X transmits an instruction to X's bank to credit a sum of money to the bank account of Y. In most cases X's bank and Y's bank are different banks. X's bank may carry out X's bank by instructing Y's bank to credit Y's account by the amount that X has requested. The instruction that X issues to its bank is a "payment order." X is the "sender" of the payment order and X's bank is the "receiving bank" with respect to X's order. Y is the "beneficiary"

CYBERLAW IN ACTION

Check Conversion

Chapter 31, Negotiable Instruments, explains that the process known as "check conversion" is utilized by a number of large retailers. The process begins with the buyer giving the seller a paper check. The seller uses special equipment to gather information from the microline on the paper check; this information includes the buyer's bank account number, the bank routing number, and the serial number of the check. The retailer then names itself as the payee, codes in the amount of the purchase, and forwards it for collection through an automated clearing house (ACH) transaction instead of the collection route for paper checks.

The Federal Reserve Board decided that the Electronic Fund Transfer Act (EFTA) and Regulation E would govern consumer "check conversion" transactions. The EFTA will govern even if the consumer gives a blank and unsigned check to the merchant. The act also governs if the merchant uses a paper check as a "source document" (source of critical account- and bank-related information) and then uses an electronic funds transfer rather than the ACH transfer mentioned above in the section titled "Check Collection."

---

of X's order. When X's bank issues an instruction to Y's bank to carry out X's payment order, X's bank "executes" X's order. With respect to that order, X's bank is the sender, Y's bank is the receiving bank, and Y is the beneficiary. The entire series of transactions is known as the "funds transfer." With respect to the funds transfer, X is the "originator," X's bank is the "originator's bank," Y is the "beneficiary" and Y's bank is the "beneficiary's bank." In more complex transactions there are one or more additional banks known as "intermediary banks" between X's bank and Y's bank.

Intermediary banks that receive payment orders and then send new payment orders to the next bank in the fund transfer sequence are known as "receiving banks."

Funds transfers have a number of advantages for those who utilize them, typically sophisticated business or financial organizations. They allow significant sums of money to move at high speed so that transactions can be completed in a very short period of time and are an effective substitute for payments made by the delivery of paper instruments. In addition, the cost of the transfers is very low compared to the amount of money being transferred. At the same time, the risk of loss can be very large if something goes wrong in the transaction. Among the possibilities are (1) a bank fails to execute the payment order of a customer; (2) a bank is late in executing a payment order; or (3) a bank makes an error in executing the payment order, either as to the amount to be paid or the identity or account number of the person to be paid or the identity of the beneficiary bank. A major policy issue in the drafting of Article 4A was the allocation of risk to the various parties in light of the price structure in the industry.

For example, if a receiving bank executes a payment order by paying more than the order calls for, or makes a duplicative payment, the bank is entitled to the amount of the payment order but is left to recover any excess or duplicative payment from the beneficiary under the common or local law governing mistake and restitution. Where banks carry out a funds transfer but are late in executing it, the banks are obligated to pay interest to either the originator or the beneficiary of the funds transfer for the period of delay caused by the improper execution. For other types of improper execution or failure to execute payment orders, banks can be liable to the originator or sender for their expenses in the transaction along with incidental expenses and interest losses due to improper execution or failure to execute. Consequential damages are recoverable only to the extent provided in an express written agreement of the receiving bank and are not otherwise recoverable under Article 4.

The Global Business Environment

International Electronic Funds Transfers

The Model Law on International Credit Transfers, adopted in 1992 by the United Nations Commission on International Trade Law, is the major international legal document concerning electronic funds transfers. The Model Law covers basically the same kind of transactions as Article 4A does, but it does require the funds transferred to have an international component and is not identical in its treatment of certain issues.

Problems and Problem Cases

1. James Drumm and Debra Brading lived together on and off for several years. Drumm was providing financial support to Brading. Brading had written numerous checks on Drumm's checking account and had access to his corporate credit cards. However, she was not an authorized signator on either his checking or savings accounts. After one particularly ugly fight between the two, Brading went to the National City Bank and withdrew $314,000 from Drumm's individual savings account. She did so by approaching a teller, giving her Drumm's account number and electronic personal identification number (PIN), and providing the teller with a driver's license bearing the name Debra Brading along with a Racquet Club membership identifying her as Debra Drumm. She was also wearing a $20,000 diamond ring, which appeared to be an engagement ring. On the basis of these facts, a teller allowed the transaction. Drumm brought suit against National City Bank for breach of contract for allowing an unauthorized transfer of funds from his account. Is National City Bank liable to Drumm?

2. Louise Kalbe drew a check in the amount of $7,260 payable to the "order of cash" on her account at the Pulaski State Bank. The check was lost or stolen, but Kalbe did not report this to the bank, nor did she attempt to stop payment on it. When the check was received by the Pulaski State Bank, Kalbe had only about $700 in her checking account. However, the bank paid the check, creating an overdraft in her account of $6,542.12. The bank then sued Kalbe to recover the amount of the overdraft. Kalbe asserted that the check was not properly payable from her account. Was the bank legally entitled to pay a check that exceeded the balance in the drawer's account and to recover the overdraft from the drawer?

3. J. E. B. Stewart received a check in the amount of $185.48 in payment of a fee from a client. Stewart presented the check, properly indorsed, to the Citizens & Southern Bank. The bank refused to cash the check even though there were sufficient funds in the drawer's account. Stewart then sued the bank for actual damages of $185.48 for its failure to cash a valid check drawn against a solvent account in the bank. Does Stewart have a good cause of action against the bank?

4. Brenda Jones, who did business as Country Kitchen, purchased some cookware from an itinerant salesman, giving him a check in the amount of $200 for the purchase price. The salesman cashed the check at the First National Bank before noon on May 22, the day of the sale. Jones later became concerned about the lack of documentation from the salesman, thinking that the cookware might be stolen, and placed a stop-payment order with her bank, the State Bank of Conway Springs, at 3:30 that afternoon. State Bank refused to honor the check when it was presented for payment through banking channels. First National Bank, claiming to be a holder in due course, then brought suit against Jones to recover the $200 value of the check. Is the drawer of a check on which a stop-payment order was placed and honored by the bank liable to pay the check to a holder in due course?

5. John Doe had a checking account at Highland National Bank in New York. Two days after John Doe died in Florida, but before Highland National knew of his death, John's sister appeared at the bank. She had a check signed by John Doe but with the amount and name of the payee left blank. She told the bank that her brother wanted to close his account. She asked how much was in the account, filled in the check for that amount, and made the check payable to herself. The bank checked her identification and verified the signature of John Doe. Then it paid the check to the sister. The executor of John Doe's estate sued Highland National Bank to recover the amount of money that was in John's account on the day he died. The executor claimed that the bank had no authority to pay checks from John Doe's account after his death. May a bank pay checks drawn on the account of a deceased customer?

6. In March 2008, Faux Themes, a corporation in the construction business, opened a checking account with Chino National Bank. Brian Peters, the president of the company, and Marilyn Charloes, its treasurer, were authorized signers on the account. Until April 2009, the average monthly balance in the account ranged from $3,000 to $5,000, and the deposits in any one month never exceeded $10,000. In March 2009, Peters received an e-mail supposedly from Husaine Norman, a citizen of Malaysia. Norman said that certain third parties in the United States and Canada owed him money; however, they were insisting that "they cannot transfer the funds to any bank account outside America continent due to their new company policy." He asked Peters to "assist me in receiving the funds and forward to me." He offered to pay Peters 12 percent of the money and Peters agreed after negotiating an increase of his fee to 15 percent.

On April 30, 2009, Faux received a check for $178,000; Peters had Charloes deposit it. On May 8, 2009, the bank confirmed the check had cleared. Charloes then had the bank wire $80,000 to a bank in Hong Kong. Also on May 8, Faux received a second check for $373,988.90, which was deposited, and on May 12 Charloes had the bank wire another $71,000 to the same bank in Hong Kong. On May 15, the bank confirmed that the second check had cleared, and Charloes had the bank wire $317,000 to a bank in China. On May 21, Faux received a third check for $257,000, which was deposited at the bank.

On May 22, 2009, the bank was notified that the name of the first check had been altered to change the name of the payee to Faux. On May 28, the bank was notified that the second and third checks had been similarly altered. Because all three checks were dishonored, the account was overdrawn in the amount of $458,782.60. When the bank got back the original checks, it found that they had been altered with an acid that was originally used by architects to remove ink from blueprints. They had no facial irregularities—no discoloration, smidges, misalignments, or disturbances of the backgrounds or watermarks. The alterations were in fonts and type sizes that were consistent with the other printing on the check. Pursuant to bank policy concerning checks over $10,000, a bank officer had reviewed the checks for irregularities and to see whether the amounts were consistent with the customer—and had initialed the deposit slips to show the procedures had been followed. Before initialing, he also had determined that the amounts of the checks were consistent with deposits made to the accounts of related entities. This is consistent with industry practice nationally.

The bank sued Peters to recover the cost of the overdraft. Peters did not dispute that he was personally responsible for any overdrafts, but contended that the bank had not followed suitable procedures in taking the checks for deposit and, therefore, its own actions substantially contributed to the losses so that it should not be entitled to charge the items back to Faux's account. On these facts, is the bank entitled to charge the items back to Faux's account?

7. Rhona Graves opened checking and savings accounts at Riggs Bank. The customer agreement with Riggs included a provision that "your [account] statement is considered correct and we will not be liable for payments made and charged to your account . . . unless you notify us of an error, including unauthorized payment or other irregularity within (a) sixty (60) calendar

days . . . of the mailing date of the earliest statement describing the charge or deposit to your account."

Prior to June 2002, Graves won a substantial amount of money in the lottery and deposited the lump sum in her accounts at Riggs Bank. On June 8, she suffered a serious stroke and thereafter was unable to communicate. She was transferred to a nursing home where she died on November 9, 2002. Between May and her death in November, someone made 73 withdrawals from her account, 72 of which were at the $500 daily limit for withdrawals. Then 21 additional withdrawals were made during the 41 days after she died, including 19 at the $500 daily maximum. Thus, $46,547 was withdrawn from the account by this method, including $10,159.50 after her death. In addition, 128 checks were written, resulting in her account being debited $84,731.61. Six of the checks (totaling $62,000) were made out to her sister and another check was written to her sister's daughter. The signatures on the checks did not match the authorized signature on file with the bank. After her stroke, Graves did not have the capacity to review bank statements, and it does not appear she received any at the hospital.

After her death, her son petitioned for letters of administration to handle her estate and received authority to open her safe-deposit box. After discovering that she had won the lottery, he sought to determine what had happened to the money, which at that point had essentially disappeared from her Riggs accounts. After asking Riggs for an investigation of the account and receiving only limited information, he filed suit on August 4, 2004, asking that her account be recredited for the unauthorized ATM withdrawals and checks. Should Riggs be required to recredit the account?

8. On August 16, Frederick Ognibene went to the ATM area at a Citibank branch and activated one of the machines with his Citibank card, provided his personal identification code, and withdrew $20. When he approached the machine a person was using the customer service telephone located between two ATMs and appeared to be telling customer service that one of the machines was malfunctioning. As Ognibene was making his withdrawal, the person said into the telephone, "I'll see if his card works in my machine." He then asked Ognibene if he could use his card to see if the other machine was working. Ognibene handed his card to him and saw him insert it into the adjoining machine at least two times while saying into the telephone, "Yes, it seems to be working." When Ognibene received his Citibank statement, it showed that two

withdrawals of $200 each from his account were made at 5:42 P.M. and 5:43 P.M., respectively, on August 16. His own $20 withdrawal was made at 5:41 P.M. At the time, Ognibene was unaware that any withdrawals from his account were being made from the adjoining machine. Ognibene sought to have his account recredited for $400, claiming that the withdrawals had been unauthorized. Citibank had been aware for some time of a scam being perpetrated against its customers by persons who observed the customer inserting his personal identification number into an ATM and then obtained access to the customer's ATM card in the same manner as Ognibene's card was obtained. After learning about the scam, Citibank posted signs in ATM areas containing a red circle approximately 2½ inches in diameter in which was written "Do Not Let Your Citicard Be Used For Any Transaction But Your Own." Was Citibank required under the Electronic Fund Transfer Act to recredit Ognibene's account on the grounds that the withdrawal of the $400 was unauthorized?

Agency Law

CHAPTER 35

The Agency Relationship

Upon graduating from college, Rita Morales was hired as a software consultant by IPQ Company, a large computer manufacturing and services company. Rita negotiated a high salary and even a nice signing bonus, yet after a few years of work she found that her spending often outstripped her earnings and savings. As her credit card bills piled up, Rita started her own consulting firm. Initially, Rita provided software consulting for her clients only on nights and weekends after she had finished her IPQ work for the day. As her business grew, she began seeing clients during normal weekday working hours and calling them from her office at IPQ. To find new clients, Rita downloaded IPQ's client information from IPQ's database. She contacted more than 200 IPQ clients and asked them to switch from IPQ to Rita's business. More than two dozen IPQ clients switched to Rita.

- Do you see any potential problems with Rita's actions?
- What legally and practically can IPQ do to prevent Rita from taking its clients?
- What would an ethical employee in Rita's position do if her income did not meet her expenses?

LO LEARNING OBJECTIVES

After studying this chapter, you should be able to:

35-1 Know when an agency relationship is created.

35-2 Understand the distinction between employees and nonemployee agents.

35-3 Recognize when an agent risks breaching a fiduciary duty.

35-4 Describe the way agency relationships are terminated.

OFTEN, BUSINESSES ARE LEGALLY bound by the actions of their employees or other representatives. For example, corporations frequently are liable on contracts their employees make or for torts their employees commit. We take such liability for granted, but why should we? A corporation is an artificial legal person distinct from the officers, employees, and other representatives who contract on its behalf and who may commit torts while on the job. Similarly, a sole proprietor and the people who work for that sole proprietor are distinct. How can these and other business actors be bound on contracts they did not make or for torts they did not commit? The reason is the law of **agency**.

Agency is a two-party relationship in which one party (the **agent**) has the power to act on behalf of, and under the control of, the other party (the **principal**). Examples include a Toyota dealership hiring a salesperson to sell cars, Google employing a software engineer to write computer code, and you engaging a real estate agent to sell your home. Agency law's most important social function has been to stimulate commercial activity. It does so by enabling businesses to increase the number of transactions they can complete within a given time. Without agency, for instance, a sole proprietor's ability to engage in trade would be limited by the need to make each purchase or sale contract in person. As artificial persons, moreover, corporations can act only through their agents.

Agency law divides into two rough categories. The first involves legal relations between the principal and the agent. These include the rules governing formation of an agency, the duties the principal and the agent owe each other, and the ways an agency can be terminated. These topics are the main concern of this chapter. Chapter 36 discusses the principal's and the agent's relations with third parties. In that chapter, our main concerns are the principal's and the agent's liability on contracts the agent enters and for torts the agent commits.

Much of the law of agency, which is largely state law in the United States, has been codified or adopted by the state legislatures or their courts in the form of the *Restatement (Third) of Agency* (2006), a project of the American Law Institute (ALI). The *Restatement (Third)* was adopted by the ALI in 2006, replacing the *Restatement (Second)*, which had been the chief source of agency law since its adoption in 1958.

Creation of an Agency

 Know when an agency relationship is created.

Formation   Agency is the fiduciary relationship that arises when one person (a principal) manifests assent to another person (an agent) that the agent will act on the principal's behalf and be subject to the principal's control. The agent must also manifest assent to the relationship or otherwise consent to act for the principal and under the principal's control. Agency is a fiduciary relationship because the principal entrusts the agent with power to make contracts for the principal and to possess and use the principal's property. As a fiduciary, the agent must use the entrusted power and property in the best interest of the principal. The Supreme Court has long-stated that "[a] fiduciary cannot serve himself first and his cestuis second, and he cannot manipulate the affairs of his corporation to the detriment of stockholders and creditors and in disregard of the standards of common decency and honesty." *Pepper v. Litton*, 308 U.S. 295, 311 (1939).

As the term *manifest* suggests, the test for an agency's existence is *objective*. If the parties' written or spoken words or other conduct indicate an agreement that one person is to act on behalf of and under the control of another, the relationship exists.

If the facts establish an agency, neither party need know about the agency's existence or subjectively desire that it exist. In fact, an agency may be present even when the parties expressly say that they do not intend to create it, or intend to create some other legal relationship instead.

Often, parties create an agency by a written contract. But an agency contract may be oral unless state law provides otherwise. Some states, for example, require written evidence of contracts to pay an agent a commission for the sale of real estate. More important, the agency relation need not be contractual at all. Thus, consideration required to form a contract is not necessary to form an agency.

The *Krakauer* case, which follows, illustrates how courts will use the objective standard of mutual assent to find that an agency relationship has been formed, even if the principal denies it.

Krakauer v. Dish Network, L.L.C.
925 F.3d 643 (4th Cir. 2019)

In May 2009, Satellite Systems Network (SSN) repeatedly called Dr. Thomas Krakauer, asking him to purchase television services through Dish Network, L.L.C. (Dish). SSN's sole business was direct marketing calls to consumers on behalf of television service providers. During the relevant time in 2009, SSN was only working for Dish.

Krakauer had registered his phone number on the national Do-Not-Call registry in 2003. The national registry was established by the Telephone Consumer Protection Act (TCPA) to prevent abusive telephone marketing practices. The TCPA prohibited calls to numbers on the national Do-Not-Call registry; thus, SSN's calls to Dr. Krakauer violated the TCPA.

Krakauer sued Dish for violating the TCPA by having SSN call on its behalf, and he sought to certify his lawsuit as a class action on behalf of all persons who, like him, had received similar calls to numbers listed on the Do-Not-Call registry.

The district court certified the class and the case proceeded to trial, which Dish Network lost.

Dish Network appealed on a number of bases, including that the district court improperly instructed the jury regarding agency law. Dish Network argued that SSN was not its agent, and, therefore, it should not be responsible for SSN's acts in violation of the TCPA.

Wilkinson, Circuit Judge

Dish does not contest that widespread violations of the TCPA occurred, nor does it dispute that these violations were made for the sole purpose of selling Dish services. Dish does not even seriously contest that it knew of the violative conduct. . . .

We first consider whether Dish was properly held liable for the calls that SSN made to members of the class. The jury concluded that it was because SSN was acting as Dish's agent when the calls were made. By its plain language, the TCPA's private right of action contemplates that a company can be held liable for calls made on its behalf, even if not placed by the company directly. . . . While we have no clear definition of "on behalf of" in the TCPA, we may, at a minimum, assume that federal statutes are written with familiar common law agency principles in mind.

Under traditional agency law, an agency relationship exists when a principal "manifests assent" to an agent "that the agent shall act on the principal's behalf and subject to the principal's control, and the agent manifests assent or otherwise consents so to act." *See Restatement (Third) of Agency, § 1.01. . . .*

The jury was asked to find whether or not SSN was Dish's agent at the time it made the calls relevant to this case. If the jury had answered that question in the negative, that would have ended the matter. The court carefully explained that Krakauer had the burden of showing such a relationship, and that the relationship required mutual assent and control by Dish. The court also instructed the jury on the scope of authority. Specifically, the court instructed the jury how to assess a situation, as we have here, wherein the principal's guidance to the agent may not be explicit, but instead arises from the principal's acquiescence to a course of conduct. As the district court explained, "to decide whether the principal acquiesced or consented, you must find that the principal knew of prior similar activities and consented or did not object to them."

In sum, the district court interpreted the statute to apply standard legal principles. The question was then presented to the jury, which ultimately held Dish liable. Despite Dish's assertions that the district court somehow engaged in legal errors on this point, its challenges bottom out on no more than a disagreement about the facts.

The evidence supporting an agency relationship between Dish and SSN is considerable. First, there are the many provisions of the contract between Dish and SSN affording Dish broad authority over SSN's business, including what technology it used and what records it retained. Second, SSN was authorized to use Dish's name and logo in carrying out its operation. Third, the jury had before it the Voluntary Compliance Agreement that Dish entered into with 46 state attorneys general, wherein Dish clearly stated its authority over SSN with regard to TCPA compliance. And on the issue of whether SSN was acting within the scope of its authority, an array of witnesses testified that Dish was aware of SSN's legal violations, took no meaningful action to ensure compliance, and profited from SSN's actions. Faced with this evidence, it was entirely reasonable for the jury to conclude both that SSN was acting as Dish's agent, and that SSN was acting pursuant to its authority when making the calls at issue in this case.

Dish . . . contends that its contract with SSN, which expressly defined the relationship between the parties, ought to outweigh the evidence on the ground. It is a familiar rule of agency, however, that parties cannot avoid the legal obligations of agency by simply contracting out of them. *See Restatement (Third) of Agency, § 1.02* ("Whether a relationship is characterized as agency in an agreement between the parties . . . is not controlling."). Agency law, including a principal's liability for acts done on his behalf, protects third parties, who themselves would receive no protection from a contractual disclaimer. This case demonstrates the need to look beyond the contract, as a failure to do so might lead to absolving a company, like Dish, that acquiesced in and benefitted from a wrongful course of conduct that was carried out on its behalf. . . .

AFFIRMED.

Capacity A person has the capacity to be a principal if that person has capacity to do the acts for which the agent has been retained. For example, a person competent to make a contract to purchase a building has the capacity to appoint an agent for that purpose.

Generally, anyone can be an agent, even if that person lacks capacity otherwise to enter contracts. An agent must merely understand that he is acting for someone else and is under that person's control.

Corporations have the capacity to appoint agents. In a partnership, each partner normally acts as the agent of the partnership in transacting partnership business, and a partnership can appoint nonpartner agents as well. In addition, corporations, partnerships, and other business organizations themselves can act as agents for other business organizations as well as individuals.

Nondelegable Obligations Certain duties or acts must be performed personally and cannot be delegated to an agent. Examples include making statements under oath, voting in public elections, and signing a will. The same is true for service contracts in which the principal's personal performance is crucial, such as certain contracts by lawyers, doctors, athletes, and entertainers. For example, the guitarist for Lady Gaga may not delegate to another guitarist his duty to perform at a Lady Gaga concert.

Agency Concepts, Definitions, and Types

Agency law includes various concepts, definitions, and distinctions. These matters often determine the rights, duties, and liabilities of the principal, the agent, and third parties.

In addition, they sometimes are important outside agency law. Because these basic topics are crucial in many different situations, we outline them together here.

Authority Although agency law lets people multiply their dealings by employing agents, a principal is not always liable for his agent's acts. Normally, an agent can bind his principal on a contract or other matter only when the agent has **authority** to do so. Authority is an agent's ability to affect his principal's legal relations. It comes in two main forms: **actual authority** and **apparent authority**. Each is based on the principal's manifested consent that the agent may act for and bind the principal. For actual authority, this consent must be communicated to the *agent*, while for apparent authority it must be communicated to the *third party*.

Actual authority comes in two forms: **express authority** and **implied authority**. *Express authority* is actual authority that the principal has manifested to the agent in very specific or detailed language. For example, a principal—a homeowner—may tell an agent—a tree removal expert—that the agent is authorized to "remove the diseased ash tree in my front yard."

Agency law also gives agents *implied authority* to bind their principals. An agent generally has implied authority to act in a way the agent reasonably believes is necessary to perform the agent's duties. For example, the tree removal expert in the example above would have authority to choose a method for removing the tree, such as topping the tree first and removing it in sections or felling the tree with one cut. Relevant factors include the principal's statements or actions, the nature of the agency, the acts reasonably necessary to carry on the agency business, and the acts customarily done when conducting that business.

Sometimes, an agent who lacks actual authority may still *appear* to have such authority, and third parties may reasonably rely on this appearance of authority. To protect third parties in such situations, agency law lets agents bind the principal on the basis of their apparent authority. *Apparent authority* arises when the *principal's* manifestations cause a third party to believe reasonably that the agent is authorized to act in a certain way.

Apparent authority depends on what the *principal* communicates to the third party—either directly or through the agent. A principal might clothe an agent through statements to the third party, telling an agent to do so, or allowing an agent to behave in a way that creates an appearance of authority. The principal's communications to the agent are irrelevant unless they become known to the third party or affect the agent's behavior. In *American Society of Mechanical Engineers, Inc. v. Hydrolevel Corp.*, 456 U.S. 556 (1982), the Supreme Court stated that apparent authority is the power to affect the legal relations of another person through transaction with a third party, professedly as agent for that other person, arising from and in accordance with that other person's manifestation to the third party. Also, *agents cannot give themselves apparent authority*, and apparent authority does not exist where an agent creates an appearance of authority without the principal's consent (direct or tacit). Finally, the third party must *reasonably* believe in the agent's authority. Trade customs and business practices can help courts determine whether such a belief is reasonable.

Authority is important in a number of agency contexts. Chapter 36 examines its most important agency application—determining a principal's liability on contracts made by his agent.

General and Special Agents Although it may be falling out of favor with courts, the blurred distinction between general agents and special agents still has some importance. A **general agent** is continuously employed to conduct a series of transactions, while a **special agent** is employed to conduct a single transaction or a small, simple group of transactions. Thus, a continuously employed general manager of a McDonald's restaurant, a construction project supervisor for homebuilder Pulte, or a buyer of women's clothing for Macy's normally is a general agent. A person employed to buy or sell a few objects on a one-shot basis usually is a special agent. General agents often serve for longer periods, perform more acts, and deal with more parties than do special agents.

Gratuitous Agents An agent who receives no compensation for his services is called a **gratuitous agent**. Gratuitous agents have the same power to bind their principals as do paid agents with the same authority. However, the fact that an agent is gratuitous sometimes lowers the duties principal and agent owe each other and also may increase the parties' ability to terminate the agency without incurring liability.

Subagents A **subagent** basically is an agent of an agent. More precisely, a subagent is a person appointed by an agent to perform tasks that the agent has undertaken to perform for his principal. For example, if you retain accounting firm PricewaterhouseCoopers LLP as your agent, the accountant actually handling your affairs is PwC's agent and your subagent. For a subagency to exist, an agent must have the authority to make the subagent *his agent* for conducting the principal's business. Sometimes, however, a party appointed by an agent is not a subagent because the appointing agent only had authority to appoint agents *for the principal*. For instance, sales agents appointed by a corporation's sales manager are agents of the corporation, not agents of the sales manager.

When an agent appoints a true subagent, the agent becomes a principal with respect to the subagent, his agent. Thus, the legal relations between agent and subagent closely parallel the legal relations between principal and agent. But a subagent is also the *original principal's* agent. Here, though, the normal rules governing principals and agents do not always apply. We occasionally refer to such situations in the pages ahead.

Employees and Nonemployee Agents

LO35-2 Understand the distinction between employees and nonemployee agents.

Many legal questions depend on whether an agent or some other party who contracts with the principal is classed as an **employee** or as a **nonemployee agent** (independent contractor). [The *Restatement (Third)* does not use the term *independent contractor* because that term can designate either an agent or a nonagent, creating further ambiguity.] No sharp line separates employees from nonemployee agents. The most important of these factors is the principal's *right to control the manner and means* of the agent's performance or work. Employees typically are subject to such control. Nonemployee agents, on the other hand, generally contract with the principal to produce a result and determine for themselves how that result will be accomplished.

Although many employees perform physical labor or are paid on an hourly basis, corporate officers who do no physical work and receive salaries usually are employees as well. Professionals such as brokers, accountants, and attorneys often are nonemployee agents of their clients, although they are employees of the brokerage, accounting, or law firms that pay their salaries. Consider the difference between a corporation represented by an attorney engaged in her own practice (a nonemployee agent) and a corporation that maintains a staff of salaried in-house counsel (employees). Finally, franchisees, like a KFC restaurant, usually are nonagents of their franchisors, like Yum! Brands.

As Chapter 36 makes clear, the employee–nonemployee agent distinction often is crucial in determining the principal's liability for an agent's torts. The distinction also helps define the coverage of some employment laws discussed in Chapter 51. Unemployment compensation, the Fair Labor Standards Act, and workers' compensation, as well as all the civil rights in employment statutes, are clear examples.

In the following case, the court determined that entertainers Janet Jackson and Justin Timberlake were not employees of CBS during the Super Bowl broadcast of their infamous halftime show.

CBS Corp. v. FCC	**535 F.3d 167 (3d Cir. 2008)**

On February 1, 2004, CBS, the television network, presented a live broadcast of the National Football League's Super Bowl XXXVIII, which included a halftime show produced by MTV Networks. Both CBS and MTV were divisions of Viacom Inc. at the time. Nearly 90 million viewers watched the show, which featured recording artists Janet Jackson and Justin Timberlake. Jackson and Timberlake performed his popular song "Rock Your Body" as the show's finale. Their performance involved sexually suggestive choreography with Timberlake seeking to dance with Jackson and she alternating between accepting and rejecting his advances. The performance ended with Timberlake singing, "gonna have you naked by the end of this song," and simultaneously tearing away part of Jackson's bustier. CBS had implemented a five-second audio delay to guard against the possibility of indecent language being transmitted on air, but it did not employ similar precautionary technology for video images. As a result, Jackson's bare right breast was exposed on camera for nine-sixteenths of one second.

Jackson's exposed breast caused a sensation and resulted in a large number of viewer complaints to the Federal Communications Commission. In response, the FCC issued a letter of inquiry asking CBS to provide more information about the broadcast. CBS issued a public statement of apology for the incident. CBS stated that Jackson and Timberlake's wardrobe stunt was unscripted and unauthorized, claiming CBS had no advance notice of any plan by the performers to deviate from the script. After its review, the FCC determined CBS was liable for a forfeiture penalty of $550,000 on several grounds, including that under the doctrine of respondeat superior, CBS was vicariously liable for the willful actions of its employees, Jackson and Timberlake. CBS asked the Third Circuit Court of Appeals to review the FCC decision.

Scirica, Chief Judge

The *respondeat superior* doctrine provides that "[a]n employer is subject to liability for torts committed by employees while acting within the scope of their employment." *Restatement (Third) of Agency* § 2.04 (2006).

But even though *the respondeat superior* doctrine may apply in this context, it is limited to the conduct of employees acting within the scope of their employment. Determining whether CBS may be liable under *respondeat superior* first requires selection of the applicable legal standard for differentiating an "employee" from an "independent contractor."

In *Cmty. for Creative Non-Violence v. Reid*, 490 U.S. 730 (1989), the Court set forth a test for determining who qualifies as an "employee" under the common law:

> In determining whether a hired party is an employee under the general common law of agency, we consider the hiring party's right to control the manner and means by which the product is accomplished. Among the other factors relevant to this inquiry are the skill required; the source of the instrumentalities and tools; the location of the work; the duration of the relationship between the parties; whether the hiring party has the right to assign additional projects to the hired party; the extent of the hired party's discretion over when and how long to work; the method of payment; the hired party's role in hiring and paying assistants; whether the work is part of the regular business of the hiring party; whether the hiring party is in business; and the tax treatment of the hired party.

While establishing that all of these factors are relevant and that "no one of these factors is determinative," *Reid* did not provide guidance on the relative weight each factor should be assigned when performing a balancing analysis. Accordingly, all of the *Reid* factors are relevant, and no one factor is decisive, but the weight each factor should be accorded depends on the context of the case. Some factors will have "little or no significance in determining whether a party is an independent contractor or an employee" on the facts of a particular case. In the present case, the FCC erred by failing to consider several important *Reid* factors when determining whether Jackson and Timberlake were employees of CBS. And rather than balancing those factors it did consider, the Commission focused almost exclusively on CBS's right of control over the performers.

Only three factors weigh in favor of a determination that Jackson and Timberlake were employees of CBS. First, CBS is in business, which increases the possibility that it would employ people. Second, CBS regularly produces shows for national broadcast in the course of its business. Both factors are relatively insignificant on balance. Third, and most significant to its argument, is the factor the FCC focused on in its orders: CBS's right to control the manner and means by which Jackson and Timberlake accomplished their Halftime Show performance. As the FCC contends, CBS, through its corporate affiliates, supervised the Halftime Show and retained the right to approve all aspects of the show's performances. But it is undisputed that CBS's actual control over the Halftime Show performances did not extend to all aspects of the performers' work. The performers, not CBS, provided their own choreography and retained substantial latitude to develop the visual performances that would accompany their songs. Similarly, as the FCC notes, CBS personnel reviewed the performers' selections of set items and wardrobes, but the performers retained discretion to make those choices in the first instance and provided some of their own materials.

CBS's control was extensive but not determinative of employment. Even though a principal's right to control is an important factor weighing in favor of a determination that an employment relationship existed, it is not dispositive when considered on balance with the rest of the *Reid* factors. Of the remaining factors significant on the facts here, all are strongly indicative of Jackson and Timberlake's independent contractor status. First, it is undisputed that both Jackson and Timberlake were hired for brief, one-time performances during the Halftime Show; CBS could not assign more work to the performers.[a] Second, Jackson and Timberlake selected and hired their own choreographers, backup dancers, and other assistants without any involvement on the part of CBS.

Third, Jackson and Timberlake were compensated by one-time, lump-sum contractual payments and "promotional considerations" rather than by salaries or other similar forms of remittances, without the provision of employee benefits. Fourth, the skill required of a performer hired to sing and dance as the headlining act for the Halftime Show—a performance during a Super Bowl broadcast, as the FCC notes, that attracted nearly 90 million viewers and was the highest-rated show during the 2003–04 television season—is substantial even relative to the job of a general entertainer, which is itself a skilled occupation.

Also weighing heavily in favor of Jackson and Timberlake's status as independent contractors is CBS's assertion in its briefs, which the FCC does not refute, that it paid no employment tax. Had the performers been employees rather than independent contractors, federal law would have required CBS to pay such taxes.

Finally, there is no evidence that Jackson, Timberlake, or CBS considered their contractual relationships to be those of employer-employee. In *Reid*, the Court incorporated the *Restatement*, describing it as "setting forth a nonexhaustive list of factors relevant to determining whether a hired party is an employee" under the common law of agency. Among the factors not explicitly listed in *Reid*, but included in the *Restatement*, is the parties' understanding of their contractual relationship. *See Restatement (Third) of Agency* § 7.07 cmt. f (including as an explicit factor in determining employment status "whether the principal and the agent believe that they are creating an employment relationship"). Although the

---

[a]This factor is accorded great weight under the common law:

> In general, employment contemplates a continuing relationship and a continuing set of duties that the employer and employee owe to each other. Agents who are retained as the need arises and who are not otherwise employees of their principal normally operate their own business enterprises and are not, except in limited respects, integrated into the principal's enterprise so that a task may be completed or a specified objective accomplished. Therefore, *respondeat superior* does not apply.

Restatement (Third) of Agency § 2.04 cmt. b (2006).

Commission did not inquire into this factor, it should have been a significant consideration in this case. Under the FCC's rationale, band members contracted to play a one-song set on a talk show or a "one-show-only" televised concert special presumably would be employees of the broadcaster. These performers—who frequently promote their work through brief contractual relationships with media outlets—would be "employees" of dozens of employers every year. Accordingly, it is doubtful that either the performers here or CBS believed their contracts created employment relationships.

On balance, the relevant factors here weigh heavily in favor of a determination that Jackson and Timberlake were independent contractors rather than employees of CBS. Accordingly, the doctrine of *respondeat superior* does not apply on these facts.

FCC order vacated in favor of CBS.

_____

[Note: A subsequent Supreme Court case vacated this decision on grounds other than the issue presented in this excerpt.]

CYBERLAW IN ACTION

In the "gig" economy, workers fill temporary positions and organizations hire people for short-term work. Gig workers include freelancers, independent contractors, workers hired to complete a particular project, and some temp workers. In the past 10 years, web-based platform businesses—like Uber, Lyft, and DoorDash, among others—have driven significant growth in the gig economy and have raised the profile of gig workers. Yet, many of those workers rely on their work for the platforms for all or significant portions of their income and have long-term working relationships for the platforms. Whether such workers are employees or nonemployee agents has been an important and contested public policy question.

In 2018, the California Supreme Court issued a landmark decision in which it adopted a new test for determining the employee status of workers for purposes of wage and hour issues under California law. *Dynamex Operations West v. Superior Court of Los Angeles,* 4 Cal. 5th 903 (2018). The new standard created a presumption that all workers are employees. The burden of proving otherwise falls on the entity that wants to claim a worker is a nonemployee agent, using the so-called ABC test. Under the ABC test, an entity must prove that the worker meets each of the following three conditions to show the worker is an independent contractor, rather than an employee:

(A) that the worker is free from the control and direction of the hiring entity in connection with the performance of the work, both under the contract for the performance of the work and in fact; *and*

(B) that the worker performs work that is outside the usual course of the hiring entity's business; *and*

(C) that the worker is customarily engaged in an independently established trade, occupation, or business of the same nature as the work performed.

Contrast this approach with that of the common law *Reid* factors described in the preceding *CBS Corp.* case.

In 2019, the California State Legislature passed Assembly Bill 5 (AB5), which codified and expanded the application of the *Dynamex* opinion and the ABC test. The governor signed AB5 into law in September 2018, and it went into effect on January 1, 2020.

After passage, platforms like Uber and Lyft indicated that they would not reclassify their drivers as employees, and they, along with other platforms like DoorDash, pledged millions of dollars to a campaign to pass a 2020 ballot initiative to reverse AB5. In August 2020, as this edition was going to press, a California Superior Court judge ruled, in a case titled *People v. Uber Technologies, Inc.,* that Uber and Lyft were required to reclassify their drivers as employees, which prompted the companies to threaten to pull out of California. An appeals court, however, granted a stay of the superior court's order, allowing the companies to continue treating drivers as nonemployee agents while they appeal.

Duties of Agent to Principal

 LO35-3 Recognize when an agent risks breaching a fiduciary duty.

An agent has a **fiduciary duty** to act loyally for the principal's benefit in all matters connected with the agency relationship. This duty supplements the duties created by an agency contract. A fiduciary duty exists because agency is a relationship of trust and confidence. The principal's many remedies

for an agent's breach of her fiduciary duty include termination of the agency and recovery of damages from the agent.

A gratuitous agent usually has the same fiduciary duty as a paid agent, but need not perform as promised. She normally can terminate the agency without incurring liability. However, a gratuitous agent *is* liable for failing to perform as promised when her promise causes the principal to rely upon her to undertake certain acts, and the principal suffers losses because he refrained from performing those acts himself.

A subagent owes the agent (his principal) all the duties agents owe their principals. A subagent who knows of the original principal's existence also owes that principal all the duties agents owe their principals, except for duties arising solely from the original principal's contract with the agent. Finally, the agent who appointed the subagent generally is liable to the original principal when the principal is harmed by the subagent's conduct.

Agent's Duty of Loyalty

Because agency is a relationship of trust and confidence, an agent has a **duty of loyalty** to his principal. Thus, an agent must subordinate his personal concerns by (1) avoiding conflicts of interest with the principal and (2) not disclosing confidential information received from the principal.

Conflicts of Interest An agent whose interests conflict with the principal's interests may be unable to represent his principal effectively. Therefore, an agent may not *acquire a material benefit* from a third party in connection with an agency transaction. When conducting the principal's business, an agent may **not engage in self-dealing**. For example, an agent authorized to sell property cannot sell that property to herself. Many courts extend the rule to include transactions with the agent's relatives or business associates or with business organizations in which the agent has an interest. However, an agent may engage in self-dealing transactions if the principal consents. For this consent to be effective, the agent must disclose all relevant facts to the principal prior to self-dealing.

Unless the principal agrees otherwise, an agent also may *not* **compete with the principal** regarding the agency business and not assist the principal's competitors during the pendency of the agency. Thus, an agent employed to purchase specific property may not buy it if the principal desires it. Furthermore, an agent ordinarily may not solicit customers for a planned competing business while still employed by the principal.

Finally, an agent who is authorized to make a certain transaction may **not act on behalf of the other party** to the transaction unless the principal knowingly consents. Thus, one ordinarily may **not act as agent for both parties** to a transaction without first disclosing the double role to, and obtaining the consent of, both principals. Here, the agent must disclose to each principal all the factors reasonably affecting that principal's decision. Occasionally, though, an agent who acts merely as a middleman may serve both parties to a transaction without notifying either. For instance, an agent may simultaneously be employed as a "finder" by a firm seeking suitable businesses to acquire and by a firm looking for prospective buyers, so long as neither principal expects the agent to advise it or negotiate for it.

An agent with a conflict of interest will not breach the duty of loyalty, however, if the agent acts in good faith, discloses to the principal all material facts regarding the conflict of interest, and deals fairly with the principal.

Confidentiality Unless otherwise agreed, an agent may not use or **communicate confidential information** of the principal for the agent's own purpose or that of a third party. Confidential information is the principal's information *entrusted* by the principal to the agent for purposes of the agent carrying out duties of the agency relationship. Confidential information includes facts that are valuable to the principal because they are not widely known or that would harm the principal's business if they became widely known. Examples include the principal's business plans, financial condition, contract bids, technological discoveries, manufacturing methods, customer files, and other trade secrets.

In the absence of an agreement to the contrary, after the agency ends, almost all fiduciary duties terminate. For example, an agent may compete with her principal after termination of the agency. As the following *North Atlantic Instruments, Inc.* case illustrates, however, the duty not to use or disclose confidential information continues after the agency ends. The former agent may, however, utilize general knowledge and skills acquired during the agency.

North Atlantic Instruments, Inc. v. Haber   188 F.3d 38 (2d Cir. 1999)

North Atlantic designs and manufactures electronics equipment utilized in the development and testing of systems used on ships, tanks, and commercial and military aircraft. On August 31, 1994, North Atlantic entered into an Asset Purchase Agreement with a related business, Transmagnetics Inc. (TMI).

At the time North Atlantic acquired TMI, Haber was a one-third owner of TMI, its president, and the head of sales—a position that allowed him to develop extensive client contacts. Shortly after the acquisition, on November 7, 1994, North Atlantic entered into an employment agreement (the Employment Agreement) with Haber. The Employment Agreement acknowledged that North Atlantic "is engaged in specialized businesses . . . and the information, research and marketing data developed by [North Atlantic] or any affiliate are confidential." In it, Haber expressly agreed

to keep secret and retain in the strictest confidence all confidential matters which relate to [North Atlantic], including, without limitation, customer lists, trade secrets, pricing policies and other confidential business affairs of [North Atlantic] . . . and any affiliate . . . and not to disclose any such confidential matter to anyone outside [North Atlantic] or any affiliate. . . .

The terms of this provision applied both "during and after his period of service with [North Atlantic]," and the agreement required that Haber turn over, upon his termination, all documents and property of North Atlantic that contained any confidential information. Haber acknowledged in the Employment Agreement that an injunction would be a permissible remedy for a material breach of the confidentiality provision because such a breach would cause "irreparable injury to [North Atlantic] and . . . money damages [would] not provide an adequate remedy to [North Atlantic]."

While Haber worked at North Atlantic, he had access to information about North Atlantic's technology and customer base, including lists of customers and contacts with their individual product needs. In July 1997, Haber left North Atlantic to join Apex Signal Corp., a company that manufactures products targeting the same niche market as North Atlantic's TMI division.

As soon as Haber left North Atlantic and began work for Apex, he began calling the client contacts he had used and developed while at North Atlantic and TMI and asking that they leave North Atlantic to do business with Apex. Indeed, Apex hired Haber specifically because his years in the business and the contacts that he had developed over those years would assist Apex in marketing its product.

North Atlantic filed its complaint on November 6, 1997, asserting that Haber and Apex misappropriated confidential business information and misused trade secrets. Also on November 6, 1997, North Atlantic moved for a temporary restraining order and preliminary injunction, seeking to enjoin Haber and Apex from misappropriating or disclosing any confidential proprietary information relating to North Atlantic's business and soliciting any customers of North Atlantic.

After a series of hearings in December 1997, the magistrate judge recommended granting the preliminary injunction in most respects and issued a Report and Recommendation to that effect on March 27, 1998. Both parties filed objections to the Report and Recommendation, and Haber and Apex filed a motion to dismiss the complaint. The district court adopted the Report and Recommendation in all material respects and denied the motion to dismiss the complaint.

Haber and Apex appealed the portion of the district court's order forbidding Haber and Apex from soliciting the contacts Haber developed while at North Atlantic and TMI. In response to Haber and Apex's appeal, the court considered North Atlantic's likelihood of success on the merits and whether it would suffer irreparable harm in the absence of an injunction.

Straub, Circuit Judge

Both this Circuit and numerous New York courts have held "that an agent has a duty 'not to use confidential knowledge acquired in his employment in competition with his principal.'" *ABKCO Music Inc. v. Harrisongs Music, Ltd.*, 722 F.2d 988, 994 (2d Cir. 1983) (quoting *Byrne v. Barrett*, 268 N.Y. 199, 206, 197 N.E. 217, 218 (1935)). Such a duty "exists as well after the employment is terminated as during its continuance." *Id.* (internal quotation marks omitted); *accord L.M. Rabinowitz & Co. v. Dasher*, 82 N.Y.S.2d 431, 435 (Sup. Ct. 1948) ("It is implied in every contract of employment that the employee will hold sacred any trade secrets or other confidential information which he acquires in the course of his employment. This is a duty that the employee assumes not only during his employment but after its termination.") (internal citations omitted).

Haber's Employment Agreement requires that he "keep secret and retain in the strictest confidence all confidential matters which relate to [North Atlantic], including, without limitation, customer lists, trade secrets, pricing policies and other confidential business affairs of [North Atlantic] . . . and any affiliate." The agreement also prohibits him from "disclos[ing] any such confidential matter to anyone." The Employment Agreement contains no limitation on its duration; rather it applies both "during [and] after his period of service with [North Atlantic]." In this way, it makes explicit an employee's implied duties under New York law with respect to confidential information.

Based upon the facts in the record, it is clear that Haber violated the duties imposed both by the Employment Agreement and by New York's laws. That is, the requirement that he "keep and retain [customer lists and trade secrets] in the strictest confidence" by its very terms precludes his using that confidential information for the benefit of a competitor business. Furthermore, common sense dictates the conclusion that the customer lists to which the Employment Agreement refers must encompass the list of client contacts at issue on this appeal.

Thus, the Employment Agreement reinforces Haber's duty under New York law not to use his former employer's trade secrets against the employer. Accordingly, we affirm on this point and therefore affirm the District Court's determination that North Atlantic has demonstrated a sufficient likelihood of success on the merits of its misappropriation of trade secrets claim.

Finally, we conclude that North Atlantic has shown that it will suffer irreparable harm in the absence of an injunction. We have held that "loss of trade secrets cannot be measured in money damages" because "[a] trade secret once lost is, of course, lost forever." *FMC Corp. v. Taiwan Tainan Giant Indus. Co.*, 730 F.2d 61, 63 (2d Cir. 1984) (per curiam). In addition, Haber acknowledged in his Employment Agreement that a breach of the confidentiality clause would cause "irreparable injury" to North Atlantic. *Cf. Ticor Title Ins. Co. v. Cohen*, 173 F.3d 63, 69 (2d Cir. 1999) (relying on a similar clause in determining irreparable injury for purposes of upholding a grant of injunctive relief).

Because North Atlantic has demonstrated a likelihood of success on the merits and because it would suffer irreparable harm in the absence of an injunction, we conclude that the District Court did not exceed its allowable discretion in granting a preliminary injunction.

Judgment in favor of North Atlantic affirmed.

Agent's Duty to Obey Instructions

Because an agent acts under the principal's control and for the principal's benefit, the agent has a duty to *act within the actual authority* granted by the principal and to obey the principal's reasonable instructions for carrying out the agency business.

There are exceptions to the duty to obey instructions. A gratuitous agent need not obey the principal's order to continue to act as an agent. Also, agents generally have no duty to obey orders to behave illegally or unethically. Thus, a sales agent need not follow directions to misrepresent the quality of the principal's goods, and professionals such as attorneys and accountants are not obligated to obey directions that conflict with the ethical rules of their professions.

Usually a principal's instructions are clear and can be easily followed. Sometimes, however, the instructions are ambiguous. For example, an instruction may have terms an agent does not understand. Or perhaps a cell phone conversation may be garbled due to poor signal strength. When a principal's instructions are unclear, the agent has a duty to communicate with the principal to clarify the instructions.

Agent's Duty to Act with Care and Skill

A paid agent must *act with the care, competence, and diligence* normally exercised by agents in similar circumstances. Paid agents who represent that they possess a higher than customary level of skill may be held to a correspondingly higher standard of performance. Similarly, an agent's duty may change if the principal and the agent agree that the agent must possess and exercise greater or lesser than customary care and skill.

Agent's Duty to Provide Information

An agent must use reasonable efforts to provide the principal with facts the agent knows, or has reason to know, when the agent knows or should know the principal wants the facts or the facts are material to the agency. The basis for the duty to notify is the principal's interest in being informed of matters that are important to the agency business.

However, the agent has no duty to notify when the agent owes a superior duty to another person. For example, a consultant may acquire confidential information from a client and thus be obligated not to disclose it to a second client. If the consultant cannot properly represent the second client without revealing this information, the agent should refuse to represent that client.

Agent's Duties of Segregation, Record-Keeping, and Accounting

An agent's cannot deal with the principal's property so that it appears to be the agent's, nor mingle the principal's property with the agent's property or anyone else's. The agent must keep accounts of the principal's money and other property, as well as accurate records and accounts of all transactions, and disclose such records to the principal once the principal makes a reasonable demand for them. Also, an agent who obtains or holds property for the principal usually may not commingle that property with the agent's property. For example, an agent ordinarily cannot deposit the principal's funds in her own name or in her own bank account.

Duty Not to Receive a Material Benefit

Other than receiving the compensation the principal gives the agent for acting as agent, an agent should not profit or receive any other benefit from acting on behalf of the principal. Improper material benefits include bribes, kickbacks, and gifts from parties with whom the agent deals on the principal's behalf. However, the principal and the agent may agree that the agent can retain certain benefits received during the agency. The Starbucks Standards of Business Conduct in the nearby Ethics and Compliance in Action box is such an example. Courts may also infer such an agreement when it is customary for agents to retain tips or accept entertainment while doing the principal's business.

Duty of Good Conduct

The *Restatement (Third)* also includes a general duty that agents act reasonably and refrain from conduct that is likely to damage the principal's enterprise. While the scope of this general duty is not entirely clear, it encompasses, for example, an employee's duty not to damage the employer's computer system by exposing the system to harmful computer viruses while visiting unauthorized websites. It could also cover an agent who makes offensive statements to customers, resulting in the principal's loss of business.

Ordinarily, if a principal suffers no monetary damages from the agent's breach of duty, it is not entitled to any recovery from the agent, although termination of the agency may be justified.

Duties of Principal to Agent

If an agency is formed by a written contract, the contract normally states the duties the principal owes the agent. In addition, the law implies certain duties from the existence of an agency relationship, however formed. The most important of these duties are the principal's obligations to *compensate* the agent, to *reimburse* the agent for money spent in the principal's service, and to *indemnify* the agent

Ethics and Compliance in Action

Corporations give special attention to rooting out conflicts of interests that result from kickbacks, bribes, and gifts to the corporations' employees. To ensure independence of auditors, auditing firms commonly have rules banning their audit staff from receiving anything of value from clients. In other contexts, most corporations permit their employees to receive items or services of nominal value only. Most firms have detailed rules, such as the following from Starbucks Corporation's Standards of Business Conduct:

Gifts and Entertainment

A gift or favor should not be accepted or given if it might create a sense of obligation, compromise your professional judgment, or create the appearance of doing so. In deciding whether a gift is appropriate, you should consider its value and whether public disclosure of the gift would embarrass you or Starbucks.

A gift of money should never be given or accepted. (Some retail partners, however, may accept customary tips for service well done.) As a general rule, partners should limit gifts to or from any one vendor or business associate to US $75 per year. A gift of nominal value may be given or accepted if it is a common business courtesy, such as coffee samples, a coffee cup, pens, or a similar token.

However, during traditional gift-giving seasons in areas where it is customary to exchange gifts of money, such as China, Japan, Malaysia, Singapore, and Thailand, partners should not solicit but may exchange cash with nongovernmental business associates in nominal amounts up to the equivalent of US $20.

Trading items of value with other businesses, including shops and restaurants, is strictly prohibited.

You may not encourage or solicit meals or entertainment from anyone with whom Starbucks does business or from anyone who desires to do business with Starbucks. Giving or accepting valuable gifts or entertainment might be construed as an improper attempt to influence the relationship.

---

for losses suffered in conducting the principal's business. These duties generally can be eliminated or modified by agreement between the parties.

Duty to Compensate Agent

If the agency contract states the compensation the agent is to receive, it usually controls questions about the agent's pay. In other cases, the relationship of the parties and the surrounding circumstances determine whether and in what amount the agent is to be compensated. Where compensation is due but its amount is not expressly stated, the amount is the market price or the customary price for the agent's services or, if neither is available, their reasonable value.

Sometimes, an agent's compensation depends on the accomplishment of a specific result. For instance, an investment banker may be retained on a contingent fee basis to find a buyer for its client's product line and be compensated with a percentage of the purchase price. In such cases, the agent is not entitled to compensation unless he achieves the result within the time stated or, if no time is stated, within a reasonable time. This is true no matter how much effort or money the agent expends. However, the principal must cooperate with the agent in achieving the result and must not do anything to frustrate the agent's efforts. Otherwise, the agent is entitled to compensation despite the failure to perform as specified.

A principal generally is not required to pay for undertakings that she did not request, services to which she did not consent, and tasks that typically are undertaken without pay. Also, a principal usually need not compensate an agent who has materially breached the agency contract or has committed a serious breach of a fiduciary duty. Of course, there is no duty to compensate a gratuitous agent.

An agent's duties to a subagent are the same as a principal's duties to an agent. If there is no agreement to the contrary, however, the original principal has no contractual liability to a subagent. For example, such a principal normally is not obligated to compensate a subagent. But a principal must reimburse and indemnify subagents as he would agents.

Duties of Reimbursement and Indemnity

If an agent makes expressly or impliedly authorized expenditures while acting on the principal's behalf, the agent normally is entitled to *reimbursement* for those expenditures. Unless otherwise agreed, for example, an agent requested to make overnight trips as part of his agency duties can recover reasonable transportation and hotel expenses.

A principal's duty of reimbursement overlaps with her duty of *indemnity*. Agency law implies a promise by the principal to indemnify an agent for losses that should fairly be borne by the principal. These include authorized payments made on the principal's behalf and payments on contracts on which the agent was authorized to become liable. A principal may also have to indemnify an agent if the agent's authorized acts constitute a breach of contract or a tort for which the agent is required to pay damages to a third party.

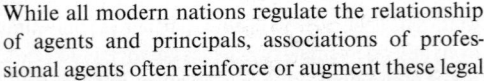

The Global Business Environment

While all modern nations regulate the relationship of agents and principals, associations of professional agents often reinforce or augment these legal duties with codes of ethics. For the real estate industry, you can find international principles of conduct for real estate agents in the 23 member countries of the International Consortium of Real Estate Associations. An excerpt from the International Principles of Conduct is below. Note how the listed rules relate to the agent's fiduciary duties we have studied.

1. Protect and promote your client's interests, and be honest with all parties.
2. Do not reveal facts that are confidential without permission from the rightful party.
3. Follow the applicable laws of representation, and disclose your legal and/or fiduciary relationship to all involved parties.
4. Respect your fellow professionals. Do not unfairly publicly discredit a competitor. Cooperate with other professionals when in the best interest of your client.
5. Agree to participate in known and organizationally supported dispute resolution systems in instances of conflict between members and/or the public.
6. Do not misrepresent yourself, or misrepresent or conceal pertinent facts regarding a property or transaction.
7. Disclose any personal interests in a transaction and avoid side deals without the informed consent of your client.
8. Provide professional service to all clients and customers.
9. Be knowledgeable and competent in the fields of practice in which you engage; seek expert assistance when providing services in a field in which you are unfamiliar.
10. Apply national codes of conduct to all relevant business relations and transactions, including those conducted in the international arena.

So long as the principal did not benefit from such behavior, however, he is *not* required to indemnify an agent for losses resulting (1) from unauthorized acts or (2) solely from the agent's negligence or other fault. Even where the principal directed the agent to commit a tortious act, moreover, there is no duty to indemnify if the agent knew the act was tortious. But the principal must indemnify the agent for tort damages resulting from authorized conduct that the agent did not believe was tortious. For example, if a principal directs his agent to repossess goods located on another's property and the agent, believing her acts legal, becomes liable for conversion or trespass, the principal must indemnify the agent for the damages the agent pays.

Termination of an Agency

LO35-4 Describe the way agency relationships are terminated.

An agency can terminate in many ways that fall under two general headings: (1) termination by act of the parties and (2) termination by operation of law.

Termination by Act of the Parties
Termination by act of the principal and/or agent occurs:

1. *At a time or upon the happening of an event stated in the agreement.* If no such time or event is stated, the agency terminates after a reasonable time.

2. *When a specified result has been accomplished, if the agency was created to accomplish a specified result.* For example, if an agency's only objective is to sell certain property, the agency terminates when the property is sold.

3. *By mutual agreement of the principal and the agent*, at any time.

4. *At the option of either party.* This is called **revocation** when done by the principal and **renunciation** when done by the agent. Revocation or renunciation occurs when either party manifests to the other a desire for the agency to end. This includes conduct inconsistent with the agency's continuance. For example, an agent may learn that the principal has hired another agent to perform the same job.

A party can revoke or renounce even if doing so violates the agency agreement. Although either party has the *power* to terminate in such cases, there is no *right* to do so. If either the agent or principal terminates the agency in violation of the agreement, that party need not continue to perform but also may be liable for damages to the other party. A gratuitous agency normally is terminable by either party without liability. Also, the terminating party is not liable when the revocation or renunciation is justified by the other party's serious breach of a fiduciary duty.

Termination by Operation of Law
Termination by operation of law usually involves situations where it is reasonable to believe that the principal would not wish the agent to act further, or where accomplishment of the

agency objectives has become impossible or illegal. Although courts may recognize exceptions in certain cases, an agency relationship usually is terminated by:

1. *The death of an individual principal.* Under the *Restatement (Third) of Agency,* this termination is effective only when the agent has notice of the principal's death.

2. *The death of an individual agent.*

3. *The principal's permanent loss of capacity.* This is a *permanent* loss of capacity occurring after creation of the agency—most often, due to the principal's loss of mental capacity. The principal's permanent incapacity ends the agency even without notice to the agent.

4. *The cessation of existence or suspension of power* of an agent or principal that is not an individual, such as the dissolution of a corporation or partnership.

5. *Upon the occurrence of circumstances* from which the agent should reasonably conclude that the *principal no longer would want the agent to take action* for the principal. Changed circumstances include:

- *Changes in the value of the agency property or subject matter* (e.g., a significant decline in the value of land to be sold by an agent).
- *Changes in business conditions* (e.g., a much lower supply and a much increased price for goods to be purchased by an agent).
- *The loss or destruction of the agency property or subject matter or the termination of the principal's interest therein* (e.g., when a house to be sold by a real estate broker burns down or is taken by a mortgage holder to satisfy a debt owed by the principal).

There are other grounds for termination not listed in the *Restatement (Third):*

1. *The agent's loss of capacity to perform the agency business.* The scope of this basis for termination is unclear. As Chapter 36 states, an agent who becomes mentally incompetent or otherwise incapacitated after the agency is formed still can bind the principal to contracts with third parties. Thus, it probably makes little sense to treat the agency as terminated in such cases. As a result, termination under this heading may be limited to such situations as the loss of a license needed to perform agency duties.

2. *Changes in the law that make the agency business illegal* (e.g., when drugs to be sold by an agent are banned by the government).

3. *The principal's bankruptcy*—as to transactions the agent should realize the principal no longer desires.

For example, consider the likely effect of the principal's bankruptcy on an agency to purchase antiques for the principal's home versus its likely effect on an agency to purchase necessities of life for the principal.

4. *The agent's bankruptcy*—where the agent's financial condition affects his ability to serve the principal. This could occur when an agent is employed to purchase goods on his own credit for the principal.

5. *Impossibility of performance by the agent.* This covers various events, some of which fall within the categories just stated, for example, (*a*) destruction of the agency subject matter, (*b*) termination of the principal's interest in the agency subject matter (as, for example, by the principal's bankruptcy), and (*c*) changes in the law or in other circumstances that make it impossible for the agent to accomplish the agency's aims. Consider that some agency relationships may have terminated in this way in the wake of the 2020 coronavirus pandemic.

6. *A serious breach of the agent's duty of loyalty.*

7. *The outbreak of war*—when this leads the agent to the reasonable belief that his services are no longer desired. An example might be the outbreak of war between the principal's country and the agent's country.

Termination of Agency Powers Given as Security

An agency power given as security for a duty owed by the principal is an exception to some of the termination rules just discussed. An important subset of an agency power given as a security is an agency coupled with an interest. Here, the agent has an interest in the subject matter of the agency that is distinct from the principal's interest and that is not exercised for the principal's benefit. This interest exists to benefit the agent or a third person by securing performance of an obligation owed by the principal.

A common example is a **power of sale**, a secured loan agreement authorizing a lender (the agent) to sell property used as security if the borrower (the principal) defaults. For instance, suppose that Allen lends Peters $500,000 and Peters gives Allen a lien or security interest on Peters's land to secure the loan. The agreement might authorize Allen to act as Peters's "agent" to sell the land if Peters fails to repay the loan.

Because the power given the "agent" in such cases is not for the principal's benefit, it sometimes is said that a power given as a security or an agency coupled with an interest is not truly an agency. In any event, courts distinguish it from genuine agency relations in which the agent is compensated from the profits or proceeds of property held for the principal's benefit. For example, if an agent is promised a commission for selling the principal's property, the relationship is not a power given as a security or an agency coupled with an interest. Here, the power exercised by the agent (selling the principal's property) benefits the principal.

Why is a power given as a security or agency coupled with an interest important? The main reason is that it is not terminated by (1) the principal's revocation, (2) the principal's or the agent's loss of capacity, (3) the agent's death, and (4) the principal's death. However, unless it is held for the benefit of a third party, the agent can voluntarily surrender it. Of course, it terminates when the principal performs her obligation.

Effect of Termination on Agent's Authority

Sometimes, former agents continue to act on their ex-principals' behalf even though the agency has ended. Once an agency terminates by any of the means just described, the agent's *actual authority* (expressed and implied) ends as well. Nonetheless, such "ex-agents" may retain *apparent authority* to bind their former principals.

Third parties who are unaware of the termination may reasonably believe that an ex-agent still has authority. To protect third parties who rely on such a reasonable appearance of authority, an agent's *apparent authority* often persists after termination. Thus, a former agent may be able to bind the principal due to apparent authority even though the agency has ended.

Notice to Third Parties Apparent authority ends only when the third party receives appropriate notice of the termination, that is, when it is no longer reasonable for a third party to believe that the agent has actual authority. Some bases for termination by operation of law (such as changed circumstances) may provide such notice.

Under the *Restatement (Third) of Agency*, an agent's apparent authority may continue even after the principal's death or loss of capacity. An agent may act with apparent authority following the principal's death or loss of capacity because the basis of apparent authority is a principal's manifestation to third parties, coupled with a third party's reasonable belief that the agent acts with actual authority. When third parties do not have notice that the principal has died or lost capacity, they may reasonably believe the agent to be authorized. The rule that the principal's death does not automatically terminate apparent authority is consistent with the interest of protecting third parties who act without knowledge of the principal's death or loss of capacity.

To protect themselves against unwanted liability, however, prudent principals will want to notify third parties that the agency has terminated and that the agent no longer acts on the principal's behalf. The required type of notification varies with the third party in question.

1. *For third parties who have previously dealt with the agent or who have begun to deal with the agent,* **actual notification** is necessary. This can be accomplished by (1) a direct personal statement to the third party or (2) a writing delivered to the third party personally, to the third party's place of business, or to some other place reasonably believed to be appropriate.

2. *For all other parties,* **constructive notification** suffices. Usually, these other parties are aware of the agency but did no business with the agent. Constructive notification normally can be accomplished by advertising the agency's termination in a newspaper of general circulation in the place where the agency business regularly was carried on. If no suitable publication exists, notification by other means reasonably likely to inform third parties—for example, posting a notice in public places or on a website—may be enough.

In the next case, a summer camp counselor's actual authority terminated when the summer season ended. His apparent authority ceased when a camper learned that he had finished his stint at the camp. For that and other reasons, the camp that previously employed the counselor was not liable for his assault of the camper.

Gniadek v. Camp Sunshine at Sebago Lake, Inc.
11 A.3d 308 (Me. 2011)

Camp Sunshine at Sebago Lake Inc. is a nonprofit corporation providing a traditional summer camp experience in Maine for children with chronic or life-threatening illnesses. To attend a session, children must be accompanied by a parent or guardian who lodges with them. Katie Gniadek, who was 17 years old at the time, attended the camp with her mother, Kimberly Cooper-Morin. Gniadek had been attending Camp Sunshine annually for four years. During their week at the camp in 2005, Gniadek and Cooper-Morin met Michael Newton, a first-year volunteer counselor. Newton was 58 years old. On Gniadek's last day of camp, Newton gave her a card and gift and asked if they could stay in touch. Gniadek agreed, and Newton gave her his contact information. Gniadek, Cooper-Morin, and Newton also obtained copies of the contact lists for that week compiled by the camp, which recorded the name, address, and phone number of the counselors and parents in attendance. The camp had begun assembling these lists at the request of campers' families. Inclusion on the list was voluntary for parents. Cooper-Morin's contact information was on the parent-camper list.

After leaving Camp Sunshine on September 9, Gniadek had no contact with Newton until November 23, when he called to invite her to go with him to New York to visit a family who had attended camp. During their call, Gniadek learned that Newton had finished volunteering at Camp Sunshine for 2005. Gniadek obtained her mother's permission and agreed to go on the trip. Camp Sunshine had no knowledge of these plans. On November 25 around 6:00 P.M., Newton picked up Gniadek, and they left for New York. Gniadek and Cooper-Morin believed that there were two possible places where Gniadek and Newton would be staying that night, and both were the homes of former Camp Sunshine volunteers in New York. However, neither Gniadek nor Cooper-Morin had contacted these volunteers about this trip. Instead of staying with other volunteers, Gniadek and Newton stopped at a Connecticut motel. During the night, Newton assaulted Gniadek.

Newton was charged with assault and consented to a charge of assault in the third degree in the Connecticut Superior Court. He was sentenced to five years in jail.

Camp Sunshine was not operating or sponsoring any sessions in Maine on November 25–26, 2005, and at that point, Gniadek had not yet applied to attend Camp Sunshine in 2006. The camp had received Newton's 2006 volunteer application but had not acted on it. After learning about the assault, the camp sent Newton a letter informing him that his volunteer services were no longer needed at Camp Sunshine. The letter also instructed him not to "solicit, recruit, speak on behalf of, or represent Camp Sunshine."

In 2008, Gniadek sued Camp Sunshine alleging, among other grounds, vicarious liability of Camp Sunshine for the acts of Newton. At the close of discovery, the trial court granted the camp's motion for summary judgment, finding that Newton was not Camp Sunshine's agent at the time of the assault. Gniadek appealed to the Supreme Judicial Court of Connecticut.

Jabar, Judge

Gniadek contends that Newton committed his tort under the apparent authority of the Camp.

Apparent authority is authority which, though not actually granted, the principal knowingly permits the agent to exercise or which he holds him out as possessing. Apparent authority exists only when the conduct of the principal leads a third party to believe that a given party is its agent. Termination of actual authority will not alone end the apparent authority held by an agent. *Restatement (Third) of Agency* § 3.11(1) (2006). Instead, apparent authority ceases when it becomes unreasonable for the third party to believe that the agent continues to act with actual authority. *Id.* § 3.11(2).

The *Restatement (Third) of Agency* § 7.08 specifically addresses tortious liability for acts of agents cloaked with apparent authority. That section states:

A principal is subject to vicarious liability for a tort committed by an agent in dealing or communicating with a third party on or purportedly on behalf of the principal when actions taken by the agent with apparent authority constitute the tort or enable the agent to conceal its commission.

The commentary explains that section 7.08 applies to torts such as "fraudulent and negligent misrepresentation, defamation, tortious institution of legal proceedings, and conversion of property obtained by an agent purportedly at the principal's direction." *Id.* § 7.08 comment a. In the commission of these torts,

there must be a "close link between an agent's tortious conduct and the agent's apparent authority" in order for the principal to be liable. *Id.* § 7.08 comment b. "Thus, a principal is not subject to liability when actions that an agent takes with apparent authority, although connected in some way to the agent's tortious conduct, do not themselves constitute the tort or enable the agent to mask its commission."

Our interpretation of a predecessor to section 7.08 recognized similar limitations. In *Mahar v. StoneWood Transport*, we interpreted the *Restatement (Second) of Agency* § 219(2)(d) (1958) as "limited in its application to cases within the apparent authority of the employee, or when the employee's conduct involves misrepresentation or deceit." 823 A.2d 540, 546 (Me. 2003). Although we had not "expressly adopted" that section, we nonetheless explained that it would not encompass assaultive and threatening conduct by an employee who did not purport to act on his employer's behalf.

Here, when Newton invited Gniadek to accompany him on a trip to New York, he told her that he had finished with Camp. By this statement, he conveyed that he was no longer acting with the actual authority of Camp Sunshine. Even assuming that after learning this, it would still be reasonable for Gniadek to believe that Newton acted on behalf of Camp Sunshine, the assault was not committed with apparent authority. Newton's conduct does not fall within the scope of section 7.08.

Judgment for Camp Sunshine affirmed.

Problems and Problem Cases

1. When Del-Mar Development Corp. failed to pay real estate taxes on an office building it owned, the building was seized by tax authorities and sold to pay the taxes. The purchaser was Euclid Plaza Associates. The sale was not valid, however, until approved by a court. After the sale and before the court's approval of the sale, Del-Mar agreed to a three-year lease of the building with African American Law Firm (AALF), which immediately began paying rent of $1,500 per month to Del-Mar. After the court approved the sale, Euclid claimed it was not bound by the lease made by Del-Mar with AALF. Euclid wanted to evict AALF unless it paid $2,033 in monthly rent. Was Del-Mar acting as Euclid's agent within Del-Mar's actual and apparent authority when Del-Mar leased the building to AALF?

2. Albert Arillotta, acting for Interstate Demolition and Environmental Corp. (IDEC), sent an e-mail to CSX Transportation, a railroad company, stating an interest in buying rail cars as scrap. Arillotta represented himself to be "from interstate demolition and recovery express." The e-mail address from which Arillotta sent this inquiry was "albert@recoveryexpress.com." The domain name of the e-mail address was assigned to Recovery Express. Arillotta did not work for Recovery Express, but he was allowed to use its offices and e-mail because he had been involved in another venture with it. CSX agreed to sell rail cars to IDEC, and they were delivered to the location specified by Arillotta. Neither Arillotta nor IDEC paid for the rail cars. CSX sued Recovery Express to recover the price of the rail cars. Did the court hold Recovery Express liable to CSX on the grounds that Arillotta had apparent authority to transact for Recovery Express?

3. Julianne Eisenberg was hired by Advance Relocation & Storage, a Danbury, Connecticut, warehouse. When she was hired, Advance did not inquire into any special skills that Eisenberg may have had, and it did not ask about her prior work experiences. Eisenberg and her coworkers were responsible for loading and unloading furniture from trucks at the Advance warehouse and customers' residences. They were paid on an hourly basis and were required to punch in and out. Eisenberg and her coworkers were occasionally sent home early if there was little to do, and they were sometimes asked to work on the weekend. At the warehouse, Advance gave Eisenberg orders, telling her where to go and what to do. At job sites, an Advance representative told the crew what objects each crew member, including

Eisenberg, was to move. Eisenberg claimed that when she worked at Advance, she was sexually harassed and subjected to a hostile work environment, in violation of the Civil Rights Act of 1964. Advance argued that she was not an employee under the act, and therefore, she could not invoke its protections. Was Eisenberg an Advance employee?

4. Merrill Lynch, the investment firm, hired Elliot Jarvin as director of wealth management services. His duties included managing a team of 10 wealth managers who advised Merrill Lynch clients regarding their investment portfolios. When Jarvin joined Merrill Lynch, he brought with him 15 very wealthy clients to whom he provided investment services on behalf of Merrill Lynch. Unknown to Merrill Lynch, Jarvin had five additional clients, the five wealthiest of his clients. Jarvin continued to advise these clients on his own, retaining for himself all fees he charged for services provided to the five clients. In addition, to help him service the five personal clients, two members of his Merrill Lynch wealth management team frequently met with Jarvin's five personal clients to create investments plans for them. Has Jarvin breached a fiduciary duty owed to Merrill Lynch?

5. Catherine Creteau and her husband contracted with a travel agency, Liberty Travel, to arrange a trip to Jamaica. While staying in Jamaica in accommodations arranged by Liberty Travel, they were robbed at gunpoint. The Creteaus alleged that Liberty Travel either knew of safety issues with the accommodations or such information was available to Liberty Travel. What duty did the Creteaus allege their agent had breached?

6. When Perry Olsen died, his children placed his ranch in Vail, Colorado, up for sale. Perry's children retained Vail Associates Real Estate, a real estate broker, to sell the land for them. Vail Associates introduced the children to Magnus Lindholm, who wanted to buy Perry's ranch along with adjacent land owned by Perry's children. The children eventually decided to sell only Perry's ranch and not the children's land. Their asking price for Perry's ranch was $400 per acre. Before committing to buying Perry's ranch (because he needed more land), Lindholm asked Vail Associates to introduce him to Del Rickstrew, whose land also abutted Perry's ranch. Rickstrew refused to negotiate the sale through a real estate agent, so Lindholm negotiated directly with Rickstrew. Vail Associates did, however, introduce Rickstrew to Lindholm and provide a model contract to Lindholm. A month later, Lindholm agreed to buy Rickstrew's land for

$6,000 per acre, subject to his buying Perry's ranch also. Vail Associates was not aware that Lindholm and Rickstrew had a contract or that the price was $6,000 per acre. Two months later, with Vail Associates's assistance, the children sold Perry's ranch to Lindholm for $400 per acre. Vail Associates received a commission from the sale. When the children discovered later that Rickstrew received 15 times as much for his acreage as did they for Perry's ranch, they sued Vail Associates for failing to disclose material information—that is, that Lindholm was negotiating with Rickstrew. Did Vail Associates breach a fiduciary duty?

7. When Nitrogen Media was acquired by General Electric's NBC Universal unit, Nitrogen's vice president of finance, Babs Grogan, was terminated as a Nitrogen employee but hired by NBCU as an outside consultant. The term of Grogan's contract was three months, and her engagement with NBCU required her to assess business opportunities presented to NBCU, such as the financial value of newly created television shows. Grogan represented to NBCU that she had an MBA degree in finance and six years of experience in financial analysis. In fact, Grogan had falsified her academic record and possessed only an undergraduate degree in political science. In addition, she had no experience as a financial analyst, having delegated such work to coworkers for the past six years, although she took credit for their work. When NBCU asked Grogan to value the new TV show *Car Shop*, she delegated the task in part to a new MBA graduate, Roger Harvey, who was recently hired by NBCU and had virtually no on-the-job experience. As a result, Grogan and Harvey failed to perform a reasonable investigation into the facts regarding the TV show's value and to use appropriate valuations tools. Did Grogan and Harvey breach their fiduciary duty?

8. Mui Luu and Cu Tu Nguyen sold their Vietnamese calendar business to Con Tu. Luu and Nguyen agreed to continue to work for Con Tu for four years as managing agents of the business. During the time they were managing agents, Luu sent an e-mail to a competing calendar company that included 1,000 names and addresses, approximately 90 percent being names and addresses of Con Tu's customers. The competing business was controlled by Luu and Nguyen. Have Luu and Nguyen breached a fiduciary duty?

9. The song "He's So Fine" is a huge hit in the United States and Great Britain. Bright Tunes Music Corporation is the copyright holder of "He's So fine" and sues ex-Beatle George Harrison and Harrisongs Music in federal court, alleging that the Harrison composition

"My Sweet Lord" infringed its copyright to "He's So Fine." Harrison's business affairs are handled by ABKCO Music and Allen Klein, ABKCO's president. Shortly after suit begins, Klein unsuccessfully tries to settle by having Harrison purchase Bright Tunes. Shortly thereafter, Bright Tunes goes into receivership, and the suit does not resume until years later. At this time, coincidentally, ABKCO's management contract with Harrison has expired; however, Klein continues his efforts to have ABKCO purchase Big Tunes. As part of these efforts, Klein gives Bright Tunes three schedules summarizing Harrison's royalty income from "My Sweet Lord," information he possessed because of his previous service to Harrison. Meanwhile Harrison's attorneys are eagerly trying to settle the copyright infringement suit with Bright Tunes, and Klein's activities of giving Bright Tunes information about the economic potential of its suit may have impeded Harrison's efforts to settle. Ultimately, Bright Tunes chooses not to settle with Harrison and at trial the court finds that Harrison has infringed on Bright Tunes's copyright. A damages hearing is set for a later date. By the time of the damages hearing, ABKCO had purchased the "He's So Fine" copyright and all rights to the infringement suit from Bright Tunes, making ABKCO the new plaintiff in the trial for damages on the suit. At trial, Harrison files a counterclaim for damages resulting from Klein and ABKCO's alleged breaches of the duty of loyalty to him. Will the court find that Klein and ABKCO breached its duty of loyalty to Harrison?

10. On March 2, Bankers Life & Casualty Co. proposed in a letter addressed to Gaston Trepanier that he accept a lump-sum settlement of $20,000 in exchange for Bankers Life's release from a disability income policy that paid Trepanier a $400-a-month benefit as long as he lived. The letter stated that should Mr. Trepanier decide "to accept our offer," he could "jot a note at the bottom of this letter and return it." Mrs. Trepanier discussed the idea with her husband, who decided to accept the offer and directed her to write a note on the bottom of the March letter as directed. She did so on April 6 and placed the letter in an envelope, intending to send it the following day. On April 7, Mr. Trepanier was hospitalized and the letter was not mailed. Mr. Trepanier fell into a coma on April 8. On April 12, Mrs. Trepanier tried to accept the offer by mailing the letter to Bankers Life. On April 14, Mr. Trepanier died. Bankers Life subsequently revoked its offer and issued a final disability payment. Was a contract formed when Mrs. Trepanier accepted the $20,000 offer on her husband's behalf?

Third-Party Relations
of the Principal
and the Agent

You are vice president of acquisitions for a medium-sized consumer food products company, Bon Vivant Foods Inc. The company's board of directors has given you authority to negotiate acquisitions of consumer food brands on behalf of Bon Vivant. The board has told you in written and oral instructions that you have the power to acquire any consumer products brand if the acquisition price is not greater than $30,000,000, which is the authority typically held by most vice presidents of acquisitions for businesses like yours. The board's written instructions also indicate, however, that you have no authority to purchase or negotiate the purchase of a cola drink brand. Others in your position in the consumer food industry typically have authority to purchase a cola drink brand for their companies. The board also tells you that the company wants to buy the Eddie's ice cream brand from its owner, Eddie Ghahraman, at a price not greater than $28,000,000. The board is fearful, however, that if Eddie knows the company wants to buy the Eddie's ice cream brand, he will demand a higher price. The board tells you, therefore, not to disclose to Eddie that you are buying for Bon Vivant, and instead to make it appear that you are buying for your own company. It suggests you make up a name for this fictitious company. You decide to use the name LHIW Inc.

Assess the risks to you and Bon Vivant. Consider the following questions:

- If you make a contract in the name of Bon Vivant to buy a snack-cracker brand for $15,000,000, will Bon Vivant be bound on that contract?
- If you make a contract in the name of Bon Vivant to buy a cola brand for $13,500,000, will Bon Vivant be bound on that contract?
- If you make a contract in the name of Bon Vivant to buy an organic canned soup brand for $40,000,000, will Bon Vivant be bound on that contract? Will Bon Vivant be bound on that contract if you present the contract to the board, the board decides to accept the contract, and then the board later rejects the contract as too costly?
- Suppose you make a contract for Bon Vivant to purchase the Eddie's ice cream brand for $26,200,000. The contract is signed by Eddie. You sign LHIW's name and also your own name as agent for LHIW. Who is liable on that contract?

LEARNING OBJECTIVES

After studying this chapter, you should be able to:

36-1 Know when an agent has authority to bind a principal to a contract.

36-2 Understand when an agent may be liable on contracts made for the principal.

36-3 Recognize when an agent is able to make a principal liable for torts committed by the agent.

BY LETTING PRINCIPALS CONTRACT through their agents and thereby multiply their dealings, agency law stimulates business activity. For this process to succeed, there must be rules for determining when the principal and the agent are liable on the agent's contracts. Principals need to predict and control their liability on agreements their agents make. Also, third parties need assurance that such agreements actually bind the principal. Furthermore, both agents and third parties have an interest in knowing when an agent is bound on these contracts. The first half of this chapter discusses the principal's and the agent's contract liability.

While acting on the principal's behalf, agents sometimes harm third parties. Normally, this makes the agent liable to the injured party in tort. Sometimes, moreover, a principal is liable for an agent's torts. Because tort judgments can be expensive, the rules for determining the principal's and the agent's tort liability are of great concern to principals, their agents, and third parties. Thus, we examine these subjects in this chapter's second half.

The law in this chapter, as in Chapter 35, reflects the rules of the *Restatement (Third) of Agency*. The *Restatement (Third)* was adopted by the American Law Institute in 2006.

Contract Liability of the Principal

 Know when an agent has authority to bind a principal to a contract.

A principal normally is liable on a contract made by an agent if the agent had *actual* or *apparent authority* to make the contract on the principal's behalf. Yet even when the agent lacks any authority to contract, a principal may be bound by later *ratifying* a contract made by an unauthorized agent.

Actual Authority
An agent has *actual authority* to take an action "designated" or "implied" in the principal's *manifestations to the agent* and *acts necessary or incidental* to achieving the principal's objectives of the agency. The agent's reasonable understanding of the principal's manifestations and objectives determines the agent's actual authority. Actual authority, therefore, is the authority the principal wants the agent to possess. It is based on communications or manifestations from the principal to the agent.

Courts separate an agent's authority into two parts: express and implied. *Express authority* is actual authority that the principal has specified in very specific or detailed language. For example, suppose that Microsoft

instructs its agent Gates to contract to sell a Windows 10 software license for $175 or more. If Gates contracts to sell the software license to Dell for $200, Microsoft is liable to Dell on the basis of Gates's express authority. However, Gates would not have express authority to sell the software license for $150 or to sell a different software license.

An agent generally has *implied authority* to do whatever it is reasonable to assume that the principal wanted the agent to do, in light of the principal's manifestations to the agent and the principal's objectives of the agency. Relevant factors include the principal's express statements, the nature of the agency, the acts reasonably necessary to carry on the agency business, the acts customarily done when conducting that business, and the relations between principal and agent.

Implied authority usually derives from a grant of express authority by the principal. On occasion, however, implied authority may exist even though there is no relevant grant of express authority. Courts generally derive implied authority from the nature of the agency business, the relations between principal and agent, customs in the trade, and other facts and circumstances. There may be implied authority to make a certain contract if the agent has made similar past contracts with the principal's knowledge and without his objection or if the agent's position usually gives an agent the power to make a certain contract.

No matter what its source, an agent's implied authority cannot contradict the principal's express statements. Thus, there is no implied authority to contract when a principal has limited her agent's authority by express statement or clear implication and the contract would conflict with that limitation. But as we will see, apparent authority may still exist in such cases.

Examples of Implied Authority Courts have created general rules or presumptions for determining the implied authority of certain agents in certain situations. For example:

1. An agent hired to *manage a business* normally has implied authority to make contracts that are reasonably necessary for conducting the business or that are customary in the business. These include contracts for obtaining equipment and supplies, making repairs, employing employees, and selling goods or services. However, a manager ordinarily has no power to borrow money or issue negotiable instruments in the principal's name unless the principal is a banking or financial concern regularly performing such activities.

2. An agent given *full control over real property* has implied authority to contract for repairs and insurance and may rent the property if this is customary. But such an agent may not sell the property or allow any third-party liens or other interests to be taken on it.

3. Agents appointed to *sell the principal's goods* may have implied authority to make customary warranties on those goods. In states that still recognize the distinction, a general agent described in Chapter 35 is more likely to have such authority than a special agent.

Apparent Authority *Apparent authority* arises
when the principal's manifestations cause a third party to form a reasonable belief that the agent is authorized to act in a certain way. In other words, apparent authority is based on (1) *manifestations by the principal* to the third party (2) that cause the *third party* to *believe reasonably* that the agent has such authority. Background factors such as trade customs and established business practices often determine whether it is reasonable for the third party to believe that the agent has authority. In other words, apparent authority exists because under the circumstances it reasonably *appears* that the agent may act for the principal, based upon the principal's words or conduct (action or inaction).

Principals can give their agents apparent authority through the statements they make, or tell their agents to make, *to third parties* and through the actions they knowingly allow their agents to take *with third parties*. Thus, a principal might create apparent authority by telling a third party that the agent has certain authority or by directing the agent to do the same. A principal might also create apparent authority by appointing an agent to a position that customarily involves the authority to make certain contracts. For instance, if Exxon makes Alba its gasoline sales agent, and if that position customarily involves the power to sell gasoline, Alba would have apparent authority to sell gasoline. Here, Exxon's behavior in appointing Alba to the position of gasoline sales agent, as reasonably interpreted in light of business customs, gives Alba apparent authority. However, because agents cannot give themselves apparent authority, there would be no such authority if, without Exxon's knowledge or permission, Alba falsely told third parties that he was Exxon's gasoline sales agent.

Apparent authority protects third parties who reasonably rely on the principal's manifestations that the agent has authority. It assumes special importance in cases where the principal has told the agent not to make certain contracts that the agent ordinarily would have actual authority to make, but the third party knows nothing about this limitation and has no reason to know about it. Suppose that Prince employs Arthur as general sales agent for its tennis racquet manufacturing business. Certain warranties customarily accompany the racquets Prince sells, and agents like Arthur ordinarily are empowered to give these warranties. But Prince tells Arthur not to make any such warranties to buyers, thus cutting off Arthur's express and implied authority. Despite Prince's orders, however, Arthur makes the usual warranties in a sale to Modell, who is familiar with customs in the trade. If Modell did not know about the limitation on Arthur's authority, Prince is bound by Arthur's warranties.

Agent's Notification and Knowledge
Sometimes, the general agency rules regarding *notification* and *knowledge* affect a principal's contract liability. If a third party gives proper notification to an agent with actual or apparent authority to receive it, the principal is bound as if the notification had been given directly to the principal. Similarly, notification to a third party by an agent with the necessary authority is considered notification by the principal.

In certain circumstances, an agent's knowledge of facts is *imputed* to the principal. This means that the principal's rights and liabilities are what they would have been if the principal had known what the agent knew. Generally, an agent's knowledge of facts or reason to know facts is imputed to a principal when it is material to the agent's duties to the principal. No imputation occurs, however, if the agent acts adversely to the principal with an intent to act solely for the agent's own purposes or those of another person. Suppose that Ames, acting on behalf of Sony, contracts with Target. Ames knows that Target is completely mistaken about a matter material to the contract to purchase TVs. Even though Sony knew nothing about Target's unilateral mistake, Target probably can avoid its contract with Sony.

Ratification Ratification is a process whereby a
principal binds himself to an unauthorized act done by an agent, or by a person purporting to act as an agent. Usually, the act in question is a contract. Ratification relates back to the time when the contract was made. It binds the principal as if the agent had possessed authority at that time.

Conduct Amounting to Ratification Ratification can be express or implied. An *express ratification* occurs when the principal manifests assent that his legal relations be affected, such as stating orally that he wishes to be bound by a contract that has already been made. *Implied ratification* arises when the principal's conduct justifies a reasonable assumption that he consents to the agent's act. Examples include the principal's part performance of a contract made by an agent or the principal's acceptance of benefits under such a contract. Sometimes, even a principal's silence, acquiescence, or failure to repudiate the transaction may constitute ratification. This can occur when the principal would be expected to object if he did not consent to the contract, the principal's silence leads the third party to believe that he does consent, and the principal is aware of all relevant facts.

Additional Requirements Even if a principal's words or conduct indicate an intent to ratify, other requirements must be met before ratification occurs. These requirements have been variously stated; the following list is typical.

1. The act ratified must be one that was *valid* at the time it was performed. For example, an agent's illegal contract cannot be made binding by the principal's subsequent ratification. However, a contract that was voidable when made due to the principal's incapacity may be ratified by a principal who has later attained or regained capacity.

2. The principal must have been *in existence* at the time the agent acted. However, as discussed in Chapter 42, corporations may bind themselves to their promoters' *preincorporation* contracts by *adopting* such contracts.

3. When the contract or other act occurred, the agent must have indicated to the third party that she was acting for a principal and not for herself. The agent need not, however, have disclosed the principal's identity.

4. The principal must have *legal capacity* at the time of ratification. For instance, an insane principal cannot ratify.

5. The principal must have *knowledge of all material facts* regarding the prior act or contract at the time it is ratified. Here, an agent's knowledge is not imputed to the principal.

6. The principal must ratify the *entire* act or contract. He cannot ratify the beneficial parts of a contract and reject those that are detrimental.

7. In ratifying, the principal must use the *same formalities* required to give the agent authority to execute the transaction. As Chapter 35 stated, few formalities normally are needed to give an agent authority. But when the original agency contract requires a writing, ratification likewise must be written.

Note that a principal's ratification is binding even if not communicated to the third party. Also, once a principal has ratified a contract, the principal is estopped from denying its ratification if the other party has been induced to make a detrimental change in position.

Intervening Events Certain events occurring after an agent's contract but before the principal's ratification may cut off the principal's power to ratify. These include (1) the third party's *withdrawal* from the contract, (2) the third party's *death or loss of capacity*, (3) the principal's *failure to ratify within a reasonable time* (assuming that the principal's silence did not already work a ratification), and (4) where it would be *inequitable* to bind the third party.

Estoppel Closely connected to but different from apparent authority and ratification is the concept of **estoppel**, that a person may be liable for an actor's transaction with a third party who justifiably is induced to make a detrimental change in position because he believed the actor had authority to act for the person. The liable person must either

1. Intentionally or carelessly cause the third party's belief or

2. Having notice that such belief might cause a third party to change his position, fail to take reasonable steps to notify the third person of the facts.

Estoppel liability is based on the same concepts as promissory estoppel, which is covered in contract law in Chapter 9.

Estoppel is different from apparent authority because it does not require that the purported principal has made any manifestation that the purported agent can act for her. For example, liability for estoppel can arise when a principal is informed that an agent is representing to a third person that the agent has authority to act for the principal, when in fact she has no such actual or apparent authority. Because the agent has made the manifestation—not the principal—no actual or apparent authority exists. If, however, the third party justifiably changes position in reliance on the agent's representation, the principal may be estopped from denying the agent's authority. It is not clear from the *Restatement (Third)* when such third-party reliance may be reasonable.

In the following *Frontier Leasing* case, the Iowa Supreme Court considered whether a golf course professional had authority to lease a beverage cart on behalf of the golf course and whether the golf course had ratified the lease or was estopped to deny the authority of the golf pro to make the lease.

Frontier Leasing Corp. v. Links Engineering, LLC
781 N.W.2d 772 (Iowa 2010)

In January 2004, Royal Links USA solicited Dave Fleming, golf professional and director of golf for Links Engineering, doing business as Bluff Creek Golf Course, to purchase a nonmotorized beverage cart. Royal Links told Fleming that advertising revenue from the beverage cart would cover Bluff Creek's monthly lease expenses for the cart. On January 21, Fleming, on behalf of Bluff Creek, applied for financing for the beverage cart and signed a Royal Links USA credit application. Royal Links sent Bluff Creek's credit application to C&J Leasing Corp., which approved Bluff Creek for credit. In February 2004, Fleming and C&J Leasing signed a lease agreement for the beverage cart.

In 2005, Bluff Creek defaulted on the lease payments. C&J Leasing sent a default letter to Bluff Creek stating that Bluff Creek could correct the default by paying $1,322. Otherwise, C&J Leasing would require payment of the entire balance of $14,636, and Bluff Creek would have to return the equipment.

Upon receiving this letter, the managing owner of Bluff Creek, Lance Clute, called C&J Leasing and learned of the lease agreement signed by Fleming. Clute requested a copy of the lease, and upon its receipt, he stopped all payments on the cart. Clute communicated to C&J Leasing that he wanted the beverage cart removed from his property. Clute submitted an affidavit stating Fleming did not have authorization to enter into financing agreements. Nonetheless, Bluff Creek had made some payments on the cart lease to C&J Leasing prior to Clute learning about the lease.

Bluff Creek was sued for breach of contract. The district court issued a summary judgment that Fleming had authority to bind Bluff Creek on the contract and that Bluff Creek was liable to the lessor, Frontier Leasing Corporation, which had acquired from C&J Leasing the rights to collect on the lease. The Iowa Court of Appeals reversed, and Frontier Leasing appealed to the Iowa Supreme Court.

Ternus, Chief Justice

An agency relationship can be established through the agent's actual or apparent authority to act on behalf of the principal.

Actual authority to act is created when a principal intentionally confers authority on the agent either by writing or through other conduct which, reasonably interpreted, allows the agent to believe that he has the power to act. Actual authority includes both express and implied authority. Express authority is derived from specific instructions by the principal in setting out duties, while implied authority is actual authority circumstantially proved. Thus, actual authority examines the principal's communications to the agent. *Restatement (Third) of Agency* § 2.01 (2006).

Apparent authority is authority the principal has knowingly permitted or held the agent out as possessing. Apparent authority focuses on the principal's communications to the third party. *Restatement (Third) of Agency* §§ 2.03, 3.03. In other words, apparent authority must be determined by what the principal does, rather than by any acts of the agent.

A principal may also be liable under the doctrines of estoppel and ratification. Under the doctrine of estoppel, the principal is liable if he (1) causes a third party to believe an agent has the authority to act, or (2) has notice that a third party believes an agent has the authority and does not take steps to notify the third party of the lack of authority. *Restatement (Third) of Agency* § 2.05. Moreover, based on principles of ratification, a principal may be liable when he knowingly accepts the benefits of a transaction entered into by one of his agents.

The district court based its ruling that Fleming had actual and apparent authority to enter into the lease on behalf of

Bluff Creek on an affidavit submitted by the director and owner of Bluff Creek, Lance Clute. Clute stated in his affidavit that Fleming was in charge of the day-to-day operations of the golf course, Clute was aware of the existence of the beverage cart and did not disavow the transaction, and Bluff Creek made payments on the cart from August 2004 through March 2005. The district court noted that Bluff Creek did not provide an affidavit from Fleming confirming the testimony of Clute. While these facts do support a finding of an agency relationship, an examination of Clute's entire affidavit could also cause one to conclude that Fleming did not have actual or apparent authority to enter into the lease and that Clute did not ratify the transaction or act in any way that would estop Bluff Creek from rejecting the transaction.

In particular, Clute's affidavit refutes the existence of actual authority with Clute's statement that Fleming was not authorized to enter into any financing agreements or transactions for the purchase, lease, or financing of capital assets like the beverage cart, especially given the lease's hefty amount of $19,000. Clute's affidavit refutes the existence of apparent authority with the statement that it is customary in the golf industry to hire a PGA golf professional to manage the day-to-day operations of a golf course, and vendors are aware that such professionals do not have authority to enter into the type of transaction at issue here. Clute's affidavit also refutes that Bluff Creek is estopped from rejecting the transaction and that Bluff Creek ratified the lease. It does so with Clute's explanation that, when he saw the cart, he thought it was an "even trade for advertisement" such as Bluff Creek[s]' practice with scorecard advertising. Clute stated that with scorecard advertisements, Bluff Creek is given the scorecards for free in exchange for the advertisements on the cards. Clute's affidavit also refutes the doctrines of estoppel and ratification with its statements that he first learned of the lease through a collection letter that was received when Fleming was no longer employed with Bluff Creek, that he immediately requested a copy of the lease when it could not be found in Bluff Creek's records, that he made the cart available for repossession after determining that the lease was a "scam," and that the cart "to this day . . . sits idle in [Bluff Creek's] garage taking up space." Finally, while Bluff Creek does not submit an affidavit

from Fleming supporting Clute's affidavit testimony, a jury nevertheless could believe Clute, finding in Bluff Creek's favor. The absence of testimony from Fleming simply goes to the weight of Bluff Creek's evidence, which is something for the jury to decide, not a court on summary judgment.

Because reasonable minds could draw different inferences from the record as to whether Fleming had authority to bind Bluff Creek to the equipment lease, we reverse the district court's grant of summary judgment.

Judgment for Bluff Creek affirmed. Remanded to the trial court.

Contracts Made by Subagents The rules governing a principal's liability for an agent's contracts generally apply to contracts made by subagents. If an agent has authorized a subagent to make a certain contract and this authorization is within the authority granted the agent by the principal, the principal is bound to the subagent's contract.

Also, a subagent contracting within the authority conferred by the principal (the agent) binds the *agent* in an appropriate case. In addition, both the principal and the agent probably can ratify the contracts of subagents.

Contract Liability of the Agent

 LO36-2 Understand when an agent may be liable on contracts made for the principal.

When are *agents* liable on contracts they make on their principals' behalf? For the most part, this question depends on a different set of variables than those determining the principal's liability. The most important of these variables is the *nature of the principal*. Thus, this section first examines the liability of agents who contract for several different kinds of principals. Then it discusses two ways that an agent can be bound after contracting for any type of principal.

The Nature of the Principal

Disclosed Principal A principal is **disclosed** if a third party knows or has reason to know (1) that the agent is acting for a principal and (2) the principal's identity. Unless subject to an agreement otherwise, an agent who represents a disclosed principal is *not liable* on authorized contracts

 **LOG ON**

http://www.unidroit.org/english /conventions/1983agency/agency-convention1983.pdf https://www.law.kuleuven.be/personal/mstorme /PECL2en.html

European Union Agency Law
Go to the first link, and you will find the "Unidroit Convention on Agency in the International Sale of Goods (1983)." The second link has "The Principles of European Contract Law." Chapter 3 covers agent's authority.

made for such a principal. Suppose that Adkins, a sales agent for Google, calls on Toyota and presents a business card clearly identifying her as Google's agent. If Adkins contracts to sell Google's advertising space to Toyota with authority to do so, Adkins is not bound because Google is a disclosed principal. This rule usually is consistent with the third party's intention to contract only with the principal.

Unidentified Principal A principal is **unidentified** if the third party (1) knows or has reason to know that the agent is acting for *a* principal but (2) lacks knowledge or reason to know the principal's *identity*. This can occur when an agent simply neglects to disclose the principal's identity. Also, a principal may tell the agent to keep secret the principal's identity in order to preserve a stronger bargaining position, such as when a national retailer tries to buy land on which to build a large store.

Among the factors affecting anyone's decision to contract are the integrity, reliability, and creditworthiness of the other party to the contract. When the principal is unidentified, the third party ordinarily cannot judge these matters. As a result, he usually depends on the agent's reliability to some degree. For this reason, and to give the third party additional protection, an agent is liable on contracts made for an unidentified principal unless the agent and the third party agree otherwise.

Undisclosed Principal A principal is **undisclosed** when the third party lacks knowledge or reason to know both the principal's existence *and* the principal's identity. This can occur when a principal judges that a better deal is more likely if the principal's existence and identity remain secret or when the agent neglects to make adequate disclosure.

A third party who deals with an agent for an undisclosed principal obviously cannot assess the principal's reliability, integrity, and creditworthiness. Indeed, here the third party reasonably believes that the *agent* is the other party to the contract. Thus, the third party may hold an agent liable on contracts made for an undisclosed principal.

The undisclosed principal is also a party to the contract. However, an undisclosed principal becomes a party to the contract *only when* the agent acts on the principal's behalf in making the contract. An undisclosed principal is not a party to the contract when the agent does not intend to act for the principal.

The third party may not usually refuse to perform the contract merely because the principal was undisclosed, unless the contract excluded the possibility of an undisclosed principal.

Nonexistent Principal Unless there is an agreement to the contrary, an agent who purports to act for a **legally nonexistent** principal, such as an unincorporated association, is personally liable when the agent knows or has reason to know the principal does not exist. Likewise, the agent is liable when the agent knows or has reason to know a principal has no capacity. This is true even when the third party knows that the principal is nonexistent or lacks capacity. See Chapter 42 for a more detailed discussion of the liability of those who transact on behalf of nonexistent corporations.

In the *Treadwell* case that follows, the court found that an agent acted for an unidentified principal when he disclosed he was transacting for a corporation, but gave the wrong corporate name to the third party with whom he transacted.

Treadwell v. J.D. Construction Co.   938 A.2d 794 (Me. 2007)

In the early 1990s, Jesse Derr created a corporation, JCDER Inc., to operate his construction business. At some point, Derr began referring to the corporation as J.D. Construction Co. Inc., but no corporation by that name was ever created. JCDER Inc. remained the official name for purposes of organization and filing with Maine's Secretary of State. Derr never filed with the Secretary of State a statement of intention to do business under the assumed name J.D. Construction Co. Inc.

In 2003, when Leah and William Treadwell decided to build a home, they were referred to Derr. The Treadwells brought their home plans to Derr's office to get a quote and left the plans with an employee, Jane Veinot. They did not meet with Derr but received a quote from him in the mail. Soon after, the Treadwells signed a contract with J.D. Construction, with work to start in May 2003. Derr signed the contract, and his signature appeared on the contract as follows:

J.D. Construction Co. Inc.
By: Jesse Derr

The name JCDER Inc. was nowhere in the contract, and the Treadwells were unaware of the existence of JCDER Inc. when they signed the agreement. None of the documents the Treadwells received from J.D. Construction indicated that the company's real name was JCDER Inc.

Mr. Treadwell testified that he spoke with Derr twice at the worksite, just as they were breaking ground. The Treadwells, who visited the site almost daily, never saw Derr again, even though they tried many times to contact him. They spoke to Veinot often, but she would tell them that Derr was at another construction site. Derr had hired subcontractors to do the work on the Treadwells' property. Around Thanksgiving 2003, the Treadwells visited the site and found that Derr had abandoned the job with the house unfinished because the company was not making any money on the job. The Treadwells had paid Derr approximately $91,000 before construction halted.

The Treadwells found many problems with the structure, including twisted studs and other lumber that had to be replaced. The Treadwells hired new contractors to fix and finish the project, for which they paid a significant sum.

To recover the additional costs, the Treadwells sued J.D. Construction Co., JCDER, and Derr for breach of contract and other grounds. The trial court awarded the Treadwells damages against J.D. Construction Co. and JCDER but found that Derr was not personally liable for the damages. The Treadwells appealed to the Supreme Judicial Court of Maine, asking that Derr also be held liable.

Alexander, Judge

The Treadwells argue that the trial court should have awarded damages against Derr individually since he signed the contract for a non-existent corporation. In the alternative, they contend that the trial court should have pierced the corporate veil and held Derr responsible because he failed to disclose the existence of JCDER, Inc.

The question presented to us is whether, as a matter of law, an individual who signs a contract, purporting to act on behalf of a corporate entity that he knows does not exist, becomes personally liable for damages arising from failure to properly perform under that contract.

An agent who makes a contract for an undisclosed principal or a partially disclosed principal will be liable as a party to the contract. In order for an agent to avoid personal liability on a contract negotiated in his principal's behalf, he must disclose not only that he is an agent but also the identity of the principal. The term "partially disclosed" principal is synonymous with "unidentified" principal. *Restatement (Third) of Agency*, § 1.04 comment b (2006). "A principal is unidentified if, when an agent and a third party interact, the third party has notice that the agent is acting for a principal but does not have notice of the principal's identity." *Restatement (Third) of Agency*, § 1.04(2)(c) (2006). To avoid liability for the agent, the third party must have actual knowledge of the identity of the principal, and does not have a duty to investigate.

In *Maine Farmers Exch. v. McGillicuddy*, 697 A.2d 1266 (Me. 1996), the son of a potato seller signed a contract with a distributor for a certain grade potato. The father/seller furnished the potatoes, which turned out to be the wrong grade. In an action by the distributor against the father and son, the trial court found them to be jointly and severally liable. They appealed the finding of joint and several liability, arguing that the distributor should have been aware that the son was acting as an agent for his father. We affirmed that finding because the son did not disclose that he was an agent for his father, and the distributor believed he was buying potatoes from the son.

In the present case, Derr organized a corporation called JCDER, Inc., which he used to operate his construction business. Both Derr and JCDER, Inc., acted under the assumed name J.D. Construction Co., Inc., Derr signed the contract on behalf of J.D. Construction, hired the subcontractors, and was purported to be the contact-person for the project, although he was not available to the Treadwells. Derr's use of an assumed trade name was not sufficient to disclose his agency relationship with JCDER, Inc. JCDER, Inc., was therefore an unidentified or partially disclosed principal. As a matter of law, Derr is personally liable for performance of contracts entered into as agent for the non-existent J.D. Construction, Co., Inc., or the undisclosed principal JCDER, Inc.

Judgment reversed in favor of the Treadwells.

Liability of Agent by Agreement

An agent may be bound to contracts made for a principal by *expressly agreeing* to be liable. This is true regardless of the principal's nature. An agent is expressly bound by (1) making the contract in the agent's name rather than in the principal's name, (2) joining the principal as an obligor on the contract, or (3) acting as surety or guarantor for the principal.

Problems of contract interpretation can arise when it is claimed that an agent has expressly promised to be bound. The two most important factors affecting the agent's liability are the wording of the contract and the way the agent has signed it. An agent who wishes to avoid liability should make no express promises in the agent's own name and should try to ensure that the agreement obligates only the principal. In addition, the agent should use a signature form that clearly identifies the principal and indicates the agent's representative capacity—for example, "Parker, by Adkins," or "Adkins, for Parker." Simply adding the word "agent" when signing her name ("Adkins, Agent") or signing without any indication of her status ("Adkins") could subject the agent to liability. Sometimes, the body of the contract suggests one result and the signature form another. In such contexts, oral evidence or other extrinsic evidence of the parties' understanding may help resolve the uncertainty.

Implied Warranty of Authority

An agent also may be liable to a third party if the agent contracts for a legally existing and competent principal while lacking authority to do so. Here, the principal is not bound on the contract. Yet it is arguably unfair to leave the third party without any recovery. Thus, an agent normally is bound by an implied warranty of the agent's authority to contract. This liability exists regardless of whether the agent is otherwise bound to the third party.

To illustrate, suppose that Allen is a salesman for Prine, who sells diamonds. Allen has actual authority to receive offers for the sale of Prine's diamonds but not to make sale contracts, which must be approved by Prine himself. Prine has long followed this practice, and it is customary in the markets where his agents work. Representing himself as Prine's agent but saying nothing about his authority, Allen contracts to sell Prine's diamonds to Thatcher on Prine's behalf. Thatcher, who should have known better, honestly believes that Allen has authority to contract to sell Prine's diamonds. Prine is not liable on Allen's contract because Allen lacked actual or apparent authority to bind him. But Allen is liable to Thatcher for breaching his implied warranty of authority.

However, an agent is *not* liable for making an unauthorized contract if any of the following applies:

1. The third party *actually knows* that the agent lacks authority. Note from the previous example, however, that the agent still is liable where the third party merely had *reason to know* that authority was lacking.

2. The principal subsequently *ratifies* the contract. Here, the principal is bound, and there is no reason to bind the agent.

3. The agent adequately *notifies* the third party that warranty of authority is being made.

In the following *DePetris & Bachrach* case, the court found the president of a dissolved corporation liable for breaching the agent's implied warranty of authority.

DePetris & Bachrach, LLP v. Srour   71 A.D.3d 460 (N.Y. App. Div. 2010)

Plaintiff law firm sued, among others, defendant attorneys, seeking to collect for fees allegedly due to the law firm for representation of defendant client. The attorneys referred the client to the law firm. The complaint alleged that the attorneys represented to the law firm that they had authority from a third party to promise payment of $75,000 of the client's fees when, in fact, they lacked such authority. Defendants-respondents moved to dismiss the complaint against them.

The Supreme Court, New York County (New York), granted the attorneys' motion to dismiss the complaint as against them and denied the law firm's cross motion for leave to serve a supplemental complaint. The law firm appealed.

Feinman, Judge

Under the doctrine of implied warranty of authority, a person who purports to make a contract, representation, or conveyance to or with a third party on behalf of another person, lacking power to bind that person, gives an implied warranty of authority to the third party and is subject to liability to the third party for damages for loss caused by breach of that warranty, including loss of the benefit expected from performance by the principal. See *Restatement (Third) of Agency* § 6.10 (2006).

In this case, the Court finds that the doctrine of apparent authority is irrelevant because the causes of action alleged are not seeking to hold the principals liable on the ground that defendants-respondents had apparent authority to make promises of payment. Rather, these causes of actions are seeking to hold the agents, defendants-respondents, liable for contracts or representations they purported to make on behalf of the principal while acting without authority from the principal. The trial court thus erred in relying on the principle of apparent authority.

Judgment modified in part and affirmed in part.

CONCEPT REVIEW

Liability of Principal and Agent: The Major Possibilities

Principal	Agent's Authority		
	Actual	**Apparent**	**None**
Disclosed	P liable on the contract. A not liable on the contract unless agrees to be liable.	P liable on the contract. A not liable on the contract unless agrees to be liable.	P not liable on the contract. A usually liable for breach of the implied warranty of authority.
Unidentified	P liable on the contract. A liable on the contract.	P liable on the contract. A liable on the contract.	P not liable on the contract. A liable on the contract or for breach of the implied warranty of authority.
Undisclosed	P liable on the contract. A liable on the contract.	Impossible.	P not liable on the contract. A liable on the contract.

Tort Liability of the Principal

 LO36-3 Recognize when an agent is able to make a principal liable for torts committed by the agent.

Besides contracting on the principal's behalf, an agent may also commit torts while acting for the principal. A principal's liability for an agent's torts may be found on either of two bases:

1. Vicarious liability, including *respondeat superior.*

2. Direct liability.

Direct liability requires that the principal be at fault; a principal's vicarious liability requires only that the agent be at fault. For some torts, a principal may have both direct and vicarious liability.

Respondeat Superior Liability

The more important type of vicarious liability is based on the doctrine of ***respondeat superior*** (let the master answer). Under this doctrine, a principal who is an ***employer*** is liable for torts committed by agents (1) who are ***employees*** and (2) who commit the tort while acting within the ***scope of their employment***. *Respondeat superior* makes the principal liable for both an employee's negligence and intentional torts. Chapter 35 outlined the main factors courts consider when determining whether an agent is an employee. The most important of these factors is a principal's right to control the manner and means of an agent's performance of work. The court in the *CBS v. FCC* case in Chapter 35 found that Janet Jackson and Justin Timberlake were not employees of CBS during their halftime performance at the Super Bowl, and therefore, CBS was not responsible for their actions under *respondeat superior.*

Respondeat superior is a rule of *imputed* or *vicarious* liability because it bases an employer's liability on its relationship with the employee rather than its own fault. This imputation of liability reflects the following beliefs: (1) that the economic burdens of employee torts can best be borne by employers; (2) that employers often can protect themselves against such burdens by self-insuring or purchasing insurance; and (3) that the resulting costs frequently can be passed on to consumers, thus "socializing" the economic risk posed by employee torts. *Respondeat superior* also motivates employers to ensure that their employees avoid tortious behavior. Because they typically control the physical details of the work, employers are fairly well positioned to do so.

Scope of Employment   *Respondeat superior*'s scope-of-employment requirement has been stated in many ways and

is notoriously ambiguous. Some courts considering this question asked whether the employee was on a "frolic" of his own or merely made a "detour" from his assigned activity. According to the *Restatement,* an employee acts within the scope of employment when performing work assigned by the employer or when engaging in a course of conduct subject to the employer's control. An employee's act is not within the scope of employment when it occurs within an independent course of conduct not intended by the employee to serve any purpose of the employer. Most courts find that an employee's conduct is within the scope of his employment if it meets each of the following four tests:

1. It was of the *kind* that the employee was employed to perform. To meet this test, an employee's conduct need only be of the same general nature as work expressly authorized or be incidental to its performance.

2. It occurred substantially within the authorized *time* period. This is simply the employee's assigned time of work. Beyond this, there is an extra period of time during which the employment may continue. For instance, a security guard whose regular quitting time is 5:00 probably meets the time test if he unjustifiably injures an intruder at 5:15. Doing the same thing three hours later, however, would probably put the guard outside the scope of employment.

3. It occurred substantially within the *location* authorized by the employer. This includes locations not unreasonably distant from the authorized location. For example, a salesperson told to limit her activities to New York City probably would satisfy the location requirement while pursuing the employer's business in New Rochelle just north of the city limits but not while pursuing the same business in Philadelphia. Generally, the smaller the authorized area of activity, the smaller the departure from that area needed to put the employee outside the scope of employment. For example, consider the different physical distance limitations that should apply to a factory worker assigned to a single building and a traveling salesperson assigned to a five-state territory.

Moreover, in today's connected economy, many employers allow some of their employees to work at the employees' homes. The scope of employment for such an employee would encompass the employee's home.

4. It was motivated *at least in part* by the *purpose* of serving the employer. This test is met when the employee's conduct was motivated *to any appreciable extent* by the desire to serve the employer. Thus, an employee's tort may be within the scope of employment even if the motives for committing it were partly personal. For example, suppose that a delivery employee is behind schedule and for that reason has an accident while speeding to make a delivery in his employer's

truck. The employee would be within the scope of employment even if another reason for his speeding was to finish work quickly so he could watch his daughter's soccer game.

In the *Corvo* case, which follows, the court determines that intentional torts committed by employees were outside the scope of their employment.

Synergies3 Tec Services, LLC v. Corvo	**2020 WL 4913636 (Ala. Aug. 21, 2020)**

Lisa Corvo and Thomas Bonds were engaged to be married. They had gotten engaged in Paris without an engagement ring. When they returned to the United States, they purchased a specially made ring in the shape of the Eiffel Tower with a diamond mounted on it. The diamond cost $40,000.

Sometime thereafter Corvo contacted DIRECTV to initiate satellite television services in her house. On February 20, 2013, Corvo and Bonds were working from home when Raymond Castro and Daniel McLaughlin arrived to perform the installation. Bonds let both men inside the house, advised them where to install the equipment, and then resumed working. At one point, while Castro and McLaughlin were still working on the installation, Corvo and Bonds experienced an interruption in their Internet access, and, as a result, Bonds went to check with Castro and McLaughlin. Corvo noticed that the door to the master bedroom was almost closed, which she thought was strange. Thus, she opened it, which startled McLaughlin, who was standing behind the door.

When the installation was complete, Castro provided Corvo and Bonds with a lengthy overview of the services. Corvo and Bonds finished paperwork associated with the installation, and Castro left.

After Castro left, Corvo went to the master bedroom to retrieve her handbag, jewelry, and shoes, and she noticed that the three-carat diamond was missing from the center of her engagement ring. The prongs on the ring were sticking out and were bent.

Corvo and Bonds sued McLaughlin, Castro, DIRECTV, and Synergies3 Tec Services (Synergies3)—which was the company contracted by DIRECTV to install services and which employed McLaughlin and Castro)—asserting claims of conversion and theft.

A jury awarded Corvo and Bonds $365,160 in damages, including mental anguish and punitive damages. DIRECTV and Synergies3 appealed the verdict on a number of grounds, including that the jury erroneously applied the doctrine of respondeat superior *to hold them vicariously liable for the actions of McLaughlin and Castro.*

STEWART, Justice

Synergies3 and DIRECTV . . . argue that a judgment as a matter of law should have been entered as to Corvo and Bonds's claim alleging vicarious liability under the doctrine of *respondeat superior*. An employer may be held vicariously liable for the intentional tort of its employee or agent if the plaintiff produces sufficient evidence showing "that [1] the agent's wrongful acts were in the scope of his employment; or [2] that the acts were in furtherance of the business of [the employer]; or [3] that [the employer] participated in, authorized, or ratified the wrongful acts." *Potts v. BE & K Constr. Co.,* 604 So. 2d 398, 400 (Ala. 1992) (quoting *Joyner v. AAA Cooper Transp.,* 477 So. 2d 364, 365 (Ala. 1985)).

> The employer is vicariously liable for acts of its employee that were done for the employer's benefit, i.e., acts done in the line and scope of employment or for acts done for the furtherance of the employer's interest. The employer is directly liable for its own conduct if it authorizes or participates in the employee's acts or ratifies the employee's conduct after it learns of the action.

Potts, 604 So. 2d at 400.

Synergies3 and DIRECTV argue that the act of stealing from customers of DIRECTV is such a marked and unusual deviation from Synergies3 and DIRECTV's business of providing satellite television service that they should have been granted a judgment as a matter of law on Corvo and Bonds's claim alleging respondeat superior liability. In support of their argument, Synergies3 and DIRECTV cite *Hendley v. Springhill Memorial Hospital,* 575 So. 2d 547 (Ala. 1990), *Hargrove v. Tree of Life Christian Day Care Center,* 699 So. 2d 1242 (Ala. 1997), and *Conner v. Magic City Trucking Service, Inc.,* 592 So. 2d 1048 (Ala. 1992).

In *Hendley,* a patient sued a hospital alleging that [a worker] who maintained medical equipment for the hospital performed an unauthorized vaginal examination on the patient. The scope of the [worker's] employment was limited to tending to certain electronic medical devices used in the hospital. In affirming the summary judgment in favor of the hospital, this Court held that the hospital could not be held liable, under the doctrine of *respondeat superior,* for the [worker's] alleged unauthorized vaginal examination of the patient because that conduct was "such a gross deviation from the purpose for which [the worker] was in [the patient's] room (monitoring her [medical device])." 575 So. 2d at 551.

In *Hargrove,* two day-care-center employees and their younger sister kidnapped the plaintiffs' child from the day-care center because one of the sisters wanted a child of her own. This court affirmed the summary judgment entered against the plaintiffs on their claims against the day-care center based on vicarious liability, holding that the sisters' "apparent plot . . . constituted, as a matter of law, a gross deviation" from the business of the day-care center. 699 So. 2d at 1246. In *Hargrove,* however, it was undisputed that "there was nothing that should have, or could have, put . . . the [day-care] [c]enter on notice that the sisters would or might kidnap one of the children." *Id.*

In *Magic City Trucking,* an employee of a trucking company, which was subcontracted by the plaintiff's employer, chased the plaintiff with a snake and eventually threw the snake on the plaintiff while the two were working in the . . . scope of their employment for their respective employers. The plaintiff sued the trucking company based on the theory of *respondeat superior,* but the trial court entered a directed verdict . . . in favor of the trucking company. 592 So. 2d at 1049. In affirming the trial court's judgment, this Court held that the trucking company's employee's "actions were a marked and unusual deviation from the business of [the trucking company]. It cannot be said that [the employee's] poor practical joke was in furtherance of [the trucking company's] business. Therefore, it was not within the scope of his employment." 592 So. 2d at 1050.

This Court, however, has recognized:

> In order to recover against a defendant under the doctrine of *respondeat superior,* the plaintiff must establish the status of [employer and employee] and that the act done was within the . . . scope of the [employee's] employment. This rule applies even where the wrong complained of was intentionally, willfully, or maliciously done in such a manner as to authorize a recovery for punitive damages. In extending the liability to a willful wrong, the motive behind the act does not defeat liability, unless it can be shown that the [employee] acted from wholly personal motives having no relation to the business of the [employer]. Whether the [employee] was actuated solely by personal motives or by the interests of his employer is a question for the jury. This is so if there is any evidence having

a tendency either directly or by reasonable inference to show that the wrong was committed while the [employee] was executing the duties assigned to him.

Meyer v. Wal-Mart Stores, Inc., 813 So. 2d 832, 834–35 (Ala. 2001) [internal quotation and citations omitted].

The evidence, viewed in the light most favorable to Corvo and Bonds, the nonmovants, indicates that Castro and McLaughlin went to Corvo's house to install DIRECTV's equipment. After Castro and McLaughlin left the house, the diamond from Corvo's engagement ring and $160 in cash were missing. A default judgment was entered against Castro and McLaughlin on Corvo and Bonds's theft and conversion claims against them. Theft and conversion are a "marked and unusual deviation" from the business of Synergies3 and DIRECTV for which Castro and McLaughlin were in Corvo's house—installing equipment for DIRECTV's satellite television service. Furthermore, there was no evidence indicating that the theft or conversion was done for Synergies3's or DIRECTV's benefit or in furtherance of their interests. Moreover, there is no evidence indicating that Synergies3 or DIRECTV authorized or participated in theft and conversion or later ratified the conduct so as to give rise to any direct liability for theft or conversion. Based on those circumstances, there was no factual dispute regarding Synergies3's and DIRECTV's vicarious or direct liability for Castro's and McLaughlin's actions that required resolution by the jury; accordingly, the trial court should have entered a judgment as a matter of law in favor of Synergies3 and DIRECTV on Corvo and Bonds's claims asserting liability based on the doctrine of *respondeat superior.*

* * *

Reversed in part; and remanded with instructions.

Ethics and Compliance in Action

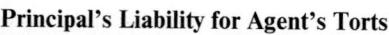

Principal's Liability for Agent's Torts

We have covered the reasons the law makes employers liable for the torts of employees under *respondeat superior,* including the ability of employers to bear the burden or to socialize the cost of paying for damages caused by an employee's tort.

- Do you think those are good reasons to make someone liable for the actions of another person? What kind of behavior is the rule of *respondeat superior* likely to foster? Does the rule encourage employers to train and supervise their employees better?

- Do you think *respondeat superior* makes employers liable for too many acts of their employees? Does the rule discourage some businesses from using employees? Does any discouragement affect both prospective employers and prospective employees?

- Do you think the law should make employers liable for all the torts of their employees?

- Do you think it is right for an employer to pay for all damages caused to others by the tort of an employee? When forming your answers, consider the ethical theories we covered in Chapter 4.

- What are compliance steps that an employer should take to avoid *respondeat superior* liability?

Direct Liability

A principal's *direct liability* for an agent's torts differs considerably from *respondeat superior* liability. Here, the principal himself is at fault, and there is no need to impute liability to him. Also, no scope-of-employment requirement exists in direct liability cases, and the agent need not be an employee. Of course, a principal might incur both direct liability and *respondeat superior* liability in cases where due to the principal's fault, an employee commits a tort within the scope of her employment.

A principal is directly liable for an agent's tortious conduct if the agent acts within her actual authority or the principal ratifies the agent's conduct. Usually, this means the principal directs the agent's conduct and intends that it occur. In such cases, the *agent's* behavior might be intentional, reckless, or negligent. For instance if Lawn Mower Company directs its agent Agnew to sell defective lawn mowers to Landscape Company, Lawn Mower Company is directly liable to Landscape Company. Likewise, Procenture Consulting Company would be liable for harm to clients caused by its ordering its consulting employees to complete an engagement in an unreasonable, substandard manner.

The typical direct liability case, however, involves harm caused by the principal's negligence regarding the agent. Examples of direct liability for negligence include (1) giving the agent improper or unclear instructions; (2) failing to make and enforce appropriate regulations to govern the agent's conduct; (3) hiring an unsuitable agent; (4) failing to discharge an unsuitable agent; (5) furnishing an agent with improper tools, instruments, or materials; and (6) failing to properly supervise an agent. Today, suits for negligent hiring are common.

Liability for Torts of Nonemployee Agents

A principal ordinarily is *not* liable for torts committed by **nonemployee agents** (independent contractors). As compared with employees, nonemployee agents are more likely to have the size and resources to insure against tort liability and to pass on the resulting costs themselves. Sometimes, therefore, the risk still can be socialized if only the nonemployee agent is held responsible. The principal does not control the manner in which a nonemployee agent's work is performed and therefore has less ability to prevent the nonemployee agent's torts than an employer has to prevent an employee's torts. Thus, imposing liability on principals for the torts of nonemployee agents may do little to eliminate the nonemployee agent's torts. However, the rule that principals are not liable for torts committed by nonemployee agents has exceptions. For example:

1. A principal can be *directly* liable for tortious behavior connected with the retention of a nonemployee agent. One example is the hiring of a dangerously incompetent nonemployee agent.

2. A principal is liable for harm resulting from the nonemployee agent's failure to perform a duty of care, which duty the principal owes to other persons but has delegated to the agent. A duty of care is a duty whose proper performance is so important that a principal cannot avoid liability by delegating it to an agent. This is often termed a *nondelegable duty*. Examples include a carrier's duty to transport its passengers safely, a municipality's duty to keep its streets in repair, a railroad's duty to maintain safe crossings, and a landlord's duties to make repairs and to use care in doing so. Thus, a landlord who retains a nonemployee agent to repair the stairs in an apartment building is liable for injuries caused by the agent's failure to repair the stairs properly.

This basis of liability also encompasses a principal's liability for a nonemployee agent's negligent failure to take the special precautions needed to conduct certain *highly dangerous* or *inherently dangerous* activities. Examples of such activities include excavations in publicly traveled areas, the clearing of land by fire, the construction of a dam, and the demolition of a building. For example, a nonemployee agent engaged in demolishing a building presumably has duties to warn pedestrians and to keep them at a safe distance. If injury results from the nonemployee agent's failure to meet these duties, the principal is liable.

Liability for Agent's Misrepresentations

Special rules apply when a third party sues a principal for **misrepresentations** made by an agent. In most cases where the principal is liable under these rules, the third party can elect to recover in tort, or to rescind the transaction.

A principal is *directly* liable for misrepresentations made by an agent during authorized transactions if the principal *intended* that the agent make the misrepresentations. In some states, a principal also may be directly liable for *negligently* allowing the agent to make misrepresentations. Even when no direct fault is established, a principal may be liable for an agent's misrepresentations if the agent had *actual or apparent authority to make true statements on the subject.* Suppose that an agent authorized to sell farmland falsely states that a stream on the land has never flooded the property when in fact it does so almost every year and that this statement induces a third party to buy the land. The principal is directly liable if she intended that the agent make this false statement. Even if the principal is personally blameless, she is liable if the agent had actual or apparent authority to make true statements about the stream.

CONCEPT REVIEW

An Outline of the Principal's Tort Liability

Respondeat Superior	1. Agent must be an employee *and* 2. Employee must act within scope of employment while committing the tort.
Direct Liability	1. Principal intends and directs agent's intentional tort, recklessness, or negligence or 2. Principal is negligent regarding hiring or training of agent.
Torts of Nonemployee Agents	1. Principal generally is *not* liable. 2. Exceptions exist for direct liability and nondelegable duties.
Misrepresentation	1. Direct liability. 2. Vicarious liability when agent has authority to make true statements on the subject of the misrepresentation. 3. An exculpatory clause may eliminate the principal's tort liability, but the third party still can rescind the contract.

After contemplating their potential liability under the rules just discussed, both honest and dishonest principals may try to escape liability for an agent's misrepresentations by including an **exculpatory clause** in contracts the agent makes with third parties. Such clauses typically state that the agent has authority only to make the representations contained in the contract and that only those representations bind the principal. Exculpatory clauses do not protect a principal who intends or expects that an agent will make false statements. Otherwise, though, they insulate the principal from *tort* liability if the agent misrepresents a material fact. But the third party still may rescind the transaction because it would be unjust to let the principal benefit from the transaction while disclaiming responsibility for it.

Tort Liability of the Agent

Agents are usually liable for their own torts. Normally, they are not absolved from tort liability just because they acted at the principal's command. However, there are exceptions to this generalization.

1. An agent can escape liability when *exercising a privilege of the principal.* Suppose that Tingle grants Parkham a right-of-way to transport his farm products over a private road crossing Tingle's land. Parkham's agent Adams would not be liable in trespass for driving across Tingle's land to transport farm products if she did so at Parkham's command. However, an agent must not exceed the scope of the privilege and must act for the purpose for which the privilege was given. Thus, Adams would not be protected if she took her Jeep on a midnight joyride across Tingle's land. Also, the privilege given the agent must be delegable in the first place. If Tingle had given the easement to Parkham exclusively, Adams would not be privileged to drive across Tingle's land.

2. A principal who is *privileged to take certain actions in defense of his person or property* may often authorize an agent to do the same. In such cases, the agent escapes liability if the principal could have done so. For example, a Walmart warehouse guard may use force to protect the property in Walmart's warehouse.

3. An agent who makes *misrepresentations* while conducting the principal's business is not liable in tort unless he either *knew or had reason to know* their falsity. Suppose Parker authorizes Arnold to sell his house, falsely telling Arnold that the house is fully insulated. Arnold does not know that the statement is false and could not discover its falsity through a reasonable inspection. If Arnold tells Thomas that the house is fully insulated and Thomas relies on this statement in purchasing the house, Parker is directly liable to Thomas, but Arnold is not liable.

4. An agent is not liable for injuries to third persons caused by *defective tools or instrumentalities* furnished by the principal unless the agent had actual knowledge or reason to know of the defect.

Tort Suits against Principal and Agent

Sometimes, both principal and agent are liable for an agent's torts. Here, the parties are *jointly and severally* liable. This means that a third party may join the principal and the agent in one suit and get a judgment against each, or may sue either or both individually and get a judgment against either or both. However, once a third party actually collects in full from either the principal or the agent, no further recovery is possible.

In some cases, therefore, either the principal or the agent has to satisfy the judgment alone despite the other party's liability. Here, the other party sometimes is required to *indemnify* the party who has satisfied the judgment. As discussed in Chapter 35, for example, sometimes a principal is required to indemnify an agent for tort liability the agent incurs. On the other hand, some torts committed by agents may involve a breach of duty to their principal, and the principal may be able to recover from an agent on this basis.

Problems and Problem Cases

1. Jonas Bravario hires Suzanne Hermano, a securities broker, to manage his $700,000 portfolio of securities. When Bravario managed his own investments, his investment strategy was to own a large number of different companies, with no one company representing more than 5 percent of his total investments. Bravario also purchased all his investments for cash and did not borrow money to finance the purchase of any investment. Hermano is aware of Bravario's historical investment strategy, which Bravario informed Hermano that he wanted to continue in the future. Nonetheless, Hermano opts to purchase 1 million shares of Enron Corporation for $70,000. To finance the purchase, Hermano sells $40,000 of Bravario's current investments and borrows $30,000 from Wells Fargo Bank in the name of Bravario. The interest rate on the loan is 10 percent. When Bravario discovers the purchase and the loan, he attempts to repudiate both contracts. Is Bravario liable on the Enron purchase and loan contracts?

2. Shelley Opp lived in California with her husband, Richard Opp, until they sought a divorce. Ten months later, Shelley contacted Soraghan Moving and Storage to move her personal property from California to Illinois. Shelley told Soraghan she wanted to insure her property for its full value of $10,000. Soraghan faxed to Shelley an "Estimate/Order for Service" form, which stated that Shelley intended to declare that the value of the goods shipped was $10,000. Shelley signed the form. According to Soraghan, it explained to Shelley that she or her representative must advise the mover at the time the shipment was picked up whether Shelley would like full replacement coverage of $10,000. According to Shelley, she was never informed that the person releasing her property in California would have to sign anything, declare any value for her property, or do anything other than give the movers access to her belongings. The estimate form also provided a location where Shelley could designate someone as her "true and lawful representative," but she made no such designation. On the day of the move, the movers in California called Shelley in Illinois to tell her they would be late arriving at the California home due to a flat tire. Shelley then phoned Richard at his office and asked him to go to the house, open the door, and let the movers in. Shelley also told Soraghan that "someone" would be at the California home to give the movers access to her property. Richard met the movers at the house, and he signed the bill of lading on a line that indicated that he was Shelley's authorized agent, and he allegedly agreed to limit the carriers' liability for her property at 60 cents per pound. Richard also signed an inventory of the property that indicated that he was its "owner or authorized agent." The truck carrying Shelley's belongings was struck by a train, damaging most of her property. Shelley inspected her damaged property and estimated its full replacement value to be over $10,000. Soraghan claimed that its liability was limited by the bill of lading to $2,625 because Richard had the actual and apparent authority to sign the bill of lading as Shelley's agent. What did the court rule?

3. Adventure Quest, a nonprofit school, was founded and operated by Peter Drutchal, its executive director and only full-time employee. From 1994 to 1996, Adventure Quest had liability coverage with Virginia Surety Company. The insurance policy included a "sexual abuse endorsement" that provided coverage for sexual abuse claims but excluded from coverage any person or entity that personally participated in committing

any sexual abuse. When Drutchal completed Adventure Quest's application for the insurance policy, he answered "no" in response to the question, "Have you ever had an incident which resulted in an allegation of sexual abuse?" In fact, Drutchal had previously sexually abused Adventure Quest's students, and additional abuse occurred during the coverage periods of the insurance policy. He kept the abuse secret from others until 2001. Drutchal's sexual abuse occurred in the course of school activities, while Drutchal was acting in his capacity as coach and chaperone. Drutchal's acts of sexual abuse were for his own purposes. The abuse was not done within the scope of his duties or authority as executive director and was not done in the best interests of Adventure Quest. Virginia Surety refused to pay for Adventure Quest's liability for Drutchal's abuse, arguing that Drutchal's knowledge of his own previous abuse was imputable to Adventure Quest, thereby excluding it from the policy's coverage. Was Virginia Surety right?

4. Richard Daynard, a Northeastern University law professor, contracted to provide tobacco litigation assistance to the Ness law firm in South Carolina. The Ness firm and the Scruggs law firm of Mississippi were plaintiffs' attorneys for tobacco litigation in Mississippi. Over a period of months, Daynard met in South Carolina and Boston, spoke over the phone, and communicated by fax with members of the Ness firm. He also communicated by phone and fax with members of the Scruggs firm. Based on their actions, Daynard believed that the Ness firm and Scruggs firm were agents of each other in directing the Mississippi tobacco litigation. In addition, both firms retained the benefits of his legal advice, which was provided in accordance with a contract he made with the Ness law firm and called for compensation equal to 5 percent of their legal fees. When the firms refused to pay Daynard, he sued in a federal district court in Massachusetts. The court had personal jurisdiction over the Ness firm because of its contacts with Massachusetts, but the Scruggs firm asserted that it had no contacts with Massachusetts. May the contacts of the Ness firm be imputed to the Scruggs firm, giving the court jurisdiction over the Scruggs firm?

5. Lee Cain was an officer and director of Timber Creek Oil Co., the operator of oil wells that it failed to plug after the Texas Railroad Commission ordered it to do so. The Commission authorized the expenditure of State of Texas funds to pay the expense of plugging the wells.

Four months later, Timber Creek failed to file its franchise-tax report. Two months later, its corporate charter was forfeited by the State of Texas, causing Timber Creek to cease to exist; the charter was never revived. Beginning one month after the charter forfeiture and continuing for six months, the Commission paid $50,000 to plug the Timber Creek wells. The state sued Cain to recover the $50,000 on a theory that he was personally liable for the Timber Creek debt. Was Cain liable for the debt?

6. Mark Bradshaw, an agent for National Foundation Life Insurance Co. (NFLIC), tried to sell a health insurance policy to Bobby Reed. Bradshaw told Reed that his health insurance coverage would begin upon signing some forms and paying the first premium. On January 7, Reed signed but did not read the forms, which included language stating that Reed understood that Bradshaw could not change any NFLIC policy or make any policy effective, that the policy would not be effective until actually issued by NFLIC, and that it could take up to two weeks for Reed's application to be processed and the policy issued. NFLIC received Reed's application, including his payment for the first premium, on January 12. On January 19, NFLIC called Reed's home and was informed he had a heart attack on January 15. NFLIC declined to issue the policy to Reed. On what grounds did Reed sue Bradshaw? Was Reed's suit against Bradshaw successful?

7. The Work Connection (Connection) was a temporary employment agency that provided workers to customers for a fee. Doyle Olson, a sales representative for Connection, contacted Universal Forest Products (Universal). Olson spoke with Ken Von Bank, Universal's production manager, who had direct supervisory authority over temporary workers. Universal hired some of Connection's employees, including Wayne DeLage, to construct fence panels at its Shakopee plant. Olson gave to Universal work verification forms that were used as employee timecards. Universal filled out and signed the forms, which contained the worker's name, date, and hours worked. Submission of a completed, signed form was required for an employee to be paid, and Connection processed the forms through its payroll department. The work verification forms contained the following language:

CUSTOMER AGREES TO THE TERMS AND CONDITIONS SET FORTH ON THE REVERSE SIDE HEREOF AND CERTIFIES THAT THE LISTED EMPLOYEES HAVE SATISFACTORILY PERFORMED SERVICES FOR THE HOURS SHOWN ABOVE.

The back of the verification form stated the following:

CONDITIONS OF UNDERTAKING: CUSTOMER agrees to indemnify, hold harmless and defend THE WORK CONNECTION against claims, damages, or penalties from any claims for bodily injury (including death), or loss of, and loss of use of, or damage to, property arising out of the use of or operation of CUSTOMER'S owned, nonowned, or leased vehicles, machinery or equipment by THE WORK CONNECTION employees.

The parties never discussed the language on the back of the work verification form. The parties' oral agreement did not include a term that required Universal to provide workers' compensation insurance for Connection's employees. Nonetheless, Von Bank signed the verification forms for Universal from March 1995 through July 1995, when the office manager, Yvonne Kohout, took over signing duties. At some point, Universal ran out of original work verification forms. Kohout simply photocopied the front side of the form and, thereafter, submitted forms that were blank on the back.

In August 1995, DeLage severed three of his fingers while operating a radial arm saw. DeLage received $75,000 in workers' compensation benefits from Connection. Connection then asked Universal to indemnify it pursuant to the language on the back of the verification form. Was Universal found liable to Connection?

8. LaVar Johnson was a retail representative for the Wheaton Company, a processor of consumer packaged goods like cereals and canned goods. Johnson's job was to visit grocery stores in his territory to ensure that each store gave adequate shelf space to all Wheaton products sold by the store. Wheaton told Johnson that maintaining good relations with the general manager and assistant manager of each store was essential. It was important, Wheaton told him, to accommodate the managers to ensure that Wheaton got the shelf space it wanted in each store.

While visiting a store in Springfield, Illinois, Johnson chatted for a few minutes with the manager, who got a phone call that his wife was in an auto accident while on her way to pick up the manager at the store. While the wife was not seriously injured, Johnson offered to take the manager to the scene of the accident, and the manager accepted. On the way to the accident scene, Johnson negligently ran a red light, resulting in his car being struck by another car. The grocery store manager received a broken leg,

arm, and pelvis. Is Wheaton liable for the manager's injuries under the doctrine of *respondeat superior*?

9. Gary McCoy ordered a pizza from a Papa John's restaurant. The restaurant was owned by RWT, a franchisee of Papa John's International. RWT did business as Papa John's Pizza. Wendell Burke, an employee of RWT, delivered the pizza and obtained payment from McCoy at his place of business. Burke lingered for almost two hours after being paid, asking McCoy for a job and viewing a hunting videotape. When Burke returned to the Papa John's restaurant, to avoid criticism for being late he concocted the story that McCoy held him against his will. The police arrested McCoy for false imprisonment, which charges were eventually dropped. McCoy sued Burke, RWT, and Papa John's International for malicious prosecution based on Burke's false statements. Does the doctrine of *respondeat superior* impose liability on the franchisor, Papa John's International, in this case?

10. Maria Millan opened two brokerage accounts at Dean Witter Reynolds. The broker for both accounts was her son Miguel, an employee of Dean Witter. Over the course of the next three years, Miguel systematically looted his mother's account, ultimately stealing from her more than $287,000. He stole checks from his mother's bathroom drawer, wrote checks on his mother's account, deposited his mother's checks into his own account, forged his mother's signature on numerous occasions, stole statements from her mailbox, created and sent bogus statements to his mother, and opened a post office box so he could receive his mother's actual statements. Dean Witter did not verify Millan's signature, as policy required. A Dean Witter supervisor also did not verify a check in the amount of $35,000, which was against Dean Witter written policy. Millan sues her son and Dean Witter for unauthorized transactions, negligence, and gross negligence. Under a theory of direct liability, who is a jury likely to find for? Under the doctrine of *respondeat superior*, is Dean Witter vicariously liable for the actions of Miguel? (*Hint:* Think about whether Miguel's actions were within his general scope of authority as a broker.)

11. Tammy Bauer hires consulting firm Accent Pointe to find a buyer for the formula and trade name of her pest repellent, NO BUGGZ. Bauer tells Accent Pointe to tell prospective buyers that NO BUGGZ is organic and has no health risks to humans. Bauer knows that NO BUGGZ has serious negative health effects on humans even when used as directed. Consequently, Accent Pointe tells Scotts Company that NO BUGGZ has

no serious negative health risks to humans when used as directed. The written purchase contract that Scotts signs with Bauer does not represent that NO BUGGZ has no health risks to humans; the contract contains an exculpatory clause stating that Bauer is not bound by Accent Pointe's representations, unless they also appear in the written contract. Two years after Scotts buys NO BUGGZ, Scotts is subjected to consumer lawsuits claiming that NO BUGGZ is causing health problems for its users. Is Bauer liable to Scotts for misrepresentation?

12. Thule Drilling sued Jacob Schimberg based on business transactions between Thule and QGM Group, a corporation for which Schimberg was the CEO. Thule's contract with QGM required QGM to do repair and construction work on three of Thule's mobile drilling rigs. Thule agreed to loan QGM funds so that QGM's work on the rigs could be completed. Thule alleged that QGM breached the contracts with Thule and that Thule was entitled to take possession of the rigs. Thule also argued that Schimberg, as the corporate agent of QGM, was personally liable to Thule because he directly denied Thule access to its rigs, committing the tort of conversion. Schimberg argued that he acted only at the behest of his QGM superiors and that he was never a party to any of the contracts between Thule and QGM. Are both QGM and Schimberg liable to Thule?

Part Nine

Partnerships

Introduction to Forms
of Business and Formation
# of Partnerships

After working for a large company for 10 years, you decide to take the leap and fulfill your lifelong dream to start your own business. Your idea is to help small businesses build their online presences—creating websites, social media profiles, etc. You envision that your business will need a capital infusion of $500,000 for the first year, during which you project the business will have a net loss of $200,000, which reflects in part your salary of $80,000. Beginning with the second year, you believe that the business will generate enough cash flow to finance internally all its normal capital expenditures. You expect second-year losses to be $100,000. Beginning with the third year, the business will be profitable.

You have $120,000 of savings that you are willing to invest in the business. You hope to obtain the remaining $380,000 of initial capital from investors. While you are willing to give a portion of the equity of the business to the investors, you want to control the business, including day-to-day operations. It is especially important that the other investors not be able to expel you from the business or its management.

- What business forms are best for your business?
- How will you modify the default rules of those business forms to make the forms work best for you?

LEARNING OBJECTIVES

After studying this chapter, you should be able to:

37-1 List the traits of each form of business.

37-2 Compare and contrast the various forms of business.

37-3 Apply the definition of *partnership* and avoid inadvertently being a partner of another person.

37-4 Appreciate the consequences of being a partner.

37-5 Understand the risks of being a purported partner and avoid being a purported partner.

37-6 Distinguish partner's property from partnership property.

37-7 List and compare the rights of a creditor having a charging order and the rights of a transferee of a partner's interest in a partnership.

IN THIS CHAPTER, YOU begin your study of business organizations. Early in this chapter, you will preview the basic characteristics of the most important forms of business and learn how to select an appropriate form for a business venture. Following that introduction, you will begin your in-depth study of partnerships, learning their characteristics and the formalities for their creation.

Types of Business Entities

One of the most important decisions made by a person beginning a business is choosing a *form of business*. This decision is important because the business owner's liability and control of the business vary greatly among the many forms of business. In addition, some business forms offer significant tax advantages to their owners.

Although other forms of business exist, usually a person starting a business will wish to organize the business as a sole proprietorship, partnership, limited liability partnership, limited partnership, corporation, or limited liability company. The rules surrounding each of these forms is a matter of state law, but the following sections give a general overview of the main features of each.

LO37-1 List the traits of each form of business.

Sole Proprietorship A **sole proprietorship** has only one owner. The sole proprietorship is merely an extension of its only owner, the **sole proprietor**.

As the only owner, the sole proprietor has the right to make all the management decisions of the business. In addition, all the profits of the business are his. A sole proprietor assumes great liability: He is personally liable for all the obligations of the business. All the debts of the business, including debts on contracts signed only in the name of the business, are his debts. If the assets of the business are insufficient to pay the claims of its creditors, the creditors may require the sole proprietor to pay the claims using his individual, nonbusiness assets such as money from his bank account and the proceeds from the sale of his house. A sole proprietor may lose everything if his business becomes insolvent. Hence, the sole proprietorship is a risky form of business for its owner.

Despite this risk, there are two reasons a person may organize a business as a sole proprietorship. First, the sole proprietorship is formed very easily and inexpensively. No formalities are necessary. Second, few people consider the business form decision. They merely begin their businesses. Thus, by default, a person going into business by herself automatically creates a sole proprietorship when she fails to choose another business form. These two reasons explain why the sole proprietorship is the most common form of business in the United States.

Because the sole proprietorship is merely an extension of its owner, it has no life apart from its owner. Therefore, while the business of a sole proprietorship may be freely sold to someone else, legally the sole proprietorship as a form of business cannot be transferred to another person.

The buyer of the business must create his own form of business to continue the business.

A sole proprietorship is not a legal entity. It cannot sue or be sued. Instead, creditors must sue the owner. The sole proprietor—in his own name—must sue those who harm the business.

A sole proprietor may hire employees for the business, but they are employees of the sole proprietor. Under the law of agency, the sole proprietor is responsible for her employees' authorized contracts and for the torts they commit in the course of their employment. Also, a sole proprietorship is not a tax-paying entity for federal income tax purposes. All of the income of a sole proprietorship is income to its owner and must be reported on the sole proprietor's individual federal income tax return. Likewise, any business losses are deductible without limit on the sole proprietor's individual tax return. This loss-deduction advantage explains why some wealthier taxpayers use the sole proprietorship for selected business investments—when losses are expected in the early years of the business, yet the risk of liability is low. Such an investor may form a sole proprietorship and hire a professional manager to operate the business.

Many sole proprietorships have trade names. For example, Caryl Stanley may operate her bagel shop under the name Caryl's Bagel Shop. Caryl would be required to file the trade name under a state statute requiring the registration of fictitious business names. If she were sued by a creditor, the creditor would address his complaint to "Caryl Stanley, doing business as Caryl's Bagel Shop."

Partnership A **partnership** has two or more owners, called **partners**, who carry on a business for a profit. There are various default rules that govern the relationship between partners. For example, partners have the right to make all the management decisions for the business and all profits and losses are shared equally among them. However, many of these rules can be modified by agreement among the partners.

Similarly, unless agreed otherwise, the partners assume personal liability for all the obligations of the business. All the debts of the business are the debts of all the partners. Likewise, partners are liable for the torts committed in the course of business by their partners or by partnership employees. If the assets of the business are insufficient to pay the claims of its creditors, the creditors may require one or more of the partners to pay the claims using their individual, nonbusiness assets. Thus, a partner may have to pay more than his share of partnership liabilities.

Like the sole proprietorship, the partnership is not a tax-paying entity for federal income tax purposes. All of the income of the partnership is income to its partners and must be reported on the individual partners' federal income tax returns whether or not it is distributed to the partners. Likewise, any business losses are deductible without limit on the partner's individual tax return.

The partnership has a life apart from its owners. When a partner dies or otherwise leaves the business, the partnership usually continues. A partner's ownership interest in a partnership is not freely transferable: A purchaser of the partner's interest is not a partner of the partnership unless the other partners agree to admit the purchaser as a partner.

Why would persons organize a business as a partnership? Formation of a partnership requires no formalities and may be formed by default. A partnership is created automatically when two or more persons own a business together without selecting another form. Also, each partner's right to manage the business and the deductibility of partnership losses on individual tax returns are attractive features.

Limited Liability Partnership   A limited liability partnership is a partnership whose partners have elected limited liability status. Reacting to the large personal liability sometimes imposed on accountants and lawyers for the professional malpractice of their partners, Texas enacted in 1991 the first statute permitting the formation of **limited liability partnerships (LLPs)**. An LLP is identical to a partnership except that an LLP partner has no liability for most LLP obligations; however, an LLP partner retains unlimited liability for his *own* wrongful acts, such as his malpractice liability to a client.

While most states recognize LLPs, the limited liability company (LLC), discussed later, is often a more popular choice for small businesses because of the additional liability protection it provides. However, because some states do not allow professional services, like law and accounting firms, to be organized as LLCs, the LLP continues to be a necessary option. Its main benefit is that it limits liability for the malpractice of other partners, while allowing all partners to both receive favorable tax treatment and participate in management.

In order to form an LLP, the partners have to file a form with the secretary of state in the state in which they wish to organize.

LLP partners may elect to have the LLP taxed like a partnership or a corporation. If an LLP is taxed like a corporation, it pays federal income tax on its income, but the partners pay federal income tax only on the compensation paid and the partnership profits distributed to the partners.

Limited Partnership   A **limited partnership** has one or more general partners and one or more limited partners. General partners have rights and liabilities similar to partners in a partnership. They manage the business of the limited partnership and have unlimited liability for the obligations of the limited partnership. Typically, however, the only general partner is a corporation, thereby protecting the human managers from unlimited liability.

Limited partners usually have no liability for the obligations of the limited partnership once they have paid their capital contributions to the limited partnership. Limited partners have no right to manage the business, but if they do manage, they nonetheless retain their limited liability.

Like an LLP, a limited partnership may elect to be taxed either as a partnership or as a corporation. If a limited partnership is taxed like a partnership, general partners report their shares of the limited partnership's income and losses on their individual federal income tax returns. For general partners, losses of the business are deductible without limit. A limited partner must pay federal income tax on his share of the profits of the business, but he may deduct his share of losses only to the extent of his investment in the business. As a passive investor, a limited partner may use the losses only to offset income from other passive investments.

If a limited partnership is taxed like a corporation, the limited partnership pays federal income tax on its net income. The partners pay federal income tax only on compensation paid and profits distributed to them.

A limited partnership may have a life apart from its owners. When a partner dies or otherwise leaves the business, the limited partnership is not dissolved, unless there is no remaining general partner or no remaining limited partner. A general or limited partner's rights may not be wholly transferred to another person unless the other partners agree to admit the new person as a partner.

Unlike a sole proprietorship or partnership—but like an LLP—a limited partnership may be created only by complying with a state statute permitting limited partnerships. Thus, no limited partnership may be created by default.

There are three main reasons persons organize a business as a limited partnership. First, by using a corporate general partner, no human will have unlimited liability for the debts of the business. Second, if the limited partnership is taxed like a partnership, losses of the business are deductible on the owners' federal income tax returns. Third, investors may contribute capital to the business yet avoid unlimited liability and the obligation to manage the business. Thus, the limited partnership has the ability to attract large amounts of capital, much more than the sole proprietorship, which has only one owner, or the partnership, whose partners' fear of unlimited liability restricts the size of the business. Hence, for a business needing millions of dollars of capital, wanting only a few owners to manage the business, and expecting to lose money in its early years, the limited partnership is a particularly good form of business.

Corporation A **corporation** is owned by shareholders who elect a board of directors to manage the business. The board of directors often selects officers to run the day-to-day affairs of the business. Consequently, ownership and management of a corporation may be completely separate: No shareholder has the right to manage, and no officer or director needs to be a shareholder.

Shareholders have limited liability for the obligations of the corporation, even if a shareholder is elected as a director or selected as an officer. Directors and officers have no liability for the contracts they or the corporation's employees sign only in the name of the corporation. While managers have liability for their own misconduct, they have no liability for corporate torts committed by other corporate managers or employees. Therefore, shareholders, officers, and directors have limited liability for the obligations of the business.

The usual corporation is a tax-paying entity for federal income tax purposes. The corporation pays taxes on its profits. Shareholders do not report their shares of corporation profits on their individual federal income tax returns. Instead, only when the corporation distributes its profits to the shareholders in the form of dividends or the shareholders sell their investments at a profit do the shareholders report income on their individual returns. This creates a double-tax possibility because profits are taxed once at the corporation level and again at the shareholder level when dividends are paid.

Also, shareholders do not deduct corporate losses on their individual returns. They may, however, deduct their investment losses after they have sold their shares of the corporation.

There is one important exception to these corporate tax rules. The shareholders may elect to have the corporation and its shareholders taxed under Subchapter S of the Internal Revenue Code. By electing **S corporation** status, the corporation and its shareholders are taxed nearly entirely like a partnership: Income and losses of the business are reported on the shareholders' individual federal income tax returns. A corporation electing S corporation status may have no more than 100 shareholders, have only one class of shares, and be owned only by individuals and trusts.

A corporation has a life separate from its owners and its managers. When a shareholder or manager dies or otherwise leaves the business, the corporation is not dissolved. A shareholder may sell his shares of the corporation to other persons without limitation unless there is a contrary agreement. The purchaser becomes a shareholder with all the rights of the selling shareholder.

There are several reasons persons organize a business as a corporation. First, no human has unlimited liability for the debts of the business. As a result, businesses in the riskiest industries—such as manufacturing—

incorporate. Second, because investors may contribute capital to the business, avoid unlimited liability, escape the obligation to manage the business, and easily liquidate their investments by selling their shares, the corporation has the ability to attract large amounts of capital, even more than the limited partnership, whose partnership interests are not as freely transferable. Thus, the corporation has the capacity to raise the largest amount of capital.

The S corporation has an additional advantage: Losses of the business are deductible on individual federal income tax returns. However, because the S corporation is limited to 100 shareholders, its ability to raise capital is severely limited. Also, while legally permitted to sell their shares, S corporation shareholders may be unable to find investors willing to buy their shares or may be restricted from selling their shares pursuant to an agreement between the shareholders.

Professional Corporation All states permit professionals such as accountants, physicians, and dentists to incorporate their professional practices. The **professional corporation** is identical to a business corporation in most respects. It is formed only by a filing with the secretary of state, and it is managed by a board of directors, unless a statute permits it to be managed like a partnership. The rigid management structure makes the professional corporation inappropriate for some smaller professional practices.

While professional shareholders have no personal liability for the obligations of the professional corporation, such as a building lease, they retain unlimited liability to their clients for their professional malpractice. A professional will have no personal liability, however, for the malpractice of a fellow shareholder or associate.

Typically, only professionals holding the same type of license to practice a profession may be shareholders of a professional corporation. For example, only physicians licensed to practice medicine may be shareholders of a professional corporation that practices medicine.

Professional corporation shareholders may elect for the corporation to be taxed like a corporation, or they may elect S corporation tax treatment.

Fewer and fewer professionals incorporate each year. All of the liability and taxation advantages of the professional corporation have been assumed by the LLP. In addition, most professionals like the flexible management structure of the LLP better.

Limited Liability Company A **limited liability company (LLC)** is a business form intended to combine the nontax advantages of corporations with the favorable tax treatment of partnerships. An LLC is owned by members, who may manage the LLC themselves or elect the manager or managers who will operate the business. Members have limited liability for the obligations of the LLC.

All states except California permit professionals to organize as LLCs. Professionals in a professional LLC have unlimited liability, however, for their own malpractice. Like an LLP, members of an LLC may elect to have the LLC taxed like a partnership or a corporation.

There is limited free transferability of the LLC members' ownership interests. Transfer of a membership interest entitles the transferee to receive only the member's distributions from the LLC, unless all members or the LLC agreement permits the transferee to become a member. The death, retirement, or bankruptcy of any member usually does not dissolve or cause the liquidation of the LLC.

LLCs are covered in detail in Chapter 40.

Benefit Corporations
A **benefit corporation** is one of the newest business forms. It is very similar to a traditional S corporation, but the purpose of a benefit corporation is to consider not only the shareholder value or the "bottom line," but the business's general public benefit. For example, Indiana's benefit corporation statute defines a public benefit, in part, as a "material positive impact on society and the environment." Ind. Code § 23-1.3-2-7. The benefit corporation is a business form adopted by over half of the states.

The reason so many states have adopted benefit corporation statutes is because, historically, the primary purpose of a corporation is to maximize shareholder value, and shareholders often have the right to sue when corporate leaders fail to protect their interests. That said, with the increase in social consciousness among businesses, which is frequently demanded by customers, many businesses have wanted the flexibility to look beyond shareholder value when making business decisions. The benefit corporation form allows for this, especially as it relates to focusing on employees, the community, and the environment.

Third-party certifications are widely available; these allow benefit corporations, and non-benefit entities for that matter, to demonstrate their commitment to the public good. However, most states do not require benefit corporations to actually obtain such certifications in order to elect benefit corporation status. The most prominent certifying body is B Lab, a nonprofit organization in Pennsylvania. The organization evaluates companies on various factors, including worker compensation, civic engagement, and environmental impact, and grants satisfactory companies B Corp Certifications. Some of the most famous benefit corporations that have B Corp Certifications include Allbirds, Kickstarter, and Patagonia.

 LO37-2 Compare and contrast the various forms of business.

See Figure 37.1 for a summary of the general characteristics of business forms.

 **LOG ON**

www.sba.gov/business-guide
The Small Business Administration has valuable resources for anyone starting a business. Under "Launch your business," you will find sections describing some forms of business and listing some of the other steps to beginning a business, as well as the tax effects of each form.

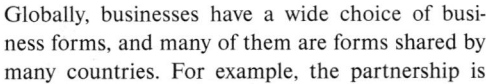 *The Global Business Environment*

Globally, businesses have a wide choice of business forms, and many of them are forms shared by many countries. For example, the partnership is recognized not only in the United States, but also in Australia, Canada, Cyprus, England, India, Israel, Russia, South Africa, Turkey, Zimbabwe, and many other nations. In the Chinese province of Hong Kong, the sole proprietorship, partnership, limited partnership, and company are the typical business forms. Limited liability partnerships do not exist in Hong Kong as yet, nor in much of the world for that matter. Limited liability companies in Hong Kong are like American corporations.

German law recognizes the public stock corporation (*AG* or *Aktiengesellschaft*). Its shares are freely transferable like those of American corporations, so it may have an unlimited number of shareholders. More common is the limited liability company (*GmbH* or *Gesellschaft mit beschrankter Haftung*), first created in 1892. It permits the owners to restrict the transfer of its shares. The majority of German subsidiaries of foreign corporations are *GmbH*s rather than *AG*s. Owners of *AG*s and *GmbH*s have liability limited to their capital contributions. The German general commercial partnership (*OHG* or *offene Handelsgesellschaft*) and the limited commercial partnership (*KG* or *Kommanditgesellschaft*) are essentially the same as the general and limited partnerships in the United States.

To find examples of forms of business in numerous countries, go to http://en.m.wikipedia.org/wiki/Types_of_business_entity.

Figure 37.1 General Characteristics of Forms of Business

	Sole Proprietorship	Partnership	Limited Liability Partnership	Limited Partnership	Benefit Corporation	Corporation	S Corporation	Limited Liability Company
Formation	When one person owns a business without forming a corporation or LLC	By agreement of owners or by default when two or more owners conduct business together without creating another business form	By agreement of owners; must comply with limited liability partnership statute	By agreement of owners; must comply with limited partnership statute	By agreement of owners; must comply with benefit corporation statute	By agreement of owners; must comply with corporation statute	By agreement of owners; must comply with corporation statute; must elect S corporation status under Internal Revenue Code	By agreement of owners; must comply with limited liability company statute
Duration	Terminates on death or withdrawal of sole proprietor	Usually unaffected by death or withdrawal of partner	Usually unaffected by death or withdrawal of partner	Unaffected by death or withdrawal of partner	Unaffected by death or withdrawal of shareholder	Unaffected by death or withdrawal of shareholder	Unaffected by death or withdrawal of shareholder	Usually unaffected by death or withdrawal of member
Management	By sole proprietor	By partners	By partners	By general partners	By board of directors	By board of directors	By board of directors	By members, unless choose to be manager-managed
Owner liability	Unlimited	Unlimited	Limited to capital contribution, except for owner's individual torts	Unlimited for general partners; limited to capital contribution for limited partners	Limited to capital contribution except for owner's individual torts	Limited to capital contribution, except for owner's individual torts	Limited to capital contribution, except for owner's individual torts	Limited to capital contribution, except for owner's individual torts
Transferability of owner's interest	None	Limited	Limited	Limited, unless agreed otherwise	Freely transferable, although shareholders may agree otherwise	Freely transferable, although shareholders may agree otherwise	Freely transferable, although shareholders usually agree otherwise	Limited, unless agreed otherwise
Federal income taxation	Only sole proprietor taxed	Only partners taxed	Usually only partners taxed; may elect to be taxed like a corporation	Usually only partners taxed; may elect to be taxed like a corporation	Corporation taxed; shareholders taxed on dividends (double tax)	Corporation taxed; shareholders taxed on dividends (double tax)	Only shareholders taxed	Usually only members taxed; may elect to be taxed like a corporation

Ethics and Compliance in Action

Two people who carefully consider which American business form to use for their business can achieve nearly any combination of attributes. For example, by choosing LLP status, they can limit their personal liability, totally control the business, and deduct business losses on their individual federal income tax returns. They can do the same with an LLC or S corporation. They will have no liability for the contracts of the business, even though they make all business decisions and make all contracts for the business. When the business becomes profitable, they can elect to have the business form taxed like a corporation, and if the corporate tax rate is lower than their individual tax rate, they will derive tax savings by retaining earnings in the business.

- Is it ethical for a business owner who controls the business to escape liability for the business's contracts and torts by hiding behind the veil of the business organization?
- Is it ethical for a business owner to select a business form and elect a tax treatment that minimizes her tax liability?

Partnerships

The basic concept of partnership is as ancient as the history of collective human activity. Partnerships were known in ancient Babylonia, ancient Greece, and the Roman Empire. Hammurabi's Code of 2300 B.C. regulated partnerships. The definition of a partnership in the 6th-century Justinian Code of the Roman Empire does not differ materially from that in our laws today. The partnership was likewise known in Asian countries, including China. During the Middle Ages, much trade between nations was carried on by partnerships.

By the close of the 17th century, the partnership was recognized in the English common law. When the United States became an independent nation and adopted the English common law in 1776, the English law of partnerships became a part of American law. In the early part of the 19th century, the partnership became the most important form of association in the United States.

Today, the American common law of partnership has been largely replaced by statutory law. Every state has a statute on partnership law. The Revised Uniform Partnership Act (RUPA) of 1994, with the 1997 amendments, is a model partnership statute that is the product of the National Conference of Commissioners on Uniform State Laws, a group of practicing lawyers, judges, and law professors. The aims of the RUPA are to codify partnership law in one document, to make that law more nearly consistent with itself, and to attain uniformity throughout the country.

In recent years, the RUPA has supplanted the Uniform Partnership Act (UPA) of 1914 as the dominant source of partnership law in the United States. While some commercially important states, such as New York, have not adopted RUPA, it is the framework we adopt for this text. In practice, do note that you will have to check the rules that are applicable to the jurisdiction in which you operate. (See Figure 37.2.)

Creation of Partnership

 LO37-3 Apply the definition of *partnership* and avoid inadvertently being a partner of another person.

No formalities are necessary to create a partnership. Two or more persons may become partners in accordance with a written partnership agreement, they may agree orally to be partners, or they may become partners merely by arranging their affairs as if they were partners. If partners conduct business under a trade name, they must file the name with the secretary of state in compliance with state statutes requiring the registration of fictitious business names.

When people decide to become partners, they should employ a lawyer to prepare a written partnership agreement. Although a partnership agreement is not required to form a partnership, it is highly desirable for the same reasons that written contracts are generally preferred. In addition, the statute of frauds requires a writing for a partnership having a term of a year or more.

More importantly, when partners do not define their relationship as partners, the default rules of the RUPA determine the rights of the partners vis-à-vis each other. While the RUPA rules are sensible and meet the needs of many partners, they may not meet the specific interests of other partners. Thus, having a written partnership agreement will allow the partners to define their rights and duties appropriately for them.

When there is no written partnership agreement, a dispute may arise over whether persons who are associated in

Figure 37.2   Principal Characteristics of Partnerships under the RUPA

1. A partnership may be created with no formalities. Two or more people merely need to agree to own and conduct a business together for a profit in order to create a partnership.
2. Partners have unlimited liability for the obligations of the business.
3. Each partner, merely by being an owner of the business, has a right to manage the business of the partnership and is an agent of the partnership and thus may make the partnership liable for contracts, torts, and crimes. Because partners are liable for all obligations of the partnership, in effect each partner is an agent of the other partners. Each partner may hire agents, and every partner is liable for the agents' authorized contracts and for torts that the agents commit in the course of their employments.
4. A partnership is not an employer of the partners, for most purposes. As a result, for example, a partner who leaves a partnership is not entitled to unemployment benefits.
5. Partners are fiduciaries of the partnership. They must act in the best interests of the partnership, not in their individual best interests.
6. The profits or losses of the business are shared by the partners, who report their shares of the profits or losses on their individual federal income tax returns because the partnership does not pay federal income taxes. Nonetheless, a partnership does keep its own financial records and must file an information return with the Internal Revenue Service.*
7. A partnership may own property in its own name.
8. A partnership may sue or be sued in its own name. The partners may also be sued on a partnership obligation.
9. A partner may sue her partners during the operation of the partnership.
10. A partner's ownership interest in a partnership is not freely transferable. A purchaser of a partner's interest does not become a partner but is entitled to receive only the partner's share of the partnership's profits.
11. Generally, a partnership has a life apart from its owners. If a partner dies, the partnership usually continues.

*The federal income tax return filed by a partnership, Schedule K-1, is merely an information return in which the partnership indicates its gross income and deductions and the names and addresses of its partners (IRC § 6031). The information return allows the Internal Revenue Service to determine whether the partners accurately report partnership income on their individual returns.

some enterprise are partners. For example, someone may assert that she is a partner and, therefore, claim a share of the value of a successful enterprise. More frequently, an unpaid creditor may seek to hold a person liable for a debt incurred by another person in the same enterprise. To determine whether there is a partnership in the absence of an express agreement, the courts use the definition of partnership in the RUPA.

 LO37-4 Appreciate the consequences of being a partner.

RUPA Definition of Partnership
The RUPA defines a *partnership* as an "association of two or more persons to carry on as co-owners of a business for profit." If the definition is satisfied, then the courts will treat those involved as partners. A relationship may meet the RUPA definition of partnership even when the parties do not believe they are a partner, and occasionally, even if the parties agree that they are not partners.

Association of Two or More Persons As an association, a partnership is a *voluntary and consensual relationship*. It cannot be imposed on a person; a person must agree expressly or impliedly to have a person associate with her. For example, a partner cannot force her partners to accept her daughter into the partnership.

No person can be a partner with herself—a partnership must have *at least two partners*. A person may be a partner with her spouse.

Nearly everyone or everything may be a partner. An individual, trust, partnership, limited partnership, corporation, or other association may be a partner.

Carrying On a Business Any trade, occupation, or profession may qualify as a business. Carrying on a business usually requires a series of transactions conducted over a period of time. For example, a group of farmers that buys supplies in quantity to get lower prices is not carrying on a business but only part of one. However, if the group buys harvesting equipment with which it intends to harvest crops for others for a fee for many years, it is carrying on a business.

Co-ownership Partners must *co-own the business* in which they associate.

The two most important factors in establishing co-ownership of the business are the sharing of profits and the sharing of management of the business. The RUPA declares that a person's ***sharing the profits*** of a business is presumptive evidence that she is a partner in the business. This means that persons sharing profits are partners, unless other evidence exists to disprove they are partners. The rationale for this rule is that a person ordinarily would not be sharing the profits of a business unless she were a co-owner. This rule brings under partnership law many persons who fail to realize that they are partners. For example, two college students who purchase college basketball tickets, resell them, and split the profits are partners.

Sharing the gross revenues of a business does not create a presumption of partnership. The profits, not the gross receipts, must be shared. For example, a broker who receives a commission on a sale of land is not a partner of the seller of that land.

Although sharing profits usually is presumptive proof of a partnership, the RUPA provides that no presumption of partnership is made when a share of profits is received in payment

1. Of a debt.
2. Of wages to an employee or services to an independent contractor.
3. Of rent.
4. Of an annuity or other retirement or health benefit to a beneficiary or representative of a deceased partner.
5. As interest on a loan.
6. For the sale of the goodwill of a business or other property.

These exceptions reflect the normal expectations of the parties that no partnership exists in such situations.

Sharing management of a business is additional evidence tending to prove the existence of a partnership. However, by itself, participation in management is not conclusive proof of the existence of a partnership. For example, a creditor may be granted considerable control in a business, such as a veto power over partnership decisions and the right of consultation, without becoming a partner. Also, a sole proprietor may hire someone to manage his business, yet the manager will not be a partner of the sole proprietor.

However, when the parties claim that they share profits for one of the six reasons given earlier, the sharing of management may overcome the presumption that they are not partners. When the parties arrange their affairs in a manner that otherwise establishes an objective intent to create a partnership, the courts find that a partnership exists. For example, when a nonmanagerial employee initially shares profits as a form of employment compensation, the employee is not a partner of his employer. But when the employer and employee modify their relationship by having the employee exercise the managerial control of a partner and fail to reaffirm that the manager is merely an employee, a partnership may exist.

Creditors occupy a special position. Many cases have permitted creditors to share profits and to exercise considerable control over a business without becoming partners. Creditor control is often justified on the grounds that it is merely reasonable protection for the creditor's risk.

For Profit The owners of an enterprise must *intend to make a profit* to create a partnership. If the enterprise suffers losses, yet the owners intend to make a profit, a partnership may result. When an endeavor is carried on by several people for charitable or other nonprofit objectives, it is not a partnership. For example, Alex and Geri operate a restaurant booth at a county fair each year to raise money for a Boy Scout troop. Their relationship is not a partnership but merely an association. (Nonetheless, like partners, they may be individually liable for the debts of the enterprise.)

Intent Frequently, courts say that there must be intent to form a partnership. This rule is more correctly stated as follows: *The parties must intend to create a relationship that the law recognizes as a partnership.* A partnership may exist even if the parties entered it inadvertently, without considering whether they had created a partnership. A written agreement to the effect that the parties do not intend to form a partnership is not conclusive if their actions provide evidence of their intent to form a relationship that meets the RUPA partnership test.

There are several important consequences of being a partner. See Figure 37.3 for a summary of the most important.

The *Rasmussen* case, which follows the next section, considered whether Iowa bison herders were partners.

Figure 37.3   Important Consequences of Being a Partner

1. Unless you agree otherwise:
   a. You share ownership of the business. For example, you want to bring an employee into your business, which is worth $250,000. If you and the employee conduct your affairs like partners, your employee will become your partner and own half of your business.
   b. You share the profits of the business.
   c. You share management of the business. Your partner must be allowed to participate in management decisions.
2. Your partner is an agent of the partnership. You are liable for your partner's torts and contracts made in the ordinary course of business.
3. You owe fiduciary duties to your partnership and your partner, such as the duties not to compete with the business, not to self-deal, and not to disclose confidential matters.
4. You have unlimited personal liability for all the obligations of the partnership.

Creation of Joint Ventures

Courts frequently distinguish **joint ventures** from partnerships. A joint venture may be found when a court is reluctant to call an arrangement a partnership because the purpose of the arrangement is not to establish an ongoing business involving many transactions; instead, it is limited to a single project. For example, an agreement to buy, develop, and resell for profit a particular piece of real estate is likely to be viewed as a joint venture rather than a partnership. In all other respects, joint ventures are created just as partnerships are created. The joint venturers may have a formal written agreement. In its absence, a court applies the RUPA definition of partnership—modified so as not to require the carrying on of a business—to determine whether a joint venture has been created.

The legal implications of the distinction between a partnership and a joint venture are not entirely clear. Generally, partnership law applies to joint ventures. For example, all of the participants in a joint venture are personally liable for its debts, and joint venturers owe each other the fiduciary duties imposed on partners. Joint ventures are treated as partnerships for federal income tax purposes. The most significant difference between joint venturers and partners is that joint venturers are usually held to have *less implied and apparent authority* to make contracts for the joint venture than partners because of the limited scope of the enterprise.

Rasmussen v. Jackson   834 N.W.2d 82 (Iowa Ct. App. 2013)

Robert Jackson, Sharon Magee, and another person agreed to raise a herd of bison. Magee owned land across the road from Jackson and purchased a 28 percent interest in the herd. She paid Jackson to manage her portion of the herd, which grazed her property as well as Jackson's. Sometime later, Galen Rasmussen became interested in the bison operation. Because Magee wanted to exit the operation, Jackson contacted Rasmussen, who bought the land from Magee. He also reached an agreement with Magee to purchase her share of the herd, although the agreement to buy her bison was never executed.

Jackson helped manage Rasmussen's land while Rasmussen was out of the country. Rasmussen, in turn, allowed the entire bison herd to graze on his property. Eventually, the friendship between the two men deteriorated. Rasmussen notified Jackson that Jackson could no longer graze the herd on Rasmussen's land and filed an action against Jackson seeking a judgment that Jackson had no rights in Rasmussen's land. Jackson counterclaimed for breach of a partnership agreement and violations of the Uniform Partnership Act. The Iowa district court found there was never a partnership between Jackson and Rasmussen. Jackson appealed to the Iowa Court of Appeals.

Viatheswaran, Judge

A partnership is "an association of two or more persons to carry on as co-owners a business for profit. . . ." Iowa Code § 486A.101(6). The term "association" signifies that the partnership is an entity separate from the partners. The term "co-owners" does not mean ownership of a business in the equity sense but the power of ultimate control.

Persons may organize a partnership informally, without any written agreement, or even by accident. All that is necessary to establish a partnership is that the parties carry on a business for profit with the intention that they share ownership (control) of the business. Uniform Partnership Act § 202, cmt. 1 (1997).

In determining whether a partnership has been formed, certain rules apply. First, joint ownership "does not by itself establish a partnership, even if the co-owners share profits made by the use of the property." Iowa Code § 486A.202(3)(a). Second, "[t]he sharing of gross returns does not by itself establish a partnership, even if the persons sharing them have a joint or common right or interest in property from which the returns are derived." Iowa Code § 486A.202(3)(b). Finally, "[a] person who receives a share of the profits of a business is presumed to be a partner in the business, unless the profits were received in payment of" certain enumerated expenses. Iowa Code. § 486A.202(3)(c).

Applying the first rule, the record reveals there was no joint ownership of property. Magee's farmland was in her name exclusively. Rasmussen purchased the property with a loan in his name alone and titled the property in his name alone. Iowa Code § 486A.204(4). ("Property acquired in the name of one or more of the partners, without an indication in the instrument transferring title to the property of the person's capacity as a partner or of the existence of a partnership and without use of partnership assets, is presumed to be separate property, even if used for partnership purposes.") The cost of maintaining the land remained Rasmussen's responsibility. While Jackson assisted with maintenance, he billed Rasmussen for the work.

As for the bison herd, Rasmussen entered into a written agreement with Magee to purchase twenty-eight percent of the herd, with the actual number of bison to be determined at a later date. Also to be determined at a later date were Jackson's fees for managing the herd. Payment for the animals was to be "a mutually beneficial and flexible agreement between Sharon Magee and Galen Rasmussen." The agreement ended with the statement, "[t]here is to be no partnership as such between Galen Rasmussen and Bob Jackson."

Ultimately, no money for the bison changed hands and no bison were identified as belonging to Rasmussen. In fact, according to Rasmussen, Jackson placed a lien on Magee's percentage of the herd, precluding a transfer of the bison to him. In short, the bison were never jointly owned by Jackson and Rasmussen.

Nor was equipment for maintenance of the herd purchased jointly. While Jackson testified that he expected Rasmussen to contribute to the purchase of additional equipment, he acknowledged that this equipment would be titled in Rasmussen's name exclusively.

To summarize, joint ownership is not conclusive evidence of a partnership, but, in this case, it was not even presumptive evidence of a partnership, because there was no evidence that Rasmussen jointly owned property with Jackson.

We turn to the second rule relating to the sharing of gross returns. Under the terms of Jackson's agreement with Magee, Magee was to pay forty percent of the expenses related to maintaining the common herd and was to receive twenty-eight percent of the proceeds. Assuming this arrangement could be characterized as a partnership, Rasmussen categorically stated he did not wish to participate in such an arrangement with Jackson. He testified, "I always intended from the beginning and stated from the beginning I wanted my own bison on my side of the road." He expressed a hope that he would have enough bison to slaughter to make payments on his farm and on the bison. That hope was not realized.

We recognize Jackson testified to discussions with Rasmussen concerning the number of bison that would be slaughtered per year. However, he presented scant, if any, evidence that they shared gross returns. Accordingly, to the extent the sharing of gross returns could constitute evidence of a partnership, this factor was not present.

This brings us to the third rule concerning receipt of a share of profits. This presumptive factor in favor of finding a partnership was not present.

Returning to the definition of a partnership as "an association of two or more persons to carry on as co-owners a business for profit," we find no evidence of an association distinct from Jackson and Rasmussen. Iowa Code § 486A.201(1). ("[P]artnership is an entity distinct from its partners.") We also find no evidence that Rasmussen had the power of ultimate control over a for-profit business distinct from his own business enterprise. Because there was no evidence of a partnership, we affirm the district court's dismissal of Jackson's counterclaims under the Uniform Partnership Act.

Judgment for Rasmussen affirmed.

Creation of Mining Partnerships
Although similar to an ordinary partnership or a joint venture, a mining partnership is recognized as a distinct relationship in a number of states. Persons who cooperate in the working of either a mine or an oil or gas well are treated as mining partners if there is (1) joint ownership of a mineral interest, (2) joint operation of the property, and (3) sharing of profits and losses. Joint operation requires more than merely financing the development of a mineral interest, but it does not require active physical participation in operations; it may be proved by furnishing labor, supplies, services, or advice. The delegation of sole operating responsibility to one of the participants does not bar treatment as a mining partnership.

Creation of Limited Liability Partnerships
Unlike an ordinary partnership, a limited liability partnership (LLP) may not be created merely by partners

conducting a business together. The partners must expressly agree to create an LLP by complying with a limited liability partnership statute. The formation of an LLP requires filing a form with the secretary of state, paying an annual fee, and adding the words "Registered Limited Liability Partnership," "Limited Liability Partnership," or the acronym "RLLP" or "LLP" to the partnership's name. Some states also require an LLP to maintain a minimum level of professional liability insurance or net worth.

Purported Partners

LO37-5 Understand the risks of being a purported partner and avoid being a purported partner.

Two persons may not be partners, yet in the eyes of a third person, they may appear to be partners. If the third person deals with one of the apparent partners, he may be harmed and seek to recover damages from both of the apparent partners. The question, then, is whether the third person may collect damages from both of the apparent partners, even though they are not partners in fact.

For example, Thomas thinks that Wilson, a wealthy person, is a partner of Porter, a poor person. Thomas decides to do business with Porter on the grounds that if Porter does not perform as agreed, he can recover damages from Wilson. If Thomas is wrong and Wilson is not Porter's partner, Thomas ordinarily has no recourse against Wilson. RUPA section 308(e) states that "persons who are not partners as to each other are not liable as partners to other persons." However, if Thomas can prove that Wilson misled him to believe that Wilson and Porter were partners, he may sue Wilson for damages suffered when Porter failed to perform as agreed. This is an application of the doctrine of **purported partners**.

The liability of a purported partner is based on substantial, detrimental reliance on the appearance of partnership. A person will be a purported partner and have liability when the three elements of RUPA section 308(a) are met:

1. A person purports to be or consents to being represented as a partner of another person or partnership.
2. A third party relies on the representation.
3. The third party transacts with the actual or purported partnership.

The third party may hold liable the persons who purported to be partners or consented to being represented as the partner of the actual or purported partnership.

Purporting to Be a Partner A person may purport to be a partner by referring to himself as another person's partner. Or he might appear frequently in the office of a purported partner and confer with him. Perhaps he and another person share office space, have one door to an office with both of their names on it, have one telephone number, and share a receptionist who answers the phone giving the names of both persons.

More difficult is determining when a person *consents* to being represented as another's partner. Mere knowledge that one is being held out as a partner is not consent. But a person's silence in response to a statement that the person is another's partner is consent.

For example, suppose Chavez tells Eaton that Gold is a partner in Birt's new restaurant. In fact, Gold is not Birt's partner. Later, Gold learns of the conversation between Chavez and Eaton. Gold does not have to seek out Chavez and Eaton to tell them that he is not Birt's partner in order to avoid being held liable as a partner for Birt's business debts. Had Chavez made the statement to Eaton in Gold's presence, however, Gold must deny the partnership relation or he will be held liable for Eaton's subsequent reliance on Gold's silence.

Note also that if a person makes a public representation that she is a partner of another, the purported partner is liable to any third person who relies on the representation, even if the purported partner is not aware of the reliance.

Reliance Resulting in a Transaction with the Partnership A purported partner is liable only to those persons who rely on the representation and enter into a transaction with the actual or purported partnership. This means that purported partnership is determined on a case-by-case basis. The third party must, in fact, rely on the appearance of partnership. For example, when Trent transacts with Doby based on Crabb's representation that Doby and Crabb are partners, Trent is able to hold both Doby and Crabb liable. If, however, Trent had dealt with Doby believing Doby was in business by herself and later discovers that Crabb had purported to be Doby's partner, only Doby would be liable to Trent because there was no reliance on Crabb's purporting to be Doby's partner when Trent transacted with Doby.

Effect of Purported Partnership Once persons are proved to be purported partners, a person who purported to be the others' partner or who consented to being represented as the others' partner is liable as though he were a partner of those persons. He is liable on contracts entered into by third parties on their belief that he was a partner. He is liable for torts committed during the course of relationships entered by third parties who believed he was a partner. In addition, a partnership that represents that a person is a partner endows the purported partner with the apparent authority to make contracts for the partnership.

Although two persons are purported partners to a person who knows of the representation and who relies on it, the purported partners are not partners in fact and do not share the profits, management, or value of the business of the purported partnership. Purported partnership is merely a device to allow creditors to sue persons who mislead the creditors into believing that a partnership exists. It does not create an actual partnership.

In the following case, *MP Nexlevel of Cal., Inc. v. CVIN*, the court found that a limited liability company was not a purported partner with another company despite federal documentation and a website where the companies refer to themselves as partners.

MP Nexlevel of Cal., Inc. v. CVIN   2014 U.S. Dist. LEXIS 142890 (E.D. Cal. Oct. 7, 2014)

This case concerns disputes that arose over a large-scale broadband infrastructure construction project (the Project) throughout California's Central Valley. The goal of the Project is to create an approximately 1,371-mile broadband fiber network through 18 Central Valley counties.

Because of various ongoing disputes that arose during the construction of the Project, plaintiff MP Nexlevel (MP) brought this suit against defendant CVIN LLC (CVIN), d/b/a Vast Networks, and defendant Corporation for Education Network Initiatives in California (CENIC), a nonprofit corporation. MP brings 47 claims against CVIN based on disputes concerning the construction of the Project. MP asserts its claims against the Member Defendants on the ground it is CVIN's partner under California Corporations Code § 16308(a) ("§ 16308(a)").

MP asserts that CVIN and CENIC were in a legal partnership such that CENIC should be liable for CVIN's alleged conduct as CVIN's partner. As proof of their purported partnership, MP points to, among other things, the joint application by CVIN and CENIC for the grant funding and various representations they made. CVIN, along with its partner CENIC, submitted an application for the grant funding (the grant application). On the grant application, CENIC was named as a proposed subrecipient of the grant by CVIN and represented that CVIN and CENIC were in a "public-private partnership." In the grant application, CVIN and CENIC represented that CVIN/CENIC would build the project and that in a public-private partnership, CVIN and CENIC would build, operate, and maintain the project.

MP alleges that CVIN and CENIC made representations in the grant application, websites, and elsewhere that demonstrate they were in a legal partnership. It is alleged that CVIN represented to various institutions that CVIN and CENIC had submitted an application for the grant funding. CENIC announced on its website that the CVIN/CENIC Central Valley Broadband Project received the grant funding. The announcement also stated that "the Project 'was designed and developed by the public-private partnership of CVIN and CENIC a non-profit corporation.'" CVIN's website also stated that "CENIC together with its private sector partner CVIN have put together a project plan designed to improve the availability of broadband networking infrastructure for 18 counties within the California Central Valley area."

The complaint stated that both CVIN and CENIC, by words on grant applications, in websites, and elsewhere, and by their conduct in jointly applying for grants, held themselves out as partners or in a partnership. Plaintiff further alleged that neither CENIC nor CVIN disclaimed their representations of being in a partnership, nor did CVIN or CENIC take any steps to publicly deny the many statements of their partnership or clarify the true nature of their relationship. MP therefore claims that because CENIC and CVIN presented themselves to the outside world as a partnership, CENIC has liability even if CENIC is not an actual partner to CVIN in the Project. MP alleges that CENIC and CVIN's representations and course of conduct indicating that they were partners, along with MP's reasonable reliance on the same, adequately supports liability of CENIC.

CENIC and Member Defendants have moved to dismiss the complaint under Fed. R. Civ. P. 12(b)(6).

O'Neill, Judge

To succeed on its claims, MP bears the burden of proving by a preponderance of the evidence that a partnership exists between CVIN and CENIC. A "purported partner is liable to the person to whom the representation is made if that person, relying on the representation, enters into a transaction with the alleged partnership." *In re Lona*, 393 B.R. 1, 16–17 (Bankr. N.D. Cal. 2008) (citing § 16308(a)). However, "the conduct of the ostensible partner must be sufficient to induce a reasonable and prudent person to believe that a partnership exists and for that person to enter into a transaction in reliance on that belief." *Id.* (citing *Armato v. Baden*, 71 Cal. App. 4th 885, 898 (1999)). In the context of a motion to dismiss, the complaint must plead sufficient facts that would support a finding that a purported partnership exists.

MP argues a partnership by estoppel exists between CVIN and CENIC for three primary reasons: (1) CVIN and CENIC publicly represented in the grant application and on their websites that they were in a "partnership"; (2) CVIN and CENIC jointly applied for the grant funding; and (3) CVIN and CENIC represented that they would jointly build, operate, maintain, and manage the Project. And because of this conduct, MP relied, in part, on the representations of both CVIN and CENIC that they were in a partnership and would jointly build and operate the Project.

MP alleges that CVIN and CENIC represented in the grant application and on their websites that they were "partners" or were in a "partnership." As other courts have noted, the term "partnership" has a colloquial meaning that describes a relationship unlike "a legal partnership of the sort that gives rise to fiduciary duties." *Love v. The Mail on Sunday*, 489 F. Supp. 2d 1100, 1108 (C.D. Cal. 2007), *aff'd*, 611 F.3d 601 (9th Cir. 2010); see also *T.G. Plastics Trading Co., Inc. v. Toray Plastics (America), Inc.*, 958 F. Supp. 2d 315, 327 (D.R.I. 2013) ("Use of the word 'partner' in the colloquial sense does not establish a legal partnership.").

MP does not provide and the Court cannot find any authority holding that two parties publicly describing themselves as "partners" or describing their relationship as a "partnership" is sufficient, without more, to establish a legal partnership, as MP suggests. Moreover, the allegations in the complaint seem to indicate that CVIN and CENIC used the words "partner" and "partnership" in the colloquial sense of the word.

Likewise, MP does not provide and the Court cannot find any authority holding that two parties jointly applying for and receiving federal grant funding, in and of itself, evinces a legal relationship, as MP suggests. Similarly, MP does not provide and the Court cannot find any authority holding that a collaboration between two parties to jointly build a project, in and of itself, evinces a legal partnership, as MP suggests. Thus, the Court finds that the complaint does not allege sufficient facts to demonstrate that MP reasonably believed a partnership existed between CVIN and CENIC.

In addition to alleging sufficient facts to demonstrate that MP reasonably believed a partnership existed between CVIN and CENIC, which MP does not do, MP must allege sufficient facts showing that it reasonably relied on that belief when entering into the contracts. The Court finds that the complaint fails to do so. Accordingly, MP's claims against CENIC fail for the additional reason that MP's alleged reliance on the conduct and representations of CVIN and CENIC was unreasonable.

Notably, MP provides no authority in its opposition for its position that it reasonably believed a partnership existed between CVIN and CENIC or that it reasonably relied on that belief when entering into the contracts. MP's alleged reliance appears particularly unreasonable given that MP alleges the following: MP entered into 14 contracts with CVIN only under which MP was CVIN's direct contractor; CVIN awarded the contracts and CVIN assured MP orally and in writing that CVIN alone would pay what was due under the contracts; and CVIN, not CENIC, allegedly "wrongfully refuses to comply with the payment terms of the Contracts." Further, MP does not allege that it had any direct interactions with CENIC when negotiating or entering the contracts with CVIN or that CVIN made any representations to MP as to CENIC's involvement with the contracts.

To find that a plaintiff reasonably relied on its belief that a purported partnership exists, courts generally require more than what MP has alleged here. The Court therefore holds, as a matter of law, MP's alleged reliance on its belief that CVIN and CENIC were legal partners when it entered into the contracts was unreasonable.

Accordingly, MP fails to allege sufficient facts to establish that it reasonably believed that CVIN and CENIC were partners or that it reasonably relied on that belief when it entered into the contracts. MP thus fails to allege facts that show CVIN and CENIC were purported partners under § 16308(a). Thus, all of MP's causes of action against CENIC fail because they are contingent on a finding that CVIN and CENIC are partners under § 16308(a).

The Court thus grants the defendant's motion to dismiss because the complaint appears futile.

Partnership Capital

When a partnership or limited liability partnership is formed, partners contribute cash or other property to the partnership. The partners' contribution is called **partnership capital**. To supplement beginning capital, other property may be contributed to the partnership as needed, such as by the partners permitting the partnership to retain some of its profits. Partnership capital is the equity of the business.

Loans made by partners to a partnership are not partnership capital but, instead, are liabilities of the business. Partners who make loans to a partnership are both owners and creditors.

Ethics and Compliance in Action

Consider the ethical basis of the doctrine of purported partnership.

• Why does Kant's categorical imperative, which we studied in Chapter 4, suggest the rule of purported partnership is the right one?

• What steps will you take to avoid being a purported partner when you carry on business with an associate who is not your partner? Are those not only legal, but also ethical acts? Is there any distinction between law and ethics in this context?

Partnership Property

 Distinguish partner's property from partnership property.

A partnership or limited liability partnership may own all or only a part of the property it uses. For example, it may own the business and perhaps a small amount of working capital in the form of cash or a checking account, yet own no other assets. All other tangible and intangible property used by the partnership may be individually or jointly owned by one or more of the partners or rented by the partnership from third parties. A determination of what is partnership property becomes essential when the partnership is dissolved and the assets are being distributed and when third persons claim that partnership property has been sold to them.

The RUPA provides that all property actually acquired by a partnership by transfer or otherwise is partnership property and, therefore, belongs to the partnership as an entity rather than to the partners. The RUPA has several rules that help determine when property is acquired by a partnership.

Property belongs to the partnership if the property is transferred (1) to the partnership in its name, (2) to any partner acting as a partner by a transfer document that names the partnership, or (3) to any partner by a transfer document indicating the partner's status as a partner or that a partnership exists. In addition, property acquired with partnership funds is presumed to be partnership property.

The presumption is very strong that property purchased with partnership funds and used in the partnership belongs to the partnership. On the other hand, property used by the partnership is presumed to belong to an individual partner when the property is purchased by a partner with her own funds and in her own name with no indication in the transfer document of the partner's status as a partner or the existence of a partnership. See this play out in the

Rasmussen case, which appears after the "Creation of Joint Ventures" section. However, in both situations, other factors such as an agreement among the partners may rebut the RUPA presumption of ownership.

The intent of the partners controls whether the partnership or an individual partner owns the property. It is best to have a written record of the partners' intent as to ownership of all property used by the partnership, such as a partnership agreement and partnership accounting records.

Examples A tax accountant discovers that a partnership is using a building to which a partner, Jacob Smith, holds title. The partnership pays rent monthly to Smith, but the partnership pays for all maintenance and repairs on the building. The accountant wants to know whether the partnership or Smith should be paying real property taxes on the building. Smith is the owner and should be paying taxes on it because his partners' intent to allow Smith to retain ownership is evidenced by the partnership's paying rent to Smith.

Changing the facts, suppose the partnership pays no rent to Smith, the partnership maintains and repairs the building, and the partnership pays real property taxes on the building, but the title is in Smith's name. Who owns the building? The property belongs to the partnership because all the objective criteria of ownership point toward partnership ownership, especially the payment of taxes. Therefore, when the partnership is liquidated, the building will be sold along with other partnership assets, and the proceeds of its sale will be distributed to partnership creditors and to all of the partners.

Need for Partnership Agreement It would be best for the partnership agreement to remove all ambiguity regarding ownership of property used by a partnership. For example, if the partnership is using a partner's building and the partners want the owning partner to retain ownership, it would be best to have a lease agreement between themselves and the partner stating that the partner owns the building; the amount of monthly rent; and who is responsible for property taxes, maintenance, and improvements to the building.

In the following case, *Finch v. Raymer*, the court held that real and personal property acquired by a cohabiting couple was a partnership and, nonetheless, property of a partnership when the couple split.

Finch v. Raymer	**2013 Tenn. App. LEXIS 319 (May 6, 2013)**

Jeffrey Finch filed this lawsuit against his former girlfriend, Tina Raymer, in May 2008. Mr. Finch's complaint alleged that he and Ms. Raymer cohabitated for several years, and during their "co-habitation/partnership," they acquired certain real and personal property as partnership property. Mr. Finch alleged that when the parties separated, Ms. Raymer ordered him to leave the residence where the parties were residing, and she refused to divide the parties' personal property. Mr. Finch sought an equal "one-half" division of the alleged partnership property, or property held in trust, and he sought an award of attorney fees. An answer to the complaint was filed denying that any of the disputed property was partnership property.

A bench trial was held on November 10, 2011, in which the trial court heard testimony. Mr. Finch testified that he and Ms. Raymer worked together renovating the properties that they bought and that they made money together. He said that both he and Ms. Raymer would search for houses, would sit down together and look at books to get ideas for house plans, and then would draw up a set of plans themselves.

The trial court found that a partnership between Mr. Finch and Ms. Raymer existed. As such, the court concluded that all of the disputed property was partnership property, and therefore, each party owned a one-half interest in the assets.

Highers, Judge

Tennessee's version of the Revised Uniform Partnership Act provides that "the association of two (2) or more persons to carry on as co-owners of a business for profit forms a partnership, whether or not the persons intend to form a partnership." Tenn. Code Ann. § 61-1-202(a). In other words, "if the parties' business brings them within the scope of a joint business undertaking for mutual profit—that is to say if they place their money, assets, labor, or skill in commerce with the understanding that profits will be shared between them—the result is a partnership whether or not the parties understood that it would be so." *Bass v. Bass*, 814 S.W.2d 38, 41 (Tenn. 1991) (citing *Pritchett v. Thomas Plater & Co.*, 144 Tenn. 406, 232 S.W. 961, 969–70 (1921)). The sharing of profits creates a rebuttable presumption of a partnership. Tenn. Code Ann. § 61-1-202(c)(3). However, in determining whether a partnership exists, no one fact or circumstance is conclusive. *Martin v. Coleman*, 19 S.W.3d 757, 761 (Tenn. 2000). "All of the relevant facts, actions, and conduct of the parties must be considered." *Id.*

"The courts regularly derive the partners' intentions and understandings by considering: (1) the parties' statements, conduct, and writings when the property was acquired, (2) the parties' course of conduct after the acquisition of the property, (3) the use of the property in the partnership business, (4) the terms of the partnership agreement, (5) the listing of the property as an asset on the partnership books and tax returns, (6) the attribution of profits or losses from the property to the partnership, and (7) the use of partnership funds to maintain the property." *Id.* (citing *Davis v. Loring*, No. 01A01-9004-CV-00149, 1991 Tenn. App. LEXIS 175, 1991 WL 32311, at *2 (Tenn. Ct. App. Mar. 13, 1991)).

Property that is "acquired by" a partnership is property of the partnership, as an entity, and not property of the partners individually. Tenn. Code Ann. § 61-1-203. The issue of when property is "acquired by" a partnership is governed by Tennessee Code Annotated section 61-1-204. The statute begins by stating, in subsection (a), that property is deemed partnership property if acquired in the name of the partnership or in the name of one or more of the partners with an indication in the instrument transferring title to the property of the person's capacity as a partner or of the existence of a partnership. Tenn. Code Ann. § 61-1-204(a). The statute goes on to provide two rebuttable presumptions that apply when the partners have failed to express their intent by referring to the existence of a partnership in the title documents.

First, subsection (c) provides that "property is presumed to be partnership property if purchased with partnership assets, even if not acquired in the name of the partnership or of one (1) or more partners with an indication in the instrument transferring title to the property of the person's capacity as a partner or the existence of a partnership." Tenn. Code Ann. § 61-1-204(c). In other words, "property purchased with partnership funds is presumed to be partnership property, notwithstanding the name in which title is held." Tenn. Code Ann. § 61-1-204 cmt. 3. The second, related presumption is found in subsection (d) of the statute, which provides that "property acquired in the name of one (1) or more of the partners, without an indication in the instrument transferring title to the property of the person's capacity as a partner or of the existence of a partnership and without use of partnership assets, is presumed to be separate property, even if used for partnership purposes." Tenn. Code Ann. § 61-1-204(d).

In this case, we derive the partners' intentions and understandings with regard to the property by considering numerous factors, mentioned above. The first two are "the parties' statements, conduct, and writings when the property was acquired" and "the parties' course of conduct after the acquisition of the property." *Leckrone v. Walker*, 2002 Tenn. App. LEXIS 309, 2002 WL 773147, at *3 (Tenn. Ct. App. Apr. 30, 2002). This Court finds it significant that the two previous houses where the parties lived, prior to Pack Hill Road, were, undisputedly, the subject of a partnership agreement between Mr. Finch and Ms. Raymer, whereby the parties would combine "their money, assets, labor, or skill" with the understanding that profits would be shared between them. It is hard for this Court to believe that every property purchased during the parties' relationship was partnership property except this one.

Although the Pack Hill Road Property was titled solely in Ms. Raymer's name, like the two properties where they lived before, Mr. Finch testified that the parties looked at the Pack Hill Road property together and made a decision together to purchase it. The parties drew up plans for the house together, and it is undisputed that Mr. Finch contributed his labor, carpentry skill, and earnings to the construction of the residence and the shop on the property. Mr. Finch and Ms. Raymer jointly executed documents regarding the homeowner's insurance policy insuring the property. Partnership funds from the joint account were used to pay the monthly mortgage payment on the Pack Hill Road residence.

Another factor for consideration is "the use of partnership funds to maintain the property." *Leckrone*, 2002 Tenn. App.

LEXIS 309, 2002 WL 773147, at *3. The profits of the partnership between 2004 and 2007 were deposited into the joint checking account, and the parties used that account, containing partnership funds, to pay for improving, insuring, and maintaining the Pack Hill Road residence.

Another relevant factor for consideration is "the use of the property in the partnership business." 2002 Tenn. App. LEXIS 309, [2002 WL 773147,] at *3. Mr. Finch reported on his individual tax returns that the business address for his carpentry business was 618 Pack Hill Road. Mr. Finch and Mrs. Raymer were co-borrowers on the home equity line of credit against the Pack Hill Road Property, which enabled them to buy and sell more real estate in their partnership dealings.

Considering all the circumstances, we conclude that the parties' conduct with regard to the Pack Hill Road residence was consistent with that of co-owners and partners. The Court, thus, finds that it was the intention of the parties that the Pack Hill Road property would be an asset of the partnership and not the individual property of Ms. Raymer. Mr. Finch established by clear and convincing evidence that the Pack Hill Road property was acquired for partnership purposes, although titled in Ms. Raymer's name alone.

As for the disputed household appliances and furnishings, the trial court found that the household items were purchased with partnership funds combined with Mr. Finch's income, and therefore, they were partnership property. The only argument raised by the defendants is that property cannot qualify as partnership assets when it is not held for sale or profit.

Finding no merit in the defendants' sole argument on appeal with regard to this property, we affirm the trial court's finding that the assets were partnership property owned one-half by each partner.

Partner's Partnership Interest

As an owner of a partnership or LLP, a partner has an ownership interest in the partnership. A partner's ownership interest is called a **partnership interest**, which embodies all a partner's rights in a partnership:

1. The partner's transferable interest.
2. The partner's management and other rights.

The first right is discussed in this section. Partners' management and other rights are discussed in Chapter 38, Operation of Partnerships and Related Forms.

Note that a partner has no individual ownership rights in partnership property. The RUPA gives ownership of

partnership property to the partnership only. Partners do, however, have the right to *use* partnership property for partnership purposes.

 LO37-7 List and compare the rights of a creditor having a charging order and the rights of a transferee of a partner's interest in a partnership.

Partner's Transferable Interest   Like a shareholder owning stock in a corporation, a partner owns his partnership interest. The only part of the partnership interest, however, that may be transferred to another person is the partner's **transferable interest**: the partner's share of profits and losses and his right to receive partnership distributions. The transferable interest may be transferred or sold to any other person. It may also be used as collateral to secure a partner's debt.

Transfer The sale or transfer of a partner's transferable interest is a voluntary act of the partner. It entitles the buyer or transferee to receive the partner's distributions from the partnership, such as a share of profits. Although the transferee is the owner of the transferable interest, the transferee does not become a partner of the partnership. The transferee has no right to inspect the partnership's books and records or to manage the partnership. The transferee's only other right is to ask a court to dissolve and wind up the partnership, but only if the partnership is at will (i.e., has no term or objective). If the partnership dissolves and is wound up, the transferee will obtain the partner's claim against the partnership's assets.

By itself a partner's transfer of his transferable interest does not dissociate the partner from the partnership or effect a dissolution; the transferring partner remains a partner and may continue to manage the partnership.

The nontransferring partners may vote to expel the transferring partner from the partnership by their unanimous agreement (unless the partner merely granted a lien in the transferable interest to the partner's creditor), even if the term or objective of the partnership has not yet been met.

Charging Order A partner's personal creditor with a judgment against the partner may ask a court to issue a **charging order**—that is, an order charging all or part of the partner's transferable partnership interest with payment of the unsatisfied amount of the judgment. Unlike a transfer, a charging order is obtained without the partner's consent. As with a transfer, however, the partner remains a partner and may manage the partnership. The charging-order creditor is a lien creditor and is entitled to receive only the partner's share of the partnership distributions. If the distributions are insufficient to pay the debt, the creditor may ask the court to order foreclosure and to sell the partner's interest to satisfy the charging order.

Neither the issuance of a charging order nor the purchase of a transferable interest at a foreclosure sale dissociates the transferring partner from the partnership. But the purchaser of a transferable interest at the foreclosure sale becomes a transferee and, therefore, may ask a court to dissolve and wind up a partnership at will. The other partners may eliminate this potential threat to the continuation of the partnership by redeeming the charging order. To redeem a charging order, the other partners must pay the creditor the amount due on the judgment against the partner. If the other partners so choose, however, they may expel the partner suffering the charging order by their unanimous agreement, even if the term or objective of the partnership has not been met.

Effect of Partnership Agreement

The partners may believe that a partner's transferring her transferable partnership interest or suffering a charging order threatens the partnership. For example, they may believe that a partner may be less motivated to work for the partnership if the partner has transferred her partnership interest to a personal creditor because she will not receive distributions from the partnership.

Consequently, the partners may restrict the transfer of a partner's transferable interest or impose negative consequences on a partner who transfers her transferable interest or suffers a charging order. For example, the partnership agreement may require a partner to offer to sell her partnership interest to the partnership prior to transferring it to any other person. Or the partnership agreement may effect a dissociation of any partner who suffers a charging order and fails to redeem the charging order within 30 days.

Note that any transfer restriction must not unreasonably limit the ability of a partner to transfer her property interest. For example, a transfer restriction that bans the transfer of a partner's interest would be unreasonable and, therefore, unenforceable against a partner. In addition, a transfer restriction will not be enforceable against a transferee who does not have notice of the restriction.

Joint Venturers and Mining Partners Transfers of interests in joint ventures are treated in the same way as transfers of partnership interests. However, a mining partner's interest is *freely transferable*. The transferee becomes a partner with all the rights of ownership and management, and the transferor loses all of his partnership rights. The other mining partners cannot object to the transfer, and their consent to a transfer is not required.

Problems and Problem Cases

1. Joan Brevig McCormick and Clark Brevig are sister and brother. When their father passes away, Joan becomes a partner with her brother in the Brevig Ranch, and eventually they become 50–50 partners. Disagreements transpire, and Joan brings suit against Clark and the partnership, alleging that Clark has converted partnership assets to his own personal use. The source of the dispute is cattle that were purchased by their mother,

Helen. Helen Brevig had purchased 10 herd of Charolais cattle to live on the ranch; the following year, she transferred ownership of the cattle to Clark and his two sons. Thereafter, these cattle were listed and treated as partnership property for all tax purposes, and proceeds from the sale of the cattle's offspring were placed into a partnership account. At the time of Joan's lawsuit against Clark, all the Charolais cattle residing on the ranch were offspring of those cattle originally purchased by Helen. Clark is now arguing that all the Charolais cattle should be regarded as separate property because his mother, who was not a partner, had given the cattle to Clark and his two sons, neither of whom were partners. Should the cattle be treated as partnership assets? Why or why not?

2. You and nine of your wealthy friends decide to purchase a local minor league baseball team. The purchase price is $15 million, 60 percent of which you contribute to the business as capital. Your nine friends will contribute the remaining $6 million. All 10 of you agree that you will be the sole general manager of the business, making all business and baseball decisions, except as you delegate them to employees of the business, such as a team manager or vice president of baseball operations. Due to the way you will account for the purchase of the team and player salaries, you expect the business not to make a profit until year 4. You expect that all 10 of you will remain owners of the business for at least 10 years, at which time you expect to sell the team at a profit. Which business form do you believe is best for your business? Why?

3. You and four of your closest professional friends agree to form a securities and real estate consulting business that advises wealthy individual investors and small companies. The business will help its clients reduce their exposure to risk by reviewing their overall investment portfolios, as well as comparing the mix of investments to an optimal portfolio. All five of you have nearly equal experience and expertise, management skills, and ability to bring clients to the business. You are concerned, however, that all of you continue to be motivated to work hard for the business and generate revenue and profit for the business. Each of you expects to devote equal amount of time and effort in attracting and servicing clients of the business. The business will have fairly low capital needs now and in the long run, no more than $300,000 for now. Each of you, therefore, will invest $60,000 in the business. You don't want to risk being liable for more than your investments in the business. All of you want only you five to own the business, unless

all of you agree to bring in a new owner. You all wish to form your company in California. Which business form do you believe is best for your business? Why?

4. Rick Yurko frequently purchased lottery tickets from Phyllis Huisel at the coffee shop she operated. Yurko bought 100 scratch-off lottery tickets, which revealed instant winners when a film covering was scratched off. Yurko asked Phyllis, Judy Fitchie, and Frances Vincent to help him scratch off the tickets. Yurko stated that if they helped him, they would be his partners and share in any winnings. Judy uncovered a ticket that gave its owner a chance to be on television and win $100,000. The owner had to complete a form on the back of the ticket and submit it for a drawing. Six tickets would be drawn for the TV appearance. Judy and Yurko urged Phyllis to fill out the ticket, but she did not want to appear on TV, so Yurko said he would. After a discussion, Frances, Judy, Phyllis, and Yurko agreed that Yurko would represent them on TV. Yurko then printed on the back of the ticket "F. J. P. Rick Yurko." F. J. P. stood for the first initials of Frances, Judy, and Phyllis. As Yurko completed the tickets, he told Phyllis that he was going to put all their initials and his name on the ticket and that they would be partners no matter what they might win.

You can predict what happened next. The ticket was drawn for the TV show, and Yurko appeared on the show and won the $100,000 prize. He did not share the winnings with the three women. Were the three women able to share the winnings by proving they were partners with Yurko? Why or why not?

5. In August 2003, Tammy Duncan began working as a waitress at Bynum's Diner, which was owned by her mother, Hazel Bynum, and stepfather, Eddie Bynum. Tammy, Hazel, and Eddie signed an agreement stating the following:

> As of September 6, 2003, I, Eddie Bynum, lease Bynum's Diner to Hazel Bynum and Tammy Duncan for $800 a month. I am completely out of it for 6 months, at which time they (Hazel Bynum and Tammy) have the option of renewing this contract for another 6 months. They are responsible for all repairs, taxes, and expenses for Bynum's Diner.

Tammy began doing paperwork and bookkeeping for the diner in addition to occasionally waiting tables and performing other duties. Tammy and Hazel's intention in their agreement was to make Tammy a co-manager and not a co-owner of the business. Tammy understood that she would take over her stepfather's duties as manager. She received wages for the performance of her duties. Although Tammy had no agreement to share in the diner's profits, Hazel believed that she and Tammy were to split half of any profit. Hazel's intent, however, was not to transfer ownership of the business to Tammy until Hazel retired, whenever that might be. On October 30, 2003, Tammy was injured when she slipped off a ladder and fell onto both knees. The diner's insurer, Cypress Insurance Company, paid Tammy temporary total disability benefits beginning in November 2003. On April 2, 2004, however, Cypress notified Tammy that it would refuse to pay her disability claim on the grounds that she was not an employee of the diner, but a co-owner. Under the diner's insurance policy with Cypress, if Tammy were an owner of the diner, she would not have been entitled to workers' compensation benefits because she did not notify Cypress that she elected to be included under the policy's coverage as a partner. Was Tammy a partner in the diner? Why or why not?

6. Don King and Scott Willson worked together on improving and selling an electronic payment system. To develop the system, they pooled their money and labor, with King providing financing and Willson contributing his time and expertise, amounting to about 2,000 hours of work over the period of a year. Willson was not paid by King for the work. Willson and King consulted with each other over pricing of equipment and services sold by the business. They made joint decisions to cut certain costs. Willson set up the invoice system used to bill customers. Willson made technical decisions on how best to assemble, repair, and maintain various aspects of the electronic payment system. King and Willson jointly addressed customer issues as they arose and jointly evaluated the systems' priorities as they went along. Willson and King also had an agreement to share profits. Are they partners? Why or why not?

7. Clint and Paige Crumley lived on a dairy farm in Hand County, South Dakota. In August 2007, Clint purchased a herd of dairy cows from James McGregor. When McGregor delivered the dairy cows to Clint's farm, Paige handed McGregor a check for payment. While at Clint's farm, McGregor observed Paige working with the dairy cows on the farm. In September 2007, Clint entered into an oral contract with McGregor about purchasing 25 more dairy cows. Clint then returned 8 cows that were substandard. McGregor then prepared a bill for the 17 cows, which listed the purchasers as Clint and Paige Crumley. When the bill was not paid, McGregor sued both Clint and Paige. Paige was not present at trial, did not testify, and was not called as a witness by either McGregor or Clint.

Clint made no admission at trial that Paige was a partner in the dairy operation. Rather, Clint's testimony was that he had entered into the business on his own and that he was solely responsible for the debts incurred in the business. Clint also testified that it was him, not Paige, who made the decision to purchase the first herd from McGregor as well as the second herd over which the dispute occurred. Should the court allow McGregor to sue Paige? Is there enough evidence to conclude that Paige is a purported partner in the dairy operation?

8. George Lawler and John Claydon were lawyers who maintained separate law practices in the same office space. They shared the expenses of that space but never shared clients, did not commingle their funds, and did not share profits or losses from their practices. A sign identified the office as "Claydon and Lawler," and the same joint listing of names appeared on stationery they both used and in their telephone listing. Claydon introduced Lawler to his clients as his partner. In phone conversations, Lawler identified himself as Claydon's partner. Is there a risk that Lawler will be liable on contracts and torts made by Claydon?

9. You are a financial and management consultant. Your client, Apple Inc., has decided to move forward with the development and manufacture of the iBrain, its next-generation data communication device. The iBrain is new, untested technology that will take billions of dollars to develop and may or may not have commercial success. Apple is developing the iBrain with SK Telecom Company, both of whom want to have equal power when making decisions regarding the iBrain's development, manufacture, and sale. Apple and SK agree to transfer their ownership of the technology and other property associated with the iBrain to a separate limited liability partnership (LLP) that is equally owned by Apple (50 percent ownership) and SK (50 percent). During the start-up phase of iBrain LLP, you are assigned by your firm to work full time on behalf of Apple, SK, and iBrain LLP. iBrain LLP gives you an office from which you conduct most of your work, which is in iBrain LLP's headquarters building. You are concerned that some of iBrain's employees and clients will think that you or your firm is a partner of Apple and SK in iBrain LLP, even though, in fact, neither you nor your firm is a partner of either Apple or SK. What is the name of the legal concept that applies when others believe you are another person's partner? What four things should you do to disabuse iBrain's employees, staff, and clients of the belief that you and your firm are partners of Apple and SK?

10. Steve Holmes and his son Mike were partners in a construction business. Steve also owned a ranch, which he contributed to the partnership, even though Steve was still listed as the owner of record. Steve learned of a low-interest loan available for the purchase of property from a parent. Solely to obtain the benefits of the low-interest loan, Steve deeded the ranch to Mike. No money exchanged hands, however, and Mike never paid Steve or the partnership for the ranch. The transfer was not treated as a sale on Steve's or Mike's books, Mike did not claim ranch income as his own, and there were no changes in ranch operation. When Steve and Mike had disagreements, Steve asked a court to dissolve the partnership and to distribute its assets. Was the ranch an asset of the partnership or Mike?

11. Demas Yan and Dong Fu made an agreement to build condominiums on Yan's land in the Chinatown section of San Francisco. Their agreement provided that Yan would own 75 percent and Fu 25 percent of the property. Yan was responsible for the initial $300,000 construction cost, and Fu the remainder. They agreed to share the proceeds of the sale or rental of the condominiums according to the ownership percentage. Fu, however, had sole power to decide whether to sell or to rent the property. Afterward, Fu assigned his interest under the agreement to Wei Suen. Thereafter, the condominiums were sold for a combined price of $2.3 million. Was Suen entitled to a share of the condominium sale proceeds?

Operation of Partnerships and Related Forms

After many years working with a large consulting partnership, you and several of your business associates and friends decide to form your own consulting business as a limited liability partnership in California. You and 5 of your close friends have 20 to 25 years' experience in the consulting field. Each of you plans to contribute capital of $400,000 to the business. Each of you has a strong national reputation and expects to attract most of the firm's clients, at least in the first few years. You 6 partners will manage only a few of the firm's consulting engagements, but you 6 will bring to the firm clients generating $40,000,000 of annual revenue for the firm. Each of you also has experience managing consulting businesses, including expertise in personnel, financial, and marketing matters.

In addition, 15 other partners with 10 to 15 years' experience will join the new firm. Each of these 15 partners will contribute capital of $200,000. Although they are expected to bring few clients to the firm at this time, they are expected to service the firm's clients and to bring in new clients as their reputations and skills expand and as the 6 older partners retire. Chiefly, these 15 partners will take charge of consulting engagements. They will directly supervise the firm's 50 associate consultants. The associate consultants will not be partners when the partnership is formed, but some expect to be offered partnership status within 5 to 10 years.

- What are the default rules regarding how the partnership will be managed?
- Why are those default rules inappropriate for this partnership?
- Write the management section of the partnership agreement. Accommodate the interests of all partners.
- What are the default rules regarding how the partners are compensated?
- Why are those default rules inappropriate for this partnership?
- Write the compensation section of the partnership agreement. Accommodate the interests of all partners.

LO LEARNING OBJECTIVES

After studying this chapter, you should be able to:

38-1 List and explain the duties partners owe to the partnership and each other.

38-2 Describe the default rules regarding partners' management and compensation rights.

38-3 Identify the impact of a partnership agreement on management and compensation issues within a partnership.

38-4 Explain the liability of partners for contracts and torts.

TWO RELATIONSHIPS ARE IMPORTANT during the operation of a partnership or limited liability partnership (LLP) business: (1) the relation of the partners to each other and the partnership and (2) the relation of the partners to third parties who are affected by the business of the partnership. In the examination of the first relationship, partners owe duties to each other and the partnership and they share the management and profits of the partnership. As for the second relation, partners have the ability to make the partnership liable to third parties for contracts and torts.

Duties of Partners to the Partnership and Each Other

 LO38-1 List and explain the duties partners owe to the partnership and each other.

The relation between partners and the partnership is a fiduciary relation of the highest order. It is one of mutual trust, confidence, and honesty. Therefore, under the Revised Uniform Partnership Act (RUPA), partners owe to the partnership and each other the highest degree of *loyalty*. In addition, partners must act consistently with the obligation of *good faith and fair dealing*. The duties partners owe each other are the same in ordinary partnerships and in limited liability partnerships.

Having Interest Adverse to Partnership

Unless there is a contrary agreement, a partner's sole compensation from partnership affairs is a share of partnership profits. Therefore, a partner may not deal with the partnership when the partner has an interest adverse to the partnership or acts on behalf of another person with any adverse interest. For example, a partner may not profit personally by receiving an undisclosed kickback from a partnership supplier. In addition, a partner may not profit secretly when she makes a contract with her partnership, such as selling a building she owns to her partnership without disclosing her ownership and her profit to her partners.

When a partner receives a secret profit, she has a conflict of interests, and there is a risk that she may prefer her own interests over those of the partnership. Therefore, the law permits a partner to profit personally from partnership transactions only if she deals in good faith, makes a full disclosure of all material facts affecting the transaction, and obtains approval from her partners. The remedy for a breach of this duty not to make a secret profit is a return of the profit that she made in the transaction with the partnership.

Competing against the Partnership

A partner may not compete against his partnership unless he obtains consent from the other partners. For example, a partner of a retail clothing store may not open a clothing store nearby. However, he may open a grocery store and not breach his fiduciary duty. The partnership has the remedy of recovering the partnership's damages caused by the competing business, often disgorgement—that is, the profits of the partner's competing venture.

Partnership agreements often define what conduct constitutes competing with the partnership. For example, a partnership agreement of a large auditing firm may state that no partner may provide auditing services except on behalf of the partnership. It may also state that a partner may provide other accounting services not offered by the partnership after disclosure to and approval by the partnership's managing partners.

In the following *McMillian* case, in which cousins were partners, the court considered the type of financial evidence that is relevant in calculating damages caused by a partner's competing against his partnership.

McMillian v. McMillian	713 S.E.2d 920 (Ga. Ct. App. 2011)

Robbie McMillian and his cousin Bruce McMillian were partners in a bulk-mail services business, Corporate Mail Management. Bruce funded the partnership's operations, pledging his personal residence as collateral to secure a business loan and to purchase equipment for the partnership. Robbie marketed its services and managed its business operations, holding himself out as the president of Corporate Mail. Despite their efforts, the partnership never made much money.

Over time, Robbie met other people who had an interest in entering the bulk-mail services business. In August 2002, Robbie met with two of these people and formed a new company with them. The new company offered the same kinds of services as Corporate Mail and, in fact, directly competed with it. At some point in 2002, Robbie told Bruce that he planned to withdraw from their partnership, ostensibly because he was tired of the bulk-mail services business and wanted to do something else altogether. Robbie never told Bruce about his new company or that it competed with Corporate Mail.

The new company, Mail Source, was formed in January 2003. Between January and April 2003, Robbie still was managing Corporate Mail and at the same time working for Mail Source, diverting to Mail Source the business opportunities that were presented to Corporate Mail. In April 2003, Robbie shut down Corporate Mail, taking all its assets and business opportunities with him to Mail Source. In its first year alone, Mail Source earned more than $245,000 from customers that previously had been customers or prospective customers of Corporate Mail.

Left with nothing but the debts of Corporate Mail, Bruce sued Robbie and Mail Source. Bruce argued that Robbie breached his fiduciary duties to Bruce and their partnership and that Mail Source wrongfully induced Robbie to breach his fiduciary duties. Bruce asked the trial court to award him monetary damages for his loss of the opportunity to profit from the prospective business opportunities that Corporate Mail lost to Mail Source.

To build his case for damages, Bruce sought to discover information from Mail Source about its finances, specifically, its revenue and profits between 2003 and the present. When Mail Source produced some financial information—a list of its sales-by-customer between 2003 and 2005—but refused to produce all the financial information Bruce had requested, Bruce asked the trial court to compel Mail Source to provide the information. The court concluded that the financial records of Mail Source were not relevant to the measure of damages and denied the motion to compel. The court said that damages for the loss of a prospective business opportunity must be based on the value that a reasonable person would have assigned to the prospective business opportunity at the time of its loss. The court concluded that the amount Mail Source earned from the business opportunities that it and Robbie misappropriated from Corporate Mail was irrelevant. Bruce appealed the decision to the Georgia Court of Appeals.

Blackwell, Judge

Bruce argues that his damages properly can be based on the revenues, or at least the profits, that Mail Source earned from any business opportunities misappropriated from Corporate Mail. If a disgorgement remedy were appropriate, it would resolve the question with which we are presented today, inasmuch as the revenues and profits of Mail Source absolutely would be relevant to damages because they would be the very measure of damages. We do not need to decide today whether the disgorgement remedy would be appropriate because, even if damages more properly are measured by reference to what Bruce lost, not what Mail Source gained, the revenues and profits of Mail Source still might be probative of damages.

When a partner wrongfully appropriates a prospective business opportunity of his partnership to his own use or that of another, the remaining partners, who are deprived of an opportunity to profit from the misappropriated business opportunity, may recover their share of the profits that the partnership would have earned from the business opportunity. Like any lost profits, a partner's share of the profits that his partnership would have earned from a lost business opportunity must be shown with reasonable certainty, and profits which are remote, or speculative, contingent or uncertain are not recoverable. That said, the rule that lost profits cannot be speculative or uncertain relates more especially to the uncertainty as to cause, rather than uncertainty as to the measure or extent of the damages. That difficulty in calculating precisely the damages sustained will not preclude their recovery is especially true when it is the conduct of the wrongdoer that prevents a more precise calculation.

If this measure of damages, rather than a disgorgement, is the more appropriate measure of damages—that is, if the measure is what Bruce lost and not what Mail Source gained—the revenues and profits earned by Mail Source from business opportunities that Corporate Mail lost to it would not be dispositive of the amount of damages Bruce might be entitled to recover. But that does not mean that the revenues and profits of Mail Source are irrelevant to the proper measure of damages. Indeed, some reasonable person might say the revenues and profits Mail Source earned from the same business opportunities could be a fair approximation of the revenues that Corporate Mail would have earned from them and are, therefore, probative of the lost revenue and profit of Corporate Mail, at least if there is some evidence that Mail Source and Corporate Mail have similar pricing structures and costs. Robbie and Mail Source would be entitled to respond, of course, that Corporate Mail could not have charged its customers the same price as Mail Source, or could not have done the same volume of work as Mail Source, or would not have earned the same profit as Mail Source, but those are all matters for a jury. At the least, the revenues earned by Mail Source might be probative of the volume of work performed by Mail Source to the extent that more revenue is earned for doing more work, something the parties do not dispute. There may be reasons in this case why such evidence ultimately might not be admitted at trial, but we are reviewing the denial of a motion to compel, not a judgment for money damages or a ruling admitting certain proof of damages at trial. It is enough to decide that the revenues and profits of Mail Source might very well have some relevance to the proper measure of damages in this case.

Judgment reversed in favor of Bruce McMillian. Remanded to the trial court.

Duty to Serve The duty to serve requires a partner to undertake his share of responsibility for running the day-to-day operations of the partnership business. The basis of this duty is the expectation that all partners will work. Sometimes, this duty is termed the duty to devote full time to the partnership.

Partners may agree to relieve a partner of the duty to serve. So-called *silent partners* merely contribute capital to the partnership. Silent partners do not have the duty to serve, but they have the same liability for partnership debts as any other partner.

The remedies for breach of the duty to serve include assessing the partner for the cost of hiring a person to do his work and paying the other partners additional compensation.

Duty of Care In transacting partnership business, each partner owes *a duty of care*. A partner is not liable to her partnership for losses resulting from honest errors in judgment, but a partner is liable for losses resulting from her gross negligence, reckless conduct, intentional misconduct, or knowing violation of the law. A partner also has an obligation of good faith and fair dealing when acting for the partnership. Collectively, these duties mean that a partner must make an *investigation* before making a decision so that she has an adequate basis for making the decision. The decision she makes must be one she has *grounds to believe is in the best interests of the partnership*.

In the partnership agreement, the partners may reduce or increase the duty of care owed to the partnership. They may not, however, eliminate the duty of care. It is common for partnership agreements to excuse partners from liability if they act in good faith and with the honest belief that their actions are in the best interests of the partnership. Such a provision is designed to encourage honest partners to take reasonable business risks without fearing liability.

Duty to Act within Actual Authority A partner has the duty not to exceed the authority granted him by the partnership agreement or, if there is no agreement, the authority normally held by partners in his position. He is responsible to the partnership for losses resulting from unauthorized transactions negotiated in the name of the partnership. For example, suppose partners agree that no partner shall purchase supplies from Jasper Supply Company, which is unaware of the limitation on the partners' authority. When one partner purchases supplies from Jasper and the partnership suffers a loss because the supplies are of low quality, the wrongdoing partner must bear the loss caused by her breach of the partnership agreement.

Duty to Account Partners have a duty to account for their use or disposal of partnership funds and partnership property, as well as their receipt of any property, benefit, or profit, without the consent of the other partners. Partnership property should be used for partnership purposes, not for a partner's personal use. In addition, a partner may not misappropriate a business opportunity in which the partnership had an interest or expectancy.

For example, when a partner of a firm that leases residential property to college students allows his daughter to live in a partnership-owned apartment, the partner must collect rent for the partnership from his daughter or risk breaching the duty to account.

Each partner owes a duty to keep a reasonable record of all business transacted by him for the partnership and to make such records available to the person keeping the partnership books. The books must be kept at the partnership's chief executive office. Every partner must at all times have access to them and may inspect and copy them.

Closely related to the duty to account is the right of a partner to be **indemnified** for payments made from personal funds and for personal liabilities incurred during the ordinary conduct of the business. For example, a partner uses her own truck to pick up some partnership supplies, which she pays for with her personal check. The partner is entitled to be reimbursed for the cost of the supplies and for her cost of picking up the supplies, including fuel.

Other Duties A partner must maintain the confidentiality of partnership information such as a trade secret or a customer list. This means a partner should not disclose to third parties confidential information of the partnership unless disclosure benefits the partnership.

On the other hand, each partner owes a duty to disclose to the other partners all information that is material to the partnership business. She also owes a duty to inform the partners of notices she has received that affect the rights of the partnership. For example, Gordon Gekko, a partner of a stock brokerage firm, learns that National Motors Corporation is projecting a loss for the current year. The projection reduces the value of National stock, which the firm has been recommending that its customers buy. Gekko has a duty to disclose the projection to his partners to allow them to advise customers of the brokerage.

In many cases you will read, the court decides upon cases involving a managing partner's liability for misusing partnership funds, self-dealing, or failing to disclose material information.

The Global Business Environment

Partner's Relations and Fiduciary Duties

All modern societies share a common set of values that are reflected not only generally in their laws, but also specifically in partnership law. Thus, there is substantial agreement from nation to nation in the duties partners owe each other under partnership law. In India and the United Kingdom, for example, partners' duties are nearly identical in name and substance to those in American law. Likewise in Canada, basic values of loyalty, good faith, honesty, and avoidance of conflicts of interest are fundamental to a partner's duties.

In other societies, there are mostly similarities but also a few differences. For example, among the Inuit and other aboriginal groups in Canada, the culture requires partners to "celebrate one another." In his book *Hunters in the Barrens: The Naskapi on the Edge of the White Man's World*, Georg Henriken notes that in a joint venture, while the Naskapi partners watch one another, examine contracts and bank statements, and even sue one another, they should respect and recognize their respective contributions.

Joint Ventures and Mining Partnerships

The fiduciary duties of partners also exist in joint ventures and mining partnerships, although there are a few special rules regarding their enforcement. For example, a joint venturer may seek an accounting in a court to settle claims between the joint venturers, or he may sue his joint venturers to recover joint property or to be indemnified for expenditures that he has made on behalf of the joint venture. A mining partner's remedy against his partners is an accounting; however, a mining partner has a lien against his partners' shares in the mining partnership for his expenditures on behalf of the mining partnership. The lien can be enforced against purchasers of his partners' shares.

Compensation of Partners

 LO38-2 Describe the default rules regarding partners' management and compensation rights.

Profits and Losses   Unless there is an agreement to the contrary, partners share partnership profits equally, according to the number of partners, and not according to their capital contributions or the amount of time that each devotes to the partnership. For example, a partnership has two partners, Juarez, who contributes $85,000 of capital to the partnership and does 35 percent of the work, and Easton, who contributes $15,000 and does 65 percent of the work. If they have made no agreement how to share profits, when the partnership makes a $50,000 profit in the first year, each partner is credited with $25,000, half of the profits.

Although the default RUPA rule allocates profits equally to partners, the partners do not necessarily *receive* profits earned by the partnership or LLP. Profits are *allocated* to each partner's capital account as profits are recognized by the business. Profits are *distributed* to partners in an amount and at a time determined by a majority of the partners. Consequently, in a partnership or LLP that is taxed like a partnership for federal income tax purposes, a partner may have taxable income despite not receiving a distribution from the partnership.

Losses   When the partnership agreement is silent on how to share losses, losses are shared in the same proportion that profits are shared. The basis of this rule is the presumption that partners want to share benefits and detriments in the same proportions. Nonetheless, the presumption does not work in reverse. If a partnership agreement specifies how losses are shared but does not specify how profits are shared, profits are shared equally by the partners, not as losses are shared.

Examples   For example, when there is no agreement regarding how profits or losses are shared, profits are shared equally, and because losses are shared like profits, losses are shared equally as well. When two partners agree to share profits 70–30 and make no agreement on losses, both profits and losses are shared 70–30.

However, when two partners make no agreement how to share profits but agree to share losses 60–40, losses are shared in that proportion, but profits are shared equally.

Partners may agree to split profits on one basis and losses on another basis for many reasons, including their making different capital and personal service contributions or a partner's having higher outside income than the other partners, which better enables him to use a partnership loss as a tax deduction.

Effect of Agreement on Creditors' Rights Each partner has unlimited personal liability to partnership creditors. Loss-sharing agreements between partners do not bind partnership creditors unless the creditors agree to be bound. For example, two partners agree to share losses 60–40, the same proportion in which they contributed capital to the partnership. After the partnership assets have been distributed to the creditors, $50,000 is still owed to them. The creditors may collect the entire $50,000 from the partner who agreed to assume only 60 percent of the losses. That partner may, however, collect $20,000—40 percent of the amount—from the other partner.

> **LO38-3** Identify the impact of a partnership agreement on management and compensation issues within a partnership.

Compensation in Large Partnerships In a large accounting or other partnership that has thousands of partners, the partnership agreement often has a detailed section on the amount of partners' compensation and when it is paid. Usually, each partner is entitled to a monthly draw or salary. The amount of each partner's draw may be established yearly by the partnership's compensation committee or be determined by a rigid formula that takes into account a partner's capital contribution to the partnership, years of service as a partner, level of partner (such as managing partner, senior partner, or junior partner), area of practice (such as consulting, auditing, or tax), and other factors.

In the following case, *Fish v. Tex. Legislative Serv., P'ship*, involving all-too-common overreaching and misconduct in a partnership with active and passive partners, the court found that based on the partnership agreement, two of the partnership's active partners were not entitled to additional compensation, absent agreement of the other partners.

Fish v. Tex. Legislative Serv., P'ship
2012 Tex. App. LEXIS 749 (Tex. App.–Austin 2012)

Russell H. Fish III, individually and on behalf of Texas Legislative Service (TLS), sued TLS partners Andrew K. Fish and John C. Fish, alleging that they violated various terms of the TLS partnership agreement.

TLS is a legislative tracking service providing subscribers with information about the activities of the Texas Legislature, including legislator voting patterns, bill histories, hearing schedules, and calendars. TLS was started in 1924 by Walter E. Long and became a family partnership in 1953. The original partnership agreement was amended from time to time, and the dispute at issue in this case involves the TLS partnership agreement executed in 1979, which remains in effect today subject to certain amendments concerning transfers of partnership interests and partner retirement payments.

In the 1979 partnership agreement, Russell and his brothers Andrew and John were named TLS partners along with other relatives, including their father Russell H. Fish Jr. and their mother Janet Long Fish. Together, Andrew and John have held a majority interest in the partnership since 1994, when they purchased equal shares of their mother's interest.

In relation to the claims in the lawsuit, the parties distinguish between "working partners," meaning those partners who work in the business, and "nonworking partners," referring to those partners who do not work in the business. Of the current partners and the partners identified in the 1979 agreement, only Andrew, John, their Uncle James, and their parents, Russell Jr. and Janet, have ever worked in the business. James held the position as manager until 1986 or 1987, when Andrew was elected the manager and James left the company. Andrew has worked continuously in the business since 1976, and John has worked continuously in the business since 1981. Currently, Andrew and John are the only partners who work at TLS, and that has been the case since their mother retired in 1994 and withdrew as a TLS partner.

During Andrew's tenure as manager, Andrew and John have set their compensation without notice to or express consent of any partners not working in the business, including their brother, Russell. Before Andrew became manager, James followed the same practice, as did Russell Jr., who preceded both Andrew and John. As specified in the 1979 partnership agreement, salaries paid to working partners are deducted from TLS's revenue before any residual profits are distributed to the partners on a pro-rata basis. Thus, compensation paid to partners working in the business directly affects the proceeds available for distribution to all partners, and that has been the case for the entire time that Russell, Andrew, and John have been TLS partners.

After Janet's death in 2008, Russell, individually and on behalf of TLS, sued Andrew and John, alleging that over the course of 20 or more years, they engaged in activities that violated various provisions of the 1979 partnership agreement. Russell asserted that Andrew and John siphoned off TLS revenue that should have been distributed pro-rata to the partners by paying themselves salaries, bonuses, and other compensation without unanimous consent of the partners as required in section 2.5 of the partnership agreement and by paying themselves more frequently than on a monthly basis.

Andrew and John challenged the allegations on a number of substantive grounds, including contending that section 2.5 of the agreement unambiguously authorizes them to set their own salaries as majority interest holders and as a majority of the partners working in the business or, alternatively, section 2.5 is ambiguous and the historical practice of allowing the working partners to set their salaries is conclusive evidence of section 2.5's intended meaning.

The trial court rendered final judgment in favor of Andrew and John on all claims. Russell appealed the trial court's ruling, contending that the trial court erroneously denied his motion for partial summary judgment on his claim that Andrew and John breached section 2.5 of the partnership agreement by paying themselves a salary, bonuses, and other compensation without the unanimous approval of all partners and paying such compensation other than on a monthly basis.

Jones, Judge

Under Texas's general partnership law, partners are not entitled to compensation for services performed on behalf of the partnership, except compensation for services rendered in winding up partnership business. However, if the partners have executed an agreement authorizing compensation, as they did in this case, the terms of that agreement govern any dispute concerning compensation. Section 2.5 of the TLS partnership agreement states, "For each fiscal year, the partners shall receive such monthly salaries as the partners mutually agree shall be paid." The heart of the dispute in this case is the proper interpretation and application of this provision and, in particular, the meaning of the phrase "partners mutually agree."

Russell argues that section 2.5 is unambiguous and does not authorize a working partner to receive any compensation absent the unanimous consent of all the partners. He further contends that section 2.5 neither authorizes salaries to be paid more frequently than on a monthly basis nor allows the payment of bonuses or any other special compensation. Russell contends that he should have been awarded summary judgment because it is undisputed that during Andrew's tenure as manager, Andrew and John were paid monthly salaries described in company financial records as "regular pay" as well as periodic payments described as "bonuses" and "special payments," all without notice to the nonworking partners and without their unanimous consent.

Andrew and John counter that section 2.5 unambiguously authorizes them to set their own compensation both as majority interest holders and as a majority of the working partners. They further assert that, although section 2.5 speaks in terms of "monthly" salary, the bonuses and special payments they received were deferred compensation, payable if and when the company's cash flow allowed for payment because the nature of TLS's business resulted in an irregular cash flow. They dispute Russell's claim that section 2.5 requires that they be paid the same amount every month in a single monthly payment and contend that any

such limitation is immaterial to the extent they have the contractual right to set their own compensation. Andrew and John also proffered the alternative argument that section 2.5 is ambiguous and that a fact issue exists regarding the proper interpretation of section 2.5 based on the historical practice of allowing the working partners with a majority interest to determine partner compensation.

The primary objective in this case is to ascertain the true intent of the parties as expressed in the partnership agreement. In section 1.1 of the partnership agreement, the "partners" are identified as all interest holders, not just those partners working in the business. The term "partners" is used repeatedly through the contract in ways that would necessarily require its interpretation to include all partnership interest holders, not just working partners and not just the holders of a majority interest. This Court rejects Andrew and John's suggestion that the term "partners" is limited to working partners or majority interest holders when used in section 2.5. Such a cabined construction of the term does not comport with either its ordinary or specifically defined meaning and is wholly lacking textual support.

The phrase "mutually agree" is not defined in the partnership agreement. Proper construction of that phrase begins with the plain, ordinary, and commonly understood meaning of the term "mutual." The plain meaning of the term "mutual," as used in section 2.5 implies unanimous agreement of the partners, not a majority in interest. This construction of section 2.5 also holds true when we consider other provisions of the agreement concerning partner decision-making.

The term "mutually agree" is used in that form or substantially similar variation in a number of other provisions in the contract. In contrast, the term "majority in interest" is specifically defined in section 3.11 of the agreement to mean "those partners owning more than fifty percent (50%) of the capital interest." The partnership agreement specifies certain situations that require more than a "majority in interest." For example, a decision to hire a non-partner as manager requires the assent of a supermajority (or two-thirds) of the partnership interests. Likewise, the partnership agreement can be altered, amended, or cancelled at any time by agreement in writing between seventy-five percent (75%) or more in interest of the partners, except that an amendment affecting the rights of a former manager or supervisor pursuant to section 2.5, which authorizes retirement payments to partners who are former managers and supervisors, in addition to governing salaries of working partners shall require the affirmative written agreement of one hundred percent (100%) of the interest of the partners.

In other words, the partnership agreement is specific in detailing with particularity the actions that may be carried out with less than unanimity of assent. Because Andrew and John's cramped construction of section 2.5 would render these provisions unnecessary, we do not believe that construction is reasonable. The fact that the agreement uses the phrase "one hundred percent (100%) of the interest of the partners" to convey a requirement of unanimity in one context,

instead of the phrase "the partners mutually agree," does not alter this Courts conclusion or create an ambiguity because that particular phrase is used in contrast to a specified circumstance in which less than unanimous agreement is required but in which a prescribed majority of partnership interest is necessary.

In conclusion, there is no definition of the term "mutually agree" that would support Andrew and John's interpretation as meaning a majority in interest or a majority of the working partners. Additionally, there is no textual support for that interpretation. Moreover, there is no evidence suggesting that at the time the partnership agreement was executed it would have been difficult or impossible to obtain unanimous consent of the partners concerning such matters on a reasonably frequent basis. Therefore, this Court concludes that section 2.5 of the 1979 partnership agreement unambiguously requires consent of all the partners in order for a partner to be compensated for working at TLS.

Judgment reversed and remanded in part.

Management Powers of Partners

 Describe the default rules regarding partners' management and compensation rights.

Individual Authority of Partners In a partnership or limited liability partnership, every partner is a general manager of the business and may make contracts that bind the partnership. This power is expressed in the RUPA, which states that a partnership is bound by the act of every partner for apparently carrying on in the ordinary course the business of the partnership or business of the kind carried on by the partnership. Such authority to make contracts derives from the nature of the business. It permits a partner to bind the partnership and his partners for acts within the ordinary course of business. The scope of this **implied authority** is determined with reference to what is usual business for partnerships of the same general type.

Implied authority of a partner may not contradict a partner's **express authority**, which is created by agreement of the partners. An agreement among the partners can expand, restrict, or even completely eliminate the implied

authority of a partner. For example, the partners in an online publishing business may agree that one partner shall have the authority to purchase a magazine business for the partnership and that another partner shall not have the authority to sell advertising space. The partners may agree also that all partners must consent to borrow money for the partnership. The partners' implied authority to be general managers is modified in accordance with these express agreements.

Express authority may be stated orally or in writing, or it may be obtained by acquiescence. Regardless of the method of agreement, all of the partners must agree to the modification of implied authority. Partners may give everyone notice of a partner's authority or limitation on a partner's authority by filing a *Statement of Partnership Authority* or *Statement of Denial* with the secretary of state or the real estate recording office. Together, a partner's express and implied authority constitute her ***actual authority***.

Apparent Authority Apparent authority exists because it reasonably appears to a third party that a partner has authority to do an act. Often, the implied authority and apparent authority of a partner are coincident. However, when a partner's implied authority is restricted or eliminated, the partnership risks the possibility that **apparent authority** to do a denied act will remain. To prevent apparent authority from continuing when there is a limitation of a partner's actual authority, third persons with whom the partner deals must have knowledge of the limitation of his actual authority or have received notification of the limitation, such as receiving an e-mail or fax or otherwise having the limitation brought to their attention. Filing a Statement of Partnership Authority or Statement of Denial may help notify third parties of a partner's limited authority. Just as a principal must notify third persons of limitations of an agent's authority, so must a partnership notify its customers, suppliers, and others of express limitations of the actual authority of partners.

Suppose that Carroll, Melton, and Ramirez are partners and that they agree that Carroll will be the only purchasing agent for the partnership. This agreement must be communicated to third parties selling goods to the partnership, or Melton and Ramirez will have apparent authority to bind the partnership on purchase contracts. Melton and Ramirez do not have express authority to purchase goods because they have agreed to such a restriction on their authority. They do not have implied authority to purchase because implied authority may not contradict express authority.

Ratification A partnership may ratify the unauthorized acts of partners. Essentially, **ratification** occurs when the partners accept an act of a partner who had no actual or apparent authority to do the act when it was done.

For example, suppose Cabrillo and Boeglin are partners in an accounting firm. They agree that only Cabrillo has authority to make contracts to perform audits of clients, an agreement known by Mantron Company. Nonetheless, Boeglin and Mantron contract for the partnership to audit Mantron's financial statements. At this point, the partnership is not liable on the contract because Boeglin has no express, implied, or apparent authority to make the contract. But suppose Boeglin takes the contract to Cabrillo, who reads it and says, "OK, we'll do this audit." Cabrillo, as the partner with express authority to make audit contracts, has ratified the contract and thereby bound the partnership to the contract.

Special Transactions
The validity of some partner's actions is affected by special partnership rules within RUPA that reflect a concern for protecting important property and the credit standing of partners. This concern is especially evident in the rules for conveying the

partnership's real property and for borrowing money in the name of the partnership.

Power to Convey Partnership's Real Property To bind the partnership, an individual partner's conveyance of a partnership's real property must be expressly, impliedly, or apparently authorized or be ratified by the partnership. For example, the partners may expressly agree that a partner may sell the partnership's real property.

The more difficult determination is whether a partner has *implied* and *apparent* authority to convey real property. A partner has implied and apparent authority to sell real property if a partnership sells real property in the usual course of the partnership business. Such would be the case with the partner of a real estate investment partnership that buys and sells land as its regular business. By contrast, a partner has no implied or apparent authority to sell the building in which the partnership's retail business is conducted. Here, unanimous agreement of the partners is required because the sale of the building may affect the ability of the firm to continue. In addition, a partner has no implied or apparent authority to sell land held for investment not in the usual course of business. A sale of such land would be authorized only if the partners concurred.

When title to partnership real property is recorded in the name of the partners and not the partnership, those partners in whose name title is recorded have apparent authority to convey title to a bona fide purchaser unaware of the partnership's interest in the real property. However, purchasers are deemed to have knowledge of a limitation on a partner's authority to convey real property that is contained in a Statement of Partnership Authority or Statement of Denial that is filed in the real estate recording office.

Borrowing Money Partnership law restricts the ability of a partner to borrow money in the name of a partnership. Essentially, a partner must possess express, implied, or apparent authority to borrow. Express authority presents few problems. Finding implied and apparent authority to borrow is more difficult.

Although the RUPA does not explicitly recognize the distinction, a number of courts have distinguished between trading and nontrading partnerships for purposes of determining whether a partner has implied or apparent authority to borrow money on behalf of the partnership. A **trading partnership** has an inventory; that is, its regular business is buying and selling merchandise, such as retailing, wholesaling, importing, or exporting. For example, a toy store and a clothing store are trading partnerships. Because there is a time lag between the date they pay for their inventory and the date they sell inventory to their customers, these firms ordinarily need to borrow to avoid cash flow problems. Therefore, a partner of a trading partnership has implied and apparent authority to borrow money for the partnership.

A **nontrading partnership** has no substantial inventory and is usually engaged in providing services—for example, accounting services or real estate brokerage. Such partnerships have no normal borrowing needs. Therefore, a partner of a nontrading partnership has no implied or apparent authority to borrow money for the partnership.

The distinction between trading and nontrading partnerships is not always clear. Businesses such as general contracting, manufacturing, and dairy farming, although not exclusively devoted to buying and selling inventory, have been held to be trading partnerships. The rationale for their inclusion in this category is that borrowing is necessary in the ordinary course of business to augment their working capital.

This suggests why the distinction between trading partnerships and nontrading partnerships is useless or misleading. There is no necessary connection between borrowing money and buying and selling. The more important inquiry should be whether a partner's borrowing is in the ordinary course of business. When borrowing is in the ordinary course of business, a partner has implied and apparent authority to borrow money. If borrowing is not in the ordinary course of business, then no individual partner has implied or apparent authority to borrow money.

If a court finds that a partner has authority to borrow money, the partnership is liable for his borrowings on behalf of the partnership. There is a limit, however, to a partner's capacity to borrow. A partner may have authority to borrow, yet not borrow beyond the ordinary needs of the business. A partnership will not be liable for any loan whose amount exceeds the ordinary needs of the business, unless otherwise agreed by the partners.

The power to borrow money on the firm's credit will ordinarily carry with it the power to grant the lender a lien or security interest in firm assets to secure the repayment of the borrowed money. Security interests are a normal part of business loan transactions.

Issuing Negotiable Instruments A partner who has the authority to borrow money also has authority to issue negotiable instruments such as promissory notes for that purpose. When a partnership has a checking account and a partner's name appears on the signature card filed with the bank, the partner has express authority to draw checks. A partner whose name is not on the signature card filed with the bank has apparent authority to issue checks, but only in respect to a third person who has no knowledge or notification of the limitation on the partner's authority.

Negotiating Instruments A partnership receives many negotiable instruments during the course of its business. For example, an accounting firm's clients often pay fees by check. Even though borrowing money and issuing negotiable instruments may be beyond a partner's implied and apparent authority, a partner usually has implied and apparent authority to transfer or negotiate instruments on behalf of the partnership.

For example, when a partnership has a bank account, a partner has implied and apparent authority to indorse and deposit in the account checks drawn payable to the partnership. As a general rule, a partner also has implied and apparent authority to indorse and cash checks drawn payable to the order of the partnership. Likewise, partners have implied authority to indorse drafts and notes payable to the order of the partnership and to sell them at a discount.

Admissions and Notice A partnership is bound by admissions or representations made by a partner concerning partnership affairs that are within her express, implied, or apparent authority. Likewise, notice to a partner is considered to be received by the partnership. Also, a partner's knowledge of material information relating to partnership affairs is **imputed** to the partnership. These rules reflect the reality that a partnership speaks, sees, and hears through its partners.

Disagreement among Partners: Ordinary Course of Business
Usually, partners will discuss management decisions among themselves before taking action, even when doing so is not required by a partnership agreement and even when a partner has the implied authority to take the action by herself. When partners discuss a prospective action, they will usually vote on what action to take. Under the default RUPA rules, each partner has one vote, regardless of the relative sizes of their partnership interests or their shares of the profits. On matters in the ordinary course of business, the vote of a majority of the partners controls ordinary business decisions and, thereby, limits the actual authority of the partners. Nonetheless, the apparent authority of the partners to bind the partnership on

contracts in the ordinary course of business is unaffected by the majority vote of partners, unless the limitation on the partners' actual authority is communicated to third parties.

When Unanimous Partners' Agreement Is Required
Some partnership actions are so important that one partner should not be able to do them by himself. To make clear that no single partner has implied or apparent authority to do certain acts, in the absence of a contrary agreement, the UPA requires unanimity for several actions. The RUPA, however, deletes such a list. Instead, the RUPA requires that any partnership act not in the ordinary course of business be approved by all partners, absent a contrary agreement of the partners.

For example, a decision to build a new executive office complex must be approved by all partners. Similarly, the decision of a small accounting partnership in Sacramento to open a second office in San Jose would require unanimity. When other actions, such as submitting a partnership claim to arbitration, are in the ordinary course of business, any partner has authority to do the actions.

Joint Ventures and Mining Partnerships
Most of the authority rules of partnerships apply to joint ventures and mining partnerships. These business organizations are in essence partnerships with limited purposes. Therefore, their members have less implied and apparent authority than do partners. Joint venturers have considerable apparent authority if third persons are unaware of the limited scope of the joint venture. A mining partner has no implied authority to borrow money or issue negotiable instruments. As with partners, joint venturers and mining partners may by agreement expand or restrict each other's agency powers.

Effect of Partnership Agreement

 Identify the impact of a partnership agreement on management and compensation issues within a partnership.

The partners may modify the rules of management by their unanimous agreement. They may agree that a partner will relinquish his management right, thus removing the partner's express and implied authority to manage the partnership. They may grant sole authority to manage the business to one or more partners. Such removals or delegations of management powers will not, however, eliminate a partner's apparent authority to bind the partnership for his

acts within the usual course of business unless a third party has knowledge or notification of the limitation.

A partnership agreement may create classes of partners, some of which will have the power to veto certain actions. Some classes of partners may be given greater voting rights. Unequal voting rights are often found in very large partnerships, such as an accounting firm with hundreds or thousands of partners.

For example, in a large accounting partnership, the partnership agreement will typically have a management section. This section usually begins with a restatement of the RUPA fiduciary duties that partners owe to the partnership, with exceptions or revisions, such as changes in the duty of care. The section also lists the duties of the partnership to the partners, such as the duty to indemnify.

Regarding the authority of partners, the management articles may give a managing partner or a managing partners' committee control over much of the firm's day-to-day management, such as the hiring, firing, and promotion of employees; investing the firm's excess cash; and drawing and indorsing partnership checks. The managing partners or a compensation committee may be given power to determine the partners' draws or salaries. Individual partners may have most of their management powers taken away but may be granted the power to hire a personal assistant or to make expenditures within limits from an expense account, such as buying a laptop computer. Other matters may require approval of all the partners (such as selling the partnership's real property and moving the partnership's place of business), a supermajority of partners (such as 75 percent approval to bind the partnership to a bank loan), a majority of partners (such as installing new carpeting), or the partners in a particular area of practice (such as requiring approval of a majority of consulting partners for a consulting engagement over $1,000,000).

In small partnerships of 10 or fewer partners, the partnership agreement often requires unanimous partners' agreement for many actions, such as hiring employees and making large contracts. In small partnerships, these and other actions have a greater impact on each partner. This impact is evident in the next case, *NBN Broadcasting*, in which a partnership agreement that was designed to prevent and resolve conflicts between the two partners eventually caused serious disagreements. The partners wanted to be equal essentially, but a deadlock provision allowed one partner to dominate, eventually causing a breakdown of the partners' relationship. It illustrates the necessity for careful drafting of partnership agreements, including anticipating that a part of the agreement may cause an undesired result.

NBN Broadcasting, Inc. v. Sheridan Broadcasting Networks, Inc.
105 F.3d 72 (2d Cir. 1997)

NBN Broadcasting, Inc. and Sheridan Broadcasting Networks, Inc. operated competing radio networks. In 1991, NBN and Sheridan agreed to form American Urban Radio Network (AURN), a Pennsylvania partnership that combined NBN's and Sheridan's networks. Sheridan owned 51 percent of the partnership; NBN owned 49 percent. They agreed to maintain NBN's offices in New York and Sheridan's offices in Pittsburgh to allow direct oversight and input by AURN's cochairmen and co-CEOs, Sydney Small (chairman of NBN) and Ronald R. Davenport (chairman of Sheridan). NBN and Sheridan wanted equal rights in management of the partnership. The partners' equal right to manage AURN was modified by the partnership agreement in sections 5.2 and 5.3. Section 5.2 created a five-member Management Committee comprising two members selected by NBN and two by Sheridan; a seat on the Management Committee was to be vacant and would be filled only when the Management Committee was deadlocked. Section 5.2 also provided:

The Management Committee shall be responsible for the following functions of the partnership and contractual arrangements relating thereto:

    (i)   Sales and marketing;
    (ii) Promotions and public relations;
    (iii) Affiliate relations and compensation;
    (iv) Network programming;
    (v) Personnel administration; and
    (vi) Budgeting, accounting, and finance.

Section 5.3 provides:

(a) In the event that three of the four members of the Management Committee are unable to reach agreement on any issue or issues relating to items (i) through (v) above and remain so unable for a period of thirty days, then Ronald R. Davenport, Chairman of Sheridan, shall have the right to fill the vacant seat on the Management Committee for the purpose of reaching an agreement, and only until an agreement is reached, on such issue or issues.

Section 5.3 did not authorize appointment of a fifth member of the Management Committee when there was a deadlock regarding budgeting, accounting, or finance or any matter other than those listed in Section 5.2(i) through (v). As to budgeting, accounting, and finance and matters not listed in Section 5.2(i) through (v), NBN and Sheridan were equal partners, and all decisions on such matters required their agreement.

At a Management Committee meeting on September 14, 1995, Davenport proposed that AURN open an expensive new office in Washington, D.C.; hire Skip Finley as chief operating officer; and employ Richard Boland. When NBN's representatives opposed opening the new office and hiring Finley and Boland, Davenport scheduled a meeting solely to appoint a fifth member to break the deadlock. On September 15, NBN asked a Pennsylvania state trial court to grant a preliminary injunction and a permanent injunction against Sheridan's opening a new AURN office in Washington and hiring Finley and Boland, on the grounds that the proposals related to budgeting, accounting, and finance and were, therefore, not subject to the deadlock voting provision. On October 13, the state trial court denied NBN's motion for a preliminary injunction. The state trial court held that Sheridan had the right to invoke the deadlock provision to "make additions to personnel" by hiring Finley and Boland. The trial court did not rule on NBN's request for a permanent injunction.

At an October 16 Management Committee meeting, Davenport appointed a fifth member of the committee. By a 3-2 vote, the Management Committee voted to hire Finley and Boland, with NBN's representatives opposing. At that meeting, Davenport also proposed to relocate AURN's New York offices from NBN's office space in New York to other office space in the New York area; to transfer to Pittsburgh from New York AURN's traffic, billing, and collection functions; and to require Finley to make cuts in AURN's New York-based marketing and research personnel. NBN's representatives opposed the proposals, and Davenport scheduled a meeting on November 28 to break the deadlock.

Sensing that the Pennsylvania state trial court would dismiss its request for a permanent injunction and hoping to litigate the issues at a later time, NBN sought to withdraw its motion for a permanent injunction. On November 28, 1995, while the state trial court judge was considering NBN's request to withdraw its lawsuit, a meeting of AURN's Management Committee was held. Davenport again invoked the deadlock provision and appointed his son as fifth member of the Management Committee. By a 3-2 vote, the Management Committee agreed to relocate AURN's New York offices from NBN's office space, to transfer AURN functions to Pittsburgh from New

York, and to authorize Finley to make cuts in AURN's New York–based marketing and research personnel. Davenport also proposed to promote Finley to chief executive officer and Boland to vice president of administration. NBN Chairman Small objected, and Davenport scheduled another meeting to break the deadlock.

On November 29 and 30, the state trial court, wanting to put "a final end to this unnecessary litigation," ordered the discontinuance of NBN's lawsuit with prejudice, meaning that NBN could appeal the ruling to an appellate court but would not be permitted to have another trial court litigate the same issues. NBN chose not to appeal the decision of the Pennsylvania state trial court.

After the November 28 meeting, Sheridan located new office space for AURN in New York and entered a new lease with a minimum annual liability of $900,000, yet Sheridan never revealed the location of the space to NBN or sought NBN approval of the relocation or new lease. On January 18, 1996, at the next Management Committee meeting, Davenport again appointed his son as the fifth member. By a 3–2 vote, with NBN's representatives opposing, the Management Committee appointed Finley as CEO and Boland as vice president of administration.

On January 31, 1996, NBN filed a federal lawsuit seeking an injunction against Sheridan's alleged violations of the equal management rights of the partners by hiring Finley and Boland, interfering with AURN's personnel and customer relations, and relocating AURN's New York offices. Sheridan asked the federal district court to dismiss the suit on the grounds of res judicata; that is, Sheridan argued that NBN was raising legal issues that the Pennsylvania state trial court had already considered or that NBN should have brought to the Pennsylvania trial court. Thus, Sheridan argued, because the Pennsylvania trial court had already dismissed NBN's request for an injunction with prejudice, the federal district court should not reconsider these issues. The federal district court agreed with Sheridan and dismissed NBN's lawsuit. NBN appealed to the federal court of appeal.

Pollack, Judge

A discontinuance with prejudice is deemed a final adjudication on the merits for res judicata purposes on the claims asserted or which could have been asserted in the suit. Any issue concerning the relocation of the New York Office could not have been raised in the State Court suit commenced on September 15, 1995, or until the voting deadlock thereon on November 28, 1995. The NBN claim on the relocation of the New York Office was a claim based on new conduct that could have only arisen long after the filing of NBN's State Court suit. Since a plaintiff has no obligation to expand its suit in order to add a claim that it could not have asserted at the time the suit was commenced, a later suit based on subsequent conduct is not barred by res judicata.

The res judicata effect is limited to those claims that had arisen at the time that NBN brought the State Court action. They did not include the relocation of the New York Office, which had not yet even been brought to an initial vote. There was no submission to the State Court of NBN's equal right to decide whether the New York Office should be moved from its existing location as part of NBN's premises.

The doctrine of res judicata embraces all claims of NBN, excluding those claims relating to the relocation of the New York Office, which were passed on by the Management Committee prior to the filing of NBN's State Court action; the claims asserted therein and the dismissal thereof on the grounds of res judicata is affirmed.

Judgment for Sheridan affirmed in part; judgment in part reversed in favor of NBN. Remanded to the district court.

LOG ON

In England and India, partnership agreements are called partnership deeds. See an example at

www.vakilno1.com/partnership-agreements.

There are several commercial websites that sell model partnership agreements. One is FindLegalForms.com. See a list of partnership agreements for sale at

www.findlegalforms.com/forms/partnership.

Liability for Torts and Crimes

 Explain the liability of partners for contracts and torts.

Torts The standards and principles of agency law's *respondeat superior* are applied in determining the liability of the partnership and of the other partners for the torts of a partner and other partnership employees. See Chapter 36. In addition, the partnership and the other partners are liable jointly and severally for the torts of a partner committed within the ordinary course of partnership business or within the authority of that partner. Finally, when a partner commits a breach of trust, the partnership and all of the partners are liable. For example, all of the partners in a stock brokerage firm are liable for a partner's embezzlement of a customer's securities and funds.

Intentional Torts While a partnership and its partners are usually liable for a partner's negligence, they usually have no liability for a partner's intentional torts. The reason for this rule is that intentional torts are not usually within the ordinary scope of business or within the ordinary authority of a partner.

A few intentional torts impose liability on a partnership and its partners. For example, a partner who repossesses consumer goods from debtors of the partnership may trespass on consumer property or batter a consumer. Such activities have been held to be in the ordinary course of business. Also, a partner who authorizes a partner to commit an intentional tort is liable for such torts.

Partners' Remedies When a partnership and the other partners are held liable for a partner's tort, they may recover the amount of their vicarious liability from the wrongdoing partner, but only if the partner fails to comply with the fiduciary duty of care.

Tort Liability and Limited Liability Partnerships

State legislatures created the limited liability partnership (LLP) as a means of reducing the personal liability of professional partners, such as accountants. Consequently, an innocent partner of an LLP has no liability for the professional malpractice of his partners. LLP statutes grant partners broad protection, eliminating an innocent partner's liability for errors, omissions, negligence, incompetence, or malfeasance of his partners or employees.

Under the RUPA, the protection afforded LLP partners is even broader. LLP partners have no liability for other debts of the business, such as a supplier's bill, lease obligations, and bank loans.

That is the limit of protection, however. The LLP itself is liable for the tort of a wrongdoing partner or employee under the doctrine of *respondeat superior*. In addition, a wrongdoing partner is liable for his own malpractice or negligence. Also, the partner supervising the work of the wrongdoing partner may have unlimited liability for the wrongdoing partner's tort. Thus, the LLP's assets, the wrongdoing partner's personal assets, and the supervising partner's personal assets are at risk.

Crimes

When a partner commits a crime in the course and scope of transacting partnership business, rarely are his partners criminally liable. But when the partners have participated in the criminal act or authorized its commission, they are liable. They may also be liable when they know of a partner's criminal tendencies yet place him in a position in which he may commit a crime.

Until recent times, a partnership could not be held liable for a crime in most states because it was not viewed as a legal entity. However, modern criminal codes usually define a partnership as a "person" that may commit a crime when a partner, acting within the scope of his authority, engages in a criminal act.

Lawsuits by and against Partnerships and Partners

Under the RUPA, a partnership may sue in its own name. Because suing someone is usually an ordinary business decision, ordinarily any partner has authority to initiate a lawsuit.

The RUPA also permits a partnership to be sued in its own name. Partners may also be sued individually on partnership obligations. Partners are jointly and severally liable for partnership obligations, whether based in contract or tort. This means that in addition to suing the partnership, a creditor may sue all of the partners (jointly) or sue fewer than all the partners (severally). If a creditor sues the partnership and all of the partners, the judgment may be satisfied from the assets of the partnership and, if partnership assets are exhausted, from the assets of the partners. If the partnership and fewer than all the partners are sued severally, the judgment may be satisfied only from the assets of the partnership and the assets of the partners sued. Again, partners cannot be required to pay until partnership assets have been exhausted.

When fewer than all the partners are sued and made to pay a partnership obligation, the partners paying may seek **indemnification** and **contribution** from the other partners for their shares of the liability.

Limited Liability Partnerships

For LLP partners, only the LLP is liable on a contractual obligation, and only the LLP may be sued on such a claim. For tort obligations, the LLP is liable as well as the partner who committed the tort. LLP partners who had no role in the commission of the tort have no liability.

In the following case, *Mortgage Grader, Inc. v. Ward & Olivo, L.L.P.*, the court held that under New Jersey LLP law, when one partner in an LLP commits malpractice, other partners in the LLP cannot be held vicariously liable for such alleged malpractice. While decided under New Jersey law, the decision would be the same under the RUPA.

Mortgage Grader, Inc. v. Ward & Olivo, L.L.P
438 N.J. Super. 202 (App. Div. 2014), *aff'd*, 139 A.3d 30 (N.J. 2016)

Ward and Olivo established defendant Ward & Olivo, L.L.P. (W&O), a law firm engaged in the practice of intellectual property law. Ward and Olivo formed W&O as a limited liability partnership (LLP) pursuant to the UPA, and W&O obtained and maintained a claims-made professional liability insurance policy.

On July 29, 2009, Mortgage Grader, Inc. (MG) retained W&O to sue various persons or entities for patent infringement. Olivo entered into a contingency fee agreement with MG and filed a lawsuit (the "underlying lawsuit") against several defendants. MG settled the underlying lawsuit ("the settlements") by giving those defendants licenses in exchange for payment of a "one-time settlement amount."

On June 30, 2011, Ward and Olivo stopped actively practicing law as W&O. Thereafter, W&O began winding up its law practice by collecting outstanding legal fees. W&O's professional liability insurance policy expired on August 8, 2011, and W&O did not purchase a tail insurance policy.

In October 2012, MG filed a legal malpractice complaint against W&O, Olivo, and Ward alleging that Olivo's legal advice harmed MG's patent rights because Olivo, among other things, failed to require that royalty rates or licensing fees be part of the settlement. In the complaint, MG further alleged that W&O and Ward were vicariously liable for Olivo's acts or omissions. By the time MG filed its complaint, W&O's claims-made policy had expired, and W&O was uninsured. Ward had no involvement in the underlying lawsuit, the settlements, or Olivo's legal representation of MG.

Ward contends that he is shielded from liability as a partner in an LLP and is, therefore, not vicariously liable for the alleged legal malpractice of his former partner, Olivo. He thus argues that MG's complaint against him should be dismissed.

Fasciale, Judge

In addressing whether Ward is shielded from Olivo's alleged malpractice, this Court looks to the statutory language to determine the Legislature's intent. When interpreting a statute, words are to be given their ordinary meaning and significance. The plain language of N.J.S.A. 42:1A-18(c) clearly expresses the Legislative intent that the partners of an LLP are shielded from liability for a fellow partner's acts as it states, "An obligation of a partnership incurred while the partnership is [an LLP], whether arising in contract, tort, or otherwise, is solely the obligation of the partnership. A partner is not personally liable, directly or indirectly, by way of contribution or otherwise, for such an obligation solely by reason of being or so acting as a partner." Without LLP status,

"all partners are liable jointly and severally for all obligations of the partnership. . . ."

Under the UPA, the status of an LLP remains effective until the LLP itself cancels its status, or the LLP's status is revoked by the Department of the Treasury in the event the LLP "fails to file an annual report when due or pay the required filling fee." Since the status of W&O remains an LLP, the court is dismissing the legal malpractice claim asserted by MG against Ward because he is not vicariously liable for the alleged malpractice of his former partner Olivo.

Judgment of the trial court is reversed; judgment affirming this decision by the Supreme Court of New Jersey.

Ethics and Compliance in Action

You and your friends consider forming a consulting partnership. If you form the business as a partnership, each partner has personal liability for all the contacts and torts of the partnership. If you form the business as an LLP, in general you and the other partners have no liability for partnership obligations beyond the assets of the LLP, that is, beyond each partner's equity interest in the business.

- As your form of business, will you choose the partnership or LLP?

- Is it ethical to be an LLP partner and to have liability limited to your equity interest in the LLP? Would a profit maximizer find it ethical to form an LLP? Would a utilitarian or rights theorist find it ethical?

- Suppose that a bank knows the business is an LLP, lends money to the LLP, but does not obtain the LLP partners' individual promises to repay the loan. Is it ethical that the LLP partners are not liable to the bank on the loan if the LLP's assets are insufficient to repay the loan?

Problems and Problem Cases

1. John Szymanowski and Michael Wheeling entered a partnership with Robert Brace and BCD Properties, Inc. The partnership, known as BSW, was to drill two gas wells in Erie County, Pennsylvania, on leaseholds held by Brace. Their one-page agreement provided:

> BCD Properties, Inc. (owner Robert H. Brace) and Michael A. Wheeling and John Szymanowski have entered into an agreement on this 1st day of October, 2002, involving two new gas wells being drilled. The two new gas wells, Dougherty #1, and Danylko #1 are located in McKean Twp. Each of the two parties entering this agreement with BCD Properties, Michael A. Wheeling and John Szymanowski, have agreed to purchase into a portion of the wells at $15,000 per well, each, making a total of $30,000 received from each contributor. This amount will be due BCD Properties at the signing of this contract. This total will account for 10 percent from each contributor per well. Each contributor will then receive 10 percent net profit after royalties, well tending fees, and operating expenses are deducted from the wells production each month.

The Gas Well Agreement did not make any express or implied reference to any other oil and gas ventures on the Danylko or Dougherty leases or elsewhere or any other kind of undertaking. The parties did discuss the possibility of additional gas well projects or ventures but no commitments of any kind were made.

Danylko #1 production peaked in October 2003 and began a steady decline thereafter until it ceased and the well was disconnected in February 2005. In April 2004, BCD drilled the two additional wells, Danylko #2 and Danylko #4, each on the same Danylko leasehold and approximately 1,100 to 1,200 feet from Danylko #1, and each modestly successful. Szymanowski and Wheeling contend that the partnership either owned the Danylko #2 and Danylko #4 gas wells or that Brace and BCD breached a fiduciary duty by drilling the wells and claiming profits from the new wells for Brace and BCD. Did the trial court require Brace and BCD to account to Szymanowski and Wheeling for the profits from these two wells?

2. Twelve accounting and financial services professionals opt to form a limited liability partnership. They have experience in the industry ranging from 15 to 35 years. Edie Fercano has the most professional and managerial experience and is bringing the most valuable clients to the business. She has one client that she has served for over 20 years. She is inclined to continue to serve that client by herself, not with the LLP's resources. What do you recommend Edie include in the partnership agreement to avoid her having liability to the LLP? Why?

3. During a pandemic, Luke and Brianna lost their jobs. Looking for ways to earn some income, they agreed to start offering landscaping and simple fence-building services to friends and family. After sending an e-mail out announcing their plans, the pair received four projects, which would give them weeks' worth of work. They also hoped that by doing great work, their friends and family would refer them to others in the community, thereby generating more projects.

Unfortunately, at the very end of the second project, Luke and Brianna had a fight, and Luke left in a huff. He didn't show up to work on the third project, the planting of some bushes, and Brianna completed the project all by herself. At the start of the fourth project, Luke showed up and apologized, and they collaborated to get the final project finished on time. Will Brianna have to share the profit from the third project ($400) with Luke? Why or why not?

4. Dennis Ranzau and William Brosseau formed a partnership to purchase the Casa T, a house in Acapulco. Their intent was to use the Casa T as a vacation home for a few weeks each year, to lease it for the remainder of each year, and to share the rental income after expenses. Ranzau soon became concerned that Brosseau was not accounting for the expenses and income of the Casa T. Brosseau refused Ranzau's requests to provide receipts for expenses Brosseau claimed to have incurred on the house. Brosseau also let his friend have "total run of the house" over Ranzau's objection. On another occasion, Ranzau's wife and her friends were locked out of the house by an agent of Brosseau and had to make other accommodation arrangements. Has Brosseau breached his fiduciary duty to Ranzau?

5. Don O'Neal, a physician, was the managing partner of a medical practice, Sulphur Springs Medical-Surgical Clinic. As managing partner, he made the day-to-day financial decisions regarding the operations of the Clinic. The other partners relied on O'Neal to make decisions concerning the operations of the enterprise and the management of the partnership assets. In 2003, O'Neal started a separate business entity with Gary Stokes, named North Campus Development Ltd. Among its activities, North Campus purchased medical equipment that it leased to the Clinic, and it acted as a recruiter of specialty physicians for the Clinic. In 2004, North Campus recruited Scott Powell, MD, to practice at the Clinic. The convoluted compensation agreement required Powell to make payments to the Clinic and required the Clinic to make payments to Powell. For seven months of his employment, Powell made

payments to the Clinic in a series of 13 checks in varying amounts, totaling $370,517. Despite the fact that each of these checks from Powell was made payable to the Clinic, O'Neal deposited each of them into his personal account and not to the account of the Clinic. Has O'Neal breached a fiduciary duty to the partnership?

6. Spector (S), Rosenberg (R), Patron (P), and Konover (K) agree to build a shopping plaza in Seymour, Connecticut. There is no written partnership agreement. The four orally form Tri Town Realty Co., a partnership in which each partner receives a 25 percent interest. S and R contribute a lease, while P and K are responsible for building, operating, and managing the shopping plaza. Initially K and P manage the shopping plaza themselves, charging the partnership for any out-of-pocket expenses they incur. Over time, K and P form K and P Management Company, which eventually is replaced by K Management Corporation, which manages Tri Town. K's duties in managing Tri Town include preparation and distribution of monthly reports to each of the partners. S believes that K's reports are not adequately explaining the finances of the partnership. S asks for an explanation of various expenses that appear on the monthly report. When S does not receive a response from K, S again reaches out to K and demands that the partnership be terminated. K never responds and stops making profit distributions to S. S hires a CPA, whose investigation reveals that K did not maintain any account dedicated solely to the Tri Town partnership. It is discovered that the Tri Town partnership funds were commingled with funds from several other K entities, and all the funds were commingled in one account called the K and R Associates Trust Fund (K and R). Not only were the funds commingled in one account, but the Tri Town funds were used by other properties owned by K. Even though Tri Town funds supposedly were kept in the K and R checking account, the balance of the entire K and R checking account was actually far less than the amount purported to be in the Tri Town partnership account. Additionally, the interest earned on Tri Town funds was not credited to Tri Town's account. K admits to diverting funds between his various entities. K said that by sharing the funds in the K and R account, K could use one property's funds to cover expenses incurred by another property. S sues K seeking damages stemming from K's alleged breaches of his fiduciary duties in managing the Tri Town partnership. Will the court find that K breached his fiduciary duties?

7. Eric Wilmot and Renee Harmeau form WH & Associates Properties LLP, a limited liability partnership in Rochester, Minnesota, to purchase and manage commercial and residential real estate in the Rochester area. WH & Associates owns five residential apartment buildings, the largest of which has 32 units on two floors and has a value of $3 million. WH & Associates also owns seven strip shopping centers, of which the biggest has 12 stores and a value of $6 million. The total value of all the apartment buildings and shopping centers owned by WH & Associates is $31 million. Most of the residential buildings and shopping centers have been purchased partly with loans for which the properties are collateral.

To escape the harsh Minnesota winters, Wilmot wants to move his home to Jacksonville, Florida. He also wants to move WH Associates's management office to Jacksonville. In addition, he has identified a mall in Jacksonville that he wants to buy for the LLP. The mall has 32 stores, and the asking price is $29 million. To purchase the mall, Wilmot wants to borrow $27 million. Does Wilmot have the authority to move WH Associates's office, to purchase the mall, and to borrow money to fund the purchase?

8. Terry Powell was a property owner in Marshall County, Kentucky. Tosh Farms General Partnership raised swine in barns on land within one mile of Terry Powell's residence. Jimmy Tosh was the general partner of Tosh Farms. Powell alleged that "recurring intolerable noxious odors" that emanated from the Tosh Farms's swine waste facilities constituted a nuisance and decreased the value of Powell's residence and real property. He alleged that both the partnership, Tosh Farms, and its general partner, Jimmy Tosh, had liability for the harm caused him by the nuisance. Was Powell correct?

9. Steven Gursky and Louis Ederer are law partners in a New York limited liability partnership, Gursky & Ederer LLP. Ederer withdraws from the LLP after a severe falling out with Gursky and because the LLP was cash-strapped and unprofitable. Ederer then sues Gursky for breaching the LLP agreement by failing to pay Ederer his 30 percent share of the LLP's profits and other compensation that Ederer earned during the last months of the LLP. Gursky claims that he, as a partner in an LLP, had no liability to Ederer because partnership law in New York shields partners in an LLP from any personal liability. The New York trial court holds that New York law placing limits on the personal liability of partners in an LLP applies to debts of the partnership or the partners to third parties and has nothing to do with a partner's duties to his partner. Was the court correct in holding this? Will the New York Appellate Division (the highest court in the state of New York) affirm or overrule this decision?

10. Upon his release from prison, Michael Clott, convicted of securities fraud and racketeering, retained a law firm partnership, Ross & Hardies, to provide Clott's company, Capital Financial Group Inc., a legal framework to do financial, securities, and banking business in Maryland. Steven Kersner was the Ross & Hardies partner primarily assigned to Clott's account. Clott created the 7.5% Program, a mortgage program designed to provide lines of credit to minority homeowners. The 7.5% Program was a fraud by which Clott stole money that was borrowed by the homeowners participating in the program. Kersner helped perpetuate the fraud by assuring homeowners that the program was legitimate, aiding Clott in transferring borrowed funds to bank accounts, opening empty accounts in the name of homeowners to deceive them that lines of credit had been opened for them, preparing false statements to make it appear that the homeowners were no longer liable on the mortgages, telling lenders with questions to contact Kersner instead of homeowners, and forging and altering checks. Did Kersner's actions make his partnership liable to homeowners under the Racketeering Influenced Corrupt Organization Act?

11. Florence and Michael Acri were married and also partners in the Acri Café, which they jointly managed. For the first 15 years of their marriage, Michael had been in and out of sanitaria for the treatment of mental disorders. Although he had beaten Florence when they had marital problems, he had not attacked anyone else. Michael and Florence separated, and Michael assumed full control and management of the café. A few months after the Acris' separation, Stephen Vrabel and a friend went into the Acri Café. Without provocation, Michael shot and killed Vrabel's companion and seriously injured Vrabel while they were seated and drinking at the café's bar. Was Florence liable for Vrabel's injuries?

Partners' Dissociation
and Partnerships'
Dissolution and Winding Up

You are planning to form a 50-person partnership for investment purposes. Knowing the attributes, weaknesses, and faults of humans, you expect that some partners will die, become ill, and act irresponsibly during the term of the partnership. You know that some partners will want to leave the partnership for good reasons, and some for bad reasons. You know that when a partner leaves the partnership, the leaving partner will want to be paid the value of her partnership interest. You also know it is human nature for partners to disagree about the value of a partnership interest. You are also concerned about how the partnership will fund its repurchase of the leaving partner's interest without causing severe liquidity problems for the firm. You know that some of the firm's clients have strong business and personal attachments to one or more firm partners; therefore, when those partners leave the partnership, the firm may lose the business of those partners' clients. Finally, you know that the firm will need to add new partners from time to time to ensure the firm's survival.

- What are the default rules that apply when partners leave and enter a partnership?
- Why may the default rules be unacceptable to you?
- Write the sections of your partnership agreement regarding partners' leaving and entering the partnership.

LO LEARNING OBJECTIVES

After studying this chapter, you should be able to:

39-1 Classify dissociation actions as wrongful or nonwrongful.

39-2 Identify the default consequences of dissociation.

39-3 Describe the causes of dissolution and the process of winding up.

39-4 Describe the default effects of continuing a partnership after dissociation.

39-5 Determine when a new member may enter a partnership and the liability of the new partner.

THIS CHAPTER IS ABOUT the death of partnerships. Four terms are important in this connection: dissociation, dissolution, winding up, and termination. *Dissociation* of a partner is a change in the relation of the partners, as when a partner dies or retires from the firm. *Dissolution* of a partnership is the commencement of the winding up process. *Winding up* is the orderly liquidation of the partnership assets and the distribution of the proceeds to those having claims against the partnership. *Termination*, the end of the partnership's existence, automatically follows winding up. A partner in a limited liability partnership dissociates from the LLP and the LLP is dissolved, wound up, and terminated in the same manner as an ordinary partnership.

Dissociation

 Classify dissociation actions as wrongful or nonwrongful.

Dissociation is defined in the Revised Uniform Partnership Act of 1997 (RUPA) as a change in the relation of the partners caused by any partner's ceasing to be associated in the carrying on of the business. A dissociation may be caused by a partner's retirement, death, expulsion, or bankruptcy filing, among other things. Whatever the cause of dissociation, however, it is characterized by a partner's **ceasing to take part in the carrying on of the partnership's business**.

Dissociation is the starting place for the dissolution, winding up (liquidation), and termination of a partnership. Although dissolution and winding up do not always follow dissociation, they often do. Winding up usually has a severe effect on a business: It usually ends the business because the assets of the business are sold and the proceeds of the sale are distributed to creditors and partners.

A partner has the *power* to dissociate from the partnership *at any time*, such as by withdrawing from the partnership. A partner does not, however, always have the *right* to dissociate.

When a partner's dissociation does not violate the partnership agreement and otherwise is nonwrongful, the partner has the right to dissociate from the partnership: Such a dissociation is **nonwrongful**. When a partner's dissociation violates the partnership agreement or otherwise is wrongful, the partner has the power—but not the right—to dissociate from the partnership: Such a dissociation is **wrongful**. The consequences that follow a nonwrongful dissociation may differ from those that follow a wrongful dissociation.

Nonwrongful Dissociation
A dissociation is nonwrongful when the dissociation does not violate the partnership agreement and is not otherwise wrongful. The following events are nonwrongful dissociations:

1. Death of a partner.

2. Withdrawal of a partner at any time from an at-will partnership. A partnership is "at will" if it does not have a partnership agreement or the partnership agreement does not specify any term or time period or undertaking to be accomplished.

3. In a partnership for a term or completion of an undertaking, withdrawal of a partner within 90 days after another partner's death, adjudicated incapacity, appointment of a custodian over his property, or wrongful dissociation. This dissociation is deemed nonwrongful to protect a partner who may think her interests are impaired by the premature departure of an important partner.

4. Withdrawal of a partner in accordance with the partnership agreement. For example, a partnership agreement allows the partners to retire at age 55. A partner who retires at age 60 has dissociated from the partnership nonwrongfully.

5. Automatic dissociation by the occurrence of an event agreed to in the partnership agreement. For example, a partnership may require a partner to retire at age 70.

6. Expulsion of a partner in accordance with the partnership agreement. For example, the removal of a partner who has been convicted of a crime causes a dissociation from the partnership if the partnership agreement allows removal on such grounds.

7. Expulsion of a partner who has transferred his transferable partnership interest or suffered a charging order against his transferable interest. Under the RUPA, such an expulsion must be approved by all the other partners, absent a contrary partnership agreement.

8. Expulsion of a partner with whom it is unlawful for the partnership to carry on its business. Under the RUPA, this expulsion must be approved by all the other partners, absent a contrary agreement.

9. A partner's assigning his assets for the benefit of creditors or consenting to the appointment of a custodian over his assets.

10. Appointment of a guardian over a partner or a judicial determination that a partner is incapable of performing as a partner. For example, a court rules that a partner who has suffered a stroke and has permanent brain damage is unable to continue as a partner of a consulting partnership.

In addition, there are a few special rules for nonwrongful dissociations of nonhuman partners, such as corporations.

 Identify the default consequences of dissociation.

Consequences of Nonwrongful Dissociation A partner who nonwrongfully dissociates from the partnership is entitled to be paid the value of her partnership interest. The partner or her representative has no power, however, to dissolve the partnership and to force winding up, unless it is a partnership at will, that is, a partnership with no term. If the partnership is not at will, the partnership will continue. If dissociation was caused by a partner's retirement in compliance with the partnership agreement, a partnership for a term may be dissolved only by all remaining partners agreeing to the dissolution. Dissociation caused by a partner's death, however, permits as few as 50 percent of the partners to dissolve a partnership for a term. See the Concept Review at the end of this chapter for a comprehensive summary of the consequences of dissociation due to death or retirement.

Wrongful Dissociation
A partner wrongfully dissociates from a partnership when she dissociates in violation of the partnership agreement or in any other wrongful way. The following are wrongful dissociations:

1. Withdrawal of a partner that breaches an express provision in the partnership agreement.

2. Withdrawal of a partner before the end of the partnership's term or completion of its undertaking, unless the partner withdraws within 90 days after another partner's death, adjudicated incapacity, appointment of a custodian over his property, or wrongful dissociation.

3. A partner's filing a bankruptcy petition or being a debtor in bankruptcy.

4. Expulsion of a partner by a court at the request of the partnership or another partner. The grounds for judicial dissociation are when

   a. A partner's wrongful conduct adversely and materially affects the partnership business,

   b. A partner willfully and persistently breaches the partnership agreement or her fiduciary duties, or

   c. A partner's conduct makes it not reasonably practicable to conduct partnership business with the partner.

For example, a partner may persistently and substantially use partnership property for his own benefit. Or three partners may refuse to allow two other partners to manage the partnership's business. The harmed partners may seek judicial dissociation. For the expelled, wrongdoing partners, the dissociation is wrongful.

In addition, there are a few wrongful dissociations that apply only to nonhuman partners, such as a corporation.

Consequences of Wrongful Dissociation A partner who wrongfully dissociates from a partnership has no right to demand that the partnership be dissolved and its business wound up. That means the remaining partners may

continue the partnership and its business. If at least 50 percent of the remaining partners so choose, however, the partnership will be wound up.

Should the other partners choose to wind up the business, the wrongfully dissociated partner has no right to perform the winding up. Nonetheless, a wrongfully dissociated partner is entitled to his share of the value of his partnership interest, minus the damages he caused the partnership. Damages may include the cost of obtaining new financing and the harm to the partnership goodwill caused by the loss of a valuable partner.

Acts Not Causing Dissociation Mere disagreements, even irreconcilable differences, between partners are expectable, and therefore by themselves are not grounds for dissociation. If the disagreements threaten the economic viability of the partnership, however, a court may order a dissolution, as will be discussed below.

Effect of Partnership Agreement The dissociations listed in the RUPA are merely default rules. The partners may limit or expand the definition of dissociation and those dissociations that are wrongful, and they may change the effects of nonwrongful and wrongful dissociations. For example, the partners may require dissociation if a partner transfers his transferable partnership interest, if a partner does not redeem a charging order within 15 days of the order, or if a partner fails to make a capital contribution required by the partnership agreement. The partnership agreement may also reduce the number of partners that must approve the expulsion of a partner, such as a two-thirds vote, and expand the grounds for expulsion. If one partner is very powerful, the partnership agreement might allow that partner to dissociate at any time without penalty.

In the following case, the court considered whether a four-person joint venture/partnership was at will or for the completion of an objective, affecting whether two partners'/joint venturers' withdrawals were wrongful. As we shall learn later, partnership law regarding dissociation applies also to joint ventures.

Dissolution and Winding Up the Partnership Business

 Describe the causes of dissolution and the process of winding up.

When a partner dissociates from a partnership, the next step may be dissolution and **winding up** of the partnership's

Meyer v. Christie   634 F.3d 1152 (10th Cir. 2011)

In March 2005, David Christie and Alexander Glenn met with Alan Meyer and John Pratt to tour potential sites for a residential housing development in Junction City, Kansas. They found an appropriate site and made an oral agreement to form a joint venture, Junction City Partners, that would purchase the land and create a residential development named The Bluffs.

They agreed that Christie and Glenn would be 50/50 partners with Meyer and Pratt, and that they would hire as a general contractor a company owned by Meyer and Pratt, Dovetail Builders.

During the next few months, Christie made a contract to purchase the land, and Dovetail began to solicit subcontractors, draft initial site plans, and purchase and lease equipment for constructing the project. Meyer and Pratt consulted with Christie and Glenn on financing and initial site plans, as well as a presentation to Junction City officials seeking financial incentives for the project. Following several meetings, the City entered into a memorandum of understanding with Junction City Partners, in which the City agreed to pay up to $15 million in financial incentives for completion of the residential development.

A few weeks later, Christie and Glenn terminated their relationship with Meyer and Pratt. They formed The Bluffs LLC, to which they assigned the contract to purchase the land. Several months later, they gave a 50 percent partnership interest in The Bluffs to two other individuals, the owners of the company that became the general contractor in the development. The Bluffs ultimately received $8 million in financial incentives from Junction City.

Meyer and Pratt sued Christie and Glenn in a federal district court alleging breach of the joint venture agreement, breach of fiduciary duty, and wrongful dissociation. The jury awarded Meyer and Pratt $9,196,345 in actual damages, including $7,170,603 in connection with their interest in the joint venture. The jury also awarded Meyer and Pratt $100 in punitive damages. Christie and Glenn appealed.

McKay, Circuit Judge

Christie and Glenn appeal the jury's finding of wrongful dissociation, arguing they did not wrongfully dissociate from the joint venture because they were free to dissociate at will.

Under Kansas law, a partner or joint venturer may disassociate at will from the partnership or joint venture agreement without liability for damages caused by the disassociation unless (1) the dissociation "is in breach of an express provision of the partnership agreement; or (2) in the case of a partnership for a definite term or particular undertaking, [the dissociation occurs] before the expiration of the term or the completion of the undertaking." Kan. Stat. Ann. 56a-602(b). Christie and Glenn argue that neither of these provisions is applicable in the instant case, as the partnership agreement included no definite terms regarding dissociation and an agreement to pursue a residential development is by its nature too speculative and uncertain to constitute an agreement for a definite term or particular undertaking.

We hold that the district court did not abuse its discretion in denying Christie and Glenn's motion for a new trial as to this issue. The jury was presented with sufficient evidence to support a finding that the joint venture agreement was one for a particular undertaking and that Christie and Glenn dissociated from the joint venture before this undertaking was completed. The jury heard evidence that the parties agreed to develop a single residential development project on a particular piece of property and intended to sell this project within a conceivable

time frame after completion. The fact the parties had not fully determined feasibility or finalized all details of the project does not mean that they necessarily could not have formed a joint venture to pursue this particular development project. We conclude the jury could reasonably have found this to be a joint venture for a particular undertaking, which had not been completed prior to Christie and Glenn's dissociation. We thus affirm the entry of judgment in favor of Meyer and Pratt on their wrongful dissociation claim.

Christie and Glenn also contend they did not breach any fiduciary duties to Meyer and Pratt because they did not breach any of the limited fiduciary duties that remain following lawful dissociation from a joint venture. Because we uphold the jury's finding that the dissociation was wrongful, we likewise reject this argument and affirm the jury's finding of breach of fiduciary duty.

We now consider Christie and Glenn's challenge to the approximately $7 million awarded to Meyer and Pratt for their interest in connection to the joint venture. Christie and Glenn contend this amount was necessarily speculative and contingent because the joint venture was terminated before the parties had acquired the land or determined whether the development project should even go forward. Because Christie and Glenn first raised this argument in their post-judgment motion for judgment as a matter of law, we review only to determine if there is any evidence to support the damage award.

Applying this standard, we affirm this award of damages to Meyer and Pratt. The jury heard expert testimony regarding the value of the property and regarding the costs and profits involved in the completed development project. The jury also heard expert testimony that the project as completed generally followed the same broad ideas contemplated by the parties prior to Christie and Glenn's wrongful dissociation. We are not persuaded by Christie and Glenn's argument that Meyer and Pratt should be prevented from recovering damages because Christie and Glenn wrongfully dissociated from the venture and conspired to take this development opportunity from them before

the parties could calculate with reasonable certainty what the project's potential costs and revenues would be. The wrongdoer may not complain of inexactness where his actions preclude precise computation to the extent of the injury. The fact that Meyer and Pratt could lose profits if they were ousted from the project was reasonably within the contemplation of the parties at the time of Christie and Glenn's wrongdoing, and the amount of profits was proven with reasonable certainty at trial. Kansas law does not require more.

Judgment for Meyer and Pratt affirmed.

business. This involves the orderly liquidation—or sale—of the assets of the business. Liquidation may be accomplished asset by asset; that is, each asset may be sold separately. It may also be accomplished by a sale of the business as a whole. Or it may be accomplished by a means somewhere between these two extremes.

Winding up does not always require the sale of the assets or the business. When a partnership has valuable assets, the partners may wish to receive the assets rather than the proceeds from their sale. Such *distributions-in-kind* are rarely permitted.

During winding up, the partners continue as fiduciaries to each other, especially in negotiating sales or making distributions of partnership assets to members of the partnership. Nonetheless, there is a termination of the fiduciary duties unrelated to winding up. For example, a partner who is not winding up the business may compete with his partnership during winding up.

Events Causing Dissolution and Winding Up

Recognizing that a partnership business is worth more as a going concern, the RUPA contemplates that the partnership business will usually continue after a partner's dissociation. Many dissociations, such as one caused by a partner's death or retirement, will *not* automatically result in the dissolution and winding up of a partnership.

Nonetheless, the RUPA provides that a partnership will be dissolved and wound up in the following situations:

1. When the partnership's term has expired.

2. When the partnership has completed the undertaking for which it was created.

3. When all the partners agree to wind up the business.

4. When an event occurs that the partnership agreement states will cause a winding up of the partnership.

5. For a partnership at will, when any partner expressly withdraws from the partnership, other than a partner who is deceased, was expelled, is a debtor in bankruptcy, assigned his assets for the benefit of creditors, had a custodian appointed over his assets, or was automatically dissociated by the occurrence of an event agreed to in the partnership agreement.

6. For a partnership for a term or completion of an undertaking, when at least half the remaining partners vote to dissolve and wind up the partnership within 90 days after a partner dies, wrongfully dissociates, assigns his property for the benefit of his creditors, or consents to the appointment of a custodian over his property.

7. When the business of the partnership is unlawful.

8. Upon the request by a partner, when a court determines that the economic purpose of the partnership is likely to be unreasonably frustrated, a partner's conduct makes it not reasonably practicable to carry on the business with that partner, or it is not reasonably practicable to conform with the partnership agreement.

9. Upon the request of a transferee of a partner's transferable interest in a partnership at will or a partnership whose term or undertaking has been completed, when a court determines that it is equitable to wind up the partnership business.

As mentioned above, when a partner of an at-will partnership wants to leave a partnership, his departure will dissolve the partnership. Therefore, as demonstrated in *Gelman v. Buehler*, the determination of whether or not the partnership is "at will" becomes very important. The *Gelman* case also once again reminds us of the importance of partnership agreements in order to avoid unwanted default rules.

Gelman v. Buehler   986 N.E.2d 914 (N.Y. 2013)

Plaintiff Geoffrey Gelman and defendant Antonio Buehler were recent business school graduates who decided to form a partnership in 2007. Buehler had proposed a plan to Gelman aimed at acquiring $600,000 from investors for the purpose of establishing a "search fund" to research and identify a business with growth potential. A second investor solicitation was contemplated to raise any additional funding needed to pay the purchase price of the targeted business. Buehler and Gelman were to manage the business with the goal of increasing its value until it could be sold at a profit—they referred to this future occurrence as the "liquidity event"—and the investors would share in the profits realized from the sale. Gelman accepted Buehler's proposal and the partnership was formed by oral agreement. Buehler and Gelman expected that the business plan would reach its objective in four to seven years.

The partners apparently pursued prospective investors for several months, but Buehler withdrew from the venture after Gelman refused his demand for majority ownership of the partnership. As relevant to this appeal, Gelman sued Buehler for breach of contract, claiming that Buehler could not unilaterally terminate his obligations under the agreement. Buehler moved to dismiss the complaint on the ground that dissolution was permissible under Partnership Law § 62(1)(b)[1] because the oral agreement did not include a "definite term or particular undertaking." The trial court, known as the State Supreme Court in New York, granted Buehler's motion to dismiss, concluding that the complaint failed to allege that the partnership agreement provided for a definite term or a defined objective.

The Appellate Division of the New York State Supreme Court reversed, reasoning that the complaint adequately described a "definite term" by its reference to the liquidity event and sufficiently alleged a "specific undertaking of acquiring a business and expanding it until the investors would receive a return on their capital investments." Two justices dissented, concluding that the partnership was dissolvable at will because the oral agreement contained neither a definite term nor a particular undertaking. Buehler appealed.

Graffeo, Judge

[New York partnership law, which reflects the Uniform Partnership Act], states that a partnership formed by oral agreement may be dissolved unilaterally if "no definite term or particular undertaking is specified" in the underlying agreement. Because the parties in this case did not sufficiently address either of these provisions in their oral contract, we conclude that there was no breach of contract when one party withdrew from the enterprise.

. . .

[Under New York law] a partnership may be dissolved "[b]y the express will of any partner when no definite term or particular undertaking is specified" in the partnership agreement. In this appeal, we are asked to decide whether the allegations in Gelman's complaint set forth a "definite term" or identify the particular objective sought to be achieved with the requisite specificity.

Since the enactment of the Partnership Law in New York, courts in other jurisdictions have held that the commonly-used statutory phrase—a "definite term"—is intended to be durational in nature and refers to an identifiable termination date. A "particular undertaking" has been defined to require a specific objective or project that may be accomplished at some future time, although the precise date need not be known or ascertainable at the time the partnership is created (*see e.g. Tropeano v. Dorman*, 441 F.3d 69, 77–78 (1st Cir. 2006) ("Business activities which may continue indefinitely are not 'particular' in nature and do not constitute particular undertakings"); *Scholastic, Inc. v. Harris,* 259 F.3d 73, 85–86 (2d Cir. 2001) . . .).

Applying similar meanings to the terminology in Partnership Law § 62(1)(b), we believe that Gelman's complaint lacks a fixed, express period of time during which the enterprise was expected to operate. Instead, the complaint alleges a flexible temporal framework: the parties were to solicit investments for an indefinite length of time; conduct an open-ended (possibly two-year) search for an unidentified business in an unknown business sector or industry; secure additional capital investments over the course of an unspecified period of time;

---

[1]The RUPA continues the UPA rule that a partner in an at-will partnership has the unilateral right to force the dissolution of the partnership.

and then purchase and operate the enterprise for an indeterminate duration (perhaps four to seven years) until a liquidity event would hopefully occur. Since the complaint does not set forth a specific or even a reasonably certain termination date, it does not satisfy the "definite term" element of section 62(1)(b).

Furthermore, when the entire scheme is considered, the alleged sequence of anticipated partnership events detailed in the complaint are too amorphous to meet the statutory "particular undertaking" standard for precluding unilateral dissolution of a partnership. The stages of the plan, as alleged by Gelman, were to: (1) raise money; (2) identify a business to buy; (3) raise more money to purchase the business; (4) "operate the business to increase its value"; (5) "achieve the liquidity event"; (6) "sell the business"; and (7) secure profit from the sale. But these objectives are fraught with uncertainty and are less definitive than the declarations referring to specific industries that have been found to be inadequate by other courts (*see e.g. Scholastic, Inc.*, 259 F.3d at 86 (objective of the partnership was the "'development, packaging, production and distribution of theatrical feature films . . .

while also involved . . . in television development and production'"); *Sanley Co. v. Louis*, 197 A.D.2d 412, 413 (1st Dept. 1993) (partnership's purpose was to acquire, manage and resell real estate)). In contrast, the Third Department ruled that the "particular undertaking" requirement was satisfied in *St. Lawrence Factory Stores v. Ogdensburg Bridge & Port Auth.*, (202 A.D.2d 844, 845 (3d Dept. 1994)) because the agreement identified the specific purpose of the partnership as the development and construction of a retail factory outlet center on an identified parcel of real property. Nothing in Gelman's complaint approaches such precision.

In the absence of a definite term of duration or a particular undertaking to be achieved, the partnership agreement at issue, however well-intended, was dissolvable at will by either partner under Partnership Law § 62(1)(b). Consequently, defendant Buehler is entitled to dismissal of the breach of contract cause of action.

Appellate Division reversed; cause of action dismissed.

Effect of Partnership Agreement   The preceding causes of winding up are the RUPA's default rules, which, except for the last three, may be changed by the partnership agreement. For example, the partnership agreement may provide that at any time two-thirds of the partners may cause a winding up or that upon the death or retirement of a partner no partner has the right to force a winding up. Partners will frequently want to limit the events that cause dissolution and winding up because they believe the business will be worth more as a going concern than by being liquidated.

In addition, if dissolution has occurred, the partners may agree to avoid winding up and to continue the business. To avoid winding up after dissolution has occurred, under the RUPA all the partners who have not wrongfully dissociated must consent to continuing the business. That means that any partner who has not wrongfully dissociated may force winding up if dissolution has occurred. That RUPA rule gives great power to one partner who wants to wind up the business when all other partners want to continue the business. Many partnership agreements, therefore, prohibit a single partner from forcing not only dissolution but also winding up of the partnership's business.

In the following case, *Urbain v. Beierling*, we return to a recurrent theme: the importance of carefully drafting partnership agreements to make sure that the partners' intent is clearly expressed. In this case, the court interpreted the partnership agreement to allow two partners to oust a third partner from the partnership because the third partner failed to show that she was damaged.

Joint Ventures and Mining Partnerships

The partnership rules of dissociation and dissolution apply to joint ventures. Mining partnerships are difficult to dissolve because of the free transferability of mining partnership interests. The death of a mining partner does not effect a dissolution. In addition, a mining partner may sell his interest to another person and dissociate from the carrying on of the mining partnership business without causing a dissolution.

 Describe the causes of dissolution and the process of winding up.

Performing Winding Up   For the well-planned partnership, the partnership agreement will indicate who

Urbain v. Beierling   835 N.W.2d 455 (Mich. Ct. App. 2013)

This case arises out of a partnership that lasted approximately four months, from November 2009 through February 2010. Defendant Beierling developed a concept for an educational software business marketing online learning games to teachers. Beierling had contacts in the software and educational arenas and wanted to stream the online games into classrooms through periodic paid subscriptions. Beierling pitched her idea to two friends, Plaintiff Katie Urbain and Defendant Maureen Clinesmith. Both Urbain and Clinesmith were interested, and the three women formed a partnership. The partnership contained no written partnership agreement.

Initially, Clinesmith orally agreed to invest $10,000 in the partnership, and for purposes of equity, Beierling's and Urbain's equity stakes were to be valued by the amount of time that each person invested in the business at an hourly rate of $25. Very shortly thereafter, Clinesmith decided to become an active partner and loaned the partnership money instead of investing money in the business. The three partners decided to be equal partners and equally divided the work, each receiving one-third of the profits after Clinesmith's loan was repaid. After Clinesmith opted to become an active partner, the partners abandoned the idea of tracking hours. Urbain testified that the first few days she worked for the partnership were the only days in which she kept track of the hours.

Over the next several months, the partners worked to create a marketing plan to sell subscriptions, write questions for game banks, and develop and design their website, ifiveeducation.com. The partners intended to launch the website in early February 2010 because they believed that was the best time for sales in the education industry. Because of several issues, however, including an apparent person- ality conflict between Beierling and Urbain, the website launch was delayed and the partnership broke down. The partners had several communications and met in person at least once, during which time Beierling told Urbain that Urbain was no longer a partner in the venture. Urbain felt that she had been ousted from the partnership and was surprised when Beierling cut off her access to a partnership e-mail account and discontinued her website administration privileges. Beierling and Clinesmith dissolved the partnership and com- menced a successor partnership, consisting of only Beierling and Clinesmith, which launched the website within weeks. Despite e-mail blasts and other targeted marketing, the partnership sold exactly one unit for a total of $69.99.

Urbain ("plaintiff") filed the instant action against defendants, alleging breach of the partnership agreement and improper dissolu- tion of the partnership.

Donofrio, Markey, and Owens, Judges (Per Curiam)

The UPA defines a partnership as "an association of 2 or more persons . . . to carry on as co-owners a business for profit." Pursuant to the UPA, "the dissolution of a partnership is the change in the relation of the partners caused by any partner ceasing to be associ- ated in the carrying on as distinguished from the winding up of the business." This dissolution of the partnership may occur by the acts of the partners, by operation of law, or by decree of the trial court. Because a partner's right to dissolve the partnership is "inseparably incident to every partnership," there can be no indis- soluble partnership.

Plaintiff argues that defendants' decision to discontinue the partnership and oust her was wrongful absent the consent of all partners. Plaintiff also alleges that discontinuing the partnership was an act that made it impossible to carry on the ordinary busi- ness of the partnership, which was required to be authorized by all partners. However, plaintiff's arguments fail to acknowledge the section of the UPA that sets forth circumstances under which a partner may dissolve a partnership. The UPA specifies that "[d]issolution is caused: (1) Without violation of the agreement between the partners: . . . (b) By the express will of any partner when no definite term of particular undertaking is specified."

Plaintiff admits that the partners did not specify a definite term for the partnership and, similarly, did not specify a particular

undertaking. Rather, plaintiff maintains that the partners agreed to carry on the partnership business indefinitely. Plaintiff also maintains that the partners agreed to work together to create, design, launch, fund, market, and make changes and improve- ments, as necessary, to the website, or other websites they may develop. Therefore, because there was no specific term set forth in the partnership agreement, which was open-ended about the partnership's undertakings with regard to developing websites then and in the future, the partnership could be dissolved by the express will of any partner pursuant to the UPA. Accordingly, neither Clinesmith nor Beierling breached the partnership agree- ment when they dissolved the partnership, and the trial court properly granted summary disposition for defendants on plain- tiff's claim alleging breach of the partnership agreement.

In respect to plaintiff's argument that she is entitled to dam- ages as a result of the dissolution, this Court acknowledges that the UPA seeks to make partners whole economically. The UPA states in part: "Each partner shall be repaid his or her contributions, whether by way of capital or advances to the partnership property and share equally in the profits and surplus remaining after all liabilities, including those to partners, are satisfied." Therefore, on dissolution of the partnership, plaintiff was entitled to be repaid her capital contribution and to share equally in all profits. However, as the trial court correctly determined, the plaintiff in the instant case did not make a capital contribution nor was there a profit to be shared. Thus, plaintiff is not entitled to damages.

Plaintiff also asserts that she had a right to account for her interests in the partnership on the date of its dissolution. Since partners who have not wrongfully dissolved the partnership have the right to wind up the partnership affairs, defendants in the instant case should have afforded plaintiff an opportunity to be involved in the winding-up of the partnership affairs. The record shows that plaintiff had no input whatsoever in the windup process because Beierling and Clinesmith took sole control of all partnership affairs, including the launch of the website and partnership finances.

Clinesmith, the partner responsible for accounting duties, testified that in regard to winding up partnership affairs, she personally looked into the financials and recognized that there were only expenses. The partnership had received no profits. Clinesmith had attempted to marshal partnership assets, value the assets at the time of dissolution, and distribute those assets. Unfortunately, there was no surplus of assets over and above the $10,000 loan from Clinesmith.

Thus, although defendants did not allow plaintiff to engage in any of the activities necessary to properly wind up the partnership, plaintiff has failed to show that she was damaged. Plaintiff testified that she was aware of the $10,000 capital loan that Clinesmith had made to the partnership and that the loan was to be repaid before any partnership assets or profits could be distributed to the partners. While it would have been wise to have a valuation of the partnership's website and other intangibles calculated at the time of the partnership's dissolution, doing so would have been a difficult task considering that the website had not yet launched. It appears that the market set value of the business after the website's launch when only one sale was generated despite extensive targeted marketing to industry professionals. While plaintiff asserts that she was a "co-owner" of partnership property, the record demonstrates that there were no assets or profits to distribute to her. Hence, the trial court properly granted summary disposition for defendants on plaintiff's dissolution-of-partnership claim.

Judgment Affirmed

may perform the process of winding up for the partnership, what the power is of the persons performing winding up, and what their compensation is for performing the service.

In the absence of a partnership agreement, the RUPA provides that any partner who has not wrongfully dissociated from the partnership may perform the winding up. A winding-up partner is entitled to reasonable compensation for her winding-up services, in addition to her usual share of profits.

Partner's Authority during Winding Up

Express and Implied Authority During winding up, a partner has the express authority to act as the partners have agreed. The implied authority of a winding-up partner is the power to do those acts *appropriate for winding up* the partnership business. That is, he has the power to bind the partnership in any transaction necessary to the liquidation of the assets. He may collect money due, sue to enforce partnership rights, prepare assets for sale, sell partnership assets, pay partnership creditors, and do whatever else is appropriate to wind up the business. He may maintain and preserve assets or enhance them for sale, for example, by painting a building or by paying a debt to prevent foreclosure on partnership land. A winding-up partner may temporarily continue the business when the effect is to preserve the value of the partnership.

Performing Executory Contracts The implied authority of a winding up partner includes the power to perform executory contracts (made before dissolution but not yet performed). A partner may not enter into *new* contracts unless the contracts aid the liquidation of the partnership's assets. For example, a partner may fulfill a contract to deliver wind turbines if the contract was made before dissolution. She may not make a new contract to deliver wind turbines unless doing so disposes of wind turbines that the partnership owns or has contracted to purchase.

Borrowing Money Usually, the implied authority of a winding-up partner includes no power to borrow money in the name of the partnership. Nonetheless, when a partner can preserve the assets of the partnership or enhance them for sale by borrowing money, he has implied authority to engage in new borrowing. For example, a partnership may have a valuable machine repossessed and sold far below its value at a foreclosure sale unless it can refinance a loan. A partner may borrow the money needed to refinance the loan, thereby preserving the asset. A partner may also borrow money to perform executory contracts.

Apparent Authority Winding-up partners have apparent authority to conduct business as they did before dissolution, when notice of dissolution is not given to those persons who knew of the partnership prior to its dissolution. For example, a construction partnership dissolves and begins winding up but does not notify anyone of its dissolution. After dissolution, a partner makes a contract with a customer to remodel the customer's building. The partner would have no implied authority to make the contract because the contract is new business and does not help liquidate assets. Nonetheless, the contract may be within the partner's apparent authority because to persons unaware of the dissolution, it appears that a partner may continue to make contracts that have been in the ordinary course of business.

To eliminate the apparent authority of a winding-up partner to conduct business in the ordinary way, the partnership must ensure that one of the following occurs:

1. A third party knows or has reason to know that the partnership has been dissolved.

2. A third party has received notification of the dissolution by delivery of a communication to the third party's place of business. For example, an e-mail message is sent to a creditor of the partnership.

3. The dissolution has come to the attention of the third party. For example, a partnership creditor was told of the dissolution by another creditor.

4. A partner has filed a Statement of Dissolution with the secretary of state, which limits the partners' authority during winding up. A third party is deemed to have notice of a limitation on a partner's authority 90 days after the filing of a Statement of Dissolution.

To be safe, a dissolved partnership should eliminate its partners' apparent authority to conduct business in the ordinary way by directly informing parties with whom it has previously conducted business, such as by e-mail, fax, or a phone call. The partnership should be able to identify such parties from its records. As for parties that may know about the partnership but with whom the partnership has not done business, the partnership should post notice of the dissolution at its place of business and in newspapers of general circulation in its area, increasing the chance that third parties will know of the dissolution. Also, the partnership should file a Statement of Dissolution: 90 days after its filing, no one should be able to rely on the apparent authority of a partner to conduct any business that is not appropriate to winding up. The partnership agreement of a well-planned partnership will require the partnership to take these steps when dissolution occurs.

Disputes among Winding-Up Partners When more than one partner has the right to wind up the partnership, the partners may disagree concerning which steps should be taken during winding up. For decisions in the ordinary course of winding up, the decision of a majority of the partners controls. When the decision is an extraordinary one, such as continuing the business for an extended period of time, unanimous partner approval is required.

In the following case, *Paciaroni v. Crane*, the court found that the business of the partnership to train and race a horse should continue during winding up. The drafters of the RUPA expressly noted that this case is a model for continuing a business during winding up.

Paciaroni v. Crane   408 A.2d 946 (Del. Ch. 1979)

Black Ace, a harness racehorse of exceptional speed, was the fourth-best pacer in the United States in 1979. He was owned by a partnership: Richard Paciaroni owned 50 percent; James Cassidy, 25 percent; and James Crane, 25 percent. Crane, a professional trainer, was in charge of the daily supervision of Black Ace, including training. It was understood that all of the partners would be consulted on the races in which Black Ace would be entered, the selection of drivers, and other major decisions; however, the recommendations of Crane were always followed by the other partners because of his superior knowledge of harness racing.

In 1979, Black Ace won $96,969 through mid-August. Seven other races remained in 1979, including the prestigious Little Brown Jug and the Messenger at Roosevelt Raceway. The purse for these races was $600,000.

A disagreement among the partners arose when Black Ace developed a ringbone condition and Crane followed the advice of a veterinarian not selected by Paciaroni and Cassidy. The ringbone condition disappeared, but later Black Ace became uncontrollable by his driver, and in a subsequent race he fell and failed to finish the race. Soon thereafter, Paciaroni and Cassidy sent a telegram to Crane dissolving the partnership and directing him to deliver Black Ace to another trainer they had selected. Crane refused to relinquish control of Black Ace, so Paciaroni and Cassidy sued him in August 1979, asking the court to appoint a receiver who would race Black Ace in the remaining 1979 stakes races and then sell the horse. Crane objected to allowing anyone other than himself to enter the horse in races. Before the trial court issued the following decision, Black Ace had entered three additional races and won $40,000.

Brown, Vice Chancellor

It is generally accepted that once dissolution occurs, the partnership continues only to the extent necessary to close out affairs and complete transactions begun but not then finished. It is not generally contemplated that new business will be generated or that new contractual commitments will be made. This, in principle, would work against permitting Black Ace to participate in the remaining few races for which he is eligible.

However, in Delaware, there have been exceptions to this. Where, because of the nature of the partnership business, a better price upon final liquidation is likely to be obtained by the temporary continuation of the business, it is permissible, during the winding up process, to have the business continue to the degree necessary to preserve or enhance its value upon liquidation, provided that such continuation is done in good faith with the intent to bring affairs to a conclusion as soon as reasonably possible. And one way to accomplish this is through an application to the Court for a winding up, which carries with it the power of the Court to appoint a receiver for that purpose.

The business purpose of the partnership was to own and race Black Ace for profit. The horse was bred to race. He has the ability to be competitive with the top pacers in the country. He is currently "racing fit" according to the evidence. He has at best only seven more races to go over a period of the next six weeks, after which time there are established horse sales at which he can be disposed of to the highest bidder. The purse for these remaining stake races is substantial. The fact that he could possibly sustain a disabling injury during this six-week period appears to be no greater than it was when the season commenced. Admittedly, an injury could occur at any time. But this is a fact of racing life which all owners and trainers are forced to accept. And the remaining stake races are races in which all three partners originally intended that he would compete, if able.

Under these circumstances, I conclude that the winding up of the partnership affairs should include the right to race Black Ace in some or all of the remaining 1979 stakes races for which he is now eligible. The final question, then, is who shall be in charge of racing him.

On this point, I rule in favor of Paciaroni and Cassidy. They may, on behalf of the partnership, continue to race the horse through their new trainer, subject, however, to the conditions hereafter set forth. Crane does have a monetary interest in the partnership assets that must be protected if Paciaroni and Cassidy are to be permitted to test the whims of providence in the name of the partnership during the next six weeks. Accordingly, I make the following ruling:

1. Paciaroni and Cassidy shall first post security in the sum of $100,000 so as to secure to Crane his share of the value of Black Ace.

2. If Paciaroni and Cassidy are unable or unwilling to meet this condition, then they shall forgo the right to act as liquidating partners. In that event, each party, within seven days, shall submit to the Court the names of two persons who they believe to be qualified, and who they know to be willing, to act as receiver for the winding up of partnership affairs.

3. In the event that no suitable person can be found to act as receiver, or in the event that the Court should deem it unwise to appoint any person from the names so submitted, then the Court reserves the power to terminate any further racing by Black Ace and to require that he simply be maintained and cared for until such time as he can be sold as a part of the final liquidation of the partnership.

Judgment for Paciaroni and Cassidy.

Distribution of Dissolved Partnership's Assets

After the partnership's assets have been sold during winding up, the proceeds are distributed to those persons who have claims against the partnership. Not only creditors but also partners have claims against the proceeds. As you might expect, the claims of creditors must be satisfied first, yet a partner who is also a creditor of the partnership is entitled to the same priority as other creditors of the partnership. Thus, a partner who has loaned money to the partnership is paid when other creditors of the partnership are paid.

After the claims of creditors have been paid, the remaining proceeds from the sale of partnership assets will be distributed to the partners according to the net amounts in their capital accounts. Over the life of a partnership, a partner's capital account is credited (increased) for any capital contributions the partner has made to the partnership plus the partner's share of partnership profits, including profits from the sale of partnership assets during winding up. The partner's capital account is charged (decreased) for the partner's share of partnership losses, including losses from the sale of partnership assets during winding up, and any distributions made to the partners, such as a distribution of profits or a return of capital. The net amount in the partner's account is distributed to the partner.

If the net amount in a partner's capital account is negative, the partner is obligated to contribute to the partnership an amount equal to the excess of charges over credits in the partner's account. Some partners may have a positive capital account balance and other partners may have a negative capital account balance. This means that during winding up, some partners may be required to contribute to enable the partnership to pay the claim of another partner.

In many partnerships that have been unprofitable, all the partners will have negative capital accounts. This means that the partnership assets have been exhausted and yet some of the partnership creditors have not been paid their claims. If partnership creditors cannot be paid from the partnership assets, the creditors may proceed against the partners, including a partner who may have already received a portion of partnership assets on account of her being a creditor also.

Because partners have liability for all the obligations of a partnership, if one partner fails to contribute the amount equal to her negative capital account balance, the other partners are obligated to contribute to the partnership in the proportions in which they share the losses of the partnership. The partner who fails to contribute as required is liable, however, to the partners who pay the defaulting partner's contribution.

The RUPA eliminates the old UPA's concept of marshaling of assets. While partnership creditors still have a priority over a partner's creditors with regard to partnership assets, partnership and partners' creditors share pro rata in the assets of individual partners.

Asset Distributions in a Limited Liability Partnership
The asset distribution rules are modified for a limited liability partnership because, in an LLP, most partners have no liability for partnership obligations beyond the partnership's assets. If the LLP has been profitable, each partner will receive the net amount in her capital account. If creditors' claims exceed the LLP's assets, however, an LLP partner is not ordinarily required to contribute an amount equal to the negative balance in her account, and the creditors may not sue the partner to force the partner to pay the debt. This result is necessary to protect the limited liability of innocent partners who did not commit a wrong against the creditors.

If, however, a partner has committed malpractice or another wrong for which LLP statutes do not provide protection from liability, that wrongdoing partner must contribute to the LLP an amount equal to her share of the unpaid liability. Creditors may sue such a partner when the LLP fails to pay the liability. If more than one partner has

liability, they must contribute to the LLP in proportion in which they share liability. If one is unable to pay, the other liable partners must contribute the shortfall. The partners who are not liable for the obligation cannot be forced to pay the debt.

Termination
After the assets of a partnership have been distributed, **termination** of the partnership occurs automatically.

When the Business Is Continued

 LO39-4 Describe the default effects of continuing a partnership after dissociation.

Dissolution and winding up need not follow a partner's dissociation from a partnership. The partners may choose not to seek dissolution and winding up, or the partnership agreement may provide that the business may be continued by the remaining partners.

When there is no winding up and the business is continued, the claims of creditors against the partnership and the partners may be affected because old partners are no longer with the business and new partners may enter the business.

Successor's Liability for Predecessor's Obligations
When the business of a partnership is continued after dissociation, creditors of the partnership are creditors of the person or partnership continuing the business. In addition, the original partners remain liable for obligations incurred prior to dissociation unless there is agreement with the creditors to the contrary. Thus, partners may not usually escape liability by forming a new partnership or a corporation to carry on the business of the partnership.

Dissociated Partner's Liability for Obligations Incurred while a Partner
Dissociated partners remain liable to partnership creditors for partnership liabilities incurred while they were partners; however, a dissociated partner's liability may be eliminated by the process of novation. **Novation** occurs when the following two conditions are met:

1. The continuing partners release a dissociated partner from liability on a partnership debt and
2. A partnership creditor releases the dissociated partner from liability on the same obligation.

The Global Business Environment

Dissolutions around the Globe

For most nations, partnership law on dissolutions is more like the old Uniform Partnership Act than the RUPA, which was drafted to create better default rules when partners leave a partnership. In countries other than the United States, dissolution is defined much like dissociation is defined under the RUPA, a change in the partners' relation. Unlike dissociation in the United States, dissolution in those countries (and in American states that still follow the UPA) often results in the end of the partnership and its business, absent a contrary agreement of the partners. Well-planned partnerships, however, have partnership agreements that in many situations provide for continuation of the partnership and its business by the remaining partners, despite dissolution.

In India, dissolution may be caused by a court, by agreement of the partners, automatically by operation of law, upon the happening of certain contingencies, and by notice. An Indian court may dissolve a partnership due to a partner's insanity, permanent incapacity, conduct that prejudicially affects carrying on the business of the firm, willful or persistent breach of the partnership agreement, and transfer of his partnership interest, or if the partnership cannot be carried on except as a loss. Partners in an Indian partnership may dissolve the partnership by their unanimous agreement. An Indian partnership dissolves automatically if its term ends or undertaking is accomplished, if a partner dies or is insolvent, or if the partnership's business is illegal. Finally, a partnership at will in India may be dissolved by action of any partner.

In Austria, a partnership is dissolved by expiration of the period for which it was entered into, by resolution of the partners, by institution of bankruptcy proceedings against the partnership assets or the assets of a partner, by death of a partner, by notice of termination by a partner, and by judicial decision.

Continuing partners are required to indemnify dissociated partners from liability on partnership obligations. To complete the requirements for novation, a dissociated partner must also secure his release by the partnership's creditors. A creditor's agreement to release an outgoing partner from liability may be express, but usually it is implied. *Implied* novation may be proved by a creditor's knowledge of a partner's withdrawal and his continued extension of credit to the partnership. In addition, a *material modification* in the nature or time of payment of an obligation operates as a novation for an outgoing partner, when the creditor has knowledge of the partner's dissociation.

When continuing partners release a dissociated partner from liability but creditors do not, there is not a novation. As a result, creditors may enforce a partnership liability against a dissociated partner. However, the outgoing partner may recover from his former partners who have indemnified him from liability.

Dissociated Partner's Liability for Obligations Incurred after Leaving the Partnership

Ordinarily, a dissociated partner has no liability for partnership obligations incurred after he leaves the partnership. Nonetheless, a third party may believe that a dissociated partner is still a partner of the continuing partnership and transact with the partnership while holding that belief. In such a context, a dissociated partner could be liable to the third party even though the dissociated partner will not benefit from the transaction between the partnership and the third party.

The RUPA makes a dissociated partner liable as a partner to a party that entered into a transaction with the continuing partnership, unless:

1. The other party did not reasonably believe the dissociated partner was still a partner.

2. The other party knew or should have known or has received notification of the partner's dissociation.

3. The transaction was entered into more than 90 days after the filing of a Statement of Dissociation with the secretary of state.

4. The transaction was entered into more than two years after the partner has dissociated.

Moreover, although a dissociated partner's right to manage the partnership has terminated upon his dissociation, unless one of the above can be proved, the dissociated partner retains his apparent authority to bind the partnership on matters in the ordinary course of business.

This means that when dissociation occurs, a partnership should take steps similar to those it took to reduce the apparent authority of a winding-up partner: that is, the partnership should directly inform parties with whom it has previously conducted business, such as by e-mail, fax, or a phone call, that the partner has dissociated. It should also post notice of the dissociation at its place of business and in newspapers of general circulation in its area. Finally, the partnership should cause the filing of a Statement of Dissociation, limiting the authority of the dissociated partner and notifying the public that the partner is no longer a partner. Taking these steps will reduce the risk that the dissociated partner will be liable for future obligations of the partnership, and it will help eliminate the apparent authority of the dissociated partner to act on behalf of the partnership. The partnership agreement of a well-planned partnership will require that these steps be taken by the partnership immediately upon the dissociation of a partner.

Effect of LLP Status In an LLP, a dissociated partner has less risk of continuing liability for contracts and torts occurring before or after the partner leaves the LLP because the partner's liability is limited to the LLP's assets. However, a buyout payment made to a dissociated LLP partner may not impair the ability of the LLP to pay its creditors. If so, the dissociated partner will be required to return some or all of the buyout payment to creditors.

Buyout of Dissociated Partners

When the partnership is continued, the partnership is required to purchase the dissociated partner's partnership interest. In well-planned partnerships, the purchase price and timing of the buyout will be included in the partnership agreement. For example, the partnership agreement may require the payment of an amount equal to the current value of the partnership multiplied by the partner's proportionate share of profits or capital. The partnership agreement may specify how to value the partnership, such as average annual profits plus partners' salaries for the last three years multiplied by seven. Many professional partnerships, however, pay a dissociated partner only her capital contribution plus her share of undistributed profits. The agreement may also permit deductions against the value of the partnership interest if the dissociated partner acted wrongly.

The agreement will state when the buyout is effected; for example, it may require the payment in a lump sum 30 days after dissociation, or it may allow the partnership to pay the amount in monthly installments over the course of three years.

In the absence of a partnership agreement, the RUPA spells outs the amount and timing of the buyout of the dissociated partner's interest. The buyout price is the greater of the amount that would have been in the dissociated partner's capital account had the partnership liquidated all its assets on the dissociation date *or* the amount in the capital account had it sold the entire business as a going concern without the dissociated partner on that date. If the partner has wrongfully dissociated from the partnership, the buyout price is reduced by any damages caused by the wrongfully dissociated partner, such as the reduction in the goodwill of the business caused by the loss of a valuable partner or hiring someone to take over duties of the partner.

When the dissociated partner has not wrongfully dissociated and there is no partnership agreement on the issue, the RUPA requires the partnership to pay the dissociated partner in cash within 120 days after she has demanded payment in writing. The buyout amount must include interest from the date of dissociation. If the dissociated partner and the partnership cannot agree on the buyout price, the partnership must, within 120 days of the written demand for payment, pay in cash to the partner the partnership's estimate of the buyout price, plus interest. The partner may challenge the sufficiency of the buyout price tendered by the partnership by asking a court to determine the buyout price.

If a partner has wrongfully dissociated, the partnership may wait to buy out the partner until the end of the partnership's term, unless the partner shows that the partnership will suffer no undue hardship by paying earlier. The buyout price must include interest from the date of the dissociation.

In the following *Dixon* case, we see again the risks of relying on the RUPA to resolve partnership issues. The case shows that the RUPA's less-than-unambiguous provision for valuing a partner's interest should be replaced in the partnership agreement by a concrete valuation method that covers every aspect of valuation the partners want to consider.

Dixon v. Crawford, McGilliard, Peterson & Yelish
262 P.3d 108 (Wash. Ct. App. 2012)

Steve Dixon was a partner in Crawford, McGilliard, Peterson & Yelish, a law firm partnership in Port Orchard, Washington. The Crawford firm had no written partnership agreement. The partners agreed orally that each of the five equity partners owned a 20 percent interest in the Crawford firm and received 20 percent of the profits annually. The equity partners each took annual draws in the range of $192,438 to $230,380. During those years, Dixon generated fee income of $231,182 to $249,434.

In 2006, Dixon left the Crawford firm. All his clients chose to follow him to his new office. Dixon asked the partnership to pay him the value of his partnership interest. To establish the value of his share in the Crawford firm, Dixon presented accounting expert Joe Lawrence. Lawrence used the capitalization of excess earnings method, which combines the income approach (for intangible assets or goodwill) and the cost approach (for tangible assets). Lawrence determined the goodwill value to be the difference between the Crawford *firm's earnings and the remaining partners' collective replacement values, adjusted for taxes and for future risk and growth (capitalization). Lawrence valued Dixon's one-fifth interest in the Crawford firm between $350,000 and $360,000, which he testified included both tangible and intangible assets.*

The Crawford firm presented three accounting experts: James Weber, Steve Kessler, and Roland Nelson. Although Nelson testified that in his experience there is no goodwill value in a law practice, both Weber and Kessler testified that goodwill value does exist in law firms. All three agreed that to the extent there is goodwill value, capitalization of excess earnings is an appropriate valuation method. Weber and Kessler each used significantly higher replacement values for the law firm's remaining partners than did Lawrence and concluded that given those replacement values, there was no goodwill value in the firm, leaving only the tangible assets. All the experts put Dixon's interest in the tangible assets between $36,000 and $48,000.

The trial court found that the Crawford firm was highly respected and had long enjoyed success as a preeminent public defense firm. Adopting the capitalization of excess earnings method and using replacement values between those suggested by the experts, the court valued the firm at $1,160,714. Dixon's one-fifth interest was therefore $232,143.

The Crawford firm appealed, contending the court erred by including goodwill in its valuation. The law firm also contended the court erred in its method of valuing goodwill, by precluding evidence of Dixon's postdissociation earnings. Dixon cross-appealed, contending the court failed to recognize his portion of the value of Crawford's tangible assets.

Ellington, Judge

Where a partner dissociates from an ongoing partnership in the absence of any agreement as to distribution of the dissociated partner's interest, the buyout price for the partnership interest is governed by Rev. Code Wash. 25.05.250(2). The buyout price of a dissociated partner's interest is the amount that would have been distributable to the dissociating partner under RCW 25.05.330(2) if, on the date of dissociation, the assets of the partnership were sold at a price equal to the greater of the liquidation value or the value based on a sale of the entire business as a going concern without the dissociated partner and the partnership were wound up as of that date. Interest must be paid from the date of dissociation to the date of payment.

The parties agree that the statute controls and that Dixon's interest should be valued under the "going concern" approach.

The value of a business typically includes the value of its intangible assets, also known as "goodwill," which is a benefit or advantage which is acquired by an establishment in consequence of the general public patronage and encouragement, which it receives from constant or habitual customers on account of its local position, or common celebrity, or reputation for skill or affluence, or punctuality, or from other accidental circumstances or necessities, or even from ancient partialities or prejudices. Essentially, goodwill is the monetary value of a reputation. It is a way of recognizing earnings not strictly attributable to the value of the work performed. It is distinguishable from the skill, education, and earning capacity of a practicing professional.

In determining goodwill value, the court adopted Lawrence's determination of Crawford's earnings. These included income from the public defense contracts. Crawford contends this amounts to the forced purchase and sale of the firm's public defense contracts, improperly treats the contracts and clients as

commodities, and allows Dixon to profit from clients to whom he had no responsibility.

These arguments are unfounded. The contract revenues were part of the firm's historical earnings, capitalized downward to account for their reduced contribution over time. Considering all the firm's earnings does not treat clients as commodities, and the court did not purport to transfer an interest in the contracts. Further, Crawford does not explain how, for purposes of valuing goodwill, public defense contracts are different from agreements to handle litigation matters for a group of employees or union members or retirees or any other client group.

Finally, the allegation that the valuation method allows Dixon to profit from clients for whom he had no responsibility ignores the fact that a dissociating partner's interest is determined as of the date of his departure. Until that moment, all the partners, including Dixon, had responsibilities to those clients. The court properly included earnings from the public defense contracts in the valuation of the firm.

Goodwill is a recognized asset of a professional practice. Here, there was no agreement among the partners excluding claims for goodwill, and the court valued the firm's goodwill to determine Dixon's share. The excess earnings method is a logical way to determine the value of Crawford's goodwill. One hundred percent of Crawford's profits were distributed equally among the partners. The capitalization of the difference between their earnings and the sum of the remaining partners' individual replacement values provide an accurate reflection of the goodwill value of the firm as a whole. Neither here nor below did Crawford suggest a more accurate means of valuation. And again, Crawford's own experts endorsed the method adopted by the court.

When Dixon dissociated from Crawford, he left Crawford's goodwill—to which he contributed—with Crawford. To the extent Dixon deprived Crawford of some of its goodwill by removing himself from the firm, the court's method recognized that by valuing Crawford without Dixon. This adheres to the requirements of RCW 25.05.250.

The trial court refused to permit discovery or consider evidence of Dixon's postdissociation earnings. Crawford contends such evidence was necessary to a fair calculation of Dixon's interest because Dixon was compensated for his contribution to Crawford's goodwill when he took his clients with him: "Plaintiff in effect received his share of any goodwill in the firm in taking a substantial portion of the firm's clients."

Crawford equates "taking a substantial portion of the firm's clients" with "taking goodwill." A firm's current clients may be evidence of the firm's "expectation of continued public patronage," but clients are not a commodity. Neither Dixon nor Crawford has a proprietary interest in the clients. Further, the experts, including Crawford's experts, agreed that the capitalization of excess earnings method was the proper methodology, and there is no place in that method for consideration of postdissociation earnings.

Under RCW 25.05.250(2), the value of a partnership must be based on the value "of the entire business as a going concern without the dissociated partner." Thus, a dissociated partner is not compensated for value taken by his or her departure from the firm. The court did not abuse its discretion in declining to permit discovery or evidence intended to value goodwill that "Mr. Dixon took with him out the door."

Dixon cross appeals from the court's finding that its valuation method includes tangible assets. He contends the court should increase the judgment to reflect his interest in the tangibles. But in both his testimony and his report, Lawrence stated that his valuation method included both tangible and intangible assets. The court adopted Lawrence's method. The court did not abuse its discretion in finding its valuation included both tangible and intangible assets.

Judgment for Dixon affirmed.

Partners Joining an Existing Partnership

 LO39-5 Determine when a new member may enter a partnership and the liability of the new partner.

Frequently, a partnership will admit new partners. For example, many of you hope to be admitted to a well-established consulting or accounting partnership after you graduate and have practiced for several years. The terms under which a new partner is admitted to a partnership are usually clearly stated in the partnership agreement and in the partner's admission agreement. The terms usually include the procedure for admission as well as the new partner's capital contribution, compensation including salary and share of profits, and power to manage the business. In the absence of a partnership agreement, the RUPA sets the rules for the partner's admission and rights and duties upon admission. For example, a new partner is admitted to a partnership only if all partners consent.

Liability of New Partners An important question is what level of liability a new partner should have for obligations of the new partnership. It makes sense for a new partner to be fully liable for all partnership obligations incurred *after* he becomes a partner, for he clearly benefits from the partnership during that time. This is the RUPA rule.

What should be his liability for partnership obligations incurred *before* he became a partner? The RUPA states that a new partner has no liability for partnership obligations incurred before he became a partner. However, many partnership agreements modify this rule by requiring a partner to assume liability for all the obligations of the business as a condition of being admitted to the partnership.

Effect of LLP Statutes If a new partner enters an LLP, however, the RUPA provides that the partner has no liability for the obligations of the LLP beyond his capital contribution, whether incurred before or after his admission, unless the new partner has committed malpractice or other wrong for which he is personally responsible. LLP partnership agreements should not change this rule.

LOG ON

www.uniformlaws.org
At the website for the National Conference of Commissioners on Uniform State Laws, you can find the complete text and comments of the RUPA of 1997. You can find the complex default rules regarding dissociation, dissolution, and buyouts of partners in Articles 6, 7, and 8. Pay particular attention to sections 601, 701, 801, and 802. Knowing the content of these sections will help you draft partnership agreement provisions dealing with a partner leaving the partnership.

Ethics and Compliance in Action

The default rules of the RUPA provide that any partner who leaves the partnership is entitled to the value of her partnership interest. The default valuation method uses the greater of the partnership's liquidation or going concern value. If a partner wrongfully dissociates, however, damages are deducted from the partner's interest and the partner need not be paid until the partnership ends.

- Why would partners want a partnership agreement that sets out a different valuation method than the default rule?
- What risk is taken by relying on the default rule? Among other things, under the default rule, a court will value a partnership interest when partners cannot agree on the valuation. Why would partners not want a court to valuate a partnership interest?
- Using profit maximization analysis, is it ethical to delay payment to a wrongfully dissociating partner for the value of her partnership interest until the partnership terminates? Does utilitarian analysis change your answer? What are the costs and benefits of delaying payment?
- When do you propose your partnership should pay a partner who dissociates due to death, disability, retirement at an expected age, and unexpected dissociations? What ethical arguments would you make to justify the rules you propose?

CONCEPT REVIEW

Consequences of Partner's Death or Retirement under the RUPA's Default Rules

Death of Partner

A. Is a nonwrongful dissociation

B. Does not by itself effect a dissolution

C. Rights of estate of deceased partner
  1. Receive the amount in the deceased partner's capital account at the time of death, valuing partnership or its assets at the greater of liquidation value or going-concern value
  2. Payment must be made within 120 days after a written demand by the estate

D. Rights of other partners
  1. In a partnership at will, any other partner may dissociate at any time and effect a dissolution
  2. In a partnership for a term
    a. Any other partner may dissociate within 90 days of death
      1) Will not dissolve the partnership
      2) Dissociated partner must be paid amount in her capital account (valued as in C.1 above) within 120 days after a written demand
    b. By a vote of at least 50 percent of partners within 90 days of death, the partnership may be dissolved and its business wound up

Retirement (Withdrawal) of Partner

A. Is a dissociation
  1. Is a nonwrongful dissociation if the partnership is at will
  2. Is a wrongful dissociation if the partnership is for a term and the term has not expired, unless the partnership agreement permits retirement before the end of the term

B. Effects a dissolution, only if a partnership at will

C. Rights of dissociated partner
  1. If nonwrongful dissociation, dissociated partner
    a. may wind up the business, if a partnership at will, or

    b. may receive the amount in the dissociated partner's capital account (valued same as for deceased partner) within 120 days after a written demand

  2. If wrongful dissociation, dissociated partner

    a. may not dissolve the partnership and

    b. may receive the amount in the dissociated partner's capital account, valuing partnership or its assets at the greater of liquidation value or going-concern value, less damages, at the end of the partnership's term, unless no undue hardship to partnership to pay the partner earlier

D. Rights of other partners

  1. In a partnership at will, any other partner may dissociate at any time and effect a dissolution or dissociate and be paid the value in his capital account (valued same as for deceased partner) within 120 days

  2. In a partnership for a term when the partner has wrongly dissociated

    a. Any other partner may dissociate within 90 days of the retirement and be paid the amount in her capital account (valued same as for deceased partner)

    b. By a vote of at least 50 percent of partners within 90 days of the retirement, the partnership may be dissolved and its business wound up

  3. In a partnership for a term when the partner has not wrongfully dissociated, the remaining partners have no rights due to the dissociation

Problems and Problem Cases

1. Horizon/CMS Healthcare Corp., a large provider of both nursing home facilities and management for nursing homes, expanded into the Kissimmee, Florida, market by entering several 20-year partnerships with Southern Oaks Health Care. Within a few years, Horizon claimed that the partners had irreconcilable differences regarding how profits were to be determined and divided, resulting in the partners' incapacity to operate in business together. Horizon asked a court to dissolve the partnerships on these grounds. Did the court grant Horizon's request? Has Horizon wrongly dissociated by seeking judicial dissolution on these grounds?

2. In 2009, Jean Pierre Maufras and William Mansfield formed a Wisconsin limited liability partnership, TideTraders LLP, to provide online training for securities market traders. In October 2012, Mansfield and Maufras exchanged several e-mails about Maufras's continued involvement in TideTraders. On October 14, 2012, Maufras wrote, "I am tired of getting no support from you. TideTraders certainly is not a rewarding venture for me and it may be time for me to move along." Mansfield responded to Maufras's statement about quitting with, "You and I both know you don't want to quit. You push yourself and the rest of us too much." Further, Mansfield encouraged Maufras to "stop talking about quitting and recognize this sort of talk as your body telling you to rest." Maufras sent a lengthy reply that started with, "I am not sure you fully understand me. I want to sell my stakes in TideTraders." Maufras articulated several business and personality differences between them, concluding that he and Mansfield "cannot get on the same page as business owners." Maufras wrote, "The bottom line is maybe someone else can better understand how to help you in this endeavor." Maufras concluded his e-mail with a description of their business model's faults, and the following comment, "Since this is of secondary importance to you, I have to respectfully bail out, because I shall not fail any longer and need to focus on the future. I will work out an arrangement to ensure a transition so you can keep TideTraders going. One that is smooth and not noticeable to subscribers."

Mansfield treated Maufras's e-mail as proof that Maufras had dissociated from the LLP. Mansfield removed Maufras's access to LLP accounts and sought to bring in another partner. Did Maufras dissociate?

3. Joe Costa and Nelson Borges orally agreed to associate together to purchase and develop a 15-acre parcel of real property located in Jerome County, Idaho. They intended to develop a subdivision with 41 residential

lots and three commercial lots. Costa was to contribute his expertise in developing the real property, and Borges was to contribute his equipment to clear and level the land. They agreed to contribute equal capital and labor, with the exception that Borges could elect to contribute additional capital to hire someone to do his share of the labor. Within two years, their relationship broke down, and they stopped communicating with each other. Costa continued working on the development and hired his son to do some of the work. Borges did not perform any further labor at the site. Costa sued Borges claiming that Borges had breached the partnership agreement and that he should be expelled from the partnership. Was Costa's suit successful?

4. Brothers Don and Harley Shoemaker formed a partnership, D & H Real Estate. After 18 years, Harley withdrew from the partnership and asked for payment of the value of his partnership interest in accordance with the following provision in the partnership agreement:

> In the event that the remaining partner(s) and the … retiring partner are unable to agree upon the value to be assigned to the partnership shares, all interested individuals shall select an appraiser and in the event they are not able to agree upon an appraiser, the remaining partner(s) and the . . . retiring partner shall be entitled to select an appraiser with the appraisers separately submitting their appraisals. If the appraisals are within ten percent of each other[,] the value shall be an average of the two appraisals. If the difference in the appraisals exceeds ten percent[,] the two appraisers shall together attempt to reach agreement on the value and if unable to do so shall obtain a third appraiser with the three appraisers together agreeing upon the value. The appraisers shall determine the value of the partnership as a going concern with all assets to be valued at their fair market value. . . . The value of the partner's interest as determined in the above section shall be paid without interest to the withdrawing or retiring partner . . . not later than 90 days after the effective date of the dissolution or termination.

When Don failed to pay the appraisal amount within 90 days of Harley's withdrawal, Harley demanded that he receive not only the amount determined by the appraisal, but also a share of the profits earned by the partnership after his withdrawal, as well as interest on the late payment. Did the court agree with Harley?

5. Labrum & Doak LLP was a law partnership that began in 1904 in Pennsylvania. John Seehousen, Jonathan Herbst, and James Hilly were partners of Labrum & Doak. They withdrew from the partnership in 1993, 1995, and 1997, respectively. They did not give creditors notice of their withdrawals from the LLP. In 1997, the LLP was dissolved. When the LLP's assets were insufficient to pay creditors' claims, the LLP's creditors argued that Seehousen, Herbst, and Hilly were liable for the malpractice of the firm's partners, which malpractice occurred after the three former partners had left the partnership. Were they found liable?

6. Bertrand Barnes was one of three partners of NMB Associates LLP, a limited liability partnership in the consulting and investment banking industries. When Barnes retired from the LLP, he sought to be released from liability on the $5,438,000 of outstanding bank loans the LLP had incurred during his tenure at NMB. Neither the partners nor the LLP nor the banks agreed to release Barnes from liability on the loans. What is the extent of Barnes's liability on the bank loans? Would his liability be different if NMB were a partnership and not an LLP?

7. Steven Schwartz, Ken Epstein, and Peter Munk enter into a partnership agreement. All are dentists by profession. Under the partnership agreement, they form Family Dental Group—Clinton Associates. Their partnership agreement provides the following:

> The partnership is to continue until the year of 2051, unless the partners agree to an early dissolution. The partners are to devote full professional attention to the partnership during the first five years of its inception. The two practicing partners . . . are to receive 35 percent of their collections from patients. Additionally, any profit beyond expenses is to be put into a profit pool of which the first 20 percent is to be divided equally between all three partners and the remaining divided equally between Schwartz and Munk.

Schwartz reduces his workload while Munk maintains a consistent, full-time work schedule. When Munk becomes aware of Schwartz's schedule change, he becomes upset. Munk is dissatisfied with Schwartz's management style and the way he conducts his practice. Munk is also displeased with both his compensation and Schwartz's refusal to expand the partnership's dental facilities. Munk wants to change the agreement to alter his compensation or alternatively terminate Schwartz as a partner. Schwartz rejects this proposal and insists that the parties submit to mediation pursuant to the agreement. The mediation results in an award of a management fee for Munk in the amount of two-thirds of 1 percent of the gross revenue. Epstein and Munk then offer to buy out Schwartz's interest in the practice, or alternatively, to keep him as a partner while eliminating his management responsibilities and his share of the profits. Schwartz rejects the offer. Shortly after, at a special meeting of the partners, Epstein and Munk vote to terminate Schwartz from the practice "without cause" and provide him with 90 days' notice pursuant to § 12(a)(i) in the partnership agreement. Section 12 of the partnership agreement is titled "Other withdrawal from practice." Section 12(a)(i) states:

> In the event that any Partner's association with the Partnership is terminated for any reason other than death or total disability, either party shall give the other not less than ninety (90) days written notice of such termination and the Partnership shall have the first option to retire the interest of the departing Partner by paying the departing Partner deferred compensation at the Formula Amount.

As a result of the termination, Schwartz has sued Munk and Epstein seeking restoration of his partnership status. Is the court likely to restore Schwartz's partnership status?

8. Wilbur and Dee Warnick and their son Randall Warnick formed Warnick Ranches general partnership to operate a ranch in Sheridan County, Wyoming. After a dispute among the partners arose, Randall dissociated from the partnership. His parents continued the business, and they offered to purchase Randall's partnership interest. Randall rejected the offer, taking his parents to court. The parents asserted that for purposes of calculating the buyout price, the value of ranch assets should be less than the amount reflected in the appraisal of those assets. Specifically, they requested that the district court deduct $50,000 for real estate commissions and expenses of sale, including those associated with selling livestock and equipment. In fact, the partnership did not sell and had no intention of selling those assets. The real estate commissions and sale expenses were hypothetical, that is, the commissions and expenses that would have been incurred if those assets were sold. To value Randall's partnership interest, should the district court deduct the hypothetical commission and expenses from the appraisal of the assets?

9. Joe Creel owned a NASCAR collectibles business named Joe's Racing Collectibles. In 1994, Creel brought Arnold Lilly and Roy Altizer into the business, which they reformed as a partnership named Joe's Racing. Creel contributed as capital to the partnership inventory and supplies of the old business, valued at $15,000. Lilly and Altizer each contributed $6,666 in cash to the partnership, and each paid $3,333 to Creel for his rights in the existing business. The partners agreed to share profits and losses with 52 percent going to Creel and 24 percent each to Lilly and Altizer. Less than a year later, Creel died and his wife sought to receive the value of his interest in the partnership. An accountant valued the partnership at $44,589.44. The partnership's creditors were the accountant for $875, Mrs. Creel $495, Lilly $2,187, and Altizer $900. What was the value of Creel's partnership interest?

10. Simon Weinberg and his brother were the only partners in Times Square Stationers LLP. The partners signed a 20-year lease with Tisch Leasing. After 12 years, Simon retired from the business and was replaced as a partner by his son, Seth. A year later, the business defaulted on its lease with Tisch Leasing. What is Seth's liability on the lease with Tisch? Would your answer change if the business were an ordinary partnership, not an LLP?

Limited Liability Companies and Limited Partnerships

Y ou are planning to start a new business that will operate "contactless" convenience stores, which will allow people to grab what they want and pay without interacting with a cashier. Due to start-up costs, you expect the business to generate losses the first two years; after that, you hope to get a 20 percent return on your investment. You prefer to own the business entirely by yourself and design the technological systems and operation methods for the stores, yet you want trustworthy people, two per store, to handle the day-to-day operations. You'd like to take a salary from the business, minimize taxes, and protect yourself from liability.

- Why is a limited liability company an especially good business form for your company?
- How might you be taxed on your salary and any profits from the business if you choose to organize as an LLC?

LEARNING OBJECTIVES

After studying this chapter, you should be able to:

40-1 Explain the attributes of a limited liability company.

40-2 Identify the default rules regarding an LLC's members' rights and responsibilities.

40-3 Explain the attributes of a limited partnership and the default rights and liabilities of partners in a limited partnership.

STATE LEGISLATURES AND THE Internal Revenue Service have cooperated to permit the creation of two business forms that offer taxation advantages similar to the sole proprietorship and the partnership, yet have simple default rules that promote management of the business by fewer than all the owners and extend limited liability to some or all of the owners. These forms are the limited liability company (LLC), limited partnership, and limited liability limited partnership (LLLP).

Limited Liability Companies

 Explain the attributes of a limited liability company.

The limited liability company (LLC) is the product of attempts by state legislators to create a new business organization that combines the nontax advantages of the corporation and the favorable tax status of the partnership. Wyoming, in 1977, passed the first LLC statute. Every state and the District of Columbia have adopted an LLC statute. The National Commissioners on Uniform State Laws has adopted the Revised Uniform Limited Liability Company Act of 2006 (RULLCA). The RULLCA provides default rules that govern an LLC in the absence of a contrary agreement of its owners. The RULLCA treats LLCs and their owners similarly to the way the Revised Uniform Partnership Act (RUPA) treats limited liability partnerships (LLPs) and their partners, with exceptions noted in this chapter. In general, the RULLCA has fewer rules than the RUPA, leaving more decisions to its members. As of

2019, 18 states and the District of Columbia have adopted or introduced the RULLCA.

LOG ON

www.uniformlaws.org
You can find the Revised Uniform Limited Liability Company Act of 2006 at the website for the National Conference of Commissioners on Uniform State Laws.

The popularity of the LLC has grown dramatically since 2000. It is the preferred form for small businesses and other businesses with few owners, including high-profile sports firms such as Yankee Global Enterprises LLC, which owns the New York Yankees baseball team. Major corporations also form some of their subsidiaries as LLCs.

Tax Treatment of LLCs
An LLC may elect to be taxed like a partnership, S corporation, or C corporation for federal income tax purposes. If LLC members elect to be recognized as a partnership or an S corporation, the LLC will pay no federal income tax. Instead, all income and losses of the LLC will be reported by the LLC's owners on their individual income tax returns.

If the LLC elects to be taxed as a partnership, none of the partners may take a salary. Instead, profits from the business are the only way they can receive compensation, and all of the profits, whether distributed or not, are subject to taxes. In addition, active members of the LLC who engage in the day-to-day affairs of the company are also subject to self-employment taxes on their percentage of the profits. These taxes are quite steep—as of 2020, they are 12.4 percent for Social security (up to a particular wage base) and a 2.9 percent Medicare tax. To minimize self-employment taxes, LLCs frequently opt to be taxed as an S corporation so that active members may receive a salary and avoid self-employment taxes based on the profits of the business. However, the requirements for qualifying as an S corporation are very stringent. For example, an S corporation may have no more than 100 owners, all owners must be U.S. citizens or residents, and there can be only one type of ownership interest.

LLCs are also tax shelters for wealthy investors. They allow such investors to reduce their taxable income by deducting LLC losses on their federal income tax returns to the extent they are *at risk,* that is, their capital contributions to the LLC. Moreover, passive investors in an LLC, like limited partners in a limited partnership, may use their shares of LLC losses to offset income from other *passive* investments.

Formation of LLCs
To create an LLC, one or more persons must file a **certificate of organization** (also called articles of organization in some jurisdictions) with the secretary of state. The certificate must include the name of the LLC and the name and address of its registered agent. The name of the LLC must include the words "limited liability company," "limited company," or an abbreviation such as "LLC" or "L.L.C.," indicating that the liability of its owners is limited.

The owners of an LLC are called members. An individual, partnership, corporation, and even another LLC may be a member of an LLC.

Although not required, an LLC will typically have an operating agreement, which is an agreement of the members. The operating agreement will usually state whether the LLC is member-managed or manager-managed. It also will cover how members share profits, manage the LLC, and withdraw from the LLC, among other things. Well-planned LLCs have detailed operating agreements that cover all aspects of the LLC's operation and members' relations, often restating much of what is contained in the RULLCA but with changes to suit the members' needs.

Once formed, an LLC may have perpetual existence and is an entity separate from its members. It may sue and be sued in its own name. It can buy, hold, and sell property. It can make contracts and incur liabilities. Figure 40.1 summarizes an LLC's characteristics.

LO40-2 Identify the default rules regarding an LLC's members' rights and responsibilities.

Members' Rights and Responsibilities

Limited Liability An LLC member has no individual liability on LLC contracts, unless she also signs LLC contracts in her personal capacity. Therefore, a member's liability is usually limited to her capital contributions to the LLC. She is, however, liable for torts she commits while acting for the LLC.

In addition, a member must make capital contributions to the LLC as she has agreed. This includes the initial capital she agreed to contribute and additional calls for capital that can be made on members according to the operating agreement.

Management Rights Under the RULLCA, an LLC may choose to be member-managed or manager-managed. If it fails to make that choice in its operating agreement, the LCC is member-managed. Each member in a member-managed LLC shares equal rights in the management of the business merely by being a member of the LLC. Each member is an agent of the LLC with implied authority to

Figure 40.1   Principal Characteristics of LLCs under the RULLCA of 2006

1. An LLC may be created only *in accordance with a statute.*

2. An LLC is owned by *members*. Members usually have *liability limited to their capital contributions* to the business.

3. LLC members *share equally in the profits* of the business, unless members agree otherwise.

4. An LLC may be *member-managed or manager-managed*. If it is member-managed, each member has an equal right to manage the business.

5. A member who manages the LLC owes *fiduciary duties* to the LLC and its members.

6. A member's ownership interest in an LLC is *not freely transferable*. A transferee of a member's distributional interest receives only the member's share of LLC distributions.

7. The death or other withdrawal of a member *does not usually dissolve an LLC.*

8. Members of an LLC may choose to have the LLC *taxed as a partnership or as a corporation.*

carry on its ordinary business. If a member-managed LLC has limited the implied authority of one of its members, that member will retain apparent authority to transact for the LLC with a third party who did not know and had no notice that the member's authority was restricted.

The LLC operating agreement may modify the default rules of the RULLCA by granting more power to some members, such as creating a class of members whose approval is required for certain contracts. The agreement could also provide that members share power in relation to their capital contributions.

Managers in a manager-managed LLC may be elected and removed *at any time* by a vote of a majority of LLC members. The powers of a manager to act for the LLC are similar to the power of members in a member-managed LLC. Each manager in a manager-managed LLC shares equal rights in the management of the business as an agent of the LLC with implied authority to carry on the LLC's ordinary business. If a manager-managed LLC has limited the implied authority of one of its managers, that manager retains apparent authority to transact for the LLC with a third party who did not know and had no notice that the manager's authority was restricted.

Under the RULLCA, most matters in an LLC may be conducted by individual managing members or managers, or by a vote of a majority of managing members or managers. This facilitates the conduct of ordinary business. Some matters, however, require the consent of all members, including amendment of the operating agreement, admission of new members, the redemption of a member's interest, and the sale of substantially all the LLC's assets.

In addition to being contractually liable for the acts of its members or managers acting within their express, implied, or apparent authority, the LLC is also liable for the torts and other wrongful acts of managing members and other managers acting within their authority. The LLC is not ordinarily liable for the wrongful acts of members not designated as managers in a manager-managed LLC.

Duties Each member in a member-managed LLC and each manager in a manager-managed LLC is a fiduciary of the LLC and its members. The managing member or manager must account for LLC property and funds and not compete with the LLC. They owe a duty to act with the care that a person in a like position would reasonably exercise and with a reasonable belief that the act is in the best interest of the LLC. Managers must comply with the business judgment rule, a rule we cover in detail in our treatment of corporation law in Chapter 43. This duty of care can be increased or it can be decreased within limits set by the RULLCA.

Nonmanaging members of a manager-managed LLC owe no fiduciary duties to the LLC. Nonetheless, whether or not they are managers, all members owe a duty of good faith and fair dealing when exercising their rights as members. This means all members must act honestly and treat each other fairly.

Most states' LLC statutes permit the LLC operating agreement to expand, restrict, or eliminate fiduciary duties of LLC managers and controlling members. In Delaware, the managers and controlling members of a limited liability company owe fiduciary duties of care and loyalty to the LLC and its members unless the LLC agreement says otherwise. The LLC agreement may not, however, eliminate the members' duty of good faith and fair dealing.

The New York LLC statute permits an LLC to eliminate or limit fiduciary duties of LLC members, except for acts or omissions that were made in bad faith, involved intentional misconduct or a knowing violation of law, or caused the manager personally to gain a financial profit or other advantage to which he was not legally entitled. In 2012, the New York Court of Appeals, without citing the New York statute, held that an LLC member who purchased the LLC interests of the other two members owed them no fiduciary duty because the relationship between the members was antagonistic, the purchase agreement provided that the two selling members had performed their own due diligence in connection with the sale, had engaged their own legal counsel, and were not relying on any representations by the buying member, and the agreement stated that the buying member had no fiduciary duty to the selling members in connection with sale.[1] The court found that the selling members, who were sophisticated businessmen represented by legal counsel, were not acting reasonably in viewing the buying member as their fiduciary.

In the following *Hecht* case, the court considered whether an LLC manager and its investment adviser can be liable for breaching a duty to the LLC by investing LLC assets in the firm of Bernard Madoff, the infamous Ponzi schemer.

---

[1]*Pappas v. Tzolis*, 982 N.E.2d 576 (N.Y. Ct. App. 2012).

Hecht v. Andover Assoc. Mgmt. Co.　　　910 N.Y.S.2d 405 (Sup. Ct. 2010)

Charles Hecht invested his money in Andover Associates LLC I, an investment company that sought funds from wealthy investors and invested the funds in a variety of investment products. Hecht was a passive investor in Andover Associates. The LLC's managing member was Andover Associates Management Company. Andover Management retained Ivy Asset Management Corporation as its investment consultant. Ivy recommended that Andover Management utilize Bernard L. Madoff Investment Securities as its investment manager. Madoff's overall fees were much lower than what investment managers typically charged, and Andover Management initially invested 100 percent of Andover Associates's funds with Madoff. For a number of years, Madoff's firm paid generous returns to Andover Associates. However, in December 2008, it became known that Madoff had been running a Ponzi scheme, whereby no profits were actually being earned, but instead earlier investors were paid returns from the capital invested by newer investors. At the time Madoff's fraud was discovered, 25 percent of Andover Associates's assets were invested with Madoff.

On behalf of Andover Associates LLC I, Hecht brought a legal action against Andover Management and Ivy on several grounds in a New York supreme court, a trial court in that state. Hecht claimed that Ivy breached the LLC's administrative services agreement by failing to reconcile Madoff's monthly statements. Hecht alleged that had Ivy attempted to reconcile Madoff's monthly statements against the trade tickets, Ivy would have discovered that there were no trade tickets because no trades were ever executed. Thus, Hecht alleged that, but for Ivy's failure to reconcile the statements, Madoff's fraud would have been discovered earlier and Andover Associates would have been able to withdraw its investment. Hecht claimed that, as a result of Ivy's breach of the administrative services agreement, Andover Associates sustained damages in the amount of $14 million, the value of its Madoff investment. Hecht also alleged that Ivy was negligent in recommending Madoff's firm without conducting a sufficient "due diligence" investigation of his operation.

Hecht asserted Andover Associates's claim against Andover Management for gross negligence in investing with Madoff without conducting its own due diligence investigation. In particular, Hecht alleged that Madoff's confirmation slips and statements reported purchases and sales of securities at prices outside the range at which the securities traded on the days in question. Hecht alleged that had Andover Management conducted a proper investigation, it would have learned that Madoff's confirmation slips and statements were false because no trades were actually being conducted. Hecht alleged that but for Andover Management's negligence in failing to react to the suspicious confirmation slips and other red flags, Andover Associates would have learned of Madoff's fraud and been able to liquidate its investment.

Andover Management asked the trial court to dismiss Hecht's complaint by citing the business judgment rule, a rule that protects from liability managers who make good-faith business decisions.

Bucaria, Judge

The business judgment rule bars judicial inquiry into actions of corporate directors taken in good faith and in the exercise of honest judgment in the lawful and legitimate furtherance of corporate purposes. Andover Management argues that the business judgment rule insulates their decisions to utilize Ivy as their investment consultant and Madoff as their investment manager.

The retaining of Ivy as the investment consultant, and the amount of compensation which Ivy was paid for investment consulting and administrative services, would ordinarily be within Andover Management's business judgment. However, administrative services included maintaining original books of entry for all Madoff activity, presumably including his fictitious trades. Hecht alleges that there were no trade tickets, or any other documentation, to substantiate the trades. Giving Hecht the benefit of every possible favorable inference, Ivy's preparing original books of entry, without the benefit of back up documentation, may have furthered Madoff's scheme or helped to avoid its detection. Accordingly, Andover Management's motion to dismiss based upon the business judgment rule is denied.

A trustee is under a duty to employ diligence and prudence in the management of the trust estate. Delegation of this duty to another is not an excuse for the failure to fulfill it by the trustee. Nor does the trustee's good faith and honesty of purpose relieve him from a breach of his fiduciary obligation. In essence, Hecht's theory is that Andover Management breached the duty of diligence and prudence by delegating management of Andover Associates' investment to Madoff without conducting an adequate investigation into his operation.

Gross negligence is the failure to exercise even slight care or slight diligence. It is conduct that is so careless as to show complete disregard for the rights and safety of others. While Andover Management denies that it knew of Madoff's scheme, it may be

inferred that Andover Management failed to exercise even slight care in failing to detect it. Similarly, it may be inferred that in entrusting Andover Associates' funds to Madoff, Andover Management showed complete disregard for Andover Associates' rights and the safety of its investment. That public regulators also failed to uncover the fraud does not establish that Andover Management was diligent. Andover Management's motion to dismiss Hecht's gross negligence claim for failure to state a cause of action is denied.

Andover Management's motion to dismiss denied in favor of Hecht.

Member's Distributions A member's most important right in an LLC is to receive distributions (usually profits) from the LLC. The RULLCA provides that members share profits and other distributions equally, regardless of differences in their capital contributions. No member, however, is entitled to a distribution of profits prior to the dissolution of the LLC unless the LLC decides to make an interim distribution. The LLC members will usually state in the LLC operating agreement how and when profits are distributed. For example, the operating agreement may simply state that managing members are entitled to salaries and that all members share profits after salaries in proportion to their capital contributions to the LLC. At the other extreme, the LLC operating agreement may have complex rules determining how profits are allocated, including factors such as hours a member works for the LLC, the revenue from clients acquired for the LLC by a member, and a member's capital contribution.

Member's Ownership Interest An LLC member's ownership interest in an LLC is the personal property of the member. However, unlike a corporation in which a shareholder may freely transfer her shares and all her rights to another person, a member has limited ability to sell or transfer her rights in the LLC. Under the RULLCA, a member may transfer her **transferable interest** in the LLC to another person; however, the transferee is not a member of the LLC. (The member remains a member despite having transferred her transferable interest.) The transferee's most important right is to receive the transferring member's right to distributions from the partnership; that is, a share of profits and the value of the member's interest

when the LLC is liquidated. A transferee has no right to manage the business and has only a limited right to information about the LLC's accounts.

The LLC operating agreement may provide that a transferee of a member's transferable interest becomes an LLC member. If so, the transferee has the rights, powers, and liabilities of the transferring member, which may include the right to manage the LLC, the right to access LLC records, and the duty to make additional capital contributions.

A personal creditor of a member may obtain from a court a charging order that charges the member's transferable interest with the payment of the debt owed to the creditor. The creditor with a charging order receives, therefore, the member's share of distributions for the life of the charging order. The creditor does not own the transferable interest, but instead only has a lien or security interest against it. To own the transferable interest and acquire all the rights of a transferee, the creditor must foreclose against the interest and purchase it at a foreclosure sale.

 Explain the attributes of a limited liability company.

Members' Dissociations and LLC Dissolution
Under the RULLCA, members dissociate from an LLC in ways similar to those by which a partner dissociates from a partnership or LLP under the RUPA. Dissolution of an LLC is also similar to that of a partnership or LLP. Therefore, generally, when an LLC member dies or otherwise withdraws from the LLC, the LLC's business will continue, preserving its going concern value.

Member Dissociations A member's dissociation is a change in the relationship among the dissociated member, the LLC, and the other members caused by a member's ceasing to be associated in the carrying on of the business. Under the RULLCA, a partner has the power to dissociate by withdrawing from the LLC at any time. Dissociations are also caused by a member's death, having a guardian appointed over her affairs, being adjudged legally incompetent by a court, being a debtor in bankruptcy, or being expelled by the other members. The other members may expel a member if it is unlawful to carry on business with her, she has suffered a charging order against her transferable interest, or she has transferred all her transferable interest in the LLC. At the request of the LLC or a member, a court may also expel a member because she has harmed the LLC's business, breached the LLC operating agreement, or engaged in conduct that makes it not practicable to carry on business with her. Judicial expulsion would be appropriate when a member persistently breaches the duty of good faith or competes against the LLC. There are also other causes of dissociation for nonhuman members.

A member's dissociation may be wrongful or nonwrongful. Wrongful dissociations breach the LLC operating agreement. Under the RULLCA, a member has wrongfully dissociated by withdrawing before an LLC's term expires, being a debtor in bankruptcy, or being expelled by a court. When dissolution is wrongful, the dissociating member is liable to the LLC for damages caused by the dissociation, such as the loss of business due to the member's withdrawal.

When a member dissociates, his right to manage the business terminates, as do his duties to the LLC, for the most part. He may, however, have apparent authority to transact for the LLC, unless notice of his dissociation is given to third parties. This apparent authority can be eliminated by giving personal notice to LLC creditors that a member has dissociated or by filing a Statement of Dissociation with the secretary of state.

Dissociation also terminates a member's status as a member. A dissociated member is treated as a transferee of a member's transferable interest.

Payment to a Dissociated Member Under the RULLCA, the dissociated member has no right after her dissociation to force the LLC to dissolve and to liquidate its assets. The RULLCA leaves such decisions to the operating agreement. In addition, a dissociated member is not entitled to receive the value of her LLC interest until the LLC dissolves, unless the members agree otherwise. The RULLCA expects members to resolve buyout issues in the operating agreement.

There is one exception. If the LLC is *at will* and is not dissolved, the LLC must purchase his interest at fair value within 120 days after the member's dissociation. If the LLC *has a term*, however, and is not dissolved, the LLC may continue its business and pay the dissociated member the value of his interest within 120 days after the end of the LLC's term.

LLC Dissolution When an LLC is dissolved, ordinarily it must be wound up. Because a business usually is worth more as a going concern, the RULLCA has few events that automatically cause dissolution of an LLC. For example, death and withdrawal of members do not by themselves cause dissolution of an LLC. Instead, the RULLCA mostly lets members decide the causes of dissolution.

The few grounds for dissolution in the RULLCA include an event making it unlawful for the LLC business to continue, judicial dissolution at the request of a member or transferee of a member's transferable interest, and administrative dissolution by the secretary of state. A member or dissociated member may ask for a judicial dissolution if, for example, the LLC cannot practicably carry on its business, the LLC is being managed illegally or oppressively, or the LLC failed to purchase a dissociated member's transferable interest on the date required. The RULLCA allows the members to state in the operating agreement the events that will dissolve the LLC. The operating agreement may also allow the members to dissolve the LLC by their vote, which may be any percentage of members that the members choose. In the absence of such a provision in the LLC agreement, all members must agree to dissolve an LLC.

When an LLC dissolves, any member who has not wrongly dissociated may wind up the business. Winding-up members should liquidate the assets, yet they may preserve the LLC's assets or business as a going concern for a reasonable time in order to optimize the proceeds from the liquidation.

The LLC is bound by the reasonable acts of its members during winding up, and may be liable for actions that continue the business and are inconsistent with winding up, unless the LLC gives third parties notice of dissolution. Notice can be given in a reasonable manner, such as by e-mail, letter, or phone call, and by filing a Notice of Dissociation with the secretary of state, which is effective against all parties 90 days after filing.

Distribution of Dissolved LLC's Assets After all the LLC assets have been sold, the proceeds will be distributed first to LLC creditors, including members who are creditors. If there are excess proceeds, members' contributions are returned next. Any remaining proceeds are distributed in proportion to how they share profits.

If the LLC's assets are insufficient to pay all creditors' claims, ordinarily creditors have no recourse because the LLC's members have liability limited to the assets of the LLC. If an LLC member has not paid in all the capital she was required to pay, however, creditors may sue the member to force the member to contribute the additional capital.

 LO40-2 Identify the default rules regarding an LLC's members' rights and responsilbilities.

Effect of Operating Agreement   The default dissociation and dissolution rules of the RULLCA may be unacceptable to members of an LLC. Therefore, a well-drafted operating agreement will cover this area completely, defining the grounds for dissociation, such as death, withdrawal, and disability of a member. The agreement should also state when a member may be expelled by the other members and a court. The RULLCA gives the members much flexibility to arrange their affairs the way they want.

The operating agreement may state the amount and timing of payments to a dissociated member for the value of her ownership interest. For example, the operating agreement may provide for a lump-sum payment within 90 days after a member dies, becomes disabled, or withdraws at age 55 or later. If a member withdraws before age 55, the agreement may provide for payment in quarterly installments over a five-year period.

The agreement may also state when dissolution and winding up occur. For example, the agreement may provide that no member has the power to seek dissolution at any time. Instead, the agreement may permit a vote of 75 percent of the members to commence winding up if any member dies or withdraws before the time permitted in the LLC operating agreement. It may require unanimous approval by the members in all other contexts. The agreement should also stipulate which members will have the right to participate in winding up.

The LLC operating agreement may also modify how proceeds are distributed to members during winding up after creditors are paid. For example, the agreement may state that all proceeds beyond creditors' claims are distributed equally to members, regardless of their capital contributions.

The following case, *McDonough v. McDonough*, discusses how a court interpreted an LLC's operating agreement after a falling out between two brothers who wished to dissolve the LLC. In denying the plaintiffs' summary judgment motion, the court in this case held that the operating agreement permitted a majority of the company's members to continue the company.

McDonough v. McDonough   153 A.3d 187 (N.H. 2016)

In 1992, brothers Mark, Matthew, and Patrick McDonough established TASC, a corporation that provides technical engineering services. In September 1995, the brothers converted TASC to a limited liability company (LLC). The brothers had a falling out, and as a result, Mark sued the defendants seeking a declaration that TASC must dissolve by September 20, 2015, pursuant to its certificate of formation and operating agreement. TASC's certificate of formation states that "[t]he latest date on which the limited liability company is to dissolve is September 30, 2015." Section 5 of TASC's operating agreement states: "The Company shall have a term beginning on the date the Certificate of Formation is filed . . . and shall continue in full force and effect for a term of twenty (20) years, unless sooner terminated or continued pursuant to the further terms of this Agreement."

Matthew and Patrick, on August 7, 2015, constituting a majority of TASC's members, voted to dissolve TASC and then immediately voted to revoke the dissolution. Both parties moved for summary judgment, and after a hearing, the trial court ruled that (1) the August 7 dissolution and revocation had no effect on TASC's governing documents and (2) TASC was not required to dissolve because its operating agreement permits a majority of its members to continue the company. As a result, summary judgment was denied to Mark and granted to the defendants. Consequently, this appeal followed.

On appeal, Mark argues that (1) the trial court erred when it determined that a majority of TASC's members could continue TASC beyond September 30, 2015, and (2) permitting a majority of TASC's members to continue the company causes him substantial harm because the company is not obligated to pay him any consideration if he withdraws.

Dalianis, Judge

Mark first argues that TASC's operating agreement and the Act required the company to dissolve by September 30, 2015. The Act requires an LLC's members to dissolve the company as provided for in the company's operating agreement. An LLC shall be dissolved as provided in the operating agreement. Section 5 of TASC's operating agreement states: "The company shall have a term beginning on the date the Certificate of Formation is filed . . . and shall continue in full force and effect for a term of twenty (20) years, unless sooner terminated or continued pursuant to the further terms of this Agreement." Mark contends that, unless amended, the plain language of TASC's operating agreement required dissolution by September 30, 2015. However, this argument overlooks the language "unless sooner terminated or continued pursuant to the further terms of this Agreement." Although Mark is correct that the members could unanimously amend section 5 of TASC's operating agreement to remove or change the dissolution clause, that does not preclude other means of continuing TASC. If TASC's members had intended that the only means of continuing the company would be an amendment of section 5, they could have explicitly said so. Instead, they chose to more broadly state that TASC would exist for 20 years unless the company was "continued pursuant to the further terms of this Agreement." TASC's operating agreement and the Act provide such a way for TASC's members to continue the company. Section 4 of TASC's operating agreement authorizes TASC to "have and exercise all powers now or hereafter conferred by [the Act]." This includes RSA 304-C:130, III (2015), which provides: "After the members have dissolved the limited liability company under RSA 304-C: 129, I, they may revoke the dissolution at any time before completing the wind-up of the limited liability company." Accordingly, TASC's members have two means to avoid the effects of the September 30, 2015 dissolution. They can either revoke the dissolution pursuant to RSA 304-C: 130, III, or unanimously amend section 5 of TASC's operating agreement. Mark also argues that a decision to revoke dissolution pursuant to RSA 304-C: 130, III requires a unanimous vote. In examining section 5 of TASC's operating agreement the agreement does not specify whether TASC may be continued by majority or unanimous vote. Likewise TASC's operating agreement is silent regarding how its members may decide to revoke dissolution. Hence, because TASC's operating agreement does not provide otherwise, RSA 304-C: 67, I controls, and TASC's members may by majority vote revoke dissolution pursuant to RSA 304-C: 130, III. Mark next argues that even if a majority of TASC's members had the power to revoke the September 30, 2015 dissolution, they have not done so yet. However, even though the trial court ruled that the August 7 voluntary dissolution and subsequent revocation had no effect on whether TASC was required to dissolve by September 30,

2015, the trial court still ruled that TASC was not required to dissolve by September 30, 2015, because its members could continue the company pursuant to the terms of the operating agreement. Matthew and Patrick represented to the trial court that they intended to continue TASC. Based upon these facts, the trial court could conclude that Matthew and Patrick intended to revoke the dissolution. Accordingly, this court cannot conclude that the trial court erred by granting summary judgment to Matthew and Patrick even though they had not yet voted to revoke TASC's dissolution. Finally, Mark argues that TASC's certificate of formation requires, without exception, that the company dissolve after 20 years. TASC's certificate of formation states that "[t]he latest date on which the limited liability company is to dissolve is September 30, 2015." However, the Act does not require an LLC's members to dissolve the company when the duration listed in the certificate of formation expires. The Act requires an LLC's members to dissolve the company only as provided in its operating agreement. Accordingly, there is no requirement that TASC's members dissolve the company after the twenty-year duration stated in its certificate of formation. The Court thus disagrees with Mark's argument that this interpretation renders the certificate of formation superfluous. Under the Act, an LLC's certificate of formation and its operating agreement are distinct documents that are separately defined and serve different purposes. The primary purpose of an LLC's operating agreement is to govern how the parties will manage the internal affairs of the LLC and the LLC's business. Rather, the primary purpose of the certificate of formation is to serve as notice to the secretary of state and the public that the company is operating as a New Hampshire LLC. The certificate of formation is not rendered superfluous just because the Act looks to an LLC's operating agreement, not its certificate of formation, to determine when the LLC's members must dissolve the company. For the reasons stated above, we hold that TASC's operating agreement and the Act permit a majority of TASC's members to continue the company beyond September 30, 2015. Accordingly, the trial court's grant of summary judgment in favor of the defendants is affirmed.

Judgment affirmed.

The Global Business Environment

The limited liability company is known in many countries throughout the world. However, LLCs formed under the laws of other nations are a bit different from American LLCs.

In Germany, which claims to be the first nation to permit them, in 1892, LLCs are known as *Gesellschaft mit beschrankter Haftung* (GmbH). Other countries soon followed Germany's lead, including Portugal (1917), Brazil (1919), Chile (1923), Turkey (1926), Uruguay (1933), Mexico (1934), and Belgium (1935). In France, the *societes de responsabilite limitee* is more popular than the more traditional stock corporation.

In these countries, LLC law confers limited liability on the members, requires use of the word *limited* in the entity's name, permits members to control admission of new members to the entity, and allows the entity to be dissolved by death of a member unless otherwise expressly stated in the articles of association. Most countries provide for management of LLCs by one or more managing directors. Many countries also limit the number of members in an LLC, making the LLC an entity inappropriate for a publicly held company. Some experts refer to these LLCs as private limited companies, which more accurately describes what they are: corporations with a limited number of owners.

Limited Partnerships

LO40-3 Explain the attributes of a limited partnership and the default rights and liabilities of partners in a limited partnership.

The partnership form—with managerial control and unlimited liability for all partners—is not acceptable for all business arrangements. Often, business managers want an infusion of capital into a business yet are reluctant to surrender managerial control to those contributing capital. Investors wish to contribute capital to a business and share in its profits yet limit their liability to the amount of their investment and be relieved of the obligation to manage the business.

As you have already seen in this chapter and the other partnership chapters, an LLC may have an operating agreement and a limited liability partnership (LLP) may have a partnership agreement that accomplishes these objectives by limiting the management right to fewer than all of the LLC's members or LLP's partners. The **limited partnership**, however, has a basic, default structure that serves these needs. The limited partnership has two classes of owners: **general partners**, who contribute capital to the business, manage it, share in its profits, and possess unlimited liability for its obligations; and **limited partners**, who contribute capital and share profits but possess no management powers and have liability limited to their investments in the business.

A variant of the limited partnership is the **limited liability limited partnership (LLLP)**. An LLLP is a limited partnership that has elected limited liability status for all its partners, including general partners. Except for the liability of general partners, limited partnerships and LLLPs are identical. For that reason, every well-planned limited partnership should eliminate the unlimited liability of its human managers by

having a corporate or LLC general partner or electing LLLP status, when available. Today, every state recognizes limited partnerships and many recognize LLLPs as well. However, with the advent of the LLC, the LLLP business form is often a rare choice. Therefore we do not examine it at length in this chapter.

The Uniform Limited Partnership Acts
In 2001, the National Conference of Commissioners on Uniform State Laws drafted a new Uniform Limited Partnership Act (ULPA) to replace the Revised Uniform Partnership Act of 1976 and its 1985 amendments. The ULPA of 2001 is the first comprehensive statement of American limited partnership law. As shown in Figure 40.2, many characteristics of a limited partnership under the ULPA are similar to those of a partnership or LLP under the Revised Uniform Partnership Act. While the ULPA copies much of the law of the RUPA, only the ULPA applies to limited partnerships.

Although most states at this time have enacted the RULPA, we will study the ULPA of 2001, which will soon be the dominant limited partnership law in the United States. As of 2020, 22 states and the District of Columbia have adopted or introduced the ULPA. The ULPA governs both limited partnerships and LLLPs. Under the ULPA, limited partnerships and LLLPs are identical except for the liability of general partners. Therefore, when this chapter addresses limited partnership law (other than the rules regarding the liability of general partners), the law applies to LLLPs as well.

Use of Limited Partnerships
The limited partnership form is used primarily in tax shelter ventures and activities such as real estate investment, oil and gas drilling, and professional sports. When the limited partnership elects to be taxed as a partnership, it operates as a tax

Figure 40.2   Principal Characteristics of Limited Partnerships and LLLPs

1. A limited partnership or LLLP may be *created only in accordance with a statute.*

2. A limited partnership or LLLP has two types of partners: *general partners* and *limited partners.* It must have one or more of each type.

3. All partners, limited and general, *share the profits* of the business *in relation to their capital contributions.*

4. Each limited partner has *liability limited to his capital contribution* to the business. Each general partner of a limited partnership has *unlimited liability* for the obligations of the business. A general partner in an LLLP, however, has *liability limited to his capital contribution.*

5. Each general partner has a *right to manage* the business, and she is an agent of the limited partnership or LLLP. A limited partner has *no right to manage* the business or to act as its agent, but she does have the right to vote on fundamental matters. A limited partner may manage the business, yet retain limited liability for partnership obligations.

6. General partners, as agents, are *fiduciaries* of the business. Limited partners are not fiduciaries.

7. A partner's rights in a limited partnership or LLLP *are not freely transferable.* A transferee of a general or limited partnership interest is not a partner but is entitled only to the transferring partner's share of capital and profits, absent a contrary agreement.

8. The death or other withdrawal of a partner does not usually dissolve a limited partnership or LLLP unless there is no surviving general partner.

9. Usually, a limited partnership or LLLP is taxed like a partnership. However, a limited partnership or LLLP may elect to be taxed like a corporation.

shelter by allowing partners to reduce their personal federal income tax liability by deducting limited partnership losses on their individual income tax returns. General partners, however, receive a greater tax shelter advantage than do limited partners. Losses of the business allocated to a general partner offset his income from any other sources. Losses of the business allocated to limited partners may be used to offset only income from other *passive* investments and only to the extent limited partners are *at risk*—that is, to the extent of their capital contributions to the limited partnership. If a limited partner has sold her limited partnership interest or the limited partnership has terminated, her loss offsets any income. Limited partnerships are also used by family businesses for estate planning purposes. The *Moser* case after the next section concerns a family limited partnership. Regardless of the use, the ULPA presumes that its partners want a highly centralized, strongly entrenched management (general partners) and passive investors with little control and little right to exit the limited partnership (limited partners).

LOG ON

www.uniformlaws.org
You can find the Uniform Limited Partnership Act of 2001 at the website for the National Conference of Commissioners on Uniform State Laws.

Creation of Limited Partnerships

A limited partnership may be created only by complying with the applicable state statute. Yet the statutory requirements of the ULPA are minimal. A **certificate of limited partnership** must be executed and submitted to the secretary of state. The certificate must be signed by all general partners. A limited partnership begins its existence at the time the certificate is filed by the office of the secretary of state. The limited partnership may ask the secretary of state to issue a Certificate of Existence, which is conclusive proof the limited partnership exists.

The ULPA requires that the limited partnership certificate submitted by the limited partnership include its address, its registered agent for service of process, and its general partners' names and addresses. The name of a limited partnership must include the words *limited partnership* or the letters *L.P.* or *LP.* The name of a limited partnership may include the name of any partner, general or limited.

It is expected that many limited partnerships will have unlimited duration. Therefore, the ULPA provides for the perpetual life of a limited partnership. The limited partnership certificate or limited partnership agreement, however, may place a limit on the limited partnership's duration.

The certificate is not required to address many other matters that are essential to the limited partnership, such as the limited partners' names, the partners' capital contributions, the partners' shares of profits and other distributions, or the acts that cause a dissolution of the limited partnership. A well-planned limited partnership will usually include those and other matters in the certificate or in a separate **limited partnership agreement**.

Any *person* may be a general or limited partner. Persons include a natural person, partnership, LLC, trust, estate, association, or corporation. Hence, as commonly occurs, a corporation or LLC may be the sole general partner of a limited partnership.

Defective Compliance with Limited Partnership Statute

The ULPA requires at least *substantial compliance* with the previously listed requirements to create a limited partnership. If the persons attempting to create a limited partnership do not substantially comply with the ULPA, a limited partnership does not exist; therefore, a limited partner may lose her limited liability and have unlimited liability for limited partnership obligations.

A lack of substantial compliance might result from failing to file a certificate of limited partnership or from filing a defective certificate. A defective certificate might, for example, misstate the name of the limited partnership.

Limited Partners Infrequently, a person will believe that she is a limited partner but discover later that she has been designated a general partner or that the general partners have not filed a certificate of limited partnership. In such circumstances and others, she may be liable as a general partner unless she in good faith believes she is a limited partner and upon discovering she is not a limited partner she either:

1. Causes a proper certificate of limited partnership (or an amendment thereto) to be filed with the secretary of state or

2. Withdraws from future equity participation in the firm by filing a certificate declaring such withdrawal with the secretary of state.

However, such a person remains liable as a general partner to third parties who previously believed in good faith that the person was a general partner.

General Partners The ULPA of 2001 has no provision protecting general partners who erroneously believe an LLLP has been formed. Consequently, a general partner in a limited partnership who believes wrongly that an LLLP has been created has unlimited liability for the obligations of the limited partnership.

In the following *Moser v. Moser* case, a husband and wife tried to use a family limited partnership to reduce taxes. Although they properly formed the limited partnership, they failed to comply with tax law and otherwise to keep the limited partnership's assets separate from themselves. Consequently, the court ruled that the husband and wife had not made a gift of the limited partnership's property to their children.

Moser v. Moser	**2007-Ohio-4109 (Ct. App. 2007)**

Terrance and Barbara Moser were married on October 11, 1980. Over the next 16 years, they had two children, Shannon and Joshua, and accumulated assets in excess of $2 million. On December 31, 1996, Terrance and Barbara signed a document creating the Moser Family Limited Partnership. A family limited partnership is an estate planning device designed to minimize tax liabilities. The Moser Family Limited Partnership was set up with Terrance, as trustee of a revocable trust holding his assets, as general partner; Barbara, as trustee of a revocable trust holding her assets, as a limited partner; and Shannon and Joshua as limited partners, with Barbara as their custodian. Typically, a family partnership is funded with assets having a high potential for appreciation. Parents will then give to their children a certain number of units or a percentage interest in the limited partnership, without tax liability, taking advantage of the gift tax exclusion. At the time the Moser Family Limited Partnership was created, the annual gift tax exclusion was $10,000. In order to function properly as an estate planning device, the gifts of partnership interest to the children had to be completed, irrevocable gifts. In this way, wealth could be transferred to children during the parents' lifetime, thus avoiding estate taxes, while the parents would be able to maintain a certain amount of control of the wealth, by virtue of the general partner's control of the partnership. After its creation, the Moser Family Limited Partnership, in conjunction with Moser Construction and other business entities previously owned and operated by the Mosers, successfully oversaw several land development ventures.

Unfortunately, Terrance and Barbara had marital problems. On January 17, 2003, Barbara filed for divorce. In addition to naming Terrance as a defendant, she also named the Moser Family Limited Partnership as an additional defendant, arguing that its assets were part of the marital estate and that she should receive a portion of the limited partnership's assets. The trial court agreed with Barbara. The court determined the total value of the marital estate to be $3,778,764, of which $1,507,663 represented the net value of the Moser Family Limited Partnership. Terrance appealed the decision to an Ohio appellate court.

Grendell, Judge

Terrance raises two arguments. The first is that the trial court erred by invalidating the gifts of partnership interest to the Moser children. The second is that the trial court erred by treating partnership assets as marital property.

As any initial assets of the Partnership were marital, Terrance and Barbara were deemed to be equal partners, *i.e.*, 50 percent owners of the partnership shares. The trial court found that transfers of interest in the Moser Family Limited Partnership to the Moser children did not occur on December 31, 1996, and January 1, 1997, as purported in the federal gift tax returns. Leslie D. Smeach is a certified public accountant who did work for Terrance. Smeach testified that the valuation of the partnership units allegedly given to the Moser children on December 31, 1996, and January 1, 1997, did not occur until April 1997. Prior to this valuation, it would have been impossible to determine the number of partnership units that could be given in accordance with the gift tax exclusion.

The trial court also found that Terrance operated the Moser Family Limited Partnership and its subsidiary companies as his own personal assets. The court noted the free transfer of funds between business entities that were part of, or associated with, the Moser Family Limited Partnership. For example, although the tax returns indicated the Moser Family Limited Partnership possessed a 50 percent interest in Rootstown Storage Partnership, Terrance continued to list Rootstown Storage as an asset on his personal financial statements. In April 2000, Terrance received a personal distribution of $55,000 from Rootstown Storage.

The trial court determined that Terrance and Barbara had not made valid, *inter vivos* gifts of their interests in the Moser Family Limited Partnership to the Moser children. In Barbara's case, the court relied upon her testimony that she did not intend to relinquish ownership interest in the Partnership until her death.

In Terrance's case, the court found the intent to make such a gift in the Memoranda of Gifts signed by Terrance on December 31, 1997. However, the court also found that there was no delivery of the Memorandum of Gift letters to the Moser children or to Barbara as their custodian. The court also concluded that Terrance had not relinquished control over his ownership interest in the Partnership in a manner consistent with the intent to make a gift.

There was considerable testimony from various witnesses at the hearings which likened Terrance's powers under the Moser Family Limited Partnership to those of "a benevolent dictator." There was also evidence at the hearings that Terrance exercised this power freely. When the marital residence was inadvertently transferred into the Partnership, Terrance transferred it out. Terrance used Partnership funds to meet the expenses of other businesses owned by him. As noted above, there was considerable "cash flow" between entities existing both within and without the Partnership.

Accordingly, the trial court had jurisdiction over the Moser Family Limited Partnership and its partners and could exercise that jurisdiction to order Terrance to assign specific partnership properties so as to effectuate a fair and equitable division of property.

Judgment for Barbara Moser affirmed.

Rights and Liabilities of Partners in Limited Partnerships

 LO40-3 Explain the attributes of a limited partnership and the default rights and liabilities of partners in a limited partnership.

The partners of a limited partnership have many rights and liabilities. Some are common to both general and limited partners, while others are not shared.

Rights and Liabilities Shared by General and Limited Partners

Capital Contributions A partner may contribute any property or other benefit to the limited partnership. This includes cash, tangible or intangible property, services rendered, a promissory note, or a promise to contribute cash, property, or services. A partner is obligated to contribute as he promised. This obligation may be enforced by the limited partnership or by any of its creditors.

Share of Profits and Losses Under the ULPA, profits and losses are shared on the basis of the value of each partner's capital contribution unless there is a written agreement to the contrary. For example, if two general partners contribute $100,000 each and 20 limited partners contribute $2,000,000 each, and the profit is $2,010,000, each general partner's share of the profits is $5,000 and each limited partner's share is $100,000.

Because most limited partnerships are tax shelters, partnership agreements often provide for limited partners to take all the losses of the business, up to the limit of their capital contributions.

Voting Rights The ULPA of 2001 requires few actions to be approved by all the partners. Only amendment of the limited partnership agreement, amendment of the limited partnership certificate, and sale or other transfer of substantially all the limited partnership's assets outside the ordinary course of business require approval of all the partners. In a well-planned limited partnership, the limited partnership agreement may require that certain transactions be approved by general partners, by limited partners, or by all the partners. The agreement may give each general partner more votes than it grants limited partners, or vice versa.

The ULPA makes it clear that limited partners have no inherent right to vote on any matter as a class. They may receive such a right only by agreement of the partners.

Admission of New Partners Under the ULPA, the default rule is that no new partner may be admitted unless each partner has consented to the admission. The limited partnership agreement may provide for other admission procedures. For example, the general partners may be given the power to admit new limited partners without the consent of existing limited partners. Usually, this power is given to general partners to facilitate the ability of the limited partnership to raise capital, but the power should be restricted to prevent any significant dilution of the ownership interests of existing limited partners.

The limited partnership agreement may also provide for the election of new general partners, such as when a general partner dies or retires. Instead of requiring approval of all partners, the agreement may provide that a majority of the partners may elect a replacement general partner. Another option is to give to limited partners the power to replace a general partner. Another alternative is to grant such power to the partners owning a majority of the limited partnership, measured by their capital contributions.

In general, the ULPA does not grant partners much power to expel other partners from the partnership. When we discuss partners' dissociations later in the chapter, we will examine the few grounds for expulsion.

Partner's Transferable Interest Each partner in a limited partnership owns a transferable interest in the limited partnership. It is his personal property. He may sell or transfer it to others, such as his personal creditors. Or his personal creditor may obtain a charging order against it. Generally, a buyer or transferee—or a creditor with a charging order—is entitled to receive only the partner's share of distributions. The ULPA treats charging orders like ordinary partnership law does.

When the limited partnership agreement so provides or all the partners consent, a buyer or transferee of a partner's transferable interest may become a partner. The new partner then assumes all the rights and liabilities of a partner, except for liabilities unknown to her at the time she became a partner.

A partner's transfer of his transferable interest has no effect on his status as a partner, absent a contrary agreement. The partner has not dissociated, and the limited partnership has not dissolved merely as a result of the transfer. However, the limited partnership agreement may create consequences, such as expulsion of the transferring partner.

Power and Right to Withdraw Partners have the power to withdraw from the limited partnership at any time. The expectation, however, is that a limited partnership will have perpetual duration. Consequently, the ULPA gives the partners no right to withdraw, absent a contrary provision in the limited partnership agreement.

One result, therefore, under the ULPA is that a withdrawing partner has no right to receive the value of her partnership interest. This means that a partner who withdraws from a limited partnership will not receive a return of her investment, unless the limited partnership agreement provides for a buyout of the withdrawing partner or the limited partnership dissolves and liquidates.

Other Rights of General Partners A general partner of a limited partnership has the same right to manage and the same agency powers as a partner in an ordinary partnership. He has the express authority to act as the partners have agreed he should and the implied authority to do what is in the ordinary course of business. In addition, he may have apparent authority to bind the partnership to contracts when his implied authority is limited yet no notice of the limitation has been given to third parties.

A general partner has no right to compensation beyond his share of the profits, absent an agreement to the contrary. Because most limited partnerships are tax shelters that are designed to lose money during their early years of operation, most limited partnership agreements provide for the payment of salaries to general partners.

Other Liabilities of General Partners

Liability A general partner in a limited partnership has unlimited liability to the creditors of the limited partnership. In an LLLP, however, a general partner's liability is limited to his capital contribution to the business.

Even so, in an LLLP a general partner may not escape liability for torts he commits in the course of the LLLP's business. Suppose a general partner drives a car on LLLP business and negligently injures a pedestrian. Not only may the LLLP be liable, but also the general partner will have personal liability to the pedestrian. Yet the LLLP form does protect the general partner from most torts of the business. For example, the general partner in an LLLP will not have personal liability for the torts of her fellow general partners or employees.

Fiduciary Duties Any general partner, whether in a limited partnership or an LLLP, is in a position of trust when she manages the business and therefore owes fiduciary duties to the limited partnership and the other partners. The general partner must account for limited partnership property, not compete against the partnership, and not self-deal with the partnership.

In addition, a general partner owes a duty of care when transacting for the partnership. The ULPA provides considerable protection for general partners under the duty of care, imposing liability to the limited partnership only if she engages in grossly negligent or reckless conduct, intentional misconduct, or knowing violations of the law. The limited partnership agreement may increase the general partners' duty of care, although that is not typical. The ULPA permits the partners to reduce the general partners' duty of care, if not unreasonable, but gives no clue to what is reasonable or unreasonable. The *Lach* case, which appears near the end of this chapter, found general partners breached their fiduciary duty by attempting to circumvent a limited partner's right to approve new general partners.

Other Rights of Limited Partners

Limited partners have the right to be informed about partnership affairs. The ULPA obligates the general partners to provide financial information and tax returns to the limited partners on demand. In addition, a limited partner may inspect and copy a list of the partners, information concerning contributions by partners, the certificate of limited partnership, tax returns, and partnership agreements.

Other Liabilities of Limited Partners

Liability Once a limited partner has contributed all of his promised capital contribution, generally he has no further liability for partnership losses or obligations.

Under the RULPA of 1976, a limited partner who participates in the control of the business may be liable to creditors of the limited partnership. Under the RULPA, a limited partner who participates in control is liable only to those persons who transact with the limited partnership reasonably believing, based on the limited partner's conduct, that the limited partner is a general partner.

The ULPA of 2001 eliminates this liability risk. The ULPA extends to limited partners the same protection given to owners who manage LLCs and LLPs: liability limited to their capital contributions, regardless whether they manage the business.

Duties No limited partner owes fiduciary duties to the limited partnership or her partners solely by being a limited partner. That means, for example, a limited partner in an oil and gas limited partnership may also invest as a limited partner in other oil and gas limited partnerships. However, all limited partners owe a duty to act in good faith and to deal fairly with the limited partnership. For example, a limited partner who lends money to the partnership is expected to disclose her interest and to transact fairly with the limited partnership. In addition, a limited partner who is an agent of the limited partnership owes the fiduciary duties imposed by agency law. For example, a limited partner who is a leasing agent for a limited partnership that owns apartment buildings owes the duty to account for rental income and a duty of skill and care.

Partners' Dissociations and Limited Partnership Dissolution

 LO40-3 Explain the attributes of a limited partnership and the default rights and liabilities of partners in a limited partnership.

The ULPA of 2001 greatly changed the law regarding dissolutions of limited partnerships. The ULPA adopts much of the terminology and framework of partnership law in the RUPA. Reflecting the intent that limited partnerships and LLLPs are for long-term businesses, the ULPA makes it harder for a limited partnership to dissolve and provides few rights for partners who dissociate from the limited partnership before the partners expect.

Partners' Dissociations Because the roles of limited partners and general partners are different in a limited partnership, the ULPA's default rules for dissociations by a limited partner are in part different from the default rules for dissociations by a general partner.

Limited Partner Dissociations A limited partner will dissociate upon the limited partner's death, withdrawal, or expulsion from the partnership.

A limited partner may be expelled by the other partners or by a court. The other partners may expel a limited partner if she has transferred all of her transferable interest or suffered a charging order against her partnership interest. She can also be expelled if it is illegal to conduct business with the limited partner, such as a securities investment firm limited partner who has been convicted of securities fraud. The other partners' vote to expel must be unanimous.

At the request of the limited partnership, a court may also expel a limited partner if she has engaged in wrongful conduct that negatively affects the business or if she has willfully and persistently breached the partnership agreement or the limited partner's duty of good faith and fair dealing.

The ULPA also defines dissociations for nonhuman limited partners, such as corporations, LLCs, and trusts. For example, the other partners may expel an LLC that has been dissolved and is winding up its business.

A dissociated limited partner is not a limited partner, has no rights as a limited partner, and is treated as a mere transferee of the dissociated limited partner's transferable interest. That means the dissociated limited partner has no right to vote or exercise any other partners' powers but does have the right to receive distributions (profits) from the limited partnership and has the right to receive the liquidation value of her transferable interest at the termination of the limited partnership.

General Partner Dissociations The ULPA treats general partners' dissociations the same as the RUPA treats partners' dissociations in a partnership. A general partner's death, withdrawal, or expulsion causes dissociation, just as with limited partners. In addition, a general partner dissociates if he becomes mentally or physically unable to care for himself (such as when a court appoints a guardian over his affairs) or he is unable to perform as a general partner (as determined by a court). A general partner also dissociates if he is a debtor in bankruptcy, assigns his assets for the benefit of creditors, or has a custodian appointed over his property. In addition, a general partner may be expelled by a vote of all the other partners or by a court for the same grounds that limited partners may be expelled. The ULPA also provides for dissociation of nonhuman general partners, such as the termination of a corporation that is a general partner.

Like a dissociated limited partner, a dissociated general partner is treated as a transferee of the dissociated general partner's transferable interest. He will receive the liquidation value of the partnership interest at the termination of the partnership.

While a general partner always has the power to dissociate, his dissociation may be wrongful. A general partner wrongfully dissociates by leaving the partnership before it terminates, violating the limited partnership agreement, being a debtor in bankruptcy, or being expelled by a court. A general partner who has wrongfully dissociated is liable to the limited partnership and other partners for damages caused by his dissociation.

Authority and Liability of Dissociated General Partners Dissociation ends a general partner's right to manage the limited partnership. The dissociated general partner is released from most of his fiduciary duties. For example, the duty not to compete would no longer apply, so the dissociated general partner could set up a competing business. The duty of confidentiality, however, exists after dissociation to protect the limited partnership's trade secrets and other proprietary information.

While a general partner's express and implied authority to act for the limited partnership terminates upon his dissociation, he may retain apparent authority to transact for the limited partnership. Moreover, his liability for partnership obligations does not terminate merely due to his dissociation. Therefore, the dissociated general partner and the limited partnership must take steps to notify creditors and other parties of the dissociation to protect the limited partnership and the dissociated general partner from liability.

The best way is for the limited partnership to give notice of the dissociation, such as by e-mail or phone calls. To give notice of a dissociation that is effective against everyone, the ULPA permits the filing of a Notice of Dissociation, which is effective 90 days after filing. In addition, two years after the dissociation, the apparent authority of a dissociated general partner automatically ends.

A dissociated general partner will remain liable on a limited partnership obligation incurred while he was a partner unless the creditor agrees to release him from liability. The dissociated general partner will not be liable for limited partnership obligations incurred after he dissociated, if notice has been given of his association or more than two years have passed since his dissociation.

Effect of Limited Partnership Agreement The partners may agree to modify the default dissociation rules in the ULPA. For example, the partners may agree that no limited partner may withdraw from the limited partnership. While such a provision will not prevent dissociation upon a limited partner's death, it would otherwise require a limited partner to remain with the limited partnership until its term ends. The partnership agreement may also state the events that cause dissociation, such as a general partner becoming a manager of a competing business. The partners may also provide grounds to expel a partner, such as when a partner fails to contribute additional capital as required by the partnership agreement. The agreement may also reduce the percentage of partners required to expel a partner, such as requiring only 80 percent approval or giving expulsion power to general partners.

While a limited partner's power to withdraw may be eliminated, the limited partnership agreement may not restrict a general partner's right to withdraw. The grounds for this distinction is that a general partner should be able to withdraw from his duties to manage the limited partnership, while the limited partner as a passive investor has no such need to be relieved of that burden.

It may be unacceptable to the partners in a limited partnership that the dissociated partners do not receive the value of their partnership interests until the partnership terminates. Therefore, the limited partnership agreement may provide for the buyout of a partner's interest. A well-written buyout agreement should state the events that trigger a buyout, the valuation method, and when and how the dissociated partner will be paid (e.g., in a lump sum 120 days after dissociation or in quarterly installments for five years). To protect creditors, the ULPA prohibits any payment to a dissociated partner if the limited partnership is insolvent.

To protect the limited partnership's competitive position, the partners' agreement may also limit a dissociated general partner's ability to compete against the partnership. For example, a noncompete agreement may prohibit a dissociated general partner from competing for five years in the geographic area served by the limited partnership.

Limited Partnership Dissolutions
Recognizing that a limited partnership is usually worth more as a going concern, the ULPA provides that a limited partnership (or LLLP) is not dissolved, its business is not wound up, and it does not terminate merely because a partner has dissociated from the limited partnership. The ULPA provides that a limited partnership is dissolved and its business wound up only if all general partners and limited partners owning a majority of the claims to limited partner distributions (such as profits) vote for dissolution, if a general partner dissociates and partners owning a majority of the claims to partners' distributions vote for dissolution, if the last general or limited partner dissociates and is not replaced within 90 days, or if a court dissolves the limited partnership because it is not reasonably practicable to carry on the business of the limited partnership. Administrative dissolution by the secretary of state is also possible if the limited

partnership fails to pay fees and taxes due to the secretary of state or fails to deliver an annual report to the secretary.

When a limited partnership dissolves, winding up of its business follows automatically. The general partners have the power to wind up the business. Dissociated general partners have no right to wind up.

If there is no remaining general partner, the limited partners may appoint a general partner to conduct the winding up. The limited partnership is bound by the acts of a general partner that are appropriate to winding up, such as selling assets of the business and completing contracts. No new business should be conducted by the winding-up general partners.

After dissolution, a general partner has no express or implied authority to continue the business, except as necessary to liquidation. The general partners may have apparent authority to continue business in the usual way, however, and therefore bind the limited partnership. To avoid liability for the act of a general partner outside the scope of winding up, the limited partnership should give notice of its dissolution to all parties. One way to give notice is by filing a certificate of dissolution, which is effective against everyone after 90 days.

Distribution of Assets After the general partners have liquidated the assets of the limited partnership, the proceeds are distributed to those having claims against the limited partnership. First paid are creditors, which may include partners who, for example, have sold goods or made loans to the limited partnership.

If the proceeds from the sale of limited partnership assets exceed creditors' claims, the remainder is paid to the partners in the same proportions that they share distributions. This modifies the RULPA rule that repaid partners' capital contributions prior to distributing the remainder according to how partners share distributions. The ULPA rule may result in a wealth transfer from partners who have disproportionately larger contributions than their shares of distributions to partners who have disproportionately larger shares of distributions in relation to their capital contributions. If this is unacceptable, the partners may modify the ULPA rule in the limited partnership agreement, such as by requiring a return of capital contributions before distributing the remaining proceeds in the manner that partners share profits.

If a limited partnership's assets are insufficient to pay a creditor's claim, the persons who were general partners when the obligation was incurred must contribute cash to allow the limited partnership to pay the obligation. The general partners contribute in the same proportions that they shared distributions (considering only distributions to general partners) when the obligation was incurred.

In an LLLP, general partners are not required to contribute additional cash when the LLLP's assets are insufficient to pay creditors' claims because the liability of general partners in an LLLP is limited to their capital contributions.

Mergers and Conversions

The ULPA and the RULLCA permit limited partnerships and LLCs to merge with other businesses, including other limited partnerships, LLCs, and corporations. All partners of a limited partnership and all members of an LLC must consent to the plan of **merger**.

In addition, those statutes also permit a limited partnership or an LLC to convert easily into another business form. For example, some limited partnerships will want to become LLCs in order to enjoy all the limited liability advantages of the LLC. By executing a plan of **conversion** to an LLC, the partners can change the form of business without the more expensive and time-consuming process of forming a new business to take over the old business and then dissolving the old one. All the owners need to do is adopt a plan of conversion to which all partners consent.

In the following *Lach* case, the court held that the general partners were not required to comply with the requirements for conversion because a new LLC was formed and the limited partnership dissolved. However, the court found that the general partners breached their fiduciary duty by transferring the assets of the limited partnership to the LLC without the consent of a limited partner.

Lach v. Man O'War, LLC	256 S.W. 3d 563 (Ky. Sup. Ct. 2008)

In 1986, Shirley Lach and her then husband, Lynwood Wiseman, formed Man O'War Limited Partnership for the purpose of leasing real property and developing and operating shopping centers. Robert Miller became a general partner along with Wiseman. Lach was one of eight limited partners. The partners' ownership percentages were Robert Miller, 1 percent; Wiseman, 32 percent; Lach, 27 percent; Jonathan Miller, 9 percent; Harry B. Miller, 12 percent; Harvey Morgan, 1 percent; Penny Miller, 3 percent; Jeffery Mullens, 1 percent; Jennifer Miller, 9 percent; and Sophie Wiseman, 5 percent. Wiseman, Lach, and Robert Miller also formed M.O.W. Place Ltd. to lease a shopping center from the joint venture. In 1988, Wiseman and Lach were divorced but continued in business together.

In the spring of 2002, Robert Miller became ill with cancer. With his approaching death, he met with Lach concerning the shopping center. Miller asked Lach to agree to naming Wiseman, Jeffery Mullens (brother-in-law of Robert Miller), and Jonathan Miller (son of Robert Miller) as the new general partners of the Partnership. Under the original Partnership agreement, new general partners could not be added without the consent of all the partners. Robert Miller also asked Lach to agree that when Wiseman died, the two remaining general partners would select a new general partner. Lach objected because it would allow the Miller family, which owned less than Lach's individual interest, to manage and control the shopping center. The Millers would have two of the three general partners while Wiseman, who was then of advancing age, was alive. Upon his death, Jonathan Miller and Jeffery Mullens would then select the third general partner. Lach proposed substituting her daughter, Sherri McVay, an attorney, as a general partner in place of Jeffery Mullens. Her proposal was rejected.

Robert Miller and Wiseman then sought to restructure the business form of the partnership to eliminate the need for Lach's consent to the proposed management change. They formed a new business entity, Man O'War Limited Liability Company. When operational, the LLC would be manager-managed and controlled only by a majority vote of the owners. The initial managers were to be Wiseman, Jonathan Miller, and Jeffery Mullens.

After forming the LLC, Robert Miller and Wiseman dissolved the Partnership, distributing its assets (the ownership of the LLC) to the partners in identical proportions to their previous ownership of the Partnership, that is—with one catch. Unless a partner signed the documents validating the restructuring, that partner would have no voting rights in the LLC. All the partners except Lach signed the agreement, leaving only Lach without any voting rights.

Lach then sued the LLC and Wiseman, among others. She asked the court to set aside the transfer of Partnership assets to the LLC on the grounds that the transfer and the Partnership's subsequent termination was a violation of KRS 362.490 and a breach by the general partners of their fiduciary duty to the Partnership and Lach. The trial court found for the LLC and Wiseman, granting them summary judgment. The Kentucky appellate court affirmed the trial court's decision. Lach appealed to the Supreme Court of Kentucky.

Scott, Justice

Lach argues that the restructuring of the Partnership business form was invalid without her consent for two reasons: (1) the restructuring was a conversion in violation of KRS 275.370, and (2) the restructuring made it impossible for the Partnership to carry on its business in violation of KRS 362.490.

KRS 275.370 provides, in pertinent part:

(1) A partnership or limited partnership may be converted to a limited liability company pursuant to this section.

(2) The terms and conditions of a conversion of a partnership or limited partnership to a limited liability company shall, in the case of a partnership, be approved by all the partners or by a number or percentage specified for conversion in the partnership agreement or, in the case of a limited partnership, by all the partners, notwithstanding any provision to the contrary in the limited partnership agreement.

While conceding that the statute, in this instance, requires the approval of all the limited partners before a limited partnership can be converted into a limited liability company, the LLC and Wiseman argue that the transformation constituted a "reorganization," not a "conversion" as envisioned under KRS 275.370(1). They illustrate their distinction of the word "conversion," by pointing out that the statute envisions a limited partnership *redesignating itself* as a limited liability company, whereas, in this instance, the limited liability company was created separately and existed concurrently with the Partnership (albeit without any assets). Thus, the fact that the LLC acquired all the assets of the Partnership and the Partnership then dissolved is simply immaterial.

KRS 275.375(1) acknowledges that "[a] partnership or limited partnership that has been converted pursuant to this chapter shall be for all purposes the same entity that existed before the conversion." KRS 275.375(2) recognizes that the property "*shall remain* vested in the converted [business entity] . . . [and] [a]ll obligations of the converting . . . limited partnership *shall continue* as obligations of the converted [business entity]." (Emphasis added.) All of which seem to confirm the LLC and Wiseman's argument that a "conversion" involves only one entity changing its legal form pursuant to statutory authorizations, rather than through interaction between *two* entities.

Looking at subsequent statutes for what light they cast on the question, we note that the Kentucky Legislature adopted the *new* Kentucky Uniform Limited Partnership Act in 2006. KRS 362.2-102, et. seq. This Act was adopted, with some changes, from the Uniform Limited Partnership Act (2001). The Act specifically provides "[i]n applying and construing this uniform act, consideration shall be given to the need to promote uniformity of the law with respect to its subject matter among states that enact it." KRS 362.2-1201.

When the need for uniformity is acknowledged, courts may consider the "Official Comments" to a Uniform Act, even where they have not been officially adopted. Looking at the Official Comments to § 1102 of the Uniform Limited Partnership Act, which, with changes, corresponds to KRS 362.2-1102, the Comment acknowledges, "[i]n contrast to a merger, which involves at least two entities, a conversion involves only one. The converting

and converted organizations are the same entity." Unif. Limited Partnership Act § 1102–1105, GA U.L.A. 107 (2006).

Having thus considered the statutory scheme, its particular language, the subsequent statute and Official Comments, we answer the question that was presented to us—that the restructuring of the business form of the Partnership, to that of the LLC, in this instance, was not a conversion under, or subject to, KRS 275.370, for reasons that a conversion deals only with one entity. We have not been asked, nor have we considered, whether the restructuring of the Partnership into the LLC constituted a merger, pursuant to KRS 362.531.

Under Kentucky law, partners owe the utmost good faith to each and every other partner. The scope of the fiduciary duty has been variously defined as one requiring utter good faith or honesty, loyalty or obedience, as well as candor, due care, and fair dealing. Indeed, it has often been said, there is no relation of trust or confidence known to law that requires of the parties a higher degree of good faith than that of a partnership. Thus, the doing of an act proscribed by law is a breach of that duty.

KRS 362.490 provides, in pertinent part:

A general partner shall have all the rights and powers and be subject to all the restrictions and liabilities of a partner in a partnership without limited partners, except that without the written consent or ratification of the specific act by all the limited partners, a general partner or all the general partners have no authority to

* * *

(2) do any act which would make it impossible to carry on the ordinary business of the partnership.

The LLC and Wiseman argue that Miller and Wiseman had the authority to perform all the acts constituting the restructuring without Lach's consent because they did not make it impossible to carry on the business of the partnership. They assert, *it was the only act which made it possible* to carry on the business of the partnership; suggesting that Lach would, by virtue of her right of rejection, have destroyed the partnership's business, something she hadn't done for the previous sixteen years. Moreover, the fact that a limited partner with significant ownership interests in a limited partnership would object to a transaction which would deprive her of her say in who might be able to successfully manage her business interest as a general partner, in return for a minority voting, or for that fact, a non-voting interest, in a limited liability company controlled by a majority vote, is not evidence that such limited partner has an interest in destroying the business, including the value of her interest therein.

They further argue that under the certificate of partnership and partnership agreement, the general partners had the absolute right to "(1) terminate the partnership, (2) execute documents agreements, contracts, leases, etc., on behalf of the partnership, and (3) to manage the partnership business in all aspects, which should include, but should not be limited to . . . take such other action, execute and deliver such other documents, and perform such other acts as the general partners may deem necessary, appropriate, or incidental to carrying out the business and affairs of the partnership." In this regard, they seek to distinguish *Mist Properties, Inc. v. Fitzsimmons Realty Co.*, 228 N.Y.S.2d 406 (Sup. Ct. 1962), in which the court approved the general partner's transfer of title to property owned by the limited partnership as against the claim of the receiver, because the limited partnership agreement allowed the general partners to do so.

Mist Properties, Inc., however, had a partnership agreement that gave the general partners the specific power to sell all of the partnership's property, subject to written approval of sixty-five percent of the limited partners. "There clearly appears to have been no violation of the statute since the conveyance was not without the written consent of the limited partners but was specifically contemplated and provided for by the agreement." *Id.* at 410. As the court recognized therein, the agreement the partners had made with themselves through their partnership agreement controlled. "There is no

intervening public policy which prevents persons dealing at arm's length from entering into an agreement such as set forth above. It has been repeatedly held that where a limited partnership agreement has been entered into the partners cannot, *inter se*, set up that their rights are not governed thereby. . . ." *Id.* at 410.

Simply put, we find that the general partners' rights under the partnership agreement to (1) terminate the partnership at any time upon agreement of the general partners, and (2) to act upon behalf of the Partnership in matters that are "necessary, appropriate, or incidental to carry out its business," can be not construed to allow them the power to transform the partnership into a limited liability company, in order to favor a majority of the partners in their selection, or substitution, of the general partners/managers of the business, without the approval of all the limited partners.

We therefore conclude that the transfer of the partnership assets to the LLC was in violation of KRS 362.490 and thus a breach of the general partners' fiduciary duty to the non-consenting limited partner.

Judgment reversed in favor of Lach.

The Global Business Environment

Limited Partnerships in Other Countries

All modern commercial countries permit the creation of limited partnerships, but almost none allow the creation of LLLPs. England and its former colonies, including the United States, Canada, Singapore, and Australia, use the term *limited partnership*. In Italy, the limited partnership form is named *Societa in accomandita semplic*e (S.a.s.); in Latin American countries, the *Sociedad en comandita*; in Austria, the *Kommanditgesellschaft* (Kg).

These business forms are mostly identical to American limited partnerships, having general partners who manage the business and possess unlimited liability and limited partners who may not manage and are granted limited liability. Most countries also permit the partners to restrict the transfer of a partner's interest and usually provide for the continuation of the business despite the death of a limited partner.

Problems and Problem Cases

1. Racing Investment Fund 2000 LLC was created in August 2000 to purchase, train, and race thoroughbred horses. The LLC's operating agreement provided for 50 membership units to be sold for an initial capital contribution of $100,000 per unit and allowed the LLC manager on an as-needed basis to call for additional capital from the members in order to pay operating, administrative, or other business expenses. Subsequently, the LLC failed to pay for insurance services provided by Clay Ward Agency. Clay Ward sued the LLC and its members and asked the court to require the LLC manager to make a call for additional capital in order to pay the debt to Clay Ward. Did the court order the call?

2. Bonnie Strickland and her husband Jake formed the Strickland Family Limited Liability Company as part of their estate plan. They transferred 83 percent of the equity shares of the LLC to their daughter Suzy Strickland Harbison. The Stricklands retained a 17 percent interest in the LLC and acted as co-managers of the LLC for the next two years. When Jake died, Bonnie became the only manager of the LLC. In 2002, Bonnie conveyed three parcels of real property belonging to the LLC to her son David Strickland. David was not a member of the LLC. Bonnie transferred the parcels

of real property for an amount Suzy believed was less than fair market value. Suzy sued Bonnie, claiming that Bonnie had breached her fiduciary duty to the LLC under the Alabama Limited Liability Company Act and that she had violated the terms of the operating agreement when she failed to make managerial decisions based on the best interests of the LLC and the equity owners. Bonnie defended by referring to the LLC's operating agreement, which clearly stated that the LLC was not formed for profit purposes:

> The managers do not, in any way guarantee a profit for the Equity Owners from the operations of the Company. Decisions with respect to the conduct, dissolution and winding up of the business of the company shall be made in the sole discretion of the Equity Owners and such other matters as the Managers consider relevant. There shall be no obligation on the part of the Managers to maximize financial gain or to make any or all of the Company Property productive.

Has Bonnie breached her fiduciary duty?

3. In 1999, Andreas Halvorsen, David Ott, and Brian Olson formed a hedge fund, Viking Global Investors LLC. The LLC's written agreement provided that the three founders would operate Viking and divide all of its profits annually. If any one of them left Viking, he would receive only his capital account balance and earned compensation that had accrued and not been paid. In August 2005, the LLC management committee terminated Olson's membership in the LLC because the returns on his portfolio of investments were disappointing. The LLC bought out Olson by returning the amount in his capital account and paying his 2005 compensation, which amounted to more than $100 million. Olson sued the LLC and the other members, alleging that subsequent to executing the written agreement, they had agreed orally to pay the fair market value of a member's interest upon his leaving the LLC. He also argued that Delaware's LLC statute required payment of fair value. Did the court agree with Olson?

4. Stephen Doherty wrote a software program called Viper for Lester Szlendak. Doherty and Szlendak, along with Peter Katris and William Hamburg (both employees of Ernst & Company), formed Viper Execution Systems LLC to exploit the software. Each member held a 25 percent interest in the LLC. Szlendak and Doherty assigned all their rights in Viper to the LLC. The operating agreement provided that the "business and affairs of the LLC shall be managed by its managers" and that the members agreed to elect Katris and Hamburg as the "sole managers" of the LLC. The operating agreement also listed the powers of the managers and the rights and obligations of the members. None of the rights and obligations of the members provided the members with any managerial authority. The operating agreement also stated it could "not be amended except by the affirmative vote of members holding a majority of the participating percentages." Katris and Hamburg, as sole managers of the LLC, adopted resolutions naming Hamburg as chief executive officer, Katris as chief financial officer, Szlendak as director of marketing, and Doherty as director of technical services. The written consent to the resolution contained signature lines for Hamburg and Katris, who were identified as "all of the managers" of the LLC. Prior to and at the time of the LLC's formation, Doherty worked as an independent contractor for Hamburg and Patrick Carroll (also an Ernst employee). In late 1997, Ernst hired Doherty to work for Carroll. Working for Carroll and Ernst, Doherty helped to adapt a software program, Worldwide Options Web (WWOW). By 2002, Katris came to believe that WWOW was functionally similar to Viper. On what grounds did Katris sue Doherty? Was his action successful?

5. Ruben Pazmino was an employee of Buena Vista Realty Group LLC, an Indiana limited liability company. From February 2008 through July 2008, law firm Bose McKinney & Evans LLP did legal work for Buena Vista at the request of Pazmino. On April 24, 2008, Buena Vista was administratively dissolved, a date after which Pazmino continued to act on behalf of Buena Vista, including requesting legal work from Bose. Pazmino was not aware of the administrative dissolution of Buena Vista. Neither Buena Vista nor Pazmino paid Bose for its services. In 2010, Bose filed a complaint against Buena Vista and Pazmino, alleging they had failed to pay for services rendered and seeking $12,580.09 plus interest from Buena Vista and $9,618.39 plus interest from Pazmino. Was Pazmino held liable to Bose?

6. Cralle Comer and Stephen Chapman form two manager-managed limited liability companies, Garrison-Ashburn LC and Garrison-Woods LC. Comer and Chapman each owns a 50 percent membership interest in each LLC. Comer is the operating manager. Chapman files a voluntary petition in bankruptcy under Chapter 11 of the U.S. Bankruptcy Code. In the course of the bankruptcy proceeding, Comer wishes to sell a parcel of land owned by Garrison-Woods. Chapman argues that Garrison-Woods cannot sell the land

without his consent on the grounds that the LLC's operating agreement requires both members to execute all deeds and sale contracts. Chapman refuses to sign the contract of sale or the deed. Comer argues that as operating manager, he is fully authorized to execute the contract. Do you think the court will find in favor of Comer or Chapman?

7. Judith Carpenter was an experienced businesswoman and served on the board of directors of a bank. In 1984, Carpenter invested in Briargate Homes, a business that owned several condominiums. She believed that Briargate was a limited partnership and that she was a limited partner. In fact, Briargate was a partnership and she was a general partner. No attempt had been made to comply with the North Carolina limited partnership statute. By 1987, Carpenter had possession of documents stating that Briargate was a partnership and she a partner. As an owner of condominiums, the partnership was liable to the condominium association for assessments for maintenance, repairs, and replacement of common areas in the complex. In 1988, the partnership failed to pay $85,000 in assessments. The partnership and its partners were sued by the condominium association. May Carpenter escape liability on the assessment because she thought she was a limited partner?

8. Virginia Partners Ltd., a limited partnership organized in Florida, was in the business of drilling oil wells. When Virginia Partners injected acid into an oil well in Kentucky, a bystander, Robert Day, was injured by acid that sprayed on him from a ruptured hose. Virginia Partners had failed to register as a foreign limited partnership in Kentucky. Are the limited partners of Virginia Partners liable to Day for his injuries?

9. Brookside Realty Ltd. was a limited partnership. In the limited partnership certificate filed with the secretary of state, four of its limited partners agreed to make capital contributions and be liable for future assessments in amounts ranging between $36,000 and $145,000. Brookside failed to pay for material Builders Steel sold to Brookside. Because the limited partners had not paid all the assessments required by the limited partnership certificate, Builders Steel claimed that it was entitled to require the limited partners to pay those assessments to the extent of the debt to Builders Steel. Did the court agree?

10. Blinder, Robinson & Co., as limited partner, and Combat Promotions Inc., as general partner, created Combat Associates to promote an eight-round exhibition match between Muhammad Ali and Lyle Alzado, the pro football player. Combat Associates promised to pay Alzado $100,000 for his participation in the match.

   Combat Promotions was owned entirely by Alzado, his accountant, and his professional agent. Alzado was also vice president of Combat Promotions. Blinder, Robinson used its Denver office as a ticket outlet for the match, gave two parties to promote the match, and provided a meeting room for Combat Associates's meetings. Meyer Blinder, president of Blinder, Robinson, personally appeared on a TV talk show and gave TV interviews to promote the match.

   Few tickets were sold, and the match was a financial debacle. Alzado received no payments for participating in the match. Alzado sued Blinder, Robinson, claiming that because it acted like a general partner, it had the liability of a general partner. The case was decided under the law of the RULPA. Was Blinder, Robinson liable to Alzado? Would Blinder, Robinson be liable to Alzado under the ULPA of 2001?

11. Joshua and Regan Bowers join Addison Barnes to form a private equity limited partnership, Kestrel Investment Partners LP. They plan to sell to wealthy investors limited partnership interests totaling $42 billion, investing the funds in small businesses that need capital infusion and management assistance to become highly successful businesses. Joshua, Regan, and Addison also form an LLC, Kestrel Management LLC, as the sole general partner of Kestrel Investment Partners LP. Each of the three own one-third of the LLC and hold equal management power as managing members of the LLC. In effect, through the LLC, the three control the management of the limited partnership. Are the three, therefore, general partners of the limited partnership? Do they have unlimited liability for the limited partnership's obligations?

Corporations

History and Nature
of Corporations

Y
ou and three friends create an online retailer, which is incorporated in California under the name Gifts&Awards.com, Inc. The website will sell awards, clocks, desk sets, and other merchandise that businesses want as gifts for their clients and as promotional items for their employees. Physically, Gifts&Awards.com will be located exclusively in San Jose, California. All its shareholders, employees, and assets will be in California. As an online retailer, however, Gifts&Awards.com's merchandise will be available to anyone, anywhere in the world. Businesses worldwide will place orders through the website, which will be filled by the Gifts&Awards.com's staff. Gifts&Awards.com will ship about 20 percent of the merchandise ordered from a warehouse it leases in California. The other 80 percent will be shipped directly from the manufacturers or importers of the items. For that 80 percent, Gifts&Awards.com will take orders from customers and direct the orders to the appropriate manufacturers or importers, some of which will be in California but most of which will be dispersed throughout the United States.

You estimate that Gifts&Awards.com will have $4,000,000 in annual sales, $60,000 of which is to customers residing in Arizona. The goods will be delivered to customers by UPS, a third-party carrier whose fee will be added to the price of the goods. Some of the goods will be shipped from Gifts&Awards.com's warehouse in California, and some from manufacturers in other states, including Arizona. Consider the following questions regarding the State of Arizona's regulation of Gifts&Awards.com, a California corporation:

- May the State of Arizona require Gifts&Awards.com to obtain a certificate of authority to do business in Arizona and collect a fee from Gifts&Awards.com for the privilege of doing business in the state?
- May the State of Arizona impose its state income tax on a portion of Gifts&Awards.com's worldwide income?
- May the State of Arizona require Gifts&Awards.com to collect the Arizona sales tax on sales to Arizona residents?
- If Gifts&Awards.com sells defective awards to a customer in Arizona, may the customer sue Gifts&Awards.com in an Arizona trial court? Will your answer affect Gifts&Awards.com's policy on customers' returns and refunds?

LO LEARNING OBJECTIVES

After studying this chapter, you should be able to:

41-1 Discuss the history of the development of corporation law.

41-2 Recognize the types of corporations.

41-3 Understand the manner in which a state may regulate a foreign or alien corporation.

41-4 Prevent a court from piercing a corporation's veil.

THE MODERN CORPORATION HAS facilitated the rapid economic development of the last 200 years by permitting businesses to attain economies of scale. Businesses organized as corporations can attain such economies because they have a greater capacity to raise capital than do other business forms. This capital-raising advantage is ensured by corporation law, which allows persons to invest their money in a corporation and become owners without imposing unlimited liability or management responsibilities on themselves. Many people are willing to invest their savings in a large, risky business if they have limited liability and no management responsibilities. Far fewer are willing to invest in a partnership or other business form in which owners have unlimited liability and management duties.

History of Corporations

 Discuss the history of the development of corporation law.

Although modern corporation law emerged only in the last 200 years, ancestors of the modern corporation existed in the times of Hammurabi, ancient Greece, and the Roman Empire. As early as 1248 in France, privileges of incorporation were given to mercantile ventures to encourage investment for the benefit of society. In England, the corporate form was used extensively before the 16th century.

The famous British trading companies—such as the Massachusetts Bay Company—were the forerunners of the modern corporation. The British government gave these companies monopolies in trade and granted them powers to govern in the areas they colonized. They were permitted to operate as corporations because of the benefits they would confer on the British empire, such as the development of natural resources. Although these trading companies were among the few corporations of the time whose owners were granted limited liability, they sought corporate status primarily because the government granted them monopolies and governmental powers.

American Corporation Law Beginning in 1776, corporation law in the United States evolved independently of English corporation law. Early American corporations received *special charters* from state legislatures. These charters were granted one at a time by special action of the legislatures and few special charters were granted.

In the late 18th century, general incorporation statutes emerged in the United States. Initially, these statutes permitted incorporation only for limited purposes beneficial to the public, such as operating toll bridges and water systems. Incorporation was still viewed as a privilege, and many restrictions were placed on corporations: Incorporation was permitted for only short periods of time; maximum limits on capitalization were low; ownership of real and personal property was often restricted.

During the last 150 years, such restrictive provisions have disappeared in most states. Today, modern incorporation statutes are mostly enabling, granting the persons who control a corporation great flexibility in establishing, financing, and operating it.

See Figure 41.1 for a summary of the characteristics of corporations.

Classifications of Corporations

LO41-2 Recognize the types of corporations.

Corporations may be divided into three classes: (1) corporations *for profit*, (2) corporations *not for profit*, and (3) *government-owned* corporations. State and federal corporation statutes establish procedures for the incorporation of each of these classes and for their operation. In addition, a large body of common law applies to all corporations.

Most business corporations are *for-profit corporations*. For-profit corporations issue stock to their shareholders, who invest in the corporation with the expectation that they will earn a profit on their investment. That profit may take the form of dividends paid by the corporation or increased market value of their shares.

Nearly all for-profit corporations are incorporated under the *general incorporation law* of a state. All of the states require professionals who wish to incorporate, such as physicians, dentists, lawyers, and accountants, to incorporate under *professional corporation acts*. In addition, for-profit corporations that especially affect the public interest, such as banks, insurance companies, and savings and loan associations, are usually required to incorporate under special statutes.

For-profit corporations range from huge international organizations such as General Electric Company to small, one-owner businesses. GE is an example of a *publicly held corporation* because its shares are generally available to public investors. The publicly held corporation tends to be managed by professional managers who own small percentages of the corporation. Nearly all the shareholders of the typical publicly held corporation are merely investors who are not concerned in the management of the corporation.

Figure 41.1   Principal Characteristics of Corporations

1. *Creation.* A corporation may be created only by *permission of a government.*

2. *Legal status.* A corporation is a legal entity independent of its owners (*shareholders*) and its managers (officers and the *board of directors*). Its life is unaffected by the retirement or death of its shareholders, officers, and directors. A corporation may be considered a person under the Constitution of the United States for certain purposes such as making political speech and involving search and seizure.

3. *Powers.* A corporation may *acquire, hold, and convey property* in its own name. A corporation may *sue and be sued* in its own name. Harm to a corporation is not harm to the shareholders; therefore, with few exceptions, a shareholder may not sue to enforce a claim of the corporation.

4. *Management.* Shareholders elect a board of directors, which manages the corporation. The board of directors may delegate management duties to officers. A shareholder has *no right or duty to manage* the business of a corporation, unless he is elected to the board of directors or is appointed an officer. The directors and officers need not be shareholders.

5. *Owners' liability.* The shareholders have *limited liability.* With few exceptions, they are not liable for the debts of a corporation after they have paid their promised capital contributions to the corporation.

6. *Transferability of owner's interest.* Generally, the ownership interest in a corporation is *freely transferable.* A shareholder may sell her shares to whomever she wants whenever she wants. The purchaser becomes a shareholder with the same rights that the seller had.

7. *Taxation.* Usually, a corporation pays *federal income taxes* on its income. Shareholders have personal income from the corporation only when the corporation makes a distribution of its income to them. For example, a shareholder would have personal income from the corporation when the corporation pays him a dividend. This creates a *double-taxation* possibility: The corporation pays income tax on its profits, and when the corporation distributes the after-tax profits as dividends, the shareholders pay tax on the dividends.

Corporations with very few shareholders whose shares are not available to the general public are called **close corporations**. In the typical close corporation, the controlling shareholders are the only managers of the business.

Usually, close corporations and publicly held corporations are subject to the same rules under state corporation law. Many states, however, allow close corporations greater latitude in the operation of their internal affairs than is granted to public corporations. For example, the shareholders of a close corporation may be permitted to dispense with the board of directors and manage the close corporation as if it were a partnership.

A Subchapter S corporation, or S **corporation**, is a special type of close corporation. It is treated nearly like a partnership for federal income tax purposes. Its shareholders report the earnings or losses of the business on their individual federal income tax returns. This means that an S corporation's profits are taxed only once—at the shareholder level, eliminating the double-taxation penalty of incorporation. All shareholders must consent to an S corporation election. The Internal Revenue Code requires an S corporation to have only one class of shares and 100 or fewer shareholders. Shareholders may be only individuals or trusts.

Not-for-profit corporations do not issue stock and do not expect to make a profit. Instead, they provide services to their members under a plan that eliminates any profit motive. These corporations have *members* rather than shareholders, and none of the surplus revenue from their operations may be distributed to their members. Because they generally pay no income tax, nonprofit corporations can reinvest a larger share of their incomes in the business than can for-profit corporations. Examples of nonprofit corporations are charities, churches, fraternal organizations, community arts councils, cooperative grocery stores, and cooperative farmers' feed and supplies stores.

Beginning in 2010, a new type of corporation has emerged that blends characteristics of traditional for-profit and not-for-profit corporations. *Benefit corporations,* also called *social purpose corporations*, are formed to make a profit and, at the same time, act in a socially conscious manner. Benefit corporations voluntarily structure themselves this way to help steer and maintain their social goals, help with branding, and attract investment. Incorporating as a benefit corporation offers the advantages of limiting liability for shareholders, officers, and directors; allows the company to make a profit for its shareholders; and permits the company to take actions that might not otherwise be beneficial to the company's bottom line. To become a benefit corporation, a company must include language in its articles of incorporation requiring consideration of all shareholders and nonfinancial interests when making business decisions. The particular language is governed by state statute, but most states require only that the company provide a general public benefit, broadly defined. Over 30 states now have statutes allowing for benefit corporations, and many well-known companies—Kickstarter, Plum Organics, Patagonia—have chosen to incorporate in this manner. Figure 41.2 shows the requirements of benefit corporations and how they compare to "Certified B Corporations," a certification given by B Lab, a nonprofit organization that has become a leader in social business certification.

Some corporations are owned by governments and perform governmental and business functions. A municipality (city) is one type of *government-owned corporation*. Other types are created to furnish more specific services—for example, school corporations and water companies. Others—such as the Tennessee Valley Authority and the Federal Deposit Insurance Corporation—operate much like for-profit corporations except that at least some of their directors are appointed by governmental officials, and some or all of their financing

frequently comes from government. The TVA and the FDIC are chartered by Congress, but government-owned corporations may also be authorized by states. Government-operated businesses seek corporate status to free themselves from governmental operating procedures, which are more cumbersome than business operating procedures.

Regulation of For-Profit Corporations

To become a corporation, a business must *incorporate* by complying with an incorporation statute. Incorporation is a fairly simple process usually requiring little more than paying a fee and filing a document with a designated government official—usually the secretary of state of the state of incorporation. Incorporation of for-profit businesses has been entrusted primarily to the governments of the 50 states.

State Incorporation Statutes State incorporation statutes set out the basic rules regarding the relationship

Figure 41.2	Comparing Benefit Corporations and B Corps.	
Issue	**Benefit Corporations**	**Certified B Corporations**
Accountability	Directors required to consider impact on all stakeholders	Same
Transparency	Must publish public report of overall social and environmental performance assessed against a third-party standard*	Same
Performance	Self-reported	Must achieve minimum verified score on B Impact Assessment
		Recertification required every three years against evolving standard
Availability	Available for corporations only in 30 U.S. states and the District of Columbia**	Available to every business regardless of corporate structure, state, or country of incorporation
Cost	State filing fees from $70–$200	B Lab certification fees from $500 to $50,000/year, based on revenues

* Delaware benefit corps are not required to report publicly or against a third party standard

** Oregon and Maryland offer benefit LLC options

Source: https://benefitcorp.net/businesses/benefit-corporations-and-certified-b-corps.

between the corporation, its shareholders, and its managers. For example, an incorporation statute sets the requirements for a business to incorporate, the procedures for shareholders' election of directors, and the duties directors and officers owe to the corporation. Although a corporation may do business in several states, usually the relationship between the corporation, its shareholders, and its managers is regulated only by the state of incorporation.

The American Bar Association's Committee on Corporate Laws has prepared a *model* statute for adoption by state legislatures. The purpose of the model statute is to improve the rationality of corporation law. It is called the **Model Business Corporation Act (MBCA).** Its last major revision was in 2016, although amendments are made nearly every year.

The revised MBCA is the basis of corporation law in 29 states and the District of Columbia. Your study of statutory corporation law in this book concentrates on the revised MBCA. Delaware, where more than 50 percent of publicly traded companies in the U.S. incorporate, and several major commercial and industrial states such as New York and California do not follow the MBCA. Therefore, selected provisions of the Delaware statute and other acts will be addressed.

Several states have special provisions or statutes that are applicable only to close corporations. The ABA's Committee on Corporate Laws has adopted the *Statutory Close Corporation Supplement to the Model Business Corporation Act.* The *Supplement* is designed to provide a rational, statutory solution to the special problems facing close corporations.

LOG ON

Go to
https://businesslawtoday.org/2017/01/model-business-corporation-act-2016-revision-launches/
You can see a listing of the most recent revisions to the MBCA.
www.corporations.uslegal.com/basics-of-corporations/state-corporation-laws
This web page lists the laws that govern corporations in each state and the District of Columbia, including the states whose laws are based on the MBCA.

State Common Law of Corporations Although nearly all of corporation law is statutory law, including the courts' interpretation of the statutes, there is a substantial body of common law of corporations (judge-made law). Most of this common law deals with creditor and shareholder rights. For example, the law of piercing the corporate veil, which you will study later in this chapter, is common law protecting creditors of corporations.

Regulation of Nonprofit Corporations

Nonprofit corporations are regulated primarily by the states. Nonprofit corporations may be created only by complying with a nonprofit incorporation statute. Incorporation under state law requires delivering articles of incorporation to the secretary of state. The existence of a nonprofit corporation begins when the secretary of state files the articles. Most states have statutes based on the revised **Model Nonprofit Corporation Act (MNCA).** Because of constitutional protection of freedom of religion, many states have special statutes regulating nonprofit religious organizations.

The law applied to nonprofit corporations is substantially similar to for-profit corporation law. At various points in the corporations chapters of this book, you will study the law of nonprofit corporations and examine how this form of business and its laws differ from the for-profit corporation and its laws. The Model Nonprofit Corporation Act will be the basis of your study of nonprofit corporation law.

Regulation of Foreign and Alien Corporations

LO41-3 Understand the manner in which a state may regulate a foreign or alien corporation.

The Global Business Environment

Corporations around the Globe

The corporate form of business is recognized throughout the world, and, regardless of the country, the form has essentially the same characteristics: limited liability for its owners, free transferability of shares, and separation of management from ownership. In Italy, the name is *Societa*

per azioni. In Zimbabwe and England, corporations are called limited companies. In Germany, the term is *Aktiengesellschaft* (AG). In Brazil, the name is *sociedade anonima.* You can learn about Canadian corporations at www.ic.gc.ca/app/scr/cc/CorporationsCanada/fdrlCrpSrch.html?locale=en_CA. This site has a guide that facilitates the incorporation process.

A corporation may be incorporated in one state yet do business in many other states in which it is not incorporated. The corporation's contacts with other persons in those states may permit the states to regulate the corporation's transactions with their citizens, to subject the corporation to suits in their courts, or to tax the corporation. The circumstances under which states may impose their laws on a business incorporated in another state is determined by the law of foreign corporations.

A corporation is a **domestic corporation** in the state that has granted its charter; it is a **foreign corporation** in all the other states in which it does business. For example, a corporation organized in Delaware and doing business in Florida is domestic in Delaware and foreign in Florida. Note that a corporation domiciled in one country is an **alien corporation** in other countries in which it does business. Many of the rules that apply to foreign corporations apply as well to alien corporations.

Generally, a state may impose its laws on a foreign corporation if such imposition does not violate the Constitution of the United States, notably the Due Process Clause of the Fourteenth Amendment and the Commerce Clause. The law discussed here also applies to foreign partnerships, LLPs, LLCs, limited partnerships, and LLLPs, forms of business discussed in Chapters 37, 38, 39, and 40.

Due Process Clause
The Due Process Clause requires that a foreign corporation have sufficient contacts with a state before a state may exercise jurisdiction over the corporation. The leading case in this area is the *International Shoe* case.[1] In that case, the Supreme Court ruled that a foreign corporation must have "certain minimum contacts" with the state such that asserting jurisdiction over the corporation does not offend "traditional notions of fair play and substantial justice." The Supreme Court justified its holding with a **benefit theory**: When a foreign corporation avails itself of the protection of a state's laws, it should suffer any reasonable burden that the state imposes as a consequence of such benefit. In other words, a foreign corporation should be required to pay for the benefits that it receives from the state.

Commerce Clause
Under the Commerce Clause, the power to regulate interstate commerce is given to the federal government. The states have no power to exclude or to discriminate against foreign corporations that are engaged solely in *interstate* commerce,

i.e., commerce existing or occurring between states. Nevertheless, a state may require a foreign corporation doing interstate business in the state to comply with its laws if the application of these laws does not unduly burden interstate commerce. When a foreign corporation enters interstate commerce to do *intrastate* business, i.e., commerce existing or occurring within the boundaries of the state, the state may regulate the corporation's activities, provided again that the regulation does not unduly burden interstate commerce.

A state law regulating the activities of a foreign corporation does not unduly burden interstate commerce if (1) the law serves a legitimate state interest, (2) the state has chosen the least burdensome means of promoting that interest, and (3) that legitimate state interest outweighs the statute's burden on interstate commerce. Because conducting intrastate business increases a corporation's contact with a state, it is easier to prove that the state has a legitimate interest and that there is no undue burden on interstate commerce when the state regulates a corporation that is conducting intrastate business.

Doing Business To aid their determination of whether a state may constitutionally impose its laws on a foreign corporation, courts have traditionally used the concept of **doing business**. Courts have generally held that a foreign corporation is subject to the laws of a state when it is doing business in the state. The activities that constitute doing business differ, however, depending on the purpose of the determination. There are four such purposes: (1) to determine whether a corporation is subject to a lawsuit in a state's courts, (2) to determine whether the corporation's activities are subject to taxation, (3) to determine whether the corporation must qualify to carry on its activities in the state, and (4) to determine whether the state may regulate the internal affairs of the corporation.

Subjecting Foreign Corporations to Suit
The Supreme Court of the United States has held that a foreign corporation may be brought into a state's court in connection with its activities within the state, provided that the state does not violate the corporation's due process rights under the Fourteenth Amendment of the Constitution and its rights under the Commerce Clause.

The *International Shoe* minimum contacts test must be met. Subjecting the corporation to suit cannot offend "traditional notions of fair play and substantial justice." A court must weigh the corporation's contacts within the state against the inconvenience to the corporation of requiring it to defend a suit within the state. The burden on the corporation must be reasonable in relation

---

[1]*International Shoe Co. v. State of Washington*, 326 U.S. 310 (1945).

to the benefit that it receives from conducting activities in the state.

Under the minimum contacts test, even an isolated event may be sufficient to confer jurisdiction on a state's courts. For example, driving a truck from Arizona through New Mexico toward a final destination in Florida provides sufficient contacts with New Mexico to permit a suit in New Mexico's courts against the foreign corporation for its driver's negligently causing an accident within New Mexico.

Most states have passed **long-arm statutes** to permit their courts to exercise jurisdiction under the decision of the *International Shoe* case. These statutes frequently specify several kinds of corporate activities that make foreign corporations subject to suit within the state, such as the commission of a tort, the making of a contract, or the ownership of property. Most of the long-arm statutes grant jurisdiction over causes of action growing out of any transaction within the state.

You may also want to read *Daimler AG v. Bauman*, which appears in Chapter 2. In that case, the Supreme Court of the United States held that 22 Argentine citizens could not bring an action in a California court against an Argentine subsidiary of Daimler AG based on another Daimler subsidiary having contacts with California when the conduct of the Argentine subsidiary took place entirely outside the United States.

Taxation
A state may tax a foreign corporation if such taxation does not violate the Due Process Clause or the Commerce Clause. Generally, a state's imposition of a tax must serve a legitimate state interest and be reasonable in relation to a foreign corporation's contacts with the state. For example, a North Carolina corporation's property located in Pennsylvania is subject to property tax in Pennsylvania. The corporation enjoys Pennsylvania's protection of private property. It may be required to pay its share of the cost of such protection.

Greater contacts are needed to subject a corporation to state income and sales taxation in a state than are needed to subject it to property taxation. A state tax does not violate the commerce clause when the tax (1) is applied to an activity with a substantial connection with the taxing state, (2) is fairly apportioned, (3) does not discriminate against interstate commerce, and (4) is fairly related to the services provided by the state.[2]

For example, New Jersey has been permitted to tax a portion of the entire net income of a corporation for the privilege of doing business, employing or owning capital or property, or maintaining an office in New Jersey when the portion of entire net income taxed is determined by an average of three ratios: in-state property to total property; in-state to total receipts; and in-state to total wages, salaries, and other employee compensation.[3] However, Pennsylvania could not assess a flat tax on the operation of all trucks on Pennsylvania highways. The flat tax imposed a disproportionate burden on interstate trucks as compared with intrastate trucks because interstate trucks traveled fewer miles per year on Pennsylvania highways.[4] Nonetheless, the Supreme Court upheld a $100 fee levied by the state of Michigan on all trucks, whether or not owned by in-state or out-of-state companies, that made point-to-point hauls between Michigan cities, on the grounds that the fee taxed purely local activity and did not tax an interstate truck's entry into Michigan or transactions spanning multiple states.[5]

State taxation of interstate Internet transactions has become a potential source for state revenue. However, in 1998 Congress placed a moratorium on new Internet access taxes. That moratorium was made permanent in 2015. The Trade Facilitation and Trade Enforcement Act established a permanent ban on the tax and made June 2020 the firm end date for seven states that currently impose a tax on Internet access.

Qualifying to Do Business
A state may require that foreign corporations **qualify** to conduct **intrastate** business in the state. The level of doing business that constitutes intrastate business for qualification purposes has been difficult to define. The MBCA lists several activities that do *not* require qualification. For example, soliciting—by mail or through employees—orders that require acceptance outside the state is not doing intrastate business requiring qualification. That exception allows a company to make sales in many states outside its home state without needing to qualify in those states. In addition, selling through independent contractors or owning real or personal property does not require qualification.

Also classified as not doing business for qualification purposes is conducting an **isolated transaction** that is completed within 30 days and is not one in the course of repeated transactions of a like nature. This isolated transaction *safe harbor* allows a tree grower to bring Christmas

[2]*Complete Auto Transit, Inc. v. Brady*, 430 U.S. 274 (1977).

[3]*Amerada Hess Corp. v. Director of Taxation*, 490 U.S. 66 (1989).

[4]*American Trucking Ass'ns, Inc. v. Scheiner*, 483 U.S. 266 (1987).

[5]*American Trucking Ass'ns, Inc. v. Michigan Public Service Commission*, 545 U.S. 429 (2005).

trees into a state to sell them to one retailer. However, a Christmas tree retailer who comes into a state for 29 days before Christmas and sells to consumers from a street corner is required to qualify. Although both merchants have consummated their transactions within 30 days, the grower has engaged in only one transaction, but the retailer has engaged in a series of transactions.

Maintaining an office to conduct intrastate business, selling personal property not in interstate commerce, entering into contracts relating to local business or sales, or owning or using real estate for general corporate purposes constitute doing intrastate business. Passive ownership of real estate for investment, however, does not.

Maintaining a stock of goods within a state from which to fill orders, even if the orders are taken or accepted outside the state, is doing intrastate business requiring qualification. Performing service activities such as machinery repair and construction work may be doing intrastate business.

Qualification Requirements If required to qualify to do intrastate business in a state, a foreign corporation must apply for a **certificate of authority** from the secretary of state, pay an application fee, maintain a registered office and a registered agent in the state, file an annual report with the secretary of state, and pay an annual fee.

Doing intrastate business without qualifying usually subjects a foreign corporation to a fine, in some states as much as $10,000. The MBCA disables the corporation to use the state's courts to bring a lawsuit until it obtains a certificate of authority. The corporation may defend itself in the state's courts, however, even if it has no certificate of authority.

LOG ON

Go to
www.usregisteredagents.com
Several online businesses have been created to relieve corporations of the burden of qualifying to do business and maintaining a registered agent in each state in which it does business. US Registered Agents is one such business. Can you find the cost of hiring US Registered Agents to be a corporation's registered agent?

In the case of *Drake Manufacturing Company, Inc. v. Polyflow, Inc.*, the court held that the seller was not exempt from the requirement to obtain a certificate of authority to conduct business in Pennsylvania. Consequently, the trial court was duty bound to rule in the buyer's favor on motions regarding the seller's failure to submit a certificate of authority into court.

Drake Manufacturing Company, Inc. v. Polyflow, Inc.
109 A.3d 250 (Pa. Super. Ct. 2015)

In 2007, Drake Manufacturing Company, Inc. ("Drake"), a Delaware corporation, entered into an agreement to sell equipment to Polyflow, Inc. ("Polyflow"). Drake shipped the equipment from its plant in Sheffield, Pennsylvania, to Polyflow's business establishment in Oaks, Pennsylvania, and other out-of-state destinations including California, Holland, and Canada. The record includes approximately 75 bills from Drake to Polyflow for equipment between August 2008 and April 2009.

In June 2009, Drake brought a civil complaint against Polyflow for breach of contract for failure to pay for the equipment delivered. In August 2009, Polyflow answered the complaint and alleged that Drake was not authorized to bring a suit in Pennsylvania as a foreign corporation. In a short nonjury trial in February 2014, Drake presented evidence of Polyflow's failure to pay. Polyflow's only defense was that Drake lacked capacity to sue because Drake failed to obtain a certificate of authority from the Department of State authorizing Drake to do business in Pennsylvania as a foreign corporation.

Drake did not possess a certificate of authority at the time of trial, and Drake failed to apply for a certificate of authority until the day of trial. At the close of trial, Polyflow moved for compulsory nonsuit due to Drake's lack of capacity to sue and its failure to submit a certificate of authority into evidence. The trial court denied Polyflow's motion for nonsuit and announced its verdict in favor of Drake in the amount of $291,766.61.

On March 5, 2014, Polyflow filed a post-trial motion seeking judgment notwithstanding the verdict (JNOV) due to Drake's failure to submit a certificate of authority into evidence. On March 17, 2014, the Department of State issued Drake a certificate of authority to do business in Pennsylvania as a foreign corporation. On April 17, 2014, almost two months after the verdict, Drake submitted its certificate of authority in response to Polyflow's post-trial motions.

On May 23, 2014, relying on Drake's delinquent certificate of authority, the trial court denied Polyflow's post-trial motions. Polyflow thereupon filed an appeal from the money judgment entered in favor of Drake for breach of contract. Additionally, Polyflow argued that the trial court erroneously denied its motion for JNOV because at the time of trial, Drake was not registered to conduct business in Pennsylvania and thus lacked capacity to sue under 15 Pa. Cons. Stat. §§ 4121, 4122, and 4141. 15 Pa. Cons. Stat. § 4121 provides:

A foreign business corporation, before doing business in this Commonwealth, shall procure a certificate of authority to do so from the Department of State, in the manner provided in this subchapter. . . .

Section 4122(a) identifies activities which do not constitute "doing business," either individually or collectively, and provides:

Without excluding other activities that may not constitute doing business in this Commonwealth, a foreign business corporation shall not be considered to be doing business in this Commonwealth for the purposes of this subchapter by reason of carrying on in this Commonwealth any one or more of the following acts:

(1) Maintaining or defending any action or administrative or arbitration proceeding or effecting the settlement thereof or the settlement of claims or disputes; (2) Holding meetings of its directors or shareholders or carrying on other activities concerning its internal affairs; (3) Maintaining bank accounts; (4) Maintaining offices or agencies for the transfer, exchange and registration of its securities or appointing and maintaining trustees or depositaries with relation to its securities; (5) Effecting sales through independent contractors; (6) Soliciting or procuring orders, whether by mail or through employees or agents or otherwise, and maintaining offices therefor, where the orders require acceptance without this Commonwealth before becoming binding contracts; (7) Creating as borrower or lender, acquiring or incurring, obligations or mortgages or other security interests in real or personal property; (8) Securing or collecting debts or enforcing any rights in property securing them; (9) Transacting any business in interstate or foreign commerce; (10) Conducting an isolated transaction completed within a period of 30 days and not in the course of a number of repeated transactions of like nature; (11) Inspecting, appraising and acquiring real estate and mortgages and other liens thereon and personal property and security interests therein, and holding, leasing, conveying and transferring them, as fiduciary or otherwise.

Section 4141(a) provides:

[A] nonqualified foreign business corporation doing business in this Commonwealth within the meaning of Subchapter B (relating to qualification) shall not be permitted to maintain any action or proceeding in any court of this Commonwealth until the corporation has obtained a certificate of authority.

The Superior Court first concluded that Polyflow appropriately preserved for appeal the issue of Drake's lack of capacity to sue. The court then considered whether Polyflow was entitled to JNOV due to Drake's failure to submit a certificate of authority.

Jenkins, Judge

Applying section 4141(a), this Court has held that a foreign corporation that failed to obtain a certificate of authority could not bring suit in Pennsylvania, because entry into contract with the defendant, a Pennsylvania corporation, and its shipment of lighting fixtures to Pennsylvania on six occasions over approximately six months constituted "doing business in this Commonwealth." *Leswat Lighting Systems, Inc. v. Lehigh Valley Restaurant Group, Inc.*, 444 Pa. Super. 281, 663 A.2d 783, 785 (1995). The evidence demonstrates that Drake failed to submit a certificate of authority into evidence prior to the verdict in violation of 15 Pa.C.S. § 4121(a); therefore, the trial court should not have allowed Drake to prosecute its action. 15 Pa.C.S. § 4141(a).

The trial court contends that Drake is exempt from the certificate of authority requirement because it merely commenced suit in Pennsylvania to collect a debt, conduct that does not constitute "doing business" under section 4122(a)(1) and (8). Drake did much more, however, than file a suit or attempt to collect debt.

Drake maintains an office in Pennsylvania to conduct local business, conduct which "[typically] require[s] a certificate of authority." 15 Pa.C.S. § 4122, Committee Comment. Drake also entered into a contract with Polyflow, and, in dozens of occasions over an eight month period, shipped equipment to Polyflow's place of business in Pennsylvania—far more than the "isolated transaction" exception under section 4122(a)(10) or the six shipments over a six-month period that the Court previously held constituted "doing business." *See Leswat Lighting Systems, supra.* In short, Drake's conduct was "more regular, systematic, [and] extensive than that described in [section 4122(a), [thus] constitut[ing] the transaction of business and requir[ing] [Drake] to obtain a certificate of authority." *See* 15 Pa.C.S. § 4122, Committee Comment.

We also hold that Drake needed a certificate of authority to sue Polyflow in Pennsylvania for Polyflow's failure to pay for out-of-state shipments in California, Canada, and Holland. A foreign corporation that "does business" in Pennsylvania within the meaning of section 4122 must obtain a certificate in order to prosecute a lawsuit in this Commonwealth, regardless of whether the lawsuit itself concerns in-state conduct or out-of-state conduct. The trial court thus erred by denying Polyfow's motion for judgment n.o.v.

The trial court relied on Drake's delinquent certificate of authority as its basis for denying Polyflow's post-trial motions; however, our Supreme Court's decision in *Claudio v. Dean Machine Co.*, 574 Pa. 359, 831 A.2d 140 (2003), prohibits Drake from submitting evidence in post-trial proceedings that it failed to submit during trial due to its own lack of reasonable diligence.

Drake had no right to submit the certificate of authority into the record in the post-trial motion stage.

For the foregoing reasons, we hold that the trial court erred in denying Polyflow's motion for judgment n.o.v. We reverse the order denying Polyflow's post-trial motions and remand for entry of judgment n.o.v. in favor of Polyflow.

Judgment reversed. Case remanded for entry of judgment n.o.v. in favor of Polyflow.

Regulation of a Corporation's Internal Affairs

Regulation of the internal affairs of a corporation—that is, the relation between the corporation and its directors, officers, and shareholders—is usually exercised only by the state of incorporation. Nonetheless, a foreign corporation may conduct most of its business in a state other than the one in which it is incorporated. Such a corporation is called a **pseudo-foreign corporation** in the state in which it conducts most of its business.

A few states subject pseudo-foreign corporations to extensive regulation of their internal affairs, regulation similar to that imposed on their domestic corporations. California's statute requires corporations that have more than 50 percent of their business and ownership in California to elect directors by cumulative voting, to hold annual directors' elections, and to comply with California's dividend payment restrictions. Foreign corporations have raised many constitutional objections to the California statute, including violations of the Commerce clause and the Due Process clause.

The Delaware Supreme Court has made it clear that the California provision violates Delaware's well-established choice of law rules and the federal Constitution, holding that the internal affairs of Delaware corporations, in particular, the voting rights of shareholders, are to be adjudicated exclusively in accordance with Delaware law.[6]

Regulation of Foreign Nonprofit Corporations

The Model Nonprofit Corporation Act and other laws impose the same requirements and penalties on nonprofit corporations as are imposed on for-profit corporations.

For example, the MNCA requires a foreign nonprofit corporation to qualify to do intrastate business in a state. The failure to qualify prevents the foreign nonprofit corporation from using the state's courts to bring lawsuits and subjects it to fines for each day it transacts intrastate business without a certificate of authority.

Piercing the Corporate Veil

 LO41-4 Prevent a court from piercing a corporation's veil.

A corporation is a legal entity separate from its shareholders. Corporation law erects an imaginary wall between a corporation and its shareholders that protects shareholders from liability for a corporation's actions. Once shareholders have made their promised capital contributions to the corporation, they have no further financial liability. This means that contracts of a corporation are not contracts of its shareholders, and debts of a corporation are not debts of its shareholders.

Nonetheless, in order *to promote justice and to prevent inequity*, courts will sometimes ignore the separateness of a corporation and its shareholders by **piercing the corporate veil**. The primary consequence of piercing the corporate veil is that a corporation's shareholders may lose their limited liability.

Two general requirements must exist for a court to pierce the corporate veil: (1) **domination** of a corporation by its shareholders and (2) use of that domination for an **improper purpose**.

As an entity separate from its shareholders, a corporation should act for itself, not for its shareholders. If a shareholder causes a corporation to act to the personal

[6]*VantagePoint Venture Partners 1996 v. Examen, Inc.*, 871 A.2d 1108 (Del. 2005).

benefit of the shareholder, *domination*—the first require-ment for piercing the corporate veil—is proved. For exam-ple, a majority shareholder's directing a corporation to pay the shareholder's personal expenses is domination. Domination is also proved if the controlling sharehold-ers cause the corporation to fail to observe corporate for-malities (such as failing to hold shareholder and director meetings or to maintain separate accounting records). Some courts say that shareholder domination makes the corporation the *alter ego* (other self) of the shareholders. Other courts say that domination makes the corporation an *instrumentality* of the shareholders.

To prove domination, it is not sufficient, or even neces-sary, to show that there is only one shareholder. Many one-shareholder corporations will never have their veils pierced. However, nearly all corporations whose veils are pierced are close corporations because domination is more easily accomplished in a close corporation than in a publicly held one with many shareholders.

In addition to domination, there must be an *improper use* of the corporation. The improper use may be any of three types: defrauding creditors, circumventing a statute, or evading an existing obligation.

Defrauding Creditors   Shareholders must organize a corporation with sufficient capital to meet the initial capital needs of the business. Inadequate capitalization, called **thin capitalization**, is proved when capitalization is very small in relation to the nature of the business of the corporation and the risks the business necessarily entails.

Thin capitalization defrauds creditors of a corporation. An example of thin capitalization is forming a business with a high debt-to-equity ratio, such as a $10 million–asset business with only $1,000 of equity capital, with the shareholders sometimes contributing the remainder of the needed capital as secured creditors. By doing so, the shareholders elevate a portion of their bankruptcy repay-ment priority to a level above that of general creditors, thereby reducing the shareholders' risk. The high debt-to-equity ratio harms nonshareholder-creditors by failing to provide an equity cushion sufficient to protect their claims. In such a situation, either the shareholders will be liable for the corporation's debts or the shareholders' loans to the corporation will be subordinated to the claims of other creditors. As a result, the nonshareholder-creditors are repaid all of their claims prior to the shareholder-creditors receiving payment from the corporation.

Transfers of corporate assets to shareholders for less than fair market value (called **looting**) also defraud credi-tors. For example, shareholder-managers loot a corporation by paying themselves excessively high salaries or by having

the corporation pay their personal credit card bills. When such payments leave insufficient assets in the corporation to pay creditors' claims, a court will hold the shareholders liable to the creditors.

Frequently, the same shareholders may control two cor-porations that transact with each other. The shareholders may cause one corporation to loot the other. When such looting occurs between corporations of common owner-ship, courts pierce the veils of these corporations. This makes each corporation liable to the creditors of the other corporation. For example, a shareholder-manager oper-ates two corporations from the same office. Corporation 1 transfers inventory to Corporation 2, but it receives less than fair market value for the inventory. Also, both corpo-rations employ the same workers, but all of the wages are paid by Corporation 1. In such a situation, the veils of the corporations will be pierced, allowing the creditors of Corporation 1 to satisfy their claims against the assets of Corporation 2.

Looting may also occur when one corporation (called the **parent corporation**) owns at least a majority of the shares of another corporation (called the **subsidiary cor-poration**). Ordinarily, the parent is liable for its own obliga-tions and the subsidiary is liable for its own obligations, but the parent is not liable for its subsidiary's debts and the subsidiary is not liable for the parent's debts. Nonetheless, because a parent corporation is able to elect the directors of its subsidiary and therefore can control the management of the subsidiary, the parent may cause its subsidiary to transact with the parent in a manner that benefits the par-ent but harms the subsidiary.

For example, a parent corporation may direct its subsid-iary to sell its assets to the parent for less than fair value. Because the subsidiary has given more assets to the par-ent than it has received from the parent, creditors of the subsidiary have been defrauded. Consequently, a court will pierce the veil between the parent and its subsidiary and hold the parent liable to the creditors of the subsidiary.

To prevent the piercing of veils between them, affiliated corporations must not commingle their assets. Each corpo-ration must have its own books of accounts. Transactions between affiliated corporations must be recorded on the books of both corporations, and such transactions must be executed at fair value.

Circumventing a Statute   A corporation should not engage in a course of conduct that is prohibited by stat-ute. For example, a city ordinance may prohibit retail busi-nesses from being open on consecutive Sundays. To avoid the statute, a retail corporation forms a subsidiary owned entirely by the retail corporation; on alternate weeks, it leases its building and inventory to the subsidiary. A court will pierce the veil because the purpose of creating the subsidiary corporation is to circumvent the statutory prohibition. Consequently, both the parent and the subsidiary will be liable for violating the statute.

Evading an Existing Obligation Sometimes, a corporation will attempt to escape liability on a contract by reincorporating or by forming a subsidiary corporation. The new corporation will claim that it is not bound by the contract, even though it is doing the same business as was done by the old corporation. In such a situation, courts pierce the corporate veil and hold the new corporation liable on the contract.

For example, to avoid an onerous labor union contract, a corporation creates a wholly owned subsidiary and sells its entire business to the subsidiary. The subsidiary will claim that it is not a party to the labor contract and may hire nonunion labor. A court will pierce the veil between the two corporations because the subsidiary was created only to avoid the union contract.

Nonprofit Corporations
Like a for-profit corporation, a nonprofit corporation is an entity separate and distinct from its members. A member is not personally liable for a nonprofit corporation's acts or liabilities merely by being a member. However, a court may pierce the veil of a nonprofit corporation if it is used to defraud creditors, circumvent a statute, or evade an existing obligation, the same grounds on which a for-profit corporation's veil may be pierced.

For a summary of the law of piercing the corporate veil, see Figure 41.3. Note that the law of veil piercing also applies to other business forms we studied in Chapters 37, 38, 39, and 40, including LLCs and LLPs.

In the following case, the court considered 12 factors in deciding whether to pierce a corporation veil and impose liability on the corporation's shareholders and affiliates.

Supply Chain Assocs., LLC v. ACT Electronics, Inc.
30 Mass. L. Rep. 12 (Super. Ct. 2012)

Supply Chain Associates, LLC and Estream Solutions LLC are manufacturer's representatives and brokers that assist in the sale of electronic products. Their services were retained by ACT Electronics, Inc., a corporation specializing in manufacturing electronic devices and components. ACT agreed to pay Supply Chain and Estream commissions of 4 percent to 5 percent on sales brokered by them, including a sale to buyer Bloomberg LP. When ACT failed to pay the commissions, Supply Chain and Estream sued not only ACT, but also other business entities affiliated with ACT: Sun Act LLC, Sun Capital Partners II LP, Sun Capital Advisors II LP, Sun Capital Partners LLC, Sun Capital Partners Inc., Sun Capital Advisors Inc., and Sun Capital Partners Management LLC. In the trial court, Supply Chain and Estream argued that the veils between ACT and the other businesses should be pierced to make them liable for the commissions that ACT failed to pay.

ACT was a Delaware corporation based in Massachusetts. From its incorporation in 2002 to its bankruptcy in 2008, ACT employed approximately 400 full-time and part-time employees who worked at one of its three manufacturing facilities.

Sun Act is a limited liability company and was ACT's majority shareholder, owning 70 percent of ACT's stock. It also held the only voting shares of ACT.

Sun Capital Partners II, a Delaware limited partnership, is an investment firm that wholly owns Sun Act. Its limited partners include approximately 70 private and public investors, including university endowments, pension funds, financial institutions, and individuals. It provided Sun Act with capital to invest and obtain a majority shareholder interest in ACT.

Sun Capital Advisors II is the general partner of Sun Capital Partners II.

Sun Capital Partners, LLC, is the general partner of Sun Capital Advisors II.

Sun Capital Partners Inc., a Florida corporation, is also a private investment firm. Entities affiliated with Sun Capital Partners Inc. raise funds to invest in underperforming or financially distressed companies. Supply Chain and Estream allege that Sun Capital Partners Inc. is the de facto parent company of all the other defendants. The defendants counter that there is no direct or indirect ownership or contractual relationship between Sun Capital Partners Inc. and any other defendant or between Sun Capital Partners Inc. and ACT.

Sun Capital Advisors Inc. is a Florida corporation that also provides consulting and advisory services to companies. Sun Capital Advisors Inc. entered into a Mastery Advisory Agreement with Sun Capital Management, contracting to provide its services to various companies, including ACT.

Sun Capital Management, a Delaware limited liability company, provides consulting services to companies. On July 2, 2002, Sun Capital Management and ACT entered into a Management Services Agreement (MSA) by which Sun Capital Management would provide services to ACT's senior corporate management in exchange for an annual fee equal to the greater of $300,000 or 8 percent of ACT's EBITDA, that is, earnings before interest, taxes, dividends, and amortization.

The Defendant shareholders and affiliates of ACT asked the court to grant them summary judgment on the grounds that ACT's corporate veil may not be pierced to make the Defendants liable for the commissions ACT failed to pay Supply Chain and Estream.

Kirpalani, Judge

There are 12 factors to consider in deciding whether to pierce the corporate veil:

(1) common ownership; (2) pervasive control; (3) confused intermingling of business activity assets, or management; (4) thin capitalization; (5) nonobservance of corporate formalities; (6) absence of corporate records; (7) no payment of dividends; (8) insolvency at the time of the litigated transaction; (9) siphoning away of corporate assets by the dominant shareholders; (10) nonfunctioning of officers and directors; (11) use of the corporation for transactions of the dominant shareholders; (12) use of the corporation in promoting fraud.

Each of these factors will be considered in turn.

(a) Common Ownership. In a veil-piercing case, courts first consider whether a corporation is operated as a separate entity. The corporation is not operated as a separate entity where there is common control of a group of separate corporations engaged in a single enterprise. Yet, common ownership of stock of two or more corporations together with common management, standing alone, will not give rise to liability on the part of one corporation for the acts of another corporation or its employees.

It appears that Defendants had some common control of ACT. For example, Sun Act owned 70% of ACT's shares. Yet, Sun Act was not in complete control of ACT; it still had a fiduciary duty to the nonvoting stockholders who held 30% of the shares. ACT had to deliver value to the buyers for which it manufactured products. In addition, Congress Financial, ACT's independent lender, approved ACT's dividend declaration. This suggests the entity that shared common control of ACT operated at arm's length with ACT.

Supply Chain and Estream allege there was common control of ACT because some of the same people who served on ACT's Board were employed by Sun Capital or one of its related entities. Of particular importance to Supply Chain and Estream is that when John M. Pino, Jr. [an ACT vice president] informed Edward Duffy [the managing member of Estream] that ACT would not pay the commissions, Mr. Terry and Rick Walter were Directors of ACT. Terry and Walter were also employees of one of the related entities. Since the parties agree that Sun Act, Sun Capital Partners II, Sun Capital Advisors II, Sun Capital Partners, LLC, Sun Capital Partners, Inc., and Sun Capital Management do not have employees, the only Sun Capital entity that could have employed Terry and Walter at that time was Sun Capital Advisors, Inc. Directors and officers, not employees, control companies. Terry and Walter, as Sun Capital Advisor, Inc., employees, could not have controlled Sun Capital Advisors, Inc., and there was thus no common control between Sun Capital Advisors, Inc., and ACT when ACT refused to pay the commissions.

(b) Pervasive Control. A court will find that a corporation has been pervasively controlled when one corporation is carrying out tasks pursuant to another corporation's command, or when one corporation seeks permission from another before taking action on its own behalf. Courts consider whether the controlled corporation had a separate mind, will, or existence of its own.

There is no evidence that Defendants ran ACT as its own candy store. ACT maintained its own headquarters, minute books, accounting records, bank accounts, and budgets separate from Defendants. It also filed its own tax returns. There is evidence that at one point, on January 22, 2003, John M. Pino, Sr., [an ACT board member] and Joseph Driscoll [an ACT officer] listed their addresses in Florida at the same business address as the Defendants. Other than this one incident in 2003, ACT and its Board members listed their addresses in Hudson, Massachusetts where ACT was located. In addition, the MSA does not show that Sun Capital Management pervasively controlled ACT. While Steven Liff [a vice president of both ACT and Sun Capital Management and an employee of Sun Capital Advisors, Inc.] might have been on both sides of the Management Sales Agreement [between ACT and Sun Capital Management], this was a conventional management sales agreement, and was approved by Congress Financial, an independent third-party lender.

(c) Confused Intermingling of Business Activity Assets, or Management. With respect to this factor, courts consider whether a business was clearly defined or whether there is a confused intermingling of activity of two or more corporations engaged in a common enterprise with substantial disregard of the separate nature of the corporate entities. *See, e.g., George Hyman Const. Co. v. Gateman*, 16 F. Supp. 2d 129, 151 (1st Cir. 1998) (company engaged in confused intermingling where used letterhead of one corporation in correspondence involving activity of another corporation and where vendors were confused about which company they were dealing with). ACT maintained separate headquarters, minute books, accounting records, bank

accounts, and budgets from Defendants, and ACT also filed its own tax returns. It is true that on January 22, 2003, ACT's Board Meeting Minutes reveal that Pino, Sr. and Driscoll listed their addresses in Florida, at the same business address as the Defendants. Supply Chain and Estream do not claim that they, or vendors, were ever confused about with whom they were dealing when they contracted with ACT. In fact, Sun Capital Partners, Inc., used Sun Capital Partner, Inc.'s letterhead in its dealings with Bloomberg. ACT used its own letterhead in its dealings with Bloomberg. Bloomberg also demanded buffer inventory from ACT; this shows Bloomberg understood that ACT, and not Sun Capital Partners, Inc., would be held liable for ACT's actions if it breached the contract with Bloomberg.

(d) Thin Capitalization. This factor focuses on whether the initial capitalization of the company was too thin. The Court considers the initial needs of the company, whether the company was given the up-front financing needed to perform its work, and whether, during its active corporate life, the company wanted for assets.

In this case, ACT was initially capitalized with over $7 million in equity and debt. ACT operated for six years after its initial capitalization, employing 400 full-time and part-time employees working at one of its three different manufacturing facilities. These factors tend to show that, based on the needs of the company, the initial capitalization was sufficient. *Evans v. Multicon Const. Corp.,* 30 Mass. App. Ct. [728,] at 734 [(1991)] ($500 was "unquestionably thin" but it was not "too thin" based on the needs of the company); *George Hyman Constr. Co.,* [v. Gateman] 16 F. Supp. 2d at [129,] 153 [(1st Cir. 1998)] ($28,000 capitalization in loan "was thin, but not anorexic" and was "not indicative of a company set up for financial failure").

(e) Nonobservance of Corporate Formalities. ACT took care to observe the corporate formalities. Separate tax returns were meticulously filed. In addition, throughout its years of activity in Massachusetts, ACT made routine filings with the Secretary of the Commonwealth.

(f) Absence of Corporate Records. ACT maintained its own corporate records, separate and apart from any of the Defendants' corporate records. Nothing in the record suggests that ACT's corporate records were ever either missing or fudged.

(g) No Payment of Dividends. Corporations in the normal course should be paying dividends, or at a minimum making conscious decisions not to do so. In this case, ACT declared a dividend to its shareholders, which resulted in SunAct's acquiring $1.86 million and ACT's other non-Defendant shareholders acquiring $1.14 million. There is nothing unusual about the payment of dividends, especially where, as here, ACT retained in excess of $1 million in cash, in addition to lines of credit, accounts receivable, and inventory. In addition, Congress Financial, ACT's independent lender, approved this distribution.

(h) Insolvency at the Time of the Litigated Transaction. The test for insolvency is whether the corporation, at any time while it was active, experienced difficulty in paying debts as they became due. The time considered for the test of insolvency is not a single point in time but rather the duration of the contested transactions between the parties. In this case, the time period considered for this factor begins on January 14, 2003, when Supply Chain entered into a Sales Representative Agreement with ACT. During ACT's first year of existence, ACT repaid all subordinated promissory notes outstanding to ACT's investors in the amount of $3 million plus accrued interest. Congress Financial approved ACT's repayment of these loans. There is no evidence on the record, other than the extrajudicial statements Bloomberg and the ACT's vendors made to Duffy, that ACT experienced difficulty in paying debts as they became due.

(i) Siphoning Away of Corporate Assets by the Dominant Shareholders. To show that there was siphoning away of corporate assets, there must be credible evidence of subterfuge or channeling excessive payments. This can be shown through, for example, payments or dividends to officers, directors or stockholders or the Internal Revenue Service challenging payments to officers or directors.

Here, it is undisputed that, after the dividend payment, ACT retained in excess of $1 million in cash in addition to lines of credit, accounts receivable, and inventory, and that Congress Financial, ACT's independent lender, was aware of, and approved, ACT's dividend payment. In addition, it is undisputed that the payment of management fees made pursuant to the MSA were also approved by Congress Financial, and that these types of agreements are common in the private equity industry. The IRS never challenged any of these payments.

(j) Non-functioning of Officers and Directors. This factor asks the court to consider whether the officers and directors functioned actively. There is nothing in the summary judgment record to support that ACT's officers and directors were non-functioning.

(k) Use of the Corporation for Transactions of the Dominant Shareholders. The test here is whether the Defendants used the corporation in aid of transactions in which they had substantial interest. ACT's one and only dividend distribution was recorded in the corporate records. The other transaction that Supply Chain and Estream consider to be evidence of abuse of the corporate form was the payment of management fees. These fees are not extravagant beyond any reasonable business usage, and, indeed, were approved by Congress Financial, ACT's third-party lender. *Contra, George Hyman Constr. Co.,* 16 F. Supp. 2d at 157

(transaction extravagant where shareholders purchased Ferrari and Mercedes for their own use through corporation).

(l) Use of the Corporation in Promoting Fraud. Finally, the court considers whether there is any basis upon which to conclude that the corporation was used to perpetrate a fraud. There is no such basis here. The record contains no evidence warranting a finding that ACT was established or operated so as to misrepresent or divert assets. The facts that in the six years that it operated, ACT employed 400 full-time and part-time employees located at one of its three manufacturing facilities, and that ACT delivered value to its customers, suggest that ACT was established to manufacture products, not to swindle sales representatives, like Supply Chain and Estream, out of money.

When determining whether to pierce the corporate veil, one examines the twelve factors to form an opinion whether the overall structure and operation misleads. There is present in the cases which have looked through the corporate form an element of dubious manipulation and contrivance, finagling, such that corporate identities are confused and third parties cannot be quite certain with what they are dealing.

Here, although Sun Act was a controlling shareholder of ACT, it did not own all of ACT's stock. It supplied ACT with some operating funds. ACT conducted some business that benefited the Defendants. But here, separate corporate boundaries were maintained, and third parties did not think of themselves as dealing with Sun Capital directly. Supply Chain and Estream in this case entered into a conventional brokering sales arrangement with ACT, and were not misled into doing so on the belief it was doing business with one of the Defendants.

In order to hold the Defendants liable for ACT's conduct, ACT's corporate veil must be pierced. Defendants have shown that, as a matter of law, Supply Chain and Estream cannot establish that the corporate veil should be pierced in this case, and therefore, the Defendants are entitled to summary judgment.

Summary judgment entered for the Defendants.

Figure 41.3   Examples of Piercing the Corporate Veil

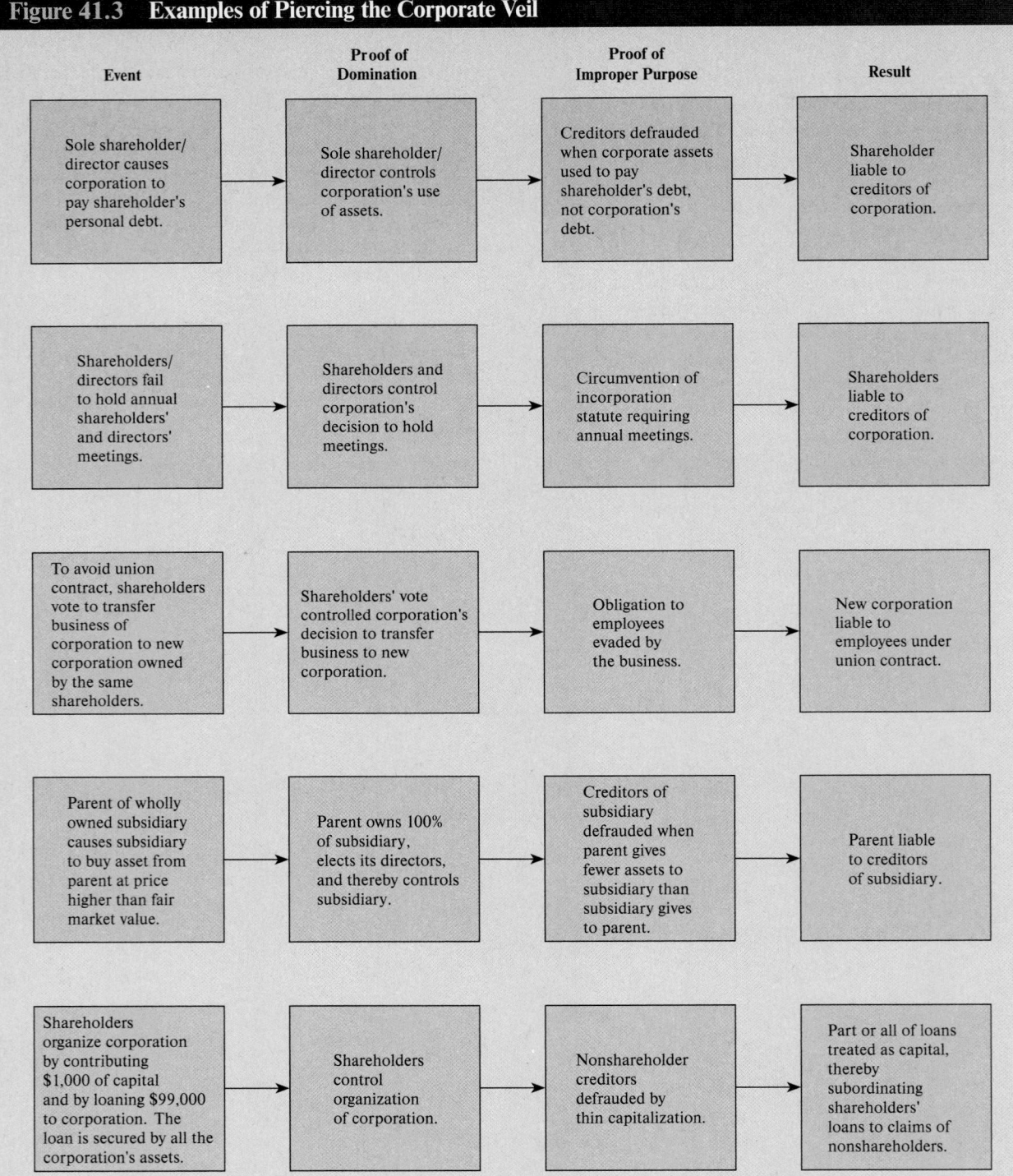

Event	Proof of Domination	Proof of Improper Purpose	Result
Sole shareholder/director causes corporation to pay shareholder's personal debt.	Sole shareholder/director controls corporation's use of assets.	Creditors defrauded when corporate assets used to pay shareholder's debt, not corporation's debt.	Shareholder liable to creditors of corporation.
Shareholders/directors fail to hold annual shareholders' and directors' meetings.	Shareholders and directors control corporation's decision to hold meetings.	Circumvention of incorporation statute requiring annual meetings.	Shareholders liable to creditors of corporation.
To avoid union contract, shareholders vote to transfer business of corporation to new corporation owned by the same shareholders.	Shareholders' vote controlled corporation's decision to transfer business to new corporation.	Obligation to employees evaded by the business.	New corporation liable to employees under union contract.
Parent of wholly owned subsidiary causes subsidiary to buy asset from parent at price higher than fair market value.	Parent owns 100% of subsidiary, elects its directors, and thereby controls subsidiary.	Creditors of subsidiary defrauded when parent gives fewer assets to subsidiary than subsidiary gives to parent.	Parent liable to creditors of subsidiary.
Shareholders organize corporation by contributing $1,000 of capital and by loaning $99,000 to corporation. The loan is secured by all the corporation's assets.	Shareholders control organization of corporation.	Nonshareholder creditors defrauded by thin capitalization.	Part or all of loans treated as capital, thereby subordinating shareholders' loans to claims of nonshareholders.

Ethics and Compliance in Action

Large multinational corporations and smaller closely held corporations use multiple corporations (and sometimes LLCs and limited partnerships) to manage their tax, contract, and tort liability. As we will learn in Chapter 42, American corporations set up subsidiaries in Delaware to take advantage of its low taxes. Also, if a corporation wants to engage in a risky new venture in a country with a volatile political climate, the corporation will almost always conduct the business in a wholly owned subsidiary.

Even in the absence of an abnormal risk, many corporations create a structure like the following, in which parts of the corporation's business, such as finance, sales, and manufacturing, are placed in separate corporations, each wholly owned by the parent corporation:

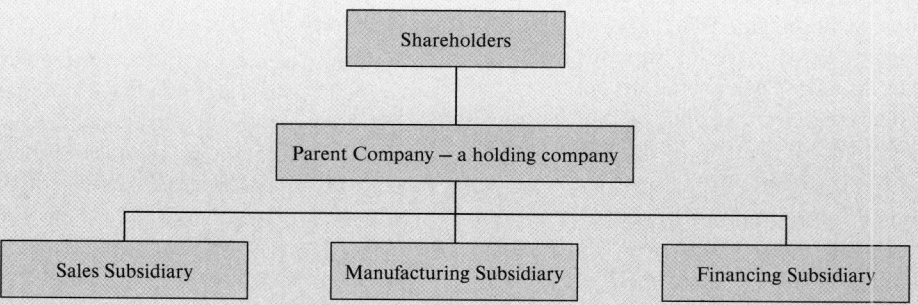

The parent company is a holding company that owns all the shares of the subsidiaries. Commonly, it also provides management services to the subsidiaries; in such cases, usually many employees working for the subsidiaries are actually employees of the parent because the employees often work for more than one subsidiary. Employees are assigned by the parent holding company, which receives a management fee from the subsidiaries and allocates employees to the subsidiaries as needed. The holding company will also be the capital-raising arm of the business because its cost of capital is usually lower than the individual subsidiaries' costs of capital due to diversification of risk.

As far as corporation law is concerned, this parent–subsidiary structure allows the business to isolate liability. Thus, if one subsidiary is unable to pay its obligations and its assets are lost, the assets of the other subsidiaries are preserved.

- Is it ethical for a business to set up such a parent–subsidiary structure? Does it matter if done for tax liability or business risk mitigation purposes? Would a profit maximizer be likely to set up such a structure? How about a stakeholder theorist?
- If a subsidiary becomes insolvent and is unable to pay its debts, would its creditors appreciate that neither the parent nor the other subsidiaries are liable to the creditors? Is it important that a creditor chose to do business with the subsidiary and could have examined its financial position before extending credit to the subsidiary?
- Would a tort victim who was injured by a product sold by the sales subsidiary appreciate that only its assets are available to pay his tort claim? Is it important that the victim is ignorant of corporation law and is not aware that the parent and subsidiaries are separate corporations? Does a tort victim have the same ability as a contract creditor to check out the corporate structure of the business before being injured by the product? Would a believer in justice theory see a difference between a contract creditor and a tort victim?

Problems and Problem Cases

1. You and four of your closest friends have decided to start a business that will purchase from banks and other financial institutions high-risk, subprime mortgage loans that are in default. You believe that you will be able to purchase the loans for no more than 40 percent of their face value. The plan is that the business will buy the loans by paying half the purchase amount in cash and the other half by issuing promissory notes due in six months to two years. You expect to turn a profit by restructuring the loans with the debtors, foreclosing against the real property securing the loans, or aggregating the loans and reselling them. You and your four friends are willing to invest $2 million each in the business. Needing an additional $10 million to start the venture, you and your four friends agree to allow 10 other investors to contribute equity of

$1 million each to the business. Only you and the four friends will be the managers of the business. The five of you want to share equally all decisions regarding the acquisition, management, and sale of the loans. You want the other 10 investors to be passive investors only with no say in the management of the business. However, the 10 other investors, who are contributing half the equity of the business, are concerned about protecting their investments. You have proposed that the business be formed as a limited liability company (LLC), but some of your friends believe that the corporation or the limited partnership is a better form. One friend says that the advantages of the corporation make it a superior business form. List the usual advantages of the corporate form of business. Explain why some of the usual advantages of the corporation are not likely to be fully available in this context.

2. Advocates of benefit corporations argue that they are resilient, offer strategic partnerships with sought-after like-minded companies, help customers identify trustworthy companies, attract capital of investors seeking socially conscience outlets for their money, and engage and retain quality employees. They point to a growing market for socially responsible investing, which is currently between $400 billion and $1 trillion. For many, benefit corporations are seen as the beginning of a historical moment in which some of the core ideas of business, and of the law that governs it, are being reconsidered. However, not everyone is so convinced. Kent Greenfield, a legal scholar who has worked for almost two decades in the corporate governance field, and has focused on many of the problems that motivate the recent move toward benefit corporations, calls himself a "skeptic." According to Greenfield, one reason that benefit corporations are problematic is because "[t]hey are based on a misreading of the law. Under current law, courts are quite deferential to the decisions of management. Under the "business judgment rule," courts will only set aside the decisions of management if they are tainted with self-interest or grossly misinformed. (And then only rarely.) So under current law, if a board wants to support charitable causes, pay employees more, or voluntarily reduce pollutive emissions, there is no doubt that they can do so without fearing legal recourse." Further, Greenfield believes that benefit corporations "do not protect companies from market pressure. Because not all companies will choose to become benefit corporations, those that do will suffer competitive disadvantage in the capital market, at least in the short term. Some shareholders may accept the lower returns implicit in the benefit corporation framework, but most

will not. So the cost of capital will be higher for benefit corporations than for their nonbenefit competitors. The problem with this is that over time, a focus on values other than shareholder profit will appear to be hurtful to a company's fortunes. The way to make sure attentiveness to social needs won't hurt a company? Level the playing field to mandate such attentiveness by all corporations. This, of course, is not what benefit corporation statutes do."[7] Do you agree with Greenfield's critiques? Is it true that benefit corporations "don't add much" from a legal and business standpoint, and may even hurt other socially conscious companies?

3. Hellyer Avenue Limited Partnership (HALP) was formed under California law for the purpose of developing, constructing, and managing a headquarters building in California for a communications company. The principal office and place of business of HALP also were in California. HALP's general partners were Mission West Properties L.P. (MWLP) and Republic Properties Corporation. The three limited partners were Steven Grigg, David Peter, and Mentmore Partners LLC. Republic, Grigg, Peter, and Mentmore sued MWLP, the managing general partner of HALP, and Mission West Properties Inc. (MWINC), the general partner of MWLP, for improperly diluting their interests in MWLP and failing to make owed distributions. The suit was brought in a Maryland state court. MWLP was formed as a limited partnership under Delaware law, but maintained its principal place of business in California. MWINC, the general partner of MWLP, was incorporated initially under the laws of California, but later was re-incorporated in 1999 under the laws of Maryland. As required under Maryland law, MWINC named a registered agent in Maryland as part of its re-incorporation under Maryland law. Were MWLP and MWINC correct in arguing that the Maryland court had no jurisdiction over them?

4. Travis Granato, a resident of Michigan, traveled to New York City to visit his brother. While there, he stopped in an electronics store in the Union Square area, 14th Street Photo, a New York corporation. 14th Street Photo's assets were entirely located in New York State. It did, however, sell its products in interstate commerce through its website, including $45,000 of merchandise sold over the web in the previous year to residents of Michigan. When a customer ordered from its website, 14th Street Photo delivered that item to the customer using either UPS or FedEx. Granato became aware of 14th Street Photo and its products by

[7]Kent Greenfield, "A Skeptic's View of Benefit Corporations," *Emory Corporate Governance and Accountability Review* 1, no.1 (2015), pp. 17–21.

searching online, and he decided to stop by 14th Street Photo's store to check out a Nikon camera in which he was interested. Granato purchased the camera at 14th Street Photo's store while he was in New York. He was given possession of the camera in New York, and he carried it back with him to Michigan. Once there, he discovered that the camera was not new, but reconditioned. He called 14th Street Photo, but it refused to refund his money. Granato sued 14th Street Photo in a Michigan trial court. Did the Michigan court have jurisdiction over 14th Street Photo?

5. Mead Corporation, an Ohio corporation in the business of producing and selling paper, packaging, and school and office supplies, also owned Lexis/Nexis, the electronic research service. Either as a separate subsidiary or as a division of Mead, Lexis was subject to Mead's oversight, but Mead did not manage its day-to-day affairs. Mead was headquartered in Ohio, while a separate management team ran Lexis out of its headquarters in Illinois. The two businesses maintained separate manufacturing, sales, and distribution facilities, as well as separate accounting, legal, human resources, credit and collections, purchasing, and marketing departments. Mead's involvement was generally limited to approving Lexis's annual business plan and any significant corporate transactions that Lexis wished to undertake. Mead managed Lexis's free cash, which was swept nightly from Lexis's bank accounts into an account maintained by Mead. The cash was reinvested in Lexis's business, but Mead decided how to invest it. Neither business was required to purchase goods or services from the other. Lexis, for example, was not required to purchase its paper supply from Mead and in fact purchased most of its paper from other suppliers. Neither received any discount on goods or services purchased from the other, and neither was a significant customer of the other.

In 1994, Mead sold Lexis for $1.5 billion, realizing a capital gain of more than $1 billion. Mead did not report any of this gain as business income on its 1994 Illinois tax return, taking the position that it was non-business income and should be allocated entirely to Mead's domestic state, Ohio. Did the Supreme Court of the United States agree with Mead?

6. B & D Shrimp, a Delaware corporation, made a contract in Texas to sell a commercial shrimp boat to Donald Gosch and Jesse Bach. Gosch and Bach paid $5,000 down and received immediate possession of the boat in Texas, where they would shrimp in the coastal waters. The contract stated that Gosch and Bach would get title to the boat after transferring a cabin cruiser to Shrimp and paying 15 percent of the cash proceeds from the boat's daily shrimp catches for the next calendar year. When Gosch and Bach defaulted on the contract, Shrimp sued Gosch and won the case. Shrimp, however, had not obtained a certificate of authority to do business in Texas. Twenty days after the judgment was entered, Gosch contested the judgment on the grounds that Shrimp, by failing to qualify to do business, could not use Texas's courts to obtain a judgment against Gosch. Shrimp decided at that time, therefore, to obtain a certificate of authority. Is the judgment for Shrimp against Gosch valid?

7. Ryan, a resident of Connecticut, is an investment banker in New York City and has an apartment in New York City. Cerullo is a resident of New York and owns Cerullo & Company, an accounting firm incorporated in New York with its principal office in Tarrytown, New York. Ryan retains Cerullo to prepare Ryan's federal, Connecticut, and New York personal income tax returns. All meetings between Ryan and Cerullo take place in New York, Ryan communicates exclusively with New York tax department personnel, and Cerullo & Company generates a majority of its revenues from persons residing or doing business in New York. Considering the tax services Cerullo provides to Ryan, is Cerullo required to qualify to do business in Connecticut?

8. Lawrence Small formed Seatwo LLC to operate a Burger King restaurant in Wyoming. Seatwo was capitalized by $500 of contributions from its three members: Small, $250; his wife, $125; one of their children, $125. Gasstop Two LLC owned real property, which it leased to Seatwo beginning June 2000. The payments would total almost $1 million over the term of the lease. Seatwo also borrowed $350,000 to obtain furniture and equipment for the new Burger King operation and had a $15,000 line of credit. Unfortunately, Seatwo never turned a profit and ceased operations in October 2003 due to its poor location and lack of customers. Despite operating at a loss, Seatwo had made rental payments to Gasstop until it ceased business in 2003. Gasstop sued Small and his wife for the remaining $237,000 payments under the lease, arguing that the veil should be pierced between the LLC and the Smalls. What grounds did Gasstop use to argue for piercing the veil? Did the court agree with Gasstop?

9. New York law required that every taxicab company carry $10,000 of accident liability insurance for each cab in its fleet. The purpose of the law was to ensure that passengers and pedestrians injured by cabs operated by these companies would be adequately compensated for their injuries. Carlton organized 10 corporations, each

owning and operating two taxicabs in New York City. Each of these corporations carried $20,000 of liability insurance. Carlton was the principal shareholder of each corporation. The vehicles, the only freely transferable assets of these corporations, were collateral for claims of secured creditors. The 10 corporations were operated more or less as a unit with respect to supplies, repairs, and employees. Walkovszky was severely injured when he was run down by one of the taxicabs. He sued Carlton personally, alleging that the multiple corporate structure amounted to fraud upon those who might be injured by the taxicabs. Should the court pierce the corporate veil to reach Carlton individually?

10. REIS Inc. owns, constructs, and manages 25 shopping malls throughout the United States and Canada. REIS is concerned that the failure of any one mall will be a substantial financial loss that will cause the entire business to fail. What parent–subsidiary structure do you recommend REIS create to solve the liability risks of operating 25 malls? What roles will the parent corporation undertake after the subsidiary structure has been established? List the dos or don'ts that will help prevent a piercing of the veils between the subsidiaries and between the parent company and its subsidiaries.

11. Castleberry, Branscum, and Byboth each owned one-third of the shares of a furniture-moving business, Texan Transfer Inc. Branscum formed Elite Moving Company, a business that competed with Texan Transfer. Castleberry objected and sued to claim part ownership of Elite Moving. Branscum threatened Castleberry that he would not receive any return on his investment in Texan Transfer unless he abandoned his claim of ownership of Elite Moving. Consequently, Castleberry sold his shares back to Texan Transfer for a $42,000 promissory note. Gradually, Elite Moving took over more and more of the business of Texan Transfer. Texan Transfer allowed Elite Moving to use its employees and trucks. Elite Moving advertised for business, while Texan Transfer did not. Elite Moving prospered, while Texan Transfer's business declined. As a result, Castleberry was paid only $1,000 of the $42,000 promissory note. Did Castleberry have any grounds to hold Branscum liable for the unpaid portion of the note?

12. John Hildreth was the sole shareholder, director, and officer of a New Jersey corporation, HCE Inc., also referred to as HCE-NJ. Engaged in the construction business, HCE-NJ began to do business in Columbia, Maryland. However, Hildreth did not register HCE-NJ as a foreign corporation in Maryland, as required by Maryland law. In September 1998, HCE-NJ and Tidewater entered negotiations for the long-term rental of a crane that HCE-NJ intended to use in connection with a construction project in Alexandria, Virginia. Hildreth made clear to Tidewater that he was acting for HCE, but neither said nor was asked where that company was incorporated. He informed Frank Kolbe, a Tidewater representative, that the company had an office in Columbia, Maryland. Kolbe visited both the Columbia office and a job site. He testified that the company "didn't appear to be a fly-by-night operation," but had "a nice office suite" and "numerous employees." The job site was also substantial, with "a huge warehouse," a rail siding, and "hundreds of metal building panels." Kolbe assumed that HCE-NJ was a Maryland corporation because it had an office in Columbia. Tidewater and HCE-NJ signed a series of daily contracts. Hildreth did not sign the contracts, which were signed on behalf of HCE-NJ by some other employee. When payments were not made in late 1998 and early 1999, Tidewater repossessed the equipment. At the time, Tidewater was owed $47,246. Tidewater sued Hildreth on the grounds Hildreth was personally liable for the debts incurred by HCE-NJ because the corporation failed to qualify to do business in Maryland and that otherwise HCE's corporate veil should be pierced. Was Hildreth found personally liable?

13. Janelle Golino controls 65 percent of the voting shares of J-Go Web Solutions Inc. Golino is also the board chair and CEO of J-Go, and she controls the board of directors, all of which she elects by exercising the voting power of her shares. Her 16-year-old daughter is a nonvoting member of the board of directors, for which service she receives annual compensation of $45,000, half the fee paid to the voting directors. J-Go's voting directors have approved the fee paid to Golino's daughter. Golino has elected her daughter to the board of directors because her daughter is extremely bright and experienced for someone of her age, having attended business meetings with her mother for the last three years and regularly discussed business decisions with her mother for the last five years. Thirty-five percent of J-Go's voting shares are owned by public investors, as are all the shares that have no right to vote in directors elections. When J-Go has a dispute with one of its creditors and fails to pay a debt, the creditor asks a court to pierce the veil of J-Go and hold Golino personally liable for the debt. Is there grounds for the court to find Golino personally liable for the obligations of J-Go?

Organization and Financial Structure of Corporations

Y ou and three friends have decided to incorporate a business that will buy and sell art online that focuses on the work of up-and-coming artists. The plan is for each of you to own equal shares of the business and manage it together. The business has not yet been incorporated.

- You and your associates identify five mixed media art pieces you want to purchase to launch the site. To reduce your personal liability on the contracts to purchase the art, what should you do prior to signing the purchase contracts?

- One of your associates says that she wants to incorporate the business because a corporation's shares are freely transferable, making it easy for shareholders to liquidate their investments. You know better. Explain to her why free transferability of the shares as a legal matter is a problem for all of you. Also explain why free transferability of the shares as a practical matter does not exist. What could you do to address the share transferability issues? Sketch the contents of a buy–sell agreement that addresses all the transferability issues.

LEARNING OBJECTIVES

After studying this chapter, you should be able to:

42-1 Appreciate the risk of liability for corporate promoters.

42-2 Understand the process for incorporating a business.

42-3 Know the appropriate sources for financing a business.

42-4 Adopt appropriate share-transfer restrictions for a variety of contexts.

A PERSON DESIRING TO incorporate a business must comply with the applicable state or federal corporation law. Failing to comply can create various problems. For example, a person may make a contract on behalf of the corporation before it is incorporated. Is the corporation liable on this contract? Is the person who made the contract on behalf of the prospective corporation liable on the contract? Do the people who thought that they were shareholders of a corporation have limited liability, or do they have unlimited liability as partners of a partnership?

Promoters and Preincorporation Transactions

 Appreciate the risk of liability for corporate promoters.

A **promoter** of a corporation incorporates a business, organizes its initial management, and raises its initial capital. Typically, a promoter creates or discovers a business or an idea to be developed, finds people who are willing to invest in the business, negotiates the contracts necessary for the initial operation of the proposed venture, incorporates the business, and helps management start the operation of the business. Consequently, a promoter may engage in many acts prior to the incorporation of the business. As a result, the promoter may have liability on the contracts he negotiates on behalf of the prospective corporation. In addition, the corporation may *not* be liable on the contracts the promoter makes on its behalf.

Corporation's Liability on Preincorporation Contracts

A nonexistent corporation has no liability on contracts made by a promoter prior to its incorporation. This is because the corporation does not yet exist.

Even when the corporation comes into existence, it does not automatically become liable on a preincorporation contract made by a promoter on its behalf. It cannot be held liable as a principal whose agent made the contracts because the promoter was not its agent and the corporation was not in existence when the contracts were made.

The only way a corporation may become bound on a promoter's preincorporation contracts is by the corporation's **adoption** of the promoter's contracts. Adoption is similar to the agency concept of ratification, which is covered in Chapter 36. For a corporation to adopt a promoter's contract, the corporation must accept the contract with knowledge of all its material facts.

Acceptance may be express or implied. The corporation's knowing receipt of the benefits of the contract is sufficient for acceptance. For example, a promoter makes a preincorporation contract with a genetic engineer, requiring the engineer to work for a prospective corporation for 3 years. After incorporation, the promoter presents the contract to the board of directors. Although the board takes no formal action to accept the contract, the board allows the engineer to work for the corporation for one year as the contract provides and pays him the salary required by the contract. The board's actions constitute an acceptance of the contract, binding the corporation to the contract for its 3-year term. The *SmithStearn* case, which appears shortly, is another example of a corporation adopting a preincorporation contract.

Promoter's Liability on Preincorporation Contracts

A promoter and her copromoters are jointly and severally liable on preincorporation contracts the promoter negotiates in the name of the nonexistent corporation. This liability exists even when the promoters' names do not appear on the contract. Promoters are also jointly and severally liable for torts committed by their copromoters prior to incorporation.

A promoter retains liability on a preincorporation contract until **novation,** the substitution of a new contract in place of an old one, occurs. For novation to occur, the corporation and the third party must agree to release the promoter from liability and to substitute the corporation for the promoter as the party liable on the contract. Usually, novation will occur by express agreement of all the parties.

If the corporation is not formed, a promoter remains liable on a preincorporation contract unless the third party releases the promoter from liability. In addition, the mere formation of the corporation does not release a promoter from liability. A promoter remains liable on a preincorporation contract even after the corporation's adoption of the contract because adoption does not automatically release the promoter. The corporation cannot by itself relieve the promoter of liability to the third party; the third party must also agree, expressly or impliedly, to release the promoter from liability.

A few courts have held that a promoter is not liable on preincorporation contracts if the third party *knew of the nonexistence* of the corporation yet insisted that the promoter sign the contract on behalf of the nonexistent corporation. Other courts have found that the promoter is not liable if the third party clearly stated that he would *look only to the prospective corporation* for performance.

Courts have held that the Model Business Corporation Act (MBCA) permits a promoter to escape liability for preincorporation contracts when the promoter has made some effort to incorporate the business and believes the corporation is in existence. The MBCA rule is discussed in the section titled "Defective Attempts to Incorporate."

Obtaining a Binding Preincorporation Contract

While it may be desirable for the promoter to escape liability on a preincorporation contract, there is one disadvantage: Only when the promoter is liable on the preincorporation contract is the other party liable on the contract. This means that when the promoter is not liable on the contract, the other party to the contract may rescind the contract at any time prior to adoption by the corporation. Once the corporation has adopted the contract, the corporation and the third party are liable on it, and the contract cannot be rescinded without the consent of both parties.

To maintain the enforceability of a preincorporation contract prior to adoption, a promoter may want to be liable on a preincorporation contract at least until the corporation comes into existence and adopts the contract. To limit his liability, however, the promoter may wish to have his liability cease automatically upon adoption. The promoter should ensure that the contract has an **automatic novation clause**. For example, a preincorporation contract may read that "the promoter's liability on this contract shall terminate upon the corporation's adoption of this contract."

Instead of using automatic novation clauses, today most well-advised promoters incorporate the business prior to making any contracts for the corporation. That is, the well-advised promoter makes *no* preincorporation contracts. Instead, she makes contracts only for existing corporations. As a result, only the corporation and the third party—and not the promoter—have liability on the contract. This approach makes sense now that creating a corporation can be done fast and efficiently, often with a few keystrokes.

Preincorporation Share Subscriptions

Promoters sometimes use *preincorporation share subscriptions* to ensure that the corporation will have adequate capital when it begins its business. Under the terms of this type of a share subscription, a prospective shareholder offers

---

SmithStearn Yachts, Inc. v. Gyrographic Communications, Inc.
2006 Conn. Super. LEXIS 1927 (June 23, 2006)

SmithStearn Yachts, Inc., a Delaware corporation providing luxury yachting services in Connecticut, agreed to a contract with Gyrographic Communications, Inc., a California company, by which Gyrographic would provide advertising, marketing, and promotional services to SmithStearn. When SmithStearn sued Gyrographic for breaching the contract, Gyrographic countered that SmithStearn was not a party to the contract because the contract was purportedly made with a limited liability company, SmithStearn Yachts LLC, not the corporation that was suing Gyrographic.

Rodriguez, Judge

Leathern Stearn, the purported promoter and president of Smith-Stearn Yachts, Inc., executed the agreement with Gyrographic on behalf of SmithStearn, LLC, an entity that never came into existence. Rather, the plaintiff, SmithStearn Yachts, Inc.[,] was formed. SmithStearn Yachts, Inc. contends that it has standing to bring this action because it assumed and ratified, both explicitly and implicitly, the agreement that was made on its behalf, prior to its formation.

Generally, a corporation is not bound by contracts entered into on its behalf prior to its existence. A corporation can, however, acquire rights and subject itself to duties with respect to preincorporation matters. A contract made in the name of an inchoate corporation can be enforced after the corporation is organized on the principle of ratification. Ratification is defined as the affirmance by a person of a prior act which did not bind him but which was done or professedly done on his account. Ratification requires acceptance of the results of the act with an intent to ratify, and with full knowledge of all the material circumstances.

A corporation may after its organization become liable on preliminary contracts made by its promoters by expressly adopting such contracts or by receiving the benefits from them. Although SmithStearn Yachts, Inc. was formed after the execution of the agreement, it received the benefit of the services pursuant to the agreement. Gyrographic worked toward developing letterheads, business cards, and other marketing material for SmithStearn Yachts, Inc. SmithStearn Yachts, Inc. made payments to Gyrographic, which SmithStearn Yachts, Inc. then recorded in its books. Thus, SmithStearn Yachts, Inc. received the benefits of the agreement and also fulfilled the obligations under it, thereby ratifying the agreement.

Furthermore, ratification, adoption, or acceptance of a preincorporation contract by a promoter need not be expressed, but may be implied from acts or acquiescence on the part of the corporation or its authorized agents. Thus, a corporation's act of suing on a preincorporation contract is in itself an adoption of the contract. SmithStearn Yachts, Inc. implicitly ratified the agreement when it brought this action. By suing under the agreement, SmithStearn Yachts, Inc. is also assuming the liabilities under it, thereby enforcing and adopting the agreement.

Motion to dismiss denied in favor of SmithStearn Yachts, Inc.

---

to buy a specific number of the corporation's shares at a stated price. Under the MBCA, a prospective shareholder may not revoke a preincorporation subscription for a six-month period, in the absence of a contrary provision in the subscription. Generally, corporate acceptance of preincorporation subscriptions occurs by action of the board of directors after incorporation.

Promoters have no liability on preincorporation share subscriptions. They have a duty, however, to make a good faith effort to bring the corporation into existence. When a corporation fails to accept a preincorporation subscription or becomes insolvent, the promoter is not liable to the disappointed subscriber, in the absence of fraud or other wrongdoing by the promoter.

Today, most promoters incorporate the business and obtain promises to buy shares from prospective shareholders. These promises, which may take the form of postincorporation subscriptions, are discussed later in this chapter.

Relation of Promoter and Prospective Corporation

A promoter of a nonexistent corporation is not an agent of the prospective corporation. A promoter is also not an agent of prospective investors in the business because they did not appoint him and they have no power to control him.

Although not an agent of the proposed corporation or its investors, a promoter owes a **fiduciary duty** to the corporation and to its prospective investors. A promoter owes such parties a duty of *full disclosure* and *honesty*. For example, a promoter breaches this duty when he diverts money received from prospective shareholders to pay his expenses, unless the shareholders agree to such payment. The fiduciary duty also prevents a promoter from diverting a business opportunity from the corporation and giving it to himself instead. In addition, the promoter may not purchase shares of the corporation at a price lower than that paid by the public shareholders.

A promoter may not profit personally by transacting secretly with the corporation in his personal capacity. The promoter's failure to disclose his interest in the transaction and the material facts permits the corporation to rescind the transaction or to recover the promoter's secret profit. On the other hand, the promoter's full disclosure of his interest and the material facts of the transaction to an independent board of directors that approves the transaction prevents the corporation from recovering the promoter's profit. Note, however, that when a promoter is a director, approval of the transaction by the board of directors may not be sufficient; the transaction may need to be intrinsically fair to the corporation.

Liability of Corporation to Promoter

Valuable as the services of a promoter may be to a prospective corporation and to society, a corporation is generally not required to compensate a promoter for her promotional services, or even her expenses, unless the corporation has agreed expressly to compensate the promoter. The justification for this rule is that the promoter is self-appointed and acts for a corporation that is not in existence.

Nonetheless, a corporation may choose to reimburse the promoter for her reasonable expenses and to pay her the value of her services to the corporation. Corporations often compensate their promoters with shares. The MBCA permits the issuance of shares for a promoter's preincorporation services.

To ensure that she is compensated for her services, a promoter may tie herself to a person or property that the corporation needs to succeed. For example, a promoter may purchase the invention that the corporation was formed to exploit. Another way to ensure compensation is by the promoter's dominating the board of directors during the early months of its life. By doing so, the promoter may direct the corporation to compensate her, but only if the compensation is reasonable and, therefore, fair to the corporation.

Incorporation

LO42-2 Understand the process for incorporating a business.

Anyone seeking to incorporate a business must decide where to do so. If the business of a proposed corporation is to be primarily *intrastate*, it is usually cheaper to incorporate in the state where the corporation's business is to be conducted. For the business that is primarily *interstate*, however, the business may benefit by incorporating in a state different from the state in which it has its principal place of business. Because few businesses qualify to incorporate under federal law, that option is rarely exercised.

Incorporation fees and taxes, annual fees, and other fees such as those on the transfer of shares or the dissolution of the corporation vary considerably from state to state. Delaware has been a popular state in which to incorporate because its fees and taxes tend to be low. It also has judges experienced in resolving corporate disputes. A majority of Fortune 500 companies are incorporated in Delaware.

Not surprisingly, promoters frequently choose to incorporate in a state whose corporation statute and court decisions grant managers broad management discretion. For example, it is easier to pay a large dividend and to effect a merger in Delaware than in many other states.

Steps in Incorporation

There are only a few requirements for incorporation. It is a fairly simple process and can be accomplished inexpensively in most cases, and even wholly online. The steps prescribed by the incorporation statutes of the different states vary, but they generally include the following, which appear in the MBCA:

1. Preparing the articles of incorporation.
2. Signing and authenticating the articles by one or more incorporators.
3. Filing the articles with the secretary of state, accompanied by the payment of specified fees.

4. Receiving a copy of the articles of incorporation stamped "Filed" by the secretary of state, accompanied by a fee receipt. (Some states retain the old MBCA rule requiring receipt of a certificate of incorporation issued by the secretary of state.)

5. Holding an organization meeting for the purpose of adopting bylaws, electing officers, and transacting other business.

Articles of Incorporation   The basic governing document of the corporation is the **articles of incorporation** (sometimes called the charter). The articles are similar to a constitution. They state many of the rights and responsibilities of the corporation, its management, and its shareholders. Figure 42.1 lists the contents of the articles.

The corporation must have a name that is distinguishable from the name of any other corporation incorporated or qualified to do business in the state. The name must include the word *corporation, incorporated, company,* or *limited,* or the abbreviation *corp., inc., co.,* or *ltd.*

The MBCA does not require the inclusion of a statement of purpose in the articles. When a purpose is stated, it is sufficient to state, alone or together with specific purposes, that the corporation may engage in "any lawful activity."

The MBCA permits a corporation to have perpetual existence. If desired, the articles of incorporation may provide for a shorter duration.

Most of the state corporation statutes require the articles to recite the initial capitalization of the business. Usually, the statutes require that there be a minimum amount of initial capital, such as $1,000. Because such a small amount of capital is rarely enough to protect creditors adequately, the MBCA dispenses with the need to recite a minimum amount of capital. Instead, the thin capitalization rule seen in Chapter 41 protects creditors.

The articles may contain additional provisions not inconsistent with law for managing the corporation, regulating the internal affairs of the corporation, and establishing the powers of the corporation and its directors and shareholders. For example, these additional provisions may contain the procedures for electing directors, the quorum requirements for shareholders' and directors' meetings, and the dividend rights of shareholders.

The MBCA specifies that one or more persons, including corporations, partnerships, and unincorporated associations, may serve as the *incorporators.* Incorporators have no function beyond lending their names and signatures to the process of bringing the corporation into existence. No special liability attaches to a person merely because she serves as an incorporator.

Filing Articles of Incorporation   The articles of incorporation must be delivered to the office of the secretary of state, and a filing fee must be paid. The office of the secretary of state reviews the articles of incorporation that are delivered to it. If the articles contain everything that is required, the secretary of state stamps the articles "Filed" and returns a copy of the stamped articles to the corporation along with a receipt for payment of incorporation fees. Some states require a duplicate filing of the articles with an office—usually the county recorder's office—in the county in which the corporation has its principal place of business.

Figure 42.1   Contents of Articles of Incorporation (pursuant to MBCA)

The following *must* be in the articles:

1. The name of the corporation.
2. The number of shares that the corporation has authority to issue.
3. The address of the initial registered office of the corporation and the name of its registered agent.
4. The name and address of each incorporator.

The following *may* be included in the articles:

1. The names and addresses of the individuals who are to serve as the initial directors.
2. The purpose of the corporation.
3. Provisions for managing the business and regulating the affairs of the corporation.
4. Provisions regarding the powers of the corporation, its board of directors, and its shareholders.
5. The par value of shares of the corporation.
6. Provisions imposing personal liability on shareholders for debts of the corporation.
7. Provisions eliminating or limiting liability of directors to the corporation.
8. Provisions regarding indemnification of directors for liability for an action taken.

Ethics and Compliance in Action

Offshore and Domestic Tax Havens

In the last 20 years, some American companies have reincorporated all or part of their businesses in countries and states that offer favorable tax treatment. For example, an owner of several consumer product brand names, like Procter & Gamble, may incorporate subsidiaries in a country or state with lower taxes. The primary function of the subsidiaries is to own the business's trademarks. The subsidiaries charge the parent company high fees to use the trademarks. This parent–subsidiary structure allows the business to transfer billions of dollars each year from high-tax countries and states like the United States and New York into countries and states where the subsidiaries pay lower taxes. Delaware is the most-used domestic tax haven, but Nevada and Florida also provide favorable tax treatment for corporations. Offshore tax havens include Ireland, the British Virgin Islands, and Bermuda.

The number of American corporations using tax havens and the total assets located offshore change constantly. But recent studies suggest the practice is growing. A 2017 report found 366 of the country's 500 largest companies maintain almost 10,000 tax haven subsidiaries holding over $2.6 trillion in accumulated profits. Apple offshored the highest amount, $246 billion, thus avoiding $76.7 billion in U.S. taxes. Goldman Sachs held $31 billion offshore in 905 subsidiaries, the most of any company. Over 500 subsidiaries were incorporated in the Cayman Islands, despite the company not having an office there. These practices are a result of U.S. tax laws that historically permitted companies to not pay taxes on profits earned overseas if the profits are not repatriated, that is, not brought back to the states. Under such laws, the offshore profits could not be used by the corporations to pay dividends to, or buy back shares from, shareholders or to invest in assets in the United States. In 2018, tax laws were rewritten to end the practice of taxing U.S. companies when they bring home foreign profits. However, companies must pay a one-time repatriation tax on the estimated $2.5 trillion of foreign profits accumulated over the past 30 years. It remains to be seen how companies will react to the changes and whether it will spur increased investment in the U.S. as hoped.

- Is it ethical and socially responsible for an American corporation to incorporate its business wholly or in part in countries or states that have low tax rates? Would a profit maximizer incorporate where tax rates are lowest? Would a believer in rights theory?
- If you were a state legislator in a state with high income taxes that is losing incorporations to foreign countries and Delaware, what legislation would you introduce? Would your answer depend on whether you were a utilitarian or a believer in justice theory?

The existence of the corporation begins when the articles are filed by the secretary of state. Filing of the articles by the secretary of state is conclusive proof of the existence of the corporation.

Because the articles of incorporation embody the basic contract between a corporation and its shareholders, shareholders must approve most changes in the articles. For example, when the articles are amended to increase the number of authorized shares, shareholder approval is required.

The Organization Meeting After the articles of incorporation have been filed by the secretary of state, an organization meeting is held. Usually, it is the first formal meeting of the directors. Frequently, only bylaws are adopted and officers elected at the meeting. The function of the bylaws is to supplement the articles of incorporation by defining more precisely the powers, rights, and responsibilities of the corporation, its managers, and its shareholders and by stating other rules under which the corporation and its activities will be governed. Common contents of bylaws listed in Figure 42.2.

Figure 42.2   Contents of the Bylaws

1. The authority of the officers and the directors, specifying what they may or may not do.
2. The time and place at which the annual shareholders' meetings will be held.
3. The procedure for calling special meetings of shareholders.
4. The procedures for shareholders' and directors' meetings, including whether more than a majority is required for approval of specified actions.
5. Provisions for special committees of the board, defining their membership and the scope of their activities.
6. The procedures for the maintenance of share records.
7. The machinery for the transfer of shares.
8. The procedures and standards for the declaration and payment of dividends.
9. Any provision not inconsistent with the law or the articles of incorporation.

The MBCA gives the incorporators or the initial directors the power to adopt the bylaws. The board of directors holds the power to repeal and to amend the bylaws, unless the articles reserve this power to the shareholders. Under the MBCA, the shareholders, as the ultimate owners of the corporation, always retain the power to amend the bylaws, even if the directors also have such power. To be valid, bylaws must be consistent with the law and with the articles of incorporation.

If the organization meeting is the first meeting of the board of directors, the board may adopt a corporate seal for use on corporate documents, approve the form of share certificates, accept share subscriptions, authorize the issuance of shares, adopt preincorporation contracts, authorize reimbursement for promoters' expenses, and fix the salaries of officers.

Filing Annual Report To retain its status as a corporation in good standing, a corporation must file an annual report with the secretary of state of the state of incorporation and pay an annual franchise fee or tax. The amount of annual franchise tax varies greatly from state to state. While the annual report includes very little information and repeats information already filed in the articles of incorporation, failure to file an annual report or pay the annual fee or tax may result in a dissolution of the corporation and an imposition of monetary penalties.

Close Corporation Elections

Close corporations face problems that normally do not affect publicly held corporations. In recognition of these problems, 20 states and the District of Columbia have separate statutes (or provisions within their traditional corporation statutes) that attend to the special needs of close corporations. For example, some corporation statutes allow a close corporation to be managed by its shareholders.

To take advantage of these close corporation statutes, most statutes require that a corporation make an *election* to be treated as a close corporation. The Statutory Close Corporation Supplement to the MBCA permits a corporation with *fewer than 50 shareholders* to elect to become a close corporation. Delaware allows no more than 30 shareholders; California, no more than 35; Missouri, no more than 50. The Close Corporation Supplement requires the articles of incorporation to state that the corporation is a statutory close corporation.

There is no penalty for a corporation's failure to make a close corporation election. The only consequence of a failure to meet the requirements is that the close corporation statutory provisions are inapplicable. Instead, statutory corporation law will treat the corporation as it treats any other general corporation.

Note, however, that even when a corporation fails to meet the statutory requirements for treatment as a close

corporation, a court may decide to apply special *common law* rules applicable only to close corporations.

Defective Attempts to Incorporate

When business managers attempt to incorporate a business, sometimes they fail to comply with all the conditions for incorporation. For example, the incorporators may not have filed articles of incorporation or the directors may not have held an organization meeting. These are examples of **defective attempts to incorporate**.

One possible consequence of defective incorporation is to make the managers and the purported shareholders *personally liable* for the obligations of the defectively formed corporation. For example, an employee of an insolvent corporation drives the corporation's truck and hits a pedestrian. If the pedestrian proves that the corporation was defectively formed, he may be able to recover damages for his injuries from the managers and the shareholders.

A second possible consequence of defective incorporation is that a party to a contract involving the purported corporation may claim nonexistence of the corporation in order to avoid a contract made in the name of the corporation. For example, a person makes an ill-advised contract with a corporation. If the person proves that the corporation was defectively formed, he may escape liability on the contract because he made a contract with a nonexistent entity, the defectively formed corporation. As an alternative, the defectively formed corporation may escape liability on the contract on the grounds that its nonexistence makes it impossible for it to have liability.

The courts have tried to determine when these two consequences should arise by making a distinction between de jure corporations, de facto corporations, corporations by estoppel, and corporations so defectively formed that they are treated as being nonexistent.

De Jure Corporation

A *de jure corporation* is formed when the promoters substantially comply with each of the **mandatory conditions precedent** to the incorporation of the business. *Mandatory* provisions are distinguished from *directory* provisions by statutory language and the purpose of the provision. Mandatory provisions are those that the corporation statute states "shall" or "must" be done or those that are necessary to protect the public interest. Directory provisions are those that "may" be done and that are unnecessary to protect the public interest.

For example, statutes provide that the incorporators shall file the articles of incorporation with the secretary of state. This is a mandatory provision, not only because of the use of the word *shall*, but also because of the importance of a filing to protect the public interest by informing the public that a business has shareholders with limited liability. Other mandatory provisions include conducting an organization meeting. Directory provisions include minor matters such as the inclusion of the incorporators' addresses in the articles of incorporation.

If a corporation has complied with each mandatory provision, it is a de jure corporation and is treated as a corporation for all purposes. The validity of a de jure corporation cannot be attacked, except in a few states in which the state, in a *quo warranto* proceeding, may attack the corporation for noncompliance with a condition subsequent to incorporation, such as a failure to file an annual report with the secretary of state.

De Facto Corporation

A *de facto corporation* exists when the incorporators fail in some material respect to comply with all of the mandatory provisions of the incorporation statute yet comply with most mandatory provisions. There are three requirements for a de facto corporation:

1. There is a valid statute under which the corporation could be organized.

2. The promoters or managers make an honest attempt to organize under the statute. This requires substantial compliance with the mandatory provisions taken as a whole.

3. The promoters or managers exercise corporate powers. That is, they act as if they were acting for a corporation.

Generally, failing to file the articles of incorporation with the secretary of state will prevent the creation of a de facto corporation. However, a de facto corporation will exist despite the lack of an organization meeting or the failure to make a duplicate filing of the articles with a county recorder.

A de facto corporation is treated as a corporation against either an attack by a third party or an attempt of the business itself to deny that it is a corporation. The state, however, may attack the claimed corporate status of the business in a *quo warranto* action.

Corporation by Estoppel

When people hold themselves out as representing a corporation or believe themselves to be dealing with a corporation, a court will estop those people from denying the existence of a corporation. This is called **corporation by estoppel**. For example, a manager states that a business has been incorporated and induces a third person to contract with the purported corporation. The manager will not be permitted to use a failure to incorporate as a defense to the contract because she has misled others to believe reasonably that a corporation exists.

Under the doctrine of estoppel, each contract must be considered individually to determine whether either party to the contract is estopped from denying the corporation's existence.

Defective Incorporation

Albeit rare, there are times when a corporation's formation is so defective that it will be deemed legally nonexistent. This occurs only when those persons attempting to organize a corporation have failed so significantly that even corporation by estoppel has not occurred. In this situation, courts generally hold such persons to be partners with unlimited liability for the contracts and torts of the business. This raises the question of liability. However, most courts impose the unlimited *contractual* liability of a partner only on those who are *actively engaged in the management* of the business or who are responsible for the defects in its organization. *Tort* liability, however, is generally imposed on everyone—the managers and the purported shareholders of the defectively formed corporation.

Modern Approaches to the Defective Incorporation Problem

As you can see, the law of defective incorporation is confusing. It becomes even more confusing when you consider that many of the defective incorporation cases look like promoter liability cases, and vice versa. A court may have difficulty deciding whether to apply the law of promoter liability or the law of defective incorporation to preincorporation contracts. It is not surprising, therefore, that modern corporation statutes have attempted to eliminate this confusion by adopting simple rules for determining the existence of a corporation and the liability of its promoters, managers, and shareholders.

The MBCA states that incorporation occurs when the articles are filed by the secretary of state. The **filing of the** articles is **conclusive proof** of the existence of the corporation, except in a proceeding brought by the state. Filing is proved by the return of a copy of the articles stamped "filed" accompanied by a receipt for payment of the incorporation fee. Consequently, the incorporators may omit even a mandatory provision, yet create a corporation, provided that the secretary of state has filed the articles of incorporation. Conversely, courts have held that a failure to obtain a filing of the articles is conclusive proof of the nonexistence of the corporation, on the grounds that the MBCA eliminates the concepts of de facto corporation and corporation by estoppel.

Liability for Defective Incorporation under the MBCA The MBCA imposes joint and several liability on those persons who purport to act on behalf of a corporation and know that there has been no incorporation. Thus, managers and shareholders who both (1) *participate* in the operational decisions of the business and (2) *know* that the

corporation does not exist are liable for the purported corporation's contracts and torts.

The MBCA releases from liability shareholders and others who either (1) take no part in the management of the defectively formed corporation *or* (2) mistakenly believe that the corporation is in existence. Consequently, *passive* shareholders have no liability for the obligations of a defectively formed corporation even when they know that the corporation has not been formed. Likewise, managers of a defectively formed corporation have no liability when they believe that the corporation exists.

The following case discusses promoter liability. The court ultimately holds that whether a person is actually a promoter is a question of fact and thus is a question that is improper for the court to determine on summary judgment.

Krupinski v. Deyesso   2016 WL 1252726 (R.I. Super. Ct. 2016)

In February 1995, Ronald Krupinski met with Frank Viola and William Deyesso to discuss investing in an adult entertainment club, to be named "Centerfolds," in Providence, Rhode Island. At the meeting, Krupinski claims it was agreed that he was to receive a 33 percent ownership interest in Centerfolds, and when the club opened, he would work as a manager and earn a salary of $52,000 annually plus bonuses.

In May 1995, Viola purchased Scharnhorst as the operating entity for Centerfolds. Viola, Deyesso, and others became officers and shareholders of Scharnhorst in December 1995 through appropriate corporate action.

Following the purchase, Krupinski began preparing the club for its opening, which officially occurred in February 1996. Due to an issue with the adult entertainment license, the club was forced to close shortly after opening. As a result of Centerfold's temporary forced closure, Krupinski agreed to reduce his ownership interest in the club to 25 percent.

Krupinski again served as a manager of the club when it reopened in August 1996. Krupinski served in that capacity until July 1997, when he claims he was terminated without cause and without justification. Krupinski did not have a written employment agreement during his tenure as manager.

Deyesso claims Krupinski was terminated due to his participation in a purported credit-card scam through the altering of customer receipts, improper conduct with the club's employees, and excessive drinking.

The site where Providence Centerfolds operated was taken by eminent domain in 2001. Once Centerfolds closed and Deyesso failed to timely locate a new building, Deyesso proceeded to open other clubs in Massachusetts under the name Centerfolds, using some of the tangible property from the Providence club. Krupinski alleges that Deyesso breached the original agreement with him by excluding him from participating in those new, additional clubs.

On October 7, 2005, Scharnhorst's corporate charter was revoked by the Rhode Island Secretary of State due to its failure to file its Annual Report for the year 2005. Krupinski's original complaint was filed on July 10, 2007, and the current, operative complaint was filed on February 8, 2012. On April 12, 2012, the court issued a decision dismissing Counts II through VIII of the complaint. Accordingly, the only remaining cause of action in this matter—which is now the subject of defendant's summary judgment motion—is Count I, setting forth a claim for breach of contract brought individually against Deyesso.

Silverstein, Judge

Deyesso argues that he was acting on behalf of Scharnhorst in his capacity as director when he terminated Krupinski's employment and is thus not personally liable. To that end, Deyesso maintains that Krupinski's employment agreement—as a claimed

preincorporation contract—subsequently became the obligation of Scharnhorst when the corporation was purchased. Scharnhorst, according to Deyesso, ratified the employment agreement at the agreed upon salary of $52,000 per year. Krupinski, in response, contends that the oral agreement was entered into with Deyesso personally. Moreover, Krupinski argues that any assumption of the agreement by Scharnhorst does not automatically relieve Deyesso of any personal liability. Essentially, to prevail on summary judgment, Deyesso must prove that he was excused from any and all liability when Scharnhorst assumed the employment agreement.

"[A] preincorporation contract may be adopted, accepted, or ratified by a corporation when properly organized, resulting in corporate liability on the contract." *Katz v. Prete*, 459 A.2d 81, 86 (R.I. 1983). A corporation impliedly adopts a preincorporation contract when it accepts the benefits of the contract and renders performance in accordance therewith. *Id*. Adoption of a preincorporation contract results in corporate liability on the contract. *Id*.

There can be no dispute that an oral agreement was made between Deyesso, Viola, and Krupinski, and that, under the terms of the agreement, Krupinski was to serve as a manager of the club. Additionally, there can be no dispute that Krupinski received compensation from Scharnhorst for services provided in accordance with the terms of the agreement. Thus, there can be no dispute that Scharnhorst accepted the benefits of the contract and thereby adopted it. In support of his Motion for Summary Judgment, Deyesso now urges the Court to find that he made the contract as Scharnhorst's promoter, and that he was released from liability upon adoption thereof.

The term "promoter" has been defined in case law as "every person acting, by whatever name, in the forming and establishing of a company at any period prior to the company becoming fully incorporated." *Gerffert Co. v. William J. Hirten Co.*, 815 F. Supp. 2d 521, 528 (D.R.I. 2011) (quoting *Dickerman v. N. Trust Co.*, 176 U.S. 181, 203–04 (1900)). This definition is consistent with the principle that "a corporation should have a full and complete organization and existence as an entity before it can enter into any kind of a contract." *Ireland v. Globe Milling & Reduction Co.*, 20 R.I. 190, 38 A. 116, 117 (1897). Under *Gerffert* and *Ireland*, it may be said that a promoter is an individual who makes a contract on behalf of an entity that lacks the capacity to enter into the transaction. Because Deyesso did not make a contract on behalf of Scharnhorst prior to the company becoming fully incorporated, under *Gerffert* and *Ireland*, he may not be considered a promoter.

However, according to the Supreme Court of Ohio, the legal principles governing the relationship between a corporation and its promoters are not based upon the principles enunciated in *Ireland*, but are instead "derived from the law of agency." *Ill. Controls, Inc. v. Langham*, 70 Ohio St. 3d 512, 522 (1994). Because a corporation may not have agents prior to becoming fully incorporated, *see, e.g., Rees v. Mosaic Techs., Inc.*, 742 F.2d 765, 768 (3d Cir. 1984), under *Ill. Controls*, a finding that a contract was made on behalf of an entity lacking legal capacity to make contracts is not a condition precedent to a determination that the individual who made the contract was acting as a corporate promoter.

For purposes of the instant dispute, this Court is not required to ascertain the nature of the rules governing Deyesso's claim. Instead, the Court finds that the motion for summary judgment may be resolved on the basis that "whether a person is actually a promoter is a question of fact to be determined by the trier of fact." *McDaniel v. Serv. Feed & Supply, Inc.*, 271 Md. 371, 376 (1974) (citing 1 Fletcher, *Cyclopedia Corporations* § 189); see also [*Indus. Nat'l Bank v. Peloso*, 121 R.I. 305, 307 (1979)].

For the foregoing reasons, Deyesso's Motion for Summary Judgment is denied with respect to the breach of contract allegations stemming from Krupinski's signing of the promissory note and his termination as manager because resolution of such issues are [sic] factual in nature and improper for the Court to determine on summary judgment.

Defendant's motion for summary judgment denied with respect to the breach of contract allegations.

[Note: There have been no further hearings regarding this case. At the end of the above opinion, the court concluded that "Counsel for Defendant shall present an order consistent herewith which shall be settled after due notice to counsel for Plaintiff."]

Incorporation of Nonprofit Corporations

Nonprofit corporations are incorporated in substantially the same manner as for-profit corporations. One or more persons serve as incorporators and deliver articles of incorporation to the secretary of state for filing. A nonprofit corporation's articles must include the name and address of the corporation and state its registered agent. Unlike a for-profit corporation, a nonprofit corporation must state that it is either a public benefit corporation, a mutual benefit corporation, or a religious corporation. A public benefit corporation is incorporated primarily for the benefit of the public—for example, a community arts council that promotes the arts. A mutual benefit corporation is designed to benefit its members—for example, a golf country club. An example of a religious corporation is a church.

A nonprofit corporation's articles must also state whether it will have members. While it is typical for nonprofit corporations to have members, the Model Nonprofit Corporation Act of 2008 (MNCA) does not require a nonprofit corporation to have members. An example of a nonprofit corporation having no members is a public benefit corporation established to promote business development in a city, whose directors are appointed by the city's mayor.

A nonprofit corporation's articles may include the purpose of the corporation, its initial directors, and any matter regarding the rights and duties of the corporation and its directors and members. Each incorporator and director named in the articles must sign the articles.

A nonprofit corporation's existence begins when the secretary of state files the articles. After incorporation, the initial directors or incorporators hold an organization meeting to adopt bylaws and conduct other business.

Liability for Preincorporation Transactions
Nonprofit corporation status normally protects the members and managers from personal liability. However, when a nonprofit corporation is not formed or is defectively formed, promoters and others who transact for the nonexistent nonprofit corporation have the same liability as promoters and others who transact for a nonexistent for-profit corporation. The MNCA states the same rule as the MBCA: Persons who act on behalf of a corporation knowing there is no corporation are jointly and severally liable for all liabilities created while so acting.

Similarly, promoters have no authority to make contracts for a nonexistent nonprofit corporation. The corporation becomes liable on preincorporation contracts when its board of directors adopts the contracts.

Financing For-Profit Corporations

 Know the appropriate sources for financing a business.

Any business needs money to operate and grow. One advantage of incorporation is the large number of sources of funds that are available to businesses that incorporate. One such source is the sale of corporate **securities**, including shares, debentures, bonds, and long-term notes payable.

In addition to obtaining funds from the sale of securities, a corporation may be financed by other sources. A bank may lend money to the corporation in exchange for the corporation's short-term promissory notes, called *commercial paper*. Earnings provide a source of funds once the corporation is operating profitably. In addition, the

corporation may use normal short-term financing, such as accounts receivable financing and inventory financing, that is, borrowing from banks or other financial institutions and using the corporation's receivables or inventory as collateral.

In this section, you will study only one source of corporate funds—a corporation's sale of securities. A corporate security may be either (1) a share in the corporation or (2) an obligation of the corporation. These two kinds of securities are called equity securities and debt securities.

Equity Securities
Every business corporation issues equity securities, which are commonly called stock or **shares**. The issuance of shares creates an ownership relationship: The holders of the shares—called stockholders or **shareholders**—are the owners of the corporation.

Modern statutes permit corporations to issue several classes of shares and to determine the rights of the various classes. Subject to minimum guarantees contained in the state business corporation law, the shareholders' rights are a matter of contract and appear in the articles of incorporation, in the bylaws, in a shareholder agreement, and on the share certificates.

Common Shares Common shares (or common stock) are a type of equity security. Ordinarily, the owners of common shares—called **common shareholders**—have the exclusive right to elect the directors, who manage the corporation.

The common shareholders often occupy a position inferior to that of other investors, notably creditors and preferred shareholders. The claims of common shareholders are subordinate to the claims of creditors and other classes of shareholders when liabilities and dividends are paid and when assets are distributed upon liquidation.

In return for this subordination, however, the common shareholders have an exclusive claim to the corporate earnings and assets that exceed the claims of creditors and other shareholders. Therefore, the common shareholders bear the major risks of the corporate venture, yet stand to profit the most if it is successful.

Preferred Shares Shares that have preferences with regard to assets or dividends over other classes of shares are called preferred shares (or preferred stock). **Preferred shareholders** are customarily given liquidation and dividend preferences over common shareholders. A corporation may have several classes of preferred shares. In such a situation, one class of preferred shares may be given preferences over another class of preferred shares. Under the MBCA, the preferences of preferred shareholders must be set out in the articles of incorporation.

The *liquidation preference* of preferred shares is usually a stated dollar amount. During a liquidation, this amount must be paid to each preferred shareholder before any common shareholder or other shareholder subordinated to the preferred class may receive his share of the corporation's assets.

Dividend preferences vary greatly. For example, the dividends may be cumulative or noncumulative. Dividends on *cumulative* preferred shares, if not paid in any year, accumulate until paid. The entire accumulation must be paid before any dividends may be paid to common shareholders. Dividends on *noncumulative* preferred shares do not accumulate if unpaid. For such shares, only the current year's dividends must be paid to preferred shareholders prior to the payment of dividends to common shareholders.

Participating preferred shares have priority up to a stated amount or percentage of the dividends to be paid by the corporation. Then, the preferred shareholders participate with the common shareholders in additional dividends paid.

Some close corporations attempt to create preferred shares with a *mandatory dividend* right. These mandatory dividend provisions have generally been held illegal as unduly restricting the powers of the board of directors. Today, a few courts and some special close corporation statutes permit mandatory dividends for shareholders of close corporations.

A **redemption** or **call** provision in the articles allows a corporation at its option to repurchase preferred shareholders' shares at a price stated in the articles, despite the shareholders' unwillingness to sell. Some statutes permit the articles to give the shareholders the right to force the corporation to redeem preferred shares.

Preferred shares may be **convertible** into another class of shares, usually common shares. A **conversion right** allows a preferred shareholder to exchange her preferred shares for another class of shares, usually common shares. The conversion rate or price is stated in the articles. A holder of preferred shares might exercise her conversion right should common shares rapidly appreciate, allowing her to give up a fixed annual income for a larger profit instead.

Preferred shares have *voting rights* unless the articles provide otherwise. Usually, most voting rights are taken from preferred shares, except for important matters such as voting for a merger or a change in preferred shareholders' dividend rights. Rarely are preferred shareholders given the right to vote for directors, except in the event of a corporation's default in the payment of dividends.

Authorized, Issued, and Outstanding Shares
Authorized shares are shares that a corporation is permitted to issue by its articles of incorporation. A corporation may not issue more shares than are authorized. **Issued shares** are shares that have been sold to shareholders. **Outstanding shares** are shares that are currently held by shareholders. The distinctions between these terms are important. For example, a corporation pays cash, property, and share dividends only on outstanding shares. Only outstanding shares may be voted at a shareholders' meeting.

Canceled Shares Sometimes, a corporation will purchase its own shares. A corporation may cancel repurchased shares. Canceled shares do not exist: They are neither authorized, issued, nor outstanding. Because canceled shares do not exist, they cannot be reissued.

Shares Restored to Unissued Status Repurchased shares may be restored to unissued status instead of being canceled. If this is done, the shares are merely authorized, and they may be reissued at a later time.

Treasury Shares If repurchased shares are neither canceled nor restored to unissued status, they are called **treasury shares.** Such shares are authorized and issued, but not outstanding. They may be sold by the corporation at a later time. The corporation may not vote them at shareholders' meetings, and it may not pay a cash or property dividend on them.

The MBCA abolishes the concept of treasury shares. It provides that repurchased shares are restored to unissued status and may be reissued, unless the articles of incorporation require cancellation.

Options, Warrants, and Rights
Equity securities include options to purchase common shares and preferred shares. The MBCA expressly permits the board of directors to issue **options** for the purchase of the corporation's shares. Options permit their holders to purchase a specific number of shares at a specified price during a specified time period, usually beginning months or years after the option is issued. Share options are often issued to top-level managers as an incentive to increase the profitability of the corporation. An increase in profitability should increase the market value of the corporation's shares, resulting in increased compensation to the employees who own and exercise share options.

Warrants are options evidenced by certificates. They are sometimes part of a package of securities sold as a unit. For example, they may be sold along with notes, bonds, or even shares. Underwriters may receive warrants as part of their compensation for aiding a corporation in selling its shares to the public.

Rights are short-term certificated options that are usually transferable. Rights are used to give present security holders an option to subscribe to a proportional quantity of the same or a different security of the corporation. They are most often issued in connection with a **preemptive right** requirement, which obligates a corporation to offer each existing shareholder the opportunity to buy the corporation's newly issued shares in the same proportion as the shareholder's current ownership of the corporation's shares.

Debt Securities

Debt Securities Corporations have inherent power to borrow money necessary for their operations by issuing debt securities. Debt securities create a debtor–creditor relationship between the corporation and the security holder. With the typical debt security, the corporation is obligated to pay interest periodically and to pay the amount of the debt (the principal) on the maturity date. Debt securities include debentures, bonds, and promissory notes.

Debentures are long-term, unsecured debt securities. Typically, a debenture has a term of 10 to 30 years. Debentures usually have indentures. An **indenture** is a contract that states the rights of the debenture holders. For example, an indenture defines what acts constitute default by the corporation and what rights the debenture holders have upon default. It may place restrictions on the corporation's right to issue other debt securities.

Bonds are long-term, secured debt securities that usually have indentures. They are identical to debentures except that bonds are secured by collateral. The collateral for bonds may be real property such as a building, or personal property such as a commercial airplane. If the debt is not paid, the bondholders may force the sale of the collateral and take the proceeds of the sale.

Generally, **notes** have a shorter duration than debentures or bonds. They seldom have terms exceeding five years. Notes may be secured or unsecured.

It is not uncommon for notes or debentures to be *convertible* into other securities, usually preferred or common shares. The right to convert belongs to the holder of the convertible note or debenture. This conversion right permits an investor to receive interest as a debt holder and, after conversion, to share in the increased value of the corporation as a shareholder.

Consideration for Shares

The board of directors has the power to issue shares on behalf of the corporation. The board must decide at what *price* and for what *type of consideration* it will issue the shares. Corporation statutes restrict the discretion of the board in accepting specified kinds of consideration and in determining the value of the shares it issues.

Quality of Consideration for Shares Not all kinds of consideration in contract law are acceptable as legal consideration for shares in corporation law. To protect creditors and other shareholders, the statutes require legal consideration to have *real value*. Modern statutes, however, place few limits on the type of consideration that may be received for shares. The MBCA permits shares to be issued in return for any tangible or intangible *property* or *benefit to the corporation*, including cash, promissory notes, services performed for the corporation, contracts for services *to be performed* for the corporation, and securities of the corporation or another corporation. The rationale for the MBCA rule is a recognition that future services and promises of future services have value that is as real as that of tangible property. Consequently, for example, a corporation may issue common shares to its president in exchange for the president's commitment to work for the corporation for three years or in exchange for bonds of the corporation or debentures issued by another corporation. In addition, the MBCA permits corporations to issue shares to their promoters in consideration for their promoters' preincorporation services. This rule acknowledges that a corporation benefits from a promoter's preincorporation services.

Several states' constitutions place stricter limits on permissible consideration for shares. They provide that shares may be issued only for money paid to the corporation, labor done for the corporation, or property actually received by the corporation. Such a rule prohibits a corporation from issuing its shares for a promise to pay money or a promise to provide services to the corporation in the future.

Quantity of Consideration for Shares The board is required to issue shares for an adequate dollar amount of consideration. Whether shares have been issued for an adequate amount of consideration depends in part on the *par value* of the shares. The more important concern, however, is whether the shares have been issued for *fair value*.

Par Value Par value is an arbitrary dollar amount that may be assigned to the shares by the articles of incorporation. Par value does not reflect the fair market value of the shares, but par value is the minimum amount of consideration for which the shares may be issued.

Shares issued for less than par value are called **discount shares**. The board of directors is liable to the corporation for issuing shares for less than par value. A shareholder who purchases shares from the corporation for less than par value is liable to the corporation for the difference between the par value and the amount she paid.

Fair Value It is not always enough for the board to issue shares for their par value. Many times, shares are worth more than par value. In addition, many shares today do not have a par value. In fact, the MBCA purports to eliminate the concept of par value as it affects the issuance of shares. In all cases, the board must exercise care to ensure that the corporation receives the *fair value* of the shares it issues. If there are no par value problems, the board's judgment as to the amount of consideration that is received for the shares is *conclusive* when the board acts in good faith, exercises the care of ordinarily prudent directors, and acts in the best interests of the corporation.

Disputes may arise concerning the value of property that the corporation receives for its shares. The board's valuation of the consideration is conclusive if it acts in good faith with the care of prudent directors and in a manner it reasonably believes to be in the best interests of the corporation. When the board impermissibly overvalues the consideration for shares, the shareholder receives **watered shares**. Both the board and the shareholder are liable to the corporation when shares are watered.

The Global Business Environment

Corporation Law Worldwide: Proper Consideration for Shares

There is substantial similarity in corporation laws from country to country. Even in many countries where corporation law is different from American law, there have been legislative attempts to modernize the law by making it more nearly consistent with U.S. law. One example is Israel, whose Knesset has adopted a corporation law in line with Western law, especially American law.

Examining the requirements to incorporate and the limits on consideration for shares, there are some differences globally, but generally not much more than one sees from state to state in the United States. For example, although the MBCA permits corporate shares to be issued for any benefit to the corporation, the laws of many countries retain the historic American rule (which is still law in many states) that certain types of benefits are improper consideration. For example, Chinese law allows shareholders to make their investments only in cash, in kind, in industrial property rights, in nonpatented technology, or in land use rights. The Kingdom of Bhutan is more limiting, however, forbidding share issuances for consideration other than cash, unless shareholders approve.

When a shareholder pays less than the amount of consideration determined by the board of directors, the corporation or its creditors may sue the shareholder to recover the deficit. When a shareholder has paid the proper amount of consideration, the shares are said to be *fully paid and nonassessable.*

In the following case involving a family corporation, the court considered whether intangible property (termed incorporeal property in Louisiana) and services rendered for a corporation may be proper consideration for shares.

Tedeton v. Tedeton   137 So. 3d 686 (La. Ct. App. 2014)

Kirk Tedeton and his father, Clayton Tedeton, incorporated Tedco Inc. on March 15, 1982. Tedco eventually sold soap products called Miracle II, the formula of which Clayton believed was divinely revealed to him in 1981. Upon this revelation and for some time after Tedco's incorporation, Clayton and his family, including Kirk, produced but did not sell the soap products. Clayton and Kirk were listed as the incorporators, registered agents, and initial directors of Tedco. Neither the articles of incorporation nor any other formative corporate documents identified the initial shareholders of the corporation.

For most of Tedco's active years, Clayton promoted the soap products in his outreach ministry. Kirk and his wife, Sue, managed the day-to-day affairs of Tedco and manufactured the soap products. The earliest tax return for Tedco was in 1993; from 1993–1995, Kirk filed the tax returns for Tedco. On those tax forms, he indicated that no person owned more than 50 percent of Tedco.

In 2007, Clayton died, and a dispute regarding ownership of Tedco arose between Kirk and his mother, Patsy, and sisters, Deborah Davis and Pamela Savage. Kirk's mother and sisters claimed that Clayton owned all the shares of Tedco at his death; therefore, they were entitled to a portion of those shares as Clayton's heirs. Kirk brought an action for a declaratory judgment against his mother and sisters, arguing he was the only shareholder of Tedco at the time of Clayton's death. The trial court held that Kirk and Clayton were 50–50 owners. Kirk appealed to the Louisiana Court of Appeals. His mother and sisters also argued on appeal that Kirk could not have been a Tedco shareholder, as he did not pay proper consideration for the shares under Louisiana corporation law.

Caraway, Judge

Section 52 of the Louisiana corporation law is entitled "Issuance of shares; consideration." La. R.S. 12:52. Relevant to this dispute, Section 52 provides that (1) the consideration for no-par value shares of the corporation may be initially fixed by the incorporators; (2) the consideration for issued shares may be paid in corporeal or incorporeal property or services actually rendered to the corporation, *see* La. R.S. 12:52(C); and (3) the directors' valuation placed upon the consideration for shares, other than cash consideration, shall be conclusive, *see* La. R.S. 12:52(D).

The trial court placed emphasis on the fact that both Clayton and Kirk were listed as incorporators in 1982. They were also listed as directors in the corporation's initial report. While there was no formal fixing of the value of the corporate shares or the issuance of stock certificates at the time, the trial court could consider the evidence of the contributions into the corporation at the inception of the corporate business activity. That evidence, circumstantial and otherwise, reveals that both Clayton and Kirk contributed in the commencement of the affairs of the business enterprise.

La. R.S. 12:52 provides that "incorporeal property" may serve as consideration for shares in corporations. La. R.S. 12:52(C). The formula for Miracle II is an incorporeal movable. The parties stipulated that Clayton transferred any and all his interest in the formula to Tedco. Therefore, it was reasonable for the trial court to conclude this transfer to Tedco was made in exchange for an ownership stake in the corporation that was created to sell Miracle II products. Therefore, Clayton contributed adequate consideration in exchange for shares in Tedco. He also received financial benefits from Tedco from the sale of the Miracle II product through the years. The trial court was not clearly wrong in determining that Clayton owned a portion of the corporation from the beginning of the business.

Whether Kirk provided adequate consideration in exchange for shares in Tedco may be less apparent, but nevertheless, the record supports the trial court's factual finding that Kirk contributed initial consideration for shares. Both Kirk and his wife, Sue, testified that they worked in the preparation of the Miracle II product in the early 1980s. Yet, during that time, the business of the corporation was not clear. However, one reasonable view of the business presented in the testimony was that beginning in 1988 and thereafter, the commercial manufacturing of Miracle II by Tedco for profit began in earnest. At that time, Clayton had lost everything from the financial difficulties of his prior businesses. He separated from his wife and began to reside on Kirk's property in a building that began to serve as Tedco's office and place of manufacture of the product.

When Tedco's corporate business is viewed as having commenced at that time, Kirk's contribution of the facility for manufacturing and his commitment to the management of the operations of the manufacturing process may also represent an adequate consideration for an ownership position in the corporation.

We view Kirk's commitment in 1988 to make Tedco a success as a contract for services and an incorporeal that may be transferred to the corporation in exchange for shares. A person may contribute incorporeal property to a corporation in exchange for shares. La. R.S. 12:52(C). Rights, obligations, and actions that apply to a movable thing are incorporeal movables. La. C.C. art. 473. When a person pledges his services to a corporation in exchange for shares, he is obligating himself to perform—specifically, to do something for the corporation.

However, we also recognize that La. R.S. 12:52(C) provides that a corporation may issue shares for "services actually rendered to the corporation." Some Louisiana appellate courts have interpreted the language in La. R.S. 12:52(C) referring to services "actually rendered" to exclude promises to provide future services to the corporation. Nevertheless, subsequent cases examining this rule hold that although a person had not already performed actual services, the subsequent rendering of those services validated the issuance of the shares.

Therefore, Kirk's promise to make Tedco a successful business along with his contribution of his house as a manufacturing and office building may act as consideration for an ownership interest in Tedco. No dilution of the existing corporate ownership occurred, as Kirk's and Clayton's contributions to Tedco occurred together at the initiation of the commercial venture.

We therefore find that the trial court's determination of the father's and son's corporate ownership of Tedco is based upon a reasonable view of the evidence and not clearly wrong. That ruling likewise does not violate the principles of Section 52 of the Louisiana corporation law. Clayton and Kirk as incorporators can be viewed from the circumstantial evidence of their relationship as having fixed the value of the consideration of the shares in Tedco and as having paid in that value capitalizing Tedco with corporeal and incorporeal properties they committed to the corporation. In a closely held corporation with complete acquiescence to informal management of the corporation between the shareholders, we find that a determination of equal ownership under the facts of this case is not manifestly erroneous.

Judgment affirmed in favor of Patsy Tedeton, Deborah Davis and Pamela Savage.

Accounting for Consideration Received The consideration received by a corporation for its equity securities appears in the equity or capital accounts in the shareholders' equity section of the corporation's balance sheet. The **stated capital** account records the product of the number of shares outstanding multiplied by the par value of each share. When the shares are sold for more than par value, the excess or surplus consideration received by the corporation is **capital surplus**.

Under the MBCA, the terms *stated capital* and *capital surplus* have been eliminated. Legally, all consideration received for shares is lumped under one accounting entry for that class of shares, such as common equity. Accounting rules may require different treatment.

Resales of Shares The par value of shares is important *only when the shares are issued* by the corporation. Because treasury shares are issued but not outstanding, the corporation does not issue treasury shares when it resells them. Therefore, the board may sell treasury shares for less than par, provided that it sells the shares for an amount equal to their fair value.

Because par value and fair value are designed to ensure only that the corporation receives adequate consideration for its shares, a shareholder may buy shares from another shareholder for less than par value or fair value and incur no liability. However, if the purchasing shareholder *knows* that the selling shareholder bought the shares from the corporation for less than par value, the purchasing shareholder is liable to the corporation for the difference between the par value and the amount paid by the selling shareholder.

Share Subscriptions

Under the terms of a **share subscription**, a prospective shareholder promises to buy a specific number of shares of a corporation at a stated price. If the subscription is accepted by the corporation and the subscriber has paid for the shares, the subscriber is a shareholder of the corporation, even if the shares have not been issued. Under the MBCA, subscriptions need not be in writing to be enforceable. Usually, however, subscriptions are written.

Promoters use written share subscriptions in the course of selling shares of a proposed corporation to ensure that equity capital will be provided once the corporation comes into existence. These are called *preincorporation subscriptions*, which were covered in this chapter's discussion of promoters. Preincorporation subscriptions are not contracts binding on the corporation and the shareholders until the corporation comes into existence and its board of directors accepts the share subscriptions.

Close corporations may use share subscriptions when they seek to sell additional shares after incorporation. These are examples of *postincorporation subscriptions*, subscription agreements made *after* incorporation. A postincorporation subscription is a contract between the corporation and the subscriber at the time the subscription agreement is made.

A subscription may provide for payment of the price of the shares on a specified day, in installments, or upon the demand of the board of directors. The board may not discriminate when it demands payment: It must demand payment from all the subscribers of a class of shares or from none of them.

A share certificate may not be issued to a share subscriber until the price of the shares has been fully paid. If the subscriber fails to pay as agreed, the corporation may sue the subscriber for the amount owed.

Issuance of Shares

Uniform Commercial Code (UCC) Article 8 regulates the issuance of securities. Under Article 8, a corporation has a duty to issue only the number of shares authorized by its articles. Overissued shares, securities issued in excess of the amount the issuer has corporate power to issue, are void. However, an overissue can generally be cured by amending the incorporation documents to allow for the issuance of more shares, and then reissuing the shares.

If a person claims she is entitled to overissued shares, the corporation may not issue them. The person has two remedies though. The corporation must obtain identical shares and deliver or register them to the person entitled to issuance (through a reissuance), or the corporation must reimburse the person for the value paid for the shares plus interest.

The directors may incur liability, including criminal liability, for an overissuance of shares. To prevent overissuance through error in the issuance or transfer of their shares, corporations often employ a bank or a trust company as a registrar.

A share certificate is evidence that a person has been issued shares, owns the shares, and is a shareholder. The certificate states the corporation's name, the shareholder's name, and the number and class of shares. A person can be a shareholder without receiving a share certificate, such as a holder of a share subscription.

Under the MBCA, a corporation is not required to issue share certificates. If a corporation does not issue share certificates, it must register the security in the name of its owner or his securities intermediary, usually a stockbroker. Today, most shareholders of public companies never receive certificates, especially those who have brokerage accounts at online brokers.

Transfer of Shares

Because share certificates are evidence of the ownership of shares, their transfer is evidence of the transfer of the ownership of shares. The MBCA and UCC Article 8 cover the registration and transfer of shares, both certificated and uncertificated.

Shares are issued in *registered* form; that is, they are registered with the corporation in the name of a specific person. The indorsement of a share certificate on its back by its registered owner and the delivery of the certificate to another person transfers ownership of the shares to the other person. The transfer of a share certificate without naming a transferee creates a *street certificate*. The transfer of a street certificate may be made by delivery without indorsement. Any holder of a street certificate is presumed to be the owner of the shares it represents. Therefore, a transferee should ask the corporation to reregister the shares in his name.

Ownership of uncertificated securities is transferred by a corporation's registering the security in the new owner's name.

Under the UCC, a corporation owes a duty to register the transfer of any registered shares presented to it for registration, provided that the shares have been properly indorsed, or in the case of uncertificated shares, the corporation has received an **instruction** from the appropriate person notifying it of the transfer of ownership. If the corporation delays or refuses to make the transfer, it is liable to the transferee for a loss caused by the unreasonable delay or refusal.

When an owner of shares claims that his registration or certificate has been lost, destroyed, or stolen, the corporation must register new shares to the owner if the corporation has not received notice that the shares have been acquired by a protected purchaser, the owner files with the corporation a sufficient indemnity bond, and the owner meets any other reasonable requirements of the corporation. A **protected purchaser** pays value for the shares, has no notice of any adverse claim against the shares, and obtains control of the shares.

If, after the issuance of the new certificated shares or registration of new uncertificated shares, a protected purchaser of the original shares presents them for registration, the corporation must register the transfer, unless overissuance would result. In addition, the corporation may recover the new certificated shares from the original owner or revoke the new registration.

Restrictions on Transferability of Shares

LO42-4 Adopt appropriate share-transfer restrictions for a variety of contexts.

Historically, a shareholder has been free to sell her shares to whomever she wants whenever she wants. Such free transferability is important to shareholders in a publicly held corporation. Because shares in a publicly held corporation are freely transferable, shareholders know that they can easily liquidate their investment by selling their shares, often on a stock exchange.

In close corporations, however, free transferability as a legal matter is a threat to the balance of power among shareholders. For example, if one of three shareholders owning a third of a corporation sells his shares to one of the other shareholders, the buying shareholder will own two-thirds of the corporation and may be able to dominate the third shareholder. In addition, as a practical matter, free transferability of close corporation shares is illusory, as few people other than existing shareholders are willing to purchase shares in a close corporation.

Consequently, many close corporations restrict the transfer of shares to ensure those in control of a corporation will continue in control. Share-transfer restrictions can also be used to guarantee a market for the shares when a shareholder dies or retires from the corporation.

The courts have been reluctant to allow restrictions on the free transferability of shares, even if the shareholder agreed to a restriction on the transfer of her shares. Gradually, the courts and the legislatures have recognized that there are good reasons to permit the use of some restrictions on the transfer of shares. Today, modern corporation statutes allow most transfer restrictions, especially for close corporations.

Types of Restrictions on Transfer There are four categories of transfer restrictions: (1) rights of first refusal and option agreements, (2) buy-and-sell agreements, (3) consent restraints, and (4) provisions disqualifying purchasers.

A **right of first refusal** grants to the corporation or the other shareholders the right to match the offer that a selling shareholder receives for her shares. An **option agreement** grants the corporation or the other shareholders an option to buy the selling shareholder's shares at a price determined by the agreement. An option agreement will usually state a formula used to calculate the price of the shares.

A **buy-and-sell agreement** compels a shareholder to sell his shares to the corporation or to the other shareholders at the price stated in the agreement. It also obligates the corporation or the other shareholders to buy the selling shareholder's shares at that price. The price of the shares is usually determined by a stated formula.

A **consent restraint** requires a selling shareholder to obtain the consent of the corporation or the other shareholders before she may sell her shares. A *provision disqualifying purchasers* may be used in rare situations to exclude unwanted persons from the corporation. For example, a transfer restriction may prohibit the shareholders from selling to a competitor of the business.

Uses of Transfer Restrictions A corporation and its shareholders may use transfer restrictions to maintain the balance of shareholder power in the corporation. For example, four persons may own 25 shares each in a corporation. No single person can control such a corporation. If one of the four can buy 26 additional shares from the other shareholders, he will acquire control. The shareholders may therefore agree that each shareholder is entitled or required to buy an equal amount of any shares sold by any selling shareholder. The right of first refusal, option agreement, or buy-and-sell agreement may serve this purpose.

A buy-and-sell agreement is the preferred transfer restriction for nearly every context in well-planned close corporations because certainty is obtained by both sides being obligated: One required to buy and the other to sell. For example, a buy-and-sell agreement may be used to guarantee a shareholder a market for his shares. In a close corporation, there may be no ready market for the shares of the corporation. To ensure that a shareholder can obtain the value of her investment when she leaves the corporation, the shareholders or the corporation may be required to buy a shareholder's shares upon the occurrence of a specific event, such as death, disability, or retirement.

A buy-and-sell agreement may also be used to determine who should be required to sell and who should be required to buy shares when there is a severe disagreement between shareholders that threatens the profitability of the corporation. It could also be worded to require majority shareholders to buy the shares of minority shareholders when a lucrative merger offer for the corporation is rejected by the majority but favored by the minority. The agreement could, but rarely does, set the buyout price as the price offered in the merger.

If minority shareholders are afraid of being frozen in a close corporation that will never go public and give shareholders a chance to sell their shares on the market and get a return on investment, a buy-and-sell agreement could require the corporation to repurchase the minority's shares if the corporation has not gone public after a specified number of years.

In a close corporation, the shareholders may want only themselves or other approved persons as shareholders.

A buy-and-sell agreement or right of first refusal may be used to prevent unwanted persons from becoming shareholders.

A provision disqualifying purchasers may be used in limited situations only, such as when the purchaser is a competitor of the business or has a criminal background.

A consent restraint is used to preserve a close corporation or Subchapter S taxation election. Close corporation statutes and Subchapter S of the Internal Revenue Code limit the number of shareholders that a close corporation or S corporation may have. A transfer restriction may prohibit the shareholders from selling shares if, as a result of the sale, there would be too many shareholders to preserve a close corporation or S corporation election. A consent restraint is also used to preserve an exemption from registration of a securities offering. Under the Securities Act of 1933 and the state securities acts, an offering of securities can be exempt from registration if the offering is to accredited investors or a limited number of qualified investors, usually 35 financially sophisticated investors. A transfer restriction may require a selling shareholder to obtain permission from the corporation's legal counsel, which will be granted upon proof that the shareholder's sale of the shares does not cause the corporation to lose its registration exemption.

Legality of Transfer Restrictions Corporation statutes permit the use of option agreements, rights of first refusal, and buy-and-sell agreements with virtually no restrictions. The MBCA authorizes transfer restrictions for any reasonable purpose. The reasonableness of a restraint is judged in light of the character and needs of the corporation.

Consent restraints and provisions disqualifying purchasers may be used if they are not *manifestly unreasonable.* The MBCA makes per se reasonable any consent restraint that maintains a corporation's status when that status is dependent on the number or identity of shareholders, as with close corporation or S corporation status. The MBCA also makes per se reasonable any restriction that preserves registration exemptions under the Securities Act of 1933 and state securities laws.

Enforceability To be enforceable against a shareholder, a transfer restriction must be contained in the articles of incorporation, the bylaws, an agreement among the shareholders, or an agreement between the corporation and the shareholders. In addition, the shareholder must either agree to the restriction or purchase the shares with notice of the restriction. Under the MBCA, a purchaser of the shares has notice of a restriction if it is noted conspicuously on the face or the back of a share certificate or a written statement provided to shareholders if no certificates were issued. A purchaser also has notice if he knows of the restriction when he buys the shares.

In the next case, *Coyle v. Schwartz*, the court enforced a buy-and-sell agreement in which the shareholders were to agree from time to time on the price to be paid for the shares. It is a good example of a poorly drafted buy–sell agreement that failed to attain the objectives of all the shareholders. For a better example of a buy–sell agreement, see Figure 42.3.

Coyle v. Schwartz   2004 Ky. App. Unpub. LEXIS 1012 (Mar. 26, 2004)

American Scale Corporation, a closely held Kentucky corporation with its principal place of business in Louisville, Kentucky, was incorporated in February 1985 to engage in the sale and repair of industrial and commercial scales. Daniel Coyle was president and Steven Schwartz was vice president. They were the sole shareholders. At the time of incorporation, Coyle and Schwartz each received 200 shares of stock in exchange for their capital contributions of $10,000.

In early March 1986, Schwartz had an automobile accident in which his passenger was seriously injured. Schwartz's passenger filed suit against American Scale because it had provided insurance coverage on Schwartz's vehicle. Coyle became concerned that Schwartz's activities would expose American Scale to further liability. He was particularly displeased with Schwartz's actions in transporting an underage female, who was purportedly Schwartz's girlfriend, in a vehicle insured by American Scale.

As a result, Coyle informed Schwartz that he no longer desired to be in a 50–50 shareholder relationship with him. Coyle told Schwartz that unless Schwartz agreed to transfer 1 percent of his shares to Coyle, thereby permitting Coyle to assume majority control of American Scale, Coyle would either seek dissolution of American Scale or withdraw and begin operating a business in competition with American Scale. On March 21, 1986, Coyle and Schwartz executed a share-transfer agreement wherein Schwartz transferred 1 percent of his American Scale shares to Coyle. The agreement specifically stated that Coyle would thereafter own a 51 percent interest in American Scale, leaving Schwartz as owner of the remaining 49 percent of American Scale's shares.

About two years later, on August 25, 1988, Coyle and Schwartz made a buy–sell agreement that they titled "Stockholders' Cross-Purchase Agreement." The agreement provided for the repurchase of a shareholder's stock in the event of death, disability, or voluntary withdrawal of that shareholder. Specifically, the agreement stated that if Coyle or Schwartz died, or otherwise attempted to dispose of his shares, the other shareholder would have the right to purchase those shares. In addition, the agreement gave the majority shareholder an option to purchase all of the minority shareholder's stock at any time upon a 60-day written notice.

The agreement provided a stock-valuation method for determining a per share price in the event either of the provisions was triggered:

Unless altered as herein provided, for the purpose of determining the purchase price to be paid for the stock of a Stockholder, the fair market value of each share of stock shall be, as of August 25, 1988, $250.

The Stockholders shall redetermine the value of the stock within 60 days following the end of each fiscal year. If the Stockholders fail to make the required annual redetermination of value for a particular year, the last previously recorded value shall control.

Over the course of the next 12 years, neither Coyle nor Schwartz attempted to revaluate the price of American Scale's shares as provided in the agreement. Hence, the initial buyout price of $250 per share was never changed.

In a letter dated November 20, 2000, Coyle informed Schwartz that he was exercising his option as majority shareholder to purchase Schwartz's stock for $250 per share. Schwartz refused to tender his shares to Coyle and filed suit against Coyle seeking to invalidate the buyout agreement. Schwartz argued that the shareholders had abandoned the agreement by not changing the buyout price for 12 years. Schwartz also argued that the buyout price was so low as to constitute a penalty. In response to Coyle's motion for summary judgment, the trial court ruled that the shareholders had not abandoned the agreement. However, the court agreed with Schwartz that forcing him to sell all of his stock at the price of $250 per share was a penalty and, therefore, unenforceable. The trial court ordered a current valuation of the stock be undertaken before Schwartz could be compelled to transfer his shares. Coyle appealed to the Kentucky Court of Appeals.

Johnson, Judge

In his appeal, Coyle argues that the trial court erred by finding that the stock-valuation provision was unenforceable as a penalty.

While Coyle and Schwartz never revaluated the stock, this fact alone does not render the provision unenforceable.

Schwartz, as owner of 49% of American Scale's outstanding shares, had the right under the corporation's bylaws to call for a special meeting to revaluate the listed price of American Scale's shares. Schwartz has admitted in his deposition testimony that he never made such a request. Hence, by sitting on his rights for over 12 years, Schwartz took the risk that Coyle would exercise the majority-purchase option at a time when the actual value of American Scale's shares was in excess of the $250 price originally listed in the stock-valuation provision. Schwartz is not entitled to have the courts rewrite the parties' agreement simply because he believes he is receiving the short end of the bargain. Accordingly, we reverse the trial court's finding that the stock-valuation provision listing a price of $250 per share was unenforceable.

The terms of the stock-valuation provision listed an original price of $250 per share. The provision further stated that the fair market value shall be $250 "unless altered as herein provided" via the "mutual agreement" revaluation method. Since the parties failed to revaluate the price of American Scale's shares, $250 is the "last recorded value" with respect to the price of the corporation's shares. Therefore, the majority-purchase option and the stock-valuation provision entitle Coyle to purchase all of Schwartz's stock at a price of $250 per share.

Finally, we address Schwartz's claim that the trial court erred by finding that Schwartz and Coyle did not abandon the stock-valuation provision of the cross-purchase agreement. Specifically, Schwartz argues that by completely ignoring the cross-purchase agreement's requirement that both shareholders "shall re-determine the value of the stock within 60 days following the end of each fiscal year" and record the same, as well as their intention to revalue their shares in American Scale, Schwartz and

Coyle unequivocally acted in a manner inconsistent with the existence of the cross-purchase agreement.

We disagree and hold that the trial court did not err by finding that Coyle and Schwartz did not abandon their rights under the stock-valuation provision. "A contract may be rescinded or discharged by acts or conduct of the parties inconsistent with the continued existence of the contract, and mutual assent to abandon a contract may be inferred from the attendant circumstances and conduct of the parties. . . . While as a general rule a contract will be treated as abandoned or rescinded where the acts and conduct of one party inconsistent with its existence are acquiesced in by the other party, to be sufficient the acts and conduct must be positive and unequivocal."

In the instant case, while Coyle and Schwartz never revaluated American Scale's stock in the years following the execution of the cross-purchase agreement, this fact, standing alone, does not constitute "positive and unequivocal" acts which could lead to a finding of abandonment. The stock-valuation provision itself provided a default price for the stock in the event the parties failed to revaluate the shares. Therefore, Coyle and Schwartz contemplated that they might not always conduct a revaluation. Accordingly, the failure of Coyle and Schwartz to conduct an annual revaluation of American Scale's shares did not constitute an abandonment of the stock-valuation provision.

Judgment reversed in favor of Coyle.

Statutory Solution to Close Corporation Share-Transfer Problems Although transfer restrictions are important to close corporations, many close corporation shareholders fail to address the share transferability problem. Therefore, a few states provide statutory resolution of the close corporation transferability problem. In these states, statutes offer solutions to the transferability problem that are similar to the solutions that the shareholders would have provided had they thought about the problem. Not all transferability problems are settled by the Close Corporation Supplement, however. For example, there is no statutory buy-and-sell provision.

Financing Nonprofit Corporations

Nonprofit corporations are financed differently from for-profit corporations. This is especially true of a public benefit corporation such as a public television station, which obtains annual financing from government sources, private

foundations, members, and public contributors. A religious corporation such as a church receives weekly offerings from its congregation and may occasionally conduct capital drives to obtain additional funding from its members. A mutual benefit corporation, such as a fraternal or social organization like an Elks Club or golf country club, obtains initial funding from its original members to build facilities and assesses its members annually and monthly to pay operating expenses. In addition, nonprofit corporations have the power to obtain debt financing, such as borrowing from a bank or issuing notes and debentures.

A nonprofit corporation may admit members whether or not they pay consideration for their memberships. There is no statutory limit on the number of members a nonprofit corporation may admit, although the articles may place a limit on the number of members. Social clubs typically limit the number of members. Members must be admitted in compliance with procedures stated in the articles or the bylaws.

Generally, memberships in a nonpublic corporation are not freely transferable. No member of a public benefit corporation or religious corporation may transfer her

Figure 42.3   Model Share Transfer Restriction

The following is a comprehensive buy–sell agreement for the shareholders in a corporation. Note that there are four essential components: the events triggering a buyout, the persons obligated to buy and shareholder required to sell, the buyout price, and the timing of payments to the selling shareholder.

The shareholders agree to provide for certain restrictions on the transfer of their shares and for the purchase by the other shareholders upon the occurrence of certain events. The shareholders agree that such restrictions are in the best interests of the shareholders and the corporation. Accordingly, the parties agree as follows:

Article 1: Events Triggering Buy-and-Sell Obligations

Upon the occurrence of any one or more of the following events or conditions, the buy-and-sell obligations of this agreement shall be invoked:

(1) the death of a shareholder;
(2) a shareholder's voluntary retirement as an employee of the corporation on or after reaching his 55th birthday;
(3) a shareholder's voluntary retirement as an employee of the corporation before reaching his 55th birthday;
(4) a shareholder's compulsory retirement as an employee of the corporation upon his reaching his 70th birthday;
(5) the for-cause termination of the shareholder's employment with the corporation by action of the corporation prior to the shareholder's reaching his 55th birthday;
(6) the for-cause termination of the shareholder's employment with the corporation by action of the corporation upon or after the shareholder's reaching his 55th birthday;
(7) the determination by a court that the shareholder is unable to undertake his responsibilities as an employee of the corporation due to mental illness or disease or disability;
(8) the filing of a petition in bankruptcy by a shareholder;
(9) the filing of an involuntary bankruptcy petition against a shareholder and the shareholder's failure to obtain dismissal of the petition within 30 days;
(10) any assignment by a shareholder of his assets for the benefit of his creditors;
(11) any transfer, award, or confirmation of any such shares to the shareholder's spouse pursuant to a decree of divorce, dissolution, or separate maintenance, or pursuant to a property settlement or separation agreement;
(12) any other event which, were it not for the provisions of this agreement, would cause any such shares, or any interest therein, to be sold, assigned, pledged, encumbered, awarded, confirmed, or otherwise transferred, for consideration or otherwise, to any person, whether voluntarily, involuntarily, or by operation of law, prior to the shareholder reaching his 55th birthday;
(13) any other event which, were it not for the provisions of this agreement, would cause any such shares, or any interest therein, to be sold, assigned, pledged, encumbered, awarded, confirmed, or otherwise transferred, for consideration or otherwise, to any person, whether voluntarily, involuntarily, or by operation of law, upon or after to the shareholder reaching his 55th birthday;
(14) the deadlock of the board of directors resulting in the inability of the board of directors to take any action on behalf of the corporation for a period of one year.

Article 2: Buy-and-Sell Obligations

(a) Upon the occurrence of any triggering event specified in Article 1, excepting section 14, the affected shareholder shall sell all his shares and the other shareholders shall purchase such shares in accordance with the provisions of Articles 3 and 4. The purchasing shareholders shall buy such shares in the same proportion in which the purchasing shareholders, between themselves, own shares of the corporation immediately prior to triggering event. In the event that any purchasing shareholder shall be required to buy a fractional share, that fractional share shall be purchased by the corporation in accordance with the provisions of Articles 3 and 4.
(b) Upon the occurrence of a deadlock of the board of directors, as defined by Article 1, section 14, shareholders Helio Castino, Kristin Katojian, and Jordan Long shall buy and the other shareholders shall sell their shares in accordance with the provisions of Articles 3 and 4. The purchasing shareholders shall buy such shares in the same proportion in which the purchasing shareholders, between themselves, own shares of the corporation immediately prior to the triggering event. In the event that any purchasing shareholder shall be required to buy a fractional share, that fractional share shall be purchased by the corporation in accordance with the provisions of Articles 3 and 4.

Article 3: Timing of Purchase of Shares

(a) Upon the death of a shareholder, the purchasing shareholders shall purchase the shares of the deceased shareholder within 60 days of a written demand to the secretary of the corporation by the administrator or executor of the deceased shareholder.
(b) Upon the occurrence of any event in Article 1, subsection 2, 4, 6, 7, 13, or 14, the purchasing shareholders shall purchase the shares of the selling shareholder in 36 equal monthly installments beginning on the first day of the first full month beginning after the occurrence of such event.
(c) Upon the occurrence of any event in Article 1, subsection 3, 5, 8 ,9, 10 ,11, or 12, the purchasing shareholders shall purchase the shares of the selling shareholder in 60 equal monthly installments beginning on the first day of the first full month beginning after the occurrence of such event.

Article 4: Valuation of Shares

(a) Upon the occurrence of any event in Article 1, subsection 1, 2, 4, 6, 7, 13, or 14, the purchasing shareholders shall purchase the shares of the selling or deceased shareholder at the following price per share: Fifteen (15) times the corporation's average net income for the two most recent fiscal years preceding the triggering event, as determined by the corporation's independent accountant, divided by the number of shares of the corporation outstanding on the date of the triggering event. The selling or deceased shareholder shall receive interest on the value of his shares equal to the six-month LIBOR as of the date of the triggering event.
(b) Upon the occurrence of any event in Article 1, subsection 3, 5, 8, 9, 10, 11 or 12, the purchasing shareholders shall purchase the shares of the selling shareholder at the following price per share: Ten (10) times the corporation's average net income for the two most recent fiscal years preceding the triggering event, as determined by the corporation's independent accountant, divided by the number of shares of the corporation outstanding on the date of the triggering event. The selling shareholder shall receive interest on the value of his shares equal to the six-month LIBOR as of the date of the triggering event.

membership or any rights she possesses as a member. A member of a mutual benefit corporation may transfer her membership and rights only if the articles or bylaws permit. When transfer rights are permitted, restrictions on transfer are valid only if approved by the members, including the affected member.

Problems and Problem Cases

1. Today, entrepreneurship has an almost cult-like worship in society. Entrepreneurs, and the companies they create, are ubiquitous. Creating a corporation to facilitate entrepreneurship is in many ways very easy; it can now occur with just the click of a mouse (although it is often undertaken with little legal advice or understanding of the corporate instrument). The difficult reality, though, is that many entrepreneurial ventures will fail, causing some companies to default on the venture's early contracts. Although the law is mostly settled as to when a promoter will be liable on a contract entered into on the business's behalf before a corporation is formed (see the concept of novation for review), what are the policy arguments for holding the promotor liable and for the converse? Consider impacts to contracting third parties, fairness to promotors, and incentives that might impact the formation of companies and the entrepreneurial ventures they support.

2. Charles McCrory has invented a new battery technology that will revolutionize the automotive power industry. To exploit the technology, McCrory seeks the financial assistance of several private equity firms, including Zoltar Partners LP, which wants to form a new corporation, to be named GoPow Inc., to exploit McCrory's invention. Zoltar wants to obtain exclusive rights to McCrory's services but is concerned that another private equity firm will preempt Zoltar by contracting with McCrory first. Therefore, Zoltar wants to bind McCrory to a contract with GoPow as soon as possible. GoPow has not yet been incorporated. Zoltar does not want to assume any liability on the contract with McCrory beyond its future capital investment in GoPow. State three options by which Zoltar may obtain McCrory's contractual commitment without imposing unlimited liability on Zoltar as a promoter making a preincorporation contract?

3. Robert Waddell decided to go into the construction business, and therefore, he signed the articles of incorporations for R. H. Waddell Construction Inc. as the incorporator on August 19, 1988. Unbeknown to Waddell, the articles were not filed by the secretary of state's office until December 9, 1988.

On September 12, 1988, Waddell entered into a contract to construct a home for Robert Valiga and signed the contract on behalf of R. H. Waddell Construction. On February 11, 1989, Waddell received a letter from Valiga expressing dissatisfaction with the slow progress and the shocking cost of the completed construction, and three days later, Waddell quit as Valiga's contractor. Subsequently, Valiga sued Waddell and others claiming there was no corporation registered in the State of Tennessee named R. H. Waddell Construction when the contract was entered into on September 12, 1988. Is Waddell personally liable as a promoter for the construction contract signed in the name of R. H. Waddell Construction?

4. Hydro-Dynamics Inc. (HDI) manufactured bed sheets, principally for waterbeds. HDI purchased cloth from Fieldcrest Cannon on credit for several years. John Meyer was an officer and director of HDI from May 22, 1987, until HDI's dissolution on September 10, 1990. After HDI's dissolution, Meyer continued to act as if HDI were a corporation, and in the name of HDI, he continued for many months to make contracts and buy cloth on credit from Fieldcrest. Fieldcrest was not aware that HDI ceased to exist. Is Meyer personally liable on the contracts he made with Fieldcrest in the name of HDI after its dissolution?

5. George Richert agreed to retain Crye-Leike Realtors as his sole and exclusive real estate agent to find a building for Richert's business. The agency contract was signed by Richert and by Colman Borosky for Crye-Leike. All parties understood that Richert would soon form a corporation that would be the actual party to lease the building found by Crye-Leike. A month later, Richert formed WDM Inc. Richert was president and CEO. WDM never formally adopted the agency contract with Crye-Leike. However, Crye-Leike contacted various landlords for WDM, showed several properties to WDM, and prepared an offer to lease space on behalf of WDM. All these efforts were done with Richert's full knowledge. When WDM hired another real estate agent, Crye-Leike sued for breach of the exclusive agency contract. WDM claimed that it was not a party to the contract between Richert and Crye-Leike. Was WDM correct?

6. Two colleagues decide to incorporate their Internet social networking business. They want complete control of the business, yet they need additional capital to expand the business. The two colleagues enter negotiations with eight friends willing to provide capital to the corporation. The friends agree that they will not be allowed to elect directors, but they want to make sure that they will receive a return on their investments by receiving payments from the corporation quarterly or semiannually. What securities with what rights should the corporation create to achieve the objectives of the friends and colleagues? For each security you create, sketch the rights of the holders.

7. For many business students, their favorite reality show is *Shark Tank*. For those who are not regular watchers, on the show entrepreneurs pitch their startup businesses to a panel of investors, including billionaire Dallas Mavericks owner Mark Cuban, fashion magnate Daymond John, and QVC star Lori Greiner. At the end of the pitch, if the "sharks" like the business, they will offer to invest for an equity stake in the company. A recent article on the popular entrepreneurial website The Hustle conducted an analysis of every deal made on the show since 2009. It determined the average deal amount was $286,000, and the average equity given up is 27%. That means small business owners pitching on the show are routinely giving up more than a quarter of their business. If you were an entrepreneur with a great business idea, what are your options for financing your company? In addition to the financial pros and cons, what are the legal considerations you should be considering? And if you did get an offer from the sharks to take an equity stake in your business, how might you structure the deal to protect your interests?

8. Pacific Coast Fisheries Corporation issued more than 5 percent of its public shares to Fujian Pelagic Fishery Group Company under the laws of the state of Washington. Fujian did not pay cash for the shares, instead issuing to Pacific Coast a promissory note committing it to pay in the future in the form of merchandise. Has Fujian paid a proper consideration for the shares?

9. Pro Brands Inc., a South Carolina corporation, hires Treena Javitz as vice president of marketing. Pro Brands and Javitz sign a written contract by which Pro Brands agrees to pay Javitz an annual salary of $450,000 and a performance bonus that could reach $400,000 a year, as well as issue to her 30,000 shares of Pro Brands common shares. The market price of the common shares is $22 per share. The board of directors agrees to issue the shares to Javitz in return for her

signing the five-year contract and a separate promissory note for $330,000. The note is due immediately if Javitz terminates the contract anytime before the end of five years. The amount that will be due to Pro Brands on the note will reduce by $5,500 for each month that Javitz works as VP of marketing for Pro Brands. If she works for Pro Brands for all five years, Javitz will owe nothing on the note. Has the board of directors issued the shares for proper consideration?

10. Seven Springs Farm is a Pennsylvania corporation that owns and operates a 5,000-acre, year-round resort, with both skiing facilities and a conference center. The shareholders signed an agreement providing that no stockholder "shall transfer, assign, sell, pledge, hypothecate, mortgage, alienate or in any other way encumber or dispose of all or any part of his stock in the Corporation . . . without first giving to all other Stockholders and the Corporation at least 30 days' written notice . . . of his intention to make a disposition of his stock. . . . Within the 30 day period a special meeting of all of the Stockholders shall be called by the Corporation. . . . At such meeting all the stock of the Stockholders . . . shall be offered for sale and shall be subject to an option to purchase or to retire on the part of the Corporation, which option shall be exercised, if at all, at the time of such meeting. . . ." In 1998, two-thirds of the shareholders voted to merge the corporation with Booth Creek Ski Holding. Due to the merger, the existing shares of Seven Springs would be "converted" into the right to receive cash and certain deferred cash payments. The dissenting shareholder, Lynda Croker, sought to purchase the shares of the shareholders who approved the merger, arguing that the merger with Booth Creek invoked the shareholders' right of first refusal. Was Croker correct?

11. Stufft Farms was a Montana corporation that owned and operated a family farm. The only shareholders were five family members. The bylaws included a share-transfer restriction stating that no shareholder had the right to sell her shares without first offering the shares to the corporation and shareholders at book value. Neil Johnson offered to purchase all of Stufft Farms's shares. His offer was contingent upon all of the shares being tendered to him. When four shareholders accepted Johnson's offer, the fifth shareholder, David Stufft, who did not accept the offer, argued that he had the right to buy the shares of the tendering four shareholders at book value. Was he correct?

12. Josh Thomas, Jack Wiley, and Will Regis are three close friends who have been offered the opportunity

to invest $100,000 each and to become 10 percent shareholders each in a closely held corporation that will be controlled by their friends Leone and Teddy Battat, who will own the remaining 70 percent of the shares. The business, to be named EZStreet .com Inc., will be an online business networking site. Leone and Teddy's plan is to amass at least 500 million users worldwide, which they estimate will take five to seven years, after which they would like to take the company public or sell it to another company, like Google. Josh is a CPA with 10 years' experience in business consulting and investment management. Jack is a software engineer who has designed more than 50 websites. Will has an MBA in consumer and business marketing with 12 years' experience in public relations and ad sales. Sketch the terms of the agreement that Josh, Jack, and Will should ask of Leone and Teddy to ensure that they will obtain returns on their investments while they are shareholders before the company goes public or is sold to another company. In addition, what type of agreement should they have to make sure they can obtain capital appreciation of their shares when the corporation goes public or is sold to another company? Sketch the contents of that agreement. How do you suggest the agreement determine the value of the shares?

CHAPTER 43

Management of Corporations

Clestra Corporation is a manufacturer of consumer products ranging from canned and packaged foods like spaghetti sauce and popcorn to over-the-counter health aids like toothpaste and mouthwash. Its annual worldwide revenues are just under $6 billion. Clestra brands are not among the top two in the industry in any of its product lines, each brand ranking from fourth to sixth in annual sales in countries in which it markets its products. Clestra's CEO has been discussing the company's future with its consultant, KRNP Consulting LLP. KRNP has suggested that Clestra consider acquiring Ballston Inc., a consumer products company with $2 billion in annual sales. Ballston's brands are complementary to Clestra's brands, and while smaller than Clestra, Ballston has a distribution system that will give Clestra access to markets in which Clestra is not currently a significant seller.

Clestra's CEO also wants to improve consumer recognition of the Clestra brand. She suggests that Clestra acquire naming rights to a stadium being built for a baseball team in northern Virginia, the Virginia Hatchets. The CEO thinks that Clestra has the inside track to acquire naming rights because the family of one of Clestra's board members owns the baseball team that will own and operate the stadium.

- What legal standard will determine whether Clestra's board of directors has acted properly when approving Clestra's acquisition of Ballston? What role may KRNP Consulting take in helping Clestra's board of directors meet its duties under that legal standard?
- What legal standard will judge whether Clestra's board of directors has acted properly when acquiring naming rights to the Virginia Hatchets's stadium? What role may KRNP Consulting take in helping Clestra's board of directors meet its duties under that legal standard?
- Suppose Clestra's CEO is concerned that Clestra may be a target for a takeover by one of the larger consumer goods companies. If Clestra wants to remain an independent company, what should Clestra's board of directors do now to increase the chances that it may fend off a hostile takeover? What legal standard will judge whether Clestra's board has acted properly in adopting defenses against a hostile takeover? What should Clestra's board do now to increase the likelihood that the board will comply with that legal standard when it opposes a hostile takeover?

LO LEARNING OBJECTIVES

After studying this chapter, you should be able to:

43-1 Understand the limits on the objectives and powers of corporations, especially the pressures corporate managers face in satisfying the interests of shareholders and other constituents.

43-2 Appreciate the roles of the board of directors and its various committees.

43-3 Describe recent developments in corporate governance.

43-4 Adapt the rules of corporate governance to the practical requirements of close corporations.

43-5 Know the legal standards that judge actions
of officers and directors and follow the steps
required to comply with each standard.

43-6 List and describe tactics a board of directors
may adopt to defend against hostile takeovers.

43-7 Explain the legal limits of corporate liability for
officers' and directors' actions.

ALTHOUGH SHAREHOLDERS OWN a corporation,
they traditionally have possessed no right to manage the
business of the corporation. Instead, shareholders elect
individuals to a *board of directors*, to which management is
entrusted. Often, the board delegates much of its management responsibilities to *officers* and other managers.

This chapter explains the legal aspects of the board's and
officers' management of the corporation. Their management of the corporation must be consistent with the objectives and powers of the corporation, and they owe duties to
the corporation to manage it prudently and in the best interests of the corporation and the shareholders as a whole.

Corporate Objectives

Understand the limits on the objectives and powers
of corporations, especially the pressures corporate
managers face in satisfying the interests of shareholders
and other constituents.

The traditional objective of the business corporation has
been to *enhance corporate profits and shareholder gain*.
According to this objective, the managers of a corporation
must seek the accomplishment of the profit objective to
the exclusion of all inconsistent goals. Interests other than
profit maximization may be considered, provided that they
do not hinder the ultimate profit objective.

Nonetheless, some courts have permitted corporations to
take *socially responsible actions* that are not strictly or obviously
aimed at the *profit maximization requirement*. In addition, every
state recognizes corporate powers that are not solely economically inspired. For example, corporations may make contributions to colleges, political campaigns, child abuse prevention
centers, literary associations, and employee benefit plans,
regardless of direct economic benefit to the corporation. Also,
every state expressly recognizes the right of shareholders to
choose freely the extent to which profit maximization captures
all of their interests and all of their sense of responsibility.

Most states have enacted **corporate constituency statutes**,
which broaden the legal objectives of corporations. Such
statutes permit or require directors to take into account the
interests of constituencies other than shareholders, including employees, suppliers, and customers. These statutes
direct the board to act in the best interests of the corporation and its stakeholders, not just short-term interests of
the shareholders, and to maximize corporate profits *over the
long term*. Such laws promote the view that a corporation is
a collection of interests working together for the purpose of
producing goods and services at a profit, and that the goal
of corporate profit maximization over the long term is not
necessarily the same as the goal of stock price maximization
over the short term. Even in the absence of a constituency
statute, however, managers have wide latitude under the
business judgment rule to maximize corporate value, which
can include taking into account the interests of stakeholders.

Ethics and Compliance in Action

Corporate Constituency Statutes

Over forty states have enacted corporate constituency stakeholder laws that explicitly *permit* directors to
weigh the interests of constituencies other than shareholders,
although no state *requires* the consideration of other constituencies. Neither the MBCA nor the Delaware statute expressly
authorizes corporate boards to consider the interests of any
persons other than the shareholders.

- Would you recommend that board members consider the
interests of stakeholders other than shareholders when making
a corporate decision?
- Which ethical theories that we studied in Chapter 4 permit
directors to consider the interests of constituencies other
than shareholders?
- Under profit maximization, what is the significance of non-
shareholders' interests? Can a corporation maximize its
profits without considering the interests of persons other
than shareholders?

Corporate Powers

The actions of management are limited not only by the objectives of business corporations but also by the *powers* granted to business corporations. Such limitations may appear in the state statute, the articles of incorporation, and the bylaws.

The primary source of a corporation's powers is the corporation statute of the state in which it is incorporated. Some state corporation statutes expressly specify the powers of corporations. These powers include making gifts for charitable and educational purposes, lending money to corporate officers and directors, and purchasing and disposing of the corporation's shares. Other state corporation statutes limit the powers of corporations, such as prohibiting the acquisition of agricultural land by corporations.

Modern statutes attempt to authorize corporations to engage in any activity. The Model Business Corporation Act (MBCA) states that a corporation has the power to do *anything that an individual may do.*

Purpose Clauses in Articles of Incorporation   Most corporations state their purposes in the articles of incorporation. The purpose is usually phrased in broad terms, even if the corporation has been formed with only one type of business in mind. Most corporations have purpose clauses stating that they may engage in any lawful business.

Under the MBCA, the inclusion of a purpose clause in the articles is optional. Any corporation incorporated under the MBCA has the purpose of engaging in any lawful business, unless the articles state a more limited purpose.

The Ultra Vires *Doctrine*   Historically, an act of a corporation beyond its powers was a nullity, as it was *ultra vires*, which is Latin for "beyond the powers." Therefore, any act not permitted by the corporation statute or by the corporation's articles of incorporation was void due to lack of capacity.

This lack of capacity or power of the corporation was a defense to a contract assertable either by the corporation or by the other party that dealt with the corporation. Often, *ultra vires* was merely a convenient justification for reneging on an agreement that was no longer considered desirable. This misuse of the doctrine has led to its near abandonment.

Today, the *ultra vires* doctrine is of small importance for two reasons. First, nearly all corporations have broad purpose clauses, thereby preventing any *ultra vires* problem. Second, the MBCA and most other statutes do not permit a corporation or the other party to an agreement to avoid an obligation on the ground that the corporate action is *ultra vires.*

Under the MBCA, *ultra vires* may be asserted by only three types of persons: (1) by a shareholder seeking to enjoin a corporation from executing a proposed action that is *ultra vires*; (2) by the corporation suing its management for damages caused by exceeding the corporation's powers; and (3) by the state's attorney general, who may have the power to enjoin an *ultra vires* act or to dissolve a corporation that exceeds its powers.

Powers of Nonprofit Corporations

Nonprofit corporations, like for-profit corporations, have the power to transact business granted by the incorporation statute, the articles, and the bylaws. The Model Nonprofit Corporation Act (MNCA), like the MBCA, grants nonprofit corporations the power to engage in any lawful activity and to do anything an individual may do. Thus, a nonprofit corporation may sue and be sued, purchase, hold, and sell real property, lend and borrow money, and make charitable and other donations, among its many powers.

Commonly, a nonprofit corporation's articles will limit its powers pursuant to a purpose clause. For example, a nonprofit corporation established to operate a junior baseball league may limit its powers to that business and matters reasonably connected to it. When a nonprofit corporation limits its powers, a risk arises that the corporation may commit an *ultra vires* act. The MNCA adopts the same rules for *ultra vires* contracts as does the MBCA: Generally, neither the corporation nor the other party may use *ultra vires* as a defense to a contract.

The Board of Directors

 LO43-2   Appreciate the roles of the board of directors and its various committees.

Traditionally, the **board of directors** has had the authority and the duty to manage the corporation. Yet in a large publicly held corporation, it is impossible for the board to manage the corporation on a day-to-day basis because many of the directors are high-level executives in other corporations who devote most of their time to their other business interests. Therefore, the MBCA permits a corporation to be managed by or *under the direction of* the board of directors. Consequently, the board of directors delegates major responsibility for management to committees of the board such as an executive committee, to individual board members such as the board chairperson, and to the officers and managers of the corporation, especially the chief executive officer (CEO). In theory, the board supervises the actions of its committees, the chairperson, and the officers and managers to ensure that the board's policies are being carried out and that the delegatees are managing the corporation prudently.

Board Authority under Corporation Statutes

A corporation's board of directors has the authority to do almost everything within the powers of the corporation. The board's authority includes not only the general power to manage or direct the corporation in the ordinary course of its business but also the power to issue shares of stock and to set the price of shares. Among its other powers, the board may repurchase shares, declare dividends, adopt and amend bylaws, elect and remove officers, and fill vacancies on the board.

Some corporate actions require *board initiative* and shareholder approval. That is, board approval is necessary to *propose such actions to the shareholders*, who then must approve the action. Board initiative is required for important changes in the corporation, such as amendment of the articles of incorporation, merger of the corporation, the sale of all or substantially all of the corporation's assets, and voluntary dissolution.

Committees of the Board

Most publicly held corporations have committees of the board of directors. These committees, which have fewer members than full board, can more efficiently handle management decisions and exercise board powers than can the entire board. Only directors may serve on board committees.

Although many board powers may be delegated to committees of the board, some decisions are so important that corporation statutes require their *approval by the board as a whole*. Under the MBCA, the powers that may not be delegated concern important corporate actions such as declaring dividends, filling vacancies on the board or its committees, adopting and amending bylaws, and approving repurchases of the corporation's shares.

The most common board committee is the **executive committee**. It is usually given authority to act for the board on most matters when the board is not in session. Generally, it consists of the *inside directors* and perhaps one or two *outside directors* who can attend a meeting on short notice. An inside director is an officer of the corporation who devotes substantially full time to the corporation. Outside directors have no such affiliation with the corporation.

Audit committees are directly responsible for the appointment, compensation, and oversight of independent public accountants. They supervise the public accountants' audit of the corporate financial records. In addition, many audit committees have oversight of regulatory compliance and risk management and mitigation activities. The Sarbanes–Oxley Act requires that all publicly held firms have audit committees comprised of independent directors. Independent directors, described more below, are those that do not accept any consulting or advisory fees from the company aside from what they are compensated as board members. That act was a response to allegations of unethical and criminal conduct by corporate CEOs and auditors at firms like Enron, World-Com, and Arthur Andersen in the 1990s and early 2000s. Rules of the New York Stock Exchange (NYSE) and the NASDAQ, which apply to firms listed on those exchanges, also require that audit committees are independent.

Nominating committees choose management's slate of directors that is to be submitted to shareholders at the annual election of directors. Nominating committees also often plan for management succession. NYSE and NASDAQ rules require that only independent directors select or recommend director nominees.

Compensation committees review and approve the salaries, bonuses, stock options, and other benefits of high-level corporate executives. Although compensation committees usually comprise directors who have no affiliation with the executives or directors whose compensation is being approved, compensation committees may also set the compensation of their members. In 2018, non-executive, directors of large public companies received annual compensation—including retainers, meeting attendance fees, and stock options—averaging more than $300,000. That amount, which can be much higher at individual firms—for example, Goldman Sachs' directors average almost $600,000—is over 40% more than it was 10 years prior.

The public and Congress have criticized board approvals of large compensation packages to CEOs and other top-level officers, including stock options and bonus plans that sometimes allowed individual officers to earn more than $100 million in a single year. In 2018, Elon Musk, Tesla's CEO, was awarded over $500 million in stock options. Disney's chairman and CEO, Bob Iger, was the third-highest-paid executive that year, earning $146 million in salary, bonus, stock, and additional compensation. Hoping that board independence would rein in such compensation, the Securities and Exchange Commission (SEC) has adopted NYSE and NASDAQ rules that require independent directors to approve executive compensation. The Dodd-Frank Wall Street Reform and Consumer Protection Act of 2010 also requires periodic shareholder approval of executive compensation. Despite this, CEO pay continues to rise, as does the difference between median CEO and worker pay.

A **shareholder litigation committee** is given the task of determining whether a corporation should sue someone who has allegedly harmed the corporation. Usually, this committee of disinterested directors is formed when a shareholder asks the board of directors to cause the corporation to sue some or all of the directors for mismanaging the corporation. Because the committee is supposed to objectively evaluate the merits of such a claim, it must be formed with the utmost care so there is no appearance that it may not be acting in the company's best interests.

Who Is an Independent Director?

Listing requirements for both the NYSE and NASDAQ provide basic checklists for director independence. Generally, independent directors are not employed by the company, do not have family members who are employed by the company, and do not have a controlling interest in the company's substantial business partners. The NYSE's listing requirements also note that independent directors have "no material relationship" with the corporation. The NASDAQ's requirements state that independent directors have no relationship that "would interfere with the exercise of independent judgment in carrying out the responsibilities of a director." When evaluating director independence, the courts consider close business or personal ties with controlling shareholders, other directors, or third parties with which the company does business; ownership of the company's stock; service on multiple boards; personal interests in past and current company business deals; and political affiliations.

Powers, Rights, and Liabilities of Directors as Individuals

A director is not an agent of the corporation *merely* by being a director. The directors may manage the corporation only when they act as a board, unless the board of directors grants agency powers to the directors individually.

A director has the *right to inspect* corporate books and records that contain corporate information essential to the director's performance of her duties. The director's right of inspection is denied when the director has an interest adverse to the corporation, as in the case of a director who plans to sell a corporation's trade secrets to a competitor.

Normally, a director does not have any personal liability for the contracts and torts of the corporation.

Election of Directors

Generally, any individual may serve as a director of a corporation. A director need not even be a shareholder. Nonetheless, a corporation is permitted to specify qualifications for directors in the articles of incorporation.

A corporation must have the number of directors required by the state corporation law. The MBCA and several state corporation statutes require a minimum of 1 director, recognizing that in close corporations with a single shareholder-manager, additional board members are superfluous. Several statutes, including the California statute, require at least 3 directors, unless there are fewer than three shareholders, in which case the corporation may have no fewer directors than it has shareholders.

A corporation may have more than the minimum number of directors required by the corporation statute. The articles of incorporation or bylaws will state the number of directors of the corporation. The size of the boards of large public corporations average just over 9 directors but can vary widely. For example, Google has 15 directors; Facebook 10; U.S. Bank, 17; Salesforce, 19; and Johnson & Johnson, 13.

Directors are elected by the shareholders at the annual shareholder meeting. Usually, each shareholder is permitted to vote for as many nominees as there are directors to be elected. The shareholder may cast as many votes for each nominee as he has shares. The top vote-getters among the nominees are elected as directors. This voting process, called **straight voting**, permits a holder of more than 50 percent of the shares of a corporation to dominate the corporation by electing a board of directors that will manage the corporation as he wants it to be managed.

To avoid domination by a large shareholder, some corporations allow class voting or cumulative voting. **Class voting** may give certain classes of shareholders the right to elect a specified number of directors. **Cumulative voting** permits shareholders to multiply the number of their shares by the number of directors to be elected and to cast the resulting total of votes for one or more directors. As a result, cumulative voting may permit minority shareholders to obtain representation on the board of directors.

Directors usually hold office for only one year, but they may have longer terms. The MBCA permits **staggered terms** for directors. A corporation may establish either two or three approximately equal classes of directors, with only one class of directors coming up for election at each annual shareholders' meeting. If there are two classes of directors, the directors serve two-year terms; if there are three classes, they serve three-year terms.

The original purpose of staggered terms was to permit continuity of management. Staggered terms also frustrate the ability of minority shareholders to use cumulative voting to elect their representatives to the board of directors.

The Proxy Solicitation Process   Most individual investors purchase corporate shares in the public market to increase their wealth, not to elect or to influence the directors of corporations. Nearly all institutional investors—such as pension funds, mutual funds, and bank trust departments—have the same profit motive. Generally, they are passive investors with little interest in exercising their shareholder right to elect directors by attending shareholder meetings.

Once public ownership of the corporation's shares exceeds 50 percent, the corporation cannot conduct any business at its shareholder meetings unless some of the shares of these passive investors are voted. This is because the corporation will have a shareholder quorum requirement, which usually requires that 50 percent or more of the shares be voted for a shareholder vote to be valid. Because passive investors rarely attend shareholder meetings, the management of the corporation must solicit **proxies** if it wishes to have a valid shareholder vote. Shareholders who will not attend a shareholder meeting must be asked to appoint someone else to vote their shares for them. This is done by furnishing each such shareholder with a proxy form to sign. The proxy designates a person who may vote the shares for the shareholder.

Management Solicitation of Proxies To ensure its perpetuation in office and the approval of other matters submitted for a shareholder vote, the corporation's management solicits proxies from shareholders for directors' elections and other important matters on which shareholders vote, such as mergers. The management designates an officer, a director, or some other person to vote the proxies received. The person who is designated to vote for the shareholder is also called a proxy. Typically, the chief executive officer (CEO) of the corporation, the president, or the chairperson of the board of directors names the person who serves as the proxy.

Usually, the proxies are merely signed and returned by the public shareholders, including the institutional shareholders. Passive investors follow the **Wall Street rule**: Either support management or sell the shares. As a result, management almost always receives enough votes from its proxy solicitation to ensure the reelection of directors and the approval of other matters submitted to the shareholders, even when other parties solicit proxies in opposition to management.

Management's solicitation of proxies may produce a result quite different from the theory of corporate management that directors serve as representatives of the shareholders. The CEO usually nominates directors of her choice, and they are almost always elected. The directors appoint officers chosen by the CEO. The CEO's nominees for director are not unduly critical of her programs or of her methods for carrying them out. This is particularly true if a large proportion of the directors are officers of the company and thus are more likely to be dominated by the CEO. In such situations, the board of directors may not function effectively as a representative of the shareholders in supervising and evaluating the CEO and the other officers of the corporation. The board members and the other officers are subordinates of the CEO, even though the CEO is not a major shareholder of the corporation.

LO43-3 Describe recent developments in corporate governance.

Proposals for improving corporate governance in public-issue corporations seek to develop a board that is capable of functioning independently of the CEO by changing the composition or operation of the board of directors. Some corporate governance critics propose that a federal agency such as the SEC appoint one or more directors to serve as watchdogs of the public interest. Other critics would require that shareholders elect at least a majority of directors without prior ties to the corporation, thus excluding shareholders, suppliers, and customers from the board.

Other proposals recommend changing the method by which directors are nominated for election. One proposal would encourage shareholders to make nominations for directors. Supporters of this proposal argue that in addition to reducing the influence of the CEO, it would also broaden the range of backgrounds represented on the board. The SEC recommends that publicly held corporations establish a nominating committee composed of outside directors. Many publicly held corporations have nomination committees.

Due to pressure from the public and Congress after the corporate scandals of the 1990s and early 2000s, the SEC approved NYSE and NASDAQ corporate governance rules that make corporate boards more nearly independent of the CEO in structure, if not in action. One rule requires boards be comprised of only independent directors. Equally important, the independent directors must meet from time to time by themselves in executive session independent of the CEO. In addition, institutional investors—including mutual funds and hedge funds—are taking increasingly active roles in director elections. This is particularly important as large index funds continue to grow, increasing the influence of a small number of fund managers over many companies' governance.

 **LOG ON**

www.issgovernance.com/
Check out the Institutional Shareholder Services website to find resources on current corporate governance issues.

In the following case, *Omnicare, Inc. v. NCS Healthcare, Inc.*, the court considered whether a merger agreement and voting agreements were valid and enforceable. In applying the business judgment rule (discussed in detail later in this chapter), the court ultimately held that the agreements were not valid and enforceable because reasonable doubt was raised as to whether the directors acted in good faith.

Omnicare, Inc. v. NCS Healthcare, Inc.   818 A.2d 914 (Del. 2003)

Genesis Health Ventures Inc. (Genesis) (defendant) entered into negotiations to acquire NCS Healthcare, Inc. (NCS) (defendant). At the urging of Genesis, the parties entered into an exclusivity agreement, which prevented NCS from engaging in any negotiations in regard to a competing acquisition or transaction. Subsequently, Omnicare, Inc. (Omnicare) (plaintiff) reached out to NCS regarding a proposed transaction; however, pursuant to the exclusivity agreement with Genesis, NCS did not respond.

Complementary to Genesis's merger proposal was a voting agreement and an agreement to omit a "fiduciary out" clause. Specifically, the proposal included a voting trust in which the two major shareholders (Jon Outcalt, chairman of the NCS board, and Kevin Shaw, NCS president and CEO) agreed to vote for the merger. In other words, this voting agreement effectively meant that NCS shareholder approval of the merger was guaranteed even if the NCS board did not recommend its approval.

The agreement to omit a "fiduciary out" clause meant that the board agreed not to consider other merger offers, would put the merger to a shareholder vote, and would allow minority shareholders to have appraisal rights. If the merger agreement had contained a fiduciary out clause, it would have given the NCS board the opportunity to opt out of the agreement if it needed to do so to discharge its fiduciary duties to the corporation.

Meanwhile, before the official, although futile, NCS shareholder vote on the Genesis merger proposal, Omnicare submitted a merger proposal that was superior to that of Genesis. It was at this point that the NCS board then withdrew its recommendation that the shareholders vote in favor of the Genesis merger agreement. However, the Genesis merger agreement provided that the proposal still must be submitted to a shareholder vote and, because of the Outcalt/Shaw voting agreement and the omission of a fiduciary out clause, that meant that the merger agreement was going to be approved no matter what. Omnicare brought suit. The Court of Chancery, New Castle County, Delaware, denied the injunction.

Holland, Judge

"The business judgment rule, as a standard of judicial review, is a common-law recognition of the statutory authority to manage a corporation that is vested in the board of directors." The business judgment rule is a "presumption that in making a business decision the directors of a corporation acted on an informed basis, in good faith and in the honest belief that the action taken was in the best interests of the company." "An application of the traditional business judgment rule places the burden on the 'party challenging the board's decision to establish facts rebutting the presumption.'" The effect of a proper invocation of the business judgment rule, as a standard of judicial review, is powerful because it operates deferentially. Unless the procedural presumption of the business judgment rule is rebutted, a "court will not substitute its judgment for that of the board if the board's decision can be 'attributed to any rational business purpose.'"

The business judgment rule embodies the deference that is accorded to managerial decisions of a board of directors. "Under normal circumstances, neither the courts nor the stockholders should interfere with the managerial decision of the directors." There are certain circumstances, however, "which mandate that a court take a more direct and active role in overseeing the decisions made and actions taken by directors. In these situations, a court subjects the directors' conduct to enhanced scrutiny to ensure that it is reasonable," "before the protections of the business judgment rule may be conferred."

The prior decisions of this Court have identified the circumstances where board action must be subjected to enhanced judicial scrutiny before the presumptive protection of the business

judgment rule can be invoked. One of those circumstances was described in *Unocal*: when a board adopts defensive measures in response to a hostile takeover proposal that the board reasonably determines is a threat to corporate policy and effectiveness. In *Moran v. Household*, we explained why a *Unocal* analysis is also applied to the adoption of a stockholder's rights plan, even in the absence of an immediate threat. Other circumstances requiring enhanced judicial scrutiny give rise to what are known as *Revlon* duties, such as when the board enters into a merger transaction that will cause a change in corporate control, initiates an active bidding process seeking to sell the corporation, or makes a breakup of the corporate entity inevitable.

Given the facts in this case, the board's action is subjected to enhanced judicial scrutiny. In applying enhanced judicial scrutiny to defensive devices designed to protect a merger agreement, a court must first determine that those measures are not preclusive or coercive before its focus shifts to the "range of reasonableness" in making a proportionality determination. The board must demonstrate that it has reasonable grounds for believing that a danger to the corporation and its stockholders exists if the merger transaction is not consummated.

Defensive measures cannot limit or circumscribe the directors' fiduciary duties. Notwithstanding a corporation's insolvent condition, the corporation's board has no authority to execute a merger agreement that subsequently prevents it from effectively discharging its ongoing fiduciary responsibilities. The NCS board was required to contract for an effective fiduciary out clause to exercise its continuing fiduciary responsibilities to the minority stockholders.

In this case, the NCS board combined two otherwise valid actions (the stockholder voting agreement and the fiduciary out clause) and caused them to operate in concert as an absolute lock up in the Genesis merger agreement. In the context of this pre-clusive and coercive lock up case, the protection of Genesis' con-tractual expectations must yield to the supervening responsibility of the directors to discharge their fiduciary duties on a continu-ing basis. The merger agreement and voting agreements, as they were combined to operate in concert in this case, are inconsistent with the NCS directors' fiduciary duties. To that extent, the Court holds that they are invalid and unenforceable.

With respect to the Fiduciary Duty Decision, the order of the Court of Chancery, denying plaintiffs' application for a prelimin-ary injunction is reversed.

Judgment REVERSED

Vacancies on the Board The MBCA permits the direc-tors to fill vacancies on the board. A majority vote of the remaining directors is sufficient to select persons to serve out unexpired terms, even though the remaining directors are less than a quorum.

Removal of Directors Modern corporation statutes per-mit shareholders to remove directors *with or without cause.* The rationale for the modern rule is that the shareholders should have the power to judge the fitness of directors at any time.

However, most corporations have provisions in their arti-cles authorizing the shareholders to remove directors *only for cause.* Cause for removal would include mismanagement or conflicts of interest. Before removal for cause, the director must be given notice and an opportunity for a hearing.

A director elected by a class of shareholders may be removed only by that class of shareholders, thereby pro-tecting the voting rights of the class. A director elected by cumulative voting may not be removed if the votes cast against her removal would have been sufficient to elect her to the board, thereby protecting the voting rights of minor-ity shareholders.

The MBCA also gives a court power to remove a dir-ector, upon petition of shareholders, when the court finds that the director engaged in fraudulent conduct with respect to the corporation or its shareholders, grossly abused the position of director, or intentionally inflicted harm on the corporation. The court must also find that removal of the director would be in the best interest of the corporation.

Directors' Meetings

For the directors to act, a *quorum* of the directors must be present. The quorum requirement ensures that the decision of the board will represent the views of a substantial por-tion of the directors. A quorum is usually a *majority* of the number of directors.

Each director has *one vote.* If a quorum is present, a vote of a majority of the directors present is an act of the board,

The Global Business Environment

Corporate Governance in Germany

Corporate governance varies somewhat from country to country. In Germany, for example, the *Aktiengesellschaft* (AG) has a **management board** and a **supervisory board**. The AG's management board represents and manages the company. Its members are not directly answer-able to shareholders but are appointed by the AG's supervisory board. All members of the management board manage the com-pany together. However, the articles may provide that the com-pany may be represented by two members of the management board.

The members of the AG's supervisory board are like the outside directors of an American company. They are elected by the AG's shareholders and, if German co-determination rules apply, by the employees. The supervisory board is charged with protecting the interests of the company, which may not coincide with those of the shareholders. To enable the supervisory board to carry out its oversight function, the management board is required to report regularly on the current status of the compa-ny's business and corporate planning. However, the supervisory board has no say in the day-to-day management of the company.

The Shop Constitution Act (*Betriebsverfassungsgesetz*) covers AGs with more than 500 employees. It provides that one-third of supervisory board members be employee representatives. Under the Co-determination Act (*Mitbestimmungsgesetz*), the super-visory boards of AGs with more than 2,000 employees must have equal numbers of shareholder and employee representatives.

unless the articles or the bylaws require the vote of a greater number of directors. Such *supermajority voting provisions* are common in close corporations but not in publicly held corporations. The use of supermajority voting provisions by close corporations is covered later in this chapter.

Directors are entitled to two days' notice of all *special meetings*, but not of regularly scheduled meetings. The MBCA does not require the notice for a special meeting to state the purpose of the meeting. A director's attendance at a meeting waives any required notice, unless at the beginning of the meeting the director objects to the lack of notice.

Traditionally, directors could act only when they were properly convened as a board. They could not vote by proxy or informally, as by telephone. This rule was based on a belief in the value of consultation and collective judgment.

Today, the corporation laws of a majority of the states and the MBCA specifically permit action by the directors without a meeting if all of the directors consent in writing to the action taken. Such authorization is useful for dealing with routine matters or for formally approving an action based on an earlier policy decision made after full discussion.

The MBCA also permits a board to meet by telephone, or virtually over the Internet. This permits a meeting of directors who may otherwise be unable to convene. The only requirement is that the directors be able to hear one another simultaneously.

Officers of the Corporation

The board of directors has the authority to appoint the officers of the corporation. Many corporation statutes provide that the officers of a corporation shall be the *president*, one or more *vice presidents*, a *secretary*, and a *treasurer*. Usually, any two or more offices may be held by the same person, except for the offices of president and secretary.

The MBCA requires only that there be an officer performing the duties normally granted to a corporate secretary. Under the MBCA, one person may hold several offices, including the offices of president and secretary.

The officers are agents of the corporation. As agents, officers have *express authority* conferred on them by the bylaws or the board of directors. In addition, officers have *implied authority* to do the things that are reasonably necessary to accomplish their express duties. Also, officers have *apparent authority* when the corporation leads third parties to believe reasonably that the officers have authority to act for the corporation. Like any principal, the corporation may *ratify* the unauthorized acts of its officers. This may be done expressly by a resolution of the board of directors or impliedly by the board's acceptance of the benefits of the officer's acts.

The most perplexing issue with regard to the authority of officers is whether an officer has *inherent authority* merely by virtue of the title of his office. Courts have held that certain official titles confer authority on officers, but such powers are much more restricted than one might expect.

Traditionally, a *president* possesses no power to bind the corporation by virtue of the office. Instead, she serves merely as the presiding officer at shareholder meetings and directors' meetings. A president with an additional title such as *general manager* or *chief executive officer* has broad implied authority to make contracts and to do other acts in the ordinary business of the corporation.

A *vice president* has no authority by virtue of that office. An executive who is vice president of a specified department, however, such as a vice president of marketing, will have the authority to transact the normal corporate business falling within the function of the department.

The *secretary* usually keeps the minutes of directors' and shareholder meetings, maintains other corporate records, retains custody of the corporate seal, and certifies corporate records as being authentic. Although the secretary has no authority to make contracts for the corporation by virtue of that office, the corporation is bound by documents certified by the secretary.

The *treasurer* has custody of the corporation's funds. He is the proper officer to receive payments to the corporation and to disburse corporate funds for authorized purposes. The treasurer binds the corporation by his receipts, checks, and indorsements, but he does not by virtue of that office alone have authority to borrow money, to issue negotiable instruments, or to make other contracts on behalf of the corporation.

Like any agent, a corporate officer ordinarily has *no liability on contracts* that he makes on behalf of his principal, the corporation, if he signs for the corporation and not in his personal capacity.

Officers serve the corporation at the pleasure of the board of directors, which may remove an officer at any time with or without cause. An officer who has been removed has no recourse against the corporation, unless the removal violates an employment contract between the officer and the corporation.

Managing Close Corporations

 Adapt the rules of corporate governance to the practical requirements of close corporations.

Many of the management formalities that you have studied in this chapter are appropriate for publicly held corporations, yet inappropriate for close corporations. For example, each close corporation shareholder may want to be *involved in management* of the corporation. If a close corporation shareholder is not involved in management, he may want to protect his interest by placing *restrictions on the managerial discretion* of those who do manage the corporation.

Modern close corporation statutes permit close corporations to dispense with most, if not all, management formalities. The Statutory Close Corporation Supplement to the MBCA permits a close corporation to *dispense with a board of directors* and to be *managed by the shareholders*. The California General Corporation Law permits the close corporation to be managed *as if it were a partnership*.

⊙ LOG ON

www.sos.ca.gov/business/corp/pdf/articles/arts-cl.pdf
This website for California's secretary of state will show you how to create a close corporation in California.

When a close corporation chooses to have a traditional board of directors, a minority shareholder may be dominated by the shareholders who control the board of directors. To protect minority shareholders, close corporations may impose **supermajority voting** requirements for board actions and *restrictions on the managerial discretion* of the board of directors.

Any corporation may require that board action be possible only with the approval of more than a majority of the directors, such as three-fourths or unanimous approval. A supermajority vote is often required to terminate the employment contract of an employee-shareholder, to reduce the level of dividends, and to change the corporation's line of business. Supermajority votes are rarely required for ordinary business matters, such as deciding with which suppliers the corporation should deal.

Traditionally, shareholders could not restrict the managerial discretion of directors. This rule recognized the traditional roles of the board as manager and of the shareholders as passive owners. Modern close corporation statutes permit shareholders to intrude into the sanctity of the boardroom. The Statutory Close Corporation Supplement grants the shareholders *unlimited* power to restrict the discretion of the board of directors. For example, the shareholders may agree that the directors may not terminate or reduce the salaries of employee-shareholders and must pay a mandatory dividend, if earned. And, as was stated above, close corporation statutes even permit the shareholders to dispense with a board of directors altogether and to manage the close corporation as if it were a partnership.

Of course, any article or bylaw protecting the rights of minority shareholders should not be changeable, unless the minority shareholders consent.

Managing Nonprofit Corporations

A nonprofit corporation is managed under the direction of a board of directors. The board of directors must have at least three directors. All corporate powers are exercised by or under the authority of the board of directors. Any person may serve as a director; however, the Model Nonprofit Corporation Act has an optional provision stating that no more than 49 percent of directors of a public service corporation may be financially interested in the business of that corporation. An interested person is, for example, the musical director of a city's symphony orchestra who receives a salary from the nonprofit corporation operating the orchestra.

If a nonprofit corporation has members, typically the members elect the directors. However, the articles may provide for the directors to be appointed or elected by other persons, such as the current directors. Directors serve for one year, unless the articles or bylaws provide otherwise. Directors who are elected may not serve terms longer than five years, but appointed directors may serve longer terms.

Directors may be elected by straight or cumulative voting and by class voting. Members may elect directors in person or by proxy. Directors may be removed at any time with or without cause by the members or other persons who elected or appointed the directors. When a director engages in fraudulent or dishonest conduct or breaches a fiduciary duty, members holding at least 5 percent of the voting power may petition a court to remove the wrongdoing director. Generally, a vacancy may be filled by the members or the board of directors; however, if a removed director was elected by a class of members or appointed by another person, only the class or person electing or appointing the director may fill the vacancy.

The board is permitted to set directors' compensation. Typically, directors of public benefit corporations and religious corporations are volunteers and receive no compensation. However, directors that serve in executive or management roles may be highly compensated, depending on the size and funding level of the organization. For example, the median salary of a nonprofit director in 2020 was $72,000, but at least 10 nonprofit CEOs made over $10 million, most of whom ran health care–related organizations.

Directors of a nonprofit corporation usually act at a meeting at which all directors may simultaneously hear each other, such as a meeting in person or by telephone conference call. The board may also act without a meeting if all directors consent in writing to the action. The board has the power to do most actions that are within the powers of the corporation, although some actions, such as mergers and amendments of the articles, require member action also. Ordinarily, an individual director has no authority to transact for a nonprofit corporation.

The board of directors of a nonprofit corporation may delegate some of its authority to committees of the board and to officers. A nonprofit corporation is not required to have officers, except for an officer performing the duties of corporate secretary. If a corporation chooses to have more officers, one person may hold more than one office. The board may remove an officer at any time with or without cause. Officers have the authority granted them by the bylaws or by board resolution.

Directors' and Officers' Duties to the Corporation

Directors and officers are in positions of trust; they are entrusted with property belonging to the corporation and with power to act for the corporation. Therefore, directors and officers owe *fiduciary duties* to the corporation. Fiduciary duties require a person to act within the authority of the position and within the objectives and powers of the corporation, to act with due care in conducting the affairs of the corporation, and to act with loyalty to the corporation.

Acting within Authority
An officer or director has a duty to *act within the authority* conferred on her by the articles of incorporation, the bylaws, and the board of directors. The directors and officers must act within the scope of the powers of the corporation. An officer or a director may be liable to the corporation if it is damaged by an act exceeding that person's or the corporation's authority.

Duty of Care

Know the legal standards that judge actions of officers and directors and follow the steps required to comply with each standard.

Directors and officers are liable for losses to the corporation resulting from their lack of *due care or due diligence.* The MBCA expressly states the standard of care that must be exercised by directors and officers. MBCA section 8.30 states:

(a) Each member of the board of directors . . . shall act:
  (1) in good faith, and
  (2) in a manner the director reasonably believes to be in the best interests of the corporation.
(b) The members of the board of directors or a committee of the board, when becoming informed in connection with their decision-making function or devoting attention to their oversight function, shall discharge their duties with the care that a person in a like position would reasonably believe appropriate under similar circumstances.

The MBCA section 8.42 imposes almost the same duty on corporate officers:

(a) An officer . . . shall act:
  (1) in good faith;
  (2) with the care that a person in a like position would reasonably exercise under similar circumstances; and
  (3) in a manner the officer reasonably believes to be in the best interests of the corporation.

Managers need merely meet the standard of the *ordinarily prudent person in the same circumstances*, a standard focusing on the basic manager attributes of common sense, practical wisdom, and informed judgment. The duty of care does not hold directors and officers to the standard of a prudent businessperson, a person of some undefined level of business skill. A director or officer's performance is evaluated at the time of the decision, thereby preventing the application of hindsight in judging her performance.

The MBCA duty of care test requires that a director or officer make a *reasonable investigation* and *honestly believe* that her decision is in the *best interests of the corporation.* For example, the board of directors decides to purchase an existing manufacturing business for $15 million without inquiring into the value of the business or examining its past financial performance. Although the directors may believe that they made a prudent decision, they have no reasonable basis for that belief. Therefore, if the plant is worth only $5 million, the directors will be liable to the corporation for its damages—$10 million—for breaching the duty of care.

The Business Judgment Rule The directors' and officers' duty of care is sometimes expressed as the **business judgment rule**: Absent bad faith, fraud, or breach of fiduciary duty, the judgment of the board of directors is conclusive. When directors and officers have complied with the business judgment rule, they are protected from liability to the corporation for their decisions, even if harmful. The business judgment rule precludes the courts from substituting their business judgment for that of the corporation's managers. The business judgment rule recognizes that the directors and officers—not the shareholders and the courts—are best able to make business judgments and should not ordinarily be vulnerable to second-guessing. Shareholders and the courts are ill equipped to make better business decisions than those made by the officers and directors of a corporation, who have more business experience and are more familiar with the day-to-day needs, strengths, and limitations of the corporation.

Three requirements must be met for the business judgment rule to protect managers from liability:

1. The managers must make an ***informed decision***. They must take the steps necessary to become informed

about the relevant facts by making a *reasonable investigation* before making a decision.

2. The managers must have *no conflicts of interest*. The managers may not benefit personally—other than as shareholders—when they transact on behalf of the corporation.

3. The managers must have a *rational basis* for believing that the decision is in the *best interests of the corporation*. The rational basis element requires only that the managers' decision have a *logical connection to the facts* revealed by a reasonable investigation or that the decision *not be manifestly unreasonable*. Some courts have held that the managers' wrongdoing must amount to *gross negligence* for the directors to lose the protection of the business judgment rule.

If the business judgment rule does not apply because one or more of its elements are missing, a court may *substitute its judgment* and that of the shareholders for the judgment of the managers.

Nonetheless, courts rarely refuse to apply the business judgment rule. As a result, the rule has been criticized frequently as providing too much protection for managers of corporations. In one famous case, the court applied the business judgment rule to protect a 1965 decision made by the board of directors of the Chicago Cubs not to install lights and not to hold night baseball games at Wrigley Field.[1] Yet, the business judgment rule is so flexible that it protected the decision of the Cubs's board of directors to install lights in 1988.

Smith v. Van Gorkom[2] is one of the few cases that has held directors liable for failing to comply with the business judgment rule. The Supreme Court of Delaware found that the business judgment rule was not satisfied by Trans Union's board when it approved an acquisition of a company for $55 per share. The board approved the acquisition after only two hours' consideration and received no documentation to support the adequacy of the $55 price. Instead, it relied entirely on a 20-minute *oral* report by the chairman of the board. No written summary of the acquisition was presented to the board. The directors failed to obtain an investment banker's report, prepared after careful consideration, that the acquisition price was fair.

In addition, the court held that the mere fact that the acquisition price exceeded the market price by $17 per share did not legitimize the board's decision. The board had frequently made statements prior to the acquisition that the market had undervalued the shares, yet the board took no steps to determine the intrinsic value of the shares; instead, it relied solely on the price negotiated by the chairman. Consequently, the court found that at a minimum, the directors had been grossly negligent.

Complying with the Business Judgment Rule While the *Van Gorkom* case created some fear among directors that they could easily be held liable for making a decision that harms the corporation, nothing could be further from the truth. The case and the business judgment rule provide a blueprint for how directors, with the assistance of investment bankers and other consultants, can properly avoid liability. First, to make an informed decision, the board must perform a reasonable investigation or reasonably rely on someone who has made a reasonable investigation, such as consultants, corporate officers, and employees. For example, few boards have the financial skills to value a product line that the corporation wants to sell, yet investment bankers are skilled at valuations. Therefore, a board will make an informed decision when an investment banker makes a reasonable investigation, informs the board of its finding in a written report delivered to the board several days prior to the board meeting, makes a presentation at the board meeting, and takes questions from the board, provided the board makes its decision after giving sufficient time and care to its deliberation of the facts.

Second, the business judgment rule will not apply unless the board has no conflicts of interest. By compiling a list of questions and quizzing the board members, consultants can help the board determine whether any member has a financial or other improper interest in the matter before the board.

Third, for the board to have a rational basis to believe that the decision is in the best interests of the corporation, the decision must fit with the firm's corporate strategy and the facts revealed by a reasonable investigation. Investment bankers and consultants can help, first by defining the corporation's strategy and second by demonstrating the fit between the course of action, the facts, and the corporate strategy.

As one can see, complying with the business judgment rule is primarily a matter of having a reasonable process when making a business decision. When directors act reasonably in acquiring and considering facts upon which a decision is based, courts grant them wide latitude in determining the action to take based on those facts.

In the following case involving Disney's hiring and firing of Michael Ovitz, the Delaware court applied the business judgment rule. This case has a good explanation of the diligence directors should exercise in acquiring information before making a decision.

[1]*Shlensky v. Wrigley*, 237 N.E.2d 776 (Ill. Ct. App. 1968).
[2]488 A.2d 858 (Del. 1985).

Brehm v. Eisner   906 A.2d 27 (Del. 2006)

From the mid-1980s to the mid-1990s, The Walt Disney Company enjoyed remarkable success under the guidance of Chairman and CEO Michael Eisner and President and Chief Operating Officer Frank Wells. In 1994, Wells died in a helicopter crash, prematurely forcing the company to consider his replacement. Eisner promoted the candidacy of his long-time friend, Michael Ovitz. Ovitz was the head of Creative Artists Agency (CAA), which he and four others had founded in 1974. By 1995, CAA had grown to be the premier Hollywood talent agency. CAA had 550 employees and an impressive roster of about 1,400 of Hollywood's top actors, directors, writers, and musicians, clients that generated $150 million in annual revenues for CAA. Ovitz drew an annual income of $20 million from CAA. He was regarded as one of the most powerful figures in Hollywood.

To leave CAA and join Disney as its president, Ovitz insisted on an employment agreement that would provide him downside risk protection if he was terminated by Disney or if he was interfered with in his performance of his duties as president. After protracted negotiations, Ovitz accepted an employment package that would provide him $23.6 million per year for the first five years of the deal, plus bonuses and stock options. The agreement guaranteed that the stock options would appreciate at least $50 million in five years or Disney would make up the difference. The Ovitz employment agreement (OEA) also provided that if Disney fired Ovitz for any reason other than gross negligence or malfeasance, Ovitz would be entitled to a non-fault termination (NFT) payment, which consisted of his remaining salary, $7.5 million a year for any unaccrued bonuses, the immediate vesting of some stock options, and a $10 million cashout payment for other stock options. While there was some opposition to the employment agreement among directors and upper management at Disney, Ovitz was hired in October 1995 largely due to Eisner's insistence.

At the end of 1995, Eisner's attitude with respect to Ovitz was positive. Eisner wrote, "1996 is going to be a great year—We are going to be a great team—We every day are working better together—Time will be on our side—We will be strong, smart, and unstoppable!!!" Eisner also wrote that Ovitz performed well during 1995, notwithstanding the difficulties Ovitz was experiencing assimilating to Disney's culture.

Unfortunately, such optimism did not last long. In January 1996, a corporate retreat was held at Walt Disney World in Orlando. At that retreat, Ovitz failed to integrate himself in the group of executives by declining to participate in group activities, insisting on a limousine when the other executives—including Eisner—were taking a bus, and making inappropriate demands of the park employees. In short, Ovitz was a little elitist for the egalitarian Disney and a poor fit with his fellow executives.

By the summer of 1996, Eisner had spoken with several directors about Ovitz's failure to adapt to the company's culture. In the fall of 1996, directors began discussing that the disconnect between Ovitz and Disney was likely irreparable and that Ovitz would have to be terminated. In December 1996, Ovitz was officially terminated by action of Eisner alone. Eisner concluded that Ovitz was terminated without cause, requiring Disney to make the costly NFT payment.

Shareholders of Disney brought a derivative action on behalf of Disney against Eisner and other Disney directors. The shareholders alleged breaches of fiduciary duty in the hiring and firing of Ovitz. Eisner and the other directors defended on the grounds that they had complied with the business judgment rule. Because Disney was incorporated in Delaware, the case was brought in the Delaware Court of Chancery. The chancery court found that Eisner and the other directors had complied with the business judgment rule. The Disney shareholders appealed to the Delaware Supreme Court.

Jacobs, Justice

The shareholders' claims are subdivisible into two groups: (A) claims arising out of the approval of the OEA and of Ovitz's election as President; and (B) claims arising out of the NFT severance payment to Ovitz upon his termination.

A. Claims Arising from the Approval of the OEA and Ovitz's Election as President

The shareholders' core argument in the trial court was that the Disney directors' approval of the OEA and election of Ovitz as President were not entitled to business judgment rule protection, because those actions were either grossly negligent or not performed in good faith. The Court of Chancery rejected these arguments, and held that the shareholders had failed to prove that the Disney defendants had breached any fiduciary duty.

Our law presumes that in making a business decision the directors of a corporation acted on an informed basis, in good faith, and in the honest belief that the action taken was in the best interests of the company. Those presumptions can be rebutted if the shareholder shows that the directors breached their fiduciary duty of care or of loyalty or acted in bad faith. If that is shown, the burden then shifts to the director defendants to demonstrate that the challenged act or transaction was entirely fair to the corporation and its shareholders.

Because no duty of loyalty claim was asserted against the Disney defendants, the only way to rebut the business judgment rule presumptions would be to show that the Disney defendants had either breached their duty of care or had not acted in good faith. The Chancellor determined that the shareholders had failed to prove either. [The Delaware Supreme Court affirmed the Chancellor's finding.]

The shareholders next challenge the Court of Chancery's determination that the full Disney board was not required to consider and approve the OEA, because the Company's governing instruments allocated that decision to the compensation committee. This challenge also cannot survive scrutiny.

Under the Company's governing documents the board of directors was responsible for selecting the corporation's officers, but under the compensation committee charter, the committee was responsible for establishing and approving the salaries, together with benefits and stock options, of the Company's CEO and President. The compensation committee also had the charter-imposed duty to "approve employment contracts, or contracts at will" for "all corporate officers who are members of the Board of Directors regardless of salary." That is exactly what occurred here. The full board ultimately selected Ovitz as President, and the compensation committee considered and ultimately approved the OEA, which embodied the terms of Ovitz's employment, including his compensation.

The Delaware General Corporation Law (DGCL) expressly empowers a board of directors to appoint committees and to delegate to them a broad range of responsibilities, which may include setting executive compensation. Nothing in the DGCL mandates that the entire board must make those decisions. At Disney, the responsibility to consider and approve executive compensation was allocated to the compensation committee, as distinguished from the full board. The Chancellor's ruling—that executive compensation was to be fixed by the compensation committee—is legally correct.

In the Court of Chancery the shareholders argued that the board had failed to exercise due care, using a director-by-director, rather than a collective analysis. In this Court, however, the shareholders argue that the Chancellor erred in following that very approach. An about-face, the shareholders now claim that in determining whether the board breached its duty of care, the Chancellor was legally required to evaluate the actions of the old board collectively.

We reject this argument, without reaching its merits, for two separate reasons. To begin with, the argument is precluded by Rule 8 of this Court [on procedural grounds]. The shareholders next challenge the Chancellor's determination that although the compensation committee's decision-making process fell far short of corporate governance "best practices," the committee members breached no duty of care in considering and approving the NFT

terms of the OEA. That conclusion is reversible error, the shareholders claim, because the record establishes that the compensation committee members did not properly inform themselves of the material facts and, hence, were grossly negligent in approving the NFT provisions of the OEA.

In our view, a helpful approach is to compare what actually happened here to what would have occurred had the committee followed a "best practices" (or "best case") scenario, from a process standpoint. In a "best case" scenario, all committee members would have received, before or at the committee's first meeting on September 26, 1995, a spreadsheet or similar document prepared by (or with the assistance of) a compensation expert (in this case, Graef Crystal). Making different, alternative assumptions, the spreadsheet would disclose the amounts that Ovitz could receive under the OEA in each circumstance that might foreseeably arise. One variable in that matrix of possibilities would be the cost to Disney of a non-fault termination for each of the five years of the initial term of the OEA. The contents of the spreadsheet would be explained to the committee members, either by the expert who prepared it or by a fellow committee member similarly knowledgeable about the subject. That spreadsheet, which ultimately would become an exhibit to the minutes of the compensation committee meeting, would form the basis of the committee's deliberations and decision.

Regrettably, the committee's informational and decisionmaking process used here was not so tidy. That is one reason why the Chancellor found that although the committee's process did not fall below the level required for a proper exercise of due care, it did fall short of what best practices would have counseled.

The Disney compensation committee met twice: on September 26 and October 16, 1995. The minutes of the September 26 meeting reflect that the committee approved the terms of the OEA (at that time embodied in the form of a letter agreement), except for the option grants, which were not approved until October 16—after the Disney stock incentive plan had been amended to provide for those options. At the September 26 meeting, the compensation committee considered a "term sheet" which, in summarizing the material terms of the OEA, relevantly disclosed that in the event of a non-fault termination, Ovitz would receive: (i) the present value of his salary ($1 million per year) for the balance of the contract term, (ii) the present value of his annual bonus payments (computed at $7.5 million) for the balance of the contract term, (iii) a $10 million termination fee, and (iv) the acceleration of his options for 3 million shares, which would become immediately exercisable at market price.

Thus, the compensation committee knew that in the event of an NFT, Ovitz's severance payment alone could be in the range of $40 million cash, plus the value of the accelerated options. Because the actual payout to Ovitz was approximately $130 million, of which roughly $38.5 million was cash, the value of the options at the time of the NFT payout would have been about $91.5 million. Thus, the issue may be framed as whether the compensation committee members knew, at the time they approved the OEA, that the value of the option component of the severance package could reach the $92 million order of magnitude if they terminated Ovitz without cause after one year. The evidentiary record shows that the committee members were so informed.

On this question the documentation is far less than what best practices would have dictated. There is no exhibit to the minutes that discloses, in a single document, the estimated value of the accelerated options in the event of an NFT termination after one year. The information imparted to the committee members on that subject is, however, supported by other evidence, most notably the trial testimony of various witnesses about spreadsheets that were prepared for the compensation committee meetings.

The compensation committee members derived their information about the potential magnitude of an NFT payout from two sources. The first was the value of the "benchmark" options previously granted to Eisner and Wells and the valuations by Raymond Watson [a Disney director, member of Disney's compensation committee, and past Disney board chairman who had helped structure Wells's and Eisner's compensation packages] of the proposed Ovitz options. Ovitz's options were set at 75% of parity with the options previously granted to Eisner and to Frank Wells. Because the compensation committee had established those earlier benchmark option grants to Eisner and Wells and were aware of their value, a simple mathematical calculation would have informed them of the potential value range of Ovitz's options. Also, in August and September 1995, Watson and Irwin Russell [a Disney director and chairman of the compensation committee] met with Crystal to determine (among other things) the value of the potential Ovitz options, assuming different scenarios. Crystal valued the options under the Black-Scholes method, while Watson used a different valuation metric. Watson recorded his calculations and the resulting values on a set of spreadsheets that reflected what option profits Ovitz might receive, based upon a range of different assumptions about stock market price increases. Those spreadsheets were shared with, and explained to, the committee members at the September meeting.

The committee's second source of information was the amount of "downside protection" that Ovitz was demanding. Ovitz required financial protection from the risk of leaving a very lucrative and secure position at CAA, of which he was a controlling partner, to join a publicly held corporation to which Ovitz was a stranger, and that had a very different culture and an environment which prevented him from completely controlling his destiny. The committee members knew that by leaving CAA and coming to Disney, Ovitz would be sacrificing "booked" CAA commissions of $150 to $200 million—an amount that Ovitz demanded as protection against the risk that his employment

relationship with Disney might not work out. Ovitz wanted at least $50 million of that compensation to take the form of an "up-front" signing bonus. Had the $50 million bonus been paid, the size of the option grant would have been lower. Because it was contrary to Disney policy, the compensation committee rejected the up-front signing bonus demand, and elected instead to compensate Ovitz at the "back end," by awarding him options that would be phased in over the five-year term of the OEA.

It is on this record that the Chancellor found that the compensation committee was informed of the material facts relating to an NFT payout. If measured in terms of the documentation that would have been generated if "best practices" had been followed, that record leaves much to be desired. The Chancellor acknowledged that, and so do we. But, the Chancellor also found that despite its imperfections, the evidentiary record was sufficient to support the conclusion that the compensation committee had adequately informed itself of the potential magnitude of the entire severance package, including the options, that Ovitz would receive in the event of an early NFT.

The OEA was specifically structured to compensate Ovitz for walking away from $150 million to $200 million of anticipated commissions from CAA over the five-year OEA contract term. This meant that if Ovitz was terminated without cause, the earlier in the contract term the termination occurred the larger the severance amount would be to replace the lost commissions. Indeed, because Ovitz was terminated after only one year, the total amount of his severance payment (about $130 million) closely approximated the lower end of the range of Ovitz's forfeited commissions ($150 million), less the compensation Ovitz received during his first and only year as Disney's President. Accordingly, the Court of Chancery had a sufficient evidentiary basis in the record from which to find that, at the time they approved the OEA, the compensation committee members were adequately informed of the potential magnitude of an early NFT severance payout.

The shareholders' final claim in this category is that the Court of Chancery erroneously held that the remaining members of the old Disney board had not breached their duty of care in electing Ovitz as President of Disney. This claim lacks merit, because the arguments shareholders advance in this context relate to a different subject—the approval of the OEA, which was the responsibility delegated to the compensation committee, not the full board.

The Chancellor found and the record shows the following: well in advance of the September 26, 1995 board meeting the directors were fully aware that the Company needed—especially in light of Wells' death and Eisner's medical problems—to hire a "number two" executive and potential successor to Eisner. There had been many discussions about that need and about potential candidates who could fill that role even before Eisner decided to try to recruit Ovitz. Before the September 26 board meeting

Eisner had individually discussed with each director the possibility of hiring Ovitz, and Ovitz's background and qualifications. The directors thus knew of Ovitz's skills, reputation and experience, all of which they believed would be highly valuable to the Company. The directors also knew that to accept a position at Disney, Ovitz would have to walk away from a very successful business—a reality that would lead a reasonable person to believe that Ovitz would likely succeed in similar pursuits elsewhere in the industry. The directors also knew of the public's highly positive reaction to the Ovitz announcement, and that Eisner and senior management had supported the Ovitz hiring. Indeed, Eisner, who had long desired to bring Ovitz within the Disney fold, consistently vouched for Ovitz's qualifications and told the directors that he could work well with Ovitz.

The board was also informed of the key terms of the OEA (including Ovitz's salary, bonus, and options). Russell reported this information to them at the September 26, 1995 executive session, which was attended by Eisner and all non-executive directors. Russell also reported on the compensation committee meeting that had immediately preceded the executive session. And, both Russell and Watson responded to questions from the

board. Relying upon the compensation committee's approval of the OEA and the other information furnished to them, the Disney directors, after further deliberating, unanimously elected Ovitz as President.

Based upon this record, we uphold the Chancellor's conclusion that, when electing Ovitz to the Disney presidency the remaining Disney directors were fully informed of all material facts, and that the shareholders failed to establish any lack of due care on the directors' part.

* * *

To summarize, the Court of Chancery correctly determined that the decisions of the Disney defendants to approve the OEA, to hire Ovitz as President, and then to terminate him on an NFT basis, were protected business judgments, made without any violations of fiduciary duty. Having so concluded, it is unnecessary for the Court to reach the shareholders' contention that the Disney defendants were required to prove that the payment of the NFT severance to Ovitz was entirely fair.

Judgment for Eisner and the other directors affirmed.

Board Opposition to Acquisition of Control of a Corporation

 List and describe tactics a board of directors may adopt to defend against hostile takeovers.

Since the early 1960s, many outsiders have attempted to acquire control of publicly held corporations. Typically, these *raiders* will make a **tender offer** for the shares of a *target* corporation. A tender offer is an offer to the shareholders to buy their shares at a price above the current market price. The raider hopes to acquire a majority of the shares, which will give it control of the target corporation.

Most tender offers are opposed by the target corporation's management. The defenses to tender offers are many and varied, and they carry colorful names, such as the Pac-Man defense, the white knight, greenmail, the poison pill, and the lock-up option. See Figure 43.1 for definitions of these defenses.

When takeover defenses are successful, shareholders of the target may lose the opportunity to sell their shares at a price up to twice the market price of the shares prior to the announcement of the hostile bid. Frequently, the loss of this opportunity upsets shareholders, who then decide to sue the directors who have opposed the tender offer.

Shareholders contend that the directors have opposed the tender offer only to preserve their corporate jobs. Shareholders also argue that the target corporation's interests would have been better served if the tender offer had succeeded.

Generally, courts have refused to find directors liable for opposing a tender offer because the business judgment rule applies to a board's decision to oppose a tender offer.

Nonetheless, the business judgment rule will not apply when the directors make a decision to oppose the tender offer before they have carefully studied it. In addition, if the directors' actions indicate that they opposed the tender offer in order to preserve their jobs, they will be liable to the corporation.

Court decisions have seemingly modified the business judgment rule as it is applied in the tender offer context. For example, in *Unocal Corp. v. Mesa Petroleum Co.*,[3] the Supreme Court of Delaware upheld the application of the business judgment rule to a board's decision to block a hostile tender offer by making a tender offer for its own shares that excluded the raider.[4] But in so ruling, the court held that the board may use only those defense tactics that are *reasonable* compared to the takeover threat. The

----

[3]493 A.2d 946 (Del. 1985).

[4]Discriminatory tender offers are now illegal pursuant to Securities Exchange Act Rule 13e-4.

Figure 43.1   Tender Offer Defenses

Greenmail

The target's repurchase of its shares from the raider at a substantial profit to the raider, upon the condition that the raider sign a standstill agreement in which it promises not to buy additional shares of the target for a stated period of time.

White Knight

A friendly tender offeror whom management prefers over the original tender offeror—called a black knight. The white knight rescues the corporation from the black knight (the raider) by offering more money for the corporation's shares.

Pac-Man

The target corporation turns the tables on the tender offeror or raider (which is often another publicly held corporation) by making a tender offer for the raider's shares. As a result, two tender offerors are trying to buy each other's shares. This is similar to the Pac-Man video game, in which Pac-Man and his enemies chase each other.

Golden Parachutes

An incentive to attract top managers, a golden parachute requires a corporation to make a large severance payment to a top-level executive such as the CEO when there is a change in control of the corporation. Payments to an individual executive may exceed $500 million.

Lock-Up Option

Used in conjunction with a white knight to ensure the success of the white knight's bid. The target and the white knight agree that the white knight will buy a highly valuable asset of the target at a very attractive price for the white knight (usually a below-market price) if the raider succeeds in taking over the target. For example, a movie company may agree to sell its film library to the white knight.

Friendly Shareholders

Establishing employee stock option plans (ESOPs), by which employees of the corporation purchase the corporation's shares, and selling the corporation's shares to other shareholders likely to be loyal to management, such as employee pension funds and people in the community in which the corporation conducts its business, may create a significant percentage of friendly shareholders who are not likely to tender their shares to a raider who may be perceived as hostile to the continuation of the corporation's business in the local community. Thus, building and maintaining a base of friendly shareholders make it easier to defeat a raider.

Poison Pill

Also called a shareholders' rights plan. There are many types, but the typical poison pill involves the target's issuance of a new class of preferred shares to its common shareholders. The preferred shares have rights (share options) attached to them. These rights allow the target's shareholders to purchase shares of the raider or shares of the target at less than fair market value. The poison pill deters hostile takeover attempts by threatening the raider and its shareholders with severe dilutions in the value of the shares they hold.

---

board may consider a variety of concerns, including the inadequacy of the price offered, nature and timing of the offer, questions of illegality, the impact on constituencies other than shareholders (i.e., creditors, customers, employees, and perhaps even the community generally), the risk of nonconsummation, and the quality of securities being offered in the exchange.

Since its decision in *Unocal*, the Supreme Court of Delaware has applied this modified business judgment rule to validate a poison pill tender offer defense tactic in *Moran v. Household Int'l, Inc.*[5] and *Versata Enterprises Inc. v. Selectica*[6] and to invalidate a lock-up option tender offer defense

in the *Revlon*[7] case. These cases confirmed the *Unocal* holding that the board of directors must show that:

1. It had reasonable grounds to believe that a danger to corporate policy and effectiveness was posed by the takeover attempt.

2. It acted primarily to protect the corporation and its shareholders from that danger.

3. The defense tactic was reasonable in relation to the threat posed to the corporation.

Such a standard appeared to impose a higher standard on directors than the rational basis requirement of

---

[5] 500 A.2d 346 (Del. 1985).
[6] 5 A.3d 586 (Del. 2010).

[7] *Revlon Inc. v. MacAndrews & Forbes Holdings, Inc.*, 506 A.2d 173 (Del. 1986).

the business judgment rule, which historically has been interpreted to require only that a decision of a board not be manifestly unreasonable. In addition, the *Revlon* case required the board to establish an auction market for the company and to sell it to the highest bidder when the directors have abandoned the long-term business objectives of the company by embracing a bust-up of the company.

In the following *Paramount v. Time* case, the Supreme Court of Delaware expanded board discretion in fighting hostile takeovers, holding that a board may oppose a hostile takeover provided the board had a *preexisting, deliberately conceived corporate plan* justifying its opposition. The existence of such a plan enabled Time's board to meet the reasonable-tactic element of the *Unocal* test.

Paramount Communications, Inc. v. Time, Inc.
571 A.2d 1140 (Del. 1989)

Since 1983, Time, Inc. had considered expanding its business beyond publishing magazines and books, owning Home Box Office and Cinemax, and operating television stations. In 1988, Time's board approved in principle a strategic plan for Time's acquisition of an entertainment company. The board gave management permission to negotiate a merger with Warner Communications Inc. The board's consensus was that a merger of Time and Warner was feasible, but only if Time controlled the resulting corporation, preserving the editorial integrity of Time's magazines. The board concluded that Warner was the superior candidate because Warner could make movies and TV shows for HBO, Warner had an international distribution system, Warner was a giant in the music business, Time and Warner would control half of New York City's cable TV system, and the Time network could promote Warner's movies.

Negotiations with Warner broke down when Warner refused to agree to Time's dominating the combined companies. Time continued to seek expansion, but informal discussions with other companies terminated when it was suggested the other companies purchase Time or control the resulting board. In January 1989, Warner and Time resumed negotiations, and on March 4, 1989, they agreed to a combination by which Warner shareholders would own 62 percent of the resulting corporation, to be named Time-Warner. To retain the editorial integrity of Time, the merger agreement provided for a board committee dominated by Time representatives.

On June 7, 1989, Paramount Communications, Inc. announced a cash tender offer for all of Time's shares at $175 per share. (The day before, Time shares traded at $126 per share.) Time's financial advisers informed the outside directors that Time's auction value was materially higher than $175 per share. The board concluded that Paramount's $175 offer was inadequate. Also, the board viewed the Paramount offer as a threat to Time's control of its own destiny and retention of the Time editorial policy; the board found that a combination with Warner offered greater potential for Time.

In addition, concerned that shareholders would not comprehend the long-term benefits of the merger with Warner, on June 16, 1989, Time's board recast its acquisition with Warner into a two-tier acquisition in which it would make a tender offer to buy 51 percent of Warner's shares for cash immediately and later buy the remaining 49 percent for cash and securities. The tender offer would eliminate the need for Time to obtain shareholder approval of the transaction.

On June 23, 1989, Paramount raised its offer to $200 per Time share. Three days later, Time's board rejected the offer as a threat to Time's survival and its editorial integrity; the board viewed the Warner acquisition as offering greater long-term value for the shareholders. Time shareholders and Paramount then sued Time and its board to enjoin Time's acquisition of Warner. The trial court held for Time. Paramount and other Time shareholders appealed to the Supreme Court of Delaware.

Horsey, Justice

Our decision does not require us to pass on the wisdom of the board's decision. That is not a court's task. Our task is simply to determine whether there is sufficient evidence to support the initial Time-Warner agreement as the product of a proper exercise of business judgment.

We have purposely detailed the evidence of the Time board's deliberative approach, beginning in 1983–84, to expand itself. Time's decision in 1988 to combine with Warner was made only after what could be fairly characterized as an exhaustive appraisal of Time's future as a corporation. Time's board was convinced that Warner would provide the best fit for Time to achieve its strategic objectives. The record attests to the zealousness of Time's executives, fully supported by their directors, in seeing to the preservation of Time's perceived editorial integrity in journalism. The Time board's decision to expand the business of the company through its March 4 merger with Warner was entitled to the protection of the business judgment rule.

The revised June 16 agreement was defense-motivated and designed to avoid the potentially disruptive effect that Paramount's offer would have had on consummation of the proposed merger were it put to a shareholder vote. Thus, we decline to apply the traditional business judgment rule to the revised transaction and instead analyze the Time board's June 16 decision under *Unocal*.

In *Unocal*, we held that before the business judgment rule is applied to a board's adoption of a defensive measure, the burden will lie with the board to prove (a) reasonable grounds for believing that a danger to corporate policy and effectiveness existed; and (b) that the defensive measure adopted was reasonable in relation to the threat posed.

Paramount argues a hostile tender offer can pose only two types of threats: the threat of coercion that results from a two-tier offer promising unequal treatment for nontendering shareholders; and the threat of inadequate value from an all-shares, all-cash offer at a price below what a target board in good faith deems to be the present value of its shares.

Paramount would have us hold that only if the value of Paramount's offer were determined to be clearly inferior to the value created by management's plan to merge with Warner could the offer be viewed—objectively—as a threat.

Paramount's position represents a fundamental misconception of our standard of review under *Unocal* principally because it would involve the court in substituting its judgment as to what is a "better" deal for that of a corporation's board of directors. The usefulness of *Unocal* as an analytical tool is precisely its flexibility in the face of a variety of fact scenarios. Thus, directors may consider, when evaluating the threat posed by a takeover bid, the inadequacy of the price offered, nature and timing of the offer, questions of illegality, the impact on constituencies other than shareholders, the risk of nonconsummation, and the quality of securities being offered in the exchange.

The Time board reasonably determined that inadequate value was not the only threat that Paramount's all-cash, all-shares offer could present. Time's board concluded that Paramount's offer posed other threats. One concern was that Time shareholders might elect to tender into Paramount's cash offer in ignorance or a mistaken belief of the strategic benefit which a business combination with Warner might produce.

Paramount also contends that Time's board had not duly investigated Paramount's offer. We find that Time explored the available entertainment companies, including Paramount, before determining that Warner provided the best strategic "fit." In addition, Time's board rejected Paramount's offer because Paramount did not serve Time's objectives or meet Time's needs. Time's board was adequately informed of the potential benefits of a transaction with Paramount. Time's failure to negotiate cannot be fairly found to have been uninformed. The evidence supporting this finding is materially enhanced by the fact that 12 of Time's 16 board members were outside independent directors.

We turn to the second part of the *Unocal* analysis. The obvious requisite to determining the reasonableness of a defensive action is a clear identification of the nature of the threat. This requires an evaluation of the importance of the corporate objective threatened; alternative methods of protecting that objective; impacts of the defensive action; and other relevant factors.

The fiduciary duty to manage a corporate enterprise includes the selection of a time frame for achievement of corporate goals. Directors are not obliged to abandon a deliberately conceived corporate plan for a short-term shareholder profit unless there is clearly no basis to sustain the corporate strategy. Time's responsive action to Paramount's tender offer was not aimed at "cramming down" on its shareholders a management-sponsored alternative, but rather had as its goal the carrying forward of a preexisting transaction in an altered form. Thus, the response was reasonably related to the threat. The revised agreement did not preclude Paramount from making an offer for the combined Time-Warner company or from changing the conditions of its offer so as not to make the offer dependent upon the nullification of the Time-Warner agreement. Thus, the response was proportionate.

Judgment for Time affirmed.

Complying with the Unocal *Test* To avoid liability when opposing a takeover of the corporation, the board of directors must act in a manner similar to which it complies with the business judgment rule. First, the board must make a reasonable investigation into the threats the takeover poses to the corporation's policies and effectiveness. Having a preexisting acquisition and expansion plan, as Time, Inc. had in the *Paramount* case, will provide a basis for determining whether there is a threat to the company's policies. An investment banker can help the company investigate the facts that reveal threats to the corporation and help define an acquisition strategy, if one does not currently exist.

Second, the board must be motivated primarily to protect the company from the raider's threat, not to save their positions as directors, including the compensation and power that go with the position of director. The *Unocal* test recognizes that directors may be conflicted by their interest in saving their jobs, yet it allows directors to oppose the takeover if they mostly are concerned about protecting the company from the takeover's threat to the company's policies, such as a preexisting acquisition or expansion strategy that would be frustrated by the takeover.

Third, the board may adopt only those takeover defenses that are reasonable in relation to the threat. While this requirement seems to limit board discretion, in practice once the board has identified a credible threat to the corporation's policies, the board may engage in nearly any legal maneuver to stop that threat. That is especially true if the threat is to a preexisting acquisition or expansion strategy, such as a long-existing corporate strategy to remain an independent company or to grow by purchasing smaller competitors.

Oversight of Legal Compliance

Directors and officers may also violate their duty of care by failing to exercise appropriate attention when managing the corporation. Sometimes couched in terms of a *duty of good faith*, courts have found that when the corporation suffers a loss based on directors' unconsidered inaction, the duty of care is implicated. This duty has its roots in the business judgment rule's requirement that managers take reasonable steps to become informed about the relevant facts before taking action. Failing to take such steps through inattention is as problematic as taking an action that is manifestly against the best interests of the corporation.

Questions of whether officers and directors have violated a duty in this way arise when companies are accused of violating the law. Because companies can only commit legal and regulatory violations through their agents, shareholders will claim that officers and directors should have known of the wrongdoing and failed to take steps to mitigate it; therefore, they are individually liable to the corporation.

The law regarding this type of oversight liability was settled for many years—directors had no affirmative duty to oversee legal compliance at a corporation absent obvious signs of employee wrongdoing. That changed in the late 1990s with the passage of the Organizational Sentencing Guidelines, federal sentencing standards for corporations. The Guidelines are structured to reduce culpability for those companies instituting corporate compliance programs aimed at uncovering and mitigating wrongdoing within the firm. Companies deemed to have an "effective" compliance program may reduce their ultimate fine by up to 95%. Given this, courts became more receptive to shareholder claims that boards should be proactive in their oversight obligations.

The following case addresses what would become known as a *"Caremark claim,"* a shareholder suit seeking to hold officers and directors liable for failing to prevent wrongdoing at the corporation by not instituting rigorous compliance protocols. Although the chances of winning a *Caremark* claim have been likened to being struck by lightening, the mere possibility of individual liability for directors caused compliance programs to proliferate across corporate America.

In re Caremark Int'l Inc. Derivative Litig.
698 A.2d 959 (Del. Ch. 1996)

Caremark International was a health care company specializing in alternative-site care. After a lengthy investigation by the Department of Justice, the company and two of its executives—but none of its board members—were indicted for paying illegal kickbacks to doctors for patient referrals. Numerous shareholder derivative suits were filed alleging that Caremark's directors breached their duty of care by failing to supervise the offending executives, thereby exposing the company to criminal and civil liability. The suits sought to recover damages from the individual board members. Caremark eventually reached a settlement with the DOJ and a host of federal agencies; the company would plead guilty and pay approximately $250 million in civil penalties but would be allowed to continue participating in federal programs. An announcement of the settlement of the derivative claims followed, but it required court approval before it could be finalized. Legendary Delaware Chancery Court judge William T. Allen had the task of approving or disapproving the settlement. In doing so, he effectively overruled the law in Delaware at the time, holding that directors had no affirmative duty to oversee legal compliance at the corporation absent clear signs of employee wrongdoing, as established in Graham v. Allis-Chalmers Manufacturing Co., *188 A.2d 125 (Del. 1963), discussed below within the case decision.*

ALLEN, Chancellor

B. Directors' Duties to Monitor Corporate Operations

The complaint charges the director defendants with breach of their duty of attention or care in connection with the on-going operation of the corporation's business. The claim is that the directors allowed a situation to develop and continue which exposed the corporation to enormous legal liability and that in so doing they violated a duty to be active monitors of corporate performance. The complaint thus does not charge either director self-dealing or the more difficult loyalty-type problems arising from cases of suspect director motivation, such as entrenchment

or sale of control contexts. The theory here advanced is possibly the most difficult theory in corporation law upon which a plaintiff might hope to win a judgment. * * *

2. *Liability for failure to monitor:* The second class of cases in which director liability for inattention is theoretically possible entail circumstances in which a loss eventuates not from a decision but, from unconsidered inaction. Most of the decisions that a corporation, acting through its human agents, makes are, of course, not the subject of director attention. Legally, the board itself will be required only to authorize the most significant corporate acts or transactions: mergers, changes in capital structure,

fundamental changes in business, appointment and compensation of the CEO, etc. As the facts of this case graphically demonstrate, ordinary business decisions that are made by officers and employees deeper in the interior of the organization can, however, vitally affect the welfare of the corporation and its ability to achieve its various strategic and financial goals. * * * Financial and organizational disasters such as [in this case] raise the question, what is the board's responsibility with respect to the organization and monitoring of the enterprise to assure that the corporation functions within the law to achieve its purposes? * * *

In 1963, the Delaware Supreme Court in [*Graham*] addressed the question of potential liability of board members for losses experienced by the corporation as a result of the corporation having violated the anti-trust laws of the United States. There was no claim in that case that the directors knew about the behavior of subordinate employees of the corporation that had resulted in the liability. Rather, as in this case, the claim asserted was that the directors ought to have known of it and if they had known they would have been under a duty to bring the corporation into compliance with the law and thus save the corporation from the loss. The Delaware Supreme Court concluded that, under the facts as they appeared, there was no basis to find that the directors had breached a duty to be informed of the ongoing operations of the firm. In notably colorful terms, the court stated that "absent cause for suspicion there is no duty upon the directors to install and operate a corporate system of espionage to ferret out wrongdoing which they have no reason to suspect exists." The Court found that there were no grounds for suspicion in that case and, thus, concluded that the directors were blamelessly unaware of the conduct leading to the corporate liability.

How does one generalize this holding today? Can it be said today that, absent some ground giving rise to suspicion of violation of law, that corporate directors have no duty to assure that a corporate information gathering and reporting systems [sic] exists which represents a good faith attempt to provide senior management and the Board with information respecting material acts, events or conditions within the corporation, including compliance with applicable statutes and regulations? I certainly do not believe so. I doubt that such a broad generalization of the *Graham* holding would have been accepted by the Supreme Court in 1963. The case can be more narrowly interpreted as standing for the proposition that, absent grounds to suspect deception, neither corporate boards nor senior officers can be charged with wrongdoing simply for assuming the integrity of employees and the honesty of their dealings on the company's behalf.

A broader interpretation of *Graham*—that it means that a corporate board has no responsibility to assure that appropriate information and reporting systems are established by management—would not, in any event, be accepted by the Delaware Supreme Court [today], in my opinion. In stating the basis for this view, I start with the recognition that in recent years the Delaware Supreme Court has made it clear—especially in its jurisprudence concerning takeovers,

from *Smith v. Van Gorkom* through *Paramount Communications*—the seriousness with which the corporation law views the role of the corporate board. Secondly, I note the elementary fact that relevant and timely information is an essential predicate for satisfaction of the board's supervisory and monitoring role under Section 141 of the Delaware General Corporation Law. Thirdly, I note the potential impact of the federal organizational sentencing guidelines on any business organization. [The guidelines set forth a uniform sentencing structure for organizations to be sentenced for violation of federal criminal statutes and offer powerful incentives for corporations to put in place compliance programs to detect violations of law, promptly to report violations to appropriate public officials when discovered, and to take prompt, voluntary remedial efforts.] Any rational person attempting in good faith to meet an organizational governance responsibility would be bound to take into account this development and the enhanced penalties and the opportunities for reduced sanctions that it offers.

In light of these developments, it would, in my opinion, be a mistake to conclude that our Supreme Court . . . means that corporate boards may satisfy their obligation to be reasonably informed concerning the corporation, without assuring themselves that information and reporting systems exist in the organization that are reasonably designed to provide to senior management and to the board itself timely, accurate information sufficient to allow management and the board, each within its scope, to reach informed judgments concerning both the corporation's compliance with law and its business performance.

Obviously the level of detail that is appropriate for such an information system is a question of business judgment. And obviously too, no rationally designed information and reporting system will remove the possibility that the corporation will violate laws or regulations, or that senior officers or directors may nevertheless sometimes be misled or otherwise fail reasonably to detect acts material to the corporation's compliance with the law. But it is important that the board exercise a good faith judgment that the corporation's information and reporting system is in concept and design adequate to assure the board that appropriate information will come to its attention in a timely manner as a matter of ordinary operations, so that it may satisfy its responsibility.

Thus, I am of the view that a director's obligation includes a duty to attempt in good faith to assure that a corporate information and reporting system, which the board concludes is adequate, exists, and that failure to do so under some circumstances may, in theory at least, render a director liable for losses caused by non-compliance with applicable legal standards. * * *

The record at this stage does not support the conclusion that the defendants either lacked good faith in the exercise of their monitoring responsibilities or conscientiously permitted a known violation of law by the corporation to occur.

Thus, the proposed settlement will be APPROVED.

Although *Caremark* remains good law and the claims it validated continue to be brought by shareholders, the doctrine has evolved. The duty of board oversight has been resituated under the duty of loyalty.[8] The duty of good faith as an independent obligation of officers and directors has diminished in the law, largely being subsumed by the duty of loyalty. Under this conception, an officer or director cannot act loyally toward the corporation unless she acts in the good faith belief that her actions are in the corporation's best interests.

Caremark claims remain very difficult to win. There are two categories of oversight claims explained in the case. One is when the directors utterly fail to implement any reporting system or controls. The other is when directors, having implemented controls, consciously fail to monitor or oversee their operation so as to ensure they are informed of risks or problems requiring their attention. Because most companies have some compliance program in place, *Caremark* claims usually proceed under the failure-to-monitor prong. To succeed, shareholders must show that directors knew that they were not discharging their fiduciary obligations of oversight, which is close to a legal impossibility when the directors are not involved in the underlying illegality themselves. While some recent cases suggest boards must engage in a risk-based analysis to clear the fiduciary bar, the difficulties of prevailing on *Caremark* claims remain.[9]

Duties of Loyalty

Directors and officers owe a duty of *utmost loyalty and fidelity* to the corporation. Judge Benjamin Cardozo conceptualized this duty as one of trust. He declared that a director

> owes loyalty and allegiance to the corporation—a loyalty that is undivided and an allegiance that is influenced by no consideration other than the welfare of the corporation. Any adverse interest of a director will be subjected to a scrutiny rigid and uncompromising. He may not profit at the expense of his corporation and in conflict with its rights; he may not for personal gain divert unto himself the opportunities which in equity and fairness belong to his corporation.[10]

Directors and officers owe the corporation the same duties of loyalty that agents owe their principals, though many of these duties have special names in corporation law. The most important of these duties of loyalty are the duties not to *self-deal*, not to *usurp a corporate opportunity*, not to *oppress minority shareholders*, and not to *trade on inside information*.

[8]*Stone v. Ritter*, 911 A.2d 362 (Del. 2006).
[9]*Marchand v. Barnhill*, 212 A.3d 805 (Del. 2019).
[10]*Meinhard v. Salmon*, 164 N.E.2d 545 (N.Y. Ct. App. 1928).

Conflicting Interest Transactions

A director or officer has a conflicting interest when a director or officer deals with his corporation. The director or officer with a **conflict of interest** may prefer his own interests over those of the corporation. The director's or officer's interest may be *direct*, such as his interest in selling his land to the corporation, or it may be *indirect*, such as his interest in having another business of which he or his family is an owner, director, or officer supply goods to the corporation. When a director has a conflict of interest, the director's transaction with the corporation may be voided or rescinded.

Under the MBCA, a director's conflicting interest transaction will not be voided merely on the grounds of a director's conflict of interest when *any one* of the following is true:

1. The transaction has been approved by a majority of informed, disinterested directors,
2. The transaction has been approved by a majority of the shares held by informed, disinterested shareholders, or
3. The transaction is fair to the corporation.

Nonetheless, even when disinterested directors' or shareholders' approval has been obtained, courts will void a conflict-of-interest transaction that is unfair to the corporation. Therefore, every corporate transaction in which a director has a conflict of interest must be fair to the corporation. If the transaction is fair, the interested director is excused from liability to the corporation. A transaction is fair if reasonable persons in an *arm's-length bargain* would have bound the corporation to it. This standard is often called the **intrinsic fairness standard**.

The function of disinterested director or disinterested shareholder approval of a conflict-of-interest transaction is merely to shift the burden of proving unfairness. The burden of proving fairness lies initially on the interested director. The burden of proof shifts to the corporation that is suing the interested officer or director if the transaction was approved by the board of directors or the shareholders. Nonetheless, when disinterested directors approve an interested person transaction, substantial deference is given to the decision in accordance with the business judgment rule, especially when the disinterested directors compose a majority of the board.

Generally, *unanimous* approval of an interested person transaction by informed shareholders *conclusively* releases an interested director or officer from liability even if the transaction is unfair to the corporation. The rationale for this rule is that fully informed shareholders should know what is best for themselves and their corporation.

Complying with the Intrinsic Fairness Standard

Complying with the intrinsic fairness standard is not much

Ethics and Compliance in Action

Sarbanes–Oxley Act of 2002 Prohibits Loans to Management

Early corporation law prohibited loans by a corporation to its officers or directors, on the grounds that such loans may result in looting of corporate assets. Today, however, the MBCA and most other general corporation statutes allow loans to directors and officers, although they require either shareholder approval or compliance with conflicting interest transaction rules.

In 2002, Congress took steps to return to the past. After it was revealed that several executives of public companies were using their corporations as personal banks to fund extravagant lifestyles—some of which loans were never repaid and some of which corporations became bankrupt—Congress included in the Sarbanes–Oxley Act of 2002 a section generally

prohibiting public companies from making loans to their directors or executive officers. This includes the company's CEO and CFO, any vice president in charge of a principal business unit or function, and any other officer or other person who performs a policy-making function. If the corporation is not a public company or if the loan is made to a nonexecutive, the Sarbanes–Oxley Act does not prohibit the corporate loan.

- Do you think that Congress has gone too far in banning loans to directors and officers? What are the ethical justifications to ban loans? What would a rights theorist argue? What would a utilitarian argue? What would a profit maximizer argue?
- Do you think that the Sarbanes–Oxley Act should have banned all corporation loans to its employees? Would you prohibit a bank from making loans to its employees, officers, and directors?

---

different than complying with the business judgment rule, despite the higher standard of conduct. The board must make a reasonable investigation to discover facts that will permit an informed decision. Almost always, the board will be aided in its investigation by officers and other employees of the corporation and by investment bankers, other consultants, and legal counsel. When relying on others' investigations, the board must receive written and oral reports in sufficient time to absorb the information, to ask questions of those who made the investigation, and to debate and to deliberate after receiving all relevant information.

Investment bankers, other consultants, and legal counsel are especially helpful in ascertaining and disclosing any director's conflict of interest. By compiling a list of questions and quizzing the board members, consultants can help the board determine the extent of a director's conflict and ensure that the conflict is fully disclosed to the board. They should also make sure that only board members who are independent of the conflicted directors approve the conflicting interest transaction.

Finally, the board must make a decision that is fair to the corporation. Investment bankers and other consultants can help with this determination by demonstrating the decision's close fit with the firm's corporate strategy and the facts revealed by a reasonable investigation. They must ensure the decision is one that a reasonable person would make acting at arm's length.

Usurpation of a Corporate Opportunity

Directors and officers may steal not only assets of their corporations (such as computer hardware and software) but also *opportunities* that their corporations could have

exploited. As fiduciaries, directors and officers are liable to their corporation for *usurping corporate opportunities*.

The opportunity must come to the director or officer *in her corporate capacity*. Clearly, opportunities received at the corporate offices are received by the manager in her corporate capacity. In addition, courts hold that CEOs and other high-level officers are nearly always acting in their corporate capacities, even when they are away from their corporate offices.

The opportunity must have a *relation or connection* to an *existing or prospective* corporate activity. Some courts apply the *line of business test*, considering how closely related the opportunity is to the lines of business in which the corporation is engaged. Other courts use the *interest or expectancy test*, requiring the opportunity to relate to property in which the corporation has an existing interest or in which it has an expectancy growing out of an existing right.

The corporation must be *able financially* to take advantage of the opportunity. Managers are required to make a good faith effort to obtain external financing for the corporation, but they are not required to use their personal funds to enable the corporation to take advantage of the opportunity.

A director or officer is free to exploit an opportunity that has been rejected by the corporation.

In the following case, *Guth v. Loft*, the court found that an opportunity to become the manufacturer of Pepsi-Cola syrup was usurped by the president of a corporation that manufactured beverage syrups and operated soda fountains. Note that the court ordered the typical remedy for usurpation: the officer's forfeiture to the corporation of all benefits the officer received.

Guth v. Loft, Inc.　　5 A.2d 503 (Del. 1939)

Loft, Inc. manufactured and sold candies, syrups, and beverages and operated 115 retail candy and soda fountain stores. Loft sold Coca-Cola at all of its stores, but it did not manufacture Coca-Cola syrup. Instead, it purchased its 30,000-gallon annual requirement of syrup and mixed it with carbonated water at its various soda fountains.

In May 1931, Charles Guth, the president and general manager of Loft, became dissatisfied with the price of Coca-Cola syrup and suggested to Loft's vice president that Loft buy Pepsi-Cola syrup from National Pepsi-Cola Company, the owner of the secret formula and trademark for Pepsi-Cola. The vice president said he was investigating the purchase of Pepsi syrup.

Before being employed by Loft, Guth had been asked by the controlling shareholder of National Pepsi, Megargel, to acquire the assets of National Pepsi. Guth refused at that time. However, a few months after Guth had suggested that Loft purchase Pepsi syrup, Megargel again contacted Guth about buying National Pepsi's secret formula and trademark for only $10,000. This time, Guth agreed to the purchase, and Guth and Megargel organized a new corporation, Pepsi-Cola Company, to acquire the Pepsi-Cola secret formula and trademark from National Pepsi. Eventually, Guth and his family's corporation owned a majority of the shares of Pepsi-Cola Company.

Very little of Megargel's or Guth's funds were used to develop the business of Pepsi-Cola. Instead, without the knowledge or consent of Loft's board of directors, Guth used Loft's working capital, credit, plant and equipment, and executives and employees to produce Pepsi-Cola syrup. In addition, Guth's domination of Loft's board of directors ensured that Loft would become Pepsi-Cola's chief customer.

By 1935, the value of Pepsi-Cola's business was several million dollars. Loft sued Guth, asking the court to order Guth to transfer to Loft his shares of Pepsi-Cola Company and to pay Loft the dividends he had received from Pepsi-Cola Company. The trial court found that Guth had usurped a corporate opportunity and ordered Guth to transfer the shares and to pay Loft the dividends. Guth appealed.

Layton, Chief Justice

Public policy demands of a corporate officer or director the most scrupulous observance of his duty to refrain from doing anything that would deprive the corporation of profit or advantage. The rule that requires an undivided and unselfish loyalty to the corporation demands that there shall be no conflict between duty and self-interest.

The real issue is whether the opportunity to secure a very substantial stock interest in a corporation to be formed for the purpose of exploiting a cola beverage on a wholesale scale was so closely associated with the existing business activities of Loft, and so essential thereto, as to bring the transaction within that class of cases where the acquisition of the property would throw the corporate officer purchasing it into competition with his company.

Guth suggests a doubt whether Loft would have been able to finance the project. The answer to this suggestion is two-fold. Loft's net asset position was amply sufficient to finance the enterprise, and its plant, equipment, executives, personnel, and facilities were adequate. The second answer is that Loft's resources were found to be sufficient, for Guth made use of no other resources to any important extent.

Guth asserts that Loft's primary business was the manufacturing and selling of candy in its own chain of retail stores, and that it never had the idea of turning a subsidiary product into a highly advertised, nationwide specialty. It is contended that the Pepsi-Cola opportunity was not in the line of Loft's activities, which essentially were of a retail nature.

Loft, however, had many wholesale activities. Its wholesale business in 1931 amounted to over $800,000. It was a large company by any standard, with assets exceeding $9 million, excluding goodwill. It had an enormous plant. It paid enormous rentals. Guth, himself, said that Loft's success depended upon the fullest utilization of its large plant facilities. Moreover, it was a manufacturer of syrups and, with the exception of cola syrup, it supplied its own extensive needs. Guth, president of Loft, was an able and experienced man in that field. Loft, then, through its own personnel, possessed the technical knowledge, the practical business experience, and the resources necessary for the development of the Pepsi-Cola enterprise. Conceding that the essential of an opportunity is reasonably within the scope of a corporation's activities, latitude should be allowed for development and expansion. To deny this would be to deny the history of industrial development.

We cannot agree that Loft had no concern or expectancy in the opportunity. Loft had a practical and essential concern with respect to some cola syrup with an established formula and trademark. A cola beverage has come to be a business necessity for soft drink establishments; and it was essential to the success of Loft to serve at its soda fountains an acceptable five-cent cola drink in order to attract into its stores the great multitude of people who have formed the habit of drinking cola beverages.

When Guth determined to discontinue the sale of Coca-Cola in the Loft stores, it became, by his own act, a matter of urgent necessity for Loft to acquire a constant supply of some satisfactory cola syrup, secure against probable attack, as a replacement; and when the Pepsi-Cola opportunity presented itself, Guth having already considered the availability of the syrup, it became impressed with a Loft interest and expectancy arising out of the circumstances and the urgent and practical need created by him as the directing head of Loft.

The fiduciary relation demands something more than the morals of the marketplace. Guth did not offer the Pepsi-Cola opportunity to Loft, but captured it for himself. He invested little or no money of his own in the venture, but commandeered for his own benefit and advantage the money, resources, and facilities of his corporation and the services of its officials. He thrust upon Loft the hazard, while he reaped the benefit. In such a manner he acquired for himself 91 percent of the capital stock of Pepsi-Cola, now worth many millions. A genius in his line he may be, but the law makes no distinction between the wrongdoing genius and the one less endowed.

Judgment for Loft affirmed.

Oppression of Minority Shareholders

Directors and officers owe a duty to manage a corporation in the best interests of the corporation and the shareholders as a whole. When, however, a group of shareholders has been isolated for beneficial treatment to the detriment of another isolated group of shareholders, the disadvantaged group may complain of **oppression**.

For example, oppression may occur when directors of a close corporation who are also the majority shareholders pay themselves high salaries yet refuse to pay dividends or to hire minority shareholders as employees of the corporation. Because there is no market for the shares of a close corporation (apart from selling to the other shareholders), these oppressed minority shareholders have investments that provide them no return. They receive no dividends or salaries, and they can sell their shares only to the other shareholders, who are usually unwilling to pay the true value of the shares.

Generally, courts treat oppression of minority shareholders the same way courts treat director self-dealing: The transaction must be intrinsically fair to the corporation and the minority shareholders.

A special form of oppression is the **freeze-out**. A freeze-out is usually accomplished by merging a corporation with a newly formed corporation under terms by which the minority shareholders do not receive shares of the new corporation but instead receive only cash or other securities. The minority shareholders are thereby *frozen out as shareholders*.

Going private is a special term for a freeze-out of shareholders of *publicly owned corporations*. Some public corporations discover that the burdens of public ownership exceed the benefits of being public. For example, the SEC requires public companies to provide to shareholders annual reports that include audited financial statements. The Sarbanes–Oxley Act has increased the cost of being public by requiring, in section 404, that annual reports include an internal control report acknowledging management's responsibility to maintain "an adequate internal control structure and procedures for financial reports."

For some small public companies (annual revenue less than $100 million), section 404 compliance consumes more than 1 percent of their revenue. Therefore, some publicly owned companies choose to freeze out their minority shareholders to avoid such burdens.

Legal Standard Often, going private transactions appear abusive because the corporation goes public at a high price and goes private at a much lower price. Some courts have adopted a fairness test and a business purpose test for freeze-outs. Most states, including Delaware, apply the **total fairness test** to freeze-outs. In the freeze-out context, total fairness has two basic aspects: *fair dealing* and *fair price*. Fair dealing requires disclosing material information to directors and shareholders and providing an opportunity for negotiation. A determination of fair value requires the consideration of all the factors relevant to the value of the shares, except speculative projections.

Some states apply the *business purpose test* to freeze-outs. This test requires that the freeze-out accomplish some legitimate business purpose and not serve the special interests of the majority shareholders or the managers.

Other courts apply the business judgment rule when a committee of independent directors approves the freeze-out. In Delaware, the test is more severe. In a 2014 decision, the Supreme Court of Delaware held that the business judgment rule applies only if the transaction is approved by both a special board committee and a majority of the minority stockholders, the special committee is independent, the committee is empowered to select freely its own advisors and to say no definitively to the freeze-out, the committee meets its duty of care in negotiating a fair price, the vote of the minority shareholders is informed, and there is no coercion of the minority shareholders.[11]

Other states place no restrictions on freeze-outs provided a shareholder has a **right of appraisal**, which permits

---

[11]*Kahn v. M&F Worldwide Corp.*, 88 A.3d 635 (Del. 2014) (overruled on other grounds).

a shareholder to require the corporation to purchase his shares at a fair price. In Delaware, for short-form mergers (when a parent corporation owns 90 percent or more of the shares of the subsidiary with which it is merging), appraisal is the exclusive remedy available to a minority stockholder who objects to the short-form merger, unless there is fraud or illegality.[12]

---

[12]*Glassman v. Unocal Exploration Corporation*, 777 A.2d. 242 (Del. 2001).

In addition, the SEC requires a *publicly held* company to make a statement on the fairness of its proposed going private transaction and to discuss in detail the material facts on which the statement is based.

In the *Coggins* case, the court required that a freeze-out of minority shareholders of the New England Patriots football team meet both the business purpose and intrinsic fairness tests. The court held that freezing out the minority shareholders merely to allow the corporation to repay the majority shareholder's personal debts was not a proper business purpose.

Coggins v. New England Patriots Football Club, Inc.
492 N.E.2d 1112 (Mass. 1986)

In 1959, the New England Patriots Football Club, Inc. (Old Patriots) was formed with one class of voting shares and one class of nonvoting shares. Each of the original 10 voting shareholders, including William H. Sullivan, purchased 10,000 voting shares for $2.50 per share. The 120,000 nonvoting shares were sold for $5 per share to the general public in order to generate loyalty to the Patriots football team. In 1974, Sullivan was ousted as president of Old Patriots. In November 1975, Sullivan succeeded in regaining control of Old Patriots by purchasing all 100,000 voting shares for $102 per share. He again became a director and president of Old Patriots.

To finance his purchase of the voting shares, Sullivan borrowed $5,350,000 from two banks. The banks insisted that Sullivan reorganize Old Patriots so that its income could be used to repay the loans made to Sullivan and its assets used to secure the loans. To make the use of Old Patriots's income and assets legal, it was necessary to freeze out the nonvoting shareholders. In November 1976, Sullivan organized a new corporation called the New Patriots Football Club Inc. (New Patriots). Sullivan was the sole shareholder of New Patriots. In December 1976, the shareholders of Old Patriots approved a merger of Old Patriots and New Patriots. Under the terms of the merger, Old Patriots went out of business, New Patriots assumed the business of Old Patriots, Sullivan became the only owner of New Patriots, and the nonvoting shareholders of Old Patriots received $15 for each share they owned.

David A. Coggins, a Patriots fan from the time of its formation and owner of 10 Old Patriots nonvoting shares, objected to the merger and refused to accept the $15 per share payment for his shares. Coggins sued Sullivan and Old Patriots to obtain rescission of the merger. The trial judge found the merger to be illegal and ordered the payment of damages to Coggins and all other Old Patriots shareholders who voted against the merger and had not accepted the $15 per share merger payment. Sullivan and Old Patriots appealed to the Massachusetts Supreme Judicial Court.

Liacos, Justice

When the director's duty of loyalty to the corporation is in conflict with his self-interest, the court will vigorously scrutinize the situation. The dangers of self-dealing and abuse of fiduciary duty are greatest in freeze-out situations like the Patriots merger, when a controlling shareholder and corporate director chooses to eliminate public ownership. Because the danger of abuse of fiduciary duty is especially great in a freeze-out merger, the court must be satisfied that the freeze-out was for the advancement of a legitimate corporate purpose. If satisfied that elimination of public ownership is in furtherance of a business purpose, the court should then proceed to determine if the transaction was fair by examining the totality of the circumstances. Consequently, Sullivan and Old

Patriots bear the burden of proving, first, that the merger was for a legitimate business purpose, and second, that, considering the totality of circumstances, it was fair to the minority.

Sullivan and Old Patriots have failed to demonstrate that the merger served any valid corporate objective unrelated to the personal interests of Sullivan, the majority shareholder. The sole reason for the merger was to effectuate a restructuring of Old Patriots that would enable the repayment of the personal indebtedness incurred by Sullivan. Under the approach we set forth above, there is no need to consider further the elements of fairness of a transaction that is not related to a valid corporate purpose.

Judgment for Coggins affirmed as modified.

Ethics and Compliance in Action

Sarbanes–Oxley Act Imposes Duties and Liabilities on Corporate Management

In the early 2000s, it was revealed that some high-level officers of public corporations reaped millions of dollars of bonuses and profits from their sale of their corporations' stock during periods in which the corporations' profits were fraudulently inflated. In the Sarbanes–Oxley Act, as amended by the Dodd-Frank Wall Street Reform and Consumer Protection Act in 2010, Congress has taken a two-barreled approach, increasing top management's responsibility for the accuracy of financial statements and eliminating management's ability to profit personally from misstated financial data.

First, the Sarbanes–Oxley Act requires the CEO and the CFO of public companies to certify that to their knowledge all financial information in annual and quarterly reports filed with the Securities and Exchange Commission fairly presents the financial condition of the company and does not include untrue or misleading material statements. The purpose of the certification requirement is to protect shareholders and investors who rely on corporate financial statements. If a CEO

or CFO certified materially false financial statements that she knew were false or misleading, she is subject to a fine of $5 million and 20 years' imprisonment. In addition, the officer could have civil liability to shareholders far exceeding the fine limitation.

Second, the act requires the executive officers of a public company to disgorge any bonus, incentive-based or equity-based compensation, and the profit from the sale of corporate securities received during the three-year period prior to which the corporation was required to restate a financial statement due to a wrongful material noncompliance with a financial reporting requirement. This reimbursement of the corporation applies to an executive officer even if the wrongdoing was by some other officer or employee and whether or not the executive officer had knowledge of the wrongdoing. In addition, the act expands the disgorgement remedy available against any wrongdoing officer who receives bonuses or stock profits during the period of time the stock price is inflated by false financial information. The act permits recovery of not only improper gains but also any other relief necessary to protect and to mitigate harm to investors.

Trading on Inside Information

Officers and directors have *confidential access* to nonpublic information about the corporation. Sometimes, directors and officers purchase their corporation's securities with knowledge of confidential information. Often, disclosure of previously nonpublic, **inside information** affects the value of the corporation's securities. Therefore, directors and officers may make a profit when the prices of the securities increase after the inside information has been disclosed publicly. Shareholders of the corporation claim that they have been harmed by such activity, either because the directors and officers misused confidential information that should have been used only for corporate purposes or because the directors and officers had an unfair informational advantage over the shareholders.

In this century, there has been a judicial trend toward finding a duty of directors and officers to disclose information that they have received confidentially from the corporation before they buy or sell the corporation's securities. As will be discussed fully in Chapter 45, insider trading is already prohibited by regulations of the Securities and Exchange Commission. However, it remains only a minority rule under state corporation law.

Duties of Directors and Officers of Nonprofit Corporations

Directors and officers of nonprofit corporations owe fiduciary duties to their corporations that are similar to the duties owed by managers of for-profit corporations. Directors and officers owe a duty of care and duties of loyalty to the nonprofit corporation. They must act in good faith, be reasonably informed, exercise the care of an ordinarily prudent person, and have a reasonable belief that they are acting in the best interests of the corporation. In addition, a director should not have a conflict of interest in any transaction of the nonprofit corporation. As with for-profit corporations, conflict-of-interest transactions must meet the intrinsic fairness standard. Finally, a nonprofit corporation may not lend money to a director.

Liability concerns of directors of nonprofit corporations, especially public benefit corporations in which directors typically receive no compensation, have made it difficult for some nonprofit corporations to find and retain directors. Therefore, the Model Nonprofit Corporation Act eliminates the monetary liability of directors of a charitable company for any action taken or not taken, unless a director receives improper financial benefits, intentionally inflicts harm, intentionally violates criminal law, or makes an unlawful distribution to the corporation's members. The articles may not limit or eliminate a director's liability for failing to act in good faith, engaging in intentional misconduct, breaching the duty of loyalty, or having a conflict of interest.

Corporate and Management Liability for Torts and Crimes

LO43-7 Explain the legal limits of corporate liability for officers' and directors' actions.

When directors, officers, and other employees of the corporation commit torts and crimes while conducting corporate affairs, the issue arises concerning who has liability. Should the individuals committing the torts and crimes be held liable, the corporation, or both?

Liability of the Corporation For **torts**, the vicarious liability rule of *respondeat superior* applies to corporations. The only issue is whether an employee acted within the scope of her employment, which encompasses not only acts the employee is authorized to commit but may also include acts that the employee is expressly instructed to avoid. Generally, under the doctrine of *respondeat superior*, a corporation is liable for an employee's tort that is reasonably connected to the authorized conduct of the employee.

For **crimes**, the traditional view was that a corporation could not be guilty because criminal guilt required intent. A corporation, not having a mind, could form no intent. Other courts held that a corporation was not a person for purposes of criminal liability.

Since the early 1900s, however, American law has allowed corporations to be held criminally liable for their employee's actions. In *New York Central & Hudson River Railroad v. United States*,[13] the Supreme Court upheld a federal statute that imposed criminal liability on corporate agents for overcharging regulated rates on common carriers like railroad companies. The Court extended tort doctrine to impute agents' illegal acts to the corporation. The Court reasoned that ruling otherwise would deny the dominant role of corporations in society and make them effectively immune from punishment. The question remains whether criminal punishment, as opposed to civil monetary liability, is necessary to achieve the same goals.

Today, criminal liability for corporations is based primarily on federal and state statutes. Modern criminal statutes either expressly provide that corporations may commit crimes or define the term *person* to include corporations. In addition, some criminal statutes designed to protect the public welfare do not require intent as an element of some crimes, thereby removing the grounds used by early courts to justify relieving corporations of criminal liability.

Although *respondeat superior* liability applies to all acts committed by a corporation's agents, when they are acting on behalf of the corporation, to benefit the corporation, and broadly within the scope of their authority, there are practical constraints. Prosecutors are especially likely to charge a corporation when the criminal act alleged is authorized or performed by:

1. The board of directors,
2. An officer,
3. Another person having responsibility for formulating company policy, or
4. A high-level administrator having supervisory responsibility over the subject matter of the offense and acting within the scope of his employment.

---

[13]212 U.S. 481 (1909).

The Global Business Environment

Directors' Duties around the Globe

The fiduciary duties that American directors owe to their corporations are echoed in corporate law throughout the world. In Brazil, for example, an officer must apply the same principles he would apply in his own business. A Brazilian director breaches the duty of loyalty if the director uses inside information for his own benefit or for that of third parties, acts negligently in the use or protection of the company's rights, or engages in a business opportunity to gain personal advantage.

For public companies, Brazil adds a duty that does not exist under American corporation law: to supply information to the shareholders and the public. In the United States, this duty is generally imposed on the corporation, not the directors.

Under German law, the management board and supervisory board of an AG owe shareholders a duty of loyalty. Members of the management board have a statutory obligation of confidentiality, and each member of the management board must exercise the care of a diligent and prudent business executive.

That said, the law allows courts to hold a corporation liable for crimes of its agent or employee even if a higher corporate official has no knowledge of the act and has not ratified it.

Directors' and Officers' Liability for Torts and Crimes

A person is always *liable for his own torts and crimes*, even when committed on behalf of his principal. Every person in our society is expected to exercise independent judgment and not merely follow orders. Therefore, directors and officers are personally liable when they commit torts or crimes during the performance of their corporate duties.

A director or officer is usually not liable for the torts of employees of the corporation because the corporation, not the director or the officer, is the principal. He will have **tort** liability, however, if he *authorizes* the tort or *participates* in its commission. A director or officer has **criminal** liability if she *requests*, *authorizes*, *conspires*, or *aids and abets* the commission of a crime by an employee.

Criminal prosecutions against officers and directors tend to be cyclical, depending on current corporate scandals. In the late 1990s and early 2000s, there were a number of high-profile criminal cases against CEOs accused of acceding to accounting irregularities or looting their companies. Bernard Ebbers, former CEO of WorldCom, was found guilty of helping to mastermind the $11 billion accounting fraud that saw the firm seek bankruptcy. Ebbers received a 25-year prison sentence. The jury rejected his defense that he knew nothing of the fraud that was orchestrated by WorldCom CFO Scott Sullivan. The jury believed that, as CEO, Ebbers must have known of the fraud and was motivated to prop up the price of WorldCom stock to increase the value of stock options he held. Sullivan, who pled guilty and testified against Ebbers, cooperated with the prosecution and received a five-year prison sentence, despite his central role in the fraud.

In 2005, Adelphia founder and former CEO John Rigas received a 15-year prison sentence, and his son and former CFO, Scott, received 20 years, after being found guilty of looting Adelphia. According to prosecutors, the Rigases used Adelphia as their "private ATM" to provide $50 million in cash advances, buy $1.6 billion in securities, and repay $252 million in margin loans. Also, Tyco's former CEO Dennis Kozlowski received up to 25 years in prison for looting Tyco, including using company funds for his wife's $2 million birthday party. Kozlowski was also fined $70 million and ordered to repay $134 million to Tyco.

More recently, Bernie Madoff and Allen Stanford, chairmen of their respective investment companies, were convicted of Ponzi schemes. Madoff's decades-long scheme was the largest in U.S. history at $65 billion in "paper" fraud. Allen's was tiny in comparison, a mere $300 million. Madoff pleaded guilty and Stanford was found guilty at trial; they were sentenced to 150 years and 110 years in prison, respectively.

Insider trading, crimes related to the financial crisis of 2008, and health care frauds surrounding opioids, blood testing, and the coronavirus pandemic have taken center stage in recent years. Although roughly 6,000 individuals and 150 companies are convicted in federal court every year of economic crimes, only a small amount make national news like Ebbers or Madoff. Yet some calculate the costs of white-collar crime, estimated between $500 billion and $1.6 trillion per year, to greatly outweigh the costs of more widely reported violent crime.

The following *Jensen* case involves a highly publicized stock options backdating case. The case is a primer on why corporations backdated options for their top executives and how courts determine an appropriate sentence, including imprisonment, for executives who willingly violate the law.

United States v. Jensen   537 F. Supp. 2d 1069 (N.D. Cal. 2008)

On March 18, 2006, The Wall Street Journal published an article analyzing how some companies were granting stock options to their executives. According to the article, companies issued a suspiciously high number of options at times when the stock price hit a periodic low, followed by a sharp price increase. The odds of these well-timed grants occurring by chance alone were astronomical— less likely than winning the lottery. Eventually, it was determined that such buy-low, sell-high returns simply could not be the product of chance. In testimony before Congress, Professor Erik Lie identified three potential strategies to account for these well-timed stock option grants. The first strategy included techniques called "spring-loading" and "bullet-dodging." The practice of "spring-loading" involved timing a stock option grant to precede an announcement of good news. The practice of "bullet-dodging" involved timing a stock option grant to follow an announcement of bad news. A second strategy included manipulating the flow of information— timing corporate announcements to match known future grant dates. A third strategy, backdating, involved cherry-picking past, and relatively low, stock prices to be the official grant date. Backdating occurs when the option's grant date is altered to an earlier date with a lower, more favorable price to the recipient.

A company grants stock options to its officers, directors, and employees at a certain "exercise price," giving the recipient the right to buy shares of the stock at that price, once the option vests. If the stock price rises after the date of the grant, the options have value. If the stock price falls after the date of the grant, the options have no value. Options with an exercise price equal to the stock's market price are called "at-the-money" options. Options with an exercise price lower than the stock's market price are called "in-the-money" options. By granting in-the-money, backdated options, a company effectively grants an employee an instant opportunity for profit.

Backdating stock options by itself is not illegal. Purposefully backdated options that are properly accounted for and disclosed are legal. On the other hand, the backdating of options that is not disclosed or does not result in the recognition of a compensation expense is fraud. A motive for fraudulent backdating may be to avoid recognizing a compensation expense, or a hit to the earnings, while awarding in-the-money options. A company's failure to account properly for in-the-money options would inflate the bottom line such that the company's net income would be higher than it should have been from an accounting perspective. As a result, the company would report excessive earnings per share, one of the more important metrics that investors used to evaluate a company's performance.

After 2002, a company's ability to backdate fraudulently option grants became much more difficult. On August 29, 2002, Congress passed the Sarbanes–Oxley Act, which instituted new reporting requirements for stock option grants. Before Sarbanes–Oxley, an employee who received a stock option grant had to file financial forms with the SEC within 45 days after the company's fiscal year-end. After Sarbanes–Oxley, an employee must file financial forms with the SEC within two days of receiving the stock option grant. A company fraudulently backdating stock options by a few weeks or months would not have filed the required SEC forms on time, raising red flags with the SEC.

There have been several highly publicized options backdating cases involving American corporations. One involved Brocade Communications issuing backdated options to its CEO Gregory Reyes. Not only were Brocade Communications and Reyes prosecuted for violating federal securities laws, but also Stephanie Jensen, a Brocade vice president and director of its human resources department. At their trial, Dr. John Garvey, an expert witness for the prosecution, provided testimony about the size of the compensation expenses that went unstated as a result of Brocade's options pricing practices. Dr. Garvey testified that Brocade failed to recognize more than $173 million of compensation expenses in 2001 and more than $161 million in 2002. He further testified that, if Brocade had properly accounted for the stock options it had backdated, then the company would have recorded a loss of $110 million in 2001, rather than the profit of $3 million it actually reported, and would have recorded a loss of $45 million in 2002, rather than the profit of nearly $60 million it actually reported.

In December 2007, a federal district court jury convicted Jensen of willingly and knowingly falsifying Brocade's records over a three-year period to conceal the actual date when stock options were granted to Reyes. The district court judge next considered whether a proper sentence for Jensen included imprisonment.

Breyer, Judge

The Securities Exchange Act's penalty provision, 15 U.S.C. § 78ff, precludes imprisonment "for the violation of any rule or regulation if [the defendant] proves that he had no knowledge of such rule or regulation." Concerned that a great mass of rules and regulations would be issued by the SEC in the wake of the Securities Act and Securities Exchange Act, Congress enacted the No Knowledge Clause, thereby rendering ludicrous a strict adherence to the fiction of presumed knowledge of the law.

The No Knowledge Clause is an affirmative defense to a sentence of imprisonment. As such, the defendant bears the burden of proving no knowledge by a preponderance of the evidence. To be more specific, Jensen bears the burden of proving that she did not know there was any applicable SEC rule prohibiting the falsification of books and records. It is not a defense for Jensen to argue that she did not know, for example, the precise number or common name of the rule, the book and page where it was to be found, or the date upon which it was promulgated.

Accordingly, the question becomes whether Jensen has satisfied her burden of proving by a preponderance that she was unaware of an SEC rule or regulation prohibiting the falsification of books and records. In the Court's opinion, she has not. Jensen argues that: (1) her background and experience are in areas that have nothing to do with SEC rules and regulations; (2) her job responsibilities had nothing to do with SEC rules or regulations; (3) Jensen had nothing to do with the SEC reporting process; (4) none of the individuals who worked with Jensen drew any connection between their work on options grants and SEC regulations; and (5) none of the more than 50 deponents in the SEC action recall discussing anything connected to any SEC rule with Jensen.

There is no smoking gun conclusively demonstrating that Jensen was aware that falsification of books was outlawed by SEC regulation. However, the circumstantial evidence that Jensen offers up is insufficient to carry her burden in light of the evidence established at trial. There is substantial evidence that Jensen knew her conduct was wrongful, including the fact that Jensen attempted to minimize the obviousness of backdated options, concealed the way options were actually dated, and directed employees not to communicate about options over the phone or email. To be sure, Jensen can only be imprisoned if she knew her conduct was unlawful *and* knew that it was prohibited by SEC rule or regulation. But in light of the evidence demonstrating that Jensen knew her conduct affected Brocade finances, the Court is assured that Jensen also knew she was violating an SEC rule or regulation.

For example, Jensen received emails establishing that options had an effect on Brocade financials and audits. On January 28, 2002, Jensen received an email from Brocade comptroller Bob Bossi, asking for the stock grant list to support an upcoming quarter-end audit from Arthur Andersen. Similarly, Jensen received an email confirming that the stock options grant lists and compensation committee meetings would be used in Brocade's year-end audit. The only reasonable conclusion to draw is that Jensen knew that stock options, and how they were priced, affected the audited results of the company.

Moreover, there was evidence at trial that after Jensen shepherded options through the pricing process, the forms were then given to the finance department so that finance could ensure that the grants were accurate. It can be reasonably assumed that as director of human resources, Jensen understood the chain for processing option grants and that stock options went from human resources directly to finance. A reasonably intelligent corporate official would understand that if the options forms went directly to finance, that was so because the forms had an effect on Brocade's financials. Falsifying options grants would therefore impair the integrity of the company's financials, which a reasonable official would know is illegal under SEC rule and regulation.

In short, the Court does not believe that Jensen was so far removed from the financial side of the process that she would not know her conduct was prohibited by the SEC. Jensen clearly knew her conduct was unlawful and, the Court believes, knew that her conduct affected Brocade's finances and audits. Under the circumstances, Jensen has not persuasively established that she was unaware her conduct violated any SEC rule or regulation.

In determining the sentence of co-defendant Gregory Reyes, the Court concluded that it would be inappropriate to enhance the sentence for loss, number of victims, and sophisticated means. The Court reaches the same conclusion with respect to Jensen's sentence. As to other enhancements, the Court will impose a two-level abuse of trust enhancement and a two-level enhancement for obstruction of justice, but rejects the government's request for an aggravating role enhancement and a public officer enhancement.

In general, the government bears the burden of proving, by a preponderance of the evidence, the facts necessary to enhance a defendant's offense level under the Sentencing Guidelines. However, when a sentencing factor has an extremely disproportionate effect on the sentence relative to the offense of conviction, due process requires that the government prove the facts underlying the enhancement by clear and convincing evidence.

The government has *not* demonstrated—at least not by clear and convincing evidence—that Jensen was the kind of Vice President who owed a heightened fiduciary duty to shareholders. Brocade proxy statements, 10-Qs, and 10-Ks frequently listed corporate officers, including the Vice Presidents in charge of Engineering, Operations, and Sales—core decisional and policy-making roles—but never Jensen. In addition, the government has identified no securities law that imposes heightened duties on executives in divisions such as human resources, as opposed to divisions more closely connected to the operational functions of the company.

To be sure, Jensen played an important *internal* role in the organization. Jensen was one of only nine executives who reported directly to Reyes, in contrast to sixteen Vice Presidents who did not. But the government has not pointed to persuasive evidence demonstrating that Jensen played the kind of role in relation to *shareholders* such that as head of Human Resources, she owed them a heightened fiduciary duty. Accordingly, the Court will not impose the four-level public officer enhancement.

Because the Court will not impose the public officer enhancement, it may consider whether to impose an enhancement for abuse of trust. To impose an enhancement for abuse of trust, the government must establish by clear and convincing evidence that: (1) Jensen occupied a position of trust; and (2) Jensen abused her position in a manner that significantly facilitated the commission or concealment of the offense.

Jensen used her managerial position to escort the backdated stock option grants through the necessary processes. It was Jensen who involved and oversaw employees in the human resources department tasked with the picking of lower dates, Jensen who ordered her employees to conceal the picking of past dates by not using email or phones, and Jensen who coordinated the signing of falsified dates by Reyes, providing the CEO with an array of earlier dates from which he could select. A lesser employee of the firm could not have accomplished these things which significantly facilitated the scheme's success and concealment.

Even if Jensen did not owe a heightened fiduciary duty to shareholders, she was entrusted with accurately maintaining books and records that affected the financials of the company. Thus, there can be no doubt that shareholders were obligated to trust that Jensen would properly maintain any books and records bearing on Brocade's assets. Because Jensen occupied a position of trust and abused that position to commit and conceal the falsification of books and records, a two-level enhancement is appropriate.

Because Jensen has not carried her burden of proving that the No Knowledge Clause controls her sentence, the Court will impose a sentence with an eye towards—among other factors—the Sentencing Guidelines. With a base offense level of six, plus two-level enhancements for abuse of trust and obstruction of justice, the Guidelines recommend a sentence of 6–12 months. The minimum term may be satisfied by a sentence of imprisonment that includes a term of supervised release with a condition that substitutes community confinement or home detention, provided that at least one month is satisfied by imprisonment.

Order entered sentencing Jensen to imprisonment.

Insurance and Indemnification

The extensive potential liability of directors may deter persons from becoming directors. The fear is that their liability for their actions as directors may far exceed their fees as directors. To encourage persons to become directors, corporations **indemnify** them for their outlays associated with defending lawsuits brought against them and paying judgments and settlement amounts. In addition, or as an alternative, corporations purchase insurance that will make such payments for the directors. Indemnification and insurance are provided for officers, also.

Mandatory Indemnification of Directors

Under the MBCA, a director is entitled to *mandatory indemnification* of her reasonable litigation expenses when she is sued and *wins completely* (is *wholly successful*). The greatest part of such expenses is attorney fees. Because indemnification is mandatory in this context, when the corporation refuses to indemnify a director who has won completely, she may ask a court to order the corporation to indemnify her.

Permissible Indemnification of Directors

Under the MBCA, a director who loses a lawsuit *may* be indemnified by the corporation. This is called *permissible indemnification* because the corporation is permitted to indemnify the director but is not required to do so.

The corporation must establish that the director acted in *good faith* and reasonably believed that she acted in the *best interests* of the corporation. When a director seeks indemnification for a *criminal* fine, the corporation must establish a third requirement—that the director had no reasonable cause to believe that her conduct was unlawful. Finally, any permissible indemnification must be approved by someone independent of the director receiving indemnification—a disinterested board of directors, disinterested shareholders, or independent legal counsel. Permissible indemnification may cover not only the director's reasonable expenses but also fines and damages that the director has been ordered to pay.

A corporation may not elect to indemnify a director who was found to have received a *financial benefit* to which he was not entitled. Such a rule tends to prevent indemnification of directors who acted from self-interest.

If a director received no financial benefit but was held liable to his corporation or paid an amount to the corporation as part of a *settlement*, the director may be indemnified only for his reasonable expenses, not for the amount that he paid to the corporation. The purpose of these rules is to avoid the circularity of having the director pay damages to the corporation and then having the corporation indemnify the director for the same amount of money.

Insurance The MBCA does not limit the ability of a corporation to purchase insurance on behalf of its directors, officers, and employees (D&O insurance). Insurance companies, however, are unwilling to insure all risks. In addition, some risks are *legally uninsurable as against public policy*. Therefore, liability for misconduct such as self-dealing, usurpation, and securities fraud is uninsurable.

Nonprofit Corporations A nonprofit corporation may obtain insurance and indemnify its officers and directors for liabilities incurred in the course of their performance of their official duties. The MNCA requires indemnification when the director or officer wins the lawsuit completely. A corporation is permitted to indemnify an officer or director who is found liable if he acted in good faith and reasonably believed he acted in the best interests of the corporation.

Ethics and Compliance in Action

News Corporation and Its Directors Agree to Largest Shareholder Suit Settlement

In April 2013, shareholder derivative litigation arising in part from News Corp.'s phone-hacking scandal was settled with a record-breaking $139 million cash settlement. The settlement was funded by directors' and officers' insurance proceeds. News Corp. shareholders argued that the company's directors approved the purchase of Shine Group Ltd. at an excessive price. Shine Group was a television and movie production company owned by the daughter of News Corp. chairman of the board Rupert Murdoch. The litigation also addressed the issue that the company's directors failed to investigate properly phone-hacking allegations that led to the end of News Corp.'s *News of the World*, a newspaper published in the United Kingdom from 1843 to 2011. A private investigator hired by the newspaper had intercepted the voicemail of a missing British teenager who was later found murdered. The paper was also alleged to have hacked into the phones of families of British service personnel killed in action.

The settlement also included several corporate governance reforms at News Corp. The agreement established a Compliance Steering Committee, responsible for setting compliance policies and overseeing their implementation, that must report at least quarterly to the Audit Committee, at least semiannually to the independent directors, and at least annually to the full board. The board's independent directors must appoint a Chief Compliance Officer reporting directly to the Audit Committee, and the company also must establish an anonymous whistleblowing hotline. Under the settlement, News Corp. also must make annual public disclosures to its shareholders of political contributions made directly by the company to state or local candidates and various political organizations.

Previous large settlements of shareholder actions include the Oracle derivative suit, settled in 2005 by CEO Larry Ellison's payment of $122 million. The Broadcom Corporation's shareholders' derivative suit regarding options backdating was settled in 2009 by a D&O insurers' agreement to pay $118 million. In 2008, the AIG shareholders' derivative action was settled by a payment of $115 million, $85.5 million of which was paid by D&O insurance.

Problems and Problem Cases

1. Tri R Angus, a closely held corporation, was owned 80 percent by Jon and Frances Neiman, who were also directors of Tri R Angus. Troy Neiman and Carol Lewis owned 12 percent of Tri R Angus's shares. Troy and Carol asked a court to remove Jon and Frances as directors of the corporation on the grounds that they authorized Tri R Angus to distribute its assets in violation of state law, inappropriately mortgaged or sold corporate assets, misused corporate earnings, and wasted corporate assets. Jon and Frances denied the allegations. At trial, Troy and Carol entered as evidence pleadings from other actions against Jon and Frances and introduced no objective evidence of current conduct by Jon or Frances. What standard of misconduct did the court require Troy and Carol to prove in order to remove Jon and Frances? Did the court find they had proved their case?

2. James Donald was the chief executive officer of DSC communications, a Delaware corporation headquartered in Plano, Texas. In 1990, DSC's board of directors entered an employment agreement with Donald, which provided that Donald "shall be responsible for the general management of the affairs of the company and report to the Board." C. L. Grimes, a DSC shareholder, sued Donald on behalf of the corporation asking the court to invalidate the employment agreement between Donald and DSC on the grounds that the agreement illegally delegated the duties and responsibilities of DSC's board of directors to Donald. Will the Court find that this is a case of abdication of the board's duties to the CEO?

3. Lillian Pritchard was a director of Pritchard & Baird Corporation, a business founded by her husband. After the death of her husband, her sons took control of the corporation. For two years, they looted the assets of the corporation through theft and improper payments. The corporation's financial statements revealed the improper payments to the sons, but Mrs. Pritchard did not read the financial statements. She did not know what her sons were doing to the corporation or that what they were doing was unlawful. When Mrs. Pritchard was sued for failing to protect the assets of the corporation, she argued that she was a figurehead director, a simple housewife who served as a director as an accommodation to her husband and sons. Was Mrs. Pritchard held liable?

4. The Chicago National League Ball Club (Chicago Cubs) operated Wrigley Field, the Cubs's home park.

Through the 1965 baseball season, the Cubs were the only major league baseball team that played no home games at night because Wrigley Field had no lights for nighttime baseball. Philip K. Wrigley, director and president of the corporation, refused to install lights because of his personal opinion that baseball was a daytime sport and that installing lights and scheduling night baseball games would result in the deterioration of the surrounding neighborhood. The other directors assented to this policy. From 1961 to 1965, the Cubs suffered losses from their baseball operations. The Chicago White Sox, whose weekday games were generally played at night, drew many more fans than did the Cubs. A shareholder sued the board of directors to force them to install lights at Wrigley Field and to schedule night games. What did the court rule? Why?

5. James Gray was the president and managing officer of Peoples Bank and Trust Company. Frank Piecara was an old customer of the bank. Piecara was president of Mirage Construction. Gray directed Peoples Bank to make a $536,000 loan to a trust managed by Piecara—the loan proceeds to be used to provide working capital for Mirage. Gray obtained a security interest in Mirage's accounts receivable and contract rights for work Mirage was to perform for Rogers Construction. Gray did not perfect the security interest or notify Rogers that it should remit payments for Mirage's work directly to Peoples Bank. Piecara and Mirage defaulted on the loan to Peoples Bank. Gray was sued by his employer for breaching his fiduciary duty. Has Gray complied with the business judgment rule?

6. Allergan, a specialty pharmaceutical manufacturer, produces Botox, a well-known drug. The FDA approved Botox for only a few conditions: crossed eyes, involuntary eyelid muscle contractions, involuntary neck muscle contractions, and excessive sweating. Although doctors are allowed to prescribe an approved pharmaceutical for purposes other than those listed by the FDA, federal law imposes numerous limits on drug manufacturers' efforts to promote such "off-label uses" of their products. Faced with allegations that it had acted illegally in marketing and labeling Botox as a cure for severe headaches, Allergan settled several lawsuits and pled guilty in a criminal case. Allergan ultimately paid a total of $600 million, in part for civil settlements and in part as a criminal fine. Allergan shareholders then filed a derivative action alleging that Allergan's directors were liable for violations of various state and federal laws, as well as for breaches of their fiduciary duties to Allergan. What type of claim are Allergan shareholders making and what specific duty are they alleging the company's directors violated? Assuming Allergan's board was aware of a series of FDA warning letters cautioning that the company was issuing "misleading statements" in Botox promotional materials and was shown a slide deck laying out a growth strategy for the company based on marketing Botox for headaches and cosmetic benefits, did the court allow the shareholder suit to go forward?

7. Simon J. Michael, a director of Shocking Technologies, was the only representative of the holders of two classes of Shocking preferred stock. Over time, significant disagreements between Michael and the other board members arose over executive compensation and whether preferred shareholders should have increased board representation. Michael argued that the company's governance problems needed to be resolved before it could attract additional equity funding, which the company desperately needed. Michael understood that Shocking's survival likely depended upon a large investment by a third party, Littelfuse. Michael spoke with Littelfuse to try to align Littelfuse's interests with his. Michael not only sought to dissuade Littelfuse from investing in Shocking, but also disclosed to Littelfuse Shocking's confidential business information that Littelfuse was the only potential investor likely to participate in the necessary fund-raising. By informing Littelfuse that there were no other options available to Shocking, Michael gave Littelfuse a significantly enhanced strategic bargaining position with Shocking. Michael believed that Shocking's resulting cash crunch would force the rest of the board to implement his objectives, which he believed served the interests of the preferred shareholders. Did Michael breach his fiduciary duty to Shocking?

8. Michael Baker and Michael Gluk were the CEO and CFO of ArthroCare Corporation, a public company. Due to fraud committed by two senior vice presidents of ArthroCare, John Raffle and David Applegate, ArthoCare misstated its earnings in various SEC filings from 2006 to 2008. Pursuant to the Sarbanes–Oxley Act and acting on behalf of ArthroCare, the SEC sought recovery from Baker and Gluk in the amount of cash bonuses, incentives, and equity-based compensation that Baker and Gluk earned during the affected periods. The SEC argued that Baker and Gluk were liable because they were the CEO and CFO at the time and thus signed the filings that required restatements. Baker and Gluk argued that they did not commit any conscious wrongdoing and did not themselves commit any violation of securities law. Did the trial court agree not to require Baker and Gluk to disgorge their compensation?

9. Selectica, a Delaware corporation, provides enterprise software solutions to business. It has never been profitable and has amassed net operating losses (NOLs) that it may use to offset future income for tax purposes. Trilogy, a Delaware corporation, also specializes in enterprise software solutions. Versata Enterprises is a Delaware corporation and a subsidiary of Trilogy, providing technology-powered business services to clients. Versata and Trilogy owned 6.7 percent of Selectica's common stock. After they intentionally triggered Selectica's Shareholder Rights Plan through the purchase of additional shares, Versata's and Trilogy's joint beneficial ownership was diluted to approximately 3.3 percent. Selectica thereafter reduced the trigger of its poison pill to 4.99 percent of Selectica's outstanding shares and capped existing shareholders who held a 5 percent or more interest to a further increase of only 0.5 percent. Selectica's reason for taking such action was to protect the company's NOL carryforwards. When Trilogy purchased shares above this cap, Selectica filed suit in the Delaware Court of Chancery, seeking a declaration that the poison pill was valid. Trilogy and its subsidiary Versata counterclaimed that the poison pill was unlawful on the grounds that, before acting, Selectica's board of directors failed to consider that its NOLs were unusable or that the poison pill was unnecessary given Selectica's unbroken history of losses and doubtful prospects of annual profits. Trilogy and Versata also asserted that the poison pill was impermissibly preclusive of a successful proxy contest for control of Selectica's board of directors, particularly when combined with Selectica's staggered director terms. What rule did the court apply to judge the actions of Selectica's board of directors? Did the court conclude that the board complied with that rule?

10. Kenneth Cole Productions (KCP), a New York corporation, designs and markets a broad range of footwear, handbags, and apparel under various brand names. Kenneth Cole has been the controlling shareholder of KCP and has served as its chairman of the board since its inception in 1982. As of February 24, 2012, Cole owned or controlled approximately 46 percent of KCP's outstanding common stock and 89 percent of its voting power. Cole's voting power resulted from his ownership and control of 100 percent of the company's super-voting Class B common stock. On February 23, 2012, Cole proposed taking KCP private. He proposed a per share price of $15 and stated that he would not entertain any other offers to sell KCP. The $15 price represented a 17 percent premium over the sale price of the KPC stock on the previous day. Cole's proposal was conditioned on the approval of a special committee of directors who were independent of him. The committee comprised four directors, which considered the proposal and negotiated the price with Cole until June 6, 2012, when a merger agreement was announced, settling on a price of $15.25 per share. Despite the publicity surrounding Cole's attempt to repurchase the stock, no competing offers to purchase KPC stock were received. The transaction was submitted for approval to the public shareholders, and 99.8 percent of the shares—more than 8 million—were cast to approve the transaction; 18,357 shares were voted against the transaction. Erie County Employees Retirement System (ECERS), the owner of common stock of KCP, sued Cole and the four special committee directors. ECERS contended that the special committee directors lacked independence because two directors were elected to the board by Cole. ECERS also alleged that the directors breached their duties by failing to solicit third-party bids. Cole was alleged to have breached his fiduciary duty as a shareholder because he was not impartial. Did the trial court agree with ECERS?

11. Ian McCarthy was president and CEO of Beazer Homes USA, a publicly held home construction company that was required to restate its quarterly and annual financial statements due to a fraudulent earnings management scheme perpetrated by Beazer's CAO, Michael Rand, to satisfy analysts' quarterly and annual earnings expectations. Rand directed and supervised a reserve accounting scheme under which reserves for certain future homebuilding expenses were improperly established, inflated, or maintained so that they could later be used in subsequent fiscal years, including 2006, to boost artificially income and earnings. In 2008, after uncovering the fraud, Beazer correctly restated its 2006 earnings. Even though McCarthy was not engaged in the fraud, the Securities and Exchange Commission demanded that McCarthy reimburse Beazer for cash bonuses, incentive and equity-based compensation, and profits from his sale of Beazer stock received during the 12-month period following the issuance of Beazer's quarterly and annual financial statements for its fiscal year 2006. Was the SEC's action successful?

12. In 1997, Peter Zaccagnino sold to investors historical bonds—issued by railroad and foreign governments—that he claimed were high-yield securities. In reality, the bonds had no value to anyone other than to collectors of historical documents. Peter obtained more than $6.8 million from the sale of these bonds. During this time, his wife, Gigi, attended meetings where her husband represented to investors that the

bonds could yield 7 to 30 percent of their valuation within a year. Zaccagnino sold the historical bonds through two corporate entities and deposited most of the sales proceeds into the corporations' accounts. One of those corporations was Wonder Glass Products, of which Gigi was the secretary, treasurer, and director. She received $5,200 a month from her employment with Wonder Glass. In March 1998, Gigi incorporated a business called Diamond in the Rough (DIR) in the British Virgin Islands, of which she was president, secretary, and director. Peter promoted DIR as a firm that placed client funds into high-yield offshore investment programs, promising investors substantial earnings. At one DIR meeting with prospective purchasers, Gigi sat at a table and made prospective investors promise that they would not record the meeting. Meanwhile, Peter told them that they could make huge sums of money with the proposed investments and that he had been arranging similar investments successfully for so long that he was ready to retire. This foreign investment scheme earned Peter millions in addition to the money from the historical bond sales. When the federal government prosecuted Peter and Gigi for conspiracy and racketeering, Gigi claimed that she became aware of the criminal conduct only in December 1999, when she overheard her husband and one of his business partners laughing about the falsity of the statements they sent to investors. Did the court accept Gigi's argument or was she found to have willfully engaged in criminal conduct while acting for the corporations?

13. The MBCA permits a corporation to expand the grounds on which it may indemnify a director, within limits. For example, the corporation may provide for indemnification of a director's liability (including a judgment paid to the corporation) when the director acted carelessly and in bad faith, but did not intend to harm the corporation or its shareholders and did not receive an improper financial benefit. Do you think it is ethical for a corporation to indemnify a careless director for the amount for which she was liable to the corporation? Would you be a shareholder in a corporation that permits indemnification in the context above? Would you be a director in a corporation if it did not indemnify you in that context? Support your answer according to rights theory, utilitarianism, or profit maximization arguments.

Shareholders' Rights
and Liabilities

Four business associates create a business that will develop and sell information technology software. The business will be incorporated. The four will provide 90 percent of the initial capital needs of the business, but none of them has the IT skills to develop marketable software. In addition, none of the four wants to be involved in the day-to-day management of the business. The four associates have found, however, an IT engineer to develop software and another person who is willing to manage the business. The engineer and the general manager each wants a 5 percent equity interest in the corporation, which the four associates are willing to grant to them. Although the engineer and the GM would each like to elect a representative to the corporation's board of directors, the four associates want to control the business absolutely, with each associate owning an equal share of the corporation and sitting on the board.

- Using classes of shares, create an equity structure for the corporation that meets the wants of the four associates, the engineer, and the GM.
- In this context, why is using classes of shares preferable to using one class of shares with cumulative voting for directors?

LO LEARNING OBJECTIVES

After studying this chapter, you should be able to:

44-1 Understand the rights and powers of shareholders and how shareholders exercise their powers.

44-2 Create classes of shares and delineate their rights to fit the needs of controlling and other shareholders.

44-3 Appreciate how shareholders may enforce corporate rights of actions, especially against corporate managers.

44-4 Explain the special liabilities of shareholders.

THE SHAREHOLDERS ARE THE owners of a corporation, but a shareholder has *no right to manage* the corporation. Instead, a corporation is managed by its board of directors and its officers for the benefit of its shareholders.

The shareholders' role in a corporation is limited to electing and removing directors; approving certain important matters; and ensuring that the actions of the corporation's managers are consistent with the applicable state corporation statute, the articles of incorporation, and the bylaws.

Shareholders also assume a few responsibilities. For example, all shareholders are required to pay the promised consideration for shares. Shareholders are liable for receiving dividends beyond the lawful amount. In addition, controlling shareholders may owe special duties to minority shareholders.

Close corporation shareholders enjoy rights and owe duties beyond the rights and duties of shareholders of publicly owned corporations. In addition, some courts have found close corporation shareholders to be fiduciaries of each other.

This chapter's study of the rights and responsibilities of shareholders begins with an examination of shareholders' meetings and voting rights.

Shareholders' Meetings

The general corporation statutes of most states and the Model Business Corporation Act (MBCA) provide that an annual meeting of shareholders shall be held. The purpose of an annual shareholders' meeting is to elect new directors and to conduct other necessary business. Often, the shareholders are asked to approve the corporation's independent auditors and to vote on shareholders' proposals.

Special meetings of shareholders may be held whenever a corporate matter arises that requires immediate shareholders' action, such as the approval of a merger that cannot wait until the next annual shareholders' meeting. Under the MBCA, a special shareholders' meeting may be called by the board of directors or by a person authorized to do so by the bylaws, usually the president or the board chair. In addition, the holders of at least 10 percent of the shares entitled to vote at the meeting may call a special meeting.

Notice of Meetings
To permit shareholders to arrange their schedules for attendance at shareholders' meetings, the MBCA requires the corporation to give shareholders notice of annual and special meetings of shareholders. Notice of a *special meeting* must list the purpose of the meeting. Under the MBCA, notice of an *annual meeting* need not include the purpose of the meeting unless shareholders will be asked to approve extraordinary corporate changes—for example, amendments to the articles of incorporation and mergers.

Notice need be given only to shareholders entitled to vote who are shareholders of record on a date fixed by the board of directors. Shareholders of record are those whose names appear on the share-transfer book of the corporation. Usually, only shareholders of record are entitled to vote at shareholders' meetings.

Conduct of Meetings
To conduct business at a shareholders' meeting, a **quorum** of the outstanding shares must be represented at the meeting. If the approval of more than one class of shares is required, a quorum of each class of shares must be present. A quorum is a majority of shares outstanding, unless a greater percentage is established in the articles. The president or the board chair usually presides at shareholders' meetings. Minutes of shareholders' meetings are usually kept by the secretary.

A majority of the votes cast at the shareholders' meeting will decide issues that are put to a vote. If the approval of more than one class of shares is required, a majority of the votes cast by each class must favor the issue. The articles may require a greater-than-majority vote. Ordinarily, a shareholder is entitled to cast as many votes as he has shares.

Shareholders have a right of *full participation* in shareholders' meetings. This includes the right to offer resolutions, to speak for and against proposed resolutions, and to ask questions of the officers of the corporation.

Typical shareholder resolutions are aimed at protecting or enhancing the interests of minority shareholders and promoting current social issues. Proposals have included limiting corporate charitable contributions, restricting the production of nuclear power, banning the manufacture of weapons, and requiring the protection of the environment.

Shareholder Action without a Meeting
Generally, shareholders can act only at a properly called meeting. However, the MBCA permits shareholders to act without a meeting if *all of the shareholders entitled to vote consent in writing* to the action.

Shareholders' Election of Directors

LO44-1 Understand the rights and powers of shareholders and how shareholders exercise their powers.

Straight Voting
The most important shareholder voting right exercised at a shareholder meeting is the right to elect the directors. Normally, directors are elected by a single class of shareholders in **straight voting**, in which each share has one vote for each new director to be elected. With straight voting, a shareholder may vote for as many nominees as there are directors to be elected; a shareholder may cast for each such nominee as many votes as she has shares. For example, in a director election in which 15 people have been nominated for five director positions, a shareholder with 100 shares can vote for up to 5 nominees and can cast up to 100 votes for each of those 5 nominees.

Under straight voting, the nominees with the most votes are elected. Consequently, straight voting allows a majority shareholder to elect the entire board of directors. Thus, minority shareholders are unable to elect any representatives to the board without the cooperation of the majority shareholder.

Straight voting is also a problem in close corporations in which a few shareholders own equal numbers of shares. In such corporations, no shareholder individually controls the corporation, yet if the holders of a majority of the shares act together, those holders will elect all of the directors and control the corporation. Such control may be exercised to the detriment of the other shareholders.

Two alternatives to straight voting aid minority shareholders' attempts to gain representation on the board and prevent harmful coalitions in close corporations: cumulative voting and classes of shares.

Cumulative Voting

With cumulative voting, a corporation allows a shareholder to cumulate her votes by multiplying the number of directors to be elected by the shareholder's number of shares. A shareholder may then allocate her votes among the nominees as she chooses. She may vote for only as many nominees as there are directors to be elected, but she may vote for fewer nominees. For example, she may choose to cast all of her votes for only one nominee.

See Figure 44.1 for a further explanation of the mechanics of cumulative voting.

Figure 44.1   Cumulative Voting Formula

The formula for determining the minimum number of shares required to elect a desired number of directors under cumulative voting is:

$$X = \frac{S \times R}{D + 1} + 1$$

X = Number of shares needed to elect the desired number of directors

S = Total number of shares voting at the shareholders' meeting

R = Number of director representatives desired

D = Total number of directors to be elected at the meeting

Example: Sarah Smiles wants to elect two of the five directors of Oates Corporation. One thousand shares will be voted. In this case:

S = 1,000
R = 2
D = 5

Therefore:

$$X = 333.33$$

Fractions are ignored; thus, Sarah will need to hold at least 333 shares to be able to elect two directors.

 LO44-2 Create classes of shares and delineate their rights to fit the needs of controlling and other shareholders.

Classes of Shares

A corporation may have several classes of shares. The two most common classes are *common shares* and *preferred shares*, but a corporation may have several classes of common shares and several classes of preferred shares. Many close corporations have two or more classes of common shares with different voting rights. Each class may be entitled to elect one or more directors in order to balance power in a corporation.

For example, suppose a corporation has four directors and 100 shares held by four shareholders—each of whom owns 25 shares. With straight voting and no classes of shares, no shareholder owns enough shares to elect himself as a director because 51 shares are necessary to elect a director. Suppose, however, that the corporation has four classes of shares, each with the right to elect one of the directors. Each class of shares is issued to only one shareholder. Now, as the sole owner of a class of shares entitling the class to elect one director, each shareholder can elect himself to the board.

Using classes of shares is the cleanest way to allocate among shareholders the power to elect directors, as well as allocate equity ownership of the corporation. To protect such allocations, however, the articles should require approval of every class of shares to change the rights of any class or to create a new class of shares.

Shareholder Control Devices

While cumulative voting and class voting are two useful methods by which shareholders can allocate or acquire voting control of a corporation, there are other devices that may also be used for these purposes: voting trusts; shareholder voting agreements; and proxies, especially irrevocable proxies.

Voting Trusts With a **voting trust**, shareholders transfer their shares to one or more voting trustees and receive voting trust certificates in exchange. The shareholders retain many of their rights, including the right to receive dividends, but the voting trustees vote for directors and other matters submitted to shareholders.

The purpose of a voting trust is to control the corporation through the concentration of shareholder voting power in the voting trustees, who often are participating shareholders. If several minority shareholders collectively own a majority of the shares of a corporation, they may create a voting trust and thereby control the corporation. You may ask why shareholders need a voting trust when they are in apparent agreement on how to vote their shares. The reason is that they may have disputes in the future that could prevent the shareholders from agreeing how to vote. The voting trust ensures that the shareholder group will control the corporation despite the emergence of differences.

The MBCA limits the duration of voting trusts to 10 years, though all or part of the participating shareholders may agree to extend the term for another 10 years. Also, a voting trust must be made public, with copies of the voting trust document available for inspection at the corporation's offices.

Shareholder Voting Agreements As an alternative to a voting trust, shareholders may merely agree how they will vote their shares. For example, shareholders collectively owning a majority of the shares may agree to vote for each other as directors, resulting in each being elected to the board of directors.

A shareholder voting agreement must be written; only shareholders signing the agreement are bound by it. When a shareholder refuses to vote as agreed, courts specifically enforce the agreement.

Shareholder voting agreements have two advantages over voting trusts. First, their duration may be *perpetual*.

Second, they may be kept secret from the other shareholders; they usually do not have to be filed in the corporation's offices.

Proxies A shareholder may appoint a **proxy** to vote his shares. If several minority shareholders collectively own a majority of the shares of a corporation, they may appoint a proxy to vote their shares and thereby control the corporation. The ordinary proxy has only a limited duration—11 months under the MBCA—unless a longer term is specified. Also, the ordinary proxy is *revocable* at any time. As a result, there is no guarantee that control agreements accomplished through the use of revocable proxies will survive future shareholder disputes.

However, a proxy is *irrevocable* if it is coupled with an interest. A proxy is coupled with an interest when, among other things, the person holding the proxy is a party to a shareholder voting agreement or a buy-and-sell agreement. The principal use of irrevocable proxies is in conjunction with shareholder voting agreements.

In the *RHCS* case, the court found that the parties created only a revocable proxy when they wanted a long-term shareholder voting agreement. The case is a good example of the need for careful drafting of corporate documents.

Reynolds Health Care Services, Inc. v. HMNH, Inc.
217 S.W.3d 797 (Ark. 2005)

John Reynolds was the sole shareholder and manager of his family's longtime business, the Hillsboro Manor Nursing Home Inc. in El Dorado, Arkansas. In 1993, Reynolds needed capital to expand the nursing home, so he approached Dr. James Sheppard, who contacted three additional investors: Sheppard's two brothers, Andrew and Courtney Sheppard, and his brother-in-law, Eugene Bilo. The Sheppards and Bilo formed a corporation called HMNH, Inc. to acquire 80 percent ownership of Hillsboro Manor. HMNH, Inc. made a contract with Reynolds Health Care Services, Inc. (RHCS), a corporation in which Reynolds was the sole shareholder. Under the contract, RHCS agreed to manage the nursing home in return for 6 percent of HMNH's gross revenues. HMNH agreed to provide adequate working capital and oversight on budgets, policies, and personnel. Of course, RHCS hired Reynolds as administrator of the facility.

To buy the nursing home, HMNH and Hillsboro Manor Nursing Home Inc. entered into a stock purchase agreement by which HMNH purchased all of the stock of Hillsboro Manor Nursing Home for $1,804,000. Hillsboro Manor Nursing Home was merged into HMNH with the three Sheppards, Bilo, and RHCS each receiving 20 shares of stock of the 100 outstanding shares of stock in HMNH. The Sheppards and Bilo also agreed to give RHCS the power to vote 7.5 of each of their shares on any matter submitted to shareholders in the next 20 years. The effect of the voting agreement was to give RHCS 50 percent voting control, which meant that Reynolds, who owned RHCS, could veto any matter submitted to HMNH's shareholders.

By 1999, HMNH had become concerned with the way Reynolds was running the nursing home. The shareholders held a meeting on September 14, 2000, at which the Sheppards and Bilo were present, but Reynolds was absent. The Sheppards voted their combined 60 shares to elect a new board of directors comprising the three Sheppards, Bilo, and Reynolds. At the directors' meeting, held immediately thereafter, all five men were elected as officers of HMNH, although Reynolds—while now present—abstained from the vote. Andrew Sheppard then made a motion that the board of directors authorize its attorney to institute a lawsuit in the name of HMNH against Reynolds and RHCS to recover damages caused by RHCS's breach of the management contract. The Sheppards and Bilo voted to adopt the resolution. On January 19, 2001, HMNH filed suit against RHCS and Reynolds, alleging that RHCS had breached the management contract. Reynolds and RHCS asked the trial court to dismiss the lawsuit on the grounds that HMNH's board had no authority to bring the lawsuit. Reynolds and RHCS argued that the directors were not properly elected because the Sheppards voted all their shares to elect the new directors, a violation of the shareholder voting agreement that gave RHCS the power to vote 7.5 of each of their shares. The trial court disagreed, ruling that the voting agreement was merely a revocable proxy, which the Sheppards revoked at the September 2000 shareholder meeting, and therefore, the Sheppards could vote all of their shares. Reynolds and RHCS appealed to the Arkansas Supreme Court.

Glaze, Justice

RHCS argues that it entered into a voting agreement with the Sheppards and Bilo when they signed a document titled "Option to Purchase Stock." In particular, RHCS points to the following language in support of its contention that a voting agreement was created:

> [HMNH] shall grant to [RHCS] a proxy to vote one-half of the issued and outstanding shares of stock of HMNH, Inc. pending the term of this option to purchase stock, which proxy shall be reduced to twenty-five percent of the issued and outstanding shares of stock of the corporation for a period of twenty years from the effective date of the Agreement to Provide Management Services to a Health Care Facility executed the 8th day of January, 1993, as set forth in paragraph IV thereof, by and between Reynolds Health Care Services, Inc., and HMNH, Inc., upon the exercise of this option and transfer to [RHCS] of the shares of stock subject to this option.

A subsequent agreement among the shareholders, dated September 19, 1996, provided that the Sheppards and Bilo "shall execute a proxy to Reynolds Health Care Services, Inc., appointing Reynolds Health Care Services, Inc. as [their] proxy to vote 7.5 shares of each of the said shareholder's stock held in HMNH, Inc." Those proxies were executed by each of the Sheppards and Bilo on October 21, 1996; the proxy agreements provided as follows:

> I, the undersigned shareholder of HMNH, Inc., an Arkansas corporation, do hereby appoint Reynolds Health Care Services, Inc., an Arkansas corporation, my true and lawful attorney and agent, for me and in my name, place and stead to vote as my proxy 7.5 shares of stock held by me in HMNH, Inc. at any stockholders' meetings to be held between the date of this proxy and 20 years from the effective date of the Agreement to Provide Management Services to a Health Care Facility dated January 7, 1993, as set forth in Paragraph IV thereof, by and between Reynolds Health

> Care Services, Inc., and HMNH, Inc., and I authorize Reynolds Health Care Services, Inc. to act for me and in my name and stead as fully as I could act if I were personally present, giving to Reynolds Health Care Services, Inc., attorney and agent, full power of substitution.

The trial court found that these agreements were not voting agreements, but rather were revocable proxies. Under Ark. Code Ann. § 4-27-722 (Repl. 2001), proxies are revocable by a shareholder "unless the appointment form conspicuously states that it is irrevocable and the appointment is coupled with an interest." An appointment coupled with an interest includes the appointment of "a party to a voting agreement created under § 4-27-731." None of the proxy agreements stated conspicuously on its face that it was irrevocable; indeed, in its reply brief, RHCS abandons its argument that the proxies were irrevocable. Nonetheless, RHCS maintains that the proxies "were merely the means of implementing the parties' foundational voting agreement," by which the Sheppards and Bilo gave RHCS the right to vote fifty percent of their shares in HMNH for twenty years.

However, we conclude that the document that RHCS calls a "voting agreement" is nothing more than a revocable appointment of proxy. The plain language of the agreement says nothing about how the stock is to be voted; it merely gives RHCS the right to vote a percentage of the stock. Because the agreement does not "provide for the manner in which" the shares are to be voted, it is not a voting agreement; it is a proxy.

Further, the proxies assigned to RHCS were revocable. Thus, the Sheppards and Bilo were acting within their rights as shareholders when they voted to revoke their proxies at the September 2000 shareholders' meeting. Accordingly, the trial court did not err when it concluded that the actions of the duly elected board of directors in voting to authorize the instant lawsuit were valid.

Judgment for HMNH affirmed.

Ethics and Compliance in Action

By using classes of shares (or a perpetual shareholder voting agreement), shareholders that individually are minority shareholders but collectively control a majority of the corporation's shares may control the corporation absolutely. For example, suppose five shareholders create a corporation and decide at incorporation that it will have five classes of shares, one for each of the five shareholders. They decide that each of the five classes will elect its own director to the board and that the consent of each class is required to amend the articles of incorporation, such as to increase the number of authorized shares of a class or to create a new class of shares. They also could agree that no shares may be issued without the consent of each class of shares. In the future, if they want to issue shares to employees of the corporation or public investors, by a vote of the five classes of shareholders they could create a class of shares that has a small (say, 20 percent) equity interest in the corporation, either has

no right to vote for directors or elects a nonvoting director, has a preferential right to dividends, and has no right to veto any action the five original classes of shares approve. The creation of the new share class would permit the five original shareholders to continue their control of the corporation while receiving an infusion of capital into the company.

- Do you think it is ethical for the five original shareholders to dominate the corporation in this way? If you were one of the five original shareholders, would you set up a different equity structure? Would you give more rights to the shareholders of the class with limited rights?
- Would you buy shares of the class that has limited rights? After you buy those shares, would it be ethical for you to argue for greater rights?
- Would your answers change if the corporation became a public company with more than 2,000 shareholders?

Fundamental Corporate Changes

Other matters besides the election of directors require shareholder action, some because they make fundamental changes in the structure or business of the corporation.

Shareholders must approve most amendments of the articles of incorporation because they embody the basic contract between a corporation and its shareholders. For example, when the articles are amended to increase the number of authorized shares or reduce the dividend rights of preferred shareholders, shareholder approval is needed.

A **merger** is a transaction in which one corporation merges into a second corporation. Usually, the first corporation dissolves; the second corporation takes all the business and assets of both corporations and becomes liable for the debts of both corporations. Usually, the shareholders of the dissolved corporation become shareholders of the surviving corporation. Ordinarily, both corporations' shareholders must approve a merger.

Corporation law allows great flexibility in the terms of a merger. For example, a merger may freeze out shareholders of the dissolved corporation by paying them cash only while allowing shareholders of the surviving corporation to remain. Freeze-outs are covered in Chapter 43.

A consolidation is similar to a merger except that both old corporations go out of existence and a new corporation takes the business, assets, and liabilities of the old corporations. Both corporations' shareholders must approve the consolidation. Modern corporate practice makes

consolidations obsolete, because it is usually desirable to have one of the old corporations survive. The MBCA does not recognize consolidations. However, the effect of a consolidation can be achieved by creating a new corporation and merging the two old corporations into it.

A share exchange is a transaction by which one corporation becomes the owner of all of the outstanding shares of a second corporation through a *compulsory* exchange of shares: The shareholders of the second corporation are compelled to exchange their shares for shares of the first corporation. The second corporation remains in existence and becomes a wholly owned subsidiary of the first corporation. Only the selling shareholders must approve the share exchange.

A sale of all or substantially all of the assets of the business other than in the regular course of business must be approved by the shareholders of the selling corporation because it drastically changes the shareholders' investment. Thus, a corporation's sale of all its real property and equipment is a sale of substantially all its assets, even though the corporation continues its business by leasing the assets back from the purchaser. However, a corporation that sells its building, but retains its machinery with the intent of continuing operations at another location, has not sold all or substantially all of its assets. Under the MBCA, a corporation that retains at least 25 percent of its business activity and either its income or revenue has not disposed of substantially all its assets.

A **dissolution** is the first step in the termination of the corporation's business. The typical dissolution requires shareholder approval. Dissolution of corporations is covered more fully at the end of this chapter.

The Global Business Environment

In recent years, shareholder activism and discontent have been exported from the United States to affect corporations based in other nations. In some cases, American shareholders of non-American corporations have exercised their rights by attempting to oppose management through the ballot box or takeovers. In other cases, citizens of other nations have taken cues from their American cousins and attempted to assert their rights as shareholders.

For example, in late 2005, VNU NV, the Netherlands-based publishing and market research firm, faced pressure from a shareholder group that included Boston-based Fidelity Investments. The shareholder group, which held 40 percent of VNU's shares, opposed VNU's bid to acquire IMS Health Inc., a Connecticut-based corporation. When shareholders first announced their opposition to the acquisition, VNU attempted to placate them by selling some assets, increasing a share buyback, and eventually replacing its CEO. Refusing to be appeased, the shareholders continued their opposition to VNU's acquisition of IMS Health.

Earlier in 2005, shareholders in Deutsche Borse AG, the German stock exchange company, prevented the company from completing an attempt to acquire London Stock Exchange PLC. The shareholders eventually forced the resignation of longtime CEO Werner Seifert. Despite Seifert's turning Deutsche Borse into the largest stock exchange during his 12-year tenure, his misjudgment of shareholder opposition to what he thought was the best strategy for the company ultimately led to his downfall.

Beginning in 2003 with HSBC's purchase of American subprime lender Household and escalating in 2007 and 2008 when HSBC suffered significant losses in the U.S. subprime loan market, U.S. activist investor Knight Vinke Asset Management engaged U.K.–based HSBC in a review of strategy. Knight Vinke called on HSBC's board to appoint independent financial advisors to review future subprime loan business, criticized its new executive compensation plan, and expressed concern about the independence of its board of directors. As a consequence of Knight Vinke's criticism that trying to be a world bank generated few cost savings, in 2011 HSBC refocused on trade and corporate banking and developed a new test for determining what businesses to acquire.

The articles of incorporation and the bylaws may require or permit other matters to be submitted for shareholder approval. For example, loans to officers, self-dealing transactions, and indemnifications of managers for litigation expenses may be approved by shareholders. Also, many of the states require shareholder approval of share option plans for high-level executive officers, but the MBCA does not.

Procedures Required Similar procedures must be met to effect each of the above fundamental changes. The procedures include approval of the board of directors; notice to all of the shareholders whether or not they are entitled to vote; and majority approval of the votes held by shareholders entitled to vote under the statute, articles, or bylaws. Majority approval will be insufficient if a corporation has a supermajority shareholder voting requirement, such as one requiring two-thirds approval.

If there are two or more classes of shares, the articles may provide that matters voted on by shareholders must be approved by each class substantially affected by the proposed transaction. For example, a merger may have to be approved by a majority of the preferred shareholders and a majority of the common shareholders. As an alternative, the articles may require only the approval of the shareholders as a whole.

Under the MBCA, voting by classes is required for mergers, share exchanges, and amendments of the articles if these would substantially affect the rights of the classes. For example, the approval of preferred shareholders is required if a merger would change the dividend rights of preferred shareholders.

In many states, no approval of shareholders of the *surviving corporation* is required for a merger *if* the merger does not fundamentally alter the character of the business or substantially reduce the shareholders' voting or dividend rights.

Also, many statutes, including the MBCA, permit a merger between a parent corporation and its subsidiary without the approval of the shareholders of either corporation. Instead, the board of directors of the parent approves the merger and sends a copy of the merger plan to the subsidiary's shareholders. This simplified merger is called a short-form merger. It is available only if the parent owns a high percentage of the subsidiary's shares—90 percent under the MBCA and the Delaware statute.

Dissenters' Rights

Many times, shareholders approve a corporate action by less than a unanimous vote, indicating that some shareholders oppose the action. For the most part, the dissenting shareholders have little recourse. The nature of a public company creates a choice for shareholders: continue owning shares despite dissenting or divest yourself of ownership by selling your shares. Their choice is to remain shareholders or to sell their shares. For close corporation shareholders, there is no choice—the dissenting close corporation shareholder has no ready market for her shares, so she will remain a shareholder.

Some corporate transactions, however, so materially change a shareholder's investment in the corporation or have such an adverse effect on the value of a shareholder's shares that it has been deemed unfair to require the dissenting shareholder either to remain a shareholder (because there is no fair market for the shares) or to suffer a loss in value when he sells his shares on a market that has been adversely affected by the news of the corporate action. Corporate law has therefore responded by creating **dissenters' rights** (right of appraisal) for shareholders who disagree with specified fundamental corporate transactions. Dissenters' rights require the corporation to pay dissenting shareholders the *fair value* of their shares.

Under the MBCA, the dissenters' rights cover mergers, short-form mergers, share exchanges, significant amendments of the articles of incorporation, and sales of all or substantially all the assets other than in the ordinary course of business. Some statutes cover consolidations also.

A dissenting shareholder seeking payment of the fair value of his shares must have the *right to vote* on the action to which he objects; however, a shareholder of a subsidiary in a short-form merger has dissenters' rights despite his lack of voting power. In addition, the shareholder must *not vote in favor* of the transaction. The shareholder may either vote against the action or abstain from voting.

The MBCA and about 70 percent of state statutes exclude from dissenters' rights shares that can be sold in a liquid market such as the New York Stock Exchange. Instead, these statutes expect a shareholder to sell his shares on the stock exchange if he dissents from the corporate action. This *market-out exception* does not apply, however, if there is an "interested transaction." About half the states, including Delaware, do not so limit the market-out exception.

Generally, a shareholder must notify the corporation of his intent to seek payment before the shareholders have voted on the action. Next, the corporation informs a dissenting shareholder how to demand payment. After the dissenting shareholder demands payment, the corporation and the shareholder negotiate a mutually acceptable price. If they cannot agree, a court will determine the fair value of the shares and order the corporation to pay that amount.

To determine fair value, most judges use the Delaware Block Method, a weighted average of several valuation techniques—such as market value, comparisons with other similar companies, net present value of future cash flows, and book value. Ironically, the Supreme Court of Delaware has abandoned the Delaware Block Method, recognizing the need for courts to value shares by methods generally considered acceptable to the financial community. The MBCA values shares using "customary and current valuation concepts and techniques generally employed for similar businesses."

The Delaware appraisal statute provides that a court:

> shall appraise the shares, determining their fair value exclusive of any element of value arising from the accomplishment or expectation of the merger or consolidation, together with interest, if any, to be paid upon the amount determined to be the fair value. In determining such fair value, the Court shall take into account all relevant factors.[1]

In *Weinberger v. UOP*,[2] the Delaware Supreme Court reconciled the dual mandates of section 262(h), which direct a court to determine fair value based upon all relevant factors, yet exclude any element of value arising from the accomplishment or expectation of the merger. In making that reconciliation, the *Weinberger* court wrote:

> Only the speculative elements of value that may arise from the "accomplishment or expectation" of the merger are excluded. We take this to be a very narrow exception to the appraisal process, designed to eliminate use of *pro forma* data and projections of a speculative variety relating to the completion of a merger. But elements of future value, including the nature of the enterprise, which are known or susceptible of proof as of the date of the merger and not the product of speculation, may be considered. When the trial court deems it appropriate, fair value also includes any damages, resulting from the taking, which the stockholders sustain as a class. If that was not the case, then the obligation to consider "all relevant factors" in the valuation process would be eroded.[3]

In the following case, the court applied the *Weinberger* test when reviewing competing valuations of minority shares. The case is a model for sophisticated financial valuations in litigation.

---

[1]8 Del. Code § 262(h).
[2]457 A.2d 701 (Del. 1983).
[3]*Id.* at 713.

Montgomery Cellular Holding Co., Inc. v. Dobler   880 A.2d 206 (Del. 2005)

Price Communications Corporation (Price) owned all the shares of Price Communications Wireless (PCW). PCW owned all the shares of Palmer Wireless Holdings Inc. (Palmer). Palmer owned controlling interests in 16 cellular telephone systems in Georgia, Florida, and Alabama, including Montgomery Cellular Holding Company (MCHC). Palmer owned 94.6 percent of MCHC stock. MCHC was a holding company with no operating assets. MCHC's sole asset was 100 percent of the stock of Montgomery Cellular Telephone Co. (Montgomery). Montgomery was a cellular telephone system located in the area around Montgomery, Alabama.

As a group, Palmer's holdings formed a valuable cluster of cellular systems in the southeastern United States. Price entered into discussions with various cellular telecommunications system operators about a possible sale of Palmer's cellular systems. Price hired the investment bank Donaldson, Lufkin & Jenrette (DLJ) to solicit interest in acquiring Palmer. Verizon emerged as the potential acquirer.

In 2000, Price agreed to sell Palmer to Verizon for $2.06 billion. Because Palmer did not control 100 percent of the stock in MCHC and other subsidiaries, the agreement obligated Price to acquire those minority shareholder interests. If Palmer failed to acquire the minority interests, the agreement allowed Verizon to reduce the purchase price by an amount equal to the minority shareholders' pro rata share of fiscal year 2000 EBITDA multiplied by 13.5. To receive the full $2.06 billion purchase price, Price would have to freeze out all the minority shareholders of MCHC. As a result of the agreement, Price had a strong incentive to squeeze out all the minority shareholders at a price that was lower than Verizon's corresponding price reduction.

On June 30, 2001, Price caused Palmer to buy out MCHC's minority shareholders by a short-form merger under Delaware law. In determining the price to be paid to MCHC's minority shareholders, Price made no effort to obtain an independent valuation, which its CEO viewed as "very costly." Instead, Palmer relied on Price's settlement of an appraisal action with the dissenting minority shareholders of a different Palmer subsidiary, Cellular Dynamics (CD).

CD, like MCHC, was the operator of a cellular telephone company in the southeastern United States and, like MCHC, was majority-owned by Price. In 1999, Price bought out the minority shareholders of CD by a short-form merger. After a lengthy negotiation using POPs as the valuation tool, the minority shareholders agreed to a settlement based upon a value of CD derived by multiplying the estimated population by $470 per POP. POP is a shorthand reference to the census population of a specific geographic area. POPs are a common cellular industry metric for valuing cellular systems.

Despite overwhelming evidence that the CD settlement was negotiated using POPs and not EBITDA, Price claimed that it had valued CD's stock using an EBITDA multiplier of 10.05 to arrive at the $8,102.23 per share price that was offered to MCHC minority shareholders as fair value. In contrast, multiplying the $470 per POP metric by MCHC's POPs (323,675) would have yielded a value of $15,212.74 per share.

Although Price had bought out MCHC minority shareholders and was entitled to receive the full agreed merger price of $2.06 billion, the initial Verizon deal was not consummated. Later, Price and Verizon agreed to a reduced purchase price of $1.7 billion. That second transaction was consummated on August 15, 2002.

Gerhard Dobler and other minority MCHC shareholders challenged the buyout price of $8,102.23 per share, and they sued Price, Palmer, and MCHC in the Delaware Court of Chancery. At the trial, the minority shareholders' expert, Marc Sherman, previously a KPMG partner in charge of its corporate transactions practice, valued MCHC at $21,346 per share. MCHC's expert, Kenneth D. Gartrell, previously an Ernst & Young auditor, testified that the stand-alone value of MCHC was $7,840 per share.

Although both experts used similar methods to value MCHC, Sherman looked to third-party experts to create his forecasts, whereas Gartrell did not consult outside appraisers or other sources of relevant information. Moreover, only Sherman performed a comparable transaction analysis.

MCHC's expert, Gartrell, employed two valuation methodologies: a comparable company analysis and a discounted cash flow (DCF) analysis. The Court of Chancery found that Gartrell's valuation approach was legally and factually flawed, and must be disregarded in its entirety, for three reasons. First, Gartrell's overall theoretical framework was invalid as a matter of law because Gartrell valued MCHC as if it were not a going concern that had contractual relationships with other cellular providers. Second, Gartrell's DCF analysis was flawed because he used a generic growth rate (the long-term growth rate of GNP) as his growth rate for MCHC without any valid, credible explanation and despite his having had access to industry-specific growth rates; Gartrell used a constant growth rate, which would yield the same value for MCHC regardless of the time frame; and Gartrell created the financial projections based entirely on his own judgment, without reference to other available sources of relevant information. Third, the Court of Chancery found that Gartrell's comparable company analysis was invalid because of his methodology and his data. Gartrell switched between the mean and the median at critical points. Had Gartrell used the mean numbers consistently throughout, the value of MCHC based on EBITDA would be more than $163 million, which, when added to the nonoperating assets, would be $183 million—a figure much closer to the value reached by the shareholders' expert.

The Court of Chancery accepted the shareholders' expert, Sherman's, valuation of MCHC with some modification, and it valued the minority shares at $19,621.74. MCHC asked the Delaware Supreme Court to review the chancery court's nearly full acceptance of Sherman's valuation. MCHC did not appeal the court's rejection of MCHC's expert's valuation.

Jacobs, Justice

The shareholders' expert, Marc Sherman, performed three different financial analyses of MCHC: a comparable transactions analysis, a DCF analysis, and a comparable company analysis. In his comparable transactions analysis, Sherman split the selected comparable transactions into three categories: similar sized transactions, the initial Verizon transaction, and the CD settlement. For the similar sized transactions category, Sherman considered five transactions that occurred between May 2000 and January 2001, each involving a cellular company with approximately the same number of POPs. The remaining two categories (the initial Verizon transaction and the CD settlement) involved single transactions that were included in the analysis because they were related to the sale of MCHC.

Sherman then analyzed each category using his four cellular system metrics (POPs, subscribers, EBITDA, and revenue). For each metric, Sherman computed a value of MCHC based on the category of comparable transactions, and then weighted these values to derive his final overall valuation. Sherman did that as follows: he first weighted the metrics based on their importance in valuing cellular companies. He then weighted the category of comparable transactions within each metric. The result of that process is shown *infra* on the table:

Category	Valuation	Metric Weighting	Category Weighting
POPs		45%	
Verizon			
Transaction	$199,278,316		20%
CD Settlement	$199,286,698		10%
Similar Sized			
Transactions	$136,352,297		15%
Subscribers		20%	
Verizon			
Transaction	$226,758,135		15%
CD Settlement	$225,865,136		5%
Operating Cash			
Flows		25%	
Verizon			
Transaction	$160,650,176		20%
CD Settlement	$226,738,142		5%
Revenue		10%	
Verizon			
Transaction	$236,517,971		7% (sic)
CD Settlement	$224,240,681		100% (sic)
Total		100%	100%

Multiplying the valuations by their respective weightings, Sherman computed a value of $192 million based on comparable transactions. To that figure he added the $20 million value of the non-operating assets to arrive at a comparable transactions value for MCHC of $212 million.

Sherman also performed a DCF analysis. Because of the lack of management projections, Sherman created forecasts of MCHC's cash flows based on predictions by others for the cellular industry and the economy. Sherman relied primarily on Paul Kagan, an outside industry expert. Sherman also looked to industry growth reports that showed an annual growth rate for the wireless industry of 16 percent.

The next step in Sherman's DCF analysis was to determine the discount rate using a weighted average cost of capital (WACC) approach. Applying that approach to the inputs he determined for each component of the WACC formula, Sherman arrived at a discount rate of 13.25 percent.

For his DCF projection period, Sherman used a ten-year period from June 1, 2001 to May 31, 2011. Before projecting the cash flows, however, Sherman first adjusted them by removing two "irregularities": (i) a nonrecurring $861,000 bad debt expense resulting from Montgomery having installed a new billing system, and (ii) the rent of $638,000 MCHC paid annually to Old North, a wholly owned subsidiary of Palmer. Lastly, using a capitalization rate of 9.25 percent and a growth rate of 4 percent, Sherman calculated a terminal value of $258 million.

From these inputs, Sherman arrived at a final enterprise (DCF) valuation of $150 million for Montgomery as a going concern, operating asset of MCHC. To that figure Sherman added the value of Montgomery's non-operating assets, which increased his valuation to $170 million. Finally, to that sum, Sherman applied a control premium of 31 percent, thereby increasing his DCF valuation to $216 million.

In his third (comparable company) analysis, Sherman found only two comparable companies, neither of which was similar in size to Montgomery. Sherman excluded companies that had international operations, multiple lines of business, or prepaid customers, as well as companies that used PCS technology. After selecting his comparable companies, Sherman applied the same metrics that he used in his comparable transactions analysis and gave them the same weight. That approach resulted in a valuation of $206 million. After adding in the value of the non-operating assets, Sherman's ultimate comparable company valuation of MCHC was $226 million.

Thus, Sherman's three analyses valued MCHC within a range of from $212 million to $226 million. Sherman derived his final fair value by combining the results of his three analyses into a weighted average, giving 80 percent weight to the comparable transactions value, 15 percent weight to the DCF value, and 5 percent weight to the comparable company value. Sherman's heavy weighting of the comparable transactions analysis reflected his judgment that the transaction data, particularly the initial Verizon transaction price, were the best indication of value for MCHC. In contrast, Sherman gave little weight to the DCF analysis because of his concerns about the reliability of MCHC's financial data and the lack of management projections. He gave even less weight to the comparable company valuation because of the scarcity of publicly traded companies to which MCHC could reliably be compared. Combining the results of the three analyses into a weighted average yielded a fair value for MCHC of $213,455,619, or $21,346 per share.

In making its independent determination of MCHC's fair value, the Court of Chancery adopted Sherman's overall valuation framework, and most of Sherman's inputs. The Court made adjustments to some of the inputs that it did not adopt. The result was to reduce Sherman's valuation of $213,455,619 ($21,346 per share) to a final valuation of MCHC of $196,217,373, or $19,621.74 per share.

First, with respect to the comparable transaction analysis, the Vice Chancellor determined that the Verizon transaction price and the CD settlement price were valid inputs. But, the Court adjusted Sherman's CD settlement price by eliminating what Sherman perceived (incorrectly, the Court determined) to be a minority discount. The Court then independently increased the CD settlement figure ($470 per POP) by 15 percent to eliminate a so-called "settlement haircut," to arrive at a value of $540.50 per POP.

Second, the Court adjusted Sherman's DCF valuation by eliminating the 31 percent control premium that Sherman had added to his DCF value. That adjustment reduced Sherman's DCF valuation of MCHC from $216 million to $170 million.

Third, and most significant, the Court adjusted the weights that Sherman had accorded to the values derived by his three valuation methods. Sherman had weighted the comparable transaction value at 80 percent of total fair value. Because the effect of that weighting was to give the Verizon transaction an overall weight of 50 percent—a weight the Court found to be "too significant"—the Vice Chancellor reduced the weight accorded to the comparable transactions valuation from 80 percent to 65 percent.

Finally, because Sherman had corrected the figures derived from MCHC's financial statements in a reasonable manner, and also had looked to third party authority for guidance on other inputs, the Court determined that the 15 percent weight Sherman had accorded to the DCF valuation should be increased to 30 percent.

On appeal, MCHC does not challenge the Court of Chancery's adoption of Sherman's overall valuation framework. Instead,

MCHC limits its attack to selected inputs to the valuation model that Sherman used.

Specifically, MCHC contends that the Court of Chancery erred in three different respects, namely by: (1) including in its comparable transactions analysis the price that Verizon Wireless initially agreed to pay to acquire Palmer; (2) adding a 15 percent premium to the price that the minority shareholders of CD, a separate Palmer subsidiary, had agreed to accept to settle their appraisal action; [and] (3) subtracting the management fees that Palmer charged to MCHC, as reported in MCHC's financial statement.

We conclude that none of the challenged findings is clearly wrong, and indeed, all have firm support in the evidentiary record.

1. The Verizon Transaction

MCHC argues that the Court of Chancery erroneously included the Verizon transaction, because the transaction price contained synergistic elements of value whose inclusion is proscribed by 8 Del. C. § 262. That statute requires the Court of Chancery to appraise the subject shares by "determining their fair value exclusive of any element of value arising from the accomplishment or expectation of the merger or consolidation." In determining statutory "fair value," the Court must value the appraisal company as a "going concern." In performing its valuation, the Court of Chancery is free to consider the price actually derived from the sale of the company being valued, but only after the synergistic elements of value are excluded from that price.

The Court found Palmer offered *no business-related* combinatorial value to MCHC, and MCHC was probably the most valuable company in Palmer's cluster. Thus, the Vice Chancellor concluded, the only synergies included in the purchase price were dealmaking—not business-related—synergies.

That conclusion is supported by the evidence. The Verizon merger with Palmer did not add any synergistic business value to MCHC because Montgomery was a metropolitan statistical area (MSA), which is generally more valuable than a rural service area (RSA), and Montgomery had superior demographics relative to Palmer's other cellular holdings. Therefore, the only synergies required to be eliminated from the Verizon transaction price were the Palmer-related "deal-making" synergies. The question became how to determine the value of those synergies.

The Court of Chancery was unable precisely to quantify those "deal-making" synergies, because MCHC did not present any reliable evidence at trial of what those synergies were worth. Having received no helpful evidence from MCHC, the Court of Chancery had to—and did—account for the synergies in a different way, namely, by reducing the total weight accorded to the comparable transactions component of the overall valuation, from 80 percent to 65 percent. Although in a perfect world that may not have been the ideal solution, in this world it was the only one permitted by the record evidence, given MCHC's failure to obtain a pre-merger valuation and to present legally reliable expert valuation testimony during the trial.

MCHC next contends that including the Verizon transaction in its comparable transaction analysis led the Court of Chancery to commit reversible error by not valuing MCHC as a going concern. Delaware law requires that in an appraisal action, a corporation must be valued as a going concern based on the "operative reality" of the company as of the time of the merger. In determining a corporation's "operative reality," the use of "speculative" elements of future value arising from the expectation or accomplishment of a merger is proscribed, but elements of future value that are known or susceptible of proof as of the date of the merger may be considered. Any facts which were known or which could be ascertained as of the date of the merger and which throw any light on future prospects of the merged corporation are not only pertinent to an inquiry as to the value of the dissenting stockholder's interest, but must be considered by the agency fixing the value.

MCHC argues that the Verizon transaction was not part of MCHC's "operative reality." At the time of the MCHC-Palmer merger, the transaction was not expected to close. MCHC characterizes the Verizon transaction as a mere "option" whose exercise was entirely within Verizon's control and which neither Price nor Verizon realistically expected to close at the time the MCHC-Palmer merger occurred.

The Vice Chancellor rejected MCHC's argument that because the Verizon–Price agreement was conditional, it was impermissibly "speculative" and did not reflect MCHC's going concern value. The Court of Chancery found that the Verizon transaction was more than an offer. Rather, it was a validly executed enforceable transaction agreement which bound Verizon to the implied covenant of good faith and fair dealing that inheres in every contract.

2. Adjustment of the CD Settlement Price to Eliminate the Settlement Discount

MCHC's second claim of error is that the Court of Chancery improperly adjusted the "CD settlement" price to eliminate what the Court regarded as a "settlement haircut."

The CD settlement was a settlement of litigation that arose out of Price's elimination, in a short form merger, of the minority shareholders of Cellular Dynamics (CD), a cellular company located in the southeastern United States. The minority shareholders of CD sued, and after protracted negotiations the parties agreed to a settlement price of $470 per POP. For purposes of valuing MCHC, both parties agreed that the CD settlement was a comparable transaction. Accordingly, Sherman utilized the $470 per POP metric in performing his comparable transactions analysis.

The Vice Chancellor upheld Sherman's use of the CD settlement price, but adjusted that price to reflect what the Court described as a "settlement haircut"; that is, a discount that reflected factors unrelated to CD's fair value, such as the costs of litigation and the uncertainty of the appraisal action's outcome. To eliminate that settlement discount, the Court of Chancery increased the CD settlement price by 15 percent, thereby reaching a value of $540.50 per POP as more fairly reflective of the value of CD. The Court then included that upwardly-adjusted CD settlement value in the comparable transactions analysis.

There was ample evidence to support the Court of Chancery's finding that the CD settlement reflected a discount from CD's fair value. The record included an exchange of several letters between Price and CD during settlement negotiations. Those letters included an offer by CD, on December 19, 2000, to settle the litigation for $500 per POP. In that December 19 letter, the CD minority shareholders specifically stated that the $500 per POP offer was less than CD's fair value, but was being made in an effort to resolve the matter quickly. That letter evidences that CD's minority shareholders were willing to settle for an amount below fair value to avoid the costs and delays of litigation.

Although there was no evidence of the precise magnitude of the actual CD settlement discount, the Court of Chancery did not err by selecting 15 percent as a reasonable measure. That percentage was based on evidence that the CD minority shareholders had accepted a price lower than CD's fair value, as well as the Court of Chancery's extensive expertise in the appraisal of corporate enterprises—an expertise that this Court has recognized on several occasions. To reiterate, where, as here, one side of the litigation presents no competent evidence to aid the Court in discharging its duty to make an independent valuation, we will defer to the Vice Chancellor's valuation approach unless it is manifestly unreasonable, *i.e.*, on its face is outside a range of reasonable values.

3. Eliminating the Management Fees Paid by MCHC to Palmer as an Input to the DCF Valuation

MCHC's third claim of error challenges the Court of Chancery's adjustment of MCHC's financial statements to eliminate from the DCF valuation the management fees Palmer had charged MCHC. The Court found that those fees were essentially a pretext, unrelated to the actual furnishing of management services.

Because there were no management projections upon which Sherman could rely to project MCHC's future cash flows, Sherman had to create his own forecasts. To do that he relied upon various sources, including MCHC's financial statements. But Sherman did not accept MCHC's financial statements at face value. In his review of those statements, he identified several irregularities.

The management fees that Palmer charged to MCHC represented one of those irregularities. The evidence established that since 1998, Palmer had charged MCHC more than $3 million in management fees, and that in the first five months of 2001 alone, those fees totaled $603,000. To determine MCHC's future cash flows more accurately, Sherman eliminated those fees.

None of Price's officers who testified were able to explain what management services Palmer had provided to MCHC, or how those management fees were calculated. Indeed, Price's CEO characterized the fees (under oath) as "accounting bullshit." The

Court was also troubled by the fact that Palmer charged management fees only to its subsidiaries that had minority shareholders, but not to those subsidiaries that Palmer wholly owned. Tellingly, after Palmer eliminated MCHC's minority shareholders in the merger, Palmer stopped charging management fees to MCHC. That evidence strongly supports the elimination of the management fees as an expense.

Judgment for Dobler affirmed in part and reversed in part. Remanded to the Chancery Court.

Shareholders' Inspection and Information Rights

 LO44-1 Understand the rights and powers of shareholders and how shareholders exercise their powers.

Inspecting a corporation's books and records is sometimes essential to the exercise of a shareholder's rights. For example, a shareholder may be able to decide how to vote in a director election only after examining corporate financial records that reveal whether the present directors are managing the corporation profitably. Also, a close corporation shareholder may need to look at the books to determine the value of his shares.

Many corporate managers are resistant to shareholders' inspecting the corporation's books and records, charging that shareholders are nuisances or that shareholders often have improper purposes for making such an inspection. Sometimes, management objects solely on the ground that it desires secrecy.

Most of the state corporation statutes specifically grant shareholders inspection rights. The purpose of these statutes is to facilitate the shareholder's inspection of the books and records of corporations whose managements resist or delay proper requests by shareholders. A shareholder's lawyer or accountant may assist the shareholder's exercise of his inspection rights.

The MBCA grants shareholders an absolute right of inspection of an alphabetical listing of the shareholders entitled to notice of a meeting, including the number of shares owned. Access to a shareholder list allows a

shareholder to contact other shareholders about important matters such as shareholder proposals.

The MBCA also grants an absolute right of inspection of, among other things, the articles, bylaws, and minutes of shareholder meetings within the past three years.

Shareholders have a qualified right to inspect other records, however. To inspect accounting records, board and committee minutes, and shareholder minutes more than three years old, a shareholder must make the demand in *good faith* and have a *proper purpose*. Proper purposes include inspecting the books of account to determine the value of shares or the propriety of dividends. On the other hand, learning business secrets and aiding a competitor are clearly improper purposes.

Shareholders also have the right to receive from the corporation **information** that is important to their voting and investing decisions. The MBCA requires a corporation to furnish its shareholders *financial statements*, including a balance sheet, an income statement, and a statement of changes in shareholders' equity. The Securities Exchange Act of 1934 also requires publicly held companies to furnish such statements, as well as other information that is important to shareholders' voting and investing decisions. The Sarbanes–Oxley Act requires the CEO and the CFO of public companies to certify that to their knowledge all financial information filed with the SEC fairly presents the financial condition of the company and does not include untrue or misleading material statements.

In the following case, *United Techs. Corp. v. Treppel*, the Delaware Supreme Court delineated some of the limits of the shareholder inspection right.

United Techs. Corp. v. Treppel   109 A.3d 553 (Del. 2014)

United Technologies Corp. is a Delaware corporation. Lawrence Treppel, a United Technologies shareholder, sent the company a litigation demand letter, seeking to "investigate, address, remedy, and commence proceedings against certain officers and directors." Treppel's claims arose out of a June 2012 investigation by the U.S. Department of Justice into violations of federal law by United Technologies in exporting software to the Chinese government for use in a military helicopter.

However, the board rejected Treppel's demand, stating that it had determined that litigation was "not in the best interests of the Company." The letter contained only two paragraphs and did not provide any additional explanation for the board's decision. Treppel then sought to use his inspection rights under § 220 to "evaluate" the board's decision to reject his litigation demand. After several unsuccessful rounds of negotiation between the parties, Treppel filed a § 220 action in the Court of Chancery, seeking access to United Technologies's books and records without any usage restrictions. United Technologies responded to Treppel's claims in the Court of Chancery with two separate, but related, arguments:

1. *That Treppel's intention to use information from his inspection to file outside of Delaware negated his proper purpose under § 200(b).*
2. *Alternatively, if Treppel's purpose was proper, the Court of Chancery should limit the use of information gained from a books and records inspection to legal action in a Delaware court, using its authority under § 200(c) to prescribe limitation or conditions in connection with granting the inspection.*

In its post-trial bench opinion, the Court of Chancery ruled that United Technologies was not entitled to the restriction it sought. The Court of Chancery determined that the limit "is not the type of restriction that 220(c) seeks to impose." The Court of Chancery also held that Treppel's purpose for inspecting United Technologies's books and records (inquiring into the board's decision to deny his litigation demand) was proper.

On appeal, United Technologies argues that the Court of Chancery erred in limiting its own authority to impose the requested restriction, and that the company is entitled to the restriction in this case.

Strine, Chief Justice

The ability to limit the use of information gathered from an inspection—not just the scope of the inspection itself—has long been recognized as within the Court of Chancery's discretion. "Delaware courts have repeatedly 'placed reasonable restrictions on shareholders' inspection rights in the context of suit brought under 8 Del. C. § 220.'"

In some cases, inspections have been denied entirely if the plaintiff's "proper purpose" for seeking books and records could not be effectuated. For example, a plaintiff would lack standing to sue if the inspection warranted further legal action. Aware of the costs of inspections, which are ultimately borne by stockholders, Delaware courts have been reluctant to grant § 220 relief when there is other pending litigation against the corporation and discovery is thus the more appropriate mechanism for obtaining relevant documents.

In restricting a stockholder's ability to use corporate books and records in certain ways, Delaware case law has consistently reflected the underlying principle that the stockholder's inspection right is a "qualified" one. Accordingly, the Court of Chancery has a wide discretion to shape the breadth and use of inspections under § 220 to protect the legitimate interests of Delaware corporations. Nothing in the text of § 220 itself or in any Delaware case law that interprets the section limits the Court of Chancery's authority to restrict the use of material from an inspection when those interests are threatened, and thus, in this case, the Court erred when it concluded that it lacked the statutory authority to impose its own preclusive limitation.

However, it should be noted that caution is still needed because use restrictions under § 220(c) have traditionally been tied to case-specific factors. For example, if a petitioner files for books and records and has a good faith purpose to investigate possible wrongdoing, and there has been no prior litigation, then the Court of Chancery might conclude that there is no reason to impose a use restriction of the kind United Technologies seeks here. In that situation, the Court of Chancery can consider in its discretion whether a forum use restriction is warranted, because the possible complications the restriction injects into the § 220 litigation may not be justified by any substantial interests of the respondent corporation. Further, the absence of pre-existing litigation would be relevant because the company and its stockholders would not have suffered the costs of defending duplicative litigation.

Judgment REVERSED and REMANDED.

Ethics and Compliance in Action

One of the most memorable scenes in the 2010 film *The Social Network* is when Facebook co-founder Eduardo Saverin confronts his business partner and now billionaire Facebook chairman, CEO, and controlling shareholder, Mark Zuckerberg. Saverin, who had just been asked to sign documents agreeing to dilute his shares in the company, storms over to Zuckerberg's desk, smashes his computer, and announces that he better "lawyer up" because Saverin is coming back to take the entire company.

Whether real life was as dramatic as the movie is not clear, but the effects of share dilution would have been for Saverin. In order to limit Saverin's role in the company, Zuckerberg created a new company to acquire the original company he and Saverin co-founded, and then distributed new shares in the new company to everybody but Saverin. This included Sean Parker, the creator of Napster and an advisor to Facebook at the time. According to the following e-mail made public after Saverin's lawsuit against Facebook was settled for an undisclosed sum (sources suggest 4–5% of the shares of the new company, now worth billions), Zuckerberg hoped to minimize the chance of Saverin knowing that his shares were being diluted.

[Redacted],

This email should probably be attorney-client privileged, not quite how to do that though. Anyhow, Sean and I have agreed that a price of one-half cent per share is the way to go for now.

We think we can maybe almost justify and if not, we'll just deal with it later.

We also agreed that if the company bonusing us the amount we need for the shares, plus tax, is a good solution to the problem of us all being completely broke.

As far as Eduardo goes, I think it's safe to ask for his permission to make grants. Especially if we do it in conjunction with raising money. It's probably even OK to say how many shares we're adding to the pool. It's probably less OK to tell him who's getting the shares, just because he might have adverse reaction initially. But I think we may even be able to make him understand that.

Is there a way to do this without making it painfully apparent to him that he's being diluted to 10%?

OK, that's all for now. I'll send you the list of grants I need made in another email in a second. Sean can send you grants for his people [later].

Hope you guys both feel better,

Mark

- Was it ethical for Zuckerberg to dilute Saverin's shares? Why did he allow Facebook's lawyers to ask for Severin's permission but ask them to withhold some information?
- What legal protections could Saverin assert in an action against Zuckerberg?
- How could Facebook have assured Saverin would not prevail in a suit over the share dilution?

Preemptive Right

The market price of a shareholder's shares will be reduced if a corporation issues additional shares at a price less than the market price. In addition, a shareholder's proportionate voting, dividend, and liquidation rights may be adversely affected by the issuance of additional shares. For example, if a corporation's only four shareholders each owns 100 shares worth $10 per share, then each shareholder has shares worth $1,000, a 25 percent interest in any dividends declared, 25 percent of the voting power, and a claim against 25 percent of the corporation's assets after creditors' claims have been satisfied. If the corporation subsequently issues 100 shares to another person for only $5 per share, the value of each shareholder's shares falls to $900 and their dividend, voting, and liquidation rights are reduced to 20 percent. In a worst-case scenario, the corporation issues 201 shares to one of the existing shareholders, giving that shareholder majority control of the corporation and reducing the other shareholders' interests to less than 17 percent each. As a result, the minority shareholders will

be dominated by the majority shareholder and will receive a greatly reduced share of the corporation's dividends.

Such harmful effects of an issuance could have been prevented if the corporation had been required to offer each existing shareholder a percentage of the new shares equal to their current proportionate ownership. If, for example, in the situation described above, the corporation had offered 50 shares to each shareholder, each shareholder could have remained a 25 percent owner of the corporation: Their interest in the corporation would not have been reduced, and their total wealth would not have been decreased.

Corporation law recognizes the importance of giving a shareholder the option of maintaining the value of her shares and retaining her proportionate interest in the corporation. This is the shareholder's **preemptive right**, an option to subscribe to a new issuance of shares in proportion to the shareholder's current interest in the corporation.

The MBCA adopts a comprehensive scheme for determining preemptive rights. It provides that the preemptive right does not exist except to the extent provided by the articles. The MBCA permits the corporation to state expressly when the preemptive right arises.

When the preemptive right exists, the corporation must notify a shareholder of her option to buy shares, the number of shares that she is entitled to buy, the price of the shares, and when the option must be exercised. Usually, the shareholder is issued a **right**, a written option that she may exercise herself or sell to a person who wishes to buy the shares.

Distributions to Shareholders

During the life of a corporation, shareholders may receive distributions of the corporation's assets. Most people are familiar with one type of distribution—dividends—but there are other important types of distributions to shareholders, including payments to shareholders upon the corporation's repurchase of its shares.

There is one crucial similarity among all the types of distributions to shareholders: Corporate assets are transferred to shareholders. Consequently, an asset transfer to shareholders may harm the corporation's creditors and others with claims against the corporation's assets. For example, a distribution of assets may impair a corporation's ability to pay its creditors. In addition, a distribution to one class of shareholders may harm another class of shareholders that has a liquidation priority over the class of shareholders receiving the distribution. The existence of these potential harms has resulted in corporation law that restricts the ability of corporations to make some distributions to shareholders.

Dividends A critical objective of a business corporation is to make a profit. Shareholders invest in a corporation primarily to share in the expected profit either through appreciation of the value of their shares or through dividends. There are two types of dividends: *cash or property dividends* and *share dividends*. Only cash or property dividends are distributions of the corporation's assets. Share dividends are *not* distributions.

Cash or Property Dividends Dividends are usually paid in cash. However, other assets of the corporation—such as airline discount coupons or shares of another corporation—may also be distributed as dividends. Cash or property dividends are declared by the board of directors and paid by the corporation on the date stated by the directors. Once declared, dividends are *debts* of the corporation, and shareholders may sue to force payment of the dividends. The board's dividend declaration, including the amount of dividend and whether to declare a dividend, is protected by the business judgment rule.

Preferred shares nearly always have a set dividend rate stated in the articles of incorporation. Even so, unless the preferred dividend is mandatory, the board has discretion to determine whether to pay a preferred dividend and what amount to pay. Most preferred shares are *cumulative preferred shares* on which unpaid dividends cumulate. The entire accumulation must be paid before common shareholders may receive any dividend. Even when preferred shares are noncumulative, the current dividend must be paid to preferred before any dividend may be paid to common shareholders.

The following *Dodge v. Ford* case is one of the few cases in which a court ordered the payment of a dividend to common shareholders. The court found that Henry Ford had the wrong motives for causing Ford Motor Company to refuse to pay a dividend.

Dodge v. Ford Motor Co.   170 N.W. 668 (Mich. 1919)

In 1916, brothers John and Horace Dodge owned 10 percent of the common shares of the Ford Motor Company. Henry Ford owned 58 percent of the outstanding common shares and controlled the corporation and its board of directors. Starting in 1911, the corporation paid a regular annual dividend of $1.2 million, which was 60 percent of its capital stock of $2 million but only about 1 percent of its total equity of $114 million. In addition, from 1911 to 1915, the corporation paid special dividends totaling $41 million.

The policy of the corporation was to reduce the selling price of its cars each year. In June 1915, the board and officers agreed to increase production by constructing new plants for $10 million, acquiring land for $3 million, and erecting an $11 million smelter. To finance the planned expansion, the board decided not to reduce the selling price of cars beginning in August 1915 and to accumulate a large surplus.

A year later, the board reduced the selling price of cars by $80 per car. The corporation was able to produce 600,000 cars annually, all of which, and more, could have been sold for $440 instead of the new $360 price, a forgone revenue of $48 million. At the same time, the corporation announced a new dividend policy of paying no special dividend. Instead, it would reinvest all earnings except the regular dividend of $1.2 million.

Henry Ford announced his justification for the new dividend policy in a press release: "My ambition is to employ still more men, to spread the benefits of this industrial system to the greatest possible number, to help them build up their lives and their homes." The corporation had a $112 million surplus, expected profits of $60 million, total liabilities of $18 million, $52.5 million in cash on hand, and municipal bonds worth $1.3 million.

The Dodge brothers sued the corporation and the directors to force them to declare a special dividend. The trial court ordered the board to declare a dividend of $19.3 million. Ford Motor Company appealed.

Ostrander, Chief Justice

It is a well-recognized principle of law that the directors of a corporation, and they alone, have the power to declare a dividend of the earnings of the corporation, and to determine its amount. Courts will not interfere in the management of the directors unless it is clearly made to appear that they are guilty of fraud or misappropriation of the corporate funds, or they refuse to declare a dividend when the corporation has a surplus of net profits which it can, without detriment to the business, divide among its stockholders, and when a refusal to do so would amount to such an abuse of discretion as would constitute a fraud, or breach of that good faith that they are bound to exercise towards the shareholders.

The testimony of Mr. Ford convinces this court that he has to some extent the attitude towards shareholders of one who has dispensed and distributed to them large gains and that they should be content to take what he chooses to give. His testimony creates the impression that he thinks the Ford Motor Company has made too much money, has had too large profits, and that, although large profits might be still earned, a sharing of them with the public, by reducing the price of the output of the company, ought to be undertaken. We have no doubt that certain sentiments, philanthropic and altruistic, creditable to Mr. Ford, had large influence in determining the policy to be pursued by the Ford Motor Company.

There should be no confusion of the duties that Mr. Ford conceives that he and the shareholders owe to the general public and the duties that in law he and his co-directors owe to protesting, minority shareholders. A business corporation is organized and carried on primarily for the profit of the shareholders. The powers of the directors are to be employed for that end.

We are not, however, persuaded that we should interfere with the proposed expansion of the Ford Motor Company. In view of the fact that the selling price of products may be increased at any time, the ultimate results of the larger business cannot be certainly estimated. The judges are not business experts. It is recognized that plans must often be made for a long future, for expected competition, for a continuing as well as an immediately profitable venture. We are not satisfied that the alleged motives of the directors, in so far as they are reflected in the conduct of the business, menace the interests of shareholders.

Assuming the general plan and policy of expansion were for the best ultimate interest of the company and therefore of its shareholders, what does it amount to in justification of a refusal to declare and pay a special dividend? The Ford Motor Company was able to estimate with nicety its income and profit. It could sell more cars than it could make. The profit upon each car depended upon the selling price. That being fixed, the yearly income and profit was determinable, and, within slight variations, was certain.

There was appropriated for the smelter $11 million. Assuming that the plans required an expenditure sooner or later of $10 million for duplication of the plant, and for land $3 million, the total is $24 million. The company was a cash business. If the total cost of proposed expenditures had been withdrawn in cash from the cash surplus on hand August 1, 1916, there would have remained $30 million.

The directors of Ford Motor Company say, and it is true, that a considerable cash balance must be at all times carried by such a concern. But there was a large daily, weekly, monthly receipt of cash. The output was practically continuous and was continuously, and within a few days, turned into cash. Moreover, the contemplated expenditures were not to be immediately made. The large sum appropriated for the smelter plant was payable over a considerable period of time. So that, without going further, it would appear that, accepting and approving the plan of the directors, it was their duty to distribute on and near the 1st of August 1916, a very large sum of money to stockholders.

Judgment for the Dodge brothers affirmed.

[Note: *Dodge v. Ford* may be the most famous lawsuit in the history of American corporate law. Academics, judges, and legal and business practitioners have used it—and misused it—for many purposes, likely because it touches on so many fundamental aspects of corporate law. The case also has a fascinating backstory that will be appreciated by anyone interested in law, business, or entrepreneurship. *See* M. Todd Henderson, *Everything Old Is New Again: Lessons from* Dodge v. Ford Motor Company, **University of Chicago Law & Economics, Olin Working Paper (2007).**]

To protect the claims of the corporation's creditors, all of the corporation statutes limit the extent to which dividends may be paid. The MBCA imposes two limits: (1) the *solvency test* and (2) the *balance sheet test*.

Solvency Test A dividend may not make a corporation insolvent; that is, unable to pay its debts as they come due in the usual course of business. This means that a corporation may pay a dividend to the extent it has *excess solvency*—that is, liquidity that it does not need to pay its currently maturing obligations. This requirement protects creditors, who are concerned primarily with the corporation's ability to pay debts as they mature.

Balance Sheet Test After the dividend has been paid, the corporation's assets must be sufficient to cover its liabilities and the liquidation preference of shareholders having a priority in liquidation over the shareholders receiving the dividend. This means that a corporation may pay a dividend to the extent it has *excess assets*—that is, assets it does not need to cover its liabilities and the liquidation preferences of shareholders having a priority in liquidation over the shareholders receiving the dividends. This requirement protects not only creditors but also preferred shareholders. It prevents a corporation from paying to common shareholders a dividend that will impair the liquidation rights of preferred shareholders.

Share Dividends and Share Splits Corporations sometimes distribute additional shares of the corporation to their shareholders. Often, this is done in order to give shareholders something instead of a cash dividend so that the cash can be retained and reinvested in the business. Such an action may be called either a *share dividend* or a *share split*.

A **share dividend** of a *specified percentage of outstanding shares* is declared by the board of directors. For example, the board may declare a 10 percent share dividend. As a result, each shareholder will receive 10 percent more shares than she currently owns. A share dividend is paid on outstanding shares only. Unlike a cash or property dividend, a share dividend may be revoked by the board after it has been declared.

A **share split** results in shareholders receiving a specified number of shares in exchange for each share that they currently own. For example, shares may be split two for one. Each shareholder will now have two shares for each share that he previously owned. A holder of 50 shares will now have 100 shares instead of 50.

The MBCA recognizes that a share split or a share dividend in the same class of shares does not affect the value of the corporation or the shareholders' wealth because no assets have been transferred from the corporation to the shareholders. The effect is like that produced by taking a pie with four pieces and dividing each piece in half. Each person may receive twice as many pieces of the pie, but each piece is worth only half as much. The total amount received by each person is unchanged.

Therefore, the MBCA permits share splits and share dividends of the same class of shares to be made merely by action of the directors. The directors merely have the corporation issue to the shareholders the number of shares needed to effect the share dividend or split. The corporation must have a sufficient number of authorized, unissued shares to effect the share split or dividend; when it does not, its articles must be amended to create the required number of additional authorized shares.

Reverse Share Split A *reverse share split* is a decrease in the number of shares of a class such that, for example, two shares become one share. Most of the state corporation statutes require shareholder action to amend the articles to effect a reverse share split because the number of authorized shares is reduced. The purpose of a reverse share split is usually to increase the market price of the shares.

A reverse share split may also be used to freeze out minority shareholders. By the setting of a high reverse split ratio, a majority shareholder will be left with whole shares while minority shareholders will have only fractional shares. Corporation law allows a corporation to repurchase fractional shares without the consent of the fractional shareholders.

Share Repurchases
Declaring a cash or property dividend is only one of the ways in which a corporation may distribute its assets. A corporation may also distribute its assets by repurchasing its shares from its shareholders. Such a repurchase may be either a *redemption* or an *open-market repurchase*.

The right of **redemption** (or a call) is usually a right of the corporation to force an *involuntary* sale by a shareholder at a fixed price. The shareholder must sell the shares to the corporation at the corporation's request; in most states, the shareholder cannot force the corporation to redeem the shares.

Under the MBCA, the right of redemption must appear in the articles of incorporation. It is common for a corporation to issue preferred shares subject to redemption at the corporation's option. Usually, common shares are not redeemable.

In addition, a corporation may repurchase its shares on the open market. A corporation is empowered to purchase its shares from any shareholder who is willing to sell them.

Such repurchases are usually *voluntary* on the shareholder's part, requiring the corporation to pay a current market price to entice the shareholder to sell. However, a corporation may force a shareholder with a fractional share to sell that fractional share back to the corporation.

A corporation's repurchase of its shares may harm creditors and other shareholders. The MBCA requires a corporation repurchasing shares to meet tests that are the same as its cash and property dividend rules, recognizing that financially a repurchase of shares is no different from a dividend or any other distribution of assets to shareholders.

Ensuring a Shareholder's Return on Investment

Obtaining a return on their investment in a corporation is important to every shareholder. In a publicly held corporation, a shareholder may receive a return in the form of dividends and more significantly an increase in the value of her shares, which she may sell in the public securities markets.

For a shareholder in a close corporation, obtaining a return on her investment is often a problem, especially for minority shareholders. The majority shareholders dominate the board of directors, who usually choose not to pay any dividend to shareholders. And because the close corporation has no publicly traded shares, minority shareholders have little if any ability to sell their shares. The majority shareholders in a close corporation do not suffer the same effect because they are usually officers and employees of the corporation and receive a return on their investment in the form of salaries.

What can a minority shareholder do? Rarely will a court, as in *Dodge v. Ford*, require the payment of a dividend. The only way a minority shareholder can protect himself is to bargain well prior to becoming a shareholder. For example, a prospective minority shareholder may insist on a mandatory dividend, that he be employed by the corporation at a salary, or that the corporation or majority shareholders be required to repurchase his shares upon the occurrence of certain events, such as the failure of the corporation to go public after five years. There is a limit to what a minority shareholder may demand, however, for the majority shareholders may refuse to sell shares to a prospective shareholder who asks too much.

Shareholders' Lawsuits

Shareholders' Individual Lawsuits A shareholder has the right to sue in his own name to prevent or redress a breach of the shareholder's contract. For example,

a shareholder may sue to recover dividends declared but not paid or dividends that should have been declared, to enjoin the corporation from committing an *ultra vires* act, to enforce the shareholder's right of inspection, and to enforce preemptive rights.

Shareholder Class Action Suits When several people have been injured similarly by the same persons in similar situations, one of the injured people may sue for the benefit of all the people injured. Likewise, if several shareholders have been similarly affected by a wrongful act of another, one of these shareholders may bring a **class action** on behalf of all the affected shareholders.

An appropriate class action under state corporation law would be an action seeking a dividend payment that has been brought by a preferred shareholder for all of the preferred shareholders. Any recovery is prorated to all members of the class.

A shareholder who successfully brings a class action is entitled to be reimbursed from the award amount for his *reasonable expenses*, including attorney fees. If the class action suit is unsuccessful and has no reasonable foundation, the court may order the suing shareholder to pay the defendants' reasonable litigation expenses, including attorney fees.

LOG ON

http://securities.stanford.edu
Stanford Law School maintains the Securities Class Action Clearinghouse. It provides detailed information relating to the prosecution, defense, and settlement of federal class action securities litigation.

Shareholders' Derivative Actions

LO44-3 Appreciate how shareholders may enforce corporate rights of actions, especially against corporate managers.

When a corporation has been harmed by the actions of another person, the right to sue belongs to the corporation, and any damages awarded by a court belong to the corporation. Hence, as a general rule, a shareholder has no right to sue in his own name when someone has harmed the corporation, and he may not recover for himself damages from that person. This is the rule even when the value of the shareholder's investment in the corporation has been impaired.

Nonetheless, one or more shareholders are permitted under certain circumstances to bring an action for the benefit of the corporation when the directors have failed to pursue a corporate cause of action. For example, if the corporation has a claim against its chief executive for wrongfully diverting corporate assets to her personal use, the corporation may not sue the chief executive because she controls the board of directors. Clearly, the CEO should not go unpunished. Consequently, corporation law authorizes a shareholder to bring a **derivative action** (or derivative suit) against the CEO on behalf of the corporation and for its benefit. Such a suit may also be used to bring a corporate claim against an outsider.

If the derivative action succeeds and damages are awarded, the damages ordinarily go to the corporate treasury for the benefit of the corporation. The suing shareholder is entitled only to reimbursement of his reasonable attorney fees that he incurred in bringing the action.

Eligible Shareholders Although allowing shareholders to bring derivative suits creates a viable procedure for suing wrongdoing officers and directors, this procedure is also susceptible to abuse. **Strike suits** (lawsuits brought to gain out-of-court settlements for the complaining shareholders personally or to earn large attorney fees, rather than to obtain a recovery for the corporation) are not uncommon. To discourage strike suits, the person bringing the action must be a current shareholder who held shares at the time the alleged wrong occurred. In addition, the shareholder must fairly and adequately represent the interests of shareholders similarly situated in enforcing the right of the corporation.

One exception to these rules is the double derivative suit, a suit brought by a shareholder of a parent corporation on behalf of a subsidiary corporation owned by the parent. Courts regularly permit double derivative suits.

Demand on Directors Because a corporation's decision to sue someone is ordinarily made by its managers, a shareholder must first **demand** that the board of directors bring the suit. A demand informs the board that the corporation may have a right of action against a person that the board, in its business judgment, may decide to pursue. Therefore, if a demand is made and the board decides to bring the suit, the shareholder may not institute a derivative suit.

Ordinarily, a shareholder's failure to make a demand on the board prevents her from bringing a derivative suit. Nonetheless, the shareholder may initiate the suit if she proves that a demand on the board would have been useless or futile. Demand is futile, and therefore excused, if the board is unable to make a disinterested decision regarding whether to sue. Futility may be proved when all or a majority of the directors are interested in the challenged transaction, such as in a suit alleging that the directors issued shares to themselves at below-market prices or committed a crime.

If a shareholder makes a demand on the board and it refuses the shareholder's demand to bring a suit, ordinarily the shareholder is not permitted to continue the derivative action. The decision to bring a lawsuit is an ordinary business decision appropriate for a board of directors to make. The business judgment rule, therefore, is available to insulate from court review a board's decision not to bring a suit.

Of course, if a shareholder's derivative suit accuses the board of harming the corporation, such as by misappropriating the corporation's assets, the board's refusal will not be protected by the business judgment rule because the board has a conflict of interest in its decision to sue. In such a situation, the shareholder may sue the directors despite the board's refusal.

Shareholder Litigation Committees In an attempt to ensure the application of the business judgment rule in demand refusal and demand futility situations, interested directors have tried to isolate themselves from the decision whether to sue by creating a special committee of the board, called a *shareholder* or *special litigation committee* (*SLC*) (or independent investigation committee) whose purpose is to decide whether to sue. A well-formed SLC should consist of directors who are not defendants in the derivative suit, are not interested in the challenged action, are independent of the defendant directors, and, if possible, were not directors at the time the alleged wrong occurred. Usually, the SLC has independent legal counsel that assists its determination whether to sue. Because the SLC is a committee of the board, its decision may be protected by the business judgment rule. Therefore, an SLC's decision not to sue may prevent a shareholder from suing.

Shareholders have challenged the application of the business judgment rule to an SLC's decision to dismiss a shareholder derivative suit against some of the directors. The suing shareholders argue that it is improper for an SLC to dismiss a shareholder derivative suit because there is a *structural bias*. That is, the SLC members are motivated by a desire to avoid hurting their fellow directors and adversely affecting future working relationships within the board.

When demand is not futile, most of the courts that have been faced with this question have upheld the decisions of special litigation committees that comply with the business judgment rule. The courts require that the SLC members be *independent* of the defendant directors, be *disinterested* with regard to the subject matter of the suit, make a *reasonable investigation* into whether to dismiss the suit, and act in *good faith*.

When demand is futile or excused, most courts faced with the decision of an SLC have applied the rule of the *Zapata* case, which follows.

The MBCA has adopted the *Zapata* rule in all contexts, whether or not an SLC is used. When a majority of directors are not independent, the corporation has the burden

Zapata Corp. v. Maldonado	430 A.2d 779 (Del. 1981)

Zapata Corporation had a share option plan that permitted its executives to purchase Zapata shares at a below-market price. Most of the directors participated in the share option plan. In 1974, the directors voted to advance the share option exercise date in order to reduce the federal income tax liability of the executives who exercised the share options, including the directors. An additional effect, however, was to increase the corporation's federal tax liability.

William Maldonado, a Zapata shareholder, believed that the board action was a breach of a fiduciary duty and that it harmed the corporation. In 1975, he instituted a derivative suit in a Delaware court on behalf of Zapata against all of the directors. He did not make a demand on the directors to sue themselves, alleging that this would be futile because they were all defendants.

The derivative suit was still pending in 1979, when four of the defendants were no longer directors. The remaining directors then appointed two new outside directors to the board and created an Independent Investigation Committee consisting solely of the two new directors. The board authorized the committee to make a final and binding decision regarding whether the derivative suit should be brought on behalf of the corporation. Following a three-month investigation, the committee concluded that Maldonado's derivative suit should be dismissed as against Zapata's best interests.

Zapata asked the Delaware court to dismiss the derivative suit. The court refused, holding that Maldonado possessed an individual right to maintain the derivative action and that the business judgment rule did not apply. Zapata appealed to the Supreme Court of Delaware.

Quillen, Justice

We find that the trial court's determination that a shareholder, once demand is made and refused, possesses an independent, individual right to continue a derivative suit for breaches of fiduciary duty over objection by the corporation, as an absolute rule, is erroneous.

Derivative suits enforce corporate rights, and any recovery obtained goes to the corporation. We see no inherent reason why a derivative suit should automatically place in the hands of the litigating shareholder sole control of the corporate right throughout the litigation. Such an inflexible rule would recognize the interest of one person or group to the exclusion of all others within the corporate entity.

When, if at all, should an authorized board committee be permitted to cause litigation, properly initiated by a derivative stockholder in his own right, to be dismissed? The problem is relatively simple. If, on the one hand, corporations can consistently wrest bona fide derivative actions away from well-meaning derivative plaintiffs through the use of the committee mechanism, the derivative suit will lose much, if not all, of its effectiveness as an intracorporate means of policing boards of directors. If, on the other hand, corporations are unable to rid themselves of meritless or harmful litigation and strike suits, the derivative action, created to benefit the corporation, will produce the opposite, unintended result. It thus appears desirable to us to find a balancing point where bona fide shareholder power to bring corporate causes of action cannot be unfairly trampled on by the board of directors, but the corporation can rid itself of detrimental litigation.

We are not satisfied that acceptance of the business judgment rationale at this stage of derivative litigation is a proper balancing point. We must be mindful that directors are passing judgment on fellow directors in the same corporation and fellow directors, in this instance, who designated them to serve both as

directors and committee members. The question naturally arises whether a "there but for the grace of God go I" empathy might not play a role. And the further question arises whether inquiry as to independence, good faith and reasonable investigation is sufficient safeguard against abuse, perhaps subconscious abuse.

We thus steer a middle course between those cases that yield to the independent business judgment of a board committee and this case as determined below, which would yield to unbridled shareholder control.

We recognize that the final substantive judgment whether a particular lawsuit should be maintained requires a balance of many factors—ethical, commercial, promotional, public relations, employee relations, fiscal, as well as legal. We recognize the danger of judicial overreaching but the alternatives seem to us to be outweighed by the fresh view of a judicial outsider.

After an objective and thorough investigation of a derivative suit, an independent committee may cause its corporation to file a motion to dismiss the derivative suit. The Court should apply a two-step test to the motion. First, the Court should inquire into the independence and good faith of the committee and the bases supporting its conclusions. The corporation should have the burden of proving independence, good faith, and reasonable investigation, rather than presuming independence, good faith, and reasonableness. If the Court determines either that the committee is not independent or has not shown reasonable bases for its conclusions, or if the Court is not satisfied for other reasons relating to the process, including but not limited to the good faith of the committee, the Court shall deny the corporation's motion to dismiss the derivative suit.

The second step provides the essential key in striking the balance between legitimate corporate claims as expressed in a derivative stockholder suit and a corporation's best interests as expressed by an independent investigating committee. The Court should determine, applying its own independent business judgment, whether the motion should be granted. The second step is intended to thwart instances where corporate actions meet the criteria of step one, but the result does not appear to satisfy its spirit, or where corporate actions would simply prematurely terminate a stockholder grievance deserving of further consideration in the corporation's interest. The Court of course must carefully consider and weigh how compelling the corporate interest in dismissal is when faced with a non-frivolous lawsuit. The

Court should, when appropriate, give special consideration to matters of law and public policy in addition to the corporation's best interests.

The second step shares some of the same spirit and philosophy of the statement of the trial court: "Under our system of law, courts and not litigants should decide the merits of litigation."

Judgment reversed in favor of Zapata. Case remanded to the trial court.

of proving that the *Zapata* test has been met: good faith and reasonable investigation by the directors making the decision to dismiss the action and a determination by those directors that the best interests of the corporation are served by dismissal. If, however, a majority of the directors are independent, the shareholders bringing the derivative action have the burden of proving that there was bad faith or no reasonable investigation, or that bringing the action is in the best interest of the corporation.

Litigation Expenses If a shareholder is successful in a derivative suit, she is entitled to a reimbursement of her reasonable litigation expenses out of the corporation's damage award. On the other hand, if the suit is unsuccessful and has been brought without reasonable cause, the shareholder must pay the defendants' expenses, including attorney fees. The purpose of this rule is to deter strike suits by punishing shareholders who litigate in bad faith.

Defense of Corporation by Shareholder

Occasionally, the officers or managers will refuse to defend a suit brought against a corporation. If a shareholder shows that the corporation has a valid defense to the suit and that the refusal or failure of the directors to defend is a breach of their fiduciary duty to the corporation, the courts will permit the shareholder to defend for the benefit of the corporation, its shareholders, and its creditors.

Shareholder Liability

LO44-4 Explain the special liabilities of shareholders.

Shareholders have many responsibilities and liabilities in addition to their many rights. In earlier chapters, we studied shareholder liability when a shareholder pays too little

consideration for shares, when a corporation is defectively formed, and when a corporation's veil is pierced. In this section, four other grounds for shareholder liability are discussed.

Shareholder Liability for Illegal Distributions Dividends and other distributions of a corporation's assets received by a shareholder with *knowledge of their illegality* may be recovered on behalf of the corporation. Under the MBCA, primary liability is placed on the directors who, failing to comply with the business judgment rule, authorized the unlawful distribution. However, the directors are entitled to contribution from shareholders who received an asset distribution knowing that it was illegally made. These liability rules enforce the limits on asset distributions that were discussed earlier in this chapter.

Shareholder Liability for Corporate Debts One of the chief attributes of a shareholder is his *limited liability*: Ordinarily, he has no liability for corporate obligations beyond his capital contribution. Defective attempts to incorporate (in Chapter 42) and piercing the corporate veil (in Chapter 41) are grounds on which a shareholder may be held liable for corporate debts beyond his capital contribution. In addition, a few states impose personal liability on shareholders for *wages owed to corporate employees*, even if the shareholders have fully paid for their shares.

Sale of a Control Block of Shares The per share value of the shares of a majority shareholder of a corporation is greater than the per share value of the shares of a minority shareholder. This difference in value is due to the majority shareholder's ability to control the corporation and to cause it to hire her as an employee at a high salary. Therefore, a majority shareholder can sell her shares for a *premium* over the fair market value of minority shares.

Ethics and Compliance in Action

After reading *Zapata Corp. v. Maldonado* and the MBCA rules for dismissal of shareholder derivative actions, you may predict that a court will almost always respect the recommendation of a special litigation committee, even when a former or existing board member is a defendant. That is not always the case because the corporation does not have a valid right of action against a director, but often because an SLC has adopted the right process (good faith and reasonable inquiry) and easily can justify that the expense of litigation and the distraction of current management outweigh the likely recovery to the corporation from the wrongdoing director.

• Do you think it is ethical for an SLC to recommend dismissal of an action against a director who has harmed the

corporation? Is that sending the right message to other directors and officers? Are there other ways to discipline a director or officer than by suing him? Are those alternatives sufficient deterrents or punishments?

• Do you think it would be justifiable for an SLC to recommend dismissal of an action against former officers who, like some top officers in Adelphia, Tyco, and Enron, either looted the corporation or caused it to overstate its earnings or understate its liabilities? Is it justifiable for a corporation not to sue directors and officers of corporations, like Apple Inc. and The Home Depot Inc., who authorized or permitted the backdating of options given to the CEO and other officers, which nearly guaranteed that the officers would profit from the options? Would a utilitarian or profit maximizer be more likely to recommend dismissal than a rights theorist?

Majority ownership is not always required for control of a corporation. In a close corporation it is required, but in a publicly held corporation with a widely dispersed, hard-to-mobilize shareholder group, minority ownership of from 5 to 30 percent may be enough to obtain control. Therefore, a holder of minority control in such a corporation will also be able to receive a premium.

Current corporation law imposes no liability on any shareholder, whether or not the shareholder is a controlling shareholder, *merely* because she is able to sell her shares for a premium. Nonetheless, if the premium is accompanied by wrongdoing, controlling shareholders have been held liable either for the amount of the premium or for the damages suffered by the corporation.

For example, a seller of control shares is liable for selling to a purchaser who harms the corporation if the seller had or should have had a *reasonable suspicion* that the purchaser would mismanage or loot the corporation. A seller may be placed on notice of a purchaser's bad motives by facts indicating the purchaser's history of *mismanagement and personal use of corporate assets*, by the purchaser's *lack of interest in the physical facilities* of the corporation, or the purchaser's great *interest in the liquid assets* of the corporation. These factors tend to indicate that the purchaser has a short-term interest in the corporation.

The mere payment of a premium is not enough to put the seller on notice. If the *premium is unduly high*, however, such as a $50 offer for shares traded for $10, a seller must doubt whether the purchaser will be able to recoup his investment without looting the corporation.

When a seller has, or should have, a reasonable suspicion that a purchaser will mismanage or loot the corporation, he must not sell to the purchaser unless a *reasonable investigation* shows there is no reasonable risk of wrongdoing.

A few courts find liability when a selling shareholder takes or sells a *corporate asset*. For example, if a purchaser wants to buy the corporation's assets and the controlling shareholder proposes that the purchaser buy her shares instead, the controlling shareholder is liable for usurping a corporate opportunity.

A more unusual situation existed in *Perlman v. Feldman*.[4] In that case, Newport Steel Corporation had excess demand for its steel production, due to the Korean War. Another corporation, in order to guarantee a steady supply of steel, bought at a premium a minority yet controlling block of shares of Newport from Feldman, its chairman and president. The court ruled that Feldman was required to share the premium with the other shareholders because he had sold a corporate asset—the ability to exploit an excess demand for steel. The court reasoned that Newport could have exploited that asset to its advantage.

Shareholders as Fiduciaries A few courts have recognized a fiduciary duty of controlling shareholders to use their ability to control the corporation in a fair, just, and equitable manner that benefits all of

---

[4]219 F.2d 173 (2d Cir. 1955).

the shareholders proportionately. This is a duty to be impartial—that is, not to prefer themselves over the minority shareholders. For example, controlling shareholders have a fiduciary duty not to cause the corporation to repurchase their own shares or to pay themselves a dividend unless the same offer is made to the minority shareholder.

One of the most common examples of impartiality is the **freeze-out** or *squeeze-out* of minority shareholders, which is wrongful because of its **oppression** of those shareholders. It occurs in close corporations when controlling shareholders pay themselves high salaries while not employing or paying dividends to noncontrolling shareholders. Because there is usually no liquid market for the shares of the noncontrolling shareholders, they have an investment that provides them no return, while the controlling shareholders reap large gains. Such actions by the majority are especially wrongful when the controlling shareholders follow with an offer to buy the minority's shares at an unreasonably low price.

Some courts have held that all close corporation shareholders—whether majority or minority owners—are fiduciaries of each other and the corporation, on the grounds that the close corporation is like an incorporated partnership. Thus, like partners, the shareholders owe fiduciary duties to act in the best interests of the corporation and the shareholders as a whole.

Some statutes, such as the Statutory Close Corporation Supplement to the MBCA, permit close corporation shareholders to dispense with a board of directors or to arrange corporate affairs as if the corporation were a partnership. The effect of these statutes is to impose management responsibilities, including the fiduciary duties of directors, on the shareholders. In essence, the shareholders are partners and owe each other fiduciary duties similar to those owed between partners of a partnership.

In the next case, *Mitchell Partners, L.P. v. Irex Corp.*, the court held that Pennsylvania's appraisal statute did not exclude separate, postmerger suits for damages alleging that majority shareholders breached their fiduciary duties to minority shareholders in the process of consummating a freeze-out merger. Additionally, the court held that the appraisal statute did not exclude the related claim that the Special Committee members aided and abetted the breach. The case was ultimately remanded to determine if there was fraud or fundamental unfairness.

Mitchell Partners, L.P. v. Irex Corp.   656 F.3d 201 (3d Cir. 2011)

Appellant Mitchell Partners, L.P., a California limited partnership, was formerly a minority shareholder of Irex Corporation (Irex), and owned more than 11,000 shares of Irex common stock. Irex was a privately held Pennsylvania corporation with its shares traded over the counter and not on a public stock exchange. Irex was also the parent corporation of several companies. A board of directors and several corporate officers, who collectively owned approximately 43 percent of Irex stock, governed Irex.

On April 26, 2006, defendant Kirk Liddell, president, CEO, and chairman of the Irex board, sent a confidential memorandum to the directors and officers outlining a plan designed to enhance their own net worth by consolidating ownership of Irex among themselves and a handful of other "participating" shareholders by buying out the minority Irex shareholders. Under the plan the insider shareholders were to create a separate holding company, North Lime Holdings Corporation, under the insiders' exclusive ownership and control. North Lime would then acquire 100 percent of Irex through a cash-out merger between Irex and a wholly owned North Lime subsidiary, Irex Acquisition Corporation. The proposal detailed that prior to the merger, the insider shareholders would exchange their Irex stock for North Lime stock. This would allow North Lime to obtain majority ownership of Irex and, at the same time, allow the insider shareholders to retain ownership of Irex indirectly through their ownership of North Lime. Under the terms of the merger, the nonparticipating, noninsider minority shareholders would be given cash in exchange for their ownership interest in Irex.

Irex's CFO informed all Irex shareholders by mail of the proposed merger. A week later, Mitchell Partners wrote back to the CFO and lodged its opposition to the proposed merger, which it viewed as a squeeze-out of minority shareholders at an unfair price. On May 31, 2006, a special meeting of the Irex board was convened to discuss the North Lime Proposal. At the meeting, the board amended its bylaws to add three supposedly disinterested directors who would form a special committee to review and comment on the fairness of the proposed merger and independently negotiate on the minority shareholders behalf. However, the new board had strong ties to the defendants. The complaint filed by the plaintiffs alleged that the defendants influenced and controlled the committee's consideration of fair value for the minority stock, thereby breaching fiduciary duties owed to minority shareholders. On October 8, 2008, Mitchell Partners filed this putative class action complaint, alleging breach of fiduciary duty against Irex, North Lime, and the individual insider directors/officers; breach of fiduciary duty and aiding and abetting breach of fiduciary duty against the Special Committee members; and unjust enrichment against Irex, North Lime, and the individual insider directors/officers. The defendants then moved to dismiss all counts for failure to state a claim. The district court granted the motion. Mitchell Partners appealed.

Sloviter, Circuit Judge

The parties do not dispute that as a general matter of Pennsylvania state law, it has long been recognized that majority shareholders have a duty to protect the interests of the minority. Majority stockholders occupy a quasi-fiduciary relation toward the minority which prevents them from using their power in such a way as to exclude the minority from their proper share of the benefits accruing from the enterprise. In *In re Jones & Laughlin Steel Corp.*, the Supreme Court of Pennsylvania recognized that freezing out of minority holders with the purpose of continuing the business for the benefit of the majority holders is a violation of the fiduciary duty owed to minority shareholders by the majority shareholders.

In applying the facts of this case to this standard, the District Court held that Mitchell Partners had stated a cognizable claim for breach of fiduciary duty against North Lime and the other insider, majority shareholders. However, in dismissing the entire complaint, the District Court held that because the lawsuit was brought after the merger had been consummated, it was barred by Pennsylvania's appraisal statute, which the District Court reasoned provided the sole post-merger remedy to dissenting minority shareholders. The narrow issue of whether a suit for damages based on breach of fiduciary duties may be brought post-merger was not directly presented to the Supreme Court; however, we predict that the Supreme Court of Pennsylvania would permit a post-merger suit for damages based on the majority shareholders' breach of their fiduciary duties. Nothing in the appraisal statute itself distinguishes between pre- and post-merger relief. Therefore, there is no reason why common law causes of action such as fiduciary breach should be permitted pre-merger, but barred post-merger. The rationale behind the appraisal statute is to prevent a dissident group of shareholders from blocking a merger desired by the majority shareholders, and a post-merger damages action would not contravene that goal.

The appraisal remedy only permits dissenters to recover from the corporation. Forbidding fiduciary duty suits against majority shareholders does not run the risk of thwarting the merger, particularly if the suit is brought after the merger is consummated. Barring such suits would do little more than insulate alleged tortfeasors from responsibility for their conduct. Further, if we were to adopt the interpretation of the statute advocated by defendants, this would mean that any shareholder who was deceived by the majority into voting for the merger would have no remedy at all for the breach of fiduciary duty.

Guided by the above analysis, we predict that the Supreme Court of Pennsylvania would hold that Pennsylvania's appraisal statute does not exclude separate, post-merger suits for damages alleging that majority shareholders breached their fiduciary duties to minority shareholders in the process of consummating a freeze out merger, nor does it exclude the related claim that the Special Committee members aided and abetted the breach.

Judgment of the District Court is reversed and case is remanded for proceedings consistent with this opinion.

[Note: The Third Circuit Court certified the question to the Pennsylvania Supreme Court for a clarification of state law. In response to the certified question, the Pennsylvania Supreme Court determined that the statute did preclude post-merger remedies unless there was fraud or fundamental unfairness. The case was then remanded to the federal district court for determination.]

Members' Rights and Duties in Nonprofit Corporations

 LO44-1 Understand the rights and powers of shareholders and how shareholders exercise their powers.

In a for-profit corporation, the shareholders' rights to elect directors and to receive dividends are their most important rights. The shareholders' duty to contribute capital as promised is the most important responsibility. By contrast, in a nonprofit corporation, the members' rights and duties—especially in a mutual benefit corporation—are defined by the ability of the members to use the facilities of the corporation (as in a social club) or to consume its output (as in a cooperative grocery store) and by their obligations to support the enterprise periodically with their money (such as dues paid to a social club) or with their labor (such as the duty to work a specified number of hours in a cooperative grocery store).

Nonprofit corporation law grants a corporation and its members considerable flexibility in determining the rights and liabilities of its members. The Model Nonprofit Corporation Act (MNCA) provides that all members of a nonprofit corporation have equal rights and obligations with respect to voting, dissolution, redemption of membership, and transfer of membership, unless the articles or bylaws establish classes of membership with different rights and obligations. For other rights and obligations, the MNCA provides that all members have the same rights and obligations, unless the articles or bylaws provide otherwise.

For example, a mutual benefit corporation that operates a golf country club may have two classes of membership. A full membership may entitle a full member to use all the club's facilities (including the swimming pool and tennis courts), grant the full member two votes on all matters submitted to members, and require the full member to pay monthly dues of $500. A limited membership may give a limited member the right to play the golf course only, grant the limited member one vote on all matters submitted to members, and require the limited members to pay monthly dues of $300 per month.

While members are primarily concerned about their consumption rights and financial obligations—such as those addressed above—that are embodied in the articles and the bylaws, they have other rights and obligations as well, including voting, inspection, and information rights similar to those held by shareholders of for-profit corporations.

Members' Meeting and Voting Rights A nonprofit corporation must hold an annual meeting of its members and may hold meetings at other times as well. Members holding at least 5 percent of the voting power may call for a special meeting of members at any time.

All members of record have one vote on all matters submitted to members, unless the articles or bylaws grant lesser or greater voting power. The articles or bylaws may provide for different classes of members. Members of one class may be given greater voting rights than the members of another class. The articles or bylaws may provide that a class has no voting power.

Members may not act at a meeting unless a quorum is present. Under the MNCA, a quorum is 10 percent of the votes entitled to be cast on a matter. However, unless at least one-third of the voting power is present at the meeting, the only matters that may be voted on are matters listed in the meeting notice sent to members. The articles or bylaws may require higher percentages.

Members may elect directors by straight or cumulative voting and by class voting. The articles or bylaws may also permit members to elect directors on the basis of chapter or other organizational unit, by region or other geographical unit, or by any other reasonable method. For example, a national humanitarian fraternity such as Lions Club may divide the United States into seven regions whose members are entitled to elect one director. Members also have the right to remove directors they have elected with or without cause.

In addition to the rights to elect and to remove directors, members have the right to vote on most amendments of the articles and bylaws, merger of the corporation with another corporation, sale of substantially all the corporation's assets, and dissolution of the corporation. Ordinarily,

members must approve such matters by two-thirds of the votes cast or a majority of the voting power, whichever is less. This requirement is more lenient than the rule applied to for-profit corporations. Combined with the 10 percent quorum requirement, members with less than 7 percent of the voting power may approve matters submitted to members.

However, the potential unfairness of such voting rules is offset by the MNCA's notice requirement. A members' meeting may not consider important matters such as mergers and articles amendments unless the corporation gave members fair and reasonable notice that such matters were to be submitted to the members for a vote.

In addition, the MNCA requires approval of each class of members whose rights are substantially affected by the matter. This requirement may increase the difficulty of obtaining member approval. For example, full members of a golf country club may not change the rights of limited members without the approval of the limited members. In addition, the articles or bylaws may require third-person approval as well. For example, a city industrial development board may not be permitted to amend its articles without the consent of the mayor.

Members may vote in person or by proxy. They may also have written voting agreements. However, member voting agreements may not have a term exceeding 10 years. Members may act without a meeting if the action is approved in writing by at least 80 percent of the voting power.

Member Inspection and Information Rights A member may not be able to exercise his voting and other rights unless he is informed. Moreover, a member must be able to communicate with other members to be able to influence the way they vote on matters submitted to members. Consequently, the MNCA grants members inspection and information rights.

Members have an absolute right to inspect and copy the articles, bylaws, board resolutions, and minutes of members' meetings. Members have a qualified right to inspect and copy a list of the members. The member's demand to inspect the members' list must be in good faith and for a proper purpose—that is, a purpose related to the member's interest as a member. Improper purposes include selling the list or using the list to solicit money. Members also have a qualified right to inspect minutes of board meetings and records of actions taken by committees of the board.

A nonprofit corporation is required to maintain appropriate accounting records, and members have a qualified right to inspect them. Upon demand, the corporation must provide to a member its latest annual financial statements,

The Global Business Environment

Chapter 43 covered some of the corporate governance differences between the United States and other countries, specifically Germany, including the makeup of corporate boards. There are many similarities but also quite a few differences in the powers of shareholders, including matters that must be submitted for shareholder approval. In Germany, the management board must obtain the approval of the shareholders to create new shares of the corporation, to transfer major assets, and to liquidate the company. The differences include German law requiring shareholder approval to declare dividends, issue new shares, and waive shareholders' preemptive right. In addition, many matters that in the United States may be included by director action in the bylaws must be included in German articles of incorporation, which cannot be modified without shareholder approval.

Shareholders of German companies have limited power to force a corporate right of action against someone who has harmed the corporation. A German corporation must sue members of the management board if a shareholders' meeting decides or if shareholders holding at least 10 percent of the shares demand the action. Beyond that, German law rarely permits an actio pro socio, the equivalent of an American derivative action. Moreover, German corporation law does not provide for direct actions by shareholders against members of the management board for breach of duty, such as wrongfully providing false financial information to shareholders.

---

including a balance sheet and statement of operations. However, the MNCA permits a religious corporation to abolish or limit the right of a member to inspect any corporate record.

Distributions of Assets Because it is not intended to make a profit, a nonprofit corporation does not pay dividends to its members. In fact, a nonprofit corporation is generally prohibited from making any distribution of its assets to its members.

Nonetheless, a mutual benefit corporation may purchase a membership and thereby distribute its assets to the selling member, but only if the corporation is able to pay its currently maturing obligations and has assets at least equal to its liabilities. For example, when a farmer joins a farmers' purchasing cooperative, he purchases a membership interest having economic value—it entitles him to purchase supplies from the cooperative at a bargain price. The mutual benefit corporation may repurchase the farmer's membership when he retires from farming. Religious and public benefit corporations may not repurchase their memberships.

Resignation and Expulsion of Members A member may resign at any time from a nonprofit corporation. When a member resigns, generally a member may not sell or transfer her membership to any other person. A member of a mutual benefit corporation may transfer her interest to a buyer if the articles or bylaws permit.

It is fairly easy for a nonprofit corporation to expel a member or terminate her membership. The corporation must follow procedures that are fair and reasonable and carried out in good faith. The MNCA does not require the corporation to have a proper purpose to expel or terminate

a member but only to follow proper procedures. The MNCA places no limits on a religious corporation's expulsion of its members.

The MNCA does not require a nonprofit corporation to purchase the membership of an expelled member, and—as explained above—permits only a mutual benefit corporation to purchase a membership. Members of mutual benefit corporations who fear expulsion should provide for repurchase rights in the articles or bylaws.

Derivative Suits Members of a nonprofit corporation have a limited right to bring derivative actions on behalf of the corporation that is almost identical to the litigation right of for-profit corporation shareholders. A derivative action may be brought by members having at least 5 percent of the voting power or by 50 members, whichever is less. Members must first demand that the directors bring the suit or establish that demand is futile. Even so, the disinterested directors' decision to dismiss the action will be accepted if backed by a reasonable investigation and a good-faith belief that the dismissal of the legal action is in the best interest of the corporation. If the action is successful, a court may require the corporation to pay the suing members' reasonable expenses. When the action is unsuccessful and has been commenced frivolously or in bad faith, a court may require the suing members to pay the other party's expenses.

Dissolution and Termination of Corporations

The MBCA provides that a corporation doing business may be dissolved by action of its directors and shareholders. The directors must adopt a dissolution resolution, and

LOG ON

www.cipe.org
The Center for International Private Enterprise is a nonprofit affiliate of the U.S. Chamber of Commerce and one of the four core institutes of the National Endowment for Democracy. CIPE advocates for market-based democratic systems in foreign countries and has adopted Corporate Governance Initiatives in the Middle East, South Asia, and North Africa to help countries and territories like the Palestinian Territories, Afghanistan, and Ethiopia advance their efforts to establish strong norms for corporate governance. Go to **www.cipe.org/region**.

a majority of the shares outstanding must be cast in favor of dissolution at a shareholders' meeting. For a voluntary dissolution to be effective, the corporation must submit articles of dissolution to the secretary of state. The dissolution is effective when the articles are filed by the secretary of state.

A corporation may also be dissolved without its consent by administrative action of the secretary of state or by judicial action of a court. The secretary of state may commence an administrative proceeding to dissolve a corporation that has not filed its annual report, paid its annual franchise tax, or appointed or maintained a registered office or agent in the state, or whose period of duration

has expired. Administrative dissolution requires that the secretary of state give written notice to the corporation of the grounds for dissolution. If, within 60 days, the corporation has not corrected the default or demonstrated that the default does not exist, the secretary dissolves the corporation by signing a certificate of dissolution.

The shareholders, secretary of state, or the creditors of a corporation may ask a court to order the involuntary dissolution of a corporation. Any **shareholder** may obtain judicial dissolution when there is a deadlock of the directors that is harmful to the corporation; when the shareholders are deadlocked and cannot elect directors for two years; or when the directors act illegally, oppressively, or fraudulently. The secretary of state may obtain judicial dissolution if it is proved that a corporation obtained its articles of incorporation by fraud or exceeded or abused its legal authority. **Creditors** may request dissolution if the corporation is insolvent.

Under the MBCA, a corporation that has not issued shares or commenced business may be dissolved by the vote of a majority of its incorporators or initial directors.

Many close corporations are nothing more than incorporated partnerships, in which all the shareholders are managers and friends or relatives. Corporation law reflects the special needs of those shareholders of close corporations who want to arrange their affairs to make

CONCEPT REVIEW

Roles of Shareholders and the Board of Directors

Corporate Action	Board's Role	Shareholders' Role
Day-to-day management	Selects officers; supervises management	Elect and remove directors
Issuance of shares	Issues shares	Protected by preemptive right
Merger and share exchange	Adopts articles of merger or share exchange	Vote to approve merger or share exchange; protected by dissenters' rights
Amendment of articles of incorporation	Proposes amendment	Vote to approve amendment
Dissolution	Proposes dissolution	Vote to approve dissolution
Dividends	Declares dividends	Receive dividends
Board of directors harms individual shareholder rights	Has harmed shareholders	Bring individual or class action against directors or the corporation
Directors harm corporation	Sues wrongdoing directors	Bring derivative action against wrongdoing directors

the close corporation more like a partnership. The Close Corporation Supplement to the MBCA recognizes that a close corporation shareholder should have more dissolution power, like a partner had under the Uniform Partnership Act. This section, like similar provisions in many states, permits the articles of incorporation to empower any shareholder to dissolve the corporation at will or upon the occurrence of a specified event such as the death of a shareholder.

Winding Up and Termination A dissolved corporation continues its corporate existence but may not carry on any business except that appropriate to winding up its affairs. Therefore, winding up (liquidation) must follow dissolution. Winding up is the orderly collection and disposal of the corporation's assets and the distribution of the proceeds of the sale of assets. From these proceeds, the claims of creditors will be paid first. Next, the liquidation preferences of preferred shareholders will be paid. Then, common shareholders receive any proceeds that remain.

After winding up has been completed, the corporation's existence terminates. A person who purports to act on behalf of a terminated corporation has the liability of a person acting for a corporation prior to its incorporation. Some courts impose similar liability on a person acting on behalf of a dissolved corporation, especially when

dissolution is obtained by the secretary of state, such as for the failure to file an annual report or to pay annual taxes.

Dissolution of Nonprofit Corporations A nonprofit corporation may be dissolved voluntarily, administratively, or judicially. Voluntary dissolution will usually require approval of both the directors and the members. However, a nonprofit corporation may also include a provision in its articles requiring the approval of a third person. For example, such a third person might be a state governor who appointed some of the directors to the board of a nonprofit corporation organized to encourage industrial development in the state. The dissolution is effective when the corporation delivers articles of dissolution to the secretary of state and the secretary of state files them. The dissolved corporation continues its existence, but only for the purpose of liquidating its assets and winding up its affairs.

The secretary of state may administratively dissolve a nonprofit corporation that fails to pay incorporation taxes or to deliver its annual report to the secretary of state, among other things. Minority members or directors may obtain judicial dissolution by a court if the directors are deadlocked, the directors in control are acting illegally or fraudulently, or the members are deadlocked and cannot elect directors for two successive elections, among other reasons.

Problems and Problem Cases

1. Wallace owned 50.25 percent of the shares of Capital Credit & Collection Service (CCCS), with Jones and Gaarde each owning 24.8 percent. Those three shareholders also constituted the board of directors. At a directors' meeting, a majority of the directors—that is, Jones and Gaarde—removed Wallace as president and elected Jones president and Gaarde secretary of the corporation. The following month at a shareholders' meeting at which Gaarde was absent, Wallace voted his majority of the shares to remove Jones and Gaarde as directors of the corporation and to replace them with Roberts and Smith. Under the Oregon Business Corporation Act, a valid shareholders' meeting required a quorum of shares equal to a majority of the shares unless a different quorum is provided in the articles of incorporation. CCCS, however, in its corporate bylaws, had a requirement that a quorum for a shareholder meeting was equal to 100 percent of the shares. Wallace had agreed to the bylaw as a shareholder and director of CCCS. Was the shareholder meeting at which Wallace

removed Jones and Gaarde invalid due to the lack of a quorum?

2. Kinetic Solutions LLC is an Internet software business with 15 members. Five members are the only managers of the business; the other 10 members are only investors. The 5 managing members want to sell part of the business to public investors. Before doing so, they opt to organize the business as a corporation. The 5 controlling shareholders want to be able to manage the corporation with little interference from other shareholders, and they want to continue to be compensated as managers of the business. The other 10 shareholders want some management control because of their sizable investments, especially if the business is not profitable. They are also concerned about being able to sell their shares at some point in the future. All 15 shareholders plan to raise an additional $50 million in capital by selling shares in the corporation to 1,000 wealthy public shareholders. The 15 original shareholders are unwilling to give the new investors any power to control the corporation or its management. The original shareholders expect that by having 1,000 new shareholders, a public

market will be created in their shares. Sketch an ownership control structure (a structure that determines how shareholders own and control the corporation through their rights as shareholders) that serves the ownership control interests of the 5 controlling shareholders and the 10 other shareholders. What is the best way for the 5 controlling shareholders to receive returns on their investment in the corporation? What is the best way for the 10 other shareholders to receive returns on their investment in the corporation?

3. The Eliason family owned a majority (5,238) of the 9,990 shares of Brosius-Eliason Co., a building and materials company, with James Eliason (3,928 shares) and his sister Sarah Englehart (1,260) holding the controlling block. The Brosius family owned a total of 3,690 shares. Frank Hewlett owned the remaining 1,062 shares. On July 31, James Eliason executed a proxy giving his daughter, Louise Eliason, authority to vote his shares. Only in the notary public's acknowledgment verifying James's signature did the proxy state that it was irrevocable. The body of the proxy, the part signed by James, did not state it was irrevocable. Two weeks later, James and his sister Sarah made a voting agreement that ensured Eliason family control over the corporation by requiring their shares to be voted as provided in the agreement. The voting agreement was irrevocable because it was coupled with an interest in each other's shares. Soon after, Sarah and Louise had a falling out when Louise tried to assert her family's control of the company. Consequently, Sarah voted her shares with the Brosiuses and Hewlett in violation of the agreement with James. She argued that she was not bound by the voting agreement with James on the grounds that James could not make the agreement because he had given Louise an irrevocable proxy two weeks earlier. Was Sarah right?

4. Axcelis Technologies is a Delaware corporation that manufactures ion implementation and semiconductor equipment. Westland is a Michigan pension fund that owns Axcelis common stock on behalf of its beneficiaries. One day, Sumitomo Heavy Industries (SHI), a Japanese company, makes an unsolicited bid to acquire Axcelis for $5.20 per share, but Axcelis's board of directors rejects SHI's proposal on the grounds that the offered price is too low. A few weeks later, SHI makes a second bid in an attempt to acquire Axcelis, this time for $6 per share, but the board again rejects SHI's proposal, feeling that it undervalues the corporation and is not within the best interests of Axcelis and its shareholders. Later that year, Axcelis receives

a letter from Westland requesting seven categories of books and records from Axcelis and its subsidiaries. Westland's purpose for this demand is to investigate Axcelis's board members' compliance with their fiduciary duty to Axcelis and its shareholders as related to SHI's acquisition proposals. Axcelis is refusing to comply with this demand. Westland is now asking the Delaware Court of Chancery to order Axcelis to provide it access to the books and records. Should the Delaware Court of Chancery grant Westland access to this information?

5. VeriFone Holdings, a Delaware corporation with its principal place of business in San Jose, California, designs, markets, and services electronic payment transaction systems. In 2006, VeriFone acquired Lipman Electronic Engineering Ltd. In 2007, VeriFone publicly announced that it would restate its reported earnings for the prior three fiscal quarters. Earnings had been materially overstated due to accounting and valuation errors made while Lipman's inventory systems were being integrated with VeriFone's. After that restatement announcement, VeriFone's stock price dropped more than 45 percent. The next day, Charles King, a VeriFone shareholder, filed a derivative action on behalf of VeriFone against certain of its officers and board of directors, asserting various federal securities fraud claims. A few months later, King demanded that VeriFone permit him to inspect the company's books and records, including VeriFone's Audit Committee Report, which contained the results of an internal investigation of VeriFone's accounting and financial controls conducted after the 2007 restatement announcement. VeriFone refused to grant to King access to the Audit Report on the grounds he lacked a proper purpose under Delaware law because he had previously elected to bring a derivative action. Was VeriFone correct?

6. Furman Nutrients Inc. is a producer of food additives for commercial and consumer use. It is dominant in its field for a number of food additives, including MSG, ETDA, lactic acid, and caramel. For each of the last 30 years, Furman has paid a quarterly dividend to its common shareholders. The annual dividend amount has averaged between 3 and 5 percent of the market price of Furman's common shares. Furman's board of directors decides to reduce the common dividend by 50 percent for the next three years, to about one-half percent of the market price of Furman's common shares. The board wants to use the cash savings to increase Furman's research and development budget as Furman attempts to identify, develop, and produce food additives that are

"more natural" and meet the "health needs and interests of our industrial and consumer users." Reducing the common share dividend will result in Furman retaining an additional $955 million of earnings and cash over a two-year period. Furman currently has retained earnings of $1.47 billion and cash of $1.26 billion. Its earnings average $610 million annually. Furman expects to spend about an additional $1.17 billion on R&D in the next four years. The board believes that the R&D expenditures will allow Furman to maintain its leadership position in the industry and maintain or increase profits in the long run, a decision backed by a report by Furman's outside financial consultants. Furman's minority shareholders sue to force the board of directors to declare a larger dividend. Will their action be successful?

7. In 2014, General Motors Company recalled nearly 29 million cars worldwide due to faulty ignition switches, which could shut off the engine during driving and thereby prevent the airbags from inflating. GM has linked 13 deaths and 31 crashes to the defective ignition switches. It counts only incidents that resulted in head-on collisions in which the airbags did not deploy. It does not include, for example, an incident where after a car's ignition switch failed, the car spun out, hydroplaned, hit an oncoming vehicle, and rolled off the road, dropping 15 feet into a creek. Also, in a collision in which two young women in a Chevrolet Cobalt were killed when the ignition switch shut off the engine, GM counts the death of only the woman in the front seat because the death of the woman in the back seat was not caused by the failure of the airbag to deploy. By contrast, Reuters published an analysis concluding that the faulty switches were responsible for 153 deaths.

GM was expected to charge $1.2 billion against its second quarter 2014 earnings as a result of its recalls, a charge that could be increased as investigations continued. The fault had been known to GM for at least a decade prior to the recall. GM shareholders who bought GM shares before the ignition switch problem was disclosed have claimed that they were deceived by GM and its management when they purchased their GM shares. They allege that they would not have bought their shares or would have paid less for the shares had the switch problem been disclosed. What type of legal action have the shareholders brought against GM and its management?

Other long-time shareholders of GM, who have been shareholders before and during the recalls, claim that GM suffered significant damages, including the

$1.2 billion charge against earnings, because GM's management and employees hid the ignition switch problem, resulting in GM's liability for recalls, as well as legal responsibility for the deaths and injuries to drivers and passengers. What type of legal action have the long-time shareholders brought against GM's management? With what processes must the shareholders comply to ensure that the lawsuit may continue?

8. Blue Co., a small company that manufactures engine overheating sensors for all-terrain vehicles, intends to issue a dividend to its shareholders. The board of directors is seeking guidance as to what dividend amount is legal under the MBCA. These are the facts presented to the board: Blue Co. has $27,000 in excess liquidity that it does not need to pay its currently maturing obligations. It has assets of $200,000 and liabilities of $160,000. It has one class of common shareholders and one class of preferred shareholders. Its one class of preferred shareholders has a liquidation preference of $15,000. Based on these facts, under the MBCA, what is the maximum cash dividend Blue Co. can distribute to its shareholders?

9. Water Works was a closely held corporation operating an automatic car wash in Wisconsin Rapids. Its 204 shares were issued to Duane and Sharon Jorgensen; their daughter, Doreen Barber, and her husband, James; and two family friends, Gary and Mary Tesch. Each received 34 shares, and each was a director. Duane was president; Sharon, Gary, and James were vice presidents; Mary was treasurer; and Doreen was secretary. The corporation's written business plan stated that Duane would be in charge of management and that the six shareholders would be permanent directors. An oral agreement of shareholders stated that Duane would oversee management as long as he lived. Each shareholder received weekly payments from the corporation, the amount of which was determined by the shareholders' agreement. In 1995, Duane discovered that some of the officers and directors were engaging in illegal activity on property owned by the corporation and using the corporation's property for their own personal benefit. When Duane demanded the activities stop, the Barbers and Tesches removed the Jorgensens from the board of directors and stopped making payments to them. The Jorgensens sued the Barbers and Tesches for breach of fiduciary duty. The Barbers and Tesches claimed they owed fiduciary duties only to the corporation and, therefore, the Jorgensens, as shareholders, could not sue in their own names. Were they right?

10. H. F. Ahmanson & Co. was the controlling share-holder of United Savings and Loan Association. There was very little trading in the Association's shares, however. To create a public market for their shares, Ahmanson and a few other shareholders of the Association incorporated United Financial Corporation and exchanged each of their Association shares for United shares. United then owned more than 85 percent of the shares of the Association. The minority shareholders of the Association were not given an opportunity to exchange their shares. United made two public offerings of its shares. As a result, trading in United shares was very active, while sales of Association shares decreased to half of the formerly low level, with United as virtually the only purchaser. United offered to purchase Association shares from the minority shareholders for $1,100 per share. Some of the minority shareholders accepted this offer. At that time, the shares held by the majority share-holders were worth $3,700. United also caused the Association to decrease its dividend payments. Has Ahmanson done anything wrong?

11. Mary Brodie, Robert Jordan, and David Barbuto were the only shareholders of Malden Centerless Grinding Co., a Massachusetts corporation. Beginning in 1984, each held one-third of the shares of the corporation, and all three served as directors. Mary's deceased husband, Walter Brodie, was one of the founding members of the company and served as its president from 1979 to 1992. Walter received compensation from the company prior to 1992, when he was voted out as president and director of Malden. Walter was paid a consultant's fee in 1994 and 1995. Neither Walter nor Mary received any compensation or other money from the corporation after 1995. When Walter died in 1997, Mary inherited his one-third interest in Malden. In July 1997, Mary attended a Malden shareholders' meeting, at which she nominated herself as a director; she was not elected because Barbuto and Jordan voted against her. At this same meeting, Mary asked Barbuto and Jordan to perform a valuation of the company so that she could value her shares, but the valuation was never performed. In 1998, Mary sued Barbuto and Jordan, claiming that they breached a fiduciary duty by freezing her out of the corporation. Will the court find that Barbuto and Jordan breached a fiduciary duty and oppressed Mary? If so, how might the court rectify the situation?

12. Sutter Ranching Corporation, an Oklahoma farming and ranching family corporation, had a provision in its articles of incorporation that provided the corporation could take action to dissolve only with the approval of 75 percent or more of the outstanding shares of the corporation. After a dispute with his sisters, Owen Sutter, owner of 30 percent of the company, sought a judicial dissolution of the corporation on the grounds of shareholder dissension and oppression by his sisters, the majority shareholders. The sisters argued that Owen could not seek a judicial dissolution because his ownership of the corporation failed to meet the 75 percent minimum for dissolution by action of the shareholders. Did the court agree with the sisters?

Securities Regulation

Y ou are the CEO of L'Malle LLC, a nonpublic company that builds and manages upscale shopping malls. L'Malle plans to raise $4,400,000 for construction of L'Malle's newest shopping center complex, Grande L'Malle Geneva (GLG). In an effort to avoid the application of the Securities Act of 1933, L'Malle's CFO has proposed that the company issue 22 profit participation plans (PPPs) to two insurance companies, four mutual funds, and 16 individual investors. Under the PPPs, each owner will contribute $200,000 cash to finance the construction of GLG and receive 3 percent of the profits generated by GLG. L'Malle will be the exclusive manager of GLG, making all decisions regarding its construction and operation, for which L'Malle will receive a fee equal to 34 percent of GLG's profits.

- Are the PPPs securities under the Securities Act of 1933?
- If the PPPs are securities, may L'Malle sell them pursuant to a registration exemption from the Securities Act of 1933 under Regulation A, Rule 504, or Rule 506?

L'Malle decides to sell the PPPs directly to investors by making a Regulation A offering. As CEO, you will accompany L'Malle's CFO and communications vice president when they visit prospective investors. During those visits, you and the other L'Malle executives will present copies of the offering circular to prospective investors and make oral reports about the offering, GLG, and L'Malle's business and prospects. You will also answer the investors' questions about L'Malle and GLG.

- Should you be fearful about having liability to the investors under Section 12(a)(2) of the 1933 Act and Rule 10b–5 of the Securities Exchange Act of 1934?

L'Malle decides to make a public offering of its common shares by registering the offering under the Securities Act of 1933 and complying with the requirements of Section 5 of the 1933 Act. The shares will be sold by a firm commitment underwriting.

- Under what legal conditions may L'Malle release earnings reports and make other normal communications with its shareholders and other investors?
- After L'Malle has filed its 1933 Act registration statement with the Securities and Exchange Commission and before the SEC has declared the registration statement effective, under what legal conditions may you (the CEO) and L'Malle's CFO conduct a road show where you pitch the shares to mutual fund investment managers in several cities?
- During that waiting period, may L'Malle post its preliminary prospectus and have an FAQ page for prospective investors at the offering's website?
- After the SEC has declared the registration statement effective, under what legal conditions may L'Malle confirm the sale of shares to an investor?
- During that post-effective period, under what legal conditions may L'Malle direct prospective investors from the offering's website to L'Malle's corporate website, where investors may obtain additional information about L'Malle?

MODERN SECURITIES REGULATION AROSE from the rubble of the great stock market crash of October 1929. After the crash, Congress studied its causes and discovered several common problems in securities transactions, the most important ones being:

1. Investors lacked the necessary information to make intelligent decisions whether to buy, sell, or hold securities.

2. Disreputable sellers of securities made outlandish claims about the expected performance of securities and sold securities in nonexistent companies.

Faced with these perceived problems, Congress chose to require securities sellers to disclose the information that investors need to make intelligent investment decisions. Congress found that investors are able to make intelligent investment decisions if they are given sufficient information about the company whose securities they are to buy. This **disclosure scheme** assumes that investors need assistance from government in acquiring information but that they need no help in evaluating information.

Purposes of Securities Regulation

 Understand why and demonstrate how the law regulates issuances and issuers of securities.

To implement its disclosure scheme, in the early 1930s Congress passed two major statutes, which are the hub of federal securities regulation in the United States today. These two statutes, the **Securities Act of 1933** and the **Securities Exchange Act of 1934**, have three basic purposes:

1. To require the disclosure of meaningful information about a security and its issuer to allow investors to make intelligent investment decisions.

2. To impose liability on those persons who make inadequate and erroneous disclosures of information.

3. To regulate insiders, professional sellers of securities, securities exchanges, and other self-regulatory securities organizations.

The crux of the securities acts is to impose on issuers of securities, other sellers of securities, and selected buyers of securities the affirmative duty to disclose important information, even if they are not asked by investors to make the disclosures. By requiring disclosure, Congress hoped to restore investor confidence in the securities markets. Congress wanted to bolster investor confidence in the honesty of the stock market and thus encourage more investors to invest in securities. Building investor confidence would increase capital formation and, it was hoped, help the American economy emerge from the Great Depression of the 1930s.

Congress has reaffirmed the purposes of the securities law many times since the 1930s by passing laws that expand investor protections. Most recent are the enactments of the Sarbanes–Oxley Act of 2002 and the Dodd–Frank Wall Street Reform and Consumer Protection Act of 2010. The Sarbanes–Oxley Act was a response to widespread misstatements and omissions in corporate financial statements, which led to accounting fraud scandals at high-profile public companies. Many public investors lost their life savings in the collapses of firms like Enron and WorldCom, while insiders profited. As we learned in Chapters 4 and 43 and will learn in this chapter and Chapter 46, the Sarbanes–Oxley Act imposes duties on corporations, their officers, and their auditors and provides for a Public Company Accounting Oversight Board to establish auditing standards.

The Dodd–Frank Act, enacted in the wake of the financial crisis of 2007, mostly regulates banks and consumer credit institutions. While this subject matter is outside the scope of the chapter, what is covered here and in Chapters 43 and 46 are the Dodd–Frank Act's provisions that impose new powers and responsibilities on the Securities and Exchange Commission, increase regulation of brokers and investment advisers, regulate asset-backed securities, require shareholder approval of executive compensation, and strengthen shareholder rights in director elections.

LOG ON

https://lawblogs.uc.edu/sld/

The Securities Lawyer's Deskbook is maintained by the Robert S. Marx Law Library at the University of Cincinnati College of Law. You can find the text of all the federal securities statutes and SEC regulations.

Securities and Exchange Commission

The Securities and Exchange Commission (SEC) was created by the 1934 Act. Its responsibility is to administer the 1933 Act, 1934 Act, and other securities statutes. Like other federal administrative agencies, the SEC has legislative, executive, and judicial functions. Its legislative branch promulgates rules and regulations; its executive branch brings enforcement actions against alleged violators of the securities statutes and their rules and regulations; its judicial branch decides whether a person has violated the securities laws.

SEC Actions   The SEC is empowered to investigate violations of the 1933 Act and 1934 Act and to hold hearings to determine whether the acts have been violated. Such hearings are held before an administrative law judge (ALJ), who is an employee of the SEC. The administrative law judge is a finder of both fact and law. Decisions of the ALJ are reviewed by the commissioners of the SEC. Decisions of the commissioners are appealed to the U.S. Court of Appeals. Most SEC actions are not litigated. Instead, the SEC issues consent orders, by which the defendant promises not to violate the securities laws in the future but does not admit to having violated them in the past.

The SEC has the power to impose civil penalties (fines) up to $500,000 and to issue *cease and desist orders*. A cease and desist order directs a defendant to stop violating the securities laws and to desist from future violations. Nonetheless, the SEC does not have the power to issue injunctions; only courts may issue injunctions. The 1933 Act and the 1934 Act empower the SEC only to ask federal district courts for injunctions against persons who have violated or are about to violate either act. The SEC may also ask the courts to grant ancillary relief, a remedy in addition to an injunction. Ancillary relief may include, for example, the disgorgement of profits that a defendant has made in a fraudulent sale or in an illegal insider trading transaction. In recent years, the SEC's disgorgement remedy has been limited, however. The Supreme Court ruled in *Kokesh v. SEC*[1] that disgorgement is a penalty subject to a five-year statute of limitations. And the Court also held in *Liu v. SEC*[2] that when disgorgement is sought as equitable relief, it may not exceeding the wrongdoer's net profits.

---

[1]137 S. Ct. 1635 (2017).
[2]Dkt. No. 18-1501, 2020 U.S. LEXIS 3374 (June 22, 2020).

Figure 45.1   A Note on *Lucia v. SEC*

In 2018, the Supreme Court heard a case, *Lucia v. SEC*, 138 S. Ct. 2044 (2018), that challenged the very nature of the SEC's functions. Six years prior, the SEC charged Raymond Lucia with violating the antifraud provisions of the Investment Advisers Act and other SEC rules. It was alleged that Lucia, an investment professional, misled potential investors in roughly 40 different retirement-planning seminars. The case was assigned to one of the SEC's five ALJs, who was appointed by SEC staff. The ALJ heard nine days of testimony, ultimately finding that Lucia had violated the Act; he recommended Lucia pay a $300,000 fine and be barred for life from the investment industry. On appeal to the SEC, Lucia argued not only that the decision was wrong on the merits, but that the ALJ was invalidly appointed and therefore lacked authority to convene a hearing, much less issue a binding decision, in his case. The question became whether the SEC's five ALJs were "Officers of the United States" or "mere employees"; if they were officers, their appointment was subject to the Appointments Clause of the Constitution and they could not be validly appointed by SEC staff.

Justice Kagan, writing for the 6-3 majority, found that the ALJs were officers. "Far from serving temporarily or episodically, SEC ALJs 'receive[] a career appointment.' And that appointment is to a position created by statute, down to its 'duties, salary, and means of appointment.'" Justice Kagan further stated that "ALJs exercise the same 'significant discretion' when carrying out the same 'important functions' as [special trial judges in tax court, which were found to be officers under *Freytag v. Commissioner*, 501 U.S. 868 (1991)]." Accordingly, Lucia's case was remanded for a rehearing by a validly appointed ALJ. More importantly, the Court's ruling called into question the appointment of some 1,900 ALJs across various federal agencies, who have collectively heard hundreds of thousands of cases. The SEC, though, made a quick fix—it reappointed its ALJs itself (as opposed to staff doing it) and thus solved the Appointments Clause issue. What long-term effects the *Lucia* decision will have beyond the SEC remains to be seen.

To reduce the risk that a securities issuer's or other person's behavior will violate the securities law and result in an SEC action, anyone may contact the SEC's staff in advance, propose a transaction or course of action, and ask the SEC to issue a ***no-action letter***. In the no-action letter, the SEC's staff states it will take no legal action against the issuer or other person if the issuer or other person acts as indicated in the no-action letter. Issuers often seek no-action letters before making exempted offerings of securities and excluding shareholder proposals from their proxy statements, issues we discuss later in the chapter. Because a no-action letter is issued by the SEC's staff and not the commissioners, it is not binding on the commissioners. Nonetheless, issuers that comply with no-action letters rarely face SEC action.

LOG ON

www.sec.gov
You can read more about the SEC at the SEC website.

What Is a Security?

LO45-2 Define a *security* and apply the definition to a variety of contracts.

The first issue in securities regulation is the definition of a security. If a transaction involves no security, then the law of securities regulation does not apply. The 1933 Act defines the term **security** broadly:

> Unless the context otherwise requires the term "security" means any note, stock, treasury stock, security future, security-based swap, bond, debenture, evidence of indebtedness, certificate of interest or participation in any profit-sharing agreement, . . . preorganization certificate or subscription, . . . investment contract, voting trust certificate, . . . fractional undivided interest in oil, gas, or mineral rights, any put, call, straddle, option, or privilege on any security, . . . or, in general, any interest or instrument commonly known as a "security" . . . or warrant or right to subscribe to or purchase, any of the foregoing.

The 1934 Act definition of security is similar but excludes notes and drafts that mature not more than nine months from the date of issuance.

While typical securities like common shares, preferred shares, bonds, and debentures are defined as securities, the definition of a security also includes many contracts that the general public may believe are not securities. This is because the term **investment contract** is broadly defined by the courts. The Supreme Court's three-part test for an investment contract, called the *Howey* test, has been the

guiding beacon in the area for more than 50 years.[3] The *Howey* test states that an investment contract is an *investment of money* in a *common enterprise* with an expectation of *profits solely from the efforts of others*.

In the *Howey* case, the sales of plots in an orange grove along with a management contract were held to be sales of securities. The purchasers had investment motives (they intended to make a profit from, not to consume, the oranges produced by the trees). There was a common enterprise because the investors provided the capital to finance the orange grove business and shared in its earnings. The sellers, not the buyers, did all of the work needed to make the plots profitable.

In other cases, sales of limited partnership interests, Scotch whisky receipts, and restaurant franchises have been held to constitute investment contracts and, therefore, securities. Even partnership interests in an ordinary partnership have been held to be securities, when the partner is a passive investor with no meaningful control over the management of the partnership.[4]

Courts define in two ways the common enterprise element of the *Howey* test. All courts permit *horizontal commonality* to satisfy the common enterprise requirement. Horizontal commonality requires that investors' funds be pooled and that profits of the enterprise be shared pro rata by investors. Some courts accept *vertical commonality*, in which the investors are similarly affected by the efforts of the person who is promoting the investment.

Courts have used the *Howey* test to hold that some contracts with names of typical securities are not securities. The courts point out that some of these contracts possess few of the characteristics of a security. For example, in *United Housing Foundation, Inc. v. Forman*,[5] the Supreme Court held that although tenants in a cooperative apartment building purchased contracts labeled as stock, the contracts were not securities. The "stock" possessed few of the typical characteristics of stock and the economic realities of the transaction bore few similarities to those of the typical stock sale: The stock gave tenants no dividend rights or voting rights in proportion to the number of shares owned, it was not negotiable, and it could not appreciate in value. More important, tenants bought the stock not for the purpose of investment but to acquire suitable living space.

However, when investors are misled to believe that the securities laws apply because a seller sold a contract bearing both the name of a typical security and significant characteristics of that security, the securities laws do apply to the sale of the security. The application of this doctrine

---

[3]*SEC v. W. J. Howey Co.*, 328 U.S. 293 (1946).
[4]*SEC v. Shields*, 744 F.3d 633 (10th Cir. 2014).
[5]421 U.S. 837 (1975).

led to the Supreme Court's rejection of the sale-of-business doctrine, which had held that the sale of 100 percent of the shares of a corporation to a single purchaser who would manage the corporation was not a security. The rationale for the sale-of-business doctrine was that the purchaser failed to meet the third element of the *Howey* test because he expected to make a profit from his own efforts in managing the business. Today, when a business sale is affected by the sale of stock, the transaction is covered by the securities acts if the stock possesses the characteristics of stock.

In 1990, the Supreme Court further extended this rationale in *Reves v. Ernst & Young*,[6] adopting the **family resemblance test** to determine whether promissory notes were securities. The Supreme Court held that it is inappropriate to apply the *Howey* test to notes. Instead, applying the family resemblance test, the Court held that notes are presumed to be securities unless they bear a "strong family resemblance" to a type of note that is not a security.

The five characteristics of notes that are not securities are:

1. There is no recognized market for the notes.
2. The note is not part of a series of notes.
3. The buyer of the note does not need the protection of the securities laws.
4. The buyer of the note has no investment intent.
5. The buyer has no expectation that the securities laws apply to the sale of the note.

Types of notes that are not securities include consumer notes, mortgage notes, short-term notes secured by a lien on a small business, short-term notes secured by accounts receivable, and notes evidencing loans by commercial banks for current operations.

In the following case, the Supreme Court applied the family resemblance test.

---

[6]494 U.S. 56 (1990).

Nye Capital Appreciation Partners, L.L.C. v. Nemchik
483 F. App'x 1 (6th Cir. 2012)

In the mid-1990s, the Nyes began making equity investments in ProPaint Plus Automobile Repairs, Systems & Services Inc. (ProPaint), a company founded by James Johnson and Jackie Nemchik. Between December 1996 and January 1997, Nemchik hired Roy Malkin as ProPaint's chief operating officer and president. In May 1997, Randy Nye became a member of ProPaint's board of directors.

After Malkin was hired, ProPaint determined it needed capital to make the company viable and to continue business operations. Malkin, Joseph Carney, and members of ProPaint's board of directors prepared a private placement memorandum (PPM) in order to produce new investors. The PPM failed to produce new investors by March 1998, so the Nyes offered to provide an $800,000 capital infusion to ProPaint in exchange for 40 percent of ProPaint's total stock in a form substantially the same as that being offered through PPM. Pursuant to this agreement, the Nyes agreed to sell shares in Nye Capital Appreciation Partners, L.L.C. (Nye Capital), an entity the Nyes created to gather investors to make equity payments in ProPaint, and use the capital raised to invest in ProPaint. ProPaint agreed to repay the Nyes $800,000 and used the remaining capital for business activities. Between March and October 1998, the Nyes, in the name of Nye Financial Group Inc. (Nye Financial), transferred a $607,000 "loan" to ProPaint. In October 1998, the Nyes raised $223,000 through Nye Capital and invested it in shares of ProPaint stock.

ProPaint continued to suffer losses through the fall of 1998. On November 15, 1998, Malkin submitted his resignation. On December 4, 1998, Randy Nye became ProPaint's chairman and senior executive and became more involved in the day-to-day operations of ProPaint. Through his involvement, Randy Nye became aware of alleged misconduct by Malkin, and shortly after, ProPaint ceased operations and filed for bankruptcy.

The Nyes filed a complaint that asserted various claims arising out of alleged fraudulent misrepresentations that led to the loss of the money they provided ProPaint. Malkin, Nemchik, and the Johnsons then filed a motion for summary judgment to dismiss, asserting that the Nyes' claims involved the sale of securities and were time-barred. In response, the Nyes filed an opposition to the summary judgment motions. They contended that the transfer of $607,000 to ProPaint constituted a loan, not a purchase or sale of securities. They argued that the claims were not time-barred because they were subject to a longer statute of limitations applicable to common law tort claims.

However, the district court granted the motions for summary judgment of the complaint on the ground that these claims were intertwined with the sale of securities and were, therefore, time-barred by the applicable statutes of limitations and repose.

On appeal, the Nyes contended that the district court erred in determining that their claims were intertwined with the purchase or sale of securities. They argued that their $607,000 cash infusion constituted "the mere making of a loan and an issuance of a promissory note."

Alarcón, Judge

To determine whether a "note" is a security, this court applies the "family resemblance" test articulated by the United States Supreme Court in *Reves v. Ernst & Young*, 494 U.S. 56, 110 S. Ct. 945 (1990). Under this test, every note is presumed to be a security, unless it falls into one of the few enumerated categories. *Reves*, 494 U.S. at 65. It is undisputed that the $607,000 loan does not fall within an enumerated category that rebuts the presumption that a note is a security.

If a note does not bear a strong resemblance to one of the enumerated categories, then courts may still weigh the following four factors to determine whether a note should be added to the list of categories of non-securities: (1) "the motivations that would prompt a reasonable seller and buyer to enter into the transaction"; (2) "the 'plan of distribution' of the instrument"; (3) "the reasonable expectations of the investing public"; and (4) "whether some factor such as the existence of another regulatory scheme significantly reduces the risk of the instrument, thereby rendering application of the Securities Acts unnecessary." *Id*. at 66–67.

With respect to the first factor, "if the seller's purpose is to raise money for the general use of a business enterprise or to finance substantial investments and the buyer is interested primarily in the profit the note is expected to generate, the instrument is likely to be a 'security.'" The Appellees sought the cash infusion to enable ProPaint to continue operating its business. The Nyes transferred the money to acquire stock in ProPaint and to generate profit by selling stock to outside investors. Accordingly, the district court did not err in determining that the first factor weighs in favor of characterizing the loan as a security.

In applying the second factor, we look to the record to "determine whether it is an instrument in which there is 'common trading for speculation or investment.'" *Id*. However, even if an instrument is not commonly distributed, "it is clear that paradigmatic securities, such as stocks, can be offered and sold to a single person, while yet remaining securities." *Bass v. Janney Montgomery Scott, Inc.*, 210 F.3d 577, 585 (6th Cir. 2000). Here, the Appellees used the PPM to generate equity interest from the Nyes. The PPM explicitly stated that the "investment in ProPaint is speculative and should be considered only by those persons who are able to bear the economic risk and could afford a complete loss of their investment." Despite the absence of common trading for speculation or investment, this solicitation of capital in exchange for stock also weighs in favor of characterizing the Nyes' loans as securities.

The record also demonstrates that the third *Reves* factor is satisfied. The Nyes referred to the $607,000 transfer to ProPaint as a "loan" but expected to receive stock in ProPaint in exchange and to convert their "loan" into an equity investment. Randy Nye wrote to Nemchik stating that the Nyes' $800,000 capital infusion to ProPaint will "initially take the form of notes and that in exchange for this funding the investment partnership or LLC will receive 40% of ProPaint." Carney also stated in a May 14, 1998 letter to Randy Nye and others, that "if ProPaint were flush with funds, we could skip the loan step and proceed directly to the investment." He laid out the steps involved in converting the loans to equity investments and added "the sooner we get equity issued the better for ProPaint."

We reject the Nyes' assertion that the district court erroneously "relied upon an interpretation of the evidence" in determining that their loan was intended as an equity investment. The district court properly reviewed the evidence on the record and "looked to the actual nature or subject matter of the case, rather than to the form in which the action was plead." The district court did not err in determining that the nature of the transaction was a sale of security and that the investing public would have reasonably perceived it as such.

The final *Reves* factor is also inapplicable because the Nyes' loan in exchange for stock in ProPaint was not collaterized or insured. The PPM warns prospective investors that their investment would be subject to financial risks, indicating the absence of any security measures. Additionally, the Nyes have not disputed Malkin's allegation that "the notes at issue here were not protected by any other regulatory scheme and were uninsured and uncollateralized." Absent a risk-reducing factor, the fourth factor supports the characterization of the Nyes' "loans" as securities.

The balance of the four factors identified in *Reves* does not support the creation of a new category of non-securities to encompass the $607,000 loan. The district court did not err in determining that the Nyes' loans were securities and that the Nyes' claims were inextricably intertwined with the sale of securities.

Judgment AFFIRMED.

Securities Act of 1933

 LO45-1 Understand why and demonstrate how the law regulates issuances and issuers of securities.

The Securities Act of 1933 (1933 Act) is concerned primarily with public distributions of securities. That is, the 1933 Act regulates the sale of securities while they are passing from the hands of the issuer into the hands of public investors. An issuer selling securities publicly must make necessary disclosures at the time the issuer sells the securities to the public.

The 1933 Act has two principal regulatory components: (1) registration provisions and (2) liability provisions. The registration requirements of the 1933 Act are designed to give investors the information they need to make intelligent decisions whether to purchase securities when an issuer sells its securities to the public. The various liability provisions in the 1933 Act impose liability on sellers of securities for misstating or omitting facts of material significance to investors.

Registration of Securities under the 1933 Act

The Securities Act of 1933 is primarily concerned with protecting investors when securities are sold by an issuer to investors. That is, the 1933 Act regulates the process during which issuers offer and sell their securities to investors, primarily public investors.

Therefore, the 1933 Act requires that *every* offering of securities be registered with the SEC prior to any offer or sale of the securities, unless the offering or the securities are exempt from registration. That is, an issuer and its underwriters may not offer or sell securities unless the securities are registered with the SEC or exempt from registration. Over the next few pages, we will cover the registration process. Then the exemptions from registration will be addressed.

 LO45-3 Comply with the communication rules that apply to a public offering of securities.

Mechanics of a Registered Offering When an issuer makes a decision to raise money by a public offering of securities, the issuer needs to obtain the assistance of securities market professionals. The issuer will contact a managing underwriter, the primary person assisting the issuer in selling the securities. The managing underwriter

will review the issuer's operations and financial statements and reach an agreement with the issuer regarding the type of securities to sell, the offering price, and the compensation to be paid to the underwriters. The issuer and the managing underwriter will determine what type of underwriting to use.

In a *standby underwriting*, the underwriters obtain subscriptions from prospective investors, but the issuer sells the securities only if there is sufficient investor interest in the securities. The underwriters receive warrants—options to purchase the issuer's securities at a bargain price—as compensation for their efforts. The standby underwriting is typically used only to sell common shares to existing shareholders pursuant to a preemptive rights offering.

With a *best efforts underwriting*, the underwriters are merely agents making their best efforts to sell the issuer's securities. The underwriters receive a commission for their selling efforts. The best efforts underwriting is used when an issuer is not well established and the underwriter is unwilling to risk being unable to sell the securities.

The classic underwriting arrangement is a *firm commitment underwriting*. Here, the managing underwriter forms an underwriting group and a selling group. The underwriting group agrees to purchase the securities from the issuer at a discount from the public offering price—for example, 25 cents per share below the offering price. The selling group agrees to buy the securities from the underwriters also at a discount—for example, $12\frac{1}{2}$ cents per share below the offering price. Consequently, the underwriting and selling groups bear much of the risk with a firm commitment underwriting, but they also stand to make the most profit under such an arrangement.

Securities Offerings on the Internet Increasingly, issuers are using the Internet to make public securities offerings, especially initial public offerings (IPOs) of companies' securities. The Internet provides issuers and underwriters the advantage of making direct offerings to all investors simultaneously—that is, selling directly to investors without the need for a selling group. The first Internet securities offering that was approved by the SEC was a firm commitment underwriting. Internet offerings have increased dramatically since 1998. The Internet is likely to become the dominant medium for marketing securities directly to investors.

Registration Statement and Prospectus

The 1933 Act requires the issuer of securities to register the securities with the SEC before the issuer or underwriters may offer or sell the securities. Registration requires filing a *registration statement* with the SEC. Historical and current data about the issuer, its business lines and the competition it faces, the material risks of the business, material litigation, its officers' and directors' experience and compensation, a description of the securities to be offered, the amount and price of the securities, the manner in which the securities will be sold, the underwriter's compensation for assisting in the sale of the securities, and the issuer's use of the proceeds of the issuance, among other information, must be included in the registration statement prepared by the issuer of the securities with the assistance of the managing underwriter, securities lawyers, and independent accountants. Generally, the registration statement must include audited balance sheets as of the end of each of the two most recent fiscal years, in addition to audited income statements and audited statements of changes in financial position for each of the last three fiscal years.

The registration statement becomes effective after it has been reviewed by the SEC. The 1933 Act provides that the registration statement becomes effective automatically on the 20th day after its filing, unless the SEC delays or advances the effective date.

The **prospectus** is the basic selling document of an offering registered under the 1933 Act. Almost all of the information in the registration statement must be included in the prospectus. It must be furnished to every purchaser of the registered security prior to or concurrently with the sale of the security to the purchaser. The prospectus enables an investor to base her investment decision on all of the relevant data concerning the issuer, not merely on the favorable information that the issuer may be inclined to disclose voluntarily.

Although some prospectuses are delivered in person or by mail, most issuers now transmit prospectuses through their own or the SEC's website.

LOG ON

Facebook Preliminary Prospectus
To see an example of a preliminary prospectus, a draft registration statement nicknamed a "red herring" because the SEC requires companies to print in red ink that indicates its preliminary nature, log on to the SEC's website and find the 2012 prospectus of Facebook, Inc.
https://www.sec.gov/Archives/edgar/
data/1326801/000119312512034517/d287954ds1.htm

Section 5: Timing, Manner, and Content of Offers and Sales
The 1933 Act restricts the issuer's and underwriter's ability to communicate with prospective purchasers of the securities. Section 5 of the 1933

Act states the basic rules regarding the timing, manner, and content of offers and sales. It creates three important periods of time in the life of a securities offering: (1) the pre-filing period, (2) the waiting period, and (3) the post-effective period.

The Pre-filing Period Prior to the filing of the registration statement (the pre-filing period), the issuer and any other person may *not offer or sell* the securities to be registered. The purpose of the pre-filing period is to prevent premature communications about an issuer and its securities, which may encourage an investor to make a decision to purchase the security before all the information she needs is available. The pre-filing period also marks the start of what is sometimes called the ***quiet period***, which continues for the full duration of the securities offering. A prospective issuer, its directors and officers, and its underwriters must avoid publicity about the issuer and the prospective issuance of securities during the pre-filing period and the rest of the quiet period.

Generally, statements made within 30 days of filing a registration statement are considered an attempt to presell securities during the quiet period. Such "gun jumping" is a violation of Section 5 and may result in liability to the issuer for violating securities laws, a delay of the public offering by the SEC, and a required disclosure in the prospectus of the potential securities law violations. Examples of gun jumping include press interviews, participation in investment banker–sponsored conferences, or new advertising campaigns; all are discouraged during the pre-filing period.

However, the SEC has created a number of safe harbors that allow issuers about to make public offerings to continue to release information to the public yet not violate Section 5. For example, under Rule 163A, an issuer can communicate *any* information about itself so long as it is more than 30 days prior to the filing of a registration statement and two conditions are met: (1) the issuer does not reference the upcoming securities offering and (2) the issuer takes reasonable steps to prevent dissemination of the information during the 30-day period before the registration statement is filed.

Rule 135 permits the issuer to publish a notice about a prospective offering during the pre-filing period. The notice may contain only basic information, such as the name of the issuer, the amount of the securities offered, a basic description of the securities and the offering, and the anticipated timing of the offering. It may not name the underwriters or state the price at which the securities will be offered. A Rule 135 notice is often referred to as a "tombstone" ad. See Figure 45.2.

Figure 45.2   Rule 134 Tombstone Ad

This announcement is neither an offer to sell nor solicitation of an offer to buy these securities. The offer is made only by the Prospectus. Copies of the Prospectus may be obtained in any State from only such of the underwriters as may lawfully offer these securities in compliance with the securities laws of such State.

September 14, 2005

$4,353,983,175

Google™

Google Inc.

14,759,265 Shares

Class A Common Stock

Price $295 Per Share

Morgan Stanley   Credit Suisse First Boston

Allen & Company LLC

Citigroup   JPMorgan
Lehman Brothers   UBS Investment Bank
Thomas Weisel Partners LLC   Blaylock & Company, Inc.

M.R. Beal & Company	William Blair & Company	CIBC World Markets
Capital Management Group Securities, LLC		Deutsche Bank Securities
Lazard Capital Markets	Loop Capital Markets, LLC	Needham & Company, LLC
Piper Jaffray	Siebert Capital Markets	The Williams Capital Group, L.P.

Under Rule 169, nonpublic issuers may release only factual business information of the type they have previously released, and the information must not be intended for investors or potential investors. The released information can only be intended for customers, suppliers, or other individuals, but not in their capacities as investors. The SEC will review the timing, manner, and form of the release of the factual information to ensure that it is consistent with prior practices of the issuing company.

Also, the Jumpstart Our Business Startups Act of 2012 (JOBS Act) created a host of new processes and disclosures for public offerings of "emerging growth companies," or EGCs. An EGC is defined as a company with total annual gross revenues of less than $1 billion during its most recently completed fiscal year. The JOBS Act is discussed in later parts of this chapter, but its disclosure safe harbors for EGCs in particular are significant.

Section 105(c) of the Act allows EGCs to "test the waters" for a registered offering by communicating with qualified institutional buyers and certain institutional investors to gauge their interest in a proposed offering. In order to be considered a qualified institutional buyer, one must own and invest $100 million of securities; to be an institutional accredited investor, one must have a minimum of $5 million in assets. So long as no securities are sold unless accompanied by a prospectus, EGCs can communicate without restrictions with these groups, and they do not have to notify the SEC.

The Waiting Period The waiting, or pre-effective, period is the time between the filing date and the effective date of the registration statement, when the issuer is waiting for the SEC to declare the registration statement effective. During the waiting period, Section 5 permits the securities to be *offered but not sold*. This distinction may sound odd, but think of it as the period when the securities are marketed. SEC rules allow only certain offerings to be made. Face-to-face oral offers (including personal phone calls) are allowed during the waiting period. However, written offers may be made only by a statutory prospectus, usually a ***preliminary prospectus***, or a free-writing prospectus. During the waiting period, the preliminary prospectus omits the price of the securities and the underwriter's compensation. (A final prospectus will be available after the registration statement becomes effective. It will contain the price of the securities and the underwriter's compensation.) The idea is to prohibit inappropriate "hyping" of the security before all investors have access to publicly available information so that they can make an informed investment decision.

The waiting period is part of the quiet period, but, as seen above, many safe harbors apply. Rule 169's protections are available during the waiting period, as is Section 105 of the JOBS Act for EGCs. Under Rule 168, public issuers are permitted to continue to release regularly released factual business and forward-looking information. The type of information, as well as the timing, manner, and form, must be similar to past releases by the public issuer. This safe harbor only applies to the release of such information by employees of the company who are historically responsible for providing such information to persons other than investors.

Rule 134 permits the issuer to communicate limited factual information about the offering after the preliminary prospectus is filed. A Rule 134 communication allows disclosure of the same information as that of Rule 135, plus the general business of the issuer, the price of the securities, and the names of the underwriters who are helping the issuer to sell the securities. In addition, Rule 134 requires the tombstone ad to state where a hard copy of a prospectus may be obtained or downloaded.

Finally, Section 105(a) of the JOBS Act eliminates restrictions on publishing analyst research while offerings are in progress. Under prior law, research reports by analysts, especially those participating in the underwriting of the issuer, could be deemed to be "offers" of those securities and could not be issued prior to the offer's completion. Section 105(a) allows publication of research reports about an EGC that is the subject of a proposed public offering of its securities, even if the broker or dealer that publishes the research is participating as an underwriter. Research is defined as any information, opinion, or recommendation about a company, made orally or in writing. No prospectus need accompany the research. As such, research providers are free to say just about anything they want to about an issuer, subject to the SEC's antifraud provisions.

Issuers making public offerings will typically send their CEOs and other top officers on the road to talk to securities analysts and institutional investors during the waiting period. These road shows are permissible, whether an investor attends in person or watches a webcast, provided it is a live, real-time road show to a live audience.

Road shows that are not viewed live in real time by a live audience are considered written offers but are permitted during the waiting period if they meet the requirements of what are known as ***free-writing prospectuses***. That means that issuers other than well-known seasoned issuers, those issuers with at least $700 million in public float (the value of its common shares held by

Communications and Information That an Issuer or Underwriter May Provide to the Public or to Investors during a Registered Offering

	Pre-filing Period		Waiting Period	Post-effective Period
More than 30 days prior to the filing date of the registration statement	Anytime during the pre-filing period	Less than 30 days prior to the filing date of the registration statement	After the filing date of the registration statement and before the SEC has declared the registration statement effective	After the SEC has declared the registration statement effective
• Any information about the issuer, provided the information does not reference the prospective securities offering (Rule 163A)	• Negotiations between the issuer and underwriters who are in privity of contract with the issuer • Formation of the Selling Group, if every member of the Selling Group is also a retail division of a member of the Underwriting Group (i.e., in privity of contract with the issuer) • Rule 135, Notice of a Prospective Offering • If the issuer is a nonpublic issuer, regularly released factual business information about the issuer, provided it is released at the regular time and with regular emphasis and does not reference the prospective securities offering, and is not intended for investors or potential investors (Rule 169) • If the issuer is a public issuer, regularly released factual or forward-looking information about the issuer, provided it is released at the regular time and with regular emphasis and does not reference the prospective securities offering • JOBS Act "test the waters" provisions for EGCs (Section 105(c))	• If the issuer is a well-known seasoned issuer, a free-writing prospectus that contains any information that does not conflict with the registration statement and contains a legend indicating that a prospectus will be available at the SEC website when the filing date arrives	• Formation of the Selling Group whether or not every member is also a member of the Underwriting Group (i.e., in privity of contract with the issuer) • Rule 135, Notice of a Prospective Offering • Rule 134, Tombstone Ad • Oral offers (face-to-face either in person or on the phone) • Preliminary Prospectus • If the issuer is a nonpublic issuer, regularly released factual business information about the issuer, provided it is released at the regular time and with regular emphasis, does not reference the prospective securities offering, and is not intended for investors or potential investors (Rule 169) • If the issuer is a public issuer, regularly released factual or forward-looking information about the issuer, provided it is released at the regular time and with regular emphasis and does not reference the prospective securities offering • A free-writing prospectus that contains any information that does not conflict with the registration statement, if investors have a preliminary prospectus or an e-mail with a hyperlink to the preliminary prospectus • If the issuer is a well-known seasoned issuer, a free-writing prospectus that contains any information that does not conflict with the registration statement, if it contains a legend indicating that a prospectus is available at the SEC website • Road show, if it is provided live to a live audience, the attendees have a copy of the preliminary prospectus, or it meets the requirements of a free-writing prospectus • Research reports by analysts, even if publisher is participating underwriter (Section 105(a) of JOBS Act)	• Rule 135, Notice of a Prospective Offering • Rule 134, Tombstone Ad • Oral offers (face-to-face either in person or on the phone) • Final Prospectus • Sales of securities, if a final prospectus is delivered to the buyer prior to or simultaneous with the confirmation of sale • Any written offer, if the offeree has received a final prospectus • If the issuer is a nonpublic issuer, regularly released factual business information about the issuer, provided it is released at the regular time and with regular emphasis, does not reference the prospective securities offering, and is not intended for investors or potential investors (Rule 169) • If the issuer is a public issuer, regularly released factual or forward-looking information about the issuer, provided it is released at the regular time and with regular emphasis and does not reference the prospective securities offering • A free-writing prospectus that contains any information that does not conflict with the registration statement, if investors have a final prospectus or an e-mail with a hyperlink to the final prospectus • If the issuer is a well-known seasoned issuer, a free-writing prospectus that contains any information that does not conflict with the registration statement, if it contains a legend indicating that a prospectus is available at the SEC website • Road show, if it is provided live to a live audience, the attendees have a copy of a final prospectus, or it meets the requirements of a free-writing prospectus • Section 105 of JOBS Act

Figure 45.3   Google's Gun Jumping

A well-known example of a gun-jumping violation of Section 5 was committed by Google, Inc. Sometime prior to the company's IPO of August 13, 2004, Google's founders Sergey Brin and Larry Page gave an interview to *Playboy* magazine. The interview was published in the September 2004 issue under the title "Playboy Interview: Google Guys." Not surprisingly, Brin and Page made favorable comments about their company but included no mention of the offering or the sale of securities. In fact, the statements the founders made about the tech company were innocuous, such as "people use Google because they trust us."

Nevertheless, the SEC found the interview was gun jumping under Section 5 for violating the quiet period. Although Google could have been required to buy back shares sold to investors in the IPO at the original purchase price for a period of one year following the violation, ultimately the company had to take three remedial actions: (1) revise its prospectus to include a risk factor warning that the *Playboy* interview violated Section 5, (2) include the full text of the article in the prospectus; and (3) address discrepancies between statistics reported in the article and the prospectus.

Note: More recently, Salesforce.com Inc. was forced to delay its IPO after the company and its CEO Marc Benioff were featured in a flattering *New York Times* article. The article drew SEC attention because it included statements from Benioff about his company that were not included in its registration statement.

nonaffiliates of the issuer), must provide a prospectus to investors who view an electronic road show that is not live. Such issuers must also make a copy of the electronic road show available to any investor or file a copy of the electronic road show with the SEC.

The waiting period is an important part of the regulatory scheme of the 1933 Act. It provides an investor with adequate time to judge the wisdom of buying the security during a period when he cannot be pressured to buy it. Not even a contract to buy the security may be made during the waiting period.

The Post-effective Period After the effective date (the date on which the SEC declares the registration effective), Section 5 permits the security to be *offered and also to be sold*, provided that the buyer has received a **final prospectus** (a preliminary prospectus is not acceptable for this purpose). Road shows and free-writing prospectuses may continue to be used. Other written offers not previously allowed are permitted during the post-effective period, but only if the offeree has received a final prospectus. During the post-effective period, the safe harbors of Rules 134, 135, and 168 and Section 105 of the JOBS Act continue to apply. The Concept Review provides a comparison of the three important periods of time in the life of a securities offering, as well as some of the applicable safe harbors.

Liability for Violating Section 5 Section 12(a)(1) of the 1933 Act imposes liability on any person who violates the provisions of Section 5. Liability extends to any *purchaser* to whom an illegal offer or sale was made. The purchaser's remedy is *rescission* of the purchase or damages if the purchaser has already resold the securities.

Exemptions from the Registration Requirements of the 1933 Act

 LO45-4   List and apply the Securities Act's exemptions from registration.

Complying with the registration requirements of the 1933 Act, including the restrictions of Section 5, is a burdensome, time-consuming, and expensive process. Planning and executing an issuer's first public offering may consume months and cost millions of dollars. Consequently, some issuers prefer to avoid registration when they sell securities. There are two types of exemptions from the registration requirements of the 1933 Act: *securities exemptions* and *transaction exemptions*.

Securities Exemptions   Exempt securities never need to be registered, regardless who sells the securities, how they are sold, or to whom they are sold. The following are the most important securities exemptions.[7]

---

[7]Excluded from the list of securities exemptions are the intrastate offering and small offering exemptions. Although the 1933 Act denotes them (except for the Section 4(a)(6) exemption) as securities exemptions, they are in practice transaction exemptions. An exempt security is exempt from registration forever. But when securities originally sold pursuant to an intrastate or small offering exemption are resold at a later date, the subsequent sales may have to be registered. The exemption of the earlier offering does not exempt a future offering. The SEC treats these two exemptions as transaction exemptions. Consequently, this chapter also treats them as transaction exemptions.

1. Securities issued or guaranteed by any government in the United States and its territories.

2. A note or draft that has a maturity date not more than nine months after its date of issuance.

3. A security issued by a nonprofit religious, charitable, educational, benevolent, or fraternal organization.

4. Securities issued by banks and by savings and loan associations.

5. An insurance policy or an annuity contract.

Although the types of securities listed above are exempt from the registration provisions of the 1933 Act, they are not exempt from the general antifraud provisions of the securities acts. For example, any fraud committed in the course of selling such securities can be attacked by the SEC and by the persons who were defrauded under Section 17(a) and Section 12(a)(2) of the 1933 Act and Section 10(b) of the 1934 Act.

Transaction Exemptions

The most important 1933 Act registration exemptions are the transaction exemptions. If a security is sold pursuant to a transaction exemption, that sale is exempt from registration. Subsequent sales, however, are not automatically exempt. Future sales must be made pursuant to a registration or another exemption.

The transaction exemptions are exemptions from the registration provisions. The general antifraud provisions of the 1933 Act and the 1934 Act apply to exempted and nonexempted transactions.

The most important transaction exemptions are those available to issuers of securities. These exemptions are the intrastate offering exemption, the private offering exemption, and the small offering exemptions.

Intrastate Offering Exemption

Under Section 3(a)(11), an offering of securities solely to investors in one state by an issuer resident and doing business in that state is exempt from the 1933 Act's registration requirements. The reason for the exemption is that there is little federal government interest in an offering that occurs in only one state. Although the offering may be exempt from SEC regulation, state securities law may require a registration. The expectation is that state securities regulation will adequately protect investors.

The SEC has defined the intrastate offering exemption more precisely in Rule 147 and Rule 147A. Under Rule 147, an issuer must be organized and have its principal place of business in the state where it offers and sells securities, and those securities can only be offered and sold to in-state residents. Resale of the securities is limited to persons within the state for six months.

Rule 147A is almost identical to Rule 147 except that it allows offers to be accessible to out-of-state residents, so long as sales are only made to those in-state and the company has its principal place of business in-state.

Private Offering Exemption

Section 4(a)(2) of the 1933 Act provides that the registration requirements of the 1933 Act "shall not apply to transactions by an issuer not involving any public offering." A private offering is an offering to a small number of purchasers who can protect themselves because they are wealthy or because they are sophisticated in investment matters and have access to the information that they need to make intelligent investment decisions.

To create greater certainty about what a private offering is, the SEC adopted Rule 506. Although an issuer may exempt a private offering under either the courts' interpretation of Section 4(a)(2) or Rule 506, the SEC tends to treat Rule 506 as the exclusive way to obtain the exemption.

Rule 506 Under Rule 506, which is part of Securities Act Regulation D, investors must be qualified to purchase the securities. The issuer must reasonably believe that each purchaser is either (a) an accredited investor or (b) an unaccredited investor who "has such knowledge and experience in financial and business matters that he is capable of evaluating the merits and risks of the prospective investment." Accredited investors include institutional investors (such as banks and mutual funds), wealthy investors, and high-level insiders of the issuer (such as executive officers, directors, and partners). Issuers should have purchasers sign an *investment letter* or *suitability letter* verifying that they are qualified.

An issuer may sell to no more than 35 unaccredited purchasers who have sufficient investment knowledge and experience; it may sell to an unlimited number of accredited purchasers, regardless of their investment sophistication.

Each purchaser must be given or have access to the information she needs to make an informed investment decision. For a public company making a nonpublic offering under Rule 506 (such as General Motors selling $5 billion of its notes to 25 mutual funds plus 5 other, unaccredited investors), purchasers must receive information in a form required by the 1934 Act, such as a 10-K or annual report. The issuer must provide the following audited financial statements: two years' balance sheets, three years' income statements, and three years' statements of changes in financial position.

For a nonpublic company making a nonpublic offering under Rule 506, the issuer must provide much of the same nonfinancial information required in a registered offering. A nonpublic company may, however, obtain some relief from the burden of providing audited financial statements to investors. When the amount of the issuance is $2 million or less, only one year's balance sheet need be audited. If the amount issued exceeds $2 million but not $7.5 million, only one year's balance sheet, one year's income statement, and one year's statement of changes in financial position need be audited. When the amount issued exceeds $7.5 million, the issuer must provide two years' balance sheets, three years' income statements, and three years' statements of changes in financial position. In any offering of any amount by a nonpublic issuer, when auditing would involve unreasonable effort or expense, only an audited balance sheet is needed. When a limited partnership issuer finds that auditing involves unreasonable effort or expense,

the limited partnership may use financial statements prepared by an independent accountant in conformance with the requirements of federal tax law.

Rule 506 prohibits the issuer from making any general public selling effort, unless all the purchasers are accredited, preventing the issuer from using the radio, newspapers, and television. However, offers to an individual one-on-one are permitted.

In addition, the issuer must take reasonable steps to ensure that the purchasers do not resell the securities in a manner that makes the issuance a public distribution rather than a private one. Usually, the investor must hold the security for a minimum of six months.

In the *Mark* case, the issuer failed to prove it was entitled to a private offering exemption under Rule 506. The case features the improper use of an investment or suitability letter.

Mark v. FSC Securities Corp.   870 F.2d 331 (6th Cir. 1989)

FSC Securities Corp., a securities brokerage, sold limited partnership interests in the Malaga Arabian Limited Partnership to Mr. and Mrs. Mark. A total of 28 investors purchased limited partnership interests in Malaga. All investors were asked to execute subscription documents, including a suitability or investment letter in which the purchaser stated his income level, that he had an opportunity to obtain relevant information, and that he had sufficient knowledge and experience in business affairs to evaluate the risks of the investment.

When the value of the limited partnership interests fell, the Marks sued FSC to rescind their purchase on the grounds that FSC sold unregistered securities in violation of the Securities Act of 1933. The jury held that the offering was exempt as an offering not involving a public offering. The Marks appealed.

Simpson, Judge

Section 4(2) [now 4(2)] of the Securities Act exempts from registration with the SEC "transactions by an issuer not involving any public offering." There are no hard and fast rules for determining whether a securities offering is exempt from registration under the general language of Section 4(2).

However, the "safe harbor" provision of Regulation D, Rule 506, deems certain transactions to be not involving any public offering within the meaning of Section 4(2). FSC had to prove that certain objective tests were met. These conditions include the general conditions not in dispute here, and the following specific conditions:

(i) Limitation on number of purchasers. The issuer shall reasonably believe that there are no more than thirty-five purchasers of securities in any offering under this Section.

(ii) Nature of purchasers. The issuer shall reasonably believe immediately prior to making any sale that each purchaser who is not an accredited investor either alone or with his purchaser representative(s) has such knowledge and experience in financial and business matters that he is capable of evaluating the merits and risks of the prospective investment.

In this case, we take the issuer to be the general partners of Malaga. FSC is required to offer evidence of the issuer's reasonable belief as to the nature of each purchaser. The only testimony at trial competent to establish the issuer's belief as to the nature of the purchasers was that of Laurence Leafer, a general partner in Malaga. By his own admission, he had no knowledge about any purchaser, much less any belief, reasonable or not, as to the purchasers' knowledge and experience in financial and business matters.

Q: What was done to determine if investors were, in fact, reasonably sophisticated?

A: Well, there were two things. Number one, we had investor suitability standards that had to be met. You had to have a certain income, be in a certain tax bracket, this kind of thing. Then in the subscription documents themselves, they, when they sign it, supposedly represented that they had received information necessary to make an informed investment decision, and that they were sophisticated. And if they were not, they relied on an offering representative who was.

Q: Did you review the subscription documents that came in for the Malaga offering?

A: No.

Q: So do you know whether all of the investors in the Malaga offering met the suitability and sophistication requirements?

A: I don't.

FSC also offered as evidence the Marks' executed subscription documents, as well as a set of documents in blank, to establish the procedure it followed in the Malaga sales offering. Although the Marks' executed documents may have been sufficient to establish the reasonableness of any belief the issuer may have had as to the Marks' particular qualifications, that does not satisfy Rule 506. The documents offered no evidence from which a jury could conclude the issuer reasonably believed each purchaser was suitable. Instead, all that was proved was the sale of 28 limited partnership interests, and the circumstances under which those sales were intended to have been made. The blank subscription documents simply do not amount to probative evidence, when it is the answers and information received from purchasers that determine whether the conditions of Rule 506 have been met.

Having concluded that the Malaga limited-partnership offering did not meet the registration exemption requirement of Rule 506 of Regulation D, we conclude that the Marks are entitled to the remedy of rescission.

Judgment reversed in favor of the Marks; remanded to the trial court.

Small Offering Exemptions

For example, several SEC rules and regulations permit an issuer to sell small amounts of securities and avoid registration. Section 3(b)(1) of the 1933 Act permits the SEC to exempt from registration any offering by an issuer not exceeding $5 million. The Jumpstart Our Business Startups Act (JOBS Act) amended the 1933 Act in Sections 3(b)(2) and 4(a)(6) to permit the SEC to exempt offerings up to $1 million, under some conditions. The rationale for these exemptions is that the dollar amount of the securities offered or the number of purchasers is too small for the federal government to be concerned with registration. State securities law may require registration, however.

Rule 504 SEC Rule 504 of Regulation D allows a nonpublic issuer to sell up to $5 million of securities in a 12-month period and avoid registration. Rule 504 sets no limits on the number of offerees or purchasers. The purchasers need not be sophisticated in investment matters, and the issuer need disclose information only as required by state securities law. Rule 504 permits general selling efforts, and purchasers are free to resell the securities at any time but only if the issuer either registers the securities under state securities law or sells only to accredited investors pursuant to a state securities law exemption.

Regulation A Regulation A allows issuers to offer and sell securities to the public, but with more limited disclosure requirements than generally required. The motivation behind the exemption is that smaller issuers in earlier stages of development may be able to raise money more cost-effectively.

Under Regulation A, issuers can raise money under two different tiers. Issuers are required to indicate the tier under which the offering is being conducted. Tier 1 issuers can raise up to $20 million in any 12-month period, but their offering circular must be filed with the SEC and securities regulators in the states where the offering is being conducted. The financial statements disclosed are not required to be audited. There are no limitations on who can invest or how much under Tier 1.

Tier 2 issuers can offer up to $50 million in any 12-month period, and their offering is subject to review and qualification only by the SEC, but financial statements disclosed must be independently audited. Tier 2 also limits those who can purchase securities and in what amounts. Accredited investors are not limited. Unaccredited entities are limited based on annual revenues and net assets. Unaccredited individual investors can invest up to no more than 10% of the *greater of* their annual income or net worth (excluding the value of the person's primary residence and any loans secured by the residence).

Regulation A's disclosure requirements also differ depending on the tier. Issuers relying on Tier 1 do not have ongoing reporting obligations other than filing a final report on the status of the offering. Tier 2 issuers have detailed ongoing reporting obligations for various disclosure forms. For example, an issuer must file an annual report within 120 days after the end of the fiscal year that includes audited financial statements for the year, a discussion of the company's financial results for the year, and information about the company's business and management, related-party transactions, and share ownership. Issuers that already publicly report, such as companies that are listed on a stock exchange, will be deemed to have met their Regulation A disclosure obligations by remaining current in their disclosures.

The JOBS Act and Regulation Crowdfunding

The JOBS Act authorizes the SEC to exempt from 1933 Act registration the use of crowdfunding to offer and sell securities. The intent of the JOBS Act is to make it easier for startups and small businesses to raise capital from a wider range of potential investors and to provide more investment opportunities for investors. The JOBS Act restricts crowdfunding to *emerging growth companies,* that is, those with less than $1 billion in total annual gross revenues. Investment companies, non-U.S. companies, and companies already required to file reports under the 1934 Act are not eligible to use the JOBS Act exemptions.

The JOBS Act established the foundation for a regulatory structure that would permit emerging growth companies to use crowdfunding and directed the SEC to write rules implementing the exemption. It also created a new entity—a funding portal—to allow Internet-based platforms or intermediaries to facilitate the offer and sale of securities without having to register with the SEC as brokers.

Under Regulation Crowdfunding, the regulation flowing from the JOBS Act, an issuer is limited in the amount of money it can raise to a maximum of $1 million in a 12-month period. Although there are no limits on the number of investors, individuals are only permitted over the course of a 12-month period to invest

- $2,000 or 5 percent of their annual income or net worth, whichever is greater, if both their annual income and net worth are less than $100,000 or
- 10 percent of their annual income or net worth, whichever is greater, if either their annual income or net worth is equal to or more than $100,000. During the 12-month period, these investors would not be able to purchase more than $100,000 of securities through crowdfunding.

Regulation Crowdfunding requires an issuer to file certain information with the SEC, provide it to investors and the broker-dealers or portals facilitating the crowdfunding offering, and make it available to potential investors. In its offering documents, the issuer must disclose the following:

- A description of the issuer's business and the use of the proceeds from the offering.
- Information about the issuer's officers and directors as well as owners of 20 percent or more of the issuer's equity securities.
- The price to the public of the securities being offered, the target offering amount, the deadline to reach the target offering amount, and whether the issuer will accept investments in excess of the target offering amount.
- A description of the financial condition of the issuer.

- Financial statements of the issuer that, depending on the amount offered and sold during a 12-month period, would have to be accompanied by a copy of the issuer's tax returns or reviewed or audited by an independent public accountant or auditor.

One of the key investor protections of the JOBS Act is the requirement that crowdfunding transactions take place through an SEC-registered intermediary: either a broker-dealer or a funding portal. Under Regulation Crowdfunding, the offerings occur exclusively online through a platform operated by a registered broker or a funding portal. These intermediaries, then, must

- Provide investors with educational materials.
- Take measures to reduce the risk of fraud.
- Make available information about the issuer and the offering.
- Provide communication channels to permit discussions about offerings on the platform.
- Facilitate the offer and sale of crowdfunded securities.

The regulation prohibits funding portals from offering investment advice or making recommendations, soliciting purchases or sales of securities on its website, and holding or processing investor assets. Regulation Crowdfunding also imposes certain restrictions on compensating people for solicitations but does allow issuers to make general solicitations to prospective investors.

Transaction Exemptions for Nonissuers

Although it is true that the registration provisions apply primarily to issuers and those who help issuers sell their securities publicly, the 1933 Act states that every person who sells a security is potentially subject to Section 5's restrictions on the timing of offers and sales. This highlights the most important rule of the 1933 Act: *Every transaction in securities must be registered with the SEC or be exempt from registration.*

This rule applies to every person, including the small investor who, through the New York Stock Exchange, sells securities that may have been registered by the issuer 15 years earlier. The small investor must either have the issuer register her sale of securities or find an exemption from registration that applies to the situation. Fortunately, most small investors who resell securities will have an exemption from the registration requirements of the 1933 Act. The transaction ordinarily used by these resellers is Section 4(a)(1) of the 1933 Act. It provides an exemption for "transactions by any person other than an issuer, underwriter, or dealer."

For example, if you buy GM common shares on the New York Stock Exchange, you may freely resell them without a registration. You are not an issuer (GM is). You are not a dealer (because you are not in the business of selling securities). And you are not an underwriter (because you are not helping GM distribute the shares to the public).

Application of this exemption when an investor sells shares that are already publicly traded is easy; however, it is more difficult to determine whether an investor can use this exemption when the investor sells *restricted securities*.

Sale of Restricted Securities
Restricted securities are securities issued pursuant to regulations that limit their resale. Restricted securities are supposed to be held by a purchaser unaffiliated with the issuer for at least six months if the issuer is a public company and one year if the issuer is not public. If they are sold earlier, the investor may be deemed an underwriter who has assisted the issuer in selling the securities to the general public. Consequently, both the issuer and the investor may have violated Section 5 of the 1933 Act by selling nonexempted securities prior to a registration of the securities with the SEC. As a result, all investors who purchased securities from the issuer in the exempted offering may have the remedy of rescission under Section 12(a)(1), resulting in the issuer being required to return to investors all the proceeds of the issuance.

For example, an investor buys 10,000 common shares issued by Arcom Corporation pursuant to a Rule 506 private

---

Ethics and Compliance in Action

JOBS Act: Ethics of Crowdfunding

While the intent of the JOBS Act seems laudatory—to make it easier for startups and small businesses to raise capital from a wider range of potential investors—it is not without its detractors. Critics charge that unless Congress reforms or repeals the law, securities crowdfunding is destined to do little more than separate mom-and-pop investors from their savings. Here's why:

From an investor's perspective, crowdfunding operates most like angel investing. Yet most crowdfunding investors will not act like successful angel investors, who invest in industries they know, exercise due diligence, spend time mentoring the companies they invest in, and diversify their investments. Even so, the majority of angel investments fail. Angel investors earn a profit only because the small percentage of successful companies make enough money to offset failures.

Moreover, crowdfunding's extensive registration and disclosure requirements not only poorly protect investors but also heavily regulate businesses. The SEC estimates that it would cost $39,000 in fees to accountants, lawyers, and the funding portal to raise just $100,000 and more than $150,000 to raise $1 million. Those capital costs are so high that companies would be better off financing their operations with a Master-Card or VISA. For comparison, consider that underwriting fees for large public offerings are usually under 4 percent.

Compared to the registration exemptions under Regulation D, crowdfunding is a poor alternative. Not only are Regulations D's disclosure requirements limited, but it also lets a company raise an unlimited amount of capital from an unlimited number of investors, provided those investors are accredited. That leaves only desperate companies using the crowdfunding rules, ones that cannot use better and cheaper exemptions from the registration provisions of the 1933 Act.

Against these criticisms, proponents of the JOBS Act point to the following:[8]

- Women have traditionally received venture capital funding at lower rates than men. One goal of the JOBS Act was to increase opportunities for female-led companies to raise capital. In a recent study, 28 percent of crowdfunding companies have a woman on their executive team, which is approximately double the percentage found in the traditional venture capital world.

- An additional goal of the JOBS Act was to geographically diversify entrepreneurs by providing them a way to seek venture capital without relocating to Silicon Valley. Some data show that companies from 44 different states participated in equity crowdfunding campaigns in recent years, suggesting that crowdfunding is living up to its promise of overcoming geographic constraints.

- Small and young startup companies were a particular focus of the JOBS Act. Data indicate that many crowdfunding companies were founded very recently (40 percent were under one year old *at* the time of key filings), and the median age of a crowdfunding company was 1.5 years. Crowdfunding companies are also very small, with a majority (55 percent) having three or fewer employees.

Given these competing perspectives, do you see the JOBS Act as overall positive or negative?

Would you use crowdfunding to raise equity capital for your business?

Would you invest your own money through crowdfunding?

If you were an investment adviser, would you recommend that a client invest through crowdfunding?

[8]The following commentary and data are drawn from Andrew A. Schwartz, "Crowdfunding Issuers in the United States," *Washington University Journal of Law & Policy* no. 61 (2020), pp. 155–71.

Issuer's Exemptions from the Registration Requirements of the Securities Act of 1933

	Type of Issuer	Amount of Offering	Number of Investors	Investor Qualifications
Regulation D (Rule 504)	Nonpublic issuer	$5,000,000 in a 12-month period	No limit	None

Regulation D (Rule 506)	Any issuer	No limit	• 35 unaccredited investors and
			• Unlimited accredited investors
				Issuer must reasonably believe that each investor is either
				• Accredited
				  • Institutional investors;
				  • High-level insiders;
				  • Net worth (excluding primary residence) > $1,000,000; or
				  • Income >$200,000 for an individual or $300,000 with a spouse
				• Nonaccredited
				  • Has such knowledge and experience in financial and business matters to be capable of evaluating the merits and risks of the investment (individually or with a purchaser representative)

Regulation A	Nonpublic issuer	• Tier 1 issuers: $20 million
		• Tier 2 issuers: $50 million
			No limit	• Tier 1 issuers: None
				• Tier 2 issuers:
				  • Accredited investors: None
				  • Nonaccredited *natural persons:* May invest no more than 10% of the greater of their annual income or net worth (excluding primary residence and loans secured by residence)
				  • Nonaccredited *entities:* May invest no more than 10% of the greater of revenue or net assets during most recently completed fiscal year

Regulation Crowdfunding (JOBS Act)	Nonpublic issuer	$1,000,000	No limit	Over 12-month period:
				• Annual income and net worth <$100,000
				  • May invest greater of $2,000 or 5% of annual income or net worth
				• Annual income or net worth is [greater than or equal to symbol] ≥ $100,000
				  • May invest greater of 10% of annual income or net worth
				  • Total investment capped at $100,000

Rule 147/147A	• For Rule 147, issuer organized and doing business in the investors' state • For Rule 147A, issuer doing business in the investors' state	No limit	No limit	All investors must reside in the issuer's state.

Disclosure Requirements	Solicitation Requirements	Resale Restrictions
None	Permitted, if the issuer registered the securities under state law or sold the securities only to accredited investors pursuant to a state securities exemption	No resale restrictions if the issuer registered the securities under state law or sold the securities only to accredited investors pursuant to a state securities exemption

If issuer sells only to accredited investors, the issuer must give the investors only the information requested.
 	
If issuer sells to any unaccredited investors, the issuer must give investors:
• The same nonfinancial information as required for a registered offering.
• Audited financial statements
  • Public issuer: 2 balance sheets, 3 income statements, 3 statements of changes in financial position.
  • Nonpublic issuer: if amount of securities sold is
    • ≤$2,000,000: 1 balance sheet.
    • >$2,000,000 but ≤$7,500,000: 1 balance sheet, 1 income statement, 1 statement of changes in financial position.
    • >$7,500,000: 2 balance sheets, 3 income statements, 3 statements of changes in financial position.
  • Nonpublic issuer, if auditing involves unreasonable effort or expense:
    • 1 balance sheet.
Any information given to one investor must be given to all investors.
	Not permitted, unless all purchasers are accredited	• Investors may not sell securities without registration.

The issuer must use an Offering Circular.
 	
Financial statements in the Offering Circular:
• Tier 1 issuers:
  • Need not be audited unless otherwise required
• Tier 2 issuers:
  • For nonpublic issuers, audited financials required, including 1 balance sheet, 2 income statements, 2 cash flow statements, 2 statements of shareholder equity
  • For public issuers, financials need not be audited unless otherwise required
	Permitted with some limitations	Investors may not resell in amount that exceeds 30% of the aggregate offering price of the offering in the first year
		
		Additionally, resale is restricted:
		• Tier 1 issuers:
		  • $6,000,000 in aggregate
		• Tier 2 issuers:
		  • $15,000,000 in aggregate

Issuer must file and update disclosure document, including • Description of issuer's financial condition • Financial statements	Permitted if made through SEC-registered broker-dealer or a funding portal	Investors may not sell securities for one year, with exceptions
Disclosures must comply with state law and include designation that offering is pursuant to Rule 147/147A and cannot be resold outside of issuer's state	• For Rule 147, offers can only be made to in-state investors • For Rule 147A, offers are permitted, but sales must be to in-state investors	Investors may not sell the securities outside the issuer's state for specified period.

Ethics and Compliance in Action

Section 5 of the 1933 Act and many of the exemptions from registration put severe limits on an issuer's ability to inform prospective investors during a registered or exempted offering. For example, during the quiet period of a registered offering, the SEC takes a dim view of an issuer's attempt to publicize itself and its business. Rule 506(b) of Regulation D prohibits general solicitations.

- Are those limitations consistent with the principles of a country that has a market-based economy and elevates freedom of speech to a constitutional right? Would a rights theorist support American securities law? How about a profit maximizer?
- Might a believer in justice theory view be more likely to support American law regulating issuances of securities? Whom would a justice theorist want to see protected?
- Who is the typical securities purchaser? Is it not someone from the wealthier classes of citizens? Is securities regulation welfare for the wealthy?

Note that Section 5 of the 1933 Act does not require that investors receive a preliminary prospectus during the waiting period. In fact, an issuer can completely avoid giving investors a prospectus until a sale is confirmed during the post-effective period. That means an investor may not receive a prospectus until he has made his purchase decision. Moreover, many investors find the prospectus overwhelming to read, and if they do read it, it is often couched in legalese that is difficult to understand. Finally, the prospectus mostly comprises historical information. It is more correctly a "retrospectus," not a prospectus, and contains information that is already in the marketplace. Yet professionals like auditors and investment bankers make millions of dollars by being involved in the preparation of the prospectus, which is not received by investors at the right time, not read, not readable, and not relevant to investment decisions.

- Is it ethical for professionals to profit enormously from their role of putting together a prospectus that provides little real value to investors?

offering exemption. One month later, the investor sells the securities to 40 other investors. The original investor has acted as an underwriter because he has helped Arcom distribute the shares to the public. The original investor may not use the issuer's private offering exemption because it exempted only the issuer's sale to him. As a result, both the original investor and Arcom have violated Section 5. The 40 investors who purchased the securities from the original investor—and all other investors who purchased common shares from the issuer in the Rule 506 offering—may rescind their purchases under Section 12(a)(1) of the 1933 Act, receiving from their seller the return of their investment.

SEC Rule 144 allows purchasers of restricted securities to resell the securities and not be deemed underwriters. The resellers must hold the securities for at least six months if the securities issuer is a public company and for one year if the issuer is nonpublic, after which the investors may sell all or part of the restricted securities. After the passage of those time periods, investors not affiliated with the issuer may sell all or part of the restricted securities they hold. For investors affiliated with the issuers, such as an officer or director, the rules are more complex. In any three-month period, the affiliated reseller may sell only a limited number of securities—the greater of 1 percent of the outstanding securities or the average weekly volume of trading. The reseller must file a notice (Form 144) with the SEC.

Consequence of Obtaining a Securities or Transaction Exemption
When an issuer has obtained an exemption from the registration provisions of the

1933 Act, the Section 5 limits on when and how offers and sales may be made do not apply. Consequently, Section 12(a)(1)'s remedy of rescission or damages is unavailable to an investor who has purchased securities in an exempt offering.

When an issuer has attempted to comply with a registration exemption and has failed to do so, any offer or sale of securities by the issuer may violate Section 5. Because the issuer has offered or sold nonexempted securities prior to filing a registration statement with the SEC, any purchaser may sue the issuer under Section 12(a)(1) of the 1933 Act.

Although the registration provisions of the 1933 Act do not apply to an exempt offering, the antifraud provisions of the 1933 Act and 1934 Act, which are discussed later, are applicable. For example, when an issuer gives false information to a purchaser in a Rule 504 offering, the issuer may have violated the antifraud provisions of the two acts. The purchaser may obtain damages from the issuer under the antifraud rules even though the transaction is exempt from registration.

Liability Provisions of the 1933 Act

 LO45-5 Engage in behavior that avoids liability under the federal securities laws.

To deter fraud, deception, and manipulation and to provide remedies to the victims of such practices, Congress included a number of liability provisions in the Securities Act of 1933.

Liability for Defective Registration Statements

Section 11 of the 1933 Act provides civil liabilities for damages when a 1933 Act registration statement on its effective date misstates or omits a material fact. A purchaser of securities issued pursuant to the defective registration statement may sue certain classes of persons that are listed in Section 11—the issuer, its chief executive officer, its chief accounting officer, its chief financial officer, the directors, other signers of the registration statement, the underwriter, and experts who contributed to the registration statement (such as auditors who issued opinions regarding the financial statements or lawyers who issued an opinion concerning the tax aspects of a limited partnership). The purchaser's remedy under Section 11 is for damages caused by the misstatement or omission. Damages are presumed to be equal to the difference between the purchase price of the securities less the price of the securities at the time of the lawsuit.

Section 11 is a radical liability section for three reasons. First, reliance is usually not required; that is, the purchaser need not show that she relied on the misstatement or omission in the registration statement. In fact, the purchaser need not have read the registration statement or have seen it. Second, privity is not required; that is, the purchaser need not prove that she purchased the securities from the defendant. All she has to prove is that the defendant is in one of the classes of persons liable under Section 11. Third, the purchaser need not prove that the defendant negligently or intentionally misstated or omitted a material fact. In other words, investors are not required to show scienter. However, defendant who otherwise would be liable under Section 11 may escape liability by proving that he exercised due diligence.

Section 11 Defenses A defendant can escape liability under Section 11 by proving that the purchaser knew of the misstatement or omission when she purchased the security. In addition, a defendant may raise the *due diligence defense*. It is the more important of the two defenses.

Any defendant except the issuer may escape liability under Section 11 by proving that he acted with due diligence in determining the accuracy of the registration statement.

CONCEPT REVIEW

Due Diligence Defenses under Section 11 of the 1933 Act

	For Expertised Portion of the Registration Statement	For Nonexpertised Portion of the Registration Statement
Expert Liable only for the expertised portion of the registration statement contributed by the expert. Examples: Auditor that issues an audit opinion regarding financial statements Geologist that issues an opinion regarding mineral reserves Lawyer that issues a tax opinion regarding the tax deductibility of losses	After a reasonable investigation, had reason to believe and did believe that there were no misstatements or omissions of material fact in the expertised portion of the registration statement contributed by the expert.	Not liable for this portion of the registration statement.
Nonexpert Liable for the entire registration statement. Examples: Directors of the issuer CEO, CFO, and CAO of the issuer Underwriters who assist in the sale of the securities and help prepare the registration statement	Had no reason to believe and did not believe that there were any misstatements or omissions of material fact in the expertised portions of the registration statement.	After a reasonable investigation, had reason to believe and did believe that there were no misstatements or omissions of material fact in the nonexpertised portion of the registration statement.

The due diligence defense basically requires the defendant to prove that he was not negligent. The exact defense varies, however, according to the class of defendant and the portion of the registration statement that is defective. Most defendants must prove that after a *reasonable investigation* they had *reasonable grounds to believe* and *did believe* that the registration statement was true and contained no omission of material fact.

Experts need to prove due diligence only in respect to the parts that they have contributed. For example, independent auditors must prove due diligence in ascertaining the accuracy of financial statements for which they issue opinions. Due diligence requires that an auditor at least comply with generally accepted auditing standards (GAAS). Experts are those who issue an opinion regarding information in the registration statement. For example, auditors of financial statements are experts under Section 11 because they issue opinions regarding the ability of the financial statements to present fairly the financial position of the companies they have audited. A geologist who issues an opinion regarding the amount of oil reserves held by an energy company is a Section 11 expert if her opinion is included in a registration statement filed by the limited partnership.

Nonexperts meet their due diligence defense for parts contributed by experts if they had no reason to believe and did not believe that the expertised parts misstated or omitted any material fact. This defense does not require the nonexpert to investigate the accuracy of expertised portions, unless something alerted the nonexpert to problems with the expertised portions.

Due Diligence Meeting Officers, directors, underwriters, accountants, and other experts attempt to reduce their Section 11 liability by holding a due diligence meeting at the end of the waiting period, just prior to the effective date of a registration statement. At the due diligence meeting, the participants obtain assurances and demand proof from each other that the registration statement contains no misstatements or omissions of material fact. If it appears from the meeting that there are inadequacies in the investigation of the information in the registration statement, the issuer will delay the effective date until an appropriate investigation is undertaken.

The *BarChris* case is the most famous case construing the due diligence defense of Section 11.

Escott v. BarChris Construction Corp.   283 F. Supp. 643 (S.D.N.Y. 1968)

BarChris Construction Corporation was in the business of constructing bowling centers. With the introduction of automatic pinsetters in 1952, there was a rapid growth in the popularity of bowling, and BarChris's sales increased from $800,000 in 1956 to more than $9 million in 1960. By 1960, it was building about 3 percent of the lanes constructed, while Brunswick Corporation and AMF were building 97 percent. BarChris contracted with its customers to construct and equip bowling alleys for them. Under the contracts, a customer was required to make a small down payment in cash. After the alleys were constructed, customers gave BarChris promissory notes for the balance of the purchase price. BarChris discounted the notes with a "factor," an intermediary agent that finances receivables. The factor kept part of the face value of the notes as a reserve until the customer paid the notes. BarChris was obligated to repurchase the notes if the customer defaulted.

In 1960, BarChris offered its customers an alternative financing method in which BarChris sold the interior of a bowling alley to a factor, James Talcott Inc. Talcott then leased the alley either to a BarChris customer (Type A financing) or to a BarChris subsidiary that then subleased to the customer (Type B financing). Under Type A financing, BarChris guaranteed 25 percent of the customer's obligation under the lease. With Type B financing, BarChris guaranteed 100 percent of its subsidiary's lease obligations. Under either financing method, BarChris made substantial expenditures before receiving payment from customers and, therefore, experienced a constant need of cash.

In early 1961, BarChris decided to issue debentures and to use part of the proceeds to help its cash position. In March 1961, BarChris filed with the SEC a registration statement covering the debentures. The registration statement became effective on May 16. The proceeds of the offering were received by BarChris on May 24, 1961. By that time, BarChris had difficulty collecting from some of its customers, and other customers were in arrears on their payments to the factors of the discounted notes. Due to overexpansion in the bowling alley industry, many BarChris customers failed. On October 29, 1962, BarChris filed a petition for bankruptcy. On November 1, it defaulted on the payment of interest on the debentures.

Escott and other purchasers of the debentures sued BarChris and its officers, directors, and auditors, among others, under Section 11 of the Securities Act of 1933. BarChris's registration statement contained material misstatements and omitted material facts. It overstated current assets by $609,689 (15.6 percent), sales by $653,900 (7.7 percent), and earnings per share by 10 cents (15.4 percent) in the 1960 balance sheet and income statement audited by Peat, Marwick, Mitchell & Co. The registration *statement also understated BarChris's contingent liabilities by $618,853 (42.8 percent) as of April 30, 1961. It overstated gross profit for the first quarter of 1961 by $230,755 (92 percent) and sales for the first quarter of 1961 by $519,810 (32.1 percent). The March 31, 1961, backlog was overstated by $4,490,000 (186 percent). The 1961 figures were not audited by Peat, Marwick.*

In addition, the registration statement reported that prior loans from officers had been repaid but failed to disclose that officers had made new loans to BarChris totaling $386,615. BarChris had used $1,160,000 of the proceeds of the debentures to pay old debts, a use not disclosed in the registration statement. BarChris's potential liability of $1,350,000 to factors due to customer delinquencies on factored notes was not disclosed. The registration statement represented BarChris's contingent liability on Type B financings as 25 percent instead of 100 percent. It misrepresented the nature of BarChris's business by failing to disclose that BarChris was already engaged and was about to become more heavily engaged in the operation of bowling alleys, including one called Capitol Lanes, as a way of minimizing its losses from customer defaults.

Trilling, BarChris's controller, signed the registration statement. Auslander, a director, signed the registration statement. Peat, Marwick consented to being named as an expert in the registration statement. All three would be liable to Escott unless they could meet the due diligence defense of Section 11.

McLean, District Judge

The question is whether Trilling, Auslander, and Peat, Marwick have proved their due diligence defenses. The position of each defendant will be separately considered.

Trilling

Trilling was BarChris's controller. He signed the registration statement in that capacity. Trilling entered BarChris's employ in October 1960. He was Kircher's [BarChris's treasurer] subordinate. When Kircher asked him for information, he furnished it.

Trilling was not a member of the executive committee. He was a comparatively minor figure in BarChris. The description of BarChris's management in the prospectus does not mention him. He was not considered to be an executive officer.

Trilling may well have been unaware of several of the inaccuracies in the prospectus. But he must have known of some of them. As a financial officer, he was familiar with BarChris's finances and with its books of account. He knew that part of the cash on deposit on December 31, 1960, had been procured temporarily by Russo [BarChris's executive vice president] for window-dressing purposes. He knew that BarChris was operating Capitol Lanes in 1960. He should have known, although perhaps through carelessness he did not know at the time, that BarChris's contingent liability on Type B lease transactions was greater than the prospectus stated. In the light of these facts, I cannot find that Trilling believed the entire prospectus to be true.

But even if he did, he still did not establish his due diligence defenses. He did not prove that as to the parts of the prospectus expertised by Peat, Marwick he had no reasonable ground to believe that it was untrue. He also failed to prove, as to the parts of the prospectus not expertised by Peat, Marwick, that he made a reasonable investigation which afforded him a reasonable ground to believe that it was true. As far as appears, he made no investigation. He did what was asked of him and assumed that others would properly take care of supplying accurate data as to the other aspects of the company's business. This would have

been well enough but for the fact that he signed the registration statement. As a signer, he could not avoid responsibility by leaving it up to others to make it accurate. Trilling did not sustain the burden of proving his due diligence defenses.

Auslander

Auslander was an outside director, i.e., one who was not an officer of BarChris. He was chairman of the board of Valley Stream National Bank in Valley Stream, Long Island. In February 1961, Vitolo [BarChris's president] asked him to become a director of BarChris. In February and early March 1961, before accepting Vitolo's invitation, Auslander made some investigation of BarChris. He obtained Dun & Bradstreet reports that contained sales and earnings figures for periods earlier than December 31, 1960. He caused inquiry to be made of certain of BarChris's banks and was advised that they regarded BarChris favorably. He was informed that inquiry of Talcott had also produced a favorable response.

On March 3, 1961, Auslander indicated his willingness to accept a place on the board. Shortly thereafter, on March 14, Kircher sent him a copy of BarChris's annual report for 1960. Auslander observed that BarChris's auditors were Peat, Marwick. They were also the auditors for the Valley Stream National Bank. He thought well of them.

Auslander was elected a director on April 17, 1961. The registration statement in its original form had already been filed, of course without his signature. On May 10, 1961, he signed a signature page for the first amendment to the registration statement which was filed on May 11, 1961. This was a separate sheet without any document attached. Auslander did not know that it was a signature page for a registration statement. He vaguely understood that it was something "for the SEC."

At the May 15 directors' meeting, however, Auslander did realize that what he was signing was a signature sheet to a registration statement. This was the first time that he had appreciated the fact. A copy of the registration statement in its earlier form as amended on May 11, 1961, was passed around at the meeting. Auslander glanced at it briefly. He did not read it thoroughly. At the May 15 meeting, Russo and Vitolo stated that everything was in order and that the prospectus was correct. Auslander believed this statement.

In considering Auslander's due diligence defenses, a distinction must be drawn between the expertised and nonexpertised portions of the prospectus. As to the former, Auslander knew that Peat, Marwick had audited the 1960 figures. He believed them to be correct because he had confidence in Peat, Marwick. He had no reasonable ground to believe otherwise.

As to the nonexpertised portions, however, Auslander is in a different position. He seems to have been under the impression that Peat, Marwick was responsible for all the figures. This impression was not correct, as he would have realized if he had read the prospectus carefully. Auslander made no investigation of the accuracy of the prospectus. He relied on the assurance of Vitolo and Russo, and upon the information he had received in answer to his inquiries back in February and early March. These inquiries were general ones, in the nature of a credit check. The information which he received in answer to them was also general, without specific reference to the statements in the prospectus, which was not prepared until some time thereafter.

It is true that Auslander became a director on the eve of the financing. He had little opportunity to familiarize himself with the company's affairs. The question is whether, under such circumstances, Auslander did enough to establish his due diligence.

Section 11 imposes liability upon a director, no matter how new he is. He is presumed to know his responsibility when he becomes a director. He can escape liability only by using that reasonable care to investigate the facts that a prudent man would employ in the management of his own property. In my opinion, a prudent man would not act in an important matter without any knowledge of the relevant facts, in sole reliance upon general information which does not purport to cover the particular case. To say that such minimal conduct measures up to the statutory standard would, to all intents and purposes, absolve new directors from responsibility merely because they are new. This is not a sensible construction of Section 11, when one bears in mind its fundamental purpose of requiring full and truthful disclosure for the protection of investors.

Auslander has not established his due diligence defense with respect to the misstatements and omissions in those portions of the prospectus other than the audited 1960 figures.

Peat, Marwick

The part of the registration statement purporting to be made upon the authority of Peat, Marwick as an expert was the 1960 figures. But because the statute requires the court to determine Peat,

Marwick's belief, and the grounds thereof, "at the time such part of the registration statement became effective," for the purposes of this affirmative defense, the matter must be viewed as of May 16, 1961, and the question is whether at that time Peat, Marwick, after reasonable investigation, had reasonable ground to believe and did believe that the 1960 figures were true and that no material fact had been omitted from the registration statement which should have been included in order to make the 1960 figures not misleading. In deciding this issue, the court must consider not only what Peat, Marwick did in its 1960 audit, but also what it did in its subsequent S–1 review. The proper scope of that review must also be determined.

The 1960 Audit

Peat, Marwick's work was in general charge of a member of the firm, Cummings, and more immediately in charge of Peat, Marwick's manager, Logan. Most of the actual work was performed by a senior accountant, Berardi, who had junior assistants, one of whom was Kennedy.

Berardi was then about 30 years old. He was not yet a CPA. He had had no previous experience with the bowling industry. This was his first job as a senior accountant. He could hardly have been given a more difficult assignment.

It is unnecessary to recount everything that Berardi did in the course of the audit. We are concerned only with the evidence relating to what Berardi did or did not do with respect to those items which I have found to have been incorrectly reported in the 1960 figures in the prospectus. More narrowly, we are directly concerned only with such of those items as I have found to be material.

First and foremost is Berardi's failure to discover that Capitol Lanes had not been sold. This error affected both the sales figure and the liability side of the balance sheet. Fundamentally, the error stemmed from the fact that Berardi never realized that Heavenly Lanes and Capitol were two different names for the same alley. Berardi assumed that Heavenly was to be treated like any other completed job.

Berardi read the minutes of the board of directors meeting of November 22, 1960, which recited that "the Chairman recommended that the Corporation operate Capitol Lanes." Berardi knew from various BarChris records that Capitol Lanes, Inc., was paying rentals to Talcott. Also, a Peat, Marwick work paper bearing Kennedy's initials recorded that Capitol Lanes, Inc., held certain insurance policies.

Berardi testified that he inquired of Russo about Capitol Lanes and that Russo told him that Capitol Lanes, Inc., was going to operate an alley someday but as yet it had no alley. Berardi testified that he understood that the alley had not been built and that he believed that the rental payments were on vacant land.

I am not satisfied with this testimony. If Berardi did hold this belief, he should not have held it. The entries as to insurance and as to "operation of alley" should have alerted him to the fact that an alley existed. He should have made further inquiry on the subject. It is apparent that Berardi did not understand this transaction.

He never identified this mysterious Capitol with the Heavenly Lanes which he had included in his sales and profit figures. The vital question is whether he failed to make a reasonable investigation which, if he had made it, would have revealed the truth.

Certain accounting records of BarChris, which Berardi testified he did not see, would have put him on inquiry. One was a job cost ledger card for job no. 6036, the job number which Berardi put on his own sheet for Heavenly Lanes. This card read "Capitol Theatre (Heavenly)." In addition, two accounts receivable cards each showed both names on the same card, Capitol and Heavenly. Berardi testified that he looked at the accounts receivable records but that he did not see these particular cards. He testified that he did not look on the job cost ledger cards because he took the costs from another record, the costs register.

The burden of proof on this issue is on Peat, Marwick. Although the question is a rather close one, I find that Peat, Marwick has not sustained that burden. Peat, Marwick has not proved that Berardi made a reasonable investigation as far as Capitol Lanes was concerned and that his ignorance of the true facts was justified.

I turn now to the errors in the current assets. As to cash, Berardi properly obtained a confirmation from the bank as to BarChris's cash balance on December 31, 1960. He did not know that part of this balance had been temporarily increased by the deposit of reserves returned by Talcott to BarChris conditionally for a limited time. I do not believe that Berardi reasonably should have known this. It would not be reasonable to require Berardi to examine all of BarChris's correspondence files [which contained correspondence indicating that BarChris was to return the cash to Talcott] when he had no reason to suspect any irregularity.

The S-1 Review

The purpose of reviewing events subsequent to the date of a certified balance sheet (referred to as an S-1 review when made with reference to a registration statement) is to ascertain whether any material change has occurred in the company's financial position which should be disclosed in order to prevent the balance sheet figures from being misleading. The scope of such a review, under generally accepted auditing standards, is limited. It does not amount to a complete audit.

Berardi made the S-1 review in May 1961. He devoted a little over two days to it, a total of 20½ hours. He did not discover any of the errors or omissions pertaining to the state of affairs in 1961, all of which were material. The question is whether, despite his failure to find out anything, his investigation was reasonable within the meaning of the statute.

What Berardi did was to look at a consolidating trial balance as of March 31, 1961, which had been prepared by BarChris, compare it with the audited December 31, 1960 figures, discuss with Trilling certain unfavorable developments which the comparison disclosed, and read certain minutes. He did not examine any important financial records other than the trial balance.

In substance, Berardi asked questions, he got answers which he considered satisfactory, and he did nothing to verify them. Since he never read the prospectus, he was not even aware that there had ever been any problem about loans from officers. He made no inquiry of factors about delinquent notes in his S-1 review. Since he knew nothing about Kircher's notes of the executive committee meetings, he did not learn that the delinquency situation had grown worse. He was content with Trilling's assurance that no liability theretofore contingent had become direct. Apparently the only BarChris officer with whom Berardi communicated was Trilling. He could not recall making any inquiries of Russo, Vitolo, or Pugliese [a BarChris vice president].

There had been a material change for the worse in BarChris's financial position. That change was sufficiently serious so that the failure to disclose it made the 1960 figures misleading. Berardi did not discover it. As far as results were concerned, his S-1 review was useless.

Accountants should not be held to a standard higher than that recognized in their profession. I do not do so here. Berardi's review did not come up to that standard. He did not take some of the steps which Peat, Marwick's written program prescribed. He did not spend an adequate amount of time on a task of this magnitude. Most important of all, he was too easily satisfied with glib answers to his inquiries.

This is not to say that he should have made a complete audit. But there were enough danger signals in the materials which he did examine to require some further investigation on his part. Generally accepted auditing standards require such further investigation under these circumstances. It is not always sufficient merely to ask questions.

Here again, the burden of proof is on Peat, Marwick. I find that burden has not been satisfied. I conclude that Peat, Marwick has not established its due diligence defense.

Judgment for Escott and the other purchasers.

The Global Business Environment

Securities Regulation of Global Issuers

All market-based economies have securities laws regulating the issuance and trading of securities. Even the Republic of China, which allows limited capitalism, has a comprehensive securities law, although not as extensive as U.S. law. All foreign laws regulate the issuance of securities, securities exchanges, and securities professionals.

Most countries' securities law applies equally to domestic and foreign issuers of securities. In the United States, for example, foreign issuers must register an issuance with the SEC in the same way a domestic company registers, under Regulation C.

Canadian securities law is similar to American law, although primarily enacted by the provinces and territories instead of the national government. Nonetheless, Canadian securities law is substantially similar throughout Canada. In general, domestic and foreign issuers must make securities offerings with a prospectus that has been filed with a securities commissioner. One exemption from registration is the private issuer exemption, which may be used by a nonpublic company with no more than 50 security holders. Another exemption is for sales to accredited investors, including individuals having net assets of at least C\$5 million. Canadian securities regulators are also considering a crowdfunding exemption like the JOBS Act in the United States. While securities qualified by a prospectus may generally be freely traded in the secondary market, securities sold through an exemption must be held by the initial purchasers for 6 to 18 months, depending on the exemption.

For more information on international securities law, visit the website of the International Organization of Securities Commissions at www.iosco.org.

Statute of Limitations Under Section 11, a defendant has liability for only a limited period of time, pursuant to a statute of limitations. A purchaser must sue the defendant within one year after the misstatement or omission was or should have been discovered by the purchaser. In addition, the purchaser may sue the defendant not more than three years after the securities were offered to the public. Although the word "offered" is used in the statute, the three-year period does not usually begin until after the registered securities are first delivered to a purchaser. The Sarbanes–Oxley Act of 2002 arguably extends the statute of limitations to two years after discovery of facts constituting a violation of Section 11 and five years after the violation.

Other Liability Provisions

Section 12(a)(2) of the 1933 Act prohibits misstatements or omissions of material fact in any written or oral communication in connection with the general distribution of any security by an issuer (except government-issued or government-guaranteed securities). Section 17(a) prohibits the use of any device or artifice to defraud, or the use of any untrue or misleading statement, in connection with the offer or sale of any security. Two of the subsections of Section 17(a) require that the defendant merely act negligently, while the third subsection requires proof of scienter. *Scienter* is the intent to deceive, manipulate, or defraud the purchaser. Some courts have held that scienter also includes recklessness.

Because these liability sections are part of federal law, there must be some connection between the illegal activity and interstate commerce for liability to exist. Section 11 merely requires the filing of a registration statement with the SEC. Sections 12(a)(1), 12(a)(2), and 17(a) require the use of the mails or other instrumentality or means of interstate communication or transportation. Chapter 46 has more information on liability under these sections.

Criminal Liability

Section 24 of the 1933 Act provides for criminal liability for any person who willfully violates the Act or its rules and regulations. The maximum penalty is a \$10,000 fine and five years' imprisonment. Criminal actions under the 1933 Act are brought by the attorney general of the United States, not by the SEC.

Securities Exchange Act of 1934

 LO45-1 Understand why and demonstrate how the law regulates issuances and issuers of securities.

The Securities Exchange Act of 1934 is chiefly concerned with requiring the disclosure of material information to investors. Unlike the 1933 Act, which is primarily a one-time disclosure statute concerned with protecting investors when an issuer sells its shares to investors, the 1934 Act requires *periodic disclosure* by issuers with publicly held equity securities. That is, the 1934 Act is primarily concerned with protecting investors after the issuer becomes a public company. An issuer with publicly traded equity securities must report annually to its shareholders and submit annual and quarterly reports to the SEC. Also, any material information about the issuer must be disclosed as the issuer obtains it, unless the issuer has a valid business purpose for withholding disclosure.

In addition, the 1934 Act regulates insiders' transactions in securities, proxy solicitations, tender offers, brokers and dealers, and securities exchanges. The 1934 Act also has several sections prohibiting fraud and manipulation in securities transactions. The ultimate purpose of the 1934 Act is to keep investors fully informed to allow them to make intelligent investment decisions at any time.

Registration of Securities under the 1934 Act

Under the 1934 Act, issuers must *register classes of securities*. This is different from the 1933 Act, which requires issuers to register issuances of securities. Under the 1933 Act, securities are registered only for the term of an issuance. Under the 1934 Act, registered classes of securities remain registered until the issuer takes steps to deregister the securities. The chief consequence of having securities registered under the 1934 Act is that the issuer is required periodically to disclose information about itself to its owners and the SEC.

Registration Requirement Two types of issuers must register securities with the SEC under the 1934 Act.

1. An issuer whose total assets exceed $10 million must register a class of equity securities held by at least 2,000 holders of record or 500 unaccredited investors, if the securities are traded in interstate commerce.

2. An issuer must register any security traded on a national security exchange, such as common shares traded on the New York Stock Exchange or NASDAQ.

To register the securities, the issuer must file a 1934 Act *registration statement* with the SEC. The information required in the 1934 Act registration statement is similar to that required in the 1933 Act registration statement, except that offering information is omitted.

Termination of Registration An issuer may avoid the expense and burden of complying with the periodic disclosure and other requirements of the 1934 Act if the issuer terminates its registration. A 1934 Act registration of a class of securities may be terminated if the issuer has fewer than 300 shareholders of that class. However, an issuer with securities listed on a national securities exchange would not be able to terminate a registration of the listed securities.

Periodic Reporting Requirement To maintain a steady flow of material information to investors, the 1934 Act requires public issuers to file periodic reports with the SEC. Three types of issuers must file such reports:

1. An issuer whose total assets exceed $10 million and who has a class of equity securities held by at least 2,000 holders of record or 500 unaccredited investors, if the securities are traded in interstate commerce.

2. An issuer whose securities are traded on a national securities exchange.

3. An issuer who has made a registered offering of securities under the 1933 Act.

The first two types of issuers—which are issuers that must also register securities under the 1934 Act—must file several periodic reports, including an annual report (Form 10-K) and a quarterly report (Form 10-Q). They must file a current report (Form 8-K) when material events occur. Comparable reports must also be sent to their shareholders. The third type of issuer—an issuer who must disclose under the 1934 Act only because it has made a registered offering under the 1933 Act—must file the same reports as the other issuers, except that it need not provide an annual report to its shareholders. The 1934 Act disclosure required of the third type of issuer is in addition to the disclosure required by the 1933 Act.

The 10-K annual report must include audited financial statements plus current information about the conduct of the business, its management, and the status of its securities. It includes management's description and analysis of the issuer's financial condition (the so-called MDA section) and the names of directors and executive officers, including their compensation (such as salary and stock options). The 10-K auditing requirements are the same as for a 1933 Act registration statement—two years' audited balance sheets, three years' audited income statements, and three years' audited statements of changes in financial position.

The quarterly report, the 10-Q, requires only a summarized, unaudited operating statement and unaudited figures on capitalization and shareholders' equity. The 8-K current report must be filed within four business days of the occurrence of the event, such as a change in the amount of securities, an acquisition or disposition of assets, a change in control of the company, a revaluation of assets, or "any materially important event."

The SEC permits issuers to file reports electronically. These electronic filings are made with the SEC's Electronic Data Gathering, Analysis, and Retrieval system (EDGAR).

LOG ON

www.sec.gov/edgar.shtml
The SEC's Internet homepage gives anyone access to the EDGAR database.

Suspension of Duty to File Reports An issuer's duty to file periodic reports with regard to a class of securities is suspended if the issuer has fewer than 300 holders of that class. However, an issuer with securities traded on a national securities exchange would remain obligated to file periodic reports with respect to those securities.

Holdings and Trading by Insiders

Section 16 of the 1934 Act is designed to promote investor confidence in the integrity of the securities markets by limiting the ability of insiders to profit from trading in the shares of their issuers. Section 16(a) requires statutory insiders to disclose their ownership of their company's securities within 10 days of becoming owners. In addition, statutory insiders must report any subsequent transaction in such securities within two business days after the trade.

A statutory insider is a person who falls into any of the following categories:

1. An officer of a corporation having equity securities registered under the 1934 Act.
2. A director of such a corporation.
3. An owner of more than 10 percent of a class of equity securities registered under the 1934 Act.

Section 16(b) prevents an insider from profiting from short-swing trading in his company's shares. Any profit made by a statutory insider is recoverable by the issuer if the profit resulted from the purchase and sale (or the sale and purchase) of any class of the issuer's equity securities within less than a six-month period. This provision was designed to stop speculative insider trading on the basis of information that "may have been obtained by such owner, director, or officer by reason of his relationship to the issuer." The application of the provision is without regard to intent to use or actual use of inside information. However, a few cases have held that sales made by a statutory insider without actual access to inside information do not violate Section 16(b).

Proxy Solicitation Regulation

In a public corporation, shareholders rarely attend and vote at shareholder meetings. Many shareholders are able to vote at shareholder meetings only by **proxy**, a document by which shareholders direct other persons to vote their shares. Just as investors need information to be able to make intelligent investment decisions, shareholders need information to make intelligent voting and proxy decisions.

The 1934 Act regulates the solicitation of proxies. Regulation 14A requires any person soliciting proxies from holders of securities registered under the 1934 Act to furnish each holder with a *proxy statement* containing voting information. Usually, the only party soliciting proxies is the corporation's management, which is seeking proxies from common shareholders to enable it to reelect itself to the board of directors.

If the management of the corporation does not solicit proxies, it must nevertheless inform the shareholders of material information affecting matters that are to be put to a vote of the shareholders. This *information statement*, which contains about the same information as a proxy statement, must be sent to all shareholders that are entitled to vote at the meeting.

The primary purpose of the SEC rules concerning information that must be included in the proxy or information statement is to permit shareholders to make informed decisions while voting for directors and considering any resolutions proposed by the management or shareholders. Information on each director nominee must include the candidate's principal occupation, his shareholdings in the corporation, his previous service as a director of the corporation, his material transactions with the corporation (such as goods or services provided), and his directorships in other corporations. The total remuneration of the five directors or officers who are highest paid—including bonuses, grants under stock option plans, fringe benefits, and other perquisites—must also be included in the proxy statement.

SEC rules regarding the content of proxies ensure that the shareholder understands how his proxy will be voted. The proxy form must indicate in boldface type on whose behalf it is being solicited—for example, the corporation's management. Generally, the proxy must permit the shareholder to vote for or against the proposal or to abstain from voting on any resolutions on the meeting's agenda. The proxy form may ask for discretionary voting authority if the proxy indicates in bold print how the shares will be voted. For directors' elections, the shareholders must be provided with a means for withholding approval for each nominee.

Modern technology has greatly increased the ease with which shareholders may participate in shareholder votes and meetings, as well as reducing the cost of counting shareholder votes. Shareholders can vote electronically by phone and on the Internet. Some companies broadcast their shareholder meetings by satellite, and others webcast their shareholder meetings.

SEC Rule 14a-9 prohibits misstatements or omissions of material fact in the course of a proxy solicitation. If a violation is proved, a court may enjoin the holding of the shareholders' meeting, void the proxies that were illegally obtained, or rescind the action taken at the shareholders' meeting.

Proxy Contests A shareholder may decide to solicit proxies in competition with management. Such a competition is called a proxy contest, and a solicitation of this kind is also subject to SEC rules. To facilitate proxy contests, the SEC

Ethics and Compliance in Action

Sarbanes–Oxley Act of 2002

In 2001 and 2002, the discovery of financial irregularities in financial statements of nearly two dozen companies—notably Enron, Global Crossing, and WorldCom—led to the bankruptcy of some companies, cost investors billions of dollars, and contributed to the bear stock market of 2001 and 2002. While many ordinary investors lost a lifetime of savings, corporate insiders received and profited from lucrative stock options, bonuses, and favorable loans that were sometimes not repaid.

Consequently, Congress passed the Sarbanes–Oxley Act of 2002 (SOX), which was designed to restore integrity to corporate financial statements and revive investor confidence in the securities markets. The Sarbanes–Oxley Act attempts to accomplish these objectives by imposing a wide array of new responsibilities on public corporations and their executives and auditors. All the provisions result from the crisis of ethics, in which some corporate officers and auditors preferred their selfish interests over those of the corporation and its shareholders, creditors, and other stakeholders.

Because some public companies were manipulating their balance sheets by omitting liabilities of certain affiliate entities, SOX requires that 10-Ks and 10-Qs filed with the SEC disclose material off-balance-sheet transactions. To increase the likelihood that auditors will not give in to corporate executives' pressure to account improperly for corporate transactions, SOX requires greater independence between the auditor and the corporation by prohibiting the audit firm from performing most types of consulting services for the corporation. Moreover, officers and directors are prohibited from coercing auditors into creating misleading financial statements. To ensure that auditors are serving the interests of shareholders and not those of corporate managers, SOX requires auditors to be hired and overseen by an audit committee whose members are independent of the CEO and other corporate executives.

In addition, the CEO and CFO of a public company must certify that the corporation's financial reports fairly present the company's operations and financial condition. To eliminate the CEO and CFO's incentive to manipulate earnings, the CEO and CFO must disgorge bonuses, other incentive-based compensation, and profits on stock sales that were received during the 12-month period before financial statements are restated due to material misstatements or omissions. Public corporations are also generally prohibited from making loans to officers and directors. To encourage the use of ethics codes, SOX requires public companies to disclose whether they have ethics codes for senior financial officers.

Finally, SOX gives the SEC several new powers, including the authority to freeze payments to officers and directors during any lawful investigation. The SEC may also bar "unfit" persons from serving as directors and officers of public companies. The previous standard was "substantial unfitness."

SOX Section 404

The most controversial part of the Sarbanes–Oxley Act has been Section 404, which requires that annual reports include an "internal control report" acknowledging management's responsibility to maintain "an adequate internal control structure and procedures for financial reports." The benefits of Section 404 are evident and substantial, yet the costs are as well. The benefits include more active participation by the board, audit committee, and management in internal controls; increased embedding of control concepts including a better understanding by operating personnel and management of their control responsibilities; improvements in the adequacy of audit trails; and a revival of basic controls, such as segregation of duties and reconciliation of accounts, that have been eroded as businesses downsized and consolidated.

The cost of initial compliance with Section 404 averaged about $3 million per company in 2004. That cost included an increase in employee hours, averaging about 26,000, when the SEC had estimated that only 383 staff hours would be required. In addition, companies paid higher fees to auditors, who have the additional Section 404 burden of attesting to the assessment made by management. One study concluded that the total private cost of Section 404 compliance was $1.4 trillion. Another study found that only 14 percent of firms believed that the benefits of Section 404 exceeded the up-front costs of Section 404 compliance.

In 2010, a study by Protiviti reported that executives found that the cost of complying with SOX had declined on average 50 percent from the first year of SOX compliance and that most executives found the benefits of SOX outweighed its costs. Protiviti's 2020 survey found that the compliance cost for large companies had increased 30 percent or more over the previous year, and 51 percent of companies reported that the hours spent on SOX compliance increased. However, 14 percent of large companies reported that they have plans in place to automate IT processes and controls, creating a substantial opportunity for future cost and manpower reductions.

Nonetheless, a study by Dr. Ivy Zhang of the University of Minnesota raises concerns about SOX. Dr. Zhang concluded that SOX contributed significantly to wiping $1.4 trillion off the value of the stock market. Zhang says some indirect costs of SOX compliance were not included in budgets by managers. "While SOX likely imposed significant direct compliance costs on firms, the indirect costs could be even greater. Executives have complained that complying with the details of the rules diverts their attention from normal business practices. Also, as SOX increases the litigation risks for executives, managers are likely to behave more conservatively than shareholders would prefer. These changes could have long-lasting and far-reaching influence on business practices."

Based on what you know about SOX, what are the three strongest pros and cons for the controversial Act?

requires the corporation either to furnish a shareholder list to shareholders who desire to wage a proxy contest or to mail the competing proxy material for them. The Dodd-Frank Act goes one step further, authorizing the SEC to issue rules permitting a shareholder to use a corporation's proxy solicitation materials to nominate persons to stand for election to the board of directors.

Perhaps the most hotly contested proxy battle ever was fought in 2002 between the management of Hewlett-Packard, which wanted to merge with Compaq, and Walter Hewitt, the son of H-P's co-founder and leader of shareholders opposed to the merger. Both sides were well organized, and each deluged shareholders with proxy solicitation material. A mere 51 percent of H-P shareholders gave the merger a narrow victory. By contrast, about 90 percent of Compaq shareholders approved the merger.

Shareholder Proposals In a large public corporation, it is very expensive for a shareholder to solicit proxies in support of a proposal for corporate action that she will offer at a shareholders' meeting. Therefore, she usually asks the management to include her proposal in its proxy statement. SEC Rule 14a-8 covers proposals by shareholders.

Under SEC Rule 14a-8, the corporation must include a shareholder's proposal in its proxy statement if, among other things, the shareholder owns at least 1 percent or $2,000 of the securities to be voted at the shareholders' meeting. A shareholder may submit only one proposal per meeting. The proposal and its supporting statement may not exceed 500 words.

Under Rule 14a-8, a corporation's management may exclude many types of shareholder proposals from its proxy statement. For example, a proposal is excludable if:

1. The proposal deals with the ordinary business operations of the corporation. For example, Pacific Telesis Group was permitted on this ground to omit a proposal that the board consider adding an environmentalist director and designate a vice president for environmental matters for each subsidiary. However, TRW Inc. was required to include in its proxy statement a proposal that it establish a shareholder advisory committee that would advise the board of directors on the interests of shareholders.

If, however, a shareholder proposal's underlying subject matter transcends the day-to-day business matters of the company and raises policy issues so significant that it would be appropriate for a shareholder vote, the SEC staff will generally not allow the proposal to be omitted. Under this rationale, the SEC staff has refused to allow companies to omit proposals requiring management to track its record of limiting greenhouse emissions, as well as document its exposure to risks of climate change.

2. The proposal relates to operations that account for less than 5 percent of a corporation's total assets and less than 5 percent of its net earnings and gross sales, and is not otherwise significantly related to the company's business. For example, Harsco Corp. could not omit a proposal that it sell its 50 percent interest in a South African firm even though the investment was arguably economically insignificant—only 4.5 percent of net earnings—because the issues raised by the proposal were significantly related to Harsco's business.

3. The proposal requires the issuer to violate a state or federal law. For example, one shareholder asked North American Bank to put a gay woman on the board of directors. The proposal was excludable because it may have required the bank to violate antidiscrimination laws.

4. The proposal relates to a personal claim or grievance. A proposal that the corporation pay the shareholder $1 million for damages that she suffered from using one of the corporation's products would be excludable.

In addition, Rule 14a-8 prevents a shareholder from submitting a proposal similar to recent proposals that have been overwhelmingly rejected by shareholders in recent years.

Liability Provisions of the 1934 Act

 LO45-5 Engage in behavior that avoids liability under the federal securities laws.

To prevent fraud, deception, or manipulation in securities transactions and to provide remedies to the victims of such practices, Congress included provisions in the 1934 Act that impose liability on persons who engage in wrongful conduct.

Liability for False Statements in Filed Documents

Section 18 is the 1934 Act counterpart to Section 11 of the 1933 Act. Section 18 imposes liability on any person responsible for a false or misleading statement of material fact in any document filed with the SEC under the 1934 Act. (Filed documents include the 10-K report, 8-K report, and proxy statements, but the 10-Q report is not considered filed for Section 18 purposes.) Any person who relies on a false or misleading statement in such a filed document may sue for damages. The purchaser need not prove that the defendant was at fault. Instead, the defendant has a defense that he acted in good faith and had no knowledge that the statement was false or misleading. This defense requires only that the defendant prove that he did not act with scienter.

Section 10(b) and Rule 10b–5

The most important liability section in the 1934 Act is Section 10(b), an extremely broad provision prohibiting the use of any manipulative or deceptive device in contravention of any rules that the SEC prescribes as "necessary or appropriate in the public interest or for the protection of investors." Rule 10b–5 was adopted by the SEC under Section 10(b). The rule states:

> It shall be unlawful for any person, directly or indirectly, by use of any means or instrumentality of interstate commerce or of the mails, or of any facility of any national securities exchange,
>
> (a) to employ any device, scheme, or artifice to defraud,
>
> (b) to make any untrue statement of a material fact or to omit to state a material fact necessary in order to make the statements made, in the light of the circumstances under which they were made, not misleading, or
>
> (c) to engage in any act, practice, or course of business which operates or would operate as a fraud or deceit upon any person,
>
> in connection with the purchase or sale of any security.

Rule 10b–5 applies to all transactions in all securities listed on an American stock exchange, and the purchase or sale of any other security in the United States,[9] whether or not registered under the 1933 Act or the 1934 Act.

Elements of a Rule 10b–5 Violation

The most important elements of a Rule 10b–5 violation are a misstatement or omission of material fact and scienter. In addition, private persons suing under the rule must be purchasers or sellers of securities who relied on the misstatement or omission. They may sue only persons who are *primarily responsible* for the misstatement or omission.

Misstatement or Omission of Material Fact Rule 10b–5 prohibits only *misstatements or omissions of material fact.* A person **misstates** material facts, for example, when a manager of an unprofitable business induces shareholders to sell their stock to him by stating that the business will fail, although he knows that the business has become potentially profitable.

Liability for an ***omission of a material fact*** arises when a person fails to disclose material facts when he has a duty to disclose. For example, a securities broker is liable to his customer for not disclosing that he owns the shares that he recommends to the customer. As an agent of the customer, he owes a fiduciary duty to his customer to disclose his conflict of interest. In addition, a person is liable for omitting to tell all of the material facts after he has chosen to disclose some of them. His incomplete disclosure creates the duty to disclose all of the material facts.

Materiality Under Rule 10b–5, the misstated or omitted fact must be **material**. In essence, material information is any information that is likely to have an impact on the price of a security in the market. A fact is material if there is a substantial likelihood that a reasonable investor would consider it important to her decision, that the fact would have assumed actual significance in the deliberations of the reasonable investor, and that the disclosure of the fact would have been viewed by the reasonable investor as having significantly altered the total mix of information made available.[10]

When there is doubt whether an important event will occur, the *Texas Gulf Sulphur*[11] case holds that materiality of the doubtful event can be determined by "a balancing of both the indicated probability that the event will occur and the anticipated magnitude of the event in light of the totality of the company activity."

Scienter Under Rule 10b–5, the defendant is not liable unless he acted with **scienter**. Scienter is an intent to deceive, manipulate, or defraud. Although the Supreme Court has not set forth a specific test for determining scienter, all courts would include gross recklessness of the defendant in ascertaining the truth of his statements. Mere negligence is not scienter, but some courts hold that simple recklessness is sufficient proof of scienter. In 1995, Congress passed the Private Litigation Securities Reform Act (PLSRA), which requires a showing of actual knowledge, as opposed to mere recklessness, in private lawsuits that relate to certain statements. The purpose of the PLSRA was to heighten the scienter requirement and thus curb what some saw as abusive practices in private securities litigation.

Other Elements Rule 10b–5 requires that private plaintiffs seeking damages be *actual purchasers or sellers* of securities. Persons who were deterred from purchasing securities by fraudulent statements may not recover lost profits under Rule 10b–5.

Under Rule 10b–5, private plaintiffs alleging damages caused by misstatements by the defendant must prove that they *relied* on the misstatement of material fact. The SEC as plaintiff need not prove reliance. For private plaintiffs, reliance is not usually required in omission cases; the investor need merely prove that the omitted fact was material. In addition, the misstatement or omission must *cause the investor's loss*. The Supreme Court has held, however, that

---

[9]*Morrison v. National Australia Bank Ltd.*, 561 U.S. 247 (2010).

[10]*TSC Industries v. Northway*, 426 U.S. 438 (1976).
[11]*SEC v. Texas Gulf Sulphur Co.*, 401 F.2d 833 (2d Cir. 1968).

proof of loss causation is not required for certification of class action status.[12]

Several courts have held that an investor's reliance on the availability of the securities on the market satisfies the reliance requirement of Rule 10b-5 because the securities market is defrauded as to the value of the securities. This *fraud-on-the-market theory* is based on the hypothesis that, in an open and developed securities market, the price of a company's stock is determined by the available material information regarding the company and its business. With the presence of a market, the market is interposed between seller and buyer and, ideally, transmits information to the investor in the processed form of a market price. Thus, the market is performing a substantial part of the valuation process performed by the investor in a face-to-face transaction. The market is acting as a type of agent of the investor, informing him that given all the information available to it, the value of the stock is the same as the market price. Misleading statements will therefore defraud purchasers of stock even if the purchasers do not directly rely on the misstatements and even if the defendants never communicated with the plaintiffs.

In *Basic, Inc. v. Levinson*,[13] the Supreme Court held that the fraud-on-the-market theory permits a court to presume an investor's reliance merely from the public availability of material misrepresentations. That presumption, however, is rebuttable, such as by evidence that an investor knew the market price was incorrect. The Supreme Court upheld the *Basic* decision in 2014, also confirming that a defendant may rebut the investor's market reliance presumption by showing that the misleading statements did not affect the price of the company's securities.[14]

For Rule 10b-5 to apply, the wrongful action must be accomplished *by the mails, with any means or instrumentality of interstate commerce,* or *on a national securities exchange.* This element satisfies the federal jurisdiction requirement. Use of the mails or a telephone within one state has been held to meet this element.

The scope of activities proscribed by Rule 10b-5 is not immediately obvious. While it is easy to understand that actual fraud and price manipulation are covered by the rule, two other areas are less easily mastered—the corporation's continuous disclosure obligation and insider trading.

---

[12]*Erica P. John Fund, Inc. v. Halliburton Co.*, 563 U.S. 804 (2011).

[13]*Basic, Inc. v. Levinson*, 485 U.S. 224 (1988).
[14]*Halliburton Co. v. Erica P. John Fund, Inc.*, 573 U.S. 258.

SRM Global Fund L.P. v. Countrywide Financial Corp.
2010 U.S. Dist. LEXIS 60108 (S.D.N.Y. June 17, 2010)

Countrywide Financial Corporation billed itself an industry leader in originating and servicing subprime mortgages—that is, mortgage loans made to borrowers who did not qualify for the best market interest rates because of their poor credit histories. Countrywide offered pay-option adjustable rate mortgages, a type of ARM designed to give buyers flexibility in paying back their mortgage. The buyer could choose, in a given month, to (1) pay down the principal, (2) make an interest-only payment, or (3) make a minimum payment lower than the interest for the period. If a buyer chose option 3, the remaining interest was added to the loan principal.

SRM Global Fund Limited Partnership was a hedge fund—that is, a private investment company that invested in a variety of assets on behalf of its clients. Over time, SRM acquired 50 million shares of Countrywide common stock and other securities. In 2008, this investment lost nearly 90 percent of its value as Countrywide's financial condition deteriorated. SRM sued Countrywide and three of its officers under Securities Exchange Act Rule 10b-5. SRM alleged that the defendants knowingly misrepresented and omitted material facts.

SRM claimed that it relied on a variety of representations by Countrywide and its officers. In Countrywide's 2006 Form 10-K, filed on March 1, 2007, Countrywide represented that it had implemented a liquidity management plan that would ensure Countrywide maintained adequate, appropriate, and cost-effective sources of liquidity under all market conditions. On May 23, 2007, Countrywide hosted a Fixed Income Investor Day meeting in New York City at which President and COO David Sambol represented that Countrywide's core fundamentals were strong. CFO Eric Sieracki's presentation at the Investor Day meeting touted Countrywide's strong asset liquidity and quality. On June 13, 2007, at Countrywide's annual shareholders meeting, Chairman and CEO Angelo Mozilo boasted of Countrywide's integration of strong capital and risk-management activities that kept the company in excellent fiscal condition. Countrywide conducted a teleconference with SRM and others on July 24, 2007, concerning its earnings for the second quarter of 2007, during which Mozilo stated that "our Company is well-positioned to capitalize on opportunities during this transitional period in the mortgage business, which we believe will enhance the Company's long-term earnings growth prospects." During this teleconference, Sieracki stated that Countrywide had "adequate diversified and reliable sources of liquidity available."

Based upon these alleged misrepresentations, among others, SRM purchased 5.5 million shares of Countrywide common stock in the week following Countrywide's second quarter 2007 earnings call on July 24, 2007.

On August 2, 2007, Countrywide issued a press release titled "Countrywide Comments on Its Strong Funding Liquidity and Financial Condition," stating that "our liquidity planning proved highly effective earlier during 2007 when market concerns first arose about subprime lending, and remains so today. Our mortgage company has significant short-term funding liquidity cushions. In fact, we have almost $50 billion of highly reliable short-term funding liquidity available as a cushion today." Countrywide's August 6, 2007, Form 8-K contained Countrywide's "Liquidity Source" schedule as of June 30, 2007, which reported that Countrywide's net available liquidity was $186.5 billion.

On August 13, 2007, Merrill Lynch issued an analyst report stating that Countrywide "has about $185 billion in available credit facilities, though the concern is that these facilities could be terminated or the terms changed meaningfully, thus impacting Countrywide's ability to operate normally. It is possible for Countrywide to go bankrupt." On August 23, 2007, Mozilo was interviewed on CNBC, and during this interview, he denounced the Merrill Lynch analysis of Countrywide as "baseless" and "irresponsible" and stated that "there is no more chance for bankruptcy today for Countrywide than there was six months ago, a year ago, two years ago. We are a very solid company."

SRM purchased more than 10.5 million shares of Countrywide common stock in the three weeks following Mozilo's CNBC interview.

On October 26, 2007, there was an unprecedented disruption in the capital markets and an abrupt loss in demand for loans and securities as well as increased credit costs related to continued deterioration in the housing market. On October 27, 2007, Countrywide issued a press release and filed a Form 8-K announcing Countrywide's financial results for the third quarter of 2007, which included a quarterly loss of $1.25 billion, or $2.85 per share and a $1 billion write-down of its loans and mortgage-backed securities. On February 29, 2008, Countrywide filed its Form 10-K for 2007 with the SEC, in which it disclosed that Countrywide held $28.42 billion of pay-option ARMs, and that the percentage of such loans that were at least 90 days past due had risen 800 percent from a year earlier, from 0.6 percent to 5.4 percent, and 71 percent of its pay-option adjustable rate mortgage borrowers were making only minimal payments that covered only part of the interest normally due, thus causing their loan principals to grow.

On December 28, 2007, SRM executives Ian Barclay, John Myers, and Jon Wood participated in a teleconference with Countrywide Investor Relations employee David Bigelow and Sieracki during which Bigelow and Sieracki confirmed Countrywide's public statements regarding Countrywide's financial condition, liquidity, and capital reserves and told SRM that Countrywide had sufficient liquidity to last for 12 months.

Based upon these misrepresentations, among others, SRM purchased more than 8.4 million shares of Countrywide in a two-week period following SRM's December 28, 2007, teleconference with Bigelow and Sieracki.

On January 11, 2008, Bank of America announced an agreement to purchase Countrywide in an all-stock transaction worth approximately $4 billion, which represented less than 30 percent of Countrywide's most recently reported book value. In SRM's view, the agreed price was too low, given Countrywide's repeated reassurances in public statements and directly to SRM regarding Countrywide's financial condition. On January 14, 2008, BOA's CEO Kenneth Lewis spoke in support of the merger, telling the investing public on behalf of Bank of America that Countrywide's bankruptcy was just "a malicious rumor" and that, after having "conducted twice as much due diligence as Bank of America ordinarily might have," Bank of America concluded that "there is great long-term value embedded in Countrywide's business" and that Countrywide "had a very impressive liquidity plan and had its backup lines in place."

On June 3, 2008, Barclay, Myers, and Wood met with Mozilo, Sambol, and Sieracki. At that meeting, Mozilo told the SRM executives that Countrywide had gone from being a viable company to being not viable during one week nearly a year before, in July 2007. Sambol told SRM that liquidity disappeared in one day, on August 2, 2007.

Beginning June 24, 2008, SRM sold its Countrywide stock and thereby suffered substantial losses. On July 1, 2008, Bank of America completed its acquisition of Countrywide.

SRM sued Countrywide, Mozilo, Sambol, and Sieracki in a New York federal district court under Securities Exchange Act § 10(b) and Rule 10b-5, as well as the state common law of fraud. SRM's lawsuit focused on a September 26, 2006, e-mail that Mozilo sent to Sambol and Sieracki, which stated, "We have no way, with any reasonable certainty, to assess the real risk of holding pay-option ARM loans on our balance sheet. The bottom line is that we are flying blind on how these loans will perform in a stressed environment of higher unemployment, reduced values and slowing home sales." SRM alleged that the e-mail shows that Countrywide and its executives knew they were "flying blind" with respect to the value of Countrywide's substantial pay-option

ARM portfolio and thus knew that Countrywide's true financial condition was precarious and had no reasonable basis for their assurances about Countrywide's financial condition.

Countrywide asked the district to dismiss the lawsuit on the ground it failed to state a claim on which relief may be granted.

Berman, Judge

To survive a motion to dismiss, a complaint must contain sufficient factual matter, accepted as true, to state a claim to relief that is plausible on its face. This standard is met when the plaintiff pleads factual content that allows the court to draw the reasonable inference that the defendant is liable for the misconduct alleged.

Section 10(b) and Rule 10b-5 Claims

To state a claim under § 10(b) and the corresponding Rule 10b-5, a plaintiff must plead that the defendant, in connection with the purchase or sale of securities, made a materially false statement or omitted a material fact, with scienter, and that the plaintiff's reliance on the defendant's action caused injury to the plaintiff.

Securities fraud actions are subject to the heightened pleading requirements of the Private Securities Litigation Reform Act of 1995, as well as those of Federal Rule of Civil Procedure 9(b), which require that plaintiffs (1) specify the statements that the plaintiff contends were fraudulent, (2) identify the speaker, (3) state where and when the statements were made, and (4) explain why the statements were fraudulent.

Each of the misrepresentations alleged in SRM's Amended Complaint were made in financial disclosures, news articles, television programs, teleconferences, or press releases which (1) specify the statements that SRM contends were fraudulent, (2) identify the speaker, and (3) state where and when the statements were made. SRM has satisfied the first three prongs of the Rule 9(b) requirements.

The "fourth prong" is critical to the analysis here. And, with respect to the fourth prong, the Court separately analyzes: (a) the flying blind email; (b) the June 3, 2008 meeting; [and] (c) Mozilo's and Lewis's denials of rumors of bankruptcy.

Flying Blind Email

It is indisputable that there can be no omission where the allegedly omitted facts are disclosed. Countrywide warned investors in its 2006 Form 10-K, filed on March 1, 2007, i.e., approximately five months before SRM's first purchase of Countrywide securities, that "due to the lack of significant historical experience at Countrywide, the credit performance of pay-option ARM loans has not been established for the Company." SRM does not explain why or how this Form 10-K disclosure was deficient. While the term "flying blind" may more colorfully convey Countrywide's "lack of significant historical experience" with pay-option ARMs, Countrywide and its executives were under no duty to employ the characterization that SRM believes is more accurate.

Countrywide made additional disclosures regarding pay-option ARMs before and during the Relevant Period. For example, on July 26, 2005, Mozilo stated that although pay-option ARMs were Countrywide's "lowest delinquency product at the moment . . . you have to wait some time for loans to mature a year, two years, even three years to determine how they're going to perform." (Transcript of Second Quarter 2005 Earnings Call, dated July 26, 2005.) Similarly, on July 25, 2006, Mozilo warned that if "interest rates continue to rise significantly, then the resets and payments shocks will be substantial" on pay-option ARMs. He further explained that "we just need time to see how this is going to play out. . . . The test will be when the resets take place and I'm not certain exactly what's going to happen there." (Transcript of Second Quarter 2006 Earnings Call, dated July 25, 2006.) And, in Countrywide's 2007 Form 10-K, filed with the SEC on February 28, 2008, Countrywide disclosed that it "has a significant investment in pay-option loans. Pay-option loans represent 32 percent and 45 percent of the Company's investment in mortgage loans held for investment at December 31, 2007 and 2006, respectively." With respect to these loans, Countrywide also disclosed in its 2007 Form 10-K that "our borrowers' ability to defer portions of the interest accruing on their loans may expose us to increased credit risk. This is because when the required monthly payments for these loans eventually increase, borrowers may be less able to pay the increased amounts and may be more likely to default than a borrower with a loan whose initial payment provides for full amortization. Our exposure to this higher credit risk is increased by the amount of deferred interest that has been added to the principal balance."

The Court is aware that whether an allegedly omitted fact was available to the market often is a fact intensive inquiry that is rarely an appropriate basis for dismissing. However, "rarely appropriate" is not the same as "never appropriate." Here, Countrywide's lack of significant historical experience with pay-option ARMs was clearly disclosed in a document filed with the SEC on March 1, 2007. (See 2006 Form 6-K, filed Mar. 1, 2007.) The facts here show that all the information SRM claims was concealed by Countrywide was publicly available and on these facts the law renders Countrywide's purported misstatements immaterial.

SRM's claim that certain statements made by the Countrywide defendants after Mozilo sent the flying blind email to Sambol and Sieracki were misleading is undermined also by the theory upon which it is based—namely, fraud-on-the-market theory—because the market price of a stock is presumed to reflect all publicly available information. Such publicly available information includes Countrywide's 2006 and 2007 Forms 10-K and statements made during a July 25, 2006 teleconference with Mozilo and analysts. Plaintiff acknowledges that the market for Countrywide securities efficiently digested current information regarding the company from all publicly available sources and reflected such information in the price of Countrywide's securities. Thus, SRM cannot use this presumption to argue that the market price reflected Countrywide's purported misstatements but not the true statements contained in its press releases and SEC filings.

June 3, 2008 Meeting

SRM's Amended Complaint does not contain any allegations of facts supporting SRM's contention that any defendant knew, prior to the June 3, 2008 meeting, that Countrywide had ceased to be a viable company in July 2007 and liquidity had disappeared on August 2, 2007. It is not sufficient for SRM to contend that Countrywide defendants must have had access to contrary facts. The compelling inference urged by SRM, i.e., that the Countrywide defendants could, nearly a year later, identify so precisely when Countrywide ceased to be viable and liquidity disappeared because they recognized those events at or about the time they happened, is unavailing because the mere disclosure of adverse information shortly after a positive statement does not support a finding that the prior statement was false at the time it was made. SRM must specifically identify the reports or statements containing this information that were allegedly available to defendants and which showed that Countrywide had ceased to be a viable company in July 2007 and liquidity had disappeared on August 2, 2007. SRM does not claim that either Mozilo or Sambol said at this meeting that they knew or believed, as of August 2007, that the company was no longer viable without liquidity. These were statements made in and as of June 2008, with the benefit of hindsight, after having lived through the mortgage and housing crisis for a year. The defendants, like so many other institutions floored by the housing market crisis, could not have been expected to anticipate the crisis with the accuracy SRM enjoys in hindsight.

Bankruptcy Rumors

SRM argues, among other things, that assurances that Countrywide's bankruptcy was "just a malicious rumor" omitted the material fact that Countrywide was not a viable company. SRM does not identify any document or statement made by any of the defendants which indicates that, during the Relevant Period, Countrywide was on the verge of or considering bankruptcy. Even assuming, arguendo, that SRM has sufficiently alleged (which it has not) that Countrywide had ceased to be a viable company in July 2007 and liquidity had disappeared on August 2, 2007, SRM fails to support its apparent assumption that bankruptcy was the only option for Countrywide as opposed, for example, to a merger (which, in fact, occurred), a sale of assets, a reduction in expenses or capital expenditures, a new business strategy, or an acquisition of additional credit lines.

Fraud

The elements of common law fraud are largely the same as those of a Rule 10b–5 claim. However, the two actions maintain meaningful distinctions. For example, common law fraud cases are to be distinguished from cases that involved a fraud-on-the-market theory or other theories in which reliance on a material omission is presumed to have existed. And, under New York law, the asserted reliance must be found to be justifiable under all the circumstances before a complaint can be found to state a cause of action in fraud. In evaluating whether a plaintiff has adequately alleged justifiable reliance, a court may consider, inter alia, the plaintiff's sophistication and expertise in finance, the existence of a fiduciary relationship, and whether the plaintiff initiated the transaction.

Countrywide's motion to dismiss is granted because SRM has failed to allege that the Countrywide defendants made a material misstatement or omission. But, even assuming, arguendo, that SRM had identified actionable misstatements or omissions, SRM has failed to state a claim for common law fraud because, as a very sophisticated investor, its reliance upon these alleged misstatements or omissions would not be considered justifiable. SRM is a multi-billion dollar hedge fund that takes a contrarian and long-term investment approach in companies or sections that have been through periods of stress and are out of favor with the market. Moreover, prior to SRM's first alleged purchase of Countrywide securities on July 24, 2007, Countrywide warned investors in its 2006 Form 10-K, filed on March 1, 2007, that "due to the lack of significant historical experience at Countrywide, the credit performance of pay-option ARM loans has not been established for the Company." As a sophisticated investor, SRM would be obligated to investigate information available to it with the care and prudence expected from people blessed with full access to information. Consequently, as a sophisticated institution contemplating the investment of tens of millions of dollars, it was unreasonable for SRM to rely upon the highly general statements alleged as misstatements in this case.

Motion to dismiss granted in favor of Countrywide, Mozilo, Sambol, and Sieracki.

A considerable amount of litigation under Rule 10b-5 arose in the wake of the credit crunch that began in 2007, including allegations that banks defrauded their shareholders and other investors who purchased their common shares and to whom they sold mortgage-backed securities. The following case involves Countrywide Financial Corporation, one of the companies hardest hit by the financial crisis. The plaintiff, a hedge fund, was unsuccessful in its lawsuit against Countrywide, in part because of the hedge fund's investment sophistication.

Continuous Disclosure Obligation The purpose of the 1934 Act is to ensure that investors have the information they need in order to make sound investment decisions at all times. The periodic reporting requirements of the 1934 Act are especially designed to accomplish this result. If important developments arise between the disclosure dates of reports, however, investors will not have all of the information they need to make intelligent decisions unless the corporation discloses the material information immediately. Rule 10b–5 requires a corporation to disclose material information immediately, unless the corporation has a valid business purpose for withholding disclosure. When a corporation chooses to disclose information or to comment on information that it has no duty to disclose, it must do so accurately.

Until 1988, courts had disagreed on whether Rule 10b–5 requires disclosure of merger and other acquisition negotiations prior to an agreement in principle. In *Basic, Inc. v. Levinson*, the Supreme Court held that materiality of merger negotiations is to be determined on a case-by-case basis. The Court held that materiality depends on the probability that the transaction will be consummated and on its significance to the issuer of the securities. In addition, the Court stated that a corporation that chooses to comment on acquisition negotiations must do so truthfully.

In response to the *Basic* decision, the SEC released guidelines to help public companies decide whether they must disclose merger negotiations. A company is not required to disclose merger negotiations if all three of the following requirements are met:

1. The company did not make any prior disclosures about the merger negotiations.
2. Disclosure is not compelled by other SEC rules.
3. Management determines that disclosure would jeopardize completion of the merger transaction.

Forward-Looking Statements Because the risk of liability has caused corporations to couch disclosures in sometimes obscure language and because companies were reluctant to provide highly valuable but difficult-to-justify predictions of the companies' future, Congress chose in the Private Securities Litigation Reform Act to provide a *safe harbor* for forward-looking statements. When a private lawsuit is based on a misstatement or omission of a material fact, no liability shall exist with respect to any forward-looking statement identified as such and accompanied by meaningful cautionary statements that actual results may differ materially from those in the forward-looking statement. A company will also not be liable if the forward-looking statement was not made by or with the approval of an executive officer of that entity or if that officer had no actual knowledge that the statement was false or misleading. Note that the safe harbor is written in the disjunctive; that is, a defendant is not liable if the forward-looking statement is **identified** *and* accompanied by **meaningful cautionary language** *or* is **immaterial** *or* it was made **without actual knowledge** that it was false or misleading.

Trading on Inside Information A potential destroyer of public confidence in the integrity of the securities market is the belief that insiders can trade securities while possessing corporate information that is not available to the general public.

Rule 10b–5 prohibits insider trading on nonpublic corporate information. A person with material, nonpublic information may not use that information when trading. He must either disclose the information before trading or refrain from trading. The difficult task in the insider trading area is determining when a person is subject to this *disclose-or-refrain* rule. And because Rule 10b–5 does not provide a comprehensive definition of insider trading, there has been much volatility in this area of the law.

Two different theories of insider trading have developed over the years. The first is the **classical theory**, which applies when a person obtains material, nonpublic information from a company and then trades on it in violation of a *direct duty* to that company's shareholders. Generally, two types of insiders (those possessing the nonpublic information) fit under the classical theory: *traditional insiders* such as corporate officers and directors, high-level employees, and others who owe a direct fiduciary duty to both the company and its shareholders and *temporary insiders* such as lawyers, accountants, and consultants who work for a company on a temporary basis and acquire a duty to the company and its shareholders because of their quasi-insider role.

The second theory of insider trading is known as the **misappropriation theory**. This theory operates when a person trades on material, nonpublic information in violation of a known fiduciary duty—not to the company per se, but to another such as an employer. For example, in one of the more famous insider trading cases, *United States v. O'Hagan,*[15] the Supreme Court approved of the misappropriation theory, holding that a defendant who was a law firm partner who bought stock in companies his firm's clients were attempting to acquire violated Rule 10b–5. Even though the defendant owed no direct duty to the companies and he was not a typical temporary insider, the Court found he had committed theft and fraud upon his law firm, which was the possessor of the nonpublic information.

_____
[15]521 U.S. 642 (1997).

These two theories may overlap. A person liable under the classical theory is also liable under the misappropriation theory. But the reverse may not be true. Misappropriators are often not liable under the classical theory because they owe no duty to the company whose stock was traded. Regardless of the theory used, it should be clear that violation of a fiduciary duty is key to insider trading law.

In the following case, *SEC v. Dorozhko,* the Second Circuit reviewed the main misappropriation cases on its way to holding that a breach of fiduciary duty is not required in every case brought under Rule 10b–5.

SEC v. Dorozhko 574 F.3d 42 (2d Cir. 2009)

The court was asked to consider whether, in a civil lawsuit brought by the SEC under Section 10(b) of the Exchange Act, computer hacking may be "deceptive" where the hacker did not breach a fiduciary duty in fraudulently obtaining material, nonpublic information used in connection with the purchase or sale of securities.

In October 2007, Oleksandr Dorozhko, a Ukrainian national, opened an online trading account with Interactive Brokers. At about the same time, IMS Health announced it would release its third-quarter earnings during an analyst conference call after trading closes on October 17. IMS had hired Thomson Financial to provide investor relations and web-hosting services, which included managing the online release of IMS's earnings reports.

Beginning the morning of the analyst call and continuing several times during the early afternoon, an anonymous computer hacker attempted to gain access to the IMS earnings report by hacking into a secure server at Thomson. That afternoon, minutes after Thomson actually received the IMS data, that hacker successfully downloaded the IMS data from Thomson's secure server. A few minutes later, Dorozhko—who had not previously used his Interactive Brokers account to trade—purchased $41,670.90 worth of IMS "put" options that would expire on October 25 and 30. These purchases represented approximately 90% of all purchases of "put" options for IMS stock for the six weeks prior to October 17. In purchasing these options, which the SEC describes as "extremely risky," Dorozhko was betting that IMS's stock price would decline precipitously.

Just slightly ahead of the analyst call, IMS announced that its earnings per share were 28% below "Street" expectations. When the market opened the next morning, IMS's stock price sank approximately 28% almost immediately. Within six minutes of the market opening, Dorozhko had sold all of his IMS options, realizing a net profit of $286,456.59 overnight.

Interactive Brokers noticed the irregular trading activity and referred the matter to the SEC, which now alleges that Dorozhko was the hacker and sought a temporary retraining order against him to freeze the proceeds of his trades. The district court ruled that computer hacking was not "deceptive" within the meaning of Section 10(b) as defined by the Supreme Court. According to the district court, a breach of a fiduciary duty of disclosure is a required element of any deceptive device under Section 10b, and that because defendant was a corporate outsider with no special relationship to IMS or Thomson, he owed no fiduciary duty to either. Although computer hacking might be fraudulent and might violate a number of federal and state criminal statutes, the district court concluded that this behavior did not violate Section 10(b) without an accompanying breach of a fiduciary duty. This appeal followed.

Cabranes, Judge

The District Court determined that the Supreme Court has interpreted the "deceptive" element of Section 10(b) to require a breach of a fiduciary duty. The District Court reached this conclusion by relying principally on three Supreme Court opinions: *Chiarella v. United States, United States v. O'Hagan,* and *SEC v. Zandford.* We consider each of these cases in turn.

In *Chiarella,* the defendant was employed by a financial printer and used information passing through his office to trade securities offered by acquiring and target companies. In a criminal prosecution, the government alleged that the defendant committed fraud by not disclosing to the market that he was trading on the basis of material, nonpublic information. The Supreme Court held that defendant's "silence," or nondisclosure, was not fraud because he was under no obligation to disclose his knowledge of inside information. "When an allegation of fraud is based upon nondisclosure, there can be no fraud absent a duty to speak. We hold that a duty to disclose under § 10(b) does not arise from the mere possession of nonpublic market information." Justice Blackmun, joined by Justice Marshall, dissented. In their view, stealing information from an employer was fraudulent within the meaning of Section 10(b) because the statute was designed as a "catchall" provision to protect investors from unknown risks.

According to Justice Blackmun, the majority had "confine[d]" the meaning of fraud "by imposition of a requirement of a 'special relationship' akin to fiduciary duty before the statute gives rise to a duty to disclose or to abstain from trading upon material, nonpublic information."

In O'Hagan, the defendant was an attorney who traded in securities based on material, nonpublic information regarding his firm's clients. As in Chiarella, the government alleged that the defendant had committed fraud through "silence" because the defendant had a duty to disclose to the source of the information (his client) that he would trade on the information. The Supreme Court agreed, noting that "[d]eception through nondisclosure is central to the theory of liability for which the Government seeks recognition." "[I]f the fiduciary discloses to the source that he plans to trade on the nonpublic information, there is no 'deceptive device' and thus no § 10(b) violation—although the fiduciary-turned-trader may remain liable under state law for breach of a duty of loyalty."

In Zandford, the defendant was a securities broker who traded under a client's account and transferred the proceeds to his own account. The Fourth Circuit held that the defendant's fraud was not "in connection with" the purchase or sale of a security because it was mere theft that happened to involve securities, rather than true securities fraud. The Supreme Court reversed in a unanimous opinion, observing that Section 10(b) "should be construed not technically and restrictively, but flexibly to effectuate its remedial purposes." Although the Court warned that not "every common-law fraud that happens to involve securities [is] a violation of § 10(b)," the defendant's scheme was a single plan to deceive, rather than a series of independent frauds, and was therefore "in connection with" the purchase or sale of a security. In a final footnote, the Court offered the following observation: "[I]f the broker told his client he was stealing the client's assets, that breach of fiduciary duty might be in connection with a sale of securities, but it would not involve a deceptive device or fraud." In the instant case, the District Court interpreted the Zandford footnote as an "explicit[ ] acknowledg[ment] that Zandford would not be liable under § 10(b) if he had disclosed to Wood that he was planning to steal his money."

In our view, none of the Supreme Court opinions relied upon by the District Court—much less the sum of all three opinions—establishes a fiduciary-duty requirement as an element of every violation of Section 10(b). In Chiarella, O'Hagan, and Zandford, the theory of fraud was silence or nondisclosure, not an affirmative misrepresentation. The Supreme Court held that remaining silent was actionable only where there was a duty to speak, arising from a fiduciary relationship. In Chiarella, the Supreme Court held that there was no deception in an employee's silence because he did not have duty to speak. In O'Hagan, an attorney who traded on client secrets had a fiduciary duty to inform his firm that he was trading on the basis of the confidential information. Even in Zandford, which dealt principally with the statutory requirement that a deceptive device be used "in connection with" the purchase or sale of a security, the defendant's fraud consisted of not telling his brokerage client—to whom he owed a fiduciary duty—that he was stealing assets from the account.

[These cases] all stand for the proposition that nondisclosure in breach of a fiduciary duty "satisfies § 10(b)'s requirement . . . [of] a 'deceptive device or contrivance.'" However, what is sufficient is not always what is necessary, and none of the Supreme Court opinions considered by the District Court require a fiduciary relationship as an element of an actionable securities claim under Section 10(b). While Chiarella, O'Hagan, and Zandford all dealt with fraud qua silence, an affirmative misrepresentation is a distinct species of fraud. Even if a person does not have a fiduciary duty to "disclose or abstain from trading," there is nonetheless an affirmative obligation in commercial dealings not to mislead. See, e.g., Basic Inc. v. Levinson, 485 U.S. 224 (1988).

In this case, the SEC has not alleged that defendant fraudulently remained silent in the face of a "duty to disclose or abstain" from trading. Rather, the SEC argues that defendant affirmatively misrepresented himself in order to gain access to material, nonpublic information, which he then used to trade. We are aware of no precedent of the Supreme Court or our Court that forecloses or prohibits the SEC's straightforward theory of fraud. Absent a controlling precedent that "deceptive" has a more limited meaning than its ordinary meaning, we see no reason to complicate the enforcement of Section 10(b) by divining new requirements. In reaching this conclusion, we are mindful of the Supreme Court's oft-repeated instruction that Section 10(b) "should be construed not technically and restrictively, but flexibly to effectuate its remedial purposes." Accordingly, we adopt the SEC's proposed interpretation of Chiarella and its progeny: "misrepresentations are fraudulent, but . . . silence is fraudulent only if there is a duty to disclose."

District Court's order denying the SEC's motion for a preliminary injunction is Vacated. The cause is Remanded for further proceedings consistent with this opinion.

In addition to insiders, another group of persons trading on material, nonpublic information can be held liable under Rule 10b-5. *Tippees* are recipients of inside information (tips) from insiders. Tippees of insiders—such as relatives and friends of insiders, stockbrokers, and securities analysts—are forbidden to trade on inside information. Their liability is derivative, or flows from, the insider. However, a tippee can be guilty of insider trading even in situations where the insider is not, if the insider that provided the tip did not herself trade on the information and did not act for personal gain. To make matters more complicated, liability may extend to others who have been tipped and trade based on information passed from the original tippee. These *remote tippee* cases have stretched the bounds of securities fraud law and created much confusion in the courts.

The standards governing tippee liability were established in *Dirks v. SEC*,[16] a Supreme Court opinion that affirmed a tippee may be liable based on a derivative breach of fiduciary duty, that is, a breach that derives from the tipper's breach (who is oftentimes, but not always, the insider). Dirks was an investment analyst who received information from a former employee of a company that was alleged to have overstated its assets. The employee told Dirks this because he believed that Dirks would make the information known and stop the company's fraud. Dirks recommended to all his clients that they sell their stock in the company and helped make the fraud public, but Dirks never traded the company's stock himself. The SEC brought a successful enforcement action against Dirks, arguing he had aided and abetted the insider trading of his clients. The theory was that Dirks obtained material, nonpublic information from the employee and passed it on to others to trade upon, when he should have disclosed the information first.

The Supreme Court reversed, holding that as a tippee of secret information, Dirks could only be liable if the tipper (here the insider employee) breached a duty to shareholders of the company. In addition, the Court held that a tipper only breaches a duty when he stands to personally benefit from passing the information. The three situations in which a personal benefit arises are when the tipper directly or indirectly profits from the trades in the form of cash, receives a reputational benefit, or is giving a gift such that it will benefit him in the future. Because the employee was a whistle-blower who did not gain financially, he breached no duty to his employer; therefore, Dirks could not be derivatively liable as a tippee.

Synthesizing the cases under the various theories of insider trading, as well as additional SEC rules,[17] reveals the following elements of tippee liability:

1. The tipper must have been an insider, temporary insider, or misappropriator.
2. The tipper must have been acting for personal gain.
3. The tippee must have acquired material, nonpublic information from the tipper.
4. The tipper must have bought or sold securities.
5. The tippee must have knowingly possessed the nonpublic information when making the trade.
6. The tippee must have acted willfully.

Tippee liability continues to evolve. The following case note includes two cases: *United States v. Newman* and *United States v. Salman*. In *Newman,* the Second Circuit Court of Appeals applied the elements for tippee liability as set forth in *Dirks v. SEC* to determine the fate of two hedge fund analysts criminally charged with insider trading. The court ultimately held that there was no personal benefit received by the tippers, and thus there could be no tipper liability from which the purported tippee liability would derive. This case is included because it shows how difficult prosecutions are in remote tippee scenarios and the struggle courts have in determining how broad insider trading liability should extend. In *Salman,* the Supreme Court rejected the Second Circuit's reading of *Dirks* and reestablished the personal gain or benefits element as originally understood. The note following the cases suggests more uncertainty to come.

Extent of Liability for Insider Trading Section 20A of the 1934 Act allows persons who traded in the securities at about the same time as the insider or tippee to recover damages from the insider or tippee. Although there may be several persons trading at about the same time, the insider or tippee's total liability cannot exceed the profit she has made or the loss she has avoided by trading on inside information.

This limitation, which merely requires disgorgement of profits, has been assailed as not adequately deterring insider trading because the defendant may realize an enormous profit if her trading is not discovered but lose nothing beyond her profits if it is. In response to this issue of liability, Congress passed an amendment to the 1934 Act permitting the SEC to seek a civil penalty of three times the profit gained or the loss avoided by trading on inside information. This

[16]463 U.S 646 (1983).

[17]C.F.R. § 240.10b5-2.

United States v. Newman	773 F.3d 438 (2d Cir. 2014)

This case arises from the government's ongoing investigation into suspected insider trading activity at hedge funds. In January 2012, the government unsealed charges against Todd Newman, Anthony Chiasson, and several other investment professionals. In February 2012, a grand jury returned an indictment.

At trial, the government presented evidence that a group of financial analysts exchanged information they obtained from company insiders, both directly and more often indirectly. Specifically, the government alleged that the analysts received information from insiders at Dell and NVIDIA, disclosing those companies' earnings numbers before they were publicly released in Dell's May 2008 and August 2008 earnings announcements and NVIDIA's May 2008 earnings announcement. The analysts then passed the inside information to their portfolio managers, including Newman and Chiasson, who, in turn, executed trades in Dell and NVIDIA stock, earning approximately $4 million and $68 million, respectively, in profits for their respective funds.

Newman and Chiasson were several steps removed from the corporate insiders, and there was no evidence that either was aware of the source of the inside information. However, the government charged that Newman and Chiasson were criminally liable for insider trading because, as sophisticated traders, they must have known that information was disclosed by insiders in breach of a fiduciary duty and not for any legitimate corporate purpose.

At the close of evidence, Newman and Chiasson moved for a judgment of acquittal, arguing that there was no evidence that the corporate insiders provided inside information in exchange for a personal benefit, which is required to establish tipper liability under Dirks v. SEC. *Newman and Chiasson also argued that, even if the corporate insiders had received a personal benefit in exchange for the inside information, there was no evidence that they knew about any such benefit. Absent such knowledge, appellants argued, they were not aware of, or participants in, the tippers' fraudulent breaches of fiduciary duties to Dell or NVIDIA and could not be convicted of insider trading under* Dirks. *In the alternative, Newman and Chiasson requested that the court instruct the jury that it must find that they knew that the corporate insiders had disclosed confidential information for personal benefit in order to find them guilty. However, the district court did not give Newman and Chiasson's proposed jury instruction. In December, 2012, the jury returned a verdict of guilty on all counts.*

Parker, Judge

In order to sustain a conviction for insider trading, the government must prove beyond a reasonable doubt that the tippee knew that an insider disclosed confidential information and that he did so in exchange for a personal benefit. The insider trading case law is not confined to insiders or misappropriators who trade for their own accounts. Courts have expanded insider trading liability to reach situations where the insider or misappropriator in possession of material nonpublic information ("the tipper") does not himself trade but discloses the information to an outsider (a "tippee") who then trades on the basis of the information before it is publicly disclosed. *See Dirks*, 463 U.S. [646, 659 (1983)]. The elements of tipping liability are the same, regardless of whether the tipper's duty arises under the "classical" or the "misappropriation" theory.

The Supreme Court was quite clear in *Dirks* of what is required to demonstrate tippee liability. First, the tippee's liability derives only from the tipper's breach of a fiduciary duty, not from trading on material, non-public information. Second, the corporate insider has committed no breach of fiduciary duty unless he receives a personal benefit in exchange for the disclosure. Third, even in the presence of a tipper's breach, a tippee is liable only if he knows or should have known of the breach.

Dirks counsels us that the exchange of confidential information for personal benefit is not separate from an insider's fiduciary breach; it is the fiduciary breach that triggers liability for securities fraud under Rule 10b–5. For purposes of insider trading liability, the insider's disclosure of confidential information, standing alone, is not a breach. Thus, without establishing that the tippee knows of the personal benefit received by the insider in exchange for the disclosure, the Government cannot meet its burden of showing that the tippee knew of a breach.

In light of *Dirks*, we find no support for the Government's contention that knowledge of a breach of the duty of confidentiality without knowledge of the personal benefit is sufficient to impose criminal liability. Although the Government might like the law to be different, nothing in the law requires a symmetry of information in the nation's securities markets. The Supreme Court has affirmatively established that insider trading liability is based on breaches of fiduciary duty, not on informational asymmetries. This is a critical limitation on insider trading liability that protects a corporation's interests in confidentiality while promoting efficiency in the nation's securities markets.

As noted above, *Dirks* clearly defines a breach of fiduciary duty as a breach of the duty of confidentiality in exchange for a personal benefit. Accordingly, we conclude that a tippee's knowledge of the insider's breach necessarily requires knowledge that the insider disclosed confidential information in exchange for personal benefit.

In sum, we hold that to sustain an insider trading conviction against a tippee, the Government must prove each of the following elements beyond a reasonable doubt: that (1) the corporate insider was entrusted with a fiduciary duty; (2) the corporate insider breached his fiduciary duty by (a) disclosing confidential information to a tippee (b) in exchange for a personal benefit; (3) the tippee knew of the tipper's breach, that is, he knew the information was confidential and divulged for personal benefit; and (4) the tippee still used that information to trade in a security or tip another individual for personal benefit.

In this case both Chiasson and Newman contested their knowledge of any benefit received by the tippers and, in fact, elicited evidence sufficient to support a contrary finding. Moreover, we conclude that the Government's evidence of any personal benefit received by the insiders was insufficient to establish tipper liability from which Chiasson and Newman's purported tippee liability would derive.

We have observed that a personal benefit is broadly defined to include not only pecuniary gain, but also any reputational benefit that will translate into future earnings and the benefit one would obtain from simply making a gift of confidential information to a trading relative or friend. This standard, although permissive, does not suggest that the Government may prove the receipt of a personal benefit by the mere fact of a friendship, particularly of a casual or social nature. If that were true, and the Government was allowed to meet its burden by proving that two individuals were alumni of the same school or attended the same church, the personal benefit requirement would be a nullity. To the extent *Dirks* suggests that a personal benefit may be inferred from a personal relationship between the tipper and tippee, where the tippee's trades resemble trading by the insider himself followed by a gift of the profits to the recipient, we hold that such an inference is impermissible in the absence of proof of a meaningfully close personal relationship that generates an exchange that is objective, consequential, and represents at least a potential gain of a pecuniary or similarly valuable nature.

Judgment vacated as to the convictions; remanded to the district court to dismiss the indictment with prejudice as it pertains to Newman and Chiasson.

United States v. Salman 137 S. Ct. 420 (2016)

Bassam Salman was indicted for federal securities fraud crimes for trading on inside information he received from a friend and relative-by-marriage, Michael Kara, who, in turn, received the information from his brother, Maher Kara, a former investment banker at Citigroup. Maher testified at Salman's trial that he shared inside information with his brother Michael to benefit him and expected him to trade on it, and Michael testified to sharing that information with Salman, who knew that it was from Maher. Salman was convicted on one count of conspiracy to commit securities fraud and four counts of securities fraud. Both Maher and Michael pleaded guilty to their own insider trading charges.

While Salman's appeal was pending in the Ninth Circuit, the Second Circuit in United States v. Newman *decided that* Dirks *does not permit a factfinder to infer a personal benefit to the tipper from a gift of confidential information to a trading relative or friend, unless there is proof of a meaningfully close personal relationship between tipper and tippee that generates an exchange that is objective, consequential, and represents at least a potential gain of a pecuniary or similarly valuable nature. The Ninth Circuit declined to follow* Newman *so far, holding that* Dirks *allowed Salman's jury to infer that the tipper breached a duty because he made a gift of confidential information to a trading relative.*

The Supreme Court granted certiorari to "resolve the tension" between the Second Circuit's Newman *decision and the Ninth Circuit's decision in this case.*

Alito, Justice

We adhere to *Dirks,* which easily resolves the narrow issue presented here.

In *Dirks,* we explained that a tippee is exposed to liability for trading on inside information only if the tippee participates in a breach of the tipper's fiduciary duty. Whether the tipper breached that duty depends in large part on the purpose of the disclosure to the tippee. The test, we explained, is whether the insider personally will benefit, directly or indirectly, from his disclosure.

Thus, the disclosure of confidential information without personal benefit is not enough. In determining whether a tipper derived a personal benefit, we instructed courts to focus on objective criteria, i.e., whether the insider receives a direct or indirect personal benefit from the disclosure, such as a pecuniary gain or a reputational benefit that will translate into future earnings. This personal benefit can often be inferred from objective facts and circumstances, we explained, such as a relationship between the insider and the recipient that suggests a quid pro quo from the latter, or an intention to benefit the particular recipient. In particular, we held that the elements of fiduciary duty and exploitation of nonpublic information also exist when an insider makes a gift of confidential information to a trading relative or friend. In such cases, the tip and trade resemble trading by the insider followed by a gift of the profits to the recipient. We then applied this gift-giving principle to resolve *Dirks* itself, finding it dispositive that the tippers received no monetary or personal benefit from their tips to Dirks, nor was their purpose to make a gift of valuable information to Dirks.

Our discussion of gift giving resolves this case. Maher, the tipper, provided inside information to a close relative, his brother Michael. *Dirks* makes clear that a tipper breaches a fiduciary duty by making a gift of confidential information to a trading relative, and that rule is sufficient to resolve the case at hand. As Salman's counsel acknowledged at oral argument, Maher would have breached his duty had he personally traded on the information here himself then given the proceeds as a gift to his brother. It is obvious that Maher would personally benefit in that situation. But Maher effectively achieved the same result by disclosing the information to Michael, and allowing him to trade on it. *Dirks* appropriately prohibits that approach, as well. *Dirks* specifies that when a tipper gives inside information to a trading relative or friend, the jury can infer that the tipper meant to provide the equivalent of a cash gift. In such situations, the tipper benefits personally because giving a gift of trading information is the same thing as trading by the tipper followed by a gift of the proceeds. Here, by disclosing confidential information as a gift to his brother with the expectation that he would trade on

it, Maher breached his duty of trust and confidence to Citigroup and its clients—a duty Salman acquired, and breached himself, by trading on the information with full knowledge that it had been improperly disclosed.

To the extent the Second Circuit held [in *Newman*] that the tipper must also receive something of a pecuniary or similarly valuable nature in exchange for a gift to family or friends, we agree with the Ninth Circuit that this requirement is inconsistent with *Dirks*.

Accordingly, the Ninth Circuit's judgment is affirmed.

Note: While *Salman* appeared to have cleared up the confusion over personal benefit created by *Newman*, the Second Circuit recently created more confusion regarding insider trading law. In *United States v. Blaszczak*,[18] the court held that the *Dirks* requirement of a personal benefit did not apply to insider trading prosecutions brought under the mail and wire fraud statutes added by the Sarbanes-Oxley Act in 18 U.S.C § 1348. In what some called an unexpected gift to prosecutors, the Second Circuit determined that the personal benefit element was a judge-made doctrine unique to securities law and that it could not be grafted onto Title 18 criminal provisions. As more insider trading cases are brought under this provision and appeals follow, a circuit split is likely to occur, potentially leading to another Supreme Court insider trading opinion.

---

[18] 947 F.3d 19 (2d Cir. 2019).

---

treble penalty is paid to the Treasury of the United States. The penalty applies only to SEC actions; it does not affect the amount of damages that may be recovered by private plaintiffs. The 1934 Act also grants the SEC power to award up to 10 percent of any triple-damage penalty as a bounty to informants who helped the SEC uncover insider trading.

Rewards to Whistle-blowers The Dodd–Frank Act attempts to increase the likelihood that persons with knowledge of securities law violations will report them to the SEC. The act requires the SEC to pay a reward to individuals who provide original information resulting in SEC enforcement monetary sanctions exceeding $1 million. The award must range from 10 to 30 percent of the amount recouped.

Liability for Aiding and Abetting Under Rule 10b-5, only a person who is *primarily responsible* for the

misstatement or omission is liable for damages to a private plaintiff. Nonetheless, actors who aid and abet another's violation of the rule may be prosecuted by the SEC. To have aiding and abetting liability, there must be (1) a primary violation by another person, (2) the aider and abettor's knowing or reckless assistance of that violation, and (3) substantial assistance by the aider and abettor in the achievement of the primary violation. Although the SEC may prosecute aiders and abettors, investors may recover their damages only from primary violators, not from aiders and abettors.

Statute of Limitations A purchaser or seller bringing an action under Rule 10b-5 must file his suit in a timely fashion or else be precluded from litigating the issue. The Sarbanes-Oxley Act of 2002 extends the statute of limitation by requiring an action under Rule 10b–5 to be commenced within two years after discovery of the facts constituting a violation of Rule 10b–5 and within five years of the violation.

For more information on Rule 10b–5, see Chapter 46.

Regulation FD
Regulation FD (Fair Disclosure) was passed by the SEC to allow general investors to have more nearly equal access to information that in the past was selectively disclosed to institutional investors and securities analysts. The regulation, which applies only to public companies, provides that when an issuer or person acting for the issuer discloses material nonpublic information to securities market professionals and holders of the issuer's securities, it must make public disclosure of that information. An *intentional* selective disclosure occurs when the discloser knows or is reckless in not knowing that the information is material and nonpublic. In such a situation, the remedy is that the issuer must make public disclosure simultaneously, that is, at the same time it discloses the information selectively. When the disclosure of material nonpublic information is *nonintentionally* selective, the issuer must make the public disclosure promptly, that is, as soon as reasonably practical after a senior official learns of the disclosure and knows it is material and nonpublic. This must be no later than 24 hours after the selective disclosure or by the commencement of the next day's trading on the NYSE, whichever is later.

The required public disclosure may be made by filing or furnishing a Form 8-K or by another method that is reasonably designed to effect broad, nonexclusionary distribution of the information to the public, such as a press release to the financial media, like CNBC and Bloomberg. In addition, in 2013 the SEC approved the use of social media, like Facebook and Twitter, to comply with Regulation FD. For an issuer to use social media, the SEC stressed two fundamental points: (1) It is critically important that a company alert the public in advance regarding the social media channels of distribution it intends to use to disseminate material, nonpublic information and (2) the company should use social media outlets that are explicitly identified with the company. While personal social media sites of company officers might be acceptable if the company has explicitly alerted investors in advance, personal sites should not be viewed as preferred vehicles for company communications.

The SEC has taken action against several firms under Regulation FD. Most make the same mistake: a material disclosure from corporate management to a select audience in private conversations or at an invitation-only meeting. In one case, the CEO said in a public conference call that the company had a negative business outlook. Three weeks later, at an invitation-only technology conference, he presented attendees with a positive view of the company's prospects, and the price of its stock immediately rose 20 percent. In fining the company $250,000, the SEC said the public did not have access to the technology conference and was unable to benefit from the information disclosed there. In another case, the SEC prosecuted one company for making material nonpublic disclosures to securities analysts following one of its investor conferences.

One other case shows the importance of taking quick action when an inadvertent selective disclosure is made. A company's CEO, working from his home, participated in a conference call with a portfolio manager and a salesperson from an investment advisory group. From her office, the company's director of investor relations also took part in the conversation. During the call, the director realized the CEO disclosed nonpublic information that the CEO unwittingly did not know was nonpublic, but she didn't interrupt him. As soon as the conference call ended, she tried to reach him by telephone but was able to leave him only a voice-mail message expressing her concern over his inadvertent selective disclosure. Not until an hour later did the CEO get her message. He then asked the other call participants to keep the information confidential, but took no further action. At the time the CEO learned of his disclosure error, he had 24 hours to publicly disseminate the material information. That much time was available because his selective release was unintentional. The next day, however, the CEO intentionally selectively disclosed the material information to analysts without issuing a press release. The second disclosure was intentionally selective because the CEO by then knew that the information was nonpublic. This intentionally selective disclosure invoked a different part of Regulation FD: It had to be accompanied by a simultaneous public announcement. The company did not meet this requirement, instead issuing a press release three hours later, thus violating the rule. By then its stock had risen nearly 15 percent since the CEO's first nonpublic disclosure.

How can companies comply with Regulation FD? They should

- Establish clear rules for the content of information that may be disclosed.
- Require previews of any material disclosure by a qualified team of executives, such as legal counsel and an investor relations officer.
- Use several mass communications outlets, including submissions to the SEC, press releases, and Internet-based sound and video presentations.

- Adopt procedures for appropriate corrective action as soon as possible after a selective disclosure occurs.

An issuer should adopt absolute rules that provide guidance to its CEO, CFO, and others who regularly communicate with securities analysts and institutional investors. Clear rules can help prevent errors in judgment that can lead to inadvertent violations during an unscripted conference call or presentation. For instance, a company may have a rule that after the CEO gives his outlook on the company earnings in a press release or conference call, the CEO does not update the earnings outlook unless the company finds that the earnings are so far off that another release is required.

As an example of a preview process, consider W. R. Grace & Co., which circulates draft press releases by e-mail to its financial, executive, and legal groups. For Grace, the process consumes only a few hours typically and only a few days when the release is about a complex subject such as quarterly earnings.

Criminal Liability Like the 1933 Act, the 1934 Act provides for liability for criminal violations of the act. Section 32 provides that individuals may be fined up to $5 million and imprisoned up to 20 years for willful violations of the 1934 Act or the related SEC rules. Businesses may be fined up to $25 million.

Tender Offer Regulation

Historically, the predominant procedure by which one corporation acquired another was the merger, a transaction requiring the cooperation of the acquired corporation's management. Since the early 1960s, the **tender offer** has become an often-used acquisition device. A tender offer is a public offer by a *bidder* to purchase a *subject company's* equity securities directly from its shareholders at a specified price for a fixed period of time. The offering price is usually well above the market price of the shares. Such offers are often made even though there is opposition from the subject company's management. Opposed offers are called hostile tender offers. The legality of efforts opposing a tender offer is covered in Chapter 43.

The Williams Act amendments to the 1934 Act require bidders and subject companies to provide a shareholder with information on which to base his decision whether to sell his shares to a bidder. The aim of the Williams Act is to protect investors and to give the bidder and the subject company equal opportunities to present their cases to the shareholder. The intent is to encourage an auction of the shares with the highest bidder purchasing the shares. The Williams Act applies only when the subject company's equity securities are registered under the 1934 Act.

The Williams Act does not define a tender offer, but the courts have compiled a list of factors to determine whether a person has made a tender offer. The greater the number of people solicited and the lower their investment sophistication, the more likely it is that the bidder will be held to have made a tender offer. Also, the shorter the offering period, the more rigid the price, and the greater the publicity concerning the offer, the more likely it is that the purchase efforts of the bidder will be treated as a tender offer. Given these factors, a person who offers to purchase shares directly from several shareholders at a set price for only a few days risks having a court treat the offer like a tender offer. The Williams Act does not regulate a tender offer unless the bidder intends to become a holder of at least 5 percent of the subject company's shares.

A bidder making a tender offer must file a tender offer statement (Schedule TO) with the SEC when the offer commences. The information in this schedule includes the terms of the offer (for example, the price), the background of the bidder, and the purpose of the tender offer (including whether the bidder intends to control the subject company).

The SEC requires the bidder to keep the tender offer open for at least 20 business days and prohibits any purchase of shares during that time. This rule gives shareholders adequate time to make informed decisions regarding whether to tender their shares. Tendering shareholders may withdraw their tendered shares during the entire term of the offer. This rule allows the highest bidder to buy the shares, as in an auction.

All tender offers, whether made by the issuer or by a third-party bidder, must be made to all holders of the targeted class of shares. When a bidder increases the offering price during the term of the tender offer, all of the shareholders must be paid the higher price even if they tendered their shares at a lower price. If more shares are tendered than the bidder offered to buy, the bidder must prorate its purchases among all of the shares tendered. This proration rule is designed to foster careful shareholder decisions about whether to sell shares. Shareholders might rush to tender their shares if the bidder could accept shares on a first-come, first-served basis.

After an initial offering period has expired, a bidder is permitted to include a "subsequent offering period" during which shareholders who tender will have no withdrawal rights. The SEC created the new offering period

The Global Business Environment

The Foreign Corrupt Practices Act

The Foreign Corrupt Practices Act (FCPA) was passed by Congress in 1977 as an amendment to the Securities Exchange Act of 1934. Its passage followed discoveries that more than 400 American corporations had given bribes or made other improper or questionable payments in connection with business abroad and within the United States. Many of these payments were bribes to high-level officials of foreign governments for the purpose of obtaining contracts for the sale of goods or services. Officers of the companies that had made the payments argued that such payments were customary and necessary in business transactions in many countries. This argument was pressed forcefully with regard to facilitating payments. Such payments were said to be essential to get lower-level government officials in a number of countries to perform their nondiscretionary or ministerial tasks, such as preparing or approving necessary import or export documents.

In a significant number of cases, bribes had been accounted for as commission payments, as normal transactions with foreign subsidiaries, or as payments for services rendered by professionals or other firms, or had in other ways been made to appear as normal business expenses. These bribes were then illegally deducted as normal business expenses in income tax returns filed with the Internal Revenue Service.

In late 2012, the Department of Justice and the SEC issued a *Resource Guide to the U.S. Foreign Corrupt Practices Act*. The 130-page guide provides insight into the DOJ and SEC's interpretation of the FCPA, including their principles for enforcement.

The Payments Prohibition

The FCPA makes it a crime for any American firm—whether or not it has securities registered under the 1934 Act—to offer, promise, or make payments or gifts of anything of value to foreign officials and certain others. Payments are prohibited if the person making the payment knows or should know that some or all of it will be used for the purpose of influencing a governmental decision, even if the offer is not accepted or the promise is not carried out. The FCPA prohibits offers or payments to foreign political parties and candidates for office as well as offers and payments to government officials. Payments of kickbacks to foreign businesses and their officers are not prohibited unless it is known or should be known that these payments will be passed on to government officials or other illegal recipients.

Facilitating or grease payments are not prohibited by the FCPA. For example, suppose a corporation applies for a radio license in Italy and makes a payment to the government official who issues the licenses. If the official grants licenses to every applicant and the payment merely speeds up the processing of the application, the FCPA is not violated.

Substantial penalties for violations may be imposed. A company may be fined up to $2 million. Directors, officers, employees, or agents participating in violations are liable for fines of up to $100,000 and prison terms of up to five years.

Record-Keeping and Internal Controls Requirements

The FCPA also establishes record-keeping and internal control requirements for firms subject to the periodic disclosure provisions of the Securities Exchange Act of 1934. The purpose of such controls is to prevent unauthorized payments and transactions and unauthorized access to company assets that may result in illegal payments.

The FCPA requires the making and keeping of records and accounts "which, in reasonable detail, accurately, and fairly reflect the transactions and dispositions of the assets of the issuer" of securities. It also requires the establishment and maintenance of a system of internal accounting controls that provides "reasonable assurances" that the firm's transactions are executed in accordance with management's authorization and that the firm's assets are used or disposed of only as authorized by management.

The SEC's focus on internal controls is shown by recent FCPA actions. For example, in 2014, Hewlett-Packard Company agreed to pay more than $108 million to settle FCPA actions brought by the SEC and the Department of Justice. These actions were based on HP's subsidiaries' alleged payments of more than $3.6 million to Russian, Polish, and Mexican government officials to obtain or maintain lucrative public contracts. In 2019, Barclays PLC paid over $6 million to settle charges that it violated the FCPA by hiring the relatives and friends of foreign government officials in order to influence them in connection with its investment banking business. The SEC found Barclays failed to maintain a system of internal accounting controls around its hiring practices to ensure "relationship hires" were not being used to bribe foreign officials.

---

to allow shareholders a last opportunity to tender into an offer.

The management of the subject company is required to inform the shareholders of its position on the tender offer, with its reasons, within 10 days after the offer has been made. It must also provide the bidder with a list of the holders of the equity securities that the bidder seeks to acquire or mail the materials for the bidder.

SEC Rule 14e–3 prohibits persons who have knowledge of an impending tender offer from using such information prior to its public disclosure. The rule limits insider trading in the tender offer context.

Private Acquisitions of Shares

The Williams Act regulates private acquisitions of shares differently from tender offers. When the bidder privately seeks a controlling block of the subject company's shares on a stock exchange or in face-to-face negotiations with only a few shareholders, no advance notice to the SEC or disclosure to shareholders is required. However, a person making a private acquisition is required to file a Schedule 13D with the SEC and to send a copy to the subject company within 10 days after he becomes a holder of 5 percent of its shares.

State Regulation of Tender Offers

Most of the states have statutes that apply to tender offers. State statutes have become highly protective of subject companies. For example, the Indiana statute gives shareholders other than the bidder the right to determine whether the shares acquired by the bidder may be voted in directors' elections and other matters. The statute, which essentially gives a subject company the power to require shareholder approval of a hostile tender offer, has been copied by several states.

Other states, such as Delaware, have adopted business combination moratorium statutes. These statutes delay the effectuation of a merger of the corporation with a shareholder owning a large percentage of shares (such as 15 percent) unless the board of directors' approval is obtained. Because the typical large shareholder in a public company is a bidder who has made a tender offer, these state statutes primarily affect the ability of a bidder to effectuate a merger after a tender offer and, therefore, may have the effect of deterring hostile acquisitions.

State Securities Law

LO45-1 Understand why and demonstrate how the law regulates issuances and issuers of securities.

State securities laws are frequently referred to as blue-sky laws, because the early state securities statutes were designed to protect investors from promoters and security salespersons who would "sell building lots in the blue sky." The first state to enact a securities law was Kansas, in 1911. All of the states now have such legislation.

The National Conference of Commissioners on Uniform State Laws has adopted the Uniform Securities Act of 1956. The act contains antifraud provisions, requires the registration of securities, and demands broker-dealer registration. About two-thirds of the states have adopted the act, but many states have made significant changes in it.

All of the state securities statutes provide penalties for fraudulent sales and permit the issuance of injunctions to protect investors from additional or anticipated fraudulent acts. Most of the statutes grant broad power to investigate fraud to some state official—usually the attorney general or his appointee as securities administrator. All of the statutes provide criminal penalties for selling fraudulent securities and conducting fraudulent transactions.

LOG ON

www.com.ohio.gov/secu

Many state securities commissioners maintain websites that warn investors of risky or fraudulent securities. Visit the Ohio Division of Securities website. Click on links under "Investors & Public" to see examples of investor warnings.

Registration of Securities

LO45-3 Comply with the communication rules that apply to a public offering of securities.

Most of the state securities statutes adopt the philosophy of the 1933 Act that informed investors can make intelligent investment decisions. The states with such statutes have a registration scheme much like the 1933 Act, with required disclosures for public offerings and exemptions from registration for small and private offerings. Other states reject the contention that investors with full information can make sound investment decisions. The securities statutes in these states have a *merit registration* requirement, giving a securities administrator power to deny registration on the merits of the security and its issuer. Only securities that are not unduly risky and promise an adequate return to investors may receive administrator approval.

All state statutes have a limited number of exemptions from registration. Most statutes have private offering exemptions that are similar to Securities Act Rule 506 of

Regulation D. In addition, a person may avoid the registration requirements of state securities laws by not offering or selling securities.

Registration by Coordination The Uniform Securities Act permits an issuer to register its securities by coordination. Instead of filing a registration statement under the Securities Act of 1933 and a different one as required by state law, registration by coordination allows an issuer to file the 1933 Act registration statement with the state securities administrator. Registration by coordination decreases an issuer's expense of complying with state law when making an interstate offering of its securities.

Problems and Problem Cases

1. Marvie, Kim, Clarence, and Goldie Tschetter purchased units in Huron Kitchen LLC, a limited liability company, which would construct and own a Country Kitchen restaurant in South Dakota. As members of an LLC, they had management powers in proportion to their contributions of capital and could elect the managers of the LLC and set the managers' responsibilities. As LLC members, the Tschetters agreed to hire Country Hospitality Corporation to do much of the operation of the LLC. The LLC Operating Agreement required that the day-to-day decisions were made by two managers, who were required to be members of the LLC and were selected by the other members. Members could authorize loans on behalf of the company by agreement. The members had the right to receive profits and distributions when warranted. The members could authorize incidental expenses within an aggregate of $12,500. The members were empowered to make any other routine actions incidental to the day-to-day activity of the LLC. The members were allowed to select officers for the LLC. Marvie, acting for all the Tschetters, exercised substantial control over the affairs of the LLC. Clarence and Goldie acquiesced in relying on Marvie and Kim for information and action. The minutes kept by the LLC showed that the Tschetters were informed and active in the LCC. Unfortunately, the restaurant failed, and the Tschetters sued the person who sold them the interests in the LLC on the grounds that the LLC interests were securities, and, therefore, the seller owed duties to them. Were the LLC interests securities?

2. Tom Hirsch, Berta Walder, Howard Walder, and Harish Shah were member managers in Radical Bunny LLC. Between 2006 and 2008, they raised nearly $190 million from investors in the name of Radical Bunny. Radical Bunny used that money to make loans to another company, Mortgages Limited. Mortgages Limited, in turn, was to make loans to developers and real estate buyers, who were to secure the repayment of the loans by deeds of trust on the land the borrowers developed or bought. The investors in Radical Bunny were to be named as beneficiaries of such deeds of trust. The LLC's member managers sent each investor a document titled "Direction to Purchase," which constituted the investor's contract with the member managers. The monetary investments each investor made pursuant to the Direction to Purchase were used for the same purpose—that is, to allow Radical Bunny to make loans to Mortgages Limited. The managers promised the investors a profit of 11 percent interest annually on their investment. The 11 percent annual payments were to be paid by Radical Bunny. All the investors' profits were to come from the member manager's efforts. Investors did not exercise any control over the loans; only the managers had the authority to manage the investments. Were the investors' purchase of LLC interests in Radical Bunny LLC held to be securities under the Securities Act of 1933?

3. AltaVerba Inc. is a nonpublic company controlled by its majority shareholder, Robyn Streel. AltaVerba wants to make an initial public offering by selling 300 million Class B common shares in a firm commitment underwriting, with Goldman Sachs acting as the lead underwriter. AltaVerba is not a public company required to file periodic reports with the SEC under the Securities Exchange Act of 1934. AltaVerba and Goldman are considering the communications they may have with existing and prospective investors and securities analysts before and during the registered offering and comply with Section 5 of the Securities Act of 1933. Seventy-two days before the 1933 Act registration statement will be filed with the SEC, AltaVerba wants to release historical information about its business and financial results. What are the restrictions on the release of such information at that time? Twenty-three days before the 1933 Act registration statement will be filed with the SEC, AltaVerba wants to release forward-looking information about its business and financial results. May AltaVerba do that? After the registration statement has been filed with the SEC, Streel and AltaVerba's vice president of finance want to speak on the phone about the issuance

with an investment manager of Fidelity Magellan Fund. Is that communication legal at that time? At the same time, AltaVerba and Goldman want to conduct a road show in five cities. Selected very wealthy investors, securities analysts, and mutual fund managers will attend the road show in person. Under what conditions may AltaVerba and Goldman conduct a legal road show? After the registration statement has been declared effective by the SEC, AltaVerba wants to use a free-writing prospectus that includes historical and forward-looking information about AltaVerba. What conditions must the free-writing prospectus meet to be legal under Section 5?

4. EMG Corp., a public corporation, decides to enter the Internet marketing business by creating a subsidiary corporation, GME Inc., that will be 51 percent owned by EMG and 49 percent owned by other investors. The plan is that GME will not be not a public corporation required to file periodic reports with the Securities and Exchange Commission under the Securities Exchange Act of 1934. GME plans to sell 100 million shares for $20 each to EMG and to the following investors:

 * An investor who has annual income of $4,080,000 and a net worth of $12,200,000.
 * GME's chief operations officer, whose annual income is $175,000 and net worth is $350,000.
 * A pension fund established for EMG's employees.
 * 14 mutual funds, each of which has assets exceeding $20 billion.

GME wants to sell its common shares to the above investors in an exemption from the registration requirements of the Securities Act of 1933 under Rule 506. Is the $2 billion amount of the offering too large for Rule 506? Is the number of purchasers a problem under Rule 506? Are the listed investors qualified purchasers under Rule 506? Under Rule 506, for how long must GME restrict the purchasers' resales of the common shares? If GME is unsure whether the offering it proposes meets the requirements of Rule 506, what document should GME request from the staff of the SEC?

5. Roxxit Corporation is in the business of providing cloud computing and other network solutions. It is incorporated and headquartered in Ames, Iowa, where all 225 of its employees are resident. It does business in 27 states, as well as Canada and Mexico. Roxxit is a nonpublic company; that is, it is not a company required to file periodic reports with the SEC under the Securities Exchange Act of 1934. Roxxit wants to raise $835,000

of capital by selling its common shares to 53 investors, mostly individuals and businesses in the Ames area, but also some investors in Omaha, Nebraska, and Chicago, Illinois. Is Roxxit eligible to make an offering that is exempt from registration under Rule 504 of the Securities Act of 1933? What must Roxxit do to comply with Rule 504?

6. Podcast Services Company is incorporated in Illinois. It has 200 employees that work in an office building leased by Podcast in Alton, Illinois. Most of Podcast's employees reside in Illinois, but a few reside in Missouri near St. Louis. All of Podcast's assets are in Illinois. It sells its services to clients in 20 states. About 35 percent of its business is conducted with clients in Missouri in the St. Louis area. Podcast wants to sell debentures to its employees, the proceeds of which will be used to purchase the building Podcast currently leases in Alton. May Podcast make the offering in compliance with Securities Act Rule 147? What must Podcast do to comply with Rule 147?

7. In 2005, The Freeman Group purchased preferred shares offered by The Royal Bank of Scotland (RBS) in an offering registered under the Securities Act of the 1933. In the prospectus by which the securities were offered, RBS disclosed that it had accumulated a significant concentration of subprime assets—that is, financial assets secured by subprime mortgages. The prospectus also disclosed that RBS was exposed to tens of billions of British pounds worth of securitized assets, including certain securitizations of residential mortgages, and identified whether the risks and rewards associated with these assets were completely held, were partially held, or had been transferred by RBS. The offering documents further described those assets, explained how RBS had calculated their value, disclosed the dangers it foresaw, and provided an account of how those dangers could affect the assets' value. These statements did not disclose the percentage of the relevant securitizations that included subprime mortgages. The prospectus stated that RBS had a strong credit quality, it had few problem loans, and its risks remained stable. When the subprime crisis hit banks, including RBS, in 2008 and 2009, the preferred shares lost 80 percent of their value. Freeman sued RBS under Sections 12(a)(2) and 11 of the 1933 Act, claiming that RBS failed to disclose a material fact—that is, the full extent of RBS's exposure to subprime mortgage risks. Was Freeman successful?

8. In 2012, Facebook Inc. filed with the SEC a registration statement under the Securities Act of 1933, pursuant to which Facebook would make a public offering of

securities. During the waiting period prior to the effective date of the registration statement, Facebook determined that, at least in the short term, it was not able to monetize its mobile application as quickly and as well as it had monetized its desktop application. That was an important discovery because Facebook users were rapidly moving to exclusive or primary use of mobile applications, especially on smartphones. What did Facebook do with the new information to ensure it complied with Section 11 of the 1933 Act?

9. Between December 4 and December 17, 2008, John Malone, a director and major shareholder of Discovery Communications Inc., sold 953,506 shares of Discovery's Series C stock and purchased 632,700 shares of Series A stock. Series A and Series C were separately registered, separately traded, nonconvertible securities. Series A holders had voting rights, while Series C holders did not. Michael Gibbons, a Discovery shareholder, filed suit under Section 16(b) of the Securities Exchange Act of 1934 seeking the recovery for Discovery of Malone's $313,573 of profits from the purchase and sale of Discovery's registered securities. Was Gibbons successful?

10. Joseph Crotty was a vice president of United Artists Communications (UA), a corporation with equity securities registered under the Securities Exchange Act of 1934. Crotty was the head film buyer of UA's western division. He had virtually complete and autonomous control of film buying for the 351 UA theaters in the western United States, including negotiating and signing movie acquisition agreements, supervising movie distribution, and settling contracts after the movies had been shown. Crotty knew how many contracts were being negotiated at any one time and the price UA was paying for the rental of each movie. Crotty was required to consult with higher officers only if he wanted to exceed a certain limit on the amount of the cash advance paid to a distributor for a movie. This occurred no more than two or three times a year. The gross revenue from Crotty's division was about 35 percent of UA's gross revenue from movie exhibitions and around 17 percent of its total gross revenue. During a six-month period, Crotty purchased 7,500 shares of UA and sold 3,500 shares, realizing a large profit. Has Crotty violated Section 16(b) of the 1934 Act?

11. PNC Financial Services Group Inc. received a request from activist investor Boston Common Asset Management to include a shareholder proposal in its upcoming annual meeting proxy statement. The proposal required PNC to report to shareholders "greenhouse gas emissions resulting from its lending portfolio and its exposure to climate change risk in its lending, investing, and financing activities." Citing SEC staff no-action letters from the mid-2000s on similar proposals, PNC requested that the SEC staff declare that it would not recommend enforcement action if PNC omitted the proposal from its proxy materials because the proposal dealt with matters related to the ordinary business of the company that are properly within the authority of a company's board of directors. PNC also argued that the proposal sought to micromanage the company by probing too deeply into matters of a complex nature upon which shareholders, as a group, would not be in a position to make an informed judgment. Did the SEC staff allow PNC to omit the shareholder proposal from its proxy statement?

12. Michael Broudo and other investors purchased stock in Dura Pharmaceuticals Inc. on the public securities market between April 15, 1997, and February 24, 1998. During this period, they allege that Dura or its officers made false statements concerning both Dura's drug profits and future Food and Drug Administration approval of a new asthmatic spray device. They also allege that Dura falsely claimed that it expected that its drug sales would prove profitable. Regarding the asthmatic spray device, they allege Dura falsely claimed that it expected the FDA would soon grant its approval. On February 24, 1998, Dura announced that its earnings would be lower than expected, principally due to slow drug sales. The next day, Dura's shares lost almost half their value, falling from about $39 per share to about $21. Eight months later in November 1998, Dura announced that the FDA would not approve Dura's new asthmatic spray device. Soon after, Broudo and the other investors sued Dura and its officers under Rule 10b–5 of the Securities Exchange Act of 1934. In their complaint, they stated that in reliance on the integrity of the market, they paid artificially inflated prices for Dura securities and suffered damages. They did not specify or attempt to calculate the amount of damages caused by the alleged misstatements made by Dura. Dura defended on the grounds that Broudo and the other investors failed adequately to allege loss causation. Did the U.S. Supreme Court agree with Dura?

13. Lululemon Athletic Inc. is a manufacturer of athletic apparel. Among its most popular products are fitness pants made from a proprietary material known as luon, an amalgamation of 86 percent nylon and 14 percent Lycra. The black luon pants were recalled

in March 2013 after customers complained that they were transparent. The recall amounted to 17 percent of the company's sales. After the recall, customers reported additional problems, including pilling, flawed seams, and continuing sheerness. The Louisiana Sheriffs' Pension & Relief Fund purchased common shares of Lululemon during the time Lululemon made representations that its apparel's quality level was the "highest in the industry," it was the "leader in technical fabrics and quality construction," and that "quality" was the company's "key differentiating factor" from its peers. After the recall, Lululemon's sales and the market price of its shares plummeted. The pension fund sued Lululemon under Securities Exchange Act Section 10(b) and Rule 10b–5, claiming that Lululemon's statements were irreconcilable with Lululemon's actual, undisclosed quality control practices. Was the pension fund's claim successful?

14. The managements of Combustion Engineering Inc. (CEI) and Basic Inc. entered negotiations regarding CEI's acquiring Basic. Despite the secrecy of the merger negotiations, there were repeated instances of abnormal trading in Basic's shares, with trading volume rising from 7,000 per day to 29,000. Basic issued a public statement that "the company knew no reason for the stock's activity and that no negotiations were under way with any company for a merger." Did Basic's statement violate Securities Exchange Act Rule 10b–5?

15. Plumbers & Steamfitters Local 773 Pension Fund sued Canadian Imperial Bank of Commerce and four of its officers on the grounds that they misled investors about CIBC's exposure to fixed-income securities backed by subprime residential mortgages. One example of a misstatement was in the 2006 Accountability Report, in which CIBC stated, "Although actual losses are not expected to be material, as of October 31, 2006, our maximum exposure to loss as a result of involvement with the CDOs [collateralized debt obligations] was approximately $729 million." Pension Fund alleges that this reference constituted false and misleading representations because CIBC's actual exposure to the U.S. real estate market was almost $12 billion. Pension Fund argued that CIBC and its officers were liable under Securities Exchange Act Rule 10b–5 because they failed to comply with generally accepted accounting principles in accounting for the CDO losses. Did the court agree?

16. In early May 2001, American Express Financial Advisors (AEFA) CEO James Cracchiolo received a fax from AEFA CFO Stuart Sedlacek advising him that AEFA was facing additional losses on its high-yield debt investments beyond those already booked. American Express Company (AMEX) COO Kenneth Chenault was advised of the situation the next day. He was told that the deterioration of the high-yield debt portfolio was so bad that "even the investment-grade CDOs [collateralized debt obligations] held by American Express showed potential deterioration" because defaults on the underlying bonds had risen so sharply. Chenault asked, "What are we talking about here?" Cracchiolo replied, "We really don't know enough to even give you a range."

In the meantime, on May 15, 2001, AMEX filed its quarterly report (Form 10-Q) for the first quarter of 2001. In it, the company reported the $182 million in first-quarter losses from AEFA's high-yield debt portfolio. The company explained, "The high-yield losses reflect the continued deterioration of the high-yield portfolio and losses associated with selling certain bonds." Importantly, it added, "Total losses on these investments for the remainder of 2001 are expected to be substantially lower than in the first quarter."

In July 2001, however, AMEX recognized that losses from the debt portfolio would be $400 million. Investors who purchased AMEX stock between the 10-Q filing and the disclosure of the actual losses sued AMEX and certain officers under Securities Act Rule 10b–5 for making erroneous forward-looking statements. Were the investors successful?

17. In March 2004, Internet broadcasting pioneer and Dallas Mavericks owner Mark Cuban acquired 600,000 shares, a 6.3 percent stake, of Mamma.com. Later that spring, Mamma.com decided to sell more of its shares through a PIPE (private investment in public equity) offering. Shares issued in PIPE offerings are typically sold below the market price of the shares. Mamma.com's CEO called Cuban to invite him to participate. Before telling Cuban about the offering of shares, the CEO told Cuban he had confidential information for him, and Cuban agreed to keep whatever information the CEO shared confidential. The CEO then told Cuban about the PIPE offering. Cuban became very upset and said, among other things, that he did not like PIPEs because they dilute the existing shareholders. At the end of the call, Cuban told the CEO, "Well, now I'm screwed. I can't sell." The CEO then sent Cuban a follow-up e-mail, encouraging him to contact Mamma.com's investment banker handling the offering. Cuban called the banker and spoke for eight minutes. During that call, the banker supplied Cuban with additional

confidential details about the PIPE. In response to Cuban's questions, the banker told him that the PIPE was being sold at a discount to the market price and that the offering included other incentives for the PIPE investors. With that information and one minute after speaking with the investment banker, Cuban called his broker and instructed him to sell his entire stake in Mamma.com. Cuban sold 10,000 shares during the evening of June 28, 2004, and the remainder during regular trading the next day. Before Cuban's sales, word had leaked into the public market that potential investors were being contacted to participate in the PIPE offering. Did Cuban illegally trade on inside information under Rule 10b–5?

18. The wife of Ching Hwa Chen was the senior tax director of Informatica, a data integration company. In late June 2012, Informatica learned it would miss its revenue guidance for the first time in 31 consecutive quarters. That revenue miss caused Chen's wife to work more than usual as the company scrambled to close its books and prepare for a potential prerelease of its quarterly revenues. Over the next several days, Chen overheard his wife's phone calls addressing the revenue miss, including on a four-hour drive to Reno, Nevada, where his wife fielded calls from the passenger seat as he drove. Early the next week, convinced that Informatica's stock would lose value, Chen bet heavily against the company, shorting its stock, buying put options, and selling call options. In early July, after announcing the miss, Informatica's stock price fell 27 percent from $43 to $31. Chen closed out all of his positions that same day, making a large profit. Was Chen found liable for insider trading under Securities Exchange Act Rule 10b–5?

19. Lawrence Polizzotto was the head of investor relations for First Solar Inc., the manufacturer and seller of solar modules. First Solar also designed, constructed, and sold complete solar power systems. Its common stock was registered with the SEC pursuant to the Securities Exchange Act, and its stock traded on the NASDAQ. Polizzotto was authorized by First Solar to speak on its behalf to investors, analysts, and other securities professionals. In June 2011, First Solar received conditional commitments from the U.S. Department of Energy for loan guarantees of approximately $4.5 billion relating to three separate First Solar projects. The loan guarantees were important to First Solar because they would allow the company to receive guaranteed low-cost financing from the federal government. However, each of the guarantees was conditioned upon First Solar meeting several requirements prior to September 30, 2011. On September 13, 2011, Polizzotto attended an investor conference with First Solar's CEO. During the conference, First Solar's CEO publicly expressed confidence that the company would receive all three loan guarantees. On September 15, 2011, Polizzotto and several other executives learned that the DOE had decided not to provide a loan guarantee with respect to one project, that is, the Topaz project. The group of employees responsible for public disclosure regarding the DOE loans, including Polizzotto and one of First Solar's in-house lawyers, began discussing how and when the company should disclose the loss of the Topaz loan guarantee. When Polizzotto arrived at work on the morning of September 21, he knew the Topaz press release had not yet been issued, and found out shortly thereafter that it would not be issued until the following morning. Nevertheless, he drafted several Topaz-related talking points, which he and a subordinate investor relations employee delivered to securities analysts and investors with whom they spoke that day. The talking points indicated that there was a lower probability the company would receive the Topaz guarantee. In addition, in certain discussions, Polizzotto told at least one analyst and one institutional investor that if they wanted to be conservative, they should assume First Solar would not receive the Topaz loan guarantee.

Later that day, First Solar executives discovered that Polizzotto had disclosed to 20 sell-side analysts and institutional investors that First Solar would not receive the loan guarantee from the DOE. The next day, First Solar finished its plans regarding the Topaz press release and issued it prior to the opening of the market on September 22. The company's stock opened that morning down 6 percent. Did First Solar comply with Regulation FD?

20. First City Financial Corp., a Canadian company controlled by the Belzberg family, was engaged in the business of investing in publicly held American corporations. Marc Belzberg identified Ashland Oil Company as a potential target, and on February 11, 1986, he secretly purchased 61,000 shares of Ashland stock for First City. By February 26, additional secret purchases of Ashland shares pushed First City's holdings to just over 4.9 percent of Ashland's stock. These last two purchases were effected for First City by Alan "Ace" Greenberg, the chief executive officer of Bear Stearns, a large Wall Street brokerage. On March 4, Belzberg called Greenberg and told him, "It wouldn't be a bad

idea if you bought Ashland Oil here." Immediately after the phone call, Greenberg purchased 20,500 Ashland shares for about $44 per share. If purchased for First City, those shares would have increased First City's Ashland holdings above 5 percent. Greenberg believed he was buying the shares for First City under a put and call agreement, under which First City had the right to buy the shares from Bear Stearns and Bear Stearns had the right to require First City to buy the shares from it. Between March 4 and 14, Greenberg purchased an additional 330,700 shares. On March 17, First City and Bear Stearns signed a formal put and call agreement covering all the shares Greenberg purchased. On March 25, First City announced publicly for the first time that it intended to make a tender offer for all of Ashland's shares. First City filed a Schedule 13D on March 26. Has First City violated the Williams Act?

21. Amenity Inc. was incorporated with 1 million authorized shares, which were issued to Capital General Corporation (CGC) for $2,000. CGC distributed 90,000 of those shares to about 900 of its clients, business associates, and other contacts to create and maintain goodwill among its clients and contacts. CGC did not receive any monetary or other direct financial consideration from those receiving the stock. Amenity had no actual business function at this time, and its sole asset was the $2,000 CGC had paid for the 1 million shares. Through CGC's efforts, Amenity was acquired by another company, which paid CGC $25,000 for its efforts. The Utah Securities Division sought to suspend the public trading of Amenity stock on the grounds that when CGC distributed the shares, it had sold them in violation of the Utah Securities Act. Was CGC's distribution a sale of securities?

22. On August 7, 2018, Elon Musk, the founder and CEO of electric carmaker Tesla, announced via tweet that he was considering taking Tesla private. His tweet, which appeared to be prompted by his frustration with short sellers driving down his company's stock price, stated the following: "Am considering taking Tesla private at $420. Funding secured." In later statements, Musk indicated that "[i]nvestor support is confirmed. Only reason why this is not certain is that it's contingent on a shareholder vote." Musk also indicated that Saudi Arabia's sovereign wealth fund was available to finance the effort. The string of tweets, which went out to Musk's 22 million followers at the time, caused Tesla's stock price to soar. But in the following weeks, the company's stock dropped 16% and the idea of taking the company private was officially abandoned on August 24. Musk explained that funding talks had stalled weeks earlier. The SEC immediately subpoenaed Musk and ultimately sued him for violating the securities laws. Did Musk violate the law?

23. Mathew Martoma worked as a portfolio manager at SAC Capital Advisors, a New York–based hedge fund. Martoma's investment portfolio was focused on pharmaceutical and health care companies. In order to obtain information about a new drug being developed to fight Alzheimer's disease, Martoma contacted expert networking firms and arranged paid consultations with doctors, including some who were working on the clinical trials of the new Alzheimer's drug. Eventually one doctor disclosed confidential information to Martoma about problems with the drug's safety and efficacy. Martoma passed this information to his superiors at SAC Capital, and the hedge fund reduced its position in two pharmaceutical companies that were jointly developing the drug. Martoma received a $9 million bonus, which was largely based on the pharmaceutical trades. Under these facts, is Martoma guilty of insider trading? Under what theory?

Legal and Professional Responsibilities of Auditors, Consultants, and Securities Professionals

Credit Deutsch First Chicago LLP (CDFC) is a financial consulting and investment banking firm. Angst & Yearn LLP (A&Y) is a public accounting firm. A client of both firms is Macrohard Corporation, a public issuer of securities required to file periodic reports with the Securities and Exchange Commission under the Securities Exchange Act of 1934. Because Macrohard has a short-term cash flow problem due to a downturn in the economy, CDFC advises Macrohard to issue 300 promissory notes, each with a face value of $10,000,000, interest of 4 percent, and a due date 11 months after issuance. CDFC recommends that the notes be sold to mutual funds, insurance companies, pension funds, and other institutional investors using the Rule 506 exemption from registration under the Securities Act of 1933.

The notes are offered in part by an offering circular, which includes financial statements audited by A&Y. A&Y's unqualified audit opinion is also included in the offering circular. A&Y receives a $6,500,000 fee for auditing Macrohard's financial statements and reviewing the financial statements for inclusion in the offering circular.

CDFC assists Macrohard with the offering of the notes by calling prospective investors on the phone, visiting investors in person, and sending e-mails to prospective investors urging them to buy the notes. In all three contacts, CDFC emphasizes that the notes carry an interest rate that is 3 percent higher than the 30-year Treasury bond rate and, therefore, offer an excellent return on investment. As compensation for its role in the notes offering, CDFC will receive 0.5 percent of the proceeds from the sale of the notes.

- What standard of care must CDFC meet when recommending that Macrohard issue promissory notes as a solution to its liquidity problems?
- If one of CDFC's managing partners during the course of the offering negligently makes false statements about Macrohard's financial position to purchasers of the notes, does CDFC have potential liability to the purchasers under Section 12(a)(2) of the Securities Act of 1933? Especially consider whether CDFC is a proper type of defendant under that section.
- Is CDFC a proper type of defendant under Rule 10b-5 of the Securities Exchange Act of 1934 due to its communications with purchasers, if one of its partners negligently makes false statements?
- Should A&Y fear liability to the note purchasers under Section 12(a)(2) of the 1933 Act?
- If A&Y negligently audited Macrohard's financial statements and as a result the financial statements materially misstate Macrohard's financial position, does A&Y have potential liability to the purchasers under Rule 10b-5 of the 1934 Act? Especially consider whether A&Y is a proper type of defendant under that rule.

- Does CDFC have potential liability to any of the note purchasers under the state law of negligent misrepresentation in a state that has adopted the *Ultramares* test?
- If A&Y knows that the audited financial statements will be used in the offering circular to sell the notes, but it does not know to which institutional investors the notes will be sold, does A&Y have potential liability to any of the note purchasers under the state law of negligent misrepresentation in a state that adopted the *Ultramares* test? How about a state that has adopted the rule of the *Restatement (Second) of Torts*?

Suppose that instead of making a Rule 506 offering, Macrohard issues preferred stock in a public offering registered under the 1933 Act. CDFC is Macrohard's underwriter for the public offering, receiving a 25-cent spread for each share sold. The financial statements audited by A&Y and its audit opinion are included in the registration statement. Unknown to CDFC and A&Y, there are material misstatements of fact in the financial statements included in the registration statement, and there are also omissions of material facts in the portions of the registration statement that describe Macrohard's business and the material risks of investing in the preferred stock.

- Is CDFC a statutory defendant under Section 11 of the 1933 Act? For what portions of the registration statement is CDFC liable under Section 11? What is CDFC's due diligence defense for errors in the financial statements audited by A&Y? What is CDFC's due diligence defense for errors in the portions of the registration statement that describe Macrohard's business and material risks?
- Is A&Y a statutory defendant under Section 11 of the 1933 Act? For what portions of the registration statement is A&Y liable under Section 11? What is A&Y's due diligence defense?
- Compile a checklist that will help CDFC and A&Y meet their due diligence defenses under Section 11.

LO LEARNING OBJECTIVES

After studying this chapter, you should be able to:

46-1 Appreciate the duties that accountants and securities professionals owe to their clients and third parties.

46-2 Engage in behavior that prevents you and your firm from having liability to clients and third parties under federal securities and other laws.

46-3 Take steps to protect a client's communications and the firm's working papers.

EACH YEAR, MANY accounting and finance students choose to become CPAs and seek jobs as auditors of public companies. Many students, however, opt for positions in consulting and other fields connected to the securities industry. Therefore, this chapter covers the legal responsibilities of not only accountants and auditors, but also consultants and securities professionals. The chapter's primary focus is on auditors of financial statements, tax accountants, consultants who provide management and financial advice to clients, investment bankers, securities underwriters, securities analysts, and securities brokers.

This chapter will first cover the general standard of performance required of professionals. Next, we will study professionals' liability to their clients, especially under state law. The largest part of this chapter comprises liability to nonclient third parties. We will also examine criminal liability of professionals and end the chapter with coverage of the law protecting the integrity of communications between professionals and their clients.

General Standard of Performance

 LO46-1 Appreciate the duties that accountants and securities professionals owe to their clients and third parties.

The general duty that auditors, consultants, and securities professionals owe to their clients and to other persons who are affected by their actions is to exercise the skill and care of the ordinarily prudent professional in the same circumstances. Hence, professionals must act carefully and diligently; they are *not* guarantors of the accuracy of their work or that the advice they give to clients will work out well. The professional's duty to exercise reasonable care is a subset of the negligence standard of tort law. Two elements compose the general duty of performance: skill and care.

A professional must have the *skill of the ordinarily prudent person in her profession*. This element focuses on education or knowledge, whether acquired formally at school or by self-instruction. For example, to audit financial records, an accountant must know generally accepted auditing standards (GAAS) and generally accepted accounting principles (GAAP). GAAS and GAAP are standards and principles embodied in the rules, releases, and pronouncements of the Securities and Exchange Commission, the American Institute of Certified Public Accountants (AICPA), the Financial Accounting Standards Board (FASB), the Public Company Accounting Oversight Board (PCAOB), and the International Accounting Standards Board (IASB). To assist a corporate client's development of an expansion strategy, a consultant must be knowledgeable of similar businesses and the opportunities for expansion. To assist a securities issuer making an initial public offering (IPO), an investment banker must know the mechanics of a public offering and the market for securities. In recommending stocks to an investor, a broker or investment adviser must know fundamental investment analysis and portfolio theory.

The care element requires a professional to act as carefully as the ordinarily prudent person in her profession. For example, in preparing a tax return, a tax accountant must discover the income exclusions, the deductions, and the tax credits that the reasonably careful accountant would find are available to the client. When recommending a corporate acquisition to a client, an investment banker must investigate the value of the acquired firm and check the acquired firm's fit with the business and strategy of the acquiring firm. A broker recommending a security to his customer must carefully investigate the security and its fit with the customer's investment goals, securities portfolio, and financial status.

Courts and legislatures usually defer to the members of a profession in determining what the ordinarily prudent professional would do. Such deference recognizes the lawmakers' lack of understanding of the nuances of professional practice. However, a profession will not be permitted to establish a standard of conduct that is harmful to the interests of clients or other members of society.

Professionals' Liability to Clients

 LO46-2 Engage in behavior that prevents you and your firm from having liability to clients and third parties under federal securities and other laws.

Professionals are sometimes sued by their clients. For example, an accountant may wrongfully claim deductions on a client's tax return. When the IRS discovers the wrongful deduction, the individual will have to pay the extra tax, interest, and perhaps a penalty. The individual may sue his accountant to recover the amount of the penalty. For another example, consider a securities broker who churns the securities account of a 92-year-old investor by executing daily trades in risky Internet stocks. When the value of the investor's portfolio declines from $500,000 to near zero as high commissions and capital losses mount, the investor may sue the broker for making imprudent investment decisions and for churning the account merely to earn the commissions.

When clients sue professionals, there are three principal bases of liability: contract, tort, and trust.

Contractual Liability As a party to a contract with her client, a professional owes a duty to the client to perform as she has agreed to perform. This includes an implied duty to perform the contract as the ordinarily prudent person in the profession would perform it. If the professional fails to perform as agreed, ordinarily she is liable only for compensatory damages and those consequential damages that are contemplated by the client and the professional at the time the contract was made, such as the client's cost of hiring another consultant or auditor to complete the work. For example, an auditor agrees to provide audited financial statements for inclusion in a client's bank loan application. The loan will be used to expand the client's business. When the auditor fails to complete the audit on time, the auditor will not ordinarily be liable for the client's lost profits from the unexecuted expansion, unless the auditor had agreed to be liable for such lost profits.

Ethics and Compliance in Action

Public Company Accounting Oversight Board

One of the main features of the Sarbanes–Oxley Act (SOX) is the creation of an independent board that oversees the audits of public companies. Congress's perception was that auditing firms were not sufficiently independent of the public companies they audited due in part to the audit firms' receiving sizable nonaudit consulting fees from their audit clients. Thus, SOX created a Public Company Accounting Oversight Board (PCAOB). Public accounting firms that audit financial statements of public companies are required to register with PCAOB and submit to its rules. The board is charged with adopting rules establishing auditing, quality control, ethics, and independence standards. It has the power to regulate the nonaudit services that audit firms may perform for their clients. The PCAOB has the power to inspect periodically public accounting firms and to issue reports of the results of the reviews. The purpose of inspections is to assess the degree of compliance with the requirements of SOX, professional

auditing standards, and the rules of the PCAOB and the SEC in the performance of audits and the issuance of audit reports of public companies. In addition, the PCAOB may investigate and discipline audit firms and their partners and employees.

The PCAOB is not a federal agency, but a nonprofit corporation with broad regulatory power like the Financial Industry Regulatory Authority (FINRA), a self-regulatory organization that regulates securities brokers and dealers. It has five members, only two of whom may be CPAs. No board member may receive any share of profits or compensation from a public accounting firm. The SEC has oversight authority over the PCAOB, including the approval of its Board's rules, standards, and budget.

- Do you think that the creation and work of the PCAOB results in greater independence of auditors of public companies?
- If auditing of financial statements is required primarily for the protection of public investors, should not all PCAOB members be taken from the investment community that uses audited financial statements?

A professional is not liable for breach of contract if the client obstructs the performance of the contract. For example, an investment banker is not liable for failing to make a timely public offering of a client's securities if the client delays giving the investment banker the information it needs to complete the securities offering registration statement.

A professional may not delegate his duty to perform a contract without the consent of the client. Delegation is not permitted because the performance of a contract for professional services depends on the skill, training, and character

of the professional. For example, PricewaterhouseCoopers, a public accounting firm, may not delegate to Ernst & Young, another public accounting firm, the contractual duty to audit the financial statements of Apple Inc., even though both firms are nearly equally skillful and careful.

Tort Liability Professionals' tort liability to their clients may be based on the common law concepts of negligence and fraud or on the violation of a statute, including federal and state securities laws.

The Global Business Environment

U.S. Moving to International Accounting Standards?

In 2008, the SEC announced that it would consider requiring American companies to comply with International Financial Reporting Standards (IFRS) adopted by the International Accounting Standards Board (IASB). The SEC proposal is designed to move the world to one set of accounting standards and, thereby, permit investors to compare more easily companies operating in differing parts of the world. The proposal, it is claimed, would also make it easier for companies to raise capital by allowing them to sell securities in securities markets anywhere in the world.

In 2011, the SEC withdrew its proposal and indicated it would not require American companies to comply with IFRS until 2015, at the earliest. In 2012, the SEC issued a report on

its IFRS work plan. The report found little support for adopting IFRS in the United States. This and subsequent SEC reports make it clear that a mandatory move to IFRS standards in the U.S is not expected anytime soon, if ever.

- From time to time, the SEC has exercised its power to block an accounting standard issued by the FASB when it deems inappropriate the treatment required or permitted by the rule. Do you think the SEC will exercise the same power when it views as wrong an IASB standard?
- Under the Securities Exchange Act of 1934, the SEC has the power to set accounting standards for U.S. public companies. Do you think the SEC abdicated its responsibility by allowing the FASB today and the IASB in the future to set American accounting standards? Whom do you trust more to adopt reasonable accounting standards: the SEC, the FASB, or the IASB? Why?

Negligence The essence of negligence is the failure of a professional to exercise the skill and care of the ordinarily prudent person in the profession. A professional is negligent when he breaches the duty to act skillfully and carefully and proximately causes damages to the client. For example, a corporate client may recover from an investment banker when the client overpays for an acquired firm due to the investment banker's careless valuation of the acquired firm.

Under the *suitability* and *know-your-customer rules* of FINRA and the stock exchanges, a securities broker is required to know the financial circumstances and investment objectives of his client before recommending securities or executing securities transactions for the client. The broker is aided by SEC rules requiring that new customers provide detailed financial information, such as their name, date of birth, address, employment status, annual income, net worth, and investment objectives, before opening accounts. A broker who does not know his customer is negligent and may be liable for losses from securities transactions that are inappropriate for the client. A broker that warns a client of the risks and inappropriateness of an investment has met his duty and is not liable, for example, to a client that disregards the risk and authorizes trading in the risky investment. The suitability and know-your-customer rules may also justify a client's action on *contract* grounds when the customer signs an account agreement that requires a broker to handle the account in accordance with industry standards.

Audit Duties Audit engagements are a unique area of professional liability. Sometimes, an accountant will audit a company, yet fail to uncover fraud, embezzlement, or other intentional wrongdoing by an employee of the company. Ordinarily, an accountant has no specific duty to uncover employee fraud or embezzlement. Nonetheless, an accountant must uncover employee fraud or embezzlement if an ordinarily prudent accountant would have discovered it. The accountant who fails to uncover such fraud or embezzlement is negligent and liable to his client. In addition, an accountant owes a duty to investigate suspicious circumstances that tend to indicate fraud, regardless of how he became aware of those circumstances. Also, an accountant has a duty to inform a proper party of his suspicions. It is *not enough* to inform or confront the person suspected of fraud.

When an accountant is hired to perform a fraud audit to investigate suspected fraud or embezzlement, she has a greater duty to investigate. She must be as skillful and careful as the ordinarily prudent auditor performing a fraud audit.

When an accountant negligently fails to discover embezzlement, generally she is liable to her client only for an amount equal to the embezzlement that occurred after she should have discovered the embezzlement. The accountant is usually not liable for any part of the embezzlement that occurred prior to the time she should have uncovered the embezzlement unless her tardy discovery prevented the client from recovering embezzled funds.

Contributory and Comparative Negligence of Client Courts are reluctant to permit a professional to escape liability to a client merely because the client was **contributorily negligent**. Because the accountant or consultant has skills superior to those of the client, courts generally allow clients to rely on an accountant's duty to discover employee fraud, a consultant's duty to make reasonable recommendations, and an underwriter's advice on what type of security to issue. The client is not required to exercise reasonable care to discover these things himself.

Nonetheless, some courts allow the defense of contributory negligence or the defense of **comparative negligence**, such as when clients negligently fail to follow a consultant's advice or when clients possess information that makes their reliance on an investment banker unwarranted.

In the following *Gold* case, the court considered the scope of an auditor's duty when conducting an audit. Although there were allegations that Deloitte had audited financial statements in a negligent manner, the court ultimately determined that there was no professional negligence because no damages resulted from Deloitte's actions.

Gold v. Deloitte & Touche, LLP (*In re* NM Holdings Co., LLC)
411 B.R. 542 (E.D. Mich. 2009)

Gold, the Chapter 7 bankruptcy trustee of 11 jointly administered bankruptcy cases, sought damages from Defendant Deloitte and Touche LLP (Deloitte). Gold alleged that Deloitte served as Venture Holding Co.'s (Venture) independent auditor from 1987 through at least May 2004. During this time, Larry Winget, Venture's sole shareholder, caused Venture to transfer tens of millions of dollars to various related entities without receiving anything in return. Winget received the benefit of these transactions because he wholly owned and/or controlled each of these related entities.

According to Gold's allegations, Deloitte audited Venture's financial statements from 1995 through 2001 in a negligent or reckless manner. Venture was required to submit various filings to the Securities and Exchange Commission because it had public debt, and these findings both failed to disclose material related-party transactions and falsely stated that other related-party transactions were fair to Venture. Furthermore, Deloitte knew that some of Venture's related-party transactions "were not bona-fide business transactions and that Venture was not receiving anything of value from those parties in exchange for the multimillion dollar payments." Nevertheless, Deloitte represented that these transactions were "on terms no less favorable to the company than would be obtained if such transactions or arrangements were arms-length transactions with non-affiliated persons." Deloitte knew that its independent auditor reports would be relied upon by Venture and third parties, and its failure to alert these parties to the improper transactions caused Venture damages in excess of $300 million.

Battani, Judge

In Michigan, to establish a prima facie case of negligence, a plaintiff must be able to prove four elements: 1) a duty owed by the defendant to the plaintiff, 2) a breach of that duty, 3) causation, and 4) damages. Proof of causation requires both cause in fact and legal, or proximate, cause. Cause in fact requires that the harmful result would not have come about but for the defendant's negligent conduct. On the other hand, legal cause or proximate cause normally involves examining the foreseeability of consequences, and whether a defendant should be held legally responsible for such consequences. When a number of actors contribute to produce an injury, one actor's negligence will not be considered a proximate cause of the harm unless it was a substantial factor in producing the injury.

This Court finds that "if nobody relied upon the audit, then the audit could not have been a substantial factor in bringing about the injury." It would make little sense to find that Deloitte's audits were a cause of the damage to Venture if nobody actually relied on the audits. Therefore, in order for Gold to establish that Deloitte was a cause of Venture's damages, he had to allege reliance upon the audits. It would be inappropriate to permit Venture (or Gold as Venture's representative) to recover from Deloitte because Deloitte's negligence prevented third parties from learning about, and stopping, improper transactions of which Venture was fully aware. Accordingly, Gold is precluded from recovering damages from Deloitte if Venture was fully aware of the transactions. Therefore, if Winget's knowledge and conduct is imputed to Venture, then Venture effectively was aware of, and in fact engaged in, the transactions itself.

This Court finds that Winget's actions and knowledge are in fact imputed to Venture, which means that Venture knowingly engaged in the related-party transactions. Thus, Venture cannot claim that Deloitte's failure to disclose the related-party transactions in the audits caused it damage because it already knew of the transactions and, therefore, it was not relying on the audits. Furthermore, the fact that third parties relied upon the audits does not establish the causation element of Gold's negligence claim.

Accordingly, the professional negligence claim must be dismissed because Gold's allegation fails to establish that Deloitte's failure to disclose the related-party transactions in the audits was the cause of any damage to Venture. As such, the Court does not need to address Deloitte's alternative argument that the wrongful conduct rule prohibits Gold's claim.

Defendant's Motion to Dismiss as to the Claim of Professional Negligence [I]s Granted.

Fraud A professional is liable to his client for fraud when he misstates or omits facts in communications with his client and acts with **scienter**. A person acts with scienter when he knows of the falsity of a statement or he recklessly disregards the truth. Thus, accountants are liable in fraud for their intentional or reckless disregard for accuracy in their work.

For example, an accountant chooses not to examine the current figures in a client's books of account but relies on last year's figures because he is behind in his work for other clients. As a result, the accountant understates the client's income on an income statement that the client uses to apply for a loan. The client obtains a loan, but he has to pay a higher interest rate because his low stated income makes the loan a higher risk for the bank. Such misconduct by the accountant proves scienter and, therefore, amounts to fraud.

Scienter also includes recklessly ignoring facts, such as an auditor's finding obvious evidence of embezzlement yet failing to notify a client of the embezzlement. An investment banker defrauds its client when it withholds information concerning the value of the client's shares and causes the client to issue the shares for too little consideration, perhaps to an affiliate of the investment banker

Ethics in and Compliance Action

The Sarbanes–Oxley Act: Auditor Independence Standards

When Congress studied the causes of financial statement irregularities in 2002, it became convinced that some auditors failed to challenge their clients' financial reporting practices for fear that the audit firms would lose lucrative consulting contracts with the clients. The belief was that firms undercharged for audit services to acquire valuable consulting clients. To ensure that audit firms are free from conflict-of-interest and lack of independence charges that can undermine the quality of their audits, the Sarbanes–Oxley Act (SOX) bans most types of services by audit firms for audit clients, including:

* Bookkeeping.
* Financial information system design.
* Appraisal or valuation services.
* Actuarial services.
* Internal audit outsourcing.
* Management or human resource services.

* Broker, dealer, investment banker, and investment adviser services.
* Legal and expert services related to the audit.
* Other services as determined by the Public Company Accounting Oversight Board.

The PCAOB also has power on a case-by-case basis to exempt services performed by an audit firm for an audit client. An audit firm may provide permissible nonaudit services for an audit client, such as tax services, only if the client's audit committee approves the services in advance.

In addition, SOX requires that the audit partner-in-charge be rotated every five years at a minimum. SOX also charges the General Accounting Office (now called the Government Accountability Office) to study whether all public companies should be required to rotate audit firms on a regular basis. Finally, no audit firm may audit a public company that within the past year has hired an audit firm employee as a CEO, CFO, or CAO.

---

who, therefore, profits unreasonably. Fraud actions are not designed to impose liability on honest professionals who sometimes make careless errors, but rather on those who act with intent or otherwise recklessly.

The chief advantage of establishing fraud is that the client may get a higher damage award than when the accountant is merely negligent. Usually, a client may receive only compensatory damages for a breach of contract or negligence. By proving fraud, a client may be awarded punitive damages as well.

In Pari Delicto   Under the doctrine of *in pari delicto*, courts refuse to intervene in a dispute between litigants when both have engaged in wrongdoing. For example, when a person has engaged in fraud, that person will not be able to sue for damages another person who was involved with the same fraudulent scheme. "[T]he law will not extend its aid to either of the parties or listen to their complaints against each other, but will leave them where their own acts have placed them."[1]

The policy behind the doctrine is that denying judicial relief to a fraudulent wrongdoer deters illegality. The equity of *in pari delicto* is most obvious when a fraudulent wrongdoer is suing someone who is alleged to be merely

negligent regarding the same scheme. The principle also applies where both parties acted fraudulently.

In cases involving a corporate plaintiff that is the client of a professional defendant, the application of *in pari delicto* is complicated by the involvement of the corporate client's agent, such as an officer, in the fraudulent behavior. Agency law, discussed in Chapter 36, generally imputes an agent's behavior to the agent's corporate principal. This means a corporation may be a fraudulent wrongdoer purely because of the fraud committed by its agent and, thus, prevented from suing a negligent or fraudulent third-party professional who had a role in the agent's wrongdoing.

Note that although an auditor or investment banker may be able to assert *in pari delicto* as a defense in an action by the client against the auditor or investment banker, the defense will not exist when on their own behalf innocent shareholders of the client sue an auditor or investment banker for causing direct harm to the shareholders.

Breach of Trust   A professional owes a duty of trust to his client. Information and assets that are entrusted to an accountant, broker, or investment banker, for example, may be used only to benefit the client. The duty of trust requires the professional to maintain the confidentiality of the client's information entrusted to the firm. Therefore, a

[1] *Stone v. Freeman*, 82 N.E.2d 571, 572 (N.Y. Ct. App. 1948).

professional may not disclose sensitive matters such as a client's income and wealth or use secret information about a client's new product to purchase the client's securities. In addition, for example, an accountant or securities broker may not use the assets of his client for his own benefit.

Securities Law Federal and state securities law creates several rights of action for persons harmed in connection with the purchase or sale of securities. These rights of action are based in tort. Although some securities law sections permit clients to sue professionals, they are rarely used for that purpose. Usually, only third parties (nonclients) sue under the securities law. Therefore, the securities law sections that apply to professionals are discussed later in this chapter.

Professionals' Liability to Third Persons: Common Law

 LO46-2 Engage in behavior that prevents you and your firm from having liability to clients and third parties under federal securities and other laws.

Other persons besides a professional's clients may use her work product. Banks may use financial statements reviewed by a loan applicant's accountant in deciding whether to make a loan to the applicant. Investors may use financial statements audited by a company's auditors in deciding whether to buy or sell the company's securities. These documents prepared by an accountant may prove incorrect, resulting in damages to the nonclients who relied on them. For example, banks may lend money to a corporation only because an income statement prepared by an accountant overstated the corporation's income. When the corporation fails to repay the loan, the bank may sue the accountant to recover the damages it suffered.

Nonclient actions are rarer outside the accountant context because the work product of nonaccounting professionals is infrequently used by others in an expectable way. For example, consulting advice is almost never passed from a client to a third party. A securities broker's client rarely relays the broker's investment advice to a friend; when the friend attempts to sue the broker if the advice turns out to be bad, the friend usually is not able to recover damages from the broker.

However, investment bankers often prepare documents for their clients that are created expressly to sell securities to nonclients, that is, shareholders and other holders of the client's securities. Therefore, purchasers who buy the client's securities based on false statements in a document prepared for investors by an investment banker may sue the investment banker.

Nonclients may sue professionals for common law negligence, common law fraud, and violations of the securities laws. In this section, common law negligence and fraud are discussed.

Negligence and Negligent Misrepresentation When a professional fails to perform as the ordinarily prudent professional would perform, she risks having liability for negligence. Many courts have restricted the ability of nonclients to sue a professional for damages proximately caused by the professional's negligent conduct. These courts limit nonclient suits on the grounds that nonclient users of a professional's work product have not contracted with the professional and, therefore, are not in **privity of contract** with her. Essentially, these courts hold that a professional owes no duty to nonclients to exercise ordinary skill and care.

This judicial stance conflicts with the usual principles of negligence law under which a negligent person is liable to all persons who are reasonably foreseeably damaged by his negligence. The rationale for the restrictive judicial stance was expressed almost 100 years ago in the *Ultramares* case,[2] a decision of the highest court in New York. In that case, Judge Benjamin Cardozo refused to hold an auditor liable to third parties for mere negligence. His rationale was stated as follows:

> If liability for negligence exists, a thoughtless slip or blunder, the failure to detect a theft or forgery beneath the cover of deceptive entries, may expose accountants to a liability in an indeterminate amount for an indeterminate time to an indeterminate class.[3]

The *Ultramares* privity requirement protects an auditor or other professional who does not know the user or the extent of use of its work product and, therefore, is unable to assess the potential dollar amount of liability or the user's propensity to sue. *Ultramares* allows auditors and other professionals to manage the known risks of their work product being used by nonclients either by insuring against the risk, increasing the client's engagement fee, or declining the engagement.

Ultramares dominated the thinking of judges for many years, and its impact is still felt today. However, many courts understand that many nonclients use and reasonably rely on the work product of professionals, especially accountants. To varying degrees, these courts have relaxed

[2]*Ultramares Corp. v. Touche*, 174 N.E. 441 (N.Y. 1931).
[3]*Id.* at 179.

the privity requirement and expanded the class of persons who may sue an accountant or other professionals for negligent conduct. Today, most courts adopt one of the following three tests to determine whether a nonclient may sue a professional for negligence.

Primary Benefit Test   The *Ultramares* court adopted a primary benefit test for imposing liability for negligence. Under this test, a professional's duty of care extends only to those persons for whose primary benefit the professional audits or prepares financial reports and other documents. The professional must actually foresee the nonclient's use and prepare the document primarily for use by a specified nonclient. That is, the nonclient must be a *foreseen user* of the professional's work product. The professional must know four things: (1) the name of the person who will use her work product; (2) the particular purpose for which that person will use the work product; (3) the extent of the use, such as the dollar amount of the nonclient's transaction; and (4) the client has the primary intent that the user use the work product.

Suppose an investment banker acts as a broker for a client issuing $100 million of securities to 10 mutual funds identified as prospective buyers. To assist the client's sale of the securities, the investment banker prepares an offering memorandum for the client, and the client tells the investment banker that the offering memo is being prepared for the benefit of the 10 mutual funds. If, due to the investment banker's negligence, the offering memorandum misstates material facts, and if the client gives the offering memorandum to the previously identified mutual funds, the investment banker may have liability to the mutual funds that relied on the misstated facts.

State supreme court cases have upheld the *Ultramares* formula for professional liability to third parties for negligent misrepresentation. The Texas Supreme Court held that liability for negligent misrepresentation is limited to situations in which the professional who provides the information is aware of the nonclient and intends that the nonclient rely on the information.[4] The court held that liability could not be premised on an auditor's general knowledge that investors might purchase the client's bonds.

The New Jersey Supreme Court held that an auditor could not be held liable to a third party who claimed to rely on audited financial statements unless the auditor had knowledge *at the time the auditor-client relationship began* that the third party would rely on its reports. "An auditor is entitled to know at the outset the scope of the work it is being requested to perform and the concomitant

risk it is being asked to assume."[5] The case arose out of a merger in which the acquiring company alleged negligence in the audit report on the acquired company's financial statements. The acquirer complained that the auditor was aware of the merger, participated in a conference call with the acquirer, and agreed to make its audit report and work papers available to the acquirer for limited agreed-upon purposes. The New Jersey court rejected the nonclient acquirer's argument that the auditor's knowledge that a third party was relying on the audited financial statements *at any time* during its engagement with the client exposed it to liability. Instead, the court held that to be liable to a third party, the auditor must know *at the outset of the engagement* that a third party will rely on the work.

Foreseen Users and Foreseen Class of Users Test   By 1965, a draft of the *Restatement (Second) of Torts* proposed that the law of professional negligence expand the class of protected persons to *foreseen users* and *users within a foreseen class of users* of reports. Under this test, the professional must know the use and extent of use to be made of the work product. The protected persons are (1) those persons who a professional knows the client intends will use the work product and (2) those persons who use the work product in a way the professional knew the client intended the work product would be used.

For example, an accountant prepares an income statement that he knows his client will use to obtain a $50 million loan at Bank X. Any bank to which the client supplies the statement to obtain a similar loan, including Bank Y, may sue the accountant for damages caused by a negligently prepared income statement. Bank X is a foreseen user, and Bank Y is in a foreseen class of users. On the other hand, if an accountant prepares an income statement for a tax return and the client, without the accountant's knowledge, uses the income statement to apply for a loan from a bank, the bank is not among the protected class of persons—the accountant did not know that the tax return would be used for that purpose.

Also, if the accountant prepared the client's income statement for the purpose of aiding the client to obtain a $50 million loan, but instead the client obtained a $200 million loan, the accountant would not be liable to the nonclient bank: The accountant did not know the extent of the bank's use—that is, the dollar amount of risk to which she was exposed.

In the securities professional context, when an underwriter prepares an offering document for a client issuing a

---

[4] *Grant Thornton LLP v. Prospect High Income Fund*, 314 S.W.3d 913 (Tex. 2010).

[5] *Cast Art Industries, LLC v. KPMG LLP*, 36 A.3d 1049, 1059 (N.J. 2012).

known amount of securities, the *Restatement* test extends an underwriter's liability for negligence to any purchaser of the securities whether known or not to the underwriter. This is because the underwriter knows the type of person who will use the offering document (i.e., buyers of the securities), the use, and the extent of the use (i.e., the dollar amount of securities to be bought).

Nonetheless, when the *Restatement* test is applied to securities brokers, liability rarely extends past the broker's client. A broker who gives investment advice to a client is rarely found liable to a nonclient who receives the advice secondhand on the grounds that investment advice is crafted specifically for the broker's client. That rationale is generally followed even in the context of a published investment newsletter, where usually only subscribers to the newsletter are permitted to sue the publisher of the newsletter.

Foreseeable Users Test A very few courts have applied traditional negligence causation principles to professional negligence. They have extended liability to **foreseeable users** of an accountant's audit and other reports who suffered damages that were proximately caused by the accountant's negligence. To be liable to a nonclient under this test, an accountant need merely be reasonably able to expect or foresee the nonclient's use of the accountant's work product. It is not necessary for the nonclient to prove that the accountant actually expected or foresaw the nonclient's use.

In the next case against accounting giant PricewaterhouseCoopers (PwC), the court reviewed the scope of *Ultramares* and other cases in the course of interpreting the Illinois statute defining those persons to whom a professional may be liable for negligent misrepresentation.

Tricontinental Industries, Ltd. v. PricewaterhouseCoopers, LLP
475 F.3d 824 (7th Cir. 2007)

Anicom Inc. was a wire distribution company founded in the early 1990s. Its stock became publicly traded, and the company adopted a strategy to increase market share and to expand its operations. Between 1995 and 1997, Anicom acquired 12 companies. Each of these transactions involved some payment in the form of Anicom stock. During this time, PricewaterhouseCoopers LLP rendered accounting, audit, and various types of consulting services to Anicom.

In 1996, Anicom began engaging in improper accounting procedures to enable it to report that it had met sales and revenue goals. The procedures included the use of fictitious sales orders or prebills for goods that were not ordered. PwC became aware of these practices in July 1997 when it was asked to investigate Anicom's billing practices. After conducting its investigation, PwC reported to Donald C. Welchco, Anicom's vice president and CFO, that improper billing had occurred at Anicom branches and that, in the absence of controls, the practice might arise at other branches as well. No mention of these irregularities was made in PwC's audits of Anicom's 1998 and 1999 financial statements. Indeed, PwC issued opinions that Anicom's financial statements were accurate, complete, and conformed with GAAP and that its audits were performed according to GAAS.

In September 1998, Anicom made an asset purchase agreement to acquire the wire and cable distribution assets of three companies: Texcan Cables Ltd. (known now as Tricontinental Distribution Ltd.), Texcan Cables Inc., and Texcan Cables International Inc. Anicom acquired those assets in exchange for cash and Anicom stock. After the transaction, Tricontinental Distribution and Texcan Cables transferred their stock to Tricontinental Industries, Ltd.

On July 18, 2000, Anicom announced that it was investigating possible accounting irregularities that could result in revision of its 1998, 1999, and first-quarter 2000 financial statements by as much as $35 million. Accordingly, Anicom announced that its 1998 and 1999 financial statements should no longer be relied upon. After conducting an internal investigation, Anicom further announced that, subject to audit, it believed that, for the period from the first quarter of 1998 to the first quarter of 2000, the company had overstated revenue by approximately $39.6 million. None of the company's announcements or disclosures ever stated that full-year 1997 revenue or net income had been materially misstated or that any of Anicom's prior financial results were inaccurate in any way. On January 5, 2001, Anicom filed for bankruptcy protection.

In July 2001, Tricontinental filed an action against PwC for negligent misrepresentation. Tricontinental maintained that PwC knew that Tricontinental was relying on Anicom's audited financial statement for 1997 and, specifically, was relying on PwC's representation that the audit was performed in a manner consistent with GAAS and that Anicom's financial statements conformed with GAAP. These statements, Tricontinental alleged, were materially false, misleading, and without reasonable basis.

PwC moved to dismiss Tricontinental's complaint on the grounds that PwC owed no duty to Tricontinental because the Illinois Public Accounting Act (IPAA) limited PwC's liability to persons who were either in privity of contract with PwC or for whose primary intent Anicom had secured PwC's services. The district court granted PwC's motion. Tricontinental appealed.

Ripple, Circuit Judge

In order to state a claim for negligent misrepresentation under Illinois law, a party must allege:

(1) a false statement of material fact; (2) carelessness or negligence in ascertaining the truth of the statement by the party making it; (3) an intention to induce the other party to act; (4) action by the other party in reliance on the truth of the statement; (5) damage to the other party resulting from such reliance; and (6) a duty on the party making the statement to communicate accurate information.

The Illinois courts have considered, on several occasions, the application of these requirements, specifically, the element of duty, as it applies to public accountants. The Illinois Appellate Court first spoke to this issue in *Brumley v. Touche, Ross & Co.*, 463 N.E.2d 195 (Ill. App. Ct. 1984) (*Brumley I*). In that case, the court reviewed the various approaches that courts around the country had adopted for accountant liability to third parties: (1) the standard set forth in *Ultramares Corp. v. Touche*, 174 N.E. 441 (N.Y. 1931), which held that public accountants could not be liable in negligence to third parties absent privity; (2) a reasonable foreseeability standard; and (3) a more limited foreseeability rule that public accountants may be liable to plaintiffs, who are not exactly identifiable, but who belong to a limited class of persons whose reliance on the accountant's representations is specifically foreseen. The appellate court held that the plaintiff's complaint was insufficient to set forth a duty on the part of defendant to plaintiff because "the complaint did not allege Touche Ross knew of plaintiff or that the report was to be used by KPK to influence plaintiff's purchase decision nor does it allege that was *the primary purpose and intent* of the preparation of the report by Touche Ross for KPK." *Id.* (emphasis added).

In *Brumley v. Touche, Ross & Company*, 487 N.E.2d 641 (Ill. App. Ct. 1985) (*Brumley II*), the court revisited this standard. In *Brumley II*, the plaintiff had argued that the Supreme Court of Illinois had altered the standard for liability for attorneys, which necessitated a change by the appellate court with respect to accountant liability. The appellate court rejected this argument: it is apparent that to be sufficient plaintiff's complaint must allege facts showing that *the purpose and intent of the accountant-client relationship* was to benefit or influence the third-party plaintiff. 487 N.E.2d at 644–45 (emphasis added).

Shortly after *Brumley II*, the Illinois legislature enacted the Illinois Public Accounting Act, 225 ILCS 450/30.1, which provides:

No person, partnership, corporation, or other entity licensed or authorized to practice under this Act . . . shall be liable to persons not in privity of contract with such person, partnership, corporation, or other entity for civil damages resulting from acts, omissions, decisions or other conduct in connection with professional services

performed by such person, partnership, corporation, or other entity, except for:
(1) such acts, omissions, decisions or conduct that constitute fraud or intentional misrepresentations, or
(2) such other acts, omissions, decisions or conduct, if such person, partnership or corporation was aware that a primary intent of the client was for the professional services to benefit or influence the particular person bringing the action; provided, however, for the purposes of this subparagraph (2), if such person, partnership, corporation, or other entity (i) identifies in writing to the client those persons who are intended to rely on the services, and (ii) sends a copy of such writing or similar statement to those persons identified in the writing or statement, then such person, partnership, corporation, or other entity or any of its employees, partners, members, officers or shareholders may be held liable only to such persons intended to so rely, in addition to those persons in privity of contract with such person, partnership, corporation, or other entity.

Following IPAA's passage, there was some question regarding the effect of the IPAA on accountant liability. We are obliged, however, to follow the interpretation given the language by the state appellate court in *Chestnut Corp. v. Pestine, Brinati, Gamer, Ltd.*, 667 N.E.2d 543, 546–47 (Ill. App. Ct. 1996). The Illinois court took the view that the first clause of subparagraph (2) states the general rule of accountant liability as set out in *Brumley* while the second clause creates a legislative exception to the general rule. Continued the court:

[T]o adopt the defendants' interpretation of the statute would require us to hold, as a matter of law, that accountants are never liable to third parties, absent fraud or intentional misrepresentation, unless they agree in writing to expose themselves to liability. The law in Illinois would have come full circle then and returned to the rationale of *Ultramares* in 1931. Absent a clear signal from the legislature or the supreme court that such a return is intended, we believe the observation of the trial court and the evolution of the law since *Ultramares* provides a useful background as one measures the statute's meaning.

Id. at 547.

Although the Supreme Court of Illinois has not spoken to the issue, Illinois Appellate Courts seem to agree that the IPAA embodies the rule applied to accountants in *Brumley II*: The plaintiff must show that a primary purpose and intent of the accountant-client relationship was to benefit or influence the third-party plaintiff.

The primary intent rule, however, has proven to be somewhat difficult to define in practical terms. For instance, disputes have arisen regarding whether the "primary intent" of the client must be contemporaneous with the accountant's work product on which the third party relies. With respect to this issue, the Illinois Appellate Court has stated:

In terms of timing, we do not read the statute to strictly require that an accountant be made aware of his client's intention to

influence or benefit a third party only at the time the work product was created as defendant contends. The standard requires
that a plaintiff prove that the primary purpose and intent of the
client was to benefit or influence the third party. In *Brumley II*,
we held that the plaintiff in that case met the standard because
he alleged that the defendant knew of the plaintiff's reliance on
the defendant's reports and that the defendant had subsequently
verified its accuracy. We do not, however, read *Brumley II* as *per
se requiring independent verification* in order to meet the standard
in *Pelham. Other conduct* may be sufficient to satisfy *Pelham*.

Builders Bank v. Barry Finkel & Assocs., 790 N.E.2d 30, 37
(Ill. App. Ct. 2003) (emphasis added).

Further, although Illinois case law has established that "independent verification" is not a per se requirement, Illinois courts have
not set forth in detail what "other conduct" may satisfy the "primary
intent" standard. The cases, however, do establish that *some* affirmative action on behalf of the defendant-accountant is necessary.
For instance, in *Builders Bank*, the record indicated that Finkel, the
accountant, was told by Urkov, the company owner, that UMC was
applying for a loan and requested that financial statements be furnished to UMC. The record further establishes that Finkel personally met with UMC on two occasions to discuss issues related to
the loan. In at least one meeting, UMC was seeking an increase of
$200,000 on a loan that had already been approved. In our view, it is
reasonable to infer that Finkel played an active role in securing the
loan or increasing the loan amount for UMC. From this evidence,
a finder of fact could conclude, pursuant to the statute, that Finkel
knew its work was being used to influence UMC at least at the time
of the second meeting and that defendant, at minimum, presented its
work as accurate. *Id.*

Similarly, in *Freeman, Freeman & Salzman, P.C. v. Lipper*, 812
N.E.2d 562 (Ill. App. Ct. 2004), the court held that the standard
had been met by the allegation that the accountant to an investment
fund had "issued clean audit opinions on each investment partner's
capital accounts for those years"; had "addressed and sent its clean
audit opinions to the partners who invested in those funds, including
plaintiffs"; and had "prepared federal income tax Schedules K-l for
plaintiffs and the limited partners each year." *Id.* at 566–67. Furthermore, "each Schedule K-1 purported to reflect each partner's proportionate share of the partnership's net income for the year, as well as
each partner's capital account balance at the beginning and end of
each year." *Id.* at 567.

Finally, in *Chestnut Corp.*, the court held that the plaintiffs had
stated a claim for negligent misrepresentation by alleging that the
plaintiff's representatives had gone to the offices of the defendant-
accountants to discuss their possible investment in the client company
and to review its financial condition. In response to specific inquiries
by the plaintiff's representatives, the defendants "stated that the audit
was accurately performed according to generally accepted auditing
standards." *Chestnut Corp.*, 667 N.E.2d at 545.

In sum, the duty owed by a professional accountant to non-client
third-parties is the standard articulated in *Brumley II* and codified in
the IPAA. The IPAA provides that an individual accountant, partnership or firm will be liable to a third party for negligence only "if such
person, partnership or corporation was aware that a primary intent
of the client was for the professional services to benefit or influence
the particular person." This "primary intent" may be demonstrated
by "independent verification" or by other affirmative actions taken
by the accountant and directed to the third party.

With this standard in mind, we turn to the allegations set forth
in the Amended Complaint to determine whether they state a
claim for relief.

With respect to the negligent misrepresentation claim,
Tricontinental alleged as follows:

163. Prior to the time that PwC conducted its 1997 audit, PwC
had assisted Anicom in raising money for acquisitions and
finding acquisition candidates. And, in 1997, PwC well knew
that Anicom was seeking to complete additional acquisitions.
PwC most certainly knew that acquisition candidates, such as
Plaintiffs, would rely on the 1997 Form 10-K in making their
decisions on whether to invest in Anicom's securities.

164. PwC knew prior to the closing of the Texcan transaction that
Plaintiffs were negotiating to sell significant assets to Anicom in
exchange in part for Anicom securities. PwC was on the circulation lists for drafts of the Asset Purchase Agreement and PwC
conducted due diligence of Texcan for Anicom. PwC knew that
Plaintiffs had received and were relying on Anicom's Form 10-K
for 1997 and, in particular, PwC's unqualified audit report, and
that Anicom intended that Plaintiffs rely on the 10-K and PwC's
audit report in assessing an investment in Anicom. Despite its
awareness of these facts, and despite its knowledge from its own
investigation and its involvement in the business of Anicom that
Anicom was engaged in improper accounting practices and
lacked adequate controls to prevent these irregular practices,
PwC intentionally or recklessly failed to withdraw its audit opinion on the 1997 financial statements. Instead, PwC allowed Plaintiffs to rely on the false and misleading information contained in
Anicom's Form 10-K for 1997.

As noted by the district court, these allegations do not demonstrate any "independent verification" provided by PwC to
Tricontinental. However, such verification to the third party is
not a per se requirement. "Other conduct" by PwC directed to
Tricontinental also may satisfy the "primary intent" requirement
of the IPAA. Tricontinental alleges that PwC knew of its reliance
on the 1997 audit opinion, knew of the misrepresentation contained in the statement and "allowed plaintiffs to rely on the false
and misleading information." However, Illinois cases, fairly read,
make clear that the IPAA requires more. In order to state a claim
under the IPAA, Tricontinental must allege that it was a primary
purpose "of the accountant-client relationship . . . to benefit or
influence" Tricontinental. None of the allegations contained in

the above-recited paragraphs support such an inference. Indeed, the opposite appears to be the case. The actions taken by PwC— assisting Anicom in raising money for acquisitions, conducting due diligence "for Anicom," and being included on the circulation lists during the transaction—are examples of Anicom's use of PwC's services for its own benefit, not that of Tricontinental. Consequently, although we agree with Tricontinental that neither privity nor independent verification need to be asserted or shown in order to state a claim, Tricontinental must set forth a short and plain statement of the claim showing that it is entitled to relief. Absent an allegation that fairly states that Anicom's primary intent in retaining and utilizing PwC's services and work product during the transaction was to influence Tricontinental, or absent factual allegations that support such an inference, Tricontinental has not stated a claim for negligent misrepresentation under Illinois law.

Judgment for PricewaterhouseCoopers affirmed.

CONCEPT REVIEW

Common Law Bases of Liability of Professional to Nonclients for Use of Professional's Work Product

Privity Test Adopted by State	Basis of Liability		
	Negligence		Fraud
Primary benefit test (*Ultramares*)	Professional liable only to foreseen users for whose primary benefit the work product was provided (professional knew name of user, purpose of the user's use, extent of the use, and that the client has the primary intent that the user use the work product)		
Restatement (Second) of Torts **test**	Professional liable to foreseen users and users in a foreseen class of users (professional knew at least the purpose and extent of the user's use)		Professional liable to all persons whose damages were caused by their reliance on professional's fraud
Foreseeable users test	Professional liable to all reasonably foreseeable users (professional can reasonably expect or foresee the purpose and extent of the user's use)		

Fraud All courts have extended a professional's liability for fraud to all foreseeable users of his work product who suffered damages that were proximately caused by the fraud. Privity of contract, therefore, is not required when a person sues a professional for fraud, even in a state that has adopted the *Ultramares* test for negligence actions. To prove fraud, a nonclient must establish that a professional acted with the mental state of scienter.

Some courts recognize a tort called constructive fraud that applies when a professional misstates a material fact. For a misstatement to amount to constructive fraud, the professional must have recklessly or grossly negligently failed to ascertain the truth of the statement. As with actual fraud, a professional's liability for constructive fraud extends to all persons who justifiably rely on the misstatement.

Professional's Liability to Third Parties: Securities Law

 Engage in behavior that prevents you and your firm from having liability to clients and third parties under federal securities and other laws.

The slow reaction of the common law in creating a negligence remedy for third parties has led to an increased use of securities law by nonclients—that is, persons not in privity with the professional. Many liability sections in these statutes either eliminate the privity requirement or expansively define privity.

Securities Act of 1933

There are several liability sections under the Securities Act of 1933 (1933 Act). The most important liability section of the Securities Act of 1933 is Section 11, but Sections 12(a)(2) and 17(a) are also important, especially for securities professionals.

Section 11 Liability Section 11 imposes liability on underwriters and experts for misstatements or omissions of material fact in Securities Act registration statements. The 1933 Act registration statement must be filed with the Securities and Exchange Commission by an issuer making a public distribution of securities. The most common expert is an auditor who issues an opinion regarding financial statements. An underwriter, although knowledgeable, skillful, and experienced in securities offerings, is not an "expert" under Section 11.

An auditor or underwriter is liable to any purchaser of securities issued pursuant to a defective registration statement. The purchaser need not establish privity of contract with an underwriter or auditor. Because the underwriter is not an expert under Section 11, the underwriter is liable for errors in the *entire* registration statement. Because an auditor is an expert, the auditor is liable only for the part of the registration statement contributed by the auditor—that is, the auditor's opinion regarding the audited financial statements and those audited financial statements. Usually, the purchaser need not prove he relied on the misstated or omitted material fact; he need not even have read or seen the defective registration statement. So long as the purchaser can show that (i) he purchased securities pursuant to a registration statement, (ii) the registration statement contained a material misstatement or omission, (iii) the auditor or underwriter is covered by the statute, and (iv) the complaint was timely brought, a Section 11 claim will be viable.

For example, an auditor issues an unqualified opinion regarding a client's income statement that overstates net income by 85 percent. The defective income statement is included in the client's registration statement pursuant to which the client sells its preferred shares. Without reading the registration statement or the income statement, a person buys from the client 1,000 preferred shares for $105 per share. After the correct income figure is released, the price of the shares drops to $25 per share. The auditor will most likely be liable to the purchaser for $80,000, unless the auditor proves the purchaser's damages were caused by other persons or factors.

Under Section 11, auditors and underwriters may escape liability by proving that they exercised due diligence. For auditors, who are experts, this **due diligence defense** requires that an auditor issuing an opinion regarding financial statements prove that she made a reasonable investigation and that she reasonably believed that there were no misstatements or omissions of material fact in the financial statements at the time the registration statement became effective. Because the effective date is often several months after an audit has been completed, an auditor must perform an additional review of the audited statements to ensure that the statements are accurate as of the effective date. In essence, due diligence means that an auditor was not negligent, which is usually proved by showing that she complied with GAAS and GAAP.

For underwriters, who are liable for the entire registration statement, the due diligence defense varies depending on the part of the registration statement. For parts of the registration statement contributed by experts (so-called expertised portions, such as an auditor's opinion and the financial statements covered by that opinion), underwriters are entitled to rely on the expert. Therefore, the underwriter's due diligence defense for errors in audited financial statements generally requires no independent investigation by the underwriter. The underwriter will have no liability for mistakes in an expertised portion if the underwriter had no reason to believe and did not believe that there were any misstatements or omissions of material fact in the audited financial statements. If, however, the underwriter has information leading her to believe that an audited financial statement misstates or omits material facts, she has a duty to investigate until she no longer has that belief and no longer has a reason to have that belief.

For errors in parts of the registration statement not contributed by experts (the nonexpertised portion), the underwriter's defense is that after a reasonable investigation, she had a reasonable belief that there were no misstatements or omissions of material fact in those parts. The nonexpertised portion constitutes the bulk of the registration statement and includes the description of the securities, the statement of the underwriter's compensation, the use of the proceeds of the securities issuance, the description of the issuer's business, the statement of the securities' material risks, and unaudited financial statements.

Standards for complying with the due diligence defense are explained more fully in *Escott v. BarChris Construction Corp.*, which appears in Chapter 45.

Section 12(a)(2) Often brought in connection with a Section 11 claim, Section 12(a)(2) imposes liability on any person who misstates or omits a material fact in connection with an offer or sale of a security that is part of a general distribution of securities by an issuer. Privity of contract between the plaintiff and the defendant is required here because Section 12(a)(2) states that the defendant is liable to the person *purchasing* the security *from him or her.*

Under Section 12(a)(2), a defendant must have direct contact with a buyer of a security to be liable. Merely performing professional services, such as auditing financial statements, is not enough for Section 12(a)(2) liability. A person must actively solicit the sale, motivated at least by a desire to serve his own financial interest. Such a financial interest is unlikely to be met by an auditor whose compensation is a fee unconnected to the proceeds of the securities sale. In addition, the *Central Bank* case[6] makes it fairly clear that auditors who merely *aid and abet* a client's Section 12(a)(2) violation will not have liability for damages under Section 12(a)(2).

Securities professionals have a greater risk of liability under Section 12(a)(2) because they frequently have direct contact with purchasers. Underwriters helping clients with public offerings sell securities or at least actively solicit sales by speaking with investors and writing the prospectus or other offering document. Because underwriters receive compensation for their services in the form of a commission or a spread (the difference between the amount underwriters pay the issuer and the price they sell at), they have the requisite financial stake in the sale. Securities brokers and dealers also are sellers or actively solicit securities sales and have a financial stake in the sale when they assist issuer distributions of securities and receive a commission or spread.

In the event that a person has sufficient contact with a purchaser to incur Section 12(a)(2) liability, the defendant may escape liability if she did not know and could not reasonably have known of the untruth or omission; that is, she was not negligent.

Section 17(a) Under Section 17(a), a purchaser of a security must prove his reliance on a misstatement or omission of material fact for which an accountant or securities professional is responsible. Under two of the subsections of Section 17(a), the investor need prove only negligence by the accountant, underwriter, broker, or adviser. Under the third, the investor must prove the accountant or securities professional acted with scienter. Whether there is a private right of action for damages under Section 17(a) is unclear. The courts of appeals are in disagreement, and the Supreme Court has not ruled on the issue.

Securities Exchange Act of 1934   Two
sections of the 1934 Act—Section 18 and Section 10(b)—especially affect the liability of professionals to nonclients.

Section 18 Section 18 of the 1934 Act imposes liability on persons who furnish misleading and false statements of material fact in any report or document filed with the Securities and Exchange Commission under the 1934 Act. Such reports or documents include the annual 10-K report—which includes auditors' opinions regarding financial statements—the 8-K current report, and proxy statements.

Under Section 18, a purchaser or seller of a security may sue an auditor if he relied on the defective statement in the filed document and it caused his damages. Usually, this means that a plaintiff must have *read and relied* on the defective statement in the filed document. The purchaser or seller may sue the auditor even if they are not in privity of contract.

An auditor may escape Section 18 liability if she acted in *good faith* and had *no knowledge* that the information was misleading. That is, she acted *without scienter*. For this reason, as well as the difficulty of proving reliance, Section 18 liability for auditors is extremely rare.

Although securities professionals, such as brokers and dealers, may file reports under the 1934 Act, those documents are not the type normally used by investors making investment decisions. Section 18 liability is, therefore, not normally an issue for securities professionals.

Section 10(b) and Rule 10b–5 Securities Exchange Act Rule 10b-5, pursuant to Section 10(b), has been the basis for most of the recent suits investors have brought against auditors and securities professionals. Rule 10b-5 prohibits any person from making a misstatement or omission of material fact in connection with the purchase or sale of any security. Rule 10b-5 applies to misstatements or omissions in any communications with investors, including the use of audited financial statements resulting in a purchase or sale of a security. The wrongful act must have a connection with interstate commerce, the mails, or a national securities exchange. Although the Act does not provide for an express private right of action to enforce Rule 10b-5, one has been implied since the mid-1940s.

A purchaser or seller of a security may sue an auditor, underwriter, or broker who has misstated or omitted a material fact. Privity is not required. The purchaser or seller must rely on the misstatement or omission. In omission cases, reliance may be inferred from materiality.

In addition, the defendant must act with scienter. In this context, scienter is an intent to deceive, manipulate, or defraud. For some courts, reckless misconduct is sufficient to prove scienter. Recklessness may be established when an auditor failed to review or check information that it had a duty to monitor, or ignored obvious signs

---

[6] *Central Bank of Denver, N.A. v. First Interstate Bank of Denver, N.A.*, 511 U.S. 164 (1994).

of fraud.[7] Negligence, however, is not enough to impose liability under Rule 10b-5.

---

[7] *Gould v. Winstar Commc'ns., Inc.*, 692 F.3d 148 (2d Cir. 2012).

In the next case, the court found that the allegations against auditor Ernst & Young did not establish that E&Y had acted with scienter. The court gives several examples of what does and does not constitute scienter.

Ferris, Baker Watts, Inc. v. Ernst & Young, LLP
395 F.3d 851 (8th Cir. 2005)

MJK Clearing Inc. (MJK) was a broker-dealer engaged in the risky business of securities borrowing. In securities borrowing, a party lent a security to MJK, which paid cash collateral slightly exceeding the value of the security. The cash collateral was "marked to market" so that if the market price of the security rose, MJK paid additional cash to the lender of the security. If the market price of the security fell, however, the lender owed MJK cash. In addition to borrowing securities, MJK was also a lender and, therefore, subject to the risk that it would be required to pay additional cash if the securities fell in value. MJK had lent securities to Ferris, Baker Watts Inc. (FBW), another broker-dealer, and received cash collateral.

By March 31, 2001, MJK had paid $ 160 million cash—representing nearly one-half of its accounts receivable and 21 percent of its total assets—to another broker-dealer, Native Nations Securities Inc., in exchange for borrowed securities. These securities were mostly from three thinly traded issuers, including GenesisIntermedia Inc. In 2001, the price of GenesisIntermedia fell, and Native Nations did not pay the cash collateral it owed MJK. As a result, MJK collapsed, and the Securities Investor Protection Corporation began the liquidation of MJK.

Consequently, FBW was unable to reclaim $20 million of cash collateral it had paid MJK. To recover its loss, FBW sued MJK's independent auditor, Ernst & Young LLP. FBW argued that it dealt with MJK relying on E&Y's audit of MJK's financial statements, as of year-end March 31, 2001. FBW alleged that E&Y's audit violated Section 10(b) of the Securities Act of 1934 and SEC Rule 10b-5 by recklessly misrepresenting that its audit met generally accepted auditing standards and that MJK's financial statements were fairly presented in accordance with generally accepted accounting principles. The district court dismissed the action, holding that the complaint insufficiently alleged that E&Y had acted with scienter. FBW appealed.

Benton, Circuit Judge

Section 10(b) and Rule 10b-5 prohibit fraudulent conduct in the sale and purchase of securities. Claims require four elements: (1) misrepresentations or omissions of material fact or acts that operated as a fraud or deceit in violation of the rule; (2) causation, often analyzed in terms of materiality and reliance; (3) scienter on the part of the defendants; and (4) economic harm caused by the fraudulent activity occurring in connection with the purchase and sale of a security. Only scienter—the intent to deceive, manipulate, or defraud—is at issue here.

Mere negligence does not violate Rule 10b-5. Severe recklessness, however, may. Recklessness is limited to those highly unreasonable omissions or misrepresentations that involve not merely simple or even inexcusable negligence, but an extreme departure from the standards of ordinary care, and that present a danger of misleading buyers or sellers which is either known to the defendant or is so obvious that the defendant must have been aware of it. This level of recklessness requires that defendants make statements that they know, or have access to information suggesting, are materially inaccurate.

FBW argues it pleaded that E&Y knew of, or had access to, facts that permit a strong inference that its audit opinion was knowingly or recklessly false or misleading. It claims E&Y falsely stated that it conducted the audit in accordance with GAAS, when: (1) E&Y's review of internal control of MJK's securities-borrowing department—the largest and most rapidly growing part of the company—revealed a complete absence of internal control, imposing a duty of heightened scrutiny that E&Y ignored; (2) E&Y failed to investigate whether the $160 million receivable from Native Nations was impaired; and (3) E&Y failed to investigate any subsequent events after the audit (but before issuance of the audit opinion) as to the collectibility of MJK's account receivable from Native Nations, which investigation would have revealed defaults.

FBW further alleges that E&Y disregarded GAAP, which a reasonable accountant follows. Thus, FBW says, a strong inference of scienter arises that E&Y's audit opinion that MJK's financial statements conformed with GAAP was a knowing or reckless misstatement of fact. Specifically, FBW alleges that the financial statements do not disclose as required by GAAP: (1) the concentration of credit risk in the $160 million receivable from Native Nations; (2) the risk that the Native Nations receivable was impaired or uncollectible; and (3) the "going concern" risk from the Native Nations receivable.

Finally, FBW alleges that E&Y failed to disclose—as required by SEC Rule 17a-5—material inadequacies in MJK's internal controls known to E&Y, permitting a strong inference that the nondisclosure was knowing or reckless.

"Allegations of GAAP violations are insufficient, standing alone, to raise an inference of scienter. Only where these allegations are coupled with evidence of corresponding fraudulent intent might they be sufficient." *In re Navarre Corp. Sec. Litig.*, 299 F.3d 735, 745 (8th Cir. 2002). *See also Kushner v. Beverly Enters., Inc.*, 317 F.3d 820, 827, 831 (8th Cir. 2003) (affirming dismissal of complaint alleging failure to establish accounting reserves); *In re K-Tel Int'l, Inc. Sec. Litig.*, 300 F.3d 881, 894-95 (8th Cir. 2002) (affirming dismissal of complaint based on overstatement of assets and "sheer magnitude" of GAAP violations).

Assuming GAAP and GAAS violations occurred here, FBW's catch-all and blanket assertions that E&Y acted recklessly or knowingly are not evidence of corresponding fraudulent intent. This is not a case like *Green Tree*, where a defendant published statements knowing that crucial information in them was based on discredited assumptions. *Florida State Bd. of Admin, v. Green Tree Fin. Corp.*, 270 F.3d 645, 665 (8th Cir. 2001).

FBW asserts that the district court misreads *Kushner, K-Tel*, and *Navarre*. In fact, the lower court follows not only this court's cases, but also those from other Circuits. *See, e.g., Novak v. Kasaks*, 216 F.3d 300, 309 (2d Cir. 2000) (allegations of GAAP violations or accounting irregularities, standing alone, are insufficient to state a securities fraud claim); *Stevelman v. Alias Research Inc.*, 174 F.3d 79, 84 (2d Cir. 1999) (allegations of a violation of GAAP provisions or SEC regulations, without corresponding fraudulent intent, are not sufficient to state a securities fraud claim; *Fidel v. Farley*, 392 F.3d 220, 230 (6th Cir. 2004) (failure to follow generally accepted accounting procedures does not in and of itself lead to an inference of scienter; *DSAM Global Value Fund v. Altris Software, Inc.*, 288 F.3d 385, 387 (9th Cir. 2002) (affirming dismissal of allegations of a "seriously botched audit" and "a compelling case of negligence—perhaps even gross negligence"); *In re Software Toolworks Inc. Sec. Litig.*, 50 F.3d 615, 627-28 (9th Cir. 1994) (affirming summary judgment for auditor, stating that "mere publication of inaccurate accounting figures, or a failure to follow GAAP, without more, does not establish scienter").

FBW repeatedly asserts that E&Y's audit was so cursory and superficial as to amount to "no audit at all." *See Software Toolworks*, 50 F.3d at 628 (auditing that is "no audit at all" shows scienter). The facts alleged here show otherwise. FBW's complaint says that E&Y was fully aware of the risks associated with MJK's securities borrowing and lending operations, and had an audit plan that recognized the need for closer testing of securities borrowing. FBW states that E&Y did confirm the account receivable with Native Nations, noting its excess over the value of the collateral securities, and its concentration in three issuers. According to the complaint, E&Y did interview MJK's securities-borrowing department manager, who described the processes and procedures, and represented that he performed credit reviews "anywhere from monthly to annually by reviewing other Broker FOCUS reports." FBW pleads that E&Y examined five files of MJK's (approximately) 60 customers for the presence of signed agreements and annual credit evaluations, inquired as to deficiencies in the files, and verified that securities-borrowing personnel prepared numerous reports, including daily "Balance Order Fail Reports." According to FBW, E&Y conducted tests of internal control activities, and identified reconciliations of balance-sheet cash accounts to bank accounts, and balance-sheet securities ledgers to securities accounts. E&Y concluded that internal controls were effective, and could be relied upon to reduce the substantive audit procedures (and increase reliance on management's representation that no subsequent events occurred after fieldwork, but before issue of the opinion). In sum, FBW alleges a poor audit, not the intent to deceive, manipulate, or defraud required for securities fraud.

Judgment for Ernst & Young affirmed.

Aiding and Abetting In 1994 in the *Central Bank* case mentioned earlier, the Supreme Court of the United States held that those who merely aid and abet Rule 10b-5 violations have no liability for damages to those injured by the fraud. The court drew a distinction between those *primarily* responsible for the fraud—who retain Rule 10b-5 liability—and those *secondarily* responsible—who no longer have liability under Rule 10b-5. The distinction between primary and secondary responsibility is unclear. Issuing unqualified opinions regarding false financial statements is primary fault and would impose Rule 10b-5 liability on the auditor. However, an independent accountant's work in connection with false unaudited statements or other financial information released by a client may be only secondary and may not impose Rule 10b-5 liability on the accountant.

The Supreme Court affirmed and explained its *Central Bank* ruling in *Stoneridge Investment Partners*.[8] You can read that case in Chapter 45.

Although auditors are not liable to private litigants for merely secondary activities, Congress has made it clear that the SEC may prosecute accountants for aiding and abetting a client's violation of Rule 10b-5.

A person is subject to SEC sanctions for aiding and abetting under Rule 10b-5 if there is (1) a primary violation by another person (such as a client fraudulently overstating its earnings), (2) the person's knowing or reckless assistance of the other person's primary violation, and (3) the person's substantial assistance in the achievement of the primary violation (such as an auditor's failure to disclose a client's fraud known by the auditor).

Securities professionals may be primarily responsible for misstatements or omissions of material facts in a variety of contexts, and therefore may have Rule 10b-5 liability to nonclients and clients. For example, an underwriter who uses its own e-mail account to solicit investors for a client's Rule 506 securities offering is primarily responsible for that document, as well the underwriter who makes oral statements about the issuer and the securities to a prospective investor. Securities brokers may have Rule 10b-5 liability for churning their clients' accounts to generate high commissions for the broker. In addition, brokers may have liability under Rule 10b-5 for giving fraudulent advice to clients.

In 2011, however, the Supreme Court held in *Janus Capital Group, Inc. v. First Derivative Traders*[9] that an investment advisor was not liable for fraudulent statements in a prospectus of a mutual fund sponsored by the investment advisor because the investment advisor was not the maker of those statements. The court came to this conclusion even though the mutual fund's officers were all employees of the advisor, and the advisor prepared and distributed the prospectus. The Supreme Court majority ruled that the advisor *did not make* the fraudulent statement because the mutual fund was a legally separate entity from the advisor and had ultimate authority over the prospectus, including its content and whether and how to communicate it. In addition, the mutual fund, not the advisor, held the statutory duty to file the prospectus, and there was nothing on the face of the prospectus indicating that any statements therein came from the advisor rather than the mutual fund.

Extent of Liability The Private Securities Litigation Reform Act limits the liability of most auditors and securities professionals to the amount of an investor's loss for which the defendant is responsible. This means that a defendant has *proportionate liability* and need no longer fear being liable for investors' entire losses when a fraudulent client is unable to pay its share of the damages. The determination of the percentage of the loss for which a defendant is responsible is a question for the jury. Note, however, the Reform Act provides that when a person knowingly commits a violation of the securities laws, the defendant may be required to pay an investor's entire loss.

State Securities Law All states have securities statutes with liability sections. Most of the states have a liability section similar to Section 12(a)(2) of the Securities Act.

Securities Analysts' Conflicts of Interest

For years, investors have known that stock recommendations and research reports by securities analysts in major investment banking firms are almost always overly optimistic. Few analysts recommend that investors sell a stock; almost all recommendations are strong buy, buy, accumulate, or hold, with a few sell recommendations sprinkled in. The reasons for such optimism vary from an unwillingness to say anything bad to a belief that a bull market will sustain rising securities prices. But the reason that caught the attention of securities regulators is that analysts may have a conflict of interest. The belief is that full-service investment firms that have securities research, brokerage, and investment banking departments discourage their securities analysts from giving poor recommendations for a public company's stock for fear that a poor recommendation will offend the company's management and cause the company to award valuable investment banking business to a more cooperative investment firm. Some investment firms even threatened to lower public companies' stock recommendations unless the companies awarded investment banking business to the firms.

The Sarbanes-Oxley Act (SOX) directed the SEC to adopt or to direct the national securities exchanges and NASDAQ to adopt rules to address research analysts' conflicts of interest. SOX requires the rules to accomplish the following:

• Restrict prepublication approval of analysts' research reports by investment banking or other nonresearch personnel in the firm.

---

[8]*Stoneridge Investment Partners, LLC v. Scientific-Atlanta, Inc.,* 552 U.S. 148 (2008).
[9]564 U.S. 135 (2011).

Ethics and Compliance in Action

Securities and Investment Banking Firms Lose and Settle Conflict of Interest Cases

Several securities firms and investment companies have settled or lost actions brought by investors, the SEC, the NASD (and its successor, FINRA), and other government and regulatory bodies in the face of allegations of conflicts of interest.

In 2003, securities firm and investment bank Goldman, Sachs & Co. agreed with the SEC, NASD, NYSE, and state regulators to pay $25 million in restitution and an additional $25 million in penalties, plus $50 million to provide the firm's clients with independent research and $10 million for investor education. The settlement stemmed from allegations that Goldman's research analysts were subject to inappropriate influence by Goldman's investment banking services. For example, Goldman required its analysts to prepare business plans that discussed the steps analysts planned to take to assist investment banking efforts. In preparing these business plans, analysts were required to answer such questions as "How much of your time will be devoted to IBD [investment banking division]?" and "How can you work more effectively with IBD to exploit the opportunities available to the firm?" In response to the question "What are the three most important goals for you in 2000?" one analyst replied, "1. Get more investment banking revenue. 2. Get more investment banking revenue. 3. Get more investment banking revenue."

A NASD arbitration panel ordered securities firm Merrill Lynch to pay $1 million to a Florida couple for failing to disclose that its analysts were recommending to Merrill Lynch customers companies that they privately disparaged. The analysts gave the companies positive recommendations in order for Merrill Lynch to obtain the companies' investment banking business.

Securities firm Morgan Stanley was charged by the NASD with improperly rewarding its brokers with tickets to concerts and sporting events in an attempt to boost sales of Morgan Stanley's mutual funds. Morgan Stanley agreed to pay a fine of $2 million.

In settlements with the SEC and state prosecutors, several mutual fund sellers, including Bank of America, FleetBoston Financial, and Putnam Investments, agreed to pay hefty fines and make restitution to investors in light of allegations their employees engaged in "market timing" of the firms' mutual funds. Market timing involves frequent trading, usually in international funds, to exploit "stale" mutual fund prices that exist due to time zone differences. The practice allegedly hurts the returns of long-term shareholders of the mutual funds. Bank of America agreed to pay $250 million in restitution and $125 million in fines; FleetBoston, $70 million in restitution and $70 million in fines; Putnam, $10 million in restitution and $100 million in fines.

In 2014, several investment banks paid fines of over $1 billion for selling mortgage-backed securities during the early 2000s credit boom without informing buyers of known problems with the loans. Deutsche Bank paid $1.93 billion; JPMorgan, $4 billion; Citigroup, $7 billion.

- Limit supervision and evaluation of securities analysts' compensation to persons not in the investment banking side of the firm.
- Prohibit investment banking personnel from retaliating against a securities analyst because of a negative research report.
- Set time periods during which firms involved in an underwriting of public issuances may not publish research reports about the issuer and its securities.
- Place information partitions to separate research analysts from review, pressure, or oversight by those whose investment banking activities might bias their judgment.
- Require securities analysts to disclose in public appearances and research reports any conflict of interest, including whether the analyst owns the issuer's securities, whether compensation has been received by the firm or analyst, and whether the issuer is currently or has been a client of the firm in the last year.

The SEC has adopted Regulation AC (Analyst Certification). Although not designed to implement the requirements of SOX, Regulation AC requires an analyst's research report to include the analyst's certification that the views expressed in the report accurately reflect her personal views. Regulation AC also requires a securities analyst to certify whether or not any part of her compensation is related to her recommendation of a security or to her views contained in a company research report. The rule also restricts the relationship between research and investment banking departments of a securities firm, as well as their relationships with companies covered by a securities firm's research reports.

The SEC also has approved NYSE and NASDAQ rules regarding analysts' conflicts of interest. The rules are substantially similar. They prohibit a securities firm from offering favorable research to a company in order to induce the company to use the securities firm's investment banking service. The rules increase analyst independence by prohibiting investment banking personnel from supervising analysts or approving research reports. Analyst compensation may not be tied to a specific investment banking services transaction. Also, an analyst is restricted in trading for his personal account in securities he recommends.

The NASDAQ and the NYSE also passed rules on analysts' conflicts of interest prior to passage of SOX. The rules are substantially similar. They ban favorable research for pay, prohibit analyst compensation based on specific investment banking services, and limit the submission of a research report to an issuer prior to publication of the report.

Dodd–Frank Act and Broker-Dealers

In 2010, Congress passed the Dodd-Frank Wall Street Reform and Consumer Protection Act. The Dodd–Frank Act specifically authorizes the SEC to issue point-of-sale disclosure rules when investors purchase investment products or services, such as mutual fund and investment management services. These disclosures include costs, risks, and conflicts of interest. In determining the disclosure rules, the act authorizes the SEC to do investor testing and rely on experts to study financial literacy among retail investors.

The Dodd–Frank Act also provides authority for the SEC to impose a fiduciary duty on broker-dealers and investment advisors in their dealings with their customer. Although the act does not create such a duty immediately, it authorizes the SEC to establish such a standard and requires that the SEC study the standards of care that broker-dealers and investment advisors apply to their customers and report the findings to Congress. Released in 2011, the SEC study recommended that the SEC adopt a uniform fiduciary standard—including a duty of loyalty and a duty of care—applying to both broker-dealers and investment advisors when providing particular investment advice to retail investors.

In addition, the Dodd–Frank Act adds new Section 9(a)(4) to the 1934 Act, making it unlawful for any broker, dealer, or other person selling or offering to sell or purchasing or offering to purchase any security (other than a government security), to make for the purpose of inducing the purchase or sale of such security any false or misleading misstatement of material fact, if the person knew or had reasonable ground to believe the statement was false or misleading. This new section tempers some of the effect of the *Janus* case, discussed in the section titled "Aiding and Abetting" earlier in this chapter.

Regulation Best Interest and Broker-Dealers

In 2019, the SEC adopted Regulation Best Interest (Reg BI) pursuant to Rule 15-1 of the Exchange Act, which requires broker-dealers to act in the best interests of their retail customers when making recommendations. Although Reg BI requires brokers to act in clients' best interests, the standard is not a fiduciary one as contemplated by Dodd–Frank. According to the SEC, Reg BI will enhance the broker-dealer standard of conduct and make it clear that a broker-dealer may not put his financial interests ahead of the interests of a retail customer when making recommendations.

Reg BI is organized around a "general obligation," which requires that broker-dealers comply with four component obligations: the disclosure obligation, the care obligation, the conflict of interest obligation, and the compliance obligation. Whether a broker-dealer has complied with each of the four component obligations is determined on a principles basis—an evaluation of the facts and circumstances of the particular recommendation and retail customer. This determination is to be made at the time of the recommendation, not in hindsight.

The general obligation suggests that when making a recommendation of any securities transaction or investment strategy involving securities (including account recommendations) to a retail customer, the broker-dealer must act in the best interest of the retail customer without placing the financial or other interest of the broker, dealer, or a natural person who is associated with the broker-dealer ahead of the interest of the retail customer. A "retail customer" is defined as a natural person, or the legal representative that person, who receives a recommendation of any securities transaction or investment strategy and uses the recommendation primarily for personal, family, or household purposes.

Notably, the term "best interest" is not defined, but SEC comments have made clear that Reg BI does not create an independent fiduciary standard. Nor is it intended to require a broker-dealer to make conflict-free recommendations to retail customers. Instead, broker-dealers must take steps to reduce the effect of conflicts that would create an incentive to place their interests ahead of those of retail customers. A broker-dealer may recommend products that are risky or costly, or that result in greater compensation to the broker-dealer, so long as each component obligation is satisfied. The following chart provides a summary of the four component obligations.

Not surprisingly, Reg BI's passage was met with immediate legal challenges. Notably, one challenge was supported by former lawmakers Dodd and Frank, who argued that Reg BI failed to create a stringent enough standard of care for broker-dealers.

CONCEPT REVIEW

Obligation	Summary	Specific Provisions

Disclosure obligation	Broker-dealers must disclose material facts about the relationship and recommendations of the products and services they provide.	• All material facts relating to the scope and terms of the relationship with the retail customer, including:
		  ○ That the broker-dealer is acting as a broker-dealer with respect to the recommendation;
		  ○ The material fees and costs that apply to the retail customer's transactions, holdings, and accounts; and
		  ○ The type and scope of services provided to the retail customer; and
		• All material facts relating to conflicts of interest that are associated with the recommendation.

Care obligation	Broker-dealers must exercise reasonable diligence, care, and skill when making a recommendation to a retail customer. The broker-dealer must understand potential risks, rewards, and costs associated with the recommendation.	• Understand the potential risks, rewards and costs associated with the recommendation, and have a reasonable basis to believe the recommendation is be in the best interest of retail customers; • Have a reasonable basis to believe that the recommendation is in the best interest of a particular retail customer based on that customer's investment profile, and does not place the financial or other interest of the broker-dealer above the interest of the retail customer; and • Have a reasonable basis to believe that a series of recommended transactions, even if in the retail customer's best interest when viewed in isolation, is not excessive.
Conflict of interest obligation	Broker-dealers must establish, maintain, and enforce written policies and procedures reasonably designed to identify and—at a minimum—disclose or eliminate conflicts of interest.	• Identify and disclose, or eliminate, all conflicts of interest associated with the recommendations; • Identify and mitigate any conflicts of interest associated with the recommendations that create an incentive for the broker-dealer to place his interest above the interest of the retail customer; • Identify and disclose any material limitations placed on the securities or investment strategies that may be recommended to a retail customer and any conflicts of interest associated with such limitations; • Prevent such limitations and associated conflicts of interest from causing the broker-dealer to make recommendations that place his interest above the interest of the retail customer; and • Identify and eliminate any sales contests, sales quotas, bonuses and noncash compensation that are based on the sales of specific securities within a limited period of time.
Compliance Obligation	Broker-dealers must establish, maintain, and enforce policies and procedures reasonably designed to achieve compliance with Reg BI as a whole.	• Establish compliance procedures reasonably designed to implement obligations of Reg BI, which would include controls, remediation of noncompliance, training, and periodic review and testing.

Liability Sections of the 1933 Act and 1934 Act

	Wrongful Conduct	Covered Communications	Who May Sue? (Proper Plaintiff)	Must the Plaintiff Prove Reliance on the Wrongful Conduct?
Securities Act of 1933 Section 11	Misstatement or omission of material fact	1933 Act registration statement only	Any purchaser of securities issued pursuant to the registration statement	No
Securities Act of 1933 Section 12(a)(2)	Misstatement or omission of material fact	Any communication in connection with a general distribution of securities by an issuer (except government-issued or guaranteed securities)	Any purchaser of the securities offered or sold	No
Securities Act of 1933 Section 17(a)	Misstatement or omission of material fact	Any communication in connection with any offer to sell or sale of any security	Any purchaser of the securities offered or sold	Yes
Securities Exchange Act of 1934 Section 10(b) and Rule 10b–5	Misstatement or omission of material fact	Any communication in connection with a purchase or sale of any security	Any purchaser or seller of the securities	Yes
Securities Exchange Act of 1934 Section 18	False or misleading statement of material fact	Any document filed with the SEC under the 1934 Act (includes the 1934 Act registration statement, 10-K, 8-K, and proxy statements)	Any purchaser or seller of a security whose price was affected by the statement	Yes

Qualified Opinions, Disclaimers of Opinion, Adverse Opinions, and Unaudited Statements

After performing an audit of financial statements, an independent auditor issues an opinion letter regarding the financial statements. The **opinion letter** expresses whether the audit has been performed in compliance with GAAS and whether, in the auditor's opinion, the financial statements fairly present the client's financial position and results of operations in conformity with GAAP. Usually, an auditor issues an unqualified *opinion*—that is, an opinion that there has been compliance with GAAS and GAAP. Sometimes, an auditor issues a qualified opinion, a disclaimer of opinion, or an adverse opinion.

Up to this point, you have studied the liability of an auditor who has issued unqualified opinions yet has not complied with GAAS and GAAP.

What liability should be imposed on an auditor who discloses that he has not complied with GAAS and GAAP? An auditor is relieved of responsibility only to the extent that a qualification or disclaimer is specifically expressed in the opinion letter. Therefore, letters that purport to disclaim liability totally for false and misleading financial statements are too general to excuse an accountant from exercising ordinary skill and care.

For example, an auditor qualifies his opinion of the ability of financial statements to present the financial position of a company by indicating that there is uncertainty about how an antitrust suit against the company may be decided. He would

Liability Sections of the 1933 Act and 1934 Act

Who May Be Sued? (Proper Defendant)	Must the Plaintiff and Defendant Be in Privity of Contract?	Defendant's Level of Fault	Who Has the Burden of Proving or Disproving Defendant's Level of Fault?
Issuer, underwriters, directors, signers (CEO, CFO, and CAO must sign), and experts who contribute to the registration statement (such as auditors of financial statements)	No	Negligence, except for the issuer; issuer is liable without regard to fault	Defendant, except issuer, may escape liability by proving due diligence. There are two defenses, but for most defendants for most parts of the registration statement, the defense is that he made a reasonable investigation and had reason to believe and did believe there were no misstatements or omissions of material fact.
Any person who sells a security or actively solicits a sale of a security	Yes (although met by a defendant who has a financial interest in a sale of securities)	Negligence	Defendant may escape liability by proving he did not know and could not reasonably have known of the misstatement or omission of material fact.
Any person responsible for the misstatement or omission	No	Negligence for some parts of Section 17(a); scienter for one part	Plaintiff must prove the defendant acted negligently or with scienter, depending on the subsection.
Any person primarily responsible for the misstatement or omission	No, but defendant must communicate with the plaintiff or know or should know plaintiff will receive the communication with the misstatement or omission	Scienter	Plaintiff must prove the defendant acted with scienter.
Any person who made or caused the statement to be made	No	Scienter	Defendant may escape liability by proving he acted in good faith with no knowledge that the statement was false or misleading.

not be held liable for damages resulting from an unfavorable verdict in the antitrust suit. He would remain liable, however, for failing to make an examination in compliance with GAAS that would have revealed other serious problems.

For another example, consider an auditor who, due to the limited scope of the audit, disclaims any opinion on the ability of the financial statements to present the financial position of the company. She would nonetheless be liable for the nondiscovery of problems that the limited audit should have revealed.

Likewise, an accountant who issued an adverse opinion that depreciation had not been calculated according to GAAP would not be liable for damages resulting from the wrongful accounting treatment of depreciation, but she would be liable for damages resulting from the wrongful treatment of receivables.

Merely preparing unaudited statements does not create a disclaimer as to their accuracy. The mere fact that the statements are unaudited only permits an accountant to exercise a lower level of inquiry. Even so, an accountant must act as the ordinarily prudent accountant would act under the same circumstances in preparing unaudited financial statements.

Criminal, Injunctive, and Administrative Proceedings

In addition to being held liable for damages to clients and third parties, a professional may be found criminally liable for his violations of securities, tax, and other laws.

For criminal violations, he may be fined and imprisoned. His wrongful conduct may also result in the issuance of an injunction, which bars him from doing the same acts in the future. In addition, his wrongful conduct may be the subject of administrative proceedings by the Securities and Exchange Commission and state licensing boards. An administrative proceeding may result in the revocation of a professional's license to practice or the suspension from practice. Finally, disciplinary proceedings may be brought by professional societies and self-regulatory organizations such as the AICPA or FINRA.

Criminal Liability under the Securities Laws

Both the Securities Act of 1933 and the Securities Exchange Act of 1934 have criminal provisions that can be applied to professionals. The 1933 Act imposes criminal liability for willful violations of any section of the 1933 Act, including Sections 11, 12(a)(2), and 17(a), or any 1933 Act rule or regulation. For example, willfully making an untrue statement or omitting any material fact in a 1933 Act registration statement subjects a person to criminal liability. The maximum penalty for a criminal violation of the 1933 Act is a $10,000 fine and five years' imprisonment.

The 1934 Act imposes criminal penalties for willful violations of any section of the 1934 Act, such as Sections 10(b) and 18, and any 1934 Act rule or regulation, such as Rule 10b–5. For example, willfully making false or misleading statements in reports that are required to be filed under the 1934 Act incurs criminal liability. Such filings include 10-Ks, 8-Ks, and proxy statements. An individual may be fined up to $5 million and imprisoned for up to 20 years for a criminal violation of the 1934 Act. A professional firm may be fined up to $25 million.

In addition, most states have statutes imposing criminal penalties on professionals who willfully falsify financial statements or other reports in filings under the securities laws and who willfully violate the state securities laws or aid and abet criminal violations of these laws by others.

In *United States v. Goyal,* the 9th Circuit Court of Appeals addressed the evidence used to convict a former CFO for securities fraud violations under the antifraud provisions of Section 10(b) of the 1934 Act. The court's discussion focuses on the elements necessary to prove that misleading material statements were made in a company's financials and to auditors. The case is notable because the government relied on the defendant's alleged failure to follow GAAP in proving its case at the trial court level. It is also notable for a concurring opinion calling into question the government's decision to prosecute Goyal.

United States v. Goyal   629 F.3d 912 (9th Cir. 2010)

Prabhat Goyal, the former CFO of software company Network Associates, appealed his convictions on 15 counts of securities fraud and making materially false statements to auditors. The government alleged that under Goyal's supervision, Network Associates violated GAAP by recognizing revenue from software sales earlier than it should have, namely by using "sell in" accounting when it should have used "sell through" accounting. The difference is that sell in accounting recognizes revenue from deals when products ship to distributors rather than when those distributors sell through to their customers, which occurs later. Goyal was indicted for concealing the allegedly improper accounting from the company's outside auditors and for filing reports with the SEC that misstated revenue. On appeal, Goyal argued that no jury could have found him guilty beyond a reasonable doubt under these facts.

Clifton, Circuit Judge

All of the securities counts—one count of securities fraud and seven counts of making false filings with the SEC—required the government to prove that Network Associates materially misstated the revenue it earned in certain quarters and years through its choice of accounting method. Network Associates' reports of allegedly inflated revenue furnished the "untrue statement of material fact" required for each of the false filing counts, as well as the "misleading statement or omission of a material fact made with scienter" needed to sustain a fraud conviction under the general antifraud provision of § 10(b) of the Securities Exchange Act of 1934.

The government's contention that Network Associates materially overstated its revenue necessarily entailed two claims: (1) that it recognized revenue at a different time than it should have; and (2) that its accounting produced artificially higher revenue figures in certain periods that "would have been viewed by the reasonable investor as having significantly altered the 'total mix' of information made available." *Basic Inc. v. Levinson,* 485 U.S. 224 (1988). The government relied on GAAP to make its case, on the first point, that sell-through accounting was required in instances where Network Associates used the sell-in method. But we need not decide whether the company actually violated GAAP, because the government clearly failed to carry its burden on the second point, materiality. The prosecution offered no evidence adequate to prove that any GAAP violations materially affected the revenue that Network Associates reported.

The government relied at trial on the parties' stipulations that applying sell-through accounting to Network Associates' entire business would have resulted in "a revenue figure that is materially less than the reported figure" for the periods charged in the false filing counts. These stipulations are fatally overbroad, however, because the government did not contend that GAAP required Network Associates to use sell-through accounting for all sales. The government only offered evidence that sell-through accounting was required for [some] buy-in transactions, and the stipulations did not provide that applying sell-through accounting to those transactions alone would have made a material difference in any given period. Without evidence of how much less revenue Network Associates would have recognized on these deals if it had used sell-through accounting, the jury had no basis to conclude that the misstatement of reported revenue resulting from the transactions was material. Even presuming, as we must, that the jury drew all reasonable inferences in the prosecution's favor, there was no way it could have properly inferred materiality from the evidence it had before it. * * * Because Goyal's jury had no competent evidence of materiality before it, it could not have properly convicted him on any of the securities counts.

The judgment of the district court is REVERSED, and the case is REMANDED for entry of judgment of acquittal on all counts.

Chief Judge Kozinski, concurring:

This case has consumed an inordinate amount of taxpayer resources, and has no doubt devastated the defendant's personal and professional life. The defendant's former employer also paid a price, footing a multimillion dollar bill for the defense. And, in the end, the government couldn't prove that the defendant engaged in any criminal conduct. This is just one of a string of recent cases in which courts have found that federal prosecutors overreached by trying to stretch criminal law beyond its proper bounds. *See Arthur Andersen LLP v. United States*, 544 U.S. 696 (2005).

This is not the way criminal law is supposed to work. Civil law often covers conduct that falls in a gray area of arguable legality. But criminal law should clearly separate conduct that is criminal from conduct that is legal. This is not only because of the dire consequences of a conviction—including disenfranchisement, incarceration and even deportation—but also because criminal law represents the community's sense of the type of behavior that merits the moral condemnation of society. When prosecutors have to stretch the law or the evidence to secure a conviction, as they did here, it can hardly be said that such moral judgment is warranted.

Mr. Goyal had the benefit of exceptionally fine advocacy on appeal, so he is spared the punishment for a crime he didn't commit. But not everyone is so lucky. The government shouldn't have brought charges unless it had clear evidence of wrongdoing, and the trial judge should have dismissed the case when the prosecution rested and it was clear the evidence could not support a conviction. Although we now vindicate Mr. Goyal, much damage has been done. One can only hope that he and his family will recover from the ordeal. And, perhaps, that the government will be more cautious in the future.

Other Criminal Law Violations

Tax Law Federal tax law imposes on professionals a wide range of penalties for a wide variety of wrongful conduct. At one end of the penalty spectrum is a $50 fine for an accountant's failing to furnish a client with a copy of his income tax return or failing to sign a client's return. At the other end is a fine of $250,000 for individuals and $500,000 for corporations and imprisonment of five years for tax fraud. In between is the penalty for promoting abusive tax shelters. The fine is $1,000, or 100 percent of the defendant's income from her participation in the tax shelter, whichever is less. In addition, all of the states impose criminal penalties for specified violations of their tax laws.

Mail Fraud Several other federal statutes also impose criminal liability on professionals. The most notable of these statutes is the general mail fraud statute, which prohibits the use of the mails to commit fraud. To be held liable, a professional must know or foresee that the mails will be used to transmit materials containing fraudulent statements provided by her.

In addition, the general false-statement-to-government-personnel statute prohibits fraudulent statements to government personnel. The false-statement-to-bank statute proscribes fraudulent statements on a loan application to a bank or other financial institution.

RICO The Racketeer Influenced and Corrupt Organizations Act (RICO) makes it a federal crime to engage in a pattern of racketeering activity. Although RICO was designed to attack the activities of organized crime enterprises, it applies to professionals who conduct or participate in the affairs of an enterprise in almost any pattern of business fraud. A pattern of fraud is proved by the commission of two predicate offenses within a 10-year period. Predicate offenses include securities law violations, mail fraud, and bribery. Individuals convicted of a RICO violation may be fined up to $250,000 or twice the gross profits from the illegal activity and imprisoned up to 20 years, as well as having seized all property acquired or maintained with funds obtained from the RICO violation.

A person who is injured in his business or property by reason of a professional's conduct or participation, directly or indirectly, in an enterprise's affairs through a pattern of racketeering activity may recover treble damages (three times his actual damages) from the professional. In *Reves v. Ernst & Young*,[10] the Supreme Court held that merely by auditing financial statements that substantially overvalued a client's assets, an accounting firm was not conducting or participating in the affairs of the client's business. The Court held that the accounting firm must participate in the "operation or management" of the enterprise itself to be liable under RICO.

Other Criminal Laws While there are many other criminal laws that may be violated by professionals, one final law bears mentioning: laws against the destruction of evidence that may be used against a professional in a criminal trial. All accounting and securities firms have rules regarding document retention and destruction. For the most part, retaining documents helps a firm prove that it has met its duty to its clients. Retained documents can establish that the firm acted in a reasonable manner when it conducted an audit or made an investment recommendation, for example.

On the other hand, documents may show that the professional or her client has acted inappropriately or even illegally. In general, professionals are not compelled to retain documents that prove their or a client's guilt, provided they do not destroy documents with the intent to obstruct a criminal prosecution. The *Andersen* case, which appears near the end of this chapter, held that Arthur Andersen LLP could not be found guilty when its employees shredded evidence regarding the Enron fraud, unless it was proved that Andersen intended to impede the prosecution of a particular criminal action at the time the shredding occurred.

Injunctions Administrative agencies such as the SEC and the IRS may bring injunctive actions against an auditor or securities professional in a federal district

court. The purpose of such an injunction is to prevent a defendant from committing a future violation of the securities or tax laws.

After an injunction has been issued by a court, violating the injunction may result in serious sanctions. Not only may penalties be imposed for contempt, but also a criminal violation may also be more easily proven.

Administrative Proceedings The SEC has the authority to bring administrative proceedings against persons who violate the provisions of the federal securities acts. In recent years, the SEC has stepped up enforcement of SEC Rule of Practice 102(e). Rule 102(e) permits the SEC to bar temporarily or permanently from practicing before the SEC a professional who has demonstrated a lack of the qualifications required to practice before it, such as an accountant who has prepared financial statements not complying with GAAP. In the Sarbanes–Oxley Act, Congress amended the 1934 Act to include the language of Rule 102(e) almost word for word.

The SEC may discipline accountants who engage in a single instance of unreasonable conduct that leads to a violation of professional accounting standards. The SEC may also discipline an accountant who engages in repeated, unreasonable conduct that results in a violation of professional accounting standards. For example, an auditor's conduct in reviewing a client's financial statements is unreasonable when the auditor knew or should have known that heightened scrutiny is warranted yet failed to exercise the additional scrutiny while conducting an audit.

For example, the SEC charged an Eide Bailly audit partner with improper professional conduct for failing to discover that its client, an insurance company, was recording revenue before it was earned. The SEC also charged the partner with failing to apply professional skepticism in gathering and evaluating audit evidence. The partner was suspended from SEC practice for three years.

Rule 102(e) also permits the SEC to take action against a professional who has willfully violated or aided and abetted another's violation of the securities acts. An SEC administrative law judge hears the case and makes an initial determination. The SEC commissioners then issue a final order, which may be appealed to a federal court of appeals.

Rule 102(e) administrative proceedings can impose severe penalties on an accountant. By suspending an accountant from practicing before it, the SEC may take away a substantial part of an accountant's practice. Also, the SEC may impose civil penalties up to $500,000.

---

[10] 507 U.S. 170 (1993).

In addition, state licensing boards may suspend or revoke an accountant's license to practice if she engages in illegal or unethical conduct. If such action is taken, an accountant may lose her entire ability to practice accounting.

Securities Exchange Act Audit Requirements

The Private Securities Litigation Reform Act of 1995 imposes significant public duties on independent auditors that audit the financial statements of public companies. In part added to the Securities Exchange Act as Section 10A, the Reform Act requires auditors to take specific steps if they learn during the course of an audit that a client may have committed an illegal act (that is, a violation of any law, rule, or regulation). First, the auditor is required to determine whether an illegal act has, in fact, occurred. If the auditor determines that the client has committed an illegal act, the auditor must calculate the prospective impact on the client's financial statements, including fines, penalties, and liability costs such as damage awards to persons harmed by the client. As soon as practical, the auditor must inform the client's management and audit committee of the auditor's determination, unless the illegal act is clearly inconsequential.

If the client's management does not take appropriate remedial action with respect to an illegal act that has a material effect on the financial statements of the client—and if the failure to take remedial action is reasonably expected to result in the auditor's issuance of a nonstandard report or resignation from the audit engagement—the auditor must make a report to the client's board of directors. The board of directors has one business day to inform the SEC of the auditor's report; if the board does not submit a report to the SEC, the auditor has one additional business day to furnish a copy of its report to the SEC, whether or not the auditor also resigns from the audit engagement.

Section 10A imposes a significant whistle-blowing duty on independent auditors, consistent with the watchdog function that Congress and the courts have continually assigned to auditors. To encourage auditors to make such reports, Section 10A also provides that an auditor will have no liability to a private litigant for any statement in the auditor's reports given to management, the board of directors, or the SEC.

Section 10A is also the repository of many of the new securities provisions enacted under the Sarbanes-Oxley Act, including the list of services audit firms may not provide for audit clients, the audit partner rotation requirement, and the standards and duties of audit committees.

SOX Section 404

The most controversial part of the Sarbanes-Oxley Act has been Section 404, which requires public issuers to include in their annual reports an "internal control report" acknowledging management's responsibility to maintain "an adequate internal control structure and procedures for financial reports." The purpose of Section 404 is to improve the quality of accounting records and financial statements, which had eroded in the 1990s as management and audit committees lost control of internal accounting processes.

SOX Section 404 requires management's internal control report to include:

- A statement of management's responsibility for establishing and maintaining adequate internal control over financial reporting for the company.
- Management's assessment of the effectiveness of the company's internal control over financial reporting.
- A statement identifying the framework used by management to evaluate the effectiveness of the company's internal control over financial reporting.
- A statement that the public accounting firm that audited the company's financial statements has issued an attestation report on management's assessment of the company's internal control over financial reporting.

Thus, SOX Section 404 requires not only that management maintain adequate internal controls, but also that auditors attest to management's assessment of internal controls. This requirement imposes new duties on auditors, yet at the same time provides new opportunities for providing services at a fee.

Auditors are experienced in performing attestation engagements on a broad variety of subjects. It was not surprising, therefore, that the rulemaking body charged with setting standards for Section 404, the Public Company Accounting Oversight Board, adopted the standard used in other contexts, SSAE No. 10, as the appropriate standard for Section 404 assessments.

Cooperation with PCAOB Investigations

Under the Sarbanes-Oxley Act, PCAOB-registered accounting firms and their associated persons are required to cooperate with PCAOB investigations of accounting rules violations, including by producing documents and providing testimony in response to PCAOB Accounting Board Demands. Under the PCAOB's policy, registered accounting firms and associated persons may receive credit for "extraordinary cooperation" with an investigation, which the PCAOB has defined as (1) voluntary and timely self-reporting, (2) voluntary and timely remedial or corrective action, or (3) voluntary and timely substantial assistance to the Board's investigative processes or to other law enforcement authorities. Such credit may include reduced charges and sanctions, language in sanctions noting the extraordinary cooperation, or in exceptional cases, no disciplinary action. The Board stressed, however, that self-reporting is not eligible for cooperation credit if it is required by legal or regulatory obligations—for example, the auditor's obligation under Section 10A of the Securities Exchange Act of 1934 to report a client's illegal acts.

LOG ON

www.aicpa.org/interestareas/
centerforauditquality.html
   The AICPA and the Center for Audit Quality maintain the Sarbanes–Oxley Act Implementation Central. Here you will find a summary of the Sarbanes–Oxley Act and articles on how to comply with SOX.

Ownership of Working Papers

LO46-3   Take steps to protect a client's communications and the firm's working papers.

The personal records that a client entrusts to a professional during an engagement, such as accounting records during an audit, remain the property of the client. A professional must return these records to his client. Nonetheless, material created by a professional, such as working papers produced by independent auditors, belong to the accountant, not the client.

Working papers are the records made during an audit. They include such items as work programs or plans for the audit, evidence of the testing of accounts, explanations of the handling of unusual matters, data reconciling the accountant's report with the client's records, and comments about the client's internal controls. The client has a right of access to the working papers. The accountant must obtain the client's permission before the working papers can be transferred to another accountant.

No doubt in reaction to the massive shredding of Enron-related documents by the Arthur Andersen audit firm, Congress included in the Sarbanes-Oxley Act a requirement that all audit or review working papers be retained for seven years. A knowing or willful violation of the document retention rule is subject to 10 years'

imprisonment, and, if corruptly done, 20 years. The *Andersen* case follows the next section.

Professional–Client Privilege

The attorney-client privilege is well established as necessary to protect confidential communications between a lawyer and her client and to permit a lawyer to perform her professional duties for her client. The privilege protects communications between clients and their attorneys from the prying eyes of courts and government agencies. It also protects a lawyer's working papers from the discovery procedures available in a lawsuit.

Although other professionals owe a duty of confidentiality to their clients, in general, communications between clients and nonlawyer professionals are not protected from judicial and administrative agency scrutiny when the professional's client is a party to legal or administrative action or the professional possesses evidence probative to an action. Thus, consultants, investment bankers, underwriters, brokers, and other securities professionals may be required to testify about client communications and produce documents concerning their clients, despite the objections of the client.

Accountants, however, enjoy a status somewhere between attorneys and other professionals. While the common law does not recognize an accountant-client privilege, a large number of states have granted such a privilege by statute. An accountant-client privilege of confidentiality protects communications between accountants and their clients as well as accountants' working papers. The provisions of the state statutes vary, but usually the privilege belongs to the client, and an accountant may not refuse to disclose the privileged material in a courtroom if the client consents to its disclosure.

Generally, the state-granted privileges are recognized in both state and federal courts deciding questions of state law. Nonetheless, federal courts do not recognize the privilege in matters involving federal questions, including antitrust, securities, and criminal matters.

In federal tax matters, for example, no privilege of confidentiality is recognized on the grounds that an accountant has a duty as a public watchdog to ensure that his client correctly reports his income tax liability. Consequently, an accountant can be required to bring his working papers into court and to testify as to matters involving the client's tax records and discussions with the client regarding tax matters. In addition, an accountant may be required by subpoena to make available his working papers involving a client who is being investigated by the IRS or who has been charged with tax irregularities. The same holds true for SEC investigations.

Although no accountant-client privilege exists in federal tax matters, an attorney-client privilege does exist. Moreover, the attorney–client privilege will protect communications between a client and a professional when the professional is assisting an attorney in rendering legal advice to the client.

As Enron Corporation's financial difficulties became public in 2001, Arthur Andersen LLP, Enron's auditor, instructed its employees to destroy Enron-related documents pursuant to its document retention policy, actions culminating in the following case. The Supreme Court mentions a concern regarding the professional-client privilege. The holding, however, focuses on when a professional can be found guilty for destroying working papers and other evidence.

Arthur Andersen LLP v. United States   544 U.S. 696 (2005)

Enron Corporation, during the 1990s, switched its business from operation of natural gas pipelines to an energy conglomerate, a move that was accompanied by aggressive accounting practices and rapid growth. Arthur Andersen LLP audited Enron's publicly filed financial statements and provided internal audit and consulting services to it. Andersen's engagement team for Enron was headed by global managing partner David Duncan. Enron's financial performance began to suffer in 2000 and continued to worsen in 2001. On August 14, 2001, Jeffrey Skilling, Enron's CEO, unexpectedly resigned. Within days, Sherron Watkins, a senior accountant at Enron, warned Kenneth Lay, Enron's newly reappointed CEO, that Enron could "implode in a wave of accounting scandals." She also informed Duncan and Michael Odom, an Andersen partner who supervised Duncan, of the problems.

A key accounting problem involved Enron's use of "Raptors," which were special-purpose entities used to engage in "off-balance-sheet" activities. Andersen's engagement team had allowed Enron to "aggregate" the Raptors for accounting purposes so that they reflected a positive return. This was a clear violation of generally accepted accounting principles.

On August 28, 2001, an article in The Wall Street Journal *suggested improprieties at Enron, and the SEC opened an informal investigation. By early September, Andersen had formed an Enron "crisis-response" team, which included Nancy Temple, an in-house lawyer. On October 8, Andersen retained outside counsel to represent it in any litigation that might arise from the Enron matter. The next day, Temple discussed Enron with other in-house lawyers. Her notes from that meeting reflect that "some SEC investigation" is "highly probable."*

On October 10, Odom spoke at a general training meeting attended by 89 employees, including 10 from the Enron engagement team. Odom urged everyone to comply with the firm's document retention policy. He added: "If it's destroyed in the course of normal policy and litigation is filed the next day, that's great. . . . We've followed our own policy, and whatever there was that might have been of interest to somebody is gone and irretrievable." On October 12, Temple entered the Enron matter into her computer, designating the "Type of Potential Claim" as "Professional Practice—Government/Regulatory Investigation." Temple also e-mailed Odom, suggesting that he "remind the engagement team of our documentation and retention policy."

Andersen's policy called for a single central engagement file, which "should contain only that information which is relevant to supporting our work." The policy stated that "in cases of threatened litigation, . . . no related information will be destroyed." It also separately provided that, if Andersen is "advised of litigation or subpoenas regarding a particular engagement, the related information should not be destroyed." The policy statement set forth "notification" procedures for whenever "professional practice litigation against Andersen or any of its personnel has been commenced, has been threatened or is judged likely to occur, or when governmental or professional investigations that may involve Andersen or any of its personnel have been commenced or are judged likely."

On October 16, Enron announced its third-quarter results, disclosing a $1.01 billion charge to earnings. The following day, the SEC notified Enron by letter that it had opened an investigation and requested certain information and documents. On October 19, Enron forwarded a copy of that letter to Andersen.

On the same day, Temple also sent an e-mail to a member of Andersen's internal team of accounting experts and attached a copy of the document retention policy. On October 20, the Enron crisis-response team held a conference call, during which Temple instructed everyone to "make sure to follow the [document] policy." On October 23, Enron CEO Lay declined to answer questions during a call with analysts because of "potential lawsuits, as well as the SEC inquiry." After the call, Duncan met with other Andersen partners on the Enron engagement team and told them that they should ensure team members were complying with the document retention policy. Another meeting for all team members followed, during which Duncan distributed the policy and told everyone to comply. These, and other smaller meetings, were followed by substantial destruction of paper and electronic documents.

On October 26, one of Andersen's senior partners circulated a New York Times *article discussing the SEC's response to Enron. His e-mail commented that "the problems are just beginning and we will be in the cross hairs. The marketplace is going to keep the pressure on this and is going to force the SEC to be tough." On October 30, the SEC opened a formal investigation and sent Enron a letter that requested accounting documents.*

Throughout this time period, Andersen continued to destroy documents, despite reservations by some of Andersen's managers. For example, on October 26, John Riley, another Andersen partner, saw Duncan shredding documents and told him "this wouldn't be the best time in the world for you guys to be shredding a bunch of stuff." On October 31, David Stulb, a forensics investigator for Andersen, met with Duncan. During the meeting, Duncan picked up a document with the words "smoking gun" written on it and began to destroy it, adding "we don't need this." Stulb cautioned Duncan on the need to maintain documents and later informed Temple that Duncan needed advice on the document retention policy.

On November 8, Enron announced that it would issue a comprehensive restatement of its earnings and assets. Also on November 8, the SEC served Enron and Andersen with subpoenas for records. On November 9, Duncan's secretary sent an e-mail that stated: "Per Dave—No more shredding. . . . We have been officially served for our documents." Enron filed for bankruptcy less than a month later. Duncan was fired and later pleaded guilty to witness tampering.

In March 2002, Andersen was indicted in the Southern District of Texas on one count of violating witness tampering provisions 18 U.S.C. §§ 1512(b)(2)(A) and (B). The indictment alleged that, between October 10 and November 9, 2001, Andersen knowingly, intentionally, and corruptly persuaded Andersen's employees, with intent to cause them to withhold documents from, and alter documents for use in, an official proceeding. The case went to a jury, which deadlocked after deliberating for seven days. The district court instructed the jury that it could find Andersen guilty if Andersen intended to "subvert, undermine, or impede" governmental factfinding by suggesting to its employees that they enforce the document retention policy. After three more days of deliberation, the jury returned a guilty verdict. Andersen appealed to the court of appeals, which affirmed the conviction. The court of appeals held that the jury instructions properly conveyed the meaning of "corruptly persuades" and "official proceeding" and that the jury need not find any consciousness of wrongdoing. The Supreme Court granted Andersen's request to review the decision.

Rehnquist, Chief Justice

Chapter 73 of Title 18 of the United States Code provides criminal sanctions for those who obstruct justice. Sections 1512(b)(2) (A) and (B), part of the witness tampering provisions, provide in relevant part:

> Whoever knowingly uses intimidation or physical force, threatens, or corruptly persuades another person, or attempts to do so, or engages in misleading conduct toward another person, with intent to . . . cause or induce any person to . . . withhold testimony, or withhold a record, document, or other object, from an official proceeding [or] alter, destroy, mutilate, or conceal an object with intent to impair the object's integrity or availability for use in an official proceeding . . . shall be fined under this title or imprisoned not more than ten years, or both.

In this case, our attention is focused on what it means to "knowingly . . . corruptly persuade" another person "with intent to . . . cause" that person to "withhold" documents from, or "alter" documents for use in, an "official proceeding."

We have traditionally exercised restraint in assessing the reach of a federal criminal statute, both out of deference to the prerogatives of Congress and out of concern that a fair warning should be given to the world in language that the common world will understand, of what the law intends to do if a certain line is passed.

Such restraint is particularly appropriate here, where the act underlying the conviction—"persuasion"—is by itself innocuous. Indeed, "persuading" a person "with intent to . . . cause" that person to "withhold" testimony or documents from a Government proceeding or Government official is not inherently malign. Consider, for instance, a mother who suggests to her son that he invoke his right against compelled self-incrimination or a wife who persuades her husband not to disclose marital confidences.

Nor is it necessarily corrupt for an attorney to "persuade" a client "with intent to . . . cause" that client to "withhold" documents from the Government. In *Upjohn Co. v. United States*, 449 U.S. 383 (1981), for example, we held that Upjohn was justified in withholding documents that were covered by the attorney-client privilege from the Internal Revenue Service. No one would suggest that an attorney who "persuaded" Upjohn to take that step acted wrongfully, even though he surely intended that his client keep those documents out of the IRS' hands.

"Document retention policies," which are created in part to keep certain information from getting into the hands of others, including the Government, are common in business. It is, of course, not wrongful for a manager to instruct his employees to comply with a valid document retention policy under ordinary circumstances.

Acknowledging this point, the parties have largely focused their attention on the word "corruptly" as the key to what may or may not lawfully be done in the situation presented here. Section 1512(b) punishes not just "corruptly persuading" another, but "*knowingly* . . . corruptly persuading" another. The Government suggests that "knowingly" does not modify "corruptly persuades," but that is not how the statute most naturally reads. It provides the *mens rea*—"knowingly"—and then a list of acts—"uses intimidation or physical force, threatens, or corruptly persuades." The Government suggests that it is questionable whether Congress would employ such an inelegant formulation as "knowingly . . . corruptly persuades." Long experience has not taught us to share the Government's doubts on this score, and we must simply interpret the statute as written.

The parties have not pointed us to another interpretation of "knowingly . . . corruptly" to guide us here. In any event, the natural meaning of these terms provides a clear answer. "Knowledge" and "knowingly" are normally associated with awareness, understanding, or consciousness. "Corrupt" and "corruptly" are normally associated with wrongful, immoral, depraved, or evil. Joining these meanings together here makes sense both linguistically and in the statutory scheme. Only persons conscious of wrongdoing can be said to "knowingly . . . corruptly persuade." And limiting criminality to persuaders conscious of their wrongdoing sensibly allows § 1512(b) to reach only those with the level of "culpability . . . we usually require in order to impose criminal liability."

The outer limits of this element need not be explored here because the jury instructions at issue simply failed to convey the requisite consciousness of wrongdoing. Indeed, it is striking how little culpability the instructions required. For example, the jury was told that, "even if Andersen honestly and sincerely believed that its conduct was lawful, you may find Andersen guilty." The instructions also diluted the meaning of "corruptly" so that it covered innocent conduct.

The District Court based its instruction on the definition of that term found in the Fifth Circuit Pattern Jury Instruction for § 1503. This pattern instruction defined "corruptly" as "knowingly and dishonestly, with the specific intent to subvert or undermine the integrity" of a proceeding. The Government, however, insisted on excluding "dishonestly" and adding the term "impede" to the phrase "subvert or undermine." The District Court agreed over Andersen's objections, and the jury was told to convict if it found Andersen intended to "subvert, undermine, or impede" governmental factfinding by suggesting to its employees that they enforce the document retention policy.

These changes were significant. No longer was any type of "dishonesty" necessary to a finding of guilt, and it was enough for petitioner to have simply "impeded" the Government's factfinding ability. "Impede" has broader connotations than "subvert" or even "undermine," and many of these connotations do not incorporate any "corruptness" at all. The dictionary defines "impede" as "to interfere with or get in the way of the progress of" or "hold up" or "detract from." By definition, anyone who innocently persuades another to withhold information from the Government "gets in the way of the progress of" the Government.

The instructions also were infirm for another reason. They led the jury to believe that it did not have to find *any* nexus between the "persuasion" to destroy documents and any particular proceeding. In resisting any type of nexus element, the Government relies heavily on § 1512(e)(1), which states that an official proceeding "need not be pending or about to be instituted at the time of the offense." It is, however, one thing to say that a proceeding "need not be pending or about to be instituted at the time of the offense," and quite another to say a proceeding need not even be foreseen. A "knowingly . . . corrupt persuader" cannot be someone who persuades others to shred documents under a document retention policy when he does not have in contemplation any particular official proceeding in which those documents might be material. If the defendant lacks knowledge that his actions are likely to affect the judicial proceeding, he lacks the requisite intent to obstruct.

For these reasons, the jury instructions here were flawed in important respects.

Judgment reversed in favor of Andersen.

Problems and Problem Cases

1. Diversified Graphics Ltd. hired Ernst & Whinney to assist it in obtaining a computer system to fit its data processing needs. DG had a long-standing relationship with E&W and developed great trust and reliance on E&W's services. Because DG lacked computer expertise, it decided to entrust E&W with the selection and implementation of an in-house computer data processing system. E&W promised to locate a "turnkey" system, which would be fully operational without the need for extensive employee training. Instead, DG received a system that was difficult to operate and failed to meet its needs. Is E&W liable to DG?

2. Al Rizek was a vice president of PaineWebber of Puerto Rico. One of his clients was Jorge Donato. Donato told Rizek that he was primarily interested in long-term bonds and the safety of his investment. In early 1993, Rizek recommended to Donato a strategy of short-term trading of zero-coupon bonds. Zero-coupon bonds are U.S. government instruments that accumulate interest until maturity, rather than paying interest periodically. The value of a zero-coupon bond is very sensitive to changes in interest rates. Rizek recommended that Donato purchase the bonds on margin, thus magnifying the potential gains and losses. Purchasing on margin meant that Donato had to make monthly margin interest payments to PaineWebber; it

also placed him at risk of being forced to sell at a loss to meet a margin call. During the 15-month period from January 1993 to March 1994, Donato's account had average monthly balances of $85,000. During this time, Rizek carried out $2 million in transactions on the account. Rizek's strategy led to losses of approximately $12,000. Rizek received about $15,000 in commissions. Donato sued Rizek and Paine Webber to recover the damages he suffered. Have Rizek and PaineWebber violated the common law of negligence or Securities Exchange Act Rule 10b-5?

3. Prospect High Income Fund and other investors bought high-yield bonds from Epic Resorts LLC, a vacation timeshare operator. The bonds were secured by Epic's assets and protected by an indenture requiring an escrow agreement that covered the interest payments on the bonds. Epic also had to obtain a statement from its auditor, Grant Thornton, confirming Epic's compliance with the indenture. Grant Thornton issued a report that showed Epic had placed more than $12 million cash in escrow at U.S. Trust and that it maintained $8.45 million at all times in escrow to cover the next required interest payment. U.S. Trust acted as the escrow agent for the benefit of Prospect and other bondholders. U.S. Trust allowed Epic to reduce the amount in the escrow account below the amount permitted by the indenture and the amount attested to by Grant Thornton. Nonetheless, U.S. Trust never objected to the absence of funds in the U.S. Trust account because Epic periodically transferred funds to U.S. Trust to make the interest payment. On June 15, 2001, Epic missed its scheduled interest payment to Prospect and other bondholders. Prospect and the other bondholders sued Grant Thornton alleging that its reports negligently or fraudulently misrepresented the escrow account's status. What was Prospect required to prove to be able to recover from Grant Thornton for negligent misrepresentation or for fraud?

4. Scioto Memorial Hospital Association planned the construction of Richmond Place, a 170-unit retirement center in Lexington, Kentucky. Scioto hired Price Waterhouse to review the work of the architect, the financial underwriter, and the marketing consultant and to recommend whether Scioto should proceed with the Richmond Place investment. PW's engagement letter represented that PW would issue a preliminary feasibility study and review a detailed financial forecast of the project. Financial forecasts represent management's judgment of the most likely set of conditions and management's most likely course of action. Instead of reviewing a financial forecast for Richmond Place, PW reviewed only a financial projection compiled by the underwriter of the construction. As PW explained in its letter to Scioto, a projection "represents management's estimate of its possible, but not necessarily most probable, future course of action." PW's final report to Scioto assumed an occupancy rate of 98 percent. Unfortunately, construction of Richmond Place was slow and delayed by a fire. While Scioto used insurance proceeds to rebuild, sales of the units were slow, and a year after opening, only 15 residents occupied Richmond Place. Scioto sued PW for negligence and breach of contract. PW defended on the grounds that Scioto's delays in construction and its lack of business interruption insurance caused Scioto's damages. Was PW found liable to Scioto?

5. Piece Goods Shops Company L.P. hired Price Waterhouse LLP to audit its 1992 financial statements. Piece Goods forwarded the audited 1992 financial statements to Marcus Brothers Textiles, Inc., which made several extensions of credit to Piece Goods up to April 1993 in reliance on the 1992 balance sheet. When Piece Goods filed for bankruptcy in April 1993, Piece Goods owed Marcus Brothers almost $300,000. Marcus Brothers sued PW for negligent misrepresentation under state law on the grounds PW negligently conducted the audit of the 1992 financial statements, which Marcus Brothers alleged contained several material misstatements. PW moved to dismiss the case on the grounds that PW did not know that Marcus Brothers would be using the financial statements to make credit extension to Piece Goods. Marcus Brothers produced evidence that PW had been Piece Goods's auditor since 1986. A PW internal memo stated that PW had historically reported on Piece Goods's financial statements and that its vendors were accustomed to receiving those financial statements. A PW audit partner signed a memo stating that some of PW's audit clients typically provided their audited financial statements to their trade creditors in reference to obtaining loans or extensions of credit. An audit manager who oversaw the audit of Piece Goods's 1992 financial statements testified that audited financial statements are used by management of the company and possibly outsiders and that such outsiders could include trade creditors such as Marcus Brothers. Piece Goods's bankruptcy filing revealed that 43 of its trade creditors had received the audited 1992 financial statements. Under the *Restatement (Second) of Torts*, is Marcus Brothers a proper plaintiff to whom PW owed a duty not to be negligent when conducting the audit?

6. Due to alleged overstatements of the value of loans held by First National Bank of Keystone (Keystone), the federal Office of the Comptroller of the Currency (OCC) began investigating Keystone. OCC required Keystone to retain an auditor to determine the appropriateness of Keystone's accounting treatments of its purchased loans and securitization of loans. Keystone hired Grant Thornton LLP to perform an audit of Keystone's financial statements. In April 1999, Grant Thornton issued an audit opinion to Keystone stating that its 1998 financial statements—which showed shareholder equity of $84 million—were fairly stated in accordance with GAAP. In fact, Keystone was insolvent. Grant Thornton's audit report stated that "This report is intended for the information and use of the Board of Directors and Management of The First National Bank of Keystone and its regulatory agencies and should not be used by third parties for any other purpose." Gary Ellis, a candidate to become Keystone's next president, reviewed in April 1999 the 1998 financial statements audited by Grant Thornton. At the time, Ellis was president of another bank and not an employee of Keystone. He became a candidate for the Keystone presidency in late March 1999. Relying on the audit, Ellis decided to accept Keystone's offer to be its president at a base salary of $375,000. He also purchased $49,500 in Keystone stock. When Keystone failed, Ellis claimed he lost more than $2 million in compensation he would have earned had he not taken the Keystone presidency, as well as losing the full amount of his investment in Keystone stock. He sued Grant Thornton for negligent misrepresentation. Under the *Restatement (Second) of Torts*, was Ellis a proper plaintiff to whom Grant Thornton owed a duty not to be negligent when conducting the audit?

7. AccentPoint LLP, an accounting firm, was hired by General Micron Company to audit its financial statements for inclusion in GMC's 1933 Act registration statement, pursuant to which GMC's common shares would be sold to investors. AccentPoint's sole compensation for performing the audit and issuing an opinion was a fee of $600,000. Due to AccentPoint's careless noncompliance with GAAS, the audited financial statements and AccentPoint's opinion contained material misstatements. AccentPoint, however, did not intentionally or recklessly mistate or omit any material fact. Does AccentPoint have potential liability to purchasers of the shares who bought GMC shares relying on AccentPoint's audit opinion under Section 12(a)(2) of the 1933 Act, Rule 10b–5 of the 1934 Act, and the common law of negligent misrepresentation? Does AccentPoint have potential liability to purchasers of the shares under Section 11 of the 1933 Act?

8. Kimon Daifotis was the lead portfolio manager of the YieldPlus Fund. In August 2007, when YieldPlus was suffering massive, unprecedented redemptions, Daifotis held two conference calls in which he allegedly falsely stated that "we've got very, very, very slight negative flows" and that "outflows have been minimal." Daifotis also allegedly made misrepresentations in YieldPlus's written materials in which he was directly quoted or in which statements were directly attributed to him, including a September 2005 brochure and a Spring 2006 brochure. When YieldPlus investors sued Daifotis for damages caused by the alleged misstatements, Daifotis argued that he had not "made" the statements and, therefore, could not be liable under Securities Exchange Act Rule 10b–5. Did the court agree?

9. Norman Cross was the independent auditor for Home-Stakes Production Company, a company that offered investors interests in oil and gas drilling programs. The programs offered investors both income and tax deductions. Cross issued unqualified opinions regarding Home-Stakes's financial statements. He prepared consolidated financial statements and start-up balance sheets for two programs. All these documents were included, with Cross's consent, in 1933 Act registration statements filed with the SEC and included in prospectuses and program books distributed to investors. When Home-Stakes collapsed after it was discovered that the oil and gas drilling programs were a classic Ponzi scheme (with investments from new investors providing the "profits" to old investors), purchasers of the programs sued Cross under Securities Exchange Act Section 10(b) and Rule 10b–5. Was Cross found liable, or was he only an aider and abettor to Home-Stakes's fraud with no Rule 10b–5 liability?

10. Danske Invest Management A/S purchased American Depositary Shares, a type of security, issued by Longtop Financial Technologies Ltd. When making the purchase, Danske relied in part on Longtop financial statements audited by Deloitte Touche Tohmatsu. When the value of the ADSs declined after disclosure that Longtop's financial results were inflated by fraudulent behavior of its employees, Danske brought an action against Deloitte under Section 10(b) and Rule 10b–5 of the Securities Exchange Act of 1934. Danske alleged that had Deloitte insisted on obtaining

third-party confirmations of Longtop's major revenue contracts in 2009, as it had done in 2008 and originally proposed to do in 2009 in e-mails to Longtop management, Deloitte would have uncovered Longtop's fraud. Danske also alleged that performing third-party confirmations of the revenue contracts was a required procedure under the circumstances and that Longtop's excuse that this procedure would delay the filing of its 2009 Form 20-F with the SEC should have increased Deloitte's professional skepticism. Danske argued that Deloitte was reckless because it agreed to perform alternative testing on revenue to confirm Longtop's major revenue contracts rather than obtaining third-party confirmations.

Deloitte did confirm Longtop's accounts receivable. Direct confirmation of revenue contracts is not a presumptively required audit step under GAAS. Deloitte initially took the position that third-party confirmation of revenue contracts was required, based on its reading of international auditing standards and a concept release proposed by the PCAOB for notice and comment, but was persuaded by Longtop's CEO, Derek Palaschuk, that under American GAAS, this procedure was not required. Palaschuk pointed out that conducting third-party confirmations of revenue contracts was not presumptively required under the GAAS and also gave numerous reasons why it was not necessary under the circumstances. He noted that Longtop (1) had no individually material contracts for the 2009 fiscal year and no long-term material contracts; (2) had never modified a contract; (3) had bad debt of less than 0.5 percent of its sales; and (4) had many contracts with and was, therefore, under the scrutiny of large companies, making fraud more difficult. Deloitte was ultimately persuaded by Palaschuk's argument, but noted that it would need to revisit the issue if new auditing standards were to be released.

Danske's argued that Palaschuk's resistance when Deloitte proposed conducting client confirmations of revenue contracts was a significant red flag and that therefore Deloitte's behavior amounted to scienter under Rule 10b–5. Did the court agree?

11. John Kinross-Kennedy, age 85, of Irvine, California, was a CPA licensed in California. Kinross was registered with the PCAOB since 2005. As of July 15, 2013, Kinross was the independent public accountant for six public companies. During 2011 and 2012, Kinross issued six audit reports containing unqualified opinions. In each of these six audit reports, Kinross represented that he conducted his audits in accordance with PCAOB standards. Kinross failed, however, to conduct each of the six audits of the issuer's financial statements in accordance with PCAOB standards. Kinross admitted to unfamiliarity with PCAOB requirements to perform certain auditing procedures, such as the annual written confirmation of his independence and communication with the predecessor auditor. He used outdated audit templates to document his audit planning and his performance of audit procedures, without any apparent effort to adapt those templates for subsequent changes in auditing standards. Kinross relied upon checklists for client acceptance, internal control evaluation, and transactional audit plans for small organizations that were published in 1993. That was the year he formed his audit practice and 10 years before the creation of the PCAOB. For one audit, Kinross instructed client personnel to select one invoice per month for the sample to be subjected to audit testing. He issued an unqualified opinion of one issuer's financial statements as of March 31, 2010, and the period from March 31, 2009, to March 31, 2010, despite the fact that he had performed no audit procedures as of March 31, 2010, or for the period from March 31, 2009, to March 31, 2010. Kinross issued an audit report containing an unqualified opinion on another issuer's August 31, 2011, financial statements. That issuer's sole operating subsidiary accounted for 100 percent of the issuer's revenues and cost of revenues and 15 percent of its expenses. Yet, Kinross performed no audit procedures on the subsidiary's revenues or its expenses. The SEC brought an action against Kinross under SEC Rule of Practice 102(e). What was the outcome of that proceeding?

12. Waters Corporation, a publicly traded manufacturer and seller of high-performance liquid chromatography systems (systems used to separate substances in a solution, here in high-tech laboratories) throughout Japan, was sued by a pension fund for intentionally failing to disclose material information to investors. The pension fund alleged that Waters omitted in public statements that Japanese drinking water testing regulations had changed, which would cause a reduction in demand for Waters' products and services. Additionally, the pension fund contended that there was a strong inference of scienter, or "a wrongful state of mind," because two of the company's senior executives sold over 600,000 shares of stock worth some $42 million around the same time. When Waters eventually disclosed the change in Japanese regulations along with its quarterly results, the price of the stock dropped by approximately 20 percent. Based on these facts, should a court allow the case to proceed or grant Waters' motion to dismiss that argues the pleading standards for scienter

and materiality have not been met? What other facts do you think the court would need to know to make the best determination?

13. AccentPoint LLP is the external auditor for E-Delphos Corporation, a public company required to file periodic reports with the SEC under the Securities Exchange Act of 1934. You are the audit partner for the engagement with E-Delphos. You want to ensure that your staff complies with Section 404 of the Sarbanes–Oxley Act. Draft a checklist of steps your staff should take to comply with SOX Section 404.

14. Ernst & Young, an accounting firm, was retained by Camelot Systems Inc. to provide tax advice. Camelot also retained a law firm to provide tax and other legal advice. At all times, E&Y was working for and paid by Camelot. When the IRS investigated a merger transaction on which E&Y had worked for Camelot, it subpoenaed E&Y's records, including communications between E&Y and Camelot. Camelot sought to quash the subpoena on grounds that the communications between Camelot and E&Y were privileged and confidential. Did the court agree?

Regulation of Business

Administrative Law

The history of attempts by the federal Food and Drug Administration (FDA) to regulate advertising of tobacco products provides a useful context in which to consider administrative law issues that you will encounter in this chapter. The story began during the mid-1990s, when the FDA adopted various regulations that restricted advertising and other marketing practices regarding tobacco products. The FDA premised these regulations on the theory that nicotine was a "drug" and cigarettes were a drug-delivery "device" for purposes of the Food, Drug, and Cosmetic Act, which gives the FDA the authority to regulate a number of matters regarding drugs and drug-delivery devices. Various tobacco companies and other parties challenged the regulations in federal court, arguing that Congress had not given the FDA authority to regulate tobacco products and that in any event, the advertising restrictions contemplated by the regulations violated the First Amendment. The litigation, which made its way to the ultimate forum—the U.S. Supreme Court—suggested fundamental questions that arise in the field of *administrative law*:

- In what subject matter area has the relevant administrative agency been granted authority to regulate by Congress or, at the state level, by the state legislature? What are the specific boundaries of that subject matter area?
- In what ways has the administrative agency been empowered by Congress or the state legislature to exercise its regulatory authority? What restrictions, if any, have been placed by Congress or the state legislature on the ways in which the agency may regulate?
- Do regulations (i.e., rules) adopted by an administrative agency have the same force of law that statutes have?
- How do constitutional provisions affect the regulatory actions that administrative agencies may take?

In *FDA v. Brown & Williamson Tobacco Corp.*, 529 U.S. 120 (2000), the Supreme Court held that in view of a series of statutes enacted over the years, Congress did not intend for the FDA to have authority to regulate tobacco as part of its otherwise broad authority in the Food, Drug, and Cosmetic Act. Because the FDA did not have authority to regulate tobacco, the tobacco advertising restrictions could not stand. The Supreme Court therefore did not need to address the full list of questions set forth above.

However, the Supreme Court's decision did not end the story. Later developments in the tobacco-regulation saga demonstrate the critical role of Congress in defining the authority of administrative agencies and shaping the direction in which administrative law is allowed to go. Changes in prevailing political winds may influence congressional decisions on whether to extend regulatory authority to an administrative agency. Authority not previously delegated by Congress can be delegated, and vice versa. That is what happened with regard to the FDA and the matter of tobacco regulation.

In 2009, nine years after the Supreme Court's decision in *FDA v. Brown & Williamson*, Congress amended existing laws and expressly granted the FDA authority to regulate tobacco products and tobacco marketing practices. Shortly thereafter, the FDA promulgated new tobacco advertising regulations that resembled the regulations it had sought to impose during the 1990s. The new FDA regulations went beyond the previously invalidated ones in an important respect, however. The regulations addressed a matter called for by the 2009 statute: the required use, on cigarette packages and in cigarette advertisements, of large and very explicit graphic images meant to depict the dangers of smoking and accompany the longstanding textual warnings about those dangers. The statute directed the FDA to develop particular graphic images that cigarette producers would have to use, on a rotating basis, on their product packages and in their advertisements. The FDA responded to the statutory directive by devising such graphic images.

Tobacco companies affected by the graphic images requirement brought First Amendment–based challenges that led to decisions by two federal courts of appeal in 2012. One court upheld, against First Amendment attack, the statutory requirement of a graphic element and the direction to the FDA to develop such images. That court, however, did not rule on the particular graphic images devised by the FDA. The Supreme Court declined review in that case. In the other case, the court ruled on the particular images devised by the FDA and concluded that the required images violated the First Amendment. Rather than seeking review by the Supreme Court, the FDA announced that it would abandon the images it had devised and would develop new ones in response to the directive from Congress. The FDA still had not yet developed new images as of the time this edition of the book went to press. Once the new images are developed, further First Amendment challenges are likely. As the foregoing discussion suggests, the graphic images controversy presents key administrative law questions of the sort identified in the bullet-pointed items that appear above.

As you study this chapter, keep such questions in mind. Your understanding of administrative law will be enhanced if you do so.

LO LEARNING OBJECTIVES

After studying this chapter, you should be able to:

47-1 Explain the role of enabling legislation in defining the legal authority of an administrative agency.

47-2 List constitutional provisions that may operate to limit what an administrative agency can do.

47-3 Explain the test courts customarily use in determining whether a broad delegation of power by Congress to an agency is constitutional.

47-4 Describe basic features of the investigative power that administrative agencies typically have.

47-5 Describe basic features of the rulemaking power that administrative agencies typically have.

47-6 Describe basic features of the adjudicatory power that administrative agencies typically have.

47-7 Identify major presidential controls that may be exerted in regard to administrative agencies.

47-8 Identify major congressional controls that may be exerted in regard to administrative agencies.

47-9 Explain what is necessary in order for a person or organization to have standing to bring a judicial challenge to administrative agency action.

47-10 Explain the major legal bases for judicially challenging administrative agency actions and identify the standards of review courts employ in such cases.

47-11 Explain essential features of the Freedom of Information Act and identify the major exemptions to the disclosure requirement it contemplates.

47-12 Describe the key arguments that have led to deregulation efforts and arguments that call for reregulation.

TODAY'S BUSINESSES OPERATE IN a highly regulated environment. The *administrative agency* serves as a primary vehicle for the creation and enforcement of modern regulation. As governmental bodies that are neither courts nor legislatures, administrative agencies have the legal power to take actions affecting the rights of private individuals and organizations. The influence of administrative agencies has become so sweeping that they are sometimes referred to as the "fourth branch" of a government that officially consists of three branches (legislative, executive, and judicial).

This chapter focuses on federal administrative agencies. It is important to remember, however, that the past century's significant growth in *federal* regulation has been accompanied by a comparable growth in *state* and *local* regulation by agencies at those levels of government.

It is difficult to think of an area of modern individual life that is not somehow touched by the actions of administrative agencies. The energy that heats and lights your home and workplace, the clothes you wear, the food you eat, the medicines you take, the design of the car you drive, the programs you watch on television, and the contents of (and label on) the pillow on which you lay your head at night are all shaped in some way by regulation. This observation is even more appropriate regarding corporations. Many significant aspects of contemporary corporate operations are regulated to the point that the legal consequences of a corporation's actions can be as important to the firm's future success as the business consequences of its decisions.

Administrative agencies have always been objects of controversy. Are they protectors of the public or impediments to business efficiency? Are they guardians of competitive market structures or shields behind which noncompetitive firms have sought refuge from more vigorous competitors? Have they been impartial, efficient agents of the public interest or are they more often overzealous, or inept, or "captives" of the industries they supposedly regulate? At various times, and where various agencies are concerned, each of the above allegations is likely to have been true. Why, then, did we resort to such controversial entities to perform the regulatory function?

Origins of Administrative Agencies

In the 19th century's latter decades, the United States was in the midst of a dramatic transformation from an agrarian nation to a major industrial power. Improved means of transportation and communication facilitated dramatic market expansions. Large business organizations acquired unprecedented economic power, and new technologies promised additional social transformations.

The tremendous growth that resulted from these developments, however, was not attained without some cost. Large organizations sometimes abused their power at the expense of their customers, distributors, and competitors. New technologies often posed risks of harm to large numbers of citizens. Yet traditional institutions of legal control, such as courts and legislatures, were not particularly well suited to the regulatory needs of an increasingly complex, interdependent society in the throes of rapid change.

Courts, after all, are passive institutions that must await a genuine case or controversy before they can act. In addition, they are constrained by rules of procedure and evidence that make litigation a time-consuming and expensive process.

Legislatures, on the other hand, are theoretically able to anticipate social problems and to act in a comprehensive fashion to minimize social harm. In reality, however, legislatures rarely act until a problem has become severe enough to generate strong political support for a regulatory solution. Legislatures may also lack (as do courts) the expertise necessary to make rational policy regarding highly technical activities.

What was needed, therefore, was a new type of governmental entity: one that would be exclusively devoted to monitoring a particular area of activity; one that could, by its exclusive focus and specialized hiring practices, develop a reservoir of expertise concerning the relevant area; and one that could provide the continuous attention and constant policy development demanded by a rapidly changing environment. Such new entities, it was thought, could best perform their regulatory tasks if they were given considerable latitude in the approaches they utilized to achieve regulatory goals.

The modern regulatory era was born in 1887 when Congress, in response to complaints about discriminatory ratemaking practices by railroads, passed the Interstate Commerce Act. This statute created the Interstate Commerce Commission and empowered it to regulate transportation industry ratemaking practices. Since then, administrative agencies have been added whenever *pressing social problems* (e.g., the threat to competition that led to the creation of the Federal Trade Commission) or *new technologies*, such as aviation (Federal Aviation Administration), communications (Federal Communications Commission), and nuclear power (Nuclear Regulatory Commission), have generated a political consensus in favor of regulation. More recently, developing scientific knowledge about the *dangers that modern technologies and*

Ethics and Compliance in Action

Controversies over the roles and actions of administrative agencies often present both legal and ethical issues. Consider the example of the federal Food and Drug Administration (FDA), whose various legal responsibilities include issuing so-called new drug approvals before newly developed medications can lawfully be sold in the United States. A pharmaceutical maker seeking a new drug approval must provide the FDA with considerable documentary information, including clinical trial results, in order to enable the FDA to determine that the medication is likely to be effective for its intended purposes without posing undue dangers to consumers who will use it.

Although the determination just mentioned is of course a legal matter, ethical questions necessarily are present as well. For instance, in deciding whether to approve a new drug, how should decision makers at the FDA balance the health benefits many consumers would be likely to receive against the harm that other consumers could experience as a result of clinically documented side effects? What are the potential consequences for society if the new medication is approved and, alternatively, if it is not approved? If a new drug appears likely to produce tremendous health benefits for most users but potentially devastating health consequences for other users, has the FDA discharged any ethical obligations it may have if it allows the new drug to be sold but requires a warning on the product's label or in its package insert?

Other questions combining legal and ethical concerns may arise if, after FDA approval occurs and a medication becomes widely used and generally successful for its intended purpose, serious health dangers for some users come to light. Such a situation arose in recent years in regard to prescription pain relievers in the COX-2 inhibitor category. After Merck & Co.'s Vioxx brand pain reliever became heavily prescribed with largely positive results, the adverse experiences of some users led to concern over possible links between long-term Vioxx use and an increased risk of heart attacks or strokes. Merck eventually withdrew Vioxx from the market on a voluntary basis, but not before some commentators criticized the FDA for supposedly devoting too many FDA resources to the initial drug approval process and not enough resources to follow-ups designed to assess the postapproval track records of pharmaceutical products. Whether fair or not in the case of Vioxx, such criticisms suggest that there may be ethical dimensions to administrative agencies' decisions on how to allocate agency resources when the agency has various responsibilities to fulfill.

Of course, other legal and ethical questions arise in regard to private parties' dealings with administrative agencies. For instance, consider the concern expressed by some observers regarding alleged failures of some COX-2 inhibitor producers to disclose adverse health indications they supposedly learned of after receiving FDA approval to market their medications. If a pharmaceutical company receives reliable information of that nature after it wins FDA approval for a new drug and begins selling it, does that company owe the FDA or the public an obligation to disclose the information?

---

industrial processes pose to the environment and to industrial workers has led to the creation of federal agencies empowered to regulate environmental pollution (Environmental Protection Agency) and promote workplace safety (Occupational Safety and Health Administration).

Sometimes, Congress may conclude that a new administrative agency need not be created to address a particular problem if an already-existing agency's lines of authority and responsibility can be stepped up (something that tends to require an increase in the agency's budget). For example, following a series of horror stories about risks to children from large numbers of lead-contaminated toys that were being imported into the United States, Congress enacted a 2008 statute that significantly increased the budget of the Consumer Product Safety Commission and charged the agency with taking a more active regulatory role.

At other times, however, the prevailing political winds lead to calls for a significant curtailing of the regulatory power and influence of certain administrative agencies, if not the outright elimination of those agencies.

The following sections examine the legal dimensions of the process by which administrative agencies are created.

Agency Creation

 LO47-1 Explain the role of enabling legislation in defining the legal authority of an administrative agency.

Enabling Legislation Administrative agencies are created when Congress passes **enabling legislation** specifying the name, composition, and powers of the agency. For example, consider the following language from Section 1 of the Federal Trade Commission Act:

> A commission is created and established, to be known as the Federal Trade Commission [FTC], which shall be composed of five commissioners, who shall be appointed by the President, by and with the advice and consent of the Senate.

Section 5 of the FTC Act prohibits "unfair methods of competition" and "unfair or deceptive acts or practices in commerce," and empowers the FTC to prevent such practices.[1] Section 5 also describes the procedures the commission must follow to charge persons or organizations with violations of the act, and provides for judicial review of agency orders. Subsequent portions of the statute give the FTC the power "to make rules and regulations for the purpose of carrying out the provisions of the Act," to conduct investigations of business practices, to require reports from interstate corporations concerning their practices and operations, to investigate possible violations of the antitrust laws,[2] to publish reports concerning its findings and activities, and to recommend new legislation to Congress.

Thus, Congress has given the FTC powers typically associated with the three traditional branches of government. The FTC may, for instance, act in a legislative fashion by *promulgating rules* that have binding legal effect on future behavior. (As will be seen, however, an agency's regulations will not have binding effect if they go beyond the scope of the power delegated to the agency by Congress.) It may also take the executive branch–like actions of *investigating* and *prosecuting* alleged violations. Finally, the FTC may act much as courts do and *adjudicate* disputes concerning alleged violations of the law. Most other federal administrative agencies have a similarly broad mix of governmental powers, making these agencies potentially powerful agents of social control.

Great power to do good things, however, may also be great power to cause harm. Regulatory bias, zeal, insensitivity, or corruption, if left unchecked, may infringe on the basic freedoms that are the essence of our system of government. Accordingly, the fundamental problem in administrative law—a problem that will surface repeatedly in this chapter—is how to design a system of control over agency action that minimizes the potential for arbitrariness and harm yet preserves the power and flexibility that make administrative agencies uniquely valuable instruments of public policy.

Administrative Agencies and the Constitution

LO47-2 List constitutional provisions that may operate to limit what an administrative agency can do.

Because administrative agencies are governmental bodies, administrative action is *governmental action* that is subject to the basic constitutional checks discussed in Chapter 3. This "fourth branch" of government is bound by basic constitutional guarantees such as *due process*, *equal protection*, and *freedom of speech*, just as the three traditional branches are. *Pearson v. Shalala*, which follows shortly, deals with First Amendment limitations on the Food and Drug Administration's regulatory authority. In dealing with the FDA's restrictions on the speech of a dietary supplement marketer, the *Pearson* court applies the intermediate scrutiny called for by the commercial speech principles discussed in Chapter 3 of the text. What if an administrative agency seeks to require *disclosures* of information (as opposed to imposing *restrictions* on speech)? The agency may have somewhat greater latitude to regulate in that fashion without violating the First Amendment, if the agency is seeking to prevent deception of consumers and perhaps when other similar motivations prompted the agency action. In *American Meat Institute v. U.S. Department of Agriculture*,[3] for instance, the court upheld a Department of Agriculture regulation requiring fairly detailed country-of-origin labels on the packaging of certain meat products. Characterizing the labeling regulation as a reasonable disclosure requirement rather than a speech restriction, the court rejected the First Amendment challenge brought by trade associations that represented livestock producers, feedlot operators, and meat packers.

[1]Section 5 of the FTC Act is discussed in detail in Chapter 48.
[2]The antitrust laws are discussed in detail in Chapters 49 and 50.

[3]730 F.3d 18 (D.C. Cir. 2014).

| **Pearson v. Shalala** | **164 F.3d 650 (D.C. Cir. 1999)** |

A federal statute prohibits marketers of dietary supplements from including on container labels any claim characterizing the relationship of the dietary supplement to the prevention or alleviation of a disease or health-related condition, unless the claim has been submitted to the Food and Drug Administration (FDA) for preapproval. According to one of its regulations, the FDA will authorize such a "health claim" only if the FDA finds "significant scientific agreement" among experts that the claim is supported by the available evidence. Dietary supplement marketers Durk Pearson and Sandy Shaw asked the FDA to authorize four separate health claims regarding their dietary supplements' preventive effects on health conditions such as cancer or heart disease.

The FDA refused to authorize any of the four health claims, not because there was a dearth of supporting evidence but because, in the FDA's view, the evidence was inconclusive and thus failed to give rise to "significant scientific agreement." The FDA declined to consider an alternative suggested by Pearson and Shaw: permitting the making of the health claims on the appropriate labels but requiring the use of a corrective disclaimer such as "The FDA has determined that the evidence supporting this claim is inconclusive."

Pearson, Shaw, and organizations representing health care practitioners and consumers of dietary supplements sought relief in the federal district court. The court rejected their arguments and upheld the FDA's action. Pearson, Shaw, and the organizations appealed to the U.S. Court of Appeals for the District of Columbia Circuit.

Silberman, Circuit Judge

Appellants raise a host of challenges to the [FDA's] action. [T]he most important are that their First Amendment rights have been impaired and that under the Administrative Procedure Act, the FDA was obliged . . . to articulate a standard a good deal more concrete than the undefined "significant scientific agreement." Normally we would discuss the non-constitutional argument first, particularly because we believe it has merit. We invert the normal order here to discuss [the argument] that the government has violated the First Amendment by declining to employ a less draconian method—the use of disclaimers—to serve the government's interests. [We do so because] even if "significant scientific agreement" were given a more concrete meaning, appellants might be entitled to make health claims that do not meet that standard—with proper disclaimers.

It is undisputed that the FDA's restrictions on appellants' health claims are [to be] evaluated under the commercial speech doctrine. The government makes two alternative arguments in response to appellants' claim that it is unconstitutional for the government to refuse to entertain a disclaimer requirement for the proposed health claims: first, that health claims lacking "significant scientific agreement" are *inherently* misleading and thus entirely outside the protection of the First Amendment; and second, that even if the claims are only *potentially* misleading, . . . the government is not obliged to consider requiring disclaimers in lieu of an outright ban on all claims that lack significant scientific agreement.

If such health claims could be thought inherently misleading, that would be the end of the inquiry. [Although nonmisleading commercial speech about lawful activities receives an intermediate degree of First Amendment protection, misleading commercial speech goes wholly unprotected by the First Amendment.] [The government's] first argument runs along the following lines: that health claims lacking "significant scientific agreement" are inherently misleading because they have such an awesome impact on consumers as to make it virtually impossible for them to exercise any judgment *at the point of sale*. It would be as if the consumers were asked to buy something while hypnotized, and therefore they are bound to be misled. We think this contention is almost frivolous. We reject it. But the government's alternative argument is more substantial. It is asserted that health claims on dietary supplements should be thought at least potentially misleading because the consumer would have difficulty in independently verifying these claims. We are told, in addition, that consumers might actually assume that the government has approved these claims.

Under *Central Hudson* [*Gas & Electric Corp. v. Public Service Commission*, 447 U.S. 557 (1980)], we are obliged to evaluate a government scheme to regulate potentially misleading commercial speech by applying a . . . test [that first asks] whether the asserted government interest is substantial. The FDA advanced two general concerns: protection of public health and prevention of consumer fraud. [In view of applicable precedent,] a substantial government interest is undeniable. The more significant questions under *Central Hudson* are the next two factors: "whether the regulation directly advances the governmental interest asserted," [quoting *Central Hudson*,] and whether the fit between the government's ends and the means chosen to accomplish those ends "is not necessarily perfect, but reasonable" [quoting *Board of Trustees of SUNY v. Fox*, 492 U.S. 469 (1989)].

[Although any advancement of the underlying public health interest may seem more indirect than direct,] the government would appear to advance directly its interest in protecting against consumer fraud through its regulatory scheme. If it can be assumed—and we think it can—that some health claims on dietary supplements will mislead consumers, it cannot be denied that requiring FDA preapproval and setting the standard extremely, perhaps even impossibly, high will surely prevent any confusion among consumers. We also recognize that the government's interest in preventing consumer fraud/confusion may well take on added importance in the context of a product, such as dietary supplements, that can affect the public's health.

The difficulty with the government's consumer fraud justification comes at the final *Central Hudson* factor: Is there a reasonable fit between the government's goals and the means chosen to advance those goals? The government insists that it is never obliged to utilize the disclaimer approach, because the commercial speech doctrine does not embody a preference for disclosure over outright suppression. Our understanding of the doctrine is otherwise. [The Supreme Court has stated that when allegedly incomplete advertising is not inherently misleading,] "the preferred remedy is more disclosure, rather than less." *Bates v. State Bar of Arizona*, 433 U.S. 350 (1977). In more recent cases, the Court has reaffirmed this principle, repeatedly pointing to disclaimers as constitutionally preferable to outright suppression. [Moreover, when] government chooses a policy of suppression over disclosure—at least where there is no showing that disclosure would not suffice to [prevent or minimize] misleadingness—government disregards a far less restrictive means. [As a result, a reasonable fit between the regulatory scheme and the underlying government interest would be lacking.]

Our rejection of the government's position that there is no general First Amendment preference for disclosure over suppression . . . does not determine that any supposed weaknesses in the [health] claims at issue can be remedied by disclaimers. [We therefore examine the particular claims.] The FDA deemed the first three claims— (1) "Consumption of antioxidant vitamins may reduce the risk of certain kinds of cancers," (2) "Consumption of fiber may reduce the risk of colorectal cancer," and (3) "Consumption of omega-3 fatty acids may reduce the risk of coronary heart disease"—to lack significant scientific agreement because existing research had examined only the relationship between consumption of *foods* containing these components and the risk of these diseases. The FDA logically determined that the specific effect of the *component* of the food constituting the dietary supplement could not be determined with certainty. But certainly this concern could be accommodated, in the first claim for example, by adding a prominent disclaimer to the label along the following lines: "The evidence is inconclusive because existing studies have been performed with *foods* containing antioxidant vitamins, and the effect of those foods on reducing the risk of cancer may result from other components in those foods." A similar disclaimer would be equally effective for the latter two claims.

The FDA's concern regarding the fourth claim—".8mg of folic acid in a dietary supplement is more effective in reducing the risk of neural tube defects than a lower amount in foods in common form"—is different from its reservations regarding the first three claims: the agency simply concluded that "the scientific literature does not support the superiority of any one source over others." [W]e suspect that a clarifying disclaimer could be added to the effect that "the evidence in support of this claim is inconclusive."

The government's general concern that . . . consumers might assume that a claim on a supplement's label is approved by the government suggests an obvious answer. The agency could require the label to state that "The FDA does not approve this claim." Similarly, the government's interest in preventing the use of labels that are true but do not mention adverse effects would seem to be satisfied—at least ordinarily—by inclusion of a prominent disclaimer setting forth those adverse effects.

The government disputes that consumers would be able to comprehend appellants' proposed health claims in conjunction with the disclaimers we have suggested. [T]his mix of information would, in the government's view, create confusion among consumers. But all the government offers in support is the FDA's pronouncement that "consumers would be considerably confused by a multitude of claims with differing degrees of reliability." Although the government may have more leeway in choosing suppression over disclosure as a response to the problem of consumer confusion where the product affects health, it must still meet its burden of justifying a restriction on speech. [H]ere, the FDA's conclusory assertion falls far short.

We do not presume to draft precise disclaimers for each of appellants' four claims; we leave that task to the agency in the first instance. Nor do we rule out the possibility that where evidence in support of a claim is outweighed by evidence against the claim, the FDA could deem it incurable by a disclaimer and ban it outright. For example, if the weight of the evidence were against the hypothetical claim that "Consumption of Vitamin E reduces the risk of Alzheimer's disease," the agency might reasonably determine that adding a disclaimer such as "The FDA has determined that *no* evidence supports this claim" would not suffice to mitigate the claim's misleadingness. Finally, while we are skeptical that the government could demonstrate with empirical evidence that disclaimers similar to the ones we suggested above would bewilder consumers and fail to correct for deceptiveness, we do not rule out that possibility.

District court decision reversed; case remanded with instructions that FDA reconsider appellants' health claims.

Separation of Powers

 LO47-3 Explain the test courts customarily use in determining whether a broad delegation of power by Congress to an agency is constitutional.

One basic constitutional principle is uniquely important when the creation of administrative agencies is at issue: the principle of *separation of powers*. A fundamental attribute of our Constitution is its allocation of governmental power among the three branches of government. Lawmaking power is given to the legislative branch, law-enforcing power to the executive branch, and law-interpreting power to the judicial branch. By limiting the powers of each branch, and by giving each branch some checks on the exercise of power by the other branches, the Constitution seeks to ensure that governmental power remains accountable to the public will.

Administrative agencies, which exercise powers resembling those of each of the three branches of government, create obvious concerns about separation of powers. In particular, the congressional delegation of legislative power to an agency in its enabling legislation may be challenged as violating the separation of powers principle if the legislation is so broadly worded as to indicate that Congress has abdicated its lawmaking responsibilities. Early judicial decisions exploring the manner in which Congress could delegate its power tended to require enabling legislation to contain fairly specific guidelines and standards limiting the exercise of agency discretion.

More recently, courts have often sustained quite broad delegations of power to administrative agencies. Section 5 of the FTC Act contains such a delegation of power. A great range of unspecified behavior falls within the statute's prohibition of "unfair methods of competition" and "unfair or deceptive acts or practices." Courts tend to approve broad delegations of power when Congress has expressed an "intelligible principle" to guide the agency's actions.[4]

The *American Trucking Associations* decision, which follows, examines the delegation of power question.

---

[4]*J. W. Hampton, Jr., & Co. v. United States,* 276 U.S. 394 (1928).

Whitman v. American Trucking Associations   531 U.S. 457 (2001)

The federal Clean Air Act requires the Environmental Protection Agency (EPA) to promulgate and periodically revise national ambient air quality standards (NAAQS) for each air pollutant that meets certain statutory criteria. Section 109 of the statute calls for the EPA to set, for each pollutant, a standard reflecting a concentration level "requisite to protect the public health" with an "adequate margin of safety." In July 1997, the EPA issued final rules revising the NAAQS for particulate matter and ozone. Various parties, including American Trucking Associations Inc., filed petitions for review in the U.S. Court of Appeals for the District of Columbia Circuit. The D.C. Circuit held, among other things, that the Clean Air Act (CAA) did not permit the EPA to consider costs of implementation in setting NAAQS, and that in any event, the challenged rules had been formulated pursuant to an unconstitutional delegation of power from Congress in CAA § 109. However, the D.C. Circuit remanded the proceedings to the EPA, in order to allow the agency to construe § 109 in a way that would cure the delegation problem.

The U.S. Supreme Court granted the EPA's petition for certiorari. In a portion of the opinion not included here, the Supreme Court agreed with the D.C. Circuit's holding that costs of implementation could not be considered by the EPA in the setting of NAAQS. The Court then turned to the delegation of power issue.

Scalia, Justice

In a delegation challenge, the constitutional question is whether the statute has delegated legislative power to the agency. Article I, § 1, of the Constitution vests "all legislative Powers herein granted . . . in a Congress of the United States." This text permits no delegation of those powers, and so we repeatedly have said that when Congress confers decision making authority upon agencies, *Congress* must "lay down by legislative act an intelligible principle to which the person or body authorized to [act] is directed to conform." *J. W. Hampton, Jr., & Co. v. United States,* 276 U.S. 394 (1928). We have never suggested that an agency can cure an unlawful delegation of legislative power by adopting in its discretion a limiting construction of the statute. Whether the statute delegates legislative power is a question for the courts, and an agency's voluntary self-denial has no bearing upon the answer.

We agree with the Solicitor General[, who argued on behalf of the United States. According to the Solicitor General's argument,] the text of § 109 of the Clean Air Act at a minimum requires that "for a discrete set of pollutants and based on published air quality criteria that reflect the latest scientific knowledge, [the] EPA must establish uniform national standards at a level that is requisite to protect public health from the adverse effects of the pollutant in the ambient air." Requisite, in [the words of the Solicitor General], "means sufficient, but not more than necessary." These limits on the EPA's discretion are strikingly similar to the ones we approved in [a 1991 decision], which permitted the Attorney General to designate a drug as a controlled substance for purposes of criminal drug enforcement if doing so was "necessary to avoid an imminent hazard to the public safety." They also resemble the Occupational Health and Safety Act provision requiring the agency to "set the standard which most adequately assures, to the extent feasible, on the basis of the best available evidence, that no employee will suffer any impairment of health"—which the Court upheld in [a 1980 decision].

The scope of discretion § 109 allows is in fact well within the outer limits of our nondelegation precedents. In the history of the Court we have found the requisite "intelligible principle" lacking in only two statutes, one of which provided literally no guidance for the exercise of discretion, and the other of which conferred authority to regulate the entire economy on the basis of no more precise a standard than stimulating the economy by assuring "fair competition." We have, on the other hand, upheld the validity of [a section of] the

Public Utility Holding Act of 1935, which gave the Securities and Exchange Commission authority to modify the structure of holding company systems so as to ensure that they are not "unduly or unnecessarily complicated" and do not "unfairly or inequitably distribute voting power among security holders." *American Power & Light Co. v. SEC,* 329 U.S. 90 (1946). We have approved the wartime conferral of agency power to fix the prices of commodities at a level that "will be generally fair and equitable and will effectuate the purposes of [the relevant statute]." *Yakus v. United States,* 321 U.S. 414 (1944). And we have found an "intelligible principle" in various statutes authorizing regulation in the "public interest." *See, e.g., National Broadcasting Co. v. United States,* 319 U.S. 190 (1943). In short, we have "almost never felt qualified to second-guess Congress regarding the permissible degree of policy judgment that can be left to those executing or applying the law." *Mistretta v. United States,* 488 U.S. 361 (1989) (Scalia, J., dissenting).

It is true enough that the degree of agency discretion that is acceptable varies according to the scope of the power congressionally conferred. While Congress need not provide any direction to the EPA regarding the manner in which it is to define "country elevators," which are to be exempt from new stationary-source regulations governing grain elevators, it must provide substantial guidance on setting air standards that affect the entire national economy. But even in sweeping regulatory schemes we have never demanded, as the Court of Appeals did here, that statutes provide a "determinate criterion" for saying "how much [of the regulated harm] is too much." [In the controlled substance designation case referred to above,] for example, we did not require the statute to decree how "imminent" was too imminent, or how "necessary" was necessary enough, or even—most relevant here—how "hazardous" was too hazardous. Similarly, the statute at issue in [another Supreme Court decision] authorized agencies to recoup "excess profits" paid under wartime government contracts, yet we did not insist that Congress specify how much profit was too much. It is therefore not conclusive for delegation purposes that, as [American Trucking Associations and the other parties challenging the NAAQS] argue, ozone and particulate matter are "nonthreshold" pollutants that inflict a continuum of adverse health effects at any airborne concentration greater than zero, and hence require the EPA to make judgments of degree. "[A] certain degree of discretion, and thus of lawmaking, inheres in most executive or judicial action." *Mistretta* (Scalia, J., dissenting).

Section 109(b)(1) of the CAA, which we interpret as requiring the EPA to set air quality standards at the level that is "requisite"—that is, not lower or higher than is necessary—to protect the public health with an adequate margin of safety, fits comfortably within the scope of discretion permitted by our precedent.

Court of Appeals decision reversed as to delegation of power issue.

Agency Types and Organization

Agency Types Administrative agencies may be found under a variety of labels. They may be called "administration," "agency," "authority," "board," "bureau," "commission," "department," "division," or "service." They sometimes have a governing body, which may be appointed or elected. They almost invariably have an administrative head (variously called "Chair," "Commissioner," "Director," etc.) and a staff. Because our focus is on federal administrative agencies, it is important to distinguish between the two basic types of federal administrative agencies: executive agencies and independent agencies.

Executive Agencies Administrative agencies that reside within the Executive Office of the President or within the executive departments of the president's cabinet are called executive agencies. Examples of such agencies and their cabinet homes are the Food and Drug Administration (Department of Health and Human Services), the Nuclear Regulatory Agency and the Federal Energy Regulatory Agency (Department of Energy), the Occupational Safety and Health Administration (Department of Labor), and the Internal Revenue Service (Treasury Department). In addition to their executive home, such agencies share one other important attribute. Their administrative heads serve "at the pleasure of the President," meaning that they are appointed and removable at the president's will.

Independent Agencies The Interstate Commerce Commission was the first independent administrative agency created by Congress. Much of the regulation businesses face emanates from independent agencies such as the FTC, the National Labor Relations Board, the Consumer Product Safety Commission, the Equal Employment Opportunity Commission, the Environmental Protection Agency, and the Securities and Exchange Commission. Independent agencies are usually headed by a board or a commission (e.g., the FTC has five commissioners) whose members are appointed by the president "with the advice and consent of the Senate." Commissioners or board members are usually appointed for fixed terms (e.g., FTC commissioners serve seven-year, staggered terms) and are removable only for cause (e.g., FTC commissioners may be removed only for "inefficiency, neglect of duty, or malfeasance in office"). Enabling legislation often requires political balance in agency appointments (e.g., the FTC Act provides that "[n]ot more than three of the commissioners shall be members of the same political party").

Department of Homeland Security In 2002, Congress enacted legislation creating the cabinet-level Department of Homeland Security. This department, whose creation had been proposed in various versions of House and Senate bills since shortly after the September 11, 2001, attacks on the United States, absorbed more than 20 different functions previously undertaken by other federal departments and agencies. The Department of Homeland Security employs roughly 170,000 workers, with the vast majority coming to that department by way of transfer from existing positions as federal government employees. With the creation of this department and the resulting reassignments of employees and areas of responsibility, the 2002 enactment called for the most sweeping governmental reorganization in more than a half-century.

Agency Organization An agency's organizational structure is largely a function of its regulatory mission. The FTC's operational side, for instance, is divided into three bureaus: the Bureau of Competition, which enforces the antitrust laws and unfair competitive practices; the Bureau of Consumer Protection, which focuses on unfair or deceptive trade practices; and the Bureau of Economics, which gathers data, compiles statistics, and furnishes technical assistance to the other bureaus. The commission is headquartered in Washington, D.C. It maintains regional offices in Atlanta, Chicago, Cleveland, Dallas, Los Angeles, New York, San Francisco, and Seattle. This regional office system enhances the commission's enforcement, investigative, and educational missions by locating commission staff closer to the public it serves.

Agency Powers and Procedures

Nature, Types, and Source of Powers

The powers administrative agencies possess may be classified in various ways. Some agencies' powers are largely *ministerial*—concerned primarily with the routine performance of duties imposed by law. The most important administrative agencies, however, have broad *discretionary* powers that necessitate the exercise of significant discretion and

judgment when they are employed. The major discretionary powers agencies can possess are investigative power, rulemaking power, and adjudicatory power.

The formal powers an agency possesses are those granted by its enabling legislation. Important federal agencies such as the FTC normally enjoy significant levels of each of the discretionary powers. However, even such powerful agencies face significant limitations on the exercise of their powers. In addition to explicit limits on agency proceedings contained in enabling legislation, basic constitutional provisions restrict agency action.

A federal agency's exercise of its rulemaking and adjudicatory powers is also constrained by the *Administrative Procedure Act (APA)*. The APA was enacted by Congress in 1946 in an attempt to standardize federal agency procedures and to respond to critics who said that administrative power was out of control. The APA applies to all federal agencies, although it will not displace stricter procedural requirements contained in a particular agency's enabling legislation. Besides specifying agency procedures, the APA plays a major role in shaping the conditions under which courts will review agency actions and the standards courts will use when conducting such a review. Most states have adopted "baby APAs" to govern the activities of state administrative agencies.

Finally, as later parts of this chapter will confirm, each of the three traditional branches of government possesses substantial powers to mold and constrain the powers of the "fourth branch." That being said, one final point should be made before we turn to a detailed examination of formal agency powers and procedures. An agency's formal powers also confer on it significant *informal* power. Agency "advice," "suggestions," or "guidelines," which technically lack the legal force of formal agency regulations or rulings, may nonetheless play a major role in shaping the behavior of regulated industries because they carry with them the implicit or explicit threat of formal agency action if they are ignored. Such gentle persuasion can be a highly effective regulatory tool—and one that is subject to far fewer constraints than formal agency action.

Investigative Power

 Describe basic features of the investigative power that administrative agencies typically have.

LO47-4

Administrative agencies need accurate information about business practices and activities not only for the detection and prosecution of regulatory violations, but also to enable the agencies to identify areas in which new rules are needed or existing rules require modification. Much of the information agencies require to do their jobs is readily available. "Public interest" groups, complaints from customers or competitors, and other regulatory agencies are all important sources of information.

However, much of the information necessary to effective agency enforcement can come only from sources that may be strongly disinclined to provide it: the individuals and business organizations subject to regulation. This reluctance may stem from the desire to avoid or delay the regulatory action that disclosure would generate. It might also be the product, however, of more legitimate concerns, such as a desire to protect personal privacy, a desire to prevent competitors from acquiring trade secrets and other sensitive information from agency files, or a reluctance to incur the costs that may accompany compliance with substantial information demands. Agencies, therefore, need the means to compel unwilling possessors of information to comply with legitimate demands for information. The two most important (and most intrusive) investigative tools employed by administrative agencies are *subpoenas* and *searches and seizures*.

Subpoenas   There are two basic types of subpoena: the subpoena *ad testificandum* and the subpoena *duces tecum*. Subpoenas *ad testificandum* may be used by an agency to compel unwilling witnesses to appear and testify at agency hearings. Subpoenas *duces tecum* may be used by an agency to compel the production of most types of documentary evidence, such as accounting records and office memoranda.

Unlimited agency subpoena power risks sacrificing individual liberty and privacy in the name of regulatory efficiency. Accordingly, courts have formulated a number of limitations that seek to balance an agency's legitimate need to know against an investigatory target's legitimate privacy interests.

Agency investigations must be *authorized by law* and *conducted for a legitimate purpose*. The former requirement means that the agency's enabling legislation must have granted the agency the investigatory power it seeks to assert. The latter requirement prohibits bad-faith investigations pursued for improper motives (e.g., Internal Revenue Service investigations undertaken solely to harass political opponents of an incumbent administration).

Even when the investigation is legally authorized and is undertaken for a legitimate purpose, the information sought must be *relevant to that purpose*. The Fourth Amendment to the Constitution provides this limitation

on agency powers. However, an agency issuing an administrative subpoena need not possess the "probable cause" that the Fourth Amendment requires in support of regular search warrants.[5] In the words of the Supreme Court, an agency "can investigate merely on the suspicion that the law is being violated, or even just because it wants assurance that it is not."[6] This lesser standard makes sense in the agency context because the only evidence of many regulatory violations is documentary and "probable cause" might be demonstrable only after inspection of the target's records. In such cases, a probable cause requirement would effectively negate agency enforcement power.

Similarly, agency information demands must be *sufficiently specific* and *not unreasonably burdensome*. This requirement derives from the Fourth Amendment's prohibition against "unreasonable searches and seizures." It means that agency subpoenas must adequately describe the information the agency seeks. It also means that the cost to the target of complying with the agency's demand (e.g., the cost of assembling and reproducing the data, the disruption of business operations, or the risk that proprietary information will be indirectly disclosed to competitors) must not be unreasonably disproportionate to the agency's interest in obtaining the information.

Finally, the information sought *must not be privileged*. Various statutory and common law privileges may, at times, limit an agency's power to compel the production of information. By far the most important privilege in this respect is the Fifth Amendment *privilege against compelled testimonial self-incrimination*, or "the right to silence." As you learned in Chapter 5, however, this privilege is subject to serious limitations in the organizational context. The right to silence in the administrative context is further limited by the fact that it is only available in *criminal* proceedings. In some regulatory contexts, the potential sanctions for violation may be labeled "civil penalties" or "forfeitures." Only when such sanctions are essentially punitive in their intent or effect will they be considered "criminal" for the purpose of allowing the invocation of the privilege.

Public policy concerns provide another subpoena power limitation that may apply even if neither the Fifth Amendment nor another privilege bars production of the documents sought by an agency. For instance, courts may conclude that an agency subpoena should not be enforced if its enforcement would tend to compromise important operations being conducted by another agency or arm of the government.

---

[5]The Fourth Amendment is discussed in Chapter 5.
[6]*United States v. Morton Salt*, 338 U.S. 632 (1950).

Searches and Seizures Sometimes the evidence necessary to prove a regulatory violation can be obtained only by entering private property such as a home, an office, or a factory. When administrative agencies seek to gather information by such an entry, the Fourth Amendment's prohibition against unreasonable searches and seizures and its warrant requirement come into play. Owners of commercial property, although afforded less Fourth Amendment protection than the owners of private dwellings, do have some legitimate expectations of privacy in their business premises.

Not all agency information-gathering efforts, however, will be considered so intrusive as to amount to a prohibited search and seizure. In *Dow Chemical Co. v. United States,*[7] for instance, the Environmental Protection Agency's warrantless aerial photography of one of Dow's plants was upheld. Furthermore, in *State of New York v. Burger,*[8] the Supreme Court upheld the constitutionality of warrantless administrative inspections of the premises of "closely regulated" businesses so long as three criteria are satisfied: (1) there must be a substantial government interest in the regulatory scheme in question, (2) the warrantless inspections must be necessary to further the scheme, and (3) the inspection program must provide a constitutionally adequate substitute for a warrant by giving owners of commercial property adequate notice that their property is subject to inspection and by limiting the discretion of inspecting officers.

Rulemaking Power

 Describe basic features of the rulemaking power that administrative agencies typically have.

An agency's rulemaking power derives from its enabling legislation. For example, the FTC Act gives the FTC the power "to make rules and regulations for the purpose of carrying out the provisions of this Act." The Administrative Procedure Act (APA) defines a rule as "an agency statement of general or particular applicability and future effect designed to complement, interpret or prescribe law or policy." All agency rules are compiled and published in the *Code of Federal Regulations.*

Types of Rules Administrative agencies create three types of rules: procedural, interpretive, and legislative. *Procedural rules* specify how the agency will conduct itself. For instance, agencies typically have procedural rules dealing with such matters as the manner in which advance notice of agency rulemaking proceedings will be communicated.

Interpretive rules are designed to advise regulated individuals and entities of the manner in which an agency interprets the statutes it enforces. For example, the FTC has promulgated a rule interpreting the term *consumer product*, as used in the Magnuson–Moss Warranty Act (a statute the FTC has the legal responsibility to enforce). Interpretive rules technically do not have the force of law. Therefore, they are not binding on businesses and the courts. Courts interpreting regulatory statutes often give agency interpretations substantial weight, however, in deference to the agency's familiarity with the statutes it administers and its presumed expertise in the general area being regulated. Businesses are also likely to pay attention to agency interpretive rules because such rules indicate the circumstances in which an agency is likely to take formal enforcement action.

If consistent with an agency's enabling legislation and the Constitution, and if created in accordance with the procedures dictated by the APA, *legislative rules* have the full force and effect of law. Legislative rules thus are binding on the courts, the public, and the agency. Federal agencies have promulgated very large numbers of legislative rules, many of which address highly specific matters. For example, an FTC legislative rule states that if a party sells a quick-freeze aerosol spray product designed for the frosting of beverage glasses and the product contains an ingredient known as fluorocarbon 12, the seller must issue a warning (on the product label) that the product should not be inhaled in concentrated form, in view of the risk that such behavior may lead to severe harm or death.

Given the greater relative importance of legislative rules, you should not be surprised to learn that the process by which they are promulgated—unlike the process by which procedural and interpretive rules are created—is highly regulated by the APA and closely scrutinized by the courts. There are three basic types of agency rulemaking: informal, formal, and hybrid.

Informal Rulemaking Informal rulemaking (or "notice and comment" rulemaking) is the method most commonly employed by administrative agencies that are not forced by their enabling legislation to follow the more stringent procedures of formal rulemaking. The informal rulemaking process commences with the publication of a "Notice of Proposed Rulemaking" in the *Federal Register.* The APA requires that such notices contain a statement of the time and place at which the proceedings will be held, a statement of the nature of the proceedings, a statement of the legal authority for the proceedings (usually the agency's enabling legislation), and either a statement of the terms of the proposed rule or a description of the matters to be addressed by the rule.

[7]476 U.S. 227 (1986).
[8]482 U.S. 691 (1987).

Publication of notice must then be followed by a *comment period* during which interested parties may submit written comments detailing their views about the proposed rule. After comments have been received and considered, the agency must publish the regulation in its final form in the *Federal Register*. As a general rule, the rule cannot become effective until at least 30 days after this final publication. The APA, however, recognizes a "good-cause" exception to the 30-day waiting period requirement, and to the notice of rulemaking requirement as well, when notice would be impractical, unnecessary, or contrary to the public interest.

Agencies tend to favor the informal rulemaking process because it allows quick and efficient regulatory action. Such quickness and efficiency, however, are purchased at a significant cost—a minimal opportunity for interested parties to participate in the rule-formation process. Giving interested parties the opportunity to be heard may, ultimately, further regulatory goals. For example, the vigorous debate about a proposed rule that a public hearing can provide may contribute to the creation of more effective rules. Also, providing interested parties an adequate opportunity to participate in the rulemaking process lends credibility to that process and the rules it produces, thereby enhancing the chances of voluntary compliance.

Formal Rulemaking Formal rulemaking is designed to give interested parties a far greater opportunity to make their views heard than that afforded by informal rulemaking. As does informal rulemaking, formal rulemaking begins with publication of a "Notice of Proposed Rulemaking" in the *Federal Register*. Unlike the notice employed to announce informal rulemaking procedures, however, this notice must include notice of a time and place at which a public hearing will be held. Such hearings resemble trials in that the agency must produce evidence justifying the proposed regulation, and interested parties are allowed to present evidence in opposition to it. Both sides may examine each other's exhibits and cross-examine each other's witnesses. At the conclusion of the proceedings, the agency must prepare a formal, written document detailing its findings based on the evidence presented at the hearing.

Although the formal rulemaking process affords interested parties greatly enhanced opportunities to be heard, this greater access is purchased at significant expense and at the risk that some parties will abuse their access rights in an effort to impede the regulatory process. By tireless cross-examination of government witnesses and lengthy presentations of their own, opponents seeking to derail or delay regulation may consume months, or even years, of agency time. A classic example of such behavior would be the Food and Drug Administration's hearings a number of years ago on a proposed rule requiring that the minimum peanut content of peanut butter be set at 90 percent. Industry forces favored an 87 percent minimum and were able to delay regulation for almost 10 years.

Hybrid Rulemaking Frustrated over the lack of access afforded by informal rulemaking and the potential for paralyzing the regulatory process that is inherent in formal rulemaking, some legislators have attempted to create a rulemaking process that combines some of the elements of informal and formal procedures. Although *hybrid rulemaking* procedures are insufficiently established and standardized at this point to permit a detailed discussion of them, some general tendencies are evident. Hybrid procedures bear some resemblance to those of formal rulemaking in that both involve some sort of hearing. Unlike formal rulemaking procedures, however, hybrid procedures tend to limit the right of interested parties to cross-examine agency witnesses.

Failure to Promulgate Rules When Congress has granted an agency rulemaking authority without specifically requiring the promulgation of regulations on a given topic, the agency normally has considerable freedom to decide not to exercise its rulemaking authority in a particular context. Despite the deference usually paid to a decision not to engage in rulemaking, failure-to-regulate decisions may sometimes be subject to judicial review—particularly if not regulating would be inconsistent with a statutory directive. *Massachusetts v. Environmental Protection Agency,*[9] provides an example. The state of Massachusetts and organizations dedicated to environmental causes sued the Environmental Protection Agency (EPA), alleging that the agency's failure to formulate regulations dealing with greenhouse-gas emissions from motor vehicles violated a congressional mandate, set forth in the Clean Air Act, to prescribe regulatory standards regarding vehicles' emissions of "any air pollutant" reasonably regarded as harmful to public health. The case made its way to the Supreme Court, which held that greenhouse-gas emissions from new vehicles would fall within the meaning of "any air pollutant" for purposes of Title II of the Clean Air Act. Accordingly, the Court concluded that Title II directed and authorized the EPA to adopt regulations dealing with such emissions from new vehicles if the agency "form[ed] a 'judgment' that such emissions contribute to climate change."[10] Following the Court's decision, the EPA promulgated regulations dealing with that subject. (The *Massachusetts* decision receives further discussion in

---

[9]549 U.S. 497 (2007).

[10]*Id.* at 528.

The Global Business Environment

With the many administrative agencies that exist at the federal, state, and sometimes even local levels, the United States surely possesses more extensive and expansive administrative law than any other nation. (Whether this is viewed as a good or bad thing may have a great deal to do with one's philosophical and political perspectives.) Many nations that lack the vast administrative agency "infrastructure" present in the United States nevertheless tend to have some regulatory—or at least advisory—bodies charged with addressing certain types of issues that, in the United States, would fall within the regulatory authority of administrative agencies.

For instance, in the European Union (EU), individual countries typically have *ministries* that may help shape governmental policy on issues falling within their respective areas of responsibility. At the EU level, the European commission's primary responsibility is to propose legislation to the Council of Ministers. The commission, however, does have limited rulemaking authority that it may exercise on its own in a manner similar to—though clearly on a lesser scale than—administrative agencies' exercising of rulemaking authority in the United States. In fulfilling its responsibilities, the commission frequently relies on the research assistance, recommendations, and other input provided by subject matter–specific advisory bodies known as the Directorates General.

---

the *Utility Air Regulatory Group* case, a 2014 Supreme Court decision that appears later in the chapter.)

Adjudicatory Power

 **LO47-6** Describe basic features of the adjudicatory power that administrative agencies typically have.

Most major federal agencies possess substantial adjudicatory powers. Besides having the authority to investigate alleged behaviors and to produce regulations that have legal effect, agencies often have the power to conduct proceedings to determine whether regulatory or statutory violations have occurred. The administrative adjudication process is at once similar to, but substantially different from, the judicial process you studied in Chapter 2.

The administrative adjudication process normally begins with a complaint filed by the agency. The party charged in the complaint (called the *respondent*) files an answer. Respondents are normally entitled to a hearing before the agency. At this hearing, they may confront and cross-examine agency witnesses and present evidence of their own. Respondents may be represented by legal counsel. No juries are present in administrative adjudications, however. The cases are heard by an agency employee usually called an administrative law judge (ALJ). Unlike criminal prosecutions, the burden of proof in administrative proceedings is normally the civil *preponderance of the evidence* standard. Constitutional procedural safeguards such as the exclusionary rule do not protect the respondent.[11]

The agency, in effect, functions as investigator, plaintiff, judge, and jury. The APA attempts to deal with the obvious potential for abuse inherent in this combination in a number of ways. First, the APA seeks to ensure that ALJs are as independent as possible by requiring internal separation between an agency's judges and its investigative and prosecutorial functions. The APA also prohibits ALJs from having private consultations with any party to an agency proceeding and shields them from agency disciplinary action other than for "good cause." Finally, insufficient separation between an agency's adjudication function and its other functions can be contrary to basic due process requirements.

After each party to the proceeding has been heard, the ALJ renders a decision stating her findings of fact and conclusions of law, and imposing whatever penalty she deems appropriate within the parameters established by the agency's enabling legislation (e.g., a fine or a cease-and-desist order). If neither party challenges the ALJ's decision, it becomes final. The losing party, however, may appeal an ALJ's decision, which will then be subjected to a **de novo review** by the governing body of the agency (e.g., appeals from FTC ALJ decisions are heard by the five FTC commissioners). *De novo* review means that the agency's governing body may treat the proceedings as if they were occurring for the first time and may ignore the ALJ's findings. Often, however, the agency's governing body will adopt the ALJ's findings. In any event, those findings will be part of the record if a disappointed respondent seeks judicial review of an agency's decision.

Finally, it is important to note that many agency proceedings are settled by a **consent order** before completion of the adjudication process. Consent orders are similar to the nolo contendere pleas discussed in Chapter 5. Respondents who sign consent orders do not admit wrongdoing, but they waive all rights to judicial review, agree to accept a specific sanction

---

[11]The exclusionary rule and the beyond a reasonable doubt standard employed in criminal cases are discussed in Chapter 5. The preponderance of the evidence standard is discussed in Chapter 6.

imposed by the agency, and commonly agree to discontinue the business practice that triggered the agency action.

Controlling Administrative Agencies

By this point in our discussion, we have already encountered certain legal controls on agency action, such as the terms of an agency's enabling legislation, the procedural requirements imposed by the APA, and the basic constraints that the Constitution places on all governmental action. The following sections continue to focus on agency control by examining the various devices through which the three traditional branches of government influence and control the actions of administrative agencies.

Presidential Controls

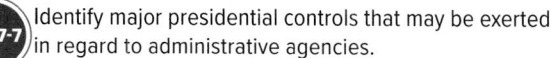 **LO47-7** Identify major presidential controls that may be exerted in regard to administrative agencies.

The executive branch has at its disposal a number of tools that may be employed to shape agency action. The most obvious among them is the president's power to appoint and remove agency administrators. This presidential power is obviously more limited in the case of independent agencies than it is where executive agencies are concerned, but the president generally has the power to appoint the heads of independent agencies and demote the prior chairpersons without cause. Skillful use of the new chair's managerial powers, probably the most important of which is the power to influence agency hiring policies, can eventually effect substantial changes in agency policy. Also, significant and sustained policy differences between an independent agency and the executive branch often eventually trigger resignations by agency commissioners, thus providing the president with the opportunity to appoint new members whose philosophies are more congruent with his own.

In addition, the president may seek to influence agency action by issuing statements that direct the agency to consider certain topics of potential regulation or deregulation. The Trump administration, for instance, issued various such directives or their informal equivalents during its early months.

The executive branch also exercises significant control over agency action through the Office of Management and Budget (OMB). The OMB plays a major role in the creation of the annual executive budget the president presents to Congress. In the process, the OMB reviews, and sometimes modifies, the budgetary requests of executive agencies. In addition, an executive order requires executive agencies to prepare cost–benefit and least-cost analyses for all major proposed rules

and to submit this information to the OMB for review prior to seeking public comments. This order and a subsequent executive order requiring agencies to give the OMB early warning of possible rule changes have made the OMB a powerful player in the rulemaking process.

Finally, the president's power to *veto* legislation concerning administrative agencies represents another point of executive influence over agency operations.

Congressional Controls

LO47-8 Identify major congressional controls that may be exerted in regard to administrative agencies.

The legislative branch possesses a number of devices, both formal and informal, by which it may influence agency action. Obvious avenues of congressional control include the Senate's "advice and consent" role in agency appointments, the power to amend an agency's enabling legislation (what Congress has given, Congress can take away), and the power to pass legislation that mandates changes in agency practices or procedures. Examples of the latter include the National Environmental Policy Act (NEPA), which dictated that administrative agencies file *environmental impact statements* for every agency action that could significantly affect the quality of the environment, and the Regulatory Flexibility Act, which ordered changes in agency rulemaking procedures designed to give small businesses improved notice of agency rulemaking activities that may have a substantial impact on them. Congress can also pass *sunset legislation* providing for the automatic expiration of an agency's authority unless Congress expressly extends it by a specified date. Such legislation ensures periodic congressional review of the initial decision to delegate legislative authority to an administrative agency.

Another tool available for controlling agencies is the Congressional Review Act (CRA), under which an agency regulation promulgated according to the procedures outlined earlier in the chapter can be nullified by a simple-majority vote in Congress if the regulation was issued within the preceding 60 legislative days. Eliminating the regulation after that point would require either that the agency go back through the lengthy promulgation process to repeal the rule or that Congress enact a statute overriding the regulation. Such a bill would be subject to the Senate's filibuster rule, however, and could be much more difficult to enact than a CRA bill that would require only a simple majority for passage. Until very recently, the CRA had languished in disuse, having been employed only one time. In the early months of the Trump administration, however, Congress (and the new president) used the CRA to eliminate roughly a dozen regulations that agencies issued near the end of the Obama administration.

Congress enjoys several other less obvious, but no less important, points of influence over agency action. For example, Congress must authorize agency budgetary appropriations. Thus, Congress may limit or deny funding for agency programs with which it disagrees. Also, the Governmental Operations Committees of both houses of Congress exercise significant oversight over agency activities. These committees review agency programs and conduct hearings concerning proposed agency appointments and appropriations. Finally, individual members of Congress may seek to influence agency action through "casework"—informal contacts with an agency on behalf of constituents who are involved with the agency.

Judicial Review

 Explain what is necessary in order for a person or organization to have standing to bring a judicial challenge to administrative agency action.

As important as the roles of the executive and legislative branches are in controlling agency action, the courts exercise the greatest control over agency behavior, perhaps because they are the branch of government most accessible to members of the public aggrieved by agency action. The APA provides for judicial review of most agency action, which takes place either in one of the U.S. courts of appeals or a U.S. district court, depending on the nature of the agency action at issue. The Supreme Court, if it chooses to grant certiorari, is the court of last resort for review of agency action.

Not all agency actions are subject to judicial review. Moreover, only certain parties may challenge those that are reviewable. An individual or organization seeking judicial review must demonstrate that the agency action being challenged is *reviewable*, that the challenging party has *standing to sue*, that *necessary administrative remedies have been exhausted*, and that the dispute is *ripe for judicial review*. These requirements are discussed in the following sections.

Reviewability Only reviewable agency actions may be challenged by dissatisfied individuals and organizations. Normally, it is not difficult for aggrieved parties to show that the agency action is reviewable because the APA creates a strong presumption in favor of reviewability. This presumption may be overcome only by a showing that "statutes preclude review" or that the decision in question is "committed to agency discretion by law." These limitations on reviewability come from Congress's power to dictate the jurisdiction of the federal courts and from judicial deference to the proper functions of the other branches of

government (e.g., a decision relating to matters of foreign policy is likely to be seen as outside the proper province of the judiciary).

Standing to Sue Once reviewability of an agency action has been established, the challenging party must demonstrate that he, she, or it has standing to sue. This means that the individual or organization seeking judicial review is "an aggrieved party" whose interests have been substantially affected by the agency action. Initially, courts took a relatively restrictive view of this basic requirement, requiring plaintiffs to show harm to a legally protected interest. More recently, however, courts have liberalized the standing requirement somewhat, requiring plaintiffs to demonstrate that they have suffered an "injury" to an interest that lies within the "zone of interests" protected by the statute or constitutional provision that serves as the basis of their challenge. Demonstrating an economic loss remains the surest way to satisfy the "injury" requirement, but emotional, aesthetic, and environmental injuries have been found sufficient on occasion.

Exhaustion and Ripeness Once standing has been established, two further obstacles—exhaustion and ripeness—confront the party challenging an agency action. Courts do not want to allow regulated parties to short-circuit the regulatory process. They also want to give agencies the chance to correct their own mistakes and to develop fully their positions in disputed matters. Accordingly, they normally insist that aggrieved parties *exhaust necessary administrative remedies* before they will grant judicial review.[12] The requirement that a dispute be *ripe* for judicial review is a general requirement emanating from the Constitution's insistence that only "cases or controversies" are judicially resolvable. In determining ripeness, the courts weigh the hardship to the parties of withholding judicial review against the degree of refinement of the issues still possible.

Legal Bases for Challenging Agency Actions

 Explain the major legal bases for judicially challenging administrative agency actions and identify the standards of review courts employ in such cases.

Assuming that the above prerequisites to judicial review are met, there are various legal theories on which agency action may be attacked. It may be alleged that the agency's action was *ultra vires* (exceeded its authority as granted by

---

[12] Necessary administrative remedies are those a statute or regulation establishes as mandatory steps to be completed before judicial review can be sought.

its enabling legislation). For example, in a 2000 case, the Supreme Court struck down the Food and Drug Administration's 1996 regulations dealing with cigarettes and smokeless tobacco. The Court held that in the Food, Drug, and Cosmetic Act, Congress neither gave, nor intended to give, the FDA authority to regulate tobacco products.[13] As noted in this chapter's introductory problem, however, Congress later amended the existing law and expressly granted the FDA the authority to regulate such products and marketing practices related to them. The FDA then reimposed restrictions on tobacco advertising. Although an *ultra vires* challenge to the FDA's regulations dealing with the marketing of tobacco products would no longer be meritorious, the regulations must still comply with constitutional constraints. (For discussion of First Amendment challenges to certain tobacco advertising restrictions set forth in the governing statute and in FDA regulations, see this chapter's introductory problem.)

In a 2005 decision, *American Library Association v. Federal Communications Commission*,[14] the U.S. Court of Appeals for the District of Columbia Circuit held that the Federal Communications Commission (FCC)

exceeded the scope of its regulatory authority when it promulgated a regulation requiring makers of televisions and computers to install "broadcast flag" technology in order to impede consumers' ability to copy digitally distributed programs. Using unusually strong language as it invalidated the regulation, the court stressed that the FCC's assertion of authority was "strained and implausible" and that "nothing in [the relevant federal] statute, its legislative history, the applicable case law, or agency practice indicat[es] that Congress meant to provide the sweeping authority the FCC now claims."[15]

Alternatively, it may be alleged that the agency *substantially deviated from procedural requirements* contained in the APA or in the agency's enabling legislation. Agency action may also be challenged as *unconstitutional* or as the product of an *erroneous interpretation of statutes*. Finally, agency action may be overturned if it is *unsubstantiated by the facts* before the agency when it acted.

In *Utility Air Regulatory Group v. Environmental Protection Agency*, a 2014 decision that follows, the Supreme Court considers whether the EPA erroneously interpreted a controlling statute when promulgating certain regulations. The Court also touches on standard-of-review questions of the sort to be discussed in a later section of the chapter.

---

[13]*Food and Drug Administration v. Brown & Williamson Tobacco Corp.*, 529 U.S. 120 (2000).

[14]406 F.3d 689 (D.C. Cir. 2005).

[15]*Id.* at 704.

Utility Air Regulatory Group v. Environmental Protection Agency
573 U.S. 302 (2014)

The federal Clean Air Act (Act) regulates pollution-generating emissions from both stationary sources, such as factories and power plants, and moving sources, such as cars, trucks, and aircraft. The act requires that stationary sources obtain, in some instances, permits from the Environmental Protection Agency (EPA) or a suitable state authority. Its "Prevention of Significant Deterioration" (PSD) provisions make it unlawful to construct or modify a "major emitting facility" in "any area to which [the PSD program] applies" unless a permit has been issued. A "major emitting facility" is a stationary source with the potential to emit 250 tons per year of "any air pollutant" (or 100 tons per year for certain types of sources). Facilities seeking a PSD permit must comply with emissions limitations that reflect the "best available control technology" (BACT) for "each pollutant subject to regulation" under the act. In addition, Title V of the act makes it unlawful to operate any "major source," wherever located, without a permit. A "major source" is a stationary source with the potential to emit 100 tons per year of "any air pollutant."

In Massachusetts v. Environmental Protection Agency, *549 U.S. 497 (2007), the Supreme Court held that the act's general definition of "air pollutant" may include greenhouse gases. In response to that decision, the EPA promulgated greenhouse-gas emission standards for new motor vehicles. The EPA also concluded that stationary sources would be subject to the PSD program and Title V on the basis of their potential to emit greenhouse gases. The EPA recognized, however, that requiring permits for all sources with greenhouse-gas emissions above the statutory thresholds would drastically expand those programs and create a huge administrative burden that Congress probably would not have wanted. Therefore, the EPA opted for a regulation meant to "tailor" the programs to accommodate greenhouse gases (hereinafter, the Tailoring Rule).*

The Tailoring Rule provided that sources would not become newly subject to the PSD and Title V permit requirements on the basis of their potential to emit greenhouse gases in amounts less than 100,000 tons per year. In addition, the Tailoring Rule stated that sources required to obtain permits anyway because of their emissions of conventional pollutants (that is, pollutants other than greenhouse-gas emissions) would need to comply with BACT as to greenhouse gases if their greenhouse-gas emissions met a certain threshold (at least 75,000 tons per year, according to the regulation). (Those sources already subject to the permit requirements will be referred to below as the "anyway" sources.) The Tailoring Rule also indicated that in future years, the EPA might choose to adjust the thresholds it had set in the regulation.

In petitions for review filed in the U.S. Court of Appeals for the D.C. Circuit, numerous parties, including several states, challenged the Tailoring Rule and related EPA regulations as inconsistent with—and unauthorized by—the Clean Air Act. For the most part, the D.C. Circuit ruled in favor of the EPA and upheld the challenged regulations. The Supreme Court granted certiorari. Further relevant facts appear in the following edited version of the Court's opinion.

Scalia, Justice

In *Massachusetts v. Environmental Protection Agency*, 549 U.S. 497 (2007), the Court held that Title II of the Clean Air Act "authorize[d] EPA to regulate greenhouse gas emissions from new motor vehicles" if the Agency "form[ed] a judgment that such emissions contribute to climate change." *Id.* at 528. EPA [then] asked the public, in a notice of proposed rulemaking, to comment on how the Agency should respond to *Massachusetts*.

In doing so, EPA explained that regulating greenhouse-gas emissions from motor vehicles could have far-reaching consequences for stationary sources. Under EPA's view, once greenhouse gases became regulated under any part of the Act, the PSD and Title V permitting requirements would apply to all stationary sources with the potential to emit greenhouse gases in excess of the statutory thresholds: 100 tons per year under Title V, and 100 or 250 tons per year under the PSD program depending on the type of source. [The notice of proposed rulemaking stated that] because greenhouse-gas emissions tend to be "orders of magnitude greater" than emissions of conventional pollutants, . . . numerous small sources not previously regulated under the Act would be swept into the PSD program and Title V, including "smaller industrial sources," "large office and residential buildings, hotels, large retail establishments, and similar facilities." [EPA] warned that this would constitute an "unprecedented expansion of EPA authority that would have a profound effect on virtually every sector of the economy and touch every household in the land," yet still be "relatively ineffective at reducing greenhouse gas concentrations."

EPA [later] announced its determination regarding the danger posed by motor vehicle greenhouse-gas emissions. Next, EPA issued its final decision regarding the prospect that motor-vehicle greenhouse-gas standards would trigger stationary-source permitting requirements. EPA announced [in its Triggering Rule] that beginning on the effective date of its [soon-to-be-issued] greenhouse-gas standards for motor vehicles, stationary sources would be subject to the PSD program and Title V on the basis of their potential to emit greenhouse gases. As expected, EPA in short order promulgated greenhouse-gas emission standards for passenger cars, light-duty trucks, and medium-duty passenger vehicles, [and stated that those standards would] take effect on January 2, 2011.

EPA then announced steps it was taking to "tailor" the PSD program and Title V to greenhouse gases. Those steps were necessary, it

said, because the PSD program and Title V were designed to regulate "a relatively small number of large industrial sources," and requiring permits for all sources with greenhouse-gas emissions above the statutory thresholds would radically expand those programs, making them both unadministrable and "unrecognizable to the Congress that designed" them. [EPA therefore issued the Tailoring Rule summarized in the above statement of facts.]

This litigation presents two distinct challenges to EPA's stance on greenhouse-gas permitting for stationary sources. First, we must decide whether EPA permissibly determined that a source may be subject to the PSD and Title V permitting requirements on the sole basis of the source's potential to emit greenhouse gases. Second, we must decide whether EPA permissibly determined that a source already subject to the PSD program because of its emission of conventional pollutants (an "anyway" source) may be required to limit its greenhouse-gas emissions by employing the "best available control technology" for greenhouse gases. The Solicitor General [(who represents the United States in cases before the Supreme Court)] joins issue on both points but evidently regards the second as more important; he informs us that "anyway" sources account for roughly 83% of American stationary-source greenhouse-gas emissions, compared to just 3% for the additional, non-"anyway" sources EPA sought to regulate [in] the Tailoring Rule.

We review EPA's interpretations of the Clean Air Act using the standard set forth in *Chevron U.S.A. Inc. v. Natural Resources Defense Council, Inc.*, 467 U.S. 837, 842–843 (1984). Under *Chevron*, we presume that when an agency-administered statute is ambiguous with respect to what it prescribes, Congress has empowered the agency to resolve the ambiguity. The question for a reviewing court is whether in doing so the agency has acted reasonably and thus has "stayed within the bounds of its statutory authority." *Arlington v. FCC*, 569 U.S. 290 (2013).

EPA thought its conclusion that a source's greenhouse-gas emissions may necessitate a PSD or Title V permit followed from the Act's unambiguous language. The Court of Appeals agreed and held that the statute "compelled" EPA's interpretation. We disagree. The statute compelled EPA's greenhouse-gas-inclusive interpretation with respect to neither the PSD program nor Title V.

The Act-wide definition says that an air pollutant is "any air pollution agent or combination of such agents, including any physical, chemical, biological, [or] radioactive . . . substance or matter which is emitted into or otherwise enters the ambient air." In *Massachusetts*, the Court held that the Act-wide definition includes greenhouse gases because it is all-encompassing; it "embraces all airborne compounds of whatever stripe." But where the term "air pollutant" appears in the Act's operative provisions, EPA has routinely given it a narrower, context-appropriate meaning.

That is certainly true of the provisions that require PSD and Title V permitting for major emitters of "any air pollutant." Since 1978, EPA's regulations have interpreted "air pollutant" in the PSD permitting trigger as limited to *regulated* air pollutants—a class much narrower than *Massachusetts'* "all airborne compounds of whatever stripe." And since 1993 EPA has informally taken the same position with regard to the Title V permitting trigger, a position the Agency ultimately incorporated into some of the regulations at issue here. It is plain as day that the Act does not envision an elaborate, burdensome permitting process for major emitters of steam, oxygen, or other harmless airborne substances. It takes some cheek for EPA to insist that it cannot possibly give "air pollutant" a reasonable, context-appropriate meaning in the PSD and Title V contexts when it has been doing precisely that for decades.

Nor are those the only places in the Act where EPA has inferred from statutory context that a generic reference to air pollutants does not encompass every substance falling within the Act-wide definition. Other examples abound. [*Author's note:* The Court went on to cite various EPA regulations that by their terms apply to a narrower range of air pollutants than what the broad act-wide definition of air pollutants would contemplate. Those further examples are omitted here.] Although these limitations are nowhere to be found in the Act-wide definition, in each instance EPA has concluded . . . that the statute is not using "air pollutant" in *Massachusetts'* broad sense to mean any airborne substance whatsoever.

Massachusetts did not invalidate all these longstanding constructions. That case did not hold that EPA must always regulate greenhouse gases as an "air pollutant" everywhere that term appears in the statute, but only that EPA must "ground its reasons for action *or inaction* in the statute," rather than on "reasoning divorced from the statutory text." EPA's inaction with regard to Title II was not sufficiently grounded in the statute, the Court said, in part because nothing in the Act suggested that regulating greenhouse gases under that Title would conflict with the statutory design. Title II would not compel EPA to regulate in any way that would be "extreme," "counterintuitive," or contrary to "common sense." At most, it would require EPA to take the modest step of adding greenhouse-gas standards to the roster of new motor vehicle emission regulations.

Massachusetts does not strip EPA of authority to exclude greenhouse gases from the class of regulable air pollutants under other parts of the Act where their inclusion would be inconsistent with the statutory scheme. The Act-wide definition to which the Court gave a

"sweeping" and "capacious" interpretation is not a command to regulate, but a description of the universe of substances EPA may *consider* regulating under the Act's operative provisions. *Massachusetts* does not foreclose the Agency's use of statutory context to infer that certain of the Act's provisions use "air pollutant" to denote not every conceivable airborne substance, but only those that may sensibly be encompassed within the particular regulatory program.

To be sure, Congress's profligate use of "air pollutant" where what is meant is obviously narrower than the Act-wide definition is not conducive to clarity. One ordinarily assumes "that identical words used in different parts of the same act are intended to have the same meaning." [Citation omitted.] In this respect (as in countless others), the Act is far from a *chef d'oeuvre* of legislative draftsmanship. But we, and EPA, must do our best, bearing in mind the "fundamental canon of statutory construction that the words of a statute must be read in their context and with a view to their place in the overall statutory scheme." *FDA v. Brown & Williamson Tobacco Corp.*, 529 U.S. 120, 133 (2000).

We need not, and do not, pass on the validity of all the limiting constructions EPA has given the term "air pollutant" throughout the Act. We merely observe that taken together, they belie EPA's rigid insistence that when interpreting the PSD and Title V permitting requirements it is bound by the Act-wide definition's inclusion of greenhouse gases, no matter how incompatible that inclusion is with those programs' regulatory structure.

Having determined that EPA was mistaken in thinking the Act *compelled* a greenhouse-gas-inclusive interpretation of the PSD and Title V triggers, we next consider the Agency's alternative position that its interpretation was justified as an exercise of its "discretion" to adopt "a reasonable construction of the statute" (quoting the Tailoring Rule). We conclude that EPA's interpretation is not permissible.

Even under *Chevron's* deferential framework, agencies must operate "within the bounds of reasonable interpretation." *Arlington*, 569 U.S. at 296. And reasonable statutory interpretation must account for both "the specific context in which . . . language is used" and "the broader context of the statute as a whole." [Citation omitted.]

EPA itself has repeatedly acknowledged that applying the PSD and Title V permitting requirements to greenhouse gases would be inconsistent with—in fact, would overthrow—the Act's structure and design. In the Tailoring Rule, EPA described the calamitous consequences of interpreting the Act in that way. Under the PSD program, annual permit applications would jump from about 800 to nearly 82,000; annual administrative costs would swell from $12 million to over $1.5 billion; and decade-long delays in issuing permits would become common, causing construction projects to grind to a halt nationwide. The picture under Title V was equally bleak: The number of sources required to have permits would jump from fewer than 15,000 to about 6.1 million; annual administrative costs would balloon from $62 million to $21 billion; and collectively the newly covered sources would face permitting costs of $147 billion.

Moreover, "the great majority of additional sources brought into the PSD and title V programs would be small sources that Congress did not expect would need to undergo permitting." EPA stated that these results would be so "contrary to congressional intent," and would so "severely undermine what Congress sought to accomplish," that they necessitated as much as a 1,000-fold increase in the permitting thresholds set forth in the statute.

Like EPA, we think it beyond reasonable debate that requiring permits for sources based solely on their emission of greenhouse gases at the 100- and 250-tons-per-year levels set forth in the statute would be incompatible with the substance of Congress' regulatory scheme. [There is] no doubt that the PSD program and Title V are designed to apply to, and cannot rationally be extended beyond, a relative handful of large sources capable of shouldering heavy substantive and procedural burdens.

The fact that EPA's greenhouse-gas-inclusive interpretation of the PSD and Title V triggers would place plainly excessive demands on limited governmental resources is alone a good reason for rejecting it; but that is not the only reason. EPA's interpretation is also unreasonable because it would bring about an enormous and transformative expansion in EPA's regulatory authority without clear congressional authorization. The power to require permits for the construction and modification of tens of thousands, and the operation of millions, of small sources nationwide falls comfortably within the class of authorizations that we have been reluctant to read into ambiguous statutory text. Moreover, in EPA's assertion of that authority, we confront a singular situation: an agency laying claim to extravagant statutory power over the national economy while at the same time strenuously asserting that the authority claimed would render the statute "unrecognizable to the Congress that designed" it (quoting the Tailoring Rule).

EPA thought that despite the foregoing problems, it could make its interpretation reasonable by adjusting the levels at which a source's greenhouse-gas emissions would oblige it to undergo PSD and Title V permitting. Although the Act, in no uncertain terms, requires permits for sources with the potential to emit more than 100 or 250 tons per year of a relevant pollutant, EPA in its Tailoring Rule wrote a new threshold of *100,000* tons per year for greenhouse gases. We conclude that EPA's rewriting of the statutory thresholds was impermissible and therefore could not validate the Agency's interpretation of the triggering provisions. An agency has no power to "tailor" legislation to bureaucratic policy goals by rewriting unambiguous statutory terms. Agencies exercise discretion only in the interstices created by statutory silence or ambiguity; they must always "give effect to the unambiguously expressed intent of Congress." *Chevron*, 467 U.S. at 843.

We reaffirm the core administrative-law principle that an agency may not rewrite clear statutory terms to suit its own sense of how the statute should operate. EPA therefore lacked authority to "tailor" the Act's unambiguous numerical thresholds to accommodate

its greenhouse-gas-inclusive interpretation of the permitting triggers. Instead, the need to rewrite clear provisions of the statute should have alerted EPA that it had taken a wrong interpretive turn.

For the reasons we have given, EPA overstepped its statutory authority when it decided that a source could become subject to PSD or Title V permitting by reason of its greenhouse-gas emissions. But what about "anyway" sources, those that would need permits based on their emissions of more conventional pollutants (such as particulate matter)? The question before us is whether EPA's decision to require BACT for greenhouse gases emitted by sources otherwise subject to PSD review is, as a general matter, a permissible interpretation of the statute under *Chevron*. We conclude that it is.

The text of the BACT provision is far less open-ended than the text of the PSD and Title V permitting triggers. It states that BACT is required "for each pollutant subject to regulation" [under the Act], a phrase that . . . "would not seem readily susceptible [of] misinterpretation." [Citation omitted.] Whereas the dubious breadth of "any air pollutant" in the permitting triggers suggests a role for agency judgment in identifying the subset of pollutants covered by the particular regulatory program at issue, the more specific phrasing of the BACT provision suggests that the necessary judgment has already been made by Congress.

Even if the text were not clear, applying BACT to greenhouse gases is not so disastrously unworkable, and need not result in such a dramatic expansion of agency authority, as to convince us that EPA's interpretation is unreasonable. We are not talking about extending EPA jurisdiction over millions of previously unregulated entities, but about moderately increasing the demands EPA (or a state permitting authority) can make of entities already subject to its regulation. And it is not yet clear that EPA's demands will be of a significantly different character from those traditionally associated with PSD review. In short, the record before us does not establish that the BACT provision as written is incapable of being sensibly applied to greenhouse gases. Our narrow holding is that nothing in the statute categorically prohibits EPA from interpreting the BACT provision to apply to greenhouse gases emitted by "anyway" sources.

To sum up: We hold that EPA exceeded its statutory authority when it interpreted the Clean Air Act to require PSD and Title V permitting for stationary sources based on their greenhouse-gas emissions. Specifically, the Agency may not treat greenhouse gases as a pollutant for purposes of defining a "major emitting facility" (or a "modification" thereof) in the PSD context or a "major source" in the Title V context. To the extent its regulations purport to do so, they are invalid. EPA may, however, continue to treat greenhouse gases as a "pollutant subject to regulation under this chapter" for purposes of requiring BACT for "anyway" sources.

Court of Appeals decision affirmed in part and reversed in part.

Standards of Review The degree of scrutiny that courts will apply to agency action depends on the nature of issues in dispute and the type of agency proceedings that produced the challenged action. Courts are least likely to defer to agency action when *questions of law* are at issue. Although courts afford substantial consideration to an agency's interpretations of the statutes it enforces, the courts are still the ultimate arbiters of the meaning of statutes and constitutional provisions. The *Utility Regulatory Air Group* decision, which appears above, serves as an example.

When *questions of fact or policy* are at issue, courts are more likely to defer to the agency because it presumably has superior expertise and because the agency fact finders who heard and viewed the evidence were better situated to judge its merit. When agency factual judgments are at stake, the APA provides for three standards of review, the most rigorous of which is *de novo* review.

When conducting a *de novo* review, courts make an independent finding of the facts after conducting a new hearing. Efficiency considerations plainly favor limited judicial review of the facts. Accordingly, *de novo* review is employed only when required by statute, when inadequate fact-finding proceedings were used in an agency adjudicatory proceeding, or when new factual issues that were not before the agency are raised in a proceeding to enforce a nonadjudicatory agency action.

When courts review formal agency adjudications or formal rulemaking, the APA calls for the application of a substantial evidence test. Only agency findings that are "unsupported by substantial evidence" will be overturned. In conducting substantial evidence reviews, courts look at the reasonableness of an agency's actions in relation to the facts before it rather than conducting an independent fact-finding hearing. The substantial evidence test also tends to be employed in hybrid rulemaking cases.

A 2015 Supreme Court decision serves as an example of judicial review of the reasonableness of an agency's actions. In *Michigan v. Environmental Protection Agency*,[16] the Supreme Court reviewed regulatory action by the Environmental Protection Agency (EPA). The EPA had been empowered under

---

[16] 135 S. Ct. 2699 (2015).

the Clean Air Act to regulate emissions of hazardous air pollutants from stationary sources such as power plants, if the EPA studied hazards to public health and concluded that emissions regulations were "appropriate and necessary." The EPA studied the matter and concluded that regulatory action was both appropriate and necessary, but refused to consider costs to power plants when it devised the regulations. The costs to the regulated plants were alleged to be considerably in excess of the quantifiable public health benefits in terms of reduction of emissions. Striking down the regulations, the Supreme Court held that in refusing to consider costs, the EPA unreasonably interpreted the Clean Air Act provision that gave the agency the authority to regulate.

The judicial standard of review often used in cases involving informal agency adjudications or rulemaking is the arbitrary and capricious test. This is the least rigorous standard of judicial review because it grants a great degree of deference to agency decisions. It is important to keep in mind that in the rulemaking context, the arbitrary and capricious test and the considerable deference it affords to the agency apply only where ambiguities in the governing statute effectively cry out for clarifying regulatory interpretations or where the statute specifically contemplates that reasonable, complementary agency regulations should be promulgated. An agency cannot adopt a regulatory interpretation that contradicts an unambiguous statutory provision and then expect deference from the courts regarding that interpretation.

In deciding whether an agency's action was arbitrary and capricious, a reviewing court should not substitute its judgment for that of the agency. Instead, it should ask whether there was an adequate factual basis for the agency's action, and should sustain actions that do not amount to a "clear error of judgment." Although the substantial evidence and arbitrary and capricious tests are separate and distinct in theory, the distinctions often tend to blur in actual practice.

In the *Mayo Foundation* case, which follows, the Supreme Court applies the arbitrary and capricious test in deciding whether to uphold a Treasury Department regulation that interpreted an Internal Revenue Code provision dealing with students. The Court also outlines the circumstances appropriate for judicial deference to agency interpretations of statutes.

Mayo Foundation for Medical Education v. United States
562 U.S. 44 (2011)

The Mayo Foundation for Medical Education and Research, the Mayo Clinic, and the Regents of the University of Minnesota offer residency programs to doctors who have graduated from medical school and seek additional instruction in a chosen specialty. (The three entities offering the residency programs will be referred to collectively as Mayo.) These programs, which typically last for three to *five years, train physicians primarily through hands-on experience. Although residents are required to take part in formal educational activities, these doctors generally spend the bulk of their time—typically 50 to 80 hours a week—caring for patients. Residents are generally supervised in this work by more senior residents and by faculty members known as attending physicians. Mayo pays its residents annual stipends (ranging from $41,000 to $56,000 at the time of the case described below) and provides them with health insurance, malpractice insurance, and paid vacation time.*

Congress enacted the Federal Insurance Contributions Act (FICA) in order to collect funds for the Social Security program. FICA requires employees and employers to pay taxes on all "wages" employees receive. The statute defines "wages" to include "all remuneration for employment." FICA also broadly defines "employment" as "any service . . . performed . . . by an employee for the person employing him." However, FICA excludes from taxation any "service performed in the employ of . . . a school, college, or university . . . if such service is performed by a student who is enrolled and regularly attending classes at [the school, college, or university]." 26 U.S.C. § 3121(b)(10). The Social Security Act, which governs workers' eligibility for benefits, contains a corresponding student exception that is nearly identical to § 3121(b)(10).

Since 1951, the U.S. Treasury Department (Department) has construed the student exception to exempt from taxation students who work for their schools "as an incident to and for the purpose of pursuing a course of study" (quoting a Treasury Department regulation). For many years, the Department determined whether an individual's work was "incident to" his studies by performing a case-by-case analysis that focused on the number of hours worked and the course load taken. Because the case-by-case approach proved to be problematic administratively and in other ways, the Department "determined that it [wa]s necessary to provide additional clarification" of the term "student," as used in § 3121(b)(10), particularly with respect to individuals who perform "services that are in the nature of on the job training" (quoting the Federal Register*).*

Therefore, after solicitation of comments and a public hearing, the Department issued a new regulation in late 2004. This regulation, referred to here as the full-time employee rule, stated that an employee's service is "incident" to his studies only when "[t]he educational aspect of the relationship between the employer and the employee, as compared to the service aspect of the relationship, [is] predominant." The full-time employee rule categorically provides that "[t]he services of a full-time employee"—which includes an employee normally scheduled to work 40 hours or more per week—"are not incident to and for the purpose of pursuing a course of study." According to the rule, this analysis "is not affected by the fact that the services . . . may have an educational, instructional, or training aspect." In addition, the rule offers the example of a medical resident whose normal schedule requires him to perform services 40 or more hours per week, and concludes that such a resident is not a student.

Mayo filed suit, asserting that the full-time employee rule was invalid. A federal district court agreed and granted summary judgment in Mayo's favor after finding the full-time employee rule inconsistent with FICA's unambiguous text. The U.S. Court of Appeals for the Eighth Circuit reversed. The Eighth Circuit concluded that the Department's regulation was a permissible interpretation of an ambiguous statute. The Supreme Court granted Mayo's petition for certiorari.

Roberts, Chief Justice

Nearly all Americans who work for wages pay taxes on those wages under the Federal Insurance Contributions Act (FICA), which Congress enacted to collect funds for Social Security. The question presented in this case is whether doctors who serve as medical residents are properly viewed as "student[s]" whose service Congress has exempted from FICA taxes under 26 U.S.C. § 3121(b)(10).

[Basic facts concerning Mayo's residency program are set forth above.] Mayo residents also take part in "a formal and structured educational program" (quoting Mayo's brief). Residents are assigned textbooks and journal articles to read and are expected to attend weekly lectures and other conferences. Residents also take written exams and are evaluated by the attending faculty physicians. But the parties do not dispute that the bulk of residents' time is spent caring for patients.

We begin our analysis [of the Treasury Department's full-time employee rule] with the first step of the two-part framework announced in *Chevron U.S.A. Inc. v. Natural Resources Defense Council, Inc.*, 467 U.S. 837, 842–43 (1984), and ask whether Congress has "directly addressed the precise question at issue." We agree with the Eighth Circuit that Congress has not done so. The statute does not define the term "student," and does not otherwise attend to the precise question whether medical residents are subject to FICA.

Mayo nonetheless contends that the full-time employee rule must be rejected under *Chevron* step one. Mayo argues that the dictionary definition of "student"—one "who engages in 'study' by applying the mind 'to the acquisition of learning, whether by means of books, observation, or experiment'"—plainly encompasses residents. Brief for Petitioners 22 (quoting *Oxford Universal Dictionary*). And, Mayo adds, residents are not excluded from that category by the only limitation on students Congress has imposed under the statute—that they "be 'enrolled and regularly attending classes at [a] school.'" *Id.* (quoting 26 U.S.C. § 3121(b)(10)).

Mayo's reading does not eliminate the statute's ambiguity as applied to working professionals. In its reply brief, Mayo acknowledges that a full-time professor taking evening classes—a person who presumably would satisfy the statute's class-enrollment requirement and apply his mind to learning—could be excluded from the exemption and taxed because he is not predominantly a student. Medical residents might likewise be excluded on the same basis; the statute itself does not resolve the ambiguity.

The district court interpreted § 3121(b)(10) as unambiguously foreclosing the Department's rule by mandating that an employee be deemed "a 'student' so long as the educational aspect of his service predominates over the service aspect of the relationship with his employer." We do not think it possible to glean so much from the little that § 3121 provides. In any event, the statutory text still would offer no insight into how Congress intended predominance to be determined or whether Congress thought that medical residents would satisfy the requirement. In sum, neither the plain text of the statute nor the district court's interpretation of the exemption "speak[s] with the precision necessary to say definitively whether [the statute] applies" to medical residents. [Citation omitted.]

[The ambiguity discussed above leads us to] *Chevron* step two, under which we may not disturb an agency rule unless it is "arbitrary or capricious in substance, or manifestly contrary to the statute." [Citation omitted.] *Chevron* recognized that "[t]he power of an administrative agency to administer a congressionally created . . . program necessarily requires the formulation of policy and the making of rules to fill any gap left, implicitly or explicitly, by Congress." 467 U.S. at 843. It acknowledged that the formulation of that policy might require "more than ordinary knowledge respecting the matters subjected to agency regulations." *Id.* at 844. Filling gaps in the Internal Revenue Code plainly requires the Treasury Department to make interpretive choices for statutory implementation. Cf. *Bob Jones Univ. v. United States*, 461 U.S. 574, 596 (1983) ("[I]n an area as complex as the tax system, the agency Congress vests with administrative responsibility must be able to exercise its authority to meet changing conditions and new problems.").

The Department issued the full-time employee rule pursuant to the explicit [statutory] authorization to "prescribe all needful rules and regulations for the enforcement" of the Internal Revenue Code. 26 U.S.C. § 7805(a). We have found such "express congressional authorizations to engage in the process of rulemaking" to be "a very good indicator of delegation meriting *Chevron* treatment." [Citation omitted.] We have explained that "the ultimate question is whether Congress would have intended, and expected, courts to treat [the regulation] as within, or outside, its delegation to the agency of 'gap-filling' authority." [Citation omitted.]

The full-time employee rule easily satisfies the second step of *Chevron*, which asks whether the Department's rule is a "reasonable interpretation" of the enacted text. 467 U.S. at 844. To begin, Mayo accepts that "the 'educational aspect of the relationship between the employer and the employee, as compared to the service aspect of the relationship, [must] be predominant'" in order for an individual to qualify for the exemption. Reply Brief for Petitioners 6–7 (quoting the full-time employee rule). Mayo objects, however, to the Department's conclusion that residents who work more than 40 hours per week categorically cannot satisfy that requirement. Because residents' employment is itself educational, Mayo argues, the hours a resident spends working make him "more of a student, not less of one." Reply Brief for Petitioners 15. Mayo contends that the Treasury Department should be required to engage in a case-by-case inquiry into "*what* [each] employee does [in his service] and *why*" he does it. *Id.* at 7. Mayo also objects that the Department has drawn an arbitrary distinction between "hands-on training" and "classroom instruction." Brief for Petitioners 35.

We disagree. Regulation, like legislation, often requires drawing lines. Mayo does not dispute that the Treasury Department reasonably sought a way to distinguish between workers who study and students who work. Focusing on the hours an individual works and the hours he spends in studies is a perfectly sensible way of accomplishing that goal. The Department explained that an individual's service and his "course of study are separate and distinct activities" in "the vast majority of cases," and reasoned that "[e]mployees who are working enough hours to be considered full-time employees . . . have filled the conventional measure of available time with work, and not study" (quoting the *Federal Register*). The Department thus did not distinguish classroom education from clinical training but rather education from service. The Department reasonably concluded that its full-time employee rule would improve administrability, and it thereby "has avoided the wasteful litigation and continuing uncertainty that would inevitably accompany any purely case-by-case approach" like the one Mayo advocates. [Citation omitted.]

As the Treasury Department has explained, moreover, the full-time employee rule has more to recommend it than administrative convenience. The Department reasonably determined that taxing residents under FICA would further the purpose of the Social Security Act and comport with this Court's precedent. As the Treasury Department appreciated, this Court has understood the terms of the Social Security Act to "import a breadth of coverage," and we have instructed that "exemptions from taxation are to be construed narrowly." [Citations omitted.] Although Mayo contends that medical residents have not yet begun their "working lives" because they are not "fully trained," Reply Brief for Petitioners 13, the Department certainly did not act irrationally in concluding that these doctors—"who work long hours, serve as highly skilled professionals, and typically share some or all of the terms of employment of career employees"—are the kind of workers that Congress intended to both contribute to and benefit from the Social Security system (quoting the *Federal Register*). The Department's rule [also] takes into account the Social Security Administration's concern that exempting residents from FICA would deprive residents and their families of vital disability and survivorship benefits that Social Security provides.

We do not doubt that Mayo's residents are engaged in a valuable educational pursuit or that they are students of their craft. The question whether they are "students" for purposes of § 3121, however, is a different matter. Because it is one to which Congress has not directly spoken, and because the Treasury Department's rule is a reasonable construction of what Congress has said, the [rule] must be [upheld].

Court of Appeals decision affirmed; full-time employee rule upheld.

CYBERLAW IN ACTION

Does a federal statute, the Telecommunications Act of 1996, require cable companies to allow other firms to use their systems in order to offer high-speed Internet access services? In answering that question "no" by enacting an agency regulation to that effect, did the Federal Communications Commission improperly interpret the federal statute? The U.S. Supreme Court took up that issue and related questions in *National Cable and Telecommunications Association v. Brand X Internet Services*, 545 U.S. 967 (2005).

The Telecommunications Act of 1996 regulates providers of telecommunications services in various ways. One provision of the statute labels firms that provide "telecommunications service" as common carriers and requires them to sell other companies access to their networks (including their basic telephone service networks and their DSL Internet access lines) on a nondiscriminatory basis. Cable Internet firms furnish broadband service, which provides faster Internet access than the dial-up Internet service offered by various providers. Dial-up service providers and consumer groups, hoping to increase competition in Internet access services—particularly concerning the faster broadband variety—began asserting that cable Internet firms were subject to the Telecommunications Act provision that required the provider of a "telecommunications service" to sell other interested parties access to that provider's network. The cable Internet firms, not wanting to be forced to open up their networks to other providers, maintained that they were not subject to the Telecommunications Act requirement.

The argument that cable Internet service is a "telecommunications service" for purposes of the federal statute rested on the notion that cable Internet service consists of two parts. One part—simple data communication—is supposedly a telecommunications service. The other part, which involves the providing of more elaborate information services, is not a telecommunications service. Dial-up firms and consumer groups argued that the telecommunications service

aspect of cable Internet service fell within the Telecommunication Act's section requiring the provider of a telecommunications service to allow, for a fee and on a nondiscriminatory basis, access to its networks.

In 2002, the Federal Communications Commission (FCC) rejected the position of the dial-up firms and consumer groups. The FCC did so by promulgating a regulation that interpreted the Telecommunications Act and its provision-of-access-to-networks provision as inapplicable to cable Internet service providers. In the FCC's view, as expressed in the regulation, cable Internet service providers were information service providers, not "telecommunications service" providers for purposes of the statute. Brand X Internet Services, a dial-up provider that believed it was entitled (for a fee) to obtain access to a cable Internet service provider's broadband network, filed suit alleging that the FCC's regulation was an invalid and incorrect interpretation of the Telecommunications Act. The U.S. Court of Appeals for the Ninth Circuit agreed with Brand X and held that the FCC regulation was invalid.

The Supreme Court, however, reversed the Ninth Circuit's decision. In an opinion authored by Justice Thomas, a six-justice majority stated that the Telecommunications Act provision at issue in the case was ambiguous and that when an appropriate administrative agency issues a reasonable interpretation of an ambiguous statute, courts must defer to the agency's interpretation. The majority noted that such deference is appropriate even if the Court thinks the agency's interpretation, though reasonable, is not necessarily the best interpretation. According to the Court, the FCC's 2002 regulation interpreting the Telecommunications Act qualified as a reasonable interpretation, so the Court deferred to it. After the *Brand X* decision, the FCC classified other types of broadband providers, including DSL and wireless, as information service providers—meaning that they would be exempt from the common carrier requirements set forth in the Telecommunications Act. Even so, the FCC left open the possibility that it might decide to regulate broadband providers in some fashion. Recent years' expressions of concern in some quarters about preserving "net neutrality" no doubt influenced the FCC's decision on whether to take regulatory action. Those advocating net neutrality wished to head off, whether through regulation or voluntary forbearance by broadband providers, the danger that providers might decide to (1) allow faster, higher-quality access to Internet sites they controlled or whose operators would pay a significant fee so that users would have the superior access and (2) provide slower, lower-quality access to sites whose operators were unwilling or unable to pay the fee.

In 2010, the FCC issued its Open Internet Order, in which it imposed disclosure, antiblocking, and antidiscrimination requirements on broadband providers. The disclosure requirements called for providers to disclose information regarding their network management policies and the terms of their broadband services. The antiblocking and antidiscrimination provisions were consistent with the goals of net-neutrality advocates, as noted above. Providers that stood to be affected by the Open Internet Order petitioned for review. In *Verizon v. FCC*, 740 F.3d 623 (D.C. Cir. 2014), the U.S. Court of Appeals for the D.C. Circuit held that under the Telecommunications Act and an earlier statute the Telecommunications Act amended, the FCC indeed has authority to regulate broadband providers—including the authority to promulgate rules governing such providers' treatment of Internet traffic. However, the court noted, the FCC must

exercise that authority in an appropriate way (i.e., without imposing common carrier requirements). The court concluded that the antiblocking and antidiscrimination provisions in the Open Internet Order were inappropriate in nature because they effectively were common carrier requirements. Given that the FCC had previously classified broadband providers in a manner that exempted them from common carrier treatment, the Open Internet Order's antiblocking and antidiscrimination provisions violated the governing statute's provisions establishing common carrier requirements only for providers of telecommunications services. The D.C. Circuit therefore vacated the Open Internet Order insofar as it set forth antiblocking and antidiscrimination provisions, and sent the FCC back to the drawing board. (The court upheld the disclosure requirements, however, because they were not in the nature of common carrier requirements.)

In 2015, the FCC responded to the *Verizon* decision by reclassifying broadband providers as common carriers and by implementing "net neutrality" rules that barred giving faster and preferential service regarding sites whose owners were willing to pay a premium price for such service. In 2017, however, a new FCC chairperson took charge of the agency. The FCC then announced a plan to reconsider the 2015 classification of broadband providers as common carries and to roll back the net neutrality rules. The proposed repeal generated over 20 million comments to the FCC. Despite a majority of these favoring a retention of the 2015 decision, the FCC still voted to repeal the Order, ending network neutrality regulation in the U.S.

Information Controls

Over roughly the last four decades, Congress has enacted three major statutes aimed at controlling administrative agencies through the regulation of information. Each of these statutes represents a compromise between competing social interests of significant importance. On one hand, we have a strong democratic preference for public disclosure of governmental operations, believing that "government in the dark" is less likely to be consistent with the public interest than is "government in the sunshine." On the other hand, we recognize that some sensitive governmental activities must be shielded from the scrutiny of unfriendly parties, and that disclosure of some information may unjustifiably invade personal privacy, hinder government law enforcement efforts, or provide the competitors of a company about which information is being disclosed with proprietary information that could be used unfairly to the competitors' advantage.

Freedom of Information Act

LO47-11 Explain essential features of the Freedom of Information Act and identify the major exemptions to the disclosure requirement it contemplates.

The *Freedom of Information Act (FOIA)* went into effect in 1967. Congress enacted it to enable private citizens to obtain access to documents in the government's possession. Agencies must normally respond to public requests for documents within 10 days after such a request has been received. An agency bears the burden of justifying a denial of any FOIA request. Denials are appealable to an appropriate federal district court. Successful plaintiffs may recover their costs and attorney fees.

Not all government-held documents are obtainable under the FOIA, however. The FOIA exempts from disclosure documents that:

1. Must be kept secret in the interest of national security.
2. Concern an agency's internal personnel rules and practices.
3. Are specifically exempted from disclosure by statute.
4. Contain trade secrets or other confidential or privileged commercial or financial information.
5. Are interagency or intra-agency memos or letters that would not be subject to discovery in litigation.
6. Appear in individual personnel or medical files, or in similar files if disclosure would constitute a clearly unwarranted invasion of personal privacy.

7. Would threaten the integrity of a law enforcement agency's investigations or jeopardize an individual's right to a fair trial.

8. Relate to the supervision or regulation of financial institutions.

9. Contain geological or geophysical data.

Frequent users of the FOIA include the media, industry trade associations, public interest groups, and companies seeking to obtain useful information about their competitors. The *Milner* case, which follows, deals with the second exemption listed above. It is important to note that although the FOIA allows agencies to refuse to disclose exempted documents, it does not impose on them the affirmative duty to do so. The Supreme Court has held that individuals cannot compel an agency to deny an FOIA request for allegedly exempt documents that contain sensitive information about them.

Milner v. Department of the Navy 562 U.S. 562 (2011)

The Freedom of Information Act (FOIA) requires federal agencies to make government records available to the public, subject to nine exemptions. Exemption 2 protects from disclosure material "related solely to the internal personnel rules and practices of an agency." This provision replaced a previous public disclosure law's exemption for "any matter relating solely to the internal management of an agency." According to the Supreme Court's decision in Department of the Air Force v. Rose, *425 U.S. 352 (1976), Congress believed that the "sweep" of the phrase "internal management" had led to excessive withholding, so Congress drafted Exemption 2 "to have a narrower reach."*

In Rose, the Court held that Exemption 2 could not be invoked as justification for withholding Air Force Academy honor and ethics hearing summaries. The exemption, the Court suggested, primarily targets material concerning employee relations or human resources. But the Court stated a possible caveat: That understanding of the provision's coverage governed "at least where the situation is not one where disclosure may risk circumvention of agency regulation." In Crooker v. Bureau of Alcohol, Tobacco & Firearms, *670 F.2d 1051 (D.C. Cir. 1981), the court relied on this caveat in concluding that Exemption 2 covers not only human resources and employee relations records but also any "predominantly internal" materials whose disclosure would "significantly ris[k] circumvention of agency regulation or statutes." Some other circuit courts of appeal also interpreted Exemption 2 in this manner; others did not. Courts that followed the Crooker approach to Exemption 2 began to use the term "Low 2" for human resources and employee relations records and the term "High 2" for records whose disclosure would risk circumvention of the law.*

Glen Milner submitted FOIA requests for explosives data and maps used by the Department of the Navy (referred to below as the Navy or as the government) in storing munitions at a naval base in the state of Washington (Milner's state of residence). Stating that disclosure would threaten the security of the base and surrounding community, the Navy invoked Exemption 2 and refused to release the data. A federal district court granted the Navy summary judgment. The U.S. Court of Appeals for the Ninth Circuit affirmed, relying on the High 2 interpretation. Disclosure of the requested material, the Ninth Circuit determined, would risk circumvention of the law by "pointing out the best targets for those bent on wreaking havoc." In light of the split among the courts of appeal regarding how to interpret Exemption 2, the Supreme Court granted Milner's petition for certiorari.

Kagan, Justice

Our consideration of Exemption 2's scope starts with its text. Judicial decisions since FOIA's enactment have analyzed and reanalyzed the meaning of the exemption. But comparatively little attention has focused on the provision's 12 simple words: "related solely to the internal personnel rules and practices of an agency."

The key word in that dozen—the one that most clearly marks the provision's boundaries—is "personnel." When used as an adjective, as it is here to modify "rules and practices," that term refers to human resources matters. "Personnel," in this common parlance, means "the selection, placement, and training of employees and . . . the formulation of policies, procedures, and relations with [or involving] employees or their representatives." *Webster's Third New International Dictionary* 1687 (1966). So, for example, a "personnel department" is "the department of a business firm that deals with problems affecting the employees of the firm and that usually interviews applicants for jobs." *Random House Dictionary* 1075 (1966). "Personnel management" is similarly "the phase of management concerned with the engagement and effective utilization of manpower to obtain optimum efficiency of human resources." *Webster's* 1687. And a "personnel agency" is "an agency for placing employable persons in jobs; employment agency." *Random House* 1075.

FOIA itself provides an additional example in Exemption 6. That exemption, just a few short paragraphs down from

Exemption 2, protects from disclosure "personnel and medical files and similar files the disclosure of which would constitute a clearly unwarranted invasion of personal privacy." Here too, the statute uses the term "personnel" as a modifier meaning "human resources." As we recognized in *Department of the Air Force v. Rose*, 425 U.S. 352 (1976), "the common and congressional meaning of . . . 'personnel file'" is the file "showing, for example, where [an employee] was born, the names of his parents, where he has lived from time to time, his . . . school records, results of examinations, [and] evaluations of his work performance." *Id.* at 377. It is the file typically maintained in the human resources office—otherwise known (to recall an example offered above) as the "personnel department."

Exemption 2 uses "personnel" in the exact same way. An agency's "personnel rules and practices" are its rules and practices dealing with employee relations or human resources. The D.C. Circuit, in a pre-*Crooker* decision, gave as examples "matters relating to pay, pensions, vacations, hours of work, lunch hours, parking, etc." [Citation omitted.] That "etc." is important; we doubt any court could know enough about the federal government's operations to formulate a comprehensive list. But all the rules and practices referenced in Exemption 2 share a critical feature: They concern the conditions of employment in federal agencies—such matters as hiring and firing, work rules and discipline, compensation, and benefits. Courts in practice have had little difficulty identifying the records that qualify for withholding under this reading: They are what now commonly fall within the Low 2 exemption. Our construction of the statutory language simply makes clear that Low 2 is all of 2 (and that High 2 is not 2 at all).

The statute's purpose reinforces this understanding of the exemption. We have often noted [FOIA's] "goal of broad disclosure" and insisted that the exemptions be "given a narrow compass." [Citations omitted.] This practice of construing FOIA exemptions narrowly stands on especially firm footing with respect to Exemption 2. As described [in the above statement of facts], Congress worded that provision to hem in [an earlier law's] exemption for "any matter relating solely to the internal management of an agency," which agencies had used to prevent access to masses of documents. See *Rose*, 425 U.S. at 362. We would ill-serve Congress's purpose by construing Exemption 2 to reauthorize the expansive withholding that Congress wanted to halt. Our reading instead gives the exemption the "narrower reach" Congress intended, *id.* at 363, through the simple device of confining the provision's meaning to its words.

The government resists giving "personnel" its plain meaning on the ground that Congress, when drafting Exemption 2, considered but chose not to enact language exempting "internal employment rules and practices." This drafting history, the Navy maintains [in its brief], proves that Congress did not wish "to limit the Exemption to employment-related matters," even if the adjective "personnel" conveys that meaning in other contexts. But we think the Navy's evidence insufficient: The scant history concerning this word change [just] as easily supports the inference that Congress merely swapped one synonym for another. Those of us who make use of legislative history believe that clear evidence of congressional intent may illuminate ambiguous text. We will not take the opposite tack of allowing ambiguous legislative history to muddy clear statutory language.

Exemption 2, as we have construed it, does not reach the information at issue here. [The requested] data and maps calculate and visually portray the magnitude of hypothetical detonations. By no stretch of imagination do they relate to "personnel rules and practices," as that term is most naturally understood. They concern the physical rules governing explosives, not the workplace rules governing sailors; they address the handling of dangerous materials, not the treatment of employees. The Navy therefore may not use Exemption 2, interpreted in accord with its plain meaning to cover human resources matters, to prevent disclosure of the requested maps and data.

[T]o support withholding the [requested] information, the Navy encourages us to adopt the construction of Exemption 2 pioneered by *Crooker*, which shields material not only if it meets the criteria set out above (Low 2), but also if it is "predominant[ly] interna[l]" and its "disclosure would significantly risk[] circumvention of federal agency functions" (High 2). But the *Crooker* interpretation, as already suggested, suffers from a patent flaw: It is disconnected from Exemption 2's text. The High 2 test . . . ignores the plain meaning of the adjective "personnel," and adopts a circumvention requirement with no basis or referent in Exemption 2's language. Indeed, the only way to arrive at High 2 is by taking a red pen to the statute—"cutting out some" words and "pasting in others" until little of the actual provision remains. [Citation omitted.] Because this is so, High 2 is better labeled "Non 2" (and Low 2, just 2).

In support of its text-light approach to the statute, the government relies primarily on legislative history, placing particular emphasis on the House Report concerning FOIA. A statement in that Report buttresses the High 2 understanding of the exemption.... But the Senate Report says exactly the opposite, [setting forth reasons] in support of a Low 2 interpretation. . . . In *Rose*, we gave reasons for thinking the Senate Report the more reliable of the two. *See* 425 U.S. at 366. But the more fundamental point is what we said before: Legislative history, for those who take it into account, is meant to clear up ambiguity, not create it. When presented, on the one hand, with clear statutory language and, on the other, with dueling committee reports, we must choose the language.

Presumably because *Crooker* so departs from Exemption 2's language, the government also offers another construction, which it says we might adopt "on a clean slate," "based on the plain text . . . alone." Brief for Respondent 15. On this reading, the exemption "encompasses records concerning an agency's internal rules and practices for its personnel to follow in the discharge of their governmental functions." *Id.* at 20. According to the government, this interpretation makes sense because "the phrase 'personnel rules and practices of an agency' is logically understood to mean an agency's rules and practices *for its personnel.*" *Id.* at 20 (emphasis added).

But the purported logic in the government's definition eludes us. We would not say, in ordinary parlance, that a "personnel file" is any file an employee uses, or that a "personnel department" is any department in which an employee serves. No more would we say that a "personnel rule or practice" is any rule or practice that assists an employee in doing her job. The use of the term "personnel" in each of these phrases connotes not that the file or department or practice/rule is *for* personnel, but rather that the file or department or practice/rule is *about* personnel—i.e., that it relates to employee relations or human resources. This case well illustrates the point. The records requested . . . are explosives data and maps showing the distances that potential blasts travel. This information no doubt assists Navy personnel in storing munitions. But that is not to say that the data and maps relate to "personnel rules and practices." No one staring at these charts of explosions and using ordinary language would describe them in this manner.

Although we cannot interpret Exemption 2 as the Government proposes, we recognize the strength of the Navy's interest in protecting [the requested] data and maps and other similar information. The government has informed us that "[p]ublicly disclosing the [requested] information would significantly risk undermining the Navy's ability to safely and securely store military ordnance," Brief for Respondent 47, and we have no reason to doubt that representation. The Ninth Circuit similarly cautioned that disclosure of this information could be used to "wrea[k] havoc" and "make catastrophe more likely." Concerns of this kind—a sense that certain sensitive information *should* be exempt from disclosure—in part led the *Crooker* court to formulate the High 2 standard. And

we acknowledge that our decision today upsets three decades of agency practice relying on *Crooker*, and therefore may force considerable adjustments.

We also note, however, that the government has other tools at hand to shield national security information and other sensitive materials. Most notably, Exemption 1 of FOIA prevents access to classified documents. The government generally may classify material even after receiving a FOIA request; an agency therefore may wait until that time to decide whether the dangers of disclosure outweigh the costs of classification. Exemption 3 also may mitigate the government's security concerns. That provision applies to records that any other statute exempts from disclosure, thus offering Congress an established, streamlined method to authorize the withholding of specific records that FOIA would not otherwise protect. And Exemption 7 protects "information compiled for law enforcement purposes" that meets one of six criteria, including if its release "could reasonably be expected to endanger the life or physical safety of any individual." The Navy argued below that the [requested] data and maps fall within Exemption 7, but the courts below did not decide whether the Navy could withhold the ESQD data under that exemption. [T]hat claim remains open for the Ninth Circuit to address on remand.

If these or other exemptions do not cover records whose release would threaten the nation's vital interests, the government may of course seek relief from Congress. All we hold today is that Congress has not enacted the FOIA exemption the government desires. We leave to Congress, as is appropriate, the question whether it should do so.

Exemption 2, consistent with the plain meaning of the term "personnel rules and practices," encompasses only records relating to issues of employee relations and human resources. The explosives maps and data requested here do not qualify for withholding under that exemption.

Court of Appeals decision reversed in favor of Milner; case remanded for further proceedings.

FOIA compliance has recently been the focus of considerable controversy on three points. First, budgetary cutbacks have combined with growing numbers of requests for information to produce agency delays as long as two years in responding to information requests. Courts tend to tolerate agency delays if the agency can show that it made a "due diligence" effort to respond. Second, the dramatic increase in computerized information storage that has occurred since the passage of the FOIA has created problems not specifically contemplated

by the statute, which focuses on information stored in documentary form. Do interested parties have the same rights of access to data stored in agency computers that they have to government documents? May the government destroy electronic mail messages, or must it save them? Future legislative or judicial action may be necessary for definitive resolution of such questions. Third, some members of Congress, media organizations, and public interest groups have criticized the federal government for what they see as excessive and unreasonable reliance on FOIA exemptions in order to keep documents under wraps. Calls for legislation to deal with this supposed problem are a possibility in the coming years.

Privacy Act of 1974 The Privacy Act of 1974 allows individuals to inspect files that agencies maintain on them and to request that erroneous or incomplete records be corrected. It also attempts to prevent agencies from gathering unnecessary information about individuals and forbids the disclosure of an individual's records without his written permission, except in certain specifically exempted circumstances. For example, records may be disclosed to employees of the agency that collected the information if those employees need the records to perform their duties (the "need to know" exception), to law enforcement agencies, to other agencies' personnel for "routine use" (uses for purposes compatible with the purpose for which the record was collected), and to persons filing legitimate FOIA requests. In addition, records may be disclosed if a court order requires disclosure.

Government in the Sunshine Act The Government in the Sunshine Act of 1976 was designed to ensure that "[e]very portion of every meeting of an agency shall be open to public observation." However, complete public access to all agency meetings could have the same negative consequences that unrestrained public access to agency records may sometimes produce. Accordingly, the Sunshine Act exempts certain agency meetings from public scrutiny under circumstances similar to those under which documents are exempt from disclosure under the FOIA.

Issues in Regulation

 Describe the key arguments that have led to deregulation efforts and arguments that call for reregulation.

"Old" Regulation versus "New" Regulation Some interested observers of regulatory developments over roughly the past 60 years have noted significant differences between the regulations that originated during the Progressive (1902 to 1914) and New Deal (1933 to 1938) eras and many regulations promulgated more recently. They argue not only that the number and scope of regulatory controls have increased substantially in recent years, but also that the focus and the impact of regulation have changed significantly.

Whereas earlier regulation often focused on business practices that harmed the economic interests of specific segments of society (e.g., workers, small-business owners, investors), many modern regulations focus on the health and safety of all citizens. Furthermore, whereas earlier regulations often focused on a particular industry or group of industries (e.g., the railroads or the securities industry), many modern regulations affect large segments of industry (e.g., Title VII of the Civil Rights Act of 1964 and regulations governing environmental pollution and workplace safety). Finally, whereas earlier congressional delegations of regulatory power tended to be quite broad, many more recent regulatory statutes have been extremely detailed.

What are the consequences of these changes in the nature of regulation? Far more businesses than ever before feel the impact of federal regulation, and far more areas of internal corporate decision making are affected by regulation. These changes tend to erode the historic distinction between "regulated" and other industries, and to heighten the importance of business–government relations. Detailed regulatory statutes also increase Congress's role in shaping regulatory policy at the expense of administrative discretion, making regulatory policy arguably more vulnerable to legislative lobbying efforts.

"Captive" Agencies and Agencies' "Shadows" Proponents of regulation have traditionally feared that regulatory agencies would become "captives" of the industries they were charged with regulating. Through "revolving door" appointments, by which key figures move back and forth between government and the private sector, and through excessive reliance on "experts" beholden to industry, the independence of administrative agencies may be compromised and their effectiveness as regulators destroyed.

More recently, commentators sympathetic to business have argued that similar dangers to agency independence exist in the form of the nonindustry "shadow" groups that public interest organizations maintain to monitor agency actions (e.g., the Center for Auto Safety, which monitors the work of the National Highway Transportation Safety Administration). Agencies may develop dependency relationships with their shadows or at least make decisions based in part on their shadows' anticipated reactions. Such informal means of shaping regulatory policy, when combined with the ability to challenge agency actions in court, have made public interest organizations important players in the contemporary regulatory process.

Is the Agency Doing Its Job? Regardless of whether agencies suffer from being captives or whether they are unduly influenced by their shadows, a fundamental question remains: Is the agency doing the job it

Ethics and Compliance in Action

As noted elsewhere in these pages, a longstanding concern about administrative agencies focuses on the prospect of a "revolving door" situation in which top agency personnel leave the agency to take positions in the industry regulated by the agency, or in which agency officials' desire for an eventual position in the industry causes them to go "soft" on businesses the agency is charged with regulating. The "revolving door" prospect may take other forms, such as where an industry executive philosophically opposed to the work of a certain administrative agency ends up being appointed to a prominent position in that agency when the White House would like to see the agency become less active. Consider these potential issues regarding the revolving door situation:

- What ethical obligations does an administrative agency official owe when she leaves her agency position to accept a job in the industry regulated by the agency?
- What ethical obligations does an executive of a corporation owe when he leaves his corporate position to accept a job with an administrative agency that regulates the industry in which the corporation does business?
- Is it ethical for an official of an administrative agency to inquire about possible employment in the very industry the agency is charged with regulating? What about the reverse of this situation?
- If the prevailing political winds lead to circumstances in which an avowed opponent of a certain administrative agency's work is appointed to a high-level position in that agency, does this new agency official have an ethical obligation to "buy in" to the work of the agency? If so, to what extent? Does this new agency official, on the other hand, have an ethical obligation to make efforts to change the agency? If so, to what extent?
- Is a revolving door between an administrative agency and its regulated industry necessarily a bad thing? May it be beneficial for the agency, the industry, and society in general? If so, in what way or ways?

is supposed to do? A recent example stems from the multifaceted legal problems General Motors has faced in regard to its failure to make adequate disclosures of ignition switch problems in certain older vehicles—problems that led to crashes, severe injuries, and deaths. The legal hot water for GM has included product liability litigation, criminal investigations by the federal government, and consequences for alleged failures to report the problems to regulators. In 2014, GM agreed to pay more than $30 billion in order to settle government claims that the automaker had fallen short on its obligations to inform the National Highway Transportation Safety Administration (NHTSA) of the ignition switch problems and the resulting dangers. But even if GM did not fulfill its disclosure obligations to the extent it should have, the automaker did make some disclosures to the NHTSA along those lines in earlier years. This fact raised further questions in the minds of some observers. Was the information GM provided to the NHTSA enough that the agency should have taken appropriate action such as calling for a recall of potentially affected vehicles? Even if GM was at fault, did the agency do its job? GM's legal troubles have rightly received considerable attention from Congress (through committee hearings), agency regulators, other government officials, courts, and the public. As time passes, however, an increasing amount of attention may be paid to the actions or inaction of the regulators themselves.

Deregulation versus Reregulation A useful axiom for understanding the process of social and legal evolution is that *the cost of the status quo is easier to perceive than the cost of change.* Few things are more illustrative of the operation of this axiom than the history of regulation in the United States.

In the latter years of the 19th century, the social costs of living in an unregulated environment were readily apparent. Large business organizations often abused their power at the expense of their customers, suppliers, employees, and distributors, and sought to increase their power by acquiring their competitors or driving them out of business. Market forces, standing alone, were apparently unable to protect the public from defective, and in some cases dangerous, products. As a result of these and numerous other social and historical factors, the 20th century witnessed a tremendous growth in government and in government regulation of business.

Regulation, too, has its costs. Regulatory bureaucracies generate their own internal momentum and have their own interests to protect. They may become insensitive to the legitimate concerns of the industries they regulate and the public they supposedly serve. They may continue to seek higher and higher levels of safety, heedless of the fact that life necessarily involves some elements of risk and that the total elimination of risk in a modern technological society may be impossible—or, if possible, obtainable at a cost that we cannot afford to pay. At a time when many Americans are legitimately concerned about economic efficiency, as well as the ability of U.S. companies to compete effectively in world markets against competitors who operate in less-regulated environments, these and other costs of regulation are also readily apparent.

As a result, in approximately the last 40 years, we have witnessed substantial deregulation in a number of industries such as the airline, banking, railroad, and trucking industries. The results of these efforts are, at best, mixed. The case of airline regulation should suffice to make the point. Proponents of deregulation cite the generally lower fares that deregulation has produced. Opponents tend to point to increased airline overbooking practices, reduced or eliminated services to smaller communities, and increased safety problems, all of which, they argue, are products of deregulation. The costs of deregulation have generated predictable calls for reregulating the airline industry. The ultimate outcome of the deregulation versus reregulation debate will depend on which costs we as a society decide we would prefer to pay.

Problems and Problem Cases

1. Title X of the Public Health Service Act provides federal funding for family-planning services. Section 1008 of the statute specifies that none of the federal funds provided under Title X are to be "used in programs where abortion is a method of family planning." In 1988, the Secretary of Health and Human Services issued new regulations that, among other things, prohibited family-planning services that receive Title X funds from engaging in counseling concerning the use of abortion as a method of family planning, referrals for abortion as a method of family planning, and activities amounting to encouragement or advocacy of abortion as a method of family planning. Various Title X grantees and physicians supervising Title X funds challenged the validity of the regulations and sought an injunction against their implementation. Were the regulations a permissible interpretation of § 1008? Did the regulations violate constitutional guarantees?

2. Section 9 of the Endangered Species Act (ESA) makes it unlawful for any person to "take" an endangered or threatened species of fish or wildlife. A definition section in the ESA states that *take* means "to harass, harm, pursue, hunt, school, wound, kill, trap, capture, or collect, or to attempt to engage in any such conduct." The Secretary of the Department of the Interior (the Secretary) promulgated a regulation that defined the term *harm* for purposes of the statutory language just quoted. This regulation stated that *harm* "means an act which actually kills or injures wildlife" and that "[s]uch act may include significant habitat modification or degradation where it actually kills or injures wildlife by significantly impairing essential behavioral patterns, including breeding, feeding or sheltering."

A declaratory judgment action attacking the validity of this regulation was brought against the Secretary by a group of landowners, logging companies, and families dependent on the forest products industries, and by organizations representing those parties' interests. The plaintiffs sought a judicial ruling that the regulation defining *harm* as including habitat modification or degradation was an unreasonable and erroneous interpretation of the ESA. The plaintiffs alleged that they had been injured economically by the government's application of the *harm* regulation to the red-cockaded woodpecker, an endangered species, and the northern spotted owl, a threatened species. Was the Department of the Interior's regulation a reasonable interpretation of the statute?

3. Commercial radio and television stations operate under licenses issued by the Federal Communications Commission (hereinafter, Commission) pursuant to a statutory framework set up by Congress. A federal statute prohibits licensees from broadcasting any "obscene, indecent, or profane language" between the hours of 6 A.M. and 10 P.M. The statute also instructs the Commission to enforce this prohibition. If the Commission concludes that the statute has been violated, it may impose civil monetary penalties on the broadcaster, revoke the broadcaster's license, or refuse to renew the license. The Commission first invoked the statutory ban on indecent broadcasts in 1975, declaring a daytime radio broadcast of comedian George Carlin's "Filthy Words" monologue actionably indecent. In that case, the Commission announced a definition that it continues to use today in enforcing the statutory ban. It defined indecent speech as "language that describes, in terms patently offensive as measured by contemporary community standards for

the broadcast medium, sexual or excretory activities or organs, at times of the day when there is a reasonable risk that children may be in the audience." In a 1978 decision, the Supreme Court upheld the Commission's order in the "Filthy Words" case.

In later indecency cases, the Commission announced and utilized enforcement standards that varied but gradually offered the potential to reach more uses of allegedly indecent language in broadcasts. For many years, however, these standards preserved a distinction between literal and nonliteral (or "expletive") uses of evocative language. The Commission explained that each literal "description or depiction of sexual or excretory functions must be examined in context to determine whether it is patently offensive," but that "deliberate and repetitive use . . . is a requisite to a finding of indecency" when a complaint focuses solely on the use of nonliteral expletives.

In 2004, however, the Commission declared for the first time that a nonliteral (expletive) use of the F-word or S-word could be actionably indecent, even when the word was used only once. The cases in which the Commission made this declaration arose from televised entertainment awards shows in which performers or award winners made one-time expletive uses of the F-word or the S-word. Broadcasters affected by the Commission's indecency finding in these cases challenged the Commission's decisions in federal court. The broadcasters argued that the Commission's change in enforcement stance occurred without adequate notice and without an adequate explanation, and that the Commission therefore had violated the federal Administrative Procedure Act. Were the broadcasters correct?

4. On December 10, 1986, a federal grand jury indicted James Mallen for allegedly making false statements to the Federal Deposit Insurance Corporation (FDIC) and for allegedly making false statements to a bank for the purposes of influencing the actions of the FDIC. Mallen was the president and a director of a federally insured bank at the time he was indicted. On January 20, 1987, the FDIC issued an ex parte order stating that Mallen's continued service could "pose a threat to the interests of the bank's depositors or threaten to impair public confidence in the bank." The order suspended Mallen as president and as a director of the bank and prohibited him "from further participation in any manner in the conduct of the affairs of the bank, or any other bank insured by the FDIC." In issuing the suspension order without first holding a hearing on the matter, the FDIC acted pursuant to a section of the Financial Institutions Supervisory Act. A copy of the FDIC's order was served on Mallen on January 26, 1987. Four days later, his attorney filed a written request for an "immediate administrative hearing" to commence no later than February 9. The FDIC scheduled a hearing for February 18, but on February 6, Mallen filed suit against the FDIC. Arguing that the FDIC's action denied him due process, Mallen sought a preliminary injunction against the suspension order. Was Mallen denied due process?

5. John Doe began work at the Central Intelligence Agency (CIA) in 1973 as a clerk-typist. Periodic fitness reports consistently rated him as an excellent or outstanding employee. By 1977, he had been promoted to covert electronics technician. In January 1982, Doe voluntarily told a CIA security officer that he was a homosexual. Almost immediately, the CIA placed Doe on paid administrative leave and began an investigation of his sexual orientation and conduct. Doe submitted to an extensive polygraph examination during which he denied having sexual relations with foreign nationals and maintained that he had not disclosed classified information to any of his sexual partners. The polygraph officer told Doe that the test results indicated that his responses had been truthful. Nonetheless, a month later Doe was told that the CIA's Office of Security had determined that his homosexuality posed a threat to security. CIA officials declined, however, to explain the nature of the danger. Doe was asked to resign. When he refused to do so he was dismissed by CIA Director William Webster, who "deemed it necessary and advisable in the interests of the United States to terminate [Doe's] employment with this Agency pursuant to § 102(c) of the National Security Act." The statutory section cited by the director allows termination of a CIA employee whenever the director "shall deem such termination necessary or advisable in the interests of the United States." Doe filed suit against the CIA, arguing that his termination was unlawful under § 102(c) and various constitutional guarantees. The CIA moved to dismiss Doe's complaint, arguing that the director's decision was a decision committed to agency discretion by law and thus was not subject to judicial review. Was the CIA's argument correct?

6. The federal Department of the Interior's Bureau of Reclamation (Reclamation) administers the Klamath Irrigation Project, which uses water from the Klamath River Basin to irrigate parts of Oregon and California. After the Department began developing the

Klamath Project Operation Plan (Plan) to provide water allocations among competing uses and users, the Department asked the Klamath and other Indian tribes (Basin Tribes) to consult with Reclamation on the matter. A memorandum of understanding between those parties called for assessment, in consultation with the Basin Tribes, of the impacts of the Plan on tribal trust resources. During roughly the same period, the Department's Bureau of Indian Affairs (Bureau) filed claims on behalf of the Klamath Tribe in an Oregon state court proceeding intended to allocate water rights. Because the Bureau is responsible for administering land and water held in trust for Indian tribes, it consulted with the Klamath Tribe. The Bureau and the Klamath Tribe then exchanged written memos on the appropriate scope of the claims ultimately submitted by the government for the benefit of the Tribe.

The Klamath Water Users Protective Association (Association) is a nonprofit organization, most of whose members receive water from the Klamath Irrigation Project. Because of the scarcity of water, most Association members have interests adverse to the tribal interests. The Association filed a series of requests with the Bureau under the Freedom of Information Act (FOIA), seeking access to communications between the Bureau and the Basin Tribes. In response, the Bureau turned over several documents but withheld others on the basis of FOIA Exemption 5. That exemption protects from disclosure "inter-agency or intra-agency memorandums or letters which would not be available by law to a party other than an agency in litigation with the agency." Arguing that Exemption 5 did not apply, the Association sued the Bureau and the Department under FOIA to compel release of the documents. Did Exemption 5 apply?

7. For many years, § 109 of the Federal Credit Union Act provided that "[f]ederal credit union membership shall be limited to groups having a common bond of occupation or association, or to groups within a well-defined neighborhood, community, or rural district." Until 1982, the National Credit Union Administration and its predecessor agencies consistently interpreted § 109 as requiring that the same common bond of occupation unite every member of an occupationally defined credit union. In 1982, however, the NCUA reversed its longstanding policy in order to permit credit unions to be composed of multiple unrelated employer groups. The NCUA thus began interpreting § 109's common bond requirement as applying only to each employer group in a multiple-group credit union, rather than to every member of that credit union. Several banks and the American Bankers Association sought judicial review of this action by the NCUA. They alleged that the NCUA's 1982 interpretation of § 109 was improper and impermissible. Were the banks and the Bankers Association correct?

8. Section 7(a)(2) of the federal Endangered Species Act of 1973 divides responsibilities concerning protection of endangered species between the secretary of the interior and the secretary of commerce. The statute also requires each federal agency to consult with the relevant secretary in order to ensure that any action funded by the agency would be unlikely to jeopardize the existence or habitat of an endangered or threatened species. In 1978, the two secretaries promulgated a joint resolution stating that the obligations imposed by § 7(a)(2) extended not only to actions taken in the United States but also to actions taken in foreign nations. A revised joint regulation, reinterpreting § 7(a)(2) to require consultation only for actions taken in the United States or on the high seas, was promulgated in 1986. Defenders of Wildlife (DOW), an organization dedicated to wildlife conservation and other environmental causes, sued the secretary of the interior, seeking a declaratory judgment that the 1986 regulation erroneously interpreted the geographic scope of § 7(a)(2). DOW also sought an injunction requiring the secretary to develop a new regulation restoring the interpretation set forth in the 1978 regulation. DOW took the position that it should be regarded as having standing to sue because the 1986 regulation's elimination of the consultation requirement concerning actions in foreign nations would hasten the endangerment and possible extinction of certain species, and would thus adversely affect DOW members' ability to observe animals of those species when the members made trips to nations elsewhere in the world. The federal district court denied the secretary's motion for summary judgment on the issue of whether DOW had standing to sue, granted DOW's motion for summary judgment on all issues, and ordered the secretary to develop a revised regulation. After the U.S. Court of Appeals for the Eighth Circuit affirmed, the U.S. Supreme Court granted certiorari. Did DOW possess standing to sue?

9. An agent of the Pennsylvania Department of Environmental Resources saw Disposal Service's loaded trash truck backing into a building that was used to compact waste to be loaded onto tractor-trailers for transportation and final disposal. Knowing the building's

purpose and that Disposal Service did not have a permit to operate it as a transfer station, as required by the state Solid Waste Management Act (SWMA), the agent entered the property, went into the building, and observed the operation. Disposal Service was later prosecuted for operating a transfer station without a permit. Disposal Service moved to suppress the agent's evidence, arguing that his warrantless entry onto the property violated the Fourth Amendment. The state argued that the SWMA's provisions allowing such warrantless inspections were constitutional. Should the evidence be suppressed?

10. Relying on the Freedom of Information Act (FOIA), Public Citizen Health Research Group asked the Food and Drug Administration (FDA) for documents relating to drug applications that had been abandoned for health or safety reasons. When the FDA denied this request, Public Citizen sued in federal court. Schering Corporation, which had submitted five investigational new drug applications (INDs) of the sort requested by Public Citizen, intervened as a defendant. The FDA and Schering contended that certain documents in the five INDs contained confidential commercial information and could therefore be withheld under Exemption 4 of the FOIA. Public Citizen argued that disclosure would prevent other drug companies "from repeating Schering's mistakes, thereby avoiding risk to human health." In addition, Public Citizen argued that under Exemption 4, the court should gauge whether the competitive harm done to the sponsor of an IND by the public disclosure of confidential information is outweighed by the strong public interest in safeguarding the health of human trial participants. Were Public Citizen's arguments regarding Exemption 4 legally correct? Were the requested documents subject to being withheld under Exemption 4?

11. The Commodity Futures Trading Commission (CFTC) was investigating Thomas Collins for possible civil violations of the federal Commodity Exchange Act. Among the violations of which Collins was suspected was the trading of commodities futures contracts other than on a commodities exchange. The CFTC's staff suspected that these trades were spurious trades, which (the staff theorized) were intended to enable Collins to reallocate losses to persons who would reap the maximum tax benefits from the losses. As part of this investigation, the CFTC issued a subpoena directing Collins to produce copies of his federal income tax returns for examination by the CFTC's staff. The staff's reasoning was that the presence of tax motives would be evidence of a likely violation of rules enforced by the CFTC. Collins resisted the subpoena on the ground that it would force him to incriminate himself. Collins argued that the tax returns contained information that could be evidence—or could lead to evidence—of felony violations of federal law. The CFTC argued that the tax returns were required records and that compelling their disclosure therefore would not violate the Fifth Amendment. (See Chapter 5's discussion of the required-records doctrine, which operates to eliminate Fifth Amendment privilege claims regarding the contents of such records.) A federal district court agreed with the CFTC and entered an enforcement order requiring Collins to obey the subpoena. Collins appealed to the U.S. Court of Appeals for the Seventh Circuit, renewing his Fifth Amendment arguments and further contending that for public policy reasons, the subpoena should not be enforceable against him. How did the Seventh Circuit rule?

CHAPTER 48

The Federal Trade Commission Act and Consumer Protection Laws

Doan's is a brand name used for more than 100 years for back pain medication sold on an over-the-counter basis. Shortly after its purchase of the *Doan's* trademark and the right to produce the underlying product, Ciba-Geigy Corporation (Ciba) conducted a marketing study concerning consumer perceptions of the *Doan's* medication for back pain. The study revealed that this medication had a weak image in comparison to the leading brands of analgesics, and indicated that Ciba would benefit from positioning *Doan's* as a more effective product that was strong enough for the types of pain typically experienced by persons susceptible to backaches.

In an effort to strengthen the image of *Doan's*, Ciba mounted a television and newspaper advertising campaign that lasted for eight years. The advertisements characterized *Doan's* as an effective remedy specifically for back pain and stated that the product contained a special ingredient (magnesium salicylate) not found in other over-the-counter analgesics. Some of the advertisements displayed images of competing over-the-counter pain remedies. The Federal Trade Commission (FTC) instituted an administrative proceeding against Ciba's successor-in-interest, Novartis Corporation, on the ground that the advertisements for *Doan's* were deceptive, in supposed violation of § 5 of the Federal Trade Commission Act. The FTC's theory was that even though the *Doan's* advertisements were truthful in stating that the product was effective for back pain and that it contained a special ingredient not present in other over-the-counter analgesics, the combination of the two literally true statements created an implied representation for which there was no substantiation: that because of its special ingredient, *Doan's* was superior to other analgesics in relieving back pain. It was this implied representation that the FTC alleged to be deceptive. Consider the following questions as you study this chapter:

- In FTC administrative proceedings, what legal test controls the determination of whether an advertisement was deceptive?
- May the FTC validly base a deceptive advertising proceeding on the theory that an advertisement consisting of literally true statements may nevertheless be deceptive in what it implies?
- If the theory just noted is valid, were the *Doan's* advertisements deceptive?
- If the *Doan's* advertisements were deceptive, what potential legal consequences could follow for Novartis? In particular, may that firm be ordered to engage in corrective advertising, or would a corrective advertising order violate the firm's right to freedom of speech?

LEARNING OBJECTIVES

After studying this chapter, you should be able to:

48-1 Identify the powers granted to the Federal Trade Commission (FTC) by § 5 of the FTC Act.

48-2 Describe key features of an FTC adjudicative proceeding.

48-3 Identify and explain the elements of the deception and unfairness tests employed by the FTC.

48-4 Describe the types of orders that the FTC may issue against a party held, in an adjudicative proceeding, to have engaged in deceptive or unfair commercial behavior.

48-5 Identify key features of the Telemarketing and Consumer Fraud and Abuse Prevention Act.

48-6 Identify key features and effects of the Do-Not-Call Registry established by federal agency regulations.

48-7 Explain the basic provisions of the Magnuson–Moss Warranty Act and related regulations.

48-8 Describe the purpose and major provisions of the Truth in Lending Act.

48-9 Describe the purpose and major provisions of the Fair Credit Reporting Act.

48-10 Explain major ways in which the FACT Act seeks to deal with the problem of identity theft.

48-11 Explain what the Equal Credit Opportunity Act seeks to prevent.

48-12 Identify the purpose of the Fair Credit Billing Act.

48-13 Identify major consumer-protection features in the Dodd–Frank Act.

48-14 Explain the purpose of the Fair Debt Collection Practices Act and describe its major requirements.

48-15 Describe ways in which the Consumer Product Safety Commission may act in order to address product safety issues.

DURING THE PAST several decades, *direct government regulation* of consumer matters has become a prominent feature of the legal landscape at the federal and state levels. This chapter addresses federal consumer protection regulation. It begins with a general discussion of America's main consumer watchdog, the Federal Trade Commission (FTC). After describing how the FTC operates, the chapter examines its regulation of anticompetitive, deceptive, and unfair business practices. Then we discuss various federal laws that deal with consumer credit and other consumer matters.

The Federal Trade Commission

The Federal Trade Commission (FTC) was formed shortly after the 1914 enactment of the Federal Trade Commission Act (FTC Act).[1] Because the FTC is an independent federal agency, it is outside the executive branch of the federal government and is less subject to political control than agencies that are executive departments. The FTC is headed by five commissioners appointed by the president and confirmed by the Senate for staggered seven-year terms. The president

designates one of the commissioners as chair of the FTC. The FTC has a Washington headquarters and several regional offices located throughout the United States.

The FTC's Powers

 LO48-1 Identify the powers granted to the Federal Trade Commission (FTC) by § 5 of the FTC Act.

The FTC's principal missions are to keep the U.S. economy both *free* and *fair*. Congress has given the commission many tools for accomplishing these missions. By far the most important, however, is § 5 of the FTC Act, which empowers the commission to prevent *unfair methods of competition* and *unfair or deceptive acts or practices*. We examine these bases of FTC authority later in this chapter. The commission also enforces a number of the consumer protection and consumer credit measures discussed in the last half of the chapter. Finally, the FTC enforces numerous other federal laws relating to specific industries or lines of commerce.

FTC Enforcement Procedures The FTC has various legal means for ensuring compliance with the

[1]See Chapter 47 for further discussion of the FTC's creation, organization, powers, and status as an independent agency.

statutes it administers. Three important FTC enforcement devices are its procedures for facilitating voluntary compliance, its issuance of trade regulation rules, and its adjudicative proceedings.

Voluntary Compliance The FTC promotes voluntary business behavior by issuing advisory opinions and industry guides. An advisory opinion is the commission's response to a private party's query about the legality of proposed business conduct. The FTC is not obligated to furnish advisory opinions. The commission may rescind a previously issued opinion when the public interest requires. When the FTC does so, however, it cannot proceed against the opinion's recipient for actions taken in good faith reliance on the opinion, unless it gives the recipient notice of the rescission and an opportunity to discontinue those actions.

Industry guides are FTC interpretations of the laws it administers. Their purpose is to encourage businesses to abandon certain unlawful practices. To further this end, industry guides are written in lay language. Although industry guides lack the force of law, behavior that violates an industry guide often violates one of the statutes or other rules the commission enforces.

Sometimes FTC guidelines that are designed to shape behavior in a particular industry depend not only on voluntary compliance by affected businesses, but also on the notion that an informed citizenry will expect such compliance. For instance, in a widely publicized 2011 effort to address the problem of childhood obesity, the FTC announced proposed guidelines for the advertising of certain food products when the ads are directed toward children and the food products possess high levels of sugar, fat, or salt. The voluntary nature of the guidelines would mean that a violator of them would not face legal liability. However, active promotion of the guidelines by the FTC and resulting public awareness of them could operate to cause companies to conclude that following the guidelines would be the "right" thing to do or would otherwise make good business sense.

Trade Regulation Rules Unlike industry guides, FTC trade regulation rules are written in legalistic language and have the force of law. Thus, the FTC can proceed directly against those who engage in practices forbidden by a trade regulation rule. This may occur through the *adjudicative proceedings* discussed immediately below. For each knowing violation of a trade regulation rule, the FTC can ask a federal district court to impose a monetary penalty on the violator.

FTC Adjudicative Proceedings

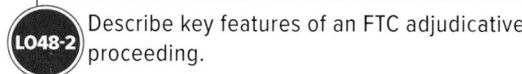

LO48-2 Describe key features of an FTC adjudicative proceeding.

Often, the FTC proceeds against violators of statutes or trade regulation rules by administrative action within the commission itself. The FTC obtains evidence of possible violations from private parties, government bodies, and its own investigations. If the FTC decides to proceed against the alleged offender (the *respondent*), it enters a formal complaint. The case is heard in a public administrative hearing called an *adjudicative proceeding.* An FTC administrative law judge presides over this proceeding.[2] The judge's decision can be appealed to the FTC's five commissioners and then to the federal courts of appeals and the U.S. Supreme Court.

The usual penalty resulting from a final decision against the respondent is an FTC cease-and-desist order. This is a command ordering the respondent to stop its illegal behavior. As you will see later in the chapter, however, FTC orders may go beyond the command to cease and desist. The civil penalty for noncompliance with a cease-and-desist order is up to $40,000 per violation. Where there is a continuing failure to obey a final order, each day that the violation continues is considered a separate violation.

Many alleged violations are never adjudicated by the FTC. Instead, they are settled through a **consent order**. This is an order approving a negotiated agreement in which the respondent promises to cease certain activities. For instance, a 2014 consent order resolved a case in which the FTC alleged that a Nissan television commercial violated FTC Act § 5's prohibition on deceptive commercial practices. (Discussion of § 5 will follow shortly, as will discussion of the case against Nissan.) Consent orders normally provide that the respondent does not admit any violation of the law. The failure to observe a consent order is punishable by civil penalties.

Actions in Court An adjudicative proceeding is not the only way the FTC can take action, however. The commission can file suit in federal court against violators of trade regulation rules or § 5 of the FTC Act (discussed below). If the commission prevails, the court can issue injunctions and other related relief, such as consumer redress taking the form of monetary recovery. Recent signs suggest that the FTC may be resorting to actions in court more frequently than was the practice for a number of years. One example is the 2014 filing

---

[2]Chapter 47 describes federal administrative proceedings.

of a suit against T-Mobile over alleged "cramming"—supposedly billing customers for premium texting services that they never requested.

FTC v. Ross, which follows, provides an illustration of an FTC decision to litigate in court rather than by way of an adjudicative proceeding. *Ross* also explores courts'

authority to order consumer redress in FTC cases regarding deceptive commercial practices, as well as key questions to which corporate executives should pay careful attention: whether they can be held individually liable for FTC Act transgressions their companies committed, and, if so, under what circumstances.

Federal Trade Commission v. Ross   743 F.3d 886 (4th Cir. 2014)

The Federal Trade Commission (Commission) filed suit in a federal district court against Innovative Marketing Inc. (IMI) and several of its high-level executives for violating the deceptive advertising prohibition set forth in the Federal Trade Commission Act (FTC Act). Kristy Ross, a vice president at IMI, was among the executives named as defendants. The Commission alleged that the defendants operated "a massive, Internet-based scheme that trick[ed] consumers into purchasing computer security software," referred to as "scareware." Under this scheme, Internet advertisements would advise consumers that a scan of their computers had detected various dangerous files, such as viruses, spyware, and "illegal" pornography. In reality, however, no scans were ever conducted.

The defendants other than Ross either settled with the Commission or did not appear in the case and had default judgments entered against them. As the case against Ross proceeded, the district court granted summary judgment in favor of the Commission on the issue of whether the IMI advertisements were deceptive. However, the court set for trial the issue of whether Ross could be held individually liable under the FTC Act. After a bench trial, the court ruled in favor of the Commission, enjoining Ross from participating in similar deceptive marketing practices and holding her jointly and severally liable (i.e., along with other defendants) for consumer redress in the amount of $163,167,539.95. Ross appealed to the U.S. Court of Appeals for the Fourth Circuit.

Davis, Circuit Judge

On appeal, Ross challenges the district court's judgment on [these] bases: the court's authority to award consumer redress; the legal standard the court applied in finding individual liability under the FTC Act; [and] the soundness of the district court's factual findings.

The FTC Act authorizes the Commission to sue in federal district court so that "in proper cases the Commission may seek, and after proper proof, the court may issue, a permanent injunction." 15 U.S.C. § 53(b). Ross contends that the district court did not have the authority to award consumer redress—a money judgment—under this provision of the statute.

Ross takes the position, correctly, that the statute's text does not expressly authorize the award of consumer redress, but precedent dictates otherwise. The Supreme Court has long held that Congress's invocation of the federal district court's equitable jurisdiction brings with it the full "power to decide all relevant matters in dispute and to award complete relief even though the decree includes that which might be conferred by a court of law." *Porter v. Warner Holding Co.*, 328 U.S. 395, 399 (1946). Once invoked by Congress in one of its duly enacted statutes, the district court's inherent equitable powers cannot be "denied or limited in the absence of a clear and valid legislative command." *Id. Porter* and its progeny thus articulate an interpretive principle that inserts a presumption into what would otherwise be the standard exercise of statutory construction: we presume that Congress, in statutorily

authorizing the exercise of the district court's injunctive power, "acted cognizant of the historic power of equity to provide complete relief in light of statutory purposes." *Mitchell v. Robert DeMario Jewelry, Inc.*, 361 U.S. 288, 291–92 (1960).

Applying this principle to the present case illuminates the legislative branch's real intent. That is, by authorizing the district court to issue a permanent injunction in the FTC Act, Congress presumably authorized the district court to exercise the full measure of its equitable jurisdiction. Accordingly, absent some countervailing indication sufficient to rebut the presumption, the court had sufficient statutory power to award "complete relief," including monetary consumer redress, which is a form of equitable relief. *Porter*, 328 U.S. at 399.

Ross makes a series of arguments about how the structure, history, and purpose of the FTC Act weigh against the conclusion that district courts have the authority to award consumer redress. Her arguments are not entirely unpersuasive, but they have ultimately been rejected by every other federal appellate court that has considered this issue. [Citations omitted.] We adopt the reasoning of those courts and reject Ross's attempt to obliterate a significant part of the Commission's remedial arsenal. A ruling in favor of Ross would forsake almost thirty years of federal appellate decisions and create a circuit split, a result that we will not countenance in the face of powerful Supreme Court authority pointing in the other direction.

The FTC Act makes it unlawful for any person, partnership, or corporation "to disseminate, or cause to be disseminated, any false advertisement" in commerce, 15 U.S.C. § 52(a), and it authorizes the Commission to bring suit in federal district court when it finds that any such person, partnership, or corporation "is engaged in, or is about to engage in, the dissemination or the causing of the dissemination of any" false advertisement. 15 U.S.C. § 53(a)(1). The district court ruled that one could be held individually liable under the FTC Act if the Commission proves that the individual (1) participated directly in the deceptive practices or had authority to control them, and (2) had knowledge of the deceptive conduct, which could be satisfied by showing evidence of actual knowledge, reckless indifference to the truth, or an awareness of a high probability of fraud combined with intentionally avoiding the truth (i.e., willful blindness).

Ross contends that the district court's standard was wrong and asks us to reject it. She proposes [in her brief] that we import from our securities fraud jurisprudence a standard that requires proof of an individual's "authority to control the specific practices alleged to be deceptive," coupled with a "failure to act within such control authority while aware of apparent fraud." Any other standard, argues Ross, would permit a finding of individual liability based on "indicia having more to do with enthusiasm for and skill at one's job [rather] than authority over specific ad campaigns, and [would] allow fault to be shown without any actual awareness of" a co-worker's misdeeds. Ross maintains that she would not have been held individually liable under her proposed standard.

Ross's proposed standard would permit the Commission to pursue individuals only when they had actual awareness of specific deceptive practices and failed to act to stop the deception, i.e., a specific intent/subjective knowledge requirement. Her proposal would effectively leave the Commission with the "futile gesture" of obtaining "an order directed to the lifeless entity of a corporation while exempting from its operation the living individuals who were responsible for the illegal practices" in the first place. *Pati-Port, Inc. v. FTC*, 313 F.2d 103, 105 (4th Cir. 1963).

We hold that one may be found individually liable under the FTC Act if she (1) participated directly in the deceptive practices or had authority to control those practices, and (2) had or should have had knowledge of the deceptive practices. The second prong of the analysis may be established by showing that the individual had actual knowledge of the deceptive conduct, was recklessly indifferent to its deceptiveness, or had an awareness of a high probability of deceptiveness and intentionally avoided learning the truth.

Our ruling maintains uniformity across the country and avoids a split in the federal appellate courts. Every other federal appellate court to resolve the issue has adopted the test we embrace today. [Citations omitted.] Ross's proposed standard, by contrast, invites us to ignore the law of every other sister court that has considered the issue, an invitation that we decline.

Ross's last contention is that the district court clearly erred in finding that she had "control" of the company, participated in any deceptive acts, and had knowledge of the deceptive advertisements. The district court did not clearly err in finding that Ross had "authority to control the deceptive acts within the meaning" of the FTC Act. In an affidavit in Canadian litigation [against one of her co-defendants], Ross swore that she was a high-level business official with duties involving, among other things, "product optimization," which the district court could reasonably have inferred afforded her authority and control over the nature and quality of the advertisements. Moreover, there was evidence that other employees requested Ross's authority to approve certain advertisements, and that she would check the design of the advertisements before approving them.

Nor did the district court clearly err in finding that Ross "directly participated in the deceptive marketing scheme." Ross's statements to other employees, as memorialized in chat logs between her and other employees were evidence that she served in a managerial role, directing the design of particular advertisements. Ross was a contact person for the purchase of advertising space for IMI, and there was evidence that Ross had the authority to discipline staff and developers when the work did not meet her standards. Given these facts, the district court could have reasonably inferred that Ross was actively and directly participating in multiple stages of the deceptive advertising scheme.

The district court did not clearly err in finding that Ross "had actual knowledge of the deceptive marketing scheme" and/or that she was "at the very least recklessly indifferent or intentionally avoided the truth." There was evidence that she edited and reviewed the content of multiple advertisements. At one point, she ordered the removal of the word "advertisement" from a set of ads. A co-defendant, the Chief Technology Officer of IMI and its sole shareholder and director, attested that Ross assumed some of his duties during his long-term illness. And although there was some indication that Ross acted in a manner suggesting that she personally did not perceive (or believe) that the advertisements were deceptive, Ross was on notice of multiple complaints about IMI's advertisements, including that they would cause consumers to automatically download unwanted IMI products.

All of this evidence paints a picture that the district court was wholly capable of accepting as a matter of fact: Ross made "countless decisions" that demonstrated her authority to control IMI. [Citation omitted.] Although a different fact-finder may have come to a contrary conclusion from that reached by the experienced district judge in this case, the rigorous clear error standard requires more than a party's simple disagreement with the court's findings.

District court's decision in favor of Commission affirmed.

Anticompetitive Behavior

Section 5 of the FTC Act empowers the commission to prevent "unfair methods of competition." This language allows the FTC to regulate anticompetitive practices made unlawful by the Sherman Act. The commission also has statutory authority to enforce the Clayton and Robinson–Patman Acts.[3]

For the most part, § 5's application to anticompetitive behavior involves the orthodox antitrust violations discussed in the following two chapters. Section 5, however, also reaches anticompetitive behavior *not covered by other antitrust statutes*. In addition, § 5 enables the FTC to proceed against *potential* or *incipient* antitrust violations.

Deception and Unfairness

LO48-3 Identify and explain the elements of the deception and unfairness tests employed by the FTC.

Section 5 of the FTC Act also prohibits "unfair or deceptive acts or practices" in commercial settings. This language enables the FTC to regulate a wide range of activities that disadvantage consumers. In doing so, the commission may seek to prove that the activity is *deceptive* or that it is *unfair*. Here, we set out the general standards that the FTC uses to define each of these § 5 violations. Much of this discussion involves FTC regulation of advertising, but the standards we outline apply to many other misrepresentations, omissions, and practices. Although their details are beyond the scope of this text, the commission also has enacted numerous trade regulation rules defining specific deceptive or unfair practices.

Deception The FTC determines the deceptiveness of advertising and other business practices on a case-by-case basis. Courts often defer to the commission's determinations. To be considered deceptive under the FTC's Policy Statement on Deception, an activity must (1) involve a *material* misrepresentation, omission, or practice (2) that

is *likely to mislead* a consumer (3) who acts *reasonably* under the circumstances.

Representation, Omission, or Practice Likely to Mislead Sometimes, sellers *expressly* make false or misleading claims in their advertisements or other representations. As revealed in the *Kraft* case, which appears shortly, an advertiser's false or misleading claims of an *implied* nature may also be challenged by the FTC. The same is true of a seller's deceptive *omissions*. Finally, certain deceptive *marketing practices* may violate § 5. In one such case, encyclopedia salespeople gained entry to the homes of potential customers by posing as surveyors engaged in advertising research.

In all of these situations, the statement, omission, or practice must be *likely to mislead* a consumer. Actual deception is not required. Determining whether an ad or practice is likely to mislead requires that the FTC evaluate the accuracy of the seller's claims. In some cases, moreover, the commission requires that sellers *substantiate* objective claims about their products by showing that they have a reasonable basis for making such claims.

The "Reasonable Consumer" Test To be deceptive, the representation, omission, or practice must also be likely to mislead *reasonable consumers under the circumstances*. This requirement aims to protect sellers from liability for every foolish, ignorant, or outlandish misconception that some consumer might entertain. As the commission noted many years ago, advertising an American-made pastry as "Danish Pastry" does not violate § 5 just because "a few misguided souls believe . . . that all Danish Pastry is made in Denmark."[4] Also, § 5 normally is not violated by statements of opinion, sales talk, or "puffing"; statements about matters that consumers can easily evaluate for themselves; and statements regarding subjective matters such as taste or smell. Such statements are unlikely to deceive reasonable consumers.

Materiality Finally, the representation, omission, or practice must be *material*. Material information is important to reasonable consumers and is likely to affect their choice of a product or service. Examples include statements or omissions regarding a product's cost, safety, effectiveness, performance, durability, quality, or warranty protection. In addition, the commission presumes that express statements are material.

Kraft v. FTC, a classic decision that follows, illustrates the application of the FTC's deception test to an advertising claim of an implied nature. *Kraft* also reveals the commission's broad discretion in fashioning appropriate orders once deceptive advertising has been proven.

---

[3]Chapter 49 discusses the Sherman Act. Chapter 50 discusses the Clayton and Robinson–Patman Acts.

[4]*Heinz v. W. Kirchner*, 63 F.T.C. 1282, 1290 (1963).

| Kraft, Inc. v. Federal Trade Commission | 970 F.2d 311 (7th Cir. 1992) |

Individually wrapped slices of cheese and cheeselike products come in two major types: process cheese food slices, which must contain at least 51 percent natural cheese according to a federal regulation, and imitation slices, which contain little or no natural cheese. Kraft Inc.'s "Kraft Singles" are process cheese food slices. In the early 1980s, Kraft began losing market share to other firms' less-expensive imitation slices. Kraft responded with its "Skimp" and "Class Picture" advertisements, which were designed to inform consumers that Kraft Singles cost more because each slice is made from 5 ounces of milk. These advertisements, which ran nationally in print and broadcast media between 1985 and 1987, also stressed the calcium content of Kraft Singles.

In the broadcast version of the Skimp advertisements, a woman stated that she bought Kraft Singles for her daughter rather than "skimping" by purchasing imitation slices. She noted that "[i]mitation slices use hardly any milk. But Kraft has 5 ounces per slice. Five ounces. So her little bones get calcium they need to grow." The commercial also showed milk being poured into a glass that bore the label "5 oz. milk slice." The glass was then transformed into part of the label on a package of Singles. In March 1987, Kraft added, as a subscript in the television commercial and as a footnote in the print media version, the disclosure that "one 3/4 ounce slice has 70% of the calcium of five ounces of milk."

The televised version of the Class Picture advertisements cited a government study indicating that "half the school kids in America don't get all the calcium recommended for growing kids." According to the commercial, "[t]hat's why Kraft Singles are important. Kraft is made from five ounces of milk per slice. So they're concentrated with calcium. Calcium the government recommends for strong bones and healthy teeth." The commercial also included the subscript disclaimer mentioned above.

The Federal Trade Commission instituted a deceptive advertising proceeding against Kraft under § 5 of the FTC Act. According to the FTC's complaint, the Skimp and Class Picture advertisements made the false implied claim that a Singles slice contains the same amount of calcium as 5 ounces of milk (the milk equivalency claim). The FTC regarded the milk equivalency claim as false even though Kraft actually uses 5 ounces of milk in making each Singles slice because roughly 30 percent of the calcium contained in the milk is lost during processing.

The administrative law judge (ALJ) concluded that the Skimp and Class Picture advertisements made the milk equivalency claim, which was false and material. He concluded that Kraft's subscript and footnote disclosures of the calcium loss were inconspicuous and confusing and therefore insufficient to dispel the misleading impression created by the advertisements. The ALJ ordered Kraft to cease and desist making the milk equivalency claim regarding any of its individually wrapped process cheese food slices or imitation slices. In addition, the ALJ ordered Kraft not to make other calcium or nutritional claims concerning its individually wrapped slices unless Kraft had reliable scientific evidence to support the claims.

Kraft appealed to the FTC commissioners (referred to here as the Commission). The Commission affirmed the ALJ's decision but modified it. According to the Commission, the Skimp and Class Picture advertisements made the false and material milk equivalency claim. The Commission modified the ALJ's orders by extending their coverage from Kraft's individually wrapped slices to "any product that is a cheese, related cheese product, imitation cheese, or substitute cheese." Kraft appealed to the U.S. Court of Appeals for the Seventh Circuit. (In a portion of the opinion not set forth here, the Seventh Circuit concluded, as had the ALJ and the Commission, that some of the Kraft advertisements made a further false claim of an implied nature: that Kraft Singles slices contain more calcium than imitation slices. The following portion of the Seventh Circuit's opinion addresses the milk equivalency claim.)

Flaum, Circuit Judge

[A]n advertisement is deceptive under [§ 5 of the FTC Act] if it is likely to mislead consumers, acting reasonably under the circumstances, in a material respect.

In determining what claims are conveyed by a challenged advertisement, the Commission relies on two sources of information: its own viewing of the ad and extrinsic evidence. Its practice is to view the ad first and, if it is unable on its own to determine with confidence what claims are conveyed . . . , to turn to extrinsic evidence. The most convincing extrinsic evidence is a [consumer] survey . . . , but the Commission also relies on other forms of extrinsic evidence including consumer testimony, expert opinion, and copy tests of ads.

Kraft has no quarrel with this approach when it comes to determining whether an ad conveys *express* claims, but contends that the FTC should be required . . . to rely on extrinsic evidence rather than its own subjective analysis in all cases involving allegedly *implied* claims. The Commissioners, Kraft argues, are simply incapable of determining what implicit messages consumers are likely to perceive. Kraft [also] asserts that the Commissioners are predisposed to find implied claims because the claims have [already] been identified in the complaint.

Here, the Commission found implied claims based solely on its own intuitive reading of the ads (although it did reinforce that conclusion by examining the proffered extrinsic evidence). Had the Commission fully and properly relied on available extrinsic evidence, Kraft argues it would have conclusively found that consumers do not perceive the milk equivalency . . . claim in the ads. Kraft's arguments . . . are unavailing as a matter of law. Courts, including the Supreme Court, have uniformly rejected imposing such a requirement on the FTC. We hold that the Commission may rely on its own reasoned analysis to determine what claims, including implied ones, are conveyed in a challenged advertisement, so long as those claims are reasonably clear from the face of the advertisement.

[Kraft relies on] the faulty premise that implied claims are inescapably subjective and unpredictable. In fact, implied claims fall on a continuum, ranging from the obvious to the barely discernible. The Commission does not have license to go on a fishing expedition to pin liability on advertisers for barely imaginable claims. However, when [implied] claims [are] conspicuous, extrinsic evidence is unnecessary because common sense and administrative experience provide the Commission with adequate tools to make its findings. The implied claims Kraft made are reasonably clear from the face of the advertisements, and hence the Commission was not required to utilize consumer surveys in reaching its decision.

Alternatively, Kraft argues that substantial evidence does not support the FTC's finding that the Class Picture ads convey a milk equivalency claim. We find substantial [supporting] evidence in the record. Although Kraft downplays the nexus in the ads between milk and calcium, the ads emphasize visually and verbally that five ounces of milk go into a slice of Kraft Singles; this image is linked to calcium content, strongly implying that the consumer gets the calcium found in five ounces of milk. Furthermore, the Class Picture ads contained one other element reinforcing the milk equivalency claim, the phrase "5 oz. milk slice" inside the image of a glass superimposed on the Singles package.

Kraft asserts that the literal truth of the . . . ads—[Kraft Singles] *are* made from five ounces of milk and they *do* have a high concentration of calcium—makes it illogical to render a finding of consumer deception. The difficulty with this argument is that even literally true statements can have misleading implications. Here, the average consumer is not likely to know that much of the calcium in five ounces of milk (30 percent) is lost in processing, which leaves consumers with a misleading impression about calcium content.

Kraft next asserts that the milk equivalency . . . claim, even if made, [is] not material to consumers. A claim is considered material if it involves information that is important to consumers and, hence, likely to affect their choice of, or conduct regarding, a product. In determining that the milk equivalency claim was material to consumers, the FTC cited Kraft surveys showing that 71 percent of respondents rated calcium content an extremely or very important factor in their decision to buy

Kraft Singles, [and that a substantial percentage of respondents] reported significant personal concerns about adequate calcium consumption. [The Commission] rationally concluded that a 30 percent exaggeration of calcium content was a nutritionally significant claim that would affect consumer purchasing decisions. This finding was supported by expert witnesses who agreed that consumers would prefer a slice of cheese with 100 percent of the calcium in five ounces of milk over one with only 70 percent. [T]he FTC [also] found evidence in the record that Kraft designed the ads with the intent to capitalize on consumer calcium deficiency concerns.

Significantly, the FTC found further evidence of materiality in Kraft's conduct. Before the ads even ran, ABC television raised a red flag when it asked Kraft to substantiate the milk and calcium claims in the ads. Kraft's ad agency also warned Kraft in a legal memorandum to substantiate the claims before running the ads. Moreover, in October 1985, a consumer group warned Kraft that it believed the Skimp ads were potentially deceptive. Nonetheless, a high-level Kraft executive recommended that the ad copy remain unaltered because the "Singles business is growing for the first time in four years due in large part to the copy." Finally, the FTC and the California Attorney General's Office independently notified the company in early 1986 that investigations had been initiated to determine whether the ads conveyed the milk equivalency claims. Notwithstanding these warnings, Kraft continued to run the ads and even rejected proposed alternatives that would have allayed concerns over their deceptive nature. From this, the FTC inferred—we believe, reasonably—that Kraft thought the challenged milk equivalency claim induced consumers to purchase Singles and hence that the claim was material to consumers.

The Commission's cease and desist order prohibits Kraft from running the Skimp and Class Picture ads, as well as from advertising any calcium or nutritional claims not supported by reliable scientific evidence. This order extends not only to the product contained in the deceptive advertisements (Kraft Singles), but to all Kraft cheeses and cheese-related products.

Kraft argues that the scope of the order is not reasonably related to Kraft's violation of the [FTC] Act because it extends to products that were not the subject of the challenged advertisements. The FTC has discretion to issue multi-product orders, so-called "fencing-in" orders, that extend beyond violations of the Act to prevent violators from engaging in similar deceptive practices in the future.

[The Commission] concluded that Kraft's violations were serious, deliberate, and easily transferable to other Kraft products, thus warranting a broad fencing-in order. We find substantial evidence to support the scope of the order. The Commission based its finding of seriousness on the size ($15 million annually) and duration (two and one-half years) of the ad campaign and on the difficulty most consumers would face in judging the truth or falsity of the calcium claims. [T]he FTC properly found that it is unreasonable to expect most consumers to perform the calculations necessary to compare the calcium content of Kraft Singles with five ounces of milk given the fact that the nutrient information given on milk cartons is not based on a five ounce serving.

As noted previously, the Commission [reasonably] found that Kraft's conduct was deliberate because it persisted in running the challenged ad copy despite repeated warnings from outside sources that the copy might be implicitly misleading. Kraft made three modifications to the ads, but two of them were implemented at the very end of the campaign, more than two years after it had begun. This dilatory response provided a sufficient basis for the Commission's conclusion. The Commission further [made the reasonable finding] that the violations were readily transferable to other Kraft cheese products given the general similarity between Singles and other Kraft cheeses.

Commission's order upheld and enforced.

Recent FTC Actions Recent FTC Actions indicate that the agency continues to make regulation of deceptive advertising a key area of emphasis. Consider, for instance, the 2014 adjudicative proceeding against Nissan, which was noted in the earlier discussion of consent orders. Visual images in the commercial appeared to show a Nissan truck pushing a dune buggy up and over a steep, sandy hill on which the dune buggy had been trapped. In reality, the FTC alleged, the truck neither performed that feat nor was capable of performing it. Both the truck and the dune buggy were dragged up the hill by cables that viewers of the commercial could not see. Moreover, the hill was made to appear steeper than it really was. As noted earlier, the case was resolved in 2014 by way of a consent order. As the second decade of the 21st century came to a close, the FTC was engrossed in a variety of actions to rein in companies from a variety of industries, including automobiles, fintech, social media influencers, data security, and manufacturers allegedly deceiving consumers with claims that their products were "Made in the USA."

Technological and communications developments and trends have often been the focus of FTC attention as the commission looks at new settings in which deceptive advertising may occur. In a 2013 industry guide, the commission issued a reminder that short-form advertisements communicated via Twitter or Facebook are no less subject to FTC regulation on deception grounds than are advertisements that appear in more traditional forms. The FTC has also expressed concern about, and has noted the possible need for investigations concerning, the deception of consumers that may result from advertisers' increasingly common practice of using so-called sponsored content. Under this practice, what is effectively an advertisement appears in a form that appears to be—but is not--a regular newscast, news story on the Internet, or news item in a newspaper or magazine. The coming years are likely to provide the FTC with opportunities to act with regard to deception in such contexts if the agency opts to do so.

Another object of the FTC's recent focus has been advertisers' potentially misleading claims that use of their products leads, or may lead, to certain beneficial health effects. The *POM Wonderful* case, which follows, illustrates the commission's approach to determining whether such claims are deceptive and whether they are adequately supported by reliable evidence. In addition, *POM Wonderful* examines the commission's power to issue remedial orders and explores the limits of the First Amendment's role when the FTC regulates advertising.

POM Wonderful, LLC v. Federal Trade Commission   777 F.3d 478 (D.C. Cir. 2015)

Beginning in 1987, Stewart and Lynda Resnick acquired and planted thousands of acres of pomegranate orchards in California. In 1998, they began collaborating with doctors and scientists to investigate the potential health benefits of pomegranate consumption. They formed POM Wonderful, LLC to make, market, and sell pomegranate-based products. The products included POM Wonderful 100% Pomegranate Juice and two dietary supplements that contained pomegranate extract in concentrated form. The Resnicks were the sole owners of POM Wonderful and an affiliated company that provided advertising and other services to POM. Those entities promoted POM products through magazine advertisements, newspaper inserts, billboards, posters, brochures, press releases, and website materials.

POM's promotional materials regularly referenced scientific support for the claimed health benefits of its pomegranate products. By 2010, the Resnicks, POM, and Roll had spent more than $35 million on pomegranate-related medical research. The case described below involved studies examining the efficacy of POM's products with regard to three particular ailments: heart disease, prostate cancer, and erectile dysfunction.

POM sponsored a number of studies examining the capacity of its products to improve cardiovascular health. One such study, led by Dr. Michael Aviram, examined the effect of pomegranate juice consumption by patients with carotid artery stenosis. Carotid artery stenosis is the narrowing of the arteries that supply oxygenated blood to the brain, usually caused by a buildup of plaque inside the arteries. The Aviram study, which was published in 2004, involved 10 carotid artery stenosis patients who consumed concentrated pomegranate juice daily for a year and 9 carotid artery stenosis patients who consumed no pomegranate juice and thus served as a control group. The investigators in the Aviram study measured the change in the patients' carotid intima-media thickness (CIMT), an indicator of plaque buildup. They found that patients who consumed pomegranate juice every day experienced a reduction in CIMT of "up to 30%" after one year, while CIMT for patients in the control group increased by 9 percent after one year. As one of POM's experts later testified in the legal proceedings described below, the Aviram study suggested a benefit from pomegranate juice consumption for patients with carotid artery stenosis, but was "not at all conclusive," in part because of the study's small sample size.

POM funded later—and larger—studies (referred to here as the "Ornish" and "Davidson" studies). The Ornish and Davidson studies found no statistically significant difference between the overall treatment group and the placebo group in terms of CIMT change. Although these studies were completed in 2005 and 2006, POM's post-2006 advertisements and other promotional materials made specific health-benefit claims based on the Aviram study, without any acknowledgment of the contrary results from the Ornish and Davidson studies and the doubt they cast on the Aviram study's findings.

For instance, POM distributed a 2007 brochure featuring a statement by Dr. Aviram that "POM Wonderful Pomegranate Juice has been proven to promote cardiovascular health," along with a description of his arterial thickness study, but with no mention of the contrary Ornish and Davidson findings. That same year, POM published a newsletter in which it asserted that "NEW RESEARCH OFFERS FURTHER PROOF OF THE HEART-HEALTHY BENEFITS OF POM WONDERFUL JUICE." The newsletter claimed a "30% DECREASE IN ARTERIAL PLAQUE" on the basis of Dr. Aviram's limited study, but again omitted any mention of the Ornish and Davidson findings. In 2008 and 2009, POM conducted a $1 million advertising campaign in which it stressed Dr. Aviram's findings—including the 30 percent figure—without any acknowledgment of the contrary Ornish and Davidson studies.

In addition to the cardiovascular studies, petitioners sponsored research on the effect of pomegranate juice consumption in prostate cancer patients. One study, led by Dr. Allan Pantuck, indicated that pomegranate juice consumption could be beneficial to such patients, but there was no control group in the study. Moreover, as Dr. Pantuck noted, all of the patients studied had already received medical treatment that could have provided an alternative explanation for the supposed health benefits. In advertisements and promotional materials from 2006 through 2009, POM made prostate cancer-related health claims based on the results of the Pantuck study, but without noting the limitations of that study and without acknowledging that medical treatments given to the patients, rather than pomegranate juice consumption, could have been the reason for the supposed health benefits revealed in the study.

POM also sponsored research on the effects of pomegranate juice consumption in men with mild to moderate erectile dysfunction. A study led by Dr. Harin Padma-Nathan utilized two alternative methods for assessing the results. One non-scientifically validated method offered some indication of a positive relationship, though it fell somewhat short of statistical significance. The other method, which was scientifically validated, led to positive benefit results that fell far short of statistical significance, given that there was a three-fourths likelihood that random chance would have produced the positive association. POM's promotional materials regarding the supposed benefits of pomegranate juice consumption by men with erectile dysfunction highlighted the Padma-Nathan study's assessment under the first method noted above, without any acknowledgment of the negative results in that same study's assessment under the second method.

In 2010, the Federal Trade Commission filed an administrative complaint alleging that POM, the affiliated company, the Resnicks, and POM's then-president had made false, misleading, and unsubstantiated representations in violation of § 5(a) of the FTC Act. The complaint identified 43 advertisements or promotional materials containing claims alleged to be false, misleading, or unsubstantiated. Following an administrative trial, the Commission's chief administrative law judge (ALJ) found that 19 of POM's advertisements and *promotional materials contained implied claims that POM products treat, prevent, or reduce the risk of heart disease, prostate cancer, or erectile dysfunction. The ALJ further concluded that POM and the related parties lacked sufficient evidence to substantiate those claims and that the claims were material to consumers. He therefore held the POM parties liable under the FTC Act and ordered them to cease and desist from making further claims about the health benefits of any food, drug, or dietary supplement unless the claims were non-misleading and supported by competent and reliable scientific evidence.*

POM and the related parties appealed to the full Commission, which affirmed the ALJ's decision to impose liability on POM and the other parties. The Commission also broadened the scope of the ALJ's order against POM and the other parties. Part I of the Commission's final order prohibited POM and the related parties from representing that any food, drug, or dietary supplement "is effective in the diagnosis, cure, mitigation, treatment, or prevention of any disease"—including but not limited to heart disease, prostate cancer, and erectile dysfunction—unless the representation is non-misleading and supported by "competent and reliable scientific evidence that, when considered in light of the entire body of relevant and reliable scientific evidence, is sufficient to substantiate that the representation is true." The order went on to say that for purposes of Part I, "competent and reliable evidence" would consist of "at least two randomized and controlled human clinical trials (RCTs)" that were double-blind in nature and resulted in statistically significant results.

Part II of the Commission's order prohibited POM and the related parties from misrepresenting the results of scientific studies in their ads. Part III barred them from making any claim about the "health benefits" of a food, drug, or dietary supplement unless the representation was non-misleading and supported by "competent and reliable scientific evidence." Unlike Part I, which applied specifically and solely to disease-related claims, Part III contained no requirement that randomized, controlled, human clinical trials support more general claims about health benefits.

POM and the related parties petitioned for review by the U.S. Court of Appeals for the District of Columbia Circuit. They contested the Commission's finding that they had violated the FTC Act and argued that the Commission's remedial order ran afoul of the statute and the First Amendment.

Srinivasan, Circuit Judge

[W]e first address petitioners' statutory challenges to the Commission's order before turning to their constitutional claims. On review of an order under the FTC Act, "[t]he findings of the Commission as to the facts, if supported by evidence, shall be conclusive." FTC Act § 5(c). The Commission "is often in a better position than are courts to determine when a practice is 'deceptive' within the meaning of the [FTC] Act," and that "admonition is especially true with respect to allegedly deceptive advertising since the finding of a § 5 violation in this field rests so heavily on inference and pragmatic judgment." *FTC v. Colgate-Palmolive Co.*, 380 U.S. 374, 385 (1965).

In determining whether an advertisement is deceptive in violation of section 5 of the FTC Act, the Commission engages in a three-step inquiry, considering: (i) what claims are conveyed in the ad, (ii) whether those claims are false, misleading, or unsubstantiated, and (iii) whether the claims are material to prospective consumers. At the first step, the Commission "will deem an advertisement to convey a claim if consumers acting reasonably under the circumstances would interpret the advertisement to contain that message." [Citation omitted.]

In identifying the claims made by an ad, the Commission distinguishes between *efficacy claims* and *establishment claims*. An efficacy claim suggests that a product successfully performs the advertised function or yields the advertised benefit, but includes no suggestion of scientific proof of the product's effectiveness.

An establishment claim, by contrast, suggests that a product's effectiveness or superiority has been scientifically established.

The distinction between efficacy claims and establishment claims gains salience at the second step of the Commission's inquiry, which calls for determining whether the advertiser's claim is false, misleading, or unsubstantiated. If an ad conveys an efficacy claim, the advertiser must possess a "reasonable basis" for the claim. See *Pfizer Inc.*, 81 F.T.C. 23, 26 (1972). The FTC examines that question under the so-called "*Pfizer* factors," including "the type of product," "the type of claim," "the benefit of a truthful claim," "the ease of developing substantiation for the claim," "the consequences of a false claim," and "the amount of substantiation experts in the field would consider reasonable."

For establishment claims, by contrast, the Commission generally does not apply the *Pfizer* factors. Rather, the amount of substantiation needed for an establishment claim depends on whether the claim is "specific" or "non-specific." [Citation omitted.] If an establishment claim "states a specific type of substantiation," the "advertiser must possess the specific substantiation claimed." [Citation omitted.] If an ad instead conveys a non-specific establishment claim—e.g., an ad stating that a product's efficacy is "medically proven" or making use of "visual aids" that "clearly suggest that the claim is based upon a foundation of scientific evidence"—the advertiser "must possess evidence sufficient to satisfy the relevant scientific community of the claim's truth." [Citation omitted.]

Even if the Commission concludes at the first step that an advertiser conveyed efficacy or establishment claims and determines at the second step that the claims qualify as false, misleading, or unsubstantiated, it can issue a finding of liability only "if the omitted information would be a material factor in the consumer's decision to purchase the product." [Citation omitted.] Here, petitioners do not dispute the materiality of POM's disease-related claims. We therefore confine our analysis to the first and second steps of the Commission's determination: its findings that petitioners' ads conveyed efficacy and establishment claims and that those claims were false, misleading, or unsubstantiated.

At the first step of its inquiry, the Commission determined that thirty-six of petitioners' advertisements and promotional materials conveyed efficacy claims asserting that POM products treat, prevent, or reduce the risk of heart disease, prostate cancer, or erectile dysfunction. The Commission further concluded that thirty-four of those ads also conveyed establishment claims representing that clinical studies substantiate the efficacy of POM products in treating, preventing, or reducing the risk of the same ailments. The Commission set forth the basis for those findings in considerable detail in an appendix to its opinion, with a separate explanation for each ad.

Those ads repeatedly claimed the benefits of POM's products in the treatment or prevention of heart disease, prostate cancer, or erectile dysfunction, and consistently touted medical studies ostensibly supporting those claimed benefits. The question whether "a claim of establishment is in fact made is a question of fact the evaluation of which is within the FTC's peculiar expertise." [Citation omitted.] [W]e perceive no basis for setting aside the Commission's carefully considered findings of efficacy and establishment claims as unsupported by substantial evidence.

As the Commission separately set forth for each ad, "these ads drew a logical connection between the study results and effectiveness for the particular diseases." Moreover, they invoked medical symbols, referenced publication in medical journals, and described the substantial funds spent on medical research, fortifying the overall sense that the referenced clinical studies establish the claimed benefits. As the Commission explained, "[w]hen an ad represents that tens of millions of dollars have been spent on medical research, it tends to reinforce the impression that the research supporting product claims is established and not merely preliminary."

At the second stage of its analysis, the Commission found petitioners' efficacy and establishment claims to be deceptive due to inadequate substantiation. "In reviewing whether there is appropriate scientific substantiation for the claims made, our task is only to determine if the Commission's finding is supported by substantial evidence on the record as a whole." [Citation omitted.] When conducting that inquiry, we are mindful of the Commission's "special expertise in determining what sort of substantiation is necessary to assure that advertising is not deceptive." [Citation omitted.]

For both petitioners' efficacy claims and their establishment claims, the Commission found that "experts in the relevant fields" would require one or more "properly randomized and controlled human clinical trials (RCTs)" in order to "establish a causal relationship between a food and the treatment, prevention, or reduction of risk" of heart disease, prostate cancer, or erectile dysfunction. Without at least one such RCT, the Commission concluded, POM's efficacy claims and its non-specific establishment claims were inadequately substantiated.

The Commission examined each of the studies invoked by petitioners in their ads, concluding that the referenced studies fail to qualify as RCTs of the kind that could afford adequate substantiation. Petitioners' claims therefore were deceptive. Moreover, in light of petitioners' selective touting of ostensibly favorable study results and nondisclosure of contrary indications from the same or a later study, the Commission found that there were "many omissions of material facts in [the] ads that consumers cannot verify independently." Petitioners, the Commission observed, "made numerous deceptive representations and were aware that they were making such representations despite the inconsistency between the results of some of their later studies and the results of earlier studies to which [they] refer in their ads."

With regard to heart disease, for instance, petitioners repeatedly touted the results of Dr. Aviram's limited CIMT study without noting the contrary findings in Drs. Ornish's and Davidson's later and larger studies. For prostate cancer, petitioners consistently relied on Dr. Pantuck's study of PSA doubling times but with no indication of the study's limitations. And in connection with erectile dysfunction, petitioners promoted the results of Dr. Padma-Nathan's study based exclusively on [one] measure, without acknowledging that the study showed no improvement according to the only scientifically validated measure used to assess the results.

Petitioners challenge the Commission's factual finding that experts in the relevant fields require RCTs to support claims about the disease-related benefits of POM's products. We conclude that the Commission's finding is supported by substantial record evidence. That evidence includes written reports and testimony from medical researchers stating that experts in the fields of cardiology and urology require randomized, double-blinded, placebo-controlled clinical trials to substantiate any claim that a product treats, prevents, or reduces the risk of disease. The Commission drew on that expert testimony to explain why the attributes of well-designed RCTs are necessary to substantiate petitioners' claims.

We acknowledge that RCTs may be costly, although we note that the petitioners nonetheless have been able to sponsor dozens of studies, including several RCTs. Yet if the cost of an RCT proves prohibitive, petitioners can choose to specify a lower level of substantiation for their claims. As the Commission observed, "the need for RCTs is driven by the claims [petitioners] have chosen to make." An advertiser who makes "express representations about the level of support for a particular claim" must "possess the level of proof claimed in the ad" and must convey that information to consumers in a non-misleading way. [Citation omitted.] An advertiser thus still may assert a health-related claim backed by medical evidence falling short of an RCT if it includes an effective disclaimer disclosing the limitations of the supporting research. Petitioners did not do so.

Having rejected petitioners' statutory claims, we now turn to their constitutional arguments. Petitioners challenge both the Commission's liability determination and its remedy on First Amendment grounds. We reject both challenges except insofar as the Commission in its remedial order imposed an across-the-board, two-RCT substantiation requirement for any future disease-related claims by petitioners.

"For commercial speech to come within [the First Amendment], it at least must concern lawful activity and not be misleading." *Central Hudson Gas & Electric Corp. v. Public Service Commission*, 447 U.S. 557, 566 (1980). In imposing liability against petitioners, the Commission found that POM's ads are entitled to no First Amendment protection because they are "deceptive and misleading." We conclude that the Commission's findings of deception are supported by substantial evidence in the record. As a result, the Commission sanctioned petitioners for misleading speech unprotected by the First Amendment.

Finally, we address petitioners' First Amendment challenge to the Commission's remedial order. Part III of the order imposes a baseline requirement applicable to all of petitioners' ads. It bars representations about a product's general health benefits "unless the representation is non-misleading" and backed by "competent and reliable scientific evidence that is sufficient in quality and quantity" to "substantiate that the representation is true." For purposes of that baseline requirement, "competent and reliable evidence" means studies that are "generally accepted in the profession to yield accurate and reliable results."

Part I of the order, meanwhile, imposes heightened requirements in the specific context of claims about the treatment or prevention of "any disease" (including, but not limited to, heart disease, prostate cancer, and erectile dysfunction). Such disease-related claims, like the broader category of health claims covered by Part III, must be "non-misleading" and supported by "competent and reliable scientific evidence." But "competent and reliable scientific evidence" is more narrowly defined for purposes of Part I to consist of "at least two randomized and controlled human clinical trials (RCTs)" that "yield statistically significant results" and are "double-blinded" whenever feasible. In short, Part III's baseline requirement for all health claims does not require RCT substantiation, whereas the specific requirements in Part I for disease-related claims not only contemplate RCT substantiation, but call for—as a categorical matter—two RCTs.

Petitioners challenge the remedial order's blanket, two-RCT-substantiation requirement under the First Amendment.

They contend, and the Commission accepts, that their challenge should be examined under the general test for commercial speech restrictions set out in *Central Hudson*, which first requires that the "asserted governmental interest [be] substantial." The Supreme Court has made clear that the governmental "interest in ensuring the accuracy of commercial information in the marketplace is substantial." [Citation omitted.] The Commission asserts that its remedial order aims to advance that concededly substantial interest, satisfying *Central Hudson*'s first prong.

With regard to the means by which the Commission seeks to further its asserted interest, *Central Hudson* requires that a challenged restriction "directly advance[] the governmental interest" and that it "is not more extensive than is necessary to serve that interest." Here, insofar as the Commission's order imposes a general RCT-substantiation requirement for disease claims—i.e., without regard to any particular number of RCTs—the order satisfies those tailoring components of *Central Hudson* review.

In finding petitioners liable for deceptive ads, the Commission determined that petitioners' efficacy and establishment claims were misleading because they were unsubstantiated by RCTs. We have upheld that approach in this opinion. Requiring RCT substantiation as a forward-looking remedy is perfectly commensurate with the Commission's assessment of liability for petitioners' past conduct: if past claims were deceptive in the absence of RCT substantiation, requiring RCTs for future claims is tightly tethered to the goal of preventing deception. To be sure, the liability determination concerned claims about three specific diseases whereas the remedial order encompasses claims about any disease. But that broadened scope is justified by petitioners' demonstrated propensity to make deceptive representations about the health benefits of their products, and also by the expert testimony supporting the necessity of RCTs to establish causation for disease-related claims generally. For purposes of *Central Hudson* scrutiny, then, the injunctive order's requirement of *some* RCT substantiation for disease claims directly advances, and is not more extensive than necessary to serve, the interest in preventing misleading commercial speech.

We reach the opposite conclusion insofar as the remedial order mandates *two* RCTs as an across-the-board requirement for any disease claim. *Central Hudson* "requires something short of a least-restrictive-means standard," *Board of Trustees v. Fox*, 492 U.S. 469, 477 (1989), but the Commission still bears the burden to demonstrate a "reasonable fit" between the particular means chosen and the government interest pursued. *Id.* at 480. Here, the Commission fails adequately to justify a categorical floor of two RCTs for any and all disease claims. It of course is true that, all else being equal, two RCTs would provide more reliable scientific evidence than one RCT, affording added assurance against misleading claims. It is equally true that three RCTs would provide more certainty than two, and four would yield more certainty still. But the Commission understandably does not claim a myopic interest in pursuing scientific certitude to the exclusion of all else, regardless of the consequences.

Here, the consequences of mandating more than one RCT bear emphasis. Requiring additional RCTs without adequate justification exacts considerable costs, and not just in terms of the substantial resources often necessary to design and conduct a properly randomized and controlled human clinical trial. If there is a categorical bar against claims about the disease-related benefits of a food product or dietary supplement in the absence of two RCTs, consumers may be denied useful, truthful information about products with a demonstrated capacity to treat or prevent serious disease. That would subvert rather than promote the objectives of the commercial speech doctrine.

Consider, for instance, a situation in which the results of a large-scale, perfectly designed and conducted RCT show that a dietary supplement significantly reduces the risk of a particular disease, with the results demonstrated to a very high degree of statistical certainty—so much so that experts in the relevant field universally regard the study as conclusively establishing clinical proof of the supplement's benefits for disease prevention. Perhaps, moreover, a wealth of medical research and evidence apart from RCTs—e.g., observational studies—reinforces the results of the blue-ribbon RCT. In that situation, there would be a substantial interest in assuring that consumers gain awareness of the dietary supplement's benefits and the supporting medical research.

The two-RCT requirement in the Commission's order brooks no exception for those circumstances. No matter how robust the results of a completed RCT, and no matter how compelling a battery of supporting research, the order would always bar any disease-related claims unless petitioners clear the magic line of two RCTs. The Commission has elsewhere explained to industry advertisers that, "[i]n most situations, the quality of studies will be more important than quantity." [Citation omitted.] The blanket, two-RCT substantiation requirement at issue here is out of step with that understanding. The Commission fails to demonstrate how such a rigid remedial rule bears the requisite "reasonable fit" with the interest in preventing deceptive speech. *Fox*, 492 U.S. at 480.

[W]e hold that the Commission's order is valid to the extent it requires disease claims to be substantiated by at least one RCT. But it fails *Central Hudson* scrutiny insofar as it categorically requires two RCTs for all disease-related claims. That is not at all to say that the Commission would be barred from imposing a two-RCT-substantiation requirement in any circumstances. Rather, the Commission has failed in this case adequately to justify an across-the-board two-RCT requirement for all disease claims by petitioners.

Commission's remedial order modified to require petitioners to possess at least one RCT before making disease claims; Commission's decision and order otherwise upheld and petition for review denied.

The Global Business Environment

In most developed nations, the problem of misleading advertising is addressed through self-regulation and through regulatory schemes established by law. Self-regulation includes voluntary action by companies and resolution of parties' advertising-related disputes under industry codes of conduct or other agreed procedures that exist outside the formal legal system.

Since the passage of a 1984 European Union (EU) Directive on Misleading Advertising, EU nations have been obligated to have domestic laws addressing misleading advertising. The domestic laws of EU nations typically have not contemplated a significant role for direct government regulation of the sort in which the Federal Trade Commission and other government agencies engage in the United States. Instead, EU countries depend more on litigation instituted by private parties—competitors and, in some countries, consumer organizations—as the chief legal means of dealing with misleading advertising. In this sense, the approach taken by EU nations resembles a different aspect of

advertising regulation in the United States: the indirect regulation that comes with private parties' false advertising lawsuits under § 43(a) of the Lanham Act. (Section 43(a) and the types of cases that may be brought under it are discussed in Chapter 8.)

Sweden and the other Scandinavian countries have established, by law, a consumer ombudsman who hears advertising complaints, resolves them when possible, and resorts to litigation if necessary. The ombudsman also has some power to promulgate advertising rules that carry legal force. In this sense, the ombudsman's role resembles that of the FTC in the United States.

Advertising laws contemplate significant regulatory roles for government agencies in New Zealand, Australia, and Japan, though industry self-regulation remains prominent in at least the latter two of those nations. In Great Britain, the traditional emphasis on self-regulation through the private Advertising Standards Authority has been supplemented during recent decades by government regulation through the office of the Director General of Fair Trading.

Unfairness   Section 5's prohibition of *unfair* acts or practices enables the FTC to attack behavior that, while not necessarily deceptive, is objectionable for other reasons. As demonstrated by the case discussed in an Ethics and Compliance in Action box that appears later in the chapter, the FTC focuses on *consumer harm* when it attacks unfair acts or practices. To violate § 5, this harm:

1. *Must be substantial.* Monetary loss and unwarranted health and safety risks usually constitute substantial harm, but emotional distress and the perceived offensiveness of certain advertisements generally do not.

2. *Must not be outweighed by any offsetting consumer or competitive benefits produced by the challenged practice.* This element requires the commission to balance the harm caused by the act or practice against its benefits to consumers and to competition generally. A seller's failure to give a consumer complex technical data about a product, for example, may disadvantage the consumer, but it may also reduce the product's price. Only when an act or practice is injurious in its *net effects* can it be unfair under § 5.

3. *Must be one that consumers could not reasonably have avoided.* An injury is considered reasonably unavoidable when a seller's actions significantly interfered with a consumer's ability to make informed decisions that would have prevented the injury. For example, a seller may have withheld otherwise unavailable information about important product features, or used high-pressure sales tactics on vulnerable consumers.

Remedies

 LO48-4   Describe the types of orders that the FTC may issue against a party held, in an adjudicative proceeding, to have engaged in deceptive or unfair commercial behavior.

Several types of orders may result from a successful FTC adjudicative proceeding attacking deceptive or unfair behavior. One possibility is an order telling the respondent to *cease* engaging in the deceptive or unfair conduct. Another is the *affirmative disclosure* of information whose absence made the advertisement deceptive or unfair. Yet another is *corrective advertising*. This requires the seller's future advertisements to correct false impressions created by its past advertisements. In certain cases, moreover, the FTC may issue an *all-products order* extending beyond the product or service whose advertisements violated § 5, and including future advertisements for other products or services marketed by the seller. The *Kraft* and *POM*

Wonderful cases, which appeared earlier, illustrate such an order. Finally, as explained earlier, the FTC may sometimes go to court to seek injunctive relief, civil penalties, or consumer redress.

Consumer Protection Laws

The term *consumer protection* includes everything from Chapter 20's product liability law to packaging and labeling regulations. Here, we examine federal regulation of telemarketing practices, product warranties, consumer credit, and product safety.

 LO48-5   Identify key features of the Telemarketing and Consumer Fraud and Abuse Prevention Act.

Telemarketing and Consumer Fraud and Abuse Prevention Act   In the Telemarketing and Consumer Fraud and Abuse Prevention Act (Telemarketing Act), Congress required the FTC to promulgate regulations defining and prohibiting *deceptive* and *abusive* telemarketing acts or practices. The FTC responded to this directive with the Telemarketing Sales Rule (TSR).

For purposes of the TSR, a *seller* is a party who (or which), in connection with a telemarketing transaction, offers or arranges to provide customers with goods or services in exchange for consideration. The TSR defines *telemarketer* as "any person who, in connection with telemarketing, initiates or receives telephone calls to or from a customer." It defines *telemarketing* as "a plan, program, or campaign which is conducted to induce the purchase of goods or services by use of one or more telephones and which involves more than one interstate telephone call." Exemptions from the telemarketing definition are provided for sellers that solicit sales through the mailing of a catalog and then receive customers' orders by telephone, and for sellers that make telephone calls of solicitation to a consumer but complete the transaction in a face-to-face meeting with the consumer.

A major feature of the TSR makes it a deceptive practice for telemarketers and sellers to fail to disclose certain information to a customer before she pays for the goods or services being telemarketed. The customer is regarded as having paid for goods or services once she provides information that may be used for billing purposes. The mandatory disclosures specified in the TSR include the total cost of the goods or services, any material restrictions or conditions on the purchase or use of the goods or services, and the terms of any refund or exchange policy mentioned in the solicitation (or, if the seller has a policy of not allowing

CYBERLAW IN ACTION

Reacting to frequently voiced concerns of e-mail users that their inboxes were being inundated by unwanted, sometimes misleading, and often offensive e-mail messages from commercial providers, Congress enacted the Controlling the Assault of Non-Solicited Pornography and Marketing Act of 2003. This statute, usually referred to as the CAN-SPAM Act, took effect on January 1, 2004.

In the CAN-SPAM Act, Congress outlawed various commercial e-mail practices, including the use of a false or misleading statement on the "from" line of a commercial message and the use of false or misleading subject headings in a commercial message. The CAN-SPAM Act also required that a sender of commercial e-mail use a functioning reply address or "opt-out" mechanism by which consumers could elect not to receive more messages from that sender, and that the sender send no further messages to a consumer more than 10 days after the consumer has opted out. In addition, the CAN-SPAM Act required that commercial e-mail messages contain three components: clear identification that the message is an advertisement or solicitation, conspicuous notice that the

recipient may decline to receive further messages from the sender, and a listing of the sender's postal address. A further CAN-SPAM Act provision required warning labels on commercial e-mail messages that feature sexually oriented material. Enforcement authority for violations of the CAN-SPAM Act was given to the FTC (which can launch adjudicative proceedings or initiate litigation in court), to state attorneys general (who can sue in federal court concerning certain violations), and to providers of Internet access services (which can sue in federal court concerning certain other violations).

The CAN-SPAM Act also required the FTC to promulgate regulations to implement the statute and further its purposes. The regulations promulgated by the FTC took effect in 2008. The CAN-SPAM Act and the related regulations have made progress toward the goals they were meant to achieve, though critics have lamented that the inbox-clutter problem remains only partially resolved. They have pointed to a continued proliferation of unwanted commercial e-mail as an indication that purveyors of such material have either ignored the legal requirements or found it relatively easy to modify their e-mail techniques enough to comply with the law while still maintaining an ability to flood inboxes with unsolicited messages.

refunds or exchanges, a disclosure of that policy). Various other disclosures are necessary if the telemarketing solicitation pertains to a prize promotion. The TSR also makes it a deceptive practice for a telemarketer or seller to misrepresent information required to be disclosed in the mandatory disclosures, or to misrepresent any other information concerning the performance, nature, or characteristics of the goods or services being offered for sale.

According to the TSR, a telemarketer or seller engages in an abusive practice if he directs threats, intimidation, or profane or obscene language toward a customer; causes the telephone to ring, or engages a person in a telephone conversation, repeatedly and with the intent to harass, abuse, or annoy a person at the called number; or initiates a call to a person who has previously stated that she does not wish to receive a call made by or on behalf of the seller whose goods or services are being offered.

The TSR also makes it an abusive practice for a telemarketer to call a person's residence at any time other than between 8:00 A.M. and 9:00 P.M. at the called person's location. In addition, the telemarketer engages in an abusive practice if, in a telephone call he initiated, he does not promptly and clearly disclose the identity of the seller, the sales purpose of the call, the nature of the goods or services, and the fact that no purchase or payment is necessary in order to win a prize or participate in a prize promotion

(if a prize or prize promotion is being offered). Still other abusive practices are enumerated in the TSR.

The FTC and state attorneys general may bring enforcement proceedings against violators of the Telemarketing Act and the TSR. Monetary civil penalties of the sort described earlier in this chapter are among the available remedies in proceedings initiated by the government. Under some circumstances, private citizens may sue violators for damages and injunctive relief.

Do-Not-Call Registry

 Identify key features and effects of the Do-Not-Call Registry established by federal agency regulations.

Regulations promulgated in 2003 by the FTC and the Federal Communications Commission created a legal mechanism by which consumers who preferred not to receive telemarketing calls of a commercial nature could have their home telephone numbers listed on a national "do-not-call" registry. Commercial telemarketers became legally obligated not to place calls to the numbers listed. The do-not-call registry became popular among consumers, with many millions taking action to have their numbers placed on the list within the first several months of its existence. The do-not-call registry's restrictions apply only to telemarketing calls made by or on behalf of sellers of goods and services. The restrictions do not apply to calls made for the purpose of charitable or political fundraising. Exceptions to the general do-not-call rule permit a seller of goods or services to call consumers who have signed up for the registry if the seller and the consumer have an established business relationship or if the consumer has provided written permission to be called.

After the registry was established, affected commercial telemarketers initiated litigation questioning the legal validity of the registry. In *Mainstream Marketing Services, Inc. v. Federal Trade Commission,*[5] the U.S. Court of Appeals for the Tenth Circuit upheld the registry as a valid exercise of statutory authority granted by Congress and rejected the telemarketers' argument that the registry violated their First Amendment rights.

Do Not Track   In recent years, the FTC has devoted attention to a perceived need to protect consumers' privacy regarding their Internet use. Rather than promulgating regulations that deal with such matters, the FTC has encouraged companies that provide Internet browsers to offer a "Do Not Track" system under which consumers can choose not to have their Internet use tracked by third parties. The FTC has also sought to educate consumers about such issues.

Although some companies began a few years ago to take steps to permit consumers to opt out of targeted

___

[5]358 F.3d 1228 (10th Cir. 2004).

advertisements, the FTC has favored a more sweeping approach under which browser providers would take further steps to allow consumers to restrict availability of their browsing history and advertising networks and websites would limit their targeted-advertising-related tracking of usage. In recent years, more companies have voluntarily moved in that direction. There also have been signs of movement toward industry adoption of a Do Not Track agreement of the sort the FTC favored. Future development will reveal whether such an agreement materializes and seems to do the job adequately, or whether the FTC will eventually seek to promulgate regulations mandating that Do Not Track systems be developed and implemented.

Magnuson–Moss Warranty Act

 LO48-7 Explain the basic provisions of the Magnuson–Moss Warranty Act and related regulations.

The Magnuson–Moss Warranty Act of 1975 mainly applies to *written warranties* for *consumer products.* Nothing in the act requires sellers to give a written warranty. Sellers who decline to provide such a warranty generally escape coverage. A consumer product is personal property that is ordinarily used for personal, family, or household purposes. In addition, many Magnuson–Moss provisions apply only when a written warranty is given in connection with the sale of a consumer product to a *consumer.* A consumer is a

___

CYBERLAW IN ACTION

Concern about uses and misuses of personal information obtained from children through their use of the Internet caused Congress to enact a 1998 statute, the Children's Online Privacy Protection Act (COPPA), and to direct the FTC to adopt related regulations. Since then, the FTC has promulgated two sets of COPPA regulations. The statute and the regulations require that if a website or online service is directed toward children under the age of 13 or the operator of the site or service knows that personal information is being collected from children under 13, the operator of the site or service must provide notice to parents and obtain their consent before collecting, using, or disclosing children's personal information. In addition, the operator must maintain security over any such information collected from children. Personal information, for purposes of the statute and the regulations, includes such information as names, phone numbers, home addresses, and e-mail addresses, as well as photos or other video or audio that could be used to identify, locate, or contact a child.

Demonstrating that the COPPA regulations have some teeth, the FTC took action in recent years against the operators of fan websites for various stars, including Justin Bieber. The operators of certain sites of that nature agreed to pay a $1 million civil penalty in 2012 in order to resolve the FTC's allegations that they had collected personal information from children in violation of COPPA and the regulations.

In an effort to make certain that the regulations kept pace with technological innovations and other developments, the FTC promulgated a further set of COPPA regulations in 2012. Those rules updated the earlier ones so that they would apply to sites and services accessed through a mobile phone or a tablet and so that they would take account of such developments as voice recognition technology and the use of online advertisements tailored to a particular user. In addition, the 2012 regulations appeared to broaden the range of companies subject to COPPA, by including advertising networks and social networks among those that must comply with the parental notice and consent requirements if those networks operate on sites regularly frequented by children.

buyer or transferee who does not use the product for resale or in his own business.

Chapter 20 discusses Magnuson–Moss's provisions giving consumers minimum warranty protection. Here, we examine its rules requiring that consumer warranties contain certain information and that this information be made available to buyers before the sale. Any failure to comply with these rules violates § 5 of the FTC Act and may trigger commission action. In addition, either the FTC or the attorney general may sue to obtain injunctive relief against such violations.

Required Warranty Information The Magnuson–Moss Act and its regulations require the simple, clear, and conspicuous presentation of certain information in written warranties to consumers for consumer products costing more than $15. That information includes (1) the persons protected by the warranty when coverage is limited to the original purchaser or is otherwise limited; (2) the products, parts, characteristics, components, or properties covered by the warranty; (3) what the warrantor will do in case of a product defect or other failure to conform to the warranty; (4) the time the warranty begins (if different from the purchase date) and its duration; and (5) the procedure the consumer should follow to obtain the performance of warranty obligations. The act also requires that a warrantor disclose (1) any limitations on the duration of implied warranties and (2) any attempt to limit consequential damages or other consumer remedies.

Presale Availability of Warranty Information The regulations accompanying Magnuson–Moss also contain detailed rules requiring that warranty terms be made available to a buyer before the sale. These rules generally govern sales to consumers of consumer products costing more than $15. They set out certain duties that must be met by sellers (usually retailers) and warrantors (usually manufacturers) of such products. For example:

1. *Sellers* must make the text of the warranty available for the prospective buyer's review before the sale, either by displaying the warranty in close proximity to the product or by furnishing the warranty upon request after posting signs informing buyers of its availability.

2. *Catalog or mail-order sellers* must clearly and conspicuously disclose in their catalog or solicitation either the full text of the warranty or the address from which a free copy can be obtained.

3. *Warrantors* must give sellers the warranty materials necessary for them to comply with the duties stated above.

Truth in Lending Act

 LO48-8 Describe the purpose and major provisions of the Truth in Lending Act.

When Congress passed the Truth in Lending Act (TILA) in 1968, its main aims were to increase consumer knowledge and understanding of credit terms by compelling their *disclosure*, and to help consumers shop for credit by commanding *uniform* disclosures. Now, however, the TILA protects consumers in other ways as well. For example, in 2018 the TILA was amended by the Economic Growth Act, discussed later in this chapter, to allow a consumer to request a financial institution to remove a default on a private student loan under certain circumstances.

Coverage Effective January 1, 2020, the TILA will apply to creditors who extend consumer credit to a debtor in an amount not exceeding $58,300. A *creditor* is a party who regularly extends consumer credit. Examples include banks, credit card issuers, and savings and loan associations. Extending credit need not be a creditor's primary business. For instance, auto dealers and retail stores are creditors if they regularly extend credit. To qualify as a creditor, the party in question must also either impose a finance charge or by agreement require payment in more than four installments. *Consumer credit* is credit enabling the purchase of goods, services, or real estate used primarily for personal, family, or household purposes—not business or agricultural purposes. The TILA *debtor* must be a natural person; the act does not protect business organizations.

Disclosure Provisions The TILA's detailed disclosure provisions break down into three categories.

1. *Open-end credit.* The TILA defines an open-end credit plan as one that contemplates repeated transactions and involves a finance charge that may be computed on the unpaid balance. Examples include credit card plans and revolving charge accounts offered by retail stores. Open-end credit plans require two forms of disclosure: (a) an *initial statement* made before the first transaction under the plan and (b) a series of *periodic statements* (usually, one for each billing cycle).

   Among the disclosures required in the initial statement are (a) when a finance charge is imposed and how it is determined, (b) the amount of any additional charges and the method for computing them, (c) the fact that the creditor has taken or will acquire a security interest in the debtor's property, and (d) the debtor's billing rights. Periodic statements require an even lengthier set of disclosures. Much of the information contained in a monthly credit card statement, for example, is compelled by the TILA.

2. *Closed-end credit.* The TILA requires a different set of disclosures for other credit plans, which generally involve closed-end credit. Closed-end credit such as a car loan or a consumer loan from a finance company is extended for a specific time period; the total amount financed, number of payments, and due dates are all agreed on at the time of the transaction. Examples of the disclosures necessary before the completion of a closed-end credit transaction include (a) the total finance charge; (b) the annual percentage rate (APR); (c) the amount financed; (d) the total number of payments, their due dates, and the amount of each payment; (e) the total dollar value of all payments; (f) any late charges imposed for past-due payments; and (g) any security interest taken by the creditor and the property that the security interest covers.

3. *Credit card applications and solicitations.* The TILA imposes disclosure requirements on credit card applications and solicitations. These elaborate requirements differ depending on whether the application or solicitation is made by direct mail, telephone, or other means such as catalogs and magazines. To take just one example, direct mail applications and solicitations must include information about matters such as the APR, annual fees, the grace period for paying without incurring a finance charge, and the method for computing the balance on which the finance charge is based.

Other TILA Provisions The TILA has provisions dealing with *consumer credit advertising.* For example, the act prevents a creditor from "baiting" customers by advertising loan or down payment amounts that it does not usually make available. To help consumers put advertised terms in perspective, if ads for open-end consumer credit plans state any of the plan's specific terms, they must state various other terms as well. For instance, an advertisement using such terms as "$100 down payment," "3 percent interest," or "$99 per month" must also state other relevant terms such as the APR.

The TILA also regulates *open-end consumer credit plans involving an extension of credit secured by a consumer's principal dwelling*—for example, the popular home equity loans. The act controls *advertisements* for such plans, requiring certain information such as the APR if the ad states any specific terms and forbidding misleading terms such as "free money." It also imposes elaborate disclosure requirements on *applications* for such plans. These include matters such as interest rates, fees, repayment options, minimum payments, and repayment periods. The act also controls the *terms* of

such a plan and the *actions* a creditor may take under it. For example, (1) if the plan involves a variable interest rate, the "index rate" to which changes in the APR are pegged must be based on some publicly available rate and must not be under the creditor's control, and (2) a creditor cannot unilaterally terminate the plan and require immediate repayment of the outstanding balance unless a consumer has made material misrepresentations, has failed to repay the balance, or has adversely affected the creditor's security.

Finally, the TILA includes rules concerning *credit cards.* The most important such rule limits a card-holder's liability for unauthorized use of the card to a maximum of $50.

Enforcement Various federal agencies enforce the TILA. Those who willfully and knowingly violate the act may face criminal prosecution. Civil actions by private parties, including class actions, are also possible.

Fair Credit Reporting Act

 LO48-9 Describe the purpose and major provisions of the Fair Credit Reporting Act.

The reports credit bureaus provide may significantly affect one's ability to obtain credit, insurance, employment, and many of life's other goods. Often, affected individuals are unaware of the influence that credit reports had on such decisions. The Fair Credit Reporting Act (FCRA) was enacted in 1970 to give people protection against abuses in the process of disseminating information about their creditworthiness. In 2018 the FCRA was amended by the Economic Growth Act, discussed later in this chapter, to include protections for student borrowers.

Duties of Consumer Reporting Agencies The FCRA imposes certain duties on consumer reporting agencies— agencies that regularly compile credit-related information on individuals for the purpose of furnishing consumer credit reports to users. A consumer reporting agency must adopt *reasonable procedures* to:

1. Ensure that *users employ* the information only for the following purposes: consumer credit sales, employment evaluations, the underwriting of insurance, the granting of a government license or other benefit, or any other business transaction where the user has a legitimate business need for the information.

2. Avoid including in a report *obsolete information* predating the report by more than a stated period. This period usually is 7 years; for a prior bankruptcy, it is 10 years. This duty does not apply to credit reports used

in connection with certain life insurance policies, large credit transactions, and applications for employment.

3. Ensure *maximum possible accuracy* regarding the personal information in credit reports. However, the act does little to limit the *types* of data included in credit reports. In fact, all kinds of information about a person's character, reputation, personal traits, and mode of living seemingly are permitted. However, medical information cannot be included without consent from the relevant consumer.

Duties of Users The FCRA also imposes disclosure duties on *users* of credit reports—mainly credit sellers, lenders, employers, and insurers. One of these duties applies to users who order an *investigative consumer report*. This is a credit report that includes information on a person's character, reputation, personal traits, or mode of living and is based on interviews with neighbors, friends, associates, and the like. If a user such as those listed earlier relies on such reports in making credit, financial, or employment decisions about applicants, the user must inform the applicant that such a report regarding him or her may be requested; obtain the applicant's permission to request the report; provide the applicant access to a copy of the report if it is to be relied upon in the user's decision; inform the applicant that the report was relied upon if that reliance led to adverse action (such as denying the application for a loan or other credit or not hiring the employment applicant); and inform the applicant about how to contact the relevant consumer reporting agency and dispute what is in the report.

Another disclosure duty arises when, because of information contained in any credit report, a user (1) rejects an applicant for consumer credit, insurance, or employment or (2) charges a higher rate for credit or insurance. Here, the user must maintain reasonable procedures for advising the affected individual that it relied on the credit report in making its decision and for stating the name and address of the consumer reporting agency that supplied the report. The *Safeco Insurance* case, which follows, deals with issues surrounding this notice requirement.

Disclosure and Correction of Credit Report Information After a request from a properly identified individual, a *consumer reporting agency* must normally disclose to that individual (1) the nature and substance of all its information about the individual, (2) the sources of this information, and (3) the recipients of any credit reports that it has furnished within certain time periods. Then, a person disputing the completeness or accuracy of the agency's information can compel it to reinvestigate. The credit bureau must delete the information from the person's file if it finds the information to be inaccurate or unverifiable. An individual who is not satisfied with the agency's investigation may file a brief statement setting forth the nature of her dispute with the agency. If so, any subsequent credit report containing the disputed information must note that it is disputed and must provide either the individual's statement or a clear and accurate summary of it. An agency may also be required to notify certain prior recipients of deleted, unverifiable, or disputed information if the individual requests this. However, there is no duty to investigate or to include the consumer's version of the facts if the credit bureau has reason to believe that the individual's request is frivolous or irrelevant. The Economic Growth Act also amends the FCRA to permit a consumer to place or remove a freeze on the consumer's credit report at no cost (at one of the "Big Three" credit bureaus—Equifax, Experian, and TransUnion) and preempts the credit freeze laws that have already been enacted in all 50 states.

Enforcement The Consumer Financial Protection Board discussed later in the chapter has primary responsibility for administering the FCRA. The FTC and other federal agencies still have enforcement roles in certain situations, however. The FCRA establishes criminal penalties for persons who knowingly and willfully obtain consumer information from a credit bureau under false pretenses. Criminal liability may also be imposed on credit bureau officers or employees who knowingly or willfully provide information to unauthorized persons. In addition, violations of the FCRA may trigger private civil suits against consumer reporting agencies and users.

Safeco Insurance Co. of America v. Burr   551 U.S. 47 (2007)

Congress enacted the Fair Credit Reporting Act (FCRA) in 1970 to ensure fair and accurate credit reporting, promote efficiency in the banking system, and protect consumer privacy. The FCRA requires, among other things, that "any person [who] takes any adverse action with respect to any consumer that is based in whole or in part on any information contained in a consumer report" must notify the affected consumer. 15 U.S.C. § 1681m(a). The FCRA defines "consumer report" as "any written, oral, or other communication of any information by a consumer reporting agency bearing on a consumer's credit worthiness, credit standing, [or] credit capacity . . . which is used or expected to be used or collected in whole or in part for the purpose of serving as a factor in establishing the consumer's eligibility for . . . credit or insurance to be used primarily for personal, family, or household purposes." § 1681a(d)(1). The notice of adverse action must point out that action, must explain how to reach the agency that reported on the consumer's credit, and must tell the consumer that he can get a free copy of the report and dispute its accuracy with the agency. § 1681m(a). As it applies to an insurance company, "adverse action" is "a denial or cancellation of, an increase in any charge for, or a reduction or other adverse or unfavorable change in the terms of coverage or amount of, any insurance, existing or applied for." § 1681a(k)(1)(B)(i).

The FCRA provides a private right of action against businesses that use consumer reports but fail to comply with the statute's requirements. If a violation is negligent in nature, the affected consumer is entitled to actual damages. § 1681o(a). If the violation is willful, however, the consumer may be entitled to added monetary relief, including punitive damages. § 1681n(a).

GEICO Corp. writes auto insurance through four subsidiaries: GEICO General, which sells "preferred" policies at low rates to low-risk customers; Government Employees, which also sells "preferred" policies, but only to government employees; GEICO Indemnity, which sells standard policies to moderate-risk customers; and GEICO Casualty, which sells nonstandard policies at higher rates to high-risk customers. (For purposes of convenience, the four subsidiaries are referred to here as GEICO.) An applicant seeking insurance from GEICO calls a toll-free number answered by a GEICO employee, who takes information and, with the applicant's permission, obtains the applicant's credit score from a credit reporting firm. (The FCRA defines a "credit score" as "a numerical value or a categorization derived from a statistical tool or modeling system used by a person who makes or arranges a loan to predict the likelihood of certain credit behaviors, including default.") The information, including the credit score, goes into GEICO's computer system, which selects the appropriate company and the particular rate at which a policy may be issued.

For some time after the FCRA went into effect, GEICO sent adverse action notices to all applicants who were not offered "preferred" policies from GEICO General or Government Employees. GEICO changed its practice, however, after a method to "neutralize" an applicant's credit score was devised. Under the neutralization method, the applicant's company and tier placements are compared with the company and tier placements he would have been assigned with a "neutral" credit score—that is, one calculated without reliance on the applicant's credit history. Under this new scheme, GEICO sends an adverse action notice only if using a neutral credit score would have put the applicant in a lower-priced tier or company. The applicant is not otherwise told if he would have received better terms with a better credit score.

Ajene Edo applied for auto insurance with GEICO. After obtaining Edo's credit score, GEICO offered him a standard policy with GEICO Indemnity (at rates higher than the most favorable), which he accepted. Because Edo's company and tier placement would have been the same with a neutral score, GEICO did not give Edo an adverse action notice. Edo later sued GEICO, alleging willful failure to give notice in violation of § 1681m(a) and seeking damages—including punitive damages—under § 1681n(a). A federal district court granted summary judgment for GEICO, concluding that there was no adverse action when "the premium charged to [Edo] ... would have been the same even if GEICO Indemnity did not consider information in [his] consumer credit history."

As does GEICO, Safeco Insurance Co. of America relies on credit reports to set initial insurance premiums. After considering their credit reports, Safeco offered insurance applicants Charles Burr and Shannon Massey higher rates than the best rates possible. Safeco sent them no adverse action notices. Burr and Massey later sued Safeco, alleging willful violation of § 1681m(a) and seeking damages under § 1681n(a). A federal district court granted summary judgment to Safeco, reasoning that offering a single, initial rate for insurance cannot be "adverse action."

The U.S. Court of Appeals for the Ninth Circuit reversed the judgments in both of the cases described above. In the case against GEICO, the Ninth Circuit held that whenever a consumer "would have received a lower rate for his insurance had the information in his consumer report been more favorable, an adverse action has been taken against him." Because a better credit score would have placed Edo with GEICO General, not GEICO Indemnity, the appeals court held that GEICO's failure to give notice was an adverse action. The Ninth Circuit also held that an insurer "willfully" fails to comply with FCRA if it acts with "reckless disregard" of a consumer's rights under the statute—a conclusion inconsistent with the position taken by certain other federal courts of appeal. The Ninth Circuit remanded the case to the district court for further proceedings concerning whether GEICO acted with reckless disregard.

In the case against Safeco, the Ninth Circuit reversed the district court's decision by relying on its (the Ninth Circuit's) reasoning in the case against GEICO (where it had held that the notice requirement applies to a single statement of an initial charge for a new policy). The Ninth Circuit also remanded the case to the district court for further proceedings on the issue of whether Safeco willfully violated the FCRA. The Supreme Court granted the petitions for certiorari in both cases and consolidated the cases for purposes of disposition.

Souter, Justice

We ... granted certiorari to resolve a conflict [among the various federal courts of appeal] as to whether § 1681n(a) reaches reckless disregard of the FCRA's obligations, and to clarify the notice requirement in § 1681m(a).

GEICO and Safeco argue that liability under § 1681n(a) for "willfully fail[ing] to comply" with the FCRA goes only to acts known to violate the Act, not to reckless disregard of statutory duty, but we think they are wrong. [W]here willfulness is a statutory condition of civil liability, we have generally taken it to cover not only knowing violations of a standard, but reckless ones as well. [Case citations omitted.] This construction reflects common law usage, which treated actions in reckless disregard of the law as willful violations. The standard civil usage thus counsels reading the phrase "willfully fails to comply" in § 1681n(a) as reaching reckless FCRA violations.

Before getting to the claims that the companies acted recklessly, we have the antecedent question whether either company violated the adverse action notice requirement at all. In both cases, respondent-plaintiffs' claims are premised on initial rates charged for new insurance policies, which are not "adverse" actions unless quoting or charging a first-time premium is "an increase in any charge for . . . any insurance, existing or applied for." § 1681a(k)(1)(B)(i).

In Safeco's case, the district court held that the initial rate for a new insurance policy cannot be an "increase" because there is no prior dealing. The phrase "increase in any charge for . . . insurance" is readily understood to mean a change in treatment for an insured, which assumes a previous charge for comparison. Since the district court understood "increase" to speak of change just as much as of comparative size or quantity, it reasoned that the statute's "increase" never touches the initial rate offer, where there is no change.

The Government takes the [position] of the Court of Appeals in construing "increase" to reach a first-time rate. It says that regular usage of the term is not as narrow as the district court thought: the point from which to measure difference can just as easily be understood without referring to prior individual dealing. The Government gives the example of a gas station owner who charges more than the posted price for gas to customers he doesn't like; it makes sense to say that the owner increases the price and that the driver pays an increased price, even if he never pulled in there for gas before. The Government implies, then, that reading "increase" requires a choice, and the chosen reading should be the broad one in order to conform to what Congress had in mind.

We think the Government's reading has the better fit with the ambitious objective set out in the FCRA's statement of purpose, which uses expansive terms to describe the adverse effects of unfair and inaccurate credit reporting and the responsibilities of consumer reporting agencies. The descriptions of systemic problem and systemic need as Congress saw them do nothing to suggest that remedies for consumers placed at a disadvantage by unsound credit ratings should be denied to first-time victims, and the legislative histories of FCRA's original enactment and [a 1996] amendment reveal no reason to confine attention to customers and businesses with prior dealings. Finally, there is nothing about insurance contracts to suggest that Congress might have meant to differentiate applicants from existing customers when it set the notice requirement; the newly insured who gets charged more owing to an erroneous report is in the same boat with the renewal applicant. We therefore hold that the "increase" required for "adverse action," 15 U.S.C. § 1681a(k)(1)(B)(i), speaks to a disadvantageous rate even with no prior dealing; the term reaches initial rates for new applicants.

Although offering the initial rate for new insurance can be an "adverse action," respondent-plaintiffs have another hurdle to clear, for § 1681m(a) calls for notice only when the adverse action is "based in whole or in part on" a credit report. GEICO argues that in order to have adverse action "based on" a credit report, consideration of the report must be a necessary condition for the increased rate. The Government and respondent-plaintiffs do not explicitly take a position on this point.

To the extent there is any disagreement on the issue, we accept GEICO's reading. In common talk, the phrase "based on" indicates a but-for causal relationship and thus a necessary logical condition. Under this most natural reading of § 1681m(a), then, an increased rate is not "based in whole or in part on" the credit report unless the report was a necessary condition of the increase.

To sum up [what has been determined so far], the difference required for an increase can be understood without reference to prior dealing (allowing a first-time applicant to sue), and considering the credit report must be a necessary condition for the difference. The remaining step in determining a duty to notify in cases like these is identifying the benchmark for determining whether a first-time rate is a disadvantageous increase. The Government and respondent-plaintiffs argue that the baseline should be the rate that the applicant would have received with the best possible credit score, while GEICO contends it is what the applicant would have had if the company had not taken his credit score into account (the "neutral score" rate GEICO used in Edo's case). We think GEICO has the better position, primarily because its "increase" baseline is more comfortable with the understanding of causation just discussed, which requires notice under § 1681m(a) only when the effect of the credit report on the initial rate offered is necessary to put the consumer in a worse position than other relevant facts would have decreed anyway. Congress was more likely concerned with the practical question whether the consumer's rate actually suffered when the company took his credit report into account than the theoretical question whether the consumer would have gotten a better rate with perfect credit.

The Government objects that this reading leaves a loophole, since it keeps first-time applicants who actually deserve better-than-neutral credit scores from getting notice, even when errors in credit reports saddle them with unfair rates. This is true; the neutral-score baseline will leave some consumers without a notice that might lead to discovering errors. But we do not know how often these cases will occur, whereas we see a more demonstrable and serious disadvantage inhering in the Government's position.

Since the best rates (the Government's preferred baseline) presumably go only to a minority of consumers, adopting the Government's view would require insurers to send slews of adverse action notices; every young applicant who had yet to establish a gilt-edged credit report, for example, would get a notice that his charge had been "increased" based on his credit report. We think that the consequence of sending out notices on this scale would undercut the obvious policy behind the notice requirement, for notices as common as these would take on the character of formalities, and formalities tend to be ignored. It would get around that new insurance usually comes with an adverse action notice, owing to some legal quirk, and instead of piquing an applicant's interest about the accuracy of his credit record, the commonplace notices would mean just about nothing and go the way of junk mail. Assuming that Congress meant a notice of adverse action to get some attention, we think the cost of closing the loophole would be too high.

In GEICO's case, the initial rate offered to Edo was the one he would have received if his credit score had not been taken into account. GEICO [therefore] owed him no adverse action notice under § 1681m(a). Safeco did not give Burr and Massey any notice because it thought § 1681m(a) did not apply to initial applications, a mistake that left the company in violation of the statute if Burr and Massey received higher rates "based in whole or in part" on their credit reports; if they did, Safeco would be liable to them on a showing of reckless conduct (or worse). The first issue we can forget, however, for although the record does not reliably indicate what rates they would have obtained if their credit reports had not been considered, it is clear enough that if Safeco did violate the statute, the company was not reckless in falling down in its duty.

While "the term recklessness is not self-defining," the common law has generally understood it in the sphere of civil liability as conduct violating an objective standard: action entailing "an unjustifiably high risk of harm that is either known or so obvious that it should be known." [Case citation omitted.] It is this high risk of harm, objectively assessed, that is the essence of recklessness at common law.

There being no indication that Congress had something different in mind, we have no reason to deviate from the common law understanding in applying the statute. Thus, a company subject to the FCRA does not act in reckless disregard of it unless the action is not only a violation under a reasonable reading of the statute's terms, but shows that the company ran a risk of violating the law substantially greater than the risk associated with a reading that was merely careless.

Here, there is no need to pinpoint the negligence/recklessness line, for Safeco's reading of the statute, albeit erroneous, was not objectively unreasonable. On the rationale that "increase" presupposes prior dealing, Safeco took the definition as excluding initial rate offers for new insurance, and so sent no adverse action notices to Burr and Massey. While we disagree with Safeco's analysis, we recognize that its reading has a foundation in the statutory text, and a sufficiently convincing justification to have persuaded the district court to adopt it and rule in Safeco's favor.

The Court of Appeals correctly held that reckless disregard of a requirement of the FCRA would qualify as a willful violation within the meaning of § 1681n(a). But there was no need for that court to remand the cases for factual development. GEICO's decision to issue no adverse action notice to Edo was not a violation of § 1681m(a), and Safeco's misreading of the statute was not reckless.

Judgments of Court of Appeals reversed, and cases remanded for further proceedings consistent with Supreme Court's opinion.

FACT Act and the Identity Theft Problem

 LO48-10 Explain major ways in which the FACT Act seeks to deal with the problem of identity theft.

In recent years, the problem of so-called identity theft has become increasingly acute. Identity theft occurs when those who improperly obtain access to other persons' Social Security number and identifying information such as credit card numbers, bank account numbers, and the like use that information to commit financial fraud by making purchases or obtaining credit in the name of those other persons. A recent FTC estimate indicates that approximately 10 million persons per year may be victims of identity theft in at least one instance and sometimes an ongoing series of instances. Hundreds of thousands of persons have made formal complaints to the FTC regarding identity theft, which is behavior that falls under the FTC's regulatory authority to address deceptive or unfair practices in commercial settings.

Congress, federal agencies, and some state legislatures have attempted to deal with the identity theft problem through statutes and regulations. In late 2003, Congress enacted the Fair and Accurate Credit Transactions Act (usually called the FACT Act) as a series of amendments to the Fair Credit Reporting Act. The FACT Act aids victims of identity theft by allowing them to file identity theft reports with consumer reporting agencies and by requiring such agencies to include "fraud alerts" in their credit reports about consumers who believe they have been victimized by someone else's fraudulent use of their financial information. The FACT Act also required the FTC and various other government agencies to promulgate regulations setting standards for appropriate disposal of financial information about consumers by companies that possess such information. "Disposal," for purposes of the standards, would include not only discarding the information but also selling the information. This FACT Act requirement was designed to minimize the chances that consumers' financial information would fall into the hands of, or be purchased by, would-be identity thieves.

Recent years also witnessed a number of high-profile instances in which security breaches and other apparent lapses at prominent firms resulted in widespread disclosure of the private financial information of huge numbers of consumers. The publicity given to such breaches and lapses and the identity theft dangers they suggested have led to calls for further legislative action. With the identity theft concern seeming to intensify, additional statutory and regulatory efforts to deal with the problem seem likely.

Equal Credit Opportunity Act

 Explain what the Equal Credit Opportunity Act seeks to prevent.

The Equal Credit Opportunity Act (ECOA) prohibits credit discrimination on the bases of sex, marital status, age, race, color, national origin, religion, and the obtaining of income from public assistance. The ECOA covers all entities that regularly arrange, extend, renew, or continue credit. Examples include banks, savings and loan associations, credit card issuers, and many retailers, auto dealers, and Realtors. The act is not limited to consumer credit; it also covers business and commercial loans.

The ECOA governs all phases of a credit transaction. As authorized by the act, the Federal Reserve Board has promulgated regulations detailing permissible and impermissible creditor behavior at each stage. Even when the regulations do not specifically prohibit certain creditor behavior, that behavior may still violate the act itself. Moreover, a credit practice that is neutral on its face may result in an ECOA violation if the practice has an adverse statistical impact on one of the ECOA's protected classes.[6]

The ECOA also requires that creditors notify applicants of the action taken on a credit application within

30 days of its receipt or any longer reasonable time stated in the regulations. If the action is unfavorable, an applicant is entitled to a statement of reasons from the creditor.

The ECOA is enforced by various federal agencies. Which agency enforces the act depends on the type of creditor or credit involved. Civil actions by aggrieved private parties, including class actions, also are possible.

Fair Credit Billing Act

 Identify the purpose of the Fair Credit Billing Act.

The Fair Credit Billing Act is primarily aimed at credit card issuers. Although the act regulates the credit card business in other ways, its most important provisions involve billing disputes. To trigger these provisions, a cardholder must give the issuer written notice of an alleged error in a billing statement within 60 days of the time that the statement is sent to the cardholder. Then, within two complete billing cycles or 90 days (whichever is less), the issuer must either (1) correct the cardholder's account or (2) send the cardholder a written statement justifying the statement's accuracy. Until the issuer takes one of these steps, it may not (1) restrict or close the cardholder's account because of her failure to pay the disputed amount, (2) try to collect the disputed amount, or (3) report or threaten to report the cardholder's failure to pay the disputed amount to a third party such as a consumer reporting agency.

Once an issuer has met the act's requirements, it must also give a cardholder at least 10 days to pay the disputed amount before making an unfavorable report to a third party. If the cardholder disputes the issuer's justification within the 10-day period allowed for payment, the issuer can make such a report only if it also tells the third party that the debt is disputed and gives the cardholder the third party's name and address. In addition, the issuer must report the final resolution of the dispute to the third party.

An issuer that fails to comply with any of these rules forfeits its right to collect $50 of the disputed amount from the cardholder. Because the issuer may still be able to collect the balance on large disputed debts, it is doubtful whether this provision does much to deter violations of the act.

The Dodd–Frank Act

 Identify major consumer-protection features in the Dodd–Frank Act.

In 2010, Congress enacted the Dodd–Frank Wall Street Reform and Consumer Protection Act. Major aspects of

---

[6]This resembles the adverse impact or disparate impact method of proof used in employment discrimination cases under Title VII of the 1964 Civil Rights Act. See Chapter 51.

Dodd–Frank's broad-ranging financial reforms receive attention in Chapters 43, 45, and 46. In addition, Dodd–Frank included significant consumer protection measures. The statute created a new agency, the Consumer Financial Protection Bureau (CFPB), and granted it authority to take regulatory action to mandate clear, accurate disclosures of information that consumers need in shopping for mortgages, credit cards, and other financial products. In addition, the CFPB was given authority to take regulatory action to prohibit hidden fees charged by a financial institution, prohibit deceptive practices by such institutions, and otherwise protect consumers in their dealings with such institutions. Dodd–Frank also granted the CFPB oversight and enforcement authority over a number of the consumer protection statutes discussed earlier in this chapter, insofar as they pertain to financial transactions involving consumers. In some instances, the CFPB assumes sole enforcement authority over such laws; in other instances, it shares such authority with agencies such as the FTC. The Fair Credit Reporting Act (discussed earlier in the chapter) and the Fair Debt Collection Practices Act (to be discussed shortly) are examples of such instances. Although Dodd–Frank specified that the CFPB is housed as part of the Federal Reserve, other measures in the statute are designed to establish a significant level of independence on the part of the bureau.

The CFPB's responsibilities also include helping consumers obtain responses to their complaints about credit cards, mortgages, bank accounts, other bank services, credit reporting, debt collection, loans, money transfers, and other similar consumer-oriented financial products or services. Upon receiving a complaint from a consumer, the CFPB contacts the relevant company and seeks to ensure that the company provides the consumer a prompt response. According to a July 2014 report, the CFPB had received approximately 400,000 complaints from consumers during the first three years of the Bureau's existence. Of those 400,000 complaints, approximately one-third pertained to mortgages. Also among the largest numbers of consumer complaints were those dealing with debt collection, credit cards, credit reporting, and bank accounts and services.

In 2018, the Economic Growth, Regulatory Relief, and Consumer Protection Act (Economic Growth Act) became law and modesty scaled back portions of the Dodd–Frank Act, including raising the threshold to $250 billion from $50 billion under which banks are deemed too important to fail. The Economic Growth Act also amended certain provisions of the Truth in Lending Act (TILA), discussed earlier in this chapter. In addition, under this new law, the CFPB is now required to provide additional guidance on the applicability of the Truth in Lending Disclosure (TRID) Rules with respect to mortgage assumption transactions and construction-to-permanent home loans.

Fair Debt Collection Practices Act

 Explain the purpose of the Fair Debt Collection Practices Act and describe its major requirements.

Concern over abusive, deceptive, and unfair practices by debt collectors led Congress to pass the Fair Debt Collection Practices Act (FDCPA) in 1977. The act applies to debts that involve money, property, insurance, or services obtained by a *consumer* for *consumer purposes*. Normally, the act covers only those who are in the business of collecting debts owed to *others*. However, creditors who collect their own debts are covered when, by using a name other than their own name, they indicate that a third party is collecting the debt.

Communication Rules Except when necessary to locate a debtor, the FDCPA generally prevents debt collectors from contacting third parties such as the debtor's employer, relatives, or friends. The act also limits a collector's contacts with the debtor himself. Unless the debtor consents, for instance, a collector cannot contact him at unusual or inconvenient times or places, or at his place of employment if the employer forbids such contacts. A collector cannot contact a debtor if it knows that the debtor is represented by an attorney, unless the attorney consents to such contact or fails to respond to the collector's communications. In addition, a collector must cease most communications with a debtor if the debtor gives the creditor written notification that he refuses to pay the debt or that he does not desire further communications.

The FDCPA also requires a collector to give a debtor certain information about the debt within five days of the collector's first communication with the debtor. The *Evory* case, which follows shortly, explains the content of this notice requirement and addresses various issues suggested by it. If the debtor disputes the debt in writing within 30 days after receiving this information, the collector must cease its collection efforts until it sends verification of the debt to the debtor.

Specific Forbidden Practices As explained in the *Evory* case, the FDCPA sets out categories of forbidden collector practices and lists specific examples of each category. The listed examples, however, do not exhaust the ways that debt collectors can violate the act. The categories are:

1. *Harassment, oppression, or abuse.* Examples include threats of violence, obscene or abusive language, and repeated phone calls.

2. *False or misleading misrepresentations.* Among the FDCPA's listed examples are statements that a debtor will be imprisoned for failure to pay, that a collector will take an action it is not legally entitled to take or does not intend to take, that a collector is affiliated with the government, and that misstate the amount of the debt.

3. *Unfair practices.* These include collecting from a debtor an amount not authorized by the agreement creating the debt, inducing a debtor to accept a collect call before revealing the call's true purpose, and falsely or unjustifiably threatening to take a debtor's property.

The FDCPA contains a provision that provides a violator of the statute's obligations a defense if the violation "was not intentional and resulted from a bona fide error notwithstanding the maintenance of procedures reasonably adapted to avoid any such error." In *Jerman v. Carlisle, McNellie, Rini, Kramer & Ulrich LPA,*[7] the Supreme Court held that this defense does not extend to mistakes regarding the legal requirements set forth in the law (i.e., mistakes of law). Rather, the statutory defense is limited to mistakes of fact and errors such as clerical errors.

Enforcement The FTC and the Consumer Financial Protection Bureau both have enforcement authority regarding the FDCPA. The statute also permits individual lawsuits and class actions to be brought by the affected debtor or debtors.

_____

[7]559 U.S. 573 (2010).

Evory v. RJM Acquisitions Funding, L.L.C.   505 F.3d 769 (7th Cir. 2007)

Section 1692g of the Fair Debt Collection Practices Act (FDCPA) provides:

Within five days after the initial communication with a consumer in connection with the collection of any debt, a debt collector shall, unless the following information is contained in the initial communication or the consumer has paid the debt, send the consumer a written notice containing—

(1) the amount of the debt;

(2) the name of the creditor to whom the debt is owed;

(3) a statement that unless the consumer, within thirty days after receipt of the notice, disputes the validity of the debt, or any portion thereof, the debt will be assumed to be valid by the debt collector;

(4) a statement that if the consumer notifies the debt collector in writing within the thirty-day period that the debt, or any portion thereof, is disputed, the debt collector will obtain verification of the debt or a copy of a judgment against the consumer and a copy of such verification or judgment will be mailed to the consumer by the debt collector; and

(5) a statement that, upon the consumer's written request within the thirty-day period, the debt collector will provide the consumer with the name and address of the original creditor, if different from the current creditor.

Other sections of the FDCPA prohibit certain debt collection practices. Section 1692d forbids "any conduct the natural consequence of which is to harass, oppress, or abuse any person in connection with the collection of a debt." Section 1692e bars a debt collector from using "any false, deceptive, or misleading representation or means in connection with the collection of any debt." Section 1692f prohibits a debt collector's use of "any unfair or unconscionable means to collect or attempt to collect any debt."

Four appeals lodged in the U.S. Court of Appeals for the Seventh Circuit presented FDCPA questions regarding debt collectors' communications with attorneys for debtors and/or debt collectors' use of allegedly deceptive, abusive, or otherwise unfair settlement offers. The four cases were Evory v. RJM Acquisitions Funding, L.L.C.; Lauer v. Mason, Silver, Wenk & Mischlin, L.L.C.; Captain v. ARS National Services, Inc.; *and* Jackson v. National Action Financial Services, Inc. *In all four cases, the plaintiffs were debtors and the defendants were debt collectors. The Seventh Circuit consolidated the four cases for decision. Further facts concerning the cases are set forth in the following edited version of the Seventh Circuit's opinion.*

Posner, Circuit Judge

We have consolidated for decision four intertwined cases that present [various] questions under the FDCPA. We shall first answer the questions and then indicate the [appropriate] disposition[s] [of the cases]. Here are the questions:

1. Whether, if the consumer (as the statute refers to the putative debtor) is represented by a lawyer, a debt collector must give the same written notice to the lawyer that section 1692g would require were the consumer unrepresented and the notice sent directly to him.

2. Whether communications to lawyers are subject to sections 1692d through 1692f, which forbid harassing, deceptive, and unfair practices in debt collection. [Federal courts of appeal have split on this question.]

3. Whether, if the answer to question 2 is yes, the standard applicable to determining whether a representation is false, deceptive, or misleading under section 1692e is the same whether the representation is made to the lawyer or to his client.

4. Whether a settlement offer contained in a letter from the debt collector to a consumer is lawful per se under section 1692f. [Federal courts of appeal have also split on this question.]

5. If it is not per se lawful, whether its lawfulness should be affected by whether it is addressed to a lawyer, rather than to the consumer directly.

6. Whether there should be a safe harbor for a debt collector accused of violating section 1692e by making such an offer.

7. Again, if such a letter is not per se lawful, what type of evidence a plaintiff must present to prove that a settlement offer violates section 1692e.

8. Whether the determination that a representation is or is not false, deceptive, or misleading under section 1692 is always to be treated as a matter of law. [Federal courts of appeal have split on this question as well.]

...

[Regarding the notice requirement set forth in § 1692g,] [i]t would be passing odd if the fact that a consumer was represented excused the debt collector from having to convey to the consumer the information to which the statute entitles him. For example, sections 1692g(a)(1) and (2) provide that the required notice must state the amount of the debt and the name of the creditor. Is it to be believed that by retaining a lawyer the debtor disentitles himself to the information? Or that the debt collector, though knowing that the debtor is represented, can communicate directly with him in defiance of the principle that once a party to a legal dispute is represented, the other party must deal with him through his lawyer, and not directly? We conclude that any written notice sent to the lawyer must contain the information that would be required by the Act if the notice were sent to the consumer directly.

The next question is whether debt collectors can, without liability, threaten, make false representations to, or commit other abusive, deceptive, or unconscionable acts against a consumer's lawyer, in violation of sections 1692d, e, or f. These sections[, which are quoted in the above statement of facts,] do not designate any class of persons, such as lawyers, who

can be abused, misled, etc., by debt collectors with impunity. It is true that a lawyer is less likely to be deceived, intimidated, harassed, and so forth (for simplicity, we shall assume that only deception is alleged) than a consumer. But that is an argument not for immunizing practices forbidden by the statute when they are directed against a consumer's lawyer, but rather for recognizing that the standard for determining whether particular conduct violates the statute is different when the conduct is aimed at a lawyer than when it is aimed at a consumer.

The courts have ruled that the statute is intended for the protection of unsophisticated consumers (sophisticated consumers presumably do not need its protection), so that in deciding whether for example a representation made in a dunning letter is misleading, the court asks whether a person of modest education and limited commercial savvy would be likely to be deceived. The standpoint is not that of the *least* intelligent consumer in this nation of 300 million people, but that of the average consumer in the lowest quartile (or some other substantial bottom fraction) of consumer competence. But if the debt collector has targeted a particularly vulnerable group—say, consumers who he knows have a poor command of English—the benchmark for deciding whether the communication is deceptive would be the competence of the substantial bottom fraction of *that* group. [Case citations omitted.]

By the same token, the "unsophisticated consumer" standpoint is inappropriate for judging communications with lawyers, just as it is inappropriate to fix a physician's standard of care at the level of that of a medical orderly. But what should the standard be? Most lawyers who represent consumers in debt collection cases are familiar with debt collection law and therefore unlikely to be deceived. But sometimes a lawyer will find himself handling a debt collection case not because he's a specialist but because a friend or relative has asked him to handle it. His sophistication in collection matters would be less than that of the specialist practitioner but much greater than that of the average unsophisticated consumer. He would not have to be an expert on the FDCPA to be able to look it up and discover what information sections 1692g(a)(3)–(5) require be disclosed to the consumer, and then compare the requirements with the content of the communication that he has received on his client's behalf. Since, therefore, most lawyers who represent consumers in debt-collection cases are knowledgeable about the law and practices of debt collection, since those who are not should be able to inform themselves sufficiently to be able to represent their consumer clients competently, and since the debt collector cannot be expected to know how knowledgeable a particular consumer's lawyer is, we conclude that a representation by a debt collector that would be unlikely to deceive a competent lawyer, even if he is not a specialist in consumer debt law, should not be actionable.

We have assumed for the sake of simplicity that the communication to the lawyer is alleged to be *deceptive*; what if instead it is alleged to be false or misleading, terms also found in section 1692e? "Misleading" is similar to "deceptive," except that it can be innocent; one intends to deceive, but one can mislead through inadvertence. A sophisticated person is less likely to be either deceived or misled than an unsophisticated one. That is less true if a statement is false. A false claim of fact in a dunning letter may be as difficult for a lawyer to see through as a consumer. Suppose the letter misrepresents the unpaid balance of the consumer's debt. The lawyer might be unable to discover the falsity of the representation without an investigation that he might be unable, depending on his client's resources, to undertake. Such a misrepresentation would be actionable whether made to the consumer directly, or indirectly through his lawyer.

We move now from the lawyer cases to the cases of settlement offers communicated directly to consumers, where there is no lawyer in the picture. But later we shall have to bring the lawyer back into the picture in order to round out our discussion of the difference between consumers and lawyers as recipients of potentially misleading statements from debt collectors.

It is apparently common for debt collectors to send letters to consumers that say such things as (these examples are all taken from the cases before us) "we would like to offer you a unique opportunity to satisfy your outstanding debt"—"a settlement of 25% OFF of your current balance. SO YOU ONLY PAY $[____] In ONE PAYMENT that must be received no later than 40 days from the date on this letter." Or "TIME'S A WASTIN'! . . . Act now and receive 30% off if you pay by March 31st." Or we are "currently able to offer you a substantial discount of *50% off* your Current Balance *if we receive payment by 05-14-2004*" (emphases in original). There is nothing improper about making a settlement offer. The concern is that unsophisticated consumers may think that if they don't pay by the deadline, they will have no further chance to settle their debt for less than the full amount; for the offers are in the idiom of limited-time or one-time sales offers, clearance sales, going-out-of-business sales, and other temporary discounts. In fact debt collectors, who naturally are averse to instituting actual collection proceedings for the often very modest sums involved in the consumer debt collection business, frequently renew their offers if the consumer fails to accept the initial offer.

The objection to allowing liability to be based on such offers is that the settlement process would disintegrate if the debt collector had to disclose the consequences of the

consumer's rejecting his initial offer. If he has to say, "We'll give you 50 percent if you pay us by May 14, but if you don't, we'll probably offer you the same or even better deal later, and if you refuse that, we'll probably give up and you'll never have to pay a cent of the debt you owe," there will be no point in making offers. As in previous cases in which we have created safe-harbor language for use in cases under the FDCPA, [case citations omitted], we think the present concern can be adequately addressed yet the unsophisticated consumer still be protected against receiving a false impression of his options by the debt collector's including with the offer the following language: "We are not obligated to renew this offer." The word "obligated" is strong and even the unsophisticated consumer will realize that there is a renewal possibility but that it is not assured.

This is not to suggest that in the absence of safe-harbor language a debt collector is per se liable for violating section 1692 if he makes the kind of settlement offer that we quoted. We see a potential for deception of the unsophisticated in those offers but we have no way of determining whether a sufficiently large segment of the unsophisticated are likely to be deceived to enable us to conclude that the statute has been violated. For that, evidence is required, the most useful sort being [a suitable] consumer survey.

Other circuits, perhaps less kindly disposed to survey evidence than we, treat the deceptive character of a debt collector's communication as a question of law, so that if the communication is not deceptive on its face, the plaintiff is forbidden to try to show that it would be likely to deceive a substantial number of its intended recipients. We disagree with that position. The intended recipients of dunning letters are not federal judges, and judges are not experts in the knowledge and understanding of unsophisticated consumers facing demands by debt collectors. We are no more entitled to rely on our intuitions in this context than we are in deciding issues of consumer confusion in trademark cases, where the use of survey evidence is routine.

But we emphasize that survey evidence in debt-collection as in trademark cases must comply with the principles of professional survey research; if it does not, it is not even admissible, let alone probative of deception. We are exceedingly doubtful that any lawyer involved in representing debtors would be deceived by the settlement offers made by debt collectors, and doubt therefore that any cases based on such offers could survive summary judgment or even a motion to dismiss were the offer directed to the consumer's lawyer rather than to the consumer. This illustrates our earlier point about the importance of distinguishing between lawyers and unsophisticated consumers in applying section 1692e.

Having answered the questions that we listed at the beginning of our opinion, we can be brief in discussing our four cases. In *Lauer*, the consumer was represented by a lawyer. The defendant debt collector did not send either the lawyer or his client the written notice required by section 1692g, but instead sent the lawyer a letter that the plaintiff characterizes as coercive because it threatened to dispose of property of the plaintiff that had a purely sentimental value, such as scrapbooks, a wedding gown, and a videotape of the arrival of his adopted child from Korea. The plaintiff doesn't explain which subsection of section 1692 the threat violates, but it could well violate d, e, f, or indeed all three. The district court dismissed the complaint on the ground that communications with a consumer's lawyer are beyond the reach of the Fair Debt Collection Practices Act. That was error.

The defendant in *Lauer* also argues that if the initial communication from the debt collector is to the consumer's lawyer rather than to the consumer himself, the notice requirement is not triggered. If you glance back at section 1692g(a) you will see that it says that the written notice is required to be sent "five days after the initial communication with a consumer." The argument is that if there is no letter sent first ("initial communication") directly to the consumer, but instead the initial communication is to the consumer's lawyer, the condition for requiring the subsequent written notice containing specified information is not satisfied and therefore such a notice need never be sent either to the lawyer or to the consumer. All that this argument shows is how unsound it would be to suppose that a communication to a person's lawyer is not a communication to the person. It would make a consumer who had a lawyer worse off than one who did not, because neither he nor his lawyer would have a right to any of the information that the statute requires be disclosed to the consumer.

In *Captain*, before realizing that the consumer was represented, the defendant sent him a letter offering a 30 percent discount off the face amount of the debt, provided payment was received by a specified date. The plaintiff claims that the letter violated section 1692e. Shortly afterward, his lawyer called the defendant and was told that if the debt wasn't paid within two weeks of the date of the initial collection letter (a deadline that had already passed), a $15 daily charge would be added to the account balance until the debt was paid in full. Such a charge, equivalent to an interest rate of 730 percent a year on the unpaid balance of the debt, would violate Indiana law. Although a violation of state law is not in itself a violation of the FDCPA, a threat to impose a penalty that the threatener knows is improper because unlawful is a good candidate for a violation of sections 1692d and e. The district court dismissed

the complaint for failure to state a claim: the settlement-offer charge on the ground that such offers are per se lawful under the Act and the challenge to the lawfulness of the $15 a day representation because it was made to a lawyer. Both rulings were erroneous.

Evory and *Jackson* . . . are pure settlement-offer cases—there were no communications to lawyers. But they are importantly different. In *Evory*, the district court dismissed the complaint, and that was error. But in *Jackson* the court granted summary judgment for the defendant. Much of the judge's opinion tracks the discussion in cases that hold that the kind of settlement offer involved in these cases is nondeceptive per se, and that is wrong. But the judge was willing to consider the survey evidence that the plaintiff had introduced. He concluded that it did not show that the settlement offer was deceptive. He was right and indeed should have ruled the evidence inadmissible. The plaintiffs lawyer at the argument of the appeal conceded that it was not a good survey. We would put the matter more strongly. The respondents in the survey were shown a letter similar to the one the plaintiff had received. The key question they were asked was, "Let's say the person getting this letter does not accept the settlement offer by the deadline date. Do you think that person would feel it is a limited-time offer, or it is not a limited-time offer?" By referring to "deadline date," the questioner signaled that it was a limited-time offer. Leading questions in surveys are improper. And "limited-time offer" was not defined. Nor should the respondents have been asked what they thought some *other* recipient of the letter would "feel," especially since they were given no information about the hypothetical recipient. They should simply have been asked, "What do you think would happen if you didn't accept the offer? Do you think it would be renewed or extended? Or do you think this would be your last chance to get a discount off the amount owed?"

There is compelling evidence that the offers in this and the other cases were not final offers. But that means only that if the offers were understood as such by the targeted recipients, they were deceptive. The anterior issue is whether they were likely to be understood as such by a substantial number of unsophisticated consumers. Maybe they were, but some evidence beyond the face of the offer was required to establish a prima facie case, and it was not presented.

District court's decision in *Jackson* affirmed; district courts' decisions in *Lauer*, *Captain*, and *Evory* reversed, and cases remanded for further proceedings.

Ethics and Compliance in Action

Since at least the early 1950s, the International Harvester Company's gasoline-powered tractors had been subject to "fuel geysering." This was a phenomenon in which hot liquid gasoline would shoot from the tractor's gas tank when the filler cap was opened. The hot gasoline could cause severe burns and could ignite and cause a fire. Over the years, at least 90 fuel geysering incidents involving International Harvester tractors occurred. At least 12 of these involved significant burn injuries, and at least one caused a death.

International Harvester discovered the full dimensions of the fuel geysering problem in 1963. In that year, it revised its owner's manuals to warn buyers of new gas-powered tractors not to remove the gas cap from a hot or running tractor. In 1976, it produced a new fuel tank decal with a similar warning. Because of an industrywide shift to diesel-powered tractors, however, this warning had a very limited distribution to buyers of new tractors, and it rarely reached former buyers. International Harvester never specifically warned either new or old buyers about the geysering problem until 1980, when it voluntarily made a mass mailing to 630,000 customers.

In 1980, the FTC issued a complaint against International Harvester, alleging that its failure to warn buyers of the fuel geysering problem for 17 years violated FTC Act § 5. Agreeing with the initial decision of an administrative law judge, the full commission held that International Harvester's failure to warn was not deceptive but was unfair for purposes of § 5. *In the Matter of International Harvester*, 104 F.T.C. 949 (1984).

Applying the three-part analysis discussed earlier in this chapter, the commission weighed the consumer injury caused by fuel geysering against the costs of providing effective warnings about it. The commission concluded that the 12 instances of serious burns and the one death caused by fuel geysering were injuries that might have been avoided by a warning and were sufficient to outweigh the $2.8 million apparently required for an effective warning. However, the commission's method clearly left open the possibility that in some cases, a practice's benefits to consumers or to competition might outweigh the harm it causes.

- Is it morally right to balance personal injury and human life against economic gain? Isn't each human life valuable beyond measure? Can decision-making processes such as the FTC's ever be justified?
- On the other hand, if you think that the commission's balancing exercise is justifiable, how is one to strike the balance? How would you have decided *International Harvester* if ethical analysis, rather than legal standards, controlled the decision?

Product Safety Regulation Yet another facet of consumer protection law is federal regulation of product safety. As discussed in Chapter 20, sellers and manufacturers of dangerously defective products may be held civilly liable to those injured by such products. Damage recoveries, however, are at best an after-the-fact remedy for injuries caused by such products. Thus, federal law also seeks to promote product safety through *direct regulation* of consumer products.

The Consumer Product Safety Act

> **LO48-15** Describe ways in which the Consumer Product Safety Commission may act in order to address product safety issues.

The most important federal product safety measure is the Consumer Product Safety Act (CPSA). The CPSA established the Consumer Product Safety Commission (CPSC), an independent regulatory agency that is the main federal body concerned with the safety of consumer products. Among the CPSC's activities are the following: (1) issuing

consumer product safety standards (which normally pertain to the performance of consumer products or require product warnings or instructions), (2) issuing rules *banning* certain *hazardous products*, (3) bringing suit in federal district court to eliminate the dangers presented by *imminently hazardous* consumer products (products that pose an immediate and unreasonable risk of death, serious illness, or severe personal injury), and (4) *ordering private parties to address "substantial product hazards"* after receiving notice of such hazards. The CPSA's remedies and enforcement devices include injunctions, the seizure of products, civil penalties, criminal penalties, and private damage suits.

In 2008, widespread media reports highlighted the harms experienced by children as a result of being exposed to toys that contained dangerous chemical elements or other dangerous substances. Many of these toys had been imported into the United States. The intense attention to toy safety issues prompted Congress to enact the first major amendments to the CPSA in a number of years. Besides including a very significant increase in the CPSC budget, the amendments instructed the CPSC to study a variety of toy safety issues and other children's product safety issues, and to appoint a Chronic Hazard Advisory Panel to advise the CPSC on the children's health effects of certain chemicals in toys and child care products. The amendments also instructed the CPSC to follow up with appropriate new regulations to address major safety concerns.

The 2008 retooling of the CPSA furnished Congress an opportunity to address long-standing concerns over the numbers of rollover accidents in which users of all-terrain vehicles (ATVs) were injured or killed. Congress directed the CPSC to develop safety regulations regarding three-wheeled and four-wheeled ATVs, with the importation

and sale of the three-wheeled ATVs being banned until the promulgation of the CPSC regulations concerning the three-wheeled variety.

Other Federal Product Safety Regulation Other federal statutes besides the CPSA regulate various specific consumer products. Among the subjects so regulated are toys, cigarette labeling and advertising, eggs, meat, poultry, smokeless tobacco, flammable fabrics, drugs, cosmetics, pesticides, and motor vehicles. Some of these laws are enforced by the CPSC and some by other bodies.

Problems and Problem Cases

1. For many years, advertisements for Listerine Antiseptic Mouthwash had impliedly claimed that Listerine was beneficial in the treatment of colds, cold symptoms, and sore throats. An FTC adjudicative proceeding concluded that these claims were false. Thus, the FTC ordered Warner-Lambert Company, the manufacturer of Listerine, to include the following statement in future Listerine advertisements: "Contrary to prior advertising, Listerine will not help prevent colds or sore throats or lessen their severity." Warner-Lambert argued that this order was invalid because it went beyond a command to simply cease and desist from illegal behavior. Was Warner-Lambert correct?

2. Pantron I Corp. sold a shampoo and conditioner known as the Helsinki Formula. Pantron promoted the Helsinki Formula as an aid in fighting male pattern baldness. According to Pantron, polysorbate was the main ingredient that made the Helsinki Formula effective in arresting hair loss and stimulating hair growth. The Federal Trade Commission filed suit against Pantron on the theory that Pantron's advertisements made deceptive representations about the effectiveness of the Helsinki Formula, as well as deceptive representations that scientific evidence supported the effectiveness claims. The FTC sought injunctive and monetary relief. The evidence showed that the Helsinki Formula was effective for some users with male pattern baldness but that this effectiveness was probably due to the "placebo effect" (i.e., the effectiveness for some users stemmed from psychological reasons rather than from the inherent merit of the product). Because there was no scientifically valid evidence indicating that polysorbate is effective in treating hair loss or in inducing hair growth, the district court

concluded that Pantron's advertisements were deceptive in representing that *scientific evidence* supported a conclusion that the Helsinki Formula was effective. The district court therefore issued an injunction that barred Pantron from representing, in its advertisements, that scientific evidence supports the alleged effectiveness of the Helsinki Formula in treating baldness or hair loss. However, because the Helsinki Formula did work for some users some of the time (whatever the reason), the district court concluded that the FTC had failed to carry its burden of proving that Pantron engaged in deceptive advertising when it represented that the Helsinki Formula was effective for persons with male pattern baldness. The court therefore refused to enjoin Pantron from making such a representation of effectiveness (i.e., a representation of effectiveness that did not go on to make the false claim of supporting scientific evidence). The court also refused to order monetary relief. In its appeal to the U.S. Court of Appeals for the Ninth Circuit, the FTC argued that when a product's effectiveness is due only to the placebo effect, an advertising claim of effectiveness is false and deceptive for purposes of the FTC Act. Was this FTC argument legally correct? Which party—the FTC or Pantron—was entitled to win the appeal?

3. Besides maintaining a private law practice, Keith Gill offered credit repair services to consumers in a business that he operated with a retired attorney, Richard Murkey. In various contexts, Gill and Murkey made representations to the effect that they could remove any accurate and nonobsolete information of a negative nature from the credit reports of consumers who used their credit repair services. The Federal Trade Commission filed suit against Gill and Murkey, alleging, among other things, that these representations violated § 5 of the Federal Trade Commission Act. Was § 5 violated?

4. Between 1966 and 1975, the Orkin Exterminating Company, the world's largest termite and pest control firm, offered its customers a "lifetime" guarantee that could be renewed each year by paying a definite amount specified in its contracts with the customers. The contracts gave no indication that the fees could be raised for any reasons other than certain narrowly specified ones. Beginning in 1980, Orkin unilaterally breached these contracts by imposing higher-than-agreed-upon annual renewal fees. Roughly 200,000 contracts were breached in this way. Orkin realized $7 million in additional revenues from customers who renewed at the higher fees. The additional fees did not purchase a higher level of service than that originally provided for in the contracts. Although some of Orkin's competitors may have been willing to assume Orkin's pre-1975 contracts at the fees stated therein, they would not have offered a fixed, locked-in "lifetime" renewal fee such as the one Orkin originally provided. Under the three-part test stated in the text, did Orkin's behavior violate FTC Act § 5's prohibition against *unfair* acts or practices?

5. Patron Aviation, an aviation company, bought an airplane engine from L&M Aircraft. The engine was assembled and shipped to L&M by Teledyne Industries. L&M installed the engine in one of Patron's airplanes. The engine turned out to be defective, so Patron sued L&M and Teledyne. One of the issues presented by the case was whether the Magnuson–Moss Act was applicable. Does the Magnuson–Moss Act apply to this transaction?

6. National Financial Services, a debt collection agency that serves magazine subscriptions clearinghouses, handled roughly 2.2 million accounts during 1986 and 1987. It sent letters to debtors whose accounts were delinquent. The average unpaid balance owed on these accounts was approximately $20. One letter sent by National Financial to a large number of debtors stated that their account "Will Be Transferred To An Attorney If It Is Unpaid After The Deadline Date!!!" Debtors who did not pay after receiving this letter received one or more letters that bore the letterhead of "N. Frank Lanocha, Attorney at Law." Lanocha prepared the text of these form letters and gave copies to National Financial's president, Smith. Smith then arranged for the letters to be prepared and mailed out. One of these letters contained the following statements: "Please Note I Am The Collection Attorney Who Represents American Family Publishers. I Have The Authority To See That Suit Is Filed Against You In This Matter." The letter also stated: "Unless This Payment Is Received In This Office Within Five Days Of The Date Of This Notice, I Will Be Compelled To Consider The Use Of The Legal Remedies That May Be Available To Effect Collection." The Federal Trade Commission sued National Financial, Smith, and Lanocha, alleging violations of the Fair Debt Collection Practices Act. How should the court rule?

7. National Credit Management Group (NCMG) offered credit monitoring and credit card services to consumers throughout the United States. NCMG used the 1-800-YES-CREDIT toll-free telephone number as the central marketing focus of its business. The company's advertisements on radio and cable television stated that persons with credit problems should call the toll-free number to receive a "confidential analysis" of their credit histories. Many of these advertisements also promised that NCMG would provide consumers with a complimentary application for a major credit card without a security deposit. In a number of the television advertisements, NCMG would flash the word "APPROVED" on the television screen or would otherwise highlight that word when the advertisement made reference to the credit card application.

NCMG received approximately 6,500 "inbound" calls per week from consumers who were responding to the radio and television advertisements. NCMG did not engage in "cold-calling" of consumers. When consumers called 1-800-YES-CREDIT, an NCMG representative offered them an initial credit analysis for an up-front fee of $95. During this phone conversation, the NCMG representative asked consumers for information—name, address, Social Security number, checking account number, employment information, and income information—that the representative stated was necessary to enable the credit analyst to gather information concerning the particular consumer's credit history. The NCMG representative also stated that the $95 fee was the charge associated with the accumulation and monitoring of the information contained in the credit profile of the consumer, and that the credit analyst would be telephoning the consumer in approximately two weeks to discuss the consumer's credit history. Between 5 and 9 percent of consumers who called the toll-free number purchased either the $95 initial credit analysis offered or other services (described below) that NCMG offered.

NCMG used the checking account information obtained by its representatives to set up an arrangement under which consumers' checking accounts would be debited in the amount of $95 if they accepted the initial credit analysis offer. Consumers who initially gave verbal authorization for the debiting arrangement later encountered great difficulty in attempting to cancel it. In the initial telephone conversation described above, the NCMG representatives did not tell consumers that when they used their "complimentary" application for a credit card (the application referred to in NCMG's advertisements), they could have to pay fees ranging from $50 to $100 to sponsoring banks. Neither were consumers informed that they were not guaranteed of receiving a credit card. Although sponsoring banks approved a high percentage of consumers who used the NCMG-provided application, not all applicants were approved for a credit card.

NCMG did not actually perform a credit analysis for paying consumers, nor did NCMG check those consumers' credit reports. When the supposed credit analyst made the above-described follow-up telephone call to a consumer, he or she did not discuss the consumer's credit history. Instead, the credit analyst attempted to sell the consumer NCMG's two-year program designed for persons who wished to establish or reestablish their credit. The two-year program, which consisted largely of NCMG's furnishing certain educational materials, ranged in cost from several hundred dollars to well over $1,000, with the NCMG caller having the discretion to set the price at what seemed an appropriate level under the circumstances. The credit analyst typically did not disclose that the earlier check-debiting arrangement would be used as the payment mechanism for persons who agreed to subscribe to the two-year program.

The Federal Trade Commission (FTC) filed suit against NCMG. Among other things, the FTC alleged that NCMG violated § 5 of the FTC Act as well as the Telemarketing Sales Rule (TSR). Did NCMG violate § 5? Did NCMG violate the TSR?

8. The owners of a certain house had listed it for rental with Gatewood Realty. Ira Simonoff, a Gatewood broker, showed the house to brothers Jonathan and Robert Scott, who offered to rent the house at a lesser monthly rate than the owners had specified. Simonoff then asked the Scotts for certain background information. Jonathan Scott responded to Simonoff's request for his Social Security number by telling Simonoff that he (Simonoff) was not authorized to make a credit check. Robert Scott added that he did not want his credit checked. During the discovery phase of the litigation

described below, Jonathan Scott testified that Simonoff assured him no credit check would be run. Both brothers testified that they understood Simonoff would not check their credit. Simonoff, however, testified that he informed the brothers of the house owners' requirement of a credit check and that one of the brothers had simply asked Simonoff not to have a credit check done "if at all possible." When Simonoff relayed the Scotts' offer to the owners, they insisted that credit checks be conducted. Simonoff therefore asked Peter Visconti, who was affiliated with Real Estate Finance Group (REFG), to check the Scotts' credit. According to later testimony by Visconti, Simonoff represented that he had written authorizations from the Scotts. (The Scotts denied that any such authorizations existed.) Visconti obtained credit reports on the Scotts by falsely representing to a computerized credit reporting service that he needed the reports to evaluate a mortgage application. He then supplied the credit reports to Simonoff. When a real estate broker working on behalf of the Scotts learned that Simonoff had obtained their credit reports, she so informed the Scotts.

The Scotts filed suit against REFG, Gatewood, and Simonoff for alleged violations of the Fair Credit Reporting Act (FCRA). After discovery, the Scotts moved for partial summary judgment against all defendants on the theory that they had obtained the Scotts' credit reports by means of false pretenses, in violation of the FCRA. Gatewood and Simonoff moved for summary judgment in their favor. The district court granted the Scotts' summary judgment motion as to REFG but not as to Gatewood and Simonoff. Instead, the court granted summary judgment in favor of Gatewood Realty and Simonoff and ordered dismissal of the Scotts' FCRA claim against them. The Scotts appealed the dismissal of their FCRA claim against Gatewood and Simonoff. How did the appellate court rule?

9. When Samuel Grant sued his landlord, the landlord filed a counterclaim. Grant later was awarded a $608 judgment against the landlord, with the landlord receiving a $476.10 judgment against Grant on the counterclaim. This left Grant with a net judgment of $131.90. Approximately one year after the above case, Texaco denied Grant's application for a credit card. Texaco did so on the basis of a credit report prepared by TRW Inc. This credit report stated that a judgment of approximately $400 had been entered against Grant in the above-described litigation between Grant and his landlord. Grant then informed TRW that the litigation

involving his landlord had resulted in a net judgment in Grant's favor. TRW eventually sent Grant an "Updated Credit Profile" showing that the $400 judgment had been deleted from his file. Several months later, Grant again applied for a Texaco credit card. Texaco again denied his application because a newly issued TRW credit report indicated that a $400 judgment had been entered against him in the case involving his landlord. Grant then sued TRW on the theory that TRW had violated the Fair Credit Reporting Act (FCRA). TRW moved to dismiss the case. Should Grant's FCRA case be dismissed?

10. Sylvia Miller, a married woman, wanted to buy a pair of loveseats from a retail furniture store. The store offered to arrange financing for her through the Public Industrial Loan Company. Public later refused to extend credit to Miller unless her husband cosigned the debt obligation. The reason was a consumer reporting agency's unfavorable credit report on Miller. Was Public's action forbidden sex discrimination under the Equal Credit Opportunity Act? In any event, what other legal remedy might Miller have?

11. John E. Koerner & Co. applied for a credit card account with the American Express Company. The application was for a company account designed for business customers. Koerner asked American Express to issue cards bearing the company's name to Louis Koerner and four other officers of the corporation.

Koerner was required to sign a company account form, under which he agreed that he would be jointly and severally liable with the company for all charges incurred through use of the company card. American Express issued the cards requested by the company. Thereafter, the cards were used almost totally for business purposes, although Koerner occasionally used his card for personal expenses. Later, a dispute regarding charges appearing on the company account arose. Does the Fair Credit Billing Act apply to this dispute?

12. Stanley Crawford owed $2,037.99 to the Heilig-Meyers furniture company on a credit account. In September 2001, LVNV Funding LLC acquired the debt from Heilig-Meyers. The last transaction on Crawford's account occurred on October 26, 2001. Although Crawford's debt went unpaid, LVNV did not file suit against Crawford over it. Accordingly, under the three-year Alabama statute of limitations that governed the account, Crawford's debt became unenforceable in October 2004. Crawford filed for Chapter 13 bankruptcy in 2008. During the bankruptcy proceeding, LVNV filed a proof of claim in an effort to collect the Heilig-Meyers debt. In response, Crawford filed a counterclaim against LVNV, alleging that LVNV's filing of a proof of claim regarding Crawford's time-barred debt violated the Fair Debt Collection Practice Act's prohibition on deceptive or unfair debt collection actions. Was Crawford correct?

CHAPTER 49

Antitrust: The Sherman Act

X YZ Inc. manufactures widgets and sells them through various wholesale dealers. Several other firms also manufacture widgets. Of course, XYZ wishes to conduct its business within the bounds of the law, including the rules of antitrust law. As you study this chapter, consider the following questions regarding possible courses of action and their treatment under antitrust law:

- Would XYZ violate antitrust law if XYZ deliberately causes its prices to match those of a competing widget manufacturer?

- If XYZ and a competing widget manufacturer agree that each will charge no more than a certain agreed amount for their widgets (i.e., a maximum price), is there an antitrust violation? What if XYZ and its competitor agree to set a minimum price in order to avoid what each sees as the potentially ruinous consequences of a price-cutting war?

- Is there an antitrust violation if XYZ and its wholesale dealers agree that the dealers will adhere to an established maximum sale price when they sell to retailers? What if the agreement between XYZ and the dealers is that the dealers will adhere to a certain minimum price when they sell to retailers?

- If XYZ and its wholesale dealers agree on exclusive sales territories within which each dealer will operate, is there an antitrust violation?

- Is there an antitrust problem if XYZ informs its dealers that it will not sell them widgets unless they also buy a certain unrelated product from XYZ, and the dealers, wanting to preserve their widget dealerships, agree to this provision?

- Would there be an antitrust violation if XYZ and some of the other widget manufacturers agree that each manufacturer has an exclusive geographic area of business operation?

- Is there an antitrust violation if XYZ and some of the other widget manufacturers agree not to purchase, from a certain supplier, materials used in making widgets?

- If XYZ's widgets acquire a public reputation for being high in quality and this perception leads, over time, to XYZ's holding a market share so large that XYZ effectively holds monopoly status, has XYZ run afoul of antitrust law?

Regardless of the legal treatment given to the behaviors referred to in the above questions, consider the ethical questions suggested by such conduct.

LO   LEARNING OBJECTIVES

After studying this chapter, you should be able to:

49-1 Describe the role an interstate or foreign commerce connection plays in the application of the federal antitrust laws.

49-2 Identify the respective types of antitrust cases that may be initiated by the government and by private parties who have standing to sue.

49-3 Explain the role of the concerted action versus unilateral action distinction in determining whether Sherman Act § 1 has been violated.

49-4 Explain the difference between per se analysis and rule of reason analysis in Sherman Act § 1 cases.

49-5 Describe what horizontal price-fixing is and identify the type of analysis (per se or rule of reason) that such behavior receives when courts determine whether it is unlawful.

49-6 Describe what vertical price-fixing is and identify the type of analysis (per se or rule of reason) that such behavior receives when courts determine whether it is unlawful.

49-7 Describe what a horizontal division of markets is and explain the approaches courts take in determining whether such behavior is unlawful.

49-8 Describe what a vertical restraint on distribution is and identify the type of analysis (per se or rule of reason) that such behavior receives when courts determine whether it is unlawful.

49-9 Explain the approaches courts take in determining the legality or illegality of group boycotts and similar refusals to deal.

49-10 Identify and explain the elements of a prohibited tying agreement.

49-11 Identify the elements of monopolization for purposes of Sherman Act § 2.

49-12 Explain what courts take into account in determining the relevant market for purposes of a monopolization case.

49-13 Describe what courts consider when they determine whether a defendant accused of monopolization possessed the requisite intent to monopolize.

49-14 Explain what is necessary for the attempted monopolization prohibited by Sherman Act § 2.

THE POST-CIVIL WAR EMERGENCE and growth of large industrial combines and trusts significantly altered the business environment of earlier years. A major feature of this phenomenon was the tendency of various large business entities to acquire dominant positions in their industries by buying up smaller competitors or engaging in practices aimed at driving those competitors out of business. This behavior led to public demands for legislation to preserve competitive market structures and prevent the accumulation of great economic power in the hands of a few firms.

Congress responded in 1890 with the Sherman Act. It supplemented this response by enacting the Clayton Act in 1914 and the Robinson–Patman Act in 1936. In enacting the antitrust statutes, Congress adopted a public policy in favor of preserving and promoting free competition as the most efficient means of allocating social resources. The Supreme Court summarized, in *Times-Picayune Co. v. United States,* 254 U.S. 594 (1953), the rationale for this faith in competition's positive effects:

> Basic to faith that a free economy best promotes the public weal is that goods must stand the cold test of competition; that the public, acting through the market's impersonal judgment, shall allocate the nation's resources and thus direct the course its economic development will take.

Congress thus presumed that competition was more likely to exist in an industrial structure characterized by a large number of competing firms than in concentrated industries dominated by a few large competitors.

Despite this long-standing policy in favor of competitive market structures, the antitrust laws have not been very successful in halting the trend toward concentration in American industry. Today's market structure in many important industries is *oligopolistic*, with the bulk of production accounted for by a few dominant firms. Traditional antitrust concepts are often difficult to apply to the behavior of firms in these highly concentrated markets. Recent years have witnessed the emergence of new ideas that challenge long-standing antitrust policy assumptions.

The Antitrust Policy Debate

Antitrust enforcement necessarily reflects fundamental public policy judgments about the economic activities to be allowed and the industrial structure best suited to foster desirable economic activity. Given the importance of such judgments to the future of the American economy, it is not surprising that antitrust policy spurs vigorous public debate.

Chicago School Theories During the past four decades, traditional antitrust assumptions have faced an effective challenge from commentators and courts advocating the application of microeconomic theory to antitrust enforcement. These methods of antitrust analysis are commonly called Chicago School theories because many of their major premises were advanced by scholars affiliated with the University of Chicago.

Chicago School advocates view *economic efficiency* as the primary, if not sole, goal of antitrust enforcement. They are far less concerned with the supposed effects of industrial concentration than are traditional antitrust thinkers. Even highly concentrated industries, they argue, may engage in significant forms of nonprice competition, such as competition in advertising, styling, and warranties. They also point out that concentration in a particular industry does not necessarily preclude *interindustry competition*. For example, a concentrated glass container industry may still face significant competition from the makers of metal, plastic, and fiberboard containers. Chicago School advocates are also quick to point out that many markets today are international in scope so that concentrated domestic industries may, nonetheless, face effective foreign competition. Moreover, they argue that the technological developments necessary for American industry to compete more effectively in international markets may require the great capital resources that result from domestic concentration.

According to the Chicago School viewpoint, the traditional antitrust focus on the structure of industry has improperly emphasized protecting *competitors* instead of protecting *competition*. Chicago School theorists argue that antitrust policy's primary thrust should feature *anticonspiracy* efforts rather than *anticoncentration* efforts. In addition, most of these theorists take a lenient view toward vertically imposed restrictions on price and distribution that have been traditionally seen as undesirable because they believe that such restrictions can promote efficiencies in distribution. Thus, they tend to be tolerant of attempts by manufacturers to control resale prices or establish exclusive distribution systems for their products.

Traditional Antitrust Theories Traditional antitrust thinkers, however, contend that even though economic efficiency is important, antitrust policy has historically embraced *political* as well as economic values. Concentrated economic power, they argue, is undesirable for a variety of noneconomic reasons. It may lead to antidemocratic concentrations of political power. Moreover, it may stimulate greater governmental intrusions into the economy in the same way that the post–Civil War activities

of the trusts led to the passage of the antitrust laws. According to the traditional view, lessening concentration enhances individual freedom by reducing the barriers to entry that confront would-be competitors and by ensuring broader input into economic decisions having important social consequences. Judge Learned Hand summed up this perspective on antitrust policy:

> Great industrial consolidations are inherently undesirable, regardless of their economic results. Throughout the history of [the Sherman Act] it has been constantly assumed that one of [its] purposes was to perpetuate and preserve, for its own sake and in spite of possible cost, an organization of industry in small units which can effectively compete with each other.[1]

Impact of Chicago School Despite the initial intentions behind antitrust policy, the Chicago School has had a significant impact on the course of antitrust enforcement in recent decades. The Supreme Court and many presidential appointees to the lower federal courts, the Department of Justice, and the Federal Trade Commission have given credence to Chicago School economic arguments during the past 30-plus years. The presence on the federal bench of so many judges who are receptive to Chicago School ideas means that those views are likely to continue to have an impact on the shape of antitrust law.

Jurisdiction, Types of Cases, and Standing

 LO49-1 Describe the role an interstate or foreign commerce connection plays in the application of the federal antitrust laws.

Jurisdiction The Sherman Act outlaws monopolization, attempted monopolization, and agreements in restraint of trade. Because the federal government's power to regulate business originates in the Commerce Clause of the U.S. Constitution (discussed in Chapter 3), the federal antitrust laws apply only to behavior having some significant impact on *interstate* or *foreign* commerce. Given the interdependent nature of our national economy, it is normally fairly easy to demonstrate that a challenged activity either involves interstate commerce (the "in commerce" jurisdiction test) or has a substantial effect on interstate commerce (the "effect on commerce" jurisdiction test). Various cases indicate that a business activity may have a

---

[1]*United States v. Aluminum Co. of America, Inc.*, 148 F.2d 416 (2d Cir. 1945).

substantial effect on interstate commerce even if the activity occurs solely within the borders of one state. Activities that are purely *intrastate* in their effects, however, are outside the scope of federal antitrust jurisdiction and must be challenged under state law.

The federal antitrust laws have been extensively applied to activities affecting the international commerce of the United States. The conduct of American firms operating outside U.S. borders may be attacked under our antitrust laws if it has an intended effect on our foreign commerce. Likewise, foreign firms "continuously engaged" in our domestic commerce are subject to federal antitrust jurisdiction. An international transaction that has a direct, substantial, and intended effect on domestic commerce may subject the firms involved to U.S. antitrust law and the jurisdiction of U.S. courts. (*United States v. Hsiung*, which appears later in the chapter, deals in part with such issues.) Determining the full extent of the extraterritorial reach of our antitrust laws often involves courts wading through difficult questions of antitrust exemptions and immunities (to be discussed in Chapter 50). The extraterritorial reach issue also suggests the troubling political prospect that aggressive expansion of antitrust law's applicability may create tension between our antitrust policy and our foreign policy in general.

Types of Cases and the Role of Pretrial Settlements

 LO49-2 Identify the respective types of antitrust cases that may be initiated by the government and by private parties who have standing to sue.

Sherman Act violations may give rise to criminal prosecutions and civil litigation instituted by the federal government (through the Department of Justice), as well as to civil cases filed by private parties. A significant percentage of the antitrust cases brought by the Department of Justice are settled without trial through *nolo contendere* pleas in criminal cases and *consent decrees* in civil cases. Although a defendant who pleads nolo contendere technically has not admitted guilt, the sentencing court is free to impose the same penalty that would be appropriate in the case of a guilty plea or a conviction at trial. Consent decrees involve a defendant's consent to remedial measures aimed at remedying the competitive harm resulting from his actions. Because neither a nolo plea nor a consent decree is admissible as proof of a violation of the Sherman Act in a private plaintiff's later civil suit, these devices are often attractive to antitrust defendants.

Criminal Prosecutions The Sherman Act provides that individuals criminally convicted of violating it may be fined up to $1 million per violation and may be imprisoned for as long as 10 years. The Act also states that corporations convicted of violating it may be fined as much as $100 million per violation. These maximum penalties reflect the past decade's statutory amendments, in which Congress significantly increased the previous penalty limits. However, the Alternative Fine Statute allows the maximum fine amounts just noted to be exceeded in certain instances in which the convicted defendant derived "pecuniary gain" from the offense or the offense caused "pecuniary loss" to someone else. In such situations, the defendant "may be fined not more than the greater of twice the gross gain or twice the gross loss," even if the amount so calculated exceeds the usual maximum figures for antitrust offenses. The *Hsiung* case, which appears later, provides an illustration. In that case, a corporation convicted of price-fixing was fined $500 million under the Alternative Fine Statute.

Before an individual may be found criminally responsible under the Sherman Act, however, the government must prove an *anticompetitive effect* flowing from the challenged activity, as well as *criminal intent* on the defendant's part. The level of criminal intent required for a violation is a "knowledge of [the challenged activity's] probable consequences" rather than a specific intent to violate the antitrust laws.[2] Civil violations of the antitrust laws may be proved, however, through evidence of either an unlawful purpose or an anticompetitive effect.

Civil Litigation The federal courts have broad injunctive powers to remedy civil antitrust violations. Courts may order convicted defendants to divest themselves of the stock or assets of acquired companies, to divorce themselves from a functional level of their operations (e.g., ordering a manufacturer to sell its captive retail outlets), to refrain from particular conduct in the future, and to cancel existing contracts. In extreme cases, courts may also enter a *dissolution decree* ordering a defendant to liquidate its assets and cease business operations. Private individuals and

---

[2]*United States v. U.S. Gypsum Co.*, 438 U.S. 422 (1978).

the Department of Justice may seek such injunctive relief regarding antitrust violations.

Treble Damages for Private Plaintiffs Section 4 of the Clayton Act discussed in detail in Chapter 50 gives private parties a significant incentive to enforce the antitrust laws by providing that private plaintiffs injured by Sherman Act or Clayton Act violations are entitled to recover treble damages plus court costs and attorney fees from the defendant. This means that once antitrust plaintiffs have demonstrated the amount of their actual losses (such as lost profits or increased costs) resulting from the challenged violation, this amount is tripled. The potential for treble damage liability plainly presents a significant deterrent threat to potential antitrust violators.

Standing Private plaintiffs who seek to enforce the antitrust laws must first demonstrate that they have **standing** to sue. This means that they must show a *direct antitrust injury* as a result of the challenged behavior. An antitrust injury results from the unlawful aspects of the challenged behavior and is of the sort Congress sought to prevent. For example, in *Brunswick Corp. v. Pueblo Bowl-o-Mat, Inc.*, 429 U.S. 477 (1977), the operator of a chain of bowling centers (Pueblo) challenged a bowling equipment manufacturer's (Brunswick's) acquisition of various competing bowling centers that had defaulted on payments owed to Brunswick for equipment purchases. In essence, Pueblo asserted that if Brunswick had not acquired them, the failing bowling centers would have gone out of business—in which event Pueblo's profits would have increased. The Supreme Court rejected Pueblo's claim because its supposed losses flowed from Brunswick's having preserved competition by acquiring the failing centers. Allowing recovery for such losses would be contrary to the antitrust purpose of promoting competition.

The antitrust injury requirement contemplates a showing that *competition* has been harmed, not merely a showing of harm to a particular *competitor*. For further discussion of this important point, see the *Suture Express* case, which appears later in the chapter.

Importance of Direct Injury Proof that an antitrust injury is *direct* is critical because the Supreme Court has held that indirect purchasers lack standing to sue for antitrust violations. In *Illinois Brick Co. v. State of Illinois*, 431 U.S. 720 (1977), the state of Illinois and other governmental entities sought treble damages from concrete block suppliers who, they alleged, had illegally fixed the price of block used in the construction of public buildings. The plaintiffs acknowledged that the builders hired to construct the buildings had actually paid the inflated prices for the blocks but argued

that these illegal costs probably had been passed on to them in the form of higher prices for building construction. The Supreme Court refused to allow recovery, holding that granting standing to indirect purchasers would create a risk of duplicative recoveries by purchasers at various levels in a product's chain of distribution. The Court also observed that affording standing to indirect purchasers would lead to difficult problems of tracing competitive injuries through several levels of distribution and assessing the extent of an indirect purchaser's actual losses.

A number of state legislatures responded to *Illinois Brick* by enacting statutes allowing indirect purchasers to sue under state antitrust statutes. The Supreme Court has held that the *Illinois Brick* holding does not preempt such statutes.

Section 1—Restraints of Trade

 LO49-3 Explain the role of the concerted action versus unilateral action distinction in determining whether Sherman Act § 1 has been violated.

Concerted Action Section 1 of the Sherman Act states that "[e]very contract, combination in the form of trust or otherwise, or conspiracy, in restraint of trade or commerce among the several states, or with foreign nations is declared to be illegal." A "contract" is any agreement, express or implied, between two or more persons or business entities to restrain competition. A combination is a continuing partnership in restraint of trade. When two or more persons or business entities join for the purpose of restraining trade, a conspiracy occurs.

The above statutory language makes obvious the conclusion that § 1 of the Sherman Act is aimed at concerted action (i.e., *joint action*) in restraint of trade. *Purely unilateral action* by a competitor, on the other hand, cannot violate § 1. This statutory section reflects the public policy that businesspersons should make important competitive decisions on their own, rather than in conjunction with competitors. In his famous book *The Wealth of Nations* (1776), Adam Smith acknowledged both the danger to competition posed by concerted action and the tendencies of competitors to engage in such action. Smith observed that "[p]eople of the same trade seldom meet together, even for merriment and diversion, [without] the conversation end[ing] in a conspiracy against the public, or in some contrivance to raise prices."

Section 1's concerted action requirement poses two major problems. First, how separate must two business entities be before their joint activities are subject to the act's prohibitions? It has long been held that a corporation cannot conspire with itself or its employees and that a corporation's employees cannot be guilty of a conspiracy in the absence of some independent party. What about conspiracies, however, among related corporate entities? In decisions several decades ago, the Supreme Court appeared to hold that a corporation could violate the Sherman Act by conspiring with a wholly owned subsidiary. However, in *Copperweld Corp. v. Independence Tube Corp.*, 467 U.S. 752 (1984), the Court repudiated the "intra-enterprise conspiracy doctrine." The Court held that a parent company is legally incapable of conspiring with a wholly owned subsidiary for Sherman Act purposes because an agreement between parent and subsidiary does not create the risk to competition that results when two independent entities act in concert. It remains to be seen whether this approach extends to corporate subsidiaries and affiliates that are not wholly owned. *Copperweld*'s logic would appear, however, to cover any subsidiary in which the parent firm has a controlling interest.

In the *American Needle* case, which follows, the Supreme Court considers whether concerted action existed for purposes of a § 1 claim when conduct alleged to have violated the statute was that of an entity established by the National Football League and its member teams to market and license the teams' intellectual property. The *American Needle* Court also comments on the nature of rule of reason analysis, a subject to be addressed in an upcoming portion of this chapter.

A second—and more difficult—problem frequently accompanies attempts to enforce § 1. This problem arises when courts are asked to infer, from the relevant circumstances, the existence of an agreement or conspiracy to restrain trade despite the lack of any overt agreement by the parties. Should parallel pricing behavior by several firms be enough, for instance, to justify the inference that a price-fixing conspiracy exists? Courts have consistently held that proof of pure *conscious parallelism*, standing alone, is not enough to establish a § 1 violation. Other evidence must be presented to show that the defendants' actions stemmed from an agreement, express or implied, rather than from independent business decisions. It therefore becomes quite difficult to attack *oligopolies* (a few large firms sharing one market) under § 1 because such firms may independently elect to follow the pricing policies of the industry "price leader" rather than risk their large market shares by engaging in vigorous price competition.

American Needle, Inc. v. National Football League
560 U.S. 183 (2010)

The National Football League (NFL) is an unincorporated association that includes 32 separately owned professional football teams. Each team has its own name, colors, and logo and owns related intellectual property. Prior to 1963, each NFL team made its own arrangements for licensing its intellectual property and marketing trademarked items such as caps and jerseys. In 1963, the teams formed National Football League Properties (NFLP) to develop, license, and market their intellectual property. Most, but not all, of the substantial revenues generated by NFLP have been shared equally among the teams.

Between 1963 and 2000, NFLP granted nonexclusive licenses to a number of vendors, permitting them to manufacture and sell apparel bearing team insignias. American Needle, Inc. was among those licensees. In December 2000, the teams voted to authorize NFLP to grant exclusive licenses. NFLP then granted Reebok International Ltd. a 10-year exclusive license to manufacture and sell trademarked headwear for all 32 teams. NFLP thereafter declined to renew American Needle's nonexclusive license.

American Needle filed suit in federal district court, alleging that the agreements among the NFL, its teams, and NFLP violated § 1 of the Sherman Act. In their answer to the complaint, the defendants contended that the teams, the NFL, and NFLP were incapable of concerted action within the meaning of § 1 because they were a single economic enterprise. The district court agreed and granted summary judgment in favor of the defendants. The U.S. Court of Appeals for the Seventh Circuit affirmed. The U.S. Supreme Court granted American Needle's petition for certiorari. (In the following edited version of the Supreme Court's opinion, the Court often refers to the defendants as "the NFL respondents.")

Stevens, Justice

As the case comes to us, we have only a narrow issue to decide: whether the NFL respondents are capable of engaging in a "contract, combination . . . , or conspiracy" as defined by § 1 of the Sherman Act, or, as we have sometimes phrased it, whether the alleged activity by the NFL respondents "must be viewed as that of a single enterprise for purposes of § 1." *Copperweld Corp. v. Independence*

Tube Corp., 467 U.S. 752, 771 (1984). Taken literally, the applicability of § 1 to "every contract, combination . . . or conspiracy" could be understood to cover every conceivable agreement, whether it be a group of competing firms fixing prices or a single firm's chief executive telling her subordinate how to price their company's product. But even though, "read literally," § 1 would address "the entire body of private contract," that is not what the statute means. [Citation omitted.] Not every instance of cooperation between two people is a potential "contract, combination . . . , or conspiracy, in restraint of trade."

The meaning of the term "contract, combination . . . or conspiracy" is informed by the basic distinction . . . "between concerted and independent action" that distinguishes § 1 of the Sherman Act from § 2. *Copperweld*, 467 U.S. at 767. Section 1 applies only to concerted action that restrains trade. Section 2, by contrast, covers both concerted and independent action, but only if that action monopolizes or threatens actual monopolization. Congress used this distinction between concerted and independent action to deter anticompetitive conduct and compensate its victims, without chilling vigorous competition through ordinary business operations. The distinction also avoids judicial scrutiny of routine, internal business decisions.

We have long held that concerted action under § 1 does not turn simply on whether the parties involved are legally distinct entities. Instead, we have eschewed such formalistic distinctions in favor of a functional consideration of how the parties involved in the alleged anticompetitive conduct actually operate. As a result, we have repeatedly found instances in which members of a legally single entity violated § 1 when the entity was controlled by a group of competitors and served, in essence, as a vehicle for ongoing concerted activity. We have similarly looked past the form of a legally "single entity" when competitors were part of professional organizations or trade groups.

Conversely, there is not necessarily concerted action simply because more than one legally distinct entity is involved. Although, under a now-defunct doctrine known as the "intraenterprise conspiracy doctrine," we once treated cooperation between legally separate entities as necessarily covered by § 1, we now embark on a more functional analysis. We reexamined the intraenterprise conspiracy doctrine in *Copperweld*, and concluded that it was inconsistent with the "basic distinction between concerted and independent action." Considering it "perfectly plain that an internal agreement to implement a single, unitary firm's policies does not raise the antitrust dangers that § 1 was designed to police," we held that a parent corporation and its wholly owned subsidiary "are incapable of conspiring with each other for purposes of § 1 of the Sherman Act." We explained that although a parent corporation and its wholly owned subsidiary are "separate" for the purposes of incorporation or formal title, they are controlled by a single center of decisionmaking and they control a single aggregation of economic power. Joint conduct by two such entities does not "depriv[e] the marketplace of independent centers of decisionmaking," and as a result, an agreement between them does not constitute a "contract, combination . . . or conspiracy" for purposes of § 1.

As *Copperweld* exemplifies, "substance, not form, should determine whether a[n] . . . entity is capable of conspiring under § 1."

This inquiry is sometimes described as asking whether the alleged conspirators are a single entity. That is perhaps a misdescription, however, because the question is not whether the defendant is a legally single entity or has a single name; nor is the question whether the parties involved seem like one firm or multiple firms in any metaphysical sense. The key is whether the alleged "contract, combination . . . , or conspiracy" is concerted action—that is, whether it joins together separate decisionmakers. The relevant inquiry, therefore, is whether there is a "contract, combination . . . or conspiracy" amongst "separate economic actors pursuing separate economic interests," such that the agreement "deprives the marketplace of independent centers of decisionmaking," . . . and thus of actual or potential competition.

The NFL teams do not possess either the unitary decisionmaking quality or the single aggregation of economic power characteristic of independent action. Each of the teams is a substantial, independently owned, and independently managed business. "[T]heir general corporate actions are guided or determined" by "separate corporate consciousnesses," and "[t]heir objectives are" not "common." *Copperweld*, 467 U.S. at 771. The teams compete with one another, not only on the playing field, but to attract fans, for gate receipts, and for contracts with managerial and playing personnel.

Directly relevant to this case, the teams compete in the market for intellectual property. To a firm making hats, the New Orleans Saints and the Indianapolis Colts are two potentially competing suppliers of valuable trademarks. When each NFL team licenses its intellectual property, it is not pursuing the common interests of the whole league but is instead pursuing interests of each corporation itself; teams are acting as separate economic actors pursuing separate economic interests, and each team therefore is a potential independent center of decisionmaking. Decisions by NFL teams to license their separately owned trademarks collectively and to only one vendor are decisions that deprive the marketplace of independent centers of decisionmaking, and therefore of actual or potential competition.

In defense, the NFL respondents argue that by forming NFLP, they have formed a single entity, akin to a merger, and market their NFL brands through a single outlet. But it is not dispositive that the teams have organized and own a legally separate entity that centralizes the management of their intellectual property. An ongoing § 1 violation cannot evade § 1 scrutiny simply by giving the ongoing violation a name and label.

The NFL respondents may be similar in some sense to a single enterprise that owns several pieces of intellectual property and licenses them jointly, but they are not similar in the relevant functional sense. Although NFL teams have common interests such as promoting the NFL brand, they are still separate, profit-maximizing entities, and their interests in licensing team trademarks are not necessarily aligned.

The NFL respondents argue that nonetheless, as the Court of Appeals held, they constitute a single entity because without their cooperation, there would be no NFL football. It is true that the clubs that make up a professional sports league are not completely independent economic competitors, as they depend upon a degree of cooperation for economic survival. But the Court of Appeals' reasoning is unpersuasive. The justification for cooperation is not relevant to whether that cooperation is concerted or independent action. A "contract, combination . . . or conspiracy" that is necessary or useful to a joint venture is still a "contract, combination . . . or conspiracy" if it deprives the marketplace of independent centers of decisionmaking. Any joint venture involves multiple sources of economic power cooperating to produce a product. And for many such ventures, the participation of others is necessary. But that does not mean that necessity of cooperation transforms concerted action into independent action; a nut and a bolt can only operate together, but an agreement between nut and bolt manufacturers is still subject to § 1 analysis. Nor does it mean that once a group of firms agree to produce a joint product, cooperation amongst those firms must be treated as independent conduct.

As discussed later, necessity of cooperation is a factor relevant to whether the agreement is subject to the Rule of Reason. In any event, it simply is not apparent that the alleged conduct was necessary at all. Although two teams are needed to play a football game, not all aspects of elaborate interleague cooperation are necessary to produce a game. Moreover, even if league-wide agreements are necessary to produce football, it does not follow that concerted activity in marketing intellectual property is necessary to produce football.

The question whether NFLP decisions can constitute concerted activity covered by § 1 is closer than whether decisions made directly by the 32 teams are covered by § 1. This is so both because NFLP is a separate corporation with its own management and because the record indicates that most of the revenues generated by NFLP are shared by the teams on an equal basis. Nevertheless we think it clear that for the same reasons the 32 teams' conduct is covered by § 1, NFLP's actions also are subject to § 1, at least with regard to its marketing of property owned by the separate teams. NFLP's licensing decisions are made by the 32 potential competitors, and each of them actually owns its share of the jointly managed assets. Apart from their agreement to cooperate in exploiting those assets, including their decisions as the NFLP, there would be nothing to prevent each of the teams from making its own market decisions relating to purchases of apparel and headwear, to the sale of such items, and to the granting of licenses to use its trademarks.

Thirty-two teams operating independently through the vehicle of the NFLP are not like the components of a single firm that act to maximize the firm's profits. The teams remain separately controlled, potential competitors with economic interests that are distinct from NFLP's financial well-being. Unlike typical decisions by corporate shareholders, NFLP licensing decisions effectively require the assent of more than a mere majority of shareholders. And each team's decision reflects not only an interest in NFLP's profits but also an interest in the team's individual profits. The 32 teams capture individual economic benefits separate and apart from NFLP profits as a result of the decisions they make for the NFLP. NFLP's decisions thus affect each team's profits from licensing its own intellectual property. In making the relevant licensing decisions, NFLP is therefore an instrumentality of the teams. [For the reasons stated here,] decisions by the NFLP regarding the teams' separately owned intellectual property constitute concerted action.

Football teams that need to cooperate are not trapped by antitrust law. The special characteristics of this industry may provide a justification for many kinds of agreements. The fact that NFL teams share an interest in making the entire league successful and profitable, and that they must cooperate in the production and scheduling of games, provides a perfectly sensible justification for making a host of collective decisions. But the conduct at issue in this case is still concerted activity under the Sherman Act that is subject to § 1 analysis.

When "restraints on competition are essential if the product is to be available at all," per se rules of illegality are inapplicable, and instead the restraint must be judged according to the flexible Rule of Reason. [Citation omitted.] In such instances, the agreement is likely to survive the Rule of Reason. And depending upon the concerted activity in question, the Rule of Reason may not require a detailed analysis; it "can sometimes be applied in the twinkling of an eye." [Citation omitted.]

Other features of the NFL may also save agreements amongst the teams. We have recognized, for example, "that the interest in maintaining a competitive balance" among athletic teams "is legitimate and important." *National Collegiate Athletic Association v. Board of Regents*, 468 U.S. 85, 117 (1984). While that same interest applies to the teams in the NFL, it does not justify treating them as a single entity for § 1 purposes when it comes to the marketing of the teams' individually owned intellectual property. It is, however, unquestionably an interest that may well justify a variety of collective decisions made by the teams. What role it properly plays in applying the Rule of Reason to the allegations in this case is a matter to be considered on remand.

Court of Appeals decision reversed; case remanded for further proceedings.

Per Se versus Rule of Reason Analysis

 LO49-4 Explain the difference between per se analysis and rule of reason analysis in Sherman Act § 1 cases.

Per Se Analysis   Although § 1's language condemns "every" contract, combination, and conspiracy in restraint of trade, the Supreme Court has long held that the Sherman Act applies only to behavior that *unreasonably* restrains competition. In addition, the Court has developed two fundamentally different approaches to analyzing behavior challenged under § 1. According to the Court, some actions always have a negative effect on competition—an effect that cannot be excused or justified. Such actions are classified as *per se* unlawful. If a particular behavior falls under the per se heading, it is conclusively presumed to violate § 1. Per se rules are thought to provide reliable guidance to business. They also simplify otherwise lengthy antitrust litigation because if per se unlawful behavior is proven, the defendant cannot assert any supposed justifications in an attempt to avoid liability.

Per se rules, however, are frequently criticized on the ground that they oversimplify complex economic realities. Recent decisions reveal that for various economic activities, the Supreme Court and the lower federal courts are moving away from per se rules and instead adopting rule of reason analysis. This trend is consistent with courts' increased inclination to consider economic theories that seek to justify behavior previously held to be per se unlawful.

Rule of Reason Analysis   Behavior not classified as per se unlawful is judged under the rule of reason. This approach requires a detailed inquiry into the actual competitive effects of the defendant's actions. It includes consideration of any justifications that the defendant may advance. If the court concludes that the challenged activity had a significant anticompetitive effect that was not offset by any positive effect on competition or other social benefit such as enhanced economic efficiency, the activity will be held to violate § 1. On the other hand, if the court concludes that the justifications advanced by the defendant outweigh the harm to competition resulting from the defendant's activity, there is no § 1 violation. For a brief discussion of the nature of rule of reason analysis, see the *American Needle* decision, which appears earlier.

In recent years, courts have sometimes employed a so-called quick-look analysis instead of a full-fledged rule of reason analysis. Quick-look analysis may be described as an intermediate type of analysis that falls somewhere between the black-and-white per se approach and the more complicated rule of reason approach. Courts may be inclined to employ quick-look analysis when they believe the behavior at issue could have both anticompetitive and procompetitive effects that can be weighed against each other without the extensive market analyses that may be necessary under full rule of reason treatment. In this sense, quick-look analysis serves as a toned-down version of the rule of reason approach.

The following subsections of this chapter examine some of the behaviors that may or will be held to violate § 1. The legal analysis given to the respective behaviors is also considered.

Horizontal Price-Fixing

 LO49-5 Describe what horizontal price-fixing is and identify the type of analysis (per se or rule of reason) that such behavior receives when courts determine whether it is unlawful.

An essential attribute of a free market is that the price of goods and services is determined by the free play of the impersonal forces of the marketplace. Attempts by competitors to interfere with market forces and control prices—called *horizontal price-fixing*—have long been held per se unlawful under § 1. Horizontal price-fixing may take the form of direct agreements among competitors about the price at which they sell or buy a particular product or service. It may also be accomplished by agreements on the quantity of goods to be produced, offered for sale, or bought. In one famous case, an agreement by major oil refiners to purchase and store the excess production of small independent refiners was held to amount to price-fixing because the purpose of the agreement was to affect the market price for gasoline by artificially limiting the available supply.[3]

Some commentators have suggested that agreements among competitors to fix *maximum* prices should be treated under a rule of reason approach rather than the harsher per se standard because, in some instances, such agreements may result in savings to consumers. In addition, lower courts have occasionally sought to craft exceptions to the rule that horizontal price-fixing triggers per se treatment. It is important to note, however, that the Supreme Court continues to adhere to the long-standing rule of per se illegality for any form of horizontal price-fixing. In *U.S. v. Hsiung*, which follows, a federal court of appeals rejects individual and corporate defendants' argument that the court should apply rule of reason treatment to the horizontal price-fixing conspiracy at issue in the case.

---

[3]*United States v. Socony-Vacuum Oil Co.*, 310 U.S. 150 (1940).

In recent years, the federal government has devoted significant regulatory attention to price-fixing. For instance, the Justice Department conducted a 2014 investigation into whether price-fixing and other collusive activity occurred in apparent attempts to manipulate benchmark rates (most notably LIBOR, the London interbank offered rate). Such rates are used in setting interest rates globally. Earlier in 2014, Bridgestone Corp. pleaded guilty to a charge of conspiring to fix prices of rubber car parts and agreed to pay a $425 million fine. In 2012 and 2013, 20 foreign companies pleaded guilty to charges of price-fixing regarding car parts and were fined hundreds of millions of dollars. Various executives of those companies were also charged, convicted, and sentenced to prison. Of course, criminal proceedings by the government do not bar civil actions by private parties (or the government) in regard to the same conduct that formed the basis of the criminal case.

United States v. Hsiung   758 F.3d 1074 (9th Cir. 2014)

AU Optronics Corporation (AUO) is a Taiwanese company. Its wholly owned subsidiary, AU Optronics Corporation of America (AUOA), serves as AUO's retailer and maintains offices in Texas and California. AUO, AUOA, and two AUO executives, Hsuan Bin Chen (president and chief operating officer) and Hui Hsiung (executive vice president), were defendants in a criminal antitrust case brought by the U.S. government in the U.S. District Court for the Northern District of California. The government alleged that the defendants participated in an international conspiracy to fix prices for display panels known as TFT-LCDs. TFT-LCD, which is an abbreviation for thin-film-transistor liquid-crystal display, is a display technology used in flat-panel computer monitors, notebook computers, flat-panel televisions, and other devices.

The government based its case on meetings that took place in Taiwan from October 2001 to January 2006 and involved representatives from six leading TFT-LCD manufacturers. Some of these manufacturers were Taiwanese firms; others were Korean firms. The meetings were designed, the government alleged, to "set the target price" and "stabilize the price" of TFT-LCDs, which were sold in the United States principally to Dell, Hewlett-Packard (HP), Compaq, Apple, and Motorola for use in consumer electronics. This series of meetings, in which Chen, Hsiung, and other AUO employees participated extensively, came to be known as the Crystal Meetings.

Following each Crystal Meeting, the participating companies produced "Crystal Meeting Reports." These reports provided pricing targets for TFT-LCD sales, which, in turn, were used by retail branches of the companies as price benchmarks for selling panels to wholesale customers. More specifically, AUOA used the Crystal Meeting Reports that AUO provided to negotiate prices for the sale of TFT-LCDs to U.S. customers, including HP, Compaq, ViewSonic, Dell, and Apple. AUOA employees and executives routinely traveled to the offices of Dell, Apple, and HP in Texas and California to discuss TFT-LCD pricing based on the targets coming out of the Crystal Meetings. Chen and Hsiung played especially important roles in settling price disputes with executives at Dell.

Crystal Meeting participants stood to make enormous profits from TFT-LCD sales to U.S. technology retailers. During the period of the alleged conspiracy, the United States comprised approximately one-third of the global market for personal computers incorporating TFT-LCDs, and sales of panels by Crystal Meeting participants to the United States generated more than $600 million in revenue. The conspiracy ended when the FBI raided AUOA's Texas office.

Following a criminal indictment and a jury trial, AUO, AUOA, Chen, and Hsiung were convicted of conspiracy to fix prices in violation of the Sherman Act. The jury also found that the "combined gross gains derived from the conspiracy by all the participants in the conspiracy" were "$500 million or more." The district court sentenced Hsiung and Chen to 36 months of imprisonment and assessed a $200,000 fine on each of them. The court sentenced the corporate defendants to a three-year term of probation with conditions. In addition, relying on a law known as the Alternative Fine Statute, the court imposed a $500 million fine on AUO. All of the defendants appealed their convictions to the U.S. Court of Appeals for the Ninth Circuit. AUO also appealed its sentence.

McKeown, Circuit Judge

The defendants' appeal raises complicated issues of first impression regarding the reach of the Sherman Act in a globalized economy. The defendants contend that the rule of reason applies to this price-fixing conspiracy because of its foreign character. [According to the defendants, the] foreign involvement [should] override the longstanding rule that a horizontal price-fixing conspiracy is subject to per se analysis under the antitrust laws. They also urge that . . . the nexus to United States commerce was insufficient [to violate] the Sherman Act.

As a preliminary matter, [however,] the defendants appeal on the basis of improper venue [i.e., that the Northern District of California was not an appropriate location for the case to be brought]. The indictment alleged that the charged conspiracy "was carried out, in part, in the Northern District of California." Trial testimony established that AUO employees negotiated prices for TFT-LCDs with HP in Cupertino, California. "It is by now well settled that venue on a conspiracy charge is proper where . . . any overt act committed in furtherance of the conspiracy occurred." [Citation omitted.] In addition to the HP negotiations, the government introduced evidence that AUOA representatives negotiated sales of price-fixed TFT-LCDs with Apple in the Northern District of California and that AUOA maintained offices in the Northern District of California from which it conducted price negotiations by e-mail and phone. This evidence is sufficient to establish . . . that overt acts in furtherance of the conspiracy occurred in the Northern District of California. Thus, venue was proper.

The Supreme Court's seminal case on antitrust and foreign conduct is *Hartford Fire Insurance v. California*, 509 U.S. 764 (1993), in which the Court held that "the Sherman Act applies to foreign conduct that was meant to produce and did in fact produce some substantial effect in the United States." *Id.* at 796. The district court instructed the jury to this effect:

> To convict the defendants you must find beyond a reasonable doubt one or both of the following: (A) that at least one member of the conspiracy took at least one action in furtherance of the conspiracy within the United States, or (B) that the conspiracy had a substantial and intended effect in the United States.

Before trial, the defendants moved to dismiss the indictment on the basis that it did not allege adequately the *Hartford Fire* "substantial and intended effects" test. At the jury instructions conference, the defendants urged the district court to give the *Hartford Fire* instruction, while also claiming that part A of the instruction was erroneous because it permitted the jury to convict on the basis of one domestic act. As to part A of the instruction, the defendants objected on the basis that it "would render *Hartford Fire* entirely nugatory, as, having proven the most minimal act in furtherance of a charged agreement, the government would never have to prove an intended and substantial effect on U.S. commerce." Although the defendants contested part A, they all concurred that part B "is a correct statement of the *Hartford Fire* requirements for establishing extraterritorial jurisdiction over foreign anticompetitive conduct, and should be given."

"In reviewing jury instructions, the relevant inquiry is whether the instructions as a whole are misleading or inadequate to guide the jury's deliberation." [Citation omitted.]

Immediately following the [above-quoted] *Hartford Fire* instruction, the district court instructed the jury that it must find the following beyond a reasonable doubt:

> [T]hat the members of the conspiracy engaged in one or both of the following activities:
>
> (A) fixing the price of TFT-LCD panels targeted by the participants to be sold in the United States or for delivery to the United States; or
>
> (B) fixing the price of TFT-LCD panels that were incorporated into finished products such as notebook computers, desktop computer monitors, and televisions, and that this conduct had a direct, substantial, and reasonably foreseeable effect on trade or commerce in those finished products sold in the United States or for delivery to the United States. In determining whether the conspiracy had such an effect, you may consider the total amount of trade or commerce in those finished products sold in the United States or for delivery to the United States; however, the government's proof need not quantify or value that effect.

The effect of foreign conduct in the United States was a central point of controversy throughout the trial. Nonetheless, the conduct always was linked, as in the above instruction, to targeting for sale or delivery in the United States. Part A of the [above] instruction required the jury to find that the defendants fixed the prices of TFT-LCDs "targeted" for sale or delivery in the United States. This "targeting" language subsumed intentionality. See *Oxford English Dictionary* 642 (2d ed. 1989) (defining "targeted" as "[d]esignated or chosen as a target"). There is no way that the defendants could have unintentionally designated or chosen the United States market as a target of the conspiracy. Viewing the instructions as a whole, nothing misled the jury as to its task.

Having determined that the prosecution was not barred by an extraterritoriality defense, we address the appropriate standard for judging liability in this price-fixing scheme. For over a century, courts have treated horizontal price-fixing as a per se violation of the Sherman Act. *See, e.g., United States v. Socony-Vacuum Oil Co.*, 310 U.S. 150, 218 (1940). [I]n recent years, the Supreme Court reiterated this principle. The directive in *Leegin Creative Leather Prods., Inc. v. PSKS, Inc.*, 551 U.S. 877, 893 (2007), is unequivocal: "A horizontal cartel among competing manufacturers or competing retailers that decreases output or reduces competition in order to increase price is, and ought to be, per se unlawful."

Consistent with Supreme Court precedent, the district court treated this price-fixing case as governed by the per se rule. The defendants claim that the district court erred by not adopting the rule of reason as the benchmark and that the indictment, jury instructions, and proof were deficient under rule of reason analysis.

We hold that the price-fixing scheme as alleged and proven is subject to per se analysis under the Sherman Act.

According to the defendants, this is not a per se case because under *Metro Industries v. Sammi Corp.*, 82 F.3d 839 (9th Cir. 1996), "application of the per se rule is not appropriate where the conduct in question occurred in another country." This approach invites us to read our circuit precedent in *Metro Industries* as out of sync with the well-established tradition of analyzing price-fixing under the per se rule and recent Supreme Court precedent emphasizing that price-fixing ought to be analyzed under the per se rule. We decline the invitation. Although the language from *Metro Industries* may have created some ambiguity based on the unusual facts of that case, we do not read the case as controlling. In any event, the Supreme Court's subsequent confirmation that courts should continue to treat horizontal price-fixing as a per se violation of the Sherman Act laid to rest any uncertainty. *See United States v. Golden Valley Elec. Ass'n*, 689 F.3d 1108, 1112 (9th Cir. 2012).

Invoking the language in *Metro Industries* to suggest that price-fixing cases involving foreign conduct always should be analyzed under the rule of reason is "clearly irreconcilable" with Supreme Court precedent. *See id.* To begin, *Metro Industries* was not a price-fixing case; rather, it involved a horizontal market division for stainless steamers by a group of Korean companies. [We noted in *Metro Industries*] that because the market division at issue was "*not* a classic horizontal market division agreement," the rule of reason applied. We then went on to write that even if [the conduct at issue] was a market division that would ordinarily be treated as a per se violation of the Sherman Act, the rule of reason applied because the allegedly unlawful conduct occurred in a foreign country. This broad statement, which was wholly superfluous, and unnecessary to the holding, has not been repeated in subsequent cases and appears to be limited to the unique facts of [*Metro Industries*]. Not surprisingly, this statement also has been the subject of scholarly criticism.

Unlike *Metro Industries*, this case centers on a classic horizontal price-fixing scheme subject to the per se rule. *See Leegin Creative*, 551 U.S. at 893. Also unlike *Metro Industries*, in which there was "no evidence of actual injury to competition in the United States," the voluminous evidence here documents substantial effects on the United States. The conduct here did not occur in a solely foreign bubble. Although the agreement to fix prices occurred in Taiwan, the sale of price-fixed TFT-LCDs occurred in large part in the United States.

In reiterating the applicability of the per se rule for horizontal price-fixing, a result that Supreme Court precedent compels, we also join the reasoning of other circuits. The district court was bound to apply the per se rule and appropriately rejected the rule of reason defense.

The final basis for the defendants' appeal is the $500 million fine the district court imposed on AUO pursuant to the Alternative Fine Statute, [which] provides: "If any person derives pecuniary gain from the offense, or if the offense results in pecuniary loss to a person other than the defendant, the defendant may be fined not more than the greater of twice the gross gain or twice the gross loss. . . ." 18 U.S.C. § 3571(d). The jury found that the collective gain to the conspiracy members was over $500 million. We [must consider] whether the fine was improper because it was based on the collective gains to all members of the conspiracy rather than the gains to AUO alone. [This is an issue] of first impression.

Whether "gross gains" under § 3571 means gross gains to the individual defendant or to the conspiracy as a whole is an issue of statutory interpretation that we review de novo. The district court instructed the jury as follows:

> In determining the gross gain from the conspiracy, [the jury] should total the gross gains to the defendants and the other participants in the conspiracy from affected sales of (1) TFT-LCD panels that were manufactured abroad and sold in the United States or for delivery to the United States; or (2) TFT-LCD panels incorporated into finished products such as notebook computers and desktop computer monitors that were sold in the United States or for delivery to the United States. Gross gain is the additional revenue to the conspirators from the conspiracy.

This instruction was proper because the statute unambiguously permits a "gross gains" calculation based on the gain attributable to the entire conspiracy. The statute does not require that the gain derive from the defendant's "own individual conduct," as AUO reads it. Indeed, AUO's interpretation reads additional provisions into the statute. AUO relies on *United States v. Pfaff*, 619 F.3d 172, 175 (2d Cir. 2010), which held that the jury must find the gain or loss amount to impose a fine beyond the limits set by § 3571. *Pfaff* is not instructive because it was not a conspiracy case; it did not address whether gross gains could include gains to all coconspirators. Nor has AUO pointed to any case that supports its suggested interpretation, which is contrary to the plain text of the statute.

AUO's offense is the conspiracy to fix prices for TFT-LCDs. The jury found $500 million in gross gains from that offense. The unambiguous language of the statute permitted the district court to impose the $500 million fine based on the gross gains to all the coconspirators.

Convictions and sentences of defendants affirmed.

A Note on *United States v. Apple*

When Apple entered the e-book market in 2010, it collaborated with five book publishers to essentially raise the price of e-books above Amazon's then price of $9.99 per book. Under the terms of Apple's agreement with publishers, publishers were allowed to set their own prices for their books instead of the retailer (e.g., Amazon). Apple called this practice "agency pricing" and suggested that it was an innovative business model. Apple also required publishers to use an agency pricing model—including with Amazon. This additional requirement opened the door to publishers, allowing them to essentially eliminate Amazon's $9.99 pricing.

The agreement between Apple and the publishers caused prices of e-books across the board to rise, and in 2012 the Department of Justice brought a case accusing Apple of horizontal price-fixing. [Note that the publishers ended up settling with the Department of Justice for their behavior through consent decrees.] A federal district court found that Apple had orchestrated a horizontal price-setting conspiracy and that the agreement was an unreasonable restraint on trade. In 2015, by a 2-to-1 vote, the U.S. Court of Appeals for the Second Circuit in *United States v. Apple, Inc.*, 791 F.3d 290 (2d Cir. 2015), upheld the district court's ruling, and the Supreme Court refused to grant certiorari to review the appellate court ruling. As a result, the appellate court's ruling stood, and Apple was required to provide $400 million in cash and credits to customers and $50 million to attorneys involved in the case.

Throughout the litigation, Apple argued, in part, that even if its conduct *did* amount to a horizontal price-fixing conspiracy, its conduct should not be condemned as a per se violation and instead the application of the rule of reason should be applied and its conduct deemed lawful. While acknowledging that there has been a shift in jurisprudence away from per se illegality for vertical restraints, the appellate court noted that the same is not true for horizontal restraints. As stated by the court, "horizontal price-fixing conspiracies traditionally have been, and remain, the 'archetypal example' of a per se unlawful restraint on trade."

Vertical Price-Fixing

 LO49-6 Describe what vertical price-fixing is and identify the type of analysis (per se or rule of reason) that such behavior receives when courts determine whether it is unlawful.

Attempts by manufacturers or suppliers to control the price of their products may also fall within the scope of § 1. This behavior is called *vertical price-fixing* or *resale price maintenance*. In determining whether vertical price-fixing occurred, the first question is whether there was only unilateral action on the part of the manufacturer or whether there was instead the concerted action contemplated by § 1. A manufacturer may lawfully state a suggested retail price for its products—an action that is unilateral and therefore not a violation of § 1. Illegality may be present, however, when there is a manufacturer–dealer agreement (express or implied) obligating the dealer to resell at a price dictated by the manufacturer.

Unilateral Refusals to Deal In *United States v. Colgate & Co.*, 250 U.S. 300 (1919), the Supreme Court held that a manufacturer could *unilaterally refuse to deal* with those who failed to follow the manufacturer's suggested resale prices. The rationale underlying this rule was that a single firm may deal or not deal with whomever it chooses without violating § 1 because unilateral action is not the joint action prohibited by the statute. Subsequent decisions, however, have narrowly construed the *Colgate* doctrine. Depending upon the facts, circumstances, and effects, manufacturers

may be held to have violated § 1 if they enlist the aid of dealers who are not price-cutting to help enforce their (the manufacturers') pricing policies, or if they engage in other concerted action to further those policies. "May be held to have violated § 1" is important language in the previous sentence, in view of the mode of analysis now required by the Supreme Court in cases of alleged resale price maintenance.

The Shift to Rule of Reason For a considerable number of years, Supreme Court decisions established that all forms of vertical price-fixing were per se violations of § 1. With per se treatment being given to such cases, defendants were not permitted to offer justifications for their behavior. Chicago School theorists argued, however, that many of the same reasons held to justify rule of reason analysis of vertical nonprice restraints on distribution (discussed later in this chapter) were equally applicable to vertical price-fixing agreements. In particular, these critics argued that vertical restrictions limiting the *maximum* price at which a dealer can resell may prevent dealers with dominant market positions from exploiting consumers through price-gouging. In *State Oil Co. v. Khan*, 522 U.S. 3 (1997), the Supreme Court agreed with the critics and overruled a long-standing precedent that had required per se treatment for vertical maximum price-fixing. The Court held in *Khan* that such behavior should instead be evaluated under the rule of reason, given that consumers could benefit when manufacturers and dealers jointly set maximum prices. The Court also recognized that there could be other sound business justifications for such agreements between manufacturers and dealers and that defendants alleged to have engaged in vertical maximum price-fixing should be given an opportunity to offer those justifications.

For 10 years after *Khan* was decided, vertical *minimum* price-fixing continued to be governed by the per se rule. Arguments for rule of reason analysis continued to resonate, however. In a 5–4 decision issued in 2007, the Supreme Court overruled a 96-year-old precedent and held that vertical minimum price-fixing would be judged under the rule of reason rather than the per se approach. The 2007 decision, *Leegin Creative Leather Products v. PSKS, Inc.*, appears below. After *Khan* and *Leegin*, all forms of vertical price-fixing now receive rule of reason analysis.

Leegin Creative Leather Products v. PSKS, Inc.
551 U.S. 877 (2007)

Leegin Creative Leather Products Inc. designs, manufactures, and distributes leather goods and accessories. In 1991, Leegin began to sell belts under the "Brighton" brand name. The Brighton brand has since expanded into a variety of women's fashion accessories. It is sold across the United States in more than 5,000 retail establishments. PSKS, Inc. operates Kay's Kloset, a women's apparel store that, in 1995, began purchasing Brighton goods from Leegin for retail sale. Brighton became the store's most important brand and once accounted for 40 to 50 percent of its profits.

In 1997, Leegin instituted the "Brighton Retail Pricing and Promotion Policy." Under this policy, Leegin refused to sell to retailers that discounted Brighton goods below suggested prices. Leegin adopted the policy to give its retailers sufficient margins to enable them to provide customers the service central to its distribution strategy. It also expressed concern that discounting harmed Brighton's brand image and reputation. In 1998, Leegin implemented a "Heart Stores" policy, under which retailers were given incentives to become Heart Stores and, in return, pledged to adhere to Leegin's suggested prices. Kay's Kloset became a Heart Store but later lost that status when a Leegin representative concluded that the store was physically unattractive. Kay's Kloset continued, however, to purchase Brighton products for resale at the store.

In December 2002, Leegin discovered that Kay's Kloset had been marking down the entire Brighton line by 20 percent. Kay's Kloset contended that it did so in order to compete with nearby retailers who also were undercutting Leegin's suggested prices. Leegin requested that Kay's Kloset cease discounting, but Kay's Kloset refused. Leegin then stopped selling to the store. The loss of the Brighton brand had a considerable negative impact on Kay's Kloset's revenues.

PSKS sued Leegin in federal district court, claiming that Leegin had violated Sherman Act § 1 by "enter[ing] into agreements with retailers to charge only those prices fixed by Leegin." Leegin planned to introduce expert testimony describing the procompetitive effects of its pricing policy. The district court excluded the testimony, however, because longstanding Supreme Court precedent extended per se treatment to vertical minimum price-fixing. At trial, PSKS argued that the Heart Store program, among other things, demonstrated that Leegin and its retailers had agreed to fix prices. Leegin responded that it had established a lawful unilateral pricing policy rather than engaging in the concerted action required for a violation of § 1. The jury agreed with PSKS and awarded it $1.2 million in damages. The district court trebled the damages and ordered reimbursement of PSKS for its attorney fees. In its appeal to the U.S. Court of Appeals for the Fifth Circuit, Leegin did not dispute that it had entered into vertical price-fixing agreements with its retailers. Rather, it contended that the rule of reason should have been applied to those agreements. Rejecting this argument because it considered itself bound by Supreme Court precedent, the Fifth Circuit affirmed the district court's decision. The U.S. Supreme Court granted Leegin's petition for a writ of certiorari.

Kennedy, Justice

In *Dr. Miles Medical Co. v. John D. Park & Sons Co.*, 220 U.S. 373 (1911), the Court established the rule that it is per se illegal under § 1 of the Sherman Act for a manufacturer to agree with its distributor to set the minimum price the distributor can charge for the manufacturer's goods. The question presented by the instant case is whether the Court should overrule the per se rule and allow resale price maintenance agreements to be judged by the rule of reason, the usual standard applied to determine if there is a violation of § 1.

Section 1 prohibits "[e]very contract, combination in the form of trust or otherwise, or conspiracy, in restraint of trade or commerce among the several States." While § 1 could be interpreted to proscribe all contracts, . . . the Court has repeated time and again that § 1 "outlaw[s] only unreasonable restraints." *State Oil Co. v. Khan*, 522 U.S. 3, 10 (1997). The rule of reason is the accepted standard for testing whether a practice restrains trade in violation of § 1. "Under this rule, the factfinder weighs all of the circumstances of a case in deciding whether a restrictive practice should be prohibited as imposing an unreasonable restraint on competition." *Continental T.V., Inc. v. GTE Sylvania, Inc.*, 433 U.S. 36, 49 (1977). Appropriate factors to take into account include "specific information about the relevant business" and "the restraint's history, nature, and effect." *Khan*, [522 U.S.] at 10. Whether the businesses involved have market power is a further, significant consideration. In its design and function the rule distinguishes between restraints with anticompetitive effect that are harmful to the consumer and restraints stimulating competition that are in the consumer's best interest.

The rule of reason does not govern all restraints. Some types are deemed unlawful per se. The per se rule, treating categories of restraints as necessarily illegal, eliminates the need to study the reasonableness of an individual restraint in light of the real market forces at work. [I]t must be acknowledged [that] the per se rule can give clear guidance for certain conduct. Restraints that are per se unlawful include horizontal agreements among competitors to fix prices or to divide markets.

Resort to per se rules is confined to restraints, like those mentioned, "that would always or almost always tend to restrict competition and decrease output." [Case citation omitted.] To justify a per se prohibition a restraint must have "manifestly anticompetitive" effects and "lack . . . any redeeming virtue." [Case citations omitted.] As a consequence, the per se rule is appropriate only after courts have had considerable experience with the type of restraint at issue, and only if courts can predict with confidence that it would be invalidated in all or almost all instances under the rule of reason. It should come as no surprise, then, that "we have expressed reluctance to adopt per se rules with regard to restraints imposed in the context of business relationships where the economic impact of certain practices is not immediately obvious." *Khan*, [522 U.S.] at 10. [A]s we have stated, "a departure from the rule of reason standard must be based upon demonstrable economic effect rather than upon formalistic line-drawing." *GTE Sylvania*, [433 U.S.] at 58–59.

The Court has interpreted *Dr. Miles* as establishing a per se rule against a vertical agreement between a manufacturer and its distributor to set minimum resale prices. In *Dr. Miles*, the plaintiff, a manufacturer of medicines, sold its products only to distributors who agreed to resell them at set prices. The Court found the manufacturer's control of resale prices to be unlawful. It relied on the common-law rule that "a general restraint upon alienation is ordinarily invalid." The Court then explained that the agreements would advantage the distributors, not the manufacturer, and were analogous to a combination among competing distributors, which the law treated as void.

The reasoning of the Court's more recent jurisprudence has rejected the rationales on which *Dr. Miles* was based. By relying on the common-law rule against restraints on alienation, the Court justified its decision based on "formalistic" legal doctrine rather than "demonstrable economic effect" [quoting *GTE Sylvania*]. The Court in *Dr. Miles* relied on a treatise published in 1628, but failed to discuss in detail the business reasons that would motivate a manufacturer situated in 1911 to make use of vertical price restraints. The Court should be cautious about putting dispositive weight on doctrines from antiquity but of slight relevance. We reaffirm that "the state of the common law 400 or even 100 years ago is irrelevant to the issue before us: the effect of the antitrust laws upon vertical distributional restraints in the American economy today." *GTE Sylvania*, [433 U.S.] at 53.

Dr. Miles, furthermore, treated vertical agreements a manufacturer makes with its distributors as analogous to a horizontal combination among competing distributors. In later cases, however, the Court rejected the approach of reliance on rules governing horizontal restraints when defining rules applicable to vertical ones. Our recent cases formulate antitrust principles in accordance with the appreciated differences in economic effect between vertical and horizontal agreements, differences the *Dr. Miles* Court failed to consider. The reasons upon which *Dr. Miles* relied do not justify a per se rule. As a consequence, it is necessary to examine, in the first instance, the economic effects of vertical agreements to fix minimum resale prices, and to determine whether the per se rule is nonetheless appropriate.

Though each side of the debate can find sources to support its position, it suffices to say here that economics literature is replete with procompetitive justifications for a manufacturer's use of resale price maintenance. The few recent studies documenting the competitive effects of resale price maintenance also cast doubt on the conclusion that the practice meets the criteria for a per se rule. The justifications for vertical price restraints are similar to those for other vertical restraints. Minimum resale price maintenance can stimulate interbrand competition—the competition among manufacturers selling different brands of the same type of product—by reducing intrabrand competition—the competition among retailers selling the same brand. The promotion of interbrand competition is important because "the primary purpose of the antitrust laws is to protect [this type of] competition." *Khan*, [522 U.S.] at 15. A single manufacturer's use of vertical price restraints tends to eliminate intrabrand price competition; this in turn encourages retailers to invest in tangible or intangible services or promotional efforts that aid the manufacturer's position as against rival manufacturers. Resale price maintenance also has the potential to give consumers more options so that they can choose among low-price, low-service brands; high-price, high-service brands; and brands that fall in between.

Absent vertical price restraints, the retail services that enhance interbrand competition might be underprovided. This is because discounting retailers can free ride on retailers who furnish services and then capture some of the increased demand those services generate. Consumers might learn, for example, about the benefits of a manufacturer's product from a retailer that invests in fine showrooms, offers product demonstrations, or hires and trains knowledgeable employees. Or consumers might decide to buy the product because they see it in a retail establishment that has a reputation for selling high-quality merchandise. If the consumer can then buy the product from a retailer that discounts because it has not spent capital providing services or developing a quality reputation, the high-service retailer will lose sales to the discounter, forcing it to cut back its services to a level lower than consumers would otherwise prefer. Minimum resale price maintenance alleviates the problem because it prevents the discounter from undercutting the service provider. With price competition decreased, the manufacturer's retailers compete among themselves over services.

While vertical agreements setting minimum resale prices can have procompetitive justifications, they may have anticompetitive effects in other cases; and unlawful price fixing, designed solely to obtain monopoly profits, is an ever-present temptation. Notwithstanding the risks of unlawful conduct, it cannot be stated with any degree of confidence that resale price maintenance always or almost always tend[s] to restrict competition and decrease output. Vertical agreements establishing minimum resale prices can have either procompetitive or anticompetitive effects, depending upon the circumstances in which they are formed. And although the empirical evidence on the topic is limited, it does not suggest efficient uses of the agreements are infrequent or hypothetical. As the rule would proscribe a significant amount of procompetitive conduct, these agreements appear ill suited for per se condemnation.

PSKS contends, nonetheless, that vertical price restraints should be per se unlawful because of the administrative convenience of per se rules. That argument suggests per se illegality is the rule rather than the exception. This misinterprets our antitrust law. Per se rules may decrease administrative costs, but that is only part of the equation. Those rules can be counterproductive. They can increase the total cost of the antitrust system by prohibiting procompetitive conduct the antitrust laws should encourage. They also may increase litigation costs by promoting frivolous suits against legitimate practices. Were the Court now to conclude that vertical price restraints should be per se illegal based on administrative costs, we would undermine, if not overrule, the traditional demanding standards for adopting per se rules. Any possible reduction in administrative costs cannot alone justify the *Dr. Miles* rule.

PSKS also argues the per se rule is justified because a vertical price restraint can lead to higher prices for the manufacturer's goods. PSKS is mistaken in relying on pricing effects absent a further showing of anticompetitive conduct. For, as has been

indicated already, the antitrust laws are designed primarily to protect interbrand competition, from which lower prices can later result. The Court, moreover, has evaluated other vertical restraints under the rule of reason even though prices can be increased in the course of promoting procompetitive effects.

The rule of reason is designed and used to eliminate anticompetitive transactions from the market. This standard principle applies to vertical price restraints. A party alleging injury from a vertical agreement setting minimum resale prices will have, as a general matter, the information and resources available to show the existence of the agreement and its scope of operation. As courts gain experience considering the effects of these restraints by applying the rule of reason over the course of decisions, they can establish the litigation structure to ensure the rule operates to eliminate anticompetitive restraints from the market and to provide more guidance to businesses.

For the foregoing reasons, we think that were the Court considering the issue as an original matter, the rule of reason, not a per se rule of unlawfulness, would be the appropriate standard to judge vertical price restraints. We do not write on a clean slate, [however,] for the decision in *Dr. Miles* is almost a century old. So there is an argument for its retention on the basis of stare decisis alone. Even if *Dr. Miles* established an erroneous rule, "[s]tare decisis reflects a policy judgment that in most matters it is more important that the applicable rule of law be settled than that it be settled right." *Khan*, [522 U.S.] at 20. And concerns about maintaining settled law are strong when the question is one of statutory interpretation.

Stare decisis is not as significant in this case, however, because the issue before us is the scope of the Sherman Act. *Khan*, [522 U.S.] at 20 ("[T]he general presumption that legislative changes should be left to Congress has less force with respect to the Sherman Act"). From the beginning the Court has treated the Sherman Act as [if it were common law]. Just as the common law adapts to modern understanding and greater experience, so too does the Sherman Act's prohibition on "restraint[s] of trade" evolve to meet the dynamics of present economic conditions. The case-by-case adjudication contemplated by the rule of reason has implemented this common-law approach. Likewise, the boundaries of the doctrine of per se illegality should not be immovable. For "[i]t would make no sense to create out of the single term 'restraint of trade' a chronologically schizoid statute, in which a 'rule of reason' evolves with new circumstance and new wisdom, but a line of per se illegality remains forever fixed where it was." [Case citation omitted.]

Stare decisis, we conclude, does not compel our continued adherence to the per se rule against vertical price restraints. As discussed earlier, respected authorities in the economics literature suggest the per se rule is inappropriate, and there is now widespread agreement that resale price maintenance can have procompetitive effects. It is also significant that both the Department of Justice and the Federal Trade Commission—the antitrust enforcement agencies with the ability to assess the long-term impacts of resale price maintenance—have recommended that this Court replace the per se rule with the traditional rule of reason. In the antitrust context the fact that a decision has been "called into serious question" justifies our reevaluation of it. *Khan*, [522 U.S.] at 21.

Other considerations reinforce the conclusion that *Dr. Miles* should be overruled. Of most relevance, "we have overruled our precedents when subsequent cases have undermined their doctrinal underpinnings." [Case citation omitted.] The Court's treatment of vertical restraints has progressed away from *Dr. Miles'* strict approach. We have distanced ourselves from the opinion's rationales. This is unsurprising, for the case was decided not long after enactment of the Sherman Act when the Court had little experience with antitrust analysis.

In more recent cases the Court . . . has continued to temper, limit, or overrule once strict prohibitions on vertical restraints. In 1977, the Court overturned the per se rule for vertical nonprice restraints, adopting the rule of reason in its stead. *GTE Sylvania*, [433 U.S.] at 57–59. [I]n 1997, after examining the issue of vertical maximum price-fixing agreements in light of commentary and real experience, the Court overruled a 29-year-old precedent treating those agreements as per se illegal. It held instead that they should be evaluated under the traditional rule of reason. *Khan*, [522 U.S.] at 22. [O]ur recent treatment of other vertical restraints justif[ies] the conclusion that *Dr. Miles* should not be retained.

The *Dr. Miles* rule is also inconsistent with a principled framework, for it makes little economic sense when analyzed with our other cases on vertical restraints. If we were to decide the procompetitive effects of resale price maintenance were

insufficient to overrule *Dr. Miles*, then cases such as . . . *GTE Sylvania* . . . would be called into question. There is yet another consideration. A manufacturer can impose territorial restrictions on distributors and allow only one distributor to sell its goods in a given region. Our cases have recognized, and the economics literature confirms, that these vertical nonprice restraints have impacts similar to those of vertical price restraints; both reduce intrabrand competition and can stimulate retailer services. The same legal standard (per se unlawfulness) applies to horizontal market division and horizontal price fixing because both have similar economic effect. There is likewise little economic justification for the current differential treatment of vertical price and nonprice restraints. Furthermore, vertical nonprice restraints may prove less efficient for inducing desired services, and they reduce intrabrand competition more than vertical price restraints by eliminating both price and service competition.

For these reasons, the Court's decision in *Dr. Miles* is now overruled. Vertical price restraints are to be judged according to the rule of reason.

Fifth Circuit decision reversed, and case remanded for further proceedings.

Breyer, Justice, dissenting

The only safe predictions to make about today's decision are that it will likely raise the price of goods at retail and that it will create considerable legal turbulence as lower courts seek to develop workable principles. I do not believe that the majority has shown new or changed conditions sufficient to warrant overruling a decision of such long standing. All ordinary stare decisis considerations indicate the contrary. For these reasons, with respect, I dissent.

Horizontal Divisions of Markets

LO49-7 Describe what a horizontal division of markets is and explain the approaches courts take in determining whether such behavior is unlawful.

It has traditionally been said that horizontal division of markets agreements—those agreements among competing firms to divide up the available market by assigning one another certain exclusive territories or certain customers—are illegal per se. Such agreements plainly represent

agreements not to compete. They result in each firm being isolated from competition in the affected market.

In *United States v. Topco Associates, Inc.*, 405 U.S. 596 (1972), the Supreme Court reaffirmed this longstanding principle by striking down a horizontal division of markets agreement among members of a cooperative association of local and regional supermarket chains. *Topco* was widely criticized, however, on the ground that its per se approach ignored an important point: that the defendants' joint activities in promoting Topco brand products were aimed at enabling them to compete more effectively with national supermarket chains. Critics argued that when such horizontal restraints were ancillary to *procompetitive* behavior, they should be judged under the rule of reason.

Naked Restraints and Ancillary Restraints Such criticism has had an impact. Several decisions by lower federal courts have distinguished between "naked" horizontal restraints (those having no other purpose or effect except restraining competition) and "ancillary" horizontal restraints (those constituting a necessary part of a larger joint undertaking serving procompetitive ends). Although these courts continue to apply the per se rule to naked horizontal restraints, they give rule of reason (or at least quick-look) treatment to ancillary restraints. In determining whether ancillary restraints are lawful, courts weigh the harm to competition resulting from such restraints against the alleged offsetting benefits to competition.

Whether the Supreme Court ultimately will endorse such departures from *Topco* remains to be seen. However, the Court's post-*Topco* tendency to discard per se rules in favor of a rule of reason approach in other areas strongly suggests that *Topco*'s critics eventually will prevail with their arguments.

Vertical Restraints on Distribution

LO49-8 Describe what a vertical restraint on distribution is and identify the type of analysis (per se or rule of reason) that such behavior receives when courts determine whether it is unlawful.

Vertical restraints on distribution (or *vertical nonprice restraints*) also fall within the scope of the Sherman Act. A manufacturer has always had the power to *unilaterally* assign exclusive territories to its dealers or to limit the dealerships it grants in a particular geographic area. However, manufacturers may run afoul of § 1 by causing dealers to *agree* not to sell outside their dealership territories or by placing other restrictions on their dealers' right to resell their products.

The Supreme Court once held that vertical restraints on distribution were per se illegal when applied to goods that the manufacturer had sold to its dealers. The Court changed course, however, in *Continental T.V., Inc. v. GTE Sylvania, Inc.*, 433 U.S. 36 (1977). In *Sylvania*, the Court abandoned the per se rule in favor of a rule of reason approach to most vertical restraints on distribution. The Court accepted many Chicago School arguments concerning the potential *economic efficiencies* that could result from vertical restraints on distribution. Most notably, such restraints were alleged to offer a chance for increased *interbrand* competition among the product lines of competing

manufacturers at the admitted cost of restraining *intrabrand* competition among dealers in a particular manufacturer's product. For further discussion of *Sylvania*, see the *Leegin* decision, which appears earlier in the chapter.

Subsequent decisions on the legality of vertical restraints on distribution have emphasized the importance of the market share of the manufacturer imposing the restraints. Restraints imposed by manufacturers with large market shares are more likely to be found unlawful under the rule of reason because the resulting harm to intrabrand competition is unlikely to be offset by significant positive effects on interbrand competition.

LO49-9 Explain the approaches courts take in determining the legality or illegality of group boycotts and similar refusals to deal.

Group Boycotts and Concerted Refusals to Deal
Under the *Colgate* doctrine, a single firm may lawfully refuse to deal with certain firms. The same is not true, however, of *agreements* by two or more business entities to refuse to deal with others, to deal with others only on certain terms and conditions, or to coerce suppliers or customers not to deal with one of their competitors. Such agreements are *joint* restraints on trade. Historically, they have been per se unlawful under § 1. For example, when a trade association of garment manufacturers agreed not to sell to retailers that sold clothing or fabrics with designs pirated from legitimate manufacturers, the agreement was held to be a per se violation of the Sherman Act.[4]

Vertical Boycotts Recent antitrust developments, however, indicate that not all concerted refusals to deal will receive per se treatment. If a manufacturer terminated a distributor in response to complaints from other distributors that the terminated distributor was selling to customers outside its prescribed sales territory, the manufacturer will be held to have violated § 1 only if the termination resulted in a significant harm to competition. This result follows logically from the *Sylvania* decision. If vertical restraints on distribution are judged under the rule of reason, the same standard should apply to a vertical boycott designed to enforce such restraints.

Even distributors claiming to have been terminated as part of a vertical price-fixing scheme have found recovery increasingly difficult to obtain in recent years. In *Monsanto v. Spray-Rite Service Corp.*, 465 U.S. 752 (1984), a

---

[4]*Fashion Originators' Guild v. FTC*, 312 U.S. 457 (1941).

manufacturer had terminated a discounting distributor after receiving complaints from its other distributors. The Supreme Court held that these facts would not trigger liability for vertical price-fixing in the absence of additional evidence tending to exclude the possibility that the manufacturer and the nonterminated distributors acted independently. In *Business Electronics Corp. v. Sharp Electronics Corp.*, 485 U.S. 717 (1988), the Court held that even proof of a conspiracy between a manufacturer and nonterminated distributors to terminate a price-cutter would not trigger liability unless it was accompanied by proof that the manufacturer and nonterminated dealers were also engaged in an unlawful vertical price-fixing conspiracy.

Horizontal Boycotts It also appears that the Supreme Court is willing to relax the per se rule for some *horizontal* boycotts. For instance, in *Northwest Wholesale Stationers, Inc. v. Pacific Stationery & Printing Co.*, 472 U.S. 284 (1985), members of an office supply retailers' purchasing cooperative had expelled a member retailer that engaged in some wholesale operations in addition to retail activities. The Court held that rule of reason treatment should be extended to the alleged boycott at issue but declined to eliminate the per se rule for all horizontal boycotts. The Court has offered only general guidance for determining which horizontal boycotts trigger rule of reason analysis (or at least quick-look analysis) and which ones amount to per se violations. The appropriate legal treatment in a given case is therefore difficult to predict.

Tying Agreements
Tying agreements occur when a seller refuses to sell a buyer a certain product (the *tying product*) unless the buyer also agrees to purchase a different product (the *tied product*) from the seller. For example, a fertilizer manufacturer refuses to sell its dealers fertilizer (the tying product) unless they also agree to buy its line of pesticides (the tied product). The potential anticompetitive effect of a tying agreement is that the seller's competitors in the sale of the tied product may be foreclosed from competing with the seller for sales to customers that have entered into tying agreements with the seller. To the extent that tying agreements are coercively imposed, they also deprive buyers of the freedom to make independent decisions concerning their purchases of the tied product. Tying agreements may be challenged under both § 1 of the Sherman Act and § 3 of the Clayton Act.[5]

---

[5]Section 3 of the Clayton Act applies, however, only when both the tying and the tied products are commodities. Chapter 50 discusses Clayton Act standards for tying agreement legality.

Elements of Prohibited Tying Agreements

 LO49-10 Identify and explain the elements of a prohibited tying agreement.

Tying agreements are sometimes said to be per se illegal under § 1. However, because a tying agreement must meet certain criteria before it is subjected to per se analysis, and because evidence of certain justifications is fairly frequently considered in tying cases, the supposed per se rule regarding tying agreements is at best a "soft" per se rule. The *Suture Express* case, which follows, illustrates an apparent trend among courts: increased willingness to apply rule of reason analysis to tying agreements.

Before a challenged tying agreement is held to violate § 1, these elements must be demonstrated: (1) the agreement involves *two* separate and distinct items rather than integrated components of a larger product, service, or system of doing business; (2) the tying product cannot be purchased unless the tied product is also purchased; (3) the seller has sufficient economic power in the market for the tying product (such as a large market share) to appreciably restrain competition in the tied product market; and (4) a "not insubstantial" amount of commerce in the tied product is affected by the seller's tying agreements.

Applying the above elements, a federal district court held in 2000 that Microsoft Corporation violated § 1 by tying its Internet Explorer web browser to versions of its Windows operating system. In a 2001 decision, however, a federal court of appeals reversed that aspect of the district court's decision and remanded the tying claim for reconsideration under the rule of reason. The appellate court concluded that in the context of software used as a platform for third-party applications, tying of the sort done by Microsoft should not necessarily be presumed to have a pernicious effect on competition. The court reasoned that in order to avoid discouraging platform software-related innovation, weighing and balancing of the tying arrangement's benefits and anticompetitive effects should be undertaken. Only the rule of reason would provide the opportunity for such weighing and balancing. The court stressed, however, that it was not changing the controlling rules for tying agreements generally or for such arrangements in computer-related settings not involving platform software. (Other aspects of the appellate court's *Microsoft* decision are addressed later in this chapter.)

The *Suture Express* case contains a discussion of the elements of prohibited tying arrangements, with a focus on the third element: *market power as to the tying product*. The case also underscores the importance of the *antitrust injury* requirement discussed earlier in the chapter.

Suture Express, Inc. v. Owens & Minor Distribution, Inc.
851 F.3d 1029 (10th Cir. 2017)

Suture Express, Inc.; Cardinal Health 200 LLC (Cardinal); and Owens & Minor Distribution, Inc. (O&M) compete in the medical-and-surgical (med-surg) supply and distribution market. Cardinal, O&M, and another company not part of this lawsuit (Medline Industries Inc.) are national broadline distributors, meaning they contract with hospitals and other acute health care providers to distribute a full line of med-surg products. This includes approximately 30 categories, ranging from custom surgical kits, bedpans, and hospital gowns to IV sets and solutions, gloves, and needles and syringes. Because many of these med-surg products are heavy or bulky, Cardinal and O&M use a network of regional distribution centers to store the inventory and then use trucks to make deliveries to the hospitals.

In 1998, Suture Express entered the med-surg market, but instead of competing as another broadline distributor, Suture Express specialized in supplying only one category of med-surg: sutures. In 2002, Suture Express also began distributing endomechanical supplies, which are used for minimally invasive or laproscopic surgeries. These two product categories, together known as suture-endo, differ from other med-surg products in that they are typically smaller and much lighter. Suture-endo products have a high-dollar value relative to their size and weight. Moreover, there exists a broader variety of these products than of any other category of med-surg.

Because of these distinctive characteristics of suture-endo, Suture Express utilized a different distribution model. Instead of using regional warehouses and delivering products by truck, Suture Express stocked all its inventory in a single warehouse and then contracted with FedEx to provide overnight delivery to ordering hospitals. By specializing in suture-endo and by using this new distribution model, Suture Express was often able to have on hand a broader variety of suture-endo than did the broadline distributors.

The market for the national distribution of med-surg products to acute care providers is divided into two broad categories: (1) suture-endo, which comprises roughly 10 percent of the overall med-surg market, and (2) other-med-surg, which includes everything else (the other 90 percent). In the case described here, Suture Express's expert witness (Professor Einer Elhauge) offered the view that the suture-endo market had grown over time, expanding from about $1.97 billion in distribution revenues in 2007 to roughly $2.36 billion in 2012. During that same time period, Suture Express was able to capture between 8 percent and 10 percent of the market. In comparison, during those six years, Cardinal's share of the suture-endo market declined from 30 percent to 26 percent, and O&M's share grew from 40 percent to 42 percent.

In the other-med-surg market, Cardinal and O&M together accounted for the majority of sales to acute care providers. Between 2007 and 2012, Cardinal's share of other-med-surg sales decreased from 31 percent to 27 percent, while O&M's share grew from 33 percent to 38 percent. The rest of the other-med-surg market was controlled by the third national broadline distributor (Medline) and regional distributors. Cardinal, O&M, and Suture Express have all won and lost contracts against Medline and certain regional distributors.

Most med-surg distributors use a "cost-plus markup" fee arrangement, under which the customer is charged the cost of the product plus a negotiated fixed percentage distribution fee. Between 2007 and 2012, average markups decreased for Cardinal, O&M, and Suture Express, as well as for some of the regional distributors. This was true both in the other-med-surg and the suture-endo markets, though markups in the other-med-surg market were higher throughout the time period. Within the suture-endo market specifically, Cardinal's and O&M's markups were always higher than Suture Express's—though, again, all declined somewhat between 2007 and 2012. Finally, overall profit margins for O&M and Cardinal declined since 2008.

After Suture Express entered the suture-endo market and steadily increased its market share, Cardinal and O&M responded by instituting bundling packages in their contracts. Though these packages took different forms, the overarching result was that the customer would pay more (usually 1 percent more) for its other-med-surg orders unless it also ordered its suture-endo through the same distributor. For instance, some Cardinal contracts required the customer to purchase all its suture-endo from Cardinal or face markups on its other-med-surg orders. O&M instituted similar packages, making the price of other-med-surg increase if the customer did not also buy its suture-endo through O&M. Medline also used similar bundling packages, as did a number of the regional distributors.

Whether viewed as a bundling discount (as Cardinal and O&M labeled it) or as a penalty (as Suture Express called it), the effect was that customers ended up paying more overall if they ordered suture-endo through Suture Express and other-med-surg through Cardinal or O&M than if they ordered everything through their broadline distributor—even though Suture Express charged less for its suture-endo than did Cardinal or O&M. For instance, before the bundling terms were put into effect, one hospital would typically buy about $750,000 worth of suture-endo per year and about $7,000,000 of other-med-surg. Buying the former from Suture Express and the latter from Cardinal would save the hospital about $18,750. But with the bundling term added, Cardinal would increase the hospital's other-med-surg markup by 1 percent if it did not also buy its suture-endo from Cardinal. Because this would translate into a $70,000 increase on the hospital's other-med-surg, the hospital might reasonably conclude that the $18,000 in suture-endo savings would not be worth the price of doing business with Suture Express.

Suture Express sued Cardinal and O&M, alleging that their bundling arrangements constituted an illegal tying practice in violation of § 1 of the Sherman Act and § 3 of the Clayton Act. A federal district court granted summary judgment in favor of Cardinal and O&M. Suture Express could not establish, the district court ruled, that either Cardinal or O&M individually possessed sufficient market power in the other-med-surg market to enable either firm to restrain trade in the suture-endo market. The court also held that even if sufficient market power had been demonstrated, Suture Express could not establish antitrust injury because it had not shown that competition itself had been harmed. Finally, the court ruled that Cardinal and O&M had cited procompetitive justifications for the bundling arrangement—justifications that would be sufficient to overcome any harm arguably caused by any anticompetitive effects resulting from the bundling arrangement. Suture Express appealed to the U.S. Court of Appeals for the Tenth Circuit.

Kelly, Circuit Judge

Section 1 of the Sherman Act prohibits unreasonable restraints of trade. Tying arrangements do not necessarily constitute illegal restraints. A tie-in exists when a seller conditions its sale of a product (the "tying" product) on the purchase of a second product (the "tied" product). In addition to outright refusals to sell two products separately, tie-ins can also include instances of discount bundling—when a seller charges less for a package of two products linked together than the sum of the prices at which it sells each product individually.

Since tying arrangements can be used for good or for ill (i.e., can have procompetitive or anticompetitive effects), the arrangement itself is only problematic when it is used to unreasonably restrain trade. Indeed, "[b]uyers often find package sales attractive; a seller's decision to offer such packages can merely be an attempt to compete effectively—conduct that is entirely consistent with the Sherman Act." *Jefferson Parish Hospital District No. 2 v. Hyde*, 466 U.S. 2, 12 (1984).

The Supreme Court has explained that illicit tying arrangements occur "when the seller has some special ability—usually called 'market power'—to force a purchaser to do something that he would not do in a competitive market." *Id.* at 13–14. Thus, "the essential characteristic of an invalid tying arrangement lies in the seller's exploitation of its control over the tying product to force the buyer into the purchase of a tied product that the buyer either did not want at all, or might have preferred to purchase elsewhere on different terms." *Id.* at 12.

As with most other antitrust claims, tying arrangements can be analyzed using a per se rule or a rule of reason. *See id.* at 15–16, 18. The four elements of a per se tying violation are: (1) two separate products are involved; (2) the sale or agreement to sell one product is conditioned on the purchase of the other; (3) the seller has sufficient economic power in the tying product market to enable it to restrain trade in the tied product market; and (4) a "not insubstantial" amount of interstate commerce in the tied product is affected.

On Cardinal and O&M's initial motion to dismiss, the district court ruled that Suture Express could not establish a plausible per se tying violation but that it was free to move forward under the rule of reason. Under the rule of reason, the plaintiff has the burden of showing that the defendant unreasonably restrained

competition in violation of the Sherman Act. This "necessarily involves an inquiry into the actual effect of the [tying arrangement] on competition." *Id.* at 29.

Beyond this general proposition, caselaw on tying claims under the rule of reason is "amazingly sparse." [However, because] the Supreme Court has continued to add more real-market analysis to the requirements of a per se tying claim, . . . the rule of reason seems to be mainly different in degree, not necessarily in kind. One difference, however, is that the rule of reason is more receptive to procompetitive justifications for the tying arrangement and more willing to examine the effects of that arrangement in both the tying and tied markets. And, as with the rule of reason in other contexts, there is a burden-shifting component to the analysis. First, the burden falls on the plaintiff to establish a prima facie showing of a substantially adverse effect on competition. If that occurs, then the burden shifts to the defendant to come forward with evidence of procompetitive justifications for the practice. Finally, the burden then shifts back to the plaintiff to rebut the defense by showing either that the proffered justification is illegitimate, that the challenged conduct is not necessary to achieve the legitimate objectives, or that the objectives can be achieved by other means that negatively affect competition far less.

Suture Express argues that Cardinal's and O&M's bundling package meets all four elements of a per se tying claim—and thus, implicitly, that the arrangement unreasonably restrains competition and violates the rule of reason. First, the two product categories involved are other-med-surg (the "tying product") and suture-endo (the "tied product"). Second, the agreement to sell other-med-surg at a favorable price is conditioned on the purchase of suture-endo. Third, Cardinal and O&M together comprise nearly 70% of the tying (other-med-surg) market, enabling them to restrain trade in the tied (suture-endo) market. Fourth, a significant amount of commerce in the suture-endo market is negatively affected, since acute care providers cannot get the better deal at Suture Express due to the bundling packages.

Applying the rule of reason on summary judgment, the district court found genuine factual disputes on the first and second factors. (Again, under rule of reason analysis, the plaintiff bears the burden of showing that the restraint of trade is, on balance, unreasonable. Thus, the per se "elements" are in fact more akin to "factors" under rule of reason analysis.) However, the court ruled for Cardinal and O&M on the third factor—that Suture Express could not prove that Cardinal or O&M individually possessed sufficient power in the other-med-surg market to allow either of them to restrain trade in the suture-endo market. The court then went on to consider whether Suture Express had established antitrust injury (no), whether any justifications for the bundling arrangement existed (yes), and the overall market effects of the bundle (procompetitive). We consider each finding in turn as necessary.

Market Power

"[I]n all cases involving a tying arrangement, the plaintiff must prove that the defendant has market power in the tying product." *Illinois Tool Works, Inc. v. Independent Ink, Inc.*, 547 U.S. 28, 46 (2006). Market power is the power "to force a purchaser to do something that he would not do in a competitive market," *Hyde*, 466 U.S. at 14, and often takes the form of a seller's ability "to raise price and restrict output." *Eastman Kodak Co. v. Image Technical Services, Inc.*, 504 U.S. 451, 464 (1992). To demonstrate market power, a plaintiff "may show evidence of either power to control prices or the power to exclude competition." [Citation omitted.] Importantly, this power over price can take the form of a tying arrangement if the price could have been raised but the tie was demanded instead.

Market power is important because if the defendant has substantial power in the tying market, then the tie has the potential of injuring competition by forcing consumers to take the tied product just to get the tying one. Without power in the tying market, we would expect that a customer would not feel obliged to take the tie, as he could simply go elsewhere to buy the tying and tied products separately. Though the majority of Supreme Court (and our) cases discussing the need to prove market power as part of a tying claim are per se cases, we see no reason why the same theoretical underpinning would not make the inquiry relevant under a rule of reason analysis.

With this said, we do think that tied market effects can be appropriate evidence of tying market power in a rule of reason case, though it cannot be dispositive. The Supreme Court suggested as much in *Eastman Kodak*. In that case, Kodak sold photocopiers, and then also sold (a) replacement parts and (b) repair service. In response to independent service agents offering repair service at a lower price, Kodak restricted the sale of replacement parts to buyers who either also purchased the Kodak repair service or who repaired their own machines. The independent agents then sued Kodak, alleging the company unlawfully restrained competition by tying the sale of service (tied market) to the sale of the parts (tying market). Kodak responded that the arrangement could not be unlawful because it lacked market power in the tying (parts) market since if it raised prices there it would suffer corresponding losses in the photocopier market. The Supreme Court rejected this proposed

legal rule and consequently denied summary judgment to Kodak, instead noting that it would at least be reasonable for a jury to infer that Kodak had market power "to raise prices and drive out competition in the aftermarkets [i.e., (a) parts and (b) service], since respondents offer direct evidence that Kodak did so." *Id.* at 477.

As Cardinal and O&M point out, *Eastman Kodak* [is not] quite on all fours with this case because the [defendant in that case] exercised a near-monopoly in the tying market. [That distinction,] however, only confirms that we should not consider direct evidence of tied market effects as conclusive—a warning the Supreme Court has also issued. *See U.S. Steel Corp. v. Fortner Enterprises*, 429 U.S. 610, 618 (1977) (finding evidence that customers paid a noncompetitive price for the tied good insufficient by itself to support illicit tying claim). That the evidence is not dispositive, however, does not mean it should not be considered. Since market power is the power to "force a purchaser to do something that he would not do in a competitive market," *Hyde*, 466 U.S. at 14, if a purchaser has indeed been coerced into doing something he would not normally do, why would it not follow that this coercion could be (though is not necessarily) because of market power in the tying market? And under the rule of reason, why should such evidence not at least be considered, especially when (as here) there exists a genuine issue of material fact as to coercion? We think it should be.

The district court held that Suture Express had not met its burden of producing evidence that demonstrated Cardinal's or O&M's ability to exclude competition or control price. As to the first, the court found that neither of the companies could exclude competition in the tying market since there was evidence the opposite was occurring, with regional and national competitors growing and expanding during the pertinent time period. Further, since Medline[, the third national broadline distributor,] and the regional distributors also offered similar bundling packages, competition was not excluded in the tied market, either: it simply took the form of bundle-to-bundle competition. These bundling packages, the court also found, did not result in prohibitively high switching costs for customers, which could be indicative of market exclusion. Though some customers noted that the cost of switching distributors required an investment of time and overhead, the court concluded that "the record is filled with examples of customers who, in fact, have switched distributors on a regular basis."

As for pricing, the court found that evidence of Cardinal's and O&M's declining profit margins in the other-med-surg market revealed that they did not have the ability to control prices in that market. The court thought the evidence showing consolidation in the buyer (i.e., acute care provider) market instead demonstrated enhanced bargaining power, which could also help explain Cardinal's and O&M's inability to control pricing. In sum, the court wrote: "[T]he undisputed facts demonstrate a market where O&M and Cardinal compete vigorously against Medline, certain regional distributors, and each other. And, after three or four years, O&M and Cardinal can retain only about half of their acute care customers. These facts preclude any triable dispute about defendants' market power."

This is persuasive evidence of a lack of market power. Suture Express contends, though, that it is not enough to settle the question as a matter of law. For instance, it notes that tying market share is very relevant to the inquiry, and contends that even if 31% and 38% market shares (Cardinal's and O&M's high points, respectively) would not be enough to win under the per se rule, it should nevertheless be enough to survive summary judgment under the rule of reason. Perhaps. Though the Supreme Court has noted that a hospital's 30% market share lacked the "kind of dominant market position that obviates the need for further inquiry into actual competitive conditions," *Hyde*, 466 U.S. at 27, courts have used that benchmark as a floor for plaintiffs seeking to prove a per se claim. In a rule of reason case, it is reasonable to conclude that other indicia can tip the balance in favor of a showing of market power, even if one begins with a lower showing of market share. But just as "market share alone is insufficient to establish market power," [citation omitted], it is also insufficient to counteract the other market realities present here that point to increased competition and lower prices.

Suture Express responds that this other evidence is actually misleading. First, it contends that Professor Elhauge's calculations that between 56% and 64% of the suture-endo market was bound by contracts with Cardinal and O&M and thus could not buy suture-endo from Suture Express constitute direct evidence of Cardinal's and O&M's power over price. This is because, it says, [if not for] the challenged conduct, buyers would have bought suture-endo from Suture Express and paid less.

We have problems accepting that [this argument reveals] significantly probative evidence by which a jury could find that Cardinal or O&M has enjoyed market power. For instance, Suture Express's contention that the acceptance of the package by 56–64% of the suture-endo market, though certainly evidence to consider, is ultimately unavailing. As the Supreme Court has explained, "this approach depends on the absence of other explanations for the willingness of buyers to purchase the package." *U.S. Steel v. Fortner*, 429 U.S. at 618. And here, other explanations abound—such as the fact that many of the acute care purchasers simply preferred consolidating their purchases and having fewer distributors to deal with.

Additionally, that Suture Express and Cardinal/O&M charged different prices does not itself show power over price. To do that, one would have to look at the costs borne by each defendant and its margins. And since the entire reason that Suture Express's business model works is that it is able to distribute suture-endo alone at a lower cost than Cardinal and O&M can distribute

other-med-surg and suture-endo together, it is logical that Cardinal's and O&M's costs would be higher. That is not a result of market power, but of different distribution models.

[There is also sufficient evidence here] of actual competition that precludes a finding of market exclusion. Medline more than doubled its med-surg sales between 2008 and 2014. Regional distributors have likewise grown. And all three parties [to this case] compete with and have won and lost contracts to these other distributors. A market in which competitors are growing and margins are shrinking is inconsistent with the claim that Cardinal and O&M can exclude competition and control prices.

In sum, we do not think a reasonable jury could conclude that either Cardinal or O&M possesses market power sufficient to force the tie. Even if there were a genuine issue as to market power, however . . . , we do not think Suture Express has carried its burden of showing antitrust injury. [We now turn to that issue.]

Antitrust Injury

As part of any claim under § 1 of the Sherman Act, the plaintiff must establish "an injury of the type the antitrust laws were intended to prevent." [Citation omitted.] The plaintiff must show the challenged restraint actually injured competition, not merely a competitor.

As evidence that it was the suture-endo market as a whole that was harmed, Suture Express offers the report of its expert witness, who examined the contract terms for a number of the largest hospital systems serviced by Cardinal and O&M. Sales under these contracts comprised roughly half of all the other-med-surg sold by the two companies. Professor Elhauge concluded that from 2007 to 2012, between 59% and 79% of suture-endo sales Cardinal made to acute care customers were under contracts that made pricing of other-med-surg contingent in some way on the purchase of suture-endo. For O&M, those percentages ranged from 95% to 97%. Multiplying these percentages by each company's share of the suture-endo market, Professor Elhauge calculated that Cardinal's bundling arrangements restrained between 18–22%, and O&M's between 38–42%, of the suture-endo market. Thus, according to Suture Express, 56–64% of the suture-endo market was restrained by their contracts from purchasing suture-endo from Suture Express. These foreclosed customers ended up paying $36 million more for suture-endo than they would have had they bought from Suture Express.

This, Suture Express [argues in its brief], is the crux of the antitrust harm inquiry, which it frames as "whether, in the but-for world without the challenged conduct, buyers would have paid less than they paid in the actual world with the conduct." The answer, it provides, is yes: "Absent Defendants' bundling terms, hospitals would have purchased from Suture Express at its lower price."

But there is a problem with this conclusion: it fails to note that the "but-for world" existed for almost half the market (since

36–44% of the market was not constrained), yet less than half of that market "purchased from Suture Express at its lower price." In 2007, Suture Express accounted for only 16% of unrestrained suture-endo sales; that number increased to 41% in 2010, and fell to 24% in 2012. We note this not because we think that every unrestrained purchase would need to take advantage of the lower price offered by Suture Express for its harm theory to be viable, but because the formulation as presented raises questions about the "but-for world" it models compared to the real-world market that actually existed—and whether it was really competition that was harmed instead of simply one competitor.

Additionally, . . . simply comparing the average price and mark-ups between the three competitors fails to show that competition itself was harmed across the market. Again, the record tends to show the opposite: overall med-surg revenues increased between 2007 and 2012, even as increased competition drove Cardinal's and O&M's profit margins down.

Accordingly, we do not think Suture Express has demonstrated substantially adverse effects on competition caused by Cardinal and O&M. What the Supreme Court said in a Sherman Act § 2 context remains true here: "The purpose of the [Sherman] Act is not to protect businesses from the working of the market; it is to protect the public from the failure of the market. The law directs itself not against conduct which is competitive, even severely so,

but against conduct which unfairly tends to destroy competition itself." *Spectrum Sports, Inc. v. McQuillan*, 506 U.S. 447, 459 (1993). The evidence in this case—the decrease in markups charged, the consolidation of buyer power, the growth of regional competitors, the success of Medline—reveals a med-surg market that is becoming more, not less, competitive. There is simply not enough probative evidence for a jury to find that Cardinal's or O&M's bundling practices constitute an injury of the kind the antitrust laws are intended to prevent. Since we affirm the district court on this point, we need not continue on to an examination of procompetitive justifications offered to support the bundling practices.

Section 3 of the Clayton Act prohibits persons engaging in commerce from making a lease or sale of goods "where the effect of such lease, sale, or contract for sale . . . may be to substantially lessen competition or tend to create a monopoly in any line of commerce." Although the language differs from that of the Sherman Act, "at least for allegations of unlawful tying arrangements, the required showings under both [acts] are identical." [Citation omitted.] Because we conclude that its Sherman Act claim should not be reinstated, Suture Express's Clayton Act claim likewise fails.

District court's grant of summary judgment in favor of Cardinal and O&M affirmed.

Possible Justifications for Tying Agreements The first two elements of a prohibited tying agreement have been particularly significant in cases involving franchisors and their franchised dealers. For example, a suit by a McDonald's franchisee alleged that McDonald's violated § 1 by requiring franchisees to lease their stores from McDonald's as a condition of acquiring a McDonald's franchise. A federal court of appeals, however, rejected the franchisee's claim and held that no tying agreement was involved. Instead, the franchise and the lease were integral components of a well-thought-out system of doing business.[6]

Courts have recognized two other possible justifications for tying agreements. First, tying arrangements that are instrumental in launching a new competitor with an otherwise uncertain future may be lawful until the new business has established itself in the marketplace. The rationale for this "new business" exception is that if a tying agreement enables a fledgling firm to become a viable competitor, the agreement's net effect on competition is positive. Second,

some courts have recognized that tying agreements sometimes may be necessary to protect the reputation of the seller's product line. For example, one of the seller's products functions properly only if used in conjunction with another of its products. To qualify for this exception, however, the seller must convince the court that a tying arrangement is the only viable means to protect its goodwill.

Chicago School Views on Tying Agreements Chicago School thinkers have long criticized the traditional judicial approach to tying agreements because they do not believe that most tie-ins result in any significant economic harm. They argue that sellers who try to impose a tie-in in competitive markets gain no increased profits as a result. This is so because instead of participating in a tying agreement, buyers may turn to substitutes for the tying product or may purchase the tying product from competing sellers. The net effect of a tie-in may therefore be that any increase in the seller's sales in the tied product is offset by a loss in sales of the tying product. Only when the seller has substantial power in the tying product market is there potential that a tie-in may be used to increase the seller's power in the tied

---

[6]*Principe v. McDonald's Corp.*, 631 F.2d 303 (4th Cir. 1980).

product market. However, even when the seller has such market power in the tying product, Chicago School thinkers argue that no harm to competition is likely to result if the seller faces strong competition in the tied product market. For these and other reasons, Chicago School thinkers favor a rule of reason approach to all tying agreements.

The Supreme Court has not formally ruled that all tying agreements should receive rule of reason analysis (or, in other words, that none of them should be given per se treatment). Some justices, however, have offered indications over the years that they may be receptive to such an approach. Given the Supreme Court's tendency in recent decades to move behaviors from the per se column to the rule of reason column, it would not be surprising if the Court were to make rule of reason analysis the controlling approach for all tying agreements. An eventual ruling of that nature by the Court would place the official stamp of approval on the previously noted trend in which lower courts have shown an increased willingness to treat certain tying agreements under the rule of reason.

Reciprocal Dealing Agreements
Under a reciprocal dealing agreement, a buyer attempts to exploit its purchasing power by conditioning its purchases from suppliers on reciprocal purchases of some product or service offered for sale by the buyer. For example, an oil company with a chain of wholly owned gas stations refuses to purchase the tires it sells in those stations unless the tire manufacturer (the would-be supplier of the tires) agrees to purchase, from the oil company, the petrochemicals used in the tire manufacturing process. Reciprocal dealing agreements are similar in motivation and effect to tying agreements. Courts therefore tend to treat them similarly. In seeking to impose the reciprocal dealing agreement on the tire manufacturer, the oil company is attempting to gain a competitive advantage over its competitors in the petrochemical market. A court judging the legality of such an agreement would examine the oil company's economic power as a purchaser of tires and the dollar amount of petrochemical sales involved.

Exclusive Dealing Agreements
Exclusive dealing agreements require buyers of a particular product or service to purchase that product or service exclusively from a particular seller. For example, Standard Lawnmower Corporation requires its retail dealers to sell only Standard brand mowers. A common variation of an exclusive dealing agreement is the *requirements contract*, under which the buyer of a particular product agrees to purchase all of its requirements for that product from a particular supplier. For example, a candy manufacturer agrees to buy all of its sugar requirements from one sugar refiner. Exclusive dealing contracts present a threat to competition similar to that involved in tying contracts—they may reduce interbrand competition by foreclosing a seller's competitors from the opportunity to compete for sales to its customers. Unlike tying contracts, however, exclusive dealing agreements may sometimes enhance efficiencies in distribution and stimulate interbrand competition. Exclusive dealing agreements reduce a manufacturer's sales costs and provide dealers with a secure source of supply. They may also encourage dealer efforts to market the manufacturer's products more effectively because a dealer selling only one product line has a greater stake in the success of that line than does a dealer who sells the products of several competing manufacturers.

Because many exclusive dealing agreements involve commodities, they may also be challenged under § 3 of the Clayton Act. The legal tests applicable to exclusive dealing agreements under both acts are identical. Therefore, we defer discussing those tests until the next chapter.

Joint Ventures by Competitors
A **joint venture** is a combined effort by two or more business entities for a limited purpose such as research. Because joint ventures may yield enhanced efficiencies through integration of the resources of more than one firm, they are commonly judged under the rule of reason. Under this approach, courts tend to ask whether any competitive restraints that are incidental to the venture are necessary to accomplish its lawful objectives and, if so, whether those restraints are offset by the venture's positive effects. Joint ventures whose primary purpose is illegal per se, however, have been given per se treatment. An example of such a case would be two competing firms that form a joint sales agency and authorize it to fix the price of their products.

National Cooperative Research and Production Act Antitrust critics have long argued that the threat of antitrust prosecution seriously inhibits the formation of joint research and development ventures, and that American firms are placed at a competitive disadvantage in world markets as a result. Such arguments have enjoyed more acceptance during roughly the past two decades. In 1984, Congress passed the National Cooperative Research Act (NCRA). This act applies to *joint research and development ventures (JRDVs)*, which are broadly defined to include basic and applied research and joint activities in the licensing of technologies developed by such research. The NCRA requires the application of a reasonableness standard, rather than a per se rule, when a JRDV's legality is determined.

Ethics and Compliance in Action

The Sherman Act's broad prohibition against "[e]very contract, combination . . . or conspiracy, in restraint of trade or commerce" has led business law scholar Inara Scott to argue that antitrust laws may indeed prevent businesses from collaborating to support environmental sustainability and human rights. For example, imagine a coffee-roasting cooperative wants to boycott a member who has engaged in human rights abuse:

1. Would such a group boycott be a per se violation of the Sherman Act?

2. Would such a group boycott be a violation of the Sherman Act under the rule of reason standard?

3. How would you change the Sherman Act in order to ensure that socially responsible collaborations are encouraged and allowed?

To read Professor Scott's full argument and a detailed discussion of the Sherman Act, see Inara Scott, "Antirust and Socially Responsible Collaboration: A Chilling Combination?," *American Business Law Journal* 53, no. 1 (2016), pp. 97–144.

It also requires firms contemplating a JRDV to provide the Department of Justice and the Federal Trade Commission with advance notice of their intent to do so. The NCRA provides that only actual (not treble) damages may be recovered for losses flowing from a JRDV ultimately found to be in violation of § 1. In addition, the NCRA contains a provision allowing the parties to a challenged JRDV to recover attorney fees from an unsuccessful challenger if the suit is shown to be "frivolous, unreasonable, without foundation, or in bad faith." Congress amended the statute in 1993 to extend its application to joint *production* ventures. In doing so, Congress renamed the statute the National Cooperative Research and Production Act.

Figure 49.1 summarizes the judicial treatment of potentially illegal practices under § 1 of the Sherman Act (as of 2020, when this book went to press).

Figure 49.1   Potentially Illegal Practices and Their Treatment under Sherman Act § 1

Potentially Illegal Practice	Judicial Treatment	
	Per Se	Rule of Reason or Quick-Look
Horizontal price-fixing	*	
Vertical price-fixing (nonmaximum)		*
Vertical maximum price-fixing		*
Horizontal division of markets	*?	*?
Vertical nonprice restraints on distribution		*
Horizontal boycotts	*	*
Vertical boycotts	*	*
Tying agreements	*?	*
Reciprocal dealing agreements	*?	*
Exclusive dealing agreements		*
Joint ventures	*	*

Note: An entry with an asterisk in both columns means the facts of the individual case determine the treatment. A question mark indicates that future treatment is in question.

Section 2—Monopolization

LO49-11 Identify the elements of monopolization for purposes of Sherman Act § 2.

Firms that acquire monopoly power in a given market have defeated the antitrust laws' objective of promoting competitive market structures. Monopolists, by definition, have the power to fix prices unilaterally because they have no effective competition. Section 2 of the Sherman Act was designed to prevent the improper acquisition and abuse of monopoly power. It provides: "Every person who shall monopolize, or attempt to monopolize, or combine or conspire with any other person to monopolize any part of trade or commerce among the several states, or with foreign nations shall be deemed guilty of a felony." Section 2 does not outlaw monopolies. Instead, it outlaws the act of *monopolization*. Under § 2, a *single firm* can be guilty of monopolizing or attempting to monopolize a part of trade or commerce. The proof of joint action required for violations of § 1 is required only when two or more firms are charged with a conspiracy to monopolize under § 2.

The Global Business Environment

U.S.-based firms that engage in international business activities must remember that they may be subject to the antitrust laws of other nations. In the European Union, for instance, the European Commission serves as chief antitrust regulator through the commission's Competition Directorate General. Articles in the Treaty of Rome contemplate bases of antitrust regulation similar, though not identical to, the legal bases in the United States under §§ 1 and 2 of the Sherman Act.

In 2004, the European Commission (EC) ruled against Microsoft in a case that dealt with some of the same types of business practices complained about in the high-profile case brought against the firm by the U.S. government and various states. (The U.S. case receives extensive treatment at various points in this chapter.) The European Union case also challenged other allegedly anticompetitive Microsoft practices that were not at issue in the U.S. case. The EC ruled that Microsoft held a dominant position in the European software market and had abused that position in various ways. The EC also fined Microsoft an amount of euros equaling roughly $689 million. In addition, the EC ordered Microsoft to allow room for competitors by offering

a version of its Windows operating system without the Media Player and by licensing confidential Windows-related information to other firms so that they could produce software compatible with Windows.

In 2006, the EC levied a further fine equating to $357 million, after concluding that Microsoft had not complied with the EC's 2004 orders. The European Court of First Instance, in a 2007 ruling, rejected Microsoft's appeal of the EC's 2004 decision. In 2008, the EC again fined Microsoft—this time in an amount of euros equaling $1.3 billion—because, in the EC's judgment, Microsoft still was in violation of the 2004 orders.

Recently, European Union regulators have shown an apparent tendency to be more aggressive than U.S. regulators in launching antitrust actions against companies with dominant market shares (Google, for instance). The Justice Department has at times offered indications that it would like to see greater coordination of international antitrust enforcement efforts, so that U.S. firms may become better able to anticipate what is, or is not, likely to trigger regulatory scrutiny from nation to nation or region to region.

Monopolization

LO49-12 Explain what courts take into account in determining the relevant market for purposes of a monopolization case.

Monopolization is "the willful acquisition or maintenance of monopoly power in a relevant market as opposed to growth as a consequence of superior product, business acumen, or historical accident."[7] This means that to be liable for monopolization, a defendant must have possessed not only monopoly power but also an intent to monopolize.

Monopoly Power *Monopoly power* is usually defined for antitrust purposes as the power to *fix prices* or *exclude competitors* in a given market. Such power is generally inferred from the fact that a firm has captured a predominant share of the relevant market. Although the exact percentage share necessary to support an inference of monopoly power remains unclear and courts often look at other economic factors (such as the existence in the industry of barriers to the entry of new competitors), market shares in excess of 70 percent have historically justified an inference of monopoly power.

Before a court can determine a defendant's market share, it must first define the relevant market. This is a crucial issue

in § 2 cases because a broad definition of the relevant market normally results in a smaller market share for the defendant and a resulting reduction in the likelihood that the defendant will be found to possess monopoly power. The two components of a relevant market determination are the relevant geographic market and the relevant product market.

Economic realities prevailing in the industry determine the relevant geographic market. In which parts of the country can the defendant effectively compete with other firms in the sale of the product in question? To whom may buyers turn for alternative sources of supply? Factors such as transportation costs may also play a critical role in relevant market determinations. Thus, the relevant market for coal may be regional in nature, but the relevant market for computer chips may be national in scope.

The relevant product market is composed of those products meeting the *functional interchangeability* test, which identifies the products "reasonably interchangeable by consumers for the same purposes." This test recognizes that a firm's ability to fix the price for its products is limited by the availability of competing products that buyers view as acceptable substitutes. In a famous antitrust case, for example, Du Pont was charged with monopolizing the national market for cellophane because it had a 75 percent share. The Supreme Court concluded, however, that the relevant market was all "flexible wrapping materials," including aluminum foil, waxed paper, and polyethylene.

---

[7]*United States v. Grinnell Corp.*, 384 U.S. 563 (1966).

Du Pont's 20 percent share of that product market was far too small to amount to monopoly power.[8]

In the highly publicized *Microsoft* decision, a portion of which follows below, a federal court of appeals held that Microsoft Corporation possessed monopoly power in the worldwide market for Intel-compatible personal computer operating systems. The court concluded that Microsoft held a 95 percent share of the market.

Intent to Monopolize

 LO49-13 Describe what courts consider when they determine whether a defendant accused of monopolization possessed the requisite intent to monopolize.

Proof of monopoly power standing alone, however, is never sufficient to prove a violation of § 2. The defendant's intent to monopolize must also be shown. Early cases required evidence that the defendant either acquired monopoly power by predatory or coercive means that violated antitrust rules (e.g., price-fixing or discriminatory pricing) or abused monopoly power in some way after acquiring it (such as by engaging in price-gouging). Contemporary courts focus on how the defendant acquired monopoly power. If the defendant *intentionally acquired it* or *attempted to maintain it* after acquiring it, the defendant possessed an intent to monopolize. Defendants are not in violation of § 2, however, if their monopoly power resulted from the superiority of their products or business decisions, or from historical accident (e.g., the owner of a professional sports franchise in an area too small to support a competing franchise).

Purposeful acquisition or maintenance of monopoly power may be demonstrated in various ways. A famous monopolization case involved Alcoa, which had a 90 percent market share of the American market for virgin aluminum ingot. Alcoa was found liable for purposefully maintaining its monopoly power by acquiring every new opportunity relating to the production or marketing of aluminum, thereby excluding potential competitors.[9] As various cases indicate, firms that develop monopoly power by acquiring ownership or control of their competitors are likely to be held to have demonstrated an intent to monopolize.

In the following portion of the *Microsoft* decision, the court concluded that Microsoft Corporation was liable for monopolization because it possessed monopoly power in the relevant market and engaged in anticompetitive behavior in order to maintain its monopoly position.

---

[8] *United States v. E. I. du Pont de Nemours & Co.*, 351 U.S. 377 (1956).

[9] *United States v. Aluminum Co. of America, Inc.*, 148 F.2d 416 (2d Cir. 1945).

United States v. Microsoft Corp.   253 F.3d 34 (D.C. Cir. 2001)

The United States, 19 individual states, and the District of Columbia brought civil antitrust actions against Microsoft Corporation. The cases were consolidated for trial. The plaintiffs charged, in essence, that Microsoft waged an unlawful campaign in defense of its monopoly position in the market for operating systems designed to run on Intel-compatible personal computers (PCs). More specifically, the plaintiffs claimed that Microsoft violated (1) § 2 of the Sherman Act by engaging in monopolization through a series of exclusionary and anticompetitive acts designed to maintain its monopoly power, (2) § 2 by engaging in attempted monopolization of the web browser market, and (3) § 1 of the Sherman Act by unlawfully tying its browser to its operating system and by entering into exclusive dealing agreements that unreasonably restrained trade. The plaintiffs other than the United States alleged that Microsoft's behavior also violated their respective antitrust laws.

The U.S. District Court for the District of Columbia held that Microsoft violated § 1 through unlawful tying arrangements but that Microsoft's exclusive dealing agreements did not run afoul of § 1. The court also held that Microsoft engaged in monopolization with regard to the market for Intel-compatible PC operating systems, as well as attempted monopolization of the web browser market, in violation of § 2 and comparable state laws. In a separate decision, the district court held that the appropriate remedy was a divestiture order splitting Microsoft into two separate companies, one for the operating systems business and the other for the applications business.

Microsoft appealed to the U.S. Court of Appeals for the District of Columbia Circuit. In portions of the opinion not included here, the D.C. Circuit affirmed the district court's holding that Microsoft's exclusive dealing agreements did not violate § 1; reversed the district court's holding that Microsoft violated § 1 through tying arrangements, and remanded the case for reconsideration of that claim under different legal standards; and reversed the district court's holding that Microsoft violated § 2 by attempting to monopolize the web browser market. The portions of the opinion set forth below deal with the D.C. Circuit's analysis of the claim that Microsoft violated § 2 by engaging in monopolization of the market for Intel-compatible PC operating systems. A nearby Cyberlaw in Action box examines the appellate court's treatment of the remedy issues and discusses later developments in the case.

Per Curiam

Section 2 of the Sherman Act makes it unlawful for a firm to "monopolize." The offense of monopolization has two elements: "(1) the possession of monopoly power in the relevant market, and (2) the willful acquisition or maintenance of that power as distinguished from growth or development as a consequence of a superior product, business acumen, or historic accident." *United States v. Grinnell Corp.*, 384 U.S. 563 (1966).

A. Monopoly Power While merely possessing monopoly power is not itself an antitrust violation, it is a necessary element of a monopolization charge. The Supreme Court defines monopoly power as the power to control prices or exclude competition. [C]ourts . . . typically examine market structure in search of circumstantial evidence of monopoly power. [M]onopoly power may be inferred from a firm's possession of a dominant share of a relevant market that is protected by entry barriers. "Entry barriers" are factors . . . that prevent new rivals from timely responding to an increase in price above the competitive level.

Because the ability of consumers to turn to other suppliers restrains a firm from raising prices above the competitive level, the relevant market must include all products "reasonably interchangeable by consumers for the same purposes." *United States v. E. I. du Pont de Nemours Co.*, 351 U.S. 377 (1956). [T]he district court defined the market as "the licensing of all Intel-compatible PC operating systems worldwide," finding that there are "currently no products—and . . . there are not likely to be any in the near future—that a significant percentage of computer users worldwide could substitute for [these operating systems] without incurring substantial costs." Calling this market definition far too narrow, Microsoft argues that the court improperly excluded . . . non-Intel compatible operating systems (primarily Apple's Macintosh operating system, Mac OS) . . . and "middleware" products.

The district court found that consumers would not switch from Windows to Mac OS in response to a substantial price increase because of the costs of acquiring the new hardware needed to run Mac OS and compatible software applications, . . . because of the effort involved in learning the new system and transferring files to its format, [and because] the Apple system . . . supports fewer applications. Microsoft . . . points to [no] evidence contradicting the district court's findings. [W]e have no basis for upsetting the court's decision to exclude Mac OS from the relevant market.

This brings us to Microsoft's main challenge to the district court's market definition: the exclusion of middleware. Because of the importance of middleware to this case, we [shall] explain what it is [and how it relates to operating systems]. Operating systems perform many functions, including allocating computer memory and . . . function[ing] as platforms for software applications. They do this by "exposing"—i.e., making available to software developers—routines or protocols that perform certain widely used functions. These are known as Application Programming Interfaces (APIs). For example, Windows contains an API that enables users to draw a box on the screen. Software developers wishing to include that function in an application need not duplicate it in their own code. Instead, they can "call"—i.e., use—the Windows API. Windows contains thousands of APIs.

"Middleware" refers to software products that expose their own APIs. Because of this, a middleware product written for Windows could take over some or all of Windows's valuable platform functions—that is, developers might begin to rely upon APIs exposed by the middleware for basic routines rather than relying upon the API set included in Windows. Ultimately, if developers could write applications relying exclusively on APIs exposed by middleware, their applications would run on any operating system on which the middleware was also present.

Microsoft argues that because middleware could usurp the operating system's platform function and might eventually take over other operating system functions . . . , the district court erred in excluding Navigator and Java from the relevant market. The court found, however, that neither Navigator, Java, nor any other middleware product could now, or would soon, expose enough APIs to serve as a platform for popular applications, much less take over all operating system functions. Whatever middleware's ultimate potential, the district court found that consumers could not now abandon their operating systems and switch to middleware in response to a sustained price for Windows above the competitive level. [B]ecause middleware is not now interchangeable with Windows, the district court had good reason for excluding middleware from the relevant market.

Having thus properly defined the relevant market, the district court found that Windows accounts for a greater than 95 percent share. The court also found that even if Mac OS were included, Microsoft's share would exceed 80 percent. [In addition], the court [properly] focused not only on Microsoft's present market share, but also on the structural barrier that protects the company's future position. That barrier—the applications barrier to entry—stems from two characteristics of the software market: (1) most consumers prefer operating systems for which a large number of applications have already been written; and (2) most developers prefer to write for operating systems that already have a substantial consumer base. This "chicken-and-egg" situation ensures that applications will continue to be written for the already dominant Windows, which in turn ensures that consumers will continue to prefer it over other operating systems.

B. Anticompetitive Conduct [After correctly] concluding that Microsoft had monopoly power, the district court held that Microsoft had violated § 2 by engaging in a variety of exclusionary acts . . . to maintain its monopoly. Whether any particular act of a monopolist is exclusionary, rather than merely a form of vigorous competition, can be difficult to discern. [T]o be condemned as exclusionary, a monopolist's act must have an anticompetitive effect. That is, it must harm the competitive *process* and thereby harm consumers. In contrast, harm to one or more *competitors* will not suffice. [Assuming that the plaintiff] establishes a *prima facie* case under § 2 by demonstrating anticompetitive effect, the monopolist may proffer a procompetitive justification. If the monopolist asserts a procompetitive justification—a nonpretextual claim that its conduct is indeed a form of competition on the merits because it involves, for example, greater efficiency or enhanced consumer appeal—then the burden shifts back to the plaintiff to rebut that claim. [I]f the monopolist's procompetitive justification stands unrebutted, then the plaintiff must demonstrate that the anticompetitive harm of the conduct outweighs the procompetitive benefit. In cases arising under § 1 of the Sherman Act, the courts routinely apply a similar balancing approach under the rubric of the "rule of reason." With these principles in mind, we now [review] the district court's holding that Microsoft violated § 2 of the Sherman Act in a variety of ways.

1. Restrictions in Licenses Issued to Original Equipment Manufacturers (OEMs)

The district court condemned a number of provisions in Microsoft's agreements licensing Windows to OEMs, because it found that Microsoft's imposition of those provisions . . . serves to reduce usage share of Netscape's browser and, hence, protect Microsoft's operating system monopoly. Browser usage share is important because [a browser] must have a critical mass of users in order to attract software developers to write applications relying upon the APIs it exposes, and away from the APIs exposed by Windows. Applications written to a particular browser's APIs . . . would run on any computer with that browser, regardless of the underlying operating system. [The district court found that the] "overwhelming majority of consumers will only use a PC operating system for which there already exists a large and varied set of . . . applications, and for which it seems relatively certain that new types of applications and new versions of existing applications will continue to be marketed." If a consumer could have access to the applications he desired—regardless of the operating system he uses—simply by installing a particular browser on his computer, then he would no longer feel compelled to select Windows in order to have access to those applications; he could select an operating system other than Windows based solely upon its quality and price. In other words, the market for operating systems would be competitive.

The restrictions Microsoft places upon OEMs are of particular importance . . . because having an OEM pre-install a browser on a computer is one of the two most cost-effective methods by

far of distributing browsing software. (The other is bundling the browser with Internet access software distributed by an Internet access provider (IAP).)

The district court concluded that [one Microsoft-imposed] license restriction—the prohibition upon the removal of desktop icons, folders, and Start menu entries—thwarts the distribution of a rival browser by preventing OEMs from removing visible means of user access to IE. The OEMs cannot practically install a second browser in addition to IE, the court found, in part because . . . a certain number of novice computer users, seeing two browser icons, will wonder which to use when and will call the OEM's support line. Support calls are extremely expensive and, in the highly competitive original equipment market, firms have a strong incentive to minimize costs. By preventing OEMs from removing visible means of user access to IE, the license restriction prevents many OEMs from pre-installing a rival browser, and therefore, protects Microsoft's monopoly from the competition that middleware might otherwise present. Therefore, we conclude that the license restriction at issue is anticompetitive.

[A] second license provision [imposed by Microsoft] prohibits OEMs from modifying the initial boot sequence—the process that occurs the first time a consumer turns on the computer. [The district court found that prior to] the imposition of that restriction, "among the programs that many OEMs inserted into the boot sequence were Internet sign-up procedures that encouraged users to choose from a list of IAPs assembled by the OEM." Microsoft's prohibition on any alteration of the boot sequence thus prevents OEMs from using that process to promote the services of IAPs, many of which—at least at the time Microsoft imposed the restriction—used Navigator rather than IE in their Internet access software. Because this prohibition has a substantial effect in protecting Microsoft's market power, and does so through a means other than competition on the merits, it is anticompetitive.

Finally, Microsoft . . . prohibits OEMs from causing any user interface other than the Windows desktop to launch automatically, from adding icons or folders different in size or shape from those supplied by Microsoft, and from using the "Active Desktop" feature to promote third-party brands. These restrictions impose significant costs upon the OEMs; prior to Microsoft's prohibiting the practice, many OEMs would change the appearance of the desktop in ways they found beneficial. The anticompetitive effect of the license restrictions is . . . that OEMs are not able to promote rival browsers, which keeps developers focused upon the APIs in Windows. This kind of promotion is not a zero-sum game; but for the restrictions in their licenses to use Windows, OEMs could promote multiple IAPs and browsers. [T]his type of license restriction . . . is anticompetitive: Microsoft reduced rival browsers' usage share not by improving its own product but, rather, by preventing OEMs from taking actions that could increase rivals' share of usage.

Microsoft argues that the license restrictions are legally justified because . . . Microsoft is simply "exercising its rights as the holder of valid copyrights." The company claims an absolute and unfettered right to use its intellectual property as it wishes: "If intellectual property rights have been lawfully acquired," it says, then, "their subsequent exercise cannot give rise to antitrust liability." That is no more correct than the proposition that use of one's personal property, such as a baseball bat, cannot give rise to tort liability. As the Federal Circuit succinctly stated: "Intellectual property rights do not confer a privilege to violate the antitrust laws." *In re Independent Service Organizations Antitrust Litigation,* 203 F.3d 1322 (Fed Cir. 2000). [Microsoft's copyright argument fails because the restrictions on OEMs are neither necessary to prevent substantial alteration of its copyrighted work nor necessary to preserve the stability of the Windows platform. Moreover,] Microsoft has not shown that the [actions OEMs otherwise would take would] reduce the value of Windows except in the sense that their promotion of rival browsers [would] undermine Microsoft's monopoly—and that is not a permissible justification for the license restrictions.

[W]e hold that . . . the OEM license restrictions represent uses of Microsoft's market power to protect its monopoly, unredeemed by any legitimate justification. The restrictions therefore violate § 2 of the Sherman Act.

2. Integration of Internet Explorer (IE) and Windows

[T]he district court found that "Microsoft's executives believed . . . its contractual restrictions placed on OEMs would not be sufficient in themselves to reverse the direction of Navigator's usage share. Consequently, . . . , Microsoft set out to bind [IE] more tightly to Windows 95." Technologically binding IE to Windows, the district court found, both prevented OEMs from pre-installing other browsers and deterred consumers from using them. [H] aving the IE software code as an irremovable part of Windows meant that pre-installing a second browser would increase an OEM's product testing costs, because an OEM must test and train its support staff to answer calls related to every software product pre-installed on the machine; moreover, pre-installing a browser in addition to IE would to many OEMs be "a questionable use of the scarce and valuable space on a PC's hard drive."

As a general rule, courts are properly very skeptical about claims that competition has been harmed by a dominant firm's product design changes. In a competitive market, firms routinely innovate in the hope of appealing to consumers, sometimes in the process making their products incompatible with those of rivals; the imposition of liability when a monopolist does the same thing will inevitably deter a certain amount of innovation. This is all the more true in a market, such as this one, in which the product itself is rapidly changing. Judicial deference to product innovation, however, does not mean that a monopolist's product design decisions are per se lawful.

The district court first condemned as anticompetitive Microsoft's decision to exclude IE from the "Add/Remove Programs" utility in Windows 98. Microsoft had included IE in the Add/Remove Programs utility in Windows 95, but when it modified Windows 95 to produce Windows 98, it took IE out of the Add/Remove Programs utility. This change reduces the usage share of rival browsers not by making Microsoft's own browser more attractive to consumers but by discouraging OEMs from distributing rival products. Because Microsoft's conduct, through something other than competition on the merits, has the effect of significantly reducing usage of rivals' products and hence protecting its own operating system monopoly, it is anticompetitive.

[T]he district court [also] condemned Microsoft's decision to bind IE to Windows 98 "by placing code specific to Web browsing in the same files as code that provided operating system functions." Putting code supplying browsing functionality into a file with code supplying operating system functionality "ensures that the deletion of any file containing browsing-specific routines would also delete vital operating system routines and thus cripple Windows." [P]reventing an OEM from removing IE deters it from installing a second browser because doing so increases the OEM's product testing and support costs; by contrast, had OEMs been able to remove IE, they might have chosen to pre-install Navigator alone.

Microsoft denies . . . that it commingled browsing and non-browsing code, and it maintains the district court's findings to the contrary are clearly erroneous. In view of the contradictory testimony in the record, some of which supports the district court's finding that Microsoft commingled browsing and nonbrowsing code, we cannot conclude that the finding was clearly erroneous. Microsoft proffers no [procompetitive] justification for . . . excluding IE from the Add/Remove Programs utility [or for] commingling browser and operating systems code. Accordingly, we hold that [those actions] constitute exclusionary conduct, in violation of § 2.

3. Agreements with Internet Access Providers (IAPs)

Microsoft concluded exclusive agreements with all the leading IAPs, including [America Online and other] major online services. [The] plaintiffs allege that, by closing to rivals a substantial percentage of the available opportunities for browser distribution, Microsoft managed to preserve its monopoly in the market for operating systems. The IAPs constitute one of the two major channels by which browsers can be distributed. [The district court found that] Microsoft has exclusive deals with "14 of the top 15 access providers in North America[, which] account for a large majority of all Internet access subscriptions in this part of the world." By ensuring that the majority of all IAP subscribers are offered IE either as the default browser or as the only browser, Microsoft's deals with the IAPs clearly have a significant effect in preserving its monopoly.

[With the plaintiffs] having demonstrated a harm to competition, the burden falls upon Microsoft to [justify] its exclusive dealing contracts with IAPs. Microsoft's only explanation . . . is that it wants to keep developers focused upon its APIs—which is to say [that] it wants to preserve its power in the operating system market. That is not an unlawful end, but neither is it a procompetitive justification. Accordingly, we affirm the district court's holding that Microsoft's exclusive contracts with IAPs are exclusionary devices, in violation of § 2 of the Sherman Act.

4. Dealings with Independent Software Vendors (ISVs) and Apple Computer

The district court held that Microsoft engages in exclusionary conduct in its dealings with . . . ISVs, which develop software. The court described Microsoft's deals with ISVs as [including promises by Microsoft to provide] "preferential support, . . . technical information, and the right to use certain Microsoft seals of approval" if, in return, the ISVs agreed to "use Internet Explorer as the default browsing software for any software they develop with a hypertext-based user interface."

The court further found that the effect of these deals is to "increase the likelihood that the millions of consumers using [applications designed by ISVs subject to agreements with Microsoft] will use Internet Explorer rather than Navigator." Although the ISVs are a relatively small channel for browser distribution, they take on greater significance because[, as revealed above,] Microsoft had largely foreclosed the two primary channels to its rivals. In that light, one can tell from the record that by affecting the applications used by "millions" of consumers, Microsoft's exclusive deals with the ISVs had a substantial effect in further foreclosing rival browsers from the market. [T]he deals [thus] have an anticompetitive effect.

[In supposed justification of its ISV agreements,] Microsoft . . . states only that [the] agreements reflect an attempt "to persuade ISVs to utilize Internet-related system services in Windows rather than Navigator." [K]eeping developers focused upon Windows—that is, preserving the Windows monopoly—is a competitively neutral goal [rather than a] procompetitive justification for [Microsoft's] exclusive dealing arrangements with the ISVs. [We therefore] hold that those arrangements violate § 2.

[T]he district court [also] held that Microsoft's dealings with Apple Computer violated the Sherman Act. Apple . . . makes both software (including an operating system, Mac OS), and hardware (the Macintosh line of computers). Microsoft primarily makes software, including, in addition to its operating system, a number of popular applications. One, called "Office," is a suite of business productivity applications that Microsoft has ported to Mac OS. The district court found that "90 percent of Mac OS users running a suite of office productivity applications [use] Microsoft's Mac Office." Further, the court found that in 1997, "Apple's

business was in steep decline" [and that] "many ISVs questioned the wisdom of continuing to spend time and money developing applications for the Mac OS. Had Microsoft announced in the midst of this atmosphere that it was ceasing to develop new versions of Mac Office, . . . ISVs, customers, developers, and investors would have interpreted the announcement as Apple's death notice."

Microsoft recognized the importance to Apple of its continued support of Mac Office. In June 1997 Microsoft Chairman Bill Gates [stated that] "Apple let us down on the browser by making Netscape the standard install" [and] that he had already called Apple's CEO to ask "how we should announce the cancellation of Mac Office." The district court further found that, within a month of Gates' call, Apple and Microsoft had reached an agreement pursuant to which [Microsoft promised] "to continue releasing up-to-date versions of Mac Office for at least five years" [and Apple] agreed to bundle the most current version [of IE] with Mac OS and make IE the default [browser]. The agreement also prohibit[ed] Apple from encouraging users to substitute another browser for IE, and state[d] that Apple [would] "encourage its employees to use [IE]."

This exclusive deal between Microsoft and Apple has a substantial effect upon the distribution of rival browsers. Pre-installation of a browser (which can be accomplished either by including the browser with the operating system or by the OEM installing the browser) is one of the two most important methods of browser distribution, and Apple had a not insignificant share of worldwide sales of operating systems. Because Microsoft's exclusive contract with Apple has a substantial effect in restricting distribution of rival browsers, and because [that effect] serves to protect Microsoft's monopoly, its deal with Apple must be regarded as anticompetitive. Microsoft offers no procompetitive justification for the exclusive dealing arrangement. It makes only the irrelevant claim that the IE-for-Mac Office deal is part of a multifaceted set of agreements between itself and Apple. Accordingly, we hold that the exclusive deal with Apple is exclusionary, in violation of § 2.

5. Java

Java, a set of technologies developed by Sun Microsystems, is another type of middleware posing a potential threat to Windows' position as the ubiquitous platform for software development. The Java technologies include: (1) a programming language; (2) a set of programs written in that language, called the "Java class libraries," which expose APIs; (3) a compiler, which translates code written by a developer into "bytecode"; and (4) a Java Virtual Machine ("JVM"), which translates bytecode into instructions to the operating system. Programs calling upon the Java APIs will run on any machine with a "Java runtime environment," that is, Java class libraries and a JVM.

In May 1995 Netscape agreed with Sun to distribute a copy of the Java runtime environment with every copy of Navigator. [The district court found that] "Navigator quickly became the principal vehicle by which Sun placed copies of its Java runtime environment on the PC systems of Windows users." Microsoft, too, agreed to promote the Java technologies—or so it seemed. For at the same time, [the district court concluded,] Microsoft took steps "to maximize the difficulty with which applications written in Java could be ported from Windows to other platforms, and vice versa." The court found that Microsoft took four steps to exclude Java from developing as a viable cross-platform threat: (a) designing a JVM incompatible with the one developed by Sun; (b) entering into contracts . . . requiring major ISVs to promote Microsoft's JVM exclusively; (c) deceiving Java developers about the Windows-specific nature of the tools it distributed to them; and (d) coercing Intel to stop aiding Sun in improving the Java technologies.

The district court [erred in holding] that Microsoft engaged in exclusionary conduct by developing and promoting its own JVM, [which was incompatible with Sun's.] A monopolist does not violate the antitrust laws simply by developing a product that is incompatible with those of its rivals. In order to violate the antitrust laws, the incompatible product must have an anticompetitive effect that outweighs any procompetitive justification for the design. Microsoft's JVM is not only incompatible with Sun's, it allows Java applications to run faster on Windows than does Sun's JVM. [Microsoft's JVM thus] does not itself have . . . anticompetitive effect.

To the extent Microsoft's [agreements] with the ISVs conditioned receipt of Windows technical information upon the ISVs' agreement to promote Microsoft's JVM exclusively, they raise a different competitive concern. The district court found that . . . the deals were exclusive in practice because they required developers to make Microsoft's JVM the default in the software they developed. [T]he record indicates that Microsoft's deals with the major ISVs had a significant effect upon JVM promotion. [T]he products of [these] ISVs reached millions of consumers. Because Microsoft's agreements foreclosed a substantial portion of the field for JVM distribution and because, in so doing, they protected Microsoft's monopoly from a middleware threat, they are anticompetitive. Because . . . Microsoft has no procompetitive justification for them, we hold that the provisions in the [ISV agreements] requiring use of Microsoft's JVM as the default are exclusionary, in violation of the Sherman Act.

Microsoft's "Java implementation" included, in addition to a JVM, a set of software development tools it created to assist ISVs in designing Java applications. The district court found that, not only were these tools incompatible with Sun's cross-platform aspirations for Java—no violation, to be sure—but Microsoft deceived Java developers regarding the Windows-specific nature of the tools. Microsoft's tools included "certain 'keywords' and 'compiler directives' that could only be executed properly by Microsoft's version of the Java runtime environment for Windows." As a result, even Java "developers who were opting for portability over performance . . . unwittingly [wrote] Java applications that [ran] only on Windows." That is, developers who relied upon Microsoft's public commitment to cooperate with Sun and who used Microsoft's tools to develop what Microsoft led them to believe were cross-platform applications ended up producing applications that would run only on the Windows operating system.

Microsoft documents confirm that Microsoft intended to deceive Java developers, and predicted that the effect of its actions would be to generate Windows-dependent Java applications that their developers believed would be cross-platform; these documents also indicate that Microsoft's ultimate objective was to thwart Java's threat to Microsoft's monopoly in the market for operating systems. One Microsoft document, for example, states as a strategic goal: "Kill cross-platform Java by growing the polluted Java market." Microsoft's conduct related to its Java developer tools served to protect its monopoly of the operating system in a manner not attributable either to the superiority of the operating system or to the acumen of its makers, and therefore was anticompetitive. Unsurprisingly, Microsoft offers no procompetitive explanation for its campaign to deceive developers. [T]his conduct is exclusionary, in violation of § 2.

The district court [properly] held that Microsoft also acted unlawfully with respect to Java by using its "monopoly power to prevent firms such as Intel from aiding in the creation of cross-platform interfaces." [The record indicates that in 1995,] Intel was in the process of developing a high-performance, Windows-compatible JVM, [that] Microsoft wanted Intel to abandon [this] effort because a fast, cross-platform JVM would threaten Microsoft's monopoly in the operating system market, [and that Microsoft threatened to cease distributing] Intel technologies bundled with Windows [if Intel] did not stop aiding Sun on the multimedia front. Intel finally capitulated in 1997, after Microsoft [kept up the pressure]. Microsoft lamely characterizes its threat to Intel as "advice." The court, however, [properly concluded] that Microsoft's "advice" to Intel to stop aiding cross-platform Java was backed by the threat of retaliation. Therefore, we affirm the conclusion that Microsoft's threats to Intel were exclusionary, in violation of § 2.

District court's decision that Microsoft committed monopolization affirmed; other portions of decision affirmed in part, reversed in part, and remanded in part; remedial order of divestiture vacated and case remanded for further proceedings regarding appropriate remedies.

CYBERLAW IN ACTION

As noted in the portion of the previous *Microsoft* decision, the federal district court (Thomas Penfield Jackson, District Judge) held that divestiture—in this instance, dividing Microsoft into two companies—was the appropriate remedy for Microsoft's Sherman Act violations. The D.C. Circuit Court of Appeals, however, reversed this determination and remanded the case for reconsideration of remedy-related issues.

The D.C. Circuit concluded that the district court erred in not holding a separate evidentiary hearing regarding remedies, and that because some of the bases of liability imposed by the district court had been reversed on appeal, the remedy of divestiture might no longer be the appropriate form of relief. Although the appellate court did not explicitly state that divestiture could not be ordered by the district court after it conducted further proceedings, the D.C. Circuit's opinion seemed to hint that divestiture was a more extreme remedy than was necessary. In remanding the case, the appellate court further ordered that the case be assigned to a district judge other than Judge Jackson, whose extensive participation in media interviews created the perception that he might not be impartial.

After the case was remanded, the United States, roughly half of the states that were plaintiffs, and Microsoft entered into a settlement agreement designed to resolve the case. District Judge Colleen Kollar-Kotelly held hearings on remedial and agreement-related issues, took under advisement the question whether to approve the agreement, and eventually issued her approval. Under the settlement agreement, Microsoft became obligated to allow computer manufacturers to add icons for Microsoft competitors' software to the desktop display for the Windows operating system. Microsoft must also employ uniform licensing agreements when dealing with software manufacturers, and must furnish technical information to Internet access providers and to software and hardware vendors so that their products will work with Windows.

Critics of the settlement agreement said it was not tough enough on Microsoft; that it would do little to benefit consumers or to curtail anticompetitive actions; and that it was, effectively, a victory for Microsoft. The U.S. Justice Department took a different view, calling the agreement a suitable and successful resolution of a case in which the plaintiffs had prevailed on their main claim of liability.

Attempted Monopolization

 LO49-14 Explain what is necessary for the attempted monopolization prohibited by Sherman Act § 2.

Firms that have not yet attained monopoly power may nonetheless be liable for an attempt to monopolize in violation of § 2 if they are dangerously close to acquiring monopoly power and are employing methods likely to result in monopoly power if left unchecked. As part of the required proof of a dangerous probability that monopoly power will be acquired, plaintiffs in attempted monopolization cases must furnish proof of the relevant market—as in monopolization cases. Attempt cases also require proof that the defendant possessed a specific intent to acquire monopoly power through anticompetitive means.

The *Microsoft* decision underscored the importance of the proof-of-relevant-market requirement in attempted monopolization cases. Although it affirmed the district court's holding that Microsoft had engaged in monopolization of the market for Intel-compatible PC operating systems, the U.S. Court of Appeals for the District of Columbia Circuit reversed the lower court's decision that Microsoft had attempted to monopolize the web browser market. The D.C. Circuit stressed that

the plaintiffs had failed to offer proof of—and that the district court had therefore made no appropriate finding regarding—the components and scope of any supposed browser market. Therefore, the lower court erred in basing its decision on conduct by Microsoft that, in the district court's view, seemed calculated to extend Microsoft's operating systems monopoly into another market. Whether Microsoft's conduct created a dangerous probability of monopoly power acquisition in that other market could not be determined without a definition of the latter market's boundaries—and no such definition had occurred.

A controversial issue that surfaces in many attempted monopolization cases concerns the role that *predatory pricing* may play in proving an intent to monopolize. The Supreme Court has defined predatory pricing as "pricing below an appropriate measure of cost for the purpose of eliminating competitors in the short run and reducing competition in the long run."[10] What constitutes "an appropriate measure of cost" in predatory pricing cases has long been a subject of debate among antitrust scholars. Although the Supreme Court has declined to resolve this debate definitively, it seems likely to take a

[10]*Cargill, Inc. & Excel Corp. v. Monfort of Colorado, Inc.*, 479 U.S. 104 (1986).

Ethics and Compliance in Action

Some of the cases in this chapter recite the statement that antitrust was designed to protect competition, not competitors. How is this statement consistent with the ethical justification of markets as the most efficient form of economic organization? Consider the case of a competitor who is driven out of business by another competitor's ultimately unsuccessful predatory pricing efforts

(unsuccessful because the predator could not maintain monopoly power long enough to recoup the profits lost through predatory pricing).

• Although competition may not suffer in such a case, does the out-of-business competitor have any *ethical* or public policy–based claim to compensation?

• Should antitrust law recognize such a claim?

---

skeptical view of predatory pricing claims in the future. The Court has described predatory pricing schemes as "rarely tried, and even more rarely successful."[11] As part of this characterization of predatory pricing schemes, the Court indicated that it agrees with economists who have argued that predatory pricing is often economically irrational because, to be successful, the predator must maintain monopoly power long enough after it has driven its competitors out of business to recoup the profits it lost through predatory pricing. The predator would be able to sustain monopoly power only if high barriers to entry prevented new competitors from being drawn into the market by the supracompetitive prices the predator would have to charge in order to recoup its losses.

---

[11]*Matsushita Electric Industrial Co., Ltd. v. Zenith Radio Corp.*, 475 U.S. 574 (1986).

Conspiracy to Monopolize When two or more business entities conspire to monopolize a relevant market, § 2 may be violated. This portion of § 2 largely overlaps § 1 because it is difficult to conceive of a conspiracy to monopolize that would not also amount to a conspiracy in restraint of trade. The lower federal courts have differed on the elements necessary to prove a conspiracy to monopolize. In addition to requiring proof of the existence of a conspiracy, some courts insist on proof of the relevant market, a specific intent to acquire monopoly power, and overt action in furtherance of the conspiracy. Other courts do not require extensive proof of the relevant market. According to these courts, a violation is established through proof that the defendants conspired to exclude competitors from, or acquire control over prices in, some significant area of commerce. An approach that deemphasizes the requirement of proof of the relevant market, however, may not be consistent with Supreme Court precedent.

Problems and Problem Cases

1. Atlantic Richfield (ARCO) is an integrated oil company that sells gasoline to consumers both directly through its own stations and indirectly through ARCO-brand dealers. USA is an independent retail marketer of gasoline that buys gasoline from major petroleum companies for resale under its own brand name. USA competes directly with ARCO dealers at the retail level. Its outlets typically are low-overhead, high-volume "discount" stations that charge less than stations selling equivalent quality gasoline under major brand names. ARCO adopted a new marketing strategy in order to compete more effectively with independents such as USA. ARCO encouraged its dealers to match the retail gasoline prices offered by independents in various ways. These included making available to its

dealers and distributors short-term discounts and reducing its dealers' costs by, for example, eliminating credit card sales. ARCO's strategy increased its sales and market share. When USA's sales dropped, it sued ARCO, charging that ARCO and its dealers were engaged in a per se illegal vertical price-fixing scheme. On these facts, could USA show an *antitrust injury* resulting from ARCO's actions (i.e., injury that flows from the unlawful aspects of the challenged behavior and is of a type that the antitrust laws were designed to prevent)? Does per se treatment apply to vertical price-fixing when the allegedly fixed price is of a *maximum* nature?

2. Co-Operative Theatres (Co-op), a Cleveland area movie theater booking agent, began seeking customers in southern Ohio. Shortly thereafter, Tri-State Theatre Services (Tri-State), a Cincinnati booking agent,

began to solicit business in the Cleveland area. Later, however, Co-op and Tri-State allegedly entered into an agreement not to solicit each other's customers. The Justice Department prosecuted them for agreeing to restrain trade in violation of § 1 of the Sherman Act. Under a government grant of immunity, Tri-State's vice president testified that Co-op's vice president had approached him at a trade convention and threatened to start taking Tri-State's accounts if Tri-State did not stop calling on Co-op's accounts. He also testified that at a luncheon meeting he attended with officials from both firms, the presidents of both firms said that it would be in the interests of both firms to stop calling on each other's accounts. Several Co-op customers testified that Tri-State had refused to accept their business because of the agreement with Co-op. The trial court found both firms guilty of a per se violation of the Sherman Act, rejecting their argument that the rule of reason should have been applied and refusing to allow them to introduce evidence that the agreement did not have a significant anticompetitive effect. Should the rule of reason have been applied?

3. Discon Inc. specialized in providing the service of removing obsolete telephone equipment. New York Telephone Company was a subsidiary of NYNEX Corporation. Another NYNEX subsidiary, Materiel Enterprises Company, was a purchasing entity that arranged for Discon to provide removal services for New York Telephone. After regularly doing business with Discon, Materiel switched its purchases of removal services from Discon to a Discon competitor, AT&T Technologies. According to Discon, Materiel did this as part of an attempt to defraud local telephone customers and regulatory authorities. Discon contended that Materiel would pay AT&T Technologies more than Discon would have charged for similar removal services; that Materiel would then pass those higher prices on to New York Telephone; and that New York Telephone would, in turn, pass those prices on to consumers in the form of higher telephone service charges that were approved by the relevant regulatory authorities. Discon further contended that at the end of the year, Materiel would receive a special rebate from AT&T Technologies and that Materiel would share this rebate with its corporate parent, NYNEX. Discon asserted that because it refused to participate in this fraudulent scheme, Materiel would not do business with Discon, which eventually went out of business. Discon sued Materiel, New York Telephone, and NYNEX, claiming that the above facts constituted a group boycott and thus a per se violation of § 1 of the Sherman Act. If Discon's allegations are true, did a per se group boycott take place?

4. Denny's Marina Inc. filed an antitrust action, described more fully below, against various defendants: the Renfro Defendants (Renfro Productions Inc.; Indianapolis Boat, Sport, and Travel Show Inc.; and individuals connected with those firms), CIMDA (the Central Indiana Marine Dealers Association), and the Dealer Defendants (various boat dealers that competed with Denny's in the sale of fishing boats, motors, trailers, and marine accessories in the central Indiana market). The Renfro Defendants operated two boat shows each year, one in the spring and one in the fall, at the Indiana State Fairgrounds. At the time of the litigation, the spring show had occurred annually for more than 30 years and was one of the top three boat shows in the United States. It attracted between 160,000 and 190,000 consumers each year. The fall show was a smaller operation that had occurred each year since 1987. Numerous boat dealers participated in the two shows. Denny's participated in the fall show in 1988, 1989, and 1990. It participated in the spring show in 1989 and 1990. According to allegations in the antitrust complaint Denny's filed, Denny's was quite successful at each of these shows, apparently because it urged customers to shop the other dealers and then return to Denny's for a lower price.

After the 1989 spring show, some of the Dealer Defendants began to complain (according to Denny's) to the Renfro Defendants about the sales methods used by Denny's. In addition, Denny's alleged, the Dealer Defendants spent a significant part of a CIMDA meeting venting frustration about similar sales tactics used by Denny's at the 1990 spring show. Denny's also asserted that the Dealer Defendants' complaints to the Renfro Defendants escalated, and that as a result, the Renfro Defendants informed Denny's after the 1990 fall show that Denny's could no longer participate in the shows. Denny's claimed that the defendants' conduct amounted to a conspiracy, prohibited by Sherman Act § 1, to exclude Denny's from participating in the boat shows because its policy was to "meet or beat" its competitors' prices at the shows. What standard— per se or rule of reason—governed the court's analysis when it decided the case? Why that standard?

5. In 1986, Market Force Inc. (MFI) began operating in the Milwaukee real estate market as a buyer's broker. MFI and prospective home buyers entered into exclusive contracts providing that MFI would receive a fee equal to 40 percent of the sales commission if it located

a house that the buyer ultimately purchased. This 40 percent commission was the same commission selling brokers (those who ultimately produced a buyer, but whose duty of loyalty was to the seller) earned when they sold property placed on the local multiple listing service (MLS) by other brokers. MFI's contracts anticipated that the buyer would ask the listing broker (the one who had listed the property for sale on behalf of its owners and who received 60 percent of the commission when the property was sold) to pay MFI the commission at the time of the sale. If the listing broker agreed to do so, the buyer had no further obligation to MFI. For some time after MFI began operations, other real estate firms treated it inconsistently; some paid the full 40 percent commission, but others paid nothing. In the fall of 1987, Wauwatosa Realty Co. and Coldwell Banker, the top two firms listing high-quality homes in Milwaukee, issued formal policies on splitting commissions with buyer's brokers. Wauwatosa said it would pay 20 percent of the selling agent's 40 percent commission. Coldwell Banker said it would pay 20 percent of the total sales commission. Several other real estate firms followed suit, setting their rates at 10 or 20 percent of the total sales commission, with the result that firms accounting for 31 percent of the annual listings of the MLS adopted policies and disseminated them to other MLS members. MFI filed suit against the brokers who had announced policies, arguing that they had conspired to restrain trade in violation of § 1 of the Sherman Act. At trial, the defendants introduced evidence of numerous business justifications for their policies and argued that their knowingly having adopted similar policies was not enough, standing alone, to justify a conclusion that the Sherman Act was violated. Was this argument correct?

6. Eastman Kodak Co. (Kodak) manufactures and sells photocopiers and micrographic equipment. In addition, Kodak provides customers with service and replacement parts for its equipment. Kodak produces some of the parts itself. The other parts are made to order for Kodak by independent original equipment manufacturers (OEMs). Rather than selling a complete system of original equipment, lifetime parts, and lifetime service for a single price, Kodak furnishes service after an initial warranty period, either through annual service contracts or on a per-call basis. Kodak provides between 80 and 95 percent of the service for Kodak machines. In the early 1980s, independent service organizations (ISOs) began repairing and servicing Kodak equipment, as well as selling parts for it. ISOs kept an inventory of parts, purchased either from

Kodak or from other sources (primarily OEMs). In 1985, Kodak adopted policies designed to limit ISOs' access to parts and to make it more difficult for ISOs to compete with Kodak in servicing Kodak equipment. Kodak began selling replacement parts only to Kodak equipment buyers who used Kodak service or repaired their own machines (i.e., buyers who did not use ISOs for service). In addition, Kodak sought to limit ISO access to other sources of Kodak parts by working out agreements with OEMs that they would sell parts for Kodak equipment to no one other than Kodak, and by pressuring Kodak equipment owners and independent parts distributors not to sell Kodak parts to ISOs.

Eighteen ISOs sued Kodak, claiming that these policies amounted to unlawful tying of the sale of service for Kodak machines to the sale of parts, in violation of Sherman Act § 1. A federal district court granted summary judgment in favor of Kodak on each of these claims. The Ninth Circuit Court of Appeals reversed, holding that summary judgment was inappropriate because there were genuine issues of material fact regarding the ISOs' claims. The U.S. Supreme Court granted certiorari. For purposes of the § 1 tying claim presented in this case, are service and parts two distinct products? If so, do the facts make it reasonable to infer that Kodak possessed sufficient market power in the parts market to force unwanted purchases of service? How did the Supreme Court rule?

7. Grinnell Corporation manufactured plumbing supplies and fire sprinkler systems. It also owned 76 percent of the stock of ADT Co., 89 percent of the stock of AFA Inc., and 100 percent of the stock of Holmes Inc. ADT provided burglary-protection and fire-protection services. AFA provided only fire-protection services. Holmes provided only burglary-protection services. Each of the three firms offered a central station service under which hazard-detecting devices installed on the protected premises automatically transmitted an electronic signal to a central station. Other companies provided forms of protection service other than the central station variety. Subscribers to an accredited central station service (i.e., one approved by insurance underwriters) received substantially greater insurance premium reductions than the premium reductions received by users of other protection services. At the relevant time in question, ADT, AFA, and Holmes were the three largest central station service companies in terms of revenue. Together, they accounted for approximately 87 percent of the central station services provided. Contending that Grinnell, ADT, AFA, and Holmes had taken various anticompetitive actions

that amounted to willful acquisition or maintenance of monopoly power, the U.S. government brought a monopolization action against Grinnell under § 2 of the Sherman Act. Concerning the first element of a monopolization claim (monopoly power in the relevant market), were fire-protection services and burglary-protection services too different to be part of the same market? What was the relevant market in this case? Were protection services other than those of the central station variety part of it?

8. Martindale Empowerment, a Virginia corporation, engaged in the business of providing commercial electronic-mail service to advertisers. Martindale regularly sent electronic advertising over the Internet in the form of e-mail to e-mail addresses throughout the United States. In September 1998, however, America Online, the largest commercial online service in the nation with more than 16,000,000 individual subscribers, implemented various mechanisms to block advertising messages that Martindale had been sending to AOL subscribers for nearly two years. AOL succeeded in blocking most of those transmissions by Martindale. Contending that Martindale was using deceptive practices in an effort to mask the source and quantity of its transmissions and thereby avoid AOL's blocking and filtering technologies, AOL sued Martindale on a variety of legal theories. AOL sought an injunction against Martindale's practice of sending unsolicited bulk e-mail advertisements to AOL subscribers. Martindale responded with a counterclaim in which it alleged that AOL had engaged in monopolization, in violation of § 2 of the Sherman Act. According to Martindale, AOL had established itself as the only entity that could advertise to AOL subscribers. For purposes of the first element of a monopolization claim—monopoly power in a relevant market—Martindale contended that the relevant product or service market was e-mail advertising. Was Martindale correct in this contention?

9. Illinois Tool Works (ITW) manufactured and marketed printing systems that included three relevant components: a patented ink-jet printhead; a patented ink container; and specially designed, but unpatented, ink. ITW sold its systems to original equipment manufacturers (OEMs). The OEMs were licensed to incorporate the printheads and containers into printers that they sell for use in printing bar codes on cartons and packaging materials. The OEMS agreed with ITW that they would purchase ink exclusively from ITW and that neither they nor their customers would refill the patented containers with ink of any kind.

Independent Ink, which had developed an ink with the same chemical composition as the ink sold by ITW, was the target of patent infringement allegations by ITW in regard to ITW's patents on the printhead system and the ink container. Independent responded by suing ITW. Besides seeking a judgment that it was not infringing ITW's patents and a judgment that the patents were invalid, Independent's complaint alleged that ITW's agreements with the OEMs amounted to unlawful tying agreements in violation of Sherman Act § 1. Regarding the § 1 claim, the federal district court concluded that Independent had not proven the necessary *market power* element of a prohibited tying agreement and therefore could not prevail. In so ruling, the district court rejected Independent's argument that ITW's patent on the printhead system gave it the necessary market power. Independent appealed to the U.S. Court of Appeals for the Federal Circuit, which reversed the lower court's decision. The Federal Circuit held that the existence of a patent on the tying product (in this instance, the printhead system) gave rise to a presumption of market power regarding the tying product. Was the Federal Circuit correct in so ruling?

10. For approximately three years, Larry and Shirley McQuillan had served as distributors of sorbothane products for a certain firm and its successor. After they lost their distributorship and their business failed, the McQuillans sued both firms, as well as other affiliated companies and individuals. The McQuillans raised various legal claims, including a claim that the defendants engaged in attempted monopolization, in violation of § 2 of the Sherman Act. The evidence produced at trial revealed various instances of unfair or predatory conduct engaged in by the defendants and directed toward the McQuillans. The jury awarded the McQuillans a very substantial damages award on their attempted monopolization claim. The defendants appealed. Relying on one of its own precedents (a 1964 decision), the U.S. Court of Appeals for the Ninth Circuit held that the evidence of the defendants' unfair or predatory conduct served to satisfy the *specific intent to monopolize* and *dangerous probability of achieving monopoly power* elements of the McQuillans' attempted monopolization claim, even though the McQuillans presented no proof of the relevant market or the defendants' market power therein. Was the Ninth Circuit's holding correct?

CHAPTER 50

The Clayton Act, the Robinson–Patman Act, and Antitrust Exemptions and Immunities

XYZ Inc., the widget manufacturer referred to at the beginning of Chapter 49, may face antitrust issues that go beyond the ones addressed in that chapter. As you study this chapter, consider these questions regarding possible courses of action in which XYZ might engage:

- If XYZ, in selling its widgets, charges different prices to different wholesale dealers, is XYZ at risk of antitrust liability? What if XYZ charges a wholesale dealer a lower price than XYZ charges a *retailer* with whom XYZ deals directly?
- If XYZ has been charging a certain price for its widgets, but XYZ learns that a competing widget manufacturer is offering its widgets at a lower price, would XYZ be at risk of violating antitrust law if it lowers its price for certain customers in order to *meet* the price offered by the competitor? What if XYZ lowers its price enough to *beat* the competitor's price?
- If XYZ and a competing widget manufacturer decide to merge, what potential hurdles might antitrust law present?
- If XYZ decides to acquire a company that produces a material used in making widgets (i.e., a noncompetitor), is antitrust law a potential obstacle to XYZ's ability to carry out the acquisition?
- If, through effective lobbying efforts, XYZ helps convince a state legislature to enact a statute that may benefit XYZ at the expense of competition in the widget market, has XYZ committed an antitrust violation?
- What ethical questions are suggested by the behaviors alluded to above?

LO LEARNING OBJECTIVES

After studying this chapter, you should be able to:

50-1 Identify the two main types of potentially anticompetitive behavior to which Clayton Act § 3 applies.

50-2 Identify the general type of potentially anticompetitive behavior to which Clayton Act § 7 applies.

50-3 Describe the role of the FTC and the Justice Department in clearing or opposing certain proposed mergers.

50-4 Explain what is taken into account in a relevant market determination when a merger is challenged as a supposed violation of § 7.

50-5 State what a horizontal merger is and describe the role of an assessment of a merger's effects in a determination of whether the merger violates § 7.

50-6 State what a vertical merger is and describe the factors taken into account in a determination of whether the merger violates § 7.

50-7 State what a conglomerate merger is and describe the factors taken into account in a determination of whether the merger violates § 7.

50-8 Identify the particular risk of anticompetitive conduct that Clayton Act § 8 is designed to address.

50-9 Describe each of the three types of price discrimination addressed by the Robinson–Patman Act (primary level, secondary level, and tertiary level).

50-10 Identify the elements of a price discrimination claim under Robinson–Patman Act § 2(a).

50-11 List the defenses to a § 2(a) price discrimination claim.

50-12 Explain what constitutes indirect price discrimination for purposes of the Robinson–Patman Act.

50-13 List the major statutory exemptions from the application of the federal antitrust laws.

50-14 Explain what is necessary for the state action exemption to apply.

50-15 Explain the operation of the *Noerr–Pennington* doctrine.

50-16 Describe the antitrust exemptions associated with foreign commerce (sovereign immunity, act of state doctrine, and sovereign compulsion doctrine).

CONCENTRATION IN THE AMERICAN economy continued despite the 1890 enactment of the Sherman Act. Restrictive judicial interpretations of § 2 of the Sherman Act limited its effectiveness against many monopolists. Critics therefore sought legislation to thwart would-be monopolists before they achieved full-blown restraint of trade or monopoly power. In 1914, Congress responded by passing the Clayton Act.

Congress envisioned the Clayton Act as a vehicle for attacking practices that monopolists historically employed to acquire monopoly power. These practices included tying and exclusive dealing arrangements designed to squeeze competitors out of the market, mergers and acquisitions aimed at reducing competition through the elimination of competitors, interlocking corporate directorates designed to reduce competition by placing competitors under common leadership, and predatory or discriminatory pricing intended to force competitors out of business. These practices will be discussed in the following pages.

In view of the congressional intent that the Clayton Act serve as a preventive measure, only a *probability* of a significant anticompetitive effect must be shown for most Clayton Act violations. Because the Clayton Act focuses on probable harms to competition, there are no criminal penalties for violating its provisions. Private plaintiffs, however, may sue for treble damages or injunctive relief if they are injured, or threatened with injury, by another party's violation of the statute. The Justice Department and the Federal Trade Commission (FTC) share responsibility for enforcing the Clayton Act. Each has the authority to seek injunctive relief to prevent or remedy violations of the statute. In addition, the FTC has the power to enforce the Clayton Act through cease and desist orders, which were discussed in Chapter 48.

Clayton Act Section 3

 LO50-1 Identify the two main types of potentially anticompetitive behavior to which Clayton Act § 3 applies.

Section 3 of the Clayton Act makes it unlawful for any person engaged in interstate commerce to *lease or sell commodities*, or to *fix a price for commodities*, on the *condition, agreement, or understanding* that the lessee or buyer will not use or deal in the commodities of the lessor's or seller's competitors, if the effect of doing so *may be* to *substantially lessen competition* or *tend to create a monopoly* in any line of commerce. Section 3 primarily targets two potentially anticompetitive behaviors: tying agreements and exclusive dealing agreements. As you learned in Chapter 49, these types of contracts may amount to restraints of trade in violation of Sherman Act § 1. The language of § 3, however, contains limitations on the Clayton Act's application to such agreements.

A major limitation is that § 3 applies only to tying agreements and exclusive dealing contracts involving the leasing or sale of *commodities*. Any such agreements involving services, real estate, or intangibles must therefore be attacked under the Sherman Act. Although § 3 speaks of sales and leases on the "condition, agreement, or understanding" that the buyer or lessee not deal in the commodities of the seller's or lessor's competitors, no formal agreement is required. Whenever a seller or lessor uses its economic power to prevent its customers from dealing with its competitors, potential Clayton Act concerns are triggered.

Tying Agreements Many tying agreements plainly fall within at least the first portion of the § 3 language. Any agreement that requires a buyer to purchase one product (the *tied product*) from a seller as a condition of purchasing another product (the *tying product*) from the same seller necessarily prevents the buyer from purchasing the tied product from the seller's competitors.

Only tying agreements that may "substantially lessen competition or tend to create a monopoly," however, violate § 3. Several decades ago, the Supreme Court appeared to indicate that a tying agreement would violate the Clayton Act if the seller either had monopoly power over the tying product or restrained a substantial volume of commerce in the tied product. Most lower federal courts today, however, require essentially the same elements for a Clayton Act violation that they require for a Sherman Act violation: The challenged agreement must involve *two separate products*; *sale of the tying product must be conditioned* on an accompanying sale of the tied product; the seller must have *sufficient economic power in the market for the tying product* to appreciably restrain competition in the tied product market; and the seller's tying arrangements must restrain a *"not insubstantial" amount of commerce in the tied product market*. The *Suture Express* case, which appears in Chapter 49, illustrates courts' usual tendency to give tying agreements that are challenged under Clayton Act § 3 the same analysis applied to such agreements when they are challenged under Sherman Act § 1. A few courts, however, continue to apply a less demanding standard for Clayton Act tying liability by dispensing with proof of the seller's economic power in the market for the tying product as long as the seller's tying arrangements involve a "not insubstantial" amount of commerce in the tied product. The defenses to tying liability under the Sherman Act (discussed in Chapter 49) are also applicable to tying claims brought under the Clayton Act.

Exclusive Dealing Agreements In the preceding chapter, we discussed the nature of exclusive dealing agreements. Such contracts clearly fall under the initial portion of the § 3 language because buyers who agree to handle one seller's product exclusively, or to purchase all of their requirements for a commodity from one seller, are also agreeing not to purchase similar items from the seller's competitors. However, not all exclusive dealing agreements are unlawful. Section 3 outlaws only those agreements that may "substantially lessen competition or tend to create a monopoly."

Exclusive dealing agreements initially were treated in much the same way as tying agreements. Courts looked at the dollar amount of commerce involved and declared illegal those agreements involving a "not insubstantial" amount of commerce. This *quantitative substantiality* test was employed

by the Supreme Court in *Standard Oil Co. v. United States,* 337 U.S. 293 (1949). Standard Oil was the largest refiner and supplier of gasoline in several western states, holding approximately 14 percent of the retail market. Roughly half of these sales were made by retail outlets owned by Standard. The remaining sales were made by independent dealers who had entered into exclusive dealing contracts with Standard. Standard's six major competitors had entered into similar contracts with their own independent dealers. The Court recognized that exclusive dealing contracts, unlike tying agreements, could benefit both buyers and sellers, but declared Standard's contracts unlawful on the ground that nearly $58 million in commerce was involved.

The *Standard Oil* decision prompted considerable criticism. In *Tampa Electric Co. v. Nashville Coal Co.,* 365 U.S. 320 (1961), the Supreme Court applied a broader *qualitative substantiality* test to gauge the legality of a long-term requirements contract for the sale of coal to an electric utility. In *Tampa Electric*, the Court looked at the "area of effective competition," which was the total market for coal in the geographic region from which the utility could reasonably purchase its coal needs. The Court then examined the percentage of this region's coal sales accounted for by the challenged contract. Because that percentage share was less than 1 percent of the region's coal sales, the Court upheld the agreement even though it represented more than $100 million in coal sales.

Tampa Electric, however, is distinguishable from *Standard Oil*, which the Court has not overruled. Unlike *Standard Oil*, *Tampa Electric* involved parties with relatively equal bargaining power and an individual agreement, rather than an industrywide practice. In addition, there were obvious reasons why an electric utility such as Tampa Electric might want to lock in its coal costs by using a long-term requirements contract. Although lower court opinions employing each test may be found, the qualitative approach employed in *Tampa Electric* almost certainly is the one the current Court would employ.

Clayton Act Section 7

 LO50-2 Identify the general type of potentially anticompetitive behavior to which Clayton Act § 7 applies.

Introduction Section 7 of the Clayton Act was designed to attack **mergers**—a term used broadly in this chapter to refer to the acquisition of one company by another. History indicates that one way monopolists acquired monopoly power was by acquiring control of their competitors. Section 7 prohibits any party engaged in commerce or in any activity affecting commerce from *acquiring the stock*

or assets of another such party if the effect, in *any line of commerce* or *any activity affecting commerce* in any section of the country, *may be to substantially lessen competition* or *tend to create a monopoly*. Rather than adopting the Sherman Act approach of waiting until a would-be monopolist has acquired monopoly power or is dangerously close to doing so, § 7 attempts to "nip monopolies in the bud" by barring mergers that *may* have an anticompetitive effect.

Although § 7 is plainly an anticoncentration device, it has also been used (as the following text indicates) to attack mergers that have had no direct effect on concentration in a particular industry. Its future evolution, however, is uncertain, given the influence of Chicago School economic theories on contemporary antitrust law and the more tolerant stance those theories take toward mergers. During the 1980s, the Justice Department signaled a more permissive approach to merger activity than the government had previously adopted. Later, Justice Department and FTC officials undertook greater scrutiny of mergers in some industries, though clearly not on an across-the-board basis.

Recent experience provides further evidence that the intensity (or lack of intensity) of federal regulatory activity regarding mergers can be likened to a swinging pendulum. During the first several years of the current century, the federal government took a generally tolerant approach toward many mergers. Then, however, there were signs of at least a partial swing the other way—that is, in the direction of a more aggressive regulatory posture. For instance, Justice Department opposition in 2011 derailed a proposed merger between AT&T Inc. and T-Mobile USA Inc., two of the nation's largest wireless carriers. Similarly, in 2015, an objection by the Justice Department derailed Comcast's plan to acquire Time Warner Cable.

That said, the pendulum has effectively begun to swing back towards tolerance. In 2018, AT&T and Time Warner Cable were given the green light to engage in a $85 million merger in a U.S. district court in Washington, D.C., despite opposition by the Trump administration. And in 2020, T-Mobile was able to acquire Sprint without much resistance.

Outside the communications sector, some large mergers have been completed with either no objection from the government or through agreed modifications that win the approval of regulators. For example, in 2013 the Justice Department withdrew its objections to a merger between American Airlines and U.S. Airways after the to-be-merged airlines agreed to give up several hundred slots at seven key airports in order to allow slots for low-cost carriers and satisfy the Justice Department's concerns about preserving competition.

Federal Filing Requirements for Mergers

 LO50-3 Describe the role of the FTC and the Justice Department in clearing or opposing certain proposed mergers.

The Hart–Scott–Rodino Antitrust Improvement Act of 1976 requires that for planned mergers involving dollar values of stock or assets exceeding certain amounts, the parties to the merger agreement must provide advance notice to the FTC and the Justice Department. The purpose of this requirement is to provide the federal government a "heads-up" warning and to give regulators a reasonable opportunity to institute a legal challenge of the merger if a challenge seems warranted. Once the statutorily specified waiting period expires and the government has cleared the merger or at least has not taken legal action to block it, the merger may proceed. The normal waiting period is 30 days from the filing of the premerger notification form, though the waiting period is sometimes subject to extension.

In the previously described case of the proposed merger between AT&T and T-Mobile, the Justice Department used the premerger review period to make a determination that it wished to take steps to block the merger. Other times, however, the premerger review may result in the government's decision to allow the merger to proceed. An example would be the 2011 decision in which the FTC and the Justice Department elected not to oppose a deal that called for General Electric Co., owner of the NBC television network, to acquire a very substantial interest in a joint venture between NBC and Comcast Corp., the owner of cable television networks, regional sports networks, and various digital properties. It should be remembered, however, that regardless of whether the government seeks to block a merger, private enforcement of § 7 is also possible.

Predictions regarding § 7's eventual judicial treatment are complicated considerably by the fact that many of the important merger cases in recent years have been settled out of court. This leaves interested observers of antitrust policy with few definitive expressions of the Supreme Court's current thinking on merger issues.

Relevant Market Determination Regardless of the treatment § 7 ultimately receives in the courts, determining the relevant market affected by a merger is likely to remain a crucial component of any § 7 case. Before a court can determine whether a particular merger will have the probable anticompetitive effect required by the Clayton Act, it must first determine the line of commerce (or *relevant product market*) and the section of the country (or *relevant geographic market*) that are likely to be affected by the merger. The court's adoption of a broad relevant market definition will usually enhance the government's or private plaintiff's difficulty in demonstrating the challenged merger's probable anticompetitive effect.

 LO50-4 Explain what is taken into account in a relevant market determination when a merger is challenged as a supposed violation of § 7.

Relevant Product Market "Line of commerce" determinations under the Clayton Act have traditionally employed *functional interchangeability* tests similar to those employed in relevant product market determinations under the Sherman Act. Which products do the acquired and acquiring firms manufacture (assuming a merger between competitors), and which products are reasonably interchangeable by consumers to serve the same purposes? The federal government's merger guidelines indicate that the relevant market includes those products that consumers view as good substitutes at prevailing prices. The guidelines also state that the relevant market includes any products to which a significant percentage of current customers would shift in the event of a "small, but significant and non-transitory increase" in price of the merged firms' products. The *ProMedica* and *Staples* cases, which appear later in the chapter, deal with the making of a relevant product market determination.

Relevant Geographic Market To determine a particular merger's probable anticompetitive effect on a section of the country, courts have traditionally asked where the effects of the merger will be direct and immediate. This means that the relevant geographic market may not be as broad as the markets in which the acquiring and acquired firms actually operate or, in the case of a merger between competitors, the markets in which they actually compete. The focus of the relevant market inquiry is on those sections of the country in which competition is most likely to be injured by the merger. As a result, the relevant geographic market could be drawn as narrowly as one metropolitan area or as broadly as the entire nation. All that is necessary to satisfy this aspect of § 7 is proof that the challenged merger may have a significant negative effect on competition in any economically significant geographic market.

The federal government's merger guidelines adopt a somewhat different approach to determining the relevant geographic market. They define the relevant geographic market as the geographic area in which a sole supplier of the product in question could profitably raise its price without causing outside suppliers to begin selling in the area. The guidelines contemplate beginning with the existing markets in which the parties to a merger compete, and then adding the markets of those suppliers that would enter the market in response to a "small, but significant and nontransitory increase" in price.

Horizontal Mergers

 LO50-5 State what a horizontal merger is and describe the role of an assessment of a merger's effects in a determination of whether the merger violates § 7.

The analytical approach employed to gauge a merger's probable effect on competition varies according to the nature of the merger in question. Horizontal mergers—mergers among firms competing in the same product and geographic markets—have traditionally been subjected to the most rigorous scrutiny because they clearly lead to increased concentration in the relevant market.

Market Share of Resulting Firm To determine the legality of such a merger, courts look at the market share of the resulting firm. In *United States v. Philadelphia National Bank*, 374 U.S. 321 (1963), the Supreme Court indicated that a horizontal merger producing a firm with an "undue percentage share" of the relevant market (33 percent in that case) and resulting in a "significant increase in concentration" of the firms in that market would be presumed illegal, absent convincing evidence that the merger would not have an anticompetitive effect.

In the past, mergers involving firms with smaller market shares than those involved in *Philadelphia National Bank* were also enjoined if other economic or historical factors pointed toward a probable anticompetitive effect. Factors that courts have traditionally considered relevant include:

1. *A trend toward concentration in the relevant market.* Has the number of competing firms decreased over time?

2. *The competitive position of the merging firms.* Are the defendants dominant firms despite their relatively small market shares?

3. *A past history of acquisitions by the acquiring firm.* Are we dealing with a would-be empire builder?

4. *The nature of the acquired firm.* Is it an aggressive, innovative competitor despite its small market share?

Recent Assessments of Merger Effects Recent developments, however, indicate that the courts and federal antitrust enforcement agencies have become increasingly less willing to presume that anticompetitive effects will result from a merger that produces a firm with a relatively large market share. Instead, a more detailed inquiry is made into the nature of the relevant market and of the merging firms in order to ascertain the likelihood of probable harm to competition as a result of a challenged merger. The federal government's merger guidelines provide that when regulators assess a horizontal merger's probable effect, the focus is on the existing concentration in the relevant market, the increase in concentration as a result of the proposed merger, and other nonmarket share factors. The more concentrated the existing market and the greater the increase in concentration that would result from the proposed merger, the more likely the merger is to be challenged by the government.

The nonmarket share factors considered by federal regulators are more traditional. They include the existence (or absence) of barriers to the entry of new competitors into the relevant market, the prior conduct of the merging firms, and the probable future competitive strength of the acquired firm. The last factor is particularly important because courts have acknowledged that a firm's current market share may not reflect its ability to compete in the future. For example, courts are sometimes willing to consider a "failing company" justification for certain mergers. If the acquired firm is a failing company and no other purchasers are interested in acquiring it, acquisition by a competitor could be held lawful under § 7. Similarly, if an acquired firm has financial problems that reflect some underlying structural weakness,

or if it lacks technologies that will be necessary if it is to compete effectively in the future, its current market share may overstate its future competitive importance.

Finally, given the increased weight being assigned to economic arguments in antitrust cases, two other merger justifications may be granted greater credence in the future. Some lower federal courts have recognized the notion that a merger between two small companies may be justifiable, despite the increase in concentration stemming from the merger, if the resulting firm is able to compete more effectively with larger competitors. In a similar vein, some commentators have argued that mergers resulting in cost savings or other enhanced economic efficiencies should sometimes be allowed even though they may have some anticompetitive impact. Though courts have not been very receptive to efficiency arguments in the past, the government's merger guidelines are flexible enough to allow the Justice Department and FTC to consider efficiency claims in deciding whether to challenge a merger.

The *ProMedica* case, which follows, addresses relevant market issues in the context of a proposed merger of competing hospital systems. In the *Staples* case, which follows immediately after *ProMedica*, the court examines a range of issues suggested by a proposed horizontal merger of competing office supply superstores.

ProMedica Health System, Inc. v. Federal Trade Commission
749 F.3d 559 (6th Cir. 2014)

Lucas County is located in northwestern Ohio. Toledo lies near the county's center; more affluent suburbs lie to the southwest. Two-thirds of the hospital patients in the county have government-provided health insurance, such as Medicare or Medicaid. Twenty-nine percent of hospital patients in the county have private health insurance, which pays significantly higher rates to hospitals than government-provided insurance does. A relatively large proportion of the county's privately insured patients reside in the county's southwestern corner.

The case described here concerns the market for general acute-care (GAC) inpatient services in Lucas County. GAC comprises four basic categories of services. The most basic is the primary services, such as hernia surgeries, radiology services, and most kinds of inpatient obstetrical (OB) services. Secondary services, such as hip replacements and bariatric surgery, require the hospital to have more specialized resources. Tertiary services, such as brain surgery and treatments for severe burns, require even more specialized resources. Quaternary services, such as major organ transplants, require the most specialized resources of all.

Different hospitals offer different levels of these services. Of the four hospital providers in Lucas County, the most dominant is ProMedica, with 46.8 percent of the county's GAC market in 2009. ProMedica operates three hospitals in the county, which together provide primary (including OB), secondary, and tertiary services. The county's second-largest provider is Mercy Health Partners, with 28.7 percent of the 2009 GAC market. Mercy likewise operates three hospitals in the county, which together provide primary (including OB), secondary, and tertiary services. The University of Toledo Medical Center (UTMC) has 13 percent of the GAC market. UTMC operates a single teaching and research hospital near downtown Toledo and focuses on tertiary and quaternary services. It does not offer OB services. The remaining provider is St. Luke's Hospital, which, before the merger discussed below, was an independent, not-for-profit hospital with 11.5 percent of the GAC market. St. Luke's offers primary (including OB) and secondary services and is located in southwestern Lucas County.

With respect to privately insured patients, hospital providers do not all receive the same rates for the same services. Each hospital negotiates its rates with private insurers (known as managed care organizations, or MCOs). The rates are determined by each party's bargaining power. An MCO's bargaining power depends primarily on the number of patients it can offer a hospital provider. The greater the number of patients an MCO can offer a provider, the greater the MCO's leverage in negotiating the hospital's rates. MCOs compete with each other just as hospitals do. To attract patients, an MCO's health care plan must offer a comprehensive range of services— primary, secondary, tertiary, and quaternary—within a geographic range that patients are willing to travel for each of those services. These criteria in turn create leverage for hospitals to raise rates: To the extent patients view a hospital's services as desirable or even essential (for instance, because of the hospital's location or its reputation for quality), the hospital's bargaining power increases. But another important criterion for a plan's competitiveness is its cost. Thus, if a hospital demands rates above a certain level—the so-called walk-away point—the MCO will try to assemble a network without that provider.

Before the merger discussed below, MCOs in Lucas County offered networks that included at least three of the four hospital provid- ers. Since 2000, every MCO offered a network that included either ProMedica or St. Luke's (and sometimes both). The likely reason MCOs found it necessary to include either ProMedica or St. Luke's in their networks is that those providers are dominant in south- western Lucas County, where St. Luke's is located. In that part of the county—relatively affluent and with a high proportion of privately insured patients—ProMedica and St. Luke's were direct competitors before the merger at issue here.

In the competition between ProMedica and St. Luke's, however, ProMedica had the upper hand. It is harder for an MCO to exclude the county's most dominant hospital system (here, ProMedica) than it is for the MCO to exclude a single hospital (here, St. Luke's) that services just one corner of the county—a corner, moreover, that the dominant system also services. That means the MCOs' walk-away point for the dominant system is higher—perhaps much higher—than it is for the single hospital. In this case, the record bore out that conclusion: ProMedica's rates before the merger discussed below were among the highest in the state, whereas St. Luke's rates did not even cover its cost of patient care. That was true even though St. Luke's quality ratings on the whole were better than ProMedica's. As a result, St. Luke's struggled in the years before the merger, losing more than $25 million between 2007 and 2009.

In late 2009, the CEO of St. Luke's recommended to the hospital's board of directors that it pursue a merger with ProMedica. The board accepted the recommendation. Six months later, ProMedica and St. Luke's signed a merger agreement. Less than two months after the agreement was signed, the Federal Trade Commission (FTC) opened an investigation into the merger's competitive effects. A month later, the FTC and ProMedica entered into a Hold Separate Agreement that allowed ProMedica to close the deal, but that, during the pendency of the FTC investigation, barred ProMedica from terminating St. Luke's contracts with MCOs, eliminating or transferring St. Luke's clinical services, or terminating St. Luke's employees without cause. With these restrictions in place, ProMedica and St. Luke's closed the merger deal in August 2010.

In January 2011, the FTC filed an administrative complaint against ProMedica. An administrative law judge (ALJ) presided over a hearing that lasted more than 30 days and produced a very large record of testimony and other evidence. In December 2011, the ALJ issued a written decision concluding that the merger likely would substantially lessen competition in violation of § 7 of the Clayton Act. As a remedy, the ALJ ordered ProMedica to divest St. Luke's. ProMedica appealed the ALJ's decision to the FTC Commissioners (Com- mission), which affirmed the ALJ's decision and ordered ProMedica to divest St. Luke's. ProMedica then filed a petition for review in the U.S. Court of Appeals for the Sixth Circuit.

Kethledge, Circuit Judge

We review the Commission's legal conclusions de novo, and its factual findings under the substantial-evidence standard. Substantial evidence is evidence that "a reasonable mind might accept as adequate to support a conclusion." [Citation omitted.]

Section 7 of the Clayton Act prohibits mergers "where in any line of commerce . . . the effect of such acquisition may be sub- stantially to lessen competition, or to tend to create a monopoly." 15 U.S.C. § 18. As its language suggests, Section 7 deals in "prob- abilities, not certainties." *Brown Shoe Co. v. United States*, 370 U.S. 294, 323 (1962).

"Merger enforcement, like other areas of antitrust, is directed at market power." [Citation omitted.] Market power is itself a term of art that the Department of Justice's Horizontal Merger Guide- lines (which we consider useful but not binding upon us here)

define as the power of "one or more firms to raise price, reduce output, diminish innovation, or otherwise harm consumers as a result of diminished competitive constraints or incentives." Hori- zontal Merger Guidelines § 1 (2010).

Often, the first steps in analyzing a merger's competitive ef- fects are to define the geographic and product markets affected by it. Here, the parties agree that the relevant geographic market is Lucas County. The relevant product market or markets, however, are more difficult. The first principle of market definition is substi- tutability: a relevant product market must "identify a set of prod- ucts that are reasonably interchangeable[.]" Horizontal Merger Guidelines § 4.1. Chevrolets and Fords might be interchangeable in this sense, but Chevrolets and Lamborghinis probably are not. "The general question is whether two products can be used for the same purpose, and if so, whether and to what extent purchasers are willing to substitute one for the other." [Citation omitted.]

By this measure, each individual medical procedure could give rise to a separate market: "If you need your hip replaced, you can't decide to have chemotherapy instead." [Citation omitted.] But nobody advocates that we analyze the effects of this merger upon hundreds if not thousands of markets for individual procedures; instead, the parties agree that we should "cluster" these markets somehow. The parties disagree, however, on the principles that should govern which services are clustered and which are not.

Two theories of clustering are pertinent here. The first—which the Commission adopted—is the "administrative-convenience" theory. (A better name might be the "similar-conditions" theory.) This theory holds, in essence, that there is no need to perform separate antitrust analyses for separate product markets when competitive conditions are similar for each. In *Brown Shoe*, for example, the Supreme Court analyzed together the markets for men's, women's, and children's shoes, because the competitive conditions for each of them were similar.

The competitive conditions for hospital services include the barriers to entry for a particular service—e.g., how difficult it might be for a new competitor to buy the equipment and sign up the professionals necessary to offer the service—as well as the hospitals' respective market shares for the service and the geographic market for the service. If these conditions are similar for a range of services, then the antitrust analysis should be similar for each of them. Thus, if the competitive conditions for, say, secondary inpatient procedures are all reasonably similar, then we can cluster those services when analyzing a merger's competitive effects.

Here, the Commission applied this theory to cluster both primary services (but excluding OB, for reasons discussed below) and secondary services for purposes of analyzing the merger's competitive effects. Substantial evidence supports that demarcation. The respective market shares for each of Lucas County's four hospital systems (ProMedica, Mercy, UTMC, St. Luke's) are similar across the range of primary and secondary services. A hospital's market share for shoulder surgery, for example, is similar to its market share for knee replacements. Barriers to entry are likewise similar across primary and secondary services. So are the services' respective geographic markets. Thus, the competitive conditions across the markets for primary and secondary services are similar enough to justify clustering those markets when analyzing the merger's competitive effects.

But the same is not true for OB services, whose competitive conditions differ in at least two respects from those for other services. First, before the merger, ProMedica's market share for OB services (71.2%) was more than half—again greater than its market share for primary and secondary services (46.8%). And the merger would drive ProMedica's share for OB services even higher, to 80.5%—no small number in this area of the law. Second, and relatedly, before the merger there were only three hospital systems that provided OB services in Lucas County (ProMedica,

Mercy, St. Luke's) rather than four; after the merger, there would be only two. The Commission therefore flagged OB as a separate relevant market for purposes of analyzing the merger's competitive effects. For the reasons just stated, substantial evidence supports that decision.

Finally, the Commission excluded tertiary services from its analysis of the merger's competitive effects. The competitive conditions for tertiary services differ from those for primary and secondary services, in part because patients are willing to travel farther for tertiary services (e.g., a liver transplant) than they are for primary or secondary services (e.g., hernia surgery). Indeed, UTMC's representative testified that, "[f]or the tertiary . . . services, we compete with . . . institutions such as the University of Michigan, the Cleveland Clinic, University Hospital in Cleveland, and the Ohio State University." The geographic market for tertiary services is therefore larger than the geographic market for primary and secondary services. Moreover, the hospitals' respective market shares for these services are different than their respective shares for primary or secondary services. Thus, the competitive conditions for tertiary services differ from those for primary and secondary services. (The same is undisputedly true for quaternary services, which the Commission likewise excluded from its analysis.)

In summary, . . . the relevant markets, for purposes of analyzing the merger's competitive effects, are what the Commission says they are: (1) a cluster market of primary (but not OB) and secondary inpatient services (hereafter, the "GAC market"), and (2) a separate market for OB services.

ProMedica's next argument is that the Commission relied too heavily on market-concentration data to establish a presumption of anticompetitive harm. Agencies typically use the Herfindahl-Hirschman Index (HHI) to measure market concentration. "The HHI is calculated by summing the squares of the individual firms' market shares, and thus gives proportionately greater weight to the larger market shares." Merger Guidelines § 5.3 at 18. Agencies use HHI data to classify markets into three types: "unconcentrated markets," which have an HHI below 1,500; "moderately concentrated markets," which have an HHI between 1,500 and 2,500; and "highly concentrated markets," which have an HHI above 2,500. The Guidelines further provide that "[m]ergers resulting in highly concentrated markets that involve an increase in the HHI of more than 200 points will be presumed to be likely to enhance market power." Thus, as a general matter, a merger that increases HHI by more than 200 points, to a total number exceeding 2,500, is presumptively anticompetitive. *Id.* § 5.3 at 19.

The merger here blew through those barriers in spectacular fashion. In the GAC market, the merger would increase the HHI by 1,078 (more than five times the increase necessary to trigger the presumption of illegality) to a total number of 4,391 (almost double the 2,500 threshold for a highly concentrated market).

The OB numbers are even worse: the merger would increase HHI by 1,323 points (almost seven times the increase necessary for the presumption of illegality) to a total number of 6,854 (almost triple the threshold for a highly concentrated market). The Commission therefore found the merger to be presumptively illegal.

[W]hat the Commission should have focused on, ProMedica says, is the extent to which consumers regard ProMedica as their next-best choice after St. Luke's, or vice-versa. And ProMedica therefore argues that the Commission was wrong to presume the merger illegal based upon HHI data alone.

The argument is one to be taken seriously. The Guidelines themselves state that "[a]gencies rely much more on the value of diverted sales [i.e., in rough terms, the extent to which the products of the merging firms are close substitutes] than on the level of HHI for diagnosing unilateral price effects in markets with differentiated products." *Id.* § 6.1 at 21. But this case is exceptional in two respects. First, even without conducting a substitutability analysis, the record already shows a strong correlation between ProMedica's prices—i.e., its ability to impose unilateral price increases—and its market share. Before the merger, ProMedica's share of the GAC market was 46.8%, followed by Mercy with 28.7%, UTMC with 13%, and St. Luke's with 11.5%. And ProMedica's prices were on average 32% higher than Mercy's, 51% higher than UTMC's, and 74% higher than St. Luke's. Thus, in this market, the higher a provider's market share, the higher its prices. In ProMedica's case, that fact is not explained by the quality of ProMedica's services or by its underlying costs. Instead, ProMedica's prices . . . are explained by *bargaining power*. As the Commission explained: "the hospital provider's bargaining leverage will depend upon how the MCO would fare if its network did not include the hospital provider (and therefore became less attractive to potential members who prefer that provider's services)." Here, the record makes clear that a network which does not include a hospital provider that services almost half the county's patients in one relevant market, and more than 70% of the county's patients in another relevant market, would be unattractive to a huge swath of potential members. Thus, the Commission had every reason to conclude that, as ProMedica's dominance in the relevant markets increases, so does the need for MCOs to include ProMedica in their networks—and thus so too does ProMedica's leverage in demanding higher rates.

The second respect in which this case is exceptional is simply the HHI numbers themselves. [A]t some point the Commission is entitled to take seriously the alarm sounded by a merger's HHI data. And here the numbers are in every respect multiples of the numbers necessary for the presumption of illegality. Before the merger, ProMedica already held dominant market shares in the relevant markets, which were themselves already highly concentrated. The merger would drive those numbers even higher— ProMedica's share of the OB market would top 80%—which

makes it extremely likely, as matter of simple mathematics, that a "significant fraction" of St. Luke's patients viewed ProMedica as a close substitute for services in the relevant markets. On this record, the Commission was entitled to put significant weight upon the market-concentration data standing alone.

These two aspects of this case—the strong correlation between market share and price, and the degree to which this merger would further concentrate markets that are already highly concentrated—converge in a manner that fully supports the Commission's application of a presumption of illegality. What ProMedica overlooks is that the "ultimate inquiry in merger analysis" is not substitutability, but "whether the merger is likely to create or enhance *market power* or facilitate its exercise." [Citation omitted.] Here, as shown above, the correlation between market share and price reflects a correlation between market share and market power; and the HHI data strongly suggest that this merger would enhance ProMedica's market power even more, to levels rarely tolerated in antitrust law. In the context of this record, therefore, the HHI data speak to our "ultimate inquiry" as directly as an analysis of substitutability would. The Commission was correct to presume the merger substantially anticompetitive.

The remaining question is whether ProMedica has rebutted that presumption. ProMedica argues on several grounds that it has; but more remarkable is what ProMedica does not argue. By way of background, the goal of antitrust law is to enhance consumer welfare. And the Merger Guidelines themselves recognize that "a primary benefit of mergers to the economy is their potential to generate significant efficiencies and thus enhance the merged firm's ability and incentive to compete, which may result in lower prices, improved quality, enhanced service, or new products." Merger Guidelines § 10 at 29. Thus, the parties to a merger often seek to overcome a presumption of illegality by arguing that the merger would create efficiencies that enhance consumer welfare. But ProMedica did not even attempt to argue before the Commission, and does not attempt to argue here, that this merger would benefit consumers (as opposed to only the merging parties themselves) in any way. To the contrary, St. Luke's CEO admitted that a merger with ProMedica might "[h]arm the community by forcing higher rates on them."

[The] Commission's best witnesses [regarding the effects of the merger] were the merging parties themselves. Those witnesses established that ProMedica and St. Luke's are direct [and strong] competitors. St. Luke's management was also candid about the merger's potential impacts on its prices: its CEO stated that a merger with ProMedica "has the greatest potential for higher hospital rates" and would bring "a lot of negotiating clout." The parties' own statements, therefore, tend to confirm the presumption rather than rebut it.

The same is true of testimony from the MCO witnesses. Those witnesses testified that a network comprising only Mercy and UTMC—the only other providers who would remain after the merger—would not be commercially viable because it would leave them with a "hole" in the suburbs of southwest Lucas County. Consequently, the MCO witnesses explained, they would have no walk-away option in post-merger negotiations with ProMedica—and thus little ability to resist ProMedica's demands for even higher rates. ProMedica responds that this testimony is self-serving, which might well be true (though one might construe Pro-Medica's response as an implicit admission of the MCOs' point). But ProMedica otherwise offers no reason to think the MCOs' predictions are wrong—and the record offers plenty of reason to think they are right. ProMedica has failed to rebut the presumption that its merger with St. Luke's would reduce competition in violation of the Clayton Act.

ProMedica argues that the Commission erred in ordering divestiture as a remedy. We review the Commission's choice of remedy for abuse of discretion. In doing so, we resolve "all doubts" in the Commission's favor. *United States v. E.I. du Pont de Nemours & Co.*, 366 U.S. 316, 334 (1961).

Once a merger is found illegal, "an undoing of the acquisition is a natural remedy." *Id.* at 329. Here, the Commission found that divestiture would be the best means to preserve competition in the relevant markets. We have no basis to dispute [that] finding. The Commission did not abuse its discretion in choosing divestiture as a remedy.

ProMedica's petition for review denied; Commission's decision regarding Clayton Act violation and divestiture remedy upheld.

Federal Trade Commission v. Staples, Inc.   970 F. Supp. 1066 (D.D.C. 1997)

Office Depot Inc. owned the nation's largest chain of retail outlets commonly known as "office supply superstores." Staples, Inc. owned the second-largest chain of this type. Each company operated more than 500 superstores, with Office Depot's outlets existing in 38 states and the District of Columbia and Staples's superstores appearing in 28 states and the District of Columbia. The only other office supply superstore firm in the United States was OfficeMax Inc. In 1996, Staples and Office Depot entered into a merger agreement. As required by law, they filed a Premerger Notification and Report Form with the Federal Trade Commission (FTC) and the Department of Justice.

Following a lengthy investigation, the FTC initiated an adjudicative proceeding against Staples and Office Depot on the theory that the planned merger violated § 7 of the Clayton Act. (Adjudicative proceedings are discussed in Chapters 47 and 48.) In an effort to prevent the merger from taking place while its legality was being determined in the adjudicative proceeding, the FTC filed suit against Staples and Office Depot and requested a preliminary injunction against the merger. The federal district court conducted an extensive evidentiary hearing.

Hogan, District Judge

Section 7 of the Clayton Act makes it illegal for two companies to merge "where in any line of commerce or in any activity affecting commerce in any section of the country, the effect of such acquisition may be substantially to lessen competition, or to tend to create a monopoly." [The FTC Act provides that if] the Commission has reason to believe that a corporation is violating, or is about to violate, § 7 . . . , the FTC may seek a preliminary injunction to prevent a merger pending the Commission's adjudication of the merger's legality.

In order to determine whether the Commission has [made the required showing of] likelihood of success on the merits, . . . the court must consider the likely competitive effects of the merger. [This requires the court to determine the relevant product and geographic markets, as well as] the transaction's probable effect on competition in the product and geographic markets. [T]he parties . . . do not disagree . . . that [more than 40 different] metropolitan areas are the appropriate geographic markets for

analyzing the competitive effects of the proposed merger. [However, the parties] sharply disagree with respect to the appropriate definition of the relevant product market. [T]o a great extent, this case hinges on the proper definition of the relevant product market.

The Commission defines the relevant product market as "the sale of consumable office supplies through office superstores," with "consumable" meaning products that consumers buy [on a recurring basis], i.e., items which "get used up" or discarded. [U]nder the Commission's definition, "consumable office supplies" would not include capital goods such as computers, fax machines, . . . or office furniture, but [would] include such products as paper, pens, file folders, post-it notes, computer disks, and toner cartridges. The defendants . . . counter that the appropriate product market within which to assess the likely competitive consequences of a Staples–Office Depot combination is simply the overall sale of office products, of which a combined Staples–Office Depot accounted for 5.5% of total sales in North America in 1996.

The general rule when determining a relevant product market is that "the outer boundaries . . . are determined by the reasonable interchangeability of use [by consumers] or the cross-elasticity of demand between the product itself and substitutes for it." *Brown Shoe Co. v. United States,* 370 U.S. 294 (1962). This case . . . is an example of perfect interchangeability. The consumable office products at issue here are identical whether they are sold by Staples or Office Depot or another seller of office supplies [such as Walmart or another retailer that is not an office supply superstore]. [A]s the government has argued, [however, the] functional interchangeability [of office supplies] should not end the court's analysis.

[In *United States v. E.I. Du Pont de Nemours and Co.,* 351 U.S. 377 (1956), the Court] did not stop after finding a high degree of functional interchangeability between cellophane and other wrapping materials. [T]he Court also found that "an element for consideration as to cross-elasticity of demand between products is the responsiveness of the sales of one product to price changes of the other." [T]he Court explained [that] "if a slight decrease in the price of cellophane causes a considerable number of customers of other flexible wrappings to switch to cellophane, it would be an indication that a high cross-elasticity of demand exists between [cellophane and other flexible wrappings, and] that the products compete in the same market." Following that reasoning . . . , the Commission has argued that a slight but significant increase in Staples–Office Depot's prices will not cause a considerable number of Staples–Office Depot's customers to purchase consumable office supplies from other non-superstore alternatives such as Wal-Mart [or] Best Buy. . . . On the other hand, the Commission has argued that an increase in price by Staples would result in consumers' turning to another office superstore, especially Office Depot, if the consumers had that option. Therefore, the Commission [contends] that the sale of consumable office supplies by office supply superstores is the . . . relevant product market in this case, and products sold by competitors such as Wal-Mart, Best Buy, . . . and others should be excluded.

The court acknowledges that there is . . . a broad market encompassing the sale of consumable office supplies by all sellers of such supplies, and that those sellers must, at some level, compete with one another. However, the mere fact that a firm may be termed a competitor in the overall marketplace does not necessarily require that it be included in the relevant product market for antitrust purposes. The Supreme Court . . . recognized [in *Brown Shoe*] that within a broad market, "well-defined submarkets may exist which, in themselves, constitute product markets for antitrust purposes." There is a possibility, therefore, that the sale of consumable office supplies by office superstores may qualify as a submarket within a large market of retailers of office supplies in general.

[T]he FTC presented evidence comparing Staples's prices in geographic markets where Staples is the only office superstore to markets where Staples competes with Office Depot or OfficeMax, or both. [I]n markets where Staples faces no office superstore competition . . . , something which was termed a one-firm market during the hearing, prices are 13 percent higher than in three-firm markets where it competes with both Office Depot and Office-Max. Similarly, the evidence showed that Office Depot's prices are . . . well over 5 percent higher in Depot-only markets than they are in three-firm markets.

[The FTC's evidence] suggests that office superstore prices are affected primarily by other office superstores and not by non-superstore competitors such as . . . Wal-Mart, Kmart, or Target, wholesale clubs . . . , computer or electronic stores . . . , mail order firms . . . , and contract stationers. Though the FTC did not present the court with evidence regarding the precise amount of non-superstore competition in each of Staples's and Office Depot's one-, two-, and three-firm markets, it is clear . . . that these competitors, albeit in different combinations and concentrations, are present in every one of these markets. For example, . . . the mail order competitors compete in all of the geographic markets at issue in this case. Despite this mail order competition, . . . Staples and Office Depot are still able to charge higher prices in their one-firm markets than they do in the two-firm markets and the three-firm markets without losing a significant number of customers to the mail order firms.

The same appears to be true with respect to Wal-Mart. [A Wal-Mart executive testified] that price-checking by Wal-Mart of Staples' prices in areas where both Staples and Wal-Mart exist showed that, on average, Staples's prices were higher than where there was a Staples and a Wal-Mart but no other superstore than where there was a Staples, a Wal-Mart, and another superstore. The evidence with respect to the wholesale club stores is consistent. There is also consistent evidence with respect to computer and/or consumer electronics stores. In addition, [the] evidence shows that the defendants [lower their prices in a given geographic area] when faced with entry of another superstore [in that area], but do not do so for other retailers. There is no evidence that . . . prices fall when another non-superstore retailer enters a geographic market.

[The FTC made] a compelling showing that a small but significant increase in Staples's prices will not cause a significant number of consumers to turn to non-superstore alternatives for purchasing their consumable office supplies. Despite the high degree of functional interchangeability between consumable office supplies sold by the office superstores and other retailers of office supplies, the evidence . . . shows that even where Staples and Office Depot charge higher prices, certain consumers do not go elsewhere for their supplies.

[In addition,] both Staples and Office Depot focus primarily on competition from other superstores. [Staples's and Office Depot's own documents] show that the merging parties evaluate their "competition" as the other office superstore firms, without reference to other retailers, mail order firms, or independent stationers. When assessing key trends and making long-range plans, Staples and Office Depot focus on the plans of other superstores. [W]hen determining whether to enter a new metropolitan area, both Staples and Office Depot evaluate the extent of office superstore competition in the market and the number of office superstores the market can support. When selecting sites and markets for new store openings, the defendants repeatedly refer to markets without office superstores as "noncompetitive," even when the new store is adjacent to or near a warehouse club, consumer electronics store, or a mass-merchandiser such as Wal-Mart.

[T]he court finds that the sale of consumable office supplies through office supply superstores is the appropriate relevant product market for purposes of considering the possible anticompetitive effects of the proposed merger. [T]he court next must consider the probable effect of a merger between Staples and Office Depot in the geographic markets previously identified. [The evidence shows] that a merged Staples–Office Depot would have a dominant market share in 42 geographic markets across the country. The combined shares of Staples and Office Depot in the office superstore market would be 100 percent in 15 metropolitan areas. In 27 other metropolitan areas, where the number of office superstore competitors would drop from three to two, the post-merger market shares would range from 45 percent to 94 percent. [T]hough the Supreme Court has established that there is no fixed threshold at which an increase in market concentration triggers the antitrust laws, this is clearly not a borderline case.

[In addition to the] market concentration evidence, [there are other] indications that a merger between Staples and Office Depot may substantially lessen competition. Much of the evidence [concerning] the relevant product market also indicates that the merger would likely have an anticompetitive effect. The evidence of the defendant's current pricing practices, for example, shows that an office superstore chain facing no competition from other superstores has the ability to profitably raise prices for consumer office supplies above competitive levels. The evidence also shows that the defendants [lower their prices] when faced with entry of another office superstore [in a particular geographic area], but do not do so for other retailers. Since prices are significantly lower in markets where Staples and Office Depot compete, eliminating this competition with one another would free the parties to charge higher prices in those markets, especially those in which the combined entity would be the sole office superstore.

In addition, allowing the defendants to merge would eliminate . . . head-to-head competition between the two . . . lowest-priced firms in the superstore market. Thus, the merger would result in the elimination of a particularly aggressive competitor in a highly concentrated market, a factor which is certainly an important consideration when analyzing possible anticompetitive effects. It is based on all of this evidence that the court finds that the Commission has shown a likelihood of success on the merits and a

reasonable probability that the proposed transaction will have an anticompetitive effect.

[T]he court finds it extremely unlikely that a new office superstore will enter the market and thereby avert the anticompetitive effects from Staples's acquisition of Office Depot. [Although the defendants also argued that] expansion [by] existing companies such as U.S. Office Products and Wal-Mart [would enhance competition in the sale of office supplies, the court] finds it unlikely that expansion by U.S. Office Products and Wal-Mart would avert the anticompetitive effects which would result from the merger. The defendants' final argument with respect to entry was that existing retailers such as Sam's Club, Kmart, and Best Buy have the capability to reallocate their shelf space to include [greater quantities and varieties] of office supplies. While [such stores may] reallocate shelf space, there is no evidence that they will in fact do this if a combined Staples–Office Depot were to raise prices . . . following a merger. In fact, the evidence indicates that [they probably] would not.

The defendants submitted an "Efficiencies Analysis" which predicted that the combined company would achieve savings of between $4.9 and $6.5 billion over the next five years. In addition, the defendants argued that the merger would also generate dynamic efficiencies. For example, the defendants argued that as suppliers become more efficient due to their increased sales volume to the combined Staples–Office Depot, they would be able to lower prices to their other retailers. Moreover, the defendants argued that two-thirds of the savings realized by the combined company would be passed along to consumers.

[T]he court credits the testimony and report of the Commission's expert over the testimony and efficiencies study of the defendants' witness, [a] Senior Vice President of Integration at Staples. [The testimony of the Commission's expert] was compelling, and the court finds, based primarily on [that expert's] testimony, that the defendants' cost savings estimates are unreliable [and far in excess of estimates by the defendants in proxy statements and in presentations to the defendants' boards of directors]. [T]he court also finds that the defendants' projected pass-through rate—the amount of the projected savings that the combined company expects to pass on to customers in the form of lower prices—is unrealistic. Staples and Office Depot have a proven track record of achieving cost savings through efficiencies, and then passing those savings to customers in the form of lower prices. However, in this case the defendants have projected a pass-through rate of two-thirds of the savings while the evidence shows that, historically, Staples has passed through only 15–17 percent.

[T]he court cannot find that the defendants have rebutted [the FTC's showing] that the merger will substantially lessen competition.

FTC's motion for preliminary injunction against merger granted.

Ethics and Compliance in Action

For decades, large technology terms—think Google, Facebook, Apple, Amazon—have acquired multiple competitors to maintain their dominance. For example, in 2012, Facebook was allowed to buy Instagram for $1 billion, and in 2014, Facebook acquired WhatsApp for $19 billion. This consolidation of power has led many politicians, scholars, and privacy advocates to consider whether these mergers were appropriate.

1. What arguments could one give that Facebook's acquisition of Instagram and WhatsApp was a violation of Section 7 of the Clayton Act?

2. Are there benefits to allowing tech firms to continue to merge? If so, what are they?

3. What are the implications for consumers in terms of privacy, if tech firms continue to acquire their competitors?

4. What would be the ethical implications if the government required big tech firms to reverse their mergers ("unmerge" so to speak) with those they have acquired?

For more information and proposals for dealing with big tech, *see* Tim Wu, "How Should Big Tech Be Reined In? Here Are 4 Prominent Ideas," *N.Y. Times,* August 20, 2019, p. B1, www.nytimes.com/2019/08/20/technology/big-tech-reined-in.html.

Vertical Mergers

 LO50-6 State what a vertical merger is and describe the factors taken into account in a determination of whether the merger violates § 7.

A vertical merger is a merger between firms that previously had, or could have had, a supplier–customer relationship. For example, a manufacturer may seek to integrate its operations by acquiring a company that controls retail outlets at which the manufacturer's products could be sold. Alternatively, the manufacturer may vertically merge by acquiring a company that makes a product the manufacturer regularly uses in its production processes. Vertical mergers, unlike horizontal mergers, do not directly result in an increase in concentration. Nonetheless, they traditionally have been thought to threaten competition in various ways.

Foreclosing Competitors in Relevant Market First, vertical mergers may foreclose competitors from a share of the relevant market. If a major customer for a product acquires a captive supplier of that product, the competitors of the acquired firm are foreclosed from competing with it for sales to the acquiring firm. Similarly, if a manufacturer acquires a captive retail outlet for its products, the manufacturer's competitors are foreclosed from competing for sales to that retail outlet. A vertical merger in the latter case may also result in reduced competition at the retail level. For instance, a shoe manufacturer acquires a retail shoe store chain that carries the brands of several competing manufacturers and has a dominant share of the retail market in certain geographic areas.

If the retail chain carries only the acquiring manufacturer's brands after the merger occurs, competition among the acquiring manufacturer and its competitors is reduced in the retail market for shoes.

Creation of Increased Market Entry Barriers A second way in which vertical mergers threaten competition is that they may lead to increased barriers to market entry for new competitors. For example, if a major purchaser of a product acquires a captive supplier of it, the merger-related contraction of the market for the product may discourage potential producers of it from commencing production.

Elimination of Potential Competition in Acquired Firm's Market Some vertical mergers threaten competition by eliminating potential competition in one of two ways. First, an acquiring firm may be perceived by existing competitors in the acquired firm's market as a likely potential entrant into that market. The threat of such a potential entrant "waiting in the wings" may moderate the behavior of existing competitors because they fear that pursuing pricing policies that exploit their current market position might cause the potential entrant to react by entering the market. The acquiring firm's entry into the market by the acquisition of an existing competitor means the end of its moderating influence as a potential entrant. Second, a vertical merger may deprive the market of the potential benefits that would have resulted if the acquiring firm had entered the market in a more competitive manner, such as by creating its own entrant into the market through internal expansion or by making a toehold acquisition of a small existing competitor and then building it into a more significant competitor.

Historically, courts seeking to determine the legality of vertical mergers have tended to look at the *share of the relevant market foreclosed to competition*. If a more than insignificant market share is foreclosed to competition, courts consider other economic and historical factors. Factors viewed as aggravating the anticompetitive potential of a vertical merger include a trend toward concentration or vertical integration in the industry, a past history of vertical integration in the industry, a past history of vertical acquisitions by the acquiring company, and significant barriers to entry resulting from the merger. This approach to determining the legality of vertical mergers has been criticized by some commentators. They argue that vertical integration may yield efficiencies of distribution and that vertical integration by merger may be more economically efficient than vertical integration by internal expansion. The Justice Department generally affords greater weight to efficiency arguments in cases involving vertical mergers than in cases involving horizontal mergers. The department generally applies the same criteria to all nonhorizontal mergers. We discuss these criteria in the upcoming section on conglomerate mergers.

LOG ON

The federal government's merger guidelines are referred to various times in this chapter. To see the actual text of the guidelines, visit the U.S. Department of Justice's website: **www.justice.gov/atr/merger-enforcement.**

Conglomerate Mergers

 State what a conglomerate merger is and describe the factors taken into account in a determination of whether the merger violates § 7.

A conglomerate merger is a merger between two firms that neither compete with each other nor have a supplier–customer relationship with each other. Conglomerate mergers may be either *market extension* mergers or *product extension* mergers. In a market extension merger, the acquiring firm expands into a new geographic market by purchasing a firm already doing business in that market. For example, a conglomerate that owns an East Coast grocery chain buys a West Coast grocery chain. In a product extension merger, the acquiring firm diversifies its operations by purchasing a

company in a new product market. For example, a conglomerate with interests in the aerospace and electronics industries purchases a department store chain.

There is considerable disagreement over the economic effects of conglomerate acquisitions. As later discussion will reveal, conglomerate mergers have been attacked with some degree of success under § 7 if they involve potential reciprocity, serve to eliminate potential competition, or give an acquired firm an unfair advantage over its competitors. Nevertheless, there is significant sentiment that the Clayton Act is not well suited to dealing with conglomerate mergers. This realization has produced calls for specific legislation on the subject. Such legislation has not been enacted, however.

Potential Reciprocity Conglomerate mergers that involve *potential reciprocity* are among those sometimes held to be prohibited by § 7. A conglomerate merger may create a risk of potential reciprocity if the acquired firm produces a product regularly purchased by the acquiring firm's suppliers. Such suppliers, eager to continue their relationship with the acquiring firm, may thereafter purchase the acquired firm's products rather than those of its competitors.

Elimination of Potential Competition Some conglomerate mergers may eliminate potential competition in ways similar to vertical mergers, and thus may be vulnerable to attack under § 7. If existing competitors perceive the acquiring company as a potential entrant in the acquired company's market, the acquiring company's entry by means of a conglomerate acquisition may result in the loss of the moderating influence that it had while waiting in the wings. In addition, when the acquiring company actually enters the new market by acquiring a well-established competitor rather than by starting a new competitor through internal expansion or by making a toehold acquisition, the market is deprived of the potential for increased competition flowing from the reduction in concentration that would have accompanied the latter strategies.

Supreme Court decisions suggest, however, that a high degree of proof is required before either of these potential competition arguments will be accepted. Arguments that a conglomerate merger eliminated a *perceived potential entrant* must be accompanied by proof that existing competitors actually perceived the acquiring firm as a potential entrant. Arguments that a conglomerate acquisition eliminated an *actual* potential entrant (and thereby deprived the market of the benefits of reduced concentration) must be accompanied by evidence that the acquiring firm had the ability to enter the market

The Global Business Environment

A planned merger involving firms whose business is international in scope may face scrutiny outside the United States even if the FTC and the Justice Department decide not to challenge the merger under U.S. law. Legal regimes for controlling mergers now exist in numerous nations, with applicable rules and enforcement approaches that do not always match those of the United States. Several years ago, for instance, legal objections lodged by the European Commission caused a highly publicized conglomerate merger-to-be involving the General Electric and Honeywell firms not to come about despite U.S. regulators' clearance of the deal.

The European Union's Merger Regulation, promulgated in furtherance of competition provisions in the Treaty of Rome, bars mergers that may "create or strengthen a [firm's] dominant position." As it has been applied, the Merger Regulation may focus somewhat more on protecting *competitors* than on preserving the *competitive process*. In this sense, the EU approach differs from the approach called for by the U.S. rule–the Clayton Act provision prohibiting mergers that may "substantially lessen competition." The U.S. approach is also likely to allow greater ability to argue that a merger may produce economic efficiencies than does the EU's Merger Regulation.

In addition, the respective enforcement mechanisms in the U.S. and the EU differ. Under U.S. law, the FTC or the Justice Department normally must take legal action in court in order to block a planned merger, whereas in the EU, the commission has considerable authority to quash a merger through its own action.

Notwithstanding the differences noted above, U.S. regulators and the European Commission fairly often reach the same conclusions regarding proposed mergers—especially those of the horizontal variety. Recent years have witnessed the development of agreements under which the EU Commission, the FTC, and the Justice Department have committed to sharing information and strategies regarding the regulation of mergers.

---

by internal expansion or a toehold acquisition and that doing so would have ultimately yielded a substantial reduction in concentration.

Unfair Advantage to Acquired Firm Finally, conglomerate mergers may violate § 7 in certain instances when the acquired firm obtains an unfair advantage over its competitors. When a large firm acquires a firm that already enjoys a significant market position, the acquired firm may gain an unfair advantage over its competitors through its ability to draw on the greater resources and expertise of its new owner. This advantage may entrench the acquired firm in its market by deterring existing competitors from actively competing with it for market share and by causing other potential competitors to be reluctant to enter the market.

Nearly all of the important conglomerate merger cases in recent years have been settled out of court. As a result, we do not have a clear indication of the Supreme Court's current thinking on conglomerate merger issues. The Justice Department takes the position that the primary theories to be used by the department in attacking all *nonhorizontal* mergers are the *elimination of perceived and actual potential competition* theories. In employing these analytical tools, the department also considers other economic factors. These include the degree of concentration in the acquired firm's market; the existence of barriers to entry into the market and the presence or absence of other firms with a comparable ability to enter; and the market share of the acquired firm (with challenges being unlikely if this is 5 percent or less and likely if it is 20 percent or more). We do not yet know whether the Supreme Court will accept this more restrictive view of § 7's scope.

Clayton Act Section 8

LO50-8 Identify the particular risk of anticompetitive conduct that Clayton Act § 8 is designed to address.

If the same individuals control theoretically competing corporations, an obvious potential exists for anticompetitive conduct such as price-fixing or division of markets. Section 8 of the Clayton Act was designed to minimize the risks posed by such interlocks. Initially, § 8 prohibited any person from serving as a director of two or more corporations (other than banks or common carriers) if each corporation had "capital, surplus, and undivided profits aggregating more than $1,000,000" and the corporations were, or had been, competitors, "so that elimination of competition by agreement between them" would violate any of the antitrust laws. The Antitrust Amendments Act of 1990 amended § 8's original language to increase the amount required to trigger the statute from $1 million to $10 million (a figure to be adjusted annually by an amount equal to the percentage increase or decrease in the gross national product). The triggering figure was $38,204,000 as of the time this book went to press.

Section 8 establishes a per se standard of liability in the sense that a violation may be demonstrated without proof that the interlock harmed competition. Until 1990, however, the statute's prohibition against interlocks was limited in scope because it barred only interlocking *directorates*. Nothing in the original language of § 8 prohibited a person from serving as an *officer* of two competing corporations, or as an officer of one firm and a director of its competitor. The Antitrust Amendments Act of 1990, however, expanded the scope of the statute by including senior officers (defined as officers elected or chosen by the board of directors) within its reach.

Although government enforcement of § 8 was historically lax, the past three-plus decades have sometimes offered signs of growing government interest in the statute. Signs of renewed government interest in § 8 produced significant concern in an era of conglomerate merger activity. Given the wide diversification that characterizes many large corporations, it would be increasingly easy to demonstrate some degree of competitive overlap among a substantial number of large, diversified corporations. Critics alleged that § 8 has operated to discourage qualified persons from serving as directors when no potential for actual competitive harm exists. In response to such criticism, the Antitrust Amendments Act of 1990 specified that individuals may serve as officers or directors of competing corporations when the "competitive overlap" between them is an insignificant part of either company's total sales. This exception took away some of § 8's potential bite.

The Robinson–Patman Act

LO50-9 Describe each of the three types of price discrimination addressed by the Robinson–Patman Act (primary level, secondary level, and tertiary level).

Section 2 of the Clayton Act originally prohibited local and territorial price discrimination by sellers, a practice monopolists frequently used to destroy smaller competitors. A large company operating in a number of geographic markets would sell at or below cost in markets where it faced local competitors and would then make up its losses by selling at higher prices in areas where it faced no competition. Faced with such tactics, the smaller local competitors might eventually be driven out of business. Section 2 was aimed at such primary level (or *first-line*) price discrimination.

During the 1930s, Congress was confronted with complaints that large chain stores were using their buying power to induce manufacturers to sell to them at prices lower than those offered to their smaller, independent competitors. Chain stores were also inclined to seek and obtain other payments and services their smaller competitors did not receive. Being able to purchase at lower prices and to obtain discriminatory payments and services arguably gave large firms a competitive advantage over their smaller competitors. Such price discrimination in sales to the competing customers of a particular seller is known as secondary level (or *second-line*) price discrimination. The *Volvo Trucks* decision, which appears later in the chapter, addresses issues that arise in secondary level price discrimination cases.

In addition, the customers of a manufacturer's favored customer (such as a wholesaler receiving a functional discount) may gain a competitive advantage over *their* competitors (e.g., other retailers purchasing directly from the manufacturer at a higher price) if the favored customer passes on all or a portion of its discount to its customers. This form of price discrimination is known as tertiary level (or *third-line*) price discrimination.

Congress responded to these problems by passing the Robinson–Patman Act in 1936. The Robinson–Patman Act preserved Clayton Act § 2's ban on primary-level price discrimination. It also amended § 2 to outlaw secondary- and tertiary-level direct price discrimination, as well as indirect price discrimination in the form of discriminatory payments and services to a seller's customers. Since its enactment, the Robinson–Patman Act has been the subject of widespread dissatisfaction and criticism. Critics have long charged that the act often protects competitors at the expense of promoting competition. Government enforcement of the act has been haphazard over the years, with prominent officials in the Justice Department and the Federal Trade Commission sometimes voicing disagreement with the act's underlying policies and assumptions. This government stance, when combined with Supreme Court decisions making private enforcement of the act difficult, raises questions about the act's future usefulness as a component of our antitrust laws.

Jurisdiction The Robinson–Patman Act applies only to discriminatory acts that occur "in commerce." This test is narrower than the "affecting commerce" test employed under the Sherman Act. At least one of the discriminatory acts complained of must take place in interstate commerce. Thus, the act probably would not apply if a Texas manufacturer discriminated in price in sales to two Texas customers. Some lower federal courts have indicated, however, that even wholly intrastate sales may be deemed sufficiently "in commerce" if the nonfavored buyer bought the goods for resale to out-of-state customers.

Section 2(a)
Section 2(a) of the Robinson–Patman Act prohibits sellers, in certain instances, from *discriminating in price* "between different purchasers of commodities of like grade or quality." Such discrimination is prohibited when its effect may be to (1) "substantially . . . lessen competition or tend to create a monopoly in any line of commerce" or (2) "injure, destroy, or prevent competition with any person who either grants [*primary level*] or knowingly receives [*secondary level*] the benefit of such discrimination, or with the customers of either of them [*tertiary level*]."

> **LO50-10** Identify the elements of a price discrimination claim under Robinson–Patman Act § 2(a).

Price Discrimination To violate § 2(a), a seller must have made two or more sales to different purchasers at different prices. Merely quoting a discriminatory price or refusing to sell except at a discriminatory price does not violate the statute because no actual purchase is involved. For the same reason, price discrimination in lease or consignment transactions is not covered by § 2(a). Actual sales at different prices to different purchasers will not be treated as discriminatory unless the sales were fairly close in time.

Section 2(a) does not directly address the legality of *functional discounts*. Such discounts are sometimes granted to buyers at various levels in a product's chain of distribution because of differences in the functions those buyers perform in the distribution system. The Supreme Court has indicated that the legality of such discounts depends on their competitive effect. If a seller charges wholesale customers lower prices than it charges retail customers, the Robinson–Patman Act is not violated unless the lower wholesale prices are somehow passed on to retailers in competition with the seller's retail customers.

Commodities of Like Grade and Quality Section 2(a) applies only to price discrimination in the sale of *commodities*. Price discrimination involving intangibles, real estate, or services must be challenged under the Sherman Act as a restraint of trade or an attempt to monopolize or

under the FTC Act as an unfair method of competition. The essence of price discrimination is that two or more buyers are charged differing prices for the *same* commodity. Sales of commodities of varying grades or quality at varying prices, therefore, do not violate § 2(a) so long as uniform prices are charged for commodities of equal quality. Some physical difference in the grade or quality of two products must be shown to justify a price differential between them. Differences solely in the brand name or label under which a product is sold—such as the seller's standard brand and a "house" brand sold to a large customer for resale under the customer's label—do not justify discriminatory pricing.

Anticompetitive Effect Only price discrimination having a probable anticompetitive effect is prohibited by § 2(a). Traditionally, courts have required a higher degree of proof of likely competitive injury in cases involving primary-level price discrimination (which may damage the seller's competitors) than in cases involving secondary- or tertiary-level discrimination (which threatens competition among the seller's customers or its customers' customers). To prove a primary-level violation, a market analysis must show that competitive harm has occurred as a result of the seller's engaging in significant and sustained price discrimination with the intent of punishing or disciplining a competitor. Proof of predatory pricing is often offered as evidence of a seller's anticompetitive intent. The *Brooke Group* case, which follows shortly, addresses predatory pricing claims under the Robinson–Patman Act and emphasizes that likely harm to competition—not merely to a competitor—remains the critical focus.

In secondary- or tertiary-level cases, courts tend to infer the existence of competitive injury from evidence of substantial price discrimination between competing purchasers over time. Some qualifications on this point are in order, however. Price discrimination for a short period of time ordinarily does not support an inference of competitive injury. Likewise, if the evidence indicates that nonfavored buyers could have purchased the same goods from other sellers at prices identical to those the defendant seller charged its favored customers, no competitive injury is inferred. Finally, buyers seeking treble damages for secondary- or tertiary-level harm must still prove that they suffered actual damages as a result of a violation of the act.

The *Volvo Trucks* decision, which appears immediately after the *Brooke Group* case, examines key issues presented in secondary-level cases.

Brooke Group Ltd. v. Brown & Williamson Tobacco Corp.
509 U.S. 209 (1993)

Brown & Williamson Tobacco Corp. (BW) and Brooke Group Ltd. (referred to here by its former corporate name, Liggett Corp.) are two of only six firms of significant consequence in the oligopolistic cigarette manufacturing industry. In 1980, BW's share of the national cigarette market was roughly 12 percent. This share placed BW a distant third behind market leaders Philip Morris and R. J. Reynolds. Liggett's share was less than half of BW's. Liggett pioneered the development of the economy segment of the national cigarette market in 1980 by introducing a popular line of "black and white" generic cigarettes (low-priced cigarettes sold in plain white packages with simple black lettering). As Liggett's sales of generic cigarettes became substantial, other cigarette manufacturers started introducing economy-priced cigarettes. In 1984, BW introduced a black and white cigarette whose net price was lower than Liggett's. BW achieved this lower price by offering volume rebates to wholesalers.

Liggett sued BW, claiming that BW's volume rebates amounted to price discrimination having a reasonable probability of injuring competition, in violation of § 2(a) of the Robinson–Patman Act. Specifically, Liggett alleged that BW's rebates were integral to a scheme of predatory pricing, under which BW reduced its net prices for generic cigarettes below average variable costs. Liggett further alleged that this pricing by BW was designed to pressure Liggett to raise its list prices on generic cigarettes so that the percentage price difference between generic and branded cigarettes would narrow. As a result, according to Liggett, the growth of the economy segment would be restrained and BW would thereby be able to preserve its supracompetitive profits on branded cigarettes. Liggett further asserted that it could not afford to reduce its wholesale rebates without losing market share to BW. Therefore, Liggett claimed that its only choice, if it wished to avoid prolonged losses on the generic line that had become its principal product, was to raise retail prices.

After a 115-day trial, the jury returned a verdict in Liggett's favor for $49.6 million in damages. The district court trebled this amount. After reviewing the trial record, however, the district court concluded that BW was entitled to prevail as a matter of law. The court therefore set aside the jury's verdict and entered judgment in BW's favor. Liggett appealed. The Fourth Circuit Court of Appeals affirmed, holding that there cannot be liability for predatory price discrimination that allegedly takes place in the context of an oligopoly such as the cigarette industry. The Supreme Court granted certiorari.

Kennedy, Justice

Liggett contends that BW's discriminatory volume rebates to wholesalers threatened substantial competitive injury by furthering a predatory pricing scheme designed to purge competition from the economy segment of the cigarette market. This type of injury, which harms direct competitors of the discriminating seller, is known as primary-line injury. [P]rimary-line competitive injury under the Robinson–Patman Act is of the same general character as the injury inflicted by predatory pricing schemes actionable under § 2 of the Sherman Act. [T]he essence of the claim under either statute is the same.

Accordingly, whether the claim alleges predatory pricing under the Sherman Act or primary-line price discrimination under the Robinson–Patman Act, two prerequisites to recovery [exist]. First, a plaintiff seeking to establish competitive injury resulting from a rival's low prices must prove that the prices complained of are below an appropriate measure of its rival's costs. [Second, the plaintiff must demonstrate] that the competitor had a reasonable prospect [if the claim is brought under the Robinson–Patman Act], or . . . a dangerous probability [if the claim is brought under § 2 of the Sherman Act], of recouping its investment in below-cost prices. Recoupment is the ultimate object of an unlawful predatory-pricing scheme; it is the means by which a predator profits from predation. Without it, predatory pricing

produces lower aggregate prices in the market, and consumer welfare is enhanced. That below-cost pricing may impose painful losses on its target is of no moment to the antitrust laws if competition is not injured.

For recoupment to occur, below-cost pricing must be capable . . . of producing the intended effects on the firm's rivals, whether driving them from the market, or, as was alleged to be the goal here, causing them to raise their prices to supracompetitive levels within a disciplined oligopoly. If circumstances indicate that below-cost pricing could likely produce its intended effect on the target, there is still the further question whether it would be likely to injure competition in the relevant market. The plaintiff must demonstrate that there is a likelihood that the predatory scheme alleged would cause a rise in prices above a competitive level that would be sufficient to compensate for the amounts expended on the predation. These prerequisites to recovery are not easy to establish, but . . . they are essential components of real market injury.

Liggett . . . allege[s] . . . that BW sought to preserve supracompetitive profits on branded cigarettes by pressuring Liggett to raise its generic cigarette prices through a process of tacit collusion with the other cigarette companies. Tacit collusion, sometimes called oligopolistic price coordination or conscious parallelism, describes the process, not in itself unlawful, by which firms in a concentrated market might in effect share monopoly power, setting their prices at a profit-maximizing, supracompetitive level by recognizing their shared economic interests and their interdependence with respect to price and output decisions.

In *Matsushita Electric Industrial Co. v. Zenith Radio Corp.*, 475 U.S. 574 (1986), we remarked upon the general implausibility of predatory pricing. *Matsushita* observed that such schemes are even more improbable when they require coordinated action among several firms. However unlikely predatory pricing by multiple firms may be when they conspire, it is even less likely when, as here, there is no express coordination. Firms that seek to recoup predatory losses through the conscious parallelism of oligopoly must rely on uncertain and ambiguous signals to achieve concerted action. The signals are subject to misinterpretation and are a blunt and imprecise means of ensuring smooth cooperation, especially in the context of changing or unprecedented market circumstances. This anticompetitive minuet is most difficult to compose and to perform, even for a disciplined oligopoly.

[O]n the whole, tacit cooperation among oligopolists must be considered the least likely means of recouping predatory losses. In addition to the difficulty of achieving effective tacit coordination and the high likelihood that any attempt to discipline will produce an outbreak of competition, the predator's present losses in a case like this fall on it alone, while the later supracompetitive profits must be shared with every other oligopolist in proportion to its market share, including the intended victim. In this case, for example, BW, with its 11-12 percent share of the cigarette market, would have had to generate around $9 in supracompetitive profits for each $1 invested in predation; the remaining $8 would belong to its competitors, who had taken no risk.

[However,] [t]o the extent that the Court of Appeals may have held that the interdependent pricing of an oligopoly may never provide a means for achieving recoupment and so may not form the basis of a primary-line injury claim, we disagree. A predatory pricing scheme designed to preserve or create a stable oligopoly, if successful, can injure consumers in the same way, and to the same extent, as one designed to bring about a monopoly. However unlikely that possibility may be as a general matter, when the realities of the market and the record facts indicate that it has occurred and was likely to have succeeded, theory will not stand in the way of liability. The Robinson–Patman Act . . . suggests no exclusion from coverage when primary-line injury occurs in an oligopoly setting. We decline to create a per se rule of nonliability [under the Robinson–Patman Act] for predatory price discrimination when recoupment is alleged to take place through supracompetitive oligopoly pricing.

Although Liggett's theory of liability, as an abstract matter, is within the reach of the statute, we agree with the [lower courts] that Liggett was not entitled to submit its case to the jury. Liggett . . . failed to demonstrate competitive injury as a matter of law. The evidence is inadequate to show that in pursuing [an alleged below-cost pricing] scheme, BW had a reasonable prospect of recovering its losses from below-cost pricing through slowing the growth of generics.

The only means by which BW is alleged to have established oligopoly pricing . . . is through tacit price coordination with the other cigarette firms. Yet the situation facing the cigarette companies in the 1980s would have made such tacit coordination unmanageable. Tacit coordination is facilitated by a stable market environment, fungible products, and a small number of variables upon which the firms seeking to coordinate their pricing may focus. By 1984, however, the cigarette market was in an obvious state of flux. The introduction of generic cigarettes in 1980 represented the first serious price competition in the cigarette market since the 1930s. This development was bound to unsettle previous expectations and patterns of market conduct and to reduce the cigarette firms' ability to predict each other's behavior. The larger number of product types and pricing variables also decreased the probability of effective parallel pricing.

Even if all the cigarette companies were willing to participate in a scheme to restrain the growth of the generic segment, they would not have been able to coordinate their actions and raise prices above a competitive level unless they understood that BW's entry into the [economy] segment was not a genuine effort to compete with Liggett. If even one other firm misinterpreted BW's entry as an effort to expand share, a chain reaction of competitive responses would almost certainly have resulted, and oligopoly discipline would have broken down, perhaps irretrievably. Liggett argues that [BW's] maintaining existing list prices while offering substantial rebates to wholesalers was a signal to the other cigarette firms that BW did not intend to attract additional smokers to the generic segment by its entry. But a reasonable jury could not conclude that this pricing structure eliminated or rendered insignificant the risk that the other firms might misunderstand BW's entry as a competitive move.

We hold that the evidence cannot support a finding that BW's alleged scheme was likely to result in oligopolistic price coordination and sustained supracompetitive pricing in the generic segment of the national cigarette market. Without this, BW had no reasonable prospect of recouping its predatory losses and could not inflict the injury to competition the antitrust laws prohibit.

Judgment for BW affirmed.

Volvo Trucks North America, Inc. v. Reeder-Simco GMC, Inc.
546 U.S. 164 (2006)

Volvo Trucks North America, Inc. (Volvo) manufactures heavy-duty trucks. Reeder-Simco GMC, Inc. (Reeder), which became an authorized dealer of Volvo trucks in 1995, generally sold Volvo trucks through a competitive bidding process. In this process, the retail customer describes its specific product requirements and invites bids from several dealers. Once a Volvo dealer receives the customer's specifications, the dealer turns to Volvo and requests a discount or "concession" off the wholesale price (set at 80 percent of the published retail price). Volvo decides on a case-by-case basis whether to offer a discount and, if so, what the discount rate will be. The dealer then uses the discount offered by Volvo in preparing its bid, and purchases trucks from Volvo only if the retail customer accepts its bid.

Reeder was one of many Volvo dealers, each assigned by Volvo to a geographic territory. Although nothing prohibits a Volvo dealer from bidding outside its territory, Reeder seldom bid against another Volvo dealer. In the atypical event that the same retail customer solicited a bid from more than one Volvo dealer, Volvo's stated policy was to provide the same price concession to each dealer competing head-to-head for the same sale. After learning that Volvo had given another dealer a price concession greater than the concessions Reeder typically received, Reeder sued Volvo. Reeder claimed that Volvo violated the Robinson–Patman Act by providing other dealers more favorable price concessions than those offered to Reeder and, in the process, adversely affecting Reeder's sales and profits.

At trial, Reeder presented evidence concerning two instances when Reeder bid against another Volvo dealer for a particular sale. In one instance, each Volvo dealer received the same concession from Volvo, and neither Volvo dealer's bid was accepted by the retail customer. The other instance involved Hiland Dairy, which solicited bids from both Reeder and Southwest Missouri Truck Center (also a Volvo dealer). In accordance with its policy, Volvo initially offered the two dealers the same concession. Hiland selected Southwest Missouri, a dealer from which Hiland had previously purchased trucks. After a later price squabble between Southwest Missouri and Hiland, Volvo increased the size of the discount it had offered Southwest Missouri in order to help make certain that the Southwest Missouri–Hiland deal would actually be accomplished.

For the most part, Reeder's evidence at trial focused on comparisons between concessions Volvo offered when Reeder bid against non-Volvo dealers and concessions accorded to other Volvo dealers similarly bidding against non-Volvo dealers for other sales. Reeder's evidence compared concessions Reeder received on four occasions when it bid successfully against non-Volvo dealers—meaning that Reeder therefore purchased Volvo trucks—with more favorable concessions that other successful Volvo dealers received in connection with bidding processes in which Reeder did not participate. In addition, Reeder identified concessions offered by Volvo on several occasions when Reeder bid unsuccessfully against non-Volvo dealers, and compared those concessions with more favorable concessions received by other Volvo dealers that gained contracts on which Reeder did not bid.

A federal district court jury found that there was a reasonable possibility that discriminatory pricing harmed competition between Reeder and other Volvo truck dealers, and that Volvo's discriminatory pricing injured Reeder to the extent of $1.3 million. The district judge tripled that amount in accordance with federal antitrust law and entered judgment accordingly. Volvo appealed, and the U.S. Court of Appeals for the Eighth Circuit affirmed. Rejecting Volvo's contention that competitive bidding situations do not give rise to claims under the Robinson–Patman Act, the court of appeals observed that Reeder was "more than an unsuccessful bidder." The instances in which Reeder "actually purchased Volvo trucks following successful bids on contracts," the court concluded, were sufficient to render Reeder a purchaser within the meaning of the statute. The court of appeals also determined that a jury could reasonably decide that Reeder was "in actual competition" with favored dealers, and that the jury could properly find from the evidence that Reeder had proven competitive injury resulting from price discrimination. The U.S. Supreme Court granted Volvo's petition for a writ of certiorari.

Ginsburg, Justice

We granted certiorari to resolve this question: May a manufacturer be held liable for secondary-line price discrimination under the Robinson–Patman Act in the absence of a showing that the manufacturer discriminated between dealers competing to resell its product to the same retail customer? Satisfied that the Court of Appeals erred in answering that question in the affirmative, we reverse the Eighth Circuit's judgment.

The Robinson–Patman Act, 15 U.S.C. § 13(a), provides, in relevant part:

It shall be unlawful for any person engaged in commerce . . . to discriminate in price between different purchasers of commodities of like grade and quality, . . . where the effect of such discrimination may be substantially to lessen competition or tend to create a monopoly in any line of commerce, or to injure, destroy, or prevent competition with any person who either grants or knowingly receives the benefit of such discrimination, or with customers of either of them. . . .

Mindful of the purposes of the Robinson–Patman Act and of the antitrust laws generally, we have explained that Robinson–Patman does not "ban all price differences charged to different purchasers of commodities of like grade and quality." *Brooke Group Ltd. v. Brown & Williamson Tobacco Corp.*, 509 U.S. 209, 220 (1993). Rather, the Act proscribes "price discrimination only to the extent that it threatens to injure competition." *Id.* Our decisions describe three categories of competitive injury that may give rise to a Robinson–Patman Act claim: primary line, secondary line, and tertiary line. Primary-line cases entail conduct—most conspicuously, predatory pricing—that injures competition at the level of the discriminating seller and its direct competitors. Secondary-line cases, of which this is one, involve price discrimination that injures competition among the discriminating seller's customers (here, Volvo's dealerships); cases in this category typically refer to "favored" and "disfavored" purchasers. Tertiary-line cases involve injury to competition at the level of the purchaser's customers.

To establish the secondary-line injury of which it complains, Reeder had to show that (1) the relevant Volvo truck sales were made in interstate commerce; (2) the trucks were of "like grade and quality"; (3) Volvo "discriminate[d] in price between" Reeder and another purchaser of Volvo trucks; and (4) "the effect of such discrimination may be . . . to injure, destroy, or prevent competition" to the advantage of a favored purchaser, i.e., one who "receive[d] the benefit of such discrimination." 15 U.S.C. § 13(a). It is undisputed that Reeder has satisfied the first and second requirements. Volvo maintains that Reeder cannot satisfy the third and fourth requirements, because Reeder has not identified any differentially priced transaction in which it was both a "purchaser" under the Act and "in actual competition" with a favored purchaser for the same customer.

A hallmark of the requisite competitive injury, our decisions indicate, is the diversion of sales or profits from a disfavored purchaser to a favored purchaser. We have also recognized that a permissible inference of competitive injury may arise from evidence that a favored competitor received a significant price reduction over a substantial period of time. Absent actual competition with a favored Volvo dealer, however, Reeder cannot establish the competitive injury required under the Act.

The evidence Reeder offered at trial falls into three categories: (1) comparisons of concessions Reeder received for four successful bids against non-Volvo dealers, with larger concessions other successful Volvo dealers received for different sales on which Reeder did not bid (purchase-to-purchase comparisons); (2) comparisons of concessions offered to Reeder in connection with several unsuccessful bids against non-Volvo dealers, with greater concessions accorded other Volvo dealers who competed successfully for different sales on which Reeder did not bid (offer-to-purchase comparisons); and (3) evidence of two occasions on which Reeder bid against another Volvo dealer (head-to-head comparisons). The Court of Appeals concluded that Reeder demonstrated competitive injury under the Act because Reeder competed with favored purchasers "at the same functional level . . . and within the same geographic market." As we see it, however, selective comparisons of the kind Reeder presented do not show the injury to competition targeted by the Robinson–Patman Act.

Both the purchase-to-purchase and the offer-to-purchase comparisons fall short, for in none of the discrete instances on which Reeder relied did Reeder compete with beneficiaries of the alleged discrimination for the same customer. Nor did Reeder even attempt to show that the compared dealers were consistently favored vis-à-vis Reeder. Reeder simply paired occasions on which it competed with non-Volvo dealers for a sale to Customer A with instances in which other Volvo dealers competed with non-Volvo dealers for a sale to Customer B. The compared incidents were tied to no systematic study and were separated in time by as many as seven months.

We decline to permit an inference of competitive injury from evidence of such a mix-and-match, manipulable quality. No similar risk of manipulation occurs in cases kin to the chainstore paradigm. Here, there is no discrete "favored" dealer comparable to a chainstore or a large independent department store—at least, Reeder's evidence is insufficient to support an inference of such a dealer or set of dealers. For all we know, Reeder, on occasion, might have gotten a better deal vis-à-vis one or more of the dealers in its comparisons.

Reeder may have competed with other Volvo dealers for the opportunity to bid on potential sales in a broad geographic area. At that initial stage, however, competition is not affected by differential pricing. A dealer in the competitive bidding process here at issue approaches Volvo for a price concession only after it has been selected by a retail customer to submit a bid. Competition for an opportunity to bid . . . is based on a variety of factors, including the existence of a relationship between the potential bidder and the customer, geography, and reputation. That Volvo dealers may bid for sales in the same geographic area does not import that they in fact competed for the same customer-tailored sales. In sum, the purchase-to-purchase and offer-to-purchase comparisons fail to show that Volvo sold at a lower price to Reeder's "competitors," hence those comparisons do not support an inference of competitive injury.

Reeder did offer evidence of two instances in which it competed head to head with another Volvo dealer. When multiple dealers bid for the business of the same customer, only one dealer will win the business and thereafter purchase the supplier's product to fulfill its contractual commitment. Because Robinson–Patman prohibits only discrimination between different purchasers, Volvo argues, the Act does not reach markets characterized by competitive bidding and special-order sales, as opposed to sales from inventory. We need not decide that question today. Assuming the Act applies to the head-to-head transactions, Reeder did not establish that it was disfavored vis-à-vis other Volvo dealers in the rare instances in which they competed for the same sale—let alone that the alleged discrimination was substantial.

Reeder's evidence showed loss of only one sale to another Volvo dealer, a sale of 12 trucks that would have generated $30,000 in gross profits for Reeder. Per its policy, Volvo initially offered Reeder and the other dealer the same concession. Volvo ultimately granted a larger concession to the other dealer, but only after it had won the bid. In the only other instance of head-to-head competition Reeder identified, Volvo increased Reeder's initial 17% discount to 18.9%, to match the discount offered to the other competing Volvo dealer; neither dealer won the bid. In short, if price discrimination between two purchasers existed at all, it was not of such magnitude as to affect substantially competition between Reeder and the "favored" Volvo dealer.

Interbrand competition, our opinions affirm, is the "primary concern of antitrust law." [Case citation omitted.] The Robinson–Patman Act signals no large departure from that main concern. Even if the Act's text could be construed in the manner urged by Reeder and embraced by the Court of Appeals, we would resist interpretation geared more to the protection of existing competitors than to the stimulation of competition. In the case before us, there is no evidence that any favored purchaser possesses market power, the allegedly favored purchasers are dealers with little resemblance to large independent department stores or chain operations, and the supplier's selective price discounting fosters competition among suppliers of different brands. By declining to extend Robinson–Patman's governance to such cases, we continue to construe the Act "consistently with broader policies of the antitrust laws." *Brooke Group*, 509 U.S. at 220.

Court of Appeals decision reversed; case remanded for further proceedings.

Defenses to Section 2(a) Liability

 List the defenses to a § 2(a) price discrimination claim.

There are three major statutory defenses to liability under § 2(a): *cost justification*, *changing conditions*, and *meeting competition in good faith*.

Cost Justification Section 2(a) legalizes price differentials that do no more than make an appropriate allowance for differences in the "cost of manufacture, sale, or delivery resulting from the differing methods or quantities" in which goods are sold or delivered to buyers. This defense recognizes the reality that it may be less costly for a seller to service some buyers than others. Sales to buyers purchasing large quantities may in some cases be more cost-effective than small-quantity sales to their competitors.

Sellers are allowed to pass on such cost savings to their customers.

Utilizing this *cost justification* defense is difficult and expensive for sellers, however, because quantity discounts must be supported by actual evidence of cost savings. Sellers are allowed to average their costs and classify their customers into categories based on their average sales costs. The customers included in any particular classification, however, must be sufficiently similar to justify similar treatment.

Changing Conditions Section 2(a) specifically exempts price discriminations that reflect "changing conditions in the market for or the marketability of the goods." The *changing conditions* defense has been narrowly confined to temporary situations caused by the physical nature of the goods. Examples include the deterioration of perishable goods and a declining market for seasonal goods. This defense also applies to forced judicial sales of the goods (such as during bankruptcy proceedings involving the seller) and to good faith sales by sellers that have decided to cease selling the goods in question.

Meeting Competition Section 2(b) of the Robinson–Patman Act states that price discrimination may be lawful if the discriminatory lower price was charged "in good faith to meet an equally low price of a competitor." This *meeting competition* defense is necessary to prevent the act from stifling the very competition it was designed to preserve. For example, suppose Sony Corporation has been selling a particular electronic device to its customers for $100 per unit. Sony then learns that Sharp Electronics is offering a comparable electronic device to Acme Appliance Stores for $80 per unit. Acme, however, competes with Better Buy Video Stores, a Sony customer that has recently been charged the $100 price. Should Sony be forced to refrain from offering the lower competitive price to Acme for fear that Better Buy will charge Sony with price discrimination if it does so? If Sony cannot offer the lower competitive price to Acme, competition between Sony and Sharp will plainly suffer.

Section 2(b) avoids this undesirable result by allowing a seller to charge a lower price to certain customers if the seller has reasonable grounds for believing that the lower price is necessary to meet an equally low price offered by a competitor. Sellers may meet competition *offensively* (to gain a new customer) or *defensively* (to keep an existing customer). The meeting competition defense is subject to significant qualifications, however. First, the lower price must be necessary to meet a lower price charged by a competitor of the *seller*, not to enable a customer of the seller to compete more effectively with that customer's competitors. Second, the seller may lawfully seek only to *meet*, not *beat*, its competitor's price. A seller cannot, however, be held in violation of the act for beating a competitor's price if it did so unknowingly in a good faith attempt to meet competition. Third, the seller may reduce its price only to meet competitors' prices for products of *similar quality*.

Courts also have held that the discriminatory price must be a response to an individual competitive situation rather than the product of a seller's wholesale adoption of a competitor's discriminatory pricing system. However, a seller's competitive response need not be on a customer-by-customer basis, so long as the lower price is offered only to those customers that the seller reasonably believes are being offered a lower price by the seller's competitors.

Indirect Price Discrimination

 Explain what constitutes indirect price discrimination for purposes of the Robinson–Patman Act.

When Congress enacted the Robinson–Patman Act, it also addressed indirect price discrimination, which takes the form of a seller's discriminating among competing buyers by making discriminatory payments to selected buyers or by furnishing certain buyers with services not made available to their competitors. Three sections of the act are designed to prevent such practices.

False Brokerage Section 2(c) prohibits sellers from granting, and buyers from receiving, any "commission, brokerage, or other compensation, or any allowance or discount in lieu thereof, except for services rendered in connection with the sale or purchase of goods." This provision prevents large buyers, either directly or through subsidiary brokerage agents, from receiving phony commissions or brokerage payments from their suppliers.

Section 2(c) establishes a per se standard of liability. No demonstration of probable anticompetitive effect is required for a violation. Neither the cost justification nor meeting competition defense is available in 2(c) cases. Individual plaintiffs still must prove that they have suffered some injury as a result of a 2(c) violation, however, before they are entitled to recover damages.

Discriminatory Payments and Services Sellers and their customers benefit from merchandising activities that customers employ to promote the sellers' products. Section 2(d) prohibits sellers from making *discriminatory payments* to competing customers for such customer-performed services as advertising and promotional activities or such customer-provided facilities as shelf space. Section 2(e) prohibits sellers from discriminating in the services they provide to competing customers, such as by providing favored customers with a display case or a demonstration kit.

A seller may lawfully make payments or provide services to customers only if the payments or services are made available to all competing customers on proportionately equal terms. This means that the seller must inform all customers of the availability of the payments or services and must distribute them on some rational basis, such as the quantity of goods bought by the customer. The seller must also devise a flexible plan that enables its various classes of customers to participate in the payment or services program in an appropriate way.

As does § 2(c), §§ 2(d), and 2(e) create a per se liability standard. No proof of probable harm to competition is required for a violation; no cost justification defense is available. The meeting competition defense is applicable, however, to actions under §§ 2(d) and 2(e).

Buyer Inducement of Discrimination

Section 2(f) of the Robinson–Patman Act makes it illegal for a buyer *knowingly to induce or receive* a discriminatory price in violation of § 2(a). The logic of the section is that buyers who are successful in demanding discriminatory prices should face liability along with the sellers charging discriminatory prices. To violate § 2(f), the buyer must know that the price the buyer received was unjustifiably discriminatory. This means that the price probably was neither cost-justified nor made in response to changing conditions. Section 2(f) does not apply to buyer inducements of discriminatory payments or services prohibited by §§ 2(d) and 2(e). Such buyer actions may, however, be attacked as unfair methods of competition under § 5 of the FTC Act.

In *Great Atlantic and Pacific Tea Co. v. FTC*, 440 U.S. 69 (1979), the Supreme Court further narrowed the effective reach of § 2(f) by holding that buyers who knowingly received a discriminatory price did not violate the act if their seller had a valid defense to the charge of violating § 2(a). The seller in *Great Atlantic* had a "meeting competition in good faith" defense. This fact was held to insulate the buyer from liability even though the buyer knew that the seller had beaten, rather than merely met, its competitor's price.

Antitrust Exceptions and Exemptions

> **LO50-13** List the major statutory exemptions from the application of the federal antitrust laws.

Many economic activities occur outside the potential reach of the antitrust laws. This is so either because these activities have been specifically exempted by statute or because courts have carved out nonstatutory exceptions designed to balance our antitrust policy in favor of competition against other social policies.

Statutory Exemptions

Labor Unions and Certain Union Activities The Clayton Act and the Norris–LaGuardia Act of 1932 provide that *labor unions* are not combinations or conspiracies in restraint of trade and exempt certain union activities, including boycotts and secondary picketing, from antitrust scrutiny. This statutory exemption does not, however, exempt union combinations with nonlabor groups aimed at restraining trade or creating a monopoly. An example of such nonexempted activity would be a labor union's agreement with Employer A to call a strike at Employer B's plants. In an attempt to accommodate the strong public policy in favor of collective bargaining, courts have also created a limited nonstatutory exemption for legitimate union–employer agreements arising from the collective bargaining context.

Agricultural Cooperatives and Certain Cooperative Actions The Clayton Act and the Capper–Volstead Act exempt the formation and collective marketing activities of *agricultural cooperatives* from antitrust liability. Courts have narrowly construed this exemption, however. Cooperatives including members not engaged in the production of agricultural commodities have been denied exempt status. One such example would be a cooperative including retailers or wholesalers who do not also produce the commodity in question. The agricultural cooperatives exemption extends only to legitimate collective marketing activities. It does not legitimize coercive or predatory practices that are unnecessary to accomplish lawful cooperative goals. For example, this exemption would not prevent the antitrust laws from being applied to a boycott designed to force nonmembers of the cooperative to adopt a pricing policy established by the cooperative.

Joint Export Activities The Webb–Pomerene Act exempts the *joint export activities* of American companies, so long as those activities do not "artificially or intentionally enhance or depress prices within the United States." The purpose of the act is to encourage export activity by allowing the formation of combinations to enable domestic firms to compete more effectively with foreign cartels. Some critics assert that this exemption is no longer needed because there are fewer foreign cartels today and American firms often play a dominant role in foreign trade. Others question whether any group of American firms enjoying significant domestic market shares in the sale of a particular product could agree on an international marketing strategy, such as the amounts that they will export, without indirectly affecting domestic supplies and prices.

Business of Insurance The McCarran–Ferguson Act exempts from federal antitrust scrutiny those aspects of the *business of insurance* that are subject to state regulation. The act provides, however, that state law cannot legitimize any agreement to boycott, coerce, or intimidate others. Because the insurance industry is extensively regulated by the states, many practices in the industry are outside the reach of the federal antitrust laws.

In recent decades, however, courts have tended to decrease the scope of this exemption by narrowly construing the meaning of "business of insurance." For example, in *Union Labor Life Insurance Co. v. Pireno*, 458 U.S. 119 (1982), the Supreme Court held that the exemption did not insulate from antitrust scrutiny a peer review system in which an insurance company used a committee established by a state chiropractic association to review the reasonableness of particular chiropractors' charges. The Court stated that to qualify for the business of insurance exemption, a challenged practice must have the effect of transferring or spreading policyholders' risk and must be an integral part of the policy relationship between the insured and the insurer. Therefore, only practices related to traditional functions of the insurance business, such as underwriting and risk-spreading, are likely to be exempt.

Calls to repeal the McCarran–Ferguson exemption—at least with regard to certain types of insurance—have been issued many times over the years, but no such repeal has occurred.

Other Regulated Industries Many other *regulated industries* enjoy various degrees of antitrust immunity. The airline, banking, utility, railroad, shipping, and securities industries traditionally have been regulated in the public interest. The regulatory agencies supervising such industries have frequently been given the power to approve industry practices such as rate-setting and mergers that would otherwise violate antitrust laws. In recent years, there has been a distinct tendency to deregulate many regulated industries. If this trend continues, a greater portion of the economic activity in these industries could be subjected to antitrust scrutiny.

State Action Exemption

(LO50-14) Explain what is necessary for the state action exemption to apply.

In *Parker v. Brown*, 317 U.S. 341 (1943), the Supreme Court held that a California state agency's regulation of the production and price of raisins was a state action exempt from the federal antitrust laws. The state action exemption developed in *Parker v. Brown* recognizes states' rights to regulate economic activity in the interest of their citizens. It also, however, may tempt business entities to seek "friendly" state regulation as a way of shielding anticompetitive activity from antitrust supervision. Recognizing

this possibility, courts have placed important limitations on the scope of the state action exemption.

First, the exemption extends only to governmental actions by a state or to actions compelled by a state acting in its sovereign capacity. Second, various decisions indicate that challenged activity cannot qualify for immunity under this exemption unless the activity is affirmatively expressed as state policy and actively supervised by the state. In other words, the price of antitrust immunity is real regulation by the state. The Supreme Court placed a further limitation on the state action exemption by holding that it does not automatically confer immunity on the actions of municipalities. Municipal conduct is immune only if it was authorized by the state legislature and its anticompetitive effects were a foreseeable result of the authorization. The Court's decision caused concern that the threat of treble damage liability might inhibit legitimate regulatory action by municipal authorities. As a result, Congress passed the Local Government Antitrust Act of 1984. This statute eliminates damage actions against municipalities and their officers, agents, and employees for antitrust violations and makes injunctive relief the sole remedy in such cases.

In the *North Carolina State Board of Dental Examiners* case, which follows shortly, the Supreme Court explains the elements that must be present in order for the protection of the state action exemption to be triggered. The Court goes on to conclude that the exemption would not apply under the circumstances presented by the case.

The *Noerr–Pennington* Doctrine

(LO50-15) Explain the operation of the *Noerr–Pennington* doctrine.

In the *Noerr* and *Pennington* cases, the Supreme Court held that "the Sherman Act does not prohibit two or more persons from associating together in an attempt to persuade the legislature or the executive to take particular action with respect to a law that would produce a restraint or a monopoly."[1] This exemption recognizes that the right to petition government provided by the Bill of Rights takes precedence over the antitrust policy favoring competition. In a later case, the Court made the *Noerr–Pennington* exemption applicable to a party's filing of a lawsuit. The exemption does not, however, extend to sham activities that are attempts to interfere with the business activities of competitors rather than legitimate attempts to influence governmental action.

---

[1]*Eastern R.R. President's Conference v. Noerr Motor Freight, Inc.*, 365 U.S. 127 (1961); *United Mine Workers v. Pennington*, 381 U.S. 657 (1965).

North Carolina State Board of Dental Examiners v. Federal Trade Commission
574 U.S. 494 (2015)

A North Carolina statute, the Dental Practice Act, established the North Carolina State Board of Dental Examiners (Board) as "the agency of the State for the regulation of the practice of dentistry." The Board's principal duty is to create, administer, and enforce a licensing system for dentists. Whereas the Board has broad authority over licensees, its authority with respect to unlicensed persons is restricted to filing suit to "perpetually enjoin any person from . . . unlawfully practicing dentistry."

The Dental Practice Act provides that six of the Board's eight members must be licensed dentists engaged in the active practice of dentistry. They are elected by other licensed dentists in North Carolina. The seventh member must be a licensed and practicing dental hygienist and is elected by other licensed hygienists. The final member, referred to by the act as a "consumer," is appointed by the governor of North Carolina. The act empowers the Board to promulgate rules and regulations governing the practice of dentistry within the state, provided that those mandates are not inconsistent with the act and are approved by the state's independent Rules Review Commission (whose members are appointed by the state legislature).

During the 1990s, North Carolina dentists started providing teeth-whitening services. Many of those who did so, including several who served on the Board during the period at issue in the case described below, earned substantial fees for those services. By 2003, non-dentists began providing teeth-whitening services and charging lower prices for those services than the dentists did. Dentists soon began to complain to the Board about their new competitors. Although some complaints warned of possible harm to consumers, most expressed a principal objection regarding the lower prices charged by non-dentists.

Responding to these complaints, the Board opened an investigation into non-dentists' offering of teeth-whitening services. The Board's investigation did not result in a formal rule or regulation. Instead, starting in 2006, the Board issued nearly 50 cease-and-desist letters on its official letterhead to non-dentist providers of teeth-whitening services and to product manufacturers. Many of those letters directed the recipient to cease "all activity constituting the practice of dentistry," warned that the unlicensed practice of dentistry is a crime, and strongly implied (or expressly stated) that teeth-whitening services constitute "the practice of dentistry"—even though the Dental Practice Act does not, by its terms, specify that teeth whitening is "the practice of dentistry." In early 2007, the Board persuaded the North Carolina Board of Cosmetic Art Examiners to warn cosmetologists against providing teeth-whitening services. Later that year, in letters sent to mall operators, the Board stated that kiosk operators who provided teeth-whitening services were violating the Dental Practice Act and that mall management should consider expelling violators from their premises. As result of these Board actions, non-dentists ceased offering teeth-whitening services in North Carolina.

In 2010, the Federal Trade Commission filed an administrative complaint in which it alleged that the Board's concerted action to exclude non-dentists from the market for teeth-whitening services in North Carolina constituted an anticompetitive and unfair method of competition, in violation of § 5 of the Federal Trade Commission Act and § 1 of the Sherman Act. The Board moved to dismiss on the theory that state-action immunity should apply. An administrative law judge (ALJ) denied the motion. On appeal, the Commission sustained the ALJ's ruling on the state-action immunity issue.

The ALJ then conducted a hearing on the merits and determined that the Board had unreasonably restrained trade in violation of antitrust law. On appeal, the Commission again sustained the ALJ's ruling. The Commission rejected the Board's public safety justification, noting the existence of "a wealth of evidence . . . suggesting that non-dentist provided teeth whitening is a safe cosmetic procedure." The Commission ordered the Board to stop sending the cease-and-desist letters or other communications asserting that non-dentists may not offer teeth-whitening services and products. It further ordered the Board to issue corrective notices to all earlier recipients of the Board's cease-and-desist orders in order to advise them of the Board's proper sphere of authority.

The Board petitioned for review in the U.S. Court of Appeals for the Fourth Circuit, which affirmed the Commission's decision in all respects. The Supreme Court granted the Board's petition for certiorari.

Kennedy, Justice

This case arises from an antitrust challenge to the actions of a state regulatory board. A majority of the board's members are engaged in the active practice of the profession it regulates. The question is whether the board's actions are protected from Sherman Act regulation under the doctrine of state-action antitrust immunity, as defined and applied in this Court's decisions beginning with *Parker v. Brown*, 317 U.S. 341 (1943).

The Sherman Act serves to promote robust competition, which in turn empowers the States and provides their citizens with opportunities to pursue their own and the public's welfare. *See FTC v. Ticor Title Insurance Co.*, 504 U.S. 621, 632 (1992).

The States, however, when acting in their respective realm, need not adhere in all contexts to a model of unfettered competition. While the States regulate their economies in many ways [that are consistent] with the antitrust laws, in some spheres they impose restrictions on occupations, confer exclusive or shared rights to dominate a market, or otherwise limit competition to achieve public objectives. If every duly enacted state law or policy were required to conform to the mandates of the Sherman Act, thus promoting competition at the expense of other values a State may deem fundamental, federal antitrust law would impose an impermissible burden on the States' power to regulate.

For these reasons, the Court in *Parker v. Brown* interpreted the antitrust laws to confer immunity on anticompetitive conduct by the States when acting in their sovereign capacity. *See* 317 U.S. at 350–351. That ruling recognized Congress's purpose to respect the federal balance and to "embody in the Sherman Act the federalism principle that the States possess a significant measure of sovereignty under our Constitution." [Citation omitted.] [In various decisions since] 1943, the Court has reaffirmed the importance of *Parker*'s central holding.

In this case, the Board argues that its members were invested by North Carolina with the power of the State and that, as a result, the Board's actions are cloaked with *Parker* immunity. This argument fails, however. A nonsovereign actor controlled by active market participants—such as the Board—enjoys *Parker* immunity only if it satisfies two requirements: "first that 'the challenged restraint . . . be one clearly articulated and affirmatively expressed as state policy,' and second that 'the policy . . . be actively supervised by the State.'" *FTC v. Phoebe Putney Health System, Inc.*, 133 S. Ct. 1003, 1010 (2013) (quoting *California Retail Liquor Dealers Association v. Midcal Aluminum, Inc.*, 445 U.S. 97, 105 (1980)). The parties have assumed that the clear articulation requirement is satisfied, and we do the same. While North Carolina prohibits the unauthorized practice of dentistry, however, its Dental Practice Act is silent on whether that broad prohibition covers teeth-whitening. Here, the Board did not receive active supervision by the State when it interpreted the Act as addressing teeth whitening and when it enforced that policy by issuing cease-and-desist letters to non-dentist teeth-whiteners.

An entity may not invoke *Parker* immunity unless the actions in question are an exercise of the State's sovereign power. *See Columbia v. Omni Outdoor Advertising, Inc.*, 499 U.S. 365, 374 (1991). State legislation and "decision[s] of a state supreme court, acting legislatively rather than judicially," will satisfy this standard, and "*ipso facto* are exempt from the operation of the antitrust laws" because they are an undoubted exercise of state sovereign authority. [Citation omitted.] But while the Sherman Act confers immunity on the States' own anticompetitive policies

out of respect for federalism, it does not always confer immunity where, as here, a State delegates control over a market to a non-sovereign actor. *See Parker*, 317 U.S. at 351. For purposes of *Parker*, a nonsovereign actor is one whose conduct does not automatically qualify as that of the sovereign State itself. State agencies are not simply by their governmental character sovereign actors for purposes of state-action immunity. *See Goldfarb v. Virginia State Bar*, 421 U.S. 773, 791 (1975) ("The fact that the State Bar is a state agency for some limited purposes does not create an antitrust shield that allows it to foster anticompetitive practices for the benefit of its members"). Immunity for state agencies, therefore, requires more than a mere facade of state involvement, for it is necessary in light of *Parker*'s rationale to ensure that the States accept political accountability for anticompetitive conduct they permit and control. *See Ticor*, 504 U.S. at 636.

Limits on state-action immunity are most essential when the State seeks to delegate its regulatory power to active market participants, for established ethical standards may blend with private anticompetitive motives in a way difficult even for market participants to discern. Dual allegiances are not always apparent to an actor. In consequence, active market participants cannot be allowed to regulate their own markets free from antitrust accountability. *See Midcal*, 445 U.S. at 106 ("The national policy in favor of competition cannot be thwarted by casting [a] gauzy cloak of state involvement over what is essentially a private price-fixing arrangement"). Indeed, prohibitions against anticompetitive self-regulation by active market participants are an axiom of federal antitrust policy. So it follows that, under *Parker* and the Supremacy Clause, the States' greater power to attain an end does not include the lesser power to negate the congressional judgment embodied in the Sherman Act through unsupervised delegations to active market participants.

Parker immunity requires that the anticompetitive conduct of nonsovereign actors, especially those authorized by the State to regulate their own profession, result from procedures that suffice to make it the State's own. The question is not whether the challenged conduct is efficient, well-functioning, or wise. Rather, it is "whether anticompetitive conduct engaged in by [nonsovereign actors] should be deemed state action and thus shielded from the antitrust laws." *Patrick v. Burget*, 486 U.S. 94, 100 (1988).

To answer this question, the Court applies the two-part test set forth in *Midcal*, a case arising from California's delegation of price-fixing authority to wine merchants. Under *Midcal*, "[a] state law or regulatory scheme cannot be the basis for antitrust immunity unless, first, the State has articulated a clear policy to allow the anticompetitive conduct, and second, the State provides active supervision of [the] anticompetitive conduct." 445 U.S. at 105. *Midcal*'s clear articulation requirement is satisfied "where the displacement of competition [is] the inherent, logical, or ordinary result of the exercise of authority delegated by the state legislature. In that scenario, the State must have foreseen and implicitly endorsed the anticompetitive effects as consistent with its policy goals." [Citation omitted.] The active supervision requirement demands, *inter alia*, "that state officials have and exercise power to review particular anticompetitive acts of private parties and disapprove those that fail to accord with state policy." *Patrick*, 486 U.S. at 101.

Midcal's supervision rule "stems from the recognition that '[w]here a private party is engaging in anticompetitive activity, there is a real danger that he is acting to further his own interests, rather than the governmental interests of the State.'" *Patrick*, 486 U.S. at 100. Concern about the private incentives of active market participants animates *Midcal*'s supervision mandate, which demands "realistic assurance that a private party's anticompetitive conduct promotes state policy, rather than merely the party's individual interests." *Patrick*, 486 U.S. at 101.

The lesson is clear: *Midcal*'s active supervision test is an essential prerequisite of *Parker* immunity for any nonsovereign entity—public or private—controlled by active market participants. State agencies controlled by active market participants, who possess singularly strong private interests, pose the very risk of self-dealing *Midcal*'s supervision requirement was created to address. This conclusion does not question the good faith of state officers but rather is an assessment of the structural risk of market participants' confusing their own interests with the State's policy goals. *See Patrick*, 486 U.S. at 100–101.

The Court applied this reasoning to a state agency in *Goldfarb*. There the Court denied immunity to a state agency (the Virginia State Bar) controlled by market participants (lawyers) because the agency had "joined in what is essentially a private anticompetitive activity" for "the benefit of its members." 421 U.S. at 791. This emphasis on the Bar's private interests explains why *Goldfarb*, though it predates *Midcal*, considered the lack of supervision by the Virginia Supreme Court to be a principal reason for denying immunity. *See id.*

The similarities between agencies controlled by active market participants and private trade associations [that might be a target of antitrust enforcement] are not eliminated simply because the former are given a formal designation by the State, vested with a measure of government power, and required to follow some procedural rules. *Parker* immunity does not derive from nomenclature alone. When a State empowers a group of active market participants to decide who can participate in its market, and on what terms, the need for supervision is manifest. The Court holds today that a state board on which a controlling number of decisionmakers are active market participants in the occupation the board regulates must satisfy *Midcal*'s active supervision requirement in order to invoke state-action antitrust immunity.

[In this case,] North Carolina delegates control over the practice of dentistry to the Board [by virtue of the Dental Practice Act]. The Act, however, says nothing about teeth-whitening, a practice that did not exist when it was passed. After receiving complaints from other dentists about the non-dentists' cheaper services, the Board's dentist members—some of whom offered whitening services—acted to expel the dentists' competitors from the market. In so doing, the Board relied upon cease-and-desist letters threatening criminal liability, rather than any of the powers at its disposal that would invoke oversight by a politically accountable official. With no active supervision by the State, North Carolina officials may well have been unaware that the Board had decided teeth-whitening constitutes "the practice of dentistry" and [was seeking] to prohibit those who competed against dentists from participating in the teeth-whitening market. Whether or not the Board exceeded its powers under North Carolina law, there is no evidence here of any decision by the State to initiate or concur with the Board's actions against the non-dentists.

The Board [did not demonstrate] that the State exercised active, or indeed any, supervision over its conduct regarding non-dentist teeth-whiteners. [As] a result, no specific supervisory systems can be reviewed here. It suffices to note that the inquiry regarding active supervision is flexible and context-dependent. Active supervision need not entail day-to-day involvement in an agency's operations or micromanagement of its every decision. Rather, the question is whether the State's review mechanisms provide "realistic assurance" that a nonsovereign actor's anticompetitive conduct "promotes state policy, rather than merely the party's individual interests." *Patrick*, 486 U.S. at 100–101.

The Court has identified only a few constant requirements of active supervision: The supervisor must review the substance of the anticompetitive decision, not merely the procedures followed to produce it; the supervisor must have the power to veto or modify particular decisions to ensure they accord with state policy; and the "mere potential for state supervision is not an adequate substitute for a decision by the State." [Citations omitted.] Further, the state supervisor may not itself be an active market participant. In general, however, the adequacy of supervision otherwise will depend on all the circumstances of a case.

The Sherman Act protects competition while also respecting federalism. It does not authorize the States to abandon markets to the unsupervised control of active market participants, whether trade associations or hybrid agencies. If a State wants to rely on active market participants as regulators, it must provide active supervision if state-action immunity under *Parker* is to be invoked.

Fourth Circuit's judgment affirmed.

Patent Licensing There is a basic tension between the antitrust objective of promoting competition and the purpose of the patent law, which, as noted in Chapter 8, seeks to promote innovation by granting a limited monopoly to those who develop new products or processes. In the early case of *United States v. General Electric Company*, 272 U.S. 476 (1926), the Supreme Court allowed General Electric to control the price at which other manufacturers sold light bulbs they had manufactured under patent licensing agreements with General Electric. The Court recognized that an important part of holding a patent was the right to license others to manufacture the patented item. This right effectively would be negated if licensees were allowed to undercut the prices that patent holders charged for their own sales of patented products.

Patent holders cannot, however, lawfully control the price at which patented items are resold by distributors purchasing them from the patent holder. Nor can patent holders use their patents to impose tying agreements on their customers by conditioning the sale of patented items on the purchase of unpatented items, unless such agreements are otherwise lawful under the Sherman and Clayton Acts. Finally, firms that seek to monopolize by acquiring most or all of the patents related to an area of commerce may face liability for violating Sherman Act § 2 or Clayton Act § 7 because a patent has been held to be an asset within the meaning of § 7.

Foreign Commerce

 Describe the antitrust exemptions associated with foreign commerce (sovereign immunity, act of state doctrine, and sovereign compulsion doctrine).

When foreign governments are involved in commercial activities affecting the domestic or international commerce of the United States, our antitrust policy may be at odds with our foreign policy. Congress and the courts have created a variety of antitrust exemptions aimed at reconciling this potential conflict. The Foreign Sovereign Immunities Act (FSIA) provides that the governmental actions of foreign sovereigns and their agents are exempt from antitrust liability. The commercial activities of foreign sovereigns, however, are not included within this sovereign immunity exemption. Significant international controversy exists concerning the proper criteria for determining whether a particular governmental act is commercial in nature. Under the FSIA, the courts employ a *nature of the act* test, holding that a commercial activity is one that an individual might customarily carry on for a profit.

The act of state doctrine provides that an American court cannot adjudicate a politically sensitive dispute whose resolution would require the court to judge the legality of a foreign government's sovereign act. This doctrine reflects judicial deference to the primary role of the executive and legislative branches in the adoption and execution of our foreign policy. The act of state doctrine recognizes (as does the doctrine of sovereign immunity) the importance of respecting the sovereignty of other nations. Unlike the doctrine of sovereign immunity, however, the act of state doctrine also reflects a fundamental attribute of our system of government: the principle of separation of powers.

Finally, the sovereign compulsion doctrine provides private parties a defense if they have been compelled by a foreign sovereign to commit, within that sovereign's territory, acts that would otherwise violate the antitrust laws because of their negative impact on our international commerce. To employ this defense successfully, a defendant must show that the challenged actions were the product of actual compulsion—as opposed to mere encouragement or approval—by a foreign sovereign.

Problems and Problem Cases

1. Mercedes-Benz of North America (MBNA), the exclusive U.S. distributor of Mercedes-Benz (Mercedes) automobiles, was a wholly owned subsidiary of Daimler-Benz Aktiengesellschaft (DBAG), the manufacturer of Mercedes automobiles. MBNA required its approximately 400 franchised Mercedes dealers to agree not to sell or use (in the repair or servicing of Mercedes automobiles) any parts other than genuine Mercedes parts. Mozart, a wholesale automotive parts distributor, filed an antitrust suit against MBNA. Mozart alleged, among other things, that MBNA had violated § 1 of the Sherman Act and § 3 of the Clayton Act by tying the sale of Mercedes parts to the sale of Mercedes automobiles. The trial court ruled in favor of MBNA. Was the trial court's ruling correct?

2. Waste Management Inc. (WMI), a company in the solid waste disposal business, acquired the stock of EMW Ventures Inc. EMW was a diversified holding company, one of whose subsidiaries was Waste Resources. WMI and Waste Resources each had subsidiaries operating in or near Dallas, Texas. The government challenged the merger on the theory that it violated § 7 of the Clayton Act. The trial court agreed. In finding a § 7 violation, the trial court defined the relevant market as including all forms of trash collection (except at single-family or multiple-family residences or small apartment complexes) in Dallas County plus a small fringe area. The combined WMI and Waste Resources subsidiaries had

a 48.8 percent share of the relevant market. The trial court held that this market share raised a presumption of illegality and that WMI had not rebutted the presumption. WMI appealed, arguing that new firms could easily enter the trash collection business in the relevant geographic area and that the trial court should have regarded this ease of entry as a sufficient rebuttal of the presumption of illegality. Was WMI correct?

3. In 1961, Ford Motor Company acquired Autolite, a manufacturer of spark plugs, in order to enter the profitable aftermarket for spark plugs sold as replacement parts. Ford and the other major automobile manufacturers had previously purchased original equipment spark plugs (those installed in new cars when they leave the factory) from independent producers such as Autolite and Champion, either at or below the producer's cost. The independents were willing to sell original equipment plugs so cheaply because aftermarket mechanics often replace original equipment plugs with the same brand of spark plug. GM had already moved into the spark plug market by developing its own division. Ford decided to do so by means of a vertical merger under which it acquired Autolite. Prior to the Autolite acquisition, Ford bought 10 percent of the total spark plug output. The merger left Champion as the only major independent spark plug producer. Champion's market share thereafter declined because Chrysler was the only major original equipment spark plug purchaser remaining in the market. The government filed a divestiture suit against Ford, arguing that Ford's acquisition of Autolite violated § 7 of the Clayton Act. Should Ford have been ordered to divest itself of Autolite?

4. Sanitizing agents are used to kill algae and bacteria in swimming pools. As of the time of the case described below, pool owners could use any of three sanitizing agents. One was liquid pool bleach; the other two were chemicals sold in dry form. These dry sanitizers are isocyanurates (ISOS) and calcium hypochlorite (CAL/HYPO). The chemical cyanuric acid (CA) is a precursor in the process of manufacturing ISOS. When CAL/HYPO is used as a sanitizer, CA is used along with it as a stabilizer. Olin Corporation was the market leader in CAL/HYPO production in the United States from 1980 through 1984, with a market share of 79 to 89 percent. Olin sought to increase its ability to produce and market ISOS. After technical problems doomed its attempts to produce CA and ISOS, Olin entered into a 1984 agreement under which it provided certain ISOS precursors to Monsanto Co., which then produced ISOS and provided them to Olin. Olin thus became a repackager of ISOS.

In 1985, Olin and FMC Corporation entered into an agreement under which Olin was to purchase FMC's swimming pool chemical business. The assets of that business included FMC's sanitizers manufacturing plant in South Charleston, West Virginia. The South Charleston plant produced both CA and ISOS. Invoking Clayton Act § 7 and FTC Act § 5, the Federal Trade Commission challenged the acquisition. To avoid a possible order that would have prohibited the acquisition, Olin agreed to maintain the acquired assets in such a way that divestiture would be possible if the FTC issued a final decision finding that the acquisition violated antitrust laws. Olin and FMC therefore were permitted to consummate their transaction, pending final review by the FTC. After a hearing, the FTC administrative law judge (ALJ) concluded that the acquisition violated the Clayton and FTC Acts because it would likely result in a substantial lessening of competition in the relevant markets. On appeal, the FTC Commissioners (Commission) upheld the ALJ's decision, including the ALJ's order of divestiture. The Commission therefore ordered Olin to divest itself of the South Charleston plant it had acquired from FMC. Olin sought review from the U.S. Court of Appeals for the Ninth Circuit. A key issue was the identification of the relevant product market or markets. Olin argued that the only relevant product market consisted of ISOS by themselves. The FTC argued that, as the ALJ and Commission had determined, there was an additional relevant product market consisting of dry sanitizers—that is, both ISOS and CAL/HYPO. Whose argument was correct, according to the Ninth Circuit?

5. The Federal Trade Commission filed an administrative complaint against six of the nation's title insurance companies. The complaint alleged that the title insurers engaged in horizontal price-fixing in their setting of uniform rates for title searches and title examinations. The challenged uniform rate-setting for title searches and title examinations occurred in various states through rating bureaus organized by the title insurers. These rating bureaus allegedly would set standard rates for search and examination services notwithstanding possible differences in efficiencies and costs as between individual title insurance companies. Though privately organized, these rating bureaus and the rates they set were potentially subject to oversight by the various states in which they operated. In Wisconsin and Montana, two of the states in which price-fixing was alleged to have occurred, the rating bureaus filed rates with state agencies that operated under the so-called negative option rule. This rule provided that the rates became effective unless they were rejected by the appropriate Wisconsin or Montana

agency within a set time. At most the state agencies checked the rate filings for mathematical accuracy. Some rates were unchecked altogether. Reviewing the administrative law judge's decision in the administrative proceeding, the FTC commissioners concluded that price-fixing occurred and that the state action exemption argued for by the title insurers did not apply. On appeal, the Third Circuit Court of Appeals held that the state action exemption shielded the title insurers' from antitrust liability for the price-fixing that occurred in Wisconsin and Montana. Was the Third Circuit correct?

6. Ricky Hasbrouck and 11 other plaintiffs were Texaco retail service station dealers in the Spokane area. They purchased gasoline directly from Texaco and resold it at retail under the Texaco trademark. Throughout the relevant time period (1972–1981), Texaco also supplied gasoline to two gasoline distributors, Dompier Oil Company and Gull Oil Company, at a price that was at various times between 2.5 cents and 5.75 cents per gallon lower than the price Hasbrouck paid. Dompier and Gull sold the gasoline they purchased from Texaco to independent retail service stations. Dompier sold the gasoline to retailers under the Texaco trademark; Gull marketed it under private brand names. Gull's customers either sold their gasoline on consignment (in which case they set their own prices) or on commission (in which case Gull set their resale prices). Gull retained title until the gas was sold to a retail customer in either case. Some of the retail stations supplied by Dompier were owned and operated by Dompier's salaried employees. Both Dompier and Gull picked up gas at the Texaco bulk plant and delivered it to their retail customers, a service for which Dompier was compensated by Texaco at the common carrier rate.

   Hasbrouck and the other dealers filed a price discrimination suit against Texaco under § 2(a) of the Robinson–Patman Act. At trial, Texaco argued that its lower prices to Gull and Dompier were lawful functional discounts. The jury awarded the plaintiffs $1,349,700 in treble damages. When the Ninth Circuit Court of Appeals affirmed the jury award, Texaco appealed. The U.S. Supreme Court granted certiorari. How did the Supreme Court rule? Were the particular functional discounts provided by Texaco lawful?

7. Indian Coffee Company, a coffee roaster in Pittsburgh, Pennsylvania, sold its Breakfast Cheer coffee in the Pittsburgh area, where it had an 18 percent market share, and in Cleveland, Ohio, where it had a significant, but smaller, market share. Late in 1971, Folger Coffee Company, then the leading seller of branded coffee west of the Mississippi, entered the Pittsburgh market for the first time. In its effort to gain market share in Pittsburgh, Folger granted retailers high promotional allowances in the form of coupons. Retail customers could use these coupons to obtain price cuts. Redeeming retailers could use the coupons as credits against invoices from Folger. For a time, Indian tried to retain its market share by matching Folger's price concessions, but because Indian operated in only two areas, it could not subsidize such sales with profits from other areas. Indian, which finally was forced out of business in 1974, later filed a Robinson–Patman suit against Folger. At trial, Indian introduced evidence that Folger's Pittsburgh promotional allowances were far higher than its allowances in other geographic areas and that Folger's Pittsburgh prices were below green (unroasted) coffee cost, below material and manufacturing costs, below total cost, and below marginal cost or average variable cost. Was the trial court's directed verdict in favor of Folger proper?

8. Bayer Corporation produced Bayferrox, a synthetic iron oxide pigment used to color paint, plastics, and building and concrete products. Hoover Color Corporation was one of several primary distributors of this pigment. Hoover therefore purchased Bayferrox from Bayer on a regular basis. For a number of years, Bayer had employed a volume-based incentive discount pricing system. Under this system, the price a distributor paid depended on the total amount of Bayferrox purchased by that distributor during the previous year. The quantities of Bayferrox purchased by Hoover were significantly smaller than those purchased by Hoover's competitors, Rockwood Industries and Landers-Segal Co. (Lansco). As a result, Hoover received smaller price discounts from Bayer than Rockwood and Lansco received. In 1992, for instance, Hoover received a 1 percent discount off Bayer's distributor market price for Bayferrox, whereas Lansco and Rockwood were given 6 percent and 10 percent discounts, respectively. Hoover sued Bayer on the theory that Bayer's volume-based incentive discount pricing system involved price discrimination, in violation of § 2(a) of the Robinson–Patman Act. Bayer contended that it set its prices in a good-faith attempt to meet competition in the marketplace and that it was thus entitled to the protection of the affirmative defense set out in § 2(b) of the statute. Holding that Bayer was entitled to the protection of the "meeting competition" defense, the district court granted summary judgment in favor of Bayer. Was the district court's decision correct?

9. Armstrong Surgical Center (the Surgical Center) wished to establish an ambulatory surgery center in Armstrong County, Pennsylvania. At the time, Armstrong County Memorial Hospital (the Hospital) was the only facility with operating rooms in Armstrong County. The Hospital's staff physicians performed the vast majority of surgeries in the county. If it had been completed, the Surgical Center's proposed facility would have provided a variety of outpatient surgical services and would have competed with the Hospital. Pennsylvania law provides that any party wishing to establish a new health care facility must first obtain a Certificate of Need (CON) from Pennsylvania's Department of Health. The Department reviews CON applications in an extensive proceeding consisting of an investigation, an evaluation of submitted materials, and a public hearing. Interested parties, including health care providers that supply similar services in an area, may submit information to the Department regarding any CON application. After extensive proceedings in which the Department reviewed the Surgical Center's application for a CON, the Department denied the application. The Surgical Center appealed this decision to a state hearing board, which upheld the Department's denial of the CON. The Surgical Center later sued the Hospital and its staff physicians for alleged antitrust violations. The plaintiff alleged that the defendants engaged in a conspiracy to deny the Surgical Center an opportunity to compete with the Hospital, that the conspiracy included the making of false statements by the defendants to the Department of Health during the proceedings on the Surgical Center's application for a CON, that the conspiracy unreasonably restrained trade in violation of Sherman Act § 1, and that the defendants engaged in monopolization in violation of Sherman Act § 2.

What defenses would potentially be available to the defendants in this antitrust case? Why those defenses? If the defendants made false statements to the Department of Health during the proceedings on the plaintiff's application for a CON, would those false statements disqualify the defendants from potential entitlement to the defenses you noted?

10. Pocahontas Coal Company filed suit against a number of other companies engaged in the mining and production of coal in West Virginia. Pocahontas alleged that the defendants were involved in a conspiracy to control the production and pricing of coal. One of Pocahontas's specific claims was that the defendants had violated § 8 of the Clayton Act by "deputizing" various persons to sit on the boards of competing subsidiaries. The defendants moved for summary judgment, noting that Pocahontas's complaint contained no factual allegations that any of the defendants were competitors, failed to name any of the alleged "deputies," and was ambiguous because it alleged that certain persons were "officers and/or directors" of competing companies. The trial court offered Pocahontas the opportunity to clarify the complaint by bringing forth additional information on these points. Did the court properly grant the defendants summary judgment when Pocahontas declined to do so?

11. Professional Real Estate Investors (PRE) operated a resort hotel in Palm Springs, California. Having installed videodisk players in the hotel's rooms and assembled a library of more than 200 motion picture titles, PRE rented videodisks to guests for in-room viewing. PRE also sought to develop a market for the sale of videodisk players to other hotels that wished to offer in-room viewing of prerecorded material. Columbia Pictures Industries and seven other major motion picture studios (referred to collectively as Columbia) owned the copyrights on the motion pictures that appeared on the videodisks PRE had purchased. Columbia also licensed the transmission of copyrighted motion pictures to hotel rooms through a wired cable system called Spectradyne. PRE therefore competed with Columbia not only for the viewing market at PRE's hotel, but also for the broader market for in-room entertainment services in hotels. Columbia sued PRE for copyright infringement on the basis of PRE's rental of videodisks for viewing in hotel rooms. PRE counterclaimed, charging Columbia with violations of §§ 1 and 2 of the Sherman Act. PRE alleged that Columbia's copyright action was a mere sham that cloaked underlying acts of monopolization and conspiracy to restrain trade. The district court granted summary judgment in favor of PRE on Columbia's copyright infringement claim. Columbia sought summary judgment on PRE's antitrust counterclaims. Columbia asserted that its copyright infringement claim had not been a sham and that the *Noerr–Pennington* doctrine therefore protected Columbia against antitrust attack. PRE opposed Columbia's motion for summary judgment on PRE's antitrust counterclaims by arguing that Columbia's copyright infringement claim was a sham because Columbia did not honestly believe that the claim was meritorious. If Columbia did not subjectively believe that the claim was meritorious but there was probable cause to bring the claim, was Columbia's claim a sham for purposes of the sham exception to the *Noerr–Pennington* doctrine's protection against liability?

Employment Law

Two residents of Wheatfield Health Care Center, a privately run nursing home, requested that only white employees provide their care. Wheatfield complied with its residents' racial preference partly due to its interpretation of a state regulation governing long-term care facilities, which supposedly gave residents the right to "choose a personal attending physician and other providers of services."

Supervisors at Wheatfield instructed Jennifer Jackson, who worked as a certified nursing assistant (CNA) and who was the only African American employee at Wheatfield, about the care restrictions for these residents. In addition, the shift assignment sheet, which Jackson received every day, included a notation next to the residents' names stating, "No Black CNA!" Jackson found this embarrassing and frustrating; however, to keep a job she badly needed, she did not complain and complied with the restriction. Nonetheless, she believed this situation contributed to a general air of hostility toward her. Several employees used vulgar racial epithets to refer to Jackson. One white employee complained loudly that Wheatfield should stop hiring Black employees because it made more work for her. Jackson's friend, Arnie Lucas, complained to the human resources department on Jackson's behalf about the coworkers' behavior. Shortly thereafter, Lucas was placed on probation, making him ineligible for overtime shifts.

Jackson badly injured her back helping a resident into bed. She required extensive surgical care, physical therapy, and rehabilitation. When she was ready to return to work, her doctor restricted how much weight she could lift. The restriction was expected to be permanent. Jackson's supervisor refused to allow her to return to work with the restriction and, eventually, Jackson was fired.

Wheatfield required all of its health care workers to submit to periodic mandatory drug tests. Not wanting Jackson to get any unemployment compensation after her termination, Wheatfield's president and CEO instructed Bettina Collins, the human resources manager, to testify falsely at Jackson's eligibility hearing that Jackson had failed her last drug test. When Collins refused to lie, she was fired.

- Was Jackson subjected to illegal discrimination by Wheatfield when it restricted her work assignments based on her race and allowed Jackson's coworkers to make derogatory statements to her?
- Can Wheatfield rely on the residents' preferences and/or the state regulations to defend a claim of race discrimination by Jackson?
- Does Lucas have any possible claim against Wheatfield for apparently punishing him for defending Jackson?
- What responsibility does Wheatfield have to Jackson regarding the medical treatment and rehabilitation she required as a result of her injury?
- Did Wheatfield violate Jackson's rights when it refused to accommodate her restrictions and ultimately fired her?
- Can Wheatfield require its health care workers to undergo periodic mandatory drug testing?
- Was Jackson entitled to unemployment compensation?
- Does Collins have any recourse to remedy her discharge for refusing to lie at the hearing?

LEARNING OBJECTIVES

After studying this chapter, you should be able to:

51-1 Explain the structure and operation of a workers' compensation regime, including the elements of a work-related injury.

51-2 Identify and describe legislation that protects workers' safety, health, and well-being; that regulates employees' wages and hours, pensions and benefits, and income security; and that governs unionized workforces.

51-3 Analyze and apply the appropriate legislation for a workplace scenario for potential unlawful discrimination and assess the possibility for liability, including an employer's potential defenses.

51-4 Distinguish the relative privacy rights of private-sector and public-sector employees.

51-5 Describe the employment-at-will doctrine and its major exceptions.

YEARS AGO, IT WAS unusual to see a separate employment law chapter in a business law text. At that time, the rights, duties, and liabilities accompanying employment usually were determined by basic legal institutions such as contract, tort, and agency. Today, these common law principles still control employer–employee relations unless displaced by government regulations or by new judge-made rules applying specifically to employment. By now, however, such rules and regulations are so numerous that they touch almost every facet of employment. This chapter discusses the most important of these modern legal controls on the employer–employee relation.

Modern U.S. employment law is so vast and complex a subject that texts designed for lawyers seldom address it in its entirety. Indeed, specialized subjects like labor law, employee benefits, and employment discrimination often get book-length treatment on their own. This chapter's overview of employment law emphasizes three topics that have attracted much recent attention—employment discrimination, employee privacy, and common law claims for wrongful discharge. But no discussion of employment law is complete without outlining certain basic regulations that significantly affect the conditions of employment for most Americans. Figure 51.1 notes these regulations and briefly states the functions they perform.

Legislation Protecting Employee Health, Safety, and Well-Being

 LO51-1 Explain the structure and operation of a workers' compensation regime, including the elements of a work-related injury.

Workers' Compensation Nineteenth-century law made it difficult for employees to recover when they sued their employer in negligence for on-the-job injuries.[1] At that time, employers had an implied assumption of risk defense under which an employee assumed all the normal and customary risks of his employment simply by taking the job. If an employee's own carelessness played some role in his injury, employers often could avoid negligence liability under the traditional rule that even a slight degree of contributory negligence is a complete defense. Another employer defense, the fellow-servant rule, excused an employer from liability when an employee's injury resulted from the negligence of a coemployee (or fellow servant). Finally, an employee sometimes had problems proving the employer's negligence. State workers' compensation statutes, which first appeared early in the 20th century, were a response to all these problems. Today all 50 states have such systems.[2]

Basic Features Workers' compensation protects only employees and not independent contractors.[3] However, many states exempt casual, agricultural, and domestic employees, among others. State and local government employees may be covered by workers' compensation or

---

[1] Chapter 7 discusses negligence law and most of the negligence defenses noted below.

[2] In addition, various federal statutes regulate on-the-job injuries suffered by employees of the federal government and other employees such as railroad workers, seamen, longshoremen, and harbor workers.

[3] Chapter 35 defines the terms *employee* and *independent contractor*.

Figure 51.1   The Ends and Means of Modern Employment Law

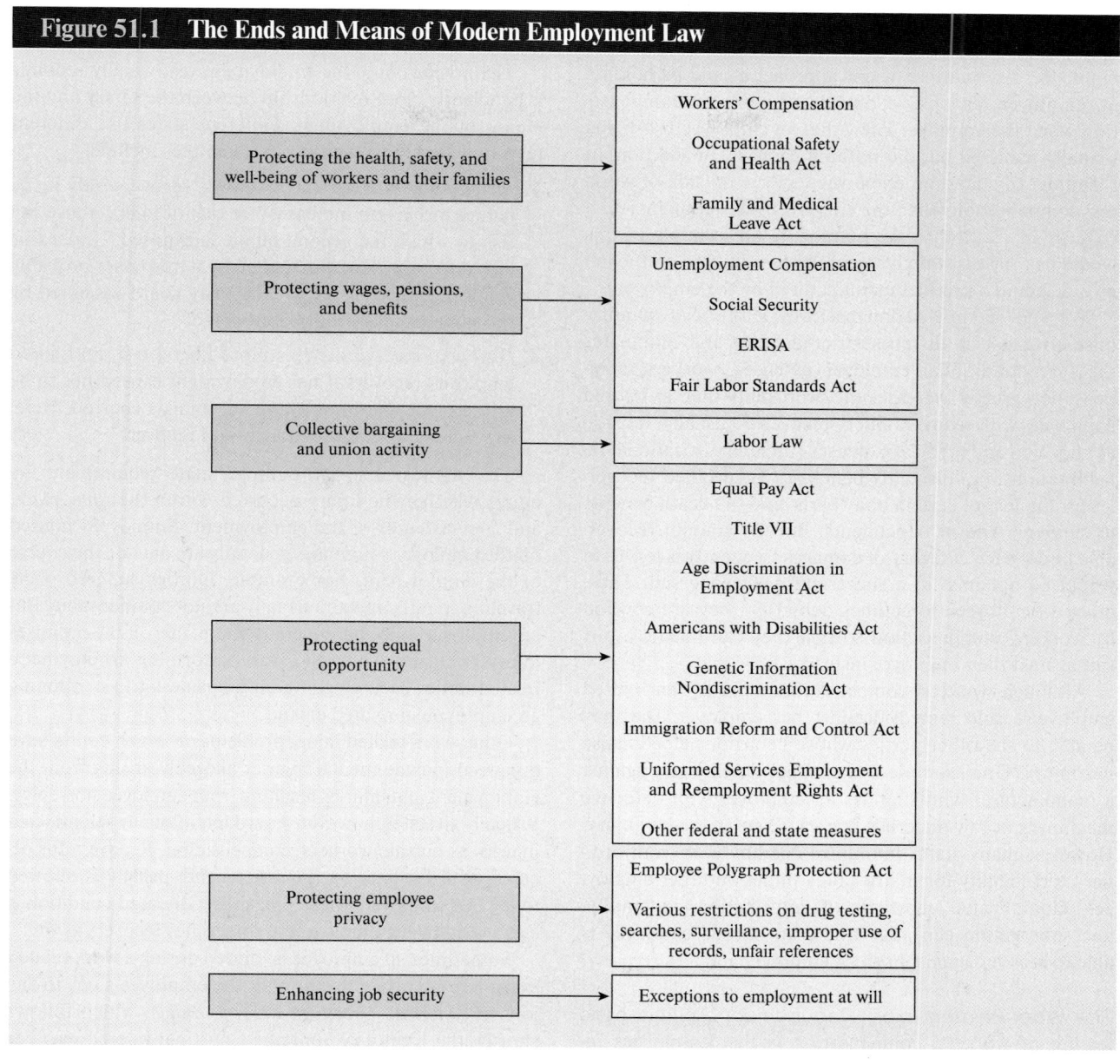

by some alternative state system. Also, states usually exempt certain employers—for example, firms employing fewer than a stated number of employees (often three).

Where they apply, however, all workers' compensation systems share certain basic features. They allow injured employees to recover under *strict liability*, thus removing any need to prove employer negligence. They also eliminate the employer's three traditional defenses: contributory negligence, assumption of risk, and the fellow-servant rule. In addition, they make workers' compensation an employee's *exclusive remedy* against her employer for covered injuries. There are some exceptions to the exclusivity of workers' compensation, however. In cases in which an employer *intentionally* injures an employee, the injured employee can usually sue the employer outside of workers' compensation. In some states, this intentional injury exception has expanded beyond intentional torts to situations in which the employer did something or maintained a condition in the workplace that the employer knew was substantially certain to harm the employee. An example of this approach would be holding an employer responsible outside of workers' compensation when the employer knew that an employee was being sexually harassed but did nothing about it. In addition, in a number of states, an employee can sue outside of workers' compensation when the employer was acting in a *dual capacity* in relation to the employee. An example of this would be a case in which an employee is injured on the job by a defect in a product manufactured by the employer.

Workers' compensation basically is a social compromise. Because it involves strict liability and eliminates the three traditional employer defenses, workers' compensation greatly increases the probability that an injured employee will recover. Such recoveries usually include (1) hospital and medical expenses (including vocational rehabilitation), (2) disability benefits, (3) specified recoveries for the loss of certain body parts, and (4) death benefits to survivors and/or dependents. But the amount recoverable under each category of damages frequently is less than would be obtained in a successful negligence suit. Thus, injured employees sometimes deny that they are covered by workers' compensation so that they can pursue a tort suit against their employer instead.

Although workers' compensation is usually an injured employee's sole remedy against her employer, she may be able to sue other parties whose behavior helped cause her injury. One example is a product liability suit against a manufacturer who supplies an employer with defective machinery or raw materials that cause an on-the-job injury. However, many states immunize coemployees from ordinary tort liability for injuries they inflict on other employees. Complicated questions of contribution, indemnity, and subrogation can arise where an injured employee is able to recover against both an employer and a third party.

The Work-Related Injury Requirement Another basic feature of workers' compensation is that employees recover only for *work-related* injuries. To be work-related, the injury must (1) arise out of the employment and (2) happen in the course of the employment. These tests have been variously interpreted.

The arising-out-of-the-employment test usually requires a sufficiently close relationship between the injury and the *nature* of the employment. Different states use different tests to define this relationship. Examples include:

1. *Increased risk.* Here, the employee recovers only if the nature of her job increases her risk of injury above the risk to which the general public is exposed. Under this test, a factory worker assaulted by a trespasser probably would not recover, while a security guard assaulted by the same trespasser probably would.

2. *Positional risk.* Under this more liberal test, an injured employee recovers if her employment caused her to be at the place and time where her injury occurred. Here, the factory worker probably would recover.

The in-the-course-of-the-employment requirement inquires whether the injury occurred within the *time, place,* and *circumstances* of the employment. Employees injured off the employer's premises generally are outside the course of the employment. For example, injuries suffered while traveling to or from work usually are not compensable. But an employee may be covered where the off-the-premises injury occurred while she was performing employment-related duties such as going on a business trip or running an employment-related errand.

Other work-related injury problems on which courts have disagreed include mental injuries allegedly arising from the employment and injuries resulting from employee horseplay. Virtually all states, however, regard intentionally self-inflicted injuries as outside workers' compensation. Recovery for occupational diseases, on the other hand, usually is allowed today. An employee whose preexisting diseased condition is aggravated by her employment sometimes recovers as well.

Sometimes an employee is injured during a work-related event but not while performing the employee's day-to-day job. In *American Greetings Corp. v. Bunch*, which follows shortly, the Kentucky Supreme Court considered whether an injury during a company-sponsored fundraiser was covered by workers' compensation.

American Greetings Corp. v. Bunch 331 S.W.3d 600 (Ky. 2010)

An employee, Sheila Bunch, injured her knee in a relay race while participating in a fundraising event for United Way, in her company cafeteria. The race was in the company cafeteria during her unpaid lunch hour. The employer, American Greetings Corp., sponsored a month-long fundraising campaign each year. Employee participation was voluntary with no penalties for not participating. Employees promoted the event (posting flyers on company bulletin boards, for example), both on and off the clock. The company donated prizes for the fundraising events, some of which were held on company property during work hours. The company encouraged employees to participate. It paid them to attend a one-hour presentation, and for employees who chose to donate, it deducted those contributions from employee paychecks.

The Kentucky Court of Appeals ruled that the injury was within the scope of employment (and therefore the employee was entitled to workers' compensation benefits). The employer appealed that decision, urging the Kentucky Supreme Court to find that the injury was outside the scope of employment. The court refers at some points to the administrative bodies that considered the case originally, the 'ALJ' (administrative law judge) and "the Board" (the state Worker's Compensation Board).

Per Curiam

An injured worker bears the burden of proof and risk of nonpersuasion with regard to every element of a claim. . . . *Smart* [*v. Georgetown Community Hospital,* 170 S.W.3d 370 (Ky. 2005),] established four independent tests to determine whether an injury that occurs during a recreational activity comes within the course and scope of the employment (*i.e.*, is work-related). *Smart* indicates that an injury occurring during a recreational activity may be viewed as being work-related if:

1. It occurs on the premises, during a lunch or recreational period, as a regular incident of the employment; or

2. The employer brings the activity within the orbit of the employment by expressly or impliedly requiring participation or by making the activity part of the service of the employee; or

3. The employer derives substantial direct benefit from the activity beyond the intangible benefit of an improvement in employee health and morale that is common to all kinds of recreation and social life; or

4. The employer exerts sufficient control over the activity to bring it within the orbit of the employment.

No single factor should receive conclusive weight when deciding whether an injury is work-related.

In *Smart* the employee's injury occurred during a picnic for hospital employees, which was held off the employer's premises and outside Ms. Smart's normal working hours. Although the employer strongly encouraged employees to attend the function, Smart did not think she was required to attend. Any benefit to the employer consisted of improving employee morale, which was intangible. Moreover, the pickup volleyball game in which she was injured was neither organized nor controlled by the employer and Smart's participation was purely voluntary. . . . [T]he court determined that such evidence did not compel a finding that an injury sustained in the volleyball game occurred within the course and scope of Smart's employment.

The ALJ determined in the present case that "the only section of the test under which the [relay race] could conceivably fall is Paragraph 1." The ALJ acknowledged that the activity took place in the cafeteria, during meal break, while employees were off work but considered it "a tremendous stretch" to view "yearly voluntary participation in a charitable event" to be a regular incident of employment. Convinced that the activity also did not come within the second, third, or fourth paragraphs of the test set forth in

Smart, the ALJ found "not a shred of evidence" that the employer required participation in United Way fundraising activities, noting that only 39 of 700 employees participated in the relay event and that the claimant did not attend the one-hour United Way presentation. The ALJ also found no evidence that the employer derived any benefit from the activity except by "being a good corporate citizen in allowing the use of its facility" and "[allowing] its employees to fulfill their sense of community responsibility."

Unlike *Smart* this case concerns an injury that occurred on the employer's premises, during normal working hours, during the claimant's lunch hour. Thus, the injury would be compensable under the first test listed in *Smart* if the activity during which it occurred was "a regular incident of the employment." The Board determined that the ALJ took an "overly narrow" view of the evidence and confined the analysis to the specific event in which the claimant was injured rather than considering the event in context, as part of the annual, month-long fundraising campaign. In other words, the Board determined that the ALJ applied an incorrect legal standard to the evidence and that the evidence compelled a favorable finding when considered under the correct standard. We agree.

An accepted and normal activity conducted on the employer's premises becomes a regular incident of the employment. The relay race in which the claimant was injured took place on the employer's premises and was not an isolated annual charitable event but part of a month-long charitable campaign that the employer allowed employees to conduct in the workplace annually. Such evidence compelled a finding that an activity conducted as part of the campaign was an incident of the employment.

The evidence that was reliable, probative, and material with respect to employer control compelled a finding that the employer exercised sufficient control to bring the claimant's injury within the orbit of her employment. An employer clearly has the right to control all activities that occur on its premises. Although the claimant's employer did not control the United Way fundraising campaign directly, it permitted the campaign to be conducted on its business premises and facilitated the campaign by permitting payroll deduction to be used for contributions; allowing workers to attend a one-hour United Way presentation while on the clock; allowing at least some organizational activities to be performed by workers while on the clock; and allowing events such as the relay race to be conducted on the premises, during the lunch hour.

The decision of the Court of Appeals is affirmed.

Administration and Funding Workers' compensation systems usually are administered by a state agency that adjudicates workers' claims and oversees the system. Its decisions on such claims normally are appealable to the state courts. The states fund workers' compensation by compelling covered employers to (1) purchase private insurance, (2) self-insure (e.g., by maintaining a contingency fund), or (3) make payments into a state insurance fund. Because employers generally pass on the costs of insurance to their customers, workers' compensation tends to spread the economic risk of workplace injuries throughout society.

The Occupational Safety and Health Act

 LO51-2 Identify and describe legislation that protects workers' safety, health, and well-being; that regulates employees' wages and hours, pensions and benefits, and income security; and that governs unionized workforces.

Although it may stimulate employers to remedy hazardous working conditions, workers' compensation does not directly forbid such conditions. The most important measure directly regulating workplace safety is the federal Occupational Safety and Health Act of 1970. With its general duty clause, the Occupational Safety and Health Act imposes a duty on employers to provide their employees with a workplace and jobs free from recognized hazards that may cause death or serious physical harm. In addition to the general duty clause requirement, employers are required to comply with many detailed regulations promulgated by the Occupational Safety and Health Administration (OSHA). One of these regulations, for example, requires employers to inform employees who could be exposed to hazardous chemicals in the workplace about the chemicals and to provide employees with training so that they can effectively protect themselves from harm. The act also requires employers to report to the secretary of labor any on-the-job injuries that require hospitalization. Because information about workplace dangers provided by employees themselves is important to the effectiveness of the act, employees who provide such information are protected from retaliation.

The Occupational Safety and Health Act applies to all employers engaged in a business affecting interstate commerce. Exempted, however, are the U.S. government, the states and their political subdivisions, and certain industries regulated by other federal safety legislation like the Mine Safety and Health Act. The Occupational Safety and Health Act mainly is administered by the Occupational Safety and Health Administration (OSHA) of the Labor Department.

It does not preempt state workplace safety regulation, but OSHA must approve any state regulatory plan.

OSHA can inspect places of employment for violations of the act and its regulations. If an employer is found to violate the act's general duty clause or any specific standard, OSHA issues a written citation.

The main sanctions for violations of the act and the regulations are various civil penalties. In addition, any employer who commits a willful violation resulting in death to an employee may suffer a fine, imprisonment, or both. Also, the secretary of labor may seek injunctive relief when an employment hazard presents an imminent danger of death or physical harm that cannot be promptly eliminated by normal citation procedures. An employee cannot sue her employer for a violation of OSHA, however. The statute provides no private right of action to covered employees.

The Family and Medical Leave Act

 LO51-2 Identify and describe legislation that protects workers' safety, health, and well-being; that regulates employees' wages and hours, pensions and benefits, and income security; and that governs unionized workforces.

After concluding that proper child-raising, family stability, and job security require that employees get reasonable work leave for family and medical reasons, Congress passed the Family and Medical Leave Act (FMLA) in 1993. In general, the act covers those employed for at least 12 months, and for 1,250 hours during those 12 months, by an employer employing 50 or more employees at the employee's work site or within a 75-mile radius of that work site. Covered employers include federal, state, and local government agencies.

Under the FMLA, covered employees are entitled to a total of 12 workweeks of leave during a 12-month period for one or more of the following reasons: (1) the birth of a child and the need to care for that child; (2) the adoption of a child; (3) the need to care for a spouse, child, or parent with a serious health condition; and (4) the employee's own serious health condition. The definition of "serious health condition" is complex. It generally requires inpatient care in a hospital or continuing care by a health care provider. Thus, ear aches, the common cold, and mild cases of influenza generally do not qualify for FMLA leave, even when a parent must stay home from work to care for a child with one of those conditions.

Usually, the leave is without pay. Upon the employee's return from leave, the employer ordinarily must put her in the same or an equivalent position and must not deny her any benefits accrued before the leave began. The National Defense Authorization Act of 2008 included provisions that revised the FMLA with respect to military families. The new provisions permit eligible employees who are employed by covered employers to take up to 12 weeks of leave because of any "qualifying exigency" arising from the fact that the employee's spouse, son, daughter, or parent is on active military duty or has been notified of an impending call to active duty status.[4]

Employers who deny any of an employee's FMLA rights are civilly liable to the affected employee for resulting lost wages or, if no wages were lost, for any other resulting monetary losses not exceeding 12 weeks' wages. Employees may also recover an additional equal amount as liquidated damages, unless the employer acted in good faith and had reasonable grounds for believing that it was not violating the act. Like the Fair Labor Standards Act (FLSA), to be discussed later in this chapter, the FMLA permits civil actions by the secretary of labor, with any sums recovered distributed to affected employees. In such actions, employees may also obtain equitable relief, including reinstatement and promotion.

On March 18, 2020, President Donald Trump signed into law the Families First Coronavirus Response Act (FFCRA), which Congress passed in response to the coronavirus pandemic. The FFCRA imposed a paid leave requirement on a broad swath of private and public employers. Eligible employees of covered employers are entitled to receive paid leave under several circumstances. First, all employees of covered employers were entitled to two weeks of sick leave at full pay when the employee was unable to work due to being officially quarantined or when the employee was experiencing symptoms of COVID-19 infection and is seeking medical diagnosis. Second, all employees of covered employers were entitled to two weeks of sick leave at two-thirds their regular rate of pay to care for an individual subject to official quarantine or to care for a child whose school or child-care provider was closed or unavailable for reasons related to the pandemic. Third, in addition to the two weeks of paid leave in the second condition, employees who had been employed by a covered employer for at least 30 calendar days were entitled to extended family and medical leave at two-thirds pay for up to 10 additional weeks when the employee was unable to work due to the need to care for a child whose school or child-care provider was closed or unavailable for reasons related to the pandemic. Covered employers included certain public employers and private employers with 500 or fewer employees. The smallest employers, with fewer than 50 employees, could apply for an exemption from the extended family leave provision, provided they could show the requirement would jeopardize the operation of their business as a going concern. Regulations regarding how employers were to count their employees were complex, but note that this law was fairly unique in that it did not cover the largest employers of more than 500 employees. As this book went to press, the FFCRA was set to expire on December 31, 2020, and Congress had taken no steps to extend it despite the ongoing impacts of the pandemic.

Legislation Protecting Wages, Pensions, and Benefits

 LO51-2 Identify and describe legislation that protects workers' safety, health, and well-being; that regulates employees' wages and hours, pensions and benefits, and income security; and that governs unionized workforces.

Social Security Today, the law requires that employers help ensure their employees' financial security after the employment ends. One example is the federal Social Security system. Social Security mainly is financed by the Federal Insurance Contributions Act (FICA). FICA imposes a flat percentage tax on all employee income below a certain base figure and requires employers to pay a matching amount. Self-employed people pay a different rate on a different wage base. FICA revenues finance various forms of financial assistance besides the old-age benefits that people usually call Social Security. These include survivors' benefits to family members of deceased workers, disability benefits, and medical and hospitalization benefits for the elderly (the Medicare system).

Unemployment Compensation Another way that the law protects employees after their employment ends is by providing unemployment compensation for discharged workers. Since 1935, federal law has authorized joint federal–state efforts in this area. Today, each state administers its own unemployment compensation system under federal guidelines. The system's costs are met by subjecting employers to federal and state unemployment compensation taxes.

Unemployment insurance plans vary from state to state but usually share certain features. States often condition the receipt of benefits on the recipient's having worked for

---

[4] This right under the FMLA for family members of active duty military personnel is different from and in addition to the reemployment and reinstatement rights that are provided by USERRA, discussed later in this chapter.

a covered employer for a specified time period, and/or having earned a certain minimum income over such a period. Generally, those who voluntarily quit work without good cause, are fired for bad conduct, fail to actively seek suitable new work, or refuse such work are ineligible for benefits. Benefit levels vary from state to state, as do the time periods during which benefits can be received.

ERISA   Many employers voluntarily contribute to their employees' postemployment income by maintaining pension plans. For years, pension plan abuses such as arbitrary termination of participation in the plan, arbitrary benefit reduction, and mismanagement of fund assets were not uncommon. The Employee Retirement Income Security Act of 1974 (ERISA) was a response to these problems. ERISA does not require employers to establish or fund pension plans and does not set benefit levels. Instead, it tries to check abuses and to protect employees' expectations that promised pension benefits will be paid.

ERISA imposes *fiduciary duties* on pension fund managers. For example, it requires that managers diversify the plan's investments to minimize the risk of large losses, unless this is clearly imprudent. ERISA also imposes *record-keeping*, *reporting*, and *disclosure* requirements. For instance, it requires that covered plans provide annual reports to their participants and specifies the contents of those reports. In addition, the act has a provision *guaranteeing employee participation* in the plan. For example, certain employees who complete one year of service with an employer cannot be denied plan participation. Furthermore, ERISA contains *funding* requirements for protecting plan participants against loss of pension income. Finally, ERISA contains complex *vesting requirements* that determine when an employee's right to receive pension benefits becomes nonforfeitable. These requirements help prevent employers from using a late vesting date to avoid pension obligations to employees who change jobs or are fired before that date. ERISA's remedies include civil suits by plan participants and beneficiaries, equitable relief, and criminal penalties.

The Fair Labor Standards Act   Although federal labor law regulates several aspects of labor–management relations, it still permits many terms of employment to be determined by private bargaining. Nonetheless, sometimes the law directly regulates such key terms of employment as wages and hours worked. The most important example is the Fair Labor Standards Act (FLSA) of 1938.

The FLSA regulates *wages and hours* by entitling covered employees to (1) a specified minimum wage whose amount changes over time and (2) a time-and-a half rate for work exceeding 40 hours per week. The FLSA's complicated coverage provisions basically enable its wages-and-hours standards to reach most significantly sized businesses that are engaged in interstate commerce or produce goods for such commerce. Also covered are the federal, state, and local governments. The many exemptions from the FLSA's wages-and-hours provisions include executive, administrative, and professional personnel.

The FLSA also forbids oppressive *child labor* by any employer engaged in interstate commerce or in the production of goods for such commerce and also forbids the interstate shipment of goods produced in an establishment where oppressive child labor occurs. Oppressive child labor includes (1) most employment of children below the age of 14; (2) employment of children aged 14–15, unless they work in an occupation specifically approved by the Department of Labor; and (3) employment of children aged 16–17 who work in occupations declared particularly hazardous by the Labor Department.

Both affected employees and the Labor Department can recover any unpaid minimum wages or overtime, plus an additional equal amount as liquidated damages, from an employer that has violated the FLSA's wages-and-hours provisions. Violations of the act's child labor provisions may result in civil penalties. Other FLSA remedies include injunctive relief and criminal liability for willful violations.

Collective Bargaining and Union Activity

 LO51-2   Identify and describe legislation that protects workers' safety, health, and well-being; that regulates employees' wages and hours, pensions and benefits, and income security; and that governs unionized workforces.

Entire legal treatises are devoted to the topic of collective bargaining by unions. What follows is only a brief historical outline of the subject. Early in the 19th century, some courts treated labor unions as illegal criminal conspiracies. After this restriction disappeared around midcentury, organized labor began its lengthy—and sometimes violent—rise to power. During the late 19th and early 20th centuries, unions' growing influence and wage earners' increasing presence in the electorate spurred the passage of many laws benefiting labor. These included statutes outlawing "yellow-dog" contracts (under which employees agreed not to join or remain a union member), minimum wage and maximum hours legislation, laws regulating the employment of women and children, factory safety measures, and workers' compensation. But during this period, some say, the courts tended to represent business interests. Perhaps for this reason, some prolabor measures were struck down on constitutional grounds. Also, some courts were quick to issue temporary and permanent injunctions to restrain union picketing and boycotts and to help quell strikes.

Organized labor's political power continued to grow during the first part of the 20th century. In 1926, Congress passed the Railway Labor Act, which regulates labor relations in the railroad industry, and which later included airlines. This was followed by the Norris–LaGuardia Act of 1932, which limited the circumstances in which federal courts could enjoin strikes and picketing in labor disputes, and also prohibited federal court enforcement of yellow-dog contracts.

The most important 20th-century American labor statute, however, was the National Labor Relations Act of 1935 (the NLRA or Wagner Act). The NLRA gave employees the *right to organize* by enabling them to form, join, and assist labor organizations. It also allowed them to *bargain collectively* through their own representatives. In addition, the Wagner Act prohibited certain *unfair labor practices* that were believed to discourage collective bargaining. These practices include (1) interfering with employees' rights to form, join, and assist labor unions; (2) dominating or interfering with the formation or administration of a labor union, or giving a union financial or other support; (3) discriminating against employees in hiring, tenure, or any term of employment due to their union membership; (4) discriminating against employees because they have filed charges or given testimony under the NLRA; and (5) refusing to bargain collectively with any duly designated employee representative. The NLRA also established the National Labor Relations Board (NLRB). The NLRB's main functions are (1) handling representation cases (which involve the process by which a union becomes the certified employee representative within a bargaining unit) and (2) deciding whether challenged employer or union activity is an unfair labor practice.

In 1947, Congress amended the NLRA by passing the Labor Management Relations Act (LMRA or Taft–Hartley Act). The act declared that certain acts by *unions* are unfair labor practices. These include (1) restraining or coercing employees in the exercise of their guaranteed bargaining rights (e.g., their right to refrain from joining a union), (2) causing an employer to discriminate against an employee who is not a union member, (3) refusing to bargain collectively with an employer, (4) conducting a secondary strike or a secondary boycott for a specified illegal

purpose,[5] (5) requiring employees covered by union-shop contracts to pay excessive or discriminatory initiation fees or dues, and (6) featherbedding (forcing an employer to pay for work not actually performed). The LMRA also established an 80-day cooling-off period for strikes that the president finds likely to endanger national safety or health. In addition, it created a Federal Mediation and Conciliation Service to assist employers and unions in settling labor disputes.

Congressional investigations during the 1950s uncovered corruption in internal union affairs and also revealed that the internal procedures of many unions were undemocratic. In response, Congress enacted the Labor Management Reporting and Disclosure Act (or Landrum–Griffin Act) in 1959. The act established a "bill of rights" for union members and attempted to make internal union affairs more democratic. It also amended the NLRA by adding to the LMRA's list of unfair union labor practices. The proportion of U.S. workers who are members of labor unions has decreased fairly steadily over the past 40 years. Today, less than 13 percent of the workforce are members of labor unions.

Two recent Supreme Court decisions appear to further weaken unions. First, in *Janus v. AFSCME,* 138 S. Ct. 2448 (2018), the Court ruled that the First Amendment prohibited public-sector unions from collecting fees from nonmembers of the union who benefit from the work of the union. Under the Taft–Hartley Act, state laws can authorize union security agreements, whereby a collective bargaining agreement can require even nonmembers to pay dues, fees, and assessments to the union. (Many states, however, prohibit union security agreements and are known euphemistically as "right-to-work" states.) *Janus,* which overruled a directly contrary precedent called *Abood v. Detroit Board of Education,* 431 U.S. 209 (1977), ruled in the context of public-sector unions that nonmembers' free speech rights under the First Amendment are violated when they are forced to pay union fees, despite any benefit they may receive from union activities.

Second, in *Epic Systems Corp. v. Lewis*, 138 S. Ct. 1612 (2018), the Supreme Court held that employers can require employees and prospective employees, as a condition of employment, to agree to submit any wage and hour or other workplace-condition claims to individual, not group, arbitration, despite the NLRA's protections for concerted and union activities. The Supreme Court determined that the Federal Arbitration Act protected employers from claims

---

[5] These are strikes or boycotts aimed at a third party with which the union has no real dispute. Their purpose is to coerce that party not to deal with an employer with which the union does have a dispute and, thus, to gain some leverage over the employer.

that they violated the NLRA in such circumstances, even though such individual arbitration agreements clearly undermine employees' attempt to engage in collective action through class arbitration actions. In other words, the Court rejected any notion that the NLRA might trump the FAA.

Equal Opportunity Legislation

LO51-3 Analyze and apply the appropriate legislation for a workplace scenario for potential unlawful discrimination and assess the possibility for liability, including an employer's potential defenses.

The Equal Pay Act The Equal Pay Act (EPA), which forbids *sex* discrimination regarding *pay*, was a 1963 amendment to the FLSA. Its coverage resembles the coverage of the FLSA's minimum wage provisions. Unlike the FLSA, however, the EPA covers executive, administrative, and professional employees.

The typical EPA case involves a woman who claims that she has received lower pay than a male employee performing substantially equal work for the same employer. The substantially equal work requirement is met if the plaintiff's job and the higher-paid male employee's job involve *each* of the following: (1) equal effort, (2) equal skill, (3) equal responsibility, and (4) similar working conditions.

Effort basically means physical or mental exertion. *Skill* refers to the experience, training, education, and ability required for the positions being compared. Here, the question is not whether the employees being compared have equal skills but whether their jobs require or utilize substantially the same skills. *Responsibility* (or accountability) involves such factors as the degree of supervision each job requires and the importance of each job to the employer. For instance, a retail sales position in which an employee may not approve customer checks probably is not equal to a sales position in which an employee has this authority. *Working conditions* refers to such factors as temperature, weather, fumes, ventilation, toxic conditions, and risk of injury. These need only be *similar*, not equal.

If the two jobs are substantially equal and they are paid unequally, an employer must prove one of the EPA's four defenses or it will lose the case. The employer has a defense if it shows that the pay disparity is based on (1) seniority, (2) merit, (3) quality or quantity of production (e.g., a piecework system), or (4) any factor other than sex. The first three defenses require an employer to show some organized, systematic, structured, and communicated rating system with predetermined criteria that apply equally to employees of each sex. The any-factor-other-than-sex

defense is a catchall category that includes shift differentials, bonuses paid because the job is part of a training program, and differences in the profitability of the products or services on which employees work, as well as employees' personal characteristics other than sex, like education and work experience. Relying on such personal characteristics, however, can be risky because they may be closely related to—or even based on—sex.

The EPA's remedial scheme resembles the FLSA's scheme. Under the EPA, however, employee suits are for the amount of back pay lost because of an employer's discrimination, not for unpaid minimum wages or overtime. An employee may also recover an equal sum as liquidated damages. The EPA is enforced by the Equal Employment Opportunity Commission (EEOC) rather than the Labor Department.[6] Unlike some of the employment discrimination statutes described later, however, the EPA does not require that private plaintiffs submit their complaints to the EEOC or a state agency before mounting suit.

In March 2019, the U.S. Women's National Soccer Team (WNT) filed a high-profile claim against the U.S. Soccer Federation (USSF) claiming a violation of the EPA and seeking $67 million in damages. Twenty-eight players on the WNT claimed that the USSF discriminated against them by engaging in "institutionalized gender discrimination" that "caused, contributed to, and perpetuated gender-based pay disparities" that manifested "in nearly every aspect of their employment."[7] The WNT players noted that they were paid significantly less than their counterparts on the U.S. Senior Men's National Soccer Team, despite the WNT's significant superior results relative to the men. In May 2020, the district court judge dismissed the EPA claim on a summary judgment ruling, finding that the pay differentials were largely a result of different collective bargaining agreements (CBAs) between USSF and the two teams, which the WNT negotiated. According to the judge:

> The WNT rejected an offer to be paid under the same pay-to-play structure as the [Senior Men's National Team] and . . . the WNT was willing to forgo higher bonuses for other benefits, such as greater base compensation and the guarantee of a higher number of contracted players. Accordingly, Plaintiffs

---

[6] The EEOC is an independent federal agency with a sizable staff and many regional offices. Its functions include (1) enforcing most of the employment discrimination laws discussed in this chapter through lawsuits that it initiates or in which it intervenes, (2) conciliating employment discrimination charges (e.g., by encouraging their negotiated settlement), (3) investigating discrimination-related matters, and (4) interpreting the statutes it enforces through regulations and guidelines.

[7] Complaint, *Morgan v. U.S. Soccer Fed'n, Inc.,* Case No. 2:19-CV-01717 (C.D. Cal. Mar. 8, 2019).

cannot now retroactively deem their CBA worse than the [men's] CBA by reference to what they would have made had they been paid under the . . . pay-to-play structure when they themselves rejected such a structure.[8]

When this book went to press, the judge rejected the WNT's request for an immediate appeal of the decision.

LOG ON

The WNT released a statement indicating they were "shocked and disappointed" by the dismissal of their EPA claim. Professor Julie Manning Magid argues that perhaps they should not have been, given shortcomings in the EPA and Title VII, which require evidentiary proof that allows real-life inequities to persist. See **https://theconversation.com/as-professional-sports-come-back-members-of-the-us-womens-soccer-team-are-still-paid-less-than-the-mens-139453**.

Title VII

LO51-3 Analyze and apply the appropriate legislation for a workplace scenario for potential unlawful discrimination and assess the possibility for liability, including an employer's potential defenses.

Employment discrimination might be defined as employer behavior that penalizes certain individuals because of personal traits that they cannot control and that bear no relation to effective job performance. Of the many employment discrimination laws in force today, the most important is Title VII of the 1964 Civil Rights Act. Unlike the Equal Pay Act, which merely forbids sex discrimination regarding pay, Title VII is a wide-ranging employment discrimination provision. It prohibits discrimination based on *race*, *color*, *religion*, *sex*, and *national origin* in hiring, firing, job assignments, pay, access to training and apprenticeship programs, and most other employment decisions.

Basic Features of Title VII In discussing Title VII, we first examine some general rules that govern all the kinds of discrimination it forbids. Then we examine each forbidden basis of discrimination in detail.

Covered Entities Title VII covers all employers employing 15 or more employees and engaging in an industry affecting interstate commerce. Employers include individuals, partnerships, corporations, colleges and universities, labor unions and employment agencies (with respect to

their own employees), and state and local governments.[9] Also, *referrals* by employment agencies are covered no matter what the size of the agency, if an employer serviced by the agency has 15 or more employees. In addition, Title VII covers certain unions—mainly those with 15 or more members—in their capacity as *employee representative*.

Procedures Although the EEOC sometimes sues to enforce Title VII, the usual Title VII suit is a private claim. The complicated procedures governing private Title VII suits are beyond the scope of this text, but a few points should be kept in mind. Private parties with a Title VII claim have no automatic right to sue. Instead, they first must file a *charge* with the EEOC, or with a state agency in states having suitable fair employment laws and enforcement schemes. This allows the EEOC or the state agency to investigate the claim, attempt conciliation if the claim has substance, or sue the employer itself. The EEOC has entered *worksharing agreements* with many of the state agencies. Among other things, the agreements relieve an employee of the hassle of separately filing charges with the EEOC and with the state agency. Instead, when an employee files a charge with a state agency that is party to a worksharing agreement, the charge is considered "dual filed" at the EEOC (and vice versa). Usually, the charge is investigated by the organization with which it was originally filed.

Regardless of whether the EEOC or a state agency conducts the investigation or attempts conciliation, at the close of the process the employee will receive a "right-to-sue letter." Until the employee receives the letter, a court has no authority to adjudicate the claim. Once the employee receives the letter, she has 90 days in which to file her lawsuit in court.

Theories of Discrimination Title VII incorporates two theories of discrimination: *disparate treatment* and *disparate impact*. Disparate treatment claims involve allegations that an employer treated an employee differently because of the employee's protected status (race, color, religion, sex, or national origin). Disparate treatment theory encompasses both individual claims by a single employee or systemic claims by a group of mistreated employees. Disparate impact claims involve allegations that an employer's policies or practices that are seemingly neutral with regard to race, color, religion, sex, or national origin have a disproportionate negative impact (or "adverse impact") on members of one of those groups. Disparate impact theory is most often used when the alleged discrimination affects many employees.

---

[8] *Morgan v. U.S. Soccer Fed'n, Inc.,* 445 F. Supp. 3d 665 (C.D. Cal. 2020).

[9] Claims of employment discrimination by federal government employees are subject to unique procedures, which are beyond the scope of this text.

How plaintiffs in Title VII cases prove that their employer discriminated against them varies depending on the theory of discrimination. Because the ability to muster sufficient proof is critical to any claim, we discuss the methods of proof under each theory in more detail here.

There are several ways a plaintiff can prove a disparate treatment claim.[10] Title VII prohibits employers from making employment decisions based, even in part, on an employee's protected status. An employee proves a disparate treatment claim if he can "demonstrate that race, color, religion, sex, or national origin was a motivating factor for any employment practice, even though other factors also motivated the practice."[11] This is often referred to as a "mixed-motives" claim, in which an employer's decision is an amalgam of both prohibited and lawful motives. As discussed briefly below, the employer may limit an employee's recovery in mixed-motives cases by proving that it would have made the same challenged employment decision even in the absence of the unlawful motive (i.e., the "same-decision defense"); nonetheless, if one of the factors in the employer's challenged decision was the employee's protected status, the employer has violated Title VII. Proving an unlawful motivating factor is easy in cases where the employer announces an express policy of disfavoring one of Title VII's protected classes. Similarly, sometimes a supervisor or manager makes an oral or written statement admitting to treating an employee differently based on her protected status. These are examples of direct evidence of a discriminatory motive. The *Gaskell v. University of Kentucky* case, which appears later in this chapter, illustrates that direct evidence need not be as explicit as these examples.

Employers often discriminate without being so obvious about it. Employees frequently rely on circumstantial evidence to prove the employer's discriminatory motive. Circumstantial evidence relies on reasonable inferences, rather than on admissions or policies, to prove the employer's unlawful motive. The Supreme Court clarified that circumstantial evidence is just as useful as direct evidence to prove claims of employment discrimination.[12]

Many Title VII plaintiffs face an uphill battle because proving an employer's discriminatory motive requires the employee to "get in the head" of the employer. Without direct evidence or strongly suggestive circumstantial evidence, proving a disparate treatment case can be difficult, especially when the employer purposefully tries to conceal its discriminatory motive. As a result, courts have adopted a specialized burden-shifting method of presenting circumstantial evidence of a cover-up upon which many Title VII plaintiffs rely. In such suits, the plaintiff is typically not proceeding under a mixed-motives approach, but rather trying to show that the only credible motive is an unlawful one. The plaintiff first must show a *prima facie case*: a case that eliminates the most common nondiscriminatory reasons for the challenged employment decision (e.g., hiring, promotion, or termination) and creates a presumption of discrimination. The proof needed for a prima facie case varies with the nature of the challenged employment decision, but usually it is not onerous and is easily made. To establish a prima facie case to challenge a hiring decision, for example, the plaintiff must prove that she applied for the job and was minimally qualified for it, that she is a member of the protected class that she claims was the unlawful motivating factor the employer considered, that she was rejected, and that the employer continued to attempt to fill the job or filled it with someone who is not a member of the relevant protected class.

Once the plaintiff establishes a prima facie case, the employer must rebut the presumption of discrimination by producing evidence that the challenged employment decision was taken for *legitimate, nondiscriminatory reasons*. If the employer refuses or fails to produce such evidence, the plaintiff automatically wins. In response to a prima facie case challenging a hiring decision, for example, the employer might produce evidence that it rejected the plaintiff because she was late to the interview.

If the employer produces satisfactory nondiscriminatory reasons, the plaintiff must then show that the discrimination actually occurred, typically by showing that the employer's reasons were a mere *pretext* for discrimination. For example, she might show that the employer has hired men for similar positions despite their tardiness for an interview.

The method of proving a disparate impact claim is more straightforward because it does not require proof of the employer's motive. Instead, disparate impact focuses on results. If a policy or practice—for example, a height, weight, or high school diploma requirement for hiring or a written test for hiring or promotion—results in an adverse impact on a protected group, the employer may have violated Title VII, even though the requirement is neutral as to Title VII's protected classes and the employer had no specific desire to discriminate against the affected employees. A prima facie case of disparate impact involves showing that the challenged, facially neutral practice has an adverse impact on the plaintiff's race, color, religion, sex, or national origin. Adverse impact is usually established by statistical evidence showing that the practice results in disproportionately

---

[10] Individual claims of disparate treatment are more common than systemic claims and, thus, are the focus of this discussion.

[11] 42 U.S.C. § 2000e-2(m) (2006).

[12] *Desert Palace, Inc. v. Costa*, 539 U.S. 90, 100 (2003).

harsher outcomes for the protected class. For example, a plaintiff may show that a standardized test that the employer uses to screen candidates for promotion has a disproportionately lower pass rate for individuals of a particular national origin than for others, or that a minimum height requirement screens out proportionally many more women than men. If the plaintiffs show a disparate impact, the employer loses unless it demonstrates that the challenged practice is *job-related for the position in question and consistent with business necessity*. For example, the employer might show that its promotion test really predicts effective job performance and that effective performance in the relevant job is necessary for its operations. Even if the employer makes this demonstration, the plaintiffs have another option: to show that the employer's legitimate business needs can be advanced by an *alternative employment practice* that is *less discriminatory than the challenged practice*. For example, the plaintiffs might show that the employer's legitimate needs can be met by a different promotion test that has less adverse impact on the protected group. If the employer refuses to adopt this practice, the plaintiffs win.

The following *Gaskell* case involves a mixed-motives claim of disparate treatment on the basis of religion, in which the court must sort out the plaintiff's evidence of a discriminatory motive and the defendant's evidence that it was motivated by nondiscriminatory reasons.

Gaskell v. University of Kentucky — 2010 WL 4867630 (E.D. Ky. Nov. 23, 2010)

In 2007, the University of Kentucky (UK) commenced a search for the founding director of its new astronomics observatory. Martin Gaskell applied for the position and, initially, was regarded by the Search Committee as the leading candidate. He was far more qualified and experienced than any of the other applicants. At the time of his application, Gaskell worked at the University of Nebraska–Lincoln (UNL), where he had secured funding for, had overseen the design and construction of, and eventually ran the student observatory.

The Search Committee conducted an initial round of phone interviews with Gaskell and several other candidates. Following the phone interviews, the committee ranked Gaskell first among the candidates.

Gaskell's candidacy hit some snags, though. When Michael Cavagnero, the chair of the Department of Physics & Astronomy and a member of the Search Committee, contacted Gaskell's supervisor at UNL, he learned that Gaskell had caused some conflict at UNL because he was sometimes obstinate. In addition, members of the Search Committee discovered articles, lecture notes, and public statements by Gaskell revolving around the theme of "Modern Astronomy, the Bible, and Creation." These raised concerns that Gaskell was a "creationist." Several Search Committee members perceived that Gaskell blended religious thought with scientific theory, which they believed would adversely affect his ability to perform the outreach functions of the job.

Cavagnero again contacted Gaskell's supervisor at UNL and asked him whether Gaskell's personal religious beliefs had interfered with his duties in the classroom and in the community at UNL. According to the supervisor, a handful of students had mentioned in their teacher evaluations that it was refreshing to have a professor who believed in God, but that otherwise, Gaskell's views on religion had not interfered with his work.

Cavagnero also asked some of his colleagues to read Gaskell's work to determine if it was "good science." Notably, members of the UK Biology Department participated in this review and determined that Gaskell's writing included scientific statements about evolution that showed a fundamental lack of appreciation for the scientific method and for well-established scientific principles. The biologists ultimately told Cavagnero that they would not work with one of "these types of individuals" if he was hired to direct the observatory.

UK ultimately hired Timothy Knauer, a former student and employee of UK's Department of Physics and Astronomy. Although UK concedes that Gaskell had more education and experience, it contends that it hired Knauer because he demonstrated more of the qualities that UK wanted in its Observatory Director.

Gaskell sued UK claiming that he was not hired because of his religion in violation of Title VII. Both parties moved for summary judgment.

Forester, Senior Judge

Title VII of the Civil Rights Act of 1964 provides that "[i]t shall be an unlawful employment practice for an employer . . . to discharge any individual, or otherwise discriminate against an individual with respect to compensation, terms, conditions, or privileges of employment, because of such individual's . . . religion." The term "religion" is defined to include "all aspects of religious observance and practice, as well as belief, unless an employer demonstrates that he is unable to reasonably accommodate to an employee's . . . religious observance or practice without undue hardship on the conduct of the employer's business."

As in any other discriminatory discharge or refusal to hire case, the plaintiff can establish that he was discharged or not hired on the basis of his religion through direct or indirect means. Direct evidence is evidence which, if believed, "requires the conclusion that unlawful discrimination was at least a motivating factor in the employer's actions." Direct evidence "does not require the factfinder to draw any inferences in order to conclude that the challenged employment action was motivated at least in part by prejudice against members of the protected group." Evidence which in and of itself suggests that the person or persons with the power to hire, fire, promote, or demote the plaintiff were animated by an illegal employment criterion amounts to direct proof of discrimination. Remarks to the effect that "I won't hire you because you're a woman," or "I'm firing you because you're not a Christian," are obvious examples of direct evidence of discrimination. However, other, less obvious remarks, have been found to be direct evidence of discrimination. Remarks and other evidence that reflect a propensity by the decisionmaker to evaluate employees based on illegal criteria can suffice as direct evidence of discrimination even if the evidence stops short of a virtual admission of illegality. Proof of this nature supports the inference that a statutorily prescribed factor such as religion was at least a motivating factor in the adverse employment action at issue.

If there is no direct evidence of discrimination, then courts rely on the framework established in the Supreme Court in *McDonnell Douglas Corp. v. Green*, 411 U.S. 792 (1973). Under this framework, the plaintiff carries the burden of proving by a preponderance of the evidence a prima facie case of discrimination. If the plaintiff is able to prove a prima facie case, then the burden shifts to the defendant "to articulate some legitimate, nondiscriminatory reason for the employee's rejection." If the defendant is able to carry this burden, then the plaintiff must prove by a preponderance of the evidence that the legitimate reasons offered were not true reasons but were a pretext for discrimination.

UK argues that it hired a different candidate for the Observatory Director for reasons that have nothing to do with Gaskell's religion. Because Gaskell has failed to show by a preponderance of the evidence that UK's reasons were a pretext for discrimination, UK contends that, based on *McDonnell Douglas* analysis, Gaskell's claims must be dismissed.

Although UK argues that the *McDonnell Douglas* framework applies to this case, Gaskell contends that he has presented direct evidence of discrimination. The record contains substantial evidence that Gaskell was a leading candidate for the position until the issue of his religion (as Gaskell calls it) or his scientific position (as UK calls it) became an issue. Specifically, he points to the e-mail written by [Professor Thomas] Troland, the Search Committee Chair, to Cavagnero just days prior to the Search Committee's vote to recommend Knauer for the position and thereby reject Gaskell. The e-mail, with the subject line "The Gaskell Affair," states:

It has become clear to me that there is virtually no way Gaskell will be offered the job despite his qualifications that stand far above those of any other applicant. Other reasons will be given

for this choice when we meet Tuesday. In the end, however, the real reason why we will not offer him the job is because of his religious beliefs in matters that are unrelated to astronomy or to any of the duties specified for this position. (For example, the job does not involve outreach in biology.) . . . If Martin were not so superbly qualified, so breathtakingly above the other applicants in background and experience, then our decision would be much simpler. We could easily choose another applicant, and we could content ourselves with the idea that Martin's religious beliefs played little role in our decision. However, this is not the case. As it is, no objective observer could possibly believe that we excluded Martin on any basis other than religious. . . .

Certainly, Troland, who was chair of the Search Committee, participated in the interviews of the candidates, discussions of the committee, [and] e-mail exchanges involving the process played an obvious and important role in the decisionmaking process. As he explained to Patty Bender, the University Equal Employment Officer who investigated [a] complaint of religious discrimination submitted by [another member of the Search Committee]:

I was part of the entire process that led to this decision. I know what observatory committee members said in meetings and privately, not just their e-mail comments. I know that the university (not your office!) chose an applicant with almost no relevant experience over one with immense experience in virtually every aspect of the observatory director's duties. And I know that this choice was made (to a significant extent) on grounds that have nothing to do with the job as advertised nor with the job as envisioned by our department.

His comments, if true, are direct evidence of religious discrimination.

Additional direct evidence of religious discrimination can be found in the deposition of Cavagnero, who stated that the debate generated by Gaskell's website and his religious beliefs, was an "element" in the decision not to hire Gaskell. Also, [another professor] testified in his deposition that Gaskell's "views of religious things in relation to reconciling what is known scientifically about how the world developed and what is represented in the Bible" was "a factor" in his decision not to support Gaskell. [Yet another] committee member stated in his deposition that religion was an "underlying theme in everything we discussed."

Gaskell points to other evidence that suggests a propensity by the Search Committee to evaluate employees based on illegal criteria, including an e-mail by a Search Committee member stating: "Clearly this man is complex and likely fascinating to talk with—but potentially evangelical." That same member also said, "If the job were solely about physics and astronomy and within the university I would strongly agree with you that Martin's beliefs on biology and religion don't matter a hoot and should not figure in the discussion at all." The negative implication is clear: because the job was not solely about physics and astronomy within the university, Gaskell's beliefs on biology and religion do matter.

Gaskell's allegations, when considered together and taken as true, raise a triable issue of fact as to whether his religious beliefs were a substantial motivating factor in UK's decision not to hire him. With the direct evidence of religious discrimination present in this case, it is not necessary for the Court to engage in the *McDonnell Douglas* burden-shifting framework.

***

Accordingly, based on Gaskell's presentation of direct evidence of discrimination, UK's motion for summary judgment will be denied. The Court now turns to Gaskell's motion for partial summary judgment.

In 1991, Title VII of the Civil Rights Act was amended to include . . . Section 2000e-2(m). This section provides as follows: an employer commits an unlawful employment practice "when the complaining party demonstrates that race, color, religion, sex, or national origin was a motivating factor for any employment practice, even though other factors also motivated the practice. [T]he purpose and effect of this section was 'to eliminate the employer's ability to escape liability in mixed-motives cases by proving that it would have made the same decision in the absence of the discriminatory motivation.'" As the Sixth Circuit has stated, "in mixed-motive cases, a plaintiff can win simply by showing that the defendant's consideration of a protected characteristic 'was *a* motivating factor for any employment practice, *even though other factors also motivated the practice.*'" The *McDonnell Douglas* burden-shifting framework does not apply to mixed-motive claims. . . . [T]o survive a defendant's motion for summary judgment, a Title VII plaintiff asserting a mixed-motive claim need only produce evidence sufficient to convince a jury that: (1) the defendant took an adverse employment action against the plaintiff; and (2) "race, color, religion, sex, or national origin was *a* motivating factor" for the defendant's adverse employment action.

There is no dispute that UK's decision not to hire Gaskell was an adverse employment action. The issue, then, is whether Gaskell's religion was "a motivating factor." As set out above, Gaskell has presented direct and other evidence which, if believed, establishes that his religion was a factor in UK's employment decision. However, UK has also come forward with other evidence that religion was not a motivating factor in its decision to hire Knauer. UK notes that the only question that was asked of Gaskell regarding his statement on evolution was posed by Cavagnero who was concerned that Gaskell would violate UK policy by representing his own opinion as that of the University should he link his university webpage to his personal webpage containing religious material. UK contends that the Search Committee did not act improperly when it considered Gaskell's comments about evolution because Gaskell made those comments public not only during his 1997 lecture at UK, but also by posting his lecture notes on his webpage. UK also contends that it did not consider Gaskell's religious beliefs, only his public comments that there were scientific problems with the theory of evolution. According to UK, the Search Committee was concerned that these publicly expressed views would impair Gaskell's ability to serve effectively as Observatory Director.

UK's motivation for its decision not to hire Gaskell is very fact intensive and difficult to determine at the summary judgment stage. Because UK has come forward with more than a scintilla of evidence to support its argument that religion was not a motivating factor in its decision, Gaskell's motion for partial summary judgment will be denied.

Gaskell's motion for partial summary judgment is denied; UK's motion for summary judgment is denied; and this matter remains pending.

Defenses Title VII provides employers several defenses, which either limit plaintiff's recovery or completely excuse the employer from liability. The most important such defenses include:

1. *Same-decision defense.* Title VII allows an employer to limit a plaintiff's recovery in a mixed-motives disparate treatment claim if the employer proves that it would have taken the same action in the absence of the unlawful motivating factor. In other words, if an employer proves it would have made the same decision regardless of the employee's protected status, the employee is not entitled to any personal recovery. The employer has violated the law and can be enjoined from continuing to do so, but the employee cannot recover money damages or be reinstated. An employee may still be entitled to recover his attorney fees for the attorney's work on the successful portion of the mixed-motives claim. In the preceding *Gaskell* case, for instance, if a jury found that UK was motivated not to choose Gaskell as Observatory Director because of his religion, the same-decision defense might allow UK to escape paying money damages (e.g., back pay, compensatory, and punitive damages) to Gaskell. For example, UK might try to prove

that it would not have hired Gaskell because of reports of his obstinacy at his previous employment, regardless of his religious beliefs.

2. *Seniority.* Title VII is not violated if the employer treats employees differently pursuant to a *bona fide seniority system.* To be bona fide, such a system at least must treat all employees equally on its face, not have been created for discriminatory reasons, and not operate in a discriminatory fashion.

3. *The various "merit" defenses.* An employer also escapes Title VII liability if it acts pursuant to a *bona fide merit system,* a system basing earnings on *quantity or quality of production,* or the results of a *professionally developed ability test.* Presumably, such systems and tests at least must meet the general standards for seniority systems stated above. Also, the EEOC has promulgated lengthy *Uniform Guidelines on Employee Selection Procedures* that speak to these and other matters.

4. *The BFOQ defense.* Finally, Title VII allows employers to discriminate on the bases of sex, religion, or national origin where one of those traits is a *bona fide occupational qualification (BFOQ) that is reasonably necessary to the business in question.* The BFOQ defense is applied to cases of disparate treatment, whereas the business necessity defense, which was discussed earlier, applies in disparate impact cases. The BFOQ defense does not protect race or color discrimination. Moreover, the defense is a narrow one. Generally, it is available only where a certain sex, religion, or national origin is necessary for effective job performance. For example, a BFOQ probably would exist where a female is employed to model women's clothing or to fit women's undergarments. But the BFOQ defense usually is unavailable where the discrimination is based on stereotypes (e.g., that women are less aggressive than men) or on the preferences of coworkers or customers (e.g., the preference of airline travelers for female rather than male flight attendants). The defense also is unavailable where the employer's discriminatory practice promotes goals, such as fetal protection, that do not concern effective job performance. In addition, required or desired traits or characteristics cannot be the basis for a BFOQ defense unless those traits or characteristics are synonymous with a particular sex, religion, or national origin. Otherwise, an individualized evaluation of the trait or characteristic in each applicant is required.

Remedies Various remedies are possible once private plaintiffs or the EEOC wins a Title VII suit. If intentional discrimination has caused lost wages, employees can obtain back pay. At the court's discretion, successful private plaintiffs also may recover reasonable attorney fees. In addition, victims of intentional discrimination can recover **compensatory damages** for harms such as emotional distress, sickness, loss of reputation, or denial of credit. Victims of intentional discrimination also can recover **punitive damages** where the defendant discriminated with malice or with reckless indifference to the plaintiff's rights. However, Title VII caps the sum of the plaintiff's recoverable compensatory and punitive damages to certain amounts that vary with the size of the employer. For example, they cannot total more than $300,000 for an employer with more than 500 employees. If a jury verdict awards a plaintiff an amount in excess of the statutory cap, a defendant can request a reduction of the award in a posttrial order by the judge.

Discrimination may also entitle successful plaintiffs to equitable relief. Examples include orders compelling hiring, reinstatement, or retroactive seniority. On occasion, moreover, the courts have ordered quotalike preferences in Title VII cases involving race and (occasionally) gender discrimination. For example, a court might order that whites and minorities be hired on a 50–50 basis until minority representation in the employer's work force reaches some specified percentage. Generally speaking, such orders are permissible if (1) an employer has engaged in severe, widespread, or longstanding discrimination; (2) the order does not unduly restrict the employment interests of white people; and (3) it does not force an employer to hire unqualified workers. Minority preferences also may appear in the **consent decrees** courts issue when approving the terms on which the parties have settled a Title VII case.

Race or Color Discrimination At this point, we consider each of Title VII's prohibited bases of discrimination in more detail. *Race or color* discrimination includes discrimination against Blacks, other racial minorities, Alaska Natives, and American Indians, among others. Title VII also prohibits racial discrimination against whites. Nonetheless, voluntary racial preferences that favor minorities who are qualified for the job in question survive a Title VII attack if they (1) are intended to correct a racial imbalance involving underrepresentation of minorities in traditionally segregated job categories, (2) do not "unnecessarily trammel" the rights of white employees or create an absolute bar to their advancement, and (3) are only temporary. Note that here our concern is not the use of minority preferences as a *remedy* for a Title VII violation, but whether such preferences *themselves* violate Title VII when voluntarily established by an employer.

National Origin Discrimination National origin discrimination includes discrimination based on (1) the country of one's or one's ancestors' origin or (2) one's possession of physical, cultural, or linguistic characteristics identified with people of a particular nation. Thus, plaintiffs in national origin discrimination cases need not have been born in the country at issue. In fact, if the discrimination is based on physical, cultural, or linguistic traits identified with a particular nation, even the plaintiff's ancestors need not have been born there. Thus, a person of pure French ancestry may have a Title VII case if she suffers discrimination because she looks like, acts like, or talks like a German.

Certain formally neutral employment practices can also constitute national origin discrimination. Employers who hire only U.S. citizens may violate Title VII if their policy has the purpose or effect of discriminating against one or more national origin groups. This could happen where the employer is located in an area where aliens of a particular nationality are heavily concentrated. Also, employment criteria such as height, weight, and fluency in English may violate Title VII if they have a disparate impact on a national origin group and are not job related.

Religious Discrimination   For Title VII purposes, the term *religion* is broadly defined. The EEOC says that it includes any set of moral beliefs that are sincerely held with the same strength as traditional religious views. Courts have followed the EEOC's expansive interpretation. In fact, Title VII forbids religious discrimination against atheists. It also forbids discrimination based on religious *observances or practices*— for example, grooming, clothing, or the refusal to work on the Sabbath. But such discrimination is permissible if an employer cannot reasonably accommodate the religious practice without suffering undue hardship. Undue hardship exists when the accommodation imposes more than a minimal burden on an employer. The Americans with Disabilities Act, discussed later in this chapter, also includes an accommodation mandate. Despite both using the same "hardship" language, courts have expected employers to shoulder substantially more inconvenience and expense to accommodate disabled employees than religious employees.

In a 2015 case, the Supreme Court clarified that a claim of failure to accommodate to an employee's religious observance or practice is simply a type of disparate treatment claim.[13] As such, the employee is not required to prove the employer had knowledge of the religious nature of the observance or practice, provided the employee can prove that the employer's negative treatment of the employee (or applicant) was motivated at least in part by the observance or practice. Practically, this ruling relieves the employee of what was sometimes an uncomfortable expectation of some courts that the employee had to notify the employer of her religiously motivated observances or practices *prior* to the employee being aware of any need for an accommodation.

Sex Discrimination   Title VII's ban on sex discrimination applies to gender discrimination against both men and women. Still, voluntary employer programs favoring women in hiring or promotion survive a Title VII attack if they meet the previous tests for voluntary racial preferences (reformulated in terms of gender). Through an important amendment to the 1964 Civil Rights Act in 1978 called the Pregnancy Discrimination Act, Title VII also forbids discrimination on the bases of pregnancy and childbirth and requires employers to treat these conditions like any other condition similarly affecting working ability in their sick leave programs, medical benefit and disability plans, and so forth. Finally, sexual stereotyping violates Title VII. This is employer behavior that either (1) denies an employee opportunities by requiring that he or she must have traits traditionally associated with his or her sex (e.g., requiring a woman to have a nurturing demeanor) or (2) penalizes him or her for lacking such traits (e.g., penalizing a man for lacking aggression or for shying away from physical confrontation).

For most of Title VII's history, courts had consistently interpreted the prohibition against sex discrimination narrowly, holding that it did not forbid discrimination on the basis of sexual orientation or gender identity.[14] Throughout the past decade, however, the EEOC and several courts departed from the traditional approach. The EEOC adopted an interpretation that discrimination on the basis of sexual orientation and/or gender identity is sex discrimination.[15] In addition, the Courts of Appeals for the Second, Sixth, and Seventh Circuits interpreted Title VII to prohibit sexual orientation discrimination as a form of sex discrimination, while the Eleventh Circuit had held the opposite. In 2019, the Supreme Court heard appeals of three such cases to resolve that split among the circuit courts. The following *Bostock* decision, issued by the Supreme Court in June 2020, ruled that Title VII's prohibition against sex discrimination in employment by necessity prohibits discrimination on the basis of sexual orientation and gender identity.

---

[13] *EEOC v. Abercrombie & Fitch Stores, Inc.*, 135 S. Ct. 2028 (2015).

[14] Even so, a number of state and municipal fair employment practices laws had long forbidden discrimination on the basis of sexual orientation. For details about the legal protections provided to LGBT people in the workplace in each state, see Lambda Legal, www.lambdalegal.org/ states-regions (providing a summary of state laws that forbid discrimination on the basis of sexual orientation).

[15] See EEOC, "What You Should Know About EEOC and the Enforcement Protections for LGBT Workers," www.eeoc.gov/eeoc/ newsroom/wysk/enforcement_protections_lgbt_workers.cfm.

Bostock v. Clayton County, Georgia   140 S. Ct. 1731 (2020)

The U.S. Supreme Court consolidated the appeal of three cases. Each began similarly: An employer fired a long-time employee shortly after the employee revealed that he or she is homosexual or transgender—and allegedly for no reason other than the employee's homosexuality or transgender status.

Gerald Bostock worked for Clayton County, Georgia, as a child welfare advocate. Under his leadership, the county won national awards for its work. After a decade with the county, Mr. Bostock began participating in a gay recreational softball league. Not long after that, influential members of the community allegedly made disparaging comments about Mr. Bostock's sexual orientation and participation in the league. Soon, he was fired for conduct "unbecoming" a county employee.

Donald Zarda worked as a skydiving instructor at Altitude Express in New York. After several seasons with the company, Mr. Zarda mentioned that he was gay and, days later, was fired.

Aimee Stephens worked at R.G. & G.R. Harris Funeral Homes in Garden City, Michigan. When she got the job, Ms. Stephens presented as a male. But two years into her service with the company, she began treatment for despair and loneliness. Ultimately, clinicians diagnosed her with gender dysphoria and recommended that she begin living as a woman. In her sixth year with the company, Ms. Stephens wrote a letter to her employer explaining that she planned to "live and work full-time as a woman" after she returned from an upcoming vacation. The funeral home fired her before she left, telling her "this is not going to work out."

Each employee brought suit under Title VII alleging unlawful discrimination on the basis of sex. In Bostock's case, the U.S. Court of Appeals for the Eleventh Circuit held that the law does not prohibit employers from firing employees for being gay. It upheld the dismissal of his suit. In Zarda's case, the U.S. Court of Appeals for the Second Circuit concluded that sexual orientation discrimination does violate Title VII and allowed his case to proceed. In Stephens's case the U.S. Court of Appeals for the Sixth Circuit held that Title VII bars employers from firing employees because of their transgender status.

The Supreme Court granted certiorari in the matters to resolve the disagreement among the courts of appeals over the scope of Title VII's protections for homosexual and transgender persons.

Gorsuch, J.

II

This Court normally interprets a statute in accord with the ordinary public meaning of its terms at the time of its enactment. After all, only the words on the page constitute the law adopted by Congress and approved by the President. If judges could add to, remodel, update, or detract from old statutory terms inspired only by extratextual sources and our own imaginations, we would risk amending statutes outside the legislative process reserved for the people's representatives. And we would deny the people the right to continue relying on the original meaning of the law they have counted on to settle their rights and obligations.

With this in mind, our task is clear. We must determine the ordinary public meaning of Title VII's command that it is "unlawful . . . for an employer to fail or refuse to hire or to discharge any individual, or otherwise to discriminate against any individual with respect to his compensation, terms, conditions, or privileges of employment, because of such individual's race, color, religion, sex, or national origin." § 2000e-2(a)(1). To do so, we orient ourselves to the time of the statute's adoption, here 1964, and begin by examining the key statutory terms in turn before assessing their impact on the cases at hand and then confirming our work against this Court's precedents.

A

The only statutorily protected characteristic at issue in today's cases is "sex"—and that is also the primary term in Title VII whose meaning the parties dispute. Appealing to roughly contemporaneous dictionaries, the employers say that, as used here, the term "sex" in 1964 referred to "status as either male or female [as] determined by reproductive biology." The employees counter by submitting that, even in 1964, the term bore a broader scope, capturing more than anatomy and reaching at least some norms concerning sex identity and sexual orientation. But because nothing in our approach to these cases turns on the outcome of the parties' debate, and because the employees concede the point for argument's sake, we proceed on the assumption that "sex" signified what the employers suggest, referring only to biological distinctions between male and female.

Still, that's just a starting point. The question isn't just what "sex" meant, but what Title VII says about it. Most notably, the statute prohibits employers from taking certain actions "because of" sex. And, as this Court has previously explained, "the ordinary meaning of 'because of' is 'by reason of' or 'on account of.'" *University of Tex. Southwestern Medical Center v. Nassar*, 570 U.S. 338, 350 (2013). In the language of law, this means that Title VII's "because of" test incorporates the "'simple'" and "traditional" standard of but-for causation. *Nassar*, 570 U.S. at 346, 360. That form of causation is established whenever a particular outcome would not have happened "but for" the purported cause. In other words, a but-for test directs us to change one thing at a time and see if the outcome changes. If it does, we have found a but-for cause.

This can be a sweeping standard. Often, events have multiple but-for causes. So, for example, if a car accident occurred *both* because the defendant ran a red light *and* because the plaintiff failed to signal his turn at the intersection, we might call each a but-for cause of the collision. When it comes to Title VII, the adoption of the traditional but-for causation standard means a defendant cannot avoid liability just by citing some *other* factor that contributed to its challenged employment decision. So long as the plaintiff's sex was one but-for cause of that decision, that is enough to trigger the law. . . .

As sweeping as even the but-for causation standard can be, Title VII does not concern itself with everything that happens "because of" sex. The statute imposes liability on employers only when they "fail or refuse to hire," "discharge," "or otherwise . . . discriminate against" someone because of a statutorily protected characteristic like sex. The employers acknowledge that they discharged the plaintiffs in today's cases, but assert that the statute's list of verbs is qualified by the last item on it: "otherwise . . . discriminate against." By virtue of the word *otherwise*, the employers suggest, Title VII concerns itself not with every discharge, only with those discharges that involve discrimination.

Accepting this point, too, for argument's sake, the question becomes: What did "discriminate" mean in 1964? As it turns out, it meant then roughly what it means today: "To make a difference in treatment or favor (of one as compared with others)." *Webster's New International Dictionary* 745 (2d ed. 1954). To "discriminate against" a person, then, would seem to mean treating that individual worse than others who are similarly situated. In so-called "disparate treatment" cases like today's, this Court has also held that the difference in treatment based on sex must be intentional. *See, e.g., Watson v. Fort Worth Bank & Trust,* 487 U.S. 977, 986 (1988). So, taken together, an employer who intentionally treats a person worse because of sex—such as by firing the person for actions or attributes it would tolerate in an individual of another sex—discriminates against that person in violation of Title VII. . . .

B
From the ordinary public meaning of the statute's language at the time of the law's adoption, a straightforward rule emerges: An employer violates Title VII when it intentionally fires an individual employee based in part on sex. It doesn't matter if other factors besides the plaintiff's sex contributed to the decision. . . . If the employer intentionally relies in part on an individual employee's sex when deciding to discharge the employee—put differently, if changing the employee's sex would have yielded a different choice by the employer—a statutory violation has occurred. Title VII's message is "simple but momentous": An individual employee's sex is "not relevant to the selection, evaluation,

or compensation of employees." *Price Waterhouse v. Hopkins,* 490 U.S. 228, 239 (1989) (plurality opinion).

The statute's message for our cases is equally simple and momentous: An individual's homosexuality or transgender status is not relevant to employment decisions. That's because it is impossible to discriminate against a person for being homosexual or transgender without discriminating against that individual based on sex. Consider, for example, an employer with two employees, both of whom are attracted to men. The two individuals are, to the employer's mind, materially identical in all respects, except that one is a man and the other a woman. If the employer fires the male employee for no reason other than the fact he is attracted to men, the employer discriminates against him for traits or actions it tolerates in his female colleague. Put differently, the employer intentionally singles out an employee to fire based in part on the employee's sex, and the affected employee's sex is a but-for cause of his discharge. Or take an employer who fires a transgender person who was identified as a male at birth but who now identifies as a female. If the employer retains an otherwise identical employee who was identified as female at birth, the employer intentionally penalizes a person identified as male at birth for traits or actions that it tolerates in an employee identified as female at birth. Again, the individual employee's sex plays an unmistakable and impermissible role in the discharge decision.

That distinguishes these cases from countless others where Title VII has nothing to say. Take an employer who fires a female employee for tardiness or incompetence or simply supporting the wrong sports team. Assuming the employer would not have tolerated the same trait in a man, Title VII stands silent. But unlike any of these other traits or actions, homosexuality and transgender status are inextricably bound up with sex. Not because homosexuality or transgender status are related to sex in some vague sense or because discrimination on these bases has some disparate impact on one sex or another, but because to discriminate on these grounds requires an employer to intentionally treat individual employees differently because of their sex. . . .

[I]ntentional discrimination based on sex violates Title VII, even if it is intended only as a means to achieving the employer's ultimate goal of discriminating against homosexual or transgender employees. There is simply no escaping the role intent plays here: Just as sex is necessarily a but-for *cause* when an employer discriminates against homosexual or transgender employees, an employer who discriminates on these grounds inescapably *intends* to rely on sex in its decisionmaking. Imagine an employer who has a policy of firing any employee known to be homosexual. The employer hosts an office holiday party and invites employees to bring their spouses. A model employee arrives and introduces a manager to Susan, the employee's wife. Will that employee be fired? If the policy works as the employer intends, the answer depends entirely on whether the model employee is a man or a woman. To be sure, that employer's ultimate goal might be to discriminate on the basis of sexual orientation. But to achieve that purpose the employer must, along the way, intentionally treat an employee worse based in part on that individual's sex.

An employer musters no better a defense by responding that it is equally happy to fire male *and* female employees who are homosexual or transgender. Title VII liability is not limited to employers who, through the sum of all of their employment actions, treat the class of men differently than the class of women. Instead, the law makes each instance of discriminating against an individual employee because of that individual's sex an independent violation of Title VII. . . .

III

What do the employers have to say in reply? For present purposes, they do not dispute that they fired the plaintiffs for being homosexual or transgender. Sorting out the true reasons for an adverse employment decision is often a hard business, but none of that is at issue here. Rather, the employers submit that even intentional discrimination against employees based on their homosexuality or transgender status supplies no basis for liability under Title VII. . . . In the end, the employers are left to retreat beyond the statute's text, where they fault us for ignoring the legislature's purposes in enacting Title VII or certain expectations about its operation. They warn, too, about consequences that might follow a ruling for the employees. But none of these contentions about what the employers think the law was meant to do, or should do, allow us to ignore the law as it is.

A

Maybe most intuitively, the employers assert that discrimination on the basis of homosexuality and transgender status aren't referred to as sex discrimination in ordinary conversation. If asked by a friend (rather than a judge) why they were fired, even today's plaintiffs would likely respond that it was because they were gay or transgender, not because of sex. According to the employers, that conversational answer, not the statute's strict terms, should guide our thinking and suffice to defeat any suggestion that the employees now before us were fired because of sex.

But this submission rests on a mistaken understanding of what kind of cause the law is looking for in a Title VII case. In conversation, a speaker is likely to focus on what seems most relevant or informative to the listener. So an employee who has just been fired is likely to identify the primary or most direct cause rather than list literally every but-for cause. To do otherwise would be

tiring at best. But these conversational conventions do not control Title VII's legal analysis, which asks simply whether sex was a but-for cause. . . .

Trying another angle, the defendants before us suggest that an employer who discriminates based on homosexuality or transgender status doesn't *intentionally* discriminate based on sex, as a disparate treatment claim requires. . . .

What . . . do the employers mean when they insist intentional discrimination based on homosexuality or transgender status isn't intentional discrimination based on sex? [T]he employers may mean that they don't perceive themselves as motivated by a desire to discriminate based on sex. But nothing in Title VII turns on the employer's labels or any further intentions (or motivations) for its conduct beyond sex discrimination. . . .

Aren't these cases different, the employers ask, given that an employer could refuse to hire a gay or transgender individual without ever learning the applicant's sex? Suppose an employer asked homosexual or transgender applicants to tick a box on its application form. The employer then had someone else redact any information that could be used to discern sex. The resulting applications would disclose which individuals are homosexual or transgender without revealing whether they also happen to be men or women. Doesn't that possibility indicate that the employer's discrimination against homosexual or transgender persons cannot be sex discrimination?

No, it doesn't. Even in this example, the individual applicant's sex still weighs as a factor in the employer's decision. Change the hypothetical ever so slightly and its flaws become apparent. Suppose an employer's application form offered a single box to check if the applicant is either Black or Catholic. If the employer refuses to hire anyone who checks that box, would we conclude the employer has complied with Title VII, so long as it studiously avoids learning any particular applicant's race or religion? Of course not: By intentionally setting out a rule that makes hiring turn on race or religion, the employer violates the law, whatever he might know or not know about individual applicants.

The same holds here. There is no way for an applicant to decide whether to check the homosexual or transgender box without considering sex. To see why, imagine an applicant doesn't know what the words homosexual or transgender mean. Then try writing out instructions for who should check the box without using the words man, woman, or sex (or some synonym). It can't be done. Likewise, there is no way an employer can discriminate against those who check the homosexual or transgender box without discriminating in part because of an applicant's sex. . . .

B

Ultimately, the employers are forced to abandon the statutory text and precedent altogether and appeal to assumptions and policy. Most pointedly, they contend that few in 1964 would have expected Title VII to apply to discrimination against homosexual and transgender persons. And whatever the text and our precedent indicate, they say, shouldn't this fact cause us to pause before recognizing liability? . . .

Because the law's ordinary meaning at the time of enactment usually governs, we must be sensitive to the possibility a statutory term that means one thing today or in one context might have meant something else at the time of its adoption or might mean something different in another context. And we must be attuned to the possibility that a statutory phrase ordinarily bears a different meaning than the terms do when viewed individually or literally. . . .

[A]s we have seen, the employers *agree* with our understanding of all the statutory language—"discriminate against any individual . . . because of such individual's . . . sex." Rather than suggesting that the statutory language bears some other *meaning,* the employers . . . merely suggest that, because few in 1964 expected today's *result,* we should not dare to admit that it follows ineluctably from the statutory text. When a new application emerges that is both unexpected and important, they would seemingly have us merely point out the question, refer the subject back to Congress, and decline to enforce the plain terms of the law in the meantime. That is exactly the sort of reasoning this Court has long rejected. . . .

The employers assert that "no one" in 1964 or for some time after would have anticipated today's result. But is that really true? Not long after the law's passage, gay and transgender employees began filing Title VII complaints, so at least *some* people foresaw this potential application. . . . And less than a decade after Title VII's passage, during debates over the Equal Rights Amendment, others counseled that its language—which was strikingly similar to Title VII's—might also protect homosexuals from discrimination. . . .

The employer's position also proves too much. If we applied Title VII's plain text only to applications some (yet-to-be-determined) group expected in 1964, we'd have more than a little law to overturn. . . . How many people in 1964 could have expected that the law would turn out to protect male employees? Let alone to protect them from harassment by other male employees? As we acknowledged at the time, "male-on-male sexual harassment in the workplace was assuredly not the principal evil Congress was concerned with when it enacted Title VII." 523 U.S. at 79. Yet the Court did not hesitate to recognize that Title VII's plain terms forbade it. Under the employer's logic, it would seem this was a mistake.

* * *

The weighty implications of the employers' argument from expectations also reveal why they cannot hide behind the no-elephants-in-mouseholes canon. That canon recognizes that Congress "does not alter the fundamental details of a regulatory scheme in vague terms or ancillary provisions." *Whitman v. American Trucking Assns., Inc.,* 531 U.S. 457, 468 (2001). But it has no relevance here. We can't deny that today's holding—that employers are prohibited from firing employees on the basis of homosexuality or transgender status—is an elephant. But where's the mousehole? Title VII's prohibition of sex discrimination in employment is a major piece of federal civil rights legislation. It is written in starkly broad terms. It has repeatedly produced unexpected applications, at least in the view of those on the receiving end of them. Congress's key drafting choices . . . virtually guaranteed that unexpected applications would emerge over time. This elephant has never hidden in a mousehole; it has been standing before us all along.

With that, the employers are left to abandon their concern for expected applications and fall back to the last line of defense for all failing statutory interpretation arguments: naked policy appeals. If we were to apply the statute's plain language, they complain, any number of undesirable policy consequences would follow. . . .

What are these consequences anyway? The employers worry that our decision will sweep beyond Title VII to other federal or state laws that prohibit sex discrimination. And, under Title VII itself, they say sex-segregated bathrooms, locker rooms, and dress codes will prove unsustainable after our decision today. But none of these other laws are before us; we have not had the benefit of adversarial testing about the meaning of their terms, and we do not prejudge any such question today. Under Title VII, too, we do not purport to address bathrooms, locker rooms, or anything else of the kind. The only question before us is whether an employer who fires someone simply for being homosexual or transgender has discharged or otherwise discriminated against that individual "because of such individual's sex. . . ." Firing employees because of a statutorily protected trait surely counts. Whether other policies and practices might or might not qualify as unlawful discrimination or find justifications under other provisions of Title VII are questions for future cases, not these.

* * *

The judgments of the Second and Sixth Circuits are affirmed. The judgment of the Eleventh Circuit is reversed, and the case is remanded for further proceedings consistent with this opinion. It is so ordered.

Sexual Harassment Even though the term "sexual harassment" does not appear in the text of Title VII, courts have long held that an employer may be liable if it allows its employees to be subjected to unwelcome sexual advances, requests for sexual favors, and other verbal or physical conduct of a sexual nature.[16] Sexual harassment is a form of disparate treatment sex discrimination because the victim is subjected to different (and disadvantageous) terms or conditions of employment because of her sex.

Recall that Title VII covers organizations (i.e., employers, employment agencies, and unions), not individuals (i.e., managers, supervisors, coworkers, or others with whom an employee comes in contact at work). Because sexual harassment is usually not the official policy or mandate of the organization, but instead is perpetrated by individuals, a plaintiff in a harassment case must establish some reason that the organization should be held responsible for the actions of the individuals. Similar to tort law, where a principal can be held vicariously or directly liable for the actions of its agents, courts have fashioned standards under which an employer can be either vicariously or directly liable for harassment perpetrated by its employees or other individuals under its control (e.g., customers or suppliers).[17] The standards vary depending on whether the perpetrator of the harassment is the victim's "supervisor."

Employers are vicariously liable for supervisory sexual harassment. A supervisor is someone who has authority to make or recommend *tangible employment decisions* (for example, termination, promotion, pay, work assignment, etc.) affecting the victim. A supervisor might be the immediate manager of the victim or someone in successively higher authority. Because an employer has given the supervisor the power to make or recommend tangible employment decisions, the supervisor acts for and on behalf of the employer in a way that other employees do not. In addition, when a supervisor engages in harassment, he is aided in his misconduct by that authority. As a result, the Supreme Court has held that an employer is automatically vicariously liable for a supervisor's harassing behavior when that harassment involves or ends in a tangible job detriment for the victim. Colloquially, this type of harassment is often referred to as *quid pro quo* sexual harassment, in which a

supervisor makes some express or implied linkage between an employee's submission to sexually oriented behavior and a tangible job consequence. For example, suppose that a supervisor fires a secretary because she refuses to have sexual relations with him or refuses to go out on a date with him. Such conduct violates Title VII whether or not the supervisor expressly tells the secretary that she will be fired for refusing to submit. Title VII is also violated when a supervisor denies a subordinate a deserved promotion or other job benefit for refusing to submit to the harassment. In such circumstances, the employer is automatically vicariously liable to the victim and has no defense.

A supervisor will not always take the drastic step of a tangible employment action when he harasses a subordinate. Title VII prohibits the employer from allowing an employee to be subjected to unwelcome, sex-related behavior that is sufficiently severe or pervasive to change the conditions of her employment and create an abusive working environment, even if no tangible job detriment accompanies it. Such conduct is often referred to as *hostile environment harassment*. The *Johnson v. J. Walter Thompson U.S.A.* case, which follows this discussion, provides an example of supervisory hostile environment harassment. Generally, the victim must show that the harassment was *unwelcome*. A victim who instigated or contributed to the offensive behavior will not recover. As discussed in the case, the behavior must be sufficiently *severe or pervasive* to create an environment that a *reasonable victim* would find hostile or abusive. The victim herself must also have subjectively experienced the harassment as abusive and hostile. Finally, the alleged harasser must have targeted his victims because of their sex. That targeting is often presumed when the perpetrator is motivated by sexual desire for his victim, but it can also be established by a showing of general animosity toward workers of the victim's sex or by differential treatment of members of the opposite sex.

If a supervisor engages in such offensive behavior, the employer will be automatically vicariously liable, unless the employer can prove (1) that the employer exercised reasonable care to prevent and correct promptly any sexually harassing behavior *and* (2) that the plaintiff unreasonably failed to take advantage of any preventive or corrective opportunities provided by the employer or otherwise to avoid harm. This two-step showing is often called the *Ellerth/Faragher* affirmative defense, after the two cases in which the Supreme Court announced the vicarious liability standard.[18] The affirmative defense places

---

[16] Harassment theory is applicable to Title VII's other protected characteristics, as well. In fact, many of the earliest cases finding unlawful harassment were based on race, not sex. Nevertheless, sexual harassment is the most common type of harassment claim and is the context in which the law largely developed. We focus on it here as a result. For the most part, this discussion is equally applicable to harassment claims based on race, color, religion, and national origin.

[17] Chapter 36 includes a detailed discussion of a principal's direct and vicarious liability for torts committed by its agent.

[18] *Burlington Industries v. Ellerth*, 524 U.S. 742 (1998); *Faragher v. Boca Raton*, 524 U.S. 775 (1998).

a premium on an employer's proactive education about and response to alleged harassment. Responsible employers accomplish this, in part, by creating, adopting, and educating their employees about specific, comprehensive policies that define and prohibit harassment, as well as provide multiple avenues of complaint for alleged victims. The affirmative defense also reinforces a victim's responsibility to notify her employer about the offending conduct and to take advantage of an employer's attempts to be proactive. The *Johnson v. Fluor Corporation* case, which follows the *J. Walter Thompson* case, provides an example of an employer that escaped liability because of the affirmative defense.

Though co-workers, customers, suppliers, and other nonsupervisors with whom an employee comes in contact in the workplace cannot threaten a victim with a tangible job detriment, they nonetheless can inflict a hostile environment. In such cases, the employer is not vicariously liable for the perpetrator's behavior. Rather, the employer can only be liable for nonsupervisory harassment under a theory of direct liability. Generally, the employer will be directly liable for harassment when the employer knew or should have known about the harassment and was negligent in responding to prevent and correct the offending behavior. The victim bears the burden of proving the employer's knowledge and negligent response.

Johnson v. J. Walter Thompson U.S.A., LLC[*]   224 F. Supp. 3d 296 (S.D.N.Y. 2016)

Erin Johnson worked at J. Walter Thompson (JWT), an international advertising agency in New York, which is owned by WPP PLC, a conglomerate of advertising, public relations, and market research firms and the world's "largest advertising company by revenue." Johnson quickly rose through the ranks of JWT. She was first the director of corporate communications for JWT New York, then director of communications for JWT North America, and finally chief communications officer of JWT. In the latter position, she oversaw global and external communications, managed a team of four employees, and managed JWT's regional communications and public relations teams around the world.

For approximately the first six years, Johnson reported to former JWT chairman and CEO Bob Jeffrey. But on January 1, 2015, Gustavo Martinez succeeded Jeffrey as JWT's worldwide chairman and CEO. According to Johnson, Martinez "made it impossible for her to do her job" because, among other things, he harassed her. His alleged campaign of harassment included making jokes about rape and sexual assault, directed at both Johnson and others; physically touching and assaulting Johnson; making routine references to sex; making comments sexualizing and demeaning women's bodies; and denigrating women, including Johnson, for being "bossy."

Johnson complained about this behavior on numerous occasions to various high-ranking officials at JWT and WPP. According to Johnson, all of these complaints were for naught.

Johnson ultimately filed suit against JWT and WPP for, among other claims, violating Title VII's prohibition against sex discrimination, alleging a hostile environment based on sex.

The defendants moved to dismiss Johnson's complaint for failure to state a claim upon which relief can be granted. The district court's ruling on that motion follows.

J. Paul Oetken, District Judge

Johnson argues that Defendants discriminated against her by creating and fostering a hostile work environment. "To state a claim for a hostile work environment in violation of Title VII, a plaintiff must plead facts that would tend to show that the complained of conduct: (1) is *objectively* severe or pervasive—that is, creates an environment that a reasonable person would find hostile or abusive; (2) creates an environment that the plaintiff *subjectively* perceives as hostile or abusive; and (3) creates such an environment because of the plaintiff's sex." *Patane v. Clark*, 508 F.3d 106, 113 (2d Cir. 2007).

[C]ourts should evaluate the facts holistically rather than "view individual incidents in isolation" or in a "piecemeal fashion." This imperative is especially important in the context of a hostile work environment claim. With this mandate in mind, the Court addresses each constituent element of Johnson's hostile work environment claim in turn.

1. Objective Hostility

The first element of a claim, "[t]he objective hostility of a work environment[,] depends on the totality of the circumstances, viewed from the perspective of a reasonable person in the plaintiff's position, considering all the circumstances including the social context in which particular behavior occurs and is experienced by its target." *Redd v. N.Y. Div. of Parole*, 678 F.3d 166, 176 (2d Cir. 2012). The alleged conduct, viewed together, must be "sufficiently severe or pervasive to alter the conditions of the victim's employment and create an abusive working environment." *Id.* at 175. "*[N]o single factor is required*," but courts may look for certain indicia, including "the *frequency* of the discriminatory conduct; its *severity*; whether it *is physically threatening or humiliating*, or a mere offensive utterance; and whether it *unreasonably interferes with an employee's work performance*." *Id.*

The Court begins by addressing the allegations that Martinez touched Johnson without her consent. The presence of any conduct that is "physically threatening or humiliating" may be especially important in determining whether a work environment is objectively hostile. This is because "even if overtly gender-based discriminatory conduct is merely episodic and not itself severe, the addition of 'physically threatening . . . behavior may cause 'offensive or boorish conduct' to cross the line into 'actionable sexual harassment.'" *Kaytor v. Elec. Boat Corp.*, 609 F.3d 537, 547 (2d Cir. 2010).

Johnson alleges that Martinez touched her routinely. . . . These allegations of physical contact plausibly allege a pattern wherein Martinez asserted physical power over Johnson without her consent. These repeated instances of nonconsensual contact, especially when coupled with offensive and explicit comments, inform the Court's understanding of the additional allegations against Martinez discussed below.

Johnson also alleges numerous potentially threatening comments by Martinez. In May 2015, for example, following an exchange with Johnson about his discussing rape at a meeting, Martinez approached Johnson at her desk and, in front of her colleagues in their shared open office, instructed her to come with him so that he could "rape [her]" in the bathroom. He then grabbed Johnson around the neck and started to laugh. That same day, Martinez interrupted a meeting with multiple female employees, including Johnson, to ask Johnson which female staff member he could rape. On a separate occasion, Martinez ushered colleagues out of his office but held Johnson behind, saying, "let's go talk about sex now . . . I am going to close the door." Johnson also learned that in spring 2015 Martinez had told another employee that a certain female senior global executive needed to be "hogtied" and "raped into submission." In the course of a business meeting, Martinez called a female JWT Director "young, willing, and ready."

Johnson further alleges that Martinez made myriad other comments about rape and sex. Defendants argue that many such comments suggest merely a lack of civility, and, in any event, were not gender-motivated because some of the comments were made in mixed company (and therefore not specifically directed at women). But Martinez's multiple comments alluding to his raping Johnson and other female employees color and make relevant his other, more generalized invocations of rape and sex, even if those comments were made in the presence of men or were not exclusively targeted at women. That is to say, these other remarks did not occur "in a vacuum[.]" On numerous occasions, Martinez used similar language to threaten female employees, including Johnson. The Court is thus especially mindful that it should

consider *all* of Martinez's comments with "a full appreciation of the social setting or the underlying threat of violence"—in part a recognition that, as compared to men, "women are disproportionately victims of rape and sexual assault." [*Ellison v. Brady*, 924 F.2d 872, 879 (9th Cir. 1991).]

Defendants argue that still other remarks allegedly made by Martinez should be discounted because they are not overtly or intentionally "sexual." But every comment underpinning a hostile work environment claim need not be "sexual in nature." *Kaytor*, 609 F.3d at 548. Certain of Martinez's comments, viewed in the context of his physically intimidating behavior and repeated sexually explicit and demeaning statements, suggest a workplace cut through with hostility. After Johnson's pregnancy, for example, Martinez made a "snide remark" about her eating at a work event, implying that she should eat less. He made similarly derogatory comments about other women's bodies. These comments, though perhaps not obviously sexual, are, considered in context, potentially sexual or sexually hostile in nature and implication.

Considering the alleged conduct in context, Johnson has pleaded enough to support a plausible inference that an objectively hostile work environment existed. . . .

2. Subjective Hostility

The second element of a hostile work environment claim is the "subjective" hostility of a work environment. "The effect on the employee's psychological well-being is . . . relevant to determining whether the plaintiff actually found the environment abusive," but such a showing is not *"required."* *Redd*, 678 F.3d at 175. Defendants do not appear to contest the effect of the alleged conduct on Johnson herself. Indeed, Johnson claims that she was "intimidate[d] and humiliate[d]" by Martinez's treatment of her. And her further reports of flagging Martinez's conduct for superiors and other colleagues evince a degree of concern and agitation about the conduct to satisfy this prong.

3. Causation

The third element, whether the hostile environment is "because of the plaintiff's sex," requires some analysis as to the nature and underlying cause of the hostility the plaintiff has pleaded. As an initial matter, Johnson alleges a fair number of interactions and comments that, on their face, were sex-based, such as commenting on women's bodies, including Johnson's, and making sexual remarks about women (including that a female employee is "young, willing, and ready").

Moreover, in the context of Johnson's collective allegations, Martinez's repeated references to sex and rape—both coupled with and divorced from physical or physically intimidating conduct—reveal a gendered component of the conduct, sometimes rising to the level of explicit gender animus. In threatening to "rape" Johnson (even jokingly) and asking which other female employees he could rape, Martinez asserted power over Johnson in an explicitly sexualized and gendered form.[a]

But it is not just Martinez's overtly sexual behavior that is plausibly viewed as undertaken because of Johnson's sex. The Second Circuit has established that "incidents that are facially sex-neutral may sometimes be used to establish a course of sex-based discrimination—for example, where the same individual is accused of multiple acts of harassment, some overtly sexual and some not." *Pucino v. Verizon Commc'ns, Inc.*, 618 F.3d 112, 118–19 (2d Cir. 2010). So while some incidents may not "directly amount" to sex discrimination "when considered alone in isolation, an inference that such conduct was gender-based could be drawn" given evidence of other sex-based conduct. *Id.* at 119. To that end, alleging some "overtly sexual comments" can be sufficient for a court to conclude that other "facially gender-neutral threats . . . were, in fact, 'because of' . . . sex." *Kaytor*, 609 F.3d at 549. The Court thus takes into account Martinez's repeatedly touching Johnson (including grabbing her by the neck and shoving her, as well as taking her apple from her hand, taking a bite, and returning it) as part of a broader effort to intimidate her physically because of her sex.

Through both his words and his actions, even if not overtly sexual, Martinez allegedly exhibited hostility toward the idea of women exercising power in the workplace. For example, Martinez's references to Johnson's being "bossy" can be understood not as a sex-neutral insult but rather as invoking a double standard for men's and women's leadership in the workplace. The view of female bosses as "bossy" is a feature of the "glass ceiling problem[ ], namely, that given the close association of 'managers' and 'leaders' with masculinity, subjects tend to dislike women whom they rate highly as managers and leaders because of 'role incongruity'—the sense that it is incongruous for women to successfully perform masculine roles as opposed to feminine roles." *Burns v. Johnson*, 829 F.3d 1, 13 n.13 (1st Cir. 2016) (quoting Joan C. Williams & Nancy Segal, *Beyond the Maternal Wall: Relief for Family Caregivers Who are Discriminated Against on the Job*, 26 Harv. Women's L.J. 77, 93 (2003)). This brand of stereotyping has been deemed impermissible under Title VII. When considered alongside his repeatedly calling Johnson "bossy," Martinez's conduct—including his physical touching and his lewd comments—can be read as a "power play[ ]," some mix of "sex-based animus" and "misdirected sexual desire," *Smith v. Sheahan*, 189 F.3d 529, 533 (7th Cir. 1999), that aimed to undermine Johnson's status at JWT because of her sex.

The totality of Martinez's alleged conduct, both overtly sex-based or sexual and not, can be read as a campaign to assert power over Johnson—to sexualize her, to demean her, to professionally diminish her, and to deprive her of bodily security—because of her sex. Johnson's Title VII hostile work environment claim therefore survives the motion to dismiss.

* * *

For the foregoing reasons, Defendants' motion[] to dismiss [is] **DENIED**.

---

[a] That Martinez apparently found his actions humorous, at one point laughing while he touched Johnson, does not, as JWT and WPP argue, belie "any claim that such conduct was 'threatening.'" To the contrary, drawing all inferences in Johnson's favor, it is plausible to infer that Martinez's cavalier attitude further undermined Johnson's physical autonomy.

---

*This case involves descriptions of a person making inappropriate comments about rape and sexual assault.

Johnson v. Fluor Corporation   181 F. Supp. 3d 325 (M.D. La. 2016)

Rose Johnson worked at the Big Cajun II power plant in New Roads, Louisiana. Her employer was Fluor Maintenance Services Inc. (FMS), which provides maintenance services and repair work to Big Canjun II during the plant's planned outages. FMS hires temporary employees like Johnson to augment its workforce during the outages and then lays them off when the work is near completion. Johnson was hired under these conditions for 13 separate periods of employment between 2009 and 2011.

In June 2011, Johnson filed a union grievance against her supervisor, Homer Jones. Pursuant to that grievance, Jones was removed from Johnson's chain of command, and Johnson subsequently reported to Jones's supervisor, Glenn Jarreau. Later in June, though, Johnson reported to her union steward that for more than a year, Jarreau had acted unprofessionally and inappropriately toward her. The union steward notified FMS management about Johnson's allegations. FMS conducted an investigation in them and terminated Jarreau's employment in early July.

Johnson filed a charge of discrimination with the EEOC, claiming that Jarreau had sexually harassed her. Following the EEOC investigation process, Johnson filed suit against FMS under Title VII claiming hostile environment sexual harassment. FMS filed a motion for summary judgment in part on the basis that the undisputed facts established that FMS was entitled to immunity under the Farragher/Ellerth *affirmative defense.*

Shelly D. Dick, Judge

The Court, assuming without finding that Johnson could establish a *prima facie* case of hostile work environment claim for sexual harassment, finds that FMS would still prevail on summary judgment as it is immune from liability under the *Ellerth/Faragher* affirmative defense. Where a supervisor's harassment does not culminate in a tangible employment action, as in the instant matter, the employer may escape liability by establishing, as an affirmative defense, that (1) the employer exercised reasonable care to prevent and correct any harassing behavior, and (2) that the plaintiff unreasonably failed to take advantage of the preventative or corrective opportunities that the employer provided.

a. FMS's Reasonable Care to Prevent and Correct Promptly Any Sexually Harassing Behavior

The Court finds that summary judgment is proper on this point because the undisputed evidence shows FMS's response to Johnson's complaint of sexual harassment was sufficient. Johnson initially expressed her concerns about Jarreau in late June of 2011 during a follow-up meeting with her Union steward regarding another grievance she filed. Upon learning of Johnson's concerns about Jarreau, FMS promptly launched its investigation in early July of 2011, by sending its Director of Employee Relations and HR Compliance, Amy Thornton, to Big Cajun II to investigate Johnson's complaint. As part of her investigation, Thornton met with Johnson and others. It is also undisputed that Johnson had no further contact with Jarreau after reporting his conduct to FMS. Based on the findings of the investigation, FMS terminated Jarreau on July 8, 2011 for his conduct. In summary, immediately upon reporting her complaints of harassment by Jarreau, Johnson was segregated from contact with him. FMS commenced an investigation, completed its investigation, and terminated Jarreau within 1 month of Johnson's complaint. Johnson has not offered any evidence to contradict these facts. Accordingly, the Court finds that Johnson has failed to show that a genuine issue of material fact exists as to whether FMS took prompt and remedial action in response to her complaint.

b. Did Johnson Unreasonably Fail to Take Advantage of Any Preventative or Corrective Opportunities Provided by FMS or to Avoid Harm Otherwise?

In *Faragher v. City of Boca Raton*, the Supreme Court stated that an employee must "avoid harm otherwise," meaning that "if damages could reasonably have been mitigated, no award against a liable employer should reward a plaintiff for what her own efforts could have avoided." The Fifth Circuit has explained that "*Faragher* implies that a plaintiff should not wait as long as it usually takes for a sexually hostile working environment to develop when the company has an effective grievance mechanism. If the plaintiff complains promptly, the then-incidental misbehavior can by stymied before it erupts into a hostile environment, and no actionable Title VII violation will have occurred." [*Indest v. Freeman Decorating, Inc.*, 164 F.3d 258, 267 (5th Cir. 1999).] Indeed, "as employers' anti-harassment policies become increasingly comprehensive and well-implemented, a plaintiff's success will often turn on whether he promptly reported the harassing conduct." [*EEOC. v. Boh Bros. Constr. Co., L.L.C.*, 731 F.3d 444, 463 n. 19 (5th Cir. 2013).] In fact, Johnson had previously successfully used the grievance procedure. "Thus, where an employer implements suitable institutional polices [sic] and educational programs regarding sexual harassment, an employee who fails to take advantage of those policies cannot recover.'" *Id.*

In this case, the uncontroverted evidence shows that Johnson acknowledged receiving FMS's project rules for workplace conduct, the Handbook, the Open-Door Policy and the Harassment Policy, and she knew she could call the Ethics Hotline. She further admitted that she understood that the Handbook, the EEO policy, Open-Door Policy, and Harassment Policy outlined the process by which employees could report problems or complaints. Johnson further acknowledged that the grievance process did not require that she report her complaint directly to Jarreau. Johnson also knew and understood that she could use the Union grievance procedure to raise concerns about her employment. Under the facts and circumstances of this case, either mechanism . . . would have constituted effective, corrective mechanisms for addressing workplace harassment. Nevertheless, the undisputed facts remain that for 17 months Johnson availed herself of neither of these mechanisms for addressing Jarreau's alleged sexually harassing conduct. No matter how loudly Johnson proclaims that she did not know of FMS's policies or the Union's grievance procedure, her actions, specifically the filing of her Union grievance against Jones before she reported Jarreau's alleged behavior, demonstrate that Johnson knew and understood FMS's grievance process. Hence, the Court finds that Johnson has failed to demonstrate that a genuine issue of material fact exists regarding her failure to take advantage of corrective opportunities.

Based on the foregoing, the Court finds that, because Johnson has failed to satisfy her evidentiary burden on summary judgment as to the *Ellerth/Faragher* affirmative defense, her hostile work environment claim shall be **dismissed**.

Section 1981 Where it applies, a post–Civil War civil rights statute called Section 1981 sets employment discrimination standards resembling those of Title VII. Section 1981 forbids public and private employment discrimination against Blacks, people of certain racially characterized national origins, and various ethnic groups. Included within such discrimination are most of the ways that an employer might disadvantage an employee.

Section 1981 is important because it gives covered plaintiffs certain advantages that Title VII does not provide. Although courts often use Title VII's methods of proof in Section 1981 cases, Title VII's limitations on covered employers and its complex procedural requirements do not apply. Also, damages are apt to be greater under Section 1981; in particular, Title VII's limits on compensatory and punitive damages are inapplicable. For these reasons, covered plaintiffs often include a Section 1981 claim along with a Title VII claim in their complaint.

The Age Discrimination in Employment Act

The 1967 Age Discrimination in Employment Act (ADEA) prohibits age-based employment discrimination against employees who are *at least 40 years of age.* In *General Dynamics Land Systems v. Cline*, 540 U.S. 581 (2004), the U.S. Supreme Court decided that it is not a violation of the ADEA for an employer to *favor* older employees over younger employees, even if the younger employees are in the 40-and-over age range.

Coverage The ADEA covers individuals, partnerships, labor organizations and employment agencies (as to their employees), and corporations that (1) engage in an industry affecting interstate commerce and (2) employ at least 20 persons. *Referrals* by an employment agency to a covered employer are within the ADEA's scope regardless of the agency's size. In addition, the ADEA reaches labor union practices affecting *union members*; usually, unions with 25 or more members are covered. The ADEA protects against age discrimination in many employment contexts, including hiring, firing, pay, job assignment, and fringe benefits.

Procedural Requirements The complex procedural requirements for an ADEA suit are beyond the scope of this text. Before she can sue in her own right, a private plaintiff must file a charge with the EEOC or with an appropriate state agency. The EEOC also may sue to enforce the ADEA; such a suit precludes private suits arising from the same alleged violation. For both government and private suits, the statute of limitations is three years from the date of an alleged *willful* violation and two years from the date of an alleged *nonwillful* violation.

Proof Like Title VII, the ADEA includes both disparate treatment and disparate impact theories of discrimination. However, the specifics of each theory diverge from Title VII. For example, the Supreme Court held that the ADEA does not incorporate mixed-motives claims of disparate treatment.[19] Plaintiffs, thus, must prove that age was the "but-for" cause of the challenged employment decision. Unless the plaintiff has direct evidence of discrimination, she will likely rely exclusively on the burden-shifting framework described earlier in this chapter.

Likewise, the Supreme Court affirmed that the disparate impact theory is available under the ADEA.[20] While it resembles a Title VII disparate impact claim, there are important differences. Most notably, when a plaintiff proves that an employer's age-neutral policy or practice results in an adverse impact on the basis of age, the employer's defense is not to prove business necessity. Rather, based on the ADEA's reasonable factors other than age defense, the employer only needs to prove that the policy or practice was reasonable under the circumstances. Obviously, because what is reasonable may not be necessary, employers generally find ADEA disparate impact claims easier to defend than analogous Title VII claims.

Defenses The *reasonable factors other than age* defense provides the employer's justification for adverse impact, as discussed above. To the extent that it is a defense to disparate treatment claims, it probably duplicates the second step of the burden-shifting framework, in which an employer is obligated to produce a legitimate, nondiscriminatory reason for a challenged employment decision. Similarly, the ADEA allows employers to discharge or otherwise discipline an employee for *good cause*. It also allows employers to observe the terms of a *bona fide seniority system*. In addition, the ADEA has a *bona fide occupational qualification* (BFOQ) defense. As a very general statement, an employer seeking to use this defense must show that its age classification is reasonably necessary to the proper performance—usually the safe performance—of the job in question. For example, an employer that refuses to hire anyone over 60 as a helicopter pilot may have a BFOQ defense if it can prove that 60-and-over helicopter pilots pose significant safety risks and that it is not feasible to test older pilots individually.

Remedies Remedies available after a successful ADEA suit include unpaid back wages and overtime pay resulting from the discrimination; an additional equal award of liquidated damages where the employer acted willfully;

---

[19] *Gross v. FBL Financial Servs., Inc.*, 557 U.S. 167 (2009).
[20] *Smith v. City of Jackson*, 544 U.S. 228 (2005).

attorney fees; and equitable relief, including hiring, reinstatement, and promotion. Most courts do not allow punitive damages and recoveries for pain, suffering, mental distress, and so forth.

The Americans with Disabilities Act

The Americans with Disabilities Act (the ADA) prohibits discrimination against people who have disabilities. Before the 1990s, federal regulation of employment discrimination against people with disabilities mainly was limited to certain federal contractors and recipients of federal financial assistance. By passing Title I of the ADA, however, Congress addressed this problem comprehensively. This portion of the ADA is primarily enforced by the EEOC, and its procedures and remedies are the same as for Title VII. The ADA's coverage basically tracks Title VII, covering employers who are engaged in interstate commerce and who employ 15 or more employees.

Substantive Protections The ADA forbids covered entities from discriminating against *qualified individuals with a disability* because of that disability. It covers disability-related discrimination regarding hiring, firing, promotion, pay, and innumerable other employment decisions. The ADA protects both individuals who can perform the essential functions of their job despite their disability and individuals who could perform the essential functions of their job if reasonable accommodation is provided. In the latter case, employers illegally discriminate if they do not provide such accommodation. *Reasonable accommodation* includes making existing facilities readily accessible and usable, acquiring new equipment, restructuring jobs, modifying work schedules, and reassigning workers to vacant positions, among other options. The *Kohl's* case later in this section discusses the accommodation requirement. Figure 51.2 displays the reasoning used in an ADA case.

However, employers need not make reasonable accommodation where such accommodation would cause them to suffer *undue hardship*. Undue hardship is an act requiring significant difficulty or expense. Among the factors used to determine its existence are the cost of accommodation, the covered entity's overall financial resources, and the accommodation's effect on the covered entity's activities. The ADA also protects employers whose allegedly discriminatory decisions are based on *job-related criteria* and *business necessity*, so long as proper job performance cannot be accomplished by reasonable accommodation.

What Is a Disability? The ADA defines a *disability* as (1) a physical or mental impairment that substantially limits one or more major life activities, or (2) a record of such

an impairment, or (3) one's being regarded as having such an impairment. (The last two categories protect those who have previously been misdiagnosed or who have recovered from earlier impairments.) Not protected, however, are those who suffer discrimination for currently engaging in the illegal use of drugs.

The Americans with Disabilities Act Amendments Act of 2008 Reacting to a series of Supreme Court opinions interpreting the ADA, Congress determined in 2008 that the Supreme Court had interpreted the definition of disability too narrowly, eliminating protections for people who Congress had intended to protect with the ADA. Congress's response was to enact the ADA Amendments Act of 2008, which clarifies the standards for determining disability. The amendments express Congress's intent that the ADA should be "construed in favor of broad coverage" and that "the question of whether an individual's impairment is a disability under the ADA should not demand extensive analysis."

The ADA amendments specify that *major life activities* include (but are not limited to) tasks such as caring for oneself, performing manual tasks, seeing, hearing, eating, sleeping, walking, standing, lifting, bending, speaking, breathing, learning, reading, concentrating, thinking, communicating, and working. They also include the operation of major bodily functions, such as (but not limited to) the operation of the immune system, normal cell growth, and digestive, bowel, bladder, neurological, brain, respiratory, circulatory, endocrine, and reproductive functions.

Directly repudiating one of the Supreme Court opinions, the amendments state that the determination of whether an impairment limits a major life activity is to be made without regard to ameliorative effects of measures that people use to cope with their mental and physical conditions, such as medication, equipment, hearing aids, prosthetic limbs, mobility devices, and oxygen therapy. The ameliorative effect of ordinary eyeglasses and contact lenses can be considered in determining whether an impairment substantially limits a major life activity. However, an employer or other covered entity cannot use qualification standards, employment tests, or other selection criteria based on an individual's uncorrected vision unless the requirement is job related and consistent with business necessity.

In response to another restrictive interpretation, the amendments state that an impairment that substantially limits one major life activity need not limit other major life activities in order to be considered a disability. Furthermore, an impairment that is episodic or in remission is a disability if it would substantially limit a major life activity when active.

Figure 51.2   A Map through the ADA

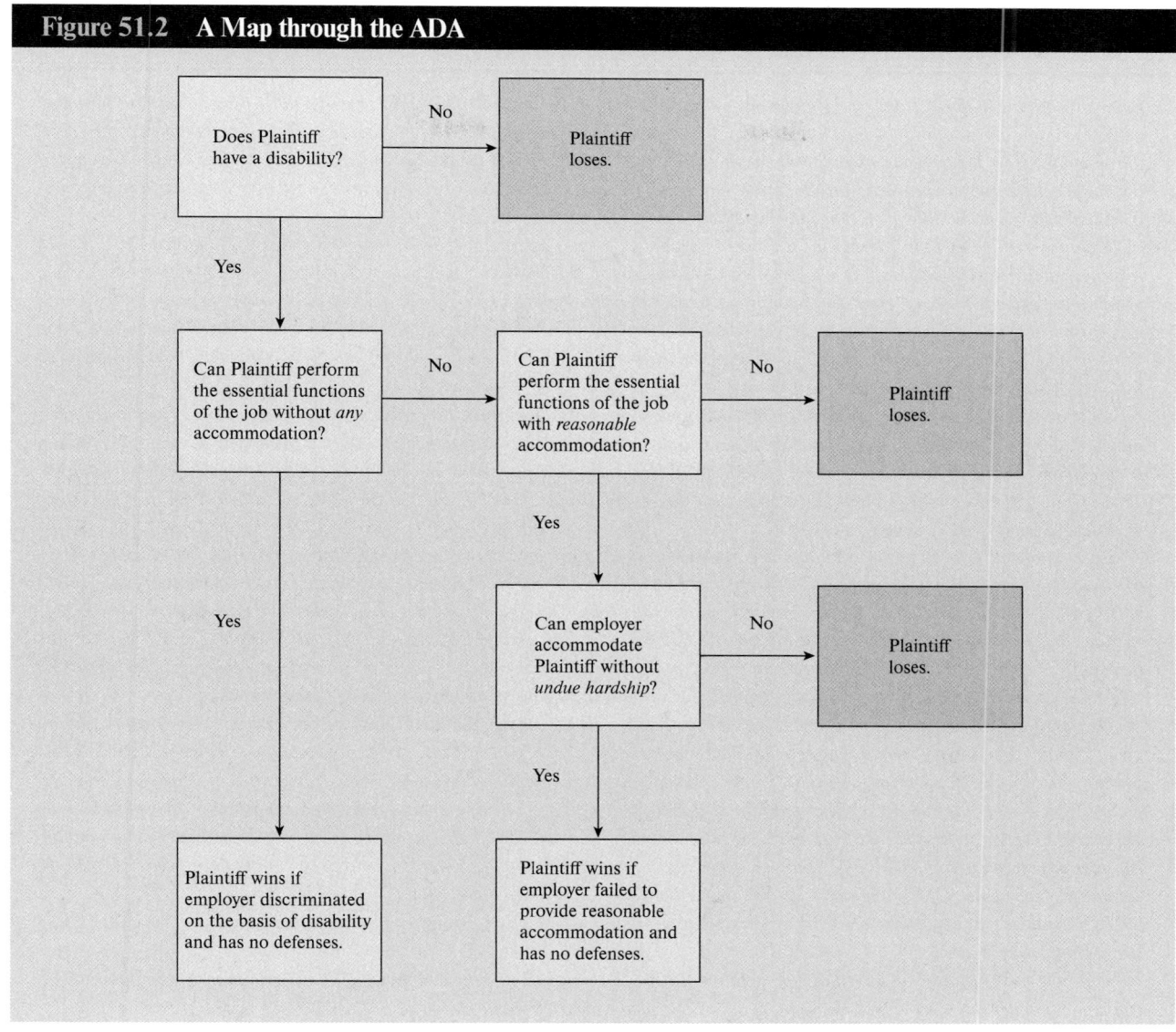

The ADA Amendments Act also states that a person meets the standard of "being regarded as having such an impairment" if he has been discriminated against because of an actual or perceived physical or mental impairment, whether or not the impairment limits or is perceived to limit a major life activity. A person is not "regarded as having such an impairment," however, if the impairment that he is perceived to have is one that is transitory or minor.

Congress intended the ADA Amendments Act to ensure that disabled citizens were protected to a greater extent than they had been in the wake of those restrictive judicial interpretations it overrode. As a result, managers have had to reorient their thinking since passage of the act when dealing with disabled employees. Particularly the ADA's accommodation mandate requires employers to abandon preexisting notions they may have about the limitations of disabled employees or their assumptions about what functions of a job can or cannot be modified to accommodate a disability. It requires open-mindedness and creative thinking. Indeed, the ADA imposes on *both* the employer and the employee a duty to engage in an "interactive process" to identify possible reasonable accommodations. As the following *EEOC v. Kohl's Department Stores* case illustrates, however, that process can be fraught.

| **EEOC v. Kohl's Dep't Stores, Inc.** | **774 F.3d 127 (1st Cir. 2014)** |

Pamela Manning suffered from type I diabetes, a chronic condition in which the pancreas produces little or no insulin, a hormone needed to allow glucose from the food one consumes to be processed at the cellular level to produce energy. Type I diabetics must carefully monitor their food intake, modulate their physical activity, regularly test their blood sugar levels, and often either take several insulin injections per day or use an insulin pump. Failure to properly treat type I diabetes can result in numerous and severe complications, including a potentially life-threatening condition known as diabetic ketoacidosis.

Manning worked at Kohl's Department Stores in Maine as a sales associate for more than three years. In January 2010, Kohl's restructured the staffing of Manning's department such that she no longer had the opportunity to fulfill her full-time work hours solely within that department. As a result, she had to supplement her hours by working in various other departments depending on the store's needs. Prior to 2010, she had worked regular, predictable shifts that usually started no earlier than 9 A.M. and ended no later than 7 P.M. With the staffing shuffle, Manning began working unpredictable shifts, including some "swing shifts" (i.e., a night shift one day followed by an early shift the next day).

In March 2010, Manning informed her immediate supervisor, Michelle Barnes, that working the erratic shifts was aggravating her diabetes and endangering her health. She asked to be scheduled for more predictable hours. Barnes instructed Manning to obtain a doctor's note to support her request, which Manning did. Her endocrinologist, Dr. Irwin Brodsky, wrote a letter to the store manager, Tricia Carr, requesting that Manning be allowed to work "a predictable day shift" so that Manning could better manage her stress, glucose level, and insulin therapy.

Carr contacted Kohl's human resources department for guidance in how to respond to Manning's request and Dr. Brosky's letter. Michael Treichler in Human Resources told Carr that Manning would still be required to work nights and weekends, but that Kohl's could ensure that she would have no swing shifts and that she always was able to take her breaks when she worked.

Carr and Barnes met with Manning on March 31, 2010, to discuss the situation. Manning requested "a steady schedule" and "a midday shift" like she had before the departmental restructuring. Manning expressed a willingness to work on weekends. Carr responded that Kohl's corporate management had not authorized her to provide a consistently steady nine-to-five schedule.

Hearing that, Manning became upset, told Carr she had no choice but to quit due to the risk her erratic schedule caused her of going into ketoacidosis or a coma, put her store keys on the table, walked out of Carr's office, and slammed the door. Carr followed Manning into the break room and asked her what she could do to help. Manning responded, "Well, you just told me Corporate wouldn't do anything for me." At that point, Carr and Manning did not discuss any other possible scheduling arrangements. Instead, Manning cleaned out her locker and left the building. A week or so later, Carr called Manning to request that she rethink her resignation and consider alternative accommodations. Manning asked about her schedule, and Carr responded that she would have to consult with the corporate office about it. Manning and Carr had no further contact after the phone call.

In none of the conversations did Carr ever mention to Manning Treichler's assurance that Manning could be scheduled to avoid swing shifts.

Manning filed a charge of discrimination with the EEOC, claiming among other things disability discrimination and failure to accommodate under the ADA. After investigation, the EEOC sued Kohl's on Manning's behalf.

The U.S. District Court for the District of Maine granted summary judgment to Kohl's, finding that Manning had failed to engage in good faith in the interactive process of determining a reasonable accommodation. The EEOC appealed to the Court of Appeals for the First Circuit. A three-judge panel heard the appeal. Below is the majority opinion joined by two of the judges followed by a dissenting opinion of one judge.

Torruella, Circuit Judge

[A]n employee's request for accommodation sometimes creates "a duty on the part of the employer to engage in an interactive process." *See Enica v. Principi*, 544 F.3d 328, 338 (1st Cir. 2008). The interactive process involves an informal dialogue between the employee and the employer in which the two parties discuss the issues affecting the employee and potential reasonable accommodations that might address those issues. It requires bilateral cooperation and communication.

We must emphasize that it is imperative that both the employer and the employee have a duty to engage in good faith, and that empty gestures on the part of the employer will not satisfy the good faith standard. If an employer engages in an interactive process with the employee, in good faith, for the purpose of discussing alternative reasonable accommodations, but the employee fails to cooperate in the process, then the employer cannot be held liable under the ADA for a failure to provide reasonable accommodations.

Here, the record shows that after Manning left the meeting on March 31, 2010, Carr pursued her, attempted to calm her down, asked her to reconsider her resignation, and requested that she con-template alternative accommodations. Manning refused, instead confirming that she quit by cleaning out her locker and departing the building. Ten days later, Carr called Manning, repeating her re-quest for Manning to reconsider her resignation and to contemplate alternative accommodations. Manning never responded to Carr.

While Kohl's response to Manning's accommodation request may well have been ham-handed, based on the undisputed facts, we cannot find that its subsequent overtures should be con-strued as empty gestures. The refusal to give Manning's specific requested accommodation does not necessarily amount to bad faith, so long as the employer makes an earnest attempt to dis-cuss other potential reasonable accommodations. Here, Kohl's refused to provide Manning's preferred schedule, but was willing to discuss other schedules that would balance Manning's needs with those of the store. Manning refused to hear what Kohl's had to offer. . . . Manning's refusal to participate in the interactive process is the reason why the record lacks facts regarding what reasonable accommodations Kohl's might have offered had Man-ning cooperated. We conclude that Kohl's acted in good faith when it initiated an interactive process and displayed its willing-ness to cooperate with Manning, not once but twice, to no effect.

Furthermore, we conclude that Manning's refusal to partici-pate in further discussions with Kohl's was not a good-faith effort to participate in an interactive process. Indeed, because Manning chose not to follow up with Carr's offer to discuss alternative ac-commodations, Manning was primarily responsible for the break-down in the interactive process. . . .

Accordingly, we hold that summary judgment against the EEOC . . . is warranted as a matter of law.

AFFIRMED.

Kayatta, Circuit Judge, dissenting

A reasonable jury could properly view the facts in this case very differently than does the majority. So viewed, those facts should preclude summary judgment unless we are to bless as a matter of law a negotiating tactic that is unfair to disabled employees who reasonably believe that they confront imminent serious harm if an accommodation is not provided. To explain why this is so, I begin with a brief example of how a reasonably competent plain-tiff's lawyer would fairly describe the well-supported facts to a jury, and I then follow with an analysis of why those facts could support a verdict in EEOC's favor. . . .

I. The Facts

Fending off the stress-induced exacerbation of a life-threatening condition, and believing that she faced imminent serious harm if she could not secure an accommodation, Manning requested less erratic work hours—especially no swing shifts—to allow her to work without suffering harmful medical consequences. Kohl's

demanded that Manning provide a note from her doctor, which she then did. Dr. Brodsky's note focused on the problem caused Manning by swing shifts in particular. . . .

Manning repeated her request for a steady work schedule and no swing shifts during the meeting with store manager Carr and assistant store manager Barnes. In response, Carr and Barnes left Manning with the impression that no individual accommodation would be forthcoming. Specifically, Carr told Manning that if she gave Manning the scheduling accommodation Manning wanted, then she would have to do that for everyone else at the store. Barnes reinforced this point by telling Manning that "we were keeping to consistency in regards to all full timers in the building and their schedules." Carr further explained that "the needs of the business dictate[d] when [Manning] work[ed]" and "would require at times shifts that are early, days, mids and closes." These statements, taken together, basically told Manning that Kohl's would not offer Man-ning any scheduling accommodation that was not both available to all other workers and compatible with a business need to have fluctuating shifts. As a concrete demonstration of this point, Carr and Barnes flatly rejected the accommodation Manning requested and, importantly, offered her no alternative accommodation even though Kohl's—through HR manager Treichler—had already ex-pressly authorized Carr to offer Manning a schedule with no swing shifts, the availability of which did not turn on its being offered to all other employees as Carr falsely told Manning.

With a vulnerable employee known to Kohl's to believe she faced imminent harm if her shifts could not be changed, the negotiating tactics employed by Carr and Barnes caused Manning to flee the one-sided discussions and announce that she had no choice but to quit. It is true that Carr chased after Manning and spoke with her in the break room, and then called her again ten days later. But in neither conver-sation did Carr propose alternative accommodations, request other information, or otherwise indicate that Kohl's had relented. In the break room, Carr failed to suggest any accommodation, including the accommodation that Carr knew she could offer and that Manning's doctor said she most needed—no swing shifts. During the second conversation, by phone on April 9, Manning asked about her work schedule after Carr asked her to consider other accommodations for full-time and part-time employment (none of which Carr actually of-fered, or even said she had authority to offer). Carr replied that she would need to consult with the corporate office about any schedule accommodations, in contradiction with the corporate office's earlier authorization for Carr to avoid scheduling Manning for swing shifts. Four times unable to get a specific counteroffer from Kohl's of any accommodation, and told that the person she was speaking to didn't even have any authority to offer one, Manning gave up and moved on.

II. The Interactive Process

My colleagues point to nothing in the foregoing presentation of the evidence that lacks support in the record. They nevertheless conclude that Manning forfeited her rights under the ADA because she was not more resilient in the face of Kohl's negotiating tactics. This conclusion misapprehends the nature of the interactive process. While Kohl's approach (as described by Manning) might be well-suited in some hard-edged business or diplomatic negotiations, it fits poorly with the type of "good faith," "interactive process" that the applicable regulations require here. The EEOC's interpretive guidance directs employers to use a "problem solving approach" to identify reasonable accommodations in consultation with the employee. Pursuit of this problem-solving approach requires that the employer, once it becomes aware of the disability of an employee, "engage in a meaningful dialogue with the employee to find the best means of accommodating that disability." *Tobin v. Liberty Mut. Ins. Co.*, 433 F.3d 100, 108 (1st Cir. 2005). Interactive discussions should involve "a flexible give-and-take with the disabled employee so that together they can determine what accommodation would enable the employee to continue working." *EEOC v. Sears, Roebuck & Co.*, 417 F.3d 789, 805 (7th Cir. 2005). Here, Kohl's did not give even what it could easily give.

[I]t seems most unfair to say that Manning forfeited her rights under the ADA. Manning communicated to Kohl's the fact that she was disabled, she provided specific medical evidence describing how the swing shifts threatened her health, and she proposed a specific but flexible accommodation. In other words, she did everything necessary to enable Kohl's to determine whether any accommodation was reasonably possible. Indeed, Kohl's did determine that an accommodation was possible; it simply never offered it.

The obligation to engage in the interactive process in good faith arises out of a need to see to it that an employer receives the information necessary to determine whether an accommodation is needed, and why. Kohl's had all that information, and required nothing more (including Manning's agreement) to offer that which it had already determined it could accommodate.

* * *

As best as I can tell, this is the first time that any circuit court has held that an employer can reject an accommodation request backed up by a doctor's note, refuse to offer an accommodation that it has determined it can make, falsely claim that any accommodation must be offered to all workers whether disabled or not, and then declare the employee's ADA rights forfeited when she gives up. Such a holding demands too much resilience and persistence on the part of a disabled and stressed-out employee, and takes away from jurors a task they are well-suited to perform.

I respectfully dissent.

Genetic Information Nondiscrimination Act

The field of human genetics has made tremendous advances in the past couple of decades. Though these advances will continue to identify genetic mutations associated with numerous serious diseases and disorders and potentially will help develop treatments or cures for them, the collection of individuals' genetic information also raises the possibility of discrimination based on genetic characteristics. In 2008, Congress addressed these concerns by passing the Genetic Information Nondiscrimination Act (GINA). The Departments of Labor, Health and Human Services, and Treasury enforce GINA's provisions dealing with health insurance, which are complex. More relevant here, GINA also prohibits employment discrimination on the basis of an individual's genetic information and prohibits employers from requesting, collecting, or purchasing genetic information. Congress allocated enforcement authority for the employment provisions to the EEOC. According to the definitions in the statute, "genetic information" includes results of genetic tests on an employee or the employee's family members, as well as the manifestation of a genetic disease or disorder in an employee's family members. It does not include information about an employee's age or sex.

Immigration Reform and Control Act

The Immigration Reform and Control Act (IRCA) prohibits employers with four or more employees from refusing to hire or terminating an employee on the basis of national origin or citizenship. This prohibition overlaps with Title VII's ban on national origin discrimination; however, a complainant cannot pursue claims under both statutes. IRCA's nondiscrimination mandate applies only to U.S. citizens and *legal* immigrants. IRCA also prohibits employers from knowingly employing or recruiting unauthorized immigrants. To aid in this process, employers are required to verify the identity and employment eligibility of every employee. You probably have personal experience with this requirement. It is the reason you must present two forms of identification (a birth certificate and a passport, for example) and fill out a federal I-9 form when you start a new job.

Uniformed Services Employment and Reemployment Rights Act

The Uniformed Services Employment and Reemployment Rights Act (USERRA) prohibits employers of any size from discriminating against members of the uniformed military service, including reservists and

Ethics and Compliance in Action

Bookworks Inc. requires employees to sign an agreement that they will settle any dispute or claim concerning employment through binding arbitration. Catherine, a Bookworks employee, alleged that her supervisor fired her for refusing to go on a date with him. She wants to file a sexual harassment case under Title VII against Bookworks, and Bookworks asserts that this is a claim that must be arbitrated rather than adjudicated in court. What are the ethical considerations involved in mandatory arbitration agreements that require employees to arbitrate discrimination and other employment-related claims?

Assume in the alternative that Bookworks and Catherine are working toward a mutually agreeable settlement to Catherine's claim; however, Bookworks insists as a condition of settlement that Catherine agree to a nondisclosure provision, whereby she would be prohibited from discussing the settlement or her claims with anyone. Why might that be ethically suspect?

Note, as a matter of compliance, that some states have recently passed laws that prohibit nondisclosure provisions in employment contracts and settlement agreements like this. New Jersey, for instance, amended its Law Against Discrimination in this way. Why might that be the case? Consider what you know about recent high-profile cases, like Harvey Weinstein, Matt Lauer, Les Moonves, and others leading to or in the wake of the #MeToo movement.

---

members of the National Guard. In addition to the general nondiscrimination mandate, USERRA also grants such employees the right of reemployment following an absence from the workplace for military service, for up to five years. As long as the employee provides the employer advance written or oral notice of the leave, receives an honorable discharge, and makes a timely request for reemployment, the employer must reinstate the employee to his rightful position upon his return. Under USERRA's "escalator principle," a returning service member's rightful position is the job that he would have attained had he not been absent for military service, with the same seniority, status, and pay, with other rights and benefits determined by seniority. The escalator principle incorporates any routine promotions and pay raises the employee would have gotten. Employers are provided limited defenses to the reemployment requirement, including (1) that a change in circumstances that renders reemployment "unreasonable or impossible" (e.g., the business closed or the position has been completely eliminated), (2) that retraining or accommodating a disabled veteran would impose an "undue hardship," or (3) that the original position carried no expectation of continued employment (e.g., seasonal or project-based employment).

Executive Order 11246

Executive Order 11246, issued in 1965 and later amended, forbids race, color, national origin, religion, and sex discrimination by certain federal contractors. The order is enforced by the Labor Department's Office of Federal Contract Compliance Programs (OFCCP). Executive Order 11246 and OFCCP regulations are the primary source of federal requirements related to affirmative action. Federal contractors must describe in an affirmative action plan the steps they take to ensure equal opportunity is provided in all aspects of their employment.

Given this limited requirement, people often misunderstand or overstate the reach and scope of affirmative action in employment as required by the federal government.

State Antidiscrimination Laws

Most states have statutes that parallel Title VII, the EPA, the ADEA, and the ADA. These statutes sometimes provide more extensive protection than their federal counterparts. In addition, some states prohibit forms of discrimination not barred by federal law. Examples include discrimination on the bases of one's marital status, physical appearance, sexual orientation, political affiliation, and off-the-job smoking.

Retaliation

Employment laws are enforced primarily by individuals who believe their or others' rights have been violated. If employers could intimidate and punish these people into staying silent, the goals of fair and equal employment would be undermined. As a result, most of the laws described specifically prohibit employers from retaliating. Title VII, for example, prohibits retaliation against individuals who oppose any practice the statute makes unlawful or who make a charge, testify, assist, or participate in any manner in a Title VII investigation, proceeding, or hearing.[21] The Supreme Court has interpreted these antiretaliation provisions extremely broadly over the past decade or so. *Kasten v. Saint-Gobain Performance Plastics Corp.*, 563 U.S. 1 (2011), provides an example of a broad interpretation of FLSA's antiretaliation provision. The Court interpreted the phrase "filed any complaint" to include both oral and written complaints. Moreover, courts have interpreted

---

[21] 42 U.S.C. 2000e-3(a) (2006).

The Federal Employment Discrimination Laws Compared

	Protected Traits	Covered Employer Decisions	Need to File Charge in Private Suit?
Equal Pay Act	Sex only	Pay only	No
Title VII	Race, color, national origin, religion, sex	Wide range	Yes
Section 1981	Race, racially characterized national origin, perhaps alienage	Wide range	No
Age Discrimination in Employment Act	Age, if victim 40 or over	Wide range	Yes
Americans with Disabilities Act	Existence of disability, if person qualified to perform job with or without reasonable accommodation	Wide range	Yes
Genetic Information Nondiscrimination Act	Genetic information	Wide range	Yes
Immigration Reform and Control Act	National origin and citizenship	Hiring and termination	No; however, procedures include hearing officer rather than court
Uniformed Services Employment and Reemployment Rights Act	Military service	Wide range	No
Executive Order 11246	Race, color, religion, national origin, sex	Wide range	Not applicable; enforced by OFCCP

laws that do not explicitly contain antiretaliation provisions to include implied antiretaliation protections, on the theory that Congress must have intended to protect individuals from retaliation because it is vital to proper enforcement of the law.[22]

Managers must appreciate how negatively courts have tended to view employers who retaliate against their employees. Even when an employee's underlying complaint or lawsuit is ultimately without merit, an employer who retaliates in response will often find itself in front of a hostile judge or jury. To be protected against retaliation, an employee need only have a good-faith belief in his claim that the employer violated the law. Thus, a manager should tread carefully in taking any arguably negative action against an employee who alleges a violation of the employment laws, regardless of how feeble the manager believes the complaint to be.

[22] E.g., CBOCS West, Inc. v. Humphries, 553 U.S. 442 (2008); Gomez-Perez v. Potter, 553 U.S. 474 (2008).

Employee Privacy

 LO51-4 Distinguish the relative privacy rights of private-sector and public-sector employees.

The term *employee privacy* describes several employment issues that have assumed increasing importance recently. Uniting these issues is a concern with protecting employees' personal dignity and increasing their freedom from intrusions, surveillance, and the revelation of personal matters.

Polygraph Testing Over the years, employers have made increasing use of polygraph and other lie detector tests—most often, to screen job applicants and to investigate employee thefts. This has led to concerns about the accuracy of such tests; the personal questions examiners sometimes ask; and the tests' impact on workers' job prospects, job security, and personal privacy. Besides

Ethics and Compliance in Action

Mike Evans, a senior at Kirkwood University, has applied for a job as an entry-level sales representative at Kelley Pharmaceuticals. In the position, he would market Axiproma, a powerful prescription painkiller, to hospice doctors and other specialists in palliative care. Kelley is understandably concerned about ensuring that its Axiproma sales people are reliable and professional, exercise sound judgment, and do not have a history of or tendency toward substance abuse. To that end, Kelley has an extensive drug testing program; however, Sandra Outten, Kelley's director of human resources, prefers to supplement its drug testing and reference checks with some Internet sleuthing. She finds social networking sites usually provide an interesting insight into the applicant's character and professionalism. Thus, when considering Evans's application, Outten asked her intern Samuel, who is also a student at Kirkwood University, to send a "friend" request to Evans on Facebook. Evans accepted the friend request and Outten asked Samuel to sign into his Facebook account on her computer so she could check out Evans's postings and pictures. What, if any, are the ethical concerns here for Outten? For Samuel?

provoking state restrictions on polygraph testing, such worries led Congress to pass the Employee Polygraph Protection Act in 1988.

The Employee Polygraph Protection Act mainly regulates lie detector tests, which include polygraph tests and certain other devices for assessing a person's honesty. Under the act, employers may not (1) require, suggest, request, or cause employees or prospective employees to take any lie detector test; (2) use, accept, refer to, or inquire about the results of any lie detector test administered to employees or prospective employees; and (3) discriminate or threaten to discriminate against employees or prospective employees because of the results of any lie detector test or because such parties failed or refused to take such a test. The act also has an antiretaliation provision.

However, certain employers and tests are exempt from these provisions. They include (1) federal, state, and local government employers; (2) certain national defense and security-related tests by the federal government; (3) certain tests by security service firms; and (4) certain tests by firms manufacturing and distributing controlled substances. The act also contains a limited exemption for private employers that use polygraph tests when investigating economic losses caused by theft, embezzlement, industrial espionage, and so forth. Finally, the act restricts the disclosure of test results by examiners and by most employers.

The Polygraph Protection Act is enforced by the Labor Department, which has issued regulations in furtherance of that mission. It does not preempt state laws that prohibit lie detector tests or that set standards stricter than those imposed by federal law. Violations of the act or its regulations can result in civil penalties, suits for equitable relief by the Labor Department, and private suits for damages and equitable relief. Workers and job applicants who succeed in a private suit can obtain employment, reinstatement, promotion, and payment of lost wages and benefits.

Drug and Alcohol Testing Due to their impact on employees' safe and effective job performance, employers have become increasingly concerned about both on-the-job and off-the-job drug and alcohol use. Thus, employers increasingly require employees and job applicants to undergo urine tests for drugs and/or alcohol. Because those who test positive may be either disciplined or induced to undergo treatment, and because the tests themselves can raise privacy concerns, some legal checks on their use have emerged.

Drug and alcohol testing by *public* employers can be attacked under the Fourth Amendment's search-and-seizure provisions. However, such tests generally are constitutional where there is a reasonable basis for suspecting that an employee is using drugs or alcohol or where drug use in a particular job could threaten the public interest or public safety. Due to the government action requirement discussed in Chapter 3, *private-sector* employees generally have no federal constitutional protection against drug and alcohol testing. Some state constitutions, however, lack a government action requirement. In addition, several states now regulate private drug and/or alcohol testing by statute. Tort suits for invasion of privacy or infliction of emotional distress may also be possible in some cases.[23]

Despite these protections, however, federal law *requires* private-sector drug testing in certain situations. Under a Defense Department rule, for example, employers who contract with the department must agree to establish a drug-testing program requiring, for instance, that employees who work in sensitive positions sometimes be tested. Also, Transportation Department regulations require random testing of public and private employees occupying safety-sensitive or security-related positions in industries such as aviation, trucking, railroads, mass transit, and others.

---

[23] Invasion of privacy and intentional infliction of emotional distress are discussed in Chapter 6, and negligent infliction of emotional distress is discussed in Chapter 7.

Employer Searches Employers concerned about theft, drug use, and other misbehavior by their employees sometimes conduct searches of those employees' offices, desks, lockers, files, briefcases, packages, vehicles, and even bodies to confirm their suspicions. The Supreme Court has held that public employees sometimes have a reasonable expectation of privacy in areas such as their offices, desks, or files. But it also held that searches of those areas are constitutional under the Fourth Amendment when they are reasonable under the circumstances. Determining reasonableness generally means balancing the employee's legitimate privacy expectations against the government's need for supervision and control of the workplace, with more intrusive searches demanding a higher degree of justification. Finally, the Court also said that neither probable cause nor a warrant is necessary for such searches to proceed.

As noted above, the U.S. Constitution ordinarily does not apply to private employment. Nonetheless, both private and public employees can mount common law invasion of privacy suits against employers who conduct searches. In such cases, courts usually try to weigh the intrusiveness of the search against the purposes justifying it and consider the availability of less intrusive alternatives that still would satisfy the employer's legitimate needs.

Records and References Many states allow both public and private employees at least some access to personnel files maintained by their employers. Also, some states limit third-party access to such records. In addition, employers who transmit such data to third parties—for example, in letters of reference—may be civilly liable for defamation or invasion of privacy.[24] However, truth is a defense in defamation cases. In both defamation and invasion of privacy suits, moreover, the employer's actions may be conditionally privileged. This defense and these privileges can protect employers who are sued for truthful, accurate, relevant, good faith statements made in references concerning former employees. Finally, a few states have allowed defamation suits for so-called compelled self-disclosure by job-seeking, wrongfully discharged employees who have been required to tell potential employers their former employer's alleged reasons for firing them.

Employer Monitoring Although employers have always monitored their employees' work, recent technological advances enable such monitoring to occur without those employees' knowledge. Examples include monitoring of computer workstations (e.g., by counting keystrokes), facial recognition and other biometric

screening, wearable technologies, and "femtech" (i.e., technologies ostensibly to improve women's health but that can track information such as women's fertility, menstrual cycles, pregnancy and nursing care, and other reproductive system health care). Some employers may provide these things as benefits of employment but then use the data collected for monitoring purposes. Such monitoring has encountered objections because employees often are unaware that it exists or may suffer stress when they do know or suspect its existence. Employers counter these objections by stressing that monitoring is highly useful in evaluating employee performance, improving efficiency, and reducing theft.

The amount of litigation and commentary about monitoring has grown as employers and employees are increasingly concerned about privacy. A variety of statutes exist on the federal and state levels concerning electronic privacy and security, and these may implicate some employer monitoring. Although employers have a significant amount of latitude in monitoring employees, telephone monitoring occasionally has been found illegal under federal wiretapping law. Although such claims have been uncommon, invasion of privacy suits may succeed in situations where an employer's need for surveillance is slight and it is conducted in areas, such as restrooms and lounges, in which employees have a reasonable expectation of privacy.

Job Security

 LO51-5 Describe the employment-at-will doctrine and its major exceptions.

The Doctrine of Employment at Will The traditional employment-at-will rule first appeared around 1870, and by the early 20th century, most state courts had adopted it.[25] The rule says that *either party can terminate an employment contract of indefinite duration without incurring any legal liability to the other party.* The termination can occur at any time and without notice. The at-will rule does not require the terminating party to have a good reason

---

[24] Defamation and invasion of privacy are discussed in Chapter 6.

[25] A modern exception is Montana, where the state legislature passed the Wrongful Discharge from Employment Act in 1987. Non-union employees in Montana who are not otherwise subject to an employment contract for a set term and who have been on the job for at least six months are covered by the act. They are protected from discharge for reasons other than good cause. "Good cause" is defined broadly, though, to include a performance deficiency or some business-related justification, like financial difficulties or a change in the focus of the business that leads to elimination of an employee's position.

Ethics and Compliance in Action

In 1997, Professor Pauline Kim of the Washington University School of Law published "Bargaining with Imperfect Information: A Study of Worker Perceptions of Legal Protection in an At-Will World" in the *Cornell Law Review*. In it, she reported the results of a survey of Missouri employees and their perceptions of protections the law provides them from losing their jobs under various circumstances. The survey revealed that the vast majority of employees were unaware of the at-will rule and erroneously believed the law protected their employment from being terminated for a variety of reasons that are clearly legally permissible under the employment-at-will default rule. For example, nearly 89 percent of respondents believed that it is unlawful for an employer to fire an employee because of the employer's personal dislike of the employee. Similarly, 87 percent of respondents believed an employer would be breaking the law if it fired an employee for erroneously concluding that the employee had stolen from the employer, even when the employee had provided proof that she had not.

Defenders of the employment-at-will rule justify it in a number of different ways. One of those is that employees who value greater job security can negotiate with employers for protection from unjustified termination of their employment (usually at the cost of a lower salary or other benefit concessions). Similarly, at least in theory, employers pay a wage premium for the labor flexibility that the at-will rule provides. However, if Professor Kim's survey is broadly representative of workers' knowledge about the at-will rule, then such employees are unlikely to value job security accurately and/or to demand an appropriate wage premium. Employers presumably have no such misunderstanding. As a result, they benefit from their employees' misapprehension of the at-will rule and some may encourage such misunderstanding in order to cultivate feelings of loyalty and security among their employees.

What, if any, ethical obligation do employers, who are at an information advantage, owe to prospective employees to ensure that they understand employment at will prior to negotiating the details of their employment?

for doing so. In other words, it can be for good cause, bad cause, or no cause. (However, discharged employees can recover for work actually done.)

As stated above, the employment-at-will rule applies to employment relationships of an indefinite term because that indefiniteness is interpreted as an indication that the parties desired the freedom to terminate the relationship at will. Employment contracts that set out a definite term for the relationship are not at will because the parties have set out a definite expectation for the duration of the relationship. Employment at will is the default rule in the United States. Thus, unless the parties are clear about their intent to create a definite-term employment contract, the relationship will be treated as terminable at will. Generally, the clarity that is required to create a definite-term contract is for the parties to be able to point to a calendar date upon which the relationship is set to end with some particularity. As a result, courts have interpreted commitments of "permanent" employment and other indicators of the parties' expectation of a long-term relationship as creating employment-at-will contracts, unless there are clearly defined beginning and end dates.

The employment-at-will rule is so entrenched in U.S. law that it is nearly always lurking in the background of courts' consideration of all kinds of employment claims, even complaints pursuant to the foregoing equal opportunity laws.

Under the rule, unfair terminations of employment are of little concern unless they violate an independent legal protection enjoyed by the employee. And courts tend to carefully limit those protections to preserve the underlying at-will rule.

The Common Law Exceptions
Because it allows employers to discharge indefinite-term employees with virtual impunity, employment at will has long been regarded as a force for economic efficiency but also as a threat to workers' job security. Although the doctrine remains important today, it has been eroded by many of the developments described in this chapter. For example, the NLRA forbids dismissal for union affiliation, and labor contracts frequently bar termination without just cause. Also, Title VII prohibits firings based on certain personal traits, the ADEA blocks discharges on the basis of age, and the ADA forbids terminations for covered disabilities.

Over the past 20 to 25 years, moreover, courts have been carving out common law exceptions to employment at will. Here we discuss the three most important such exceptions. Although a few states do not recognize any of these exceptions, most states have adopted one or more of them. In such states, a terminated employee sometimes can recover against her employer for wrongful discharge or unjust dismissal. The remedies in successful wrongful discharge suits depend heavily on whether the plaintiff's claim sounds in contract or in tort, with tort remedies being more advantageous for plaintiffs.

The Public Policy Exception The public policy exception to employment at will, which has been recognized by over four-fifths of the states, is the most common basis for a wrong-ful discharge suit. It usually is a tort claim. In public policy cases, the terminated employee argues that his discharge was unlawful because it violated the state's public policy. How do courts determine the content of this public policy? The mere fact that a discharge is unfounded or unfair does not mean that the public policy theory applies. Although there is some disagreement on the subject, most courts limit "public policy" to the policies furthered by existing laws such as constitutional provisions, statutes, and perhaps administrative regulations and common law rules. For this reason, employees often fail to recover where they are fired for ethical objections to job assignments or employer practices.

Successful suits under the public policy exception usually involve firings caused by an employee's (1) refusal to commit an unlawful act (e.g., committing perjury or violating the anti-trust laws), (2) performance of an important public obligation (e.g., jury duty or whistleblowing),[26] or (3) exercise of a legal right or privilege (e.g., making a workers' compensation claim or refusing to take an illegal polygraph test). A prima facie case of wrongful termination in contravention of public policy typi-cally includes three elements. A plaintiff must show (1) that the state has a *clear and substantial* public policy related to the plaintiff's conduct; (2) that the termination would discourage the plaintiff's conduct and thereby *jeopardize* the public policy; and (3) that the plaintiff's conduct, which supports the public policy, *caused* the termination. A plaintiff who proves these elements will win unless the employer can prove that it was justified in terminating the plaintiff's employment based on le-gitimate business reasons.

The *Peterson* case at the end of the chapter illustrates that the public policy exception is often quite narrow and is not intended to remedy run-of-the-mill "unfair" treatment.

---

[26] Whistleblowers are employees who publicly disclose dangerous, illegal, or improper behavior. Most states have passed statutes protecting the employment rights of certain whistleblowers.

The Implied Covenant of Good Faith and Fair Dealing

A wrongful discharge suit based on the implied covenant of good faith and fair dealing usually is a contract claim. Here, the employee argues that her discharge was unlawful because it was not made in good faith or did not amount to fair deal-ing, thus breaching the implied contract term. Nevertheless, the implied covenant of good faith and fair dealing does not impose a general duty that employers behave fairly toward employees or that terminations must be for cause. Instead, a successful claim pursuant to this exception is usually based on a bad-faith termination that has the effect of denying an employee benefits or compensation to which she is entitled. For instance, an employee who is terminated just before she would have received a bonus, and who can prove her termi-nation was intended to deny her that bonus payment, would have a claim for breach of the implied covenant in states that recognize this exception. Only about 25 percent of the states have, and most of these give it a narrow scope.

Promises by Employers

Using various legal theories, courts have increasingly made employers liable for breaking promises to their employees regarding termination policy. Such promises typically are express statements made by em-ployers during hiring or employee orientation, or in their em-ployee manuals, handbooks, personnel policies, and benefit plans. Occasionally such promises are implied from business custom and usage as well. Here, our concern is with express or implied employer promises involving matters such as dis-charge policies and discharge procedures. If the employer fails to follow those promises when it fires an employee, it is liable for breach of contract. At least two-thirds of the states rec-ognize this exception to employment at will. As the *Peterson* case illustrates, courts tend not to modify an at-will contract without convincing evidence of specific and definite promises. Moreover, employers often succeed in avoiding liability under this theory by inserting disclaimers of job security in employ-ment applications and employment manuals.

Peterson v. AT&T Mobility Services, LLC   134 F. Supp. 3d 112 (D.D.C. 2015)

John Peterson began working for AT&T in October 2004. He was originally in an hourly position covered by a collective bargaining agreement, which called for graduated disciplinary measures before a covered employee could be fired. He excelled in the position and, after about three years, was promoted to a salaried managerial position, which was not covered by any collective bargaining agreement. Even though he resigned from the union at that point and understood he would no longer be represented by the union or subject to the agreement, he claimed to "clearly remember" that his manager at the time assured him that graduated disciplinary measures still applied. AT&T both denied that Peterson was told the latter and claimed that there was no graduated disciplinary policy for salaried management employees.

That dispute was relevant because in October 2010 (at which point Peterson had been promoted twice and was serving as a national retail account executive), AT&T fired Peterson without any graduated discipline process. As a national retail account executive, Peterson was required to travel by car regularly in his territory, on average driving about 250 miles per week.

Peterson was nominally fired for violating a company policy, included in AT&T's Code of Business Conduct, which required all employees "regardless of their job duties" to report "any driving-related offense that involves intoxication" and employees "whose job involves operation of a company-owned" or leased vehicle to "also report [a]ll tickets, citations, arrests, charges, convictions, guilty pleas . . . for any driving-related offense other than parking tickets, equipment violations or other non-moving violations." Peterson had several infractions encompassed by the latter.

Peterson had a contentious relationship with his immediate supervisor. While she was on leave in August 2010, Peterson made an off-hand comment to his acting supervisor that he had a poor driving record. That comment prompted the acting supervisor to investigate Peterson's driving record. That investigation uncovered Peterson's infractions, which he had otherwise not reported to AT&T. His supervisor fired him as a result.

Peterson sued AT&T for breach of contract and wrongful termination. AT&T moved for summary judgment.

Beryl A. Howell, U.S. District Judge

The parties agree that no written employment agreement exists between the parties, but the plaintiff nevertheless contends that AT&T breached an employment agreement by terminating him without first applying graduated disciplinary measures, which a former supervisor allegedly orally conveyed to him when he was first promoted to a managerial position. The plaintiff also claims wrongful termination because he was not provided with, or made aware of, the company policy requiring the reporting of "all traffic infractions, whether or not the ticket even results in a fine or conviction," the violation of which policy led to his dismissal. AT&T contends that, as an at-will employee, the plaintiff was subject to termination at any time for any reason, and that the nature of this employment relationship was never qualified by any oral agreement. Consequently, AT&T argues that both of the plaintiff's claims fail as a matter of law since no breach of contract occurred and his termination was not wrongful because AT&T simply exercised its right to terminate the plaintiff, not in violation of any "clear mandate of public policy," and, in any event, was justified in doing so due to the plaintiff's violation of company policy. Each of the plaintiff's claims is discussed . . . below.

A. Breach of Contract

The plaintiff premises his breach of contract claim on an alleged oral promise, made by his then-manager when he accepted a managerial position, that the right he enjoyed as a union employee to verbal and written warnings prior to termination would nonetheless continue. AT&T counters that it is entitled to summary judgment on this claim because, after ample discovery, the plaintiff has failed to provide any admissible evidence to support this claim, other than his own self-serving statement in his affidavit about an oral promise, which is contradicted by his deposition testimony. The Court agrees with AT&T.

Under District of Columbia law, employment is presumed to be terminable at will by either party, and the presumption is rebuttable by "a showing that 'the parties intended that termination be

subject to specific preconditions.'" *Futrell v. Dep't of Labor Federal Credit Union*, 816 A.2d 793, 806 (D.C. 2003). Employee personnel or policy manuals may create contractual rights for the employee but "such implied contractual rights can be disclaimed, and 'the legal effect of such a disclaimer, is in the first instance, a question for the court to decide.'" *Id.* "The facts and circumstances surrounding the hiring and the conduct of the parties may provide evidence sufficient to rebut the presumption." *Nickens v. Labor Agency of Metro. Wash.*, 600 A.2d 813, 816 (D.C. 1991).

In the instant case, the plaintiff seeks to imply a contractual right to specific termination preconditions based on a "promise" received from a former supervisor when he was first promoted to a managerial position, two jobs prior to the one he had when he was ultimately terminated in October 2010. The only evidence he presents, however, is his own affidavit, despite months of discovery, stating that "I clearly remember [my supervisor at the time] saying that the same sort of graduated response for discipline—verbal warning, written warning and final written discharge—applied to the new job." Plaintiff presents no corroboration for this recollection, such as an affidavit or deposition testimony from the former supervisor, who allegedly made the statement, or any other witness.

[T]he veracity of the plaintiff's recollection is significantly undermined by the plaintiff's clear deposition testimony that he fully understood that his new managerial position would require forfeit of all of his rights that he may have had under the union, which would include the collective bargaining agreement's requirement of graduated warnings.

The plausibility of the purported oral precondition applying to the plaintiff is also undermined by the plaintiff's admissions at his deposition that, while he received documentation regarding performance quotas, he never received "any document that discussed disciplinary procedures" for "policy violations." Given the lack of corroboration of the alleged oral precondition, as well as the plaintiff's own testimony, at both his deposition and in his affidavit, acknowledging that, as a manager, he was no longer subject to union protection, the plaintiff's recollection of an oral precondition, without more, is insufficient to create a genuine issue of material fact on which a reasonable jury could conclude that the plaintiff's at-will employment was specially conditioned for him to receive the graduated warnings prior to termination to which union members were entitled.

Accordingly, AT&T is entitled to summary judgment on the plaintiff's breach of contract claim.

B. Wrongful Termination

The plaintiff apparently believes that the "real issue which led to [his] termination had nothing to do with driving or failing to report anything or violating any rules" and that the "idea that [he] was fired for not reporting one or more speeding tickets is simply not the true reason." Consequently, he argues his supervisor's "single-minded objective" was to terminate his employment and she "did not care what the reason was." Even if the plaintiff's belief and argument are correct, this is not sufficient to sustain a wrongful termination claim.

"It has long been the common law in this jurisdiction that an at-will employee may be discharged 'at any time and for any reason, or for no reason at all.'" *Rosella v. Long Rap, Inc.*, 121 A.3d 775, 777 (D.C. 2015) (quoting *Adams v. George W. Cochran & Co.*, 597 A.2d 28, 30 (D.C. 1991)). In *Adams*, the D.C. Court of Appeals recognized a "very narrow" non-statutory exception to this doctrine when "an employer's discharge of an employee for the employee's refusal to violate a statute is a wrongful discharge in violation of public policy." 597 A.2d at 34. Thus, to bring a wrongful termination claim in the District of Columbia, the plaintiff must demonstrate that his discharge violates a clear mandate of public policy, as expressed in statute, regulations or the Constitution.

The plaintiff was terminated for violation of a company policy requiring immediate reporting of any driving offenses. The plaintiff argues that his termination was wrongful because it was "mean-spirited," illegitimate because he was unaware of the policies he violated, and mistaken because the plaintiff was ultimately awarded unemployment benefits over the objection of AT&T that he was fired for cause. The plaintiff, however, fails to explain—and the Court cannot discern—how his discharge, even if it were "trumped-up," violated a "clear mandate of public policy" implicit in "statutes or municipal regulations, or in the Constitution." To the contrary, AT&T's enforcement of its internal policies and standards for safe driving serve as a means of monitoring the driving records and, thereby, minimizing the driving risks posed by its employees, particularly those engaged in driving on company business, where accidents could result in liability and reputational harm to AT&T. As such, these internal policies carry public policy benefits.

At the same time, the plaintiff's distress is understandable that, after six years of successive advancement in positions at AT&T, his employment at the company was abruptly terminated. Even if the plaintiff's [sic] correctly perceives that AT&T "overreacted and adopted a hair-trigger approach" to his driving offenses, however, "[i]t is not the Judiciary's place to micro-manage an employer's" enforcement of its internal policies since, "[a]s the Supreme Court has stated, '[c]ourts are generally less competent than employers to restructure business practices, and unless mandated to do so by Congress they should not attempt it.'" *Brady v. Office of the Sergeant at Arms*, 520 F.3d 490, 496 (D.C. Cir. 2008) (quoting *Furnco Constr. Corp. v. Waters*, 438 U.S. 567, 578 (1978)).

Accordingly, AT&T is entitled to summary judgment on the plaintiff's wrongful termination claim.

Conclusion

For the foregoing reasons, AT&T's motion for summary judgment is granted. . . .

Problems and Problem Cases

1. Adam Childers worked as a cook at Boston's Gourmet Pizza. While on duty, he was struck in the back by a heavy freezer door, seriously injuring his lower back. As a result of the injury, Childers suffered from severe lower back, hip, and leg pain. He was treated with pain medication and physical therapy, but his condition worsened over several months. He wanted to have spinal fusion surgery, but the doctors recommended against it. At the time of the injury, Childers was 25 years old, six feet tall, and weighed approximately 340 pounds. Due to his age and weight, the surgery was extremely risky. Furthermore, Childers's weight ballooned to 380 pounds in the months after his injury because he was depressed and inactive. Though he tried to lose weight by adjusting his diet, he failed. A doctor ultimately recommended that Childers undergo lap band or other weight reduction surgery so that either his resulting weight loss would alleviate his pain

symptoms or his lowered body weight would allow him safely to have back fusion surgery. Boston's Gourmet Pizza admitted that Childers's back injury was work-related and did not dispute that treatment for the injury was covered under the applicable workers' compensation law. It argued, though, that it was not obligated to provide the precursor surgery (i.e., lap band for weight reduction) that would allow Childers to undergo the treatment for his work-related injury. Rather, the employer asserted that Childers's weight problem was a preexisting condition that relieved it of responsibility for Childers's treatment under the workers' compensation law. Is the employer's argument correct?

2. Edwin Graning is an ordained Christian minister, who is opposed to abortion on religious grounds. He also worked for the Capital Area Rural Transportation System as a bus driver. He did not drive a fixed route; instead, Graning's bus acted more like a taxi, picking up riders in the nonurban areas around Austin, Texas, at the instruction of a central dispatcher, and delivering them to specified locations. In January 2010, Graning was dispatched to pick up several women and take them to a Planned Parenthood clinic. Graning called his supervisor to inform her that "in good conscience, [I can]not take someone to have an abortion" and that, in taking women to Planned Parenthood, he was concerned that he might be transporting a client to undergo an abortion. His supervisor responded that either he could pick up the women and take them to Planned Parenthood or he could resign. Graning did not want to quit his job, but he refused to drive the women to the clinic. As a result, he was told to drive his bus back to the office. When he arrived there, he was fired. Did the Capital Area Rural Transportation System violate Title VII by refusing to accommodate Graning's religion? What additional facts might help you in making a determination?

3. At approximately 4:00 A.M. on July 14, 2000, a woman wearing a mask and pointing a firearm demanded that 7-Eleven employees at a store in Berkeley County, West Virginia, give her the store's money. Antonio Feliciano was working that morning as a sales clerk. While other employees emptied the cash register and the woman was focused on them, Feliciano grabbed and disarmed her. He continued to restrain the would-be robber until local law enforcement authorities arrived on the scene and apprehended her. No one was physically injured in the incident. Nevertheless, shortly thereafter, 7-Eleven terminated Feliciano's at-will employment. 7-Eleven explained to

Feliciano that he was being fired because he violated a company policy that prohibits employees from subduing a robber or otherwise interfering with a store robbery. Feliciano subsequently filed a lawsuit against 7-Eleven alleging that he had been wrongfully discharged in contravention of the West Virginia public policy favoring an individual's right to self-defense. Is Feliciano correct that the public policy exception to employment at will renders his termination wrongful?

4. In March 2006, Lindsay Fleck suffered a chronic ankle injury, resulting in her inability to stand for prolonged periods of time or walk significant distances. In August 2007, she began working at the Attleboro Nursing and Rehabilitation Center as a part-time employee. At the time she was able to meet her job requirements with the use of a walking cast on her leg. In November 2008, Fleck had surgery on her leg and utilized FMLA leave until it ran out in February 2009. Prior to her scheduled return to work, Fleck obtained a doctor's note indicating that she could work four hours each day as opposed to her previous eight-hour day. The note further explained that she could gradually increase her hours to a full eight-hour day over the course of six weeks. Fleck's supervisor informed her that she would be terminated if she could not work eight hours each day she was scheduled to work immediately upon her return. Fleck then submitted an alternative suggestion from her doctor that indicated she could work for eight hours if she took a break every hour. In the absence of either of the previous two accommodations, Fleck requested to take unpaid leave until she was able to return for her full eight-hour shifts. Attleboro refused to consider any alternative to a full return to work, and Fleck was fired. Fleck sued Attleboro for failure to accommodate and discriminatory discharge under the ADA. Attleboro defended by arguing that Fleck was not a qualified individual with a disability. Should Fleck prevail on her claim?

5. KellyMarie Griffin works for the City of Portland, Oregon, as a clerical employee in the Parks and Recreation Department. She complains of conflict with her coworkers. In particular, Therea Lareau, the "lead" clerical employee at the same location, has made comments that are derogatory about or offensive to Griffin's Christian faith. Ms. Lareau has referred to Griffin as "a wacko" because of her beliefs and, on at least one occasion, told Griffin that God was "a figment of [her] imagin[ation]" and that Griffin was "praying to something that didn't exist." Griffin also complains that many of her coworkers frequently

use "God" and "Jesus Christ" as swear words, which she finds offensive due to her religious beliefs. Griffin, however, admits that when she has informed her coworkers about how the swearing offends her, they have made efforts to avoid doing so in her presence—even Lareau. Despite that, things have deteriorated. Recently, Griffin and Lareau found themselves in a particularly tense encounter. While another coworker was gathering her things to leave for lunch, Griffin sneezed loudly. This apparently startled the coworker, because she exclaimed, "Jesus Christ!" The coworker then left for lunch. The exclamation offended Griffin, so she commented to Lareau, the only other clerical worker in the office at the time, "I said that I objected to profanity of God's name. I said that this type of language is not professional, I find it personally distasteful, and it is in violation of my religious convictions. I said if it didn't stop, I would make a complaint with management." Lareau responded in a loud, angry voice, "I'm sick of your Christian attitude, your Christian [expletive] all over your desk, and your Christian [expletive] all over the place." She further accused Griffin of using her Christian religion to get "attention." If Griffin files a complaint with the City claiming a violation of her rights under Title VII, how should the City respond to this complaint? Can it avoid liability under Title VII at this point?

6. Brian Petty was both a police office in Nashville, Tennessee, and an officer in the Army Reserve. In October, he informed the department that he would be deployed to Iraq at the end of the year. While in Iraq, Petty was charged with a violation of the Military Code of Justice. He resigned his commission and received an honorable discharge in lieu of a court martial. Upon his return to the United States a little over a year after his deployment, he requested reinstatement to his position as patrol sergeant. The police department commenced its customary return-to-work process for all officers who have been away from the department for extended periods of time. The process required Petty to complete a personal history update questionnaire, a medical examination, a computer voice stress analysis, a drug screening, and a debriefing with a psychologist. Petty received no pay or benefits for three weeks while the return-to-work process ran its course. At that point, Petty was reinstated to a "desk" job and not his former position as patrol sergeant, due to an ongoing investigation into his military discharge and his alleged untruthful answers on the return-to-work questionnaire

about the discharge. Has the police department complied with its responsibilities under USERRA in its interactions with Petty?

7. Maetta Vance, an African American woman, worked at Ball State University as a catering assistant in the University Banquet and Catering Division of Dining Services. Over the course of her employment with Ball State, she lodged numerous complaints of racial discrimination and retaliation. She had a particularly acrimonious relationship with Saundra Davis, a white woman who was employed as a catering specialist in the Banquet and Catering Division. Vance complained that Davis "gave her a hard time at work by glaring at her, slamming pots and pans around her, and intimidating her." She alleged that she was "left alone in the kitchen with Davis, who smiled at her"; that Davis "blocked" her on an elevator and "stood there with her cart smiling"; and that Davis often gave Vance "weird" looks. Vance filed an EEOC charge and, ultimately, a lawsuit in federal court against Ball State, claiming violations of Title VII for racial harassment. Davis, as a catering specialist, had some leadership responsibilities in the Division. She would give instructions and assign tasks to others, including Vance, in the kitchen. As a result, Davis wielded some significant control over various aspects of Vance's day-to-day tasks and experiences as an employee of Ball State. Davis did not, however, have the power to hire, fire, demote, promote, transfer, or discipline Vance. If Vance were to prove that the environment in which she worked was racially hostile, would Ball State face the possibility of vicarious liability?

8. Jill Beaver was an employee at RGIS Inventory Specialists. She became ill while on vacation with acute sinusitis, bronchitis, and an ear infection. She was prescribed an antibiotic by a physician, who indicated that she should not fly on an airplane due to the danger it poses to her eardrum. Beaver did not advise her company of the situation until the day before her planned return date and did not give them the details of her diagnosis. Due to complications rescheduling her flight, Beaver could not return to work until almost a week after she was scheduled. She was fired upon her return. She filed a lawsuit against RGIS alleging that the termination of her employment violated the FMLA. Did it?

9. In 1972, Randy Counts began his employment with Shell at its Belpre, Ohio, plant. Counts was laid off within a month of starting work but was rehired in

1974. Counts states that upon returning to Shell in 1974, he was promised by three individuals during the interview process that his term of employment would continue for life or until he accrued retirement benefits. In 2000, Kraton Polymers LLC purchased the assets of Shell and offered jobs to all Shell employees, including Counts. As part of the employment relationship, Kraton agreed to provide all employees in the Belpre plant with a three-step procedure for resolving disagreements and disputes. The Dispute Resolution Procedure was intended to provide "all employees of the Belpre Plant with a means of obtaining a definitive response to questions, complaints, misunderstandings, or disagreements involving personnel policies and procedures and create a forum for the employee to resolve a dispute." On October 30, 2000, Kraton provided Counts with a written "Offer of Employment" stating in part:

> I wish to welcome you to Kraton Polymers under the terms set out in this letter. . . . Although we hope you choose to have a long career with Kraton Polymers, any employment relationship by law is one that requires the mutual consent of both employee and employer. This offer is not to be, and may not be considered, a contract of employment for a specific period of duration. Employment is "at will" and either the company or the employee may terminate the employment relationship at any time.

Counts signed the Offer of Employment, thereby agreeing to its terms.

Counts worked in safety and environmentally sensitive positions. Therefore, he was required to undergo random substance abuse testing. In May 2000, prior to Kraton's takeover, Counts underwent a drug test and tested positive for cocaine, which he admitted having used. He was instructed by Shell to contact one of its drug counselors. The counselor informed Counts that in order to continue his employment, he had to satisfy certain conditions. Counts signed a return-to-work agreement on May 24, 2000, which required him to submit to periodic substance abuse testing for 48 months following his return to work. The agreement provided that "[t]he results of these tests must be negative," and that termination could result from a failed test. On December 6, 2002, Counts's direct supervisor told him to report to the plant nurse's office for a substance abuse test. Counts reported there, went into the office's private bathroom, and thereafter handed the nurse a purported urine sample,

which she split into separate sealed containers for submission to an independent, third-party drug testing lab. Approximately one week later the lab, Quest Diagnostics, reported that Counts's sample was "Substituted." Pursuant to Kraton's drug testing policy, the still-sealed second sample container was sent to another independent drug analysis company, LabOne, which also found that Counts's sample was "Substituted" and was "[n]ot consistent with normal human urine." When confronted, Counts denied having tampered with the sample. He was sent home from work, and later his employment was officially terminated. Kraton's Substance Abuse Policy stated that "[t]ermination of employment will normally occur" after "[a] second positive test following a prior Company initiated positive test where employment has been continued." Did Kraton violate its (or Shell's) contractual obligations to Counts?

10. Johnson Controls manufactures batteries. Lead is a primary ingredient in that manufacturing process. A pregnant female employee's occupational exposure to lead involves a risk of harm to a fetus that she is carrying. For this reason, Johnson Controls excluded women who are pregnant or *who are capable of bearing children* from jobs that involve exposure to lead. Numerous plaintiffs, including a woman who had chosen to be sterilized to avoid losing her job, filed a class action against Johnson Controls under Title VII. Is Johnson Controls entitled to use the BFOQ defense?

11. The Pillsbury Company maintained an electronic mail communication system. The company repeatedly assured its employees that all e-mail communications on the system would remain confidential. Pillsbury further assured its employees that it would not intercept e-mail communications and use them as grounds for terminating or reprimanding employees. Smyth, a Pillsbury employee, received e-mails from his supervisor over Pillsbury's e-mail system on his home computer. Relying on Pillsbury's assurances, Smyth exchanged some blunt e-mails with his supervisor. One of them apparently contained a threat to "kill the back-stabbing bastards," and another seemingly referred to a firm holiday party as the "Jim Jones Kool-aid affair." Later, Pillsbury retrieved or intercepted these messages and fired Smyth for what it deemed inappropriate and unprofessional comments over the e-mail system. Smyth sued Pillsbury for wrongful discharge under the public policy theory, alleging that public policy precludes an employer from firing an employee in violation of his privacy. Will Smyth win?

12. Mary Delaney worked as a data entry clerk at Signature Health Care Foundation, a nonprofit organization that provides physical therapy services to its clients. Shortly after she began her employment, she learned that her brother needed a kidney transplant in order to survive a condition that was causing his kidneys to fail. Delaney underwent testing and learned that she was a match to donate her kidney to her brother. She informed Signature that she was going to proceed with the donation and that she would require four weeks of leave from work for the surgery and recovery. Signature initially approved the request; however, three days before the scheduled surgery, Signature changed course and notified Delaney that it could not hold open her position for four weeks. It then discharged Delaney. Does Delaney have a viable claim for wrongful discharge?

Environmental Regulation

The B-P Paper Company is planning to build a new papermaking facility on property it owns in the Atlanta, Georgia, area that borders on the Chattahoochee River. The facility will have an industrial boiler that burns wood wastes to generate process steam for plant operation and will emit sulfur oxides, nitrogen oxides, and particulate emissions to the air. The company plans to draw water from the river to use in the papermaking process and will return it to the river after some in-house treatment to remove some of the pollutants that have been added by the process. Significant quantities of sludge from the papermaking process will have to be disposed of, as well as empty containers in which the chlorine used at the facility was delivered.

- What major requirements will the facility have to meet to control its anticipated air emissions?
- What major requirements will the facility have to meet to control its discharge of wastewater to the Chattahoochee River?
- What major requirements will the company have to meet in dealing with the waste sludge and containers?
- If the company realizes that some materials it releases into the environment pose a hazard to human health or the environment but are not currently subject to regulation, does the company have an ethical obligation to take steps to protect against those hazards?

LO LEARNING OBJECTIVES

After studying this chapter, you should be able to:

52-1 Explain when an environmental impact statement must be prepared and what it must contain.

52-2 List and briefly discuss the major provisions in the Clean Air Act.

52-3 Assess how governmental action to deal with greenhouse gas emission and global climate change may affect businesses.

52-4 List and briefly discuss the major provisions in the Clean Water Act.

52-5 Explain why Congress passed the Oil Pollution Act of 1990 and list its major provisions.

52-6 List and briefly discuss the purpose of the Resource Conservation and Recovery Act.

52-7 Discuss the purpose of the Comprehensive Environmental Response, Compensation, and Liability Act ("Superfund").

52-8 Identify the two statutory authorities the EPA has to protect the public against unreasonable risks posed by new and existing chemicals.

TODAY'S BUSINESSPERSON MUST BE concerned not only with competing effectively against competitors, but also with complying with a myriad of regulatory requirements. For many businesses, particularly those that manufacture goods or that generate wastes, the environmental laws and regulations loom large in terms of the requirements and costs they impose. They can have a significant effect on the way businesses have to be conducted as well as on their profitability. This area of the law has expanded dramatically over the last five decades, and environmental issues are a major concern of people and governments around the world. This chapter will briefly discuss the development of environmental law and will outline the major federal statutes that have been enacted to control pollution of air, water, and land.

Historical Perspective

Historically, people assumed that the air, water, and land around them would absorb their waste products. However, over time it has become clear that nature's capacity to assimilate people's wastes is not infinite. Burgeoning population, economic growth, and the products of our industrial society can pose risks to human health and the environment. The societal challenge is to accommodate economic activity and growth and at the same time provide reasonable protection of human health and the environment.

Concern about the environment is not a recent phenomenon. In medieval England, Parliament passed smoke control acts making it illegal to burn soft coal at certain times of the year. Where the owner or operator of a piece of property is using it in such a manner as to unreasonably interfere with another owner's (or the public's) health or enjoyment of his property, the courts have long entertained suits to abate the nuisance. Nuisance actions, which are discussed in Chapter 24, Real Property, are frequently not ideal vehicles for dealing with widespread pollution problems. Rather than a hit-or-miss approach, a comprehensive across-the-board approach may be required.

Realizing this, the federal government, as well as many state and local governments, had passed laws to abate air and water pollution by the late 1950s and 1960s. As the 1970s began, concern over the quality and future of the environment produced new laws and fresh public demands for action. During the 1980s, these laws were refined, and in some cases, their coverage was extended. Environmental concerns continue to be prominent around the globe, and many countries, both individually and collectively, have programs in place to address them. Accordingly, it is important that the businessperson be cognizant of the legal requirements and the public's environmental concerns in operating a business. These requirements and concerns not only may pose challenges to businesses but can provide opportunities for them as well.

The Environmental Protection Agency In 1970, the Environmental Protection Agency was created to consolidate the federal government's environmental responsibilities. This was an explicit recognition that the problems of air and water pollution, solid waste disposal, water supply, and pesticide and radiation control were interrelated and required a consolidated approach.

Congress subsequently passed comprehensive new legislation covering, among other things, air and water pollution, drinking water, pesticides, ocean dumping, and waste disposal. Among the considerations prompting these laws were protection of human health, aesthetics, economic costs of continued pollution, and protection of natural systems.

EPA, in concert with the states, was charged with implementing and enforcing much of that legislation. Part of the agency's role is to promulgate regulations that serve to flesh out the detail on the statutory framework established by Congress. It does so through a public process known as informal—or notice and comment—rulemaking, whereby it provides notice to the public of what it is proposing to do, takes public comment on those proposals, and then finalizes its decision. Over time, this process has become increasingly complex as interest groups weigh in with their particular analyses of the science, technology, and financial considerations involved in the rules.

During the 1980s Congress made a number of midcourse corrections and added additional elements to the laws as they had been initially enacted. As was the case with the initial legislation, these changes were passed by large, bipartisan majorities in Congress. Thus, by 1990 the comprehensive regulatory schemes to address environmental concerns were largely in place, and the country made significant progress in dealing with many of its environmental and public health issues.

During this period, there were some changes in the tools and approaches used by the government to deal with environmental problems. Much of the initial effort to address problems involved what is known as command and control regulation, an approach that is heavily prescriptive and relies on an intensive enforcement presence to ensure the regulations are followed. In the 1990s, however, the government looked to supplement—or to replace in part—the command and control system with alternative approaches that instead rely on economic incentives or allow the regulatory community flexibility as long as the desired results are achieved. The highly competitive world market places a premium on companies' ability to rapidly change their products or production methods—and this can be frustrated by a cumbersome or slow regulatory regime. The tensions between public health and the environment, the desire to be supportive of domestic companies in a global competitive business climate, and the costs of compliance with environmental requirements will dominate the public policy debate in this area for years to come.

Moreover, today many of the laws are in serious need of being updated to take account of changing circumstances and emerging issues. Between 1970 and 1990, Congress acted on a bipartisan aim of crafting solutions to known problems. However, in recent years, the environment has become much more politicized, with bipartisan consensus hard to come by and with markedly different approaches being taken at EPA, depending on which party holds the presidency. The resulting gridlock, and swings in policy between administrations, can make it challenging for businesses to plan in an era of uncertainty.

The National Environmental Policy Act

 LO52-1 Explain when an environmental impact statement must be prepared and what it must contain.

The National Environmental Policy Act (NEPA) was signed into law on January 1, 1970. The act required that an **environmental impact statement** be prepared for every recommendation or report on legislation and for every *major federal action significantly affecting the quality of the environment.* The environmental impact statement must (1) describe the environmental impact of the proposed action, (2) discuss impacts that cannot be avoided, (3) discuss the alternatives to the proposed action, (4) indicate differences between short- and long-term impacts, and (5) detail any irreversible commitments of resources.

NEPA requires a federal agency to consider the environmental impact of a project before the project is undertaken. Other federal, state, and local agencies, as well as interested citizens, have an opportunity to comment on the environmental impact of a project before the agency can proceed. Where the process is not followed, citizens can and have gone to court to force compliance with NEPA. A number of states and local governments have passed their own environmental impact laws requiring NEPA-type statements for major public and private developments.

While the federal and state laws requiring the preparation of environmental impact statements appear directed at government actions, it is important to note that the government actions covered often include the granting of permits to private parties. Thus, businesspeople may readily find themselves involved in the preparation of an environmental impact statement—for example, in connection with a marina to be built in a navigable waterway, a resort development that will impact wetlands, both of which require permits from the U.S. Army Corps of Engineers, or for the construction of an oil or natural gas pipeline, or a wind farm. Similarly, a developer seeking a local zoning change so she can build a major commercial or residential development may find that she is asked to finance a study of the potential environmental impact of her proposed project.

Air Pollution

 LO52-2 List and briefly discuss the major provisions in the Clean Air Act.

Background Fuel combustion, industrial processes, and solid waste disposal are the major contributors to air pollution. People's initial concern with air pollution related to what they could see—visible or smoke pollution. For instance, in the 1880s, Chicago and Cincinnati enacted smoke control ordinances. As the technology became available to deal with smoke and particulate emissions, attention focused on other, less-visible gases that could adversely affect human health and vegetation or that could increase the acidity of lakes, thus making them unsuitable for fish.

Clean Air Act The Clean Air Act—enacted in 1970 and amended in 1977 and 1990—provides the basis for the present approach to air pollution control.

Ambient Air Control Standards The Clean Air Act established a comprehensive approach for dealing with air pollution. EPA is required to set **national ambient air quality standards** for the major pollutants that have an adverse impact on human health—that is, to regulate the amount of a given pollutant that may be present in the air around us. The ambient air quality standards are set at two levels: (1) primary standards are designed to protect the public's health from harm and (2) secondary standards are designed to protect vegetation, materials, climate, visibility, and economic values. Pursuant to this statutory mandate, EPA has set national ambient air quality standards for carbon monoxide, nitrogen oxide, sulfur oxide, ozone, lead, and particulate matter.

Each state is required to develop a **state implementation plan** for meeting national ambient air quality standards. This necessitates an inventory of the various sources of air pollution and their contribution to the total air pollution in the air quality region. The major emitters of pollutants are then required to reduce their emissions to a level that ensures that overall air quality meets the national standards. For example, a factory may be required to limit its emissions of volatile organic compounds (a contributor to ozone or smog) to a certain amount per unit of production or hour of operation; similarly, a power plant might have its emissions of sulfur oxides and nitrogen oxides limited to so many pounds per Btu of energy produced. The states have the responsibility for selecting which activities must be regulated or curtailed so that air pollution at any point in the state or area does not exceed the national standards.

Because by the late 1980s many of the nation's major urban areas were still not in compliance with the health-based standards for ozone and carbon monoxide, Congress, in its 1990 amendments, imposed an additional set of requirements on the areas that had not attained the national standards. Thus, citizens living in the areas and existing businesses, as well as prospective businesses seeking to locate in the designated areas, face increasingly stringent control measures designed to bring the areas into attainment with the national standards. These new requirements mean that businesses such as bakeries that are generally not thought of as major polluters of the air have to further control their emissions and that paints and other products that contain solvents may have to be reformulated.

Acid Rain Controls

Responding to the 1970 Clean Air Act, which sought to protect the air in the area near sources of air pollution, many electric generating facilities built tall smokestacks—some as high as 500 feet—so that the emissions were dispersed over a broader area. Unwittingly, this contributed to long-range transport of some of the pollutants, which changed chemically en route and fell to earth many miles away in the form of acid rain, snow, fog, or dry deposition. For a number of years, a considerable debate ensued over acid rain, in particular as to whether it was a problem, what kind of damage it caused, whether anything should be done about it, and who should pay for the cost of limiting it. The 1990 amendments addressed acid deposition by, among other things, placing a cap on the overall emissions of the contributors to it (the oxides of sulfur and nitrogen) and requiring electric utilities to reduce their emissions to specified levels in two steps over the next decade. This required most electric generating facilities in the country to install large control devices known as scrubbers, to switch to lower-sulfur coal, or to install so-called clean coal technologies. The 1990 amendments also provide an innovative system whereby companies whose emissions are cleaner than required by law can sell their rights to emit more sulfur oxide—known as *allowances*—to other companies that may be finding it more difficult to meet the standards. This emission trading scheme has worked well to achieve reductions in emissions in an economically efficient way.

Control of Hazardous Air Pollutants

The 1970 Clean Air Act also required EPA to regulate the emission of **hazardous air pollutants**. Under this authority, EPA initially set standards only for asbestos, beryllium,

mercury, vinyl chloride, benzene, and radionuclides. Unhappy with the slow pace of regulation of hazardous air pollutants, Congress in 1990 specified a list of 189 chemicals for which EPA is required to issue regulations requiring the installation of the **maximum available control technology**. The regulations are to be developed and the control technology installed by industry in phases. Thus, while many hazardous emissions had largely gone unregulated, that situation has changed. In addition, a number of chemical companies have announced they are voluntarily reducing their emissions of hazardous chemicals to levels below those they are required to meet by law.

New Source Controls

The Clean Air Act requires that new stationary sources such as factories and power plants install the **best available technology** for reducing air pollution. EPA is required to establish the standards to be met by new stationary sources and has done so for the major stationary sources of air pollution. This means that a new facility covered by the regulations must install state-of-the-art control technology, even if it is locating in an area where the air quality is better than that required by law. Two major policy objectives underlie this requirement: (1) to provide a level playing field for new industry irrespective of where it locates and (2) to gradually improve air quality by requiring state-of-the-art controls whenever a new facility is built.

The act also requires that facilities that undergo major modifications—defined as physical changes that result in significant increases in emissions of air pollutants—must go through a preconstruction review, obtain a permit, and meet the same new source performance standards or limits on emissions that must be met by new facilities. The rationale for imposing these standards when a new facility is built, or an existing facility undergoes a major modification, is that is the easiest time to design and incorporate state-of-the-art environmental controls into the facility. Routine maintenance, repair, and replacement activities, increases in hours of production, and physical changes that are not accompanied by increases in emissions are excluded from the definition of modification.

The preconstruction review process that is required—known as new source review—is the subject of very contentious debate and various proposals to modify it. Industry is concerned that the process slows down its ability to make changes to increase efficiency, take advantage of new technologies, or gain a competitive edge, while environmentalists claim that some companies are increasing emissions and avoiding the installation of required controls on emissions.

In the case that follows, *United States v. Ohio Edison Company*, the court rejected a utility's argument that its work on its coal-fired electric generating units was "routine maintenance, repair, and replacement" and thus exempt from the preconstruction review and permitting requirements applicable to facilities that are "modified," resulting in a significant increase in their emissions.

United States v. Ohio Edison Company   276 F. Supp. 2d 829 (S.D. Ohio 2003)

The Sammis Plant is a coal-fired electric generating plant owned by the Ohio Edison Company and situated along the Ohio River in the Village of Stratton, Ohio. The plant consists of seven separate generating units, numbered 1 through 7. Units 1 through 4 were placed in service from 1959 to 1962, Unit 5 in 1967, Unit 6 in 1969, and Unit 7 in 1971.

Coal-fired power plants, such as the Sammis Plant, generate electricity using three major components: the boiler, turbine, and generator. The boiler is a large building-like structure (150–200 feet high) in which coal is burned inside the furnace and the energy from the combustion process is converted to water to produce steam. The steam is then directed to the turbine, where it is further converted to mechanical energy in the form of a spinning turbine shaft, which in turn drives the generator that produces electricity. The walls, roof, and floor of the boiler are comprised of tubes, as are the other major components of the boiler, which are made up of densely packed assemblies of tubes that incrementally raise the temperature of the steam before it leaves the boiler to generate electricity.

The Sammis units are fueled by pulverized coal (coal that has been ground to a powdery consistency) that is fed through pipes to burners, where it is ignited and combusts within the furnace area of the boiler. In the combustion of coal, chemical energy, gas by-products, and particulate matter are released. The gases are known as flue gas. The flue gases produced from the combustion process form carbon dioxide, carbon monoxide, sulfur dioxide, and nitrogen oxides. The flue gases are discharged to the atmosphere. At the time the seven units were built, Ohio Edison installed electrostatic precipitators to collect fly ash coming out of the boilers. At the time of installations, the precipitators were state-of-the-art technology. Over time, the tubing that is in contact with the flue gases, combusting coal, and water inside the tubing deteriorates and periodically must be replaced.

Fossil fuel-fired generating stations have traditionally been built with an assumed nominal design and economic life of about 30 years. The implicit expectation was that these units would be replaced at the end of this period with new units that would meet load requirements and, through the use of technological improvements, produce power at lower cost, higher availability, and higher efficiency. For a number of reasons, these expectations have not been realized, and many utility companies have undertaken so-called life extension projects that offer the prospect of retaining units in service for 50 to 60 years or longer.

In the 1980s and 1990s, Ohio Edison developed a program and undertook 11 projects at the Sammis with the purpose of extending the life of the seven units and making them more efficient. The projects went beyond the normal replacement of tubing and focused on other components that would require repair or replacement in the next 30 years. All of the projects involved replacement of major components that had never before been replaced on the particular units. The total cost of the projects was approximately $136.4 million. By replacing aging or deficient components, Ohio Edison intended and achieved a significant increase in the operation and output of the units. In turn, the amount of emission of sulfur dioxide, nitrogen oxides, and particulate matter also increased. The vast majority of the expenditures were treated for accounting purposes as capital, as opposed to maintenance, expenses. Most of the work was performed by outside contractors, as opposed to in-house maintenance crews.

Sargus, Judge

This case highlights an abysmal breakdown in the administrative process following the passage of the landmark Clean Air Act in 1970. For thirty-three years, various administrations have wrestled with and, to a great extent, have avoided a fundamental issue addressed in the Clean Air Act, that is, at what point plants built before 1970 must comply with new air pollution standards. The Clean Air Act requires plants constructed after 1970 to meet stringent air quality standards, but the Act exempts old facilities from compliance with the law, unless such sites undergo what the law identifies as a "modification." Decades later, the United

States Environmental Protection Agency, together with the States of Connecticut, New Jersey, and New York, ask this Court to find that eleven construction projects undertaken between 1984 and 1998 on the seven electric generating units at the Sammis Plant constituted modifications, requiring Ohio Edison to bring the units into compliance with current ambient air quality standards.

By any standard, the enforcement of the Clean Air Act with regard to the Sammis Plant has been disastrous. From a public health perspective, thirty-three years after passage of the Act, the plant to this day emits on an annual basis 145,000 tons of sulphur dioxide, a pollutant injurious to the public health. From an employment perspective, Ohio Edison has chosen to meet other statewide and regional air quality standards by switching to out-of-state, low-sulphur coal, a strategy which in conjunction with other utilities has caused a huge loss of coal mining and related jobs in Ohio. From the standpoint of Ohio Edison, since 1970 the company has invested over $450 million to install pollution control devices on the Sammis units yet still fails to meet the new source pollution standards. Thirty-three years later, the air is still not clean, tens of thousands of jobs have been lost, and enforcement by the EPA has been highly inconsistent.

As is described in detail below, the original and current language of the Clean Air Act requires that an older plant undergoing a modification thereafter comply with new air quality standards. Regulations issued under the Clean Air Act by the U.S. EPA may not conflict with statutory language enacted into law by Congress. EPA regulations give further definition as to what types of projects are to be viewed as modifications which trigger the application of new air quality standards to an older facility. These statutory and regulatory definitions are at issue here.

With regard to this case, the parties have litigated at this juncture whether the eleven projects at the Sammis units have triggered application of the standards set forth in the 1977 amendments to the Clean Air Act. The questions resolved today by this Court are legal in nature. In contrast, in the next phase of this case, the remedies the Court may consider and impose involve a much broader, equitable analysis, requiring the Court to consider air quality, public health, economic impact, and employment consequences. The Court may also consider the less than consistent efforts of the EPA to apply and enforce the Clean Air Act.

The issues presented in this lawsuit turn on an interpretation of the term "modification." Congress provided in the Clean Air Act that any modification of a plant triggered application of the Act and later amendments. The Administrator of the EPA has refined, by regulation, the definition of modification to include only activities which involve both a physical change to a unit and a resulting significant increase in emissions. Excluded from the definition of modification are projects involving only "routine maintenance, repair or replacement."

In this case, Ohio Edison undertook eleven construction projects at the seven Sammis Units. The total cost of the projects was approximately $136.4 million. The documents prepared to justify the expenditures described the various purposes of the projects to include replacement of major components to increase both the life and the reliability of the units. A primary goal of the projects was to prevent or at least diminish the number and duration of outages, meaning unplanned periods of time when the unit was offline and unproductive.

By physically replacing aging or deficient components, Ohio Edison intended and achieved a significant increase in the operation and output of the units. In turn, the amount of emission of sulphur dioxide, nitrogen oxides, and particulate matter also increased.

If the projects were modifications, as used in the Clean Air Act, Ohio Edison was required prior to construction to project and calculate postconstruction emissions to determine if the new standards applied. Further, if the projects were modifications, Ohio Edison was required to obtain a preconstruction permit. Because the company contended the projects were not modifications but were instead "routine maintenance, repair and replacement," neither of those courses was pursued. The EPA and state plaintiffs contend that all eleven projects constituted modifications.

While the analysis required to distinguish between a modification sufficient to trigger compliance from routine maintenance, repair and replacement is complex, the distinction is hardly subtle. Routine maintenance, repair and replacement occurs regularly, involves no permanent improvements, is typically limited in expense, is usually performed in large plants by in-house employees, and is treated for accounting purposes as an expense. In contrast to routine maintenance stand capital improvements which generally involve more expense, are large in scope, often involve outside contractors, involve an increase of value to the unit, are usually not undertaken with regular frequency, and are treated for accounting purposes as capital expenditures on the balance sheet. The only two courts which have addressed this issue have essentially adopted this same analysis.

The projects were all intended to result in increased hours of operation as a result of a reduction in the number and length of forced outages, or shutdown for repair or maintenance. A significant decrease in outages results in a significant increase in both production and emissions. Given the actual goals placed on the construction projects by Ohio Edison, and the substantial increase in emissions certain to follow, the company was required to project future emissions. If those projected increases were substantial, as defined by regulations noted below, preconstruction approval, which was never sought, was required by law.

The eleven projects at issue in this case were extensive, involving a combined outlay of $136.4 million. The vast majority of the expenditures were treated for accounting purposes as capital, as opposed to maintenance, expenses. Most of the work was performed by outside contractors, as opposed to in-house maintenance crews. The purpose of the projects was to extend the lives of units built before 1970, not simply to perform routine preventative care on components of the units. Finally, all of the projects involved replacement of major components which had never before been replaced on the particular units. As a result, the projects were not routine in any sense of the term, and could have been projected to significantly increase the emission of pollutants.

Congress expressly intended the Clean Air Act and the 1977 Amendments to become applicable to preexisting plants, as such facilities were modified. As noted by the United States Court of Appeals for the Seventh Circuit in *Wisconsin Electric Power Company v. Reilly* [, 893 F.2d 901, 909 (7th Cir.]1990):

> Congress did not permanently exempt existing plants from these requirements . . . existing plants that have been modified are subject to the Clean Air Act programs at issue here.

Further, as at least one member of the Sixth Circuit has observed:

> The purpose of the "modification" rule is to ensure that pollution control measures are undertaken when they can be most effective, at the time of new or modified construction.

National-Southwire Aluminum Co. v. EPA, 835, 843 (6th Cir. 1988) (Boggs, J., dissenting).

The eleven projects at issue in this case were major modifications sufficient to trigger application of the Clean Air Act and subsequent amendments.

Judgment for United States and other plaintiffs.

CYBERLAW IN ACTION

Online Permitting

The Clean Air Act, the Clean Water Act, and the Resource Conservation and Recovery Act, as well as a number of other federal and local environmental laws, require certain businesses to obtain permits and to periodically report their discharges and/or other information to administrative agencies by filing permits or monitoring reports. Now the EPA and most, if not all, states make permit applications and motoring report forms available online. In addition, some states make specific companies' reports, or permit files, available to the public on their websites. Online permit and report transactions can streamline the process of complying with environmental law and regulations. Also, businesses can quickly access information on their competition's compliance with environmental standards by viewing, or ordering, their competitors' monitoring reports and permits on the Internet. Such information might provide insight into what materials another company is using in its processes—or how product volume may be changing over time. Moreover, the online permitting and reporting systems make environmental regulations more transparent, which helps ensure that businesses and regulatory agencies remain accountable to the public.

Permits In the 1990 amendments to the Clean Air Act, Congress established a permit system whereby major sources of air pollution—particularly those subject to the New Source Performance Standards, hazardous air pollutants standards (NESHAPS), and the nonattainment and acid rain provisions of the act—as well as certain other sources—have to obtain permits that specify the limits on emissions from the sources. The permits also contain monitoring and reporting requirements. Once a state permitting program is approved by EPA, the permits are issued by the state in which a facility is located. A controversial issue in the permitting regulations is when a source has to seek a modification of a permit because of process or operational changes that might increase emissions. If a modification to a permit is required by an anticipated change, this can greatly complicate the timely execution of business plans.

Enforcement The primary responsibility for enforcing air quality standards lies with the states, but the federal government has the right to enforce the standards where the states fail to do so. The Clean Air Act also provides for suits by citizens to force industry or the government to fully comply with the act's provisions.

The Clean Air Act—like the other major acts that deal with water pollution and the management of hazardous waste—provides three types of enforcement authority and possible sanctions: (1) administrative, (2) civil, and (3) criminal. Enforcement actions involving compliance orders and the imposition of penalties using the administrative authority are handled entirely within the administrative agency (EPA or the counterpart state agency). Enforcement actions using the civil sanctions are brought, at the federal level, by the Department of Justice in a federal district court and can result in injunctions requiring certain compliance actions and/or in the imposition of civil penalties. In assessing the penalties, the government tries, as a minimum, to deprive the alleged violator of any economic benefit the entity realized by not complying; in addition, the penalty assessed will depend on the gravity of the

Ethics and Compliance in Action

If It's Legal, Is It Ethical?

Suppose a manufacturing facility emits into the air a chemical that it has reason to believe is inadequately regulated by EPA and that poses a significant threat to nearby residents even at levels lower than permitted by EPA. As manager of the facility, would you be satisfied to meet the EPA-required level or would you install the additional controls you believe necessary to achieve a reasonably safe level?

---

offense, the extent of harm it caused, and whether the entity is a repeat violator. For the most serious or egregious violations, a criminal action seeking a fine or, in the case of individuals, imprisonment may be brought at the federal level by the Department of Justice—or at the state level by the state attorney general.

Enforcement actions often begin with an inspection by the relevant agency, followed by a notice of violation where any violations of the statutes or regulations are noted and an indication of what action is required and what, if any, penalties are being sought. Some of the environmental regulatory schemes require monitoring of discharges to the environment and the submission of reports under oath; these self-reports may show violations of permits and, in turn, serve as the basis for enforcement actions.

Automobile Pollution

The Clean Air Act provides specifically for air pollution controls on transportation sources such as automobiles. The major pollutants from automobiles are carbon monoxide, hydrocarbons, and nitrogen oxides. Carbon monoxide is a colorless, odorless gas that can dull mental performance and even cause death when inhaled in large quantities. Hydrocarbons, in the form of unburned fuel, are part of a category of air pollutants known as volatile organic compounds (VOCs). VOCs combine with nitrogen oxides under the influence of sunlight to become ozone—we know it as smog.

The 1970 Clean Air Act required a reduction of 90 percent of the carbon monoxide and hydrocarbons emitted by automobiles by 1975 and a 90 percent reduction in the nitrogen oxides emitted by 1976. At the time, these requirements were "technology forcing"—that is, the manufacturers could not rely on already-existing technology to meet the standards but, rather, had to develop new technology. Ultimately, most manufacturers had to go beyond simply making changes in engine design and utilize pollution control devices known as catalytic converters.

Subsequently, Congress addressed the question of setting even more stringent limits on automobile emissions while, at the same time, requiring that the new automobiles get better gas mileage. The 1990 amendments required further limitations on emissions from tailpipes, the development of so-called clean-fueled vehicles (such as electric and natural gas–fueled vehicles) for use in cities with dirty air, and the availability of oxygenated fuels (which are cleaner burning) in specified areas of the country that are having difficulty meeting the air quality limits at least part of the year. These requirements have significant ramifications for the oil and automobile industries.

Under the Clean Air Act, no manufacturer may sell vehicles subject to emission standards without prior certification from EPA that the vehicles meet the required standards. The tests are performed on prototype vehicles and if they pass, a certificate of conformity covering that type of engine and vehicle is issued. EPA subsequently can test vehicles on the assembly line to make sure that the production vehicles covered by the certificate are meeting the standards. The manufacturers are required to warrant that the vehicle, if properly maintained, will comply with the emission standards for its useful life. If EPA discovers that vehicles in actual use exceed the emission standards, it may order the manufacturer to recall and repair the defective models; this is a power that EPA has exercised on a number of occasions.

Recently, Volkswagen was subjected to large fines of more than $22 billion by EPA and Germany for an emissions cheating scheme to mask the emissions from its diesel engines that did not comply with the legal requirements.

The act also provides for the regulation and registration of fuel additives such as lead. In the 1980s, lead was largely phased out of use in gasoline as an octane enhancer in gasoline. As indicated previously, the 1990 amendments also provide for the availability of alternative fuels based on ethanol and methanol.

Subsequently, EPA and the Department of Transportation promulgated regulations requiring automobile and light-duty trucks sold after January 1, 2011, to meet restricted fuel economy standards for new cars and light trucks that will have the additional benefit of reducing emissions, including those of greenhouse gases. They also promulgated even more restrictive fuel economy standards for 2017–2025 model vehicles. In March 2020, the Trump EPA and DOT published regulations significantly pulling back on the standards applicable from 2011 to 2025. The State of California—which to date has been exempt from the federal preemption for regulation of motor vehicle emissions and has issued its own stringent regulations—along with other states, some automobile manufacturers, and environmental and other public interest groups have opposed that move by the Trump administration and have challenged the action in court.

International Air Problems

 LO52-3 Assess how governmental action to deal with greenhouse gas emission and global climate change may affect businesses.

Stratospheric Ozone Depletion During the late 1970s and 1980s, concern developed that the release of chlorine-containing substances such as chlorofluorocarbons (CFCs) used in air conditioning, refrigeration, and certain foam products was depleting the stratospheric ozone layer, which could lead to more ultraviolet radiation reaching the earth and, in turn, more skin cancer. Subsequently, a number of nations, acting under the aegis of the United Nations, signed a treaty agreeing first to limit any increases in production of CFCs and ultimately to phase out their use. The 1990 amendments to the Clean Air Act implement the obligations of the United States under the treaty and provide for the phase-down and phase-out of a number of chlorofluorocarbons; accordingly, many businesses have developed or located substitutes for those chemicals that are henceforth available only in reduced quantities, if at all.

Climate Change Currently, the issue of global warming/climate change is the focus of considerable debate, discussion, and some action by governments and private entities. The crux of the issue is whether human activity—primarily in the form of increased emissions of carbon dioxide to the atmosphere—is creating conditions that, over time, are resulting in the warming of the earth's atmosphere, a rise in sea level, an increase in number and severity of various weather events, and changes in the climate in many parts of the world. An international treaty known as the Kyoto Protocol was drafted with the intention of addressing this issue through collective international action. Although it was signed by many nations, it generated significant controversy in many countries, including the United States, and it did not prove an effective mechanism for addressing global climate change. The most recent international effort was a meeting of some 200 nations in Paris in late 2015 that produced an agreement with goals of limiting future warming and the

countries making nonbinding commitments to reduce their emissions of greenhouse gases.

The issue raises important concerns for many kinds of businesses, including insurance companies, producers and users of fossil fuels, and producers of products such as motor vehicles that emit carbon dioxide and may, at some point, be subjected to controls under either domestic or international regimes. The implications turn on the extent, nature, pace, and location of possible warming-induced changes, as well as on the reactions and policy decisions of individuals, businesses, and governments to those changes. The issue also holds potential business opportunities for individuals and firms, and many are developing business plans to try to take advantage of the issue.

The next few years will likely see continued debate and discussion of global warming/climate change and the appropriate responses to it. As of 2020, the United States does not have a comprehensive legal regime in place to address environmental and energy-related aspects of the issue. In the absence of such a federal response, a number of organizations and state and local governments have sought to use litigation to force the federal government to take some steps using existing authority. The case that follows, *Massachusetts v. EPA*, illustrates such an effort, which ended with the Supreme Court, in a 5–4 vote, agreeing that the EPA had not provided sufficient legal justification to refuse to exercise the legal authority it had to regulate greenhouse gas emission from automobiles.

Following the decision of the Supreme Court in *Massachusetts v. EPA*, EPA issued a formal finding that greenhouse gas emissions from mobile sources threaten public health and welfare. It also required large emitters of greenhouse gases to report their annual emissions and announced that major emitters will have to address greenhouse gases in the permit they obtain under the Clean Air Act.

EPA also promulgated a Clean Power Plan that establishes carbon emission budgets for states that will require them to develop plans to reduce the emission of greenhouse gases from power plants. It also establishes carbon emission standards for new power plants. However, the Trump administration has withdrawn those requirements and proposed significantly scaling back the Obama EPA regulations for coal-fired power plants. As this text went to print, both the earlier standards and the withdrawal have been challenged in court by some states and industries. Because this is an evolving area, you and your instructor will need to be alert for further legislative and regulatory developments in this area.

Massachusetts v. Environmental Protection Agency   549 U.S. 497 (2007)

On October 20, 1999, a group of 19 private organizations filed a rulemaking petition asking EPA to regulate "greenhouse gas emissions from new motor vehicles under § 202 of the Clean Air Act." Petitioners maintained that 1998 was the "warmest year on record"; that carbon dioxide, methane, nitrous oxide, and hydrofluorocarbons are "heat trapping greenhouse gases"; and that greenhouse gas emissions have significantly accelerated climate change. They also noted that in a 1995 report, the Intergovernmental Panel on Climate Change, a multinational scientific body organized under the auspices of the United Nations, warned that "carbon dioxide remains the most important contributor to [man-made] forcing of climate change." The petition further alleged that climate change will have serious adverse effects on human health and the environment. As to EPA's statutory authority, the petition observed that the agency itself had already confirmed that it had the power to regulate carbon dioxide. In 1998, Jonathan Z. Cannon, then EPA's general counsel, prepared a legal opinion concluding that "CO_2 emissions are within the scope of EPA's authority to regulate," even as he recognized that EPA had so far declined to exercise that authority. Cannon's successor, Gary S. Guzy, reiterated that opinion before a congressional committee just two weeks before the rulemaking petition was filed.

Fifteen months after the petition's submission, EPA requested public comment on "all the issues raised in [the] petition," adding a "particular" request for comments on "any scientific, technical, legal, economic or other aspect of these issues that may be relevant to EPA's consideration of this petition." EPA received more than 50,000 comments over the next five months.

Before the close of the comment period, the White House sought "assistance in identifying the areas in the science of climate change where there are the greatest certainties and uncertainties" from the National Research Council, asking for a response "as soon as possible." The result was a 2001 report titled Climate Change: An Analysis of Some Key Questions *(NRC Report), which, drawing heavily on the 1995 IPCC report, concluded that "[g]reenhouse gases are accumulating in Earth's atmosphere as a result of human activities, causing surface air temperatures and subsurface ocean temperatures to rise. Temperatures are, in fact, rising."*

On September 8, 2003, EPA entered an order denying the rulemaking petition. The agency gave two reasons for its decision: (1) that contrary to the opinions of its former general counsels, the Clean Air Act does not authorize EPA to issue mandatory regulations to address global climate change and (2) that even if the agency had the authority to set greenhouse gas emission standards, it would be unwise to do so at this time.

The petitioners, joined by a number of states and local governments, sought review of EPA's order in the U.S. Court of Appeals for the District of Columbia Circuit. Although each of the three judges on the panel wrote a separate opinion, two judges agreed that the EPA administrator properly exercised his discretion under section 202(a)(1) in denying the petition for rulemaking. The court therefore denied the petition for review. The Supreme Court granted a petition for certiorari and agreed to hear the case.

Stevens, Justice

Section 202(a)(1) of the Clean Air Act provides:

The [EPA] Administrator shall by regulation prescribe (and from time to time revise) in accordance with the provisions of this section, standards applicable to the emission of any air pollutant from any class or classes of new motor vehicles or new motor vehicle engines, which in his judgment cause, or contribute to, air pollution which may reasonably be anticipated to endanger public health or welfare. . . .

The Act defines "air pollutant" to include "any air pollution agent or combination of such agents, including any physical, chemical, biological, radioactive . . . substance or matter which is emitted into or otherwise enters the ambient air." "Welfare" is also defined broadly: among other things, it includes "effects on . . . weather . . . and climate."

On the merits, the first question is whether § 202(a)(1) of the Clean Air Act authorizes EPA to regulate greenhouse gas emissions from new motor vehicles in the event that it forms a "judgment" that such emissions contribute to climate change. We have little trouble concluding that it does. In relevant part, § 202(a)(1) provides that EPA "shall by regulation prescribe . . . standards applicable to the emission of any air pollutant from any class or classes of new motor vehicles or new motor vehicle engines, which in [the Administrator's] judgment cause, or contribute to, air pollution which may reasonably be anticipated to endanger public health or welfare." Because EPA believes that Congress did not intend it to regulate substances that contribute to climate change, the agency maintains that carbon dioxide is not an "air pollutant" within the meaning of the provision.

The statutory text forecloses EPA's reading. The Clean Air Act's sweeping definition of "air pollutant" includes "*any* air pollution agent or combination of such agents, including *any* physical, chemical . . . substance or matter which is emitted into or otherwise enters the ambient air. . . ." (emphasis added). On its face, the definition embraces all airborne compounds of whatever stripe, and underscores that intent through the repeated use of the word "any." Carbon dioxide, methane, nitrous oxide, and hydrofluorocarbons are without a doubt "physical [and] chemical . . . substance[s] which [are] emitted into . . . the ambient air." The statute is unambiguous.

Rather than relying on statutory text, EPA invokes post-enactment congressional actions and deliberations it views as tantamount to a congressional command to refrain from regulating greenhouse gas emissions. Even if such postenactment legislative history could shed light on the meaning of an otherwise-unambiguous statute, EPA never identifies any action remotely suggesting that Congress meant to curtail its power to treat greenhouse gases as air pollutants. That subsequent Congresses have eschewed enacting binding emissions limitations to combat global warming tells us nothing about what Congress meant when it amended § 202(a)(1) in 1970 and 1977. And unlike EPA, we have no difficulty reconciling Congress' various efforts to promote interagency collaboration and research to better understand climate change with the agency's preexisting mandate to regulate "any air pollutant" that may endanger the public welfare. Collaboration and research do not conflict with any thoughtful regulatory effort; they complement it.

EPA finally argues that it cannot regulate carbon dioxide emissions from motor vehicles because doing so would require it to tighten mileage standards, a job (according to EPA) that Congress has assigned to DOT. But that DOT sets mileage standards in no way licenses EPA to shirk its environmental responsibilities. EPA has been charged with protecting the public's "health" and "welfare," a statutory obligation wholly independent of DOT's mandate to promote energy efficiency. The two obligations may overlap, but there is no reason to think the two agencies cannot both administer their obligations and yet avoid inconsistency.

While the Congresses that drafted § 202(a)(1) might not have appreciated the possibility that burning fossil fuels could lead to global warming, they did understand that without regulatory flexibility, changing circumstances and scientific developments would soon render the Clean Air Act obsolete. The broad language of § 202(a)(1) reflects an intentional effort to confer the flexibility necessary to forestall such obsolescence. Because greenhouse gases fit well within the Clean Air Act's capacious definition of "air pollutant," we hold that EPA has the statutory authority to regulate the emission of such gases from new motor vehicles.

The alternative basis for EPA's decision—that even if it does have statutory authority to regulate greenhouse gases, it would be unwise to do so at this time—rests on reasoning divorced from the statutory text. While the statute does condition the exercise of EPA's authority on its formation of a "judgment," that judgment must relate to whether an air pollutant "cause[s], or contribute[s]

to, air pollution which may reasonably be anticipated to endanger public health or welfare." Put another way, the use of the word "judgment" is not a roving license to ignore the statutory text. It is but a direction to exercise discretion within defined statutory limits.

If EPA makes a finding of endangerment, the Clean Air Act requires the agency to regulate emissions of the deleterious pollutant from new motor vehicles. EPA no doubt has significant latitude as to the manner, timing, content, and coordination of its regulations with those of other agencies. But once EPA has responded to a petition for rulemaking, its reasons for action or inaction must conform to the authorizing statute. Under the clear terms of the Clean Air Act, EPA can avoid taking further action only if it determines that greenhouse gases do not contribute to climate change or if it provides some reasonable explanation as to why it cannot or will not exercise its discretion to determine whether they do. To the extent that this constrains agency discretion to pursue other priorities of the Administrator or the President, this is the congressional design.

EPA has refused to comply with this clear statutory command. Instead, it has offered a laundry list of reasons not to regulate. For example, EPA said that a number of voluntary executive branch programs already provide an effective response to the threat of global warming, that regulating greenhouse gases might impair the President's ability to negotiate with "key developing nations" to reduce emissions, and that curtailing motor-vehicle emissions would reflect "an inefficient, piecemeal approach to address the climate change issue."

Although we have neither the expertise nor the authority to evaluate these policy judgments, it is evident they have nothing to do with whether greenhouse gas emissions contribute to climate change. Still less do they amount to a reasoned justification for declining to form a scientific judgment. In particular, while the President has broad authority in foreign affairs, that authority does not extend to the refusal to execute domestic laws. In the Global Climate Protection Act of 1987, Congress authorized the State Department—not EPA—to formulate United States foreign policy with reference to environmental matters relating to climate. EPA has made no showing that it issued the ruling in question here after consultation with the State Department. Congress did direct EPA to consult with other agencies in the formulation of its policies and rules, but the State Department is absent from that list.

Nor can EPA avoid its statutory obligation by noting the uncertainty surrounding various features of climate change and concluding that it would therefore be better not to regulate at this time. If the scientific uncertainty is so profound that it precludes EPA from making a reasoned judgment as to whether greenhouse gases contribute to global warming, EPA must say so. That EPA would prefer not to regulate greenhouse gases because of some residual uncertainty is irrelevant. The statutory question is whether sufficient information exists to make an endangerment finding.

In short, EPA has offered no reasoned explanation for its refusal to decide whether greenhouse gases cause or contribute to climate change. Its action was therefore arbitrary, capricious, or otherwise not in accordance with law. We need not and do not reach the question whether on remand EPA must make an endangerment finding, or whether policy concerns can inform EPA's actions in the event that it makes such a finding. We hold only that EPA must ground its reasons for action or inaction in the statute.

The judgment of the Court of Appeals is reversed, and the case is remanded for further proceedings consistent with this opinion.

Water Pollution

 LO52-4 List and briefly discuss the major provisions in the Clean Water Act.

Background History is replete with plagues and epidemics brought on by poor sanitation and polluted water. Indeed, preventing waterborne disease has always been the major reason for combating water pollution. In the early 1970s, fishing and swimming were prohibited in many bodies of water, and game fish could no longer survive in some waters where they had formerly thrived. Lake Erie was becoming choked with algae and considered to be dying. The nation recognized that water pollution could affect public health, recreation, commercial fishing, agriculture, water supplies, and aesthetics. During the 1970s, Congress enacted three major statutes to protect our water resources: the Clean Water Act; the Marine Protection, Research, and Sanctuaries Act; and the Safe Drinking Water Act.

Early Federal Legislation Federal water pollution legislation dates back to the 19th century when Congress enacted the River and Harbor Act of 1886. In fact, this statute, recodified in the River and Harbor Act of 1899, often referred to as the "Refuse Act," furnished the legal basis for EPA's initial enforcement actions against polluters. The act provided that people had to obtain a discharge permit from the Army Corps of Engineers to deposit or discharge refuse into a navigable waterway. This act was designed to protect navigation rather than water quality—for example, from construction of docks and using a waterway as a means of transporting logs to a mill. Under some contemporary court decisions, even hot water discharged from nuclear power plants was considered refuse. The permit system established pursuant to the Refuse Act was replaced in 1972 by a more comprehensive permit system now administered by EPA.

Clean Water Act The 1972 amendments to the Federal Water Pollution Control Act (FWPCA)—known as the Clean Water Act—were as comprehensive in the water pollution field as the 1970 Clean Air Act was in the air pollution field. They proclaimed two general goals for this country: (1) to achieve wherever possible by July 1, 1983, water clean enough for swimming and other recreational uses and clean enough for the protection and propagation of fish, shellfish, and wildlife and (2) to have no discharges of pollutants into the nation's waters by 1985. These goals reflected a national frustration with the lack of progress in dealing with water pollution and a commitment to end such pollution. The new law set out a series of specific actions that federal, state, and local governments and industry were to take by certain dates and also provided strong enforcement provisions to back up the deadlines. In 1977 and again in 1987, Congress modified the 1972 act by adjusting some of the deadlines and otherwise fine-tuning the act.

Under the Clean Water Act, the states have the primary responsibility for preventing, reducing, and eliminating water pollution. The states have to do this within a national framework, and EPA is empowered to move in if the states do not fulfill their responsibilities.

Discharge Permits The keystone of the Clean Water Act is a prohibition against persons discharging pollutants from "point sources" into "waters of the United States" except in compliance with the requirements of the act; these requirements normally include obtaining a permit from the federal or state government for the discharge. Thus, anyone who discharges industrial wastewater (wastewater that contains pollutants) from a point source (such as a pipe or ditch) into a river must obtain a National Pollution Discharge Elimination System (NPDES) permit from the state where the discharge takes place or from EPA. Similarly, anyone who discharges wastewater, other than just domestic sewage, to a publicly owned treatment works (POTW) must obtain what is known as an industrial discharge permit from the local sewage treatment plant where the discharge is being sent or from the state.

Typically, these permits (1) establish limits on the concentration and amount of various pollutants that can be discharged and (2) require the discharger to keep records, to install equipment to monitor the discharges, and to report the monitoring results to the state environmental agency. All of the permits contain limits established by EPA in the form of nationally applicable, technology-based effluent limits. In the case of the industrial discharge permits, the limitations are known as pretreatment standards because they normally require the discharger to provide some onsite treatment of the wastewater before it enters the sewer system. For industries that discharge directly into rivers, the technology-based limits established by EPA can be tightened if necessary to ensure that the water quality standards established by the state for that body of water are met and the designated uses protected.

Water Quality Standards
The act continued and expanded the previously established system of setting *water quality standards* by designating, and establishing, limits to protect the uses of specific bodies of water for recreation, public water supply, propagation of fish and wildlife, and agricultural and industrial water supply. Then, the maximum daily loads of various pollutants are set so that the water is suitable for the designated use. The final step is to establish limits on individual dischargers of pollutants so that the water quality standards will be met.

Water quality standards are established by states using guidance documents provided by EPA and are subject to approval by EPA. Once approved, they are enforceable by either the state or the federal government.

Enforcement
Both civil and criminal sanctions are included in the act. Criminal penalties for violating the law range from a minimum of $2,500 for a first offense up to $50,000 per day and two years in prison for subsequent violations. The act is enforced by federal and state governments. In addition, any citizen or group of citizens whose interests are adversely affected has the right to bring a court action against anyone violating an effluent standard, limitation, or order issued by EPA or a state. A significant number of cases have been brought by citizen-action groups against firms whose wastewater discharges exceeded the limits of their discharge permits. Citizens also have the right to take court action against EPA if it fails to carry out mandatory provisions of the law.

In the case that follows, *United States v. Hopkins*, a corporate officer was convicted and sentenced to prison for falsifying reports to the government concerning the discharge of pollutants.

United States v. Hopkins	**53 F.3d 533 (2d Cir. 1995)**

Spirol International Corporation is a manufacturer of metal shims and fasteners located in northeastern Connecticut. Spirol's manufacturing operation involves a zinc-based plating process that generates substantial amounts of wastewater containing zinc and other toxic materials; this wastewater is discharged into the nearby Five Mile River. The U.S. Environmental Protection Agency (EPA) has delegated to the State of Connecticut's Department of Environmental Protection (DEP) the authority to administer the Clean Water Act provisions applicable to Spirol's discharges into the river. In 1987, Spirol entered into a consent order with DEP requiring Spirol to pay a $30,000 fine for past violations and to comply in the future with discharge limitations specified in the order. In February 1989, DEP issued a modified "wastewater discharge permit" imposing more restrictive limits on the quantity of zinc and other substances that Spirol was permitted to release into the river.

From 1987 through September 6, 1990, Robert Hopkins was Spirol's vice president for manufacturing. Hopkins signed the 1987 consent decree on behalf of Spirol and had the corporate responsibility for ensuring compliance with the order and the DEP permit. The DEP permit required Spirol each week to collect a sample of its wastewater and send it to an independent laboratory by Friday morning of that week. Spirol was required to report the laboratory results to DEP in a discharge monitoring report once a month. Under the DEP permit, the concentrations of zinc in Spirol's wastewater were not to exceed 2.0 milligrams per liter in any weekly sample, nor to average more than 1 milligram per liter in any month.

During the period March 1989 to September 1990, Spirol began its weekly sampling process on Monday. A composite sample was taken and analyzed in house. If it contained less than 1 milligram of zinc, it was sent to the independent laboratory with a "chain of custody" record signed by Hopkins. However, if it exceeded 1 milligram of zinc, it was discarded and another sample taken and tested the following day. In 54 of the 78 weeks, the samples were sent to the laboratory later than Tuesday. If the Wednesday sample also failed the in-house test, Hopkins would sometimes order that it be discarded and another taken on Thursday, but more often he instructed his subordinates doing the testing to dilute the sample with tap water or to reduce the zinc concentration using an ordinary coffee filter. Any

Friday sample that failed the in-house test was always diluted or filtered so that a good sample could be sent to the laboratory by the Friday deadline. In some samples sent to the laboratory, there was more tap water than wastewater.

During this period, Hopkins filed with DEP monthly discharge monitoring reports consolidating the weekly tests from the independent laboratory. The reports showed no zinc concentrations above 1 milligram per liter. On each report, Hopkins signed the following certification.

I certify under penalty of law that this document and all attachments were prepared under my direction or supervision in accordance with a system designed to assure that qualified personnel properly gather and evaluate the information submitted. Based on my inquiry of the person or persons who administer the system, or those persons directly responsible for gathering the information, the information is, to the best of my knowledge and belief, true, accurate and complete. I am aware that there are significant penalties for submitting false information, including the possibility of fine and imprisonment for knowing violations.

Contrary to Hopkins's certifications, his subordinates testified that he had caused the samples to be tampered with about 40 percent of the time. On some 25–30 occasions when he had been told that a satisfactory sample had finally been obtained by means of dilution or filtration, Hopkins responded, "I know nothing, I hear nothing." Hopkins was told that the testing procedures were improper, yet he continued to sign the certifications, and Spirol continued its discharges into the river.

In December 1993, Hopkins was charged in a three-count indictment alleging (1) that he had knowingly falsified or tampered with Spirol's discharge sampling methods, (2) that he had knowingly violated the conditions of the permit, and (3) that he had conspired to commit those offenses. Hopkins was convicted following a jury trial and sentenced to 21 months in prison, with two years' probation following that, and a $7,500 fine. Hopkins appealed, arguing that the government should have been required to prove that he intended to violate the law and that he had specific knowledge of the particular statutory, regulatory, or permit requirements imposed under the Clean Water Act. The government contended that it was enough to prove that he had acted voluntarily or intentionally to falsify, tamper with, or render inaccurate a monitoring method—or to violate the permit—and that he did not do so by mistake, accident, or other innocent reason.

Kearse, Circuit Judge

Subsection (2) of section 1319(c), whose violation was alleged in count two of the indictment, establishes criminal penalties, including fines of up to $50,000 per day and imprisonment for up to three years, for "any person" who, inter alia, *knowingly violates* section 1311, 1312, 1316, 1317, 1318, 1321(b)(3), 1328, or 1345 of [Title 33], or any permit condition or limitation implementing any of such sections in a permit issued under [the Clean Water Act] by the Administrator or by a State.

Hopkins contends that the district court should have instructed the jury that it could not find him guilty of violating this section unless it found that he knew he was acting in violation of the CWA or the DEP permit. We disagree.

Section 1319(c)(2)(A) itself does not expressly state whether the adverb "knowingly" is intended to require proof that the defendant had actual knowledge that his conduct violated any of the statutory provisions that follow the phrase "knowingly violates" or had actual knowledge that his conduct violated a permit condition. As a matter of abstract logic, it would seem that a statute making it unlawful to "knowingly violate" a given statutory or permit provision would require proof that the defendant both violated and knew that he violated that provision. In defining the mental state required for conviction under a given statute, however, the courts must seek the proper "inference of the intent of Congress."

In *United States v. International Minerals & Chemical Corp.* ("*International Minerals*"), the Court construed a statute that authorized the Interstate Commerce Commission ("ICC") to promulgate regulations governing the transport of corrosive liquids and imposed criminal penalties on those who "knowingly violated any such regulation." The Court held that the quoted phrase required the government to prove only that the defendant knew the nature of his acts, not that he knew his acts violated an ICC regulation. The Court stated that "where . . . dangerous or deleterious devices or products or obnoxious waste materials are involved, the probability of regulation is so great that anyone who is aware that he is in possession of them or dealing with them must be presumed to be aware of the regulation." Applying this presumption of awareness, the Court concluded that the phrase "knowingly violated any [ICC] regulation" was meant to be a "shorthand" method of referring to the acts or omissions contemplated by the statute.

Noting the general rule that ignorance of the law is no excuse, the court declined to attribute to Congress the inaccurate view that use of the word "knowingly" would require proof of knowledge of the law, as well as the facts. The mens rea presumption requires knowledge only of the facts that make the defendant's conduct illegal, lest it conflict with the related presumption, deeply rooted in the American legal system, that ordinarily ignorance of the law or a mistake of law is no defense to criminal prosecution.

This court in *United States v. Laughlin* applied the *International Minerals* "presumption of awareness of regulation" in construing provisions of the Resource Conservation and Recovery Act ("RCRA") and the Comprehensive Environmental Response, Compensation and Liability Act ("CERCLA"). RCRA provides for the imposition of criminal penalties against any person who "knowingly treats, stores, or disposes of any hazardous waste identified or listed under [RCRA]" without a permit. We held that this provision did not require the government to prove that the defendant knew that the waste he dealt with was identified or listed under RCRA or that he lacked a disposal permit. Rather, we held that the government need prove only that the defendant knew the nature of the hazardous waste matter with which he dealt.

For several reasons, we view the presumption of awareness of regulation, applied to the ground-pollution offenses in *Laughlin*, to be equally applicable to the phrase "knowingly violates [the specified sections or permit]" in section 1319(c)(2)(A). Congress considered discharges of hazardous waste onto the ground, which are regulated in RCRA, as no less serious than such discharges into water. Further, the CWA sections to which section 1319(c)(2)(A) refers regulate a broad range of pollutant discharges, including "water quality related effluents," "toxic pollutants" listed in accordance with section 1317(a), "oil and hazardous substances," and "sewage sludge." The vast majority of these substances are of the type that would alert any ordinary user to the likelihood of stringent regulation. Moreover, the very fact that a governmental permit has been issued enhances the user's awareness of the existence of regulation.

Thus, we conclude that the purpose and legislative history of section 1319(c)(2)(A) indicate that Congress meant that that section would be violated if the defendant's acts were proscribed, even if the defendant was not aware of the proscription.

Judgment of conviction affirmed.

The Global Business Environment

International Voluntary Consensus Standards and Certification: ISO 14000 Environmental Management Standards

Today, national and international companies competing in a global economy face a daunting array of challenges, including complying with increasingly complex environmental regulations in those countries in which they operate or do business. And differing national standards may not only create nontariff trade barriers, but also increase costs and the difficulty of doing business. Managers who want to be proactive in systematically improving the environmental performance of their organization can adopt and follow the ISO 14000 series of environmental management standards.

The ISO, located in Geneva, Switzerland, was founded in 1947 to promote the development of international manufacturing, trade, and communication standards. The ISO standards—which are international voluntary consensus standards—are developed with input from industry, government, and other interested parties. The standards have legal standing only if actually adopted by a country—but they have been utilized by many organizations on a voluntary basis. In addition to the performance enhancement that can be obtained by following the standards, in some instances certification of compliance with the standards can lead to competitive advantages and/or may be necessary to do certain types of business.

The most prominent of the ISO standards is the worldwide quality standard, ISO 9000. The standard provides organizations with a process for producing quality products through a systems approach that involves all phases of production. You may have encountered these standards in other business school classes. They have been adopted by many countries and utilized by many organizations—and as of 2020, more than one million organizations have been certified.

Development of the ISO 14000 series of standards began in 1993, and the initial set of standards was finalized in 1996. These include (1) ISO 14001, Environmental management systems—specification with guidance for use; (2) ISO 14004, Environmental management systems—general guidelines on principles, systems, and supporting techniques; (3) ISO 14010, Guidelines for environmental auditing—general principles; (4) ISO 14011, Guidelines for environmental auditing—audit procedures—Part 1: Auditing of environmental management programs; (5) ISO Guidelines for environmental auditing—qualification criteria for environmental auditors; (6) ISO 14024, Environmental labeling—guidance principles, practices, and criteria for multiple criteria-based practitioner programs (Type 1)—guide for certification procedures; (7) ISO 14040, Life-cycle assessment—principles and guidelines; and (8) ISO Guide for the inclusion of environmental aspects in product standards.

Organizations can be certified that they comply with ISO 14001. Certification is a procedure by which a third party gives written assurance that a product, process, or service conforms to the specific requirements of the ISO standard. An organization that obtains ISO certification can claim that it has an environmental management system (EMS) meeting the ISO standards that has been implemented and is being consistently followed. This certification would be based on an audit of the EMS system by the third-party certifier. It should be noted that the certification goes to the nature of the management system employed by the organization—and does not give it a basis for claiming that its products or services are environmentally superior to those of other organizations. However, such certification can be either a matter of competitive advantage—or of necessity—as some companies will only do business with ISO-certified entities. In the United States, the American National Standards Institute (ANSI) is the organization responsible for certifying that an organization meets the requirements of ISO 14001.

Wetlands

Another aspect of the Clean Water Act having the potential to affect businesses as well as individual property owners are the wetlands provisions. Commonly, wetlands are transition zones between land and open water. Under section 404 of the act, any *dredging or filling* activity in a wetland that is connected to the waters of the United States—as well as in any water of the United States—requires a permit before any activity begins. The permit program is administered by the Army Corps of Engineers, with the involvement of the Environmental Protection Agency.

The requirement that a permit be obtained before engaging in any significant deposit of soil or other fill in wetlands can be an important consideration for residential or commercial development in coastal areas or other areas adjacent to bodies of water that contain marshy areas that meet the definition of wetlands.[1] To obtain a permit, an applicant must establish that there are no alternatives available to the developer that would have less adverse impact on the aquatic environment. Practicable alternatives can include other property not owned by the applicant but that might be obtained and would achieve the objectives of the proposed project. Where the project is not water-dependent (i.e., is something other than, say, a marina, which does require water access and would be considered "water-dependent"), the permit applicant must overcome a presumption that other alternatives are available and that they would have less environmental impact.

Where the property owner is not able to get a permit to fill a wetland and is effectively deprived of being able to make any economically viable use of his property, the landowner may be able to pursue a claim for regulatory taking and receive compensation from the government for the fair market value of the interest that was taken. The basis for such a claim is the clause in the Fifth Amendment that forbids the government to take private property for public use unless it pays the owner for the value of the property interest taken by the government.

Waters of the United States

In enacting what we know as the Clean Water Act, Congress stated that its objective was to restore and maintain "the chemical, physical, and biological integrity of the Nation's waters." While the act applies to activities affecting the "waters of the United States," the precise reach of this authority remains elusive today some 49 years after the act was passed in 1972. Despite numerous court decisions and efforts by the Environmental Protection Agency and the Army Corps of Engineers, the issue continues to be a source of great frustration and extensive litigation. Clearly the act is applicable to navigable waters; interstate waters; non-navigable tributaries to navigable waters that are relatively permanent, containing water at least seasonally; and wetlands that are adjacent to those water bodies. However, beyond those waters, there are a wide range of aquatic areas that arguably affect the physical, chemical, or biological integrity of those waters that private property owners also contend strongly should not be subject to the act. Legal challenges to the most recent set of EPA and Corps regulations seeking to delineate the Waters of the United States (WOTUS) are unlikely to be resolved in the next few years, and a resolution by Congress appears even more unlikely.

Ocean Dumping

The Marine Protection, Research, and Sanctuaries Act of 1972 set up a permit system regulating the dumping of all types of materials into ocean waters. EPA has the responsibility for designating disposal sites and for establishing the rules governing ocean disposal. The Ocean Dumping Ban Act of 1987 required that all ocean dumping of municipal sewage sludge and industrial wastes be terminated by December 31, 1991. Thus, the major remaining questions of ocean dumping concern the disposal of dredge spoils from dredging to keep harbors open.

[1] The question of which wetlands fall within the jurisdictional reach of the Clean Water Act and the authority of the Army Corps of Engineers to require a permit before any filling activity takes place has been the focus of three major decisions by the Supreme Court. *See United States v. Riverside Bayview Homes, Inc.*, 474 U.S. 121 (1985); *Solid Waste Agency of Northern Cook County v. United States Army Corps of Engineers*, 531 U.S. 159 (2001); and *Rapanos v. United States*, 547 U.S. 715 (2006).

Liability for Oil Spills

LO52-5 Explain why Congress passed the Oil Pollution Act of 1990 and list its major provisions.

In March 1989, the supertanker *Exxon Valdez* ran aground on a reef in Alaska's scenic Prince William Sound, spilling 11 million gallons of crude oil in an environmentally sensitive area. The accident occurred after the tanker's captain, who had a history of alcohol abuse and had a high blood-alcohol level 11 hours after the spill, inexplicitly exited the bridge, leaving a tricky course correction to unlicensed subordinates. The massive spill and the subsequent efforts to deal with its consequences focused attention on the then-current legal mechanisms for dealing with such spills. At that time, the liability for oil spills in U.S. waters was governed by a patchwork maze of five federal laws, three international conventions, private international agreements, and numerous state laws. In general, those laws and agreements were designed to limit the liability of ship owners in case of a major spill. One of those laws—the Limitation of Liability Act of 1851—limited the liability to the value of a ship after an accident occurred. Some of the laws focused on where the oil came from (e.g., a ship or the Trans-Alaska Pipeline), while others focused on where the oil was spilled (e.g., in a port or on the Outer-Continental Shelf).

Exxon spent an estimated $2.1 billion in cleanup costs, pled guilty to criminal violations that resulted in fines, settled a civil action by the United States and Alaska for some $900 million, and paid another $303 million in voluntary payments to private parties. A number of civil actions against Exxon and the captain seeking recovery for economic losses sustained as a result of the spill were consolidated into a single lawsuit that found its way to the U.S. Supreme Court in 2008, some 19 years after the spill occurred. The issues in that case, *Exxon Shipping Co. v. Baker*, which follows, focused on whether the recovery was barred by the Clean Water Act and whether the multi-billion-dollar punitive damage award against Exxon was excessive as a matter of federal maritime law.

Following the Exxon disaster, Congress enacted the Oil Pollution Prevention, Response, Liability and Compensation Act of 1990. Among other things, the act created a $1 billion trust fund, the Oil Spill Liability Trust Fund, funded by a five-cent-per-barrel tax on oil to pay for cleanup costs in excess of the liability limit in the act. The act provides for fines of $1,000 for every barrel spilled, with the amount increasing to $3,000 per barrel if negligence can be shown. Those entities found responsible for oil spills are liable for the costs of cleanup and for economic damages, such as those for damage to fisheries, up to $75 million. However, that cap does not apply if the loss was proximately caused by gross negligence or willful misconduct or violation of a federal regulation. Moreover, it is important to note that the federal law does not preempt state laws, which may provide for additional liability for such accidents.

The explosion and fire that led to the sinking of the Deepwater Horizon drilling rig in April 2010 resulted in a massive oil spill in the Gulf of Mexico, with widespread damage to the coastal estuaries, fishing grounds, and economies of the region. In the wake of that accident and the investigations into the causes, we have seen considerable litigation as well as proposed changes in the laws and regulations concerning offshore oil drilling.

One of the cases in Chapter 22, Remedies for Breach of Sales Contracts, *Cahaba Disaster Recovery v. Rogers*, deals with the sale of a product supposedly designed to contain the oil spill, but which failed to meet the representations made for it.

Exxon Shipping Co. v. Baker   554 U.S. 471 (2008)

On March 24, 1989, the supertanker Exxon Valdez *grounded on Bligh Reef off the Alaskan coast, fracturing its hull and spilling millions of gallons of crude oil into Prince William Sound. The tanker was more than 900 feet long and was being used by Exxon to carry crude oil from the end of the Trans-Alaska Pipeline in Valdez, Alaska, to the lower 48 states. On the night of the spill, it was carrying 53 million gallons of crude oil, or more than a million barrels. Its captain, Joseph Hazelwood, had recently completed a 28-day alcohol treatment program while employed by Exxon but had dropped out of a prescribed follow-up program. Witnesses testified that before the ship left port on the night of the disaster, the captain downed at least five double vodkas in waterfront bars of Valdez, an intake of about 15 ounces of 80-proof alcohol. Eleven hours after the tanker hit the reef, his blood-alcohol level was .061, three times the legal limit for driving in most states.*

A state-licensed pilot guided the ship through the Valdez Narrows and then, two hours into the voyage, the captain took command. However, just as the ship was about to execute a very difficult maneuver near a reef, the captain inexplicably left the deck and went to his cabin to "do paperwork." He was the only person on board licensed to maneuver the boat in this part of Prince William Sound. With an unlicensed pilot at the helm, the ship ran aground and split open, resulting in a spill of 11 million gallons of crude oil.

In addition to seeking cleanup costs from Exxon, the United States charged the company with criminal violations of the Clean Water Act, the Refuse Act of 1899, the Migratory Bird Treaty Act, the Ports and Waterways Safety Act, and the Dangerous Cargo Act. The company pled guilty to violations of the Clean Water Act, the Refuse Act, and the Migratory Bird Treaty Act and agreed to pay a $150 million fine, later reduced to $25 million plus restitution of $100 million. A civil action brought by the United States and Alaska for environmental harms ended with a consent decree for Exxon to pay $900 million toward restoring natural resources, and Exxon paid another $303 million in voluntary settlements with fishermen, property owners, and other private parties.

A number of other civil cases were consolidated into one case where the plaintiffs seeking damages were divided into three classes: commercial fishermen, Native Americans, and landowners. At Exxon's request, the court also certified a mandatory class of all plaintiffs seeking punitive damages, whose number topped 32,000. For purposes of the case, Exxon stipulated to its negligence in the Valdez disaster and its ensuing liability for compensatory damages. The trial court divided the trial into several phases: Phase I considered Exxon's and the captain's recklessness and thus their potential for punitive damages; Phase II set compensatory damages for commercial fishermen and Native Americans; and Phase III determined the amount of punitive damages for which Exxon and the captain were each liable.

In Phase I, the judge instructed the jury that a corporation is responsible for the reckless acts of those employees who are employed in a managerial capacity while acting in the scope of their employment. Exxon did not dispute that the captain was a managerial employee under the definition of managerial employee used by the judge, and the jury found both the captain and Exxon reckless, and thus potentially liable for punitive damages. In Phase II, the jury awarded $287 million in compensatory damages to the commercial fishermen, and the Native Americans settled their compensatory claims. In Phase III, the court instructed the jurors that the purpose of punitive damages was not to provide compensatory relief but rather to punish and deter the defendants. The courts charged the jury to consider the reprehensibility of the defendants' conduct, their financial condition, the magnitude of the harm, and any mitigating facts. The jury awarded $5,000 in punitive damages against Hazelwood and $5 billion against Exxon.

The Ninth Circuit upheld the Phase I jury instructions on corporate liability for acts of managerial agents and, after twice remanding the case for adjustments to the amount of punitive damages, adjusted the award to $2.5 billion. The U.S. Supreme Court agreed to review the case to consider (1) whether maritime law allows corporate liability for punitive damages on the basis of acts of managerial agents, (2) whether the Clean Water Act forecloses the award of punitive damages in maritime spill cases, and (3) whether the punitive damages awarded against Exxon were excessive as a matter of maritime common law.

Souter, Justice

There are three questions of maritime law before us: whether a ship owner may be liable for punitive damages without acquiescence in the actions causing harm, whether punitive damages have been barred explicitly by federal statutory law, and whether the award of $2.5 billion in this case is greater than maritime law should allow in the circumstances. We are equally divided on the owner's derivative liability, and hold that the federal statutory law does not bar a punitive damage award on top of damages for economic loss, but that the award here should be limited to an amount equal to compensatory damages.

In Phase I, the jury heard extensive testimony about Hazelwood's alcoholism and his conduct on the night of the spill, as well as conflicting testimony about Exxon officials' knowledge of Hazelwood's backslide. At the close of Phase I, the Court instructed the jury in part that

A corporation is responsible for the reckless acts of those employees who are employed in a managerial capacity while acting in the scope of their employment. The reckless act or omission of a managerial officer or employee of a corporation, in the course and scope of the performance of his duties, is held in law to be the reckless act or omission of the corporation.

The Court went on that "an employee of a corporation is employed in a managerial capacity if the employee supervises other employees and has responsibility for, and authority over, a particular aspect of the corporation's business." Exxon did not dispute that Hazelwood was a managerial employee under this definition, and the jury found both Hazelwood and Exxon reckless and thus potentially liable for punitive damages.

[*Because the Supreme Court was split 4–4 on the issue of whether the corporation had derivative liability for punitive damages for the acts of its employees, it left undisturbed the Ninth Circuit's affirmation of the trial court's instructions. The court also rejected Exxon's contention that the Clean Water Act preempts any common law punitive-damages remedies.*]

Finally, Exxon raises an issue of first impression about punitive damages in maritime law, which falls within a federal court's jurisdiction to decide in the manner of a common law court, subject to the authority of Congress to legislate otherwise if it disagrees with the judicial result. Exxon challenges the size of the remaining $2.5 billion punitive award. Other than the preemption argument, it does not offer a legal ground for concluding that maritime law should never award punitive damages, or that none should be awarded in this case, but it does argue that this award exceeds the bounds justified by the punitive damages goal of deterring reckless (or worse) behavior and the consequently heightened threat of harm. The claim goes to our understanding of the place of punishment in modern civil law and reasonable standards of process in administering punitive law, subjects that call for starting with a brief account of the history behind today's punitive damages.

[*After recounting the history of punitive damages over the last several hundred years, the process by which such awards are established, statutory limits in other contexts, and studies of compensatory damage awards by juries, the Court concluded: (1) that the current rationale for punitive damages is not compensation but aimed rather at retribution and deterring harmful conduct and (2) that a 1:1 rule of punitive damages to compensatory damages was a fair and necessary upper limit to protect against the possibility (the disruptive cost to the legal system) of awards that are unpredictable and unnecessary, for either deterrence or measured retribution.*]

The provision of the Clean Water Act respecting daily fines confirms our judgment that anything greater would be excessive here and in cases of this type. Congress set criminal penalties of up to $25,000 per day for negligent violations of pollution restrictions and up to $50,000 per day for knowing ones. Discretion to double the penalties for knowing action compares to discretion to double the civil liability on conduct going beyond negligence and meriting punitive treatment. And our explanation of the constitutional upper limit confirms that the 1:1 ratio is not too low. In *State Farm Mutual Automobile Insurance Co. v. Campbell*, we said that single-digit maximum is appropriate in all but the most exceptional of cases, and when compensatory damages are substantial, then a lesser ratio, perhaps only equal to compensatory damages, can reach the outermost limit of the due process guarantee.

Applying this standard to the present case, we take for granted the district court's calculation of the total relevant compensatory damages at $507.5 million. A punitive-to-compensatory ratio of 1:1 thus yields maximum punitive damages in that amount.

Case remanded to the Court of Appeals to revise the punitive damage award accordingly.

Drinking Water

In 1974, Congress passed, and in 1986 and in 1996 amended, the Safe Drinking Water Act that is designed to protect and enhance the quality of our drinking water. Under the act, EPA sets *primary drinking water standards*, minimum levels of quality for water consumed by humans. The act also establishes a program governing the injection of wastes into wells. The primary responsibility for complying with the federally established standards lies with the states. Where the states fail to enforce the drinking water standards, the federal government has the right to enforce them.

A significant number of suppliers of drinking water are privately owned—and they, as well as the publicly owned systems, have to be concerned with meeting the federal standards. In addition, factories, trailer parks, schools, and other entities that draw drinking water from wells and provide it within their facility can find that they are also subject to the drinking water regulations.

Waste Disposal

Background

Historically, concern about the environment focused on decreasing air and water pollution as well as protecting natural resources and wildlife. People paid relatively little attention to the disposal of wastes on land. Until the early 1970s, much of the solid and hazardous waste generated was disposed of in open dumps and landfills. Although some of the waste we produce can be disposed of without presenting significant health or environmental problems, some industrial, agricultural, and mining wastes—and even some household wastes—are hazardous and can present serious problems. Unless wastes are properly disposed of, they can cause air, water, and land pollution as well as contamination of the underground aquifers from which much of our drinking water is drawn. Once aquifers have been contaminated, they can take a very long time to cleanse themselves of pollutants.

In the 1970s, the discovery of abandoned dump sites such as Love Canal in New York and the Valley of the Drums in Kentucky heightened public concern about the disposal of toxic and hazardous wastes. Congress has enacted several laws regulating the generation and disposal of hazardous waste: The Resource Conservation and Recovery Act mandates proper management and disposal of wastes currently generated and the Comprehensive Environmental Response, Compensation, and Liability Act focuses on cleaning up past disposal sites threatening public health and the environment.

The Resource Conservation and Recovery Act

 LO52-6 List and briefly discuss the purpose of the Resource Conservation and Recovery Act.

Congress originally enacted the Resource Conservation and Recovery Act (RCRA) in 1976 and significantly amended it in 1984. RCRA provides the federal government and the states with the authority to regulate facilities that generate, treat, store, and dispose of hazardous waste. Most of the wastes defined as hazardous are subject to a "cradle-to-the-grave" tracking system and must be handled and disposed of in defined ways. RCRA requires persons who generate, treat, store, or transport hazardous waste to meet certain standards and follow specified procedures in the handling of the wastes, to keep records, and, in some instances, to obtain permits. Figure 52.1 illustrates the form known as a *manifest* that must accompany all shipments of hazardous waste from the point of generation until its final treatment or disposal.

In addition, operators of land waste disposal facilities must meet financial responsibility requirements and monitor groundwater quality. EPA determines whether certain wastes should be banned entirely from land disposal; a significant number of wastes must be treated before they can be disposed of in land disposal units.

Underground Storage Tanks

In 1984, Congress directed that EPA also regulate underground product storage tanks such as gasoline tanks to prevent and respond to leaks that might contaminate underground water. The regulations that EPA issued to implement these requirements impose significant costs on many businesses such as gasoline stations that utilize such storage tanks. Owners of such tanks have had to upgrade them or replace them with tanks that are corrosion resistant and can be monitored for leaks. New tanks must meet stringent standards, and any leaks must promptly be addressed.

State Responsibilities

EPA sets minimum requirements for state RCRA programs and then delegates the responsibility for conducting programs to the states when they have the legal ability and interest to administer them. Until a state assumes partial or complete responsibility for an RCRA program, the federal government administers the program.

Enforcement

Failure to comply with the hazardous waste regulations promulgated under RCRA can subject violators to civil and criminal penalties. In the *United States v. Southern Union Co.* case, which follows, a company that stored hazardous waste without an RCRA permit was held criminally liable.

United States v. Southern Union Co.   643 F. Supp. 2d 201 (D.R.I. 2009)

Southern Union Company is a Delaware corporation, based in Texas and primarily engaged in the business of transporting and distributing natural gas. In 2000, Southern Union acquired several separate gas companies in Rhode Island and Massachusetts, consolidated those companies, and formed the New England Gas Company (NEGC). Through NEGC, Southern Union supplied natural gas to Rhode Island and parts of southeastern Massachusetts. In connection with this business, it owned a vacated, dilapidated, and frequently vandalized facility at the end of Tidewater Street in Pawtucket, Rhode Island. Located along the Seekonk River, the Tidewater facility consisted of several buildings and two unused natural gas storage tanks.

After forming NEGC in June 2001, Southern Union started a mercury reclamation program at Tidewater known as the Mercury-Sealed Regulator Removal Program. Prior to the 1960s, many of the homes in the NEGC service area used gas meters that operated with mercury-sealed regulators, or MSRs. Recognizing that mercury is a dangerous substance, Southern Union began a program by which workers went to customers' homes and replaced MSRs with nonmercury regulators. The work crews would then transport the MSRs and any recovered liquid mercury to the Tidewater facility. There, it employed an environmental services company, International Environmental Trading Company Inc. (IETC), to pour off the liquid mercury from inside the regulators into special containers, which were shipped to a reclamation facility in Pennsylvania. The MSR housings were decontaminated through a rinsing process, and IETC also ensured that all mercury contaminated rags, protective clothing, and cleaning agents were properly disposed.

In November 2001, Southern Union stopped removing MSRs from customers' homes but kept IETC at the Tidewater site to finish processing the remaining MSRs through the end of the year. In the spring of 2002, Southern Union again began removing MSRs from customers' homes; however, it did not re-contract with IETC to ensure the proper reclamation of the liquid mercury. Instead, it stored the MSRs removed from customers' homes in one of the vacant buildings at the Tidewater facility. To prevent the spillage of liquid mercury into the environment, Southern Union double-bagged each MSR in heavy-duty plastic bags and then piled those bags in plastic "kiddie" swimming pools. Liquid mercury that was spilt during the removal process was kept in assorted containers (e.g., paint cans, plastic jugs, glass bottles) and stored inside the building in a plywood cabinet secured by a hasp and padlock.

Southern Union accumulated MSRs and liquid mercury at the Tidewater facility over the course of 2002, 2003, and 2004. Despite drafting several requests for proposals to solicit bids from contractors to dispose of the liquid mercury, it did not restart the reclamation component to the MSR Removal Program.

Throughout this time period, the Tidewater facility (including the mercury storage building) was in a state of utter disrepair, and Southern Union was aware of the shoddy security conditions. Although it periodically stationed a security guard at the facility, graffiti covered the building, the doors and windows were broken, the perimeter security fencing contained numerous gaps, and the site was subject to repeated break-ins and had become the periodic home to several homeless people.

In September 2004, three youths broke into the mercury storage building. Once inside, they removed several containers of waste liquid mercury and proceeded to spill the mercury throughout the building and the outside grounds. The vandals also brought some of the liquid mercury to a nearby residential apartment complex where they littered it in and around the parking lots and outdoor common areas.

The spilled liquid mercury lay undiscovered on the Tidewater property for approximately three weeks. On October 19, 2004, an employee discovered the spill and a cleanup was conducted. The ensuing investigation then led to the discovery of the second spill at the apartment complex.

The United States charged Southern Union in a three-count criminal indictment with, among other things, violating the Resource Conservation and Recovery Act (RCRA) by storing a hazardous waste (i.e., liquid mercury) without a permit at the Tidewater facility. A jury returned a verdict of guilty, and Southern Union moved for judgment of acquittal or, in the alternative, for a new trial.

Smith, District Judge

Congress enacted RCRA to address the nation's problems with hazardous waste disposal. The intent behind RCRA is to facilitate the safe management of hazardous waste from the time it is generated to its ultimate disposal, to protect human health and the environment from the dangers of hazardous waste, and to encourage the conservation and recovery of natural resources.

The Defendant attacks the weight of the evidence used to convict it of (storing liquid mercury without a permit). Its argument for a new trial on this point has two themes: first, that the Government failed to prove that the liquid mercury the Defendant stored was a *waste*; and second, that the weight of the evidence does not support finding it *knowingly* stored a waste.

A key question at trial was whether the liquid mercury was a waste (so said the Government) or a "commercial chemical product" (so said the Defendant). At the heart of this dispute is what, if anything, the Defendant intended to do with the mercury (nothing said the Government; recycle it said the Defendant). The Defendant claims the jury could not have found the mercury was a waste because the evidence "clearly" showed it could be poured and was at least 99% pure mercury. And, it argues, employee testimony, contemporaneous documents, and company actions all demonstrate an intent to recycle.

The evidence presented to the jury was such that reasonable minds could differ. As to whether the mercury was "pure," the Government showed some degree of contamination and established that some degree of re-processing would have been necessary to make this mercury truly a pure commercial grade.

The more important point is the Defendant's intent. Here, the jury sided with the Government as to what the evidence showed: that the company did not intend to recycle and stored the mercury at Tidewater in lieu of disposal. There was more than ample evidence to support the jury's conclusion; for example, the storage and security conditions at Tidewater, the employee testimony that items were stored at Tidewater "instead of" throwing them away, and numerous references in company documents to the mercury as "waste" and to Tidewater as a "disposal area."

The Defendant next argues that the record did not support a finding that it *knowingly* stored a waste. In essence, this is but a slightly different flavor of the weight of the evidence argument discussed above regarding the company's intent—that it "considered" the mercury a product (because it planned to recycle it) and thus could not have knowingly stored it as a waste. For the reasons already discussed, this argument is unpersuasive. All in all, what the mercury was and what the company intended to do with it were hot button issues at trial. Given the evidence presented on both sides of the issue, there was nothing clearly erroneous about the jury's decision.

Defendant's motion for judgment of acquittal and, in the alternative, its motion for new trial are denied.

Figure 52.1 Sample Uniform Hazardous Waste Manifest Form

Please print or type. (Form designed for use on elite (12-pitch) typewriter.)

Form Approved. OMB No. 2050-0039

UNIFORM HAZARDOUS WASTE MANIFEST	1. Generator ID Number	2. Page 1 of	3. Emergency Response Phone	4. Manifest Tracking Number

5. Generator's Name and Mailing Address

Generator's Site Address (if different than mailing address)

Generator's Phone:

6. Transporter 1 Company Name — U.S. EPA ID Number

7. Transporter 2 Company Name — U.S. EPA ID Number

8. Designated Facility Name and Site Address — U.S. EPA ID Number

Facility's Phone:

9a. HM	9b. U.S. DOT Description (including Proper Shipping Name, Hazard Class, ID Number, and Packing Group (if any))	10. Containers No.	Type	11. Total Quantity	12. Unit Wt./Vol.	13. Waste Codes
	1.					
	2.					
	3.					
	4.					

14. Special Handling Instructions and Additional Information

15. GENERATOR'S/OFFEROR'S CERTIFICATION: I hereby declare that the contents of this consignment are fully and accurately described above by the proper shipping name, and are classified, packaged, marked and labeled/placarded, and are in all respects in proper condition for transport according to applicable international and national governmental regulations. If export shipment and I am the Primary Exporter, I certify that the contents of this consignment conform to the terms of the attached EPA Acknowledgment of Consent.

I certify that the waste minimization statement identified in 40 CFR 262.27(a) (if I am a large quantity generator) or (b) (if I am a small quantity generator) is true.

Generator's/Offeror's Printed/Typed Name — Signature — Month Day Year

16. International Shipments ☐ Import to U.S. ☐ Export from U.S. Port of entry/exit: _____

Transporter signature (for exports only): _____ Date leaving U.S.: _____

17. Transporter Acknowledgment of Receipt of Materials

Transporter 1 Printed/Typed Name — Signature — Month Day Year

Transporter 2 Printed/Typed Name — Signature — Month Day Year

18. Discrepancy

18a. Discrepancy Indication Space ☐ Quantity ☐ Type ☐ Residue ☐ Partial Rejection ☐ Full Rejection

Manifest Reference Number:

18b. Alternate Facility (or Generator) — U.S. EPA ID Number

Facility's Phone:

18c. Signature of Alternate Facility (or Generator) — Month Day Year

19. Hazardous Waste Report Management Method Codes (i.e., codes for hazardous waste treatment, disposal, and recycling systems)

1.	2.	3.	4.

20. Designated Facility Owner or Operator: Certification of receipt of hazardous materials covered by the manifest except as noted in Item 18a

Printed/Typed Name — Signature — Month Day Year

EPA Form 8700-22 (Rev. 3-05) Previous editions are obsolete.

DESIGNATED FACILITY TO DESTINATION STATE (IF REQUIRED)

GENERATOR — TRANSPORTER INT'L — DESIGNATED FACILITY

The Global Business Environment

Extended Producer Responsibility

Extended producer responsibility (EPR) for consumer packaging is a part of doing business in many countries, particularly developed countries other than the United States. EPR shifts the financial burden of recycling products back to the seller or manufacturer of the products. Commonly, the consumer ends up paying a fee on packaging materials that is used to support recycling programs. The concept has been adopted close to the United States as Quebec and Ontario Provinces in Canada began EPR programs in 2004. And, while there has been no broadscale adoption of such programs in the United States, in 2003, the state of California did enact EPR legislation addressing electronic products. The Electronic Waste Recycling Act of 2003 requires retailers and manufacturers to include a fee on each covered product to finance recycling and requires that manufacturers reduce the amount of toxic materials used in electronic devices.

Solid Waste

Mining, commercial, and household activities generate a large volume of waste material that can present problems if not properly disposed of. As population density has increased, causing a corresponding increase in the total volume of waste, it has become more difficult to find land or incinerators where the waste material can be disposed of properly. RCRA authorizes EPA to set minimum standards for such disposal, but states and local governments bear the primary responsibility for the siting and regulation of such activity.

As the cost and difficulty of disposing of waste increase, public attention focuses on reducing the waste to be disposed of, on looking for opportunities to recycle some of the waste material, and on changing the characteristics of the material that must ultimately be disposed of so that it poses fewer environmental problems. One of the significant challenges faced by tomorrow's businessperson will be in designing products, packaging, and production processes so as to minimize the waste products that result. A significant problem for both government and industry is the difficulty in trying to site new waste facilities. The NIMBY, or not-in-my-backyard, syndrome is pervasive as people almost universally desire to have the wastes from their everyday lives and from the economic activity in their community disposed of in someone else's neighborhood—any place but their own. As governments try to cope with the reality of finding places to dispose of wastes in an environmentally safe manner and, at the same time, cope with public opposition to siting new facilities, the temptation is strong to try to bar wastes from other areas from being disposed of in local facilities.

In the 1978 landmark case *City of Philadelphia v. New Jersey*,[2] the U.S. Supreme Court struck down an attempt by the state of New Jersey to prohibit the importation of most solid waste originating outside the state. An ironic twist is that decades later, we found a number of other eastern and midwestern states trying to find ways to block the importation of wastes from New Jersey into their states. Subsequently, the Supreme Court has had occasion to reiterate its holding in *City of Philadelphia v. New Jersey* in a series of new cases involving efforts by states to block or limit the flow of solid and hazardous waste from outside their state to disposal sites within the state.

Superfund

 LO52-7 Discuss the purpose of the Comprehensive Environmental Response, Compensation, and Liability Act ("Superfund").

In 1980, Congress passed the Comprehensive Environmental Response, Compensation, and Liability Act (CERCLA), commonly known as Superfund, to deal with the problem of uncontrolled or abandoned hazardous waste sites. In 1986, it strengthened and expanded the law. Under the Superfund law, EPA identified and assessed the sites in the United States where hazardous wastes had been spilled, stored, or abandoned.

Currently, EPA has identified more than 36,000 such sites. The sites are ranked on the basis of the type, quantity, and toxicity of the wastes; the number of people potentially exposed to the wastes; the different ways (e.g., in the air or drinking water) in which they might be exposed; the risks to contamination of aquifers; and other factors. The sites with the highest ranking are put on the National Priority List to receive priority federal and/or state attention for cleanup. At these sites, EPA makes careful scientific and engineering studies to determine the most appropriate cleanup plans. Once a site has been cleaned up, the state is responsible for managing it to prevent future environmental problems. EPA also has the authority to quickly initiate actions at hazardous waste sites—whether or not the site is on the priority list—to address imminent hazards such as the risk of fire, explosion, or contamination of drinking water.

[2] 437 U.S. 617 (1978).

The cleanup activity was initially financed by a federal tax on chemicals and feedstocks, but Congress subsequently suspended the tax. Today, federal general revenues, along with costs the government recovers from those responsible for contamination, are the primary funding sources. However, EPA is authorized to require that a site be cleaned up by those persons responsible for contaminating it, either as the owner or operator of the site, a transporter of wastes to the site, or the owner of wastes deposited at the site. Where EPA expends money to clean up a site, it has the legal authority to recover its costs from those who were responsible for the problem. The courts have held that such persons are "jointly and severally responsible for the cost of cleanup." Chapter 7, Negligence and Strict Liability, discusses the concept of joint liability. Of concern to many businesspeople is the fact that this stringent and potentially very expensive liability can, in some instances, be imposed on a current owner of a site who had nothing to do with the contamination, such as a subsequent purchaser of the land.

In the case that follows, *United States v. Domenic Lombardi Realty*, a subsequent purchaser was held liable for cleaning up a property that had been contaminated, in part, by the actions of its predecessor in title.

United States v. Domenic Lombardi Realty
290 F. Supp. 2d 198 (D.R.I. 2003)

During the early 1980s, Armand Allen acquired 31 acres of property located off of Robin Hollow Road in West Greenwich, Rhode Island. Allen began construction of a home on the property but never completed the structure. Allen, along with his wife, lived in a 60-foot trailer on the site. Although he never obtained the licenses required to operate a junkyard, Allen stored a number of junk cars and trucks in various states of disrepair on the property. The Town of West Greenwich denied Allen's multiple applications for a junkyard license but never ordered him to clean up his property.

In the fall of 1986 Domenic Lombardi, an employee of Lombardi Realty, approached Allen regarding a "For Sale" sign that was posted at the site. Allen indicated that his price for the property was $135,000 but that he was willing to drop the price to $85,000 in order to make a quick sale. Lombardi later testified that while he was on the property, he noticed stripped down cars and trucks as well as other solid waste. Lombardi instructed his real estate agent, Ray Walsh, to make an offer on the property of $85,000, which Allen immediately accepted on December 11, 1986.

Lombardi testified that Allen informed him that at one time, he stripped electrical transformers on the site to recover copper from them. He also had a witness who claimed he had taken a load of transformers to the site sometime between 1982 and 1986; this witness was a convicted felon with a history of lying in court. Moreover, this testimony was contradicted by Allen's wife that she never saw any transformers brought on site.

Walsh testified that in preparation for the purchase, he obtained a plat map from the city in order to estimate the future assessment of taxes that Lombardi would incur, but he did not perform any additional background investigation, such as an environmental assessment or a walk around the property, nor did he contact authorities concerning the prior use of the property.

After the purchase, Lombardi completed work on the partially constructed, single-family home. He also began renting out the trailer. The tenant testified that within a few months after she began renting the trailer, she saw transformers among the solid waste debris on the property. Other neighbors testified that they witnessed Lombardi Realty trucks dumping trash, including electrical transformers, on the site.

In November 1987, the Rhode Island Department of Environmental Management (RIDEM), believing that Lombardi Realty was permitting the property to be used for the disposal of solid waste without a permit, issued Lombardi Realty a notice of violation and ordered it to remove all solid waste that had been disposed of at the site. Subsequently, RIDEM discovered the presence of oil containing PCBs at the site. RIDEM ordered Lombardi to—among other things—submit and implement a sampling plan, to contract for the removal of all hazardous wastes from the site, and to submit and implement a cleanup plan. Lombardi Realty did not comply with any of the orders until 1989, when it arranged for the excavation of some of the PCB-contaminated soil, which it put in uncovered piles on the site.

In 1991, John Lombardi became president of Lombardi Realty when Dominic was sent to prison for the arson of the trailer on the site. John Lombardi knew little about the seriousness of the contamination on the site prior to becoming president, never having been informed about it by his father. The information withheld included the fact that children were using the piles as ramps for their dirt bikes.

In November 1994, EPA became involved at the request of RIDEM. From February through July of 1995, EPA removed the contaminated soil from the site and replaced it with clean backfill. In total, EPA excavated about 900 tons of soil. EPA then initiated an action against Lombardi Realty to recover the $481,068 "response costs" incurred in removing the hazardous substances from the site. Lombardi Realty asserted that it was an "innocent landowner" and that it should not be liable for the response costs.

Smith, Judge

The Comprehensive Environmental Response, Compensation, and Liability Act (CERCLA) provides the EPA a mechanism to compel parties associated with contaminated property to clean-up, or pay for the clean-up, of the contaminated property. In order for the EPA to successfully pursue its CERCLA claim against Lombardi Realty, it must prove (1) a release or threatened release of hazardous waste has occurred; (2) at a facility; (3) causing the EPA to incur response costs; and (4) that the defendant is a responsible party as defined by 42 U.S.C. § 9607(a). Here, it is either uncontested, or has been established at the summary judgment stage, that the EPA has met its burden with respect to these requirements. Accordingly, unless Lombardi Realty can take advantage of one of CERCLA's affirmative defenses, it will be held liable for the clean-up costs incurred by the EPA.

The affirmative defense asserted in this case is the innocent landowner defense. In 1986, Congress amended CERCLA by enacting the Superfund Amendments and Reauthorization Act ("SARA"). In these amendments, Congress provided an affirmative defense for landowners who, innocently and in good faith, purchase property without knowledge that a predecessor in the chain of title had allowed hazardous substances to be disposed on the property. The innocent landowner defense provides a statutory defense to liability where the release of hazardous substances was due to "an act or omission of a third party other than an employee or agent of the defendant, or than one whose act or omission occurs in connection with a contractual relationship, existing directly or indirectly, with the defendant. . . ."

In order to assert this defense, the statute provided that a party must demonstrate, by a preponderance of the evidence, that (1) the contamination occurred prior to the defendant's purchase of the land; (2) the defendant had "no reason to know" that the property was contaminated; (3) the defendant took "all appropriate inquiry into the previous ownership and uses of the property consistent with good commercial or customary practice" in an effort to minimize liability; and (4) once the contamination was discovered, the defendant exercised due care with respect to the hazardous substances concerned.

Subsequent to the initiation of this lawsuit, Congress enacted the Small Business Relief and Brownfields Revitalization Act ("Brownfields Amendments"), which altered elements of CERCLA's innocent landowner defense. In part, this Act was intended to encourage the purchase and development of "brownfields" by attempting to eliminate the fear of CERCLA liability often associated with the purchase of such land. The Act altered CERCLA's innocent landowner defense in three significant ways. First, the Act changed the "all appropriate inquiries" standard from one that must be "consistent with good commercial or customary practice" to one that must be "in accordance with generally accepted good commercial and customary standards and practices." Second, it

established criteria for determining whether a defendant has made "all appropriate inquiries" regarding the past ownership and usage of a property. Third, a party must now demonstrate to the court that it took reasonable steps to stop any continuing release, prevent any future release, and prevent or limit exposure to any previously released hazardous substance.

In order to take advantage of the innocent landowner defense, Lombardi Realty must first meet the threshold burden of proving that the contamination at the Site was caused "*solely* by an act or omission of a third party." Accordingly, Lombardi Realty cannot avail itself of the protection of the innocent landowner defense if it contributed to the release of PCBs at the Site.

While Lombardi Realty attempted to establish that Allen had disposed of transformers on the property, that testimony was rife with credibility problems. While there is evidence to indicate that Allen operated a junk or scrap yard, there is none to establish that he contaminated the Site with PCBs. The Government, on the other hand, offered testimony from numerous credible witnesses regarding the presence of transformers on the Site during Lombardi Realty's ownership. First, Haroldean Allen testified that she never saw her husband dispose of transformers at the Robin Hollow Road property. Second, another witness testified that she witnessed Lombardi with transformers on the property on several different occasions. Third, another witness also testified that she saw broken transformers "with some kind of oil stuff" and "oil around" them. Accordingly, Lombardi Realty has not proven that the PCB contamination was caused solely by Allen or any other third party. Therefore, this Court holds that Lombardi Realty cannot avail itself of the protections of the innocent landowner defense.

Even if Lombardi Realty could establish that the release was caused solely by the act or omission of a third party, it would still be unable to prove the other elements of the innocent landowner defense. Lombardi Realty failed to offer sufficient evidence that it "had no reason to know" of the presence of PCBs on the Site. While Lombardi Realty presented no evidence as to what constituted "good commercial or customary practices" for purchasing property in Rhode Island in 1986, the Government proffered expert testimony indicating that an environmental assessment of the property would have been required. Lombardi Realty never performed an environmental assessment of the Site, nor does this Court find that Lombardi Realty made any other meaningful inquiry into the Site's environmental state. Accordingly, Lombardi Realty cannot prove that it carried out all appropriate inquiry into the prior use of the property as required.

Lombardi Realty also failed to meet its burden of establishing that it took "due care" with respect to the PCB contaminated soil. As early as 1989, RIDEM issued an NOV ordering Lombardi Realty to, *inter alia*, inform all visitors to the property of the soil contamination and its hazards. At trial, the Government submitted unrebutted testimony which established that Lombardi Realty never informed visitors or tenants living on the property of the contamination. Furthermore, the Government established that Lombardi Realty never properly stored the contaminated soil following its removal. On numerous occasions, witnesses observed the piles of soil in an uncovered state. Lombardi Realty also failed to obtain a "roll-off" container to store the contaminated soil despite the EPA's orders. Lombardi Realty is therefore unable to prove that it acted with due care in regard to the contaminated soil.

Judgment in favor of United States granting it the costs it incurred cleaning up the site.

Community Right to Know and Emergency Cleanup
As part of its 1986 amendments to Superfund, Congress enacted a series of requirements for emergency planning, notification of spills and accidents involving hazardous materials, disclosure by industry to the community of the presence of certain listed chemicals, and notification of the amounts of various chemicals being routinely released into the environment in the area of a facility. This legislation was in response to the industrial accident at Bhopal, India, in 1984 that killed 2,500 people and injured thousands more—and to several similar incidents in the United States. Firms subject to the requirements have to carefully plan how they will communicate with the surrounding community what chemicals are being regularly released and what precautions the facility has taken to protect the community from regular or accidental releases. Mindful of the difficulty of explaining to a community why large emissions of hazardous substances are taking place, a significant number of companies have undertaken to reduce those emissions below levels they are currently required to meet by law.

Regulation of Chemicals

 LO52-8 Identify the two statutory authorities the EPA has to protect the public against unreasonable risks posed by new and existing chemicals.

Background   More than 80,000 chemical substances are manufactured in the United States and used in a variety of products. Although these chemicals contribute much to the standard of living we enjoy, some of them are toxic or have the potential to cause cancer, birth defects, reproductive failures, and other health-related problems. These risks may be posed in the manufacturing process, during the use of a product, or as a result of the manner of disposal of the chemical or product. EPA has two statutory authorities that give it the ability to prevent or restrict the manufacture and use of new and existing chemicals to remove unreasonable risks to human health or the environment. These authorities are the Federal Insecticide, Fungicide, and Rodenticide Act and the Toxic Substances Control Act.

Regulation of Agricultural Chemicals
The vast increase in the American farmer's productivity over the past few decades has been in large measure attributable to the farmer's use of chemicals to kill the insects, pests, and weeds that have historically competed with the farmer for crops. Some of these chemicals, such as pesticides and herbicides, were a mixed blessing. They enabled people to dramatically increase productivity and to conquer disease. On the other hand, dead fish and birds provided evidence that chemicals were not only building up in the food chain but also proving fatal to some species. Unless such chemicals are carefully used and disposed of, they can present a danger to the applier and to the consumer of the food and water. Gradually, people realized the need to focus on the effects of using such chemicals.

Ethics and Compliance in Action

Environmental Standards for International Operations

Suppose that a multinational chemical company with its primary manufacturing facilities in the United States plans to build a manufacturing facility in a developing country where there are few, if any, real state-imposed environmental regulations. Is it sufficient for the company to simply meet the environmental requirements of the host country? Is there any ethical obligation to do more—for example, to build the facility to meet the requirements it would have to meet in this country?

EPA enforces the Federal Insecticide, Fungicide, and Rodenticide Act (FIFRA). This act gives EPA the authority to register pesticides before they can be sold, to provide for the certification of appliers of pesticides designated for restrictive use, to set limits on the pesticide residue permitted on crops that provide food for people or animals, and to register and inspect pesticide manufacturing establishments.

When the EPA administrator has reason to believe that continued use of a particular pesticide poses an "imminent hazard," he may suspend its registration and remove the product from the market. When the administrator believes that there is a less-than-imminent hazard but that the environmental risks of continuing to use a pesticide outweigh its benefits, the administrator may initiate a cancellation of registration proceeding. This proceeding affords all interested persons—manufacturers, distributors, users, environmentalists, and scientists—an opportunity to present evidence on the proposed cancellation. Cancellation of the registration occurs when the administrator finds that the product causes unreasonable adverse effects on the environment.

Companion regulations promulgated by EPA and enforced by the Food and Drug Administration control the amount of pesticide residue that can remain on raw and processed food intended for human or animal consumption. These regulations establish what are known as "tolerances."

Those involved in the food production and distribution process must keep a close watch on regulatory developments at EPA concerning the registration, cancellation, and suspension of products as well as actions it takes concerning permissible residues of pesticide on food products. During the 1980s, the agency took highly publicized actions concerning the use of ethylene dibromide (EDB), a fumigant, on citrus and grain products, sulfites on table grapes, alar on apples, and chlordane as a treatment against termite infestation. In each instance, the economic well-being of many businesses was at risk if they did not adequately anticipate and/or deal with the EPA's action and the publicity that resulted from these actions.

Toxic Substances Control Act

The other major statute regulating chemical use focuses on toxic substances—such as asbestos and PCBs—and on the new chemical compounds that are developed each year. The Toxic Substances Control Act (TSCA) was enacted in 1976 and extensively amended in 2016. The initial enactment required that new chemicals be tested by manufacturers or processors to determine their effect on human health or the environment. At the same time, some 62,000 existing chemicals were grandfathered. EPA did have the authority to regulate chemical substances or mixtures that present an unreasonable risk of injury to health or the environment and to take action against such substances or mixtures that pose an imminent hazard. The action could include bans, limitations, and additional testing.

Over the next 40 years, it became increasingly apparent that the act had not been successful in ensuring chemical safety and protecting human health because very few existing chemicals were assessed and new chemicals came into commerce without an affirmative finding they did not pose an unreasonable risk.

The 2016 amendments require EPA to establish a risk-based process to determine which chemicals it will prioritize for assessment, identifying them as high- or low-priority substances. High-priority designation triggers a requirement and deadline for EPA to complete a risk evaluation on that chemical to determine its safety. The act also establishes a minimum number of ongoing risk evaluations. Chemicals are evaluated against a risk-based safety standard that excludes consideration of costs or nonrisk factors and must consider risks to susceptible and highly exposed populations. When unreasonable risks are identified, EPA must take risk management action within a certain period, but it can consider costs and availability of alternatives in determining what is appropriate action. When reviewing new chemicals before they are allowed to be put on the market, EPA must make an affirmative finding on the safety of a new chemical or significant new use of an existing chemical.

Finally, recognizing that some states, like California, have been much more aggressive in addressing risks from chemicals, existing state requirements (as of 2003) are grandfathered, and states can establish requirements to control risks of any chemical or use that EPA has not, or is not currently, addressing.

International Developments Concerning Regulation of Toxic Substances

In 2007, the European Union put in place new restrictions on producers of chemicals that are linked to various health problems. The provisions, which were be phased in over an eleven-year period, were strongly opposed by the chemical industry in the United States and will require changes in the way that chemical products are developed, produced, and marketed abroad, particularly in Europe. Canada, too, has a new chemical regulatory program that will affect the way that U.S firms can do business there.

The European Union regulatory scheme is premised on what is known as the "precautionary principle," which requires companies to demonstrate that a chemical is safe

Major Environmental Laws

Act	Focus
Clean Air Act	Protects quality of ambient (outdoor) air through national ambient air quality standards, state implementation plans, control of hazardous air pollutants, new source performance standards, and controls on automobiles and fuels
Clean Water Act	Protects and enhances quality of surface waters by setting water quality standards and limiting discharges by industry and municipalities to those waters through permit system; also regulates dredging and filling of wetlands
Safe Drinking Water Act	Protects and enhances quality of our drinking water; also regulates disposal of wastes in wells
Resource Conservation and Recovery Act (RCRA)	Establishes a cradle-to-grave regulatory system for handling and disposal of hazardous wastes; also deals with solid waste
Comprehensive Environmental Response, Compensation, and Liability Act (Superfund)	Provides a program to deal with hazardous waste that was inadequately disposed of in the past
Federal Insecticide, Fungicide, and Rodenticide Act (FIFRA)	Regulates the sale and use of chemicals to be used as pesticides and herbicides; companion legislation regulates residues permitted on crops intended for use as food
Toxic Substances Control Act (TSCA)	Requires preclearance of new chemicals and provides for regulation of existing chemicals that pose an unreasonable risk to health or the environment

before it is produced and distributed. While the United States requires some premanufacture screening of new chemicals and new chemical uses, it essentially requires regulators to show that products or their uses present an *unreasonable risk* to human health or the environment before they can be regulated or taken off the market.

The EU's REACH program mandates the creation of a list of "substances of very high concern" (those suspected of causing cancer or other significant health effects) and requires that manufacturers wishing to produce or sell chemicals on the list receive authorization to do so. The EU program will require U.S. producers to provide data on thousands of chemicals and chemical constituents in products. The manufacturers will need to study and report on the risks posed by various chemicals, and the data will be made publicly available to consumers and regulators as

CYBERLAW IN ACTION

The Toxic Release Inventory Is Available Online

In 1986, the Emergency Planning and Community Right-to-Know Act (EPCRA) was enacted. A primary purpose of this legislation was to ensure that communities and citizens were aware of chemical hazards in their area. Under section 313 of the EPCRA, the EPA and the states must annually collect data on releases and transfers of certain toxic chemicals from specific facilities. In turn, the data must be made available to the general public in a Toxic Release Inventory (TRI).

Now, much of the EPCRA information and data, including data in the TRI program, are easily accessible online through the EPA website. In addition, many individual state environmental agency websites provide information on TRI for facilities within their particular state. A company's detailed toxic release data can be useful information for the company's competitors. A company could use the TRI information to determine how much of a particular chemical is being produced by its competitors or to gain insight into what production process is being used by the competition. For more information about the TRI program, visit **www.epa.gov/tri/**.

well as to those engaged in product-related litigation. The EU regulatory scheme will also require companies to reformulate or redesign various products if they want to be able to sell them in the European market.

Biotechnology
The development of techniques to genetically manipulate organisms—often referred to generally as **biotechnology**—offers considerable promise to aid our ability to provide food and health care and to generate a range of new products and production processes. At the same time, the new techniques raise concerns about their potential to adversely affect human health or the environment. Responsibility for regulating research and use of biotechnology is shared in the federal government among the Food and Drug Administration, the Department of Agriculture, the Environmental Protection Agency, and the National Institutes of Health. Generally, a review is required of such activity before it takes place. This process is of considerable import to companies that develop genetically engineered organisms for commercial purposes; it can affect both the speed at which they are able to get the products to market and the public's confidence that release of the organisms does not pose an unreasonable risk.

Because consumers in other countries—and their governments—may not share the U.S. view of the safety of such bioengineered foods and products, other countries may impose barriers to entry, triggering trade disputes as to the legitimacy of the health/environmental concerns and/or of the trade restrictions.

Problems and Problem Cases

1. The U.S. Forest Service is responsible for managing the Cabinet Mountain Wilderness Area in northwestern Montana. The wilderness area consists of approximately 94,272 acres and is part of the Cabinet-Yank ecosystem, one of only six ecosystems in the continental United States that supports populations of grizzly bears. The bears are listed as an endangered species under the Endangered Species Act. ASARCO, which holds 149 unpatented mining claims (covering 2,980 acres) located in the wilderness area, has applied to the Forest Service for permission to conduct exploratory drilling to assess the extent of copper and silver deposits in the area. ASARCO proposes to drill 36 drill holes on 22 sites in a portion of the wilderness area with a similar level of activity in each of the next three years. Each drill site is limited to an area of 20 feet by 20 feet. Over the four-year period, these sites will occupy a combined area of about 0.5 acre.

   During the time drilling is being conducted, the drilling equipment, personnel, and supplies would be brought in by helicopter, and the company has proposed that the workers would camp overnight at the site while the drilling was being conducted. It is estimated that only about a dozen grizzly bears may inhabit the portion of the wilderness area where the drilling will take place. If the exploratory drilling reveals significant deposits of copper or silver at any particular site, the company might seek a permit to conduct developmental exploration or mineral extraction at the site. This would have some potential to impact the feeding and denning activities of the bears—and, in turn, their reproductive success—depending on where the activity is conducted, when it is conducted, and how substantial the activity is.

   Should issuance of the requested exploratory drilling permit to ASARCO be considered "a major federal action significantly affecting the environment," thus requiring the Forest Service to prepare an environmental impact statement (EIS) pursuant to the National Environmental Policy Act (NEPA)?

2. In July, Vanguard Corporation began operating a metal furniture manufacturing plant in Brooklyn, New York. The plant is located in an area that has not attained the national ambient air quality standards for ozone. The plant is a major stationary source (i.e., has the potential to emit more than 100 tons a year) of volatile organic compounds that contribute to the production of ozone in the atmosphere. The New York state implementation plan (SIP) requires that metal-coating facilities use paint that contains less than three pounds of organic solvent (minus water) per gallon at the time of coating. EPA notified Vanguard that it was not in compliance with the SIP provision concerning coatings and issued it a notice of violation. Vanguard sought to defend against the notice of violation on the grounds that it had used its best faith efforts to comply but that full compliance was technologically and economically infeasible. It indicated that it wanted 18 more months to come into compliance. Should Vanguard be held to be in violation of the Clean Air Act?

3. In August, Tzavah Urban Renewal Corporation purchased from the city of Newark a building formerly known as the Old Military Park Hotel. While the buyer was given an opportunity to inspect the building, it was not informed by the city that the building was

permeated with asbestos-containing material. At the time of the purchase, the building was in great disrepair and had been uninhabited for many years. Its proposed renovation was to be a major urban renewal project. In the following June, Tzavah contracted with Greer Industrial Corporation to "gut" the building. While the work was going on, an EPA inspector visited the site and concluded that the hotel was contaminated with asbestos. He observed Greer employees throwing asbestos-laced objects out of the windows of the building and noted an uncovered refuse pile next to the hotel that contained asbestos. The workers were not wetting the debris before heaving it out the windows and the refuse pile was also dry. As a result, asbestos dust was being released into the air. Although the hotel was located in a commercial district, there were private homes nearby. Renovation of buildings contaminated with asbestos is regulated under the Clean Air Act. The EPA regulations require building owners or operators to notify EPA before commencing renovation or demolition and prescribe various procedures for storage and removal of the asbestos. Tzavah failed to provide the required notice or to comply with procedures required. After being notified by EPA of the violation of the law, Tzavah stopped the demolition work, left the building unsecured, and left the waste piles dry and uncovered. EPA tried informally to get Tzavah to complete the work in accordance with the asbestos regulations; when Tzavah did not take action, EPA brought a lawsuit against Tzavah to do so. Should the court issue an injunction requiring Tzavah to abate the hazard posed by the dry asbestos remaining in the hotel?

4. Villegas was co-owner and vice president of Plaza Health Laboratories, a blood testing laboratory in Brooklyn, New York. On two occasions between April and September, Villegas loaded containers of numerous vials of human blood generated from his business into his personal car and drove to his residence in a condominium complex in Edgewater, New Jersey. There he removed the containers from his car and carried them to the edge of the Hudson River, where he placed them in a bulkhead that separates his condominium complex from the river. The vials were placed during low tide in a crevice in the bulkhead that was below the high-water line.

In May, a group of eighth-graders on a field trip on Staten Island discovered numerous glass vials containing human blood along the shore and in the water. Ultimately, 70 vials were recovered; some of them were cracked and others remained intact. The vials, some of which contained blood infected with hepatitis-B virus, were traced back to Plaza Health Laboratories. In September, a maintenance worker at the condominium complex discovered other vials wedged in the bulkhead; they were also traced back to Plaza Health Laboratories.

The United States brought a criminal action against Villegas, charging him with "knowingly discharging pollutants from a point source into a water of the United States." The Clean Water Act defines "point source" to be a "discernable, confined and discrete conveyance, including but not limited to any pipe, ditch, tunnel, conduit, well, discrete fissure . . ." but does not enumerate human beings among the enumerated items. After Villegas was convicted by a jury, he appealed, contending that the government had not established one necessary element of the crime with which he was charged—namely, that the discharge had come from a "point source" as that term is used in the statute. Should his conviction be reversed on the grounds there was no discharge from a point source?

5. Mall Properties was an organization that, for many years, sought to develop a shopping mall in the Town of North Haven, Connecticut, a suburb of New Haven. Because the proposed development would require the filling of some wetlands, Mall Properties was required to obtain a permit from the Corps of Engineers pursuant to section 404 of the Clean Water Act. The City of New Haven opposed development of the mall—and the granting of the permit—on the grounds it would jeopardize the fragile economy of New Haven. The Corps of Engineers found the net loss of wetlands would be substantially compensated for by a proposed onsite wetland creation. Relying primarily on the socioeconomic concerns of the City of New Haven, the district engineer rejected the proposed permit. Mall Properties then brought suit against the Corps of Engineers, claiming that the decision was arbitrary and capricious. Should the district engineer have relied on socioeconomic factors unrelated to the project's environmental impacts in making a decision on the permit?

6. The General Metal Fabricators (GMF) facility in Erwin, Tennessee, was engaged in metal stamping, plating, and painting. The facility utilized hazardous chemicals and generated hazardous waste. No RCRA permit had been sought for the GMF facility. The hazardous waste disposal practices at GMF were discovered by chance by state waste-management authorities whose attention was caught, while driving to an appointment at another facility, by two 55-gallon drums abandoned among weeds on GMF's property.

Gale Dean, the production manager, had day-to-day supervision of GMF's production process and employees. Among his duties was the instruction of employees on hazardous waste handling and disposal. Numerous practices at GMF violated RCRA. GMF's plating operations utilized rinse baths, contaminated with hazardous chemicals, which were drained through a pipe into an earthen lagoon outside the facility. In addition, Dean instructed employees to shovel various kinds of solid wastes from the tanks into 55-gallon drums. Dean ordered the construction of a pit, concealed behind the facility, into which 38 drums of such hazardous waste were tossed. The contents spilled onto the soil from open or corroded drums. Chemical analyses of soil and solid wastes revealed that the lagoon and the pit were contaminated with chromium. In addition, the pit was contaminated with toluene and xylene solvents. All of these substances are hazardous. Drums of spent chromic acid solution were also illegally stored on the premises.

Dean was familiar with the chemicals used in each of the tanks on the production lines and described to authorities the manner in which the contents of the rinse tanks were deposited in the lagoon. Material Safety Data Sheets (MSDS) provided to GMF by the chemical manufacturer clearly stated that various chemicals in use at GMF were hazardous and were subject to state and federal pollution control laws. The MSDS were given to investigators by Dean, who demonstrated his knowledge of their contents. The MSDS delivered with the chromic acid made specific reference to RCRA and to related EPA regulations. Dean informed investigators that he "had read this RCRA waste code but thought it was a bunch of bull****."

RCRA makes it a crime for "Any person to . . . knowingly treat, store, or dispose of any hazardous waste . . . without a permit. . . ." Dean and the plant managers and owners of the company were indicted for conspiracy to violate RCRA and, individually, for violations of various sections of the statute. Dean was convicted of, among other things, knowingly storing, and disposing of, hazardous wastes without a permit. He appealed the conviction, contending that (1) RCRA requires that the owner of a facility have a permit and that because he was not the owner, he should not have been convicted of storing and disposing without a permit and (2) the materials were not hazardous because of the way he had stored or disposed of them. Has Dean stated sound reasons his conviction should be reversed?

7. The Royal McBee Corporation manufactured typewriters at a factory in Springfield, Missouri. As a part of the manufacturing process, Royal McBee generated cyanide-based electroplating wastes, sludge from the bottom of electroplating tanks, and spent plating bath solution. As part of their duties, Royal McBee employees dumped the wastes onto the surface of the soil on a vacant lot adjoining the factory. This took place between 1959 and 1962. Over time, the waste materials migrated outward and downward from the original dumping site, contaminating a large area. In 1970, the manufacturing facility and lot were sold to General Electric, which operated the plant but did not engage in the dumping of wastes on the vacant lot. In the mid-1980s, General Electric was required by EPA and the state of Missouri, under the authority of the federal Superfund law, to clean up the contamination at the site. General Electric then brought a lawsuit against the successor corporation of Royal McBee's typewriter business, Litton Business Systems, to recover for the costs incurred in cleaning up the site. Under the Superfund law, "any person who at the time of disposal of any hazardous substance owned or operated any facilities at which such hazardous substances were disposed of, shall be liable for any other necessary costs of response incurred by any other person" consistent with the Superfund law and regulations. Is General Electric entitled to recover its cleanup costs from Litton?

A

abstract of title   A summary of the conveyances, transfers, and other facts relied on as evidence of title, together with all such facts appearing of record that may impair its validity.

abuse of process   An intentional tort designed to protect against the initiation of legal proceedings for a primary purpose other than the one for which such proceedings were designed.

acceptance   The actual or implied receipt and retention of that which is tendered or offered.

accession   The acquisition of property by its incorporation or union with other property.

accommodation party   A person who signs a negotiable instrument for the purpose of adding his name and liability to another party to the instrument.

accord and satisfaction   A legally binding agreement to settle a disputed claim for a definite amount.

actual authority   An agent's ability to affect the principal's legal relations. Consent must be communicated to the agent.

actual damages   Reputional injury and other harm such as emotional distress.

actual notification   For third parties who have previously dealt with the agent or who have begun to deal with the agent. This can be accomplished by (1) a direct personal statement to the third party or (2) a writing delivered to the third party personally, to his place of business, or to some other place reasonably believed to be appropriate.

adjudicate   To adjudge; to settle by judicial decree.

administrator   The personal representative appointed by a probate court to settle the estate of a deceased person who died intestate (without leaving a valid will).

adoption   In corporation law, a corporation's acceptance of a preincorporation contract by action of its board of directors, by which the corporation becomes liable on the contract.

advance directive   A written document such as a living will or durable power of attorney that directs others how future health care decisions should be made in the event that the individual becomes incapacitated.

adverse possession   Open and notorious possession of real property over a given length of time that denies ownership in any other claimant.

advised letter of credit   The seller's bank acts as the seller's agent to collect against the letter of credit issued by the buyer's bank.

affirmative defense   A fact or set of facts offered by a defendant in response to allegations in a complaint, which, if proven by the defendant, allows the defendant to escape or mitigate the legal consequences of the facts alleged in the complaint, even if they are true and otherwise unlawful.

after-acquired property   Property of the debtor that is obtained after a security interest in the debtor's property has been created.

agency   A legal relationship in which an agent acts under the direction of a principal for the principal's benefit. Also used to refer to government regulatory bodies of all kinds.

agent   One who acts under the direction of a principal for the principal's benefit in a legal relationship known as agency. See also *principal.*

alien corporation   A corporation incorporated in one country that is doing business in another country. See also *foreign corporation.*

alternative dispute resolution (ADR)   A general name applied to the many nonjudicial means of settling private disputes.

American legal realism   A school of jurisprudence and philosophy of law dating from the early twentieth century, which defines law with reference to the actual practice of legal authorities (judges, law enforcement officers, etc.) rather than what they say they are doing or the language of the legal enactments upon which they purportedly rely.

ancillary covenant not to compete   A promise that is ancillary to (part of) a valid contract whereby one party to a contract agrees not to compete with the other party for a specified time and within a specified location. Also called *noncompetition clause.*

answer   The pleading of a defendant in which he or she may deny any or all the facts set out in the plaintiff's declaration or complaint.

anticipatory breach   A contracting party's indication before the time for performance that he cannot or will not perform the contract.

apparent authority   An agent's ability to affect the principal's legal relations. Consent must be communicated to the third party.

articles of incorporation   A document that must be filed with a secretary of state to create a corporation. Usually, it includes the basic rights and responsibilities of the corporation and the shareholders.

artisan's lien   A common law possessory security interest arising out of the improvement of property by one skilled in some mechanical art or craft; the lien entitles the improver of the property to retain possession in order to secure the agreed-on price or the value of the work performed.

assault   An intentional tort that prohibits any attempt or offer to cause harmful or offensive contact with another if it results in a well-grounded apprehension of imminent battery in the mind of the threatened person.

assignee   A person to whom an assignment is made.

assignment   A transfer of property or some right or interest.

assignor   The maker of an assignment.

assumption of risk   A traditional defense to negligence liability based on the argument that the plaintiff voluntarily exposed himself to a known danger created by the defendant's negligence.

assurance To provide confidence or to inform positively.

attachment In general, the process of taking a person's property under an appropriate judicial order by an appropriate officer of the court. Used for a variety of purposes, including the acquisition of jurisdiction over the property seized and the securing of property that may be used to satisfy a debt.

attorney in fact An agent who is given express, written authorization by his principal to do a particular act or series of acts on behalf of the principal.

audit committee In corporation law, a committee of the board that recommends and supervises the public accountant who audits the corporation's financial records.

authority In agency law, an agent's ability to affect his principal's legal relations with third parties. Also used to refer to an actor's legal power or ability to do something. In addition, sometimes used to refer to a statute, case, or other legal source that justifies a particular result.

authorized shares Shares that a corporation is empowered to issue by its articles of incorporation.

Automated Clearing Hours System (ACH) A nationwide network through which depository institutions send each other batches of electronic credit and debit transfers (either on a one-time or recurring basis), such as credits for payroll direct deposits, social security benefits, or tax refunds and debits for mortgages or utility bills.

automatic novation clause A contractual clause wherein all parties agree to automatically substitute a new contract or contractual obligation for an old one.

automatic stay Under the Bankruptcy Act, the suspension of all litigation against the debtor and his property, which is triggered by the filing of a bankruptcy petition.

B

bailee The person to whom a bailment is made.

bailment The transfer of personal property by its owner to another person with the understanding that the property will be returned to the owner in the future.

bailor The owner of bailed property; the one who delivers personal property to another to be held in bailment.

bankruptcy The state of a person who is unable to pay his or her debts without respect to time; one whose liabilities exceed his or her assets.

battery An intentional tort that prohibits the harmful or offensive touching of another without his consent.

beneficiary The person for whose benefit an insurance policy, trust, will, or contract is established. In the case of a contract, the beneficiary is called a *third-party beneficiary*.

benefit corporation A type of corporation with modified obligations committing it to higher standards of purpose, accountability, and transparency than traditional corporations.

bequest In a will, a gift of personal property or money. Also called a *legacy*.

best available technology The Clean Air Act requires that new stationary sources such as factories and power plants install the best available technology for reducing air pollution. Two major policy objectives underlie this requirement: (1) to provide a level playing field for new industry irrespective of where it locates and (2) to gradually improve air quality by requiring state-of-the-art controls whenever a new facility is built.

bicameral legislature A legislative body made up of two branches or chambers, like the House of Representatives and the Senate in the U.S. Congress.

bilateral contract A contract in which the promise of one of the parties forms the consideration for the promise of the other.

bill of lading A written acknowledgment of the receipt of goods to be transported to a designated place and delivery to a named person or to his or her order.

biotechnology The development of techniques to genetically manipulate organisms.

bona fide purchaser An innocent buyer for valuable consideration who purchases goods without notice of any defects in the title of the goods acquired.

bond A long-term debt security that is secured by collateral.

business judgment rule A rule protecting business managers from liability for making bad decisions when they have acted prudently and in good faith.

buy-and-sell agreement A share transfer restriction compelling a shareholder to sell his shares to the other shareholders or the corporation and obligating the other shareholders or the corporation to buy the shareholder's shares.

buyer in ordinary course of business A person who, in good faith and without knowledge that the sale to him is in violation of a third party's ownership rights or security interest in the goods, buys in ordinary course from a person who is in the business of selling goods of that kind.

C

call A type of option permitting a person to buy a fixed number of securities at a fixed price at a specified time. See also *redemption*.

cancellation The act of crossing out a writing. The operation of destroying a written instrument.

capacity The ability to incur legal obligations and acquire legal rights.

capital surplus A balance sheet account; the portion of shareholders' contributions exceeding the par or stated value of shares. Also called *additional paid-in capital*.

case law reasoning A form of analogical legal reasoning whereby decisions from prior cases are used to resolve similar current disputes by extending or distinguishing the rulings in those prior cases. See also *precedent*.

cashier's check A draft (including a check) drawn by a bank on itself and accepted by the act of issuance.

caveat emptor "Let the buyer beware."

certificate of deposit An acknowledgment by a bank of the receipt of money with an engagement to pay it back.

certificate of limited partnership A document that must be filed with a secretary of state to create a limited partnership.

certificate of organization (or articles of organization, depending on the jurisdiction) A document filed with the secretary of state (in some states) to form a limited liability company (LLC).

charging order A court's order granting rights in a partner's transferable interest to a personal creditor of the partner; a creditor with a charging order is entitled to the partner's share of partnership distributions.

check A written order on a bank or banker payable on demand to the person named or his order or bearer and drawn by virtue of credits due the drawer from the bank created by money deposited with the bank.

checks and balances A fundamental principle of American government, guaranteed by the Constitution, whereby each branch of the government (executive, judicial, and legislative) has some measure of influence over the other branches and may choose to block procedures of the other branches.

civil law The body of law applicable to lawsuits involving two private parties.

class action An action brought on behalf of the plaintiff and others similarly situated.

classical theory Theory of liability for insider trading offense that applies when a person obtains material, nonpublic information from a company and then trades on it in violation of a fiduciary duty to that company's shareholders.

close corporation A corporation with few shareholders generally having a close personal relationship to each other and participating in the management of the business.

codicil Some addition to or qualification of one's last will and testament.

commercial impracticability The standards used by the UCC, replacing the common law doctrine of impossibility, to define when a party is relieved of his or her contract obligations because of the occurrence of unforeseeable, external events beyond his or her control.

commercial paper Negotiable paper such as promissory notes, drafts, and checks that provides for the payment of money and can readily be transferred to other parties.

commercial speech Speech communicated by or on behalf of a company or individual for the purpose of promoting a product, service, or business. It is economic in nature and usually has the intent of convincing the audience to partake in a particular action, such as purchasing a specific product.

commercial unit Under the UCC, any unit of goods that is treated by commercial usage as a single whole. It may, for example, be a single article or a set of articles such as a dozen, bale, gross, or carload.

common law The law that is made and applied by judges.

common shareholders Shareholders who claim the residual profits and assets of a corporation, and usually have the exclusive power and right to elect the directors of the corporation.

comparative fault Often used synonymously with *comparative negligence*. But also sometimes used to refer to a defense that operates like comparative negligence but considers the plaintiff's and the defendant's overall fault rather than either's negligence alone.

comparative negligence The contemporary replacement for the traditional doctrine of contributory negligence. The basic idea is that damages are apportioned between the parties to a negligence action in proportion to their relative fault. The details vary from state to state.

compensatory damages Damages that will compensate a party for direct losses due to an injury suffered.

complaint The pleading in a civil case in which the plaintiff states his claim and requests relief.

concealment In contract law, taking active steps to prevent another from learning the truth.

concurrent Running with; simultaneously with.

condition In contract law, a future, uncertain event that creates or extinguishes a duty of performance; a provision or clause in a contract that operates to suspend or rescind a party's duty to perform.

condition precedent A condition that operates to give rise to a contracting party's duty to perform.

condition subsequent A condition that operates to relieve or discharge one from his obligation under a contract.

confirmed letter of credit The seller's bank agrees to assume liability on the letter of credit issued by the buyer's bank.

confusion The inseparable intermixture of property belonging to different owners.

consent decree or consent order Used to refer to the order courts or administrative agencies issue when approving the settlement of a lawsuit or administrative action against some party.

consent restraint A security transfer restriction requiring a shareholder to obtain the consent of the corporation or its shareholders prior to the shareholder's sale of her shares.

consequential damages Damages that do not flow directly and immediately from an act but rather flow from the results of the act; damages that are indirect consequences of a breach of contract or certain other legal wrongs. Examples include personal injury, damage to property, and lost profits.

consideration In contract law, a basic requirement for an enforceable agreement under traditional contract principles, defined in this text as legal value, bargained for and given in exchange for an act or promise. In corporation law, cash or property contributed to a corporation in exchange for shares, or a promise to contribute such cash or property.

constructive eviction In landlord–tenant law, a breach of duty by the landlord that makes the premises uninhabitable or otherwise deprives the tenant of the benefit of the lease and gives rise to the tenant's right to vacate the property and terminate the lease.

constructive notification For third parties who have previously dealt with the agent or who have begun to deal with the agent.

This is accomplished by advertising the agency's termination in a newspaper of general circulation in the place where the agency business regularly was carried on.

continuation statement   A document, usually a multicopy form, filed in a public office to indicate the continuing viability of a financing statement. See also *financing statement.*

contract   A legally enforceable promise or set of promises.

contract of adhesion   A contract in which a stronger party is able to dictate terms to a weaker party, leaving the weaker party no practical choice but to adhere to the terms. If the stronger party has exploited its bargaining power to achieve unfair terms, the contract is against public policy.

contribution   In business organization law, the cash or property contributed to a business by its owners.

contributory negligence   A traditional defense to negligence liability based on the plaintiff's failure to exercise reasonable care for his own safety.

conversion   Any distinct act of dominion wrongfully exerted over another's personal property in denial of or inconsistent with his rights therein. That tort committed by a person who deals with chattels not belonging to him in a manner that is inconsistent with the ownership of the lawful owner.

conversion right   Right allowing a preferred shareholder to exchange that class of shares for another class, usually common shares.

convertible   Securities giving their holders the power to exchange those securities for other securities without paying any additional consideration.

corporate constituency statutes   A statute that expands the traditional view that directors and officers of a corporation have a duty to make business decisions primarily or exclusively to maximize shareholders' interests by explicitly permitting the consideration of non-shareholder interests. Those interests may vary but often include the environment, corporate employees, customers, creditors, suppliers, and local community.

corporation   A form of business organization that is owned by owners, called shareholders, who have no inherent right to manage the business, and is managed by a board of directors that is elected by the shareholders.

corporation by estoppel   A doctrine that prevents persons from denying that a corporation exists when the persons hold themselves out as representing a corporation or believe themselves to be dealing with a corporation.

counterclaim   A legal claim made in response to the plaintiff's initial claim in a civil suit. Unlike a defense, the counterclaim is the defendant's affirmative attempt to obtain legal relief; in effect, it states a cause of action entitling the defendant to such relief. Often, the counterclaim must arise out of the occurrence that forms the basis for the plaintiff's claim.

cover   To obtain substitute or equivalent goods.

cram down   When the court forces dissenting creditors whose claims would be impaired by a proposed plan to accept the plan when the court can find that it is fair and equitable to the class of creditors whose claims are impaired.

creditor   A person to whom a debt or legal obligation is owed and who has the right to enforce payment of that debt or obligation.

crime   An act prohibited by the state; a public wrong.

criminal law   The body of law setting out public wrongs that the government attempts to correct by prosecuting wrongdoers.

cumulative voting   A procedure for voting for a corporation's directors that permits a shareholder to multiply the number of shares he or she owns by the number of directors to be elected and to cast the resulting total of votes for one or more directors. See also *straight voting.*

curtesy   At common law, a husband's right in property owned by his wife during her life.

cy pres   As near as possible. In the law of trusts, a doctrine applied to prevent a charitable trust from failing when the application of trust property to the charitable beneficiary designated by the settlor becomes illegal or impossible to carry out; in such a case, cy pres allows the court to redirect the distribution of trust property for some purpose that is as near as possible to the settlor's general charitable intent.

D

de novo **review**   Anew; over again; a second time. A trial *de novo*, for example, is a new trial in which the entire case is retried.

debenture   A long-term, unsecured debt security.

deceit   A tort involving intentional misrepresentation or cheating by means of some device.

declaratory judgment   One that expresses the opinion of a court on a question of law without ordering anything to be done.

deed   A writing, sealed and delivered by the parties; an instrument conveying real property.

deed of trust   A three-party instrument used to create a security interest in real property in which the legal title to the real property is placed in one or more trustees to secure the repayment of a sum of money or the performance of other conditions.

defenses   Legal arguments made in the context of a claim brought by a plaintiff. See *contributory negligence; assumption of risk; comparative negligence; comparative fault.*

delegation   In constitutional law and administrative law, a process whereby a legislature effectively hands over some of its legislative power to an administrative agency that it has created, thus giving the agency power to make law within the limits set by the legislature. In contract law, a transaction whereby a person who owes a legal duty to perform under a contract appoints someone else to carry out his performance.

demand   A claim; a legal obligation; a request to perform an alleged obligation; a written statement of a claim. In corporation law, a request that the board of directors sue a person who has harmed the corporation; a prerequisite to a shareholder derivative suit.

demurrer   A civil motion that attacks the plaintiff's complaint by assuming the truth of the facts stated in the complaint for purposes of the motion, and by arguing that even if these facts are true, there is no rule of law entitling the plaintiff to recovery. Roughly similar to the motion to dismiss for failure to state a claim on which relief can be granted.

derivative suit   A suit to enforce a corporate right of action brought on behalf of a corporation by one or more of its shareholders. Also called *derivative action.*

devise   In a will, a gift of real property.

directed verdict   A verdict issued by a judge who has, in effect, taken the case away from the jury by directing a verdict for one party. Usually, the motion for a directed verdict is made at trial by one party after the other party has finished presenting his evidence.

disaffirmance   The right for minors to avoid contracts as a means of protecting against their own improvidence and against overreaching by adults.

discharge   Release from liability.

disclaimer   A term in a contract whereby a party attempts to relieve itself of some potential liability associated with the contract. The most common example is the seller's attempt to disclaim liability for defects in goods that it sells.

discount shares   Shares issued for less than par value.

discovery   A process of information gathering that takes place before a civil trial.

dishonor   The failure to pay or accept a negotiable instrument that has been properly presented.

dissenter's rights   A shareholder's right to receive the fair value of his or her shares from his or her corporation when he or she objects to a corporate transaction that significantly alters his or her rights in the corporation.

dissociation   In partnership law, the change in the relation of the partners caused by any partner ceasing to be associated with the carrying on of the business.

dissolution   In partnership law, the commencement of the winding up process.

diversity jurisdiction   One of two bases for a case to be litigated in federal court, satisfied when the case (1) is between citizens of different states and (2) the amount in controversy exceeds $75,000.

domestic corporation   A corporation is deemed a domestic corporation in the state that has granted its charter. If the corporation does business in other states, it is considered a foreign corporation in the other states.

domicile   A place where a person lives or has his home; in a strict legal sense, the place where he has his true, fixed, permanent home and principal establishment, and to which place he has, whenever he is absent, the intention of returning.

donee   A person to whom a gift is made.

donor   A person who makes a gift.

dower   The legal right or interest that a wife has in her husband's real estate by virtue of their marriage.

draft   A written order drawn on one person by another, requesting him to pay money to a designated third person.

drawee   A person on whom a draft is drawn by the drawer.

drawer   The maker of a draft.

due process   The principle that an individual cannot be deprived of life, liberty, or property without appropriate legal procedures and safeguards.

durable power of attorney   A power of attorney that is not affected by the principal's incapacity. See also *attorney in fact.*

durable power of attorney for health care   A durable power of attorney in which the principal specifically gives the attorney in fact the authority to make health care decisions for her in the event that the principal should become incompetent. Also called *health care representative.*

duty of loyalty   An agent must subordinate his personal concerns by (1) avoiding conflicts of interest with the principal and (2) not disclosing confidential information received from the principal.

easement   The right to make certain uses of another person's property or to prevent another person from making certain uses of his own property.

emancipation   The termination of a parent's right to control a child and receive services and wages from him or her.

eminent domain   A governmental power whereby the government can take or condemn private property for a public purpose on the payment of just compensation.

employee   Someone who is classified as a paid worker for a principal.

enabling legislation   The statute by which a legislative body creates an administrative agency.

enumerated powers   Specific powers granted to Congress as outlined in Article 1, Section 8 of the U.S. Constitution.

environmental impact statement   A document that the National Environmental Policy Act requires federal agencies to prepare in connection with any legislative proposals or proposed actions that will significantly affect the environment.

equity   A system of justice that developed in England separate from the common law courts. Few states in the United States still maintain separate equity courts, though most apply equity principles and procedures when remedies derived from the equity courts are sought. A broader meaning denotes fairness and justice. In business organization law, the capital contributions of owners plus profits that have not been distributed to the owners; stated capital plus capital surplus plus earned surplus.

equity of redemption   The right of a mortgagee to discharge the mortgage when due and to have title to the mortgaged property free and clear of the mortgage debt.

escheat   The reversion of land to the state in the event that a decedent dies leaving no heirs.

estate   An interest in land. Property owned by a decedent at the time of his death.

estoppel   That state of affairs that arises when one is forbidden by law from alleging or denying a fact because of his previous action or inaction.

eviction   Depriving the tenant of the possession of leased premises.

exculpatory clause   A clause in a contract or trust instrument that excuses a party from some duty.

executive order   A legal rule issued by a chief executive (e.g., the president or a state governor), usually pursuant to a delegation of power from the legislature.

executor   The personal representative appointed to administer the estate of a person who died leaving a valid will.

executory   Not yet executed; not yet fully performed, completed, fulfilled, or carried out; to be performed wholly or in part.

exemption   A release from some burden, duty, or obligation; a grace; a favor; an immunity; taken out from under the general rule, not to be like others who are not exempt.

express authority   Actual authority that the principal has manifested to the agent in very specific or detailed language.

express warranty   A warranty made in words, either oral or written.

F

false imprisonment   An intentional tort that prohibits the unlawful confinement of another for an appreciable time without his consent.

FAS   An abbreviation for the expression *free alongside ship*.

federal question jurisdiction   One of two bases for a case to be litigated in federal court, satisfied when the case arises under the Constitution, laws, or treaties of the United States.

federal supremacy   The ability of federal laws to defeat inconsistent state laws in case they conflict.

federalism   Government marked by mixed or compound levels, including a central of federal level and one or more regional levels, in a single system.

fee simple absolute   The highest form of land ownership, which gives the owner the right to possess and use the land for an unlimited period of time, subject only to governmental or private restrictions, and unconditional power to dispose of the property during his lifetime or upon his death.

felony   As a general rule, all crimes punishable by death or by imprisonment in a state prison.

fictitious payee   A person identified in a UCC Article 3 negotiable instrument that is not intended to have any interest in the instrument or a person identified as the payee of a negotiable instrument who is created by the person whose intent determines to whom the instrument is payable under UCC §3-110(a), even if some person or entity by that name may exist somewhere.

fiduciary duty   Someone who is required to act for the benefit of another person on all matters within the scope of their relationship; one who owes to another the duties of good faith, loyalty, due care, and disclosure.

field warehousing arrangement   A method of protecting a security interest in the inventory of a debtor whereby the creditor or his agent retains the physical custody of the debtor's inventory, which is released to the debtor as he complies with the underlying security agreement.

financing statement   A document, usually a multicopy form, filed in a public office serving as constructive notice to the world that a creditor claims a security interest in collateral that belongs to a certain named debtor.

firm offer   Under the Uniform Commercial Code, a signed, written offer by a merchant containing assurances that it will be held open, and which is not revocable for the time stated in the offer, or for a reasonable time if no such time is stated.

fixture   A thing that was originally personal property and that has been actually or constructively affixed to the soil itself or to some structure legally a part of the land.

FOB   An abbreviation of *free on board*.

foreign corporation   A corporation incorporated in one state doing business in another state. See also *alien corporation*.

fraudulent indorsement   A forged indorsement purporting to be that of the employer in the case of an instrument payable to the employer; a forged indorsement purporting to be that of the person intended as the payee in the case of an instrument with respect to which the employer is the issuer.

freeze-out   In corporation law, a type of oppression by which only minority shareholders are forced to sell their shares.

fundamental rights   A group of rights that have been recognized by the Supreme Court as requiring a high degree of protection from government encroachment. These rights are specifically identified in the Constitution, especially in the Bill of Rights, or have been found under due process.

future advances   Money or other value provided to a debtor by a creditor subsequent to the time a security interest in the debtor's collateral is taken by that creditor.

G

general agent   An agent that is continuously employed to conduct a series of transactions.

general partner   An owner of a limited partnership who has a right to manage the business and is direct and joint liability for the limited partnership's obligations.

general partnership   See *partnership*.

gift   A voluntary transfer of property for which the donor receives no consideration in return.

good faith   Honesty in fact; an honest intention to abstain from taking an unfair advantage of another.

good-faith purchaser   One who has in good faith—that is, consistent with reasonable commercial standards of fair dealing in the trade—paid valuable consideration without any notice of another's claim or any defects in the seller's ability to sell.

gratuitous agent   An agent who receives no compensation for his or her services.

gray market goods   Goods lawfully bearing trademarks or using patented or copyrighted material, but imported into a foreign market without the authorization of the owner of the trademark, patent, or copyright.

hazardous air pollutants   The 1970 Clean Air Act, enacted by the Environmental Protection Agency (EPA), initially required set standards only for asbestos, beryllium, mercury, vinyl chloride, benzene, and radionuclides.

health care representative   An advance directive in which the principal gives the attorney-in-fact the authority to make certain health care decisions for the principal should the principal become incompetent. See *durable power of attorney for health care.*

holder   A person in possession of a document of title or an instrument payable or indorsed to him, his order, or bearer.

holder in due course   A person who is a holder of a negotiable instrument who took the instrument for value, in good faith, without notice that it is overdue or has been dishonored or that there is any uncured default with respect to payment of another instrument issued as part of the same series, without notice that the instrument contains an unauthorized signature or has been altered, without notice of any claim of a property or possessory interest in it, and without notice that any party has any defense against it or claim in recoupment to it.

holographic will   A will written in the handwriting of the testator.

I

implied authority   Actual authority given to an agent to bind his or her principals and to act in a way that the agent reasonably believes is necessary to perform his or her duties.

implied warranty   A warranty created by operation of law.

implied warranty of habitability   Implied warranty arising in lease or sale of residential real estate that the property will be fit for human habitation.

impossibility   A doctrine under which a party to a contract is relieved of his or her duty to perform when that performance has become impossible because of the occurrence of an event unforeseen at the time of contracting.

imposter   A person who pretends to be someone else in order to deceive others.

in personam   Against a person. For example, in personam jurisdiction.

in rem   Against a thing and not against a person; concerning the condition or status of a thing; for example, in rem jurisdiction.

incidental damages   Collateral damages that result from a breach of contract, including all reasonable expenses that are incurred because of the breach; damages that compensate a person injured by a breach of contract for reasonable costs he incurs in an attempt to avoid further loss.

indemnify   To reimburse or promise to reimburse another from loss. To act as security or protection against a loss.

indenture   A contract between a corporation and the holders of bonds or debentures issued by the corporation stating the rights of the holders and duties of the corporation.

independent checks   Limits put in place by the Constitution limiting both state and federal power. They establish that even if Congress has an enumerated power to legislate on a particular matter or a state constitution authorizes a state to take certain actions, there are still certain protected spheres into which neither the federal government nor the state government may reach.

indorsement   Writing on the back of an instrument; the contract whereby the holder of an instrument (such as a draft, check, or note) or a document (such as a warehouse receipt or bill of lading) transfers to another person his right to such instrument and incurs the liabilities incident to the transfer.

information   A written accusation of crime brought by a public prosecuting officer to a court without the intervention of a grand jury.

injunction   An equitable remedy whereby the defendant is ordered to perform certain acts or to desist from certain acts.

inside information   Confidential information possessed by a person due to his or her relationship with a business.

instructions   In the context of a jury trial, typically written by a judge for use by a jury as the only guidance that a jury is supposed to consider during its deliberations regarding the facts and law presented during the trial.

insurable interest   Any interest in property such that the owner would experience a benefit from the continued existence of the property or a loss from its destruction.

inter vivos   A transaction between living persons.

intestate   Having died without leaving a valid will.

intrastate   Within a particular state.

investment contract   In securities law, a type of security encompassing any contract by which an investor invests in a common enterprise with an expectation of profits solely from the efforts of persons other than the investor.

irrevocable letter of credit   The issuing bank may not revoke the letter of credit issued by the buyer's bank.

issue   Lineal descendants such as children and grandchildren. This category of persons includes adopted children.

issued shares   A corporation's shares that a corporation has sold to its shareholders. Includes shares repurchased by the corporation and retained as treasury shares, but not shares canceled or returned to unissued status.

J

joint tenancy   An estate held by two or more jointly, with an equal right in all to share in the enjoyments of the land during their lives. An incident of joint tenancy is the right of survivorship.

joint venture   A form of business organization identical to a partnership, except that it is engaged in a single project, not carrying on a business.

judgment notwithstanding the verdict   A judgment made by a judge contrary to a prior jury verdict whereby the judge effectively overrules the jury's verdict. Also called the *j.n.o.v.* or the *judgment* *non obstante veredicto.* Similar to the directed verdict, except that it occurs after the jury has issued its verdict.

judicial review   The courts' power to declare the actions of the other branches of government unconstitutional.

jurisdiction   The power of a court to hear and decide a case.

jurisprudence   The philosophy of law. Also sometimes used to refer to the collected positive law of some jurisdiction.

L

land contract   A conditional agreement for the sale and purchase of real estate in which the legal title to the property is retained by the seller until the purchaser has fulfilled the agreement, usually by completing the payment of the agreed-on purchase price.

lease   A contract for the possession and use of land or other property, including goods, on one side, and a recompense of rent or other income on the other; a conveyance to a person for life, or years, or at will in consideration of a return of rent or other recompense.

legacy   A bequest; a testamentary gift of personal property. Sometimes incorrectly applied to a testamentary gift of real property.

legal   According to the principles of law; according to the method required by statute; by means of judicial proceedings; not equitable.

legal positivism   A school of jurisprudential thought and philosophy of law that defines law by reference to positive norms as determined by the commands of a recognized political authority.

legally nonexistent   An agent who purports to act for a principal, such as an unincorporated association, is personally liable when the agent knows or has reason to know the principal does not exist.

libel   The defamation action appropriate to printed or written defamations, or to those that have a physical form.

license   A personal privilege to do some act or series of acts on the land of another, without possessing any ownership interest in the land. A permit or authorization to do something that, without a license, would be unlawful.

lien   In its most extensive meaning, it is a charge on property for the payment or discharge of a debt or duty; a qualified right; a proprietary interest that, in a given case, may be exercised over the property of another.

life estate   A property interest that gives a person the right to possess and use property for a time that is measured by his lifetime or that of another person.

limited liability company (LLC)   A business form intended to combine the nontax advantages of corporations with the favorable tax treatment of partnerships. An LLC is owned by members, who may manage the LLC themselves or elect the manager or managers who will operate the business. Members have limited liability for the obligations of the LLC.

limited liability limited partnership (LLLP)   A limited partnership that has elected to obtain limited liability status for all of its partners, including general partners, by filing with the secretary of state.

limited liability partnership (LLP)   A partnership that has elected to obtain limited liability for its partners by filing with the secretary of state.

limited partner   An owner of a limited partnership who has no right to manage the business but who possesses liability limited to his capital contribution to the business.

limited partnership   A form of business organization that has one or more general partners who manage the business and have unlimited liability for the obligations of the business and one or more limited partners who do not manage and have limited liability.

liquidated damages   The stipulation by the parties to a contract of the sum of money to be recovered by the aggrieved party in the event of a breach of the contract by the other party.

liquidated debt   A debt that is due and certain. That is, one that is not the subject of a bona fide dispute as to either its existence or the amount that is owed.

living will   A document executed with specific legal formalities stating a person's preference that heroic life support measures should not be used if there is no hope of the person's recovery.

long-arm statute   A state statute that grants to a state's courts broad authority to exercise jurisdiction over out-of-state persons who have contacts with the state.

looting   In corporation law, the transfer of a corporation's assets to its managers or controlling shareholders at less than fair value.

M

Magnetic Ink Character Recognition (MICR)   A technology used to verify the legitimacy or originality of paper documents using special ink, which is sensitive to magnetic fields to print the characters.

maker   A person who makes or executes an instrument. The signer of an instrument.

malicious prosecution   An intentional tort designed to protect against the wrongful initiation of criminal proceedings.

material   Important. In securities law, a fact is material if a reasonable person would consider it important in his decision to purchase shares or to vote shares.

maximum available control technology   In 1990, Congress specified a list of 189 chemicals for which EPA is required to issue regulations requiring the installation of maximum available control technology. The regulations are to be developed and the control technology installed by industry in phases.

means-end test   A judicially created test developed by the Supreme Court. These tests were created because no constitutional right is absolute and because judges, therefore, must weigh individual rights against the social purposes served by laws that restrict those rights.

merchant   Under the Uniform Commercial Code, one who regularly deals in goods of the kind sold in the contract at issue, or holds himself out as having special knowledge or skill relevant to such goods, or who makes the sale through an agent who regularly deals in such goods or claims such knowledge or skill.

merger   In corporation law, traditionally, a transaction by which one corporation acquires another corporation, with the acquiring corporation being owned by the shareholders of both corporations and the acquired corporation going out of existence. Today, loosely applied to any negotiated acquisition of one corporation by another.

merger clause   A contract clause providing that the written contract is the complete expression of the parties' agreement. Also called *integration clause.*

misappropriation theory   Theory of liability for insider trading offense in which a person trades on material, nonpublic information in violation of a known fiduciary duty. However, unlike with the classical theory, the fiduciary duty is not owed to the company per se, but to another such as an employer.

misdemeanor   Any crime that is punishable neither by death nor by imprisonment in a state prison.

misrepresentation   The assertion of a fact that is not in accord with the truth. A contract can be rescinded on the ground of misrepresentation when the assertion relates to a material fact or is made fraudulently and the other party actually and justifiably relies on the assertion.

mortgage   A conveyance of property to secure the performance of some obligation, the conveyance to be void on the due performance thereof.

mortgagee   The creditor to whom property has been mortgaged to secure the performance of an obligation.

mortgagor   The owner of the property that has been mortgaged or pledged as security for a debt.

motion for judgment on the pleadings   A motion made after time has passed for filing any additional pleadings, based on insufficiency of allegations in the complaint and underlying merits of the claim.

motion to dismiss   A motion made by the defendant in a civil case to defeat the plaintiff's case, usually after the complaint or all the pleadings have been completed. The most common form of motion to dismiss is the motion to dismiss for failure to state a claim on which relief can be granted, which attacks the legal sufficiency of the plaintiff's complaint. See also *demurrer.*

N

national ambient air quality standards   Federally established air pollution standards designed to protect the public health and welfare.

natural law   A body of allegedly existing ethical rules or principles that is morally superior to positive law and that prevails over positive law in case of a clash between it and the natural law.

necessaries   That which is reasonably necessary for a minor's proper and suitable maintenance, in view of the income level and social position of the minor's family.

negligence   The omission to do something that a reasonable person, guided by those considerations that ordinarily regulate human affairs, would do, or doing something that a prudent and reasonable person would not do.

negligence per se   The doctrine that provides that a conclusive presumption of breach of duty arises when a defendant has violated a statute and thereby caused a harm the statute was designed to prevent to a person the statute was designed to protect.

negotiation   The transfer of an instrument in such form that the transferee becomes a holder.

nominal damages   Damages that are recoverable when a legal right is to be vindicated against an invasion that has produced no actual present loss.

nonemployee agent   A nonemployee agent typically contracts with the principal to produce a result and determines for himself or herself how that result will be accomplished. Also called an *independent contractor.*

nontrading partnership   A partnership whose business has no substantial inventory and is usually engaged in providing services.

novation   A mutual agreement, between all parties concerned, for the discharge of a valid existing obligation by the substitution of a new valid obligation on the part of the debtor or another, or a like agreement for the discharge of a debtor to his creditor by the substitution of a new creditor.

nuisance   That which endangers life or health, gives offense to the senses, violates the laws of decency, or obstructs the reasonable and comfortable use of property.

obligee   A person to whom another is bound by a promise or other obligation; a promisee.

obligor   A person who is bound by a promise or other obligation; a promisor.

offer   A proposal by one person to another that is intended to create legal relations on acceptance by the person to whom it is made.

offeree   The party to whom an offer is made.

offeror   The party who makes an offer.

opinion letter   A document issued by an auditor after the completion of auditing financial statements. This letter expresses whether the audit has been performed in compliance with GAAS and whether, in the auditor's opinion, the financial statements fairly present the client's financial position and results of operations in conformity with GAAP.

oppression   The officers, directors, or controlling shareholder's isolation of one group of shareholders for disadvantageous treatment to the benefit of another group of shareholders.

option   A separate contract in which an offeror agrees not to revoke her offer for a stated period of time in exchange for some valuable consideration.

option agreement   A share transfer restriction granting a corporation or its shareholders an option to buy a selling shareholder's shares at a price determined by the agreement.

ordinance A legislative enactment of a county or an incorporated city or town.

original jurisdiction The power to decide a case as a trial court.

outstanding shares A corporation's shares currently held by shareholders.

overdue When an instrument is not paid when due or at maturity.

P

parent corporation A corporation that owns a controlling interest of another corporation, called a *subsidiary corporation.*

parol evidence Where a written contract exists, evidence about promises or statements made prior to or during the execution of the writing that are not contained in the written contract.

partners The owners of a partnership.

partnership A form of business organization; specifically, an association of two or more persons to carry on a business as co-owners for profit.

partnership capital When a partnership or limited liability partnership is formed, partners contribute cash or other property to the partnership.

partnership interest A partner's ownership interest in a partnership that embodies the partner's transferable interest and the partner's management and other rights.

patentee The holder of a patent.

payee A person to whom a payment is made or is made payable.

per capita A distribution of property in which each member of a group shares equally.

per stirpes A distribution in which each surviving descendant divides the share that his or her parent would have taken if the parent had survived. Also called *by right of representation.*

perfection The process or method by which a secured party obtains a priority in certain collateral belonging to a debtor against creditors or claimants of a debtor; it usually entails giving notice of the security interest, such as by taking possession or filing a financial statement.

periodic tenancy The tenancy that exists when the landlord and tenant agree that rent will be paid in regular successive intervals until notice to terminate is given but do not agree on a specific duration of the lease. A typical periodic tenancy is a tenancy from month to month.

personal property All objects and rights, other than real property, that can be owned. See also *real property.*

piercing the corporate veil Holding a shareholder responsible for acts of a corporation due to a shareholder's domination and improper use of the corporation.

pleadings The documents the parties file with the court when they state their claims and counterarguments early in a civil case. Examples include the complaint and the answer.

police power The states' power to regulate to promote the public health, safety, morals, and welfare.

power of sale A secured loan agreement authorizing a lender (the agent) to sell property used as security if the borrower (the principal) defaults.

precedent A past judicial decision relied on as authority in a present case.

preemptive right A shareholder's option to purchase new issuances of shares in proportion to the shareholder's current ownership of the corporation.

preferred shareholders Shareholders who have dividend and liquidation preferences over other classes of shareholders, usually common shareholders.

presentment A demand made by or on behalf of a person entitled to enforce an instrument either (i) to pay the instrument made to the drawee or a party obliged to pay the instrument or, in the case of a note or accepted draft payable at a bank, to the bank, or (ii) to accept a draft made to the drawee.

pretermitted In the law of wills, an heir born after the execution of the testator's will.

pretrial conference A relatively informal meeting between the judge and attorneys for the parties to a lawsuit during which the judge attempts to craft an agreement among the parties to agree to resolution of certain issues in order to simplify the trial.

principal In agency law, one under whose direction an agent acts and for whose benefit that agent acts.

priority The right of one creditor to take first claim on the property of its debtor even when there are multiple creditors with claims against the debtor or to specific items of tangible or intangible property of the debtor.

privity of contract The existence of a direct contractual relation between two parties.

procedural due process A principle required by the Constitution that when the state or federal government acts in such a way that denies a citizen of a life, liberty, or property interest, the person must first be given notice and the opportunity to be heard.

procedural law The body of law controlling public bodies such as courts, as they create and enforce rules of substantive law. See also *substantive law.*

proceeds Whatever is received on the sale, exchange, collection, or other disposition of collateral.

professional corporation Identical to a business corporation in most respects. A professional corporation is formed by filing with the secretary of state, and it is managed by a board of directors, unless a statute permits it to be managed like a partnership. The rigid management structure makes the professional corporation inappropriate for some smaller professional practices.

profit An interest in land giving a person the right to enter land owned by another and remove natural resources (e.g., timber) from the land. Also called *profit à prendre.*

promissory estoppel An equitable doctrine that protects those who foreseeably and reasonably rely on the promises of others by enforcing such promises when enforcement is necessary to avoid injustice, even though one or more of the elements normally required for an enforceable agreement is absent.

promissory note Commercial paper or instrument in which the maker promises to pay a specific sum of money to another person, to his order, or to bearer.

promoter A person who incorporates a business, organizes its initial management, and raises its initial capital.

property Something that is capable of being owned. A right or interest associated with something that gives the owner the ability to exercise dominion over it.

prospectus In securities law, a document given to prospective purchasers of a security that contains information about an issuer of securities and the securities being issued.

proxy A person who is authorized to vote the shares of another person. Also, the written authorization empowering a person to vote the shares of another person.

public accommodation Business and nonbusiness enterprises, buildings, and other places and organizations that are generally open to the public, which are subject to regulation, including non-discrimination requirements on various bases, by federal, state, and local laws. Definitions vary somewhat under each specific law, but generally exclude private clubs and religious organizations.

punitive damages Damages designed to punish flagrant wrongdoers and to deter them and others from engaging in similar conduct in the future.

purchase money security interest (PMSI) A security interest that is (1) taken or retained by the seller of collateral to secure all or part of its purchase price or (2) taken by a debtor to acquire rights in or the use of the collateral if the value is so used.

purported partnership The appearance of partnership when there is no partnership; it arises when a person misleads a second person into believing that the first person is a partner of a third person; a theory that allows the second person to recover from the first person all reasonable damages the second person has suffered due to his reliance on the appearance of partnership.

quasi-contract The doctrine by which courts imply, as a matter of law, a promise to pay the reasonable value of goods or services when the party receiving such goods or services has knowingly done so under circumstances that make it unfair to retain them without paying for them.

quitclaim deed A deed conveying only the right, title, and interest of the grantor in the property described, as distinguished from a deed conveying the property itself.

quorum That number of persons, shares represented, or officers who may lawfully transact the business of a meeting called for that purpose.

ratification The adoption or affirmance by a person of a prior act that did not bind him.

real property The earth's crust and all things firmly attached to it.

redemption The buying back of one's property after it has been sold. The right to redeem property sold under an order or decree of court is purely a privilege conferred by, and does not exist independently of, statute.

reformation An equitable remedy in which a court effectively rewrites the terms of a contract.

rejection In contract law, an express or implied manifestation of an offeree's unwillingness to contract on the terms of an offer. In sales law, a buyer's refusal to accept goods because they are defective or nonconforming.

remainderman One who is entitled to the remainder of the estate after a particular estate carved out of it has expired.

renunciation Occurs when either party manifests to the other that he does not wish the agency to continue. This is done by the agent.

reply A plaintiff's point-by-point response to the allegations in the answer or counterclaim.

res The thing; the subject matter of a suit; the property involved in the litigation; a matter; property; the business; the affair; the transaction.

res ipsa loquitur Literally, the thing speaks for itself. A doctrine that, in some circumstances, gives rise to an inference that a defendant was negligent and that his negligence was the cause of the plaintiff's injury.

rescind As the word is applied to contracts, to terminate the contract as to future transactions or to annul the contract from the beginning.

rescission The rescinding or cancellation of a contract or transaction. In general, its effect is to restore the parties to their original precontractual position.

residue Residuary; all that portion of the estate of a testator of which no effectual disposition has been made by his will otherwise than in the residuary clause.

respondeat superior A legal doctrine making an employer (or master) liable for the torts of an employee (servant) that are committed within the scope of the employee's employment.

restitution A remedy whereby one is able to obtain the return of that which he has given the other party, or an amount of money equivalent to that which he has given the other party.

restrictive covenant An agreement restricting the use of real property.

revocation In general, the recalling or voiding of a prior action. In contract law, the withdrawal of an offer by the offeror prior to effective acceptance by the offeree.

right An interest given and protected by law. In corporation law, an option to purchase shares given to existing shareholders, permitting them to buy quantities of newly issued securities in proportion to their current ownership.

right of appraisal See *dissenter's rights.*

right of exoneration The right of the surety or guarantor to require the debtor to make good on his commitment to the creditor when he (1) is able to do so and (2) does not have a valid defense against payment.

right of first refusal In corporation law, a share transfer restriction granting a corporation or its shareholders an option to match the offer that a selling shareholder receives for her shares. See also *option agreement*.

right of subrogation When a surety has to perform or pay the principal's obligation, the surety then acquires all of the rights that the creditor had against the principal.

right of survivorship A feature of some types of co-ownership of property causing a co-owner's interest in property to be transferred on his death immediately and by operation of law to his surviving co-owner(s). See also *tenancy by the entirety* and *joint tenancy*.

right to contribution When several people act as cosureties for another and pay the entire obligation on behalf of another. The payor is entitled to collect one-third from all parties because they paid more than their prorated share.

right to reimbursement When the surety performs or pays the principal's obligation, the surety is entitled to recover those costs from the principal.

S

S corporation A close corporation whose shareholders have elected to be taxed essentially like partners are taxed under federal income tax law. Also called *subchapter S corporation*.

sale of goods The transfer of ownership to tangible personal property in exchange for money, other goods, or the performance of service.

sale on approval A conditional sale that is to become final only in case the buyer, after a trial, approves or is satisfied with the article sold.

sale or return A contract in which the seller delivers a quantity of goods to the buyer on the understanding that if the buyer desires to retain, use, or sell any portion of the goods, he will consider such part as having been sold to him, and that he will return the balance or hold it as bailee for the seller.

scienter In cases of fraud and deceit, the word means knowledge on the part of the person making the representations, at the time when they are made, that they are false. In an action for deceit, scienter must be proved.

Securities Act of 1933 The first major federal legislation to regulate the offer and sale of securities. Prior to this act, regulation of securities was chiefly governed by state laws, commonly referred to as blue sky laws. When Congress enacted this act, it left existing state securities laws ("blue sky laws") in place.

Securities Exchange Act of 1934 The Securities Exchange Act of 1934 was created to govern securities transactions on the secondary market, after issue, ensuring greater financial transparency and accuracy and less fraud or manipulation. This act authorized the formation of the Securities and Exchange Commission (SEC), the regulatory arm of the Securities Exchange Act (SEA). The SEC has the power to oversee securities, such as stocks, bonds and over-the-counter securities, markets, and the conduct of financial professionals including brokers, dealers, and investment advisors, and monitor the financial reports that publicly traded companies are required to disclose.

security An instrument commonly dealt with in the securities markets or commonly recognized as a medium of investment and evidencing an obligation of an issuer or a share, participation, or other interest in an enterprise.

security interest A lien given by a debtor to his creditor to secure payment or performance of a debt or obligation.

separation of powers A characteristic of government that vests the executive, legislative, and judicial powers in separate bodies.

settlor A person who creates a trust. Also called *trustor*.

share An equity security, representing a shareholder's ownership of a corporation.

share dividend The distribution of some of a company's earnings to the holders of a certain class of shares, which can be in the form of cash or additional shares.

share split Traditionally, a corporation's dividing existing shares into two or more shares, thereby increasing the number of authorized, issued, and outstanding shares and reducing their par value. In modern corporation law, treated like a share dividend. Also called *stock split*.

share subscription A promise by a person to purchase a specified number of shares at a specified price.

shareholder An owner of a corporation who has no inherent right to manage the corporation but has liability limited to his capital contribution. Also called *stockholder*.

slander The defamation action appropriate to oral defamation.

sociological jurisprudence A philosophical approach to law that focuses on the social effects of legal institutions, doctrines, and practices, by examining how the law influences society and how social phenomena impact the law.

sole proprietor The owner of a sole proprietorship.

sole proprietorship A form of business under which one person owns and controls the business.

special agent An agent that is employed to conduct a single transaction or a small, simple group of transactions.

special damages Actual damages that would not necessarily but because of special circumstances do in fact flow from an injury.

specific performance A contract remedy whereby the defendant is ordered to perform according to the terms of his contract.

stale check A check that is more than 90 days past the date on its face; banks do not owe a duty to their customers to pay any such checks more than six months past the dates on their face.

standing The legal requirement that anyone seeking to challenge a particular action in court must demonstrate that such action substantially affects his or her legitimate interests before he or she will be entitled to bring suit.

state implementation plan A document prepared by states in which the emissions to the air from individual sources are limited legally so that the area will meet the national ambient air quality standards.

stated capital A balance sheet account; shareholders' capital contributions representing the par value of par shares or stated value of no-par shares. Also called *capital stock.*

statute of limitations A statute that requires that certain classes of lawsuits must be brought within defined limits of time after the right to begin them accrued or the right to bring the lawsuit is lost.

straight voting A form of voting for directors that ordinarily permits a shareholder to cast a number of votes equal to the number of shares he or she owns for as many nominees as there are directors to be elected. See also *cumulative voting.*

strict liability Legal responsibility placed on an individual for the results of his actions irrespective of whether he was culpable or at fault.

strike suit In corporation law, a derivative suit motivated primarily by an intent to gain an out-of-court settlement for the suing shareholder personally or to earn large attorney fees for lawyers, rather than to obtain a recovery for the corporation.

subagent An agent of an agent, or a person who is appointed by an agent to perform tasks that the agent has undertaken to perform for the principal.

sublease A transfer of some but not all of a tenant's remaining right to possess property under a lease.

subsidiary corporation A corporation owned and controlled by another corporation, called a *parent corporation.*

substantive due process A principle allowing courts to protect certain rights deemed fundamental from government interference, even where procedural protections are present or where those rights are not specifically mentioned elsewhere in the Constitution.

substantive law The body of law setting out rights and duties that affect how people behave in organized social life. See also *procedural law.*

summary judgment A method of reaching a judgment in a civil case before trial. The standard for granting a motion for summary judgment is that there be no significant issue of material fact and that the moving party be entitled to judgment as a matter of law.

summons A writ or process issued and served on a defendant in a civil action for the purpose of securing his appearance in the action.

supermajority voting The board needs more than a simple majority of directors to vote in favor of an action before the action is possible; for example, it may require a 2/3 or unanimous vote prior to action.

surety A person who promises to perform the same obligation as another person (the principal) and who is jointly liable along with the principal for that obligation's performance.

suspect classes A class of individuals that have been historically subject to discrimination. Any statute that makes a distinction between individuals based on any of the suspect classifications (i.e., alienage, race) will be subject to a strict scrutiny standard of review before the Supreme Court.

T

Takings Clause The Fifth Amendment states that "private property [shall not] be taken for public use, without just compensation." This clause has been incorporated within the Fourteenth Amendment due process, so it also applies to the states.

tenancy General term indicating a possessory interest in property. In landlord–tenant law, a property owner's conveyance to another person of the right to possess the property exclusively for a period of time.

tenancy at sufferance The leasehold interest that occurs when a tenant remains in possession of property after the expiration of a lease.

tenancy at will A leasehold interest that occurs when property is leased for an indefinite period of time and is terminable at the will of either landlord or tenant.

tenancy by the entirety A form of co-ownership of property by a married couple that gives the owners a right of survivorship and cannot be severed during life by the act of only one of the parties.

tenancy for a term A leasehold interest that results when the landlord and tenant agree on a specific duration for a lease and fix the date on which the tenancy will terminate.

tenancy in common A form of co-ownership of property that is freely disposable both during life and at death, and in which the co-owners have undivided interests in the property and equal rights to possess the property.

tenancy in partnership A form of co-ownership created when a partnership takes title to a property in the partnership's name.

tender offer A public offer by a bidder to purchase a subject company's shares directly from its shareholders at a specified price for a fixed period of time.

testator A deceased person who died leaving a will.

thin capitalization In corporation law, a ground for piercing the corporate veil due to the shareholders' contributing too little capital to the corporation in relation to its needs.

third-party beneficiary A person who is not a party to a contract but who has the right to enforce it because the parties to the contract made the contract with the intent to benefit him.

tort A private (civil) wrong against a person or his property.

trade fixtures Articles of personal property that have been annexed to real property leased by a tenant during the term of the lease and that are necessary to the carrying on of a trade.

trade secret A secret formula, pattern, process, program, device, method, technique, or compilation of information that is used in its owner's business and affords that owner a competitive advantage. Trade secrets are protected by state law.

trademark A distinctive word, name, symbol, device, or combination thereof, which enables consumers to identify favored products or services and which may find protection under state or federal law.

trading partnership A partnership that has an inventory; that is, its regular business is buying and selling merchandise, such as retailing, wholesaling, importing, or exporting.

transferable interest   In partnership law, a partner's share of the partnership's profits and losses and right to receive partnership distributions.

treasury shares   Previously outstanding shares repurchased by a corporation that are not canceled or restored to unissued status.

treaty   A formally negotiated and ratified agreement between or among countries.

trespass   An unauthorized entry on another's property.

trust   A legal relationship in which a person who has legal title to property has the duty to hold it for the use or benefit of another person. The term is also used in a general sense to mean confidence reposed in one person by another.

trustee   A person in whom property is vested in trust for another.

U

unconscionable   In contract law, a contract that is grossly unfair or one-sided; one that "shocks the conscience of the court."

undisclosed principal   In agency law, a principal whom a third party lacks knowledge or the reason to know the principal's existence and identity.

unidentified principal   In agency law, a principal whom a third party knows or has reason to know exists but who lacks knowledge or reason to know the principal's identity.

uniform acts   Model statutes drafted by private bodies of lawyers and scholars.

unilateral contract   A contract formed by an offer or a promise on one side for an act to be done on the other, and a doing of the act by the other by way of acceptance of the offer or promise; that is, a contract wherein the only acceptance of the offer that is necessary is the performance of the act.

V

value   Under the UCC (except for negotiable instruments and bank collections), generally any consideration sufficient to support a simple contract.

venue   A requirement distinct from jurisdiction that the court be geographically situated so that it is the most appropriate and convenient court to try the case.

verdict   Usually, the decision made by a jury and reported to the judge on the matters or questions submitted to it at trial. In some situations, however, the judge may be the party issuing a verdict, as, for example, in the motion for a directed verdict. See also *directed verdict*.

void   That which is entirely null. A void act is one that is not binding on either party and that is not susceptible of ratification.

voidable   Capable of being made void; not utterly null, but annullable, and hence may be either voided or confirmed. See also *void*.

voidable title   A title that is capable of, or subject to, being judged invalid or void.

voting trust   A type of shareholder voting arrangement by which shareholders transfer their voting rights to a voting trustee.

waiver   The intentional relinquishment of a known right. It is a voluntary act and implies an election by the party to dispense with something of value, or to forgo some advantage that he or she might have demanded and insisted on.

warrant   An order authorizing a payment of money by another person to a third person. Also, an option to purchase a security. As a verb, the word means to defend; to guarantee; to enter into an obligation of warranty.

warranty   An undertaking relating to characteristics of a thing being sold; a guaranty.

warranty deed   A deed that guarantees a clear title to the purchaser of real property.

waste   The material alteration, abuse, or destructive use of property by one in rightful possession of it that results in injury to one having an underlying interest in it.

watered shares   Shares issued in exchange for property that has been overvalued. Also called *watered stock*. See also *discount shares*.

will   A document executed with specific legal formalities that contains a person's instructions about the disposition of his property at his death.

winding up   In partnership and corporation law, the orderly liquidation of the business's assets.

wrongful use of civil proceedings   An intentional tort designed to protect against the wrongful initiation of civil proceedings.

The Constitution of the United States of America

Preamble

We the People of the United States, in Order to form a more perfect Union, establish Justice, insure domestic Tranquility, provide for the common defense, promote the general Welfare, and secure the Blessings of Liberty to ourselves and our Posterity, do ordain and establish this Constitution for the United States of America.

Article I

Section 1. All legislative Powers herein granted shall be vested in a Congress of the United States, which shall consist of a Senate and House of Representatives.

Section 2. The House of Representatives shall be composed of Members chosen every second Year by the People of the several States, and the Electors in each State shall have the Qualifications requisite for Electors of the most numerous Branch of the State Legislature.

No Person shall be a Representative who shall not have attained to the age of twenty five Years, and been seven Years a Citizen of the United States, and who shall not, when elected, be an Inhabitant of that State in which he shall be chosen.

Representatives and direct Taxes shall be apportioned among the several States which may be included within this Union, according to their respective Numbers, which shall be determined by adding to the whole Number of free Persons, including those bound to Service for a Term of Years, and excluding Indians not taxed, three fifths of all other Persons.[1] The actual Enumeration shall be made within three Years after the first Meeting of the Congress of the United States, and within every subsequent Term of ten Years, in such Manner as they shall by Law direct. The Number of Representatives shall not exceed one for every thirty Thousand, but each State shall have at Least one Representative; and until such enumeration shall be made, the State of New Hampshire shall be entitled to choose three, Massachusetts eight, Rhode-Island and Providence Plantations one, Connecticut five, New York six, New Jersey four, Pennsylvania eight, Delaware one, Maryland six, Virginia ten, North Carolina five, South Carolina five, and Georgia three.

When vacancies happen in the Representation from any State, the Executive Authority thereof shall issue Writs of Election to fill such Vacancies.

The House of Representatives shall chuse their Speaker and other Officers; and shall have the sole Power of Impeachment.

Section 3. The Senate of the United States shall be composed of two Senators from each State, chosen by the Legislature thereof,[2] for six Years; and each Senator shall have one Vote.

Immediately after they shall be assembled in Consequence of the first Election, they shall be divided as equally as may be into three Classes. The Seats of the Senators of the first Class shall be vacated at the Expiration of the second Year, of the second Class at the Expiration of the fourth Year, and of the third Class at the Expiration of the sixth Year, so that one third may be chosen every second Year; and if Vacancies happen by Resignation, or otherwise, during the Recess of the Legislature of any State, the Executive thereof may make temporary Appointments until the next Meeting of the Legislature, which shall then fill such Vacancies.[3]

No Person shall be a Senator who shall not have attained to the Age of thirty Years, and been nine Years a Citizen of the United States, and who shall not, when elected, be an Inhabitant of that State for which he shall be chosen.

The Vice President of the United States shall be President of the Senate, but shall have no Vote, unless they be equally divided.

The Senate shall chuse their other Officers, and also a President pro tempore, in the Absence of the Vice

---

[1]Changed by the Fourteenth Amendment.

[2]Changed by the Seventeenth Amendment.
[3]Changed by the Seventeenth Amendment.

President, or when he shall exercise the Office of President of the United States.

The Senate shall have the sole Power to try all Impeachments. When sitting for that Purpose, they shall be on Oath or Affirmation. When the President of the United States is tried, the Chief Justice shall preside: And no Person shall be convicted without the Concurrence of two thirds of the Members present.

Judgment in Cases of Impeachment shall not extend further than to removal from Office, and disqualification to hold and enjoy any Office of honor, Trust or Profit under the United States: but the Party convicted shall nevertheless be liable and subject to Indictment, Trial, Judgment and Punishment, according to Law.

Section 4. The Times, Places and Manner of holding Elections for Senators and Representatives, shall be prescribed in each State by the Legislature thereof; but the Congress may at any time by Law make or alter such Regulations, except as to the Places of chusing Senators.

The Congress shall assemble at least once in every Year, and such Meeting shall be on the first Monday in December, unless they shall by Law appoint a different Day.[4]

Section 5. Each House shall be the Judge of the Elections, Returns and Qualifications of its own Members, and a Majority of each shall constitute a Quorum to do Business; but a smaller Number may adjourn from day to day, and may be authorized to compel the Attendance of absent Members, in such Manner, and under such Penalties as each House may provide.

Each House may determine the Rules of its Proceedings, punish its Members for disorderly Behaviour, and with the Concurrence of two thirds, expel a Member.

Each House shall keep a Journal of its Proceedings, and from time to time publish the same, excepting such Parts as may in their Judgment require Secrecy; and the Yeas and Nays of the Members of either House on any question shall, at the Desire of one fifth of those Present, be entered on the Journal.

Neither House, during the Session of Congress, shall, without the Consent of the other, adjourn for more than three days, nor to any other Place than that in which the two Houses shall be sitting.

Section 6. The Senators and Representatives shall receive a Compensation for their Services, to be ascertained by Law, and paid out of the Treasury of the United States. They shall in all Cases, except Treason, Felony and Breach of the Peace, be privileged from Arrest during their Attendance at the Session of their respective Houses, and in going to and returning from the same; and for any Speech or Debate in either House, they shall not be questioned in any other Place.

No Senator or Representative shall, during the Time for which he was elected, be appointed to any civil Office under the Authority of the United States, which shall have been created, or the Emoluments whereof shall have been encreased during such time; and no Person holding any Office under the United States, shall be a Member of either House during his Continuance in Office.

Section 7. All Bills for raising Revenue shall originate in the House of Representatives; but the Senate may propose or concur with Amendments as on other Bills.

Every Bill which shall have passed the House of Representatives and the Senate, shall, before it becomes a Law, be presented to the President of the United States; If he approves he shall sign it, but if not he shall return it, with his Objections to that House in which it shall have originated, who shall enter the Objections at large on their Journal, and proceed to reconsider it. If after such Reconsideration two thirds of that House shall agree to pass the Bill, it shall be sent, together with the Objections, to the other House, by which it shall likewise be reconsidered, and if approved by two thirds of that House, it shall become a Law. But in all such Cases the Votes of both Houses shall be determined by Yeas and Nays, and the Names of the Persons voting for and against the Bill shall be entered on the Journal of each House respectively. If any Bill shall not be returned by the President within ten Days (Sundays excepted) after it shall have been presented to him, the Same shall be a Law, in like Manner as if he had signed it, unless the Congress by their Adjournment prevent its Return, in which Case it shall not be a Law.

Every Order, Resolution, or Vote to which the Concurrence of the Senate and House of Representatives may be necessary (except on a question of Adjournment) shall be presented to the President of the United States; and before the Same shall take Effect, shall be approved by him, or being disapproved by him, shall be repassed by two thirds of the Senate and House of Representatives, according to the Rules and Limitations prescribed in the Case of a Bill.

Section 8. The Congress shall have Power To lay and collect Taxes, Duties, Imposts and Excises, to pay the Debts and provide for the common Defence and general Welfare of the United States; but all Duties, Imposts, and Excises shall be uniform throughout the United States.

To borrow Money on the credit of the United States;

To regulate Commerce with foreign Nations, and among the several States, and with the Indian Tribes;

---

[4]Changed by the Twentieth Amendment.

To establish an uniform Rule of Naturalization, and uniform Laws on the subject of Bankruptcies throughout the United States;

To coin Money, regulate the Value thereof, and of foreign Coin, and fix the Standard of Weights and Measures;

To provide for the Punishment of counterfeiting the Securities and current Coin of the United States;

To establish Post Offices and post Roads;

To promote the Progress of Science and useful Arts, by securing for limited Times to Authors and Inventors the exclusive Right to their respective Writings and Discoveries;

To constitute Tribunals inferior to the supreme Court;

To define and punish Piracies and Felonies committed on the high Seas, and Offences against the Law of Nations;

To declare War, grant Letters of Marque and Reprisal, and make Rules concerning Captures on Land and Water;

To raise and support Armies, but no Appropriation of Money to that Use shall be for a longer Term than two Years;

To provide and maintain a Navy;

To make Rules for the Government and Regulation of the land and naval Forces;

To provide for calling forth the Militia to execute the Laws of the Union, suppress Insurrections and repel Invasions;

To provide for organizing, arming, and disciplining, the Militia, and for governing such Part of them as may be employed in the Service of the United States, reserving to the States respectively, the Appointment of the Officers, and the Authority of training the Militia according to the discipline prescribed by Congress;

To exercise exclusive Legislation in all Cases whatsoever, over such District (not exceeding ten Miles square) as may, by Cession of particular States, and the Acceptance of Congress, become the Seat of the Government of the United States, and to exercise like Authority over all Places purchased by the Consent of the Legislature of the State in which the Same shall be, for the Erection of Forts, Magazines, Arsenals, dock-Yards, and other needful Buildings;—And

To make all Laws which shall be necessary and proper for carrying into Execution the foregoing Powers, and all other Powers vested by this Constitution in the Government of the United States, or in any Department or Officer thereof.

Section 9. The Migration or Importation of such Persons as any of the States now existing shall think proper to admit, shall not be prohibited by the Congress prior to the Year one thousand eight hundred and eight, but a Tax or duty may be imposed on such Importation, not exceeding ten dollars for each Person.

The Privilege of the Writ of Habeas Corpus shall not be suspended, unless when in Cases of Rebellion or Invasion the public Safety may require it.

No Bill of Attainder or ex post facto Law shall be passed.

No Capitation, or other direct, Tax shall be laid, unless in Proportion to the Census of Enumeration herein before directed to be taken.[5]

No Tax or Duty shall be laid on Articles exported from any State.

No Preference shall be given by any Regulation of Commerce or Revenue to the Ports of one State over those of another: nor shall Vessels bound to, or from, one State, be obliged to enter, clear, or pay Duties in another.

No Money shall be drawn from the Treasury, but in Consequence of Appropriations made by Law; and a regular Statement and Account of the Receipts and Expenditures of all public Money shall be published from time to time.

No Title of Nobility shall be granted by the United States: And no Person holding any Office of Profit or Trust under them, shall, without the Consent of the Congress, accept of any present, Emolument, Office, or Title, of any kind whatever, from any King, Prince, or foreign State.

Section 10. No State shall enter into any Treaty, Alliance, or Confederation; grant Letters of Marque and Reprisal; coin Money; emit Bills of Credit; make any Thing but gold and silver coin a Tender in Payment of Debts; pass any Bill of Attainder, ex post facto Law, or Law impairing the Obligation of Contracts, or grant any Title of Nobility.

No State shall, without the Consent of the Congress, lay any Imposts or Duties on Imports or Exports, except what may be absolutely necessary for executing its inspection Laws: and the net Produce of all Duties and Imposts, laid by any State on Imports or Exports, shall be for the Use of the Treasury of the United States; and all such Laws shall be subject to the Revision and Control of the Congress.

No State shall, without the consent of Congress, lay any Duty of Tonnage, keep Troops, or Ships of War in time of Peace, enter into any Agreement or Compact with another State, or with a foreign Power, or engage in War, unless actually invaded, or in such imminent Danger as will not admit of delay.

---

[5]Changed by the Sixteenth Amendment.

Article II

Section 1. The executive Power shall be vested in a President of the United States of America. He shall hold his Office during the Term of four Years, and, together with the Vice President, chosen for the same Term, be elected, as follows

Each state shall appoint, in such Manner as the Legislature thereof may direct, a Number of Electors, equal to the whole Number of Senators and Representatives to which the State may be entitled in Congress: but no Senator or Representative, or Person holding an Office of Trust or Profit under the United States, shall be appointed an Elector.

The Electors shall meet in their respective States, and vote by Ballot for two Persons, of whom one at least shall not be an inhabitant of the same State with themselves. And they shall make a List of all the Persons voted for, and of the Number of Votes for each; which List they shall sign and certify, and transmit sealed to the Seat of the Government of the United States, directed to the President of the Senate. The President of the Senate shall, in the Presence of the Senate and House of Representatives, open all the Certificates, and the Votes shall then be counted. The Person having the greatest Number of Votes shall be the President, if such Number be a Majority of the whole Number of Electors appointed; and if there be more than one who have such Majority, and have an equal Number of Votes, then the House of Representatives shall immediately chuse by Ballot one of them for President; and if no Person have a Majority, then from the five highest on the List the said House shall in like Manner chuse the President. But in chusing the President, the Votes shall be taken by States, the Representation from each State having one Vote; A quorum for this purpose shall consist of a Member or Members from two thirds of the States, and a Majority of all the States shall be necessary to a Choice. In every Case, after the Choice of the President, the Person having the greatest Number of Votes of the Electors shall be the Vice President. But if there should remain two or more who have equal Votes, the Senate shall chuse from them by Ballot the Vice President.[6]

The Congress may determine the Time of chusing the Electors, and the Day on which they shall give their Votes; which Day shall be the same throughout the United States.

No Person except a natural born Citizen, or a Citizen of the United States, at the time of the Adoption of this Constitution, shall be eligible to the Office of President; neither shall any Person be eligible to that Office who shall not have attained to the Age of thirty five Years, and been fourteen Years a Resident within the United States.

In Case of the Removal of the President from Office, or of his Death, Resignation, or Inability to discharge the Powers and Duties of the said Office, the Same shall devolve on the Vice President, and the Congress may by Law provide for the Case of Removal, Death, Resignation or Inability, both of the President and Vice President, declaring what Officer shall then act as President, and such Officer shall act accordingly, until the Disability be removed, or a President shall be elected.[7]

The President shall, at stated Times, receive for his Services, a Compensation, which shall neither be encreased nor diminished during the Period for which he shall have been elected, and he shall not receive within that Period any other Emolument from the United States, or any of them.

Before he enter on the Execution of his Office, he shall take the following Oath or Affirmation:—"I do solemnly swear (or affirm) that I will faithfully execute the Office of President of the United States, and will to the best of my Ability, preserve, protect, and defend the Constitution of the United States."

Section 2. The President shall be Commander in Chief of the Army and Navy of the United States, and of the Militia of the several States, when called into the actual Service of the United States; he may require the Opinion, in writing, of the principal Officer in each of the executive Departments, upon any Subject relating to the Duties of their respective Offices, and he shall have Power to grant Reprieves and Pardons for Offences against the United States, except in Cases of Impeachment.

He shall have Power, by and with the Advice and Consent of the Senate, to make Treaties, provided two thirds of the Senators present concur; and he shall nominate, and by and with the Advice and Consent of the Senate, shall appoint Ambassadors, other public Ministers and Consuls, Judges of the supreme Court, and all other Officers of the United States, whose Appointments are not herein otherwise provided for, and which shall be established by Law; but the Congress may by Law vest the Appointment of such inferior Officers, as they think proper, in the President alone, in the Courts of Law, or in the Heads of Departments.

The President shall have Power to fill up all Vacancies that may happen during the Recess of the Senate, by granting Commissions which shall expire at the End of their next Session.

---

[6]Changed by the Twelfth Amendment.

[7]Changed by the Twenty-fifth Amendment.

Section 3. He shall from time to time give to the Congress Information of the State of the Union, and recommend to their Consideration such Measures as he shall judge necessary and expedient; he may, on extraordinary Occasions, convene both Houses, or either of them, and in Case of Disagreement between them, with Respect to the Time of Adjournment, he may adjourn them to such Time as he shall think proper; he shall receive Ambassadors and other public Ministers; he shall take Care that the Laws be faithfully executed, and shall Commission all the Officers of the United States.

Section 4. The President, Vice President and all civil Officers of the United States, shall be removed from Office on Impeachment for, and Conviction of, Treason, Bribery, or other high Crimes and Misdemeanors.

Article III

Section 1. The judicial Power of the United States, shall be vested in one supreme Court, and in such inferior Courts as the Congress may from time to time ordain and establish. The Judges, both of the supreme and inferior Courts, shall hold their Offices during good Behaviour, and shall, at stated Times, receive for their Services, a Compensation, which shall not be diminished during their Continuance in Office.

Section 2. The judicial Power shall extend to all Cases, in Law and Equity, arising under this Constitution, the Laws of the United States, and Treaties made, or which shall be made, under their Authority;—to all Cases affecting Ambassadors, other public Ministers and Consuls;—to all Cases of admiralty and maritime Jurisdiction;—to Controversies to which the United States shall be a party;—to Controversies between two or more States;—between a State and Citizens of another State;[8]—between Citizens of different States;—between Citizens of the same State claiming Lands under Grants of different States, and between a State, or the Citizens thereof, and foreign States, Citizens or Subjects.

In all Cases affecting Ambassadors, other public Ministers and Consuls, and those in which a State shall be Party, the supreme Court shall have original Jurisdiction. In all the other Cases before mentioned, the supreme Court shall have appellate Jurisdiction, both as to Law and Fact, with such Exceptions, and under such Regulations as the Congress shall make.

The Trial of all Crimes, except in Cases of Impeachment, shall be by Jury: and such Trial shall be held in the State where the said Crimes shall have been committed; but when not committed within any State, the Trial shall

be at such Place or Places as the Congress may by Law have directed.

Section 3. Treason against the United States, shall consist only in levying War against them, or in adhering to their Enemies, giving them Aid and Comfort. No Person shall be convicted of Treason unless on the Testimony of two Witnesses to the same overt Act, or on Confession in open Court.

The Congress shall have Power to declare the Punishment of Treason, but no Attainder of Treason shall work Corruption of Blood, or Forfeiture except during the Life of the Person attainted.

Article IV

Section 1. Full Faith and Credit shall be given in each State to the public Acts, Records, and judicial Proceedings of every other State. And the Congress may by general Laws prescribe the Manner in which such Acts, Records and Proceedings shall be proved, and the Effect thereof.

Section 2. The Citizens of each State shall be entitled to all Privileges and Immunities of Citizens in the several States.

A Person charged in any State with Treason, Felony, or other Crime, who shall flee from Justice, and be found in another State, shall on Demand of the executive Authority of the State from which he fled, be delivered up, to be removed to the State having Jurisdiction of the Crime.

No Person held to Service or Labour in one State, under the Laws thereof, escaping into another, shall, in Consequence of any Law or Regulation therein, be discharged from such Service or Labour, but shall be delivered up on Claim of the Party to whom such Service or Labour may be due.[9]

Section 3. New States may be admitted by the Congress into this Union; but no new State shall be formed or erected within the Jurisdiction of any other State; nor any State be formed by the Junction of two or more States, or Parts of States, without the Consent of the Legislatures of the States concerned as well as of the Congress.

The Congress shall have Power to dispose of and make all needful Rules and Regulations respecting the Territory or other Property belonging to the United States; and nothing in this Constitution shall be so construed as to Prejudice any Claims of the United States, or of any particular State.

Section 4. The United States shall guarantee to every State in this Union a Republican Form of Government, and shall protect each of them against Invasion; and on

---

[8]Changed by the Eleventh Amendment.

[9]Changed by the Thirteenth Amendment.

Application of the Legislature, or of the Executive (when the Legislature cannot be convened) against domestic Violence.

Article V

The Congress, whenever two thirds of both Houses shall deem it necessary, shall propose Amendments to this Constitution, or, on the Application of the Legislatures of two thirds of the several States, shall call a Convention for proposing Amendments, which, in either Case, shall be valid to all Intents and Purposes, as Part of this Constitution, when ratified by the legislatures of three fourths of the several States, or by Conventions in three fourths thereof, as the one or the other Mode of Ratification may be proposed by the Congress; Provided that no Amendment which may be made prior to the Year One thousand eight hundred and eight shall in any Manner affect the first and fourth Clauses in the Ninth Section of the first Article; and that no State, without its Consent, shall be deprived of its equal Suffrage in the Senate.

Article VI

All Debts contracted and Engagements entered into, before the Adoption of this Constitution, shall be as valid against the United States under this Constitution, as under the Confederation.

The Constitution, and the Laws of the United States which shall be made in Pursuance thereof; and all Treaties made, or which shall be made, under the Authority of the United States, shall be the supreme Law of the Land; and the Judges in every State shall be bound thereby, any Thing in the Constitution or Laws of any State to the Contrary notwithstanding.

The Senators and Representatives before mentioned, and the Members of the several State Legislatures, and all executive and judicial Officers, both of the United States and of the several States, shall be bound by Oath or Affirmation, to support this Constitution; but no religious Test shall ever be required as a Qualification to any Office or public Trust under the United States.

Article VII

The Ratification of the Conventions of nine States, shall be sufficient for the Establishment of this Constitution between the States so ratifying the Same.

Done in Convention by the Unanimous Consent of the States present the Seventeenth Day of September in the Year of our Lord one thousand seven hundred and eighty

seven and of the Independance of the United States of America the Twelfth. In witness whereof We have hereunto subscribed our Names.

Amendments

[The first 10 amendments are known as the "Bill of Rights."]

Amendment 1 (Ratified 1791) Congress shall make no law respecting an establishment of religion, or prohibiting the free exercise thereof; or abridging the freedom of speech, or of the press; or the right of the people peaceably to assemble, and to petition the Government for a redress of grievances.

Amendment 2 (Ratified 1791) A well regulated Militia, being necessary to the security of a free State, the right of the people to keep and bear Arms, shall not be infringed.

Amendment 3 (Ratified 1791) No Soldier shall, in time of peace be quartered in any house, without the consent of the Owner, nor in time of war, but in a manner to be prescribed by law.

Amendment 4 (Ratified 1791) The right of the people to be secure in their persons, houses, papers, and effects, against unreasonable searches and seizures, shall not be violated, and no Warrants shall issue, but upon probable cause, supported by Oath or affirmation, and particularly describing the place to be searched, and the persons or things to be seized.

Amendment 5 (Ratified 1791) No person shall be held to answer for a capital, or otherwise infamous crime, unless on a presentment or indictment of a Grand Jury, except in cases arising in the land or naval forces, or in the Militia, when in actual service in time of War or public danger; nor shall any person be subject for the same offence to be twice put in jeopardy of life or limb; nor shall be compelled in any criminal case to be a witness against himself, nor be deprived of life, liberty, or property, without due process of law; nor shall private property be taken for public use, without just compensation.

Amendment 6 (Ratified 1791) In all criminal prosecutions, the accused shall enjoy the right to a speedy and public trial, by an impartial jury of the State and district wherein the crime shall have been committed, which district shall have been previously ascertained by law, and to be informed of the nature and cause of the accusation; to be confronted with the witnesses against him; to have compulsory process for obtaining Witnesses in his favor, and to have assistance of counsel for his defence.

Amendment 7 (Ratified 1791) In Suits at common law, where the value in controversy shall exceed twenty dollars, the right of trial by jury shall be preserved, and no fact tried by a jury, shall be otherwise re-examined in any Court of the United States, than according to the rules of the common law.

Amendment 8 (Ratified 1791) Excessive bail shall not be required, nor excessive fines imposed, nor cruel and unusual punishments inflicted.

Amendment 9 (Ratified 1791) The enumeration in the Constitution, of certain rights, shall not be construed to deny or disparage others retained by the people.

Amendment 10 (Ratified 1791) The powers not delegated to the United States by the Constitution, nor prohibited by it to the States, are reserved to the States respectively, or to the people.

Amendment 11 (Ratified 1795) The Judicial power of the United States shall not be construed to extend to any suit in law or equity, commenced or prosecuted against one of the United States by Citizens of another State, or by Citizens or Subjects of any Foreign State.

Amendment 12 (Ratified 1804) The Electors shall meet in their respective states, and vote by ballot for President and Vice-President, one of whom, at least, shall not be an inhabitant of the same state with themselves; they shall name in their ballots the person voted for as President, and in distinct ballots the person voted for as Vice-President, and they shall make distinct lists of all persons voted for as President, and of all persons voted for as Vice-President, and of the number of votes for each, which lists they shall sign and certify, and transmit sealed to the seat of the government of the United States, directed to the President of the Senate;—The President of the Senate shall, in the presence of the Senate and House of Representatives, open all the certificates and the votes shall then be counted;—The person having the greatest number of votes for President, shall be the President, if such number be a majority of the whole number of Electors appointed; and if no person have such majority, then from the persons having the highest numbers not exceeding three on the list of those voted for as President, the House of Representatives

shall choose immediately, by ballot, the President. But in choosing the President, the votes shall be taken by states, the representation from each state having one vote; a quorum for this purpose shall consist of a member or members from two-thirds of the states, and a majority of all the states shall be necessary to a choice. And if the House of Representatives shall not choose a President whenever the right of choice shall devolve upon them, before the fourth day of March next following, then the Vice-President shall act as president, as in the case of the death or other constitutional disability of the President.[10]—The person having the greatest number of votes as Vice-President, shall be the Vice-President, if such number be a majority of the whole number of Electors appointed, and if no person have a majority, then from the two highest numbers on the list, the Senate shall choose the Vice-President; a quorum for the purpose shall consist of two-thirds of the whole number of Senators, and a majority of the whole number shall be necessary to a choice. But no person constitutionally ineligible to the office of President shall be eligible to that of Vice-President of the United States.

Amendment 13 (Ratified 1865) Section 1. Neither slavery nor involuntary servitude, except as a punishment for crime whereof the party shall have been duly convicted, shall exist within the United States, or any place subject to their jurisdiction.

Section 2. Congress shall have power to enforce this article by appropriate legislation.

Amendment 14 (Ratified 1868) Section 1. All persons born or naturalized in the United States, and subject to the jurisdiction thereof, are citizens of the United States and of the State wherein they reside. No State shall make or enforce any law which shall abridge the privileges or immunities of citizens of the United States; nor shall any State deprive any person of life, liberty, or property, without due process of law; nor deny to any person within its jurisdiction the equal protection of the laws.

Section 2. Representatives shall be apportioned among the several States according to their respective numbers, counting the whole number of persons in each State, excluding Indians not taxed. But when the right to vote at any election for the choice of electors for President and Vice President of the United States, Representatives in Congress, the Executive and Judicial officers of a State, or the members of the Legislature thereof, is denied to any

---

[10]Changed by the Twentieth Amendment.

of the male inhabitants of such State, being twenty-one[11] years of age, and citizens of the United States, or in any way abridged except for participation in rebellion, or other crime, the basis of representation therein shall be reduced in the proportion which the number of such male citizens shall bear to the whole number of male citizens twenty-one years of age in such State.

Section 3. No person shall be a Senator or Representative in Congress, or elector of President and Vice President, or hold any office, civil or military, under the United States, or under any State, who, having previously taken an oath, as a member of Congress, or as an officer of the United States, or as a member of any State legislature, or as an executive or judicial officer of any State, to support the Constitution of the United States, shall have engaged in insurrection or rebellion against the same, or given aid or comfort to the enemies thereof. But Congress may by a vote of two-thirds of each House, remove such disability.

Section 4. The validity of the public debt of the United States, authorized by law, including debts incurred for payment of pensions and bounties for services in suppressing insurrection or rebellion, shall not be questioned. But neither the United States nor any State shall assume or pay any debt or obligation incurred in aid of insurrection or rebellion against the United States, or any claim for the loss or emancipation of any slave; but all such debts, obligations and claims shall be held illegal and void.

Section 5. The Congress shall have power to enforce, by appropriate legislation, the provisions of this article.

Amendment 15 (Ratified 1870) **Section 1.**
The right of citizens of the United States to vote shall not be denied or abridged by the United States or by any State on account of race, color, or previous condition of servitude.

Section 2. The Congress shall have power to enforce this article by appropriate legislation.

Amendment 16 (Ratified 1913) The Congress
shall have power to lay and collect taxes on incomes, from whatever source derived, without apportionment among the several States, and without regard to any census or enumeration.

Amendment 17 (Ratified 1913) The Senate of
the United States shall be composed of two Senators from each State, elected by the people thereof, for six years; and each Senator shall have one vote. The electors in each State shall have the qualifications requisite for electors of the most numerous branch of the State legislatures.

When vacancies happen in the representation of any State in the Senate, the executive authority of such State shall issue writs of election to fill such vacancies: *Provided,* That the legislature of any State may empower the executive thereof to make temporary appointments until the people fill the vacancies by election as the legislature may direct.

This amendment shall not be so construed as to affect the election or term of any Senator chosen before it becomes valid as part of the Constitution.

Amendment 18 (Ratified 1919; Repealed 1933) **Section 1.** After one year from the ratification of
this article the manufacture, sale, or transportation of intoxicating liquors within, the importation thereof into, or the exportation thereof from the United States and all territory subject to the jurisdiction thereof for beverage purposes is hereby prohibited.

Section 2. The Congress and the several States shall have concurrent power to enforce this article by appropriate legislation.

Section 3. This article shall be inoperative unless it shall have been ratified as an amendment to the Constitution by the legislatures of the several States, as provided in the Constitution, within seven years from the date of the submission hereof to the States by the Congress.[12]

Amendment 19 (Ratified 1920) The right of
citizens of the United States to vote shall not be denied or abridged by the United States or by any State on account of sex.

Congress shall have power to enforce this article by appropriate legislation.

Amendment 20 (Ratified 1933) **Section 1.**
The terms of the President and Vice President shall end at noon on the 20th day of January, and the terms of Senators and Representatives at noon on the 3rd day of January, of the years in which such terms would have ended if this article had not been ratified; and the terms of their successors shall then begin.

Section 2. The Congress shall assemble at least once in every year, and such meeting shall begin at noon on the 3rd day of January, unless they shall by law appoint a different day.

---

[11]Changed by the Twenty-sixth Amendment.

[12]Repealed by the Twenty-first Amendment.

Section 3. If, at the time fixed for the beginning of the term of the President, the President elect shall have died, the Vice President elect shall become President. If a President shall not have been chosen before the time fixed for the beginning of his term, or if the President elect shall have failed to qualify, then the Vice President elect shall act as President until a President shall have qualified; and the Congress may by law provide for the case wherein neither a President elect nor a Vice President elect shall have qualified, declaring who shall then act as President, or the manner in which one who is to act shall be selected, and such person shall act accordingly until a President or Vice President shall have qualified.

Section 4. The Congress may by law provide for the case of the death of any of the persons from whom the House of Representatives may choose a President whenever the right of choice shall have devolved upon them, and for the case of the death of any of the persons from whom the Senate may choose a Vice President whenever the right of choice shall have devolved upon them.

Section 5. Sections 1 and 2 shall take effect on the 15th day of October following the ratification of this article.

Section 6. This article shall be inoperative unless it shall have been ratified as an amendment to the Constitution by the legislatures of three-fourths of the several States within seven years from the date of its submission.

Amendment 21 (Ratified 1933) Section 1.

The eighteenth article of amendment to the Constitution of the United States is hereby repealed.

Section 2. The transportation or importation into any State, Territory, or possession of the United States for delivery or use therein of intoxicating liquors, in violation of the laws thereof, is hereby prohibited.

Section 3. This article shall be inoperative unless it shall have been ratified as an amendment to the Constitution by conventions in the several States, as provided in the Constitution, within seven years from the date of the submission hereof to the States by the Congress.

Amendment 22 (Ratified 1951) Section 1.

No person shall be elected to the office of the President more than twice, and no person who has held the office of President, or acted as President, for more than two years of a term to which some other person was elected President shall be elected to the office of the President more than once. But this Article shall not apply to any person holding the office of President when this Article was proposed by the Congress, and shall not prevent any person who may be holding the office of President, or acting as President, during the term within which this

Article becomes operative from holding the office of President or acting as President during the remainder of such term.

Section 2. This Article shall be inoperative unless it shall have been ratified as an amendment to the Constitution by the legislatures of three-fourths of the several States within seven years from the date of its submission to the States by the Congress.

Amendment 23 (Ratified 1961) Section 1.

The District constituting the seat of Government of the United States shall appoint in such manner as the Congress may direct:

A number of electors of President and Vice President equal to the whole number of Senators and Representatives in Congress to which the District would be entitled if it were a State, but in no event more than the least populous State; they shall be in addition to those appointed by the States, but they shall be considered, for the purposes of the election of President and Vice President, to be electors appointed by a State; and they shall meet in the District and perform such duties as provided by the twelfth article of amendment.

Section 2. The Congress shall have power to enforce this article by appropriate legislation.

Amendment 24 (Ratified 1964) Section 1.

The right of citizens of the United States to vote in any primary or other election for President or Vice President, for electors for President or Vice President, or for Senator or Representative in Congress, shall not be denied or abridged by the United States or any State by reason of failure to pay any poll tax or other tax.

Section 2. The Congress shall have power to enforce this article by appropriate legislation.

Amendment 25 (Ratified 1967) Section 1.

In case of the removal of the President from office or of his death or resignation, the Vice President shall become President.

Section 2. Whenever there is a vacancy in the office of the Vice President, the President shall nominate a Vice President who shall take office upon confirmation by a majority vote of both Houses of Congress.

Section 3. Whenever the President transmits to the President pro tempore of the Senate and the Speaker of the House of Representatives his written declaration that he is unable to discharge the powers and duties of his office, and until he transmits to them a written declaration to the contrary, such powers and duties shall be discharged by the Vice President as Acting President.

Section 4. Whenever the Vice President and a majority of either the principal officers of the executive departments or of such other body as Congress may by law provide, transmit to the President pro tempore of the Senate and the Speaker of the House of Representatives their written declaration that the President is unable to discharge the powers and duties of his office, the Vice President shall immediately assume the powers and duties of the office as Acting President.

Thereafter, when the President transmits to the President pro tempore of the Senate and the Speaker of the House of Representatives his written declaration that no inability exists, he shall resume the powers and duties of his office unless the Vice President and a majority of either the principal officers of the executive department or of such other body as Congress may by law provide, transmit within four days to the President pro tempore of the Senate and the Speaker of the House of Representatives their written declaration that the President is unable to discharge the powers and duties of his office. Thereupon Congress shall decide the issue, assembling within forty-eight hours for that purpose if not in session. If the Congress, within twenty-one days after receipt of the latter written declaration, or, if Congress is not in session, within twenty-one days after Congress is required to assemble, determines by two-thirds vote of both Houses that the President is unable to discharge the powers and duties of his office, the Vice President shall continue to discharge the same as Acting President; otherwise, the President shall resume the powers and duties of his office.

Amendment 26 (Ratified 1971) Section 1.

The right of citizens of the United States, who are eighteen years of age or older, to vote shall not be denied or abridged by the United States or by any State on account of age.

Section 2. The Congress shall have power to enforce this article by appropriate legislation.

Amendment 27 (Ratified 1992) No law,

varying the compensation for the services of the Senators and Representatives, shall take effect, until an election of Representatives shall have intervened.

Uniform Commercial Code

The Uniform Commercial Code, or UCC, was developed by the American Law Institute (ALI) and the National Conference of Commissioners on Uniform State Laws (NCCUSL) as a body of rules intended to make the application of law to commercial transactions consistent across fifty states. The UCC has been adopted in whole by all but one state legislature, Louisiana, which adopts only certain sections. Such widespread use of the UCC, even with the minor deviations some jurisdictions make from the official code, makes possible more efficient and more confident transactions across state lines. The UCC can be accessed here: www.law.cornell.edu/ucc.

Index

P